The National Hockey League

Official Guide & Record Book 2018

THE NATIONAL HOCKEY LEAGUE
Official Guide & Record Book/2018

Copyright © 2017 by the National Hockey League. All rights reserved.

The National Hockey League owns, and retains ownership of, the data contained in this book to the extent permitted by law.

To obtain a license for commercial use of this data, please contact: Christopher Golier (cgolier@nhl.com).

Compiled by the NHL Public Relations Department and the 31 NHL Club Public Relations Directors.

Printed in the United States of America. All rights reserved under the Pan-American and International Copyright Conventions.

Trade edition published in the United States
and distributed in Canada by: Triumph Books, 814 N. Franklin Street, Chicago, Illinois 60610
ISBN 978-1-62937-477-2

NHL and media edition published by: Dan Diamond and Associates, Inc., 194 Dovercourt Road, Toronto, Ontario M6J 3C8 Canada
ISBN 978-1-894801-34-8

Staff

For the NHL: Dave McCarthy; Supervising Editor: Greg Inglis; Statistician: Benny Ercolani;
Editorial Staff: Dave Baker, John Dellapina, David Keon, Jennifer Moad, Kelley Rosset, Susan Snow, Julie Young.

Senior Managing Editor: Ralph Dinger
Associate Managing Editor: Paul Bontje
Production Editors: John Pasternak, Alex Dubiel
Photo Editor: Eric Zweig
International Editor: Igor Kuperman
Publisher: Dan Diamond

Data Management and Typesetting: Caledon Data Management, Vienna, Ontario
Printing Consultant: Sunrise Consulting Inc., Toronto, Ontario
Printed in the United States of America by Ripon Printers, Ripon, Wisconsin
Production Management: Dan Diamond and Associates, Inc., Toronto, Ontario
Contributors and Photo Credits: see page 679

Distribution

Trade sales and distribution in the United States by:
Triumph Books, 814 North Franklin Street, Chicago, Illinois 60610   800/335-5323; Fax 312/663-3557

Trade sales and distribution in Canada by:
Canadian Manda Group, 664 Annette Street, Toronto, Ontario M6S 2C8   416/516/0911 info@mandagroup.cpm

International distribution:
For information on international distrtibution opportunities, contact Dan Diamond at dda.nhl@sympatico.ca

The National Hockey League
1185 Avenue of the Americas, 14th Floor, New York, New York 10036
1800 McGill College Ave., Suite 2600, Montreal, Quebec H3A 3J6
50 Bay Street, 11th Floor, Toronto, Ontario M5J 2X8

www.nhlofficialguide.com

Table of Contents

Table of Contents *continued*

Introduction

WELCOME TO THE 86TH EDITION OF *THE NATIONAL HOCKEY LEAGUE OFFICIAL GUIDE & RECORD BOOK*. 2016-17 was the 16th and final season in which the NHL operated with 30 clubs. As the League continues its centennial celebration in 2017-18, it will do so as a 31-team league when the Vegas Golden Knights begin play in League game #15 in Dallas on Friday, October 6, 2017. Playing in the Pacific Division of the Western Conference, the Golden Knights will be the NHL's first new franchise since 2000-01 when Minnesota and Columbus began play. *(The various expansions that have seen the League grow from four to 31 teams are described on pages 9 and 10. See the inside front cover for a list of teams in each division and information on the makeup of the regular-season schedule. Information about the Vegas Golden Knights begins on page 127.)*

Nine teams finished the 2016-17 season with 100 points or more, topped by the Presidents' Trophy-winning Washington Capitals with 120. No Division winner reached the Stanley Cup Final for the fourth consecutive playoff year, the last one to do so being the Central Division champion Chicago Blackhawks in 2013. In the 2017 playoffs, the second-place team from the Metropolitan Division (Pittsburgh, 111 points) defeated the second wildcard team from the Western Conference (Nashville, 94 points). The Predators' success lit up the city of Nashville starting with their sweep of the defending Cup-champion Blackhawks in the First Round. This was the Penguins' fifth championship and second in a row, making them the first club to repeat as Cup champions since the Detroit Red Wings in 1997 and 1998. If today's Penguins could win a third consecutive title they would become the first club to do so since the New York Islanders, winners of four in a row beginning in 1980. *(See page 137 for the 2016-17 Final Standings and page 243 for playoff scores. The names of the players on each Cup winner spanning back to 1893 can be found on pages 247 to 254. Year-by-year Cup winners are listed on page 246.)*

Pittsburgh captain Sidney Crosby repeated as playoff MVP, winning the Conn Smythe Trophy in 2017. Crosby also won the Rocket Richard Trophy as the League's top regular-season goal scorer. Second-year superstar Connor McDavid of the Edmonton Oilers was the League's only 100-point scorer and won both the Art Ross and Hart trophies as the League's top scorer and most valuable player while Toronto super-rookie Auston Matthews won the Calder Trophy with a 40-goal debut season that began with four goals in his first game. Crosby, Matthews and Tampa Bay's Nikita Kucherov were the only players to score 40-or-more goals in 2016-17. *(Detailed statistics on the regular season begin on page 137; trophy descriptions and winners on page 206.)*

Outdoor games continued to be popular in 2016-17 with more than 185,000 fans attending games played in Winnipeg, Toronto, St. Louis and Pittsburgh. With three more scheduled for 2017-18 (including the League's "NHL 100 Classic" centennial game set for Ottawa in December), a total of 25 outdoor regular-season NHL games will have been played. *(A complete list of all outdoor games including scores, attendance and temperature is found on page 13.)*

The modern *NHL Official Guide & Record Book* has seen numerous improvements in content and useability throughout 34-year history and the 2018 edition is no exception. Several new features have been added.

The Draft section *(beginning on page 214)* now treats the United States Hockey League as a separate player source. This Tier 1 U.S.-based junior league has been an important player source for more than 20 years. Previously, it had been listed in the "Other" category along with lower-tier U.S. and Canadian junior leagues. The USHL has separated itself from this pack with more than 20 players drafted in each of the last eight years including a league-high 33 in 2017. *(A breakdown of drafted players by USHL club is found on page 215.)*

The 2018 *Guide & Record Book* will also reflect a recent and welcome decision by the NHL to apply today's standard to earlier years, identifying players who played the majority of the regular-season for teams that would go on to win the Stanley Cup. Previously, these players were not considered to be official Cup winners. This has changed. The following six players have now been added to their club's list of Stanley Cup-winners: Vic Stasiuk (Detroit 1954), Jackie Leclair (Montreal 1957), Kent Douglas (Toronto 1964), John Brenneman (Toronto 1967) and Don Awrey and John Van Boxmeer (Montreal 1976). *(Cup-winning rosters spanning 1954 to 1971 are found on pages 251 and 252.)*

As always, the *NHL Official Guide & Record Book* contains data on every one of the more than 7,000 players who have appeared in an NHL game, plus more than 1,000 prospects who have yet to do so. See the Prospect Register *(page 279)*, Active Player Register *(351)* and Goaltender Register *(589)* in addition to the Retired Players *(616)* and Retired Goaltenders *(665)*. A key to the abbreviations and symbols used in individual player and goaltender data panels, along with useful information on how to use the Registers, is found on page 278. Each NHL club's minor-pro affiliates are found on page 12. A list of league abbreviations used in the Prospect, Player and Goaltender Registers is found on page 678.

Thanks to readers, correspondents, members of the media and hockey communications professionals throughout the game who make good use of what we produce.

Best wishes,

Dan Diamond
Publisher

ACCURACY REMAINS THE *GUIDE & RECORD BOOK*'S TOP PRIORITY.
We appreciate comments and clarification from our readers. Please direct these to:
- Ralph Dinger — Senior Managing Editor, 194 Dovercourt Road, Toronto, Ontario M6J 3C8. e-mail: ralph.dda@sympatico.ca.
- Greg Inglis — 1185 Avenue of the Americas, New York, New York 10036 . . . or . . .
- David Keon — 50 Bay Street, 11th Floor, Toronto, Ontario, M5J 2X8

Your involvement makes a better book.

NATIONAL HOCKEY LEAGUE

New York
1185 Avenue of the Americas
New York, NY 10036
212/789-2000, Fax: 212/789-2020

Montréal
1800 McGill College Avenue
Suite 2600
Montréal, Québec, H3A 3J6
514/841-9220, Fax: 514/841-1040

Toronto
50 Bay Street
11th Floor
Toronto, Ontario, M5J 2X8
416/359-7900, Fax: 416/981-2779

League and Club websites: www.nhl.com • Twitter: @NHL

Executive

Commissioner ....Gary B. Bettman
Deputy Commissioner ....William Daly
Senior Executive Vice President of Hockey Operations ....Colin Campbell

Commissioner and League Presidents

Gary B. Bettman

Gary B. Bettman took office as the NHL's first Commissioner on February 1, 1993. Since the League was formed in 1917, there have been five League Presidents.

NHL President	Years in Office
Frank Calder	1917-1943
Mervyn "Red" Dutton	1943-1946
Clarence Campbell	1946-1977
John A. Ziegler, Jr.	1977-1992
Gil Stein	1992-1993

Hockey Hall of Fame

Hockey Hall of Fame
Brookfield Place
30 Yonge Street, Toronto, Ontario M5E 1X8
Phone: 416/360-7735 • Executive Fax: 416/360-1501

Lanny McDonald – Chairman of the Board
Jeff Denomme – President and CEO
Craig Baines – Vice-President, Development & Building Operations
Peter Jagla – Vice-President, Marketing & Attraction Services
Ron Ellis - Program Director, HHOF Development Association
Kelly Masse – Director, Corporate & Media Relations
Craig Beckim – Manager, Merchandising & Retail Operations
Darren Boyko – Manager, Special Projects & International Business
Jackie Schwartz – Manager, Marketing & Promotions

D.K. (Doc) Seaman Resource Centre and Archives
400 Kipling Avenue, Toronto, Ontario M8V 3L1
Phone: 416/360-7735 • Fax: 416/251-5770
www.hhof.com, www.imagesonice.net

Phil Pritchard – Vice President, Resource Centre and Curator
Craig Campbell – Manager, Resource Centre and Archives
Izak Westgate – Manager, Outreach and Asst. Curator
Steve Poirier – Coordinator, HHOF Images and Archival Services
Miragh Bitove – Archivist & Collections Registrar

National Hockey League Players' Association

10 Bay Street, Suite 1200, Toronto, Ontario M5J 2R8
Phone: 416/313-2300 • Fax: 416/313-2301
www.nhlpa.com

Robert DeGregory ....Associate Counsel, Labour
Maria Dennis ....Associate Counsel, Labour
Donald Fehr ....Executive Director
Stephen Frank...............Director, Technology & Security
Roland Lee ....Director, Salary Cap & Marketplace and Senior Counsel
Jasmine Lew ....Director, Business Ops & Associate Counsel
Bruce Meyer ....Sr. Director, Collective Bargaining, Policy & Legal
Sandra Monteiro............Chief of Global Business Strategies
Kim Murdoch.................Director, Player Insurance & Pensions
Mike Ouellet.................Senior Business & Association Counsel
Joe Reekie ....Divisional Player Representative
Mathieu Schneider.........Special Assistant to the Exec. Director
Richard Smit ....Director, Finance and HRR
Devin Smith ....Director, Mktg. & Community Relations
Roman Stoykewych ....Senior Counsel, Labour
Jonathan Weatherdon ....Director, Communications
Steve Webb ....Divisional Player Representative
Rob Zamuner.................Divisional Player Representative
Don Zavelo ....General Counsel

BOARD OF GOVERNORS

CHAIRMAN OF THE BOARD – JEREMY M. JACOBS

Anaheim Ducks

Henry Samueli	Governor
Susan Samueli	Alternate Governor
Michael Schulman	Alternate Governor
Tim Ryan	Alternate Governor
Bob Murray	Alternate Governor

Arizona Coyotes

Andrew Barroway	Governor
Ahron Cohen	Alternate Governor
John Chayka	Alternate Governor

Boston Bruins

Jeremy M. Jacobs	Governor
Charles Jacobs	Alternate Governor
Jeremy Jacobs, Jr.	Alternate Governor
Louis Jacobs	Alternate Governor
Harry J. Sinden	Alternate Governor
Cam Neely	Alternate Governor
Don Sweeney	Alternate Governor

Buffalo Sabres

Terry Pegula	Governor
Kim Pegula	Alternate Governor
Russ Brandon	Alternate Governor

Calgary Flames

N. Murray Edwards	Governor
Ken King	Alternate Governor
Alvin Libin	Alternate Governor
Brian Burke	Alternate Governor

Carolina Hurricanes

Peter Karmanos, Jr.	Governor
Ron Francis	Alternate Governor
Don Waddell	Alternate Governor

Chicago Blackhawks

W. Rockwell Wirtz	Governor
Robert J. Pulford	Alternate Governor
John McDonough	Alternate Governor

Colorado Avalanche

Josh Kroenke	Governor
Mark Waggoner	Alternate Governor
Joe Sakic	Alternate Governor

Columbus Blue Jackets

John P. McConnell	Governor
Mike Priest	Alternate Governor
John Davidson	Alternate Governor
Jarmo Kekalainen	Alternate Governor

Dallas Stars

Tom Gaglardi	Governor
Jim Lites	Alternate Governor
Jim Nill	Alternate Governor
Jason Farris	Alternate Governor

Detroit Red Wings

Christopher Ilitch	Governor
Jim Devellano	Alternate Governor
Ken Holland	Alternate Governor
Rob Carr	Alternate Governor
Tom Wilson	Alternate Governor

Edmonton Oilers

Daryl Katz	Governor
Kevin Lowe	Alternate Governor
Bob Nicholson	Alternate Governor
Peter Chiarelli	Alternate Governor

Florida Panthers

Vinnie Viola	Governor
Bill Torrey	Alternate Governor
Doug Cifu	Alternate Governor
Dale Tallon	Alternate Governor
Peter Luukko	Alternate Governor
Matthew Caldwell	Alternate Governor
Rory Babich	Alternate Governor

Los Angeles Kings

Philip F. Anschutz	Governor
Luc Robitaille	Alternate Governor
Dan Beckerman	Alternate Governor
Kelly Cheeseman	Alternate Governor

Minnesota Wild

Craig Leipold	Governor
Matt Majka	Alternate Governor
Chuck Fletcher	Alternate Governor

Montréal Canadiens

Geoff Molson	Governor
Fred Steer	Alternate Governor
Michael Andlauer	Alternate Governor
Andrew T. Molson	Alternate Governor
Marc Bergevin	Alternate Governor
France-Margaret Belanger	Alternate Governor

Nashville Predators

Tom Cigarran	Governor
Herbert Fritch	Alternate Governor
David Poile	Alternate Governor
Sean Henry	Alternate Governor
Joel Dobberpuhl	Alternate Governor

New Jersey Devils

Josh Harris	Governor
David Blitzer	Alternate Governor
Scott O'Neil	Alternate Governor
Ray Shero	Alternate Governor

New York Islanders

Scott Malkin	Governor
Charles Wang	Alternate Governor
Arthur J. McCarthy	Alternate Governor
Garth Snow	Alternate Governor
Jon Ledecky	Alternate Governor

New York Rangers

James L. Dolan	Governor
Glen Sather	Alternate Governor

Ottawa Senators

Eugene Melnyk	Governor
Sheldon Plener	Alternate Governor
Tom Anselmi	Alternate Governor

Philadelphia Flyers

Dave Scott	Governor
Philip I. Weinberg	Alternate Governor
Paul Holmgren	Alternate Governor
Shawn Tilger	Alternate Governor
Ron Hextall	Alternate Governor

Pittsburgh Penguins

David Morehouse	Governor
Ronald Burkle	Alternate Governor
Anthony Liberati	Alternate Governor
Travis Williams	Alternate Governor
Mario Lemieux	Alternate Governor

St. Louis Blues

Thomas Stillman	Governor
Doug Armstrong	Alternate Governor
Chris Zimmerman	Alternate Governor

San Jose Sharks

Hasso Plattner	Governor
Doug Wilson	Alternate Governor
John Tortora	Alternate Governor

Tampa Bay Lightning

Jeff Vinik	Governor
Steve Yzerman	Alternate Governor
Steve Griggs	Alternate Governor

Toronto Maple Leafs

Larry Tanenbaum	Governor
Dale Lastman	Alternate Governor
Brendan Shanahan	Alternate Governor

Vancouver Canucks

Francesco Aquilini	Governor
Paolo Aquilini	Alternate Governor
Roberto Aquilini	Alternate Governor
Victor de Bonis	Alternate Governor
Trevor Linden	Alternate Governor
Jeff Stipec	Alternate Governor

Vegas Golden Knights

Bill Foley	Governor
George McPhee	Alternate Governor
Gavin Maloof	Alternate Governor
John Breslow	Alternate Governor

Washington Capitals

Ted Leonsis	Governor
Richard M. Patrick	Alternate Governor
Brian MacLellan	Alternate Governor

Winnipeg Jets

Mark Chipman	Governor
Kevin Cheveldayoff	Alternate Governor
Patrick Phillips	Alternate Governor

Top to bottom: Referees Eric Furlatt, Tom Kowal, Chris Lee and Chris Rooney and all reached the 1,000-game milestone in 2016-17. Linesmen Steve Barton, David Brisebois, Jonny Murray and Vaughan Rody also worked their 1,000th regular-season games during this past season.

NHL On-Ice Officials
*Age at start of 2017-18 season.

Total NHL Games and 2016-17 Games columns count regular-season games only.

Referees

#	Name	*Age	Birthplace	First NHL Game	Total NHL Games	2016-17 Games
49	Reid Anderson	28	Calgary, AB		40	37
26	Jacob Brenk	35	Detroit Lakes, MN	Dec. 11/15	40	37
6	Francis Charron	34	Ottawa, ON	Apr. 5/10	332	40
18	Tom Chmielewski	30	Colorado Springs, CO	Apr. 8/14	76	37
19	Gord Dwyer	40	Halifax, NS	Nov. 19/05	795	75
27	Eric Furlatt	46	Trois-Rivieres, QC	Oct. 8/01	1026	75
14	Trevor Hanson	33	Richmond, BC	Oct. 24/13	176	74
22	Ghislain Hebert	36	Bathurst, NB	Mar. 2/09	442	75
15	Jean Hebert	37	Moncton, NB	Mar. 30/11	325	76
8	Dave Jackson	52	Montreal, QC	Dec. 22/90	1483	2
25	Marc Joannette	48	Verdun, QC	Oct. 1/99	1152	75
32	Tom Kowal	49	Vernon, BC	Oct. 29/99	1033	73
40	Steve Kozari	44	Penticton, BC	Oct. 15/05	745	57
47	Pierre Lambert	29	Greenfield Park, QC	Nov. 17/16	12	12
17	Frederick L'Ecuyer	40	Trois-Rivieres, QC	Oct. 11/07	554	75
28	Chris Lee	47	Saint John, NB	Apr. 2/00	1011	75
21	Thomas John Luxmore	32	Timmins, ON	Nov. 19/13	173	75
45	Peter MacDougall	32	Lumsden, SK	Apr. 8/17	1	1
4	Wes McCauley	45	Georgetown, ON	Jan. 20/03	886	75
2	Jon McIsaac	33	Truro, NS	Nov. 21/13	106	74
34	Brad Meier	50	Dayton, OH	Oct. 23/99	1151	75
36	Dean Morton	49	Peterborough, ON	Nov. 11/00	676	72
30	Kendrick Nicholson	35	Stratford, ON	Jan. 17/15	107	75
13	Dan O'Halloran	53	Essex, ON	Oct. 1/95	1303	75
9	Dan O'Rourke	45	Calgary, AB	Oct. 2/99	[1]869	74
20	Tim Peel	51	Toronto, ON	Oct. 21/99	1155	75
16	Brian Pochmara	40	Detroit, MI	Dec. 23/05	693	75
33	Kevin Pollock	47	Kincardine, ON	Mar. 28/00	1156	75
7	Garrett Rank	30	Kitchener, ON	Jan. 15/15	114	75
10	Kyle Rehman	39	Stettler, AB	Jan. 22/08	533	75
39	Evgeny Romasko	35	Tver, Russia	Mar. 9/15	56	25
5	Chris Rooney	42	Boston, MA	Nov. 22/00	1014	38
48	Chris Schlenker	33	Medicine Hat, AB	Oct. 24/16	28	28
24	Graham Skilliter	33	La Ronge, SK	Jan. 28/13	255	75
44	Furman South	29	Sewickley, PA	Apr. 6/17	1	1
38	Francois St. Laurent	40	Greenfield Park, QC	Nov. 10/05	602	75
12	Justin St. Pierre	45	Dolbeau, QC	Nov. 9/05	793	75
11	Kelly Sutherland	46	Richmond, BC	Dec. 19/00	1081	74
41	Cameron Voss	30	St. Paul, MN	Apr. 4/17	1	1
29	Ian Walsh	45	Philadelphia, PA	Oct. 14/00	995	75
23	Brad Watson	56	Regina, SK	Mar. 7/96	1252	74

[1] plus 120 games as a linesman.

Linesmen

#	Name	*Age	Birthplace	First NHL Game	Total NHL Games	2016-17 Games
52	Shandor Alphonso	33	Orangeville, ON	Oct. 17/14	169	77
75	Derek Amell	49	Port Colborne, ON	Oct. 11/97	1297	76
59	Steve Barton	45	Vankleek Hill, ON	Nov. 1/00	1071	76
87	Devin Berg	27	Kitchener, ON	Oct. 15/15	124	77
96	David Brisebois	41	Sudbury, ON	Oct. 11/99	1036	76
74	Lonnie Cameron	53	Victoria, BC	Oct. 5/96	1410	76
50	Scott Cherrey	41	Drayton, ON	Oct. 6/07	694	77
76	Michel Cormier	43	Trois-Rivieres, QC	Oct. 10/03	937	77
81	Ryan Daisy	29	Newton, MA	Oct. 13/16	48	48
54	Greg Devorski	48	Guelph, ON	Oct. 9/93	1570	77
68	Scott Driscoll	49	Seaforth, ON	Oct. 10/92	1632	77
82	Ryan Galloway	45	Winnipeg, MB	Oct. 17/02	962	77
64	Brandon Gawryletz	34	Trail, BC	Oct. 14/15	118	76
58	Ryan Gibbons	32	Vancouver, BC	Oct. 8/15	149	76
66	Darren Gibbs	51	Edmonton, AB	Oct. 1/97	1268	83
55	Shane Heyer	53	Summerland, BC	Oct. 6/88	[2]1561	77
63	Trent Knorr	31	Powell River, BC	Feb. 26/14	[3]215	77
71	Brad Kovachik	46	Woodstock, ON	Oct. 10/96	1371	76
78	Brian Mach	43	Little Falls, MN	Oct. 7/00	1139	76
83	Matt MacPherson	34	Antigonish, NS	Oct. 11/11	399	77
89	Steve Miller	45	Stratford, ON	Oct. 11/00	1124	76
53	Bevan Mills	29	Langley, BC	Nov. 29/16	29	29
79	Kiel Murchison	32	Cloverdale, BC	Jan. 21/13	330	77
93	Brian Murphy	52	Dover, NH	Oct. 7/88	[4]1775	77
95	Jonny Murray	43	Beauport, QC	Oct. 7/00	1065	77
97	Kory Nagy	28	London, ON	Oct. 12/16	37	37
70	Derek Nansen	45	Ottawa, ON	Oct. 11/02	912	0
77	Tim Nowak	50	Buffalo, NY	Oct. 8/93	1583	77
94	Bryan Pancich	35	Great Falls, MT	Oct. 3/09	519	75
65	Pierre Racicot	50	Verdun, QC	Oct. 12/93	1613	77
73	Vaughan Rody	48	Winnipeg, MB	Oct. 8/00	1022	76
84	Anthony Sericolo	49	Troy, NY	Oct. 21/98	1235	77
92	Mark Shewchyk	42	Waterdown, ON	Oct. 9/03	933	77
51	Andrew Smith	26	Kitchener, ON			
60	Libor Suchanek	28	Stod, Czech.			
56	Mark Wheler	52	North Battleford, SK	Oct. 10/92	1673	77

[2] plus 386 games as a referee. [3] plus 2 games as a referee. [4] plus 88 games as a referee.

NHL History

1917 — National Hockey League organized November 26 in Montreal following suspension of operations by the National Hockey Association of Canada Limited (NHA). Montreal Canadiens, Montreal Wanderers, Ottawa Senators and Quebec Bulldogs attended founding meeting. Delegates decided to use NHA rules.

Toronto Arenas were later admitted as fifth team; Quebec decided not to operate during the first season. Quebec players allocated to remaining four teams.

Frank Calder elected president and secretary-treasurer.

First NHL games played December 19, with Toronto only arena with artificial ice. Clubs played 22-game split schedule.

1918 — Emergency meeting held January 3 due to destruction by fire of Montreal Arena which was home ice for both Canadiens and Wanderers.

Wanderers withdrew, reducing the NHL to three teams; Canadiens played remaining home games at 3,250-seat Jubilee rink.

Quebec franchise sold to P.J. Quinn of Toronto on October 18 on the condition that the team operate in Quebec City for 1918-19 season. Quinn did not attend the November League meeting and Quebec did not play in 1918-19.

1919-20 — NHL reactivated Quebec Bulldogs franchise. Former Quebec players returned to the club. New Mount Royal Arena became home of Canadiens. Toronto Arenas changed name to St. Patricks. Clubs played 24-game split schedule.

1920-21 — H.P. Thompson of Hamilton, Ontario made application for the purchase of an NHL franchise. Quebec franchise shifted to Hamilton with other NHL teams providing players to strengthen the club.

1921-22 — Split schedule abandoned. First and second place teams at the end of full schedule to play for championship.

1922-23 — Clubs agreed that players could not be sold or traded to clubs in any other league without first being offered to all other clubs in the NHL. Norman Albert made the first broadcast of a hockey game on February 8, 1923. The first NHL game was broadcast on February 14, 1923. Foster Hewitt called his first game on February 16, 1923. All games were broadcast on Toronto radio station CFCA.

1923-24 — Ottawa's new 10,000-seat arena opened. First U.S. franchise granted to Boston for following season.

Dr. Cecil Hart Trophy donated to NHL to be awarded to the player judged most useful to his team.

1924-25 — New franchises granted to Boston and Montreal (later named Maroons). NHL now six team league with two clubs in Montreal. Inaugural game in new Montreal Forum played November 29, 1924 as Canadiens defeated Toronto 7-1. Hamilton finished first in the standings, receiving a bye into the finals. But Hamilton players, demanding $200 each for additional games in the playoffs, went on strike. The NHL suspended all players, fining them $200 each. Stanley Cup finalist to be the winner of NHL semi-final between Toronto and Canadiens.

Lady Byng Trophy donated to NHL.

Clubs played 30-game schedule.

1925-26 — Hamilton club dropped from NHL. Players signed by new New York Americans franchise. Pittsburgh Pirates granted franchise. Prince of Wales Trophy donated to NHL.

Clubs played 36-game schedule.

1926-27 — New York Rangers granted franchise May 15, 1926. Chicago Black Hawks and Detroit Cougars granted franchises September 25, 1926. NHL now ten-team league with an American and a Canadian Division.

Stanley Cup came under the control of NHL. In previous seasons, winners of the now-defunct Western or Pacific Coast leagues would play NHL champion in Cup finals.

Toronto franchise sold to a new company controlled by Hugh Aird and Conn Smythe. Name changed from St. Patricks to Maple Leafs.

Clubs played 44-game schedule.

The Montreal Canadiens donated the Vezina Trophy to be awarded to the team allowing the fewest goals-against in regular season play. The winning team would, in turn, present the trophy to the goaltender playing in the greatest number of games during the season.

1930-31 — Detroit franchise changed name from Cougars to Falcons. Pittsburgh transferred to Philadelphia for one season. Pirates changed name to Philadelphia Quakers. Trading deadline for teams set at February 15 of each year. NHL approved operation of farm teams by Rangers, Americans, Falcons and Bruins. Four-sided electric arena clock first demonstrated.

1931-32 — Philadelphia dropped out. Ottawa withdrew for one season. New Maple Leaf Gardens completed.

Clubs played 48-game schedule.

1932-33 — Detroit franchise changed name from Falcons to Red Wings. Franchise application received from St. Louis but refused because of additional travel costs. Ottawa team resumed play.

1933-34 — First All-Star Game played as a benefit for injured player Ace Bailey. Leafs defeated All-Stars 7-3 in Toronto.

1934-35 — Ottawa franchise transferred to St. Louis. Team called St. Louis Eagles and consisted largely of Ottawa's players.

1935-36 — Ottawa-St. Louis franchise terminated. Montreal Canadiens finished season with very poor record. To strengthen the club, NHL gave Canadiens first call on the services of all French-Canadian players for three seasons.

1937-38 — Second benefit All-Star game staged November 2 in Montreal in aid of the family of the late Canadiens star Howie Morenz.

Montreal Maroons withdrew from the NHL on June 22, 1938, leaving seven clubs in the League.

1938-39 — Expenses for each club regulated at $5 per man per day for meals and $2.50 per man per day for accommodation.

1939-40 — Benefit All-Star Game played October 29, 1939 in Montreal for the children of the late Albert (Babe) Siebert.

1940-41 — Ross-Tyer puck adopted as the official puck of the NHL. Early in the season it was apparent that this puck was too soft. The Spalding puck was adopted in its place.

On May 16, 1941, Arthur Ross, NHL governor from Boston, donated a perpetual trophy to be awarded annually to the player voted outstanding in the league. Due to wartime restrictions, the trophy was never awarded.

1941-42 — New York Americans changed name to Brooklyn Americans.

1942-43 — Brooklyn Americans withdrew from NHL, leaving six teams: Boston, Chicago, Detroit, Montreal, New York and Toronto. Playoff format saw first-place team play third-place team and second play fourth.

Clubs played 50-game schedule.

Frank Calder, president of the NHL since its inception, died in Montreal. Meryn "Red" Dutton, former manager of the New York Americans, became president. The NHL commissioned the Calder Memorial Trophy to be awarded to the League's outstanding rookie each year.

1945-46 — Philadelphia, Los Angeles and San Francisco applied for NHL franchises.

The Philadelphia Arena Company of the American Hockey League applied for an injunction to prevent the possible operation of an NHL franchise in that city.

1946-47 — Mervyn Dutton retired as president of the NHL prior to the start of the season. He was succeeded by Clarence S. Campbell.

Individual trophy winners and all-star team members to receive $1,000 awards.

Playoff guarantees for players introduced.

Clubs played 60-game schedule.

1947-48 — The first annual All-Star Game for the benefit of the players' pension fund was played when the All-Stars defeated the Stanley Cup Champion Toronto Maple Leafs 4-3 in Toronto on October 13, 1947.

Criteria for awarding Art Ross Trophy changed. Now awarded to top scorer. Elmer Lach was its first winner.

Philadelphia and Los Angeles franchise applications refused.

National Hockey League Pension Society formed.

1949-50 — Clubs played 70-game schedule.

First intra-league draft held April 30, 1950. Clubs allowed to protect 30 players. Remaining players available for $25,000 each.

1951-52 — Referees included in the League's pension plan.

1952-53 — In May of 1952, City of Cleveland applied for NHL franchise. Application denied. In March of 1953, the Cleveland Barons of the AHL challenged the NHL champions for the Stanley Cup. The NHL governors did not accept this challenge.

1953-54 — The James Norris Memorial Trophy presented to the NHL for annual presentation to the League's best defenseman.

Intra-league draft rules amended to allow teams to protect 18 skaters and two goaltenders, claiming price reduced to $15,000.

1954-55 — Each arena to operate an "out-of-town" scoreboard.

1956-57 — Referees and linesmen to wear shirts of black and white vertical stripes. Standardized signals for referees and linesmen introduced.

1960-61 — Canadian National Exhibition, City of Toronto and NHL reach agreement for the construction of a Hockey Hall of Fame on the CNE grounds. Hall opens on August 26, 1961.

1963-64 — Player development league established with clubs operated by NHL franchises located in Minneapolis, St. Paul, Indianapolis, Omaha and, beginning in 1964-65, Tulsa. First universal amateur draft took place. All players of qualifying age (17) unaffected by sponsorship of junior teams available to be drafted.

1964-65 — Conn Smythe Trophy presented to the NHL to be awarded annually to the outstanding player in the Stanley Cup playoffs.

Minimum age of players subject to amateur draft changed to 18.

1965-66 — NHL announced expansion plans for a second six-team division to begin play in 1967-68.

1966-67 — Fourteen applications for NHL franchises received.

Lester Patrick Trophy presented to the NHL to be awarded annually for outstanding service to hockey in the United States.

NHL sponsorship of junior teams ceased, making all players of qualifying age not already on NHL-sponsored lists eligible for the amateur draft.

1967-68 — Six new teams added: California Seals, Los Angeles Kings, Minnesota North Stars, Philadelphia Flyers, Pittsburgh Penguins, St. Louis Blues. New teams to play in West Division. Remaining six teams to play in East Division.

Minimum age of players subject to amateur draft changed to 20.

Clubs played 74-game schedule.

Clarence S. Campbell Trophy awarded to team finishing the regular season in first place in West Division.

California Seals change name to Oakland Seals on December 8, 1967.

1968-69 — Clubs played 76-game schedule.

Amateur draft expanded to cover any amateur player of qualifying age throughout the world.

1970-71 — Two new teams added: Buffalo Sabres and Vancouver Canucks. These teams joined East Division: Chicago switched to West Division. Oakland Seals change name to California Golden Seals prior to season.

Clubs played 78-game schedule.

1971-72 — Playoff format amended. In each division, first to play fourth; second to play third.

1972-73 — Soviet Nationals and Canadian NHL stars play eight pre-season games. Canadians win 4-3-1.

Two new teams added. Atlanta Flames join West Division; New York Islanders join East Division.

1974-75 — Two new teams added: Kansas City Scouts and Washington Capitals. Teams realigned into two nine-team conferences, the Prince of Wales made up of the Norris and Adams Divisions, and the Clarence Campbell made up of the Smythe and Patrick Divisions.

Clubs played 80-game schedule.

1976-77 — California franchise transferred to Cleveland. Team named Cleveland Barons. Kansas City franchise transferred to Denver. Team named Colorado Rockies.

1977-78 — Clarence S. Campbell retires as NHL president. Succeeded by John A. Ziegler, Jr.

1978-79 — Cleveland and Minnesota franchises merge, leaving NHL with 17 teams. Merged team placed in Adams Division, playing home games in Minnesota.

Minimum age of players subject to amateur draft changed to 19.

1979-80 — Four new teams added: Edmonton Oilers, Hartford Whalers, Quebec Nordiques and Winnipeg Jets.

Minimum age of players subject to NHL Draft changed to 18.

1980-81 — Atlanta franchise shifted to Calgary, retaining "Flames" name.

1981-82 — Teams realigned within existing divisions. New groupings based on geographical areas. Unbalanced schedule adopted.

1982-83 — Colorado Rockies franchise shifted to East Rutherford, New Jersey. Team named New Jersey Devils. Franchise moved to Patrick Division from Smythe; Winnipeg moved to Smythe from Norris.

1991-92 — San Jose Sharks added, making the NHL a 22-team league. NHL celebrates 75th Anniversary Season. The 1991-92 regular season suspended due to a players' strike on April 1, 1992. Play resumed April 12, 1992.

1992-93 — Gil Stein named NHL president (October, 1992). Gary Bettman named first NHL Commissioner (February, 1993). Ottawa Senators and Tampa Bay Lightning added, making the NHL a 24-team league. NHL celebrates Stanley Cup Centennial. Clubs played 84-game schedule.

NHL History — *continued*

1993-94 — Mighty Ducks of Anaheim and Florida Panthers added, making the NHL a 26-team league. Minnesota franchise shifted to Dallas, team named Dallas Stars. Prince of Wales and Clarence Campbell Conferences renamed Eastern and Western. Adams, Patrick, Norris and Smythe Divisions renamed Northeast, Atlantic, Central and Pacific. Winnipeg moved to Central Division from Pacific; Tampa Bay moved to Atlantic Division from Central; Pittsburgh moved to Northeast Division from Atlantic.

1994-95 — A lockout resulted in the cancellation of 468 games from October 1, 1994 to January 19, 1995. Clubs played a 48-game schedule that began January 20, 1995 and ended May 3, 1995. No inter-conference games were played.

1995-96 — Quebec franchise transferred to Denver. Team named Colorado Avalanche and placed in Pacific Division of Western Conference. Clubs to play 82-game schedule.

1996-97 — Winnipeg franchise transferred to Phoenix. Team named Phoenix Coyotes and placed in Central Division of Western Conference.

1997-98 — Hartford franchise transferred to Raleigh. Team named Carolina Hurricanes and remains in Northeast Division of Eastern Conference.

1998-99 — The addition of the Nashville Predators made the NHL a 27-team league and brought about the creation of two new divisions and a League-wide realignment in preparation for further expansion to 30 teams by 2000-2001. Nashville was added to the Central Division of the Western Conference, while Toronto moved into the Northeast Division of the Eastern Conference. Pittsburgh was shifted from the Northeast to the Atlantic, while Carolina left the Northeast for the newly created Southeast Division of the Eastern Conference. Florida, Tampa Bay and Washington also joined the Southeast. In the Western Conference, Calgary, Colorado, Edmonton and Vancouver make up the new Northwest Division. Dallas and Phoenix moved from the Central to the Pacific Division.

The NHL retired uniform number 99 in honor of all-time scoring leader Wayne Gretzky who retired at the end of the season.

1999-2000 — Atlanta Thrashers added, making the NHL a 28-team league.

2000-01 — Columbus Blue Jackets and Minnesota Wild added, making the NHL a 30-team league.

2003-04 — First outdoor NHL game. 57,167 attend Heritage Classic at Edmonton's Commonwealth Stadium. Montreal defeated Edmonton 4-3, November 22, 2003.

2004-05 — A lockout resulted in the cancellation of the season.

2007-08 — NHL-record crowd of 71,217 fills Buffalo's Ralph Wilson Stadium on New Year's Day for the 2008 Winter Classic, the first NHL outdoor game in the United States. Sidney Crosby's shootout goal gives the Pittsburgh Penguins a 2-1 win over the Buffalo Sabres.

2011-12 — Atlanta franchise transferred to Winnipeg. Team named Winnipeg Jets.

2012-13 — A lockout resulted in the cancellation of 510 games from October 11, 2012 to January 18, 2013. Clubs played a 48-game schedule that began January 19, 2013 and ended April 27, 2013. No inter-conference games were played.

2013-14 — The NHL's clubs are re-aligned into two conferences each consisting of two divisions. The new alignment places several clubs in more geographically appropriate groupings. The Eastern Conference is made up of the Atlantic and Metropolitan divisions, each with eight teams. The Western Conference is made up of the Central and Pacific divisions, each with seven teams. All 30 teams play in all 30 arenas at least once a season.

2014-15 — Phoenix franchise renamed Arizona Coyotes.

2015-16 — Las Vegas franchise added, to begin play in 2017-18. The team will be placed in the Pacific Division of the Western Conference.

Major Rule Changes

1910-11 — Game changed from two 30-minute periods to three 20-minute periods.

1911-12 — National Hockey Association (forerunner of the NHL) originated six-man hockey, replacing seven-man game.

1917-18 — Goalies permitted to fall to the ice to make saves. Previously a goaltender was penalized for dropping to the ice.

1918-19 — Penalty rules amended. For minor fouls, substitutes not allowed until penalized player had served three minutes. For major fouls, no substitutes for five minutes. For match fouls, no substitutes allowed for the remainder of the game.

With the addition of two lines painted on the ice twenty feet from center, three playing zones were created, producing a forty-foot neutral center ice area in which forward passing was permitted. Kicking the puck was permitted in this neutral zone.

Tabulation of assists began.

1921-22 — Goaltenders allowed to pass the puck forward up to their own blue line.

Overtime limited to twenty minutes.

Minor penalties changed from three minutes to two minutes.

1923-24 — Match foul defined as actions deliberately injuring or disabling an opponent. For such actions, a player was fined not less than $50 and ruled off the ice for the balance of the game. A player assessed a match penalty may be replaced by a substitute at the end of 20 minutes. Match penalty recipients must meet with the League president who can assess additional punishment.

1925-26 — Delayed penalty rules introduced. Each team must have a minimum of four players on the ice at all times.

Two rules were amended to encourage offense: No more than two defensemen permitted to remain inside a team's own blue line when the puck has left the defensive zone. A faceoff to be called for ragging the puck unless shorthanded.

Team captains only players allowed to talk to referees.

Goaltender's leg pads limited to 12-inch width.

Timekeeper's gong to mark end of periods rather than referee's whistle. Teams to dress a maximum of 12 players for each game from a roster of no more than 14 players.

1926-27 — Blue lines repositioned to sixty feet from each goal-line, thereby enlarging the neutral zone and standardizing distance from blue line to goal.

Uniform goal nets adopted throughout NHL with goal posts securely fastened to the ice.

1927-28 — To further encourage offense, forward passes allowed in defending and neutral zones and goaltender's pads reduced in width from 12 to 10 inches.

Game standardized at three twenty-minute periods of stop-time separated by ten-minute intermissions.

Teams to change ends after each period.

Ten minutes of sudden-death overtime to be played if the score is tied after regulation time.

Minor penalty to be assessed to any player other than a goaltender for deliberately picking up the puck while it is in play. Minor penalty to be assessed for deliberately shooting the puck out of play.

The Art Ross goal net adopted as the official net of the NHL.

Maximum length of hockey sticks limited to 53 inches measured from heel of blade to end of handle. No minimum length stipulated.

Home teams given choice of end to defend at start of game.

1928-29 — Forward passing permitted in defensive and neutral zones and into attacking zone if pass receiver is in neutral zone when pass is made. No forward passing allowed inside attacking zone.

Minor penalty to be assessed to any player who delays the game by passing the puck back into his defensive zone.

Ten-minute overtime without sudden-death provision to be played in games tied after regulation time. Games tied after this overtime period declared a draw.

Exclusive of goaltenders, team to dress at least 8 and no more than 12 skaters.

NHL Attendance

| Season | Regular Season | | Playoffs | | Total |
	Games	Attendance	Games	Attendance	Attendance
2016-17	1,230	21,545,024	87	1,606,364	23,151,388
2015-16	1,230	21,615,397	91	1,685,451	23,300,848
2014-15	1,230	21,533,419	89	1,701,336	23,234,755
2013-14	1,230	21,758,902	93	1,775,557	23,534,459
2012-13	720 [4]	12,792,707	86	1,631,683	14,424,390
2011-12	1,230	21,468,121	86	1,591,856	23,059,977
2010-11	1,230	21,112,139	89	1,667,624	22,779,763
2009-10	1,230	20,996,455	89	1,702,371	22,698,826
2008-09	1,230	21,475,223	87	1,639,602	23,114,825
2007-08	1,230	21,236,255	85	1,587,054	22,823,309
2006-07	1,230	20,861,787	81	1,496,501	22,358,288
2005-06	1,230	20,854,169	83	1,530,405	22,384,574
2004-05	....	....	....	....	....
2003-04	1,230	20,356,199	89	1,708,691	22,064,890
2002-03	1,230	20,408,704	89	1,636,120	22,044,824
2001-02	1,230	20,614,613	90	1,691,174	22,305,787
2000-01	1,230	20,373,379	86	1,584,011	21,957,390
1999-2000	1,148	18,800,139	83	1,524,629	20,324,768
1998-99	1,107	18,001,741	86	1,509,411	19,511,152
1997-98	1,066	17,264,678	82	1,507,416	18,772,094
1996-97	1,066	17,640,529	82	1,494,878	19,135,407
1995-96	1,066 [3]	17,041,614	86	1,540,140	18,581,754
1994-95	624 [3]	9,233,884	81	1,329,130	10,563,014
1993-94	1,092	16,105,604 [2]	90	1,440,095	17,545,699
1992-93	1,008	14,158,177 [1]	83	1,346,034	15,504,211
1991-92	880	12,769,676	86	1,327,920	14,097,596
1990-91	840	12,343,897	92	1,442,203	13,786,100
1989-90	840	12,579,651	85	1,355,593	13,935,244
1988-89	840	12,417,969	82	1,327,214	13,745,183
1987-88	840	12,117,512	83	1,336,901	13,454,413
1986-87	840	11,855,880	87	1,383,967	13,239,847
1985-86	840	11,621,000	72	1,152,503	12,773,503
1984-85	840	11,633,730	70	1,107,500	12,741,230
1983-84	840	11,359,386	70	1,107,400	12,466,786
1982-83	840	11,020,610	66	1,088,222	12,028,832
1981-82	840	10,710,894	71	1,058,948	11,769,842
1980-81	840	10,726,198	68	966,390	11,692,588
1979-80	840	10,533,623	67	976,699	11,510,322
1978-79	680	7,758,053	45	694,521	8,452,574
1977-78	720	8,526,564	45	686,634	9,213,198
1976-77	720	8,563,890	44	646,279	9,210,169
1975-76	720	9,103,761	48	726,279	9,830,040

NHL Expansion: the NHL operated as a six-team league from 1942-43 to 1966-67. Six teams were added in 1967-68: California (later to move to Cleveland), Los Angeles, Minnesota (later to move to Dallas), Philadelphia, Pittsburgh and St. Louis. In 1970-71: Buffalo and Vancouver. In 1972-73: Atlanta (later to move to Calgary) and NY Islanders. In 1974-75: Kansas City (later to move to Colorado and then to New Jersey) and Washington. In 1979-80, Hartford (later to move to Carolina), Edmonton, Quebec (later to move to Colorado) and Winnipeg (later to move to Phoenix). In 1991-92, San Jose. In 1992-93, Ottawa and Tampa Bay. In 1993-94, Anaheim and Florida. In 1998-99, Nashville. In 1999-2000, Atlanta (later to move to Winnipeg). In 2000-01, Columbus and Minnesota.

[1] Includes 24 neutral site games • [2] Includes 26 neutral site games
[3] Lockout resulted in the cancellation of 468 games. • [4] Lockout resulted in the cancellation of 510 games.

Major Rule Changes — *continued*

1929-30 — Forward passing permitted inside all three zones but not permitted across either blue line.

Kicking the puck allowed, but a goal cannot be scored by kicking the puck in.

No more than three players including the goaltender may remain in their defensive zone when the puck has gone up ice. Minor penalties to be assessed for the first two violations of this rule in a game; major penalties thereafter.

Goaltenders forbidden to hold the puck. Pucks caught must be cleared immediately. For infringement of this rule, a faceoff to be taken ten feet in front of the goal with no player except the goaltender standing between the faceoff spot and the goal-line.

Highsticking penalties introduced.

Maximum number of players in uniform increased from 12 to 15.

December 21, 1929 — Forward passing rules instituted at the beginning of the 1929-30 season more than doubled number of goals scored. Partway through the season, these rules were further amended to read, "No attacking player allowed to precede the play when entering the opposing defensive zone." This is similar to modern offside rule.

1930-31 — A player without a complete stick ruled out of play and forbidden from taking part in further action until a new stick is obtained. A player who has broken his stick must obtain a replacement at his bench.

A further refinement of the offside rule stated that the puck must first be propelled into the attacking zone before any player of the attacking side can enter that zone; for infringement of this rule a faceoff to take place at the spot where the infraction took place.

1931-32 — Though there is no record of a team attempting to play with two goaltenders on the ice, a rule was instituted which stated that each team was allowed only one goaltender on the ice at one time.

Attacking players forbidden to impede the movement or obstruct the vision of opposing goaltenders.

Defending players with the exception of the goaltender forbidden from falling on the puck within 10 feet of the net.

1932-33 — Each team to have captain on the ice at all times. Maximum number of players in uniform reduced to 14 from 15.

If the goaltender is removed from the ice to serve a penalty, the manager of the club to appoint a substitute.

Match penalty with substitution after five minutes instituted for kicking another player.

1933-34 — Number of players permitted to stand in defensive zone restricted to three including goaltender.

Visible time clocks required in each rink.

Two referees replace one referee and one linesman.

1934-35 — Penalty shot awarded when a player is tripped and thus prevented from having a clear shot on goal, having no player to pass to other than the offending player. Shot taken from inside a 10-foot circle located 38 feet from the goal. The goaltender must not advance more than one foot from his goal-line when the shot is taken.

1937-38 — Rules introduced governing icing the puck.

Penalty shot awarded when a player other than a goaltender falls on the puck within 10 feet of the goal.

1938-39 — Penalty shot modified to allow puck carrier to skate in before shooting.

One referee and one linesman replace two referee system.

Blue line widened to 12 inches.

Maximum number of players in uniform increased from 14 to 15.

1939-40 — A substitute replacing a goaltender removed from ice to serve a penalty may use a goaltender's stick and gloves but no other goaltending equipment.

1940-41 — Flooding ice surface between periods made obligatory.

1941-42 — Penalty shots classified as minor and major. Minor shot to be taken from a line 28 feet from the goal. Major shot, awarded when a player is tripped with only the goaltender to beat, permits the player taking the penalty shot to skate right into the goalkeeper and shoot from point-blank range.

One referee and two linesmen employed to officiate games.

For playoffs, standby minor league goaltenders employed by NHL as emergency substitutes.

1942-43 — Because of wartime restrictions on train scheduling, regular-season overtime was discontinued on November 21, 1942.

Player limit reduced from 15 to 14. Minimum of 12 men in uniform abolished.

1943-44 — Red line at center ice introduced to speed up the game and reduce offside calls. This rule is considered to mark the beginning of the modern era in the NHL.

1945-46 — Goal indicator lights synchronized with official time clock required at all rinks.

1946-47 — System of signals by officials to indicate infractions introduced.

Linesmen from neutral cities employed for all games.

1947-48 — Goal awarded when a player with the puck has an open net to shoot at and a thrown stick prevents the shot on goal. Major penalty to any player who throws his stick in any zone other than defending zone. If a stick is thrown by a player in his defending zone but the thrown stick is not considered to have prevented a goal, a penalty shot is awarded.

All playoff games played until a winner determined, with 20-minute sudden-death overtime periods separated by 10-minute intermissions.

1949-50 — Ice surface painted white.

Clubs allowed to dress 17 players exclusive of goaltenders.

Major penalties incurred by goaltenders served by a member of the goaltender's team instead of resulting in a penalty shot.

1950-51 — Each team required to provide an emergency goaltender in attendance with full equipment at each game for use by either team in the event of illness or injury to a regular goaltender.

1951-52 — Home teams to wear basic white uniforms; visiting teams basic colored uniforms.

Goal crease enlarged from 3 × 7 feet to 4 × 8 feet.

Number of players in uniform reduced to 15 plus goaltenders.

Faceoff circles enlarged from 10-foot to 15-foot radius.

1952-53 — Teams permitted to dress 15 skaters on the road and 16 at home.

1953-54 — Number of players in uniform set at 16 plus goaltenders.

1954-55 — Number of players in uniform set at 18 plus goaltenders up to December 1 and 16 plus goaltenders thereafter. Teams agree to wear colored uniforms at home and white uniforms on the road.

1956-57 — Player serving a minor penalty allowed to return to ice when a goal is scored by opposing team.

1959-60 — Players prevented from leaving their benches to enter into an altercation. Substitutions permitted providing substitutes do not enter into altercation.

1960-61 — Number of players in uniform set at 16 plus goaltenders.

1961-62 — Penalty shots to be taken by the player against whom the foul was committed. In the event of a penalty shot called in a situation where a particular player hasn't been fouled, the penalty shot to be taken by any player on the ice when the foul was committed.

1964-65 — No body contact on faceoffs.

In playoff games, each team to have its substitute goaltender dressed in his regular uniform except for leg pads and body protector. All previous rules governing standby goaltenders terminated.

1965-66 — Teams required to dress two goaltenders for each regular-season game. Maximum stick length increased to 55 inches.

1966-67 — Substitution allowed on coincidental major penalties.

Between-periods intermissions fixed at 15 minutes.

1967-68 — If a penalty incurred by a goaltender is a co-incident major, the penalty to be served by a player of the goaltender's team on the ice at the time the penalty was called. Limit of curvature of hockey stick blade set at 1½ inches.

1969-70 — Limit of curvature of hockey stick blade set at 1 inch.

1970-71 — Home teams to wear basic white uniforms; visiting teams to wear basic colored uniforms.

Limit of curvature of hockey stick blade set at ½ inch.

Minor penalty for deliberately shooting the puck out of the playing area.

1971-72 — Number of players in uniform set at 17 plus 2 goaltenders.

Third man to enter an altercation assessed an automatic game misconduct penalty.

1972-73 — Minimum width of stick blade reduced to 2 inches from 2½ inches.

1974-75 — Bench minor penalty imposed if a penalized player does not proceed directly and immediately to the penalty box.

1976-77 — Rule dealing with fighting amended to provide a major and game misconduct penalty for any player who is clearly the instigator of a fight.

1977-78 — Teams requesting a stick measurement to be assessed a minor penalty in the event that the measured stick does not violate the rules.

1979-80 — Wearing of helmets made mandatory for players entering the NHL.

1980-81 — Maximum stick length increased to 58 inches.

1981-82 — If both of a team's listed goaltenders are incapacitated, the team can dress and play any eligible goaltender who is available.

1982-83 — Number of players in uniform set at 18 plus 2 goaltenders.

1983-84 — Five-minute sudden-death overtime to be played in regular-season games that are tied at the end of regulation time.

1985-86 — Substitutions allowed in the event of co-incidental minor penalties. Maximum stick length increased to 60 inches.

1986-87 — Delayed off-side is no longer in effect once the players of the offending team have cleared the opponents' defensive zone.

1990-91 — The goal lines, blue lines, defensive zone face-off circles and markings all moved one foot out from the end boards, creating 11 feet of room behind the nets and shrinking the neutral zone from 60 to 58 feet.

1991-92 — Video replays employed to assist referees in goal/no goal situations. Size of goal crease increased. Crease changed to semi-circular configuration. Time clock to record tenths of a second in last minute of each period and overtime. Major and game misconduct penalty for checking from behind into boards. Penalties added for crease infringement and unnecessary contact with goaltender. Goal disallowed if puck enters net while a player of the attacking team is standing on the goal crease line, is in the goal crease or places his stick in the goal crease.

1992-93 — No substitutions allowed in the event of coincidental minor penalties called when both teams are at full strength. Minor penalty for attempting to draw a penalty ("diving"). Major and game misconduct penalty for checking from behind into goal frame. Game misconduct penalty for instigating a fight. High sticking redefined to include any use of the stick above waist-height. Previous rule stipulated shoulder-height.

1993-94 — High sticking redefined to allow goals scored with a high stick below the height of the crossbar of the goal frame.

1996-97 — Maximum stick length increased to 63 inches. All players must be clear of the attacking zone prior to the puck being shot into that zone. The opportunity to "tag-up" and return into the zone has been removed.

1998-99 — The league instituted a two-referee system with each team to play 20 regular-season games with two referees and a pair of linesmen. Goal line moved to 13 feet from end boards. Goal crease altered to extend one foot beyond each goal post (eight feet across in total. Sides of crease squared off, extending 4'6". Only the top of the crease remains rounded. Only the top of the crease remains rounded.

1999-2000 — Each team to play 25 home and 25 road games using the two-referee system. Crease rule revised to implement a "no harm, no foul, no video review" standard. Teams to play with four skaters and a goaltender in regular-season overtime. If a goal is scored in regular-season overtime, the winner is awarded two points and the loser one point. In no goal is scored in overtime, both teams are awarded one point.

2000-01 — All games to be played using the two-referee system.

2002-03 — "Hurry-up" faceoff and line-change rules implemented.

2003-04 — Home teams to wear basic colored uniforms; visiting teams to wear basic white uniforms. Maximum length of goaltender's pads set at 38 inches.

2005-06 — The NHL adopted a comprehensive package of rule changes that included the following:

Goal line moved to 11 feet from end boards; blue lines moved to 75 feet from end boards, reducing neutral zone from 54 feet to 50 feet. Center red line eliminated for two-line passes. "Tag-up" off-side rule reinstituted. Goaltender not permitted to play the puck outside a designated trapezoid-shaped area behind the net. A team that ices the puck is not permitted to make any player substitutions prior to the ensuing faceoff. A player who instigates a fight in the final five minutes of regulation time or at any time of overtime to receive a minor, a major, a misconduct and an automatic one-game suspension. The size of goaltender equipment reduced. If a game remains tied after five minutes of overtime, winner determined by shootout.

2011-12 — Rules and penalties modified to address contact with the head.

2015-16 — Teams to play with three skaters and a goaltender in regular-season overtime. Coaches may request video review of off-sides or goaltender interference when a goal is scored.

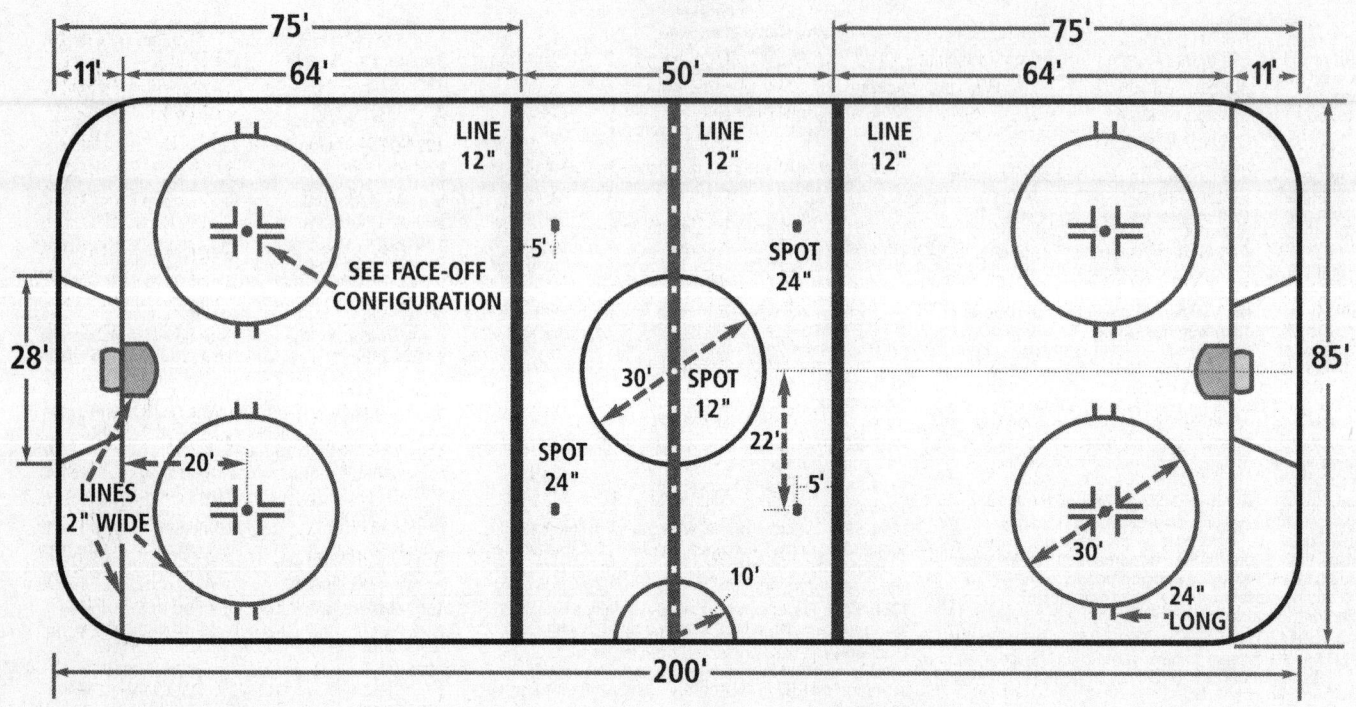

NHL RINK DIMENSIONS

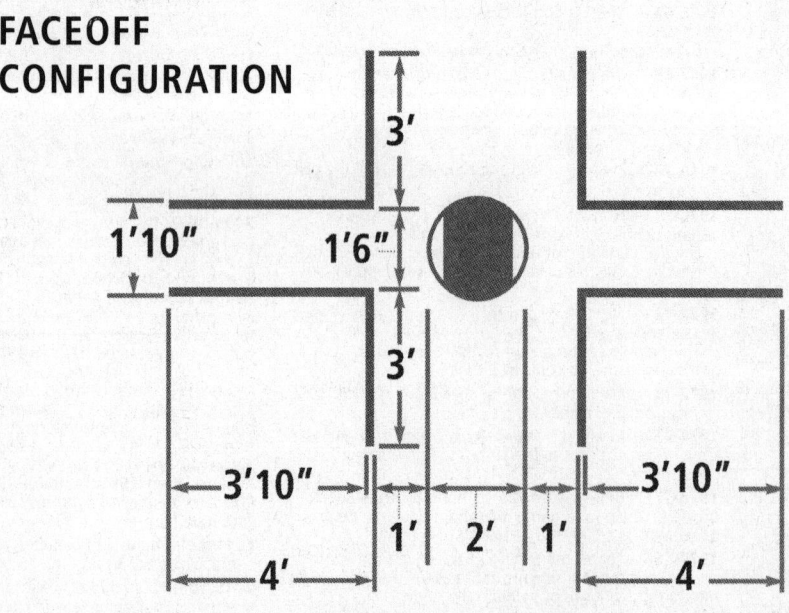

FACEOFF
CONFIGURATION

ALL LINES 2" IN WIDTH

Regular-Season NHL Outdoor Games

Date	Location	Venue	Attendance	Final Score				Game-Winning Goal	Time of GWG	Temperature
Nov. 22, 2003[¶]	Edmonton, Alberta	Commonwealth Stadium	57,167	Montreal	4	Edmonton	3	Richard Zednik	14:18 (3rd)	0°F/–18°C
Jan. 1, 2008*	Buffalo, New York	Ralph Wilson Stadium	71,217	Pittsburgh	2	Buffalo	1	Sidney Crosby	Shootout	33°F/+1°C
Jan. 1, 2009*	Chicago, Illinois	Wrigley Field	40,818	Detroit	6	Chicago	4	Brian Rafalski	3:07 (3rd)	32°F/0°C
Jan. 1, 2010*	Boston, Massachusetts	Fenway Park	38,112	Boston	2	Philadelphia	1	Marco Sturm	1:57 (OT)	35°F/+2°C
Jan. 1, 2011*	Pittsburgh, Pennsylvania	Heinz Field	68,111	Washington	3	Pittsburgh	1	Eric Fehr	11:59 (3rd)	50°F/+10°C
Feb. 20, 2011[¶]	Calgary, Alberta	McMahon Stadium	41,022	Calgary	4	Montreal	0	Rene Bourque	8:09 (1st)	18°F/–8°C
Jan. 2, 2012*	Philadelphia, Pennsylvania	Citizens Bank Park	46,967	NY Rangers	3	Philadelphia	2	Brad Richards	5:21 (3rd)	41°F/+5°C
Jan. 1, 2014*	Ann Arbor, Michigan	Michigan Stadium	105,491	Toronto	3	Detroit	2	Tyler Bozak	Shootout	13°F/–11°C
Jan. 25, 2014[§]	Los Angeles, California	Dodger Stadium	54,099	Anaheim	3	Los Angeles	0	Corey Perry	2:45 (1st)	62°F/+17°C
Jan. 26, 2014[§]	New York, New York	Yankee Stadium	50,105	NY Rangers	7	New Jersey	3	Mats Zuccarello	12:44 (2nd)	25°F/–4°C
Jan. 29, 2014[§]	New York, New York	Yankee Stadium	50,027	NY Rangers	2	NY Islanders	1	Daniel Carcillo	4:36 (3rd)	22°F/–6°C
Mar. 1, 2014[§]	Chicago, Illinois	Soldier Field	62,921	Pittsburgh	1	Chicago	5	Jonathan Toews	10:47 (2nd)	17°F/–8°C
Mar. 2, 2014[¶]	Vancouver, B.C.	BC Place[•]	54,194	Ottawa	4	Vancouver	2	Cody Ceci	10:11 (2nd)	37°F/+3°C
Jan. 1, 2015*	Washington, D.C.	Nationals Park	43,832	Chicago	3	Washington	2	Troy Brouwer	19:48 (3rd)	37°F/+3°C
Feb. 21, 2015[§]	Santa Clara, California	Levi's Stadium	70,205	Los Angeles	2	San Jose	1	Marian Gaborik	4:04 (3rd)	57°F/+14°C
Jan. 1, 2016*	Foxborough, Mass.	Gillette Stadium	67,246	Montreal	5	Boston	1	Paul Byron	2:00 (2nd)	41°F/+5°C
Feb. 21, 2016[§]	Minneapolis, Minnesota	TCF Bank Stadium	50,426	Minnesota	6	Chicago	1	Thomas Vanek	7:10 (1st)	37°F/+3°C
Feb. 27, 2016[§]	Denver, Colorado	Coors Field	50,095	Detroit	5	Colorado	3	Brad Richards	19:00 (3rd)	65°F/+18°C
Oct. 23, 2016[¶]	Winnipeg, Manitoba	Investors Group Field	33,230	Edmonton	3	Winnipeg	0	Mark Letestu	9:24 (2nd)	50°F/+10°C
Jan. 1. 2017[‡]	Toronto, Ontario	BMO Field	40,148	Detroit	4	Toronto	5	Auston Matthews	3:40 (OT)	37°F/+3°C
Jan. 2, 2017[§]	St. Louis, Missouri	Busch Stadium	46,556	Chicago	1	St. Louis	4	Vladimir Tarasenko	12:05 (3rd)	33°F/+1°C
Feb. 25, 2017[§]	Pittsburgh, Pennsylvania	Heinz Field	67,318	Philadelphia	2	Pittsburgh	4	Mark Cullen	1:50 (3rd)	46°F/+8°C
Dec. 16, 2017[‡‡]	Ottawa, Ontario	Lansdowne Park	**24,000	Montreal		Ottawa				
Jan. 1, 2018*	New York, New York	Citi Field	**41,922	Buffalo		NY Rangers				
Mar. 3, 2018[§]	Annapolis, Maryland	Navy-Marine Corps Memorial Stadium	**34,000	Toronto		Washington				

** - seating capacity

* - Bridgestone Winter Classic   [¶] - Tim Hortons Heritage Classic   [§] - Coors Light NHL Stadium Series   [‡] - Centennial Classic   [•] - retractable roof closed   [‡‡] - Scotiabank NHL 100 Classic

Regular-Season NHL Games Played Outside North America

Date	Location	Venue	Attendance	Final Score				Game-Winning Goal	Time of GWG
Oct. 3, 1997	Tokyo, Japan	Yoyogi Arena	10,500	Vancouver	3	Anaheim	2	Pavel Bure	14:41 (2nd)
Oct. 4, 1997	Tokyo, Japan	Yoyogi Arena	10,500	Anaheim	3	Vancouver	2	J.J. Daigneault	13:38 (3rd)
Oct. 9, 1998	Tokyo, Japan	Yoyogi Arena	10,000	San Jose	3	Calgary	3	...	...
Oct. 10, 1998	Tokyo, Japan	Yoyogi Arena	10,000	Calgary	5	San Jose	3	Dave Roche	11:41 (2nd)
Oct. 7, 2000	Saitama, Japan	Saitama Super Arena	13,849	Nashville	3	Pittsburgh	1	Vitali Yachmanev	8:01 (2nd)
Oct. 8, 2000	Saitama, Japan	Saitama Super Arena	13,426	Pittsburgh	3	Nashville	1	Martin Straka	16:16 (3rd)
Sept. 29, 2007	London, England	O2 Arena	17,551	Los Angeles	4	Anaheim	1	Rob Blake	10:15 (2nd)
Sept. 30, 2007	London, England	O2 Arena	17,300	Anaheim	4	Los Angeles	1	Chris Kunitz	15:19 (1st)
Oct. 4, 2008	Prague, Czech Republic	O2 Arena	17,085	NY Rangers	2	Tampa Bay	1	Brandon Dubinsky	14:16 (3rd)
Oct. 4, 2008	Stockholm, Sweden	Ericsson Globe	13,699	Pittsburgh	4	Ottawa	3	Tyler Kennedy	4:35 (OT)
Oct. 5, 2008	Prague, Czech Republic	O2 Arena	17,085	NY Rangers	2	Tampa Bay	1	Scott Gomez	12:12 (2nd)
Oct. 5, 2008	Stockholm, Sweden	Ericsson Globe	13,699	Ottawa	3	Pittsburgh	1	Dany Heatley	12:17 (3rd)
Oct. 2, 2009	Helsinki, Finland	Hartwell Arena	12,056	Florida	4	Chicago	3	Ville Koistinen	Shootout
Oct. 2, 2009	Stockholm, Sweden	Ericsson Globe	13,850	St. Louis	4	Detroit	3	Paul Kariya	17:36 (2nd)
Oct. 3, 2009	Helsinki, Finland	Hartwell Arena	11,526	Chicago	4	Florida	0	Brian Campbell	3:05 (1st)
Oct. 3, 2009	Stockholm, Sweden	Ericsson Globe	13,850	St. Louis	5	Detroit	3	Patrick Berglund	13:37 (2nd)
Oct. 7, 2010	Helsinki, Finland	Hartwell Arena	12,355	Carolina	4	Minnesota	3	Brandon Sutter	18:03 (2nd)
Oct. 8, 2010	Helsinki, Finland	Hartwell Arena	13,465	Carolina	2	Minnesota	1	Jeff Skinner	Shootout
Oct. 8, 2010	Stockholm, Sweden	Ericsson Globe	11,324	San Jose	3	Columbus	2	Logan Couture	10:15 (3rd)
Oct. 9, 2010	Stockholm, Sweden	Ericsson Globe	11,324	Columbus	3	San Jose	2	Ethan Moreau	1:56 (OT)
Oct. 9, 2010	Prague, Czech Republic	O2 Arena	15,299	Phoenix	5	Boston	2	Scottie Upshall	15:02 (2nd)
Oct. 10, 2010	Prague, Czech Republic	O2 Arena	12,990	Boston	3	Phoenix	0	Milan Lucic	12:11 (2nd)
Oct. 7, 2011	Helsinki, Finland	Hartwell Arena	13,349	Buffalo	4	Anaheim	2	Ville Leino	8:30 (1st)
Oct. 7, 2011	Stockholm, Sweden	Ericsson Globe	13,800	Los Angeles	3	NY Rangers	2	Jack Johnson	4:08 (OT)
Oct. 8, 2011	Stockholm, Sweden	Ericsson Globe	13,800	Anaheim	2	NY Rangers	1	Bobby Ryan	Shootout
Oct. 8, 2011	Berlin, Germany	O2 World	14,300	Buffalo	4	Los Angeles	2	Paul Gaustad	13:19 (2nd)
Nov. 10, 2017	Stockholm, Sweden	Ericsson Globe	**16,000	Ottawa		Colorado			
Nov. 11, 2017	Stockholm, Sweden	Ericsson Globe	**16,000	Colorado		Ottawa			

NHL Clubs' Minor-League Affiliations, 2017-18

NHL CLUB	MINOR-LEAGUE AFFILIATES
Anaheim	San Diego Gulls (AHL)
	Utah Grizzlies (ECHL)
Arizona	Tucson Roadrunners (AHL)
	Fort Wayne Komets (ECHL)
Boston	Providence Bruins (AHL)
	Atlanta Gladiators (ECHL)
Buffalo	Rochester Americans (AHL)
	Cincinnati Cyclones (ECHL)
Calgary	Stockton Heat (AHL)
	Kansas City Mavericks (ECHL)
Carolina	Charlotte Checkers (AHL)
	Florida Everblades (ECHL)
Chicago	Rockford IceHogs (AHL)
	Indy Fuel (ECHL)
Colorado	San Antonio Rampage (AHL)
	Colorado Eagles (ECHL)
Columbus	Cleveland Monsters (AHL)
Dallas	Texas Stars (AHL)
	Idaho Steelheads (ECHL)
Detroit	Grand Rapids Griffins (AHL)
	Toledo Walleye (ECHL)
Edmonton	Bakersfield Condors (AHL)
	Wichita Thunder (ECHL)
Florida	Springfield Thunderbirds (AHL)
Los Angeles	Ontario Reign (AHL)
	Manchester Monarchs (ECHL)
Minnesota	Iowa Wild (AHL)
	Rapid City Rush (ECHL)

NHL CLUB	MINOR-LEAGUE AFFILIATES
Montreal	Rocket de Laval (AHL)
	Brampton Beast (ECHL)
Nashville	Milwaukee Admirals (AHL)
	Norfolk Admirals (ECHL)
New Jersey	Binghamton Devils (AHL)
	Adirondack Thunder (ECHL)
NY Islanders	Bridgeport Sound Tigers (AHL)
	Worcester Railers (ECHL)
NY Rangers	Hartford Wolf Pack (AHL)
	Greenville Swamp Rabbits (ECHL)
Ottawa	Belleville Senators (AHL)
	Wichita Thunder (ECHL)
Philadelphia	Lehigh Valley Phantoms (AHL)
	Reading Royals (ECHL)
Pittsburgh	Wilkes-Barre/Scranton Penguins (AHL)
	Wheeling Nailers (ECHL)
St. Louis	*various* (AHL)
	Tulsa Oilers (ECHL)
San Jose	San Jose Barracuda (AHL)
	Allen Americans (ECHL)
Tampa Bay	Syracuse Crunch (AHL)
	Kalamazoo Wings (ECHL)
Toronto	Toronto Marlies (AHL)
	Orlando Solar Bears (ECHL)
Vancouver	Utica Comets (AHL)
	Kalamazoo Wings (ECHL)
Vegas	Chicago Wolves (AHL)
	Quad City Mallards (ECHL)
Washington	Hershey Bears (AHL)
	South Carolina Stingrays (ECHL)
Winnipeg	Manitoba Moose (AHL)
	Jacksonville IceMen (ECHL)

Anaheim Ducks

2016-17 Results: 46w-23l-10otl-3sol 105pts
1st, Pacific Division • 2nd, Western Conference

2017-18 Schedule

Oct.	Thu.	5	Arizona		Thu.	4	at Edmonton
	Sat.	7	Philadelphia		Sat.	6	at Calgary
	Mon.	9	Calgary		Sat.	13	at Los Angeles
	Wed.	11	NY Islanders		Mon.	15	at Colorado*
	Fri.	13	at Colorado		Wed.	17	Pittsburgh
	Sun.	15	Buffalo		Fri.	19	Los Angeles
	Fri.	20	Montreal		Sun.	21	San Jose
	Tue.	24	at Philadelphia		Tue.	23	NY Rangers
	Thu.	26	at Florida		Thu.	25	Winnipeg
	Sat.	28	at Tampa Bay		Tue.	30	at Boston
	Sun.	29	at Carolina*	**Feb.**	Thu.	1	at Ottawa
Nov.	Wed.	1	Toronto		Sat.	3	at Montreal*
	Fri.	3	Nashville		Mon.	5	at Toronto
	Sat.	4	at San Jose		Tue.	6	at Buffalo
	Tue.	7	Los Angeles		Fri.	9	at Edmonton
	Thu.	9	Vancouver		Sun.	11	San Jose*
	Sun.	12	Tampa Bay*		Tue.	13	at Detroit
	Wed.	15	Boston		Thu.	15	at Chicago
	Sun.	19	Florida*		Sat.	17	at Minnesota*
	Mon.	20	at San Jose		Mon.	19	at Vegas
	Wed.	22	Vegas		Wed.	21	Dallas
	Fri.	24	Winnipeg*		Sat.	24	at Arizona
	Sat.	25	at Los Angeles		Sun.	25	Edmonton*
	Mon.	27	at Chicago	**Mar.**	Fri.	2	Columbus
	Wed.	29	at St. Louis		Sun.	4	Chicago*
Dec.	Fri.	1	at Columbus		Tue.	6	Washington
	Sat.	2	at Nashville		Thu.	8	at Nashville
	Tue.	5	at Vegas		Fri.	9	at Dallas
	Wed.	6	Ottawa		Mon.	12	St. Louis
	Fri.	8	Minnesota		Wed.	14	Vancouver
	Mon.	11	Carolina		Fri.	16	Detroit
	Thu.	14	at St. Louis*		Sun.	18	New Jersey
	Sat.	16	at Washington		Wed.	21	at Calgary
	Mon.	18	at New Jersey		Fri.	23	at Winnipeg
	Tue.	19	at NY Rangers		Sun.	25	at Edmonton
	Thu.	21	at NY Islanders		Tue.	27	at Vancouver
	Sat.	23	at Pittsburgh		Fri.	30	Los Angeles
	Wed.	27	Vegas	**Apr.**	Sun.	1	Colorado
	Fri.	29	Calgary		Wed.	4	Minnesota
	Sun.	31	Arizona*		Fri.	6	Dallas
Jan.	Tue.	2	at Vancouver		Sat.	7	at Arizona

* Denotes afternoon game.

Retired Numbers

8 Teemu Selanne 1996-2001, 2005-14

PACIFIC DIVISION
25th NHL Season

Franchise date: June 15, 1993

Year-by-Year Record

Season	GP	Home W	L	T	OL	Road W	L	T	OL	Overall W	L	T	OL	GF	GA	Pts.	Div. Fin.	Conf. Fin.	Playoff Result
2016-17	82	29	8	....	4	17	15	....	9	46	23	....	13	223	200	105	1st, Pac.	2nd, West	Lost Conf. Final
2015-16	82	25	10	....	6	21	15	....	5	46	25	....	11	218	192	103	1st, Pac.	4th, West	Lost First Round
2014-15	82	26	12	....	3	25	12	....	4	51	24	....	7	236	226	109	1st, Pac.	1st, West	Lost Conf. Final
2013-14	82	29	8	....	4	25	12	....	4	54	20	....	8	266	209	116	1st, Pac.	1st, West	Lost Second Round
2012-13	48	16	7	....	1	14	5	....	5	30	12	....	6	140	118	66	1st, Pac.	2nd, West	Lost Conf. Quarter-Final
2011-12	82	21	18	....	2	13	18	....	10	34	36	....	12	204	231	80	5th, Pac.	13th, West	– out of playoffs –
2010-11	82	26	13	....	2	21	17	....	3	47	30	....	5	239	235	99	2nd, Pac.	4th, West	Lost Conf. Quarter-Final
2009-10	82	25	11	....	5	14	21	....	6	39	32	....	11	238	251	89	4th, Pac.	11th, West	– out of playoffs –
2008-09	82	20	18	....	3	22	15	....	4	42	33	....	7	245	238	91	2nd, Pac.	8th, West	Lost Conf. Semi-Final
2007-08	82	28	9	....	4	19	18	....	4	47	27	....	8	205	191	102	2nd, Pac.	4th, West	Lost Conf. Quarter-Final
2006-07	82	26	6	....	9	22	14	....	5	48	20	....	14	258	208	110	1st, Pac.	2nd, West	**Won Stanley Cup**
2005-06*	82	26	10	....	5	17	17	....	7	43	27	....	12	254	229	98	3rd, Pac.	6th, West	Lost Conf. Final
2004-05*	....	....				....				....									
2003-04*	82	19	11	7	4	10	24	3	4	29	35	10	8	184	213	76	4th, Pac.	12th, West	– out of playoffs –
2002-03*	82	22	10	7	2	18	17	2	4	40	27	9	6	203	193	95	2nd, Pac.	7th, West	Lost Final
2001-02*	82	15	19	5	2	14	23	3	1	29	42	8	3	175	198	69	5th, Pac.	13th, West	– out of playoffs –
2000-01*	82	15	20	4	2	10	21	7	3	25	41	11	5	188	245	66	5th, Pac.	15th, West	– out of playoffs –
1999-2000*	82	19	13	7	2	15	20	5	1	34	33	12	3	217	227	83	5th, Pac.	9th, West	– out of playoffs –
1998-99*	82	21	14	6	....	14	20	7	....	35	34	13	....	215	206	83	3rd, Pac.	6th, West	Lost Conf. Quarter-Final
1997-98*	82	12	23	6	....	14	20	7	....	26	43	13	....	205	261	65	6th, Pac.	12th, West	– out of playoffs –
1996-97*	82	23	12	6	....	13	21	7	....	36	33	13	....	245	233	85	2nd, Pac.	4th, West	Lost Conf. Semi-Final
1995-96*	82	22	15	4	....	13	24	4	....	35	39	8	....	234	247	78	4th, Pac.	9th, West	– out of playoffs –
1994-95*	48	11	9	4	....	5	18	1	....	16	27	5	....	125	164	37	6th, Pac.	12th, West	– out of playoffs –
1993-94*	84	14	26	2	....	19	20	3	....	33	46	5	....	229	251	71	4th, Pac.	9th, West	– out of playoffs –

* Mighty Ducks of Anaheim

Rickard Rakell led the Ducks with a career-high 33 goals in 2016-17. He's improved from 9 to 20 to 33 goals over the past three seasons and his 10 game-winning goals in 2016-17 led the NHL.

2017-18 Player Personnel

FORWARDS	HT	WT	*Age	Birthplace	S	2016-17 Club
BOLL, Jared	6-3	209	31	Charlotte, NC	R	Anaheim
COGLIANO, Andrew	5-10	184	30	Toronto, ON	L	Anaheim
EAVES, Patrick	6-0	200	33	Calgary, AB	R	Dallas-Anaheim
GETZLAF, Ryan	6-4	221	32	Regina, SK	R	Anaheim
KASE, Ondrej	6-0	180	21	Kadan, Czech Rep.	L	Anaheim-San Diego
KERDILES, Nicolas	6-2	191	23	Lewisville, TX	L	Anaheim-San Diego
KESLER, Ryan	6-2	202	33	Livonia, MI	R	Anaheim
KOSSILA, Kalle	5-11	175	24	Kauniainen, Finland	L	Anaheim-San Diego
NATTINEN, Julius	6-2	191	20	Jyvaskyla, Finland	L	Windsor
PERRY, Corey	6-3	210	32	Peterborough, ON	R	Anaheim
RAKELL, Rickard	6-2	201	24	Sundbyberg, Sweden	R	Anaheim
RASMUSSEN, Dennis	6-3	205	27	Vasteras, Sweden	L	Chicago
RITCHIE, Nick	6-2	232	21	Orangeville, ON	L	Anaheim
ROY, Kevin	5-9	174	24	Greenfield Park, QC	L	San Diego
SHAW, Logan	6-3	202	24	Glace Bay, NS	R	Sprfld-Ana-San Diego
SILFVERBERG, Jakob	6-2	196	26	Gavle, Sweden	R	Anaheim
TROPP, Corey	6-0	185	28	Grosse Pointe, MI	R	Anaheim-San Diego
WAGNER, Chris	6-0	195	26	Wellesley, MA	R	Anaheim-San Diego
DEFENSEMEN						
BIEKSA, Kevin	6-1	200	36	Grimsby, ON	R	Anaheim
FOWLER, Cam	6-1	207	25	Windsor, ON	L	Anaheim
HOLZER, Korbinian	6-3	215	29	Munich, West Germany	R	Anaheim
LINDHOLM, Hampus	6-3	205	23	Helsingborg, Sweden	L	Anaheim
MANSON, Josh	6-3	215	25	Prince Albert, SK	R	Anaheim
MEGNA, Jaycob	6-6	225	24	Plantation, FL	L	Anaheim-San Diego
MONTOUR, Brandon	6-0	192	23	Brantford, ON	R	Anaheim-San Diego
OLEKSY, Steve	6-0	190	31	Chesterfield, MI	R	Pit-Wilkes-Barre-Tor (AHL)
THOMPSON, Keaton	6-0	182	22	Edina, MN	L	San Diego-Utah
VATANEN, Sami	5-10	183	26	Jyvaskyla, Finland	R	Anaheim
WELINSKI, Andy	6-1	196	24	Duluth, MN	R	San Diego

GOALTENDERS	HT	WT	*Age	Birthplace	C	2016-17 Club
BERRA, Reto	6-4	210	30	Bulach, Switzerland	L	Florida-Springfield
BOYLE, Kevin	6-2	200	25	Manalapan, NJ	L	San Diego-Utah
GIBSON, John	6-3	226	24	Pittsburgh, PA	L	Anaheim
MILLER, Ryan	6-2	168	37	East Lansing, MI	L	Vancouver
TOKARSKI, Dustin	6-0	205	28	Watson, SK	L	Anaheim-San Diego

* – Age at start of 2017-18 season

Bob Murray

Executive Vice President and General Manager

Born: Kingston, ON, November 26, 1954.

Bob Murray was named executive vice president and general manager of the Anaheim Ducks on November 12, 2008 after 3 1/2 years as senior vice president of hockey operations. He was named to that original position on July 14, 2005. Murray's astute judgment of hockey talent and player evaluation were instrumental in several trades and acquisitions the Ducks made over his tenure, highlighted by a Stanley Cup championship in 2007. Anahiem has won five consecutive division titles under Murray from 2012-13 to 2016-17, and he was named NHL General Manager of the Year in 2014.

Murray's responsibilities include overseeing all aspects of player development, playing a key role in the club's professional scouting efforts, contract negotiations and all matters relating to the National Hockey League. He has been instrumental in the organization's success at both the NHL and AHL level.

Prior to joining the Ducks, Murray worked as a professional scout with the Vancouver Canucks from 1999 to 2005 under then-general manager Brian Burke (1998 to 2004). Murray's scouting expertise helped to build teams that recorded 100+ point season two years in a row (2002-03 and 2003-04) and advanced to the Stanley Cup playoffs four seasons in a row (2001 to 2004). Before his stint in Vancouver, he served as a scouting consultant for Anaheim during the 1998-99 season.

Murray was a member of the Chicago Blackhawks organization for 25 years, serving as general manager from 1997 to 1999. He was promoted to the post after serving as assistant general manager under Bob Pulford for two seasons. Before joining upper management, Murray was named the director of player personnel in 1991 and was largely responsible for the club's Draft choices over eight seasons.

Drafted by the Blackhawks in 1974, Murray spent his entire 1,008-game, 15-year career in a Chicago uniform. He became just the fourth player in Blackhawks history to reach the 1,000-game plateau. In addition, he became the first defenseman in club history to appear in 100 postseason contests, reaching the mark during the 1990 Stanley Cup playoffs. In all, Murray had 132 goals and 382 assists for 514 points, and currently ranks second in all-time points among Blackhawk defensemen. He was named to both the 1981 and 1983 NHL All-Star Games. Murray retired at the conclusion of the 1989-90 season. Known for his work ethic, intelligence and determination as a player, Murray remained with the organization as a professional scout following his retirement in 1990.

2016-17 Scoring

* – rookie

Regular Season

Pos	#	Player	Team	GP	G	A	Pts	TOI	+/–	PIM	PP	SH	GW	S	S%
C	15	Ryan Getzlaf	ANA	74	15	58	73	21:04	7	49	6	2	3	138	10.9
C	17	Ryan Kesler	ANA	82	22	36	58	21:18	8	83	8	0	2	186	11.8
R	10	Corey Perry	ANA	82	19	34	53	17:42	2	76	5	0	3	215	8.8
R	67	Rickard Rakell	ANA	71	33	18	51	17:23	10	12	5	0	10	177	18.6
R	18	Patrick Eaves	DAL	59	21	16	37	16:38	–10	16	11	0	1	154	13.6
			ANA	20	11	3	14	15:42	8	8	2	0	1	55	20.0
			Total	79	32	19	51	16:24	–2	24	13	0	2	209	15.3
R	33	Jakob Silfverberg	ANA	79	23	26	49	18:29	10	20	5	1	5	227	10.1
D	4	Cam Fowler	ANA	80	11	28	39	24:50	7	20	5	1	3	186	5.9
C	7	Andrew Cogliano	ANA	82	16	19	35	15:08	11	26	0	3	2	178	9.0
L	37	Nick Ritchie	ANA	77	14	14	28	12:59	4	62	1	0	3	149	9.4
C	50	Antoine Vermette	ANA	72	9	19	28	15:54	–7	42	5	0	1	88	10.2
D	45	Sami Vatanen	ANA	71	3	21	24	21:39	3	30	2	0	0	117	2.6
D	47	Hampus Lindholm	ANA	66	6	14	20	22:26	13	36	1	0	2	94	6.4
D	42	Josh Manson	ANA	82	5	12	17	18:37	14	82	0	1	1	88	5.7
R	86 *	Ondrej Kase	ANA	53	5	10	15	11:47	–1	18	0	0	2	77	6.5
D	2	Kevin Bieksa	ANA	81	3	11	14	18:45	0	63	1	0	1	94	3.2
R	48	Logan Shaw	ANA	55	3	7	10	9:42	3	10	0	1	1	59	5.1
D	53 *	Shea Theodore	ANA	34	2	7	9	17:18	–6	28	1	0	1	60	3.3
R	21	Chris Wagner	ANA	43	6	1	7	9:21	2	6	0	0	0	40	15.0
D	5	Korbinian Holzer	ANA	32	2	5	7	13:30	0	23	0	0	0	14	14.3
D	71 *	Brandon Montour	ANA	27	2	4	6	17:22	11	14	0	0	0	50	4.0
C	16	Ryan Garbutt	ANA	27	2	1	3	9:09	–3	20	0	0	1	26	7.7
D	3	Clayton Stoner	ANA	14	1	2	3	17:33	0	28	0	0	0	16	6.3
R	40	Jared Boll	ANA	51	0	3	3	5:48	–3	87	0	0	0	13	0.0
C	44	Nate Thompson	ANA	30	1	1	2	10:23	4	14	0	0	0	19	5.3
R	59 *	Nick Sorensen	ANA	5	0	1	1	10:53	–1	2	0	0	0	7	0.0
R	41	Corey Tropp	ANA	1	0	0	0	9:28	–1	0	0	0	0	0	0.0
D	6	Simon Despres	ANA	1	0	0	0	16:08	0	0	0	0	0	1	0.0
L	58 *	Nicolas Kerdiles	ANA	1	0	0	0	11:08	1	0	0	0	0	0	0.0
D	75 *	Jaycob Megna	ANA	1	0	0	0	15:20	1	0	0	0	0	0	0.0
C	83 *	Kalle Kossila	ANA	1	0	0	0	6:54	0	0	0	0	0	1	0.0
R	26	Emerson Etem	ANA	3	0	0	0	8:48	1	2	0	0	0	0	0.0
L	39	Mason Raymond	ANA	4	0	0	0	8:54	–2	0	0	0	0	3	0.0
D	51 *	Jacob Larsson	ANA	4	0	0	0	16:25	–1	2	0	0	0	2	0.0

Goaltending

No.	Goaltender	GPI	Mins	Avg	W	L	OT	EN	SO	GA	SA	Sv%	G	A	PIM
30	Dustin Tokarski	1	10	0.00	0	0	0	0	0	0	5	1.000	0	0	0
36	John Gibson	52	2950	2.22	25	16	9	3	6	109	1437	.924	0	1	4
1	Jonathan Bernier	39	1993	2.50	21	7	4	2	2	83	982	.915	0	0	4
	Totals	**82**	**4980**	**2.37**	**46**	**23**	**13**	**5**	**8**	**197**	**2429**	**.919**			

Playoffs

Pos	#	Player	Team	GP	G	A	Pts	TOI	+/–	PIM	PP	SH	GW	OT	S	S%
C	15	Ryan Getzlaf	ANA	17	8	11	19	24:10	7	8	3	0	1	0	53	15.1
R	33	Jakob Silfverberg	ANA	17	9	5	14	19:53	–4	6	2	0	2	1	61	14.8
R	67	Rickard Rakell	ANA	15	7	6	13	19:03	13	0	0	0	0	0	48	14.6
R	10	Corey Perry	ANA	17	4	7	11	17:52	4	34	1	0	3	3	43	9.3
D	4	Cam Fowler	ANA	13	2	7	9	26:30	–6	2	0	0	0	0	26	7.7
D	53 *	Shea Theodore	ANA	14	2	6	8	17:25	1	4	0	0	0	0	24	8.3
C	17	Ryan Kesler	ANA	17	1	7	8	21:21	–6	32	0	0	0	0	45	2.2
D	71 *	Brandon Montour	ANA	17	0	7	7	19:11	12	4	0	0	0	0	37	0.0
C	44	Nate Thompson	ANA	17	2	4	6	11:28	6	6	0	0	1	0	12	16.7
D	45	Sami Vatanen	ANA	12	1	5	6	22:07	–5	4	1	0	0	0	22	4.5
L	37	Nick Ritchie	ANA	15	4	0	4	13:26	–1	46	0	0	2	0	27	14.8
R	18	Patrick Eaves	ANA	7	2	2	4	16:53	0	6	0	0	0	0	19	10.5
D	47	Hampus Lindholm	ANA	17	1	3	4	22:00	8	10	0	0	0	0	24	4.2
D	2	Kevin Bieksa	ANA	8	0	4	4	16:56	5	23	0	0	0	0	10	0.0
R	21	Chris Wagner	ANA	17	3	0	3	10:59	1	6	0	0	1	0	18	16.7
C	50	Antoine Vermette	ANA	17	1	2	3	13:59	–3	2	0	0	0	0	30	3.3
C	7	Andrew Cogliano	ANA	17	1	2	3	13:49	–3	9	0	0	0	0	32	3.1
D	42	Josh Manson	ANA	17	0	3	3	20:32	–2	20	0	0	0	0	27	0.0
R	86 *	Ondrej Kase	ANA	9	2	0	2	10:32	2	4	0	0	0	0	12	16.7
L	58 *	Nicolas Kerdiles	ANA	4	0	1	1	9:22	1	2	0	0	0	0	1	0.0
D	5	Korbinian Holzer	ANA	5	0	0	0	11:51	0	18	0	0	0	0	0	0.0
R	40	Jared Boll	ANA	8	0	0	0	4:30	–1	5	0	0	0	0	3	0.0
R	48	Logan Shaw	ANA	9	0	0	0	9:31	0	4	0	0	0	0	7	0.0

Goaltending

No.	Goaltender	GPI	Mins	Avg	W	L	EN	SO	GA	SA	Sv%	G	A	PIM
36	John Gibson	16	879	2.59	9	5	1	0	38	466	.918	0	0	0
1	Jonathan Bernier	4	183	3.28	1	2	3	0	10	79	.873	0	0	0
	Totals	**17**	**1069**	**2.92**	**10**	**7**	**4**	**0**	**52**	**549**	**.905**			

Captains' History

Troy Loney, 1993-94; Randy Ladouceur, 1994-95, 1995-96; Paul Kariya, 1996-97; Paul Kariya and Teemu Selanne, 1997-98; Paul Kariya, 1998-99 to 2002-03; Steve Rucchin, 2003-04; Scott Niedermayer, 2005-06, 2006-07; Chris Pronger, 2007-08; Scott Niedermayer, 2008-09, 2009-10; Ryan Getzlaf, 2010-11 to date.

Coaching History

Ron Wilson, 1993-94 to 1996-97; Pierre Page, 1997-98; Craig Hartsburg, 1998-99, 1999-2000; Craig Hartsburg and Guy Charron, 2000-01; Bryan Murray, 2001-02; Mike Babcock, 2002-03 to 2004-05; Randy Carlyle, 2005-06 to 2010-11; Randy Carlyle and Bruce Boudreau, 2011-12; Bruce Boudreau, 2012-13 to 2015-16; Randy Carlyle, 2016-17 to date.

Club Records

Team

(Figures in brackets for season records are games played; records for fewest points, wins, ties, losses, goals, goals against are for 70 or more games)

Most Points **116** 2013-14 (82)
Most Wins **54** 2013-14 (82)
Most Ties **13** 1996-97 (82), 1997-98 (82), 1998-99 (82)
Most Losses **46** 1993-94 (84)
Most Goals **266** 2013-14 (82)
Most Goals Against **261** 1997-98 (82)
Fewest Points **65** 1997-98 (82)
Fewest Wins **25** 2000-01 (82)
Fewest Ties **5** 1993-94 (84)
Fewest Losses **20** 2006-07 (82), 2013-14 (82)
Fewest Goals **175** 2001-02 (82)
Fewest Goals Against **191** 2007-08 (82)
Longest Winning Streak
Overall .... **11** Feb. 13-Mar. 5/16
Home .... **13** Jan. 26-Mar. 20/13
Away .... **7** Nov. 28-Dec. 13/06
Longest Team Point Streak
Overall .... **14** Feb. 9-Mar. 7/16 (9W, 2OTW, 1SOW, 2SOL)
Home .... **14** Feb. 12-Apr. 9/97 (10W, 4T)
Away .... **7** Nov. 28-Dec. 13/06 (6W, 1OTW)
Longest Losing Streak
Overall .... **8** Oct. 12-30/96, Nov. 3-20/05
Home .... **8** Jan. 10-Feb. 9/01
Away .... **13** Oct. 29-Dec. 22/11
Longest Winless Streak
Overall .... **9** Nov. 21-Dec. 10/95 (6L, 3T), Oct. 10-30/96 (8L, 1T), Nov. 7-24/01 (7L, 2T)
Home .... **11** Jan. 5-Feb. 14/01 (8L, 3T)
Away .... **13** Nov. 1-Dec. 27/03 (8L, 3OTL, 2T)
Most Shutouts, Season **9** 2002-03 (82)
Most PIM, Season **1,843** 1997-98 (82)
Most Goals, Game .... **8** Jan. 21/98 (Fla. 3 at Ana. 8), Mar. 21/04 (Det. 6 at Ana. 8)

Individual

Most Seasons .... **15** Teemu Selanne
Most Games .... **966** Teemu Selanne
Most Goals, Career .... **457** Teemu Selanne
Most Assists, Career .... **531** Teemu Selanne
Most Points, Career .... **988** Teemu Selanne (457G, 531A)
Most PIM, Career .... **1,012** Corey Perry
Most Shutouts, Career .... **32** Jean-Sebastien Giguere
Longest Consecutive Games Streak .... **458** Andrew Cogliano (Oct. 7/11-to date)
Most Goals, Season .... **52** Teemu Selanne (1997-98)
Most Assists, Season .... **66** Ryan Getzlaf (2008-09)
Most Points, Season .... **109** Teemu Selanne (1996-97; 51G, 58A)
Most PIM, Season .... **285** Todd Ewen (1995-96)
Most Points, Defenseman, Season .... **69** Scott Niedermayer (2006-07; 15G, 54A)
Most Points, Center, Season .... **91** Ryan Getzlaf (2008-09; 25G, 66A)
Most Points, Right Wing, Season .... **109** Teemu Selanne (1996-97; 51G, 58A)
Most Points, Left Wing, Season .... **108** Paul Kariya (1995-96; 50G, 58A)
Most Points, Rookie, Season .... **57** Bobby Ryan (2008-09; 31G, 26A)
Most Shutouts, Season .... **8** Jean-Sebastien Giguere (2002-03)
Most Goals, Game .... **3** Forty times
Most Assists, Game .... **5** Dmitri Mironov (Dec. 12/97), Teemu Selanne (Nov. 19/06), Ryan Getzlaf (Oct. 29/08)
Most Points, Game .... **5** Fifteen times

General Managers' History

Jack Ferreira, 1993-94 to 1997-98; Pierre Gauthier, 1998-99 to 2001-02; Bryan Murray, 2002-03, 2003-04; Al Coates, 2004-05; Brian Burke, 2005-06 to 2007-08; Brian Burke and Bob Murray, 2008-09; Bob Murray, 2009-10 to date.

All-time Record vs. Other Clubs

Regular Season

	Total								At Home								On Road							
	GP	W	L	T	OL	GF	GA	PTS	GP	W	L	T	OL	GF	GA	PTS	GP	W	L	T	OL	GF	GA	PTS
Arizona	124	70	35	5	14	373	325	159	63	39	16	3	5	195	156	86	61	31	19	2	9	178	169	73
Boston	32	17	9	2	4	94	82	40	16	8	4	2	2	43	38	20	16	9	5	0	2	51	44	20
Buffalo	34	14	15	3	2	83	92	33	17	8	8	0	1	39	44	17	17	6	7	3	1	44	48	16
Calgary	101	56	36	7	2	307	277	121	50	36	8	6	0	178	119	78	51	20	28	1	2	129	158	43
Carolina	34	18	13	2	1	97	97	39	17	10	6	1	0	55	56	21	17	8	7	1	1	42	41	18
Chicago	89	47	31	5	6	223	208	105	43	24	14	3	2	116	94	53	46	23	17	2	4	107	114	52
Colorado	85	40	33	7	5	233	226	92	43	22	16	3	2	116	109	49	42	18	17	4	3	117	117	43
Columbus	55	26	20	1	8	153	151	61	28	14	9	1	4	85	76	33	27	12	11	0	4	68	75	28
Dallas	119	44	64	5	6	274	349	99	59	28	27	3	1	152	159	60	60	16	37	2	5	122	190	39
Detroit	83	26	45	7	5	196	252	64	42	19	19	4	0	103	107	42	41	7	26	3	5	93	145	22
Edmonton	101	55	36	2	8	272	241	120	51	30	17	2	2	147	128	64	50	25	19	0	6	125	113	56
Florida	31	13	14	3	1	81	89	30	16	7	8	1	0	46	50	15	15	6	6	2	1	35	39	15
Los Angeles	132	63	45	11	13	382	360	150	66	36	15	7	8	218	175	87	66	27	30	4	5	164	185	63
Minnesota	59	30	20	2	7	139	142	69	30	18	9	0	3	79	68	39	29	12	11	2	4	60	74	30
Montreal	30	14	12	2	2	87	89	32	15	8	5	0	2	46	41	18	15	6	7	2	0	41	48	14
Nashville	67	38	22	2	5	187	160	83	34	25	6	0	3	110	71	53	33	13	16	2	2	77	89	30
New Jersey	32	14	14	1	3	80	85	32	17	9	6	1	1	53	41	20	15	5	8	0	2	27	44	12
NY Islanders	32	12	12	4	4	83	89	32	17	6	5	3	3	42	47	18	15	6	7	1	1	41	42	14
NY Rangers	33	17	10	1	5	97	92	40	16	10	4	0	2	57	44	22	17	7	6	1	3	40	48	18
Ottawa	31	17	9	3	2	80	73	39	16	9	4	2	1	42	30	21	15	8	5	1	1	38	43	18
Philadelphia	32	17	8	5	2	101	95	41	17	9	4	2	2	64	58	22	15	8	4	3	0	37	37	19
Pittsburgh	32	11	18	2	1	90	107	25	15	8	6	0	1	45	46	17	17	3	12	2	0	45	61	8
St. Louis	87	40	36	5	6	241	259	91	43	25	15	2	1	126	113	53	44	15	21	3	5	115	146	38
San Jose	132	61	59	4	8	341	370	134	66	31	29	2	4	175	184	68	66	30	30	2	4	166	186	66
Tampa Bay	32	16	14	1	1	80	80	34	16	9	6	1	0	43	38	19	16	7	8	0	1	37	42	15
Toronto	40	12	22	5	1	103	126	30	18	8	9	1	0	54	48	17	22	4	13	4	1	49	78	13
Vancouver	102	45	38	9	10	287	291	109	50	20	17	7	6	141	141	53	52	25	21	2	4	146	150	56
Washington	33	16	12	1	4	98	89	37	16	7	6	1	2	52	50	17	17	9	6	0	2	46	39	20
Winnipeg	26	16	7	0	3	84	70	35	13	7	4	0	2	42	38	16	13	9	3	0	1	42	32	19
Totals	**1820**	**865**	**709**	**107**	**139**	**4946**	**4966**	**1976**	**910**	**490**	**302**	**58**	**60**	**2664**	**2369**	**1098**	**910**	**375**	**407**	**49**	**79**	**2282**	**2597**	**878**

Playoffs

	Series	W	L	GP	W	L	T	GF	GA	Last Mtg.	Rnd.	Result
Arizona	1	1	0	7	4	3	0	17	17	1997	CQF	W 4-3
Calgary	3	3	0	16	12	4	0	50	34	2017	FR	W 4-0
Chicago	1	0	1	7	3	4	0	22	24	2015	CF	L 3-4
Colorado	1	1	0	4	4	0	0	16	4	2006	CSF	W 4-0
Dallas	3	2	1	18	10	8	0	47	52	2014	FR	W 4-2
Detroit	6	2	4	32	14	18	0	78	93	2013	CQF	L 3-4
Edmonton	2	1	1	12	5	7	0	34	40	2017	SR	W 4-3
Los Angeles	1	0	1	7	3	4	0	15	19	2014	SR	L 3-4
Minnesota	2	2	0	9	8	1	0	21	10	2007	CQF	W 4-1
Nashville	3	0	3	19	7	12	0	53	55	2017	CF	L 2-4
New Jersey	1	0	1	7	3	4	0	12	19	2003	F	L 3-4
Ottawa	1	1	0	5	4	1	0	16	11	2007	F	W 4-1
San Jose	1	1	0	6	4	2	0	18	10	2009	CQF	W 4-2
Vancouver	1	1	0	5	4	1	0	14	8	2007	CSF	W 4-1
Winnipeg	1	1	0	4	4	0	0	16	9	2015	FR	W 4-0
Totals	**28**	**16**	**12**	**158**	**89**	**69**	**0**	**429**	**405**			

Playoff Results 2017-2013

Year	Round	Opponent	Result	GF	GA
2017	CF	Nashville	L 2-4	15	19
	SR	Edmonton	W 4-3	21	24
	FR	Calgary	W 4-0	14	9
2016	FR	Nashville	L 3-4	18	14
2015	CF	Chicago	L 3-4	22	24
	SR	Calgary	W 4-1	19	9
	FR	Winnipeg	W 4-0	16	9
2014	SR	Los Angeles	L 3-4	15	19
	FR	Dallas	W 4-2	20	18
2013	CQF	Detroit	L 3-4	21	18

Abbreviations: Round: F – Final; **CF** – conference final; **CSF** – conference semi-final; **SR** – second round; **CQF** – conference quarter-final; **FR** – first round.

Carolina totals include Hartford, 1993-94 to 1996-97.
Phoenix totals include Winnipeg, 1993-94 to 1995-96.
Colorado totals include Quebec, 1993-94 to 1994-95.
Winnipeg totals include Atlanta Thrashers, 1999-2000 to 2010-11.

2016-17 Results

Oct.	13	at Dallas	2-4		8	Minnesota	1-2
	15	at Pittsburgh	2-3		10	Dallas	2-0
	16	at NY Islanders	2-3*		12	at Colorado	4-1
	18	at New Jersey	1-2		14	at Arizona	3-0
	20	at Philadelphia	3-2		15	St. Louis	1-2*
	23	Vancouver	4-2		17	Tampa Bay	2-1*
	25	at San Jose	1-2*		19	Colorado	2-1
	26	Nashville	6-1		21	at Minnesota	3-5
	28	Columbus	0-4		23	at Winnipeg	3-2
Nov.	1	at Los Angeles	4-0		25	Edmonton	0-4
	2	Pittsburgh	1-5		31	Colorado	5-1
	4	Arizona	5-1	**Feb.**	3	at Florida	1-2
	6	Calgary	4-1		4	at Tampa Bay	2-3†
	9	at Columbus	2-3*		7	at NY Rangers	1-4
	10	at Carolina	4-2		9	at Buffalo	5-2
	12	at Nashville	0-5		11	at Washington	4-6
	15	Edmonton	4-1		14	at Minnesota	1-0
	17	New Jersey	3-2		17	Florida	1-4
	20	Los Angeles	2-3		19	Los Angeles	1-0
	22	NY Islanders	2-3†		20	at Arizona	2-3
	25	Chicago	2-3		22	Boston	5-3
	26	at San Jose	3-2		25	at Los Angeles	1-4
	29	Montreal	2-1	**Mar.**	3	Toronto	5-2
Dec.	1	at Vancouver	3-1		5	Vancouver	1-2
	3	at Edmonton	2-3*		7	Nashville	4-3†
	4	at Calgary	3-8		9	at Chicago	1-0
	7	Carolina	6-5†		10	at St. Louis	3-4
	9	San Jose	3-2		12	Washington	5-2
	11	Ottawa	5-1		15	St. Louis	2-1
	13	at Dallas	2-6		17	Buffalo	1-2†
	15	at Boston	4-3		18	at San Jose	2-1
	17	at Detroit	4-6		22	Edmonton	4-3
	19	at Toronto	3-2		24	Winnipeg	3-1
	20	at Montreal	1-5		26	NY Rangers	6-3
	22	at Ottawa	1-2*		28	at Vancouver	4-1
	27	San Jose	2-3*		30	at Winnipeg	3-4*
	29	at Calgary	3-1	**Apr.**	1	at Edmonton	2-3*
	30	at Vancouver	2-3*		2	at Calgary	4-3
Jan.	1	Philadelphia	4-3†		4	Calgary	3-1
	4	Detroit	2-0		6	Chicago	4-0
	6	Arizona	3-2*		9	Los Angeles	4-3*

* – Overtime † – Shootout

NHL Draft Selections 2017-2003

Name in bold denotes played in NHL.

2017
Pick
50 Maxime Comtois
60 Antoine Morand
91 Jack Badini
122 Kyle Olson
153 Olle Eriksson Ek

2016
Pick
24 Max Jones
30 Sam Steel
85 Joshua Mahura
93 Jack Kopacka
115 Alex Dostie
205 Tyler Soy

2015
Pick
27 **Jacob Larsson**
59 Julius Nattinen
80 Brent Gates
84 Deven Sideroff
148 Troy Terry
178 Steven Ruggiero
179 Garrett Metcalf

2014
Pick
10 **Nick Ritchie**
38 Marcus Pettersson
55 **Brandon Montour**
123 Matthew Berkovitz
205 **Ondrej Kase**

2013
Pick
26 **Shea Theodore**
45 **Nick Sorensen**
87 Keaton Thompson
147 Grant Besse
177 Miro Aaltonen

2012
Pick
6 **Hampus Lindholm**
36 **Nicolas Kerdiles**
87 **Frederik Andersen**
97 Kevin Roy
108 Andrew O'Brien
127 Brian Cooper
187 Kenton Helgesen
210 **Jaycob Megna**

2011
Pick
30 **Rickard Rakell**
39 **John Gibson**
53 **William Karlsson**
65 **Joseph Cramarossa**
83 Andy Welinski
143 **Max Friberg**
160 **Josh Manson**

2010
Pick
12 **Cam Fowler**
29 **Emerson Etem**
42 **Devante Smith-Pelly**
122 **Chris Wagner**
132 **Tim Heed**
161 Andreas Dahlstrom
177 Kevin Lind
192 Brett Perlini

2009
Pick
15 **Peter Holland**
26 **Kyle Palmieri**
37 **Mat Clark**
76 Igor Bobkov
106 **Sami Vatanen**
136 Radoslav Illo
166 Scott Valentine

2008
Pick
17 **Jake Gardiner**
35 **Nicolas Deschamps**
39 **Eric O'Dell**
43 **Justin Schultz**
71 Josh Brittain
83 Marco Cousineau
85 **Brandon McMillan**
113 Ryan Hegarty
143 Stefan Warg
208 Nick Pryor

2007
Pick
19 Logan MacMillan
42 **Eric Tangradi**
63 **Maxime Macenauer**
92 Justin Vaive
93 **Steven Kampfer**
98 Sebastian Stefaniszin
121 Mattias Modig
151 Brett Morrison

2006
Pick
19 Mark Mitera
38 Bryce Swan
83 John de Gray
112 **Matt Beleskey**
172 **Petteri Wirtanen**

2005
Pick
2 **Bobby Ryan**
31 **Brendan Mikkelson**
63 Jason Bailey
127 Bobby Bolt
141 **Brian Salcido**
197 Jean-Philippe Levasseur

2004
Pick
9 **Ladislav Smid**
39 Jordan Smith
74 Kyle Klubertanz
75 **Tim Brent**
172 Matt Auffrey
203 Gabriel Bouthillette
236 Matt Christie
269 **Janne Pesonen**

2003
Pick
19 **Ryan Getzlaf**
28 **Corey Perry**
86 Shane Hynes
90 Juha Alen
119 Nathan Saunders
186 **Drew Miller**
218 Dirk Southern
250 **Shane O'Brien**
280 Ville Mantymaa

Randy Carlyle

Head Coach

Born: Sudbury, ON, April 19, 1956.

Randy Carlyle was hired for his second stint as head coach of the Ducks on June 14, 2016. He returned to Anaheim as the team's all-time winningest head coach from his original tenure and extended his record to 319-205-74 in 2016-17. Carlyle was originally named the seventh head coach in team history on August 1, 2005. He led Anaheim to a four straight playoff appearances from 2006 to 2009, made two trips to the Conference Finals (2006 and 2007) and became the first coach to lead a California team to the Stanley Cup in 2007. Carlyle, who coached the Toronto Maple Leafs from 2011 to 2015, led Anaheim to the Conference Finals again in 2017.

Before coaching in the NHL, Carlyle spent the 2004-05 season as head coach of the Manitoba Moose, Vancouver's primary development affiliate in the American Hockey League. In all, he spent six seasons (1996 to 2001 and 2004-05) as head coach in Manitoba (both in the International and American Hockey Leagues) and had the additional duties of general manager of the Moose from 1996 to 2000, adding the title of club president for the 2001-02 season. The Sudbury, Ontario, native helped the Moose to a 47-21-14 record for 108 points in 1998-99, for which he was named the IHL's General Manager of the Year. Following the 2001-02 season, Carlyle joined the coaching staff of the Washington Capitals. He served as an assistant coach with Washington for two years (2002 to 2004), helping the organization return to the Stanley Cup playoffs in his first season before rejoining Manitoba in 2004-05.

Carlyle played 17 seasons in the NHL with Toronto, Pittsburgh and Winnipeg. He appeared in 1,055 games and earned 148 goals and 499 assists for 647 points. Known as a fiery, tough-nosed defenseman, he was selected to play in four NHL All-Star Games and won the Norris Trophy as the league's top defenseman in 1981. He set a career high with 82 points in 1980-81, appearing in 76 games with Pittsburgh that season. In all, Carlyle had five seasons in which he topped the 50-point plateau. He appeared in 69 NHL postseason games as a player, earning 9 goals and 24 assists for 33 points. At the conclusion of his playing career in 1993, Carlyle remained with the Winnipeg organization's hockey operations staff, eventually becoming an assistant coach for the 1995-96 season.

Coaching Record

			Regular Season				Playoffs			
Season	Team	League	GC	W	L	O/T	GC	W	L	T
1996-97	Manitoba	IHL	32	16	14	2	....	....	....	....
1997-98	Manitoba	IHL	82	39	36	7	3	0	3	....
1998-99	Manitoba	IHL	82	47	21	14	5	2	3	....
99-2000	Manitoba	IHL	82	37	31	14	2	0	2	....
2000-01	Manitoba	IHL	82	39	31	12	13	6	7	....
2004-05	Manitoba	AHL	80	44	26	10	14	6	8	....
2005-06	**Anaheim**	**NHL**	**82**	**43**	**27**	**12**	**16**	**9**	**7**	....
2006-07 ♦	**Anaheim**	**NHL**	**82**	**48**	**20**	**14**	**21**	**16**	**5**	....
2007-08	**Anaheim**	**NHL**	**82**	**47**	**27**	**8**	**6**	**2**	**4**	....
2008-09	**Anaheim**	**NHL**	**82**	**42**	**33**	**7**	**13**	**7**	**6**	....
2009-10	**Anaheim**	**NHL**	**82**	**39**	**32**	**11**	....	....	....	....
2010-11	**Anaheim**	**NHL**	**82**	**47**	**30**	**5**	**6**	**2**	**4**	....
2011-12	**Anaheim**	**NHL**	**24**	**7**	**13**	**4**	....	....	....	....
2011-12	**Toronto**	**NHL**	**18**	**6**	**9**	**3**	....	....	....	....
2012-13	**Toronto**	**NHL**	**48**	**26**	**17**	**5**	**7**	**3**	**4**	....
2013-14	**Toronto**	**NHL**	**82**	**38**	**36**	**8**	....	....	....	....
2014-15	**Toronto**	**NHL**	**40**	**21**	**16**	**3**	....	....	....	....
2016-17	**Anaheim**	**NHL**	**82**	**46**	**23**	**13**	**17**	**10**	**7**	....
	NHL Totals		**786**	**410**	**283**	**93**	**86**	**49**	**37**	....

♦ Stanley Cup win.

Club Directory

Honda Center

Anaheim Ducks
Honda Center
2695 E. Katella Ave.
Anaheim, CA 92806
Phone **714/940-2900**
FAX 714/940-2953
Ticket Information 877/WILDWING
www.anaheimducks.com
Capacity: 17,174

Executive Management
Owners .... Henry and Susan Samueli
Chief Executive Officer .... Michael Schulman
Executive Vice President/General Manager .... Bob Murray
Executive Vice President/Chief Operating Officer .... Tim Ryan
Senior Vice President, Hockey Operations .... David McNab
Chief Financial Officer .... Bill Foltz
Chief Human Resources Officer .... Jay Scott
Vice President, Human Resources .... Gina Galasso
Vice President/COO, Anaheim Arena .... Kevin Starkey
Vice President, Chief Marketing Officer .... Aaron Teats
Chief Commercial Officer .... Bill Pedigo
Administrative Services Manager/Executive Asst. .... Cheryl Gorman
Executive Assistant .... Janet Conley

Coaching Staff
Head Coach .... Randy Carlyle
Assistant Coaches .... Steve Konowalchuk, Mark Morrison, Rich Preston, Trent Yawney
Goaltending Coach / Skating Coach .... Sudarshan Maharaj / Larry Barron
Video Coach .... Joe Piscotty

Hockey Operations
Consultant to the General Manager .... Dave Nonis
Director of Player Personnel .... Rick Paterson
Assistant to the General Manager .... Dave Baseggio
Director of Player Development .... Todd Marchant
Director of Scouting, Amateur / Pro .... Martin Madden
Director of Player Evaluation .... Bruce Franklin
Player Development, Off-Ice .... Scott Niedermayer
Scouting Staff .... Glen Cochrane, Jan-Åke Danielson, Steve Lyons, Martin Madden, Sr., Kevin Murray, Stephane Pilotte, Jim Sandlak, Mike Stapleton
Director of Team Services .... Ryan Lichtenfels
Team Services Mgr. / Coordinator .... Chase Flanigan / Josh Schlichter
Hockey Ops. Exec. Asst. / Intern .... Colleen MacKinnon / Connor Hanrahan
Strength & Conditioning Coach .... Mark Fitzgerald
Athletic Trainers, Head / Assistant .... Joe Huff / Mike Hannegan
Physical Therapist .... Kevin Taylor
Equipment Manager / Asst. Managers .... Doug Shearer / Chris Aldrich, Matt Brayfield, Jeff Tyni
Medical Director / Orthopedic Surgeon .... Orr Limpisvasti / Brian Schulz
Oral Surgeon / Neuropsychologists .... Bao-Thy Grant / Josh Johnson
Foot & Ankle Surgeon / Hand Surgeon .... Ken Jung / David Hay
Internal Medicine / Primary Care Physicians .... Satoshi Kamada / Kenton Fibel, Chris Kroner

Legal
General Counsel / Asst. General Counsel .... Bernard Schneider / Katie Rodin

Broadcasting
TV: FSN Prime Ticket (Cable) .... John Ahlers, Brian Hayward
Radio: KLAA AM 830 & Ducks Radio Network .... Steve Carroll, Dan Wood
Host-Producer / Postgame Radio Host .... Kent French / Josh Brewster
Broadcasting Associate / Coordinator .... Tiffany Spiritosanto / Julia Walter

Communications
Director of Media & Communications .... Alex Gilchrist
Media & Communications Manager / Publicist .... Steve Hoem / Keren Lynch
Game Night Communications Staff .... Chelsea Gonye, Larry Woodard, Blake Kaprelyan

Community Relations
Community Relations Director / Manager .... Wendy Arciero / Jesse Bryson
Community Relations Manager / Coordinators .... Laura McNary / Ashley Brown, Kelly Williams

Corporate Partnerships
Director of Corporate Partnerships .... Graham Siderius
Corporate Partnerships Managers .... Jason Andrea, Deanna Christensen, Aaron Cook, Chris Wilson

Corporate Partnership Activation
Sr. Manager, Corp. Partnership Activation .... Sarah Morales
Mgr. of Corp Partnership Development / Coordinator... Brett Miller / Allison Beltran
Activation Associates / Coordinator .... Randy Bernabe, Andrea Berryman / Samantha Luehrs

Entertainment
Director of Production & Entertainment .... Rich Cooley
Entertainment Manager / Associate .... Davin Maske / Sarah Moews
Producers / Video Producer .... Peter Uvalle, Gabe Suarez/Joseph Schwehr
Digital Content Associate .... Paul Janicki

Finance
Controller / Asst. Controller / Payroll .... Melody Martin / Rosanna Sitzman / Regina Terrana
Accounts Receivable / Accounts Payable / Ticketing Acct. .. Rob Dumlao / Lou Rae Campbell / Robert Slaby

Human Resources
Human Resources Managers / Business Partner .... Wendy Mulhall, Donna Vass / Angel Montes
Human Resources Analyst / Associate .... Christian Young / Lisa Monson

Marketing/Brand Management
Director of Marketing & Brand Management .... Merit Tully
Fan Development Marketing Sr. Manager / Manager ... Joseph Hwang / Jason Cooper
Youth Hockey Associate / Fan Development Coordinator .. Ryan Herrman / Molly Schaus
Senior Marketing Manager / Marketing Project Manager .. Trent Nielsen / Cindy Iwami
The Rinks, Marketing Director .... Jesse Chatfield
Associate / Coordinator .... Craig Appleby / Kirstie Bender, Tanner Privia, Amy Wesson
Digital Marketing Manager .... G.M. Ciallella
Senior Graphic Designer/ Graphic Designer .... Jeff Ipjian / Wes Tiongco

Merchandise, Team Store
Director of Merchandising .... Jill Bauer
Retail Store Operations Manager / Store Manager/Warehouse Mgr. Ricardo Silva / Lizette Gutierrez/Josh McCord

Publications and New Media
Director of Publications & Digital Content .... Adam Brady
Digital Content Producers .... Anthony Manderichio/Kyle Shohara

Premium Sales and Service
Director of Premium Sales & Service .... Tim Thompson
Premium Sales Managers .... Geoff Matthews, Branden Moran, Timothy Ravenstahl
Manager, Premium Services / Associate/Coordinators ... Jana Cannavo / Kathryn Baker/Samantha Wilson, Sanaz Tavassol

Signature Programs & Events
Director of Integrated Projects & Programming .... Kris Loomis
Signature Events & Projects Manager / Coordinator .... Jamie Minkler / David Schenker

Ticket Sales and Customer Service
Director of Ticket Sales .... Chris Kenyon
Group & Inside Sales Manager .... Matt Payne

Ticketing
Senior Manager of Ticket Operations .... Gina Bradshaw
Manager of Ticketing Operations / Assistant Mgr .... Kameron Kwok / Jonas Calicdan
Season Ticketing Rep / Group Ticketing Rep .... Meghan Murphy / Nick Vassar
Premium Ticket Representatives .... John Watson, Ashley Gorvetzian

Key Off-Season Signings/Acquisitions

2017

June 16 • Acquired C **Nick Cousins** and G **Merrick Madsen** from Philadelphia for LW **Brendan Warren** and a 5th-round pick in 2018 NHL Draft.

17 • Acquired D **Brandon Hickey**, G **Chad Johnson** and a conditional 3rd-round pick in 2018 NHL Draft from Calgary for G **Mike Smith**.

23 • Acquired C **Derek Stepan** and G **Antti Raanta** from NY Rangers for D **Tony DeAngelo** and a 1st-round pick in 2017 NHL Draft.

23 • Acquired D **Niklas Hjalmarsson** from Chicago for D **Connor Murphy** and C **Laurent Dauphin**.

July 1 • Signed C **Zac Rinaldo**, RW **Mike Sislo**, D **Adam Clendening**, D **Andrew Campbell** and D **Joel Hanley**.

4 • Signed C **Michael Latta**.

5 • Signed LW **Emerson Etem**.

11 • Named **Rick Tocchet** head coach.

22 • Re-signed C **Tyler Gaudet** and LW **Jordan Martinook**.

26 • Named **John MacLean** and **Scott Allen** assistant coaches.

2017-18 Schedule

Oct.	Thu.	5	at Anaheim		
	Sat.	7	Vegas		
	Tue.	10	at Vegas		
	Thu.	12	Detroit		
	Sat.	14	Boston		
	Tue.	17	at Dallas		
	Thu.	19	Dallas		
	Sat.	21	Chicago		
	Tue.	24	at NY Islanders		
	Thu.	26	at NY Rangers		
	Sat.	28	at New Jersey		
	Mon.	30	at Philadelphia		
	Tue.	31	at Detroit		
Nov.	Thu.	2	Buffalo		
	Sat.	4	Carolina		
	Mon.	6	at Washington		
	Tue.	7	at Pittsburgh		
	Thu.	9	at St. Louis*		
	Sat.	11	Winnipeg		
	Tue.	14	at Winnipeg		
	Thu.	16	at Montreal		
	Sat.	18	at Ottawa*		
	Mon.	20	at Toronto		
	Wed.	22	San Jose		
	Fri.	24	Los Angeles		
	Sat.	25	Vegas		
	Tue.	28	at Edmonton		
	Thu.	30	at Calgary		
Dec.	Sat.	2	New Jersey		
	Sun.	3	at Vegas*		
	Thu.	7	at Boston		
	Sat.	9	at Columbus		
	Sun.	10	at Chicago		
	Thu.	14	Tampa Bay		
	Sat.	16	Pittsburgh		
	Tue.	19	Florida		
	Fri.	22	Washington		
	Sat.	23	Colorado		
	Wed.	27	at Colorado		
	Thu.	28	Toronto		
	Sun.	31	at Anaheim*		
Jan.	Thu.	4	Nashville		
	Sat.	6	NY Rangers		
	Fri.	12	Edmonton		
	Sat.	13	at San Jose		
	Tue.	16	San Jose		
	Thu.	18	at Nashville		
	Sat.	20	at St. Louis*		
	Mon.	22	NY Islanders		
	Thu.	25	Columbus		
Feb.	Thu.	1	Dallas		
	Sat.	3	at Los Angeles		
	Tue.	6	at Winnipeg		
	Thu.	8	at Minnesota		
	Sat.	10	Philadelphia		
	Mon.	12	Chicago		
	Tue.	13	at San Jose		
	Thu.	15	Montreal		
	Sat.	17	Edmonton*		
	Thu.	22	Calgary		
	Sat.	24	Anaheim		
	Sun.	25	Vancouver		
Mar.	Thu.	1	Minnesota		
	Sat.	3	Ottawa		
	Mon.	5	at Edmonton		
	Wed.	7	at Vancouver		
	Sat.	10	at Colorado*		
	Sun.	11	Vancouver		
	Tue.	13	Los Angeles		
	Thu.	15	Nashville		
	Sat.	17	Minnesota		
	Mon.	19	Calgary		
	Wed.	21	at Buffalo		
	Thu.	22	at Carolina		
	Sat.	24	at Florida		
	Mon.	26	at Tampa Bay		
	Wed.	28	at Vegas		
	Thu.	29	at Los Angeles		
	Sat.	31	St. Louis		
Apr.	Tue.	3	at Calgary		
	Thu.	5	at Vancouver		
	Sat.	7	Anaheim		

* Denotes afternoon game.

Retired Numbers

7	Keith Tkachuk	1991-2001
9	Bobby Hull*	1972-1980°
10	Dale Hawerchuk*	1981-1990
25	Thomas Steen*	1981-1995
27	Teppo Numminen*	1988-2003
97	Jeremy Roenick	1996-2001

* Winnipeg Jets ° Includes WHA

PACIFIC DIVISION
39th NHL Season

Franchise date: June 22, 1979

Transferred from Winnipeg to Phoenix, July 1, 1996.
Team name changed from Phoenix to Arizona, June 27, 2014.

Arizona Coyotes

2016-17 Results: 30w-42L-8OTL-2SOL 70PTS
6TH, Pacific Division • 12TH, Western Conference

Year-by-Year Record

Season	GP	Home W	L	T	OL	Road W	L	T	OL	Overall W	L	T	OL	GF	GA	Pts.	Div. Fin.	Conf. Fin.	Playoff Result
2016-17	82	18	18	....	5	12	24	....	5	30	42	....	10	197	260	70	6th, Pac.	12th, West	– out of playoffs –
2015-16	82	22	15	....	4	13	24	....	4	35	39	....	8	209	245	78	4th, Pac.	10th, West	– out of playoffs –
2014-15	82	11	25	....	5	13	25	....	3	24	50	....	8	170	272	56	4th, Pac.	14th, West	– out of playoffs –
2013-14	82	22	14	....	5	15	16	....	10	37	30	....	15	216	231	89	4th, Pac.	9th, West	– out of playoffs –
2012-13	48	14	8	....	2	7	10	....	7	21	18	....	9	125	131	51	4th, Pac.	10th, West	– out of playoffs –
2011-12	82	22	13	....	6	20	14	....	7	42	27	....	13	216	204	97	1st, Pac.	3rd, West	Lost Conf. Final
2010-11	82	21	13	....	7	22	13	....	6	43	26	....	13	231	226	99	3rd, Pac.	6th, West	Lost Conf. Quarter-Final
2009-10	82	29	10	....	2	21	15	....	5	50	25	....	7	225	202	107	2nd,Pac.	4th, West	Lost Conf. Quarter-Final
2008-09	82	23	15	....	3	13	24	....	4	36	39	....	7	208	252	79	4th, Pac.	13th, West	– out of playoffs –
2007-08	82	17	20	....	4	21	17	....	3	38	37	....	7	214	231	83	4th, Pac.	12th, West	– out of playoffs –
2006-07	82	18	20	....	3	13	26	....	2	31	46	....	5	216	284	67	5th, Pac.	15th, West	– out of playoffs –
2005-06	82	19	18	....	4	19	21	....	1	38	39	....	5	246	271	81	5th, Pac.	12th, West	– out of playoffs –
2004-05	....																		
2003-04	82	11	19	7	4	11	17	11	2	22	36	18	6	188	245	68	5th, Pac.	13th, West	– out of playoffs –
2002-03	82	17	16	6	2	14	19	5	3	31	35	11	5	204	230	78	4th, Pac.	11th, West	– out of playoffs –
2001-02	82	27	8	3	3	13	19	6	3	40	27	9	6	228	210	95	2nd, Pac.	6th, West	Lost Conf. Quarter-Final
2000-01	82	21	11	7	2	14	16	10	1	35	27	17	3	214	212	90	4th, Pac.	9th, West	– out of playoffs –
1999-2000	82	22	16	2	1	17	15	6	3	39	31	8	4	232	228	90	3rd, Pac.	6th, West	Lost Conf. Quarter-Final
1998-99	82	23	13	5	....	16	18	7	....	39	31	12	....	205	197	90	4th, Pac.	4th, West	Lost Conf. Quarter-Final
1997-98	82	19	16	6	....	16	19	6	....	35	35	12	....	224	227	82	4th, Cen.	6th, West	Lost Conf. Quarter-Final
1996-97	82	15	19	7	....	23	18	0	....	38	37	7	....	240	243	83	3rd, Cen.	6th, West	Lost Conf. Quarter-Final
1995-96*	82	22	16	3	....	14	24	3	....	36	40	6	....	275	291	78	5th, Cen.	8th, West	Lost Conf. Quarter-Final
1994-95*	48	10	10	4	....	6	15	3	....	16	25	7	....	157	177	39	6th, Cen.	10th, West	– out of playoffs –
1993-94*	84	15	23	4	....	9	28	5	....	24	51	9	....	245	344	57	6th, Cen.	12th, West	– out of playoffs –
1992-93*	84	23	16	3	....	17	21	4	....	40	37	7	....	322	320	87	4th, Smythe		Lost Div. Semi-Final
1991-92*	80	18	13	9	....	13	18	9	....	33	32	15	....	251	244	81	4th, Smythe		Lost Div. Semi-Final
1990-91*	80	17	18	5	....	9	25	6	....	26	43	11	....	260	288	63	5th, Smythe		– out of playoffs –
1989-90*	80	22	13	5	....	15	19	6	....	37	32	11	....	298	290	85	3rd, Smythe		Lost Div. Semi-Final
1988-89*	80	17	18	5	....	9	24	7	....	26	42	12	....	300	355	64	5th, Smythe		– out of playoffs –
1987-88*	80	20	14	6	....	13	22	5	....	33	36	11	....	292	310	77	3rd, Smythe		Lost Div. Semi-Final
1986-87*	80	25	12	3	....	15	20	5	....	40	32	8	....	279	271	88	3rd, Smythe		Lost Div. Final
1985-86*	80	18	19	3	....	8	28	4	....	26	47	7	....	295	372	59	3rd, Smythe		Lost Div. Semi-Final
1984-85*	80	21	13	6	....	22	14	4	....	43	27	10	....	358	332	96	2nd, Smythe		Lost Div. Final
1983-84*	80	17	15	8	....	14	23	3	....	31	38	11	....	340	374	73	4th, Smythe		Lost Div. Semi-Final
1982-83*	80	22	16	2	....	11	23	6	....	33	39	8	....	311	333	74	4th, Smythe		Lost Div. Semi-Final
1981-82*	80	18	13	9	....	15	20	5	....	33	33	14	....	319	332	80	2nd, Norris		Lost Div. Semi-Final
1980-81*	80	7	25	8	....	2	32	6	....	9	57	14	....	246	400	32	6th, Smythe		– out of playoffs –
1979-80*	80	13	19	8	....	7	30	3	....	20	49	11	....	214	314	51	5th, Smythe		– out of playoffs –

* Winnipeg Jets

In his first season with the Coyotes in 2016-17, defenseman Alex Goligoski was the only player on the team to see action in all 82 games. His 30 assists led all Arizona blueliners and ranked him second on the team overall.

2017-18 Player Personnel

FORWARDS	HT	WT	*Age	Birthplace	S	2016-17 Club
COUSINS, Nick	5-10	188	24	Belleville, ON	L	Philadelphia
CROUSE, Lawson	6-4	220	20	Mt. Brydges, ON	L	Arizona
DOMI, Max	5-10	198	22	Winnipeg, MB	L	Arizona
DUCLAIR, Anthony	5-11	185	22	Pointe-Claire, QC	L	Arizona-Tucson
DVORAK, Christian	6-0	198	21	Palos, IL	L	Arizona
ETEM, Emerson	6-1	212	25	Long Beach, CA	L	Anaheim-San Diego
FISCHER, Christian	6-2	212	20	Chicago, IL	R	Arizona-Tucson
GAUDET, Tyler	6-3	205	24	Hamilton, ON	L	Arizona-Tucson
KELLER, Clayton	5-10	169	19	Chesterfield, MO	L	Boston University-Arizona
LATTA, Michael	6-0	207	26	Kitchener, ON	R	Ontario-Rockford
MARTINOOK, Jordan	6-0	202	25	Brandon, MB	L	Arizona
McGINN, Jamie	6-1	205	29	Fergus, ON	L	Arizona
PERLINI, Brendan	6-4	207	21	Guildford, UK	L	Arizona-Tucson
RICHARDSON, Brad	6-0	197	32	Belleville, ON	L	Arizona
RIEDER, Tobias	5-11	185	24	Landshut, Germany	L	Arizona
RINALDO, Zac	5-10	188	27	Mississauga, ON	L	Providence (AHL)
SISLO, Mike	5-11	190	29	Superior, WI	R	San Antonio-Toronto (AHL)
STEPAN, Derek	6-0	196	27	Hastings, MN	R	NY Rangers
STROME, Dylan	6-3	197	20	Mississauga, ON	L	Arizona-Erie

DEFENSEMEN						
CAMPBELL, Andrew	6-4	206	29	Caledonia, ON	L	Toronto (AHL)
CHYCHRUN, Jakob	6-3	200	19	Boca Raton, FL	L	Arizona
CLENDENING, Adam	6-0	196	24	Niagara Falls, NY	R	NY Rangers
CONNAUTON, Kevin	6-2	205	27	Edmonton, AB	L	Arizona-Tucson
EKMAN-LARSSON, Oliver	6-2	200	24	Karlskrona, Sweden	L	Arizona
GOLIGOSKI, Alex	5-11	185	32	Grand Rapids, MN	L	Arizona
HANLEY, Joel	6-0	193	26	Keswick, ON	L	Montreal-St. John's
HJALMARSSON, Niklas	6-3	197	30	Eksjo, Sweden	L	Chicago
SCHENN, Luke	6-2	229	27	Saskatoon, SK	R	Arizona
WOOD, Kyle	6-5	235	21	Waterloo, ON	R	Tucson

GOALTENDERS	HT	WT	*Age	Birthplace	C	2016-17 Club
DOMINGUE, Louis	6-3	210	25	St-Hyacinthe, QC	R	Arizona
RAANTA, Antti	6-0	193	28	Rauma, Finland	L	NY Rangers

* – Age at start of 2017-18 season

2016-17 Scoring

* – rookie

Regular Season

Pos	#	Player	Team	GP	G	A	Pts	TOI	+/-	PIM	PP	SH	GW	S	S%
R	17	Radim Vrbata	ARI	81	20	35	55	16:53	−18	16	4	0	4	233	8.6
D	23	Oliver Ekman-Larsson	ARI	79	12	27	39	24:36	−25	48	8	0	1	145	8.3
C	16	Max Domi	ARI	59	9	29	38	16:58	−9	40	1	0	1	108	8.3
D	33	Alex Goligoski	ARI	82	6	30	36	23:19	−9	28	1	1	0	112	5.4
C	8	Tobias Rieder	ARI	80	16	18	34	17:18	−8	6	2	1	1	155	10.3
L	18	* Christian Dvorak	ARI	78	15	18	33	15:37	7	22	2	0	1	88	17.0
R	19	Shane Doan	ARI	74	6	21	27	15:02	−3	48	3	0	4	144	4.2
L	48	Jordan Martinook	ARI	77	11	14	25	15:40	−8	40	1	1	2	109	10.1
L	29	* Brendan Perlini	ARI	57	14	7	21	14:50	−4	20	3	0	2	92	15.2
D	6	* Jakob Chychrun	ARI	68	7	13	20	16:40	−4	47	1	0	0	86	8.1
L	88	Jamie McGinn	ARI	72	9	8	17	13:10	−23	23	0	0	2	116	7.8
D	5	Connor Murphy	ARI	77	2	15	17	19:10	−13	45	0	1	1	81	2.5
C	91	Alexander Burmistrov	WPG	23	0	2	2	11:02	−6	6	0	0	0	13	0.0
			ARI	26	5	9	14	15:24	−1	6	4	0	0	32	15.6
			Total	49	5	11	16	13:21	−7	12	4	0	0	45	11.1
L	10	Anthony Duclair	ARI	58	5	10	15	13:17	−7	14	0	0	1	76	6.6
D	77	* Tony DeAngelo	ARI	39	5	9	14	17:05	−13	37	2	0	1	60	8.3
C	13	Peter Holland	TOR	8	0	1	1	10:43	−2	4	0	0	0	13	0.0
			ARI	40	5	6	11	13:09	−14	18	1	0	0	66	7.6
			Total	48	5	7	12	12:45	−16	22	1	0	0	79	6.3
L	67	* Lawson Crouse	ARI	72	5	7	12	11:53	−20	48	0	1	2	84	6.0
R	86	Josh Jooris	NYR	12	1	1	2	8:36	1	6	0	0	0	11	9.1
			ARI	42	3	7	10	13:13	−3	10	0	0	0	64	4.7
			Total	54	4	8	12	12:11	−2	16	0	0	0	75	5.3
R	15	Brad Richardson	ARI	16	5	4	9	15:20	−1	15	0	2	0	25	20.0
D	2	Luke Schenn	ARI	78	1	7	8	18:02	−9	85	0	0	0	94	1.1
R	36	* Christian Fischer	ARI	7	3	0	3	12:19	0	0	0	0	1	10	30.0
D	76	Laurent Dauphin	ARI	24	2	1	3	10:54	−2	12	0	0	0	32	6.3
L	12	Teemu Pulkkinen	MIN	9	1	0	1	9:23	−1	2	0	0	0	4	25.0
			ARI	4	1	0	1	9:45	−1	0	0	0	0	6	16.7
			Total	13	2	0	2	9:30	−2	2	0	0	0	10	20.0
C	14	* Clayton Keller	ARI	3	0	2	2	12:40	−3	0	0	0	0	0	0.0
C	32	* Tyler Gaudet	ARI	1	0	1	1	12:59	0	0	0	0	0	3	0.0
C	20	* Dylan Strome	ARI	7	0	1	1	13:41	−5	0	0	0	0	6	0.0
D	44	Kevin Connauton	ARI	24	0	1	1	13:07	−1	24	0	0	0	21	0.0
D	4	Zbynek Michalek	ARI	3	0	0	0	17:39	1	0	0	0	0	3	0.0
D	21	Jamie McBain	ARI	3	0	0	0	16:40	+/-	0	0	0	0	0	0.0

Goaltending

No.	Goaltender	GPI	Mins	Avg	W	L	OT	EN	SO	GA	SA	Sv%	G	A	PIM
41	Mike Smith	55	3202	2.92	19	26	9	8	3	156	1819	.914	0	0	14
35	Louis Domingue	31	1599	3.08	11	15	1	3	0	82	888	.908	0	0	0
40	Justin Peters	3	133	3.16	0	1	0	1	0	7	70	.900	0	0	0
30	* Marek Langhamer	1	16	3.75	0	0	0	0	0	1	8	.875	0	0	0
	Totals	82	4986	3.10	30	42	10	12	3	258	2797	.908			

Rookie Christian Dvorak scored 15 goals in 2016-17 and led the Coyotes in plus-minus.

Rick Tocchet
Head Coach
Born: Scarborough, ON, April 9, 1964.

Arizona Coyotes general manager John Chayka announced on July 11, 2017, that Rick Tocchet had signed a multiyear contract to serve as the club's head coach. Tocchet is the 18th man to serve as head coach in franchise history. He joined the Coyotes following three seasons and back-to-back Stanley Cup championships as an assistant coach with the Pittsburgh Penguins. The Penguins of 2016 and 2017 became the first team since the 1997 and 1998 Detroit Red Wings to win consecutive Stanley Cup titles.

Tocchet began his coaching career as an assistant with the Colorado Avalanche from 2002 to 2004. He spent one season as an assistant with the Coyotes in 2005-06 before joining the Tampa Bay Lightning as an assistant coach in 2008. He was named interim head coach of the Lightning on November 14 and later head coach following the 2008-09 season.

The former winger played 18 NHL seasons including parts of three seasons with the Coyotes (1997 to 2000). Tocchet totaled 64 goals and 66 assists for 130 points with 371 penalty minutes in 213 games with Phoenix. He finished second on the team with 26 goals in both 1997-98 and 1998-99. The four-time NHL All-Star won the Stanley Cup with the Penguins in 1992 and played in the 1987 Stanley Cup Final with the Philadelphia Flyers. Tocchet totaled 440 goals and 512 assists for 952 with 2,972 penalty minutes in 1,144 career NHL games with the Flyers, Penguins, Coyotes, Los Angeles Kings, Boston Bruins and Washington Capitals. His best season came in 1992-93 when he played alongside Mario Lemieux in Pittsburgh and totaled 48 goals and 61 assists for 109 points with 252 penalty minutes. Tocchet is one of just three players in NHL history to record 400-plus goals and 2,500 penalty minutes. He also registered five 30-plus goal seasons and three seasons with 40-plus goals. Tocchet was originally drafted by the Flyers in the sixth round (125th overall) in the 1983 NHL Draft. He also represented Canada on multiple occasions including the 1990 and 1991 World Championships and won Canada Cup titles in 1987 and 1991.

Coaching Record

Season	Team	League	Regular Season				Playoffs			
			GC	W	L	O/T	GC	W	L	T
2008-09	Tampa Bay	NHL	66	19	33	14	....	....	....	....
2009-10	Tampa Bay	NHL	82	34	36	12	....	....	....	....
	NHL Totals		148	53	69	26				

Posted a 2-3-0 record as replacement coach for the Coyotes when Wayne Gretzky was sidelined due to a death in the family, December 17-28, 2005. Games are credited to Gretzky's coaching record.

Captains' History

Lars-Erik Sjoberg, 1979-80; Morris Lukowich and Scott Campbell, 1980-81; Dave Christian and Barry Long, 1981-82; Dave Christian and Lucien DeBlois, 1982-83; Lucien DeBlois, 1983-84; Dale Hawerchuk, 1984-85 to 1988-89; Randy Carlyle, Dale Hawerchuk and Thomas Steen (tri-captains), 1989-90; Randy Carlyle and Thomas Steen (co-captains), 1990-91; Troy Murray, 1991-92; Troy Murray and Dean Kennedy, 1992-93; Dean Kennedy and Keith Tkachuk, 1993-94; Keith Tkachuk, 1994-95; Kris King, 1995-96; Keith Tkachuk, 1996-97 to 2000-01; Teppo Numminen, 2001-02, 2002-03; Shane Doan, 2003-04 to 2016-17.

Coaching History

Tom McVie and Bill Sutherland, 1979-80; Tom McVie, Bill Sutherland and Mike Smith, 1980-81; Tom Watt, 1981-82, 1982-83; Tom Watt and Barry Long, 1983-84; Barry Long, 1984-85; Barry Long and John Ferguson, 1985-86; Dan Maloney, 1986-87, 1987-88; Dan Maloney and Rick Bowness, 1988-89; Bob Murdoch, 1989-90, 1990-91; John Paddock, 1991-92 to 1993-94; John Paddock and Terry Simpson, 1994-95; Terry Simpson, 1995-96; Don Hay, 1996-97; Jim Schoenfeld, 1997-98, 1998-99; Bob Francis, 1999-2000 to 2002-03; Bob Francis and Rick Bowness, 2003-04; Rick Bowness, 2004-05; Wayne Gretzky, 2005-06 to 2008-09; Dave Tippett, 2009-10 to 2016-17; Rick Tocchet, 2017-18.

Club Records

Team

(Figures in brackets for season records are games played; records for fewest points, wins, ties, losses, goals, goals against are for 70 or more games)

Most Points	107	2009-10 (82)
Most Wins	50	2009-10 (82)
Most Ties	18	2003-04 (82)
Most Losses	57	1980-81 (80)
Most Goals	358	1984-85 (80)
Most Goals Against	400	1980-81 (80)
Fewest Points	32	1980-81 (80)
Fewest Wins	9	1980-81 (80)
Fewest Ties	6	1995-96 (82)
Fewest Losses	25	2009-10 (82)
Fewest Goals	170	2014-15 (82)
Fewest Goals Against	197	1998-99 (82)
Longest Winning Streak		
Overall	9	Mar. 8-27/85, Mar. 4-21/10
Home	10	Nov. 21-Dec. 29/09
Away	8	Feb. 25-Apr. 6/85
Longest Team Point Streak		
Overall	14	Oct. 25-Nov. 28/98 (12W, 2T)
Home	11	Dec. 23/83-Feb. 5/84 (6W, 5T), Oct. 15-Dec. 20/98 (10W, 1T)
Away	9	Feb. 25-Apr. 7/85 (8W, 1T), Dec. 7/03-Jan. 9/04 (5W, 4T)
Longest Losing Streak		
Overall	10	Nov. 30-Dec. 20/80, Feb. 6-25/94, Feb. 10-Mar. 3/15
Home	6	Oct. 6-Nov. 3/07, Jan. 27-Feb. 16/09, Mar. 12-30/15
Away	13	Jan. 26-Apr. 14/94
Longest Winless Streak		
Overall	*30	Oct. 19-Dec. 20/80 (23L, 7T)
Home	14	Oct. 19-Dec. 14/80 (9L, 5T)
Away	18	Oct. 10-Dec. 20/80 (16L, 2T)
Most Shutouts, Season	9	1998-99 (82), 2010-11 (82)
Most PIM, Season	2,278	1987-88 (80)
Most Goals, Game	12	Feb. 25/85 (Wpg. 12 at NYR 5)

Individual

Most Seasons	21	Shane Doan
Most Games	1,540	Shane Doan
Most Goals, Career	402	Shane Doan
Most Assists, Career	570	Shane Doan
Most Points, Career	972	Shane Doan (402G, 570A)
Most PIM, Career	1,508	Keith Tkachuk
Most Shutouts, Career	22	Mike Smith
Longest Consecutive Games Streak	475	Dale Hawerchuk (Dec. 19/82-Dec. 10/88)
Most Goals, Season	76	Teemu Selanne (1992-93)
Most Assists, Season	79	Phil Housley (1992-93)
Most Points, Season	132	Teemu Selanne (1992-93; 76G, 56A)
Most PIM, Season	347	Tie Domi (1993-94)
Most Points, Defenseman, Season	97	Phil Housley (1992-93; 18G, 79A)
Most Points, Center, Season	130	Dale Hawerchuk (1984-85; 53G, 77A)
Most Points, Right Wing, Season	132	Teemu Selanne (1992-93; 76G, 56A)
Most Points, Left Wing, Season	98	Keith Tkachuk (1995-96; 50G, 48A)
Most Points, Rookie, Season	*132	Teemu Selanne (1992-93; 76G, 56A)
Most Shutouts, Season	8	Nikolai Khabibulin (1998-99), Ilya Bryzgalov (2009-10), Mike Smith (2011-12)
Most Goals, Game	5	Willy Lindstrom (Mar. 2/82), Alexei Zhamnov (Apr. 1/95)
Most Assists, Game	5	Dale Hawerchuk (Mar. 6/84), (Mar. 18/89), (Mar. 4/90), Phil Housley (Jan. 18/93), Keith Tkachuk (Feb. 23/01)
Most Points, Game	6	Willy Lindstrom (Mar. 2/82; 5G, 1A), Dale Hawerchuk (Dec. 14/83; 3G, 3A), (Mar. 5/88; 2G, 4A), (Mar. 18/89; 1G, 5A), Thomas Steen (Oct. 24/84; 2G, 4A), Ed Olczyk (Dec. 21/91; 2G, 4A)

* NHL Record.

Records include Winnipeg Jets, 1979-80 through 1995-96.

All-time Record vs. Other Clubs

Regular Season

	Total								At Home								On Road							
	GP	W	L	T	OL	GF	GA	PTS	GP	W	L	T	OL	GF	GA	PTS	GP	W	L	T	OL	GF	GA	PTS
Anaheim	124	49	59	5	11	325	373	114	61	28	26	2	5	169	178	63	63	21	33	3	6	156	195	51
Boston	75	21	46	7	1	219	283	50	38	14	20	3	1	115	127	32	37	7	26	4	0	104	156	18
Buffalo	76	24	43	7	2	201	269	57	37	15	19	2	1	103	116	33	39	9	24	5	1	98	153	24
Calgary	192	80	88	20	4	622	678	184	95	47	36	11	1	330	306	106	97	33	52	9	3	292	372	78
Carolina	76	30	33	8	5	244	263	73	38	15	17	2	4	130	139	36	38	15	16	6	1	114	124	37
Chicago	141	56	64	15	6	396	483	133	72	35	29	5	3	224	231	78	69	21	35	10	3	172	252	55
Colorado	124	53	51	12	8	408	404	126	62	27	23	7	5	211	201	66	62	26	28	5	3	197	203	60
Columbus	55	28	20	4	3	154	138	63	28	16	8	3	1	87	66	36	27	12	12	1	2	67	72	27
Dallas	173	71	79	13	10	496	553	165	86	39	39	4	4	257	264	86	87	32	40	9	6	239	289	79
Detroit	139	48	61	22	8	425	488	126	69	23	27	14	5	201	222	65	70	25	34	8	3	224	266	61
Edmonton	194	80	95	11	8	682	771	179	96	45	42	5	4	370	379	99	98	35	53	6	4	312	392	80
Florida	32	17	10	3	2	84	83	39	17	9	3	3	2	48	42	23	15	8	7	0	0	36	41	16
Los Angeles	222	110	79	25	8	791	739	253	112	61	37	11	3	417	350	136	110	49	42	14	5	374	389	117
Minnesota	59	25	27	3	4	138	153	57	30	13	14	1	2	72	75	29	29	12	13	2	2	66	78	28
Montreal	72	16	44	9	3	195	300	44	36	11	16	7	2	115	134	31	36	5	28	2	1	80	166	13
Nashville	67	31	24	2	10	177	193	74	33	20	9	0	4	98	93	44	34	11	15	2	6	79	100	30
New Jersey	74	39	25	9	1	236	217	88	38	26	9	3	0	135	100	55	36	13	16	6	1	101	117	33
NY Islanders	75	27	35	12	1	230	264	67	38	17	16	4	1	125	123	39	37	10	19	8	0	105	141	28
NY Rangers	76	25	40	6	5	247	288	61	38	15	18	4	1	124	129	35	38	10	22	2	4	123	159	26
Ottawa	35	15	16	2	2	107	126	34	17	7	7	1	2	52	61	17	18	8	9	1	0	55	65	17
Philadelphia	77	30	43	2	2	226	279	64	38	18	18	2	0	121	122	38	39	12	25	0	2	105	157	26
Pittsburgh	76	30	41	3	2	232	276	65	38	18	15	3	2	135	127	41	38	12	26	0	0	97	149	24
St. Louis	144	56	68	18	2	399	471	132	72	33	32	7	0	214	236	73	72	23	36	11	2	185	235	59
San Jose	139	61	61	7	10	376	415	139	71	35	28	3	5	202	198	78	68	26	33	4	5	174	217	61
Tampa Bay	37	17	20	0	0	103	116	34	20	9	11	0	0	49	54	18	17	8	9	0	0	54	62	16
Toronto	96	52	35	8	1	371	332	113	46	25	15	6	0	186	159	56	50	27	20	2	1	185	173	57
Vancouver	191	73	91	20	7	567	655	173	94	46	36	10	2	312	308	104	97	27	55	10	5	255	347	69
Washington	75	30	31	12	2	236	266	74	37	20	9	7	1	132	122	48	38	10	22	5	1	104	144	26
Winnipeg	28	16	8	1	3	83	72	36	15	11	2	1	1	50	33	24	13	5	6	0	2	33	39	12
Totals	**2944**	**1210**	**1337**	**266**	**131**	**8970**	**9948**	**2817**	**1472**	**698**	**581**	**131**	**62**	**4784**	**4695**	**1589**	**1472**	**512**	**756**	**135**	**69**	**4186**	**5253**	**1228**

Playoffs

	Series	W	L	GP	W	L	T	GF	GA	Last Mtg.	Rnd.	Result
Anaheim	1	0	1	7	3	4	0	17	17	1997	CQF	L 3-4
Calgary	3	2	1	13	7	6	0	45	43	1987	DSF	W 4-2
Chicago	1	1	0	6	4	2	0	17	12	2012	CQF	W 4-2
Colorado	1	0	1	5	1	4	0	10	17	2000	CQF	L 1-4
Detroit	4	0	4	23	7	16	0	56	88	2011	CQF	L 0-4
Edmonton	6	0	6	26	4	22	0	75	120	1990	DSF	L 3-4
Los Angeles	1	0	1	5	1	4	0	8	14	2012	CF	L 1-4
Nashville	1	1	0	5	4	1	0	12	9	2012	CSF	W 4-1
St. Louis	2	0	2	11	4	7	0	29	39	1999	CQF	L 3-4
San Jose	1	0	1	5	1	4	0	7	13	2002	CQF	L 1-4
Vancouver	2	0	2	13	5	8	0	34	50	1993	DSF	L 2-4
Totals	**23**	**4**	**19**	**119**	**41**	**78**	**0**	**310**	**422**			

Calgary totals include Atlanta Flames, 1979-80.
Colorado totals include Quebec, 1979-80 to 1994-95.
New Jersey totals include Colorado Rockies, 1979-80 to 1981-82.
Carolina totals include Hartford, 1979-80 to 1996-97.
Dallas totals include Minnesota North Stars, 1979-80 to 1992-93.
Winnipeg totals include Atlanta Thrashers, 1999-2000 to 2010-11.

Playoff Results 2017-2013

(Last playoff appearance: 2012)

Abbreviations: Round: CF – conference final; **CSF** – conference semi-final; **CQF** – conference quarter-final; **DSF** – division semi-final.

2016-17 Results

Oct.	15	Philadelphia	4-3*		14	Anaheim	0-3
	18	at Ottawa	4-7		16	at Edmonton	1-3
	20	at Montreal	2-5		18	at Winnipeg	3-6
	21	at NY Islanders	2-3		19	at Minnesota	3-4
	23	at NY Rangers	2-3		21	Tampa Bay	5-3
	25	at New Jersey	3-5		23	Florida	3-2*
	27	at Philadelphia	5-4		26	Vancouver	3-0
	29	Colorado	2-3		31	Los Angeles	2-3
Nov.	1	San Jose	3-2	**Feb.**	2	Chicago	3-4
	3	Nashville	3-2†		4	at San Jose	3-2†
	4	at Anaheim	1-5		9	Montreal	4-5*
	8	at Colorado	4-2		11	Pittsburgh	4-3*
	10	Winnipeg	2-3		13	at Calgary	5-0
	12	Boston	1-2		14	at Edmonton	2-5
	16	at Calgary	1-2*		16	at Los Angeles	5-3
	17	at Vancouver	2-3*		18	San Jose	1-4
	19	San Jose	3-2*		20	Anaheim	3-2
	23	Vancouver	1-4		23	at Chicago	3-6
	25	Edmonton	3-2†		24	at Dallas	2-5
	27	at Edmonton	2-1		26	Buffalo	3-2
	29	at San Jose	1-2*		28	at Boston	1-4
Dec.	1	Los Angeles	3-4	**Mar.**	2	at Buffalo	3-6
	3	Columbus	2-3†		3	at Carolina	4-2
	5	at Columbus	1-4		5	Carolina	1-2
	6	at Chicago	0-4		9	Ottawa	2-3*
	8	Calgary	1-2*		11	New Jersey	5-4
	10	Nashville	4-1		13	Colorado	1-0
	12	at Pittsburgh	0-7		14	at Los Angeles	3-2†
	13	at Detroit	4-1		16	Detroit	4-5†
	15	at Toronto	3-2†		18	St. Louis	0-3
	17	at Minnesota	1-4		20	at Nashville	1-3
	19	Calgary	2-4		21	at Tampa Bay	5-3
	21	Edmonton	2-3		23	at Florida	1-3
	23	Toronto	1-4		25	at Washington	1-4
	27	Dallas	2-3		27	at St. Louis	1-4
	29	NY Rangers	3-6		29	St. Louis	1-3
	31	at Calgary	2-4		31	Washington	6-3
Jan.	4	at Vancouver	0-3	**Apr.**	2	at Los Angeles	2-1
	6	at Anaheim	2-3*		4	at Dallas	2-3*
	7	NY Islanders	2-1†		6	Vancouver	4-3
	13	Winnipeg	4-3		8	Minnesota	1-3

* – Overtime † – Shootout

NHL Draft Selections 2017-2003

Name in bold denotes played in NHL.

2017 Pick		2014 Pick		2010 Pick		2006 Pick	
23	Pierre-Olivier Joseph	12	**Brendan Perlini**	13	**Brandon Gormley**	8	**Peter Mueller**
44	Filip Westerlund	43	Ryan MacInnis	27	**Mark Visentin**	29	**Chris Summers**
69	Mackenzie Entwistle	58	**Christian Dvorak**	52	Phil Lane	88	Jonas Ahnelov
75	Nate Schnarr	87	Anton Karlsson	57	**Oscar Lindberg**	130	Brett Bennett
82	Cameron Crotty	117	Michael Bunting	138	**Louis Domingue**	131	Martin Latal
108	Noel Hoefenmayer	133	Dysin Mayo			152	Jordan Bendfeld
126	Michael Karow	163	David Westlund	**2009**		188	Chris Frank
128	Tyler Steenbergen	191	Jared Fiegl	**Pick**		196	**Benn Ferriero**
190	Erik Walli-Walterholm	193	Edgars Kulda	6	**Oliver Ekman-Larsson**		
				36	**Chris Brown**	**2005**	
2016		**2013**		91	**Mike Lee**	**Pick**	
Pick		**Pick**		97	**Jordan Szwarz**	17	**Martin Hanzal**
7	**Clayton Keller**	12	**Max Domi**	105	Justin Weller	59	Pier-Olivier Pelletier
16	**Jakob Chychrun**	39	**Laurent Dauphin**	157	Evan Bloodoff	105	**Keith Yandle**
68	Cam Dineen	62	Pavel Laplante			148	Anton Krysanov
158	Patrick Kudla	133	Connor Clifton	**2008**		212	Pat Brosnihan
188	Dean Stewart	163	Brendan Burke	**Pick**			
		193	Jedd Soleway	8	**Mikkel Boedker**	**2004**	
2015				28	**Viktor Tikhonov**	**Pick**	
Pick		**2012**		49	**Jared Staal**	5	**Blake Wheeler**
3	**Dylan Strome**	**Pick**		69	**Michael Stone**	35	Logan Stephenson
30	Nick Merkley	27	**Henrik Samuelsson**	76	Mathieu Brodeur	50	**Enver Lisin**
32	**Christian Fischer**	58	**Jordan Martinook**	99	Colin Long	103	Roman Tomanek
63	Kyle Capobianco	88	James Melindy	159	Brett Hextall	119	**Kevin Porter**
76	Adin Hill	102	Rhett Holland	189	Tim Billingsley	168	Kevin Cormier
81	Brendan Warren	148	Niklas Tikkinen			199	**Chad Kolarik**
83	Jens Looke	178	Hunter Fejes	**2007**		240	**Aaron Gagnon**
123	Conor Garland	184	**Marek Langhamer**	**Pick**		261	Will Engasser
183	Erik Kallgren	208	Justin Hache	3	**Kyle Turris**	265	**Daniel Winnik**
				30	Nick Ross		
		2011		32	**Brett Maclean**	**2003**	
		Pick		36	Joel Gistedt	**Pick**	
		20	**Connor Murphy**	103	Vladimir Ruzicka	77	Tyler Redenbach
		51	Alexander Ruuttu	123	Maxim Goncharov	80	Dmitri Pestunov
		56	**Lucas Lessio**	153	**Scott Darling**	115	Liam Lindstrom
		84	Harrison Ruopp			178	Ryan Gibbons
		111	Kale Kessy			208	Randall Gelech
		141	Darian Dziurzynski			242	Eduard Lewandowski
		155	Andrew Fritsch			272	Sean Sullivan
		196	Zac Larraza			290	Loic Burkhalter

General Managers' History

John Ferguson, 1979-80 to 1987-88; John Ferguson and Mike Smith, 1988-89; Mike Smith, 1989-90 to 1992-93; Mike Smith and John Paddock, 1993-94; John Paddock, 1994-95, 1995-96; John Paddock and Bobby Smith, 1996-97; Bobby Smith, 1997-98 to 1999-2000; Bobby Smith and Cliff Fletcher, 2000-01; Michael Barnett, 2001-02 to 2006-07; Don Maloney, 2007-08 to 2015-16; John Chayka, 2016-17 to date.

John Chayka
General Manager

Born: St. Catherines, ON, June 9, 1989.

John Chayka was named as the general manager of the Arizona Coyotes on May 5, 2016. At 26 years old, he became the youngest general manager in NHL and North American major sports history.

Chayka joined the Coyotes in 2015-16 as assistant general manager, analytics. He was involved in all areas of hockey operations including NHL, minor league and amateur player evaluation as well as player development and coaching support. Prior to joining the Coyotes, Chayka co-founded and served as director of hockey operations at Stathletes Inc. since 2009. Stathletes is a hockey analytics firm that tracks data through an intensive video analysis process and breaks down the game to provide objective insight into player and team performance tendencies.

The native of Jordan Station, Ontario, earned his bachelor's degree in business administration from the Richard Ivey School of Business at the University of Western Ontario in 2014. Chayka was drafted to the Ontario Hockey League but committed to going to college instead. He played Junior A hockey in Canada and was a top scorer in the Maritime Junior A League. He also played briefly in the BCHL before suffering a career ending injury

Club Directory

Gila River Arena

Arizona Coyotes
Gila River Arena
9400 W. Maryland Avenue
Glendale, AZ 85305
Phone **623/772-3200**
FAX 623/872-2000
Tickets 480/563-PUCK
www.ArizonaCoyotes.com
Capacity: 17,125

Club Officers and Executives
Owner, Chairman & Governor . . . . Andrew Barroway
President, CEO & Alternate Governor . . . . Steve Patterson
President of Hockey Operations, G.M. & Alt. Governor . . John Chayka
COO, General Counsel & Alternate Governor . . . . . Ahron Cohen
Chief Financial Officer. . . . . Gregg Olson
Executive VP, Corporate & Premium Seating . . . . . John Knebel
Executive VP, Ticket Sales & Strategy . . . . Jeff Morander
Executive VP, Communications & Broadcasting . . . . Rich Nairn

Hockey Operations
Head Coach . . . . Rick Tocchet
Assistant General Managers . . . . Steve Sullivan / Chris O'Hearn
Assistant Coaches. . . . . John MacLean, Scott Allen
Goaltending Coaches . . . . Jon Elkin, Corey Schwab
Player Development Coach . . . . Alex Henry
Strength & Conditioning Coach . . . . JP Major
Assistant Coach, Video . . . . Steve Peters
Dir. of Hockey Operations . . . . Jake Goldberg
Dir. of Statistical Analysis . . . . Brad Rossen
Hockey Operations Coord. . . . . Al Ambrosia
Executive Assistant, Hockey Ops . . . . Kara Montgomery
Head Athletic Trainer / Assistant Athletic Trainer . . . Dave Zenobi / Donnie Fuller
Manual Therapist . . . . Eric Ford
Equipment: Head Mgr. / Mgr. / Asst. Mgrs. . . . . . . Stan Wilson / Tony Silva / Jason Rudee, Denver Wilson
Team Services Manager / Coord & Security . . . . . . Dave Griffiths / Jim O'Neal
Director, Amateur Scouting. . . . . Tim Bernhardt
Asst. Director of Amateur Scouting. . . . . Jeff Twohey
Professional Scouts . . . . Craig Cunningham, Mark Bell
European Scouts . . . . Thomas Carlsson, Max Kolu, Sergei Kuznetsov, Robert Neuhauser
Amateur Scouts . . . . Trevor Hanson, Rob Pulford, Mike Sands, Glen Zacharias, Jim Hammett. Rick Beckfeld
Team Internist / Orthopedic Surgeons . . . . . Drs. Robert Luberto / Brian Shafer, Gary Waslewski
Ophthalmologists . . . . Drs. George Reiss, Jeffery Edelstein

Broadcasting
Director of Broadcasting . . . . Doug Cannon
TV Play-by-Play / Color / Host . . . . Matt McConnell / Tyson Nash / Todd Walsh
Radio Play-By-Play Announcer / Analyst / Host. . . . Bob Heethuis / Paul Bissonnette / Luke Lapinski

Communications
Director of News Content . . . . Dave Vest
Media Relations Manager / Coordinator . . . . Greg Dillard / Jeffrey Sanders

Community Relations
Exec. Dir. of Arizona Coyotes Foundation /
   Community Relations Director . . . . Olivia Matos
Community Relations Mgr. / Foundation Mgr. . . . . Natalia Protopopoff / Katrina Hinsberg
Mascot Coordinator . . . . Jeph Harris

Corporate Partnerships & Service
Sr. Advisor, Business Dev. & Alumni Relations . . . . Cale Hulse
Corporate Partnerships Manager. . . . . Mike Akers
Corporate Partnerships Service Managers . . . . . . Lindsay Foletta, Matt Carnot
Partnership Activation Coordinator . . . . Blake Pangman

Finance & Legal
Controller . . . . David Montgomery
Dir. Financial Planning/Analysis . . . . Craig Wolman
Accounting Coord. / Payroll Admin. . . . . Craig Scott / Debi Leal
Staff Accountants . . . . Chris Shelley, Jessica Fuentes
Associate General Counsel . . . . Marina Mercer

Game Presentation
Game Presentation Director / Coordinator . . . . . . Lamont Buford / Dave Ellsworth

Human Resources
Sr. Director, HR / Receptionist . . . . Patty Frankenfield / Ivette Servin

Marketing
Director, Marketing Analytics . . . . Ben Wang
Sr. Manager, Creative & Web Services. . . . . Scott Jenner
Social Media Strategy Mgr. . . . . Marissa O'Connor
Events & Marketing Manager . . . . Rachel Olish
Marketing Coordinator . . . . Jessica Isner

Premium & Suite Sales
Sr. Director of Premium & Suite Sales . . . . Grant Buckborough
Sr. Business Development Executive . . . . Mike Briody
Premium Seating & Suite Sales Mgrs. . . . . Matt McClelland, Dave Paris
Service Manager . . . . Matt Herold

Production
Sr. Manager of Production . . . . Jon Kingston
Video Graphics Manager . . . . Robert Clark
Motion Graphics Coord. / Shooter/Editor . . . . Courtney Orner / Tim Page

Technology
IT Director / Tech / Support . . . . Monty Low / Justin Ferguson / Michael Wenzel

Ticket Operations
Director, Ticket Operations . . . . Jim Bakken
Ticket Operations Coordinators . . . . Jackie Purcell, Laura Anderson, Tyler Oberg

Ticket Sales & Service
Vice President of Ticket Sales & Service . . . . Bill Makris
Sr. Director, Client Services & Guest Experience. . . . Lindsay Kray
Director, Business Development . . . . Sam Bays

Tucson Roadrunners (AHL)
President . . . . Bob Hoffman
Head Coach . . . . Mike Van Ryn
Assistant Coaches. John Slaney, Steve Potvin
Athletic Trainer / Equipment Manager . . . . Todd Daniels / Eric Bechtol
Radio Play by Play . . . . Tom Callahan
Director of Game Operations . . . . Mark Iralson

Team Information
Regional Sports Network / Radio Station . . . . FOX Sports Arizona / Arizona Sports 98.7 FM
Team Photographer . . . . Norm Hall

Boston Bruins

2016-17 Results: 44W-31L-4OTL-3SOL 95PTS
3RD, Atlantic Division • 6TH, Eastern Conference

Key Off-Season Signings/Acquisitions

2017

June 13 • Named **Kevin Dean** assistant coach.
14 • Re-signed D **Tommy Cross**.
28 • Re-signed C **Noel Acciari**.
July 1 • Signed LW **Kenny Agostino**, RW **Jordan Szwarz** and D **Paul Postma**.
5 • Re-signed C **Tim Schaller**.
14 • Re-signed G **Zane McIntyre** and G **Malcolm Subban**.
18 • Re-signed C **Austin Czarnik**.
26 • Re-signed C **Ryan Spooner**.

2017-18 Schedule

Oct.	Thu.	5	Nashville		Sat.	13	at Montreal
	Mon.	9	Colorado*		Mon.	15	Dallas*
	Wed.	11	at Colorado		Wed.	17	Montreal
	Sat.	14	at Arizona		Thu.	18	at NY Islanders
	Sun.	15	at Vegas*		Sat.	20	at Montreal
	Thu.	19	Vancouver		Tue.	23	New Jersey
	Sat.	21	Buffalo		Thu.	25	at Ottawa
	Thu.	26	San Jose		Tue.	30	Anaheim
	Sat.	28	Los Angeles	**Feb.**	Thu.	1	St. Louis
	Mon.	30	at Columbus		Sat.	3	Toronto
Nov.	Thu.	2	Vegas		Tue.	6	at Detroit
	Sat.	4	Washington		Wed.	7	at NY Rangers
	Mon.	6	Minnesota		Sat.	10	Buffalo
	Wed.	8	at NY Rangers		Sun.	11	at New Jersey
	Fri.	10	at Toronto		Tue.	13	Calgary
	Sat.	11	Toronto		Sat.	17	at Vancouver
	Wed.	15	at Anaheim		Mon.	19	at Calgary*
	Thu.	16	at Los Angeles		Tue.	20	at Edmonton
	Sat.	18	at San Jose		Sat.	24	at Toronto
	Wed.	22	at New Jersey		Sun.	25	at Buffalo*
	Fri.	24	Pittsburgh*		Tue.	27	Carolina
	Sun.	26	Edmonton*	**Mar.**	Thu.	1	Pittsburgh
	Wed.	29	Tampa Bay		Sat.	3	Montreal*
Dec.	Sat.	2	at Philadelphia*		Tue.	6	Detroit
	Mon.	4	at Nashville		Thu.	8	Philadelphia
	Thu.	7	Arizona		Sat.	10	Chicago*
	Sat.	9	NY Islanders		Sun.	11	at Chicago*
	Wed.	13	at Detroit		Tue.	13	at Carolina
	Thu.	14	Washington		Thu.	15	at Florida
	Sat.	16	NY Rangers*		Sat.	17	at Tampa Bay
	Mon.	18	Columbus		Mon.	19	Columbus
	Tue.	19	at Buffalo		Wed.	21	at St. Louis*
	Thu.	21	Winnipeg		Fri.	23	at Dallas
	Sat.	23	Detroit*		Sun.	25	at Minnesota
	Wed.	27	Ottawa		Tue.	27	at Winnipeg
	Thu.	28	at Washington		Thu.	29	Tampa Bay
	Sat.	30	at Ottawa		Sat.	31	Florida*
Jan.	Tue.	2	at NY Islanders	**Apr.**	Sun.	1	at Philadelphia*
	Thu.	4	Florida		Tue.	3	at Tampa Bay
	Sat.	6	Carolina		Thu.	5	at Florida
	Sun.	7	at Pittsburgh		Sat.	7	Ottawa

* Denotes afternoon game.

Retired Numbers

2	Eddie Shore	1926-1940
3	Lionel Hitchman	1925-1934
4	Bobby Orr	1966-1976
5	Dit Clapper	1927-1947
7	Phil Esposito	1967-1975
8	Cam Neely	1986-1996
9	John Bucyk	1957-1978
15	Milt Schmidt	1936-1955
24	Terry O'Reilly	1971-1985
77	Raymond Bourque	1979-2000

ATLANTIC DIVISION
94th NHL Season
Franchise date: November 1, 1924

Year-by-Year Record

		Home				Road				Overall									
Season	GP	W	L	T	OL	W	L	T	OL	W	L	T	OL	GF	GA	Pts.	Div. Fin.	Conf. Fin.	Playoff Result
2016-17	82	23	17	....	1	21	14	....	6	44	31	....	7	234	212	95	3rd, Atl.	6th, East	Lost First Round
2015-16	82	17	18	....	6	25	13	....	3	42	31	....	9	240	230	93	4th, Atl.	9th, East	– out of playoffs –
2014-15	82	24	10	....	7	17	17	....	7	41	27	....	14	213	211	96	5th, Atl.	9th, East	– out of playoffs –
2013-14	82	31	7	....	3	23	12	....	6	54	19	....	9	261	177	117	1st, Atl.	1st, East	Lost Second Round
2012-13	48	16	5	....	3	12	9	....	3	28	14	....	6	131	109	62	2nd, NE	4th, East	Lost Final
2011-12	82	24	14	....	3	25	15	....	1	49	29	....	4	269	202	102	1st, NE	2nd, East	Lost Conf. Quarter-Final
2010-11	**82**	**22**	**13**	....	**6**	**24**	**12**	....	**5**	**46**	**25**	....	**11**	**246**	**195**	**103**	**1st, NE**	**3rd, East**	**Won Stanley Cup**
2009-10	82	18	17	....	6	21	13	....	7	39	30	....	13	206	200	91	3rd, NE	6th, East	Lost Conf. Semi-Final
2008-09	82	29	6	....	6	24	13	....	4	53	19	....	10	274	196	116	1st, NE	1st, East	Lost Conf. Semi-Final
2007-08	82	21	16	....	4	20	13	....	8	41	29	....	12	212	222	94	3rd, NE	8th, East	Lost Conf. Quarter-Final
2006-07	82	18	19	....	4	17	22	....	2	35	41	....	6	219	289	76	5th, NE	13th, East	– out of playoffs –
2005-06	82	16	15	....	10	13	22	....	6	29	37	....	16	230	266	74	5th, NE	13th, East	– out of playoffs –
2004-05	....	....	....	....	....	....	....	....	....	....	....	....	....	....	....	....			
2003-04	82	18	12	9	2	23	7	6	5	41	19	15	7	209	188	104	1st, NE	2nd, East	Lost Conf. Quarter-Final
2002-03	82	23	11	5	2	13	20	6	2	36	31	11	4	245	237	87	3rd, NE	7th, East	Lost Conf. Quarter-Final
2001-02	82	23	11	2	5	20	13	4	4	43	24	6	9	236	201	101	1st, NE	1st, East	Lost Conf. Quarter-Final
2000-01	82	21	12	5	3	15	18	3	5	36	30	8	8	227	249	88	4th, NE	9th, East	– out of playoffs –
1999-2000	82	12	17	11	1	12	16	8	5	24	33	19	6	210	248	73	5th, NE	12th, East	– out of playoffs –
1998-99	82	22	10	9	....	17	20	4	....	39	30	13	....	214	181	91	3rd, NE	6th, East	Lost Conf. Semi-Final
1997-98	82	19	16	6	....	20	14	7	....	39	30	13	....	221	194	91	2nd, NE	5th, East	Lost Conf. Quarter-Final
1996-97	82	14	20	7	....	12	27	2	....	26	47	9	....	234	300	61	6th, NE	13th, East	– out of playoffs –
1995-96	82	22	14	5	....	18	17	6	....	40	31	11	....	282	269	91	2nd, NE	5th, East	Lost Conf. Quarter-Final
1994-95	48	15	7	2	....	12	11	1	....	27	18	3	....	150	127	57	3rd, NE	4th, East	Lost Conf. Quarter-Final
1993-94	84	20	14	8	....	22	15	5	....	42	29	13	....	289	252	97	2nd, NE	4th, East	Lost Conf. Semi-Final
1992-93	84	29	10	3	....	22	16	4	....	51	26	7	....	332	268	109	1st, Adams		Lost Div. Semi-Final
1991-92	80	23	11	6	....	13	21	6	....	36	32	12	....	270	275	84	2nd, Adams		Lost Conf. Final
1990-91	80	26	9	5	....	18	15	7	....	44	24	12	....	299	264	100	1st, Adams		Lost Conf. Final
1989-90	80	23	13	4	....	23	12	5	....	46	25	9	....	289	232	101	1st, Adams		Lost Final
1988-89	80	17	15	8	....	20	14	6	....	37	29	14	....	289	256	88	2nd, Adams		Lost Div. Final
1987-88	80	24	13	3	....	20	17	3	....	44	30	6	....	300	251	94	2nd, Adams		Lost Final
1986-87	80	25	11	4	....	14	23	3	....	39	34	7	....	301	276	85	3rd, Adams		Lost Div. Semi-Final
1985-86	80	24	9	7	....	13	22	5	....	37	31	12	....	311	288	86	3rd, Adams		Lost Div. Semi-Final
1984-85	80	21	15	4	....	15	19	6	....	36	34	10	....	303	287	82	4th, Adams		Lost Div. Semi-Final
1983-84	80	25	12	3	....	24	13	3	....	49	25	6	....	336	261	104	1st, Adams		Lost Div. Semi-Final
1982-83	80	28	6	6	....	22	14	4	....	50	20	10	....	327	228	110	1st, Adams		Lost Conf. Final
1981-82	80	24	12	4	....	19	15	6	....	43	27	10	....	323	285	96	2nd, Adams		Lost Div. Final
1980-81	80	26	10	4	....	11	20	9	....	37	30	13	....	316	272	87	2nd, Adams		Lost Prelim. Round
1979-80	80	27	9	4	....	19	12	9	....	46	21	13	....	310	234	105	2nd, Adams		Lost Quarter-Final
1978-79	80	25	10	5	....	18	13	9	....	43	23	14	....	316	270	100	1st, Adams		Lost Semi-Final
1977-78	80	29	6	5	....	22	12	6	....	51	18	11	....	333	218	113	1st, Adams		Lost Final
1976-77	80	27	7	6	....	22	16	2	....	49	23	8	....	312	240	106	1st, Adams		Lost Final
1975-76	80	27	5	8	....	21	10	9	....	48	15	17	....	313	237	113	1st, Adams		Lost Semi-Final
1974-75	80	29	5	6	....	11	21	8	....	40	26	14	....	345	245	94	2nd, Adams		Lost Prelim. Round
1973-74	78	33	4	2	....	19	13	7	....	52	17	9	....	349	221	113	1st, East		Lost Final
1972-73	78	27	10	2	....	24	12	3	....	51	22	5	....	330	235	107	2nd, East		Lost Quarter-Final
1971-72	**78**	**28**	**4**	**7**	....	**26**	**9**	**4**	....	**54**	**13**	**11**	....	**330**	**204**	**119**	**1st, East**		**Won Stanley Cup**
1970-71	78	33	4	2	....	24	10	5	....	57	14	7	....	399	207	121	1st, East		Lost Quarter-Final
1969-70	**76**	**27**	**3**	**8**	....	**13**	**14**	**11**	....	**40**	**17**	**19**	....	**277**	**216**	**99**	**2nd, East**		**Won Stanley Cup**
1968-69	76	29	3	6	....	13	15	10	....	42	18	16	....	303	221	100	2nd, East		Lost Semi-Final
1967-68	74	22	9	6	....	15	18	4	....	37	27	10	....	259	216	84	3rd, East		Lost Quarter-Final
1966-67	70	10	21	4	....	7	22	6	....	17	43	10	....	182	253	44	6th		– out of playoffs –
1965-66	70	15	17	3	....	6	26	3	....	21	43	6	....	174	275	48	5th		– out of playoffs –
1964-65	70	12	17	6	....	9	26	0	....	21	43	6	....	166	253	48	6th		– out of playoffs –
1963-64	70	13	15	7	....	5	25	5	....	18	40	12	....	170	212	48	6th		– out of playoffs –
1962-63	70	7	18	10	....	7	21	7	....	14	39	17	....	198	281	45	6th		– out of playoffs –
1961-62	70	9	22	4	....	6	25	4	....	15	47	8	....	177	306	38	6th		– out of playoffs –
1960-61	70	13	17	5	....	2	25	8	....	15	42	13	....	176	254	43	6th		– out of playoffs –
1959-60	70	21	11	3	....	7	23	5	....	28	34	8	....	220	241	64	5th		– out of playoffs –
1958-59	70	21	11	3	....	11	18	6	....	32	29	9	....	205	215	73	2nd		Lost Semi-Final
1957-58	70	15	14	6	....	12	14	9	....	27	28	15	....	199	194	69	4th		Lost Final
1956-57	70	20	9	6	....	14	15	6	....	34	24	12	....	195	174	80	3rd		Lost Final
1955-56	70	14	14	7	....	9	20	6	....	23	34	13	....	147	185	59	5th		– out of playoffs –
1954-55	70	16	10	9	....	7	16	12	....	23	26	21	....	169	188	67	4th		Lost Semi-Final
1953-54	70	22	8	5	....	10	20	5	....	32	28	10	....	177	181	74	4th		Lost Semi-Final
1952-53	70	19	10	6	....	9	19	7	....	28	29	13	....	152	172	69	3rd		Lost Final
1951-52	70	15	12	8	....	10	17	8	....	25	29	16	....	162	176	66	4th		Lost Semi-Final
1950-51	70	13	12	10	....	9	18	8	....	22	30	18	....	178	197	62	4th		Lost Semi-Final
1949-50	70	15	12	8	....	7	20	8	....	22	32	16	....	198	228	60	5th		– out of playoffs –
1948-49	60	18	10	2	....	11	13	6	....	29	23	8	....	178	163	66	2nd		Lost Semi-Final
1947-48	60	12	8	10	....	11	16	3	....	23	24	13	....	167	168	59	3rd		Lost Semi-Final
1946-47	60	18	7	5	....	8	16	6	....	26	23	11	....	190	175	63	3rd		Lost Semi-Final
1945-46	50	11	5	4	....	13	13	4	....	24	18	8	....	167	156	56	2nd		Lost Final
1944-45	50	11	12	2	....	5	18	2	....	16	30	4	....	179	219	36	4th		Lost Semi-Final
1943-44	50	15	8	2	....	4	18	3	....	19	26	5	....	223	268	43	5th		– out of playoffs –
1942-43	50	17	3	5	....	7	14	4	....	24	17	9	....	195	176	57	2nd		Lost Final
1941-42	48	17	4	3	....	8	13	3	....	25	17	6	....	160	118	56	3rd		Lost Semi-Final
1940-41	**48**	**15**	**4**	**5**	....	**12**	**4**	**8**	....	**27**	**8**	**13**	....	**168**	**102**	**67**	**1st**		**Won Stanley Cup**
1939-40	48	20	3	1	....	11	9	4	....	31	12	5	....	170	98	67	1st		Lost Semi-Final
1938-39	**48**	**20**	**2**	**2**	....	**16**	**8**	**0**	....	**36**	**10**	**2**	....	**156**	**76**	**74**	**1st**		**Won Stanley Cup**
1937-38	48	18	3	3	....	12	8	4	....	30	11	7	....	142	89	67	1st, Amn.		Lost Semi-Final
1936-37	48	9	11	4	....	14	7	3	....	23	18	7	....	120	110	53	2nd, Amn.		Lost Quarter-Final
1935-36	48	15	8	1	....	7	12	5	....	22	20	6	....	92	83	50	2nd, Amn.		Lost Quarter-Final
1934-35	48	17	7	0	....	9	9	6	....	26	16	6	....	129	112	58	1st, Amn.		Lost Semi-Final
1933-34	48	11	11	2	....	7	14	3	....	18	25	5	....	111	130	41	4th, Amn.		– out of playoffs –
1932-33	48	19	2	3	....	6	13	5	....	25	15	8	....	124	88	58	1st, Amn.		Lost Semi-Final
1931-32	48	11	10	3	....	4	11	9	....	15	21	12	....	122	117	42	4th, Amn.		– out of playoffs –
1930-31	44	16	1	5	....	12	9	1	....	28	10	6	....	143	90	62	1st, Amn.		Lost Semi-Final
1929-30	44	21	1	0	....	17	4	1	....	38	5	1	....	179	98	77	1st, Amn.		Lost Final
1928-29	**44**	**15**	**6**	**1**	....	**11**	**7**	**4**	....	**26**	**13**	**5**	....	**89**	**52**	**57**	**1st, Amn.**		**Won Stanley Cup**
1927-28	44	13	4	5	....	7	9	6	....	20	13	11	....	77	70	51	1st, Amn.		Lost Semi-Final
1926-27	44	15	7	0	....	6	13	3	....	21	20	3	....	97	89	45	2nd, Amn.		Lost Final
1925-26	36	10	7	1	....	7	8	3	....	17	15	4	....	92	85	38	4th		– out of playoffs –
1924-25	30	3	12	0	....	3	12	0	....	6	24	0	....	49	119	12	6th		– out of playoffs –

2017-18 Player Personnel

FORWARDS	HT	WT	*Age	Birthplace	S	2016-17 Club
ACCIARI, Noel	5-10	208	25	Johnston, RI	R	Boston-Providence (AHL)
AGOSTINO, Kenny	6-0	205	25	Morristown, NJ	L	St. Louis-Chicago (AHL)
BACKES, David	6-3	221	33	Blaine, MN	R	Boston
BELESKEY, Matt	6-0	203	29	Windsor, ON	L	Boston
BERGERON, Patrice	6-1	195	32	Ancienne-Lorette, QC	R	Boston
BJORK, Anders	6-0	186	21	Mequon, WI	L	U. of Notre Dame
BLIDH, Anton	6-0	201	22	Molnlycke, Sweden	L	Boston-Providence (AHL)
CAVE, Colby	6-1	200	22	Battleford, SK	L	Providence (AHL)
CEHLARIK, Peter	6-3	202	22	Zilina, Slovakia	L	Boston-Providence (AHL)
CZARNIK, Austin	5-9	167	24	Washington, MI	R	Boston-Providence (AHL)
DeBRUSK, Jake	6-0	183	20	Edmonton, AB	L	Providence (AHL)
FORSBACKA KARLSSON, Jakob	6-1	184	20	Stockholm, Sweden	R	Boston University-Boston
HEINEN, Danton	6-1	193	22	Langley, BC	L	Boston-Providence (AHL)
KREJCI, David	6-0	186	31	Sternberk, Czech.	R	Boston
KURALY, Sean	6-2	212	24	Lewiston, NY	L	Boston-Providence (AHL)
MARCHAND, Brad	5-9	181	29	Halifax, NS	L	Boston
NASH, Riley	6-1	200	28	Consort, AB	R	Boston
PASTRNAK, David	6-0	181	21	Havirov, Czech Rep.	R	Boston
SCHALLER, Tim	6-2	219	26	Merrimack, NH	L	Boston
SPOONER, Ryan	5-10	184	25	Ottawa, ON	L	Boston
SZWARZ, Jordan	5-11	196	26	Burlington, ON	R	Providence (AHL)
VATRANO, Frank	5-9	201	23	East Longmeadow, MA	L	Boston-Providence (AHL)

DEFENSEMEN	HT	WT	*Age	Birthplace	S	2016-17 Club
CARLO, Brandon	6-5	203	20	Colorado Springs, CO	R	Boston
CHARA, Zdeno	6-9	250	40	Trencin, Czechoslovakia	L	Boston
CROSS, Tommy	6-3	205	28	Hartford, CT	L	Providence (AHL)-Boston
GRZELCYK, Matt	5-9	174	23	Charlestown, MA	L	Boston-Providence (AHL)
KRUG, Torey	5-9	186	26	Livonia, MI	L	Boston
LILES, John-Michael	5-10	185	36	Indianapolis, IN	L	Boston
McAVOY, Charlie	6-1	208	19	Long Beach, NY	R	Boston University-Boston
McQUAID, Adam	6-4	212	30	Charlottetown, PE	R	Boston
MILLER, Kevan	6-2	210	29	Los Angeles, CA	R	Boston
O'GARA, Rob	6-4	207	24	Massapequa, NY	L	Boston-Providence (AHL)
POSTMA, Paul	6-3	195	28	Red Deer, AB	R	Winnipeg

GOALTENDERS	HT	WT	*Age	Birthplace	C	2016-17 Club
KHUDOBIN, Anton	5-11	195	31	Ust-Kamenogorsk, USSR	L	Boston-Providence (AHL)
McINTYRE, Zane	6-2	206	25	Grand Forks, ND	L	Boston-Providence (AHL)
RASK, Tuukka	6-2	185	30	Savonlinna, Finland	L	Boston
SUBBAN, Malcolm	6-2	222	23	Toronto, ON	L	Boston-Providence (AHL)

* – Age at start of 2017-18 season

Bruce Cassidy

Head Coach

Born: Ottawa, ON, May 20, 1965.

The Boston Bruins announced on April 26, 2017, that Bruce Cassidy would remain as the team's head coach after having been named interim head coach on February 7. The Bruins went 18-8-1 under Cassidy and finished in third place in the Atlantic Division to qualify for the playoffs for the first time since 2013-14. Under Cassidy, the Bruins ranked first in the NHL in goals per game (3.37) and fewest shots allowed (741), and tied for second in the league in wins (18) and power-play percentage (27.8). Boston was also third in goals allowed per game (2.30) and tied for fifth in faceoff percentage (53.6).

Cassidy became an assistant coach in Boston on May 24, 2016 following eight seasons in the organization with the Providence Bruins, Boston's American Hockey League affiliate. He first joined the organization in 2008 as an assistant coach in Providence and was named the tenth head coach in that team's history on June 25, 2011. He compiled a 207-128-45 record at the helm of the AHL Bruins, including the best record in the AHL in 2012-13 at 50-21-5.

The native of Ottawa, Ontario has a lengthy resume from both his playing and coaching careers. Selected 18th overall by the Chicago Blackhawks in the first round of the 1983 NHL Draft, Cassidy played with the Blackhawks and their affiliates from 1985 to 1990, including 36 Chicago games (four goals, 13 assists). He then played three seasons in Europe, suiting up for Alleghe HC in Italy and Kaufbeuren in Germany. He retired with the International Hockey League's Indianapolis Ice in 1996 to accept a head-coaching job with the Jacksonville Lizard Kings of the East Coast Hockey League (ECHL). Cassidy was promoted to head coach of the team in Indianapolis during the 1998-99 season and went on to coach the ECHL's Trenton Titans and the IHL's Grand Rapids Griffins before being hired as head coach of the Washington Capitals in 2002-03.

Cassidy signed with Chicago in June 2004 as an assistant coach, working with the AHL's Norfolk Admirals during the 2004-05 NHL lockout season and then with the Blackhawks in 2005-06. He again became a head coach with OHL's Kingston Frontenacs in 2006-07.

Coaching Record

			Regular Season				Playoffs			
Season	Team	League	GC	W	L	O/T	GC	W	L	T
1996-97	Jacksonville	ECHL	50	15	25	10	....	....	....	....
1997-98	Jacksonville	ECHL	70	35	29	6	....	....	....	....
1998-99	Indianapolis	IHL	82	33	37	12	7	3	4	....
99-2000	Trenton	ECHL	70	37	29	4	14	8	6	....
2000-01	Grand Rapids	IHL	82	53	22	7	10	6	4	....
2001-02	Grand Rapids	AHL	80	42	27	11	5	2	3	....
2002-03	**Washington**	**NHL**	**82**	**39**	**29**	**14**	**6**	**2**	**4**	....
2003-04	**Washington**	**NHL**	**28**	**8**	**18**	**2**	....	....	....	....
2006-07	Kingston	OHL	68	31	30	7	5	1	4	....
2007-08	Kingston	OHL	12	2	9	1	....	....	....	....
2011-12	Providence	AHL	76	35	34	7	....	....	....	....
2012-13	Providence	AHL	76	50	21	5	12	6	6	....
2013-14	Providence	AHL	76	40	25	11	12	6	6	....
2014-15	Providence	AHL	76	41	26	9	5	2	3	....
2015-16	Providence	AHL	76	41	22	13	3	0	3	....
2016-17	**Boston**	**NHL**	**27**	**18**	**8**	**1**	**6**	**2**	**4**	....
	NHL Totals		**137**	**65**	**55**	**17**	**12**	**4**	**8**	....

2016-17 Scoring

* – rookie

Regular Season

Pos	#	Player	Team	GP	G	A	Pts	TOI	+/-	PIM	PP	SH	GW	S	S%
C	63	Brad Marchand	BOS	80	39	46	85	19:26	18	81	9	3	8	226	17.3
R	88	David Pastrnak	BOS	75	34	36	70	17:58	11	34	10	0	6	262	13.0
C	46	David Krejci	BOS	82	23	31	54	18:15	–12	26	8	0	3	158	14.6
C	37	Patrice Bergeron	BOS	79	21	32	53	19:25	12	24	8	0	7	302	7.0
D	47	Torey Krug	BOS	81	8	43	51	21:36	–10	37	6	0	1	208	3.8
C	51	Ryan Spooner	BOS	78	11	28	39	14:05	–8	14	3	0	3	145	7.6
R	42	David Backes	BOS	74	17	21	38	17:07	2	69	2	0	2	175	9.7
D	33	Zdeno Chara	BOS	75	10	19	29	23:19	18	59	1	2	0	136	7.4
C	28	Dominic Moore	BOS	82	11	14	25	12:56	2	44	0	3	1	96	11.5
R	19	Drew Stafford	WPG	40	4	9	13	13:17	–2	12	2	0	1	68	5.9
			BOS	18	4	4	8	14:16	8	12	1	0	2	41	9.8
			Total	58	8	13	21	13:36	6	24	3	0	3	109	7.3
C	72	Frank Vatrano	BOS	44	10	8	18	13:28	–3	14	4	0	1	116	8.6
C	20	Riley Nash	BOS	81	7	10	17	13:48	–1	14	0	1	2	125	5.6
D	25*	Brandon Carlo	BOS	82	6	10	16	20:48	9	59	0	1	0	88	6.8
C	59	Tim Schaller	BOS	59	7	7	14	12:16	–6	23	0	0	2	89	7.9
D	6	Colin Miller	BOS	61	6	7	13	15:48	0	55	1	0	0	85	7.1
C	27*	Austin Czarnik	BOS	49	5	8	13	13:00	–10	12	0	0	1	66	7.6
D	86	Kevan Miller	BOS	58	3	10	13	17:47	1	50	0	0	1	49	6.1
D	54	Adam McQuaid	BOS	77	2	8	10	18:14	4	71	0	0	1	64	3.1
L	39	Matt Beleskey	BOS	49	3	5	8	13:15	–10	47	0	0	0	79	3.8
C	55*	Noel Acciari	BOS	29	2	3	5	10:22	3	16	0	0	0	24	8.3
R	11	Jimmy Hayes	BOS	58	2	3	5	9:13	–3	29	0	0	1	74	2.7
D	26	John-Michael Liles	BOS	36	0	5	5	16:12	1	4	0	0	0	36	0.0
L	81*	Anton Blidh	BOS	19	1	1	2	8:46	–2	7	0	0	0	26	3.8
L	83*	Peter Cehlarik	BOS	11	0	2	2	13:54	0	0	0	0	0	8	0.0
C	52*	Sean Kuraly	BOS	8	0	1	1	9:12	–1	2	0	0	0	11	0.0
D	45	Joe Morrow	BOS	17	0	1	1	15:31	–4	8	0	0	0	19	0.0
C	23*	Jakob Forsbacka-Karlsson	BOS	1	0	0	0	8:25	0	0	0	0	0	0	0.0
D	48*	Matt Grzelcyk	BOS	2	0	0	0	12:29	0	2	0	0	0	4	0.0
D	44*	Rob O'Gara	BOS	3	0	0	0	16:00	1	0	0	0	0	2	0.0
C	43*	Danton Heinen	BOS	8	0	0	0	13:14	–3	2	0	0	0	7	0.0

Goaltending

No.	Goaltender	GPI	Mins	Avg	W	L	OT	EN	SO	GA	SA	Sv%	G	A	PIM
40	Tuukka Rask	65	3680	2.23	37	20	5	8	8	137	1610	.915	0	2	0
35	Anton Khudobin	16	885	2.64	7	6	1	0	0	39	405	.904	0	1	2
31	* Zane McIntyre	8	333	3.96	0	4	1	0	0	22	155	.858	0	0	0
70	* Malcolm Subban	1	31	5.81	0	1	0	0	0	3	16	.813	0	0	0
	Totals	**82**	**4964**	**2.53**	**44**	**31**	**7**	**8**	**8**	**209**	**2194**	**.905**			

Playoffs

Pos	#	Player	Team	GP	G	A	Pts	TOI	+/-	PIM	PP	SH	GW	OT	S	S%
C	37	Patrice Bergeron	BOS	6	2	2	4	22:51	2	2	1	0	0	0	19	10.5
R	88	David Pastrnak	BOS	6	2	2	4	21:04	1	6	1	0	0	0	10	20.0
R	42	David Backes	BOS	6	1	3	4	17:41	2	2	0	0	0	0	14	7.1
C	63	Brad Marchand	BOS	6	1	3	4	23:30	1	6	0	0	1	0	18	5.6
D	73*	Charlie McAvoy	BOS	6	0	3	3	26:11	–2	2	0	0	0	0	5	0.0
C	52*	Sean Kuraly	BOS	4	2	0	2	12:24	0	4	0	0	1	1	10	20.0
R	19	Drew Stafford	BOS	6	2	0	2	13:44	–2	2	1	0	0	0	14	14.3
C	51	Ryan Spooner	BOS	4	0	2	2	13:02	–2	0	0	0	0	0	2	0.0
D	26	John-Michael Liles	BOS	6	0	2	2	16:28	1	0	0	0	0	0	5	0.0
C	20	Riley Nash	BOS	6	0	2	2	17:27	0	2	0	0	0	0	9	0.0
C	55*	Noel Acciari	BOS	4	1	0	1	19:03	0	2	0	0	0	0	4	25.0
C	59	Tim Schaller	BOS	6	1	0	1	13:28	2	2	0	1	0	0	7	14.3
C	72	Frank Vatrano	BOS	6	1	0	1	11:20	–1	4	0	0	0	0	7	14.3
D	54	Adam McQuaid	BOS	2	0	1	1	11:48	0	0	0	0	0	0	2	0.0
D	6	Colin Miller	BOS	4	0	1	1	15:33	1	2	0	0	0	0	5	0.0
D	45	Joe Morrow	BOS	5	0	1	1	22:12	1	2	0	0	0	0	6	0.0
D	33	Zdeno Chara	BOS	6	0	1	1	28:45	–3	2	0	0	0	0	8	0.0
C	28	Dominic Moore	BOS	6	0	1	1	16:08	0	4	0	0	0	0	5	0.0
C	46	David Krejci	BOS	3	0	0	0	13:24	–1	0	0	0	0	0	3	0.0
L	39	Matt Beleskey	BOS	3	0	0	0	7:59	–2	4	0	0	0	0	3	0.0
D	86	Kevan Miller	BOS	6	0	0	0	25:14	0	4	0	0	0	0	9	0.0

Goaltending

No.	Goaltender	GPI	Mins	Avg	W	L	EN	SO	GA	SA	Sv%	G	A	PIM
40	Tuukka Rask	6	402	2.24	2	4	0	0	15	187	.920	0	0	0
	Totals	**6**	**405**	**2.22**	**2**	**4**	**0**	**0**	**15**	**187**	**.920**			

Coaching History

Art Ross, 1924-25 to 1933-34; Frank Patrick, 1934-35, 1935-36; Art Ross, 1936-37 to 1938-39; Cooney Weiland, 1939-40, 1940-41; Art Ross, 1941-42 to 1944-45; Dit Clapper, 1945-46 to 1948-49; George Boucher, 1949-50; Lynn Patrick, 1950-51 to 1953-54; Lynn Patrick and Milt Schmidt, 1954-55; Milt Schmidt, 1955-56 to 1960-61; Phil Watson, 1961-62; Phil Watson and Milt Schmidt, 1962-63; Milt Schmidt, 1963-64 to 1965-66; Harry Sinden, 1966-67 to 1969-70; Tom Johnson, 1970-71, 1971-72; Tom Johnson and Bep Guidolin, 1972-73; Bep Guidolin, 1973-74; Don Cherry, 1974-75 to 1978-79; Fred Creighton and Harry Sinden, 1979-80; Gerry Cheevers, 1980-81 to 1983-84; Gerry Cheevers and Harry Sinden, 1984-85; Butch Goring, 1985-86; Butch Goring and Terry O'Reilly, 1986-87; Terry O'Reilly, 1987-88, 1988-89; Mike Milbury, 1989-90, 1990-91; Rick Bowness, 1991-92; Brian Sutter, 1992-93 to 1994-95; Steve Kasper, 1995-96, 1996-97; Pat Burns, 1997-98 to 1999-2000; Pat Burns and Mike Keenan, 2000-01; Robbie Ftorek, 2001-02; Robbie Ftorek and Mike O'Connell, 2002-03; Mike Sullivan, 2003-04 to 2005-06; Dave Lewis, 2006-07; Claude Julien, 2007-08 to 2015-16; Claude Julien and Bruce Cassidy, 2016-17; Bruce Cassidy, 2017-18.

Club Records

Team

(Figures in brackets for season records are games played; records for fewest points, wins, ties, losses, goals, goals against are for 70 or more games)

Most Points	**121**	1970-71 (78)
Most Wins	**57**	1970-71 (78)
Most Ties	**21**	1954-55 (70)
Most Losses	**47**	1961-62 (70), 1996-97 (82)
Most Goals	**399**	1970-71 (78)
Most Goals Against	**306**	1961-62 (70)
Fewest Points	**38**	1961-62 (70)
Fewest Wins	**14**	1962-63 (70)
Fewest Ties	**5**	1972-73 (78)
Fewest Losses	**13**	1971-72 (78)
Fewest Goals	**147**	1955-56 (70)
Fewest Goals Against	**172**	1952-53 (70)
Longest Winning Streak		
Overall	**14**	Dec. 3/29-Jan. 9/30
Home	**20**	Dec. 3/29-Mar. 18/30
Away	**9**	Mar. 2-30/14
Longest Team Point Streak		
Overall	**23**	Dec. 22/40-Feb. 23/41 (15W, 8T)
Home	**27**	Nov. 22/70-Mar. 20/71 (26W, 1T)
Away	**15**	Dec. 22/40-Mar. 16/41 (9W, 6T)
Longest Losing Streak		
Overall	**11**	Dec. 3/24-Jan. 5/25
Home	**11**	Dec. 8/24-Feb. 17/25
Away	**14**	Dec. 27/64-Feb. 21/65
Longest Winless Streak		
Overall	**20**	Jan. 28-Mar. 11/62 (16L, 4T)
Home	**11**	Dec. 8/24-Feb. 17/25 (11L)
Away	**14**	Three times
Most Shutouts, Season	**15**	1927-28 (44)
Most PIM, Season	**2,443**	1987-88 (80)
Most Goals, Game	**14**	Jan. 21/45 (NYR 3 at Bos. 14)

Individual

Most Seasons	**21**	John Bucyk, Raymond Bourque
Most Games	**1,518**	Raymond Bourque
Most Goals, Career	**545**	John Bucyk
Most Assists, Career	**1,111**	Raymond Bourque
Most Points, Career	**1,506**	Raymond Bourque (395G, 1,111A)
Most PIM, Career	**2,095**	Terry O'Reilly
Most Shutouts, Career	**74**	Tiny Thompson
Longest Consecutive Games Streak	**418**	John Bucyk (Jan. 23/69-Mar. 2/75)
Most Goals, Season	**76**	Phil Esposito (1970-71)
Most Assists, Season	**102**	Bobby Orr (1970-71)
Most Points, Season	**152**	Phil Esposito (1970-71; 76G, 76A)
Most PIM, Season	**302**	Jay Miller (1987-88)
Most Points, Defenseman, Season	***139**	Bobby Orr (1970-71; 37G, 102A)
Most Points, Center, Season	**152**	Phil Esposito (1970-71; 76G, 76A)
Most Points, Right Wing, Season	**105**	Ken Hodge (1970-71; 43G, 62A), (1973-74; 50G, 55A) Rick Middleton (1983-84; 47G, 58A)
Most Points, Left Wing, Season	**116**	John Bucyk (1970-71; 51G, 65A)
Most Points, Rookie, Season	**102**	Joe Juneau (1992-93; 32G, 70A)
Most Shutouts, Season	**15**	Hal Winkler (1927-28)
Most Goals, Game	**4**	Twenty one times
Most Assists, Game	**6**	Ken Hodge (Feb. 9/71) Bobby Orr (Jan. 1/73)
Most Points, Game	**7**	Bobby Orr (Nov. 15/73; 3G, 4A) Phil Esposito (Dec. 19/74; 3G, 4A) Barry Pederson (Apr. 4/82; 3G, 4A) Cam Neely (Oct. 16/88; 3G, 4A)

* NHL Record.

All-time Record vs. Other Clubs

Regular Season

	Total								At Home								On Road							
	GP	W	L	T	OL	GF	GA	PTS	GP	W	L	T	OL	GF	GA	PTS	GP	W	L	T	OL	GF	GA	PTS
Anaheim	32	13	16	2	1	82	94	29	16	7	8	0	1	44	51	15	16	6	8	2	0	38	43	14
Arizona	75	47	20	7	1	283	219	102	37	26	6	4	1	156	104	57	38	21	14	3	0	127	115	45
Buffalo	285	135	110	29	11	919	902	310	141	79	44	14	4	503	408	176	144	56	66	15	7	416	494	134
Calgary	105	58	33	10	4	363	318	130	54	33	13	6	2	190	139	74	51	25	20	4	2	173	179	56
Carolina	197	104	70	16	7	664	570	231	99	57	32	7	3	335	256	124	98	47	38	9	4	329	314	107
Chicago	586	265	238	79	4	1841	1773	613	292	166	92	34	0	1045	823	366	294	99	146	45	4	796	950	247
Colorado	142	72	53	15	2	543	459	161	69	31	28	9	1	248	210	72	73	41	25	6	1	295	249	89
Columbus	24	15	7	0	2	79	60	32	11	7	4	0	0	33	27	14	13	8	3	0	2	46	33	18
Dallas	135	79	30	23	3	526	357	184	67	44	11	10	2	280	165	100	68	35	19	13	1	246	192	84
Detroit	596	246	251	95	4	1801	1780	591	299	162	92	43	2	1049	790	369	297	84	159	52	2	752	990	222
Edmonton	73	45	19	6	3	270	212	99	37	26	7	3	1	151	92	56	36	19	12	3	2	119	120	43
Florida	92	51	30	6	5	267	225	113	47	24	16	4	3	134	104	55	45	27	14	2	2	133	121	58
Los Angeles	139	84	38	13	4	552	430	185	70	48	13	6	3	306	197	105	69	36	25	7	1	246	233	80
Minnesota	20	6	13	0	1	37	56	13	10	2	8	0	0	17	31	4	10	4	5	0	1	20	25	9
Montreal	738	275	351	103	9	1944	2233	662	369	166	141	56	6	1076	1004	394	369	109	210	47	3	868	1229	268
Nashville	25	13	7	1	4	68	58	31	12	8	3	1	0	38	24	17	13	5	4	0	4	30	34	14
New Jersey	152	82	41	19	10	505	404	193	78	45	19	8	6	279	220	104	74	37	22	11	4	226	184	89
NY Islanders	163	84	54	21	4	553	476	193	81	44	24	11	2	285	222	101	82	40	30	10	2	268	254	92
NY Rangers	643	291	246	97	9	2017	1872	688	320	170	102	42	6	1120	885	388	323	121	144	55	3	897	987	300
Ottawa	134	74	41	8	11	420	340	167	69	40	20	5	4	230	178	89	65	34	21	3	7	190	162	78
Philadelphia	192	103	60	21	8	633	561	235	97	57	24	11	5	342	265	130	95	46	36	10	3	291	296	105
Pittsburgh	201	111	62	21	7	765	615	250	99	67	22	6	4	410	273	144	102	44	40	15	3	355	342	106
St. Louis	133	64	42	18	9	487	395	155	66	36	17	9	4	259	181	85	67	28	25	9	5	228	214	70
San Jose	36	19	12	5	0	114	100	43	18	10	5	3	0	62	55	23	18	9	7	2	0	52	45	20
Tampa Bay	94	60	24	9	1	315	242	130	48	35	7	6	0	177	110	76	46	25	17	3	1	138	132	54
Toronto	666	295	262	98	11	1967	1980	699	333	183	98	47	5	1089	885	418	333	112	164	51	6	878	1095	281
Vancouver	117	72	29	15	1	463	327	160	59	41	10	7	1	234	141	90	58	31	19	8	0	229	186	70
Washington	154	76	47	21	10	501	428	183	77	42	22	9	4	257	202	97	77	34	25	12	6	244	226	86
Winnipeg	59	35	17	2	5	188	166	77	29	20	5	2	2	104	83	44	30	15	12	0	3	84	83	33
Defunct Clubs	328	191	106	31	0	1021	746	413	164	112	39	13	0	525	306	237	164	79	67	18	0	496	440	176
Totals	**6336**	**3065**	**2329**	**791**	**151**	**20188**	**18398**	**7072**	**3168**	**1788**	**932**	**376**	**72**	**10978**	**8431**	**4024**	**3168**	**1277**	**1397**	**415**	**79**	**9210**	**9967**	**3048**

Playoffs

	Series	W	L	GP	W	L	T	GF	GA	Last Mtg.	Rnd.	Result
Buffalo	8	6	2	45	25	20	0	155	145	2010	CQF	W 4-2
Carolina	4	3	1	26	15	11	0	80	64	2009	CSF	L 3-4
Chicago	7	5	2	28	18	9	1	112	80	2013	F	L 2-4
Colorado	2	1	1	11	6	5	0	37	36	1983	DSF	W 3-1
Dallas	1	0	1	3	0	3	0	13	20	1981	PR	L 0-3
Detroit	8	5	3	38	23	15	0	110	104	2014	FR	W 4-1
Edmonton	2	0	2	9	1	8	0	20	41	1990	F	L 1-4
Florida	1	0	1	5	1	4	0	16	22	1996	CQF	L 1-4
Los Angeles	2	2	0	13	8	5	0	56	38	1977	QF	W 4-2
Montreal	34	9	25	177	71	106	0	436	531	2014	SR	L 3-4
New Jersey	4	1	3	23	8	15	0	60	68	2003	CQF	L 1-4
NY Islanders	2	0	2	11	3	8	0	35	49	1983	CF	L 2-4
NY Rangers	10	7	3	47	26	19	2	130	114	2013	CSF	W 4-1
Ottawa	1	0	1	6	2	4	0	13	15	2017	FR	L 2-4
Philadelphia	6	3	3	31	18	13	0	100	86	2011	CSF	W 4-0
Pittsburgh	5	3	2	23	13	10	0	74	69	2013	CF	W 4-0
St. Louis	2	2	0	8	8	0	0	48	15	1972	SF	W 4-0
Tampa Bay	1	1	0	7	4	3	0	21	21	2011	CF	W 4-3
Toronto	14	6	8	69	34	34	1	175	168	2013	CQF	W 4-3
Vancouver	1	1	0	7	4	3	0	23	8	2011	F	W 4-3
Washington	3	1	2	17	9	8	0	43	37	2012	CQF	L 3-4
Defunct Clubs	3	1	2	11	4	5	2	20	20			
Totals	**121**	**57**	**64**	**615**	**301**	**308**	**6**	**1777**	**1751**			

Calgary totals include Atlanta Flames, 1972-73 to 1979-80.
Carolina totals include Hartford, 1979-80 to 1996-97.
Colorado totals include Quebec, 1979-80 to 1994-95.
Dallas totals include Minnesota North Stars, 1967-68 to 1992-93.
New Jersey totals include Kansas City, 1974-75, 1975-76, and Colorado Rockies, 1976-77 to 1981-82.
Phoenix totals include Winnipeg, 1979-80 to 1995-96.
Winnipeg totals include Atlanta Thrashers, 1999-2000 to 2010-11.

Playoff Results 2017-2013

Year	Round	Opponent	Result	GF	GA
2017	FR	Ottawa	L 2-4	13	15
2014	SR	Montreal	L 3-4	16	20
	FR	Detroit	W 4-1	14	6
2013	F	Chicago	L 2-4	15	17
	CF	Pittsburgh	W 4-0	12	2
	CSF	NY Rangers	W 4-1	16	10
	CQF	Toronto	W 4-3	22	18

Abbreviations: Round: F – Final; **CF** – conference final; **CSF** – conference semi-final; **SR** – second round; **CQF** – conference quarter-final; **FR** – first round; **DSF** – division semi-final; **SF** – semi-final; **QF** – quarter-final; **PR** – preliminary round.

2016-17 Results

Month	Day	Game	Score	Month	Day	Game	Score
Oct.	13	at Columbus	6-3		7	at Florida	4-0
	15	at Toronto	1-4		8	at Carolina	3-4*
	17	at Winnipeg	4-1		10	at St. Louis	5-3
	20	New Jersey	2-1		12	at Nashville	1-2
	22	Montreal	2-4		14	Philadelphia	6-3
	25	Minnesota	0-5		16	NY Islanders	0-4
	26	at NY Rangers	2-5		18	at Detroit	5-6†
	29	at Detroit	1-0		20	Chicago	0-1
Nov.	1	at Florida	2-1		22	at Pittsburgh	1-5
	3	at Tampa Bay	4-3†		24	Detroit	4-3*
	5	NY Rangers	2-5		26	Pittsburgh	4-3
	7	Buffalo	4-0		31	at Tampa Bay	4-3
	8	at Montreal	2-3	**Feb.**	1	at Washington	3-5
	10	Columbus	5-2		4	Toronto	5-6
	12	at Arizona	2-1		9	San Jose	6-3
	13	at Colorado	2-0		11	Vancouver	4-3
	17	at Minnesota	0-1		12	Montreal	4-0
	19	Winnipeg	4-1		19	at San Jose	2-1*
	22	St. Louis	2-4		22	at Anaheim	3-5
	24	at Ottawa	1-3		23	at Los Angeles	4-1
	25	Calgary	1-2		26	at Dallas	6-3
	27	Tampa Bay	4-1		28	Arizona	4-1
	29	at Philadelphia	2-3†	**Mar.**	2	NY Rangers	1-2
Dec.	1	Carolina	2-1†		4	New Jersey	3-2
	3	at Buffalo	2-1		6	at Ottawa	2-4
	5	Florida	4-3*		8	Detroit	6-1
	7	at Washington	3-4*		11	Philadelphia	2-1
	8	Colorado	2-4		13	at Vancouver	6-3
	10	Toronto	1-4		15	at Calgary	5-2
	12	at Montreal	2-1*		16	at Edmonton	4-7
	14	at Pittsburgh	3-4*		20	at Toronto	2-4
	15	Anaheim	3-4		21	Ottawa	2-3
	18	Los Angeles	1-0		23	Tampa Bay	3-6
	20	NY Islanders	2-4		25	at NY Islanders	2-1
	22	at Florida	3-1		28	Nashville	4-1
	23	at Carolina	2-3*		30	Dallas	2-0
	27	at Columbus	3-4	**Apr.**	1	Florida	5-2
	29	at Buffalo	4-2		2	at Chicago	3-2
	31	Buffalo	3-1		4	Tampa Bay	4-0
Jan.	2	at New Jersey	0-3		6	Ottawa	1-2†
	5	Edmonton	3-4		8	Washington	1-3

* – Overtime † – Shootout

NHL Draft Selections 2017-2003

Name in bold denotes played in NHL.

2017

Pick	
18	Urho Vaakanainen
53	Jack Studnicka
111	Jeremy Swayman
173	Cedric Pare
195	Victor Berglund
204	Daniel Bukac

2016

Pick	
14	**Charles McAvoy**
29	Trent Frederic
49	Ryan Lindgren
135	Joona Koppanen
136	Cameron Clarke
165	Oskar Steen

2015

Pick	
13	Jakub Zboril
14	Jake Debrusk
15	Zach Senyshyn
37	**Brandon Carlo**
45	**Jakob Forsbacka-Karlsson**
52	Jeremy Lauzon
75	Dan Vladar
105	Jesse Gabrielle
165	Cameron Hughes
195	Jack Becker

2014

Pick	
25	**David Pastrnak**
56	Ryan Donato
116	**Danton Heinen**
146	Anders Bjork
206	Emil Johansson

2013

Pick	
60	Linus Arnesson
90	**Peter Cehlarik**
120	Ryan Fitzgerald
150	Wiley Sherman
180	**Anton Blidh**
210	Mitchell Dempsey

2012

Pick	
24	**Malcolm Subban**
85	**Matthew Grzelcyk**
131	**Seth Griffith**
145	Cody Payne
175	**Matthew Benning**
205	Colton Hargrove

2011

Pick	
9	**Dougie Hamilton**
40	**Alex Khokhlachev**
81	Anthony Camara
121	**Brian Ferlin**
151	**Rob O'Gara**
181	Lars Volden

2010

Pick	
2	**Tyler Seguin**
32	Jared Knight
45	**Ryan Spooner**
97	**Craig Cunningham**
135	**Justin Florek**
165	**Zane McIntyre**
195	Maxim Chudinov
210	**Zach Trotman**

2009

Pick	
25	**Jordan Caron**
86	Ryan Button
112	**Lane MacDermid**
176	**Tyler Randell**
206	Ben Sexton

2008

Pick	
16	**Joe Colborne**
47	**Max Sauve**
77	**Michael Hutchinson**
97	**Jamie Arniel**
173	Nick Tremblay
197	Mark Goggin

2007

Pick	
8	**Zach Hamill**
35	**Tommy Cross**
130	Denis Reul
159	Alain Goulet
169	Radim Ostrcil
189	Jordan Knackstedt

2006

Pick	
5	**Phil Kessel**
37	Yury Alexandrov
50	**Milan Lucic**
71	**Brad Marchand**
128	**Andrew Bodnarchuk**
158	Levi Nelson

2005

Pick	
22	**Matt Lashoff**
39	**Petr Kalus**
83	**Mikko Lehtonen**
100	**Jonathan Sigalet**
106	**Vladimir Sobotka**
154	Wacey Rabbit
172	Lukas Vantuch
217	Brock Bradford

2004

Pick	
63	**David Krejci**
64	**Martins Karsums**
108	Ashton Rome
134	**Kris Versteeg**
160	**Ben Walter**
224	**Matt Hunwick**
255	Anton Hedman

2003

Pick	
21	**Mark Stuart**
45	**Patrice Bergeron**
66	**Masi Marjamaki**
107	**Byron Bitz**
118	Frank Rediker
129	Patrik Valcak
153	Mike Brown
183	**Nate Thompson**
247	Benoit Mondou
277	Kevin Regan

Captains' History

No captain, 1924-25; Sprague Cleghorn, 1925-26, 1926-27; Lionel Hitchman, 1927-28 to 1930-31; George Owen, 1931-32; Dit Clapper, 1932-33 to 1937-38; Cooney Weiland, 1938-39; Dit Clapper, 1939-40 to 1945-46; Dit Clapper and John Crawford, 1946-47; John Crawford 1947-48 to 1949-50; Milt Schmidt, 1950-51 to 1953-54; Milt Schmidt, Ed Sanford, 1954-55; Fern Flaman, 1955-56 to 1960-61; Don McKenney, 1961-62, 1962-63; Leo Boivin, 1963-64 to 1965-66; John Bucyk, 1966-67; no captain, 1967-68 to 1972-73; John Bucyk, 1973-74 to 1976-77; Wayne Cashman, 1977-78 to 1982-83; Terry O'Reilly, 1983-84, 1984-85; Raymond Bourque, Rick Middleton (co-captains) 1985-86 to 1987-88; Raymond Bourque, 1988-89 to 1999-2000; Jason Allison, 2000-01; no captain, 2001-02; Joe Thornton, 2002-03 to 2004-05; Joe Thornton and no captain, 2005-06; Zdeno Chara, 2006-07 to date.

General Managers' History

Art Ross, 1924-25 to 1953-54; Lynn Patrick, 1954-55 to 1964-65; Hap Emms, 1965-66, 1966-67; Milt Schmidt, 1967-68 to 1971-72; Harry Sinden, 1972-73 to 1999-2000; Harry Sinden and Mike O'Connell, 2000-01; Mike O'Connell, 2001-02 to 2004-05; Mike O'Connell and Jeff Gorton, 2005-06; Peter Chiarelli, 2006-07 to 2014-15; Don Sweeney, 2015-16 to date.

Don Sweeney

General Manager

Born: St. Stevens, NB, August 17, 1966.

Don Sweeney was named general manager of the Boston Bruins on May 20, 2015. He is the eighth man to hold the position, is the fourth who also played for the team (joining Hap Emms, Milt Schmidt and Mike O'Connell) and is the first former Boston draft pick to rise to the post. He oversees all aspects of the team's hockey operations and he also serves the club as an alternate governor on the NHL's Board of Governors.

Sweeney's ascension to the head of the club's hockey operations continues his long legacy with the club, beginning as the team's eighth pick, 166th overall, in the 1984 NHL Draft. He moved through the organization as a player for 15 seasons and in various front office capacities for the previous nine years. In his six seasons as the team's assistant general manager beginning in 2009, he oversaw the development of the team's drafted prospects at the AHL, junior hockey, college and European levels in addition to having a supervisory role in the day-to-day operations of the hockey department. He also oversaw all hockey operations matters for Boston's AHL affiliate in Providence. Sweeney began his front office career in June, 2006, when he was named the team's director of player development.

After being drafted by the Bruins as their eighth pick, Sweeney went on to play four seasons at Harvard University. He earned both NCAA East All-American and ECAC First Team All-Star honors with the Crimson and played in the 1986 NCAA Finals before graduating with a degree in Economics.

The defenseman played 16 seasons in the National Hockey League, including 15 in a Bruins uniform. He is one of just two defensemen and four players in team history to play over 1,000 games in a Boston sweater and he still ranks third on the team's all-time games played list. He also ranks in the top ten of the club's all-time list in career assists by a defenseman. He played his final NHL season with the Dallas Stars in 2003-04.

Club Directory

TD Garden

Boston Bruins
TD Garden
100 Legends Way
Boston, MA 02114
Phone **617/624-BEAR (2327)**
FAX 617/523-7184
www.bostonbruins.com
Capacity: 17,565

Ownership

Owner & Governor, Boston Bruins; Chairman, NHL Board of Governors	Jeremy M. Jacobs
CEO, Delaware North Boston Holdings	Charlie Jacobs
Alternate Governors	Charlie Jacobs, Jeremy Jacobs, Jr., Louis Jacobs, Harry Sinden, Cam Neely, Don Sweeney
Senior Advisor to the Owner	Harry Sinden

Executive

President	Cam Neely
Chief Revenue Officer	Glen Thornborough
Vice President, Finance	Jim Bednarek
Vice President, Communications & Marketing	Matthew Chmura
Vice President, Human Resources	Shauna K. Gilhooly
Vice President, Corporate Partnerships	Chris Johnson
Vice President, Strategy	Joshua Brickman
Vice President, Premium Sales & Service	Leah Leahy
Director of Administration	Dale Hamilton-Powers
Executive / Administrative Assistants	Rita Brandano, Maria Poirier / Karen Ondo

Hockey Operations

General Manager	Don Sweeney
Assistant General Manager	Scott Bradley
Executive Director of Player Personnel	John Ferguson
Directors, Legal Affairs	Evan Gold
Development Coach	Jamie Langenbrunner
Goaltender Development Coach	Mike Dunham
Amateur Scouting Director / Asst. Director	TBD / Scott Fitzgerald
Scouting Staff	P. J. Axelsson, Alain Bissonnette, Dennis Bonvie, Adam Creighton, Ryan Hardy, Matt Lindblad, Dean Malkoc, Mike McGraw, Tom McVie, Victor Nyblad, Erkki Rajamaki, Blair Reid, Andrew Shaw, Svenake Svensson, Bob Wetick
Director of Hockey Operations/Analytics	Ryan Nadeau
Hockey Ops Asst. / Travel & Services Coord.	Jeremy Rogalski / Whitney Delorey
Ambassador	John Bucyk

Coaching

Head Coach	Bruce Cassidy
Assistant Coaches	Joe Sacco, Jay Pandolfo, TBD
Goaltending Coach / Video Coordinator	Bob Essensa / J. P. Buckley

Medical, Training and Equipment

Director of Sports Performance & Rehab	Paul Whissel
Athletic Trainer / Head Physical Therapist	Don DelNegro / Sean Jordan
Sports Performance Coaches	Kenneth Pitts, Mike Macchioni
Equipment Manager / Assistant Managers	Keith Robinson / Jim "Beets" Johnson, Matt Falconer
Head Team Physician/Orthopedist	Dr. Peter Asnis
Team Internist / Dentist	Dr. David Finn / Dr. Edwin Riley
Sports Nutritionist	Julie Nicoletti

Communications

Director of Communications & Content	Brandon McNelis
Director of Publications & Information	Heidi Holland
Communications Manager / Specialist	Tom Brewster / Sarah McMahon
Specialists, Digital Content / Content	Caryn Switaj / Travis Basciotta
Content Administrator / Graduate Assistant	Eric Russo / Michael Tolvo
Web Video Producer	Mike Penhollow

Marketing and Community Relations

Directors, Marketing / Digital and Creative	Chris DiPierro / Jenna Camann
Platform Manager	Jon Spiris
Creative Marketing & Game Presentation Manager	Renee Riva
Marketing Managers, Activation / Strategic	Lindsay Sparling / Yelena Cashion
Digital Specialist, Engagement	Kelsey Ohman
Marketing Activation	Sam Nunes
Designers, Graphic, Assoc. Graphic	Jason Petrie / Carley Johnson

Community Relations and Alumni Office

Community Relations Director / Coordinator	Kerry Collins / Brooke Pinkham
Youth Hockey Manager / Coordinator	Mike Dargin / Julia Wardwell
Boston Bruins Alumni Coordinator	Karen Wonoski

Boston Bruins Foundation

Executive Director, Boston Bruins Foundation	Bob Sweeney
Foundation Manager / Coordinator	Zack Fitzgerald / Leandra Murphy

Sales, Fan Relations and Retail

Ticket Sales Director / Manager	Mark Rodrigues / Kevin Stone
Retail Manager / Buyer	Mark Maimone / Lauma Cerlins
Managers, Retail Warehouse / Fan Relations	Jenny Bartlett / Keith Ricci
Season Sales Account Executives	Matt Gulley, Tina Zettel, Kate Sullivan
Group Sales Account Executives	Alexandra Bottone, Rachel Hansen, Jonathan Leite
Fan Relations Representatives	Brian Joyce, Billy Ricci, Richard Yutkins, Matthew Dario, Patricia Bradle

Finance, Legal, Human Resources and Box Office

Controller / Staff Accountant	Rick McGlinchey / Linda Bartlett
Accounting Manager / Coordinator	Sean Sullivan / Rick McGlinchey, Jr.
Payroll & Benefits Manager / Business Analyst	Botin Bou-James / Casey Burnham
Assistant General Counsel / Paralegal	Matt Reece / Kristin DiRocco
Director of Human Resources	Amela Hadziahmetovic
Box Office Director / Manager	TBD / Courtney McNeice
Asst. Director, Ticket Ops / Ticket Office Receptionist	Jim Foley / Jo-Ann Connolly-White

Broadcasting

TV Rightsholder	New England Sports Network (NESN)
TV play-by-play / analyst	Jack Edwards / Andy Brickley
TV studio host / producer	Dale Arnold / Brian Zechello
Radio Rightsholder	98.5 The Sports Hub (CBS Radio Boston)
Radio play-by-play / analyst	Dave Goucher / Bob Beers

Buffalo Sabres

2016-17 Results: 33W-37L-6OTL-6SOL 78PTS
8TH, Atlantic Division • 15TH, Eastern Conference

Key Off-Season Signings/Acquisitions

2017

May 11 • Named **Jason Botterill** general manager.
June 13 • Re-signed G **Linus Ullmark**.
15 • Named **Phil Housley** head coach.
17 • Acquired D **Nathan Beaulieu** from Montreal for Buffalo's 3rd-round pick in 2017 NHL Draft.
26 • Re-signed D **Taylor Fedun**.
30 • Acquired D **Marco Scandella**, RW **Jason Pominville** and a 4th-round pick in 2018 NHL Draft from Minnesota for C **Tyler Ennis**, LW **Marcus Foligno** and a 3rd-round pick in 2018 NHL Draft.
July 1 • Signed G **Chad Johnson**, C **Jacob Josefson**, C **Kevin Porter**, C **Seth Griffith**, LW **Benoit Pouliot** and D **Matt Tennyson**.
5 • Named **Davis Payne** associate coach.
8 • Re-signed C **Johan Larsson**.
17 • Named **Chris Hajt** assistant coach.
25 • Re-signed G **Robin Lehner**.
27 • Re-signed LW **Evan Rodrigues**.

2017-18 Schedule

Oct.	Thu.	5	Montreal		Sun.	7	at Philadelphia*
	Sat.	7	at NY Islanders		Tue.	9	Winnipeg
	Mon.	9	New Jersey*		Thu.	11	Columbus
	Thu.	12	at San Jose		Thu.	18	at NY Rangers
	Sat.	14	at Los Angeles		Sat.	20	Dallas*
	Sun.	15	at Anaheim		Mon.	22	at Calgary
	Tue.	17	at Vegas		Tue.	23	at Edmonton
	Fri.	20	Vancouver		Thu.	25	at Vancouver
	Sat.	21	at Boston		Tue.	30	New Jersey
	Tue.	24	Detroit	**Feb.**	Thu.	1	Florida
	Wed.	25	at Columbus		Sat.	3	St. Louis
	Sat.	28	San Jose*		Tue.	6	Anaheim
Nov.	Thu.	2	at Arizona		Thu.	8	NY Islanders
	Sat.	4	at Dallas		Sat.	10	at Boston
	Tue.	7	Washington		Sun.	11	Colorado
	Fri.	10	Florida		Tue.	13	Tampa Bay
	Sat.	11	at Montreal		Thu.	15	at Ottawa
	Tue.	14	at Pittsburgh		Sat.	17	Los Angeles*
	Fri.	17	at Detroit		Mon.	19	Washington*
	Sat.	18	Carolina		Thu.	22	at Detroit
	Mon.	20	Columbus		Sat.	24	at Washington
	Wed.	22	Minnesota		Sun.	25	Boston*
	Fri.	24	Edmonton		Wed.	28	at Tampa Bay
	Sat.	25	at Montreal	**Mar.**	Fri.	2	at Florida
	Tue.	28	Tampa Bay		Mon.	5	Toronto
Dec.	Fri.	1	Pittsburgh		Wed.	7	Calgary
	Sat.	2	at Pittsburgh		Thu.	8	at Ottawa
	Tue.	5	at Colorado		Sat.	10	Vegas*
	Fri.	8	at Chicago		Thu.	15	Toronto
	Sun.	10	at St. Louis*		Sat.	17	Chicago*
	Tue.	12	Ottawa		Mon.	19	Nashville
	Thu.	14	at Philadelphia		Wed.	21	Arizona
	Fri.	15	Carolina		Fri.	23	Montreal
	Tue.	19	Boston		Sat.	24	at NY Rangers
	Fri.	22	Philadelphia		Mon.	26	at Toronto
	Sat.	23	at Carolina		Thu.	29	Detroit
	Wed.	27	at NY Islanders		Sat.	31	at Nashville
	Fri.	29	at New Jersey	**Apr.**	Mon.	2	at Toronto
Jan.	Mon.	1	NY Rangers*		Wed.	4	Ottawa
	Thu.	4	at Minnesota		Fri.	6	at Tampa Bay
	Fri.	5	at Winnipeg		Sat.	7	at Florida

* Denotes afternoon game.

Retired Numbers

2	Tim Horton	1972-1974
7	Rick Martin	1971-1981
11	Gilbert Perreault	1970-1987
14	Rene Robert	1971-1979
16	Pat LaFontaine	1991-1996
18	Danny Gare	1974-1981

ATLANTIC DIVISION
48th NHL Season
Franchise date: May 22, 1970

Jack Eichel (15) and Ryan O'Reilly celebrate a goal at the Buffalo bench. They were the top two scorers for the Sabres for the second season in a row in 2016-17.

Year-by-Year Record

Season	GP	Home W	L	T	OL	Road W	L	T	OL	Overall W	L	T	OL	GF	GA	Pts.	Div. Fin.	Conf. Fin.	Playoff Result
2016-17	82	20	15	....	6	13	22	....	6	33	37	....	12	201	237	78	8th, Atl.	15th, East	– out of playoffs –
2015-16	82	16	19	....	6	19	17	....	5	35	36	....	11	201	222	81	7th, Atl.	14th, East	– out of playoffs –
2014-15	82	14	22	....	5	9	29	....	3	23	51	....	8	161	274	54	8th, Atl.	16th, East	– out of playoffs –
2013-14	82	13	21	....	7	8	30	....	3	21	51	....	10	157	248	52	8th, Atl.	16th, East	– out of playoffs –
2012-13	48	11	10	....	3	10	11	....	3	21	21	....	6	125	143	48	5th, NE	12th, East	– out of playoffs –
2011-12	82	21	12	....	8	18	20	....	3	39	32	....	11	218	230	89	3rd, NE	9th, East	– out of playoffs –
2010-11	82	21	16	....	4	22	13	....	6	43	29	....	10	245	229	96	3rd, NE	7th, East	Lost Conf. Quarter-Final
2009-10	82	25	10	....	6	20	17	....	4	45	27	....	10	235	207	100	1st, NE	3rd, East	Lost Conf. Quarter-Final
2008-09	82	23	15	....	4	18	17	....	6	41	32	....	9	250	234	91	3rd, NE	10th, East	– out of playoffs –
2007-08	82	20	15	....	6	19	16	....	6	39	31	....	12	255	242	90	4th, NE	10th, East	– out of playoffs –
2006-07	82	28	10	....	3	25	12	....	4	53	22	....	7	308	242	113	1st, NE	1st, East	Lost Conf. Final
2005-06	82	27	11	....	3	25	13	....	3	52	24	....	6	281	239	110	2nd, NE	4th, East	Lost Conf. Final
2004-05	....																		
2003-04	82	21	13	4	3	16	21	3	1	37	34	7	4	220	221	85	5th, NE	9th, East	– out of playoffs –
2002-03	82	18	16	5	2	9	21	5	6	27	37	10	8	190	219	72	5th, NE	12th, East	– out of playoffs –
2001-02	82	20	16	5	0	15	19	6	1	35	35	11	1	213	200	82	5th, NE	10th, East	– out of playoffs –
2000-01	82	26	12	3	0	20	18	2	1	46	30	5	1	218	184	98	2nd, NE	5th, East	Lost Conf. Semi-Final
1999-2000	82	21	14	5	1	14	18	6	3	35	32	11	4	213	204	85	3rd, NE	8th, East	Lost Conf. Quarter-Final
1998-99	82	23	12	6	....	14	16	11	....	37	28	17	....	207	175	91	4th, NE	7th, East	Lost Final
1997-98	82	20	13	8	....	16	16	9	....	36	29	17	....	211	187	89	3rd, NE	6th, East	Lost Conf. Final
1996-97	82	24	11	6	....	16	19	6	....	40	30	12	....	237	208	92	1st, NE	3rd, East	Lost Conf. Semi-Final
1995-96	82	19	15	7	....	14	25	2	....	33	42	7	....	247	262	73	5th, NE	11th, East	– out of playoffs –
1994-95	48	15	8	1	....	7	11	6	....	22	19	7	....	130	119	51	4th, NE	6th, East	Lost Conf. Quarter-Final
1993-94	84	22	17	3	....	21	15	6	....	43	32	9	....	282	218	95	4th, NE	6th, East	Lost Conf. Quarter-Final
1992-93	84	25	15	2	....	13	21	8	....	38	36	10	....	335	297	86	4th, Adams		Lost Div. Final
1991-92	80	22	15	3	....	9	24	7	....	31	37	12	....	289	299	74	3rd, Adams		Lost Div. Semi-Final
1990-91	80	15	13	12	....	16	17	7	....	31	30	19	....	292	278	81	3rd, Adams		Lost Div. Semi-Final
1989-90	80	27	11	2	....	18	16	6	....	45	27	8	....	286	248	98	2nd, Adams		Lost Div. Semi-Final
1988-89	80	25	12	3	....	13	23	4	....	38	35	7	....	291	299	83	3rd, Adams		Lost Div. Semi-Final
1987-88	80	19	14	7	....	18	18	4	....	37	32	11	....	283	305	85	3rd, Adams		Lost Div. Semi-Final
1986-87	80	18	18	4	....	10	26	4	....	28	44	8	....	280	308	64	5th, Adams		– out of playoffs –
1985-86	80	23	16	1	....	14	21	5	....	37	37	6	....	296	291	80	5th, Adams		– out of playoffs –
1984-85	80	23	10	7	....	15	18	7	....	38	28	14	....	290	237	90	3rd, Adams		Lost Div. Semi-Final
1983-84	80	25	9	6	....	23	16	1	....	48	25	7	....	315	257	103	2nd, Adams		Lost Div. Semi-Final
1982-83	80	25	7	8	....	13	22	5	....	38	29	13	....	318	285	89	3rd, Adams		Lost Div. Final
1981-82	80	25	7	8	....	14	19	7	....	39	26	15	....	307	273	93	3rd, Adams		Lost Div. Semi-Final
1980-81	80	21	7	12	....	18	13	9	....	39	20	21	....	327	250	99	1st, Adams		Lost Quarter-Final
1979-80	80	27	5	8	....	20	12	8	....	47	17	16	....	318	201	110	1st, Adams		Lost Semi-Final
1978-79	80	19	13	8	....	17	15	8	....	36	28	16	....	280	263	88	2nd, Adams		Lost Prelim. Round
1977-78	80	25	7	8	....	19	12	9	....	44	19	17	....	288	215	105	2nd, Adams		Lost Quarter-Final
1976-77	80	27	8	5	....	21	16	3	....	48	24	8	....	301	220	104	2nd, Adams		Lost Quarter-Final
1975-76	80	28	7	5	....	18	14	8	....	46	21	13	....	339	240	105	2nd, Adams		Lost Quarter-Final
1974-75	80	28	6	6	....	21	10	9	....	49	16	15	....	354	240	113	1st, Adams		Lost Final
1973-74	78	23	10	6	....	9	24	6	....	32	34	12	....	242	250	76	5th, East		– out of playoffs –
1972-73	78	30	6	3	....	7	21	11	....	37	27	14	....	257	219	88	4th, East		Lost Quarter-Final
1971-72	78	11	19	9	....	5	24	10	....	16	43	19	....	203	289	51	6th, East		– out of playoffs –
1970-71	78	16	13	10	....	8	26	5	....	24	39	15	....	217	291	63	5th, East		– out of playoffs –

2017-18 Player Personnel

FORWARDS	HT	WT	*Age	Birthplace	S	2016-17 Club
DESLAURIERS, Nicolas	6-1	212	26	LaSalle, QC	L	Buffalo
EICHEL, Jack	6-2	201	20	North Chelmsford, MA	R	Buffalo
GIRGENSONS, Zemgus	6-1	203	23	Riga, Latvia	L	Buffalo
GRIFFITH, Seth	5-9	191	24	Wallaceburg, ON	R	Tor-Tor (AHL)-Fla
JOSEFSON, Jacob	6-0	190	26	Stockholm, Sweden	L	New Jersey
KANE, Evander	6-2	204	26	Vancouver, BC	L	Buffalo
LARSSON, Johan	5-11	200	25	Lau, Sweden	L	Buffalo
MOULSON, Matt	6-1	212	33	North York, ON	L	Buffalo
OKPOSO, Kyle	6-0	217	29	St. Paul, MN	R	Buffalo
O'REILLY, Ryan	6-1	210	26	Clinton, ON	L	Buffalo
POMINVILLE, Jason	6-0	184	34	Repentigny, QC	R	Minnesota
POULIOT, Benoit	6-3	200	31	Alfred, ON	L	Edmonton
REINHART, Sam	6-1	189	21	North Vancouver, BC	R	Buffalo

DEFENSEMEN						
ANTIPIN, Victor	5-11	179	24	Ust-Kamenogorsk, Kazakh.	L	Magnitogorsk
BEAULIEU, Nathan	6-2	205	24	Strathroy, ON	L	Montreal
BOGOSIAN, Zach	6-3	219	27	Massena, NY	R	Buffalo
FALK, Justin	6-5	224	28	Snowflake, MB	L	Buffalo-Rochester
FEDUN, Taylor	6-0	200	29	Edmonton, AB	R	Buffalo-Rochester
GORGES, Josh	6-1	203	33	Kelowna, BC	L	Buffalo
McCABE, Jake	6-0	214	23	Eau Claire, WI	L	Buffalo
RISTOLAINEN, Rasmus	6-4	207	22	Turku, Finland	R	Buffalo
SCANDELLA, Marco	6-3	211	27	Montreal, QC	L	Minnesota
TENNYSON, Matt	6-2	205	27	Pleasanton, CA	R	Carolina-Charlotte

GOALTENDERS	HT	WT	*Age	Birthplace	C	2016-17 Club
JOHNSON, Chad	6-3	196	31	Calgary, AB	L	Calgary
LEHNER, Robin	6-5	240	26	Goteborg, Sweden	L	Buffalo

* – Age at start of 2017-18 season

Coaching History

Punch Imlach, 1970-71; Punch Imlach, Floyd Smith and Joe Crozier, 1971-72; Joe Crozier, 1972-73, 1973-74; Floyd Smith, 1974-75 to 1976-77; Marcel Pronovost, 1977-78; Marcel Pronovost and Billy Inglis, 1978-79; Scotty Bowman, 1979-80; Roger Neilson, 1980-81; Jim Roberts and Scotty Bowman, 1981-82; Scotty Bowman 1982-83 to 1984-85; Jim Schoenfeld and Scotty Bowman, 1985-86; Scotty Bowman, Craig Ramsay and Ted Sator, 1986-87; Ted Sator, 1987-88, 1988-89; Rick Dudley, 1989-90, 1990-91; Rick Dudley and John Muckler, 1991-92; John Muckler, 1992-93 to 1994-95; Ted Nolan, 1995-96, 1996-97; Lindy Ruff, 1997-98 to 2011-12; Lindy Ruff and Ron Rolston, 2012-13; Ron Rolston and Ted Nolan, 2013-14; Ted Nolan, 2014-15; Dan Bylsma, 2015-16, 2016-17; Phil Housley, 2017-18.

Phil Housley
Head Coach
Born: St. Paul, MN, March 9, 1964.

The Buffalo Sabres announced on June 15, 2017, that Phil Housley had become the 18th man to serve as head coach in franchise history. The Hockey Hall of Famer and former Sabres defenseman is the seventh alumnus to serve as the team's head coach. Housley joined the Sabres after helping to guide the Nashville Predators to their first Stanley Cup Final appearance in franchise history.

Named an assistant coach in Nashville on May 22, 2013, Housley was a driving force behind one of the NHL's best defensive groups throughout his tenure. During his four seasons in Nashville, the Predators ranked in the top two in the league in goals by defensemen every season and finished in the top half in fewest goals allowed in each of the last three seasons. Under Housley's tutelage, Nashville had at least one player finish in the top five in voting for the James Norris Memorial Trophy every season from 2013-14 to 2015-16.

A native of South St. Paul, Minnesota, Housley began his coaching career in 2004 as head coach of Stillwater Area High School in Minnesota. During his nine seasons at the helm, Housley turned around the school's program while also accepting numerous opportunities to coach for Team USA at the international level. Throughout his time with USA Hockey, Housley has served as an assistant coach at two World Junior Championships and three World Championships. Most notably, he served as the head coach when Team USA won the gold medal at the 2013 World Junior Championship. He was also an assistant coach for Team USA at the 2016 World Cup of Hockey.

Drafted by the Sabres in the first round (sixth overall) of the 1982 NHL Draft, Housley went on to play 21 seasons in the NHL. His 1,232 career points (338 goals, 894assists) rank third among American players and fourth among defensemen all-time. He is also the Sabres' career and individual-season leader in goals, assists and points by a defenseman. Each of his eight seasons in Buffalo rank among the top 10 single-season point totals by a Sabres defensemen. Internationally, Housley was a part of Team USA's gold medal team at the 1996 World Cup of Hockey, as well as the American squad that took home silver at the 2002 Winter Olympics. He also represented the United States at six World Championships, one World Junior Championship and two Canada Cup tournaments.

A member of the Buffalo Sabres, USA Hockey and IIHF Halls of Fame, Housley was inducted into the Hockey Hall of Fame in 2015. During his career, he played in seven All-Star Games and was named to the first All-Rookie Team in 1983.

Coaching Record

Season	Team	League	Regular Season GC	W	L	O/T	Playoffs GC	W	L	T
2004-05	Stillwater	High-MN	25	8	12	5	1	0	1	....
2005-06	Stillwater	High-MN	25	12	11	2	1	0	1	....
2006-07	Stillwater	High-MN	25	12	11	2	1	0	1	....
2007-08	Stillwater	High-MN	25	9	15	1	1	0	1	....
2008-09	Stillwater	High-MN	25	11	11	3	3	2	1	....
2009-10	Stillwater	High-MN	25	14	9	2	2	1	1	....
2010-11	Stillwater	High-MN	25	16	7	2	2	1	1	....
2011-12	Stillwater	High-MN	25	12	11	2	2	1	1	....
2012-13	Stillwater	High-MN	25	9	14	2	1	0	1	....
2012-13	USA	WJC	4	2	2	0	3	3	0	....

2016-17 Scoring
*– rookie

Regular Season

Pos	#	Player	Team	GP	G	A	Pts	TOI	+/-	PIM	PP	SH	GW	S	S%
C	15	Jack Eichel	BUF	61	24	33	57	19:55	-13	22	10	0	4	249	9.6
C	90	Ryan O'Reilly	BUF	72	20	35	55	21:27	-1	10	8	1	3	189	10.6
C	23	Sam Reinhart	BUF	79	17	30	47	17:13	-11	8	9	0	3	178	9.6
R	21	Kyle Okposo	BUF	65	19	26	45	18:58	-7	24	7	0	2	156	12.2
D	55	Rasmus Ristolainen	BUF	79	6	39	45	26:28	-9	58	1	0	2	186	3.2
L	9	Evander Kane	BUF	70	28	15	43	19:12	-17	113	3	0	5	260	10.8
R	12	Brian Gionta	BUF	82	15	20	35	16:36	-11	22	3	1	3	149	10.1
L	26	Matt Moulson	BUF	81	14	18	32	11:36	-4	10	11	0	2	134	10.4
L	82	Marcus Foligno	BUF	80	13	10	23	15:28	-1	73	0	1	0	97	13.4
D	29	Jake McCabe	BUF	76	3	17	20	20:42	-7	26	1	0	1	79	3.8
D	6	Cody Franson	BUF	68	3	16	19	18:28	-5	34	1	0	0	93	3.2
C	28	Zemgus Girgensons	BUF	75	7	9	16	13:09	-7	18	0	0	0	112	6.3
C	63	Tyler Ennis	BUF	51	5	8	13	12:50	-10	12	0	0	1	89	5.6
L	22	Johan Larsson	BUF	36	6	5	11	16:51	-7	20	1	0	2	49	12.2
D	47	Zach Bogosian	BUF	56	2	9	11	20:05	-17	46	0	0	1	73	2.7
L	48 *	William Carrier	BUF	41	5	3	8	9:00	-1	21	0	0	1	50	10.0
D	41	Justin Falk	BUF	52	0	8	8	13:41	-3	29	0	0	0	33	0.0
D	38	Taylor Fedun	BUF	27	0	7	7	13:21	3	14	0	0	0	24	0.0
C	71 *	Evan Rodrigues	BUF	30	4	2	6	12:55	-7	4	1	0	0	51	7.8
D	4	Josh Gorges	BUF	66	1	5	6	18:27	-3	50	0	0	0	40	2.5
D	77	Dmitry Kulikov	BUF	47	2	3	5	21:54	-26	26	1	0	0	42	4.8
R	73 *	Nicholas Baptiste	BUF	14	3	1	4	9:14	1	6	0	0	0	16	18.8
R	56 *	Justin Bailey	BUF	32	2	2	4	10:37	0	4	0	0	1	36	5.6
C	27	Derek Grant	BUF	35	0	3	3	10:12	-3	19	0	0	0	31	0.0
			NSH	6	0	1	1	8:41	-2	5	0	0	0	6	0.0
			BUF	5	0	0	0	7:56	0	0	0	0	0	3	0.0
			Total	46	0	4	4	9:45	-5	24	0	0	0	40	0.0
L	44	Nicolas Deslauriers	BUF	42	0	2	2	7:24	-6	38	0	0	0	26	0.0
L	49 *	C.J. Smith	BUF	2	0	1	1	11:32	-1	0	0	0	0	0	0.0
L	10	Cole Schneider	BUF	4	0	1	1	7:08	2	0	0	0	0	6	0.0
L	70 *	Alexander Nylander	BUF	4	0	1	1	12:19	-2	0	0	0	0	4	0.0
R	52 *	Hudson Fasching	BUF	10	0	1	1	10:24	-1	2	0	0	0	6	0.0
C	19	Cal O'Reilly	BUF	11	0	1	1	7:55	-6	0	0	0	0	3	0.0
C	42 *	Sean Malone	BUF	1	0	0	0	12:12	0	0	0	0	0	1	0.0
D	46 *	Erik Burgdoerfer	BUF	2	0	0	0	11:10	-1	0	0	0	0	0	0.0
D	45 *	Brendan Guhle	BUF	3	0	0	0	16:21	1	0	0	0	0	4	0.0
D	67 *	Brady Austin	BUF	5	0	0	0	16:05	0	4	0	0	0	8	0.0
D	34 *	Casey Nelson	BUF	11	0	0	0	12:36	-3	4	0	0	0	10	0.0

Goaltending

No.	Goaltender	GPI	Mins	Avg	W	L	OT	EN	SO	GA	SA	Sv%	G	A	PIM
31	Anders Nilsson	26	1484	2.67	10	10	4	3	1	66	857	.923	0	0	0
40	Robin Lehner	59	3405	2.68	23	26	8	6	2	152	1910	.920	0	1	6
35	* Linus Ullmark	1	59	3.05	0	1	0	1	0	3	36	.917	0	0	0
	Totals	82	4985	2.78	33	37	12	10	3	231	2813	.918			

Rasmus Ristolainen ranked seventh among NHL defensemen with 39 assists in 2016-17.

Captains' History

Floyd Smith, 1970-71; Gerry Meehan, 1971-72 to 1973-74; Gerry Meehan and Jim Schoenfeld, 1974-75; Jim Schoenfeld, 1975-76, 1976-77; Danny Gare, 1977-78 to 1980-81; Danny Gare and Gilbert Perreault, 1981-82; Gilbert Perreault, 1982-83 to 1985-86; Gilbert Perreault and Lindy Ruff, 1986-87; Lindy Ruff, 1987-88; Lindy Ruff and Mike Foligno, 1988-89; Mike Foligno, 1989-90; Mike Foligno and Mike Ramsey, 1990-91; Mike Ramsey, 1991-92; Mike Ramsey and Pat LaFontaine, 1992-93; Pat LaFontaine and Alexander Mogilny, 1993-94; Pat LaFontaine, 1994-95 to 1996-97; Donald Audette and Michael Peca, 1997-98; Michael Peca, 1998-99, 1999-2000; no captain, 2000-01; Stu Barnes, 2001-02, 2002-03; Miroslav Satan, Chris Drury, James Patrick, J.P. Dumont, Daniel Briere, 2003-04; Daniel Briere and Chris Drury, 2005-06, 2006-07; Jochen Hecht, Toni Lydman, Brian Campbell, Jaroslav Spacek, Jason Pominville, 2007-08; Craig Rivet, 2008-09 to 2010-11; Jason Pominville, 2011-12, 2012-13; no captain, 2013-14; Brian Gionta, 2014-15 to 2016-17.

Club Records

Team

(Figures in brackets for season records are games played; records for fewest points, wins, ties, losses, goals, goals against are for 70 or more games)

Most Points **113** 1974-75 (80), 2006-07 (82)
Most Wins **53** 2006-07 (82)
Most Ties **21** 1980-81 (80)
Most Losses **44** 1986-87 (80)
Most Goals **354** 1974-75 (80)
Most Goals Against **308** 1986-87 (80)
Fewest Points **51** 1971-72 (78)
Fewest Wins **16** 1971-72 (78)
Fewest Ties **5** 2000-01 (82)
Fewest Losses **16** 1974-75 (80)
Fewest Goals **157** 2013-14 (82)
Fewest Goals Against **175** 1998-99 (82)

Longest Winning Streak
Overall .... **10** Jan. 4-23/84, Oct. 4-26/06
Home .... **12** Nov. 12/72-Jan. 7/73, Oct. 13-Dec. 10/89
Away .... **10** Dec. 10/83-Jan. 23/84, Oct. 4-Nov. 13/06

Longest Team Point Streak
Overall .... **14** Mar. 6-Apr. 6/80 (8W, 6T)
Home .... **21** Oct. 8/72-Jan. 7/73 (18W, 3T)
Away .... **10** Dec. 10/83-Jan. 23/84 (10W), Oct. 4-Nov. 13/06 (5W, 2OTW, 3SOW)

Longest Losing Streak
Overall .... **14** Dec. 29/14-Jan. 30/15
Home .... **9** Oct. 4-Nov. 2/13
Away .... **12** Dec. 17/11-Jan. 21/12

Longest Winless Streak
Overall .... **12** Nov. 23-Dec. 20/91 (8L, 4T), Oct. 25-Nov. 19/02 (10L, 1OTL, 1T)
Home .... **12** Jan. 27-Mar. 10/91 (7L, 5T)
Away .... **23** Oct. 30/71-Feb. 19/72 (15L, 8T)

Most Shutouts, Season **13** 1997-98 (82)
Most PIM, Season ***2,713** 1991-92 (80)
Most Goals, Game .... **14** Jan. 21/75 (Wsh. 2 at Buf. 14), Mar. 19/81 (Tor. 4 at Buf. 14)

Individual

Most Seasons .... **17** Gilbert Perreault
Most Games .... **1,191** Gilbert Perreault
Most Goals, Career .... **512** Gilbert Perreault
Most Assists, Career .... **814** Gilbert Perreault
Most Points, Career .... **1,326** Gilbert Perreault (512G, 814A)
Most PIM, Career .... **3,189** Rob Ray
Most Shutouts, Career .... **55** Dominik Hasek
Longest Consecutive Games Streak .... **776** Craig Ramsay (Mar. 27/73-Feb. 10/83)
Most Goals, Season .... **76** Alexander Mogilny (1992-93)
Most Assists, Season .... **95** Pat LaFontaine (1992-93)
Most Points, Season .... **148** Pat LaFontaine (1992-93; 53G, 95A)
Most PIM, Season .... **354** Rob Ray (1991-92)
Most Points, Defenseman, Season .... **81** Phil Housley (1989-90; 21G, 60A)
Most Points, Center, Season .... **148** Pat LaFontaine (1992-93; 53G, 95A)
Most Points, Right Wing, Season .... **127** Alexander Mogilny (1992-93; 76G, 51A)
Most Points, Left Wing, Season .... **95** Rick Martin (1974-75; 52G, 43A)
Most Points, Rookie, Season .... **74** Rick Martin (1971-72; 44G, 30A)
Most Shutouts, Season .... **13** Dominik Hasek (1997-98)
Most Goals, Game .... **5** Dave Andreychuk (Feb. 6/86)
Most Assists, Game .... **5** Gilbert Perreault (Feb. 1/76), (Mar. 9/80), (Jan. 4/84); Dale Hawerchuk (Jan. 15/92); Pat LaFontaine (Mar. 19/92), (Dec. 31/92), (Feb. 10/93)
Most Points, Game .... **7** Gilbert Perreault (Feb. 1/76; 2G, 5A)

* NHL Record.

All-time Record vs. Other Clubs

Regular Season

	Total								At Home								On Road							
	GP	W	L	T	OL	GF	GA	PTS	GP	W	L	T	OL	GF	GA	PTS	GP	W	L	T	OL	GF	GA	PTS
Anaheim	34	17	14	3	0	92	83	37	17	8	6	3	0	48	44	19	17	9	8	0	0	44	39	18
Arizona	76	45	22	7	2	269	201	99	39	25	7	5	2	153	98	57	37	20	15	2	0	116	103	42
Boston	285	121	120	29	15	902	919	286	144	73	48	15	8	494	416	169	141	48	72	14	7	408	503	117
Calgary	105	51	36	16	2	370	326	120	52	33	13	5	1	211	145	72	53	18	23	11	1	159	181	48
Carolina	198	102	71	18	7	671	575	229	98	58	32	7	1	378	279	124	100	44	39	11	6	293	296	105
Chicago	119	53	51	13	2	368	352	121	60	34	18	7	1	214	158	76	59	19	33	6	1	154	194	45
Colorado	141	61	56	20	4	480	482	146	70	38	21	9	2	265	226	87	71	23	35	11	2	215	256	59
Columbus	26	10	14	1	1	69	76	22	14	6	7	0	1	38	40	13	12	4	7	1	0	31	36	9
Dallas	120	56	47	17	0	382	353	129	59	33	15	11	0	211	157	77	61	23	32	6	0	171	196	52
Detroit	133	58	57	13	5	441	439	134	65	36	19	8	2	252	193	82	68	22	38	5	3	189	246	52
Edmonton	73	24	38	10	1	231	263	59	37	14	15	7	1	127	128	36	36	10	23	3	0	104	135	23
Florida	92	48	36	4	4	257	229	104	47	27	16	3	1	134	106	58	45	21	20	1	3	123	123	46
Los Angeles	121	59	43	18	1	444	373	137	60	35	16	9	0	248	166	79	61	24	27	9	1	196	207	58
Minnesota	20	9	10	0	1	42	57	19	10	2	7	0	1	16	33	5	10	7	3	0	0	26	24	14
Montreal	275	126	110	31	8	805	840	291	137	72	39	19	7	413	363	170	138	54	71	12	1	392	477	121
Nashville	23	9	10	1	3	58	68	22	11	1	6	1	3	28	40	6	12	8	4	0	0	30	28	16
New Jersey	151	74	51	17	9	482	429	174	76	40	25	8	3	260	221	91	75	34	26	9	6	222	208	83
NY Islanders	165	80	62	18	5	494	468	183	83	44	27	9	3	270	233	100	82	36	35	9	2	224	235	83
NY Rangers	177	81	62	25	9	565	547	196	90	48	28	10	4	333	274	110	87	33	34	15	5	232	273	86
Ottawa	133	65	49	10	9	368	342	149	65	35	22	3	5	194	156	78	68	30	27	7	4	174	186	71
Philadelphia	173	67	82	20	4	508	552	158	85	42	33	8	2	280	244	94	88	25	49	12	2	228	308	64
Pittsburgh	185	65	78	35	7	598	603	172	92	41	29	17	5	323	257	104	93	24	49	18	2	275	346	68
St. Louis	116	46	54	13	3	351	390	108	59	31	22	6	0	212	185	68	57	15	32	7	3	139	205	40
San Jose	37	24	7	4	2	138	102	54	19	17	1	0	1	81	50	35	18	7	6	4	1	57	52	19
Tampa Bay	94	52	34	5	3	278	244	112	46	24	17	2	3	136	130	53	48	28	17	3	0	142	114	59
Toronto	206	113	67	18	8	736	572	252	104	69	27	6	2	405	269	146	102	44	40	12	6	331	303	106
Vancouver	118	48	51	19	0	387	391	115	59	31	20	8	0	210	172	70	59	17	31	11	0	177	219	45
Washington	155	87	48	15	5	541	411	194	77	46	22	6	3	286	200	101	78	41	26	9	2	255	211	93
Winnipeg	59	26	22	1	10	195	173	63	30	17	9	0	4	119	80	38	29	9	13	1	6	76	93	25
Defunct Clubs	46	25	13	8	0	191	139	58	23	13	5	5	0	94	63	31	23	12	8	3	0	97	76	27
Totals	**3656**	**1702**	**1415**	**409**	**130**	**11713**	**10999**	**3943**	**1828**	**993**	**572**	**197**	**66**	**6433**	**5126**	**2249**	**1828**	**709**	**843**	**212**	**64**	**5280**	**5873**	**1694**

Playoffs

	Series	W	L	GP	W	L	T	GF	GA	Last Mtg.	Rnd.	Result
Boston	8	2	6	45	20	25	0	145	155	2010	CQF	L 2-4
Carolina	1	0	1	7	3	4	0	17	22	2006	CF	L 3-4
Chicago	2	2	0	9	8	1	0	36	17	1980	QF	W 4-0
Colorado	2	0	2	8	2	6	0	27	35	1985	DSF	L 2-3
Dallas	3	1	2	13	5	8	0	37	39	1999	F	L 2-4
Montreal	7	3	4	35	17	18	0	111	124	1998	CSF	W 4-0
New Jersey	1	0	1	7	3	4	0	14	14	1994	CQF	L 3-4
NY Islanders	4	1	3	21	8	13	0	62	70	2007	CQF	W 4-1
NY Rangers	2	2	0	9	6	3	0	28	19	2007	CSF	W 4-2
Ottawa	4	3	1	21	13	8	0	52	47	2007	CF	L 1-4
Philadelphia	9	3	6	50	21	29	0	141	146	2011	CQF	L 3-4
Pittsburgh	2	0	2	10	4	6	0	26	26	2001	CSF	L 3-4
St. Louis	1	1	0	3	2	1	0	7	8	1976	PR	W 2-1
Toronto	1	1	0	5	4	1	0	21	16	1999	CF	W 4-1
Vancouver	2	2	0	7	6	1	0	28	14	1981	PR	W 3-0
Washington	1	0	1	6	2	4	0	11	13	1998	CF	L 2-4
Totals	**50**	**21**	**29**	**256**	**124**	**132**	**0**	**763**	**765**			

Playoff Results 2017-2013

(Last playoff appearance: 2011)

Abbreviations: Round: F – Final; **CF** – conference final; **CSF** – conference semi-final; **CQF** – conference quarter-final; **DSF** – division semi-final; **QF** – quarter-final; **PR** – preliminary round.

Calgary totals include Atlanta Flames, 1972-73 to 1979-80.
Carolina totals include Hartford, 1979-80 to 1996-97.
Colorado totals include Quebec, 1979-80 to 1994-95.
Dallas totals include Minnesota North Stars, 1970-71 to 1992-93.
New Jersey totals include Kansas City, 1974-75, 1975-76, and Colorado Rockies, 1976-77 to 1981-82.
Phoenix totals include Winnipeg, 1979-80 to 1995-96.
Winnipeg totals include Atlanta Thrashers, 1999-2000 to 2010-11.

2016-17 Results

Oct.	13	Montreal	1-4
	16	at Edmonton	6-2
	18	at Calgary	3-4*
	20	at Vancouver	1-2
	25	at Philadelphia	3-4†
	27	Minnesota	0-4
	29	Florida	3-0
	30	at Winnipeg	3-1
Nov.	1	at Minnesota	2-1
	3	Toronto	1-2
	5	at Ottawa	2-1
	7	at Boston	0-4
	9	Ottawa	1-2†
	11	New Jersey	1-2*
	12	at New Jersey	2-4
	15	at St. Louis	1-4
	17	Tampa Bay	1-4
	19	Pittsburgh	2-1†
	21	Calgary	4-2
	23	Detroit	1-2†
	25	at Washington	1-3
	29	at Ottawa	5-4
Dec.	1	NY Rangers	4-3
	3	Boston	1-2
	5	at Washington	2-3*
	6	Edmonton	4-3*
	9	Washington	1-4
	13	Los Angeles	6-3
	16	NY Islanders	3-2*
	17	at Carolina	1-2†
	20	at Florida	3-4†
	22	Carolina	1-3
	23	at NY Islanders	1-5
	27	at Detroit	4-3
	29	Boston	2-4
	31	at Boston	1-3
Jan.	3	at NY Rangers	4-1
	5	at Chicago	3-4*
	7	Winnipeg	4-3
	10	Philadelphia	4-1
	12	at Tampa Bay	2-4
	13	at Carolina	2-5
	16	Dallas	4-1
	17	at Toronto	3-4
	20	Detroit	3-2*
	21	at Montreal	3-2*
	24	at Nashville	5-4*
	26	at Dallas	3-4
	31	at Montreal	2-5
Feb.	2	NY Rangers	1-2*
	4	Ottawa	4-0
	6	at New Jersey	1-2
	7	San Jose	5-4*
	9	Anaheim	2-5
	11	at Toronto	3-1
	12	Vancouver	2-4
	14	at Ottawa	3-2
	16	Colorado	2-0
	18	St. Louis	3-2
	19	Chicago	1-5
	25	at Colorado	3-5
	26	at Arizona	2-3
	28	Nashville	4-5*
Mar.	2	Arizona	6-3
	4	Tampa Bay	1-2†
	5	at Pittsburgh	3-4
	7	Philadelphia	3-6
	10	at Columbus	3-4
	11	Columbus	5-3
	14	at San Jose	1-4
	16	at Los Angeles	0-2
	17	at Anaheim	2-1†
	20	at Detroit	2-1
	21	Pittsburgh	1-3
	25	Toronto	5-2
	27	Florida	4-2
	28	at Columbus	1-3
Apr.	2	NY Islanders	2-4
	3	Toronto	2-4
	5	Montreal	2-1
	8	at Florida	0-3
	9	at Tampa Bay	2-4

* – Overtime † – Shootout

NHL Draft Selections 2017-2003

Name in bold denotes played in NHL.

2017
Pick	
8	Casey Mittelstadt
37	Marcus Davidsson
54	Ukko-Pekka Luukkonen
89	Oskari Laaksonen
99	Jacob Bryson
192	Linus Weissbach

2016
Pick	
8	**Alexander Nylander**
33	Rasmus Asplund
69	Cliff Pu
86	Casey Fitzgerald
99	Brett Murray
129	Philip Nyberg
130	Vojtech Budik
159	Brandon Hagel
189	Austin Osmanski
190	Vasili Glotov

2015
Pick	
2	**Jack Eichel**
51	**Brendan Guhle**
92	William Borgen
122	Devante Stephens
152	Giorgio Estephan
182	Ivan Chukarov

2014
Pick	
2	**Sam Reinhart**
31	Brendan Lemieux
44	Eric Cornel
49	Vaclav Karabacek
61	Jonas Johansson
74	Brycen Martin
121	Max Willman
151	Christopher Brown
181	Victor Olofsson

2013
Pick	
8	**Rasmus Ristolainen**
16	**Nikita Zadorov**
35	**J.T. Compher**
38	Connor Hurley
52	**Justin Bailey**
69	**Nicholas Baptiste**
129	Cal Petersen
130	Gustav Possler
143	Anthony Florentino
159	**Sean Malone**
189	Eric Locke

2012
Pick	
12	**Mikhail Grigorenko**
14	**Zemgus Girgensons**
44	**Jake McCabe**
73	Justin Kea
133	Logan Nelson
163	**Linus Ullmark**
193	**Brady Austin**
204	Judd Peterson

2011
Pick	
16	**Joel Armia**
77	**Daniel Catenacci**
107	Colin Jacobs
137	Alex Lepkowski
167	**Nathan Lieuwen**
197	Brad Navin

2010
Pick	
23	**Mark Pysyk**
68	Jerome Leduc
75	Kevin Sundher
83	Matt MacKenzie
98	Steven Shipley
143	Gregg Sutch
173	Cedrick Henley
203	Christian Isackson
208	Riley Boychuk

2009
Pick	
13	**Zack Kassian**
66	**Brayden McNabb**
104	**Marcus Foligno**
134	Mark Adams
164	**Connor Knapp**
194	Maxime Legault

2008
Pick	
12	**Tyler Myers**
26	**Tyler Ennis**
44	**Luke Adam**
81	Corey Fienhage
101	Justin Jokinen
104	Jordon Southorn
134	Jacob Lagace
164	Nick Crawford

2007
Pick	
31	**T.J. Brennan**
59	Drew Schiestel
89	**Corey Tropp**
139	Brad Eidsness
147	Jean-Simon Allard
179	**Paul Byron**
187	Nick Eno
209	Drew Mackenzie

2006
Pick	
24	Dennis Persson
46	**Jhonas Enroth**
57	**Mike Weber**
117	Felix Schutz
147	**Alex Biega**
207	Benjamin Breault

2005
Pick	
13	Marek Zagrapan
48	Philip Gogulla
87	**Marc-Andre Gragnani**
96	**Chris Butler**
142	**Nathan Gerbe**
182	Adam Dennis
191	Vyacheslav Buravchikov
208	Matt Generous
227	Andrew Orpik

2004
Pick	
13	**Drew Stafford**
43	**Michael Funk**
71	**Andrej Sekera**
145	Michal Valent
176	**Patrick Kaleta**
207	**Mark Mancari**
241	**Mike Card**
273	Dylan Hunter

2003
Pick	
5	**Thomas Vanek**
65	Branislav Fabry
74	**Clarke MacArthur**
106	**Jan Hejda**
114	Denis Ezhov
150	Thomas Morrow
172	Pavel Voroshnin
202	**Nathan Paetsch**
235	Jeff Weber
266	Louis-Philippe Martin

General Managers' History

Punch Imlach, 1970-71 to 1977-78; Punch Imlach and John Anderson, 1978-79; Scotty Bowman, 1979-80 to 1985-86; Scotty Bowman and Gerry Meehan, 1986-87; Gerry Meehan, 1987-88 to 1992-93; John Muckler, 1993-94 to 1996-97; Darcy Regier, 1997-98 to 2012-13; Darcy Regier and Tim Murray, 2013-14; Tim Murray, 2014-15 to 2016-17; Jason Botterill, 2017-18.

Jason Botterill

General Manager

Born: Edmonton, AB, May 19, 1976.

Buffalo Sabres owner Terry Pegula announced on May 11, 2017, that the team had hired Jason Botterill as general manager. Botterill joined the Sabres after spending the previous 10 seasons as a member of the Pittsburgh Penguins organization, where he played an integral role in building the roster of three Stanley Cup champion teams (2008-09, 2015-16 and 2016-17).

Botterill joined the Penguins as their director of hockey administration in July 2007 after serving as a scout for the Dallas Stars in 2006-07. He was later promoted to assistant general manager in 2009 before serving as associate general manager from 2014 to 2017. As associate general manager in Pittsburgh, Botterill was involved in scouting, player development, contract negotiations and salary cap management. He also served as general manager of the American Hockey League's Wilkes-Barre/Scranton Penguins from 2009-10 to 2016-17, guiding the team to two division titles and eight consecutive playoff appearances.

A native of Edmonton, Alberta, Botterill developed a championship pedigree during his playing career. He won a gold medal as a member of the Canadian World Junior Championship team in 1994, 1995 and 1996, and was a part of the University of Michigan's NCAA Championship squad in 1996. Botterill later won a Calder Cup in 2001 as a member of the St. John Flames.

Selected by the Dallas Stars in the first round (20th overall) in the 1994 NHL Draft, Botterill played in the Sabres organization during his final three professional seasons, posting eight points (three goals, five assists) in 36 games for the Sabres and 100 points (59 goals, 41 assists) in 118 games for the Rochester Americans (AHL) from 2002 to 2005.

Club Directory

KeyBank Center

Buffalo Sabres
KeyBank Center
One Seymour H. Knox III Plaza
Buffalo, NY 14203
Phone **716/855-4100**
Fax 716/855-4110
Tickets, U.S.: 888/GO-SABRES
Canada: 888/669-GOAL
www.sabres.com
Capacity: 19,070

Executive	
Owners	Terrence M. Pegula, Kim Pegula
President	Russ Brandon
Chief Operating Officer, PSE	Bruce Popko
E.V.P. of Creative Services, PSE	Frank Cravotta
E.V.P. of Finance, PSE	Chuck LaMattina
E.V.P. of Business Development, PSE	Erica Muhleman
E.V.P. of Media & Content, PSE	Mark Preisler
E.V.P. of Marketing & Brand Strategy, PSE	Brent Rossi
E.V.P. & General Counsel, PSE	Gregg Brandon
Executive Assistant	Toni Addeo
Administration	
Senior V.P.	Michael Gilbert
Director of World Junior Championship	Rob Crean
Team Concierge/Executive Assistant	Nadine Leone
Hockey Department	
General Manager	Jason Botterill
Assistant General Managers	Randy Sexton, Steve Greeley
V.P., Hockey Administration	Mark Jakubowski
Director / Asst. Director Amateur Scouting	Ryan Jankowski / Jeff Crisp
Head, Collegiate Scouting	Jerry Forton
Director of Player Personnel	Kevin Devine
Pro Scouts	Jeremiah Crowe, Mark Mowers, John Van Boxmeer
Amateur Scouts	Jan Axel-Alavaara, Cory Banika, Kevin Devine, Scott Halpenny, Frank Musil, Teemu Numminen, Tom O'Connor, Ron Pyette, Rob Riley, Mike Rooney, Matt Tiesling
Scouting Coordinators, Pro/Amateur	Graham Beamish / Austin Dunne
Coordinator, Hockey Analytics	Jason Nightingale
Coordinators, Team Services / Hockey Administration	Cole Burkhalter, Brett Ruff
Head, Hockey IT	Kyle Kiebzak
Coaching Staff	
Head Coach	Phil Housley
Associate Coach	Davis Payne
Assistant Coaches	Chris Hajt, Tom Ward
Goaltending Coach / Video Coach	Andrew Allen / Mat Myers
Strength & Conditioning Coaches	Ed Gannon / J.T. Allaire
Dietitian & Sports Nutritionist	Ashley Charlebois
Head Athletic Trainer	Rich Stinziano
Assistant Athletic Trainer/Physical Therapist	Michael Adesso
Equipment Managers	Dave Williams, Rip Simonick
Assistant Equipment Manager / Equipment Assistant	George Babcock / Keith Hayes
Player Development	
Player Development Coaches	Adam Mair, Krys Barch, Mike Komisarek
Goaltending Development Coach	Seamus Kotyk
Medical	
Medical Director	Marc Fineberg, M.D.
Team Physician / Dentist	William Hartrich, M.D. / David Croglio
Legal, Finance and Human Resources	
E.V.P., Finance & Business Operations	Chuck LaMattina
V.P.s, Legal Affairs / Human Resources	Dave Zygaj / Christie Joseph
Paralegal	Kim Szymanoski
Human Resources Managers / Sr. Coordinator	Holly Weiskerger, Erin Fierle / Terri O'Brien
HRMS Analyst/Project Lead	Gina Reagan
Human Resources Coordinator / Assistant	Kayla Collins / Amanda Westfall
Corporate Controller / Accounting Managers	Kristin Zirnheld / Lynn Slanovich, Eric McGuire
Recruiter / Senior Payroll Manager	Annmarie Schneider / Martha Kaeding
Payroll Specialists	Dena Fowler, Birgid Haensel, Christy Hardwick
Accounts Payable Coordinator / Accounting Staff	Kim Binkley / John Kolkowski, Marilyn McCabe, Maggie Stewart, Gabrielle Wilson
Finance Business Administrator	Amy Terranova
Broadcast and Game Presentation	
E.V.P., Content and Media	Mark Preisler
V.P., Broadcasting	Chrisanne Bellas
TV Producer / TV Director	Joe Pinter / Eric Grossman
Production Manager / Assistant	Jason Wiese / Tom Meka
Game Presentation Director / Coordinator	Kelsey Schneider / Kelsey Landers
Videoboard Director	Jeff Hill
Broadcast Team	Rick Jeanneret (Play-by-Play), Rob Ray (Color), Dan Dunleavy (Play-by-Play/Reporter), Brian Duff (Studio Host), Marty Biron (Studio Analyst)
Merchandise	
Director, Merchandise	Mike Kaminska
Merchandise Mgrs., Inventory / Event Sales	Glenn Barker, Jeff Smith
Store Manager / Assistant Managers	Theresa Cerabone / Dashawn Richardson, Jonathon Calarco
Marketing	
E.V.P., Marketing & Brand Strategy	Brent Rossi
Database Marketing Manager	Tom Matheny
Marketing Manager	Cara Foligno
Content Marketing Manager / Coordinator	Chris Ryndak / Jourdon LaBarber
Media and Community Relations	
V.P., Media Relations	Chris Bandura
Manager / Coordinator, Media Relations	Ian Ott / Chris Dierken
V.P., Community Relations	Rich Jureller
Community Relations Manager / Coordinator	Teresa Belbas / Nick Fearby
Youth Hockey Manager / Ambassador	Ed Grudzinski / Patrick Kaleta
Team Photographer / Director, Alumni Relations	Bill Wippert / Larry Playfair
Ticket Sales and Operations	
V.P., Tickets & Service	John Sinclair
Director, Ticket Ops	Marty Maloney
Box Office Manager / Coordinator	Paul Barker / Gretchen Knott
Ticket Administrator	Melissa Rugg
Ticket Sales Representatives	Casey Jenkins, Greg Metzen
Account Services Reps.	Roxanne Anderson, Melissa Eagen, Chris Miller, Dan Ristine, Nate Shively
Receptionist	Saralynn Ruhland
Information Technology	
Director of Information Technology	Todd Henzler
Support Specialists, Advanced / IT	Nate Brozyna, Michael Walker
KeyBank Center Staff	
V.P., Arena Operation	Stan Makowski, Jr.
Director, Arena Operations	Beth Giuliani Gatto
Event Managers	Laura Hettrick, Dave Kutter, Robert Neumann
Directors, Security / Building Services	Marc Brenner / Dennis Hooper
Managers, Technical Communications	Mike Queeno, Trevor Ecklund
Chief Engineer	Bruce Johnson

Calgary Flames

2016-17 Results: 45w-33L-2oTL-2soL 94pts
4TH, Pacific Division • 7TH, Western Conference

Key Off-Season Signings/Acquisitions

2017

June 17 • Acquired G **Mike Smith** from Arizona for G **Chad Johnson**, D **Brandon Hickey** and a conditional 3rd-round pick in 2018 NHL Draft.

24 • Acquired D **Travis Hamonic** and a 4th-round pick in 2019 or 2020 NHL Draft from NY Islanders for Calgary's 1st- and 2nd-round picks in 2018 NHL Draft and a 2nd-round pick in 2019 or 2020 NHL Draft.

29 • Acquired G **Eddie Lack**, D **Ryan Murphy** and a 7th-round pick in 2019 NHL Draft from Carolina for D **Keegan Kanzig** and a 6th-round pick in 2019 NHL Draft.

30 • Re-signed D **Michael Stone**.

July 1 • Signed LW **Marek Hrivik**.

2 • Signed LW **Luke Gazdic**.

13 • Re-signed LW **Micheal Ferland**.

14 • Re-signed C **Curtis Lazar**.

20 • Re-signed RW **Garnet Hathaway**.

2017-18 Schedule

Oct.	Wed.	4	at Edmonton
	Sat.	7	Winnipeg
	Mon.	9	at Anaheim
	Wed.	11	at Los Angeles
	Fri.	13	Ottawa
	Sat.	14	at Vancouver
	Thu.	19	Carolina
	Sat.	21	Minnesota
	Tue.	24	at Nashville
	Wed.	25	at St. Louis*
	Fri.	27	Dallas
	Sun.	29	Washington
Nov.	Thu.	2	Pittsburgh
	Sun.	5	New Jersey
	Tue.	7	Vancouver
	Thu.	9	Detroit
	Mon.	13	St. Louis
	Wed.	15	at Detroit
	Sat.	18	at Philadelphia*
	Mon.	20	at Washington
	Wed.	22	at Columbus
	Fri.	24	at Dallas
	Sat.	25	at Colorado
	Tue.	28	Toronto
	Thu.	30	Arizona
Dec.	Sat.	2	Edmonton
	Mon.	4	Philadelphia
	Wed.	6	at Toronto
	Thu.	7	at Montreal
	Sat.	9	Vancouver
	Tue.	12	at Minnesota
	Thu.	14	San Jose
	Sat.	16	Nashville
	Sun.	17	at Vancouver*
	Wed.	20	St. Louis
	Fri.	22	Montreal
	Thu.	28	at San Jose
	Fri.	29	at Anaheim
	Sun.	31	Chicago
Jan.	Thu.	4	Los Angeles
	Sat.	6	Anaheim

	Tue.	9	at Minnesota
	Thu.	11	at Tampa Bay
	Fri.	12	at Florida
	Sun.	14	at Carolina*
	Sat.	20	Winnipeg*
	Mon.	22	Buffalo
	Wed.	24	Los Angeles
	Thu.	25	at Edmonton
	Tue.	30	Vegas
Feb.	Thu.	1	Tampa Bay
	Sat.	3	Chicago
	Tue.	6	at Chicago
	Thu.	8	at New Jersey
	Fri.	9	at NY Rangers
	Sun.	11	at NY Islanders
	Tue.	13	at Boston
	Thu.	15	at Nashville
	Sat.	17	Florida
	Mon.	19	Boston*
	Wed.	21	at Vegas
	Thu.	22	at Arizona
	Sat.	24	Colorado*
	Tue.	27	at Dallas
	Wed.	28	at Colorado
Mar.	Fri.	2	NY Rangers
	Mon.	5	at Pittsburgh
	Wed.	7	at Buffalo
	Fri.	9	at Ottawa
	Sun.	11	NY Islanders*
	Tue.	13	Edmonton
	Fri.	16	San Jose
	Sun.	18	at Vegas*
	Mon.	19	at Arizona
	Wed.	21	Anaheim
	Sat.	24	at San Jose*
	Mon.	26	at Los Angeles
	Thu.	29	Columbus
	Sat.	31	Edmonton
Apr.	Tue.	3	Arizona
	Thu.	5	at Winnipeg
	Sat.	7	Vegas

* Denotes afternoon game.

Retired Numbers

9	Lanny McDonald	1981-1989
30	Mike Vernon	1982-1994; 2000-2002

Honored Numbers

2	Al MacInnis	1981-1994
25	Joe Nieuwendyk	1986-1995

PACIFIC DIVISION
46th NHL Season

Franchise date: June 6, 1972

Transferred from Atlanta to Calgary, June 24, 1980.

Sean Monahan and Johnny Gaudreau celebrate a goal during a 2-1 victory in Dallas on December 6, 2016. Monahan led the Flames with 27 goals in 2016-17, while Gaudreau topped the team with 43 assists and 61 points.

Year-by-Year Record

Season	GP	Home W	L	T	OL	Road W	L	T	OL	Overall W	L	T	OL	GF	GA	Pts.	Div. Fin.	Conf. Fin.	Playoff Result
2016-17	82	24	17	....	0	21	16	....	4	45	33	....	4	226	221	94	4th, Pac.	7th, West	Lost First Round
2015-16	82	21	16	....	4	14	24	....	3	35	40	....	7	231	260	77	5th, Pac.	12th, West	– out of playoffs –
2014-15	82	23	13	....	5	22	17	....	2	45	30	....	7	241	216	97	3rd, Pac.	8th, West	Lost Second Round
2013-14	82	19	19	....	3	16	21	....	4	35	40	....	7	209	241	77	6th, Pac.	13th, West	– out of playoffs –
2012-13	48	13	9	....	2	6	16	....	2	19	25	....	4	128	160	42	4th, NW	13th, West	– out of playoffs –
2011-12	82	23	12	....	6	14	17	....	10	37	29	....	16	202	226	90	2nd, NW	9th, West	– out of playoffs –
2010-11	82	23	13	....	5	18	16	....	7	41	29	....	12	250	237	94	2nd, NW	10th, West	– out of playoffs –
2009-10	82	20	17	....	4	20	15	....	6	40	32	....	10	204	210	90	3rd, NW	10th, West	– out of playoffs –
2008-09	82	27	10	....	4	19	20	....	2	46	30	....	6	254	248	98	2nd, NW	5th, West	Lost Conf. Quarter-Final
2007-08	82	21	11	....	9	21	19	....	1	42	30	....	10	229	227	94	3rd, NW	7th, West	Lost Conf. Quarter-Final
2006-07	82	30	9	....	2	13	20	....	8	43	29	....	10	258	226	96	3rd, NW	8th, West	Lost Conf. Quarter-Final
2005-06	82	30	7	....	4	16	18	....	7	46	25	....	11	218	200	103	1st, NW	3rd, West	Lost Conf. Quarter-Final
2004-05	....																		
2003-04	82	21	14	5	1	21	16	2	2	42	30	7	3	200	176	94	3rd, NW	6th, West	Lost Final
2002-03	82	14	16	10	1	15	20	3	3	29	36	13	4	186	228	75	5th, NW	12th, West	– out of playoffs –
2001-02	82	20	14	5	2	12	21	7	1	32	35	12	3	201	220	79	4th, NW	11th, West	– out of playoffs –
2000-01	82	12	18	9	2	15	18	6	2	27	36	15	4	197	236	73	4th, NW	11th, West	– out of playoffs –
1999-2000	82	20	14	6	1	11	22	4	4	31	36	10	5	211	256	77	4th, NW	10th, West	– out of playoffs –
1998-99	82	15	20	6	....	15	20	6	....	30	40	12	....	211	234	72	3rd, NW	9th, West	– out of playoffs –
1997-98	82	18	17	6	....	8	24	9	....	26	41	15	....	217	252	67	5th, Pac.	11th, West	– out of playoffs –
1996-97	82	21	18	2	....	11	23	7	....	32	41	9	....	214	239	73	5th, Pac.	10th, West	– out of playoffs –
1995-96	82	18	18	5	....	16	19	6	....	34	37	11	....	241	240	79	2nd, Pac.	6th, West	Lost Conf. Quarter-Final
1994-95	48	15	7	2	....	9	10	5	....	24	17	7	....	163	135	55	1st, Pac.	3rd, West	Lost Conf. Quarter-Final
1993-94	84	25	12	5	....	17	17	8	....	42	29	13	....	302	256	97	1st, Pac.	3rd, West	Lost Conf. Quarter-Final
1992-93	84	23	14	5	....	20	16	6	....	43	30	11	....	322	282	97	2nd, Smythe		Lost Div. Semi-Final
1991-92	80	19	14	7	....	12	23	5	....	31	37	12	....	296	305	74	5th, Smythe		– out of playoffs –
1990-91	80	29	8	3	....	17	18	5	....	46	26	8	....	344	263	100	2nd, Smythe		Lost Div. Semi-Final
1989-90	80	28	7	5	....	14	16	10	....	42	23	15	....	348	265	99	1st, Smythe		Lost Div. Semi-Final
1988-89	80	32	4	4	....	22	13	5	....	54	17	9	....	354	226	117	**1st, Smythe**		**Won Stanley Cup**
1987-88	80	26	11	3	....	22	12	6	....	48	23	9	....	397	305	105	1st, Smythe		Lost Div. Final
1986-87	80	25	13	2	....	21	18	1	....	46	31	3	....	318	289	95	2nd, Smythe		Lost Div. Semi-Final
1985-86	80	23	11	6	....	17	20	3	....	40	31	9	....	354	315	89	2nd, Smythe		Lost Final
1984-85	80	23	11	6	....	18	16	6	....	41	27	12	....	363	302	94	3rd, Smythe		Lost Div. Semi-Final
1983-84	80	22	11	7	....	12	21	7	....	34	32	14	....	311	314	82	2nd, Smythe		Lost Div. Final
1982-83	80	21	12	7	....	11	22	7	....	32	34	14	....	321	317	78	2nd, Smythe		Lost Div. Semi-Final
1981-82	80	20	11	9	....	9	23	8	....	29	34	17	....	334	345	75	3rd, Smythe		Lost Div. Semi-Final
1980-81	80	25	5	10	....	14	22	4	....	39	27	14	....	329	298	92	3rd, Patrick		Lost Semi-Final
1979-80*	80	18	15	7	....	17	17	6	....	35	32	13	....	282	269	83	4th, Patrick		Lost Prelim. Round
1978-79*	80	25	11	4	....	16	20	4	....	41	31	8	....	327	280	90	4th, Patrick		Lost Prelim. Round
1977-78*	80	20	13	7	....	14	14	12	....	34	27	19	....	274	252	87	3rd, Patrick		Lost Prelim. Round
1976-77*	80	22	11	7	....	12	23	5	....	34	34	12	....	264	265	80	3rd, Patrick		Lost Prelim. Round
1975-76*	80	19	14	7	....	16	19	5	....	35	33	12	....	262	237	82	3rd, Patrick		Lost Prelim. Round
1974-75*	80	24	9	7	....	10	22	8	....	34	31	15	....	243	233	83	4th, Patrick		– out of playoffs –
1973-74*	78	17	15	7	....	13	19	7	....	30	34	14	....	214	238	74	4th, West		Lost Quarter-Final
1972-73*	78	16	16	7	....	9	22	8	....	25	38	15	....	191	239	65	7th, West		– out of playoffs –

* Atlanta Flames

2017-18 Player Personnel

FORWARDS	HT	WT	*Age	Birthplace	S	2016-17 Club
BACKLUND, Mikael	6-1	199	28	Vasteras, Sweden	L	Calgary
BENNETT, Sam	6-1	186	21	Holland Landing, ON	L	Calgary
BROUWER, Troy	6-3	215	32	Vancouver, BC	R	Calgary
FERLAND, Micheal	6-2	210	25	Swan River, MB	L	Calgary
FROLIK, Michael	6-1	194	29	Kladno, Czech.	L	Calgary
GAUDREAU, Johnny	5-9	157	24	Salem, NJ	L	Calgary
GAZDIC, Luke	6-4	225	28	Toronto, ON	L	New Jersey-Albany
HAMILTON, Freddie	6-1	195	25	Toronto, ON	R	Calgary
HATHAWAY, Garnet	6-2	207	25	Kennebunkport, ME	R	Calgary-Stockton
LAZAR, Curtis	6-0	209	22	Salmon Arm, BC	R	Ott-Binghamton-Cgy
MONAHAN, Sean	6-3	195	22	Brampton, ON	L	Calgary
STAJAN, Matt	6-1	195	33	Mississauga, ON	L	Calgary
TKACHUK, Matthew	6-2	202	19	Scottsdale, AZ	L	Calgary
VERSTEEG, Kris	5-11	176	31	Lethbridge, AB	R	Calgary
DEFENSEMEN						
BARTKOWSKI, Matt	6-1	196	29	Pittsburgh, PA	L	Calgary-Providence (AHL)
BRODIE, T.J.	6-1	182	27	Chatham, ON	L	Calgary
GIORDANO, Mark	6-0	198	34	Toronto, ON	L	Calgary
HAMILTON, Dougie	6-6	210	24	Toronto, ON	R	Calgary
HAMONIC, Travis	6-2	205	27	St. Malo, MB	R	NY Islanders
STONE, Michael	6-3	215	27	Winnipeg, MB	R	Arizona-Calgary

GOALTENDERS	HT	WT	*Age	Birthplace	C	2016-17 Club
LACK, Eddie	6-4	200	29	Norrtalje, Sweden	L	Carolina-Charlotte
SMITH, Mike	6-4	215	35	Kingston, ON	L	Arizona

* – Age at start of 2017-18 season

Glen Gulutzan

Head Coach

Born: The Pas, MB, August 12, 1971.

The Calgary Flames announced on June 17, 2016 that they had named Glen Gulutzan as head coach. He brought 15 years of coaching experience to the club. Gulutzan had spent the previous three seasons as an assistant coach with the Vancouver Canucks. He led the Flames back to the playoffs in his first season behind the bench in 2016-17 after Calgary missed the postseason the previous year.

Born in The Pas, Manitoba, but raised in Hudson Bay, Saskatchewan, Gulutzan was the head coach of the Dallas Stars for the 2011-12 and 2012-13 seasons. Before that, he led the American Hockey League's Texas Stars for a pair of campaigns. In 2009-10, he took the Stars to the Calder Cup finals.

Gulutzan played junior hockey in the Western Hockey League with Moose Jaw, Brandon and Saskatoon, then two years with the University of Saskatchewan, before playing professionally for seven seasons. His coaching career began in the final four seasons of his playing career when he served as a player-assistant coach for the Fresno Falcons of the West Coast Hockey League, including in 2001-02 when they won the league's championship.

Gulutzan took over the reigns as head coach for the East Coast Hockey League's Las Vegas Wranglers in 2003-04. He has a familiarity with the Flames organization as all six years he spent with the Wranglers they were Calgary's ECHL affiliate. Gulutzan had a record of 254-124-55 over his half-dozen seasons in Las Vegas, including three straight where the Wranglers had 100+ points (2005-06 to 2007-08) – a first for any ECHL team. He also won the ECHL's coach of the year honors in 2005-06.

In 2009, the Stars organization bought Iowa's defunct American Hockey League franchise and moved it to Austin where it became the Texas Stars. Glen Gulutzan was named the first head coach of the club and held that role for two seasons, including 2009-10's Calder Cup final campaign. He then assumed the head coaching position with the NHL's Stars for the 2011-12 and 2012-13 seasons. After Gulutzan and the team parted ways in 2013, he was quickly brought on board in Vancouver.

Coaching Record

			Regular Season				Playoffs			
Season	Team	League	GC	W	L	O/T	GC	W	L	T
2003-04	Las Vegas	ECHL	72	43	22	7	5	2	3	....
2004-05	Las Vegas	ECHL	72	31	33	8	....	....	....	....
2005-06	Las Vegas	ECHL	72	53	13	6	13	6	7	....
2006-07	Las Vegas	ECHL	72	46	12	14	10	6	4	....
2007-08	Las Vegas	ECHL	72	47	13	12	21	14	7	....
2008-09	Las Vegas	ECHL	73	34	31	8	18	8	10	....
2009-10	Texas	AHL	80	46	27	7	24	14	10	....
2010-11	Texas	AHL	80	41	29	10	6	2	4	....
2011-12	**Dallas**	**NHL**	**82**	**42**	**35**	**5**	....	....	....	....
2012-13	**Dallas**	**NHL**	**48**	**22**	**22**	**4**	....	....	....	....
2016-17	**Calgary**	**NHL**	**82**	**45**	**33**	**4**	**4**	**0**	**4**	....
	NHL Totals		**212**	**109**	**90**	**13**	**4**	**0**	**4**	....

2016-17 Scoring

* – rookie

Regular Season

Pos	#	Player	Team	GP	G	A	Pts	TOI	+/–	PIM	PP	SH	GW	S	S%
L	13	Johnny Gaudreau	CGY	72	18	43	61	18:29	–7	4	4	0	3	182	9.9
C	23	Sean Monahan	CGY	82	27	31	58	17:34	–1	20	8	1	4	199	13.6
C	11	Mikael Backlund	CGY	81	22	31	53	17:36	9	36	7	0	7	197	11.2
D	27	Dougie Hamilton	CGY	81	13	37	50	19:41	12	64	2	0	5	222	5.9
L	19	* Matthew Tkachuk	CGY	76	13	35	48	14:39	14	105	3	0	2	142	9.2
R	67	Michael Frolik	CGY	82	17	27	44	17:04	13	58	3	2	1	202	8.4
D	5	Mark Giordano	CGY	81	12	27	39	23:34	22	59	3	2	4	151	7.9
R	10	Kris Versteeg	CGY	69	15	22	37	14:43	–3	46	8	0	1	136	11.0
D	7	T.J. Brodie	CGY	82	6	30	36	23:34	–16	24	1	1	2	78	7.7
C	93	Sam Bennett	CGY	81	13	13	26	14:59	–16	75	4	0	0	122	10.7
L	79	Micheal Ferland	CGY	76	15	10	25	11:33	–1	50	2	0	1	106	14.2
R	36	Troy Brouwer	CGY	74	13	12	25	16:13	–11	31	5	1	2	86	15.1
R	39	Alex Chiasson	CGY	81	12	12	24	13:23	–6	46	0	1	1	104	11.5
C	18	Matt Stajan	CGY	81	6	17	23	12:40	3	40	0	0	3	59	10.2
D	6	Dennis Wideman	CGY	57	5	13	18	20:13	–6	32	2	0	1	87	5.7
D	29	Deryk Engelland	CGY	81	4	12	16	18:19	2	85	0	0	2	107	3.7
D	26	Michael Stone	ARI	45	1	8	9	20:13	–5	12	1	0	0	57	1.8
			CGY	19	2	4	6	18:51	5	20	0	0	0	24	8.3
			Total	64	3	12	15	19:49	0	32	1	0	0	81	3.7
L	17	Lance Bouma	CGY	61	3	4	7	11:20	–2	35	0	0	1	53	5.7
R	64	* Garnet Hathaway	CGY	26	1	4	5	9:08	0	44	0	0	0	22	4.5
C	20	Curtis Lazar	OTT	33	0	1	1	8:48	–10	4	0	0	0	24	0.0
			CGY	4	1	2	3	11:46	2	0	0	0	0	2	50.0
			Total	37	1	3	4	9:08	–8	4	0	0	0	26	3.8
D	61	* Brett Kulak	CGY	21	0	3	3	14:14	–3	12	0	0	0	19	0.0
C	25	Freddie Hamilton	CGY	26	2	0	2	9:46	–3	8	0	0	1	30	6.7
D	44	Matt Bartkowski	CGY	24	1	1	2	15:23	–4	26	0	0	0	16	6.3
C	49	* Hunter Shinkaruk	CGY	7	0	1	1	10:35	–3	2	0	0	0	5	0.0
C	77	* Mark Jankowski	CGY	1	0	0	0	10:18	0	0	0	0	0	0	0.0
D	54	* Rasmus Andersson	CGY	1	0	0	0	18:33	–1	0	0	0	0	0	0.0
D	8	Nicklas Grossmann	CGY	3	0	0	0	13:00	–4	2	0	0	0	3	0.0
R	16	Linden Vey	CGY	4	0	0	0	11:01	–2	0	0	0	0	1	0.0
D	26	Tyler Wotherspoon	CGY	4	0	0	0	10:54	–2	0	0	0	0	4	0.0

Goaltending

No.	Goaltender	GPI	Mins	Avg	W	L	OT	EN	SO	GA	SA	Sv%	G	A	PIM
32	* Jon Gillies	1	60	1.00	1	0	0	0	0	1	28	.964	0	0	0
1	Brian Elliott	49	2844	2.55	26	18	3	7	2	121	1338	.910	0	0	4
31	Chad Johnson	36	2013	2.59	18	15	1	2	3	87	969	.910	0	0	0
33	* David Rittich	1	20	3.00	0	0	0	0	0	1	10	.900	0	0	0
	Totals	**82**	**4974**	**2.64**	**45**	**33**	**4**	**9**	**5**	**219**	**2354**	**.907**			

Playoffs

Pos	#	Player	Team	GP	G	A	Pts	TOI	+/–	PIM	PP	SH	GW	OT	S	S%
C	23	Sean Monahan	CGY	4	4	1	5	18:30	–4	0	4	0	0	0	9	44.4
R	10	Kris Versteeg	CGY	4	1	3	4	15:19	–2	4	1	0	0	0	12	8.3
D	7	T.J. Brodie	CGY	4	0	4	4	22:19	–1	2	0	0	0	0	10	0.0
C	11	Mikael Backlund	CGY	4	1	2	3	19:48	–3	0	0	1	0	0	14	7.1
C	93	Sam Bennett	CGY	4	2	0	2	13:39	–1	4	1	0	0	0	10	20.0
R	36	Troy Brouwer	CGY	4	0	2	2	14:03	–1	0	0	0	0	0	11	0.0
L	13	Johnny Gaudreau	CGY	4	0	2	2	19:51	–4	0	0	0	0	0	8	0.0
D	26	Michael Stone	CGY	4	1	0	1	18:46	–1	0	0	0	0	0	5	20.0
D	5	Mark Giordano	CGY	4	0	1	1	25:30	–2	2	0	0	0	0	6	0.0
R	67	Michael Frolik	CGY	4	0	1	1	18:48	–2	0	0	0	0	0	7	0.0
D	27	Dougie Hamilton	CGY	4	0	1	1	22:16	–3	8	0	0	0	0	10	0.0
C	25	Freddie Hamilton	CGY	1	0	0	0	6:40	0	0	0	0	0	0	1	0.0
C	20	Curtis Lazar	CGY	1	0	0	0	7:16	0	0	0	0	0	0	0	0.0
C	18	Matt Stajan	CGY	3	0	0	0	10:15	–1	0	0	0	0	0	1	0.0
L	17	Lance Bouma	CGY	3	0	0	0	9:59	–1	2	0	0	0	0	3	0.0
D	29	Deryk Engelland	CGY	4	0	0	0	15:16	–3	2	0	0	0	0	2	0.0
D	44	Matt Bartkowski	CGY	4	0	0	0	12:44	–5	0	0	0	0	0	6	0.0
R	39	Alex Chiasson	CGY	4	0	0	0	12:48	–1	2	0	0	0	0	2	0.0
L	79	Micheal Ferland	CGY	4	0	0	0	12:28	–4	7	0	0	0	0	15	0.0
L	19	* Matthew Tkachuk	CGY	4	0	0	0	15:31	–2	4	0	0	0	0	6	0.0

Goaltending

No.	Goaltender	GPI	Mins	Avg	W	L	EN	SO	GA	SA	Sv%	G	A	PIM
31	Chad Johnson	1	52	1.15	0	1	1	0	1	21	.952	0	0	0
1	Brian Elliott	4	185	3.89	0	3	0	0	12	100	.880	0	0	0
	Totals	**4**	**242**	**3.47**	**0**	**4**	**1**	**0**	**14**	**122**	**.885**			

Captains' History

Keith McCreary, 1972-73 to 1974-75; Pat Quinn, 1975-76, 1976-77; Tom Lysiak, 1977-78, 1978-79; Jean Pronovost, 1979-80; Brad Marsh, 1980-81; Phil Russell, 1981-82, 1982-83; Lanny McDonald, Doug Risebrough, 1983-84; Lanny McDonald, Doug Risebrough, Jim Peplinski, 1984-85 to 1986-87; Lanny McDonald, Jim Peplinski, 1987-88; Lanny McDonald, Jim Peplinski, Tim Hunter, 1988-89; Brad McCrimmon, 1989-90; alternating captains, 1990-91; Joe Nieuwendyk, 1991-92 to 1994-95; Theoren Fleury, 1995-96, 1996-97; Todd Simpson, 1997-98, 1998-99; Steve Smith, 1999-2000; Steve Smith and Dave Lowry, 2000-01; Dave Lowry; Bob Boughner and Craig Conroy, 2001-02; Bob Boughner and Craig Conroy, 2002-03; Jarome Iginla, 2003-04 to 2012-13; Mark Giordano, 2013-14 to date.

Club Records

Team

(Figures in brackets for season records are games played; records for fewest points, wins, ties, losses, goals, goals against are for 70 or more games)

Most Points 117 1988-89 (80)
Most Wins 54 1988-89 (80)
Most Ties 19 1977-78 (80)
Most Losses 41 1996-97 (82), 1997-98 (82), 1999-2000 (82)
Most Goals 397 1987-88 (80)
Most Goals Against 345 1981-82 (80)
Fewest Points 65 1972-73 (78)
Fewest Wins 25 1972-73 (78)
Fewest Ties 3 1986-87 (80)
Fewest Losses 17 1988-89 (80)
Fewest Goals 186 2002-03 (82)
Fewest Goals Against 176 2003-04 (82)
Longest Winning Streak
Overall .... 10 Oct. 14-Nov. 3/78
Home .... 11 Nov. 5-Dec. 27/15
Away .... 7 Nov. 10-Dec. 4/88
Longest Team Point Streak
Overall .... 13 Nov. 10-Dec. 8/88 (12W, 1T)
Home .... 18 Dec. 29/90-Mar. 14/91 (17W, 1T)
Away .... 9 Feb. 20-Mar. 21/88 (6W, 3T), Nov. 11-Dec. 16/90 (6W, 3T)
Longest Losing Streak
Overall .... 11 Dec. 14/85-Jan. 7/86
Home .... 9 Dec. 27/13-Jan. 16/14
Away .... 13 Feb. 18-Apr. 6/13
Longest Winless Streak
Overall .... 11 Dec. 14/85-Jan. 7/86 (11L), Jan. 5-26/93 (9L, 2T)
Home .... 10 Oct. 21-Dec. 4/00 (4L, 2OTL, 4T)
Away .... 15 Nov. 11/79-Jan. 9/80 (11L, 4T), Jan. 7-Mar. 2/03 (11L, 2OTL, 2T)
Most Shutouts, Season 11 2003-04 (82)
Most PIM, Season 2,643 1991-92 (80)
Most Goals, Game .... 13 Feb. 10/93 (S.J. 1 at Cgy. 13)

Individual

Most Seasons .... 16 Jarome Iginla
Most Games .... 1,219 Jarome Iginla
Most Goals, Career .... 525 Jarome Iginla
Most Assists, Career .... 609 Al MacInnis
Most Points, Career .... 1,095 Jarome Iginla (525G, 570A)
Most PIM, Career .... 2,405 Tim Hunter
Most Shutouts, Career .... 41 Miikka Kiprusoff
Longest Consecutive Games Streak .... 441 Jarome Iginla (Oct. 4/07-Mar. 26/13)
Most Goals, Season .... 66 Lanny McDonald (1982-83)
Most Assists, Season .... 82 Kent Nilsson (1980-81)
Most Points, Season .... 131 Kent Nilsson (1980-81; 49G, 82A)
Most PIM, Season .... 375 Tim Hunter (1988-89)
Most Points, Defenseman, Season .... 103 Al MacInnis (1990-91; 28G, 75A)
Most Points, Center, Season .... 131 Kent Nilsson (1980-81; 49G, 82A)
Most Points, Right Wing, Season .... 110 Joe Mullen (1988-89; 51G, 59A)
Most Points, Left Wing, Season .... 90 Gary Roberts (1991-92; 53G, 37A)
Most Points, Rookie, Season .... 92 Joe Nieuwendyk (1987-88; 51G, 41A)
Most Shutouts, Season .... 10 Miikka Kiprusoff (2005-06)
Most Goals, Game .... 5 Joe Nieuwendyk (Jan. 11/89)
Most Assists, Game .... 6 Guy Chouinard (Feb. 25/81), Gary Suter (Apr. 4/86)
Most Points, Game .... 7 Sergei Makarov (Feb. 25/90; 2G, 5A)

Records include Atlanta Flames, 1972-73 through 1979-80.

All-time Record vs. Other Clubs

Regular Season

	Total								At Home								On Road							
	GP	W	L	T	OL	GF	GA	PTS	GP	W	L	T	OL	GF	GA	PTS	GP	W	L	T	OL	GF	GA	PTS
Anaheim	101	38	48	7	8	277	307	91	51	30	19	1	1	158	129	62	50	8	29	6	7	119	178	29
Arizona	192	92	73	20	7	678	622	211	97	55	31	9	2	372	292	121	95	37	42	11	5	306	330	90
Boston	105	37	58	10	0	318	363	84	51	22	25	4	0	179	173	48	54	15	33	6	0	139	190	36
Buffalo	105	38	48	16	3	326	370	95	53	24	18	11	0	181	159	59	52	14	30	5	3	145	211	36
Carolina	71	43	20	7	1	288	221	94	36	27	7	2	0	167	105	56	35	16	13	5	1	121	116	38
Chicago	167	66	70	26	5	482	521	163	84	37	31	13	3	255	250	90	83	29	39	13	2	227	271	73
Colorado	158	73	57	20	8	523	493	174	79	40	25	9	5	271	229	94	79	33	32	11	3	252	264	80
Columbus	55	25	23	0	7	138	147	57	27	14	7	0	6	76	67	34	28	11	16	0	1	62	80	23
Dallas	167	75	60	25	7	519	505	182	83	43	22	14	4	268	216	104	84	32	38	11	3	251	289	78
Detroit	158	70	67	16	5	513	508	161	80	44	28	6	2	277	228	96	78	26	39	10	3	236	280	65
Edmonton	233	117	92	19	5	814	761	258	116	66	40	9	1	440	369	142	117	51	52	10	4	374	392	116
Florida	31	17	9	3	2	91	78	39	15	8	5	1	1	48	41	18	16	9	4	2	1	43	37	21
Los Angeles	235	119	90	21	5	856	772	264	119	70	35	12	2	483	371	154	116	49	55	9	3	373	401	110
Minnesota	86	46	26	4	10	198	200	106	43	26	9	3	5	106	91	60	43	20	17	1	5	92	109	46
Montreal	113	39	57	15	2	316	373	95	58	23	27	7	1	179	185	54	55	16	30	8	1	137	188	41
Nashville	68	32	30	4	2	189	192	70	33	17	11	3	2	98	83	39	35	15	19	1	0	91	109	31
New Jersey	101	64	24	11	2	386	270	141	49	33	7	8	1	207	128	75	52	31	17	3	1	179	142	66
NY Islanders	114	45	46	20	3	348	376	113	56	27	16	11	2	194	166	67	58	18	30	9	1	154	210	46
NY Rangers	115	55	40	15	5	434	368	130	56	31	13	10	2	237	171	74	59	24	27	5	3	197	197	56
Ottawa	39	19	13	4	3	124	102	45	20	13	6	1	0	71	45	27	19	6	7	3	3	53	57	18
Philadelphia	117	46	57	12	2	379	407	106	59	28	21	9	1	224	190	66	58	18	36	3	1	155	217	40
Pittsburgh	104	42	43	18	1	368	348	103	53	29	15	8	1	220	162	67	51	13	28	10	0	148	186	36
St. Louis	169	77	74	14	4	519	522	172	84	42	34	5	3	263	237	92	85	35	40	9	1	256	285	80
San Jose	117	61	43	8	5	357	334	135	58	33	18	4	3	191	148	73	59	28	25	4	2	166	186	62
Tampa Bay	34	15	14	1	4	107	103	35	17	8	7	0	2	51	48	18	17	7	7	1	2	56	55	17
Toronto	132	62	57	12	1	485	449	137	70	42	23	5	0	272	212	89	62	20	34	7	1	213	237	48
Vancouver	269	131	90	33	15	903	846	310	133	74	39	15	5	490	388	168	136	57	51	18	10	413	458	142
Washington	93	43	36	13	1	332	295	100	45	26	12	7	0	172	119	59	48	17	24	6	1	160	176	41
Winnipeg	25	14	10	1	0	79	63	29	12	10	2	0	0	50	27	20	13	4	8	1	0	29	36	9
Defunct Clubs	26	15	7	4	0	94	67	34	13	8	4	1	0	51	34	17	13	7	3	3	0	43	33	17
Totals	**3500**	**1616**	**1382**	**379**	**123**	**11441**	**10983**	**3734**	**1750**	**950**	**557**	**188**	**55**	**6251**	**5063**	**2143**	**1750**	**666**	**825**	**191**	**68**	**5190**	**5920**	**1591**

Playoffs

	Series	W	L	GP	W	L	T	GF	GA	Last Mtg.	Rnd.	Result
Anaheim	3	0	3	16	4	12	0	34	50	2017	FR	L 0-4
Arizona	3	1	2	13	6	7	0	43	45	1987	DSF	L 2-4
Chicago	4	2	2	18	9	9	0	53	54	2009	CQF	L 2-4
Dallas	1	0	1	6	2	4	0	18	25	1981	SF	L 2-4
Detroit	3	1	2	14	6	8	0	26	38	2007	CQF	L 2-4
Edmonton	5	1	4	30	11	19	0	96	132	1991	DSF	L 3-4
Los Angeles	6	2	4	26	13	13	0	112	105	1993	DSF	L 2-4
Montreal	2	1	1	11	5	6	0	32	31	1989	F	W 4-2
NY Rangers	1	0	1	4	1	3	0	8	14	1980	PR	L 1-3
Philadelphia	2	1	1	11	4	7	0	28	43	1981	QF	W 4-3
St. Louis	1	1	0	7	4	3	0	28	22	1986	CF	W 4-3
San Jose	3	1	2	20	10	10	0	68	57	2008	CQF	L 3-4
Tampa Bay	1	0	1	7	3	4	0	14	13	2004	F	L 3-4
Toronto	1	0	1	2	0	2	0	5	9	1979	PR	L 0-2
Vancouver	7	5	2	38	21	17	0	119	110	2015	FR	W 4-2
Totals	**43**	**16**	**27**	**223**	**99**	**124**	**0**	**684**	**748**			

Playoff Results 2017-2013

Year	Round	Opponent	Result	GF	GA
2017	FR	Anaheim	L 0-4	9	14
2015	SR	Anaheim	L 1-4	9	19
	FR	Vancouver	W 4-2	18	14

Abbreviations: Round: F – Final; **CF** – conference final; **SR** – second round; **CQF** – conference quarter-final; **FR** – first round; **DSF** – division semi-final; **SF** – semi-final; **QF** – quarter-final; **PR** – preliminary round.

Carolina totals include Hartford, 1979-80 to 1996-97.
Colorado totals include Quebec, 1979-80 to 1994-95.
Dallas totals include Minnesota North Stars, 1972-73 to 1992-93.
New Jersey totals include Kansas City, 1974-75, 1975-76, and Colorado Rockies, 1976-77 to 1981-82.
Phoenix totals include Winnipeg, 1979-80 to 1995-96.
Winnipeg totals include Atlanta Thrashers, 1999-2000 to 2010-11.

2016-17 Results

Oct.	12	at Edmonton	4-7
	14	Edmonton	3-5
	15	at Vancouver	1-2†
	18	Buffalo	4-3*
	20	Carolina	2-4
	22	St. Louis	4-6
	24	at Chicago	3-2†
	25	at St. Louis	4-1
	28	Ottawa	5-2
	30	Washington	1-3
Nov.	1	at Chicago	1-5
	3	at San Jose	3-2
	5	at Los Angeles	0-5
	6	at Anaheim	1-4
	10	Dallas	2-4
	12	NY Rangers	1-4
	15	at Minnesota	1-0
	16	Arizona	2-1*
	18	Chicago	2-3
	20	at Detroit	3-2
	21	at Buffalo	2-4
	23	at Columbus	2-0
	25	at Boston	2-1
	27	at Philadelphia	3-5
	28	at NY Islanders	1-2*
	30	Toronto	3-0
Dec.	2	Minnesota	3-2†
	4	Anaheim	8-3
	6	at Dallas	2-1
	8	at Arizona	2-1*
	10	Winnipeg	6-2
	14	Tampa Bay	3-6
	16	Columbus	1-4
	19	at Arizona	4-2
	20	at San Jose	1-4
	23	Vancouver	4-1
	27	at Colorado	6-3
	29	Anaheim	1-3
	31	Arizona	4-2
Jan.	4	Colorado	4-1
	6	at Vancouver	2-4
	7	Vancouver	3-1
	9	at Winnipeg	0-2
	11	San Jose	3-2
	13	New Jersey	1-2
	14	at Edmonton	1-2†
	17	Florida	5-2
	19	Nashville	3-4
	21	Edmonton	3-7
	23	at Toronto	0-4
	24	at Montreal	1-5
	26	at Ottawa	3-2*
Feb.	1	Minnesota	5-1
	3	at New Jersey	4-3*
	5	at NY Rangers	3-4
	7	at Pittsburgh	3-2†
	13	Arizona	0-5
	15	Philadelphia	3-1
	18	at Vancouver	1-2*
	21	at Nashville	6-5*
	23	at Tampa Bay	3-2
	24	at Florida	4-2
	26	at Carolina	3-1
	28	Los Angeles	2-1*
Mar.	3	Detroit	3-2*
	5	NY Islanders	5-2
	9	Montreal	5-0
	11	at Winnipeg	3-0
	13	Pittsburgh	4-3†
	15	Boston	2-5
	17	Dallas	3-1
	19	Los Angeles	5-2
	21	at Washington	2-4
	23	at Nashville	1-3
	25	at St. Louis	3-2*
	27	Colorado	4-2
	29	Los Angeles	1-4
	31	San Jose	5-2
Apr.	2	Anaheim	3-4
	4	at Anaheim	1-3
	6	at Los Angeles	4-1
	8	at San Jose	1-3

* – Overtime † – Shootout

NHL Draft Selections 2017-2003

Name in bold denotes played in NHL.

2017

Pick	
16	Juuso Valimaki
109	Adam Ruzicka
140	Zach Fischer
171	D'artagnan Joly
202	Filip Sveningsson

2016

Pick	
6	**Matthew Tkachuk**
54	Tyler Parsons
56	Dillon Dube
66	Adam Fox
96	Linus Lindstrom
126	Mitchell Mattson
156	Eetu Tuulola
166	Matthew Phillips
186	Stepan Falkovsky

2015

Pick	
53	**Rasmus Andersson**
60	**Oliver Kylington**
136	Pavel Karnaukhov
166	Andrew Mangiapane
196	Riley Bruce

2014

Pick	
4	**Sam Bennett**
34	Mason McDonald
54	Hunter Smith
64	Brandon Hickey
175	Adam Ollas Mattsson
184	Austin Carroll

2013

Pick	
6	**Sean Monahan**
22	**Emile Poirier**
28	Morgan Klimchuk
67	Keegan Kanzig
135	Eric Roy
157	Tim Harrison
187	Rushan Rafikov
198	John Gilmour

2012

Pick	
21	**Mark Jankowski**
42	**Patrick Sieloff**
75	**Jon Gillies**
105	**Brett Kulak**
124	Ryan Culkin
165	Coda Gordon
186	Matthew Deblouw

2011

Pick	
13	**Sven Baertschi**
45	**Markus Granlund**
57	**Tyler Wotherspoon**
104	**Johnny Gaudreau**
164	**Laurent Brossoit**

2010

Pick	
64	**Max Reinhart**
73	Joey Leach
103	**John Ramage**
108	**Bill Arnold**
133	**Micheal Ferland**
193	**Patrick Holland**

2009

Pick	
23	**Tim Erixon**
74	Ryan Howse
111	Henrik Bjorklund
141	Spencer Bennett
171	**Joni Ortio**
201	Gaelan Patterson

2008

Pick	
25	**Greg Nemisz**
48	Mitch Wahl
78	**Lance Bouma**
108	Nicholas Larson
114	**T.J. Brodie**
168	Ryley Grantham
198	Alexander Deilert

2007

Pick	
24	**Mikael Backlund**
70	**John Negrin**
116	**Keith Aulie**
143	Mickey Renaud
186	C.J. Severyn

2006

Pick	
26	**Leland Irving**
87	John Armstrong
89	Aaron Marvin
118	Hugo Carpentier
149	Juuso Puustinen
179	Jordan Fulton
187	Devin Didiomete
209	Per Jonsson

2005

Pick	
26	**Matt Pelech**
69	Gord Baldwin
74	Dan Ryder
111	J.D. Watt
128	Kevin Lalande
158	**Matt Keetley**
179	**Brett Sutter**
221	Myles Rumsey

2004

Pick	
24	**Kris Chucko**
70	**Brandon Prust**
98	**Dustin Boyd**
118	Aki Seitsonen
121	Kris Hogg
173	**Adam Pardy**
182	Fred Wikner
200	Matt Schneider
213	James Spratt
279	**Adam Cracknell**

2003

Pick	
9	**Dion Phaneuf**
39	**Tim Ramholt**
97	Ryan Donally
112	**Jamie Tardif**
143	**Greg Moore**
173	Tyler Johnson
206	Thomas Bellemare
240	Cam Cunning
270	Kevin Harvey

Coaching History

Bernie Geoffrion, 1972-73, 1973-74; Bernie Geoffrion and Fred Creighton, 1974-75; Fred Creighton, 1975-76 to 1978-79; Al MacNeil, 1979-80 to 1981-82; Bob Johnson, 1982-83 to 1986-87; Terry Crisp, 1987-88 to 1989-90; Doug Risebrough, 1990-91; Doug Risebrough and Guy Charron, 1991-92; Dave King, 1992-93 to 1994-95; Pierre Page, 1995-96, 1996-97; Brian Sutter, 1997-98 to 1999-2000; Don Hay and Greg Gilbert, 2000-01; Greg Gilbert, 2001-02; Greg Gilbert, Al MacNeil and Darryl Sutter, 2002-03; Darryl Sutter, 2003-04 to 2005-06; Jim Playfair, 2006-07; Mike Keenan, 2007-08, 2008-09; Brent Sutter, 2009-10 to 2011-12; Bob Hartley, 2012-13 to 2015-16; Glen Gulutzan, 2016-17 to date.

General Managers' History

Cliff Fletcher, 1972-73 to 1990-91; Doug Risebrough, 1991-92 to 1994-95; Doug Risebrough and Al Coates, 1995-96; Al Coates, 1996-97 to 1999-2000; Craig Button, 2000-01 to 2002-03; Darryl Sutter, 2003-04 to 2009-10; Darryl Sutter and Jay Feaster, 2010-11; Jay Feaster, 2011-12 to 2013-14; Brad Treliving, 2014-15 to date.

Brad Treliving

General Manager

Born: Penticton, BC, August 18, 1969.

Brad Treliving joined the Calgary Flames organization as general manager on April 28, 2014. In his first season with the Flames in 2014-15, Calgary reached the playoffs for the first time since 2008-09. They made the playoffs again in 2016-17. Treliving reports directly to president of hockey operations Brian Burke. He is responsible for all team personnel decisions, both players and staff; managing the amateur and pro scouting staffs; as well as other administrative duties. He is also responsible for all player personnel assignments with Flames' minor league affiliates.

Treliving served as the vice president of hockey operations and assistant general manager with the Phoenix (now Arizona) Coyotes for seven seasons prior to coming to Calgary. He worked closely with general manager Don Maloney on the day-to-day administration of the Coyotes' hockey operations. Treliving also served as general manager of the club's American Hockey League affiliate, the Portland Pirates.

Prior to his role with the Coyotes, Treliving served as the president of the Central Hockey League (CHL) for seven years. During his tenure, he guided the CHL to remarkable growth and development including the establishment of numerous successful expansion franchises. In 1996 Treliving co-founded the Western Professional Hockey League (WPHL) and served as the league's vice president and director of hockey operations for five seasons. He played an integral role in the merger of the WPHL and the CHL in May 2001 upon which he began his tenure as president of the league.

Prior to his front office career, Treliving played five seasons of professional hockey from 1990-91 to 1994-95 in the IHL, the AHL and the ECHL. A defenseman, Treliving registered 17 goals and 85 assists for 102 points and 811 penalty minutes in 243 games in the ECHL. As a junior, the native of Penticton, British Columbia, played in the BCJHL and two years in the WHL

Club Directory

Scotiabank Saddledome

Calgary Flames
Scotiabank Saddledome
P.O. Box 1540 Station M
Calgary, Alberta T2P 3B9
Phone **403/777-2177**
FAX 403/777-2195
www.calgaryflames.com
Capacity: 19,289

Owners . . . N. Murray Edwards (Chairman), Alvin G. Libin, Allan P. Markin, Jeff McCaig, Clayton H. Riddell

Executive Management

President & Chief Executive Officer	Ken King
Chief Operating Officer	John Bean
President, Hockey Operations	Brian Burke
General Manager	Brad Treliving
Chief Financial Officer	Cameron Olson
V.P., Sales, Ticket Operations & Customer Service	Rollie Cyr
V.P., Sports Property Sales and Marketing	Gordon Norrie
V.P., Building Operations	Libby Raines
V.P., Finance and Administration	Ken Zaba
V.P., Communications	Peter Hanlon
V.P., Business Development	Jim Peplinski
Sr. Directors, Business Intelligence & Special Projects / Human Resources / IT & Food and Beverage	Deniece Kennedy / Helen Pozsonyi / Ziad Mehio
Directors, Retail / Building Ops / Benefits & Rewards	Brent Gibbs / Trent Anderson / Betty Mah

Hockey Club Personnel

President, Hockey Operations	Brian Burke
General Manager	Brad Treliving
Assistant General Manager	Craig Conroy
Assistant General Manager	Brad Pascall
Vice-President of Hockey Operations	Don Maloney
Director, Hockey Administration	Mike Burke
Director, Player Development	Ray Edwards
Director of Pro Personnel	Derek MacKinnon
Director, Amateur Scouting	Tod Button
Director, Team Operations	Sean O'Brien
Director, Hockey Analysis	Chris Snow
Player Development	Ron Sutter
Head Coach	Glen Gulutzan
Assistant Coaches	Dave Cameron, Paul Jerrard, Martin Gelinas
Assistant Coach, Video	Jamie Pringle
Goaltending Coach	Jordan Sigalet
Exec. Asst. to President, Hockey Ops and G.M.	Brenda Koyich
Exec. Asst., Hockey Operations	Anita Cranston
Pro Scout	Steve Pleau
Assistant Directors of Scouting	Fred Parker, Rob Sumner

Scouts. . . . Jim Cummins, Terry Doran, Ari Haanpaa, Bobbie Hagelin, Bob MacMillan, Allister MacNeil, Eric Soltys, Robert Neuhauser (Europe), Darren Kruger, Reid Jackson, Billy Powers

Medical/Medical and Training Staff

Strength & Conditioning Coach	Ryan van Asten
Athletic Therapist / Asst. Athletic Therapist	Kent Kobelka / Mike Gudmundson
Equipment Manager / Asst. Equipment Manager	Mark DePasquale / Corey Osmak
Massage / Rehab Therapist	Domenic Manchisi / Kevin Wagner
Dressing Room Attendant	Ben Dumaine
Head Physician	Dr. Ian Auld
Team Physicians	Dr. Jim Thorne, Dr. David Manning
Team Orthopedic Surgeons	Dr. Richard Boorman, Dr. Stephen French
Team Dentist	Dr. Kristin Yont

Stockton Heat

Head Coach	Ryan Huska
Assistant Coaches	Cail MacLean, Domenic Pittis
Goaltending Development Coach	Colin Zulianello
Strength and Conditioning Coach	Alan Selby
Equipment Manager / Asst. Equipment Manager	Peter Bureaux / Mitch MacLeod
Athletic Therapist	James Borrelli
Video Analyst and Team Services Manager	Kohl Schultz

Communications

Vice-President, Communications	Peter Hanlon
Director, Communications & Media Relations	Sean Kelso
Coordinator, Public Relations	Dalton Ulrich
Assistant, Communications	Kelsey McCay

Calgary Flames Foundation

Executive Director	Candice Goudie
Manager, Community Relations	Blake Heynen

Administration

Chief Operating Officer	John Bean
Chief Financial Officer	Cameron Olson
V.P., Finance and Administration	Ken Zaba
Sr. Director, Business Intelligence & Special Projects	Deniece Kennedy
Human Resources	Helen Pozsonyi / Betty Mah
Director, Retail	Brent Gibbs
Exec. Asst. to President/CEO	Judy O'Brien
Exec. Asst. to COO	Coralie Baun

Marketing

V.P. Sports Property Sales and Marketing	Gordon Norrie
V.P. Business Development	Jim Peplinski
Sr. Director National Partnerships & Broadcast	Kevin Gross
Sr. Director, Game Presentation, Events & Community Relations	Geordie Macleod
Sr. Director, Partnership Sales Leader	Mark Stiles
Senior Account Executive, Partnership Sales	Pat Halls
Manager, Marketing / Game Presentation	Ryan Popowich / Steve Edgar
Director, Digital and Social Media	Ty Pilson
Sr. Director, Broadcast & Production	Carlo Petrini
Executive Assistant Marketing	Lori McCarry

Ticketing, Suites and Customer Service

V.P. Sales, Ticket Operations & Customer Service	Rollie Cyr
Executive Assistant to V.P. of Sales, Ticket Operations & Customer Service	Tracy Wood
Director, Sales and Luxury Suites	Marc Leost
Manager, Customer Service & Retention	Caitlin Bell

Miscellaneous

Radio Affiliate	The FAN 960 (960 AM)
TV Affiliate	Rogers Sportsnet, CBC-TV, TSN

Carolina Hurricanes

2016-17 Results: 36w-31L-9OTL-6SOL 87PTS
7TH, Metropolitan Division • 12TH, Eastern Conference

Key Off-Season Signings/Acquisitions

2017

April 21 • Re-signed D **Klas Dahlbeck**.
28 • Acquired G **Scott Darling** from Chicago for a 3rd-round pick in 2017 NHL Draft.
June 13 • Re-signed C **Andrew Miller**.
15 • Re-signed LW **Teuvo Teravainen**.
22 • Acquired D **Trevor van Riemsdyk** and a 7th-round pick in 2018 NHL Draft from Vegas for a 2nd-round pick in 2017 NHL Draft.
26 • Re-signed C **Derek Ryan** and D **Trevor Carrick**.
27 • Re-signed C **Patrick Brown** and D **Jake Chelios**.
28 • Re-signed LW **Brock McGinn** and D **Philip Samuelsson**.
29 • Acquired D **Keegan Kanzig** and a 6th-round pick in 2019 NHL Draft from Calgary for G **Eddie Lack**, D **Ryan Murphy** and a 7th-round pick in 2019 NHL Draft.
July 1 • Signed RW **Justin Williams**, RW **Josh Jooris**, G **Jeremy Smith** and D **Brenden Kichton**.
1 • Re-signed D **Dennis Robertson**.
4 • Acquired C **Marcus Kruger** from Vegas for a 5th-round pick in 2018 NHL Draft.
12 • Re-signed D **Jaccob Slavin**.
27 • Re-signed LW **Phillip Di Giuseppe**.
Aug. 1 • Re-signed D **Brett Pesce**.

2017-18 Schedule

Oct.	Sat.	7	Minnesota	Tue.	9	at Tampa Bay
	Tue.	10	Columbus	Thu.	11	at Washington
	Sat.	14	at Winnipeg	Fri.	12	Washington
	Tue.	17	at Edmonton	Sun.	14	Calgary*
	Thu.	19	at Calgary	Sat.	20	at Detroit
	Sat.	21	at Dallas	Sun.	21	Vegas*
	Tue.	24	Tampa Bay	Tue.	23	at Pittsburgh
	Thu.	26	at Toronto	Thu.	25	at Montreal
	Fri.	27	St. Louis	Tue.	30	Ottawa
	Sun.	29	Anaheim*	**Feb.** Thu.	1	Montreal
Nov.	Thu.	2	at Colorado	Fri.	2	Detroit
	Sat.	4	at Arizona	Sun.	4	San Jose*
	Tue.	7	Florida	Tue.	6	Philadelphia
	Fri.	10	at Columbus	Fri.	9	Vancouver
	Sat.	11	Chicago	Sat.	10	Colorado
	Mon.	13	Dallas	Tue.	13	Los Angeles
	Thu.	16	at NY Islanders	Thu.	15	at New Jersey
	Sat.	18	at Buffalo	Fri.	16	NY Islanders
	Sun.	19	NY Islanders*	Sun.	18	New Jersey*
	Wed.	22	NY Rangers	Fri.	23	Pittsburgh
	Fri.	24	Toronto	Sat.	24	at Detroit
	Sun.	26	Nashville*	Tue.	27	at Boston
	Tue.	28	at Columbus	**Mar.** Thu.	1	at Philadelphia
Dec.	Fri.	1	at NY Rangers	Fri.	2	New Jersey
	Sat.	2	Florida	Sun.	4	Winnipeg
	Tue.	5	at Vancouver	Tue.	6	at Minnesota
	Thu.	7	at San Jose	Thu.	8	at Chicago
	Sat.	9	at Los Angeles	Mon.	12	at NY Rangers
	Mon.	11	at Anaheim	Tue.	13	Boston
	Tue.	12	at Vegas	Sat.	17	Philadelphia
	Fri.	15	at Buffalo	Sun.	18	at NY Islanders*
	Sat.	16	Columbus	Tue.	20	Edmonton
	Tue.	19	at Toronto*	Thu.	22	Arizona
	Thu.	21	at Nashville	Sat.	24	at Ottawa
	Sat.	23	Buffalo	Mon.	26	Ottawa
	Wed.	27	Montreal	Tue.	27	at New Jersey
	Fri.	29	Pittsburgh	Fri.	30	at Washington
	Sat.	30	at St. Louis*	Sat.	31	NY Rangers
Jan.	Tue.	2	Washington	**Apr.** Mon.	2	at Florida
	Thu.	4	at Pittsburgh	Thu.	5	at Philadelphia
	Sat.	6	at Boston	Sat.	7	Tampa Bay

* Denotes afternoon game.

Retired Numbers

2	Glen Wesley	1994-2008
10	Ron Francis	1981-1991; 1998-2004
17	Rod Brind'Amour	2000-2010

METROPOLITAN DIVISION
39th NHL Season

Franchise date: June 22, 1979

Transferred from Hartford to Carolina, June 25, 1997.

Jeff Skinner established a new career standard with 37 goals in 2016-17. His 63 points equalled the career-high reached in his Calder Trophy-winning rookie season of 2010-11.

Year-by-Year Record

Season	GP	Home W	L	T	OL	Road W	L	T	OL	Overall W	L	T	OL	GF	GA	Pts.	Div. Fin.	Conf. Fin.	Playoff Result
2016-17	82	23	12	....	6	13	19	....	9	36	31	....	15	215	236	87	7th, Met.	12th, East	– out of playoffs –
2015-16	82	19	15	....	7	16	16	....	9	35	31	....	16	198	226	86	6th, Met.	10th, East	– out of playoffs –
2014-15	82	18	16	....	7	12	25	....	4	30	41	....	11	188	226	71	8th, Met.	14th, East	– out of playoffs –
2013-14	82	18	17	....	6	18	18	....	5	36	35	....	11	207	230	83	7th, Met.	13th, East	– out of playoffs –
2012-13	48	9	14	....	1	10	11	....	3	19	25	....	4	128	160	42	3rd, SE	13th, East	– out of playoffs –
2011-12	82	20	14	....	7	13	19	....	9	33	33	....	16	213	243	82	5th, SE	12th, East	– out of playoffs –
2010-11	82	22	14	....	5	18	17	....	6	40	31	....	11	236	239	91	3rd, SE	9th, East	– out of playoffs –
2009-10	82	21	17	....	3	14	20	....	7	35	37	....	10	230	256	80	3rd, SE	11th, East	– out of playoffs –
2008-09	**82**	**26**	**14**	**....**	**1**	**19**	**16**	**....**	**6**	**45**	**30**	**....**	**7**	**239**	**226**	**97**	**2nd, SE**	**6th, East**	**Lost Conf. Final**
2007-08	82	24	13	....	4	19	20	....	2	43	33	....	6	252	249	92	2nd, SE	9th, East	– out of playoffs –
2006-07	82	21	16	....	4	19	18	....	4	40	34	....	8	241	253	88	3rd, SE	11th, East	– out of playoffs –
2005-06	**82**	**31**	**8**	**....**	**2**	**21**	**14**	**....**	**6**	**52**	**22**	**....**	**8**	**294**	**260**	**112**	**1st, SE**	**2nd, East**	**Won Stanley Cup**
2004-05																			
2003-04	82	13	18	8	2	15	16	6	3	28	34	14	6	172	209	76	3rd, SE	11th, East	– out of playoffs –
2002-03	82	12	17	9	3	10	26	2	3	22	43	11	6	171	240	61	5th, SE	15th, East	– out of playoffs –
2001-02	82	15	13	11	2	20	13	5	3	35	26	16	5	217	217	91	1st, SE	3rd, East	Lost Final
2000-01	82	23	15	3	0	15	17	6	3	38	32	9	3	212	225	88	2nd, SE	8th, East	Lost Conf. Quarter-Final
1999-2000	82	20	15	5	0	17	19	5	0	37	35	10	0	217	216	84	3rd, SE	9th, East	– out of playoffs –
1998-99	82	20	12	9	....	14	18	9	....	34	30	18	....	210	202	86	1st, SE	3rd, East	Lost Conf. Quarter-Final
1997-98	82	16	18	7	....	17	23	1	....	33	41	8	....	200	219	74	6th, NE	9th, East	– out of playoffs –
1996-97*	82	23	15	3	....	9	24	8	....	32	39	11	....	226	256	75	5th, NE	10th, East	– out of playoffs –
1995-96*	82	22	15	4	....	12	24	5	....	34	39	9	....	237	259	77	4th, NE	10th, East	– out of playoffs –
1994-95*	48	12	10	2	....	7	14	3	....	19	24	5	....	127	141	43	5th, NE	13th, East	– out of playoffs –
1993-94*	84	14	22	5	....	13	26	3	....	27	48	9	....	227	288	63	6th, NE	13th, East	– out of playoffs –
1992-93*	84	14	25	5	....	12	27	1	....	26	52	6	....	284	369	58	5th, Adams		– out of playoffs –
1991-92*	80	13	17	10	....	13	24	3	....	26	41	13	....	247	283	65	4th, Adams		Lost Div. Semi-Final
1990-91*	80	18	16	6	....	13	22	5	....	31	38	11	....	238	276	73	4th, Adams		Lost Div. Semi-Final
1989-90*	80	17	18	5	....	21	15	4	....	38	33	9	....	275	268	85	4th, Adams		Lost Div. Semi-Final
1988-89*	80	21	17	2	....	16	21	3	....	37	38	5	....	299	290	79	4th, Adams		Lost Div. Semi-Final
1987-88*	80	21	14	5	....	14	24	2	....	35	38	7	....	249	267	77	4th, Adams		Lost Div. Semi-Final
1986-87*	80	26	9	5	....	17	21	2	....	43	30	7	....	287	270	93	1st, Adams		Lost Div. Semi-Final
1985-86*	80	21	17	2	....	19	19	2	....	40	36	4	....	332	302	84	4th, Adams		Lost Div. Final
1984-85*	80	17	18	5	....	13	23	4	....	30	41	9	....	268	318	69	5th, Adams		– out of playoffs –
1983-84*	80	19	16	5	....	9	26	5	....	28	42	10	....	288	320	66	5th, Adams		– out of playoffs –
1982-83*	80	13	22	5	....	6	32	2	....	19	54	7	....	261	403	45	5th, Adams		– out of playoffs –
1981-82*	80	13	17	10	....	8	24	8	....	21	41	18	....	264	351	60	5th, Adams		– out of playoffs –
1980-81*	80	14	17	9	....	7	24	9	....	21	41	18	....	292	372	60	4th, Norris		– out of playoffs –
1979-80*	80	22	12	6	....	5	22	13	....	27	34	19	....	303	312	73	4th, Norris		Lost Prelim. Round

* Hartford Whalers

2017-18 Player Personnel

FORWARDS	HT	WT	*Age	Birthplace	S	2016-17 Club
AHO, Sebastian	5-11	172	20	Rauma, Finland	L	Carolina
BROWN, Patrick	6-1	210	25	Bloomfield Hills, MI	R	Carolina-Charlotte
Di GIUSEPPE, Phil	6-0	200	23	Toronto, ON	L	Carolina-Charlotte
JOORIS, Josh	6-1	197	27	Burlington, ON	R	NY Rangers-Arizona
KRUGER, Marcus	6-0	186	27	Stockholm, Sweden	L	Chicago
LINDHOLM, Elias	6-1	192	22	Boden , Sweden	R	Carolina
McGINN, Brock	6-0	185	23	Fergus, ON	L	Carolina-Charlotte
NORDSTROM, Joakim	6-1	189	25	Tyreso, Sweden	L	Carolina
RASK, Victor	6-2	200	24	Leksand, Sweden	L	Carolina
RYAN, Derek	5-10	170	30	Spokane, WA	R	Carolina-Charlotte
SKINNER, Jeff	5-11	200	25	Markham, ON	L	Carolina
STAAL, Jordan	6-4	220	29	Thunder Bay, ON	L	Carolina
STEMPNIAK, Lee	5-11	195	34	Buffalo, NY	R	Carolina
TERAVAINEN, Teuvo	5-11	178	23	Helsinki, Finland	L	Carolina
WILLIAMS, Justin	6-1	186	36	Cobourg, ON	R	Washington

DEFENSEMEN	HT	WT	*Age	Birthplace	S	2016-17 Club
DAHLBECK, Klas	6-3	207	26	Katrineholm, Sweden	L	Carolina-Charlotte
FAULK, Justin	6-0	215	25	South St. Paul, MN	R	Carolina
FLEURY, Haydn	6-3	221	21	Carlyle, SK	L	Charlotte
HANIFIN, Noah	6-3	206	20	Boston, MA	L	Carolina
PESCE, Brett	6-3	200	22	Tarrytown, NY	R	Carolina
SLAVIN, Jaccob	6-3	205	23	Denver, CO	L	Carolina
van RIEMSDYK, Trevor	6-2	188	26	Middletown, NJ	R	Chicago

GOALTENDERS	HT	WT	*Age	Birthplace	C	2016-17 Club
DARLING, Scott	6-6	232	28	Lemont, IL	L	Chicago
SMITH, Jeremy	6-0	177	28	Dearborn, MI	L	Colorado-San Antonio
WARD, Cam	6-1	185	33	Saskatoon, SK	L	Carolina

* – Age at start of 2017-18 season

Coaching History

Don Blackburn, 1979-80; Don Blackburn and Larry Pleau, 1980-81; Larry Pleau, 1981-82; Larry Kish, Larry Pleau and John Cuniff, 1982- 83; Jack Evans, 1983-84 to 1986-87; Jack Evans and Larry Pleau, 1987-88; Larry Pleau, 1988-89; Rick Ley, 1989-90, 1990-91; Jim Roberts, 1991-92; Paul Holmgren, 1992-93; Paul Holmgren and Pierre Maguire, 1993-94; Paul Holmgren, 1994-95; Paul Holmgren and Paul Maurice, 1995-96; Paul Maurice, 1996-97 to 2002-03; Paul Maurice and Peter Laviolette, 2003-04; Peter Laviolette, 2004-05 to 2007-08; Peter Laviolette and Paul Maurice, 2008-09; Paul Maurice, 2009-10, 2010-11; Paul Maurice and Kirk Muller, 2011-12; Kirk Muller, 2012-13, 2013-14; Bill Peters, 2014-15 to date.

Bill Peters
Head Coach
Born: Three Hills, AB, January 13, 1965.

Bill Peters began his tenure as head coach of the Carolina Hurricane on June 19, 2014. He is the 13th person to serve as head coach in franchise history, and the fourth since the team's arrival in North Carolina in 1997. This is Peters' first head coaching positon in the NHL.

Prior to joining the Hurricanes, Peters served as assistant coach for the Detroit Red Wings for three seasons, working primarily with Detroit's defensemen and penalty kill units. Before joining Detroit's staff, Peters served as head coach of Rockford of the American Hockey League, guiding the Ice Hogs to consecutive 40-win seasons and Calder Cup playoff appearances in 2008-09 and 2009-10. In his final season with Rockford in 2010-11, Peters directed the second-youngest team in the AHL. He helped 28 Rockford players reach the NHL during his three seasons with the club. Eight players who played under Peters for Rockford went on to win the Stanley Cup with Chicago in 2010 or 2013 – Niklas Hjalmarsson, Jordan Henry, Antti Niemi, Corey Crawford, Bryan Bickell, Nick Leddy, Brandon Bollig and Ben Smith.

Before beginning his AHL coaching career, Peters spent three seasons with Spokane of the Western Hockey League, leading the Chiefs to the Memorial Cup title in 2008. Spokane established franchise records with 50 wins and 107 points that season before winning 16 of 21 WHL playoff games to capture the Ed Chynoweth Cup as WHL champions. Peters then guided the Chiefs to four consecutive victories at the Memorial Cup, topping the host Kitchener Rangers 4-1 in the championship game.

Peters got his first experience as a head coach at the University of Lethbridge, serving as the Proghorns' head coach for three seasons from 2002 to 2005. Prior to that, he served as assistant coach for Spokane for four seasons, helping the Chiefs to a 47-win, 100-point campaign and the WHL Western Conference championship in 1999-2000 under current Red Wings' head coach Mike Babcock.

Peters also has gained international head coaching experience for Canada, capturing the gold medal at the 2008 Under-18 World Championship and at the 2016 World Championship. He also served as an assistant coach for Canada at the 2016 World Cup of Hockey.

Coaching Record

Season	Team	League	Regular Season GC	W	L	O/T	Playoffs GC	W	L	T
2002-03	U of Lethbridge	CWUAA	28	10	16	2	3	1	2	0
2003-04	U of Lethbridge	CWUAA	28	4	20	4	....	....	....	....
2004-05	U of Lethbridge	CWUAA	28	3	23	2	....	....	....	....
2005-06	Spokane	WHL	72	25	39	8	....	....	....	....
2006-07	Spokane	WHL	72	36	28	8	6	2	4	0
2007-08	Spokane	WHL	72	50	15	7	21	16	5	0
2007-08	Spokane	M-Cup	....	....	....	....	4	4	0	0
2008-09	Rockford	AHL	80	40	34	6	4	0	4	0
2009-10	Rockford	AHL	80	44	30	6	4	0	4	0
2010-11	Rockford	AHL	80	38	33	9	....	....	....	....
2014-15	Carolina	NHL	82	30	41	11	....	....	....	....
2015-16	Carolina	NHL	82	35	31	16	....	....	....	....
2016-17	Carolina	NHL	82	36	31	15	....	....	....	....
	NHL Totals		246	101	103	42	....	....	....	....

2016-17 Scoring
* – rookie

Regular Season

Pos	#	Player	Team	GP	G	A	Pts	TOI	+/-	PIM	PP	SH	GW	S	S%
C	53	Jeff Skinner	CAR	79	37	26	63	17:44	-3	28	7	0	4	281	13.2
R	20 *	Sebastian Aho	CAR	82	24	25	49	16:47	-1	26	6	1	4	214	11.2
C	11	Jordan Staal	CAR	75	16	29	45	18:39	-1	38	4	1	3	164	9.8
C	49	Victor Rask	CAR	82	16	29	45	17:17	-10	16	4	0	3	186	8.6
C	16	Elias Lindholm	CAR	72	11	34	45	18:10	-2	16	2	1	0	151	7.3
L	86	Teuvo Teravainen	CAR	81	15	27	42	16:14	-6	16	5	0	2	169	8.9
R	21	Lee Stempniak	CAR	82	16	24	40	15:50	-2	32	2	0	2	131	12.2
D	27	Justin Faulk	CAR	75	17	20	37	23:08	-18	32	4	0	2	225	7.6
D	74	Jaccob Slavin	CAR	82	5	29	34	23:26	23	12	0	1	0	99	5.1
C	33	Derek Ryan	CAR	67	11	18	29	14:53	-8	22	4	1	3	73	15.1
D	5	Noah Hanifin	CAR	81	4	25	29	17:55	-19	26	2	0	1	108	3.7
D	22	Brett Pesce	CAR	82	2	18	20	21:12	23	20	0	0	0	109	1.8
L	23 *	Brock McGinn	CAR	57	7	9	16	11:59	-11	6	0	0	1	74	9.5
C	42	Joakim Nordstrom	CAR	82	7	5	12	12:43	-12	17	0	1	2	104	6.7
C	18	Jay McClement	CAR	65	5	3	8	11:22	-8	18	0	1	1	37	13.5
L	34	Phil Di Giuseppe	CAR	36	1	4	5	12:17	-12	15	0	0	1	68	1.5
D	6	Klas Dahlbeck	CAR	43	2	4	6	13:53	-12	30	0	0	0	37	5.4
D	26	Matt Tennyson	CAR	45	0	6	6	13:17	-13	6	0	0	0	36	0.0
C	15	Andrej Nestrasil	CAR	19	1	4	5	10:54	-3	2	0	0	0	27	3.7
C	71 *	Lucas Wallmark	CAR	8	0	2	2	10:52	1	2	0	0	0	11	0.0
R	8	Ty Rattie	STL	4	0	0	0	7:20	0	0	0	0	0	1	0.0
			CAR	5	0	2	2	13:27	-2	0	0	0	0	9	0.0
			Total	9	0	2	2	10:44	-2	0	0	0	0	10	0.0
D	7	Ryan Murphy	CAR	27	0	2	2	13:10	-11	8	0	0	0	17	0.0
L	39 *	Valentin Zykov	CAR	2	1	0	1	6:15	1	0	0	0	0	3	33.3
L	29	Bryan Bickell	CAR	11	1	0	1	10:26	-4	4	1	0	1	8	12.5
L	61 *	Sergey Tolchinsky	CAR	2	0	1	1	11:28	0	0	0	0	0	2	0.0
R	91 *	Martin Frk	CAR	2	0	0	0	8:20	-3	0	0	0	0	1	0.0
C	57 *	Andrew Poturalski	CAR	2	0	0	0	12:16	-3	0	0	0	0	1	0.0
D	14	Jakub Nakladal	CAR	3	0	0	0	14:30	-4	0	0	0	0	4	0.0
C	36	Patrick Brown	CAR	14	0	0	0	9:42	-6	0	0	0	0	12	0.0

Goaltending

No.	Goaltender	GPI	Mins	Avg	W	L	OT	EN	SO	GA	SA	Sv%	G	A	PIM
35	* Alex Nedeljkovic	1	30	0.00	0	0	0	0	0	0	17	1.000	0	0	2
40	Jorge Alves	1	0	0.00	0	0	0	0	0	0	0	.000	0	0	0
31	Eddie Lack	20	1090	2.64	8	7	3	3	1	48	492	.902	0	0	0
30	Cam Ward	61	3618	2.69	26	22	12	5	2	162	1711	.905	0	1	6
32	Michael Leighton	4	210	3.43	2	2	0	0	0	12	92	.870	0	1	0
	Totals	82	4993	2.76	36	31	15	8	3	230	2320	.901			

Sebastien Aho finished third in goals (24) and fifth in points (49) among rookie scorers in the NHL in 2016-17.

Captains' History

Rick Ley, 1979-80; Rick Ley and Mike Rogers, 1980-81; Dave Keon, 1981-82; Russ Anderson, 1982-83; Mark Johnson, 1983-84; Mark Johnson and Ron Francis, 1984-85; Ron Francis, 1985-86 to 1990-91; Randy Ladouceur, 1991-92; Pat Verbeek, 1992-93 to 1994-95; Brendan Shanahan, 1995-96; Kevin Dineen, 1996-97, 1997-98; Keith Primeau, 1998-99; Keith Primeau and Ron Francis, 1999-2000; Ron Francis, 2000-01 to 2003-04; Rod Brind'Amour, 2005-06 to 2008-09; Rod Brind'Amour and Eric Staal, 2009-10; Eric Staal, 2010-11 to 2015-16; no captain, 2016-17.

Club Records

Team

(Figures in brackets for season records are games played; records for fewest points, wins, ties, losses, goals, goals against are for 70 or more games)

Most Points	112	2005-06 (82)
Most Wins	52	2005-06 (82)
Most Ties	19	1979-80 (80)
Most Losses	54	1982-83 (80)
Most Goals	332	1985-86 (80)
Most Goals Against	403	1982-83 (80)
Fewest Points	45	1982-83 (80)
Fewest Wins	19	1982-83 (80)
Fewest Ties	4	1985-86 (80)
Fewest Losses	22	2005-06 (82)
Fewest Goals	171	2002-03 (82)
Fewest Goals Against	202	1998-99 (82)

Longest Winning Streak

Overall	9	Oct. 22-Nov. 11/05, Dec. 31/05-Jan. 19/06, Mar. 18-Apr. 07/09
Home	12	Feb. 20-Apr. 7/09
Away	6	Nov. 10-Dec. 7/90

Longest Team Point Streak

Overall	10	Jan. 20-Feb. 10/82 (6W, 4T)
Home	12	Feb. 20-Apr. 7/09 (10W, 1OTW, 1SOW)
Away	8	Nov. 11-Dec. 5/96 (4W, 4T)

Longest Losing Streak

Overall	14	Oct. 10-Nov. 13/09
Home	8	Mar. 14-Apr. 9/13
Away	13	Dec. 18/82-Feb. 5/83, Oct. 3-Nov. 28/09

Longest Winless Streak

Overall	14	Jan. 4-Feb. 9/92 (8L, 6T), Oct. 10-Nov. 13/09 (10L, 3OTL, 1SOL)
Home	10	Oct. 21-Dec. 4/00 (4L, 2OTL, 4T)
Away	13	Feb. 3-Mar. 29/73 (10L, 3T), Feb. 18-Apr. 6/13 (12L, 1OTL)

Most Shutouts, Season	8	1998-99 (82)
Most PIM, Season	2,354	1992-93 (84)
Most Goals, Game	11	Feb. 12/84 (Edm. 0 at Hfd. 11), Oct. 19/85 (Mtl. 6 at Hfd. 11), Jan. 17/86 (Que. 6 at Hfd. 11), Mar. 15/86 (Chi. 4 at Hfd. 11)

Individual

Most Seasons	16	Ron Francis
Most Games	1,186	Ron Francis
Most Goals, Career	382	Ron Francis
Most Assists, Career	793	Ron Francis
Most Points, Career	1,175	Ron Francis (382G, 793A)
Most PIM, Career	1,439	Kevin Dineen
Most Shutouts, Career	25	Cam Ward
Longest Consecutive Games Streak	419	Dave Tippett (Mar. 3/84-Oct. 7/89)
Most Goals, Season	56	Blaine Stoughton (1979-80)
Most Assists, Season	69	Ron Francis (1989-90)
Most Points, Season	105	Mike Rogers (1979-80; 44G, 61A), (1980-81; 40G, 65A)
Most PIM, Season	358	Torrie Robertson (1985-86)

Most Points, Defenseman, Season	69	Dave Babych (1985-86; 14G, 55A)
Most Points, Center, Season	105	Mike Rogers (1979-80; 44G, 61A), (1980-81; 40G, 65A)
Most Points, Right Wing, Season	100	Blaine Stoughton (1979-80; 56G, 44A)
Most Points, Left Wing, Season	89	Geoff Sanderson (1992-93; 46G, 43A)
Most Points, Rookie, Season	72	Sylvain Turgeon (1983-84; 40G, 32A)
Most Shutouts, Season	6	Arturs Irbe (1998-99), (2000-01) Kevin Weekes (2003-04) Cam Ward (2008-09)
Most Goals, Game	4	Jordy Douglas (Feb. 3/80) Ron Francis (Feb. 12/84) Eric Staal (Mar. 7/09)
Most Assists, Game	6	Ron Francis (Mar. 5/87)
Most Points, Game	6	Paul Lawless (Jan. 4/87; 2G, 4A) Ron Francis (Mar. 5/87; 6A), (Oct. 8/89; 3G, 3A) Eric Staal (Mar. 7/09; 4G, 2A)

Records include Hartford Whalers, 1979-80 through 1996-97.

All-time Record vs. Other Clubs

Regular Season

		Total								At Home								On Road						
	GP	W	L	T	OL	GF	GA	PTS	GP	W	L	T	OL	GF	GA	PTS	GP	W	L	T	OL	GF	GA	PTS
Anaheim	34	14	14	2	4	97	97	34	17	8	7	1	1	41	42	18	17	6	7	1	3	56	55	16
Arizona	76	38	30	8	0	263	244	84	38	17	15	6	0	124	114	40	38	21	15	2	0	139	130	44
Boston	197	77	99	16	5	570	664	175	98	42	44	9	3	314	329	96	99	35	55	7	2	256	335	79
Buffalo	198	78	96	18	6	575	671	180	100	45	41	11	3	296	293	104	98	33	55	7	3	279	378	76
Calgary	71	21	42	7	1	221	288	50	35	14	16	5	0	116	121	33	36	7	26	2	1	105	167	17
Chicago	73	31	33	7	2	217	242	71	37	19	13	4	1	120	106	43	36	12	20	3	1	97	136	28
Colorado	142	48	70	21	3	432	529	120	70	30	26	12	2	225	230	74	72	18	44	9	1	207	299	46
Columbus	30	16	12	0	2	77	83	34	16	9	5	0	2	44	45	20	14	7	7	0	0	33	38	14
Dallas	77	27	41	6	3	229	285	63	40	16	20	4	0	122	139	36	37	11	21	2	3	107	146	27
Detroit	79	30	38	8	3	234	256	71	39	20	16	1	2	124	108	43	40	10	22	7	1	110	148	28
Edmonton	74	24	36	12	2	250	258	62	36	16	13	7	0	141	112	39	38	8	23	5	2	109	146	23
Florida	115	56	42	11	6	308	321	129	57	36	16	3	2	174	140	77	58	20	26	8	4	134	181	52
Los Angeles	75	31	34	8	2	256	281	72	38	19	13	5	1	128	132	44	37	12	21	3	1	128	149	28
Minnesota	22	9	7	2	4	59	60	24	9	6	1	0	2	21	17	14	13	3	6	2	2	38	43	10
Montreal	196	68	102	20	6	555	701	162	99	40	44	13	2	287	333	95	97	28	58	7	4	268	368	67
Nashville	25	10	11	1	3	59	66	24	13	7	2	1	3	35	33	18	12	3	9	0	0	24	33	6
New Jersey	137	53	67	12	5	391	429	123	69	29	31	8	1	195	206	67	68	24	36	4	4	196	223	56
NY Islanders	137	70	48	9	10	452	419	159	69	34	25	5	5	240	221	78	68	36	23	4	5	212	198	81
NY Rangers	136	54	66	7	9	367	443	124	67	35	25	3	4	209	202	77	69	19	41	4	5	158	241	47
Ottawa	99	52	34	8	5	273	255	117	48	31	11	4	2	144	110	68	51	21	23	4	3	129	145	49
Philadelphia	136	41	67	14	14	379	486	110	68	23	31	9	5	202	232	60	68	18	36	5	9	177	254	50
Pittsburgh	142	60	64	11	7	478	507	138	72	34	30	5	3	247	245	76	70	26	34	6	4	231	262	62
St. Louis	78	29	39	5	5	226	255	68	39	16	19	2	2	113	119	36	39	13	20	3	3	113	136	32
San Jose	36	19	17	0	0	111	115	38	18	11	7	0	0	55	41	22	18	8	10	0	0	56	74	16
Tampa Bay	118	51	47	10	10	334	354	122	60	31	19	7	3	176	175	72	58	20	28	3	7	158	179	50
Toronto	116	62	38	11	5	404	355	140	58	31	18	6	3	212	180	71	58	31	20	5	2	192	175	69
Vancouver	73	26	32	9	6	212	253	67	36	16	14	5	1	118	122	38	37	10	18	4	5	94	131	29
Washington	166	60	82	14	10	443	516	144	83	32	38	10	3	233	243	77	83	28	44	4	7	210	273	67
Winnipeg	86	32	42	8	4	272	244	111	43	22	16	1	4	124	129	49	43	28	9	3	148	115	62
Totals	**2944**	**1205**	**1333**	**263**	**143**	**8744**	**9677**	**2816**	**1472**	**689**	**576**	**147**	**60**	**4580**	**4519**	**1585**	**1472**	**516**	**757**	**116**	**83**	**4164**	**5158**	**1231**

Playoffs

	Series	W	L	GP	W	L	T	GF	GA	Last Mtg.	Rnd.	Result
Boston	4	1	3	26	11	15	0	64	80	2009	CSF	W 4-3
Buffalo	1	1	0	7	4	3	0	22	17	2006	CF	W 4-3
Colorado	2	1	1	9	5	4	0	35	34	1987	DSF	L 2-4
Detroit	1	0	1	5	1	4	0	7	14	2002	F	L 1-4
Edmonton	1	1	0	7	4	3	0	19	16	2006	F	W 4-3
Montreal	7	2	5	39	16	23	0	106	125	2006	CQF	W 4-2
New Jersey	4	3	1	24	14	10	0	51	56	2009	CQF	W 4-2
Pittsburgh	1	0	1	4	0	4	0	9	20	2009	CF	L 0-4
Toronto	1	1	0	6	4	2	0	10	6	2002	CF	W 4-2
Totals	**22**	**10**	**12**	**127**	**59**	**68**	**0**	**323**	**368**			

Calgary totals include Atlanta Flames, 1979-80.
Dallas totals include Minnesota North Stars, 1979-80 to 1992-93.
Phoenix totals include Winnipeg, 1979-80 to 1995-96.

Colorado totals include Quebec, 1979-80 to 1994-95.
New Jersey totals include Colorado Rockies, 1979-80 to 1981-82.
Winnipeg totals include Atlanta Thrashers, 1999-2000 to 2010-11.

Playoff Results 2017-2013

(Last playoff appearance: 2009)

Abbreviations: Round: F – Final;
CF – conference final; CSF – conference semi-final;
CQF – conference quarter-final;
DSF – division semi-final.

2016-17 Results

Oct.	13	at Winnipeg	4-5*		13	Buffalo	5-2
	16	at Vancouver	3-4*		14	NY Islanders	7-4
	18	at Edmonton	2-3		17	at Columbus	1-4
	20	at Calgary	4-2		20	Pittsburgh	1-7
	22	at Philadelphia	3-6		21	at Columbus	2-3
	25	at Detroit	2-4		23	at Washington	1-6
	28	NY Rangers	3-2		26	Los Angeles	3-5
	30	Philadelphia	3-4		31	Philadelphia	5-1
Nov.	1	at Ottawa	1-2*	Feb.	3	Edmonton	2-1
	5	at Nashville	3-2†		4	at NY Islanders	5-4*
	6	New Jersey	1-4		7	at Washington	0-5
	8	at New Jersey	2-3†		11	at Dallas	2-5
	10	Anaheim	2-4		17	Colorado	1-2*
	12	Washington	5-1		19	Toronto	0-4
	15	San Jose	1-0		21	Pittsburgh	1-3
	18	Montreal	3-2		24	Ottawa	3-0
	20	Winnipeg	3-1		26	Calgary	1-3
	22	at Toronto	2-1		28	at Florida	2-3†
	24	at Montreal	1-2	Mar.	1	at Tampa Bay	3-4*
	26	at Ottawa	1-2		3	Arizona	2-4
	27	Florida	3-2		5	at Arizona	2-1
	29	at NY Rangers	2-3		7	at Colorado	1-3
Dec.	1	at Boston	1-2†		9	NY Rangers	4-3
	3	at NY Rangers	2-4		11	Toronto	2-3*
	4	Tampa Bay	1-0*		13	at NY Islanders	8-4
	7	at Anaheim	5-6†		14	NY Islanders	2-3*
	8	at Los Angeles	3-1		16	Minnesota	3-1
	10	at San Jose	3-4		18	Nashville	3-0
	13	Vancouver	8-6		19	at Philadelphia	3-4*
	16	Washington	3-4†		21	at Florida	4-3
	17	Buffalo	2-1†		23	at Montreal	4-1
	22	at Buffalo	3-1		25	at New Jersey	3-1
	23	Boston	3-2*		27	Detroit	3-4*
	28	at Pittsburgh	2-3		28	Detroit	4-1
	30	Chicago	3-2		30	Columbus	2-1*
	31	at Tampa Bay	1-3	Apr.	1	Dallas	0-3
Jan.	3	New Jersey	1-3		2	at Pittsburgh	2-3†
	5	at St. Louis	4-2		4	at Minnesota	3-5
	6	at Chicago	1-2		6	NY Islanders	0-3
	8	Boston	4-3*		8	St. Louis	4-5†
	10	Columbus	5-3		9	at Philadelphia	4-3†

* – Overtime † – Shootout

NHL Draft Selections 2017-2003

Name in bold denotes played in NHL.

2017 Pick		2014 Pick		2010 Pick		2006 Pick	
12	Martin Necas	7	Haydn Fleury	7	Jeff Skinner	63	Jamie McBain
42	Eetu Luostarinen	37	Alex Nedeljkovic	37	Justin Faulk	93	Harrison Reed
52	Luke Martin	67	Warren Foegele	53	Mark Alt	123	Bobby Hughes
67	Morgan Geekie	96	Josh Wesley	67	Danny Biega	153	Stefan Chaput
73	Stelio Mattheos	97	Lucas Wallmark	85	Austin Levi	183	Nick Dodge
104	Eetu Makiniemi	127	Clark Bishop	105	Justin Shugg	213	Justin Krueger
166	Brendan De Jong	187	Kyle Jenkins	157	Tyler Stahl		
197	Ville Rasanen			187	Frederik Andersen	**2005** Pick	
		2013 Pick				3	Jack Johnson
2016 Pick		5	Elias Lindholm	**2009** Pick		58	Nate Hagemo
13	Jake Bean	66	Brett Pesce	27	Philippe Paradis	64	Joe Barnes
21	Julien Gauthier	126	Brent Pedersen	51	Brian Dumoulin	94	Jakub Vojta
43	Janne Kuokkanen	156	Tyler Ganly	88	Mattias Lindstrom	123	Ondrej Otcenas
67	Matt Filipe			131	Matt Kennedy	145	Tim Kunes
74	Hudson Elynuik	**2012** Pick		178	Rasmus Rissanen	159	Risto Korhonen
75	Jack LaFontaine	38	Phil Di Giuseppe	208	Tommi Kivisto	192	Nicolas Blanchard
104	Max Zimmer	47	Brock McGinn			198	Kyle Lawson
134	Jeremy Helvig	69	Daniel Altshuller	**2008** Pick			
164	Noah Carroll	99	Erik Karlsson	14	Zach Boychuk	**2004** Pick	
		115	Trevor Carrick	45	Zac Dalpe	4	Andrew Ladd
2015 Pick		120	Jaccob Slavin	105	Michal Jordan	38	Justin Peters
5	Noah Hanifin	129	Brendan Woods	165	Mike Murphy	69	Casey Borer
35	Sebastian Aho	159	Collin Olson	195	Samuel Morneau	109	Brett Carson
93	Callum Booth	189	Brendan Collier			137	Magnus Akerlund
96	Nicolas Roy			**2007** Pick		202	Ryan Pottruff
126	Luke Stevens	**2011** Pick		11	Brandon Sutter	235	Jonas Fiedler
138	Spencer Smallman	12	Ryan Murphy	72	Drayson Bowman	268	Martin Vagner
156	Jake Massie	42	Victor Rask	102	Justin McCrae		
169	David Cotton	73	Keegan Lowe	132	Chris Terry	**2003** Pick	
186	Steven Lorentz	103	Gregory Hofmann	162	Brett Bellemore	2	Eric Staal
		163	Matt Mahalak			31	Danny Richmond
		193	Brody Sutter			102	Aaron Dawson
						126	Kevin Nastiuk
						130	Matej Trojovsky
						137	Tyson Strachan
						198	Shay Stephenson
						230	Jamie Hoffmann
						262	Ryan Rorabeck

General Managers' History

Jack Kelley, 1979-80; Jack Kelley and Larry Pleau, 1980-81; Larry Pleau, 1981-82, 1982-83; Emile Francis, 1983-84 to 1988-89; Eddie Johnston, 1989-90 to 1991-92; Brian Burke, 1992-93; Paul Holmgren, 1993-94; Jim Rutherford, 1994-95 to 2013-14; Ron Francis, 2014-15 to date.

Ron Francis

Executive Vice President and General Manager

Born: Sault Ste. Marie, ON, March 1, 1963.

Ron Francis was named the eighth general manager in franchise history, and just the second since the team has been located in Carolina, on April 28, 2014. He is the second person to serve as general manager after also playing for the team. Francis spent the previous eight seasons in management with Carolina, most recently serving as vice president of hockey operations. Francis is responsible for all of the team's hockey decisions and also serves as one of the teams' alternate governors.

Following a career in which he established himself as the greatest player in Hurricanes franchise history, Francis re-joined the organization in November 2006 as the team's director of player development. He was promoted to assistant general manager on October 4, 2007, but returned to the team's locker room on December 3, 2008, when he joined new head coach Paul Maurice behind the bench as associate head coach. While serving as a coach, Francis maintained a voice in the Hurricanes' front office decision-making, serving as the team's director of player personnel. He returned to the front office full-time in June 2011, accepting the role of director of hockey operations.

Francis announced his retirement as a player on September 14, 2005, following a 23-year NHL career with Hartford, Pittsburgh, Carolina and Toronto. In 1,731 NHL regular-season games, Francis scored 549 goals and earned 1,249 assists (1,798 points), to rank him fourth all-time on the league's points list behind Wayne Gretzky, Mark Messier and Gordie Howe. Francis' 1,249 assists rank second only to Gretzky (1,963), and he ranks third on the games-played list behind Howe (1,767) and Messier (1,756). The Hartford Whalers drafted Francis in the first round, fourth overall, in the 1981 NHL Draft. He played with the Whalers for 10 seasons before joining Pittsburgh at the trading deadline of the 1990-91 season, helping them win the Stanley Cup in 1991 and 1992. He spent seven full seasons with the Penguins before rejoining the organization that drafted him, when the relocated Carolina Hurricanes signed him as a free agent on July 13, 1998. In 16 seasons with the Hartford/Carolina franchise, Francis played in 1,186 games, scoring 382 goals and earning 793 assists for 1,175 points – all of which are franchise records. The Hurricanes officially retired his number 10 jersey to the arena's rafters on January 28, 2006, and on November 12, 2007, Francis was inducted into the Hockey Hall of Fame. The impact Francis had for the sport of hockey in North Carolina was further recognized on May 2, 2013, when he became the first hockey player inducted into the North Carolina Sports Hall of Fame.

Club Directory

PNC Arena

Carolina Hurricanes
1400 Edwards Mill Rd.
Raleigh, NC 27607
Phone **919/467-7825**
FAX 919/462-0123
Tickets 1.866.NHL.CANES
www.carolinahurricanes.com
Capacity: 18,680

Executive Management
Chief Executive Officer/Owner/Governor . . . . Peter Karmanos, Jr.
President . . . . Don Waddell
Chief Financial Officer . . . . Dennis Moore
Executive Vice President/General Manager . . . . Ron Francis
Executive Vice President/General Manager, PNC Arena . . Davin Olsen

Hockey Operations
Assistant GM / Dir of Hockey Ops . . . . Mike Vellucci
Assistant General Managers . . . . Ricky Olczyk, Brian Tatum
Head Coach . . . . Bill Peters
Assistant Coaches . . . . Rod Brind'Amour, Steve Smith
Goaltending Coach . . . . Mike Bales
Video Coaches . . . . Chris Huffine / L.J. Scarpace
Defensemen / Forwards Development . . . . Glen Wesley / Sergei Samsonov
Manager of Scouting . . . . Darren Yorke
Manager of Analytics / Ops Coordinator . . . . Eric Tulsky / Beth Carter
Goaltending Consultant. . . . . Curtis Joseph
Head Athletic Trainer / Assistant Athletic Trainer . . . . . Doug Bennett / Brian Maddox
Head Strength and Conditioning Coach . . . . Bill Burniston
Equipment Managers . . . . Skip Cunningham, Bob Gorman, Jorge Alves, Darren Yorke, Eric Tulsky, Beth Carter
Director of Amateur Scouting . . . . Tony MacDonald
Head North American / European Scout . . . . Sheldon Ferguson / Robert Kron
Amateur Scouts. . . . . Rob Beatty, Mike Dawson, Daniel Eklund, Don Elland, Ron Ferguson, Robert Kron, Bob Luccini, Bert Marshall, Rob Papineau, Joni Pitkanen
Manager of Pro Scouting . . . . Jeff Daniels
Pro Scout / Advisor . . . . Joe Nieuwendyk
Pro Scouts. . . . . Mark Craig, Dave Hunter, Ray Whitney
Charlotte Checkers Head Coach / Asst Coach . . . . Mike Vellucci / Peter Andersson
Charlotte Checkers Head Athletic Trainer. . . . . TBD
Charlotte Checkers Video Coach . . . . Myles Fee
Charlotte Checkers Strength & Conditioning Coach . . . . Bryn-Marc Conaway
Charlotte Checkers Equipment Managers . . . . Steve Latin, Donny White, Derek Wilkinson

Arena Operations
Vice President, Guest Relations, PNC Arena . . . . Larry Perkins
Director, Arena Marketing / Event and Guest Services. . . Crystal Pace / Barbara Nichols
Executive Asst / Customer Care Coord . . . . Sarah Woo / Kimberly Jenkins
Director, Safety and Security / Parking and Traffic. . . . . Clinton Peterson / Jared Wright
Senior Director, Premium Sales . . . . Jack Brockman
Premium Services Director / Coord . . . . Jonathan Kramer / Allyson Buckmeier
Production Director / Manager. . . . . Rob Douglas / Alfred Fought
Marketing Coordinator . . . . Lindsey Hall
Production / Event Coordinator . . . . Kim Chandler
Senior Director, Facilities and Operations . . . . Alan Wobbleton
Director / Manager / Supervisor, Operations . . . . Craig Stover / Melvin Terrell / Alan Sykes
Facilities Systems Manager. . . . . Sean Sollace
Ticket Operations Vice President / Asst. Manager . . . . . Bill Nowicki / Chris Jovino
Arena Box Office Director / Manager . . . . Joe Sousa / Erin Latore
Ice Technician / Receptionist . . . . Jared Dupre / Janet Davis

Broadcasters
Television Play-by-Play / Analyst . . . . John Forslund / Tripp Tracy
Radio Play-by-Play . . . . Chuck Kaiton
TV/Web Host. . . . . Mike Maniscalco

Communications
Vice President Communications and Team Services . . . . Mike Sundheim
Manager of Communications and Team Services . . . . . . Pace Sagester
Team Photographer. . . . . Gregg Forwerck

Finance/Information Technology
Senior Vice President/General Counsel . . . . William Traurig
Director of Finance / Senior Accountant . . . . Shaun Nicholson / Tracy Pyrak
Accounts Payable / Receivable . . . . Michael Arrington / Patty Hilliard, Temika Smith-Harris
Payroll / Human Resources. . . . . Crystal DeDitius, Keitha Stanley
Assistant to the CFO . . . . Cris Folmar
Vice President, Information Technology . . . . Glenn Johnson
Director, IT Services / Client/Server Tech., Devel. . . . . . . Myatt Williams / Larry Kelly / Jacob Doiron

Food and Beverage
Vice President, VAB Catering . . . . Chris Diamond
Director, Concessions / Director, Catering . . . . Rick Rhodes / Frankie McGee
Manager / Asst. Mgr., Suites Food and Beverage . . . . . Hollie Hawkins
Manager, F&B Financials and In-Seat Services . . . . Lori Holtz
Managers, Commissary / Catering . . . . Gary Berry / Melissa Fulkerson
Chefs . . . . Michael Flood, Dennis Atkinson, Kevin Heintz, Lecan Huynh, Pete Aiello
Concessions Manager / Asst. Manager. . . . . Jim OlBrien / Barbara Couch

Marketing
. . . . Doug Warf
Director, Marketing . . . . Mike Forman
Dir., Canesvision and In-Game Marketing. . . . . Chris Greenley
Dir., Community Relations and Promotions . . . . Jon Chase
Senior Web Producer/Writer . . . . Michael Smith
Managers, Creative Services / Digital & Social Marketing . . Lauren Baxter / Coop Elias
Coordinators, Marketing / Social Media . . . . Nikki Stoudt / Derrick Holt
Graphic Designers . . . . Kyle Fowlkes, Ashley Knappenberger
Coordinators, Youth & Amateur Hockey / Mascot . . . . . Shane Willis / George Brown
Promotions/Fan Development Coordinator . . . . Jonathan Boggs
Community Relations Coord/
Kids 'N Community Foundation Grant Specialist . . . . . . Gabby Pinto
Community Relations Coordinator . . . . Laura Fazzina

CanesVision and Wolfpack TV
Producers . . . . Nathan Hess, Zak Miklusak, Christine Williams
Graphics Producer . . . . April Caroselli

Merchandise
Director, Merchandise / Assistant, Merchandise . . . . James Blitch / Erin Murray

Sales
VP / Manager, Corporate Partnerships . . . . Jim Ballweg / Justin Buck
Senior Corporate Sales Executives . . . . Johnny Gill
Corporate Sales Executive . . . . Lane Cody, Doug Dickman, Ryan Martin
Senior Manager of Client Services . . . . Marie Bobalik
Vice President, Ticket Sales / Assistant . . . . Sara Daniel / Karen Prince, Tamara Mires
Director of Client Retention & Group Sales. . . . . Ryan Erdman
CR Database/ Database Coordinator . . . . Jenna Jones
Inside Sales Manager . . . . Dennis Fryer
Senior Business Development Account Representative . . . Greg Perna
Account Executives/Business Development . . . . . Tim Campbell, Dean Lucero, Anthony Marino, Tyler Wallace, Derek Allan, Jimmy Naughton, Jenna Jones
Client Relations Representative . . . . Christina Coleman, Michael Musialowski, Max Szilagyi, Joe Welch
Group Sales Managers, Hurricanes / PNC Arena . . . . . . Brian Kaputa / Brian Slais, Rich Davis
Group Sales Representatives . . . . Paul Friedlander, Christina Monterosso

Chicago Blackhawks

2016-17 Results: 50W-23L-8OTL-1SOL 109PTS
1ST, Central Division • 1ST, Western Conference

Key Off-Season Signings/Acquisitions

2017

May 11 • Re-signed RW **Richard Panik**.
27 • Re-signed D **Michal Kempny**.

June 15 • Named **Ulf Samuelsson** and **Don Granato** assistant coaches.
23 • Acquired D **Connor Murphy** and C **Laurent Dauphin** from Arizona for D **Niklas Hjalmarsson**.
23 • Acquired LW **Brandon Saad**, G **Anton Forsberg** and a 5th-round pick in 2018 NHL Draft from Columbus for LW **Artemi Panarin**, LW **Tyler Motte** and a 6th-round pick in 2017 NHL Draft.
27 • Re-signed D **Ville Pokka**.

July 1 • Signed LW **Patrick Sharp**, LW **Lance Bouma**, C **Tommy Wingels**, D **Jordan Oesterle** and G **Jean-Francois Berube**.
14 • Re-signed D **Erik Gustafsson**.

2017-18 Schedule

Month	Day	Date	Opponent
Oct.	Thu.	5	Pittsburgh
	Sat.	7	Columbus
	Mon.	9	at Toronto
	Tue.	10	at Montreal
	Thu.	12	Minnesota
	Sat.	14	Nashville
	Wed.	18	at St. Louis*
	Thu.	19	Edmonton
	Sat.	21	at Arizona
	Tue.	24	at Vegas
	Fri.	27	Nashville
	Sat.	28	at Colorado
Nov.	Wed.	1	Philadelphia
	Sat.	4	at Minnesota
	Sun.	5	Montreal
	Thu.	9	at Philadelphia
	Sat.	11	at Carolina
	Sun.	12	New Jersey
	Wed.	15	NY Rangers
	Sat.	18	at Pittsburgh
	Wed.	22	at Tampa Bay
	Sat.	25	at Florida
	Mon.	27	Anaheim
	Tue.	28	at Nashville
	Thu.	30	Dallas
Dec.	Sat.	2	at Dallas
	Sun.	3	Los Angeles
	Wed.	6	at Washington
	Fri.	8	Buffalo
	Sun.	10	Arizona
	Tue.	12	Florida
	Thu.	14	at Winnipeg
	Sun.	17	Minnesota
	Thu.	21	at Dallas
	Sat.	23	at New Jersey
	Thu.	28	at Vancouver
	Fri.	29	at Edmonton
	Sun.	31	at Calgary
Jan.	Wed.	3	at NY Rangers
	Fri.	5	Vegas
	Sun.	7	Edmonton*
	Tue.	9	at Ottawa
	Wed.	10	Minnesota
	Fri.	12	Winnipeg
	Sun.	14	Detroit
	Sat.	20	NY Islanders
	Mon.	22	Tampa Bay
	Wed.	24	Toronto
	Thu.	25	at Detroit
	Tue.	30	at Nashville
Feb.	Thu.	1	at Vancouver
	Sat.	3	at Calgary
	Tue.	6	Calgary
	Thu.	8	Dallas
	Sat.	10	at Minnesota
	Mon.	12	at Arizona
	Tue.	13	at Vegas
	Thu.	15	Anaheim
	Sat.	17	Washington
	Mon.	19	Los Angeles
	Wed.	21	Ottawa
	Fri.	23	San Jose
	Sat.	24	at Columbus
Mar.	Thu.	1	at San Jose
	Sat.	3	at Los Angeles*
	Sun.	4	at Anaheim*
	Tue.	6	Colorado
	Thu.	8	Carolina
	Sat.	10	at Boston*
	Sun.	11	Boston*
	Thu.	15	at Winnipeg
	Sat.	17	at Buffalo*
	Sun.	18	St. Louis
	Tue.	20	Colorado
	Thu.	22	Vancouver
	Sat.	24	at NY Islanders
	Mon.	26	San Jose
	Thu.	29	Winnipeg
	Fri.	30	at Colorado
Apr.	Wed.	4	at St. Louis*
	Fri.	6	St. Louis
	Sat.	7	at Winnipeg

* Denotes afternoon game.

Retired Numbers

1	Glenn Hall	1957-1967
3	Pierre Pilote	1955-1968
	Keith Magnuson	1969-1980
9	Bobby Hull	1957-1972
18	Denis Savard	1980-1990, 1995-1997
21	Stan Mikita	1958-1980
35	Tony Esposito	1969-1984

CENTRAL DIVISION
92nd NHL Season

Franchise date: September 25, 1926

Year-by-Year Record

		Home				Road				Overall									
Season	GP	W	L	T	OL	W	L	T	OL	W	L	T	OL	GF	GA	Pts.	Div. Fin.	Conf. Fin.	Playoff Result
2016-17	82	26	10	....	5	24	13	....	4	50	23	....	9	244	213	109	1st, Cen.	1st, West	Lost First Round
2015-16	82	26	11	....	4	21	15	....	5	47	26	....	9	235	209	103	3rd, Cen.	3rd, West	Lost First Round
2014-15	**82**	**24**	**12**	....	**5**	**24**	**16**	....	**1**	**48**	**28**	....	**6**	**229**	**189**	**102**	**3rd, Cen.**	**4th, West**	**Won Stanley Cup**
2013-14	82	27	7	....	7	19	14	....	8	46	21	....	15	267	220	107	3rd, Cen.	5th, West	Lost Conf. Final
2012-13	**48**	**18**	**3**	....	**3**	**18**	**4**	....	**2**	**36**	**7**	....	**5**	**155**	**102**	**77**	**1st, Cen.**	**1st, West**	**Won Stanley Cup**
2011-12	82	27	8	....	6	18	18	....	5	45	26	....	11	248	238	101	4th, Cen.	6th, West	Lost Conf. Quarter-Final
2010-11	82	24	17	....	0	20	12	....	9	44	29	....	9	258	225	97	3rd, Cen.	8th, West	Lost Conf. Quarter-Final
2009-10	**82**	**29**	**8**	....	**4**	**23**	**14**	....	**4**	**52**	**22**	....	**8**	**271**	**209**	**112**	**1st, Cen.**	**2nd, West**	**Won Stanley Cup**
2008-09	82	24	9	....	8	22	15	....	4	46	24	....	12	264	216	104	2nd, Cen.	4th, West	Lost Conf. Final
2007-08	82	23	16	....	2	17	18	....	6	40	34	....	8	239	235	88	3rd, Cen.	10th, West	– out of playoffs –
2006-07	82	17	20	....	4	14	22	....	5	31	42	....	9	201	258	71	5th, Cen.	13th, West	– out of playoffs –
2005-06	82	16	19	....	6	10	24	....	7	26	43	....	13	211	285	65	4th, Cen.	14th, West	– out of playoffs –
2004-05	....	....	....	....	....	....	....	....	....	....	....	....	....	....	....	....			
2003-04	82	13	17	6	5	7	26	5	3	20	43	11	8	188	259	59	5th, Cen.	15th, West	– out of playoffs –
2002-03	82	17	15	7	2	13	18	6	4	30	33	13	6	207	226	79	3rd, Cen.	9th, West	– out of playoffs –
2001-02	82	28	7	5	1	13	20	8	0	41	27	13	1	216	207	96	3rd, Cen.	5th, West	Lost Conf. Quarter-Final
2000-01	82	14	21	4	2	15	19	4	3	29	40	8	5	210	246	71	4th, Cen.	12th, West	– out of playoffs –
1999-2000	82	16	19	5	1	17	18	5	1	33	37	10	2	242	245	78	3rd, Cen.	11th, West	– out of playoffs –
1998-99	82	20	17	4	....	9	24	8	....	29	41	12	....	202	248	70	3rd, Cen.	10th, West	– out of playoffs –
1997-98	82	14	19	8	....	16	20	5	....	30	39	13	....	192	199	73	5th, Cen.	9th, West	– out of playoffs –
1996-97	82	16	21	4	....	18	14	9	....	34	35	13	....	223	210	81	5th, Cen.	8th, West	Lost Conf. Quarter-Final
1995-96	82	22	13	6	....	18	15	8	....	40	28	14	....	273	220	94	2nd, Cen.	3rd, West	Lost Conf. Semi-Final
1994-95	48	11	10	3	....	13	9	2	....	24	19	5	....	156	115	53	3rd, Cen.	4th, West	Lost Conf. Final
1993-94	84	21	16	5	....	18	20	4	....	39	36	9	....	254	240	87	5th, Cen.	6th, West	Lost Conf. Quarter-Final
1992-93	84	25	11	6	....	22	14	6	....	47	25	12	....	279	230	106	1st, Norris		Lost Div. Semi-Final
1991-92	80	23	9	8	....	13	20	7	....	36	29	15	....	257	236	87	2nd, Norris		Lost Final
1990-91	80	28	8	4	....	21	15	4	....	49	23	8	....	284	211	106	1st, Norris		Lost Div. Semi-Final
1989-90	80	25	13	2	....	16	20	4	....	41	33	6	....	316	294	88	1st, Norris		Lost Conf. Final
1988-89	80	16	14	10	....	11	27	2	....	27	41	12	....	297	335	66	4th, Norris		Lost Conf. Final
1987-88	80	21	17	2	....	9	24	7	....	30	41	9	....	284	328	69	3rd, Norris		Lost Div. Semi-Final
1986-87	80	18	13	9	....	11	24	5	....	29	37	14	....	290	310	72	3rd, Norris		Lost Div. Semi-Final
1985-86	80	23	12	5	....	16	21	3	....	39	33	8	....	351	349	86	1st, Norris		Lost Div. Semi-Final
1984-85	80	22	16	2	....	16	19	5	....	38	35	7	....	309	299	83	2nd, Norris		Lost Conf. Final
1983-84	80	25	13	2	....	5	29	6	....	30	42	8	....	277	311	68	4th, Norris		Lost Div. Semi-Final
1982-83	80	29	8	3	....	18	15	7	....	47	23	10	....	338	268	104	1st, Norris		Lost Conf. Final
1981-82	80	20	13	7	....	10	25	5	....	30	38	12	....	332	363	72	4th, Norris		Lost Conf. Final
1980-81	80	21	11	8	....	10	22	8	....	31	33	16	....	304	315	78	2nd, Smythe		Lost Prelim. Round
1979-80	80	21	12	7	....	13	15	12	....	34	27	19	....	241	250	87	1st, Smythe		Lost Quarter-Final
1978-79	80	18	12	10	....	11	24	5	....	29	36	15	....	244	277	73	1st, Smythe		Lost Quarter-Final
1977-78	80	20	9	11	....	12	20	8	....	32	29	19	....	230	220	83	1st, Smythe		Lost Quarter-Final
1976-77	80	19	16	5	....	7	27	6	....	26	43	11	....	240	298	63	3rd, Smythe		Lost Prelim. Round
1975-76	80	17	15	8	....	15	15	10	....	32	30	18	....	254	261	82	1st, Smythe		Lost Quarter-Final
1974-75	80	24	12	4	....	13	23	4	....	37	35	8	....	268	241	82	3rd, Smythe		Lost Quarter-Final
1973-74	78	20	6	13	....	21	8	10	....	41	14	23	....	272	164	105	2nd, West		Lost Semi-Final
1972-73	78	26	9	4	....	16	18	5	....	42	27	9	....	284	225	93	1st, West		Lost Final
1971-72	78	28	3	8	....	18	14	7	....	46	17	15	....	256	166	107	1st, West		Lost Semi-Final
1970-71	78	30	6	3	....	19	14	6	....	49	20	9	....	277	184	107	1st, West		Lost Final
1969-70	76	26	7	5	....	19	15	4	....	45	22	9	....	250	170	99	1st, East		Lost Semi-Final
1968-69	76	20	14	4	....	14	19	5	....	34	33	9	....	280	246	77	6th, East		– out of playoffs –
1967-68	74	20	13	4	....	12	13	12	....	32	26	16	....	212	222	80	4th, East		Lost Semi-Final
1966-67	70	24	5	6	....	17	12	6	....	41	17	12	....	264	170	94	1st		Lost Semi-Final
1965-66	70	21	8	6	....	16	17	2	....	37	25	8	....	240	187	82	2nd		Lost Semi-Final
1964-65	70	20	13	2	....	14	15	6	....	34	28	8	....	224	176	76	3rd		Lost Final
1963-64	70	26	4	5	....	10	18	7	....	36	22	12	....	218	169	84	2nd		Lost Semi-Final
1962-63	70	17	9	9	....	15	12	8	....	32	21	17	....	194	178	81	2nd		Lost Semi-Final
1961-62	70	20	10	5	....	11	16	8	....	31	26	13	....	217	186	75	3rd		Lost Final
1960-61	**70**	**20**	**6**	**9**	....	**9**	**18**	**8**	....	**29**	**24**	**17**	....	**198**	**180**	**75**	**3rd**		**Won Stanley Cup**
1959-60	70	18	11	6	....	10	18	7	....	28	29	13	....	191	180	69	3rd		Lost Semi-Final
1958-59	70	14	12	9	....	14	17	4	....	28	29	13	....	197	208	69	3rd		Lost Semi-Final
1957-58	70	15	17	3	....	9	22	4	....	24	39	7	....	163	202	55	5th		– out of playoffs –
1956-57	70	12	15	8	....	4	24	7	....	16	39	15	....	169	225	47	6th		– out of playoffs –
1955-56	70	9	19	7	....	10	20	5	....	19	39	12	....	155	216	50	6th		– out of playoffs –
1954-55	70	6	21	8	....	7	19	9	....	13	40	17	....	161	235	43	6th		– out of playoffs –
1953-54	70	8	21	6	....	4	30	1	....	12	51	7	....	133	242	31	6th		– out of playoffs –
1952-53	70	14	11	10	....	13	17	5	....	27	28	15	....	169	175	69	4th		Lost Semi-Final
1951-52	70	9	19	7	....	8	25	2	....	17	44	9	....	158	241	43	6th		– out of playoffs –
1950-51	70	8	22	5	....	5	25	5	....	13	47	10	....	171	280	36	6th		– out of playoffs –
1949-50	70	13	18	4	....	9	20	6	....	22	38	10	....	203	244	54	6th		– out of playoffs –
1948-49	60	13	12	5	....	8	19	3	....	21	31	8	....	173	211	50	5th		– out of playoffs –
1947-48	60	10	17	3	....	10	17	3	....	20	34	6	....	195	225	46	6th		– out of playoffs –
1946-47	60	10	17	3	....	9	20	1	....	19	37	4	....	193	274	42	6th		– out of playoffs –
1945-46	50	15	5	5	....	8	15	2	....	23	20	7	....	200	178	53	3rd		Lost Semi-Final
1944-45	50	9	14	2	....	4	16	5	....	13	30	7	....	141	194	33	5th		– out of playoffs –
1943-44	50	15	6	4	....	7	17	1	....	22	23	5	....	178	187	49	4th		Lost Final
1942-43	50	14	3	8	....	3	15	7	....	17	18	15	....	179	180	49	5th		– out of playoffs –
1941-42	48	15	8	1	....	7	15	2	....	22	23	3	....	145	155	47	4th		Lost Quarter-Final
1940-41	48	11	10	3	....	5	15	4	....	16	25	7	....	112	139	39	5th		Lost Semi-Final
1939-40	48	15	7	2	....	8	12	4	....	23	19	6	....	112	120	52	4th		Lost Quarter-Final
1938-39	48	5	13	6	....	7	15	2	....	12	28	8	....	91	132	32	7th		– out of playoffs –
1937-38	**48**	**10**	**10**	**4**	....	**4**	**15**	**5**	....	**14**	**25**	**9**	....	**97**	**139**	**37**	**3rd, Amn.**		**Won Stanley Cup**
1936-37	48	8	13	3	....	6	14	4	....	14	27	7	....	99	131	35	4th, Amn.		– out of playoffs –
1935-36	48	15	7	2	....	6	12	6	....	21	19	8	....	93	92	50	3rd, Amn.		Lost Quarter-Final
1934-35	48	12	9	3	....	14	8	2	....	26	17	5	....	118	88	57	2nd, Amn.		Lost Quarter-Final
1933-34	**48**	**13**	**4**	**7**	....	**7**	**13**	**4**	....	**20**	**17**	**11**	....	**88**	**83**	**51**	**2nd, Amn.**		**Won Stanley Cup**
1932-33	48	12	7	5	....	4	13	7	....	16	20	12	....	88	101	44	4th, Amn.		– out of playoffs –
1931-32	48	13	5	6	....	5	14	5	....	18	19	11	....	86	101	47	2nd, Amn.		Lost Quarter-Final
1930-31	44	13	8	1	....	11	9	2	....	24	17	3	....	108	78	51	2nd, Amn.		Lost Final
1929-30	44	12	9	1	....	9	9	4	....	21	18	5	....	117	111	47	2nd, Amn.		Lost Quarter-Final
1928-29	44	3	13	6	....	4	16	2	....	7	29	8	....	33	85	22	5th, Amn.		– out of playoffs –
1927-28	44	2	18	2	....	5	16	1	....	7	34	3	....	68	134	17	5th, Amn.		– out of playoffs –
1926-27	44	12	8	2	....	7	14	1	....	19	22	3	....	115	116	41	3rd, Amn.		Lost Quarter-Final

2017-18 Player Personnel

FORWARDS	HT	WT	*Age	Birthplace	S	2016-17 Club
ANISIMOV, Artem	6-4	198	29	Yaroslavl, Russia	L	Chicago
BOUMA, Lance	6-2	208	27	Provost, AB	L	Calgary
DAUPHIN, Laurent	6-1	180	22	Repentigny, QC	L	Arizona-Tucson
HARTMAN, Ryan	6-0	181	23	Hilton Head Island, SC	R	Chicago
HAYDEN, John	6-3	223	22	Chicago, IL	R	Yale-Chicago
HINOSTROZA, Vinnie	5-9	173	23	Chicago, IL	R	Chicago-Rockford
HOSSA, Marian	6-1	207	38	Stara Lubovna, Slovakia	L	Chicago
JURCO, Tomas	6-2	188	24	Kosice, Slovakia	L	Det-Grand Rapids-Chi
KANE, Patrick	5-11	177	28	Buffalo, NY	L	Chicago
KERO, Tanner	6-0	185	25	Hancock, MI	L	Chicago-Rockford
PANIK, Richard	6-1	208	26	Martin, Slovakia	L	Chicago
SAAD, Brandon	6-1	206	24	Pittsburgh, PA	L	Columbus
SCHMALTZ, Nick	6-0	177	21	Madison, WI	R	Chicago-Rockford
SHARP, Patrick	6-1	200	35	Winnipeg, MB	R	Dallas
TOEWS, Jonathan	6-2	201	29	Winnipeg, MB	L	Chicago
TOOTOO, Jordin	5-9	195	34	Churchill, MB	R	Chicago
WINGELS, Tommy	6-0	200	29	Evanston, IL	R	San Jose-Ottawa
DEFENSEMEN						
FORSLING, Gustav	6-0	186	21	Linkoping, Sweden	L	Chicago-Rockford
GUSTAFSSON, Erik	6-0	176	25	Nynashamn, Sweden	L	Rockford
KEITH, Duncan	6-1	192	34	Winnipeg, MB	L	Chicago
KEMPNY, Michal	6-0	194	27	Hodonin, Czech.	L	Chicago
MURPHY, Connor	6-4	212	24	Dublin, OH	R	Arizona
OESTERLE, Jordan	6-0	182	25	Dearborn Heights, MI	L	Edmonton-Bakersfield
POKKA, Ville	6-0	214	23	Tornio, Finland	R	Rockford
ROZSIVAL, Michal	6-1	210	39	Vlasim, Czech.	R	Chicago
RUTTA, Jan	6-3	200	27	Pisek, Czech.	R	Chomutov
SEABROOK, Brent	6-3	220	32	Richmond, BC	R	Chicago

GOALTENDERS	HT	WT	*Age	Birthplace	C	2016-17 Club
BERUBE, Jean-Francois	6-1	177	26	Repentigny, QC	L	NY Islanders
CRAWFORD, Corey	6-2	216	32	Montreal, QC	L	Chicago
FORSBERG, Anton	6-3	192	24	Harnosand, Sweden	L	Columbus-Cleveland

* – Age at start of 2017-18 season

Coaching History

Pete Muldoon, 1926-27; Barney Stanley and Hugh Lehman, 1927-28; Herb Gardiner and Dick Irvin, 1928-29; Tom Shaughnessy and Bill Tobin, 1929-30; Dick Irvin, 1930-31; Godfrey Matheson, 1931*; Emil Iverson, 1931-32; Emil Iverson and Tommy Gorman, 1932-33; Tommy Gorman, 1933-34; Clem Loughlin, 1934-35 to 1936-37; Bill Stewart, 1937-38; Bill Stewart and Paul Thompson, 1938-39; Paul Thompson, 1939-40 to 1943-44; Paul Thompson and Johnny Gottselig, 1944-45; Johnny Gottselig, 1945-46, 1946-47; Johnny Gottselig and Charlie Conacher, 1947-48; Charlie Conacher, 1948-49, 1949-50; Ebbie Goodfellow, 1950-51, 1951-52; Sid Abel, 1952-53, 1953-54; Frank Eddolls, 1954-55; Dick Irvin, 1955-56; Tommy Ivan, 1956-57; Tommy Ivan and Rudy Pilous, 1957-58; Rudy Pilous, 1958-59 to 1962-63; Billy Reay, 1963-64 to 1975-76; Billy Reay and Bill White, 1976-77; Bob Pulford, 1977-78, 1978-79; Eddie Johnston, 1979-80; Keith Magnuson, 1980-81; Keith Magnuson and Bob Pulford, 1981-82; Orval Tessier, 1982-83, 1983-84; Orval Tessier and Bob Pulford, 1984-85; Bob Pulford, 1985-86, 1986-87; Bob Murdoch, 1987-88; Mike Keenan, 1988-89 to 1991-92; Darryl Sutter, 1992-93 to 1994-95; Craig Hartsburg, 1995-96 to 1997-98; Dirk Graham and Lorne Molleken, 1998-99; Lorne Molleken and Bob Pulford, 1999-2000; Alpo Suhonen, 2000-01; Brian Sutter, 2001-02 to 2004-05; Trent Yawney, 2005-06; Trent Yawney and Denis Savard, 2006-07; Denis Savard, 2007-08; Denis Savard and Joel Quenneville, 2008-09; Joel Quenneville, 2009-10 to date.

* Named coach on October 14, 1931, but replaced after training camp due to health reasons.

Joel Quenneville

Head Coach

Born: Windsor, ON, September 15, 1958.

Joel Quenneville was named the 37th head coach in Chicago Blackhawks history on October 16, 2008. He has led Chicago to Stanley Cup titles 2010, 2013 and 2015. On January 14, 2016, Quenneville won his 783rd coaching victory, moving him past Al Arbour into second place in NHL coaching victories behind only Scotty Bowman. On February 21, 2017, Quenneville become the second coach in Blackhawks history to win 400 games. His 413 victories trail only Billy Reay (516) in club history. Quenneville originally joined the Blackhawks as a pro scout in September 2008. He has been a proven winner throughout his career as a head coach in the NHL, including seven seasons with the St. Louis Blues (1996 to 2004) and three with the Colorado Avalanche (2005 to 2008).

One of only two men in the history of the NHL (along with Jacques Lemaire) to have played in 800 or more games and coached 1,000 or more, Quenneville is the winningest coach in Blues history, having compiled a 307-191-95 record. He won the 2000 Jack Adams Award as the league's top coach. Quenneville was drafted by the Toronto Maple Leafs in the first round (21st overall) of the 1978 NHL Draft. He spent 13 seasons as an NHL defenseman, netting 54 goals, 136 assists, 190 points and 705 penalty minutes in 803 career games with the Toronto Maple Leafs, Colorado Rockies, New Jersey Devils, Hartford Whalers and Washington Capitals.

Quenneville retired as an active player after the 1991-92 season, when he served as a player-coach for the American Hockey League's St. John's Maple Leafs. Quenneville broke into coaching with the AHL's Springfield Indians before serving as an assistant coach for the Quebec Nordiques/Colorado Avalanche organization for two and a half seasons. He helped Colorado capture the 1996 Stanley Cup in that position before accepting his first NHL head coaching job with St. Louis for the 1996-97 campaign. Internationally, Quenneville served as an assistant coach with Team Canada at the 2016 World Cup of Hockey.

2016-17 Scoring

* – rookie

Regular Season

Pos	#	Player	Team	GP	G	A	Pts	TOI	+/–	PIM	PP	SH	GW	S	S%
R	88	Patrick Kane	CHI	82	34	55	89	21:23	11	32	7	0	5	292	11.6
C	72	Artemi Panarin	CHI	82	31	43	74	19:28	18	21	9	0	5	211	14.7
C	19	Jonathan Toews	CHI	72	21	37	58	20:09	7	35	6	0	5	199	10.6
D	2	Duncan Keith	CHI	80	6	47	53	25:37	22	16	2	0	2	183	3.3
R	81	Marian Hossa	CHI	73	26	19	45	16:51	7	8	5	1	7	167	15.6
C	15	Artem Anisimov	CHI	64	22	23	45	17:50	9	30	4	0	7	105	21.0
R	14	Richard Panik	CHI	82	22	22	44	14:44	14	58	4	0	5	155	14.2
D	7	Brent Seabrook	CHI	79	3	36	39	21:53	5	26	2	0	0	131	2.3
R	38 *	Ryan Hartman	CHI	76	19	12	31	12:46	13	70	1	0	4	170	11.2
C	8 *	Nick Schmaltz	CHI	61	6	22	28	13:15	10	6	0	0	0	66	9.1
D	4	Niklas Hjalmarsson	CHI	73	5	13	18	21:29	12	20	0	0	0	61	8.2
C	16	Marcus Kruger	CHI	70	5	12	17	14:01	7	34	0	0	0	83	6.0
D	51	Brian Campbell	CHI	80	5	12	17	18:25	12	24	2	0	1	74	6.8
C	67 *	Tanner Kero	CHI	47	6	10	16	13:29	15	8	0	0	0	60	10.0
D	57	Trevor van Riemsdyk	CHI	58	5	11	16	18:24	17	29	0	0	2	73	6.8
C	48 *	Vinnie Hinostroza	CHI	49	6	8	14	11:58	–1	17	0	0	2	76	7.9
D	27	Johnny Oduya	DAL	37	1	6	7	18:10	–2	10	0	0	0	24	4.2
			CHI	15	1	1	2	18:31	–2	8	0	0	0	13	7.7
			Total	52	2	7	9	18:16	–4	18	0	0	0	37	5.4
C	70	Dennis Rasmussen	CHI	68	4	4	8	11:49	–4	12	0	0	0	77	5.2
D	6	Michal Kempny	CHI	50	2	6	8	14:57	1	22	0	0	0	67	3.0
C	64 *	Tyler Motte	CHI	33	4	3	7	11:23	2	14	0	0	0	46	8.7
D	42 *	Gustav Forsling	CHI	38	2	3	5	14:49	3	4	0	0	0	48	4.2
C	40 *	John Hayden	CHI	12	1	3	4	11:41	3	4	0	0	0	22	4.5
R	22	Jordin Tootoo	CHI	50	2	1	3	6:44	–6	28	0	0	0	43	4.7
D	32	Michal Rozsival	CHI	22	1	2	3	15:29	–3	14	0	0	1	16	6.3
R	13	Tomas Jurco	DET	16	0	0	0	10:02	–8	2	0	0	0	12	0.0
			CHI	13	1	0	1	11:22	–4	2	0	0	0	23	4.3
			Total	29	1	0	1	10:38	–12	4	0	0	0	35	2.9
C	11	Andrew Desjardins	CHI	46	0	1	1	9:24	–6	22	0	0	0	46	0.0
L	24	Spencer Abbott	CHI	1	0	0	0	8:34	0	0	0	0	0	1	0.0

Goaltending

No.	Goaltender	GPI	Mins	Avg	W	L	OT	EN	SO	GA	SA	Sv%	G	A	PIM
33	Scott Darling	32	1689	2.38	18	5	5	1	2	67	877	.924	0	0	0
50	Corey Crawford	55	3247	2.55	32	18	4	6	2	138	1691	.918	0	1	2
	Totals	**82**	**4980**	**2.55**	**50**	**23**	**9**	**7**	**4**	**212**	**2575**	**.918**			

Playoffs

Pos	#	Player	Team	GP	G	A	Pts	TOI	+/–	PIM	PP	SH	GW	OT	S	S%
C	19	Jonathan Toews	CHI	4	1	1	2	20:33	–5	0	1	0	0	0	10	10.0
R	88	Patrick Kane	CHI	4	1	1	2	23:55	–3	2	1	0	0	0	23	4.3
C	70	Dennis Rasmussen	CHI	3	1	0	1	13:36	–2	0	0	0	0	0	5	20.0
D	2	Duncan Keith	CHI	4	0	1	1	25:33	–6	2	0	0	0	0	6	0.0
R	14	Richard Panik	CHI	4	0	1	1	15:45	–3	2	0	0	0	0	6	0.0
C	16	Marcus Kruger	CHI	4	0	1	1	15:19	–2	2	0	0	0	0	7	0.0
C	72	Artemi Panarin	CHI	4	0	1	1	20:51	–4	0	0	0	0	0	11	0.0
C	48 *	Vinnie Hinostroza	CHI	1	0	0	0	6:48	–2	0	0	0	0	0	0	0.0
C	40 *	John Hayden	CHI	1	0	0	0	5:39	0	0	0	0	0	0	0	0.0
D	6	Michal Kempny	CHI	1	0	0	0	8:51	0	0	0	0	0	0	1	0.0
R	22	Jordin Tootoo	CHI	2	0	0	0	6:13	0	0	0	0	0	0	2	0.0
R	81	Marian Hossa	CHI	4	0	0	0	19:00	–4	2	0	0	0	0	15	0.0
D	51	Brian Campbell	CHI	4	0	0	0	16:10	–2	0	0	0	0	0	2	0.0
D	27	Johnny Oduya	CHI	4	0	0	0	19:20	–3	0	0	0	0	0	3	0.0
D	7	Brent Seabrook	CHI	4	0	0	0	22:24	–3	2	0	0	0	0	7	0.0
D	4	Niklas Hjalmarsson	CHI	4	0	0	0	22:29	–4	2	0	0	0	0	1	0.0
C	15	Artem Anisimov	CHI	4	0	0	0	17:21	–2	0	0	0	0	0	6	0.0
R	38 *	Ryan Hartman	CHI	4	0	0	0	11:33	–3	14	0	0	0	0	6	0.0
D	57	Trevor van Riemsdyk	CHI	4	0	0	0	19:02	–4	0	0	0	0	0	9	0.0
C	8 *	Nick Schmaltz	CHI	4	0	0	0	15:22	–2	2	0	0	0	0	2	0.0
C	67 *	Tanner Kero	CHI	4	0	0	0	13:38	–2	0	0	0	0	0	4	0.0

Goaltending

No.	Goaltender	GPI	Mins	Avg	W	L	EN	SO	GA	SA	Sv%	G	A	PIM
50	Corey Crawford	4	254	2.83	0	4	1	0	12	123	.902	0	0	0
	Totals	**4**	**257**	**3.04**	**0**	**4**	**1**	**0**	**13**	**124**	**.895**			

Coaching Record

			Regular Season				Playoffs			
Season	Team	League	GC	W	L	O/T	GC	W	L	T
1993-94	Springfield	AHL	80	29	38	13	6	2	4	....
1996-97	**St. Louis**	**NHL**	**40**	**18**	**15**	**7**	**6**	**2**	**4**	....
1997-98	**St. Louis**	**NHL**	**82**	**45**	**29**	**8**	**10**	**6**	**4**	....
1998-99	**St. Louis**	**NHL**	**82**	**37**	**32**	**13**	**13**	**6**	**7**	....
99-2000	**St. Louis**	**NHL**	**82**	**51**	**19**	**12**	**7**	**3**	**4**	....
2000-01	**St. Louis**	**NHL**	**82**	**43**	**22**	**17**	**15**	**9**	**6**	....
2001-02	**St. Louis**	**NHL**	**82**	**43**	**27**	**12**	**10**	**5**	**5**	....
2002-03	**St. Louis**	**NHL**	**82**	**41**	**24**	**17**	**7**	**3**	**4**	....
2003-04	**St. Louis**	**NHL**	**61**	**29**	**23**	**9**	....	....	....	....
2004-05	**Colorado**				SEASON CANCELLED					
2005-06	**Colorado**	**NHL**	**82**	**43**	**30**	**9**	**9**	**4**	**5**	....
2006-07	**Colorado**	**NHL**	**82**	**44**	**31**	**7**	....	....	....	....
2007-08	**Colorado**	**NHL**	**82**	**44**	**31**	**7**	**10**	**4**	**6**	....
2008-09	**Chicago**	**NHL**	**78**	**45**	**22**	**11**	**17**	**9**	**8**	....
2009-10♦	**Chicago**	**NHL**	**82**	**52**	**22**	**8**	**22**	**16**	**6**	....
2010-11	**Chicago**	**NHL**	**82**	**44**	**29**	**9**	**7**	**3**	**4**	....
2011-12	**Chicago**	**NHL**	**82**	**45**	**26**	**11**	**6**	**2**	**4**	....
2012-13♦	**Chicago**	**NHL**	**48**	**36**	**7**	**5**	**23**	**16**	**7**	....
2013-14	**Chicago**	**NHL**	**82**	**46**	**21**	**15**	**19**	**11**	**8**	....
2014-15♦	**Chicago**	**NHL**	**82**	**48**	**28**	**6**	**23**	**16**	**7**	....
2015-16	**Chicago**	**NHL**	**82**	**47**	**26**	**9**	**7**	**3**	**4**	....
2016-17	**Chicago**	**NHL**	**82**	**50**	**23**	**9**	**4**	**0**	**4**	....
	NHL Totals		**1539**	**851**	**487**	**201**	**215**	**118**	**97**	....

♦ Stanley Cup win.
Jack Adams Award (2000)
Assistant coach Mike Haviland posted a 3-1-0 record as replacement coach when Joel Quenneville was sidelined with an ulcer, February 16 to 23, 2011. All games are credited to Quenneville's coaching record.

Club Records

Team

(Figures in brackets for season records are games played; records for fewest points, wins, ties, losses, goals, goals against are for 70 or more games)

Most Points	**112**	2009-10 (82)
Most Wins	**52**	2009-10 (82)
Most Ties	**23**	1973-74 (78)
Most Losses	**56**	2005-06 (82)
Most Goals	**351**	1985-86 (80)
Most Goals Against	**363**	1981-82 (80)
Fewest Points	**31**	1953-54 (70)
Fewest Wins	**12**	1953-54 (70)
Fewest Ties	**6**	1989-90 (80)
Fewest Losses	**14**	1973-74 (78)
Fewest Goals	***133**	1953-54 (70)
Fewest Goals Against	**164**	1973-74 (78)
Longest Winning Streak		
Overall	**12**	Dec. 29/15-Jan. 19/16
Home	**13**	Nov. 11-Dec. 20/70
Away	**8**	Feb. 2-Mar. 4/17
Longest Team Point Streak		
Overall	**15**	Jan. 14-Feb. 16/67 (12W, 3T), Oct. 29-Dec. 3/75 (6W, 9T)
Home	**18**	Oct. 11-Dec. 20/70 (16W, 2T)
Away	**12**	Nov. 2-Dec. 16/67 (6W, 6T)
Longest Losing Streak		
Overall	**12**	Feb. 25-Mar. 25/51
Home	**10**	Jan. 29-Mar. 21/28
Away	**19**	Nov. 10/03-Jan. 29/04
Longest Winless Streak		
Overall	**21**	Dec. 17/50-Jan. 28/51 (18L, 3T)
Home	**15**	Dec. 16/28-Feb. 28/29 (11L, 4T)
Away	**22**	Dec. 19/50-Mar. 25/51 (20L, 2T)
Most Shutouts, Season	**15**	1969-70 (76)
Most PIM, Season	**2,663**	1991-92 (80)
Most Goals, Game	**12**	Jan. 30/69 (Chi. 12 at Phi. 0)

Individual

Most Seasons	**22**	Stan Mikita
Most Games	**1,394**	Stan Mikita
Most Goals, Career	**604**	Bobby Hull
Most Assists, Career	**926**	Stan Mikita
Most Points, Career	**1,467**	Stan Mikita (541G, 926A)
Most PIM, Career	**1,495**	Chris Chelios
Most Shutouts, Career	**74**	Tony Esposito
Longest Consecutive Games Streak	**884**	Steve Larmer (Oct. 6/82-Apr. 15/93)
Most Goals, Season	**58**	Bobby Hull (1968-69)
Most Assists, Season	**87**	Denis Savard (1981-82, 1987-88)
Most Points, Season	**131**	Denis Savard (1987-88; 44G, 87A)
Most PIM, Season	**408**	Mike Peluso (1991-92)
Most Points, Defenseman, Season	**85**	Doug Wilson (1981-82; 39G, 46A)
Most Points, Center, Season	**131**	Denis Savard (1987-88; 44G, 87A)
Most Points, Right Wing, Season	**106**	Patrick Kane (2015-16; 46G, 60A)
Most Points, Left Wing, Season	**107**	Bobby Hull (1968-69; 58G, 49A)
Most Points, Rookie, Season	**90**	Steve Larmer (1982-83; 43G, 47A)
Most Shutouts, Season	**15**	Tony Esposito (1969-70)
Most Goals, Game	**5**	Grant Mulvey (Feb. 3/82)
Most Assists, Game	**6**	Pat Stapleton (Mar. 30/69)
Most Points, Game	**7**	Max Bentley (Jan. 28/43; 4G, 3A), Grant Mulvey (Feb. 3/82; 5G, 2A)

* NHL Record.

General Managers' History

Major Frederic McLaughlin, 1926-27 to 1931-32; Major Frederic McLaughlin and Tommy Gorman, 1932-33; Tommy Gorman, 1933-34; Clem Loughlin, 1934-35, 1935-36; Bill Tobin, 1936-37 to 1953-54; Tommy Ivan, 1954-55 to 1976-77; Bob Pulford, 1977-78 to 1989-90; Mike Keenan, 1990-91, 1991-92; Mike Keenan and Bob Pulford, 1992-93; Bob Pulford, 1993-94 to 1996-97; Bob Murray, 1997-98, 1998-99; Bob Murray and Bob Pulford, 1999-2000; Mike Smith, 2000-01 to 2002-03; Mike Smith and Bob Pulford, 2003-04; Bob Pulford, 2004-05; Dale Tallon, 2005-06 to 2008-09; Stan Bowman, 2009-10 to date.

All-time Record vs. Other Clubs

Regular Season

	Total								At Home								On Road							
	GP	W	L	T	OL	GF	GA	PTS	GP	W	L	T	OL	GF	GA	PTS	GP	W	L	T	OL	GF	GA	PTS
Anaheim	89	37	44	5	3	208	223	82	46	21	20	2	3	114	107	47	43	16	24	3	0	94	116	35
Arizona	141	70	47	15	9	483	396	164	69	38	16	10	5	252	172	91	72	32	31	5	4	231	224	73
Boston	586	242	263	79	2	1773	1841	565	294	150	97	45	2	950	796	347	292	92	166	34	0	823	1045	218
Buffalo	119	53	52	13	1	352	368	120	59	34	18	6	1	194	154	75	60	19	34	7	0	158	214	45
Calgary	167	75	60	26	6	521	482	182	83	41	26	13	3	271	227	98	84	34	34	13	3	250	255	84
Carolina	73	35	30	7	1	242	217	78	36	21	11	3	1	136	97	46	37	14	19	4	0	106	120	32
Colorado	130	58	54	9	9	419	438	134	66	34	23	3	6	216	198	77	64	24	31	6	3	203	240	57
Columbus	81	47	25	2	7	273	223	103	40	25	12	1	2	128	92	53	41	22	13	1	5	145	131	50
Dallas	273	137	102	31	3	921	826	308	135	79	41	15	0	495	366	173	138	58	61	16	3	426	460	135
Detroit	733	282	356	84	11	2020	2277	659	368	169	141	51	7	1102	1036	396	365	113	215	33	4	918	1241	263
Edmonton	132	65	50	12	5	465	443	147	66	35	20	7	4	246	214	81	66	30	30	5	1	219	229	66
Florida	35	21	9	3	2	111	85	47	18	11	4	2	1	59	45	25	17	10	5	1	1	52	40	22
Los Angeles	192	93	75	17	7	628	576	210	97	50	36	9	2	323	265	111	95	43	39	8	5	305	311	99
Minnesota	66	27	29	1	9	173	187	64	32	14	14	1	3	84	88	32	34	13	15	0	6	89	99	32
Montreal	563	157	299	103	4	1426	1856	421	280	100	125	55	0	756	774	255	283	57	174	48	4	670	1082	166
Nashville	105	55	38	4	8	304	300	122	53	32	18	1	2	156	140	67	52	23	20	3	6	148	160	55
New Jersey	109	49	36	21	3	364	313	122	54	29	14	10	1	203	147	69	55	20	22	11	2	161	166	53
NY Islanders	110	49	39	20	2	349	364	120	56	32	18	5	1	188	177	70	54	17	21	15	1	161	187	50
NY Rangers	587	248	238	98	3	1709	1666	597	294	131	117	43	3	884	808	308	293	117	121	55	0	825	858	289
Ottawa	32	20	9	2	1	91	86	43	15	10	3	2	0	41	33	22	17	10	6	0	1	50	53	21
Philadelphia	136	46	59	30	1	405	417	123	67	30	18	19	0	233	189	79	69	16	41	11	1	172	228	44
Pittsburgh	133	72	42	17	2	471	397	163	67	45	11	10	1	261	169	101	66	27	31	7	1	210	228	62
St. Louis	306	147	114	35	10	1008	927	339	154	89	42	18	5	553	433	201	152	58	72	17	5	455	494	138
San Jose	94	41	40	5	8	272	274	95	47	25	17	2	3	149	140	55	47	16	23	3	5	123	134	40
Tampa Bay	40	17	12	5	6	114	106	45	21	12	6	2	1	62	48	27	19	5	6	3	5	52	58	18
Toronto	647	265	286	96	0	1846	1939	626	325	163	120	42	0	998	845	368	322	102	166	54	0	848	1094	258
Vancouver	186	87	67	22	10	587	504	206	92	56	23	7	6	323	225	125	94	31	44	15	4	264	279	81
Washington	95	42	39	11	3	316	311	98	47	26	13	6	2	177	138	60	48	16	26	5	1	139	173	38
Winnipeg	31	19	12	0	0	90	79	38	15	7	8	0	0	35	35	14	16	12	4	0	0	55	44	24
Defunct Clubs	279	131	107	41	0	724	614	303	139	79	40	20	0	408	268	178	140	52	67	21	0	316	346	125
Totals	**6270**	**2687**	**2633**	**814**	**136**	**18665**	**18735**	**6324**	**3135**	**1588**	**1072**	**410**	**65**	**9997**	**8426**	**3651**	**3135**	**1099**	**1561**	**404**	**71**	**8668**	**10309**	**2673**

Playoffs

	Series	W	L	GP	W	L	T	GF	GA	Last Mtg.	Rnd.	Result
Anaheim	1	1	0	7	4	3	0	24	22	2015	CF	W 4-3
Arizona	1	0	1	6	2	4	0	12	17	2012	CQF	L 2-4
Boston	7	2	5	28	9	18	1	80	112	2013	F	W 4-2
Buffalo	2	0	2	9	1	8	0	17	36	1980	QF	L 0-4
Calgary	4	2	2	18	9	9	0	54	53	2009	CQF	W 4-2
Colorado	2	0	2	12	4	8	0	28	49	1997	CQF	L 2-4
Dallas	6	4	2	33	19	14	0	120	118	1991	DSF	L 2-4
Detroit	16	9	7	81	43	38	0	236	224	2013	CSF	W 4-3
Edmonton	4	1	3	20	8	12	0	77	102	1992	CF	W 4-0
Los Angeles	3	2	1	17	11	6	0	47	46	2014	CF	L 3-4
Minnesota	3	3	0	15	12	3	0	45	27	2015	SR	W 4-0
Montreal	17	5	12	81	29	50	2	185	261	1976	QF	L 0-4
Nashville	3	2	1	16	8	8	0	39	49	2017	FR	L 0-4
NY Islanders	2	0	2	6	0	6	0	6	21	1979	QF	L 0-4
NY Rangers	5	4	1	24	14	10	0	66	54	1973	SF	W 4-1
Philadelphia	2	2	0	10	8	2	0	45	30	2010	F	W 4-2
Pittsburgh	2	1	1	8	4	4	0	24	23	1992	F	L 0-4
St. Louis	12	8	4	63	35	28	0	211	175	2016	FR	L 3-4
San Jose	1	1	0	4	4	0	0	13	7	2010	CF	W 4-0
Tampa Bay	1	1	0	6	4	2	0	13	10	2015	F	W 4-2
Toronto	9	3	6	38	15	22	1	89	111	1995	CQF	W 4-3
Vancouver	5	3	2	28	16	12	0	92	77	2011	CQF	L 3-4
Defunct Clubs	4	2	2	9	5	3	1	16	15			
Totals	**112**	**56**	**56**	**539**	**264**	**270**	**5**	**1539**	**1639**			

Playoff Results 2017-2013

Year	Round	Opponent	Result	GF	GA
2017	FR	Nashville	L 0-4	3	13
2016	FR	St. Louis	L 3-4	20	19
2015	**F**	**Tampa Bay**	**W 4-2**	**13**	**10**
	CF	Anaheim	W 4-3	24	22
	SR	Minnesota	W 4-0	13	7
	FR	Nashville	W 4-2	19	21
2014	CF	Los Angeles	L 3-4	23	28
	SR	Minnesota	W 4-2	15	13
	FR	St. Louis	W 4-2	20	14
2013	**F**	**Boston**	**W 4-2**	**17**	**15**
	CF	Los Angeles	W 4-1	14	11
	CSF	Detroit	W 4-3	16	15
	CQF	Minnesota	W 4-1	17	7

Abbreviations: Round: F – Final;
CF – conference final; **CSF** – conference semi-final;
SR – second round; **CQF** – conference quarter-final;
FR – first round; **DSF** – division semi-final;
SF – semi-final; **QF** – quarter-final.

Calgary totals include Atlanta Flames, 1972-73 to 1979-80.
Carolina totals include Hartford, 1979-80 to 1996-97.
Colorado totals include Quebec, 1979-80 to 1994-95.
Dallas totals include Minnesota North Stars, 1967-68 to 1992-93.
New Jersey totals include Kansas City, 1974-75, 1975-76, and Colorado Rockies, 1976-77 to 1981-82.
Phoenix totals include Winnipeg, 1979-80 to 1995-96.
Winnipeg totals include Atlanta Thrashers, 1999-2000 to 2010-11.

2016-17 Results

Oct.	12	St. Louis	2-5
	14	at Nashville	2-3
	15	Nashville	5-3
	18	Philadelphia	7-4
	21	at Columbus	2-3
	22	Toronto	5-4†
	24	Calgary	2-3†
	28	at New Jersey	3-2*
	30	Los Angeles	3-0
Nov.	1	Calgary	5-1
	3	Colorado	4-0
	5	at Dallas	3-2
	6	Dallas	4-3*
	9	at St. Louis	2-1*
	11	Washington	2-3*
	13	Montreal	3-2
	15	at Winnipeg	0-4
	18	at Calgary	3-2
	19	at Vancouver	4-3*
	21	at Edmonton	0-5
	23	at San Jose	1-2
	25	at Anaheim	3-2
	26	at Los Angeles	1-2*
	29	Florida	2-1†
Dec.	1	New Jersey	4-3*
	3	at Philadelphia	1-3
	4	Winnipeg	1-2
	6	Arizona	4-0
	9	NY Rangers	0-1*
	11	Dallas	3-1
	13	at NY Rangers	2-1
	15	at NY Islanders	5-4
	17	at St. Louis	6-4
	18	San Jose	4-1
	20	Ottawa	3-4
	23	Colorado	1-2*
	27	Winnipeg	1-3
	29	at Nashville	3-2
	30	at Carolina	2-3
Jan.	2	at St. Louis	1-4
	5	Buffalo	4-3*
	6	Carolina	2-1
	8	Nashville	5-2
	10	Detroit	4-3*
	13	at Washington	0-6
	15	Minnesota	2-3
	17	at Colorado	6-4
	20	at Boston	1-0
	22	Vancouver	4-2
	24	Tampa Bay	2-5
	26	Winnipeg	3-5
	31	at San Jose	1-3
Feb.	2	at Arizona	4-3
	4	at Dallas	5-3
	8	at Minnesota	4-3*
	10	at Winnipeg	5-2
	11	at Edmonton	5-1
	18	Edmonton	1-3
	19	at Buffalo	5-1
	21	at Minnesota	5-3
	23	Arizona	6-3
	26	St. Louis	4-2
Mar.	1	Pittsburgh	4-1
	3	NY Islanders	2-1†
	4	at Nashville	5-3
	9	Anaheim	0-1
	10	at Detroit	2-4
	12	Minnesota	4-2
	14	at Montreal	4-2
	16	at Ottawa	2-1
	18	at Toronto	2-1*
	19	Colorado	6-3
	21	Vancouver	4-5*
	23	Dallas	3-2†
	25	at Florida	0-7
	27	at Tampa Bay	4-5*
	29	at Pittsburgh	5-1
	31	Columbus	3-1
Apr.	2	Boston	2-3
	4	at Colorado	3-4*
	6	at Anaheim	0-4
	8	at Los Angeles	2-3*

* – Overtime † – Shootout

NHL Draft Selections 2017-2003

Name in bold denotes played in NHL.

2017 Pick		2013 Pick		2009 Pick		2005 Pick	
29	Henri Jokiharju	30	**Ryan Hartman**	28	**Dylan Olsen**	7	**Jack Skille**
57	Ian Mitchell	51	Carl Dahlstrom	59	**Brandon Pirri**	43	**Mike Blunden**
70	Andrei Altybarmakyan	74	**John Hayden**	89	Dan Delisle	54	Dan Bertram
90	Evan Barratt	111	Robin Norell	119	**Byron Froese**	68	**Evan Brophey**
112	Tim Soderlund	121	**Tyler Motte**	149	**Marcus Kruger**	108	**Niklas Hjalmarsson**
119	Roope Laavainen	134	Luke Johnson	177	David Pacan	113	Nathan Davis
144	Parker Foo	181	Anthony Louis	195	Paul Phillips	117	Denis Istomin
150	Jakub Galvas	211	Robin Press	209	David Gilbert	134	Brennan Turner
215	Josh Ess					167	Joe Fallon
						188	Joe Charlebois
2016 Pick		**2012** Pick		**2008** Pick		202	David Kuchejda
39	Alexander DeBrincat	18	**Teuvo Teravainen**	11	Kyle Beach	203	Adam Hobson
45	Chad Krys	48	Dillon Fournier	68	**Shawn Lalonde**		
50	Artur Kayumov	79	Chris Calnan	132	Teigan Zahn	**2004** Pick	
83	Wouter Peeters	139	Garret Ross	162	Jonathan Carlsson	3	**Cam Barker**
110	Lucas Carlsson	149	Travis Brown	169	**Ben Smith**	32	**Dave Bolland**
113	Nathan Noel	169	**Vincent Hinostroza**	179	Braden Birch	41	**Bryan Bickell**
143	Mathias From	191	Brandon Whitney	192	Joe Gleason	45	Ryan Garlock
173	Blake Hillman	199	Matt Tomkins			54	Jakub Sindel
203	Jake Ryczek			**2007** Pick		68	**Adam Berti**
		2011 Pick		1	**Patrick Kane**	120	Mitch Maunu
2015 Pick		18	**Mark McNeill**	38	**Bill Sweatt**	123	Karel Hromas
54	Graham Knott	26	**Phillip Danault**	56	**Akim Aliu**	131	Trevor Kell
91	Dennis Gilbert	36	**Adam Clendening**	69	Maxime Tanguay	140	**Jake Dowell**
121	Ryan Shea	43	**Brandon Saad**	86	Josh Unice	165	Scott McCulloch
151	Radovan Bondra	70	**Michael Paliotta**	126	Joe Lavin	196	**Petri Kontiola**
164	Roy Radke	79	**Klas Dahlbeck**	156	Richard Greenop	214	**Troy Brouwer**
181	Joni Tuulola	109	Maxim Shalunov			223	Jared Walker
211	John Dahlstrom	139	**Andrew Shaw**	**2006** Pick		229	Eric Hunter
		169	Sam Jardine	3	**Jonathan Toews**	256	Matthew Ford
2014 Pick		199	Alex Broadhurst	33	Igor Makarov	260	Marko Anttila
20	**Nick Schmaltz**	211	Johan Mattsson	61	Simon Danis-Pepin		
83	Matt Iacopelli			76	Tony Lagerstrom	**2003** Pick	
88	Beau Starrett	**2010** Pick		95	Ben Shutron	14	**Brent Seabrook**
98	Fredrik Olofsson	24	**Kevin Hayes**	96	Joe Palmer	52	**Corey Crawford**
141	Luc Snuggerud	35	Ludvig Rensfeldt	156	Jan-Mikael Juutilainen	59	**Michal Barinka**
148	Andreas Soderberg	54	Justin Holl	169	Chris Auger	151	**Lasse Kukkonen**
178	Dylan Sikura	58	**Kent Simpson**	186	**Peter Leblanc**	156	Alexei Ivanov
179	Ivan Nalimov	60	**Stephen Johns**			181	Johan Andersson
208	Jack Ramsey	90	**Joakim Nordstrom**			211	**Mike Brodeur**
		120	Rob Flick			245	**Dustin Byfuglien**
		151	Mirko Hoefflin			275	Michael Grenzy
		180	Nick Mattson			282	**Chris Porter**
		191	Mac Carruth				

Captains' History

Dick Irvin, 1926-27 to 1928-29; Duke Dukowski, 1929-30; Ty Arbour, 1930-31; Cy Wentworth, 1931-32; Helge Bostrom and Teddy Graham, 1932-33; Charlie Gardiner, 1933-34; no captain, 1934-35; Johnny Gottselig, 1935-36 to 1939-40; Earl Seibert, 1940-41, 1941-42; Doug Bentley, 1942-43, 1943-44; Clint Smith 1944-45; John Mariucci, 1945-46; Red Hamill, 1946-47; John Mariucci, 1947-48; Gaye Stewart, 1948-49; Doug Bentley, 1949-50; Jack Stewart, 1950-51, 1951-52; Bill Gadsby, 1952-53, 1953-54; Gus Mortson, 1954-55 to 1956-57; no captain, 1957-58; Ed Litzenberger, 1958-59 to 1960-61; Pierre Pilote, 1961-62 to 1967-68, no captain, 1968-69; Pat Stapleton, 1969-70; no captain, 1970-71 to 1974-75; Stan Mikita and Pit Martin, 1975-76; Stan Mikita, Pit Martin and Keith Magnuson, 1976-77; Keith Magnuson, 1977-78, 1978-79; Keith Magnuson and Terry Ruskowski, 1979-80; Terry Ruskowski, 1980-81, 1981-82; Darryl Sutter, 1982-83 to 1984-85; Darryl Sutter and Bob Murray, 1985-86; Darryl Sutter, 1986-87; no captain, 1987-88; Denis Savard and Dirk Graham, 1988-89; Dirk Graham, 1989-90 to 1994-95; Chris Chelios, 1995-96 to 1998-99; Doug Gilmour, 1999-2000; Tony Amonte, 2000-01, 2001-02; Alex Zhamnov, 2002-03, 2003-04; Adrian Aucoin and Martin Lapointe, 2005-06, 2006-07; no captain, 2007-08; Jonathan Toews, 2008-09 to date.

Stan Bowman

Senior Vice President and General Manager

Born: Montreal, QC, June 28, 1973.

Stan Bowman was named general manager of the Chicago Blackhawks on July 14, 2009. In his first season on the job in 2009-10, the Blackhawks won the Stanley Cup for the first time since 1961. They won it again in 2013 and 2015. Prior to being named to the position, Bowman had served for eight years in the Blackhawks operations department.

Bowman originally joined the Blackhawks in 2001, serving for four seasons as special assistant to the G.M. before being promoted to director of hockey operations from 2005 to 2007. As assistant G.M. from 2007 to 2009, Bowman attended to the day-to-day administration of the hockey operations department including contract negotiations, free agency, salary arbitration, player movement and player assignment. He also tracked the progress of the Blackhawks prospects at the club's minor league affiliate in Rockford, Illinois and assisted with player evaluation, prospect development and scouting.

Bowman graduated from the University of Notre Dame in 1995 with degrees in Finance and Computer Applications. He was born in Montreal where his father, current Blackhawks senior advisor and Hall of Fame member Scotty Bowman, was coaching at the time.

Club Directory

United Center

Chicago Blackhawks
United Center
1901 W. Madison Street
Chicago, IL 60612
Phone **312/455-7000**
FAX 312/455-7042
www.chicagoblackhawks.com
Capacity: 19,717

Chairman	W. Rockwell "Rocky" Wirtz
President & CEO	John F. McDonough
Executive Vice President	Jay Blunk
Senior Vice President/General Manager	Stan Bowman
Senior Vice President, Hockey Operations	Al MacIsaac
Vice President, Amateur Scouting	Mark Kelley
Vice President, Ticketing and Customer Relations	Chris Werner
Vice President, Finance	T.J. Skattum
Vice President, Marketing	Pete Hassen
Vice President, Human Resources	Marie Sutera
Vice President, Corporate Sponsorships	Steve Waight
Vice President, Communications	Adam Rogowin
Vice President, Digital Content	Adam Kempenaar
Assistant General Manager	Norm Maciver

Coaching Staff

Head Coach	Joel Quenneville
Assistant Coaches	Kevin Dineen, Don Granato, Ulf Samuelsson
Goaltending Coach	Jimmy Waite
Video Coach	Matt Meacham
Strength and Conditioning Coach	Paul Goodman
Skating and Skills Development	Kevin Delaney
Development Coaches	Christian Burrus, Yanic Perreault, Derek Plante, Anders Sorensen, Mikael Samuelsson (European)

Training/Equipment Staff

Athletic Trainers, Head / Assistant	Mike Gapski / Jeff Thomas
Massage Therapist	Pawel Prylinski
Equipment Manager / Asst. Manager / Assistants	Troy Parchman / Jim Heintzelman / D.J. Kogut, Jeff Uyeno

Medical

Head Team Physician, Orthopedics	Dr. Michael Terry
Team Physicians	Drs. George Chiampas, Angelo Costas, Lou Hiotis, Bradley Merk
Team Dentists	DDS Russ Baer, Martin Marcus, Michael Marcus
Mental Skills Coaches	James Gary, David Marks
Nutritionist	Julie Burns
Chiropractors	Brian Allen, Stuart Yoss

Hockey Operations and Scouting

Senior Advisor, Hockey Operations	Scotty Bowman
Senior Director, Minor League Affiliations	Mark Bernard
Director, Player Personnel	Pierre Gauthier
Directors, Player Development / Pro Scouting	Mark Eaton / Ryan Stewart
Directors, Player Evaluation / Recruitment	Barry Smith / Ron Anderson
Senior Director, Team Services	Tony Ommen
Manager, Player Development	Ian Gentile
Hockey Ops Manager / Assistant	Kyle Davidson / Lyle Gregory
Player Recruitment	Rick Comley
Head Western Canada Scout	Darrell May
Head Eastern Canada Scout	Jim McKellar
Head USA Scout	Mike Doneghey
Amateur Scouts	Rob Facca, Kirt Hill, Peter Nevin, Andrei Nikolishin, Alexandre Rouleau
European Scouting, Director / Head / Scout	Mats Hallin / Niklas Blomgren / Karel Pavlik, Peter Sundstrom
Pro Scouts	Matt Bardsley, Derek Booth, Wade Brookbank, Alex Brooks, Gord Donnelly, Michael Grier, Richard Kromm, Don Lever, Mike MacPherson, Michel Mottau, Allan Power, Anatoly Semenov, Tom Younghans
Goaltending Scout	Dan Ellis
Scouting Coordinator	Hudson Chodos
Director, Team Security	Brian Higgins
Hockey Analytics/Video Analyst	Andrew Contis

Communications

Director, Media Relations / PR Manager	John Steinmiller / Lyndsey Stroope
Coordinator, Media Relations	Nate Haeni
Assistant, Media Relations	Will Chukerman

Broadcasters

Television Play-By-Play / Analyst / Studio Host	Pat Foley / Eddie Olczyk / Steve Konroyd
Radio Play-By-Play / Analyst / Studio Host	John Wiedeman / Troy Murray / Judd Sirott

Marketing, Fan Development and Community Relations

Foundation Director	Tovah McCord
GM, Community Ice Arena	Andrea Hahn
Director / Assistants, Community Relations	Ashley Hinton / Sara Olson, Meghan Pollock
Charitable Partnerships Manager	Kelly Doody
Sr. Director / Manager, Fan Development	Annie Camins / Spencer Montgomery
Assistants, Fan Development	Laura Jordan, Samantha Ratty
Director, Merchandising	Laura Clawson
Director, Production and Content Marketing	A.J. Dolan
Manager, Game Presentation	Mike Horn
Mascot Coordinator	Joe Doyle
Sr. Manager / Assistant, Events Marketing	Brian Howe / Paul Unruh
Sr. Manager / Assistants, Marketing	Brian Dahm / Amber Hughes, Corinne Harris
Community Liaison / Special Advisor, Bus./Hockey Ops.	Jamal Mayers / Brian Campbell

Finance

Director of Finance	Michael Dorsch
Payroll Director / Accounting Manager	Patricia Walsh / Andrew LeFevour

Human Resources

Sr. Manager / Coordinator, H.R. & Office Admin.	Kyleen Howe / Leanne Mayville
Manager, Executive Projects	Jillian Smith
Exec. Asst. to Sr. VP/GM & Hockey Ops	Meghan Hunter
Business Operations Executive Coordinator	Molly Connelly
Receptionist	Lauren Bozzi

Corporate Sponsorships

Director	Sara Bailey
Sr. Manager, Client Services	Kelly Smith
Client Service Managers / Coordinator	Kayla Roan, Brian Szubrych / Dan Cluchey
Sr. Manager / Manager / Account Exec	Greg Zinsmeister / Ryan Gallante / Phil Carden

Digital Content

Creative Director / Social Media Manager	John Sandberg / Leah Hendrickson
Manager, Team Photography	Chase Agnello-Dean
Sr. Graphic Designer / Graphic Designer	Sean Grady / Missy Wilson
Digital Content Coordinator / Analyst / Assistant	Emerald Gao / Chris Levine / Leah Pascarella
Reporter, New Media / Team Historian	Eric Lear / Bob Verdi

Tickets Ops, Customer Relations, Arena Ops

Exec. Director, Ticket Operations	Jim Bare
Exec. Director / Sr. Manager, Ticket Sales and Service	Dan Rozenblat / T.R. Johnson
Directors, Service and Retention / Group Sales	Julie Lovins / Steve DiLenardi
Coordinator, Ticket Operations	Allison Ferrara
Sr. Account Exec, Ticket Sales	Andrew Roan, Jake Tuton
Account Execs., Youth Hockey / Ticket Sales	Matt Brooks / Kevin Kowynia
Sr. Execs., Customer Service	Neil Desmond, Lindsay Dresser, Kevin LeClair, Kathie Raimondi, Shilpa Rupani
Customer Service Execs.	Rebecca Goldstein, Josh Helton, Heather Larson, Shannon Pyrz, Rebecca Roy, Connor Spurlin

Colorado Avalanche

2016-17 Results: 22w-56l-2otl-2sol 48pts
7th, Central Division • 14th, Western Conference

Nathan MacKinnon played in all 82 games for Colorado in 2016-17 for the first time since his Calder Trophy-winning season in 2013-14. He led the team in scoring for the first time in his career.

2017-18 Schedule

Oct.	Thu.	5	at NY Rangers
	Sat.	7	at New Jersey
	Mon.	9	at Boston*
	Wed.	11	Boston
	Fri.	13	Anaheim
	Sat.	14	at Dallas
	Tue.	17	at Nashville
	Thu.	19	St. Louis
	Tue.	24	Dallas
	Fri.	27	at Vegas*
	Sat.	28	Chicago
Nov.	Thu.	2	Carolina
	Sat.	4	at Philadelphia
	Sun.	5	at NY Islanders
	Fri.	10	Ottawa†
	Sat.	11	at Ottawa†
	Thu.	16	Washington
	Sat.	18	at Nashville
	Sun.	19	at Detroit
	Wed.	22	Dallas
	Fri.	24	at Minnesota*
	Sat.	25	Calgary
	Wed.	29	Winnipeg
Dec.	Fri.	1	New Jersey
	Sun.	3	Dallas
	Tue.	5	Buffalo
	Thu.	7	at Tampa Bay
	Sat.	9	at Florida
	Mon.	11	at Pittsburgh
	Tue.	12	at Washington
	Thu.	14	Florida
	Sat.	16	Tampa Bay
	Mon.	18	Pittsburgh
	Thu.	21	at Los Angeles
	Sat.	23	at Arizona
	Wed.	27	Arizona
	Fri.	29	Toronto
	Sun.	31	NY Islanders
Jan.	Tue.	2	Winnipeg
	Thu.	4	Columbus
	Sat.	6	Minnesota*

	Sat.	13	at Dallas
	Mon.	15	Anaheim*
	Thu.	18	San Jose
	Sat.	20	NY Rangers*
	Mon.	22	at Toronto
	Tue.	23	at Montreal
	Thu.	25	at St. Louis*
	Tue.	30	at Vancouver
Feb.	Thu.	1	at Edmonton
	Sat.	3	at Winnipeg
	Tue.	6	San Jose
	Thu.	8	at St. Louis*
	Sat.	10	at Carolina
	Sun.	11	at Buffalo
	Wed.	14	Montreal
	Fri.	16	at Winnipeg
	Sun.	18	Edmonton*
	Tue.	20	at Vancouver
	Thu.	22	at Edmonton
	Sat.	24	at Calgary*
	Mon.	26	Vancouver
	Wed.	28	Calgary
Mar.	Fri.	2	Minnesota
	Sun.	4	Nashville*
	Tue.	6	at Chicago
	Thu.	8	at Columbus
	Sat.	10	Arizona*
	Tue.	13	at Minnesota
	Thu.	15	at St. Louis*
	Fri.	16	Nashville
	Sun.	18	Detroit*
	Tue.	20	at Chicago
	Thu.	22	Los Angeles
	Sat.	24	Vegas*
	Mon.	26	at Vegas
	Wed.	28	Philadelphia
	Fri.	30	Chicago
Apr.	Sun.	1	at Anaheim
	Mon.	2	at Los Angeles
	Thu.	5	at San Jose
	Sat.	7	St. Louis

* Denotes afternoon game.
† Game played in Stockholm, Sweden.

Retired Numbers

3	J.C. Tremblay*	1972-1979°
8	Marc Tardif*	1974-1983°
16	Michel Goulet*	1979-1990
19	Joe Sakic	1988-2009
21	Peter Forsberg	1994-04, 07-08, 2010-11
26	Peter Stastny*	1980-1990
33	Patrick Roy	1995-2003
52	Adam Foote	1991-04, 08-11
77	Raymond Bourque	2000-2001

* Quebec Nordiques   ° Includes WHA

CENTRAL DIVISION
39th NHL Season

Franchise date: June 22, 1979

Transferred from Quebec to Denver, June 21, 1995.

Year-by-Year Record

		Home				Road				Overall									
Season	GP	W	L	T	OL	W	L	T	OL	W	L	T	OL	GF	GA	Pts.	Div. Fin.	Conf. Fin.	Playoff Result
2016-17	82	13	26	....	2	9	30	....	2	22	56	....	4	166	278	48	7th, Cen.	14th, West	– out of playoffs –
2015-16	82	17	20	....	4	22	19	....	0	39	39	....	4	216	240	82	6th, Cen.	9th, West	– out of playoffs –
2014-15	82	23	15	....	3	16	16	....	9	39	31	....	12	219	227	90	7th, Cen.	11th, West	– out of playoffs –
2013-14	82	26	11	....	4	26	11	....	4	52	22	....	8	250	220	112	1st, Cen.	2nd, West	Lost First Round
2012-13	48	12	9	....	3	4	16	....	4	16	25	....	7	116	152	39	5th, NW	15th, West	– out of playoffs –
2011-12	82	22	17	....	2	19	18	....	4	41	35	....	6	208	220	88	3rd, NW	11th, West	– out of playoffs –
2010-11	82	16	21	....	4	14	23	....	4	30	44	....	8	227	288	68	4th, NW	14th, West	– out of playoffs –
2009-10	82	24	14	....	3	19	16	....	6	43	30	....	9	244	233	95	2nd, NW	8th, West	Lost Conf. Quarter-Final
2008-09	82	18	21	....	2	14	24	....	3	32	45	....	5	199	257	69	5th, NW	15th, West	– out of playoffs –
2007-08	82	27	12	....	2	17	19	....	5	44	31	....	7	231	219	95	2nd, NW	6th, West	Lost Conf. Semi-Final
2006-07	82	22	16	....	3	22	15	....	4	44	31	....	7	272	251	95	4th, NW	9th, West	– out of playoffs –
2005-06	82	25	10	....	6	18	20	....	3	43	30	....	9	283	257	95	2nd, NW	7th, West	Lost Conf. Semi-Final
2004-05	....																		
2003-04	82	19	14	6	2	21	8	7	5	40	22	13	7	236	198	100	2nd, NW	4th, West	Lost Conf. Semi-Final
2002-03	82	21	9	8	3	21	10	15	5	42	19	13	8	251	194	105	1st, NW	3rd, West	Lost Conf. Quarter-Final
2001-02	82	24	12	4	1	21	16	4	0	45	28	8	1	212	169	99	1st, NW	2nd, West	Lost Conf. Final
2000-01	82	28	6	5	2	24	10	5	2	52	16	10	4	270	192	118	1st, NW	**1st, West**	**Won Stanley Cup**
1999-2000	82	25	12	4	0	17	16	7	1	42	28	11	1	233	201	96	1st, NW	3rd, West	Lost Conf. Final
1998-99	82	21	14	6	....	23	14	4	....	44	28	10	....	239	205	98	1st, NW	2nd, West	Lost Conf. Final
1997-98	82	21	10	10	....	18	16	7	....	39	26	17	....	231	205	95	1st, Pac.	4th, West	Lost Conf. Quarter-Final
1996-97	82	26	10	5	....	23	14	4	....	49	24	9	....	277	205	107	1st, Pac.	1st, West	Lost Conf. Final
1995-96	82	24	10	7	....	23	15	3	....	47	25	10	....	326	240	104	1st, Pac.	2nd, West	**Won Stanley Cup**
1994-95*	48	19	1	4	....	11	12	1	....	30	13	5	....	185	134	65	1st, NE	1st, East	Lost Conf. Quarter-Final
1993-94*	84	19	17	6	....	15	17	10	....	34	42	8	....	277	292	76	5th, NE	11th, East	– out of playoffs –
1992-93*	84	23	17	2	....	24	10	8	....	47	27	10	....	351	300	104	2nd, Adams		Lost Div. Semi-Final
1991-92*	80	18	19	3	....	2	29	9	....	20	48	12	....	255	318	52	5th, Adams		– out of playoffs –
1990-91*	80	9	23	8	....	7	27	6	....	16	50	14	....	236	354	46	5th, Adams		– out of playoffs –
1989-90*	80	8	24	8	....	4	35	1	....	12	61	7	....	240	407	31	5th, Adams		– out of playoffs –
1988-89*	80	16	20	4	....	11	26	3	....	27	46	7	....	269	342	61	5th, Adams		– out of playoffs –
1987-88*	80	15	23	2	....	17	20	3	....	32	43	5	....	271	306	69	5th, Adams		– out of playoffs –
1986-87*	80	20	13	7	....	11	26	3	....	31	39	10	....	267	276	72	4th, Adams		Lost Div. Final
1985-86*	80	23	13	4	....	20	18	2	....	43	31	6	....	330	289	92	1st, Adams		Lost Div. Semi-Final
1984-85*	80	23	14	3	....	18	17	5	....	41	30	9	....	323	275	91	2nd, Adams		Lost Div. Final
1983-84*	80	24	11	5	....	18	17	5	....	42	28	10	....	360	278	94	3rd, Adams		Lost Div. Final
1982-83*	80	23	10	7	....	11	24	5	....	34	34	12	....	343	336	80	4th, Adams		Lost Div. Semi-Final
1981-82*	80	24	13	3	....	9	18	13	....	33	31	16	....	356	345	82	4th, Adams		Lost Conf. Final
1980-81*	80	18	11	11	....	12	21	7	....	30	32	18	....	314	318	78	4th, Adams		Lost Prelim. Round
1979-80*	80	17	16	7	....	8	28	4	....	25	44	11	....	248	313	61	5th, Adams		– out of playoffs –

* Quebec Nordiques

2017-18 Player Personnel

FORWARDS

	HT	WT	*Age	Birthplace	S	2016-17 Club
AGOZZINO, Andrew	5-10	187	26	Kleinburg, ON	L	Chicago (AHL)
ANDRIGHETTO, Sven	5-10	188	24	Zurich, Switz.	L	Mtl-St. John's-Col
BEAUDIN, J.C.	6-1	185	20	Longueuil, QC	R	Rouyn-Noranda
BOURQUE, Gabriel	5-10	206	27	Rimouski, QC	L	Colorado-San Antonio
COLBORNE, Joe	6-5	221	27	Calgary, AB	L	Colorado
COMEAU, Blake	6-1	202	31	Meadow Lake, SK	R	Colorado
COMPHER, J.T.	6-0	193	22	Northbrook, IL	R	Colorado-San Antonio
DUCHENE, Matt	5-11	195	26	Haliburton, ON	L	Colorado
GIRARD, Felix	5-10	197	23	Levis, QC	R	Milwaukee-San Antonio
GREER, A.J.	6-3	204	20	Joliette, QC	L	Colorado-San Antonio
GRIMALDI, Rocco	5-6	180	24	Anaheim, CA	R	Colorado-San Antonio
JOST, Tyson	5-11	191	19	St. Albert, AB	L	North Dakota-Colorado
LANDESKOG, Gabriel	6-1	215	24	Stockholm, Sweden	L	Colorado
MacKINNON, Nathan	6-0	205	22	Halifax, NS	L	Colorado
NANTEL, Julien	6-0	193	21	Laval, QC	L	San Antonio-Colorado
NIETO, Matt	5-11	190	24	Long Beach, CA	L	San Jose-Colorado
PETRYK, Reid	6-1	205	24	Edmonton, AB	R	San Antonio
RANTANEN, Mikko	6-4	211	20	Nousiainen, Finland	L	Colorado-San Antonio
SODERBERG, Carl	6-3	210	31	Malmo, Sweden	L	Colorado
VOGELHUBER, Trent	6-2	185	29	Dublin, OH	R	San Antonio
WILSON, Colin	6-1	221	27	Greenwich, CT	L	Nashville
YAKUPOV, Nail	5-11	195	23	Nizhnekamsk, Russia	L	St. Louis

DEFENSEMEN

	HT	WT	*Age	Birthplace	S	2016-17 Club
BARBERIO, Mark	6-1	207	27	Montreal, QC	L	Mtl-St. John's-Col
BARRIE, Tyson	5-10	190	26	Victoria, BC	R	Colorado
BIGRAS, Chris	6-1	190	22	Orillia, ON	L	San Antonio
BOIKOV, Sergei	6-2	200	21	Khabarovsk, Russia	L	San Antonio-Colorado
GEERTSEN, Mason	6-4	215	22	Drayton Valley, AB	L	San Antonio-Colorado
GRAHAM, Jesse	6-0	184	23	Oshawa, ON	R	Bridgeport-Missouri
JOHNSON, Erik	6-4	225	29	Bloomington, MN	R	Colorado
LINDHOLM, Anton	5-11	191	22	Skelleftea, Sweden	L	Colorado-San Antonio
MELOCHE, Nicolas	6-3	204	20	LaSalle, QC	R	Gatineau-Charlottetown
MIRONOV, Andrei	6-3	194	23	Moscow, Russia	L	Dynamo Moscow
SIEMENS, Duncan	6-3	210	24	Edmonton, AB	L	Colorado-San Antonio
TYUTIN, Fedor	6-2	221	34	Izhevsk, USSR	L	Colorado
WARSOFSKY, David	5-9	170	27	Marshfield, MA	L	Pittsburgh-Wilkes-Barre
ZADOROV, Nikita	6-5	230	22	Moscow, Russia	L	Colorado

GOALTENDERS

	HT	WT	*Age	Birthplace	C	2016-17 Club
BERNIER, Jonathan	6-0	184	29	Laval, QC	L	Anaheim
CANNATA, Joe	6-1	200	27	Wakefield, MA	L	Her-South Carolina-San Antonio
MARTIN, Spencer	6-3	210	22	Oakville, ON	L	Colorado-San Antonio
VARLAMOV, Semyon	6-2	209	29	Kuybyshev, USSR	L	Colorado

* – Age at start of 2017-18 season

2016-17 Scoring

* – rookie

Regular Season

Pos	#	Player	Team	GP	G	A	Pts	TOI	+/-	PIM	PP	SH	GW	S	S%
C	29	Nathan MacKinnon	COL	82	16	37	53	19:56	-14	16	2	2	4	251	6.4
C	9	Matt Duchene	COL	77	18	23	41	18:18	-34	12	3	1	3	160	11.3
R	96	* Mikko Rantanen	COL	75	20	18	38	18:03	-25	22	4	0	2	133	15.0
D	4	Tyson Barrie	COL	74	7	31	38	23:18	-34	18	1	0	2	182	3.8
L	92	Gabriel Landeskog	COL	72	18	15	33	18:46	-25	62	5	1	2	169	10.7
R	10	Sven Andrighetto	MTL	27	2	6	8	11:28	1	4	0	0	0	31	6.5
			COL	19	5	11	16	17:29	0	8	2	0	0	37	13.5
			Total	46	7	17	24	13:58	1	12	2	0	0	68	10.3
C	25	Mikhail Grigorenko	COL	75	10	13	23	14:05	-14	18	0	0	1	85	11.8
L	14	Blake Comeau	COL	77	8	12	20	14:59	-19	58	2	1	1	103	7.8
R	17	Rene Bourque	COL	65	12	6	18	13:56	-19	56	2	0	2	111	10.8
D	32	Francois Beauchemin	COL	81	5	13	18	21:30	-14	32	0	0	1	132	3.8
D	6	Erik Johnson	COL	46	2	15	17	22:04	-6	9	0	0	1	96	2.1
C	34	Carl Soderberg	COL	80	6	8	14	13:26	-26	22	1	0	0	128	4.7
L	83	Matt Nieto	S.J.	16	0	2	2	12:12	-3	4	0	0	0	24	0.0
			COL	43	7	4	11	15:56	-9	4	0	0	1	61	11.5
			Total	59	7	6	13	14:55	-12	8	0	0	1	85	8.2
D	45	Mark Barberio	MTL	26	0	4	4	15:07	1	10	0	0	0	28	0.0
			COL	34	2	7	9	20:39	-6	4	1	0	0	52	3.8
			Total	60	2	11	13	18:15	-5	14	1	0	0	80	2.5
D	51	Fedor Tyutin	COL	69	1	12	13	18:56	-25	38	0	0	0	46	2.2
D	28	Patrick Wiercioch	COL	57	4	8	12	16:39	-18	23	0	0	0	63	6.3
D	16	Nikita Zadorov	COL	56	0	10	10	19:02	-20	73	0	0	0	61	0.0
C	8	Joe Colborne	COL	62	4	4	8	10:41	-21	34	2	0	0	48	8.3
C	7	John Mitchell	COL	65	3	4	7	12:33	-12	45	0	0	1	57	5.3
L	37	* J.T. Compher	COL	21	3	2	5	14:55	0	4	1	0	1	30	10.0
D	18	Cody Goloubef	COL	33	0	5	5	16:59	-11	25	0	0	0	35	0.0
R	42	* Samuel Henley	COL	1	1	0	1	5:18	1	2	0	0	0	1	100.0
C	27	* Tyson Jost	COL	6	1	0	1	15:40	-5	0	0	0	0	9	11.1
C	22	Rocco Grimaldi	COL	4	0	1	1	11:00	-3	2	0	0	0	11	0.0
L	46	* A.J. Greer	COL	5	0	1	1	13:39	-2	4	0	0	0	8	0.0
D	44	Eric Gelinas	COL	27	0	1	1	11:34	-4	12	0	0	0	29	0.0
D	15	* Duncan Siemens	COL	9	0	0	0	12:18	-2	2	0	0	0	4	0.0
L	57	Gabriel Bourque	COL	6	0	0	0	11:12	0	0	0	0	0	4	0.0
D	54	* Anton Lindholm	COL	12	0	0	0	14:45	-8	2	0	0	0	7	0.0

Goaltending

No.	Goaltender	GPI	Mins	Avg	W	L	OT	EN	SO	GA	SA	Sv%	G	A	PIM
31	Calvin Pickard	50	2820	2.98	15	31	2	7	2	140	1461	.904	0	2	2
1	Semyon Varlamov	24	1348	3.38	6	17	0	5	1	76	745	.898	0	1	0
40	Jeremy Smith	10	543	3.54	1	6	1	3	0	32	286	.888	0	0	0
30	* Spencer Martin	3	179	4.36	0	2	1	0	0	13	96	.865	0	0	0
	Totals	82	4954	3.34	22	56	4	15	3	276	2603	.894			

Joe Sakic
Executive Vice President/General Manager
Born: Burnaby, BC, July 7, 1969.

Former Avalanche captain Joe Sakic was named executive vice president of hockey operations on May 10, 2013 and was given responsibility for overseeing all hockey-related decisions. The Avalanche won the 2013-14 Central Division championship and tied a franchise record with 52 wins. On September 19, 2014, the Avalanche officially announced that Sakic was the club's new general manager.

Sakic announced his retirement from the NHL on July 9, 2009, following a career that spanned 20 seasons and 1,378 games with the same organization. He wore the 'C' as team captain for 16 consecutive seasons (17 seasons overall), making him the second-longest serving captain in NHL history. Sakic led the Avalanche to two Stanley Cup titles (1996, 2001) including the city of Denver's first major professional sports championship in 1996. He captured the franchise's first Hart Trophy as league MVP in 2001, won the Conn Smythe Trophy as playoff MVP in 1996, earned the Lester B. Pearson Award (NHLPA MVP) and Lady Byng Trophy (sportsmanship) in 2001 and was named to the NHL's First All-Star Team on three occasions (2001, 2002 and 2004).

Sakic was elected to the Hockey Hall of Fame in 2012, his first year of eligibility. Selected by the Quebec Nordiques in the first round (15th overall) of the 1987 NHL Draft, he retired as the eighth-highest scorer in NHL history with 1,641 career points. He ranked seventh all-time in both playoff goals (84) and playoff points (188-tied), and still holds the NHL record for postseason overtime goals with eight.

Jared Bednar
Head Coach
Born: Yorkton, SK, February 28, 1972.

Jared Bednar was named head coach of the Colorado Avalanche on August 25, 2016. He is the seventh head coach of the Avalanche and the 15th in franchise history. This is his first NHL coaching position. Bednar spent the previous two seasons as a head coach in the American Hockey League. He guided the Columbus Blue Jackets' AHL affiliate, the Lake Erie Monsters, to the 2016 Calder Cup championship. The Monsters finished second in the Central Division with a 43-22-6-5 record (97 points) and then proceeded to go 15-2 during the postseason, sweeping both the Western Conference Final and Calder Cup Final.

Prior to leading the Monsters to their title, Bednar served as the head coach of the Blue Jackets' previous AHL affiliate, the Springfield Falcons, in 2014-15. He also spent two seasons as the head coach of the AHL's Peoria Rivermen from 2010 to 2012. Bednar began his coaching career as an assistant with the South Carolina Stingrays of the ECHL in 2002-03. He took over the Stingrays' head coaching job in 2007-08 and in his second season led South Carolina to the 2009 Kelly Cup as ECHL champions. Bednar was also an AHL assistant coach with Abbotsford in 2009-10 and Springfield from 2012 to 2014.

Prior to his time behind the bench, Bednar played nine seasons of professional hockey in a career that spanned parts of six seasons in the ECHL, with the Huntington Blizzard and South Carolina Stingrays (1993 to 2002), parts of three seasons in the AHL, with the St. John's Maple Leafs and Rochester Americans (1996 to 2000), and one season in the International Hockey League, with the Grand Rapids Griffins in 1998-99. The defenseman was part of two Kelly Cup championship teams as a player, 1997 and 2001, with South Carolina. Before turning pro, Bednar spent three seasons in the Western Hockey League from 1990 to 1993, competing with the Saskatoon Blades, Spokane Chiefs, Medicine Hat Tigers and Prince Albert Raiders.

Coaching Record

Season	Team	League	Regular Season				Playoffs			
			GC	W	L	O/T	GC	W	L	T
2007-08	South Carolina	ECHL	72	47	22	3	20	10	10	....
2008-09	South Carolina	ECHL	71	42	23	6	23	16	7	....
2010-11	Peoria	AHL	80	42	30	8	4	0	4	....
2011-12	Peoria	AHL	76	39	33	4	....	....	....	....
2014-15	Springfield	AHL	76	38	28	10	....	....	....	....
2015-16	Lake Erie	AHL	76	43	22	11	17	15	2	....
2016-17	**Colorado**	**NHL**	82	22	56	4	....	....	....	....
	NHL Totals		82	22	56	4	....	....	....	....

Club Records

Team

(Figures in brackets for season records are games played; records for fewest points, wins, ties, losses, goals, goals against are for 70 or more games)

Most Points **118** 2000-01 (82)
Most Wins **52** 2000-01 (82), 2013-14 (82)
Most Ties **18** 1980-81 (80)
Most Losses **61** 1989-90 (80)
Most Goals **360** 1983-84 (80)
Most Goals Against **407** 1989-90 (80)
Fewest Points **31** 1989-90 (80)
Fewest Wins **12** 1989-90 (80)
Fewest Ties **5** 1987-88 (80)
Fewest Losses **16** 2000-01 (82)
Fewest Goals **166** 2016-17 (82)
Fewest Goals Against **169** 2001-02 (82)

Longest Winning Streak
Overall .... **12** Jan. 10-Feb. 7/99
Home .... **10** Nov. 26/83-Jan. 10/84, Mar. 6-Apr. 16/95
Away .... **7** Jan. 10-Feb. 7/99

Longest Team Point Streak
Overall .... **12** Dec. 23/96-Jan. 20/97 (9W, 3T), Jan. 10-Feb. 7/99 (12W)
Home .... **14** Nov. 19/83-Jan. 21/84 (11W, 3T)
Away .... **10** Jan. 10-Mar. 3/99 (8W, 2T)

Longest Losing Streak
Overall .... **14** Oct. 21-Nov. 19/90
Home .... **10** Nov. 23-Dec. 31/16
Away .... **18** Jan. 18-Apr. 1/90

Longest Winless Streak
Overall .... **17** Oct. 21-Nov. 25/90 (15L, 2T)
Home .... **11** Nov. 14-Dec. 26/89 (7L, 4T)
Away .... **33** Oct. 8/91-Feb. 27/92 (25L, 8T)

Most Shutouts, Season **11** 2001-02 (82)
Most PIM, Season **2,104** 1989-90 (80)
Most Goals, Game .... **12** Feb. 1/83 (Hfd. 3 at Que. 12), Oct. 20/84 (Que. 12 at Tor. 3), Dec. 5/95 (S.J. 2 at Col. 12)

Individual

Most Seasons .... **20** Joe Sakic
Most Games .... **1,378** Joe Sakic
Most Goals, Career .... **625** Joe Sakic
Most Assists, Career .... **1,016** Joe Sakic
Most Points, Career .... **1,641** Joe Sakic (625G, 1,016A)
Most PIM, Career .... **1,562** Dale Hunter
Most Shutouts, Career .... **37** Patrick Roy
Longest Consecutive Games Streak .... **312** Dale Hunter (Oct. 9/80-Mar. 13/84)
Most Goals, Season .... **57** Michel Goulet (1982-83)
Most Assists, Season .... **93** Peter Stastny (1981-82)
Most Points, Season .... **139** Peter Stastny (1981-82; 46G, 93A)
Most PIM, Season .... **301** Gord Donnelly (1987-88)
Most Points, Defenseman, Season .... **82** Steve Duchesne (1992-93; 20G, 62A)
Most Points, Center, Season .... **139** Peter Stastny (1981-82; 46G, 93A)
Most Points, Right Wing, Season .... **103** Jacques Richard (1980-81; 52G, 51A)
Most Points, Left Wing, Season .... **121** Michel Goulet (1983-84; 56G, 65A)
Most Points, Rookie, Season .... **109** Peter Stastny (1980-81; 39G, 70A)
Most Shutouts, Season .... **9** Patrick Roy (2001-02)
Most Goals, Game .... **5** Mats Sundin (Mar. 5/92), Mike Ricci (Feb. 17/94)
Most Assists, Game .... **5** Eight times
Most Points, Game .... **8** Peter Stastny (Feb. 22/81; 4G, 4A), Anton Stastny (Feb. 22/81; 3G, 5A)

Records include Quebec Nordiques, 1979-80 through 1994-95.

All-time Record vs. Other Clubs

Regular Season

	Total								At Home								On Road							
	GP	W	L	T	OL	GF	GA	PTS	GP	W	L	T	OL	GF	GA	PTS	GP	W	L	T	OL	GF	GA	PTS
Anaheim	85	38	31	7	9	226	233	92	42	20	17	4	1	117	117	45	43	18	14	3	8	109	116	47
Arizona	124	59	47	12	6	404	408	136	62	31	22	5	4	203	197	71	62	28	25	7	2	201	211	65
Boston	142	55	72	15	0	459	543	125	73	26	41	6	0	249	295	58	69	29	31	9	0	210	248	67
Buffalo	141	60	59	20	2	482	480	142	71	37	22	11	1	256	215	86	70	23	37	9	1	226	265	56
Calgary	158	65	71	20	2	493	523	152	79	35	32	11	1	264	252	82	79	30	39	9	1	229	271	70
Carolina	142	73	45	21	3	529	432	170	72	45	17	9	1	299	207	100	70	28	28	12	2	230	225	70
Chicago	130	63	53	9	5	438	419	140	64	34	21	6	3	240	203	77	66	29	32	3	2	198	216	63
Columbus	55	37	14	1	3	186	113	78	28	19	8	0	1	98	62	39	27	18	6	1	2	88	51	39
Dallas	132	63	48	12	9	423	385	147	66	38	16	7	5	234	164	88	66	25	32	5	4	189	221	59
Detroit	121	50	61	5	5	362	409	110	61	26	27	4	4	192	201	60	60	24	34	1	1	170	208	50
Edmonton	158	74	72	8	4	522	560	160	80	41	34	4	1	279	270	87	78	33	38	4	3	243	290	73
Florida	37	21	10	3	3	120	106	48	18	8	6	3	1	50	47	20	19	13	4	0	2	70	59	28
Los Angeles	128	54	61	8	5	434	449	121	63	32	27	3	1	239	208	68	65	22	34	5	4	195	241	53
Minnesota	94	43	39	3	9	246	248	98	47	23	20	2	2	124	118	50	47	20	19	1	7	122	130	48
Montreal	141	56	70	15	0	461	532	127	70	37	28	5	0	237	236	79	71	19	42	10	0	224	296	48
Nashville	74	31	32	5	6	203	220	73	38	18	16	2	2	97	103	40	36	13	16	3	4	106	117	33
New Jersey	86	42	35	8	1	282	272	93	42	24	14	4	0	145	108	52	44	18	21	4	1	137	164	41
NY Islanders	81	39	36	4	2	270	273	84	42	25	12	3	2	144	112	55	39	14	24	1	0	126	161	29
NY Rangers	84	38	39	7	0	279	309	83	42	22	17	3	0	162	153	47	42	16	22	4	0	117	156	36
Ottawa	47	28	15	4	0	183	137	60	22	16	5	1	0	95	68	33	25	12	10	3	0	88	69	27
Philadelphia	84	30	38	14	2	257	288	76	43	18	12	12	1	150	143	49	41	12	26	2	1	107	145	27
Pittsburgh	84	39	35	7	3	328	314	88	40	20	16	2	2	161	147	44	44	19	19	5	1	167	167	44
St. Louis	131	59	57	11	4	395	395	133	67	37	21	7	2	221	174	83	64	22	36	4	2	174	221	50
San Jose	90	44	34	5	7	283	254	100	44	25	13	4	2	148	108	56	46	19	21	1	5	135	146	44
Tampa Bay	41	22	14	3	2	130	104	49	21	14	4	2	1	75	49	31	20	8	10	1	1	55	55	18
Toronto	78	39	29	9	1	285	254	88	36	19	12	5	0	133	122	43	42	20	17	4	1	152	132	45
Vancouver	158	72	62	15	9	508	478	168	79	37	29	8	5	248	226	87	79	35	33	7	4	260	252	81
Washington	81	31	41	9	0	244	290	71	41	17	19	5	0	122	141	39	40	14	22	4	0	122	149	32
Winnipeg	37	17	14	1	5	99	106	40	19	10	6	0	3	54	50	23	18	7	8	1	2	45	56	17
Totals	**2944**	**1342**	**1234**	**261**	**107**	**9531**	**9534**	**3052**	**1472**	**754**	**534**	**138**	**46**	**5036**	**4496**	**1692**	**1472**	**588**	**700**	**123**	**61**	**4495**	**5038**	**1360**

Playoffs

	Series	W	L	GP	W	L	T	GF	GA	Last Mtg.	Rnd.	Result
Anaheim	1	0	1	4	0	4	0	4	16	2006	CSF	L 0-4
Arizona	1	1	0	5	4	1	0	17	10	2000	CQF	W 4-1
Boston	2	1	1	11	5	6	0	36	37	1983	DSF	L 1-3
Buffalo	2	2	0	8	6	2	0	35	27	1985	DSF	W 3-2
Carolina	2	1	1	9	4	5	0	34	35	1987	DSF	W 4-2
Chicago	2	2	0	12	8	4	0	49	28	1997	CQF	W 4-2
Dallas	4	2	2	24	14	10	0	66	62	2006	CQF	W 4-1
Detroit	6	3	3	34	17	17	0	88	97	2008	CSF	L 0-4
Edmonton	2	1	1	12	7	5	0	35	30	1998	CQF	L 3-4
Florida	1	1	0	4	4	0	0	15	4	1996	F	W 4-0
Los Angeles	2	2	0	14	8	6	0	33	23	2002	CQF	W 4-3
Minnesota	3	1	2	20	10	10	0	54	50	2014	FR	L 3-4
Montreal	5	2	3	31	14	17	0	85	105	1993	DSF	L 2-4
New Jersey	1	1	0	7	4	3	0	19	11	2001	F	W 4-3
NY Islanders	1	0	1	4	0	4	0	9	18	1982	CF	L 0-4
NY Rangers	1	0	1	6	2	4	0	19	25	1995	CQF	L 2-4
Philadelphia	2	0	2	11	4	7	0	29	39	1985	CF	L 2-4
St. Louis	1	1	0	5	4	1	0	17	11	2001	CF	W 4-1
San Jose	4	2	2	25	12	13	0	62	71	2010	CQF	L 2-4
Vancouver	2	2	0	10	8	2	0	40	26	2001	CQF	W 4-0
Totals	**45**	**25**	**20**	**256**	**135**	**121**	**0**	**746**	**725**			

Playoff Results 2017-2013

Year	Round	Opponent	Result	GF	GA
2014	FR	Minnesota	L 3-4	20	22

Abbreviations: Round: F – Final; **CF** – conference final; **CSF** – conference semi-final; **CQF** – conference quarter-final; **FR** – first round; **DSF** – division semi-final.

Calgary totals include Atlanta Flames, 1979-80.
Dallas totals include Minnesota North Stars, 1979-80 to 1992-93.
Phoenix totals include Winnipeg, 1979-80 to 1995-96.
Carolina totals include Hartford, 1979-80 to 1996-97.
New Jersey totals include Colorado Rockies, 1979-80 to 1981-82.
Winnipeg totals include Atlanta Thrashers, 1999-2000 to 2010-11.

2016-17 Results

Oct.	15	Dallas	6-5		17	Chicago	4-6
	17	at Pittsburgh	4-3*		19	at Anaheim	1-2
	18	at Washington	0-3		21	at San Jose	2-3*
	20	at Tampa Bay	4-0		23	San Jose	2-5
	22	at Florida	2-5		25	Vancouver	2-3
	28	Winnipeg	0-1		31	at Anaheim	1-5
	29	at Arizona	3-2	**Feb.**	1	at Los Angeles	0-5
Nov.	1	Nashville	1-5		4	Winnipeg	5-2
	3	at Chicago	0-4		7	Montreal	4-0
	5	Minnesota	1-0		9	Pittsburgh	1-4
	6	at St. Louis	1-5		11	at NY Rangers	2-4
	8	Arizona	2-4		12	at NY Islanders	1-5
	11	Winnipeg	3-2*		14	at New Jersey	2-3
	13	Boston	0-2		16	at Buffalo	0-2
	15	Los Angeles	4-1		17	at Carolina	2-1*
	17	at Dallas	2-3		19	Tampa Bay	2-3*
	19	at Minnesota	3-2		21	Los Angeles	1-2
	21	at Columbus	3-2*		23	at Nashville	2-4
	23	Edmonton	3-6		25	Buffalo	5-3
	26	Vancouver	2-3†		28	at Philadelphia	0-4
	29	Nashville	3-5	**Mar.**	2	at Ottawa	1-2
Dec.	1	Columbus	2-3		4	at Winnipeg	1-6
	3	Dallas	0-3		5	St. Louis	0-3
	6	at Nashville	3-4		7	Carolina	3-1
	8	at Boston	4-2		9	New Jersey	3-2
	10	at Montreal	1-10		11	Ottawa	2-4
	11	at Toronto	3-1		13	at Arizona	0-1
	14	Philadelphia	3-4		15	Detroit	3-1
	16	Florida	1-3		18	at Detroit	1-5
	18	at Winnipeg	1-4		19	at Chicago	3-6
	20	at Minnesota	0-2		21	St. Louis	2-4
	22	Toronto	0-6		23	Edmonton	4-7
	23	at Chicago	2-1*		25	at Edmonton	1-4
	27	Calgary	3-6		27	at Calgary	2-4
	29	at Dallas	2-4		29	Washington	3-5
	31	NY Rangers	2-6		31	St. Louis	2-1†
Jan.	2	at Vancouver	2-3	**Apr.**	2	at Minnesota	2-5
	4	at Calgary	1-4		4	Chicago	4-3*
	6	NY Islanders	2-1*		6	Minnesota	3-4
	12	Anaheim	1-4		8	at Dallas	3-4†
	14	Nashville	2-3		9	at St. Louis	2-3

* – Overtime † – Shootout

NHL Draft Selections 2017-2003

Name in bold denotes played in NHL.

2017 Pick		2013 Pick		2009 Pick		2005 Pick	
4	Cale Makar	1	**Nathan MacKinnon**	3	**Matt Duchene**	34	**Ryan Stoa**
32	Conor Timmins	32	**Chris Bigras**	33	**Ryan O'Reilly**	44	**Paul Stastny**
94	Nick Henry	63	**Spencer Martin**	49	**Stefan Elliott**	47	Tom Fritsche
114	Petr Kvaca	93	Mason Geertsen	64	**Tyson Barrie**	52	Chris Durand
125	Igor Shvyrev	123	Will Butcher	124	Kieran Millan	88	**T.J. Hensick**
156	Denis Smirnov	153	Ben Storm	154	Brandon Maxwell	124	**Ray Macias**
187	Nick Leivermann	183	Wilhelm Westlund	184	Gus Young	166	Jason Lynch
						168	Justin Mercier
						222	Kyle Cumiskey

2016 Pick		2012 Pick		2008 Pick		2004 Pick	
10	**Tyson Jost**	41	Mitchell Heard	50	**Cameron Gaunce**	21	**Wojtek Wolski**
40	Cam Morrison	72	Troy Bourke	61	Peter Delmas	55	**Victor Oreskovich**
71	Josh Anderson	132	Michael Clarke	110	Kelsey Tessier	72	Denis Parshin
131	Adam Werner	162	**Joseph Blandisi**	140	**Mark Olver**	154	Richard Demen-Willaume
161	Nate Clurman	192	**Colin Smith**	167	Joel Chouinard	184	**Derek Peltier**
191	Travis Barron			170	**Jonas Holos**	215	Ian Keserich
				200	Nate Condon	239	**Brandon Yip**
						249	J.D. Corbin
						281	Steve McClellan

2015 Pick		2011 Pick		2007 Pick		2003 Pick	
10	**Mikko Rantanen**	2	**Gabriel Landeskog**	14	**Kevin Shattenkirk**	63	**David Liffiton**
39	**A.J. Greer**	11	**Duncan Siemens**	45	**Colby Cohen**	131	David Svagrovsky
40	Nicolas Meloche	93	Joachim Nermark	49	Trevor Cann	146	Mark McCutcheon
71	J.C. Beaudin	123	Garrett Meurs	55	**TJ Galiardi**	163	**Brad Richardson**
101	Andrei Mironov	153	Gabriel Beaupre	105	**Brad Malone**	204	Linus Videll
161	Sergei Boikov	183	Dillon Donnelly	113	Kent Patterson	225	Brett Hemingway
191	Gustav Olhaver			135	**Paul Carey**	257	Darryl Yacboski
				155	Jens Hellgren	288	**David Jones**
				195	Johan Alcen		

2014 Pick		2010 Pick		2006 Pick	
23	Conner Bleackley	17	**Joey Hishon**	18	**Chris Stewart**
84	Kyle Wood	49	**Calvin Pickard**	51	Nigel Williams
93	Nick Magyar	71	**Michael Bournival**	59	Codey Burki
114	Alexis Pepin	95	Stephen Silas	81	Mike Carman
144	**Anton Lindholm**	107	**Sami Aittokallio**	110	Kevin Montgomery
174	Maximilian Pajpach	137	Troy Rutkowski	201	Billy Sauer
204	Julien Nantel	139	Luke Walker		
		197	Luke Moffatt		

Selected tenth overall in the 2015 NHL Draft, Mikko Rantanen scored 20 goals for Colorado in his first full NHL season in 2016-17.

Club Directory

Pepsi Center

Colorado Avalanche
Pepsi Center
1000 Chopper Circle
Denver, CO 80204
Phone **303/405-1100**
FAX 303/893-0614
Press Box 303/575-1926
www.coloradoavalanche.com
Capacity: 17,809

Executive
Owner/Chairman, Kroenke Sports & Entertainment . . E. Stanley Kroenke
President & Governor . . . . Josh Kroenke
Exec. Vice President/General Manager/Alt. Governor . Joe Sakic
Assistant General Managers . . . . Craig Billington, Chris MacFarland
Vice President of Hockey Administration . . . . Charlotte Grahame

Coaching Staff
Head Coach . . . . Jared Bednar
Assistant Coaches . . . . Ray Bennett, Nolan Pratt
Goaltending Coach . . . . Jussi Parkkila
Video Coach . . . . Brett Heimlich

Medical Staff
Head Athletic Trainer . . . . Matthew Sokolowski
Assistant Athletic Trainer/Physical Therapist . . . . . . Scott Woodward
Assistant Medical Trainer . . . . Dusty Hibdon

Equipment Staff
Head Equipment Manager . . . . Mark Miller
Assistant Equipment Managers . . . . Cliff Halstead, Brad Lewkow
Inventory Manager . . . . Wayne Flemming

Strength & Conditioning/Massage Staff
Strength & Conditioning Coach . . . . Casey Bond
Massage Therapist . . . . Gregorio Pradera

Pro Scouting Staff
Director, Reserve List Scouting . . . . Brad Smith
Sr. Pro Scout . . . . Garth Joy
Pro Scouts . . . . Dan Laperriere, Terry Martin, Mike Battaglia
Pro Scout (Europe) . . . . Miroslav Zalesak
Hockey Analyst . . . . Arik Parnass

Amateur Scouting Staff
Director of Amateur Scouting . . . . Alan Hepple
Head, European Scouting . . . . Joni Lehto
Scouts . . . . Anton Edlund, John Funk, Wade Klippenstein, Jerome Mesonero, Don Paarup, Norm Robert, Neil Shea, Lyle Wingert

Player Development Staff
Director of Player Development . . . . David Oliver
Development Consultants . . . . Brett Clark, Adam Foote, Brian Willsie
Skating Coach . . . . Tracy Tutton

Communications/Team Services/Website Staff
Sr. VP, Communications & Team Services . . . . Jean Martineau
Exec. Director of Media Services . . . . Brendan McNicholas
Director of Team Services & Immigration . . . . Erin DeGraff
Website Coordinator . . . . Ron Knabenbauer
Media Relations Assistant . . . . Danielle Bernstein

San Antonio Rampage (AHL affiliate)
Head Coach . . . . Eric Veilleux
Assistant Coach . . . . Randy Ladouceur
Goaltending Coach . . . . Jean-Ian Filiatrault
Business/Video Coordinator . . . . Steven Petrovek
Head Athletic Trainer . . . . Brent Woodside
Strength & Conditioning Coach . . . . Tim Martin
Head Equipment Manager . . . . Steven Passineau
Assistant Equipment Manager . . . . Jack Markwardt

Team Information
Practice Facility . . . . South Suburban Family Sports Center
Television Outlet . . . . Altitude Sports & Entertainment Network
Radio . . . . Altitude Radio Network (Altitude Sports Radio 950 AM)

Captains' History

Marc Tardif, 1979-80, 1980-81; Robbie Ftorek and Andre Dupont, 1981-82; Mario Marois, 1982-83 to 1984-85; Mario Marois and Peter Stastny, 1985-86; Peter Stastny, 1986-87 to 1989-90; Joe Sakic and Steven Finn, 1990-91; Mike Hough, 1991-92; Joe Sakic, 1992-93 to 2008-09; Adam Foote, 2009-10, 2010-11; Milan Hejduk, 2011-12; Gabriel Landeskog, 2012-13 to date.

Coaching History

Jacques Demers, 1979-80; Maurice Filion and Michel Bergeron, 1980-81; Michel Bergeron, 1981-82 to 1986-87; Andre Savard and Ron Lapointe, 1987-88; Ron Lapointe and Jean Perron, 1988-89; Michel Bergeron, 1989-90; Dave Chambers, 1990-91; Dave Chambers and Pierre Page, 1991-92; Pierre Page, 1992-93, 1993-94; Marc Crawford, 1994-95 to 1997-98; Bob Hartley, 1998-99 to 2001-02; Bob Hartley and Tony Granato, 2002-03; Tony Granato, 2003-04; Joel Quenneville, 2004-05 to 2007-08; Tony Granato, 2008-09; Joe Sacco, 2009-10 to 2012-13; Patrick Roy, 2013-14 to 2015-16; Jared Bednar, 2016-17 to date.

General Managers' History

Maurice Filion, 1979-80 to 1987-88; Martin Madden, 1988-89; Martin Madden and Maurice Filion, 1989-90; Pierre Page, 1990-91 to 1993-94; Pierre Lacroix, 1994-95 to 2005-06; Francois Giguere, 2006-07 to 2008-09; Greg Sherman, 2009-10 to 2013-14; Joe Sakic, 2014-15 to date.

Columbus Blue Jackets

2016-17 Results: 50w-24l-6otl-2sol 108pts
3rd, Metropolitan Division • 4th, Eastern Conference

Key Off-Season Signings/Acquisitions

2017

June 9 • Re-signed C **Zac Dalpe** and G **Joonas Korpisalo**.

23 • Acquired LW **Artemi Panarin**, LW **Tyler Motte** and a 6th-round pick in 2017 NHL Draft from Chicago for LW **Brandon Saad**, G **Anton Forsberg** and a 5th-round pick in 2018 NHL Draft.

23 • Acquired C **Jordan Schroeder** from Minnesota for C **Dante Salituro**.

July 1 • Signed D **Andre Benoit** and D **Cameron Gaunce**.

Year-by-Year Record

Season	GP	Home W	L	T	OL	Road W	L	T	OL	Overall W	L	T	OL	GF	GA	Pts.	Div. Fin.	Conf. Fin.	Playoff Result
2016-17	82	28	12	....	1	22	12	....	7	50	24	....	8	249	195	108	3rd, Met.	4th, East	Lost First Round
2015-16	82	18	17	....	6	16	23	....	2	34	40	....	8	219	252	76	8th, Met.	15th, East	– out of playoffs –
2014-15	82	19	20	....	3	23	15	....	3	42	35	....	5	236	250	89	5th, Met.	11th, East	– out of playoffs –
2013-14	82	22	15	....	4	21	17	....	3	43	32	....	7	231	216	93	4th, Met.	7th, East	Lost First Round
2012-13	48	14	5	....	5	10	12	....	2	24	17	....	7	120	119	55	4th, Cen.	9th, West	– out of playoffs –
2011-12	82	17	21	....	3	12	25	....	4	29	46	....	7	202	262	65	5th, Cen.	15th, West	– out of playoffs –
2010-11	82	17	19	....	5	17	16	....	8	34	35	....	13	215	258	81	5th, Cen.	14th, West	– out of playoffs –
2009-10	82	20	12	....	9	12	23	....	6	32	35	....	15	216	259	79	5th, Cen.	14th, West	– out of playoffs –
2008-09	82	25	13	....	3	16	18	....	7	41	31	....	10	226	230	92	4th, Cen.	7th, West	Lost Conf. Quarter-Final
2007-08	82	20	14	....	7	14	22	....	5	34	36	....	12	193	218	80	4th, Cen.	13th, West	– out of playoffs –
2006-07	82	18	19	....	4	15	23	....	3	33	42	....	7	201	249	73	4th, Cen.	11th, West	– out of playoffs –
2005-06	82	23	18	....	0	12	25	....	4	35	43	....	4	223	279	74	3rd, Cen.	13th, West	– out of playoffs –
2004-05	....																		
2003-04	82	17	18	4	2	8	27	4	2	25	45	8	4	177	238	62	4th, Cen.	14th, West	– out of playoffs –
2002-03	82	20	14	5	2	9	28	3	1	29	42	8	3	213	263	69	5th, Cen.	15th, West	– out of playoffs –
2001-02	82	14	18	5	4	8	29	3	1	22	47	8	5	164	255	57	5th, Cen.	15th, West	– out of playoffs –
2000-01	82	19	15	4	3	9	24	5	3	28	39	9	6	190	233	71	5th, Cen.	13th, West	– out of playoffs –

2017-18 Schedule

Oct.	Fri.	6	NY Islanders		Thu.	4	at Colorado
	Sat.	7	at Chicago		Sun.	7	Florida*
	Tue.	10	at Carolina		Mon.	8	at Toronto
	Fri.	13	NY Rangers		Thu.	11	at Buffalo
	Sat.	14	at Minnesota		Fri.	12	Vancouver
	Tue.	17	at Winnipeg		Thu.	18	Dallas
	Thu.	19	Tampa Bay		Tue.	23	at Vegas
	Sat.	21	Los Angeles		Thu.	25	at Arizona
	Wed.	25	Buffalo		Tue.	30	Minnesota
	Fri.	27	Winnipeg	**Feb.**	Fri.	2	San Jose
	Sat.	28	at St. Louis*		Sat.	3	at NY Islanders
	Mon.	30	Boston		Tue.	6	Washington
Nov.	Thu.	2	at Florida		Fri.	9	at Washington
	Sat.	4	at Tampa Bay		Sat.	10	New Jersey
	Mon.	6	at NY Rangers		Tue.	13	at NY Islanders
	Tue.	7	Nashville		Wed.	14	at Toronto
	Fri.	10	Carolina		Fri.	16	Philadelphia
	Sat.	11	at Detroit		Sun.	18	Pittsburgh
	Tue.	14	at Montreal		Tue.	20	at New Jersey
	Fri.	17	NY Rangers		Thu.	22	at Philadelphia
	Mon.	20	at Buffalo		Sat.	24	Chicago
	Wed.	22	Calgary		Mon.	26	Washington
	Fri.	24	Ottawa	**Mar.**	Thu.	1	at Los Angeles
	Mon.	27	at Montreal		Fri.	2	at Anaheim
	Tue.	28	Carolina		Sun.	4	at San Jose
Dec.	Fri.	1	Anaheim		Tue.	6	Vegas
	Sat.	2	at Washington		Thu.	8	Colorado
	Tue.	5	New Jersey		Fri.	9	Detroit
	Fri.	8	at New Jersey		Mon.	12	Montreal
	Sat.	9	Arizona		Thu.	15	at Philadelphia
	Tue.	12	Edmonton		Sat.	17	Ottawa
	Thu.	14	NY Islanders		Mon.	19	at Boston
	Sat.	16	at Carolina		Tue.	20	at NY Rangers
	Mon.	18	at Boston		Thu.	22	Florida
	Wed.	20	Toronto		Sat.	24	St. Louis
	Thu.	21	at Pittsburgh		Tue.	27	at Edmonton
	Sat.	23	Philadelphia		Thu.	29	at Calgary
	Wed.	27	at Pittsburgh		Sat.	31	at Vancouver*
	Fri.	29	at Ottawa	**Apr.**	Tue.	3	Detroit
	Sun.	31	Tampa Bay		Thu.	5	Pittsburgh
Jan.	Tue.	2	at Dallas		Sat.	7	at Nashville

* Denotes afternoon game.

Cam Atkinson established career highs with 35 goals, 27 assists, and 62 points in 2016-17 to help Columbus establish new club records with 50 wins and 108 points.

METROPOLITAN DIVISION
18th NHL Season

Franchise date: June 25, 1997

2017-18 Player Personnel

FORWARDS	HT	WT	*Age	Birthplace	S	2016-17 Club
ANDERSON, Josh	6-3	221	23	Burlington, ON	R	Columbus
ATKINSON, Cam	5-8	180	28	Riverside, CT	R	Columbus
BJORKSTRAND, Oliver	6-0	177	22	Herning, Denmark	R	Columbus-Cleveland
CALVERT, Matt	5-11	188	27	Brandon, MB	L	Columbus
DALPE, Zac	6-2	200	27	Paris, ON	R	Minnesota-Iowa-Cleveland
DUBINSKY, Brandon	6-2	216	31	Anchorage, AK	L	Columbus
DUBOIS, Pierre-Luc	6-3	215	19	Ste-Agathe-des-Monts, QC	L	Cape Breton-Blainville-Bois.
FOLIGNO, Nick	6-0	205	29	Buffalo, NY	L	Columbus
HANNIKAINEN, Markus	6-2	189	24	Helsinki, Finland	L	Columbus-Cleveland
JENNER, Boone	6-2	215	24	Dorchester, ON	L	Columbus
MILANO, Sonny	6-1	196	21	Massapequa, NY	L	Columbus-Cleveland
MOTTE, Tyler	5-9	188	22	Port Huron, MI	L	Chicago-Rockford
PANARIN, Artemi	5-11	170	25	Korkino, USSR	R	Chicago
SCHROEDER, Jordan	5-9	184	27	Lakeville, MN	R	Minnesota-Iowa
SEDLAK, Lukas	6-0	213	24	Ceske Budejovice, Czech Rep.	L	Columbus
WENNBERG, Alexander	6-2	197	23	Stockholm, Sweden	L	Columbus
DEFENSEMEN						
BENOIT, Andre	5-11	191	33	St. Albert, ON	L	Malmo
CARLSSON, Gabriel	6-4	191	20	Orebro, Sweden	L	Linkoping-CBJ-Cleveland
GAUNCE, Cameron	6-1	210	27	Sudbury, ON	L	Pittsburgh-Wilkes-Barre
HARRINGTON, Scott	6-2	216	24	Kingston, ON	L	Columbus-Cleveland
JOHNSON, Jack	6-1	230	30	Indianapolis, IN	L	Columbus
JONES, Seth	6-4	208	23	Arlington, TX	R	Columbus
KUKAN, Dean	6-2	198	24	Volketswil, Switzerland	L	Cleveland
MURRAY, Ryan	6-1	208	24	Regina, SK	L	Columbus
NUTIVAARA, Markus	6-1	185	23	Oulu, Finland	L	Columbus
RAMAGE, John	6-0	200	26	Mississauga, ON	R	Cleveland
SAVARD, David	6-2	227	26	St. Hyacinthe, QC	R	Columbus
WERENSKI, Zach	6-2	218	20	Grosse Pointe, MI	L	Columbus

GOALTENDERS	HT	WT	*Age	Birthplace	C	2016-17 Club
BOBROVSKY, Sergei	6-2	182	29	Novokuznetsk, USSR	L	Columbus
KORPISALO, Joonas	6-3	191	23	Pori, Finland	L	Columbus-Cleveland

* – Age at start of 2017-18 season

Coaching History

Dave King, 2000-01, 2001-02; Dave King and Doug MacLean, 2002-03; Doug MacLean and Gerard Gallant, 2003-04; Gerard Gallant, 2004-05, 2005-06; Gerard Gallant, Gary Agnew and Ken Hitchcock, 2006-07; Ken Hitchcock, 2007-08, 2008-09; Ken Hitchcock and Claude Noel, 2009-10; Scott Arniel, 2010-11; Scott Arniel and Todd Richards, 2011-12; Todd Richards, 2012-13 to 2014-15; Todd Richards and John Tortorella, 2015-16; John Tortorella, 2016-17 to date.

John Tortorella

Head Coach

Born: Boston, MA, June 24, 1958.

The Columbus Blue Jackets named John Tortorella the club's new head coach on October 21, 2015. Under his leadership in 2016-17, the Blue Jackets set club records with 50 wins and 108 points and Tortorella was rewarded with the Jack Adams Award as coach of the year for the second time in his career. With Columbus on March 19, 2016, Tortorella became the first American to coach in 1,000 NHL games. On December 18, 2016, he became the first American-born coach with 500 victories.

After finishing out the 1999-2000 season as interim coach of the New York Rangers, Tortorella joined Tampa Bay as an associate coach in the summer of 2000 and took over head coaching duties on January 6, 2001. He compiled a 239-222-74 record in 535 games during six-plus seasons with the club from 2001 to 2008 and led the Lightning to the Southeast Division title in 2002-03 and 2003-04. In the latter campaign, he won the Jack Adams Award as the NHL's coach of the year as the club went 46-22-14 (106 points) and won the Stanley Cup.

Tortorella returned to the Rangers in February, 2009 and posted a 171-118-30 record in 319 games with the club, including his four-game stint as interim coach. In 2011-12, he guided the Rangers to the third-best regular season in franchise history with a 51-24-7 mark (109 points) and a spot in the Eastern Conference Final. He joined the Canucks prior to the 2013-14 campaign and guided the club to a 36-35-11 mark.

Tortorella's coaching career began in 1986-87 with the Virginia Lancers of the Atlantic Coast Hockey League, leading the club to a championship and winning coach of the year honors in back-to-back seasons in 1986-87 and 1987-88. He returned to coaching with the American Hockey League's Rochester Americans from 1995 to 1997 and won the 1996 Calder Cup championship in his first season. He went on to serve as an assistant coach with the Buffalo Sabres, Phoenix Coyotes and Rangers.

Internationally, Tortorella served as head coach of the U.S. team at the 2016 World Cup of Hockey. He was an assistant coach with Team USA at the 2010 Olympic Games and helped the club capture a silver medal. He also served as the squad's head coach at the 2008 World Championships and was an assistant coach for Team USA at the 2005 World Championships.

2016-17 Scoring

* – rookie

Regular Season

Pos	#	Player	Team	GP	G	A	Pts	TOI	+/–	PIM	PP	SH	GW	S	S%
R	13	Cam Atkinson	CBJ	82	35	27	62	18:05	13	22	10	3	9	240	14.6
C	10	Alexander Wennberg	CBJ	80	13	46	59	18:22	9	21	2	0	5	109	11.9
L	20	Brandon Saad	CBJ	82	24	29	53	17:01	23	8	1	0	4	210	11.4
L	71	Nick Foligno	CBJ	79	26	25	51	18:25	–4	55	11	0	5	185	14.1
C	89	Sam Gagner	CBJ	81	18	32	50	13:42	10	22	8	0	1	178	10.1
D	8 *	Zach Werenski	CBJ	78	11	36	47	20:54	17	14	4	0	1	188	5.9
D	3	Seth Jones	CBJ	75	12	30	42	23:24	6	24	1	0	3	152	7.9
C	17	Brandon Dubinsky	CBJ	80	12	29	41	17:53	16	91	1	1	5	115	10.4
L	43	Scott Hartnell	CBJ	78	13	24	37	12:03	14	63	2	0	1	104	12.5
C	38	Boone Jenner	CBJ	82	18	16	34	16:03	14	52	0	2	4	211	8.5
R	34	Josh Anderson	CBJ	78	17	12	29	12:01	12	89	0	0	3	119	14.3
C	25	William Karlsson	CBJ	81	6	19	25	13:23	10	10	1	0	3	96	6.3
D	58	David Savard	CBJ	74	6	17	23	21:50	33	44	0	0	0	135	4.4
D	7	Jack Johnson	CBJ	82	5	18	23	21:49	23	32	1	0	1	116	4.3
L	29	Lauri Korpikoski	DAL	60	8	12	20	13:01	5	10	0	0	0	104	7.7
			CBJ	9	0	0	0	8:14	0	0	0	0	0	4	0.0
			Total	69	8	12	20	12:24	5	10	0	0	0	108	7.4
L	11	Matt Calvert	CBJ	65	10	5	15	13:20	–4	48	0	3	1	92	10.9
D	26	Kyle Quincey	N.J.	53	4	8	12	18:38	4	39	0	0	0	61	6.6
			CBJ	20	2	1	3	15:55	0	12	0	0	0	18	11.1
			Total	73	6	9	15	17:53	4	51	0	0	0	79	7.6
C	45 *	Lukas Sedlak	CBJ	62	7	6	13	9:43	10	25	0	1	0	57	12.3
R	28 *	Oliver Bjorkstrand	CBJ	26	6	7	13	14:05	4	6	0	0	2	55	10.9
D	27	Ryan Murray	CBJ	60	2	9	11	18:19	3	24	0	0	0	52	3.8
D	65 *	Markus Nutivaara	CBJ	66	2	5	7	13:12	7	6	0	0	0	66	3.0
D	54	Scott Harrington	CBJ	22	1	2	3	13:00	3	10	0	0	0	16	6.3
L	33 *	Markus Hannikainen	CBJ	10	1	1	2	9:07	0	6	0	0	0	8	12.5
D	53 *	Gabriel Carlsson	CBJ	2	0	1	1	17:07	–2	0	0	0	0	3	0.0
C	49 *	TJ Tynan	CBJ	3	0	0	0	7:29	–1	0	0	0	0	3	0.0
L	22 *	Sonny Milano	CBJ	4	0	0	0	11:41	–3	0	0	0	0	2	0.0

Goaltending

No.	Goaltender	GPI	Mins	Avg	W	L	OT	EN	SO	GA	SA	Sv%	G	A	PIM
72	Sergei Bobrovsky	63	3707	2.06	41	17	5	5	7	127	1854	.931	0	0	8
35	Curtis McElhinney	7	376	2.39	2	1	2	0	0	15	198	.924	0	0	0
70	Joonas Korpisalo	14	791	2.88	7	5	1	3	1	38	401	.905	0	0	0
31	* Anton Forsberg	1	59	4.07	0	1	0	1	0	4	27	.852	0	0	0
	Totals	**82**	**4970**	**2.33**	**50**	**24**	**8**	**9**	**8**	**193**	**2489**	**.922**			

Playoffs

Pos	#	Player	Team	GP	G	A	Pts	TOI	+/–	PIM	PP	SH	GW	OT	S	S%
R	13	Cam Atkinson	CBJ	5	2	1	3	19:34	–3	0	0	0	0	0	14	14.3
C	38	Boone Jenner	CBJ	5	2	1	3	17:48	–2	14	1	0	1	0	16	12.5
C	25	William Karlsson	CBJ	5	2	1	3	16:05	4	0	0	0	0	0	12	16.7
L	20	Brandon Saad	CBJ	5	1	2	3	15:58	–5	0	0	0	0	0	10	10.0
D	65 *	Markus Nutivaara	CBJ	2	1	1	2	11:55	3	0	0	0	0	0	7	14.3
L	11	Matt Calvert	CBJ	4	1	1	2	14:13	4	4	0	0	0	0	9	11.1
C	17	Brandon Dubinsky	CBJ	5	1	1	2	17:56	–2	6	0	0	0	0	8	12.5
D	7	Jack Johnson	CBJ	5	1	1	2	25:52	–3	0	0	0	0	0	15	6.7
R	34	Josh Anderson	CBJ	5	1	1	2	13:43	2	2	0	0	0	0	11	9.1
L	71	Nick Foligno	CBJ	4	0	2	2	20:24	–3	6	0	0	0	0	12	0.0
C	89	Sam Gagner	CBJ	5	0	2	2	12:39	–3	2	0	0	0	0	12	0.0
D	3	Seth Jones	CBJ	5	0	2	2	26:03	–4	0	0	0	0	0	12	0.0
D	8 *	Zach Werenski	CBJ	3	1	0	1	23:29	–2	0	1	0	0	0	14	7.1
D	26	Kyle Quincey	CBJ	2	0	1	1	19:01	–1	2	0	0	0	0	1	0.0
D	58	David Savard	CBJ	5	0	1	1	24:53	–4	4	0	0	0	0	10	0.0
R	28 *	Oliver Bjorkstrand	CBJ	5	0	1	1	12:51	–2	0	0	0	0	0	10	0.0
C	10	Alexander Wennberg	CBJ	5	0	1	1	19:26	–3	2	0	0	0	0	10	0.0
L	22 *	Sonny Milano	CBJ	1	0	0	0	6:47	0	0	0	0	0	0	0	0.0
C	45 *	Lukas Sedlak	CBJ	2	0	0	0	8:16	–1	0	0	0	0	0	2	0.0
D	54	Scott Harrington	CBJ	3	0	0	0	12:27	0	10	0	0	0	0	3	0.0
L	43	Scott Hartnell	CBJ	4	0	0	0	10:39	–2	0	0	0	0	0	4	0.0
D	53 *	Gabriel Carlsson	CBJ	5	0	0	0	10:57	1	0	0	0	0	0	2	0.0

Goaltending

No.	Goaltender	GPI	Mins	Avg	W	L	EN	SO	GA	SA	Sv%	G	A	PIM
72	Sergei Bobrovsky	5	309	3.88	1	4	1	0	20	170	.882	0	0	0
	Totals	**5**	**313**	**4.03**	**1**	**4**	**1**	**0**	**21**	**171**	**.877**			

Coaching Record

			Regular Season				Playoffs			
Season	Team	League	GC	W	L	O/T	GC	W	L	T
1995-96	Rochester	AHL	80	37	34	9	19	15	4	....
1996-97	Rochester	AHL	80	40	30	10	10	6	4	....
99-2000	**NY Rangers**	**NHL**	**4**	**0**	**3**	**1**	....	....	....	....
2000-01	**Tampa Bay**	**NHL**	**43**	**12**	**27**	**4**	....	....	....	....
2001-02	**Tampa Bay**	**NHL**	**82**	**27**	**40**	**15**	....	....	....	....
2002-03	**Tampa Bay**	**NHL**	**82**	**36**	**25**	**21**	**11**	**5**	**6**	....
2003-04♦	**Tampa Bay**	**NHL**	**82**	**46**	**22**	**14**	**23**	**16**	**7**	....
2004-05	**Tampa Bay**		SEASON CANCELLED							
2005-06	**Tampa Bay**	**NHL**	**82**	**43**	**33**	**6**	**5**	**1**	**4**	....
2006-07	**Tampa Bay**	**NHL**	**82**	**44**	**33**	**5**	**6**	**2**	**4**	....
2007-08	**Tampa Bay**	**NHL**	**82**	**31**	**42**	**9**	....	....	....	....
2008-09	**NY Rangers**	**NHL**	**21**	**12**	**7**	**2**	**7**	**3**	**4**	....
2009-10	**NY Rangers**	**NHL**	**82**	**38**	**33**	**11**	....	....	....	....
2010-11	**NY Rangers**	**NHL**	**82**	**44**	**33**	**5**	**5**	**1**	**4**	....
2011-12	**NY Rangers**	**NHL**	**82**	**51**	**24**	**7**	**20**	**10**	**10**	....
2012-13	**NY Rangers**	**NHL**	**48**	**26**	**18**	**4**	**12**	**5**	**7**	....
2013-14	**Vancouver**	**NHL**	**82**	**36**	**35**	**11**	....	....	....	....
2015-16	**Columbus**	**NHL**	**75**	**34**	**33**	**8**	....	....	....	....
2016-17	**Columbus**	**NHL**	**82**	**50**	**24**	**8**	**5**	**1**	**4**	....
	NHL Totals		**1093**	**530**	**432**	**131**	**94**	**44**	**50**	....

♦ Stanley Cup win.

Jack Adams Award (2004, 2017)

Jim Schoenfeld posted an 0-1 playoff record as replacement coach when Tortorella was suspended, April 26, 2009. Loss is credited to Tortorella's coaching record. Craig Hartsburg posted a 2-0-1 record as replacement coach when Tortorella missed three games after breaking a rib, January 22, 2016. Games are credited to Tortorella's coaching record. Brad Larsen and Brad Shaw had an 0-1 record as replacement coach when Tortorella missed a game on January 26, 2017. Loss is credited to Tortorella's coaching record.

Club Records

Team

(Figures in brackets for season records are games played.)

Most Points	108	2016-17 (82)
Most Wins	50	2016-17 (82)
Most Ties	9	2000-01 (82)
Most Losses	47	2001-02 (82)
Most Goals	249	2016-17 (82)
Most Goals Against	279	2005-06 (82)
Fewest Points	57	2001-02 (82)
Fewest Wins	22	2001-02 (82)
Fewest Ties	8	2001-02 (82), 2002-03 (82), 2003-04 (82)
Fewest Losses	24	2016-17 (82)
Fewest Goals	164	2001-02 (82)
Fewest Goals Against	195	2016-17 (82)

Longest Winning Streak
- Overall . . . . 16 — Nov. 29/16-Jan. 3/17
- Home . . . . 9 — Nov. 29/16-Jan. 3/17
- Away . . . . 8 — Mar. 6-28/15, Dec. 1-31/16

Longest Team Point Streak
- Overall . . . . 18 — Nov. 25/16-Jan. 3/17 (14w, 1oTw, 2sow, 1soL)
- Home . . . . 8 — Oct. 21-Nov. 21/16 (4w, 3oTw, 1oTL), Nov. 29/16-Jan. 3/17 (7w, 1sow)
- Away . . . . 11 — Nov. 20-Dec. 31/16 (8w, 1oTw, 1sow, 1soL)

Longest Losing Streak
- Overall . . . . 9 — Dec. 10-26/09 (7L, 2soL), Oct. 24-Nov. 11/14 (8L, 1oTL)
- Home . . . . 7 — Jan. 29-Mar. 7/08 (4L, 2oTL, 1soL)
- Away . . . . 13 — Nov. 21/09-Jan. 5/10

Longest Winless Streak
- Overall . . . . 9 — Dec. 4-23/03 (6L, 3oTL), Dec. 10-26/09 (7L, 2soL), Oct. 24-Nov. 11/14 (8L, 1oTL)
- Home . . . . 8 — Oct. 4-Nov. 9/01 (6L, 2T), Dec. 4-31/03 (6L, 1oTL, 1T)
- Away . . . . 14 — Oct. 9-Dec. 20/03 (11L, 2oTL, 1T)

Most Shutouts, Season	11	2007-08 (82), 2008-09 (82)
Most PIM, Season	1,505	2002-03 (82)
Most Goals, Game	10	Nov. 4/16 (Mtl. 0 at CBJ 10)

Individual

Most Seasons	10	Rostislav Klesla
Most Games	674	Rick Nash
Most Goals, Career	289	Rick Nash
Most Assists, Career	258	Rick Nash
Most Points, Career	547	Rick Nash (289G, 258A)
Most PIM, Career	1,195	Jared Boll
Most Shutouts, Career	19	Steve Mason, Sergei Bobrovsky

Longest Consecutive Games Streak . . . . 288 — RJ Umberger (Oct. 10/08-Jan. 10/12)

Most Goals, Season . . . . 41 — Rick Nash (2003-04)

Most Assists, Season	52	Ray Whitney (2002-03)
Most Points, Season	79	Rick Nash (2008-09; 40G, 39A)
Most PIM, Season	249	Jody Shelley (2002-03)
Most Points, Defenseman, Season	51	James Wisniewski (2013-14; 7G, 44A)
Most Points, Center, Season	71	Ryan Johansen (2014-15; 26G, 45A)
Most Points, Right Wing, Season	65	David Vyborny (2005-06; 22G, 43A)
Most Points, Left Wing, Season	79	Rick Nash (2008-09; 40G, 39A)
Most Points, Rookie, Season	47	Zach Werenski (2016-17; 11G, 36A)
Most Shutouts, Season	10	Steve Mason (2008-09)
Most Goals, Game	4	Geoff Sanderson (Mar. 29/03)
Most Assists, Game	5	Espen Knutsen (Mar. 24/01)
Most Points, Game	5	Espen Knutsen (Mar. 24/01; 5A); Geoff Sanderson (Mar. 29/03; 4G, 1A); Andrew Cassels (Mar. 29/03; 1G, 4A); David Vyborny (Feb. 28/04; 1G, 4A)

Captains' History

Lyle Odelein, 2000-01, 2001-02; Ray Whitney, 2002-03; Luke Richardson, 2003-04; Luke Richardson and Adam Foote, 2005-06; Adam Foote, 2006-07; Adam Foote and Rick Nash, 2007-08; Rick Nash, 2008-09 to 2011-12; no captain, 2012-13 to 2014-15; Nick Foligno, 2015-16 to date.

All-time Record vs. Other Clubs

Regular Season

		Total								At Home								On Road					
	GP	W	L	T	OL	GF	GA	PTS	GP	W	L	T	OL	GF	GA	PTS	GP	W	L	T	OL	GF	GA	PTS
Anaheim	55	28	23	1	3	151	153	60	27	15	11	0	1	75	68	31	28	13	12	1	2	76	85	29
Arizona	55	23	26	4	2	138	154	52	27	14	11	1	1	72	67	30	28	9	15	3	1	66	87	22
Boston	24	9	9	0	6	60	79	24	13	5	5	0	3	33	46	13	11	4	4	0	3	27	33	11
Buffalo	26	15	10	1	0	76	69	31	12	7	4	1	0	36	31	15	14	8	6	0	0	40	38	16
Calgary	55	30	19	0	6	147	138	66	28	17	7	0	4	80	62	38	27	13	12	0	2	67	76	28
Carolina	30	14	13	0	3	83	77	31	14	7	6	0	1	38	33	15	16	7	7	0	2	45	44	16
Chicago	81	32	39	2	8	223	273	74	41	18	17	1	5	131	145	42	40	14	22	1	3	92	128	32
Colorado	55	17	32	1	5	113	186	40	27	8	15	1	3	51	88	20	28	9	17	0	2	62	98	20
Dallas	55	22	27	0	6	132	158	50	28	11	13	0	4	70	83	26	27	11	14	0	2	62	75	24
Detroit	86	31	42	1	12	198	266	75	44	18	18	1	7	97	128	44	42	13	24	0	5	101	138	31
Edmonton	55	21	28	3	3	145	192	48	28	14	10	3	1	83	90	32	27	7	18	0	2	62	102	16
Florida	24	15	7	0	2	68	56	32	12	9	2	0	1	35	23	19	12	6	5	0	1	33	33	13
Los Angeles	55	23	26	1	5	129	162	52	27	14	10	0	3	73	83	31	28	9	16	1	2	56	79	21
Minnesota	54	28	22	1	3	133	128	60	26	17	8	1	0	69	52	35	28	11	14	0	3	64	76	25
Montreal	23	11	9	1	2	61	51	25	11	5	4	0	1	33	23	11	13	6	5	1	1	28	28	14
Nashville	82	25	46	1	10	182	255	61	40	17	18	0	5	94	112	39	42	8	28	1	5	88	143	22
New Jersey	29	15	12	1	1	74	68	32	15	9	6	0	0	44	38	18	14	6	6	1	1	30	30	14
NY Islanders	31	17	8	1	5	102	89	40	17	11	2	1	3	62	40	26	14	6	6	0	2	40	49	14
NY Rangers	29	12	13	1	3	89	88	28	16	7	9	0	0	47	43	14	13	5	4	1	3	42	45	14
Ottawa	23	8	13	2	0	62	74	18	11	4	6	1	0	30	37	9	12	4	7	1	0	32	37	9
Philadelphia	28	15	10	3	0	77	78	33	14	10	2	2	0	39	26	22	14	5	8	1	0	38	52	11
Pittsburgh	31	12	15	0	4	86	98	28	16	8	5	0	3	51	46	19	15	4	10	0	1	35	52	9
St. Louis	81	30	36	3	12	214	250	75	40	20	13	2	5	118	106	47	41	10	23	1	7	96	144	28
San Jose	55	20	30	0	5	130	158	45	28	14	11	0	3	77	62	31	27	6	19	0	2	53	96	14
Tampa Bay	25	10	12	1	2	55	62	23	13	6	5	1	0	29	28	13	13	4	7	0	2	26	34	10
Toronto	22	11	10	1	0	64	64	23	10	4	6	0	0	31	36	8	12	7	4	1	0	33	28	15
Vancouver	55	19	27	2	7	136	189	47	28	10	13	2	3	64	92	25	27	9	14	0	4	72	97	22
Washington	32	11	14	1	6	87	104	29	17	7	7	0	3	54	56	17	15	4	7	1	3	33	48	12
Winnipeg	22	11	11	0	0	60	57	22	11	5	6	0	0	28	28	10	11	6	5	0	0	32	29	12
Totals	1278	535	589	33	121	3275	3776	1224	639	311	250	18	60	1744	1772	700	639	224	339	15	61	1531	2004	524

Playoffs

	Series	W	L	GP	W	L	T	GF	GA	Last Mtg.	Rnd.	Result
Detroit	1	0	1	4	0	4	0	7	18	2009	CQF	L 0-4
Pittsburgh	2	0	2	11	3	8	0	31	42	2017	FR	L 1-4
Totals	3	0	3	15	3	12	0	38	60			

Winnipeg totals include Atlanta Thrashers, 1999-2000 to 2010-11.

Playoff Results 2017-2013

Year	Round	Opponent	Result	GF	GA
2017	FR	Pittsburgh	L 1-4	13	21
2014	FR	Pittsburgh	L 2-4	18	21

Abbreviations: Round: CQF – conference quarter-final; **FR** – first round.

2016-17 Results

Oct. 13	Boston	3-6	14	at Florida	3-4
15	San Jose	2-3	17	Carolina	4-1
21	Chicago	3-2	19	Ottawa	0-2
22	at Dallas	3-0	21	Carolina	3-2
25	at Los Angeles	2-3*	22	at Ottawa	7-6*
27	at San Jose	1-3	24	at NY Islanders	2-4
28	at Anaheim	4-0	26	at Nashville	3-4
Nov. 1	Dallas	3-2*	31	at NY Rangers	6-4
4	Montreal	10-0	Feb. 3	at Pittsburgh	3-4*
5	at St. Louis	1-2*	4	New Jersey	1-5
9	Anaheim	3-2*	7	at Detroit	3-2*
10	at Boston	2-5	9	Vancouver	0-3
12	St. Louis	8-4	11	Detroit	2-1
15	Washington	2-1*	13	NY Rangers	2-3
18	NY Rangers	4-2	15	Toronto	5-2
20	at Washington	3-2	17	Pittsburgh	2-1*
21	Colorado	2-3*	19	Nashville	3-2
23	Calgary	0-2	25	NY Islanders	7-0
25	at Tampa Bay	5-3	26	at NY Rangers	5-2
26	at Florida	1-2†	28	at Montreal	0-1*
28	Tampa Bay	5-1	Mar. 2	Minnesota	1-0
Dec. 1	at Colorado	3-2	4	at Ottawa	2-3
3	at Arizona	3-2†	5	at New Jersey	3-0
5	Arizona	4-1	7	New Jersey	2-0
9	at Detroit	4-1	10	Buffalo	2-3
10	NY Islanders	6-2	11	at Buffalo	3-5
13	at Edmonton	3-1	13	at Philadelphia	5-3
16	at Calgary	4-1	16	Florida	2-1
18	at Vancouver	4-3*	18	at NY Islanders	3-2*
20	Los Angeles	3-2†	19	at New Jersey	4-5
22	Pittsburgh	7-1	22	Toronto	2-5
23	Montreal	2-1	23	at Washington	1-2†
27	Boston	4-3	25	Philadelphia	1-0
29	at Winnipeg	5-3	28	Buffalo	5-2
31	at Minnesota	4-2	30	at Carolina	1-2*
Jan. 3	Edmonton	3-1	31	at Chicago	1-3
5	at Washington	0-5	Apr. 2	Washington	2-3
7	NY Rangers	4-5	4	at Pittsburgh	0-5
8	Philadelphia	2-1*	6	Winnipeg	4-5
10	at Carolina	3-5	8	at Philadelphia	2-4
13	at Tampa Bay	3-1	9	at Toronto	3-2

* – Overtime † – Shootout

NHL Draft Selections 2017-2003

Name in bold denotes played in NHL.

2017
Pick	
45	Alexandre Texier
86	Daniil Tarasov
117	Emil Bemstrom
148	Kale Howarth
170	Jonathan Davidsson
179	Carson Meyer
210	Robbie Stucker

2016
Pick	
3	Pierre-Luc Dubois
34	Andrew Peeke
65	Vitaly Abramov
155	Peter Thome
185	Calvin Thurkauf

2015
Pick	
8	**Zach Werenski**
29	**Gabriel Carlsson**
38	Paul Bittner
58	Kevin Stenlund
69	Keegan Kolesar
129	Sam Ruopp
141	Veeti Vainio
159	Vladislav Gavrikov
189	**Markus Nutivaara**

2014
Pick	
16	**Sonny Milano**
47	Ryan Collins
76	Elvis Merzlikins
77	Blake Siebenaler
107	Julien Pelletier
137	Tyler Bird
197	Olivier LeBlanc

2013
Pick	
14	**Alexander Wennberg**
19	**Kerby Rychel**
27	**Marko Dano**
50	Dillon Heatherington
89	**Oliver Bjorkstrand**
105	Nick Moutrey
165	Markus Soberg
195	Peter Quenneville

2012
Pick	
2	**Ryan Murray**
31	Oscar Dansk
62	**Joonas Korpisalo**
95	**Josh Anderson**
152	Daniel Zaar
182	Gianluca Curcuruto

2011
Pick	
37	**Boone Jenner**
66	**TJ Tynan**
98	**Mike Reilly**
128	Seth Ambroz
158	**Lukas Sedlak**
188	**Anton Forsberg**

2010
Pick	
4	**Ryan Johansen**
34	Dalton Smith
55	**Petr Straka**
94	Brandon Archibald
102	Mathieu Corbeil
124	Austin Madaisky
154	**Dalton Prout**
184	Martin Ouellette

2009
Pick	
21	**John Moore**
56	Kevin Lynch
94	**David Savard**
137	Thomas Larkin
167	Anton Blomqvist
197	Kyle Neuber

2008
Pick	
6	**Nikita Filatov**
37	**Cody Goloubef**
107	Steven Delisle
118	Drew Olson
127	**Matt Calvert**
135	**Tomas Kubalik**
137	**Brent Regner**
157	**Cam Atkinson**
187	**Sean Collins**

2007
Pick	
7	**Jakub Voracek**
37	Stefan Legein
53	Will Weber
68	Jake Hansen
94	**Maksim Mayorov**
158	**Allen York**
211	Trent Vogelhuber

2006
Pick	
6	**Derick Brassard**
69	**Steve Mason**
85	**Tom Sestito**
113	Ben Wright
129	Robert Nyholm
136	Nick Sucharski
142	Maxime Frechette
159	Jesse Dudas
189	**Derek Dorsett**
194	Matt Marquardt

2005
Pick	
6	**Gilbert Brule**
55	**Adam McQuaid**
67	**Kris Russell**
101	**Jared Boll**
131	**Tomas Popperle**
177	Derek Reinhart
189	Kirill Starkov
201	Trevor Hendrikx

2004
Pick	
8	**Alexandre Picard**
46	**Adam Pineault**
59	Kyle Wharton
93	**Dan LaCosta**
96	Andrey Plekhanov
133	Petr Pohl
167	Rob Page
190	**Lennart Petrell**
198	Justin Vienneau
231	Brian McGuirk
233	Matt Greer
271	**Grant Clitsome**

2003
Pick	
4	**Nikolai Zherdev**
46	**Dan Fritsche**
71	Dmitry Kosmachev
103	Kevin Jarman
104	**Philippe Dupuis**
138	Arsi Piispanen
168	**Marc Methot**
200	Alexander Guskov
233	Mathieu Gravel
283	Trevor Hendrikx

General Managers' History

Doug MacLean, 2000-01 to 2006-07; Scott Howson, 2007-08 to 2011-12; Scott Howson and Jarmo Kekalainen, 2012-13; Jarmo Kekalainen, 2013-14 to date.

Jarmo Kekalainen

General Manager

Born: Tampere, Finland, July 3, 1966.

Jarmo Kekalainen was named the third general manager in Columbus Blue Jackets history on February 13, 2013. He joined Columbus after serving as the president and general manager of Jokerit in the Finnish Elite League since 2010 and works closely with Blue Jackets president of hockey operations John Davidson on all hockey-related matters involving the club. In Kekalainen's first full season with the club in 2013-14, the Blue Jackets established new franchise highs with 43 wins and 93 points. They broke those records with 50 wins and 108 points in 2016-17. He owns a bachelor's degree in management from Clarkson University and earned a master's in business marketing from the University of Tampere.

Prior to his stint with Jokerit, Kekalainen spent eight seasons with the St. Louis Blues from 2002 to 2010. He joined the Blues as director of amateur scouting and was named assistant general manager as well in 2005. Kekalainen was involved in all facets of hockey operations, including professional scouting efforts and overseeing the club's amateur scouting and draft preparations. During his eight years in St. Louis, the Blues drafted players such as David Backes, Roman Polak, David Perron, T.J. Oshie, Patrik Berglund and Alex Pietrangelo.

Kekalainen was a member of the Ottawa Senators hockey operations department from 1995 to 2002 and served in a variety of roles with the club. He served as Ottawa's director of player personnel for three years and also oversaw the amateur draft and the club's scouting efforts in Europe. Among the players selected by Ottawa during this time were Jason Spezza, Marian Hossa, Martin Havlat, Antoine Vermette and Ray Emery. While working with the Senators, he also served as general manager of HIFK Helsinki in the Finnish Elite League from 1995 to 1999 and led the club to the league championship in 1998.

As a player, Kekalainen appeared in 55 career NHL games with the Senators and Boston Bruins during his career. He also played in the American Hockey League and his native Finland before wrapping up his playing career with Vasteras IK in the Swedish Elite League in 1994-95. Before signing with the Bruins, Kekalainen played two seasons at Clarkson University from 1987 to 1989. He was named to the Eastern Collegiate Athletic Conference First All-Star Team after tallying 19 goals and 25 assists for 44 points in 31 games during the 1988-89 season. He also represented Finland at the 1986 World Junior Championship and the 1991 Canada Cup Tournament. He served as assistant general manager for Finland at the 2016 World Cup of Hockey.

Club Directory

Nationwide Arena

Columbus Blue Jackets
Nationwide Arena
200 W. Nationwide Blvd.
Columbus, Ohio 43215
Phone **614/246-4625**
FAX 614/246-4007
www.BlueJackets.com
Capacity: 18,144

Ownership/Senior Management

Majority Owner/Governor	John P. McConnell
President/Alternate Governor	Mike Priest
President, Hockey Operations/Alternate Governor	John Davidson

Executive Staff – Business Operations

Senior Vice President/General Counsel	Greg Kirstein
Senior Vice President/Chief Revenue Officer	Cameron Scholvin
Senior Vice President/Chief Financial Officer	T.J. LaMendola
Vice President, Communications & Team Services	Todd Sharrock
Vice President, Community Relations/ Exec. Dir. CBJ Foundation	Kathryn Dobbs
Vice President, Digital Marketing & Media	Marc Gregory
Vice President, Marketing	J.D. Kershaw
Vice President, Ticket Sales & Service	Joe Andrade
Vice President, Corporate Partnerships	Ryan Shirk

Hockey Operations

General Manager	Jarmo Kekalainen
Assistant General Manager	Bill Zito
Assistant to the General Manager	Tom Bark
Director of Player Personnel	Basil McRae
Director of Hockey Administration	Josh Flynn
Director of High Performance	Nelson Ayotte
Hockey Operations Advisor	Fredrik Modin
Assistant General Manager, Cleveland Monsters	Blake Geoffrion
Director of Amateur Scouting	Ville Siren
Director of European Scouting	Josef Boumedienne
Assistant Director of Amateur Scouting	Chris Morehouse
Amateur Scouts	Mike Antonovich, Simon Barrette, Marshall Davidson, Greg Drechsel, Derek Ginnell, Stephane Leblanc, Phil McRae, Rob Riley, Milan Tichy
Pro Scouts	Peter Dineen, Bob Halkidis, John Hill, Doug MacDonald, Sam McMaster, Rich Sutter
Scout / Pro Video Coordinator	Craig Hartsburg / Jim Viers
Athletic Trainers, Head / Assistants	Mike Vogt / Nates Goto, Chris Strickland
Equipment Manager / Assistant Mgr. / Assistant	Tim LeRoy / Jamie Healy / Jason Stypinski
Executive Assistant, Hockey Operations	Beth Carlisle Ebright

Coaching Staff

Head Coach	John Tortorella
Assistant Coaches / Goaltending Coach	Brad Larsen, Kenny McCudden, Brad Shaw / Ian Clark
Strength & Conditioning Coach	Kevin Collins
Video Assistant Coach	Dan Singleton
Development Coaches / Eur. Development Coach	Gregory Campbell, Chris Clark / Jarkko Ruutu
Skating Consultant	Lee Harris

Corporate Development and Premium Seating

Senior Director of Partner Activation/Premium Service	Becky Coffey
Director of Corporate Partnerships	Craig Smith
Corporate Partnership Account Executives	Justin Baldinger, Marc Gosselin, Sam Morgan, Doug Vinci
Partnership Activation Specialists	Samantha Hagan, Caleb Horsley, Molly Taylor, Victoria King
Premium Seating Manager	Trent Gerhart
Premium Seating Account Executive	Morgan Obendorfer
Premium Seating Specialists	Brenna Frattaroli, Paige Shepherd

Communications and Team Services

Director of Communications	Karen Davis
Managers, Communications / Team Services	Glenn Odebralski / Julie Gamble

Community Relations

Director of Fan Development & Community Programs	Andee Boiman
Managers, Mascot Services / CBJ Foundation	Jason Zumpano / Darla Owens
Manager, Fan Development	Joel Siegman
Manager, Education & Community Partnerships	Michelle Brueggeman
Community Relations & Foundation Coordinator	Meredith Bush

Game Operations and Event Presentation

Exec. Producer & Senior Director of Event Presentation	Derek Dawley
Managers, Senior Event Presentation / Production	Lynn Truitt / Andy Hookman
Senior Editor-Producer / Broadcast Engineer	David Traube / Rick Shepherd
Producer/Videographer	Tanner Smith

Marketing

Director, Marketing	Jim Riley
Managers, Marketing / Advertising & Creative Services	Ben Harrison / Jack Lyttle
Graphics, Senior Designer / Designer	Jason Duignan / Cassie Good

Digital Marketing & Media

Director, Digital Marketing & Analytics	Jeff Eldersveld
Manager, CRM	Amy French
Coordinators, Digital & Social Media	Allie Dosmann / Carson Reider
Coordinators, CRM / Digital Media	Mary Lynn Berilla / Adam Carro

Human Resources and Legal

Director, Human Resources	Becky Magaw
Senior Payroll Manager / Assistant	Christine Phipps / Karen Albert
Staff Counsel / Paralegal	Pete Lovins / Ken Erney
Human Resources Generalist	Katherine Schuette
Administrative Assistant	Heidi Gibbs

Finance and Information Technology

Director of Finance & Controller	Joe Rudolf
Accountants, Senior / Staff	Zachary Kramer / Nora Ludwig
Director of IT / Systems Analyst	Jim Connolly / Matthew DeStephen
Technical Support Specialist	Brad Zarnoch
Accounts Payable Coordinator	Heather Benintendi

Ticket Sales and Operations

Senior Director, Ticket Sales	Drew Ribarchak
Directors, Ticket Ops / Service & Retention	Mark Metz / Kelly Jones
Managers, Ticket Operations / Season Ticket Services	Kevin O'Malley / Carmelo Marzullo
Managers, Inside Sales / Group Sales	Justin Dunn / Dani Nell
Season Ticket Sales Execs.	Noah Heiber, Matthew Hogan, Joshua Latzko, Jacob Welter
Group Event Specialists	Leah Cover, Alexa Edwards, Grant Jamieson, Matt Menard, Patrick Reilly, Malinda Smith
Season Ticket Account Specialists	Emily Auker, Maxwell Cohen, Cody Craig, Amanda Crandell, Jared Crockett, Richard Crimshaw
Coordinators, Ticket Operations / Ticket Sales	Stephen Humphries, Matt Kill / Kayla Constantino

Broadcasting

Director of Broadcasting	Russ Mollohan
FOX Sports Ohio Play-By-Play / Color	Jeff Rimer / Jody Shelley
Radio Play-By-Play Announcer	Bob McElligott
FOX Sports Ohio Hosts/Reporters	Bill Davidge, Brian Giesenschlag, Dave Maetzold

Dallas Stars

Key Off-Season Signings/Acquisitions

2017

April 13 • Named **Ken Hitchcock** head coach.
27 • Re-signed C **Mattias Janmark**.
May 9 • Acquired G **Ben Bishop** from Los Angeles for a 4th-round pick in 2017 NHL Draft.
June 22 • Named **Rick Wilson** and **Stu Barnes** assistant coaches.
26 • Acquired D **Marc Methot** from Vegas for G **Dylan Ferguson** and a 2nd-round pick in 2020 NHL Draft.
26 • Re-signed C **Mark McNeill** and D **Esa Lindell**.
July 1 • Signed C **Martin Hanzal**, C **Brian Flynn**, D **Tyler Pitlick**, D **Brent Regner** and G **Mike McKenna**.
1 • Re-signed D **Patrik Nemeth**.
3 • Signed RW **Alexander Radulov**.
6 • Re-signed RW **Brett Ritchie**.
10 • Re-signed C **Radek Faksa**.
11 • Re-signed C **Gemel Smith**.
Aug. 4 • Re-signed D **Jamie Oleksiak**.

2017-18 Schedule

Oct.	Fri.	6	Vegas		Thu.	4	New Jersey
	Sat.	7	at St. Louis*		Sat.	6	Edmonton*
	Tue.	10	Detroit		Sat.	13	Colorado
	Thu.	12	at Nashville		Mon.	15	at Boston*
	Sat.	14	Colorado		Tue.	16	at Detroit
	Tue.	17	Arizona		Thu.	18	at Columbus
	Thu.	19	at Arizona		Sat.	20	at Buffalo*
	Sat.	21	Carolina		Tue.	23	Florida
	Tue.	24	at Colorado		Thu.	25	Toronto
	Thu.	26	at Edmonton		Tue.	30	Los Angeles
	Fri.	27	at Calgary	**Feb.**	Thu.	1	at Arizona
	Mon.	30	at Vancouver		Sat.	3	Minnesota
Nov.	Thu.	2	at Winnipeg		Mon.	5	NY Rangers
	Sat.	4	Buffalo		Thu.	8	at Chicago
	Mon.	6	Winnipeg		Fri.	9	Pittsburgh
	Fri.	10	NY Islanders		Sun.	11	Vancouver*
	Mon.	13	at Carolina		Fri.	16	St. Louis
	Tue.	14	at Florida		Sun.	18	at San Jose
	Thu.	16	at Tampa Bay		Wed.	21	at Anaheim
	Sat.	18	Edmonton*		Thu.	22	at Los Angeles
	Tue.	21	Montreal		Sat.	24	Winnipeg
	Wed.	22	at Colorado		Tue.	27	Calgary
	Fri.	24	Calgary	**Mar.**	Thu.	1	Tampa Bay
	Tue.	28	at Vegas		Sat.	3	St. Louis*
	Thu.	30	at Chicago		Mon.	5	Ottawa
Dec.	Sat.	2	Chicago		Tue.	6	at Nashville
	Sun.	3	at Colorado		Fri.	9	Anaheim
	Tue.	5	Nashville		Sun.	11	at Pittsburgh
	Thu.	7	at St. Louis*		Tue.	13	at Montreal
	Sat.	9	Vegas		Wed.	14	at Toronto
	Mon.	11	at NY Rangers		Fri.	16	at Ottawa
	Wed.	13	at NY Islanders		Sun.	18	at Winnipeg
	Fri.	15	at New Jersey		Tue.	20	at Washington
	Sat.	16	at Philadelphia		Fri.	23	Boston
	Tue.	19	Washington		Sun.	25	Vancouver
	Thu.	21	Chicago		Tue.	27	Philadelphia
	Sat.	23	Nashville		Thu.	29	at Minnesota
	Wed.	27	at Minnesota		Sat.	31	Minnesota
	Fri.	29	St. Louis	**Apr.**	Tue.	3	at San Jose
	Sun.	31	San Jose		Fri.	6	at Anaheim
Jan.	Tue.	2	Columbus		Sat.	7	at Los Angeles

* Denotes afternoon game.

Retired Numbers

7	Neal Broten	1980-1995, 1996-1997
8	Bill Goldsworthy*	1967-1976
9	Mike Modano	1989-2010
19	Bill Masterton*	1967-1968
26	Jere Lehtinen**	1995-2010

* Minnesota North Stars
** Ceremony to take place on November 24, 2017

CENTRAL DIVISION
51st NHL Season

Franchise date: June 5, 1967

Transferred from Minnesota to Dallas, June 9, 1993.

2016-17 Results: 34w-37l-9otl-2sol 79pts
6th, Central Division • 11th, Western Conference

Tyler Seguin played in all 82 games for the first time in his career in 2016-17. He tied Jamie Benn for the Dallas team lead with 26 goals and led the team with 46 assists and 72 points.

Year-by-Year Record

		Home				Road				Overall									
Season	GP	W	L	T	OL	W	L	T	OL	W	L	T	OL	GF	GA	Pts.	Div. Fin.	Conf. Fin.	Playoff Result
2016-17	82	22	13	....	6	12	24	....	5	34	37	....	11	223	262	79	6th, Cen.	11th, West	Lost Second Round
2015-16	82	28	11	....	2	22	12	....	7	50	23	....	9	267	230	109	1st, Cen.	1st, West	Lost Second Round
2014-15	82	17	16	....	8	24	15	....	2	41	31	....	10	261	260	92	6th, Cen.	10th, West	— out of playoffs —
2013-14	82	23	11	....	7	17	20	....	4	40	31	....	11	235	228	91	5th, Cen.	8th, West	Lost First Round
2012-13	48	11	11	....	3	11	11	....	2	22	22	....	4	130	142	48	5th, Pac.	11th, West	— out of playoffs —
2011-12	82	22	16	....	3	20	19	....	2	42	35	....	5	211	222	89	4th, Pac.	10th, West	— out of playoffs —
2010-11	82	22	11	....	8	20	18	....	3	42	29	....	11	227	233	95	5th, Pac.	9th, West	— out of playoffs —
2009-10	82	23	11	....	7	14	20	....	7	37	31	....	14	237	254	88	5th, Pac.	12th, West	— out of playoffs —
2008-09	82	20	16	....	5	16	19	....	6	36	35	....	11	230	257	83	3rd, Pac.	12th, West	— out of playoffs —
2007-08	82	23	16	....	2	22	14	....	5	45	30	....	7	242	207	97	3rd, Pac.	5th, West	Lost Conf. Final
2006-07	82	28	11	....	2	22	14	....	5	50	25	....	7	226	197	107	3rd, Pac.	6th, West	Lost Conf. Quarter-Final
2005-06	82	28	11	....	2	25	12	....	4	53	23	....	6	265	218	112	1st, Pac.	2nd, West	Lost Conf. Quarter-Final
2004-05																			
2003-04	82	26	7	8	0	15	19	5	2	41	26	13	2	194	175	97	2nd, Pac.	5th, West	Lost Conf. Quarter-Final
2002-03	82	28	5	6	2	18	12	9	2	46	17	15	4	245	169	111	1st, Pac.	1st, West	Lost Conf. Semi-Final
2001-02	82	18	13	6	4	18	15	7	1	36	28	13	5	215	213	90	4th, Pac.	10th, West	— out of playoffs —
2000-01	82	26	10	5	0	22	14	3	2	48	24	8	2	241	187	106	1st, Pac.	3rd, West	Lost Conf. Semi-Final
1999-2000	82	21	11	5	4	22	12	5	2	43	23	10	6	211	184	102	1st, Pac.	2nd, West	Lost Final
1998-99	82	29	8	4	....	22	11	8	....	51	19	12	....	236	168	114	1st, Pac.	1st, West	Won Stanley Cup
1997-98	82	26	7	8	....	23	14	4	....	49	22	11	....	242	167	109	1st, Cen.	1st, West	Lost Conf. Final
1996-97	82	25	13	3	....	23	13	5	....	48	26	8	....	252	198	104	1st, Cen.	2nd, West	Lost Conf. Quarter-Final
1995-96	82	24	18	9	....	12	24	5	....	26	42	14	....	227	280	66	6th, Cen.	11th, West	— out of playoffs —
1994-95	48	9	10	5	....	8	13	3	....	17	23	8	....	136	135	42	5th, Cen.	8th, West	Lost Conf. Quarter-Final
1993-94	84	23	12	7	....	19	17	6	....	42	29	13	....	286	265	97	3rd, Cen.	4th, West	Lost Conf. Semi-Final
1992-93*	84	18	17	7	....	18	21	3	....	36	38	10	....	272	293	82	5th, Norris		— out of playoffs —
1991-92*	80	20	16	4	....	12	26	2	....	32	42	6	....	246	278	70	4th, Norris		Lost Div. Semi-Final
1990-91*	80	19	15	6	....	8	24	8	....	27	39	14	....	256	266	68	4th, Norris		Lost Final
1989-90*	80	26	12	2	....	10	28	2	....	36	40	4	....	284	291	76	4th, Norris		Lost Div. Semi-Final
1988-89*	80	17	15	8	....	10	22	8	....	27	37	16	....	258	278	70	3rd, Norris		Lost Div. Semi-Final
1987-88*	80	10	24	6	....	9	24	7	....	19	48	13	....	242	349	51	5th, Norris		— out of playoffs —
1986-87*	80	17	20	3	....	13	20	7	....	30	40	10	....	296	314	70	5th, Norris		— out of playoffs —
1985-86*	80	21	15	4	....	17	18	5	....	38	33	9	....	327	305	85	2nd, Norris		Lost Div. Semi-Final
1984-85*	80	14	19	7	....	11	24	5	....	25	43	12	....	268	321	62	4th, Norris		Lost Div. Final
1983-84*	80	22	14	4	....	17	17	6	....	39	31	10	....	345	344	88	1st, Norris		Lost Conf. Final
1982-83*	80	23	6	11	....	17	18	5	....	40	24	16	....	321	290	96	2nd, Norris		Lost Div. Final
1981-82*	80	21	7	12	....	16	16	8	....	37	23	20	....	346	288	94	1st, Norris		Lost Div. Semi-Final
1980-81*	80	23	10	7	....	12	18	10	....	35	28	17	....	291	263	87	3rd, Adams		Lost Final
1979-80*	80	25	8	7	....	11	20	9	....	36	28	16	....	311	253	88	3rd, Adams		Lost Semi-Final
1978-79*	80	19	15	6	....	9	25	6	....	28	40	12	....	257	289	68	4th, Adams		— out of playoffs —
1977-78*	80	12	24	4	....	6	29	5	....	18	53	9	....	218	325	45	5th, Smythe		— out of playoffs —
1977-78**	80	14	17	9	....	8	28	4	....	22	45	13	....	230	325	57	4th, Adams		— out of playoffs —
1976-77*	80	17	14	9	....	6	25	9	....	23	39	18	....	240	310	64	2nd, Smythe		Lost Prelim. Round
1976-77**	80	14	17	9	....	11	25	4	....	25	42	13	....	240	292	63	4th, Adams		— out of playoffs —
1975-76*	80	15	22	3	....	5	31	4	....	20	53	7	....	195	303	47	4th, Smythe		— out of playoffs —
1975-76***	80	16	19	5	....	11	23	6	....	27	42	11	....	250	278	65	4th, Adams		— out of playoffs —
1974-75*	80	17	20	3	....	6	30	4	....	23	50	7	....	221	341	53	4th, Smythe		— out of playoffs —
1974-75***	80	15	15	10	....	4	33	3	....	19	48	13	....	212	316	51	4th, Adams		— out of playoffs —
1973-74*	78	18	15	6	....	5	23	11	....	23	38	17	....	235	275	63	7th, West		— out of playoffs —
1973-74***	78	11	18	10	....	2	37	0	....	13	55	10	....	195	342	36	8th, West		— out of playoffs —
1972-73*	78	18	15	6	....	11	22	6	....	37	30	11	....	254	230	85	3rd, West		Lost Quarter-Final
1972-73***	78	11	15	13	....	5	31	3	....	16	46	16	....	213	323	48	8th, West		— out of playoffs —
1971-72*	78	22	11	6	....	15	18	6	....	37	29	12	....	212	191	86	2nd, West		Lost Quarter-Final
1971-72***	78	14	12	13	....	7	27	5	....	21	39	18	....	216	288	60	6th, West		— out of playoffs —
1970-71*	78	16	15	8	....	12	19	8	....	28	34	16	....	191	223	72	4th, West		Lost Semi-Final
1970-71***	78	17	21	1	....	3	32	4	....	20	53	5	....	199	320	45	7th, West		— out of playoffs —
1969-70*	76	11	16	11	....	8	19	11	....	19	35	22	....	224	257	60	3rd, West		Lost Quarter-Final
1969-70†	76	15	16	7	....	7	24	7	....	22	40	14	....	169	243	58	4th, West		Lost Quarter-Final
1968-69*	76	11	21	6	....	7	22	9	....	18	43	15	....	189	270	51	6th, West		— out of playoffs —
1968-69†	76	14	17	7	....	12	18	8	....	29	36	11	....	219	251	69	2nd, West		Lost Quarter-Final
1967-68*	74	17	12	8	....	10	20	7	....	27	32	15	....	191	226	69	4th, West		Lost Semi-Final
1967-68††	74	12	16	9	....	3	26	8	....	15	42	17	....	153	219	47	6th, West		— out of playoffs —

* Minnesota North Stars; ** Cleveland Barons; *** California Golden Seals; † Oakland Seals; †† California/Oakland Seals California transferred to Cleveland, July 14, 1976. Cleveland and Minnesota merged prior to the 1978-79 season.

2017-18 Player Personnel

FORWARDS	HT	WT	*Age	Birthplace	S	2016-17 Club
BENN, Jamie	6-2	210	28	Victoria, BC	L	Dallas
CRACKNELL, Adam	6-2	210	32	Prince Albert, SK	R	Dallas
FAKSA, Radek	6-3	210	23	Vitkov, Czech Rep.	L	Dallas
FLYNN, Brian	6-1	183	29	Lynnfield, MA	R	Montreal
HANZAL, Martin	6-6	226	30	Pisek, Czech.	L	Arizona-Minnesota
JANMARK, Mattias	6-1	195	24	Stockholm, Sweden	L	Dallas
McKENZIE, Curtis	6-2	205	26	Golden, BC	L	Dallas
McNEILL, Mark	6-2	214	24	Langley, BC	R	Rockford-Dallas-Texas
NICHUSHKIN, Valeri	6-4	205	22	Chelyabinsk, Russia	L	CSKA
RADULOV, Alexander	6-1	200	31	Nizhny Tagil, USSR	L	Montreal
RITCHIE, Brett	6-3	220	24	Orangeville, ON	R	Dallas
ROUSSEL, Antoine	6-0	200	27	Roubaix, France	L	Dallas
SEGUIN, Tyler	6-1	200	25	Brampton, ON	R	Dallas
SPEZZA, Jason	6-3	220	34	Mississauga, ON	R	Dallas
DEFENSEMEN						
HAMHUIS, Dan	6-1	209	34	Smithers, BC	L	Dallas
HEISKANEN, Miro	6-1	172	18	Espoo, Finland	L	HIFK
JOHNS, Stephen	6-4	225	25	Ellwood City, PA	R	Dallas-Texas
KLINGBERG, John	6-2	180	25	Lerum, Sweden	R	Dallas
LINDELL, Esa	6-3	210	23	Vantaa, Finland	L	Dallas-Texas
METHOT, Marc	6-3	228	32	Ottawa, ON	L	Ottawa
NEMETH, Patrik	6-3	230	25	Stockholm, Sweden	L	Dallas-Texas
OLEKSIAK, Jamie	6-7	260	24	Toronto, ON	L	Dallas
PATERYN, Greg	6-2	223	27	Sterling Heights, MI	R	Montreal-Dallas
GOALTENDERS	**HT**	**WT**	***Age**	**Birthplace**	**C**	**2016-17 Club**
BISHOP, Ben	6-7	216	30	Denver, CO	L	Tampa Bay-Los Angeles
LEHTONEN, Kari	6-4	205	33	Helsinki, Finland	L	Dallas

* – Age at start of 2017-18 season

Captains' History

* – indicates Cal/Oak/Cle

Bob Woytowich, 1967-68; *Bobby Baun, 1967-68; Moose Vasko, 1968-69; Claude Larose, 1969-70; *Ted Hampson, 1969-70 to 1970-71; Ted Harris, 1970-71 to 1973-74; *Carol Vadnais, 1971-72; *Bert Marshall, 1972-73; *no captain, 1973-74; *Joey Johnston, 1974-75; Bill Goldsworthy, 1974-75, 1975-76; *Jim Neilson and Bob Stewart, 1975-76 to 1977-78 (co-captains); Bill Hogaboam, 1976-77; Nick Beverley, 1977-78; J.P. Parise, 1978-79; Paul Shmyr, 1979-80, 1980-81; Tim Young, 1981-82; Craig Hartsburg, 1982-83; Craig Hartsburg and Brian Bellows, 1983-84; Craig Hartsburg, 1984-85 to 1987-88; Curt Fraser, Bob Rouse and Curt Giles, 1988-89; Curt Giles, 1989-90, 1990-91; Mark Tinordi,1991-92 to 1993-94; Neal Broten and Derian Hatcher, 1994-95; Derian Hatcher,1995-96 to 2002-03; Mike Modano, 2003-04 to 2005-06; Brenden Morrow, 2006-07 to 2012-13; Jamie Benn, 2013-14 to date.

Ken Hitchcock

Head Coach

Born: Edmonton, AB, December 17, 1951.

Dallas Stars general manager Jim Nill announced on April 13, 2017 that Ken Hitchcock had be named head coach. This is Hitchcock's second stint as head coach of the Stars, having previously spent the first seven seasons of his NHL head coaching career behind the Dallas bench from 1996 to 2002.

In his first tour with Dallas, Hitchcock earned a 277-154-72 record in 503 games. He currently ranks first in Stars franchise history in games coached, wins and points percentage (.622). Hitchcock also amassed a 47-33 record in 80 Stanley Cup playoff games during his first tenure with the Stars, making five appearances in the postseason and leading the Stars to the franchise's first Stanley Cup championship in 1999.

The native of Edmonton, Alberta, owns a record of 781-474-199 in 1,454 career games coached over 21 seasons with Dallas, Philadelphia, Columbus and St. Louis. Hitchcock's 1,454 games behind the bench rank fifth in NHL history, while he ranks fourth with 781 and is one win away from tying Al Arbour for third on the league's all-time wins list. The bench boss guided his teams to eight division titles (1996-97, 1997-98, 1998-99, 1999-2000, 2000-01, 2003-04, 2011-12 and 2014-15) and two Presidents' Trophies (1997-98 and 1998-99). Hitchcock was also named the Jack Adams Award winner in 2011-12. Hitchcock ranks eighth all-time in postseason games coached (168) and ninth in postseason wins (86), while he ranks third among all active NHL coaches in both categories. He made five trips to the Conference Finals (1998, 1999, 2000, 2004 and 2016), continuing to two Stanley Cup Finals (1999 and 2000) and winning the Stanley Cup in 1999 with Dallas.

Hitchcock began his professional coaching career as an assistant coach with the Philadelphia Flyers from 1990 to 1993 before spending two-plus seasons as the head coach of the Kalamazoo Wings/Michigan K-Wings, Dallas' International Hockey League affiliate. Previously, Hitchcock was one of the winningest coaches in the Western Hockey League with the Kamloops Blazers from 1984 to 1990.

On the international stage, Hitchcock has represented Team Canada on several occasions. He was named to Team Canada for the 2008 World Championship, leading the squad to the silver medal. Additionally, Hitchcock has served as an associate coach on Team Canada five times in 2002, 2004, 2006, 2010 and 2014, while he helped his teams win gold at the 2002, 2010 and 2014 Winter Olympics. He was also named an assistant coach for Canada at the 2002 World Championships and at the 1987 World Junior Championships, with his teams taking home the gold medal at both.

2016-17 Scoring

* – rookie

Regular Season

Pos	#	Player	Team	GP	G	A	Pts	TOI	+/-	PIM	PP	SH	GW	S	S%
C	91	Tyler Seguin	DAL	82	26	46	72	18:27	–15	22	11	0	4	301	8.6
L	14	Jamie Benn	DAL	77	26	43	69	19:22	–9	66	12	1	4	201	12.9
C	90	Jason Spezza	DAL	68	15	35	50	16:10	–18	29	2	1	4	149	10.1
D	3	John Klingberg	DAL	80	13	36	49	23:21	2	34	4	0	3	124	10.5
C	17 *	Devin Shore	DAL	82	13	20	33	14:08	–4	14	1	0	0	115	11.3
C	12	Radek Faksa	DAL	80	12	21	33	16:10	–6	67	0	0	0	132	9.1
L	21	Antoine Roussel	DAL	60	12	15	27	15:31	1	115	0	0	3	82	14.6
R	25	Brett Ritchie	DAL	78	16	8	24	12:53	11	38	1	0	2	167	9.6
L	10	Patrick Sharp	DAL	48	8	10	18	15:56	–22	31	1	1	0	146	5.5
D	23 *	Esa Lindell	DAL	73	6	12	18	21:52	8	22	0	0	2	99	6.1
R	27	Adam Cracknell	DAL	69	10	6	16	10:27	9	12	0	1	2	87	11.5
L	11	Curtis McKenzie	DAL	53	6	10	16	10:51	5	72	0	0	3	66	9.1
D	2	Dan Hamhuis	DAL	79	1	15	16	19:21	–7	23	1	0	0	83	1.2
C	20	Cody Eakin	DAL	60	3	9	12	16:48	–7	49	0	0	1	82	3.7
R	22	Jiri Hudler	DAL	32	3	8	11	11:51	–3	4	1	0	1	27	11.1
D	28 *	Stephen Johns	DAL	61	4	6	10	18:15	–10	36	0	0	1	91	4.4
D	29	Greg Pateryn	MTL	24	1	5	6	14:22	1	4	0	0	0	28	3.6
			DAL	12	0	3	3	17:30	–2	6	0	0	0	14	0.0
			Total	36	1	8	9	15:25	–1	10	0	0	0	42	2.4
D	5	Jamie Oleksiak	DAL	41	5	2	7	16:12	–4	37	0	0	1	33	15.2
R	83	Ales Hemsky	DAL	15	4	3	7	14:25	–1	0	1	0	0	30	13.3
L	40 *	Remi Elie	DAL	18	1	6	7	15:37	5	8	0	0	0	15	6.7
C	46 *	Gemel Smith	DAL	17	3	3	6	13:35	–1	21	0	1	0	19	15.8
D	6 *	Julius Honka	DAL	16	1	4	5	16:52	–4	4	0	0	1	34	2.9
D	15	Patrik Nemeth	DAL	40	0	3	3	15:46	–4	14	0	0	0	46	0.0
C	16 *	Jason Dickinson	DAL	10	2	0	2	11:47	–3	0	0	0	0	9	22.2
C	37 *	Justin Dowling	DAL	9	0	2	2	10:28	0	2	0	0	0	11	0.0
C	38 *	Mark McNeill	DAL	1	0	0	0	13:49	–1	0	0	0	0	1	0.0
R	34 *	Denis Gurianov	DAL	1	0	0	0	13:06	–1	0	0	0	0	0	0.0

Goaltending

No.	Goaltender	GPI	Mins	Avg	W	L	OT	EN	SO	GA	SA	Sv%	G	A	PIM
32	Kari Lehtonen	59	3177	2.85	22	25	7	10	3	151	1546	.902	0	1	4
31	Antti Niemi	37	1729	3.30	12	12	4	4	0	95	880	.892	0	0	0
	Totals	**82**	**4960**	**3.15**	**34**	**37**	**11**	**14**	**3**	**260**	**2440**	**.893**			

Coaching History

* – indicates Cal/Oak/Cle

Wren Blair, 1967-68; *Bert Olmstead and Gord Fashoway, 1967-68; Wren Blair and John Muckler, 1968-69; *Fred Glover, 1968-69 to 1970-71; Wren Blair and Charlie Burns, 1969-70; Jack Gordon, 1970-71 to 1972-73; *Fred Glover and Vic Stasiuk, 1971-72; *Garry Young and Fred Glover, 1972-73; Jack Gordon and Parker MacDonald, 1973-74; *Fred Glover and Marshall Johnston, 1973-74; Jack Gordon and Charlie Burns, 1974-75; *Marshall Johnston and Bill McCreary, Sr., 1974-75; Ted Harris,1975-76, 1976-77; *Jack Evans, 1975-76 to 1977-78; Ted Harris, André Beaulieu and Lou Nanne, 1977-78; Harry Howell and Glen Sonmor, 1978-79; Glen Sonmor, 1979-80 to 1981-82; Glen Sonmor and Murray Oliver, 1982-83; Bill Mahoney, 1983-84, 1984-85; Lorne Henning, 1985-86; Lorne Henning and Glen Sonmor, 1986-87; Herb Brooks,1987-88; Pierre Page, 1988-89, 1989-90; Bob Gainey, 1990-91 to 1994-95; Bob Gainey and Ken Hitchcock, 1995-96; Ken Hitchcock, 1996-97 to 2000-01; Ken Hitchcock and Rick Wilson, 2001-02; Dave Tippett, 2002-03 to 2008-09; Marc Crawford, 2009-10, 2010-11; Glen Gulutzan, 2011-12, 2012-13; Lindy Ruff, 2013-14 to 2016-17; Ken Hitchcock, 2017-18.

Coaching Record

			Regular Season				Playoffs			
Season	Team	League	GC	W	L	O/T	GC	W	L	T
1984-85	Kamloops	WHL	71	52	17	2	15	10	5	....
1985-86	Kamloops	WHL	72	49	19	4	16	14	2	....
1985-86	Kamloops	M-Cup	....	....	....	....	4	1	3	....
1986-87	Kamloops	WHL	72	55	14	3	13	8	5	....
1987-88	Kamloops	WHL	72	45	26	1	18	12	6	....
1988-89	Kamloops	WHL	72	34	33	5	16	8	8	....
1989-90	Kamloops	WHL	72	56	16	0	17	14	3	....
1989-90	Kamloops	M-Cup	....	....	....	....	3	0	3	....
1993-94	Kalamazoo	IHL	81	48	26	7	5	1	4	....
1994-95	Kalamazoo	IHL	81	43	24	14	16	10	6	....
1995-96	Michigan	IHL	40	19	10	11	....	....	....	....
1995-96	**Dallas**	**NHL**	**43**	**15**	**23**	**5**	....	....	....	....
1996-97	**Dallas**	**NHL**	**82**	**48**	**26**	**8**	**7**	**3**	**4**	....
1997-98	**Dallas**	**NHL**	**82**	**49**	**22**	**11**	**17**	**10**	**7**	....
1998-99 ♦	**Dallas**	**NHL**	**82**	**51**	**19**	**12**	**23**	**16**	**7**	....
99-2000	**Dallas**	**NHL**	**82**	**43**	**23**	**16**	**23**	**14**	**9**	....
2000-01	**Dallas**	**NHL**	**82**	**48**	**24**	**10**	**10**	**4**	**6**	....
2001-02	**Dallas**	**NHL**	**50**	**23**	**17**	**10**	....	....	....	....
2002-03	**Philadelphia**	**NHL**	**82**	**45**	**20**	**17**	**13**	**6**	**7**	....
2003-04	**Philadelphia**	**NHL**	**82**	**40**	**21**	**21**	**18**	**11**	**7**	....
2004-05	**Philadelphia**				SEASON CANCELLED					
2005-06	**Philadelphia**	**NHL**	**82**	**45**	**26**	**11**	**6**	**2**	**4**	....
2006-07	**Philadelphia**	**NHL**	**8**	**1**	**6**	**1**	....	....	....	....
2006-07	**Columbus**	**NHL**	**62**	**28**	**29**	**5**	....	....	....	....
2007-08	**Columbus**	**NHL**	**82**	**34**	**36**	**12**	....	....	....	....
2008-09	**Columbus**	**NHL**	**82**	**41**	**31**	**10**	**4**	**0**	**4**	....
2009-10	**Columbus**	**NHL**	**58**	**22**	**27**	**9**	....	....	....	....
2011-12	**St. Louis**	**NHL**	**69**	**43**	**15**	**11**	**9**	**4**	**5**	....
2012-13	**St. Louis**	**NHL**	**48**	**29**	**17**	**2**	**6**	**2**	**4**	....
2013-14	**St. Louis**	**NHL**	**82**	**52**	**23**	**7**	**6**	**2**	**4**	....
2014-15	**St. Louis**	**NHL**	**82**	**51**	**24**	**7**	**6**	**2**	**4**	....
2015-16	**St. Louis**	**NHL**	**82**	**49**	**24**	**9**	**20**	**10**	**10**	....
2016-17	**St. Louis**	**NHL**	**50**	**24**	**21**	**5**	....	....	....	....
	NHL Totals		**1454**	**781**	**474**	**199**	**168**	**86**	**82**	....

♦ Stanley Cup win.
Jack Adams Award (2012)

Club Records

Team

(Figures in brackets for season records are games played; records for fewest points, wins, ties, losses, goals, goals against are for 70 or more games)

Most Points .... 114 — 1998-99 (82)
Most Wins .... 53 — 2005-06 (82)
Most Ties .... 22 — 1969-70 (76)
Most Losses .... 55 — 1973-74 (78) California
.... 53 — 1975-76 (80), 1977-78 (80)
Most Goals .... 346 — 1981-82 (80)
Most Goals Against .... 349 — 1987-88 (80)
Fewest Points .... 36 — 1973-74 (78) California
.... 45 — 1977-78 (80)
Fewest Wins .... 13 — 1973-74 (78) California
.... 18 — 1968-69 (76), 1977-78 (80)
Fewest Ties .... 4 — 1989-90 (80)
Fewest Losses .... 19 — 1998-99 (82)
Fewest Goals .... 153 — 1967-68 (74) Cal./Oakland
.... 189 — 1968-69 (76)
Fewest Goals Against .... 167 — 1997-98 (82)
Longest Winning Streak
Overall .... 7 — Mar. 16-28/80, Mar. 16-Apr. 2/97, Nov. 22-Dec. 5/97, Jan. 29-Feb. 11/08
Home .... 11 — Nov. 4-Dec. 27/72
Away .... 8 — Dec. 13/10-Jan. 20/11
Longest Team Point Streak
Overall .... 15 — Dec. 6/98-Jan. 6/99 (12W, 3T)
Home .... 17 — Jan. 23-Mar. 20/04 (13W, 4T)
Away .... 11 — Dec. 27/02-Feb. 27/03 (7W, 3T, 1OTL)
Longest Losing Streak
Overall .... 10 — Feb. 1-20/76
Home .... 6 — Jan. 17-Feb. 4/70, Feb. 21-Mar. 8/09
Away .... 10 — Dec. 12/09-Jan. 21/10
Longest Winless Streak
Overall .... 20 — Jan. 15-Feb. 28/70 (15L, 5T)
Home .... 12 — Jan. 17-Feb. 25/70 (8L, 4T)
Away .... 24 — Nov. 21/73-Feb. 20/74 (24L) California
.... 23 — Oct. 25/74-Jan. 28/75 (19L, 4T)
Most Shutouts, Season .... 11 — 2000-01 (82), 2002-03 (82)
Most PIM, Season .... 2,303 — 1987-88 (80)
Most Goals, Game .... 15 — Nov. 11/81 (Wpg. 2 at Min. 15)

Individual

Most Seasons .... 21 — Mike Modano
Most Games .... 1,459 — Mike Modano
Most Goals, Career .... 557 — Mike Modano
Most Assists, Career .... 802 — Mike Modano
Most Points, Career ...... 1,359 — Mike Modano (557G, 802A)
Most PIM, Career .... 1,883 — Shane Churla
Most Shutouts, Career .... 40 — Marty Turco
Longest Consecutive Games Streak .... 442 — Danny Grant (Dec. 4/68-Apr. 7/74)
Most Goals, Season .... 55 — Dino Ciccarelli (1981-82), Brian Bellows (1989-90)
Most Assists, Season .... 76 — Neal Broten (1985-86)
Most Points, Season .... 114 — Bobby Smith (1981-82; 43G, 71A)
Most PIM, Season .... 382 — Basil McRae (1987-88)
Most Points, Defenseman, Season .... 77 — Craig Hartsburg (1981-82; 17G, 60A)
Most Points, Center, Season .... 114 — Bobby Smith (1981-82; 43G, 71A)
Most Points, Right Wing, Season .... 106 — Dino Ciccarelli (1981-82; 55G, 51A)
Most Points, Left Wing, Season .... 99 — Brian Bellows (1989-90; 55G, 44A)
Most Points, Rookie, Season .... 98 — Neal Broten (1981-82; 38G, 60A)
Most Shutouts, Season .... 9 — Ed Belfour (1997-98), Marty Turco (2003-04)
Most Goals, Game .... 5 — Tim Young (Jan. 15/79)
Most Assists, Game .... 5 — Murray Oliver (Oct. 24/71), Larry Murphy (Oct. 17/89), Brad Richards (Feb. 28/08), Jamie Benn (Nov. 14/13)
Most Points, Game .... 7 — Bobby Smith (Nov. 11/81; 4G, 3A)

Records include Minnesota North Stars, 1967-68 through 1992-93 and California/Oakland/Cleveland, 1967-68 through 1977-78. Cleveland and Minnesota merged prior to the 1978-79 season.

All-time Record vs. Other Clubs

Regular Season

	Total								At Home								On Road							
	GP	W	L	T	OL	GF	GA	PTS	GP	W	L	T	OL	GF	GA	PTS	GP	W	L	T	OL	GF	GA	PTS
Anaheim	119	70	34	5	10	349	274	155	60	42	12	2	4	190	122	90	59	28	22	3	6	159	152	65
Arizona	173	89	65	13	6	553	496	197	87	46	30	9	2	289	239	103	86	43	35	4	4	264	257	94
Boston	135	33	79	23	0	357	526	89	68	20	35	13	0	192	246	53	67	13	44	10	0	165	280	36
Buffalo	120	47	54	17	2	353	382	113	61	32	22	6	1	196	171	71	59	15	32	11	1	157	211	42
Calgary	167	67	66	25	9	505	519	168	84	41	26	11	6	289	251	99	83	26	40	14	3	216	268	69
Carolina	77	44	27	6	0	285	229	94	37	24	11	2	0	146	107	50	40	20	16	4	0	139	122	44
Chicago	273	105	128	31	9	826	921	250	138	64	54	16	4	460	426	148	135	41	74	15	5	366	495	102
Colorado	132	57	56	12	7	385	423	133	66	36	19	5	6	221	189	83	66	21	37	7	1	164	234	50
Columbus	55	33	16	0	6	158	132	72	27	16	9	0	2	75	62	34	28	17	7	0	4	83	70	38
Detroit	251	105	108	34	4	807	848	248	125	59	44	18	4	420	380	140	126	46	64	16	0	387	468	108
Edmonton	132	69	43	15	5	443	416	158	66	39	18	7	2	233	178	87	66	30	25	8	3	210	238	71
Florida	33	15	12	3	3	93	91	36	16	5	7	2	2	44	56	14	17	10	5	1	1	49	35	22
Los Angeles	231	112	76	32	11	749	679	267	116	67	33	13	3	410	314	150	115	45	43	19	8	339	365	117
Minnesota	66	38	22	1	5	196	173	82	34	24	6	1	3	125	81	52	32	14	16	0	2	71	92	30
Montreal	131	34	74	21	2	339	494	91	66	21	32	12	1	180	222	55	65	13	42	9	1	159	272	36
Nashville	75	42	29	1	3	207	176	88	37	27	9	0	1	118	67	55	38	15	20	1	2	89	109	33
New Jersey	106	54	40	9	3	338	310	120	54	32	14	6	2	190	135	72	52	22	26	3	1	148	175	48
NY Islanders	110	39	53	16	2	322	402	96	54	21	24	8	1	159	192	51	56	18	29	8	1	163	210	45
NY Rangers	138	42	73	22	1	395	479	107	68	22	34	11	1	208	241	56	70	20	39	11	0	187	238	51
Ottawa	34	21	11	0	2	114	93	44	18	11	7	0	0	68	55	22	16	10	4	0	2	46	38	22
Philadelphia	149	43	72	32	2	409	512	120	74	31	25	16	2	240	233	80	75	12	47	16	0	169	279	40
Pittsburgh	142	63	65	12	2	462	493	140	72	42	22	6	2	269	230	92	70	21	43	6	0	193	263	48
St. Louis	282	107	121	43	11	853	902	268	140	66	46	22	6	463	406	160	142	41	75	21	5	390	496	108
San Jose	123	64	45	5	9	340	319	142	61	30	23	4	4	175	160	68	62	34	22	1	5	165	159	74
Tampa Bay	38	23	12	3	0	122	99	49	18	10	7	1	0	60	53	21	20	13	5	2	0	62	46	28
Toronto	212	91	91	28	2	727	703	212	104	54	38	11	1	390	325	120	108	37	53	17	1	337	378	92
Vancouver	185	92	67	22	4	597	577	210	93	52	29	12	0	322	260	116	92	40	38	10	4	275	317	94
Washington	95	49	27	16	3	334	265	117	48	26	11	8	3	177	130	63	47	23	16	8	0	157	135	54
Winnipeg	33	20	11	0	2	104	100	42	16	10	5	0	1	42	36	21	17	10	6	0	1	62	64	21
Defunct Clubs	65	29	24	12	0	207	191	70	33	19	8	6	0	123	86	44	32	10	16	6	0	84	105	26
Totals	**3882**	**1697**	**1601**	**459**	**125**	**11929**	**12224**	**3978**	**1941**	**989**	**660**	**228**	**64**	**6474**	**5653**	**2270**	**1941**	**708**	**941**	**231**	**61**	**5455**	**6571**	**1708**

Cal/Oak/Cle results other than those vs. Minnesota North Stars not included. Results vs. North Stars listed under Defunct Clubs.

Playoffs

	Series	W	L	GP	W	L	T	GF	GA	Last Mtg.	Rnd.	Result
Anaheim	3	1	2	18	8	10	0	52	47	2014	FR	L 2-4
Boston	1	1	0	3	3	0	0	20	13	1981	PR	W 3-0
Buffalo	3	2	1	13	8	5	0	39	37	1999	F	W 4-2
Calgary	1	1	0	6	4	2	0	25	18	1981	SF	W 4-2
Chicago	6	2	4	33	14	19	0	118	120	1991	DSF	W 4-2
Colorado	4	2	2	24	10	14	0	62	66	2006	CQF	L 1-4
Detroit	4	0	4	24	8	16	0	50	72	2008	CF	L 2-4
Edmonton	8	6	2	42	27	15	0	118	104	2003	CQF	W 4-2
*Los Angeles	2	1	1	14	7	7	0	51	44	1969	QF	L 3-4
Minnesota	1	1	0	6	4	2	0	21	17	2016	FR	W 4-2
Montreal	2	1	1	13	6	7	0	37	48	1980	QF	W 4-3
New Jersey	1	0	1	6	2	4	0	9	15	2000	F	L 2-4
NY Islanders	1	0	1	5	1	4	0	16	26	1981	F	L 1-4
Philadelphia	2	0	2	11	3	8	0	26	41	1980	SF	L 1-4
*Pittsburgh	2	0	2	10	2	8	0	22	41	1991	F	L 2-4
St. Louis	13	6	7	73	37	36	0	211	212	2016	SR	L 3-4
San Jose	3	3	0	17	12	5	0	46	30	2008	CSF	W 4-2
Toronto	2	2	0	7	6	1	0	35	26	1983	DSF	W 3-1
Vancouver	2	0	2	12	4	8	0	23	31	2007	CQF	L 3-4
Totals	**61**	**29**	**32**	**337**	**166**	**171**	**0**	**981**	**1008**			

* Includes Oakland playoff results.

Calgary totals include Atlanta Flames, 1972-73 to 1979-80. Carolina totals include Hartford, 1979-80 to 1996-97.
Colorado totals include Quebec, 1979-80 to 1994-95.
New Jersey totals include Kansas City, 1974-75, 1975-76, and Colorado Rockies, 1976-77 to 1981-82.
Phoenix totals include Winnipeg, 1979-80 to 1995-96. Winnipeg totals include Atlanta Thrashers, 1999-2000 to 2010-11.

Playoff Results 2017-2013

Year	Round	Opponent	Result	GF	GA
2016	SR	St. Louis	L 3-4	14	25
	FR	Minnesota	W 4-2	21	17
2014	FR	Anaheim	L 2-4	18	20

Abbreviations: Round: F – Final; **CF** – conference final; **CSF** – conference semi-final; **SR** – second round; **CQF** – conference quarter-final; **FR** – first round; **DSF** – division semi-final; **SF** – semi-final; **QF** – quarter-final; **PR** – preliminary round.

2016-17 Results

Oct.	13	Anaheim	4-2		10	at Anaheim	0-2
	15	at Colorado	5-6		12	Detroit	5-2
	18	at Nashville	2-1		14	Minnesota	4-5
	20	Los Angeles	3-4*		16	at Buffalo	1-4
	22	Columbus	0-3		17	at NY Rangers	7-6
	25	Winnipeg	3-2		19	at NY Islanders	0-3
	27	at Winnipeg	1-4		21	Washington	3-4*
	29	at Minnesota	0-4		24	Minnesota	2-3†
Nov.	1	at Columbus	2-3*		26	Buffalo	4-3
	3	St. Louis	6-2		31	Toronto	6-3
	5	Chicago	2-3	**Feb.**	2	Winnipeg	3-4
	6	at Chicago	3-4*		4	Chicago	3-5
	8	at Winnipeg	2-8		7	at Toronto	1-3
	10	at Calgary	4-2		9	at Ottawa	2-3
	11	at Edmonton	3-2		11	Carolina	5-2
	13	at Vancouver	4-5*		12	at Nashville	3-5
	15	New Jersey	1-2*		14	at Winnipeg	2-5
	17	Colorado	3-2		16	at Minnesota	1-3
	19	Edmonton	2-5		18	Tampa Bay	4-3*
	21	Minnesota	3-2*		24	Arizona	5-2
	23	at Nashville	2-5		26	Boston	3-6
	25	Vancouver	2-1		28	Pittsburgh	3-2
	28	at St. Louis	3-4*	**Mar.**	2	NY Islanders	4-5
	29	at Detroit	1-3		4	at Florida	2-1
Dec.	1	at Pittsburgh	2-6		6	at Washington	4-2
	3	at Colorado	3-0		8	Ottawa	2-5
	6	Calgary	1-2		12	at San Jose	1-5
	8	Nashville	5-2		14	at Edmonton	1-7
	10	at Philadelphia	2-4		16	at Vancouver	4-2
	11	at Chicago	1-3		17	at Calgary	1-3
	13	Anaheim	6-2		20	San Jose	1-0
	15	NY Rangers	0-2		23	at Chicago	2-3†
	17	Philadelphia	3-1		24	San Jose	6-1
	20	St. Louis	2-3*		26	at New Jersey	2-1*
	23	Los Angeles	3-2*		28	at Montreal	1-4
	27	at Arizona	3-2		30	at Boston	0-2
	29	Colorado	4-2	**Apr.**	1	at Carolina	3-0
	31	Florida	1-3		2	at Tampa Bay	3-6
Jan.	4	Montreal	3-4*		4	Arizona	3-2*
	7	at St. Louis	3-4		6	Nashville	3-7
	9	at Los Angeles	6-4		8	Colorado	4-3†

* – Overtime † – Shootout

NHL Draft Selections 2017-2003

Name in bold denotes played in NHL.

2017

Pick	
3	Miro Heiskanen
26	Jake Oettinger
39	Jason Robertson
79	Lane Zablocki
101	Liam Hawel
132	Jacob Peterson
163	Brett Davis
194	Dylan Ferguson

2016

Pick	
25	Riley Tufte
90	Fredrik Karlstrom
116	Rhett Gardner
128	Colton Point
146	Nicholas Caamano
176	Jakob Stenqvist

2015

Pick	
12	**Denis Gurianov**
49	Roope Hintz
103	Chris Martenet
133	Joseph Cecconi
163	Markus Ruusu

2014

Pick	
14	**Julius Honka**
45	Brett Pollock
75	Alex Peters
105	Michael Prapavessis
115	Brent Moran
135	Miro Karjalainen
154	Aaron Haydon
165	John Nyberg
195	Patrick Sanvido

2013

Pick	
10	**Valeri Nichushkin**
29	**Jason Dickinson**
40	**Remi Elie**
54	Philippe Desrosiers
68	Niklas Hansson
101	**Nick Paul**
131	Cole Ully
149	Matej Paulovic
182	Aleksi Makela

2012

Pick	
13	**Radek Faksa**
43	Ludwig Bystrom
54	Mike Winther
61	**Devin Shore**
74	**Esa Lindell**
104	**Gemel Smith**
134	Branden Troock
144	Henri Kiviaho
183	Dmitry Sinitsyn

2011

Pick	
14	**Jamie Oleksiak**
44	**Brett Ritchie**
105	Emil Molin
135	Troy Vance
165	Matej Stransky
195	**Jyrki Jokipakka**

2010

Pick	
11	**Jack Campbell**
41	**Patrik Nemeth**
77	Alexander Guptill
109	Alex Theriau
131	**John Klingberg**

2009

Pick	
8	**Scott Glennie**
38	**Alex Chiasson**
69	**Reilly Smith**
129	**Tomas Vincour**
159	**Curtis McKenzie**

2008

Pick	
59	Tyler Beskorowany
89	Scott Winkler
149	**Philip Larsen**
176	Matthew Tassone
209	Mike Bergin

2007

Pick	
50	Nico Sacchetti
64	Sergei Korostin
112	**Colton Sceviour**
128	Austin Smith
129	**Jamie Benn**
136	Ondrej Roman
149	Michael Neal
172	**Luke Gazdic**

2006

Pick	
27	**Ivan Vishnevskiy**
90	Aaron Snow
120	**Richard Bachman**
138	**David McIntyre**
150	Max Warn

2005

Pick	
28	**Matt Niskanen**
33	**James Neal**
71	**Rich Clune**
75	**Perttu Lindgren**
146	**Tom Wandell**
160	**Matt Watkins**
223	Pat McGann

2004

Pick	
28	**Mark Fistric**
34	Johan Fransson
52	**Raymond Sawada**
56	**Nicklas Grossmann**
86	John Lammers
104	Fredrik Naslund
183	Trevor Ludwig
218	Sergei Kukushkin
248	Lukas Vomela
280	Matt McKnight

2003

Pick	
33	**Loui Eriksson**
36	**Vojtech Polak**
54	**B.J. Crombeen**
99	Matt Nickerson
134	Alexander Naurov
144	Eero Kilpelainen
165	Gino Guyer
185	**Francis Wathier**
195	**Drew Bagnall**
196	Elias Granath
259	Niko Vainio

General Managers' History

* – indicates Cal/Oak/Cle

*Rudy Pilous, until June 1967; Wren Blair, 1967-68 to 1973-74; *Bert Olmstead, 1967-68; *Frank Selke Jr. 1968-69, 1969-70; *Frank Selke Jr., Bill Torrey and Fred Glover, 1970-71; *Garry Young, 1971-72; *Garry Young and Fred Glover, 1972-73; *Fred Glover and Garry Young, 1973-74; Jack Gordon, 1974-75 to 1976-77; *Bill McCreary Sr., 1974-75, 1975-76; *Bill McCreary Sr. and Harry Howell, 1976-77; Jack Gordon and Lou Nanne, 1977-78; *Harry Howell, 1977-78; Lou Nanne, 1978-79 to 1986-87; Lou Nanne and Jack Ferreira, 1987-88; Jack Ferreira, 1988-89, 1989-90; Bob Clarke, 1990-91, 1991-92; Bob Gainey, 1992-93 to 2000-01; Bob Gainey and Doug Armstrong, 2001-02; Doug Armstrong, 2002-03 to 2006-07; Doug Armstrong and Brett Hull/Les Jackson, 2007-08; Brett Hull/Les Jackson, 2008-09; Joe Nieuwendyk, 2009-10 to 2012-13; Jim Nill, 2013-14 to date.

Jim Nill

General Manager

Born: Hanna, AB, April 11, 1958.

Jim Nill was appointed general manager of the Dallas Stars on April 29, 2013. He is the 11th General Manager in franchise history and the sixth since the team moved to Dallas. In his first season with the club in 2013-14, Dallas returned to the playoffs for the first time since 2007-08. In 2015-16, the Stars had the second-best record in the NHL with 109 points.

Before coming to Dallas, Nill concluded his 15th season as assistant general manager of the Detroit Red Wings, and his 19th season overall as a member of the management team, in 2012-13. His responsibilities with Detroit included directing the amateur scouting department and overseeing all selections at the annual NHL Draft, as well as managing the development of the organization's prospects at both the professional and amateur levels. During Nill's tenure in Detroit, the Red Wings had more wins than any other franchise in the NHL, won the Stanley Cup four times (1997, 1998, 2002 and 2008), the Presidents' Trophy six times (1995, 1996, 2002, 2004, 2006 and 2008), the Central Division title 12 times, and won seven regular season Western Conference titles while never missing the playoffs. He was an integral part of Detroit's drafting of Pavel Datsyuk, Henrik Zetterberg, Niklas Kronwall, Valtteri Filppula, Jimmy Howard and Johan Franzen. Nill was also general manager of Team Canada for the 2004 World Championship, winning a gold medal.

Nill joined the Red Wings' front office in the summer of 1994 following three seasons with the Ottawa Senators. Previously, Nill enjoyed a nine-season NHL career as a right winger with the Boston Bruins, Vancouver Canucks, St. Louis Blues, Winnipeg Jets and Red Wings. He collected 58 goals, 87 assists and 854 penalty minutes in 524 regular season games. Nill later went to Adirondack of the American Hockey League as a player/coach, retiring as a player after the 1990-91 season. A member of the 1979-80 Canadian national and Olympic team, he was a fifth-round pick of the St. Louis Blues (89th overall) in the 1978 NHL Draft.

Club Directory

American Airlines Center

Dallas Stars
Office Address:
2601 Avenue of the Stars
Frisco, TX 75034
Phone **214/387-5500**
FAX 214/387-5564
Ticket Information 214/GO STARS
www.dallasstars.com
Capacity: 18,532

Executives	
Owner and Governor	R. Thomas Gaglardi
President, CEO and Alternate Governor	James R. Lites
Executive Vice President, Chief Revenue Officer	Brad Alberts
Executive Vice President, Chief Operating Officer	Jason Farris
Executive Assistant to the President	Brittany McMullen
Hockey Operations	
General Manager	Jim Nill
Senior Advisor to the General Manager	Les Jackson
Assistant General Manager/Texas Stars G.M.	Scott White
Assistant General Manager	Mark Janko
Head Coach	Ken Hitchcock
Assistant Coaches	Stu Barnes / Curt Fraser / Rick Wilson
Goaltending Coach / Video Coach	Jeff Reese / Kelly Forbes
Skills Coach / Goaltending Development Coach	Stan Tugolukov / Jim Bedard
Coordinators, Player Development	J.J. McQueen / Rich Peverley
Director, Team Services	Jason Rademan
Directors, Amateur / European Scouting	Joe McDonnell / Kari Takko
Head Professional Scout	Paul McIntosh
Professional Scouts	Craig Bonner, Alex Lepore, Danny O'Brien
Amateur Scouts	Dennis Holland, Jiri Hrdina, Jimmy Johnston, David Kolb, Mark Leach, Rickard Oquist, Buddy Powers, Borys Protsenko, Evgueni Tsybouk, Shane Turner
Athletic Trainers, Head / Associate	Dave Zeis / Craig Lowry
Equipment Manager / Asst. Mgr. / Assistant	Steve Sumner / Dennis Soetaert / Ryan Martin
Strength and Conditioning / Massage	Brad Jellis / Daniel Garcia
Executive Assistant, Hockey Operations	Lisa Smail
Medical Staff	
Head Team Physician	Dr. William J. Robertson
Team Doctors	Drs. Wayne Bowman, Kathy Coyner, Robert J. Dimeff, Alexander Eastman, S. Marshal Isaacs, Jeffery M. Kenkel, Jeffrey C. Metzger, Shane Miller
Dentist / Neuropsychologist	Dr. Wayne Scott / Munro Cullum
Physical Therapy / Chiropractor	Ross Quesry / Mary Collings
Production and Entertainment	
Vice President, Brand Development & Broadcasting	Dan Stuchal
Play-By-Play / Analysts / Host	David Strader / Daryl Reaugh / Craig Ludwig / Josh Bogorad
Producer / Director/Producer / Assoc. Director	Mike Leary / Mark Vittorio / Doug Foster
Broadcast Manager / Digital Content Manager	John Sponsler / Cody Eastwood
Radio Analysts	Bruce LeVine, Owen Newkirk
Sr. Dir., Game Entertainment / Dir., Visual Effects	Jason Danby / Jeff Neal
Director, Production	Jerry Miranda
Editors	Hunter Harrington, Kevin Harp
Digital Content Director / Editor	Jeff Toates / Chandler Smith
Art Director / Graphic Designer	Chase Hargrove / Gabriella Pineda
Director, Event Operations	Steve Phillips
Ice Girls Director	Christina Swanson
Manager, Promotions	Kevin Hardey
Coordinators, Production / Mascot	Shae Bryan / Wade Schapp
Communications	
Vice President, Communications	Tom Holy
Managers, Media Relations / Corporate Comm.	Ben Fromstein / Joe Calvillo
Manager, Player Relations	Christa Melia
Team Photographers	Glenn James, Tim Heitman, Brandon Colston
Dallas Stars Foundation	
Executive Director	Grady Raskin
Director, Development of the Foundation	Brett Dougherty
Coordinators, Foundation / Education / 50/50 Raffle	Katherine Markland / Allie Helm / Cheryl Swain
Assistant	Chelsea Livingston
Corporate Partnerships	
Vice President, Corporate Partnerships	Grady Raskin
Directors, Corporate Partnerships	Shay Butler, Christopher Hart
Account Executives	Geoffrey Aultz, Jenifer Guerrero
Activation Director / Managers / Coordinator	Lisa Wile / Caroline Morehead, Kimberly Skrepcinski / Ann Marie Hickey
Business Development	
Directors, Business Development	Marty Turco, Chase Smith
Finance and Administration	
Chief Financial Officer / Senior Director, Finance	Toni May / Ruth Hill
Managers, Accounting / Accounts Payable	Michael Beener / Tina Forbes
Sr. Staff Accountant / Staff Accountants	Matthew Lillestol / Maren Garcia, Lindsey Pacatte
Accounts Payable / Payroll Administrator	Joshua Webb / Jenny Thompson
Legal and Human Resources	
Vice President and General	Alana Newhook
Associate Legal Counsel	Cara Martin
Human Resources Director / Generalist	Lindsay Dowdy / Megan Lippe
Corporate Operations	
Vice President/Chief Information Officer	Dan Doggendorf
Technology Engineers	Alex Cheng, Jonathan Geremia, Jchon Paradise, Zacchary Phifer
Business Ops. Asst. / Archivist/Warehouse Coord.	Jessica Nemergut / Jeremy Rasmussen
Director, Facility Improvement / Facility Engineer	Jerid Nemergut / Lee Savage
Front Desk Receptionist	Jamie Silva
Marketing	
Vice President, Sales and Marketing	Matt Bowman
Director, Marketing	Trent Morton
Manager, Marketing and Brand Affiliate	Sheryll Gomez
Managers, Digital & Social Media / Website	Bryan Renahan / Colleen Hamilton
Administrator, Sales & Marketing	Robbyn Dougherty
Alumni Association	
Director, Alumni Association	Bob Bassen
Ticket Sales and Operations	
Senior Director, Ticket Sales & Service	Daniel Venegas
Director, New Business & Premium Sales	Michael Montgomery
Director, Ticket Operations	Mac Amin
Dr Pepper StarCenters and Arena	
Vice President, Dr Pepper StarCenters	Damon Boettcher
Assistant Vice President, Programming	Aanya Montgomery
Hockey Development Director / Coordinator	Dwight Mullins / Jesse Fraser
Director, Operations	David Copland

Detroit Red Wings

Key Off-Season Signings/Acquisitions

2017

June 27 • Re-signed C **Ben Street**.
29 • Re-signed D **Brian Lashoff** and D **Dylan McIlrath**.
July 1 • Signed D **Trevor Daley** and D **Luke Witkowski**.
3 • Re-signed D **Xavier Ouellet**.
18 • Re-signed RW **Martin Frk**.
21 • Re-signed LW **Tomas Tatar**.

2016-17 Results: 33W-36L-13OTL-0SOL 79PTS

7TH, Atlantic Division • 14TH, Eastern Conference

2017-18 Schedule

Month	Day	Date	Opponent
Oct.	Thu.	5	Minnesota
	Sat.	7	at Ottawa
	Tue.	10	at Dallas
	Thu.	12	at Arizona
	Fri.	13	at Vegas
	Mon.	16	Tampa Bay
	Wed.	18	at Toronto
	Fri.	20	Washington
	Sun.	22	Vancouver
	Tue.	24	at Buffalo
	Thu.	26	at Tampa Bay
	Sat.	28	at Florida
	Tue.	31	Arizona
Nov.	Thu.	2	at Ottawa
	Sun.	5	at Edmonton*
	Mon.	6	at Vancouver
	Thu.	9	at Calgary
	Sat.	11	Columbus
	Wed.	15	Calgary
	Fri.	17	Buffalo
	Sun.	19	Colorado
	Wed.	22	Edmonton
	Fri.	24	at NY Rangers
	Sat.	25	New Jersey
	Tue.	28	Los Angeles
	Thu.	30	Montreal
Dec.	Sat.	2	at Montreal
	Tue.	5	Winnipeg
	Sat.	9	St. Louis*
	Mon.	11	Florida
	Wed.	13	Boston
	Fri.	15	Toronto
	Tue.	19	at NY Islanders
	Wed.	20	at Philadelphia
	Sat.	23	at Boston*
	Wed.	27	at New Jersey
	Fri.	29	NY Rangers
	Sun.	31	Pittsburgh
Jan.	Wed.	3	Ottawa
	Fri.	5	Florida
	Sun.	7	Tampa Bay
	Sat.	13	at Pittsburgh*
	Sun.	14	at Chicago
	Tue.	16	Dallas
	Sat.	20	Carolina
	Mon.	22	at New Jersey
	Tue.	23	Philadelphia
	Thu.	25	Chicago
	Wed.	31	San Jose
Feb.	Fri.	2	at Carolina
	Sat.	3	at Florida
	Tue.	6	Boston
	Fri.	9	at NY Islanders
	Sun.	11	at Washington*
	Tue.	13	Anaheim
	Thu.	15	at Tampa Bay
	Sat.	17	at Nashville
	Sun.	18	Toronto
	Tue.	20	Nashville
	Thu.	22	Buffalo
	Sat.	24	Carolina
	Sun.	25	at NY Rangers
	Wed.	28	at St. Louis*
Mar.	Fri.	2	at Winnipeg
	Sun.	4	at Minnesota
	Tue.	6	at Boston
	Thu.	8	Vegas
	Fri.	9	at Columbus
	Mon.	12	at San Jose
	Thu.	15	at Los Angeles
	Fri.	16	at Anaheim
	Sun.	18	at Colorado*
	Tue.	20	Philadelphia
	Thu.	22	Washington
	Sat.	24	at Toronto
	Mon.	26	at Montreal
	Tue.	27	Pittsburgh
	Thu.	29	at Buffalo
	Sat.	31	Ottawa*
Apr.	Tue.	3	at Columbus
	Thu.	5	Montreal
	Sat.	7	NY Islanders

* Denotes afternoon game.

Retired Numbers

1	Terry Sawchuk	1949-55, 57-64, 1968-69
5	Nicklas Lidstrom	1991-2012
7	Ted Lindsay	1944-57, 64-65
9	Gordie Howe	1946-1971
10	Alex Delvecchio	1951-1973
12	Sid Abel	1938-43, 45-52
19	Steve Yzerman	1983-2006

ATLANTIC DIVISION
92nd NHL Season

Franchise date: September 25, 1926

Year-by-Year Record

Season	GP	Home W	Home L	Home T	Home OL	Road W	Road L	Road T	Road OL	Overall W	Overall L	Overall T	Overall OL	GF	GA	Pts.	Div. Fin.	Conf. Fin.	Playoff Result
2016-17	82	17	17	....	7	16	19	....	6	33	36	....	13	207	244	79	7th, Atl.	14th, East	– out of playoffs –
2015-16	82	22	13	....	6	19	17	....	5	41	30	....	11	211	224	93	3rd, Atl.	8th, East	Lost First Round
2014-15	82	22	10	....	9	21	15	....	5	43	25	....	14	235	221	100	3rd, Atl.	6th, East	Lost First Round
2013-14	82	18	13	....	10	21	15	....	5	39	28	....	15	222	230	93	4th, Atl.	8th, East	Lost First Round
2012-13	48	13	7	....	4	11	9	....	4	24	16	....	8	124	115	56	3rd, Cen.	7th, West	Lost Conf. Semi-Final
2011-12	82	31	7	....	3	17	21	....	3	48	28	....	6	248	203	102	3rd, Cen.	5th, West	Lost Conf. Quarter-Final
2010-11	82	21	14	....	6	26	11	....	4	47	25	....	10	261	241	104	1st, Cen.	3rd, West	Lost Conf. Semi-Final
2009-10	82	25	10	....	6	19	14	....	8	44	24	....	14	229	216	102	2nd, Cen.	5th, West	Lost Conf. Semi-Final
2008-09	82	27	9	....	5	24	12	....	5	51	21	....	10	295	244	112	1st, Cen.	2nd, West	Lost Final
2007-08	**82**	**29**	**9**	....	**3**	**25**	**12**	....	**4**	**54**	**21**	....	**7**	**257**	**184**	**115**	**1st, Cen.**	**1st, West**	**Won Stanley Cup**
2006-07	82	29	4	....	8	21	15	....	5	50	19	....	13	254	199	113	1st, Cen.	1st, West	Lost Conf. Final
2005-06	82	27	9	....	5	31	7	....	3	58	16	....	8	305	209	124	1st, Cen.	1st, West	Lost Conf. Quarter-Final
2004-05	....	....	....	....	....	....	....	....	....	....	....	....	....	....	....	....			
2003-04	82	30	7	4	0	18	14	7	2	48	21	11	2	255	189	109	1st, Cen.	1st, West	Lost Conf. Semi-Final
2002-03	82	28	6	5	2	20	14	5	2	48	20	10	4	269	203	110	1st, Cen.	2nd, West	Lost Conf. Quarter-Final
2001-02	**82**	**28**	**7**	**5**	**1**	**23**	**10**	**5**	**3**	**51**	**17**	**10**	**4**	**251**	**187**	**116**	**1st, Cen.**	**1st, West**	**Won Stanley Cup**
2000-01	82	27	9	3	2	22	11	6	2	49	20	9	4	253	202	111	1st, Cen.	2nd, West	Lost Conf. Quarter-Final
1999-2000	82	28	9	3	1	20	13	7	1	48	22	10	2	278	210	108	2nd, Cen.	4th, West	Lost Conf. Semi-Final
1998-99	82	27	12	2	....	16	20	5	....	43	32	7	....	245	202	93	1st, Cen.	3rd, West	Lost Conf. Semi-Final
1997-98	**82**	**25**	**8**	**8**	....	**19**	**15**	**7**	....	**44**	**23**	**15**	....	**250**	**196**	**103**	**2nd, Cen.**	**2nd, West**	**Won Stanley Cup**
1996-97	**82**	**20**	**12**	**9**	....	**18**	**14**	**9**	....	**38**	**26**	**18**	....	**253**	**197**	**94**	**2nd, Cen.**	**3rd, West**	**Won Stanley Cup**
1995-96	82	36	3	2	....	26	10	5	....	62	13	7	....	325	181	131	1st, Cen.	1st, West	Lost Conf. Final
1994-95	48	17	4	3	....	16	7	1	....	33	11	4	....	180	117	70	1st, Cen.	1st, West	Lost Final
1993-94	84	23	13	6	....	23	17	2	....	46	30	8	....	356	275	100	1st, Cen.	1st, West	Lost Conf. Quarter-Final
1992-93	84	25	14	3	....	22	14	6	....	47	28	9	....	369	280	103	2nd, Norris		Lost Div. Semi-Final
1991-92	80	24	12	4	....	19	13	8	....	43	25	12	....	320	256	98	1st, Norris		Lost Div. Final
1990-91	80	26	14	0	....	8	24	8	....	34	38	8	....	273	298	76	3rd, Norris		Lost Div. Semi-Final
1989-90	80	20	14	6	....	8	24	8	....	28	38	14	....	288	323	70	5th, Norris		– out of playoffs –
1988-89	80	20	14	6	....	14	20	6	....	34	34	12	....	313	316	80	1st, Norris		Lost Div. Semi-Final
1987-88	80	24	10	6	....	17	18	5	....	41	28	11	....	322	269	93	1st, Norris		Lost Conf. Final
1986-87	80	20	14	6	....	14	22	4	....	34	36	10	....	260	274	78	2nd, Norris		Lost Conf. Final
1985-86	80	10	26	4	....	7	31	2	....	17	57	6	....	266	415	40	5th, Norris		– out of playoffs –
1984-85	80	19	14	7	....	8	27	5	....	27	41	12	....	313	357	66	3rd, Norris		Lost Div. Semi-Final
1983-84	80	18	20	2	....	13	22	5	....	31	42	7	....	298	323	69	3rd, Norris		Lost Div. Semi-Final
1982-83	80	14	19	7	....	7	25	8	....	21	44	15	....	263	344	57	5th, Norris		– out of playoffs –
1981-82	80	15	19	6	....	6	28	6	....	21	47	12	....	270	351	54	6th, Norris		– out of playoffs –
1980-81	80	16	15	9	....	3	28	9	....	19	43	18	....	252	339	56	5th, Norris		– out of playoffs –
1979-80	80	14	21	5	....	12	22	6	....	26	43	11	....	268	306	63	5th, Norris		– out of playoffs –
1978-79	80	15	17	8	....	8	24	8	....	23	41	16	....	252	295	62	5th, Norris		– out of playoffs –
1977-78	80	22	11	7	....	10	23	7	....	32	34	14	....	252	266	78	2nd, Norris		Lost Quarter-Final
1976-77	80	12	22	6	....	4	33	3	....	16	55	9	....	183	309	41	5th, Norris		– out of playoffs –
1975-76	80	17	15	8	....	9	29	2	....	26	44	10	....	226	300	62	4th, Norris		– out of playoffs –
1974-75	80	17	17	6	....	6	28	6	....	23	45	12	....	259	335	58	4th, Norris		– out of playoffs –
1973-74	78	21	12	6	....	8	27	4	....	29	39	10	....	255	319	68	6th, East		– out of playoffs –
1972-73	78	22	12	5	....	15	17	7	....	37	29	12	....	265	243	86	5th, East		– out of playoffs –
1971-72	78	25	11	3	....	8	24	7	....	33	35	10	....	261	262	76	5th, East		– out of playoffs –
1970-71	78	17	15	7	....	5	30	4	....	22	45	11	....	209	308	55	7th, East		– out of playoffs –
1969-70	76	20	11	7	....	20	10	8	....	40	21	15	....	246	199	95	3rd, East		Lost Quarter-Final
1968-69	76	23	8	7	....	10	23	5	....	33	31	12	....	239	221	78	5th, East		– out of playoffs –
1967-68	74	18	15	4	....	9	20	8	....	27	35	12	....	245	257	66	6th, East		– out of playoffs –
1966-67	70	21	11	3	....	6	28	1	....	27	39	4	....	212	241	58	5th		– out of playoffs –
1965-66	70	20	8	7	....	11	19	5	....	31	27	12	....	221	194	74	4th		Lost Final
1964-65	70	25	7	3	....	15	16	4	....	40	23	7	....	224	175	87	1st		Lost Semi-Final
1963-64	70	23	9	3	....	7	20	8	....	30	29	11	....	191	204	71	4th		Lost Final
1962-63	70	19	10	6	....	13	15	7	....	32	25	13	....	200	194	77	4th		Lost Final
1961-62	70	17	11	7	....	6	22	7	....	23	33	14	....	184	219	60	5th		– out of playoffs –
1960-61	70	15	13	7	....	10	16	9	....	25	29	16	....	195	215	66	4th		Lost Final
1959-60	70	18	14	3	....	8	15	12	....	26	29	15	....	186	197	67	4th		Lost Semi-Final
1958-59	70	13	17	5	....	12	20	3	....	25	37	8	....	167	218	58	6th		– out of playoffs –
1957-58	70	16	11	8	....	13	18	4	....	29	29	12	....	176	207	70	3rd		Lost Semi-Final
1956-57	70	23	7	5	....	15	13	7	....	38	20	12	....	198	157	88	1st		Lost Semi-Final
1955-56	70	21	6	8	....	9	18	8	....	30	24	16	....	183	148	76	2nd		Lost Final
1954-55	**70**	**25**	**5**	**5**	....	**17**	**12**	**6**	....	**42**	**17**	**11**	....	**204**	**134**	**95**	**1st**		**Won Stanley Cup**
1953-54	**70**	**24**	**4**	**7**	....	**13**	**15**	**7**	....	**37**	**19**	**14**	....	**191**	**132**	**88**	**1st**		**Won Stanley Cup**
1952-53	70	20	5	10	....	16	11	8	....	36	16	18	....	222	133	90	1st		Lost Semi-Final
1951-52	**70**	**24**	**7**	**4**	....	**20**	**7**	**8**	....	**44**	**14**	**12**	....	**215**	**133**	**100**	**1st**		**Won Stanley Cup**
1950-51	70	25	3	7	....	19	10	6	....	44	13	13	....	236	139	101	1st		Lost Semi-Final
1949-50	**70**	**19**	**9**	**7**	....	**18**	**10**	**7**	....	**37**	**19**	**14**	....	**229**	**164**	**88**	**1st**		**Won Stanley Cup**
1948-49	60	21	6	3	....	13	13	4	....	34	19	7	....	195	145	75	1st		Lost Final
1947-48	60	16	9	5	....	14	9	7	....	30	18	12	....	187	148	72	2nd		Lost Final
1946-47	60	14	10	6	....	8	17	5	....	22	27	11	....	190	193	55	4th		Lost Semi-Final
1945-46	50	16	5	4	....	4	15	6	....	20	20	10	....	146	159	50	4th		Lost Semi-Final
1944-45	50	19	5	1	....	12	9	4	....	31	14	5	....	218	161	67	2nd		Lost Final
1943-44	50	18	5	2	....	8	13	4	....	26	18	6	....	214	177	58	2nd		Lost Semi-Final
1942-43	**50**	**16**	**4**	**5**	....	**9**	**10**	**6**	....	**25**	**14**	**11**	....	**169**	**124**	**61**	**1st**		**Won Stanley Cup**
1941-42	48	14	7	3	....	5	18	1	....	19	25	4	....	140	147	42	5th		Lost Final
1940-41	48	14	5	5	....	7	11	6	....	21	16	11	....	112	102	53	3rd		Lost Final
1939-40	48	11	10	3	....	5	16	3	....	16	26	6	....	90	126	38	5th		Lost Semi-Final
1938-39	48	14	8	2	....	4	16	4	....	18	24	6	....	107	128	42	5th		Lost Semi-Final
1937-38	48	8	10	6	....	4	15	5	....	12	25	11	....	99	133	35	4th, Amn.		– out of playoffs –
1936-37	**48**	**14**	**5**	**5**	....	**11**	**9**	**4**	....	**25**	**14**	**9**	....	**128**	**102**	**59**	**1st, Amn.**		**Won Stanley Cup**
1935-36	**48**	**14**	**5**	**5**	....	**10**	**11**	**3**	....	**24**	**16**	**8**	....	**124**	**103**	**56**	**1st, Amn.**		**Won Stanley Cup**
1934-35	48	11	8	5	....	8	14	2	....	19	22	7	....	127	114	45	4th, Amn.		– out of playoffs –
1933-34	48	15	5	4	....	9	9	6	....	24	14	10	....	113	98	58	1st, Amn.		Lost Final
1932-33*	48	17	3	4	....	8	12	4	....	25	15	8	....	111	93	58	2nd, Amn.		Lost Semi-Final
1931-32	48	15	3	6	....	3	17	4	....	18	20	10	....	95	108	46	3rd, Amn.		Lost Quarter-Final
1930-31**	44	10	7	5	....	6	14	2	....	16	21	7	....	102	105	39	4th, Amn.		– out of playoffs –
1929-30	44	9	10	3	....	5	14	3	....	14	24	6	....	117	133	34	4th, Amn.		– out of playoffs –
1928-29	44	11	6	5	....	8	10	4	....	19	16	9	....	72	63	47	3rd, Amn.		Lost Quarter-Final
1927-28	44	9	10	3	....	10	9	3	....	19	19	6	....	88	79	44	4th, Amn.		– out of playoffs –
1926-27***	44	5	16	0	....	7	12	4	....	12	28	4	....	76	105	28	5th, Amn.		– out of playoffs –

* Team name changed to Red Wings. ** Team name changed to Falcons. *** Team named Cougars.

2017-18 Player Personnel

FORWARDS	HT	WT	*Age	Birthplace	S	2016-17 Club
ABDELKADER, Justin	6-2	218	30	Muskegon, MI	L	Detroit
ATHANASIOU, Andreas	6-2	192	23	London, ON	L	Detroit
FRANZEN, Johan	6-4	232	37	Landsbro, Sweden	L	Detroit
GLENDENING, Luke	5-11	199	28	Grand Rapids, MI	R	Detroit
HELM, Darren	6-0	196	30	Winnipeg, MB	L	Detroit
LARKIN, Dylan	6-1	190	21	Waterford, MI	L	Detroit
MANTHA, Anthony	6-5	221	23	Longueuil, QC	L	Detroit-Grand Rapids
NIELSEN, Frans	6-1	188	33	Herning, Denmark	L	Detroit
NYQUIST, Gustav	5-11	183	28	Halmstad, Sweden	L	Detroit
SHEAHAN, Riley	6-3	226	25	St. Catharines, ON	L	Detroit
TATAR, Tomas	5-10	185	26	Ilava, Czech.	L	Detroit
ZETTERBERG, Henrik	6-0	195	36	Njurunda, Sweden	L	Detroit

DEFENSEMEN						
DALEY, Trevor	5-11	195	33	Toronto, ON	L	Pittsburgh
DeKEYSER, Danny	6-3	191	27	Detroit, MI	L	Detroit
ERICSSON, Jonathan	6-4	220	33	Karlskrona, Sweden	L	Detroit
GREEN, Mike	6-1	207	31	Calgary, AB	R	Detroit
JENSEN, Nick	6-0	200	27	St. Paul, MN	R	Detroit-Grand Rapids
KRONWALL, Niklas	6-0	194	36	Stockholm, Sweden	L	Detroit
OUELLET, Xavier	6-1	200	24	Bayonne, France	L	Detroit
SPROUL, Ryan	6-4	211	24	Mississauga, ON	R	Detroit
WITKOWSKI, Luke	6-2	200	27	Holland, MI	R	Tampa Bay-Syracuse

GOALTENDERS	HT	WT	*Age	Birthplace	C	2016-17 Club
HOWARD, Jimmy	6-1	218	33	Syracuse, NY	L	Detroit-Grand Rapids
MRAZEK, Petr	6-2	183	25	Ostrava, Czech.	L	Detroit

* – Age at start of 2017-18 season

2016-17 Scoring

* – rookie

Regular Season

Pos	#	Player	Team	GP	G	A	Pts	TOI	+/-	PIM	PP	SH	GW	S	S%
L	40	Henrik Zetterberg	DET	82	17	51	68	19:43	15	22	2	0	0	195	8.7
C	14	Gustav Nyquist	DET	76	12	36	48	17:26	0	18	2	0	2	165	7.3
C	21	Tomas Tatar	DET	82	25	21	46	17:16	-8	26	5	0	5	166	15.1
C	51	Frans Nielsen	DET	79	17	24	41	17:08	-19	18	4	2	0	162	10.5
R	39 *	Anthony Mantha	DET	60	17	19	36	15:54	10	53	4	0	3	133	12.8
D	25	Mike Green	DET	72	14	22	36	23:33	-20	40	3	0	2	125	11.2
C	71	Dylan Larkin	DET	80	17	15	32	16:09	-28	37	5	1	1	178	9.6
C	72	Andreas Athanasiou	DET	64	18	11	29	13:27	-7	28	1	0	3	120	15.0
L	8	Justin Abdelkader	DET	64	7	14	21	16:39	-20	50	5	0	1	104	6.7
C	43	Darren Helm	DET	50	8	9	17	15:22	-6	20	2	0	1	98	8.2
C	41	Luke Glendening	DET	74	3	11	14	12:54	-10	26	0	0	0	76	3.9
D	3 *	Nick Jensen	DET	49	4	9	13	17:45	-7	12	0	0	0	59	6.8
D	55	Niklas Kronwall	DET	57	2	11	13	19:27	-7	32	0	0	0	67	3.0
C	15	Riley Sheahan	DET	80	2	11	13	13:58	-29	14	1	0	0	109	1.8
D	65	Danny Dekeyser	DET	82	4	8	12	21:56	-22	33	0	0	2	85	4.7
D	61 *	Xavier Ouellet	DET	66	3	9	12	17:58	2	51	0	0	0	89	3.4
D	52	Jonathan Ericsson	DET	51	1	8	9	19:13	-2	63	0	0	0	43	2.3
L	20	Drew Miller	DET	55	5	2	7	10:16	-12	18	0	0	1	43	11.6
D	48 *	Ryan Sproul	DET	27	1	6	7	15:08	-8	6	1	0	0	46	2.2
L	83 *	Tomas Nosek	DET	11	1	0	1	10:07	-1	2	0	0	0	19	5.3
R	22 *	Matt Lorito	DET	2	0	1	1	14:26	0	0	0	0	0	6	0.0
C	46	Ben Street	DET	6	0	1	1	8:15	1	0	0	0	0	8	0.0
D	77	Dan Renouf	DET	1	0	0	0	13:35	0	0	0	0	0	1	0.0
L	37 *	Evgeny Svechnikov	DET	2	0	0	0	13:08	0	0	0	0	0	4	0.0
R	57 *	Mitch Callahan	DET	4	0	0	0	6:48	0	0	0	0	0	2	0.0
D	23	Brian Lashoff	DET	5	0	0	0	12:30	-3	0	0	0	0	1	0.0
L	59 *	Tyler Bertuzzi	DET	7	0	0	0	9:06	-1	0	0	0	0	3	0.0
D	18 *	Robbie Russo	DET	19	0	0	0	16:04	2	2	0	0	0	18	0.0

Goaltending

No.	Goaltender	GPI	Mins	Avg	W	L	OT	EN	SO	GA	SA	Sv%	G	A	PIM
35	Jimmy Howard	26	1397	2.10	10	11	1	2	1	49	675	.927	0	0	2
34	Petr Mrazek	50	2858	3.04	18	21	9	6	1	145	1462	.901	0	0	2
31	* Jared Coreau	14	712	3.46	5	4	3	1	2	41	362	.887	0	0	0
	Totals	82	5019	2.92	33	36	13	9	4	244	2508	.903	0		0

Jeff Blashill

Head Coach

Born: Southfield, MI, December 10, 1973.

The Detroit Red Wings announced on June 9, 2015, that Jeff Blashill had been named the 27th head coach in franchise history. In his first season behind the bench in 2015-16, the Detroit reached the playoffs for the 25th consecutive season. Blashill joined the organization in 2011-12, spending one season behind the Red Wings' bench as an assistant coach before being named head coach of the Grand Rapids Griffins, Detroit's American Hockey League affiliate, on June 25, 2012.

With the Griffins, Blashill led the club to three of the most successful campaigns in franchise history, highlighted by a 2012-13 campaign that saw Grand Rapids capture a regular-season Midwest Division title and eventually the first Calder Cup championship in the franchise's 17-year history. In 2014-15, the Griffins won the Midwest Division after reaching 100 points for the first time during Blashill's tenure. The club advanced to the Western Conference Finals for the second time in three seasons before falling to the Utica Comets in six games.

Born in Detroit and raised in Sault Ste. Marie, Michigan, Blashill won the Louis A.R. Pieri Memorial Award as the AHL's most outstanding coach in 2013-14 and was named head coach for the 2014 AHL All-Star Classic. In his three seasons with Grand Rapids, he compiled a 134-71-23 regular-season record and a 29-21 mark in the postseason, winning seven of nine playoff series. He is the only coach in Griffins history to qualify for the playoffs in three consecutive seasons, leading the team to 92 points or better each year.

Twenty-four players who skated for the Griffins between 2012 and 2015 went on to play at least one NHL game, including Joakim Andersson, Danny DeKeyser, Luke Glendening, Tomas Jurco, Petr Mrazek, Gustav Nyquist, Riley Sheahan and Tomas Tatar, who all moved up to full-time roles with Detroit after winning the Calder Cup with Blashill in 2013. A total of 15 players who appeared for Detroit in 2014-15 spent time in Grand Rapids over the past three years. Additionally, 11 current Red Wings were also regulars in 2011-12, which Blashill spent as an assistant coach in Detroit, helping the team to a 12th consecutive 100-point season.

Blashill joined the Red Wings' organization after one season as the head coach at Western Michigan University in 2010-11, where he doubled the Broncos' win total from the previous season and led the school to its first appearance in the CCHA championship game since 1986. He finished as a finalist for CCHA coach of the year, and was named national coach of the year by College Hockey News, Inside College Hockey and USCHO.com. Blashill made his head coaching debut with the United States Hockey League's Indiana Ice, compiling a 72-43-5 mark as head coach and general manager from 2008 to 2010. The Ice earned a franchise-record 39 wins in 2008-09 and won the Clark Cup as champions of the USHL.

A former goaltender at Ferris State University, Blashill was the Bulldogs' rookie of the year in 1994-95 and earned a spot on the CCHA all-academic team in 1996-97. He began his coaching career with four seasons as an assistant coach for Ferris State from 1998 to 2002, followed by six seasons in the same role with Miami University in which the RedHawks qualified for the NCAA tournament four times. Blashill represented the United States as an assistant coach at international tournaments on three occasions: the 2009 World Junior A Challenge (gold medal), the 2009 World Junior Championship (fifth place) and the 2006 Ivan Hlinka Memorial Tournament (silver medal).

Captain Henrik Zetterberg confers with center Tomas Tatar. Tatar led the Red Wings with 25 goals in 2016-17, while Zetterberg topped the team with 51 assists and 68 points.

Coaching Record

			Regular Season				Playoffs			
Season	Team	League	GC	W	L	O/T	GC	W	L	T
2008-09	Indiana	USHL	60	39	19	2	13	9	4	....
2009-10	Indiana	USHL	60	33	24	3	9	4	5	....
2010-11	Western Michigan	CCHA	42	19	13	10	....	....	....	....
2012-13	Grand Rapids	AHL	76	42	26	8	24	15	9	....
2013-14	Grand Rapids	AHL	76	46	23	7	10	5	5	....
2014-15	Grand Rapids	AHL	76	46	22	8	16	9	7	....
2015-16	Detroit	NHL	82	41	30	11	5	1	4	....
2016-17	Detroit	NHL	82	33	36	13				
	NHL Totals		164	74	66	24	5	1	4	....

Club Records

Team

(Figures in brackets for season records are games played; records for fewest points, wins, ties, losses, goals, goals against are for 70 or more games)

Most Points **131** 1995-96 (82)
Most Wins ***62** 1995-96 (82)
Most Ties **18** 1952-53 (70), 1980-81 (80), 1996-97 (82)
Most Losses **57** 1985-86 (80)
Most Goals **369** 1992-93 (84)
Most Goals Against **415** 1985-86 (80)
Fewest Points **40** 1985-86 (80)
Fewest Wins **16** 1976-77 (80)
Fewest Ties **4** 1966-67 (70)
Fewest Losses **13** 1950-51 (70), 1995-96 (82)
Fewest Goals **167** 1958-59 (70)
Fewest Goals Against **132** 1953-54 (70)
Longest Winning Streak
Overall .... **9** Seven times
Home .... ***23** Nov. 5/11-Feb. 19/12
Away .... ***12** Mar. 1-Apr. 15/06
Longest Team Point Streak
Overall .... **15** Nov. 27-Dec. 28/52 (8W, 7T)
Home .... **19** Dec. 31/00-Apr.7/01 (14W, 3OTW, 2T)
Away .... **15** Oct. 18-Dec. 20/51 (10W, 5T)
Longest Losing Streak
Overall .... **14** Feb. 24-Mar. 25/82
Home .... **7** Feb. 20-Mar. 25/82
Away .... **14** Oct. 19-Dec. 21/66
Longest Winless Streak
Overall .... **19** Feb. 26-Apr. 3/77 (18L, 1T)
Home .... **10** Dec. 11/85-Jan. 18/86 (9L, 1T)
Away .... **26** Dec. 15/76-Apr. 3/77 (23L, 3T)
Most Shutouts, Season **13** 1953-54 (70)
Most. PIM, Season **2,393** 1985-86 (80)
Most Goals, Game .... **15** Jan. 23/44 (NYR 0 at Det. 15)

Individual

Most Seasons .... **25** Gordie Howe
Most Games .... **1,687** Gordie Howe
Most Goals, Career .... **786** Gordie Howe
Most Assists, Career .... **1,063** Steve Yzerman
Most Points, Career .... **1,809** Gordie Howe (786G, 1,023A)
Most PIM, Career .... **2,090** Bob Probert
Most Shutouts, Career .... **85** Terry Sawchuk
Longest Consecutive Games Streak .... **548** Alex Delvecchio (Dec. 13/56-Nov. 11/64)
Most Goals, Season .... **65** Steve Yzerman (1988-89)
Most Assists, Season .... **90** Steve Yzerman (1988-89)
Most Points, Season .... **155** Steve Yzerman (1988-89; 65G, 90A)
Most PIM, Season .... **398** Bob Probert (1987-88)
Most Points, Defenseman, Season .... **80** Nicklas Lidstrom (2005-06; 16G, 64A)
Most Points, Center, Season .... **155** Steve Yzerman (1988-89; 65G, 90A)
Most Points, Right Wing, Season .... **103** Gordie Howe (1968-69; 44G, 59A)
Most Points, Left Wing, Season .... **105** John Ogrodnick (1984-85; 55G, 50A)
Most Points, Rookie, Season .... **87** Steve Yzerman (1983-84; 39G, 48A)
Most Shutouts, Season .... **12** Terry Sawchuk (1951-52), (1953-54), (1954-55) Glenn Hall (1955-56)
Most Goals, Game .... **6** Syd Howe (Feb. 3/44)
Most Assists, Game .... ***7** Billy Taylor (Mar. 16/47)
Most Points, Game .... **7** Carl Liscombe (Nov. 5/42; 3G, 4A), Don Grosso (Feb. 3/44; 1G, 6A), Billy Taylor (Mar. 16/47; 7A)

* NHL Record.

All-time Record vs. Other Clubs

Regular Season

	Total								At Home								On Road							
	GP	W	L	T	OL	GF	GA	PTS	GP	W	L	T	OL	GF	GA	PTS	GP	W	L	T	OL	GF	GA	PTS
Anaheim	83	50	23	7	3	252	196	110	41	31	7	3	0	145	93	65	42	19	16	4	3	107	103	45
Arizona	139	69	44	22	4	488	425	164	70	37	23	8	2	266	224	84	69	32	21	14	2	222	201	80
Boston	596	255	242	95	4	1780	1801	609	297	161	82	52	2	990	752	376	299	94	160	43	2	790	1049	233
Buffalo	133	62	55	13	3	439	441	140	68	41	21	5	1	246	189	88	65	21	34	8	2	193	252	52
Calgary	158	72	67	16	3	508	513	163	78	42	25	10	1	280	236	95	80	30	42	6	2	228	277	68
Carolina	79	41	30	8	0	256	234	90	40	23	10	7	0	148	110	53	39	18	20	1	0	108	124	37
Chicago	733	367	268	84	14	2277	2020	832	365	219	107	33	6	1241	918	477	368	148	161	51	8	1036	1102	355
Colorado	121	66	42	5	8	409	362	145	60	35	17	1	7	208	170	78	61	31	25	4	1	201	192	67
Columbus	86	54	22	1	9	266	198	118	42	29	8	0	5	138	101	63	44	25	14	1	4	128	97	55
Dallas	251	112	99	34	6	848	807	264	126	64	43	16	3	468	387	147	125	48	56	18	3	380	420	117
Edmonton	127	64	39	13	11	458	410	152	64	40	17	3	4	240	185	87	63	24	22	10	7	218	225	65
Florida	40	20	8	5	7	119	104	52	19	7	4	3	5	55	49	22	21	13	4	2	2	64	55	30
Los Angeles	198	87	82	27	2	682	684	203	99	51	35	13	0	376	324	115	99	36	47	14	2	306	360	88
Minnesota	55	35	11	3	6	179	133	79	28	19	4	1	4	106	67	43	27	16	7	2	2	73	66	36
Montreal	585	207	278	96	4	1492	1774	514	292	136	101	53	2	832	744	327	293	71	177	43	2	660	1030	187
Nashville	93	55	26	4	8	294	234	122	47	32	8	2	5	168	108	71	46	23	18	2	3	126	126	51
New Jersey	99	48	38	11	2	331	311	109	50	32	16	2	0	200	151	66	49	16	22	9	2	131	160	43
NY Islanders	109	52	49	6	2	349	354	112	54	29	22	2	1	185	157	61	55	23	27	4	1	164	197	51
NY Rangers	587	265	214	103	5	1780	1608	638	294	170	77	45	2	1027	721	387	293	95	137	58	3	753	887	251
Ottawa	42	26	13	1	2	135	109	55	20	12	7	0	1	66	50	25	22	14	6	1	1	69	59	30
Philadelphia	136	51	61	21	3	429	475	126	69	37	20	10	2	242	206	86	67	14	41	11	1	187	269	40
Pittsburgh	151	67	64	16	4	515	528	154	75	45	16	12	2	289	218	104	76	22	48	4	2	226	310	50
St. Louis	281	123	113	37	8	898	855	291	141	69	51	17	4	495	412	159	140	54	62	20	4	403	443	132
San Jose	90	54	28	4	4	316	244	116	44	31	9	1	3	157	88	66	46	23	19	3	1	159	156	50
Tampa Bay	50	29	15	2	4	172	134	64	24	17	3	1	3	79	45	38	26	12	12	1	1	93	89	26
Toronto	661	283	279	93	6	1872	1898	665	333	173	110	46	4	994	815	396	328	110	169	47	2	878	1083	269
Vancouver	170	90	55	18	7	603	534	205	85	52	20	8	5	336	241	117	85	38	35	10	2	267	293	88
Washington	113	49	44	16	4	358	366	118	57	27	17	11	2	187	160	67	56	22	27	5	2	171	206	51
Winnipeg	22	13	7	0	2	85	70	28	12	7	3	0	2	42	34	16	10	6	4	0	0	43	36	12
Defunct Clubs	282	125	103	54	0	794	682	304	141	76	40	25	0	430	307	177	141	49	63	29	0	364	375	127
Totals	**6270**	**2891**	**2419**	**815**	**145**	**19384**	**18504**	**6742**	**3135**	**1744**	**923**	**390**	**78**	**10636**	**8262**	**3956**	**3135**	**1147**	**1496**	**425**	**67**	**8748**	**10242**	**2786**

Playoffs

	Series	W	L	GP	W	L	T	GF	GA	Last Mtg.	Rnd.	Result
Anaheim	6	4	2	32	18	14	0	93	78	2013	CQF	W 4-3
Arizona	4	4	0	23	16	7	0	88	56	2011	CQF	W 4-0
Boston	8	3	5	38	15	23	0	104	110	2014	FR	L 1-4
Calgary	3	2	1	14	8	6	0	38	26	2007	CQF	W 4-2
Carolina	1	1	0	5	4	1	0	14	7	2002	F	W 4-1
Chicago	16	7	9	81	38	43	0	224	236	2013	CSF	L 3-4
Colorado	6	3	3	34	17	17	0	97	88	2008	CSF	W 4-0
Columbus	1	1	0	4	4	0	0	18	7	2009	CQF	W 4-0
Dallas	4	4	0	24	16	8	0	72	50	2008	CF	W 4-2
Edmonton	3	0	3	16	4	12	0	43	58	2006	CQF	L 2-4
Los Angeles	2	1	1	10	6	4	0	32	21	2001	CQF	L 2-4
Montreal	12	7	5	62	29	33	0	149	161	1978	QF	L 1-4
Nashville	3	2	1	17	9	8	0	38	34	2012	CQF	L 1-4
New Jersey	1	0	1	4	0	4	0	7	16	1995	F	L 0-4
NY Rangers	5	4	1	23	13	10	0	57	49	1950	F	W 4-3
Philadelphia	1	1	0	4	4	0	0	16	6	1997	F	W 4-0
Pittsburgh	2	1	1	13	7	6	0	34	24	2009	F	L 3-4
St. Louis	7	5	2	40	24	16	0	125	103	2002	CSF	W 4-1
San Jose	5	2	3	29	15	14	0	99	69	2011	CSF	L 3-4
Tampa Bay	2	0	2	12	4	8	0	23	29	2016	FR	L 1-4
Toronto	23	11	12	117	59	58	0	321	311	1993	DSF	L 3-4
Vancouver	1	1	0	6	4	2	0	22	16	2002	CQF	W 4-2
Washington	1	1	0	4	4	0	0	13	7	1998	F	W 4-0
Defunct Clubs	4	3	1	10	7	2	1	21	13			
Totals	**121**	**68**	**53**	**622**	**325**	**296**	**1**	**1748**	**1575**			

Calgary totals include Atlanta Flames, 1972-73 to 1979-80.
Colorado totals include Quebec, 1979-80 to 1994-95.
New Jersey totals include Kansas City, 1974-75, 1975-76, and Colorado Rockies, 1976-77 to 1981-82.
Phoenix totals include Winnipeg, 1979-80 to 1995-96.
Carolina totals include Hartford, 1979-80 to 1996-97.
Dallas totals include Minnesota North Stars, 1967-68 to 1992-93.
Winnipeg totals include Atlanta Thrashers, 1999-2000 to 2010-11.

Playoff Results 2017-2013

Year	Round	Opponent	Result	GF	GA
2016	FR	Tampa Bay	L 1-4	8	12
2015	FR	Tampa Bay	L 3-4	15	17
2014	FR	Boston	L 1-4	6	14
2013	CSF	Chicago	L 3-4	15	16
	CQF	Anaheim	W 4-3	18	21

Abbreviations: Round: F – Final; **CF** – conference final; **CSF** – conference semi-final; **CQF** – conference quarter-final; **FR** – first round; **DSF** – division semi-final; **QF** – quarter-final.

2016-17 Results

Oct.	13	at Tampa Bay	4-6		12	at Dallas	2-5
	15	at Florida	1-4		14	Pittsburgh	6-3
	17	Ottawa	5-1		16	Montreal	1-0
	19	at NY Rangers	2-1		18	Boston	6-5†
	21	Nashville	5-3		20	at Buffalo	2-3*
	22	San Jose	3-0		22	NY Rangers	0-1*
	25	Carolina	4-2		24	at Boston	3-4*
	27	at St. Louis	2-1†		25	Toronto	0-4
	29	Boston	0-1		31	New Jersey	3-4
	30	Florida	2-5	**Feb.**	3	NY Islanders	5-4
Nov.	2	at Philadelphia	3-4*		4	at Nashville	1-0
	4	Winnipeg	3-5		7	Columbus	2-3*
	6	Edmonton	1-2		9	at Washington	3-6
	8	at Philadelphia	3-2†		11	at Columbus	1-2
	10	Vancouver	3-1		12	at Minnesota	3-6
	12	at Montreal	0-5		15	St. Louis	0-2
	15	Tampa Bay	3-4		18	Washington	3-2†
	18	at Washington	0-1		19	at Pittsburgh	5-2
	20	Calgary	2-3		21	NY Islanders	1-3
	23	at Buffalo	2-1†		28	at Vancouver	3-2*
	25	at New Jersey	5-4*	**Mar.**	3	at Calgary	2-3*
	26	Montreal	1-2*		4	at Edmonton	3-4
	29	Dallas	3-1		7	at Toronto	2-3
Dec.	1	Florida	1-2*		8	at Boston	1-6
	3	at Pittsburgh	3-5		10	Chicago	4-2
	4	at NY Islanders	4-3*		12	NY Rangers	1-4
	6	at Winnipeg	4-3†		15	at Colorado	1-3
	9	Columbus	1-4		16	at Arizona	5-4†
	11	Philadelphia	0-1*		18	Colorado	5-1
	13	Arizona	1-4		20	Buffalo	1-2
	15	Los Angeles	1-4		21	at Montreal	2-1*
	17	Anaheim	6-4		24	Tampa Bay	1-2*
	20	at Tampa Bay	1-4		26	Minnesota	3-2*
	23	at Florida	4-3†		27	at Carolina	4-3*
	27	Buffalo	3-4		28	at Carolina	1-4
	29	at Ottawa	3-2*		30	at Tampa Bay	3-5
Jan.	1	at Toronto	4-5*	**Apr.**	1	Toronto	4-5
	4	at Anaheim	0-2		3	Ottawa	5-4†
	5	at Los Angeles	4-0		4	at Ottawa	0-2
	7	at San Jose	3-6		8	Montreal	2-3*
	10	at Chicago	3-4*		9	New Jersey	4-1

* – Overtime † – Shootout

NHL Draft Selections 2017-2003

Name in bold denotes played in NHL.

2017
Pick
9	Michael Rasmussen
38	Gustav Lindstrom
71	Kasper Kotkansalo
83	Zach Gallant
88	Keith Petruzzelli
100	Malte Setkov
131	Cole Fraser
162	John Adams
164	Reilly Webb
193	Brady Gilmour

2016
Pick
20	Dennis Cholowski
46	Givani Smith
53	Filip Hronek
107	Alfons Malmstrom
137	Jordan Sambrook
167	Filip Larsson
197	Mattias Elfstrom

2015
Pick
19	**Evgeni Svechnikov**
73	Vili Saarijarvi
110	Joren Van Pottelberghe
140	Chase Pearson
170	Patrick Holway
200	Adam Marsh

2014
Pick
15	**Dylan Larkin**
63	Dominic Turgeon
106	Christoffer Ehn
136	Chase Perry
166	Julius Vahatalo
196	Axel Holmstrom
201	Alexander Kadeykin

2013
Pick
20	**Anthony Mantha**
48	Zach Nastasiuk
58	**Tyler Bertuzzi**
79	**Mattias Janmark**
109	David Pope
139	Mitchell Wheaton
169	Marc McNulty
199	Hampus Melen

2012
Pick
49	**Martin Frk**
80	Jake Paterson
110	**Andreas Athanasiou**
140	Mike McKee
170	James De Haas
200	Rasmus Bodin

2011
Pick
35	**Tomas Jurco**
48	**Xavier Ouellet**
55	**Ryan Sproul**
85	**Alan Quine**
115	Marek Tvrdon
145	Philippe Hudon
146	Mattias Backman
175	Richard Nedomlel
205	**Alexey Marchenko**

2010
Pick
21	**Riley Sheahan**
51	**Calle Jarnkrok**
81	Louis-Marc Aubry
111	**Teemu Pulkkinen**
141	**Petr Mrazek**
171	Brooks Macek
201	Ben Marshall

2009
Pick
32	**Landon Ferraro**
60	**Tomas Tatar**
75	Andrej Nestrasil
90	Gleason Fournier
150	**Nick Jensen**
180	**Mitch Callahan**
210	**Adam Almqvist**

2008
Pick
30	Tom McCollum
91	Max Nicastro
121	**Gustav Nyquist**
151	Julien Cayer
181	Stephen Johnston
211	Jesper Samuelsson

2007
Pick
27	**Brendan Smith**
88	**Joakim Andersson**
148	Randy Cameron
178	Zack Torquato
208	Bryan Rufenach

2006
Pick
41	**Cory Emmerton**
47	**Shawn Matthias**
62	Dick Axelsson
92	Daniel Larsson
182	**Jan Mursak**
191	Nick Oslund
212	Logan Pyett

2005
Pick
19	**Jakub Kindl**
42	**Justin Abdelkader**
80	Christofer Lofberg
103	**Mattias Ritola**
132	**Darren Helm**
137	Johan Ryno
151	Jeff May
175	Juho Mielonen
214	Bretton Stamler

2004
Pick
97	**Johan Franzen**
128	Evan McGrath
151	Sergei Kolosov
162	Tyler Haskins
192	Anton Axelsson
226	Steven Covington
257	Gennady Stolyarov
290	Nils Backstrom

2003
Pick
64	**Jimmy Howard**
132	**Kyle Quincey**
164	Ryan Oulahen
170	Andreas Sundin
194	Stefan Blom
226	Tomas Kollar
258	Vladimir Kutny
289	Mikael Johansson

General Managers' History

Art Duncan, 1926-27; Jack Adams, 1927-28 to 1961-62; Sid Abel, 1962-63 to 1969-70; Sid Abel and Ned Harkness, 1970-71; Ned Harkness, 1971-72, 1972-73; Ned Harkness and Jimmy Skinner, 1973-74; Alex Delvecchio, 1974-75, 1975-76; Alex Delvecchio and Ted Lindsay, 1976-77; Ted Lindsay, 1977-78 to 1979-80; Jimmy Skinner, 1980-81, 1981-82; Jim Devellano, 1982-83 to 1989-90; Bryan Murray, 1990-91 to 1993-94; Jim Devellano (Senior Vice President/Hockey), 1994-95 to 1996-97; Ken Holland, 1997-98 to date.

Ken Holland
Executive Vice President and General Manager
Born: Vernon, BC, November 10, 1955.

Ken Holland has served in the Red Wings front office since 1985, and has been the club's general manager since July 18, 1997 after serving three seasons as the club's assistant general manager. He has established himself as one of the most innovative and aggressive GMs in the National Hockey League. Detroit's Stanley Cup victory in 2008 marked the team's third championship under his leadership and he has a gold medal as part of the management group for Team Canada at the 2014 Sochi Winter Olympics. The Red Wings made the playoffs for 25 consecutive seasons from 1990-91 through 2015-16.

Holland oversees all aspects of hockey operations including all matters relating to player personnel, development, contract negotiations and player movements, though he now takes a less prominent role in the NHL draft than he did during his seven years as the club's director of amateur scouting.

At the conclusion of his playing days as a goaltender, spending most of his pro career at the American Hockey League level, Holland began his off-ice career in 1985 as a western Canada scout followed by five years as an amateur scouting director before promotions led to his current position as general manager.

A native of Vernon, British Columbia, Holland played in the junior ranks for Medicine Hat (WHL) in 1974-75. He was Toronto's 13th pick (188th overall) in the 1975 NHL Draft but never saw action with the Maple Leafs. Holland twice signed with NHL teams as a free agent — in 1980 with Hartford and 1983 with Detroit. He spent most of his pro career with AHL clubs in Binghamton and Springfield, along with Adirondack, but did appear in four NHL games, making his debut with Hartford in 1980-81 and playing three contests for Detroit in 1983-84.

Club Directory

Little Caesars Arena

Detroit Red Wings
Little Caesars Arena
2645 Woodward Avenue
Detroit, MI 48201
Phone **313/471-7000**
FAX PR: 313/567-0296
Media Hotline: 313/471-7599
www.detroitredwings.com
Capacity: TBD

Owner	Mike Ilitch (1929-2017)
Owner/Secretary-Treasurer	Marian Ilitch
Governor	Christopher Ilitch
Senior Vice President/Alternate Governor	Jim Devellano
Executive Vice President/General Manager	Ken Holland
Assistant General Manager	Ryan Martin
Assistant to the General Manager	Kris Draper
Director of Player Evaluation	Jiri Fischer
Director of Player Development	Shawn Horcoff
Group President, Sports and Entertainment	Chris Granger
President and CEO, Olympia Entertainment/ Alternate Governor Red Wings	Tom Wilson
Vice President Olympia Entertainment/ General Counsel Red Wings	Robert E. Carr
Head Coach	Jeff Blashill
Assistant Coaches	John Torchetti, Doug Houda, Pat Ferschweiler, Chris Chelios
Goaltending Coach	Jeff Salajko
Assistant Coach/Video	Adam Nightingale
Assistant Video Coach	Jeff Weintraub
Director of Pro Scouting	Mark Howe
Pro Scouts	Bruce Haralson, Archie Henderson, Kirk Maltby, Glenn Merkosky
Director of Amateur Scouting	Tyler Wright
Chief Amateur Scout	Jeff Finley
Amateur Scouts	Andrew Dickson, Kelly Harper, Sam Lites, Mario Marois, Mark Mullen, Len Quesnelle, Marty Stein
Director of European Scouting	Hakan Andersson
European Scouts	Vladimir Havluj, Antonin Routa, Nikolai Vakourov
Vice President of Finance	Paul MacDonald
Executive Assistant	Kim Brodie
Team Travel Coordinator	Lisa Wright
Head Equipment Manager	Paul Boyer
Assistant Equipment Managers	John Remejes, Brady Munger
Head Athletic Therapist	Piet Van Zant
Assistant Athletic Therapist	Russ Baumann
Team Masseurs	Sergei Tchekmarev, Ainars Treiguts
Strength and Conditioning Coach	Mike Kadar
Director of Public Relations	Todd Beam
Communications Professionals	Kyle Kujawa, Alex DiFilippo
Director of Community Relations and DRW Foundation	Kevin Brown
Community Relations Manager	Anne Bowlby
Community Relations Coordinator	Merideth Gokey
Community Relations Assistant	Rachael Hille
Detroit Red Wings Foundation Coordinator	Kelsey Rentner
Medical Director	Dr. Donald Weaver
Team Physicians	Dr. Anthony Colucci, Dr. Doug Plagens
Team Dentists	Dr. Jeffrey Boogren, Dr. Randy Freij
Team Photographer	Dave Reginek
Radio Announcers, 97.1 The Ticket	Ken Kal, Paul Woods
Television Announcers, FOX Sports Detroit	Ken Daniels, Mickey Redmond

Coaching History

Art Duncan and Duke Keats, 1926-27; Jack Adams, 1927-28 to 1946-47; Tommy Ivan, 1947-48 to 1953-54; Jimmy Skinner, 1954-55 to 1956-57; Jimmy Skinner and Sid Abel, 1957-58; Sid Abel, 1958-59 to 1967-68; Bill Gadsby, 1968-69; Bill Gadsby and Sid Abel, 1969-70; Ned Harkness and Doug Barkley, 1970-71; Doug Barkley and Johnny Wilson, 1971-72; Johnny Wilson, 1972-73; Ted Garvin and Alex Delvecchio, 1973-74; Alex Delvecchio, 1974-75; Doug Barkley and Alex Delvecchio, 1975-76; Alex Delvecchio and Larry Wilson, 1976-77; Bobby Kromm, 1977-78, 1978-79; Bobby Kromm and Ted Lindsay, 1979-80; Ted Lindsay and Wayne Maxner, 1980-81; Wayne Maxner and Billy Dea, 1981-82; Nick Polano, 1982-83 to 1984-85; Harry Neale and Brad Park, 1985-86; Jacques Demers, 1986-87 to 1989-90; Bryan Murray, 1990-91 to 1992-93; Scotty Bowman, 1993-94 to 1997-98; Dave Lewis, Barry Smith (co-coaches) and Scotty Bowman, 1998-99; Scotty Bowman, 1999-2000 to 2001-02; Dave Lewis, 2002-03 to 2004-05; Mike Babcock, 2005-06 to 2014-15; Jeff Blashill, 2015-16 to date.

Captains' History

Art Duncan, 1926-27; Reg Noble, 1927-28 to 1929-30; George Hay, 1930-31; Carson Cooper, 1931-32; Larry Aurie, 1932-33; Herbie Lewis, 1933-34; Ebbie Goodfellow, 1934-35; Doug Young, 1935-36 to 1937-38; Ebbie Goodfellow, 1938-39 to 1940-41; Ebbie Goodfellow and Syd Howe, 1941-42; Sid Abel, 1942-43; Mud Bruneteau, Flash Hollett, 1943-44; Flash Hollett, 1944-45; Flash Hollett and Sid Abel, 1945-46; Sid Abel, 1946-47 to 1951-52; Ted Lindsay, 1952-53 to 1955-56; Red Kelly, 1956-57, 1957-58; Gordie Howe, 1958-59 to 1961-62; Alex Delvecchio, 1962-63 to 1972-73; Alex Delvecchio, Nick Libett, Red Berenson, Gary Bergman, Ted Harris, Mickey Redmond and Larry Johnston, 1973-74; Marcel Dionne, 1974-75; Danny Grant and Terry Harper, 1975-76; Danny Grant and Dennis Polonich, 1976-77; Dan Maloney and Dennis Hextall, 1977-78; Dennis Hextall, Nick Libett and Paul Woods, 1978-79; Dale McCourt, 1979-80; Errol Thompson and Reed Larson, 1980-81; Reed Larson, 1981-82; Danny Gare, 1982-83 to 1985-86; Steve Yzerman, 1986-87 to 2005-06; Nicklas Lidstrom, 2006-07 to 2011-12; Henrik Zetterberg, 2012-13 to date.

Edmonton Oilers

Key Off-Season Signings/Acquisitions

2017

June 16 • Re-signed LW **Jujhar Khaira**.
22 • Acquired C **Ryan Strome** from NY Islanders for C **Jordan Eberle**.
23 • Re-signed D **Kris Russell**.
26 • Re-signed RW **Zack Kassian**.
27 • Re-signed D **Eric Gryba**.
July 1 • Signed RW **Mitch Callahan**, C **Grayson Downing**, RW **Brian Ferlin**, RW **Ty Rattie**, D **Ryan Stanton**, D **Keegan Lowe** and G **Edward Pasquale**.
3 • Signed C **Brad Malone**.
5 • Re-signed C **Connor McDavid**.
7 • Signed LW **Jussi Jokinen**.
10 • Signed D **Yohann Auvitu**.

2016-17 Results: 47w-26l-4otl-5sol 103pts
2nd, Pacific Division • 4th, Western Conference

2017-18 Schedule

Oct.	Wed.	4	Calgary	Sat.	6	at Dallas*
	Sat.	7	at Vancouver	Sun.	7	at Chicago*
	Mon.	9	Winnipeg	Tue.	9	at Nashville
	Sat.	14	Ottawa	Fri.	12	at Arizona
	Tue.	17	Carolina	Sat.	13	at Vegas
	Thu.	19	at Chicago	Sat.	20	Vancouver
	Sat.	21	at Philadelphia*	Tue.	23	Buffalo
	Tue.	24	at Pittsburgh	Thu.	25	Calgary
	Thu.	26	Dallas	Feb. Thu.	1	Colorado
	Sat.	28	Washington	Mon.	5	Tampa Bay
Nov.	Wed.	1	Pittsburgh	Wed.	7	at Los Angeles
	Fri.	3	New Jersey	Fri.	9	at Anaheim
	Sun.	5	Detroit*	Sat.	10	at San Jose
	Tue.	7	at NY Islanders	Mon.	12	Florida
	Thu.	9	at New Jersey	Thu.	15	at Vegas
	Sat.	11	at NY Rangers	Sat.	17	at Arizona*
	Sun.	12	at Washington	Sun.	18	at Colorado*
	Tue.	14	Vegas	Tue.	20	Boston
	Thu.	16	St. Louis	Thu.	22	Colorado
	Sat.	18	at Dallas*	Sat.	24	at Los Angeles
	Tue.	21	at St. Louis*	Sun.	25	at Anaheim*
	Wed.	22	at Detroit	Tue.	27	at San Jose
	Fri.	24	at Buffalo	Mar. Thu.	1	Nashville
	Sun.	26	at Boston*	Sat.	3	NY Rangers
	Tue.	28	Arizona	Mon.	5	Arizona
	Thu.	30	Toronto	Thu.	8	NY Islanders
Dec.	Sat.	2	at Calgary	Sat.	10	Minnesota
	Wed.	6	Philadelphia	Tue.	13	at Calgary
	Sat.	9	at Montreal	Wed.	14	San Jose
	Sun.	10	at Toronto	Sat.	17	at Florida*
	Tue.	12	at Columbus	Sun.	18	at Tampa Bay*
	Thu.	14	Nashville	Tue.	20	at Carolina
	Sat.	16	at Minnesota*	Thu.	22	at Ottawa
	Mon.	18	San Jose	Sat.	24	Los Angeles
	Thu.	21	St. Louis	Sun.	25	Anaheim
	Sat.	23	Montreal*	Tue.	27	Columbus
	Wed.	27	at Winnipeg	Thu.	29	at Vancouver
	Fri.	29	Chicago	Sat.	31	at Calgary
	Sun.	31	Winnipeg*	Apr. Mon.	2	at Minnesota
Jan.	Tue.	2	Los Angeles	Thu.	5	Vegas
	Thu.	4	Anaheim	Sat.	7	Vancouver

* Denotes afternoon game.

Year-by-Year Record

Season	GP	Home W	L	T	OL	Road W	L	T	OL	Overall W	L	T	OL	GF	GA	Pts.	Div. Fin.	Conf. Fin.	Playoff Result
2016-17	82	25	12	....	4	22	14	....	5	47	26	....	9	247	212	103	2nd, Pac.	4th, West	Lost Second Round
2015-16	82	19	20	....	2	12	23	....	6	31	43	....	8	203	245	70	7th, Pac.	14th, West	– out of playoffs –
2014-15	82	15	23	....	3	9	21	....	11	24	44	....	14	198	283	62	6th, Pac.	13th, West	– out of playoffs –
2013-14	82	18	22	....	3	13	22	....	6	29	44	....	9	203	270	67	7th, Pac.	14th, West	– out of playoffs –
2012-13	48	9	11	....	4	10	11	....	3	19	22	....	7	125	134	45	3rd, NW	12th, West	– out of playoffs –
2011-12	82	18	17	....	6	14	23	....	4	32	40	....	10	212	239	74	5th, NW	14th, West	– out of playoffs –
2010-11	82	13	22	....	6	12	23	....	6	25	45	....	12	193	269	62	5th, NW	15th, West	– out of playoffs –
2009-10	82	18	19	....	4	9	28	....	4	27	47	....	8	214	284	62	5th, NW	15th, West	– out of playoffs –
2008-09	82	18	17	....	6	20	18	....	3	38	35	....	9	234	248	85	4th, NW	11th, West	– out of playoffs –
2007-08	82	23	17	....	1	18	18	....	5	41	35	....	6	235	251	88	4th, NW	9th, West	– out of playoffs –
2006-07	82	19	19	....	3	13	24	....	4	32	43	....	7	195	248	71	5th, NW	15th, West	– out of playoffs –
2005-06	82	20	15	....	6	21	13	....	7	41	28	....	13	256	251	95	3rd, NW	8th, West	Lost Final
2004-05	....																		
2003-04	82	22	12	4	3	14	17	8	2	36	29	12	5	221	208	89	4th, NW	9th, West	– out of playoffs –
2002-03	82	20	12	5	4	16	14	6	5	36	26	11	9	231	230	92	4th, NW	8th, West	Lost Conf. Quarter-Final
2001-02	82	23	14	4	0	15	14	8	4	38	28	12	4	205	182	92	3rd, NW	9th, West	– out of playoffs –
2000-01	82	23	9	7	2	16	19	5	1	39	28	12	3	243	222	93	2nd, NW	6th, West	Lost Conf. Quarter-Final
1999-2000	82	18	11	9	3	14	15	7	5	32	26	16	8	226	212	88	2nd, NW	7th, West	Lost Conf. Quarter-Final
1998-99	82	17	19	5	....	16	18	7	....	33	37	12	....	230	226	78	2nd, NW	7th, West	Lost Conf. Quarter-Final
1997-98	82	20	16	5	....	15	21	5	....	35	37	10	....	215	224	80	3rd, Pac.	7th, West	Lost Conf. Semi-Final
1996-97	82	21	16	4	....	15	21	5	....	36	37	9	....	252	247	81	3rd, Pac.	7th, West	Lost Conf. Semi-Final
1995-96	82	21	15	5	....	15	23	3	....	30	44	8	....	240	304	68	5th, Pac.	10th, West	– out of playoffs –
1994-95	48	11	12	1	....	6	15	3	....	17	27	4	....	136	183	38	5th, Pac.	11th, West	– out of playoffs –
1993-94	84	17	22	3	....	8	23	11	....	25	45	14	....	261	305	64	6th, Pac.	11th, West	– out of playoffs –
1992-93	84	16	21	5	....	10	29	3	....	26	50	8	....	242	337	60	5th, Smythe		– out of playoffs –
1991-92	80	22	13	5		14	21	5		36	34	10		295	297	82	3rd, Smythe		Lost Conf. Final
1990-91	80	22	15	3		15	22	3		37	37	6		272	272	80	3rd, Smythe		Lost Conf. Final
1989-90	80	23	11	6		15	17	8		38	28	14		315	283	90	2nd, Smythe		**Won Stanley Cup**
1988-89	80	21	16	3		17	18	5		38	34	8		325	306	84	3rd, Smythe		Lost Div. Semi-Final
1987-88	80	28	8	4		16	17	7		44	25	11		363	288	99	2nd, Smythe		**Won Stanley Cup**
1986-87	80	29	6	5		21	18	1		50	24	6		372	284	106	1st, Smythe		**Won Stanley Cup**
1985-86	80	32	6	2		24	11	5		56	18	6		426	310	119	1st, Smythe		Lost Div. Final
1984-85	80	26	7	7		23	13	4		49	20	11		401	298	109	1st, Smythe		**Won Stanley Cup**
1983-84	80	31	5	4		26	13	1		57	18	5		446	314	119	1st, Smythe		**Won Stanley Cup**
1982-83	80	25	9	6		22	12	6		47	21	12		424	315	106	1st, Smythe		Lost Final
1981-82	80	31	5	4		17	12	11		48	17	15		417	295	111	1st, Smythe		Lost Div. Semi-Final
1980-81	80	17	13	10		12	22	6		29	35	16		328	327	74	4th, Smythe		Lost Quarter-Final
1979-80	80	17	14	9		11	25	4		28	39	13		301	322	69	4th, Smythe		Lost Prelim. Round

Retired Numbers

3	Al Hamilton	1972-1980°
7	Paul Coffey	1980-1987
9	Glenn Anderson	1980-91, 1996
11	Mark Messier	1980-1991
17	Jari Kurri	1980-1990
31	Grant Fuhr	1981-1991
99	Wayne Gretzky	1979-1988

° Includes WHA

PACIFIC DIVISION
39th NHL Season
Franchise date: June 22, 1979

Connor McDavid's league-leading 100 points in 2016-17 and Cam Talbot's 42 wins were a huge reason why Edmonton posted its first 100-point season since its dynasty days and returned to the playoffs for the first time since 2005-06.

2017-18 Player Personnel

FORWARDS	HT	WT	*Age	Birthplace	S	2016-17 Club
CAGGIULA, Drake	5-10	185	23	Pickering, ON	L	Edmonton
DRAISAITL, Leon	6-1	214	21	Cologne, Germany	L	Edmonton
JOKINEN, Jussi	5-11	198	34	Kalajoki, Finland	L	Florida
KASSIAN, Zack	6-3	207	26	Windsor, ON	R	Edmonton
KHAIRA, Jujhar	6-4	219	23	Surrey, BC	L	Edmonton-Bakersfield
LETESTU, Mark	5-10	197	32	Elk Point, AB	R	Edmonton
LUCIC, Milan	6-3	236	29	Vancouver, BC	L	Edmonton
MAROON, Patrick	6-3	227	29	St Louis, MO	L	Edmonton
McDAVID, Connor	6-1	200	20	Richmond Hill, ON	L	Edmonton
NUGENT-HOPKINS, Ryan	6-0	196	24	Burnaby, BC	L	Edmonton
PAKARINEN, Iiro	6-1	215	26	Suonenjoki, Finland	R	Edmonton-Bakersfield
PULJUJARVI, Jesse	6-4	203	19	Alvkarleby, Sweden	R	Edmonton-Bakersfield
SLEPYSHEV, Anton	6-2	218	23	Penza, Russia	R	Edmonton-Bakersfield
STROME, Ryan	6-1	199	24	Mississauga, ON	R	NY Islanders
DEFENSEMEN						
AUVITU, Yohann	5-11	191	28	Ivry-sur-Seine, France	L	New Jersey-Albany
BENNING, Matt	6-1	195	23	Edmonton, AB	R	Edmonton-Bakersfield
FAYNE, Mark	6-3	212	30	Nashua, NH	R	Edmonton-Bakersfield
GRYBA, Eric	6-4	225	29	Saskatoon, SK	R	Edmonton
KLEFBOM, Oscar	6-3	220	24	Karlstad, Sweden	L	Edmonton
LARSSON, Adam	6-3	215	24	Skelleftea, Sweden	R	Edmonton
NURSE, Darnell	6-4	213	22	Hamilton, ON	L	Edmonton
RUSSELL, Kris	5-10	170	30	Caroline, AB	L	Edmonton
SEKERA, Andrej	6-0	198	31	Bojnice, Czech.	L	Edmonton

GOALTENDERS	HT	WT	*Age	Birthplace	C	2016-17 Club
BROSSOIT, Laurent	6-3	204	24	Port Alberni, BC	L	Edmonton-Bakersfield
TALBOT, Cam	6-3	199	30	Caledonia, ON	L	Edmonton

* – Age at start of 2017-18 season

Captains' History

Ron Chipperfield, 1979-80; Blair MacDonald and Lee Fogolin, Jr., 1980-81; Lee Fogolin, Jr., 1981-82, 1982-83; Wayne Gretzky, 1983-84 to 1987-88; Mark Messier, 1988-89 to 1990-91; Kevin Lowe, 1991-92; Craig MacTavish, 1992-93, 1993-94; Shayne Corson, 1994-95; Kelly Buchberger, 1995-96 to 1998-99; Doug Weight, 1999-2000, 2000-01; Jason Smith, 2001-02 to 2006-07; Ethan Moreau, 2007-08 to 2009-10; Shawn Horcoff, 2010-11 to 2012-13; Andrew Ference, 2013-14, 2014-15; no captain, 2015-16; Connor McDavid, 2016-17 to date.

Coaching History

Glen Sather, 1979-80; Bryan Watson and Glen Sather, 1980-81; Glen Sather, 1981-82 to 1988-89; John Muckler, 1989-90, 1990-91; Ted Green, 1991-92, 1992-93; Ted Green and Glen Sather, 1993-94; George Burnett and Ron Low, 1994-95; Ron Low, 1995-96 to 1998-99; Kevin Lowe, 1999-2000; Craig MacTavish, 2000-01 to 2008-09; Pat Quinn, 2009-10; Tom Renney, 2010-11, 2011-12; Ralph Krueger, 2012-13; Dallas Eakins, 2013-14; Dallas Eakins, Craig MacTavish and Todd Nelson, 2014-15; Todd McLellan, 2015-16 to date.

Todd McLellan

Head Coach

Born: Melville, SK, October 3, 1967.

The Edmonton Oilers announced on May 19, 2015 that Todd McLellan had been appointed as the club's new head coach. McLellan is the 14th head coach in Oilers franchise history. He was hired after serving as the head coach of Team Canada at the 2015 World Hockey Championship, leading Canada to their first gold medal since 2007 with an undefeated record of 10-0. Before the start of the 2016-17 season, McLellan was head coach of Team North America at the World Cup of Hockey. He then led Edmonton into the playoffs for the first time since 2005-06 as the Oilers topped 100 points for the first time since 1986-87.

Before being hired in Edmonton, McLellan spent the previous seven seasons as head coach of the San Jose Sharks, posting a record of 311-163-66 in 540 games. During that span, McLellan led the Sharks to six playoff appearances, four 40-plus win seasons, three 100-point seasons, captured the Presidents' Trophy (2009), three Pacific Division titles and made back-to-back appearances in the Western Conference Final (2010, 2011). No head coach in NHL history has won more games in their first four seasons behind the bench than the 195 collected by Todd McLellan. In 2010 he became just the third coach in NHL history to record 50-plus wins in his first two seasons as head coach. He was named a finalist for the NHL's Jack Adams Award in 2008-09 and became just the sixth NHL coach (first since 1990) to lead his team to the Presidents' Trophy in his first season as a head coach.

Prior to joining San Jose, McLellan spent three seasons as an assistant coach with the Detroit Red Wings. One of McLellan's key responsibilities was Detroit's power play, which finished first in the NHL in 2005-06 (22.1) and third in 2007-08 (20.7). McLellan won a Stanley Cup in 2008 with the Red Wings, as well as two Presidents' Trophies (2006, 2008). Before entering the NHL coaching ranks, McLellan spent four seasons as a head coach with the American Hockey League's Houston Aeros, capturing the 2003 Calder Cup Championship and being named Minor coach of the year by The Hockey News. He was also selected to coach two AHL All-Star Games during his tenure in Houston. McLellan also spent the 2000-01 season as head coach of the Cleveland Lumberjacks of the International Hockey League.

McLellan spent six seasons in junior hockey as head coach with the Swift Current Broncos of the Western Hockey League, where he also served as the general manager in his final four seasons. He was named the WHL executive of the year in 1997 and WHL coach of the year in 2000. The Broncos also captured division titles in 1996 and 2000 under McLellan. He played his junior hockey in the WHL with the Saskatoon Blades and was drafted by the New York Islanders in the fifth round (106th overall) in the 1986 NHL Draft. He played parts of two seasons with Springfield in the AHL and played in five games with the Islanders in 1987-88, posting two points (one goal, one assist) before a shoulder injury ended his career.

2016-17 Scoring

* – rookie

Regular Season

Pos	#	Player	Team	GP	G	A	Pts	TOI	+/–	PIM	PP	SH	GW	S	S%
C	97	Connor McDavid	EDM	82	30	70	100	21:07	27	26	3	1	6	251	12.0
C	29	Leon Draisaitl	EDM	82	29	48	77	18:53	7	20	10	0	5	172	16.9
C	14	Jordan Eberle	EDM	82	20	31	51	16:46	3	16	4	0	0	208	9.6
L	27	Milan Lucic	EDM	82	23	27	50	17:09	–3	50	12	0	3	175	13.1
C	93	Ryan Nugent-Hopkins	EDM	82	18	25	43	17:41	–10	29	5	0	4	200	9.0
L	19	Patrick Maroon	EDM	81	27	15	42	16:44	13	95	3	0	5	178	15.2
D	77	Oscar Klefbom	EDM	82	12	26	38	22:22	7	6	3	0	3	201	6.0
C	55	Mark Letestu	EDM	78	16	19	35	14:14	–2	17	11	2	6	120	13.3
D	2	Andrej Sekera	EDM	80	8	27	35	21:28	14	18	1	1	1	128	6.3
R	44	Zack Kassian	EDM	79	7	17	24	12:18	4	101	0	0	0	110	6.4
D	6	Adam Larsson	EDM	79	4	15	19	20:08	21	55	0	0	0	85	4.7
C	36 *	Drake Caggiula	EDM	60	7	11	18	13:14	3	16	2	0	2	93	7.5
D	83 *	Matthew Benning	EDM	62	3	12	15	16:36	8	29	1	0	0	69	4.3
L	67	Benoit Pouliot	EDM	67	8	6	14	14:03	–5	34	0	0	1	77	10.4
C	13	David Desharnais	MTL	31	4	6	10	13:06	5	6	0	0	1	30	13.3
			EDM	18	2	2	4	11:20	–1	6	0	0	0	16	12.5
			Total	49	6	8	14	12:27	4	12	0	0	1	46	13.0
D	4	Kris Russell	EDM	68	1	12	13	21:13	5	23	0	0	1	68	1.5
C	15	Tyler Pitlick	EDM	31	8	3	11	9:55	0	6	0	0	1	54	14.8
D	25	Darnell Nurse	EDM	44	5	6	11	17:01	0	33	0	0	0	85	5.9
L	42 *	Anton Slepyshev	EDM	41	4	6	10	11:06	5	4	0	0	0	55	7.3
R	98 *	Jesse Puljujarvi	EDM	28	1	7	8	11:15	5	10	1	0	0	41	2.4
C	23	Matt Hendricks	EDM	42	4	3	7	10:44	–3	29	0	0	1	42	9.5
D	62	Eric Gryba	EDM	40	2	4	6	16:08	–5	65	0	0	2	45	4.4
R	26	Iiro Pakarinen	EDM	14	2	2	4	8:55	2	2	0	0	1	15	13.3
C	51	Anton Lander	EDM	22	1	3	4	9:46	2	6	0	0	0	12	8.3
D	5	Mark Fayne	EDM	4	0	2	2	7:55	1	0	0	0	0	4	0.0
L	54 *	Jujhar Khaira	EDM	10	1	0	1	9:15	1	2	0	0	1	10	10.0
D	82	Jordan Oesterle	EDM	2	0	0	0	17:17	–1	0	0	0	0	2	0.0
D	79 *	Dillon Simpson	EDM	3	0	0	0	10:53	0	2	0	0	0	2	0.0

Goaltending

No.	Goaltender	GPI	Mins	Avg	W	L	OT	EN	SO	GA	SA	Sv%	G	A	PIM
1	* Laurent Brossoit	8	332	1.99	4	1	0	1	0	11	153	.928	0	0	0
33	Cam Talbot	73	4294	2.39	42	22	8	6	7	171	2117	.919	0	0	4
50	Jonas Gustavsson	7	329	3.10	1	3	1	1	0	17	139	.878	0	0	0
	Totals	**82**	**4991**	**2.49**	**47**	**26**	**9**	**8**	**7**	**207**	**2417**	**.914**			

Playoffs

Pos	#	Player	Team	GP	G	A	Pts	TOI	+/–	PIM	PP	SH	GW	OT	S	S%
C	29	Leon Draisaitl	EDM	13	6	10	16	19:32	8	19	1	0	1	0	22	27.3
C	55	Mark Letestu	EDM	13	5	6	11	17:35	–4	2	4	0	0	0	33	15.2
C	97	Connor McDavid	EDM	13	5	4	9	22:24	3	2	1	1	0	0	37	13.5
L	19	Patrick Maroon	EDM	13	3	5	8	17:21	2	28	1	0	1	0	33	9.1
L	27	Milan Lucic	EDM	13	2	4	6	17:02	–5	20	2	0	0	0	17	11.8
D	6	Adam Larsson	EDM	13	2	4	6	23:43	–4	4	0	0	1	0	15	13.3
D	77	Oscar Klefbom	EDM	12	2	3	5	23:10	–2	0	0	0	0	0	25	8.0
C	13	David Desharnais	EDM	13	1	3	4	9:31	3	0	0	0	1	1	6	16.7
D	4	Kris Russell	EDM	13	0	4	4	22:01	2	4	0	0	0	0	16	0.0
C	93	Ryan Nugent-Hopkins	EDM	13	0	4	4	18:25	–3	2	0	0	0	0	33	0.0
L	42 *	Anton Slepyshev	EDM	12	3	0	3	11:20	1	4	0	0	1	0	16	18.8
R	44	Zack Kassian	EDM	13	3	0	3	13:29	1	27	0	1	2	0	19	15.8
C	36 *	Drake Caggiula	EDM	13	3	0	3	15:22	0	25	0	0	0	0	22	13.6
D	2	Andrej Sekera	EDM	11	1	2	3	21:10	–1	2	0	0	0	0	18	5.6
D	83 *	Matthew Benning	EDM	12	0	3	3	17:08	3	12	0	0	0	0	9	0.0
C	14	Jordan Eberle	EDM	13	0	2	2	14:32	–6	2	0	0	0	0	22	0.0
D	25	Darnell Nurse	EDM	13	0	2	2	17:24	0	6	0	0	0	0	18	0.0
D	8	Griffin Reinhart	EDM	1	0	1	1	13:23	0	0	0	0	0	0	1	0.0
R	26	Iiro Pakarinen	EDM	1	0	0	0	8:26	–1	0	0	0	0	0	0	0.0
D	62	Eric Gryba	EDM	3	0	0	0	14:08	–1	4	0	0	0	0	0	0.0
L	67	Benoit Pouliot	EDM	13	0	0	0	12:40	–2	4	0	0	0	0	18	0.0

Goaltending

No.	Goaltender	GPI	Mins	Avg	W	L	EN	SO	GA	SA	Sv%	G	A	PIM
33	Cam Talbot	13	799	2.48	7	6	0	2	33	437	.924	0	1	0
1	* Laurent Brossoit	1	27	4.44	0	0	0	0	2	8	.750	0	0	0
	Totals	**13**	**829**	**2.53**	**7**	**6**	**0**	**2**	**35**	**445**	**.921**			

Coaching Record

			Regular Season				Playoffs			
Season	Team	League	GC	W	L	O/T	GC	W	L	T
1994-95	Swift Current	WHL	72	31	34	7	6	2	4	....
1995-96	Swift Current	WHL	72	36	31	5	6	2	4	....
1996-97	Swift Current	WHL	72	44	23	5	10	4	4	....
1997-98	Swift Current	WHL	72	44	19	9	12	7	5	....
1998-99	Swift Current	WHL	72	34	32	6	6	2	4	....
99-2000	Swift Current	WHL	72	47	18	7	12	6	6	....
2000-01	Cleveland	IHL	82	43	32	7	4	0	4	....
2001-02	Houston	AHL	80	39	26	15	14	8	6	....
2002-03	Houston	AHL	80	47	23	10	23	15	8	....
2003-04	Houston	AHL	80	28	34	18	2	0	2	....
2004-05	Houston	AHL	80	40	28	12	5	1	4	....
2008-09	**San Jose**	**NHL**	**82**	**53**	**18**	**11**	**6**	**2**	**4**	....
2009-10	**San Jose**	**NHL**	**82**	**51**	**20**	**11**	**15**	**8**	**7**	....
2010-11	**San Jose**	**NHL**	**82**	**48**	**25**	**9**	**18**	**9**	**9**	....
2011-12	**San Jose**	**NHL**	**82**	**43**	**29**	**10**	**5**	**1**	**4**	....
2012-13	**San Jose**	**NHL**	**48**	**25**	**16**	**7**	**11**	**7**	**4**	....
2013-14	**San Jose**	**NHL**	**82**	**51**	**22**	**9**	**7**	**3**	**4**	....
2014-15	**San Jose**	**NHL**	**82**	**40**	**33**	**9**	....	....	....	....
2015-16	**Edmonton**	**NHL**	**82**	**31**	**43**	**8**	....	....	....	....
2016-17	**Edmonton**	**NHL**	**82**	**47**	**26**	**9**	**13**	**7**	**6**	....
	NHL Totals		**704**	**389**	**232**	**83**	**75**	**37**	**38**	....

Assistant coaches Matt Shaw and Jay Woodcrofl posted an 1-2-0 record as replacement coach when Todd McLellan was sidelined due to a concussion suffered February 26, 2012. McLellan returned March 5. Games are credited to McLellan's coaching record.

Club Records

Team

(Figures in brackets for season records are games played; records for fewest points, wins, ties, losses, goals, goals against are for 70 or more games)

Most Points .... 119 — 1983-84 (80), 1985-86 (80)
Most Wins .... 57 — 1983-84 (80)
Most Ties .... 16 — 1980-81 (80), 1999-2000 (82)
Most Losses .... 50 — 1992-93 (84)
Most Goals .... *446 — 1983-84 (80)
Most Goals Against .... 337 — 1992-93 (84)
Fewest Points .... 60 — 1992-93 (84)
Fewest Wins .... 25 — 1993-94 (84)
Fewest Ties .... 5 — 1983-84 (80)
Fewest Losses .... 17 — 1981-82 (80), 1985-86 (80)
Fewest Goals .... 193 — 2010-11 (82)
Fewest Goals Against .... 182 — 2001-02 (82)
Longest Winning Streak
Overall .... 9 — Feb. 20-Mar. 13/01
Home .... 9 — Mar. 14-Apr. 9/17
Away .... 8 — Dec. 9/86-Jan. 17/87
Longest Team Point Streak
Overall .... 15 — Oct. 11-Nov. 9/84 (12W, 3T)
Home .... 14 — Nov. 15/89-Jan. 6/90 (11W, 3T)
Away .... 9 — Jan. 17-Mar. 2/82 (6W, 3T), Nov. 23/82-Jan. 18/83 (7W, 2T)
Longest Losing Streak
Overall .... 13 — Dec. 31/09-Jan. 30/10
Home .... 9 — Oct. 16-Nov. 24/93
Away .... 11 — Dec. 23/09-Feb. 10/10
Longest Winless Streak
Overall .... 14 — Oct. 11-Nov. 7/93 (13L, 1T)
Home .... 9 — Oct. 16-Nov. 24/93 (9L)
Away .... 11 — Dec. 18/01-Feb. 8/02 (7L, 4T), Dec. 23/09-Feb. 10/10 (11L)
Most Shutouts, Season .... 8 — 1997-98 (82); 2000-01 (82); 2001-02 (82)
Most PIM, Season .... 2,173 — 1987-88 (80)
Most Goals, Game .... 13 — Nov. 19/83 (N.J. 4 at Edm. 13), Nov. 8/85 (Van. 0 at Edm. 13)

Individual

Most Seasons .... 15 — Kevin Lowe
Most Games .... 1,037 — Kevin Lowe
Most Goals, Career .... 583 — Wayne Gretzky
Most Assists, Career .... 1,086 — Wayne Gretzky
Most Points, Career .... 1,669 — Wayne Gretzky (583G, 1,086A)
Most PIM, Career .... 1,747 — Kelly Buchberger
Most Shutouts, Career .... 23 — Tommy Salo
Longest Consecutive Games Streak .... 518 — Craig MacTavish (Oct. 12/86-Jan. 2/93)
Most Goals, Season .... *92 — Wayne Gretzky (1981-82)
Most Assists, Season .... *163 — Wayne Gretzky (1985-86)
Most Points, Season .... *215 — Wayne Gretzky (1985-86; 52G, 163A)
Most PIM, Season .... 286 — Steve Smith (1987-88)
Most Points, Defenseman, Season .... 138 — Paul Coffey (1985-86; 48G, 90A)
Most Points, Center, Season .... *215 — Wayne Gretzky (1985-86; 52G, 163A)
Most Points, Right Wing, Season .... 135 — Jari Kurri (1984-85; 71G, 64A)
Most Points, Left Wing, Season .... 106 — Mark Messier (1982-83; 48G, 58A)
Most Points, Rookie, Season .... 75 — Jari Kurri (1980-81; 32G, 43A)
Most Shutouts, Season .... 8 — Curtis Joseph (1997-98), Tommy Salo (2000-01)
Most Goals, Game .... 5 — Wayne Gretzky (Feb. 18/81), (Dec. 30/81), (Dec. 15/84), (Dec. 6/87); Jari Kurri (Nov. 19/83); Pat Hughes (Feb. 3/84)
Most Assists, Game .... *7 — Wayne Gretzky (Feb. 15/80), (Dec. 11/85), (Feb. 14/86)
Most Points, Game .... 8 — Wayne Gretzky (Nov. 19/83; 3G, 5A), (Jan. 4/84; 4G, 4A); Paul Coffey (Mar. 14/86; 2G, 6A); Sam Gagner (Feb. 2/12; 4G, 4A)

* NHL Record.

All-time Record vs. Other Clubs

Regular Season

	Total								At Home								On Road							
	GP	W	L	T	OL	GF	GA	PTS	GP	W	L	T	OL	GF	GA	PTS	GP	W	L	T	OL	GF	GA	PTS
Anaheim	101	44	50	2	5	241	272	95	50	25	21	0	4	113	125	54	51	19	29	2	1	128	147	41
Arizona	194	103	67	11	13	771	682	230	98	57	31	6	4	392	312	124	96	46	36	5	9	379	370	106
Boston	73	22	42	6	3	212	270	53	36	14	17	3	2	120	119	33	37	8	25	3	1	92	151	20
Buffalo	73	39	22	10	2	263	231	90	36	23	10	3	0	135	104	49	37	16	12	7	2	128	127	41
Calgary	233	97	109	19	8	761	814	221	117	56	45	10	6	392	374	128	116	41	64	9	2	369	440	93
Carolina	74	38	24	12	0	258	250	88	38	25	8	5	0	146	109	55	36	13	16	7	0	112	141	33
Chicago	132	55	62	12	3	443	465	125	66	31	29	5	1	229	219	68	66	24	33	7	2	214	246	57
Colorado	158	76	64	8	10	560	522	170	78	41	28	4	5	290	243	91	80	35	36	4	5	270	279	79
Columbus	55	31	14	3	7	192	145	72	27	20	5	0	2	102	62	42	28	11	9	3	5	90	83	30
Dallas	132	48	60	15	9	416	443	120	66	28	23	8	7	238	210	71	66	20	37	7	2	178	233	49
Detroit	127	50	57	13	7	410	458	120	63	29	22	10	2	225	218	70	64	21	35	3	5	185	240	50
Florida	30	17	10	3	0	90	71	37	14	8	5	1	0	42	31	17	16	9	5	2	0	48	40	20
Los Angeles	204	92	79	30	3	777	728	217	103	50	38	15	0	404	345	115	101	42	41	15	3	373	383	102
Minnesota	85	31	40	4	10	187	233	76	43	16	20	3	4	94	112	39	42	15	20	1	6	93	121	37
Montreal	83	39	37	4	3	269	269	85	44	24	20	0	0	148	137	48	39	15	17	4	3	121	132	37
Nashville	68	26	33	3	6	185	193	61	33	14	15	0	4	87	96	32	35	12	18	3	2	98	97	29
New Jersey	78	37	26	9	6	277	252	89	38	18	12	6	2	153	128	44	40	19	14	3	4	124	124	45
NY Islanders	74	30	29	14	1	251	254	75	36	22	9	5	0	128	99	49	38	8	20	9	1	123	155	26
NY Rangers	72	32	29	9	2	248	253	75	35	15	17	3	0	116	115	33	37	17	12	6	2	132	138	42
Ottawa	39	17	15	4	3	114	109	41	20	8	9	2	1	57	59	19	19	9	6	2	2	57	50	22
Philadelphia	73	32	32	8	1	230	251	73	35	20	8	6	1	124	99	47	38	12	24	2	0	106	152	26
Pittsburgh	74	38	30	4	2	308	259	82	37	24	11	1	1	161	116	50	37	14	19	3	1	147	143	32
St. Louis	131	56	60	11	4	421	437	127	65	31	28	4	2	211	214	68	66	25	32	7	2	210	223	59
San Jose	115	51	45	12	7	337	336	121	58	29	20	7	2	171	149	67	57	22	25	5	5	166	187	54
Tampa Bay	35	19	13	2	1	101	97	41	17	12	5	0	0	49	40	24	18	7	8	2	1	52	57	17
Toronto	98	43	43	8	4	381	354	98	52	26	18	6	2	200	166	60	46	17	25	2	2	181	188	38
Vancouver	236	119	83	19	15	866	765	272	118	68	37	7	6	459	351	149	118	51	46	12	9	407	414	123
Washington	72	30	35	6	1	250	251	67	36	19	13	4	0	140	110	42	36	11	22	2	1	110	141	25
Winnipeg	25	14	5	1	5	83	61	34	13	7	3	1	2	45	35	17	12	7	2	0	3	38	26	17
Totals	**2944**	**1326**	**1215**	**262**	**141**	**9902**	**9725**	**3055**	**1472**	**760**	**527**	**125**	**60**	**5171**	**4497**	**1705**	**1472**	**566**	**688**	**137**	**81**	**4731**	**5228**	**1350**

Playoffs

	Series	W	L	GP	W	L	T	GF	GA	Last Mtg.	Rnd.	Result
Anaheim	2	1	1	12	7	5	0	40	34	2017	SR	L 3-4
Arizona	6	6	0	26	22	4	0	120	75	1990	DSF	W 4-3
Boston	2	2	0	9	8	1	0	41	20	1990	F	W 4-1
Calgary	5	4	1	30	19	11	0	132	96	1991	DSF	W 4-3
Carolina	1	0	1	7	3	4	0	16	19	2006	F	L 3-4
Chicago	4	3	1	20	12	8	0	102	77	1992	CF	L 0-4
Colorado	2	1	1	12	5	7	0	30	35	1998	CQF	W 4-3
Dallas	8	2	6	42	15	27	0	104	118	2003	CQF	L 2-4
Detroit	3	3	0	16	12	4	0	58	43	2006	CQF	W 4-2
Los Angeles	7	5	2	36	24	12	0	154	127	1992	DSF	W 4-2
Montreal	1	1	0	3	3	0	0	15	6	1981	PR	W 3-0
NY Islanders	3	1	2	15	6	9	0	47	58	1984	F	W 4-1
Philadelphia	3	2	1	15	8	7	0	49	44	1987	F	W 4-3
San Jose	2	2	0	12	8	4	0	31	26	2017	FR	W 4-2
Vancouver	2	2	0	9	7	2	0	35	20	1992	DF	W 4-2
Totals	**51**	**35**	**16**	**264**	**159**	**105**	**0**	**974**	**798**			

Calgary totals include Atlanta Flames, 1979-80.
Colorado totals include Quebec, 1979-80 to 1994-95.
New Jersey totals include Colorado Rockies, 1979-80 to 1981-82.
Winnipeg totals include Atlanta Thrashers, 1999-2000 to 2010-11.
Carolina totals include Hartford, 1979-80 to 1996-97.
Dallas totals include Minnesota North Stars, 1979-80 to 1992-93.
Phoenix totals include Winnipeg, 1979-80 to 1995-96.

Playoff Results 2017-2013

Year	Round	Opponent	Result	GF	GA
2017	SR	Anaheim	L 3-4	24	21
	FR	San Jose	W 4-2	12	14

Abbreviations: Round: F – Final; **CF** – conference final; **CSF** – conference semi-final; **CQF** – conference quarter-final; **DF** – division final; **DSF** – division semi-final; **PR** – preliminary round.

2016-17 Results

Month	Day	Opponent	Score	Month	Day	Opponent	Score
Oct.	12	Calgary	7-4		8	at Ottawa	3-5
	14	at Calgary	5-3		10	San Jose	3-5
	16	Buffalo	2-6		12	New Jersey	3-2*
	18	Carolina	3-2		14	Calgary	2-1†
	20	St. Louis	3-1		16	Arizona	3-1
	23	at Winnipeg	3-0		18	Florida	4-3*
	26	Washington	4-1		20	Nashville	2-3†
	28	at Vancouver	2-0		21	at Calgary	7-3
	30	Ottawa	0-2		25	at Anaheim	4-0
Nov.	1	at Toronto	2-3*		26	at San Jose	4-1
	3	at NY Rangers	3-5		31	Minnesota	2-5
	5	at NY Islanders	4-3†	**Feb.**	2	at Nashville	0-2
	6	at Detroit	2-1		3	at Carolina	1-2
	8	at Pittsburgh	3-4		5	at Montreal	1-0†
	11	Dallas	2-3		11	Chicago	1-5
	13	NY Rangers	1-3		14	Arizona	5-2
	15	at Anaheim	1-4		16	Philadelphia	6-3
	17	at Los Angeles	2-4		18	at Chicago	3-1
	19	at Dallas	5-2		21	at Tampa Bay	1-4
	21	Chicago	5-0		22	at Florida	4-3
	23	at Colorado	6-3		24	at Washington	1-2
	25	at Arizona	2-3†		26	at Nashville	4-5
	27	Arizona	1-2		28	at St. Louis	2-1
	29	Toronto	2-4	**Mar.**	4	Detroit	4-3
Dec.	1	at Winnipeg	6-3		7	NY Islanders	1-4
	3	Anaheim	3-2*		10	Pittsburgh	2-3†
	4	Minnesota	1-2*		12	Montreal	1-4
	6	at Buffalo	3-4*		14	Dallas	7-1
	8	at Philadelphia	5-6		16	Boston	7-4
	9	at Minnesota	2-3†		18	Vancouver	2-0
	11	Winnipeg	3-2		20	Los Angeles	2-0
	13	Columbus	1-3		22	at Anaheim	3-4
	17	Tampa Bay	3-2†		23	at Colorado	7-4
	19	at St. Louis	3-2*		25	Colorado	4-1
	21	at Arizona	3-2		28	Los Angeles	2-1
	23	at San Jose	2-3*		30	San Jose	3-2
	29	Los Angeles	3-1	**Apr.**	1	Anaheim	3-2*
	31	Vancouver	2-3†		4	at Los Angeles	4-6
Jan.	3	at Columbus	1-3		6	at San Jose	4-2
	5	at Boston	4-3		8	at Vancouver	3-2
	7	at New Jersey	2-1*		9	Vancouver	5-2

* – Overtime † – Shootout

NHL Draft Selections 2017-2003

Name in bold denotes played in NHL.

2017
Pick
22 Kailer Yamamoto
78 Stuart Skinner
84 Dmitri Samorukov
115 Ostap Safin
146 Kirill Maximov
177 Skyler Brind'Amour
208 Philip Kemp

2016
Pick
4 **Jesse Puljujarvi**
32 Tyler Benson
63 Markus Niemelainen
84 Matthew Cairns
91 Filip Berglund
123 Dylan Wells
149 Graham McPhee
153 Aapeli Rasanen
183 Vincent Desharnais

2015
Pick
1 **Connor McDavid**
117 Caleb Jones
124 Ethan Bear
154 John Marino
208 Miroslav Svoboda
209 Ziyat Paigin

2014
Pick
3 **Leon Draisaitl**
91 William Lagesson
111 Zach Nagelvoort
130 Liam Coughlin
153 Tyler Vesel
183 Keven Bouchard

2013
Pick
7 **Darnell Nurse**
56 Marc-Olivier Roy
83 **Bogdan Yakimov**
88 **Anton Slepyshev**
94 Jackson Houck
96 Kyle Platzer
113 Aidan Muir
128 Evan Campbell
158 Ben Betker
188 Gregory Chase

2012
Pick
1 **Nail Yakupov**
32 Mitchell Moroz
63 **Jujhar Khaira**
91 Daniil Zharkov
93 **Erik Gustafsson**
123 Joey Laleggia
153 John McCarron

2011
Pick
1 **Ryan Nugent-Hopkins**
19 **Oscar Klefbom**
31 **David Musil**
62 Samu Perhonen
74 Travis Ewanyk
92 **Dillon Simpson**
114 **Tobias Rieder**
122 Martin Gernat
182 Frans Tuohimaa

2010
Pick
1 **Taylor Hall**
31 **Tyler Pitlick**
46 **Martin Marincin**
48 **Curtis Hamilton**
61 Ryan Martindale
91 Jeremie Blain
121 **Tyler Bunz**
162 **Brandon Davidson**
166 Drew Czerwonka
181 Kristians Pelss
202 Kellen Jones

2009
Pick
10 **Magnus Paajarvi**
40 **Anton Lander**
71 Troy Hesketh
82 Cameron Abney
99 Kyle Bigos
101 Toni Rajala
133 Olivier Roy

2008
Pick
22 **Jordan Eberle**
103 **Johan Motin**
133 **Philippe Cornet**
163 **Teemu Hartikainen**
193 Jordan Bendfeld

2007
Pick
6 **Sam Gagner**
15 **Alex Plante**
21 **Riley Nash**
97 **Linus Omark**
127 **Milan Kytnar**
157 William Quist

2006
Pick
45 **Jeff Petry**
75 **Theo Peckham**
133 Bryan Pitton
140 Cody Wild
170 Alexander Bumagin

2005
Pick
25 **Andrew Cogliano**
36 **Taylor Chorney**
81 **Danny Syvret**
86 Robby Dee
97 **Chris VandeVelde**
120 Viacheslav Trukhno
157 Fredrik Pettersson
220 Matthew Glasser

2004
Pick
14 **Devan Dubnyk**
25 **Rob Schremp**
44 Roman Tesliuk
57 Geoff Paukovich
112 **Liam Reddox**
146 **Bryan Young**
177 Max Gordichuk
208 Stephane Goulet
242 Tyler Spurgeon
274 Bjorn Bjurling

2003
Pick
22 **Marc Pouliot**
51 **Colin McDonald**
68 **Jean-Francois Jacques**
72 Mikhail Zhukov
94 **Zack Stortini**
147 Kalle Olsson
154 David Rohlfs
184 Dragan Umicevic
214 **Kyle Brodziak**
215 **Mathieu Roy**
248 Josef Hrabal
278 **Troy Bodie**

General Managers' History

Larry Gordon, 1979-80; Glen Sather, 1980-81 to 1999-2000; Kevin Lowe, 2000-01 to 2007-08; Steve Tambellini, 2008-09 to 2011-12; Steve Tambellini and Craig MacTavish, 2012-13; Craig MacTavish, 2013-14, 2014-15; Peter Chiarelli, 2015-16 to date.

Peter Chiarelli
President of Hockey Operations and General Manager

Born: Nepean, ON, August 5, 1964.

Peter Chiarelli was appointed president of hockey operations and general manager on April 24, 2015. He reports to CEO Bob Nicholson, and is responsible for all aspects of hockey operations. Shortly after Chiarelli came on board, Edmonton won the 2015 NHL Draft Lottery and made Connor McDavid the number-one pick. In 2016-17, the Oilers returned to the playoffs for the first time since 2005-06 and topped 100 points for the first time since 1986-87.

Before coming to Edmonton, Chiarelli served as the general manager of the Boston Bruins for eight seasons. He guided the Bruins to the Stanley Cup Final twice during his tenure in Boston, including winning the Stanley Cup in 2011. Chiarelli has also served as a member of the management group for Hockey Canada's national men's team, including the 2014 Winter Olympics and the 2013 Men's World Championships. He was general manager of Team North America at the 2016 World Cup of Hockey.

Chiarelli graduated from Harvard University with an Economics degree in 1987 and he played for the Harvard men's hockey team from 1983 to 1987. He began his career in hockey after graduating with a law degree from the University of Ottawa and was hired as the director of legal relations for the Ottawa Senators in 2000. In 2004, Chiarelli was promoted to assistant general manager of the Senators and he served in that role until being hired by the Boston Bruins in 2006.

Club Directory

Rogers Place

Edmonton Oilers
300, 10214-104 Avenue NW
Edmonton, Alberta T5J 0H6
Phone **780/414-GOAL(4625)**
Press Box 780/409-3780
Media Lounge 780/409-3778
FAX 780/409-5890
www.edmontonoilers.com
Capacity: 18,550

Executive
Owner & Governor . . . . Daryl A. Katz
Chief Executive Officer & Vice Chair . . . . Bob Nicholson
Vice Chairs . . . . Wayne Gretzky, Kevin Lowe
EVP Corporate Strategy & Business Development . . Darryl Boessenkool
EVP of Revenue . . . . Stew MacDonald
EVP of KGRE & OEG Special Projects . . . . Bob Black
EVP of Finance . . . . Jason Quilley
EVP of Rogers Place . . . . Susan Darrington
Executive Assistants . . . . Amanda Bacon, Salli Bruno

Hockey Operations
President of Hockey Operations & General Manager . . Peter Chiarelli
Senior Vice President, Hockey Operations . . . . Craig MacTavish
Assistant General Manager . . . . Keith Gretzky
VPs, Player Development / Player Personnel . . . . . . Scott Howson / Duane Sutter
Head Coach . . . . Todd McLellan
Assistant Coach . . . . Ian Herbers, Jim Johnson, Jay Woodcroft
Goalie Coach / Assistant Goalie Coach . . . . Dustin Schwartz / Sylvain Rodrigue
Skating Coach / Video Coach . . . . David Pelletier / Jeremy Coupal
Senior Director, Player Development . . . . Rick Carriere
Senior Director, Hockey Communications
& Media Relations . . . . JJ Hebert
Directors, High Performance / Player Personnel . . . . Simon Bennett / Bob Green
Director, Cap Compliance & Asst. to
President Hockey Ops . . . . Bill Scott
Director, Research, Analysis &
Software Development . . . . Sean Draper
Manager of Team Services . . . . Patrick Garland
Manager, Hockey Communications and Research . . Andre Brin
Manager, Hockey Communications and
Media Relations . . . . Shawn May
Manager, Hockey Analysis . . . . Justin Mahe
Senior Coordinator, Medical Services . . . . Ken Lowe
Senior Coordinator, Video Analysis . . . . Brian Ross
Coordinator, Player Development . . . . Shaun Mahe

Medical and Training Staff
Head Athletic Therapist. TD Forss
Head Equipment Manager . . . . Jeff Lang
Assistant Medical Trainer . . . . Chris Davie
Assistant Equipment Manager. . . . . Brad Harrison
Massage Therapist . . . . Stephen Lines
Head Strength and Conditioning Coach . . . . Chad Drummond
Assistant Strength and Conditioning Coach . . . . . . Joel Schneider
Assistant Equipment Manager. . . . . Shane Olmsted
Assistant Athletic Therapist. . . . . Ryan Williams
Family Liaison . . . . Jill Metz
Dressing Room Attendant. . . . . Joey Moss

Marketing
Senior Vice President, Marketing. . . . . Jeff Harrop
Vice President, Content. Michael Bobroff
Senior Advisor, OEG . . . . Don Metz
Directors. . . . . Marc Ciampa, Dan Cote-Rosen, Ryan Frankson,
Rich Meyers, Christine McAnally, Bryce York
Senior Manager, Fan Development . . . . Brad Ellard
Managers . . . . PJ Aucoin, Andrew Baer, Jessica Bromley,
Avery Hardy, James McCurdy, Jeff Nash,
Chris Schultz, Barrie Stafford, Heather Weigum
Reporter, EdmontonOilers.com and Oilers TV . . . . . Tom Gazzola
Oilers Head Writer / Senior Producer . . . . Chris Wescott / Gord Redel
Producers, Oilers Video . . . . Blaine Sayers, Ryan Hrycun
Coordinator, Oilers Video . . . . Kassidy Collins
Coordinators . . . . Sean Adams, Derek Fullerton, Paul Gazzola,
Jessica Kent, Sabrina Licata, Cait MacPhail, Karli
Paterson, Emily Pavelich, Dylan Retz, Meg Tilley
Creative Design, Lead / Intermediate . . . . Joey Angeles / Cristoval Castillon
Motion Graphics . . . . Dion Coursen, Jeremy Webb
Librarian / Archivist . . . . Lorraine Cousineau

Broadcast
Play by Play / Color Commentator . . . . Jack Michaels / Bob Stauffer

Corporate Sales
Vice President, Corporate Sales . . . . Steve Violetta
Senior Directors, Corporate Partnerships . . . . J.F. Amyot, Lisa Munro, Abe Hajar
Senior Director, Corporate Service. . . . . Brad Bissonette
Director, Partnership Service . . . . Brent Frew
Director, Digital and Media Sales. . . . . Brennan Watts
Manager, Corporate Partnerships . . . . Erik Hapke

Ticketing Sales and Service
Group Director, Ticket Services and Operations . . . . Jody Young
Directors, Ticket Sales and Service . . . . Jared Ginsburg, Bob Haromy, Mathew Johnson,
Gavin Morton
Supervisor, Ticket Event Services . . . . Brienne Patton
Managers . . . . Keenyn Bijou, Jessica Hanlon, Dianne Haydey,
Derek Perchaluk, Melissa Smart, Daniel Troiani

Operations
Senior VP / Manager, Operations . . . . Stu Ballantyne / Gilbert Da Silva
Senior Vice President, Enterprise Security
and Risk Mgmt. . . . . Kevin Galvin
Vice President, Corp. Communications
& Govt. Relations . . . . Tim Shipton
Vice President, Operations & Facilities . . . . Tom Cornwall
Vice President & G.M. / Asst. G.M., Rogers Place. . Susan Darrington / Michael McFaul
Vice President, Information Technology . . . . Kevin Flemming
Vice President, Human Resources . . . . Adam Barrie
Assistant G.M., Guest Experience & Events . . . . . . Steinunn Parsons
Senior Legal Counsels. . . . . Keely Brown, Imran Hussainly
Executive Director, EOCF . . . . Natalie Minckler
Director, Business Intelligence . . . . Sharon Lyseng

Florida Panthers

2016-17 Results: 35w-36L-5OTL-6SOL 81PTS
6TH, Atlantic Division • 13TH, Eastern Conference

Key Off-Season Signings/Acquisitions

2017

June 12 • Named **Bob Boughner** head coach.
23 • Named **Jack Capuano** associate coach.
24 • Named **Paul McFarland** assistant coach.
July 1 • Signed RW **Radim Vrbata**, RW **Evgeny Dadonov** and C **Micheal Haley**.
1 • Re-signed D **Alex Petrovic**.
3 • Signed RW **Alexandre Grenier**.
6 • Re-signed D **Mark Pysyk**.
Aug. 3 • Re-signed D **MacKenzie Weegar**.

Year-by-Year Record

Season	GP	Home W	L	T	OL	Road W	L	T	OL	Overall W	L	T	OL	GF	GA	Pts.	Div. Fin.	Conf. Fin.	Playoff Result
2016-17	82	19	19	....	3	16	17	....	8	35	36	....	11	210	237	81	6th, Atl.	13th, East	– out of playoffs –
2015-16	82	25	11	....	5	22	15	....	4	47	26	....	9	239	203	103	1st, Atl.	3rd, East	Lost First Round
2014-15	82	21	13	....	7	17	16	....	8	38	29	....	15	206	223	91	6th, Atl.	10th, East	– out of playoffs –
2013-14	82	16	20	....	5	13	25	....	3	29	45	....	8	196	268	66	7th, Atl.	15th, East	– out of playoffs –
2012-13	48	8	11	....	5	7	16	....	1	15	27	....	6	112	171	36	5th, SE	15th, East	– out of playoffs –
2011-12	82	21	9	....	11	17	17	....	7	38	26	....	18	203	227	94	1st, SE	3rd, East	Lost Conf. Quarter-Final
2010-11	82	16	17	....	8	14	23	....	4	30	40	....	12	195	229	72	5th, SE	15th, East	– out of playoffs –
2009-10	82	16	16	....	9	16	21	....	4	32	37	....	13	208	244	77	5th, SE	14th, East	– out of playoffs –
2008-09	82	22	12	....	7	19	18	....	4	41	30	....	11	234	231	93	3rd, SE	9th, East	– out of playoffs –
2007-08	82	18	15	....	8	20	20	....	1	38	35	....	9	216	226	85	3rd, SE	11th, East	– out of playoffs –
2006-07	82	23	12	....	6	12	19	....	10	35	31	....	16	247	257	86	4th, SE	12th, East	– out of playoffs –
2005-06	82	25	11	....	5	12	23	....	6	37	34	....	11	240	257	85	4th, SE	11th, East	– out of playoffs –
2004-05	....	....	....	....	....	....	....	....	....	....	....	....	....	....	....	....	....	....	
2003-04	82	16	15	7	3	12	20	8	1	28	35	15	4	188	221	75	4th, SE	12th, East	– out of playoffs –
2002-03	82	8	21	7	5	16	15	6	4	24	36	13	9	176	237	70	4th, SE	13th, East	– out of playoffs –
2001-02	82	11	23	3	4	11	21	7	2	22	44	10	6	180	250	60	4th, SE	14th, East	– out of playoffs –
2000-01	82	12	18	7	4	10	20	6	5	22	38	13	9	200	246	66	3rd, SE	12th, East	– out of playoffs –
1999-2000	82	26	9	4	2	17	18	2	4	43	27	6	6	244	209	98	2nd, SE	5th, East	Lost Conf. Quarter-Final
1998-99	82	17	17	7	....	13	17	11	....	30	34	18	....	210	228	78	2nd, SE	9th, East	– out of playoffs –
1997-98	82	11	24	6	....	13	19	9	....	24	43	15	....	203	256	63	6th, Atl.	12th, East	– out of playoffs –
1996-97	82	21	12	8	....	14	16	11	....	35	28	19	....	221	201	89	3rd, Atl.	4th, East	Lost Conf. Quarter-Final
1995-96	82	25	12	4	....	16	19	6	....	41	31	10	....	254	234	92	3rd, Atl.	4th, East	Lost Final
1994-95	48	9	12	3	....	11	10	3	....	20	22	6	....	115	127	46	5th, Atl.	9th, East	– out of playoffs –
1993-94	84	15	18	9	....	18	16	8	....	33	34	17	....	233	233	83	5th, Atl.	9th, East	– out of playoffs –

2017-18 Schedule

Oct.
Fri. 6 at Tampa Bay
Sat. 7 Tampa Bay
Thu. 12 St. Louis
Sat. 14 at Pittsburgh
Tue. 17 at Philadelphia
Fri. 20 Pittsburgh
Sat. 21 at Washington
Tue. 24 at Montreal
Thu. 26 Anaheim
Sat. 28 Detroit
Mon. 30 Tampa Bay

Nov.
Thu. 2 Columbus
Sat. 4 NY Rangers
Tue. 7 at Carolina
Fri. 10 at Buffalo
Sat. 11 at New Jersey
Tue. 14 Dallas
Thu. 16 at San Jose
Sat. 18 at Los Angeles*
Sun. 19 at Anaheim*
Wed. 22 Toronto
Sat. 25 Chicago
Mon. 27 at New Jersey
Tue. 28 at NY Rangers

Dec.
Fri. 1 San Jose
Sat. 2 at Carolina
Mon. 4 NY Islanders
Thu. 7 Winnipeg
Sat. 9 Colorado
Mon. 11 at Detroit
Tue. 12 at Chicago
Thu. 14 at Colorado
Sun. 17 at Vegas*
Tue. 19 at Arizona
Fri. 22 Minnesota
Sat. 23 Ottawa
Thu. 28 Philadelphia
Sat. 30 Montreal

Jan.
Tue. 2 at Minnesota
Thu. 4 at Boston
Fri. 5 at Detroit

Sun. 7 at Columbus*
Tue. 9 at St. Louis*
Fri. 12 Calgary
Fri. 19 Vegas
Sat. 20 at Nashville
Tue. 23 at Dallas
Thu. 25 Washington
Tue. 30 at NY Islanders

Feb.
Thu. 1 at Buffalo
Sat. 3 Detroit
Tue. 6 Vancouver
Fri. 9 Los Angeles
Mon. 12 at Edmonton
Wed. 14 at Vancouver
Sat. 17 at Calgary
Sun. 18 at Winnipeg
Tue. 20 at Toronto
Thu. 22 Washington
Sat. 24 Pittsburgh
Tue. 27 Toronto

Mar.
Thu. 1 New Jersey
Fri. 2 Buffalo
Sun. 4 Philadelphia*
Tue. 6 at Tampa Bay
Thu. 8 Montreal
Sat. 10 NY Rangers
Mon. 12 Ottawa
Thu. 15 Boston
Sat. 17 Edmonton*
Mon. 19 at Montreal
Tue. 20 at Ottawa
Thu. 22 at Columbus
Sat. 24 Arizona
Mon. 26 at NY Islanders
Wed. 28 at Toronto
Thu. 29 at Ottawa
Sat. 31 at Boston*

Apr.
Mon. 2 Carolina
Tue. 3 Nashville
Thu. 5 Boston
Sat. 7 Buffalo

* Denotes afternoon game.

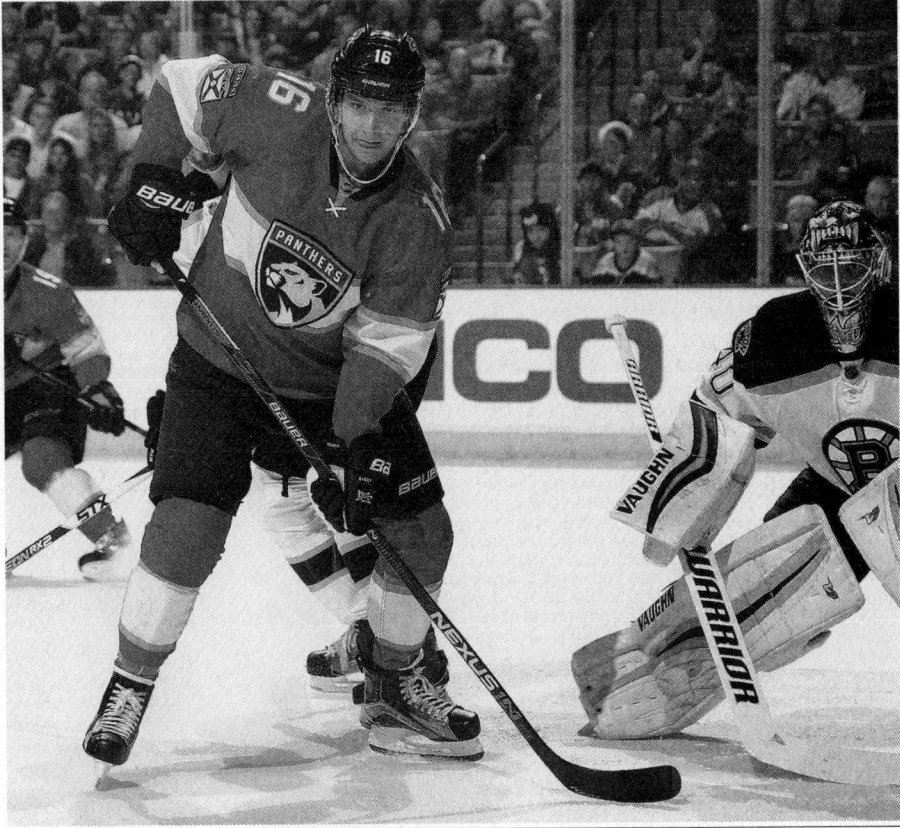

Aleksander Barkov (setting up in front of Boston goalie Tuukka Rask) played just 61 games in 2016-17 but had 21 goals and 31 assists and led the Panthers in plus-minus at +13.

ATLANTIC DIVISION
25th NHL Season

Franchise date: June 14, 1993

2017-18 Player Personnel

FORWARDS	HT	WT	*Age	Birthplace	S	2016-17 Club
BARKOV, Aleksander	6-3	213	22	Tampere, Finland	L	Florida
BJUGSTAD, Nick	6-6	218	25	Minneapolis, MN	R	Florida
DADONOV, Evgenii	5-11	184	28	Chelyabinsk, USSR	L	St. Petersburg
HAAPALA, Henrik	5-9	165	23	Lempaala, Finland	L	Tappara
HALEY, Micheal	5-10	205	31	Guelph, ON	L	San Jose
HUBERDEAU, Jonathan	6-1	188	24	Saint-Jerome, QC	L	Florida
MacKENZIE, Derek	5-11	181	36	Sudbury, ON	L	Florida
MALGIN, Denis	5-9	177	20	Olten, Switzerland	R	Florida-Springfield
MAMIN, Maxim	6-2	191	22	Moscow, Russia	L	CSKA-Zvezda Chekhov
McCANN, Jared	6-1	198	21	London, ON	L	Florida-Springfield
SCEVIOUR, Colton	6-0	195	28	Red Deer, AB	R	Florida
TROCHECK, Vincent	5-10	182	24	Pittsburgh, PA	R	Florida
VRBATA, Radim	6-1	194	36	Mlada Boleslav, Czech.	R	Arizona

DEFENSEMEN	HT	WT	*Age	Birthplace	S	2016-17 Club
DEMERS, Jason	6-1	200	29	Dorval, QC	R	Florida
EKBLAD, Aaron	6-4	216	21	Windsor, ON	R	Florida
MATHESON, Mike	6-2	192	23	Pointe-Claire, QC	L	Florida
McCOSHEN, Ian	6-3	217	22	Anaheim, CA	L	Florida-Springfield
PETROVIC, Alex	6-4	206	25	Edmonton, AB	R	Florida
PYSYK, Mark	6-1	192	25	Edmonton, AB	R	Florida
WEEGAR, MacKenzie	6-0	212	23	Ottawa, ON	R	Florida-Springfield
YANDLE, Keith	6-1	196	31	Boston, MA	L	Florida

GOALTENDERS	HT	WT	*Age	Birthplace	C	2016-17 Club
LUONGO, Roberto	6-3	217	38	Montreal, QC	L	Florida
REIMER, James	6-2	217	29	Morweena, MB	L	Florida

* – Age at start of 2017-18 season

General Managers' History

Bob Clarke, 1993-94; Bryan Murray, 1994-95 to 1999-2000; Bryan Murray and Bill Torrey, 2000-01; Bill Torrey and Chuck Fletcher, 2001-02; Rick Dudley, 2002-03, 2003-04; Mike Keenan, 2004-05, 2005-06; Jacques Martin, 2006-07 to 2008-09; Randy Sexton, 2009-10; Dale Tallon, 2010-11 to 2015-16; Tom Rowe, 2016-17; Dale Tallon, 2017-18.

Dale Tallon

President Hockey Ops / General Manager

Born: Noranda, QC, October 19, 1950.

Florida Panthers chairman and governor Vincent Viola announced on April 10, 2017 that Dale Tallon had been appointed the club's general manager. Tallon, who previously served as the team's general manager from May 2010 through to May 2016, retains his title as president of Hockey Operations. Tallon oversees all aspects of hockey operations in his role including scouting, player acquisition and development.

During his tenure with the Panthers, Tallon has been responsible for reshaping the club's hockey operations department, as well as the team's player personnel. He has led the franchise to a pair of division titles and two playoff appearances. In 2015-16, the Panthers set franchise records for wins (47) and points (103) on the way to winning the Atlantic Division. In addition, the team won a franchise record 12 consecutive games from December 15 to January 10. Florida completed the 2014-15 season as the NHL's most improved team, finishing the season with a 38-29-15 record and 91 points, a 25-point improvement from the previous year. The Panthers won the franchise's first Southeast Division championship in 2011-12 season and Tallon was runner up as the NHL's General Manager of the Year. He has been responsible for drafting two Calder Memorial Trophy winners in defenseman Aaron Ekblad (2015) and forward Jonathan Huberdeau (2013). Among Tallon's group of highly-regarded draft selections during his tenure are Erik Gudbranson (3rd overall, 2010), Nick Bjugstad (19th overall, 2010), Huberdeau (3rd overall, 2011), Vincent Trocheck (64th overall, 2011), Michael Matheson (23rd overall, 2012), Aleksander Barkov (2nd overall, 2013), Ekblad (1st overall, 2014) and Lawson Crouse (11th overall, 2015).

Prior to joining the Panthers, Tallon spent 33 years with the Chicago Blackhawks organization as a front office executive, player and broadcast personality. He served as Chicago's General Manager from 2005-09, and assistant GM from 2003-05. He was responsible for drafting or acquiring many of the Blackhawks' top players who won the 2010 Stanley Cup. Tallon spent the 2009-10 season serving as a Senior Advisor of Hockey Operations for the Blackhawks. He also served four years (1998-2002) as director of player personnel before returning to the radio and television booth prior to the 2002-03 season.

A defenseman, Tallon was Vancouver's first-round selection (2nd overall) in the 1970 NHL Draft. He played in 642 NHL contests with Vancouver (1970-73), Chicago (1973-78) and Pittsburgh (1978-80), registering 336 points (98-238-336) and 568 PIM. Tallon recorded a career-high 17 goals in 69 games with Vancouver during the 1971-72 season and appeared in the 1971 and 1972 NHL All-Star Games. In 1972, Tallon was picked as an alternate for Team Canada at the 1972 Summit Series against the USSR.

2016-17 Scoring

* – rookie

Regular Season

Pos	#	Player	Team	GP	G	A	Pts	TOI	+/-	PIM	PP	SH	GW	S	S%
C	21	Vincent Trocheck	FLA	82	23	31	54	20:49	–13	43	2	0	2	230	10.0
C	16	Aleksander Barkov	FLA	61	21	31	52	19:24	13	10	3	0	5	142	14.8
C	81	Jonathan Marchessaul	FLA	75	30	21	51	16:54	–21	38	8	0	6	193	15.5
L	26	Thomas Vanek	DET	48	15	23	38	14:37	2	16	5	0	2	99	15.2
			FLA	20	2	8	10	13:53	–7	6	0	0	0	34	5.9
			Total	68	17	31	48	14:24	–5	22	5	0	2	133	12.8
R	68	Jaromir Jagr	FLA	82	16	30	46	16:59	2	56	8	0	2	181	8.8
D	3	Keith Yandle	FLA	82	5	36	41	22:02	–6	39	2	0	0	178	2.8
R	18	Reilly Smith	FLA	80	15	22	37	18:21	–13	17	6	1	3	160	9.4
L	36	Jussi Jokinen	FLA	69	11	17	28	17:24	–15	39	4	1	2	118	9.3
D	55	Jason Demers	FLA	81	9	19	28	19:36	–14	53	0	0	2	98	9.2
C	11	Jonathan Huberdeau	FLA	31	10	16	26	17:55	–2	13	3	0	2	86	11.6
C	7	Colton Sceviour	FLA	80	9	15	24	14:38	–16	25	1	3	1	172	5.2
D	5	Aaron Ekblad	FLA	68	10	11	21	21:27	–23	58	4	1	2	225	4.4
D	19 *	Michael Matheson	FLA	81	7	10	17	21:03	–5	36	0	0	0	179	3.9
D	13	Mark Pysyk	FLA	82	4	13	17	18:33	0	10	0	0	0	86	4.7
C	17	Derek MacKenzie	FLA	82	6	10	16	12:33	–7	50	0	2	1	91	6.6
C	27	Nick Bjugstad	FLA	54	7	7	14	13:09	–19	22	1	0	1	91	7.7
D	6	Alex Petrovic	FLA	49	1	13	14	18:09	–1	79	0	0	0	55	1.8
C	62 *	Denis Malgin	FLA	47	6	4	10	11:14	–5	8	2	0	1	67	9.0
C	48 *	Michael Sgarbossa	ANA	9	0	2	2	9:28	–2	0	0	0	0	7	0.0
			FLA	29	2	5	7	11:40	–3	9	1	0	0	26	7.7
			Total	38	2	7	9	11:09	–5	9	1	0	0	33	6.1
C	90	Jared McCann	FLA	29	1	6	7	11:38	–1	4	0	0	0	44	2.3
C	24	Seth Griffith	TOR	3	0	0	0	9:28	0	0	0	0	0	3	0.0
			FLA	21	0	5	5	13:12	6	8	0	0	0	18	0.0
			Total	24	0	5	5	12:44	6	8	0	0	0	21	0.0
L	22	Shawn Thornton	FLA	50	2	2	4	7:41	–7	67	0	0	0	42	4.8
D	46	Jakub Kindl	FLA	39	0	4	4	14:41	–11	28	0	0	0	41	0.0
R	38	Shane Harper	FLA	14	2	1	3	10:18	–1	18	0	0	0	13	15.4
C	92 *	Kyle Rau	FLA	24	2	1	3	9:36	–3	4	0	0	0	21	9.5
R	15	Paul Thompson	FLA	21	0	3	3	7:54	–4	22	0	0	0	19	0.0
D	8	Dylan McIlrath	NYR	1	0	0	0	9:14	0	4	0	0	0	0	0.0
			FLA	5	1	0	1	9:34	–2	10	0	0	0	3	33.3
			Total	6	1	0	1	9:31	–2	14	0	0	0	3	33.3
D	12 *	Ian McCoshen	FLA	3	0	1	1	13:15	0	0	0	0	0	0	0.0
D	52 *	MacKenzie Weegar	FLA	3	0	0	0	17:26	0	4	0	0	0	3	0.0

Goaltending

No.	Goaltender	GPI	Mins	Avg	W	L	OT	EN	SO	GA	SA	Sv%	G	A	PIM
34	James Reimer	43	2325	2.53	18	16	5	5	3	98	1222	.920	0	0	2
1	Roberto Luongo	40	2327	2.68	17	15	6	3	1	104	1217	.915	0	1	4
20	Reto Berra	7	313	3.45	0	5	0	3	0	18	145	.876	0	0	0
	Totals	**82**	**5007**	**2.77**	**35**	**36**	**11**	**11**	**4**	**231**	**2595**	**.911**			

Coaching History

Roger Neilson, 1993-94, 1994-95; Doug MacLean, 1995-96, 1996-97; Doug MacLean and Bryan Murray, 1997-98; Terry Murray, 1998-99, 1999-2000; Terry Murray and Duane Sutter, 2000-01; Duane Sutter and Mike Keenan, 2001-02; Mike Keenan, 2002-03; Mike Keenan, Rick Dudley and John Torchetti, 2003-04; Jacques Martin, 2004-05 to 2007-08; Peter DeBoer, 2008-09 to 2010-11; Kevin Dineen, 2011-12, 2012-13; Kevin Dineen and Peter Horachek, 2013-14; Gerard Gallant, 2014-15, 2015-16; Gerard Gallant and Tom Rowe, 2016-17; Bob Boughner, 2017-18.

Bob Boughner

Head Coach

Born: Windsor, ON, March 8, 1971.

Bob Boughner was named the 15th head coach of the Florida Panthers on June 12, 2017. Boughner served the previous two seasons as an assistant coach for the San Jose Sharks (2015 to 2017), helping them advance to the postseason twice and the Stanley Cup Final in 2016. He began his NHL coaching career as an assistant coach with the Columbus Blue Jackets in 2010-11.

The native of Windsor, Ontario, served as head coach of his hometown Windsor Spitfires of the Ontario Hockey League for eight seasons, winning two consecutive John Ross Robertson Cups and two consecutive Memorial Cups (2009, 2010). Boughner was named the OHL and the Canadian Hockey League's coach of the year in 2007-08 and 2008-09. In 2006, Boughner headed an ownership group to purchase the Spitfires and served as the organization's president until being hired by Florida. Under Boughner's leadership, the Spitfires won three Memorial Cups (2009, 2010, 2017).

A defenseman in the NHL for 10 seasons (1996 to 2006), Boughner appeared in 630 NHL games for the Buffalo Sabres, Nashville Predators, Pittsburgh Penguins, Calgary Flames, Carolina Hurricanes and Colorado Avalanche. Boughner originally was selected by the Detroit Red Wings in the second round (32nd overall) of the 1989 NHL Draft. On July 25, 1994, Boughner signed with the Panthers and played for two seasons for their minor league affiliates, the Cincinnati Cyclones of the International Hockey League (1994-95) and the Carolina Monarchs (1995-96) of the American Hockey League.

Coaching Record

			Regular Season				Playoffs			
Season	Team	League	GC	W	L	O/T	GC	W	L	T
2006-07	Windsor	OHL	68	18	43	7	....	....	....	....
2007-08	Windsor	OHL	68	41	15	12	5	1	4	....
2008-09	Windsor	OHL	68	57	10	1	20	16	4	....
2008-09	Windsor	M-Cup	....	....	....	....	6	4	2	....
2009-10	Windsor	OHL	68	50	12	6	19	16	3	....
2009-10	Windsor	M-Cup	....	....	....	....	4	4	0	....
2011-12	Windsor	OHL	68	29	32	7	4	0	4	....
2012-13	Windsor	OHL	68	26	33	9	....	....	....	....
2013-14	Windsor	OHL	68	37	28	3	4	0	4	....
2014-15	Windsor	OHL	68	24	40	4	....	....	....	....

Club Records

Team

(Figures in brackets for season records are games played; records for fewest points, wins, ties, losses, goals, goals against are for 70 or more games)

Most Points	103	2015-16 (82)
Most Wins	47	2015-16 (82)
Most Ties	19	1996-97 (82)
Most Losses	45	2013-14 (82)
Most Goals	254	1995-96 (82)
Most Goals Against	268	2013-14 (82)
Fewest Points	60	2001-02 (82)
Fewest Wins	22	2000-01 (82), 2001-02 (82)
Fewest Ties	6	1999-2000 (82)
Fewest Losses	26	2011-12 (82), 2015-16 (82)
Fewest Goals	176	2002-03 (82)
Fewest Goals Against	201	1996-97 (82)

Longest Winning Streak

Overall	12	Dec. 15/15-Jan. 10/16
Home	7	Dec. 18/15-Jan. 3/16
Away	6	Dec. 15/15-Jan. 10/16

Longest Team Point Streak

Overall	12	Oct. 5-30/96 (8W, 4T)
Home	8	Nov. 5-26/95 (7W, 1T)
Away	7	Dec. 7-29/93 (5W, 2T); Oct. 5-29/96 (4W, 3T); Feb. 2-Mar. 2/16 (4W, 1OTW, 1OTL, 1SOL)

Longest Losing Streak

Overall	13	Feb. 7-Mar. 23/98
Home	6	Feb. 25-Mar. 23/98
Away	13	Oct. 27-Dec. 17/05

Longest Winless Streak

Overall	15	Feb. 1-Mar. 23/98 (14L, 1T)
Home	13	Feb. 5-Mar. 24/03 (10L, 1OTL, 2T)
Away	16	Jan. 2-Mar. 21/98 (12L, 4T)

Most Shutouts, Season	9	2008-09 (82)
Most PIM, Season	1,994	2001-02 (82)
Most Goals, Game	10	Nov. 26/97 (Bos. 5 at Fla. 10)

Individual

Most Seasons	11	Stephen Weiss
Most Games	654	Stephen Weiss
Most Goals, Career	188	Olli Jokinen
Most Assists, Career	249	Stephen Weiss
Most Points, Career	419	Olli Jokinen (188G, 231A)
Most PIM, Career	1,702	Paul Laus
Most Shutouts, Career	34	Roberto Luongo

Longest Consecutive Games Streak .... 376 Olli Jokinen (Dec. 27/02-Apr. 5/08), Brian Campbell (Oct. 8/11-Apr. 9/16)

Most Goals, Season	59	Pavel Bure (2000-01)
Most Assists, Season	53	Viktor Kozlov (1999-2000)
Most Points, Season	94	Pavel Bure (1999-2000; 58G, 36A)
Most PIM, Season	354	Peter Worrell (2001-02)

Most Points, Defenseman, Season .... 57 Robert Svehla (1995-96; 8G, 49A)

Most Points, Center, Season .... 91 Olli Jokinen (2006-07; 39G, 52A)

Most Points, Right Wing, Season .... 94 Pavel Bure (1999-2000; 58G, 36A)

Most Points, Left Wing, Season .... 71 Ray Whitney (1999-2000; 29G, 42A)

Most Points, Rookie, Season .... 50 Jesse Belanger (1993-94; 17G, 33A)

Most Shutouts, Season .... 7 Roberto Luongo (2003-04) Tomas Vokoun (2009-10)

Most Goals, Game .... 4 Mark Parrish (Oct. 30/98) Pavel Bure (Jan. 1/00), (Feb. 10/01)

Most Assists, Game .... 4 Eight times

Most Points, Game .... 6 Olli Jokinen (Mar. 17/07; 2G, 4A)

Captains' History

Brian Skrudland, 1993-94 to 1996-97; Scott Mellanby, 1997-98 to 2000-01; Pavel Bure, 2001-02; no captain, 2002-03; Olli Jokinen, 2003-04 to 2007-08; no captain, 2008-09; Bryan McCabe, 2009-10, 2010-11; no captain, 2011-12; Ed Jovanovski, 2012-13, 2013-14; Willie Mitchell, 2014-15, 2015-16; Derek MacKenzie, 2016-17 to date.

All-time Record vs. Other Clubs

Regular Season

			Total							At Home							On Road				
	GP	W	L	T	OL	GF	GA	PTS	GP	W	L	T	OL	GF	GA	PTS	GP	W	L	T	OL	GF	GA	PTS
Anaheim	31	15	11		3	89	81	35	15	7	6		2	39	35	16	16	8	5		1	50	46	19
Arizona	32	12	13	3	4	83	84	31	15	7	7	0	1	41	36	15	17	5	6	3	3	42	48	16
Boston	92	35	43	6	8	225	267	84	45	16	21	2	6	121	133	40	47	19	22	4	2	104	134	44
Buffalo	92	40	41	4	7	229	257	91	45	23	18	1	3	123	123	50	47	17	23	3	4	106	134	41
Calgary	31	11	13	4	3	78	91	29	16	5	7	2	2	37	43	14	15	6	6	1	2	41	48	15
Carolina	115	48	45	11	11	321	308	118	58	30	12	8	8	181	134	76	57	18	33	3	3	140	174	42
Chicago	35	11	17	3	4	85	111	29	17	6	8	1	2	40	52	15	18	5	9	2	2	45	59	14
Colorado	37	13	18	3	3	106	120	32	19	6	12	0	1	59	70	13	18	7	6	3	2	47	50	19
Columbus	24	9	9	0	6	56	68	24	12	6	2	0	4	33	33	16	12	3	7	0	2	23	35	8
Dallas	33	15	14	3	1	91	93	34	17	6	9	1	1	35	49	14	16	9	5	2	0	56	44	20
Detroit	40	15	16	5	4	104	119	39	21	6	10	2	3	55	64	17	19	9	6	3	1	49	55	22
Edmonton	30	10	11	3	6	71	90	29	16	5	4	2	5	40	48	17	14	5	7	1	1	31	42	12
Los Angeles	32	11	17	3	1	77	93	26	15	6	5	3	1	36	40	16	17	5	12	0	0	41	53	10
Minnesota	21	5	13	1	2	36	66	13	11	4	6	1	0	23	34	9	10	1	7	1	1	13	32	4
Montreal	91	42	32	6	11	225	238	101	47	21	18	3	5	123	126	50	44	21	14	3	6	102	112	51
Nashville	26	11	7	3	5	66	66	30	13	7	2	1	3	36	32	18	13	4	5	2	2	30	34	12
New Jersey	92	33	45	7	7	205	258	80	46	20	24	4	4	111	117	48	46	13	27	3	3	94	141	32
NY Islanders	93	47	30	8	8	273	252	110	46	25	12	6	3	146	132	59	47	22	18	2	5	127	120	51
NY Rangers	92	35	43	6	8	215	272	84	46	19	18	2	7	112	128	47	46	16	25	4	1	103	144	37
Ottawa	92	37	48	3	4	247	283	81	47	19	26	1	1	135	147	40	45	18	22	2	3	112	136	41
Philadelphia	92	34	44	7	7	227	269	82	45	15	25	1	4	114	148	35	47	19	19	6	3	113	121	47
Pittsburgh	88	36	37	4	11	240	253	87	44	23	17	1	3	127	118	50	44	13	20	3	8	113	135	37
St. Louis	33	9	19	3	2	58	89	23	16	4	8	2	2	33	43	12	17	5	11	1	0	25	46	11
San Jose	32	12	17	1	2	81	95	32	16	5	5	1	0	40	44	16	16	7	7	2	0	41	51	16
Tampa Bay	126	64	39	10	13	387	339	151	62	37	12	4	9	199	158	87	64	27	27	6	4	188	181	64
Toronto	80	34	33	7	6	239	231	81	41	18	15	5	3	125	113	44	39	16	18	2	3	114	118	37
Vancouver	31	10	11	6	4	75	90	30	15	7	5	1	2	40	46	17	16	3	6	5	2	35	44	13
Washington	120	48	53	6	13	305	354	115	60	27	23	4	6	162	165	64	60	21	30	3	6	143	189	51
Winnipeg	87	35	34	5	13	236	278	88	44	21	16	1	6	120	125	49	43	14	18	4	7	116	153	39
Totals	**1820**	**737**	**768**	**142**	**173**	**4730**	**5215**	**1789**	**910**	**401**	**347**	**65**	**97**	**2486**	**2536**	**964**	**910**	**336**	**421**	**77**	**76**	**2244**	**2679**	**825**

Playoffs

	Series	W	L	GP	W	L	T	GF	GA	Last Mtg.	Rnd.	Result
Boston	1	1	0	5	4	1	0	22	16	1996	CQF	W 4-1
Colorado	1	0	1	4	0	4	0	4	15	1996	F	L 0-4
New Jersey	2	0	2	11	3	8	0	23	30	2012	CQF	L 3-4
NY Islanders	1	0	1	6	2	4	0	14	15	2016	FR	L 2-4
NY Rangers	1	0	1	5	1	4	0	10	13	1997	CQF	L 1-4
Philadelphia	1	1	0	6	4	2	0	15	11	1996	CSF	W 4-2
Pittsburgh	1	1	0	7	4	3	0	20	15	1996	CF	W 4-3
Totals	**8**	**3**	**5**	**44**	**18**	**26**	**0**	**108**	**115**			

Colorado totals include Quebec, 1993-94 to 1994-95.
Phoenix totals include Winnipeg, 1993-94 to 1995-96.
Carolina totals include Hartford, 1993-94 to 1996-97.
Winnipeg totals include Atlanta Thrashers, 1999-2000 to 2010-11.

Playoff Results 2017-2013

Year	Round	Opponent	Result	GF	GA
2016	FR	NY Islanders	L 2-4	14	15

Abbreviations: Round: F – Final;
CF – conference final; **CSF** – conference semi-final;
CQF – conference quarter-final; **FR** – first round.

2016-17 Results

Oct.	13	New Jersey	2-1*		9	at New Jersey	3-0
	15	Detroit	4-1		11	at NY Islanders	2-1
	18	at Tampa Bay	3-4†		13	NY Islanders	2-5
	20	Washington	2-4		14	Columbus	4-3
	22	Colorado	5-2		17	at Calgary	2-5
	25	at Pittsburgh	2-3		18	at Edmonton	3-4*
	27	at Toronto	2-3		20	at Vancouver	1-2
	29	at Buffalo	0-3		23	at Arizona	2-3*
	30	at Detroit	5-2		26	Tampa Bay	2-1*
Nov.	1	Boston	1-2		31	Ottawa	6-5
	3	New Jersey	4-3*	Feb.	3	Anaheim	2-1
	5	at Washington	1-3		9	Los Angeles	3-6
	7	Tampa Bay	3-1		11	at Nashville	7-4
	10	San Jose	2-4		15	at San Jose	6-5*
	12	NY Islanders	3-2*		17	at Anaheim	4-1
	15	at Montreal	4-3*		18	at Los Angeles	3-2
	17	at Toronto	1-6		20	at St. Louis	2-1
	19	at Ottawa	4-1		22	Edmonton	3-4
	20	at NY Rangers	3-2†		24	Calgary	2-4
	22	Philadelphia	1-3		26	Ottawa	1-2
	26	Columbus	2-1†		28	Carolina	3-2†
	27	at Carolina	2-3	Mar.	2	at Philadelphia	1-2†
	29	at Chicago	1-2†		4	Dallas	1-2
Dec.	1	at Detroit	2-1*		7	NY Rangers	2-5
	3	at Ottawa	0-2		10	Minnesota	4-7
	5	at Boston	3-4*		11	at Tampa Bay	2-3
	6	at Philadelphia	2-3*		14	Toronto	7-2
	8	Pittsburgh	1-5		16	at Columbus	1-2
	10	Vancouver	4-2		17	at NY Rangers	4-3†
	13	at Minnesota	1-5		19	at Pittsburgh	0-4
	15	at Winnipeg	3-4†		21	Carolina	3-4
	16	at Colorado	3-1		23	Arizona	3-1
	20	Buffalo	4-3†		25	Chicago	7-0
	22	Boston	1-3		27	at Buffalo	2-4
	23	Detroit	3-4†		28	at Toronto	2-3
	28	Toronto	2-3†		30	at Montreal	2-6
	29	Montreal	2-3*	Apr.	1	at Boston	2-5
	31	at Dallas	3-1		3	Montreal	1-4
Jan.	4	Winnipeg	1-4		6	St. Louis	3-6
	6	Nashville	2-1		8	Buffalo	3-0
	7	Boston	0-4		9	at Washington	2-0

* – Overtime   † – Shootout

NHL Draft Selections 2017-2003

Name in bold denotes played in NHL.

2017
Pick
10	Owen Tippett
40	Aleksi Heponiemi
66	Maxwell Gildon
133	Tyler Inamoto
184	Sebastian Repo

2016
Pick
23	Henrik Borgstrom
38	Adam Mascherin
89	Linus Nassen
94	Jonathan Ang
114	Riley Stillman
175	Maxim Mamin
195	Benjamin Finkelstein

2015
Pick
11	**Lawson Crouse**
77	Sam Montembeault
88	Thomas Schemitsch
102	**Denis Malgin**
132	Karch Bachman
162	Chris Wilkie
192	Patrick Shea
206	Ryan Bednard

2014
Pick
1	**Aaron Ekblad**
32	Jayce Hawryluk
65	Juho Lammikko
92	Joe Wegwerth
143	Miguel Fidler
182	Hugo Fagerblom

2013
Pick
2	**Aleksander Barkov**
31	**Ian McCoshen**
92	Evan Cowley
97	Michael Downing
98	Matt Buckles
122	Christopher Clapperton
152	Josh Brown
206	**MacKenzie Weegar**

2012
Pick
23	**Michael Matheson**
84	Steven Hodges
114	Alexander Delnov
174	Francis Beauvillier
194	Jonatan Nielsen

2011
Pick
3	**Jonathan Huberdeau**
33	**Rocco Grimaldi**
59	Rasmus Bengtsson
64	**Vincent Trocheck**
76	**Logan Shaw**
87	**Jonathan Racine**
91	**Kyle Rau**
124	Yaroslav Kosov
154	Eddie Wittchow
184	**Iiro Pakarinen**

2010
Pick
3	**Erik Gudbranson**
19	**Nick Bjugstad**
25	**Quinton Howden**
33	**John McFarland**
36	**Alex Petrovic**
50	**Connor Brickley**
69	Joe Basaraba
93	Ben Gallacher
99	**Joonas Donskoi**
123	**Zach Hyman**
153	Corey Durocher
183	Ronald Boyd

2009
Pick
14	**Dmitry Kulikov**
44	**Drew Shore**
67	Josh Birkholz
107	**Garrett Wilson**
135	**Corban Knight**
138	**Wade Megan**
165	Scott Timmins

2008
Pick
31	**Jacob Markstrom**
46	**Colby Robak**
80	Adam Comrie
100	A.J. Jenks
190	**Matt Bartkowski**

2007
Pick
10	**Keaton Ellerby**
40	**Michal Repik**
71	**Evgeni Dadonov**
101	Matt Rust
131	John Lee
181	Corey Syvret
191	Ryan Watson
202	Sergei Gayduchenko

2006
Pick
10	**Michael Frolik**
73	Brady Calla
103	**Michael Caruso**
116	Derrick Lapoint
155	Peter Aston
193	Marc Cheverie

2005
Pick
20	**Kenndal McArdle**
32	Tyler Plante
90	Dan Collins
93	Olivier Legault
104	Matt Duffy
161	**Brian Foster**
164	Roman Derlyuk
224	Zach Bearson

2004
Pick
7	**Rostislav Olesz**
37	David Shantz
53	**David Booth**
105	Evan Schafer
152	Bret Nasby
267	Spencer Dillon
283	Luke Beaverson

2003
Pick
3	**Nathan Horton**
25	**Anthony Stewart**
38	**Kamil Kreps**
55	**Stefan Meyer**
105	**Martin Lojek**
124	James Pemberton
141	Dan Travis
162	Martin Tuma
171	Denis Stasyuk
223	Dany Roussin
234	Petr Kadlec
264	John Hecimovic
265	**Tanner Glass**

Selected with the 64th pick in the 2011 NHL Draft, Vincent Trocheck led the Panthers with 54 points in 2016-17.

Club Directory

BB&T Center

Florida Panthers
BB&T Center
One Panther Parkway
Sunrise, FL 33323
Phone **954/835-7000**
FAX 954/835-7700
www.floridapanthers.com
Twitter @FlaPanthers
Capacity: 19,250

Ownership
Chairman, Owner & Governor . . . . Vincent J. Viola

Executive
Vice Chairman, Partner & Alternate Governor . . . . . Douglas A. Cifu
Executive Chairman . . . . Peter Luukko
President & CEO . . . . Matthew Caldwell
President of Hockey Operations & General Manager . . Dale Tallon
Asst. General Manager, GM of Springfield (AHL) . . . Eric Joyce
Senior Advisor to the President of Hockey Operations . . Chris Pronger
Special Advisor to the GM/Alternate Governor . . . . William Torrey
Special Advisor to the General Manager . . . . Tom Rowe
Chief of Staff . . . . Sean McCaffrey
Executive Vice President . . . . Charlie Turano
Executive Vice President, Sales . . . . Jim Willits
Chief Financial Officer . . . . Amy Perry
Chief Technology Officer . . . . John Spade
Vice President, Hockey Ops and Special Projects . . . Travis Viola
Vice President, Broadcasting and Panthers Alumni . . Randy Moller
Vice President, Event Programming . . . . Kevin Grove
Vice President, Human Resources/Payroll . . . . Lane Miller
Vice President, Communications & Public Relations . . Thomas Drance
Vice President, Marketing . . . . Genya Adesso
Vice President, Finance/Controller . . . . Scott Levine
Vice President, Event Ops. & Security . . . . Tom Embrey
Executive Director, Florida Panthers Foundation . . . . Lauren Simone
General Counsel . . . . Ed Wildermuth
Executive Assistant . . . . Lindsay Bohlen

Hockey Operations
Sr. Advisor to the President, Hockey Ops. . . . . Chris Pronger
Director, Player Personnel . . . . Bryan McCabe
Director, Hockey Operations . . . . Braden Birch
Director, Hockey Analytics . . . . Brian MacDonald
Team Services Manager . . . . Stiles Burr

Scouting Staff
Head Pro Scout . . . . Al Tuer
Special Advisor to Ownership/Pro Scout . . . . Peter Mahovlich
Pro Scouts . . . . Neil Little, Richard Pollock
Director, Amateur Scouting . . . . Jason Bukala,
Amateur Scouts . . . . Fred Bandel, Wes Clark, Mike Fairman,
 Rhys Jessop, Bill Ryan
Director, European Scouting . . . . Jari Kekalainen
European Scouts . . . . Vadim Podrezov, Patrik Hall
Prospect Consultant Specialists . . . . Cam Lawrence, Josh Weissbock

Coaching Staff
Head Coach . . . . Bob Boughner
Associate Coach . . . . Jack Capuano
Assistant Coaches . . . . Paul McFarland, Ben Cooper (video)
Goaltending Coach . . . . Robb Tallas
Strength & Conditioning Coach . . . . Tommy Powers

Training Staff
Head Athletic Trainer . . . . Dave DiNapoli
Assistant Athletic Trainer . . . . Tommy Alva
Director of Sports Science/Physical Therapist . . . . . Tim Wittenauer
Head Equipment Manager . . . . Teddy Richards
Equipment Assistants . . . . Brian Godin, Dakota King, Thomas Anderson

Public Relations and Communications
Director, Communications & Digital Media . . . . Adelyn Biedenbach
Media Relations Coordinator . . . . Mike Lewis
Public Relations Coordinator . . . . Chrissy Parente

Broadcasting
Television . . . . FOX Sports Florida
Radio . . . . Florida Panthers Radio Network
TV Play-By-Play / Color Analyst . . . . Steve Goldstein / Denis Potvin
Television Analyst . . . . Randy Moller
Radio Play-By-Play / Color Analyst . . . . Doug Plagens / Bill Lindsay

Key Off-Season Signings/Acquisitions

2017

April	10	• Named **Rob Blake** General Manager.
	23	• Named **John Stevens** head coach.
May	9	• Re-signed LW **Tanner Pearson**.
	30	• Named **Dave Lowry** assistant coach.
June	7	• Re-signed RW **Tyler Toffoli**.
	22	• Named **Don Nachbaur** assistant coach.
	24	• Re-signed LW **Andy Andreoff**.
July	1	• Signed C **Michael Cammalleri**, D **Christian Folin** and G **Darcy Kuemper**.
	6	• Re-signed C **Nick Shore**.
	10	• Named **Pierre Turgeon** assistant coach.
	14	• Re-signed C **Jonny Brodzinski**, D **Kevin Gravel** and D **Paul LaDue**.

Los Angeles Kings

2016-17 Results: 39w-35L-4OTL-4SOL 86PTS
5TH, Pacific Division • 10TH, Western Conference

2017-18 Schedule

Oct.	Thu.	5	Philadelphia	Sat.	6	Nashville
	Sat.	7	at San Jose	Sat.	13	Anaheim
	Wed.	11	Calgary	Mon.	15	San Jose*
	Sat.	14	Buffalo	Thu.	18	Pittsburgh
	Sun.	15	NY Islanders	Fri.	19	at Anaheim
	Wed.	18	Montreal	Sun.	21	NY Rangers
	Sat.	21	at Columbus	Tue.	23	at Vancouver
	Mon.	23	at Toronto	Wed.	24	at Calgary
	Tue.	24	at Ottawa	Tue.	30	at Dallas
	Thu.	26	at Montreal	**Feb.** Thu.	1	at Nashville
	Sat.	28	at Boston	Sat.	3	Arizona
	Mon.	30	at St. Louis*	Wed.	7	Edmonton
Nov.	Thu.	2	Toronto	Fri.	9	at Florida
	Sat.	4	Nashville	Sat.	10	at Tampa Bay
	Tue.	7	at Anaheim	Tue.	13	at Carolina
	Thu.	9	Tampa Bay	Thu.	15	at Pittsburgh
	Sun.	12	San Jose	Sat.	17	at Buffalo*
	Tue.	14	Vancouver	Mon.	19	at Chicago
	Thu.	16	Boston	Tue.	20	at Winnipeg
	Sat.	18	Florida*	Thu.	22	Dallas
	Sun.	19	at Vegas*	Sat.	24	Edmonton
	Wed.	22	Winnipeg	Mon.	26	Vegas
	Fri.	24	at Arizona	Tue.	27	at Vegas
	Sat.	25	Anaheim	**Mar.** Thu.	1	Columbus
	Tue.	28	at Detroit	Sat.	3	Chicago*
	Thu.	30	at Washington	Thu.	8	Washington
Dec.	Fri.	1	at St. Louis*	Sat.	10	St. Louis*
	Sun.	3	at Chicago	Mon.	12	Vancouver
	Tue.	5	Minnesota	Tue.	13	at Arizona
	Thu.	7	Ottawa	Thu.	15	Detroit
	Sat.	9	Carolina	Sat.	17	New Jersey*
	Tue.	12	at New Jersey	Mon.	19	at Minnesota
	Fri.	15	at NY Rangers	Tue.	20	at Winnipeg
	Sat.	16	at NY Islanders	Thu.	22	at Colorado
	Mon.	18	at Philadelphia	Sat.	24	at Edmonton
	Thu.	21	Colorado	Mon.	26	Calgary
	Sat.	23	at San Jose	Thu.	29	Arizona
	Thu.	28	Vegas	Fri.	30	at Anaheim
	Sat.	30	at Vancouver	**Apr.** Mon.	2	Colorado
Jan.	Tue.	2	at Edmonton	Thu.	5	Minnesota
	Thu.	4	at Calgary	Sat.	7	Dallas

* Denotes afternoon game.

Retired Numbers

4	Rob Blake	1990-01, 06-08
16	Marcel Dionne	1975-1987
18	Dave Taylor	1977-1994
20	Luc Robitaille	1986-94, 97-01, 2003-2006
30	Rogie Vachon	1971-1978
99	Wayne Gretzky	1988-1996

PACIFIC DIVISION
51st NHL Season

Franchise date: June 5, 1967

Jeff Carter's team-leading 32 goals and 66 points for Los Angeles in 2016-17 were his best totals since collecting 36 goals and 66 points for the Philadelphia Flyers back in 2010-11.

Year-by-Year Record

Season	GP	Home W	L	T	OL	Road W	L	T	OL	Overall W	L	T	OL	GF	GA	Pts.	Div. Fin.	Conf. Fin.	Playoff Result
2016-17	82	23	16	....	2	16	19	....	6	39	35	....	8	201	205	86	5th, Pac.	10th, West	– out of playoffs –
2015-16	82	26	12	....	3	22	16	....	3	48	28	....	6	225	195	102	2nd, Pac.	5th, West	Lost First Round
2014-15	82	25	9	....	7	15	18	....	8	40	27	....	15	220	205	95	4th, Pac.	9th, West	– out of playoffs –
2013-14	82	23	14	....	4	23	14	....	4	46	28	....	8	206	174	100	3rd, Pac.	6th, West	Won Stanley Cup
2012-13	48	19	4	....	1	8	12	....	4	27	16	....	5	133	118	59	2nd, Pac.	5th, West	Lost Conf. Final
2011-12	82	22	14	....	5	18	13	....	10	40	27	....	15	194	179	95	3rd, Pac.	8th, West	Won Stanley Cup
2010-11	82	25	13	....	3	21	17	....	3	46	30	....	6	219	198	98	4th, Pac.	7th, West	Lost Conf. Quarter-Final
2009-10	82	22	13	....	6	24	14	....	3	46	27	....	9	241	219	101	3rd, Pac.	6th, West	Lost Conf. Quarter-Final
2008-09	82	18	15	....	8	16	22	....	3	34	37	....	11	207	234	79	5th, Pac.	14th, West	– out of playoffs –
2007-08	82	17	21	....	3	15	22	....	4	32	43	....	7	231	266	71	5th, Pac.	15th, West	– out of playoffs –
2006-07	82	16	16	....	9	11	25	....	5	27	41	....	14	227	283	68	4th, Pac.	14th, West	– out of playoffs –
2005-06	82	26	14	....	1	16	21	....	4	42	35	....	5	249	270	89	4th, Pac.	10th, West	– out of playoffs –
2004-05	....	....	....	....	....	....	....	....	....	....	....	....	....	....	....	....			
2003-04	82	15	16	9	1	13	13	7	8	28	29	16	9	205	217	81	3rd, Pac.	11th, West	– out of playoffs –
2002-03	82	19	19	2	1	14	18	4	5	33	37	6	6	203	221	78	3rd, Pac.	10th, West	– out of playoffs –
2001-02	82	22	12	6	1	18	15	5	3	40	27	11	4	214	190	95	3rd, Pac.	7th, West	Lost Conf. Quarter-Final
2000-01	82	20	12	8	1	18	16	5	2	38	28	13	3	252	228	92	3rd, Pac.	7th, West	Lost Conf. Semi-Final
1999-2000	82	21	13	5	2	18	14	7	2	39	27	12	4	245	228	94	2nd, Pac.	5th, West	Lost Conf. Quarter-Final
1998-99	82	18	20	3	....	14	25	3	....	32	45	5	....	189	222	69	5th, Pac.	11th, West	– out of playoffs –
1997-98	82	22	16	3	....	16	17	8	....	38	33	11	....	227	225	87	2nd, Pac.	5th, West	Lost Conf. Quarter-Final
1996-97	82	18	16	7	....	10	27	4	....	28	43	11	....	214	268	67	6th, Pac.	12th, West	– out of playoffs –
1995-96	82	16	16	9	....	8	24	9	....	24	40	18	....	256	302	66	6th, Pac.	12th, West	– out of playoffs –
1994-95	48	7	11	6	....	9	12	3	....	16	23	9	....	142	174	41	4th, Pac.	9th, West	– out of playoffs –
1993-94	84	18	19	5	....	9	26	7	....	27	45	12	....	294	322	66	5th, Pac.	10th, West	– out of playoffs –
1992-93	84	22	15	5	....	17	20	5	....	39	35	10	....	338	340	88	3rd, Smythe		Lost Final
1991-92	80	20	11	9	....	15	20	5	....	35	31	14	....	287	296	84	2nd, Smythe		Lost Div. Semi-Final
1990-91	80	26	9	5	....	20	15	5	....	46	24	10	....	340	254	102	1st, Smythe		Lost Div. Final
1989-90	80	21	16	3	....	13	23	4	....	34	39	7	....	338	337	75	4th, Smythe		Lost Div. Final
1988-89	80	25	12	3	....	17	19	4	....	42	31	7	....	376	335	91	2nd, Smythe		Lost Div. Final
1987-88	80	19	18	3	....	11	24	5	....	30	42	8	....	318	359	68	4th, Smythe		Lost Div. Semi-Final
1986-87	80	20	17	3	....	11	24	5	....	31	41	8	....	318	341	70	4th, Smythe		Lost Div. Semi-Final
1985-86	80	9	27	4	....	14	22	4	....	23	49	8	....	284	389	54	5th, Smythe		– out of playoffs –
1984-85	80	20	14	6	....	14	18	8	....	34	32	14	....	339	326	82	4th, Smythe		Lost Div. Semi-Final
1983-84	80	13	19	8	....	10	25	5	....	23	44	13	....	309	376	59	5th, Smythe		– out of playoffs –
1982-83	80	20	13	7	....	7	28	5	....	27	41	12	....	308	365	66	5th, Smythe		– out of playoffs –
1981-82	80	19	15	6	....	5	26	9	....	24	41	15	....	314	369	63	4th, Smythe		Lost Div. Final
1980-81	80	22	11	7	....	21	13	6	....	43	24	13	....	337	290	99	2nd, Norris		Lost Prelim. Round
1979-80	80	18	13	9	....	12	23	5	....	30	36	14	....	290	313	74	2nd, Norris		Lost Prelim. Round
1978-79	80	20	13	7	....	14	21	5	....	34	34	12	....	292	286	80	3rd, Norris		Lost Prelim. Round
1977-78	80	18	16	6	....	13	18	9	....	31	34	15	....	243	245	77	3rd, Norris		Lost Prelim. Round
1976-77	80	20	13	7	....	14	18	8	....	34	31	15	....	271	241	83	2nd, Norris		Lost Quarter-Final
1975-76	80	22	13	5	....	16	20	4	....	38	33	9	....	263	265	85	2nd, Norris		Lost Quarter-Final
1974-75	80	27	7	11	....	20	10	10	....	42	17	21	....	269	185	105	2nd, Norris		Lost Prelim. Round
1973-74	78	22	13	4	....	11	20	8	....	33	33	12	....	233	231	78	3rd, West		Lost Quarter-Final
1972-73	78	21	11	7	....	10	25	4	....	31	36	11	....	232	245	73	6th, West		– out of playoffs –
1971-72	78	14	23	2	....	6	26	7	....	20	49	9	....	206	305	49	7th, West		– out of playoffs –
1970-71	78	17	14	8	....	8	26	5	....	25	40	13	....	239	303	63	6th, West		– out of playoffs –
1969-70	76	12	22	4	....	2	30	6	....	14	52	10	....	168	290	38	6th, West		– out of playoffs –
1968-69	76	19	14	5	....	5	28	5	....	24	42	10	....	185	260	58	4th, West		Lost Semi-Final
1967-68	74	20	13	4	....	11	20	6	....	31	33	10	....	200	224	72	2nd, West		Lost Quarter-Final

2017-18 Player Personnel

FORWARDS

	HT	WT	*Age	Birthplace	S	2016-17 Club
ANDREOFF, Andy	6-1	203	26	Pickering, ON	L	Los Angeles
BRODZINSKI, Jonny	6-0	202	24	Ham Lake, MN	R	Los Angeles-Ontario
BROWN, Dustin	6-0	206	32	Ithaca, NY	R	Los Angeles
CAMMALLERI, Michael	5-9	185	35	Toronto, ON	L	New Jersey
CARTER, Jeff	6-4	215	32	London, ON	R	Los Angeles
CLIFFORD, Kyle	6-2	206	26	Ayr, ON	L	Los Angeles
DOWD, Nic	6-2	195	27	Huntsville, AL	R	Los Angeles
GABORIK, Marian	6-1	205	35	Trencin, Czech.	L	Los Angeles
KEMPE, Adrian	6-1	187	21	Kramfors, Sweden	L	Los Angeles-Ontario
KOPITAR, Anze	6-3	224	30	Jesenice, Yugoslavia	L	Los Angeles
LEWIS, Trevor	6-1	199	30	Salt Lake City, UT	L	Los Angeles
NOLAN, Jordan	6-3	219	28	Garden River First Nation, ON	L	Los Angeles
PEARSON, Tanner	6-1	208	25	Kitchener, ON	L	Los Angeles
SHORE, Nick	6-1	194	25	Denver, CO	L	Los Angeles
TOFFOLI, Tyler	6-1	200	25	Scarborough, ON	R	Los Angeles

DEFENSEMEN

DOUGHTY, Drew	6-1	195	27	London, ON	R	Los Angeles
FOLIN, Christian	6-4	219	26	Gothenburg, Sweden	R	Minnesota
FORBORT, Derek	6-4	216	25	Duluth, MN	L	Los Angeles
GRAVEL, Kevin	6-4	199	25	Kingsford, MI	L	Los Angeles-Ontario
LADUE, Paul	6-1	186	25	Grand Forks, ND	R	Los Angeles-Ontario
MARTINEZ, Alec	6-1	210	30	Rochester Hills, MI	L	Los Angeles
MUZZIN, Jake	6-3	216	28	Woodstock, ON	L	Los Angeles

GOALTENDERS

	HT	WT	*Age	Birthplace	C	2016-17 Club
KUEMPER, Darcy	6-5	212	27	Saskatoon, SK	L	Minnesota
QUICK, Jonathan	6-1	218	31	Milford, CT	L	Los Angeles
ZATKOFF, Jeff	6-2	179	30	Detroit, MI	L	Los Angeles-Ontario

* – Age at start of 2017-18 season

2016-17 Scoring
* – rookie

Regular Season

Pos	#	Player	Team	GP	G	A	Pts	TOI	+/–	PIM	PP	SH	GW	S	S%
C	77	Jeff Carter	L.A.	82	32	34	66	18:01	2	41	10	1	9	250	12.8
C	11	Anze Kopitar	L.A.	76	12	40	52	20:45	-10	28	5	0	0	150	8.0
L	70	Tanner Pearson	L.A.	80	24	20	44	16:19	5	13	3	1	5	187	12.8
D	8	Drew Doughty	L.A.	82	12	32	44	27:08	8	46	5	0	1	181	6.6
D	27	Alec Martinez	L.A.	82	9	30	39	21:38	-17	24	2	1	3	144	6.3
L	23	Dustin Brown	L.A.	82	14	22	36	16:00	4	22	4	1	1	175	8.0
C	73	Tyler Toffoli	L.A.	63	16	18	34	16:35	6	22	4	0	2	165	9.7
D	6	Jake Muzzin	L.A.	82	9	19	28	22:17	-21	46	4	0	1	184	4.9
R	88	Jarome Iginla	COL	61	8	10	18	14:44	-21	54	4	0	4	120	6.7
			L.A.	19	6	3	9	16:20	-9	16	3	0	4	33	18.2
			Total	80	14	13	27	15:07	-30	70	7	0	4	153	9.2
C	22	Trevor Lewis	L.A.	82	12	12	24	14:16	-6	30	1	0	3	145	8.3
C	26	Nic Dowd	L.A.	70	6	16	22	12:27	-15	25	1	0	2	78	7.7
R	12	Marian Gaborik	L.A.	56	10	11	21	14:47	-4	18	3	0	3	123	8.1
D	24 *	Derek Forbort	L.A.	82	2	16	18	20:06	8	54	0	0	0	100	2.0
C	21	Nick Shore	L.A.	70	6	11	17	12:47	-2	20	0	1	1	79	7.6
L	13	Kyle Clifford	L.A.	73	6	6	12	10:43	-2	92	0	0	0	122	4.9
R	10	Devin Setoguchi	L.A.	45	4	8	12	12:26	-5	14	0	0	0	60	6.7
C	71	Jordan Nolan	L.A.	46	4	4	8	10:51	-3	44	0	0	0	39	10.3
D	38 *	Paul Ladue	L.A.	22	0	8	8	15:24	-5	4	0	0	0	27	0.0
D	53 *	Kevin Gravel	L.A.	49	1	6	7	14:09	3	6	0	0	0	52	1.9
L	39 *	Adrian Kempe	L.A.	25	2	4	6	12:13	-3	6	0	0	1	32	6.3
D	14	Tom Gilbert	L.A.	18	1	4	5	15:27	-4	6	0	0	0	12	8.3
D	3	Brayden McNabb	L.A.	49	2	2	4	15:03	1	54	0	0	0	47	4.3
D	2	Matt Greene	L.A.	26	1	1	2	13:10	3	19	0	0	0	14	7.1
C	76 *	Jonny Brodzinski	L.A.	6	0	2	2	12:17	2	2	0	0	0	17	0.0
R	9	Teddy Purcell	L.A.	12	0	2	2	12:53	0	0	0	0	0	10	0.0
C	15	Andy Andreoff	L.A.	36	0	0	0	10:35	-2	70	0	0	0	38	0.0

Goaltending

No.	Goaltender	GPI	Mins	Avg	W	L	OT	EN	SO	GA	SA	Sv%	G	A	PIM
1	* Jack Campbell	1	20	0.00	0	0	0	0	0	0	5	1.000	0	0	0
31	Peter Budaj	53	3029	2.12	27	20	3	11	7	107	1286	.917	0	1	0
32	Jonathan Quick	17	931	2.26	8	5	2	2	2	35	421	.917	0	0	2
31	Ben Bishop	7	410	2.49	2	3	2	1	0	17	170	.900	0	0	2
37	Jeff Zatkoff	13	550	2.95	2	7	1	1	0	27	223	.879	0	0	0
	Totals	**82**	**4978**	**2.42**	**39**	**35**	**8**	**15**	**9**	**201**	**2120**	**.905**			

John Stevens
Head Coach
Born: Campbellton, NB, December 30, 1965.

John Stevens was named head coach of the Los Angeles Kings on April 23, 2017. He had spent the previous seven seasons with the organization serving as the club's associate head coach where he helped play a critical coaching role in the club's two Stanley Cup championships, three trips to the Western Conference Finals and five playoff appearances. On the defensive end in particular, Stevens has helped direct the Kings to top-10 finishes in fewest goals allowed per game in every year he has been with the Kings and since he was hired in 2010-11, the Kings hold the lowest goals against per game average in the league. In 2013-14, the Kings won the William M. Jennings Trophy as the team with the lowest goals-against-average in the league for the first time in franchise history.

Stevens is officially the 27th head coach in Kings history with 24 different men – including Stevens – having served as head coach. He initially served as the Kings' head coach for four games during the 2011-12 regular season (December 13-19), replacing Terry Murray (whose last game was December 10, 2011) before Darryl Sutter was hired (his first game was December 22, 2011).

The native of Campbellton, New Brunswick, assumed his first NHL head coaching job with the Philadelphia Flyers on October 22, 2006, after beginning the 2006-07 campaign as the club's assistant coach. The Flyers were 21-42-11 under Stevens in 2006-07, before having a great turnaround in 2007-08. The Flyers had an NHL-best 39-point improvement from the year before, and following that season The Hockey News honored Stevens with their coach of the year award.

Before his NHL coaching tenure, Stevens was the head coach of the Philadelphia Phantoms (the Flyers' American Hockey League affiliate) for six years (2000-01 through 2005-06). His Phantoms made the playoffs four times and won the Calder Cup championship in 2005. In 2012, he was inducted into the AHL Hall of Fame.

Stevens was drafted by the Flyers (third round, 47th overall) in the 1984 NHL Draft and played parts of five seasons with Philadelphia and Hartford, totaling 10 points (10 assists) and 48 penalty minutes in 53 NHL regular season games. In 834 career AHL games Stevens, a defenseman, had 188 points (21 goals, 167 assists), 1,397 penalty minutes and won three Calder Cups: 1988 with Hershey, 1991 with Springfield (team captain) and 1998 with the Phantoms (team captain).

Coaching Record

				Regular Season				Playoffs			
Season	Team	League	GC	W	L	O/T	GC	W	L	T
2000-01	Philadelphia	AHL	80	36	34	10	10	5	5	....
2001-02	Philadelphia	AHL	80	33	27	20	5	2	3	....
2002-03	Philadelphia	AHL	80	33	33	14	....	....	....	....
2003-04	Philadelphia	AHL	80	46	25	9	12	6	6	....
2004-05	Philadelphia	AHL	80	48	25	7	21	16	5	....
2006-07	Philadelphia	NHL	74	21	42	11	....	....	....	....
2007-08	Philadelphia	NHL	82	42	29	11	17	9	8	....
2008-09	Philadelphia	NHL	82	44	27	11	6	2	4	....
2009-10	Philadelphia	NHL	25	13	11	1	....	....	....	....
2011-12	Los Angeles	NHL	4	2	2	0	....	....	....	....
	NHL Totals		**267**	**122**	**111**	**34**	**23**	**11**	**12**	....

In his fourth NHL season, Tanner Pearson established new career highs with 80 games played, 24 goals and 44 points.

Coaching History
Red Kelly, 1967-68, 1968-69; Hal Laycoe and Johnny Wilson, 1969-70; Larry Regan, 1970-71; Larry Regan and Fred Glover, 1971-72; Bob Pulford, 1972-73 to 1976-77; Ron Stewart, 1977-78; Bob Berry, 1978-79 to 1980-81; Parker MacDonald and Don Perry, 1981-82; Don Perry, 1982-83; Don Perry, Rogie Vachon and Roger Neilson, 1983-84; Pat Quinn, 1984-85, 1985-86; Pat Quinn and Mike Murphy 1986-87; Mike Murphy, Rogie Vachon and Robbie Ftorek, 1987-88; Robbie Ftorek, 1988-89; Tom Webster, 1989-90 to 1991-92; Barry Melrose, 1992-93, 1993-94; Barry Melrose and Rogie Vachon, 1994-95; Larry Robinson, 1995-96 to 1998-99; Andy Murray, 1999-2000 to 2004-05; Andy Murray and John Torchetti, 2005-06; Marc Crawford, 2006-07, 2007-08; Terry Murray, 2008-09 to 2010-11; Terry Murray, John Stevens and Darryl Sutter, 2011-12; Darryl Sutter, 2012-13 to 2016-17; John Stevens, 2017-18.

Club Records

Team

(Figures in brackets for season records are games played; records for fewest points, wins, ties, losses, goals, goals against are for 70 or more games)

Most Points **105** 1974-75 (80)
Most Wins **48** 2015-16 (82)
Most Ties **21** 1974-75 (80)
Most Losses **52** 1969-70 (76)
Most Goals **376** 1988-89 (80)
Most Goals Against **389** 1985-86 (80)
Fewest Points **38** 1969-70 (76)
Fewest Wins **14** 1969-70 (76)
Fewest Ties **5** 1998-99 (82)
Fewest Losses **17** 1974-75 (80)
Fewest Goals **168** 1969-70 (76)
Fewest Goals Against **174** 2013-14 (82)
Longest Winning Streak
Overall .... **9** Jan. 21-Feb. 6/10
Home .... **12** Oct. 10-Dec. 5/92
Away .... **8** Dec. 18/74-Jan. 16/75, Feb. 26-Mar. 27/14
Longest Team Point Streak
Overall .... **11** Feb. 28-Mar. 24/74 (9W, 2T), Jan. 22-Feb.17/11 (8W, 1OTL, 2SOL), Nov. 7-27/13 (7W, 2OTL, 2SOL)
Home .... **13** Oct. 10-Dec. 8/92 (12W, 1T)
Away .... **11** Oct. 10-Dec. 11/74 (6W, 5T)
Longest Losing Streak
Overall .... **11** Mar. 16-Apr. 4/04
Home .... **9** Feb. 8-Mar. 12/86
Away .... **11** Jan. 11-Feb. 15/70
Longest Winless Streak
Overall .... **17** Jan. 29-Mar. 5/70 (13L, 4T)
Home .... **9** Jan. 29-Mar. 5/70 (8L, 1T), Feb. 8-Mar. 12/86 (9L)
Away .... **20** Jan. 11-Apr. 3/70 (16L, 4T)
Most Shutouts, Season **13** 2013-14 (82)
Most PIM, Season **2,247** 1992-93 (84)
Most Goals, Game .... **12** Nov. 29/84 (Van. 1 at L.A. 12)

Individual

Most Seasons .... **17** Dave Taylor
Most Games .... **1,111** Dave Taylor
Most Goals, Career .... **557** Luc Robitaille
Most Assists, Career .... **757** Marcel Dionne
Most Points Career .... **1,307** Marcel Dionne (550G, 757A)
Most PIM, Career .... **1,846** Marty McSorley
Most Shutouts, Career .... **44** Jonathan Quick
Longest Consecutive Games Streak .... **330** Anze Kopitar (Mar. 21/07-Mar. 26/11)
Most Goals, Season .... **70** Bernie Nicholls (1988-89)
Most Assists, Season .... **122** Wayne Gretzky (1990-91)
Most Points, Season .... **168** Wayne Gretzky (1988-89; 54G, 114A)
Most PIM, Season .... **399** Marty McSorley (1992-93)
Most Points, Defenseman, Season .... **76** Larry Murphy (1980-81; 16G, 60A)
Most Points, Center, Season .... **168** Wayne Gretzky (1988-89; 54G, 114A)
Most Points, Right Wing, Season .... **112** Dave Taylor (1980-81; 47G, 65A)
Most Points, Left Wing, Season .... ***125** Luc Robitaille (1992-93; 63G, 62A)
Most Points, Rookie, Season .... **84** Luc Robitaille (1986-87; 45G, 39A)
Most Shutouts, Season .... **10** Jonathan Quick (2011-12)
Most Goals, Game .... **4** Seventeen times
Most Assists, Game .... **6** Bernie Nicholls (Dec. 1/88), Tomas Sandstrom (Oct. 9/93)
Most Points, Game .... **8** Bernie Nicholls (Dec. 1/88; 2G, 6A)

* NHL Record.

Captains' History

Bob Wall, 1967-68, 1968-69; Larry Cahan, 1969-70, 1970-71; Bob Pulford, 1971-72, 1972-73; Terry Harper, 1973-74, 1974-75; Mike Murphy, 1975-76 to 1980-81; Dave Lewis, 1981-82, 1982-83; Terry Ruskowski, 1983-84, 1984-85; Dave Taylor, 1985-86 to 1988-89; Wayne Gretzky, 1989-90 to 1991-92; Wayne Gretzky and Luc Robitaille, 1992-93; Wayne Gretzky, 1993-94, 1994-95; Wayne Gretzky and Rob Blake, 1995-96; Rob Blake, 1996-97 to 2000-01; Mattias Norstrom, 2001-02 to 2006-07; Rob Blake, 2007-08; Dustin Brown, 2008-09 to 2015-16; Anze Kopitar, 2016-17 to date.

All-time Record vs. Other Clubs

Regular Season

	Total								At Home								On Road							
	GP	W	L	T	OL	GF	GA	PTS	GP	W	L	T	OL	GF	GA	PTS	GP	W	L	T	OL	GF	GA	PTS
Anaheim	132	58	49	11	14	360	382	141	66	35	20	4	7	185	164	81	66	23	29	7	7	175	218	60
Arizona	222	87	101	25	9	739	791	208	110	47	46	14	3	389	374	111	112	40	55	11	6	350	417	97
Boston	139	42	83	13	1	430	552	98	69	26	35	7	1	233	246	60	70	16	48	6	0	197	306	38
Buffalo	121	44	57	18	2	373	444	108	61	28	24	9	0	207	196	65	60	16	33	9	2	166	248	43
Calgary	235	95	111	21	8	772	856	219	116	58	46	9	3	401	373	128	119	37	65	12	5	371	483	91
Carolina	75	36	29	8	2	281	256	82	37	22	12	3	0	149	128	47	38	14	17	5	2	132	128	35
Chicago	192	82	88	17	5	576	628	186	95	44	40	8	3	311	305	99	97	38	48	9	2	265	323	87
Colorado	128	66	50	8	4	449	434	144	65	38	19	5	3	241	195	84	63	28	31	3	1	208	239	60
Columbus	55	31	19	1	4	162	129	67	28	18	9	1	0	79	56	37	27	13	10	0	4	83	73	30
Dallas	231	87	103	32	9	679	749	215	115	51	42	19	3	365	339	124	116	36	61	13	6	314	410	91
Detroit	198	84	82	27	5	684	682	200	99	49	35	14	1	360	306	113	99	35	47	13	4	324	376	87
Edmonton	204	82	83	30	9	728	777	203	101	44	36	15	6	383	373	109	103	38	47	15	3	345	404	94
Florida	32	18	11	3	0	93	77	39	17	12	5	0	0	53	41	24	15	6	6	3	0	40	36	15
Minnesota	59	26	19	5	9	145	140	66	29	14	9	2	4	73	69	34	30	12	10	3	5	72	71	32
Montreal	143	32	90	20	1	395	588	85	72	22	40	9	1	217	278	54	71	10	50	11	0	178	310	31
Nashville	67	34	25	3	5	191	173	76	34	17	14	0	3	102	98	37	33	17	11	3	2	89	75	39
New Jersey	101	55	31	11	4	383	308	125	50	31	11	6	2	217	152	70	51	24	20	5	2	166	156	55
NY Islanders	105	47	44	12	2	326	330	108	52	27	17	7	1	183	151	62	53	20	27	5	1	143	179	46
NY Rangers	133	48	66	16	3	411	488	115	68	27	29	10	2	218	236	66	65	21	37	6	1	193	252	49
Ottawa	33	20	11	2	0	115	85	42	17	13	3	1	0	69	35	27	16	7	8	1	0	46	50	15
Philadelphia	145	44	84	15	2	380	505	105	74	23	43	8	0	209	247	54	71	21	41	7	2	171	258	51
Pittsburgh	156	75	59	18	4	528	484	172	76	47	18	8	3	284	202	105	80	28	41	10	1	244	282	67
St. Louis	199	75	98	22	4	577	625	176	99	48	37	12	2	330	276	110	100	27	61	10	2	247	349	66
San Jose	146	64	63	7	12	399	429	147	73	39	27	4	3	211	197	85	73	25	36	3	9	188	232	62
Tampa Bay	35	13	18	2	2	74	92	30	18	5	11	2	0	39	50	12	17	8	7	0	2	35	42	18
Toronto	147	65	59	21	2	497	487	153	72	38	24	10	0	251	205	86	75	27	35	11	2	246	282	67
Vancouver	246	108	102	32	4	818	789	252	125	66	41	16	2	463	366	150	121	42	61	16	2	355	423	102
Washington	108	58	35	13	2	403	369	131	55	34	14	6	1	214	159	75	53	24	21	7	1	189	210	56
Winnipeg	26	14	5	0	7	91	79	35	13	9	0	0	4	58	39	22	13	5	5	0	3	33	40	13
Defunct Clubs	69	38	20	11	0	232	185	87	35	27	6	2	0	141	76	56	34	11	14	9	0	91	109	31
Totals	**3882**	**1628**	**1695**	**424**	**135**	**12291**	**12913**	**3815**	**1941**	**959**	**713**	**211**	**58**	**6635**	**5932**	**2187**	**1941**	**669**	**982**	**213**	**77**	**5656**	**6981**	**1628**

Playoffs

	Series	W	L	GP	W	L	T	GF	GA	Last Mtg.	Rnd.	Result
Anaheim	1	1	0	7	4	3	0	19	15	2014	SR	W 4-3
Arizona	1	1	0	5	4	1	0	14	8	2012	CF	W 4-1
Boston	2	0	2	13	5	8	0	38	56	1977	QF	L 2-4
Calgary	6	4	2	26	13	13	0	105	112	1993	DSF	W 4-2
Chicago	3	1	2	17	6	11	0	46	47	2014	CF	W 4-3
Colorado	2	0	2	14	6	8	0	23	33	2002	CQF	L 3-4
*Dallas	2	1	1	14	7	7	0	44	51	1969	QF	W 4-3
Detroit	2	1	1	10	4	6	0	21	32	2001	CQF	W 4-2
Edmonton	7	2	5	36	12	24	0	127	154	1992	DSF	L 2-4
Montreal	1	0	1	5	1	4	0	12	15	1993	F	L 1-4
New Jersey	1	1	0	6	4	2	0	16	8	2012	F	W 4-2
NY Islanders	1	0	1	4	1	3	0	10	21	1980	PR	L 1-3
NY Rangers	3	1	2	11	5	6	0	29	42	2014	F	W 4-1
St. Louis	4	2	2	18	8	10	0	40	48	2013	CQF	W 4-2
San Jose	4	2	2	25	11	14	0	71	68	2016	FR	L 1-4
Toronto	3	1	2	12	5	7	0	31	41	1993	CF	W 4-3
Vancouver	5	3	2	28	15	13	0	96	93	2012	CQF	W 4-1
Totals	**48**	**21**	**27**	**251**	**111**	**140**	**0**	**742**	**844**			

* Includes series with Oakland 1969.

Calgary totals include Atlanta Flames, 1972-73 to 1979-80.
Colorado totals include Quebec, 1979-80 to 1994-95.
New Jersey totals include Kansas City, 1974-75, 1975-76, and Colorado Rockies, 1976-77 to 1981-82.
Phoenix totals include Winnipeg, 1979-80 to 1995-96.
Carolina totals include Hartford, 1979-80 to 1996-97.
Dallas totals include Minnesota North Stars, 1967-68 to 1992-93.
Winnipeg totals include Atlanta Thrashers, 1999-2000 to 2010-11.

Playoff Results 2017-2013

Year	Round	Opponent	Result	GF	GA
2016	FR	San Jose	L 1-4	11	16
2014	**F**	**NY Rangers**	**W 4-1**	**15**	**10**
	CF	Chicago	W 4-3	28	23
	SR	Anaheim	W 4-3	19	15
	FR	San Jose	W 4-3	26	22
2013	CF	Chicago	L 1-4	11	14
	CSF	San Jose	W 4-3	14	10
	CQF	St. Louis	W 4-2	12	10

Abbreviations: Round: F – Final; **CF** – conference final; **CSF** – conference semi-final; **SR** – second round; **CQF** – conference quarter-final; **FR** – first round; **DSF** – division semi-final; **QF** – quarter-final; **PR** – preliminary round.

2016-17 Results

Oct.	12	at San Jose	1-2		12	St. Louis	5-1
	14	Philadelphia	2-4		14	Winnipeg	3-2*
	18	at Minnesota	3-6		16	Tampa Bay	1-2
	20	at Dallas	4-3*		18	San Jose	2-3
	22	Vancouver	4-3†		21	at NY Islanders	2-4
	25	Columbus	3-2*		23	at NY Rangers	2-3
	27	Nashville	3-2*		24	at New Jersey	3-1
	29	at St. Louis	0-1		26	at Carolina	3-0
	30	at Chicago	0-3		31	at Arizona	3-2
Nov.	1	Anaheim	0-4	**Feb.**	1	Colorado	5-0
	3	Pittsburgh	3-2*		4	at Philadelphia	1-0*
	5	Calgary	5-0		5	at Washington	0-5
	8	at Toronto	7-0		7	at Tampa Bay	0-5
	10	at Montreal	1-4		9	at Florida	6-3
	11	at Ottawa	1-2		16	Arizona	3-5
	13	at Winnipeg	2-3†		18	Florida	2-3
	15	at Colorado	1-4		19	at Anaheim	0-1
	17	Edmonton	4-2		21	at Colorado	2-1
	19	New Jersey	4-2		23	Boston	1-4
	20	at Anaheim	3-2		25	Anaheim	4-1
	23	NY Islanders	4-2		27	at Minnesota	4-5*
	26	Chicago	2-1*		28	at Calgary	1-2*
	30	San Jose	1-4	**Mar.**	2	Toronto	3-2†
Dec.	1	at Arizona	4-3		4	Vancouver	3-4
	4	Montreal	4-5†		9	Nashville	3-2*
	8	Carolina	1-3		11	Washington	4-2
	10	Ottawa	4-1		13	St. Louis	1-3
	13	at Buffalo	3-6		14	Arizona	2-3†
	15	at Detroit	4-1		16	Buffalo	2-0
	16	at Pittsburgh	1-0*		19	at Calgary	2-5
	18	at Boston	0-1		20	at Edmonton	0-2
	20	at Columbus	2-3†		23	Winnipeg	5-2
	22	at Nashville	4-0		25	NY Rangers	0-3
	23	at Dallas	2-3*		28	at Edmonton	1-2
	28	at Vancouver	1-2		29	at Calgary	4-1
	29	at Edmonton	1-3		31	at Vancouver	2-0
	31	San Jose	3-2	**Apr.**	2	Arizona	1-2
Jan.	3	at San Jose	2-1*		4	Edmonton	6-4
	5	Detroit	0-4		6	Calgary	1-4
	7	Minnesota	4-3*		8	Chicago	3-2*
	9	Dallas	4-6		9	at Anaheim	3-4*

* – Overtime † – Shootout

NHL Draft Selections 2017-2003

Name in bold denotes played in NHL.

2017
Pick
11	Gabriel Vilardi
41	Jaret Anderson-Dolan
72	Matt Villalta
103	Michael Anderson
118	Markus Phillips
134	Cole Hults
138	Drake Rymsha

2016
Pick
51	Kale Clague
112	Jacob Moverare
142	Mikey Eyssimont
202	Jacob Friend

2015
Pick
43	Erik Cernak
74	Alexander Dergachev
99	Austin Wagner
134	Matt Schmalz
187	Chaz Reddekopp
194	Matt Roy

2014
Pick
29	**Adrian Kempe**
50	Roland McKeown
60	Alex Lintuniemi
90	Mike Amadio
120	Steven Johnson
150	Alec Dillon
157	Jake Marchment
180	Matthew Mistele
209	Spencer Watson
210	Jacob Middleton

2013
Pick
37	**Valentin Zykov**
103	Justin Auger
118	**Hudson Fasching**
146	Patrik Bartosak
148	**Jonny Brodzinski**
178	Zachary Leslie
191	Dominik Kubalik

2012
Pick
30	**Tanner Pearson**
121	Nikolay Prokhorkin
151	**Colin Miller**
171	Tomas Hyka
181	**Paul Ladue**
211	Nick Ebert

2011
Pick
49	**Christopher Gibson**
80	**Andy Andreoff**
82	**Nick Shore**
110	**Michael Mersch**
140	Joel Lowry
200	Michael Schumacher

2010
Pick
15	**Derek Forbort**
47	**Tyler Toffoli**
70	**Jordan Weal**
148	**Kevin Gravel**
158	Maxim Kitsyn

2009
Pick
5	**Brayden Schenn**
35	**Kyle Clifford**
84	**Nicolas Deslauriers**
95	**Jean-Francois Berube**
96	**Linden Vey**
126	David Kolomatis
156	Michael Pelech
179	**Brandon Kozun**
186	Jordan Nolan
198	**Nic Dowd**

2008
Pick
2	**Drew Doughty**
13	**Colten Teubert**
32	**Slava Voynov**
63	Robert Czarnik
74	**Andrew Campbell**
88	Geordie Wudrick
123	**Andrei Loktionov**
153	Justin Azevedo
183	Garrett Roe

2007
Pick
4	**Thomas Hickey**
52	**Oscar Moller**
61	**Wayne Simmonds**
82	Bryan Cameron
95	**Alec Martinez**
109	**Dwight King**
124	Linden Rowat
137	Joshua Turnbull
184	Josh Kidd
188	Matt Fillier

2006
Pick
11	**Jonathan Bernier**
17	**Trevor Lewis**
48	Joe Ryan
74	**Jeff Zatkoff**
86	**Bud Holloway**
114	Niclas Andersen
134	David Meckler
144	Martin Nolet
164	Constantin Braun

2005
Pick
11	**Anze Kopitar**
50	Dany Roussin
60	T.J. Fast
72	**Jonathan Quick**
139	Patrik Hersley
184	Ryan McGinnis
206	Josh Meyers
226	John Seymour

2004
Pick
11	**Lauri Tukonen**
95	Paul Baier
110	Ned Lukacevic
143	Eric Neilson
174	**Scott Parse**
205	Mike Curry
221	**Daniel Taylor**
238	Yutaka Fukufuji
264	Valtteri Tenkanen

2003
Pick
13	**Dustin Brown**
26	**Brian Boyle**
27	**Jeff Tambellini**
44	Konstantin Pushkarev
82	Ryan Munce
152	**Brady Murray**
174	Esa Pirnes
231	**Matt Zaba**
244	Mike Sullivan
274	Marty Guerin

General Managers' History

Larry Regan, 1967-68 to 1972-73; Larry Regan and Jake Milford, 1973-74; Jake Milford, 1974-75 to 1976-77; George Maguire, 1977-78 to 1982-83; George Maguire and Rogie Vachon, 1983-84; Rogie Vachon, 1984-85 to 1991-92; Nick Beverley, 1992-93, 1993-94; Sam McMaster, 1994-95 to 1996-97; Dave Taylor, 1997-98 to 2005-06; Dean Lombardi, 2006-07 to 2016-17; Rob Blake, 2017-18.

Rob Blake

Vice President and General Manager

Born: Simcoe, ON, December 10, 1969.

Rob Blake was named vice president and general manager of the Los Angeles Kings on April 10, 2017, making him responsible for all day-to-day hockey operations for the organization. Blake, who is a member of the Hockey Hall of Fame, becomes the ninth general manager in team history. He had been named vice president/assistant general manager in 2013 and held that position for four seasons. Prior to that, Blake worked in the National Hockey League's player safety department for three years.

During his time as an executive with the Kings, Blake has also served as the general manager of the team's primary minor league affiliate, the Ontario Reign of the American Hockey League. (That franchise won the Calder Cup Championship in 2015). In addition, Blake served as general manager of Canada's national men's team for the 2014 World Championship, and he worked on the management staff for Team Canada's winning entry at the 2016 World Cup of Hockey.

Selected by Los Angeles in the fourth round (70th overall) of the 1988 NHL Draft, Blake spent 20 seasons as an NHL player, including 14 with the Kings. He took over as the Kings' captain from Wayne Gretzky in 1996 and wore the 'C' until he was traded to the Colorado Avalanche in 2001. Blake recorded 777 points (240 goals, 537 assists) during his career and won the Stanley Cup with Colorado in 2001. He was in his front office role with the Kings when Los Angeles won the Stanley Cup in 2014, and he had his jersey retired by the Kings in 2015.

Club Directory

STAPLES Center

Los Angeles Kings
STAPLES Center
1111 South Figueroa Street
Los Angeles, CA 90015
Phone **213/742-7100**
GM FAX 310/535-4525
www.lakings.com
Capacity: 18,230

Ownership
Owner	Philip F. Anschutz
Owner	Edward P. Roski, Jr.
Alternate Governor	Dan Beckerman
Executive Assistant to the Alternate Governor	Tanya Brice

Kings Executive
President, Alt. Governor	Luc Robitaille
Chief Operating Officer, Alternate Governor	Kelly Cheeseman
Executive Assistant, President	Kehly Sloane
Manager, Hockey Administration	Eva Bassett
Executive Assistant, Chief Operating Officer	Alicia Briones
Senior Office Administrator	Kiki Oldani

Hockey Operations
Vice President and General Manager	Rob Blake
Exec. V.P./Hockey Ops and Legal Affairs	Jeff Solomon
Assistant General Manager	Michael Futa
Senior Advisor to the GM/Development	Mike O'Connell
Sr. Advisor	Jack Ferreira

Coaches
Head Coach	John Stevens
Assistant Coaches	Dave Lowry, Don Nachbaur, Pierre Turgeon
Goaltending Coach	Bill Ranford
Video	Samson Lee, Brooks Bertsch

Player Development
Director of Player Development	Nelson Emerson
Player Development	Mike Donnelly
Player Development	Glen Murray
Player Development	Sean O'Donnell
Goaltender Development	Dusty Imoo
Player Assistance	Brantt Myhres
Player Development	Jarret Stoll

Training Staff – Medical
Head Athletic Trainer	Chris Kingsley
Assistant Athletic Trainer	Myles Hirayama
Head Strength and Conditioning Coach	Matt Price
Assistant Strength and Conditioning Coach	Trent Frey
Massage Therapist	Nathan Schmit

Training Staff – Equipment
Head Equipment Manager	Darren Granger
Equipment Assistant Managers / Assistant	Dana Bryson, Joe Alexander / Bobby Halfacre

Medical
Team Physician / Internist	Dr. Ronald Kvitne / Dr. Michael Mellman
Team Dentist / Opthalmologist	Dr. Ken Ochi / Dr. Jane Semel

Scouts/Hockey Operations
Scouting Operations Coordinator	Lee Callans
Senior Pro Scout / Pro Scout	Rob Laird / Mark Osborne, David Torrie
Scouting Directors, Amateur / Europe	Mark Yannetti / Christian Ruuttu
Amateur Scouts	Niklas Andersson, Chris Byrne, Bryan Denny, Denis Fugere, Tony Gasparini, Brent McEwen, Jussi-Kari Koskinen, Ted Belisle

Communications and Content
Senior VP, Communications and Broadcasting	Michael Altieri
Senior Director, Communications and Heritage	Jeff Moeller
Director, Communications and Media Services	Mike Kalinowski
Manager, Communications and Media Services	Eddie Fischermann
Beat Reporter	Jon Rosen

Broadcasters
TV Station / Play-by-Play / Analyst	FOX Sports West / Alex Faust / Jim Fox
Radio Flagship / Play-by-Play / Analyst	KABC 790 / Nick Nickson / Daryl Evans

Minnesota Wild

Key Off-Season Signings/Acquisitions

2017

June 23 • Acquired C **Dante Salituro** from Columbus for C **Jordan Schroeder**.

24 • Named **Bob Woods** assistant coach.

27 • Re-signed C **Patrick Cannone**.

30 • Acquired C **Tyler Ennis**, LW **Marcus Foligno** and a 3rd-round pick in 2018 NHL Draft from Buffalo for D **Marco Scandella**, RW **Jason Pominville** and a 4th-round pick in 2018 NHL Draft.

July 1 • Signed D **Kyle Quincey**, C **Kyle Rau**, C **Cal O'Reilly**, C **Landon Ferraro**, D **Ryan Murphy**, D **Alex Grant** and G **Niklas Svedberg**.

3 • Re-signed D **Mike Reilly**.

10 • Re-signed RW **Kurtis Gabriel** and RW **Zack Mitchell**.

30 • Re-signed RW **Nino Niederreiter**.

Aug. 1 • Re-signed C **Mikael Granlund**.

2016-17 Results: 49w-25L-6otl-2sol 106pts
2nd, Central Division • 3rd, Western Conference

Year-by-Year Record

		Home				Road				Overall								Div. Fin.	Conf. Fin.	Playoff Result
Season	GP	W	L	T	OL	W	L	T	OL	W	L	T	OL	GF	GA	Pts.				
2016-17	82	27	12	....	2	22	13	....	6	49	25	....	8	266	208	106	2nd, Cen.	3rd, West	Lost First Round
2015-16	82	21	16	....	4	17	17	....	7	38	33	....	11	216	206	87	5th, Cen.	8th, West	Lost First Round
2014-15	82	22	13	....	6	24	15	....	2	46	28	....	8	231	201	100	4th, Cen.	6th, West	Lost Second Round
2013-14	82	26	10	....	5	17	17	....	7	43	27	....	12	207	206	98	4th, Cen.	7th, West	Lost Second Round
2012-13	48	14	8	....	2	12	11	....	1	26	19	....	3	122	127	55	2nd, NW	8th, West	Lost Conf. Quarter-Final
2011-12	82	20	17	....	4	15	19	....	7	35	36	....	11	177	226	81	4th, NW	12th, West	– out of playoffs –
2010-11	82	19	17	....	5	20	18	....	3	39	35	....	8	206	233	86	3rd, NW	12th, West	– out of playoffs –
2009-10	82	25	12	....	4	13	24	....	4	38	36	....	8	219	246	84	4th, NW	13th, West	– out of playoffs –
2008-09	82	23	11	....	7	17	22	....	2	40	33	....	9	219	200	89	3rd, NW	9th, West	– out of playoffs –
2007-08	82	25	11	....	5	19	17	....	5	44	28	....	10	223	218	98	1st, NW	3rd, West	Lost Conf. Quarter-Final
2006-07	82	29	7	....	5	19	19	....	3	48	26	....	8	235	191	104	2nd, NW	7th, West	Lost Conf. Quarter-Final
2005-06	82	23	16	....	2	15	20	....	6	38	36	....	8	231	215	84	5th, NW	11th, West	– out of playoffs –
2004-05	....																		
2003-04	82	19	13	7	....	11	16	13	1	30	29	20	3	188	183	83	5th, NW	10th, West	– out of playoffs –
2002-03	82	25	13	3	0	17	16	7	1	42	29	10	1	198	178	95	3rd, NW	6th, West	Lost Conf. Final
2001-02	82	14	14	8	5	12	21	4	4	26	35	12	9	195	238	73	5th, NW	12th, West	– out of playoffs –
2000-01	82	14	13	10	4	11	26	3	1	25	39	13	5	168	210	68	5th, NW	14th, West	– out of playoffs –

2017-18 Schedule

Oct.							
Thu.	5	at Detroit		Sat.	6	at Colorado*
Sat.	7	at Carolina		Tue.	9	Calgary
Thu.	12	at Chicago		Wed.	10	at Chicago
Sat.	14	Columbus		Sat.	13	Winnipeg
Fri.	20	at Winnipeg		Sun.	14	Vancouver
Sat.	21	at Calgary		Sat.	20	Tampa Bay
Tue.	24	Vancouver		Mon.	22	Ottawa
Thu.	26	NY Islanders		Thu.	25	at Pittsburgh
Sat.	28	Pittsburgh		Tue.	30	at Columbus
Tue.	31	Winnipeg	Feb.	Fri.	2	Vegas
Nov. Thu.	2	Montreal		Sat.	3	at Dallas
Sat.	4	Chicago		Tue.	6	at St. Louis*
Mon.	6	at Boston		Thu.	8	Arizona
Wed.	8	at Toronto		Sat.	10	Chicago
Thu.	9	at Montreal		Tue.	13	NY Rangers
Sat.	11	at Philadelphia		Thu.	15	Washington
Tue.	14	Philadelphia		Sat.	17	Anaheim*
Thu.	16	Nashville		Mon.	19	at NY Islanders*
Sat.	18	at Washington		Thu.	22	at New Jersey
Mon.	20	New Jersey		Fri.	23	at NY Rangers
Wed.	22	at Buffalo		Sun.	25	San Jose
Fri.	24	Colorado*		Tue.	27	St. Louis
Sat.	25	at St. Louis*	**Mar.**	Thu.	1	at Arizona
Mon.	27	at Winnipeg		Fri.	2	at Colorado
Thu.	30	Vegas		Sun.	4	Detroit
Dec. Sat.	2	St. Louis*		Tue.	6	Carolina
Tue.	5	at Los Angeles		Fri.	9	at Vancouver
Fri.	8	at Anaheim		Sat.	10	at Edmonton
Sun.	10	at San Jose		Tue.	13	Colorado
Tue.	12	Calgary		Fri.	16	at Vegas
Thu.	14	Toronto		Sat.	17	at Arizona
Sat.	16	Edmonton*		Mon.	19	Los Angeles
Sun.	17	at Chicago		Sat.	24	Nashville
Tue.	19	at Ottawa		Sun.	25	Boston
Fri.	22	at Florida		Tue.	27	at Nashville
Sat.	23	at Tampa Bay		Thu.	29	Dallas
Wed.	27	Dallas		Sat.	31	at Dallas
Fri.	29	Nashville	**Apr.**	Mon.	2	Edmonton
Sat.	30	at Nashville		Wed.	4	at Anaheim
Jan. Tue.	2	Florida		Thu.	5	at Los Angeles
Thu.	4	Buffalo		Sat.	7	at San Jose

* Denotes afternoon game.

CENTRAL DIVISION
18th NHL Season

Franchise date: June 25, 1997

Jason Zucker (16) and Ryan Suter tied for the NHL lead in plus-minus with a +34 rating in 2016-17. Suter was busy as usual, playing in all 82 games and trailing only Drew Doughty in total ice time.

2017-18 Player Personnel

FORWARDS	HT	WT	*Age	Birthplace	S	2016-17 Club
COYLE, Charlie	6-3	221	25	E. Weymouth, MA	R	Minnesota
ENNIS, Tyler	5-9	160	27	Edmonton, AB	L	Buffalo
ERIKSSON EK, Joel	6-2	198	20	Karlstad, Sweden	L	Minnesota-Iowa-Farjestad
FERRARO, Landon	6-0	186	26	Trail, BC	R	Chicago (AHL)
FOLIGNO, Marcus	6-3	228	26	Buffalo, NY	L	Buffalo
GABRIEL, Kurtis	6-4	212	24	Newmarket, ON	R	Minnesota-Iowa
GRANLUND, Mikael	5-10	184	25	Oulu, Finland	L	Minnesota
KOIVU, Mikko	6-3	215	34	Turku, Finland	L	Minnesota
NIEDERREITER, Nino	6-2	211	25	Chur, Switzerland	L	Minnesota
O'REILLY, Cal	6-0	191	31	Toronto, ON	L	Buf-Roch-Tor (AHL)
PARISE, Zach	5-11	196	33	Minneapolis, MN	L	Minnesota
RAU, Kyle	5-8	178	24	Eden Prairie, MN	L	Florida-Springfield
STAAL, Eric	6-4	205	32	Thunder Bay, ON	L	Minnesota
STEWART, Chris	6-2	231	29	Toronto, ON	R	Minnesota
ZUCKER, Jason	5-11	185	25	Newport Beach, CA	L	Minnesota
DEFENSEMEN						
BRODIN, Jonas	6-1	193	24	Karlstad, Sweden	L	Minnesota
DUMBA, Matt	6-0	183	23	Regina, SK	R	Minnesota
GRANT, Alex	6-4	205	28	Antigonish, NS	R	Providence (AHL)
MURPHY, Ryan	5-11	185	24	Aurora, ON	R	Carolina-Charlotte
OLOFSSON, Gustav	6-3	197	22	Boras, Sweden	L	Minnesota-Iowa
QUINCEY, Kyle	6-2	216	32	Kitchener, ON	L	New Jersey-Columbus
REILLY, Mike	6-2	191	24	Chicago, IL	L	Minnesota-Iowa
SPURGEON, Jared	5-9	164	27	Edmonton, AB	R	Minnesota
SUTER, Ryan	6-2	206	32	Madison, WI	L	Minnesota

GOALTENDERS	HT	WT	*Age	Birthplace	C	2016-17 Club
DUBNYK, Devan	6-6	212	31	Regina, SK	L	Minnesota
STALOCK, Alex	6-0	190	30	St. Paul, MN	L	Minnesota-Iowa

* – Age at start of 2017-18 season

Bruce Boudreau

Head Coach

Born: Toronto, ON, January 9, 1955.

Minnesota Wild general manager Chuck Fletcher announced the signing of Bruce Boudreau as the team's new head coach on May 7, 2016. In his first season behind the bench in 2016-17, the Wild set club records with 49 wins and 106 points. Boudreau previously coached the Washington Capitals and the Anaheim Ducks. He became the fastest coach in NHL history to reach the 400-win milestone (663 games) on March 5, 2016 and leads active NHL coaches in win percentage. Boudreau led Anaheim to four straight Pacific Division titles through 2015-16 and club records in wins (54), points (116), and goals (266) in a season in 2013-14. He won the Presidents' Trophy with Washington in 2009-10 when the Capitals set club records with 121 points and 313 goals.

Boudreau's NHL coaching career began when he was named interim head coach of the Capitals on November 22, 2007. On that date, Washington was 30th in the NHL standings. He led the club to a 37-17-7 finish as the Capitals won the Southeast Division. Boudreau was rewarded with the 2008 Jack Adams Award. Before joining the Capitals, Boudreau spent parts of nine seasons as a head coach in the American Hockey League. He won the 2006 Calder Cup and advanced to the 2007 Calder Cup Final. Boudreau began his coaching career in the Colonial Hockey League with Muskegon (1992-93) and won the Commissioners' Trophy as the International Hockey League coach of the year in 1993-94 with Fort Wayne. He also served as head coach and director of hockey operations for Mississippi (ECHL), where he won the 1999 Kelly Cup championship.

Boudreau played parts of eight NHL seasons (1976 to 1986) with the Toronto Maple Leafs and Chicago Blackhawks recording 70 points (28 goals, 42 assists) in 141 career games. He ranks 12th all-time in AHL scoring with 799 points (316 goals, 483 assists) in 634 games. No AHL player in the 1980s notched more points than Boudreau who was inducted into the AHL Hall of Fame in 2009.

Coaching Record

			Regular Season				Playoffs			
Season	Team	League	GC	W	L	O/T	GC	W	L	T
1992-93	Muskegon	CoHL	60	28	27	5	7	3	4	....
1993-94	Fort Wayne	IHL	81	41	29	11	18	10	8	....
1994-95	Fort Wayne	IHL	39	15	21	3	....	....	....	....
1996-97	Mississippi	ECHL	70	34	26	10	3	0	3	....
1997-98	Mississippi	ECHL	70	34	27	9	....	....	....	....
1998-99	Mississippi	ECHL	70	41	22	7	18	14	4	....
99-2000	Lowell	AHL	80	33	36	11	7	3	4	....
2000-01	Lowell	AHL	80	35	35	10	4	1	3	....
2001-02	Manchester	AHL	80	38	28	14	5	2	3	....
2002-03	Manchester	AHL	80	40	23	17	3	0	3	....
2003-04	Manchester	AHL	80	40	28	12	6	2	4	....
2004-05	Manchester	AHL	80	51	21	8	6	2	4	....
2005-06	Hershey	AHL	80	44	21	15	21	16	5	....
2006-07	Hershey	AHL	80	51	17	12	19	13	6	....
2007-08	Hershey	AHL	15	8	7	0	....	....	....	....
2007-08	**Washington**	**NHL**	**61**	**37**	**17**	**7**	**7**	**3**	**4**	....
2008-09	**Washington**	**NHL**	**82**	**50**	**24**	**8**	**14**	**7**	**7**	....
2009-10	**Washington**	**NHL**	**82**	**54**	**15**	**13**	**7**	**3**	**4**	....
2010-11	**Washington**	**NHL**	**82**	**48**	**23**	**11**	**9**	**4**	**5**	....
2011-12	**Washington**	**NHL**	**22**	**12**	**9**	**1**	....	....	....	....
2011-12	**Anaheim**	**NHL**	**58**	**27**	**23**	**8**	....	....	....	....
2012-13	**Anaheim**	**NHL**	**48**	**30**	**12**	**6**	**7**	**3**	**4**	....
2013-14	**Anaheim**	**NHL**	**82**	**54**	**20**	**8**	**13**	**7**	**6**	....
2014-15	**Anaheim**	**NHL**	**82**	**51**	**24**	**7**	**16**	**11**	**5**	....
2015-16	**Anaheim**	**NHL**	**82**	**46**	**25**	**11**	**7**	**3**	**4**	....
2016-17	**Minnesota**	**NHL**	**82**	**49**	**25**	**8**	**5**	**1**	**4**	....
	NHL Totals		**763**	**458**	**217**	**88**	**85**	**42**	**43**	....

Jack Adams Award (2008)

2016-17 Scoring

* – rookie

Regular Season

Pos	#	Player	Team	GP	G	A	Pts	TOI	+/–	PIM	PP	SH	GW	S	S%
C	64	Mikael Granlund	MIN	81	26	43	69	18:49	23	12	7	3	4	177	14.7
C	12	Eric Staal	MIN	82	28	37	65	18:36	17	34	4	1	8	211	13.3
C	9	Mikko Koivu	MIN	80	18	40	58	19:06	27	34	2	0	4	139	12.9
R	22	Nino Niederreiter	MIN	82	25	32	57	15:04	17	53	8	0	3	186	13.4
C	3	Charlie Coyle	MIN	82	18	38	56	16:42	13	36	4	0	5	159	11.3
L	16	Jason Zucker	MIN	79	22	25	47	15:17	34	30	1	0	3	172	12.8
R	29	Jason Pominville	MIN	78	13	34	47	14:13	2	4	0	0	2	176	7.4
L	11	Zach Parise	MIN	69	19	23	42	17:25	–3	30	6	0	4	194	9.8
D	20	Ryan Suter	MIN	82	9	31	40	26:55	34	36	4	1	1	164	5.5
C	19	Martin Hanzal	ARI	51	16	10	26	18:35	–15	43	4	0	2	126	12.7
			MIN	20	4	9	13	15:31	–2	10	1	0	0	43	9.3
			Total	71	20	19	39	17:43	–17	53	5	0	2	169	11.8
D	46	Jared Spurgeon	MIN	76	10	28	38	24:01	33	20	1	0	2	144	6.9
D	24	Matt Dumba	MIN	76	11	23	34	20:19	15	59	6	0	1	131	8.4
L	56	Erik Haula	MIN	72	15	11	26	13:48	5	28	1	0	4	134	11.2
D	25	Jonas Brodin	MIN	68	3	22	25	19:34	5	20	2	0	2	85	3.5
R	7	Chris Stewart	MIN	79	13	8	21	10:23	3	94	0	0	0	82	15.9
C	21	Ryan White	ARI	46	7	6	13	10:57	–8	70	0	0	1	43	16.3
			MIN	19	2	1	3	9:56	–8	14	0	0	0	17	11.8
			Total	65	9	7	16	10:39	–16	84	0	0	1	60	15.0
C	10	Jordan Schroeder	MIN	37	6	7	13	9:46	5	0	0	0	0	37	16.2
D	6	Marco Scandella	MIN	71	4	9	13	18:20	–2	25	0	0	0	88	4.5
C	44 *	Tyler Graovac	MIN	52	7	2	9	9:50	7	10	0	0	2	48	14.6
D	5	Christian Folin	MIN	51	2	6	8	14:56	10	26	0	0	0	39	5.1
C	14 *	Joel Eriksson Ek	MIN	15	3	4	7	10:36	1	4	0	0	1	15	20.0
D	39	Nate Prosser	MIN	39	2	5	7	12:43	0	12	0	0	0	20	10.0
C	27	Zac Dalpe	MIN	9	1	2	3	8:33	0	9	0	0	0	8	12.5
D	23 *	Gustav Olofsson	MIN	13	0	3	3	13:28	–1	2	0	0	0	7	0.0
D	4	Mike Reilly	MIN	17	1	0	1	12:22	1	2	0	0	0	19	5.3
C	47 *	Christoph Bertschy	MIN	5	0	1	1	8:08	0	4	0	0	0	5	0.0
R	63 *	Kurtis Gabriel	MIN	13	0	1	1	5:49	0	29	0	0	0	3	0.0
C	42	Patrick Cannone	MIN	3	0	0	0	7:53	0	0	0	0	0	2	0.0
R	53 *	Alex Tuch	MIN	6	0	0	0	10:42	–3	0	0	0	0	8	0.0
R	59 *	Zack Mitchell	MIN	11	0	0	0	8:25	–1	0	0	0	0	10	0.0

Goaltending

No.	Goaltender	GPI	Mins	Avg	W	L	OT	EN	SO	GA	SA	Sv%	G	A	PIM
32	Alex Stalock	2	119	1.51	1	1	0	1	0	3	54	.944	0	0	0
40	Devan Dubnyk	65	3758	2.25	40	19	5	4	5	141	1842	.923	0	0	10
35	Darcy Kuemper	18	1053	3.13	8	5	3	2	0	55	562	.902	0	1	4
	Totals	**82**	**4967**	**2.49**	**49**	**25**	**8**	**7**	**5**	**206**	**2465**	**.916**			

Playoffs

Pos	#	Player	Team	GP	G	A	Pts	TOI	+/–	PIM	PP	SH	GW	OT	S	S%
L	11	Zach Parise	MIN	5	2	1	3	19:27	–4	8	1	0	0	0	19	10.5
D	20	Ryan Suter	MIN	5	1	2	3	29:06	–3	10	1	0	0	0	15	6.7
C	3	Charlie Coyle	MIN	5	2	0	2	17:11	–1	2	0	0	1	0	14	14.3
C	9	Mikko Koivu	MIN	5	1	1	2	20:09	–1	0	1	0	0	0	6	16.7
C	64	Mikael Granlund	MIN	5	0	2	2	20:32	0	2	0	0	0	0	10	0.0
C	19	Martin Hanzal	MIN	5	1	0	1	18:44	–2	0	0	0	0	0	10	10.0
L	16	Jason Zucker	MIN	5	1	0	1	17:15	–1	2	0	0	0	0	20	5.0
D	39	Nate Prosser	MIN	3	0	1	1	9:47	0	2	0	0	0	0	4	0.0
L	56	Erik Haula	MIN	4	0	1	1	15:24	–2	0	0	0	0	0	9	0.0
R	29	Jason Pominville	MIN	5	0	1	1	14:05	1	0	0	0	0	0	11	0.0
C	12	Eric Staal	MIN	5	0	1	1	18:54	–1	0	0	0	0	0	12	0.0
D	46	Jared Spurgeon	MIN	5	0	1	1	25:20	–1	0	0	0	0	0	13	0.0
R	22	Nino Niederreiter	MIN	5	0	1	1	15:58	–2	2	0	0	0	0	7	0.0
D	25	Jonas Brodin	MIN	5	0	1	1	19:00	–3	0	0	0	0	0	5	0.0
D	5	Christian Folin	MIN	2	0	0	0	11:23	–2	2	0	0	0	0	1	0.0
C	21	Ryan White	MIN	3	0	0	0	7:04	0	4	0	0	0	0	2	0.0
C	14 *	Joel Eriksson Ek	MIN	3	0	0	0	7:34	0	0	0	0	0	0	5	0.0
R	7	Chris Stewart	MIN	5	0	0	0	7:50	0	0	0	0	0	0	2	0.0
D	6	Marco Scandella	MIN	5	0	0	0	22:55	–1	2	0	0	0	0	10	0.0
D	24	Matt Dumba	MIN	5	0	0	0	23:53	–1	2	0	0	0	0	7	0.0

Goaltending

No.	Goaltender	GPI	Mins	Avg	W	L	EN	SO	GA	SA	Sv%	G	A	PIM
40	Devan Dubnyk	5	322	1.86	1	4	1	1	10	133	.925	0	0	0
	Totals	**5**	**328**	**2.01**	**1**	**4**	**1**	**1**	**11**	**134**	**.918**			

Club Records

Team

(Figures in brackets for season records are games played.)

Most Points	106	2016-17 (82)
Most Wins	49	2016-17 (82)
Most Ties	20	2003-04 (82)
Most Losses	39	2000-01 (82)
Most Goals	266	2016-17 (82)
Most Goals Against	246	2009-10 (82)
Fewest Points	68	2000-01 (82)
Fewest Wins	25	2000-01 (82)
Fewest Ties	10	2002-03 (82)
Fewest Losses	25	2016-17 (82)
Fewest Goals	168	2000-01 (82)
Fewest Goals Against	178	2002-03 (82)

Longest Winning Streak
Overall . . . 12 Dec. 4-29/16
Home . . . 8 Oct. 5-Nov. 2/06, Dec. 5/06-Jan. 2/07, Nov. 23-Dec. 29/16
Away . . . 12 Feb. 18-Apr. 9/15

Longest Team Point Streak
Overall . . . 13 Dec. 2-27/16 (9W, 2OTW, 1SOW, 1SOL)
Home . . . 10 Feb. 19-Apr. 10/09 (5W, 3OTL, 1SOL), Jan. 16-Mar. 15/14 (5W, 2OTW, 3SOW)
Away . . . 14 Dec. 2/16-Jan. 31/17 (9W, 2OTW, 1SOW, 1OTL, 1SOL)

Longest Losing Streak
Overall . . . 8 Mar. 10-26/11
Home . . . 5 Feb. 28-Mar. 13/12, Apr. 1-21/13
Away . . . 11 Nov. 20/06-Jan. 9/07, Dec. 13/11-Jan. 19/12

Longest Winless Streak
Overall . . . 12 Mar. 11-Apr. 4/01 (7L, 2OTL, 3T)
Home . . . 8 Feb. 26-Mar. 28/01 (3L, 2OTL, 3T), Jan. 7-Feb. 13/16 (5L, 2OTL, 1SOL)
Away . . . 12 Dec. 18/03-Jan. 31/04 (4L, 1OTL, 7T)

Most Shutouts, Season . . . 8 2006-07 (82), 2008-09 (82), 2013-14 (82), 2014-15 (82), 2015-16 (82)
Most PIM, Season . . . 1,209 2001-02 (82), 2005-06 (82)
Most Goals, Game . . . 8 Mar. 25/04 (Min. 8 at Chi. 2) Apr. 10/09 (Nsh. 2 at Min. 8)

Individual

Most Seasons . . . 12 Mikko Koivu
Most Games . . . 843 Mikko Koivu
Most Goals, Career . . . 219 Marian Gaborik
Most Assists, Career . . . 435 Mikko Koivu
Most Points, Career . . . 614 Mikko Koivu (179G, 435A)
Most PIM, Career . . . 698 Matt Johnson
Most Shutouts, Career . . . 28 Niklas Backstrom
Longest Consecutive Games Streak . . . 313 Charlie Coyle (Nov. 5/13 to date)
Most Goals, Season . . . 42 Marian Gaborik (2007-08)
Most Assists, Season . . . 50 Pierre-Marc Bouchard (2007-08)
Most Points, Season . . . 83 Marian Gaborik (2007-08; 42G, 41A)
Most PIM, Season . . . 201 Matt Johnson (2002-03)

Most Points, Defenseman, Season . . . 51 Ryan Suter (2015-16; 8G, 43A)
Most Points, Center, Season . . . 71 Mikko Koivu (2009-10; 22G, 49A)
Most Points, Right Wing, Season . . . 83 Marian Gaborik (2007-08; 42G, 41A)
Most Points, Left Wing, Season . . . 79 Brian Rolston (2005-06; 34G, 45A)
Most Points, Rookie, Season . . . 36 Marian Gaborik (2000-01; 18G, 18A)
Most Shutouts, Season . . . 8 Niklas Backstrom (2008-09)
Most Goals, Game . . . 5 Marian Gaborik (Dec. 20/07)
Most Assists, Game . . . 4 Andrew Brunette (Mar. 10/02), Marian Gaborik (Oct. 26/02), Pascal Dupuis (Mar. 25/04), Eric Belanger (Nov. 15/07), Mikko Koivu (Oct. 16/08, Jan. 2/11)
Most Points, Game . . . 6 Marian Gaborik (Oct. 26/02; 2G, 4A), (Dec. 20/07; 5G, 1A)

Captains' History

Sean O'Donnell, Scott Pellerin, Wes Walz, Brad Bombardir, Darby Hendrickson, 2000-01; Jim Dowd, Filip Kuba, Brad Brown, Andrew Brunette, 2001-02; Brad Bombardir, Matt Johnson, Sergei Zholtok, 2002-03; Brad Brown, Andrew Brunette, Richard Park, Brad Bombardir, Jim Dowd, 2003-04; Alex Henry, Filip Kuba, Willie Mitchell, Brian Rolston, Wes Walz, 2005-06; Brian Rolston, Keith Carney, Mark Parrish, 2006-07; Pavol Demitra, Brian Rolston, Mark Parrish, Nick Schultz, Marian Gaborik, 2007-08; Mikko Koivu, Kim Johnsson, Andrew Brunette, 2008-09; Mikko Koivu, 2009-10 to date.

General Managers' History

Doug Risebrough, 2000-01 to 2008-09; Chuck Fletcher, 2009-10 to date.

Coaching History

Jacques Lemaire, 2000-01 to 2008-09; Todd Richards, 2009-10, 2010-11; Mike Yeo, 2011-12 to 2014-15; Mike Yeo and John Torchetti, 2015-16; Bruce Boudreau, 2016-17 to date.

All-time Record vs. Other Clubs

Regular Season

	Total								At Home								On Road							
	GP	W	L	T	OL	GF	GA	PTS	GP	W	L	T	OL	GF	GA	PTS	GP	W	L	T	OL	GF	GA	PTS
Anaheim	59	27	27	2	3	142	139	59	29	15	10	2	2	74	60	34	30	12	17	0	1	68	79	25
Arizona	59	31	21	3	4	153	138	69	29	15	10	2	2	78	66	34	30	16	11	1	2	75	72	35
Boston	20	14	4	0	2	56	37	30	10	6	2	0	2	25	20	14	10	8	2	0	0	31	17	16
Buffalo	20	11	7	0	2	57	42	24	10	3	5	0	2	24	26	8	10	8	2	0	0	33	16	16
Calgary	86	36	37	4	9	200	198	85	43	22	14	1	6	109	92	51	43	14	23	3	3	91	106	34
Carolina	22	11	7	2	2	60	59	26	13	8	3	2	0	43	38	18	9	3	4	0	2	17	21	8
Chicago	66	38	24	1	3	187	173	80	34	21	11	0	2	99	89	44	32	17	13	1	1	88	84	36
Colorado	94	48	35	3	8	248	246	107	48	26	16	1	4	130	122	57	47	22	19	2	4	118	124	50
Columbus	54	25	21	1	7	128	133	58	28	17	7	0	4	76	64	38	26	8	14	1	3	52	69	20
Dallas	66	27	27	1	11	173	196	66	32	18	10	0	4	92	71	40	34	9	17	1	7	81	125	26
Detroit	55	17	26	3	9	133	179	46	27	9	9	2	7	66	73	27	28	8	17	1	2	67	106	19
Edmonton	85	50	25	4	6	233	187	110	42	26	13	1	2	121	93	55	43	24	12	3	4	112	94	55
Florida	21	15	3	1	2	66	36	33	10	8	0	1	1	32	13	18	11	7	3	0	1	34	23	15
Los Angeles	59	28	18	5	8	140	145	69	30	15	8	3	4	71	72	37	29	13	10	2	4	69	73	32
Montreal	19	10	6	1	2	55	56	23	9	6	2	0	1	27	24	13	10	4	4	1	1	28	32	10
Nashville	66	30	28	5	3	178	182	68	33	17	12	3	1	105	94	38	33	13	16	2	2	73	88	30
New Jersey	20	5	9	2	4	52	64	16	10	4	4	1	1	31	27	10	10	1	5	1	3	21	37	6
NY Islanders	22	12	9	0	1	69	63	25	11	7	3	0	1	37	28	15	11	5	6	0	0	32	29	10
NY Rangers	22	8	13	0	1	61	68	17	12	5	6	0	1	35	35	11	10	3	7	0	0	26	33	6
Ottawa	19	6	9	1	3	44	58	16	10	3	5	1	1	25	31	8	9	3	4	0	2	19	27	8
Philadelphia	21	6	13	1	1	36	62	14	9	3	4	1	1	17	25	8	12	3	9	0	0	19	37	6
Pittsburgh	21	12	8	1	0	65	51	25	10	5	4	1	0	29	15	11	11	7	4	0	0	36	26	14
St. Louis	66	29	23	5	9	163	160	72	34	19	9	2	4	98	73	44	32	10	14	3	5	65	87	28
San Jose	59	25	27	2	5	137	160	57	29	15	10	1	3	74	72	34	30	10	17	1	2	63	88	23
Tampa Bay	22	13	6	1	2	60	48	29	11	9	2	0	0	35	21	18	11	4	4	1	2	25	27	11
Toronto	18	10	8	0	0	40	41	20	8	6	2	0	0	20	12	12	10	4	6	0	0	20	29	8
Vancouver	85	37	34	5	9	229	228	88	43	22	16	2	3	127	107	49	42	15	18	3	6	102	121	39
Washington	20	9	9	1	1	42	45	20	10	7	2	0	1	29	22	15	10	2	7	1	0	16	28	5
Winnipeg	32	17	10	1	4	91	87	39	16	9	4	1	2	42	35	21	16	8	6	0	2	49	52	18
Totals	1278	607	494	55	122	3301	3286	1391	639	346	203	28	62	1771	1536	782	639	261	291	27	60	1530	1750	609

Playoffs

	Series	W	L	GP	W	L	T	GF	GA	Last Mtg.	Rnd.	Result
Anaheim	2	0	2	9	1	8	0	10	21	2007	CQF	L 1-4
Chicago	3	0	3	15	3	12	0	27	45	2015	SR	L 0-4
Colorado	3	2	1	20	10	10	0	50	54	2014	FR	W 4-3
Dallas	1	0	1	6	2	4	0	17	21	2016	FR	L 2-4
St. Louis	2	1	1	11	5	6	0	25	25	2017	FR	L 1-4
Vancouver	1	1	0	7	4	3	0	26	17	2003	CSF	W 4-3
Totals	12	4	8	68	25	43	0	155	183			

Winnipeg totals include Atlanta Thrashers, 1999-2000 to 2010-11.

Playoff Results 2017-2013

Year	Round	Opponent	Result	GF	GA
2017	FR	St. Louis	L 1-4	8	11
2016	FR	Dallas	L 2-4	17	21
2015	SR	Chicago	L 0-4	7	13
	FR	St. Louis	W 4-2	17	14
2014	SR	Chicago	L 2-4	13	15
	FR	Colorado	W 4-3	22	20
2013	CQF	Chicago	L 1-4	7	17

Abbreviations: Round: CSF – conference semi-final; **SR** – second round; **CQF** – conference quarter-final; **FR** – first round.

2016-17 Results

Oct.	13	at St. Louis	2-3
	15	Winnipeg	4-3
	18	Los Angeles	6-3
	20	Toronto	3-2
	22	at New Jersey	1-2*
	23	at NY Islanders	3-6
	25	at Boston	5-0
	27	at Buffalo	4-0
	29	Dallas	4-0
Nov.	1	Buffalo	1-2
	5	at Colorado	0-1
	10	at Pittsburgh	4-2
	12	at Philadelphia	2-3
	13	at Ottawa	2-1*
	15	Calgary	0-1
	17	Boston	1-0
	19	Colorado	2-3
	21	at Dallas	2-3*
	23	Winnipeg	3-1
	25	Pittsburgh	6-2
	26	at St. Louis	3-4†
	29	at Vancouver	4-5
Dec.	2	at Calgary	2-3†
	4	at Edmonton	2-1*
	7	at Toronto	3-2
	9	Edmonton	3-2†
	11	St. Louis	3-1
	13	Florida	5-1
	15	at Nashville	5-2
	17	Arizona	4-1
	20	Colorado	2-0
	22	at Montreal	4-2
	23	at NY Rangers	7-4
	27	at Nashville	3-2*
	29	NY Islanders	6-4
	31	Columbus	2-4
Jan.	5	at San Jose	5-4
	7	at Los Angeles	3-4*
	8	at Anaheim	2-1
	12	Montreal	7-1
	14	at Dallas	5-4

Oct.	15	at Chicago	3-2
	17	New Jersey	3-4
	19	Arizona	4-3
	21	Anaheim	5-3
	22	Nashville	2-4
	24	at Dallas	3-2†
	26	St. Louis	5-1
	31	at Edmonton	3-1
Feb.	1	at Calgary	1-5
	4	at Vancouver	6-3
	7	at Winnipeg	4-2
	8	Chicago	3-4*
	10	Tampa Bay	2-1†
	12	Detroit	6-3
	14	Anaheim	0-1
	16	Dallas	3-1
	18	Nashville	5-2
	21	Chicago	3-5
	27	Los Angeles	5-4*
	28	at Winnipeg	6-5
Mar.	2	at Columbus	0-1
	5	San Jose	3-1
	7	St. Louis	1-2
	9	at Tampa Bay	1-4
	10	at Florida	7-4
	12	at Chicago	2-4
	14	at Washington	2-4
	16	at Carolina	1-3
	18	NY Rangers	2-3
	19	at Winnipeg	4-5
	21	San Jose	3-2
	23	Philadelphia	1-3
	25	Vancouver	2-4
	26	at Detroit	2-3*
	28	Washington	4-5*
	30	Ottawa	5-1
Apr.	1	at Nashville	0-3
	2	Colorado	5-3
	4	Carolina	5-3
	6	at Colorado	4-3
	8	at Arizona	3-1

* – Overtime   † – Shootout

NHL Draft Selections 2017-2003

Name in bold denotes played in NHL.

2017 Pick		2013 Pick		2009 Pick		2005 Pick	
85	Ivan Lodnia	46	**Gustav Olofsson**	16	**Nick Leddy**	4	**Benoit Pouliot**
97	Mason Shaw	81	**Kurtis Gabriel**	77	**Matt Hackett**	57	**Matt Kassian**
116	Bryce Misley	107	Dylan Labbe	103	**Kris Foucault**	65	Kristofer Westblom
147	Jacob Golden	137	Carson Soucy	116	Alex Fallstrom	110	Kyle Bailey
178	Andrei Svetlakov	167	Avery Peterson	161	**Darcy Kuemper**	122	Morten Madsen
209	Nick Swaney	197	Nolan De Jong	163	Jere Sallinen	129	Anthony Aiello
		200	Alexandre Belanger	182	**Erik Haula**	199	Riley Emmerson
2016 Pick				193	Anthony Hamburg		
15	Luke Kunin	**2012 Pick**				**2004 Pick**	
106	Brandon Duhaime	7	**Matt Dumba**	**2008 Pick**		12	A.J. Thelen
196	Dmitri Sokolov	46	Raphael Bussieres	23	**Tyler Cuma**	42	Roman Voloshenko
204	Brayden Chizen	68	John Draeger	55	**Marco Scandella**	78	**Peter Olvecky**
		98	Adam Gilmour	115	Sean Lorenz	79	**Clayton Stoner**
2015 Pick		128	Daniel Gunnarsson	145	Eero Elo	111	**Ryan Jones**
20	**Joel Eriksson Ek**	158	Christoph Bertschy			114	**Patrick Bordeleau**
50	Jordan Greenway	188	Louis Nanne	**2007 Pick**		117	Julien Sprunger
111	Ales Stezka			16	**Colton Gillies**	161	Jean-Claude Sawyer
135	Kirill Kaprizov	**2011 Pick**		110	**Justin Falk**	175	Aaron Boogaard
171	Nicholas Boka	10	**Jonas Brodin**	140	**Cody Almond**	195	Jean-Michel Rizk
201	Gustav Bouramman	28	Zack Phillips	170	Harri Ilvonen	206	**Anton Khudobin**
204	Jack Sadek	60	Mario Lucia	200	**Carson McMillan**	272	**Kyle Wilson**
		131	Nick Seeler				
2014 Pick		161	Steve Michalek	**2006 Pick**		**2003 Pick**	
18	**Alex Tuch**	191	**Tyler Graovac**	9	**James Sheppard**	20	**Brent Burns**
80	Louis Belpedio			40	Ondrej Fiala	56	**Patrick O'Sullivan**
109	Kaapo Kahkonen	**2010 Pick**		72	**Cal Clutterbuck**	78	**Danny Irmen**
139	Tanner Faith	9	**Mikael Granlund**	102	Kyle Medvec	157	Marcin Kolusz
160	Pontus Sjalin	39	**Brett Bulmer**	132	Niko Hovinen	187	Miroslav Kopriva
167	Chase Lang	56	**Johan Larsson**	162	Julian Walker	207	Georgy Misharin
169	Reid Duke	59	**Jason Zucker**	192	Chris Hickey	219	Adam Courchaine
199	Pavel Jenys	159	Johan Gustafsson			251	Mathieu Melanson
		189	Dylen McKinlay			281	Jean-Michel Bolduc

Chuck Fletcher

General Manager and Executive Vice President

Born: Montreal, QC, April 29, 1967.

The Minnesota Wild announced the hiring of Chuck Fletcher as the second general manager in club history on May 22, 2009. During the summer of 2012, Fletcher made his mark with the acquisition of Zach Parise and Ryan Suter, two of the biggest names available on the free-agent market, and the Wild made their first playoff appearance since 2008 in the spring of 2013. They have returned to the playoffs again every season since then, setting club records with 49 wins and 106 points in 2016-17.

Fletcher has been to the Stanley Cup Final in management with three different teams (Florida, Anaheim and Pittsburgh). With the Penguins from 2006 to 2009, he worked closely with general manager Ray Shero on all hockey-related matters, including scouting, overseeing the development of young prospects and contract negotiations. Fletcher also managed hockey operations for the club's American Hockey League affiliate, the Wilkes-Barre/Scranton Penguins. Under his leadership, Wilkes-Barre/Scranton reached the AHL's Calder Cup finals in 2007-08, and the division finals in 2008-09.

Fletcher, the son of Hockey Hall of Famer Cliff Fletcher, had extensive NHL management experience before he joined the Penguins in July 2006 – including a four-year stint with the Anaheim Ducks from 2003 to 2006 as director of hockey operations, assistant general manager, and vice president of amateur scouting and player development.

The Montreal native also spent nine years in the front office of the Florida Panthers from 1993 to 2002, working seven seasons as assistant general manager and part of one season (2001-02) as interim general manager. In 1996, the Panthers advanced to the Stanley Cup Final.

Fletcher graduated from Harvard in 1990 and spent one year as the sales and merchandising coordinator for Hockey Canada and two years as a player representative for Newport Sports Management before making the transition to the front office.

Club Directory

Xcel Energy Center

Minnesota Wild
317 Washington Street
St. Paul, MN 55102
Phone **651/602-6000**
FAX 651/222-1055
Tickets 651/222-9453
www.wild.com
Capacity: 17,954

Board Members
Craig Leipold (Owner/Governor), Kyle Leipold, Quinn Martin, Mark Pacchini and Jac Sperling

Investors in MSE
Craig Leipold (Owner/Governor); Limited Partners: Robert Hubbard, Stanley E. Hubbard, Stanley S. Hubbard, Horace H. Irvine III, Robert Marvin Jr., Ford Nicholson, Todd Nicholson, Vance Opperman and Michael Reilly

Owner/Governor . . . . Craig Leipold
General Manager and EVP . . . . Chuck Fletcher
President and Alternate Governor . . . . Matt Majka
Chief Financial Officer and EVP . . . . Jeff Pellegrom
Executive VP of Business Development . . . . Jamie Spencer
Senior Vice President Corp. Partnerships
  and Retail Mgmt. . . . . Carin Anderson
Senior Vice President, Marketing and Ticket Sales . . Mitch Helgerson
Vice President, Facility Admin. / G.M., RiverCentre . . Jim Ibister
Vice President / G.M., Xcel Energy Center . . . . . . Jack Larson
Vice President, Brand, Broadcast and Production . . . John Maher
Vice President, Customer Service and Retention . . Maria Troje
Vice President, General Counsel . . . . Steve Weinreich
Executive Assistants . . . . Deb Hanson, Stephanie Huseby

Hockey Operations
Senior Vice President of Hockey Operations . . . . Brent Flahr
Assistant General Managers . . . . Andrew Brunette / Shep Harder
Head Coach . . . . Bruce Boudreau
Assistant Coaches . . . . John Anderson, Darby Hendrickson, Bob Woods
Goalie Coach . . . . Bob Mason
Video Coach . . . . Jonas Plumb
Strength and Conditioning Coach . . . . Sean Skahan
Directors, Player Personnel / Development . . . . . . Blair Mackasey / Brad Bombardir
Chief of Amateur Scouting . . . . Guy Lapointe
Hockey Ops Administrator . . . . Cindy Sweiger
Director of Team Operations and Player Relations . . Andrew Heydt
Video Scouting Coordinator . . . . Tom Minton
Lead Hockey Researcher . . . . Andrew C. Thomas
Hockey Operations Analyst . . . . Alexandra Mandrycky
Media Relations Director . . . . Aaron Sickman
Media Relations Sr. Coordinator / Coordinator . . . Carly Peters / Megan Kogut
Scouts . . . . Craig Channell, Paul Charles, Martin Gendron, Christopher Hamel, Jamie Hislop, Brian Hunter, Chris Kelleher, Martin Nanne, Ivan Nepryaeu, Ricard Persson, Pavel Routa, Ernie Vargas, Darren Yopyk
Head Athletic Trainer / Assistant . . . . John Worley / Chad Krawiec
Head Equipment Manager / Assistants . . . . Tony DaCosta / Matt Benz, Rick Bronwell
Massage Therapist . . . . Travis Green
Medical Staff . . . . Drs. Sheldon Burns, Joel Boyd, Brad Nelson, Dan Peterson, Sonia Coelho Mosch
Craniofacial Surgeon / Team Dentists . . . . David Hamlar / Kyle Edlund, Mike Pelke

Ticket Sales and Service
Senior Manager, Customer Service and Retention . . Erica McKenzie
Director, Ticket Operations and Business Analytics . . Chris Turns

Marketing Intelligence
Marketing Manager . . . . Bridget Johnson
Sr. Business Analyst . . . . Bjorn Kadlec
Business Analyst . . . . Matt Bergstrom

Retail Operation
Retail Operations Manager / Buyer . . . . Scott Sarkis / Jen Meyers

Corporate Partnerships and Suite Sales
Director, Corporate Partnerships . . . . Bryan Bellows
Director, Corporate Partnerships Activation . . . . . . Ed Souter
Account Executive . . . . Jeff Hunsaker/Trent Michaels
Suite Sales Manager . . . . Mark Fasching

Brand Content and Communications/Broadcasting
Manager, Broadcasting and Production . . . . Maggie Kukar
Manager, Game Presentation . . . . Paul Loomis
Manager, Production Facilities Operations . . . . Hank Dolan
Coordinators, Radio Ops / Production Services . . . . Kevin Falness / Dustin Peterson
Radio Play-By-Play / Analyst . . . . Bob Kurtz / Tom Reid
Television Play-By-Play / Analyst . . . . Anthony LaPanta / Mike Greenlay
Manager, Web and Creative Services . . . . Matt Minnichsoffer
Digital Content Manager / Coordinator . . . . Phil Ervin / Dan Myers
Social and Digital Media Coordinator . . . . Katlyn Gambill
Senior Graphic Designer / Graphic Designer . . . . . Allison Thompson / Dakota Perock
Team Curator / Mascot Coordinator . . . . Roger Godin / Robert Hathaway

Community Relations
Executive Director, Wild Foundation . . . . Rachel Schuldt
Director, Community Relations
  and Hockey Partnerships . . . . Wayne Petersen
Development Assistant . . . . Jessica Blum

Finance and Accounting
Controller . . . . Trevor Shannon

Human Resources
Director, HR and Organizational Development . . . . Monica Laurent
Human Resources Generalists . . . . Rachel Link / Lacie Ausland

Information Technology
Senior IT Manager / IT Generalists . . . . Mike Vevea / Josh Kielbasa / Rick Jacobson

Miscellaneous
Radio Network Flagship . . . . KFAN 100.3 FM
Television Network . . . . FOX Sports North
Team Photographer / Public Address Announcer . . . Bruce Kluckhohn / Adam Abrams

Key Off-Season Signings/Acquisitions

2017

June 5 • Re-signed LW **Andreas Martinsen**.
15 • Acquired LW **Jonathan Drouin** and a conditional pick in 2018 NHL Draft from Tampa Bay for D **Mikhail Sergachev** and a conditional pick in 2018 NHL Draft.
15 • Re-signed LW **Charles Hudon**.
22 • Acquired D **David Schlemko** from Vegas for a 5th-round pick in 2019 NHL Draft.
28 • Re-signed LW **Jacob De La Rose**.
July 1 • Signed D **Karl Alzner**, C **Peter Holland**, C **Byron Froese**, D **Joe Morrow** and D **Matt Taormina**.
2 • Re-signed G **Carey Price**.
3 • Signed RW **Ales Hemsky**.
5 • Re-signed C **Alex Galchenyuk**.
25 • Signed D **Mark Streit**.

2017-18 Schedule

Oct.	Thu.	5	at Buffalo
	Sat.	7	at Washington
	Sun.	8	at NY Rangers
	Tue.	10	Chicago
	Sat.	14	Toronto
	Tue.	17	at San Jose
	Wed.	18	at Los Angeles
	Fri.	20	at Anaheim
	Tue.	24	Florida
	Thu.	26	Los Angeles
	Sat.	28	NY Rangers
	Mon.	30	at Ottawa
Nov.	Thu.	2	at Minnesota
	Sat.	4	at Winnipeg
	Sun.	5	at Chicago
	Tue.	7	Vegas
	Thu.	9	Minnesota
	Sat.	11	Buffalo
	Tue.	14	Columbus
	Thu.	16	Arizona
	Sat.	18	Toronto
	Tue.	21	at Dallas
	Wed.	22	at Nashville
	Sat.	25	Buffalo
	Mon.	27	Columbus
	Wed.	29	Ottawa
	Thu.	30	at Detroit
Dec.	Sat.	2	Detroit
	Tue.	5	St. Louis
	Thu.	7	Calgary
	Sat.	9	Edmonton
	Thu.	14	New Jersey
	Sat.	16	at Ottawa
	Tue.	19	at Vancouver
	Fri.	22	at Calgary
	Sat.	23	at Edmonton*
	Wed.	27	at Carolina
	Thu.	28	at Tampa Bay
	Sat.	30	at Florida
Jan.	Tue.	2	San Jose
	Thu.	4	Tampa Bay
	Sun.	7	Vancouver
	Sat.	13	Boston
	Mon.	15	NY Islanders
	Wed.	17	at Boston
	Fri.	19	at Washington
	Sat.	20	Boston
	Tue.	23	Colorado
	Thu.	25	Carolina
	Tue.	30	at St. Louis*
Feb.	Thu.	1	at Carolina
	Sat.	3	Anaheim*
	Sun.	4	Ottawa*
	Thu.	8	at Philadelphia
	Sat.	10	Nashville
	Wed.	14	at Colorado
	Thu.	15	at Arizona
	Sat.	17	at Vegas*
	Tue.	20	at Philadelphia
	Thu.	22	NY Rangers
	Sat.	24	Tampa Bay
	Mon.	26	Philadelphia
	Wed.	28	NY Islanders
Mar.	Fri.	2	at NY Islanders
	Sat.	3	at Boston*
	Tue.	6	at New Jersey
	Thu.	8	at Florida
	Sat.	10	at Tampa Bay*
	Mon.	12	at Columbus
	Tue.	13	Dallas
	Thu.	15	Pittsburgh
	Sat.	17	at Toronto
	Mon.	19	Florida
	Wed.	21	at Pittsburgh
	Fri.	23	at Buffalo
	Sat.	24	Washington
	Mon.	26	Detroit
	Sat.	31	at Pittsburgh
Apr.	Sun.	1	New Jersey
	Tue.	3	Winnipeg
	Thu.	5	at Detroit
	Sat.	7	at Toronto

* Denotes afternoon game.

Retired Numbers

1	Jacques Plante	1952-1963
2	Doug Harvey	1947-1961
3	Butch Bouchard	1941-1956
4	Jean Béliveau	1950-1971
5	Bernard Geoffrion	1950-1964
	Guy Lapointe	1968-1982
7	Howie Morenz	1923-1937
9	Maurice Richard	1942-1960
10	Guy Lafleur	1971-1984
12	Dickie Moore	1951-1963
	Yvan Cournoyer	1963-1979
16	Henri Richard	1955-1975
	Elmer Lach	1940-1954
18	Serge Savard	1966-1981
19	Larry Robinson	1972-1989
23	Bob Gainey	1973-1989
29	Ken Dryden	1970-1979
33	Patrick Roy	1984-1995

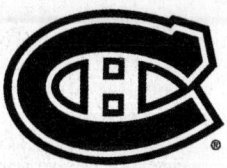

ATLANTIC DIVISION
101st NHL Season

Franchise date: November 26, 1917

Montreal Canadiens

2016-17 Results: 47W-26L-7OTL-2SOL 103PTS
1ST, Atlantic Division • 2ND, Eastern Conference

Year-by-Year Record

Season	GP	Home W	Home L	Home T	Home OL	Road W	Road L	Road T	Road OL	Overall W	Overall L	Overall T	Overall OL	GF	GA	Pts.	Div. Fin.	Conf. Fin.	Playoff Result
2016-17	82	24	12	....	5	23	14	....	4	47	26	....	9	226	200	103	1st, Atl.	2nd, East	Lost First Round
2015-16	82	22	16	....	3	16	22	....	3	38	38	....	6	221	236	82	6th, Atl.	13th, East	– out of playoffs –
2014-15	82	26	9	....	6	24	13	....	4	50	22	....	10	221	189	110	1st, Atl.	2nd, East	Lost Second Round
2013-14	82	23	13	....	5	23	15	....	3	46	28	....	8	215	204	100	3rd, Atl.	4th, East	Lost Conf. Final
2012-13	48	14	7	....	3	15	7	....	2	29	14	....	5	149	126	63	1st, NE	2nd, East	Lost Conf. Quarter-Final
2011-12	82	16	15	....	10	15	20	....	6	31	35	....	16	212	226	78	5th, NE	15th, East	– out of playoffs –
2010-11	82	24	11	....	6	20	19	....	2	44	30	....	8	216	209	96	2nd, NE	6th, East	Lost Conf. Quarter-Final
2009-10	82	20	16	....	5	19	17	....	5	39	33	....	10	217	223	88	4th, NE	8th, East	Lost Conf. Final
2008-09	82	24	10	....	7	17	20	....	4	41	30	....	11	249	247	93	2nd, NE	8th, East	Lost Conf. Quarter-Final
2007-08	82	22	13	....	6	25	12	....	4	47	25	....	10	262	222	104	1st, NE	1st, East	Lost Conf. Semi-Final
2006-07	82	26	12	....	3	16	22	....	3	42	34	....	6	245	256	90	4th, NE	10th, East	– out of playoffs –
2005-06	82	24	13	....	4	18	18	....	5	42	31	....	9	243	247	93	3rd, NE	7th, East	Lost Conf. Quarter-Final
2004-05	....	....	....	....	....	....	....	....	....	....	....	....	....	....	....	....			
2003-04	82	23	13	4	1	18	17	3	3	41	30	7	4	208	192	93	4th, NE	7th, East	Lost Conf. Semi-Final
2002-03	82	16	16	5	4	14	19	3	5	30	35	8	9	206	234	77	4th, NE	10th, East	– out of playoffs –
2001-02	82	21	13	6	1	15	18	6	2	36	31	12	3	207	209	87	4th, NE	8th, East	Lost Conf. Semi-Final
2000-01	82	15	20	4	2	13	20	4	4	28	40	8	6	206	232	70	5th, NE	11th, East	– out of playoffs –
1999-2000	82	18	17	5	1	17	17	4	3	35	34	9	4	196	194	83	4th, NE	10th, East	– out of playoffs –
1998-99	82	21	15	5	....	11	24	6	....	32	39	11	....	184	209	75	5th, NE	11th, East	– out of playoffs –
1997-98	82	15	17	9	....	22	15	4	....	37	32	13	....	235	208	87	4th, NE	7th, East	Lost Conf. Semi-Final
1996-97	82	17	17	7	....	14	19	8	....	31	36	15	....	249	276	77	4th, NE	8th, East	Lost Conf. Quarter-Final
1995-96	82	23	12	6	....	17	20	4	....	40	32	10	....	265	248	90	3rd, NE	6th, East	Lost Conf. Quarter-Final
1994-95	48	15	5	4	....	3	18	3	....	18	23	7	....	125	148	43	6th, NE	11th, East	– out of playoffs –
1993-94	84	26	12	4	....	15	17	10	....	41	29	14	....	283	248	96	3rd, NE	5th, East	Lost Conf. Quarter-Final
1992-93	**84**	**27**	**13**	**2**	....	**21**	**17**	**4**	....	**48**	**30**	**6**	....	**326**	**280**	**102**	**3rd, Adams**		**Won Stanley Cup**
1991-92	80	27	8	5	....	14	20	6	....	41	28	11	....	267	207	93	1st, Adams		Lost Div. Final
1990-91	80	23	12	5	....	16	18	6	....	39	30	11	....	273	249	89	2nd, Adams		Lost Div. Final
1989-90	80	26	8	6	....	15	20	5	....	41	28	11	....	288	234	93	3rd, Adams		Lost Div. Final
1988-89	80	30	6	4	....	23	12	5	....	53	18	9	....	315	218	115	1st, Adams		Lost Final
1987-88	80	26	8	6	....	19	14	7	....	45	22	13	....	298	238	103	1st, Adams		Lost Div. Final
1986-87	80	27	9	4	....	14	20	6	....	41	29	10	....	277	241	92	2nd, Adams		Lost Conf. Final
1985-86	**80**	**25**	**11**	**4**	....	**15**	**22**	**3**	....	**40**	**33**	**7**	....	**330**	**280**	**87**	**2nd, Adams**		**Won Stanley Cup**
1984-85	80	24	10	6	....	17	17	6	....	41	27	12	....	309	262	94	1st, Adams		Lost Div. Final
1983-84	80	19	19	2	....	16	21	3	....	35	40	5	....	286	295	75	4th, Adams		Lost Conf. Final
1982-83	80	25	6	9	....	17	18	5	....	42	24	14	....	350	286	98	2nd, Adams		Lost Div. Semi-Final
1981-82	80	25	6	9	....	21	11	8	....	46	17	17	....	360	223	109	1st, Adams		Lost Div. Semi-Final
1980-81	80	31	7	2	....	14	15	11	....	45	22	13	....	332	232	103	1st, Norris		Lost Prelim. Round
1979-80	80	30	7	3	....	17	13	10	....	47	20	13	....	328	240	107	1st, Norris		Lost Quarter-Final
1978-79	**80**	**29**	**6**	**5**	....	**23**	**11**	**6**	....	**52**	**17**	**11**	....	**337**	**204**	**115**	**1st, Norris**		**Won Stanley Cup**
1977-78	**80**	**32**	**4**	**4**	....	**27**	**6**	**7**	....	**59**	**10**	**11**	....	**359**	**183**	**129**	**1st, Norris**		**Won Stanley Cup**
1976-77	**80**	**33**	**1**	**6**	....	**27**	**7**	**6**	....	**60**	**8**	**12**	....	**387**	**171**	**132**	**1st, Norris**		**Won Stanley Cup**
1975-76	**80**	**32**	**3**	**5**	....	**26**	**8**	**6**	....	**58**	**11**	**11**	....	**337**	**174**	**127**	**1st, Norris**		**Won Stanley Cup**
1974-75	80	27	8	5	....	20	6	14	....	47	14	19	....	374	225	113	1st, Norris		Lost Semi-Final
1973-74	78	24	12	3	....	21	12	6	....	45	24	9	....	293	240	99	2nd, East		Lost Quarter-Final
1972-73	**78**	**29**	**4**	**6**	....	**23**	**6**	**10**	....	**52**	**10**	**16**	....	**329**	**184**	**120**	**1st, East**		**Won Stanley Cup**
1971-72	78	29	3	7	....	17	13	9	....	46	16	16	....	307	205	108	3rd, East		Lost Quarter-Final
1970-71	**78**	**29**	**7**	**3**	....	**13**	**16**	**10**	....	**42**	**23**	**13**	....	**291**	**216**	**97**	**3rd, East**		**Won Stanley Cup**
1969-70	76	21	9	8	....	17	13	8	....	38	22	16	....	244	201	92	5th, East		– out of playoffs –
1968-69	**76**	**26**	**7**	**5**	....	**20**	**12**	**6**	....	**46**	**19**	**11**	....	**271**	**202**	**103**	**1st, East**		**Won Stanley Cup**
1967-68	**74**	**26**	**5**	**6**	....	**16**	**17**	**4**	....	**42**	**22**	**10**	....	**236**	**167**	**94**	**1st, East**		**Won Stanley Cup**
1966-67	70	19	9	7	....	13	16	6	....	32	25	13	....	202	188	77	2nd		Lost Final
1965-66	**70**	**23**	**11**	**1**	....	**18**	**10**	**7**	....	**41**	**21**	**8**	....	**239**	**173**	**90**	**1st**		**Won Stanley Cup**
1964-65	**70**	**20**	**8**	**7**	....	**16**	**15**	**4**	....	**36**	**23**	**11**	....	**211**	**185**	**83**	**2nd**		**Won Stanley Cup**
1963-64	70	22	7	6	....	14	14	7	....	36	21	13	....	209	167	85	1st		Lost Semi-Final
1962-63	70	15	10	10	....	13	9	13	....	28	19	23	....	225	183	79	3rd		Lost Semi-Final
1961-62	70	26	2	7	....	16	12	7	....	42	14	14	....	259	166	98	1st		Lost Semi-Final
1960-61	70	24	6	5	....	17	13	5	....	41	19	10	....	254	188	92	1st		Lost Semi-Final
1959-60	**70**	**23**	**4**	**8**	....	**17**	**14**	**4**	....	**40**	**18**	**12**	....	**255**	**178**	**92**	**1st**		**Won Stanley Cup**
1958-59	**70**	**21**	**8**	**6**	....	**18**	**10**	**7**	....	**39**	**18**	**13**	....	**258**	**158**	**91**	**1st**		**Won Stanley Cup**
1957-58	**70**	**23**	**8**	**4**	....	**20**	**9**	**6**	....	**43**	**17**	**10**	....	**250**	**158**	**96**	**1st**		**Won Stanley Cup**
1956-57	**70**	**23**	**6**	**6**	....	**12**	**17**	**6**	....	**35**	**23**	**12**	....	**210**	**155**	**82**	**2nd**		**Won Stanley Cup**
1955-56	**70**	**29**	**5**	**1**	....	**16**	**10**	**9**	....	**45**	**15**	**10**	....	**222**	**131**	**100**	**1st**		**Won Stanley Cup**
1954-55	70	26	5	4	....	15	13	7	....	41	18	11	....	228	157	93	2nd		Lost Final
1953-54	70	27	5	3	....	8	19	8	....	35	24	11	....	195	141	81	2nd		Lost Final
1952-53	**70**	**18**	**12**	**5**	....	**10**	**11**	**14**	....	**28**	**23**	**19**	....	**155**	**148**	**75**	**2nd**		**Won Stanley Cup**
1951-52	70	22	8	5	....	12	18	5	....	34	26	10	....	195	164	78	2nd		Lost Final
1950-51	70	17	10	8	....	8	20	7	....	25	30	15	....	173	184	65	3rd		Lost Final
1949-50	70	17	8	10	....	12	14	9	....	29	22	19	....	172	150	77	2nd		Lost Semi-Final
1948-49	60	19	8	3	....	9	15	6	....	28	23	9	....	152	126	65	3rd		Lost Semi-Final
1947-48	60	13	13	4	....	7	16	7	....	20	29	11	....	147	169	51	5th		– out of playoffs –
1946-47	60	19	6	5	....	15	10	5	....	34	16	10	....	189	138	78	1st		Lost Final
1945-46	**50**	**16**	**6**	**3**	....	**12**	**11**	**2**	....	**28**	**17**	**5**	....	**172**	**134**	**61**	**1st**		**Won Stanley Cup**
1944-45	50	21	2	2	....	17	6	2	....	38	8	4	....	228	121	80	1st		Lost Semi-Final
1943-44	**50**	**22**	**0**	**3**	....	**16**	**5**	**4**	....	**38**	**5**	**7**	....	**234**	**109**	**83**	**1st**		**Won Stanley Cup**
1942-43	50	14	4	7	....	5	15	5	....	19	19	12	....	181	191	50	4th		Lost Semi-Final
1941-42	48	12	10	2	....	6	17	1	....	18	27	3	....	134	173	39	6th		Lost Quarter-Final
1940-41	48	11	9	4	....	5	17	2	....	16	26	6	....	121	147	38	6th		Lost Quarter-Final
1939-40	48	5	14	5	....	5	19	0	....	10	33	5	....	90	167	25	7th		– out of playoffs –
1938-39	48	8	11	5	....	7	13	4	....	15	24	9	....	115	146	39	6th		Lost Quarter-Final
1937-38	48	13	4	7	....	5	13	6	....	18	17	13	....	123	128	49	3rd, Cdn.		Lost Quarter-Final
1936-37	48	16	8	0	....	8	10	6	....	24	18	6	....	115	111	54	1st, Cdn.		Lost Semi-Final
1935-36	48	5	11	8	....	6	15	3	....	11	26	11	....	82	123	33	4th, Cdn.		– out of playoffs –
1934-35	48	11	11	2	....	8	12	4	....	19	23	6	....	110	145	44	3rd, Cdn.		Lost Quarter-Final
1933-34	48	16	6	2	....	6	14	4	....	22	20	6	....	99	101	50	2nd, Cdn.		Lost Quarter-Final
1932-33	48	15	5	4	....	3	20	1	....	18	25	5	....	92	115	41	3rd, Cdn.		Lost Quarter-Final
1931-32	48	18	3	3	....	7	13	4	....	25	16	7	....	128	111	57	1st, Cdn.		Lost Semi-Final
1930-31	**44**	**15**	**3**	**4**	....	**11**	**7**	**4**	....	**26**	**10**	**8**	....	**129**	**89**	**60**	**1st, Cdn.**		**Won Stanley Cup**
1929-30	**44**	**13**	**5**	**4**	....	**8**	**9**	**5**	....	**21**	**14**	**9**	....	**142**	**114**	**51**	**2nd, Cdn.**		**Won Stanley Cup**
1928-29	44	12	4	6	....	10	3	9	....	22	7	15	....	71	43	59	1st, Cdn.		Lost Semi-Final
1927-28	44	12	7	3	....	14	4	4	....	26	11	7	....	116	48	59	1st, Cdn.		Lost Semi-Final
1926-27	44	15	5	2	....	13	9	0	....	28	14	2	....	99	67	58	2nd, Cdn.		Lost Semi-Final
1925-26	36	5	12	1	....	6	12	0	....	11	24	1	....	79	108	23	7th		– out of playoffs –
1924-25	30	10	5	0	....	7	6	2	....	17	11	2	....	93	56	36	3rd		Lost Final
1923-24	**24**	**10**	**2**	**0**	....	**3**	**9**	**0**	....	**13**	**11**	**0**	....	**59**	**48**	**26**	**2nd**		**Won Stanley Cup**
1922-23	24	10	2	0	....	3	7	2	....	13	9	2	....	73	61	28	2nd		Lost NHL Final
1921-22	24	8	3	1	....	4	8	0	....	12	11	1	....	88	94	25	3rd		– out of playoffs –
1920-21	24	9	3	0	....	4	8	0	....	13	11	0	....	112	99	26	3rd and 2nd*		– out of playoffs –
1919-20	24	8	4	0	....	5	7	0	....	13	11	0	....	129	113	26	2nd and 3rd*		– out of playoffs –
1918-19	18	7	2	0	....	3	6	0	....	10	8	0	....	88	78	20	1st and 2nd*		Cup Final/No Decision
1917-18	22	8	3	0	....	5	6	0	....	13	9	0	....	115	84	26	1st and 3rd*		Lost NHL Final

* Season played in two halves with no combined standing at end.
From 1917-18 through 1925-26, NHL champions played against PCHA/WCHL champions for Stanley Cup.

2017-18 Player Personnel

FORWARDS	HT	WT	*Age	Birthplace	S	2016-17 Club
BYRON, Paul	5-9	160	28	Ottawa, ON	L	Montreal
DANAULT, Phillip	6-0	193	24	Victoriaville, QC	L	Montreal
DROUIN, Jonathan	5-11	188	22	Ste-Agathe, QC	L	Tampa Bay
FROESE, Byron	6-0	201	26	Winkler, MB	R	Tor-Tor(AHL)-T.B.-Syr
GALCHENYUK, Alex	6-1	210	23	Milwaukee, WI	L	Montreal
GALLAGHER, Brendan	5-9	182	25	Edmonton, AB	R	Montreal
HEMSKY, Ales	6-0	185	34	Pardubice, Czech.	R	Dallas
HOLLAND, Peter	6-2	201	26	Toronto, ON	L	Toronto-Arizona
LEHKONEN, Artturi	6-0	182	22	Piikkio, Finland	L	Montreal
MARTINSEN, Andreas	6-3	220	27	Baerum, Norway	L	Colorado-Montreal
MITCHELL, Torrey	5-11	190	32	Greenfield Park, QC	R	Montreal
PACIORETTY, Max	6-2	215	28	New Canaan, CT	L	Montreal
PLEKANEC, Tomas	5-11	196	34	Kladno, Czech.	L	Montreal
SHAW, Andrew	5-11	179	26	Belleville, ON	R	Montreal
DEFENSEMEN						
ALZNER, Karl	6-3	219	29	Burnaby, BC	L	Washington
BENN, Jordie	6-2	200	30	Victoria, BC	L	Dallas-Montreal
DAVIDSON, Brandon	6-2	210	26	Lethbridge, AB	L	Edmonton-Montreal
MORROW, Joe	6-0	199	24	Edmonton, AB	L	Boston-Providence (AHL)
PETRY, Jeff	6-3	204	29	Ann Arbor, MI	R	Montreal
SCHLEMKO, David	6-0	190	30	Edmonton, AB	L	San Jose
STREIT, Mark	5-11	191	39	Bern, Switz.	L	Philadelphia-Pittsburgh
WEBER, Shea	6-4	232	32	Sicamous, BC	R	Montreal
GOALTENDERS	**HT**	**WT**	***Age**	**Birthplace**	**C**	**2016-17 Club**
MONTOYA, Al	6-2	209	32	Chicago, IL	L	Montreal
PRICE, Carey	6-3	226	30	Anahim Lake, BC	L	Montreal

* – Age at start of 2017-18 season

Captains' History

Jack Laviolette, 1909-10; Newsy Lalonde, 1910-11; Jack Laviolette, 1911-12; Newsy Lalonde, 1912-13; Jimmy Gardner, 1913-14, 1914-15; Howard McNamara, 1915-16; Newsy Lalonde, 1916-17 to 1921-22; Sprague Cleghorn, 1922-23 to 1924-25; Bill Coutu, 1925-26; Sylvio Mantha, 1926-27 to 1931-32; George Hainsworth, 1932-33; Sylvio Mantha, 1933-34 to 1935-36; Babe Siebert, 1936-37 to 1938-39; Walt Buswell, 1939-40; Toe Blake, 1940-41 to 1946-47; Toe Blake and Bill Durnan, 1947-48; Butch Bouchard, 1948-49 to 1955-56; Maurice Richard, 1956-57 to 1959-60; Doug Harvey, 1960-61; Jean Béliveau, 1961-62 to 1970-71; Henri Richard, 1971-72 to 1974-75; Yvan Cournoyer, 1975-76 to 1977-78; Yvan Cournoyer and Serge Savard (interim), 1978-79; Serge Savard, 1979-80, 1980-81; Bob Gainey, 1981-82 to 1988-89; Guy Carbonneau and Chris Chelios, 1989-90; Guy Carbonneau, 1990-91 to 1993-94; Kirk Muller and Mike Keane, 1994-95; Mike Keane and Pierre Turgeon, 1995-96; Pierre Turgeon and Vincent Damphousse, 1996-97; Vincent Damphousse, 1997-98, 1998-99; Saku Koivu, 1999-2000 to 2008-09; no captain, 2009-10; Brian Gionta, 2010-11 to 2013-14; no captain, 2014-15; Max Pacioretty, 2015-16 to date.

Coaching History

Jack Laviolette, 1909-10; Adolphe Lecours, 1910-11; Napoleon Dorval, 1911-12, 1912-13; Jimmy Gardner, 1913-14, 1914-15; Newsy Lalonde, 1915-16 to 1920-21; Newsy Lalonde and Léo Dandurand, 1921-22; Léo Dandurand, 1922-23 to 1925-26; Cecil Hart, 1926-27 to 1931-32; Newsy Lalonde, 1932-33, 1933-34; Newsy Lalonde and Léo Dandurand, 1934-35; Sylvio Mantha, 1935-36; Cecil Hart, 1936-37, 1937-38; Cecil Hart and Jules Dugal, 1938-39; Babe Siebert, 1939*; Pit Lepine, 1939-40; Dick Irvin 1940-41 to 1954-55; Toe Blake, 1955-56 to 1967-68; Claude Ruel, 1968-69, 1969-70; Claude Ruel and Al MacNeil, 1970-71; Scotty Bowman, 1971-72 to 1978-79; Bernie Geoffrion and Claude Ruel, 1979-80; Claude Ruel, 1980-81; Bob Berry, 1981-82, 1982-83; Bob Berry and Jacques Lemaire, 1983-84; Jacques Lemaire, 1984-85; Jean Perron, 1985-86 to 1987-88; Pat Burns, 1988-89 to 1991-92; Jacques Demers, 1992-93 to 1994-95; Jacques Demers, Jacques Laperriere, Mario Tremblay, 1995-96; Mario Tremblay, 1996-97; Alain Vigneault, 1997-98 to 1999-2000; Alain Vigneault and Michel Therrien, 2000-01; Michel Therrien, 2001-02; Michel Therrien and Claude Julien, 2002-03; Claude Julien, 2003-04, 2004-05; Claude Julien and Bob Gainey, 2005-06; Guy Carbonneau, 2006-07, 2007-08; Guy Carbonneau and Bob Gainey, 2008-09; Jacques Martin, 2009-10, 2010-11; Jacques Martin and Randy Cunneyworth, 2011-12; Michel Therrien, 2012-13 to 2015-16; Michel Therrien and Claude Julien, 2016-17; Claude Julien, 2017-18.

* Named coach in summer but died before 1939-40 season began.

Marc Bergevin

Executive Vice President and General Manager

Born: Montreal, QC, August 11, 1965.

The Montreal Canadiens announced the appointment of Marc Bergevin as executive vice president and general manager on May 2, 2012. Bergevin became the 17th general manager in Canadiens history after having spent the previous seven seasons with the Chicago Blackhawks where he was the assistant general manager under Stan Bowman in 2011-12. After finishing 15th in the Eastern Conference in 2011-12, the Canadiens won a division title in 2012-13 and Bergevin finished third in voting as NHL General Manager of the Year. He finished second in voting in 2013-14 after the Canadiens posted a 100-point season and reached the Eastern Conference Final. Montreal has won division titles again in 2014-15 and 2016-17.

Bergevin held various positions within the Blackhawks organization, including director of player personnel for two seasons (2009 to 2011), and won the Stanley Cup in 2009-10. He served as an assistant coach on Joel Quenneville's staff during the 2008-09 campaign and also spent three years on the Blackhawks scouting staff (2005 to 2008), including one season as director of professional scouting (2007-08).

Originally selected by the Blackhawks in the third round (59th overall) in the 1983 NHL Draft, Bergevin enjoyed a 20-season career as a defenseman in the National Hockey League, collecting 181 points (36 goals, 145 assists) in 1,191 regular season games with Chicago, the New York Islanders, Hartford Whalers, Tampa Bay Lightning, Detroit Red Wings, St. Louis Blues, Pittsburgh Penguins and Vancouver Canucks. Bergevin also skated in 80 playoff contests, reaching the Conference Finals in 1996 (Detroit) and in 2001 (Pittsburgh). He played his junior hockey in the Quebec Major Junior Hockey League with the Chicoutimi Sagueneens, from 1982 to 1984.

2016-17 Scoring

* – rookie

Regular Season

Pos	#	Player	Team	GP	G	A	Pts	TOI	+/–	PIM	PP	SH	GW	S	S%
L	67	Max Pacioretty	MTL	81	35	32	67	19:10	15	38	8	1	7	268	13.1
R	47	Alexander Radulov	MTL	76	18	36	54	18:17	10	62	6	0	2	147	12.2
C	27	Alex Galchenyuk	MTL	61	17	27	44	15:55	–5	24	6	0	6	104	16.3
L	41	Paul Byron	MTL	81	22	21	43	15:04	21	29	0	1	6	96	22.9
D	6	Shea Weber	MTL	78	17	25	42	25:03	20	38	12	0	4	183	9.3
L	24	Phillip Danault	MTL	82	13	27	40	15:34	5	35	0	0	3	133	9.8
D	79	Andrei Markov	MTL	62	6	30	36	21:50	18	16	1	0	1	98	6.1
C	65	Andrew Shaw	MTL	68	12	17	29	15:12	4	110	1	0	1	127	9.4
R	11	Brendan Gallagher	MTL	64	10	19	29	15:05	7	39	1	0	2	187	5.3
L	62 *	Artturi Lehkonen	MTL	73	18	10	28	13:51	–1	8	2	1	3	158	11.4
C	14	Tomas Plekanec	MTL	78	10	18	28	16:49	10	24	3	2	3	139	7.2
D	26	Jeff Petry	MTL	80	8	20	28	22:06	3	22	2	0	1	172	4.7
D	28	Nathan Beaulieu	MTL	74	4	24	28	19:28	8	44	2	0	1	118	3.4
C	17	Torrey Mitchell	MTL	78	8	9	17	12:36	5	38	0	0	1	68	11.8
D	89	Nikita Nesterov	T.B.	35	3	9	12	16:35	–3	20	1	0	0	46	6.5
			MTL	13	1	4	5	15:28	3	4	0	0	0	17	5.9
			Total	48	4	13	17	16:17	0	24	1	0	0	63	6.3
D	8	Jordie Benn	DAL	58	2	13	15	18:36	–3	24	0	0	0	59	3.4
			MTL	13	2	0	2	16:50	–1	4	0	0	1	9	22.2
			Total	71	4	13	17	18:17	–4	28	0	0	1	68	5.9
L	21	Dwight King	L.A.	63	8	7	15	14:59	0	10	0	0	1	89	9.0
			MTL	17	1	0	1	12:14	–2	2	0	0	0	21	4.8
			Total	80	9	7	16	14:24	–2	12	0	0	1	110	8.2
C	32	Brian Flynn	MTL	51	6	4	10	12:03	2	4	0	0	0	47	12.8
D	74	Alexei Emelin	MTL	76	2	8	10	21:19	1	71	0	0	0	82	2.4
L	43 *	Daniel Carr	MTL	33	2	7	9	10:15	4	6	0	0	1	44	4.5
C	92	Steve Ott	DET	42	3	3	6	10:27	–6	63	0	0	0	33	9.1
			MTL	11	0	1	1	11:55	–2	17	0	0	0	12	0.0
			Total	53	3	4	7	10:45	–8	80	0	0	0	45	6.7
L	37	Andreas Martinsen	COL	55	3	4	7	9:38	–10	32	0	0	0	59	5.1
			MTL	9	0	0	0	11:54	–4	0	0	0	0	14	0.0
			Total	64	3	4	7	9:57	–14	32	0	0	0	73	4.1
R	34 *	Michael McCarron	MTL	31	1	4	5	9:53	–4	41	0	0	0	31	3.2
D	20	Zach Redmond	MTL	16	0	5	5	12:18	6	2	0	0	0	12	0.0
L	15	Chris Terry	MTL	14	2	2	4	9:53	–1	4	0	0	0	15	13.3
D	88	Brandon Davidson	EDM	28	0	1	1	15:23	1	16	0	0	0	29	0.0
			MTL	10	0	2	2	16:37	–3	4	0	0	0	13	0.0
			Total	38	0	3	3	15:43	–2	20	0	0	0	42	0.0
L	54 *	Charles Hudon	MTL	3	0	2	2	11:55	1	2	0	0	0	3	0.0
R	38 *	Nikita Scherbak	MTL	3	1	0	1	11:22	1	0	1	0	0	3	33.3
D	36 *	Brett Lernout	MTL	2	0	0	0	18:59	–1	0	0	0	0	3	0.0
R	44	Bobby Farnham	MTL	3	0	0	0	8:16	0	17	0	0	0	4	0.0
D	22 *	Mikhail Sergachev	MTL	4	0	0	0	12:07	1	0	0	0	0	2	0.0
D	71 *	Joel Hanley	MTL	7	0	0	0	10:09	–3	4	0	0	0	5	0.0
D	89 *	Ryan Johnston	MTL	7	0	0	0	9:52	–3	4	0	0	0	3	0.0
L	25	Jacob de La Rose	MTL	9	0	0	0	10:54	–3	4	0	0	0	4	0.0

Goaltending

No.	Goaltender	GPI	Mins	Avg	W	L	OT	EN	SO	GA	SA	Sv%	G	A	PIM
40	* Charlie Lindgren	2	122	1.48	2	0	0	0	0	3	59	.949	0	0	0
31	Carey Price	62	3708	2.23	37	20	5	6	3	138	1794	.923	0	1	4
35	Al Montoya	19	1125	2.67	8	6	4	1	2	50	569	.912	0	2	2
	Totals	**82**	**4987**	**2.38**	**47**	**26**	**9**	**7**	**5**	**198**	**2429**	**.918**			

Playoffs

Pos	#	Player	Team	GP	G	A	Pts	TOI	+/–	PIM	PP	SH	GW	OT	S	S%
R	47	Alexander Radulov	MTL	6	2	5	7	19:54	0	6	0	0	1	1	9	22.2
L	62 *	Artturi Lehkonen	MTL	6	2	2	4	15:32	–1	2	1	0	0	0	19	10.5
C	14	Tomas Plekanec	MTL	6	1	2	3	18:31	–4	0	0	0	0	0	15	6.7
D	6	Shea Weber	MTL	6	1	2	3	27:58	1	5	1	0	1	0	15	6.7
R	11	Brendan Gallagher	MTL	6	1	2	3	17:21	–3	8	1	0	0	0	19	5.3
C	27	Alex Galchenyuk	MTL	6	0	3	3	16:35	0	4	0	0	0	0	13	0.0
L	24	Phillip Danault	MTL	6	0	2	2	16:38	1	2	0	0	0	0	10	0.0
D	74	Alexei Emelin	MTL	2	1	0	1	17:54	1	2	0	0	0	0	2	50.0
C	17	Torrey Mitchell	MTL	3	1	0	1	11:32	1	0	0	0	0	0	4	25.0
D	26	Jeff Petry	MTL	6	1	0	1	24:44	–3	2	0	0	0	0	12	8.3
L	41	Paul Byron	MTL	6	1	0	1	16:47	–3	0	0	0	0	0	8	12.5
D	28	Nathan Beaulieu	MTL	5	0	1	1	17:32	–3	0	0	0	0	0	5	0.0
D	79	Andrei Markov	MTL	6	0	1	1	26:09	–1	10	0	0	0	0	8	0.0
L	67	Max Pacioretty	MTL	6	0	1	1	20:44	–2	7	0	0	0	0	28	0.0
C	32	Brian Flynn	MTL	1	0	0	0	15:33	0	0	0	0	0	0	2	0.0
R	34 *	Michael McCarron	MTL	1	0	0	0	6:54	–1	0	0	0	0	0	0	0.0
D	89	Nikita Nesterov	MTL	2	0	0	0	14:28	–1	0	0	0	0	0	1	0.0
L	37	Andreas Martinsen	MTL	2	0	0	0	10:12	–1	0	0	0	0	0	3	0.0
D	88	Brandon Davidson	MTL	3	0	0	0	12:46	–1	0	0	0	0	0	2	0.0
C	65	Andrew Shaw	MTL	5	0	0	0	15:01	–2	7	0	0	0	0	13	0.0
C	92	Steve Ott	MTL	6	0	0	0	12:22	0	0	0	0	0	0	3	0.0
L	21	Dwight King	MTL	6	0	0	0	12:32	–1	0	0	0	0	0	6	0.0
D	8	Jordie Benn	MTL	6	0	0	0	20:20	–3	6	0	0	0	0	9	0.0

Goaltending

No.	Goaltender	GPI	Mins	Avg	W	L	EN	SO	GA	SA	Sv%	G	A	PIM
31	Carey Price	6	387	1.86	2	4	2	0	12	179	.933	0	0	0
	Totals	**6**	**393**	**2.14**	**2**	**4**	**2**	**0**	**14**	**181**	**.923**			

General Managers' History

Jack Laviolette and Joseph Cattarinich, 1909-10; George Kennedy, 1910-11 to 1920-21; Leo Dandurand, 1921-22 to 1934-35; Ernest Savard, 1935-36; Cecil Hart, 1936-37, 1937-38; Cecil Hart and Jules Dugal, 1938-39; Jules Dugal, 1939-40; Tom P. Gorman, 1940-41 to 1945-46; Frank J. Selke, 1946-47 to 1963-64; Sam Pollock, 1964-65 to 1977-78; Irving Grundman, 1978-79 to 1982-83; Serge Savard, 1983-84 to 1994-95; Serge Savard and Réjean Houle, 1995-96; Réjean Houle, 1996-97 to 1999-2000; Réjean Houle and Andre Savard, 2000-01; Andre Savard, 2001-02, 2002-03; Bob Gainey, 2003-04 to 2008-09; Bob Gainey and Pierre Gauthier, 2009-10; Pierre Gauthier, 2010-11, 2011-12; Marc Bergevin, 2012-13 to date.

Club Records

Team

(Figures in brackets for season records are games played; records for fewest points, wins, ties, losses, goals, goals against are for 70 or more games)

Most Points	***132**	1976-77 (80)
Most Wins	**60**	1976-77 (80)
Most Ties	**23**	1962-63 (70)
Most Losses	**40**	1983-84 (80), 2000-01 (82)
Most Goals	**387**	1976-77 (80)
Most Goals Against	**295**	1983-84 (80)
Fewest Points	**65**	1950-51 (70)
Fewest Wins	**25**	1950-51 (70)
Fewest Ties	**5**	1983-84 (80)
Fewest Losses	***8**	1976-77 (80)
Fewest Goals	**155**	1952-53 (70)
Fewest Goals Against	***131**	1955-56 (70)
Longest Winning Streak		
Overall	**12**	Jan. 6-Feb. 3/68
Home	**13**	Nov. 2/43-Jan. 8/44, Jan. 30-Mar. 26/77
Away	**8**	Dec. 18/77-Jan. 18/78, Jan. 21-Feb. 21/82
Longest Team Point Streak		
Overall	**28**	Dec. 18/77-Feb. 23/78 (23W, 5T)
Home	***34**	Nov. 1/76-Apr. 2/77 (28W, 6T)
Away	***23**	Nov. 27/74-Mar. 12/75 (14W, 9T)
Longest Losing Streak		
Overall	**12**	Feb. 13-Mar. 13/26
Home	**7**	Dec. 16/39-Jan. 18/40, Oct. 28-Nov. 25/00
Away	**10**	Jan. 16-Mar. 13/26
Longest Winless Streak		
Overall	**12**	Feb. 13-Mar. 13/26 (12L), Nov. 28-Dec. 29/35 (8L, 4T)
Home	**15**	Dec. 16/39-Mar. 7/40 (12L, 3T)
Away	**12**	Nov. 26/33-Jan. 28/34 (8L, 4T), Oct. 20-Dec. 13/51 (8L, 4T)
Most Shutouts, Season	***22**	1928-29 (44)
Most PIM, Season	**1,847**	1995-96 (82)
Most Goals, Game	***16**	Mar. 3/20 (Mtl. 16 at Que. 3)

Individual

Most Seasons	**20**	Henri Richard, Jean Béliveau
Most Games	**1,256**	Henri Richard
Most Goals, Career	**544**	Maurice Richard
Most Assists, Career	**728**	Guy Lafleur
Most Points, Career	**1,246**	Guy Lafleur (518G, 728A)
Most PIM, Career	**2,248**	Chris Nilan
Most Shutouts, Career	**75**	George Hainsworth
Longest Consecutive Games Streak	**560**	Doug Jarvis (Oct. 8/75-Apr. 4/82)
Most Goals, Season	**60**	Steve Shutt (1976-77), Guy Lafleur (1977-78)
Most Assists, Season	**82**	Pete Mahovlich (1974-75)
Most Points, Season	**136**	Guy Lafleur (1976-77; 56G, 80A)
Most PIM, Season	**358**	Chris Nilan (1984-85)
Most Points, Defenseman, Season	**85**	Larry Robinson (1976-77; 19G, 66A)
Most Points, Center, Season	**117**	Pete Mahovlich (1974-75; 35G, 82A)
Most Points, Right Wing, Season	**136**	Guy Lafleur (1976-77; 56G, 80A)
Most Points, Left Wing, Season	**110**	Mats Naslund (1985-86; 43G, 67A)
Most Points, Rookie, Season	**71**	Mats Naslund (1982-83; 26G, 45A), Kjell Dahlin (1985-86; 32G, 39A)
Most Shutouts, Season	***22**	George Hainsworth (1928-29)
Most Goals, Game	**6**	Newsy Lalonde (Jan. 10/20)
Most Assists, Game	**6**	Elmer Lach (Feb. 6/43)
Most Points, Game	**8**	Maurice Richard (Dec. 28/44; 5G, 3A), Bert Olmstead (Jan. 9/54; 4G, 4A)

* NHL Record.

All-time Record vs. Other Clubs

Regular Season

	Total								At Home								On Road							
	GP	W	L	T	OL	GF	GA	PTS	GP	W	L	T	OL	GF	GA	PTS	GP	W	L	T	OL	GF	GA	PTS
Anaheim	30	14	12	2	2	89	87	32	15	7	5	2	1	48	41	17	15	7	7	0	1	41	46	15
Arizona	72	47	16	9	0	300	195	103	36	29	5	2	0	166	80	60	36	18	11	7	0	134	115	43
Boston	738	360	267	103	8	2233	1944	831	369	213	105	47	4	1229	868	477	369	147	162	56	4	1004	1076	354
Buffalo	275	118	110	31	16	840	805	283	138	72	45	12	9	477	392	165	137	46	65	19	7	363	413	118
Calgary	113	59	38	15	1	373	316	134	55	31	16	8	0	188	137	70	58	28	22	7	1	185	179	64
Carolina	196	108	62	20	6	701	555	242	97	62	26	7	2	368	268	133	99	46	36	13	4	333	287	109
Chicago	563	303	156	103	1	1856	1426	710	283	178	57	48	0	1082	670	404	280	125	99	55	1	774	756	306
Colorado	141	70	53	15	3	532	461	158	71	42	17	10	2	296	224	96	70	28	36	5	1	236	237	62
Columbus	23	11	8	1	3	51	61	26	13	6	4	1	2	28	28	15	10	5	4	0	1	23	33	11
Dallas	131	76	34	21	0	494	339	173	65	43	13	9	0	272	159	95	66	33	21	12	0	222	180	78
Detroit	585	282	203	96	4	1774	1492	664	293	179	68	43	3	1030	660	404	292	103	135	53	1	744	832	260
Edmonton	83	40	33	4	6	269	269	90	39	20	11	4	4	132	121	48	44	20	22	0	2	137	148	42
Florida	91	43	37	6	5	238	225	97	44	20	16	3	5	112	102	48	47	23	21	3	0	126	123	49
Los Angeles	143	91	31	20	1	588	395	203	71	50	10	11	0	310	178	111	72	41	21	9	1	278	217	92
Minnesota	19	8	9	1	1	56	55	18	10	5	4	1	0	32	28	11	9	3	5	0	1	24	27	7
Nashville	22	12	6	1	3	52	59	28	11	7	2	0	2	28	25	16	11	5	4	1	1	24	34	12
New Jersey	151	76	60	10	5	475	412	167	75	40	26	6	3	227	190	89	76	36	34	4	2	248	222	78
NY Islanders	163	88	52	15	8	523	458	199	81	49	18	9	5	286	220	112	82	39	34	6	3	237	238	87
NY Rangers	623	335	191	94	3	2095	1609	767	312	206	65	40	1	1199	716	453	311	129	126	54	2	896	893	314
Ottawa	134	66	52	5	11	387	391	148	68	37	23	4	4	203	186	82	66	29	29	1	7	184	205	66
Philadelphia	190	87	71	30	2	602	566	206	96	50	31	14	1	329	280	115	94	37	40	16	1	273	286	91
Pittsburgh	207	120	56	23	8	799	588	271	103	70	20	10	3	443	272	153	104	50	36	13	5	356	316	118
St. Louis	130	74	29	22	5	486	350	175	66	43	13	7	3	272	180	96	64	31	16	15	2	214	170	79
San Jose	36	15	15	4	2	93	96	36	18	11	5	2	0	53	34	24	18	4	10	2	2	40	62	12
Tampa Bay	93	46	35	6	6	252	232	104	46	24	16	1	5	128	112	54	47	22	19	5	1	124	120	50
Toronto	736	355	285	88	8	2254	2033	806	368	218	102	43	5	1273	922	484	368	137	183	45	3	981	1111	322
Vancouver	126	82	28	13	3	493	327	180	62	45	11	5	1	270	151	96	64	37	17	8	2	223	176	84
Washington	162	76	61	17	8	509	419	177	82	42	28	8	4	280	198	96	80	34	33	9	4	229	221	81
Winnipeg	59	37	15	2	5	182	131	81	30	21	6	0	3	103	66	45	29	16	9	2	2	79	65	36
Defunct Clubs	461	246	155	60	0	1365	1075	552	231	148	58	25	0	779	469	321	230	98	97	35	0	586	606	231
Totals	**6496**	**3345**	**2180**	**837**	**134**	**20961**	**17371**	**7661**	**3248**	**1968**	**826**	**382**	**72**	**11643**	**7977**	**4390**	**3248**	**1377**	**1354**	**455**	**62**	**9318**	**9394**	**3271**

Playoffs

	Series	W	L	GP	W	L	T	GF	GA	Last Mtg.	Rnd.	Result
Boston	34	25	9	177	106	71	0	531	436	2014	SR	W 4-3
Buffalo	7	4	3	35	18	17	0	124	111	1998	CSF	L 0-4
Calgary	2	1	1	11	6	5	0	31	32	1989	F	L 2-4
Carolina	7	5	2	39	23	16	0	125	106	2006	CQF	L 2-4
Chicago	17	12	5	81	50	29	2	261	185	1976	QF	W 4-0
Colorado	5	3	2	31	17	14	0	105	85	1993	DSF	W 4-2
Dallas	2	1	1	13	7	6	0	48	37	1980	QF	L 3-4
Detroit	12	5	7	62	33	29	0	161	149	1978	QF	W 4-1
Edmonton	1	0	1	3	0	3	0	6	15	1981	PR	L 0-3
Los Angeles	1	1	0	5	4	1	0	15	12	1993	F	W 4-1
New Jersey	1	0	1	5	1	4	0	11	22	1997	CQF	L 1-4
NY Islanders	4	3	1	22	14	8	0	64	55	1993	CF	W 4-1
NY Rangers	16	7	9	73	38	33	2	214	192	2017	FR	L 2-4
Ottawa	2	1	1	11	5	6	0	21	32	2015	FR	W 4-2
Philadelphia	6	3	3	31	16	15	0	93	89	2010	CF	L 1-4
Pittsburgh	2	2	0	13	8	5	0	37	33	2010	CSF	W 4-3
St. Louis	3	3	0	12	12	0	0	42	14	1977	QF	W 4-0
Tampa Bay	3	1	2	14	6	8	0	34	41	2015	SR	L 2-4
Toronto	15	8	7	71	42	29	0	215	160	1979	QF	W 4-0
Vancouver	1	1	0	5	4	1	0	20	9	1975	QF	W 4-1
Washington	1	1	0	7	4	3	0	20	22	2010	CQF	W 4-3
Defunct Clubs	10*	5	4	28	15	9	4	70	71			
Totals	**152***	**92**	**59**	**749**	**429**	**312**	**8**	**2248**	**1908**			

* 1919 Final incomplete due to influenza epidemic.

Playoff Results 2017-2013

Year	Round	Opponent	Result	GF	GA
2017	FR	NY Rangers	L 2-4	11	14
2015	SR	Tampa Bay	L 2-4	13	17
	FR	Ottawa	W 4-2	12	12
2014	CF	NY Rangers	L 2-4	15	20
	SR	Boston	W 4-3	20	16
	FR	Tampa Bay	W 4-0	16	10
2013	CQF	Ottawa	L 1-4	9	20

Abbreviations: Round: F – Final; **CF** – conference final; **CSF** – conference semi-final; **SR** – second round; **CQF** – conference quarter-final; **FR** – first round; **DSF** – division semi-final; **QF** – quarter-final; **PR** – preliminary round.

Calgary totals include Atlanta Flames, 1972-73 to 1979-80.
Colorado totals include Quebec, 1979-80 to 1994-95.
New Jersey totals include Kansas City, 1974-75, 1975-76, and Colorado Rockies, 1976-77 to 1981-82.
Phoenix totals include Winnipeg, 1979-80 to 1995-96.
Carolina totals include Hartford, 1979-80 to 1996-97.
Dallas totals include Minnesota North Stars, 1967-68 to 1992-93.
Winnipeg totals include Atlanta Thrashers, 1999-2000 to 2010-11.

2016-17 Results

Month	Day	Opponent	Score	Month	Day	Opponent	Score
Oct.	13	at Buffalo	4-1		11	at Winnipeg	7-4
	15	at Ottawa	3-4†		12	at Minnesota	1-7
	18	Pittsburgh	4-0		14	NY Rangers	5-4
	20	Arizona	5-2		16	at Detroit	0-1
	22	at Boston	4-2		18	Pittsburgh	1-4
	24	Philadelphia	3-1		20	at New Jersey	3-1
	26	at NY Islanders	3-2		21	Buffalo	2-3*
	27	Tampa Bay	3-1		24	Calgary	5-1
	29	Toronto	2-1		26	at NY Islanders	1-3
Nov.	2	Vancouver	3-0		31	Buffalo	5-2
	4	at Columbus	0-10	Feb.	2	at Philadelphia	1-3
	5	Philadelphia	5-4		4	Washington	2-3
	8	Boston	3-2		5	Edmonton	0-1†
	10	Los Angeles	4-1		7	at Colorado	0-4
	12	Detroit	5-0		9	at Arizona	5-4*
	13	at Chicago	2-3		11	St. Louis	2-4
	15	Florida	3-4*		12	at Boston	0-4
	18	at Carolina	2-3		18	Winnipeg	1-3
	19	Toronto	2-1		21	at NY Rangers	3-2†
	22	Ottawa	3-4		23	NY Islanders	0-3
	24	Carolina	2-1		25	at Toronto	3-2*
	26	at Detroit	2-1*		27	at New Jersey	4-3*
	29	at Anaheim	1-2		28	Columbus	1-0*
Dec.	2	at San Jose	1-2	Mar.	2	Nashville	2-1
	4	at Los Angeles	5-4†		4	at NY Rangers	4-1
	6	at St. Louis	2-3*		7	at Vancouver	2-1*
	8	New Jersey	5-2		9	at Calgary	0-5
	10	Colorado	10-1		12	at Edmonton	4-1
	12	Boston	1-2*		14	Chicago	2-4
	16	San Jose	2-4		18	at Ottawa	4-3†
	17	at Washington	2-1		19	Ottawa	4-1
	20	Anaheim	5-1		21	Detroit	1-2*
	22	Minnesota	2-4		23	Carolina	1-4
	23	at Columbus	1-2		25	Ottawa	3-1
	28	at Tampa Bay	3-4*		28	Dallas	4-1
	29	at Florida	3-2*		30	Florida	6-2
	31	at Pittsburgh	3-4*	Apr.	1	at Tampa Bay	2-1*
Jan.	3	at Nashville	2-1*		3	at Florida	4-1
	4	at Dallas	4-3*		5	at Buffalo	1-2
	7	at Toronto	5-3		7	Tampa Bay	2-4
	9	Washington	1-4		8	at Detroit	3-2*

* – Overtime † – Shootout

NHL Draft Selections 2017-2003

Name in bold denotes played in NHL.

2017

Pick	
25	Ryan Poehling
56	Josh Brook
58	Joni Ikonen
68	Scott Walford
87	Cale Fleury
149	Jarret Tyszka
199	Cayden Primeau

2016

Pick	
9	**Mikhail Sergachev**
70	Will Bitten
100	Victor Mete
124	Casey Staum
160	Michael Pezzetta
187	Arvid Henrikson

2015

Pick	
26	Noah Juulsen
87	Lukas Vejdemo
131	Matthew Bradley
177	Simon Bourque
207	Jeremiah Addison

2014

Pick	
26	**Nikita Scherbak**
73	**Brett Lernout**
125	Nikolas Koberstein
147	Daniel Audette
177	Hayden Hawkey
207	Jake Evans

2013

Pick	
25	**Michael McCarron**
34	**Jacob de La Rose**
36	Zachary Fucale
55	**Artturi Lehkonen**
71	Connor Crisp
86	**Sven Andrighetto**
116	Martin Reway
176	Jeremy Gregoire

2012

Pick	
3	**Alex Galchenyuk**
33	Sebastian Collberg
51	Dalton Thrower
64	Tim Bozon
94	Brady Vail
122	**Charles Hudon**
154	Erik Nystrom

2011

Pick	
17	**Nathan Beaulieu**
97	Josiah Didier
108	Olivier Archambault
113	Magnus Nygren
138	**Darren Dietz**
168	Daniel Pribyl
198	Colin Sullivan

2010

Pick	
22	**Jarred Tinordi**
113	Mark MacMillan
117	**Morgan Ellis**
147	**Brendan Gallagher**
207	John Westin

2009

Pick	
18	**Louis Leblanc**
65	**Joonas Nattinen**
79	Mac Bennett
109	Alexander Avtsin
139	**Gabriel Dumont**
169	Dustin Walsh
199	Michael Cichy
211	Petteri Simila

2008

Pick	
56	Danny Kristo
86	Steve Quailer
116	Jason Missiaen
138	Maxim Trunev
206	Patrick Johnson

2007

Pick	
12	**Ryan McDonagh**
22	**Max Pacioretty**
43	**P.K. Subban**
65	Olivier Fortier
73	**Yannick Weber**
133	Joe Stejskal
142	Andrew Conboy
163	Nichlas Torp
192	Scott Kishel

2006

Pick	
20	David Fischer
49	**Ben Maxwell**
53	**Mathieu Carle**
66	**Ryan White**
139	Pavel Valentenko
199	Cameron Cepek

2005

Pick	
5	**Carey Price**
45	**Guillaume Latendresse**
121	Juraj Mikus
130	Mathieu Aubin
190	**Matt D'Agostini**
200	**Sergei Kostitsyn**
229	Philippe Paquet

2004

Pick	
18	**Kyle Chipchura**
84	**Alexei Emelin**
100	**J.T. Wyman**
150	**Mikhail Grabovski**
181	Loic Lacasse
212	Jon Gleed
246	**Greg Stewart**
262	**Mark Streit**
278	Alex Dulac-Lemelin

2003

Pick	
10	**Andrei Kostitsyn**
40	Cory Urquhart
61	**Maxim Lapierre**
79	**Ryan O'Byrne**
113	**Corey Locke**
123	Danny Stewart
177	Chris Heino-Lindberg
188	**Mark Flood**
217	Oskari Korpikari
241	Jimmy Bonneau
271	**Jaroslav Halak**

Claude Julien

Head Coach

Born: Blind River, ON, April 23, 1960.

Montreal Canadiens general manager Marc Bergevin announced the appointment of Claude Julien as the club's new head coach on February 14, 2017. Julien is in his second tour of duty with the Canadiens after holding the role of head coach from January 2003 to January 2006 with a record of 72-62-25 in 159 regular season games (a .531 winning percentage).

Julien became the winningest coach in Boston Bruins history with his 388th win on March 7, 2016, but was relieved of his coaching duties in Boston on February 7, 2017. He had a record of 419-246-94 in 759 regular season games over 10 years for a .614 winning percentage and led the Bruins to the Stanley Cup in 2011. He also reached the Stanley Cup Final in 2013 and led the Bruins to the Presidents' Trophy in 2013-14 after racking up 117 points in the standings. Julien won the Jack Adams Award winner as the NHL's coach of the year in 2008-09. In 2006-07, he coached the New Jersey Devils but was fired with three games to go in the season despite his team being in first place in its division.

Born in Blind River, Ontario, but raised in the Ottawa suburb of Orleans, Julien began his coaching career behind the bench of the Hull Olympiques in the QMJHL in 1996 and later spent three seasons coaching Montreal's American Hockey League affiliate in Hamilton from 2000 to 2003. Julien has also coached at the international level, winning a bronze medal as head coach of Team Canada at the 2000 World Junior Championship and a silver medal as an assistant coach at the 2006 World Championship. He won a gold medal as an associate coach for Canada at the 2014 Sochi Winter Olympics and as an assistant coach at the 2016 World Cup of Hockey.

As a player, Julien played 12 pro seasons as a defenseman from 1980 to 1992, highlighted by 14 games with the Quebec Nordiques between 1984 and 1986.

Coaching Record

			Regular Season				Playoffs			
Season	Team	League	GC	W	L	O/T	GC	W	L	T
....			....	....	....	....	....	....	....	....
1996-97	Hull	QMJHL	70	48	19	3	14	12	2	....
1996-97	Hull	M-Cup	....	....	....	....	5	3	2	....
1997-98	Hull	QMJHL	70	32	37	1	11	6	5	....
1998-99	Hull	QMJHL	70	23	38	9	23	15	8	....
99-2000	Hull	QMJHL	72	42	24	6	15	9	6	....
2000-01	Hamilton	AHL	80	28	41	11	....	....	....	....
2001-02	Hamilton	AHL	80	37	30	13	15	10	5	....
2002-03	Hamilton	AHL	45	33	9	3	....	....	....	....
2002-03	**Montreal**	**NHL**	**36**	**12**	**16**	**8**	....	....	....	....
2003-04	**Montreal**	**NHL**	**82**	**41**	**30**	**11**	**11**	**4**	**7**	....
2004-05	**Montreal**				SEASON CANCELLED					
2005-06	**Montreal**	**NHL**	**41**	**19**	**16**	**6**	....	....	....	....
2006-07	**New Jersey**	**NHL**	**79**	**47**	**24**	**8**	....	....	....	....
2007-08	**Boston**	**NHL**	**82**	**41**	**29**	**12**	**7**	**3**	**4**	....
2008-09	**Boston**	**NHL**	**82**	**53**	**19**	**10**	**11**	**7**	**4**	....
2009-10	**Boston**	**NHL**	**82**	**39**	**30**	**13**	**13**	**7**	**6**	....
2010-11♦	**Boston**	**NHL**	**82**	**46**	**25**	**11**	**25**	**16**	**9**	....
2011-12	**Boston**	**NHL**	**82**	**49**	**29**	**4**	**7**	**3**	**4**	....
2012-13	**Boston**	**NHL**	**48**	**28**	**14**	**6**	**22**	**14**	**8**	....
2013-14	**Boston**	**NHL**	**82**	**54**	**19**	**9**	**12**	**7**	**5**	....
2014-15	**Boston**	**NHL**	**82**	**41**	**27**	**14**	....	....	....	....
2015-16	**Boston**	**NHL**	**82**	**42**	**31**	**9**	....	....	....	....
2016-17	**Boston**	**NHL**	**55**	**26**	**23**	**6**	....	....	....	....
2016-17	**Montreal**	**NHL**	**24**	**16**	**7**	**1**	**6**	**2**	**4**	....
	NHL Totals		**1021**	**554**	**339**	**128**	**114**	**63**	**51**	....

♦ Stanley Cup win.
Jack Adams Award (2009)

Club Directory

Bell Centre

Club de hockey Canadien
1909, avenue des
Canadiens-de-Montréal
Montréal, QC H3B 5E8
Phone: **514/932-2582**
Media Hotline: 514/989-2835
www.canadiens.nhl.com
Twitter: @CanadiensMTL
PR Twitter: @chcinfomedia
Capacity: 21,288

Executive Management
Owner, President and CEO, Club de hockey Canadien, Bell Centre & evenko ... Geoff Molson
Executive VP Hockey and General Manager, Hockey ... Marc Bergevin
Executive VP, Commercial and Corporate Affairs ... France Margaret Bélanger
Executive VP and Chief Financial Officer ... Fred Steer, Anna Martini
Executive VP and General Manager, Facilities Ops. ... Alain Gauthier
President, Effix – Advertising and Sponsorship Sales ... François Seigneur
Executive VP & Chief Operating Officer, evenko ... Jacques Aubé
Senior Vice President, Communications ... Donald Beauchamp
Presidents, Canadiens Alumni / Place Bell Amphitheatre ... Réjean Houle / Vincent Lucier
Executive Assistant to the Owner, President and CEO ... Rolande Bernier
Administrative Assistant to the Executive Vice President, Commercial and Corporate Affairs ... Maria Carreira

Hockey Operations
Senior VP, Hockey Operations ... Rick Dudley
Assistant General Managers ... Scott Mellanby, Trevor Timmins
Sr. Advisor Hockey Ops. and GM Laval Rocket ... Larry Carrière
Director of Player Personnel ... Martin Lapointe
VP Hockey Operations and Legal Affairs ... John Sedgwick
Directors, Pro / Amateur Scouting / Player Development ... Eric Crawford / Shane Churla / Rob Ramage
Player Development Coach ... Francis Bouillon
Director of Goalie Development & Pro Scout ... Vincent Riendeau
Professional Scouts ... Sean Burke, Scott Masters, Mark Mowers, Reid Simpson, Dave Starman
Amateur Scouting Staff ... Donald Audette, Alvin Backus, Elmer Benning, Andy Bezeau, Serge Boisvert, Bobby Kinsella, Michal Krupa, Hannu Laine, Steve Ludzik Jr., Ken Morin, Vic Posa, Christer Rockstrom, Artem Telepin, Pat Westrum
Executive Assistant to the General Manager ... Susan Cryans
Team Services & Hockey Admin. Manager / Coordinator ... Claudine Crépin / Alain Gagnon
Head Coach ... Claude Julien
Associate Coach ... Kirk Muller
Assistant Coaches/Goaltending Coach ... Dan Lacroix, Jean-Jacques Daigneault / Stéphane Waite
Video Coach / IT Support Video Coaches ... Mario Leblanc / Éric Gravel

Medical and Training Staff
Head Team Physician ... Dr. David S. Mulder
Assistant to Head Team Physician ... Dr. Dan Deckelbaum
Team Physicians ... Dr. Tarek Razek, Dr. Kosar Khwaja, Jeremy Grushka
Head Orthopedic Surgeon ... Dr. Paul Martineau
Dentist / Consultant, Ophthalmology ... Dr. Jean-François Desjardins / Dr. John Little
TBC ... Pierre Allard
Strength & Conditioning Coach ... Patrick Delisle-Houle
Consultants, Sports Psychology / Nutrition ... Dr. David Scott / Martin Fréchette
Consultant, Skills & Skating ... Sébastien Bordeleau
Head Athletic Therapist / Massage Therapist ... Graham Rynbend / Claude Thériault
TBC ... Donald Balmforth
Consultants, Osteopathy / Physiotherapy ... Dave Campbell / Steve Villeneuve
Head Equipment Manager ... Pierre Gervais
Assistants to the Equipment Manager ... Patrick Langlois, Pierre Ouellette, Richard Généreux

Communications
Executive Director, Media Relations ... Dominick Saillant
Executive Assistant to the Sr VP Communications ... Sylvie Lambert
Communications Manager ... François Marchand
Manager, Research and Translation ... Carl Lavigne

Montreal Canadiens Children's Foundation / Community Relations / Minor Hockey
Exec. Dir., Foundation and Community Relations ... Geneviève Paquette
Manager, Fundraising & Partnerships, Foundation ... Ryan Frank
Managers, Development & Programs / Youth Hockey ... Patrick Mahoney / Stéphane Verret
Coords., Foundation / Comm. Rels. / Youth Hockey ... Caroline Benoit, Mélanie Bergeron, Sylvie Nadeau, Marie-Pier Perron / Laurence Beaulieu / Francis Payant

Ticketing and Suite Services
Executive Director, Sales ... Gilbert Brault
Executive Director / Director, Luxury Suites & Services ... Richard Primeau / Sabina D'Ascoli
Coordinators, Sales & Services / Luxury Suite & Services ... Sarah Jasmin / Marie-Claude Quesnel

Marketing / Creative Services/Game Operations
Executive Director, Marketing ... Jon Trzcienski
Executive Director, Creative Services and Video ... Jean Simard
Director, Digital Media ... Alexandre Harvey
Group Manager, HabsTV and Editorial ... Shauna Denis
Group Manager, Advertising and Fan Development ... Kim Marois
Manager, Consumer Products ... Maxime St. Laurent
Manager, Marketing Operations & Events ... Dave McGinnis
Senior Coordinator, Promotions & Events ... Vanessa Harrison
Managers, Media Planning / Creative Services ... Jonathan B. Mailhot / David Bayreuther, Claudia Marin, Eric Pelletier
Sr. Coordinators Publications and Editorial ... Hugo Fontaine, Joanie Godin
Coords., Game Presentation / Video / Photo / Branding ... Carl Abran / Cynthia Paquin-Lepage / Florence Labelle / Anne-Frédérique Laporte

Building Operations
Adm. Asst. to the Exec. VP and GM, Facilities Ops ... Marie-France Beaulieu
Vice Presidents, Operations / Food Services / Customer Satisfaction / Ticket Operations ... Xavier Luydlin / Alec Beaudry / Caroline Hamel / Cathy D'Ascoli
Exec. Dirs., Guests & Security Services / Building Services ... Réjean Toutant / Patrick Auger
Dirs, F&B Supplies & Control / F&B Event Management / Merchandising ... Daniel Michaud / Nathalie Vincent / Cindy Haché
Asst. Directors, Ticketing / Guests & Security Services ... Lucie Masse / Alain Simoneau

Information Technology
Vice President, Info and Communication Technology ... Pierre-Éric Belzile
Director, Info and Communication Technology ... Jacques Farand
Senior IT Analyst, Development ... Louis Pennimpede

Human Resources / Finance
Vice President, Human Resources / Admin. Assistant ... Maryse Landry / Laurie Meloche
Executive Assistant to the Executive VP and CFO ... Christine Ouellette
Controller / Assistant Controller / Payroll Admin. ... Raymond Lamarche / Bernadette Kajjouni / Teresa Nola

Broadcasting
Play-by-play TV/Radio ... Pierre Houde (RDS), TBC (TSN), Félix Séguin (TVA Sports), Martin McGuire (Cogéco 98.5 FM), Dan Robertson (TSN Radio 690)
Color TV/Radio ... Marc Denis (RDS), TBC (TSN), Patrick Lalime (TVA Sports), Dany Dubé (Cogéco 98.5 FM), Sergio Momesso (TSN Radio 690)
Radio/television flagships ... RDS (Cable), TSN (Cable), TVA Sports (Cable), Cogéco (98.5 FM), TSN Radio (690 AM)

Nashville Predators

2016-17 Results: 41w-29L-8OTL-4SOL 94PTS
4TH, Central Division • 8TH, Western Conference

Acquired in a blockbuster deal for Shea Weber, P.K. Subban was limited to 66 games during the 2016-17 regular season, but was a workhorse in the playoffs helping Nashville reach the Stanley Cup Final for the first time.

Key Off-Season Signings/Acquisitions

2017

June 13 • Re-signed D **Yannick Weber**.

July 1 • Signed C **Nick Bonino**, LW **Scott Hartnell** and G **Anders Lindback**.

1 • Acquired D **Alexei Emelin** from Vegas for a 3rd-round pick in 2019 NHL Draft.

17 • Re-signed C **Frederick Gaudreau**.

18 • Re-signed LW **Pontus Aberg**.

21 • Re-signed G **Marek Mazanec**.

21 • Named **Dan Muse** assistant coach.

22 • Re-signed LW **Viktor Arvidsson**.

24 • Re-signed LW **Austin Watson**.

28 • Re-signed C **Ryan Johansen**.

Year-by-Year Record

Season	GP	Home				Road				Overall						Div. Fin.	Conf. Fin.	Playoff Result
		W	L	T	OL	W	L	T	OL	W	L	T	OL	GF	GA	Pts.			
2016-17	82	24	9	....	8	17	20	....	4	41	29	....	12	240	224	94	4th, Cen.	8th, West	Lost Final
2015-16	82	23	11	....	7	18	16	....	7	41	27	....	14	228	215	96	4th, Cen.	7th, West	Lost Second Round
2014-15	82	28	9	....	4	19	16	....	6	47	25	....	10	232	208	104	2nd, Cen.	3rd, West	Lost First Round
2013-14	82	19	17	....	5	19	15	....	7	38	32	....	12	216	242	88	6th, Cen.	10th, West	– out of playoffs –
2012-13	48	11	9	....	4	5	14	....	5	16	23	....	9	111	139	41	5th, Cen.	14th, West	– out of playoffs –
2011-12	82	26	10	....	5	22	16	....	3	48	26	....	8	237	210	104	2nd, Cen.	4th, West	Lost Conf. Semi-Final
2010-11	82	24	9	....	8	20	18	....	3	44	27	....	11	219	194	99	2nd, Cen.	5th, West	Lost Conf. Semi-Final
2009-10	82	24	14	....	3	23	15	....	3	47	29	....	6	225	225	100	3rd, Cen.	7th, West	Lost Conf. Quarter-Final
2008-09	82	24	13	....	4	16	21	....	4	40	34	....	8	213	233	88	5th, Cen.	10th, West	– out of playoffs –
2007-08	82	23	14	....	4	18	18	....	5	41	32	....	9	230	229	91	2nd, Cen.	8th, West	Lost Conf. Quarter-Final
2006-07	82	28	8	....	5	23	15	....	3	51	23	....	8	272	212	110	2nd, Cen.	4th, West	Lost Conf. Quarter-Final
2005-06	82	32	8	....	1	17	17	....	7	49	25	....	8	259	227	106	2nd, Cen.	4th, West	Lost Conf. Quarter-Final
2004-05	....																		
2003-04	82	22	10	7	2	16	19	4	2	38	29	11	4	216	217	91	3rd, Cen.	8th, West	Lost Conf. Quarter-Final
2002-03	82	18	17	5	1	9	18	8	6	27	35	13	7	183	206	74	4th, Cen.	13th, West	– out of playoffs –
2001-02	82	17	16	8	0	11	25	5	0	28	41	13	0	196	230	69	4th, Cen.	14th, West	– out of playoffs –
2000-01	82	16	18	7	0	18	18	2	3	34	36	9	3	186	200	80	3rd, Cen.	14th, West	– out of playoffs –
1999-2000	82	15	21	3	2	13	19	4	5	28	40	7	7	199	240	70	4th, Cen.	13th, West	– out of playoffs –
1998-99	82	15	22	4	....	13	25	3	....	28	47	7	....	190	261	63	4th, Cen.	12th, West	– out of playoffs –

2017-18 Schedule

Oct.	Thu.	5	at Boston
	Sat.	7	at Pittsburgh
	Tue.	10	Philadelphia
	Thu.	12	Dallas
	Sat.	14	at Chicago
	Tue.	17	Colorado
	Thu.	19	at Philadelphia
	Sat.	21	at NY Rangers*
	Tue.	24	Calgary
	Fri.	27	at Chicago
	Sat.	28	NY Islanders
Nov.	Wed.	1	at San Jose
	Fri.	3	at Anaheim
	Sat.	4	at Los Angeles
	Tue.	7	at Columbus
	Sat.	11	Pittsburgh
	Tue.	14	Washington
	Thu.	16	at Minnesota
	Sat.	18	Colorado
	Mon.	20	Winnipeg
	Wed.	22	Montreal
	Fri.	24	at St. Louis*
	Sun.	26	at Carolina*
	Tue.	28	Chicago
	Thu.	30	Vancouver
Dec.	Sat.	2	Anaheim
	Mon.	4	Boston
	Tue.	5	at Dallas
	Fri.	8	Vegas
	Wed.	13	at Vancouver
	Thu.	14	at Edmonton
	Sat.	16	at Calgary
	Tue.	19	Winnipeg
	Thu.	21	Carolina
	Wed.	27	at St. Louis*
	Sat.	23	at Dallas
	Fri.	29	at Minnesota
	Sat.	30	Minnesota
Jan.	Tue.	2	at Vegas
	Thu.	4	at Arizona
	Sat.	6	at Los Angeles

	Tue.	9	Edmonton
	Tue.	16	Vegas
	Thu.	18	Arizona
	Sat.	20	Florida
	Tue.	23	Tampa Bay
	Thu.	25	at New Jersey
	Tue.	30	Chicago
Feb.	Thu.	1	Los Angeles
	Sat.	3	NY Rangers
	Mon.	5	at NY Islanders
	Wed.	7	at Toronto
	Thu.	8	at Ottawa
	Sat.	10	at Montreal
	Tue.	13	St. Louis
	Thu.	15	Calgary
	Sat.	17	Detroit
	Mon.	19	Ottawa
	Tue.	20	at Detroit
	Thu.	22	San Jose
	Sun.	25	St. Louis*
	Tue.	27	at Winnipeg
Mar.	Thu.	1	at Edmonton
	Fri.	2	at Vancouver
	Sun.	4	at Colorado*
	Tue.	6	Dallas
	Thu.	8	Anaheim
	Sat.	10	New Jersey
	Tue.	13	Winnipeg
	Thu.	15	at Arizona
	Fri.	16	at Colorado
	Mon.	19	at Buffalo
	Thu.	22	Toronto
	Sat.	24	at Minnesota
	Sun.	25	at Winnipeg
	Tue.	27	Minnesota
	Thu.	29	San Jose
	Sat.	31	Buffalo
Apr.	Sun.	1	at Tampa Bay
	Tue.	3	at Florida
	Thu.	5	at Washington
	Sat.	7	Columbus

* Denotes afternoon game.

CENTRAL DIVISION
20th NHL Season

Franchise date: June 25, 1997

2017-18 Player Personnel

FORWARDS	HT	WT	*Age	Birthplace	S	2016-17 Club
ABERG, Pontus	5-11	196	24	Stockholm, Sweden	R	Nashville-Milwaukee
ARVIDSSON, Viktor	5-9	180	24	Skelleftea, Sweden	R	Nashville
BASS, Cody	6-0	205	30	Owen Sound, ON	R	Nashville-Milwaukee
BONINO, Nick	6-1	196	29	Hartford, CT	L	Pittsburgh
FIALA, Kevin	5-10	193	21	St. Gallen, Switzerland	L	Nashville-Milwaukee
FORSBERG, Filip	6-1	205	23	Ostervala, Sweden	R	Nashville
GAUDREAU, Frederick	6-0	192	24	Bromont, QC	R	Nashville-Milwaukee
HARTNELL, Scott	6-2	214	35	Regina, SK	L	Columbus
JARNKROK, Calle	5-11	186	26	Gavle, Sweden	R	Nashville
JOHANSEN, Ryan	6-3	218	25	Port Moody, BC	R	Nashville
KAMENEV, Vladislav	6-2	194	21	Orsk, Russia	L	Nashville-Milwaukee
McLEOD, Cody	6-2	210	33	Binscarth, MB	L	Colorado-Nashville
SALOMAKI, Miikka	5-11	203	24	Raahe, Finland	L	Nashville-Milwaukee
SISSONS, Colton	6-1	200	23	North Vancouver, BC	R	Nashville
SMITH, Craig	6-1	208	28	Madison, WI	R	Nashville
WATSON, Austin	6-4	204	25	Ann Arbor, MI	R	Nashville-Milwaukee
DEFENSEMEN						
BITETTO, Anthony	6-1	210	27	Island Park, NY	L	Nashville-Milwaukee
CARRIER, Alexandre	5-11	174	20	Quebec City, QC	R	Nashville-Milwaukee
EKHOLM, Mattias	6-4	215	27	Borlange, Sweden	L	Nashville
ELLIS, Ryan	5-10	180	26	Hamilton, ON	R	Nashville
EMELIN, Alexei	6-2	216	31	Togliatti, USSR	L	Montreal
GRANBERG, Petter	6-3	200	25	Gallivare, Sweden	R	Nashville-Milwaukee
IRWIN, Matt	6-1	207	29	Brentwood Bay, BC	L	Nashville-Milwaukee
JOSI, Roman	6-1	201	27	Bern, Switzerland	L	Nashville
SUBBAN, P.K.	6-0	210	28	Toronto, ON	R	Nashville
WEBER, Yannick	5-11	200	29	Morges, Switz.	R	Nashville

GOALTENDERS	HT	WT	*Age	Birthplace	C	2016-17 Club
LINDBACK, Anders	6-6	215	29	Gavle, Sweden	L	Ontario-Rogle-Rogle
MAZANEC, Marek	6-4	187	26	Pisek, Czech.	R	Nashville-Milwaukee
RINNE, Pekka	6-5	217	34	Kempele, Finland	L	Nashville
SAROS, Juuse	5-11	180	22	Forssa, Finland	L	Nashville-Milwaukee

* – Age at start of 2017-18 season

Peter Laviolette

Head Coach

Born: Norwood, MA, December 7, 1964.

The Nashville Predators hired Peter Laviolette as the second head coach in team history on May 6, 2014. In his first season with the club in 2014-15, the Predators posted 104 points and returned to the playoffs after a two-year absence. Laviolette finished third in voting for the Jack Adams Award as coach of the year. Nashville made the playoffs again in 2015-16, and reached the Stanley Cup Final for the first time in franchise history in 2016-17. Laviolette, who won the Stanley Cup with Carolina in 2006 and reached the Final with Philadelphia in 2010, joined Dick Irvin, Scotty Bowman and Mike Keenan as the only coaches in NHL history to lead three different teams to the Final.

Prior to Nashville, Laviolette spent parts of 12 seasons with the New York Islanders (2001 to 2003), Carolina Hurricanes (2003 to 2009) and Philadelphia Flyers (2009 to 2014) and each of the three teams improved exponentially in the first full season after he took the helm. Laviolette won 52 games in his first full season with Carolina in 2005-06 – earning him runner-up honors for the Jack Adams Award in the closest vote in award history – and winning the Stanley Cup. Laviolette's offensive-minded philosophy is evidenced by his teams' often ranking about the NHL's top 10 in goals scored. Multiple young, developing players who have gone on to become dependable NHL players and in some cases superstars were cultivated under Laviolette's watch, including Eric Staal in Carolina and Claude Giroux in Philadelphia.

Second in wins among U.S.-born NHL coaches, Laviolette has led the United States' entry at the World Championships in 2004 (bronze), 2005 and 2014. He has also represented his country in four Olympic Games, first as a player in the 1988 Calgary Games and the 1994 Lillehammer Games, then as a head coach at the 2006 Torino Games, and as an assistant at the 2014 Sochi Games.

After amassing 268 points (78 goals, 190 assists) in 594 minor-league games in the American and International hockey leagues (Indianapolis, Colorado, Denver, Flint, Binghamton, Providence and San Diego) from 1986 to 1997, and appearing in 12 games for the New York Rangers in 1988-89, Laviolette began his coaching career with the ECHL's Wheeling Nailers in 1997. After posting a 37-24-9 record and reaching the conference finals in his rookie coaching season, he was hired as head coach of the AHL's Providence Bruins, and led the team to an AHL-best 56 wins and a Calder Cup in 1998-99, just one season after the team had won just 19 games and finished last in the league. Following the 1999-2000 season, the 1999 AHL Coach of the Year was promoted to assistant coach of the parent Boston Bruins, which he held for a single campaign (2000-01) before starting his NHL head coaching career with the Islanders in 2001-02.

Coaching Record

			Regular Season				Playoffs			
Season	Team	League	GC	W	L	O/T	GC	W	L	T
1997-98	Wheeling	ECHL	70	37	24	9	15	8	7	....
1998-99	Providence	AHL	80	56	16	8	19	15	4	....
99-2000	Providence	AHL	80	33	38	9	14	10	4	....
2001-02	**NY Islanders**	**NHL**	**82**	**42**	**28**	**12**	**7**	**3**	**4**	....
2002-03	**NY Islanders**	**NHL**	**82**	**35**	**34**	**13**	**5**	**1**	**4**	....
2003-04	**Carolina**	**NHL**	**52**	**20**	**22**	**10**	....	....	....	....
2004-05	**Carolina**				SEASON CANCELLED					
2005-06♦	**Carolina**	**NHL**	**82**	**52**	**22**	**8**	**25**	**16**	**9**	....
2006-07	**Carolina**	**NHL**	**82**	**40**	**34**	**8**	....	....	....	....
2007-08	**Carolina**	**NHL**	**82**	**43**	**33**	**6**	....	....	....	....
2008-09	**Carolina**	**NHL**	**25**	**12**	**11**	**2**	....	....	....	....
2009-10	**Philadelphia**	**NHL**	**57**	**28**	**24**	**5**	**23**	**14**	**9**	....
2010-11	**Philadelphia**	**NHL**	**82**	**47**	**23**	**12**	**11**	**4**	**7**	....
2011-12	**Philadelphia**	**NHL**	**82**	**47**	**26**	**9**	**11**	**5**	**6**	....
2012-13	**Philadelphia**	**NHL**	**48**	**23**	**22**	**3**	....	....	....	....
2013-14	**Philadelphia**	**NHL**	**3**	**0**	**3**	**0**	....	....	....	....
2014-15	**Nashville**	**NHL**	**82**	**47**	**25**	**10**	**6**	**2**	**4**	....
2015-16	**Nashville**	**NHL**	**82**	**41**	**27**	**14**	**14**	**7**	**7**	....
2016-17	**Nashville**	**NHL**	**82**	**41**	**29**	**12**	**22**	**14**	**8**	....
	NHL Totals		**1005**	**518**	**363**	**124**	**124**	**66**	**58**	....

♦ Stanley Cup win.

2016-17 Scoring

* – rookie

Regular Season

Pos	#	Player	Team	GP	G	A	Pts	TOI	+/–	PIM	PP	SH	GW	S	S%
L	38	Viktor Arvidsson	NSH	80	31	30	61	17:09	16	28	4	5	6	246	12.6
C	92	Ryan Johansen	NSH	82	14	47	61	18:50	1	60	4	1	3	154	9.1
L	9	Filip Forsberg	NSH	82	31	27	58	18:31	–4	32	3	3	9	234	13.2
D	59	Roman Josi	NSH	72	12	37	49	25:04	7	18	7	0	1	217	5.5
C	12	Mike Fisher	NSH	72	18	24	42	16:37	1	55	7	0	3	120	15.0
L	18	James Neal	NSH	70	23	18	41	17:41	–10	35	5	0	5	202	11.4
D	76	P.K. Subban	NSH	66	10	30	40	24:24	–8	44	3	0	2	142	7.0
D	4	Ryan Ellis	NSH	71	16	22	38	23:57	17	29	4	1	3	140	11.4
C	33	Colin Wilson	NSH	70	12	23	35	14:57	7	18	6	0	0	113	10.6
C	19	Calle Jarnkrok	NSH	81	15	16	31	15:43	–1	25	2	1	1	134	11.2
C	15	Craig Smith	NSH	78	12	17	29	13:49	7	30	2	0	1	155	7.7
R	11	PA Parenteau	N.J.	59	13	14	27	14:59	–16	35	4	0	2	109	11.9
			NSH	8	0	1	1	12:33	–2	0	0	0	0	14	0.0
			Total	67	13	15	28	14:41	–18	35	4	0	2	123	10.6
C	63	Mike Ribeiro	NSH	46	4	21	25	15:58	–5	14	2	0	0	38	10.5
D	14	Mattias Ekholm	NSH	82	3	20	23	23:27	4	34	0	0	1	120	2.5
L	51	Austin Watson	NSH	77	5	12	17	12:25	14	99	0	0	0	90	5.6
L	56 *	Kevin Fiala	NSH	54	11	5	16	13:30	1	18	0	0	1	114	9.6
D	52	Matt Irwin	NSH	74	3	11	14	16:16	15	26	0	0	1	98	3.1
C	10	Colton Sissons	NSH	58	8	2	10	11:07	11	12	0	1	1	42	19.0
D	7	Yannick Weber	NSH	73	1	7	8	11:55	1	25	0	0	1	72	1.4
D	2	Anthony Bitetto	NSH	29	0	7	7	11:48	–1	25	0	0	0	17	0.0
L	55	Cody McLeod	COL	28	1	0	1	5:52	–2	52	0	0	0	12	8.3
			NSH	31	4	1	5	8:19	–1	93	0	0	0	18	22.2
			Total	59	5	1	6	7:09	–3	145	0	0	0	30	16.7
D	24	Brad Hunt	STL	9	1	4	5	13:35	–2	2	1	0	0	12	8.3
			NSH	3	0	1	1	17:13	1	0	0	0	0	2	0.0
			Total	12	1	5	6	14:30	–1	2	1	0	0	14	7.1
L	26	Harry Zolnierczyk	NSH	24	2	2	4	8:52	–2	10	0	0	0	19	10.5
L	83	Vernon Fiddler	N.J.	39	1	2	3	12:14	–11	29	0	1	0	37	2.7
			NSH	20	1	0	1	10:30	–4	37	0	0	0	11	9.1
			Total	59	2	2	4	11:39	–15	66	0	1	0	48	4.2
L	46 *	Pontus Aberg	NSH	15	1	1	2	12:20	–2	4	0	0	0	12	8.3
D	25	Matt Carle	NSH	6	0	1	1	13:08	–1	0	0	0	0	2	0.0
C	32 *	Frederick Gaudreau	NSH	9	0	1	1	8:39	1	0	0	0	0	8	0.0
C	23	Trevor Smith	NSH	1	0	0	0	7:20	0	0	0	0	0	0	0.0
L	17	Mike Liambas	NSH	1	0	0	0	4:42	–1	0	0	0	0	0	0.0
C	50 *	Vladislav Kamenev	NSH	2	0	0	0	10:03	–1	2	0	0	0	1	0.0
D	73 *	Alexandre Carrier	NSH	2	0	0	0	10:23	1	0	0	0	0	1	0.0
D	5	Adam Pardy	NSH	4	0	0	0	10:59	–1	6	0	0	0	4	0.0
R	20	Miikka Salomaki	NSH	5	0	0	0	12:12	–1	2	0	0	0	3	0.0
C	16	Cody Bass	NSH	9	0	0	0	6:46	–1	19	0	0	0	1	0.0
D	8	Petter Granberg	NSH	10	0	0	0	9:37	0	10	0	0	0	4	0.0

Goaltending

No.		Goaltender	GPI	Mins	Avg	W	L	OT	EN	SO	GA	SA	Sv%	G	A	PIM
74	*	Juuse Saros	21	1200	2.35	10	8	3	6	1	47	614	.923	0	1	0
35		Pekka Rinne	61	3568	2.42	31	19	9	9	3	144	1757	.918	0	0	4
39	*	Marek Mazanec	4	178	4.72	0	2	0	0	0	14	87	.839	0	1	0
		Totals	**82**	**4986**	**2.65**	**41**	**29**	**12**	**15**	**4**	**220**	**2473**	**.911**			

Playoffs

Pos	#	Player	Team	GP	G	A	Pts	TOI	+/–	PIM	PP	SH	GW	OT	S	S%
L	9	Filip Forsberg	NSH	22	9	7	16	19:59	14	14	1	0	0	0	71	12.7
D	59	Roman Josi	NSH	22	6	8	14	25:45	2	12	2	0	1	0	76	7.9
D	4	Ryan Ellis	NSH	22	5	8	13	23:25	4	12	2	0	1	0	48	10.4
C	92	Ryan Johansen	NSH	14	3	10	13	20:45	12	12	0	0	1	0	15	20.0
L	38	Viktor Arvidsson	NSH	22	3	10	13	18:39	3	19	0	0	1	0	49	6.1
C	10	Colton Sissons	NSH	22	6	6	12	15:03	7	16	1	0	2	0	28	21.4
D	76	P.K. Subban	NSH	22	2	10	12	25:32	5	29	0	0	0	0	39	5.1
D	14	Mattias Ekholm	NSH	22	1	10	11	25:20	6	38	1	0	0	0	33	3.0
L	18	James Neal	NSH	22	6	3	9	17:54	–8	14	1	0	2	1	67	9.0
L	51	Austin Watson	NSH	22	4	5	9	13:40	3	28	0	0	0	0	28	14.3
C	19	Calle Jarnkrok	NSH	21	2	5	7	16:59	–2	2	0	0	0	0	26	7.7
L	46 *	Pontus Aberg	NSH	16	2	3	5	12:54	–1	2	0	0	1	0	23	8.7
C	33	Colin Wilson	NSH	14	2	2	4	15:16	–1	2	2	0	0	0	20	10.0
C	12	Mike Fisher	NSH	20	0	4	4	17:17	–6	2	0	0	0	0	34	0.0
C	32 *	Frederick Gaudreau	NSH	8	3	0	3	11:29	2	0	0	0	2	0	7	42.9
C	15	Craig Smith	NSH	10	1	2	3	12:50	2	2	0	0	0	0	21	4.8
L	26	Harry Zolnierczyk	NSH	11	1	2	3	8:49	3	0	0	0	0	0	6	16.7
L	56 *	Kevin Fiala	NSH	5	2	0	2	13:54	0	0	1	0	1	1	12	16.7
L	83	Vernon Fiddler	NSH	9	1	1	2	8:02	–4	25	0	0	1	0	7	14.3
D	52	Matt Irwin	NSH	22	0	2	2	11:54	–1	4	0	0	0	0	10	0.0
L	55	Cody McLeod	NSH	15	1	0	1	6:49	–1	27	0	0	1	0	11	9.1
D	7	Yannick Weber	NSH	22	0	1	1	11:09	0	5	0	0	0	0	12	0.0
R	11	PA Parenteau	NSH	5	0	0	0	9:22	0	0	0	0	0	0	6	0.0
R	20	Miikka Salomaki	NSH	6	0	0	0	8:12	0	2	0	0	0	0	4	0.0

Goaltending

No.		Goaltender	GPI	Mins	Avg	W	L	EN	SO	GA	SA	Sv%	G	A	PIM
35		Pekka Rinne	22	1289	1.96	14	8	3	2	42	599	.930	0	3	0
74	*	Juuse Saros	2	57	3.16	0	0	0	0	3	17	.824	0	0	0
		Totals	**22**	**1357**	**2.12**	**14**	**8**	**3**	**2**	**48**	**619**	**.922**			

Captains' History

Tom Fitzgerald, 1998-99 to 2001-02; Greg Johnson, 2002-03 to 2005-06; Kimmo Timonen, 2006-07; Jason Arnott, 2007-08 to 2009-10; Shea Weber, 2010-11 to 2015-16; Mike Fisher, 2016-17.

Coaching History

Barry Trotz, 1998-99 to 2013-14; Peter Laviolette, 2014-15 to date.

Club Records

Team

(Figures in brackets for season records are games played; records for fewest points, wins, ties, losses, goals, goals against are for 70 or more games)

Most Points	110	2006-07 (82)
Most Wins	51	2006-07 (82)
Most Ties	13	2001-02 (82), 2002-03 (82)
Most Losses	47	1998-99 (82)
Most Goals	272	2006-07 (82)
Most Goals Against	261	1998-99 (82)
Fewest Points	63	1998-99 (82)
Fewest Wins	27	2002-03 (82)
Fewest Ties	7	1998-99 (82)
		1999-2000 (82)
Fewest Losses	23	2006-07 (82)
Fewest Goals	183	2002-03 (82)
Fewest Goals Against	194	2010-11 (82)

Longest Winning Streak

Overall	8	Oct. 5-25/05
Home	9	Dec. 16/14-Feb. 3/15
Away	7	Oct. 16-Nov. 4/06

Longest Team Point Streak

Overall	9	Oct. 5-26/05 (5W, 3SOW, 1OTL)
Home	11	Dec. 20/03-Jan. 31/04 (7W, 2OTW, 2T), Nov. 3-Dec. 23/01 (9W, 2T)
Away	7	Oct. 16-Nov. 4/06 (5W, 2SOW)

Longest Losing Streak

Overall	8	Apr. 4-19/13
Home	6	Jan. 21-Feb. 15/99, Feb. 26-Mar. 21/02, Feb. 21-Mar. 20/08, Apr. 4-15/13, Mar. 1-25/14, Dec. 15/16-Jan. 3/17
Away	10	Mar. 14-Apr. 27/13

Longest Winless Streak

Overall	15	Mar. 10-Apr. 6/03 (10L, 2OTL, 3T)
Home	9	Jan. 21-Mar. 2/99 (8L, 1T)
Away	10	Mar. 14-Apr. 27/13 (7L, 2OTL, 1SOL)

Most Shutouts, Season	11	2006-07 (82)
Most PIM, Season	1,533	2005-06 (82)
Most Goals, Game	9	Mar. 4/04 (Nsh. 9 at Pit. 4), Mar. 18/06 (Cgy. 4 at Nsh. 9), Nov. 18/14 (Nsh. 9 at Tor. 2)

Individual

Most Seasons	15	David Legwand
Most Games	956	David Legwand
Most Goals, Career	210	David Legwand
Most Assists, Career	356	David Legwand
Most Points, Career	566	David Legwand (210G, 356A)
Most PIM, Career	725	Jordin Tootoo
Most Shutouts, Career	43	Pekka Rinne

Longest Consecutive Games Streak	269	Karlis Skrastins (Feb. 21/00-Apr. 6/03)
Most Goals, Season	33	Jason Arnott (2008-09), Filip Forsberg (2015-16)
Most Assists, Season	54	Paul Kariya (2005-06)
Most Points, Season	85	Paul Kariya (2005-06; 31G, 54A)
Most PIM, Season	242	Patrick Cote (1998-99)
Most Points, Defenseman, Season	61	Roman Josi (2015-16; 14G, 47A)

Most Points, Center, Season	72	Jason Arnott (2007-08; 28G, 44A)
Most Points, Right Wing, Season	72	J.P. Dumont (2007-08; 29G, 43A)
Most Points, Left Wing, Season	85	Paul Kariya (2005-06; 31G, 54A)
Most Points, Rookie, Season	63	Filip Forsberg (2014-15; 26G, 37A)
Most Shutouts, Season	7	Pekka Rinne (2008-09), (2009-10)
Most Goals, Game	4	Eric Nystrom (Jan. 24/14)
Most Assists, Game	5	Marek Zidlicky (Feb. 18/04)
Most Points, Game	5	Marek Zidlicky (Feb. 18/04; 5A) Dan Hamhuis (Mar. 4/04; 1G, 4A) J.P. Dumont (Oct. 22/09; 1G, 4A)

All-time Record vs. Other Clubs

Regular Season

	Total								At Home								On Road							
	GP	W	L	T	OL	GF	GA	PTS	GP	W	L	T	OL	GF	GA	PTS	GP	W	L	T	OL	GF	GA	PTS
Anaheim	67	27	29	2	9	160	187	65	33	18	10	2	3	89	77	41	34	9	19	0	6	71	110	24
Arizona	67	34	26	2	5	193	177	75	34	21	10	2	1	100	79	45	33	13	16	0	4	93	98	30
Boston	25	11	11	1	2	58	68	25	13	8	5	0	0	34	30	16	12	3	6	1	2	24	38	9
Buffalo	23	13	7	1	2	68	58	29	12	4	6	0	2	28	30	10	11	9	1	1	0	40	28	19
Calgary	68	32	22	4	10	192	189	78	35	19	10	1	5	109	91	44	33	13	12	3	5	83	98	34
Carolina	25	14	8	1	2	66	59	31	12	9	2	0	1	33	24	19	13	5	6	1	1	33	35	12
Chicago	105	46	47	4	8	300	304	104	52	26	20	3	3	160	148	58	53	20	27	1	5	140	156	46
Colorado	74	38	28	5	3	220	203	84	36	20	12	3	1	117	106	44	38	18	16	2	2	103	97	40
Columbus	82	56	19	1	6	255	182	119	42	33	5	1	3	143	88	70	40	23	14	0	3	112	94	49
Dallas	75	32	38	1	4	176	207	69	38	22	13	1	2	109	89	47	37	10	25	0	2	67	118	22
Detroit	93	34	46	4	9	234	294	81	46	21	20	2	3	126	126	47	47	13	26	2	6	108	168	34
Edmonton	68	39	23	3	3	193	185	84	35	20	12	3	0	97	98	43	33	19	11	0	3	96	87	41
Florida	26	12	10	3	1	66	66	28	13	7	4	2	0	34	30	16	13	5	6	1	1	32	36	12
Los Angeles	67	30	26	3	8	173	191	71	33	13	15	3	2	75	89	31	34	17	11	0	6	98	102	40
Minnesota	66	31	22	5	8	182	178	75	33	18	9	2	4	88	73	42	33	13	13	3	4	94	105	33
Montreal	22	9	6	1	6	59	52	25	11	5	1	1	4	34	24	15	11	4	5	0	2	25	28	10
New Jersey	25	11	9	0	5	64	73	27	13	4	5	0	4	32	39	12	12	7	4	0	1	32	34	15
NY Islanders	23	13	7	0	3	62	57	29	12	8	3	0	1	33	27	17	11	5	4	0	2	29	30	12
NY Rangers	24	10	11	1	2	54	68	23	11	4	5	1	1	26	34	10	13	6	6	0	1	28	34	13
Ottawa	23	12	10	0	1	66	64	25	11	6	4	0	1	29	25	13	12	6	6	0	0	37	39	12
Philadelphia	24	9	9	3	3	53	69	24	11	4	4	2	1	27	29	11	13	5	5	1	2	26	40	13
Pittsburgh	25	11	10	2	2	73	69	26	13	7	4	0	2	41	30	16	12	4	6	2	0	32	39	10
St. Louis	105	49	41	4	11	238	265	113	53	27	17	3	6	123	124	63	52	22	24	1	5	115	141	50
San Jose	67	32	26	2	7	173	170	73	33	19	11	1	2	95	81	41	34	13	15	1	5	78	89	32
Tampa Bay	24	12	8	2	2	71	67	28	13	8	4	0	1	39	34	17	11	4	4	2	1	32	33	11
Toronto	21	11	8	1	1	63	54	24	8	4	3	0	1	20	21	9	13	7	5	1	0	43	33	15
Vancouver	68	27	33	2	6	170	199	62	35	15	13	1	6	95	93	37	33	12	20	1	0	75	106	25
Washington	25	11	9	1	4	68	70	27	13	7	3	1	2	40	34	17	12	4	6	0	2	28	36	10
Winnipeg	35	20	11	1	3	102	87	44	17	12	5	0	0	58	39	24	18	8	6	1	3	44	48	20
Totals	**1442**	**686**	**560**	**60**	**136**	**3852**	**3912**	**1568**	**721**	**389**	**235**	**34**	**63**	**2034**	**1812**	**875**	**721**	**297**	**325**	**26**	**73**	**1818**	**2100**	**693**

Winnipeg totals include Atlanta Thrashers, 1999-2000 to 2010-11.

Playoffs

	Series	W	L	GP	W	L	T	GF	GA	Last Mtg.	Rnd.	Result
Anaheim	3	3	0	19	12	7	0	55	53	2017	CF	W 4-2
Arizona	1	0	1	5	1	4	0	9	12	2012	CSF	L 1-4
Chicago	3	1	2	16	8	8	0	49	39	2017	FR	W 4-0
Detroit	3	1	2	17	8	9	0	34	38	2012	CQF	W 4-1
Pittsburgh	1	0	1	6	2	4	0	13	19	2017	F	L 2-4
St. Louis	1	1	0	6	4	2	0	15	11	2017	SR	W 4-2
San Jose	3	0	3	15	5	12	0	41	58	2016	SR	L 3-4
Vancouver	1	0	1	6	1	5	0	11	14	2011	CSF	L 2-4
Totals	**16**	**6**	**10**	**92**	**42**	**50**	**0**	**227**	**244**			

Playoff Results 2017-2013

Year	Round	Opponent	Result	GF	GA
2017	F	Pittsburgh	L 2-4	13	19
	CF	Anaheim	W 4-2	19	15
	SR	St. Louis	W 4-2	15	11
	FR	Chicago	W 4-0	13	3
2016	SR	San Jose	L 3-4	17	25
	FR	Anaheim	W 4-3	14	18
2015	FR	Chicago	L 2-4	21	19

Abbreviations: Round: F – Final;
CF – conference final; **CSF** – conference semi-final;
SR – second round; **CQF** – conference quarter-final;
FR – first round.

2016-17 Results

Oct.	14	Chicago	3-2		12	Boston	2-1
	15	at Chicago	3-5		14	at Colorado	3-2
	18	Dallas	1-2		17	at Vancouver	0-1
	21	at Detroit	3-5		19	at Calgary	4-3
	22	Pittsburgh	5-1		20	at Edmonton	3-2†
	26	at Anaheim	1-6		22	at Minnesota	4-2
	27	at Los Angeles	2-3*		24	Buffalo	4-5*
	29	at San Jose	1-4		26	Columbus	4-3
Nov.	1	at Colorado	5-1		31	at Pittsburgh	2-4
	3	at Arizona	2-3†	Feb.	2	Edmonton	2-0
	5	Carolina	2-3†		4	Detroit	0-1
	8	Ottawa	3-1		7	Vancouver	4-2
	10	St. Louis	3-1		9	at NY Rangers	3-4
	12	Anaheim	5-0		11	Florida	4-7
	15	at Toronto	2-6		13	Dallas	5-3
	17	at Ottawa	5-1		18	at Minnesota	2-5
	19	at St. Louis	1-3		19	at Columbus	4-3
	21	Tampa Bay	3-1		21	Calgary	5-6*
	23	Dallas	5-2		23	Colorado	4-2
	25	Winnipeg	5-1		25	Washington	5-2
	27	at Winnipeg	0-3		26	Edmonton	5-4
	29	at Colorado	5-3		28	at Buffalo	5-4*
Dec.	3	New Jersey	4-5*	Mar.	2	at Montreal	1-2
	4	Philadelphia	2-4		4	Chicago	3-5
	6	Colorado	4-3		7	at Anaheim	3-4†
	8	at Dallas	2-5		9	at Los Angeles	2-3*
	10	at Arizona	1-4		11	at San Jose	3-1
	13	St. Louis	6-3		13	Winnipeg	5-4*
	15	Minnesota	2-5		16	at Washington	2-1*
	17	NY Rangers	1-2†		18	at Carolina	2-4
	19	at Philadelphia	2-1†		20	Arizona	3-1
	20	at New Jersey	5-1		23	Calgary	3-1
	22	Los Angeles	0-4		25	San Jose	7-2
	27	Minnesota	2-3*		27	at NY Islanders	3-1
	29	Chicago	2-3		28	at Boston	1-4
	30	at St. Louis	4-0		30	Toronto	1-3
Jan.	3	Montreal	1-2*	Apr.	1	Minnesota	3-0
	5	at Tampa Bay	6-1		2	at St. Louis	1-4
	6	at Florida	1-2		4	NY Islanders	1-2*
	8	at Chicago	2-5		6	at Dallas	7-3
	10	Vancouver	2-1*		8	at Winnipeg	1-2

* – Overtime   † – Shootout

NHL Draft Selections 2017-2003

Name in bold denotes played in NHL.

2017

Pick	
30	Eeli Tolvanen
61	Grant Mismash
92	David Farrance
154	Tomas Vomacka
176	Pavel Koltygin
216	Jacob Paquette

2016

Pick	
17	Dante Fabbro
47	Samuel Girard
76	Rem Pitlick
78	Frederic Allard
108	Hardy Haman Aktell
138	Patrick Harper
168	Konstantin Volkov
198	Adam Smith

2015

Pick	
55	Yakov Trenin
85	Thomas Novak
100	Anthony Richard
115	**Alexandre Carrier**
145	Karel Vejmelka
175	Tyler Moy
205	Evan Smith

2014

Pick	
11	**Kevin Fiala**
42	**Vladislav Kamenev**
51	Jack Dougherty
62	Justin Kirkland
112	**Viktor Arvidsson**
132	Joonas Lyytinen
162	Aaron Irving

2013

Pick	
4	**Seth Jones**
64	Jonathan Diaby
95	Felix Girard
99	**Juuse Saros**
125	Saku Maenalanen
140	Teemu Kivihalme
155	Emil Pettersson
171	Tommy Veilleux
185	Wade Murphy
203	Janne Juvonen

2012

Pick	
37	**Pontus Aberg**
50	**Colton Sissons**
66	**Jimmy Vesey**
89	**Brendan Leipsic**
112	Zach Stepan
118	Mikko Vainonen
164	Simon Fernholm
172	Max Gortz
179	**Marek Mazanec**

2011

Pick	
38	**Magnus Hellberg**
52	**Miikka Salomaki**
94	Josh Shalla
112	Garrett Noonan
142	Simon Karlsson
170	Chase Balisy
202	Brent Andrews

2010

Pick	
18	**Austin Watson**
78	Taylor Aronson
126	Patrick Cehlin
168	**Anthony Bitetto**
194	David Elsner
198	**Joonas Rask**

2009

Pick	
11	**Ryan Ellis**
41	Zach budish
42	Charles-Olivier Roussel
70	**Taylor Beck**
72	**Michael Latta**
98	**Craig Smith**
102	**Mattias Ekholm**
110	Nick Oliver
132	**Gabriel Bourque**
192	Cam Reid

2008

Pick	
7	**Colin Wilson**
18	Chet Pickard
38	**Roman Josi**
136	Taylor Stefishen
166	Jeff Foss
201	Jani Lajunen
207	**Anders Lindback**

2007

Pick	
23	**Jonathon Blum**
54	**Jeremy Smith**
58	**Nick Spaling**
81	**Ryan Thang**
114	Ben Ryan
119	Mark Santorelli
144	**Andreas Thuresson**
174	Robert Dietrich
204	Atte Engren

2006

Pick	
56	**Blake Geoffrion**
105	Niko Snellman
146	**Mark Dekanich**
176	Ryan Flynn
206	Viktor Sjodin

2005

Pick	
18	**Ryan Parent**
78	**Teemu Laakso**
79	**Cody Franson**
150	**Cal O'Reilly**
176	Ryan Maki
213	Scott Todd
230	**Patric Hornqvist**

2004

Pick	
15	**Alexander Radulov**
81	Vaclav Meidl
107	Nick Fugere
139	Kyle Moir
147	**Janne Niskala**
178	**Mike Santorelli**
193	Kevin Schaeffer
209	Stanislav Balan
243	Denis Kulyash
258	**Pekka Rinne**
275	Craig Switzer

2003

Pick	
7	**Ryan Suter**
35	Konstantin Glazachev
37	**Kevin Klein**
49	**Shea Weber**
76	Richard Stehlik
89	Paul Brown
92	**Alexander Sulzer**
98	Grigory Shafigulin
117	Teemu Lassila
133	Rustam Sidikov
210	Andrei Mukhachev
213	Miroslav Hanuljak
268	Lauris Darzins

General Managers' History

David Poile, 1998-99 to date.

David Poile

President of Hockey Operations and General Manager

Born: Toronto, ON, February 14, 1949.

Hired as the first general manager in franchise history on July 9, 1997, David Poile saw the Predators reach the Stanley Cup Final for the first time in 2016-17 and was rewarded as the NHL General Manager of the Year.

Over the years, Poile has been committed to building the team through the NHL Draft. In 2003-04, Nashville reached the playoffs for the first time in franchise history. During the 2006-07 season, the team was in contention for first overall in the NHL, setting club records with 51 wins and 110 points. Though forced to rebuild the roster for 2007-08, the Predators reached the playoffs for the fourth year in a row. Poile has an impressive reputation as an NHL leader and in 2001 he received the Lester Patrick Trophy for his contributions to hockey in the United States. His father, Norman "Bud" Poile, had won the honor in 1989. He served as Associate G.M. for the 2010 U.S. Olympic Team and U.S. squads for the 2009 and 2010 IIHF World Championships and was the general manager of the 2014 U.S. Olympic team at Sochi. He was a finalist for the NHL's inaugural G.M. of the Year Award in 2010 and was a finalist for the award again in 2011 and 2012.

Prior to joining Nashville, Poile spent 15 seasons as vice president/general manager of the Washington Capitals. During his tenure in Washington, the Capitals made 14 postseason appearances, winning their only Patrick Division title in 1989 and advancing to the Conference Finals in 1990. During Poile's 15 years in Washington, the Capitals compiled a record of 594-454-132, finished second in the Patrick Division seven times and recorded 90-or-more points seven different seasons.

Poile started his professional hockey career as an administrative assistant for the Atlanta Flames in 1972, shortly after graduating from Northeastern University in Boston. At Northeastern, he was hockey team captain, leading scorer and most valuable player for two years. In 1977, he was named assistant general manager of the Atlanta Flames (who moved to Calgary in 1980), serving as the manager and coordinator of the Flames farm club.

Poile was instrumental in the NHL's adoption of the instant replay rule in 1991. He was awarded *Inside Hockey*'s man of the year for his leadership on the issue. He has also been honored three times as *The Sporting News* NHL executive of the year in 1982-83, 1983-84 and 2006-07. Poile served as general manager of the 1998 and 1999 U.S. national teams for the World Championships.

Club Directory

Bridgestone Arena

Nashville Predators
Bridgestone Arena
501 Broadway
Nashville, TN 37203
Phone **615/770-2300**
FAX 615/770-2309
Ticket Information 615/770-PUCK
www.nashvillepredators.com
Capacity: 17,113

Owner	Predators Holdings LLC
Investor Group	Christopher Cigarran, Thomas Cigarran, Joel and Holly Dobberpuhl, David Freeman, Herbert Fritch, DeWitt Thompson V, John Thompson, W. Brett Wilson & Warren Woo
Chairman and Governor	Thomas Cigarran
Pres. of Hockey Ops/G.M./Alt. Gov.	David Poile
President/CEO/Alt. Gov	Sean Henry
Exec. V.P., General Counsel and CFO	Michelle Kennedy
Exec. V.P., Chief Revenue Officer	Chris Junghans
Sr. V.P., Ticket/Premium Sales, Youth Hockey	Nat Harden
Sr. V.P., Senior Advisor	Gerry Helper
Sr. V.P.s, Booking / Finance	David Kells / Keith Hegger

Hockey Operations

Assistant General Manager	Paul Fenton
Director of Hockey Operations	Brian Poile
Hockey Operations Manager / Assistant	Brandon Walker / Jeff Zavatsky
Hockey Ops Systems Analyst / Analytics Coord	Paul Cook / Matt Hamann
Head Coach	Peter Laviolette
Assistant Coaches	Kevin McCarthy, Dan Muse
Goaltending Coach	Ben Vanderklok
Strength and Conditioning Coach	David Good
Video Coach / Coordinators	Lawrence Feloney / Andrew Meloche, Nick Lubrano
Player Development Director / Asst. Director	Scott Nichol / Wade Redden
Chief Amateur Scout	Jeff Kealty
Professional Scouts	Nick Beverley, Rob Cowie, Shawn Dineen
North American Amateur Scouts	J-P Glaude, Tom Nolan, Ryan Rezmierski, Glen Sanders, David Westby
European Scouts	Martin Bakula, Lucas Bergman, Janne Kekalainen
Head Athletic Trainer / Assistant Trainers	Andy Hosler / D.J. Amadio, Jeff Biddle
Equipment Manager / Asst. Manager	Pete Rogers / Jeff Camelio
Equipment Assistant / Locker Room Attendant	Brad Peterson / Craig "Partner" Baugh

Medical Staff

Team Doctors	Drs. John E. Kuhn, Paul J. Rummo, Charles L. Cox, Alex Diamond, Brian Drolet, Kevin Dabrowski, Daniel Weikert, Sean Donahue, Gary Solomon, Joseph Fredi, Stephane Braun, Christopher Ellis, Kent Higdon, Blair Summitt, Wesley Thayer & Cliff Brown

Marketing & Communications

Vice President, Marketing & Communications	Danny Shaklan
Communications Director / Manager	Kevin Wilson / XXXXXXXXX
Dir., Mktg. Entertainment / Digital Manager, Producer	Adam DeVault / Thomas Willis
Marketing Managers / Coordinator / Asst.	Sandy Weaver, Claire Francis / Sean Hochberg / Alexandria DiDomenico
Corp. Comm. / Comm. & Content Coordinator	Natalie Aronson / Brooks Bratten
Social Media / Promotion & Event Coordinator	Megan Garrett / Maverick Whited
Director, Creative Services	Chuck Stephens
Sr. Graphic Designer / Graphics Assistants	Jackie Fisher / Chris LoBosco, James O'Hara
Team Photographer	John Russell

Community Relations

Community Relations Sr. Dir. / Mgr. / Coordinators	Rebecca King / Kristen Finch / Krystin Fisher, Taylor Bartz

Corporate Partnerships/Development

Vice President, Corporate Partnerships / Directors	Delmar Smith / Jeremy Burson, Jack Burk
Sr. Account Service Mgrs., Corporate Partnerships	Jennifer Maxwell, Paige Ciuffo
Account Managers, Corporate Partnerships	Marilu Hagen, Robin Lee & Jordan Wright

Premium Seats

Vice President of Service and Retention / Sr. Director	Britt Kincheloe / Marty Mulford
Club Services Coordinators	Zach Preston & Whitney Snyder
Premium Seats Service Coordinators	Braydon Brown & MacKenzie Hood

Finance & Human Resources

VP of Human Resources	Laurie Scott
Human Resources Sr. Dir. / Coordinator	Courtni Mosley / Bre Laabs
Controller	Jane Avinger
Sr. Director, Operations	Kyle Clayton
Accounting Mgr. / Coord. / Staff Accountant	Matt Loftus / Brandon Koehler / Brianna Gefre
Director, Payroll / Manager, Payroll	Susan Charnley / Amber Stone
Assistant General Counsel / Counsel	Heidi Bundren / Jill Ormandy
Exec. Assistant / Administrative Assistant	Beth DeGrandis / Pier Vaughn

Information Technology

IT Sr. Director / Director / Coord.	Casey Millar / Michael Paul / Tommy Nelson

Broadcast & Entertainment

Broadcast and Entertainment, Sr. Dir. / Producer	Bob Kohl / David White
Director, Event Presentation / Coordinator	Brian Campbell / Colleen Flynn
Video Production Manager / Creative Content Producer	Mitch Jordan / Shane Blindert
Associate Producer / Feature Producer	Brett Newkirk / Lynne Koester
Television Play-by-Play Announcer / Color	Willy Daunic / Chris Mason
Radio Play-by-Play Announcer / Color	Pete Weber / Hal Gill, Brent Peterson
Television Pre and Postgame Hosts	Mark Howard, Terry Crisp
Rinkside Reporter	Lyndsay Rowley

Ticket Operations

Directors Ticket Sales / Business Strategy	Brad Gillispie / JT Louviere
Premium Sales Dir. / Sr. Manager	Chris Burton / Tim Wilson
Business Analytics Mgr. / Business Intelligence Mgr.	Lindsay Rutledge / Michael Rust
Group Sales Manager	Dan Schaefer
Corp. Development Managers	Alex Garmezy, Mickey Hock, AJ Rockwell & Josh Wolf

Key Off-Season Signings/Acquisitions

2017

June 17 • Acquired D **Mirco Mueller** and a 5th-round pick in 2017 NHL Draft from San Jose for 2nd- and 4th-round picks in 2017 NHL Draft.

29 • Re-signed G **Keith Kinkaid**.

July 1 • Signed C **Brian Boyle** and D **Brian Strait**.

2 • Acquired LW **Marcus Johansson** from Washington for 2nd- and 3rd-round picks in 2018 NHL Draft.

25 • Re-signed LW **Joseph Blandisi**, D **Mirco Mueller** and G **Scott Wedgewood**.

26 • Re-signed RW **Stefan Noesen**, C **Kevin Rooney** and LW **Ben Thomson**.

New Jersey Devils

2016-17 Results: 28W-40L-11OTL-3SOL 70PTS
8TH, Metropolitan Division • 16TH, Eastern Conference

Celebrating a goal against the rival Rangers in a 3-2 Devils win on March 21, 2017, Taylor Hall (left) and Kyle Palmieri were New Jersey's two top scorers in 2016-17.

2017-18 Schedule

Oct.	Sat.	7	Colorado		Sat.	13	Philadelphia
	Mon.	9	at Buffalo*		Tue.	16	at NY Islanders
	Wed.	11	at Toronto		Thu.	18	Washington
	Fri.	13	Washington		Sat.	20	at Philadelphia*
	Sat.	14	at NY Rangers		Mon.	22	Detroit
	Tue.	17	Tampa Bay		Tue.	23	at Boston
	Thu.	19	at Ottawa		Thu.	25	Nashville
	Fri.	20	San Jose		Tue.	30	at Buffalo
	Fri.	27	Ottawa	**Feb.**	Thu.	1	Philadelphia
	Sat.	28	Arizona		Sat.	3	Pittsburgh
Nov.	Wed.	1	at Vancouver		Tue.	6	at Ottawa
	Fri.	3	at Edmonton		Thu.	8	Calgary
	Sun.	5	at Calgary		Sat.	10	at Columbus
	Tue.	7	St. Louis		Sun.	11	Boston
	Thu.	9	Edmonton		Tue.	13	at Philadelphia
	Sat.	11	Florida		Thu.	15	Carolina
	Sun.	12	at Chicago		Sat.	17	at Tampa Bay
	Thu.	16	at Toronto		Sun.	18	at Carolina*
	Sat.	18	at Winnipeg*		Tue.	20	Columbus
	Mon.	20	at Minnesota		Thu.	22	Minnesota
	Wed.	22	Boston		Sat.	24	NY Islanders
	Fri.	24	Vancouver		Tue.	27	at Pittsburgh
	Sat.	25	at Detroit	**Mar.**	Thu.	1	at Florida
	Mon.	27	Florida		Fri.	2	at Carolina
Dec.	Fri.	1	at Colorado		Sun.	4	Vegas*
	Sat.	2	at Arizona		Tue.	6	Montreal
	Tue.	5	at Columbus		Thu.	8	Winnipeg
	Fri.	8	Columbus		Sat.	10	at Nashville
	Sat.	9	at NY Rangers		Wed.	14	at Vegas
	Tue.	12	Los Angeles		Sat.	17	at Los Angeles*
	Thu.	14	at Montreal		Sun.	18	at Anaheim
	Fri.	15	Dallas		Tue.	20	at San Jose
	Mon.	18	Anaheim		Fri.	23	at Pittsburgh
	Thu.	21	NY Rangers		Sat.	24	Tampa Bay
	Sat.	23	Chicago		Tue.	27	Carolina
	Wed.	27	Detroit		Thu.	29	Pittsburgh
	Fri.	29	Buffalo		Sat.	31	NY Islanders
	Sat.	30	at Washington	**Apr.**	Sun.	1	at Montreal
Jan.	Tue.	2	at St. Louis*		Tue.	3	NY Rangers
	Thu.	4	at Dallas		Thu.	5	Toronto
	Sun.	7	at NY Islanders*		Sat.	7	at Washington

* Denotes afternoon game.

Retired Numbers

3	Ken Daneyko	1982-2003
4	Scott Stevens	1991-2005
27	Scott Niedermayer	1991-2004
30	Martin Brodeur	1992-2014

METROPOLITAN DIVISION
44th NHL Season

Franchise date: June 11, 1974

Transferred from Denver to New Jersey, June 30, 1982.
Transferred from Kansas City to Denver, August 25, 1976.

Year-by-Year Record

Season	GP	Home W	L	T	OL	Road W	L	T	OL	Overall W	L	T	OL	GF	GA	Pts.	Div. Fin.	Conf. Fin.	Playoff Result
2016-17	82	16	17	....	8	12	23	....	6	28	40		14	183	244	70	8th, Met.	16th, East	– out of playoffs –
2015-16	82	19	17	....	5	19	19	....	3	38	36		8	184	208	84	7th, Met.	12th, East	– out of playoffs –
2014-15	82	19	14	....	8	13	22	....	6	32	36		14	181	216	78	7th, Met.	13th, East	– out of playoffs –
2013-14	82	21	11	....	9	14	18	....	9	35	29		18	197	208	88	6th, Met.	10th, East	– out of playoffs –
2012-13	48	13	9	....	2	6	10	....	8	19	19		10	112	129	48	5th, Atl.	11th, East	– out of playoffs –
2011-12	82	24	13	....	4	24	15	....	2	48	28		6	228	209	102	4th, Atl.	6th, East	**Lost Final**
2010-11	82	22	16	....	3	16	23	....	2	38	39		5	174	209	81	4th, Atl.	11th, East	– out of playoffs –
2009-10	82	27	10	....	4	21	17	....	3	48	27		7	222	191	103	1st, Atl.	2nd, East	Lost Conf. Quarter-Final
2008-09	82	28	12	....	1	23	15	....	3	51	27		4	244	209	106	1st, Atl.	3rd, East	Lost Conf. Quarter-Final
2007-08	82	25	14	....	2	21	15	....	5	46	29		7	206	197	99	2nd, Atl.	4th, East	Lost Conf. Quarter-Final
2006-07	82	25	10	....	6	24	14	....	3	49	24		9	216	201	107	1st, Atl.	2nd, East	Lost Conf. Semi-Final
2005-06	82	27	11	....	3	19	16	....	6	46	27		9	242	229	101	1st, Atl.	3rd, East	Lost Conf. Semi-Final
2004-05	....																		
2003-04	82	22	13	5	1	21	12	7	1	43	25	12	2	213	164	100	2nd, Atl.	6th, East	Lost Conf. Quarter-Final
2002-03	**82**	**25**	**11**	**3**	**2**	**21**	**9**	**7**	**4**	**46**	**20**	**10**	**6**	**216**	**166**	**108**	**1st, Atl.**	**2nd, East**	**Won Stanley Cup**
2001-02	82	22	13	4	2	19	15	5	2	41	28	9	4	205	187	95	3rd, Atl.	6th, East	Lost Conf. Quarter-Final
2000-01	82	24	11	6	0	24	8	6	3	48	19	12	3	295	195	111	1st, Atl.	1st, East	Lost Final
1999-2000	**82**	**28**	**9**	**3**	**1**	**17**	**15**	**5**	**4**	**45**	**24**	**8**	**5**	**251**	**203**	**103**	**2nd, Atl.**	**4th, East**	**Won Stanley Cup**
1998-99	82	28	10	3	....	19	14	8	....	47	24	11		248	196	105	1st, Atl.	1st, East	Lost Conf. Quarter-Final
1997-98	82	29	10	2	....	19	13	9	....	48	23	11		225	166	107	1st, Atl.	1st, East	Lost Conf. Quarter-Final
1996-97	82	23	9	9	....	22	14	5	....	45	23	14		231	182	104	1st, Atl.	1st, East	Lost Conf. Semi-Final
1995-96	82	22	17	2	....	15	16	10	....	37	33	12		215	202	86	6th, Atl.	9th, East	– out of playoffs –
1994-95	**48**	**14**	**4**	**6**	....	**8**	**14**	**2**	....	**22**	**18**	**8**		**136**	**121**	**52**	**2nd, Atl.**	**5th, East**	**Won Stanley Cup**
1993-94	84	29	11	2	....	18	14	10	....	47	25	12		306	220	106	2nd, Atl.	2nd, East	Lost Conf. Final
1992-93	84	24	14	4	....	16	23	3	....	40	37	7		308	299	87	4th, Patrick		Lost Div. Semi-Final
1991-92	80	24	12	4	....	14	19	3	....	38	31	11		289	259	87	4th, Patrick		Lost Div. Semi-Final
1990-91	80	23	10	7	....	9	23	8	....	32	33	15		272	264	79	4th, Patrick		Lost Div. Semi-Final
1989-90	80	22	15	3	....	15	19	6	....	37	34	9		295	288	83	2nd, Patrick		Lost Div. Semi-Final
1988-89	80	17	18	5	....	10	23	7	....	27	41	12		281	325	66	5th, Patrick		– out of playoffs –
1987-88	80	23	16	1	....	15	20	5	....	38	36	6		295	296	82	4th, Patrick		Lost Conf. Final
1986-87	80	20	17	3	....	9	28	3	....	29	45	6		293	368	64	6th, Patrick		– out of playoffs –
1985-86	80	17	21	2	....	11	28	1	....	28	49	3		300	374	59	6th, Patrick		– out of playoffs –
1984-85	80	13	21	6	....	9	27	4	....	22	48	10		264	346	54	5th, Patrick		– out of playoffs –
1983-84	80	10	28	2	....	7	28	5	....	17	56	7		231	350	41	5th, Patrick		– out of playoffs –
1982-83	80	11	20	9	....	6	29	5	....	17	49	14		230	338	48	5th, Patrick		– out of playoffs –
1981-82**	80	14	21	5	....	4	28	8	....	18	49	13		241	362	49	5th, Smythe		– out of playoffs –
1980-81**	80	15	16	9	....	7	29	4	....	22	45	13		258	344	57	6th, Smythe		– out of playoffs –
1979-80**	80	12	20	8	....	7	28	5	....	19	48	13		234	308	51	6th, Smythe		– out of playoffs –
1978-79**	80	8	24	8	....	7	29	4	....	15	53	12		210	331	42	4th, Smythe		– out of playoffs –
1977-78	**80**	**17**	**14**	**9**	....	**2**	**26**	**12**	....	**19**	**40**	**21**		**257**	**305**	**59**	**2nd, Smythe**		**Lost Prelim. Round**
1976-77**	80	12	20	8	....	8	26	6	....	20	46	14		226	307	54	5th, Smythe		– out of playoffs –
1975-76*	80	12	20	8	....	4	32	4	....	12	56	12		190	351	36	5th, Smythe		– out of playoffs –
1974-75*	80	12	20	8	....	3	34	3	....	15	54	11		184	328	41	5th, Smythe		– out of playoffs –

* Kansas City Scouts. ** Colorado Rockies.

2017-18 Player Personnel

FORWARDS	HT	WT	*Age	Birthplace	S	2016-17 Club
BADDOCK, Brandon	6-4	215	22	Vermilion, AB	L	Adirondack
BASTIAN, Nathan	6-4	205	19	Kitchener, ON	R	Mississauga
BLANDISI, Joseph	6-0	200	23	Markham, ON	L	New Jersey-Albany
BOYLE, Brian	6-6	245	32	Hingham, MA	L	Tampa Bay-Toronto
BRATT, Jesper	5-10	175	19	Stockholm, Sweden	L	AIK Jr.-AIK
COLEMAN, Blake	5-11	200	25	Plano, TX	L	New Jersey-Albany
GIBBONS, Brian	5-8	175	29	Braintree, MA	L	Albany
GIGNAC, Brandon	5-11	180	19	Repentigny, QC	L	Shawinigan-Albany
HALL, Taylor	6-1	205	25	Calgary, AB	L	New Jersey
HENRIQUE, Adam	6-0	195	27	Brantford, ON	L	New Jersey
HISCHIER, Nico	6-1	175	18	Brig, Switz.	L	Halifax
JOHANSSON, Marcus	6-1	205	26	Landskrona, Sweden	L	Washington
KEARNS, Bracken	6-0	195	36	West Vancouver, BC	L	NY Islanders-Bridgeport
KUJAWINSKI, Ryan	6-2	205	22	Kirkland Lake, ON	L	Albany
LAPPIN, Nick	6-1	175	24	Geneva, IL	R	New Jersey-Albany
McLEOD, Michael	6-2	195	19	Mississauga, ON	R	Mississauga
NOESEN, Stefan	6-1	205	24	Plano, TX	R	Ana-San Diego-N.J.
PALMIERI, Kyle	5-11	185	26	Smithtown, NY	R	New Jersey
PIETILA, Blake	5-11	200	24	Milford, MI	L	New Jersey-Albany
QUENNEVILLE, John	6-1	195	21	Edmonton, AB	L	New Jersey-Albany
ROONEY, Kevin	6-2	190	24	Canton, MA	L	New Jersey-Albany
SPEERS, Blake	5-11	185	20	Sault Ste. Marie, ON	R	N.J.-Sault Ste. Marie-Alb
THOMSON, Ben	6-3	205	24	Brampton, ON	L	New Jersey-Albany
WOOD, Miles	6-2	195	22	Buffalo, NY	L	New Jersey-Albany
ZACHA, Pavel	6-3	210	20	Brno, Czech Rep.	L	New Jersey
ZAJAC, Travis	6-2	185	32	Winnipeg, MB	R	New Jersey
DEFENSEMEN						
DYBLENKO, Yaroslav	6-2	195	23	Surgut, Russia	L	Spartak
GREENE, Andy	5-11	190	34	Trenton, MI	L	New Jersey
JACOBS, Joshua	6-2	200	21	Shelby Township, MI	R	Albany-Adirondack
KAPLA, Michael	6-0	200	23	Eau Claire, WI	L	U. Mass Lowell-New Jersey
LOOV, Viktor	6-3	210	24	Sodertalje, Sweden	L	Toronto (AHL)-Albany
LOVEJOY, Ben	6-1	205	33	Concord, NH	R	New Jersey
MOORE, John	6-3	210	26	Winnetka, IL	L	New Jersey
MUELLER, Mirco	6-3	210	22	Winterthur, Switz.	L	San Jose-San Jose (AHL)
PROUT, Dalton	6-3	230	27	Kingsville, ON	R	CBJ-Cleveland-N.J.
SANTINI, Steven	6-2	205	22	Bronxville, NY	R	New Jersey-Albany
SEVERSON, Damon	6-2	205	23	Melville, SK	R	New Jersey
SISSONS, Colby	6-2	190	19	Edmonton, AB	L	Swift Current
STRAIT, Brian	6-1	205	29	Boston, MA	L	Winnipeg-Manitoba
WHITE, Colton	6-1	195	20	London, ON	L	Sault Ste. Marie
GOALTENDERS	HT	WT	*Age	Birthplace	C	2016-17 Club
APPLEBY, Ken	6-4	210	22	North Bay, ON	L	Albany-Adirondack
BLACKWOOD, Mackenzie	6-4	225	20	Thunder Bay, ON	L	Albany
KINKAID, Keith	6-3	195	28	Farmingville, NY	L	New Jersey
SCHNEIDER, Cory	6-3	200	31	Marblehead, MA	L	New Jersey
WEDGEWOOD, Scott	6-2	195	25	Brampton, ON	L	Albany

* – Age at start of 2017-18 season

General Managers' History

Sid Abel, 1974-75; Sid Abel and Baz Bastien, 1975-76; Ray Miron, 1976-77 to 1980-81; Bill MacMillan, 1981-82, 1982-83; Bill MacMillan and Max McNab, 1983-84; Max McNab 1984-85 to 1986-87; Lou Lamoriello, 1987-88 to 2014-15; Ray Shero, 2015-16 to date.

Ray Shero
Executive Vice President/General Manager
Born: St. Paul, MN, July 28, 1962.

Ray Shero was named the fourth general manager in New Jersey Devils history on May 4, 2015.

Shero spent eight seasons, 2006-07 through 2013-14, as executive vice president and general manager of the Pittsburgh Penguins. During that time, the team compiled a 373-193-56 (.645) mark, won the 2009 Stanley Cup championship, two consecutive Eastern Conference titles in 2007-08 and 2008-09 and had three first-place divisional finishes. He was named the 2012-13 recipient of the General Manager of the Year Award, as voted on by the 30 NHL general managers, a panel of NHL executives, as well as print and broadcast media. Previously, Shero spent 14 seasons as an assistant general manager with the Ottawa Senators (1993 to 1998) and Nashville Predators (1998 to 2006). Shero has been actively involved with USA Hockey, is a member of its national team advisory board, and most recently served as associate general manager for the 2014 Winter Olympic Games. He also spent seven seasons as a player agent prior to making the transition to the front office.

A forward in his playing days, Shero was drafted by Los Angeles in the 11th round (216th overall) of the 1982 NHL Draft. He played four seasons collegiately at St. Lawrence University (Canton, New York), and served as the team's captain on two occasions. He led the school in scoring twice, and graduated in 1984 as one of the top-ten scorers in Saints' history. The son of the late Hockey Hall of Fame head coach Fred Shero, Ray and his dad are one of the few father-son tandems to both have their names engraved on the Stanley Cup. Fred Shero served as the Devils' radio commentator in the 1980s.

2016-17 Scoring
* – rookie

Regular Season

Pos	#	Player	Team	GP	G	A	Pts	TOI	+/-	PIM	PP	SH	GW	S	S%
C	21	Kyle Palmieri	N.J.	80	26	27	53	17:20	2	46	8	1	4	192	13.5
L	9	Taylor Hall	N.J.	72	20	33	53	19:19	-9	32	7	0	4	238	8.4
C	19	Travis Zajac	N.J.	80	14	31	45	19:43	-8	33	6	1	1	126	11.1
C	14	Adam Henrique	N.J.	82	20	20	40	18:10	-20	38	6	2	2	142	14.1
L	13	Michael Cammalleri	N.J.	61	10	21	31	17:21	-9	21	1	0	3	142	7.0
D	28	Damon Severson	N.J.	80	3	28	31	20:21	-31	58	0	0	1	125	2.4
C	37	* Pavel Zacha	N.J.	70	8	16	24	14:18	-17	19	5	0	2	83	9.6
D	2	John Moore	N.J.	63	12	10	22	18:58	-7	39	1	0	1	102	11.8
R	8	Beau Bennett	N.J.	65	8	11	19	13:33	-3	20	1	0	1	101	7.9
L	44	* Miles Wood	N.J.	60	8	9	17	12:51	-21	86	2	0	0	105	7.6
D	6	Andy Greene	N.J.	66	4	9	13	21:56	-16	8	1	1	1	83	4.8
R	23	* Stefan Noesen	ANA	12	2	0	2	6:33	2	2	0	0	0	12	16.7
			N.J.	32	6	2	8	12:50	4	22	0	0	0	51	11.8
			Total	44	8	2	10	11:07	6	24	0	0	0	63	12.7
C	16	Jacob Josefson	N.J.	38	1	9	10	12:14	-1	16	0	0	1	44	2.3
C	25	Devante Smith-Pelly	N.J.	53	4	5	9	13:30	-19	12	0	0	0	76	5.3
C	64	Joseph Blandisi	N.J.	27	3	6	9	13:21	-10	26	1	0	2	24	12.5
R	36	* Nick Lappin	N.J.	43	4	3	7	11:43	-17	17	0	0	0	57	7.0
C	34	* Steven Santini	N.J.	38	2	5	7	16:05	-6	14	0	0	0	46	4.3
D	12	Ben Lovejoy	N.J.	82	1	6	7	20:46	-7	39	0	0	1	84	1.2
D	7	Jon Merrill	N.J.	51	1	5	6	18:33	-9	24	0	0	0	48	2.1
D	47	Dalton Prout	CBJ	15	0	3	3	13:03	4	14	0	0	0	6	0.0
			N.J.	14	0	3	3	14:56	-5	30	0	0	0	7	0.0
			Total	29	0	6	6	13:58	-1	44	0	0	0	13	0.0
D	33	Yohann Auvitu	N.J.	25	2	2	4	15:36	1	2	0	0	0	54	3.7
C	51	Sergey Kalinin	N.J.	43	2	2	4	12:47	-14	15	0	0	0	38	5.3
C	42	* John Quenneville	N.J.	12	1	3	4	13:41	1	2	1	0	0	21	4.8
C	46	Karl Stollery	N.J.	11	0	3	3	16:55	-5	13	0	0	0	11	0.0
C	40	* Blake Coleman	N.J.	23	1	2	3	12:50	-7	27	0	0	0	29	3.4
D	39	Seth Helgeson	N.J.	9	1	0	1	13:28	2	15	0	0	0	3	33.3
L	56	* Blake Pietila	N.J.	10	0	1	1	13:02	-5	4	0	0	0	9	0.0
L	43	* Ben Thomson	N.J.	8	0	1	1	10:53	-4	7	0	0	0	7	0.0
C	74	* Blake Speers	N.J.	3	0	0	0	9:29	0	0	0	0	0	3	0.0
C	58	* Kevin Rooney	N.J.	4	0	0	0	10:11	-3	4	0	0	0	2	0.0
D	32	* Michael Kapla	N.J.	5	0	0	0	17:26	-1	0	0	0	0	3	0.0
L	20	Luke Gazdic	N.J.	11	0	0	0	7:07	-2	12	0	0	0	3	0.0

Goaltending

No.	Goaltender	GPI	Mins	Avg	W	L	OT	EN	SO	GA	SA	Sv%	G	A	PIM
1	Keith Kinkaid	26	1476	2.64	8	13	3	4	1	65	778	.916	0	1	0
35	Cory Schneider	60	3473	2.82	20	27	11	9	2	163	1781	.908	0	0	0
	Totals	82	4988	2.90	28	40	14	13	3	241	2572	.906			

Captains' History

Simon Nolet, 1974-75 to 1976-77; Wilf Paiement, 1977-78; Gary Croteau, 1978-79; Mike Christie, Rene Robert and Lanny McDonald, 1979-80; Lanny McDonald, 1980-81; Lanny McDonald and Rob Ramage, 1981-82; Don Lever, 1982-83; Don Lever and Mel Bridgman, 1983-84; Mel Bridgman, 1984-85 to 1986-87; Kirk Muller, 1987-88 to 1990-91; Bruce Driver, 1991-92; Scott Stevens, 1992-93 to 2002-03; Scott Stevens and Scott Niedermayer, 2003-04; no captain, 2005-06; Patrik Elias, 2006-07; Patrik Elias and Jamie Langenbrunner, 2007-08; Jamie Langenbrunner, 2008-09 to 2010-11; Zach Parise, 2011-12; Bryce Salvador, 2012-13 to 2014-15; Andy Greene, 2015-16 to date.

In his first season with the Devils in 2016-17, Ben Lovejoy played a full 82 games for the first time in his carer and led the team in time on ice.

Club Records

Team

(Figures in brackets for season records are games played; records for fewest points, wins, ties, losses, goals, goals against are for 70 or more games)

Most Points	111	2000-01 (82)
Most Wins	51	2008-09 (82)
Most Ties	*21	1977-78 (80)
	15	1990-91 (80)
Most Losses	56	1975-76 (80), 1983-84 (80)
Most Goals	308	1992-93 (84)
Most Goals Against	374	1985-86 (80)
Fewest Points	*36	1975-76 (80)
	41	1983-84 (80)
Fewest Wins	*12	1975-76 (80)
	17	1982-83 (80), 1983-84 (80)
Fewest Ties	3	1985-86 (80)
Fewest Losses	19	2000-01 (82)
Fewest Goals	174	2010-11 (82)
Fewest Goals Against	164	2003-04 (82)

Longest Winning Streak
Overall............ 13 Feb. 26-Mar. 23/01
Home.............. 11 Feb. 9-Mar. 20/09
Away.............. 10 Feb. 27-Apr. 7/01

Longest Team Point Streak
Overall............ 13 Four times
Home.............. 15 Jan. 8-Mar. 15/97
(9w, 6т)
Away.............. 10 Feb. 27-Apr. 7/01
(9w, 1oTw)

Longest Losing Streak
Overall............ *14 Dec. 30/75-Jan. 29/76
.... 10 Oct. 14-Nov. 4/83
Home.............. 9 Dec. 22/85-Feb. 6/86
Away.............. 12 Oct. 19-Dec. 1/83

Longest Winless Streak
Overall............ *27 Feb. 12-Apr. 4/76
(21L, 6т)
.... 18 Oct. 20-Nov. 26/82
(14L 4т)
Home.............. *14 Feb. 12-Mar. 30/76
(10L, 4т),
Feb. 4-Mar. 31/79
(12L, 2т)
.... 9 Dec. 22/85-Feb. 6/86
(9L)
Away.............. *32 Nov. 12/77-Mar. 15/78
(22L, 10т)
.... 14 Dec. 26/82-Mar. 5/83
(13L, 1т)

Most Shutouts, Season	14	2003-04 (82)
Most PIM, Season	2,494	1988-89 (80)
Most Goals, Game	9	Nine times

Individual

Most Seasons	21	Martin Brodeur
Most Games	1,283	Ken Daneyko
Most Goals, Career	408	Patrik Elias
Most Assists, Career	617	Patrik Elias
Most Points, Career	1,025	Patrik Elias (408G, 617A)
Most PIM, Career	2,516	Ken Daneyko
Most Shutouts, Career	124	Martin Brodeur

Longest Consecutive
Games Streak............ 401 Travis Zajac
(Oct. 26/06-Apr. 10/11)

Most Goals, Season	48	Brian Gionta (2005-06)
Most Assists, Season	60	Scott Stevens (1993-94)
Most Points, Season	96	Patrik Elias (2000-01; 40G, 56A)
Most PIM, Season	295	Krzysztof Oliwa (1997-98)
Most Points, Defenseman, Season	78	Scott Stevens (1993-94; 18G, 60A)
Most Points, Center, Season	94	Kirk Muller (1987-88; 37G, 57A)
Most Points, Right Wing, Season	89	Brian Gionta (2005-06; 48G, 41A)
Most Points, Left Wing, Season	96	Patrik Elias (2000-01; 40G, 56A)
Most Points, Rookie, Season	70	Scott Gomez (1999-2000; 19G, 51A)
Most Shutouts, Season	12	Martin Brodeur (2006-07)
Most Goals, Game	4	Six times
Most Assists, Game	5	Greg Adams (Oct. 10/85) Kirk Muller (Mar. 25/87) Tom Kurvers (Feb. 13/89) Scott Gomez (Mar. 30/03)
Most Points, Game	6	Kirk Muller (Oct. 29/86; 3G, 3A)

* Records include Kansas City Scouts and Colorado Rockies, 1974-75 through 1981-82.

All-time Record vs. Other Clubs

Regular Season

	Total								At Home								On Road							
	GP	W	L	T	OL	GF	GA	PTS	GP	W	L	T	OL	GF	GA	PTS	GP	W	L	T	OL	GF	GA	PTS
Anaheim	32	17	13	1	1	85	80	36	15	10	4	0	1	44	27	21	17	7	9	1	0	41	53	15
Arizona	74	26	38	9	1	217	236	62	36	17	12	6	1	117	101	41	38	9	26	3	0	100	135	21
Boston	152	51	75	19	7	404	505	128	74	26	35	11	2	184	226	65	78	25	40	8	5	220	279	63
Buffalo	151	60	67	17	7	429	482	144	75	32	32	9	2	208	222	75	76	28	35	8	5	221	260	69
Calgary	101	26	61	11	3	270	386	66	52	18	30	3	1	142	179	40	49	8	31	8	2	128	207	26
Carolina	137	72	50	12	3	429	391	159	68	40	23	4	1	223	196	85	69	32	27	8	2	206	195	74
Chicago	109	39	44	21	5	313	364	104	55	24	17	11	3	166	161	62	54	15	27	10	2	147	203	42
Colorado	86	36	38	8	4	272	282	84	44	22	16	4	2	164	137	50	42	14	22	4	2	108	145	34
Columbus	29	13	12	1	3	68	74	30	14	7	5	1	1	30	30	16	15	6	7	0	2	38	44	14
Dallas	106	43	50	9	4	310	338	99	52	27	19	3	3	175	148	60	54	16	31	6	1	135	190	39
Detroit	99	40	45	11	3	311	331	94	49	24	14	9	2	160	131	59	50	16	31	6	1	151	200	35
Edmonton	78	32	34	9	3	252	277	76	40	18	18	3	1	124	124	40	38	14	16	6	2	128	153	36
Florida	92	52	28	7	5	258	205	116	46	30	12	3	1	141	94	64	46	22	16	4	4	117	111	52
Los Angeles	101	35	53	11	2	308	383	83	51	22	24	5	0	156	166	49	50	13	29	6	2	152	217	34
Minnesota	20	13	5	2	0	64	52	28	10	8	1	1	0	37	21	17	10	5	4	1	0	27	31	11
Montreal	151	65	71	10	5	412	475	145	76	36	33	4	3	222	248	79	75	29	38	6	2	190	227	66
Nashville	25	14	8	0	3	73	64	31	12	5	6	0	1	34	32	11	13	9	2	0	2	39	32	20
NY Islanders	239	87	119	22	11	686	814	207	118	52	49	11	6	366	375	121	121	35	70	11	5	320	439	86
NY Rangers	239	98	104	27	10	705	786	233	121	63	46	7	5	392	371	138	118	35	58	20	5	313	415	95
Ottawa	90	52	28	5	5	232	209	114	45	27	15	2	1	123	103	57	45	25	13	3	4	109	106	57
Philadelphia	238	109	105	18	6	704	772	242	119	68	40	8	3	397	358	147	119	41	65	10	3	307	414	95
Pittsburgh	230	111	97	17	5	739	744	244	116	61	40	10	2	391	349	137	114	50	57	4	3	348	395	107
St. Louis	106	37	53	14	2	320	362	90	53	23	22	7	1	159	144	54	53	14	31	7	1	161	218	36
San Jose	37	19	13	2	3	111	92	43	20	7	1	2	1	64	50	23	17	7	5	1	2	47	42	20
Tampa Bay	94	55	26	7	6	298	219	123	48	32	12	2	2	164	107	68	46	23	14	5	4	134	112	55
Toronto	137	48	59	20	10	407	443	126	67	28	20	15	4	225	207	75	70	20	39	5	6	182	236	51
Vancouver	110	36	53	17	4	312	370	93	56	24	23	6	3	170	176	57	54	12	30	11	1	142	194	36
Washington	206	88	101	13	4	583	674	193	102	51	41	7	3	299	293	112	104	37	60	6	1	284	381	81
Winnipeg	59	32	18	3	6	172	139	73	30	16	9	1	4	84	69	37	29	16	9	2	2	88	70	36
Defunct Clubs	16	6	5	5	0	44	46	17	8	4	2	2	0	25	19	10	8	2	3	3	0	19	27	7
Totals	3344	1412	1473	328	131	9788	10595	3283	1672	825	627	159	61	5186	4864	1870	1672	587	846	169	70	4602	5731	1413

Playoffs

	Series	W	L	GP	W	L	T	GF	GA	Last Mtg.	Rnd.	Result
Anaheim	1	1	0	7	4	3	0	19	12	2003	F	W 4-3
Boston	4	3	1	23	15	8	0	68	60	2003	CQF	W 4-3
Buffalo	1	1	0	7	4	3	0	14	14	1994	CQF	W 4-3
Carolina	4	1	3	24	10	14	0	56	51	2009	CQF	L 3-4
Colorado	1	0	1	7	3	4	0	11	19	2001	F	L 3-4
Dallas	1	1	0	6	4	2	0	15	9	2000	F	W 4-2
Detroit	1	1	0	4	4	0	0	16	7	1995	F	W 4-0
Florida	2	2	0	11	8	3	0	30	23	2012	CQF	W 4-3
Los Angeles	1	0	1	6	2	4	0	8	16	2012	F	L 2-4
Montreal	1	1	0	5	4	1	0	22	11	1997	CQF	W 4-1
NY Islanders	1	1	0	6	4	2	0	23	18	1988	DSF	W 4-2
NY Rangers	6	2	4	34	16	18	0	90	93	2012	CF	W 4-2
Ottawa	3	1	2	18	7	11	0	40	41	2007	CSF	L 1-4
Philadelphia	6	3	3	30	14	16	0	77	75	2012	CSF	W 4-1
Pittsburgh	5	2	3	29	15	14	0	86	80	2001	CF	W 4-1
Tampa Bay	2	2	0	11	8	3	0	33	22	2007	CQF	W 4-2
Toronto	2	2	0	13	8	5	0	37	27	2001	CSF	W 4-3
Washington	2	1	1	10	7	3	0	43	44	1990	DSF	L 2-4
Totals	44	25	19	254	136	118	0	688	622			

Calgary totals include Atlanta Flames, 1974-75 to 1979-80.
Colorado totals include Quebec, 1979-80 to 1994-95.
Phoenix totals include Winnipeg, 1979-80 to 1995-96.

Carolina totals include Hartford, 1979-80 to 1996-97.
Dallas totals include Minnesota North Stars, 1974-75 to 1992-93.
Winnipeg totals include Atlanta Thrashers, 1999-2000 to 2010-11.

Playoff Results 2017-2013

(Last playoff appearance: 2012)

Abbreviations: Round: F – Final;
CF – conference final; **CSF** – conference semi-final;
CQF – conference quarter-final; **DSF** – division semi-final.

NHL Draft Selections 2017-2003

Name in bold denotes played in NHL.

2017
Pick
1 Nico Hischier
36 Jesper Boqvist
63 Fabian Zetterlund
81 Reilly Walsh
98 Nikita Popugayev
129 Gilles Senn
143 Marian Studenic
160 Aarne Talvitie
191 Jocktan Chainey
205 Yegor Zaitsev
214 Matthew Hellickson

2016
Pick
12 Michael McLeod
41 Nathan Bastian
73 Joey Anderson
80 Brandon Gignac
102 Mikhail Maltsev
105 Evan Cormier
132 Yegor Rykov
162 Jesper Bratt
192 Jeremy Davies

2015
Pick
6 **Pavel Zacha**
42 **Mackenzie Blackwood**
67 **Blake Speers**
97 Colton White
157 Brett Seney

2014
Pick
30 **John Quenneville**
41 Joshua Jacobs
71 Connor Chatham
131 Ryan Rehill
152 J.D. Dudek
161 Brandon Baddock

2013
Pick
42 **Steven Santini**
73 Ryan Kujawinski
100 **Miles Wood**
160 Myles Bell
208 Anthony Brodeur

2012
Pick
29 **Stefan Matteau**
60 **Damon Severson**
90 Ben Johnson
96 **Ben Thomson**
135 Graham Black
150 Alexander Kerfoot
180 Artur Gavrus

2011
Pick
4 **Adam Larsson**
69 forfeited pick
75 **Blake Coleman**
99 **Reid Boucher**
129 **Blake Pietila**
159 Reece Scarlett
189 Patrick Daly

2010
Pick
38 **Jon Merrill**
84 **Scott Wedgewood**
114 Joe Faust
174 Maxime Clermont
204 Mauro Jorg

2009
Pick
20 **Jacob Josefson**
54 **Eric Gelinas**
73 **Alexander Urbom**
114 **Seth Helgeson**
144 Derek Rodwell
174 Ashton Bernard
204 Curtis Gedig

2008
Pick
24 **Mattias Tedenby**
52 Brandon Burlon
54 **Patrice Cormier**
82 **Adam Henrique**
112 Matt Delahey
142 Kory Nagy
172 David Wohlberg
202 Harry Young
205 Jean-Sebastien Berube

2007
Pick
57 Mike Hoeffel
79 **Nick Palmieri**
87 Corbin McPherson
117 **Matt Halischuk**
177 Vili Sopanen
207 Ryan Molle

2006
Pick
30 **Matthew Corrente**
58 **Alexander Vasyunov**
67 Kirill Tulupov
77 **Vladimir Zharkov**
107 Tyler Miller
148 **Olivier Magnan**
178 Tony Romano
208 Kyell Henegan

2005
Pick
23 **Niclas Bergfors**
38 **Jeff Frazee**
84 **Mark Fraser**
99 **Patrick Davis**
155 **Mark Fayne**
170 Sean Zimmerman
218 Alexander Sundstrom

2004
Pick
20 **Travis Zajac**
155 Alexander Mikhailishin
185 Josh Disher
216 **Pierre-Luc Letourneau-Leblond**
217 **Tyler Eckford**
250 Nathan Perkovich
282 Valeri Klimov

2003
Pick
17 **Zach Parise**
42 Petr Vrana
93 Ivan Khomutov
167 Zach Tarkir
197 Jason Smith
261 **Joey Tenute**
292 Arseny Bondarev

John Hynes
Head Coach

Born: Warwick, RI, February 10, 1975.

The New Jersey Devils named John Hynes as the 17th head coach in team history. The announcement was made by Devils' general manager Ray Shero on June 2, 2015.

Hynes joined the Devils after spending the previous six seasons with Wilkes-Barre/Scranton (American Hockey League), including five years, 2010-11 through 2014-15, as head coach. During that time, he led the Penguins to a 231-126-27 (.637) mark, including five straight 40-plus victory campaigns. Hynes guided Wilkes-Barre/Scranton to five consecutive playoff berths, including consecutive AHL Eastern Conference finals appearances in 2012-13 and 2013-14. His teams allowed the league's fewest goals in four of the five years. In Hynes' first season behind the Pens' bench, he was named the 2010-11 coach of the year after finishing with the AHL's best record. Hynes became the second-fastest coach in AHL history to reach the 100 career wins mark, doing so in just 152 games. In the second round of the 2013 Calder Cup playoffs, the Pens became the first team in league history to overcome a 3-0 deficit by winning games six and seven on the road. Hynes originally joined the organization as an assistant coach in 2009-10.

Hynes spent six seasons from 2003 to 2009 as head coach of USA Hockey's national team development program, posting an overall record of 188-131-26. He led the U.S. under-18 national team to three medals at the World Under-18 Championships, winning the gold in 2006, silver in 2004 and bronze in 2008. Hynes also served as assistant coach on the U.S. squad that won gold at the 2004 World Junior tourney. In 2016, he coached the U.S. team at the World Championship.

Hynes began his coaching career as a graduate assistant at Boston University under legendary coach Jack Parker. He later worked as an assistant coach at UMass-Lowell in 2000-01 and Wisconsin in 2002-03. As a player, he was a forward for four seasons at Boston U., participating in four straight NCAA Frozen Fours, and was a member of the Terriers' 1995 NCAA Championship Team.

Coaching Record

Season	Team	League	GC	W	L	O/T	GC	W	L	T
				Regular Season				Playoffs		
2003-04	USNTDP	U18	55	29	19	7	....	....	....	....
2004-05	USNTDP	U17	53	31	18	4	....	....	....	....
2005-06	USNTDP	U18	53	31	19	3	....	....	....	....
2006-07	USNTDP	U17	62	22	36	4	....	....	....	....
2007-08	USNTDP	U17	57	33	22	2	....	....	....	....
2008-09	USNTDP	U17	65	42	17	6	....	....	....	....
2010-11	Wilkes-Barre/Scranton	AHL	80	58	21	1	12	6	6	
2011-12	Wilkes-Barre/Scranton	AHL	76	44	25	7	12	6	6	
2012-13	Wilkes-Barre/Scranton	AHL	76	42	30	4	15	8	7	
2013-14	Wilkes-Barre/Scranton	AHL	76	42	26	8	17	9	8	
2014-15	Wilkes-Barre/Scranton	AHL	76	45	24	7	8	4	4	
2015-16	New Jersey	NHL	82	38	36	8	....	....	....	....
2016-17	New Jersey	NHL	82	28	40	14	....	....	....	....
	NHL Totals		**164**	**66**	**76**	**22**	....	....	....	....

Club Directory

New Jersey Devils
Prudential Center
25 Lafayette Street
Newark, NJ 07102
Phone **973/757-6100**
FAX 973/757-6399
www.newjerseydevils.com
Capacity: 16,514

Prudential Center

Owner/Chairman/Governor . . . . Joshua Harris
Owner/Vice Chairman/Alternate Governor . . . . David Blitzer
Co-Owners . . . . Marc Leder, Michael Rubin
CEO, NJ Devils & Prudential Center/Alt. Governor . Scott O'Neil
President, NJ Devils & Prudential Center . . . . Hugh Weber
Exec. V.P./General Manager/Alt. Governor . . . . . . Ray Shero
Assistant General Manager/G.M. Binghamton . . . . Tom Fitzgerald
Sr. Director, Player Personnel. . . . . Dan MacKinnon
Vice President, Hockey Operations . . . . Stephen Pellegrini

Club Personnel
Head Coach . . . . John Hynes
Assistant Coaches . . . . Geoff Ward, Alain Nasreddine, Ryane Clowe
Goaltending Coach . . . . Roland Melanson
Consultant . . . . Jacques Laperriere
Director, Amateur Scouting . . . . Paul Castron
Asst. Dir., Amateur Scouting . . . . Gates Orlando
Amateur Scouting Staff . . . . Ryan Breen, Glen Dirk, Joe Ferras, Scott Lachance, Jan Ludvig, Jim Mill, Pierre Mondou, Lou Reycroft, Andy Schneider, Steve Smith, Geoff Stevens
Amateur Scouting Staff – Europe . . . . Timo Blomqvist, Drake Braun, Niklas Evertsson, Misha Manchik, Vaclav Slansky, Jr.
Pro Scouting Staff . . . . Bob Hoffmeyer, Peter Horachek, Claude Noel, Andre Savard, Nick Vitucci
European Scout . . . . Greg Royce
Player Development Coaches . . . . Patrick Rissmiller, Eric Weinrich
Goaltending Development Coach . . . . Scott Clemmensen
Development/Skills Coach . . . . Pertti Hasanen
Director of Player and Team Development . . . . Dr. Aimee Kimball
Manager of Player Information and Video . . . . Scott Harris
Video Coach . . . . Mike Regan
Head Athletic Trainer . . . . Kevin Morley
Assistant Athletic Trainer . . . . Steve Ruhmel
Head Equipment Manager . . . . Christopher Scoppetto
Assistant Equipment Managers . . . . Jason McGrath, Andrew Schmidt
Strength/Conditioning Coach / Asst. Coach . . . . . Joe Lorincz / Jaime Rodriguez
Massage Therapist . . . . Brian Smith
Chief Medical Officer . . . . Dr. Jonathan L. Glashow
Team Orthopedist. . . . . Dr. Michael Shindle
Sports Medicine Internist. . . . . Dr. Michael Farber
Team Dentist . . . . Dr. Jason Schepis
Video Consultant . . . . Mitch Kaufman
Head Coach, Binghamton . . . . Rick Kowalsky
Assistant Coach, Binghamton . . . . Sergei Brylin
Video Coordinator, Binghamton . . . . Ryan Durocher
Athletic Trainer, Binghamton . . . . Scott Stanhibel
Equipment Manager / Asst. Manager, Binghamton . Jared Mycyk / TBD
Strength/Conditioning Coach, Binghamton . . . . . . John Sardos

Executive Vice President / General Manager's Office
Director of Hockey Administration . . . . Marie Carnevale
Exec. Asst. to EVP/GM & Hockey Ops. . . . . Christine Garcia
Director of Hockey Finance . . . . Kristin Farina

Hockey Analytics
Director, Hockey Analytics. . . . . Sunny Mehta

Hockey Communications
V.P., Hockey Communications/Team Operations . . . Pete Albietz
Director, Hockey Communications/Content. . . . . . . Sarah Baicker
Mgr., Hockey Communications/Team Operations . . James Stolfi
Assistant, Hockey Operations/Communications . . . . Scott Litwack

Alumni Representatives
Ken Daneyko, Bruce Driver, Grant Marshall, Jim Dowd, Colin White, Bryce Salvador

Television/Radio
Television Outlet . . . . MSG Plus
TV Play-by-Play / Color . . . . Steve Cangialosi / Ken Daneyko
Radio Outlet . . . . Sports Radio 66 AM/101.9 FM WFAN / The One Jersey Network
Radio Play-by-Play / Color . . . . Matt Loughlin / TBD

Coaching History

Bep Guidolin, 1974-75; Bep Guidolin, Sid Abel and Eddie Bush, 1975-76; Johnny Wilson, 1976-77; Pat Kelly, 1977-78; Pat Kelly and Aldo Guidolin, 1978-79; Don Cherry, 1979-80; Bill MacMillan, 1980-81; Bert Marshall and Marshall Johnston, 1981-82; Bill MacMillan, 1982-83; Bill MacMillan and Tom McVie, 1983-84; Doug Carpenter, 1984-85 to 1986-87; Doug Carpenter and Jim Schoenfeld, 1987-88; Jim Schoenfeld, 1988-89; Jim Schoenfeld and John Cunniff, 1989-90; John Cunniff and Tom McVie, 1990-91; Tom McVie, 1991-92; Herb Brooks, 1992-93; Jacques Lemaire, 1993-94 to 1997-98; Robbie Ftorek, 1998-99; Robbie Ftorek and Larry Robinson, 1999-2000; Larry Robinson, 2000-01; Larry Robinson and Kevin Constantine, 2001-02; Pat Burns, 2002-03 to 2004-05; Larry Robinson and Lou Lamoriello, 2005-06; Claude Julien and Lou Lamoriello, 2006-07; Brent Sutter, 2007-08, 2008-09; Jacques Lemaire, 2009-10; John MacLean and Jacques Lemaire, 2010-11; Peter DeBoer, 2011-12 to 2014-15; John Hynes, 2015-16 to date.

New York Islanders

2016-17 Results: 41W-29L-8OTL-4SOL 94PTS
5TH, Metropolitan Division • 9TH, Eastern Conference

Josh Bailey and Anders Lee celebrate a 4-2 Islanders victory over Buffalo on April 2, 2017. Bailey set career highs in assists (43) and points (56) in 2016-17, while Lee reached highs in goals (34) and points (52).

Key Off-Season Signings/Acquisitions

2017

April	24	• Re-signed D **Dennis Seidenberg**.
May	18	• Named **Luke Richardson** assistant coach.
	30	• Named **Scott Gomez** assistant coach.
June	22	• Acquired C **Jordan Eberle** from Edmonton for C **Ryan Strome**.
July	1	• Signed D **Seth Helgeson**.
	1	• Acquired G **Kristers Gudlevskis** from Tampa Bay for C **Carter Verhaeghe**.
	11	• Named **Kelly Buchberger** assistant coach.
	14	• Re-signed G **Christopher Gibson**.
	24	• Re-signed D **Adam Pelech**.
	27	• Re-signed C **Connor Jones**.
Aug.	2	• Re-signed D **Calvin de Haan**.

2017-18 Schedule

Oct.	Fri.	6	at Columbus
	Sat.	7	Buffalo
	Mon.	9	St. Louis*
	Wed.	11	at Anaheim
	Sat.	14	at San Jose
	Sun.	15	at Los Angeles
	Thu.	19	at NY Rangers
	Sat.	21	San Jose
	Tue.	24	Arizona
	Thu.	26	at Minnesota
	Sat.	28	at Nashville
	Mon.	30	Vegas
Nov.	Thu.	2	at Washington
	Sun.	5	Colorado
	Tue.	7	Edmonton
	Fri.	10	at Dallas
	Sat.	11	at St. Louis*
	Thu.	16	Carolina
	Sat.	18	at Tampa Bay
	Sun.	19	at Carolina*
	Wed.	22	Philadelphia
	Fri.	24	at Philadelphia*
	Sat.	25	at Ottawa
	Tue.	28	Vancouver
Dec.	Fri.	1	Ottawa
	Mon.	4	at Florida
	Tue.	5	at Tampa Bay
	Thu.	7	at Pittsburgh
	Sat.	9	at Boston
	Mon.	11	Washington
	Wed.	13	Dallas
	Thu.	14	at Columbus
	Sat.	16	Los Angeles
	Tue.	19	Detroit
	Thu.	21	Anaheim
	Sat.	23	Winnipeg*
	Wed.	27	Buffalo
	Fri.	29	at Winnipeg
	Sun.	31	at Colorado
Jan.	Tue.	2	Boston
	Thu.	4	at Philadelphia

	Fri.	5	Pittsburgh
	Sun.	7	New Jersey*
	Sat.	13	at NY Rangers*
	Mon.	15	at Montreal
	Tue.	16	New Jersey
	Thu.	18	Boston
	Sat.	20	at Chicago
	Mon.	22	at Arizona
	Thu.	25	at Vegas
	Tue.	30	Florida
	Wed.	31	at Toronto
Feb.	Sat.	3	Columbus
	Mon.	5	Nashville
	Thu.	8	at Buffalo
	Fri.	9	Detroit
	Sun.	11	Calgary
	Tue.	13	Columbus
	Thu.	15	NY Rangers
	Fri.	16	at Carolina
	Mon.	19	Minnesota*
	Thu.	22	at Toronto
	Sat.	24	at New Jersey
	Wed.	28	at Montreal
Mar.	Fri.	2	Montreal
	Sat.	3	at Pittsburgh*
	Mon.	5	at Vancouver
	Thu.	8	at Edmonton
	Sun.	11	at Calgary*
	Thu.	15	Washington
	Fri.	16	at Washington
	Sun.	18	Carolina*
	Tue.	20	Pittsburgh
	Thu.	22	Tampa Bay
	Sat.	24	Chicago
	Mon.	26	Florida
	Tue.	27	at Ottawa
	Fri.	30	Toronto
	Sat.	31	at New Jersey
Apr.	Tue.	3	Philadelphia
	Thu.	5	NY Rangers
	Sat.	7	at Detroit

* Denotes afternoon game.

Retired Numbers

5	Denis Potvin	1973-1988
9	Clark Gillies	1974-1986
19	Bryan Trottier	1975-1990
22	Mike Bossy	1977-1987
23	Bob Nystrom	1972-1986
31	Billy Smith	1972-1989

METROPOLITAN DIVISION
46th NHL Season

Franchise date: June 6, 1972

Year-by-Year Record

Season	GP	Home W	L	T	OL	Road W	L	T	OL	Overall W	L	T	OL	GF	GA	Pts.	Div. Fin.	Conf. Fin.	Playoff Result
2016-17	82	22	12	....	7	19	17	....	5	41	29	....	12	241	242	94	5th, Met.	9th, East	– out of playoffs –
2015-16	82	25	11	....	5	20	16	....	5	45	27	....	10	232	216	100	4th, Met.	5th, East	Lost Second Round
2014-15	82	25	14	....	2	22	14	....	5	47	28	....	7	252	230	101	3rd, Met.	5th, East	Lost First Round
2013-14	82	13	19	....	9	21	18	....	2	34	37	....	11	225	267	79	8th, Met.	14th, East	– out of playoffs –
2012-13	48	10	11	....	3	14	6	....	4	24	17	....	7	139	139	55	3rd, Atl.	8th, East	Lost Conf. Quarter-Final
2011-12	82	17	18	....	6	17	19	....	5	34	37	....	11	203	255	79	5th, Atl.	14th, East	– out of playoffs –
2010-11	82	17	18	....	6	13	21	....	7	30	39	....	13	229	264	73	5th, Atl.	14th, East	– out of playoffs –
2009-10	82	23	14	....	4	11	23	....	7	34	37	....	11	222	264	79	5th, Atl.	13th, East	– out of playoffs –
2008-09	82	17	18	....	6	9	29	....	3	26	47	....	9	201	279	61	5th, Atl.	15th, East	– out of playoffs –
2007-08	82	22	13	....	6	18	17	....	6	40	30	....	12	248	240	92	4th, Atl.	8th, East	Lost Conf. Quarter-Final
2006-07	82	20	18	....	3	16	22	....	3	36	40	....	6	230	278	78	4th, Atl.	12th, East	Lost Conf. Quarter-Final
2005-06	82																		
2004-05	....																		
2003-04	82	25	11	4	1	13	18	7	3	38	29	11	4	237	210	91	3rd, Atl.	8th, East	Lost Conf. Quarter-Final
2002-03	82	18	18	5	0	17	16	6	2	35	34	11	2	224	231	83	3rd, Atl.	8th, East	Lost Conf. Quarter-Final
2001-02	82	21	13	5	2	21	15	3	2	42	28	8	4	239	220	96	2nd, Atl.	5th, East	Lost Conf. Quarter-Final
2000-01	82	12	27	1	1	9	24	6	2	21	51	7	3	185	268	52	5th, Atl.	15th, East	– out of playoffs –
1999-2000	82	10	25	5	1	14	23	4	0	24	48	9	1	194	275	58	5th, Atl.	13th, East	– out of playoffs –
1998-99	82	11	23	7	....	13	25	3	....	24	48	10	....	194	244	58	5th, Atl.	13th, East	– out of playoffs –
1997-98	82	17	18	6	....	13	21	7	....	30	41	11	....	212	225	71	4th, Atl.	10th, East	– out of playoffs –
1996-97	82	19	18	4	....	10	23	8	....	29	41	12	....	240	250	70	7th, Atl.	12th, East	– out of playoffs –
1995-96	82	14	21	6	....	8	29	4	....	22	50	10	....	229	315	54	7th, Atl.	12th, East	– out of playoffs –
1994-95	48	10	11	3	....	5	17	2	....	15	28	5	....	126	158	35	7th, Atl.	13th, East	– out of playoffs –
1993-94	84	23	15	4	....	13	21	8	....	36	36	12	....	282	264	84	4th, Atl.	8th, East	Lost Conf. Quarter-Final
1992-93	84	20	19	3	....	20	18	4	....	40	37	7	....	335	297	87	3rd, Patrick		Lost Conf. Final
1991-92	80	20	15	5	....	14	20	6	....	34	35	11	....	291	299	79	5th, Patrick		– out of playoffs –
1990-91	80	15	19	6	....	10	26	4	....	25	45	10	....	223	290	60	6th, Patrick		– out of playoffs –
1989-90	80	15	17	8	....	16	21	3	....	31	38	11	....	281	288	73	4th, Patrick		Lost Div. Semi-Final
1988-89	80	19	18	3	....	9	29	2	....	28	47	5	....	265	325	61	6th, Patrick		– out of playoffs –
1987-88	80	24	10	6	....	15	21	4	....	39	31	10	....	308	267	88	1st, Patrick		Lost Div. Semi-Final
1986-87	80	20	15	5	....	15	18	7	....	35	33	12	....	279	281	82	3rd, Patrick		Lost Div. Final
1985-86	80	22	11	7	....	17	18	5	....	39	29	12	....	327	284	90	3rd, Patrick		Lost Div. Semi-Final
1984-85	80	26	11	3	....	14	23	3	....	40	34	6	....	345	312	86	3rd, Patrick		Lost Div. Final
1983-84	80	26	11	3	....	24	15	1	....	50	26	4	....	357	269	104	1st, Patrick		Lost Final
1982-83	80	26	11	3	....	16	15	9	....	42	26	12	....	302	226	96	2nd, Patrick		**Won Stanley Cup**
1981-82	80	33	3	4	....	21	13	6	....	54	16	10	....	385	250	118	1st, Patrick		**Won Stanley Cup**
1980-81	80	23	6	11	....	25	12	3	....	48	18	14	....	355	260	110	1st, Patrick		**Won Stanley Cup**
1979-80	80	26	9	5	....	13	19	8	....	39	28	13	....	281	247	91	2nd, Patrick		**Won Stanley Cup**
1978-79	80	31	3	6	....	20	12	8	....	51	15	14	....	358	214	116	1st, Patrick		Lost Semi-Final
1977-78	80	29	3	8	....	19	14	7	....	48	17	15	....	334	210	111	1st, Patrick		Lost Quarter-Final
1976-77	80	24	11	5	....	23	10	7	....	47	21	12	....	288	193	106	2nd, Patrick		Lost Semi-Final
1975-76	80	24	8	8	....	18	13	9	....	42	21	17	....	297	190	101	2nd, Patrick		Lost Semi-Final
1974-75	80	22	11	7	....	11	19	10	....	33	25	22	....	264	221	88	3rd, Patrick		Lost Semi-Final
1973-74	78	13	17	9	....	6	24	9	....	19	41	18	....	182	247	56	8th, East		– out of playoffs –
1972-73	78	10	25	4	....	2	35	2	....	12	60	6	....	170	347	30	8th, East		– out of playoffs –

2017-18 Player Personnel

FORWARDS	HT	WT	*Age	Birthplace	S	2016-17 Club
BAILEY, Josh	6-1	210	28	Bowmanville, ON	L	NY Islanders
BARZAL, Matthew	6-0	182	20	Coquitlam, BC	R	NY Islanders-Seattle
BEAUVILLIER, Anthony	5-11	176	20	Sorel-Tracy, QC	L	NY Islanders
CHIMERA, Jason	6-3	216	38	Edmonton, AB	L	NY Islanders
CIZIKAS, Casey	5-11	201	26	Toronto, ON	L	NY Islanders
CLUTTERBUCK, Cal	5-11	218	29	Welland, ON	R	NY Islanders
DAL COLLE, Michael	6-3	198	21	Richmond Hill, ON	L	Bridgeport
EBERLE, Jordan	5-11	181	27	Regina, SK	R	Edmonton
HO-SANG, Joshua	6-0	175	21	Toronto, ON	R	NY Islanders-Bridgeport
JONES, Connor	5-9	176	27	Montrose, BC	L	NY Islanders-Bridgeport
KULEMIN, Nikolay	6-1	225	31	Magnitogorsk, USSR	L	NY Islanders
LADD, Andrew	6-3	200	31	Maple Ridge, BC	L	NY Islanders
LEE, Anders	6-3	228	27	Edina, MN	L	NY Islanders
NELSON, Brock	6-3	206	25	Warroad, MN	L	NY Islanders
PRINCE, Shane	5-11	185	24	Rochester, NY	L	NY Islanders
QUINE, Alan	6-0	200	24	Orleans, ON	L	NY Islanders
TAVARES, John	6-1	211	27	Mississauga, ON	L	NY Islanders

DEFENSEMEN						
BOYCHUK, Johnny	6-2	227	33	Edmonton, AB	R	NY Islanders
de HAAN, Calvin	6-1	197	26	Carp, ON	L	NY Islanders
HICKEY, Thomas	6-0	189	28	Calgary, AB	L	NY Islanders
LEDDY, Nick	6-0	199	26	Eden Prairie, MN	L	NY Islanders
MAYFIELD, Scott	6-4	224	24	St. Louis, MO	R	NY Islanders-Bridgeport
PELECH, Adam	6-3	210	23	Toronto, ON	L	NY Islanders-Bridgeport
PULOCK, Ryan	6-2	215	22	Dauphin, MB	R	NY Islanders-Bridgeport
SEIDENBERG, Dennis	6-0	198	36	Schwenningen, W. Germany	L	NY Islanders
TOEWS, Devon	6-1	181	23	Abbotsford, BC	L	Bridgeport

GOALTENDERS	HT	WT	*Age	Birthplace	C	2016-17 Club
GIBSON, Christopher	6-1	188	24	Karkkila, Finland	L	Bridgeport
GREISS, Thomas	6-1	228	31	Fussen, West Germany	L	NY Islanders
GUDLEVSKIS, Kristers	6-3	223	25	Aizkraukle, Latvia	L	Tampa Bay-Syracuse
HALAK, Jaroslav	5-11	181	32	Bratislava, Czech.	L	NY Islanders-Bridgeport

* – Age at start of 2017-18 season

2016-17 Scoring

* – rookie

Regular Season

Pos	#	Player	Team	GP	G	A	Pts	TOI	+/-	PIM	PP	SH	GW	S	S%
C	91	John Tavares	NYI	77	28	38	66	20:25	4	38	7	1	3	260	10.8
C	12	Josh Bailey	NYI	82	13	43	56	18:22	5	12	3	0	1	173	7.5
C	27	Anders Lee	NYI	81	34	18	52	15:35	9	56	9	0	6	191	17.8
D	2	Nick Leddy	NYI	81	11	35	46	22:43	-2	12	3	0	1	137	8.0
C	29	Brock Nelson	NYI	81	20	25	45	15:38	-6	36	1	0	4	173	11.6
L	25	Jason Chimera	NYI	82	20	13	33	13:03	1	40	0	1	2	121	16.5
L	16	Andrew Ladd	NYI	78	23	8	31	16:10	-14	45	3	1	4	142	16.2
C	18	Ryan Strome	NYI	69	13	17	30	14:36	-8	40	2	0	2	114	11.4
C	53	Casey Cizikas	NYI	59	8	17	25	13:54	9	30	0	0	1	82	9.8
D	44	Calvin de Haan	NYI	82	5	20	25	19:50	15	36	1	0	1	116	4.3
L	72	* Anthony Beauvillier	NYI	66	9	15	24	13:01	1	10	0	0	2	101	8.9
L	86	Nikolay Kulemin	NYI	72	12	11	23	13:49	3	18	1	1	4	74	16.2
C	55	Johnny Boychuk	NYI	66	6	17	23	20:43	11	19	1	1	2	155	3.9
D	4	Dennis Seidenberg	NYI	73	5	17	22	19:25	25	32	0	0	0	89	5.6
R	15	Cal Clutterbuck	NYI	66	5	15	20	13:59	-2	28	0	0	1	115	4.3
D	14	Thomas Hickey	NYI	76	4	16	20	17:31	-1	35	0	0	2	87	4.6
C	11	Shane Prince	NYI	50	5	13	18	12:58	-9	18	1	0	2	71	7.0
C	10	* Alan Quine	NYI	61	5	13	18	12:31	-2	8	2	0	1	82	6.1
D	3	Travis Hamonic	NYI	49	3	11	14	20:27	-21	60	0	0	0	74	4.1
C	66	* Joshua Ho-Sang	NYI	21	4	6	10	16:27	1	12	1	0	0	22	18.2
D	50	* Adam Pelech	NYI	44	3	7	10	16:50	-5	6	0	0	0	40	7.5
D	42	* Scott Mayfield	NYI	25	2	7	9	14:08	-1	35	0	0	0	39	5.1
R	24	Stephen Gionta	NYI	26	1	5	6	11:12	9	2	0	0	0	17	5.9
D	6	* Ryan Pulock	NYI	1	0	0	0	3:57	1	0	0	0	0	0	0.0
C	38	Bracken Kearns	NYI	2	0	0	0	11:11	-1	2	0	0	0	3	0.0
C	13	* Mathew Barzal	NYI	2	0	0	0	9:45	-2	6	0	0	0	0	0.0
C	48	Connor Jones	NYI	4	0	0	0	11:50	1	0	0	0	0	2	0.0

Goaltending

No.	Goaltender	GPI	Mins	Avg	W	L	OT	EN	SO	GA	SA	Sv%	G	A	PIM
1	Thomas Greiss	51	2813	2.69	26	18	5	1	3	126	1453	.913	0	1	0
41	Jaroslav Halak	28	1605	2.80	12	9	5	3	2	75	885	.915	0	1	0
30	* Jean-Francois Berube	14	527	3.42	3	2	2	3	0	30	271	.889	0	0	0
	Totals	82	4979	2.87	41	29	12	7	5	238	2616	.909			

Coaching History

Phil Goyette and Earl Ingarfield, 1972-73; Al Arbour, 1973-74 to 1985-86; Terry Simpson, 1986-87, 1987-88; Terry Simpson and Al Arbour, 1988-89; Al Arbour, 1989-90 to 1993-94; Lorne Henning, 1994-95; Mike Milbury, 1995-96; Mike Milbury and Rick Bowness, 1996-97; Rick Bowness and Mike Milbury, 1997-98; Mike Milbury and Bill Stewart, 1998-99; Butch Goring, 1999-2000; Butch Goring and Lorne Henning, 2000-01; Peter Laviolette, 2001-02, 2002-03; Steve Stirling, 2003-04, 2004-05; Steve Stirling and Brad Shaw, 2005-06; Ted Nolan, 2006-07, 2007-08; Scott Gordon, 2008-09, 2009-10; Scott Gordon and Jack Capuano, 2010-11; Jack Capuano, 2011-12 to 2015-16; Jack Capuano and Doug Weight, 2016-17; Doug Weight, 2017-18.

Doug Weight
Head Coach and Assistant General Manager
Born: Warren, MI, January 21, 1971.

The New York Islanders announced that Doug Weight had been named head coach on April 12, 2017. Weight was named the club's interim head coach midway through the 2016-17 season and led the team to a 24-12-4 record over the final 40 games. From Weight's first game on January 19, 2017, to the end of the season, the Islanders posted the second-best record in the National Hockey League with 24 wins and 52 points. The club also registered the most hits in the league during that stretch and scored the fourth-most goals (120). Weight is the 19th head coach in Islanders history, and will continue to serve as the team's assistant general manager. Prior to filling the interim position, he had served as an assistant coach and assistant GM.

Weight, a four-time NHL All-Star, was named the 12th captain in Islanders history on October 2, 2009. Originally drafted by the New York Rangers in the second round (34th overall) of the 1990 NHL Draft, Weight amassed 278 goals and 755 assists in a career that included stints with the Rangers, Edmonton Oilers, St. Louis Blues, Carolina Hurricanes, Anaheim Ducks and the Islanders. Weight was inducted into the USA Hockey Hall of Fame in 2013. He won the 2011 King Clancy Memorial Trophy, presented annually to the player who "best exemplifies leadership qualities on and off the ice and has made a noteworthy humanitarian contribution in his community."

On the international stage, Weight won a silver medal with the United States at the 2002 Winter Olympics and also skated with the 1998 and 2006 United States Olympic teams. He helped the United Stats win the inaugural World Cup of Hockey in 1996 and also played at the 2004 tournament. Weight appeared in one World Junior Championship in 1991, leading the entire tournament in scoring, and he also played in the 1993, 1994 and 2005 World Championships for the United States. Upon retiring as a player on May 26, 2011, Weight was named Islanders assistant coach and senior advisor to the general manager.

Thomas Greiss firmly established himself as the Islanders' number-one goaltender in 2016-17.

Coaching Record

			Regular Season					Playoffs			
Season	Team	League	GC	W	L	O/T		GC	W	L	T
2016-17	NY Islanders	NHL	40	24	12	4		....	....	....	....
	NHL Totals		40	24	12	4		....	....	....	....

Club Records

Team

(Figures in brackets for season records are games played; records for fewest points, wins, ties, losses, goals, goals against are for 70 or more games)

Most Points	**118**	1981-82 (80)
Most Wins	**54**	1981-82 (80)
Most Ties	**22**	1974-75 (80)
Most Losses	**60**	1972-73 (78)
Most Goals	**385**	1981-82 (80)
Most Goals Against	**347**	1972-73 (78)
Fewest Points	**30**	1972-73 (78)
Fewest Wins	**12**	1972-73 (78)
Fewest Ties	**4**	1983-84 (80)
Fewest Losses	**15**	1978-79 (80)
Fewest Goals	**170**	1972-73 (78)
Fewest Goals Against	**190**	1975-76 (80)
Longest Winning Streak		
Overall	**15**	Jan. 21-Feb. 20/82
Home	**14**	Jan. 2-Feb. 25/82
Away	**8**	Feb. 27-Mar. 29/81
Longest Team Point Streak		
Overall	**15**	Three times
Home	**23**	Oct. 17/78-Jan. 20/79 (19W, 4T), Jan. 2-Apr. 3/82 (21W, 2T)
Away	**8**	Three times
Longest Losing Streak		
Overall	**14**	Oct. 23-Nov. 24/10
Home	**8**	Nov. 27-Dec. 28/13
Away	**15**	Jan. 20-Mar. 31/73
Longest Winless Streak		
Overall	**15**	Nov. 22-Dec. 21/72 (12L, 3T)
Home	**9**	Mar. 2-Apr. 6/99 (7L, 2T)
Away	**20**	Nov. 3/72-Jan. 13/73 (19L, 1T)
Most Shutouts, Season	**10**	1975-76 (80)
Most PIM, Season	**1,857**	1986-87 (80)
Most Goals, Game	**11**	Dec. 20/83 (Pit. 3 at NYI 11), Mar. 3/84 (NYI 11 at Tor. 6)

Individual

Most Seasons	**17**	Billy Smith
Most Games	**1,123**	Bryan Trottier
Most Goals, Career	**573**	Mike Bossy
Most Assists, Career	**853**	Bryan Trottier
Most Points, Career	**1,353**	Bryan Trottier (500G, 853A)
Most PIM, Career	**1,879**	Mick Vukota
Most Shutouts, Career	**25**	Glenn Resch
Longest Consecutive Games Streak	**576**	Billy Harris (Oct. 7/72-Nov. 30/79)
Most Goals, Season	**69**	Mike Bossy (1978-79)
Most Assists, Season	**87**	Bryan Trottier (1978-79)
Most Points, Season	**147**	Mike Bossy (1981-82; 64G, 83A)
Most PIM, Season	**356**	Brian Curran (1986-87)
Most Points, Defenseman, Season	**101**	Denis Potvin (1978-79; 31G, 70A)
Most Points, Center, Season	**134**	Bryan Trottier (1978-79; 47G, 87A)
Most Points, Right Wing, Season	**147**	Mike Bossy (1981-82; 64G, 83A)
Most Points, Left Wing, Season	**100**	John Tonelli (1984-85; 42G, 58A)
Most Points, Rookie, Season	**95**	Bryan Trottier (1975-76; 32G, 63A)
Most Shutouts, Season	**7**	Glenn Resch (1975-76)
Most Goals, Game	**5**	Bryan Trottier (Dec. 23/78), (Feb. 13/82) John Tonelli (Jan. 6/81)
Most Assists, Game	**6**	Mike Bossy (Jan. 6/81)
Most Points, Game	**8**	Bryan Trottier (Dec. 23/78; 5G, 3A)

Captains' History

Ed Westfall, 1972-73 to 1975-76; Ed Westfall and Clark Gillies, 1976-77; Clark Gillies, 1977-78, 1978-79; Denis Potvin, 1979-80 to 1986-87; Brent Sutter, 1987-88 to 1990-91; Brent Sutter and Pat Flatley, 1991-92; Pat Flatley, 1992-93 to 1995-96; no captain, 1996-97; Bryan McCabe and Trevor Linden, 1997-98; Trevor Linden, 1998-99; Kenny Jonsson, 1999-2000, 2000-01; Michael Peca, 2001-02 to 2003-04; Alexei Yashin, 2005-06, 2006-07; Bill Guerin, 2007-08; Bill Guerin and no captain, 2008-09; Doug Weight, 2009-10, 2010-11; Mark Streit, 2011-12, 2012-13; John Tavares, 2013-14 to date.

All-time Record vs. Other Clubs

Regular Season

	Total								At Home								On Road							
	GP	W	L	T	OL	GF	GA	PTS	GP	W	L	T	OL	GF	GA	PTS	GP	W	L	T	OL	GF	GA	PTS
Anaheim	32	16	11	4	1	89	83	37	15	8	6	1	0	42	41	17	17	8	5	3	1	47	42	20
Arizona	75	36	25	12	2	264	230	86	37	19	9	8	1	141	105	47	38	17	16	4	1	123	125	39
Boston	163	58	81	21	3	476	553	140	82	32	40	10	0	254	268	74	81	26	41	11	3	222	285	66
Buffalo	165	67	71	18	9	468	494	161	82	37	32	9	4	235	224	87	83	30	39	9	5	233	270	74
Calgary	114	49	45	20	0	376	348	118	58	31	18	9	0	210	154	71	56	18	27	11	0	166	194	47
Carolina	137	58	65	9	5	419	452	130	68	28	33	4	3	198	212	63	69	30	32	5	2	221	240	67
Chicago	110	41	45	20	4	364	349	106	54	22	15	15	2	187	161	61	56	19	30	5	2	177	188	45
Colorado	81	38	36	4	3	273	270	83	39	24	14	1	0	161	126	49	42	14	22	3	3	112	144	34
Columbus	31	13	11	1	6	89	102	33	14	8	2	0	4	49	40	20	17	5	9	1	2	40	62	13
Dallas	110	55	36	16	3	402	322	129	56	30	16	8	2	210	163	70	54	25	20	8	1	192	159	59
Detroit	109	51	49	6	3	354	349	111	55	28	20	4	3	197	164	63	54	23	29	2	0	157	185	48
Edmonton	74	30	28	14	2	254	251	76	38	21	7	9	1	155	123	52	36	9	21	5	1	99	128	24
Florida	93	38	42	8	5	252	273	89	47	23	21	2	1	120	127	49	46	15	21	6	4	132	146	40
Los Angeles	105	46	46	12	1	330	326	105	53	28	19	5	1	179	143	62	52	18	27	7	0	151	183	43
Minnesota	22	10	10	0	2	63	69	22	11	6	4	0	1	29	32	13	11	4	6	0	1	34	37	9
Montreal	163	60	86	15	2	458	523	137	82	37	38	6	1	238	237	81	81	23	48	9	1	220	286	56
Nashville	23	10	12	0	1	57	62	21	11	6	4	0	1	30	29	13	12	4	8	0	0	27	33	8
New Jersey	239	130	79	22	8	814	686	290	121	75	32	11	3	439	320	164	118	55	47	11	5	375	366	126
NY Rangers	262	118	119	19	6	845	872	261	131	69	50	8	4	461	406	150	131	49	69	11	2	384	466	111
Ottawa	90	27	48	11	4	242	311	69	46	14	25	6	1	135	168	35	44	13	23	5	3	107	143	34
Philadelphia	262	100	129	26	7	793	864	233	133	60	53	15	5	441	403	140	129	40	76	11	2	352	461	93
Pittsburgh	244	106	102	22	14	850	861	248	120	62	41	8	9	455	398	141	124	44	61	14	5	395	463	107
St. Louis	111	51	36	20	4	379	348	126	57	29	14	11	3	208	153	72	54	22	22	9	1	171	195	54
San Jose	37	16	16	3	2	115	106	37	18	8	7	2	1	61	57	19	19	8	9	1	1	54	49	18
Tampa Bay	94	45	40	3	6	271	262	99	47	26	18	1	2	141	123	55	47	19	22	2	4	130	139	44
Toronto	151	75	62	7	7	534	492	164	74	42	25	3	4	280	220	91	77	33	37	4	3	254	272	73
Vancouver	108	53	38	13	4	366	331	123	54	28	13	10	3	189	155	69	54	25	25	3	1	177	176	54
Washington	210	93	90	13	14	685	659	213	105	53	43	2	7	371	325	115	105	40	47	11	7	314	334	98
Winnipeg	59	33	20	2	4	213	172	72	29	14	15	0	0	97	84	28	30	19	5	2	4	116	88	44
Defunct Clubs	26	15	5	6	0	110	74	36	13	11	0	2	0	75	33	24	13	4	5	4	0	35	41	12
Totals	**3500**	**1538**	**1483**	**347**	**132**	**11205**	**11094**	**3555**	**1750**	**879**	**634**	**170**	**67**	**5988**	**5194**	**1995**	**1750**	**659**	**849**	**177**	**65**	**5217**	**5900**	**1560**

Playoffs

	Series	W	L	GP	W	L	T	GF	GA	Last Mtg.	Rnd.	Result
Boston	2	2	0	11	8	3	0	49	35	1983	CF	W 4-2
Buffalo	4	3	1	21	13	8	0	70	62	2007	CQF	L 1-4
Chicago	2	2	0	6	6	0	0	21	6	1979	QF	W 4-0
Colorado	1	1	0	4	4	0	0	18	9	1982	CF	W 4-0
Dallas	1	1	0	5	4	1	0	26	16	1981	F	W 4-1
Edmonton	3	2	1	15	9	6	0	58	47	1984	F	L 1-4
Florida	1	1	0	6	4	2	0	15	14	2016	FR	W 4-2
Los Angeles	1	1	0	4	3	1	0	21	10	1980	PR	W 3-1
Montreal	4	1	3	22	8	14	0	55	64	1993	CF	L 1-4
New Jersey	1	0	1	6	2	4	0	18	23	1988	DSF	L 2-4
NY Rangers	8	5	3	39	20	19	0	129	132	1994	CQF	L 0-4
Ottawa	1	0	1	5	1	4	0	7	13	2003	CQF	L 1-4
Philadelphia	4	1	3	25	11	14	0	69	83	1987	DF	L 3-4
Pittsburgh	4	3	1	25	13	12	0	84	83	2013	CQF	L 2-4
Tampa Bay	2	0	2	10	2	8	0	16	30	2016	SR	L 1-4
Toronto	3	1	2	17	9	8	0	54	42	2002	CQF	L 3-4
Vancouver	2	2	0	6	6	0	0	26	14	1982	F	W 4-0
Washington	7	5	2	37	21	16	0	114	104	2015	FR	L 3-4
Totals	**51**	**31**	**20**	**264**	**144**	**120**	**0**	**850**	**787**			

Playoff Results 2017-2013

Year	Round	Opponent	Result	GF	GA
2016	SR	Tampa Bay	L 1-4	11	18
	FR	Florida	W 4-2	15	14
2015	FR	Washington	L 3-4	15	16
2013	CQF	Pittsburgh	L 2-4	17	25

Abbreviations: Round: F – Final; **CF** – conference final; **SR** – second round; **CQF** – conference quarter-final; **FR** – first round; **DF** – division final; **DSF** – division semi-final; **QF** – quarter-final; **PR** – preliminary round.

Calgary totals include Atlanta Flames, 1972-73 to 1979-80.
Carolina totals include Hartford, 1979-80 to 1996-97.
Colorado totals include Quebec, 1979-80 to 1994-95.
Dallas totals include Minnesota North Stars, 1972-73 to 1992-93.
New Jersey totals include Kansas City, 1974-75, 1975-76, and Colorado Rockies, 1976-77 to 1981-82.
Phoenix totals include Winnipeg, 1979-80 to 1995-96.
Winnipeg totals include Atlanta Thrashers, 1999-2000 to 2010-11.

2016-17 Results

Oct.	13	at NY Rangers	3-5		16	at Boston	4-0
	15	at Washington	1-2		19	Dallas	3-0
	16	Anaheim	3-2*		21	Los Angeles	4-2
	18	San Jose	2-3		22	Philadelphia	2-3*
	21	Arizona	3-2		24	Columbus	4-2
	23	Minnesota	6-3		26	Montreal	3-1
	26	Montreal	2-3		31	Washington	3-2
	27	at Pittsburgh	2-4	**Feb.**	3	at Detroit	4-5
	30	Toronto	5-1		4	Carolina	4-5*
Nov.	1	Tampa Bay	1-6		6	Toronto	6-5*
	3	Philadelphia	2-3†		9	at Philadelphia	3-1
	5	Edmonton	3-4†		11	at Ottawa	0-3
	7	Vancouver	4-2		12	Colorado	5-1
	10	at Tampa Bay	1-4		14	at Toronto	1-7
	12	at Florida	2-3*		16	NY Rangers	4-2
	14	Tampa Bay	0-4		18	at New Jersey	2-3
	18	Pittsburgh	2-3*		19	New Jersey	6-4
	22	at Anaheim	3-2†		21	at Detroit	3-1
	23	at Los Angeles	2-4		23	at Montreal	3-0
	25	at San Jose	2-3		25	at Columbus	0-7
	28	Calgary	2-1*	**Mar.**	2	at Dallas	5-4
	30	Pittsburgh	5-3		3	at Chicago	1-2†
Dec.	1	at Washington	3-0		5	at Calgary	2-5
	4	Detroit	3-4*		7	at Edmonton	4-1
	6	NY Rangers	4-2		9	at Vancouver	4-3*
	8	St. Louis	3-2		11	at St. Louis	3-4
	10	at Columbus	2-6		13	Carolina	4-8
	13	Washington	2-4		14	at Carolina	3-2*
	15	Chicago	4-5		16	Winnipeg	2-4
	16	at Buffalo	2-3*		18	Columbus	2-3*
	18	Ottawa	2-6		22	at NY Rangers	3-2
	20	at Boston	4-2		24	at Pittsburgh	4-3†
	23	Buffalo	5-1		25	Boston	1-2
	27	Washington	4-3		27	Nashville	1-3
	29	at Minnesota	4-6		30	at Philadelphia	3-6
	31	at Winnipeg	6-2		31	New Jersey	2-1
Jan.	6	at Colorado	1-2*	**Apr.**	2	at Buffalo	4-2
	7	at Arizona	1-2†		4	at Nashville	2-1*
	11	Florida	1-2		6	at Carolina	3-0
	13	at Florida	5-2		8	at New Jersey	4-2
	14	at Carolina	4-7		9	Ottawa	4-2

* – Overtime † – Shootout

NHL Draft Selections 2017-2003

Name in bold denotes played in NHL.

2017 Pick		2012 Pick		2008 Pick		2005 Pick	
46	Robin Salo	4	**Griffin Reinhart**	9	**Josh Bailey**	15	**Ryan O'Marra**
77	Ben Mirageas	34	Ville Pokka	36	Corey Trivino	46	**Dustin Kohn**
139	Sebastian Aho	65	**Adam Pelech**	40	**Aaron Ness**	76	Shea Guthrie
165	Arnaud Durandeau	103	Loic Leduc	53	**Travis Hamonic**	144	**Masi Marjamaki**
201	Logan Cockerill	125	Doyle Somerby	66	David Toews	180	Tyrell Mason
		155	Jesse Graham	72	Jyri Niemi	196	Nick Tuzzolino
2016		185	Jake Bischoff	73	Kirill Petrov	210	Luciano Aquino
Pick				96	**Matt Donovan**		
19	Kieffer Bellows	**2011**		102	**David Ullstrom**	**2004**	
95	Anatoli Golyshev	**Pick**		126	Kevin Poulin	**Pick**	
120	Otto Koivula	5	**Ryan Strome**	148	**Matt Martin**	16	**Petteri Nokelainen**
170	Collin Adams	34	**Scott Mayfield**	156	**Jared Spurgeon**	47	**Blake Comeau**
193	Nick Pastujov	50	**Johan Sundstrom**	175	**Justin Dibenedetto**	82	Sergei Ogorodnikov
200	David Quenneville	63	**Andrey Pedan**			115	Wes O'Neill
		95	**Robbie Russo**	**2007**		148	**Steve Regier**
2015		125	**John Persson**	**Pick**		179	Jaroslav Mrazek
Pick		127	Brenden Kichton	62	**Mark Katic**	210	Emil Axelsson
16	**Mathew Barzal**	185	Mitchell Theoret	76	Jason Gregoire	227	**Chris Campoli**
28	**Anthony Beauvillier**			106	Maxim Gratchev	244	Jason Pitton
82	Mitchell Vande Sompel	**2010**		166	Blake Kessel	276	Sylvain Michaud
112	Parker Wotherspoon	**Pick**		196	Simon Lacroix		
147	Ryan Pilon	5	**Nino Niederreiter**			**2003**	
172	Andong Song	30	**Brock Nelson**	**2006**		**Pick**	
202	Petter Hansson	65	Kirill Kabanov	**Pick**		15	**Robert Nilsson**
		82	Jason Clark	7	**Kyle Okposo**	48	Dmitri Chernykh
2014		125	Tony Dehart	60	**Jesse Joensuu**	53	Evgeny Tunik
Pick		185	Cody Rosen	70	Robin Figren	58	**Jeremy Colliton**
5	Michael Dal Colle			100	**Rhett Rakhshani**	120	Stefan Blaho
28	**Joshua Ho-Sang**	**2009**		108	Jase Weslosky	182	**Bruno Gervais**
78	Ilya Sorokin	**Pick**		115	Tomas Marcinko	212	Denis Rehak
95	Linus Soderstrom	1	**John Tavares**	119	Doug Rogers	238	Cody Blanshan
108	Devon Toews	12	**Calvin de Haan**	126	**Shane Sims**	246	Igor Volkov
155	Kyle Schempp	31	**Mikko Koskinen**	141	Kim Johansson		
200	Lukas Sutter	62	**Anders Nilsson**	160	**Andrew MacDonald**		
		92	**Casey Cizikas**	171	Brian Day		
2013		122	Anton Klementyev	177	Stefan Ridderwall		
Pick		152	**Anders Lee**	190	Troy Mattila		
15	**Ryan Pulock**						
70	Eamon McAdam						
76	Taylor Cammarata						
106	Stephon Williams						
136	Victor Crus-Rydberg						
166	**Alan Quine**						
196	Kyle Burroughs						

General Managers' History

Bill Torrey, 1972-73 to 1991-92; Don Maloney, 1992-93 to 1994-95; Don Maloney, Darcy Regier and Mike Milbury, 1995-96; Mike Milbury, 1996-97 to 2005-06; Neil Smith and Garth Snow, 2006-07; Garth Snow, 2007-08 to date.

Garth Snow
President and General Manager
Born: Wrentham, MA, June 28, 1969.

Former Islanders' goaltender Garth Snow retired as a player on July 18, 2006 to become the fifth general manager of the New York Islanders. In his first season as general manager, Snow successfully bolstered the lineup with several key additions that helped to propel the Islanders into the postseason for the first time since the 2003–04 season and earned Snow the title of NHL Executive of the Year from *Sports Illustrated.*

Snow spent four seasons with the Islanders and 12 in the NHL. The goaltender was 135-147-44 with a 2.80 goals-against average and .901 save percentage over 368 games with Quebec, Philadelphia, Vancouver, Pittsburgh and the Islanders. Originally selected in the sixth round by Quebec in the 1987 NHL Draft, the native of Wrentham, Massachusetts signed with the Islanders as a free agent on July 1, 2001.

Club Directory

Barclays Center

New York Islanders
Executive Office and Practice Facility:
Northwell Health Ice Center
200 Merrick Avenue
East Meadow, NY 11554
Phone 516/441-0070
www.newyorkislanders.com
Arena:
Barclays Center
620 Atlantic Ave.
Brooklyn, NY 11217
Capacity: 15,795

Islanders Ownership and Executive Management
Co-Owner and Alternate Governor	Jon Ledecky
Co-Owner and Governor	Scott Malkin
Co-Owner and Alternate Governor	Charles B. Wang
Co-Owner	Dewey Shay
President, GM & Alternate Governor	Garth Snow
Alternate Governor	Art McCarthy
General Counsel	Jay Itzkowitz
President, Bridgeport Sound Tigers	Michael Picker

Barclays Center Executive Management
Barclays Center CEO	Brett Yormark
Barclays Center CBO	Drew Cloud
Barclays Center EVP, Business Operation/CFO	Charlie Mierswa

Islanders Hockey Operations
Manager, Hockey Administration	Joanne Holewa
Assistant G.M. & Head Coach	Doug Weight
Director of Pro Scouting	Ken Morrow
Director of Player Personnel	Chris Lamoriello
Assistant to the General Manager	Kerry Gwydir
Hockey Operations Consultant	Claude Loiselle
Associate Coach	Greg Cronin
Assistant Coaches	Luke Richardson, Scott Gomez, Matt Bertani
Goalie Coaches	Fred Brathwaite, Marc Champagne
Skill Development Coach	Bernie Cassell
Director of Sports Performance	Sean Donellan
Strength and Conditioning Coach	Derrek Douglas
Head Amateur Scout	Vellu Kautonen
Director of Player Development	Eric Cairns
Player Development	Marty Reasoner
Equipment Manager / Asst. Manager / Assistants	Scott Boggs / Richard Krouse / Kevin Putzig, Arthur Verdi
Head Athletic Trainer / Assistant Trainer	Damien Hess / Jody Green
Massage Therapist	Jim Miccio
Scouts	Trent Klatt, Tim Maclean, Mario Saraceno, Dennis Maxwell, Jeff Napierala, Don McDuff, Chris O'Sullivan, Jeremy Bachusz, Derrick Kemp, Matti Kautto

Islanders Administration
New York Hockey Holdings Director	Nick Pizzutello
New York Hockey Holdings Manager/Coordinator	Dana Schraudner/Heather Cohen
Sr. Vice President of Sales & Marketing	Paul Lancey
Vice President, Ticket Sales	Ralph Sellitti
Deputy General Counsel	Zachary Klein
Human Resources Manager / Coordinator	Michele Finkelstein / Megan Lynch
IT Manager	Pawel Tauter
Receptionist / Office Assistant	Bonnie Dreher

Islanders Media Relations / Communications
Director of Communications	Kimber Auerbach
Communications Manager / Coordinator	Jesse Eisenberg / Kelly Keogh
Video Producer	Alex Leafer

Islanders Community Relations, Fan Development, Marketing and Operations
Community Relations Director	Ann Rina
Director of Family Services	Allison Weight
Event Operations Coordinator	Ryan McLear
Manager, Amateur Hockey Development	Jocelyne Cummings

Islanders Retail and Merchandise Operations
Islanders Pro Shop Manager / Asst. Manager	Tim Murray / Nicolo Valenti
Retail Manager	Robert Marsala

Islanders Finance
Controller / Accounting Manager	Frank Romano / Chris Vardaro
Payroll Manager / A/P Coordinator	Christine Bowler / Janet Nelson
Staff Accountant	Lisa Rodolitz

Islanders Practice Facility
General Manager / Assistant Manager	A.J. Congero / Christina Mott
Arena Operations / Registrar	Joseph Fu / Jessica Higgins
Figure Skating Director / Hockey Director	Valerie Murray / Bob Thornton

Barclays Center Administration
EVP Business Affairs/Chief Legal Officer	Jeff Gewirtz
VP Assistant General Counsel	Kari Cohen

Barclays Center Communications
Communications Director	Mandy Gutmann
Communications Manager	Stuart Bryan

Barclays Center Ticket Sales and Operations
Senior VP, Ticket Sales	John Baier
Vice President of Sales and Service	Mike DeMarino
Executive Director, Group Sales	Kirk King
Vice President, Sports Ticketing	Paul Kavanaugh
Senior Director of Ticket Sales	Emmanuel Jacobo
Director of Ticket Sales	Ashley Faust
Director of Group Sales	Daivd Nosti
Manager, Sports Ticketing Operations	Meghan Garvey
Senior Account Executive	Brian Frankel
Manager, Inside Sales	Adam Metzendorf
Account Executives, Ticket Sales	Maxwell Bloch, Claire Chen, George Hirsch, Brody Mankus, Robert Nogueras, Tanner Woods
Inside Sales Representatives	Zach Cohen, Krista Lamoreaux, Brittany McDonald, Nicole Medvitz, Max Padway, Rob Palomba, Steven Persaud, Talia Rosenhaus, Daniel Singer
Director, Premium Sales	Bryan Nadell
Senior Manager, VIP Services	Rachel Low
Account Managers, VIP Services	Marc Gerstein, David Koblentz , Ryan Koerner, Leah Papalia, Steven Weiss, Zachary Schwartz
Coordinator of Member Services	Bobby Stroud
Senior Account Manager, Group Sales	Anthony Infante
Account Manager, Group Sales	Patrick Bogan, Victoria Natoli, Zachary Pleeter
Coordinator, Group Sales	Deena Sena
Coordinator, Ticket Sales	Lauren Herzlich
Coordinator, Sports Ticketing Operations	Christopher Zabady

Barclays Center Marketing and Sponsorship
Executive VP, Global Partnerships	Mike Zavodsky
Sr. VP, Partnership Marketing	Joshua Pruss
Vice President, Analytics & Business Strategy	Randy Lewis
Vice President, Content and Creative	Jeff Gamble
Vice President, Global Partnerships	Chris Lombardo
Sr. Director, Partnership Marketing	Howard Seif
Sr. Director, Global Partnerships	Daniel Gaiman
Director, Business Strategy and Analytics	Michael Shear
Social Media Coordinator / Web Content Producer	Rachel Schwartz / Cory Wright
Marketing Manager / Coordinator	Joseph Paciullo / Derick Beresford

New York Rangers

2016-17 Results: 48W-28L-2OTL-4SOL 102PTS
4TH, Metropolitan Division • 7TH, Eastern Conference

Key Off-Season Signings/Acquisitions

2017

June 14 • Re-signed LW **Matt Puempel**.
23 • Acquired D **Tony DeAngelo** and a 1st-round pick in 2017 NHL Draft from Arizona for C **Derek Stepan** and G **Antti Raanta**.
29 • Re-signed D **Brendan Smith**.
July 1 • Signed D **Kevin Shattenkirk**, G **Ondrej Pavelec**, C **Paul Carey** and LW **Cole Schneider**.
5 • Signed C **David Desharnais**.
5 • Re-signed RW **Jesper Fast**.
10 • Named **Lindy Ruff** assistant coach.
25 • Re-signed C **Mika Zibanejad**.

2017-18 Schedule

Oct.	Thu.	5	Colorado		Sun.	7	at Vegas
	Sat.	7	at Toronto		Sat.	13	NY Islanders*
	Sun.	8	Montreal		Sun.	14	at Pittsburgh*
	Tue.	10	St. Louis		Tue.	16	Philadelphia
	Fri.	13	at Columbus		Thu.	18	Buffalo
	Sat.	14	New Jersey		Sat.	20	at Colorado*
	Tue.	17	Pittsburgh		Sun.	21	at Los Angeles
	Thu.	19	NY Islanders		Tue.	23	at Anaheim
	Sat.	21	Nashville*		Thu.	25	at San Jose
	Mon.	23	San Jose	**Feb.**	Thu.	1	Toronto
	Thu.	26	Arizona		Sat.	3	at Nashville
	Sat.	28	at Montreal		Mon.	5	at Dallas
	Tue.	31	Vegas		Wed.	7	Boston
Nov.	Thu.	2	at Tampa Bay		Fri.	9	Calgary
	Sat.	4	at Florida		Sun.	11	at Winnipeg*
	Mon.	6	Columbus		Tue.	13	at Minnesota
	Wed.	8	Boston		Thu.	15	at NY Islanders
	Sat.	11	Edmonton*		Sat.	17	at Ottawa*
	Wed.	15	at Chicago		Sun.	18	Philadelphia*
	Fri.	17	at Columbus		Thu.	22	at Montreal
	Sun.	19	Ottawa		Fri.	23	Minnesota
	Wed.	22	at Carolina		Sun.	25	Detroit
	Fri.	24	Detroit		Wed.	28	at Vancouver
	Sun.	26	Vancouver*	**Mar.**	Fri.	2	at Calgary
	Tue.	28	Florida		Sat.	3	at Edmonton
Dec.	Fri.	1	Carolina		Tue.	6	Winnipeg
	Tue.	5	at Pittsburgh		Thu.	8	at Tampa Bay
	Fri.	8	at Washington		Sat.	10	at Florida
	Sat.	9	New Jersey		Mon.	12	Carolina
	Mon.	11	Dallas		Wed.	14	Pittsburgh
	Wed.	13	at Ottawa		Sat.	17	at St. Louis*
	Fri.	15	Los Angeles		Tue.	20	Columbus
	Sat.	16	at Boston*		Thu.	22	at Philadelphia
	Tue.	19	Anaheim		Sat.	24	Buffalo
	Thu.	21	at New Jersey		Mon.	26	Washington
	Sat.	23	Toronto		Wed.	28	at Washington
	Wed.	27	Washington		Fri.	30	Tampa Bay
	Fri.	29	at Detroit		Sat.	31	at Carolina
Jan.	Mon.	1	at Buffalo*	**Apr.**	Tue.	3	at New Jersey
	Wed.	3	Chicago		Thu.	5	at NY Islanders
	Sat.	6	at Arizona		Sat.	7	at Philadelphia*

* Denotes afternoon game.

Retired Numbers

1	Ed Giacomin	1965-1975
2	Brian Leetch	1987-2004
3	Harry Howell	1952-1969
7	Rod Gilbert	1960-1977
9	Andy Bathgate	1952-1964
	Adam Graves	1991-2001
11	Mark Messier	1991-97; 2000-04
35	Mike Richter	1989-2003

METROPOLITAN DIVISION
92nd NHL Season

Franchise date: May 15, 1926

Year-by-Year Record

		Home				Road				Overall									
Season	**GP**	**W**	**L**	**T**	**OL**	**W**	**L**	**T**	**OL**	**W**	**L**	**T**	**OL**	**GF**	**GA**	**Pts.**	**Div. Fin.**	**Conf. Fin.**	**Playoff Result**
2016-17	82	21	16	....	4	27	12	....	2	48	28	....	6	256	220	102	4th, Met.	7th, East	Lost Second Round
2015-16	82	27	10	....	4	19	17	....	5	46	27	....	9	236	217	101	3rd, Met.	4th, East	Lost First Round
2014-15	82	25	11	....	5	28	11	....	2	53	22	....	7	252	192	113	1st, Met.	1st, East	Lost Conf. Final
2013-14	82	20	17	....	4	25	14	....	2	45	31	....	6	218	193	96	2nd, Met.	5th, East	Lost Final
2012-13	48	16	6	....	2	10	12	....	2	26	18	....	4	130	112	56	2nd, Atl.	6th, East	Lost Conf. Semi-Final
2011-12	82	27	12	....	2	24	12	....	5	51	24	....	7	226	187	109	1st, Atl.	1st, East	Lost Conf. Final
2010-11	82	20	17	....	4	24	16	....	1	44	33	....	5	233	198	93	3rd, Atl.	8th, East	Lost Conf. Quarter-Final
2009-10	82	18	17	....	6	20	16	....	5	38	33	....	11	222	218	87	4th, Atl.	9th, East	– out of playoffs –
2008-09	82	26	11	....	4	17	19	....	5	43	30	....	9	210	218	95	4th, Atl.	7th, East	Lost Conf. Quarter-Final
2007-08	82	25	13	....	3	17	14	....	10	42	27	....	13	213	199	97	3rd, Atl.	5th, East	Lost Conf. Semi-Final
2006-07	82	21	15	....	5	21	15	....	5	42	30	....	10	242	216	94	3rd, Atl.	6th, East	Lost Conf. Semi-Final
2005-06	82	25	10	....	6	19	16	....	6	44	26	....	12	257	215	100	3rd, Atl.	6th, East	Lost Conf. Quarter-Final
2004-05	....	....	....	....	....	....	....	....	....	....	....	....	....	....	....	....			
2003-04	82	13	21	3	4	14	19	4	4	27	40	7	8	206	250	69	4th, Atl.	13th, East	– out of playoffs –
2002-03	82	17	18	4	2	15	18	6	2	32	36	10	4	210	231	78	4th, Atl.	9th, East	– out of playoffs –
2001-02	82	19	19	2	1	17	19	2	3	36	38	4	4	227	258	80	4th, Atl.	11th, East	– out of playoffs –
2000-01	82	17	20	3	1	16	23	2	0	33	43	5	1	250	290	72	4th, Atl.	10th, East	– out of playoffs –
1999-2000	82	15	20	5	1	14	18	7	2	29	38	12	3	218	246	73	4th, Atl.	11th, East	– out of playoffs –
1998-99	82	17	19	5	....	16	19	6	....	33	38	11	....	217	227	77	4th, Atl.	10th, East	– out of playoffs –
1997-98	82	14	18	9	....	11	21	9	....	25	39	18	....	197	231	68	5th, Atl.	11th, East	– out of playoffs –
1996-97	82	21	14	6	....	17	20	4	....	38	34	10	....	258	231	86	4th, Atl.	5th, East	Lost Conf. Final
1995-96	82	22	10	9	....	19	17	5	....	41	27	14	....	272	237	96	2nd, Atl.	3rd, East	Lost Conf. Semi-Final
1994-95	48	11	10	3	....	11	13	0	....	22	23	3	....	139	134	47	4th, Atl.	8th, East	Lost Conf. Semi-Final
1993-94	**84**	**28**	**8**	**6**	....	**24**	**16**	**2**	....	**52**	**24**	**8**	....	**299**	**231**	**112**	**1st, Atl.**	**1st, East**	**Won Stanley Cup**
1992-93	84	20	17	5	....	14	22	6	....	34	39	11	....	304	308	79	6th, Patrick		– out of playoffs –
1991-92	80	28	8	4	....	22	17	1	....	50	25	5	....	321	246	105	1st, Patrick		Lost Div. Final
1990-91	80	22	11	7	....	14	20	6	....	36	31	13	....	297	265	85	2nd, Patrick		Lost Div. Semi-Final
1989-90	80	20	11	9	....	16	20	4	....	36	31	13	....	279	267	85	1st, Patrick		Lost Div. Final
1988-89	80	21	17	2	....	16	18	6	....	37	35	8	....	310	307	82	3rd, Patrick		Lost Div. Semi-Final
1987-88	80	22	13	5	....	14	21	5	....	36	34	10	....	300	283	82	5th, Patrick		– out of playoffs –
1986-87	80	18	18	4	....	16	20	4	....	34	38	8	....	307	323	76	4th, Patrick		Lost Div. Semi-Final
1985-86	80	20	18	2	....	16	20	4	....	36	38	6	....	280	276	78	4th, Patrick		Lost Conf. Final
1984-85	80	16	18	6	....	10	26	4	....	26	44	10	....	295	345	62	4th, Patrick		Lost Div. Semi-Final
1983-84	80	27	12	1	....	15	17	8	....	42	29	9	....	314	304	93	4th, Patrick		Lost Div. Semi-Final
1982-83	80	24	13	3	....	11	22	7	....	35	35	10	....	306	287	80	4th, Patrick		Lost Div. Final
1981-82	80	19	15	6	....	20	12	8	....	39	27	14	....	316	306	92	2nd, Patrick		Lost Div. Final
1980-81	80	17	13	10	....	13	23	4	....	30	36	14	....	312	317	74	4th, Patrick		Lost Semi-Final
1979-80	80	22	10	8	....	16	22	2	....	38	32	10	....	308	284	86	3rd, Patrick		Lost Quarter-Final
1978-79	80	19	13	8	....	21	16	3	....	40	29	11	....	316	292	91	3rd, Patrick		Lost Final
1977-78	80	18	15	7	....	12	22	6	....	30	37	13	....	279	280	73	4th, Patrick		Lost Prelim. Round
1976-77	80	17	18	5	....	12	19	9	....	29	37	14	....	272	310	72	4th, Patrick		– out of playoffs –
1975-76	80	16	16	8	....	13	26	1	....	29	42	9	....	262	333	67	4th, Patrick		– out of playoffs –
1974-75	80	21	11	8	....	16	18	6	....	37	29	14	....	319	276	88	2nd, Patrick		Lost Prelim. Round
1973-74	78	26	7	6	....	14	17	8	....	40	24	14	....	300	251	94	3rd, East		Lost Semi-Final
1972-73	78	26	8	5	....	21	15	3	....	47	23	8	....	297	208	102	3rd, East		Lost Semi-Final
1971-72	78	26	6	7	....	22	11	6	....	48	17	13	....	317	192	109	2nd, East		Lost Final
1970-71	78	30	2	7	....	19	16	4	....	49	18	11	....	259	177	109	2nd, East		Lost Semi-Final
1969-70	76	22	8	8	....	16	14	8	....	38	22	16	....	246	189	92	4th, East		Lost Quarter-Final
1968-69	76	27	7	4	....	14	19	5	....	41	26	9	....	231	196	91	3rd, East		Lost Quarter-Final
1967-68	74	22	8	7	....	17	15	5	....	39	23	12	....	226	183	90	2nd, East		Lost Quarter-Final
1966-67	70	18	12	5	....	12	16	7	....	30	28	12	....	188	189	72	4th		Lost Semi-Final
1965-66	70	12	16	7	....	6	25	4	....	18	41	11	....	195	261	47	6th		– out of playoffs –
1964-65	70	8	19	8	....	12	19	4	....	20	38	12	....	179	246	52	5th		– out of playoffs –
1963-64	70	14	13	8	....	8	25	2	....	22	38	10	....	186	242	54	5th		– out of playoffs –
1962-63	70	12	17	6	....	10	19	6	....	22	36	12	....	211	233	56	5th		– out of playoffs –
1961-62	70	16	11	8	....	10	21	4	....	26	32	12	....	195	207	64	4th		Lost Semi-Final
1960-61	70	15	15	5	....	7	23	5	....	22	38	10	....	204	248	54	5th		– out of playoffs –
1959-60	70	10	15	10	....	7	23	5	....	17	38	15	....	187	247	49	6th		– out of playoffs –
1958-59	70	14	16	5	....	12	16	7	....	26	32	12	....	201	217	64	5th		– out of playoffs –
1957-58	70	14	15	6	....	18	10	7	....	32	25	13	....	195	188	77	2nd		Lost Semi-Final
1956-57	70	15	12	8	....	11	18	6	....	26	30	14	....	184	227	66	4th		Lost Semi-Final
1955-56	70	20	7	8	....	12	21	2	....	32	28	10	....	204	203	74	3rd		Lost Semi-Final
1954-55	70	10	12	13	....	7	23	5	....	17	35	18	....	150	210	52	5th		– out of playoffs –
1953-54	70	18	12	5	....	11	19	5	....	29	31	10	....	161	182	68	5th		– out of playoffs –
1952-53	70	11	14	10	....	6	23	6	....	17	37	16	....	152	211	50	6th		– out of playoffs –
1951-52	70	16	13	6	....	7	21	7	....	23	34	13	....	192	219	59	5th		– out of playoffs –
1950-51	70	14	11	10	....	6	18	11	....	20	29	21	....	169	201	61	5th		– out of playoffs –
1949-50	70	19	12	4	....	9	19	7	....	28	31	11	....	170	189	67	4th		Lost Final
1948-49	60	13	12	5	....	5	19	6	....	18	31	11	....	133	172	47	6th		– out of playoffs –
1947-48	60	11	12	7	....	10	14	6	....	21	26	13	....	176	201	55	4th		Lost Semi-Final
1946-47	60	11	14	5	....	11	18	1	....	22	32	6	....	167	186	50	5th		– out of playoffs –
1945-46	50	8	12	5	....	5	16	4	....	13	28	9	....	144	191	35	6th		– out of playoffs –
1944-45	50	7	11	7	....	4	18	3	....	11	29	10	....	154	247	32	6th		– out of playoffs –
1943-44	50	4	17	4	....	2	22	1	....	6	39	5	....	162	310	17	6th		– out of playoffs –
1942-43	50	7	13	5	....	4	18	3	....	11	31	8	....	161	253	30	6th		– out of playoffs –
1941-42	48	15	8	1	....	14	9	1	....	29	17	2	....	177	143	60	1st		Lost Semi-Final
1940-41	48	13	7	4	....	8	12	4	....	21	19	8	....	143	125	50	4th		Lost Quarter-Final
1939-40	**48**	**17**	**4**	**3**	....	**10**	**7**	**7**	....	**27**	**11**	**10**	....	**136**	**77**	**64**	**2nd**		**Won Stanley Cup**
1938-39	48	13	8	3	....	13	8	3	....	26	16	6	....	149	105	58	2nd		Lost Semi-Final
1937-38	48	15	5	4	....	12	10	2	....	27	15	6	....	149	96	60	2nd, Amn.		Lost Quarter-Final
1936-37	48	9	7	8	....	10	13	1	....	19	20	9	....	117	106	47	3rd, Amn.		Lost Final
1935-36	48	11	6	7	....	8	11	5	....	19	17	12	....	91	96	50	4th, Amn.		– out of playoffs –
1934-35	48	11	8	5	....	11	12	1	....	22	20	6	....	137	139	50	3rd, Amn.		Lost Semi-Final
1933-34	48	11	7	6	....	10	12	2	....	21	19	8	....	120	113	50	3rd, Amn.		Lost Quarter-Final
1932-33	**48**	**12**	**7**	**5**	....	**11**	**10**	**3**	....	**23**	**17**	**8**	....	**135**	**107**	**54**	**3rd, Amn.**		**Won Stanley Cup**
1931-32	48	13	7	4	....	10	10	4	....	23	17	8	....	134	112	54	1st, Amn.		Lost Final
1930-31	44	10	9	3	....	9	7	6	....	19	16	9	....	106	87	47	3rd, Amn.		Lost Semi-Final
1929-30	44	11	5	6	....	6	12	4	....	17	17	10	....	136	143	44	3rd, Amn.		Lost Semi-Final
1928-29	44	12	6	4	....	9	7	6	....	21	13	10	....	72	65	52	2nd, Amn.		Lost Final
1927-28	**44**	**10**	**8**	**4**	....	**9**	**8**	**5**	....	**19**	**16**	**9**	....	**94**	**79**	**47**	**2nd, Amn.**		**Won Stanley Cup**
1926-27	44	13	5	4	....	12	8	2	....	25	13	6	....	95	72	56	1st, Amn.		Lost Quarter-Final

2017-18 Player Personnel

FORWARDS	HT	WT	*Age	Birthplace	S	2016-17 Club
BUCHNEVICH, Pavel	6-2	193	22	Cherepovets, Russia	L	NY Rangers-Hartford
DESHARNAIS, David	5-7	180	31	Laurier-Station, QC	L	Montreal-Edmonton
FAST, Jesper	6-0	190	25	Nassjo, Sweden	R	NY Rangers
GRABNER, Michael	6-1	185	29	Villach, Austria	L	NY Rangers
HAYES, Kevin	6-5	215	25	Dorchester, MA	L	NY Rangers
KREIDER, Chris	6-3	228	26	Boxford, MA	L	NY Rangers
MILLER, J.T.	6-1	206	24	East Palestine, OH	L	NY Rangers
NASH, Rick	6-4	212	33	Brampton, ON	L	NY Rangers
NIEVES, Cristoval	6-3	219	23	Syracuse, NY	L	NY Rangers-Hartford
PUEMPEL, Matt	6-1	205	24	Windsor, ON	L	Ottawa-NY Rangers
VESEY, Jimmy	6-3	207	24	North Reading, MA	L	NY Rangers
ZIBANEJAD, Mika	6-2	215	24	Huddinge, Sweden	R	NY Rangers
ZUCCARELLO, Mats	5-8	179	30	Oslo, Norway	L	NY Rangers
DEFENSEMEN						
BEREGLAZOV, Alexei	6-4	205	23	Magnitogorsk, Russia	L	Magnitogorsk
DeANGELO, Tony	5-11	183	21	Sewell, NJ	R	Arizona-Tucson
HOLDEN, Nick	6-4	214	30	St. Albert, AB	L	NY Rangers
KAMPFER, Steven	5-11	192	29	Ann Arbor, MI	R	NYR-Hart-Fla
McDONAGH, Ryan	6-1	216	28	St.Paul, MN	L	NY Rangers
SHATTENKIRK, Kevin	6-0	200	28	New Rochelle, NY	R	St. Louis-Washington
SKJEI, Brady	6-3	211	23	Lakeville, MN	L	NY Rangers
SMITH, Brendan	6-2	211	28	Mimico, ON	L	Detroit-NY Rangers
STAAL, Marc	6-4	209	30	Thunder Bay, ON	L	NY Rangers

GOALTENDERS	HT	WT	*Age	Birthplace	C	2016-17 Club
LUNDQVIST, Henrik	6-1	188	35	Are, Sweden	L	NY Rangers
PAVELEC, Ondrej	6-3	215	30	Kladno, Czech.	L	Winnipeg-Manitoba

* – Age at start of 2017-18 season

Alain Vigneault

Head Coach

Born: Quebec City, QC, May 14, 1961.

The New York Rangers officially named Alain Vigneault as the club's head coach on June 21, 2013. He is the 35th head coach in franchise history. A three-time Jack Adams Award finalist, and the 2007 winner of the award presented to the NHL's top coach, Vigneault joined the Rangers after spending seven seasons with the Vancouver Canucks. In his first season in New York, Vigneault led the Rangers to the Stanley Cup Finals. In 2014-15, the Rangers won the Presidents' Trophy and Vigneault was runner-up for the Jack Adams Award. He previously coached the Canucks to a pair of Presidents' Trophy wins – in 2010-11 and 2011-12 – six Northwest Division titles, five seasons with 100 or more points, and an appearance in the 2011 Stanley Cup Final, where Vancouver lost in seven games to the Boston Bruins. Vigneault is Vancouver's all-time leader in coaching victories with 313.

After being a successful head coach in the Quebec Major Junior Hockey League and as an assistant with the Ottawa Senators, Vigneault earned his first NHL head coaching job with the Canadiens in 1997-98. Vigneault led the Canadiens to the second round of the playoffs that season, before missing out on the postseason the next two years – although he still earned a Jack Adams nomination for his outstanding work in 1999-2000. After being relieved of his duties by Montreal 20 games into the 2000-01 campaign, Vigneault coached once again in the QMJHL and then in the minor leagues for Vancouver before becoming the Canucks head coach prior to the 2006-07 season. His most successful season behind the bench in Vancouver was 2010-11 when the Canucks won 54 games, totaled 117 points, captured the Presidents' Trophy as the top team in the league over the regular season, and then fell just one victory shy of winning the Stanley Cup. A year later Vigneault's Canucks edged the Rangers by just two points, 111 to 109, to win the Presidents' Trophy again.

Coaching Record

			Regular Season				Playoffs			
Season	Team	League	GC	W	L	O/T	GC	W	L	T
1986-87	Trois-Rivieres	QMJHL	70	28	40	2	....	....	....	....
1987-88	Hull	QMJHL	70	43	23	4	19	12	7	....
1987-88	Hull	M-Cup	....	....	....	....	4	1	3	....
1988-89	Hull	QMJHL	70	40	25	5	9	5	4	....
1989-90	Hull	QMJHL	70	36	29	5	11	4	7	....
1990-91	Hull	QMJHL	70	36	27	7	6	2	4	....
1991-92	Hull	QMJHL	70	41	24	5	6	2	4	....
1995-96	Beauport	QMJHL	31	19	7	5	20	13	7	....
1996-97	Beauport	QMJHL	70	24	44	2	4	1	3	....
1997-98	**Montreal**	**NHL**	**82**	**37**	**32**	**13**	**10**	**4**	**6**	....
1998-99	**Montreal**	**NHL**	**82**	**32**	**39**	**11**	....	....	....	....
99-2000	**Montreal**	**NHL**	**82**	**35**	**34**	**13**	....	....	....	....
2000-01	**Montreal**	**NHL**	**20**	**5**	**13**	**2**	....	....	....	....
2003-04	PEI	QMJHL	70	40	19	11	11	6	5	....
2004-05	PEI	QMJHL	70	24	39	7	....	....	....	....
2005-06	Manitoba	AHL	80	44	24	12	13	7	6	....
2006-07	**Vancouver**	**NHL**	**82**	**49**	**26**	**7**	**12**	**5**	**7**	....
2007-08	**Vancouver**	**NHL**	**82**	**39**	**33**	**10**	....	....	....	....
2008-09	**Vancouver**	**NHL**	**82**	**45**	**27**	**10**	**10**	**6**	**4**	....
2009-10	**Vancouver**	**NHL**	**82**	**49**	**28**	**5**	**12**	**6**	**6**	....
2010-11	**Vancouver**	**NHL**	**82**	**54**	**19**	**9**	**25**	**15**	**10**	....
2011-12	**Vancouver**	**NHL**	**82**	**51**	**22**	**9**	**5**	**1**	**4**	....
2012-13	**Vancouver**	**NHL**	**48**	**26**	**15**	**7**	**4**	**0**	**4**	....
2013-14	**NY Rangers**	**NHL**	**82**	**45**	**31**	**6**	**25**	**13**	**12**	....
2014-15	**NY Rangers**	**NHL**	**82**	**53**	**22**	**7**	**19**	**11**	**8**	....
2015-16	**NY Rangers**	**NHL**	**82**	**46**	**27**	**9**	**5**	**1**	**4**	....
2016-17	**NY Rangers**	**NHL**	**82**	**48**	**28**	**6**	**12**	**6**	**6**	....
	NHL Totals		**1134**	**614**	**396**	**124**	**139**	**68**	**71**	....

Jack Adams Award (2007)

2016-17 Scoring

* – rookie

Regular Season

Pos	#	Player	Team	GP	G	A	Pts	TOI	+/-	PIM	PP	SH	GW	S	S%
C	36	Mats Zuccarello	NYR	80	15	44	59	18:49	15	26	5	0	3	189	7.9
C	10	J.T. Miller	NYR	82	22	34	56	16:21	17	21	2	3	6	132	16.7
C	21	Derek Stepan	NYR	81	17	38	55	18:36	19	16	4	1	2	209	8.1
C	20	Chris Kreider	NYR	75	28	25	53	17:00	6	58	6	0	4	186	15.1
R	13	Kevin Hayes	NYR	76	17	32	49	16:33	10	18	1	1	4	143	11.9
D	27	Ryan McDonagh	NYR	77	6	36	42	24:21	20	37	1	1	1	153	3.9
R	40	Michael Grabner	NYR	76	27	13	40	14:05	22	10	0	1	3	162	16.7
D	76 *	Brady Skjei	NYR	80	5	34	39	17:27	11	42	0	0	0	127	3.9
L	61	Rick Nash	NYR	67	23	15	38	16:27	9	26	6	1	3	195	11.8
C	93	Mika Zibanejad	NYR	56	14	23	37	17:04	9	16	4	0	2	119	11.8
D	22	Nick Holden	NYR	80	11	23	34	20:36	13	35	3	0	2	84	13.1
L	26 *	Jimmy Vesey	NYR	80	16	11	27	13:38	–13	26	5	0	6	116	13.8
R	19	Jesper Fast	NYR	68	6	15	21	13:47	6	16	0	0	1	56	10.7
L	89 *	Pavel Buchnevich	NYR	41	8	12	20	13:15	6	13	1	0	0	55	14.5
C	24	Oscar Lindberg	NYR	65	8	12	20	10:49	2	32	0	0	1	86	9.3
C	73	Brandon Pirri	NYR	60	8	10	18	12:16	–8	25	5	0	3	96	8.3
D	5	Dan Girardi	NYR	63	4	11	15	19:06	8	16	0	1	3	56	7.1
D	8	Kevin Klein	NYR	60	3	11	14	17:38	5	31	0	0	0	54	5.6
D	4	Adam Clendening	NYR	31	2	9	11	15:48	3	17	1	0	0	38	5.3
D	18	Marc Staal	NYR	72	3	7	10	19:10	9	34	0	0	0	70	4.3
L	12	Matt Puempel	OTT	13	0	0	0	8:34	–5	7	0	0	0	12	0.0
			NYR	27	6	3	9	10:09	–6	4	3	0	1	32	18.8
			Total	40	6	3	9	9:38	–11	11	3	0	1	44	13.6
D	42	Brendan Smith	DET	33	2	3	5	18:44	–1	34	1	0	1	39	5.1
			NYR	18	1	3	4	20:09	2	29	0	0	0	23	4.3
			Total	51	3	6	9	19:14	1	63	1	0	1	62	4.8
L	15	Tanner Glass	NYR	11	1	1	2	10:54	0	17	0	0	0	8	12.5
D	43	Steven Kampfer	FLA	1	0	0	0	16:48	–1	4	0	0	0	0	0.0
			NYR	10	1	1	2	12:54	–1	2	0	0	0	10	10.0
			Total	11	1	1	2	13:15	–2	6	0	0	0	10	10.0
L	46 *	Marek Hrivik	NYR	16	0	2	2	10:25	–3	2	0	0	0	15	0.0
C	67 *	Cristoval Nieves	NYR	1	0	0	0	11:44	–1	0	0	0	0	0	0.0
L	28	Taylor Beck	EDM	3	0	0	0	5:53	–1	4	0	0	0	0	0.0
			NYR	2	0	0	0	13:12	–2	0	0	0	0	5	0.0
			Total	5	0	0	0	8:48	–3	4	0	0	0	5	0.0
L	39 *	Nicklas Jensen	NYR	7	0	0	0	9:13	–2	0	0	0	0	8	0.0

Goaltending

No.	Goaltender	GPI	Mins	Avg	W	L	OT	EN	SO	GA	SA	Sv%	G	A	PIM
45	* Magnus Hellberg	2	79	1.52	1	0	0	0	0	2	28	.929	0	0	0
32	Antti Raanta	30	1617	2.26	16	8	2	2	4	61	782	.922	0	1	0
30	Henrik Lundqvist	57	3240	2.74	31	20	4	3	2	148	1650	.910	0	1	0
	Totals	**82**	**4974**	**2.61**	**48**	**28**	**6**	**5**	**7**	**216**	**2465**	**.912**			

Henrik Lundqvist and Antti Raanta shared a shutout vs. DAL on Dec. 15, 2016

Playoffs

Pos	#	Player	Team	GP	G	A	Pts	TOI	+/-	PIM	PP	SH	GW	OT	S	S%
C	93	Mika Zibanejad	NYR	12	2	7	9	17:52	4	0	0	0	1	1	34	5.9
C	36	Mats Zuccarello	NYR	12	4	3	7	20:32	0	16	1	0	1	0	25	16.0
D	27	Ryan McDonagh	NYR	12	2	5	7	27:20	0	12	1	0	0	0	26	7.7
R	40	Michael Grabner	NYR	12	4	2	6	14:01	4	0	0	1	1	0	26	15.4
R	19	Jesper Fast	NYR	12	3	3	6	14:58	4	0	0	1	0	0	13	23.1
C	21	Derek Stepan	NYR	12	2	4	6	20:59	–3	4	0	1	0	0	33	6.1
D	76 *	Brady Skjei	NYR	12	4	1	5	19:14	6	10	0	0	0	0	19	21.1
L	61	Rick Nash	NYR	12	3	2	5	18:24	1	4	0	0	1	0	44	6.8
L	26 *	Jimmy Vesey	NYR	12	1	4	5	14:26	0	9	0	0	0	0	15	6.7
C	20	Chris Kreider	NYR	12	3	1	4	16:52	1	18	1	0	0	0	30	10.0
C	24	Oscar Lindberg	NYR	12	3	1	4	9:54	3	2	0	0	1	0	17	17.6
D	22	Nick Holden	NYR	11	2	2	4	19:20	–3	4	0	0	0	0	22	9.1
L	15	Tanner Glass	NYR	7	1	3	4	9:52	–1	7	0	0	1	0	5	20.0
D	42	Brendan Smith	NYR	12	0	4	4	19:41	8	20	0	0	0	0	11	0.0
R	13	Kevin Hayes	NYR	12	0	3	3	17:43	0	4	0	0	0	0	21	0.0
C	10	J.T. Miller	NYR	12	0	3	3	16:32	1	21	0	0	0	0	17	0.0
D	5	Dan Girardi	NYR	12	0	2	2	22:06	–1	2	0	0	0	0	16	0.0
D	8	Kevin Klein	NYR	1	0	1	1	18:15	0	0	0	0	0	0	0	0.0
L	89 *	Pavel Buchnevich	NYR	5	0	1	1	12:17	1	0	0	0	0	0	10	0.0
D	18	Marc Staal	NYR	12	0	0	0	19:15	–1	2	0	0	0	0	12	0.0

Goaltending

No.	Goaltender	GPI	Mins	Avg	W	L	EN	SO	GA	SA	Sv%	G	A	PIM
30	Henrik Lundqvist	12	775	2.25	6	6	1	1	29	395	.927	0	0	0
	Totals	**12**	**782**	**2.30**	**6**	**6**	**1**	**1**	**30**	**396**	**.924**			

Coaching History

Lester Patrick, 1926-27 to 1938-39; Frank Boucher, 1939-40 to 1947-48; Frank Boucher and Lynn Patrick, 1948-49; Lynn Patrick, 1949-50; Neil Colville, 1950-51; Neil Colville and Bill Cook, 1951-52; Bill Cook, 1952-53; Frank Boucher and Muzz Patrick, 1953-54; Muzz Patrick, 1954-55; Phil Watson, 1955-56 to 1958-59; Phil Watson, Muzz Patrick and Alf Pike, 1959-60; Alf Pike, 1960-61; Doug Harvey, 1961-62; Muzz Patrick and Red Sullivan, 1962-63; Red Sullivan, 1963-64, 1964-65; Red Sullivan and Emile Francis, 1965-66; Emile Francis, 1966-67, 1967-68; Bernie Geoffrion and Emile Francis, 1968-69; Emile Francis, 1969-70 to 1972-73; Larry Popein and Emile Francis, 1973-74; Emile Francis, 1974-75; Ron Stewart and John Ferguson, 1975-76; John Ferguson, 1976-77; Jean-Guy Talbot, 1977-78; Fred Shero, 1978-79, 1979-80; Fred Shero and Craig Patrick, 1980-81; Herb Brooks, 1981-82 to 1983-84; Herb Brooks and Craig Patrick, 1984-85; Ted Sator, 1985-86; Ted Sator, Tom Webster and Phil Esposito, 1986-87; Michel Bergeron, 1987-88; Michel Bergeron and Phil Esposito, 1988-89; Roger Neilson, 1989-90 to 1991-92; Roger Neilson and Ron Smith, 1992-93; Mike Keenan, 1993-94; Colin Campbell, 1994-95 to 1996-97; Colin Campbell and John Muckler, 1997-98; John Muckler, 1998-99; John Muckler and John Tortorella, 1999-2000; Ron Low, 2000-01, 2001-02; Bryan Trottier and Glen Sather, 2002-03; Glen Sather and Tom Renney, 2003-04; Tom Renney, 2004-05 to 2007-08; Tom Renney and John Tortorella, 2008-09; John Tortorella, 2009-10 to 2012-13; Alain Vigneault, 2013-14 to date.

Club Records

Team

(Figures in brackets for season records are games played; records for fewest points, wins, ties, losses, goals, goals against are for 70 or more games)

Most Points 113 2014-15 (82)
Most Wins 53 2014-15 (82)
Most Ties 21 1950-51 (70)
Most Losses 44 1984-85 (80)
Most Goals 321 1991-92 (80)
Most Goals Against 345 1984-85 (80)
Fewest Points 47 1965-66 (70)
Fewest Wins 17 1952-53 (70), 1954-55 (70), 1959-60 (70)
Fewest Ties 4 2001-02 (82)
Fewest Losses 17 1971-72 (78)
Fewest Goals 150 1954-55 (70)
Fewest Goals Against 177 1970-71 (78)

Longest Winning Streak
- Overall .... 10 Dec. 19/39-Jan. 13/40, Jan. 19-Feb. 10/73
- Home .... 14 Dec. 19/39-Feb. 25/40
- Away .... 7 Jan. 12-Feb. 12/35, Oct. 28-Nov. 29/78

Longest Team Point Streak
- Overall .... 19 Nov. 23/39-Jan. 13/40 (14W, 5T)
- Home .... 24 Oct. 14/70-Jan. 31/71 (18W, 6T), Oct. 24/95-Feb.15/96 (18W, 6T)
- Away .... 11 Nov. 5/39-Jan. 13/40 (6W, 5T)

Longest Losing Streak
- Overall .... 11 Oct. 30-Nov. 27/43
- Home .... 7 Oct. 20-Nov. 14/76, Mar. 24-Apr. 14/93
- Away .... 10 Oct. 30-Dec. 23/43, Feb. 8-Mar. 15/61

Longest Winless Streak
- Overall .... 21 Jan. 23-Mar. 19/44 (17L, 4T)
- Home .... 10 Jan. 30-Mar. 19/44 (7L, 3T)
- Away .... 16 Oct. 9-Dec. 20/52 (12L, 4T)

Most Shutouts, Season 13 1928-29 (44)
Most PIM, Season 2,018 1989-90 (80)
Most Goals, Game .... 12 Nov. 21/71 (Cal. 1 at NYR 12)

Individual

Most Seasons .... 18 Rod Gilbert
Most Games .... 1,160 Harry Howell
Most Goals, Career .... 406 Rod Gilbert
Most Assists, Career .... 741 Brian Leetch
Most Points, Career .... 1,021 Rod Gilbert (406G, 615A)
Most PIM, Career .... 1,226 Ron Greschner
Most Shutouts, Career .... 61 Henrik Lundqvist
Longest Consecutive Games Streak .... 560 Andy Hebenton (Oct. 7/55-Mar. 24/63)
Most Goals, Season .... 54 Jaromir Jagr (2005-06)
Most Assists, Season .... 80 Brian Leetch (1991-92)
Most Points, Season .... 123 Jaromir Jagr (2005-06; 54G, 69A)
Most PIM, Season .... 305 Troy Mallette (1989-90)
Most Points, Defenseman, Season .... 102 Brian Leetch (1991-92; 22G, 80A)
Most Points, Center, Season .... 109 Jean Ratelle (1971-72; 46G, 63A)
Most Points, Right Wing, Season .... 123 Jaromir Jagr (2005-06; 54G, 69A)
Most Points, Left Wing, Season .... 106 Vic Hadfield (1971-72; 50G, 56A)
Most Points, Rookie, Season .... 76 Mark Pavelich (1981-82; 33G, 43A)
Most Shutouts, Season .... 13 John Ross Roach (1928-29)
Most Goals, Game .... 5 Don Murdoch (Oct. 12/76), Mark Pavelich (Feb. 23/83)
Most Assists, Game .... 5 Walt Tkaczuk (Feb. 12/72), Rod Gilbert (Mar. 2/75), (Mar. 30/75), (Oct. 8/76), Don Maloney (Jan. 3/87), Brian Leetch (Apr. 18/95), Wayne Gretzky (Feb. 15/99)
Most Points, Game .... 7 Steve Vickers (Feb. 18/76; 3G, 4A)

Captains' History

Bill Cook, 1926-27 to 1936-37; Art Coulter, 1937-38 to 1941-42; Ott Heller, 1942-43 to 1944-45; Neil Colville 1945-46 to 1948-49; Buddy O'Connor, 1949-50; Frank Eddolls, 1950-51; Frank Eddolls and Allan Stanley, 1951-52; Allan Stanley, 1952-53; Allan Stanley and Don Raleigh, 1953-54; Don Raleigh, 1954-55; Harry Howell, 1955-56, 1956-57; Red Sullivan, 1957-58 to 1960-61; Andy Bathgate, 1961-62, 1962-63; Andy Bathgate and Camille Henry, 1963-64; Camille Henry and Bob Nevin, 1964-65; Bob Nevin 1965-66 to 1970-71; Vic Hadfield, 1971-72 to 1973-74; Brad Park, 1974-75; Brad Park and Phil Esposito, 1975-76; Phil Esposito, 1976-77, 1977-78; Dave Maloney, 1978-79, 1979-80; Dave Maloney, Walt Tkaczuk and Barry Beck, 1980-81; Barry Beck, 1981-82 to 1985-86; Ron Greschner, 1986-87; Ron Greschner and Kelly Kisio, 1987-88; Kelly Kisio, 1988-89 to 1990-91; Mark Messier, 1991-92 to 1996-97; Brian Leetch, 1997-98 to 1999-2000; Mark Messier, 2000-01 to 2003-04; no captain, 2005-06; Jaromir Jagr, 2006-07, 2007-08; Chris Drury, 2008-09 to 2010-11; Ryan Callahan, 2011-12, 2012-13; Ryan Callahan and no captain, 2013-14; Ryan McDonagh, 2014-15 to date.

All-time Record vs. Other Clubs

Regular Season

	Total								At Home								On Road							
	GP	W	L	T	OL	GF	GA	PTS	GP	W	L	T	OL	GF	GA	PTS	GP	W	L	T	OL	GF	GA	PTS
Anaheim	33	15	16	1	1	92	97	32	17	9	7	1	0	48	40	19	16	6	9	0	1	44	57	13
Arizona	76	45	25	6	0	288	247	96	38	26	10	2	0	159	123	54	38	19	15	4	0	129	124	42
Boston	643	255	289	97	2	1872	2017	609	323	147	121	55	0	987	897	349	320	108	168	42	2	885	1120	260
Buffalo	177	71	76	25	5	547	565	172	87	39	30	15	3	273	232	96	90	32	46	10	2	274	333	76
Calgary	115	45	54	15	1	368	434	106	59	30	24	5	0	197	197	65	56	15	30	10	1	171	237	41
Carolina	136	75	52	7	2	443	367	159	69	46	17	4	2	241	158	98	67	29	35	3	0	202	209	61
Chicago	587	241	246	98	2	1666	1709	582	293	121	117	55	0	858	825	297	294	120	129	43	2	808	884	285
Colorado	84	39	32	7	6	309	279	91	42	22	13	4	3	156	117	51	42	17	19	3	3	153	162	40
Columbus	29	16	11	1	1	88	89	34	13	7	4	1	1	45	42	16	16	9	7	0	0	43	47	18
Dallas	138	74	40	22	2	479	395	172	70	39	19	11	1	238	187	90	68	35	21	11	1	241	208	82
Detroit	587	219	262	103	3	1608	1780	544	293	140	95	58	0	887	753	338	294	79	167	45	3	721	1027	206
Edmonton	72	31	30	9	2	253	248	73	37	14	16	6	1	138	132	35	35	17	14	3	1	115	116	38
Florida	92	51	29	6	6	272	215	114	46	26	14	4	2	144	103	58	46	25	15	2	4	128	112	56
Los Angeles	133	69	45	16	3	488	411	157	65	38	20	6	1	252	193	83	68	31	25	10	2	236	218	74
Minnesota	22	14	8	0	0	68	61	28	10	7	3	0	0	33	26	14	12	7	5	0	0	35	35	14
Montreal	623	194	330	94	5	1609	2095	487	311	128	127	54	2	893	896	312	312	66	203	40	3	716	1199	175
Nashville	24	13	8	1	2	68	54	29	13	6	5	1	1	34	28	14	11	7	3	0	1	34	26	15
New Jersey	239	114	89	27	9	786	705	264	118	63	31	20	4	415	313	150	121	51	58	7	5	371	392	114
NY Islanders	262	125	110	19	8	872	845	277	131	71	44	11	5	466	384	158	131	54	66	8	3	406	461	119
Ottawa	89	40	42	3	4	237	248	87	44	17	25	0	2	117	128	36	45	23	17	3	2	120	120	51
Philadelphia	289	130	114	37	8	856	847	305	144	68	49	23	4	451	403	163	145	62	65	14	4	405	444	142
Pittsburgh	271	126	109	23	13	955	909	288	137	70	52	9	6	507	448	155	134	56	57	14	7	448	461	133
St. Louis	139	79	43	16	1	488	374	175	67	47	13	6	1	266	160	101	72	32	30	10	0	222	214	74
San Jose	37	24	9	3	1	133	100	52	17	12	4	1	0	66	44	25	20	12	5	2	1	67	56	27
Tampa Bay	95	47	36	5	7	298	277	106	49	26	17	2	4	161	135	58	46	21	19	3	3	137	142	48
Toronto	608	230	276	95	7	1758	1922	562	305	132	113	56	4	946	894	324	303	98	163	39	3	812	1028	238
Vancouver	119	78	32	8	1	483	338	165	61	41	14	5	1	258	162	88	58	37	18	3	0	225	176	77
Washington	214	96	93	18	7	718	727	217	107	52	42	9	4	385	355	117	107	44	51	9	3	333	372	100
Winnipeg	59	28	20	1	10	169	165	67	30	11	12	1	6	80	86	29	29	17	8	0	4	89	79	38
Defunct Clubs	278	169	64	45	0	901	581	383	139	87	30	22	0	460	290	196	139	82	34	23	0	441	291	187
Totals	**6270**	**2753**	**2590**	**808**	**119**	**19172**	**19101**	**6433**	**3135**	**1542**	**1088**	**447**	**58**	**10161**	**8751**	**3589**	**3135**	**1211**	**1502**	**361**	**61**	**9011**	**10350**	**2844**

Playoffs

	Series	W	L	GP	W	L	T	GF	GA	Last Mtg.	Rnd.	Result
Boston	10	3	7	47	19	26	2	114	130	2013	CSF	L 1-4
Buffalo	2	0	2	9	3	6	0	19	28	2007	CSF	L 2-4
Calgary	1	1	0	4	3	1	0	14	8	1980	PR	W 3-1
Chicago	5	1	4	24	10	14	0	54	66	1973	SF	L 1-4
Colorado	1	1	0	6	4	2	0	25	19	1995	CQF	W 4-2
Detroit	5	1	4	23	10	13	0	49	57	1950	F	L 3-4
Florida	1	1	0	5	4	1	0	13	10	1997	CQF	W 4-1
Los Angeles	3	2	1	11	6	5	0	42	29	2014	F	L 1-4
Montreal	16	9	7	73	33	38	2	192	214	2017	FR	W 4-2
New Jersey	6	4	2	34	18	16	0	93	90	2012	CF	L 2-4
NY Islanders	8	3	5	39	19	20	0	132	129	1994	CQF	W 4-0
Ottawa	2	1	1	13	6	7	0	34	32	2017	SR	L 2-4
Philadelphia	11	5	6	54	24	30	0	172	173	2014	FR	W 4-3
Pittsburgh	7	2	5	37	13	24	0	93	122	2016	FR	L 1-4
St. Louis	1	1	0	6	4	2	0	29	22	1981	QF	W 4-2
Tampa Bay	1	0	1	7	3	4	0	21	21	2015	CF	L 3-4
Toronto	8	5	3	35	19	16	0	86	86	1971	QF	W 4-2
Vancouver	1	1	0	7	4	3	0	21	19	1994	F	W 4-3
Washington	9	5	4	55	27	28	0	134	144	2015	SR	W 4-3
Winnipeg	1	1	0	4	4	0	0	17	6	2007	CQF	W 4-0
Defunct Clubs	9	6	3	22	11	7	4	43	29			
Totals	**108**	**53**	**55**	**515**	**244**	**263**	**8**	**1397**	**1434**			

Calgary totals include Atlanta Flames, 1972-73 to 1979-80.
Colorado totals include Quebec, 1979-80 to 1994-95.
New Jersey totals include Kansas City, 1974-75, 1975-76, and Colorado Rockies, 1976-77 to 1981-82.
Phoenix totals include Winnipeg, 1979-80 to 1995-96.
Carolina totals include Hartford, 1979-80 to 1996-97.
Dallas totals include Minnesota North Stars, 1967-68 to 1992-93.
Winnipeg totals include Atlanta Thrashers, 1999-2000 to 2010-11.

Playoff Results 2017-2013

Year	Round	Opponent	Result	GF	GA
2017	SR	Ottawa	L 2-4	20	19
	FR	Montreal	W 4-2	14	11
2016	FR	Pittsburgh	L 1-4	10	21
2015	CF	Tampa Bay	L 3-4	21	21
	SR	Washington	W 4-3	13	12
	FR	Pittsburgh	W 4-1	11	8
2014	F	Los Angeles	L 1-4	10	15
	CF	Montreal	W 4-2	20	15
	SR	Pittsburgh	W 4-3	15	14
	FR	Philadelphia	W 4-3	19	16
2013	CSF	Boston	L 1-4	10	16
	CQF	Washington	W 4-3	16	12

Abbreviations: Round: F – Final; **CF** – conference final; **CSF** – conference semi-final; **SR** – second round; **CQF** – conference quarter-final; **FR** – first round; **SF** – semi-final; **QF** – quarter-final; **PR** – preliminary round.

2016-17 Results

Oct.	13	NY Islanders	5-3
	15	at St. Louis	2-3
	17	San Jose	7-4
	19	Detroit	1-2
	22	at Washington	4-2
	23	Arizona	3-2
	26	Boston	5-2
	28	at Carolina	2-3
	30	Tampa Bay	6-1
Nov.	1	St. Louis	5-0
	3	Edmonton	5-3
	5	at Boston	5-2
	6	Winnipeg	5-2
	8	Vancouver	3-5
	12	at Calgary	4-1
	13	at Edmonton	3-1
	15	at Vancouver	7-2
	18	at Columbus	2-4
	20	Florida	2-3†
	21	at Pittsburgh	5-2
	23	Pittsburgh	1-6
	25	at Philadelphia	3-2
	27	Ottawa	0-2
	29	Carolina	3-2
Dec.	1	at Buffalo	3-4
	3	Carolina	4-2
	6	at NY Islanders	2-4
	8	at Winnipeg	2-1
	9	at Chicago	1-0*
	11	New Jersey	5-0
	13	Chicago	1-2
	15	at Dallas	2-0
	17	at Nashville	2-1†
	18	New Jersey	3-2†
	20	at Pittsburgh	2-7
	23	Minnesota	4-7
	27	Ottawa	4-3
	29	at Arizona	6-3
	31	at Colorado	6-2
Jan.	3	Buffalo	1-4
	4	at Philadelphia	5-2
	7	at Columbus	5-4
	13	Toronto	2-4
	14	at Montreal	4-5
	17	Dallas	6-7
	19	at Toronto	5-2
	22	at Detroit	1-0*
	23	Los Angeles	3-2
	25	Philadelphia	0-2
	31	Columbus	4-6
Feb.	2	at Buffalo	2-1*
	5	Calgary	4-3
	7	Anaheim	4-1
	9	Nashville	4-3
	11	Colorado	4-2
	13	at Columbus	3-2
	16	at NY Islanders	2-4
	19	Washington	2-1
	21	Montreal	2-3†
	23	at Toronto	2-1†
	25	at New Jersey	4-3*
	26	Columbus	2-5
	28	Washington	1-4
Mar.	2	at Boston	2-1
	4	Montreal	1-4
	6	at Tampa Bay	1-0*
	7	at Florida	5-2
	9	at Carolina	3-4
	12	at Detroit	4-1
	13	Tampa Bay	2-3
	17	Florida	3-4†
	18	at Minnesota	3-2
	21	at New Jersey	2-3*
	22	NY Islanders	2-3
	25	at Los Angeles	3-0
	26	at Anaheim	3-6
	28	at San Jose	4-5*
	31	Pittsburgh	3-4†
Apr.	2	Philadelphia	4-3
	5	at Washington	0-2
	8	at Ottawa	1-3
	9	Pittsburgh	3-2

* – Overtime † – Shootout

NHL Draft Selections 2017-2003

Name in bold denotes played in NHL.

2017

Pick	
7	Lias Andersson
21	Filip Chytil
123	Brandon Crawley
145	Calle Sjalin
157	Dominik Lakatos
174	Morgan Barron
207	Patrik Virta

2016

Pick	
81	Sean Day
98	Tarmo Reunanen
141	Tim Gettinger
171	Gabriel Fontaine
174	Tyler Wall
201	Ty Ronning

2015

Pick	
41	Ryan Gropp
62	Robin Kovacs
79	Sergey Zborovskiy
89	Aleksi Saarela
113	Brad Morrison
119	Daniel Bernhardt
184	Adam Huska

2014

Pick	
59	Brandon Halverson
85	Keegan Iverson
104	Ryan Mantha
118	Igor Shesterkin
122	Richard Nejezchleb
140	Daniel Walcott
142	Tyler Nanne

2013

Pick	
65	Adam Tambellini
75	**Pavel Buchnevich**
80	**Anthony Duclair**
110	Ryan Graves
170	**Mackenzie Skapski**

2012

Pick	
28	**Brady Skjei**
59	**Cristoval Nieves**
119	Calle Andersson
142	Thomas Spelling

2011

Pick	
15	**J.T. Miller**
72	Steven Fogarty
106	Michael St. Croix
134	Shane McColgan
136	Samuel Noreau
172	Peter Ceresnak

2010

Pick	
10	**Dylan McIlrath**
40	**Christian Thomas**
100	Andrew Yogan
130	Jason Wilson
157	**Jesper Fast**
190	Randy McNaught

2009

Pick	
19	**Chris Kreider**
47	Ethan Werek
80	**Ryan Bourque**
127	**Roman Horak**
140	Scott Stajcer
170	Dan Maggio
200	Mikhail Pashnin

2008

Pick	
20	**Michael Del Zotto**
51	**Derek Stepan**
75	**Evgeny Grachev**
90	**Tomas Kundratek**
111	**Dale Weise**
141	Chris Doyle
171	Mitch Gaulton

2007

Pick	
17	Alexei Cherepanov
48	Antoine Lafleur
138	Max Campbell
168	**Carl Hagelin**
193	David Skokan
198	Danny Hobbs

2006

Pick	
21	**Bobby Sanguinetti**
54	**Artem Anisimov**
84	Ryan Hillier
104	David Kveton
137	Tomas Zaborsky
174	Eric Hunter
204	Lukas Zeliska

2005

Pick	
12	**Marc Staal**
40	**Michael Sauer**
56	**Marc-Andre Cliche**
66	**Brodie Dupont**
77	Dalyn Flatt
107	**Tom Pyatt**
147	Trevor Koverko
178	Greg Beller
211	**Ryan Russell**

2004

Pick	
6	**Al Montoya**
19	**Lauri Korpikoski**
36	Darin Olver
48	**Dane Byers**
51	Bruce Graham
60	**Brandon Dubinsky**
73	Zdenek Bahensky
80	Billy Ryan
127	**Ryan Callahan**
135	Roman Psurny
169	Jordan Foote
247	Jonathan Paiement
266	**Jakub Petruzalek**

2003

Pick	
12	**Hugh Jessiman**
50	**Ivan Baranka**
75	Ken Roche
122	**Corey Potter**
149	**Nigel Dawes**
176	Ivan Dornic
179	Philippe Furrer
180	**Chris Holt**
209	**Dylan Reese**
243	Jan Marek

General Managers' History

Lester Patrick, 1926-27 to 1944-45; Lester Patrick and Frank Boucher, 1945-46; Frank Boucher, 1946-47 to 1954-55; Muzz Patrick, 1955-56 to 1963-64; Muzz Patrick and Emile Francis, 1964-65; Emile Francis, 1965-66 to 1974-75; Emile Francis and John Ferguson, 1975-76; John Ferguson, 1976-77, 1977-78; Fred Shero, 1978-79, 1979-80; Fred Shero and Craig Patrick, 1980-81; Craig Patrick, 1981-82 to 1985-86; Phil Esposito, 1986-87 to 1988-89; Neil Smith, 1989-90 to 1999-2000; Glen Sather, 2000-01 to 2014-15; Jeff Gorton, 2015-16 to date.

Jeff Gorton

General Manager

Born: Melrose, MA, June 6, 1968.

New York Rangers president Glen Sather announced on July 1 that Jeff Gorton had been named the 11th general manager in franchise history. Gorton had been a member of the Rangers organization for the previous eight seasons and served as the team's assistant general manager over the last four seasons. He joined the Rangers in 2007 as a professional scout, and served three seasons as assistant director, player personnel before becoming the team's assistant general manager.

During Gorton's tenure with the Rangers, he has played a key role in the selection of such players as Derek Stepan, Chris Kreider, Jesper Fast, and J.T. Miller in the NHL Draft. Gorton was vital in the Rangers' acquisitions of Ryan McDonagh, Rick Nash, Derick Brassard, and Keith Yandle through trades, as well as the signing of free agents Kevin Shattenkirk, Kevin Hayes and Mats Zuccarello.

Prior to joining the Rangers, Gorton spent 15 seasons with the Boston Bruins organization, serving as the Bruins' assistant general manager during the final seven years of his tenure. In that role, he was involved in contract negotiations, scouting operations and the team's American Hockey League affiliate in Providence. Gorton served as Boston's interim general manager from March 27 to July 8, 2006, directing the Bruins' efforts at the 2006 NHL Draft and negotiating contracts and trades at the start of the 2006 free agency period. At the 2006 NHL Draft, Gorton was instrumental in landing Bruins' star players Brad Marchand and Tuukka Rask (in a trade), as well as former Bruins' stars Phil Kessel and Milan Lucic. He also acquired All-Star free agents Zdeno Chara and Marc Savard.

Gorton originally joined the Bruins organization in their public relations department at the beginning of the 1992-93 season. He became the Bruins' director of scouting information in October 1994, where he created the scouting database which networks the club's scouts via computer, and coordinated video on prospects in preparation of scouting assignments and the annual NHL Draft. Gorton holds a degree in physical education from Bridgewater State College, and a Masters in sports management from Springfield College.

Club Directory

Madison Square Garden

New York Rangers
14th Floor
2 Pennsylvania Plaza
New York, New York 10121
Phone **212/465-6486**
PR FAX 212/465-6494
www.newyorkrangers.com
Capacity: 18,006

Team Executive Management	
Exec. Chairman, The Madison Square Garden Company	James L. Dolan
President & Chief Executive Officer, The Madison Square Garden Company	David O'Connor
President and Alternate Governor, New York Rangers	Glen Sather
General Manager, New York Rangers	Jeff Gorton
Exec. V.P., MSG Sports	Jordan Solomon
Sr. V.P., Legal & Business Affairs, Team & Sports Ops.	Jamaal Lesane
Sr. V.P., Legal & Business Affairs, Sports Ops	John Master
Sr. V.P., Finance	Jeanine McGrory
Sr. V.P., Sports Team Operations	Mark Piazza
Sr. V.P., Public Relations & Player Recruitment	John Rosasco
Deputy General Counsel & Sr. V.P., Legal & Business Affairs, Team Operations	Marc Schoenfeld
Hockey Club Personnel	
Sr. V.P. & Assistant General Manager	Jim Schoenfeld
Assistant G.M., & G.M., Hartford Wolf Pack	Chris Drury
Head Coach	Alain Vigneault
Associate Coach	Scott Arniel
Assistant Coaches	Lindy Ruff, Darryl Williams
Assistant Coach & Goaltending Coach	Benoit Allaire
Video Coach	Jerry Dineen
Video Assistant	Shawn Roche
Skills Coach	Mark Ciaccio
Dir., Player Care & Development/Analytics & Hockey Tech	Jim Sullivan
Director, Player Personnel	Gordie Clark
Director of Professional Scouting	Kevin Maxwell
Director of Player Development	Jed Ortmeyer
Senior Advisor to the President	Mike Barnett
Hockey Consultant	Doug Risebrough
Hockey & Business Operations	Adam Graves
Director of European Scouting	Nickolai Bobrov
European Scouts	Mikko Eloranta, Jan Gajdosik, Oto Hascak, Patric Kjellberg, Vladimir Lutchenko
Amateur Scouts	Larry Bernard, Rich Brown, Brendon Clark, Daniel Dore, Eric Doyle, Kim Gellert, Jamie Herrington Peter Stephan
Professional Scouts	Steve Eminger, Rick Kehoe, Gilles Leger, Justin Sather
Head Athletic Trainer & Director of Sports Medicine	Jim Ramsay
Assistant Trainer	Sean Murdoch
Equipment Manager / Asst. Managers	Acacio Marques / Billy Southard / Timothy Webb
Massage Therapist/Assistant Trainer	Bruce Lifrieri
Strength & Cond. Coach / Asst. Strength & Cond. Coach.	Reg Grant / Pete Draovitch
Performance Analyst	Adam Virgile
Strength & Conditioning Consultant	Ben Prentiss
Strength & Conditioning Consultant, Europe	Daniel Hedin
Director, MSG Training Center Operations	Alex Case
Sports Team Operations	
Vice President, Sports Team Ops	Jason Vogel
Director, Sports Team Ops	Brian Wendth
Director, MSG Sports Travel	Sharon Toledo
Manager, Sports Team Ops	Caroline Notaro
Coordinator, Sports Team Ops	Mary Clare Condon
Hockey Operations	
Directors, Scouting Info / Hockey Admin	Victor Saljanin / Katie Condon
Building Operations	
Vice President, Building Ops, MSG Training Center	Miguel Vazquez
Security Supervisor, MSG Training Center	Kevin Deegan
Manager, Building Operations, MSG Training Center	Steve Kaminski
Coordinator, Building Operations, MSG Training Center	Jennifer LaGrippo
Medical Staff	
Chief Medical Officer & Sr. V.P., Player Care	Dr. Lisa Callahan
Head Team Physician	Dr. Bryan Kelly
Team Sports Dietitian	Erika Whitman
Team Dentist / Assistant Team Dentist	Dr. Don Salomon / Dr. Joseph V. Esposito
Communications	
Vice President, Communications, MSG Sports	Ryan Watson
Director, Public Relations	Ryan Nissan
Manager, Communications, MSG Sports	Mallory Kwitter
Manager / Coordinator, Public Relations	Lindsay Hayes / Michael Rappaport
Marketing	
Vice President, Marketing Strategy	Jeanie Baumgartner
Director, Digital	Adam Skollar
Manager, Marketing	Greer O'Keefe
Manager, Website Production & Analytics	Lisa Hayward
Manager, Digital Content	Matt Calamia
Digital Content Producer	Amanda Borges
Coordinator, Marketing	Robert Winston
Senior Design Director	Joanecy Kagalingan
Event Presentation	
Senior Vice President & Executive Producer	Marc Bauman
Vice President, Event Presentation	Greg Kwizak
Music Director, Event Presentation	Ray Castoldi
Director / Coordinator, Event Presentation	Justin Casserly / Amanda Librot
Manager, Video Production	Cory Gershon
Community Relations, Fan Development, and Youth Programming	
Vice President, Youth Programs	Rick Nadeau
Director, Community Programs	David Martella
Manager, Youth Programs	Mike Fasulo
Manager, Business Operations	Felicia Ganthier
Coordinator, Fan Development and Engagement	Madeleine Peake
Coordinator, Alumni Relations	Michael Ali
Director, Special Projects & Community Relations Representative	Rod Gilbert
MSG Photo Services	
Official Photographer of Madison Square Garden	George Kalinsky
Vice President, MSG Photo Services	Rebecca Taylor
Editor / Manager, MSG Photo Services	Carly Boyle / Zachary Lane
Coordinator, MSG Photo Services	Taylor Wilder
Additional Information	
Television / Radio Network	MSG Network / MSG Radio

Ottawa Senators

2016-17 Results: 44W-28L-6OTL-4SOL 98PTS
2ND, Atlantic Division • 5TH, Eastern Conference

Key Off-Season Signings/Acquisitions

2017

June 26 • Re-signed LW **Tom Pyatt**.
28 • Re-signed G **Mike Condon**.
July 1 • Signed C **Nate Thompson**.
5 • Re-signed G **Chris Driedger**.
17 • Re-signed C **Jean-Gabriel Pageau**.
21 • Re-signed LW **Ryan Dzingel**.
24 • Signed D **Johnny Oduya**.

2017-18 Schedule

Oct.	Thu.	5	Washington	Wed.	10	at Toronto
	Sat.	7	Detroit	Thu.	18	St. Louis
	Tue.	10	at Vancouver	Sat.	20	Toronto
	Fri.	13	at Calgary	Mon.	22	at Minnesota
	Sat.	14	at Edmonton	Tue.	23	at St. Louis*
	Tue.	17	Vancouver	Thu.	25	Boston
	Thu.	19	New Jersey	Tue.	30	at Carolina
	Sat.	21	Toronto	Feb. Thu.	1	Anaheim
	Tue.	24	Los Angeles	Sat.	3	at Philadelphia*
	Thu.	26	Philadelphia	Sun.	4	at Montreal*
	Fri.	27	at New Jersey	Tue.	6	New Jersey
	Mon.	30	Montreal	Thu.	8	Nashville
Nov.	Thu.	2	Detroit	Sat.	10	at Toronto
	Sat.	4	Vegas*	Tue.	13	at Pittsburgh
	Fri.	10	at Colorado†	Thu.	15	Buffalo
	Sat.	11	Colorado†	Sat.	17	NY Rangers*
	Thu.	16	Pittsburgh	Mon.	19	at Nashville
	Sat.	18	Arizona*	Wed.	21	at Chicago
	Sun.	19	at NY Rangers	Thu.	22	Tampa Bay
	Wed.	22	at Washington	Sat.	24	Philadelphia*
	Fri.	24	at Columbus	Tue.	27	at Washington
	Sat.	25	NY Islanders	Mar. Fri.	2	at Vegas
	Wed.	29	at Montreal	Sat.	3	at Arizona
Dec.	Fri.	1	at NY Islanders	Mon.	5	at Dallas
	Sun.	3	at Winnipeg	Thu.	8	Buffalo
	Wed.	6	at Anaheim	Fri.	9	Calgary
	Thu.	7	at Los Angeles	Mon.	12	at Florida
	Sat.	9	at San Jose	Tue.	13	at Tampa Bay
	Tue.	12	at Buffalo	Fri.	16	Dallas
	Wed.	13	NY Rangers	Sat.	17	at Columbus
	Sat.	16	Montreal	Tue.	20	Florida
	Tue.	19	Minnesota	Thu.	22	Edmonton
	Thu.	21	at Tampa Bay	Sat.	24	Carolina
	Sat.	23	at Florida	Mon.	26	at Carolina
	Wed.	27	at Boston	Tue.	27	NY Islanders
	Fri.	29	Columbus	Thu.	29	Florida
	Sat.	30	Boston	Sat.	31	at Detroit*
Jan.	Wed.	3	at Detroit	Apr. Mon.	2	Winnipeg
	Fri.	5	San Jose	Wed.	4	at Buffalo
	Sat.	6	Tampa Bay	Fri.	6	at Pittsburgh
	Tue.	9	Chicago	Sat.	7	at Boston

*Denotes afternoon game.
† Game played in Stockholm, Sweden.

Year-by-Year Record

Season	GP	Home W	L	T	OL	Road W	L	T	OL	Overall W	L	T	OL	GF	GA	Pts.	Div. Fin.	Conf. Fin.	Playoff Result
2016-17	82	22	11	....	8	22	17	....	2	44	28	....	10	212	214	98	2nd, Atl.	5th, East	Lost Conf. Final
2015-16	82	21	14	....	6	17	21	....	3	38	35	....	9	236	247	85	5th, Atl.	11th, East	– out of playoffs –
2014-15	82	23	13	....	5	20	13	....	8	43	26	....	13	238	215	99	4th, Atl.	7th, East	Lost First Round
2013-14	82	18	17	....	6	19	14	....	8	37	31	....	14	236	265	88	5th, Atl.	11th, East	– out of playoffs –
2012-13	48	15	6	....	3	10	11	....	3	25	17	....	6	116	104	56	4th, NE	7th, East	Lost Conf. Semi-Final
2011-12	82	20	17	....	4	21	14	....	6	41	31	....	10	249	240	92	2nd, NE	8th, East	Lost Conf. Quarter-Final
2010-11	82	16	20	....	5	16	20	....	5	32	40	....	10	192	250	74	5th, NE	13th, East	– out of playoffs –
2009-10	82	26	11	....	4	18	21	....	2	44	32	....	6	225	238	94	2nd, NE	5th, East	Lost Conf. Quarter-Final
2008-09	82	22	12	....	7	14	23	....	4	36	35	....	11	217	237	83	4th, NE	11th, East	– out of playoffs –
2007-08	82	22	15	....	4	21	16	....	4	43	31	....	8	261	247	94	2nd, NE	7th, East	Lost Conf. Quarter-Final
2006-07	82	25	13	....	3	23	12	....	6	48	25	....	9	288	222	105	2nd, NE	4th, East	Lost Final
2005-06	82	29	9	....	3	23	12	....	6	52	21	....	9	314	211	113	1st, NE	1st, East	Lost Conf. Semi-Final
2004-05	....																		
2003-04	82	23	8	5	5	20	15	5	1	43	23	10	6	262	189	102	3rd, NE	5th, East	Lost Conf. Quarter-Final
2002-03	82	28	9	3	1	24	12	5	0	52	21	8	1	263	182	113	1st, NE	1st, East	Lost Conf. Final
2001-02	82	21	13	3	4	18	14	6	3	39	27	9	7	243	208	94	3rd, NE	7th, East	Lost Conf. Semi-Final
2000-01	82	26	7	5	3	22	14	4	1	48	21	9	4	274	205	109	1st, NE	2nd, East	Lost Conf. Quarter-Final
1999-2000	82	24	10	5	2	17	18	6	0	41	28	11	2	244	210	95	4th, NE	6th, East	Lost Conf. Quarter-Final
1998-99	82	22	11	8	....	22	12	7	....	44	23	15	....	239	179	103	1st, NE	2nd, East	Lost Conf. Quarter-Final
1997-98	82	18	16	7	....	16	17	8	....	34	33	15	....	193	200	83	5th, NE	8th, East	Lost Conf. Semi-Final
1996-97	82	16	17	8	....	15	19	7	....	31	36	15	....	226	234	77	3rd, NE	7th, East	Lost Conf. Quarter-Final
1995-96	82	8	28	5	....	10	31	0	....	18	59	5	....	191	291	41	7th, NE	13th, East	– out of playoffs –
1994-95	48	5	16	3	....	4	18	2	....	9	34	5	....	117	174	23	7th, NE	14th, East	– out of playoffs –
1993-94	84	8	30	4	....	6	31	5	....	14	61	9	....	201	397	37	7th, NE	14th, East	– out of playoffs –
1992-93	84	9	29	4	....	1	41	0	....	10	70	4	....	202	395	24	6th, Adams		– out of playoffs –

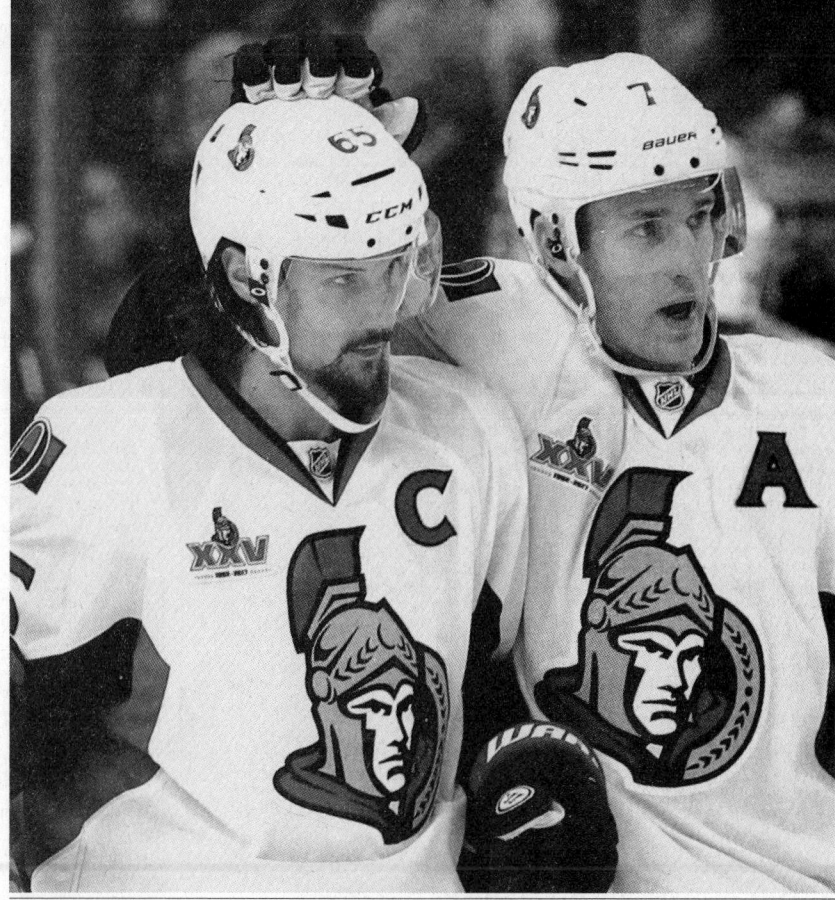

Senators captain Erik Karlsson continued to prove himself among the best defensemen in the NHL in 2016-17 and was a standout in the playoffs. Kyle Turris established a new career high with 27 goals during the regular season.

Retired Numbers

8	Frank Finnigan	1924-1934
11	Daniel Alfredsson	1995-2013

ATLANTIC DIVISION
26th NHL Season

Franchise date: December 16, 1991

2017-18 Player Personnel

FORWARDS	HT	WT	*Age	Birthplace	S	2016-17 Club
BRASSARD, Derick	6-1	205	30	Hull, QC	L	Ottawa
BURROWS, Alexandre	6-1	188	36	Pincourt, QC	L	Vancouver-Ottawa
DZINGEL, Ryan	6-0	190	25	Wheaton, IL	L	Ottawa
HOFFMAN, Mike	6-1	180	27	Kitchener, ON	L	Ottawa
MacARTHUR, Clarke	6-0	185	32	Lloydminster, AB	L	Ottawa
McCORMICK, Max	5-11	188	25	De Pere, WI	L	Ottawa-Binghamton
PAGEAU, Jean-Gabriel	5-10	180	24	Ottawa, ON	R	Ottawa
PAUL, Nick	6-4	221	22	Mississauga, ON	L	Ottawa-Binghamton
PYATT, Tom	5-11	188	30	Thunder Bay, ON	L	Ottawa
RYAN, Bobby	6-2	209	30	Cherry Hill, NJ	R	Ottawa
SMITH, Zack	6-2	209	29	Medicine Hat, AB	L	Ottawa
STONE, Mark	6-3	205	25	Winnipeg, MB	R	Ottawa
THOMPSON, Nate	6-0	212	32	Anchorage, AK	L	Anaheim-San Diego
TURRIS, Kyle	6-1	190	28	New Westminster, BC	R	Ottawa
WHITE, Colin	6-1	185	20	Boston, MA	R	Bos Coll-Ott-Binghamton
DEFENSEMEN						
BOROWIECKI, Mark	6-2	205	28	Ottawa, ON	L	Ottawa
CECI, Cody	6-3	205	23	Ottawa, ON	R	Ottawa
CHABOT, Thomas	6-2	190	20	Sainte-Marie, QC	L	Ottawa-Saint John
CLAESSON, Fredrik	6-1	205	24	Stockholm, Sweden	L	Ottawa-Binghamton
HARPUR, Ben	6-6	225	22	Hamilton, ON	L	Ottawa-Binghamton
KARLSSON, Erik	6-0	192	27	Landsbro, Sweden	R	Ottawa
ODUYA, Johnny	6-0	195	36	Stockholm, Sweden	L	Dallas-Chicago
PHANEUF, Dion	6-3	227	32	Edmonton, AB	L	Ottawa
WIDEMAN, Chris	5-10	180	27	St. Louis, MO	R	Ottawa

GOALTENDERS	HT	WT	*Age	Birthplace	C	2016-17 Club
ANDERSON, Craig	6-2	184	36	Park Ridge, IL	L	Ottawa
CONDON, Mike	6-2	197	27	Holliston, MA	L	Pittsburgh-Ottawa
HAMMOND, Andrew	6-1	220	29	Surrey, BC	L	Ottawa-Binghamton

* – Age at start of 2017-18 season

Coaching History

Rick Bowness, 1992-93 to 1994-95; Rick Bowness, Dave Allison and Jacques Martin, 1995-96; Jacques Martin, 1996-97 to 2000-01; Jacques Martin and Roger Neilson, 2001-02; Jacques Martin, 2002-03, 2003-04; Bryan Murray, 2004-05 to 2006-07; John Paddock and Bryan Murray, 2007-08; Craig Hartsburg and Cory Clouston, 2008-09; Cory Clouston, 2009-10, 2010-11; Paul MacLean, 2011-12 to 2013-14, Paul MacLean and Dave Cameron, 2014-15; Dave Cameron, 2015-16; Guy Boucher, 2016-17 to date.

Guy Boucher

Head Coach

Born: Notre-Dame-du-Lac, QC, August 3, 1971.

Ottawa Senators general manager Pierre Dorion announced the hiring of Guy Boucher as the club's head coach on May 8, 2016. Boucher agreed to terms on a three-year agreement with the Senators and became the 12th head coach in Senators franchise history. In his first season with the club in 2016-17, Boucher led the team back into the playoffs and all the way to the Eastern Conference Finals. Before arriving in Ottawa, he spent parts of the previous three seasons as the head coach of SC Bern of the National League A in Switzerland. Prior to that, he spent two-plus seasons as the head coach of the National Hockey League's Tampa Bay Lightning, posting a 97-78-20 record in 195 games. Boucher led the Lightning to the Eastern Conference Final in 2010-11.

In addition to his time with the Lightning and SC Bern, Boucher spent one season as head coach of the American Hockey League's Hamilton Bulldogs, leading them to a North Division championship in 2009-10. For his efforts, he was awarded the AHL's Louis A. R. Pieri Award as its coach of the year. Prior to coaching Hamilton, Boucher was the head coach of the Quebec Major Junior Hockey League's Drummondville Voltigeurs for three seasons. Boucher led Drummondville to QMJHL regular-season and playoff championships and a berth in the Memorial Cup in 2008-09.

Boucher has also represented his country internationally on several occasions, including winning a goal medal as an assistant coach at the 2009 World Junior Championship. He was the head coach for Team Canada at Spengler Cup in 2014 and 2015, winning gold in 2015. He was an assistant coach with Canada's national men's under-18 team on three occasions, including 2008 when the team won a gold medal.

A native of Notre-Dame-du-Lac, Quebec, Boucher graduated from Montreal's McGill University where he also played with the Redmen hockey club from 1991 to 1995. Boucher has degrees in four different disciplines: sports psychology, biosystems engineering, environmental biology and history.

Coaching Record

			Regular Season				Playoffs			
Season	Team	League	GC	W	L	O/T	GC	W	L	T
2006-07	Drummondville	QMJHL	70	37	26	7	12	7	5	....
2007-08	Drummondville	QMJHL	70	14	51	5	....	....	....	....
2008-09	Drummondville	QMJHL	68	54	10	4	19	16	3	....
2008-09	Drummondville	M-Cup	....	....	....	....	4	2	2	....
2009-10	Hamilton	AHL	80	52	11	11	19	11	8	....
2010-11	**Tampa Bay**	**NHL**	**82**	**46**	**25**	**11**	**18**	**11**	**7**	....
2011-12	**Tampa Bay**	**NHL**	**82**	**38**	**36**	**8**	....	....	....	....
2012-13	**Tampa Bay**	**NHL**	**31**	**13**	**17**	**1**	....	....	....	....
2013-14	SC Bern	Swiss	6	2	4	0	....	....	....	....
2014-15	SC Bern	Swiss	50	32	13	5	11	4	7	....
2015-16	SC Bern	Swiss	22	10	12	0	....	....	....	....
2016-17	**Ottawa**	**NHL**	**82**	**44**	**28**	**10**	**19**	**11**	**8**	....
	NHL Totals		**277**	**141**	**106**	**30**	**37**	**22**	**15**	....

2016-17 Scoring

* – rookie

Regular Season

Pos	#	Player	Team	GP	G	A	Pts	TOI	+/-	PIM	PP	SH	GW	S	S%
D	65	Erik Karlsson	OTT	77	17	54	71	26:50	10	28	4	0	5	218	7.8
C	68	Mike Hoffman	OTT	74	26	35	61	17:35	17	51	13	0	8	224	11.6
C	7	Kyle Turris	OTT	78	27	28	55	19:30	–3	47	6	0	6	185	14.6
R	61	Mark Stone	OTT	71	22	32	54	18:33	12	25	6	0	5	134	16.4
C	19	Derick Brassard	OTT	81	14	25	39	17:22	12	24	3	0	3	195	7.2
C	44	Jean-Gabriel Pageau	OTT	82	12	21	33	16:07	13	24	0	0	2	169	7.1
C	15	Zack Smith	OTT	74	16	16	32	16:22	6	61	1	4	1	137	11.7
C	18	Ryan Dzingel	OTT	81	14	18	32	14:23	7	30	1	1	1	123	11.4
L	14	Alexandre Burrows	VAN	55	9	11	20	14:57	–3	53	0	0	1	114	7.9
			OTT	20	6	5	11	13:47	6	9	1	0	1	29	20.7
			Total	75	15	16	31	14:38	3	62	1	0	2	143	10.5
D	2	Dion Phaneuf	OTT	81	9	21	30	23:02	–6	100	4	1	2	156	5.8
R	9	Bobby Ryan	OTT	62	13	12	25	15:32	–3	24	2	0	0	111	11.7
C	10	Tom Pyatt	OTT	82	9	14	23	15:37	9	16	0	0	1	95	9.5
D	6	Chris Wideman	OTT	76	5	12	17	13:57	7	46	1	0	1	123	4.1
D	5	Cody Ceci	OTT	79	2	15	17	23:12	–11	20	0	0	0	143	1.4
L	24	Viktor Stalberg	CAR	57	9	3	12	11:41	–6	33	0	2	2	71	12.7
			OTT	18	2	2	4	13:47	–3	8	1	0	0	30	6.7
			Total	75	11	5	16	12:12	–9	41	1	2	2	101	10.9
C	57	Tommy Wingels	S.J.	37	5	3	8	10:03	–2	15	0	0	2	42	11.9
			OTT	36	2	2	4	10:57	–9	12	0	0	0	39	5.1
			Total	73	7	5	12	10:30	–11	27	0	0	2	81	8.6
C	22	Chris Kelly	OTT	82	5	7	12	11:56	–17	23	0	1	2	85	5.9
D	3	Marc Methot	OTT	68	0	12	12	19:49	13	24	0	0	0	69	0.0
D	33	* Fredrik Claesson	OTT	33	3	8	11	13:08	5	4	0	0	0	25	12.0
D	23	Jyrki Jokipakka	CGY	38	1	5	6	14:25	–3	12	0	0	0	29	3.4
			OTT	3	0	0	0	14:27	–1	0	0	0	0	0	0.0
			Total	41	1	5	6	14:26	–4	12	0	0	0	29	3.4
R	25	Chris Neil	OTT	53	1	3	4	7:34	–11	63	0	0	0	42	2.4
D	74	Mark Borowiecki	OTT	70	1	2	3	14:00	–3	154	0	0	0	50	2.0
L	13	* Nick Paul	OTT	1	0	0	0	16:29	–2	0	0	0	0	4	0.0
D	72	* Thomas Chabot	OTT	1	0	0	0	7:09	–2	0	0	0	0	1	0.0
R	14	Mike Blunden	OTT	2	0	0	0	8:07	0	4	0	0	0	1	0.0
C	82	* Colin White	OTT	2	0	0	0	13:42	0	0	0	0	0	1	0.0
C	49	Christopher DiDomenico	OTT	3	0	0	0	11:01	0	6	0	0	0	5	0.0
L	16	Clarke MacArthur	OTT	4	0	0	0	13:29	–1	0	0	0	0	5	0.0
R	55	* Buddy Robinson	OTT	4	0	0	0	6:56	0	2	0	0	0	4	0.0
D	39	* Andreas Englund	OTT	5	0	0	0	10:37	–3	2	0	0	0	3	0.0
D	67	* Ben Harpur	OTT	6	0	0	0	17:48	–1	0	0	0	0	3	0.0
C	81	Phil Varone	OTT	7	0	0	0	7:58	–3	2	0	0	0	1	0.0
L	89	* Max McCormick	OTT	7	0	0	0	6:45	–3	0	0	0	0	7	0.0
C	37	* Casey Bailey	OTT	7	0	0	0	7:59	–1	0	0	0	0	10	0.0

Goaltending

No.	Goaltender	GPI	Mins	Avg	W	L	OT	EN	SO	GA	SA	Sv%	G	A	PIM
41	Craig Anderson	40	2421	2.28	25	11	4	0	5	92	1247	.926	0	1	0
1	Mike Condon	40	2304	2.50	19	14	6	4	5	96	1115	.914	0	0	4
30	Andrew Hammond	6	206	4.08	0	2	0	0	0	14	86	.837	0	0	0
32	* Chris Driedger	1	40	6.00	0	1	0	0	0	4	15	.733	0	0	0
	Totals	**82**	**4994**	**2.52**	**44**	**28**	**10**	**4**	**10**	**210**	**2467**	**.915**			

Playoffs

Pos	#	Player	Team	GP	G	A	Pts	TOI	+/-	PIM	PP	SH	GW	OT	S	S%
D	65	Erik Karlsson	OTT	19	2	16	18	28:07	13	10	0	0	2	0	53	3.8
R	9	Bobby Ryan	OTT	19	6	9	15	17:13	1	14	3	0	3	2	42	14.3
C	68	Mike Hoffman	OTT	19	6	5	11	18:22	3	10	1	0	1	0	49	12.2
C	19	Derick Brassard	OTT	19	4	7	11	18:11	–3	8	0	0	0	0	49	8.2
C	44	Jean-Gabriel Pageau	OTT	19	8	2	10	18:18	5	16	0	0	1	1	44	18.2
C	7	Kyle Turris	OTT	19	4	6	10	21:18	2	25	0	0	1	1	46	8.7
L	16	Clarke MacArthur	OTT	19	3	6	9	15:10	5	12	2	0	1	1	32	9.4
R	61	Mark Stone	OTT	19	5	3	8	20:41	5	20	0	0	0	0	43	11.6
C	15	Zack Smith	OTT	19	1	5	6	16:10	–5	12	0	0	0	0	25	4.0
D	2	Dion Phaneuf	OTT	19	1	4	5	23:18	–3	17	0	0	1	1	29	3.4
L	14	Alexandre Burrows	OTT	15	0	5	5	14:23	0	18	0	0	0	0	20	0.0
D	3	Marc Methot	OTT	18	2	2	4	22:13	5	10	0	0	1	0	16	12.5
D	6	Chris Wideman	OTT	15	1	3	4	13:00	–4	4	0	0	0	0	24	4.2
C	18	Ryan Dzingel	OTT	15	2	1	3	12:08	–1	4	1	0	0	0	8	25.0
D	33	* Fredrik Claesson	OTT	14	0	3	3	14:49	3	4	0	0	0	0	7	0.0
C	10	Tom Pyatt	OTT	14	2	0	2	13:15	–3	0	0	0	0	0	10	20.0
D	67	* Ben Harpur	OTT	9	0	2	2	18:28	–3	4	0	0	0	0	8	0.0
L	24	Viktor Stalberg	OTT	17	0	2	2	13:45	–8	2	0	0	0	0	31	0.0
D	5	Cody Ceci	OTT	19	0	1	1	23:36	–7	2	0	0	0	0	23	0.0
C	82	* Colin White	OTT	1	0	0	0	2:39	0	0	0	0	0	0	0	0.0
R	25	Chris Neil	OTT	2	0	0	0	2:07	0	12	0	0	0	0	0	0.0
C	22	Chris Kelly	OTT	2	0	0	0	5:25	0	0	0	0	0	0	1	0.0
D	74	Mark Borowiecki	OTT	2	0	0	0	10:24	0	2	0	0	0	0	1	0.0
C	57	Tommy Wingels	OTT	9	0	0	0	9:53	0	4	0	0	0	0	13	0.0

Goaltending

No.	Goaltender	GPI	Mins	Avg	W	L	EN	SO	GA	SA	Sv%	G	A	PIM
41	Craig Anderson	19	1178	2.34	11	8	0	1	46	590	.922	0	1	0
1	Mike Condon	2	61	3.93	0	0	0	0	4	32	.875	0	0	0
	Totals	**19**	**1244**	**2.41**	**11**	**8**	**0**	**1**	**50**	**622**	**.920**			

Club Records

Team

(Figures in brackets for season records are games played; records for fewest points, wins, ties, losses, goals, goals against are for 70 or more games)

Record		
Most Points	113	2002-03 (82), 2005-06 (82)
Most Wins	52	2002-03 (82), 2005-06 (82)
Most Ties	15	1996-97 (82), 1997-98 (82), 1998-99 (82)
Most Losses	70	1992-93 (84)
Most Goals	312	2005-06 (82)
Most Goals Against	397	1993-94 (84)
Fewest Points	24	1992-93 (84)
Fewest Wins	10	1992-93 (84)
Fewest Ties	4	1992-93 (84)
Fewest Losses	21	2000-01 (82), 2002-03 (82), 2005-06 (82)
Fewest Goals	191	1995-96 (82)
Fewest Goals Against	179	1998-99 (82)
Longest Winning Streak		
Overall	11	Jan. 14-Feb. 4/10
Home	9	Mar. 5-Apr. 7/09
Away	6	Mar. 18-Apr. 5/03, Jan. 14-Feb. 3/10
Longest Team Point Streak		
Overall	11	Four times
Home	23	Dec. 18/03-Jan. 24/04 (15W, 2OTW, 3T, 3OTL)
Away	7	Three times
Longest Losing Streak		
Overall	14	Mar. 2-Apr. 7/93
Home	11	Oct. 27-Dec. 8/93
Away	*38	Oct. 10/92-Apr. 3/93**
Longest Winless Streak		
Overall	21	Oct. 10-Nov. 23/92 (20L, 1T)
Home	*17	Oct. 28/95-Jan. 27/96 (15L, 2T)
Away	*38	Oct. 10/92-Apr. 3/93 (38L)
Most Shutouts, Season	10	2001-02 (82), 2016-17 (82)
Most PIM, Season	1,716	1992-93 (84)
Most Goals, Game	11	Nov. 13/01 (Ott. 11 at Wsh. 5)

Individual

Record		
Most Seasons	18	Chris Phillips
Most Games, Career	1,179	Chris Phillips
Most Goals, Career	426	Daniel Alfredsson
Most Assists, Career	682	Daniel Alfredsson
Most Points, Career	1,108	Daniel Alfredsson (426G, 682A)
Most PIM, Career	2,522	Chris Neil
Most Shutouts, Career	30	Patrick Lalime
Longest Consecutive Games Streak	324	Erik Karlsson (Apr. 25/13-Mar. 28/17)
Most Goals, Season	50	Dany Heatley (2005-06), (2006-07)
Most Assists, Season	71	Jason Spezza (2005-06)
Most Points, Season	105	Dany Heatley (2006-07; 50G, 55A)
Most PIM, Season	318	Mike Peluso (1992-93)
Most Points, Defenseman, Season	82	Erik Karlsson (2015-16; 16G, 66A)
Most Points, Center, Season	94	Alexei Yashin (1998-99; 44G, 50A)
Most Points, Right Wing, Season	103	Daniel Alfredsson (2005-06; 43G, 60A)
Most Points, Left Wing, Season	105	Dany Heatley (2006-07; 50G, 55A)
Most Points, Rookie, Season	79	Alexei Yashin (1993-94; 30G, 49A)
Most Shutouts, Season	8	Patrick Lalime (2002-03)
Most Goals, Game	4	Marian Hossa (Jan. 2/03); Dany Heatley (Oct. 29/05); Daniel Alfredsson (Nov. 2/05); Martin Havlat (Nov. 2/05); Alex Kovalev (Jan. 3/10)
Most Assists, Game	5	Marian Hossa (Jan. 4/01)
Most Points, Game	7	Daniel Alfredsson (Jan. 24/08; 3G, 4A)

* NHL Record.

** NHL records do not include neutral site games.

General Managers' History

Mel Bridgman, 1992-93; Randy Sexton, 1993-94, 1994-95; Randy Sexton and Pierre Gauthier, 1995-96; Pierre Gauthier, 1996-97, 1997-98; Rick Dudley, 1998-99; Marshall Johnston, 1999-2000 to 2001-02; John Muckler, 2002-03 to 2006-07; Bryan Murray, 2007-08 to 2015-16; Pierre Dorion, 2016-17 to date.

Captains' History

Laurie Boschman, 1992-93; Brad Shaw, Mark Lamb and Gord Dineen, 1993-94; Randy Cunneyworth, 1994-95 to 1997-98; Alexei Yashin, 1998-99; Daniel Alfredsson, 1999-2000 to 2012-13; Jason Spezza, 2013-14; Erik Karlsson, 2014-15 to date.

All-time Record vs. Other Clubs

Regular Season

	Total								At Home								On Road							
	GP	W	L	T	OL	GF	GA	PTS	GP	W	L	T	OL	GF	GA	PTS	GP	W	L	T	OL	GF	GA	PTS
Anaheim	31	11	14	3	3	73	80	28	15	6	5	1	3	43	38	16	16	5	9	2	0	30	42	12
Arizona	35	18	14	2	1	126	107	39	18	9	7	1	1	65	55	20	17	9	7	1	0	61	52	19
Boston	134	52	68	8	6	340	420	118	65	28	31	3	3	162	190	62	69	24	37	5	3	178	230	56
Buffalo	133	58	51	10	14	342	368	140	68	31	22	7	8	186	174	77	65	27	29	3	6	156	194	63
Calgary	39	16	16	4	3	102	124	39	19	10	4	3	2	57	53	25	20	6	12	1	1	45	71	14
Carolina	99	39	46	8	6	255	273	92	51	26	18	4	3	145	129	59	48	13	28	4	3	110	144	33
Chicago	32	10	15	2	5	86	91	27	17	7	7	0	3	53	50	17	15	3	8	2	2	33	41	10
Colorado	47	15	25	4	3	137	183	37	25	10	12	3	0	69	88	23	22	5	13	1	3	68	95	14
Columbus	23	13	5	2	3	74	62	31	12	7	2	1	2	37	32	17	11	6	3	1	1	37	30	14
Dallas	34	13	20	0	1	93	114	27	16	6	9	0	1	38	46	13	18	7	11	0	0	55	68	14
Detroit	42	15	20	1	6	109	135	37	22	7	10	1	4	59	69	19	20	8	10	0	2	50	66	18
Edmonton	39	18	16	4	1	109	114	41	19	8	8	2	1	50	57	19	20	10	8	2	0	59	57	22
Florida	92	52	33	3	4	283	247	111	45	25	16	2	2	136	112	54	47	27	17	1	2	147	135	57
Los Angeles	33	11	18	2	2	85	115	26	16	8	6	1	1	50	46	18	17	3	12	1	1	35	69	8
Minnesota	19	12	4	1	2	58	44	27	9	6	2	0	1	27	19	13	10	6	2	1	1	31	25	14
Montreal	134	63	58	5	8	391	387	139	66	36	25	1	4	205	184	77	68	27	33	4	4	186	203	62
Nashville	23	11	9	0	3	64	66	25	12	6	3	0	3	39	37	15	11	5	6	0	0	25	29	10
New Jersey	90	33	42	5	10	209	232	81	45	17	20	3	5	106	109	42	45	16	22	2	5	103	123	39
NY Islanders	90	52	21	11	6	311	242	121	44	26	10	5	3	143	107	60	46	26	11	6	3	168	135	61
NY Rangers	89	46	36	3	4	248	237	99	45	19	21	3	2	120	120	43	44	27	15	0	2	128	117	56
Philadelphia	90	38	40	8	4	254	275	88	45	22	16	6	1	136	129	51	45	16	24	2	3	118	146	37
Pittsburgh	97	36	44	9	8	285	322	89	49	20	19	5	5	151	155	50	48	16	25	4	3	134	167	39
St. Louis	33	16	14	2	1	89	105	35	17	7	9	0	1	38	58	15	16	9	5	2	0	51	47	20
San Jose	32	14	12	4	2	89	84	34	16	6	5	4	1	51	47	17	16	8	7	0	1	38	37	17
Tampa Bay	94	54	33	2	5	319	251	115	46	30	15	0	1	160	105	61	48	24	18	2	4	159	146	54
Toronto	112	59	41	3	9	332	318	130	56	32	18	1	5	166	155	70	56	27	23	2	4	166	163	60
Vancouver	39	16	17	2	4	88	113	38	19	9	8	1	1	43	52	20	20	7	9	1	3	45	61	18
Washington	90	41	40	5	4	270	272	91	45	26	17	1	1	152	123	54	45	15	23	4	3	118	149	37
Winnipeg	59	34	16	2	7	218	173	77	30	17	7	1	5	111	76	40	29	17	9	1	2	107	97	37
Totals	**1904**	**866**	**788**	**115**	**135**	**5439**	**5554**	**1982**	**952**	**467**	**352**	**60**	**73**	**2798**	**2615**	**1067**	**952**	**399**	**436**	**55**	**62**	**2641**	**2939**	**915**

Playoffs

	Series	W	L	GP	W	L	T	GF	GA	Last Mtg.	Rnd.	Result
Anaheim	1	0	1	5	1	4	0	11	16	2007	F	L 1-4
Boston	1	1	0	6	4	2	0	15	13	2017	FR	W 4-2
Buffalo	4	1	3	21	8	13	0	47	52	2007	CF	W 4-1
Montreal	2	1	1	11	6	5	0	32	21	2015	FR	L 2-4
New Jersey	3	2	1	18	11	7	0	41	40	2007	CSF	W 4-1
NY Islanders	1	1	0	5	4	1	0	13	7	2003	CQF	W 4-1
NY Rangers	2	1	1	13	7	6	0	32	34	2017	SR	W 4-2
Philadelphia	2	2	0	11	8	3	0	28	12	2003	CSF	W 4-2
Pittsburgh	5	1	4	27	10	17	0	66	89	2017	CF	L 3-4
Tampa Bay	1	1	0	5	4	1	0	23	13	2006	CQF	W 4-1
Toronto	4	0	4	24	8	16	0	42	57	2004	CQF	L 3-4
Washington	1	0	1	5	1	4	0	7	18	1998	CSF	L 1-4
Totals	**27**	**11**	**16**	**151**	**72**	**79**	**0**	**357**	**372**			

Playoff Results 2017-2013

Year	Round	Opponent	Result	GF	GA
2017	CF	Pittsburgh	L 3-4	13	17
	SR	NY Rangers	W 4-2	19	20
	FR	Boston	W 4-2	15	13
2015	FR	Montreal	L 2-4	12	12
2013	CSF	Pittsburgh	L 1-4	11	22
	CQF	Montreal	W 4-1	20	9

Abbreviations: Round: F – Final; **CF** – conference final; **CSF** – conference semi-final; **CQF** – conference quarter-final; **FR** – first round.

Colorado totals include Quebec, 1992-93 to 1994-95.
Dallas totals include Minnesota North Stars, 1992-93.
Winnipeg totals include Atlanta Thrashers, 1999-2000 to 2010-11.
Carolina totals include Hartford, 1992-93 to 1996-97.
Phoenix totals include Winnipeg, 1992-93 to 1995-96.

2016-17 Results

Month	Day	Opponent	Score	Month	Day	Opponent	Score
Oct.	12	Toronto	5-4*		17	at St. Louis	6-4
	15	Montreal	4-3†		19	at Columbus	2-0
	17	at Detroit	1-5		21	at Toronto	3-2†
	18	Arizona	7-4		22	Columbus	6-7*
	22	Tampa Bay	1-4		24	Washington	3-0
	25	at Vancouver	3-0		26	Calgary	2-3*
	28	at Calgary	2-5		31	at Florida	5-6
	30	at Edmonton	2-0	**Feb.**	2	at Tampa Bay	5-2
Nov.	1	Carolina	2-1*		4	at Buffalo	0-4
	3	Vancouver	1-0		7	St. Louis	0-6
	5	Buffalo	1-2		9	Dallas	3-2
	8	at Nashville	1-3		11	NY Islanders	3-0
	9	at Buffalo	2-1†		14	Buffalo	2-3
	11	Los Angeles	2-1		16	at New Jersey	3-0
	13	Minnesota	1-2*		18	at Toronto	6-3
	15	at Philadelphia	3-2†		19	Winnipeg	2-3
	17	Nashville	1-5		21	at New Jersey	2-1
	19	Florida	1-4		24	at Carolina	0-3
	22	at Montreal	4-3		26	at Florida	2-1
	24	Boston	3-1		27	at Tampa Bay	1-5
	26	Carolina	2-1	**Mar.**	2	Colorado	2-1
	27	at NY Rangers	2-0		4	Columbus	3-2
	29	Buffalo	4-5		6	Boston	4-2
Dec.	1	Philadelphia	2-3*		8	at Dallas	5-2
	3	Florida	2-0		9	at Arizona	3-2*
	5	at Pittsburgh	5-8		11	at Colorado	4-2
	7	at San Jose	4-2		14	Tampa Bay	1-2*
	10	at Los Angeles	1-4		16	Chicago	1-2
	11	at Anaheim	1-5		18	Montreal	3-4†
	14	San Jose	3-4†		19	at Montreal	1-4
	17	New Jersey	3-1		21	at Boston	3-2
	18	at NY Islanders	6-2		23	Pittsburgh	2-1†
	20	at Chicago	4-3		25	at Montreal	1-3
	22	Anaheim	2-1*		28	at Philadelphia	2-3†
	27	at NY Rangers	3-4		30	at Minnesota	1-5
	29	Detroit	2-3*	**Apr.**	1	at Winnipeg	2-4
Jan.	1	at Washington	1-2		3	at Detroit	4-5†
	7	Washington	0-1		4	Detroit	2-0
	8	Edmonton	5-3		6	at Boston	2-1†
	12	Pittsburgh	4-1		8	NY Rangers	3-1
	14	Toronto	2-4		9	at NY Islanders	2-4

* – Overtime † – Shootout

NHL Draft Selections 2017-2003

Name in bold denotes played in NHL.

2017
Pick
28 Shane Bowers
47 Alex Formenton
121 Drake Batherson
183 Jordan Hollett

2016
Pick
11 Logan Brown
42 Jonathan Dahlen
103 Todd Burgess
133 Maxime Lajoie
163 Markus Nurmi

2015
Pick
18 **Thomas Chabot**
21 **Colin White**
36 Gabriel Gagne
48 Filip Chlapik
107 Christian Wolanin
109 Filip Ahl
139 Christian Jaros
199 Joel Daccord

2014
Pick
40 **Andreas Englund**
70 Miles Gendron
100 Shane Eiserman
189 Kelly Summers
190 Francis Perron

2013
Pick
17 **Curtis Lazar**
78 Marcus Hogberg
102 **Tobias Lindberg**
108 **Ben Harpur**
138 Vincent Dunn
161 Chris Leblanc
168 Quentin Shore

2012
Pick
15 **Cody Ceci**
76 **Chris Driedger**
82 Jarrod Maidens
106 Tim Boyle
136 Robert Baillargeon
166 Francois Brassard
196 Mikael Wikstrand

2011
Pick
6 **Mika Zibanejad**
21 **Stefan Noesen**
24 **Matt Puempel**
61 **Shane Prince**
96 **Jean-Gabriel Pageau**
126 **Fredrik Claesson**
156 Darren Kramer
171 **Max McCormick**
186 Jordan Fransoo
204 **Ryan Dzingel**

2010
Pick
76 Jakub Culek
106 **Marcus Sorensen**
178 **Mark Stone**
196 Bryce Aneloski

2009
Pick
9 **Jared Cowen**
39 **Jakob Silfverberg**
46 **Robin Lehner**
100 **Chris Wideman**
130 **Mike Hoffman**
146 Jeff Costello
160 Corey Cowick
190 Brad Peltz
191 Michael Sdao

2008
Pick
15 **Erik Karlsson**
42 **Patrick Wiercioch**
79 **Zack Smith**
109 **Andre Petersson**
119 **Derek Grant**
139 **Mark Borowiecki**
199 Emil Sandin

2007
Pick
29 **Jim O'Brien**
60 Ruslan Bashkirov
90 Louie Caporusso
120 Ben Blood

2006
Pick
28 **Nick Foligno**
68 **Eric Gryba**
91 **Kaspars Daugavins**
121 Pierre-Luc Lessard
151 Ryan Daniels
181 Kevin Koopman
211 **Erik Condra**

2005
Pick
9 **Brian Lee**
70 Vitali Anikeyenko
95 **Cody Bass**
98 **Ilya Zubov**
115 Janne Kolehmainen
136 Tomas Kudelka
186 Dmitri Megalinsky
204 **Colin Greening**

2004
Pick
23 **Andrej Meszaros**
58 Kirill Lyamin
77 Shawn Weller
87 **Peter Regin**
89 Jeff Glass
122 **Alexander Nikulin**
141 Jim McKenzie
156 **Roman Wick**
219 Joe Cooper
251 Matthew McIlvane
284 John Wikner

2003
Pick
29 **Patrick Eaves**
67 Igor Mirnov
100 Philippe Seydoux
135 Mattias Karlsson
142 Tim Cook
166 Sergei Gimayev
228 Will Colbert
260 Ossi Louhivaara
291 **Brian Elliott**

Canadian Tire Centre

A lot of Ottawa's late draft picks have had great success in the NHL. Ryan Dzingel was chosen 204th overall in 2011.

Pierre Dorion
General Manager
Born: Ottawa, ON, July 6, 1972.

Ottawa Senators owner and chief executive officer Eugene Melnyk announced the appointment of Pierre Dorion as the team's new general manager on April 10, 2016. Dorion became the eighth general manager in team history after having spent nine seasons with the Senators. In his first season as general manager in 2016-17, the Senators returned to the playoffs and went all the way to the Eastern Conference Finals.

An Ottawa native, Dorion spent two-plus seasons as assistant general manager with a focus on NHL contracts, player personnel and leading the club's professional and amateur scouting activities. Before taking on the assistant general manager role in January of 2014, Dorion spent four-plus seasons as director of player personnel and also served two seasons as the Senators' chief amateur scout. As director of player personnel, Dorion was responsible for managing the Senators scouting staff, both professional and amateur, and oversaw all facets of evaluation for players both inside and outside of the organization.

Dorion originally joined the Senators in July of 2007 after spending the previous two seasons as an amateur scout for the New York Rangers and the prior 11 seasons with the Montreal Canadiens, where he served as an amateur scouting coordinator and as chief scout.

Club Directory

Ottawa Senators
Canadian Tire Centre
1000 Palladium Drive
Ottawa, Ontario
K2V 1A5
Phone **613/599-0250**
FAX 613/599-5562
www.ottawasenators.com
Capacity: 18,572

Executive
Owner, Governor and Chairman . . . . Eugene Melnyk
President. . . . . Tom Anselmi
V.P., Human Resources . . . . Mardi Walker
V.P., Strategic Development. Geoff Publow
V.P. and Executive Director, Canadian Tire Centre . . . Tom Conroy
Exec. Assistant to the President . . . . Amanda Clements

Hockey Operations
General Manager . . . . Pierre Dorion
Assistant General Manager . . . . Randy Lee
Manager of Hockey Administration . . . . Allison Vaughan
Director, Team Services . . . . Jordan Silmser
Player Development Coach . . . . Shean Donovan
Coordinator, Hockey Operations . . . . Sean McCauley
Hockey Operations Assistant, Analytics and Research . . Tim Pattyson
Head Coach . . . . Guy Boucher
Associate Coach . . . . Marc Crawford
Assistant Coaches . . . . Rob Cookson, Martin Raymond
Goaltending Coach . . . . Pierre Groulx
Video Coach . . . . Kristopher Young
Conditioning Coach. . . . . Chris Schwarz
Assistant Conditioning Coach . . . . Rob Mouland
Director of Sports Medicine . . . . Gerry Townend
Head Athletic Therapist . . . . Domenic Nicoletta
Assistant Athletic Therapist . . . . Jean-Sebastien Hartell
Equipment Manager . . . . John Forget
Assistant Equipment Manager . . . . Ian Cox
Massage Therapist. . . . . Shawn Markwick

Scouts
Chief Amateur Scout. . . . . Trent Mann
Amateur Scouts. . . . . Jimmy Blixt, Dan Boeser, Don Boyd,
George Fargher, Bob Janecyk, Justin Murray,
Anders Östberg, Todd Stirling, Bobby Strumm
Chief European Scout . . . . Mikko Ruutu
Chief Professional Scout . . . . Jim Clark
Pro Scouts. . . . . Michael Abbamont, John Perpich, Steve Stirling

Communications
Senior Director, Communications. . . . . Brian Morris
Manager, Communications . . . . Chris Moore
Coordinator, Communications. . . . . Brett Varey
Translator . . . . Eric Tremblay

Legal
Senior Legal Council . . . . Richard Stacey

Corporate Partnerships, Premium Client Services and Ticketing
Sr. V.P., Corporate Strategy and Sales . . . . Mark Bonneau
EA to Sr. V.P., Corporate Strategy and Sales
  & V.P. Strategic Development. . . . . Brooke Brown
Sr. Director of Sales, Corporate Partnerships . . . . Bill Courchaine
Director, Corporate Partnerships . . . . Steve Chestnut
Sr. Corporate Account Manager . . . . Steve Katzman
Sr. Director, Corporate Partnerships & Activations . . . Gina Gianetto
Director, Regional Corporate Sales & Partnerships . . . Chris Atack
Director, Ticket Sales & Service. . . . . Geoff Ross
Manager, Sales . . . . Daniel Julien
Manager, Premium Sales . . . . Brendan Du Vall
Manager, Group Sales and Service . . . . Devon Hogan
Director, Premium Services. . . . . Christine Clancy
Manager, Suite Operations . . . . Tracey Bonner
Manager, Premium Client Services . . . . Kristin Wood

Data Management and Analytics
Director, Data & Analytics . . . . Tom Gillis
System Administrator . . . . Darren Isnor
CRM &Ticketing Analyst . . . . Rick Hardy Cheam

Finance
Senior Director, Finance. . . . . Marcello Pecora
Corporate Controller, Capital Sports & Entertainment . . Andrea Tunks
Controller, Capital Sports Properties Inc . . . . Kris Quarrington
Exec. Assistant to the CFO . . . . Colette Hiscott

Information Technology
IT Director / Architect. . . . . Darren Just / Don Morin

Marketing
Senior Director, Marketing. . . . . Michael Wallace
Director, Game Entertainment . . . . Paul Gallant
Director, Fan and Community Development . . . . Aaron Robinson
Manager, Digital Production . . . . Alex Forbes
Manager, Brand Integration. Dana Telfer
Social Content Producer . . . . Craig Medaglia
Video Producers . . . . Nick Gilmore, Adam Wood
Art Director . . . . Edtmun Jasvins
Manager, Marketing & Administration . . . . Deborah Wilson

Operations and Events
Assistant to the V.P. and Executive Director . . . . Linda Julian
Director, Engineering and Operations. . . . . Ed Healy
Director, Canadian Tire Centre Marketing . . . . Krista Galbraith
Managers, Engineering / Event Production / Operations . . Konstantinos Capordelis / Tim Swords / Alex Gagnon

Merchandise
Director, Merchandise Operations . . . . Kevin Lawton

Sens Foundation
President . . . . Danielle Robinson
V.P., Corp. Relations & Fundraising Partnerships . . . . . Jonathan Bodden
Director, Communications & Community Investments . . Brad Weir

Miscellaneous
Radio . . . . TSN 1200 (English), 94,5 FM (French)
Television . . . . TSN and RDS
Team Photographer. . . . . Freestyle Photography (Andre Ringuette)
Mascot . . . . Spartacat

Philadelphia Flyers

2016-17 Results: 39W-33L-5OTL-5SOL 88PTS
6TH, Metropolitan Division • 11TH, Eastern Conference

Key Off-Season Signings/Acquisitions

2017
June **7** • Named **Kris Knoblauch** assistant coach.
   9 • Re-signed D **Shayne Gostisbehere**.
   16 • Acquired LW **Brendan Warren** and a 5th-round pick in 2018 NHL Draft from Arizona for C **Nick Cousins** and G **Merrick Madsen**.
   23 • Acquired C **Jori Lehtera**, a 1st-round pick in 2017 NHL Draft and a conditional pick in 2018 NHL Draft from St. Louis for C **Brayden Schenn**.
   29 • Re-signed C **Jordan Weal**.
July **1** • Signed G **Brian Elliott**.
   11 • Re-signed C **Scott Laughton**.
   14 • Re-signed LW **Taylor Leier**.

2017-18 Schedule

Oct.	Wed.	4	at San Jose	Sun.	7	Buffalo*
	Thu.	5	at Los Angeles	Sat.	13	at New Jersey
	Sat.	7	at Anaheim	Tue.	16	at NY Rangers
	Tue.	10	at Nashville	Thu.	18	Toronto
	Sat.	14	Washington	Sat.	20	New Jersey*
	Tue.	17	Florida	Sun.	21	at Washington*
	Thu.	19	Nashville	Tue.	23	at Detroit
	Sat.	21	Edmonton*	Thu.	25	Tampa Bay
	Tue.	24	Anaheim	Wed.	31	at Washington
	Thu.	26	at Ottawa	Feb. Thu.	1	at New Jersey
	Sat.	28	at Toronto	Sat.	3	Ottawa*
	Mon.	30	Arizona	Tue.	6	at Carolina
Nov.	Wed.	1	at Chicago	Thu.	8	Montreal
	Thu.	2	at St. Louis*	Sat.	10	at Arizona
	Sat.	4	Colorado	Sun.	11	at Vegas*
	Thu.	9	Chicago	Tue.	13	New Jersey
	Sat.	11	Minnesota	Fri.	16	at Columbus
	Tue.	14	at Minnesota	Sun.	18	at NY Rangers*
	Thu.	16	at Winnipeg	Tue.	20	Montreal
	Sat.	18	Calgary*	Thu.	22	Columbus
	Tue.	21	Vancouver	Sat.	24	at Ottawa*
	Wed.	22	at NY Islanders	Mon.	26	at Montreal
	Fri.	24	NY Islanders*	Mar. Thu.	1	Carolina
	Mon.	27	at Pittsburgh	Sat.	3	at Tampa Bay*
	Tue.	28	San Jose	Sun.	4	at Florida*
Dec.	Sat.	2	Boston*	Wed.	7	Pittsburgh
	Mon.	4	at Calgary	Thu.	8	at Boston
	Wed.	6	at Edmonton	Sat.	10	Winnipeg*
	Thu.	7	at Vancouver	Mon.	12	Vegas
	Tue.	12	Toronto	Thu.	15	Columbus
	Thu.	14	Buffalo	Sat.	17	at Carolina
	Sat.	16	Dallas	Sun.	18	Washington*
	Mon.	18	Los Angeles	Tue.	20	at Detroit
	Wed.	20	Detroit	Thu.	22	NY Rangers
	Fri.	22	at Buffalo	Sun.	25	at Pittsburgh*
	Sat.	23	at Columbus	Tue.	27	at Dallas
	Thu.	28	at Florida	Wed.	28	at Colorado
	Fri.	29	at Tampa Bay	Apr. Sun.	1	Boston*
Jan.	Tue.	2	Pittsburgh	Tue.	3	at NY Islanders
	Thu.	4	NY Islanders	Thu.	5	Carolina
	Sat.	6	St. Louis*	Sat.	7	NY Rangers*

* Denotes afternoon game.

Retired Numbers

1	Bernie Parent	1967-1971, 1973-1979
2	Mark Howe	1982-1992
4	Barry Ashbee	1970-1974
7	Bill Barber	1972-1985
16	Bobby Clarke	1969-1984

METROPOLITAN DIVISION
51st NHL Season
Franchise date: June 5, 1967

Year-by-Year Record

Season	GP	Home				Road				Overall						Div. Fin.	Conf. Fin.	Playoff Result
		W	L	T	OL	W	L	T	OL	W	L	T	OL	GF	GA	Pts.			
2016-17	82	25	11	....	5	14	22	....	5	39	33	....	10	219	236	88	6th, Met.	11th, East	– out of playoffs –
2015-16	82	23	10	....	8	18	17	....	6	41	27	....	14	214	218	96	5th, Met.	7th, East	Lost First Round
2014-15	82	23	11	....	7	10	20	....	11	33	31	....	18	215	234	84	6th, Met.	12th, East	– out of playoffs –
2013-14	82	24	14	....	3	18	16	....	7	42	30	....	10	236	235	94	3rd, Met.	6th, East	Lost First Round
2012-13	48	15	7	....	2	8	15	....	1	23	22	....	3	133	141	49	4th, Atl.	10th, East	– out of playoffs –
2011-12	82	22	13	....	6	25	13	....	3	47	26	....	9	264	232	103	3rd, Atl.	5th, East	Lost Conf. Semi-Final
2010-11	82	22	12	....	7	25	11	....	5	47	23	....	12	259	223	106	1st, Atl.	2nd, East	Lost Conf. Semi-Final
2009-10	82	24	14	....	4	17	21	....	3	41	35	....	6	236	225	88	3rd, Atl.	7th, East	Lost Final
2008-09	82	24	13	....	4	20	14	....	7	44	27	....	11	264	238	99	3rd, Atl.	5th, East	Lost Conf. Quarter-Final
2007-08	82	21	14	....	6	21	15	....	5	42	29	....	11	248	233	95	4th, Atl.	6th, East	Lost Conf. Final
2006-07	82	10	24	....	7	12	24	....	5	22	48	....	12	214	303	56	5th, Atl.	15th, East	– out of playoffs –
2005-06	82	22	13	....	6	23	13	....	5	45	26	....	11	267	259	101	2nd, Atl.	5th, East	Lost Conf. Quarter-Final
2004-05	....																		
2003-04	82	24	11	3	3	16	10	12	3	40	21	15	6	229	186	101	1st, Atl.	3rd, East	Lost Conf. Final
2002-03	82	21	10	8	2	24	10	5	2	45	20	13	4	211	166	107	2nd, Atl.	4th, East	Lost Conf. Semi-Final
2001-02	82	20	13	5	3	22	14	5	0	42	27	10	3	234	192	97	1st, Atl.	2nd, East	Lost Conf. Quarter-Final
2000-01	82	26	11	4	0	17	14	7	3	43	25	11	3	240	207	100	2nd, Atl.	4th, East	Lost Conf. Quarter-Final
1999-2000	82	25	6	7	3	20	16	5	0	45	22	12	3	237	179	105	1st, Atl.	1st, East	Lost Conf. Final
1998-99	82	21	9	11	....	16	17	8	....	37	26	19	....	231	196	93	2nd, Atl.	5th, East	Lost Conf. Quarter-Final
1997-98	82	24	11	6	....	18	18	5	....	42	29	11	....	242	193	95	1st, Atl.	3rd, East	Lost Conf. Quarter-Final
1996-97	82	23	12	6	....	22	12	7	....	45	24	13	....	274	217	103	2nd, Atl.	2nd, East	Lost Final
1995-96	82	27	9	5	....	18	15	8	....	45	24	13	....	282	208	103	1st, Atl.	1st, East	Lost Conf. Semi-Final
1994-95	48	16	7	1	....	12	9	3	....	28	16	4	....	150	132	60	1st, Atl.	3rd, East	Lost Conf. Final
1993-94	84	19	20	3	....	16	19	7	....	35	39	10	....	294	314	80	6th, Atl.	10th, East	– out of playoffs –
1992-93	84	23	14	5	....	13	23	6	....	36	37	11	....	319	319	83	5th, Patrick		– out of playoffs –
1991-92	80	22	11	7	....	10	26	4	....	32	37	11	....	252	273	75	6th, Patrick		– out of playoffs –
1990-91	80	18	16	6	....	15	21	4	....	33	37	10	....	252	267	76	5th, Patrick		– out of playoffs –
1989-90	80	17	19	4	....	13	20	7	....	30	39	11	....	290	297	71	6th, Patrick		– out of playoffs –
1988-89	80	22	15	3	....	14	21	5	....	36	36	8	....	307	285	80	4th, Patrick		Lost Conf. Final
1987-88	80	20	14	6	....	18	19	3	....	38	33	9	....	292	292	85	3rd, Patrick		Lost Div. Semi-Final
1986-87	80	29	9	2	....	17	17	6	....	46	26	8	....	310	245	100	1st, Patrick		Lost Final
1985-86	80	33	6	1	....	20	17	3	....	53	23	4	....	335	241	110	1st, Patrick		Lost Div. Semi-Final
1984-85	80	32	4	4	....	21	16	3	....	53	20	7	....	348	241	113	1st, Patrick		Lost Final
1983-84	80	25	10	5	....	19	16	5	....	44	26	10	....	350	290	98	3rd, Patrick		Lost Div. Semi-Final
1982-83	80	29	8	3	....	20	15	5	....	49	23	8	....	326	240	106	1st, Patrick		Lost Div. Semi-Final
1981-82	80	25	10	5	....	13	21	6	....	38	31	11	....	325	313	87	3rd, Patrick		Lost Div. Semi-Final
1980-81	80	23	9	8	....	18	15	7	....	41	24	15	....	313	249	97	2nd, Patrick		Lost Quarter-Final
1979-80	80	27	5	8	....	21	7	12	....	48	12	20	....	327	254	116	1st, Patrick		Lost Final
1978-79	80	26	10	4	....	14	15	11	....	40	25	15	....	281	248	95	2nd, Patrick		Lost Quarter-Final
1977-78	80	29	6	5	....	16	14	10	....	45	20	15	....	296	200	105	2nd, Patrick		Lost Semi-Final
1976-77	80	33	6	1	....	15	10	15	....	48	16	16	....	323	213	112	1st, Patrick		Lost Semi-Final
1975-76	80	36	2	2	....	15	11	14	....	51	13	16	....	348	209	118	1st, Patrick		Lost Final
1974-75	80	32	6	2	....	19	12	9	....	51	18	11	....	293	181	113	1st, Patrick		**Won Stanley Cup**
1973-74	78	28	6	5	....	22	10	7	....	50	16	12	....	273	164	112	1st, West		**Won Stanley Cup**
1972-73	78	27	8	4	....	10	22	7	....	37	30	11	....	296	256	85	2nd, West		Lost Semi-Final
1971-72	78	19	13	7	....	7	25	7	....	26	38	14	....	200	236	66	5th, West		– out of playoffs –
1970-71	78	20	10	9	....	8	23	8	....	28	33	17	....	207	225	73	3rd, West		Lost Quarter-Final
1969-70	76	11	14	13	....	6	21	11	....	17	35	24	....	197	225	58	5th, West		– out of playoffs –
1968-69	76	14	16	8	....	6	19	13	....	20	35	21	....	174	225	61	3rd, West		Lost Quarter-Final
1967-68	74	17	13	7	....	14	19	4	....	31	32	11	....	173	179	73	1st, West		Lost Quarter-Final

Wayne Simmonds topped 30 goals for the second straight season in 2016-17 and scored the 200th of his career on March 15, 2017.

2017-18 Player Personnel

FORWARDS	HT	WT	*Age	Birthplace	S	2016-17 Club
COUTURIER, Sean	6-3	211	24	Phoenix, AZ	L	Philadelphia
FILPPULA, Valtteri	6-0	196	33	Vantaa, Finland	L	Tampa Bay-Philadelphia
GIROUX, Claude	5-11	185	29	Hearst, ON	R	Philadelphia
KONECNY, Travis	5-10	177	20	London, ON	R	Philadelphia
LAUGHTON, Scott	6-1	190	23	Oakville, ON	L	Philadelphia-Lehigh Valley
LEHTERA, Jori	6-2	210	29	Helsinki, Finland	L	St. Louis
RAFFL, Michael	6-0	200	28	Villach, Austria	L	Philadelphia
READ, Matt	5-10	185	31	Ilderton, ON	R	Philadelphia
SIMMONDS, Wayne	6-2	185	29	Scarborough, ON	R	Philadelphia
VORACEK, Jakub	6-2	214	28	Kladno, Czech.	R	Philadelphia
WEAL, Jordan	5-10	179	25	North Vancouver, BC	R	Philadelphia-Lehigh Valley
WEISE, Dale	6-2	206	29	Winnipeg, MB	R	Philadelphia

DEFENSEMEN						
BRENNAN, T.J.	6-1	216	28	Willingboro, NJ	L	Lehigh Valley
GOSTISBEHERE, Shayne	5-11	180	24	Pembroke Pines, FL	L	Philadelphia
GUDAS, Radko	6-0	204	27	Prague, Czech.	R	Philadelphia
HAGG, Robert	6-2	201	22	Uppsala, Sweden	L	Philadelphia-Lehigh Valley
MacDONALD, Andrew	6-1	204	31	Judique, NS	L	Philadelphia
MANNING, Brandon	6-1	205	27	Prince George, BC	L	Philadelphia
MORIN, Samuel	6-7	227	22	Lac-Beauport, QC	L	Philadelphia-Lehigh Valley
O'NEILL, Will	6-1	190	29	Boston, MA	L	Lehigh Valley
PROVOROV, Ivan	6-0	200	20	Yaroslavl, Russia	L	Philadelphia

GOALTENDERS	HT	WT	*Age	Birthplace	C	2016-17 Club
ELLIOTT, Brian	6-2	209	32	Newmarket, ON	L	Calgary
NEUVIRTH, Michal	6-1	209	29	Usti nad Labem, Czech.	L	Philadelphia

* – Age at start of 2017-18 season

Coaching History

Keith Allen, 1967-68, 1968-69; Vic Stasiuk, 1969-70, 1970-71; Fred Shero, 1971-72 to 1977-78; Bob McCammon and Pat Quinn, 1978-79; Pat Quinn, 1979-80, 1980-81; Pat Quinn and Bob McCammon, 1981-82; Bob McCammon, 1982-83, 1983-84; Mike Keenan, 1984-85 to 1987-88; Paul Holmgren, 1988-89 to 1990-91; Paul Holmgren and Bill Dineen, 1991-92; Bill Dineen, 1992-93; Terry Simpson, 1993-94; Terry Murray, 1994-95 to 1996-97; Wayne Cashman and Roger Neilson, 1997-98; Roger Neilson, 1998-99, 1999-2000; Craig Ramsay and Bill Barber, 2000-01; Bill Barber, 2001-02; Ken Hitchcock, 2002-03 to 2005-06; Ken Hitchcock and John Stevens, 2006-07; John Stevens, 2007-08, 2008-09; John Stevens and Peter Laviolette, 2009-10; Peter Laviolette, 2010-11 to 2012-13; Peter Laviolette and Craig Berube, 2013-14; Craig Berube, 2014-15; Dave Hakstol, 2015-16 to date.

Dave Hakstol
Head Coach
Born: Warburg, AB, July 30, 1968.

Philadelphia Flyers general manager Ron Hextall announced on May 18, 2015 that Dave Hakstol had been named the 19th head coach in Flyers history. In his first season in 2015-16, Hakstol led Philadelphia back into the playoffs after missing out in 2014-15.

Hakstol joined the Flyers from the University of North Dakota where he spent the previous 11 seasons compiling an overall record of 289-143-43 with a .654 winning percentage in 475 games. In 2014-15, he led North Dakota to a 29-10-3 record with a .726 winning percentage and a berth in the NCAA Frozen Four. North Dakota made the NCAA tournament in every one of Hakstol's 11 seasons and reached the Frozen Four seven times in that span, which is the most of any program in the country during that period. Hakstol led North Dakota to an overall postseason record of 54-24 for a .692 winning percentage, including a 17-11 record in the NCAA tournament, during his tenure. He joined the school's coaching staff in 2000 as an assistant coach, and took over the head coaching job four years later. Under Hakstol's watch, North Dakota won three regular season conference championships – two in the Western Collegiate Hockey Association (2008-09, 2010-11) and one in the National Collegiate Hockey Conference (2014-15). North Dakota also won WCHA playoff championships in 2005-06, 2009-10, 2010-11 and 2011-12. Hakstol received conference coach of the year honors twice, in the WCHA in 2008-09 and in the NCHC in 2014-15. He was also an eight-time finalist for the Spencer Penrose Award as national coach of the year.

Hakstol's program produced 20 NHL players and a total of 46 that have played professionally at some level. His former players include Jonathan Toews, Matt Greene, T.J. Oshie, Travis Zajac, Drew Stafford and Chris VandeVelde. He has also had seven players named Hobey Baker Award finalists, including Ryan Duncan who won the award in 2007, and 11 players named All-Americans.

Coaching Record

				Regular Season				Playoffs			
Season	Team	League	GC	W	L	O/T	GC	W	L	T	
1996-97	Sioux City	USHL	53	8	43	2	....				
1997-98	Sioux City	USHL	56	35	18	3	5	1	4	....	
1998-99	Sioux City	USHL	56	34	19	3	5	2	3	....	
99-2000	Sioux City	USHL	58	27	26	5	5	2	3	....	
2004-05	North Dakota	WCHA	45	25	15	5	....				
2005-06	North Dakota	WCHA	46	29	16	1	....				
2006-07	North Dakota	WCHA	43	24	14	5	....				
2007-08	North Dakota	WCHA	43	28	11	4	....				
2008-09	North Dakota	WCHA	43	24	15	4	....				
2009-10	North Dakota	WCHA	43	25	13	5	....				
2010-11	North Dakota	WCHA	44	32	9	3	....				
2011-12	North Dakota	WCHA	42	26	13	3	....				
2012-13	North Dakota	WCHA	42	22	13	7	....				
2013-14	North Dakota	NCHC	42	25	14	3	....				
2014-15	North Dakota	NCHC	42	29	10	3	....				
2015-16	Philadelphia	NHL	82	41	27	14	6	2	4	....	
2016-17	Philadelphia	NHL	82	39	33	10					
	NHL Totals		164	80	60	24	6	2	4	....	

2016-17 Scoring
* – rookie

Regular Season

Pos	#	Player	Team	GP	G	A	Pts	TOI	+/-	PIM	PP	SH	GW	S	S%
R	93	Jakub Voracek	PHI	82	20	41	61	19:05	–24	56	5	0	3	253	7.9
R	28	Claude Giroux	PHI	82	14	44	58	19:07	–15	38	5	0	3	199	7.0
C	10	Brayden Schenn	PHI	79	25	30	55	17:48	–13	38	17	0	7	178	14.0
R	17	Wayne Simmonds	PHI	82	31	23	54	18:58	–18	122	16	2	4	224	13.8
C	51	Valtteri Filppula	T.B.	59	7	27	34	17:30	1	24	0	0	1	74	9.5
			PHI	20	5	3	8	17:07	–2	2	0	0	0	23	21.7
			Total	79	12	30	42	17:24	–1	26	0	0	1	97	12.4
D	53	Shayne Gostisbehere	PHI	76	7	32	39	19:35	–21	32	2	0	1	198	3.5
C	14	Sean Couturier	PHI	66	14	20	34	18:26	12	33	0	2	1	120	11.7
D	9	* Ivan Provorov	PHI	82	6	24	30	21:58	–7	34	0	0	1	161	3.7
C	11	* Travis Konecny	PHI	70	11	17	28	14:05	–2	49	3	0	0	133	8.3
D	3	Radko Gudas	PHI	67	6	17	23	19:17	8	93	0	0	0	113	5.3
R	24	Matt Read	PHI	63	10	9	19	13:47	3	8	2	1	2	92	10.9
D	15	Michael Del Zotto	PHI	51	6	12	18	19:30	–5	28	0	0	0	92	6.5
D	47	Andrew MacDonald	PHI	73	2	16	18	20:06	–5	26	0	0	0	65	3.1
C	25	Nick Cousins	PHI	60	6	10	16	12:00	–6	31	1	0	0	99	6.1
R	22	Dale Weise	PHI	64	8	7	15	12:52	1	39	1	0	2	94	8.5
C	76	Chris Vandevelde	PHI	81	6	9	15	11:33	–5	16	0	0	0	69	8.7
C	40	* Jordan Weal	PHI	23	8	4	12	14:18	5	10	1	0	1	49	16.3
D	23	Brandon Manning	PHI	65	3	9	12	18:03	–12	83	0	1	1	84	3.6
L	12	Michael Raffl	PHI	52	8	3	11	13:15	–7	20	0	0	3	63	12.7
L	78	Pierre Bellemare	PHI	82	4	4	8	12:58	–1	20	0	0	0	90	4.4
L	13	* Roman Lyubimov	PHI	47	4	2	6	9:34	–2	8	0	1	0	41	9.8
D	55	Nick Schultz	PHI	28	0	4	4	15:15	1	10	0	0	0	25	0.0
L	58	* Taylor Leier	PHI	10	1	1	2	9:03	–4	0	0	0	0	7	14.3
R	36	Colin McDonald	PHI	3	1	0	1	9:01	1	0	0	0	0	5	20.0
C	27	Boyd Gordon	PHI	13	1	0	1	8:10	–5	2	0	0	0	8	12.5
D	48	* Robert Hagg	PHI	1	0	0	0	21:19	0	0	0	0	0	5	0.0
D	50	* Samuel Morin	PHI	1	0	0	0	17:47	0	0	0	0	0	2	0.0
L	21	Scott Laughton	PHI	2	0	0	0	10:14	0	0	0	0	0	1	0.0
R	74	* Mike Vecchione	PHI	2	0	0	0	8:30	–1	0	0	0	0	1	0.0

Goaltending

No.	Goaltender	GPI	Mins	Avg	W	L	OT	EN	SO	GA	SA	Sv%	G	A	PIM
41	* Anthony Stolarz	7	376	2.07	2	1	1	0	1	13	181	.928	0	0	0
35	Steve Mason	58	3225	2.66	26	21	8	7	3	143	1556	.908	0	1	0
30	Michal Neuvirth	28	1364	2.82	11	11	1	4	0	64	586	.891	0	0	2
	Totals	82	5008	2.77	39	33	10	11	5	231	2334	.901			

Michal Neuvirth and Anthony Stolarz shared a shutout vs. N.J. on Apr. 1, 2017

Claude Giroux and Jakub Voracek were the two top point-getters in Philadelphia in 2016-17.

Captains' History

Lou Angotti, 1967-68; Ed Van Impe, 1968-69 to 1971-72; Ed Van Impe and Bobby Clarke, 1972-73; Bobby Clarke, 1973-74 to 1978-79; Mel Bridgman, 1979-80, 1980-81; Bill Barber, 1981-82; Bill Barber and Bobby Clarke, 1982-83; Bobby Clarke, 1983-84; Dave Poulin, 1984-85 to 1988-89; Dave Poulin and Ron Sutter, 1989-90; Ron Sutter, 1990-91; Rick Tocchet, 1991-92; no captain, 1992-93; Kevin Dineen, 1993-94; Eric Lindros, 1994-95 to 1998-99; Eric Lindros and Eric Desjardins, 1999-2000; Eric Desjardins, 2000-01; Eric Desjardins and Keith Primeau, 2001-02; Keith Primeau, 2002-03, 2003-04; Keith Primeau and Derian Hatcher, 2005-06; Peter Forsberg, 2006-07; Jason Smith, 2007-08; Mike Richards, 2008-09 to 2010-11; Chris Pronger, 2011-12; Claude Giroux, 2012-13 to date.

Club Records

Team

(Figures in brackets for season records are games played; records for fewest points, wins, ties, losses, goals, goals against are for 70 or more games)

Most Points 118 1975-76 (80)
Most Wins 53 1984-85 (80), 1985-86 (80)
Most Ties *24 1969-70 (76)
Most Losses 48 2006-07 (82)
Most Goals 350 1983-84 (80)
Most Goals Against 319 1992-93 (84)
Fewest Points 56 2006-07 (82)
Fewest Wins 17 1969-70 (76)
Fewest Ties 4 1985-86 (80)
Fewest Losses 12 1979-80 (80)
Fewest Goals 173 1967-68 (74)
Fewest Goals Against 164 1973-74 (78)
Longest Winning Streak
Overall .... 13 Oct. 19-Nov. 17/85
Home .... 20 Jan. 4-Apr. 3/76
Away .... 8 Dec. 22/82-Jan. 16/83
Longest Team Point Streak
Overall .... *35 Oct. 14/79-Jan. 6/80 (25W, 10T)
Home .... 26 Oct. 11/79-Feb. 3/80 (19W, 7T)
Away .... 16 Oct. 20/79-Jan. 6/80 (11W, 5T)
Longest Losing Streak
Overall .... 9 Dec. 8-27/06
Home .... 13 Nov. 29/06-Feb. 8/07
Away .... 8 Oct. 25-Nov. 26/72, Mar. 3-29/88
Longest Winless Streak
Overall .... 12 Feb. 24-Mar. 16/99 (8L, 4T)
Home .... 13 Nov. 29/06-Feb. 8/07 (13L)
Away .... 19 Oct. 23/71-Jan. 27/72 (15L, 4T)
Most Shutouts, Season 13 1974-75 (80)
Most PIM, Season 2,621 1980-81 (80)
Most Goals, Game .... 13 Mar. 22/84 (Pit. 4 at Phi. 13), Oct. 18/84 (Van. 2 at Phi. 13)

Individual

Most Seasons .... 15 Bobby Clarke
Most Games .... 1,144 Bobby Clarke
Most Goals, Career .... 420 Bill Barber
Most Assists, Career .... 852 Bobby Clarke
Most Points, Career .... 1,210 Bobby Clarke (358G, 852A)
Most PIM, Career .... 1,817 Rick Tocchet
Most Shutouts, Career .... 50 Bernie Parent
Longest Consecutive Game Streak .... 484 Rod Brind'Amour (Feb. 24/93-Apr. 18/99)
Most Goals, Season .... 61 Reggie Leach (1975-76)
Most Assists, Season .... 89 Bobby Clarke (1974-75), (1975-76)
Most Points, Season .... 123 Mark Recchi (1992-93; 53G, 70A)
Most PIM, Season .... *472 Dave Schultz (1974-75)
Most Points, Defenseman, Season .... 82 Mark Howe (1985-86; 24G, 58A)
Most Points, Center, Season .... 119 Bobby Clarke (1975-76; 30G, 89A)
Most Points, Right Wing, Season .... 123 Mark Recchi (1992-93; 53G, 70A)
Most Points, Left Wing, Season .... 112 Bill Barber (1975-76; 50G, 62A)
Most Points, Rookie, Season .... 82 Mikael Renberg (1993-94; 38G, 44A)
Most Shutouts, Season .... 12 Bernie Parent (1973-74), (1974-75)
Most Goals, Game .... 4 Sixteen times
Most Assists, Game .... 6 Eric Lindros (Feb. 26/97)
Most Points, Game .... 8 Tom Bladon (Dec. 11/77; 4G, 4A)

* NHL Record.

All-time Record vs. Other Clubs

Regular Season

	Total								At Home								On Road							
	GP	W	L	T	OL	GF	GA	PTS	GP	W	L	T	OL	GF	GA	PTS	GP	W	L	T	OL	GF	GA	PTS
Anaheim	32	10	12	5	5	95	101	30	15	4	6	3	2	37	37	13	17	6	6	2	3	58	64	17
Arizona	77	45	28	2	2	279	226	94	39	27	11	0	1	157	105	55	38	18	17	2	1	122	121	39
Boston	192	68	93	21	10	561	633	167	95	39	42	10	4	296	291	92	97	29	51	11	6	265	342	75
Buffalo	173	86	60	20	7	552	508	199	88	51	20	12	5	308	228	119	85	35	40	8	2	244	280	80
Calgary	117	59	42	12	4	407	379	134	58	37	15	3	3	217	155	80	59	22	27	9	1	190	224	54
Carolina	136	81	33	14	8	486	379	184	68	45	13	5	5	254	177	100	68	36	20	9	3	232	202	84
Chicago	136	60	46	30	0	417	405	150	69	42	16	11	0	228	172	95	67	18	30	19	0	189	233	55
Colorado	84	40	25	14	5	288	257	99	41	27	10	2	2	145	107	58	43	13	15	12	3	143	150	41
Columbus	28	10	10	3	5	78	77	28	14	8	5	1	0	52	38	17	14	2	5	2	5	26	39	11
Dallas	149	74	43	32	0	512	409	180	75	47	12	16	0	279	169	110	74	27	31	16	0	233	240	70
Detroit	136	64	50	21	1	475	429	150	67	42	13	11	1	269	187	96	69	22	37	10	0	206	242	54
Edmonton	73	33	31	8	1	251	230	75	38	24	12	2	0	152	106	50	35	9	19	6	1	99	124	25
Florida	92	51	29	7	5	269	227	114	47	22	15	6	4	121	113	54	45	29	14	1	1	148	114	60
Los Angeles	145	86	39	15	5	505	380	192	71	43	17	7	4	258	171	97	74	43	22	8	1	247	209	95
Minnesota	21	14	5	1	1	62	36	30	12	9	2	0	1	37	19	19	9	5	3	1	0	25	17	11
Montreal	190	73	80	30	7	566	602	183	94	41	34	16	3	286	273	101	96	32	46	14	4	280	329	82
Nashville	24	12	4	3	5	69	53	32	13	7	2	1	3	40	26	18	11	5	2	2	2	29	27	14
New Jersey	238	111	97	18	12	772	704	252	119	68	35	10	6	414	307	152	119	43	62	8	6	358	397	100
NY Islanders	262	136	90	26	10	864	793	308	129	78	34	11	6	461	352	173	133	58	56	15	4	403	441	135
NY Rangers	289	122	121	37	9	847	856	290	145	69	56	14	6	444	405	158	144	53	65	23	3	403	451	132
Ottawa	90	44	31	8	7	275	254	103	45	27	13	2	3	146	118	59	45	17	18	6	4	129	136	44
Pittsburgh	281	153	90	30	8	1013	857	344	140	97	31	8	4	556	366	206	141	56	59	22	4	457	491	138
St. Louis	149	87	42	17	3	515	380	194	74	50	14	10	0	283	168	110	75	37	28	7	3	232	212	84
San Jose	39	15	15	4	5	102	108	39	19	7	6	2	4	55	58	20	20	8	9	2	1	47	50	19
Tampa Bay	94	46	36	8	4	281	266	104	46	23	14	7	2	145	118	55	48	23	22	1	2	136	148	49
Toronto	177	94	57	22	4	610	488	214	88	54	25	8	1	319	211	117	89	40	32	14	3	291	277	97
Vancouver	119	73	33	13	0	477	349	159	61	40	20	1	0	252	182	81	58	33	13	12	0	225	167	78
Washington	211	111	73	19	8	719	635	249	108	67	33	6	2	398	305	142	103	44	40	13	6	321	330	107
Winnipeg	59	39	12	3	5	214	157	86	29	19	5	2	3	114	83	43	30	20	7	1	2	100	74	43
Defunct Clubs	69	37	18	14	0	239	156	88	34	24	4	6	0	137	67	54	35	13	14	8	0	102	89	34
Totals	**3882**	**1934**	**1345**	**457**	**146**	**12800**	**11334**	**4471**	**1941**	**1138**	**535**	**193**	**75**	**6860**	**5114**	**2544**	**1941**	**796**	**810**	**264**	**71**	**5940**	**6220**	**1927**

Playoffs

	Series	W	L	GP	W	L	T	GF	GA	Last Mtg.	Rnd.	Result
Boston	6	3	3	31	13	18	0	86	100	2011	CSF	L 0-4
Buffalo	9	6	3	50	29	21	0	146	141	2011	CQF	W 4-3
Calgary	2	1	1	11	7	4	0	43	28	1981	QF	L 3-4
Chicago	2	0	2	10	2	8	0	30	45	2010	F	L 2-4
Colorado	2	2	0	11	7	4	0	39	29	1985	CF	W 4-2
Dallas	2	2	0	11	8	3	0	41	26	1980	SF	W 4-1
Detroit	1	0	1	4	0	4	0	6	16	1997	F	L 0-4
Edmonton	3	1	2	15	7	8	0	44	49	1987	F	L 3-4
Florida	1	0	1	6	2	4	0	11	15	1996	CSF	L 2-4
Montreal	6	3	3	31	15	16	0	89	93	2010	CF	W 4-1
New Jersey	6	3	3	30	16	14	0	75	77	2012	CSF	L 1-4
NY Islanders	4	3	1	25	14	11	0	83	69	1987	DF	W 4-3
NY Rangers	11	6	5	54	30	24	0	173	172	2014	FR	L 3-4
Ottawa	2	0	2	11	3	8	0	12	28	2003	CSF	L 2-4
Pittsburgh	6	4	2	35	19	16	0	121	115	2012	CQF	W 4-2
St. Louis	2	0	2	11	3	8	0	20	34	1969	QF	L 0-4
Tampa Bay	2	1	1	13	7	6	0	45	34	2004	CF	L 3-4
Toronto	6	5	1	36	22	14	0	119	85	2004	CSF	W 4-2
Vancouver	1	1	0	3	2	1	0	15	9	1979	PR	W 2-1
Washington	5	2	3	29	13	16	0	84	99	2016	FR	L 2-4
Totals	**79**	**43**	**36**	**427**	**219**	**208**	**0**	**1282**	**1264**			

Calgary totals include Atlanta Flames, 1972-73 to 1979-80. Carolina totals include Hartford, 1979-80 to 1996-97.
Colorado totals include Quebec, 1979-80 to 1994-95. Dallas totals include Minnesota North Stars, 1967-68 to 1992-93.
New Jersey totals include Kansas City, 1974-75, 1975-76, and Colorado Rockies, 1976-77 to 1981-82.
Phoenix totals include Winnipeg, 1979-80 to 1995-96. Winnipeg totals include Atlanta Thrashers, 1999-2000 to 2010-11.

Playoff Results 2017-2013

Year	Round	Opponent	Result	GF	GA
2016	FR	Washington	L 2-4	6	14
2014	FR	NY Rangers	L 3-4	16	19

Abbreviations: Round: F – Final;
CF – conference final; **CSF** – conference semi-final;
CQF – conference quarter-final; **FR** – first round;
DF – division final; **SF** – semi-final; **QF** – quarter-final;
PR – preliminary round.

2016-17 Results

Oct.	14	at Los Angeles	4-2		8	at Columbus	1-2*
	15	at Arizona	3-4*		10	at Buffalo	1-4
	18	at Chicago	4-7		12	Vancouver	5-4†
	20	Anaheim	2-3		14	at Boston	3-6
	22	Carolina	6-3		15	at Washington	0-5
	24	at Montreal	1-3		21	New Jersey	1-4
	25	Buffalo	4-3†		22	at NY Islanders	3-2*
	27	Arizona	4-5		25	at NY Rangers	2-0
	29	Pittsburgh	4-5		26	Toronto	2-1
	30	at Carolina	4-3		31	at Carolina	1-5
Nov.	2	Detroit	4-3*	**Feb.**	2	Montreal	3-1
	3	at NY Islanders	3-2†		4	Los Angeles	0-1*
	5	at Montreal	4-5		6	St. Louis	0-2
	8	Detroit	2-3†		9	NY Islanders	1-3
	11	at Toronto	3-6		11	San Jose	2-1*
	12	Minnesota	3-2		15	at Calgary	1-3
	15	Ottawa	2-3†		16	at Edmonton	3-6
	17	Winnipeg	5-2		19	at Vancouver	3-2
	19	Tampa Bay	0-3		22	Washington	1-4
	22	at Florida	3-1		25	at Pittsburgh	2-4
	23	at Tampa Bay	2-4		28	Colorado	4-0
	25	NY Rangers	2-3	**Mar.**	2	Florida	2-1†
	27	Calgary	5-3		4	at Washington	1-2*
	29	Boston	3-2†		7	at Buffalo	6-3
Dec.	1	at Ottawa	3-2*		9	at Toronto	2-4
	3	Chicago	3-1		11	at Boston	1-2
	4	at Nashville	4-2		13	Columbus	3-5
	6	Florida	3-2*		15	Pittsburgh	4-0
	8	Edmonton	6-5		16	at New Jersey	2-6
	10	Dallas	4-2		19	Carolina	4-3*
	11	at Detroit	1-0*		21	at Winnipeg	2-3
	14	at Colorado	4-3		23	at Minnesota	3-1
	17	at Dallas	1-3		25	at Columbus	0-1
	19	Nashville	1-2†		26	at Pittsburgh	6-2
	21	Washington	3-2†		28	Ottawa	3-2†
	22	at New Jersey	0-4		30	NY Islanders	6-3
	28	at St. Louis	3-6	**Apr.**	1	New Jersey	3-0
	30	at San Jose	0-2		2	at NY Rangers	3-4
Jan.	1	at Anaheim	3-4†		4	at New Jersey	0-1*
	4	NY Rangers	2-5		8	Columbus	4-2
	7	Tampa Bay	4-2		9	Carolina	3-4†

* – Overtime † – Shootout

NHL Draft Selections 2017-2003

Name in bold denotes played in NHL.

2017

Pick	
2	Nolan Patrick
27	Morgan Frost
35	Isaac Ratcliffe
80	Kirill Ustimenko
106	Matthew Strome
107	Maxim Sushko
137	Noah Cates
168	Olle Lycksell
196	Wyatt Kalynuk

2016

Pick	
22	German Rubtsov
36	Pascal Laberge
48	Carter Hart
52	Wade Allison
82	Carsen Twarynski
109	Connor Bunnaman
139	Linus Hogberg
169	Tanner Laczynski
172	Anthony Salinitri
199	David Bernhardt

2015

Pick	
7	**Ivan Provorov**
24	**Travis Konecny**
70	Felix Sandstrom
90	Matej Tomek
98	Samuel Dove-McFalls
104	Mikhail Vorobyev
128	David Kase
158	Cooper Marody
188	Ivan Fedotov

2014

Pick	
17	Travis Sanheim
48	Nicolas Aube-Kubel
86	Mark Friedman
138	Oskar Lindblom
168	Radel Fazleev
198	Jesper Pettersson

2013

Pick	
11	**Samuel Morin**
41	**Robert Hagg**
72	Tyrell Goulbourne
132	Terrance Amorosa
162	Merrick Madsen
192	David Drake

2012

Pick	
20	**Scott Laughton**
45	**Anthony Stolarz**
78	**Shayne Gostisbehere**
111	Fredric Larsson
117	**Taylor Leier**
141	Reece Willcox
201	Valeri Vasiliev

2011

Pick	
8	**Sean Couturier**
68	**Nick Cousins**
116	Colin Suellentrop
118	Marcel Noebels
176	Petr Placek
206	Derek Mathers

2010

Pick	
89	**Michael Chaput**
119	**Tye McGinn**
149	Michael Parks
179	Nick Luukko
206	Ricard Blidstrand
209	**Brendan Ranford**

2009

Pick	
81	Adam Morrison
87	Simon Bertilsson
142	Nic Riopel
153	Dave Labrecque
172	**Eric Wellwood**
196	**Oliver Lauridsen**

2008

Pick	
19	**Luca Sbisa**
67	**Marc-Andre Bourdon**
84	Jacob Deserres
178	**Zac Rinaldo**
196	**Joacim Eriksson**

2007

Pick	
2	**James van Riemsdyk**
41	**Kevin Marshall**
66	Garrett Klotz
122	Mario Kempe
152	**Jon Kalinski**
161	**Patrick Maroon**
182	Brad Phillips

2006

Pick	
22	**Claude Giroux**
39	**Andreas Nodl**
42	Mike Ratchuk
55	Denis Bodrov
79	**Jon Matsumoto**
101	Joonas Lehtivuori
109	Jakub Kovar
145	**Jon Rheault**
175	Michael Dupont
205	Andrei Popov

2005

Pick	
29	**Steve Downie**
91	**Oskars Bartulis**
119	**Jeremy Duchesne**
152	Josh Beaulieu
174	John Flatters
215	Matt Clackson

2004

Pick	
92	Rob Bellamy
101	R.J. Anderson
124	**David Laliberte**
144	Chris Zarb
149	Gino Pisellini
170	Ladislav Scurko
171	Frederik Cabana
232	**Martin Houle**
253	Travis Gawryletz
286	**Triston Grant**
291	John Carter

2003

Pick	
11	**Jeff Carter**
24	**Mike Richards**
69	**Colin Fraser**
81	**Stefan Ruzicka**
85	**Alexandre Picard**
87	**Ryan Potulny**
95	Rick Kozak
108	Kevin Romy
140	David Tremblay
191	Rejean Beauchemin
193	Ville Hostikka

General Managers' History

Bud Poile, 1967-68, 1968-69; Bud Poile and Keith Allen, 1969-70; Keith Allen, 1970-71 to 1982-83; Bob McCammon, 1983-84; Bob Clarke, 1984-85 to 1989-90; Russ Farwell, 1990-91 to 1993-94; Bob Clarke, 1994-95 to 2005-06; Bob Clarke and Paul Holmgren, 2006-07; Paul Holmgren, 2007-08 to 2013-14; Ron Hextall, 2014-15 to date.

Ron Hextall

General Manager

Born: Brandon, MB, May 3, 1964.

Ron Hextall was named general manager of the Philadelphia Flyers on May 7, 2014 after serving as assistant GM and director of hockey operations during the 2013-14 season. Hextall returned to the Flyers after spending the previous seven seasons with the Los Angeles Kings, where he held the title of vice president and assistant general manager. In Los Angeles, Hextall assisted in all facets of the Kings' hockey operations department while helping the team win the 2012 Stanley Cup championship. He also served as the general manager of the Manchester Monarchs, Los Angeles's primary affiliate in the American Hockey League.

Prior to joining the Kings, Hextall spent seven seasons in the Flyers front office. He became a pro scout in 1999 upon his retirement as a player, and served in that role for three seasons before being promoted to director of pro player personnel in 2002. In his front office positions with the Flyers, Hextall was instrumental in the club's three Atlantic Division titles and two trips to the Eastern Conference Finals while the club averaged nearly 102 points per season.

Hextall played 11 years of his 13-year career with the Flyers, while also playing a year each with Quebec and the New York Islanders. He led the Flyers to the Stanley Cup Final in his rookie season of 1986-87, winning the Vezina Trophy as the NHL's top goaltender and the Conn Smythe Trophy as Most Valuable Player in the 1987 Stanley Cup playoffs, despite losing to the Edmonton Oilers in seven games. He was also named to both the NHL All-Rookie and NHL First All-Star Teams that season. Hextall played for the Flyers until 1992 and then returned to Philadelphia from 1994 until his retirement in 1999, making another trip to the Stanley Cup Final in 1997. He is the franchise's all-time leader among goaltenders in games played (489) and wins (240), while ranking third in shutouts (18). His NHL career included a total of 608 regular season games, a 296-214-69 record including 23 shutouts, a 2.97 goals-against-average and a .895 save-percentage. On December 8, 1987, he became the first goaltender in the history of the NHL to score a goal by shooting the puck into the net as the Flyers defeated the Boston Bruins by a score of 5-2 at the Spectrum. On April 11, 1989, during a Flyers 8-5 playoff victory against the Washington Capitals at the Capital Centre, he collected his second career goal and became the first goalie to score a goal in an NHL playoff game.

A native of Brandon, Manitoba, Hextall was originally selected by the Flyers in the sixth-round (119th overall) of the 1982 NHL Draft. He is the fourth Hextall to play in the NHL following his father, Bryan Jr., his grandfather, Hall of Famer Bryan, Sr., and his uncle Dennis, who played for the Kings during the 1969-70 season. His son Brett was drafted by the Phoenix Coyotes in the sixth-round of the 2008 NHL Draft.

Club Directory

Wells Fargo Center

Philadelphia Flyers
Wells Fargo Center
3601 South Broad Street
Philadelphia, PA 19148-5290
Phone **215/465-4500**
PR FAX 215/218-7837
www.philadelphiaflyers.com
Capacity: 19,605

Executive Management	
President and COO, Comcast-Spectacor, Governor	Dave Scott
President, Philadelphia Flyers	Paul Holmgren
Executive Vice President/General Manager	Ron Hextall
Senior Vice President	Bob Clarke
Alternate Governors	Paul Holmgren, Shawn Tilger, Phil Weinberg
COO, Business Operations	Shawn Tilger
Executive Assistants	Sharon Allison, Cheri Arnao, Ann Marie Nasuti
Hockey Club Personnel	
Assistant General Manager	Barry Hanrahan
Head Coach	Dave Hakstol
Assistant Coaches	Gord Murphy, Ian Laperriere, Kris Knoblauch
Goaltending Coach / Video Coach	Kim Dillabaugh / Adam Patterson
Director of Scouting	Chris Pryor
Head Pro Scout	Dave Brown
Pro Scouts	John Chapman, Ross Fitzpatrick, Al Hill, Ilkka Sinisalo
College Scout	Wade Clarke
Amateur Scouts	Mark Greig, Joakim Grundberg, Todd Hearty, Ken Hoodikoff, Jack McIlhargey, Simon Nolet, Dennis Patterson, Rick Pracey, Nick Pryor
Scouting Consultant	Bill Barber
Player Development	Kjell Samuelsson, John Riley, Brady Robinson
Director of Team Services	Bryan Hardenbergh
Manager of Hockey Analytics	Ian Anderson
Hockey Operations Assistant	Jacob Hurlbut
Executive Asst. / Administrative Asst.	Kelly Flanagan / Jody Clarke
Medical/Training	
Director of Medical Services	Jim McCrossin
Assistant Athletic Trainer	Sal Raffa
Strength & Conditioning Coach	Chris Osmond
Director of Sports Science	Ben Peterson
Massage Therapist	Jack Kelly
Team Physicians	Peter DeLuca, M.D.; Gary Dorshimer, M.D.; Guy Lanzi, D.M.D.; Frank Brady, D.C.
Head Equipment Manager	Derek Settlemyre
Equipment Managers	Harry Bricker, Anthony Oratorio
Assistant Equipment Trainer	Mike Craytor
Business Development	
Director, Business Development	Steve Coskey
Communications	
Senior Director, Communications	Zack Hill
Director, Public Relations	Joe Siville
Manager, Broadcasting & Media Services	Brian Smith
Customer Service	
Vice President, Revenue Support	Cindy Stutman
Senior Manager, Customer Service	Courtney Sams
Customer Service Account Managers	Vincent Galasso, Niles McFate, Chris McClendon, Sean Naylor, Michelle Siporin
Client Communications Manager	Shannon Bowes
Season Ticket Holder Programs/Services Coord.	Amanda Perkins
Finance	
Chief Financial Officer	Angelo Cardone
Director of Accounting / Senior Accountant	Stephen Stout / Chris Boyer
Manager, Accounting and Reporting	Ryan Gillies
Staff Accountants	Eric Wojciechowski, Candy McKnight
Payroll Accountant / Accounting Clerk	Renee Eiler / Michele Dominic
Marketing	
Vice President, Marketing	Joe Heller
Game Presentation Senior Director / Manager	Anthony Gioia / Corinne Yamada
Director, Marketing	Sarah Fergus
Director, Community Development	Brad Marsh
Senior Manager, Community Relations	Jason Tempesta
Manager, Youth & Amateur Hockey	Rob Baer
Digital Media Manager	Christine Mina
Manager, Marketing	Hung Tran
Production Coordinator	Max Farrara
Digital Media Specialist	Lauren Robins
Ambassadors of Hockey	Bob Kelly, Bernie Parent
Fan Relations Assistant	Jerry Callahan
Producer/Director	Artie Halstead
Graphics Designers	Mike Cahill, Matthew Stalker
Video Editors	Chris Shay, Kevin Sutton, Lauren Tancredi
Public Address Announcer / Anthem Singer	Lou Nolan / Lauren Hart
Ticket Sales	
Senior Vice President, Sales	Bryan Anton
Ticket Sales Director / Coordinator	Ilkka Kortesluoma / Sarah Kurtz
Direct Marketing Manager	Justine Pletnick
Managers, Sales / Client Development	Josh Wentz, Nick Marchesiello / James Darlington
Sr. Account Exec. / Sr. Client Development Exec.	Charlie Wanner / Fran Walmsley
Account Executives	John Kramer, Ryan Pirrone, Will Spellman
Group Sales Account Executive	Steve Luongo
Client Development Executives	Juliana Carfagno, Cameron Lucas, Vicki Rees-Jones, Rick Halverson, David Tierno
Sales Associates	Mike Miller, Michelle Shames, Alexis Cochran, Alex Bergen, Patrick Tobey
Ticketing	
Director, Ticketing	Dan McGinnes
Ticket Office Manager / Asst. Manager / Coord.	Linda Fleischer / Tyler Wolford / Kris Hourin
Broadcast	
TV Rightsholders	Comcast SportsNet, The Comcast Network (TCN)
TV Play-by-Play / Color	Jim Jackson / Keith Jones, Bill Clement
Rinkside Analyst	Chris Therien
Radio Rightsholder / Play-by-Play / Color	97.5 The Fanatic / Tim Saunders / Steve Coates

Pittsburgh Penguins

2016-17 Results: 50w-21L-6OTL-5SOL 111PTS
2ND, Metropolitan Division • 3RD, Eastern Conference

Key Off-Season Signings/Acquisitions

2017

June 22 • Re-signed D **Chad Ruhwedel**.

23 • Acquired RW **Ryan Reaves** and a 2nd-round pick in 2017 NHL Draft from St. Louis for C **Oscar Sundqvist** and a 1st-round pick in 2017 NHL Draft.

July 1 • Signed G **Antti Niemi**, D **Matt Hunwick**, D **Chris Summers**, D **Jarred Tinordi**, D **Zach Trotman** and C **Greg McKegg**.

1 • Re-signed D **Justin Schultz** and LW **Garrett Wilson**.

11 • Named **Mark Recchi** assistant coach.

12 • Named **Sergei Gonchar** assistant coach.

12 • Re-signed RW **Josh Archibald** and D **Derrick Pouliot**.

24 • Re-signed D **Brian Dumoulin**.

30 • Re-signed LW **Conor Sheary**.

2017-18 Schedule

Oct.	Wed.	4	St. Louis	Thu.	4	Carolina
	Thu.	5	at Chicago	Fri.	5	at NY Islanders
	Sat.	7	Nashville	Sun.	7	Boston
	Wed.	11	at Washington	Sat.	13	Detroit*
	Thu.	12	at Tampa Bay	Sun.	14	NY Rangers*
	Sat.	14	Florida	Wed.	17	at Anaheim
	Tue.	17	at NY Rangers	Thu.	18	at Los Angeles
	Fri.	20	at Florida	Sat.	20	at San Jose
	Sat.	21	at Tampa Bay	Tue.	23	Carolina
	Tue.	24	Edmonton	Thu.	25	Minnesota
	Thu.	26	Winnipeg	Tue.	30	San Jose
	Sat.	28	at Minnesota	**Feb.** Fri.	2	Washington
	Sun.	29	at Winnipeg	Sat.	3	at New Jersey
Nov.	Wed.	1	at Edmonton	Tue.	6	Vegas
	Thu.	2	at Calgary	Fri.	9	at Dallas
	Sat.	4	at Vancouver	Sun.	11	at St. Louis*
	Tue.	7	Arizona	Tue.	13	Ottawa
	Fri.	10	at Washington	Thu.	15	Los Angeles
	Sat.	11	at Nashville	Sat.	17	Toronto
	Tue.	14	Buffalo	Sun.	18	at Columbus
	Thu.	16	at Ottawa	Fri.	23	at Carolina
	Sat.	18	Chicago	Sat.	24	at Florida
	Wed.	22	Vancouver	Tue.	27	New Jersey
	Fri.	24	at Boston*	**Mar.** Thu.	1	at Boston
	Sat.	25	Tampa Bay	Sat.	3	NY Islanders*
	Mon.	27	Philadelphia	Mon.	5	Calgary
Dec.	Fri.	1	at Buffalo	Wed.	7	at Philadelphia
	Sat.	2	Buffalo	Sat.	10	at Toronto
	Tue.	5	NY Rangers	Sun.	11	Dallas
	Thu.	7	NY Islanders	Wed.	14	at NY Rangers
	Sat.	9	Toronto	Thu.	15	at Montreal
	Mon.	11	Colorado	Tue.	20	at NY Islanders
	Thu.	14	at Vegas	Wed.	21	Montreal
	Sat.	16	at Arizona	Fri.	23	New Jersey
	Mon.	18	at Colorado	Sun.	25	Philadelphia*
	Thu.	21	Columbus	Tue.	27	at Detroit
	Sat.	23	Anaheim	Thu.	29	at New Jersey
	Wed.	27	Columbus	Sat.	31	Montreal
	Fri.	29	at Carolina	**Apr.** Sun.	1	Washington
	Sun.	31	at Detroit	Thu.	5	at Columbus
Jan.	Tue.	2	at Philadelphia	Fri.	6	Ottawa

* Denotes afternoon game.

Retired Numbers

21	Michel Brière	1969-1970
66	Mario Lemieux	1984-2006

METROPOLITAN DIVISION
51st NHL Season

Franchise date: June 5, 1967

Sidney Crosby displays the puck from his 1,000th career point on February 16, 2017. Crosby and the Penguins would later celebrate the NHL's first Stanley Cup repeat since the Detroit Red Wings in 1997 and 1998.

Year-by-Year Record

		Home				Road				Overall							
Season	GP	W	L	T	OL	W	L	T	OL	W	L	T	OL	GF	GA	Pts.	Div. Fin.	Conf. Fin.	Playoff Result
2016-17	82	31	6	....	4	19	15	....	7	50	21	....	11	282	234	111	2nd, Met.	3rd, East	Won Stanley Cup
2015-16	82	26	11	....	4	22	15	....	4	48	26	....	8	245	203	104	2nd, Met.	2nd, East	Won Stanley Cup
2014-15	82	23	14	....	4	20	13	....	8	43	27	....	12	221	210	98	4th, Met.	8th, East	Lost First Round
2013-14	82	28	9	....	4	23	15	....	3	51	24	....	7	249	207	109	1st, Met.	2nd, East	Lost Second Round
2012-13	48	18	6	....	0	18	6	....	0	36	12	....	0	165	119	72	1st, Atl.	1st, East	Lost Conf. Final
2011-12	82	29	10	....	2	22	15	....	4	51	25	....	6	282	221	108	2nd, Atl.	4th, East	Lost Conf. Quarter-Final
2010-11	82	25	14	....	2	24	11	....	6	49	25	....	8	238	199	106	4th, Atl.	4th, East	Lost Conf. Quarter-Final
2009-10	82	25	12	....	4	22	16	....	3	47	28	....	7	257	237	101	2nd, Atl.	4th, East	Lost Conf. Quarter-Final
2008-09	82	25	13	....	3	20	15	....	6	45	28	....	9	264	239	99	2nd, Atl.	4th, East	Won Stanley Cup
2007-08	82	26	10	....	5	21	17	....	3	47	27	....	8	247	216	102	1st, Atl.	2nd, East	Lost Final
2006-07	82	26	10	....	5	21	14	....	6	47	24	....	11	277	246	105	2nd, Atl.	5th, East	Lost Conf. Quarter-Final
2005-06	82	12	21	....	8	10	25	....	6	22	46	....	14	244	316	58	5th, Atl.	15th, East	– out of playoffs –
2004-05																			
2003-04	82	13	22	6	0	10	25	2	4	23	47	8	4	190	303	58	5th, Atl.	15th, East	– out of playoffs –
2002-03	82	15	22	2	2	12	22	4	3	27	44	6	5	189	255	65	5th, Atl.	14th, East	– out of playoffs –
2001-02	82	16	20	4	1	12	21	4	4	28	41	8	5	198	249	69	5th, Atl.	12th, East	– out of playoffs –
2000-01	82	24	15	2	0	18	13	7	3	42	28	9	3	281	256	96	3rd, Atl.	6th, East	Lost Conf. Final
1999-2000	82	23	11	7	0	14	20	1	6	37	31	8	6	241	236	88	3rd, Atl.	7th, East	Lost Conf. Semi-Final
1998-99	82	21	10	10	....	17	20	4	....	38	30	14	....	242	225	90	3rd, Atl.	8th, East	Lost Conf. Semi-Final
1997-98	82	21	10	10	....	19	14	8	....	40	24	18	....	228	188	98	1st, NE	2nd, East	Lost Conf. Quarter-Final
1996-97	82	25	11	5	....	13	25	3	....	38	36	8	....	285	280	84	2nd, NE	6th, East	Lost Conf. Quarter-Final
1995-96	82	32	9	0	....	17	20	4	....	49	29	4	....	362	284	102	1st, NE	2nd, East	Lost Conf. Final
1994-95	48	18	5	1	....	11	11	2	....	29	16	3	....	181	158	61	2nd, NE	2nd, East	Lost Conf. Semi-Final
1993-94	84	25	9	8	....	19	18	5	....	44	27	13	....	299	285	101	1st, NE	3rd, East	Lost Conf. Quarter-Final
1992-93	84	32	6	4	....	24	15	3	....	56	21	7	....	367	268	119	1st, Patrick		Lost Div. Final
1991-92	80	21	13	6	....	18	19	3	....	39	32	9	....	343	308	87	3rd, Patrick		Won Stanley Cup
1990-91	80	25	12	3	....	16	21	3	....	41	33	6	....	342	305	88	1st, Patrick		Won Stanley Cup
1989-90	80	22	15	3	....	10	25	5	....	32	40	8	....	318	359	72	5th, Patrick		– out of playoffs –
1988-89	80	24	13	3	....	16	20	4	....	40	33	7	....	347	349	87	2nd, Patrick		Lost Div. Final
1987-88	80	22	12	6	....	14	23	3	....	36	35	9	....	319	316	81	6th, Patrick		– out of playoffs –
1986-87	80	19	15	6	....	11	23	6	....	30	38	12	....	297	290	72	5th, Patrick		– out of playoffs –
1985-86	80	20	15	5	....	14	23	3	....	34	38	8	....	313	305	76	5th, Patrick		– out of playoffs –
1984-85	80	17	20	3	....	7	31	2	....	24	51	5	....	276	385	53	6th, Patrick		– out of playoffs –
1983-84	80	7	29	4	....	9	29	2	....	16	58	6	....	254	390	38	6th, Patrick		– out of playoffs –
1982-83	80	14	22	4	....	4	31	5	....	18	53	9	....	257	394	45	6th, Patrick		– out of playoffs –
1981-82	80	21	11	8	....	10	25	5	....	31	36	13	....	310	337	75	4th, Patrick		Lost Div. Semi-Final
1980-81	80	21	16	3	....	9	21	10	....	30	37	13	....	302	345	73	3rd, Norris		Lost Prelim. Round
1979-80	80	20	13	7	....	10	24	6	....	30	37	13	....	251	303	73	3rd, Norris		Lost Prelim. Round
1978-79	80	23	12	5	....	13	19	8	....	36	31	13	....	281	279	85	2nd, Norris		Lost Quarter-Final
1977-78	80	16	15	9	....	9	22	9	....	25	37	18	....	254	321	68	4th, Norris		– out of playoffs –
1976-77	80	22	12	6	....	12	21	7	....	34	33	13	....	240	252	81	3rd, Norris		Lost Prelim. Round
1975-76	80	23	11	6	....	12	22	6	....	35	33	12	....	339	303	82	3rd, Norris		Lost Prelim. Round
1974-75	80	25	5	10	....	12	23	5	....	37	28	15	....	326	289	89	3rd, Norris		Lost Quarter-Final
1973-74	78	15	18	6	....	13	23	3	....	28	41	9	....	242	273	65	5th, West		– out of playoffs –
1972-73	78	24	11	4	....	8	26	5	....	32	37	9	....	257	265	73	5th, West		– out of playoffs –
1971-72	78	18	15	6	....	8	23	8	....	26	38	14	....	220	258	66	4th, West		Lost Quarter-Final
1970-71	78	18	12	9	....	3	25	11	....	21	37	20	....	221	240	62	6th, West		– out of playoffs –
1969-70	76	17	13	8	....	9	25	4	....	26	38	12	....	182	238	64	2nd, West		Lost Semi-Final
1968-69	76	12	20	6	....	8	25	5	....	20	45	11	....	189	252	51	5th, West		– out of playoffs –
1967-68	74	15	12	10	....	12	22	3	....	27	34	13	....	195	216	67	5th, West		– out of playoffs –

2017-18 Player Personnel

FORWARDS	HT	WT	*Age	Birthplace	S	2016-17 Club
ARCHIBALD, Josh	5-10	176	24	Regina, SK	R	Pittsburgh-Wilkes-Barre
ASTON-REESE, Zach	6-0	190	23	Staten Island, NY	L	Wilkes-Barre-Northeastern
BLUEGER, Teddy	6-0	185	23	Riga, Latvia	L	Wilkes-Barre
CROSBY, Sidney	5-11	200	30	Cole Harbour, NS	L	Pittsburgh
DEA, Jean-Sebastien	6-11	175	23	Laval, QC	R	Pittsburgh-Wilkes-Barre
DI PAULI, Thomas	5-11	188	23	Woodbridge, IL	L	Wilkes-Barre
GUENTZEL, Jake	5-10	167	22	Omaha, NE	L	Pittsburgh-Wilkes-Barre
HAGELIN, Carl	5-11	186	29	Sodertalje, Sweden	L	Pittsburgh
HORNQVIST, Patric	5-11	189	30	Sollentuna, Sweden	R	Pittsburgh
JOHNSON, Adam	6-0	175	23	Hibbing, MN	L	U. Minn-Duluth
KESSEL, Phil	6-0	202	30	Madison, WI	R	Pittsburgh
KUHNHACKL, Tom	6-2	196	25	Landshut, Germany	L	Pittsburgh
MALKIN, Evgeni	6-3	195	31	Magnitogorsk, USSR	L	Pittsburgh
McKEGG, Greg	6-0	191	25	St.Thomas, ON	L	Fla-Sprfld-T.B.
REAVES, Ryan	6-1	224	30	Winnipeg, MB	R	St. Louis
ROWNEY, Carter	6-2	200	28	Grand Prairie, AB	R	Pittsburgh-Wilkes-Barre
RUST, Bryan	5-11	192	25	Pontiac, MI	R	Pittsburgh
SESTITO, Tom	6-5	228	30	Rome, NY	L	Pittsburgh-Wilkes-Barre
SHEARY, Conor	5-8	175	25	Melrose, MA	L	Pittsburgh
SIMON, Dominik	5-11	176	23	Prague, Czech Rep.	L	Pittsburgh-Wilkes-Barre
SPRONG, Daniel	6-0	180	20	Amsterdam, Netherlands	R	Charlottetown
TIFFELS, Frederik	6-0	192	22	Cologne, Germany	L	Western Mich.
WILSON, Garrett	6-2	199	26	Barrie, ON	L	Wilkes-Barre
WILSON, Scott	5-11	183	25	Oakville, ON	L	Pittsburgh
DEFENSEMEN						
BENGTSSON, Lukas	5-11	172	23	Stockholm, Sweden	R	Wilkes-Barre
COLE, Ian	6-1	219	28	Ann Arbour, MI	L	Pittsburgh
CORRADO, Frank	6-0	195	24	Woodbridge, ON	R	Tor-Tor (AHL)-Pit-Wilkes-Barre
CZUCZMAN, Kevin	6-2	206	26	Port Elgin, ON	L	Manitoba
DUMOULIN, Brian	6-4	207	26	Biddeford, ME	L	Pittsburgh
HUNWICK, Matt	5-11	191	32	Warren, MI	L	Toronto
LETANG, Kris	6-0	201	30	Montreal, QC	R	Pittsburgh
MAATTA, Olli	6-2	206	23	Jyvaskyla, Finland	L	Pittsburgh
POULIOT, Derrick	6-0	208	23	Estevan, SK	L	Pittsburgh-Wilkes-Barre
PROW, Ethan	6-0	185	24	Sauk Rapids, MN	R	Wilkes-Barre-Wheeling
RUHWEDEL, Chad	5-11	191	27	San Diego, CA	R	Pittsburgh-Wilkes-Barre
SCHULTZ, Justin	6-2	193	27	Kelowna, BC	R	Pittsburgh
SUMMERS, Chris	6-2	209	29	Ann Arbor, MI	L	Hartford
TAYLOR, Jeff	5-11	181	23	Albany, NY	L	Union College-Wilkes-Barre
TINORDI, Jarred	6-6	230	25	Burnsville, MN	L	Tucson
TROTMAN, Zach	6-3	217	27	Novi, MI	R	Ontario

GOALTENDERS	HT	WT	*Age	Birthplace	C	2016-17 Club
DESMITH, Casey	6-0	181	26	Rochester, NH	L	Wilkes-Barre
JARRY, Tristan	6-2	194	22	Surrey, BC	L	Pittsburgh-Wilkes-Barre
MURRAY, Matt	6-4	178	23	Thunder Bay, ON	L	Pittsburgh
NIEMI, Antti	6-2	210	34	Vantaa, Finland	L	Dallas

* – Age at start of 2017-18 season

Mike Sullivan

Head Coach

Born: Marshfield, MA, February 27, 1968.

Mike Sullivan was announced as the new head coach of the Pittsburgh Penguins by general manager Jim Rutherford on December 12, 2015. Sullivan was in his first season as head coach of the Penguins' American Hockey League affiliate in Wilkes-Barre/Scranton when he was promoted to the Pittsburgh post. At the time, Pittsburgh had a record of 15-10-3. Under Sullivan, the Penguins finished on a roll with a 33-16-5 record to close out the regular season and went on to win the Stanley Cup. He led the Penguins to the Stanley Cup again in 2016-17, making the Penguins the first back-to-back winners since the Detroit Red Wings in 1997 and 1998.

Prior to joining the Penguins organization, Sullivan was head coach of the Boston Bruins from 2003 to 2006 and was an NHL assistant coach for eight seasons with the Bruins (2002-03), Tampa Bay Lightning (2007 to 2009), New York Rangers (2009 to 2013) and Vancouver Canucks (2013-14). He spent the 2014-15 season as player development coach for the Stanley Cup champion Chicago Blackhawks. He also was an assistant coach for the United States at the 2006 Olympics, the 2007 World Championship and the 2016 World Cup of Hockey.

Sullivan played 709 NHL games over 11 seasons with the San Jose Sharks, Calgary Flames, Boston Bruins and Phoenix Coyotes. A center who specialized in killing penalties, he produced 54 goals and 136 points. Sixteen of his goals came shorthanded. He was named head coach of the AHL Providence Bruins immediately after retiring as a player in 2002 before being promoted to an assistant coaching role in Boston late that same season.

Sullivan played college hockey at Boston University and was named team captain as a senior in 1989-90. He played for the United States at the 1988 World Junior Championships and the 1997 World Championships.

Coaching Record

			Regular Season				Playoffs			
Season	Team	League	GC	W	L	O/T	GC	W	L	T
2003-04	**Boston**	**NHL**	**82**	**41**	**19**	**22**	**7**	**3**	**4**	....
2004-05	**Boston**				SEASON CANCELLED					
2005-06	**Boston**	**NHL**	**82**	**29**	**37**	**16**	....	....	....	....
2015-16	Wilkes-Barre	AHL	23	18	5	0	....	....	....	....
2015-16♦	**Pittsburgh**	**NHL**	**54**	**33**	**16**	**5**	**24**	**16**	**8**	....
2016-17♦	**Pittsburgh**	**NHL**	**82**	**50**	**21**	**11**	**25**	**16**	**9**	....
	NHL Totals		**300**	**153**	**93**	**54**	**56**	**35**	**21**	....

♦ Stanley Cup win.

2016-17 Scoring

* – rookie

Regular Season

Pos	#	Player	Team	GP	G	A	Pts	TOI	+/–	PIM	PP	SH	GW	S	S%
C	87	Sidney Crosby	PIT	75	44	45	89	19:52	17	24	14	0	5	255	17.3
C	71	Evgeni Malkin	PIT	62	33	39	72	18:37	18	77	11	0	6	191	17.3
C	81	Phil Kessel	PIT	82	23	47	70	17:56	3	20	8	0	4	229	10.0
L	43	Conor Sheary	PIT	61	23	30	53	15:56	24	22	2	0	6	154	14.9
D	4	Justin Schultz	PIT	78	12	39	51	20:26	27	34	3	0	1	154	7.8
R	72	Patric Hornqvist	PIT	70	21	23	44	15:57	16	28	10	0	6	223	9.4
C	13	Nick Bonino	PIT	80	18	19	37	16:39	–5	16	6	1	1	142	12.7
D	58	Kris Letang	PIT	41	5	29	34	25:31	2	32	2	0	2	122	4.1
C	59 *	Jake Guentzel	PIT	40	16	17	33	15:53	7	10	1	0	0	81	19.8
C	7	Matt Cullen	PIT	72	13	18	31	13:55	4	30	2	2	2	93	14.0
L	14	Chris Kunitz	PIT	71	9	20	29	15:30	0	36	0	0	3	134	6.7
R	17	Bryan Rust	PIT	57	15	13	28	13:38	4	8	0	0	1	110	13.6
D	32	Mark Streit	PHI	49	5	16	21	19:23	–10	22	1	0	1	88	5.7
			PIT	19	1	5	6	17:06	–2	6	0	0	1	26	3.8
			Total	68	6	21	27	18:44	–12	28	1	0	2	114	5.3
C	23 *	Scott Wilson	PIT	78	8	18	26	10:56	0	32	0	0	1	127	6.3
D	28	Ian Cole	PIT	81	5	21	26	19:49	26	72	0	0	1	89	5.6
L	62	Carl Hagelin	PIT	61	6	16	22	15:29	10	16	0	0	2	128	4.7
D	6	Trevor Daley	PIT	56	5	14	19	20:22	7	37	1	0	0	84	6.0
D	65	Ron Hainsey	PIT	72	4	13	17	22:01	–8	21	0	1	1	71	5.6
R	34	Tom Kuhnhackl	PIT	57	4	12	16	10:39	8	18	0	1	0	49	8.2
D	8	Brian Dumoulin	PIT	70	1	14	15	20:32	0	14	0	0	0	78	1.3
D	2	Chad Ruhwedel	PIT	34	2	8	10	17:20	9	8	0	0	0	45	4.4
R	37	Carter Rowney	PIT	27	3	4	7	10:58	2	4	0	0	1	24	12.5
D	3	Olli Maatta	PIT	55	1	6	7	18:03	17	12	0	0	0	66	1.5
D	24	Cameron Gaunce	PIT	12	1	3	4	12:31	1	13	0	0	0	8	12.5
R	45 *	Josh Archibald	PIT	10	3	0	3	10:51	3	4	0	1	0	11	27.3
L	25	Tom Sestito	PIT	13	0	2	2	5:31	0	48	0	0	0	3	0.0
C	49 *	Dominik Simon	PIT	2	0	1	1	13:02	–1	0	0	0	0	2	0.0
D	5	David Warsofsky	PIT	7	0	1	1	15:44	–3	6	0	0	0	14	0.0
D	61	Steve Oleksy	PIT	11	0	1	1	13:41	2	24	0	0	0	11	0.0
C	39 *	Jean-Sebastien Dea	PIT	1	0	0	0	11:18	0	2	0	0	0	1	0.0
C	11	Kevin Porter	PIT	2	0	0	0	11:15	–1	0	0	0	0	0	0.0
D	20	Frank Corrado	TOR	2	0	0	0	14:00	0	6	0	0	0	2	0.0
			PIT	2	0	0	0	7:32	–1	2	0	0	0	1	0.0
			Total	4	0	0	0	10:46	–1	8	0	0	0	3	0.0
C	40 *	Oskar Sundqvist	PIT	10	0	0	0	9:10	–4	2	0	0	0	9	0.0
D	51	Derrick Pouliot	PIT	11	0	0	0	14:53	–4	4	0	0	0	11	0.0

Goaltending

No.	Goaltender	GPI	Mins	Avg	W	L	OT	EN	SO	GA	SA	Sv%	G	A	PIM
1	Mike Condon	1	20	0.00	0	0	0	0	0	0	7	1.000	0	0	0
30	* Matt Murray	49	2766	2.41	32	10	4	3	4	111	1450	.923	0	2	0
29	Marc-Andre Fleury	38	2125	3.02	18	10	7	5	1	107	1181	.909	0	0	6
35	* Tristan Jarry	1	59	3.05	0	1	0	0	0	3	25	.880	0	0	0
	Totals	**82**	**4990**	**2.75**	**50**	**21**	**11**	**8**	**5**	**229**	**2671**	**.914**			

Playoffs

Pos	#	Player	Team	GP	G	A	Pts	TOI	+/–	PIM	PP	SH	GW	OT	S	S%
C	71	Evgeni Malkin	PIT	25	10	18	28	18:03	9	53	1	0	0	0	60	16.7
C	87	Sidney Crosby	PIT	24	8	19	27	19:23	4	10	4	0	0	0	63	12.7
C	81	Phil Kessel	PIT	25	8	15	23	17:32	12	2	5	0	2	0	68	11.8
C	59 *	Jake Guentzel	PIT	25	13	8	21	17:29	1	10	1	1	5	1	52	25.0
D	4	Justin Schultz	PIT	21	4	9	13	19:44	3	4	3	0	2	0	26	15.4
L	14	Chris Kunitz	PIT	20	2	9	11	14:51	6	27	0	0	1	1	28	7.1
R	17	Bryan Rust	PIT	23	7	2	9	15:56	5	10	0	0	2	0	42	16.7
R	72	Patric Hornqvist	PIT	19	5	4	9	14:16	6	18	1	0	1	0	44	11.4
C	7	Matt Cullen	PIT	25	2	7	9	14:19	–1	24	0	1	0	0	22	9.1
D	28	Ian Cole	PIT	25	0	9	9	18:50	2	22	0	0	0	0	23	0.0
D	65	Ron Hainsey	PIT	25	2	6	8	21:06	5	6	0	0	0	0	29	6.9
D	3	Olli Maatta	PIT	25	2	6	8	20:36	8	12	0	0	1	0	35	5.7
C	13	Nick Bonino	PIT	21	4	3	7	16:51	4	2	0	0	1	0	33	12.1
L	43	Conor Sheary	PIT	22	2	5	7	14:08	–5	4	0	0	0	0	44	4.5
C	23 *	Scott Wilson	PIT	20	3	3	6	11:58	4	11	0	0	0	0	28	10.7
D	8	Brian Dumoulin	PIT	25	1	5	6	21:59	9	6	0	0	1	0	25	4.0
D	6	Trevor Daley	PIT	21	1	4	5	19:06	7	24	1	0	0	0	26	3.8
R	37	Carter Rowney	PIT	20	0	3	3	12:17	3	4	0	0	0	0	22	0.0
L	62	Carl Hagelin	PIT	15	2	0	2	12:08	–2	19	0	0	0	0	20	10.0
R	34	Tom Kuhnhackl	PIT	11	1	1	2	11:36	2	4	0	0	0	0	11	9.1
D	32	Mark Streit	PIT	3	0	2	2	15:03	–1	0	0	0	0	0	2	0.0
R	45 *	Josh Archibald	PIT	4	0	0	0	7:51	–1	2	0	0	0	0	4	0.0
D	2	Chad Ruhwedel	PIT	6	0	0	0	14:06	–3	4	0	0	0	0	11	0.0

Goaltending

No.	Goaltender	GPI	Mins	Avg	W	L	EN	SO	GA	SA	Sv%	G	A	PIM
30	* Matt Murray	11	669	1.70	7	3	1	3	19	303	.937	0	0	0
29	Marc-Andre Fleury	15	867	2.56	9	6	0	2	37	490	.924	0	0	0
	Totals	**25**	**1547**	**2.21**	**16**	**9**	**1**	**5**	**57**	**794**	**.928**			

Coaching History

Red Sullivan, 1967-68, 1968-69; Red Kelly, 1969-70 to 1971-72; Red Kelly and Ken Schinkel, 1972-73; Ken Schinkel and Marc Boileau, 1973-74; Marc Boileau, 1974-75; Marc Boileau and Ken Schinkel, 1975-76; Ken Schinkel, 1976-77; Johnny Wilson, 1977-78 to 1979-80; Eddie Johnston, 1980-81 to 1982-83; Lou Angotti, 1983-84; Bob Berry, 1984-85 to 1986-87; Pierre Creamer, 1987-88; Gene Ubriaco, 1988-89; Gene Ubriaco and Craig Patrick, 1989-90; Bob Johnson, 1990-91; Scotty Bowman, 1991-92, 1992-93; Eddie Johnston, 1993-94 to 1995-96; Eddie Johnston and Craig Patrick, 1996-97; Kevin Constantine, 1997-98, 1998-99; Kevin Constantine and Herb Brooks, 1999-2000; Ivan Hlinka, 2000-01; Ivan Hlinka and Rick Kehoe, 2001-02; Rick Kehoe, 2002-03; Ed Olczyk, 2003-04, 2004-05; Ed Olczyk and Michel Therrien, 2005-06; Michel Therrien, 2006-07, 2007-08; Michel Therrien and Dan Bylsma, 2008-09; Dan Bylsma, 2009-10 to 2013-14; Mike Johnston, 2014-15; Mike Johnston and Mike Sullivan, 2015-16; Mike Sullivan, 2016-17 to date.

Club Records

Team

(Figures in brackets for season records are games played; records for fewest points, wins, ties, losses, goals, goals against are for 70 or more games)

Most Points	**119**	1992-93 (84)
Most Wins	**56**	1992-93 (84)
Most Ties	**20**	1970-71 (78)
Most Losses	**58**	1983-84 (80)
Most Goals	**367**	1992-93 (84)
Most Goals Against	**394**	1982-83 (80)
Fewest Points	**38**	1983-84 (80)
Fewest Wins	**16**	1983-84 (80)
Fewest Ties	**4**	1995-96 (82)
Fewest Losses	**21**	1992-93 (84)
Fewest Goals	**182**	1969-70 (76)
Fewest Goals Against	**188**	1997-98 (82)
Longest Winning Streak		
Overall	***17**	Mar. 9-Apr. 10/93
Home	**13**	Nov. 15/13-Jan. 15/14
Away	**8**	Mar. 11-Apr. 7/16
Longest Team Point Streak		
Overall	**18**	Mar. 9-Apr. 14/93 (17W, 1T)
Home	**20**	Nov. 30/74-Feb. 22/75 (12W, 8T)
Away	**8**	Mar. 14-Apr. 14/93 (7W, 1T)
Longest Losing Streak		
Overall	**18**	Jan. 13-Feb. 22/04
Home	***14**	Dec. 31/03-Feb. 22/04
Away	**18**	Dec. 23/82-Mar. 4/83
Longest Winless Streak		
Overall	**18**	Jan. 2-Feb. 10/83 (17L, 1T), Jan. 13-Feb. 22/04 (18L)
Home	**16**	Dec. 31/03-Mar. 4/04 (15L, 1T)
Away	**18**	Oct. 25/70-Jan. 14/71 (11L, 7T), Dec. 23/82-Mar. 4/83 (18L)
Most Shutouts, Season	**10**	2014-15 (82)
Most PIM, Season	**2,670**	1988-89 (80)
Most Goals, Game	**12**	Mar. 15/75 (Wsh. 1 at Pit. 12), Dec. 26/91 (Tor. 1 at Pit. 12)

Individual

Most Seasons	**17**	Mario Lemieux
Most Games	**915**	Mario Lemieux
Most Goals, Career	**690**	Mario Lemieux
Most Assists, Career	**1,033**	Mario Lemieux
Most Points, Career	**1,723**	Mario Lemieux (690G, 1,033A)
Most PIM, Career	**1,048**	Kevin Stevens
Most Shutouts, Career	**44**	Marc-Andre Fleury
Longest Consecutive Games Streak	**313**	Ron Schock (Oct. 24/73-Apr. 3/77)
Most Goals, Season	**85**	Mario Lemieux (1988-89)
Most Assists, Season	**114**	Mario Lemieux (1988-89)
Most Points, Season	**199**	Mario Lemieux (1988-89; 85G, 114A)
Most PIM, Season	**409**	Paul Baxter (1981-82)
Most Points, Defenseman, Season	**113**	Paul Coffey (1988-89; 30G, 83A)
Most Points, Center, Season	**199**	Mario Lemieux (1988-89; 85G, 114A)
Most Points, Right Wing, Season	***149**	Jaromir Jagr (1995-96; 62G, 87A)
Most Points, Left Wing, Season	**123**	Kevin Stevens (1991-92; 54G, 69A)
Most Points, Rookie, Season	**102**	Sidney Crosby (2005-06; 39G, 63A)
Most Shutouts, Season	**10**	Marc-Andre Fleury (2014-15)
Most Goals, Game	**5**	Mario Lemieux (Dec. 31/88), (Apr. 9/93), (Mar. 26/96)
Most Assists, Game	**6**	Ron Stackhouse (Mar. 8/75) Greg Malone (Nov. 28/79) Mario Lemieux (Oct. 15/88), (Dec. 5/92), (Nov. 1/95)
Most Points, Game	**8**	Mario Lemieux (Oct. 15/88; 2G, 6A), (Dec. 31/88; 5G, 3A)

* NHL Record.

Captains' History

Ab McDonald, 1967-68; Earl Ingarfield and no captain, 1968-69; no captain, 1969-70 to 1972-73; Ron Schock, 1973-74 to 1976-77; Jean Pronovost, 1977-78; Orest Kindrachuk, 1978-79 to 1980-81; Randy Carlyle, 1981-82 to 1983-84; Mike Bullard, 1984-85, 1985-86; Mike Bullard and Terry Ruskowski, 1986-87; Dan Frawley and Mario Lemieux, 1987-88; Mario Lemieux, 1988-89 to 1993-94; Ron Francis, 1994-95; Mario Lemieux, 1995-96, 1996-97; Ron Francis, 1997-98; Jaromir Jagr, 1998-99 to 2000-01; Mario Lemieux, 2001-02 to 2004-05; Mario Lemieux and no captain, 2005-06; no captain, 2006-07; Sidney Crosby, 2007-08 to date.

All-time Record vs. Other Clubs

Regular Season

	Total								At Home								On Road							
	GP	W	L	T	OL	GF	GA	PTS	GP	W	L	T	OL	GF	GA	PTS	GP	W	L	T	OL	GF	GA	PTS
Anaheim	32	19	9	2	2	107	90	42	17	12	3	2	0	61	45	26	15	7	6	0	2	46	45	16
Arizona	76	43	29	3	1	276	232	90	38	26	12	0	0	149	97	52	38	17	17	3	1	127	135	38
Boston	201	69	106	21	5	615	765	164	102	43	41	15	3	342	355	104	99	26	65	6	2	273	410	60
Buffalo	185	85	62	35	3	603	598	208	93	51	23	18	1	346	275	121	92	34	39	17	2	257	323	87
Calgary	104	44	40	18	2	348	368	108	51	28	12	10	1	186	148	67	53	16	28	8	1	162	220	41
Carolina	142	71	54	11	6	507	478	159	70	38	25	6	1	262	231	83	72	33	29	5	5	245	247	76
Chicago	133	44	67	17	5	397	471	110	66	32	24	7	3	228	210	74	67	12	43	10	2	169	261	36
Colorado	84	38	37	7	2	314	328	85	44	20	18	5	1	167	167	46	40	18	19	2	1	147	161	39
Columbus	31	19	8	0	4	98	86	42	15	11	4	0	0	52	35	22	16	8	4	0	4	46	51	20
Dallas	142	67	62	12	1	493	462	147	70	43	21	6	0	263	193	92	72	24	41	6	1	230	269	55
Detroit	151	68	64	16	3	528	515	155	76	50	22	4	0	310	226	104	75	18	42	12	3	218	289	51
Edmonton	74	32	35	4	3	259	308	71	37	20	13	3	1	143	147	44	37	12	22	1	2	116	161	27
Florida	88	48	31	4	5	253	240	105	44	28	12	3	1	135	113	60	44	20	19	1	4	118	127	45
Los Angeles	156	63	71	18	4	484	528	148	80	42	26	10	2	282	244	96	76	21	45	8	2	202	284	52
Minnesota	21	8	11	1	1	51	65	18	11	4	6	0	1	26	36	9	10	4	5	1	0	25	29	9
Montreal	207	64	112	23	8	588	799	159	104	41	47	13	3	316	356	98	103	23	65	10	5	272	443	61
Nashville	25	12	10	2	1	69	73	27	12	6	3	2	1	39	32	15	13	6	7	0	0	30	41	12
New Jersey	230	102	103	17	8	744	739	229	114	60	46	4	4	395	348	128	116	42	57	13	4	349	391	101
NY Islanders	244	116	98	22	8	861	850	262	124	66	40	14	4	463	395	150	120	50	58	8	4	398	455	112
NY Rangers	271	122	116	23	10	909	955	277	134	64	51	14	5	461	448	147	137	58	65	9	5	448	507	130
Ottawa	97	52	31	9	5	322	285	118	48	28	13	4	3	167	134	63	49	24	18	5	2	155	151	55
Philadelphia	281	98	146	30	7	857	1013	233	141	63	55	22	1	491	457	149	140	35	91	8	6	366	556	84
St. Louis	143	53	67	18	5	443	474	129	71	34	23	12	2	252	208	82	72	19	44	6	3	191	266	47
San Jose	37	16	14	3	4	132	102	39	16	8	5	1	2	58	46	19	21	8	9	2	2	74	56	20
Tampa Bay	89	48	31	5	5	294	251	106	45	29	10	3	3	173	114	64	44	19	21	2	2	121	137	42
Toronto	179	83	72	17	7	640	625	190	90	49	33	6	2	354	289	106	89	34	39	11	5	286	336	84
Vancouver	114	65	37	11	1	452	390	142	57	37	13	7	0	246	189	81	57	28	24	4	1	206	201	61
Washington	217	106	90	16	5	783	768	233	107	60	38	7	2	400	336	129	110	46	52	9	3	383	432	104
Winnipeg	59	45	11	0	3	226	154	93	29	25	3	0	1	127	75	51	30	20	8	0	2	99	79	42
Defunct Clubs	69	35	16	18	0	256	194	88	35	22	6	7	0	148	93	51	34	13	10	11	0	108	101	37
Totals	**3882**	**1735**	**1640**	**383**	**124**	**12909**	**13206**	**3977**	**1941**	**1040**	**648**	**205**	**48**	**7042**	**6042**	**2333**	**1941**	**695**	**992**	**178**	**76**	**5867**	**7164**	**1644**

Playoffs

	Series	W	L	GP	W	L	T	GF	GA	Last Mtg.	Rnd.	Result
Boston	5	2	3	23	10	13	0	69	74	2013	CF	L 0-4
Buffalo	2	2	0	10	6	4	0	26	26	2001	CSF	W 4-3
Carolina	1	1	0	4	4	0	0	20	9	2009	CF	W 4-0
Chicago	2	1	1	8	4	4	0	23	24	1992	F	W 4-0
Columbus	2	2	0	11	8	3	0	42	31	2017	FR	W 4-1
*Dallas	2	2	0	10	8	2	0	41	22	1991	F	W 4-2
Detroit	2	1	1	13	6	7	0	24	34	2009	F	W 4-3
Florida	1	0	1	7	3	4	0	15	20	1996	CF	L 3-4
Montreal	2	0	2	13	5	8	0	33	37	2010	CSF	L 3-4
Nashville	1	1	0	6	4	2	0	19	13	2017	F	W 4-2
New Jersey	5	3	2	29	14	15	0	80	86	2001	CF	L 1-4
NY Islanders	4	1	3	25	12	13	0	83	84	2013	CQF	W 4-2
NY Rangers	7	5	2	37	24	13	0	122	93	2016	FR	W 4-1
Ottawa	5	4	1	27	17	10	0	89	66	2017	CF	W 4-3
Philadelphia	6	2	4	35	16	19	0	115	121	2012	CQF	L 2-4
St. Louis	3	1	2	13	6	7	0	40	45	1981	PR	L 2-3
San Jose	1	1	0	6	4	2	0	15	12	2016	F	W 4-2
Tampa Bay	2	1	1	14	7	7	0	35	40	2016	CF	W 4-3
Toronto	3	0	3	12	4	8	0	27	39	1999	CSF	L 2-4
Washington	10	9	1	62	38	24	0	200	176	2017	SR	W 4-3
Totals	**66**	**39**	**27**	**365**	**200**	**165**	**0**	**1118**	**1052**			

* Includes series with Oakland 1980.

Calgary totals include Atlanta Flames, 1972-73 to 1979-80.
Carolina totals include Hartford, 1979-80 to 1996-97.
Colorado totals include Quebec, 1979-80 to 1994-95.
Dallas totals include Minnesota North Stars, 1967-68 to 1992-93.
New Jersey totals include Kansas City, 1974-75, 1975-76, and Colorado Rockies, 1976-77 to 1981-82.
Phoenix totals include Winnipeg, 1979-80 to 1995-96.
Winnipeg totals include Atlanta Thrashers, 1999-2000 to 2010-11.

Playoff Results 2017-2013

Year	Round	Opponent	Result	GF	GA
2017	**F**	**Nashville**	**W 4-2**	**19**	**13**
	CF	Ottawa	W 4-3	17	13
	SR	Washington	W 4-3	20	18
	FR	Columbus	W 4-1	21	13
2016	**F**	**San Jose**	**W 4-2**	**15**	**12**
	CF	Tampa Bay	W 4-3	21	18
	SR	Washington	W 4-2	16	15
	FR	NY Rangers	W 4-1	21	10
2015	FR	NY Rangers	L 1-4	8	11
2014	SR	NY Rangers	L 3-4	14	15
	FR	Columbus	W 4-2	21	18
2013	CF	Boston	L 0-4	2	12
	CSF	Ottawa	W 4-1	22	11
	CQF	NY Islanders	W 4-2	25	17

Abbreviations: Round: F – Final; **CF** – conference final; **CSF** – conference semi-final; **SR** – second round; **CQF** – conference quarter-final; **FR** – first round; **PR** – preliminary round.

2016-17 Results

Oct.	13	Washington	3-2†
	15	Anaheim	3-2
	17	Colorado	3-4*
	18	at Montreal	0-4
	20	San Jose	3-2
	22	at Nashville	1-5
	25	Florida	3-2
	27	NY Islanders	4-2
	29	at Philadelphia	5-4
Nov.	2	at Anaheim	5-1
	3	at Los Angeles	2-3*
	5	at San Jose	5-0
	8	Edmonton	4-3
	10	Minnesota	2-4
	12	Toronto	4-1
	16	at Washington	1-7
	18	at NY Islanders	3-2*
	19	at Buffalo	1-2†
	21	NY Rangers	2-5
	23	at NY Rangers	6-1
	25	at Minnesota	2-6
	26	New Jersey	4-3†
	30	at NY Islanders	3-5
Dec.	1	Dallas	6-2
	3	Detroit	5-3
	5	Ottawa	8-5
	8	at Florida	5-1
	10	at Tampa Bay	4-3
	12	Arizona	7-0
	14	Boston	4-3*
	16	Los Angeles	0-1*
	17	at Toronto	1-2*
	20	NY Rangers	7-2
	22	at Columbus	1-7
	23	New Jersey	4-1
	27	at New Jersey	5-2
	28	Carolina	3-2
	31	Montreal	4-3*
Jan.	8	Tampa Bay	6-2
	11	at Washington	2-5
	12	at Ottawa	1-4
	14	at Detroit	3-6
	16	Washington	8-7*
	18	at Montreal	4-1
	20	at Carolina	7-1
	22	Boston	5-1
	24	St. Louis	0-3
	26	at Boston	3-4
	31	Nashville	4-2
Feb.	3	Columbus	4-3*
	4	at St. Louis	4-1
	7	Calgary	2-3†
	9	at Colorado	4-1
	11	at Arizona	3-4*
	14	Vancouver	4-0
	16	Winnipeg	4-3*
	17	at Columbus	1-2*
	19	Detroit	2-5
	21	at Carolina	3-1
	25	Philadelphia	4-2
	28	at Dallas	2-3
Mar.	1	at Chicago	1-4
	3	Tampa Bay	5-2
	5	Buffalo	4-3
	8	at Winnipeg	7-4
	10	at Edmonton	3-2†
	11	at Vancouver	3-0
	13	at Calgary	3-4†
	15	at Philadelphia	0-4
	17	New Jersey	6-4
	19	Florida	4-0
	21	at Buffalo	3-1
	23	at Ottawa	1-2†
	24	NY Islanders	3-4†
	26	Philadelphia	2-6
	29	Chicago	1-5
	31	at NY Rangers	4-3†
Apr.	2	Carolina	3-2
	4	Columbus	4-1
	6	at New Jersey	7-4
	8	at Toronto	3-5
	9	at NY Rangers	2-3

* – Overtime † – Shootout

NHL Draft Selections 2017-2003

Name in bold denotes played in NHL.

2017 Pick		2013 Pick		2009 Pick		2005 Pick	
51	Zachary Lauzon	44	**Tristan Jarry**	30	**Simon Despres**	1	**Sidney Crosby**
93	Clayton Phillips	77	**Jake Guentzel**	61	**Philip Samuelsson**	61	Michael Gergen
152	Jan Drozg	119	Ryan Segalla	63	**Ben Hanowski**	62	**Kris Letang**
155	Linus Olund	164	Dane Birks	121	Nick Petersen	125	Tommi Leinonen
186	Antti Palojarvi	179	Blaine Byron	123	Alex Velischek	126	Tim Crowder
217	William Reilly	209	Troy Josephs	151	Andy Bathgate	194	Jean-Philippe Paquet
				181	Viktor Ekbom	195	**Joe Vitale**

2016 Pick		2012 Pick		2008 Pick		2004 Pick	
55	Filip Gustavsson	8	**Derrick Pouliot**	120	Nathan Moon	2	**Evgeni Malkin**
61	Kasper Bjorkqvist	22	**Olli Maatta**	150	**Alexander Pechurski**	31	Johannes Salmonsson
77	Connor Hall	52	Teddy Blueger	180	Patrick Killeen	61	**Alex Goligoski**
121	Ryan Jones	81	**Oscar Sundqvist**	210	Nick D'Agostino	67	**Nick Johnson**
151	Niclas Almari	83	**Matt Murray**			85	Brian Gifford
181	Joe Masonius	92	Matia Marcantuoni	**2007 Pick**		99	**Tyler Kennedy**
		113	Sean Maguire	20	Angelo Esposito	130	Michal Sersen
2015 Pick		143	Clark Seymour	51	Keven Veilleux	164	Moises Gutierrez
46	**Daniel Sprong**	173	Anton Zlobin	78	**Robert Bortuzzo**	194	Chris Peluso
137	**Dominik Simon**			80	Casey Pierro-Zabotel	222	Jordan Morrison
167	Frederik Tiffels	**2011 Pick**		111	**Luca Caputi**	228	David Brown
197	Nikita Pavlychev	23	**Joe Morrow**	118	Alex Grant	259	Brian Ihnacak
		54	**Scott Harrington**	141	**Jake Muzzin**		
2014 Pick		144	Dominik Uher	171	**Dustin Jeffrey**	**2003 Pick**	
22	**Kasperi Kapanen**	174	**Josh Archibald**			1	**Marc-Andre Fleury**
113	Sam Lafferty	209	**Scott Wilson**	**2006 Pick**		32	**Ryan Stone**
145	Anthony Angello			2	**Jordan Staal**	70	**Jonathan Filewich**
173	Jaden Lindo	**2010 Pick**		32	**Carl Sneep**	73	**Daniel Carcillo**
203	Jeff Taylor	20	**Beau Bennett**	65	**Brian Strait**	121	**Paul Bissonnette**
		80	**Bryan Rust**	125	**Chad Johnson**	161	Evgeni Isakov
		110	**Tom Kuhnhackl**	185	Timo Seppanen	169	Lukas Bolf
		140	**Kenny Agostino**			199	**Andy Chiodo**
		152	Joe Rogalski			229	Stephen Dixon
		170	Reid McNeill			232	**Joe Jensen**
						263	**Matt Moulson**

General Managers' History

Jack Riley, 1967-68 to 1969-70; Red Kelly, 1970-71; Red Kelly and Jack Riley, 1971-72; Jack Riley, 1972-73; Jack Riley and Jack Button, 1973-74; Jack Button, 1974-75; Wren Blair, 1975-76; Wren Blair and Baz Bastien, 1976-77; Baz Bastien, 1977-78 to 1982-83; Eddie Johnston, 1983-84 to 1987-88; Tony Esposito, 1988-89; Tony Esposito and Craig Patrick, 1989-90; Craig Patrick, 1990-91 to 2005-06; Ray Shero, 2006-07 to 2013-14; Jim Rutherford, 2014-15 to date.

Jim Rutherford

Executive Vice President and General Manager

Born: Beeton, ON, February 17, 1949.

Jim Rutherford was named general manager of the Pittsburgh Penguins on June 6, 2014. In his second season in charge in 2015-16, Rutherford used the trade and free-agent markets to add veteran forwards Nick Bonino, Matt Cullen, Eric Fehr and Phil Kessel over the summer plus forward Carl Hagelin and defenseman Trevor Daley during the campaign. Rutherford's retooled roster and midseason coaching change spurred the Penguins to a sizzling regular-season finish and a playoff run that carried them to the fourth Stanley Cup in franchise history. He was named the NHL General Manager of the Year for 2016, and in 2016-17, the Penguins became the first team since the 1997 and 1998 Detroit Red Wings to win back-to-back Stanley Cup championships.

Rutherford, one of the most respected executives in hockey, was general manager of the Hartford/Carolina franchise for 20 years and led the Carolina Hurricanes to the Stanley Cup in 2006. He stepped down from that position in April of 2014. He had been expected to continue in an advisory role with the Hurricanes until the Penguins opportunity arose.

Rutherford was named general manager of the NHL's Hartford Whalers on June 28, 1994 and helped transition the club to Carolina in 1997. He also served as team president. He was named the NHL's Executive of the Year by The Hockey News in 2002 and 2006 and by The Sporting News in 2006. Under Rutherford's leadership, the Hurricanes made two trips to the Stanley Cup Final, winning the Eastern Conference championship in 2002 and 2006, reached the conference finals in 2009 and captured three division titles.

Rutherford played 13 seasons in the NHL as a goaltender, including parts of three seasons with the Penguins from 1971 to 1974. He was a first-round draft pick of the Detroit Red Wings in 1969 and played in the NHL from 1970 to 1983 with Detroit, Pittsburgh, Toronto and Los Angeles. He appeared in 115 games with the Penguins, posting a 44-49-14 record and a 3.14 goals-against average.

When his playing career ended, Rutherford joined the Compuware Sports Corporation as director of hockey operations in 1983. He oversaw youth and junior hockey for the Detroit-based company and was named general manager of the Windsor Spitfires of the Ontario Hockey League after Compuware bought the major junior franchise in 1984. He was honored as the OHL's Executive of the Year in 1987 and 1988.

Club Directory

PPG Paints Arena

Pittsburgh Penguins
PPG Paints Arena
1001 Fifth Avenue
Pittsburgh, PA 15219
Phone **412/642-1300**
PR FAX 412/255-1988
www.pittsburghpenguins.com
Capacity: 18,387

Executive Management
Co-Owner/Chairman . . . . Mario Lemieux
Co-Owner . . . . Ron Burkle
CEO/President . . . . David Morehouse
COO/General Counsel . . . . Travis Williams

Hockey Operations
Executive V.P./General Manager . . . . Jim Rutherford
Assistant General Managers . . . . Bill Guerin, Jason Karmanos
Head Coach . . . . Mike Sullivan
Assistant Coaches . . . . Sergei Gonchar, Jacques Martin, Mark Recchi
Goaltending Coach / Video Coach . . . . Mike Buckley / Andy Saucier
Directors, Team Operations / Hockey Research . . Jim Britt / Sam Ventura
Hockey Ops Asst. / Exec. Asst. to the EVP/GM . . . Erik Heasley / Michele Colaianni
Player Development Director / Coach . . . . Scott Young / Jarrod Skalde
Goaltending Development Coach . . . . Brendan Sullivan
AHL Head Coach / Assistant Coaches . . . . Clark Donatelli / J.D. Forrest, Tim Army
Head Equipment Mgr. / Asst. Mgrs. . . . . Dana Heinze / JC Ihrig, Jon Taglianetti, Daniel Kroll
Head Athletic Trainer . . . . Chris Stewart
Director of Sports Performance . . . . Curtis Bell
Assistant Athletic Trainer . . . . Patrick Steidle
Head Team Physician / Assistant Team Physician . . Dr. Dharmesh Vyas / Dr. Melissa McLane
Director, Sport Science . . . . Andy O'Brien
Strength & Conditioning Coach . . . . Alex Trinca

Scouting
Director of Pro Scouting . . . . Derek Clancey
Professional Scouts . . . . Al Santilli, Ryan Bowness
Director of Amateur Scouting . . . . Patrik Allvin
Amateur Scouts . . . . . Colin Alexander, Brian Fitzgerald, Luc Gauthier, Frank Golden, Jay Heinbuck, Jamie Huffman, Wayne Meier, Casey Torres, Warren Young
European Scouts . . . . Tommy Westlund, Petri Pakaslahti
Special Assignment Scout . . . . Gilles Meloche

Administration
Exec. Administrator/Director, Events & Hospitality . . Kat Smerdel
Executive Assistants . . . . Susan Carper, Nicole Schaaf, Molly Trunzo
Shipping/Receiving Coordinator / Receptionist . . . . Brett Hart / Kelly Hart
Manager, Ice Operations . . . . Brandon Radeke

Partnership Sales
Senior Vice President, Sales & Broadcasting . . . . . . Terry Kalna
Sr. Director, Partnership Sales . . . . George Manias
Sr. Director, Partnership Marketing . . . . Ross Miller
Sr. Director, Partnership Sales & Media . . . . Mark Turley
Director, Partnership Marketing / Partnership Sales . . Lori Wineland / Jack Tipton
Manager, Partnership Sales . . . . Brett Baur
Managers, Partnership Marketing . . . . . Devin Beahm, Matt Dentinger, Paige Hancher, Jim Meyer
Partnership Sales Liaison . . . . Pierre Larouche

Communications
Vice President, Communications . . . . Tom McMillan
Communications Senior Director / Manager . . . . . Jennifer Bullano / Jason Seidling
Executive Director, Penguins Radio / Producer . . . . David Reynolds / Wayne Anderson
Radio Play-by-Play / Color . . . . Mike Lange / Phil Bourque
Penguins Radio Network & PensTV Host . . . . Josh Getzoff
Communications Specialist . . . . Paul Steigerwald

New Media
Content Director / Manager . . . . Sam Kasan / Michelle Crechiolo
Manager, New Media . . . . Andi Perelman
New Media Coordinators . . . . Jonathan Kabana, Jamie Louden, Evan Schall

Marketing
Vice President, Marketing . . . . James Santilli
Sr. Director, Creative Services & Publications . . . . . Barbara Pilarski
Director, Marketing . . . . Leo McCafferty
Manager, Publications / Graphic Designer . . . . . . Erin Halley / Dave Scheponik
Director, Fan Development & Special Events . . . . . Jill Shipley
Manager, Fan Development / Marketing Coord. . . . Laura Spencer / Christine King

Game Entertainment
Sr. Director, Production and Game Presentation . . . Rod Murray
Directors, Event Presentation / Production Ops. . . . . Bill Wareham / Mike Davenport
New Media Video Producer . . . . Mark Cottington
In The Room Producers / Producer . . . . Andrew McIntyre, Jon Otte / Meghan McManimon
Senior Designer, Motion Graphics . . . . Aaron Spiegel
Producers, Motion Graphics . . . . Dave Distilli, Ethan Mansberger
Producer/Host of PensTV / P.A. Announcer . . . . . Celina Pompeani / Ryan Mill

Finance
Senior Vice President, Finance . . . . Kevin Hart
Director, Finance . . . . Mark Kuczinski
Sr. Accountant / Financial Analyst . . . . Troy Ussack / Derek Bacon
Payroll Manager / Accounts Payable . . . . Andrea Winschel / Tawni Love

Technology
Sr. Director, Technology . . . . Erik Watts
Building Audio/Video Specialists . . . . Aaron Miller, Drew Warren
Systems Administrator / Jr. Administrator . . . . Jason Henry / Justin Mellor
Manager, CRM . . . . Mark Walczak

Ticketing
Vice President, Ticketing . . . . Chad Slencak
Sr. Directors, Premium Seating / Ticket Sales . . . . . Brian Magness / George Murphy
Managers, Premium Seating / Premium Services . . . Kyle Lux, Jon Seelnacht / Julia Ivery
Managers, Group Sales / Ticket Sales . . . . Ashley Smith, Mike Zatchey / Nicole Rudy
Ticket Sales Account Executives . . . . George Birman, Bonnie Golinski
Managers, Box Office / Box Office Operations . . . . Carol Coulson, Kelly Gabany / Jason Onufer
Director, Customer Service / Customer Service Reps. . . Kathy Davis / Holly Bandish, Jeff Blizman
Sr. Director / Manager, Database Marketing . . . . . . Erin Exley / Danny Gardner
Inside Sales Representatives . . . . Derek Leto, Kevin Devine, Auguste DeRose-Jones, Paige Wise

Penguins Foundation
President, Penguins Foundation . . . . David Soltesz
Director / Coordinators, Foundation . . . . . Amanda Susko / Abbey Braddock, Madison Connelly
Director / Liason, Community/Alumni Relations . . . . Cindy Himes / Ed Johnston

Key Off-Season Signings/Acquisitions

2017

May 24 • Named **Darryl Sydor** assistant coach.

25 • Named **Steve Ott** assistant coach.

June 15 • Named **Craig Berube** associate coach and **Daniel Tkaczuk** assistant coach.

23 • Acquired C **Brayden Schenn** from Philadelphia for C **Jori Lehtera**, a 1st-round pick in 2017 NHL Draft and a conditional pick in 2018 NHL Draft.

23 • Acquired C **Oscar Sundqvist** and a 1st-round pick in 2017 NHL Draft from Pittsburgh for RW **Ryan Reaves** and a 2nd-round pick in 2017 NHL Draft.

28 • Re-signed D **Chris Butler**.

29 • Re-signed LW **Magnus Paajarvi**.

July 1 • Signed RW **Chris Thorburn** and RW **Beau Bennett**.

20 • Re-signed D **Colton Parayko**.

Aug. 3 • Signed D **Nate Prosser**.

2017-18 Schedule

Oct.	Wed.	4	at Pittsburgh	Jan.	Tue. 2	New Jersey*
	Sat.	7	Dallas*		Thu. 4	Vegas*
	Mon.	9	at NY Islanders*		Sat. 6	at Philadelphia*
	Tue.	10	at NY Rangers		Sun. 7	at Washington*
	Thu.	12	at Florida		Tue. 9	Florida*
	Sat.	14	at Tampa Bay		Tue. 16	at Toronto
	Wed.	18	Chicago*		Thu. 18	at Ottawa
	Thu.	19	at Colorado		Sat. 20	Arizona*
	Sat.	21	at Vegas		Tue. 23	Ottawa*
	Wed.	25	Calgary*		Thu. 25	Colorado*
	Fri.	27	at Carolina		Tue. 30	Montreal*
	Sat.	28	Columbus*	Feb.	Thu. 1	at Boston
	Mon.	30	Los Angeles*		Sat. 3	at Buffalo
Nov.	Thu.	2	Philadelphia*		Tue. 6	Minnesota*
	Sat.	4	Toronto*		Thu. 8	Colorado*
	Tue.	7	at New Jersey		Fri. 9	at Winnipeg
	Thu.	9	Arizona*		Sun. 11	Pittsburgh*
	Sat.	11	NY Islanders*		Tue. 13	at Nashville
	Mon.	13	at Calgary		Fri. 16	at Dallas
	Thu.	16	at Edmonton		Tue. 20	San Jose*
	Sat.	18	at Vancouver		Fri. 23	Winnipeg*
	Tue.	21	Edmonton*		Sun. 25	at Nashville*
	Fri.	24	Nashville*		Tue. 27	at Minnesota
	Sat.	25	Minnesota*		Wed. 28	Detroit*
	Wed.	29	Anaheim*	Mar.	Sat. 3	at Dallas*
Dec.	Fri.	1	Los Angeles*		Thu. 8	at San Jose
	Sat.	2	at Minnesota*		Sat. 10	at Los Angeles*
	Tue.	5	at Montreal		Mon. 12	at Anaheim
	Thu.	7	Dallas*		Thu. 15	Colorado*
	Sat.	9	at Detroit*		Sat. 17	NY Rangers*
	Sun.	10	Buffalo*		Sun. 18	at Chicago
	Tue.	12	Tampa Bay*		Wed. 21	Boston*
	Thu.	14	Anaheim*		Fri. 23	Vancouver*
	Sat.	16	Winnipeg*		Sat. 24	at Columbus
	Sun.	17	at Winnipeg*		Tue. 27	San Jose*
	Wed.	20	at Calgary		Fri. 30	at Vegas
	Thu.	21	at Edmonton		Sat. 31	at Arizona
	Wed.	27	Nashville*	Apr.	Mon. 2	Washington*
	Sat.	23	at Vancouver		Wed. 4	Chicago*
	Fri.	29	at Dallas		Fri. 6	at Chicago
	Sat.	30	Carolina*		Sat. 7	at Colorado

Denotes afternoon game.

Retired Numbers

2	Al MacInnis	1994-2004
3	Bob Gassoff	1973-1977
8	Barclay Plager	1967-1977
11	Brian Sutter	1976-1988
16	Brett Hull	1987-1998
24	Bernie Federko	1976-1989

CENTRAL DIVISION
51st NHL Season

Franchise date: June 5, 1967

St. Louis Blues

2016-17 Results: 46w-29l-5otl-2sol 99pts
3rd, Central Division • 5th, Western Conference

The St. Louis Blues hosted the 2017 NHL Winter Classic at Busch Stadium, home of the St. Louis Cardinals.

Year-by-Year Record

Season	GP	Home W	L	T	OL	Road W	L	T	OL	Overall W	L	T	OL	GF	GA	Pts.	Div. Fin.	Conf. Fin.	Playoff Result
2016-17	82	24	12	....	5	22	17	....	2	46	29	....	7	235	218	99	3rd, Cen.	5th, West	Lost Second Round
2015-16	82	24	13	....	4	25	11	....	5	49	24	....	9	224	201	107	2nd, Cen.	2nd, West	Lost Conf. Final
2014-15	82	27	12	....	2	24	12	....	5	51	24	....	7	248	201	109	1st, Cen.	2nd, West	Lost First Round
2013-14	82	28	9	....	4	24	14	....	3	52	23	....	7	248	191	111	2nd, Cen.	3rd, West	Lost First Round
2012-13	48	15	8	....	1	14	9	....	1	29	17	....	2	129	115	60	2nd, Cen.	4th, West	Lost Conf. Quarter-Final
2011-12	82	30	6	....	5	19	16	....	6	49	22	....	11	210	165	109	1st, Cen.	2nd, West	Lost Conf. Semi-Final
2010-11	82	23	13	....	5	15	20	....	6	38	33	....	11	240	234	87	4th, Cen.	11th, West	– out of playoffs –
2009-10	82	18	18	....	5	22	14	....	5	40	32	....	10	225	223	90	4th, Cen.	9th, West	– out of playoffs –
2008-09	82	23	13	....	5	18	18	....	5	41	31	....	10	233	233	92	3rd, Cen.	6th, West	Lost Conf. Quarter-Final
2007-08	82	20	15	....	6	13	21	....	7	33	36	....	13	205	237	79	5th, Cen.	14th, West	– out of playoffs –
2006-07	82	18	19	....	4	16	16	....	9	34	35	....	13	214	254	81	5th, Cen.	10th, West	– out of playoffs –
2005-06	82	12	23	....	6	9	23	....	9	21	46	....	15	197	292	57	5th, Cen.	15th, West	– out of playoffs –
2004-05	.....	....		....		....		....		....		....		....	....	....	....		
2003-04	82	23	11	7	0	16	19	4	2	39	30	11	2	191	198	91	2nd, Cen.	7th, West	Lost Conf. Quarter-Final
2002-03	82	23	11	4	3	18	13	7	3	41	24	11	6	253	222	99	2nd, Cen.	5th, West	Lost Conf. Quarter-Final
2001-02	82	27	12	1	1	16	15	7	3	43	27	8	4	227	188	98	2nd, Cen.	4th, West	Lost Conf. Semi-Final
2000-01	82	28	5	5	3	15	17	7	2	43	22	12	5	249	195	103	2nd, Cen.	4th, West	Lost Conf. Final
1999-2000	82	24	9	7	1	27	10	4	0	51	19	11	1	248	165	114	1st, Cen.	1st, West	Lost Conf. Quarter-Final
1998-99	82	18	17	6		19	15	7		37	32	13	....	237	209	87	2nd, Cen.	5th, West	Lost Conf. Semi-Final
1997-98	82	26	10	5		19	19	3		45	29	8	....	256	204	98	3rd, Cen.	3rd, West	Lost Conf. Semi-Final
1996-97	82	17	20	4		19	15	7		36	35	11	....	236	239	83	4th, Cen.	6th, West	Lost Conf. Quarter-Final
1995-96	82	15	17	9		17	17	7		32	34	16	....	219	248	80	4th, Cen.	6th, West	Lost Conf. Semi-Final
1994-95	48	16	6	2		12	9	3		28	15	5	....	178	135	61	2nd, Cen.	2nd, West	Lost Conf. Quarter-Final
1993-94	84	23	11	8		17	22	3		40	33	11	....	270	283	91	4th, Cen.	5th, West	Lost Conf. Quarter-Final
1992-93	84	22	13	7		15	23	4		37	36	11	....	282	278	85	4th, Norris		Lost Div. Final
1991-92	80	25	12	3		11	21	8		36	33	11	....	279	266	83	3rd, Norris		Lost Div. Semi-Final
1990-91	80	24	9	7		23	13	4		47	22	11	....	310	250	105	2nd, Norris		Lost Div. Final
1989-90	80	20	15	5		17	19	4		37	34	9	....	295	279	83	2nd, Norris		Lost Div. Final
1988-89	80	22	11	7		11	24	5		33	35	12	....	275	285	78	2nd, Norris		Lost Div. Final
1987-88	80	18	17	5		16	21	3		34	38	8	....	278	294	76	2nd, Norris		Lost Div. Final
1986-87	80	21	12	7		11	21	8		32	33	15	....	281	293	79	1st, Norris		Lost Div. Semi-Final
1985-86	80	23	11	6		14	23	3		37	34	9	....	302	291	83	3rd, Norris		Lost Conf. Final
1984-85	80	21	12	7		16	19	5		37	31	12	....	299	288	86	1st, Norris		Lost Div. Semi-Final
1983-84	80	23	14	3		9	27	4		32	41	7	....	293	316	71	2nd, Norris		Lost Div. Final
1982-83	80	16	16	8		9	24	7		25	40	15	....	285	316	65	4th, Norris		Lost Div. Semi-Final
1981-82	80	22	14	4		10	26	4		32	40	8	....	315	349	72	3rd Norris		Lost Div. Final
1980-81	80	29	7	4		16	11	13		45	18	17	....	352	281	107	1st, Smythe		Lost Quarter-Final
1979-80	80	20	13	7		14	21	5		34	34	12	....	266	278	80	2nd, Smythe		Lost Prelim. Round
1978-79	80	14	20	6		4	30	6		18	50	12	....	249	348	48	3rd, Smythe		– out of playoffs –
1977-78	80	12	20	8		8	27	5		20	47	13	....	195	304	53	4th, Smythe		– out of playoffs –
1976-77	80	22	13	5		10	27	3		32	39	9	....	239	276	73	1st, Smythe		Lost Quarter-Final
1975-76	80	20	12	8		9	25	6		29	37	14	....	249	290	72	3rd, Smythe		Lost Prelim. Round
1974-75	80	23	14	3		12	18	10		35	31	14	....	269	267	84	2nd, Smythe		Lost Prelim. Round
1973-74	78	16	16	7		10	24	5		26	40	12	....	206	248	64	6th, West		– out of playoffs –
1972-73	78	21	11	7		11	23	5		32	34	12	....	233	251	76	4th, West		Lost Quarter-Final
1971-72	78	17	17	5		11	22	6		28	39	11	....	208	247	67	3rd, West		Lost Semi-Final
1970-71	78	23	7	9		11	18	10		34	25	19	....	223	208	87	2nd, West		Lost Quarter-Final
1969-70	76	24	9	5		13	18	7		37	27	12	....	224	179	86	1st, West		Lost Final
1968-69	76	21	8	9		16	17	5		37	25	14	....	204	157	88	1st, West		Lost Final
1967-68	74	18	12	7		9	19	9		27	31	16	....	177	191	70	3rd, West		Lost Final

2017-18 Player Personnel

FORWARDS	HT	WT	*Age	Birthplace	S	2016-17 Club
BARBASHEV, Ivan	6-0	180	21	Moscow, Russia	L	St. Louis-Chicago (AHL)
BENNETT, Beau	6-2	195	25	Gardena, CA	R	New Jersey
BERGLUND, Patrik	6-3	217	29	Vasteras, Sweden	L	St. Louis
BRODZIAK, Kyle	6-2	212	33	St. Paul, AB	R	St. Louis
FABBRI, Robby	5-10	180	21	Mississauga, ON	L	St. Louis
JASKIN, Dmitrij	6-2	217	24	Omsk, Russia	L	St. Louis
PAAJARVI, Magnus	6-3	208	26	Norrkoping, Sweden	L	St. Louis-Chicago (AHL)
SANFORD, Zach	6-3	185	22	Salem, MA	L	Wsh-Her-St.L.-Chi (AHL)
SCHENN, Brayden	6-1	195	26	Saskatoon, SK	L	Philadelphia
SCHWARTZ, Jaden	5-10	190	25	Melfort, SK	L	St. Louis
SOBOTKA, Vladimir	5-10	197	30	Trebic, Czech.	L	Omsk-St. Louis
STASTNY, Paul	6-0	205	31	Quebec City, QC	L	St. Louis
STEEN, Alexander	5-11	212	33	Winnipeg, MB	L	St. Louis
SUNDQVIST, Oskar	6-3	209	23	Boden, Sweden	R	Pittsburgh-Wilkes-Barre
TARASENKO, Vladimir	6-0	219	25	Yaroslavl, USSR	L	St. Louis
THORBURN, Chris	6-3	235	34	Sault Ste. Marie, ON	R	Winnipeg

DEFENSEMEN	HT	WT	*Age	Birthplace	S	2016-17 Club
BORTUZZO, Robert	6-4	215	28	Thunder Bay, ON	R	St. Louis
BOUWMEESTER, Jay	6-4	212	34	Edmonton, AB	L	St. Louis
BUTLER, Chris	6-1	196	30	St. Louis, MO	L	St. Louis-Chicago (AHL)
EDMUNDSON, Joel	6-4	207	24	Brandon, MB	L	St. Louis
GUNNARSSON, Carl	6-2	196	30	Orebro, Sweden	L	St. Louis
LINDBOHM, Petteri	6-3	198	24	Helsinki, Finland	L	St. Louis-Chicago (AHL)
PARAYKO, Colton	6-6	226	24	St. Albert, AB	R	St. Louis
PIETRANGELO, Alex	6-3	210	27	King City, ON	R	St. Louis
PROSSER, Nate	6-2	202	31	Elk River, MN	R	Minnesota
SCHMALTZ, Jordan	6-2	190	23	Madison, WI	R	St. Louis-Chicago (AHL)

GOALTENDERS	HT	WT	*Age	Birthplace	C	2016-17 Club
ALLEN, Jake	6-2	195	27	Fredericton, NB	L	St. Louis
HUTTON, Carter	6-1	201	31	Thunder Bay, ON	L	St. Louis

* – Age at start of 2017-18 season

Vladimir Tarasenko and goalie Jake Allen celebrate a victory during the first round of the playoffs.

Mike Yeo

Head Coach

Born: North Bay, ON, July 31, 1973.

Mike Yeo joined the St. Louis Blues as an associate coach on June 13, 2016 and was named head coach on February 1, 2017. He is the 25th coach in Blues history. The team went 22-8-2 in 32 games under Yeo in 2016-17.

Prior to joining the Blues, Yeo spent the majority of five seasons as the head coach of the Minnesota Wild before being fired on February 13, 2015. He went 173-132-44 with the Wild, the second-best record in team history. In four full seasons he coached the Wild to the playoffs three times, including back-to-back trips to the second round in 2014 and 2015.

Before his stint in Minnesota, Yeo spent one season as the head coach of the American Hockey League's Houston Aeros, where he led the club to the 2011 Calder Cup Final. He also spent 10 seasons in the Pittsburgh Penguins organization, including four seasons as an assistant coach, and helped the Pittsburgh Penguins win the Stanley Cup in 2009 as a member of Dan Bylsma's coaching staff.

As a player, Yeo spent five seasons with Houston (1994 to 1999) and was captain of the Aeros' 1999 International Hockey League Turner Cup championship team. Before that, he played four seasons with the Ontario Hockey League with the Sudbury Wolves. Yeo joined the Wilkes-Barre/Scranton Penguins for the 1999-2000 season and played in 19 games before suffering a career-ending knee injury. After the injury, he joined the coaching staff and spent six seasons as an assistant coach before joining the NHL coaching staff in Pittsburgh in December of 2005.

Coaching Record

			Regular Season				Playoffs			
Season	Team	League	GC	W	L	O/T	GC	W	L	T
2010-11	Houston	AHL	80	46	28	6	24	14	10	....
2011-12	**Minnesota**	**NHL**	**82**	**35**	**36**	**11**	....	....	....	....
2012-13	**Minnesota**	**NHL**	**48**	**26**	**19**	**3**	**5**	**1**	**4**	....
2013-14	**Minnesota**	**NHL**	**82**	**43**	**27**	**12**	**13**	**6**	**7**	....
2014-15	**Minnesota**	**NHL**	**82**	**46**	**28**	**8**	**10**	**4**	**6**	....
2015-16	**Minnesota**	**NHL**	**55**	**23**	**22**	**10**	....	....	....	....
2016-17	**St. Louis**	**NHL**	**32**	**22**	**8**	**2**	**11**	**6**	**5**	....
	NHL Totals		**381**	**195**	**140**	**46**	**39**	**17**	**22**	....

2016-17 Scoring

* – rookie

Regular Season

Pos	#	Player	Team	GP	G	A	Pts	TOI	+/–	PIM	PP	SH	GW	S	S%
R	91	Vladimir Tarasenko	STL	82	39	36	75	18:28	–1	12	9	0	8	286	13.6
C	17	Jaden Schwartz	STL	78	19	36	55	18:54	14	18	3	0	4	179	10.6
L	20	Alexander Steen	STL	76	16	35	51	19:18	–2	53	3	0	2	117	13.7
D	27	Alex Pietrangelo	STL	80	14	34	48	25:16	3	24	6	0	4	181	7.7
L	57	David Perron	STL	82	18	28	46	17:17	–2	54	3	1	3	151	11.9
C	26	Paul Stastny	STL	66	18	22	40	19:08	4	36	5	0	5	112	16.1
D	55	Colton Parayko	STL	81	4	31	35	21:11	7	32	4	0	2	188	2.1
C	21	Patrik Berglund	STL	82	23	11	34	15:59	–7	32	4	0	5	153	15.0
C	15	Robby Fabbri	STL	51	11	18	29	15:36	–16	27	4	0	0	91	12.1
C	12	Jori Lehtera	STL	64	7	15	22	15:10	–6	34	0	0	1	67	10.4
R	10	Scottie Upshall	STL	73	10	8	18	10:59	–1	45	0	2	1	85	11.8
C	28	Kyle Brodziak	STL	69	8	7	15	11:12	2	27	0	0	2	55	14.5
D	6	Joel Edmundson	STL	69	3	12	15	17:46	11	60	0	0	1	81	3.7
D	19	Jay Bouwmeester	STL	81	1	14	15	22:24	6	28	0	0	0	106	0.9
L	56	Magnus Paajarvi	STL	32	8	5	13	12:09	9	6	1	0	3	51	15.7
R	75	Ryan Reaves	STL	80	7	6	13	8:53	4	104	0	0	1	58	12.1
C	49 *	Ivan Barbashev	STL	30	5	7	12	11:47	5	2	0	0	1	20	25.0
R	23	Dmitrij Jaskin	STL	51	1	10	11	11:33	5	18	0	0	0	55	1.8
R	64	Nail Yakupov	STL	40	3	6	9	10:38	–3	14	0	0	0	35	8.6
L	82 *	Zach Sanford	WSH	26	2	1	3	10:08	0	6	0	0	1	23	8.7
			STL	13	2	3	5	12:14	2	4	0	0	1	13	15.4
			Total	39	4	4	8	10:50	2	10	0	0	2	36	11.1
D	4	Carl Gunnarsson	STL	56	0	6	6	13:35	–5	4	0	0	0	32	0.0
D	41	Robert Bortuzzo	STL	38	1	3	4	14:05	11	15	0	0	0	45	2.2
L	73 *	Kenny Agostino	STL	7	1	2	3	12:46	0	2	0	0	0	17	5.9
D	43 *	Jordan Schmaltz	STL	9	0	2	2	14:20	0	4	0	0	0	5	0.0
C	71	Vladimir Sobotka	STL	1	1	0	1	16:41	0	0	0	0	0	2	50.0
C	61	Wade Megan	STL	3	1	0	1	8:48	1	0	0	0	0	6	16.7
D	25	Chris Butler	STL	1	0	0	0	21:28	0	0	0	0	0	1	0.0
D	48	Petteri Lindbohm	STL	7	0	0	0	12:59	–4	4	0	0	0	10	0.0

Goaltending

No.	Goaltender	GPI	Mins	Avg	W	L	OT	EN	SO	GA	SA	Sv%	G	A	PIM
40	Carter Hutton	30	1459	2.39	13	8	2	7	4	58	663	.913	0	1	4
34	Jake Allen	61	3418	2.42	33	20	5	8	4	138	1620	.915	0	1	4
30	* Pheonix Copley	1	59	5.08	0	1	0	0	0	5	29	.828	0	0	0
	Totals	**82**	**4965**	**2.61**	**46**	**29**	**7**	**15**	**8**	**216**	**2327**	**.907**			

Playoffs

Pos	#	Player	Team	GP	G	A	Pts	TOI	+/–	PIM	PP	SH	GW	OT	S	S%
C	17	Jaden Schwartz	STL	11	4	5	9	21:32	4	2	1	0	3	0	33	12.1
L	20	Alexander Steen	STL	10	3	4	7	19:12	1	4	0	0	0	0	20	15.0
R	91	Vladimir Tarasenko	STL	11	3	3	6	20:49	2	0	1	0	1	0	44	6.8
D	6	Joel Edmundson	STL	11	3	3	6	21:06	12	14	0	0	1	1	9	33.3
C	71	Vladimir Sobotka	STL	11	2	4	6	17:26	4	2	0	0	0	0	13	15.4
D	55	Colton Parayko	STL	11	2	3	5	23:43	6	2	0	0	0	0	27	7.4
C	12	Jori Lehtera	STL	8	1	3	4	12:05	5	4	0	0	0	0	5	20.0
C	21	Patrik Berglund	STL	11	0	4	4	16:46	–1	10	0	0	0	0	14	0.0
D	27	Alex Pietrangelo	STL	11	0	4	4	28:16	–3	8	0	0	0	0	29	0.0
C	26	Paul Stastny	STL	7	2	1	3	21:24	4	2	0	0	0	0	14	14.3
L	56	Magnus Paajarvi	STL	8	1	2	3	12:36	1	2	0	0	1	1	9	11.1
C	28	Kyle Brodziak	STL	10	0	2	2	12:18	–3	2	0	0	0	0	8	0.0
R	23	Dmitrij Jaskin	STL	2	1	0	1	14:02	–1	4	0	0	0	0	9	11.1
L	57	David Perron	STL	11	0	1	1	14:27	–1	8	0	0	0	0	17	0.0
D	43 *	Jordan Schmaltz	STL	1	0	0	0	9:18	0	0	0	0	0	0	0	0.0
L	82 *	Zach Sanford	STL	4	0	0	0	10:55	0	0	0	0	0	0	6	0.0
C	49 *	Ivan Barbashev	STL	6	0	0	0	12:48	–1	2	0	0	0	0	4	0.0
D	41	Robert Bortuzzo	STL	10	0	0	0	11:31	–1	4	0	0	0	0	5	0.0
R	10	Scottie Upshall	STL	11	0	0	0	11:34	–2	8	0	0	0	0	11	0.0
D	19	Jay Bouwmeester	STL	11	0	0	0	24:15	–5	4	0	0	0	0	8	0.0
R	75	Ryan Reaves	STL	11	0	0	0	9:34	–1	8	0	0	0	0	8	0.0
D	4	Carl Gunnarsson	STL	11	0	0	0	11:52	–1	2	0	0	0	0	3	0.0

Goaltending

No.	Goaltender	GPI	Mins	Avg	W	L	EN	SO	GA	SA	Sv%	G	A	PIM
34	Jake Allen	11	675	1.96	6	5	1	0	22	336	.935	0	0	0
	Totals	**11**	**688**	**2.01**	**6**	**5**	**1**	**0**	**23**	**337**	**.932**			

Coaching History

Lynn Patrick and Scotty Bowman, 1967-68; Scotty Bowman, 1968-69, 1969-70; Al Arbour and Scotty Bowman, 1970-71; Sid Abel, Bill McCreary and Al Arbour, 1971-72; Al Arbour and Jean-Guy Talbot, 1972-73; Jean-Guy Talbot and Lou Angotti, 1973-74; Lou Angotti, Lynn Patrick and Garry Young, 1974-75; Garry Young, Lynn Patrick and Leo Boivin, 1975-76; Emile Francis, 1976-77; Leo Boivin and Barclay Plager, 1977-78; Barclay Plager, 1978-79; Barclay Plager and Red Berenson, 1979-80; Red Berenson, 1980-81; Red Berenson and Emile Francis, 1981-82; Emile Francis and Barclay Plager, 1982-83; Jacques Demers, 1983-84 to 1985-86; Jacques Martin, 1986-87, 1987-88; Brian Sutter, 1988-89 to 1991-92; Bob Plager and Bob Berry, 1992-93; Bob Berry, 1993-94; Mike Keenan, 1994-95, 1995-96; Mike Keenan, Jim Roberts and Joel Quenneville, 1996-97; Joel Quenneville, 1997-98 to 2002-03; Joel Quenneville and Mike Kitchen, 2003-04; Mike Kitchen, 2004-05, 2005-06; Mike Kitchen and Andy Murray, 2006-07; Andy Murray, 2007-08, 2008-09; Andy Murray and Davis Payne, 2009-10; Davis Payne, 2010-11; Davis Payne and Ken Hitchcock, 2011-12; Ken Hitchcock, 2012-13 to 2015-16; Ken Hitchcock and Mike Yeo, 2016-17; Mike Yeo, 2017-18.

Club Records

Team

(Figures in brackets for season records are games played; records for fewest points, wins, ties, losses, goals, goals against are for 70 or more games)

Most Points	**114**	1999-2000 (82)
Most Wins	**52**	2013-14 (82)
Most Ties	**19**	1970-71 (78)
Most Losses	**50**	1978-79 (80)
Most Goals	**352**	1980-81 (80)
Most Goals Against	**349**	1981-82 (80)
Fewest Points	**48**	1978-79 (80)
Fewest Wins	**18**	1978-79 (80)
Fewest Ties	**7**	1983-84 (80)
Fewest Losses	**18**	1980-81 (80)
Fewest Goals	**177**	1967-68 (74)
Fewest Goals Against	**157**	1968-69 (76)
Longest Winning Streak		
Overall	**10**	Jan. 3-23/02
Home	**9**	Jan. 26-Feb. 26/91
Away	**10**	Jan. 21-Mar. 2/00
Longest Team Point Streak		
Overall	**12**	Nov. 10-Dec. 8/68 (5W, 7T), Nov. 24-Dec. 26/00 (10W, 1OTW, 1T)
Home	**14**	Oct. 27-Dec. 15/16 (7W, 3OTW, 2OTL, 1SOW, 1SOL)
Away	**11**	Jan. 21-Mar. 4/00 (10W, 1T)
Longest Losing Streak		
Overall	**13**	Mar. 16-Apr. 8/06
Home	**7**	Oct. 22-Nov. 26/05, Nov. 25-Dec. 17/06
Away	**10**	Jan. 20-Mar. 8/82, Dec. 29/05-Feb. 1/06, Feb. 16-Mar. 15/08
Longest Winless Streak		
Overall	**13**	Mar. 16-Apr. 8/06 (13L)
Home	**7**	Dec. 28/82-Jan. 25/83 (5L, 2T), Oct. 22-Nov. 26/05 (7L)
Away	**17**	Jan. 23-Apr. 7/74 (14L, 3T)
Most Shutouts, Season	**15**	2011-12 (82)
Most PIM, Season	**2,041**	1990-91 (80)
Most Goals, Game	**11**	Feb. 26/94 (St.L. 11 at Ott. 1)

Individual

Most Seasons	**13**	Bernie Federko
Most Games	**927**	Bernie Federko
Most Goals, Career	**527**	Brett Hull
Most Assists, Career	**721**	Bernie Federko
Most Points, Career	**1,073**	Bernie Federko (352G, 721A)
Most PIM, Career	**1,786**	Brian Sutter
Most Shutouts, Career	**25**	Brian Elliott
Longest Consecutive Games Streak	**662**	Garry Unger (Feb. 7/71-Apr. 8/79)
Most Goals, Season	**86**	Brett Hull (1990-91)
Most Assists, Season	**90**	Adam Oates (1990-91)
Most Points, Season	**131**	Brett Hull (1990-91; 86G, 45A)
Most PIM, Season	**306**	Bob Gassoff (1975-76)
Most Points, Defenseman, Season	**78**	Jeff Brown (1992-93; 25G, 53A)
Most Points, Center, Season	**115**	Adam Oates (1990-91; 25G, 90A)
Most Points, Right Wing, Season	**131**	Brett Hull (1990-91; 86G, 45A)
Most Points, Left Wing, Season	**102**	Brendan Shanahan (1993-94; 52G, 50A)
Most Points, Rookie, Season	**73**	Jorgen Pettersson (1980-81; 37G, 36A)
Most Shutouts, Season	**9**	Brian Elliott (2011-12)
Most Goals, Game	**6**	Red Berenson (Nov. 7/68)
Most Assists, Game	**5**	Brian Sutter (Nov. 22/83), Bernie Federko (Feb. 27/88), Adam Oates (Jan. 26/91), Dallas Drake (Oct. 29/03)
Most Points, Game	**7**	Red Berenson (Nov. 7/68; 6G, 1A), Garry Unger (Mar. 13/71; 3G, 4A)

All-time Record vs. Other Clubs

Regular Season

	Total								At Home								On Road							
	GP	W	L	T	OL	GF	GA	PTS	GP	W	L	T	OL	GF	GA	PTS	GP	W	L	T	OL	GF	GA	PTS
Anaheim	87	42	33	5	7	259	241	96	44	26	10	3	5	146	115	60	43	16	23	2	2	113	126	36
Arizona	144	70	51	18	5	471	399	163	72	38	22	11	1	235	185	88	72	32	29	7	4	236	214	75
Boston	133	51	64	18	0	395	487	120	67	30	28	9	0	214	228	69	66	21	36	9	0	181	259	51
Buffalo	116	57	46	13	0	390	351	127	57	35	15	7	0	205	139	77	59	22	31	6	0	185	212	50
Calgary	169	78	70	14	7	522	519	177	85	41	32	9	3	285	256	94	84	37	38	5	4	237	263	83
Carolina	78	44	28	5	1	255	226	94	39	23	12	3	1	136	113	50	39	21	16	2	0	119	113	44
Chicago	306	124	134	35	13	927	1008	296	152	77	54	17	4	494	455	175	154	47	80	18	9	433	553	121
Colorado	131	61	52	11	7	395	395	140	64	38	20	4	2	221	174	82	67	23	32	7	5	174	221	58
Columbus	81	48	27	3	3	250	214	102	41	30	9	1	1	144	96	62	40	18	18	2	2	106	118	40
Dallas	282	132	102	43	5	902	853	312	142	80	40	21	1	496	390	182	140	52	62	22	4	406	463	130
Detroit	281	121	113	37	10	855	898	289	140	66	48	20	6	443	403	158	141	55	65	17	4	412	495	131
Edmonton	131	64	49	11	7	437	421	146	66	34	21	7	4	223	210	79	65	30	28	4	3	214	211	67
Florida	33	21	9	3	0	89	58	45	17	11	5	1	0	46	25	23	16	10	4	2	0	43	33	22
Los Angeles	199	102	72	22	3	625	577	229	100	63	26	10	1	349	247	137	99	39	46	12	2	276	330	92
Minnesota	66	32	23	5	6	160	163	75	32	19	7	3	3	87	65	44	34	13	16	2	3	73	98	31
Montreal	130	34	73	22	1	350	486	91	64	18	30	15	1	170	214	52	66	16	43	7	0	180	272	39
Nashville	105	52	36	4	13	265	238	121	52	29	17	1	5	141	115	64	53	23	19	3	8	124	123	57
New Jersey	106	55	36	14	1	362	320	125	53	32	13	7	1	218	161	72	53	23	23	7	0	144	159	53
NY Islanders	111	40	47	20	4	348	379	104	54	23	19	9	3	195	171	58	57	17	28	11	1	153	208	46
NY Rangers	139	44	77	16	2	374	488	106	72	30	31	10	1	214	222	71	67	14	46	6	1	160	266	35
Ottawa	33	15	12	2	4	105	89	36	16	5	6	2	3	47	51	15	17	10	6	0	1	58	38	21
Philadelphia	149	45	83	17	4	380	515	111	75	31	35	7	2	212	232	71	74	14	48	10	2	168	283	40
Pittsburgh	143	72	50	18	3	474	443	165	72	47	18	6	1	266	191	101	71	25	32	12	2	208	252	64
San Jose	95	55	33	2	5	288	241	117	50	26	22	1	1	143	130	54	45	29	11	1	4	145	111	63
Tampa Bay	39	24	10	3	2	135	106	53	18	15	3	0	0	67	42	30	21	9	7	3	2	68	64	23
Toronto	215	97	90	25	3	689	686	222	109	62	31	14	2	370	296	140	106	35	59	11	1	319	390	82
Vancouver	186	95	63	18	10	613	523	218	92	53	25	9	5	328	254	120	94	42	38	9	5	285	269	98
Washington	95	41	41	12	1	322	314	95	48	23	17	8	0	183	154	54	47	18	24	4	1	139	160	41
Winnipeg	34	19	8	1	6	97	87	45	16	9	4	0	3	45	39	21	18	10	4	1	3	52	48	24
Defunct Clubs	65	36	14	15	0	226	155	87	32	25	4	3	0	131	55	53	33	11	10	12	0	95	100	34
Totals	**3882**	**1771**	**1546**	**432**	**133**	**11960**	**11880**	**4107**	**1941**	**1039**	**624**	**218**	**60**	**6454**	**5428**	**2356**	**1941**	**732**	**922**	**214**	**73**	**5506**	**6452**	**1751**

Playoffs

	Series	W	L	GP	W	L	T	GF	GA	Last Mtg.	Rnd.	Result
Arizona	2	2	0	11	7	4	0	39	29	1999	CQF	W 4-3
Boston	2	0	2	8	0	8	0	15	48	1972	SF	L 0-4
Buffalo	1	0	1	3	1	2	0	8	7	1976	PR	L 1-2
Calgary	1	0	1	7	3	4	0	22	28	1986	CF	L 3-4
Chicago	12	4	8	63	28	35	0	175	211	2016	FR	W 4-3
Colorado	1	0	1	5	1	4	0	11	17	2001	CF	L 1-4
Dallas	13	7	6	73	36	37	0	212	211	2016	SR	W 4-3
Detroit	7	2	5	40	16	24	0	103	125	2002	CSF	L 1-4
Los Angeles	4	2	2	18	10	8	0	48	40	2013	CQF	L 2-4
Minnesota	2	1	1	11	6	5	0	25	25	2017	FR	W 4-1
Montreal	3	0	3	12	0	12	0	14	42	1977	QF	L 0-4
Nashville	1	0	1	6	2	4	0	11	15	2017	SR	L 2-4
NY Rangers	1	0	1	6	2	4	0	22	29	1981	QF	L 2-4
Philadelphia	2	2	0	11	8	3	0	34	20	1969	QF	W 4-0
Pittsburgh	3	2	1	13	7	6	0	45	40	1981	PR	W 3-2
San Jose	5	2	3	29	14	15	0	74	73	2016	CF	L 2-4
Toronto	5	3	2	31	17	14	0	88	90	1996	CQF	W 4-2
Vancouver	3	0	3	18	6	12	0	53	55	2009	CQF	L 0-4
Totals	**68**	**27**	**41**	**365**	**164**	**201**	**0**	**999**	**1105**			

Playoff Results 2017-2013

Year	Round	Opponent	Result	GF	GA
2017	SR	Nashville	L 2-4	11	15
	FR	Minnesota	W 4-1	11	8
2016	CF	San Jose	L 2-4	13	22
	SR	Dallas	W 4-3	25	14
	FR	Chicago	W 4-3	19	20
2015	FR	Minnesota	L 2-4	14	17
2014	FR	Chicago	L 2-4	14	20
2013	CQF	Los Angeles	L 2-4	10	12

Abbreviations: Round: CF – conference final; **CSF** – conference semi-final; **SR** – second round; **CQF** – conference quarter-final; **FR** – first round; **SF** – semi-final; **QF** – quarter-final; **PR** – preliminary round.

Calgary totals include Atlanta Flames, 1972-73 to 1979-80. Carolina totals include Hartford, 1979-80 to 1996-97.
Colorado totals include Quebec, 1979-80 to 1994-95. Dallas totals include Minnesota North Stars, 1967-68 to 1992-93.
New Jersey totals include Kansas City, 1974-75, 1975-76, and Colorado Rockies, 1976-77 to 1981-82.
Phoenix totals include Winnipeg, 1979-80 to 1995-96. Winnipeg totals include Atlanta Thrashers, 1999-2000 to 2010-11.

2016-17 Results

Oct.	12	at Chicago	5-2		12	at Los Angeles	1-5
	13	Minnesota	3-2		14	at San Jose	4-0
	15	NY Rangers	3-2		15	at Anaheim	2-1*
	18	at Vancouver	1-2*		17	Ottawa	4-6
	20	at Edmonton	1-3		19	Washington	3-7
	22	at Calgary	6-4		21	at Winnipeg	3-5
	25	Calgary	1-4		24	at Pittsburgh	3-0
	27	Detroit	1-2†		26	at Minnesota	1-5
	29	Los Angeles	1-0		31	Winnipeg	3-5
Nov.	1	at NY Rangers	0-5	**Feb.**	2	Toronto	5-1
	3	at Dallas	2-6		4	Pittsburgh	1-4
	5	Columbus	2-1*		6	at Philadelphia	2-0
	6	Colorado	5-1		7	at Ottawa	6-0
	9	Chicago	1-2*		9	at Toronto	2-1*
	10	at Nashville	1-3		11	at Montreal	4-2
	12	at Columbus	4-8		15	at Detroit	2-0
	15	Buffalo	4-1		16	Vancouver	4-3
	17	San Jose	3-2		18	at Buffalo	2-3
	19	Nashville	3-1		20	Florida	1-2
	22	at Boston	4-2		26	at Chicago	2-4
	23	at Washington	3-4		28	Edmonton	1-2
	26	Minnesota	4-3†	**Mar.**	3	at Winnipeg	0-3
	28	Dallas	4-3*		5	at Colorado	3-0
Dec.	1	Tampa Bay	5-4		7	at Minnesota	2-1
	3	Winnipeg	2-3*		10	Anaheim	4-3
	6	Montreal	3-2*		11	NY Islanders	4-3
	8	at NY Islanders	2-3		13	at Los Angeles	3-1
	9	at New Jersey	4-1		15	at Anaheim	1-2
	11	at Minnesota	1-3		16	at San Jose	4-1
	13	at Nashville	3-6		18	at Arizona	3-0
	15	New Jersey	5-2		21	at Colorado	4-2
	17	Chicago	4-6		23	Vancouver	4-1
	19	Edmonton	2-3*		25	Calgary	2-3*
	20	at Dallas	3-2*		27	Arizona	4-1
	22	at Tampa Bay	2-5		29	at Arizona	3-1
	28	Philadelphia	6-3		31	at Colorado	1-2†
	30	Nashville	0-4	**Apr.**	2	Nashville	4-1
Jan.	2	Chicago	4-1		4	Winnipeg	2-5
	5	Carolina	2-4		6	at Florida	6-3
	7	Dallas	4-3		8	at Carolina	5-4†
	10	Boston	3-5		9	Colorado	3-2

* – Overtime † – Shootout

NHL Draft Selections 2017-2003

Name in bold denotes played in NHL.

2017
Pick
20 Robert Thomas
31 Klim Kostin
113 Alexei Toropchenko
130 David Noel
175 Trenton Bourque
206 Anton Andersson

2016
Pick
26 Tage Thompson
35 Jordan Kyrou
59 Evan Fitzpatrick
119 Tanner Kaspick
125 Nolan Stevens
144 Conner Bleackley
209 Nikolaj Krag Christensen
211 Filip Helt

2015
Pick
56 Vince Dunn
94 Adam Musil
116 Glenn Gawdin
127 Niko Mikkola
146 Luke Opilka
176 Liam Dunda

2014
Pick
21 **Robby Fabbri**
33 **Ivan Barbashev**
52 Maxim Letunov
82 Jake Walman
94 Ville Husso
110 Austin Poganski
124 Jaedon Descheneau
172 C.J. Yakimowicz
176 Samuel Blais
202 Dwyer Tschantz

2013
Pick
47 Thomas Vannelli
57 **William Carrier**
112 Zach Pochiro
173 Santeri Saari

2012
Pick
25 **Jordan Schmaltz**
56 Sam Kurker
67 Mackenzie MacEachern
86 **Colton Parayko**
116 Nicholas Walters
146 Francois Tremblay
176 **Petteri Lindbohm**
206 Tyrel Seaman

2011
Pick
32 **Ty Rattie**
41 **Dmitrij Jaskin**
46 **Joel Edmundson**
88 **Jordan Binnington**
102 Yannick Veilleux
132 Niklas Lundstrom
162 Ryan Tesink
192 Teemu Eronen

2010
Pick
14 **Jaden Schwartz**
16 **Vladimir Tarasenko**
44 Sebastian Wannstrom
74 Max Gardiner
104 Jani Hakanpaa
134 Cody Beach
164 Stephen Macaulay

2009
Pick
17 **David Rundblad**
48 Brett Ponich
78 Sergei Andronov
108 Tyler Shattock
168 David Shields
202 Max Tardy

2008
Pick
4 **Alex Pietrangelo**
33 **Philip McRae**
34 **Jake Allen**
65 **Jori Lehtera**
70 James Livingston
87 Ian Schultz
95 **David Warsofsky**
125 Kristofer Berglund
155 Anthony Nigro
185 Paul Karpowich

2007
Pick
13 **Lars Eller**
18 **Ian Cole**
26 **David Perron**
39 Simon Hjalmarsson
44 **Aaron Palushaj**
85 Brett Sonne
96 **Cade Fairchild**
100 Travis Erstad
160 **Anthony Peluso**
190 Trevor Nill

2006
Pick
1 **Erik Johnson**
25 **Patrik Berglund**
31 **Tomas Kana**
64 **Jonas Junland**
94 Ryan Turek
106 **Reto Berra**
124 Andy Sackrison
154 Matthew McCollem
184 Alexander Hellstrom

2005
Pick
24 **T.J. Oshie**
37 **Scott Jackson**
85 **Ben Bishop**
156 **Ryan Reaves**
169 Mike Gauthier
171 **Nick Drazenovic**
219 Nikolai Lemtyugov

2004
Pick
17 **Marek Schwarz**
49 **Carl Soderberg**
83 Viktor Alexandrov
116 Michal Birner
136 **Nikita Nikitin**
180 **Roman Polak**
211 David Fredriksson
277 Jonathan Michel Boutin

2003
Pick
30 **Shawn Belle**
62 **David Backes**
84 Konstantin Barulin
88 **Zack Fitzgerald**
101 Konstantin Zakharov
127 **Alexandre Bolduc**
148 **Lee Stempniak**
159 **Chris Beckford-Tseu**
189 Jonathan Lehun
221 Evgeny Skachkov
253 Andrei Pervyshin
284 Juhamatti Aaltonen

General Managers' History

Lynn Patrick, 1967-68; Scotty Bowman, 1968-69 to 1970-71; Lynn Patrick and Sid Abel, 1971-72; Sid Abel, 1972-73; Charles Catto, 1973-74; Gerry Ehman and Dennis Ball, 1974-75; Dennis Ball, 1975-76; Emile Francis, 1976-77 to 1982-83; Ron Caron, 1983-84 to 1993-94; Mike Keenan, 1994-95, 1995-96; Mike Keenan and Ron Caron, 1996-97; Larry Pleau, 1997-98 to 2009-10; Doug Armstrong, 2010-11 to date.

Captains' History

Al Arbour, 1967-68 to 1969-70; Red Berenson and Barclay Plager, 1970-71; Barclay Plager, 1971-72 to 1975-76; no captain, 1976-77; Red Berenson, 1977-78; Barry Gibbs, 1978-79; Brian Sutter, 1979-80 to 1987-88; Bernie Federko, 1988-89; Rick Meagher, 1989-90; Scott Stevens, 1990-91; Garth Butcher, 1991-92; Brett Hull, 1992-93 to 1994-95; Brett Hull, Shayne Corson and Wayne Gretzky, 1995-96; no captain, 1996-97; Chris Pronger, 1997-98 to 2001-02; Al MacInnis, 2002-03, 2003-04; Dallas Drake, 2005-06, 2006-07; Eric Brewer, 2007-08 to 2010-11; David Backes, 2011-12 to 2015-16; Alex Pietrangelo, 2016-17 to date.

Doug Armstrong

President of Hockey Operations and General Manager

Born: Sarnia, ON, September 24, 1964.

Doug Armstrong was named the Blues' executive vice president and general manager on July 1, 2010 after serving two seasons with the club as vice president of player personnel. In his second season on the job in 2011-12, Armstrong was the NHL G.M. of the Year after his moves helped the team rebound from a slow start to post a 109-point season. The Blues set a club record with 52 wins in 2013-14 and had 111 points. They won the Central Division title in 2014-15 and had the third-best record in the NHL in 2015-16.

Prior to being hired in St. Louis, Armstrong spent 17 years with the Dallas Stars organization and the last six seasons (from January 25, 2002, to 2008) as the club's general manager. He was a part of the Stars' organization since the club moved to Dallas in 1993 and helped lead the franchise to two Presidents' Trophies, two Western Conference titles and the 1999 Stanley Cup championship. Prior to being named the team's seventh general manager, Armstrong served nine years as the assistant general manager under Bob Gainey. As Gainey's assistant, Armstrong worked on contract negotiations and season scheduling, and handled the day-to-day operations of the hockey department.

In international play, Armstrong was part of Team Canada's management at the 2010 and 2014 Winter Olympics, winning gold at both events. He was G.M. for Team Canada when they won the 2016 World Cup of Hockey and at the 2009 World Championships, where Canada earned a silver medal. Armstrong was an assistant G.M. at the World Championships in 2002 and 2008 (silver), and a special advisor in 2007 (gold). He is the son of former NHL linesman Neil Armstrong who was inducted into the Hockey Hall of Fame in 1991.

Club Directory

Scottrade Center

St. Louis Blues
Scottrade Center
1401 Clark Avenue at Brett Hull Way
St. Louis, MO 63103
Phone **314/622-2500**
FAX 314/622-2582
www.stlouisblues.com
Capacity: 19,150

Ownership
Tom Stillman, Jerald Kent, Donn Lux, James Cooper, Jo Ann Taylor Kindle, Steve Maritz, Edward Potter, Mr. & Mrs. Andrew Taylor, David Steward, James Kavanaugh, John Danforth, Christopher Danforth, Jim Johnson III, Scott McCuaig, John Ross, Jr., Tom Schlafly

Executive	
Chairman and Governor	Tom Stillman
President of Hockey Operations/G.M./Alt. Governor	Doug Armstrong
President and CEO, Business Operations	Chris Zimmerman
Group V.P., Ticketing & Guest Experience	Josh Bender
Group V.P., Brand, Community & Partnership Development	Steve Chapman
Group V.P., Sports & Entertainment Operations	Alex Rodrigo
Group V.P., Chief Financial Officer	Phil Siddle
Executive V.P.s	Bruce Affleck, Brett Hull
Sr. V.P., Marketing and Public Relations	Mike Caruso
Sr. V.P., Corporate Sponsorship	Eric Stisser
Vice President, Corporate Sponsorship	Bryan Lucas
Vice President, Hockey Operations	Dave Taylor
Exec. Asst. to the G.M.	Donna Lembke
Exec. Asst. to the Chairman & CEO	Lisa Cwiklowski
Hockey Operations	
Assistant General Manager	Martin Brodeur
Assistant General Manager	Kevin McDonald
Senior Advisor to the General Manager	Al MacInnis
Senior Advisor for Amateur Scouting	Larry Pleau
Head Coach	Mike Yeo
Associate Coach	Craig Berube
Assistant Coaches	Steve Ott, Darryl Sydor, Daniel Tkaczuk
Goaltending Coach / Video Coach	David Alexander / Sean Ferrell
Strength and Conditioning Coach	Eric Renaghan
Sr. Director, Media Relations/Team Services	Rich Jankowski
Scouting Directors, Amateur / Pro	Bill Armstrong / Rob DiMaio
Directors, Hockey Administration / Player Development	Ryan Miller / Tim Taylor
Sports Psychologist	Dr. Scot McFadden
Player Development Coach	Barret Jackman
Assistant Director, Media Relations	Dan O'Neill
Head of European Scouting	Jan Vopat
Amateur Scouts	Tony Feltrin, Dan Ginnell, J Niemiec, Michel Picard, Timo Koskela, Jesse Wallin
Part-Time Amateur Scouts	Corey Banika, , Bill Bestwick, Stefan Elvenes, Ian MacLellan, Vincent Montalbano, Blair Nicholson, Keith Tkachuk
Director of Hockey Analytics	Thomas Cason
Training	
Head Medical Trainer / Asst. Athletic Trainer	Ray Barile / Dustin Flynn
Equipment Manager / Asst. Manager / Assistant	Joel Farnsworth / Andrew Dvorak / Rich Mathews
Massage Therapist	Steve Squier
Medical	
Orthopedic Surgeons	Drs. Matt Matava, Rick Wright
Internists	Drs. Aaron Birenbaum, William Birenbaum
Neurosurgeon	Dr. Ralph Dacey
General / Plastic Surgeons	Dr. Michael Brunt / Dr. Tom Francel
Dentist / Oral Surgeon	Dr. Ron Sherstoff / Dr. Ken Kram
Ophthalmologist / Optometrist	Dr. Gill Grand / Dr. David Seibel
Chiropractor	Dr. Michael Murphy
Broadcasting	
Radio / Television Stations	KMOX 1120 AM / FOX Sports Midwest
V.P., Broadcast and Content Development	Chris Kerber
Radio Color Analyst, Community Relations	Kelly Chase
Community Relations, KMOX Radio 1120 AM	Bob Plager
Television Play-by-Play / Color	John Kelly / Darren Pang, Bernie Federko
FOX Sports Midwest Analyst / Host	Sara Dayley / Andy Strickland / Scott Warmann
Marketing	
Sr. Director, Event Presentation	Chris Frome
Sr. Director, Promotions/Digital Strategy	Matt Gardner
Sr. Director, Advertising/Event Marketing	Megan Little
Director, Community Relations/Blues 14 Fund	Randy Girsch
Director, Game Entertainment/Amateur Hockey	Jason Pippi
Director, Digital Media	Chris Pinkert
Director, Branding and Creative	Brenda Wilbur
Executive Producer, Video & Content Development	Trevor Nickerson
Director, Alumni Relations	Terry Yake
Event Operations	
Public Address Announcer	Tom Calhoun
Organist / Music Coordinator	Jeremy Boyer / Carl Middleman
Video Producer / In-Game Host	Eric Siders / Angella Sharpe
Sponsorship	
Director, Corporate Sponsorships	Mary Greener, Jackie Miller, Matt Polling
Director, Sponsorship Services	Amy Johnson
Ticket Sales and Service	
Director, Association and Promotional Sales	Jennifer Nevins
Sr. Director, Premium Seating & Suite Sales	Nick Wierciak
Director, Group and Event Suite Sales	Kari Takmajian
Director, Premium Seating & Suite Service	Melissa Gale
Director, Retention & Guest Experience	Ashley Hoffman
CRM & Analytics	
Director, CRM & Analytics / Database Manager	Keira Hertz / Michael Peterson
Ticket Operations	
Director, Ticket Operations	Greg Rapini
Managers, Ticket Operations	Justin Malmberg, Tiffany Stamper
Ticket Sales	Juanita Hall, Jeff Jovanovic, Brittany Bommarito, Todd Morris, Debbie Nyberg, Peggie O'Connor
Finance	
Finance Controller	Stephen Kruse
Senior Accountants	Kristy Atwater, Craig Bryant, Brent Lester
Manager, IT	Larry Womack
Coordinator, Accounts Payable	Mindy Wallace
Retail	
Retail Director	George Pavlik
Retail Managers / Store Manager	Amy Dugan / Matt Tierney
Guest Services	
Director, Public Safety	Dave Gilbert
Manager, Public Safety	Nick Bellamy
Manager, Guest Services and Event Operations	Lauren Carro
Human Resources	
Senior Director of Human Resources	Jamie Sackman
HR Generalist	Tiffany Stern
Manager / Assistant Manager, Payroll	Pam Di Rie / Crystal Strasburg
Building Operations	
Director Building Operations	Doug Waugh
Assistant Director of Building Operations	Phillip Ransford
Event Operations Manager	Kyle Worman

San Jose Sharks

2016-17 Results: 46w-29L-6OTL-1SOL 99PTS
3RD, Pacific Division • 6TH, Western Conference

Year-by-Year Record

Season	GP	Home W	L	T	OL	Road W	L	T	OL	Overall W	L	T	OL	GF	GA	Pts.	Div. Fin.	Conf. Fin.	Playoff Result
2016-17	82	26	11	....	4	20	18	....	3	46	29	....	7	221	201	99	3rd, Pac.	6th, West	Lost First Round
2015-16	82	18	20	....	3	28	10	....	3	46	30	....	6	241	210	98	3rd, Pac.	6th, West	Lost Final
2014-15	82	19	17	....	5	21	16	....	4	40	33	....	9	228	232	89	5th, Pac.	12th, West	– out of playoffs –
2013-14	82	29	7	....	5	22	15	....	4	51	22	....	9	249	200	111	2nd, Pac.	4th, West	Lost First Round
2012-13	48	17	2	....	5	8	14	....	2	25	16	....	7	124	116	57	3rd, Pac.	6th, West	Lost Conf. Semi-Final
2011-12	82	26	12	....	3	17	17	....	3	43	29	....	10	228	210	96	2nd, Pac.	7th, West	Lost Conf. Quarter-Final
2010-11	82	25	11	....	5	23	14	....	4	48	25	....	9	248	213	105	1st, Pac.	2nd, West	Lost Conf. Final
2009-10	82	27	6	....	8	24	14	....	3	51	20	....	11	264	215	113	1st, Pac.	1st, West	Lost Conf. Final
2008-09	82	32	5	....	4	21	13	....	7	53	18	....	11	257	204	117	1st, Pac.	1st, West	Lost Conf. Quarter-Final
2007-08	82	22	13	....	6	27	10	....	4	49	23	....	10	222	193	108	1st, Pac.	2nd, West	Lost Conf. Semi-Final
2006-07	82	25	12	....	4	26	14	....	1	51	26	....	5	258	199	107	2nd, Pac.	5th, West	Lost Conf. Semi-Final
2005-06	82	25	9	....	7	19	18	....	4	44	27	....	11	266	242	99	2nd, Pac.	5th, West	Lost Conf. Semi-Final
2004-05	....																		
2003-04	82	24	8	7	2	19	13	5	4	43	21	12	6	219	183	104	1st, Pac.	2nd, West	Lost Conf. Final
2002-03	82	17	16	5	3	11	21	4	5	28	37	9	8	214	239	73	5th, Pac.	14th, West	– out of playoffs –
2001-02	82	25	11	3	2	19	16	5	1	44	27	8	3	248	199	99	1st, Pac.	3rd, West	Lost Conf. Semi-Final
2000-01	82	22	14	4	1	18	13	8	2	40	27	12	3	217	192	95	2nd, Pac.	5th, West	Lost Conf. Quarter-Final
1999-2000	82	21	14	3	3	14	16	7	4	35	30	10	7	225	214	87	4th, Pac.	8th, West	Lost Conf. Semi-Final
1998-99	82	17	15	9	....	14	18	9	....	31	33	18	....	196	191	80	4th, Pac.	7th, West	Lost Conf. Quarter-Final
1997-98	82	17	19	5	....	17	19	5	....	34	38	10	....	210	216	78	4th, Pac.	8th, West	Lost Conf. Quarter-Final
1996-97	82	14	23	4	....	13	24	4	....	27	47	8	....	211	278	62	7th, Pac.	13th, West	– out of playoffs –
1995-96	82	12	26	3	....	8	29	4	....	20	55	7	....	252	357	47	7th, Pac.	13th, West	– out of playoffs –
1994-95	48	10	13	1	....	9	12	3	....	19	25	4	....	129	161	42	3rd, Pac.	7th, West	Lost Conf. Semi-Final
1993-94	84	19	13	10	....	14	22	6	....	33	35	16	....	252	265	82	3rd, Pac.	8th, West	Lost Conf. Semi-Final
1992-93	84	8	33	1	....	3	38	1	....	11	71	2	....	218	414	24	6th, Smythe		– out of playoffs –
1991-92	80	14	23	3	....	3	35	2	....	17	58	5	....	219	359	39	6th, Smythe		– out of playoffs –

2017-18 Schedule

Oct.					
Wed.	4	Philadelphia	Mon.	15	at Los Angeles*
Sat.	7	Los Angeles	Tue.	16	at Arizona
Thu.	12	Buffalo	Thu.	18	at Colorado
Sat.	14	NY Islanders	Sat.	20	Pittsburgh
Tue.	17	Montreal	Sun.	21	at Anaheim
Fri.	20	at New Jersey	Tue.	23	Winnipeg
Sat.	21	at NY Islanders	Thu.	25	NY Rangers
Mon.	23	at NY Rangers	Tue.	30	at Pittsburgh
Thu.	26	at Boston	Wed.	31	at Detroit
Sat.	28	at Buffalo*	**Feb.** Fri.	2	at Columbus
Mon.	30	Toronto	Sun.	4	at Carolina*
Nov. Wed.	1	Nashville	Tue.	6	at Colorado
Sat.	4	Anaheim	Thu.	8	Vegas
Wed.	8	Tampa Bay	Sat.	10	Edmonton
Sat.	11	Vancouver	Sun.	11	at Anaheim*
Sun.	12	at Los Angeles	Tue.	13	Arizona
Thu.	16	Florida	Thu.	15	Vancouver
Sat.	18	Boston	Sun.	18	Dallas
Mon.	20	Anaheim	Tue.	20	at St. Louis*
Wed.	22	at Arizona	Thu.	22	at Nashville
Fri.	24	at Vegas	Fri.	23	at Chicago
Sat.	25	Winnipeg	Sun.	25	at Minnesota
Tue.	28	at Philadelphia	Tue.	27	Edmonton
Dec. Fri.	1	at Florida	**Mar.** Thu.	1	Chicago
Sat.	2	at Tampa Bay	Sun.	4	Columbus
Mon.	4	at Washington	Thu.	8	St. Louis
Thu.	7	Carolina	Sat.	10	Washington*
Sat.	9	Ottawa	Mon.	12	Detroit
Sun.	10	Minnesota	Wed.	14	at Edmonton
Thu.	14	at Calgary	Fri.	16	at Calgary
Fri.	15	at Vancouver	Sat.	17	at Vancouver
Mon.	18	at Edmonton	Tue.	20	New Jersey
Thu.	21	Vancouver	Thu.	22	Vegas
Sat.	23	Los Angeles	Sat.	24	Calgary*
Thu.	28	Calgary	Mon.	26	at Chicago
Sun.	31	at Dallas	Tue.	27	at St. Louis*
Jan. Tue.	2	at Montreal	Thu.	29	at Nashville
Thu.	4	at Toronto	Sat.	31	at Vegas
Fri.	5	at Ottawa	**Apr.** Tue.	3	Dallas
Sun.	7	at Winnipeg*	Thu.	5	Colorado
Sat.	13	Arizona	Sat.	7	Minnesota

* Denotes afternoon game.

Brent Burns set franchise records for goals and points by a defenseman for the second consecutive season in 2016-17. He posted 29 goals and 47 assists to top all NHL blueliners with 76 points and won the Norris Trophy.

**PACIFIC DIVISION
27th NHL Season**

Franchise date: May 9, 1990

2017-18 Player Personnel

FORWARDS	HT	WT	*Age	Birthplace	S	2016-17 Club
BOEDKER, Mikkel	6-0	210	27	Brondby, Denmark	L	San Jose
BOLLIG, Brandon	6-2	230	30	St. Charles, MO	L	Stockton
CARPENTER, Ryan	6-0	195	26	Oviedo, FL	R	San Jose-San Jose (AHL)
COUTURE, Logan	6-1	200	28	Guelph, ON	L	San Jose
DONSKOI, Joonas	6-0	190	25	Raahe, Finland	R	San Jose
GOODROW, Barclay	6-2	215	24	Aurora, ON	L	San Jose-San Jose (AHL)
HANSEN, Jannik	6-1	195	31	Rodovre, Denmark	R	Vancouver-San Jose
HERTL, Tomas	6-2	215	23	Prague, Czech Rep.	L	San Jose
KARLSSON, Melker	6-0	180	27	Lycksele, Sweden	R	San Jose
LABANC, Kevin	5-11	185	21	Brooklyn, NY	R	San Jose-San Jose (AHL)
MEIER, Timo	6-0	210	20	St. Gallen, Switzerland	L	San Jose-San Jose (AHL)
O'REGAN, Daniel	5-9	180	23	Berlin, Germany	R	San Jose-San Jose (AHL)
PAVELSKI, Joe	5-11	190	33	Plover, WI	R	San Jose
SORENSEN, Marcus	5-11	175	25	Sodertalje, Sweden	L	San Jose-San Jose (AHL)
THORNTON, Joe	6-4	220	38	London, ON	L	San Jose
TIERNEY, Chris	6-1	195	23	Keswick, ON	L	San Jose
WARD, Joel	6-1	225	36	Toronto, ON	R	San Jose
DEFENSEMEN						
BRAUN, Justin	6-2	205	30	St. Paul, MN	R	San Jose
BURNS, Brent	6-5	230	32	Ajax, ON	R	San Jose
DeMELO, Dylan	6-1	195	24	London, ON	R	San Jose
DILLON, Brenden	6-3	220	26	Surrey, BC	L	San Jose
HEED, Tim	5-11	175	26	Gothenburg, Sweden	R	San Jose-San Jose (AHL)
MARTIN, Paul	6-1	200	36	Minneapolis, MN	L	San Jose
RYAN, Joakim	5-11	185	24	Rumson, NJ	L	San Jose (AHL)
VLASIC, Marc-Edouard	6-1	205	30	Montreal, QC	L	San Jose

GOALTENDERS	HT	WT	*Age	Birthplace	C	2016-17 Club
DELL, Aaron	6-0	205	28	Airdrie, AB	L	San Jose
GROSENICK, Troy	6-1	185	28	Brookfield, WI	L	San Jose (AHL)
JONES, Martin	6-4	190	27	North Vancouver, BC	L	San Jose

* – Age at start of 2017-18 season

Peter DeBoer

Head Coach

Born: Dunnville, ON, June 13, 1968.

San Jose Sharks general manager Doug Wilson announced on May 28, 2015, that Peter DeBoer had been named the eighth head coach in Sharks franchise history. In his 21st consecutive season as a head coach, serving at both the NHL and Canadian Hockey League levels, DeBoer led the Sharks to the Stanley Cup Final for the first time in franchise history in his first season behind the bench in San Jose in 2015-16.

DeBoer spent the previous three-plus seasons as head coach of the New Jersey Devils. In 248 games coached with New Jersey, DeBoer posted a 114-93-41 record and ranks as the second-winningest coach in Devils franchise history, behind Jacques Lemaire. In 2011-12, after finishing with 102 points, he led the team to the Stanley Cup final, alongside current Sharks director of player development Larry Robinson, who served as assistant coach on DeBoer's staff. The Devils fell to the Los Angeles Kings in six games. Prior to coaching in New Jersey, DeBoer spent three seasons as head coach of the Florida Panthers. In 2008-09, his first season as an NHL head coach, he coached the Panthers to their then second-best season in franchise history with 93 points. In 246 games coached with Florida, DeBoer posted a 103-107-36 record.

Prior to coaching in the NHL, DeBoer was one of the most distinguished coaches in Ontario Hockey League history. He spent 13 seasons coaching with Detroit, Plymouth and Kitchener in the OHL, won the Memorial Cup in 2003 and the OHL championship in 2003 and 2008 with Kitchener. Winner of the OHL coach of the year award in 1999 and 2000 with Plymouth, he was also named the Canadian Hockey League coach of the year in 2000. During his time in the OHL, he led his team to the league's best overall record four times (1998-99, 1999-2000, 2002-03, 2007-08) and is one of only eight coaches in OHL history to reach the 500+ win mark.

Internationally, DeBoer has frequently been selected to represent his native Canada, including serving as an assistant coach for the Canadian World Championship squad in 2015 (gold medal), 2014 and 2010. Additionally, he was a member of the coaching staff for Canada's World Junior Championship team in 2005 (gold medal) and 1998. He also served on the Team Canada coaching staff for the 2007 Canada-Russia Super Series. DeBoer was selected by the Toronto Maple Leafs in the 1988 NHL Draft (12th round, 237th overall) while playing for the Windsor Spitfires (OHL). He played three seasons (1989 to 1991) professionally with the Milwaukee Admirals of the International Hockey League. DeBoer holds a law degree from the University of Windsor and University of Detroit through the Dual J.D. Program.

2016-17 Scoring

* – rookie

Regular Season

Pos	#	Player	Team	GP	G	A	Pts	TOI	+/–	PIM	PP	SH	GW	S	S%
D	88	Brent Burns	S.J.	82	29	47	76	24:51	19	40	8	0	6	320	9.1
C	8	Joe Pavelski	S.J.	81	29	39	68	19:07	11	34	7	1	7	233	12.4
C	39	Logan Couture	S.J.	73	25	27	52	17:36	11	12	11	0	3	174	14.4
C	19	Joe Thornton	S.J.	79	7	43	50	18:03	7	51	1	0	0	81	8.6
C	12	Patrick Marleau	S.J.	82	27	19	46	17:09	4	28	7	0	6	190	14.2
R	42	Joel Ward	S.J.	78	10	19	29	15:56	–2	30	1	2	2	105	9.5
D	44	Marc-Edouard Vlasic	S.J.	75	6	22	28	21:14	4	35	1	0	2	144	4.2
L	89	Mikkel Boedker	S.J.	81	10	16	26	14:20	0	10	0	1	2	122	8.2
D	7	Paul Martin	S.J.	81	4	22	26	19:13	10	20	0	0	1	57	7.0
C	50	Chris Tierney	S.J.	80	11	12	23	14:36	0	6	1	1	2	90	12.2
C	68	Melker Karlsson	S.J.	67	11	11	22	12:48	7	22	0	2	1	73	15.1
C	48	Tomas Hertl	S.J.	49	10	12	22	17:13	–8	14	1	0	4	100	10.0
R	36	Jannik Hansen	VAN	28	6	7	13	16:20	2	27	0	0	1	56	10.7
			S.J.	15	2	5	7	15:30	0	7	0	0	0	17	11.8
			Total	43	8	12	20	16:03	2	34	0	0	1	73	11.0
R	62	* Kevin Labanc	S.J.	55	8	12	20	13:40	9	22	0	0	2	70	11.4
D	5	David Schlemko	S.J.	62	2	16	18	16:44	4	14	1	0	1	118	1.7
R	27	Joonas Donskoi	S.J.	61	6	11	17	13:48	–5	10	1	0	0	95	6.3
D	61	Justin Braun	S.J.	81	4	9	13	20:04	1	28	0	0	0	95	4.2
C	38	Micheal Haley	S.J.	58	2	10	12	9:10	6	128	0	0	1	37	5.4
D	4	Brenden Dillon	S.J.	81	2	8	10	16:28	–2	60	0	0	0	86	2.3
D	74	Dylan Demelo	S.J.	25	1	7	8	15:53	2	14	0	0	0	32	3.1
R	28	* Timo Meier	S.J.	34	3	3	6	12:28	1	10	0	0	1	85	3.5
C	40	* Ryan Carpenter	S.J.	11	2	2	4	10:23	5	4	0	0	0	20	10.0
L	20	* Marcus Sorensen	S.J.	19	1	3	4	10:48	–1	4	0	0	1	27	3.7
D	41	Mirco Mueller	S.J.	4	1	1	2	9:35	2	0	0	0	0	3	33.3
C	65	* Daniel O'Regan	S.J.	3	1	0	1	11:33	–2	0	1	0	0	5	20.0
C	23	Barclay Goodrow	S.J.	3	0	1	1	11:18	0	0	0	0	0	3	0.0
D	72	* Tim Heed	S.J.	1	0	0	0	16:29	0	0	0	0	0	1	0.0

Goaltending

No.	Goaltender	GPI	Mins	Avg	W	L	OT	EN	SO	GA	SA	Sv%	G	A	PIM
30	Aaron Dell	20	1111	2.00	11	6	1	3	1	37	533	.931	0	0	0
31	Martin Jones	65	3800	2.40	35	23	6	8	2	152	1725	.912	0	0	0
	Totals	**82**	**4956**	**2.42**	**46**	**29**	**7**	**11**	**3**	**200**	**2269**	**.912**			

Playoffs

Pos	#	Player	Team	GP	G	A	Pts	TOI	+/–	PIM	PP	SH	GW	OT	S	S%
C	12	Patrick Marleau	S.J.	6	3	1	4	19:07	–1	0	1	0	0	0	12	25.0
C	8	Joe Pavelski	S.J.	6	2	2	4	21:12	–1	0	1	0	1	0	16	12.5
R	42	Joel Ward	S.J.	6	1	3	4	14:43	0	4	1	0	0	0	9	11.1
D	5	David Schlemko	S.J.	6	2	1	3	16:49	2	2	1	0	0	0	9	22.2
C	39	Logan Couture	S.J.	6	2	1	3	18:18	–1	0	1	0	0	0	10	20.0
D	88	Brent Burns	S.J.	6	0	3	3	25:03	–1	6	0	0	0	0	28	0.0
D	44	Marc-Edouard Vlasic	S.J.	6	0	3	3	23:16	–1	2	0	0	0	0	9	0.0
L	89	Mikkel Boedker	S.J.	4	1	1	2	14:04	0	2	0	0	0	0	5	20.0
L	20	* Marcus Sorensen	S.J.	6	1	1	2	10:57	1	0	0	0	0	0	5	20.0
C	19	Joe Thornton	S.J.	4	0	2	2	18:49	–1	0	0	0	0	0	4	0.0
R	27	Joonas Donskoi	S.J.	5	0	2	2	13:06	–3	0	0	0	0	0	5	0.0
C	48	Tomas Hertl	S.J.	6	0	2	2	19:17	0	2	0	0	0	0	15	0.0
D	7	Paul Martin	S.J.	6	1	0	1	19:24	–1	4	0	0	0	0	5	20.0
C	68	Melker Karlsson	S.J.	6	1	0	1	14:16	0	6	0	0	1	1	7	14.3
R	36	Jannik Hansen	S.J.	6	0	1	1	15:41	0	0	0	0	0	0	10	0.0
D	61	Justin Braun	S.J.	6	0	1	1	22:07	–1	0	0	0	0	0	6	0.0
D	4	Brenden Dillon	S.J.	6	0	1	1	16:29	1	4	0	0	0	0	3	0.0
C	50	Chris Tierney	S.J.	6	0	1	1	13:50	0	0	0	0	0	0	4	0.0
R	28	* Timo Meier	S.J.	5	0	0	0	12:04	0	2	0	0	0	0	11	0.0

Goaltending

No.	Goaltender	GPI	Mins	Avg	W	L	EN	SO	GA	SA	Sv%	G	A	PIM
31	Martin Jones	6	377	1.75	2	4	1	1	11	168	.935	0	0	0
	Totals	**6**	**382**	**1.88**	**2**	**4**	**1**	**1**	**12**	**169**	**.929**			

Coaching Record

			Regular Season				Playoffs			
Season	Team	League	GC	W	L	O/T	GC	W	L	T
1995-96	Detroit	OHL	66	40	22	4	17	9	8	....
1996-97	Detroit	OHL	66	26	34	6	5	1	4	....
1997-98	Plymouth	OHL	66	37	22	7	15	8	7	....
1998-99	Plymouth	OHL	66	51	13	4	11	7	4	....
99-2000	Plymouth	OHL	68	45	18	5	23	15	8	....
2000-01	Plymouth	OHL	68	43	15	10	19	14	5	....
2001-02	Kitchener	OHL	68	35	22	11	4	0	4	....
2002-03	Kitchener	OHL	68	46	14	8	21	16	5	....
2002-03	Kitchener	M-Cup	....	....	....	....	4	4	0	....
2003-04	Kitchener	OHL	68	34	26	8	5	1	4	....
2004-05	Kitchener	OHL	68	35	20	13	15	9	6	....
2005-06	Kitchener	OHL	68	47	19	2	5	1	4	....
2006-07	Kitchener	OHL	68	47	17	4	9	5	4	....
2007-08	Kitchener	OHL	68	53	11	4	20	16	4	....
2007-08	Kitchener	M-Cup	....	....	....	....	5	2	3	....
2008-09	**Florida**	**NHL**	**82**	**41**	**30**	**11**	....	....	....	....
2009-10	**Florida**	**NHL**	**82**	**32**	**37**	**13**	....	....	....	....
2010-11	**Florida**	**NHL**	**82**	**30**	**40**	**12**	....	....	....	....
2011-12	**New Jersey**	**NHL**	**82**	**48**	**28**	**6**	**24**	**14**	**10**	....
2012-13	**New Jersey**	**NHL**	**48**	**19**	**19**	**10**	....	....	....	....
2013-14	**New Jersey**	**NHL**	**82**	**35**	**29**	**18**	....	....	....	....
2014-15	**New Jersey**	**NHL**	**36**	**12**	**17**	**7**	....	....	....	....
2015-16	**San Jose**	**NHL**	**82**	**46**	**30**	**6**	**24**	**14**	**10**	....
2016-17	**San Jose**	**NHL**	**82**	**46**	**29**	**7**	**6**	**2**	**4**	....
	NHL Totals		**658**	**309**	**259**	**90**	**54**	**30**	**24**	....

Club Records

Team

(Figures in brackets for season records are games played; records for fewest points, wins, ties, losses, goals, goals against are for 70 or more games)

Most Points **117** 2008-09 (82)
Most Wins **53** 2008-09 (82)
Most Ties **18** 1998-99 (82)
Most Losses ***71** 1992-93 (84)
Most Goals **266** 2005-06 (82)
Most Goals Against **414** 1992-93 (84)
Fewest Points **24** 1992-93 (84)
Fewest Wins **11** 1992-93 (84)
Fewest Ties ***2** 1992-93 (84)
Fewest Losses **18** 2008-09 (82)
Fewest Goals **196** 1998-99 (82)
Fewest Goals Against **183** 2003-04 (82)
Longest Winning Streak
  Overall .... **11** Feb. 21-Mar. 14/08
  Home .... **9** Oct. 9-Nov. 8/08
  Away .... **10** Nov. 14-Dec. 31/07
Longest Team Point Streak
  Overall .... **10** Nov. 27-Dec. 19/01 (8W, 1OTW, 1T)
  Home .... **11** Nov. 15-Dec. 29/03 (7W, 4T)
  Away .... **10** Dec. 26/00-Feb. 16/01 (5W, 1OTW, 4T)
Longest Losing Streak
  Overall .... ***17** Jan. 4-Feb. 12/93
  Home .... **9** Nov. 19-Dec. 19/92
  Away .... **19** Nov. 27/92-Feb. 12/93
Longest Winless Streak
  Overall .... **20** Dec. 29/92-Feb. 12/93 (19L, 1T)
  Home .... **9** Nov. 19-Dec. 19/92 (9L), Oct. 16-Nov. 18/03 (4L, 1OTL, 4T)
  Away .... **19** Nov. 27/92-Feb. 12/93 (19L)
Most Shutouts, Season **11** 2003-04 (82), 2006-07 (82)
Most PIM, Season **2,124** 1992-93 (84)
Most Goals, Game .... **10** Jan. 13/96 (S.J. 10 at Pit. 8), Mar. 30/02 (CBJ 2 at S.J. 10)

Individual

Most Seasons .... **19** Patrick Marleau
Most Games, Career .... **1,493** Patrick Marleau
Most Goals, Career .... **508** Patrick Marleau
Most Assists, Career .... **722** Joe Thornton
Most Points, Career .... **1,082** Patrick Marleau (508G, 574A)
Most PIM, Career .... **1,001** Jeff Odgers
Most Shutouts, Career .... **50** Evgeni Nabokov
Longest Consecutive Games Streak .... **624** Patrick Marleau (Apr. 9/09-to date)
Most Goals, Season .... **56** Jonathan Cheechoo (2005-06)
Most Assists, Season .... **92** Joe Thornton (2006-07)
Most Points, Season .... **114** Joe Thornton (2006-07; 22G, 92A)
Most PIM, Season .... **326** Link Gaetz (1991-92)
Most Points, Defenseman, Season .... **76** Brent Burns (2016-17; 29G, 47A)
Most Points, Center, Season .... **114** Joe Thornton (2006-07; 22G, 92A)
Most Points, Right Wing, Season .... **93** Jonathan Cheechoo (2005-06; 56G, 37A)
Most Points, Left Wing, Season .... **83** Patrick Marleau (2009-10; 44G, 39A)
Most Points, Rookie, Season .... **59** Pat Falloon (1991-92; 25G, 34A)
Most Shutouts, Season .... **9** Evgeni Nabokov (2003-04)
Most Goals, Game .... **4** Owen Nolan (Dec. 19/95), Tomas Hertl (Oct. 8/13). Patrick Marleau (Jan. 23/17)
Most Assists, Game .... **4** Nineteen times
Most Points, Game .... **6** Owen Nolan (Oct. 4/99; 3G, 3A)

* NHL Record.

Captains' History

Doug Wilson, 1991-92, 1992-93; Bob Errey, 1993-94; Bob Errey and Jeff Odgers, 1994-95; Jeff Odgers, 1995-96; Todd Gill, 1996-97, 1997-98; Owen Nolan, 1998-99 to 2002-03; Mike Ricci, Vincent Damphousse, Alyn McCauley, Patrick Marleau, 2003-04; Patrick Marleau, 2005-06 to 2008-09; Rob Blake, 2009-10; Joe Thornton, 2010-11 to 2013-14; no captain, 2014-15; Joe Pavelski, 2015-16 to date.

Coaching History

George Kingston, 1991-92, 1992-93; Kevin Constantine, 1993-94, 1994-95; Kevin Constantine and Jim Wiley, 1995-96; Al Sims, 1996-97; Darryl Sutter, 1997-98 to 2001-02; Darryl Sutter, Cap Raeder and Ron Wilson, 2002-03; Ron Wilson, 2003-04 to 2007-08; Todd McLellan, 2008-09 to 2014-15; Peter DeBoer, 2015-16 to date.

General Managers' History

Jack Ferreira, 1991-92; Chuck Grillo (V.P. Director of Player Personnel), 1992-93 to 1995-96; Chuck Grillo and Dean Lombardi, 1996-97; Dean Lombardi, 1997-98 to 2002-03; Doug Wilson, 2003-04 to date.

All-time Record vs. Other Clubs

Regular Season

	Total								At Home								On Road							
	GP	W	L	T	OL	GF	GA	PTS	GP	W	L	T	OL	GF	GA	PTS	GP	W	L	T	OL	GF	GA	PTS
Anaheim	132	67	53	4	8	370	341	146	66	34	27	2	3	186	166	73	66	33	26	2	5	184	175	73
Arizona	139	71	49	7	12	415	376	161	68	38	17	4	9	217	174	89	71	33	32	3	3	198	202	72
Boston	36	12	17	5	2	100	114	31	18	7	7	2	2	45	52	18	18	5	10	3	0	55	62	13
Buffalo	37	9	21	4	3	102	138	25	18	7	6	4	1	52	57	19	19	2	15	0	2	50	81	6
Calgary	117	48	54	8	7	334	357	111	59	27	24	4	4	186	166	62	58	21	30	4	3	148	191	49
Carolina	36	17	17	0	2	115	111	36	18	10	6	0	2	74	56	22	18	7	11	0	0	41	55	14
Chicago	94	48	33	5	8	274	272	109	47	28	14	3	2	134	123	61	47	20	19	2	6	140	149	48
Colorado	90	41	38	5	6	254	283	93	46	26	19	1	0	146	135	53	44	15	19	4	6	108	148	40
Columbus	55	35	16	0	4	158	130	74	27	21	4	0	2	96	53	44	28	14	12	0	2	62	77	30
Dallas	123	54	51	5	13	319	340	126	62	27	25	1	9	159	165	64	61	27	26	4	4	160	175	62
Detroit	90	32	49	4	5	244	316	73	46	20	21	3	2	156	159	45	44	12	28	1	3	88	157	28
Edmonton	115	52	42	12	9	336	337	125	57	30	17	5	5	187	166	70	58	22	25	7	4	149	171	55
Florida	32	13	9	7	3	95	81	36	16	7	4	2	3	51	41	19	16	6	5	5	0	44	40	17
Los Angeles	146	75	55	7	9	429	399	166	73	45	21	3	4	232	188	97	73	30	34	4	5	197	211	69
Minnesota	59	32	19	2	6	160	137	72	30	19	8	1	2	88	63	41	29	13	11	1	4	72	74	31
Montreal	36	17	14	4	1	96	93	39	18	12	3	2	1	62	40	27	18	5	11	2	0	34	53	12
Nashville	67	33	26	2	6	170	173	74	34	20	9	1	4	89	78	45	33	13	17	1	2	81	95	29
New Jersey	37	16	17	2	2	92	111	36	17	7	8	1	1	42	47	16	20	9	9	1	1	50	64	20
NY Islanders	37	18	13	3	3	106	115	42	19	10	6	1	2	49	54	23	18	8	7	2	1	57	61	19
NY Rangers	37	10	22	3	2	100	133	25	20	6	11	2	1	56	67	15	17	4	11	1	1	44	66	10
Ottawa	32	14	13	4	1	84	89	33	16	8	7	0	1	37	38	17	16	6	6	4	0	47	51	16
Philadelphia	39	20	14	4	1	108	102	45	20	10	8	2	0	50	47	22	19	10	6	2	1	58	55	23
Pittsburgh	37	18	14	3	2	102	132	41	21	11	8	2	0	56	74	24	16	7	6	1	2	46	58	17
St. Louis	95	38	49	2	6	241	288	84	45	15	25	1	4	111	145	35	50	23	24	1	2	130	143	49
Tampa Bay	38	19	15	2	2	125	106	42	18	9	8	1	0	66	53	19	20	10	7	1	2	59	53	23
Toronto	47	22	20	5	0	134	137	49	22	11	8	3	0	61	52	25	25	11	12	2	0	73	85	24
Vancouver	116	54	48	9	5	337	337	122	59	25	25	5	4	170	168	59	57	29	23	4	1	167	169	63
Washington	39	27	9	1	2	131	96	57	19	13	3	1	2	68	47	29	20	14	6	0	0	63	49	28
Winnipeg	26	17	5	2	2	85	59	38	13	8	4	1	0	43	30	17	13	9	1	1	2	42	29	21
Totals	**1984**	**929**	**802**	**121**	**132**	**5616**	**5703**	**2111**	**992**	**511**	**353**	**58**	**70**	**2969**	**2704**	**1150**	**992**	**418**	**449**	**63**	**62**	**2647**	**2999**	**961**

Playoffs

	Series	W	L	GP	W	L	T	GF	GA	Last Mtg.	Rnd.	Result
Anaheim	1	0	1	6	2	4	0	10	18	2009	CQF	L 2-4
Arizona	1	1	0	5	4	1	0	13	7	2002	CQF	W 4-1
Calgary	3	2	1	20	10	10	0	57	68	2008	CQF	W 4-3
Chicago	1	0	1	4	0	4	0	7	13	2010	CF	L 0-4
Colorado	4	2	2	25	13	12	0	71	62	2010	CQF	W 4-2
Dallas	3	0	3	17	5	12	0	30	46	2008	CSF	L 2-4
Detroit	5	3	2	29	14	15	0	69	99	2011	CSF	W 4-3
Edmonton	2	0	2	12	4	8	0	26	31	2017	FR	L 2-4
Los Angeles	4	2	2	25	14	11	0	68	71	2016	FR	W 4-1
Nashville	3	3	0	17	12	5	0	58	41	2016	SR	W 4-3
Pittsburgh	1	0	1	6	2	4	0	12	15	2016	F	L 2-4
St. Louis	5	3	2	29	15	14	0	73	74	2016	CF	W 4-2
Toronto	1	0	1	7	3	4	0	21	26	1994	CSF	L 3-4
Vancouver	2	1	1	9	5	4	0	28	28	2013	CQF	W 4-0
Totals	**36**	**17**	**19**	**211**	**103**	**108**	**0**	**543**	**599**			

Carolina totals include Hartford, 1991-92 to 1996-97.
Dallas totals include Minnesota North Stars, 1991-92 to 1992-93.
Winnipeg totals include Atlanta Thrashers, 1999-2000 to 2010-11.
Colorado totals include Quebec, 1991-92 to 1994-95.
Phoenix totals include Winnipeg, 1991-92 to 1995-96.

Playoff Results 2017-2013

Year	Round	Opponent	Result	GF	GA
2017	FR	Edmonton	L 2-4	14	12
2016	F	Pittsburgh	L 2-4	12	15
	CF	St. Louis	W 4-2	22	13
	SR	Nashville	W 4-3	25	17
	FR	Los Angeles	W 4-1	16	11
2014	FR	Los Angeles	L 3-4	22	26
2013	CSF	Los Angeles	L 3-4	10	14
	CQF	Vancouver	W 4-0	15	8

Abbreviations: Round: F – Final; **CF** – conference final; **CSF** – conference semi-final; **SR** – second round; **CQF** – conference quarter-final; **FR** – first round.

2016-17 Results

Oct.	12	Los Angeles	2-1		11	at Calgary	2-3
	15	at Columbus	3-2		14	St. Louis	0-4
	17	at NY Rangers	4-7		16	Winnipeg	5-2
	18	at NY Islanders	3-2		18	at Los Angeles	3-2
	20	at Pittsburgh	2-3		19	Tampa Bay	2-1
	22	at Detroit	0-3		21	Colorado	3-2*
	25	Anaheim	2-1*		23	at Colorado	5-2
	27	Columbus	3-1		24	at Winnipeg	4-3
	29	Nashville	4-1		26	Edmonton	1-4
Nov.	1	at Arizona	2-3		31	Chicago	3-1
	3	Calgary	2-3	**Feb.**	2	at Vancouver	4-1
	5	Pittsburgh	0-5		4	Arizona	2-3†
	8	at Washington	3-0		7	at Buffalo	4-5*
	10	at Florida	4-2		9	at Boston	3-6
	12	at Tampa Bay	3-1		11	at Philadelphia	1-2*
	15	at Carolina	0-1		12	at New Jersey	4-1
	17	at St. Louis	2-3		15	Florida	5-6*
	19	at Arizona	2-3*		18	at Arizona	4-1
	21	New Jersey	4-0		19	Boston	1-2*
	23	Chicago	2-1		25	at Vancouver	4-1
	25	NY Islanders	3-2		28	Toronto	3-1
	26	Anaheim	2-3	**Mar.**	2	Vancouver	3-1
	29	Arizona	2-1*		5	at Minnesota	1-3
	30	at Los Angeles	4-1		6	at Winnipeg	3-2
Dec.	2	Montreal	2-1		9	Washington	4-2
	7	Ottawa	2-4		11	Nashville	1-3
	9	at Anaheim	2-3		12	Dallas	5-1
	10	Carolina	4-3		14	Buffalo	4-1
	13	at Toronto	3-2†		16	St. Louis	1-4
	14	at Ottawa	4-3†		18	Anaheim	1-2
	16	at Montreal	4-2		20	at Dallas	0-1
	18	at Chicago	1-4		21	at Minnesota	2-3
	20	Calgary	4-1		24	at Dallas	1-6
	23	Edmonton	3-2*		25	at Nashville	2-7
	27	at Anaheim	3-2*		28	NY Rangers	5-4*
	30	Philadelphia	2-0		30	at Edmonton	2-3
	31	at Los Angeles	2-3		31	at Calgary	2-5
Jan.	3	Los Angeles	1-2*	**Apr.**	2	at Vancouver	3-1
	5	Minnesota	4-5		4	Vancouver	3-1
	7	Detroit	6-3		6	Edmonton	2-4
	10	at Edmonton	5-3		8	Calgary	3-1

* – Overtime † – Shootout

NHL Draft Selections 2017-2003

Name in bold denotes played in NHL.

2017 Pick		2013 Pick		2009 Pick		2005 Pick	
19	Joshua Norris	18	**Mirco Mueller**	43	William Wrenn	8	**Devin Setoguchi**
49	Mario Ferraro	49	Gabryel Boudreau	57	Taylor Doherty	35	**Marc-Edouard Vlasic**
102	Scott Reedy	117	Fredrik Bergvik	147	**Phil Varone**	112	**Alex Stalock**
159	Jacob McGrew	141	Michael Brodzinski	189	Marek Viedensky	140	Taylor Dakers
185	Sasha Chmelevski	151	Gage Ausmus	207	Dominik Bielke	149	**Derek Joslin**
212	Ivan Chekhovich	201	Jacob Jackson			162	P.J. Fenton
		207	Emil Galimov	**2008** Pick		183	Will Colbert
2016 Pick				62	Justin Daniels	193	Tony Lucia
60	Dylan Gambrell	**2012** Pick		92	Samuel Groulx		
111	Noah Gregor	17	**Tomas Hertl**	106	Harri Sateri	**2004** Pick	
150	Manuel Wiederer	55	**Chris Tierney**	146	Julien Demers	22	**Lukas Kaspar**
180	Mark Shoemaker	109	Christophe Lalancette	177	**Tommy Wingels**	94	**Thomas Greiss**
210	Joachim Blichfeld	138	**Daniel O'Regan**	186	**Jason Demers**	126	**Torrey Mitchell**
		168	Clifford Watson	194	Drew Daniels	129	Jason Churchill
2015 Pick		198	Joakim Ryan			153	**Steven Zalewski**
9	**Timo Meier**			**2007** Pick		201	**Mike Vernace**
31	Jeremy Roy	**2011** Pick		9	**Logan Couture**	225	David MacDonald
86	Mike Robinson	47	**Matt Nieto**	28	**Nicholas Petrecki**	234	Derek MacIntyre
106	Adam Helewka	89	Justin Sefton	83	Timo Pielmeier	288	Brian Mahoney-Wilson
130	Karlis Cukste	133	**Sean Kuraly**	91	Tyson Sexsmith	289	Christian Jensen
142	Rudolfs Balcers	166	Daniil Sobchenko	165	Patrik Zackrisson		
160	Adam Parsells	179	**Dylan DeMelo**	173	**Nick Bonino**	**2003** Pick	
190	Marcus Vela	194	Colin Blackwell	201	**Justin Braun**	6	**Milan Michalek**
193	Jake Kupsky			203	**Frazer McLaren**	16	**Steve Bernier**
		2010 Pick				43	Josh Hennessy
2014 Pick		28	**Charlie Coyle**	**2006** Pick		47	**Matt Carle**
27	**Nikolay Goldobin**	88	Max Gaede	16	**Ty Wishart**	139	Patrick Ehelechner
46	Julius Bergman	127	Cody Ferriero	36	**Jamie McGinn**	201	Jonathan Tremblay
53	Noah Rod	129	**Freddie Hamilton**	98	James Delory	205	**Joe Pavelski**
72	Alex Schoenborn	136	Isaac MacLeod	143	Ashton Rome	216	Kai Hospelt
81	Dylan Sadowy	163	Konrad Abeltshauser	202	**John McCarthy**	236	Alexander Hult
102	Alexis Vanier	188	Lee Moffie	203	Jay Barriball	267	Brian O'Hanley
149	Rourke Chartier	200	Chris Crane			276	Carter Lee
171	**Kevin Labanc**						

Doug Wilson
General Manager
Born: Ottawa, ON, July 5, 1957.

Since taking charge of the Sharks hockey department on May 13, 2003, Doug Wilson has guided the team to its most successful era since the franchise's inception, capturing the Presidents' Trophy (2009) and five Pacific Division titles (2004, 2008, 2009, 2010, 2011). Under Wilson, the Sharks advanced to the Western Conference Final in 2004, 2010 and 2011 and reached the Stanley Cup Final for the first time in franchise history in 2016.

Wilson has overall authority regarding all hockey-related operations. He oversees player personnel decisions, contract negotiation, scouting, player evaluation and draft day preparation. In his previous role as the team's director of pro development (1997 to 2003), the 16-year NHL veteran's responsibilities included evaluating talent at all professional and minor league levels and continuous assessment of the Sharks roster and reserve list. Working closely with the entire hockey department, Wilson has played a major role in creating a positive atmosphere in the Sharks dressing room.

Wilson draws on a vast amount of hockey knowledge. He was an integral member of the NHL Players' Association for four years (1993 to 1997) and is a past president of the NHLPA and served as a consultant to Team Canada, winners of four consecutive World Junior gold medals in the 1990s. His brother Murray was a member of four Stanley Cup championship teams with Montreal in the 1970s. With the Ottawa 67s in junior, Wilson played for Hall of Famer Hec Kilrea, junior hockey's winningest coach.

In 2004, Wilson was named to the NHL's Game Committee, a panel of players, coaches, executives and media responsible for examining all aspects of the game. This committee included Hall of Fame Coach Scotty Bowman, Pittsburgh's Mario Lemieux and St. Louis Blues President of Hockey Operations John Davidson, among others.

A first-round draft choice (sixth overall) by the Blackhawks in 1977 after a stellar junior career, Wilson played 14 seasons in Chicago and still ranks as that club's highest scoring defenseman with 225 goals and 554 assists for 779 points. He led all Blackhawks defensemen in scoring for 10 consecutive seasons (1980-81 through 1990-91) and captured the 1982 James Norris Memorial Trophy, as the League's top defenseman, when he tallied 39 goals and 85 points — still Blackhawks single-season records for goals and points for a defenseman.

Acquired by San Jose from Chicago just before the Sharks inaugural season (1991-92), Wilson brought instant credibility and respect to the young franchise. He played two seasons for the Sharks, serving as the franchise's first team captain (1991 to 1993). He played his 1,000th NHL game on Nov. 21, 1992 and was named San Jose's nominee (1992 and 1993) for the King Clancy Award for leadership and humanitarian contributions both on-and-off-the-ice.

Wilson announced his retirement as a member of the Sharks during training camp in 1993-94 after playing 1,024 regular-season and 95 playoff games. He played in seven NHL All-Star Games (six with Chicago and one with San Jose) and earned one First and two Second Team All-Star selections.

Club Directory

SAP Center at San Jose

San Jose Sharks
SAP Center at San Jose
525 West Santa Clara Street
San Jose, CA 95113
Phone **408/287-7070**
FAX 408/999-5797
www.sjsharks.com
twitter.com/sanjosesharks
facebook.com/sanjosesharks
Capacity: 17,562

Ownership Group
Hasso Plattner, Gary Valenzuela, Gordon Russell, Rudy Staedler
Sharks Sports & Entertainment Advisory Board
Hasso Plattner, Gary Valenzuela, Scott McNealy, Rouven Westphal
Hockey Operations
General Manager . . . . Doug Wilson
Vice President & Assistant General Manager . . . . Joe Will
Head Coach . . . . Peter DeBoer
Assistant Coaches . . . . Steve Spott, Rob Zettler, Dave Barr
Assistant Coach / Goaltending Coach . . . . Johan Hedberg
Director of Hockey Operations . . . . Doug Wilson Jr.
Development Coach . . . . Mike Ricci
Goaltending Development & Special Assignment Scout . . Evgeni Nabokov
Video Coach . . . . Dan Darrow
Director of Scouting . . . . Tim Burke
Supervisor of European Scouting . . . . Shin Larsson
Scouts . . . . Michael Chiasson, Gilles Cote, Pat Funk, Rob Grillo, Brian Gross, Bryan Marchment, Ryan Russell, Niklas Sundstrom, Mike Yandle
Pro Scout . . . . Dirk Graham, Jimmy Bonneau
Pro Scouting Analyst . . . . Charlie Townsend
Director, Hockey Admin. / Sr. Team Services Mgr. . . . Rosemary Tebaldi / Ryan Stenn
Head / Assistant Athletic Trainer . . . . Ray Tufts, ATC / Wes Howard, ATC
Strength & Conditioning Coordinator . . . . Mike Potenza
Assistant Strength & Conditioning Coach . . . . Kevin Neeld
Skating Consultant / Massage Therapist . . . . Luke Chilcott / Arnulfo Aguirre, CMT, ART
Equipment / Assistant Equipment Manager . . . . Mike Aldrich / Vinny Ferraiuolo, John Peters
Equipment Assistant & Equipment Transportation . . . Roy Sneesby
Cleaning Specialist . . . . Norma Hernandez
Team Physicians . . . . Dr. Mark Davies, Dr. Scott Crow & Dr. Anthony Abene
Team Internists/Family Practice . . . . Dr. AJ Uy, Dr. Chris Fowler, Dr. Harley Goldberg & Dr. Katherine Gray
ER Medicine . . . . Dr. Young Yoon & Dr. David Nix
Team Dentist / Chiropractic Consultant . . . . Don Goudy, D.D.S. / Mike McMurray, D.C.
Buiness & Building Operations
Chief Operating Officer . . . . John Tortora
Executive Vice President, Governmental Affairs . . . . . . Jim Goddard
Executive Vice President, Chief Sales & Marketing Officer . . Flavil Hampsten
Vice President, SSE Marketing & Digital . . . . Doug Bentz
Vice President, Sales & Service . . . . John Castro
Vice President, Finance . . . . Ken Caveney
Vice President, Media Relations & Broadcasting . . . . . Scott Emmert
Vice President, Sharks Ice & San Jose Barracuda . . . . . Jon Gustafson
Vice President, Booking & Events . . . . Steve Kirsner
Vice President, Building Operations . . . . Rich Sotelo
Vice President, Business Intelligence . . . . Neda Tabatabaie
Executive Assistants . . . . Rebeca Davichick, Kelley Hutton, Mary Grace Miller
Ticket Sales
Director of Special Event Sales . . . . Mike Nieves
Director, Ticket Sales / Client Development & Ticket Ops. . Brian Towers / Jamie Weinstein
Ticket Operations / Client Development . . . . Matt Gulino / Jake Carlson
Group Sales / Sr. Account Sales / Inside Sales Manager . Kyle Brant / Eric Manuta / Frank Batres-Landaeta
Business Intelligence
Business Intelligence Coordinator . . . . Darion Afshar-Gomez
Corporate Partnerships
Dir., Corp. Partnership Sales & Service / Bus. Development . . Jennifer Birmingham / Jon Carpenter
Senior Service Manager, Corporate Partnerships . . . . . Jennifer De Carlo
Suite Sales & Service
Director of Suite Sales & Service . . . . Bruce Ross
Executive Suite & Premium Sales / Suites Services Mgr. . . Ted Chuba / Julie Kennedy
Event Presentation
Director of Event Presentation . . . . Steve Maroni
Event Presentation Manager . . . . Tina Divilio
Motion Graphics Designer / Editor/Videographer . . . . . Jamie McNeill / Taylor Hone
Marketing & Digital Media
Director of Marketing . . . . Casey Lepannen
Marketing / CRM Marketing Manager . . . . Courtney Jankovich / Stacy McGranor
Graphic Designers . . . . Caitlynn Steinberg, Laurence Roman
Director of Content Production . . . . Dustin Lamendola
Digital Media Production Coordinators . . . . Nathan Hone, Austin Webb
Digital Media Mgr. / Digital Media Coordinators . . Patrick Hooper / Ann Frazier, Nicole Grazioli, Casey Krygier
Marketing / Arena Marketing Coordinator . . . . Amanda Behrendt / Megan Ebeck
Media Relations
Media Relations Manager / Coordinator . . . . Ben Guerrero / Nicolas Carrillo
Broadcast Operations and Media Relations Manager . . . Joanna Schimmel
Public Relations & Fan development / Sharls Foundation
Director of Public Relations, Business Operations . . . . . . Jim Sparaco
Mascot Operations Manager . . . . Tim Patnode
Fan Development Coordinators . . . . Amber Cottle, Stephanie Dubin
Sharks Foundation Dir. / Coordinators . . . . . . Heather Hooper / Jenne Johnson, Missy Zielinski, Lisa Vestal
Broadcasting
Television Play-By-Play Broadcaster / Color Analyst . . . . . Randy Hahn / Jamie Baker
Radio Play-By-Play Broadcaster / Color Analysts . . . . . . Dan Rusanowsky / Bret Hedican, David Maley
Building Operations
Director of Booking & Events / Building Services . . . . . James Hamnett / Monte Chavez
Director of Ticket Operations / Guest Services . . . . Patrick Doherty / Mike McCarroll
Ticket Operations Manager . . . . Darryl Washington
Facilities Technical Director / Chief Engineer . . . . Jason Lemiere / Eric Gold
Building Services Managers . . . . Bruce Tharaldson, Ray Romero
Ushering & Emergency Medical Manager . . . . Ryan Osenton
Fianance
Controller . . . . Stephanie Reitz
Information Technology
Director of Information Technologies . . . . Allison Aiello
IT Systems Manager / Systems Support Specialist . . . . . Cara Browning / Tony Harrell
Human Resources
Business Partners . . . . Karen Aasen, Jeannine Young
Legal
Counsel . . . . Andrew Koehler
Miscellaneous
Television Station / Radio Network Flagship . . . . NBC Sports California / 98.5/102.1 FM KFOX (KUFX)
Team Photographers . . . . Don Smith, Rocky Widner
P.A. Announcer / Mascot . . . . Danny Miller / S.J. Sharkie

Tampa Bay Lightning

2016-17 Results: 42w-30L-7otl-3sol 94pts
5th, Atlantic Division • 10th, Eastern Conference

Year-by-Year Record

Season	GP	Home W	L	T	OL	Road W	L	T	OL	Overall W	L	T	OL	GF	GA	Pts.	Div. Fin.	Conf. Fin.	Playoff Result
2016-17	82	23	14	....	4	19	16	....	6	42	30	....	10	234	227	94	5th, Atl.	10th, East	– out of playoffs –
2015-16	82	25	13	....	3	21	18	....	2	46	31	....	5	227	201	97	2nd, Atl.	6th, East	Lost Conf. Final
2014-15	82	32	8	....	1	18	16	....	7	50	24	....	8	262	211	108	2nd, Atl.	3rd, East	Lost Final
2013-14	82	25	10	....	6	21	17	....	3	46	27	....	9	240	215	101	2nd, Atl.	3rd, East	Lost First Round
2012-13	48	12	10	....	2	6	16	....	2	18	26	....	4	148	150	40	4th, SE	14th, East	– out of playoffs –
2011-12	82	25	14	....	2	13	22	....	6	38	36	....	8	235	281	84	3rd, SE	10th, East	– out of playoffs –
2010-11	82	25	11	....	5	21	14	....	6	46	25	....	11	247	240	103	2nd, SE	5th, East	Lost Conf. Final
2009-10	82	21	14	....	6	13	22	....	6	34	36	....	12	217	260	80	4th, SE	12th, East	– out of playoffs –
2008-09	82	12	18	....	11	12	22	....	7	24	40	....	18	210	279	66	5th, SE	14th, East	– out of playoffs –
2007-08	82	20	18	....	3	11	24	....	6	31	42	....	9	223	267	71	5th, SE	15th, East	– out of playoffs –
2006-07	82	22	18	....	1	22	15	....	4	44	33	....	5	253	261	93	2nd, SE	7th, East	Lost Conf. Quarter-Final
2005-06	82	25	14	....	2	18	19	....	4	43	33	....	6	252	260	92	2nd, SE	8th, East	Lost Conf. Quarter-Final
2004-05	....	....	....	....	....	....	....	....	....	....	....	....	....	....	....	....			
2003-04	82	24	10	4	3	22	12	4	3	46	22	8	6	245	192	106	1st, SE	1st, East	Won Stanley Cup
2002-03	82	22	9	7	3	14	16	9	2	36	25	16	5	219	210	93	1st, SE	3rd, East	Lost Conf. Semi-Final
2001-02	82	16	17	5	3	11	23	6	1	27	40	11	4	178	219	69	3rd, SE	13th, East	– out of playoffs –
2000-01	82	17	19	3	2	7	28	3	3	24	47	6	5	201	280	59	5th, SE	14th, East	– out of playoffs –
1999-2000	82	13	20	4	4	6	27	5	3	19	47	9	7	204	310	54	5th, SE	14th, East	– out of playoffs –
1998-99	82	12	25	4	....	7	29	5	....	19	54	9	....	179	292	47	4th, SE	14th, East	– out of playoffs –
1997-98	82	11	23	7	....	6	32	3	....	17	55	10	....	151	269	44	7th, Atl.	13th, East	– out of playoffs –
1996-97	82	15	18	8	....	17	22	2	....	32	40	10	....	217	247	74	4th, Atl.	11th, East	– out of playoffs –
1995-96	82	22	14	5	....	16	18	7	....	38	32	12	....	238	248	88	5th, Atl.	8th, East	Lost Conf. Quarter-Final
1994-95	48	10	14	0	....	7	14	3	....	17	28	3	....	120	144	37	6th, Atl.	12th, East	– out of playoffs –
1993-94	84	14	22	6	....	16	21	5	....	30	43	11	....	224	251	71	7th, Atl.	12th, East	– out of playoffs –
1992-93	84	12	27	3	....	11	27	4	....	23	54	7	....	245	332	53	6th, Norris		– out of playoffs –

2017-18 Schedule

Oct.	Fri.	6	Florida
	Sat.	7	at Florida
	Mon.	9	Washington
	Thu.	12	Pittsburgh
	Sat.	14	St. Louis
	Mon.	16	at Detroit
	Tue.	17	at New Jersey
	Thu.	19	at Columbus
	Sat.	21	Pittsburgh
	Tue.	24	at Carolina
	Thu.	26	Detroit
	Sat.	28	Anaheim
	Mon.	30	at Florida
Nov.	Thu.	2	NY Rangers
	Sat.	4	Columbus
	Wed.	8	at San Jose
	Thu.	9	at Los Angeles
	Sun.	12	at Anaheim*
	Thu.	16	Dallas
	Sat.	18	NY Islanders
	Wed.	22	Chicago
	Fri.	24	at Washington*
	Sat.	25	at Pittsburgh
	Tue.	28	at Buffalo
	Wed.	29	at Boston
Dec.	Sat.	2	San Jose
	Tue.	5	NY Islanders
	Thu.	7	Colorado
	Sat.	9	Winnipeg
	Tue.	12	at St. Louis*
	Thu.	14	at Arizona
	Sat.	16	at Colorado
	Tue.	19	at Vegas
	Thu.	21	Ottawa
	Sat.	23	Minnesota
	Thu.	28	Montreal
	Fri.	29	Philadelphia
	Sun.	31	at Columbus
Jan.	Tue.	2	at Toronto
	Thu.	4	at Montreal
	Sat.	6	at Ottawa
	Sun.	7	at Detroit
	Tue.	9	Carolina
	Thu.	11	Calgary
	Thu.	18	Vegas
	Sat.	20	at Minnesota
	Mon.	22	at Chicago
	Tue.	23	at Nashville
	Thu.	25	at Philadelphia
	Tue.	30	at Winnipeg
Feb.	Thu.	1	at Calgary
	Sat.	3	at Vancouver
	Mon.	5	at Edmonton
	Thu.	8	Vancouver
	Sat.	10	Los Angeles
	Mon.	12	at Toronto
	Tue.	13	at Buffalo
	Thu.	15	Detroit
	Sat.	17	New Jersey
	Tue.	20	at Washington
	Thu.	22	at Ottawa
	Sat.	24	at Montreal
	Mon.	26	Toronto
	Wed.	28	Buffalo
Mar.	Thu.	1	at Dallas
	Sat.	3	Philadelphia*
	Tue.	6	Florida
	Thu.	8	NY Rangers
	Sat.	10	Montreal*
	Tue.	13	Ottawa
	Sat.	17	Boston
	Sun.	18	Edmonton*
	Tue.	20	Toronto
	Thu.	22	at NY Islanders
	Sat.	24	at New Jersey
	Mon.	26	Arizona
	Thu.	29	at Boston
	Fri.	30	at NY Rangers
Apr.	Sun.	1	Nashville
	Tue.	3	Boston
	Fri.	6	Buffalo
	Sat.	7	at Carolina

* Denotes afternoon game.

Nikita Kucherov established himself as a top star in 2016-17, tying for second in the NHL with 40 goals and finishing fifth in the league with 85 points.

ATLANTIC DIVISION
26th NHL Season
Franchise date: December 16, 1991

2017-18 Player Personnel

FORWARDS	HT	WT	*Age	Birthplace	S	2016-17 Club
BROWN, J.T.	5-10	175	27	High Point, NC	R	Tampa Bay
CALLAHAN, Ryan	5-10	186	32	Rochester, NY	R	Tampa Bay
CONACHER, Cory	5-8	180	27	Burlington, ON	L	Tampa Bay-Syracuse
CONDRA, Erik	5-11	183	31	Trenton, MI	R	Tampa Bay-Syracuse
JOHNSON, Tyler	5-8	185	27	Spokane, WA	R	Tampa Bay
KILLORN, Alex	6-2	198	28	Halifax, NS	L	Tampa Bay
KUCHEROV, Nikita	5-11	178	24	Maikop, Russia	L	Tampa Bay
KUNITZ, Chris	6-0	195	38	Regina, SK	L	Pittsburgh
NAMESTNIKOV, Vladislav	5-11	180	24	Zhukovsky, Russia	L	Tampa Bay
PALAT, Ondrej	6-0	188	26	Frydek-Mistek, Czech.	L	Tampa Bay
PAQUETTE, Cedric	6-1	199	24	Gaspe, QC	L	Tampa Bay
STAMKOS, Steven	6-1	194	27	Markham, ON	R	Tampa Bay

DEFENSEMEN						
COBURN, Braydon	6-5	226	32	Calgary, AB	L	Tampa Bay
DOTCHIN, Jake	6-2	207	23	Cambridge, ON	R	Tampa Bay-Syracuse
GIRARDI, Dan	6-1	208	33	Welland, ON	R	NY Rangers
HEDMAN, Victor	6-6	223	26	Ornskoldsvik, Sweden	L	Tampa Bay
KOEKKOEK, Slater	6-2	198	23	Winchester, ON	L	Tampa Bay-Syracuse
SERGACHEV, Mikhail	6-3	223	19	Nizhnekamsk, Russia	L	Montreal-Windsor
STRALMAN, Anton	5-11	190	31	Tibro, Sweden	R	Tampa Bay
SUSTR, Andrej	6-7	220	26	Plzen, Czech.	R	Tampa Bay

GOALTENDERS	HT	WT	*Age	Birthplace	C	2016-17 Club
BUDAJ, Peter	6-1	192	35	Banska Bystrica, Czech.	L	Los Angeles-Tampa Bay
LEIGHTON, Michael	6-3	186	36	Petrolia, ON	L	Carolina-Charlotte
VASILEVSKIY, Andrei	6-3	207	23	Tyumen, Russia	L	Tampa Bay

* – Age at start of 2017-18 season

2016-17 Scoring

* – rookie

Regular Season

Pos	#	Player	Team	GP	G	A	Pts	TOI	+/-	PIM	PP	SH	GW	S	S%
R	86	Nikita Kucherov	T.B.	74	40	45	85	19:26	13	38	17	0	7	246	16.3
D	77	Victor Hedman	T.B.	79	16	56	72	24:30	3	47	4	0	5	166	9.6
L	27	Jonathan Drouin	T.B.	73	21	32	53	17:42	-13	16	9	0	6	183	11.5
L	18	Ondrej Palat	T.B.	75	17	35	52	19:07	8	39	5	0	3	162	10.5
C	9	Tyler Johnson	T.B.	66	19	26	45	18:49	-5	28	6	0	3	130	14.6
C	21	* Brayden Point	T.B.	68	18	22	40	17:07	4	14	5	0	2	122	14.8
C	17	Alex Killorn	T.B.	81	19	17	36	18:00	-9	66	4	1	4	176	10.8
C	90	Vladislav Namestnikov	T.B.	74	10	18	28	14:47	-4	31	3	0	0	114	8.8
D	6	Anton Stralman	T.B.	73	5	17	22	22:54	1	20	1	0	0	130	3.8
C	91	Steven Stamkos	T.B.	17	9	11	20	17:52	3	14	3	0	1	58	15.5
D	62	Andrej Sustr	T.B.	80	3	11	14	17:35	-10	43	0	0	1	93	3.2
D	55	Braydon Coburn	T.B.	80	5	7	12	16:44	-1	50	0	1	0	102	4.9
D	59	* Jake Dotchin	T.B.	35	0	11	11	18:25	10	35	0	0	0	50	0.0
C	13	Cedric Paquette	T.B.	58	4	6	10	11:31	-6	80	0	0	0	68	5.9
D	5	Jason Garrison	T.B.	70	1	8	9	18:33	-8	14	0	0	0	96	1.0
C	65	* Yanni Gourde	T.B.	20	6	2	8	15:22	-1	8	0	1	1	30	20.0
C	33	* Greg McKegg	FLA	31	3	3	6	10:12	-5	11	0	0	0	28	10.7
			T.B.	15	0	1	1	9:16	2	11	0	0	0	8	0.0
			Total	46	3	4	7	9:54	-3	22	0	0	0	36	8.3
R	23	J.T. Brown	T.B.	64	3	3	6	10:22	-7	73	0	1	1	67	4.5
R	24	Ryan Callahan	T.B.	18	2	2	4	14:08	-4	23	0	0	1	22	9.1
C	61	* Gabriel Dumont	T.B.	39	2	2	4	9:40	1	29	0	0	0	34	5.9
C	19	Cory Conacher	T.B.	11	1	3	4	11:33	0	4	1	0	0	16	6.3
D	29	* Slater Koekkoek	T.B.	29	0	4	4	12:59	-4	8	0	0	0	27	0.0
D	28	* Luke Witkowski	T.B.	34	0	4	4	9:52	-1	39	0	0	0	24	0.0
L	73	* Adam Erne	T.B.	26	3	0	3	11:48	-9	11	0	0	0	40	7.5
L	15	Michael Bournival	T.B.	19	2	1	3	10:08	-3	2	0	0	0	25	8.0
R	92	* Joel Vermin	T.B.	18	0	3	3	10:55	2	4	0	0	0	12	0.0
C	63	* Matthew Peca	T.B.	10	1	1	2	11:26	-3	2	0	0	0	9	11.1
C	38	* Tanner Richard	T.B.	3	0	0	0	12:42	-2	2	0	0	0	0	0.0
C	78	Byron Froese	TOR	2	0	0	0	8:00	0	1	0	0	0	2	0.0
			T.B.	4	0	0	0	11:49	-3	4	0	0	0	4	0.0
			Total	6	0	0	0	10:33	-3	5	0	0	0	6	0.0
R	22	Erik Condra	T.B.	13	0	0	0	9:38	-4	0	0	0	0	8	0.0

Goaltending

No.	Goaltender	GPI	Mins	Avg	W	L	OT	EN	SO	GA	SA	Sv%	G	A	PIM
50	* Kristers Gudlevskis	1	11	0.00	0	0	0	0	0	0	3	1.000	0	0	0
31	Ben Bishop	32	1813	2.55	16	12	3	2	1	77	870	.911	0	0	8
88	Andrei Vasilevski	50	2831	2.61	23	17	7	8	2	123	1480	.917	0	2	2
31	Peter Budaj	7	279	2.80	3	1	0	1	0	13	128	.898	0	0	0
	Totals	**82**	**4988**	**2.69**	**42**	**30**	**10**	**11**	**3**	**224**	**2492**	**.910**			

Victor Hedman led all NHL defensemen with 56 assists in 2016-17, which placed him fourth in the league overall.

Coaching History

Terry Crisp, 1992-93 to 1996-97; Terry Crisp, Rick Paterson and Jacques Demers, 1997-98; Jacques Demers, 1998-99; Steve Ludzik, 1999-2000; Steve Ludzik and John Tortorella, 2000-01; John Tortorella, 2001-02 to 2007-08; Barry Melrose and Rick Tocchet, 2008-09; Rick Tocchet, 2009-10; Guy Boucher, 2010-11, 2011-12; Guy Boucher and Jon Cooper, 2012-13; Jon Cooper, 2013-14 to date.

Jon Cooper

Head Coach

Born: Prince George, BC, August 23, 1967.

The Tampa Bay Lightning named Jon Cooper as the eighth head coach in franchise history on March 25, 2013. In his first full season with the club in 2013-14, Cooper led the Lightning back to the playoffs after a two-year absence. The team tied a club record with 46 wins and he finished third in voting for the Jack Adams Award as coach of the year. In 2014-15, the Lightning set club records with 50 wins and 108 points and reached the Stanley Cup Final.

Cooper joined the Lightning after having spent the previous three seasons behind the bench of Tampa Bay's top minor league affiliate, the Norfolk Admirals, from 2010 to 2012 and the Syracuse Crunch in 2012-13. He compiled a 133-62-26 regular-season record (.661) in 221 games in the American Hockey League.

Cooper was awarded the Louis A.R. Pieri Memorial Award as the AHL's top coach in 2011-12 after guiding the Admirals to a franchise-record 55 wins and 113 points en route to the team's first Calder Cup Championship. Along the way, Cooper and his team set a North American professional hockey record, winning a remarkable 28 consecutive games. Norfolk also earned the Macgregor Kilpatrick Trophy as the AHL's regular-season points champion, while capturing the league's East Division title. Cooper led Norfolk to a 94-44-18 record in the regular season and a 17-7 mark in the playoffs during two seasons behind the bench. In 2012-13, he led the Syracuse Crunch to a 39-18-8 record, the best in the AHL at the time, despite a number of key players being recalled to the Lightning before he himself was summoned to Tampa Bay.

Before joining the AHL ranks, Cooper also found success in the United States Hockey League with the Green Bay Gamblers, posting an 84-27-9 record in two seasons. Under Cooper's guidance the Gamblers posted back-to-back seasons with the best record in the USHL and won the 2010 Clark Cup. In his first season in 2008-09, Green Bay saw a 50-point improvement from the previous year, setting a USHL record for largest single-season improvement. He was rewarded with the 2009 and 2010 USHL General Manager of the Year Awards, as well as being named the 2010 USHL Coach of the Year.

Cooper played high school hockey at Notre Dame in Wilcox, Saskatchewan. He then moved on to Hofstra University in the NCAA, where he played four seasons of Division I lacrosse and spent one season on Hofstra's hockey team. He then went on to earn a law degree from Thomas M. Cooley Law School in Lansing, Michigan, eventually closing his practice in 2003 to pursue a career in coaching.

Coaching Record

Season	Team	League	Regular Season				Playoffs			
			GC	W	L	O/T	GC	W	L	T
2003-04	Texarkana	NAHL	56	30	24	2	4	0	4	0
2004-05	Texarkana	NAHL	56	36	15	5	9	4	5	0
2005-06	Texarkana	NAHL	58	42	12	4	8	3	5	0
2006-07	St. Louis	NAHL	62	43	14	5	12	9	3	0
2007-08	St. Louis	NAHL	58	47	9	2	11	9	1	1
2008-09	Green Bay	USHL	60	39	17	4	7	4	3	....
2009-10	Green Bay	USHL	60	45	10	5	12	9	3	....
2010-11	Norfolk	AHL	80	39	26	15	6	2	4	....
2011-12	Norfolk	AHL	76	55	18	3	18	15	3	....
2012-13	Syracuse	AHL	65	39	18	8	....	....	....	....
2012-13*	Tampa Bay	NHL	15	4	8	3	....	....	....	....
2013-14	Tampa Bay	NHL	82	46	27	9	4	0	4	
2014-15	Tampa Bay	NHL	82	50	24	8	26	14	12	
2015-16	Tampa Bay	NHL	82	46	31	5	17	11	6	
2016-17	Tampa Bay	NHL	82	42	30	10				
	NHL Totals		**343**	**188**	**120**	**35**	**47**	**25**	**22**	

* Hired by Tampa Bay on March 25, 2013 but did not appear behind the bench until March 29. Assistant coaches Dan Lacroix, Martin Raymond, and Steve Thomas worked a 3-2 loss at Winnipeg on March 24. Lacroix and Thomas worked a 2-1 win vs. Buffalo on March 26.

Club Records

Team

(Figures in brackets for season records are games played; records for fewest points, wins, ties, losses, goals, goals against are for 70 or more games)

Most Points 108 2014-15 (82)
Most Wins 50 2014-15 (82)
Most Ties 16 2002-03 (82)
Most Losses 55 1997-98 (82)
Most Goals 262 2014-15 (82)
Most Goals Against 332 1992-93 (84)
Fewest Points 44 1997-98 (82)
Fewest Wins 17 1997-98 (82)
Fewest Ties 6 2000-01 (82)
Fewest Losses 22 2003-04 (82)
Fewest Goals 151 1997-98 (82)
Fewest Goals Against 192 2003-04 (82)

Longest Winning Streak
Overall . . . . 9 Feb. 18-Mar. 5/16
Home . . . . 10 Dec. 11/14-Jan. 31/15
Away . . . . 7 Jan. 7-Feb. 1/07

Longest Team Point Streak
Overall . . . . 18 Feb. 5-Mar. 12/04
(13W, 1OTW, 2T, 2OTL)
Home . . . . 13 Jan. 3-Mar. 12/04
(10W, 1OTW, 1T, 1OTL)
Away . . . . 10 Feb. 5-Mar. 10/04
(7W, 1T, 2OTL)

Longest Losing Streak
Overall . . . . 13 Jan. 3-Feb. 2/98
Home . . . . 10 Jan. 3-Feb. 26/98
Away . . . . 11 Oct. 24-Dec. 10/97

Longest Winless Streak
Overall . . . . 16 Oct. 10-Nov. 17/97
(15L, 1T),
Jan. 2-Feb. 5/98
(14L, 2T)
Home . . . . 11 Jan. 2-Feb. 26/98
(10L, 1T)
Away . . . . 17 Dec. 2/99-Feb. 19/00
(12L, 2OTL, 3T)

Most Shutouts, Season 9 2001-02 (82)
Most PIM, Season 1,823 1997-98 (82)
Most Goals, Game . . . . 9 Nov. 8/03
(Pit. 0 at T.B. 9)

Individual

Most Seasons . . . . 14 Vincent Lecavalier
Most Games, Career . . . . . 1,037 Vincent Lecavalier
Most Goals, Career . . . . 383 Vincent Lecavalier
Most Assists, Career . . . . 588 Martin St. Louis
Most Points, Career . . . . 953 Martin St. Louis
(365G, 588A)
Most PIM, Career . . . . 828 Chris Gratton
Most Shutouts, Career . . . . . . 17 Ben Bishop

Longest Consecutive
Games Streak . . . . 499 Martin St. Louis
(Nov. 17/05-Dec. 6/11)
Most Goals, Season . . . . 60 Steven Stamkos
(2011-12)

Most Assists, Season . . . . 68 Brad Richards
(2005-06),
Martin St. Louis
(2010-11)
Most Points, Season . . . . 108 Vincent Lecavalier
(2006-07; 52G, 56A)
Most PIM, Season . . . . 265 Zenon Konopka
(2009-10)
Most Points, Defenseman,
Season . . . . 72 Victor Hedman
(2016-17; 16G, 56A)
Most Points, Center,
Season . . . . 108 Vincent Lecavalier
(2006-07; 52G, 56A)
Most Points, Right Wing,
Season . . . . 102 Martin St. Louis
(2006-07; 43G, 59A)
Most Points, Left Wing,
Season . . . . 80 Cory Stillman
(2003-04; 25G, 55A)
Vinny Prospal
(2005-06; 25G, 55A)
Most Points, Rookie,
Season . . . . 62 Brad Richards
(2000-01; 21G, 41A)
Most Shutouts, Season . . . . 7 Nikolai Khabibulin
(2001-02)
Most Goals, Game . . . . 4 Chris Kontos (Oct. 7/92),
Martin St. Louis (Jan. 18/14)
Most Assists, Game . . . . 5 Mark Recchi
(Mar. 1/09),
Martin St. Louis
(Nov. 18/10)
Most Points, Game . . . . 6 Doug Crossman
(Nov. 7/92; 3G, 3A)

Captains' History

No captain, 1992-93 to 1994-95; Paul Ysebaert, 1995-96, 1996-97; Paul Ysebaert and Mikael Renberg, 1997-98; Rob Zamuner, 1998-99; Bill Houlder, Chris Gratton and Vincent Lecavalier, 1999-2000; Vincent Lecavalier, 2000-01; no captain, 2001-02; Dave Andreychuk, 2002-03 to 2004-05; Dave Andreychuk and no captain, 2005-06; Tim Taylor, 2006-07, 2007-08; Vincent Lecavalier, 2008-09 to 2012-13; Martin St. Louis and Steven Stamkos, 2013-14; Steven Stamkos, 2014-15 to date.

All-time Record vs. Other Clubs

Regular Season

	Total							At Home							On Road						
	GP	W	L	T	OL	GF	GA	PTS	GP	W	L	T	OL	GF	GA	PTS	GP	W	L	T	OL	GF	GA	PTS
Anaheim	32	15	11	1	5	80	80	36	16	9	6	0	1	42	37	19	16	6	5	1	4	38	43	17
Arizona	37	20	16	0	1	116	103	41	17	9	7	0	1	62	54	19	20	11	9	0	0	54	49	22
Boston	94	25	51	9	9	242	315	68	46	18	20	3	5	132	138	44	48	7	31	6	4	110	177	24
Buffalo	94	37	45	5	7	244	278	86	48	17	24	3	4	114	142	41	46	20	21	2	3	130	136	45
Calgary	34	18	14	1	1	103	107	38	17	9	7	1	0	55	56	19	17	9	7	0	1	48	51	19
Carolina	118	57	45	10	6	354	334	130	58	35	19	3	1	179	158	74	60	22	26	7	5	175	176	56
Chicago	40	18	14	5	3	106	114	44	19	11	4	3	1	58	52	26	21	7	10	2	2	48	62	18
Colorado	41	16	18	3	4	104	130	39	20	11	6	1	2	55	55	25	21	5	12	2	2	49	75	14
Columbus	25	14	10	1	0	62	55	29	13	9	4	0	0	34	26	18	12	5	6	1	0	28	29	11
Dallas	38	12	20	3	3	99	122	30	20	5	12	2	1	46	62	13	18	7	8	1	2	53	60	17
Detroit	50	19	28	2	1	134	172	41	26	13	11	1	1	89	93	28	24	6	17	1	0	45	79	13
Edmonton	35	14	16	2	3	97	101	33	18	9	6	2	1	57	52	21	17	5	10	0	2	40	49	12
Florida	126	52	51	10	13	339	387	127	64	31	21	6	6	181	188	74	62	21	30	4	7	158	199	53
Los Angeles	35	20	11	2	2	92	74	44	17	9	6	0	2	42	35	20	18	11	5	2	0	50	39	24
Minnesota	22	8	11	1	2	48	60	19	11	6	3	1	1	27	25	14	11	2	8	0	1	21	35	5
Montreal	93	41	37	6	9	232	252	97	47	20	15	5	7	120	124	52	46	21	22	1	2	112	128	45
Nashville	24	10	10	2	2	67	71	24	11	5	4	2	0	33	32	12	13	5	6	0	2	34	39	12
New Jersey	94	32	48	7	7	219	298	78	46	18	20	5	3	112	134	44	48	14	28	2	4	107	164	34
NY Islanders	94	46	39	3	6	262	271	101	47	26	15	2	4	139	130	58	47	20	24	1	2	123	141	43
NY Rangers	95	43	42	5	5	277	298	96	46	22	18	3	3	142	137	50	49	21	24	2	2	135	161	46
Ottawa	94	38	46	2	8	251	319	86	48	22	21	2	3	146	159	49	46	16	25	0	5	105	160	37
Philadelphia	94	40	43	8	3	266	281	91	48	24	21	1	2	148	136	51	46	16	22	7	1	118	145	40
Pittsburgh	89	36	45	5	3	251	294	80	44	23	19	2	0	137	121	48	45	13	26	3	3	114	173	32
St. Louis	39	12	21	3	3	106	135	30	21	9	8	3	1	64	68	22	18	3	13	0	2	42	67	8
San Jose	38	17	19	2	0	106	125	36	20	9	10	1	0	53	59	19	18	8	9	1	0	53	66	17
Toronto	89	35	45	2	7	232	287	79	44	18	22	1	3	105	129	40	45	17	23	1	4	127	158	39
Vancouver	32	11	16	2	3	89	118	27	16	7	7	1	1	36	59	16	16	4	9	2	1	37	61	11
Washington	122	39	69	6	8	315	421	92	61	24	33	2	2	160	191	52	61	15	36	4	6	155	230	40
Winnipeg	86	45	29	4	8	276	244	102	43	27	11	1	4	152	108	59	43	18	18	3	4	124	136	43
Totals	**1904**	**790**	**870**	**112**	**132**	**5169**	**5846**	**1824**	**952**	**455**	**380**	**56**	**61**	**2736**	**2758**	**1027**	**952**	**335**	**490**	**56**	**71**	**2433**	**3088**	**797**

Playoffs

	Series	W	L	GP	W	L	T	GF	GA	Last Mtg.	Rnd.	Result
Boston	1	0	1	7	3	4	0	21	21	2011	CF	L 3-4
Calgary	1	1	0	7	4	3	0	13	14	2004	F	W 4-3
Chicago	1	0	1	6	2	4	0	10	13	2015	F	L 2-4
Detroit	2	2	0	8	8	4	0	29	23	2016	FR	W 4-1
Montreal	3	2	1	14	8	6	0	41	34	2015	SR	W 4-2
New Jersey	2	0	2	11	3	8	0	22	33	2007	CQF	L 2-4
NY Islanders	2	2	0	10	8	2	0	30	16	2016	SR	W 4-1
NY Rangers	1	1	0	7	4	3	0	21	21	2015	CF	W 4-3
Ottawa	1	0	1	5	1	4	0	13	23	2006	CQF	L 1-4
Philadelphia	2	1	1	13	7	6	0	34	45	2004	CF	W 4-3
Pittsburgh	2	1	1	14	7	7	0	40	35	2016	CF	L 3-4
Washington	2	2	0	10	8	2	0	30	25	2011	CSF	W 4-0
Totals	**20**	**12**	**8**	**116**	**62**	**54**	**0**	**304**	**303**			

Carolina totals include Hartford, 1992-93 to 1996-97.
Dallas totals include Minnesota North Stars, 1992-93.
Winnipeg totals include Atlanta Thrashers, 1999-2000 to 2010-11.
Colorado totals include Quebec, 1992-93 to 1994-95.
Phoenix totals include Winnipeg, 1992-93 to 1995-96.

Playoff Results 2017-2013

Year	Round	Opponent	Result	GF	GA
2016	CF	Pittsburgh	L 3-4	18	21
	SR	NY Islanders	W 4-1	18	11
	FR	Detroit	W 4-1	12	8
2015	F	Chicago	L 2-4	10	13
	CF	NY Rangers	W 4-3	21	21
	SR	Montreal	W 4-2	17	13
	FR	Detroit	W 4-3	17	15
2014	FR	Montreal	L 0-4	10	16

Abbreviations: Round: F – Final;
CF – conference final; **CSF** – conference semi-final;
SR – second round; **CQF** – conference quarter-final;
FR – first round.

NHL Draft Selections 2017-2003

Name in bold denotes played in NHL.

2017

Pick	
14	Cal Foote
48	Alexander Volkov
76	Alexei Lipanov
169	Nicklaus Perbix
180	Cole Guttman
200	Samuel Walker

2016

Pick	
27	Brett Howden
37	Libor Hajek
44	Boris Katchouk
58	Taylor Raddysh
88	Connor Ingram
118	Ross Colton
148	Chris Paquette
178	Oleg Sosunov
206	Otto Somppi
208	Ryan Lohin

2015

Pick	
33	Mitchell Stephens
44	Matthew Spencer
64	Dennis Yan
72	Anthony Cirelli
118	Jonne Tammela
120	Mathieu Joseph
150	Ryan Zuhlsdorf
153	Kristian Oldham
180	Boko Imama

2014

Pick	
19	**Anthony DeAngelo**
35	Dominik Masin
57	Johnathan MacLeod
79	**Brayden Point**
119	Ben Thomas
170	Cristiano DiGiacinto
185	Cameron Darcy

2013

Pick	
3	**Jonathan Drouin**
33	**Adam Erne**
124	**Kristers Gudlevskis**
154	Henri Ikonen
184	Saku Salminen
186	**Joel Vermin**

2012

Pick	
10	**Slater Koekkoek**
19	**Andrei Vasilevskiy**
40	Dylan Blujus
53	Brian Hart
71	**Tanner Richard**
101	**Cedric Paquette**
161	**Jake Dotchin**
202	Nikita Gusev

2011

Pick	
27	**Vladislav Namestnikov**
58	**Nikita Kucherov**
148	**Nikita Nesterov**
178	Adam Wilcox
201	**Matthew Peca**
208	**Ondrej Palat**

2010

Pick	
6	**Brett Connolly**
63	Brock Beukeboom
66	**Radko Gudas**
72	Adam Janosik
96	Geoffrey Schemitsch
118	Jimmy Mullin
156	Brendan O'Donnell
186	Teigan Zahn

2009

Pick	
2	**Victor Hedman**
29	**Carter Ashton**
52	**Richard Panik**
93	Alex Hutchings
148	Michael Zador
162	Jaroslav Janus
183	Kirill Gotovets

2008

Pick	
1	**Steven Stamkos**
117	**James Wright**
122	**Dustin Tokarski**
147	Kyle DeCoste
152	**Mark Barberio**
160	**Luke Witkowski**
182	Matias Sointu
203	David Carle

2007

Pick	
47	**Dana Tyrell**
75	Luca Cunti
77	**Alex Killorn**
107	Mitch Fadden
150	Matt Marshall
167	**Johan Harju**
183	Torrie Jung
197	Michael Ward
210	Justin Courtnall

2006

Pick	
15	**Riku Helenius**
78	**Kevin Quick**
168	Dane Crowley
198	Denis Kazionov

2005

Pick	
30	**Vladimir Mihalik**
73	**Radek Smolenak**
89	Chris Lawrence
92	Marek Bartanus
102	**Blair Jones**
133	Stanislav Lascek
163	Marek Kvapil
165	Kevin Beech
225	John Wessbecker

2004

Pick	
30	Andy Rogers
65	Mark Tobin
102	**Mike Lundin**
158	Brandon Elliott
163	Dusty Collins
188	Jan Zapletal
191	**Karri Ramo**
245	Justin Keller

2003

Pick	
34	Mike Egener
41	**Matt Smaby**
96	Jonathan Boutin
192	**Doug O'Brien**
224	**Gerald Coleman**
227	**Jay Rosehill**
255	Raimonds Danilics
256	Brady Greco
273	Albert Vishnyakov
286	Zbynek Hrdel
287	**Nick Tarnasky**

General Managers' History

Phil Esposito, 1992-93 to 1997-98; Phil Esposito and Jacques Demers, 1998-99; Rick Dudley, 1999-2000, 2000-01; Rick Dudley and Jay Feaster, 2001-02; Jay Feaster, 2002-03 to 2007-08; Brian Lawton, 2008-09, 2009-10; Steve Yzerman, 2010-11 to date.

Steve Yzerman

Vice President and General Manager

Born: Cranbrook, BC, May 9, 1965.

Steve Yzerman – the iconic Detroit Red Wing player and executive – was named the sixth general manager in Lightning history on May 25, 2010. In his first season with the club in 2010-11 Yzerman was a finalist for the G.M of the Year award as Tampa Bay returned to the playoffs for the first time since 2006-07 and reached the Eastern Conference Final after tying a club record with 46 wins during the regular season. In 2014-15, Tampa Bay set new club records with 50 wins and 108 points en route to reaching the Stanley Cup Final and Yzerman was rewarded as G.M of the year.

Before joining the Lightning Yzerman spent four seasons as vice president with the Red Wings, working closely with general manager Ken Holland, senior vice president Jim Devellano and assistant general manager Jim Nill on evaluating talent at both the professional and amateur levels. He also contributed valuable input on trades, free agent signings and at the NHL Draft each summer. Yzerman served as general manager for Canada at the 2007 and 2008 World Championships, bringing home gold and silver respectively. He then led Canada to an Olympic gold medal victory on home ice in Vancouver at the 2010 Winter Olympics as executive director, and won gold again in that role at the 2014 Sochi Olympics. Yzerman also won an Olympic gold medal as a player with Canada in 2002.

Yzerman is a four-time Stanley Cup champion, winning three as a player (1997, 1998 and 2002) and another as a member of Detroit's management team (2008). Overall he spent 27 seasons with the franchise. He was inducted into the Hockey Hall of Fame in 2009, his first year of eligibility. Recognized as one of the best centers in NHL history, Yzerman retired on July 3, 2006 after a remarkable 22-year NHL career with the Red Wings. He ranks among the NHL's all-time leaders with 1,514 career games, 692 goals, 1,063 assists and 1,755 career points. Even more impressive than his career statistics may be his 20-year run as captain in Detroit, the longest tenure in NHL and major sports history. Yzerman was named captain of the Red Wings prior to the 1986-87 season, making him the youngest captain in franchise history at 21-years-old.

During his illustrious career Yzerman was selected to the NHL All-Star Game on nine occasions. He also won the Bill Masterton Trophy (perseverance, sportsmanship and dedication to hockey) in 2003, the Frank J. Selke Trophy (best defensive forward) in 2000, the Conn Smythe Trophy (playoff MVP) in 1998, the Lester B. Pearson Award (the NHLPA's top player) in 1989 and was also selected to the NHL All-Rookie Team in 1984.

Club Directory

Amalie Arena

Tampa Bay Lightning
Amalie Arena
401 Channelside Drive
Tampa, FL 33602
Phone **813/301-6500**
FAX 813/301-1480
Ticket Info. 813/301-6600
www.tampabaylightning.com
Capacity: 19,092

Executive Staff	
Owner, Governor & Chairman	Jeff Vinik
Chief Executive Officer and Alternate Governor	Steve Griggs
Chief Revenue Officer, TBSE	Jarrod Dillon
VP, General Manager, and Alternate Governo	Steve Yzerman
EVP of Communications	Bill Wickett
EVP and General Counsel	Jim Shimberg
EVP, TBEP Business Development	Bill Abercrombie
EVP & G.M., Amalie Arena	Darryl Benge
Sr. V.P. of Event Management	Kevin Preast
VPs, Finance / Innovation & Technology Services	Doug Riefler / Sean Walker
VPs, Corporate Relations / Game Presentation	Phil Esposito / John Franzone
VPs, H.R. / Corporate & Community Affairs	Keith Harris / Dave Andreychuk
VPs, Guest Experience and Blue Ribbon Service	Mary Milne
Ticket Ops	Jim Mannino
Sr. VP. Philanthropy and Community Initiatives	Elizabeth Frazier
VP of Community Hockey Development	Jay Feaster
VP, Partnership Development and Activation	Mike Harrison
Executive Assistant	Connie Van Horn
Coaching Staff	
Head Coach	Jon Cooper
Associate Coach / Assistant Coaches	Rick Bowness / Todd Richards, Brad Lauer
Coaches, Goaltending / Video / Player Development	Frantz Jean / Nigel Kirwan / Stacy Roest
Strength & Conditioning Coach / Manual Therapist	Mark Lambert / Christian Rivas
Hockey Operations	
Asst. G.M., G.M., Syracuse Crunch	Julien BriseBois
Asst. G.M., Director of Player Personnel	Pat Verbeek
Sr. Advisor to the G.M. / Director of Team Services	Tom Kurvers / Ryan Belec
Amateur Scouting Director / Head Scout	Al Murray / Darryl Plandowski
Manager of Hockey Admin / Statistical Analyst	Liz Koharski / Michael Peterson
Head Athletic Trainer / Assistant Trainer	Tom Mulligan / Mike Poirier
Equipment Manager / Assistant Managers	Ray Thill / Rob Kennedy, Jason Berger
Public Relations	
Director, Public Relations / Editorial Content Mgr.	Brian Breseman / Trevor Van Knotsenburg
Beat Writer / Team Photographer	Bryan Burns / Scott Audette
Digital / Hockey Reporter/ Alumni Coordinator	Gabe Marte / Caley Chelios / Rachel Kilman
Community Relations and Lightning Foundation	
Senior Director of Community Relations	Kasey Smith
Community Rep. / Hockey Manager	Brian Bradley / Tom Garavaglia
Finance	
VP, Business Strategy	Chris Kamke
Finance Dir. / Mgr. / Staff Accountant / Sr. Accountant	Michelle Davidson / Tim Ennis / Scott Peterson/ Molly Venters
Business Analysts	Kristen Riker, Allie MacLeod, Laura Mooradin
Managers, Business Intelligence/ AP / AR	Brendan Russell/ Donna Clark / Cara Jessa
Human Resources	
Associate General Counsel/ Shipping Coordinator	Jessica Merrick/Angelina Evans
Director of H.R. / Generalist / Assistant	Nicole Parente / Charlea Jackson / Molly Weisbrod
Talent Coord. / Front Desk Administrator	Autumn Chamberlain / Kelsey Yelich
Information Technology	
Technology Services Manager	Jay Young
Help Desk Technician / Network Engineer	Ryan Bamford / Peter Oswalt
Ticket Office	
Ticket Supervisors, Sports / Event Manager	Helen Junker / Bobby Loman
Premium and Staffing Supervisor	Missy Davis
Client Sales and Services	
Sr. Dir. of Suite Sales & Service / Mgrs. / Specialist	Matt Hill, Toni Connor, Erin Bailey-Wilson, Adam Laws, Mike Sarage, Toni Connor
Membership Services Execs.	Shannon Dixie, Dan Schlindwein, Leslie Redfield, Megan Iacofano, Nathan Black, Hannah Landes, Daniel Lozada, Jason Hill, Danny Rowan, Paige Westlake, Justyn Carlson
Manager of Member Services / Asst. Mgrs.	Lakisha Sharpe / Thomas Gregory, Jason Hill
Customer Service Supervisor	Clark Brooks
Corporate Partnership & Activation	
Sr. Director of Partnership Activation	Sheri Anderson
Sr. Manager of Partnership Development / Managers	Casey Cole / Joshua Korlin
Partnership Activation & Development Mgrs. / Coord.	Shannon Burrows, Michael Wozney, Savannah Deiserling, Justin Versaggi / Reece Anderson
Partnership Activation Account Executives	Dan Williams, Madeline Hooper
Ticket Sales	
VP, Ticket Sales & Service	Travis Pelleymounter
Sr. Director of New Business Development	Ryan Bringger
Directors, Corporate Sales/ Group Sales	Ryan Cook / Ryan Niemeyer
Corporate Sales Managers	TJ Abone, Tommy Curtis, John Curry, Nicky Gordan, Colin Cook
Manager of Corporate Sales/Inside Sales	Jim VanDam/ Adam Lawson
Group Sales	Brian Boksen, Danny Rowen, Tyler Thompson, Kyle Laga, Benjamin Salo, Dean Dickinson, Sam Reiner
Inside Sales	Jennifer Babcock, Jonathan Conde, Chloe Laniado, Nikki Gregory
Marketing	
Managers, Digital Media / Live Events	Andrew DeWitt / Kelli Yeloushan
Sr. Manager of Event Marketing / Director of Marketing	Angela Lanza / Brittany Austin
Creative Services Manager / Senior / Graphic Designers	Jenna Baldwin / Carolina Brinkley / Nick Meader, Matt Turner
Digital Marketing Manager / Promotions Manager	Patrick Abts / Justin Savoie
Manger of Social Media / Media Buyer	Kinsey Janke / Samantha Krone
Arena Management	
G.M., SportService	Bruce Ground
Directors, Arena Departments	Daryl Niles, Steve Butler, Susan Danielik
Managers, Arena Departments	Steven Butler, Amy Ford, Michael O'Donnell, Tom Miracle, Stevan Simms, Brendon Hite, Michael Silva, Tom Dacey, Susan Danielik, Justin Bechtold, Kim Seeley, Samantha Nemeroff
Ice Operations Manager	Tom Miracle
Security Supervisors	Russ Snyder, Jackie Mills, Kevin Eshleman
Coordinators / Operations Analyst	Keisha Ray, Jordan Fisher/ Sam Carr
Broadcast & Game Presentation	
Director of Broadcasting/Programming	Matt Sammon
Managers A/V / Production Systems	JC Kent / Andrew Samel, Deni Brave
Flagship Station, Television	Fox Sports Sun
Radio Stations	WFLA 970 AM, WDCF 1350 AM, WZHR 1400 AM, WSRQ 1220 AM/106.9 FM/98.9 FM, WDBO 580 AM, WKFL 1220 AM, WWJB 1450 AM/103.9 FM/101.1 FM, WKII 1070 AM
TV Play-by-Play / Color / Reporter	Rick Peckham / Brian Engblom / Paul Kennedy
Radio Play-by-Play / Analyst	David Mishkin / Phil Esposito
Manager / Coordinators	Brian Fink / Ryan Bushey, Jim Wilson, Bryce Huffman, Stephen Frey Catherine Schwaninger, Felicia Sablan, Tyler Flood

Toronto Maple Leafs

2016-17 Results: 40W-27L-7OTL-8SOL 95PTS
4TH, Atlantic Division • 8TH, Eastern Conference

Key Off-Season Signings/Acquisitions

2017

May 2 • Re-signed D **Nikita Zaitsev** and RW **Ben Smith**.

July 1 • Signed D **Ron Hainsey** and C **Dominic Moore**.

1 • Re-signed G **Curtis McElhinney** and G **Garret Sparks**.

2 • Signed C **Patrick Marleau**.

5 • Re-signed C **Zach Hyman**.

2017-18 Schedule

Month	Day	Date	Opponent
Oct.	Wed.	4	at Winnipeg
	Sat.	7	NY Rangers
	Mon.	9	Chicago
	Wed.	11	New Jersey
	Sat.	14	at Montreal
	Tue.	17	at Washington
	Wed.	18	Detroit
	Sat.	21	at Ottawa
	Mon.	23	Los Angeles
	Thu.	26	Carolina
	Sat.	28	Philadelphia
	Mon.	30	at San Jose
Nov.	Wed.	1	at Anaheim
	Thu.	2	at Los Angeles
	Sat.	4	at St. Louis*
	Mon.	6	Vegas
	Wed.	8	Minnesota
	Fri.	10	Boston
	Sat.	11	at Boston
	Thu.	16	New Jersey
	Sat.	18	at Montreal
	Mon.	20	Arizona
	Wed.	22	at Florida
	Fri.	24	at Carolina
	Sat.	25	Washington
	Tue.	28	at Calgary
	Thu.	30	at Edmonton
Dec.	Sat.	2	at Vancouver*
	Wed.	6	Calgary
	Sat.	9	at Pittsburgh
	Sun.	10	Edmonton
	Tue.	12	at Philadelphia
	Thu.	14	at Minnesota
	Fri.	15	at Detroit
	Tue.	19	Carolina*
	Wed.	20	at Columbus
	Sat.	23	at NY Rangers
	Thu.	28	at Arizona
	Fri.	29	at Colorado
	Sun.	31	at Vegas*
Jan.	Tue.	2	Tampa Bay
	Thu.	4	San Jose
	Sat.	6	Vancouver
	Mon.	8	Columbus
	Wed.	10	Ottawa
	Tue.	16	St. Louis
	Thu.	18	at Philadelphia
	Sat.	20	at Ottawa
	Mon.	22	Colorado
	Wed.	24	at Chicago
	Thu.	25	at Dallas
	Wed.	31	NY Islanders
Feb.	Thu.	1	at NY Rangers
	Sat.	3	at Boston
	Mon.	5	Anaheim
	Wed.	7	Nashville
	Sat.	10	Ottawa
	Mon.	12	Tampa Bay
	Wed.	14	Columbus
	Sat.	17	at Pittsburgh
	Sun.	18	at Detroit
	Tue.	20	Florida
	Thu.	22	NY Islanders
	Sat.	24	Boston
	Mon.	26	at Tampa Bay
	Tue.	27	at Florida
Mar.	Sat.	3	at Washington
	Mon.	5	at Buffalo
	Sat.	10	Pittsburgh
	Wed.	14	Dallas
	Thu.	15	at Buffalo
	Sat.	17	Montreal
	Tue.	20	at Tampa Bay
	Thu.	22	at Nashville
	Sat.	24	Detroit
	Mon.	26	Buffalo
	Wed.	28	Florida
	Fri.	30	at NY Islanders
	Sat.	31	Winnipeg
Apr.	Mon.	2	Buffalo
	Thu.	5	at New Jersey
	Sat.	7	Montreal

* Denotes afternoon game.

Retired Numbers

1	Turk Broda	1936-43, 1945-52
	Johnny Bower	1958-1970
4	Hap Day	1926-1937
	Red Kelly	1959-1967

(continued on page 121)

Year-by-Year Record

Season	GP	Home W	L	T	OL	Road W	L	T	OL	Overall W	L	T	OL	GF	GA	Pts.	Div. Fin.	Conf. Fin.	Playoff Result
2016-17	82	21	13	....	7	19	14	....	8	40	27	....	15	251	242	95	4th, Atl.	8th, East	Lost First Round
2015-16	82	14	18	....	9	15	24	....	2	29	42	....	11	198	246	69	8th, Atl.	16th, East	– out of playoffs –
2014-15	82	22	17	....	2	8	27	....	6	30	44	....	8	211	262	68	7th, Atl.	15th, East	– out of playoffs –
2013-14	82	24	16	....	1	14	20	....	7	38	36	....	8	231	256	84	6th, Atl.	12th, East	– out of playoffs –
2012-13	48	13	9	....	2	13	8	....	3	26	17	....	5	145	133	57	3rd, NE	5th, East	Lost Conf. Quarter-Final
2011-12	82	18	16	....	7	17	21	....	3	35	37	....	10	231	264	80	4th, NE	13th, East	– out of playoffs –
2010-11	82	18	15	....	8	19	19	....	3	37	34	....	11	218	251	85	4th, NE	10th, East	– out of playoffs –
2009-10	82	18	17	....	6	12	21	....	8	30	38	....	14	214	267	74	5th, NE	15th, East	– out of playoffs –
2008-09	82	16	16	....	9	18	19	....	4	34	35	....	13	250	293	81	5th, NE	12th, East	– out of playoffs –
2007-08	82	18	17	....	6	18	18	....	5	36	35	....	11	231	260	83	5th, NE	12th, East	– out of playoffs –
2006-07	82	21	15	....	5	19	16	....	6	40	31	....	11	258	269	91	3rd, NE	9th, East	– out of playoffs –
2005-06	82	26	12	....	3	15	21	....	5	41	33	....	8	257	270	90	4th, NE	9th, East	– out of playoffs –
2004-05	....	....	....	....	....	....	....	....	....	....	....	....	....	....	....	....			
2003-04	82	22	14	3	2	23	10	7	1	45	24	10	3	242	204	103	2nd, NE	4th, East	Lost Conf. Semi-Final
2002-03	82	24	13	4	0	20	15	3	3	44	28	7	3	236	208	98	2nd, NE	5th, East	Lost Conf. Quarter-Final
2001-02	82	24	11	6	0	19	14	4	4	43	25	10	4	249	207	100	2nd, NE	4th, East	Lost Conf. Final
2000-01	82	19	11	7	4	18	18	4	1	37	29	11	5	232	207	90	3rd, NE	7th, East	Lost Conf. Semi-Final
1999-2000	82	24	12	5	0	21	15	2	3	45	27	7	3	246	222	100	1st, NE	3rd, East	Lost Conf. Semi-Final
1998-99	82	23	13	5	....	22	17	2	....	45	30	7	....	268	231	97	2nd, NE	4th, East	Lost Conf. Final
1997-98	82	16	20	5	....	14	23	4	....	30	43	9	....	194	237	69	6th, Cen.	10th, West	– out of playoffs –
1996-97	82	18	20	3	....	12	24	5	....	30	44	8	....	230	273	68	6th, Cen.	11th, West	– out of playoffs –
1995-96	82	19	15	7	....	15	21	5	....	34	36	12	....	247	252	80	3rd, Cen.	4th, West	Lost Conf. Quarter-Final
1994-95	48	15	7	2	....	6	12	6	....	21	19	8	....	135	146	50	4th, Cen.	5th, West	Lost Conf. Quarter-Final
1993-94	84	23	15	4	....	20	14	8	....	43	29	12	....	280	243	98	2nd, Cen.	2nd, West	Lost Conf. Final
1992-93	84	25	11	6	....	19	18	5	....	44	29	11	....	288	241	99	3rd, Norris		Lost Conf. Final
1991-92	80	21	16	3	....	9	27	4	....	30	43	7	....	234	294	67	5th, Norris		– out of playoffs –
1990-91	80	15	21	4	....	8	25	7	....	23	46	11	....	241	318	57	5th, Norris		– out of playoffs –
1989-90	80	24	14	2	....	14	24	2	....	38	38	4	....	337	358	80	3rd, Norris		Lost Div. Semi-Final
1988-89	80	15	20	5	....	13	26	1	....	28	46	6	....	259	342	62	5th, Norris		– out of playoffs –
1987-88	80	14	20	6	....	7	29	4	....	21	49	10	....	273	345	52	4th, Norris		Lost Div. Semi-Final
1986-87	80	22	14	4	....	10	28	2	....	32	42	6	....	286	319	70	4th, Norris		Lost Div. Final
1985-86	80	16	21	3	....	9	27	4	....	25	48	7	....	311	386	57	4th, Norris		Lost Div. Final
1984-85	80	10	28	2	....	10	24	6	....	20	52	8	....	253	358	48	5th, Norris		– out of playoffs –
1983-84	80	17	16	7	....	9	29	2	....	26	45	9	....	303	387	61	5th, Norris		– out of playoffs –
1982-83	80	20	15	5	....	8	25	7	....	28	40	12	....	293	330	68	3rd, Norris		Lost Div. Semi-Final
1981-82	80	12	20	8	....	8	24	8	....	20	44	16	....	298	380	56	5th, Norris		– out of playoffs –
1980-81	80	14	21	5	....	14	16	10	....	28	37	15	....	322	367	71	5th, Adams		Lost Prelim. Round
1979-80	80	17	19	4	....	18	21	1	....	35	40	5	....	304	327	75	4th, Adams		Lost Prelim. Round
1978-79	80	20	12	8	....	14	21	5	....	34	33	13	....	267	252	81	3rd, Adams		Lost Quarter-Final
1977-78	80	21	13	6	....	20	16	4	....	41	29	10	....	271	237	92	3rd, Adams		Lost Semi-Final
1976-77	80	18	13	9	....	15	19	6	....	33	32	15	....	301	285	81	3rd, Adams		Lost Quarter-Final
1975-76	80	23	12	5	....	11	19	10	....	34	31	15	....	294	276	83	3rd, Adams		Lost Quarter-Final
1974-75	80	19	12	9	....	12	21	7	....	31	33	16	....	280	309	78	3rd, Adams		Lost Quarter-Final
1973-74	78	21	11	7	....	14	16	9	....	35	27	16	....	274	230	86	4th, East		Lost Quarter-Final
1972-73	78	20	12	7	....	7	29	3	....	27	41	10	....	247	279	64	6th, East		– out of playoffs –
1971-72	78	21	11	7	....	12	20	7	....	33	31	14	....	209	208	80	4th, East		Lost Quarter-Final
1970-71	78	24	9	6	....	13	24	2	....	37	33	8	....	248	211	82	4th, East		Lost Quarter-Final
1969-70	76	18	13	7	....	11	21	6	....	29	34	13	....	222	242	71	6th, East		– out of playoffs –
1968-69	76	20	8	10	....	15	18	5	....	35	26	15	....	234	217	85	4th, East		Lost Quarter-Final
1967-68	74	24	9	4	....	9	22	6	....	33	31	10	....	209	176	76	5th, East		– out of playoffs –
1966-67	70	21	8	6	....	11	19	5	....	32	27	11	....	204	211	75	3rd		**Won Stanley Cup**
1965-66	70	22	9	4	....	12	16	7	....	34	25	11	....	208	187	79	3rd		Lost Semi-Final
1964-65	70	17	15	3	....	13	11	11	....	30	26	14	....	204	173	74	4th		Lost Semi-Final
1963-64	70	22	7	6	....	11	18	6	....	33	25	12	....	192	172	78	3rd		**Won Stanley Cup**
1962-63	70	21	8	6	....	14	15	6	....	35	23	12	....	221	180	82	1st		**Won Stanley Cup**
1961-62	70	25	5	5	....	12	17	6	....	37	22	11	....	232	180	85	2nd		**Won Stanley Cup**
1960-61	70	21	6	8	....	18	13	4	....	39	19	12	....	234	176	90	2nd		Lost Semi-Final
1959-60	70	20	9	6	....	15	17	3	....	35	26	9	....	199	195	79	2nd		Lost Final
1958-59	70	17	13	5	....	10	19	6	....	27	32	11	....	189	201	65	4th		Lost Final
1957-58	70	12	16	7	....	9	22	4	....	21	38	11	....	192	226	53	6th		– out of playoffs –
1956-57	70	12	16	7	....	9	18	8	....	21	34	15	....	174	192	57	5th		– out of playoffs –
1955-56	70	19	10	6	....	5	23	7	....	24	33	13	....	153	181	61	4th		Lost Semi-Final
1954-55	70	14	10	11	....	10	14	11	....	24	24	22	....	147	135	70	3rd		Lost Semi-Final
1953-54	70	22	6	7	....	10	18	7	....	32	24	14	....	152	131	78	3rd		Lost Semi-Final
1952-53	70	17	12	6	....	10	18	7	....	27	30	13	....	156	167	67	5th		– out of playoffs –
1951-52	70	17	10	8	....	12	15	8	....	29	25	16	....	168	157	74	3rd		Lost Semi-Final
1950-51	70	22	8	5	....	19	8	8	....	41	16	13	....	212	138	95	2nd		**Won Stanley Cup**
1949-50	70	18	9	8	....	13	18	4	....	31	27	12	....	176	173	74	3rd		Lost Semi-Final
1948-49	60	12	8	10	....	10	17	3	....	22	25	13	....	147	161	57	4th		**Won Stanley Cup**
1947-48	60	22	3	5	....	10	12	8	....	32	15	13	....	182	143	77	1st		**Won Stanley Cup**
1946-47	60	20	8	2	....	11	11	8	....	31	19	10	....	209	172	72	2nd		**Won Stanley Cup**
1945-46	50	10	13	2	....	9	11	5	....	19	24	7	....	174	185	45	5th		– out of playoffs –
1944-45	50	13	9	3	....	11	13	1	....	24	22	4	....	183	161	52	3rd		**Won Stanley Cup**
1943-44	50	13	11	1	....	10	12	3	....	23	23	4	....	214	174	50	3rd		Lost Semi-Final
1942-43	50	17	6	2	....	5	13	7	....	22	19	9	....	198	159	53	3rd		Lost Semi-Final
1941-42	48	18	6	0	....	9	12	3	....	27	18	3	....	158	136	57	2nd		**Won Stanley Cup**
1940-41	48	16	5	3	....	12	9	3	....	28	14	6	....	145	99	62	2nd		Lost Semi-Final
1939-40	48	15	3	6	....	10	14	0	....	25	17	6	....	134	110	56	3rd		Lost Final
1938-39	48	13	8	3	....	6	12	6	....	19	20	9	....	114	107	47	3rd		Lost Final
1937-38	48	13	6	5	....	11	9	4	....	24	15	9	....	151	127	57	1st, Cdn.		Lost Final
1936-37	48	14	9	1	....	8	12	4	....	22	21	5	....	119	115	49	3rd, Cdn.		Lost Quarter-Final
1935-36	48	15	4	5	....	8	15	1	....	23	19	6	....	126	106	52	2nd, Cdn.		Lost Final
1934-35	48	16	6	2	....	14	8	2	....	30	14	4	....	157	111	64	1st, Cdn.		Lost Final
1933-34	48	19	2	3	....	7	11	6	....	26	13	9	....	174	119	61	1st, Cdn.		Lost Semi-Final
1932-33	48	16	4	4	....	8	14	2	....	24	18	6	....	119	111	54	1st, Cdn.		Lost Final
1931-32	48	17	4	3	....	6	14	4	....	23	18	7	....	155	127	53	2nd, Cdn.		**Won Stanley Cup**
1930-31	44	15	4	3	....	7	9	6	....	22	13	9	....	118	99	53	2nd, Cdn.		Lost Quarter-Final
1929-30	44	10	8	4	....	7	13	2	....	17	21	6	....	116	124	40	4th, Cdn.		– out of playoffs –
1928-29	44	15	5	2	....	6	13	3	....	21	18	5	....	85	69	47	3rd, Cdn.		Lost Semi-Final
1927-28	44	9	8	5	....	9	10	3	....	18	18	8	....	89	88	44	4th, Cdn.		– out of playoffs –
1926-27*	44	10	10	2	....	5	14	3	....	15	24	5	....	79	94	35	5th, Cdn.		– out of playoffs –
1925-26	36	11	5	2	....	1	16	1	....	12	21	3	....	92	114	27	6th		– out of playoffs –
1924-25	30	10	5	0	....	9	6	0	....	19	11	0	....	90	84	38	2nd		Lost NHL S-Final
1923-24	24	7	5	0	....	3	9	0	....	10	14	0	....	59	85	20	3rd		– out of playoffs –
1922-23	24	10	1	1	....	3	9	0	....	13	10	1	....	82	88	27	3rd		– out of playoffs –
1921-22	24	8	4	0	....	5	6	1	....	13	10	1	....	98	97	27	2nd		**Won Stanley Cup**
1920-21	24	9	3	0	....	6	6	0	....	15	9	0	....	105	100	30	2nd and 1st***		Lost NHL Final
1919-20**	24	8	4	0	....	4	8	0	....	12	12	0	....	119	106	24	3rd and 2nd***		– out of playoffs –
1918-19	18	5	4	0	....	0	9	0	....	5	13	0	....	64	92	10	3rd and 3rd***		– out of playoffs –
1917-18	22	10	1	0	....	3	8	0	....	13	9	0	....	108	109	26	2nd and 1st***		**Won Stanley Cup**

* Name changed from St. Patricks to Maple Leafs (February, 1927). ** Name changed from Arenas to St. Patricks.

*** Season played in two halves with no combined standing at end.

From 1917-18 through 1925-26, NHL champions played against PCHA/WCHL champions for Stanley Cup.

ATLANTIC DIVISION
101st NHL Season

Franchise date: November 26, 1917

2017-18 Player Personnel

FORWARDS	HT	WT	*Age	Birthplace	S	2016-17 Club
AALTONEN, Miro	5-11	176	24	Joensuu, Finland	L	Chekhov Vityaz
BOZAK, Tyler	6-1	196	31	Regina, SK	R	Toronto
BRACCO, Jeremy	5-10	190	20	Freeport, NY	R	Windsor-Kitchener
BROOKS, Adam	5-10	175	21	Winnipeg, MB	L	Regina
BROWN, Connor	6-0	185	23	Toronto, ON	R	Toronto
FEHR, Eric	6-4	212	32	Winkler, MB	R	Pittsburgh-Toronto
GAUTHIER, Frederik	6-5	232	22	Laval, QC	L	Toronto-Toronto (AHL)
GREENING, Colin	6-2	210	31	St. John's, NL	L	Toronto (AHL)
GRUNDSTROM, Carl	6-0	194	19	Umea, Sweden	L	Frolunda-Toronto (AHL)
HORTON, Nathan	6-2	229	32	Welland, ON	R	did not play
HYMAN, Zach	6-0	202	25	Toronto, ON	R	Toronto
JOHNSSON, Andreas	5-10	184	22	Gavle, Sweden	L	Toronto (AHL)
KADRI, Nazem	6-0	192	26	London, ON	L	Toronto
KAPANEN, Kasperi	6-0	185	21	Kuopio, Finland	R	Toronto-Toronto (AHL)
KOMAROV, Leo	5-11	211	30	Narva, USSR	L	Toronto
LEIVO, Josh	6-2	205	24	Innisfil, ON	R	Toronto-Toronto (AHL)
LINDBERG, Tobias	6-3	227	22	Stockholm, Sweden	L	Toronto (AHL)
LUPUL, Joffrey	6-1	211	34	Fort Saskatchewan, AB	R	did not play
MARLEAU, Patrick	6-2	215	38	Swift Current, SK	L	San Jose
MARNER, Mitch	5-11	160	20	Markham, ON	R	Toronto
MARTIN, Matt	6-3	220	28	Windsor, ON	L	Toronto
MATTHEWS, Auston	6-2	216	20	San Ramon, CA	L	Toronto
MOORE, Dominic	6-0	192	37	Sarnia, ON	L	Boston
MOORE, Trevor	5-10	183	22	Thousand Oaks, CA	L	Toronto (AHL)
MUELLER, Chris	5-11	210	31	West Seneca, NY	R	Tucson
NYLANDER, William	5-11	190	21	Calgary, AB	R	Toronto
RYCHEL, Kerby	6-1	213	22	Torrance, CA	L	Toronto (AHL)
SMITH, Ben	5-11	198	29	Winston-Salem, NC	R	Colorado-Toronto
SOSHNIKOV, Nikita	5-11	190	23	Nizhny Tagil, Russia	L	Toronto-Toronto (AHL)
TIMASHOV, Dmytro	5-10	194	21	Kirovograd, Ukraine	L	Toronto (AHL)
van RIEMSDYK, James	6-3	209	28	Middletown, NJ	L	Toronto
DEFENSEMEN						
BORGMAN, Andreas	6-0	205	22	Stockholm, Sweden	L	HV 71 Jonkoping
CARRICK, Connor	5-11	193	23	Orland Park, IL	R	Toronto
DERMOTT, Travis	5-11	215	20	Newmarket, ON	L	Toronto (AHL)
GARDINER, Jake	6-2	197	27	Minnetonka, MN	L	Toronto
HAINSEY, Ron	6-3	210	36	Bolton, CT	L	Carolina-Pittsburgh
HOLL, Justin	6-3	199	25	Tonka Bay, MN	R	Toronto (AHL)
LILJEGREN, Timothy	6-0	191	18	Kristianstad, Sweden	R	Rogle BK (Jr.,Sr.,U18)-Timra IK
LoVERDE, Vincent	5-11	205	28	Chicago, IL	R	Ontario
MARCHENKO, Alexey	6-3	210	25	Moscow, Russia	R	Detroit-Toronto
MARINCIN, Martin	6-4	201	25	Kosice, Czech.	L	Toronto
NIELSEN, Andrew	6-3	220	20	Red Deer, AB	R	Toronto (AHL)
RIELLY, Morgan	6-1	214	23	Vancouver, BC	L	Toronto
ROSEN, Calle	6-0	175	23	Vaxjo, Sweden	L	Vaxjo HC
VALIEV, Rinat	6-2	214	22	Niznekamsk, Russia	L	Toronto (AHL)
ZAITSEV, Nikita	6-2	196	25	Moscow, USSR	R	Toronto

GOALTENDERS	HT	WT	*Age	Birthplace	C	2016-17 Club
ANDERSEN, Frederik	6-4	220	28	Herning, Denmark	L	Toronto
KASKISUO, Kasimir	6-3	195	24	Vantaa, Finland	L	Toronto (AHL)-Orlando
McELHINNEY, Curtis	6-3	205	34	London, ON	L	Columbus-Toronto
SPARKS, Garret	6-2	207	24	Elmhurst, IL	L	Toronto (AHL)

* – Age at start of 2017-18 season

Mike Babcock

Head Coach

Born: Manitouwadge, ON, April 29, 1963.

Mike Babcock was named the 30th head coach in Leafs' history on May 20, 2015. Babcock joined the Leafs after serving as head coach of the Detroit Red Wings for the previous 10 seasons. He has been part of a rebuilding effort in Toronto that saw the Maple Leafs return to the playoffs in 2016-17. Babcock finished second in voting for the Jack Adams Award as coach of the year that season.

In Detroit, Babcock posted a 458-223-105 regular season record as he became the franchise leader in games coached (786) and wins. In his time with the Red Wings, the club twice captured the Presidents' Trophy as the NHL's regular-season champion and made the playoffs in each of his 10 seasons. In 2007-08, Babcock led the Red Wings to a Stanley Cup championship.

Prior to joining the Red Wings, Babcock spent two seasons with the Mighty Ducks of Anaheim (2002 to 2004), where in his first season as head coach he led the Ducks to their first appearance in the Stanley Cup final. He spent two seasons (2000 to 2002) as head coach of the Cincinnati Mighty Ducks of the American Hockey League. He had moved to Cincinnati following a six-year run at the helm of the Spokane Chiefs of the Western Hockey League (1994-95 through 1999-2000).

In international play, Babcock has represented Canada at several competitions, including the 2016 World Cup of Hockey. Most notably, he became the only coach in hockey history to lead Canada to gold medals in consecutive Olympic appearances after guiding Canada in Vancouver (2010) and Sochi, Russia (2014). In 2004, he led Team Canada to a gold medal at the World Championships. In 1997, he took part in his first international coaching experience at the World Junior Championships as Canada also captured gold. Babcock is the only coach in the "Triple Gold Club," having captured the three most prestigious championships in hockey (a World Championship, an Olympic gold medal and the Stanley Cup).

Coaching Record see page 671

2016-17 Scoring

* – rookie

Regular Season

Pos	#	Player	Team	GP	G	A	Pts	TOI	+/–	PIM	PP	SH	GW	S	S%
C	34	* Auston Matthews	TOR	82	40	29	69	17:37	2	14	8	0	8	279	14.3
L	25	James van Riemsdyk	TOR	82	29	33	62	15:53	–2	37	6	0	5	238	12.2
C	43	Nazem Kadri	TOR	82	32	29	61	16:34	–7	95	12	0	6	236	13.6
C	29	* William Nylander	TOR	81	22	39	61	16:00	–3	32	9	0	2	205	10.7
C	16	* Mitch Marner	TOR	77	19	42	61	16:48	0	38	4	0	5	176	10.8
C	42	Tyler Bozak	TOR	78	18	37	55	16:25	–1	30	7	0	1	145	12.4
D	51	Jake Gardiner	TOR	82	9	34	43	21:32	24	34	2	0	2	127	7.1
R	12	* Connor Brown	TOR	82	20	16	36	16:12	3	10	2	1	4	139	14.4
D	22	* Nikita Zaitsev	TOR	82	4	32	36	22:01	–22	38	1	0	0	106	3.8
C	47	Leo Komarov	TOR	82	14	18	32	17:04	6	31	4	1	1	114	12.3
C	11	* Zach Hyman	TOR	82	10	18	28	16:41	2	30	0	4	3	156	6.4
D	44	Morgan Rielly	TOR	76	6	21	27	22:10	–20	21	1	0	1	171	3.5
C	24	Brian Boyle	T.B.	54	13	9	22	13:41	5	48	3	0	2	109	11.9
			TOR	21	0	3	3	11:19	–2	18	0	0	0	22	0.0
			Total	75	13	12	25	13:01	3	66	3	0	2	131	9.9
D	2	Matt Hunwick	TOR	72	1	18	19	17:58	8	18	0	0	0	73	1.4
C	23	Eric Fehr	PIT	52	6	5	11	10:55	3	14	0	0	3	61	9.8
			TOR	1	0	0	0	10:44	–1	0	0	0	0	1	0.0
			Total	53	6	5	11	10:55	2	14	0	0	3	62	9.7
D	46	Roman Polak	TOR	75	4	7	11	17:55	10	65	0	0	1	64	6.3
L	32	Josh Leivo	TOR	13	2	8	10	12:34	2	4	1	0	0	27	7.4
R	26	* Nikita Soshnikov	TOR	56	5	4	9	10:50	1	16	0	0	0	70	7.1
L	15	Matt Martin	TOR	82	5	4	9	8:53	0	123	0	0	0	66	7.6
D	8	Connor Carrick	TOR	67	2	6	8	16:20	8	51	1	0	0	89	2.2
D	3	Alexey Marchenko	DET	30	0	6	6	17:58	6	12	0	0	0	27	0.0
			TOR	11	1	1	2	14:08	1	0	0	0	0	9	11.1
			Total	41	1	7	8	16:57	7	12	0	0	0	36	2.8
D	52	Martin Marincin	TOR	25	1	6	7	18:02	3	16	0	0	0	22	4.5
R	18	Ben Smith	COL	4	0	0	0	10:46	–2	0	0	0	0	1	0.0
			TOR	36	2	2	4	11:32	–5	4	0	0	0	29	6.9
			Total	40	2	2	4	11:27	–7	4	0	0	0	30	6.7
C	33	* Frederik Gauthier	TOR	21	2	1	3	9:41	2	23	0	0	0	15	13.3
L	18	Milan Michalek	TOR	5	1	1	2	14:16	–2	2	0	0	0	6	16.7
R	28	* Kasperi Kapanen	TOR	8	1	0	1	10:41	–2	0	0	0	0	11	9.1

Goaltending

No.	Goaltender	GPI	Mins	Avg	W	L	OT	EN	SO	GA	SA	Sv%	G	A	PIM
30	* Antoine Bibeau	2	121	1.98	1	1	0	1	0	4	55	.927	0	0	0
31	Frederik Andersen	66	3799	2.67	33	16	14	4	4	169	2052	.918	0	1	16
35	Curtis McElhinney	14	759	2.85	6	7	0	2	1	36	418	.914	0	0	0
31	Jhonas Enroth	6	274	3.94	0	3	1	0	0	18	141	.872	0	0	0
	Totals	**82**	**4992**	**2.81**	**40**	**27**	**15**	**7**	**5**	**234**	**2673**	**.912**			

Playoffs

Pos	#	Player	Team	GP	G	A	Pts	TOI	+/–	PIM	PP	SH	GW	OT	S	S%
C	34	* Auston Matthews	TOR	6	4	1	5	20:18	2	0	0	0	0	0	16	25.0
D	44	Morgan Rielly	TOR	6	1	4	5	26:53	1	2	1	0	0	0	16	6.3
C	42	Tyler Bozak	TOR	6	2	2	4	18:45	0	4	1	0	1	1	14	14.3
C	11	* Zach Hyman	TOR	6	1	3	4	18:28	0	4	0	0	0	0	13	7.7
C	29	* William Nylander	TOR	6	1	3	4	18:40	4	2	0	0	0	0	23	4.3
C	16	* Mitch Marner	TOR	6	1	3	4	17:47	1	0	0	0	0	0	9	11.1
L	25	James van Riemsdyk	TOR	6	2	1	3	17:37	3	0	1	0	0	0	23	8.7
D	51	Jake Gardiner	TOR	6	1	2	3	28:38	2	4	0	0	0	0	9	11.1
R	28	* Kasperi Kapanen	TOR	6	2	0	2	10:47	–2	0	0	0	1	1	8	25.0
C	43	Nazem Kadri	TOR	6	1	1	2	19:21	0	8	0	0	0	0	18	5.6
C	24	Brian Boyle	TOR	6	0	2	2	12:26	–2	6	0	0	0	0	14	0.0
L	15	Matt Martin	TOR	6	0	2	2	9:57	–2	6	0	0	0	0	4	0.0
D	2	Matt Hunwick	TOR	6	0	1	1	25:38	–3	2	0	0	0	0	10	0.0
C	47	Leo Komarov	TOR	6	0	1	1	19:36	–1	2	0	0	0	0	10	0.0
R	12	* Connor Brown	TOR	6	0	1	1	18:13	0	0	0	0	0	0	8	0.0
D	46	Roman Polak	TOR	2	0	0	0	17:36	1	0	0	0	0	0	1	0.0
D	22	* Nikita Zaitsev	TOR	4	0	0	0	21:44	–4	0	0	0	0	0	5	0.0
D	52	Martin Marincin	TOR	6	0	0	0	16:52	2	2	0	0	0	0	9	0.0
D	8	Connor Carrick	TOR	6	0	0	0	12:16	0	4	0	0	0	0	3	0.0

Goaltending

No.	Goaltender	GPI	Mins	Avg	W	L	EN	SO	GA	SA	Sv%	G	A	PIM
31	Frederik Andersen	6	403	2.68	2	4	0	0	18	211	.915	0	0	0
	Totals	**6**	**406**	**2.66**	**2**	**4**	**0**	**0**	**18**	**211**	**.915**			

Coaching History

Dick Carroll, 1917-18, 1918-19; Frank Heffernan and Harry Sproule, 1919-20; Frank Carroll, 1920-21; George O'Donohue, 1921-22; George O'Donohue and Charles Querrie, 1922-23; Charles Querrie, 1923-24; Eddie Powers, 1924-25, 1925-26; Charles Querrie, Mike Rodden and Alex Romeril, 1926-27; Conn Smythe, 1927-28 to 1929-30; Conn Smythe and Art Duncan, 1930-31; Art Duncan, Conn Smythe and Dick Irvin, 1931-32; Dick Irvin, 1932-33 to 1939-40; Hap Day, 1940-41 to 1949-50; Joe Primeau, 1950-51 to 1952-53; King Clancy, 1953-54 to 1955-56; Howie Meeker, 1956-57; Billy Reay, 1957-58; Billy Reay and Punch Imlach, 1958-59; Punch Imlach, 1959-60 to 1968-69; John McLellan, 1969-70 to 1972-73; Red Kelly, 1973-74 to 1976-77; Roger Neilson, 1977-78, 1978-79; Floyd Smith, Dick Duff and Punch Imlach, 1979-80; Joe Crozier and Mike Nykoluk, 1980-81; Mike Nykoluk, 1981-82 to 1983-84; Dan Maloney, 1984-85, 1985-86; John Brophy, 1986-87, 1987-88; John Brophy and George Armstrong, 1988-89; Doug Carpenter, 1989-90; Doug Carpenter and Tom Watt, 1990-91; Tom Watt, 1991-92; Pat Burns, 1992-93 to 1994-95; Pat Burns and Nick Beverley, 1995-96; Mike Murphy, 1996-97, 1997-98; Pat Quinn, 1998-99 to 2005-06; Paul Maurice, 2006-07, 2007-08; Ron Wilson, 2008-09 to 2010-11; Ron Wilson and Randy Carlyle, 2011-12; Randy Carlyle, 2012-13, 2013-14; Randy Carlyle and Peter Horachek, 2014-15; Mike Babcock, 2015-16 to date.

Club Records

Team

(Figures in brackets for season records are games played; records for fewest points, wins, ties, losses, goals, goals against are for 70 or more games)

Most Points **103** 2003-04 (82)
Most Wins **45** 1998-99 (82), 1999-2000 (82), 2003-04 (82)
Most Ties **22** 1954-55 (70)
Most Losses **52** 1984-85 (80)
Most Goals **337** 1989-90 (80)
Most Goals Against **387** 1983-84 (80)
Fewest Points **48** 1984-85 (80)
Fewest Wins **20** 1981-82 (80), 1984-85 (80)
Fewest Ties **4** 1989-90 (80)
Fewest Losses **16** 1950-51 (70)
Fewest Goals **147** 1954-55 (70)
Fewest Goals Against ***131** 1953-54 (70)

Longest Winning Streak
Overall .... **10** Oct. 7-28/93
Home .... **9** Nov. 11-Dec. 26/53, Mar. 6-Apr. 7/07
Away .... **7** Nov. 14-Dec. 15/40, Dec. 4/60-Jan. 5/61, Jan. 29-Feb. 22/03

Longest Team Point Streak
Overall .... **11** Oct. 15-Nov. 8/50 (8W, 3T), Jan. 6-Feb. 1/94 (7W, 4T)
Home .... **18** Nov. 28/33-Mar. 10/34 (15W, 3T), Oct. 31/53-Jan. 23/54 (16W, 2T)
Away .... **11** Dec. 3/16-Jan. 25/17 (7W, 1OTW, 1OTL, 1SOW, 1SOL)

Longest Losing Streak
Overall .... **10** Jan. 15-Feb. 8/67
Home .... **7** Nov. 11-Dec. 5/84
Away .... **11** Feb. 20-Apr. 1/88

Longest Winless Streak
Overall .... **15** Dec. 26/87-Jan. 25/88 (11L, 4T)
Home .... **11** Dec. 19/87-Jan. 25/88 (7L, 4T), Feb. 11-Mar. 29/12 (8L, 1OTL, 2SOL)
Away .... **18** Oct. 6/82-Jan. 5/83 (13L, 5T)

Most Shutouts, Season **13** 1953-54 (70)
Most PIM, Season **2,419** 1989-90 (80)
Most Goals, Game .... **14** Mar. 16/57 (NYR 1 at Tor. 14)

Individual

Most Seasons .... **21** George Armstrong
Most Games .... **1,187** George Armstrong
Most Goals, Career .... **420** Mats Sundin
Most Assists, Career .... **620** Borje Salming
Most Points, Career .... **987** Mats Sundin (420G, 567A)
Most PIM, Career .... **2,265** Tie Domi
Most Shutouts, Career .... **62** Turk Broda
Longest Consecutive Games Streak .... **486** Tim Horton (Feb. 11/61-Feb. 4/68)
Most Goals, Season .... **54** Rick Vaive (1981-82)
Most Assists, Season .... **95** Doug Gilmour (1992-93)
Most Points, Season .... **127** Doug Gilmour (1992-93; 32G, 95A)
Most PIM, Season .... **365** Tie Domi (1997-98)
Most Points, Defenseman, Season .... **79** Ian Turnbull (1976-77; 22G, 57A)
Most Points, Center, Season .... **127** Doug Gilmour (1992-93; 32G, 95A)
Most Points, Right Wing, Season .... **97** Wilf Paiement (1980-81; 40G, 57A)
Most Points, Left Wing, Season .... **99** Dave Andreychuk (1993-94; 53G, 46A)
Most Points, Rookie, Season .... **69** Auston Matthews (2016-17; 40G, 29A)
Most Shutouts, Season .... **13** Harry Lumley (1953-54)
Most Goals, Game .... **6** Corb Denneny (Jan. 26/21), Darryl Sittler (Feb. 7/76)
Most Assists, Game .... **6** Babe Pratt (Jan. 8/44), Doug Gilmour (Feb. 13/93)
Most Points, Game .... ***10** Darryl Sittler (Feb. 7/76; 6G, 4A)

* NHL Record.

Retired Numbers *(continued from page 119)*

5	Bill Barilko	1946-1951
6	Ace Bailey	1926-1934
7	King Clancy	1930-1937
	Tim Horton	1949-50, 1951-70
9	Charlie Conacher	1929-1938
	Ted Kennedy	1942-55, 1956-57
10	Syl Apps	1936-43, 1945-48
	George Armstrong	1949-50, 1951-71
13	Mats Sundin	1994-2008
14	Dave Keon	1960-1975
17	Wendel Clark	1985-94, 96-98, 2000
21	Borje Salming	1973-1989
27	Frank Mahovlich	1956-1968
	Darryl Sittler	1970-1982
93	Doug Gilmour	1992-97, 2003

All-time Record vs. Other Clubs

Regular Season

	Total								At Home								On Road							
	GP	W	L	T	OL	GF	GA	PTS	GP	W	L	T	OL	GF	GA	PTS	GP	W	L	T	OL	GF	GA	PTS
Anaheim	40	23	11	5	1	126	103	52	22	14	3	4	1	78	49	33	18	9	8	1	0	48	54	19
Arizona	96	36	50	8	2	332	371	82	50	21	25	2	2	173	185	46	46	15	25	6	0	159	186	36
Boston	666	273	285	98	10	1980	1967	654	333	170	109	51	3	1095	878	394	333	103	176	47	7	885	1089	260
Buffalo	206	75	102	18	11	572	736	179	102	46	39	12	5	303	331	109	104	29	63	6	6	269	405	70
Calgary	132	58	58	12	4	449	485	132	62	35	18	7	2	237	213	79	70	23	40	5	2	212	272	53
Carolina	116	43	55	11	7	355	404	104	58	22	29	5	2	175	192	51	58	21	26	6	5	180	212	53
Chicago	647	286	262	96	3	1939	1846	671	322	166	100	54	2	1094	848	388	325	120	162	42	1	845	998	283
Colorado	78	30	37	9	2	254	285	71	42	18	19	4	1	132	152	41	36	12	18	5	1	122	133	30
Columbus	22	10	9	1	2	64	64	23	12	4	6	1	1	28	33	10	10	6	3	0	1	36	31	13
Dallas	212	93	90	28	1	703	727	215	108	54	37	17	0	378	337	125	104	39	53	11	1	325	390	90
Detroit	661	285	280	93	3	1898	1872	666	328	171	108	47	2	1083	878	391	333	114	172	46	1	815	994	275
Edmonton	98	47	42	8	1	354	381	103	46	27	17	2	0	188	181	56	52	20	25	6	1	166	200	47
Florida	80	39	32	7	2	231	239	87	39	21	15	2	1	118	114	45	41	18	17	5	1	113	125	42
Los Angeles	147	61	63	21	2	487	497	145	75	37	26	11	1	282	246	86	72	24	37	10	1	205	251	59
Minnesota	18	8	9	0	1	41	40	17	10	6	4	0	0	29	20	12	8	2	5	0	1	12	20	5
Montreal	736	293	341	88	14	2033	2254	688	368	186	128	45	9	1111	981	426	368	107	213	43	5	922	1273	262
Nashville	21	9	10	1	1	54	63	20	13	5	7	1	0	33	43	11	8	4	3	0	1	21	20	9
New Jersey	137	69	39	20	9	443	407	167	70	45	16	5	4	236	182	99	67	24	23	15	5	207	225	68
NY Islanders	151	69	65	7	10	492	534	155	77	40	29	4	4	272	254	88	74	29	36	3	6	220	280	67
NY Rangers	608	283	221	95	9	1922	1758	670	303	166	94	39	4	1028	812	375	305	117	127	56	5	894	946	295
Ottawa	112	50	48	3	11	318	332	114	56	27	20	2	7	163	166	63	56	23	28	1	4	155	166	51
Philadelphia	177	61	90	22	4	488	610	148	89	35	37	14	3	277	291	87	88	26	53	8	1	211	319	61
Pittsburgh	179	79	76	17	7	625	640	182	89	44	31	11	3	336	286	102	90	35	45	6	4	289	354	80
St. Louis	215	93	93	25	4	686	689	215	106	60	31	11	4	390	319	135	109	33	62	14	0	296	370	80
San Jose	47	20	20	5	2	137	134	47	25	12	9	2	2	85	73	28	22	8	11	3	0	52	61	19
Tampa Bay	89	52	29	2	6	287	232	112	45	27	14	1	3	158	127	58	44	25	15	1	3	129	105	54
Vancouver	142	57	61	22	2	482	486	138	69	32	25	11	1	249	227	76	73	25	36	11	1	233	259	62
Washington	141	60	67	10	4	470	488	134	69	37	25	6	1	273	225	81	72	23	42	4	3	197	263	53
Winnipeg	57	30	18	1	8	199	160	69	28	16	8	1	3	102	83	36	29	14	10	0	5	97	77	33
Defunct Clubs	465	242	173	50	0	1467	1260	534	232	158	53	21	0	860	515	337	233	84	120	29	0	607	745	197
Totals	**6496**	**2834**	**2736**	**783**	**143**	**19888**	**20064**	**6594**	**3248**	**1702**	**1082**	**393**	**71**	**10966**	**9241**	**3868**	**3248**	**1132**	**1654**	**390**	**72**	**8922**	**10823**	**2726**

Playoffs

	Series	W	L	GP	W	L	T	GF	GA	Last Mtg.	Rnd.	Result
Boston	14	8	6	69	34	34	1	168	175	2013	CQF	L 3-4
Buffalo	1	0	1	5	1	4	0	16	21	1999	CF	L 1-4
Calgary	1	1	0	2	2	0	0	9	5	1979	PR	W 2-0
Carolina	1	0	1	6	2	4	0	6	10	2002	CF	L 2-4
Chicago	9	6	3	38	22	15	1	111	89	1995	CQF	L 3-4
Dallas	2	0	2	7	1	6	0	26	35	1983	DSF	L 1-3
Detroit	23	12	11	117	58	59	0	311	321	1993	DSF	W 4-3
Los Angeles	3	2	1	12	7	5	0	41	31	1993	CF	L 3-4
Montreal	15	7	8	71	29	42	0	160	215	1979	QF	L 0-4
New Jersey	2	0	2	13	5	8	0	27	37	2001	CSF	L 3-4
NY Islanders	3	2	1	17	8	9	0	42	54	2002	CQF	W 4-3
NY Rangers	8	3	5	35	16	19	0	86	86	1971	QF	L 2-4
Ottawa	4	4	0	24	16	8	0	57	42	2004	CQF	W 4-3
Philadelphia	6	1	5	36	14	22	0	85	119	2004	CSF	L 2-4
Pittsburgh	3	3	0	12	8	4	0	39	27	1999	CSF	W 4-2
St. Louis	5	2	3	31	14	17	0	90	88	1996	CQF	L 2-4
San Jose	1	1	0	7	4	3	0	26	21	1994	CSF	W 4-3
Vancouver	1	0	1	5	1	4	0	9	16	1994	CF	L 1-4
Washington	1	0	1	6	2	4	0	16	18	2017	FR	L 2-4
Defunct Clubs	8	6	2	24	12	10	2	59	57			
Totals	**111**	**58**	**53**	**537**	**256**	**277**	**4**	**1384**	**1467**			

Playoff Results 2017-2013

Year	Round	Opponent	Result	GF	GA
2017	FR	Washington	L 2-4	16	18
2013	CQF	Boston	L 3-4	18	22

Abbreviations: Round: CF – conference final; **CSF** – conference semi-final; **CQF** – conference quarter-final; **DSF** – division semi-final; **QF** – quarter-final; **PR** – preliminary round.

Calgary totals include Atlanta Flames, 1972-73 to 1979-80.
Colorado totals include Quebec, 1979-80 to 1994-95.
New Jersey totals include Kansas City, 1974-75, 1975-76, and Colorado Rockies, 1976-77 to 1981-82.
Phoenix totals include Winnipeg, 1979-80 to 1995-96.
Carolina totals include Hartford, 1979-80 to 1996-97.
Dallas totals include Minnesota North Stars, 1967-68 to 1992-93.
Winnipeg totals include Atlanta Thrashers, 1999-2000 to 2010-11.

2016-17 Results

Oct.	12	at Ottawa	4-5*
	15	Boston	4-1
	19	at Winnipeg	4-5*
	20	at Minnesota	2-3
	22	at Chicago	4-5†
	25	Tampa Bay	3-7
	27	Florida	3-2
	29	at Montreal	1-2
	30	at NY Islanders	1-5
Nov.	1	Edmonton	3-2*
	3	at Buffalo	2-1
	5	Vancouver	6-3
	8	Los Angeles	0-7
	11	Philadelphia	6-3
	12	at Pittsburgh	1-4
	15	Nashville	6-2
	17	Florida	6-1
	19	at Montreal	1-2
	22	Carolina	1-2
	23	at New Jersey	4-5†
	26	Washington	4-2
	29	at Edmonton	4-2
	30	at Calgary	0-3
Dec.	3	at Vancouver	2-3†
	7	Minnesota	2-3
	10	at Boston	4-1
	11	Colorado	1-3
	13	San Jose	2-3†
	15	Arizona	2-3†
	17	Pittsburgh	2-1*
	19	Anaheim	2-3
	22	at Colorado	6-0
	23	at Arizona	4-1
	28	at Florida	3-2†
	29	at Tampa Bay	3-2*
Jan.	1	Detroit	5-4*
	3	at Washington	5-6*
	6	at New Jersey	4-2
	7	Montreal	3-5
	13	at NY Rangers	4-2
	14	at Ottawa	4-2
	17	Buffalo	4-3
	19	NY Rangers	2-5
	21	Ottawa	2-3†
	23	Calgary	4-0
	25	at Detroit	4-0
	26	at Philadelphia	1-2
	31	at Dallas	3-6
Feb.	2	at St. Louis	1-5
	4	at Boston	6-5
	6	at NY Islanders	5-6*
	7	Dallas	3-1
	9	St. Louis	1-2*
	11	Buffalo	1-3
	14	NY Islanders	7-1
	15	at Columbus	2-5
	18	Ottawa	3-6
	19	at Carolina	4-0
	21	Winnipeg	5-4*
	23	NY Rangers	1-2†
	25	Montreal	2-3*
	28	at San Jose	1-3
Mar.	2	at Los Angeles	2-3†
	3	at Anaheim	2-5
	7	Detroit	3-2
	9	Philadelphia	4-2
	11	at Carolina	3-2*
	14	at Florida	2-7
	16	at Tampa Bay	5-0
	18	Chicago	1-2*
	20	Boston	4-2
	22	at Columbus	5-2
	23	New Jersey	4-2
	25	at Buffalo	2-5
	28	Florida	3-2
	30	at Nashville	3-1
Apr.	1	at Detroit	5-4
	3	at Buffalo	4-2
	4	Washington	1-4
	6	Tampa Bay	1-4
	8	Pittsburgh	5-3
	9	Columbus	2-3

* – Overtime † – Shootout

NHL Draft Selections 2017-2003

Name in bold denotes played in NHL.

2017 Pick		2014 Pick		2010 Pick		2006 Pick	
17	Timothy Liljegren	8	**William Nylander**	43	**Brad Ross**	13	**Jiri Tlusty**
59	Eemeli Rasanen	68	**Rinat Valiev**	62	**Greg McKegg**	44	**Nikolay Kulemin**
110	Ian Scott	103	J.J. Piccinich	79	Sondre Olden	99	**James Reimer**
124	Vladislav Kara	128	Dakota Joshua	116	**Petter Granberg**	111	**Korbinian Holzer**
141	Fedor Gordeev	158	**Nolan Vesey**	144	**Sam Carrick**	161	**Viktor Stalberg**
172	Ryan McGregor	188	Pierre Engvall	146	Daniel Brodin	166	Tyler Ruegsegger
203	Ryan O'Connell			182	Josh Nicholls	180	**Leo Komarov**

2016 Pick		2013 Pick		2009 Pick		2005 Pick	
1	**Auston Matthews**	21	**Frederik Gauthier**	7	**Nazem Kadri**	21	**Tuukka Rask**
31	Yegor Korshkov	82	Carter Verhaeghe	50	Kenny Ryan	82	**Phil Oreskovic**
57	Carl Grundstrom	142	Fabrice Herzog	58	Jesse Blacker	153	Alex Berry
62	Joseph Woll	172	**Antoine Bibeau**	68	Jamie Devane	173	Johan Dahlberg
72	J.D. Greenway	202	Andreas Johnson	128	Eric Knodel	216	**Anton Stralman**
92	Adam Brooks			158	Jerry D'Amigo	228	Chad Rau
101	Keaton Middleton	**2012 Pick**		188	Barron Smith		
122	Vladimir Bobylev	5	**Morgan Rielly**			**2004 Pick**	
152	Jack Walker	35	Matt Finn	**2008 Pick**		90	**Justin Pogge**
179	Nicolas Mattinen	126	Dominic Toninato	5	**Luke Schenn**	113	Roman Kukumberg
182	Nikolai Chebykin	156	**Connor Brown**	60	**Jimmy Hayes**	157	Dmitri Vorobiev
		157	Ryan Rupert	98	Mikhail Stefanovich	187	**Robbie Earl**
2015 Pick		209	**Viktor Loov**	128	**Greg Pateryn**	220	Maxim Semenov
4	**Mitch Marner**			129	Joel Champagne	252	Jan Steber
34	**Travis Dermott**	**2011 Pick**		130	Jerome Flaake	285	Pierce Norton
61	Jeremy Bracco	22	Tyler Biggs	158	Grant Rollheiser		
65	Andrew Nielsen	25	**Stuart Percy**	188	**Andrew MacWilliam**	**2003 Pick**	
68	Martins Dzierkals	86	**Josh Leivo**			57	John Doherty
95	Jesper Lindgren	100	Tom Nilsson	**2007 Pick**		91	Martin Sagat
125	Dmytro Timashov	130	Tony Cameranesi	74	Dale Mitchell	125	Konstantin Volkov
155	Stephen Desrocher	152	**David Broll**	99	**Matt Frattin**	158	**John Mitchell**
185	Nikita Korostelev	173	Dennis Robertson	104	Ben Winnett	220	**Jeremy Williams**
		190	**Garret Sparks**	134	Juraj Mikus	237	Shaun Landolt
		203	Max Everson	164	**Chris Didomenico**		
				194	**Carl Gunnarsson**		

General Managers' History

Charles Querrie, 1917-18 to 1926-27; Conn Smythe, 1927-28 to 1953-54; Conn Smythe and Hap Day, 1954-55; Hap Day, 1955-56, 1956-57; Howie Meeker, summer 1957; Stafford Smythe 1957-58; Stafford Smythe and Punch Imlach, 1958-59; Punch Imlach, 1959-60 to 1968-69; Jim Gregory, 1969-70 to 1978-79; Punch Imlach, 1979-80, 1980-81; Punch Imlach and Gerry McNamara, 1981-82; Gerry McNamara, 1982-83 to 1986-87; Gerry McNamara and Gord Stellick, 1987-88; Gord Stellick, 1988-89; Floyd Smith, 1989-90, 1990-91; Cliff Fletcher, 1991-92 to 1996-97; Ken Dryden, 1997-98, 1998-99; Pat Quinn, 1999-2000 to 2002-03; John Ferguson Jr., 2003-04 to 2006-07; John Ferguson Jr. and Cliff Fletcher, 2007-08; Cliff Fletcher and Brian Burke, 2008-09; Brian Burke, 2009-10 to 2011-12; Brian Burke and Dave Nonis, 2012-13; Dave Nonis, 2013-14, 2014-15; Lou Lamoriello, 2015-16 to date.

Lou Lamoriello
General Manager
Born: Providence, RI, October 21, 1942.

Brendan Shanahan, president and alternate governor of the Toronto Maple Leafs, announced on July 23, 2015 that Lou Lamoriello had been named the 16th general manager in the club's history. Lamoriello joined the Leafs after spending the previous 28 years in the New Jersey Devils organization. He has been part of a rebuilding effort in Toronto that saw the Maple Leafs fall to last overall in the standings in 2015-16, select Auston Matthews first overall in the 2016 NHL Draft to augment a solid group of young talent, and return to the playoffs in 2016-17.

Lamoriello first joined the Devils as president and general manager in 1987. Under his leadership, New Jersey went to the Stanley Cup playoffs 21 times, won nine division titles, went to the Stanley Cup Final five times and won the Cup on three occasions (1995, 2000 and 2003). The Devils also made 13 consecutive postseason berths from 1997 to 2010 and finished with a winning record every season from 1992-93 through 2009-10.

Lamoriello also served as interim head coach during three different seasons – most recently the 2014-15 season as he served as co-coach alongside Scott Stevens and Adam Oates for the final 46 games of the regular season (20-19-7). On May 4, 2015, Ray Shero was introduced as the Devils' new general manager while Lamoriello remained in his role as president of hockey operations. He finished as the longest serving general manager of any one team in the history of the NHL at 28 years (1987 to 2015).

In 1996, Lamoriello served as general manager for Team USA as they won the World Cup of Hockey. He was also general manager of Team USA at the 1998 Nagano Winter Olympics. His many accomplishments have earned him a number of prestigious awards, including induction into the Hockey Hall of Fame in the Builder category in 2009 and into the U.S. Hockey Hall of Fame in 2012.

Coaching Record

| Season | Team | League | Regular Season | | | | | Playoffs | | | |
			GC	W	L	O/T	GC	W	L	T
2005-06	New Jersey	NHL	50	32	14	4	9	5	4	....
2006-07	New Jersey	NHL	3	2	0	1	11	5	6	....
2014-15	New Jersey	NHL	....	....	....	....	....	....	....	....
	NHL Totals		**53**	**34**	**14**	**5**	**20**	**10**	**10**	**....**

Posted an 0-1 playoff record as replacement coach with New Jersey when Jim Schoenfeld was suspended, May 10, 1988. Loss is credited to Schoenfeld's coaching record.
Shared a 20-19-7 record with Adam Oates and Scott Stevens while serving as co-head coaches with New Jersey from December 27, 2014 to the end of the 2014-15 season. The games are not officially credited to anyone's coaching record.

Club Directory

Air Canada Centre

Toronto Maple Leafs
Air Canada Centre
40 Bay St.
Toronto, Ontario M5J 2X2
Phone **416/815-5700**
FAX 416/359-9331
mapleleafs.nhl.com
Capacity: 18,819

Board of Directors
Lawrence M. Tanenbaum, George Cope, Dale Lastman, Edward Rogers, Anthony Staffieri, Siim Vanaselja, Bernard Le Duc

Maple Leaf Sports & Entertainment
Chairman, NHL Governor	Lawrence M. Tanenbaum
Alternate NHL Governor	Dale Lastman
President & CEO	Michael Friisdahl
Chief Commercial Officer	Dave Hopkinson
Chief Legal & Development Officer	Peter Miller
Chief Financial Officer	Cynthia Devine
Chief Venues & Operations Officer	Nick Eaves
Senior VP, Marketing & Fan Experience	Shannon Hosford
Senior VP, Music and Live Events	Wayne Zronik
VP, Ticket Sales & Service	Tom Pistore
VP, Information Technology	Sasha Puric
VP, Global Partnerships	Jeff Deline
VP, Human Resources	Kim Carter

Hockey Operations
President & Alternate Governor	Brendan Shanahan
General Manager	Lou Lamoriello
Assistant General Manager	Kyle Dubas
Assistant General Manager	Mark Hunter
Assistant to the General Manager	Brandon Pridham
Senior Advisor	Cliff Fletcher
Head Coach	Mike Babcock
Assistant Coaches	Jim Hiller, D.J. Smith and Andrew Brewer
Goaltending Coach	Steve Briere
Special Assignment Coach	Jacques Lemaire
Director, Hockey and Scouting Operations	Reid Mitchell
Director of Player Evaluation	Jim Paliafito
Director of Team Services, Hockey Operations	Brad Lynn
Director of Pro Scouting	Dave Morrison
Director of United States Scouting	John Lilley
Director of Eastern Area Scouting	Lindsay Hofford
Director of Western Area Scouting	Tim Speltz
Director of European Scouting	Ari Vuori
Pro Scouts	Tommy Albelin, Troy Bodie, Mike Penny, Bryan Stewart, Tom Watt
Amateur Scouts	Thommie Bergman, Patrick Charbonneau, Dale Derkatch, Radim Jelinek, Nikolai Ladygin, Mike Gerritts John Lilley, Garth Malarchuk, Tony Martino, Robert Nordmark, Real Paiement, Jim Vesey
Director, Hockey Research and Development	Darryl Metcalf
Hockey Research and Development Analysts	Cam Charron, Bruce Peter, Rob Pettapiece
Director of Player Development	Scott Pellerin
Player Development Consultant	Darryl Belfry
Skating Development Consultant	Barb Underhill
Skill Development Consultant	Mike Ellis
Goaltending Consultant	Brian Daccord
Video and Technical Services Analyst	Adam Jancelewicz
Video Analyst	Jordan Bean
Administrative Assistant, Hockey Operations	Leanne Hederson
Exec. Assistant to the President and Alt. Governor	Laura Patterson
Exec. Assistant to the GM	Meghan Arnoldi
Director, Finance	Stephen Hare
Community Representatives	Wendel Clark, Darryl Sittler, George Armstrong

Medical and Training Staff
Director of Sports Science and Performance	Dr. Jeremy Bettle
Strength and Conditioning Coach	Matthew J. Herring
Director, Rehabilitation	Ryan Morrison
Head Athletic Therapist	Paul Ayotte
Assistant Athletic Therapist	Jon Geller
Massage Therapist	Todd Bean
Nutritionist	Jennifer Sygo
Equipment Manager	Brian Papineau
Assistant Equipment Managers	Tom Blatchford, Bobby Hastings
Medical Director, Maple Leafs and Marlies	Dr. Noah Forman
Orthopedic Consultant	Dr. John Theodoropoulos
Team Dentists	Dr. Marvin Lean, Dr. Charles Goldberg

Communications
Director, Media Relations	Steve Keogh
Senior Manager, Media Relations	Scott McNaughton
Coordinator, Media Relations	Chris Lund

Broadcasting
Talent, Leafs TV	Joe Bowen, Paul Hendrick, Bob McGill
Radio, Play-By-Play / Colour	Joe Bowen, Jim Ralph
Chief Engineer & Manager, Ice Operations	Derek King

Captains' History

Ken Randall, 1917-18, 1918-19; Frank Heffernan, 1919-20; Reg Noble, 1920-21, 1921-22; Reg Noble and Jack Adams, 1922-23; Jack Adams, 1923-24; John Ross Roach, 1924-25; Babe Day, 1925-26; Bert Corbeau, 1926-27; Hap Day, 1927-28 to 1936-37; Charlie Conacher, 1937-38; Red Horner, 1938-39, 1939-40; Syl Apps, 1940-41 to 1942-43; Bob Davidson, 1943-44, 1944-45; Syl Apps, 1945-46 to 1947-48; Ted Kennedy, 1948-49 to 1954-55; Sid Smith, 1955-56; Jimmy Thomson, Ted Kennedy, 1956-57; George Armstrong, 1957-58 to 1968-69; Dave Keon, 1969-70 to 1974-75; Darryl Sittler, 1975-76 to 1980-81; Rick Vaive, 1981-82 to 1985-86; no captain, 1986-87 to 1988-89; Rob Ramage, 1989-90, 1990-91; Wendel Clark, 1991-92 to 1993-94; Doug Gilmour, 1994-95 to 1996-97; Mats Sundin, 1997-98 to 2007-08; no captain, 2008-09, 2009-10; Dion Phaneuf, 2010-11 to 2014-15; Dion Phaneuf and no captain, 2015-16; no captain, 2016-17.

Vancouver Canucks

2016-17 Results: 30W-43L-7OTL-2SOL 69PTS
7TH, Pacific Division • 13TH, Western Conference

Key Off-Season Signings/Acquisitions

2017

April 26 • Named **Travis Green** head coach.

June 7 • Named **Newell Brown** and **Nolan Baumgartner** assistant coaches.

July 1 • Signed C **Sam Gagner**, C **Alexander Burmistrov** and D **Michael Del Zotto**.

1 • Re-signed RW **Anton Rodin**.

7 • Re-signed C **Joseph LaBate**.

13 • Re-signed C **Michael Chaput**.

24 • Re-signed C **Reid Boucher**.

2017-18 Schedule

Oct.	Sat.	7	Edmonton	Sun.	7	at Montreal
	Tue.	10	Ottawa	Tue.	9	at Washington
	Thu.	12	Winnipeg	Fri.	12	at Columbus
	Sat.	14	Calgary	Sun.	14	at Minnesota
	Tue.	17	at Ottawa	Sat.	20	at Edmonton
	Thu.	19	at Boston	Sun.	21	at Winnipeg
	Fri.	20	at Buffalo	Tue.	23	Los Angeles
	Sun.	22	at Detroit	Thu.	25	Buffalo
	Tue.	24	at Minnesota	Tue.	30	Colorado
	Thu.	26	Washington	**Feb.** Thu.	1	Chicago
	Mon.	30	Dallas	Sat.	3	Tampa Bay
Nov.	Wed.	1	New Jersey	Tue.	6	at Florida
	Sat.	4	Pittsburgh	Thu.	8	at Tampa Bay
	Mon.	6	Detroit	Fri.	9	at Carolina
	Tue.	7	at Calgary	Sun.	11	at Dallas*
	Thu.	9	at Anaheim	Wed.	14	Florida
	Sat.	11	at San Jose	Thu.	15	at San Jose
	Tue.	14	at Los Angeles	Sat.	17	Boston
	Thu.	16	Vegas	Tue.	20	Colorado
	Sat.	18	St. Louis	Fri.	23	at Vegas
	Tue.	21	at Philadelphia	Sun.	25	at Arizona
	Wed.	22	at Pittsburgh	Mon.	26	at Colorado
	Fri.	24	at New Jersey	Wed.	28	NY Rangers
	Sun.	26	at NY Rangers*	**Mar.** Fri.	2	Nashville
	Tue.	28	at NY Islanders	Mon.	5	NY Islanders
	Thu.	30	at Nashville	Wed.	7	Arizona
Dec.	Sat.	2	Toronto*	Fri.	9	Minnesota
	Tue.	5	Carolina	Sun.	11	at Arizona
	Thu.	7	Philadelphia	Mon.	12	at Los Angeles
	Sat.	9	at Calgary	Wed.	14	at Anaheim
	Mon.	11	at Winnipeg	Sat.	17	San Jose
	Wed.	13	Nashville	Tue.	20	at Vegas
	Fri.	15	San Jose	Thu.	22	at Chicago
	Sun.	17	Calgary*	Fri.	23	at St. Louis*
	Tue.	19	Montreal	Sun.	25	at Dallas
	Thu.	21	at San Jose	Tue.	27	Anaheim
	Sat.	23	St. Louis	Thu.	29	Edmonton
	Thu.	28	Chicago	Sat.	31	Columbus*
	Sat.	30	Los Angeles	**Apr.** Tue.	3	Vegas
Jan.	Tue.	2	Anaheim	Thu.	5	Arizona
	Sat.	6	at Toronto	Sat.	7	at Edmonton

* Denotes afternoon game.

Retired Numbers

10	Pavel Bure	1991-1998
12	Stan Smyl	1978-1991
16	Trevor Linden	1988-1998; 2001-2008
19	Markus Naslund	1996-2008

PACIFIC DIVISION
48th NHL Season

Franchise date: May 22, 1970

Bo Horvat had a team-best 20 goals and 52 points in 2016-17, making him the first player other than a Sedin to lead the Canucks in scoring since Markus Naslund in 2005-06.

Year-by-Year Record

		Home				Road				Overall						Div. Fin.	Conf. Fin.	Playoff Result
Season	GP	W	L	T	OL	W	L	T	OL	W	L	T	OL	GF	GA	Pts.			
2016-17	82	18	17	....	6	12	26	....	3	30	43	....	9	182	243	69	7th, Pac.	13th, West	– out of playoffs –
2015-16	82	15	21	....	5	16	17	....	8	31	38	....	13	191	243	75	6th, Pac.	13th, West	– out of playoffs –
2014-15	82	24	15	....	2	24	14	....	3	48	29	....	5	242	222	101	2nd, Pac.	5th, West	Lost First Round
2013-14	82	20	15	....	6	16	20	....	5	36	35	....	11	196	223	83	5th, Pac.	12th, West	– out of playoffs –
2012-13	48	15	6	....	3	11	9	....	4	26	15	....	7	127	121	59	1st, NW	3rd, West	Lost Conf. Quarter-Final
2011-12	82	27	10	....	4	24	12	....	5	51	22	....	9	249	198	111	1st, NW	1st, West	Lost Conf. Quarter-Final
2010-11	82	27	9	....	5	27	10	....	4	54	19	....	9	262	185	117	1st, NW	1st, West	Lost Final
2009-10	82	30	8	....	3	19	20	....	2	49	28	....	5	272	222	103	1st, NW	3rd, West	Lost Conf. Semi-Final
2008-09	82	24	12	....	5	21	15	....	5	45	27	....	10	246	220	100	1st, NW	3rd, West	Lost Conf. Semi-Final
2007-08	82	21	15	....	5	18	18	....	5	39	33	....	10	213	215	88	1st, NW	11th, West	– out of playoffs –
2006-07	82	26	11	....	4	23	15	....	3	49	26	....	7	222	201	105	1st, NW	3rd, West	Lost Conf. Semi-Final
2005-06	82	25	10	....	6	17	22	....	2	42	32	....	8	256	255	92	4th, NW	9th, West	– out of playoffs –
2004-05																			
2003-04	82	21	13	7	0	22	11	3	5	43	24	10	5	235	194	101	1st, NW	3rd, West	Lost Conf. Quarter-Final
2002-03	82	22	13	6	0	23	10	7	1	45	23	13	1	264	208	104	2nd, NW	4th, West	Lost Conf. Semi-Final
2001-02	82	23	11	5	2	19	19	2	1	42	30	7	3	254	211	94	2nd, NW	8th, West	Lost Conf. Quarter-Final
2000-01	82	21	12	5	3	15	16	6	4	36	28	11	7	239	238	90	3rd, NW	8th, West	Lost Conf. Quarter-Final
1999-2000	82	16	14	5	6	14	15	10	2	30	29	15	8	227	237	83	3rd, NW	10th, West	– out of playoffs –
1998-99	82	14	21	6	....	9	26	6	....	23	47	12	....	192	258	58	4th, NW	13th, West	– out of playoffs –
1997-98	82	15	22	4	....	10	21	10	....	25	43	14	....	224	273	64	7th, Pac.	13th, West	– out of playoffs –
1996-97	82	20	17	4	....	15	23	3	....	35	40	7	....	257	273	77	4th, Pac.	9th, West	– out of playoffs –
1995-96	82	15	19	7	....	17	16	8	....	32	35	15	....	278	278	79	3rd, Pac.	7th, West	Lost Conf. Quarter-Final
1994-95	48	10	8	6	....	8	10	6	....	18	18	12	....	153	148	48	2nd, Pac.	6th, West	Lost Conf. Semi-Final
1993-94	84	20	19	3	....	21	27	0	....	41	40	3	....	279	276	85	2nd, Pac.	7th, West	Lost Final
1992-93	84	27	11	4	....	19	18	5	....	46	29	9	....	346	278	101	1st, Smythe		Lost Div. Final
1991-92	80	23	10	7	....	19	16	5	....	42	26	12	....	285	250	96	1st, Smythe		Lost Div. Final
1990-91	80	18	17	5	....	10	26	4	....	28	43	9	....	243	315	65	4th, Smythe		Lost Div. Semi-Final
1989-90	80	13	16	11	....	12	25	3	....	25	41	14	....	245	306	64	5th, Smythe		– out of playoffs –
1988-89	80	19	15	6	....	14	24	2	....	33	39	8	....	251	253	74	4th, Smythe		Lost Div. Semi-Final
1987-88	80	15	20	5	....	10	26	4	....	25	46	9	....	272	320	59	5th, Smythe		– out of playoffs –
1986-87	80	17	19	4	....	12	24	4	....	29	43	8	....	282	314	66	5th, Smythe		– out of playoffs –
1985-86	80	17	18	5	....	6	26	8	....	23	44	13	....	282	333	59	4th, Smythe		Lost Div. Semi-Final
1984-85	80	15	21	4	....	10	25	5	....	25	46	9	....	284	401	59	5th, Smythe		– out of playoffs –
1983-84	80	20	16	4	....	12	23	5	....	32	39	9	....	306	328	73	3rd, Smythe		Lost Div. Semi-Final
1982-83	80	20	12	8	....	10	23	7	....	30	35	15	....	303	309	75	3rd, Smythe		Lost Div. Semi-Final
1981-82	80	20	8	12	....	10	25	5	....	30	33	17	....	290	286	77	2nd, Smythe		Lost Final
1980-81	80	17	12	11	....	11	20	9	....	28	32	20	....	289	301	76	3rd, Smythe		Lost Prelim. Round
1979-80	80	14	17	9	....	13	20	7	....	27	37	16	....	256	281	70	3rd, Smythe		Lost Prelim. Round
1978-79	80	15	18	7	....	10	24	6	....	25	42	13	....	217	291	63	2nd, Smythe		Lost Prelim. Round
1977-78	80	13	15	12	....	7	28	5	....	20	43	17	....	239	320	57	3rd, Smythe		– out of playoffs –
1976-77	80	13	21	6	....	12	11	7	....	25	42	13	....	235	294	63	4th, Smythe		– out of playoffs –
1975-76	80	22	11	7	....	11	21	8	....	33	32	15	....	271	272	81	2nd, Smythe		Lost Prelim. Round
1974-75	80	23	12	5	....	15	20	5	....	38	32	10	....	271	254	86	1st, Smythe		Lost Quarter-Final
1973-74	78	14	18	7	....	10	25	4	....	24	43	11	....	224	296	59	7th, East		– out of playoffs –
1972-73	78	17	18	4	....	5	29	5	....	22	47	9	....	233	339	53	7th, East		– out of playoffs –
1971-72	78	14	20	5	....	6	30	3	....	20	50	8	....	203	297	48	7th, East		– out of playoffs –
1970-71	78	17	18	4	....	7	28	4	....	24	46	8	....	229	296	56	6th, East		– out of playoffs –

2017-18 Player Personnel

FORWARDS	HT	WT	*Age	Birthplace	S	2016-17 Club
BAERTSCHI, Sven	5-11	190	24	Bern, Switzerland	L	Vancouver
BOESER, Brock	6-1	191	20	Burnsville, MN	R	North Dakota-Vancouver
BOUCHER, Reid	5-10	195	24	Lansing, MI	L	N.J.-Nsh-Milwaukee-Van
BURMISTROV, Alexander	6-1	180	25	Kazan, Russia	L	Winnipeg-Arizona
CHAPUT, Michael	6-2	204	25	Ile Bizard, QC	L	Vancouver-Utica
DORSETT, Derek	6-0	192	30	Kindersley, SK	R	Vancouver
ERIKSSON, Loui	6-2	183	32	Goteborg, Sweden	L	Vancouver
GAGNER, Sam	5-11	202	28	London, ON	R	Columbus
GAUNCE, Brendan	6-2	207	23	Markham, ON	L	Vancouver-Utica
GOLDOBIN, Nikolay	5-11	185	21	Moscow, Russia	L	S.J.-S.J. (AHL)-Van-Utica
GRANLUND, Markus	6-0	178	24	Oulu, Finland	L	Vancouver
HORVAT, Bo	6-0	206	22	Rodney, ON	L	Vancouver
MEGNA, Jayson	6-1	195	27	Fort Lauderdale, FL	R	Vancouver-Utica
RODIN, Anton	5-11	181	26	Stockholm, Sweden	L	Vancouver-Utica
SEDIN, Daniel	6-1	187	37	Ornskoldsvik, Sweden	L	Vancouver
SEDIN, Henrik	6-2	188	37	Ornskoldsvik, Sweden	L	Vancouver
SUTTER, Brandon	6-3	190	28	Huntington, NY	R	Vancouver
VIRTANEN, Jake	6-1	208	21	New Westminster, BC	R	Vancouver-Utica

DEFENSEMEN						
BIEGA, Alex	5-10	187	29	Montreal, QC	R	Vancouver-Utica
DEL ZOTTO, Michael	6-0	195	27	Stouffville, ON	L	Philadelphia
EDLER, Alexander	6-3	215	31	Ostersund, Sweden	L	Vancouver
GUDBRANSON, Erik	6-5	216	25	Ottawa, ON	R	Vancouver
HUTTON, Ben	6-2	183	24	Prescott, ON	L	Vancouver
PEDAN, Andrey	6-5	213	24	Kaunas, Lithuania	L	Utica
STECHER, Troy	5-11	191	23	Richmond, BC	R	Vancouver-Utica
TANEV, Chris	6-2	185	27	Toronto, ON	R	Vancouver
WIERCIOCH, Patrick	6-5	202	27	Burnaby, BC	L	Colorado

GOALTENDERS	HT	WT	*Age	Birthplace	C	2016-17 Club
MARKSTROM, Jacob	6-6	196	27	Gavle, Sweden	L	Vancouver
NILSSON, Anders	6-5	229	27	Lulea, Sweden	L	Buffalo

* – Age at start of 2017-18 season

2016-17 Scoring

* – rookie

Regular Season

Pos	#	Player	Team	GP	G	A	Pts	TOI	+/-	PIM	PP	SH	GW	S	S%
C	53	Bo Horvat	VAN	81	20	32	52	18:01	-7	27	3	2	1	158	12.7
C	33	Henrik Sedin	VAN	82	15	35	50	19:02	-27	28	1	0	0	99	15.2
L	22	Daniel Sedin	VAN	82	15	29	44	18:23	-16	32	6	0	3	216	6.9
L	47	Sven Baertschi	VAN	68	18	17	35	15:52	-6	8	2	0	5	114	15.8
C	20	Brandon Sutter	VAN	81	17	17	34	18:48	-20	12	4	1	0	160	10.6
C	60	Markus Granlund	VAN	69	19	13	32	17:18	-19	14	3	0	3	122	15.6
L	21	Loui Eriksson	VAN	65	11	13	24	18:40	-9	8	5	0	1	132	8.3
D	51 *	Troy Stecher	VAN	71	3	21	24	19:58	-16	25	1	0	0	125	2.4
D	23	Alexander Edler	VAN	68	6	15	21	24:18	-20	36	2	0	0	138	4.3
D	27	Ben Hutton	VAN	71	5	14	19	20:29	-22	31	2	0	1	130	3.8
D	5	Luca Sbisa	VAN	82	2	11	13	18:58	-1	40	0	0	1	75	2.7
C	24	Reid Boucher	N.J.	9	0	2	2	12:15	0	2	0	0	0	12	0.0
			NSH	3	1	0	1	8:42	1	0	0	0	0	3	33.3
			VAN	27	5	2	7	12:10	-7	6	1	0	0	55	9.1
			Total	39	6	4	10	11:55	-6	8	1	0	0	70	8.6
C	26 *	Joseph Cramarossa	ANA	49	4	6	10	9:48	-1	51	0	0	1	26	15.4
			VAN	10	0	0	0	10:35	-1	9	0	0	0	10	0.0
			Total	59	4	6	10	9:56	0	60	0	0	1	36	11.1
D	8	Chris Tanev	VAN	53	2	8	10	20:20	3	14	0	0	1	39	5.1
R	9	Jack Skille	VAN	55	5	4	9	8:47	0	12	0	0	0	73	6.8
C	45	Michael Chaput	VAN	68	4	5	9	11:01	-12	29	0	0	0	64	6.3
C	88 *	Nikita Tryamkin	VAN	66	2	7	9	16:44	-7	64	0	0	0	65	3.1
C	46	Jayson Megna	VAN	58	4	4	8	12:26	-4	6	0	0	0	72	5.6
D	63	Philip Larsen	VAN	26	1	5	6	16:27	-8	4	0	0	0	32	3.1
D	44	Erik Gudbranson	VAN	30	1	5	6	20:20	-14	18	0	0	1	40	2.5
R	6 *	Brock Boeser	VAN	9	4	1	5	16:12	0	0	2	0	1	25	16.0
C	50 *	Brendan Gaunce	VAN	57	0	5	5	9:29	-2	33	0	0	0	51	0.0
R	15	Derek Dorsett	VAN	14	1	3	4	9:55	-6	33	0	0	0	24	4.2
R	82 *	Nikolay Goldobin	S.J.	2	0	0	0	9:49	-1	0	0	0	0	4	0.0
			VAN	12	3	0	3	11:37	1	0	1	0	0	10	30.0
			Total	14	3	0	3	11:22	0	0	1	0	0	14	21.4
D	55	Alex Biega	VAN	36	0	3	3	13:10	-4	18	0	0	0	37	0.0
C	42	Drew Shore	VAN	14	0	2	2	11:57	-3	4	0	0	0	11	0.0
R	17 *	Anton Rodin	VAN	3	0	1	1	8:54	1	0	0	0	0	2	0.0
R	18	Jake Virtanen	VAN	10	0	1	1	10:08	1	2	0	0	0	13	0.0
D	61 *	Evan McEneny	VAN	1	0	0	0	15:08	-1	0	0	0	0	0	0.0
L	40 *	Mike Zalewski	VAN	1	0	0	0	8:03	-1	0	0	0	0	0	0.0
C	64 *	Borna Rendulic	VAN	1	0	0	0	4:51	0	0	0	0	0	1	0.0
R	65 *	Alexandre Grenier	VAN	3	0	0	0	6:29	-1	0	0	0	0	1	0.0
C	13 *	Griffen Molino	VAN	5	0	0	0	10:35	-2	0	0	0	0	6	0.0
C	62 *	Joseph Labate	VAN	13	0	0	0	6:45	-2	21	0	0	0	5	0.0

Goaltending

No.	Goaltender	GPI	Mins	Avg	W	L	OT	EN	SO	GA	SA	Sv%	G	A	PIM
25	Jacob Markstrom	26	1417	2.63	10	11	3	6	0	62	692	.910	0	0	2
32	Richard Bachman	5	295	2.64	2	3	0	0	0	13	162	.920	0	0	0
30	Ryan Miller	54	3212	2.80	18	29	6	10	3	150	1737	.914	0	1	22
	Totals	**82**	**4980**	**2.90**	**30**	**43**	**9**	**16**	**3**	**241**	**2607**	**.908**			

Coaching History

Hal Laycoe, 1970-71, 1971-72; Vic Stasiuk, 1972-73; Bill McCreary and Phil Maloney, 1973-74; Phil Maloney, 1974-75, 1975-76; Phil Maloney and Orland Kurtenbach, 1976-77; Orland Kurtenbach, 1977-78; Harry Neale, 1978-79 to 1980-81; Harry Neale and Roger Neilson, 1981-82; Roger Neilson, 1982-83; Roger Neilson and Harry Neale, 1983-84; Bill Laforge and Harry Neale, 1984-85; Tom Watt, 1985-86, 1986-87; Bob McCammon, 1987-88 to 1989-90; Bob McCammon and Pat Quinn, 1990-91; Pat Quinn, 1991-92 to 1993-94; Rick Ley, 1994-95; Rick Ley and Pat Quinn, 1995-96; Tom Renney, 1996-97; Tom Renney and Mike Keenan, 1997-98; Mike Keenan and Marc Crawford, 1998-99; Marc Crawford, 1999-2000 to 2005-06; Alain Vigneault, 2006-07 to 2012-13; John Tortorella, 2013-14; Willie Desjardins, 2014-15 to 2016-17; Travis Green, 2017-18.

Travis Green
Head Coach

Born: Castlegar, BC, December 20, 1970.

Vancouver Canucks general manager Jim Benning announced on April 26, 2017 that the team had named Travis Green as head coach. Green became the 19th man to coach the Canucks in team history after being promoted from his role as head coach of the club's American Hockey League affiliate, the Utica Comets.

Green was named the first head coach in Comets history in 2013 and built a record of 155-110-39 in 304 games coached over four seasons. In 2014-15, his second season, Green led the Comets to a 47-20-9 record, a North Division Championship and Calder Cup Final berth. Prior to joining the Comets, Green was interim head coach of the Portland Winterhawks in 2012-13, leading the team to a 37-8-2 record, a Western Hockey League championship title and a berth in the 2013 Memorial Cup Final. He began his coaching career with the Winterhawks as an assistant coach and assistant general manager in the 2009-10 season.

Green played 14 seasons in the NHL and a final professional season with EV Zug in Switzerland. He recorded 455 career points (193 goals, 262 assists) and 764 penalty minutes in 970 career games with the New York Islanders, Anaheim Ducks, Phoenix Coyotes, Toronto Maple Leafs and Boston Bruins. In 56 career playoff games Green scored 21 points (10 goals, 11 assists) and added 60 penalty minutes. Green was originally selected by the New York Islanders in the second round, 23rd overall, in the 1989 NHL Draft.

Coaching Record

				Regular Season					Playoffs			
Season	Team	League	GC	W	L	O/T		GC	W	L	T
2012-13	Portland	WHL	47	37	8	2		21	16	5	....
2012-13	Portland	M-Cup	....	....	....	....		5	3	2	....
2013-14	Utica	AHL	76	35	32	9		....	....	....	....
2014-15	Utica	AHL	76	47	20	9		23	12	11	....
2015-16	Utica	AHL	76	38	26	12		4	1	3	....
2016-17	Utica	AHL	76	35	32	9		....	....	....	....

Brandon Sutter was limited to 20 games due to injuries in 2015-16 but bounced back to play 81 games in 2016-17 and post 34 points.

Captains' History

Orland Kurtenbach, 1970-71 to 1973-74; no captain, 1974-75; Andre Boudrias, 1975-76; Chris Oddleifson, 1976-77; Don Lever, 1977-78, 1978-79; Kevin McCarthy, 1979-80 to 1981-82; Stan Smyl, 1982-83 to 1989-90; Dan Quinn, Doug Lidster and Trevor Linden, 1990-91; Trevor Linden, 1991-92 to 1996-97; Mark Messier, 1997-98 to 1999-2000; Markus Naslund, 2000-01 to 2007-08; Roberto Luongo, 2008-09, 2009-10; Henrik Sedin, 2010-11 to date.

Club Records

Team

(Figures in brackets for season records are games played; records for fewest points, wins, ties, losses, goals, goals against are for 70 or more games)

Most Points **117** 2010-11 (82)
Most Wins **54** 2010-11 (82)
Most Ties **20** 1980-81 (80)
Most Losses **50** 1971-72 (78)
Most Goals **346** 1992-93 (84)
Most Goals Against **401** 1984-85 (80)
Fewest Points **48** 1971-72 (78)
Fewest Wins **20** 1971-72 (78), 1977-78 (80)
Fewest Ties **3** 1993-94 (84)
Fewest Losses **19** 2010-11 (82)
Fewest Goals **182** 2016-17 (82)
Fewest Goals Against **185** 2010-11 (82)

Longest Winning Streak
Overall .... **10** Nov. 9-30/02
Home .... **11** Feb. 3-Mar. 19/09
Away .... **9** Mar. 5-29/11

Longest Team Point Streak
Overall **14** Jan.26-Feb. 25/03 (7W, 3OTW, 4T)
Home .... **18** Nov. 4/92-Jan. 16/93 (14W, 4T)
Away .... **9** Feb. 4-Mar. 3/03 (4W, 2OTW, 3T), Mar. 5-29/11 (7W, 1OTW, 1SOW)

Longest Losing Streak
Overall .... **10** Oct. 23-Nov. 11/97
Home .... **12** Feb. 19-Apr. 8/17
Away .... **12** Nov. 28/81-Feb. 6/82

Longest Winless Streak
Overall .... **13** Nov. 9-Dec. 7/73 (10L, 3T)
Home .... **12** Feb. 19-Apr. 8/17 (9L, 3OTL)
Away .... **20** Jan. 2-Apr. 2/86 (14L, 6T)

Most Shutouts, Season **10** 2008-09 (82)
Most PIM, Season **2,326** 1992-93 (84)
Most Goals, Game .... **11** Mar. 28/71 (Cal. 5 at Van. 11), Nov. 25/86 (L.A. 5 at Van. 11), Mar. 1/92 (Cgy. 0 at Van. 11)

Individual

Most Seasons .... **16** Trevor Linden, Daniel Sedin, Henrik Sedin
Most Games .... **1,248** Henrik Sedin
Most Goals, Career .... **370** Daniel Sedin
Most Assists, Career .... **783** Henrik Sedin
Most Points, Career .... **1,020** Henrik Sedin (237G, 783A)
Most PIM, Career .... **2,127** Gino Odjick
Most Shutouts, Career .... **38** Roberto Luongo
Longest Consecutive Games Streak .... **679** Henrik Sedin (Mar. 21/04-Jan. 18/13)
Most Goals, Season .... **60** Pavel Bure (1992-93), (1993-94)
Most Assists, Season .... **83** Henrik Sedin (2009-10)
Most Points, Season .... **112** Henrik Sedin (2009-10; 29G, 83A)
Most PIM, Season .... **372** Donald Brashear (1997-98)
Most Points, Defenseman, Season .... **63** Doug Lidster (1986-87; 12G, 51A)
Most Points, Center, Season .... **112** Henrik Sedin (2009-10; 29G, 83A)
Most Points, Right Wing, Season .... **110** Pavel Bure (1992-93; 60G, 50A)
Most Points, Left Wing, Season .... **104** Markus Naslund (2002-03; 48G, 56A), Daniel Sedin (2010-11; 41G, 63A)
Most Points, Rookie, Season .... **60** Ivan Hlinka (1981-82; 23G, 37A), Pavel Bure (1991-92; 34G, 26A)
Most Shutouts, Season .... **9** Roberto Luongo (2008-09)
Most Goals, Game .... **4** Twelve times
Most Assists, Game .... **6** Patrik Sundstrom (Feb. 29/84)
Most Points, Game .... **7** Patrik Sundstrom (Feb. 29/84; 1G, 6A)

All-time Record vs. Other Clubs

Regular Season

	Total								At Home								On Road							
	GP	W	L	T	OL	GF	GA	PTS	GP	W	L	T	OL	GF	GA	PTS	GP	W	L	T	OL	GF	GA	PTS
Anaheim	102	48	40	9	5	291	287	110	52	25	23	2	2	150	146	54	50	23	17	7	3	141	141	56
Arizona	191	98	66	20	7	655	567	223	97	60	26	10	1	347	255	131	94	38	40	10	6	308	312	92
Boston	117	30	70	15	2	327	463	77	58	19	30	8	1	186	229	47	59	11	40	7	1	141	234	30
Buffalo	118	51	46	19	2	391	387	123	59	31	17	11	0	219	177	73	59	20	29	8	2	172	210	50
Calgary	269	105	125	33	6	846	903	249	136	61	52	18	5	458	413	145	133	44	73	15	1	388	490	104
Carolina	73	36	26	11	0	253	212	83	37	21	10	6	0	131	94	48	36	15	16	5	0	122	118	35
Chicago	186	77	81	22	6	504	587	182	94	48	30	15	1	279	264	112	92	29	51	7	5	225	323	70
Colorado	158	71	62	15	10	478	508	167	79	37	30	7	5	252	260	86	79	34	32	8	5	226	248	81
Columbus	55	34	11	2	8	189	136	78	27	18	4	0	5	97	72	41	28	16	7	2	3	92	64	37
Dallas	185	71	84	22	8	577	597	172	92	42	37	10	3	317	275	97	93	29	47	12	5	260	322	75
Detroit	170	62	82	18	8	534	603	150	85	37	33	10	5	293	267	89	85	25	49	8	3	241	336	61
Edmonton	236	98	109	19	10	765	866	225	118	55	46	12	5	414	407	127	118	43	63	7	5	351	459	98
Florida	31	15	7	6	3	90	75	39	16	8	2	5	1	44	35	22	15	7	5	1	2	46	40	17
Los Angeles	246	106	99	32	9	789	818	253	121	63	37	16	5	423	355	147	125	43	62	16	4	366	463	106
Minnesota	85	43	29	5	8	228	229	99	42	24	9	3	6	121	102	57	43	19	20	2	2	107	127	42
Montreal	126	31	80	13	2	327	493	77	64	19	36	8	1	176	223	47	62	12	44	5	1	151	270	30
Nashville	68	39	24	2	3	199	170	83	33	20	11	1	1	106	75	42	35	19	13	1	2	93	95	41
New Jersey	110	57	34	17	2	370	312	133	54	31	11	11	1	194	142	74	56	26	23	6	1	176	170	59
NY Islanders	108	42	50	13	3	331	366	100	54	26	24	3	1	176	177	56	54	16	26	10	2	155	189	44
NY Rangers	119	33	77	8	1	338	483	75	58	18	37	3	0	176	225	39	61	15	40	5	1	162	258	36
Ottawa	39	21	15	2	1	113	88	45	20	12	7	1	0	61	45	25	19	9	8	1	1	52	43	20
Philadelphia	119	33	69	13	4	349	477	83	58	13	31	12	2	167	225	40	61	20	38	1	2	182	252	43
Pittsburgh	114	38	61	11	4	390	452	91	57	25	25	4	3	201	206	57	57	13	36	7	1	189	246	34
St. Louis	186	73	93	18	2	523	613	166	94	43	41	9	1	269	285	96	92	30	52	9	1	254	328	70
San Jose	116	53	48	9	6	337	337	121	57	24	24	4	5	169	167	57	59	29	24	5	1	168	170	64
Tampa Bay	32	19	9	2	2	118	89	42	16	10	2	2	2	61	37	24	16	9	7	0	0	57	52	18
Toronto	142	63	55	22	2	486	482	150	73	37	23	11	2	259	233	87	69	26	32	11	0	227	249	63
Washington	93	40	42	9	2	296	298	91	46	23	17	5	1	160	143	52	47	17	25	4	1	136	155	39
Winnipeg	24	13	9	1	1	69	62	28	12	8	3	1	0	37	26	17	12	5	6	0	1	32	36	11
Defunct Clubs	38	24	11	3	0	153	116	51	19	14	3	2	0	82	48	30	19	10	8	1	0	71	68	21
Totals	**3656**	**1524**	**1614**	**391**	**127**	**11316**	**12076**	**3566**	**1828**	**872**	**681**	**210**	**65**	**6025**	**5608**	**2019**	**1828**	**652**	**933**	**181**	**62**	**5291**	**6468**	**1547**

Playoffs

	Series	W	L	GP	W	L	T	GF	GA	Last Mtg.	Rnd.	Result
Anaheim	1	0	1	5	1	4	0	8	14	2007	CSF	L 1-4
Arizona	2	2	0	13	8	5	0	50	34	1993	DSF	W 4-2
Boston	1	0	1	7	3	4	0	8	23	2011	F	L 3-4
Buffalo	2	0	2	7	1	6	0	14	28	1981	PR	L 0-3
Calgary	7	2	5	38	17	21	0	110	119	2015	FR	L 2-4
Chicago	5	2	3	28	12	16	0	77	92	2011	CQF	W 4-3
Colorado	2	0	2	10	2	8	0	26	40	2001	CQF	L 0-4
Dallas	2	2	0	12	8	4	0	31	23	2007	CQF	W 4-3
Detroit	1	0	1	6	2	4	0	16	22	2002	CQF	L 2-4
Edmonton	2	0	2	9	2	7	0	20	35	1992	DF	L 2-4
Los Angeles	5	2	3	28	13	15	0	93	96	2012	CQF	L 1-4
Minnesota	1	0	1	7	3	4	0	17	26	2003	CSF	L 3-4
Montreal	1	0	1	5	1	4	0	9	20	1975	QF	L 1-4
Nashville	1	1	0	6	4	2	0	14	11	2011	CSF	W 4-2
NY Islanders	2	0	2	6	0	6	0	14	26	1982	F	L 0-4
NY Rangers	1	0	1	7	3	4	0	19	21	1994	F	L 3-4
Philadelphia	1	0	1	3	1	2	0	9	15	1979	PR	L 1-2
St. Louis	3	3	0	18	12	6	0	55	53	2009	CQF	W 4-0
San Jose	2	1	1	9	4	5	0	28	28	2013	CQF	L 0-4
Toronto	1	1	0	5	4	1	0	16	9	1994	CF	W 4-1
Totals	**43**	**16**	**27**	**229**	**101**	**128**	**0**	**634**	**735**			

Calgary totals include Atlanta Flames, 1972-73 to 1979-80.
Colorado totals include Quebec, 1979-80 to 1994-95.
New Jersey totals include Kansas City, 1974-75, 1975-76, and Colorado Rockies, 1976-77 to 1981-82.
Phoenix totals include Winnipeg, 1979-80 to 1995-96.
Carolina totals include Hartford, 1979-80 to 1996-97.
Dallas totals include Minnesota North Stars, 1970-71 to 1992-93.
Winnipeg totals include Atlanta Thrashers, 1999-2000 to 2010-11.

Playoff Results 2017-2013

Year	Round	Opponent	Result	GF	GA
2015	FR	Calgary	L 2-4	14	18
2013	CQF	San Jose	L 0-4	8	15

Abbreviations: Round: F – Final;
CF – conference final; **CSF** – conference semi-final;
SR – second round; **CQF** – conference quarter-final;
FR – first round; **DF** – division final;
DSF – division semi-final; **QF** – quarter-final;
PR – preliminary round.

2016-17 Results

Oct.	15	Calgary	2-1†		7	at Calgary	1-3
	16	Carolina	4-3*		10	at Nashville	1-2*
	18	St. Louis	2-1*		12	at Philadelphia	4-5†
	20	Buffalo	2-1		15	New Jersey	1-2*
	22	at Los Angeles	3-4†		17	Nashville	1-0
	23	at Anaheim	2-4		20	Florida	2-1
	25	Ottawa	0-3		22	at Chicago	2-4
	28	Edmonton	0-2		25	at Colorado	3-2
	29	Washington	2-5		26	at Arizona	0-3
Nov.	2	at Montreal	0-3	**Feb.**	2	San Jose	1-4
	3	at Ottawa	0-1		4	Minnesota	3-6
	5	at Toronto	3-6		7	at Nashville	2-4
	7	at NY Islanders	2-4		9	at Columbus	3-0
	8	at NY Rangers	5-3		11	at Boston	3-4
	10	at Detroit	1-3		12	at Buffalo	4-2
	13	Dallas	5-4*		14	at Pittsburgh	0-4
	15	NY Rangers	2-7		16	at St. Louis	3-4
	17	Arizona	3-2*		18	Calgary	2-1*
	19	Chicago	3-4*		19	Philadelphia	2-3
	23	at Arizona	4-1		25	San Jose	1-4
	25	at Dallas	1-2		28	Detroit	2-3*
	26	at Colorado	3-2†	**Mar.**	2	at San Jose	1-3
	29	Minnesota	5-4		4	at Los Angeles	4-3
Dec.	1	Anaheim	1-3		5	at Anaheim	2-1
	3	Toronto	3-2†		7	Montreal	1-2*
	6	at New Jersey	2-3		9	NY Islanders	3-4*
	8	at Tampa Bay	5-1		11	Pittsburgh	0-3
	10	at Florida	2-4		13	Boston	3-6
	11	at Washington	0-3		16	Dallas	2-4
	13	at Carolina	6-8		18	at Edmonton	0-2
	16	Tampa Bay	4-2		21	at Chicago	5-4*
	18	Columbus	3-4*		23	at St. Louis	1-4
	20	Winnipeg	4-1		25	at Minnesota	4-2
	22	Winnipeg	1-4		26	at Winnipeg	1-2
	23	at Calgary	1-4		28	Anaheim	1-4
	28	Los Angeles	2-1		31	Los Angeles	0-2
	30	Anaheim	3-2*	**Apr.**	2	San Jose	1-3
	31	at Edmonton	3-2†		4	at San Jose	1-3
Jan.	2	Colorado	3-2		6	at Arizona	3-4
	4	Arizona	3-0		8	Edmonton	2-3
	6	Calgary	4-2		9	at Edmonton	2-5

* – Overtime † – Shootout

NHL Draft Selections 2017-2003

Name in bold denotes played in NHL.

2017
Pick
5	Elias Pettersson
33	Kole Lind
55	Jonah Gadjovich
64	Michael Dipietro
95	Jack Rathbone
135	Kristoffer Gunnarsson
181	Petrus Palmu
188	Matt Brassard

2016
Pick
5	Olli Juolevi
64	William Lockwood
140	Cole Candella
154	Jakob Stukel
184	Rodrigo Abols
194	Brett McKenzie

2015
Pick
23	**Brock Boeser**
66	Guillaume Brisebois
114	Dmitri Zhukenov
144	Carl Neill
149	Adam Gaudette
174	Lukas Jasek
210	Tate Olson

2014
Pick
6	**Jake Virtanen**
24	**Jared McCann**
36	Thatcher Demko
66	**Nikita Tryamkin**
126	**Gustav Forsling**
156	Kyle Pettit
186	Mackenze Stewart

2013
Pick
9	**Bo Horvat**
24	**Hunter Shinkaruk**
85	Cole Cassels
115	Jordan Subban
145	Anton Cederholm
175	Mike Williamson
205	Miles Liberati

2012
Pick
26	**Brendan Gaunce**
57	Alexandre Mallet
147	**Ben Hutton**
177	Wesley Myron
207	Matthew Beattie

2011
Pick
29	**Nicklas Jensen**
71	David Honzik
90	**Alexandre Grenier**
101	**Joseph Labate**
120	Ludwig Blomstrand
150	**Frank Corrado**
180	Pathrik Westerholm
210	Henrik Tommernes

2010
Pick
115	Patrick McNally
145	Adam Polasek
172	**Alex Friesen**
175	Jonathan Iilahti
205	Sawyer Hannay

2009
Pick
22	**Jordan Schroeder**
53	**Anton Rodin**
83	**Kevin Connauton**
113	Jeremy Price
143	Peter Andersson
173	Joe Cannata
187	Steven Anthony

2008
Pick
10	**Cody Hodgson**
41	**Yann Sauve**
131	Prab Rai
161	Mats Froshaug
191	Morgan Clark

2007
Pick
25	Patrick White
33	Taylor Ellington
145	Charles-Antoine Messier
146	Ilja Kablukov
176	Taylor Matson
206	Dan Gendur

2006
Pick
14	**Michael Grabner**
82	Daniel Rahimi
163	**Sergei Shirokov**
167	Juraj Simek
197	Evan Fuller

2005
Pick
10	**Luc Bourdon**
51	**Mason Raymond**
114	Alexandre Vincent
138	Matt Butcher
185	**Kris Fredheim**
205	Mario Bliznak

2004
Pick
26	**Cory Schneider**
91	**Alexander Edler**
125	Andrew Sarauer
159	**Mike Brown**
189	Julien Ellis
254	David Schulz
287	**Jannik Hansen**

2003
Pick
23	**Ryan Kesler**
60	Marc-Andre Bernier
111	**Brandon Nolan**
128	Ty Morris
160	Nicklas Danielsson
190	Chad Brownlee
222	Francois-Pierre Guenette
252	Sergei Topol
254	**Nathan McIver**
285	Matthew Hansen

General Managers' History

Bud Poile, 1970-71, 1971-72; Bud Poile and Hal Laycoe, 1972-73; Hal Laycoe and Phil Maloney, 1973-74; Phil Maloney, 1974-75 to 1976-77; Jake Milford, 1977-78 to 1981-82; Harry Neale, 1982-83 to 1984-85; Jack Gordon, 1985-86, 1986-87; Pat Quinn, 1987-88 to 1996-97; Pat Quinn and Mike Keenan, 1997-98; Brian Burke, 1998-99 to 2003-04; David Nonis, 2004-05 to 2007-08; Mike Gillis, 2008-09 to 2013-14; Jim Benning, 2014-15 to date.

Jim Benning
General Manager
Born: Edmonton, AB, April 29, 1963.

Vancouver Canucks president of hockey operations Trevor Linden confirmed at a Canucks' Town Hall Meeting on May 21, 2014 that Jim Benning had been named general manager of the team. Benning was officially introduced on May 23, 2014. In his first season in the role in 2014-15 the Canucks returned to the playoffs after having missed the postseason the previous year.

Benning is the 11th general manager in club history. He joined Vancouver after serving as the Boston Bruins assistant general manager for seven years. In that role he acted as an advisor to general manager Peter Chiarelli on all matters pertaining to player evaluation, trades and free agent signings, in addition to assisting the general manager in overseeing all individuals in their specific duties for the Bruins. Benning initially joined the Bruins as director of player personnel in 2006.

The Edmonton, Alberta native also previously held a 12-year tenure with the Buffalo Sabres. For eight of those seasons, Benning served as the team's director of amateur scouting. In that position, he oversaw the club's scouting staff and led the team at the annual NHL Draft, in addition to scouting prospects at the high school, college and junior hockey levels as well as in Europe.

A former defenceman, Benning was drafted by the Toronto Maple Leafs with their first pick, sixth overall, in the 1981 NHL Draft and played nine seasons in the National Hockey League with the Maple Leafs and Vancouver Canucks. Benning accumulated 243 points (52 goals, 191 assists) and 461 penalty minutes in 605 career games. He played one season in Europe before retiring as a player in 1992 and attended college for one year before joining the Anaheim organization as an amateur scout.

Club Directory

Rogers Arena

Vancouver Canucks
Arena & Practice Facility:
Rogers Arena
800 Griffiths Way
Vancouver, B.C. V6B 6G1
Office:
89 West Georgia
Vancouver, B.C. V6B 0N8
Phone **604/899-4600**
FAX 604/899-4640
www.canucks.com
Capacity: 18,865

Executive Directory – Vancouver Canucks Limited Partnership
Chairman, Canucks L.P. and Governor, NHL	Francesco Aquilini
Alternate Governors, NHL	Roberto Aquilini, Paolo Aquilini
President, Hockey Operations & Alt. Governor, NHL	Trevor Linden
General Manager	Jim Benning
Assistant General Manager	John Weisbrod
Chief Operating Officer and Alt. Governor, NHL	Jeff Stipec
President, Hospitality and Live Entertainment	Michael Doyle
Executive Vice President, Sales and Service	Trent Carroll
Executive Vice President, Operations and CFO	Todd Kobus
Vice President, Hockey Administration, Entertainment and Content	TC Carling
Vice President and General Counsel	Chris Gear
Vice President, Communications and Community Partnerships	Chris Brumwell
Vice President, Ticket and Suite Sales and Service	Michael Cosentino
Vice President, Information Services	Kelly Gilchrist

Hockey Operations
President and Alt. Governor, NHL	Trevor Linden
General Manager	Jim Benning
Assistant General Manager	John Weisbrod
Sr. Advisor to GM and Director, Collegiate Scouting	Stan Smyl
Vice President, Hockey Administration, Entertainment and Content	TC Carling
Vice President and General Counsel	Chris Gear
Sr. Director, Hockey Operations and Analytics	Jonathan Wall
Utica Comets G.M. & Dir., Player Development	Ryan Johnson
Consultant, Player Development	Scott Walker
Consultant, Power Skating	Ryan Lounsbury
Manager, Team Services	Mike Brown
Executive Assistant	Andrea Lobo
Executive Office Coordinator	Melanie Taplin

Coaching Staff
Head Coach	Travis Green
Assistant Coaches	Nolan Baumgartner, Newell Brown, Doug Jarvis, Manny Malhotra
Goaltending Coach / Video Coach	Dan Cloutier / Darryl Seward
Skill Coach	Glenn Carnegie

Utica Comets (AHL Affiliate)
Head Coach, Utica Comets	Trent Cull
Assistant Coaches, Utica Comets	Jason King, Gary Agnew

Communications and Community Partnerships
Vice President, Communications and Community Partnerships	Chris Brumwell
Director, Media Relations and Team Operations	Ben Brown
Manager, Media Relations and Publications	Stephanie Maniago
Coordinator, Media Relations	Alfred De Vera
Senior Director, Community Partnerships	Alex Oxenham
Sr. Manager, Canucks for Kids Fund Events, 50/50	Diana Campbell
Manager, Hockey Development and Alumni Liaison	Rod Brathwaite
Managers, Community Partnerships	Jessica Hoffman, Tara Clarke
Coordinator, Community Partnerships and Mascot Liaison	Paul Buckley
Canucks Ambassador	Kirk McLean
Program Coordinator 50/50	Nikki Matwiv

Scouting Staff
Director, Amateur Scouting	Judd Brackett
Chief Amateur Scout	Ron Delorme
Associate Chief Scout	Thomas Gradin
Amateur Scouts	Sergei Chibisov, Ted Hampson, Inge Hammarstrom, Wyatt Smith, Dan Palango, Chris MacDonald, Tim Lenardon, Brandon Benning, Jonathan Bates, Todd Harvey, Paul Gallagher, Doug Gasper, Vincent Montalbano
Director, Professional Scouting	Brett Henning
Professional Scouts	Neil Komadoski, Lars Lindgren, Lou Crawford, Brian Chapman, David Volek

Human Performance
Director, Rehabilitation	Dr. Rick Celebrini
Head Athletic Therapist / Asst.	Jon Sanderson / Dave Zarn
Strength & Conditioning Coach / Asst.	Roger Takahashi / Bryan Marshall
Rehab Therapist	Graeme Poole
Team Physician	Dr. Bill Regan
Primary Team Physician	Dr. Jim Bovard
Team Dentist	Dr. Jeffrey Norden
Sports Psychologist	Dr. David Cox
Team Chiropractor	Dr. Glenn Cashman
Team Optometrist	Dr. Alan R. Boyco

Training Staff
Equipment Manager	Pat O'Neill
Assistant Equipment Manager	Brian Hamilton
Trainer's Assistant	Mackenzie Stewart
Game Dressing Room Attendants	John Jukich, Ron Shute, Ferdie De Guzman, Trevor Penrose

Broadcast
Senior Director, Content & Game Presentation	Ryan Nicholas
Director, Game Presentation	Mike Hall
Senior Producer, Game & Events	Art Green
Manager, Game Entertainment & Events	Cam Goudreau
Manager, Content / Writer	Briana Griffith / Derek Jory
Senior Producer / Editor	Jason Steensma / Gayla Anderson
Program Manager, Game Entertainment & Community Events	Rebecca Grant
Senior Broadcast Technician	Greg Story
Canucks TV Reporter	Joey Kenward
Editor / Content Producer	Lawren Cody / Paul Albi
Segment Producers	Jessica McNeill / Shawn Edstrom

Vegas Golden Knights

NHL/Vegas Expansion Draft

2017

Player	Drafted From
Forwards	
Pierre-Edouard Bellemare	Philadelphia
Connor Brickley	Carolina
William Carrier	Buffalo
Cody Eakin	Dallas
Erik Haula	Minnesota
William Karlsson	Columbus
Brendan Leipsic	Toronto
Oscar Lindberg	NY Rangers
Jonathan Marchessault	Florida
James Neal	Nashville
Tomas Nosek	Detroit
David Perron	St. Louis
Teemu Pulkkinen	Arizona
Chris Thorburn	Winnipeg
Defensemen	
Alexei Emelin	Montreal
Deryk Engelland	Calgary
Jason Garrison	Tampa Bay
Brayden McNabb	Los Angeles
Jon Merrill	New Jersey
Marc Methot	Ottawa
Colin Miller	Boston
Griffin Reinhart	Edmonton
Luca Sbisa	Vancouver
David Schlemko	San Jose
Nate Schmidt	Washington
Clayton Stoner	Anaheim
Trevor van Riemsdyk	Chicago
Goaltenders	
J.F. Berube	NY Islanders
Marc-Andre Fleury	Pittsburgh
Calvin Pickard	Colorado

2017-18 Schedule

Oct.							
Fri.	6	at Dallas		Sat.	13	Edmonton
Sat.	7	at Arizona		Tue.	16	at Nashville
Tue.	10	Arizona		Thu.	18	at Tampa Bay
Fri.	13	Detroit		Fri.	19	at Florida
Sun.	15	Boston*		Sun.	21	at Carolina*
Tue.	17	Buffalo		Tue.	23	Columbus
Sat.	21	St. Louis		Thu.	25	NY Islanders
Tue.	24	Chicago		Tue.	30	at Calgary
Fri.	27	Colorado*	**Feb.** Thu.	1	at Winnipeg
Mon.	30	at NY Islanders		Fri.	2	at Minnesota
Tue.	31	at NY Rangers		Sun.	4	at Washington*
Nov. Thu.	2	at Boston		Tue.	6	at Pittsburgh
Sat.	4	at Ottawa*		Thu.	8	at San Jose
Mon.	6	at Toronto		Sun.	11	Philadelphia*
Tue.	7	at Montreal		Tue.	13	Chicago
Fri.	10	Winnipeg		Thu.	15	Edmonton
Tue.	14	at Edmonton		Sat.	17	Montreal*
Thu.	16	at Vancouver		Mon.	19	Anaheim
Sun.	19	Los Angeles*		Wed.	21	Calgary
Wed.	22	at Anaheim		Fri.	23	Vancouver
Fri.	24	San Jose		Mon.	26	at Los Angeles
Sat.	25	at Arizona		Tue.	27	Los Angeles
Tue.	28	Dallas	**Mar.** Fri.	2	Ottawa
Thu.	30	at Minnesota		Sun.	4	at New Jersey*
Dec. Fri.	1	at Winnipeg		Tue.	6	at Columbus
Sun.	3	Arizona*		Thu.	8	at Detroit
Tue.	5	Anaheim		Sat.	10	at Buffalo*
Fri.	8	at Nashville		Mon.	12	at Philadelphia
Sat.	9	at Dallas		Wed.	14	New Jersey
Tue.	12	Carolina		Fri.	16	Minnesota
Thu.	14	Pittsburgh		Sun.	18	Calgary*
Sun.	17	Florida*		Tue.	20	Vancouver
Tue.	19	Tampa Bay		Thu.	22	at San Jose
Sat.	23	Washington*		Sat.	24	at Colorado*
Wed.	27	at Anaheim		Mon.	26	Colorado
Thu.	28	at Los Angeles		Wed.	28	Arizona
Sun.	31	Toronto*		Fri.	30	St. Louis
Jan. Tue.	2	Nashville		Sat.	31	San Jose
Thu.	4	at St. Louis	**Apr.** Tue.	3	at Vancouver
Fri.	5	at Chicago		Thu.	5	at Edmonton
Sun.	7	NY Rangers		Sat.	7	at Calgary

* Denotes afternoon game.

PACIFIC DIVISION
1st NHL Season

Franchise date: March 1, 2017

2017-18 Player Personnel

FORWARDS	HT	WT	*Age	Birthplace	S	2016-17 Club
BELLEMARE, Pierre-Edouard	6-0	198	32	Paris, France	L	Philadelphia
CARRIER, William	6-2	212	22	La Salle, QC	L	Buffalo-Rochester
CLARKSON, David	6-0	207	33	Toronto, ON	R	Columbus
EAKIN, Cody	6-0	190	26	Winnipeg, MB	L	Dallas
GRABOVSKI, Mikhail	5-11	186	33	Potsdam, East Germany	L	did not play
HAULA, Erik	6-0	193	26	Pori, Finland	L	Minnesota
KARLSSON, William	6-1	188	24	Marsta, Sweden	L	Columbus
LEIPSIC, Brendan	5-9	165	23	Winnipeg, MB	L	Toronto (AHL)
LINDBERG, Oscar	6-1	195	25	Skelleftea, Sweden	L	NY Rangers
MARCHESSAULT, Jonathan	5-9	174	26	Cap-Rouge, QC	R	Florida
NEAL, James	6-2	221	30	Whitby, ON	L	Nashville
PERRON, David	6-0	200	29	Sherbrooke, QC	R	St. Louis
PULKKINEN, Teemu	5-11	183	25	Vantaa, Finland	R	Minnesota-Iowa-Arizona
SHIPACHEV, Vadim	6-1	190	30	Cherepovets, USSR	L	St. Petersburg
SMITH, Reilly	6-0	185	26	Toronto, ON	L	Florida
DEFENSEMEN						
ENGELLAND, Deryk	6-2	214	35	Edmonton, AB	R	Calgary
GARRISON, Jason	6-2	223	32	White Rock, BC	L	Tampa Bay
McNABB, Brayden	6-4	216	26	Davidson, SK	L	Los Angeles
MERRILL, Jon	6-3	205	25	Oklahoma City, OK	L	New Jersey
MILLER, Colin	6-1	196	24	Sault Ste. Marie, ON	R	Boston
REINHART, Griffin	6-4	212	23	North Vancouver, BC	L	Bakersfield-Edmonton
SBISA, Luca	6-2	198	27	Ozieri, Italy	L	Vancouver
SCHMIDT, Nate	6-0	191	26	St. Cloud, MN	L	Washington
STONER, Clayton	6-4	216	32	Port McNeill, BC	L	Anaheim-San Diego
THEODORE, Shea	6-2	195	22	Langley, BC	L	Anaheim-San Diego
GOALTENDERS	HT	WT	*Age	Birthplace	C	2016-17 Club
FLEURY, Marc-Andre	6-2	180	32	Sorel, QC	L	Pittsburgh
PICKARD, Calvin	6-1	200	25	Moncton, NB	L	Colorado

* – Age at start of 2017-18 season

George McPhee
General Manager

Born: Wallaceburg, ON, July 2, 1958.

On July 13, 2016, George McPhee became the first president of Hockey Operations and general manager of the Vegas Golden Knights. In his position, he oversees the team's day-to-day business including development, with an emphasis on scouting, drafting and overseeing the coaching staff. McPhee has created a team-first culture in his short time with the franchise and has hired staff around him who share that philosophy.

McPhee was tasked with putting together a competitive team in the short-term but also building for long-term success. Contributing to both of those goals was a successful Expansion Draft, which saw him select three-time Stanley Cup champion goaltender Marc-Andre Fleury from the Pittsburgh Penguins as well other players who will immediately compete for playing time. The Expansion Draft was not the only place where McPhee and his staff were successful. Through the expansion process, the Golden Knights made agreements with other teams and benefited by having three first-round draft picks in the 2017 NHL Draft and 13 overall picks in the draft. The team ended up making 12 selections, the most of any team in the 2017 Draft.

McPhee joined the Golden Knights after having most recently served as special advisor to New York Islanders general manager Garth Snow in 2015. Prior to his time with the Islanders, McPhee served as the vice president and general manager of the Washington Capitals for 17 seasons. Under his guidance, the Capitals grew from a lottery team to a perennial contender with multiple Southeast Division championships and the Presidents' Trophy in 2009-10. The Capitals reached the playoffs 10 times during McPhee's tenure in Washington, including six straight seasons from 2007-08 to 2012-13. Under his leadership, the team claimed seven Southeast Division titles and he oversaw the Capitals' first trip to the Stanley Cup Final in 1997-98, McPhee's first season with the franchise. During his tenure, the team also saw success through the NHL Draft as Washington held 15 first-round draft picks from 2004 to 2013, the most of any NHL team. His most notable selection was the number one overall pick in 2004, Alex Ovechkin, the league's only active three-time MVP. Those prospects flourished under McPhee's direction as the Capitals affiliate of the American Hockey League, the Hershey Bears, were Calder Cup champions in 2006, 2009 and 2010.

Prior to his time in Washington, McPhee spent five seasons as the vice president and director of hockey operations as well as alternate governor for the Vancouver Canucks, assisting then general manager Pat Quinn with all hockey-related matters. In his time with the Canucks, the team enjoyed four trips to the playoffs, a division championship and a trip to the 1994 Stanley Cup Final.

McPhee began his playing career in his hometown of Guelph, Ontario, with the Ontario Junior Hockey League's Guelph Platers, leading them to the 1978 Centennial Cup, which was then Canada's Tier II championship. Following his stint with the Platers, McPhee attended Bowling Green State University of the Central Collegiate Hockey Association, where he became one of college hockey's most decorated players. A four-year letter-winner from 1978 to 1982, he was the recipient of the 1982 Hobey Baker Memorial Award, given to the top player in college hockey. His other accolades included a first-team All-CCHA selection in 1982, second-team All-CCHA honors in 1979 and 1981 and his selection as the CCHA's Rookie of the Year in 1979. Earning a degree in business, he became the first player to be named to the CCHA All-Academic Team in three consecutive seasons. Upon the completion of his college career, McPhee signed as a free agent with the New York Rangers and started his NHL career during the 1982 Stanley Cup playoffs. Following his seven seasons with the Rangers and New Jersey Devils, McPhee earned his law degree from Rutgers University in 1992. In 2016, his son Graham was selected by the Edmonton Oilers in the fifth round of the NHL Draft.

NHL Draft Selections 2017

2017 Pick	
6	Cody Glass
13	Nick Suzuki
15	Erik Brannstrom
34	Nicolas Hague
62	Jake Leschyshyn
65	Jonas Rondbjerg
96	Maxim Zhukov
127	Lucas Elvenes
142	Jack Dugan
158	Nick Campoli
161	Jiri Patera
189	Ben Jones

General Managers' History

George McPhee, 2017-18.

Coaching History

Gerard Gallant, 2017-18.

Vegas chose Cody Glass from Portland of the Western Hockey League.

Gerard Gallant

Head Coach

Born: Summerside, PEI, September 2, 1963.

Vegas Golden Knights general manager George McPhee announced on April 13, 2017, that Gerard Gallant had been hired as the first head coach in team history. Gallant joins the Golden Knights after his most recent head coaching tenure with the Florida Panthers. During his first season behind Florida's bench in 2014-15, Gallant guided the Panthers to a 38-29-15 record and 91 points, a 25-point improvement from the previous season. In his second season, Gallant helped lead the Panthers to 103 points and a first-place regular season finish in the Atlantic Division. He was named a Jack Adams Award finalist (coach of the year) for his efforts.

Prior to joining the Panthers, Gallant spent two seasons (2012 to 2014) as an assistant coach with the Montreal Canadiens, helping the team advance to the postseason each year, including the 2014 Eastern Conference Finals. During his two years as an assistant coach, Montreal posted a 75-42-13 mark, including their first 100-point season since 2007-2008.

Before coaching in Montreal, Gallant spent three seasons (2009 to 2012) as the head coach of the Saint John Sea Dogs of the Quebec Major Junior Hockey League. During his three seasons with Saint John, he compiled a 159-34-9 record and led the Sea Dogs to three first-place finishes, three league final appearances, back-to-back QMJHL championships (2011 and 2012) and one Memorial Cup (2011). Gallant was also named the QMJHL and Canadian Hockey League coach of the year twice (2010 and 2011).

Gallant served as head coach of the Columbus Blue Jackets for parts of three seasons from 2003 to 2007 after serving as an assistant coach with the Blue Jackets from 2000 to 2003. He also was an assistant coach with the New York Islanders (2007 to 2009), the International Hockey League's Fort Wayne Komets (1998-99) and the American Hockey League's Louisville Panthers (1999-2000). Gallant began his coaching career in 1995-96 with the Summerside Capitals of the Maritime Junior Hockey League and led the team to the Royal Bank Cup in 1997.

At the international level, Gallant was part of Team Canada's gold medal-winning coaching staff at the 2007 World Championship and silver medal winners at the 2017 World Championship. He also served as an assistant coach for Team North America during the 2016 World Cup of Hockey.

As a player, Gallant was selected by the Detroit Red Wings in the sixth round (107th overall) in the 1981 NHL Draft. He played in 615 NHL games for Detroit (1984 to1993) and Tampa Bay (1993 to 1995) registering 211 goals and 269 assists for 480 points and 1,674 penalty minutes. Gallant recorded four 70-plus point seasons, including his most successful year in 1988-1989 when he registered a career high 93 points (39 goals, 54 assists) and was selected as an NHL Second Team All-Star.

Coaching Record

			Regular Season				Playoffs			
Season	Team	League	GC	W	L	O/T	GC	W	L	T
1995-96	Summerside	MrJHL	12	6	5	1	....	....	....	....
1996-97	Summerside	MrJHL	55	35	14	6	20	12	8	0
1996-97	Summerside	RB-Cup	....	....	....	....	6	3	2	1
1997-98	Summerside	MrJHL	37	9	22	6	....	....	....	....
2003-04	**Columbus**	**NHL**	**45**	**16**	**24**	**5**	....	....	....	....
2004-05	**Columbus**			SEASON CANCELLED						
2005-06	**Columbus**	**NHL**	**82**	**35**	**43**	**4**	....	....	....	....
2006-07	**Columbus**	**NHL**	**15**	**5**	**9**	**1**	....	....	....	....
2009-10	Saint John	QMJHL	67	52	15	0	21	14	7	....
2010-11	Saint John	QMJHL	67	57	10	0	19	16	3	....
2010-11	Saint John	M-Cup	....	....	....	....	4	3	1	....
2011-12	Saint John	QMJHL	67	50	17	0	17	16	1	....
2011-12	Saint John	M-Cup	....	....	....	....	4	2	2	....
2014-15	**Florida**	**NHL**	**82**	**38**	**29**	**15**	....	....	....	....
2015-16	**Florida**	**NHL**	**82**	**47**	**26**	**9**	**6**	**2**	**4**	....
2016-17	**Florida**	**NHL**	**22**	**11**	**10**	**1**	....	....	....	....
	NHL Totals		**328**	**152**	**141**	**35**	**6**	**2**	**4**	....

Club Directory

T-Mobile Arena

Vegas Golden Knights
T-Mobile Arena
3780 S. Las Vegas Blvd.
Las Vegas, NV 89158
Phone **702/790-2663**
Ticket Information 702/645-4259
www.vegasgoldenknights.com
Capacity: 17,500

Owner

Chairman, CEO and Governor	Bill Foley

Hockey Operations

President, General Manager, Alt. Governor	George McPhee
Executive Vice President, Assistant GM	Kelly McCrimmon
Senior Vice President	Murray Craven
Director of Hockey Operations / Administration	Misha Donskov / Katy Boettinger
Director of Hockey Legal Affairs	Andrew Lugerner
Special Advisor to Hockey Operations	David Conte
Director of Team Services	Rick Braunstein
Hockey Operations Analyst / Assistants	Tom Poraszka / Keith Veronesi, Robert Foley
Chicago Wolves Head Coach / Assistant Coach	Rocky Thompson / Chris Dennis

Executives

President and COO	Kerry Bubolz
General Counsel	Peter Sadowski
Chief Financial Officer	Joleen Legakes
Senior Vice President and CMO	Brian Killingsworth
Senior Vice President and Chief Sales Officer	Jim Frevola
Executive Assistants	Shelly Kellum, Kristina Crunk

Coaching Staff

Head Coach	Gerard Gallant
Assistant Coaches	Mike Kelly, Ryan Craig, Ryan McGill
Video Coach	Tommy Cruz
Goaltending Coach/Director of Goaltending	David Prior

Medical Staff

Dir. of Sports Performance/Head Athletic Trainer	Jay Mellette
Associate Head Athletic Trainer	Kyle Moore
Assistant Athletic Trainer	Mike Muir
Strength & Conditioning Coach / Massage Therapist	Doug Davidson / Raul Durantes
Medical Director	Dr. James Dettling
Team Physicians	Drs. Mike Gunter, William Rosenberg, Chad Hanson, Brandon Snead
Team Dentist	Dr. Byron Blasco

Equipment Staff

Head Equipment Manager	Chris Davidson-Adams
Asst. Equipment Manager / Equipment Assistant	J.W. Aiken / Pat Maino

Scouting Staff

Director of Player Personnel	Vaughn Karpan
Assistant Director of Player Personnel	Bob Lowes
Scouting Director, Amateur / European	Scott Luce / Vojtech Kucera
Director of Player Development	Wil Nichol
Scout/Player Development	Mike Levine
Professional Scouts	Kelly Kisio, Jim McKenzie, Vaclav Nedomansky, Vince Williams
Amateur Scouts	Bruno Campese, Erin Ginell, Kent Hawley, Raphael Pouliot, Peter Ward, Mark Workman
European Scouts	Peter Ahola, Alex Godynyuk

City National Arena Operations

General Manager	Dan Patterson
Director, Hockey and Asst. Manager	Robbert McDonald
Director, Guest Services/Events/Admin.	Ashley Andrich
Director, Skating / Operations	Chad Goodwin / Christian Glowinski
Sr. Supervisor	Nick Salami

Communications

Vice President of Communications & Content	Eric Tosi
Director of Communications	Sage Sammons
Public Relations Coordinator / VGK Insider	Alyssa Girardi / Gary Lawless
Senior Writer / Web Video Coordinator	Dan Marrazza / Tyler Pico

Finance / Legal

Controller / Payroll Manager	Danielle Thomason / Melanie Long
Senior Accountant / Director of Finance	Jen Jones / Justin Klein

Entertainment

Vice President of Events and Entertainment	Jonny Greco
Senior Director, Events	Ayron Sequeira
Directors, Post / Live Video Production	Andrew Abrams / Jim Dittman
Lead Video Editor / Motion Graphic Designer	Patrick Ruhlig / Trent Bailey
Events and Entertainment Coordinator	Haley Craven
Entertainment Producer	Tyler Cofer
Video Producer & Shooter	Rob Depew

Marketing

Vice President of Marketing	Kim Frank
Manager of Marketing and Events	Carley Sisolak
Community Relations Coordinator	TBD
Manager Fan Development/Youth Hockey	TBD
Art Director / Digital Marketing Manager	David Lopez / Nil Sasha
Mascot Coordinator	TBD

Ticket Sales and Service

Vice President, Ticketing & Suites	Todd Pollock
Director, Ticketing & Suites	Chase Jolesch
Director, Group & Event Suite Sales	Nicholas Zombolas
Directors, Ticket Ops. / Membership Services	Gene Tinner / Jerrett Burke
Manager, Premium Services	TBD

Corporate Sponsorships

Vice President of Global Partnerships	Mike Mungiello
Sr. Director Corporate Activations	Danielle Sergeant
Directors, Corporate Partnerships	Dan Hanneke, Steve Duffy, Brendan Dolby
Manager, Partner Activation	Brittany Usmail
Account Manager & Partnership Activation	Lindsay Berezen

Administration

IT Directors / Systems Administrator	Kenny Akodu, George Guevara / Leo Deguire
Receptionist	Donna Alcantra

Miscellaneous

Television Rights Holder	AT&T SportsNet
Television Play-by-Play / Analyst	Dave Goucher / Shane Hnidy
Radio Rightsholders	Fox Sports 1340/98.9 / ESPN Deportes 1460
Radio Play-by-Play	Dan D'Uva
Spanish Radio Play-by-Play / Analyst	TBD / TBD

Washington Capitals

Key Off-Season Signings/Acquisitions

2017

June 14 • Acquired C **Tyler Graovac** from Minnesota for a 5th-round pick in 2018 NHL Draft.

23 • Re-signed RW **T.J. Oshie**.

29 • Re-signed C **Chandler Stephenson**.

30 • Re-signed D **Dmitry Orlov**.

July 1 • Signed RW **Anthony Peluso**.

1 • Re-signed LW **Brett Connolly**.

2 • Re-signed C **Evgeny Kuznetsov**.

3 • Signed RW **Devante Smith-Pelly**.

4 • Re-signed LW **Andre Burakovsky**.

6 • Re-signed G **Philipp Grubauer**.

14 • Re-signed C **Liam O'Brien**.

2016-17 Results: 55w-19L-3OTL-5SOL 118PTS
1ST, Metropolitan Division • 1ST, Eastern Conference

Alex Ovechkin, with teammates Nicklas Backstrom (left) and T.J. Oshie (right), poses with the puck from his 1,000th career point from his first period goal in a 5-2 win over Pittsburgh in Washington on January 11, 2017.

2017-18 Schedule

Oct.	Thu.	5	at Ottawa		Sun.	7	St. Louis*
	Sat.	7	Montreal		Tue.	9	Vancouver
	Mon.	9	at Tampa Bay		Thu.	11	Carolina
	Wed.	11	Pittsburgh		Fri.	12	at Carolina
	Fri.	13	at New Jersey		Thu.	18	at New Jersey
	Sat.	14	at Philadelphia		Fri.	19	Montreal
	Tue.	17	Toronto		Sun.	21	Philadelphia*
	Fri.	20	at Detroit		Thu.	25	at Florida
	Sat.	21	Florida		Wed.	31	Philadelphia
	Thu.	26	at Vancouver	**Feb.**	Fri.	2	at Pittsburgh
	Sat.	28	at Edmonton		Sun.	4	Vegas*
	Sun.	29	at Calgary		Tue.	6	at Columbus
Nov.	Thu.	2	NY Islanders		Fri.	9	Columbus
	Sat.	4	at Boston		Sun.	11	Detroit*
	Mon.	6	Arizona		Tue.	13	at Winnipeg
	Tue.	7	at Buffalo		Thu.	15	at Minnesota
	Fri.	10	Pittsburgh		Sat.	17	at Chicago
	Sun.	12	Edmonton		Mon.	19	at Buffalo*
	Tue.	14	at Nashville		Tue.	20	Tampa Bay
	Thu.	16	at Colorado		Thu.	22	at Florida
	Sat.	18	Minnesota		Sat.	24	Buffalo
	Mon.	20	Calgary		Mon.	26	at Columbus
	Wed.	22	Ottawa		Tue.	27	Ottawa
	Fri.	24	Tampa Bay*	**Mar.**	Sat.	3	Toronto
	Sat.	25	at Toronto		Tue.	6	at Anaheim
	Thu.	30	Los Angeles		Thu.	8	at Los Angeles
Dec.	Sat.	2	Columbus		Sat.	10	at San Jose*
	Mon.	4	San Jose		Mon.	12	Winnipeg
	Wed.	6	Chicago		Thu.	15	at NY Islanders
	Fri.	8	NY Rangers		Fri.	16	NY Islanders
	Mon.	11	at NY Islanders		Sun.	18	at Philadelphia*
	Tue.	12	Colorado		Tue.	20	Dallas
	Thu.	14	at Boston		Thu.	22	at Detroit
	Sat.	16	Anaheim		Sat.	24	at Montreal
	Tue.	19	at Dallas		Mon.	26	at NY Rangers
	Fri.	22	at Arizona		Wed.	28	NY Rangers
	Sat.	23	at Vegas*		Fri.	30	Carolina
	Wed.	27	at NY Rangers	**Apr.**	Sun.	1	at Pittsburgh
	Thu.	28	Boston		Mon.	2	at St. Louis*
	Sat.	30	New Jersey		Thu.	5	Nashville
Jan.	Tue.	2	at Carolina		Sat.	7	New Jersey

* Denotes afternoon game.

Retired Numbers

5	Rod Langway	1982-1993
7	Yvon Labre	1974-1981
11	Mike Gartner	1979-1989
32	Dale Hunter	1987-1999

METROPOLITAN DIVISION
44th NHL Season

Franchise date: June 11, 1974

Year-by-Year Record

Season	GP	Home W	L	T	OL	Road W	L	T	OL	Overall W	L	T	OL	GF	GA	Pts.	Div. Fin.	Conf. Fin.	Playoff Result
2016-17	82	32	7	....	2	23	12	....	6	55	19	....	8	263	182	118	1st, Met.	1st, East	Lost Second Round
2015-16	82	29	8	....	4	27	10	....	4	56	18	....	8	252	193	120	1st, Met.	1st, East	Lost Second Round
2014-15	82	23	13	....	5	22	13	....	6	45	26	....	11	242	203	101	2nd, Met.	4th, East	Lost Second Round
2013-14	82	21	13	....	7	17	17	....	7	38	30	....	14	235	240	90	5th, Met.	9th, East	– out of playoffs –
2012-13	48	15	8	....	1	12	10	....	2	27	18	....	3	149	130	57	1st, SE	3rd, East	Lost Conf. Quarter-Final
2011-12	82	26	11	....	4	16	21	....	4	42	32	....	8	222	230	92	2nd, SE	7th, East	Lost Conf. Semi-Final
2010-11	82	25	8	....	8	23	15	....	3	48	23	....	11	224	197	107	1st, SE	1st, East	Lost Conf. Semi-Final
2009-10	82	30	5	....	6	24	10	....	7	54	15	....	13	318	233	121	1st, SE	1st, East	Lost Conf. Quarter-Final
2008-09	82	29	9	....	3	21	15	....	5	50	24	....	8	272	245	108	1st, SE	2nd, East	Lost Conf. Semi-Final
2007-08	82	23	15	....	3	20	16	....	5	43	31	....	8	242	231	94	1st, SE	3rd, East	Lost Conf. Quarter-Final
2006-07	82	17	17	....	7	11	23	....	7	28	40	....	14	235	286	70	5th, SE	14th, East	– out of playoffs –
2005-06	82	16	18	....	7	13	23	....	5	29	41	....	12	237	306	70	5th, SE	14th, East	– out of playoffs –
2004-05	....																		
2003-04	82	13	20	6	2	10	26	4	1	23	46	10	3	186	253	59	5th, SE	14th, East	– out of playoffs –
2002-03	82	24	13	2	2	15	16	6	4	39	29	8	6	224	220	92	2nd, SE	6th, East	Lost Conf. Quarter-Final
2001-02	82	21	12	6	2	15	21	5	0	36	33	11	2	228	240	85	2nd, SE	9th, East	– out of playoffs –
2000-01	82	24	9	6	2	17	18	4	2	41	27	10	4	233	211	96	1st, SE	3rd, East	Lost Conf. Quarter-Final
1999-2000	82	26	5	8	2	18	19	4	0	44	24	12	2	227	194	102	1st, SE	2nd, East	Lost Conf. Quarter-Final
1998-99	82	16	23	2	....	15	22	4	....	31	45	6	....	200	218	68	3rd, SE	12th, East	– out of playoffs –
1997-98	82	23	12	6	....	17	18	6	....	40	30	12	....	219	202	92	3rd, Atl.	4th, East	Lost Final
1996-97	82	19	17	5	....	14	23	4	....	33	40	9	....	214	231	75	5th, Atl.	9th, East	– out of playoffs –
1995-96	82	21	15	5	....	18	17	6	....	39	32	11	....	234	204	89	4th, Atl.	6th, East	Lost Conf. Quarter-Final
1994-95	48	15	6	3	....	7	12	5	....	22	18	8	....	136	120	52	3rd, Atl.	6th, East	Lost Conf. Semi-Final
1993-94	84	21	15	6	....	22	19	1	....	39	35	10	....	277	263	88	3rd, Atl.	7th, East	Lost Conf. Semi-Final
1992-93	84	21	15	6	....	22	19	1	....	43	34	7	....	325	286	93	2nd, Patrick		Lost Div. Semi-Final
1991-92	80	25	12	3	....	20	15	5	....	45	27	8	....	330	275	98	2nd, Patrick		Lost Div. Semi-Final
1990-91	80	21	14	5	....	16	22	2	....	37	36	7	....	258	258	81	3rd, Patrick		Lost Div. Final
1989-90	80	19	18	3	....	17	20	3	....	36	38	6	....	284	275	78	3rd, Patrick		Lost Conf. Final
1988-89	80	25	12	3	....	16	19	5	....	41	29	10	....	305	259	92	1st, Patrick		Lost Div. Semi-Final
1987-88	80	22	14	4	....	16	19	5	....	38	33	9	....	281	249	85	2nd, Patrick		Lost Div. Final
1986-87	80	22	15	3	....	16	17	7	....	38	32	10	....	285	278	86	2nd, Patrick		Lost Div. Semi-Final
1985-86	80	30	8	2	....	20	15	5	....	50	23	7	....	315	272	107	2nd, Patrick		Lost Div. Final
1984-85	80	27	11	2	....	19	14	7	....	46	25	9	....	322	240	101	2nd, Patrick		Lost Div. Semi-Final
1983-84	80	26	11	3	....	22	16	2	....	48	27	5	....	308	226	101	2nd, Patrick		Lost Div. Semi-Final
1982-83	80	22	12	6	....	17	13	10	....	39	25	16	....	306	283	94	3rd, Patrick		Lost Div. Semi-Final
1981-82	80	16	16	8	....	10	25	5	....	26	41	13	....	319	338	65	5th, Patrick		– out of playoffs –
1980-81	80	16	17	7	....	10	19	11	....	26	36	18	....	286	317	70	5th, Patrick		– out of playoffs –
1979-80	80	20	14	6	....	7	26	7	....	27	40	13	....	261	293	67	5th, Patrick		– out of playoffs –
1978-79	80	15	19	6	....	9	22	9	....	24	41	15	....	273	338	63	4th, Norris		– out of playoffs –
1977-78	80	10	23	7	....	7	26	7	....	17	49	14	....	195	321	48	4th, Norris		– out of playoffs –
1976-77	80	17	15	8	....	7	27	6	....	24	42	14	....	221	307	62	4th, Norris		– out of playoffs –
1975-76	80	6	26	8	....	5	33	2	....	11	59	10	....	224	394	32	5th, Norris		– out of playoffs –
1974-75	80	7	28	5	....	1	39	0	....	8	67	5	....	181	446	21	5th, Norris		– out of playoffs –

2017-18 Player Personnel

FORWARDS	HT	WT	*Age	Birthplace	S	2016-17 Club
BACKSTROM, Nicklas	6-1	213	29	Gavle, Sweden	L	Washington
BEAGLE, Jay	6-3	210	31	Calgary, AB	R	Washington
BURAKOVSKY, Andre	6-3	188	22	Klagenfurt , Austria	L	Washington
CONNOLLY, Brett	6-2	193	25	Prince George, BC	R	Washington
ELLER, Lars	6-2	207	28	Rodovre, Denmark	L	Washington
GRAOVAC, Tyler	6-5	212	24	Brampton, ON	L	Minnesota-Iowa
KUZNETSOV, Evgeny	6-0	192	25	Chelyabinsk, Russia	L	Washington
OSHIE, T.J.	5-11	189	30	Mt. Vernon, WA	R	Washington
OVECHKIN, Alex	6-3	239	32	Moscow, USSR	R	Washington
PELUSO, Anthony	6-3	235	28	North York, ON	R	Manitoba
STEPHENSON, Chandler	5-11	190	23	Saskatoon, SK	L	Washington-Hershey
VRANA, Jakub	5-11	185	21	Prague, Czech Rep.	L	Washington-Hershey
WALKER, Nathan	5-8	179	23	Cardiff, Wales	L	Hershey
WILSON, Tom	6-4	215	23	Toronto, ON	R	Washington
DEFENSEMEN						
CARLSON, John	6-3	215	27	Natick, MA	R	Washington
CHORNEY, Taylor	6-1	190	30	Thunder Bay, ON	L	Washington
DJOOS, Christian	5-11	158	23	Gothenburg, Sweden	L	Hershey
NESS, Aaron	5-10	187	27	Roseau, MN	L	Washington-Hershey
NISKANEN, Matt	6-0	200	30	Virginia, MN	R	Washington
ORLOV, Dmitry	6-0	212	26	Novokuznetsk, USSR	L	Washington
ORPIK, Brooks	6-2	221	37	San Francisco, CA	L	Washington

GOALTENDERS	HT	WT	*Age	Birthplace	C	2016-17 Club
GRUBAUER, Philipp	6-1	182	25	Rosenheim, Germany	L	Washington
HOLTBY, Braden	6-2	217	28	Lloydminster, SK	L	Washington

* – Age at start of 2017-18 season

2016-17 Scoring

* – rookie

Regular Season

Pos	#	Player	Team	GP	G	A	Pts	TOI	+/–	PIM	PP	SH	GW	S	S%
C	19	Nicklas Backstrom	WSH	82	23	63	86	18:15	17	38	8	0	5	162	14.2
L	8	Alex Ovechkin	WSH	82	33	36	69	18:21	6	50	17	0	7	313	10.5
C	92	Evgeny Kuznetsov	WSH	82	19	40	59	16:57	18	46	3	0	4	170	11.2
L	90	Marcus Johansson	WSH	82	24	34	58	16:59	25	10	5	0	5	129	18.6
R	77	T.J. Oshie	WSH	68	33	23	56	17:51	28	36	7	1	4	143	23.1
D	22	Kevin Shattenkirk	STL	61	11	31	42	19:51	–11	37	7	0	0	115	9.6
			WSH	19	2	12	14	20:12	4	10	1	0	2	46	4.3
			Total	80	13	43	56	19:56	–7	47	8	0	2	161	8.1
R	14	Justin Williams	WSH	80	24	24	48	15:28	14	50	5	0	4	167	14.4
D	2	Matt Niskanen	WSH	78	5	34	39	22:10	20	32	1	0	2	154	3.2
D	74	John Carlson	WSH	72	9	28	37	22:42	7	10	3	0	3	180	5.0
L	65	Andre Burakovsky	WSH	64	12	23	35	13:15	13	14	2	0	1	111	10.8
D	9	Dmitry Orlov	WSH	82	6	27	33	19:32	30	51	1	0	0	125	4.8
C	83	Jay Beagle	WSH	81	13	17	30	13:37	20	22	0	1	4	100	13.0
C	26	Daniel Winnik	WSH	72	12	13	25	12:54	15	49	0	2	3	82	14.6
C	20	Lars Eller	WSH	81	12	13	25	13:54	15	36	0	1	2	115	10.4
R	10	Brett Connolly	WSH	66	15	8	23	10:41	20	40	1	0	3	81	18.5
R	43	Tom Wilson	WSH	82	7	12	19	12:55	9	133	0	0	0	95	7.4
D	88	Nate Schmidt	WSH	60	3	14	17	15:28	22	16	0	0	0	60	5.0
D	44	Brooks Orpik	WSH	79	0	14	14	17:47	32	48	0	0	0	93	0.0
D	27	Karl Alzner	WSH	82	3	10	13	19:47	23	28	0	0	0	81	3.7
L	13*	Jakub Vrana	WSH	21	3	3	6	11:06	2	2	3	0	2	32	9.4
D	4	Taylor Chorney	WSH	18	1	4	5	14:15	8	11	0	0	1	19	5.3
R	76*	Garrett Mitchell	WSH	1	0	0	0	8:48	0	0	0	0	0	0	0.0
C	87*	Liam O'Brien	WSH	1	0	0	0	6:08	0	0	0	0	0	0	0.0
D	55	Aaron Ness	WSH	2	0	0	0	12:50	–1	0	0	0	0	0	0.0
R	24*	Riley Barber	WSH	3	0	0	0	8:34	0	0	0	0	0	2	0.0
C	18*	Chandler Stephenson	WSH	4	0	0	0	8:52	0	0	0	0	0	3	0.0
C	28	Paul Carey	WSH	6	0	0	0	10:28	–2	0	0	0	0	8	0.0

Goaltending

No.	Goaltender	GPI	Mins	Avg	W	L	OT	EN	SO	GA	SA	Sv%	G	A	PIM
31	Philipp Grubauer	24	1265	2.04	13	6	2	5	3	43	585	.926	0	0	0
70	Braden Holtby	63	3680	2.07	42	13	6	2	9	127	1690	.925	0	0	0
	Totals	**82**	**4973**	**2.14**	**55**	**19**	**8**	**7**	**12**	**177**	**2282**	**.922**			

Playoffs

Pos	#	Player	Team	GP	G	A	Pts	TOI	+/–	PIM	PP	SH	GW	OT	S	S%
C	19	Nicklas Backstrom	WSH	13	6	7	13	20:44	0	2	1	0	1	0	26	23.1
R	77	T.J. Oshie	WSH	13	4	8	12	20:53	2	4	2	0	1	0	27	14.8
C	92	Evgeny Kuznetsov	WSH	13	5	5	10	19:49	–1	8	0	0	1	0	43	11.6
R	14	Justin Williams	WSH	13	3	6	9	18:38	0	6	1	0	1	1	29	10.3
L	8	Alex Ovechkin	WSH	13	5	3	8	19:29	–4	8	2	0	0	0	49	10.2
L	90	Marcus Johansson	WSH	13	2	6	8	19:29	–1	2	0	0	1	1	23	8.7
L	65	Andre Burakovsky	WSH	13	3	3	6	14:19	5	2	0	0	0	0	27	11.1
D	22	Kevin Shattenkirk	WSH	13	1	5	6	18:27	–4	6	1	0	1	1	36	2.8
C	20	Lars Eller	WSH	13	0	5	5	14:17	–2	10	0	0	0	0	22	0.0
D	74	John Carlson	WSH	13	2	2	4	22:24	1	4	2	0	0	0	38	5.3
D	88	Nate Schmidt	WSH	11	1	3	4	16:38	6	4	0	0	0	0	17	5.9
D	2	Matt Niskanen	WSH	13	1	3	4	22:38	0	19	1	0	0	0	24	4.2
R	43	Tom Wilson	WSH	13	3	0	3	13:51	–2	34	0	0	1	1	19	15.8
D	9	Dmitry Orlov	WSH	13	0	3	3	21:24	–1	2	0	0	0	0	21	0.0
D	44	Brooks Orpik	WSH	13	0	2	2	15:55	–7	11	0	0	0	0	15	0.0
C	28	Paul Carey	WSH	1	0	0	0	5:40	0	0	0	0	0	0	0	0.0
D	27	Karl Alzner	WSH	7	0	0	0	15:45	–1	2	0	0	0	0	1	0.0
R	10	Brett Connolly	WSH	7	0	0	0	8:34	–2	0	0	0	0	0	6	0.0
C	26	Daniel Winnik	WSH	13	0	0	0	10:58	–4	0	0	0	0	0	11	0.0
C	83	Jay Beagle	WSH	13	0	0	0	11:41	–5	4	0	0	0	0	6	0.0

Goaltending

No.	Goaltender	GPI	Mins	Avg	W	L	EN	SO	GA	SA	Sv%	G	A	PIM
70	Braden Holtby	13	803	2.47	7	6	0	0	33	364	.909	0	0	2
31	Philipp Grubauer	1	19	6.32	0	0	1	0	2	9	.778	0	0	0
	Totals	**13**	**830**	**2.60**	**7**	**6**	**1**	**0**	**36**	**374**	**.904**			

Barry Trotz

Head Coach

Born: Winnipeg, MB, July 15, 1962.

Majority owner Ted Leonsis and president Dick Patrick announced on May 26, 2014 that they had named Barry Trotz as the team's head coach. Trotz is the 17th coach in Capitals history and joined Washington after spending 15 seasons as coach of the Nashville Predators. In his first season with the Capitals in 2014-15, the team had 101 points and returned to the playoffs. In 2015-16, Washington won the Presidents' Trophy with 120 points and Trotz earned the Jack Adams Award as coach of the year. AfterTrotz served as an assisant coach with Team Canada at the World Cup of Hockey in 2016, the Capitals won the Presidents' Trophy again with 118 points in 2016-17.

Trotz was previously the longest tenured coach in the NHL and only coach in the Predators history. Trotz has put himself among some legendary names, ranking third all-time in both games coached (1,196) and wins (557) with a single franchise. He is one of just six coaches in all four major North American sports leagues to have coached or managed each of a team's first 15 seasons of existence (MLB: Connie Mack - 50, Philadelphia (AL); NFL Curly Lambeau - 29, Green Bay, Tom Landry - 29, Dallas, Hank Stram - 15, Kansas City, Paul Brown - 15, Cleveland). Trotz has also been the finalist for the Jack Adams Award, awarded annually to the NHL's top head coach, twice (2010 and 2011) while finishing in the top five on four other occasions since 2006.

Prior to joining the Predators, Trotz spent five seasons (1992 to 1997) as the coach of the Capitals' primary developmental affiliate in the American Hockey League. He was named coach of the Baltimore Skipjacks in 1992 after one season as an assistant coach. Following the franchise's relocation to Portland, Maine, in 1993, he led the Portland Pirates to two Calder Cup finals appearances during the next four seasons. In 1994-95, Trotz coached Portland to a Calder Cup championship and a league-best 43-27-10 record and captured AHL Coach of the Year honors. In 2006 he was honored with election to the Pirates' Hall of Fame.

Trotz earned the first of his back-to-back Jack Adams nominations in 2009-10 when he was runner-up for the award after leading his club to a 100-point season (47-29-6) despite the NHL's 28th-highest payroll. Trotz was again nominated for the award in 2010-11 after guiding the Predators to the fifth seed in the Western Conference (44-27-11) despite losing 348 man-games due to injury, a number that ranked among the top three in the league, and being the fifth youngest roster down the stretch and the youngest among playoff teams. That success continued in 2011-12 when he finished fifth in Adams voting after steering the team to their third-best record in franchise history and to top 10 rankings in goals for (eighth), goals against (eighth), power-play percentage (first) and penalty-kill percentage (10th). On November 12, 2011, against the Montreal Canadiens, he hit the 1,000-game milestone, and on March 30, 2012, reached the 500-win mark. He moved into the top 10 in all-time NHL coaching victories during the 2015-16 season.

Coaching Record

			Regular Season				Playoffs			
Season	Team	League	GC	W	L	O/T	GC	W	L	T
1992-93	Baltimore	AHL	80	28	40	12	7	3	4	....
1993-94	Portland	AHL	80	43	27	10	8	6	2	....
1994-95	Portland	AHL	80	46	22	12	7	3	4	....
1995-96	Portland	AHL	80	32	34	14	24	14	10	....
1996-97	Portland	AHL	80	37	26	17	5	2	3	....
1998-99	**Nashville**	**NHL**	**82**	**28**	**47**	**7**	....	....	....	....
99-2000	**Nashville**	**NHL**	**82**	**28**	**40**	**14**	....	....	....	....
2000-01	**Nashville**	**NHL**	**82**	**34**	**36**	**12**	....	....	....	....
2001-02	**Nashville**	**NHL**	**82**	**28**	**41**	**13**	....	....	....	....
2002-03	**Nashville**	**NHL**	**82**	**27**	**35**	**20**	....	....	....	....
2003-04	**Nashville**	**NHL**	**82**	**38**	**29**	**15**	**6**	**2**	**4**	....
2004-05	**Nashville**				SEASON CANCELLED					
2005-06	**Nashville**	**NHL**	**82**	**49**	**25**	**8**	**5**	**1**	**4**	....
2006-07	**Nashville**	**NHL**	**82**	**51**	**23**	**8**	**5**	**1**	**4**	....
2007-08	**Nashville**	**NHL**	**82**	**41**	**32**	**9**	**6**	**2**	**4**	....
2008-09	**Nashville**	**NHL**	**82**	**40**	**34**	**8**	....	....	....	....
2009-10	**Nashville**	**NHL**	**82**	**47**	**29**	**6**	**6**	**2**	**4**	....
2010-11	**Nashville**	**NHL**	**82**	**44**	**27**	**11**	**12**	**6**	**6**	....
2011-12	**Nashville**	**NHL**	**82**	**48**	**26**	**8**	**10**	**5**	**5**	....
2012-13	**Nashville**	**NHL**	**48**	**16**	**23**	**9**	....	....	....	....
2013-14	**Nashville**	**NHL**	**82**	**38**	**32**	**12**	....	....	....	....
2014-15	**Washington**	**NHL**	**82**	**45**	**26**	**11**	**14**	**7**	**7**	....
2015-16	**Washington**	**NHL**	**82**	**56**	**18**	**8**	**12**	**6**	**6**	....
2016-17	**Washington**	**NHL**	**82**	**55**	**19**	**8**	**13**	**7**	**6**	....
	NHL Totals		**1442**	**713**	**542**	**187**	**89**	**39**	**50**	....

Jack Adams Award (2016)

Club Records

Team

(Figures in brackets for season records are games played; records for fewest points, wins, ties, losses, goals, goals against are for 70 or more games)

Most Points **121** 2009-10 (82)
Most Wins **56** 2015-16 (82)
Most Ties **18** 1980-81 (80)
Most Losses **67** 1974-75 (80)
Most Goals **330** 1991-92 (80)
Most Goals Against ***446** 1974-75 (80)
Fewest Points ***21** 1974-75 (80)
Fewest Wins ***8** 1974-75 (80)
Fewest Ties **5** 1974-75 (80), 1983-84 (80)
Fewest Losses **15** 2009-10 (82)
Fewest Goals **181** 1974-75 (80)
Fewest Goals Against **182** 2016-17 (82)

Longest Winning Streak
Overall .... **14** Jan. 13-Feb. 7/10
Home .... **15** Jan. 1-Mar. 14/17
Away .... **6** Feb. 26-Apr. 1/84, Feb. 20-Mar. 15/11

Longest Team Point Streak
Overall .... **14** Nov. 24-Dec. 23/82 (9W, 5T), Jan. 17-Feb. 18/84 (13W, 1T), Jan. 13-Feb. 7/10 (12W, 1OTW, 1SOW)
Home .... **15** Jan. 1-Mar. 14/17 (13W, 2OTW)
Away .... **10** Nov. 24/82-Jan. 8/83 (6W, 4T)

Longest Losing Streak
Overall .... ***17** Feb. 18-Mar. 26/75
Home .... **11** Feb. 18-Mar. 30/75
Away .... **37** Oct. 9/74-Mar. 26/75

Longest Winless Streak
Overall .... **25** Nov. 29/75-Jan. 21/76 (22L, 3T)
Home .... **14** Dec. 3/75-Jan. 21/76 (11L, 3T)
Away .... **37** Oct. 9/74-Mar. 26/75 (37L)

Most Shutouts, Season **9** 1995-96 (82), 2014-15 (82)
Most PIM, Season **2,204** 1989-90 (80)
Most Goals, Game .... **12** Feb. 6/90 (Que. 2 at Wsh. 12), Jan. 11/03 (Fla. 2 at Wsh. 12)

Individual

Most Seasons .... **16** Olie Kolzig
Most Games .... **983** Calle Johansson
Most Goals, Career .... **558** Alex Ovechkin
Most Assists, Career .... **540** Nicklas Backstrom
Most Points, Career .... **1,035** Alex Ovechkin (558G, 477A)
Most PIM, Career .... **2,003** Dale Hunter
Most Shutouts, Career .... **35** Olie Kolzig
Longest Consecutive Games Streak .... **540** Karl Alzner (Oct. 8/10-Apr. 9/17)
Most Goals, Season .... **65** Alex Ovechkin (2007-08)
Most Assists, Season .... **76** Dennis Maruk (1981-82)
Most Points, Season .... **136** Dennis Maruk (1981-82; 60G, 76A)
Most PIM, Season .... **339** Alan May (1989-90)
Most Points, Defenseman, Season .... **81** Larry Murphy (1986-87; 23G, 58A)
Most Points, Center, Season .... **136** Dennis Maruk (1981-82; 60G, 76A)
Most Points, Right Wing, Season .... **102** Mike Gartner (1984-85; 50G, 52A)
Most Points, Left Wing, Season .... **112** Alex Ovechkin (2007-08; 65G, 47A)
Most Points, Rookie, Season .... **106** Alex Ovechkin (2005-06; 52G, 54A)
Most Shutouts, Season .... **9** Jim Carey (1995-96), Braden Holtby (2014-15), (2016-17)
Most Goals, Game .... **5** Bengt Gustafsson (Jan. 8/84) Peter Bondra (Feb. 5/94)
Most Assists, Game .... **6** Mike Ridley (Jan. 7/89)
Most Points, Game .... **7** Dino Ciccarelli (Mar. 18/89; 4G, 3A) Jaromir Jagr (Jan. 11/03; 3G, 4A)

* NHL Record.

All-time Record vs. Other Clubs

Regular Season

	Total								At Home								On Road							
	GP	W	L	T	OL	GF	GA	PTS	GP	W	L	T	OL	GF	GA	PTS	GP	W	L	T	OL	GF	GA	PTS
Anaheim	33	16	15	1	1	89	98	34	17	8	8	0	1	39	46	17	16	8	7	1	0	50	52	17
Arizona	75	33	28	12	2	266	236	80	38	23	9	5	1	144	104	52	37	10	19	7	1	122	132	28
Boston	154	57	68	21	8	428	501	143	77	31	30	12	4	226	244	78	77	26	38	9	4	202	257	65
Buffalo	155	53	82	15	5	411	541	126	78	28	38	9	3	211	255	68	77	25	44	6	2	200	286	58
Calgary	93	37	41	13	2	295	332	89	48	25	15	6	2	176	160	58	45	12	26	7	0	119	172	31
Carolina	166	92	52	14	8	516	443	206	83	51	24	4	4	273	210	110	83	41	28	10	4	243	233	96
Chicago	95	42	41	11	1	311	316	96	48	27	15	5	1	173	139	60	47	15	26	6	0	138	177	36
Colorado	81	41	30	9	1	290	244	92	40	22	13	4	1	149	122	49	41	19	17	5	0	141	122	43
Columbus	32	20	7	1	4	104	87	45	15	10	2	1	2	48	33	23	17	10	5	0	2	56	54	22
Dallas	95	30	48	16	1	265	334	77	47	16	22	8	1	135	157	41	48	14	26	8	0	130	177	36
Detroit	113	48	45	16	4	366	358	116	56	29	22	5	0	206	171	63	57	19	23	11	4	160	187	53
Edmonton	72	36	29	6	1	251	250	79	36	23	10	2	1	141	110	49	36	13	19	4	0	110	140	30
Florida	120	63	39	9	9	354	305	144	60	34	16	5	5	189	143	78	60	29	23	4	4	165	162	66
Los Angeles	108	37	55	13	3	369	403	90	53	22	23	7	1	210	189	52	55	15	32	6	2	159	214	38
Minnesota	20	11	8	0	1	50	45	23	10	8	2	0	0	28	16	16	10	3	6	0	1	22	29	7
Montreal	162	69	71	17	5	419	509	160	80	37	32	9	2	221	229	85	82	32	39	8	3	198	280	75
Nashville	25	13	9	1	2	70	68	29	12	8	3	0	1	36	28	17	13	5	6	1	1	34	40	12
New Jersey	206	105	74	13	14	674	583	237	104	61	29	6	8	381	284	136	102	44	45	7	6	293	299	101
NY Islanders	210	104	87	13	6	659	685	227	105	54	37	11	3	334	314	122	105	50	50	2	3	325	371	105
NY Rangers	214	100	90	18	6	727	718	224	107	54	40	9	4	372	333	121	107	46	50	9	2	355	385	103
Ottawa	90	44	36	5	5	272	270	98	45	26	13	4	2	149	118	58	45	18	23	1	3	123	152	40
Philadelphia	211	81	101	19	10	635	719	191	103	46	41	13	3	330	321	108	108	35	60	6	7	305	398	83
Pittsburgh	217	95	97	16	9	768	783	215	110	55	41	9	5	432	383	124	107	40	56	7	4	336	400	91
St. Louis	95	42	40	12	1	314	322	97	47	25	18	4	0	160	139	54	48	17	22	8	1	154	183	43
San Jose	39	11	24	1	3	96	131	26	20	6	11	0	3	49	63	15	19	5	13	1	0	47	68	11
Tampa Bay	122	77	31	6	8	421	315	168	61	42	11	4	4	230	155	92	61	35	20	2	4	191	160	76
Toronto	141	71	54	10	6	488	470	158	72	45	21	4	2	263	197	96	69	26	33	6	4	225	273	62
Vancouver	93	44	39	9	1	298	296	98	47	26	17	4	0	155	136	56	46	18	22	5	1	143	160	42
Winnipeg	87	48	26	5	8	284	244	109	43	28	9	3	3	158	123	62	44	20	17	2	5	126	121	47
Defunct Clubs	20	6	13	1	0	58	81	13	10	2	8	0	0	28	42	4	10	4	5	1	0	30	39	9
Totals	**3344**	**1526**	**1380**	**303**	**135**	**10548**	**10687**	**3490**	**1672**	**872**	**580**	**153**	**67**	**5646**	**4964**	**1964**	**1672**	**654**	**800**	**150**	**68**	**4902**	**5723**	**1526**

Playoffs

	Series	W	L	GP	W	L	T	GF	GA	Last Mtg.	Rnd.	Result
Boston	3	2	1	17	8	9	0	37	43	2012	CQF	W 4-3
Buffalo	1	1	0	6	4	2	0	13	11	1998	CF	W 4-2
Detroit	1	0	1	4	0	4	0	7	13	1998	F	L 0-4
Montreal	1	0	1	7	3	4	0	22	20	2010	CQF	L 3-4
New Jersey	2	1	1	13	7	6	0	44	43	1990	DSF	W 4-2
NY Islanders	7	2	5	37	16	21	0	104	114	2015	FR	W 4-3
NY Rangers	9	4	5	55	28	27	0	144	134	2015	SR	L 3-4
Ottawa	1	1	0	5	4	1	0	18	7	1998	CSF	W 4-1
Philadelphia	5	3	2	29	16	13	0	99	84	2016	FR	W 4-2
Pittsburgh	10	1	9	62	24	38	0	176	200	2017	SR	L 3-4
Tampa Bay	2	0	2	10	2	8	0	25	30	2011	CSF	L 0-4
Toronto	1	1	0	6	4	2	0	18	16	2017	FR	W 4-2
Totals	**43**	**16**	**27**	**251**	**116**	**135**	**0**	**707**	**715**			

Playoff Results 2017-2013

Year	Round	Opponent	Result	GF	GA
2017	SR	Pittsburgh	L 3-4	18	20
	FR	Toronto	W 4-2	18	16
2016	SR	Pittsburgh	L 2-4	15	16
	FR	Philadelphia	W 4-2	14	6
2015	SR	NY Rangers	L 3-4	12	13
	FR	NY Islanders	W 4-3	16	15
2013	CQF	NY Rangers	L 3-4	12	16

Abbreviations: Round: F – Final; **CF** – conference final; **CSF** – conference semi-final; **SR** – second round; **CQF** – conference quarter-final; **FR** – first round; **DSF** – division semi-final.

Calgary totals include Atlanta Flames, 1974-75 to 1979-80.
Colorado totals include Quebec, 1979-80 to 1994-95.
New Jersey totals include Kansas City, 1974-75, 1975-76, and Colorado Rockies, 1976-77 to 1981-82.
Phoenix totals include Winnipeg, 1979-80 to 1995-96.
Carolina totals include Hartford, 1979-80 to 1996-97.
Dallas totals include Minnesota North Stars, 1974-75 to 1992-93.
Winnipeg totals include Atlanta Thrashers, 1999-2000 to 2010-11.

2016-17 Results

Month	Day	Opponent	Score	Month	Day	Opponent	Score
Oct.	13	at Pittsburgh	2-3†		13	Chicago	6-0
	15	NY Islanders	2-1		15	Philadelphia	5-0
	18	Colorado	3-0		16	at Pittsburgh	7-8*
	20	at Florida	4-2		19	at St. Louis	7-3
	22	NY Rangers	2-4		21	at Dallas	4-3*
	26	at Edmonton	1-4		23	Carolina	6-1
	29	at Vancouver	5-2		24	at Ottawa	0-3
	30	at Calgary	3-1		26	at New Jersey	5-2
Nov.	1	at Winnipeg	3-2		31	at NY Islanders	2-3
	3	Winnipeg	4-3*	**Feb.**	1	Boston	5-3
	5	Florida	4-2		4	at Montreal	3-2
	8	San Jose	0-3		5	Los Angeles	5-0
	11	at Chicago	3-2*		7	Carolina	5-0
	12	at Carolina	1-5		9	Detroit	6-3
	15	at Columbus	1-2*		11	Anaheim	6-4
	16	Pittsburgh	7-1		18	at Detroit	2-3†
	18	Detroit	1-0		19	at NY Rangers	1-2
	20	Columbus	2-3		22	at Philadelphia	4-1
	23	St. Louis	4-3		24	Edmonton	2-1
	25	Buffalo	3-1		25	at Nashville	2-5
	26	at Toronto	2-4		28	at NY Rangers	4-1
Dec.	1	NY Islanders	0-3	**Mar.**	2	New Jersey	1-0
	3	at Tampa Bay	1-2†		4	Philadelphia	2-1*
	5	Buffalo	3-2*		6	Dallas	2-4
	7	Boston	4-3*		9	at San Jose	2-4
	9	at Buffalo	4-1		11	at Los Angeles	2-4
	11	Vancouver	3-0		12	at Anaheim	2-5
	13	at NY Islanders	4-2		14	Minnesota	4-2
	16	at Carolina	4-3†		16	Nashville	1-2*
	17	Montreal	1-2		18	at Tampa Bay	5-3
	21	at Philadelphia	2-3†		21	Calgary	4-2
	23	Tampa Bay	4-0		23	Columbus	2-1†
	27	at NY Islanders	3-4		25	Arizona	4-1
	29	New Jersey	1-2†		28	at Minnesota	5-4*
	31	at New Jersey	6-2		29	at Colorado	5-3
Jan.	1	Ottawa	2-1		31	at Arizona	3-6
	3	Toronto	6-5*	**Apr.**	2	at Columbus	3-2
	5	Columbus	5-0		4	at Toronto	4-1
	7	at Ottawa	1-0		5	NY Rangers	2-0
	9	at Montreal	4-1		8	at Boston	3-1
	11	Pittsburgh	5-2		9	Florida	0-2

* – Overtime † – Shootout

NHL Draft Selections 2017-2003

Name in bold denotes played in NHL.

2017 Pick		2012 Pick		2008 Pick		2005 Pick	
120	Tobias Geisser	11	**Filip Forsberg**	21	Anton Gustafsson	14	Sasha Pokulok
151	Sebastian Walfridsson	16	**Tom Wilson**	27	**John Carlson**	27	**Joe Finley**
182	Benton Maass	77	**Chandler Stephenson**	57	Eric Mestery	109	Andrew Thomas
213	Kristian Roykas	100	Thomas Di Pauli	58	Dmitry Kugryshev	118	Patrick McNeill
	Marthinsen	107	Austin Wuthrich	93	**Braden Holtby**	143	Daren Machesney
		137	**Connor Carrick**	144	Joel Broda	181	**Tim Kennedy**
2016		167	**Riley Barber**	174	Greg Burke	209	Viktor Dovgan
Pick		195	Christian Djoos	204	**Stefan Della Rovere**		
28	Lucas Johansen	197	Jaynen Rissling			**2004**	
87	Garrett Pilon	203	Sergey Kostenko	**2007**		Pick	
117	Damien Riat			Pick		1	**Alex Ovechkin**
145	Beck Malenstyn	**2011**		5	**Karl Alzner**	27	**Jeff Schultz**
147	Axel Jonsson-Fjallby	Pick		34	Josh Godfrey	29	**Mike Green**
177	Chase Priskie	117	Steffen Soberg	46	Theo Ruth	33	**Chris Bourque**
207	Dmitri Zaitsev	147	Patrick Koudys	84	Phil Desimone	62	Mikhail Yunkov
		177	Travis Boyd	108	Brett Bruneteau	66	**Sami Lepisto**
2015		207	Garrett Haar	125	Brett Leffler	88	Clayton Barthel
Pick				154	Dan Dunn	132	Oscar Hedman
22	**Ilya Samsonov**	**2010**		180	Justin Taylor	138	Pasi Salonen
57	Jonas Siegenthaler	Pick		185	Nick Larson	166	Peter Guggisberg
143	Connor Hobbs	26	**Evgeny Kuznetsov**	199	Andrew Glass	197	**Andrew Gordon**
173	Colby Williams	86	**Stanislav Galiev**			230	Justin Mrazek
		112	**Philipp Grubauer**	**2006**		263	**Travis Morin**
2014		142	Caleb Herbert	Pick			
Pick		176	Samuel Carrier	4	**Nicklas Backstrom**	**2003**	
13	**Jakub Vrana**			23	**Semyon Varlamov**	Pick	
39	Vitek Vanecek	**2009**		34	**Michal Neuvirth**	18	**Eric Fehr**
89	Nathan Walker	Pick		35	Francois Bouchard	83	Steve Werner
134	Shane Gersich	24	**Marcus Johansson**	52	Keith Seabrook	109	Andreas Valdix
159	Steven Spinner	55	**Dmitry Orlov**	97	**Oskar Osala**	155	Josh Robertson
194	Kevin Elgestal	85	**Cody Eakin**	122	Luke Lynes	249	**Andrew Joudrey**
		115	**Patrick Wey**	127	Maxime Lacroix	279	Mark Olafson
2013		145	Brett Flemming	157	Brent Gwidt		
Pick		175	**Garrett Mitchell**	177	**Mathieu Perreault**		
23	**Andre Burakovsky**	205	Benjamin Casavant				
53	Madison Bowey						
61	**Zach Sanford**						
144	Blake Heinrich						
174	Brian Pinho						
204	Tyler Lewington						

General Managers' History

Milt Schmidt, 1974-75; Milt Schmidt and Max McNab, 1975-76; Max McNab, 1976-77 to 1980-81; Max McNab and Roger Crozier, 1981-82; David Poile, 1982-83 to 1996-97; George McPhee, 1997-98 to 2013-14; Brian MacLellan, 2014-15 to date.

Brian MacLellan

Senior Vice President and General Manager

Born: Guelph, ON, October 27, 1958.

Majority owner Ted Leonsis and president Dick Patrick announced on May 26, 2014 that the Washington Capitals had promoted Brian MacLellan to senior vice president and general manager. MacLellan is the sixth general manager in Capitals history after spending the previous 13 seasons with Washington, seven as the team's assistant general manager, player personnel. In his first season as general manager in 2014-15, the team had 101 points and returned to the playoffs. In 2015-16, the Capitals had 120 points and won the Presidents' Trophy. They won the Presidents' Trophy again with 118 points in 2016-17.

In his previous role, MacLellan oversaw the club's professional scouting staff and worked closely with the team's American Hockey League affiliate, the Hershey Bears, who won the Calder Cup in 2006, 2009 and 2010. MacLellan, who served as a pro scout for the Capitals from 2000 to 2003 and then was promoted to director of player personnel, assisted and advised the general manager in all player-related matters.

MacLellan, who won a Stanley Cup with the Calgary Flames in 1989, had a 10-year NHL career in which he skated for the Los Angeles Kings, New York Rangers, Minnesota North Stars, Calgary Flames and Detroit Red Wings. A forward who played 606 NHL games, MacLellan recorded 172 goals, and 241 assists for 413 points. He also won a silver medal with Team Canada at the 1985 World Championship in Prague.

The Guelph, Ontario, native played hockey at Bowling Green State University from 1978 to 1982, where he graduated with a bachelor of science in business administration. In 1982 he was named an All-America defenseman and First-Team All-CCHA. MacLellan earned his MBA in finance from the University of St. Thomas in 1995 and went on to work for an investment consulting firm in Minneapolis before joining the Capitals as a pro scout.

Club Directory

Capital One Arena

Washington Capitals
627 N. Glebe Road, Suite 850
Arlington, VA 22203
Phone **202/266-2200**
PR FAX 202/266-2360
www.washingtoncaps.com
Capacity: 18,506

Ownership
Owner	Monumental Sports & Entertainment
Founder, Chairman, Majority Owner and CEO	Ted Leonsis
Vice Chairman and President, COO	Dick Patrick
Vice Chairmen	Raul Fernandez, Sheila Johnson
MSE Partners	David Blair, Scott Brickman, Neil D. Cohen, Jack Davies, Richard Fairbank, Michelle D. Freeman, Richard Kay, Jeong Kim, Mark D. Lerner, Roger Mody, Anthony Nader, Fred Schaufeld, Earl Stafford, George Stamas, Cliff White

Hockey Operations
Senior Vice President, General Manager & Alternate Governor	Brian MacLellan
Assistant General Manager	Ross Mahoney
Assistant General Manager, Director of Legal Affairs	Don Fishman
Director of Player Personnel	Chris Patrick
Director of Hockey Operations	Kris Wagner
Director of Player Development	Steve Richmond
Director of Hockey Analytics	Tim Barnes
Director of Team Services	Rob Tillotson
Hockey Operations Assistant	HT Lenz
Hockey Operations	Jeremy Sinton

Scouting Staff
Head Amateur Scout	Steve Bowman
Pro Scout/Minor League Operations	Jason Fitzsimmons
Scouts	Darrell Baumgartner, Matt Bradley, Danny Brooks, Alan Haworth, Phil Horner, Peter Ihnacak, Ed McColgan, Martin Pouliot, Terry Richardson, Brian Sutherby, A.J. Toews, Mats Weiderstal

Coaching Staff
Head Coach	Barry Trotz
Associate Coach	Todd Reirden
Assistant Coaches	Lane Lambert, Blaine Forsythe
Director of Goaltending	Mitch Korn
Goaltending Coach	Scott Murray
Video Coach	Brett Leonhardt
Hockey Ops Analyst	Tim Ohashi

Medical Staff
Head Athletic Trainer	Jason Serbus
Assistant Trainer	Michael Booi
Massage Therapist	TBD
Strength & Conditioning Coach	Mark Nemish

Training Staff
Head Equipment Manager	Brock Myles
Assistant Equipment Manager	Craig Leydig
Equipment Assistant	Dave Marin
Locker Room Assistant	Ray Straccia

Hershey Bears (AHL Affiliate)
Vice President of Hockey Operations	Bryan Helmer
Head Coach	Troy Mann
Assistant Coaches	Reid Cashman, Ryan Murphy
Video Coach	Mike King
Pro Development Coach	Olie Kolzig

Communications
Vice President of Communications	Sergey Kocharov
Manager of Media Relations & Content	Tommy Chalk
Manager of Communications & Publicity	Megan Eichenberg
Senior Editor & Content Strategist	Mike Vogel
Director of Digital Media	James Heuser

Broadcasting
Radio Rightsholder	Caps Radio 24/7
Radio Play-by-Play / Analyst	John Walton / Ken Sabourin
Television Rightsholder	Comcast SportsNet
Television Play-by-Play / Analyst	Joe Beninati / Craig Laughlin
Television Reporters / Studio Analyst	Al Koken, Jill Sorenson / Alan May

Captains' History

Doug Mohns, 1974-75; Bill Clement and Yvon Labre, 1975-76; Yvon Labre, 1976-77, 1977-78; Guy Charron, 1978-79; Ryan Walter, 1979-80 to 1981-82; Rod Langway, 1982-83 to 1991-92; Rod Langway and Kevin Hatcher, 1992-93; Kevin Hatcher, 1993-94; Dale Hunter, 1994-95 to 1998-99; Adam Oates, 1999-2000, 2000-01; Brendan Witt and Steve Konowalchuk, 2001-02; Steve Konowalchuk, 2002-03; Steve Konowalchuk and no captain, 2003-04; Jeff Halpern, 2005-06; Chris Clark, 2006-07 to 2008-09; Chris Clark and Alex Ovechkin, 2009-10; Alex Ovechkin, 2010-11 to date.

Coaching History

Jim Anderson, Red Sullivan and Milt Schmidt, 1974-75; Milt Schmidt and Tom McVie, 1975-76; Tom McVie, 1976-77, 1977-78; Danny Belisle, 1978-79; Danny Belisle and Gary Green, 1979-80; Gary Green, 1980-81; Gary Green, Roger Crozier and Bryan Murray, 1981-82; Bryan Murray, 1982-83 to 1988-89; Bryan Murray and Terry Murray, 1989-90; Terry Murray, 1990-91 to 1992-93; Terry Murray and Jim Schoenfeld, 1993-94; Jim Schoenfeld, 1994-95 to 1996-97; Ron Wilson, 1997-98 to 2001-02; Bruce Cassidy, 2002-03; Bruce Cassidy and Glen Hanlon, 2003-04; Glen Hanlon, 2004-05 to 2006-07; Glen Hanlon and Bruce Boudreau, 2007-08; Bruce Boudreau, 2008-09 to 2010-11; Bruce Boudreau and Dale Hunter, 2011-12; Adam Oates, 2012-13, 2013-14; Barry Trotz, 2014-15 to date.

Winnipeg Jets

Key Off-Season Signings/Acquisitions

2017

June 13 • Re-signed C **Marko Dano**.

24 • Re-signed D **Ben Chiarot**.

July 1 • Signed G **Steve Mason**, D **Dmitry Kulikov**, RW **Buddy Robinson** and C **Michael Sgarbossa**.

10 • Re-signed LW **Brandon Tanev**.

13 • Re-signed C **Andrew Copp**.

17 • Re-signed RW **JC Lipon**.

24 • Re-signed G **Connor Hellebuyck**.

2016-17 Results: 40w-35l-6otl-1sol 87pts
5th, Central Division • 9th, Western Conference

Year-by-Year Record

Season	GP	Home				Road				Overall							Div. Fin.	Conf. Fin.	Playoff Result
		W	L	T	OL	W	L	T	OL	W	L	T	OL	GF	GA	Pts.			
2016-17	82	22	18	....	1	18	17	....	6	40	35	....	7	249	256	87	5th, Cen.	9th, West	– out of playoffs –
2015-16	82	18	19	....	4	17	20	....	4	35	39	....	8	215	239	78	7th, Cen.	11th, West	– out of playoffs –
2014-15	82	23	13	....	5	20	13	....	8	43	26	....	13	230	210	99	5th, Cen.	7th, West	**Lost First Round**
2013-14	82	18	17	....	6	19	18	....	4	37	35	....	10	227	237	84	7th, Cen.	11th, West	– out of playoffs –
2012-13	48	13	10	....	1	11	11	....	2	24	21	....	3	128	144	51	2nd, SE	9th, East	– out of playoffs –
2011-12	82	23	13	....	5	14	22	....	5	37	35	....	10	225	246	84	4th, SE	11th, East	– out of playoffs –
2010-11*	82	17	17	....	7	17	19	....	5	34	36	....	12	223	269	80	4th, SE	12th, East	– out of playoffs –
2009-10*	82	19	16	....	6	16	18	....	7	35	34	....	13	234	256	83	2nd, SE	10th, East	– out of playoffs –
2008-09*	82	18	21	....	2	17	20	....	4	35	41	....	6	257	280	76	4th, SE	13th, East	– out of playoffs –
2007-08*	82	19	19	....	3	15	21	....	4	34	40	....	8	216	272	76	4th, SE	14th, East	– out of playoffs –
2006-07*	82	23	12	....	6	20	16	....	5	43	28	....	11	246	245	97	**1st, SE**	**3rd, East**	**Lost Conf. Quarter-Final**
2005-06*	82	24	13	....	4	17	20	....	4	41	33	....	8	281	275	90	3rd, SE	10th, East	– out of playoffs –
2004-05*	....																		
2003-04*	82	18	17	4	2	15	20	4	2	33	37	8	4	214	243	78	2nd, SE	10th, East	– out of playoffs –
2002-03*	82	15	19	4	3	16	20	3	2	31	39	7	5	226	284	74	3rd, SE	11th, East	– out of playoffs –
2001-02*	82	11	21	9	0	8	26	2	5	19	47	11	5	187	288	54	4th, SE	15th, East	– out of playoffs –
2000-01*	82	10	23	6	2	13	22	6	0	23	45	12	2	211	289	60	4th, SE	13th, East	– out of playoffs –
1999-2000*	82	9	26	3	3	5	31	4	1	14	57	7	4	170	313	39	5th, SE	15th, East	– out of playoffs –

* Atlanta Thrashers

2017-18 Schedule

Oct.
- Wed. 4 Toronto
- Sat. 7 at Calgary
- Mon. 9 at Edmonton
- Thu. 12 at Vancouver
- Sat. 14 Carolina
- Tue. 17 Columbus
- Fri. 20 Minnesota
- Thu. 26 at Pittsburgh
- Fri. 27 at Columbus
- Sun. 29 Pittsburgh
- Tue. 31 at Minnesota

Nov.
- Thu. 2 Dallas
- Sat. 4 Montreal
- Mon. 6 at Dallas
- Fri. 10 at Vegas
- Sat. 11 at Arizona
- Tue. 14 Arizona
- Thu. 16 Philadelphia
- Sat. 18 New Jersey*
- Mon. 20 at Nashville
- Wed. 22 at Los Angeles
- Fri. 24 at Anaheim*
- Sat. 25 at San Jose
- Mon. 27 Minnesota
- Wed. 29 at Colorado

Dec.
- Fri. 1 Vegas
- Sun. 3 Ottawa
- Tue. 5 at Detroit
- Thu. 7 at Florida
- Sat. 9 at Tampa Bay
- Mon. 11 Vancouver
- Thu. 14 Chicago
- Sat. 16 at St. Louis*
- Sun. 17 St. Louis*
- Tue. 19 at Nashville
- Thu. 21 at Boston
- Sat. 23 at NY Islanders*
- Wed. 27 Edmonton
- Fri. 29 NY Islanders
- Sun. 31 at Edmonton*

Jan.
- Tue. 2 at Colorado

- Fri. 5 Buffalo
- Sun. 7 San Jose*
- Tue. 9 at Buffalo
- Fri. 12 at Chicago
- Sat. 13 at Minnesota
- Sat. 20 at Calgary*
- Sun. 21 Vancouver
- Tue. 23 at San Jose
- Thu. 25 at Anaheim
- Tue. 30 Tampa Bay

Feb.
- Thu. 1 Vegas
- Sat. 3 Colorado
- Tue. 6 Arizona
- Fri. 9 St. Louis
- Sun. 11 NY Rangers*
- Tue. 13 Washington
- Fri. 16 Colorado
- Sun. 18 Florida
- Tue. 20 Los Angeles
- Fri. 23 at St. Louis*
- Sat. 24 at Dallas
- Tue. 27 Nashville

Mar.
- Fri. 2 Detroit
- Sun. 4 at Carolina
- Tue. 6 at NY Rangers
- Thu. 8 at New Jersey
- Sat. 10 at Philadelphia*
- Mon. 12 at Washington
- Tue. 13 at Nashville
- Thu. 15 Chicago
- Sun. 18 Dallas
- Tue. 20 Los Angeles
- Fri. 23 Anaheim
- Sun. 25 Nashville
- Tue. 27 Boston
- Thu. 29 at Chicago
- Sat. 31 at Toronto

Apr.
- Mon. 2 at Ottawa
- Tue. 3 at Montreal
- Thu. 5 Calgary
- Sat. 7 Chicago

* Denotes afternoon game.

Selected second overall in the 2016 NHL Draft, Patrik Laine scored 36 goals in 2016-17 (second among rookies) and was second in Calder Trophy voting.

CENTRAL DIVISION
19th NHL Season

Franchise date: June 25, 1997

Transferred from Atlanta to Winnipeg, June 21, 2011.

2017-18 Player Personnel

FORWARDS	HT	WT	*Age	Birthplace	S	2016-17 Club
ARMIA, Joel	6-3	205	24	Pori, Finland	R	Winnipeg
CONNOR, Kyle	6-1	182	20	Shelby Twp., MI	L	Winnipeg-Manitoba
COPP, Andrew	6-1	206	23	Ann Arbor, MI	L	Winnipeg-Manitoba
DANO, Marko	5-11	183	22	Eisenstadt , Austria	L	Winnipeg-Manitoba
EHLERS, Nikolaj	6-0	172	21	Aalborg, Denmark	L	Winnipeg
LAINE, Patrik	6-5	204	19	Tampere, Finland	R	Winnipeg
LITTLE, Bryan	6-0	191	29	Edmonton, AB	R	Winnipeg
LOWRY, Adam	6-5	210	24	St. Louis, MO	L	Winnipeg
MATTHIAS, Shawn	6-4	231	29	Mississauga, ON	L	Winnipeg
PERREAULT, Mathieu	5-10	188	29	Drummondville, QC	L	Winnipeg
PETAN, Nic	5-9	179	22	Delta, BC	L	Winnipeg-Manitoba
SCHEIFELE, Mark	6-3	207	24	Kitchener, ON	R	Winnipeg
SGARBOSSA, Michael	6-0	186	25	Campbellville, ON	L	Ana-San Diego-Fla-Sprfld
TANEV, Brandon	6-0	180	25	Toronto, ON	L	Winnipeg-Manitoba
WHEELER, Blake	6-5	225	31	Plymouth, MN	R	Winnipeg

DEFENSEMEN	HT	WT	*Age	Birthplace	S	2016-17 Club
BYFUGLIEN, Dustin	6-5	260	32	Roseau, MN	R	Winnipeg
CHIAROT, Ben	6-3	219	26	Hamilton, ON	L	Winnipeg
ENSTROM, Toby	5-10	180	32	Nordingra, Sweden	L	Winnipeg
KULIKOV, Dmitry	6-1	204	26	Lipetsk, USSR	L	Buffalo
MORRISSEY, Josh	6-0	195	22	Calgary, AB	L	Winnipeg
MYERS, Tyler	6-8	229	27	Houston, TX	R	Winnipeg
TROUBA, Jacob	6-3	202	23	Rochester, MI	R	Winnipeg

GOALTENDERS	HT	WT	*Age	Birthplace	C	2016-17 Club
HELLEBUYCK, Connor	6-4	207	24	Commerce, MI	L	Winnipeg
HUTCHINSON, Michael	6-3	202	27	Barrie, ON	R	Winnipeg
MASON, Steve	6-4	210	29	Oakville, ON	R	Philadelphia

* – Age at start of 2017-18 season

2016-17 Scoring

* – rookie

Regular Season

Pos	#	Player	Team	GP	G	A	Pts	TOI	+/-	PIM	PP	SH	GW	S	S%
C	55	Mark Scheifele	WPG	79	32	50	82	20:33	18	38	7	0	5	160	20.0
R	26	Blake Wheeler	WPG	82	26	48	74	20:08	6	47	5	2	4	259	10.0
R	29 *	Patrik Laine	WPG	73	36	28	64	17:54	7	26	9	0	5	204	17.6
L	27	Nikolaj Ehlers	WPG	82	25	39	64	17:29	1	38	5	0	4	204	12.3
D	33	Dustin Byfuglien	WPG	80	13	39	52	27:26	10	117	1	0	1	241	5.4
C	18	Bryan Little	WPG	59	21	26	47	17:33	–7	18	6	0	3	119	17.6
C	85	Mathieu Perreault	WPG	65	13	32	45	16:17	–11	30	3	0	3	134	9.7
D	8	Jacob Trouba	WPG	60	8	25	33	24:57	4	54	2	0	1	154	5.2
L	17	Adam Lowry	WPG	82	15	14	29	16:02	1	52	5	0	1	122	12.3
D	44 *	Josh Morrissey	WPG	82	6	14	20	19:29	6	38	1	0	3	99	6.1
R	40	Joel Armia	WPG	57	10	9	19	15:08	–8	20	0	4	1	111	9.0
C	9	Andrew Copp	WPG	68	6	11	17	12:20	8	18	0	1	1	77	11.7
D	39	Toby Enstrom	WPG	60	1	13	14	21:54	–7	42	0	1	0	46	2.2
D	4	Paul Postma	WPG	65	1	13	14	10:51	3	15	0	0	0	50	2.0
C	19	Nic Petan	WPG	54	1	12	13	10:54	–13	12	0	0	0	57	1.8
C	16	Shawn Matthias	WPG	45	8	4	12	13:33	0	13	0	1	1	51	15.7
D	7	Ben Chiarot	WPG	59	2	10	12	15:19	2	33	0	0	0	49	4.1
C	56	Marko Dano	WPG	38	4	7	11	10:41	0	10	2	0	0	44	9.1
D	57	Tyler Myers	WPG	11	2	3	5	22:12	5	13	0	0	0	16	12.5
L	81 *	Kyle Connor	WPG	20	2	3	5	12:13	–7	4	0	0	1	24	8.3
R	22	Chris Thorburn	WPG	64	3	1	4	6:58	–7	95	0	1	0	36	8.3
D	5	Mark Stuart	WPG	42	2	2	4	12:27	4	27	0	0	1	24	8.3
L	13 *	Brandon Tanev	WPG	51	2	2	4	10:40	–6	26	0	0	1	54	3.7
L	47	Brian Strait	WPG	5	0	2	2	15:55	–1	0	0	0	0	5	0.0
D	71 *	Julian Melchiori	WPG	18	0	2	2	18:22	0	8	0	0	0	15	0.0
C	52 *	Jack Roslovic	WPG	1	0	0	0	8:24	–1	0	0	0	0	1	0.0
C	21	Quinton Howden	WPG	5	0	0	0	8:39	1	0	0	0	0	5	0.0
D	62 *	Nelson Nogier	WPG	10	0	0	0	11:42	–1	5	0	0	0	8	0.0

Goaltending

No.	Goaltender	GPI	Mins	Avg	W	L	OT	EN	SO	GA	SA	Sv%	G	A	PIM
37	Connor Hellebuyck	56	3034	2.89	26	19	4	9	4	146	1572	.907	0	0	0
34	Michael Hutchinso	28	1378	2.92	9	12	3	2	1	67	690	.903	0	0	0
31	Ondrej Pavelec	8	440	3.55	4	4	0	1	0	26	233	.888	0	0	0
1 *	Eric Comrie	1	59	4.07	1	0	0	0	0	4	39	.897	0	0	0
	Totals	82	4965	3.08	40	35	7	12	5	255	2546	.900			

With 50 assists and 82 points in 2016-17, Mark Scheifele led the Jets in scoring and ranked eighth and seventh in the NHL overall in those categories.

Paul Maurice
Head Coach
Born: Sault Ste. Marie, ON, January 30, 1967.

The Winnipeg Jets announced on January 12, 2014 that Paul Maurice had been hired as their head coach. He is the second head coach in franchise history since the team's move from Atlanta to Winnipeg in 2011. In his first full season behind the bench in 2014-15, Maurice led the Jets to the playoffs for just the second time in franchise history. He served as an assistant coach with Team Europe at the 2016 World Cup of Hockey.

Before being hired in Winnipeg, Maurice had earned a career NHL coaching record of 460-457-167 in 14 seasons with the Carolina Hurricanes/Hartford Whalers and the Toronto Maple Leafs. He won his 400th career NHL game when the Hurricanes defeated the Buffalo Sabres in overtime on February 11, 2010, and on November 28, 2010, he became the 19th coach, and the youngest in history, to coach 1,000 NHL games. In his first head coaching stint with the Hurricanes, Maurice guided Carolina to the 2002 Eastern Conference title and two Southeast Division crowns as well as four consecutive winning seasons from 1998 to 2002. On March 16, 2010, he became just the 10th coach in NHL history to spend more than 800 games behind the bench for one franchise.

Prior to re-joining the Hurricanes, the Sault Ste. Marie, Ontario native collected a record of 76-66-22 during two full seasons as head coach of the Toronto Maple Leafs from 2006 to 2008. Maurice began with Toronto during the 2006-07 season, leading the Maple Leafs to 40 victories, and recording his 300th NHL victory on March 6, 2007.

Before moving to the NHL level during the summer of 1995 as an assistant coach with the Hartford Whalers, Maurice spent two seasons as head coach of the Ontario Hockey League's Detroit Jr. Red Wings. While in Detroit, he compiled a regular-season record of 86-38-8 and led the team to the 1995 OHL Championship and an appearance in the Memorial Cup. That season, he finished second in voting to Guelph's Craig Hartsburg for the Matt Leyden Trophy, which is annually awarded to the OHL's Coach of the Year.

Maurice played his junior hockey with the OHL's Windsor Spitfires (1984 to 1988) and was Philadelphia's 12th choice, 252nd overall, in the 1985 NHL Draft. Maurice had his career cut short due to an eye injury, and began coaching as an assistant with the Jr. Red Wings shortly thereafter.

Coaching Record

			Regular Season					Playoffs			
Season	Team	League	GC	W	L	O/T		GC	W	L	T
1993-94	Detroit	OHL	66	42	20	4		17	11	6	....
1994-95	Detroit	OHL	44	18	4	....		21	16	5	....
1994-95	Detroit	M-Cup	....	....	....	....		5	3	2	....
1995-96	Hartford	NHL	70	29	33	8		....	....	....	....
1996-97	Hartford	NHL	82	32	39	11		....	....	....	....
1997-98	Carolina	NHL	82	33	41	8		....	....	....	....
1998-99	Carolina	NHL	82	34	30	18		6	2	4	....
99-2000	Carolina	NHL	82	37	35	10		....	....	....	....
2000-01	Carolina	NHL	82	38	32	12		6	2	4	....
2001-02	Carolina	NHL	82	35	26	21		23	13	10	....
2002-03	Carolina	NHL	82	22	43	17		....	....	....	....
2003-04	Carolina	NHL	30	8	12	10		....	....	....	....
2005-06	Toronto	AHL	80	41	29	10		5	1	4	....
2006-07	Toronto	NHL	82	40	31	11		....	....	....	....
2007-08	Toronto	NHL	82	36	35	11		....	....	....	....
2008-09	Carolina	NHL	57	33	19	5		18	8	10	....
2009-10	Carolina	NHL	82	35	37	10		....	....	....	....
2010-11	Carolina	NHL	82	40	31	11		....	....	....	....
2011-12	Carolina	NHL	25	8	13	4		....	....	....	....
2012-13	Magnitogorsk	KHL	52	27	13	12		7	3	4	....
2013-14	Winnipeg	NHL	35	18	12	5		....	....	....	....
2014-15	Winnipeg	NHL	82	43	26	13		4	0	4	....
2015-16	Winnipeg	NHL	82	35	39	8		....	....	....	....
2016-17	Winnipeg	NHL	82	40	35	7		....	....	....	....
	NHL Totals		1365	596	569	200		57	25	32	

Club Records

Team

(Figures in brackets for season records are games played.)

Most Points 99   2014-15 (82)
Most Wins 43   2006-07 (82),
                                2014-15 (82)
Most Ties 12   2000-01 (82)
Most Losses 57   1999-2000 (82)
Most Goals 281   2005-06 (82)
Most Goals Against 313   1999-2000 (82)
Fewest Points 39   1999-2000 (82)
Fewest Wins 14   1999-2000 (82)
Fewest Ties 7   1999-2000 (82), 2002-03 (82)
Fewest Losses 28   2006-07 (82)
Fewest Goals 170   1999-2000 (82)
Fewest Goals Against 210   2014-15 (82)

Longest Winning Streak

Overall 7   Mar. 26-Apr. 8/17
Home 7   Mar. 2-18/07
Away 4   Jan. 13-Feb. 7/03,
                                Nov. 3-21/07,
                                Feb. 3-16/09,
                                Nov. 12-Dec. 5/09,
                                Jan. 15-Feb. 3/16,
                                Dec. 22/16-Jan. 4/17

Longest Team Point Streak

Overall 9   Dec. 9-28/05
                                (5W, 1OTW, 1OTL, 2SOL)
Home 11   Dec. 9/05-Jan. 13/06
                                (7W, 1OTW, 1OTL, 2SOL)
Away 8   Nov. 16-Dec. 27/14
                                (4W, 1OTW, 2OTL, 1SOL)

Longest Losing Streak

Overall 12   Jan. 24-Feb. 20/00
Home 11   Jan. 24-Mar. 16/00
Away 10   Oct. 6-Nov. 18/01,
                                Feb. 16-Mar. 18/08

Longest Winless Streak

Overall 16   Jan. 16-Feb. 20/00
                                (13L, 1OTL, 2T)
Home . . . . *17   Jan. 19-Mar. 29/00
                                (14L, 1OTL, 2T)
Away 16   Oct. 6-Nov. 18/01
                                (10L),
                                Feb. 16-Mar. 18/08
                                (7L, 1OTL, 2SOL)

Most Shutouts, Season 7   2014-15 (82)
Most PIM, Season 1,505   2003-04 (82)
Most Goals, Game 9   Nov. 12/05
                                (Atl. 9 at Car. 0)

Individual

Most Seasons 10   Jim Slater,
                                Toby Enstrom,
                                Bryan Little,
                                Chris Thorburn
Most Games 709   Chris Thorburn
Most Goals, Career 328   Ilya Kovalchuk
Most Assists, Career 287   Ilya Kovalchuk
Most Points, Career 615   Ilya Kovalchuk
                                (328G, 287A)
Most PIM, Career 832   Chris Thorburn
Most Shutouts, Career 17   Ondrej Pavelec

Longest Consecutive

Games Streak 252   Vyacheslav Kozlov
                                (Jan. 9/07-Jan. 21/10)

Most Goals, Season 52   Ilya Kovalchuk
                                (2005-06), (2007-08)
Most Assists, Season 69   Marc Savard
                                (2005-06)
Most Points, Season 100   Marian Hossa
                                (2006-07; 43G, 57A)
Most PIM, Season 226   Jeff Odgers
                                (2000-01)

Most Points, Defenseman,
  Season 56   Dustin Byfuglien
                                (2013-14; 20G, 36A)

Most Points, Center,
  Season 97   Marc Savard
                                (2005-06; 28G, 69A)

Most Points, Right Wing,
  Season 100   Marian Hossa
                                (2006-07; 43G, 57A)

Most Points, Left Wing,
  Season 98   Ilya Kovalchuk
                                (2005-06; 52G, 46A)

Most Points, Rookie,
  Season 67   Dany Heatley
                                (2001-02; 26G, 41A)

Most Shutouts, Season 5   Ondrej Pavelec
                                (2014-15)

Most Goals, Game 4   Pascal Rheaume
                                (Jan. 19/02),
                                Ilya Kovalchuk
                                (Nov. 11/05)

Most Assists, Game 4   Nine times
Most Points, Game 5   Seven times

* NHL Record.

Records include Atlanta Thrashers, 1999-2000 through 2010-11.

Captains' History

Kelly Buchberger, 1999-2000; Steve Staios, 2000-01; Ray Ferraro, 2001-02; Shawn McEachern, 2002-03, 2003-04; Scott Mellanby, 2005-06, 2006-07; Bobby Holik, 2007-08; no captain and Ilya Kovalchuk, 2008-09; Ilya Kovalchuk, 2009-10; Andrew Ladd, 2010-11 to 2015-16; Blake Wheeler, 2016-17 to date.

Coaching History

Curt Fraser, 1999-2000 to 2001-02; Curt Fraser, Don Waddell and Bob Hartley, 2002-03; Bob Hartley, 2003-04 to 2006-07; Bob Hartley and Don Waddell, 2007-08; John Anderson, 2008-09, 2009-10; Craig Ramsay, 2010-11; Claude Noel, 2011-12, 2012-13; Claude Noel and Paul Maurice, 2013-14; Paul Maurice, 2014-15 to date.

General Managers' History

Don Waddell, 1999-2000 to 2009-10; Rick Dudley, 2010-11; Kevin Cheveldayoff, 2011-12 to date.

All-time Record vs. Other Clubs

Regular Season

	Total							At Home							On Road						
	GP	W	L	T	OL	GF	GA	PTS	GP	W	L	T	OL	GF	GA	PTS	GP	W	L	T	OL	GF	GA	PTS
Anaheim	26	10	12	0	4	70	84	24	13	4	7	0	2	32	42	10	13	6	5	0	2	38	42	14
Arizona	28	11	13	1	3	72	83	26	13	8	3	0	2	39	33	18	15	3	10	1	1	33	50	8
Boston	59	22	29	2	6	166	188	52	30	15	14	0	1	83	84	31	29	7	15	2	5	83	104	21
Buffalo	59	32	21	1	5	173	195	70	29	19	6	1	3	93	76	42	30	13	15	0	2	80	119	28
Calgary	25	10	13	1	1	63	79	22	13	8	3	1	1	36	29	18	12	2	10	0	0	27	50	4
Carolina	86	32	41	4	9	244	272	77	43	12	24	3	4	115	148	31	43	20	17	1	5	129	124	46
Chicago	31	12	14	0	5	79	90	29	16	4	8	0	4	44	55	12	15	8	6	0	1	35	35	17
Colorado	37	19	10	1	7	106	99	46	18	10	5	1	2	56	45	23	19	9	5	0	5	50	54	23
Columbus	22	11	10	0	1	57	60	23	11	5	6	0	0	29	32	10	11	6	4	0	1	28	28	13
Dallas	33	13	18	0	2	100	104	28	17	7	9	0	1	64	62	15	16	6	9	0	1	36	42	13
Detroit	22	9	10	0	3	70	85	21	10	4	5	0	1	36	43	9	12	5	5	0	2	34	42	12
Edmonton	25	10	14	1	0	61	83	21	12	5	7	0	0	26	38	10	13	5	7	1	0	35	45	11
Florida	87	47	27	5	8	278	236	107	43	25	10	4	4	153	116	58	44	22	17	1	4	125	120	49
Los Angeles	26	12	13	0	1	79	91	25	13	8	5	0	0	40	33	16	13	4	8	0	1	39	58	9
Minnesota	32	14	15	1	2	87	91	31	16	8	7	0	1	52	49	17	16	6	8	1	1	35	42	14
Montreal	59	20	33	2	4	131	182	46	29	11	14	2	2	65	79	26	30	9	19	0	2	66	103	20
Nashville	35	14	16	1	4	87	102	33	18	9	6	1	2	48	44	21	17	5	10	0	2	39	58	12
New Jersey	59	24	27	3	5	139	172	56	29	11	15	2	1	70	88	25	30	13	12	1	4	69	84	31
NY Islanders	59	24	27	2	6	172	213	56	30	9	14	2	5	88	116	25	29	15	13	0	1	84	97	31
NY Rangers	59	30	25	1	3	165	169	64	29	12	15	0	2	79	89	26	30	18	10	1	1	86	80	38
Ottawa	59	23	33	2	1	173	218	49	29	11	17	1	0	97	107	23	30	12	16	1	1	76	111	26
Philadelphia	59	17	33	3	6	157	214	43	30	9	16	1	4	74	100	23	29	8	17	2	2	83	114	20
Pittsburgh	59	14	38	0	7	154	226	35	30	10	17	0	3	79	99	23	29	4	21	0	4	75	127	12
St. Louis	34	14	15	1	4	87	97	33	18	7	8	1	2	48	52	17	16	7	7	0	2	39	45	16
San Jose	26	7	17	2	0	59	85	16	13	3	9	1	0	29	42	7	13	4	8	1	0	30	43	9
Tampa Bay	86	37	30	4	15	244	276	93	43	22	11	3	7	136	124	54	43	15	19	1	8	108	152	39
Toronto	57	26	24	1	6	160	199	59	29	15	12	0	2	77	97	32	28	11	12	1	4	83	102	27
Vancouver	24	10	11	1	2	62	69	23	12	7	4	0	1	36	32	15	12	3	7	1	1	26	37	8
Washington	87	34	39	5	9	244	284	82	44	22	17	2	3	121	126	49	43	12	22	3	6	123	158	33
Totals	**1360**	**558**	**628**	**45**	**129**	**3739**	**4346**	**1290**	**680**	**300**	**294**	**26**	**60**	**1945**	**2080**	**686**	**680**	**258**	**334**	**19**	**69**	**1794**	**2266**	**604**

Playoffs

	Series	W	L	GP	W	L	T	GF	GA	Last Mtg.	Rnd.	Result
Anaheim	1	0	1	4	0	4	0	9	16	2015	FR	L 0-4
NY Rangers	1	0	1	4	0	4	0	6	17	2007	CQF	L 0-4
Totals	**2**	**0**	**2**	**8**	**0**	**8**	**0**	**15**	**33**			

Playoff Results 2017-2013

Year	Round	Opponent	Result	GF	GA
2015	FR	Anaheim	L 0-4	9	16

Abbreviations: Round: CQF – conference quarter-final; **FR** – first round.

NHL Draft Selections 2017-2003

Name in bold denotes played in NHL.

2017
Pick
24	Kristian Vesalainen
43	Dylan Samberg
74	Johnny Kovacevic
105	Santeri Virtanen
136	Leon Gawanke
167	Arvid Holm
198	Skyler McKenzie
211	Croix Evingson

2016
Pick
2	**Patrik Laine**
18	Logan Stanley
79	Luke Green
97	Jacob Cederholm
127	Jordan Stallard
157	Mikhail Berdin

2015
Pick
17	**Kyle Connor**
25	**Jack Roslovic**
47	Jansen Harkins
78	Erik Foley
108	Michael Spacek
168	Mason Appleton
198	Sami Niku
203	Matteo Gennaro

2014
Pick
9	**Nikolaj Ehlers**
69	Jack Glover
99	**Chase De Leo**
101	**Nelson Nogier**
129	C.J. Franklin
164	Pavel Kraskovsky
192	Matt Ustaski

2013
Pick
13	**Josh Morrissey**
43	**Nic Petan**
59	**Eric Comrie**
84	Jimmy Lodge
91	**JC Lipon**
104	**Andrew Copp**
114	Jan Kostalek
127	Tucker Poolman
190	Brenden Kichton
194	Marcus Karlstrom

2012
Pick
9	**Jacob Trouba**
39	Lukas Sutter
70	**Scott Kosmachuk**
130	**Connor Hellebuyck**
160	Ryan Olsen
190	Jamie Phillips

2011
Pick
7	**Mark Scheifele**
67	**Adam Lowry**
78	Brennan Serville
119	Zachary Yuen
149	Austen Brassard
157	**Jason Kasdorf**
187	Aaron Harstad

2010
Pick
8	**Alexander Burmistrov**
87	**Julian Melchiori**
101	Ivan Telegin
128	Fredrik Pettersson-Wentzel
150	Yasin Cisse
155	Kendall McFaull
160	Tanner Lane
169	Sebastian Owuya
199	Peter Stoykewych

2009
Pick
4	**Evander Kane**
34	**Carl Klingberg**
45	**Jeremy Morin**
117	Eddie Pasquale
120	**Ben Chiarot**
125	Cody Sol
155	Jimmy Bubnick
185	Levko Koper
203	Jordan Samuels-Thomas

2008
Pick
3	**Zach Bogosian**
29	Daultan Leveille
64	Danick Paquette
94	Vinny Saponari
124	Nicklas Lasu
154	Chris Carrozzi
184	**Zach Redmond**

2007
Pick
67	**Spencer Machacek**
115	Niclas Lucenius
175	**John Albert**
205	**Paul Postma**

2006
Pick
12	**Bryan Little**
43	Riley Holzapfel
80	Michael Forney
135	Alex Kangas
165	Jonas Enlund
195	Jesse Martin
200	**Arturs Kulda**
210	Will O'Neill

2005
Pick
16	Alex Bourret
41	**Ondrej Pavelec**
49	Chad Denny
53	Andrew Kozek
116	**Jordan Smotherman**
135	Tomas Pospisil
187	**Andrei Zubarev**
207	Myles Stoesz

2004
Pick
10	**Boris Valabik**
40	**Grant Lewis**
76	**Scott Lehman**
106	Chad Painchaud
142	Juraj Gracik
186	Dan Turple
204	Miikka Tuomainen
237	Mitch Carefoot
270	Matt Siddall

2003
Pick
8	**Braydon Coburn**
110	Jim Sharrow
116	**Guillaume Desbiens**
136	Michael Vannelli
145	**Brett Sterling**
175	Mike Hamilton
203	Denis Loginov
239	**Toby Enstrom**
269	Rylan Kaip

Club Directory

Bell MTS Place

Winnipeg Jets
Bell MTS Place
345 Graham Avenue
Winnipeg, Manitoba, R3C 5S6
Phone **204/987-7825**
FAX 204/926-5555
www.winnipegjets.com
Twitter @NHLJets
Capacity: 15,294

Senior Management
Executive Chairman & Governor	Mark Chipman
Executive VP & Chief Operating Officer	John Olfert
Executive VP & General Manager	Kevin Cheveldayoff
President, TN Development	Jim Ludlow
Senior VP & Assistant General Manager	Craig Heisinger
Senior VP, Venues & Entertainment	Kevin Donnelly
Senior VP, Sales & Marketing	Norva Riddell
VP, Finance & CFO	Lorna Daniels
VP, Marketing	Dorian Morphy
VP, Human Resources	Dawn Haus
VP, AHL Operations & General Counsel	Dan Hursh
VP, Communications & Community Engagement	Rob Wozny
VP & Assistant General Manager	Larry Simmons
VP, Facilities Operations	Ed Meichsner

Hockey Operations
Executive VP & General Manager	Kevin Cheveldayoff
Senior VP & Assistant General Manager	Craig Heisinger
VP & Assistant General Manager	Larry Simmons
Executive Assistant, Hockey Operations	Katie Ferniuk
Head Coach	Paul Maurice
Assistant Coaches	Charlie Huddy, Jamie Kompon, Todd Woodcroft
Goaltending Coach	Wade Flaherty
Video Coach	Matt Prefontaine
Head Equipment Manager	Jason McMaster
Assistant Equipment Managers	Mark Grehan, Mike Flaman
Head Athletic Therapist	Rob Milette
Assistant Athletic Therapist	Brad Shaw
Director of Fitness	Dr. Craig Slaunwhite
Massage Therapist	Al Pritchard
Coordinator, Team Travel	Silvana Gosgnach
Director Security, Winnipeg Jets	Ken Shipley
Coordinator, Team Services	Chris Kreviazuk
Scouting Coordinator	Barrett Leganchuk
Research & Data Analysis Coordinator	Max Erenberg

Scouting Staff
Director, Pro Scouting	Mark Dobson
Director, Amateur Scouting	Mark Hillier
Pro Scouts	Jack Birch, Bruce Southern, Peter Ratchuk, Mark White, Jari Gronstrand
Amateur Scouts	Evgeny Bogdanovich, Pat Carmichael, Chris Snell, Scott Scoville, Bob Owen, Yanick Lemay, Brian Renfrew, Vladimir Havluj, Scott Robson, Max Giese, Marcel Comeau, Dan Shrader, Kjell Dahlin
Coordinator, Player Development	Jimmy Roy
Player Development	Mike Keane

Medical Staff
Head Physician	Dr. Peter MacDonald
Assistant Physicians	Dr. Greg Stranges, Dr. Jamie Dubberley
Primary Care	Dr. Mike MacKay, Dr. Swee Teo
Team Dentist	Dr. Gene Solmundson

Marketing & Communications
Senior Director, Game Production & Broadcast Services	Kyle Balharry
Director, Creative & Marketing Services	Josh Dudych
Director, Digital & Marketing Services	Andrew Wilkinson
Senior Director, Hockey Communications	Scott Brown
Manager, Hockey Communications	Greger Buer
Coordinator, Hockey Communications	Scott Unger
Manager, Visual Media	Steve Godkin
Video & Motion Graphics Producers	Curtis Robson, Dylann Bobei, Aiden Padgett Reimer
Manager, Digital Content	Ryan Dittrick
Coordinator, Digital Content	Mitchell Clinton, Tyler Esquivel
Coordinator, Digital Media	Fabio Bellisario, Kristina Ung
Senior Graphic Designer	Jessie Greenwood
Graphic Designers	Allison Ferley, Marc Gomez

Sales
Senior Director, Corporate Partnerships	JP Adams
Director, Consumer Technology & Analytics	Mitch Brennan
Director, Ticket Sales & Account Service	Linzy Jones
Director, Partnership Services	Collin Farrell

Retail Operations
Director, Retail Operations	Dave Blackmore
Director, Retail Development	Dan Suga

Community Relations
Director, Community Relations	Barrett Paulsen
Director, Player & Alumni Relations	Anders Strome
Marketing & Community Relations Coordinator	Katie Dicks

Finance
VP, Finance & CFO	Lorna Daniels
Controllers	Lindsay McLean, Ashley Paluk, Jace Cowan

Information Systems
Director, Information Technology	Dan Gill
Senior Systems Administrator	Darryl Elyk
Systems Administrator	Patrick Momotiuk

True North Youth Foundation
Executive Director, TNYF	Dwayne Green

Building Operations
VP, Facility Operations	Ed Meichsner

Kevin Cheveldayoff

Executive Vice President and General Manager

Born: Blaine Lake, SK, February 4, 1970.

Kevin Cheveldayoff was given his first assignment as general manager of an NHL hockey club when he was named to the position by the Winnipeg Jets on June 8, 2011. In 2014-15 the Jets reached the playoffs for the first time.

Prior to joining the Jets, Cheveldayoff had spent two seasons with the Chicago Blackhawks and served as the club's assistant general manager/senior director, hockey operations in 2010-11. During his tenure in Chicago, the Blackhawks won the 2010 Stanley Cup championship, the team's first since 1961.

Before joining the Blackhawks on August 3, 2009, Cheveldayoff spent the previous 12 seasons as the general manager of the Chicago Wolves, guiding the franchise to four league championships, which included the 2002 and 2008 Calder Cup titles in the American Hockey League and the 1998 and 2000 International Hockey League's Turner Cup. Overall, Cheveldayoff was a part of seven league championships during his 15-year management career before being hired in Winnipeg, including two Turner Cup titles in three seasons as the assistant vice president of hockey operations and assistant coach for the Denver and Utah Grizzlies (1994 to 1997).

Cheveldayoff was the architect of 12 Wolves teams that compiled a .615 regular-season winning percentage (544-320-114) and 10 postseason berths from 1997 to 2009. Eight of those clubs reached the 100-point mark during the regular season while earning four division titles and six postseason conference championships.

Cheveldayoff was originally drafted by the New York Islanders with their first pick (16th overall) in the 1988 NHL Draft. He began his career in the AHL with the Springfield Indians at the end of the 1989-90 season. He then played with the Capital District Islanders beginning in 1990, serving as the alternate captain from 1991 to 1993. He held the same role with the Salt Lake Golden Eagles in 1993-94, earning the team's "Unsung Hero Award" after racking up a career-high 216 penalty minutes in 73 games. Known as a defensive defenseman during his playing days, a knee injury cut his professional career short after five seasons.

2016-17 Final Standings

Standings

Abbreviations: GP - games played; **W** - wins; **L** - losses; **OT** - overtime and shootout losses; **GF** - goals for; **GA** - goals against; **PTS** - points.
Note: teams receive two points for a Win (W), one point for an Overtime or Shootout Loss (OT)

EASTERN CONFERENCE

Atlantic Division

		GP	W	L	OT	GF	GA	PTS
Montreal	(A1)	82	47	26	9	226	200	103
Ottawa	(A2)	82	44	28	10	212	214	98
Boston	(A3)	82	44	31	7	234	212	95
Toronto	(W2)	82	40	27	15	251	242	95
Tampa Bay		82	42	30	10	234	227	94
Florida		82	35	36	11	210	237	81
Detroit		82	33	36	13	207	244	79
Buffalo		82	33	37	12	201	237	78

Metropolitan Division

		GP	W	L	OT	GF	GA	PTS
Washington	(M1)	82	55	19	8	263	182	118
Pittsburgh	(M2)	82	50	21	11	282	234	111
Columbus	(M3)	82	50	24	8	249	195	108
NY Rangers	(W1)	82	48	28	6	256	220	102
NY Islanders		82	41	29	12	241	242	94
Philadelphia		82	39	33	10	219	236	88
Carolina		82	36	31	15	215	236	87
New Jersey		82	28	40	14	183	244	70

WESTERN CONFERENCE

Central Division

		GP	W	L	OT	GF	GA	PTS
Chicago	(C1)	82	50	23	9	244	213	109
Minnesota	(C2)	82	49	25	8	266	208	106
St. Louis	(C3)	82	46	29	7	235	218	99
Nashville	(W2)	82	41	29	12	240	224	94
Winnipeg		82	40	35	7	249	256	87
Dallas		82	34	37	11	223	262	79
Colorado		82	22	56	4	166	278	48

Pacific Division

		GP	W	L	OT	GF	GA	PTS
Anaheim	(P1)	82	46	23	13	223	200	105
Edmonton	(P2)	82	47	26	9	247	212	103
San Jose	(P3)	82	46	29	7	221	201	99
Calgary	(W1)	82	45	33	4	226	221	94
Los Angeles		82	39	35	8	201	205	86
Arizona		82	30	42	10	197	260	70
Vancouver		82	30	43	9	182	243	69

Sidney Crosby celebrates his third goal of the night with Conor Sheary in a 4-0 win over Florida on March 19, 2017. Crosby led the NHL with 44 goals in 2016-17, marking the second time in his career that he won the Maurice Richard Trophy.

INDIVIDUAL LEADERS

Goal Scoring

Player	Team	GP	G
Sidney Crosby	Pittsburgh	75	44
Nikita Kucherov	Tampa Bay	74	40
*Auston Matthews	Toronto	82	40
Brad Marchand	Boston	80	39
Vladimir Tarasenko	St. Louis	82	39
Jeff Skinner	Carolina	79	37
*Patrik Laine	Winnipeg	73	36
Max Pacioretty	Montreal	81	35
Cam Atkinson	Columbus	82	35
David Pastrnak	Boston	75	34
Anders Lee	NY Islanders	81	34
Patrick Kane	Chicago	82	34
Evgeni Malkin	Pittsburgh	62	33
T.J. Oshie	Washington	68	33
Rickard Rakell	Anaheim	71	33
Alex Ovechkin	Washington	82	33
Patrick Eaves	Dal-Ana	79	32
Mark Scheifele	Winnipeg	79	32
Jeff Carter	Los Angeles	82	32
Nazem Kadri	Toronto	82	32

Assists

Player	Team	GP	A
Connor McDavid	Edmonton	82	70
Nicklas Backstrom	Washington	82	63
Ryan Getzlaf	Anaheim	74	58
Victor Hedman	Tampa Bay	79	56
Patrick Kane	Chicago	82	55
Erik Karlsson	Ottawa	77	54
Henrik Zetterberg	Detroit	82	51
Mark Scheifele	Winnipeg	79	50
Blake Wheeler	Winnipeg	82	48
Leon Draisaitl	Edmonton	82	48
Duncan Keith	Chicago	80	47
Brent Burns	San Jose	82	47
Phil Kessel	Pittsburgh	82	47
Ryan Johansen	Nashville	82	47
Brad Marchand	Boston	80	46
Alexander Wennberg	Columbus	80	46
Tyler Seguin	Dallas	82	46
Nikita Kucherov	Tampa Bay	74	45
Sidney Crosby	Pittsburgh	75	45

Power-play Goals

Player	Team	GP	PP
Nikita Kucherov	Tampa Bay	74	17
Brayden Schenn	Philadelphia	79	17
Alex Ovechkin	Washington	82	17
Wayne Simmonds	Philadelphia	82	16
Sidney Crosby	Pittsburgh	75	14

Shorthand Goals

Player	Team	GP	SH
Viktor Arvidsson	Nashville	80	5
Joel Armia	Winnipeg	57	4
Zack Smith	Ottawa	74	4
*Zach Hyman	Toronto	82	4
9 players tied with			3

Game-winning Goals

Player	Team	GP	GW
Rickard Rakell	Anaheim	71	10
Jeff Carter	Los Angeles	82	9
Cam Atkinson	Columbus	82	9
Filip Forsberg	Nashville	82	9
5 players tied with			8

Shots

Player	Team	GP	S
Brent Burns	San Jose	82	320
Alex Ovechkin	Washington	82	313
Patrice Bergeron	Boston	79	302
Tyler Seguin	Dallas	82	301
Patrick Kane	Chicago	82	292

Shooting Percentage

(minimum 82 shots)

Player	Team	GP	G	S	S%
T.J. Oshie	Washington	68	33	143	23.1
Paul Byron	Montreal	81	22	96	22.9
Artem Anisimov	Chicago	64	22	105	21.0
Mark Scheifele	Winnipeg	79	32	160	20.0
Rickard Rakell	Anaheim	71	33	177	18.6
Marcus Johansson	Washington	82	24	129	18.6

Plus/Minus

Player	Team	GP	+/-
Jason Zucker	Minnesota	79	34
Ryan Suter	Minnesota	82	34
David Savard	Columbus	74	33
Jared Spurgeon	Minnesota	76	33
Brooks Orpik	Washington	79	32

* – rookie eligible for Calder Trophy

Individual Leaders

Abbreviations: GP – games played; **G** – goals; **A** – assists; **Pts** – points; **+/–** – difference between Goals For (**GF**) scored when a player is on the ice with his team at even strength or shorthanded and Goals Against (**GA**) scored when the same player is on the ice with his team at even strength or on a power play; **PIM** – penalties in minutes; **PP** – power play goals; **SH** – shorthanded goals; **GW** – game-winning goals; **S** – shots on goal; **S%** – percentage of shots on goal resulting in goals.

Individual Scoring Leaders for Art Ross Trophy

Player	Team	GP	G	A	Pts	+/–	PIM	PP	SH	GW	S	S%
Connor McDavid	Edmonton	82	30	70	100	27	26	3	1	6	251	12.0
Sidney Crosby	Pittsburgh	75	44	45	89	17	24	14	0	5	255	17.3
Patrick Kane	Chicago	82	34	55	89	11	32	7	0	5	292	11.6
Nicklas Backstrom	Washington	82	23	63	86	17	38	8	0	1	162	14.2
Nikita Kucherov	Tampa Bay	74	40	45	85	13	38	17	0	7	246	16.3
Brad Marchand	Boston	80	39	46	85	18	81	9	3	8	226	17.3
Mark Scheifele	Winnipeg	79	32	50	82	18	38	7	0	5	160	20.0
Leon Draisaitl	Edmonton	82	29	48	77	7	20	10	0	5	172	16.9
Brent Burns	San Jose	82	29	47	76	19	40	8	0	6	320	9.1
Vladimir Tarasenko	St. Louis	82	39	36	75	–1	12	9	0	8	286	13.6
Artemi Panarin	Chicago	82	31	43	74	18	21	9	0	5	211	14.7
Blake Wheeler	Winnipeg	82	26	48	74	6	47	5	2	4	259	10.0
Ryan Getzlaf	Anaheim	74	15	58	73	7	49	6	2	3	138	10.9
Evgeni Malkin	Pittsburgh	62	33	39	72	18	77	11	0	6	191	17.3
Tyler Seguin	Dallas	82	26	46	72	–15	22	11	0	4	301	8.6
Victor Hedman	Tampa Bay	79	16	56	72	3	47	4	0	5	166	9.6
Erik Karlsson	Ottawa	77	17	54	71	10	28	4	0	5	218	7.8
David Pastrnak	Boston	75	34	36	70	11	34	10	0	4	262	13.0
Phil Kessel	Pittsburgh	82	23	47	70	3	20	8	0	4	229	10.0
*Auston Matthews	Toronto	82	40	29	69	2	14	8	0	8	279	14.3
Alex Ovechkin	Washington	82	33	36	69	6	50	17	0	7	313	10.5
Jamie Benn	Dallas	77	26	43	69	–9	66	12	1	4	201	12.9
Mikael Granlund	Minnesota	81	26	43	69	23	12	7	3	4	177	14.7
Joe Pavelski	San Jose	81	29	39	68	11	34	7	1	7	233	12.4
Henrik Zetterberg	Detroit	82	17	51	68	15	22	2	0	0	195	8.7

Defensemen Scoring Leaders

Player	Team	GP	G	A	Pts	+/–	PIM	PP	SH	GW	S	S%
Brent Burns	San Jose	82	29	47	76	19	40	8	0	6	320	9.1
Victor Hedman	Tampa Bay	79	16	56	72	3	47	4	0	5	166	9.6
Erik Karlsson	Ottawa	77	17	54	71	10	28	4	0	5	218	7.8
Kevin Shattenkirk	St.L.-Wsh.	80	13	43	56	–7	47	8	0	2	161	8.1
Duncan Keith	Chicago	80	6	47	53	22	16	2	0	2	183	3.3
Dustin Byfuglien	Winnipeg	80	13	39	52	10	117	1	0	1	241	5.4
Justin Schultz	Pittsburgh	78	12	39	51	27	34	3	0	1	154	7.8
Torey Krug	Boston	81	8	43	51	–10	37	6	0	1	208	3.8
Dougie Hamilton	Calgary	81	13	37	50	12	64	2	0	5	222	5.9
John Klingberg	Dallas	80	13	36	49	2	34	4	0	3	124	10.5
Roman Josi	Nashville	72	12	37	49	7	18	7	0	1	217	5.5
Alex Pietrangelo	St. Louis	80	14	34	48	3	24	6	0	4	181	7.7
*Zach Werenski	Columbus	78	11	36	47	17	14	4	0	1	188	5.9
Nick Leddy	NY Islanders	81	11	35	46	–3	12	3	0	1	137	8.0
Rasmus Ristolainen	Buffalo	79	6	39	45	–9	58	1	0	2	186	3.2
Drew Doughty	Los Angeles	82	12	32	44	8	46	5	0	1	181	6.6
Jake Gardiner	Toronto	82	9	34	43	24	34	2	0	2	127	7.1
Shea Weber	Montreal	78	17	25	42	20	38	12	0	4	183	9.3
Seth Jones	Columbus	75	12	30	42	6	24	1	0	3	152	7.9
Ryan McDonagh	NY Rangers	77	6	36	42	20	37	1	1	1	153	3.9
Keith Yandle	Florida	82	5	36	41	–6	39	2	0	0	178	2.8
P.K. Subban	Nashville	66	10	30	40	–8	44	3	0	2	142	7.0
Ryan Suter	Minnesota	82	9	31	40	34	36	4	1	1	164	5.5

CONSECUTIVE SCORING STREAKS

Goals

Games	Player	Team	G
6	Jeff Skinner	Carolina	8
6	James Neal	Nashville	7
5	Filip Forsberg	Nashville	10
5	Nikita Kucherov	Tampa Bay	7
5	Patrick Eaves	Dallas	6
5	Mikael Backlund	Calgary	6
5	Artemi Panarin	Chicago	6
5	*Auston Matthews	Toronto	6
5	Sidney Crosby	Pittsburgh	5
5	*Jake Guentzel	Pittsburgh	5
5	Sean Monahan	Calgary	5

Assists

Games	Player	Team	A
9	Jack Eichel	Buffalo	10
8	Ryan McDonagh	NY Rangers	9
7	Claude Giroux	Philadelphia	9
7	Johnny Gaudreau	Calgary	9
7	Andrei Markov	Montreal	8
7	Drew Doughty	Los Angeles	7
6	Leon Draisaitl	Edmonton	10
6	Nicklas Backstrom	Washington	9
6	Mats Zuccarello	NY Rangers	9
6	Evgeny Kuznetsov	Washington	8
6	Johnny Gaudreau	Calgary	8
6	Connor McDavid	Edmonton	8
6	Erik Karlsson	Ottawa	7
6	*Zach Hyman	Toronto	7
6	Mikael Granlund	Minnesota	7
6	*Brady Skjei	NY Rangers	7
6	David Pastrnak	Boston	7
6	Dustin Byfuglien	Winnipeg	6
6	Rasmus Ristolainen	Buffalo	6
6	*Pavel Zacha	New Jersey	6
6	*Matthew Tkachuk	Calgary	6

Points

Games	Player	Team	G	A	PTS
14	Connor McDavid	Edmonton	7	18	25
12	Mikael Granlund	Minnesota	5	12	17
12	*William Nylander	Toronto	4	10	14
11	Leon Draisaitl	Edmonton	5	14	19
11	Artem Anisimov	Chicago	8	9	17
11	Jack Eichel	Buffalo	5	11	16
11	David Pastrnak	Boston	6	9	15
10	Nicklas Backstrom	Washington	4	13	17
10	James Van Riemsdyk	Toronto	3	11	14
10	Claude Giroux	Philadelphia	2	11	13
10	Radim Vrbata	Arizona	4	8	12
10	Sean Monahan	Calgary	5	7	12
10	Elias Lindholm	Carolina	4	7	11
9	Artemi Panarin	Chicago	5	10	15
9	Sidney Crosby	Pittsburgh	7	7	14
9	Cam Atkinson	Columbus	7	7	14
9	Patrick Marleau	San Jose	8	5	13
9	Eric Staal	Minnesota	5	7	12
9	*Auston Matthews	Toronto	8	4	12
9	*Matthew Tkachuk	Calgary	1	9	10

*— rookie eligible for Calder Trophy

Connor McDavid (right) celebrates his 100th point with teammate Leon Draisaitl during Edmonton's 5-2 win over Vancouver on the final day of the 2016-17 season.

Individual Rookie Scoring Leaders

Player	Team	GP	G	A	Pts	+/–	PIM	PP	SH	GW	S	S%
Auston Matthews	Toronto	82	40	29	69	2	14	8	0	8	279	14.3
Patrik Laine	Winnipeg	73	36	28	64	7	26	9	0	5	204	17.6
William Nylander	Toronto	81	22	39	61	–3	32	9	0	2	205	10.7
Mitch Marner	Toronto	77	19	42	61	0	38	4	0	5	176	10.8
Sebastian Aho	Carolina	82	24	25	49	–1	26	6	1	4	214	11.2
Matthew Tkachuk	Calgary	76	13	35	48	14	105	3	0	2	142	9.2
Zach Werenski	Columbus	78	11	36	47	17	14	4	0	1	188	5.9
Brayden Point	Tampa Bay	68	18	22	40	4	14	5	0	2	122	14.8
Brady Skjei	NY Rangers	80	5	34	39	11	42	0	0	0	127	3.9
Mikko Rantanen	Colorado	75	20	18	38	–25	22	4	0	2	133	15.0
Connor Brown	Toronto	82	20	16	36	3	10	2	1	4	139	14.4
Anthony Mantha	Detroit	60	17	19	36	10	53	1	0	3	133	12.8
Nikita Zaitsev	Toronto	82	4	32	36	–22	38	1	0	0	106	3.8
Jake Guentzel	Pittsburgh	40	16	17	33	7	10	1	0	0	81	19.8
Christian Dvorak	Arizona	78	15	18	33	7	22	2	0	1	88	17.0
Devin Shore	Dallas	82	13	20	33	–4	14	1	0	0	115	11.3
Ryan Hartman	Chicago	76	19	12	31	13	70	1	0	4	170	11.2
Ivan Provorov	Philadelphia	82	6	24	30	–7	34	0	0	1	161	3.7
Artturi Lehkonen	Montreal	73	18	10	28	–1	8	2	1	3	158	11.4
Travis Konecny	Philadelphia	70	11	17	28	–2	49	3	0	0	133	8.3
Zach Hyman	Toronto	82	10	18	28	2	30	0	4	3	156	6.4
Nick Schmaltz	Chicago	61	6	22	28	10	6	0	0	0	66	9.1
Jimmy Vesey	NY Rangers	80	16	11	27	–13	26	5	0	6	116	13.8
Scott Wilson	Pittsburgh	78	8	18	26	0	32	0	0	1	127	6.3

Goal Scoring

Player	Team	GP	G
Auston Matthews	Toronto	82	40
Patrik Laine	Winnipeg	73	36
Sebastian Aho	Carolina	82	24
William Nylander	Toronto	81	22
Mikko Rantanen	Colorado	75	20
Connor Brown	Toronto	82	20
Ryan Hartman	Chicago	76	19
Mitch Marner	Toronto	77	19
Brayden Point	Tampa Bay	68	18
Artturi Lehkonen	Montreal	73	18

Assists

Player	Team	GP	A
Mitch Marner	Toronto	77	42
William Nylander	Toronto	81	39
Zach Werenski	Columbus	78	36
Matthew Tkachuk	Calgary	76	35
Brady Skjei	NY Rangers	80	34
Nikita Zaitsev	Toronto	82	32
Auston Matthews	Toronto	82	29
Patrik Laine	Winnipeg	73	28
Sebastian Aho	Carolina	82	25
Ivan Provorov	Philadelphia	82	24

Power-play Goals

Player	Team	GP	PP
Patrik Laine	Winnipeg	73	9
William Nylander	Toronto	81	9
Auston Matthews	Toronto	82	8
Sebastian Aho	Carolina	82	6
Brayden Point	Tampa Bay	68	5
Pavel Zacha	New Jersey	70	5
Jimmy Vesey	NY Rangers	80	5
Mikko Rantanen	Colorado	75	4
Mitch Marner	Toronto	77	4
Zach Werenski	Columbus	78	4

Shorthand Goals

Player	Team	GP	SH
Zach Hyman	Toronto	82	4
Josh Archibald	Pittsburgh	10	1
Gemel Smith	Dallas	17	1
Yanni Gourde	Tampa Bay	20	1
Laurent Dauphin	Arizona	24	1
Lukas Sedlak	Columbus	62	1
Lawson Crouse	Arizona	72	1
Artturi Lehkonen	Montreal	73	1
Connor Brown	Toronto	82	1
Sebastian Aho	Carolina	82	1
Brandon Carlo	Boston	82	1

Game-winning Goals

Player	Team	GP	GW
Auston Matthews	Toronto	82	8
Jimmy Vesey	NY Rangers	80	6
Patrik Laine	Winnipeg	73	5
Mitch Marner	Toronto	77	5
Ryan Hartman	Chicago	76	4
Connor Brown	Toronto	82	4
Sebastian Aho	Carolina	82	4

Shots

Player	Team	GP	S
Auston Matthews	Toronto	82	279
Sebastian Aho	Carolina	82	214
William Nylander	Toronto	81	205
Patrik Laine	Winnipeg	73	204
Zach Werenski	Columbus	78	188

Shooting Percentage
(minimum 82 shots)

Player	Team	GP	G	S	S%
Patrik Laine	Winnipeg	73	36	204	17.6
Christian Dvorak	Arizona	78	15	88	17.0
Brendan Perlini	Arizona	57	14	92	15.2
Mikko Rantanen	Colorado	75	20	133	15.0
Brayden Point	Tampa Bay	68	18	122	14.8

Plus/Minus

Player	Team	GP	+/–
Zach Werenski	Columbus	78	17
Tanner Kero	Chicago	47	15
Matthew Tkachuk	Calgary	76	14
Ryan Hartman	Chicago	76	13
Brandon Montour	Anaheim	27	11
Brady Skjei	NY Rangers	80	11

Three-or-More-Goal Games

Player	Team	Date		Final Score				G
*Sebastian Aho	Carolina	Jan	31	Phi	1	Car	5	3
Viktor Arvidsson	Nashville	Feb	11	Fla	7	Nsh	4	3
Patrik Berglund	St. Louis	Feb	11	St.L.	4	Mtl	2	3
Mikkel Boedker	San Jose	Jan	10	S.J.	5	Edm	3	3
Nick Bonino	Pittsburgh	Mar	08	Pit	7	Wpg	4	3
Michael Cammalleri	New Jersey	Nov	06	N.J.	4	Car	1	3
Joe Colborne	Colorado	Oct	15	Dal	5	Col	6	3
Adam Cracknell	Dallas	Mar	24	S.J.	1	Dal	6	3
Sidney Crosby	Pittsburgh	Mar	19	Fla	0	Pit	4	3
Jordan Eberle	Edmonton	Apr	09	Van	2	Edm	5	3
Robby Fabbri	St. Louis	Dec	28	Phi	3	St.L.	6	3
Filip Forsberg	Nashville	Feb	21	Cgy	2	Nsh	4	3
Filip Forsberg	Nashville	Feb	23	Col	2	Nsh	4	3
Michael Grabner	NY Rangers	Oct	30	T.B.	1	NYR	6	3
Michael Grabner	NY Rangers	Jan	07	NYR	5	CBJ	4	3
Mikael Granlund	Minnesota	Feb	04	Min	6	Van	3	3
Mike Green	Detroit	Oct	17	Ott	1	Det	5	3
*Ryan Hartman	Chicago	Jan	08	Nsh	2	Chi	5	3
Scott Hartnell	Columbus	Dec	22	Pit	1	CBJ	7	3
Mike Hoffman	Ottawa	Nov	29	Buf	5	Ott	4	3
Patrick Kane	Chicago	Feb	23	Ari	3	Chi	6	3

Player	Team	Date		Final Score				G
Patrick Kane	Chicago	Mar	01	Pit	1	Chi	4	3
Ryan Kesler	Anaheim	Jan	01	Phi	3	Ana	4	3
Chris Kreider	NY Rangers	Dec	31	NYR	6	Col	2	3
Nikita Kucherov	Tampa Bay	Feb	27	Ott	1	T.B.	5	3
Nikita Kucherov	Tampa Bay	Mar	23	T.B.	6	Bos	3	3
*Patrik Laine	Winnipeg	Oct	19	Tor	4	Wpg	5	3
*Patrik Laine	Winnipeg	Nov	08	Dal	2	Wpg	8	3
*Patrik Laine	Winnipeg	Feb	14	Dal	2	Wpg	5	3
Milan Lucic	Edmonton	Apr	06	Edm	4	S.J.	2	3
Evgeni Malkin	Pittsburgh	Jan	16	Wsh	7	Pit	8	3
Brad Marchand	Boston	Mar	13	Bos	6	Van	3	3
Jonathan Marchessault	Florida	Mar	25	Chi	0	Fla	7	3
Patrick Marleau	San Jose	Jan	23	S.J.	5	Col	2	4
Patrick Maroon	Edmonton	Jan	05	Edm	4	Bos	3	3
*Auston Matthews	Toronto	Oct	12	Tor	4	Ott	5	4
Connor McDavid	Edmonton	Nov	19	Edm	5	Dal	2	3
*William Nylander	Toronto	Feb	04	Tor	6	Bos	3	3
T.J. Oshie	Washington	Mar	18	Wsh	5	T.B.	3	3
Alex Ovechkin	Washington	Nov	23	St.L.	3	Wsh	4	3
Alex Ovechkin	Washington	Mar	28	Wsh	5	Min	4	3
Max Pacioretty	Montreal	Dec	10	Col	1	Mtl	10	4

Player	Team	Date		Final Score				G
Max Pacioretty	Montreal	Jan	31	Buf	2	Mtl	5	3
Richard Panik	Chicago	Oct	15	Nsh	3	Chi	5	3
David Perron	St. Louis	Oct	22	St.L.	6	Cgy	4	3
Matt Puempel	NY Rangers	Dec	29	NYR	6	Ari	3	3
*Mikko Rantanen	Colorado	Feb	07	Mtl	0	Col	4	3
Antoine Roussel	Dallas	Feb	18	T.B	3	Dal	4	3
Bryan Rust	Pittsburgh	Dec	05	Ott	5	Pit	8	3
Colton Sceviour	Florida	Oct	30	Fla	5	Det	2	3
Brayden Schenn	Philadelphia	Dec	10	Dal	2	Phi	4	3
Colton Sissons	Nashville	Jan	05	Nsh	6	T.B.	1	3
Jaccob Slavin	Carolina	Mar	13	Car	8	NYI	4	3
Vladimir Tarasenko	St. Louis	Dec	01	T.B	4	St.L.	5	3
Tomas Tatar	Detroit	Dec	17	Ana	4	Det	6	3
John Tavares	NY Islanders	Jan	13	NYI	5	Fla	2	3
Jonathan Toews	Chicago	Feb	21	Chi	5	Min	3	3
James Van Riemsdyk	Toronto	Nov	15	Nsh	2	Tor	6	3
Travis Zajac	New Jersey	Dec	01	N.J.	3	Chi	4	3

* — rookie eligible for Calder Trophy

2016-17 Penalty Shots

(For shootout statistics, see page 145.)

Scored

Connor McDavid (Edm.) scored against Brian Elliott (Cgy.), Oct. 3. Final score: Cgy. 4 at Edm. 7

Jakub Voracek (Phi.) scored against Marc-Andre Fleury (Pit.), Oct. 29. Final score: Pit. 5 at Phi. 4

Brad Marchand (Bos.) scored against Roberto Luongo (Fla.), Nov. 1. Final score: Bos. 2 at Fla. 1

Andy Greene (N.J.) scored against Anders Nilsson (Buf.), Nov. 11. Final score: N.J. 2 at Buf. 1

Ben Hutton (Van.) scored against Louis Domingue (Ari.), Nov. 17. Final score: Ari. 2 at Van. 3

Bryan Rust (Pit.) scored against Craig Anderson (Ott.), Dec. 5. Final score: Ott. 5 at Pit. 8

Radim Vrbata (Ari.) scored against Kari Lehtonen (Dal.), Dec. 27. Final score: Dal. 3 at Ari. 2

Nikolaj Ehlers (Wpg.) scored against Andrei Vasilevskiy (T.B.), Jan. 3. Final score: Wpg. 6 at T.B. 4

Brandon Sutter (Van.) scored against Mike Smith (Ari.), Jan. 4. Final score: Ari. 0 at Van. 3

Melker Karlsson (S.J.) scored against Ondrej Pavelec (Wpg.), Jan. 24. Final score: S.J. 4 at Wpg. 3

Jason Chimera (NYI) scored against Frederik Andersen (Tor.), Feb. 14. Final score: NYI 1 at Tor. 7

Jeff Skinner (Car.) scored against Thomas Greiss (NYI) Mar. 13. Final score: Car. 8 at NYI 4

Brandon Dubinsky (CBJ) scored against Cory Schneider (N.J.), Mar. 19. Final score: CBJ 4 at N.J. 1

Lukas Sedlak (CBJ) scored against Cory Schneider (N.J.) Mar. 19. Final score: CBJ 4 at N.J. 1

Stopped

Cory Schneider (N.J.) stopped Chris Wagner (Ana.), Oct. 18. Final score: Ana 1 at N.J. 2

Kari Lehtonen (Dal.) stopped Cam Atkinson (CBJ), Oct 22. Final score: CBJ 3 at Dal. 0

Anders Nilsson (Buf.) stopped Vincent Trocheck (Fla.), Oct 29. Final score: Fla. 0 at Buf. 3

John Gibson (Ana.) stopped Scott Wilson (Pit.), Nov. 2. Final score: Pit. 5 at Ana 1

Ben Bishop (T.B.) stopped Joonas Donskoi (S.J.), Nov. 12. Final score: S.J. 3 at T.B. 1

Thomas Greiss (NYI) stopped Joe Thornton (S.J.), Nov. 25. Final score: NYI 2 at S.J. 3

Connor Hellebuyck (Wpg.) stopped Miles Wood (N.J.), Nov. 29. Final score: N.J. 2 at Wpg. 3

Tuukka Rask (Bos.) stopped Jakub Voracek (Phi.), Nov. 29. Final score: Bos. 2 at Phi. 3

Pekka Rinne (Nsh.) stopped Shane Doan (Ari.), Dec. 10. Final score: Nsh. 1 at Ari. 4

Frederik Andersen (Tor.) stopped Carl Hagelin (Pit.), Dec. 17. Final score: Pit. 1 at Tor. 2

Semyon Varlamov (Col.) stopped Eric Staal (Min.), Dec. 20. Final score: Col. 0 at Min. 2

Mike Condon (Ott.) stopped Marcus Kruger (Chi.), Dec. 20. Final score: Ott. 4 at Chi. 3

Frederik Andersen (Tor.) stopped Denis Malgin (Fla.), Dec. 28. Final score: Tor. 3 at Fla. 2

Jared Coreau (Det.) stopped Tanner Pearson (L.A.), Jan. 5. Final score: Det. 4 at L.A. 0

Thomas Greiss (NYI) stopped Matt Nieto (Col.), Jan. 6. Final score: NYI 1 at Col. 2

Chad Johnson (Cgy.) stopped Mikkel Boedker (S.J.), Jan. 11. Final score: S.J. 2 at Cgy. 3

Connor Hellebuyck (Wpg.) stopped Mikael Granlund (Min.), Feb. 7. Final score: Min. 4 at Wpg. 2

Kari Lehtonen (Dal.) stopped Craig Smith (Nsh.), Feb. 12. Final score: Dal. 3 at Nsh. 5

Roberto Luongo (Fla.) stopped Joe Pavelski (S.J.), Feb. 15. Final score: Fla. 6 at S.J. 5

Cory Schneider (N.J.) stopped John Tavares (NYI), Feb. 18. Final score: NYI 2 at N.J. 3

Henrik Lundqvist (NYR) stopped Brandon Saad (CBJ), Feb. 26. Final score: CBJ 5 at NYR 2

Steve Mason (Phi.) stopped Mikko Rantanen (Col.), Feb. 28. Final score: Col. 0 at Phi. 4

Ryan Miller (Van.) stopped Chris Tierney (S.J.), Mar. 2. Final score: Van. 1 at S.J. 3

John Gibson (Ana.) stopped Ryan Reaves (St.L.), Mar. 10. Final score: Ana 3 at STL 4

Mike Smith (Ari.) stopped Taylor Hall (N.J.), Mar. 11. Final score: N.J. 4 at Ari. 5

Jimmy Howard (Det.) stopped Gabriel Landeskog (Col.), Mar. 15. Final score: Det. 1 at Col. 3

Keith Kinkaid (N.J.) stopped Phil Kessel (Pit.), Mar. 17. Final score: N.J. 4 at Pit. 6

Robin Lehner (Buf.) stopped Reilly Smith (Fla.), Mar. 27. Final score: Fla. 2 at Buf. 4

Ryan Miller (Van.) stopped Max Domi (Ari.), Apr. 6. Final score: Van. 3 at Ari. 4

Cam Talbot (Edm.) stopped Marcus Sorensen (S.J.), Apr. 6. Final score: Edm. 4 at S.J. 2

Total Shots: 44
Total Goals: 14
Total Saves: 30

Brandon Sutter of Vancouver prepares to backhand the puck past Arizona's Mike Smith on a penalty shot on January 4, 2017. The Canucks beat the Coyotes 3-0.

Goaltending Leaders

Minimum 25 games

Goals Against Average

Goaltender	Team	GP	MINS	GA	Avg
Sergei Bobrovsky	Columbus	63	3707	127	**2.06**
Braden Holtby	Washington	63	3680	127	**2.07**
Jimmy Howard	Detroit	26	1397	49	**2.10**
Peter Budaj	L.A.-T.B.	60	3308	120	**2.18**
John Gibson	Anaheim	52	2950	109	**2.22**

Save Percentage

Goaltender	Team	GP	MINS	GA	SA	Sv%	W	L	OT
Sergei Bobrovsky	Columbus	63	3707	127	1854	**.931**	41	17	5
Jimmy Howard	Detroit	26	1397	49	675	**.927**	10	11	1
Craig Anderson	Ottawa	40	2421	92	1247	**.926**	25	11	4
Braden Holtby	Washington	63	3680	127	1690	**.925**	42	13	6
John Gibson	Anaheim	52	2950	109	1437	**.924**	25	16	9
Scott Darling	Chicago	32	1689	67	877	**.924**	18	5	5

Wins

Goaltender	Team	GP	W	L	OT
Braden Holtby	Washington	63	**42**	13	6
Cam Talbot	Edmonton	73	**42**	22	8
Sergei Bobrovsky	Columbus	63	**41**	17	5
Devan Dubnyk	Minnesota	65	**40**	19	5
Tuukka Rask	Boston	65	**37**	20	5
Carey Price	Montreal	62	**37**	20	5

Shutouts

Goaltender	Team	GP	MINS	SO	W	L	OT
Braden Holtby	Washington	63	3680	**9**	42	13	6
Tuukka Rask	Boston	65	3680	**8**	37	20	5
Peter Budaj	L.A.-T.B	60	3308	**7**	30	21	3
Sergei Bobrovsky	Columbus	63	3707	**7**	41	17	5
Cam Talbot	Edmonton	73	4294	**7**	42	22	8

* — rookie eligible for Calder Trophy

Team-by-Team Point Totals

2012-13 to 2016-17
(Ranked by five-year point %)

Team	16-17	15-16	14-15	13-14	12-13	Pts%
Anaheim	105	103	109	116	66	.664
Chicago	109	103	102	107	77	.662
Pittsburgh	111	104	98	109	72	.657
Washington	118	120	101	90	57	.646
St. Louis	99	107	109	111	60	.646
NY Rangers	102	101	113	96	56	.622
Boston	95	93	96	117	62	.616
Montreal	103	82	110	100	63	.609
San Jose	99	98	89	111	57	.604
Minnesota	106	87	100	98	55	.593
Los Angeles	86	102	95	100	59	.588
Tampa Bay	94	97	108	101	40	.585
NY Islanders	94	100	101	79	55	.570
Ottawa	98	85	99	88	56	.566
Nashville	94	96	104	88	41	.562
Columbus	108	76	89	93	55	.560
Detroit	79	93	100	93	56	.560
Dallas	79	109	92	91	48	.557
Philadelphia	88	96	84	94	49	.547
Winnipeg	87	78	99	84	51	.531
Calgary	94	77	97	77	42	.515
Vancouver	69	75	101	83	59	.515
Florida	81	103	91	66	36	.501
Toronto	95	69	68	84	57	.496
Colorado	48	82	90	112	39	.493
Carolina	87	86	71	83	42	.491
New Jersey	70	84	78	88	48	.498
Edmonton	103	70	62	67	45	.461
Arizona	70	78	56	89	51	.457
Buffalo	78	81	54	52	48	.416

Team Record When Scoring First Goal of a Game

Team	FG	W	L	OT	Win%
Washington	58	46	7	5	.793
Ottawa	38	29	6	3	.763
Edmonton	41	31	7	3	.756
Montreal	44	33	6	5	.750
San Jose	47	35	11	1	.745
Chicago	50	37	8	5	.740
Anaheim	45	33	7	5	.733
Minnesota	48	35	8	5	.729
Calgary	38	27	10	1	.711
Columbus	50	35	10	5	.700
Boston	46	32	9	5	.696
St. Louis	45	31	10	4	.689
Los Angeles	31	21	5	5	.677
Dallas	37	25	9	3	.676
Nashville	37	25	4	8	.676
NY Rangers	45	30	13	2	.667
Tampa Bay	33	22	9	2	.667
Toronto	45	29	7	9	.644
Pittsburgh	47	30	10	7	.638
Winnipeg	40	25	13	2	.625
NY Islanders	44	27	9	8	.614
Florida	42	25	11	6	.595
Philadelphia	34	20	10	4	.588
Vancouver	29	17	9	3	.586
Carolina	34	18	9	7	.529
Arizona	40	21	14	5	.525
Buffalo	41	21	12	8	.512
Detroit	36	18	9	9	.500
Colorado	24	12	12	0	.500
New Jersey	41	19	13	9	.463

Team Plus/Minus Differential

Team	GF	PPGF	Net GF	GA	PPGA	Net GA	Goal Differential
Washington	263	57	206	182	44	138	+68
Columbus	249	42	207	195	39	156	+51
Minnesota	266	47	219	208	37	171	+48
Pittsburgh	282	60	222	234	52	182	+40
Chicago	244	42	202	213	47	166	+36
NY Rangers	256	47	209	220	45	175	+34
Montreal	226	45	181	200	47	153	+28
Edmonton	247	56	191	212	43	169	+22
San Jose	221	41	180	201	41	160	+20
Anaheim	223	47	176	200	43	157	+19
Nashville	240	49	191	224	46	178	+13
Winnipeg	249	48	201	256	62	194	+7
St. Louis	235	50	185	218	40	178	+7
Boston	234	53	181	212	38	174	+7
NY Islanders	241	35	206	242	41	201	+5
Ottawa	212	43	169	214	50	164	+5
Calgary	226	52	174	221	51	170	+4
Toronto	251	58	193	242	44	198	−5
Tampa Bay	234	62	172	227	48	179	−7
Los Angeles	201	46	155	205	38	167	−12
Dallas	223	46	177	262	65	197	−20
Philadelphia	219	54	165	236	50	186	−21
Carolina	215	41	174	236	32	204	−30
Detroit	207	38	169	244	45	199	−30
Florida	210	45	165	237	36	201	−36
Buffalo	201	57	144	237	53	184	−40
Vancouver	182	32	150	243	52	191	−41
Arizona	197	38	159	260	59	201	−42
New Jersey	183	44	139	244	53	191	−52
Colorado	166	30	136	278	64	214	−78

Team Record When Leading, Trailing, Tied

Team	Leading after 1 period W	L	OT	Leading after 2 periods W	L	OT	Trailing after 1 period W	L	OT	Trailing after 2 periods W	L	OT	Tied after 1 period W	L	OT	Tied after 2 periods W	L	OT
Anaheim	23	6	3	33	2	2	4	9	6	2	19	7	19	8	4	11	2	4
Arizona	16	6	0	19	0	4	5	22	5	6	33	2	9	14	5	5	9	4
Boston	23	4	4	34	0	2	4	11	2	3	23	3	17	16	1	7	8	2
Buffalo	15	8	5	20	2	5	8	18	2	7	31	3	10	11	5	6	4	4
Calgary	23	4	1	33	0	1	12	20	2	4	27	2	10	9	1	8	6	1
Carolina	16	5	6	20	2	6	7	15	3	6	22	1	13	11	6	10	7	8
Chicago	26	4	3	30	2	3	7	11	3	7	17	3	17	8	3	13	4	3
Colorado	7	7	0	11	8	0	6	33	4	3	41	3	9	16	0	8	7	1
Columbus	28	8	1	33	1	3	5	12	2	4	18	3	17	4	5	13	5	2
Dallas	15	4	2	22	2	4	7	22	3	3	27	2	12	11	6	9	8	5
Detroit	13	6	3	20	3	4	8	21	4	3	30	1	12	9	6	10	3	8
Edmonton	18	4	2	29	2	1	9	15	2	7	17	3	20	7	5	11	7	5
Florida	17	8	3	24	1	4	7	21	5	1	25	5	11	7	3	10	10	2
Los Angeles	13	1	3	19	1	2	11	21	2	5	31	1	15	13	3	15	3	5
Minnesota	27	4	2	33	3	3	7	11	3	3	15	3	15	10	3	13	7	2
Montreal	21	2	2	26	1	3	7	17	3	11	20	4	19	7	3	10	5	2
Nashville	15	2	5	29	2	6	11	17	3	7	21	0	15	10	4	5	6	6
New Jersey	11	6	8	19	0	8	5	19	4	6	33	3	12	15	2	3	6	3
NY Islanders	21	4	4	30	0	5	4	17	2	4	22	3	16	8	6	7	7	4
NY Rangers	20	5	2	27	4	0	9	10	1	5	19	3	19	13	3	16	5	3
Ottawa	18	5	1	29	2	2	6	14	2	3	16	4	20	9	7	10	6	5
Philadelphia	12	1	2	19	2	2	8	16	3	5	22	2	19	16	5	15	9	6
Pittsburgh	21	4	2	37	1	1	13	10	1	8	16	4	16	7	8	5	4	6
San Jose	26	3	1	33	3	2	5	12	3	1	22	1	15	14	3	12	4	4
St. Louis	20	4	2	29	2	2	9	14	2	4	21	1	17	11	3	13	6	4
Tampa Bay	19	4	0	27	3	1	11	14	2	6	24	2	12	12	8	9	3	7
Toronto	25	1	9	31	1	9	3	17	3	3	22	3	12	9	3	6	4	4
Vancouver	12	5	1	17	2	2	7	22	5	5	34	6	11	16	4	8	7	1
Washington	34	4	4	41	1	1	6	7	1	3	14	5	11	3	1	11	4	2
Winnipeg	17	7	2	23	2	2	9	19	3	8	28	2	14	9	2	9	5	3

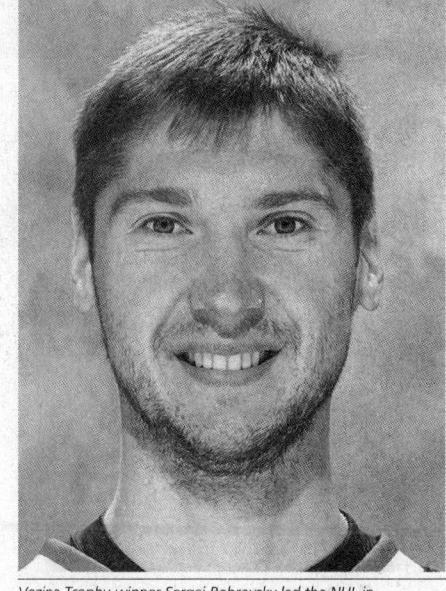

Vezina Trophy-winner Sergei Bobrovsky led the NHL in goals-against average and save percentage in 2016-17. He also ranked among the leaders with a career-best 41 wins and seven shutouts.

Team Statistics

TEAMS' HOME AND ROAD RECORD

Eastern Conference

Team			Home							Road				
	GP	W	L	OT	GF	GA	PTS	GP	W	L	OT	GF	GA	PTS
BOS	41	23	17	1	118	100	47	41	21	14	6	116	112	48
BUF	41	20	15	6	107	111	46	41	13	22	6	94	126	32
CAR	41	23	12	6	110	107	52	41	13	19	9	105	129	35
CBJ	41	28	12	1	130	87	57	41	22	12	7	119	108	51
DET	41	17	17	7	105	110	41	41	16	19	6	102	134	38
FLA	41	19	19	3	111	120	41	41	16	17	8	99	117	40
MTL	41	24	12	5	122	88	53	41	23	14	4	104	112	50
N.J.	41	16	17	8	94	121	40	41	12	23	6	89	123	30
NYI	41	22	12	7	128	119	51	41	19	17	5	113	123	43
NYR	41	21	16	4	129	123	46	41	27	12	2	127	97	56
OTT	41	22	11	8	102	97	52	41	22	17	2	110	117	46
PHI	41	25	11	5	123	105	55	41	14	22	5	96	131	33
PIT	41	31	6	4	158	110	66	41	19	15	7	124	124	45
T.B.	41	23	14	4	128	118	50	41	19	16	6	106	109	44
TOR	41	21	13	7	124	116	49	41	19	14	8	127	126	46
WSH	41	32	7	2	134	68	66	41	23	12	6	129	114	52
TOTAL	656	367	211	78	1923	1700	812	656	298	265	93	1760	1902	689

Western Conference

Team	GP	W	L	OT	GF	GA	PTS	GP	W	L	OT	GF	GA	PTS
ANA	41	18	18	5	104	117	41	41	17	15	9	101	116	43
ARI	41	22	15	4	122	113	48	41	12	24	5	93	143	29
CGY	41	24	17	0	131	112	48	41	21	16	4	95	109	46
CHI	41	26	10	5	130	97	57	41	24	13	4	114	116	52
COL	41	13	26	2	96	136	28	41	9	30	2	70	142	20
DAL	41	22	13	6	130	118	50	41	12	24	5	93	144	29
EDM	41	25	12	4	120	100	54	41	22	14	5	127	112	49
L.A.	41	23	16	2	115	106	48	41	16	19	6	86	99	38
MIN	41	27	12	2	139	93	56	41	22	13	6	127	115	50
NSH	41	24	9	8	131	103	56	41	17	20	4	109	121	38
ST.L.	41	24	12	5	124	113	53	41	22	17	2	111	105	46
S.J.	41	26	11	4	111	90	56	41	20	18	3	110	111	43
VAN	41	18	17	6	89	115	42	41	12	26	3	93	128	27
WPG	41	22	18	1	131	123	45	41	18	17	6	118	133	42
TOTAL	574	321	199	54	1673	1507	696	574	244	266	64	1447	1694	552
	1230	688	410	132	3596	3207	1508	1230	542	531	157	3207	3596	1241

TEAMS' DIVISIONAL RECORD

Atlantic Division

Team	Total	vs. EAST vs. Atl.	vs. Met	Total	vs. WEST vs. Cen	vs. Pac	Total Pts.
MTL	32-15-7	19-5-6	13-10-1	15-11-2	6-7-1	9-4-1	103
OTT	29-18-7	14-12-4	15-6-3	15-10-3	6-7-1	9-3-2	98
BOS	27-20-7	18-10-2	9-10-5	17-11-0	8-6-0	9-5-0	95
TOR	30-17-7	18-9-3	12-8-4	10-10-8	5-5-4	5-5-4	95
T.B.	30-18-6	19-7-4	11-11-2	12-12-4	7-5-2	5-7-2	94
FLA	22-25-7	11-14-5	11-11-2	13-11-4	7-5-2	6-6-2	81
DET	19-24-11	8-15-7	11-9-4	14-12-2	8-5-1	6-7-1	79
BUF	19-26-9	13-13-4	6-13-5	14-11-3	7-5-2	7-6-1	78

Metropolitan Division

Team	Total	vs. Atl.	vs. Met	Total	vs. Cen	vs. Pac	Total Pts.
WSH	36-11-7	18-4-2	18-7-5	19-8-1	11-2-1	8-6-0	118
PIT	35-14-5	15-6-3	20-8-2	15-7-6	6-7-1	9-0-5	111
CBJ	33-16-5	15-7-2	18-9-3	17-8-3	8-4-2	9-4-1	108
NYR	27-22-5	12-9-3	15-13-2	21-6-1	10-4-0	11-2-1	102
NYI	26-20-8	11-10-3	15-10-5	15-9-4	7-5-2	8-4-2	94
PHI	25-23-6	13-9-2	12-14-4	14-10-4	8-5-1	6-5-3	88
CAR	24-20-10	13-5-6	11-15-4	12-11-5	6-5-3	6-6-2	87
N.J.	18-29-7	7-13-4	11-16-3	10-11-7	5-5-4	5-6-3	70

Central Division

Team	Total	vs. Atl.	vs. Met	Total	vs. Cen	vs. Pac	Total Pts.
CHI	20-9-3	10-5-1	10-4-2	30-14-6	19-8-2	11-6-4	109
MIN	18-11-3	13-2-1	5-9-2	31-14-5	17-9-3	14-5-2	106
ST.L.	19-12-1	10-5-1	9-7-0	27-17-6	14-12-3	13-5-3	99
NSH	14-12-6	6-8-2	8-4-4	27-17-6	16-12-1	11-5-5	94
WPG	14-14-4	8-6-2	6-8-2	26-21-3	19-8-2	7-13-1	87
DAL	12-16-4	5-10-1	7-6-3	22-21-7	9-15-5	13-6-2	79
COL	12-19-1	6-9-1	6-10-0	10-37-3	8-21-1	2-16-2	48

Pacific Division

Team	Total	vs. Atl.	vs. Met	Total	vs. Cen	vs. Pac	Total Pts.
ANA	16-10-6	9-4-3	7-6-3	30-13-7	12-7-2	18-6-5	105
EDM	14-15-3	8-6-2	6-9-1	33-11-6	13-5-3	20-6-3	103
S.J.	21-7-4	10-3-3	11-4-1	25-22-3	9-11-0	16-11-3	99
CGY	18-13-1	11-5-0	7-8-1	27-20-3	14-7-0	13-13-3	94
L.A.	15-15-2	6-9-1	9-6-1	24-20-6	12-6-3	12-14-3	86
ARI	13-15-4	6-7-3	7-8-1	17-27-6	5-15-1	12-12-5	70
VAN	9-17-6	6-8-2	3-9-4	21-26-3	10-9-2	11-17-1	69

Alexander Wennberg celebrates a goal with Seth Jones, Zach Werenski and Brandon Saad during a 5-1 win over Tampa Bay on November 29, 2016. It was the first of 16-straight wins for the Columbus Blue Jackets; one short of the all-time NHL record set by Pittsburgh in 1992-93.

TEAM STREAKS

Consecutive Wins

Games	Team	From	To
16	Columbus	Nov. 29	Jan. 3
12	Minnesota	Dec. 4	Dec. 29
10	Philadelphia	Nov. 27	Dec. 14
10	Calgary	Feb. 21	Mar. 13
9	Washington	Dec. 31	Jan. 15
8	Montreal	Oct. 18	Nov. 2
7	Chicago	Oct. 28	Nov. 9
7	Pittsburgh	Dec. 1	Dec. 14
7	Chicago	Feb. 19	Mar. 4
7	Winnipeg	Mar. 26	Apr. 8

Consecutive Home Wins

Games	Team	From	To
15	Washington	Jan. 1	Mar. 4
10	Montreal	Oct. 18	Nov. 12
9	Edmonton	Mar. 14	Apr. 9
8	Minnesota	Nov. 23	Dec. 29
8	Columbus	Nov. 29	Jan. 3
7	Columbus	Oct. 21	Nov. 18
7	Carolina	Nov. 12	Dec. 13
7	Pittsburgh	Dec. 20	Jan. 22
6	NY Rangers	Oct. 23	Nov. 6
6	Los Angeles	Nov. 3	Nov. 26
6	Nashville	Nov. 8	Nov. 25
6	St. Louis	Nov. 15	Dec. 1
6	Pittsburgh	Nov. 26	Dec. 14
6	Philadelphia	Nov. 27	Dec. 10
6	Calgary	Feb. 15	Mar. 13
6	Philadelphia	Mar. 15	Apr. 8
6	Winnipeg	Mar. 19	Apr. 8
6	Anaheim	Mar. 22	Apr. 9

Consecutive Road Wins

Games	Team	From	To
8	Columbus	Dec. 1	Dec. 31
8	Chicago	Feb. 2	Mar. 4
7	Minnesota	Dec. 4	Jan. 5
6	New Jersey	Jan. 13	Feb. 4
5	Toronto	Dec. 10	Dec. 29
5	Minnesota	Jan. 8	Jan. 31
5	St. Louis	Feb. 6	Feb. 15
5	Florida	Feb. 11	Feb. 20
5	Calgary	Feb. 21	Mar. 11
5	Montreal	Feb. 21	Mar. 7
5	NY Rangers	Feb. 23	Mar. 7
5	Tampa Bay	Mar. 4	Mar. 24

TEAM PENALTIES

Abbreviations: GP – games played; **PEN** – total penalty minutes including bench minutes; **BMI** – total bench minor minutes; **AVG** – average penalty minutes/game calculated by dividing total penalty minutes by games played

Team	GP	PEN	BMI	AVG	Team	GP	PEN	BMI	AVG
CAR	82	476	26	5.8	COL	82	767	20	9.4
CHI	82	584	18	7.1	TOR	82	799	18	9.7
NYR	82	593	14	7.2	DAL	82	810	20	9.9
S.J.	82	642	20	7.8	FLA	82	813	16	9.9
NYI	82	648	10	7.9	ARI	82	809	14	9.9
VAN	82	648	10	7.9	N.J.	82	817	14	10.0
MIN	82	669	16	8.2	BOS	82	831	14	10.1
PIT	82	703	18	8.6	NSH	82	833	14	10.2
CBJ	82	714	8	8.7	WPG	82	835	18	10.2
DET	82	718	16	8.8	OTT	82	848	24	10.3
BUF	82	741	16	9.0	PHI	82	844	18	10.3
EDM	82	738	14	9.0	T.B.	82	875	18	10.7
ST.L.	82	734	28	9.0	ANA	82	934	10	11.4
WSH	82	750	12	9.1	CGY	82	956	16	11.7
L.A.	82	754	18	9.2	**TOT**	**1230**	**22642**	**490**	**18.4**
MTL	82	759	12	9.3					

Viktor Arvidsson of the Nashville Predators led the NHL with five shorthand goals in 2016-17. Nashville led the league with 12 shorthand goals on the season.

TEAMS' POWER-PLAY RECORD

Abbreviations: ADV – total advantages; **PPGF** – power-play goals for; **%** – calculated by dividing number of power-play goals by total advantages.

Overall

	Team	GP	ADV	PPGF	%
1	BUF	82	233	57	24.5
2	TOR	82	244	58	23.8
3	PIT	82	260	60	23.1
4	WSH	82	247	57	23.1
5	EDM	82	245	56	22.9
6	T.B.	82	272	62	22.8
7	BOS	82	244	53	21.7
8	ST.L.	82	235	50	21.3
9	MIN	82	224	47	21.0
10	CGY	82	257	52	20.2
11	NYR	82	233	47	20.2
12	CBJ	82	211	42	19.9
13	MTL	82	229	45	19.7
14	PHI	82	277	54	19.5
15	L.A.	82	241	46	19.1
16	NSH	82	259	49	18.9
17	ANA	82	251	47	18.7
18	WPG	82	264	48	18.2
19	CHI	82	233	42	18.0
20	DAL	82	257	46	17.9
21	CAR	82	231	41	17.7
22	N.J.	82	251	44	17.5
23	OTT	82	253	43	17.0
24	FLA	82	265	45	17.0
25	S.J.	82	246	41	16.7
26	ARI	82	235	38	16.2
27	DET	82	252	38	15.1
28	NYI	82	234	35	15.0
29	VAN	82	227	32	14.1
30	COL	82	239	30	12.6
	TOTALS	**1230**	**7349**	**1405**	**19.1**

Home

Team	GP	ADV	PPGF	%
BUF	41	127	35	27.6
MIN	41	113	31	27.4
PIT	41	132	35	26.5
T.B.	41	149	36	24.2
L.A.	41	128	30	23.4
NSH	41	127	28	22.0
CGY	41	140	30	21.4
WSH	41	131	28	21.4
BOS	41	136	29	21.3
PHI	41	146	31	21.2
EDM	41	130	27	20.8
TOR	41	130	26	20.0
CBJ	41	111	22	19.8
ST.L.	41	124	24	19.4
N.J.	41	134	26	19.4
ANA	41	129	24	18.6
S.J.	41	126	23	18.3
MTL	41	120	22	18.3
DET	41	138	25	18.1
CHI	41	122	22	18.0
DAL	41	134	24	17.9
ARI	41	124	22	17.7
NYR	41	116	20	17.2
WPG	41	152	26	17.1
FLA	41	140	22	15.7
CAR	41	119	18	15.1
OTT	41	124	18	14.5
VAN	41	112	15	13.4
NYI	41	120	16	13.3
COL	41	131	15	11.5
1230		**3865**	**750**	**19.4**

Road

Team	GP	ADV	PPGF	%
TOR	41	114	32	28.1
EDM	41	115	29	25.2
WSH	41	116	29	25.0
ST.L.	41	111	26	23.4
NYR	41	117	27	23.1
BOS	41	108	24	22.2
MTL	41	109	23	21.1
T.B.	41	123	26	21.1
BUF	41	106	22	20.8
CAR	41	112	23	20.5
CBJ	41	100	20	20.0
WPG	41	112	22	19.6
PIT	41	128	25	19.5
OTT	41	129	25	19.4
ANA	41	122	23	18.9
CGY	41	117	22	18.8
FLA	41	125	23	18.4
CHI	41	111	20	18.0
DAL	41	123	22	17.9
PHI	41	131	23	17.6
NYI	41	114	19	16.7
NSH	41	132	21	15.9
N.J.	41	117	18	15.4
S.J.	41	120	18	15.0
VAN	41	115	17	14.8
MIN	41	111	16	14.4
ARI	41	111	16	14.4
L.A.	41	113	16	14.2
COL	41	108	15	13.9
DET	41	114	13	11.4
1230		**3484**	**655**	**18.8**

SHORTHAND GOALS FOR

Overall

	Team	GP	SHGF
1	NSH	82	12
2	CBJ	82	10
3	BOS	82	10
4	WPG	82	10
5	CAR	82	10
6	NYR	82	9
7	ANA	82	9
8	CGY	82	8
9	FLA	82	8
10	ARI	82	8
11	OTT	82	7
12	S.J.	82	7
13	TOR	82	6
14	N.J.	82	6
15	L.A.	82	6
16	MTL	82	5
17	NYI	82	5
18	PIT	82	5
19	WSH	82	5
20	MIN	82	5
21	DAL	82	5
22	COL	82	5
23	EDM	82	5
24	T.B.	82	4
25	PHI	82	4
26	ST.L.	82	3
27	BUF	82	3
28	DET	82	3
29	VAN	82	2
30	CHI	82	1
	1230		**184**

Home

Team	GP	SHGF
WPG	41	6
NSH	41	6
BOS	41	6
S.J	41	5
L.A	41	5
ANA	41	5
OTT	41	4
TOR	41	4
NYI	41	4
MTL	41	4
CGY	41	3
WSH	41	3
ARI	41	3
CAR	41	3
BUF	41	2
PIT	41	2
CBJ	41	2
T.B	41	2
FLA	41	2
DAL	41	1
COL	41	1
EDM	41	1
NYR	41	1
MIN	41	1
VAN	41	1
DET	41	1
N.J	41	1
PHI	41	1
CHI	41	0
STL	41	0
1230		**82**

Road

Team	GP	SHGF
NYR	41	8
CBJ	41	8
CAR	41	7
NSH	41	6
FLA	41	6
CGY	41	5
N.J	41	5
ARI	41	5
BOS	41	4
MIN	41	4
ANA	41	4
WPG	41	4
STL	41	3
EDM	41	3
PHI	41	3
DAL	41	3
COL	41	3
OTT	41	3
PIT	41	3
TOR	41	2
WSH	41	2
DET	41	2
S.J	41	2
T.B	41	2
MTL	41	1
NYI	41	1
CHI	41	1
BUF	41	1
VAN	41	1
L.A	41	0
1230		**102**

TEAMS' PENALTY KILLING RECORD

Abbreviations: TSH – total times shorthanded; **PPGA** – power-play goals against; **%** – calculated by dividing times short minus power-play goals against by times short.

Overall

	Team	GP	TSH	PPGA	%
1	BOS	82	265	38	85.7
2	FLA	82	245	36	85.3
3	STL	82	263	40	84.8
4	ANA	82	281	43	84.7
5	L.A.	82	246	38	84.6
6	CAR	82	202	32	84.2
7	WSH	82	272	44	83.8
8	MIN	82	217	37	82.9
9	TOR	82	251	44	82.5
10	CBJ	82	223	39	82.5
11	NYI	82	227	41	81.9
12	CGY	82	277	51	81.6
13	T.B	82	258	48	81.4
14	MTL	82	249	47	81.1
15	DET	82	235	45	80.9
16	NSH	82	241	46	80.9
17	EDM	82	223	43	80.7
18	S.J	82	212	41	80.7
19	NYR	82	223	45	79.8
20	PIT	82	257	52	79.8
21	PHI	82	247	50	79.8
22	OTT	82	246	50	79.7
23	N.J.	82	260	53	79.6
24	CHI	82	211	47	77.7
25	BUF	82	237	53	77.6
26	WPG	82	275	62	77.5
27	ARI	82	260	59	77.3
28	VAN	82	223	52	76.7
29	COL	82	274	64	76.6
30	DAL	82	249	65	73.9
	TOTALS	**1230**	**7349**	**1405**	**80.9**

Home

Team	GP	TSH	PPGA	%
BOS	41	125	15	88.0
WSH	41	129	15	86.8
OTT	41	117	17	85.5
MTL	41	124	18	85.5
STL	41	134	20	85.1
ANA	41	133	20	85.0
MIN	41	99	15	84.8
FLA	41	118	18	84.7
CAR	41	95	15	84.2
CBJ	41	102	17	83.3
PIT	41	119	20	83.2
EDM	41	102	17	82.4
T.B	41	125	22	82.4
PHI	41	107	19	82.2
DET	41	112	21	81.3
CGY	41	137	26	81.0
L.A	41	109	21	80.7
NYI	41	114	22	80.7
COL	41	131	26	80.2
BUF	41	110	22	80.0
S.J	41	99	20	79.8
TOR	41	127	27	78.7
NSH	41	121	26	78.5
ARI	41	125	28	77.6
NYR	41	104	24	76.9
CHI	41	100	24	76.0
DAL	41	116	28	75.9
WPG	41	133	33	75.2
VAN	41	99	25	74.7
N.J	41	118	31	73.7
1230		**3484**	**655**	**81.2**

Road

Team	GP	TSH	PPGA	%
L.A	41	137	17	87.6
TOR	41	124	17	86.3
FLA	41	127	18	85.8
STL	41	129	20	84.5
N.J	41	142	22	84.5
ANA	41	148	23	84.5
CAR	41	107	17	84.1
BOS	41	140	23	83.6
NSH	41	120	20	83.3
NYI	41	113	19	83.2
NYR	41	119	21	82.4
CGY	41	140	25	82.1
CBJ	41	121	22	81.8
MIN	41	118	22	81.4
S.J	41	113	21	81.4
WSH	41	143	27	81.1
DET	41	123	24	80.5
T.B	41	133	26	80.5
WPG	41	142	29	79.6
CHI	41	111	23	79.3
EDM	41	121	25	79.3
VAN	41	124	27	78.2
PHI	41	140	31	77.9
ARI	41	135	31	77.0
MTL	41	125	29	76.8
PIT	41	138	32	76.8
BUF	41	127	31	75.6
OTT	41	129	33	74.4
COL	41	143	38	73.4
DAL	41	133	37	72.2
1230		**3865**	**750**	**80.6**

SHORTHAND GOALS AGAINST

Overall

	Team	GP	SHGA
1	CBJ	82	2
2	COL	82	2
3	OTT	82	3
4	L.A.	82	3
5	WSH	82	3
6	MIN	82	3
7	BUF	82	4
8	ST.L.	82	5
9	EDM	82	5
10	CGY	82	5
11	NYR	82	5
12	S.J.	82	6
13	MTL	82	6
14	BOS	82	6
15	CAR	82	6
16	NSH	82	6
17	VAN	82	6
18	TOR	82	7
19	CHI	82	7
20	NYI	82	7
21	PIT	82	7
22	ANA	82	7
23	ARI	82	7
24	T.B.	82	8
25	FLA	82	8
26	DET	82	9
27	WPG	82	9
28	PHI	82	9
29	DAL	82	11
30	N.J.	82	12
	1230		**184**

Home

Team	GP	SHGA
NYR	41	0
OTT	41	1
CBJ	41	1
MIN	41	1
COL	41	1
BUF	41	1
NSH	41	2
WSH	41	2
VAN	41	2
CHI	41	3
EDM	41	3
S.J	41	3
STL	41	3
CGY	41	3
L.A	41	3
ARI	41	3
ANA	41	3
PIT	41	4
FLA	41	4
DAL	41	4
NYI	41	4
MTL	41	4
T.B	41	5
TOR	41	5
BOS	41	5
PHI	41	5
CAR	41	5
WPG	41	7
DET	41	7
N.J	41	7
1230		**102**

Road

Team	GP	SHGA
L.A	41	0
WSH	41	1
BOS	41	1
CAR	41	1
COL	41	1
CBJ	41	1
TOR	41	2
STL	41	2
CGY	41	2
MTL	41	2
DET	41	2
MIN	41	2
EDM	41	2
WPG	41	2
BUF	41	2
OTT	41	2
NYI	41	3
S.J	41	3
PIT	41	3
T.B	41	3
ANA	41	4
CHI	41	4
PHI	41	4
NSH	41	4
ARI	41	4
FLA	41	4
VAN	41	5
N.J	41	5
NYR	41	7
DAL	41	7
1230		**82**

Regular-Season Overtime Results

2016-17 to 1996-97

Team	2016-17				2015-16				2014-15				2013-14				2012-13			
	GP	W	L	SO	GP	W	L	SO	GP	W	L	SO	GP	W	L	SO	GP	W	L	SO
ANA	19	6	10	3	18	4	7	7	23	8	2	13	18	7	2	9	13	1	3	9
ARI/PHX/WPG	20	10	8	2	14	5	7	2	18	5	3	10	24	3	8	13	14	1	3	10
BOS	13	6	4	3	18	5	7	6	27	9	4	14	16	4	3	9	11	1	3	7
BUF	20	8	6	6	17	4	4	9	17	1	3	13	20	3	5	12	14	1	2	11
CGY	17	13	2	2	18	9	4	5	20	9	4	7	21	7	4	10	6	2	1	3
CAR/HFD	23	8	9	6	26	8	11	7	17	1	4	12	17	4	7	6	6	1	3	2
CHI	22	13	8	1	16	2	4	10	18	3	3	12	22	1	7	14	16	5	0	11
COL/QUE	12	8	2	2	20	10	7	3	24	2	8	14	23	10	4	9	12	3	5	4
CBJ	19	11	6	2	10	2	4	4	19	5	3	11	15	3	5	7	17	5	3	9
DAL/MIN	17	6	9	2	17	6	7	4	18	4	7	7	17	2	6	9	8	2	3	3
DET	29	16	13	0	22	9	6	7	25	7	4	14	24	4	6	14	12	2	3	7
EDM	19	10	4	5	19	7	5	7	21	2	7	12	18	5	6	7	11	2	4	5
FLA	23	12	5	6	17	1	6	10	24	1	5	18	16	0	2	14	10	1	5	4
L.A.	22	14	4	4	20	12	3	5	18	1	7	10	20	4	2	14	8	1	1	6
MIN	15	7	6	2	15	1	9	5	16	4	5	7	23	3	4	16	10	3	1	6
MTL	23	14	7	2	14	3	3	8	23	6	5	12	21	7	5	9	10	2	3	5
NSH	18	6	8	4	20	2	12	6	24	8	4	12	17	3	3	11	14	3	3	8
N.J.	24	10	11	3	19	9	2	8	20	1	7	12	27	9	5	13	13	1	3	9
NYI	20	8	8	4	21	6	5	10	20	6	1	13	24	4	5	15	13	2	4	7
NYR	14	8	2	4	16	4	7	5	17	6	2	9	12	2	3	7	12	4	0	8
OTT	20	10	6	4	21	6	3	12	26	7	6	13	24	3	7	14	12	2	2	8
PHI	24	14	5	5	27	10	6	11	26	5	7	14	17	4	2	11	6	2	1	3
PIT	21	10	6	5	18	6	4	8	22	6	6	10	18	4	4	10	5	2	0	3
ST.L.	15	8	5	2	22	8	5	9	21	5	3	13	23	4	2	17	15	0	3	12
S.J.	15	8	6	1	15	5	3	7	15	2	3	10	19	3	4	12	11	4	1	6
T.B.	20	10	7	3	15	7	2	6	15	4	3	8	23	6	3	14	6	1	1	4
TOR	22	7	7	8	20	3	5	12	16	3	3	10	22	5	4	13	7	2	0	5
VAN	20	11	7	2	22	4	9	9	17	6	3	8	22	6	4	12	13	1	1	11
WSH	14	7	6	1	14	3	5	6	21	5	7	9	28	4	3	21	10	4	3	3
WPG/ATL	18	10	3	5	19	7	6	6	24	4	7	13	23	5	4	14	9	4	0	5
Totals	**289**	**190**		**99**	**275**	**168**		**107**	**306**	**136**		**170**	**307**	**129**		**178**	**162**	**65**		**97**

Team	2011-12				2010-11				2009-10				2008-09				2007-08			
	GP	W	L	SO	GP	W	L	SO	GP	W	L	SO	GP	W	L	SO	GP	W	L	SO
ANA	17	2	5	10	18	9	3	6	19	3	3	13	19	5	4	10	20	4	1	15
ARI/PHX/WPG	22	3	3	16	20	2	7	11	26	5	1	20	11	1	4	6	16	4	1	11
BOS	15	2	1	12	14	1	5	8	27	4	4	19	17	3	4	10	21	3	5	13
BUF	23	5	4	14	25	10	9	6	20	6	4	10	19	2	4	13	21	5	3	13
CGY	21	2	7	12	23	2	5	16	15	2	3	10	12	3	4	5	16	3	7	6
CAR/HFD	20	3	10	7	22	6	6	10	19	5	5	9	17	7	2	8	13	5	3	5
CHI	22	4	4	14	19	4	4	11	23	6	2	15	22	6	5	11	17	4	4	9
COL/QUE	22	7	4	11	20	6	7	7	18	2	4	12	17	3	1	13	18	4	4	10
CBJ	13	2	2	9	23	5	5	13	20	3	5	12	21	5	3	13	17	2	4	11
DAL/MIN	16	4	1	11	21	5	4	12	23	2	4	17	22	5	5	12	15	3	4	8
DET	18	3	3	12	23	9	6	8	25	5	5	15	19	3	6	10	14	2	2	10
EDM	17	2	3	12	16	2	3	11	17	1	2	14	16	1	5	10	25	4	2	19
FLA	25	1	7	17	22	6	5	11	21	2	3	16	18	4	3	11	18	4	3	11
L.A.	24	3	6	15	17	1	4	12	23	4	1	18	19	3	3	13	14	2	4	8
MIN	24	2	2	20	16	5	3	8	18	5	1	12	17	3	6	8	19	6	2	11
MTL	23	2	4	17	16	5	5	6	25	8	5	12	22	4	4	14	20	5	4	11
NSH	16	3	3	10	19	2	7	10	20	6	2	12	20	6	3	11	17	5	4	8
N.J.	22	4	2	16	15	7	3	5	15	2	2	11	19	9	2	8	22	7	3	12
NYI	21	3	7	11	24	7	7	10	25	6	5	14	15	3	4	8	19	5	6	8
NYR	19	8	2	9	17	3	2	12	15	1	7	7	22	3	3	16	25	4	4	17
OTT	21	5	6	10	14	2	5	7	16	5	1	10	18	3	5	10	14	3	3	8
PHI	19	6	2	11	18	3	5	10	12	2	3	7	21	6	5	10	17	3	5	9
PIT	17	2	3	12	23	5	5	13	21	6	5	10	21	6	3	12	16	1	4	11
ST.L.	22	3	5	14	18	3	5	10	20	3	5	12	20	4	4	12	17	1	8	8
S.J.	18	3	1	14	19	5	4	10	19	1	5	13	21	4	6	11	19	3	4	12
T.B.	21	10	5	6	25	8	5	12	21	5	5	11	23	2	8	13	13	2	8	3
TOR	19	5	5	9	18	2	5	11	23	5	10	8	23	4	6	13	19	5	7	7
VAN	24	7	2	15	17	4	4	9	13	4	1	8	18	5	3	10	20	4	1	15
WSH	19	7	4	8	25	9	5	11	24	6	7	11	18	6	3	9	19	7	4	8
WPG/ATL	20	6	6	8	27	10	5	12	19	2	7	10	17	4	5	8	23	6	2	15
Totals	**300**	**119**		**181**	**297**	**148**		**149**	**301**	**117**		**184**	**282**	**123**		**159**	**272**	**116**		**156**

Team	2006-07				2005-06				2003-04				2002-03				2001-02			
	GP	W	L	SO	GP	W	L	SO	GP	W	L	T	GP	W	L	T	GP	W	L	T
ANA	23	5	4	14	18	3	5	10	22	4	8	10	21	6	6	9	14	3	3	8
ARI/PHX/WPG	12	2	3	7	15	6	2	7	29	5	6	18	20	4	5	11	19	4	6	9
BOS	19	4	2	13	22	4	8	10	30	8	7	15	21	6	4	11	24	9	9	6
BUF	22	5	3	14	17	6	1	10	13	2	4	7	21	3	8	10	16	4	1	11
CGY	15	2	5	8	15	2	4	9	13	3	3	7	19	2	6	11	17	2	3	12
CAR/HFD	14	6	3	5	20	4	6	10	25	5	6	14	15	4	3	8	27	6	5	16
CHI	18	3	2	13	22	7	7	8	23	4	8	11	23	6	4	13	17	3	1	13
COL/QUE	15	3	3	9	15	3	3	9	28	8	7	13	23	4	6	13	13	4	1	8
CBJ	16	4	2	10	18	6	1	11	18	6	4	8	28	7	8	13	15	2	5	8
DAL/MIN	22	6	3	13	21	3	5	13	18	3	2	13	24	5	4	15	21	3	5	13
DET	18	3	5	10	15	3	5	7	20	7	2	11	21	7	4	10	24	10	4	10
EDM	11	1	4	6	26	6	4	16	23	6	5	12	27	7	9	11	19	3	4	12
FLA	21	3	8	10	23	8	6	9	24	5	4	15	26	4	9	13	16	0	6	10
L.A.	20	2	8	10	15	4	4	7	27	2	9	16	19	6	7	6	18	3	4	11
MIN	25	7	1	17	14	1	5	8	24	1	3	20	19	8	1	10	21	0	9	12
MTL	14	2	1	11	18	7	6	5	16	5	4	7	19	2	9	8	17	2	3	12
NSH	17	3	3	11	17	3	5	9	22	7	4	11	24	8	6	10	18	5	0	13
N.J.	22	3	1	18	22	4	5	13	21	7	2	12	25	5	7	13	19	6	4	9
NYI	22	2	7	13	18	3	3	12	17	2	4	11	18	5	2	11	18	6	4	8
NYR	22	3	5	14	23	4	8	11	18	3	8	7	20	6	4	10	13	5	4	4
OTT	13	2	3	8	13	2	3	8	19	3	6	10	16	7	1	8	19	3	7	9
PHI	16	3	6	7	22	7	5	10	23	2	6	15	23	6	4	13	16	3	3	10
PIT	27	6	5	16	19	4	8	7	19	7	4	8	14	3	5	6	20	7	5	8
ST.L.	23	4	7	12	22	3	7	12	24	11	2	11	19	2	8	9	18	6	4	8
S.J.	8	1	3	4	21	9	4	8	21	3	6	12	23	6	6	11	13	2	3	8
T.B.	20	5	3	12	18	6	2	10	18	4	6	8	23	2	5	16	19	4	4	11
TOR	19	4	4	11	18	7	1	10	17	4	3	10	17	7	3	7	17	3	4	10
VAN	24	12	3	9	16	4	4	8	26	11	5	10	19	5	1	13	14	4	3	7
WSH	19	4	3	12	21	2	6	13	14	1	3	10	20	6	6	8	19	6	2	11
WPG/ATL	25	7	7	11	18	5	3	10	18	6	4	8	19	7	5	7	19	3	5	11
Totals	**281**	**117**		**164**	**281**	**136**		**145**	**315**	**145**		**170**	**313**	**156**		**157**	**270**	**121**		**149**

Team	2000-01				1999-2000				1998-99				1997-98				1996-97			
	GP	W	L	T	GP	W	L	T	GP	W	L	T	GP	W	L	T	GP	W	L	T
ANA	20	4	5	11	18	3	3	12	17	1	3	13	20	3	4	13	16	3	0	13
ARI/PHX/WPG	23	3	3	17	16	4	4	8	15	2	1	12	14	0	2	12	16	5	4	7
BOS	20	4	8	8	26	1	6	19	17	2	2	13	17	3	1	13	15	3	3	9
BUF	10	4	1	5	20	5	4	11	23	3	3	17	21	3	1	17	21	5	4	12
CGY	22	3	4	15	26	11	5	10	16	3	1	12	22	4	3	15	16	3	4	9
CAR/HFD	18	6	3	9	14	4	0	10	24	1	5	18	12	2	2	8	18	3	4	11
CHI	15	2	5	8	17	5	2	10	15	1	2	12	18	1	4	13	19	1	5	13
COL/QUE	20	6	4	10	17	5	1	11	12	2	0	10	22	2	3	17	15	2	3	10
CBJ	18	3	6	9	...	...	...	...	...	...	...	...	...	...	...	...	...	...	...	...
DAL/MIN	16	6	2	8	19	3	6	10	16	3	1	12	17	5	1	11	15	4	3	8
DET	23	10	4	9	16	4	2	10	10	2	1	7	15	0	0	15	27	7	2	18
EDM	20	5	3	12	27	3	8	16	20	3	5	12	15	3	2	10	16	1	6	9
FLA	24	2	9	13	15	3	6	6	21	1	2	18	20	3	2	15	26	3	4	19
L.A.	19	3	3	13	21	5	4	12	12	5	2	5	16	3	2	11	14	0	3	11
MIN	22	4	5	13	...	...	...	...	...	...	...	...	...	...	...	...	...	...	...	...
MTL	16	2	6	8	17	4	4	9	15	0	4	11	20	3	4	13	21	2	4	15
NSH	17	5	3	9	18	4	7	7	10	1	2	7	...	...	...	...	...	...	...	...
N.J.	20	5	3	12	16	3	5	8	15	3	1	11	16	2	3	11	17	1	2	14
NYI	12	2	3	7	15	5	1	9	17	1	6	10	13	0	2	11	17	3	2	12
NYR	11	5	1	5	21	6	3	12	19	5	3	11	24	2	4	18	13	3	0	10
OTT	16	3	4	9	15	2	2	11	18	1	2	15	17	2	0	15	17	0	2	15
PHI	19	5	3	11	21	6	3	12	24	2	3	19	15	3	1	11	18	3	2	13
PIT	15	3	3	9	17	3	6	8	22	7	1	14	23	3	2	18	13	1	4	8
ST.L.	23	6	5	12	17	5	1	11	15	1	1	13	12	2	2	8	13	1	1	11
S.J.	22	7	3	12	21	4	7	10	21	1	2	18	12	0	2	10	12	3	1	8
T.B.	13	2	5	6	16	0	7	9	12	1	2	9	13	0	3	10	16	4	2	10
TOR	19	3	5	11	17	7	3	7	14	6	1	7	10	1	0	9	10	1	1	8
VAN	23	5	7	11	27	4	8	15	13	0	1	12	17	0	3	14	14	5	2	7
WSH	16	2	4	10	19	5	2	12	11	2	3	6	17	4	1	12	13	2	2	9
WPG/ATL	16	2	2	12	11	0	4	7	...	...	...	...	...	...	...	...	...	...	...	...
Totals	**274**	**122**		**152**	**260**	**114**		**146**	**222**	**60**		**162**	**219**	**54**		**165**	**214**	**70**		**144**

Abbreviations: GP – overtime games played; **W** – overtime win; **L** – overtime loss;
SO – game tied after overtime. Game decided in shootout. (2005-06 to date); See page 145.
T – game tied after overtime. (Up to and including 2003-04.)

2016-17 Shootout Summary

Team Shootout Statistics

	GP	W	L	W%	G	S	S%	GA	SA	Sv%
Anaheim	6	3	3	.500	13	42	.310	13	42	.690
Arizona	8	6	2	.750	11	28	.393	6	28	.786
Boston	5	2	3	.400	6	28	.214	7	27	.741
Buffalo	8	2	6	.250	6	27	.222	14	26	.462
Calgary	6	4	2	.667	5	19	.263	4	22	.818
Carolina	9	3	6	.333	8	25	.320	13	27	.519
Chicago	5	4	1	.800	8	19	.421	3	17	.824
Colorado	4	2	2	.500	4	11	.364	3	10	.700
Columbus	3	1	2	.333	2	9	.222	2	6	.667
Dallas	3	1	2	.333	4	10	.400	5	11	.545
Detroit	9	9	0	1.000	15	37	.405	6	39	.846
Edmonton	9	4	5	.444	10	27	.370	11	27	.593
Florida	11	5	6	.455	12	34	.353	11	36	.694
Los Angeles	6	2	4	.333	7	27	.259	9	27	.667
Minnesota	5	3	2	.600	8	21	.381	7	20	.650
Montreal	5	3	2	.600	8	18	.444	6	17	.647
Nashville	6	2	4	.333	3	16	.188	6	17	.647
New Jersey	6	3	3	.500	6	18	.333	4	16	.750
NY Islanders	6	2	4	.333	7	27	.259	11	27	.593
NY Rangers	7	3	4	.429	7	20	.350	9	20	.550
Ottawa	10	6	4	.600	10	35	.286	8	37	.784
Philadelphia	12	7	5	.583	13	46	.283	10	45	.778
Pittsburgh	9	4	5	.444	9	26	.346	10	24	.583
St. Louis	4	2	2	.500	4	18	.222	5	19	.737
San Jose	3	2	1	.667	3	9	.333	2	9	.778
Tampa Bay	7	4	3	.571	11	32	.344	9	32	.719
Toronto	9	1	8	.111	5	28	.179	12	26	.538
Vancouver	6	4	2	.667	5	17	.294	3	19	.842
Washington	4	3	1	.750	6	15	.400	4	16	.750
Winnipeg	7	2	5	.286	8	24	.333	11	24	.542
Totals	**99**				**224**	**713**	**.314**			

Team Shootout Leaders

Wins

	W	L	W%
Detroit	9	0	1.000
Philadelphia	7	5	.583
Arizona	6	2	.750
Ottawa	6	4	.600
Florida	5	6	.455

six teams tied with **4**

Goals Scored

	G	S	S%
Detroit	15	37	.405
Anaheim	13	42	.310
Philadelphia	13	46	.283
Florida	12	34	.353
Arizona	11	28	.393
Tampa Bay	11	32	.344
Edmonton	10	27	.370
Ottawa	10	35	.286
Pittsburgh	9	26	.346

Fewest Goals Against

	GA	SA	Sv%
San Jose	2	9	.778
Columbus	2	6	.667
Vancouver	3	19	.842
Chicago	3	17	.824
Colorado	3	10	.700
Calgary	4	22	.818
New Jersey	4	16	.750
Washington	4	16	.750

two teams tied with **5**

Winning Percentage

	W%	W	L
Detroit	**1.000**	9	0
Chicago	**.800**	4	1
Arizona	**.750**	6	2
Washington	**.750**	3	1
Vancouver	**.667**	4	2
Calgary	**.667**	4	2
San Jose	**.667**	2	1
Ottawa	**.600**	6	4
Montreal	**.600**	3	2
Minnesota	**.600**	3	2

Shootout Abbreviations

G ....Goals Scored
GA ......Goals Against
GDG ...Game Deciding Goals
S ....Shots Taken
SA ......Shots Against
S% ....Goal Scoring %
Sv%....Save %
W% ....Win %

Shootout Games

	GP	W	L
Philadelphia	12	7	5
Florida	11	5	6
Ottawa	10	6	4
Detroit	9	9	0
Edmonton	9	4	5
Pittsburgh	9	4	5
Carolina	9	3	6
Toronto	9	1	8
Arizona	8	6	2
Buffalo	8	2	6

Individual Shootout Leaders
Goaltenders

Goaltender Shootout Wins

	Team	W	L
Petr Mrazek	Det.	6	0
Steve Mason	Phi.	5	4
Cam Talbot	Edm.	4	5
Louis Domingue	Ari.	3	0
Carey Price	Mtl.	3	0
Corey Crawford	Chi.	3	1
Mike Condon	Ott.	3	1
Connor Hellebuyck	Wpg.	3	1
Mike Smith	Ari.	3	2
Devan Dubnyk	Min.	3	2
Ben Bishop	Dal.	3	2
Craig Anderson	Ott.	3	3
Henrik Lundqvist	NYR	3	3
Roberto Luongo	Fla.	3	4

Goaltender Shootout Shots Against

	Team	SA	GA	Sv%
Steve Mason	Phi.	36	8	.778
Jonathan Bernier	Ana.	33	11	.667
Petr Mrazek	Det.	30	4	.867
Ben Bishop	T.B.-L.A.	28	8	.714
Cam Talbot	Edm.	27	11	.593
Craig Anderson	Ott.	24	5	.792
Cam Ward	Car.	24	12	.500
Tuukka Rask	Bos.	24	6	.750
Frederik Andersen	Tor.	23	11	.522
Roberto Luongo	Fla.	22	7	.682
Braden Holtby	Wsh.	22	11	.500
Devan Dubnyk	Min.	20	7	.650

Goaltender Shootout Save Percentage

(min. 10 shots faced)

	Team	Sv%	SA	GA
Louis Domingue	Ari.	**.933**	15	1
Petr Mrazek	Det.	**.867**	30	4
Corey Crawford	Chi.	**.857**	14	2
Brian Elliott	Cgy.	**.833**	12	2
Ryan Miller	Van.	**.800**	10	2
Chad Johnson	Cgy.	**.800**	10	2
Andrei Vasilevskiy	T.B.	**.800**	15	3
Craig Anderson	Ott.	**.792**	24	5
Steve Mason	Phi.	**.778**	36	8
Mike Condon	Ott.	**.769**	13	3
Connor Hellebuyck	Wpg.	**.750**	16	4
Tuukka Rask	Bos.	**.750**	24	6

Individual Shootout Leaders – Skaters

Shootout Goals Scored

	Team	G	S	S%
Aleksander Barkov	Fla.	7	10	.700
Thomas Vanek	Det.	5	5	1.000
Brayden Point	T.B.	5	7	.714
Jakub Voracek	Phi.	5	11	.455
Kris Versteeg	Cgy.	4	5	.800
Artemi Panarin	Chi.	4	5	.800
Alexander Radulov	Mtl.	4	5	.800
T.J. Oshie	Wsh.	4	6	.667
Mats Zuccarello	NYR	4	7	.571
Radim Vrbata	Ari.	4	8	.500
Mark Letestu	Edm.	4	9	.444
Kyle Turris	Ott.	4	10	.400
Vincent Trocheck	Fla.	4	11	.364
Claude Giroux	Phi.	4	12	.333

Shootout Shots Taken

	Team	S	G	S%
Claude Giroux	Phi.	12	4	.333
Jakub Voracek	Phi.	11	5	.455
Vincent Trocheck	Fla.	11	4	.364
Aleksander Barkov	Fla.	10	7	.700
Kyle Turris	Ott.	10	4	.400
Mark Letestu	Edm.	9	4	.444
Radim Vrbata	Ari.	8	4	.500
Bobby Ryan	Ott.	8	3	.375
Mitch Marner	Tor.	8	3	.375
Sidney Crosby	Pit.	8	3	.375
Frans Nielsen	Det.	8	2	.250
Auston Matthews	Tor.	8	2	.250

Shootout Scoring Percentage

(min. 5 shots taken)

	Team	S%	S	G
Thomas Vanek	Fla.	**1.000**	5	5
Artemi Panarin	Chi.	**.800**	5	4
Alexander Radulov	Mtl.	**.800**	5	4
Kris Versteeg	Cgy.	**.800**	5	4
Brayden Point	T.B.	**.714**	7	5
Aleksander Barkov	Fla.	**.700**	10	7
T.J. Oshie	Wsh.	**.667**	6	4
Ryan Getzlaf	Ana.	**.600**	5	3
Mats Zuccarello	NYR	**.571**	7	4
Radim Vrbata	Ari.	**.500**	8	4
Gustav Nyquist	Det.	**.500**	6	3
Leon Draisaitl	Edm.	**.500**	6	3
Phil Kessel	Pit.	**.500**	6	3

Shootout Game-Deciding Goals

	Team	GDG	S	G
Paul Byron	Mtl.	3	4	3
Henrik Zetterberg	Det.	3	4	3
Kris Versteeg	Cgy.	3	5	4
Artemi Panarin	Chi.	3	5	4
Phil Kessel	Pit.	3	6	3
Aleksander Barkov	Fla.	3	10	7
Claude Giroux	Phi.	3	12	4
Brian Boyle	T.B.	2	3	2
Ryan Ellis	Nsh.	2	3	2
Bo Horvat	Van.	2	4	2
Erik Karlsson	Ott.	2	5	2
T.J. Oshie	Wsh.	2	6	4
Leon Draisaitl	Edm.	2	6	3
Anthony Duclair	Ari.	2	6	2
Brayden Point	T.B.	2	7	5
Frans Nielsen	Det.	2	8	2
Kyle Turris	Ott.	2	10	4
Vincent Trocheck	Fla.	2	11	4

Shootout Register, 2016-17

Skaters

Player	Team	S	G	S%	GDG
Sven Andrighetto	Mtl.	4	2	.500	2
Sebastian Aho	Car.	5	2	.400	0
Artem Anisimov	Chi.	1	0	.000	0
Viktor Arvidsson	Nsh.	1	0	.000	0
Andreas Athanasiou	Det.	6	1	.167	1
Cam Atkinson	CBJ	4	2	.500	1
David Backes	Bos.	1	0	.000	0
Mikael Backlund	Cgy.	1	0	.000	0
Nicklas Backstrom	Wsh.	5	1	.200	0
Sven Baertschi	Van.	2	0	.000	0
Josh Bailey	NYI	2	0	.000	0
Aleksander Barkov	Fla.	10	7	.700	3
Anthony Beauvillier	NYI	2	1	.500	0
Jamie Benn	Dal.	3	1	.333	0
Sam Bennett	Cgy.	2	0	.000	0
Patrice Bergeron	Bos.	2	0	.000	0
Patrik Berglund	St.L.	2	1	.500	0
Bryan Bickell	Car.	1	1	1.000	0
Kevin Bieksa	Ana.	1	0	.000	0
Nick Bjugstad	Fla.	3	0	.000	0
Mikkel Boedker	S.J.	1	0	.000	0
Nick Bonino	Pit.	3	0	.000	0
Johnny Boychuk	NYI	1	0	.000	0
Brian Boyle	T.B.	3	2	.667	2
Tyler Bozak	Tor.	3	0	.000	0
Derick Brassard	Ott.	2	0	.000	0
Troy Brouwer	Cgy.	1	0	.000	0
Dustin Brown	L.A.	2	0	.000	0
Brent Burns	S.J.	1	0	.000	0
Alexandre Burrows	Van.-Ott.	3	0	.000	0
Paul Byron	Mtl.	4	3	.750	3
Ryan Callahan	T.B.	1	0	.000	0
Michael Cammalleri	N.J.	4	2	.500	1
Jeff Carter	L.A.	4	3	.750	0
Jason Chimera	NYI	2	0	.000	0
Jakob Chychrun	Ari.	1	0	.000	0
Casey Cizikas	NYI	1	0	.000	0
Cal Clutterbuck	NYI	2	0	.000	0
Andrew Cogliano	Ana.	1	0	.000	0
Brett Connolly	Wsh.	1	0	.000	0
Nick Cousins	Phi.	6	0	.000	0
Logan Couture	S.J.	2	2	1.000	1
Sean Couturier	Phi.	1	0	.000	0
Charlie Coyle	Min.	3	0	.000	0
Sidney Crosby	Pit.	8	3	.375	0
Austin Czarnik	Bos.	1	0	.000	0
Tony DeAngelo	Ari.	1	1	1.000	1
David Desharnais	Mtl.	1	0	.000	0
Shane Doan	Ari.	1	0	.000	0
Max Domi	Ari.	1	0	.000	0
Drew Doughty	L.A.	1	0	.000	0
Nic Dowd	L.A.	2	0	.000	0
Leon Draisaitl	Edm.	6	3	.500	2
Jonathan Drouin	T.B.	5	2	.400	0
Matt Duchene	Col.	3	1	.333	1
Anthony Duclair	Ari.	6	2	.333	2
Christian Dvorak	Ari.	1	0	.000	0
Ryan Dzingel	Ott.	1	0	.000	0
Patrick Eaves	Ana.	3	2	.667	1
Jordan Eberle	Edm.	3	1	.333	0
Nikolaj Ehlers	Wpg.	1	0	.000	0
Jack Eichel	Buf.	3	0	.000	0
Aaron Ekblad	Fla.	1	0	.000	0
Oliver Ekman-Larsson	Ari.	3	1	.333	1
Ryan Ellis	Nsh.	3	2	.667	2
Tyler Ennis	Buf.	1	0	.000	0
Loui Eriksson	Van.	3	0	.000	0
Robby Fabbri	St.L.	2	0	.000	0
Valtteri Filppula	T.B.	2	0	.000	0
Brian Flynn	Mtl.	2	1	.500	0
Filip Forsberg	Nsh.	3	0	.000	0
Cam Fowler	Ana.	3	1	.333	0
Marian Gaborik	L.A.	3	0	.000	0
Sam Gagner	CBJ	4	2	.500	1
Alex Galchenyuk	Mtl.	2	0	.000	0
Ryan Garbutt	Ana.	1	0	.000	0
Johnny Gaudreau	Cgy.	3	0	.000	0
Ryan Getzlaf	Ana.	5	3	.600	0
Brian Gionta	Buf.	2	0	.000	0
Mark Giordano	Cgy.	1	0	.000	0
Zemgus Girgensons	Buf.	1	1	1.000	1
Claude Giroux	Phi.	12	4	.333	3
Shayne Gostisbehere	Phi.	3	1	.333	1
Michael Grabner	NYR	1	0	.000	0
Markus Granlund	Van.	4	2	.500	1
Mikael Granlund	Min.	1	0	.000	0
Seth Griffith	Tor.	2	0	.000	0
Taylor Hall	N.J.	3	1	.333	0
Noah Hanifin	Car.	1	0	.000	0
Jimmy Hayes	Bos.	2	1	.500	1
Kevin Hayes	NYR	1	1	1.000	1
Victor Hedman	T.B.	1	0	.000	0
Darren Helm	Det.	1	0	.000	0
Ales Hemsky	Dal.	1	0	.000	0
Matt Hendricks	Edm.	1	0	.000	0
Thomas Hickey	NYI	1	1	1.000	0
Joshua Ho-Sang	NYI	1	0	.000	0
Mike Hoffman	Ott.	1	0	.000	0
Peter Holland	Tor.-Ari.	3	1	.333	1
Bo Horvat	Van.	3	2	.667	2
Marian Hossa	Chi.	1	0	.000	0
Jonathan Huberdeau	Fla.	2	1	.500	0
Jarome Iginla	L.A.	1	0	.000	0
Dmitrij Jaskin	St.L.	1	0	.000	0
Ryan Johansen	Nsh.	5	0	.000	0
Marcus Johansson	Wsh.	1	0	.000	0
Tyler Johnson	T.B.	1	0	.000	0
Jussi Jokinen	Fla.	2	0	.000	0
Jacob Josefson	N.J.	3	2	.667	1
Tyson Jost	Col.	1	0	.000	0
Nazem Kadri	Tor.	2	0	.000	0
Evander Kane	Buf.	1	0	.000	0
Patrick Kane	Chi.	5	1	.200	0
Erik Karlsson	Ott.	5	2	.400	2
Ondrej Kase	Ana.	3	2	.667	1
Adrian Kempe	L.A.	1	0	.000	0
Ryan Kesler	Ana.	2	0	.000	0
Phil Kessel	Pit.	6	3	.500	3
Alex Killorn	T.B.	1	0	.000	0
Dwight King	L.A.	1	1	1.000	0
Mikko Koivu	Min.	4	2	.500	1
Travis Konecny	Phi.	3	0	.000	0
Anze Kopitar	L.A.	5	2	.400	1
David Krejci	Bos.	2	0	.000	0
Torey Krug	Bos.	2	0	.000	0
Nikita Kucherov	T.B.	6	2	.333	0
Nikolay Kulemin	NYI	2	1	.500	0
Evgeny Kuznetsov	Wsh.	7	3	.429	0
Kevin Labanc	S.J.	1	1	1.000	1
Andrew Ladd	NYI	4	0	.000	0
Patrik Laine	Wpg.	4	3	.750	1
Dylan Larkin	Det.	2	0	.000	0
Nick Leddy	NYI	2	1	.500	0
Anders Lee	NYI	1	0	.000	0
Kris Letang	Pit.	4	2	.500	1
Mark Letestu	Edm.	9	4	.444	1
Trevor Lewis	L.A.	1	0	.000	0
Hampus Lindholm	Ana.	1	0	.000	0
Bryan Little	Wpg.	2	1	.500	0
Roman Lyubimov	Phi.	1	0	.000	0
Nathan MacKinnon	Col.	3	1	.333	0
Evgeni Malkin	Pit.	5	1	.200	0
Brad Marchand	Bos.	4	2	.500	0
Jonathan Marchessault	Fla.	1	0	.000	0
Patrick Marleau	S.J.	1	0	.000	0
Mitch Marner	Tor.	8	3	.375	1
Patrick Maroon	Edm.	1	0	.000	0
Auston Matthews	Tor.	8	2	.250	0
Connor McDavid	Edm.	4	2	.500	1
Brock McGinn	Car.	1	1	1.000	1
J.T. Miller	NYR	1	0	.000	0
Sean Monahan	Cgy.	6	1	.167	0
Brandon Montour	Ana.	1	1	1.000	0
Dominic Moore	Bos.	1	0	.000	0
Matt Moulson	Buf.	1	0	.000	0
Vladislav Namestnikov	T.B.	1	0	.000	0
Riley Nash	Bos.	2	1	.500	0
James Neal	Nsh.	2	1	.500	0
Chris Neil	Ott.	1	0	.000	0
Brock Nelson	NYI	1	0	.000	0
Nino Niederreiter	Min.	1	0	.000	0
Frans Nielsen	Det.	8	2	.250	2
Ryan Nugent-Hopkins	Edm.	3	0	.000	0
William Nylander	Tor.	2	0	.000	0
Gustav Nyquist	Det.	6	3	.500	1
Cal O'Reilly	Buf.	2	1	.500	1
Ryan O'Reilly	Buf.	3	1	.333	0
Kyle Okposo	Buf.	5	0	.000	0
T.J. Oshie	Wsh.	6	4	.667	2
Alex Ovechkin	Wsh.	3	0	.000	0
Max Pacioretty	Mtl.	4	0	.000	0
Ondrej Palat	T.B.	1	0	.000	0
Artemi Panarin	Chi.	5	4	.800	3
Richard Panik	Chi.	2	1	.500	0
PA Parenteau	Nsh.	4	1	.250	1
Zach Parise	Min.	4	0	.000	0
David Pastrnak	Bos.	4	1	.250	1
Joe Pavelski	S.J.	3	0	.000	0
Tanner Pearson	L.A.	4	1	.250	1
Brendan Perlini	Ari.	3	2	.667	0
Mathieu Perreault	Wpg.	1	1	1.000	1
David Perron	St.L.	3	1	.333	0
Corey Perry	Ana.	6	1	.167	1
Brandon Pirri	NYR	1	0	.000	0
Brayden Point	T.B.	7	5	.714	2
Jason Pominville	Min.	4	3	.750	0
Tom Pyatt	Ott.	3	1	.333	1
John Quenneville	N.J.	1	0	.000	0
Alan Quine	NYI	1	0	.000	0
Alexander Radulov	Mtl.	5	4	.800	0
Rickard Rakell	Ana.	5	2	.400	0
Mikko Rantanen	Col.	2	0	.000	0
Matt Read	Phi.	1	0	.000	0
Sam Reinhart	Buf.	6	2	.333	0
Tobias Rieder	Ari.	1	0	.000	0
Rasmus Ristolainen	Buf.	1	1	1.000	0
Nick Ritchie	Ana.	2	0	.000	0
Evan Rodrigues	Buf.	1	0	.000	0
Bobby Ryan	Ott.	8	3	.375	1
Zach Sanford	St.L.	1	0	.000	0
Mark Scheifele	Wpg.	3	1	.333	1
Brayden Schenn	Phi.	2	0	.000	0
Nick Schmaltz	Chi.	1	0	.000	0
Tyler Seguin	Dal.	3	2	.667	1
Devin Setoguchi	L.A.	1	0	.000	0
Damon Severson	N.J.	1	0	.000	0
Patrick Sharp	Dal.	1	0	.000	0
Kevin Shattenkirk	L.A.	2	0	.000	0
Riley Sheahan	Det.	1	0	.000	0
Jakob Silfverberg	Ana.	6	1	.167	0
Wayne Simmonds	Phi.	3	1	.333	0
Jeff Skinner	Car.	5	0	.000	0
Jaccob Slavin	Car.	6	2	.333	1
Craig Smith	Nsh.	2	0	.000	0
Reilly Smith	Fla.	2	0	.000	0
Nikita Soshnikov	Tor.	2	0	.000	0
Jason Spezza	Dal.	1	0	.000	0
Ryan Spooner	Bos.	5	1	.200	0
Eric Staal	Min.	1	1	1.000	1
Drew Stafford	Wpg.-Bos.	2	0	.000	0
Steven Stamkos	T.B.	2	0	.000	0
Alexander Steen	St.L.	2	1	.500	0
Lee Stempniak	Car.	3	2	.667	1
Derek Stepan	NYR	2	0	.000	0
Chris Stewart	Min.	2	2	1.000	1
Mark Stone	Ott.	2	0	.000	0
Anton Stralman	T.B.	1	0	.000	0
Ryan Strome	NYI	1	1	1.000	0
Brandon Sutter	Van.	3	1	.333	1
Evgeny Svechnikov	Det.	1	1	1.000	1
Vladimir Tarasenko	St.L.	4	1	.250	1
Tomas Tatar	Det.	3	0	.000	0
John Tavares	NYI	3	2	.667	1
Teuvo Teravainen	Car.	2	0	.000	0
Shea Theodore	Ana.	1	1	1.000	0
Jonathan Toews	Chi.	4	2	.500	1
Tyler Toffoli	L.A.	1	0	.000	0
Sergey Tolchinsky	Car.	1	0	.000	0
Vincent Trocheck	Fla.	11	4	.364	2
Kyle Turris	Ott.	10	4	.400	2
James van Riemsdyk	Tor.	2	0	.000	0
Thomas Vanek	Det..	5	5	1.000	1
Frank Vatrano	Bos.	1	0	.000	0
Antoine Vermette	Ana.	2	0	.000	0
Kris Versteeg	Cgy.	5	4	.800	3
Jimmy Vesey	NYR	3	1	.333	1
Jakub Voracek	Phi.	11	5	.455	1
Radim Vrbata	Ari.	8	4	.500	1
Jordan Weal	Phi.	3	2	.667	1
Alexander Wennberg	CBJ	3	0	.000	0
Blake Wheeler	Wpg.	3	0	.000	0
Colin White	Ott.	1	0	.000	0
Justin Williams	Wsh.	1	0	.000	0
Nail Yakupov	St.L.	1	0	.000	0
Pavel Zacha	N.J.	1	0	.000	0
Travis Zajac	N.J.	1	0	.000	0
Henrik Zetterberg	Det.	4	3	.750	3
Mika Zibanejad	NYR	4	1	.250	1
Mats Zuccarello	NYR	7	4	.571	0
Jason Zucker	Min.	1	0	.000	0

Goaltenders

Goaltender	Team	W	L	SA	GA	Sv %
Jake Allen	St.L.	1	2	15	4	.733
Frederik Andersen	Tor.	1	7	23	11	.522
Craig Anderson	Ott.	3	3	24	5	.792
Jonathan Bernier	Ana.	1	3	33	11	.667
Ben Bishop	T.B.-L.A.	3	2	28	8	.714
Sergei Bobrovsky	CBJ	0	2	5	2	.600
Peter Budaj	L.A.-T.B.	1	3	13	7	.462
Mike Condon	Ott.	3	1	13	3	.769
Jared Coreau	Det.	1	0	3	1	.667
Corey Crawford	Chi.	3	1	14	2	.857
Scott Darling	Car.	1	0	3	1	.667
Louis Domingue	Ari.	3	0	15	1	.933
Devan Dubnyk	Min.	3	2	20	7	.650
Brian Elliott	Cgy.	2	1	12	2	.833
Jhonas Enroth	Ana.	0	1	3	1	.667
Marc-Andre Fleury	Pit.	2	3	15	7	.533
John Gibson	Ana.	2	0	9	2	.778
Thomas Greiss	NYI	1	2	19	8	.579
Philipp Grubauer	Wsh.	1	0	2	0	1.000
Jaroslav Halak	NYI	1	2	8	3	.625
Connor Hellebuyck	Wpg.	3	1	16	4	.750
Braden Holtby	Wsh.	1	5	22	11	.500
Jimmy Howard	Det.	2	0	6	1	.833
Carter Hutton	St.L.	1	0	4	1	.750
Chad Johnson	Cgy.	2	1	10	2	.800
Martin Jones	S.J.	2	1	9	2	.778
Anton Khudobin	Bos.	1	0	3	1	.667
Keith Kinkaid	N.J.	1	1	5	1	.800
Eddie Lack	Car.	1	0	3	1	.667
Robin Lehner	Buf.	0	4	8	8	.000
Kari Lehtonen	Dal.	1	2	11	5	.546
Henrik Lundqvist	NYR	3	3	18	8	.556
Roberto Luongo	Fla.	3	4	22	7	.682
Jacob Markstrom	Van.	2	1	9	1	.889
Steve Mason	Phi.	5	4	36	8	.778
Curtis McElhinney	Tor.	2	0	5	1	.800
Ryan Miller	Van.	2	1	10	2	.800
Al Montoya	Mtl.	0	2	6	3	.500
Petr Mrazek	Det.	6	0	30	4	.867
Matt Murray	Pit.	2	2	9	3	.667
Michal Neuvirth	Phi.	2	0	6	0	1.000
Anders Nilsson	Buf.	2	2	18	6	.667
Calvin Pickard	Col.	1	1	4	1	.750
Carey Price	Mtl.	3	0	11	3	.727
Jonathan Quick	L.A.	1	0	3	0	1.000
Antti Raanta	NYR	0	1	2	1	.500
Tuukka Rask	Bos.	1	3	24	6	.750
James Reimer	Fla.	2	2	14	4	.714
Pekka Rinne	Nsh.	2	3	15	4	.733
Juuse Saros	Nsh.	0	1	2	2	.000
Cory Schneider	N.J.	2	2	11	3	.727
Jeremy Smith	Col.	0	1	2	1	.500
Mike Smith	Ari.	3	2	13	5	.615
Anthony Stolarz	Phi.	0	1	3	2	.333
Cam Talbot	Edm.	4	5	27	11	.593
Andrei Vasilevskiy	T.B.	1	2	15	3	.800
Cam Ward	Car.	2	6	24	12	.500

NHL Record Book

Year-By-Year Final Standings & Leading Scorers

*Stanley Cup winner

1917-18

First Half

Team	GP	W	L	T	GF	GA	PTS
Montreal	14	10	4	0	81	47	20
Toronto	14	8	6	0	71	75	16
Ottawa	14	5	9	0	67	79	10
**Mtl. Wanderers	6	1	5	0	17	35	2

**Montreal Arena burned down and Wanderers forced to withdraw from League. Montreal Canadiens and Toronto each counted a win for defaulted games with Wanderers.

Second Half

Team	GP	W	L	T	GF	GA	PTS
*Toronto	8	5	3	0	37	34	10
Ottawa	8	4	4	0	35	35	8
Montreal	8	3	5	0	34	37	6

Leading Scorers

Player	Team	GP	G	A	PTS	PIM
Joe Malone	Montreal	20	44	4	48	30
Cy Denneny	Ottawa	20	36	10	46	80
Reg Noble	Toronto	20	30	10	40	35
Newsy Lalonde	Montreal	14	23	7	30	51
Corb Denneny	Toronto	21	20	9	29	14
Harry Cameron	Toronto	21	17	10	27	28
Didier Pitre	Montreal	20	17	6	23	29
Eddie Gerard	Ottawa	20	13	7	20	26
Jack Darragh	Ottawa	18	14	5	19	26
Frank Nighbor	Ottawa	10	11	8	19	6
Harry Meeking	Toronto	21	10	9	19	28

1918-19

First Half

Team	GP	W	L	T	GF	GA	PTS
• Montreal	10	7	3	0	57	50	14
Ottawa	10	5	5	0	39	39	10
Toronto	10	3	7	0	42	49	6

Second Half

Team	GP	W	L	T	GF	GA	PTS
Ottawa	8	7	1	0	32	14	14
Montreal	8	3	5	0	31	28	6
Toronto	8	2	6	0	22	43	4

• NHL Champion. Stanley Cup not awarded due to influenza epidemic.

Leading Scorers

Player	Team	GP	G	A	PTS	PIM
Newsy Lalonde	Montreal	17	22	10	32	40
Odie Cleghorn	Montreal	17	22	6	28	22
Frank Nighbor	Ottawa	18	19	9	28	27
Cy Denneny	Ottawa	18	18	4	22	58
Didier Pitre	Montreal	17	14	5	19	12
Alf Skinner	Toronto	17	12	4	16	26
Harry Cameron	Tor., Ott.	14	11	3	14	35
Jack Darragh	Ottawa	14	11	3	14	33
Ken Randall	Toronto	15	8	6	14	27
Sprague Cleghorn	Ottawa	18	7	6	13	27

1919-20

First Half

Team	GP	W	L	T	GF	GA	PTS
Ottawa	12	9	3	0	59	23	18
Montreal	12	8	4	0	62	51	16
Toronto	12	5	7	0	52	62	10
Quebec	12	2	10	0	44	81	4

Second Half

Team	GP	W	L	T	GF	GA	PTS
*Ottawa	12	10	2	0	62	41	20
Toronto	12	7	5	0	67	44	14
Montreal	12	5	7	0	67	62	10
Quebec	12	2	10	0	47	96	4

All-Time Standings of NHL Teams

(ranked by percentage)

Active Teams

Team	Games	Wins	Losses	Ties	OT Losses	SO Losses	Goals For	Goals Against	Points	Pts %	First Season
Montreal	6496	3345	2180	837	78	56	20961	17371	7661	.590	1917-18
Philadelphia	3882	1934	1345	457	71	75	12800	11334	4471	.576	1967-68
Boston	6336	3065	2329	791	84	67	20188	18398	7072	.558	1924-25
Minnesota	1278	607	494	55	63	59	3301	3286	1391	.544	2000-01
Nashville	1442	686	560	60	78	58	3852	3912	1568	.544	1998-99
Anaheim	1820	865	709	107	74	65	4946	4966	1976	.543	1993-94
Buffalo	3656	1702	1415	409	66	64	11713	10999	3943	.539	1970-71
Detroit	6270	2891	2419	815	80	65	19384	18504	6742	.538	1926-27
Calgary	3500	1616	1382	379	69	54	11441	10983	3734	.533	1972-73
San Jose	1984	929	802	121	75	57	5616	5703	2111	.532	1991-92
St. Louis	3882	1771	1546	432	73	60	11960	11880	4107	.529	1967-68
Washington	3344	1526	1380	303	71	64	10548	10687	3490	.522	1974-75
Ottawa	1904	866	788	115	70	65	5439	5554	1982	.520	1992-93
Edmonton	2944	1326	1215	262	78	63	9902	9725	3055	.519	1979-80
Colorado	2944	1342	1234	261	70	37	9531	9534	3052	.518	1979-80
NY Rangers	6270	2753	2590	808	65	54	19172	19101	6433	.513	1926-27
Dallas	3882	1697	1601	459	77	48	11929	12224	3978	.512	1967-68
Pittsburgh	3882	1735	1640	383	76	48	12909	13206	3977	.512	1967-68
NY Islanders	3500	1538	1483	347	76	56	11205	11094	3555	.508	1972-73
Toronto	6496	2834	2736	783	75	68	19888	20064	6594	.508	1917-18
Chicago	6270	2687	2633	814	75	61	18665	18735	6324	.504	1926-27
Florida	1820	737	768	142	92	81	4730	5215	1789	.491	1993-94
Los Angeles	3882	1628	1695	424	74	61	12291	12913	3815	.491	1967-68
New Jersey	3344	1412	1473	328	66	65	9788	10595	3283	.491	1974-75
Vancouver	3656	1524	1614	391	66	61	11316	12076	3566	.488	1970-71
Tampa Bay	1904	790	870	112	79	53	5169	5846	1824	.479	1992-93
Columbus	1278	535	589	33	61	60	3275	3776	1224	.479	2000-01
Arizona	2944	1210	1337	266	74	57	8970	9948	2817	.478	1979-80
Carolina	2944	1205	1333	263	89	54	8744	9677	2816	.478	1979-80
Winnipeg	1360	558	628	45	77	52	3739	4346	1290	.474	1999-2000

Defunct Teams

Team	Games	Wins	Losses	Ties	Goals For	Goals Against	Points	Pts %	First Season	Last Season
Ottawa Senators	542	258	221	63	1458	1333	579	.534	1917-18	1933-34
Montreal Maroons	622	271	260	91	1474	1405	633	.509	1924-25	1937-38
NY/Brooklyn Americans	784	255	402	127	1643	2182	637	.406	1925-26	1941-42
Hamilton Tigers	126	47	78	1	414	475	95	.377	1920-21	1924-25
Cleveland Barons	160	47	87	26	470	617	120	.375	1976-77	1977-78
Pittsburgh Pirates	212	67	122	23	376	519	157	.370	1925-26	1929-30
Calif./Oakland Seals	698	182	401	115	1826	2580	479	.343	1967-68	1975-76
St. Louis Eagles	48	11	31	6	86	144	28	.292	1934-35	1934-35
Quebec Bulldogs	24	4	20	0	91	177	8	.167	1919-20	1919-20
Montreal Wanderers	6	1	5	0	17	35	2	.167	1917-18	1917-18
Philadelphia Quakers	44	4	36	4	76	184	12	.136	1930-31	1930-31

Calgary totals include Atlanta Flames, 1972-73 to 1979-80.
Carolina totals include Hartford, 1979-80 to 1996-97.
Colorado totals include Quebec, 1979-80 to 1994-95.
Dallas totals include Minnesota North Stars, 1967-68 to 1992-93.
Detroit totals include Cougars, 1926-27 to 1929-30, and Falcons, 1930-31 to 1931-32.
New Jersey totals include Kansas City, 1974-75 to 1975-76, and Colorado Rockies, 1976-77 to 1981-82.
Phoenix totals include Winnipeg, 1979-80 to 1995-96.
Toronto totals include Arenas, 1917-18 to 1918-19, and St. Patricks, 1919-20 to 1925-26.
Winnipeg totals include Atlanta Thrashers, 1999-2000 to 2010-11.

Leading Scorers

Player	Team	GP	G	A	PTS	PIM
Joe Malone	Quebec	24	39	10	49	12
Newsy Lalonde	Montreal	23	37	9	46	34
Frank Nighbor	Ottawa	23	26	15	41	18
Corb Denneny	Toronto	24	24	12	36	20
Jack Darragh	Ottawa	23	22	14	36	22
Reg Noble	Toronto	24	24	9	33	52
Amos Arbour	Montreal	22	21	5	26	13
Cully Wilson	Toronto	23	20	6	26	86
Didier Pitre	Montreal	22	14	12	26	6
Punch Broadbent	Ottawa	21	19	6	25	40

1920-21

First Half

Team	GP	W	L	T	GF	GA	PTS
*Ottawa	10	8	2	0	49	23	16
Toronto	10	5	5	0	39	47	10
Montreal	10	4	6	0	37	51	8
Hamilton	10	3	7	0	34	38	6

Second Half

Team	GP	W	L	T	GF	GA	PTS
Toronto	14	10	4	0	66	53	20
Montreal	14	9	5	0	75	48	18
Ottawa	14	6	8	0	48	52	12
Hamilton	14	3	11	0	58	94	6

Leading Scorers

Player	Team	GP	G	A	PTS	PIM
Newsy Lalonde	Montreal	24	33	10	43	36
Babe Dye	Ham., Tor.	24	35	5	40	32
Cy Denneny	Ottawa	24	34	5	39	10
Joe Malone	Hamilton	20	28	9	37	6
Frank Nighbor	Ottawa	24	19	10	29	10
Reg Noble	Toronto	24	19	8	27	54
Harry Cameron	Toronto	24	18	9	27	35
Goldie Prodger	Hamilton	24	18	9	27	8
Corb Denneny	Toronto	20	19	7	26	29
Jack Darragh	Ottawa	24	11	15	26	20

1921-22

Team	GP	W	L	T	GF	GA	PTS
Ottawa	24	14	8	2	106	84	30
*Toronto	24	13	10	1	98	97	27
Montreal	24	12	11	1	88	94	25
Hamilton	24	7	17	0	88	105	14

Leading Scorers

Player	Team	GP	G	A	PTS	PIM
Punch Broadbent	Ottawa	24	32	14	46	28
Cy Denneny	Ottawa	22	27	12	39	20
Babe Dye	Toronto	24	31	7	38	39
Harry Cameron	Toronto	24	18	17	35	22
Joe Malone	Hamilton	24	24	7	31	4
Corb Denneny	Toronto	24	19	9	28	28
Reg Noble	Toronto	24	17	11	28	19
Sprague Cleghorn	Montreal	24	17	9	26	80
George Boucher	Ottawa	23	13	12	25	12
Odie Cleghorn	Montreal	23	21	3	24	26

1922-23

Team	GP	W	L	T	GF	GA	PTS
*Ottawa	24	14	9	1	77	54	29
Montreal	24	13	9	2	73	61	28
Toronto	24	13	10	1	82	88	27
Hamilton	24	6	18	0	81	110	12

Leading Scorers

Player	Team	GP	G	A	PTS	PIM
Babe Dye	Toronto	22	26	11	37	19
Cy Denneny	Ottawa	24	23	11	34	28
Billy Boucher	Montreal	24	24	7	31	55
Jack Adams	Toronto	23	19	9	28	42
Mickey Roach	Hamilton	24	17	10	27	8
Odie Cleghorn	Montreal	24	19	6	25	18
George Boucher	Ottawa	24	14	9	23	58
Reg Noble	Toronto	24	12	11	23	47
Cully Wilson	Hamilton	23	16	5	21	46
Aurel Joliat	Montreal	24	12	9	21	37

1923-24

Team	GP	W	L	T	GF	GA	PTS
Ottawa	24	16	8	0	74	54	32
*Montreal	24	13	11	0	59	48	26
Toronto	24	10	14	0	59	85	20
Hamilton	24	9	15	0	63	68	18

Leading Scorers

Player	Team	GP	G	A	PTS	PIM
Cy Denneny	Ottawa	22	22	2	24	10
George Boucher	Ottawa	21	13	10	23	38
Billy Boucher	Montreal	23	16	6	22	48
Billy Burch	Hamilton	24	16	6	22	6
Aurel Joliat	Montreal	24	15	5	20	27
Babe Dye	Toronto	19	16	3	19	23
Jack Adams	Toronto	22	14	4	18	51
Reg Noble	Toronto	24	12	5	17	79
Frank Nighbor	Ottawa	20	11	6	17	16
Howie Morenz	Montreal	24	13	3	16	20
King Clancy	Ottawa	24	8	8	16	26

1924-25

Team	GP	W	L	T	GF	GA	PTS
Hamilton	30	19	10	1	90	60	39
Toronto	30	19	11	0	90	84	38
• Montreal	30	17	11	2	93	56	36
Ottawa	30	17	12	1	83	66	35
Mtl. Maroons	30	9	19	2	45	65	20
Boston	30	6	24	0	49	119	12

• NHL Champion (Stanley Cup won by Victoria Cougars, WCHL)

Leading Scorers

Player	Team	GP	G	A	PTS	PIM
Babe Dye	Toronto	29	38	8	46	41
Cy Denneny	Ottawa	29	27	15	42	16
Aurel Joliat	Montreal	25	30	11	41	85
Howie Morenz	Montreal	30	28	11	39	46
Red Green	Hamilton	30	19	15	34	81
Jack Adams	Toronto	27	21	10	31	67
Billy Boucher	Montreal	30	17	13	30	92
Billy Burch	Hamilton	27	20	7	27	10
Jimmy Herberts	Boston	30	17	7	24	55
Hooley Smith	Ottawa	30	10	13	23	81

1925-26

Team	GP	W	L	T	GF	GA	PTS
Ottawa	36	24	8	4	77	42	52
*Mtl. Maroons	36	20	11	5	91	73	45
Pittsburgh	36	19	16	1	82	70	39
Boston	36	17	15	4	92	85	38
NY Americans	36	12	20	4	68	89	28
Toronto	36	12	21	3	92	114	27
Montreal	36	11	24	1	79	108	23

Leading Scorers

Player	Team	GP	G	A	PTS	PIM
Nels Stewart	Mtl. Maroons	36	34	8	42	119
Cy Denneny	Ottawa	36	24	12	36	18
Carson Cooper	Boston	36	28	3	31	10
Jimmy Herberts	Boston	36	26	5	31	47
Howie Morenz	Montreal	31	23	3	26	39
Jack Adams	Toronto	36	21	5	26	52
Aurel Joliat	Montreal	35	17	9	26	52
Billy Burch	NY Americans	36	22	3	25	33
Hooley Smith	Ottawa	28	16	9	25	53
Frank Nighbor	Ottawa	35	12	13	25	40

1926-27

Canadian Division

Team	GP	W	L	T	GF	GA	PTS
*Ottawa	44	30	10	4	86	69	64
Montreal	44	28	14	2	99	67	58
Mtl. Maroons	44	20	20	4	71	68	44
NY Americans	44	17	25	2	82	91	36
Toronto	44	15	24	5	79	94	35

American Division

Team	GP	W	L	T	GF	GA	PTS
NY Rangers	44	25	13	6	95	72	56
Boston	44	21	20	3	97	89	45
Chicago	44	19	22	3	115	116	41
Pittsburgh	44	15	26	3	79	108	33
Detroit	44	12	28	4	76	105	28

Leading Scorers

Player	Team	GP	G	A	PTS	PIM
Bill Cook	NY Rangers	44	33	4	37	58
Dick Irvin	Chicago	43	18	18	36	34
Howie Morenz	Montreal	44	25	7	32	49
Frank Fredrickson	Det., Bos.	41	18	13	31	46
Babe Dye	Chicago	41	25	5	30	14
Ace Bailey	Toronto	42	15	13	28	82
Frank Boucher	NY Rangers	44	13	15	28	17
Billy Burch	NY Americans	43	19	8	27	40
Harry Oliver	Boston	42	18	6	24	17
Duke Keats	Bos., Det.	42	16	8	24	52

1927-28

Canadian Division

Team	GP	W	L	T	GF	GA	PTS
Montreal	44	26	11	7	116	48	59
Mtl. Maroons	44	24	14	6	96	77	54
Ottawa	44	20	14	10	78	57	50
Toronto	44	18	18	8	89	88	44
NY Americans	44	11	27	6	63	128	28

American Division

Team	GP	W	L	T	GF	GA	PTS
Boston	44	20	13	11	77	70	51
*NY Rangers	44	19	16	9	94	79	47
Pittsburgh	44	19	17	8	67	76	46
Detroit	44	19	19	6	88	79	44
Chicago	44	7	34	3	68	134	17

Leading Scorers

Player	Team	GP	G	A	PTS	PIM
Howie Morenz	Montreal	43	33	18	51	66
Aurel Joliat	Montreal	44	28	11	39	105
Frank Boucher	NY Rangers	44	23	12	35	15
George Hay	Detroit	42	22	13	35	20
Nels Stewart	Mtl. Maroons	41	27	7	34	104
Art Gagne	Montreal	44	20	10	30	75
Bun Cook	NY Rangers	44	14	14	28	45
Bill Carson	Toronto	32	20	6	26	36
Frank Finnigan	Ottawa	38	20	5	25	34
Bill Cook	NY Rangers	43	18	6	24	42
Duke Keats	Det., Chi.	38	14	10	24	60

1928-29

Canadian Division

Team	GP	W	L	T	GF	GA	PTS
Montreal	44	22	7	15	71	43	59
NY Americans	44	19	13	12	53	53	50
Toronto	44	21	18	5	85	69	47
Ottawa	44	14	17	13	54	67	41
Mtl. Maroons	44	15	20	9	67	65	39

American Division

Team	GP	W	L	T	GF	GA	PTS
*Boston	44	26	13	5	89	52	57
NY Rangers	44	21	13	10	72	65	52
Detroit	44	19	16	9	72	63	47
Pittsburgh	44	9	27	8	46	80	26
Chicago	44	7	29	8	33	85	22

Leading Scorers

Player	Team	GP	G	A	PTS	PIM
Ace Bailey	Toronto	44	22	10	32	78
Nels Stewart	Mtl. Maroons	44	21	8	29	74
Carson Cooper	Detroit	43	18	9	27	14
Howie Morenz	Montreal	42	17	10	27	47
Andy Blair	Toronto	44	12	15	27	41
Frank Boucher	NY Rangers	44	10	16	26	8
Harry Oliver	Boston	43	17	6	23	24
Bill Cook	NY Rangers	43	15	8	23	41
Jimmy Ward	Mtl. Maroons	43	14	8	22	46

Seven players tied with 19 points

1929-30

Canadian Division

Team	GP	W	L	T	GF	GA	PTS
Mtl. Maroons	44	23	16	5	141	114	51
*Montreal	44	21	14	9	142	114	51
Ottawa	44	21	15	8	138	118	50
Toronto	44	17	21	6	116	124	40
NY Americans	44	14	25	5	113	161	33

American Division

Team	GP	W	L	T	GF	GA	PTS
Boston	44	38	5	1	179	98	77
Chicago	44	21	18	5	117	111	47
NY Rangers	44	17	17	10	136	143	44
Detroit	44	14	24	6	117	133	34
Pittsburgh	44	5	36	3	102	185	13

Leading Scorers

Player	Team	GP	G	A	PTS	PIM
Cooney Weiland	Boston	44	43	30	73	27
Frank Boucher	NY Rangers	42	26	36	62	16
Dit Clapper	Boston	44	41	20	61	48
Bill Cook	NY Rangers	44	29	30	59	56
Hec Kilrea	Ottawa	44	36	22	58	72
Nels Stewart	Mtl. Maroons	44	39	16	55	81
Howie Morenz	Montreal	44	40	10	50	72
Normie Himes	NY Americans	44	28	22	50	15
Joe Lamb	Ottawa	44	29	20	49	119
Dutch Gainor	Boston	42	18	31	49	39

1930-31

Canadian Division

Team	GP	W	L	T	GF	GA	PTS
*Montreal	44	26	10	8	129	89	60
Toronto	44	22	13	9	118	99	53
Mtl. Maroons	44	20	18	6	105	106	46
NY Americans	44	18	16	10	76	74	46
Ottawa	44	10	30	4	91	142	24

American Division

Team	GP	W	L	T	GF	GA	PTS
Boston	44	28	10	6	143	90	62
Chicago	44	24	17	3	108	78	51
NY Rangers	44	19	16	9	106	87	47
Detroit	44	16	21	7	102	105	39
Philadelphia	44	4	36	4	76	184	12

Leading Scorers

Player	Team	GP	G	A	PTS	PIM
Howie Morenz	Montreal	39	28	23	51	49
Ebbie Goodfellow	Detroit	44	25	23	48	32
Charlie Conacher	Toronto	37	31	12	43	78
Bill Cook	NY Rangers	43	30	12	42	39
Ace Bailey	Toronto	40	23	19	42	46
Joe Primeau	Toronto	38	9	32	41	18
Nels Stewart	Mtl. Maroons	42	25	14	39	75
Frank Boucher	NY Rangers	44	12	27	39	20
Cooney Weiland	Boston	44	25	13	38	14
Bun Cook	NY Rangers	44	18	17	35	72
Aurel Joliat	Montreal	43	13	22	35	73

1931-32

Canadian Division

Team	GP	W	L	T	GF	GA	PTS
Montreal	48	25	16	7	128	111	57
*Toronto	48	23	18	7	155	127	53
Mtl. Maroons	48	19	22	7	142	139	45
NY Americans	48	16	24	8	95	142	40

American Division

Team	GP	W	L	T	GF	GA	PTS
NY Rangers	48	23	17	8	134	112	54
Chicago	48	18	19	11	86	101	47
Detroit	48	18	20	10	95	108	46
Boston	48	15	21	12	122	117	42

Leading Scorers

Player	Team	GP	G	A	PTS	PIM
Busher Jackson	Toronto	48	28	25	53	63
Joe Primeau	Toronto	46	13	37	50	25
Howie Morenz	Montreal	48	24	25	49	46
Charlie Conacher	Toronto	44	34	14	48	66
Bill Cook	NY Rangers	48	34	14	48	33
Dave Trottier	Mtl. Maroons	48	26	18	44	94
Hooley Smith	Mtl. Maroons	43	11	33	44	49
Babe Siebert	Mtl. Maroons	48	21	18	39	64
Dit Clapper	Boston	48	17	22	39	21
Aurel Joliat	Montreal	48	15	24	39	46

1932-33

Canadian Division

Team	GP	W	L	T	GF	GA	PTS
Toronto	48	24	18	6	119	111	54
Mtl. Maroons	48	22	20	6	135	119	50
Montreal	48	18	25	5	92	115	41
NY Americans	48	15	22	11	91	118	41
Ottawa	48	11	27	10	88	131	32

American Division

Team	GP	W	L	T	GF	GA	PTS
Boston	48	25	15	8	124	88	58
Detroit	48	25	15	8	111	93	58
*NY Rangers	48	23	17	8	135	107	54
Chicago	48	16	20	12	88	101	44

Leading Scorers

Player	Team	GP	G	A	PTS	PIM
Bill Cook	NY Rangers	48	28	22	50	51
Busher Jackson	Toronto	48	27	17	44	43
Baldy Northcott	Mtl. Maroons	48	22	21	43	30
Hooley Smith	Mtl. Maroons	48	20	21	41	66
Paul Haynes	Mtl. Maroons	48	16	25	41	18
Aurel Joliat	Montreal	48	18	21	39	53
Marty Barry	Boston	48	24	13	37	40
Bun Cook	NY Rangers	48	22	15	37	35
Nels Stewart	Boston	47	18	18	36	62
Howie Morenz	Montreal	46	14	21	35	32
Johnny Gagnon	Montreal	48	12	23	35	64
Eddie Shore	Boston	48	8	27	35	102
Frank Boucher	NY Rangers	46	7	28	35	4

1933-34

Canadian Division

Team	GP	W	L	T	GF	GA	PTS
Toronto	48	26	13	9	174	119	61
Montreal	48	22	20	6	99	101	50
Mtl. Maroons	48	19	18	11	117	122	49
NY Americans	48	15	23	10	104	132	40
Ottawa	48	13	29	6	115	143	32

American Division

Team	GP	W	L	T	GF	GA	PTS
Detroit	48	24	14	10	113	98	58
*Chicago	48	20	17	11	88	83	51
NY Rangers	48	21	19	8	120	113	50
Boston	48	18	25	5	111	130	41

Leading Scorers

Player	Team	GP	G	A	PTS	PIM
Charlie Conacher	Toronto	42	32	20	52	38
Joe Primeau	Toronto	45	14	32	46	8
Frank Boucher	NY Rangers	48	14	30	44	4
Marty Barry	Boston	48	27	12	39	12
Cecil Dillon	NY Rangers	48	13	26	39	10
Nels Stewart	Boston	48	21	17	38	68
Busher Jackson	Toronto	38	20	18	38	38
Aurel Joliat	Montreal	48	22	15	37	27
Hooley Smith	Mtl. Maroons	47	18	19	37	58
Paul Thompson	Chicago	48	20	16	36	17

1934-35

Canadian Division

Team	GP	W	L	T	GF	GA	PTS
Toronto	48	30	14	4	157	111	64
*Mtl. Maroons	48	24	19	5	123	92	53
Montreal	48	19	23	6	110	145	44
NY Americans	48	12	27	9	100	142	33
St. Louis	48	11	31	6	86	144	28

American Division

Team	GP	W	L	T	GF	GA	PTS
Boston	48	26	16	6	129	112	58
Chicago	48	26	17	5	118	88	57
NY Rangers	48	22	20	6	137	139	50
Detroit	48	19	22	7	127	114	45

Leading Scorers

Player	Team	GP	G	A	PTS	PIM
Charlie Conacher	Toronto	47	36	21	57	24
Syd Howe	St.L., Det.	50	22	25	47	34
Larry Aurie	Detroit	48	17	29	46	24
Frank Boucher	NY Rangers	48	13	32	45	2
Busher Jackson	Toronto	42	22	22	44	27
Herbie Lewis	Detroit	47	16	27	43	26
Art Chapman	NY Americans	47	9	34	43	4
Marty Barry	Boston	48	20	20	40	33
Sweeney Schriner	NY Americans	48	18	22	40	6
Nels Stewart	Boston	47	21	18	39	45
Paul Thompson	Chicago	48	16	23	39	20

1935-36

Canadian Division

Team	GP	W	L	T	GF	GA	PTS
Mtl. Maroons	48	22	16	10	114	106	54
Toronto	48	23	19	6	126	106	52
NY Americans	48	16	25	7	109	122	39
Montreal	48	11	26	11	82	123	33

American Division

Team	GP	W	L	T	GF	GA	PTS
*Detroit	48	24	16	8	124	103	56
Boston	48	22	20	6	92	83	50
Chicago	48	21	19	8	93	92	50
NY Rangers	48	19	17	12	91	96	50

Leading Scorers

Player	Team	GP	G	A	PTS	PIM
Sweeney Schriner	NY Americans	48	19	26	45	8
Marty Barry	Detroit	48	21	19	40	16
Paul Thompson	Chicago	45	17	23	40	19
Bill Thoms	Toronto	48	23	15	38	29
Charlie Conacher	Toronto	44	23	15	38	74
Hooley Smith	Mtl. Maroons	47	19	19	38	75
Doc Romnes	Chicago	48	13	25	38	6
Art Chapman	NY Americans	47	10	28	38	14
Herbie Lewis	Detroit	45	14	23	37	25
Baldy Northcott	Mtl. Maroons	48	15	21	36	41

1936-37

Canadian Division

Team	GP	W	L	T	GF	GA	PTS
Montreal	48	24	18	6	115	111	54
Mtl. Maroons	48	22	17	9	126	110	53
Toronto	48	22	21	5	119	115	49
NY Americans	48	15	29	4	122	161	34

American Division

Team	GP	W	L	T	GF	GA	PTS
*Detroit	48	25	14	9	128	102	59
Boston	48	23	18	7	120	110	53
NY Rangers	48	19	20	9	117	106	47
Chicago	48	14	27	7	99	131	35

Leading Scorers

Player	Team	GP	G	A	PTS	PIM
Sweeney Schriner	NY Americans	48	21	25	46	17
Syl Apps	Toronto	48	16	29	45	10
Marty Barry	Detroit	48	17	27	44	6
Larry Aurie	Detroit	45	23	20	43	20
Busher Jackson	Toronto	46	21	19	40	12
Johnny Gagnon	Montreal	48	20	16	36	38
Bob Gracie	Mtl. Maroons	47	11	25	36	18
Nels Stewart	Bos., NYA	43	23	12	35	37
Paul Thompson	Chicago	47	17	18	35	28
Bill Cowley	Boston	46	13	22	35	4

1937-38

Canadian Division

Team	GP	W	L	T	GF	GA	PTS
Toronto	48	24	15	9	151	127	57
NY Americans	48	19	18	11	110	111	49
Montreal	48	18	17	13	123	128	49
Mtl. Maroons	48	12	30	6	101	149	30

American Division

Team	GP	W	L	T	GF	GA	PTS
Boston	48	30	11	7	142	89	67
NY Rangers	48	27	15	6	149	96	60
*Chicago	48	14	25	9	97	139	37
Detroit	48	12	25	11	99	133	35

Leading Scorers

Player	Team	GP	G	A	PTS	PIM
Gordie Drillon	Toronto	48	26	26	52	4
Syl Apps	Toronto	47	21	29	50	9
Paul Thompson	Chicago	48	22	22	44	14
Georges Mantha	Montreal	47	23	19	42	12
Cecil Dillon	NY Rangers	48	21	18	39	6
Bill Cowley	Boston	48	17	22	39	8
Sweeney Schriner	NY Americans	49	21	17	38	22
Bill Thoms	Toronto	48	14	24	38	14
Clint Smith	NY Rangers	48	14	23	37	0
Nels Stewart	NY Americans	48	19	17	36	29
Neil Colville	NY Rangers	45	17	19	36	11

1938-39

Team	GP	W	L	T	GF	GA	PTS
*Boston	48	36	10	2	156	76	74
NY Rangers	48	26	16	6	149	105	58
Toronto	48	19	20	9	114	107	47
NY Americans	48	17	21	10	119	157	44
Detroit	48	18	24	6	107	128	42
Montreal	48	15	24	9	115	146	39
Chicago	48	12	28	8	91	132	32

Leading Scorers

Player	Team	GP	G	A	PTS	PIM
Toe Blake	Montreal	48	24	23	47	10
Sweeney Schriner	NY Americans	48	13	31	44	20
Bill Cowley	Boston	34	8	34	42	2
Clint Smith	NY Rangers	48	21	20	41	2
Marty Barry	Detroit	48	13	28	41	4
Syl Apps	Toronto	44	15	25	40	4
Tom Anderson	NY Americans	48	13	27	40	14
Johnny Gottselig	Chicago	48	16	23	39	15
Paul Haynes	Montreal	47	5	33	38	27
Roy Conacher	Boston	47	26	11	37	12
Lorne Carr	NY Americans	46	19	18	37	16
Neil Colville	NY Rangers	48	18	19	37	12
Phil Watson	NY Rangers	48	15	22	37	42

1939-40

Team	GP	W	L	T	GF	GA	PTS
Boston	48	31	12	5	170	98	67
*NY Rangers	48	27	11	10	136	77	64
Toronto	48	25	17	6	134	110	56
Chicago	48	23	19	6	112	120	52
Detroit	48	16	26	6	90	126	38
NY Americans	48	15	29	4	106	140	34
Montreal	48	10	33	5	90	167	25

Leading Scorers

Player	Team	GP	G	A	PTS	PIM
Milt Schmidt	Boston	48	22	30	52	37
Woody Dumart	Boston	48	22	21	43	16
Bobby Bauer	Boston	48	17	26	43	2
Gordie Drillon	Toronto	43	21	19	40	13
Bill Cowley	Boston	48	13	27	40	24
Bryan Hextall	NY Rangers	48	24	15	39	52
Neil Colville	NY Rangers	48	19	19	38	22
Syd Howe	Detroit	46	14	23	37	17
Toe Blake	Montreal	48	17	19	36	48
Murray Armstrong	NY Americans	48	16	20	36	12

1940-41

Team	GP	W	L	T	GF	GA	PTS
*Boston	48	27	8	13	168	102	67
Toronto	48	28	14	6	145	99	62
Detroit	48	21	16	11	112	102	53
NY Rangers	48	21	19	8	143	125	50
Chicago	48	16	25	7	112	139	39
Montreal	48	16	26	6	121	147	38
NY Americans	48	8	29	11	99	186	27

Leading Scorers

Player	Team	GP	G	A	PTS	PIM
Bill Cowley	Boston	46	17	45	62	16
Bryan Hextall	NY Rangers	48	26	18	44	16
Gordie Drillon	Toronto	42	23	21	44	2
Syl Apps	Toronto	41	20	24	44	6
Lynn Patrick	NY Rangers	48	20	24	44	12
Syd Howe	Detroit	48	20	24	44	8
Neil Colville	NY Rangers	48	14	28	42	28
Eddie Wiseman	Boston	48	16	24	40	10
Bobby Bauer	Boston	48	17	22	39	2
Sweeney Schriner	Toronto	48	24	14	38	6
Roy Conacher	Boston	40	24	14	38	7
Milt Schmidt	Boston	44	13	25	38	23

1941-42

Team	GP	W	L	T	GF	GA	PTS
NY Rangers	48	29	17	2	177	143	60
*Toronto	48	27	18	3	158	136	57
Boston	48	25	17	6	160	118	56
Chicago	48	22	23	3	145	155	47
Detroit	48	19	25	4	140	147	42
Montreal	48	18	27	3	134	173	39
Brooklyn	48	16	29	3	133	175	35

Leading Scorers

Player	Team	GP	G	A	PTS	PIM
Bryan Hextall	NY Rangers	48	24	32	56	30
Lynn Patrick	NY Rangers	47	32	22	54	18
Don Grosso	Detroit	48	23	30	53	13
Phil Watson	NY Rangers	48	15	37	52	48
Sid Abel	Detroit	48	18	31	49	45
Toe Blake	Montreal	47	17	28	45	19
Bill Thoms	Chicago	47	15	30	45	8
Gordie Drillon	Toronto	48	23	18	41	6
Syl Apps	Toronto	38	18	23	41	0
Tom Anderson	Brooklyn	48	12	29	41	54

1942-43

Team	GP	W	L	T	GF	GA	PTS
*Detroit	50	25	14	11	169	124	61
Boston	50	24	17	9	195	176	57
Toronto	50	22	19	9	198	159	53
Montreal	50	19	19	12	181	191	50
Chicago	50	17	18	15	179	180	49
NY Rangers	50	11	31	8	161	253	30

Leading Scorers

Player	Team	GP	G	A	PTS	PIM
Doug Bentley	Chicago	50	33	40	73	18
Bill Cowley	Boston	48	27	45	72	10
Max Bentley	Chicago	47	26	44	70	2
Lynn Patrick	NY Rangers	50	22	39	61	28
Lorne Carr	Toronto	50	27	33	60	15
Billy Taylor	Toronto	50	18	42	60	2
Bryan Hextall	NY Rangers	50	27	32	59	28
Toe Blake	Montreal	48	23	36	59	28
Elmer Lach	Montreal	45	18	40	58	14
Buddy O'Connor	Montreal	50	15	43	58	2

1943-44

Team	GP	W	L	T	GF	GA	PTS
*Montreal	50	38	5	7	234	109	83
Detroit	50	26	18	6	214	177	58
Toronto	50	23	23	4	214	174	50
Chicago	50	22	23	5	178	187	49
Boston	50	19	26	5	223	268	43
NY Rangers	50	6	39	5	162	310	17

Leading Scorers

Player	Team	GP	G	A	PTS	PIM
Herb Cain	Boston	48	36	46	82	4
Doug Bentley	Chicago	50	38	39	77	22
Lorne Carr	Toronto	50	36	38	74	9
Carl Liscombe	Detroit	50	36	37	73	17
Elmer Lach	Montreal	48	24	48	72	23
Clint Smith	Chicago	50	23	49	72	4
Bill Cowley	Boston	36	30	41	71	12
Bill Mosienko	Chicago	50	32	38	70	10
Art Jackson	Boston	49	28	41	69	8
Gus Bodnar	Toronto	50	22	40	62	18

1944-45

Team	GP	W	L	T	GF	GA	PTS
Montreal	50	38	8	4	228	121	80
Detroit	50	31	14	5	218	161	67
*Toronto	50	24	22	4	183	161	52
Boston	50	16	30	4	179	219	36
Chicago	50	13	30	7	141	194	33
NY Rangers	50	11	29	10	154	247	32

Leading Scorers

Player	Team	GP	G	A	PTS	PIM
Elmer Lach	Montreal	50	26	54	80	37
Maurice Richard	Montreal	50	50	23	73	36
Toe Blake	Montreal	49	29	38	67	15
Bill Cowley	Boston	49	25	40	65	2
Ted Kennedy	Toronto	49	29	25	54	14
Bill Mosienko	Chicago	50	28	26	54	0
Joe Carveth	Detroit	50	26	28	54	6
Ab DeMarco	NY Rangers	50	24	30	54	10
Clint Smith	Chicago	50	23	31	54	0
Syd Howe	Detroit	46	17	36	53	6

1945-46

Team	GP	W	L	T	GF	GA	PTS
*Montreal	50	28	17	5	172	134	61
Boston	50	24	18	8	167	156	56
Chicago	50	23	20	7	200	178	53
Detroit	50	20	20	10	146	159	50
Toronto	50	19	24	7	174	185	45
NY Rangers	50	13	28	9	144	191	35

Leading Scorers

Player	Team	GP	G	A	PTS	PIM
Max Bentley	Chicago	47	31	30	61	6
Gaye Stewart	Toronto	50	37	15	52	8
Toe Blake	Montreal	50	29	21	50	2
Clint Smith	Chicago	50	26	24	50	2
Maurice Richard	Montreal	50	27	21	48	50
Bill Mosienko	Chicago	40	18	30	48	12
Ab DeMarco	NY Rangers	50	20	27	47	20
Elmer Lach	Montreal	50	13	34	47	34
Alex Kaleta	Chicago	49	19	27	46	17
Billy Taylor	Toronto	48	23	18	41	14
Pete Horeck	Chicago	50	20	21	41	34

1946-47

Team	GP	W	L	T	GF	GA	PTS
Montreal	60	34	16	10	189	138	78
*Toronto	60	31	19	10	209	172	72
Boston	60	26	23	11	190	175	63
Detroit	60	22	27	11	190	193	55
NY Rangers	60	22	32	6	167	186	50
Chicago	60	19	37	4	193	274	42

Leading Scorers

Player	Team	GP	G	A	PTS	PIM
Max Bentley	Chicago	60	29	43	72	12
Maurice Richard	Montreal	60	45	26	71	69
Billy Taylor	Detroit	60	17	46	63	35
Milt Schmidt	Boston	59	27	35	62	40
Ted Kennedy	Toronto	60	28	32	60	27
Doug Bentley	Chicago	52	21	34	55	18
Bobby Bauer	Boston	58	30	24	54	4
Roy Conacher	Detroit	60	30	24	54	6
Bill Mosienko	Chicago	59	25	27	52	2
Woody Dumart	Boston	60	24	28	52	12

1947-48

Team	GP	W	L	T	GF	GA	PTS
*Toronto	60	32	15	13	182	143	77
Detroit	60	30	18	12	187	148	72
Boston	60	23	24	13	167	168	59
NY Rangers	60	21	26	13	176	201	55
Montreal	60	20	29	11	147	169	51
Chicago	60	20	34	6	195	225	46

Leading Scorers

Player	Team	GP	G	A	PTS	PIM
Elmer Lach	Montreal	60	30	31	61	72
Buddy O'Connor	NY Rangers	60	24	36	60	8
Doug Bentley	Chicago	60	20	37	57	16
Gaye Stewart	Tor., Chi.	61	27	29	56	83
Max Bentley	Chi., Tor.	59	26	28	54	14
Bud Poile	Tor., Chi.	58	25	29	54	17
Maurice Richard	Montreal	53	28	25	53	89
Syl Apps	Toronto	55	26	27	53	12
Ted Lindsay	Detroit	60	33	19	52	95
Roy Conacher	Chicago	52	22	27	49	4

1948-49

Team	GP	W	L	T	GF	GA	PTS
Detroit	60	34	19	7	195	145	75
Boston	60	29	23	8	178	163	66
Montreal	60	28	23	9	152	126	65
*Toronto	60	22	25	13	147	161	57
Chicago	60	21	31	8	173	211	50
NY Rangers	60	18	31	11	133	172	47

Leading Scorers

Player	Team	GP	G	A	PTS	PIM
Roy Conacher	Chicago	60	26	42	68	8
Doug Bentley	Chicago	58	23	43	66	38
Sid Abel	Detroit	60	28	26	54	49
Ted Lindsay	Detroit	50	26	28	54	97
Jim Conacher	Det., Chi.	59	26	23	49	43
Paul Ronty	Boston	60	20	29	49	11
Harry Watson	Toronto	60	26	19	45	0
Billy Reay	Montreal	60	22	23	45	33
Gus Bodnar	Chicago	59	19	26	45	14
Johnny Peirson	Boston	59	22	21	43	45

1949-50

Team	GP	W	L	T	GF	GA	PTS
*Detroit	70	37	19	14	229	164	88
Montreal	70	29	22	19	172	150	77
Toronto	70	31	27	12	176	173	74
NY Rangers	70	28	31	11	170	189	67
Boston	70	22	32	16	198	228	60
Chicago	70	22	38	10	203	244	54

Leading Scorers

Player	Team	GP	G	A	PTS	PIM
Ted Lindsay	Detroit	69	23	55	78	141
Sid Abel	Detroit	69	34	35	69	46
Gordie Howe	Detroit	70	35	33	68	69
Maurice Richard	Montreal	70	43	22	65	114
Paul Ronty	Boston	70	23	36	59	8
Roy Conacher	Chicago	70	25	31	56	16
Doug Bentley	Chicago	64	20	33	53	28
Johnny Peirson	Boston	57	27	25	52	49
Metro Prystai	Chicago	65	29	22	51	31
Bep Guidolin	Chicago	70	17	34	51	42

1950-51

Team	GP	W	L	T	GF	GA	PTS
Detroit	70	44	13	13	236	139	101
*Toronto	70	41	16	13	212	138	95
Montreal	70	25	30	15	173	184	65
Boston	70	22	30	18	178	197	62
NY Rangers	70	20	29	21	169	201	61
Chicago	70	13	47	10	171	280	36

Leading Scorers

Player	Team	GP	G	A	PTS	PIM
Gordie Howe	Detroit	70	43	43	86	74
Maurice Richard	Montreal	65	42	24	66	97
Max Bentley	Toronto	67	21	41	62	34
Sid Abel	Detroit	69	23	38	61	30
Milt Schmidt	Boston	62	22	39	61	33
Ted Kennedy	Toronto	63	18	43	61	32
Ted Lindsay	Detroit	67	24	35	59	110
Tod Sloan	Toronto	70	31	25	56	105
Red Kelly	Detroit	70	17	37	54	24
Sid Smith	Toronto	70	30	21	51	10
Cal Gardner	Toronto	66	23	28	51	42

1951-52

Team	GP	W	L	T	GF	GA	PTS
*Detroit	70	44	14	12	215	133	100
Montreal	70	34	26	10	195	164	78
Toronto	70	29	25	16	168	157	74
Boston	70	25	29	16	162	176	66
NY Rangers	70	23	34	13	192	219	59
Chicago	70	17	44	9	158	241	43

Leading Scorers

Player	Team	GP	G	A	PTS	PIM
Gordie Howe	Detroit	70	47	39	86	78
Ted Lindsay	Detroit	70	30	39	69	123
Elmer Lach	Montreal	70	15	50	65	36
Don Raleigh	NY Rangers	70	19	42	61	14
Sid Smith	Toronto	70	27	30	57	6
Bernie Geoffrion	Montreal	67	30	24	54	66
Bill Mosienko	Chicago	70	31	22	53	10
Sid Abel	Detroit	62	17	36	53	32
Ted Kennedy	Toronto	70	19	33	52	33
Milt Schmidt	Boston	69	21	29	50	57
Johnny Peirson	Boston	68	20	30	50	30

1952-53

Team	GP	W	L	T	GF	GA	PTS
Detroit	70	36	16	18	222	133	90
*Montreal	70	28	23	19	155	148	75
Boston	70	28	29	13	152	172	69
Chicago	70	27	28	15	169	175	69
Toronto	70	27	30	13	156	167	67
NY Rangers	70	17	37	16	152	211	50

Leading Scorers

Player	Team	GP	G	A	PTS	PIM
Gordie Howe	Detroit	70	49	46	95	57
Ted Lindsay	Detroit	70	32	39	71	111
Maurice Richard	Montreal	70	28	33	61	112
Wally Hergesheimer	NY Rangers	70	30	29	59	10
Alex Delvecchio	Detroit	70	16	43	59	28
Paul Ronty	NY Rangers	70	16	38	54	20
Metro Prystai	Detroit	70	16	34	50	12
Red Kelly	Detroit	70	19	27	46	8
Bert Olmstead	Montreal	69	17	28	45	83
Fleming Mackell	Boston	65	27	17	44	63
Jim McFadden	Chicago	70	23	21	44	29

1953-54

Team	GP	W	L	T	GF	GA	PTS
*Detroit	70	37	19	14	191	132	88
Montreal	70	35	24	11	195	141	81
Toronto	70	32	24	14	152	131	78
Boston	70	32	28	10	177	181	74
NY Rangers	70	29	31	10	161	182	68
Chicago	70	12	51	7	133	242	31

Leading Scorers

Player	Team	GP	G	A	PTS	PIM
Gordie Howe	Detroit	70	33	48	81	109
Maurice Richard	Montreal	70	37	30	67	112
Ted Lindsay	Detroit	70	26	36	62	110
Bernie Geoffrion	Montreal	54	29	25	54	87
Bert Olmstead	Montreal	70	15	37	52	85
Red Kelly	Detroit	62	16	33	49	18
Dutch Reibel	Detroit	69	15	33	48	18
Ed Sandford	Boston	70	16	31	47	42
Fleming Mackell	Boston	67	15	32	47	60
Ken Mosdell	Montreal	67	22	24	46	64
Paul Ronty	NY Rangers	70	13	33	46	18

1954-55

Team	GP	W	L	T	GF	GA	PTS
*Detroit	70	42	17	11	204	134	95
Montreal	70	41	18	11	228	157	93
Toronto	70	24	24	22	147	135	70
Boston	70	23	26	21	169	188	67
NY Rangers	70	17	35	18	150	210	52
Chicago	70	13	40	17	161	235	43

Leading Scorers

Player	Team	GP	G	A	PTS	PIM
Bernie Geoffrion	Montreal	70	38	37	75	57
Maurice Richard	Montreal	67	38	36	74	125
Jean Béliveau	Montreal	70	37	36	73	58
Dutch Reibel	Detroit	70	25	41	66	15
Gordie Howe	Detroit	64	29	33	62	68
Red Sullivan	Chicago	69	19	42	61	51
Bert Olmstead	Montreal	70	10	48	58	103
Sid Smith	Toronto	70	33	21	54	14
Ken Mosdell	Montreal	70	22	32	54	82
Danny Lewicki	NY Rangers	70	29	24	53	8

1955-56

Team	GP	W	L	T	GF	GA	PTS
*Montreal	70	45	15	10	222	131	100
Detroit	70	30	24	16	183	148	76
NY Rangers	70	32	28	10	204	203	74
Toronto	70	24	33	13	153	181	61
Boston	70	23	34	13	147	185	59
Chicago	70	19	39	12	155	216	50

Leading Scorers

Player	Team	GP	G	A	PTS	PIM
Jean Béliveau	Montreal	70	47	41	88	143
Gordie Howe	Detroit	70	38	41	79	100
Maurice Richard	Montreal	70	38	33	71	89
Bert Olmstead	Montreal	70	14	56	70	94
Tod Sloan	Toronto	70	37	29	66	100
Andy Bathgate	NY Rangers	70	19	47	66	59
Bernie Geoffrion	Montreal	59	29	33	62	66
Dutch Reibel	Detroit	68	17	39	56	10
Alex Delvecchio	Detroit	70	25	26	51	24
Dave Creighton	NY Rangers	70	20	31	51	43
Bill Gadsby	NY Rangers	70	9	42	51	84

1956-57

Team	GP	W	L	T	GF	GA	PTS
*Detroit	70	38	20	12	198	157	88
*Montreal	70	35	23	12	210	155	82
Boston	70	34	24	12	195	174	80
NY Rangers	70	26	30	14	184	227	66
Toronto	70	21	34	15	174	192	57
Chicago	70	16	39	15	169	225	47

Leading Scorers

Player	Team	GP	G	A	PTS	PIM
Gordie Howe	Detroit	70	44	45	89	72
Ted Lindsay	Detroit	70	30	55	85	103
Jean Béliveau	Montreal	69	33	51	84	105
Andy Bathgate	NY Rangers	70	27	50	77	60
Ed Litzenberger	Chicago	70	32	32	64	48
Maurice Richard	Montreal	63	33	29	62	74
Don McKenney	Boston	69	21	39	60	31
Dickie Moore	Montreal	70	29	29	58	56
Henri Richard	Montreal	63	18	36	54	71
Norm Ullman	Detroit	64	16	36	52	47

1957-58

Team	GP	W	L	T	GF	GA	PTS
*Montreal	70	43	17	10	250	158	96
NY Rangers	70	32	25	13	195	188	77
Detroit	70	29	29	12	176	207	70
Boston	70	27	28	15	199	194	69
Chicago	70	24	39	7	163	202	55
Toronto	70	21	38	11	192	226	53

Leading Scorers

Player	Team	GP	G	A	PTS	PIM
Dickie Moore	Montreal	70	36	48	84	65
Henri Richard	Montreal	67	28	52	80	56
Andy Bathgate	NY Rangers	65	30	48	78	42
Gordie Howe	Detroit	64	33	44	77	40
Bronco Horvath	Boston	67	30	36	66	71
Ed Litzenberger	Chicago	70	32	30	62	63
Fleming Mackell	Boston	70	20	40	60	72
Jean Béliveau	Montreal	55	27	32	59	93
Alex Delvecchio	Detroit	70	21	38	59	22
Don McKenney	Boston	70	28	30	58	22

1958-59

Team	GP	W	L	T	GF	GA	PTS
*Montreal	70	39	18	13	258	158	91
Boston	70	32	29	9	205	215	73
Chicago	70	28	29	13	197	208	69
Toronto	70	27	32	11	189	201	65
NY Rangers	70	26	32	12	201	217	64
Detroit	70	25	37	8	167	218	58

Leading Scorers

Player	Team	GP	G	A	PTS	PIM
Dickie Moore	Montreal	70	41	55	96	61
Jean Béliveau	Montreal	64	45	46	91	67
Andy Bathgate	NY Rangers	70	40	48	88	48
Gordie Howe	Detroit	70	32	46	78	57
Ed Litzenberger	Chicago	70	33	44	77	37
Bernie Geoffrion	Montreal	59	22	44	66	30
Red Sullivan	NY Rangers	70	21	42	63	56
Andy Hebenton	NY Rangers	70	33	29	62	8
Don McKenney	Boston	70	32	30	62	20
Tod Sloan	Chicago	59	27	35	62	79

1959-60

Team	GP	W	L	T	GF	GA	PTS
*Montreal	70	40	18	12	255	178	92
Toronto	70	35	26	9	199	195	79
Chicago	70	28	29	13	191	180	69
Detroit	70	26	29	15	186	197	67
Boston	70	28	34	8	220	241	64
NY Rangers	70	17	38	15	187	247	49

Leading Scorers

Player	Team	GP	G	A	PTS	PIM
Bobby Hull	Chicago	70	39	42	81	68
Bronco Horvath	Boston	68	39	41	80	60
Jean Béliveau	Montreal	60	34	40	74	57
Andy Bathgate	NY Rangers	70	26	48	74	28
Henri Richard	Montreal	70	30	43	73	66
Gordie Howe	Detroit	70	28	45	73	46
Bernie Geoffrion	Montreal	59	30	41	71	36
Don McKenney	Boston	70	20	49	69	28
Vic Stasiuk	Boston	69	29	39	68	121
Dean Prentice	NY Rangers	70	32	34	66	43

1960-61

Team	GP	W	L	T	GF	GA	PTS
Montreal	70	41	19	10	254	188	92
Toronto	70	39	19	12	234	176	90
*Chicago	70	29	24	17	198	180	75
Detroit	70	25	29	16	195	215	66
NY Rangers	70	22	38	10	204	248	54
Boston	70	15	42	13	176	254	43

Leading Scorers

Player	Team	GP	G	A	PTS	PIM
Bernie Geoffrion	Montreal	64	50	45	95	29
Jean Béliveau	Montreal	69	32	58	90	57
Frank Mahovlich	Toronto	70	48	36	84	131
Andy Bathgate	NY Rangers	70	29	48	77	22
Gordie Howe	Detroit	64	23	49	72	30
Norm Ullman	Detroit	70	28	42	70	34
Red Kelly	Toronto	64	20	50	70	12
Dickie Moore	Montreal	57	35	34	69	62
Henri Richard	Montreal	70	24	44	68	91
Alex Delvecchio	Detroit	70	27	35	62	26

1961-62

Team	GP	W	L	T	GF	GA	PTS
Montreal	70	42	14	14	259	166	98
*Toronto	70	37	22	11	232	180	85
Chicago	70	31	26	13	217	186	75
NY Rangers	70	26	32	12	195	207	64
Detroit	70	23	33	14	184	219	60
Boston	70	15	47	8	177	306	38

Leading Scorers

Player	Team	GP	G	A	PTS	PIM
Bobby Hull	Chicago	70	50	34	84	35
Andy Bathgate	NY Rangers	70	28	56	84	44
Gordie Howe	Detroit	70	33	44	77	54
Stan Mikita	Chicago	70	25	52	77	97
Frank Mahovlich	Toronto	70	33	38	71	87
Alex Delvecchio	Detroit	70	26	43	69	18
Ralph Backstrom	Montreal	66	27	38	65	29
Norm Ullman	Detroit	70	26	38	64	54
Bill Hay	Chicago	60	11	52	63	34
Claude Provost	Montreal	70	33	29	62	22

1962-63

Team	GP	W	L	T	GF	GA	PTS
*Toronto	70	35	23	12	221	180	82
Chicago	70	32	21	17	194	178	81
Montreal	70	28	19	23	225	183	79
Detroit	70	32	25	13	200	194	77
NY Rangers	70	22	36	12	211	233	56
Boston	70	14	39	17	198	281	45

Leading Scorers

Player	Team	GP	G	A	PTS	PIM
Gordie Howe	Detroit	70	38	48	86	100
Andy Bathgate	NY Rangers	70	35	46	81	54
Stan Mikita	Chicago	65	31	45	76	69
Frank Mahovlich	Toronto	67	36	37	73	56
Henri Richard	Montreal	67	23	50	73	57
Jean Béliveau	Montreal	69	18	49	67	68
John Bucyk	Boston	69	27	39	66	36
Alex Delvecchio	Detroit	70	20	44	64	8
Bobby Hull	Chicago	65	31	31	62	27
Murray Oliver	Boston	65	22	40	62	38

1963-64

Team	GP	W	L	T	GF	GA	PTS
Montreal	70	36	21	13	209	167	85
Chicago	70	36	22	12	218	169	84
*Toronto	70	33	25	12	192	172	78
Detroit	70	30	29	11	191	204	71
NY Rangers	70	22	38	10	186	242	54
Boston	70	18	40	12	170	212	48

Leading Scorers

Player	Team	GP	G	A	PTS	PIM
Stan Mikita	Chicago	70	39	50	89	146
Bobby Hull	Chicago	70	43	44	87	50
Jean Béliveau	Montreal	68	28	50	78	42
Andy Bathgate	NYR, Tor.	71	19	58	77	34
Gordie Howe	Detroit	69	26	47	73	70
Kenny Wharram	Chicago	70	39	32	71	18
Murray Oliver	Boston	70	24	44	68	41
Phil Goyette	NY Rangers	67	24	41	65	15
Rod Gilbert	NY Rangers	70	24	40	64	62
Dave Keon	Toronto	70	23	37	60	6

1964-65

Team	GP	W	L	T	GF	GA	PTS
Detroit	70	40	23	7	224	175	87
*Montreal	70	36	23	11	211	185	83
Chicago	70	34	28	8	224	176	76
Toronto	70	30	26	14	204	173	74
NY Rangers	70	20	38	12	179	246	52
Boston	70	21	43	6	166	253	48

Leading Scorers

Player	Team	GP	G	A	PTS	PIM
Stan Mikita	Chicago	70	28	59	87	154
Norm Ullman	Detroit	70	42	41	83	70
Gordie Howe	Detroit	70	29	47	76	104
Bobby Hull	Chicago	61	39	32	71	32
Alex Delvecchio	Detroit	68	25	42	67	16
Claude Provost	Montreal	70	27	37	64	28
Rod Gilbert	NY Rangers	70	25	36	61	52
Pierre Pilote	Chicago	68	14	45	59	162
John Bucyk	Boston	68	26	29	55	24
Ralph Backstrom	Montreal	70	25	30	55	41
Phil Esposito	Chicago	70	23	32	55	44

1965-66

Team	GP	W	L	T	GF	GA	PTS
*Montreal	70	41	21	8	239	173	90
Chicago	70	37	25	8	240	187	82
Toronto	70	34	25	11	208	187	79
Detroit	70	31	27	12	221	194	74
Boston	70	21	43	6	174	275	48
NY Rangers	70	18	41	11	195	261	47

Leading Scorers

Player	Team	GP	G	A	PTS	PIM
Bobby Hull	Chicago	65	54	43	97	70
Stan Mikita	Chicago	68	30	48	78	58
Bobby Rousseau	Montreal	70	30	48	78	20
Jean Béliveau	Montreal	67	29	48	77	50
Gordie Howe	Detroit	70	29	46	75	83
Norm Ullman	Detroit	70	31	41	72	35
Alex Delvecchio	Detroit	70	31	38	69	16
Bob Nevin	NY Rangers	69	29	33	62	10
Henri Richard	Montreal	62	22	39	61	47
Murray Oliver	Boston	70	18	42	60	30

1966-67

Team	GP	W	L	T	GF	GA	PTS
Chicago	70	41	17	12	264	170	94
Montreal	70	32	25	13	202	188	77
*Toronto	70	32	27	11	204	211	75
NY Rangers	70	30	28	12	188	189	72
Detroit	70	27	39	4	212	241	58
Boston	70	17	43	10	182	253	44

Leading Scorers

Player	Team	GP	G	A	PTS	PIM
Stan Mikita	Chicago	70	35	62	97	12
Bobby Hull	Chicago	66	52	28	80	52
Norm Ullman	Detroit	68	26	44	70	26
Kenny Wharram	Chicago	70	31	34	65	21
Gordie Howe	Detroit	69	25	40	65	53
Bobby Rousseau	Montreal	68	19	44	63	58
Phil Esposito	Chicago	69	21	40	61	40
Phil Goyette	NY Rangers	70	12	49	61	6
Doug Mohns	Chicago	61	25	35	60	58
Henri Richard	Montreal	65	21	34	55	28
Alex Delvecchio	Detroit	70	17	38	55	10

1967-68
East Division

Team	GP	W	L	T	GF	GA	PTS
*Montreal	74	42	22	10	236	167	94
NY Rangers	74	39	23	12	226	183	90
Boston	74	37	27	10	259	216	84
Chicago	74	32	26	16	212	222	80
Toronto	74	33	31	10	209	176	76
Detroit	74	27	35	12	245	257	66

West Division

Team	GP	W	L	T	GF	GA	PTS
Philadelphia	74	31	32	11	173	179	73
Los Angeles	74	31	33	10	200	224	72
St. Louis	74	27	31	16	177	191	70
Minnesota	74	27	32	15	191	226	69
Pittsburgh	74	27	34	13	195	216	67
Oakland	74	15	42	17	153	219	47

Leading Scorers

Player	Team	GP	G	A	PTS	PIM
Stan Mikita	Chicago	72	40	47	87	14
Phil Esposito	Boston	74	35	49	84	21
Gordie Howe	Detroit	74	39	43	82	53
Jean Ratelle	NY Rangers	74	32	46	78	18
Rod Gilbert	NY Rangers	73	29	48	77	12
Bobby Hull	Chicago	71	44	31	75	39
Norm Ullman	Det., Tor.	71	35	37	72	28
Alex Delvecchio	Detroit	74	22	48	70	14
John Bucyk	Boston	72	30	39	69	8
Kenny Wharram	Chicago	74	27	42	69	18

1968-69
East Division

Team	GP	W	L	T	GF	GA	PTS
*Montreal	76	46	19	11	271	202	103
Boston	76	42	18	16	303	221	100
NY Rangers	76	41	26	9	231	196	91
Toronto	76	35	26	15	234	217	85
Detroit	76	33	31	12	239	221	78
Chicago	76	34	33	9	280	246	77

West Division

Team	GP	W	L	T	GF	GA	PTS
St. Louis	76	37	25	14	204	157	88
Oakland	76	29	36	11	219	251	69
Philadelphia	76	20	35	21	174	225	61
Los Angeles	76	24	42	10	185	260	58
Pittsburgh	76	20	45	11	189	252	51
Minnesota	76	18	43	15	189	270	51

Leading Scorers

Player	Team	GP	G	A	PTS	PIM
Phil Esposito	Boston	74	49	77	126	79
Bobby Hull	Chicago	74	58	49	107	48
Gordie Howe	Detroit	76	44	59	103	58
Stan Mikita	Chicago	74	30	67	97	52
Ken Hodge	Boston	75	45	45	90	75
Yvan Cournoyer	Montreal	76	43	44	87	31
Alex Delvecchio	Detroit	72	25	58	83	8
Red Berenson	St. Louis	76	35	47	82	43
Jean Béliveau	Montreal	69	33	49	82	55
Frank Mahovlich	Detroit	76	49	29	78	38
Jean Ratelle	NY Rangers	75	32	46	78	26

1969-70
East Division

Team	GP	W	L	T	GF	GA	PTS
Chicago	76	45	22	9	250	170	99
*Boston	76	40	17	19	277	216	99
Detroit	76	40	21	15	246	199	95
NY Rangers	76	38	22	16	246	189	92
Montreal	76	38	22	16	244	201	92
Toronto	76	29	34	13	222	242	71

West Division

Team	GP	W	L	T	GF	GA	PTS
St. Louis	76	37	27	12	224	179	86
Pittsburgh	76	26	38	12	182	238	64
Minnesota	76	19	35	22	224	257	60
Oakland	76	22	40	14	169	243	58
Philadelphia	76	17	35	24	197	225	58
Los Angeles	76	14	52	10	168	290	38

Leading Scorers

Player	Team	GP	G	A	PTS	PIM
Bobby Orr	Boston	76	33	87	120	125
Phil Esposito	Boston	76	43	56	99	50
Stan Mikita	Chicago	76	39	47	86	50
Phil Goyette	St. Louis	72	29	49	78	16
Walt Tkaczuk	NY Rangers	76	27	50	77	38
Jean Ratelle	NY Rangers	75	32	42	74	28
Red Berenson	St. Louis	67	33	39	72	38
Jean-Paul Parise	Minnesota	74	24	48	72	72
Gordie Howe	Detroit	76	31	40	71	58
Frank Mahovlich	Detroit	74	38	32	70	59
Dave Balon	NY Rangers	76	33	37	70	100
John McKenzie	Boston	72	29	41	70	114

1970-71

East Division

Team	GP	W	L	T	GF	GA	PTS
Boston	78	57	14	7	399	207	121
NY Rangers	78	49	18	11	259	177	109
*Montreal	78	42	23	13	291	216	97
Toronto	78	37	33	8	248	211	82
Buffalo	78	24	39	15	217	291	63
Vancouver	78	24	46	8	229	296	56
Detroit	78	22	45	11	209	308	55

West Division

Team	GP	W	L	T	GF	GA	PTS
Chicago	78	49	20	9	277	184	107
St. Louis	78	34	25	19	223	208	87
Philadelphia	78	28	33	17	207	225	73
Minnesota	78	28	34	16	191	223	72
Los Angeles	78	25	40	13	239	303	63
Pittsburgh	78	21	37	20	221	240	62
California	78	20	53	5	199	320	45

Leading Scorers

Player	Team	GP	G	A	PTS	PIM
Phil Esposito	Boston	78	76	76	152	71
Bobby Orr	Boston	78	37	102	139	91
John Bucyk	Boston	78	51	65	116	8
Ken Hodge	Boston	78	43	62	105	113
Bobby Hull	Chicago	78	44	52	96	32
Norm Ullman	Toronto	73	34	51	85	24
Wayne Cashman	Boston	77	21	58	79	100
John McKenzie	Boston	65	31	46	77	120
Dave Keon	Toronto	76	38	38	76	4
Jean Béliveau	Montreal	70	25	51	76	40
Fred Stanfield	Boston	75	24	52	76	12

1971-72

East Division

Team	GP	W	L	T	GF	GA	PTS
*Boston	78	54	13	11	330	204	119
NY Rangers	78	48	17	13	317	192	109
Montreal	78	46	16	16	307	205	108
Toronto	78	33	31	14	209	208	80
Detroit	78	33	35	10	261	262	76
Buffalo	78	16	43	19	203	289	51
Vancouver	78	20	50	8	203	297	48

West Division

Team	GP	W	L	T	GF	GA	PTS
Chicago	78	46	17	15	256	166	107
Minnesota	78	37	29	12	212	191	86
St. Louis	78	28	39	11	208	247	67
Pittsburgh	78	26	38	14	220	258	66
Philadelphia	78	26	38	14	200	236	66
California	78	21	39	18	216	288	60
Los Angeles	78	20	49	9	206	305	49

Leading Scorers

Player	Team	GP	G	A	PTS	PIM
Phil Esposito	Boston	76	66	67	133	76
Bobby Orr	Boston	76	37	80	117	106
Jean Ratelle	NY Rangers	63	46	63	109	4
Vic Hadfield	NY Rangers	78	50	56	106	142
Rod Gilbert	NY Rangers	73	43	54	97	64
Frank Mahovlich	Montreal	76	43	53	96	36
Bobby Hull	Chicago	78	50	43	93	24
Yvan Cournoyer	Montreal	73	47	36	83	15
John Bucyk	Boston	78	32	51	83	4
Bobby Clarke	Philadelphia	78	35	46	81	87
Jacques Lemaire	Montreal	77	32	49	81	26

1972-73

East Division

Team	GP	W	L	T	GF	GA	PTS
*Montreal	78	52	10	16	329	184	120
Boston	78	51	22	5	330	235	107
NY Rangers	78	47	23	8	297	208	102
Buffalo	78	37	27	14	257	219	88
Detroit	78	37	29	12	265	243	86
Toronto	78	27	41	10	247	279	64
Vancouver	78	22	47	9	233	339	53
NY Islanders	78	12	60	6	170	347	30

West Division

Team	GP	W	L	T	GF	GA	PTS
Chicago	78	42	27	9	284	225	93
Philadelphia	78	37	30	11	296	256	85
Minnesota	78	37	30	11	254	230	85
St. Louis	78	32	34	12	233	251	76
Pittsburgh	78	32	37	9	257	265	73
Los Angeles	78	31	36	11	232	245	73
Atlanta	78	25	38	15	191	239	65
California	78	16	46	16	213	323	48

Leading Scorers

Player	Team	GP	G	A	PTS	PIM
Phil Esposito	Boston	78	55	75	130	87
Bobby Clarke	Philadelphia	78	37	67	104	80
Bobby Orr	Boston	63	29	72	101	99
Rick MacLeish	Philadelphia	78	50	50	100	69
Jacques Lemaire	Montreal	77	44	51	95	16
Jean Ratelle	NY Rangers	78	41	53	94	12
Mickey Redmond	Detroit	76	52	41	93	24
John Bucyk	Boston	78	40	53	93	12
Frank Mahovlich	Montreal	78	38	55	93	51
Jim Pappin	Chicago	76	41	51	92	82

1973-74

East Division

Team	GP	W	L	T	GF	GA	PTS
Boston	78	52	17	9	349	221	113
Montreal	78	45	24	9	293	240	99
NY Rangers	78	40	24	14	300	251	94
Toronto	78	35	27	16	274	230	86
Buffalo	78	32	34	12	242	250	76
Detroit	78	29	39	10	255	319	68
Vancouver	78	24	43	11	224	296	59
NY Islanders	78	19	41	18	182	247	56

West Division

Team	GP	W	L	T	GF	GA	PTS
*Philadelphia	78	50	16	12	273	164	112
Chicago	78	41	14	23	272	164	105
Los Angeles	78	33	33	12	233	231	78
Atlanta	78	30	34	14	214	238	74
Pittsburgh	78	28	41	9	242	273	65
St. Louis	78	26	40	12	206	248	64
Minnesota	78	23	38	17	235	275	63
California	78	13	55	10	195	342	36

Leading Scorers

Player	Team	GP	G	A	PTS	PIM
Phil Esposito	Boston	78	68	77	145	58
Bobby Orr	Boston	74	32	90	122	82
Ken Hodge	Boston	76	50	55	105	43
Wayne Cashman	Boston	78	30	59	89	111
Bobby Clarke	Philadelphia	77	35	52	87	113
Rick Martin	Buffalo	78	52	34	86	38
Syl Apps Jr.	Pittsburgh	75	24	61	85	37
Darryl Sittler	Toronto	78	38	46	84	55
Lowell MacDonald	Pittsburgh	78	43	39	82	14
Brad Park	NY Rangers	78	25	57	82	148
Dennis Hextall	Minnesota	78	20	62	82	138

1974-75

PRINCE OF WALES CONFERENCE

Norris Division

Team	GP	W	L	T	GF	GA	PTS
Montreal	80	47	14	19	374	225	113
Los Angeles	80	42	17	21	269	185	105
Pittsburgh	80	37	28	15	326	289	89
Detroit	80	23	45	12	259	335	58
Washington	80	8	67	5	181	446	21

Adams Division

Team	GP	W	L	T	GF	GA	PTS
Buffalo	80	49	16	15	354	240	113
Boston	80	40	26	14	345	245	94
Toronto	80	31	33	16	280	309	78
California	80	19	48	13	212	316	51

CLARENCE CAMPBELL CONFERENCE

Patrick Division

Team	GP	W	L	T	GF	GA	PTS
*Philadelphia	80	51	18	11	293	181	113
NY Rangers	80	37	29	14	319	276	88
NY Islanders	80	33	25	22	264	221	88
Atlanta	80	34	31	15	243	233	83

Smythe Division

Team	GP	W	L	T	GF	GA	PTS
Vancouver	80	38	32	10	271	254	86
St. Louis	80	35	31	14	269	267	84
Chicago	80	37	35	8	268	241	82
Minnesota	80	23	50	7	221	341	53
Kansas City	80	15	54	11	184	328	41

Leading Scorers

Player	Team	GP	G	A	PTS	PIM
Bobby Orr	Boston	80	46	89	135	101
Phil Esposito	Boston	79	61	66	127	62
Marcel Dionne	Detroit	80	47	74	121	14
Guy Lafleur	Montreal	70	53	66	119	37
Pete Mahovlich	Montreal	80	35	82	117	64
Bobby Clarke	Philadelphia	80	27	89	116	125
Rene Robert	Buffalo	74	40	60	100	75
Rod Gilbert	NY Rangers	76	36	61	97	22
Gilbert Perreault	Buffalo	68	39	57	96	36
Rick Martin	Buffalo	68	52	43	95	72

1975-76

PRINCE OF WALES CONFERENCE

Norris Division

Team	GP	W	L	T	GF	GA	PTS
*Montreal	80	58	11	11	337	174	127
Los Angeles	80	38	33	9	263	265	85
Pittsburgh	80	35	33	12	339	303	82
Detroit	80	26	44	10	226	300	62
Washington	80	11	59	10	224	394	32

Adams Division

Team	GP	W	L	T	GF	GA	PTS
Boston	80	48	15	17	313	237	113
Buffalo	80	46	21	13	339	240	105
Toronto	80	34	31	15	294	276	83
California	80	27	42	11	250	278	65

CLARENCE CAMPBELL CONFERENCE

Patrick Division

Team	GP	W	L	T	GF	GA	PTS
Philadelphia	80	51	13	16	348	209	118
NY Islanders	80	42	21	17	297	190	101
Atlanta	80	35	33	12	262	237	82
NY Rangers	80	29	42	9	262	333	67

Smythe Division

Team	GP	W	L	T	GF	GA	PTS
Chicago	80	32	30	18	254	261	82
Vancouver	80	33	32	15	271	272	81
St. Louis	80	29	37	14	249	290	72
Minnesota	80	20	53	7	195	303	47
Kansas City	80	12	56	12	190	351	36

Leading Scorers

Player	Team	GP	G	A	PTS	PIM
Guy Lafleur	Montreal	80	56	69	125	36
Bobby Clarke	Philadelphia	76	30	89	119	136
Gilbert Perreault	Buffalo	80	44	69	113	36
Bill Barber	Philadelphia	80	50	62	112	104
Pierre Larouche	Pittsburgh	76	53	58	111	33
Jean Ratelle	Bos., NYR	80	36	69	105	18
Pete Mahovlich	Montreal	80	34	71	105	76
Jean Pronovost	Pittsburgh	80	52	52	104	24
Darryl Sittler	Toronto	79	41	59	100	90
Syl Apps Jr.	Pittsburgh	80	32	67	99	24

1976-77

PRINCE OF WALES CONFERENCE

Norris Division

Team	GP	W	L	T	GF	GA	PTS
*Montreal	80	60	8	12	387	171	132
Los Angeles	80	34	31	15	271	241	83
Pittsburgh	80	34	33	13	240	252	81
Washington	80	24	42	14	221	307	62
Detroit	80	16	55	9	183	309	41

Adams Division

Team	GP	W	L	T	GF	GA	PTS
Boston	80	49	23	8	312	240	106
Buffalo	80	48	24	8	301	220	104
Toronto	80	33	32	15	301	285	81
Cleveland	80	25	42	13	240	292	63

CLARENCE CAMPBELL CONFERENCE

Patrick Division

Team	GP	W	L	T	GF	GA	PTS
Philadelphia	80	48	16	16	323	213	112
NY Islanders	80	47	21	12	288	193	106
Atlanta	80	34	34	12	264	265	80
NY Rangers	80	29	37	14	272	310	72

Smythe Division

Team	GP	W	L	T	GF	GA	PTS
St. Louis	80	32	39	9	239	276	73
Minnesota	80	23	39	18	240	310	64
Chicago	80	26	43	11	240	298	63
Vancouver	80	25	42	13	235	294	63
Colorado	80	20	46	14	226	307	54

Leading Scorers

Player	Team	GP	G	A	PTS	PIM
Guy Lafleur	Montreal	80	56	80	136	20
Marcel Dionne	Los Angeles	80	53	69	122	12
Steve Shutt	Montreal	80	60	45	105	28
Rick MacLeish	Philadelphia	79	49	48	97	42
Gilbert Perreault	Buffalo	80	39	56	95	30
Tim Young	Minnesota	80	29	66	95	58
Jean Ratelle	Boston	78	33	61	94	22
Lanny McDonald	Toronto	80	46	44	90	77
Darryl Sittler	Toronto	73	38	52	90	89
Bobby Clarke	Philadelphia	80	27	63	90	71

1977-78

PRINCE OF WALES CONFERENCE

Norris Division

Team	GP	W	L	T	GF	GA	PTS
*Montreal	80	59	10	11	359	183	129
Detroit	80	32	34	14	252	266	78
Los Angeles	80	31	34	15	243	245	77
Pittsburgh	80	25	37	18	254	321	68
Washington	80	17	49	14	195	321	48

Adams Division

Team	GP	W	L	T	GF	GA	PTS
Boston	80	51	18	11	333	218	113
Buffalo	80	44	19	17	288	215	105
Toronto	80	41	29	10	271	237	92
Cleveland	80	22	45	13	230	325	57

CLARENCE CAMPBELL CONFERENCE

Patrick Division

NY Islanders	80	48	17	15	334	210	111
Philadelphia	80	45	20	15	296	200	105
Atlanta	80	34	27	19	274	252	87
NY Rangers	80	30	37	13	279	280	73

Smythe Division

Chicago	80	32	29	19	230	220	83
Colorado	80	19	40	21	257	305	59
Vancouver	80	20	43	17	239	320	57
St. Louis	80	20	47	13	195	304	53
Minnesota	80	18	53	9	218	325	45

Leading Scorers

Player	Team	GP	G	A	PTS	PIM
Guy Lafleur	Montreal	78	60	72	132	26
Bryan Trottier	NY Islanders	77	46	77	123	46
Darryl Sittler	Toronto	80	45	72	117	100
Jacques Lemaire	Montreal	76	36	61	97	14
Denis Potvin	NY Islanders	80	30	64	94	81
Mike Bossy	NY Islanders	73	53	38	91	6
Terry O'Reilly	Boston	77	29	61	90	211
Gilbert Perreault	Buffalo	79	41	48	89	20
Bobby Clarke	Philadelphia	71	21	68	89	83
Lanny McDonald	Toronto	74	47	40	87	54
Wilf Paiement	Colorado	80	31	56	87	114

1978-79

PRINCE OF WALES CONFERENCE

Norris Division

Team	GP	W	L	T	GF	GA	PTS
*Montreal	80	52	17	11	337	204	115
Pittsburgh	80	36	31	13	281	279	85
Los Angeles	80	34	34	12	292	286	80
Washington	80	24	41	15	273	338	63
Detroit	80	23	41	16	252	295	62

Adams Division

Boston	80	43	23	14	316	270	100
Buffalo	80	36	28	16	280	263	88
Toronto	80	34	33	13	267	252	81
Minnesota	80	28	40	12	257	289	68

CLARENCE CAMPBELL CONFERENCE

Patrick Division

NY Islanders	80	51	15	14	358	214	116
Philadelphia	80	40	25	15	281	248	95
NY Rangers	80	40	29	11	316	292	91
Atlanta	80	41	31	8	327	280	90

Smythe Division

Chicago	80	29	36	15	244	277	73
Vancouver	80	25	42	13	217	291	63
St. Louis	80	18	50	12	249	348	48
Colorado	80	15	53	12	210	331	42

Leading Scorers

Player	Team	GP	G	A	PTS	PIM
Bryan Trottier	NY Islanders	76	47	87	134	50
Marcel Dionne	Los Angeles	80	59	71	130	30
Guy Lafleur	Montreal	80	52	77	129	28
Mike Bossy	NY Islanders	80	69	57	126	25
Bob MacMillan	Atlanta	79	37	71	108	14
Guy Chouinard	Atlanta	80	50	57	107	14
Denis Potvin	NY Islanders	73	31	70	101	58
Bernie Federko	St. Louis	74	31	64	95	14
Dave Taylor	Los Angeles	78	43	48	91	124
Clark Gillies	NY Islanders	75	35	56	91	68

1979-80

PRINCE OF WALES CONFERENCE

Norris Division

Team	GP	W	L	T	GF	GA	PTS
Montreal	80	47	20	13	328	240	107
Los Angeles	80	30	36	14	290	313	74
Pittsburgh	80	30	37	13	251	303	73
Hartford	80	27	34	19	303	312	73
Detroit	80	26	43	11	268	306	63

Adams Division

Buffalo	80	47	17	16	318	201	110
Boston	80	46	21	13	310	234	105
Minnesota	80	36	28	16	311	253	88
Toronto	80	35	40	5	304	327	75
Quebec	80	25	44	11	248	313	61

CLARENCE CAMPBELL CONFERENCE

Patrick Division

Philadelphia	80	48	12	20	327	254	116
*NY Islanders	80	39	28	13	281	247	91
NY Rangers	80	38	32	10	308	284	86
Atlanta	80	35	32	13	282	269	83
Washington	80	27	40	13	261	293	67

Smythe Division

Chicago	80	34	27	19	241	250	87
St. Louis	80	34	34	12	266	278	80
Vancouver	80	27	37	16	256	281	70
Edmonton	80	28	39	13	301	322	69
Winnipeg	80	20	49	11	214	314	51
Colorado	80	19	48	13	234	308	51

Leading Scorers

Player	Team	GP	G	A	PTS	PIM
Marcel Dionne	Los Angeles	80	53	84	137	32
Wayne Gretzky	Edmonton	79	51	86	137	21
Guy Lafleur	Montreal	74	50	75	125	12
Gilbert Perreault	Buffalo	80	40	66	106	57
Mike Rogers	Hartford	80	44	61	105	10
Bryan Trottier	NY Islanders	78	42	62	104	68
Charlie Simmer	Los Angeles	64	56	45	101	65
Blaine Stoughton	Hartford	80	56	44	100	16
Darryl Sittler	Toronto	73	40	57	97	62
Blair MacDonald	Edmonton	80	46	48	94	6
Bernie Federko	St. Louis	79	38	56	94	24

1980-81

PRINCE OF WALES CONFERENCE

Norris Division

Team	GP	W	L	T	GF	GA	PTS
Montreal	80	45	22	13	332	232	103
Los Angeles	80	43	24	13	337	290	99
Pittsburgh	80	30	37	13	302	345	73
Hartford	80	21	41	18	292	372	60
Detroit	80	19	43	18	252	339	56

Adams Division

Buffalo	80	39	20	21	327	250	99
Boston	80	37	30	13	316	272	87
Minnesota	80	35	28	17	291	263	87
Quebec	80	30	32	18	314	318	78
Toronto	80	28	37	15	322	367	71

CLARENCE CAMPBELL CONFERENCE

Patrick Division

*NY Islanders	80	48	18	14	355	260	110
Philadelphia	80	41	24	15	313	249	97
Calgary	80	39	27	14	329	298	92
NY Rangers	80	30	36	14	312	317	74
Washington	80	26	36	18	286	317	70

Smythe Division

St. Louis	80	45	18	17	352	281	107
Chicago	80	31	33	16	304	315	78
Vancouver	80	28	32	20	289	301	76
Edmonton	80	29	35	16	328	327	74
Colorado	80	22	45	13	258	344	57
Winnipeg	80	9	57	14	246	400	32

Leading Scorers

Player	Team	GP	G	A	PTS	PIM
Wayne Gretzky	Edmonton	80	55	109	164	28
Marcel Dionne	Los Angeles	80	58	77	135	70
Kent Nilsson	Calgary	80	49	82	131	26
Mike Bossy	NY Islanders	79	68	51	119	32
Dave Taylor	Los Angeles	72	47	65	112	130
Peter Stastny	Quebec	77	39	70	109	37
Charlie Simmer	Los Angeles	65	56	49	105	62
Mike Rogers	Hartford	80	40	65	105	32
Bernie Federko	St. Louis	78	31	73	104	47
Jacques Richard	Quebec	78	52	51	103	39
Rick Middleton	Boston	80	44	59	103	16
Bryan Trottier	NY Islanders	73	31	72	103	74

1981-82

CLARENCE CAMPBELL CONFERENCE

Norris Division

Team	GP	W	L	T	GF	GA	PTS
Minnesota	80	37	23	20	346	288	94
Winnipeg	80	33	33	14	319	332	80
St. Louis	80	32	40	8	315	349	72
Chicago	80	30	38	12	332	363	72
Toronto	80	20	44	16	298	380	56
Detroit	80	21	47	12	270	351	54

Smythe Division

Edmonton	80	48	17	15	417	295	111
Vancouver	80	30	33	17	290	286	77
Calgary	80	29	34	17	334	345	75
Los Angeles	80	24	41	15	314	369	63
Colorado	80	18	49	13	241	362	49

PRINCE OF WALES CONFERENCE

Adams Division

Montreal	80	46	17	17	360	223	109
Boston	80	43	27	10	323	285	96
Buffalo	80	39	26	15	307	273	93
Quebec	80	33	31	16	356	345	82
Hartford	80	21	41	18	264	351	60

Patrick Division

*NY Islanders	80	54	16	10	385	250	118
NY Rangers	80	39	27	14	316	306	92
Philadelphia	80	38	31	11	325	313	87
Pittsburgh	80	31	36	13	310	337	75
Washington	80	26	41	13	319	338	65

Leading Scorers

Player	Team	GP	G	A	PTS	PIM
Wayne Gretzky	Edmonton	80	92	120	212	26
Mike Bossy	NY Islanders	80	64	83	147	22
Peter Stastny	Quebec	80	46	93	139	91
Dennis Maruk	Washington	80	60	76	136	128
Bryan Trottier	NY Islanders	80	50	79	129	88
Denis Savard	Chicago	80	32	87	119	82
Marcel Dionne	Los Angeles	78	50	67	117	50
Bobby Smith	Minnesota	80	43	71	114	82
Dino Ciccarelli	Minnesota	76	55	51	106	138
Dave Taylor	Los Angeles	78	39	67	106	130

1982-83

CLARENCE CAMPBELL CONFERENCE

Norris Division

Team	GP	W	L	T	GF	GA	PTS
Chicago	80	47	23	10	338	268	104
Minnesota	80	40	24	16	321	290	96
Toronto	80	28	40	12	293	330	68
St. Louis	80	25	40	15	285	316	65
Detroit	80	21	44	15	263	344	57

Smythe Division

Edmonton	80	47	21	12	424	315	106
Calgary	80	32	34	14	321	317	78
Vancouver	80	30	35	15	303	309	75
Winnipeg	80	33	39	8	311	333	74
Los Angeles	80	27	41	12	308	365	66

PRINCE OF WALES CONFERENCE

Adams Division

Boston	80	50	20	10	327	228	110
Montreal	80	42	24	14	350	286	98
Buffalo	80	38	29	13	318	285	89
Quebec	80	34	34	12	343	336	80
Hartford	80	19	54	7	261	403	45

Patrick Division

Philadelphia	80	49	23	8	326	240	106
*NY Islanders	80	42	26	12	302	226	96
Washington	80	39	25	16	306	283	94
NY Rangers	80	35	35	10	306	287	80
New Jersey	80	17	49	14	230	338	48
Pittsburgh	80	18	53	9	257	394	45

Leading Scorers

Player	Team	GP	G	A	PTS	PIM
Wayne Gretzky	Edmonton	80	71	125	196	59
Peter Stastny	Quebec	75	47	77	124	78
Denis Savard	Chicago	78	35	86	121	99
Mike Bossy	NY Islanders	79	60	58	118	20
Marcel Dionne	Los Angeles	80	56	51	107	22
Barry Pederson	Boston	77	46	61	107	47
Mark Messier	Edmonton	77	48	58	106	72
Michel Goulet	Quebec	80	57	48	105	51
Glenn Anderson	Edmonton	72	48	56	104	70
Kent Nilsson	Calgary	80	46	58	104	10
Jari Kurri	Edmonton	80	45	59	104	22

1983-84

CLARENCE CAMPBELL CONFERENCE

Norris Division

Team	GP	W	L	T	GF	GA	PTS
Minnesota	80	39	31	10	345	344	88
St. Louis	80	32	41	7	293	316	71
Detroit	80	31	42	7	298	323	69
Chicago	80	30	42	8	277	311	68
Toronto	80	26	45	9	303	387	61

Smythe Division

*Edmonton	80	57	18	5	446	314	119
Calgary	80	34	32	14	311	314	82
Vancouver	80	32	39	9	306	328	73
Winnipeg	80	31	38	11	340	374	73
Los Angeles	80	23	44	13	309	376	59

PRINCE OF WALES CONFERENCE

Adams Division

Boston	80	49	25	6	336	261	104
Buffalo	80	48	25	7	315	257	103
Quebec	80	42	28	10	360	278	94
Montreal	80	35	40	5	286	295	75
Hartford	80	28	42	10	288	320	66

Patrick Division

NY Islanders	80	50	26	4	357	269	104
Washington	80	48	27	5	308	226	101
Philadelphia	80	44	26	10	350	290	98
NY Rangers	80	42	29	9	314	304	93
New Jersey	80	17	56	7	231	350	41
Pittsburgh	80	16	58	6	254	390	38

Leading Scorers

Player	Team	GP	G	A	PTS	PIM
Wayne Gretzky	Edmonton	74	87	118	205	39
Paul Coffey	Edmonton	80	40	86	126	104
Michel Goulet	Quebec	75	56	65	121	76
Peter Stastny	Quebec	80	46	73	119	73
Mike Bossy	NY Islanders	67	51	67	118	8
Barry Pederson	Boston	80	39	77	116	64
Jari Kurri	Edmonton	64	52	61	113	14
Bryan Trottier	NY Islanders	68	40	71	111	59
Bernie Federko	St. Louis	79	41	66	107	43
Rick Middleton	Boston	80	47	58	105	14

1984-85

CLARENCE CAMPBELL CONFERENCE

Norris Division

Team	GP	W	L	T	GF	GA	PTS
St. Louis	80	37	31	12	299	288	86
Chicago	80	38	35	7	309	299	83
Detroit	80	27	41	12	313	357	66
Minnesota	80	25	43	12	268	321	62
Toronto	80	20	52	8	253	358	48

Smythe Division

Team	GP	W	L	T	GF	GA	PTS
*Edmonton	80	49	20	11	401	298	109
Winnipeg	80	43	27	10	358	332	96
Calgary	80	41	27	12	363	302	94
Los Angeles	80	34	32	14	339	326	82
Vancouver	80	25	46	9	284	401	59

PRINCE OF WALES CONFERENCE

Adams Division

Team	GP	W	L	T	GF	GA	PTS
Montreal	80	41	27	12	309	262	94
Quebec	80	41	30	9	323	275	91
Buffalo	80	38	28	14	290	237	90
Boston	80	36	34	10	303	287	82
Hartford	80	30	41	9	268	318	69

Patrick Division

Team	GP	W	L	T	GF	GA	PTS
Philadelphia	80	53	20	7	348	241	113
Washington	80	46	25	9	322	240	101
NY Islanders	80	40	34	6	345	312	86
NY Rangers	80	26	44	10	295	345	62
New Jersey	80	22	48	10	264	346	54
Pittsburgh	80	24	51	5	276	385	53

Leading Scorers

Player	Team	GP	G	A	PTS	PIM
Wayne Gretzky	Edmonton	80	73	135	208	52
Jari Kurri	Edmonton	73	71	64	135	30
Dale Hawerchuk	Winnipeg	80	53	77	130	74
Marcel Dionne	Los Angeles	80	46	80	126	46
Paul Coffey	Edmonton	80	37	84	121	97
Mike Bossy	NY Islanders	76	58	59	117	38
John Ogrodnick	Detroit	79	55	50	105	30
Denis Savard	Chicago	79	38	67	105	56
Bernie Federko	St. Louis	76	30	73	103	27
Mike Gartner	Washington	80	50	52	102	71

1985-86

CLARENCE CAMPBELL CONFERENCE

Norris Division

Team	GP	W	L	T	GF	GA	PTS
Chicago	80	39	33	8	351	349	86
Minnesota	80	38	33	9	327	305	85
St. Louis	80	37	34	9	302	291	83
Toronto	80	25	48	7	311	386	57
Detroit	80	17	57	6	266	415	40

Smythe Division

Team	GP	W	L	T	GF	GA	PTS
Edmonton	80	56	17	7	426	310	119
Calgary	80	40	31	9	354	315	89
Winnipeg	80	26	47	7	295	372	59
Vancouver	80	23	44	13	282	333	59
Los Angeles	80	23	49	8	284	389	54

PRINCE OF WALES CONFERENCE

Adams Division

Team	GP	W	L	T	GF	GA	PTS
Quebec	80	43	31	6	330	289	92
*Montreal	80	40	33	7	330	280	87
Boston	80	37	31	12	311	288	86
Hartford	80	40	36	4	332	302	84
Buffalo	80	37	37	6	296	291	80

Patrick Division

Team	GP	W	L	T	GF	GA	PTS
Philadelphia	80	53	23	4	335	241	110
Washington	80	50	23	7	315	272	107
NY Islanders	80	39	29	12	327	284	90
NY Rangers	80	36	38	6	280	276	78
Pittsburgh	80	34	38	8	313	305	76
New Jersey	80	28	49	3	300	374	59

Leading Scorers

Player	Team	GP	G	A	PTS	PIM
Wayne Gretzky	Edmonton	80	52	163	215	52
Mario Lemieux	Pittsburgh	79	48	93	141	43
Paul Coffey	Edmonton	79	48	90	138	120
Jari Kurri	Edmonton	78	68	63	131	22
Mike Bossy	NY Islanders	80	61	62	123	14
Peter Stastny	Quebec	76	41	81	122	60
Denis Savard	Chicago	80	47	69	116	111
Mats Naslund	Montreal	80	43	67	110	16
Dale Hawerchuk	Winnipeg	80	46	59	105	44
Neal Broten	Minnesota	80	29	76	105	47

1986-87

CLARENCE CAMPBELL CONFERENCE

Norris Division

Team	GP	W	L	T	GF	GA	PTS
St. Louis	80	32	33	15	281	293	79
Detroit	80	34	36	10	260	274	78
Chicago	80	29	37	14	290	310	72
Toronto	80	32	42	6	286	319	70
Minnesota	80	30	40	10	296	314	70

Smythe Division

Team	GP	W	L	T	GF	GA	PTS
*Edmonton	80	50	24	6	372	284	106
Calgary	80	46	31	3	318	289	95
Winnipeg	80	40	32	8	279	271	88
Los Angeles	80	31	41	8	318	341	70
Vancouver	80	29	43	8	282	314	66

PRINCE OF WALES CONFERENCE

Adams Division

Team	GP	W	L	T	GF	GA	PTS
Hartford	80	43	30	7	287	270	93
Montreal	80	41	29	10	277	241	92
Boston	80	39	34	7	301	276	85
Quebec	80	31	39	10	267	276	72
Buffalo	80	28	44	8	280	308	64

Patrick Division

Team	GP	W	L	T	GF	GA	PTS
Philadelphia	80	46	26	8	310	245	100
Washington	80	38	32	10	285	278	86
NY Islanders	80	35	33	12	279	281	82
NY Rangers	80	34	38	8	307	323	76
Pittsburgh	80	30	38	12	297	290	72
New Jersey	80	29	45	6	293	368	64

Leading Scorers

Player	Team	GP	G	A	PTS	PIM
Wayne Gretzky	Edmonton	79	62	121	183	28
Jari Kurri	Edmonton	79	54	54	108	41
Mario Lemieux	Pittsburgh	63	54	53	107	57
Mark Messier	Edmonton	77	37	70	107	73
Doug Gilmour	St. Louis	80	42	63	105	58
Dino Ciccarelli	Minnesota	80	52	51	103	92
Dale Hawerchuk	Winnipeg	80	47	53	100	54
Michel Goulet	Quebec	75	49	47	96	61
Tim Kerr	Philadelphia	75	58	37	95	57
Raymond Bourque	Boston	78	23	72	95	36

1987-88

CLARENCE CAMPBELL CONFERENCE

Norris Division

Team	GP	W	L	T	GF	GA	PTS
Detroit	80	41	28	11	322	269	93
St. Louis	80	34	38	8	278	294	76
Chicago	80	30	41	9	284	328	69
Toronto	80	21	49	10	273	345	52
Minnesota	80	19	48	13	242	349	51

Smythe Division

Team	GP	W	L	T	GF	GA	PTS
Calgary	80	48	23	9	397	305	105
*Edmonton	80	44	25	11	363	288	99
Winnipeg	80	33	36	11	292	310	77
Los Angeles	80	30	42	8	318	359	68
Vancouver	80	25	46	9	272	320	59

PRINCE OF WALES CONFERENCE

Adams Division

Team	GP	W	L	T	GF	GA	PTS
Montreal	80	45	22	13	298	238	103
Boston	80	44	30	6	300	251	94
Buffalo	80	37	32	11	283	305	85
Hartford	80	35	38	7	249	267	77
Quebec	80	32	43	5	271	306	69

Patrick Division

Team	GP	W	L	T	GF	GA	PTS
NY Islanders	80	39	31	10	308	267	88
Washington	80	38	33	9	281	249	85
Philadelphia	80	38	33	9	292	292	85
New Jersey	80	38	36	6	295	296	82
NY Rangers	80	36	34	10	300	283	82
Pittsburgh	80	36	35	9	319	316	81

Leading Scorers

Player	Team	GP	G	A	PTS	PIM
Mario Lemieux	Pittsburgh	77	70	98	168	92
Wayne Gretzky	Edmonton	64	40	109	149	24
Denis Savard	Chicago	80	44	87	131	95
Dale Hawerchuk	Winnipeg	80	44	77	121	59
Luc Robitaille	Los Angeles	80	53	58	111	82
Peter Stastny	Quebec	76	46	65	111	69
Mark Messier	Edmonton	77	37	74	111	103
Jimmy Carson	Los Angeles	80	55	52	107	45
Hakan Loob	Calgary	80	50	56	106	47
Michel Goulet	Quebec	80	48	58	106	56

1988-89

CLARENCE CAMPBELL CONFERENCE

Norris Division

Team	GP	W	L	T	GF	GA	PTS
Detroit	80	34	34	12	313	316	80
St. Louis	80	33	35	12	275	285	78
Minnesota	80	27	37	16	258	278	70
Chicago	80	27	41	12	297	335	66
Toronto	80	28	46	6	259	342	62

Smythe Division

Team	GP	W	L	T	GF	GA	PTS
*Calgary	80	54	17	9	354	226	117
Los Angeles	80	42	31	7	376	335	91
Edmonton	80	38	34	8	325	306	84
Vancouver	80	33	39	8	251	253	74
Winnipeg	80	26	42	12	300	355	64

PRINCE OF WALES CONFERENCE

Adams Division

Team	GP	W	L	T	GF	GA	PTS
Montreal	80	53	18	9	315	218	115
Boston	80	37	29	14	289	256	88
Buffalo	80	38	35	7	291	299	83
Hartford	80	37	38	5	299	290	79
Quebec	80	27	46	7	269	342	61

Patrick Division

Team	GP	W	L	T	GF	GA	PTS
Washington	80	41	29	10	305	259	92
Pittsburgh	80	40	33	7	347	349	87
NY Rangers	80	37	35	8	310	307	82
Philadelphia	80	36	36	8	307	285	80
New Jersey	80	27	41	12	281	325	66
NY Islanders	80	28	47	5	265	325	61

Leading Scorers

Player	Team	GP	G	A	PTS	PIM
Mario Lemieux	Pittsburgh	76	85	114	199	100
Wayne Gretzky	Los Angeles	78	54	114	168	26
Steve Yzerman	Detroit	80	65	90	155	61
Bernie Nicholls	Los Angeles	79	70	80	150	96
Rob Brown	Pittsburgh	68	49	66	115	118
Paul Coffey	Pittsburgh	75	30	83	113	193
Joe Mullen	Calgary	79	51	59	110	16
Jari Kurri	Edmonton	76	44	58	102	69
Jimmy Carson	Edmonton	80	49	51	100	36
Luc Robitaille	Los Angeles	78	46	52	98	65

1989-90

CLARENCE CAMPBELL CONFERENCE

Norris Division

Team	GP	W	L	T	GF	GA	PTS
Chicago	80	41	33	6	316	294	88
St. Louis	80	37	34	9	295	279	83
Toronto	80	38	38	4	337	358	80
Minnesota	80	36	40	4	284	291	76
Detroit	80	28	38	14	288	323	70

Smythe Division

Team	GP	W	L	T	GF	GA	PTS
Calgary	80	42	23	15	348	265	99
*Edmonton	80	38	28	14	315	283	90
Winnipeg	80	37	32	11	298	290	85
Los Angeles	80	34	39	7	338	337	75
Vancouver	80	25	41	14	245	306	64

PRINCE OF WALES CONFERENCE

Adams Division

Team	GP	W	L	T	GF	GA	PTS
Boston	80	46	25	9	289	232	101
Buffalo	80	45	27	8	286	248	98
Montreal	80	41	28	11	288	234	93
Hartford	80	38	33	9	275	268	85
Quebec	80	12	61	7	240	407	31

Patrick Division

Team	GP	W	L	T	GF	GA	PTS
NY Rangers	80	36	31	13	279	267	85
New Jersey	80	37	34	9	295	288	83
Washington	80	36	38	6	284	275	78
NY Islanders	80	31	38	11	281	288	73
Pittsburgh	80	32	40	8	318	359	72
Philadelphia	80	30	39	11	290	297	71

Leading Scorers

Player	Team	GP	G	A	PTS	PIM
Wayne Gretzky	Los Angeles	73	40	102	142	42
Mark Messier	Edmonton	79	45	84	129	79
Steve Yzerman	Detroit	79	62	65	127	79
Mario Lemieux	Pittsburgh	59	45	78	123	78
Brett Hull	St. Louis	80	72	41	113	24
Bernie Nicholls	L.A., NYR	79	39	73	112	86
Pierre Turgeon	Buffalo	80	40	66	106	29
Pat LaFontaine	NY Islanders	74	54	51	105	38
Paul Coffey	Pittsburgh	80	29	74	103	95
Joe Sakic	Quebec	80	39	63	102	27
Adam Oates	St. Louis	80	23	79	102	30

1990-91

CLARENCE CAMPBELL CONFERENCE
Norris Division

Team	GP	W	L	T	GF	GA	PTS
Chicago	80	49	23	8	284	211	106
St. Louis	80	47	22	11	310	250	105
Detroit	80	34	38	8	273	298	76
Minnesota	80	27	39	14	256	266	68
Toronto	80	23	46	11	241	318	57

Smythe Division

Team	GP	W	L	T	GF	GA	PTS
Los Angeles	80	46	24	10	340	254	102
Calgary	80	46	26	8	344	263	100
Edmonton	80	37	37	6	272	272	80
Vancouver	80	28	43	9	243	315	65
Winnipeg	80	26	43	11	260	288	63

PRINCE OF WALES CONFERENCE
Adams Division

Team	GP	W	L	T	GF	GA	PTS
Boston	80	44	24	12	299	264	100
Montreal	80	39	30	11	273	249	89
Buffalo	80	31	30	19	292	278	81
Hartford	80	31	38	11	238	276	73
Quebec	80	16	50	14	236	354	46

Patrick Division

Team	GP	W	L	T	GF	GA	PTS
*Pittsburgh	80	41	33	6	342	305	88
NY Rangers	80	36	31	13	297	265	85
Washington	80	37	36	7	258	258	81
New Jersey	80	32	33	15	272	264	79
Philadelphia	80	33	37	10	252	267	76
NY Islanders	80	25	45	10	223	290	60

Leading Scorers

Player	Team	GP	G	A	PTS	PIM
Wayne Gretzky	Los Angeles	78	41	122	163	16
Brett Hull	St. Louis	78	86	45	131	22
Adam Oates	St. Louis	61	25	90	115	29
Mark Recchi	Pittsburgh	78	40	73	113	48
John Cullen	Pit., Hfd.	78	39	71	110	101
Joe Sakic	Quebec	80	48	61	109	24
Steve Yzerman	Detroit	80	51	57	108	34
Theoren Fleury	Calgary	79	51	53	104	136
Al MacInnis	Calgary	78	28	75	103	90
Steve Larmer	Chicago	80	44	57	101	79

1991-92

CLARENCE CAMPBELL CONFERENCE
Norris Division

Team	GP	W	L	T	GF	GA	PTS
Detroit	80	43	25	12	320	256	98
Chicago	80	36	29	15	257	236	87
St. Louis	80	36	33	11	279	266	83
Minnesota	80	32	42	6	246	278	70
Toronto	80	30	43	7	234	294	67

Smythe Division

Team	GP	W	L	T	GF	GA	PTS
Vancouver	80	42	26	12	285	250	96
Los Angeles	80	35	31	14	287	296	84
Edmonton	80	36	34	10	295	297	82
Winnipeg	80	33	32	15	251	244	81
Calgary	80	31	37	12	296	305	74
San Jose	80	17	58	5	219	359	39

PRINCE OF WALES CONFERENCE
Adams Division

Team	GP	W	L	T	GF	GA	PTS
Montreal	80	41	28	11	267	207	93
Boston	80	36	32	12	270	275	84
Buffalo	80	31	37	12	289	299	74
Hartford	80	26	41	13	247	283	65
Quebec	80	20	48	12	255	318	52

Patrick Division

Team	GP	W	L	T	GF	GA	PTS
NY Rangers	80	50	25	5	321	246	105
Washington	80	45	27	8	330	275	98
*Pittsburgh	80	39	32	9	343	308	87
New Jersey	80	38	31	11	289	259	87
NY Islanders	80	34	35	11	291	299	79
Philadelphia	80	32	37	11	252	273	75

Leading Scorers

Player	Team	GP	G	A	PTS	PIM
Mario Lemieux	Pittsburgh	64	44	87	131	94
Kevin Stevens	Pittsburgh	80	54	69	123	254
Wayne Gretzky	Los Angeles	74	31	90	121	34
Brett Hull	St. Louis	73	70	39	109	48
Luc Robitaille	Los Angeles	80	44	63	107	95
Mark Messier	NY Rangers	79	35	72	107	76
Jeremy Roenick	Chicago	80	53	50	103	23
Steve Yzerman	Detroit	79	45	58	103	64
Brian Leetch	NY Rangers	80	22	80	102	26
Adam Oates	St.L., Bos.	80	20	79	99	22

1992-93

CLARENCE CAMPBELL CONFERENCE
Norris Division

Team	GP	W	L	T	GF	GA	PTS
Chicago	84	47	25	12	279	230	106
Detroit	84	47	28	9	369	280	103
Toronto	84	44	29	11	288	241	99
St. Louis	84	37	36	11	282	278	85
Minnesota	84	36	38	10	272	293	82
Tampa Bay	84	23	54	7	245	332	53

Smythe Division

Team	GP	W	L	T	GF	GA	PTS
Vancouver	84	46	29	9	346	278	101
Calgary	84	43	30	11	322	282	97
Los Angeles	84	39	35	10	338	340	88
Winnipeg	84	40	37	7	322	320	87
Edmonton	84	26	50	8	242	337	60
San Jose	84	11	71	2	218	414	24

PRINCE OF WALES CONFERENCE
Adams Division

Team	GP	W	L	T	GF	GA	PTS
Boston	84	51	26	7	332	268	109
Quebec	84	47	27	10	351	300	104
*Montreal	84	48	30	6	326	280	102
Buffalo	84	38	36	10	335	297	86
Hartford	84	26	52	6	284	369	58
Ottawa	84	10	70	4	202	395	24

Patrick Division

Team	GP	W	L	T	GF	GA	PTS
Pittsburgh	84	56	21	7	367	268	119
Washington	84	43	34	7	325	286	93
NY Islanders	84	40	37	7	335	297	87
New Jersey	84	40	37	7	308	299	87
Philadelphia	84	36	37	11	319	319	83
NY Rangers	84	34	39	11	304	308	79

Leading Scorers

Player	Team	GP	G	A	PTS	PIM
Mario Lemieux	Pittsburgh	60	69	91	160	38
Pat LaFontaine	Buffalo	84	53	95	148	63
Adam Oates	Boston	84	45	97	142	32
Steve Yzerman	Detroit	84	58	79	137	44
Teemu Selanne	Winnipeg	84	76	56	132	45
Pierre Turgeon	NY Islanders	83	58	74	132	26
Alexander Mogilny	Buffalo	77	76	51	127	40
Doug Gilmour	Toronto	83	32	95	127	100
Luc Robitaille	Los Angeles	84	63	62	125	100
Mark Recchi	Philadelphia	84	53	70	123	95

1993-94

EASTERN CONFERENCE
Northeast Division

Team		GP	W	L	T	GF	GA	PTS
Pittsburgh	(2)	84	44	27	13	299	285	101
Boston	(4)	84	42	29	13	289	252	97
Montreal	(5)	84	41	29	14	283	248	96
Buffalo	(6)	84	43	32	9	282	218	95
Quebec		84	34	42	8	277	292	76
Hartford		84	27	48	9	227	288	63
Ottawa		84	14	61	9	201	397	37

Atlantic Division

Team		GP	W	L	T	GF	GA	PTS
*NY Rangers	(1)	84	52	24	8	299	231	112
New Jersey	(3)	84	47	25	12	306	220	106
Washington	(7)	84	39	35	10	277	263	88
NY Islanders	(8)	84	36	36	12	282	264	84
Florida		84	33	34	17	233	233	83
Philadelphia		84	35	39	10	294	314	80
Tampa Bay		84	30	43	11	224	251	71

WESTERN CONFERENCE
Central Division

Team		GP	W	L	T	GF	GA	PTS
Detroit	(1)	84	46	30	8	356	275	100
Toronto	(3)	84	43	29	12	280	243	98
Dallas	(4)	84	42	29	13	286	265	97
St. Louis	(5)	84	40	33	11	270	283	91
Chicago	(6)	84	39	36	9	254	240	87
Winnipeg		84	24	51	9	245	344	57

Pacific Division

Team		GP	W	L	T	GF	GA	PTS
Calgary	(2)	84	42	29	13	302	256	97
Vancouver	(7)	84	41	40	3	279	276	85
San Jose	(8)	84	33	35	16	252	265	82
Anaheim		84	33	46	5	229	251	71
Los Angeles		84	27	45	12	294	322	66
Edmonton		84	25	45	14	261	305	64

Leading Scorers

Player	Team	GP	G	A	PTS	PIM
Wayne Gretzky	Los Angeles	81	38	92	130	20
Sergei Fedorov	Detroit	82	56	64	120	34
Adam Oates	Boston	77	32	80	112	45
Doug Gilmour	Toronto	83	27	84	111	105
Pavel Bure	Vancouver	76	60	47	107	86
Jeremy Roenick	Chicago	84	46	61	107	125
Mark Recchi	Philadelphia	84	40	67	107	46
Brendan Shanahan	St. Louis	81	52	50	102	211
Dave Andreychuk	Toronto	83	53	46	99	98
Jaromir Jagr	Pittsburgh	80	32	67	99	61

1994-95

EASTERN CONFERENCE
Northeast Division

Team		GP	W	L	T	GF	GA	PTS
Quebec	(1)	48	30	13	5	185	134	65
Pittsburgh	(3)	48	29	16	3	181	158	61
Boston	(4)	48	27	18	3	150	127	57
Buffalo	(7)	48	22	19	7	130	119	51
Hartford		48	19	24	5	127	141	43
Montreal		48	18	23	7	125	148	43
Ottawa		48	9	34	5	117	174	23

Atlantic Division

Team		GP	W	L	T	GF	GA	PTS
Philadelphia	(2)	48	28	16	4	150	132	60
*New Jersey	(5)	48	22	18	8	136	121	52
Washington	(6)	48	22	18	8	136	120	52
NY Rangers	(8)	48	22	23	3	139	134	47
Florida		48	20	22	6	115	127	46
Tampa Bay		48	17	28	3	120	144	37
NY Islanders		48	15	28	5	126	158	35

WESTERN CONFERENCE
Central Division

Team		GP	W	L	T	GF	GA	PTS
Detroit	(1)	48	33	11	4	180	117	70
St. Louis	(3)	48	28	15	5	178	135	61
Chicago	(4)	48	24	19	5	156	115	53
Toronto	(5)	48	21	19	8	135	146	50
Dallas	(8)	48	17	23	8	136	135	42
Winnipeg		48	16	25	7	157	177	39

Pacific Division

Team		GP	W	L	T	GF	GA	PTS
Calgary	(2)	48	24	17	7	163	135	55
Vancouver	(6)	48	18	18	12	153	148	48
San Jose	(7)	48	19	25	4	129	161	42
Los Angeles		48	16	23	9	142	174	41
Edmonton		48	17	27	4	136	183	38
Anaheim		48	16	27	5	125	164	37

Leading Scorers

Player	Team	GP	G	A	PTS	PIM
Jaromir Jagr	Pittsburgh	48	32	38	70	37
Eric Lindros	Philadelphia	46	29	41	70	60
Alex Zhamnov	Winnipeg	48	30	35	65	20
Joe Sakic	Quebec	47	19	43	62	30
Ron Francis	Pittsburgh	44	11	48	59	18
Theoren Fleury	Calgary	47	29	29	58	112
Paul Coffey	Detroit	45	14	44	58	72
Mikael Renberg	Philadelphia	47	26	31	57	20
John LeClair	Mtl., Phi.	46	26	28	54	30
Mark Messier	NY Rangers	46	14	39	53	40
Adam Oates	Boston	48	12	41	53	8

1995-96

EASTERN CONFERENCE
Northeast Division

Team		GP	W	L	T	GF	GA	PTS
Pittsburgh	(2)	82	49	29	4	362	284	102
Boston	(5)	82	40	31	11	282	269	91
Montreal	(6)	82	40	32	10	265	248	90
Hartford		82	34	39	9	237	259	77
Buffalo		82	33	42	7	247	262	73
Ottawa		82	18	59	5	191	291	41

Atlantic Division

Team		GP	W	L	T	GF	GA	PTS
Philadelphia	(1)	82	45	24	13	282	208	103
NY Rangers	(3)	82	41	27	14	272	237	96
Florida	(4)	82	41	31	10	254	234	92
Washington	(7)	82	39	32	11	234	204	89
Tampa Bay	(8)	82	38	32	12	238	248	88
New Jersey		82	37	33	12	215	202	86
NY Islanders		82	22	50	10	229	315	54

WESTERN CONFERENCE
Central Division

Team		GP	W	L	T	GF	GA	PTS
Detroit	(1)	82	62	13	7	325	181	131
Chicago	(3)	82	40	28	14	273	220	94
Toronto	(4)	82	34	36	12	247	252	80
St. Louis	(5)	82	32	34	16	219	248	80
Winnipeg	(8)	82	36	40	6	275	291	78
Dallas		82	26	42	14	227	280	66

Pacific Division

Team		GP	W	L	T	GF	GA	PTS
*Colorado	(2)	82	47	25	10	326	240	104
Calgary	(6)	82	34	37	11	241	240	79
Vancouver	(7)	82	32	35	15	278	278	79
Anaheim		82	35	39	8	234	247	78
Edmonton		82	30	44	8	240	304	68
Los Angeles		82	24	40	18	256	302	66
San Jose		82	20	55	7	252	357	47

Leading Scorers

Player	Team	GP	G	A	PTS	PIM
Mario Lemieux	Pittsburgh	70	69	92	161	54
Jaromir Jagr	Pittsburgh	82	62	87	149	96
Joe Sakic	Colorado	82	51	69	120	44
Ron Francis	Pittsburgh	77	27	92	119	56
Peter Forsberg	Colorado	82	30	86	116	47
Eric Lindros	Philadelphia	73	47	68	115	163
Paul Kariya	Anaheim	82	50	58	108	20
Teemu Selanne	Wpg., Ana.	79	40	68	108	22
Alexander Mogilny	Vancouver	79	55	52	107	16
Sergei Fedorov	Detroit	78	39	68	107	48

1996-97
EASTERN CONFERENCE
Northeast Division

Team		GP	W	L	T	GF	GA	PTS
Buffalo	(2)	82	40	30	12	237	208	92
Pittsburgh	(6)	82	38	36	8	285	280	84
Ottawa	(7)	82	31	36	15	226	234	77
Montreal	(8)	82	31	36	15	249	276	77
Hartford		82	32	39	11	226	256	75
Boston		82	26	47	9	234	300	61

Atlantic Division

Team		GP	W	L	T	GF	GA	PTS
New Jersey	(1)	82	45	23	14	231	182	104
Philadelphia	(3)	82	45	24	13	274	217	103
Florida	(4)	82	35	28	19	221	201	89
NY Rangers	(5)	82	38	34	10	258	231	86
Washington		82	33	40	9	214	231	75
Tampa Bay		82	32	40	10	217	247	74
NY Islanders		82	29	41	12	240	250	70

WESTERN CONFERENCE
Central Division

Team		GP	W	L	T	GF	GA	PTS
Dallas	(2)	82	48	26	8	252	198	104
*Detroit	(3)	82	38	26	18	253	197	94
Phoenix	(5)	82	38	37	7	240	243	83
St. Louis	(6)	82	36	35	11	236	239	83
Chicago	(8)	82	34	35	13	223	210	81
Toronto		82	30	44	8	230	273	68

Pacific Division

Team		GP	W	L	T	GF	GA	PTS
Colorado	(1)	82	49	24	9	277	205	107
Anaheim	(4)	82	36	33	13	245	233	85
Edmonton	(7)	82	36	37	9	252	247	81
Vancouver		82	35	40	7	257	273	77
Calgary		82	32	41	9	214	239	73
Los Angeles		82	28	43	11	214	268	67
San Jose		82	27	47	8	211	278	62

Leading Scorers

Player	Team	GP	G	A	PTS	PIM
Mario Lemieux	Pittsburgh	76	50	72	122	65
Teemu Selanne	Anaheim	78	51	58	109	34
Paul Kariya	Anaheim	69	44	55	99	6
John LeClair	Philadelphia	82	50	47	97	58
Wayne Gretzky	NY Rangers	82	25	72	97	28
Jaromir Jagr	Pittsburgh	63	47	48	95	40
Mats Sundin	Toronto	82	41	53	94	59
Ziggy Palffy	NY Islanders	80	48	42	90	43
Ron Francis	Pittsburgh	81	27	63	90	20
Brendan Shanahan	Hfd., Det.	81	47	41	88	131

1997-98
EASTERN CONFERENCE
Northeast Division

Team		GP	W	L	T	GF	GA	PTS
Pittsburgh	(2)	82	40	24	18	228	188	98
Boston	(5)	82	39	30	13	221	194	91
Buffalo	(6)	82	36	29	17	211	187	89
Montreal	(7)	82	37	32	13	235	208	87
Ottawa	(8)	82	34	33	15	193	200	83
Carolina		82	33	41	8	200	219	74

Atlantic Division

Team		GP	W	L	T	GF	GA	PTS
New Jersey	(1)	82	48	23	11	225	166	107
Philadelphia	(3)	82	42	29	11	242	193	95
Washington	(4)	82	40	30	12	219	202	92
NY Islanders		82	30	41	11	212	225	71
NY Rangers		82	25	39	18	197	231	68
Florida		82	24	43	15	203	256	63
Tampa Bay		82	17	55	10	151	269	44

WESTERN CONFERENCE
Central Division

Team		GP	W	L	T	GF	GA	PTS
Dallas	(1)	82	49	22	11	242	167	109
*Detroit	(3)	82	44	23	15	250	196	103
St. Louis	(4)	82	45	29	8	256	204	98
Phoenix	(6)	82	35	35	12	224	227	82
Chicago		82	30	39	13	192	199	73
Toronto		82	30	43	9	194	237	69

Pacific Division

Team		GP	W	L	T	GF	GA	PTS
Colorado	(2)	82	39	26	17	231	205	95
Los Angeles	(5)	82	38	33	11	227	225	87
Edmonton	(7)	82	35	37	10	215	224	80
San Jose	(8)	82	34	38	10	210	216	78
Calgary		82	26	41	15	217	252	67
Anaheim		82	26	43	13	205	261	65
Vancouver		82	25	43	14	224	273	64

Leading Scorers

Player	Team	GP	G	A	PTS	PIM
Jaromir Jagr	Pittsburgh	77	35	67	102	64
Peter Forsberg	Colorado	72	25	66	91	94
Pavel Bure	Vancouver	82	51	39	90	48
Wayne Gretzky	NY Rangers	82	23	67	90	28
John LeClair	Philadelphia	82	51	36	87	32
Ziggy Palffy	NY Islanders	82	45	42	87	34
Ron Francis	Pittsburgh	81	25	62	87	20
Teemu Selanne	Anaheim	73	52	34	86	30
Jason Allison	Boston	81	33	50	83	60
Jozef Stumpel	Los Angeles	77	21	58	79	53

1998-99
EASTERN CONFERENCE
Northeast Division

Team		GP	W	L	T	GF	GA	PTS
Ottawa	(2)	82	44	23	15	239	179	103
Toronto	(4)	82	45	30	7	268	231	97
Boston	(6)	82	39	30	13	214	181	91
Buffalo	(7)	82	37	28	17	207	175	91
Montreal		82	32	39	11	184	209	75

Atlantic Division

Team		GP	W	L	T	GF	GA	PTS
New Jersey	(1)	82	47	24	11	248	196	105
Philadelphia	(5)	82	37	26	19	231	196	93
Pittsburgh	(8)	82	38	30	14	242	225	90
NY Rangers		82	33	38	11	217	227	77
NY Islanders		82	24	48	10	194	244	58

Southeast Division

Team		GP	W	L	T	GF	GA	PTS
Carolina	(3)	82	34	30	18	210	202	86
Florida		82	30	34	18	210	228	78
Washington		82	31	45	6	200	218	68
Tampa Bay		82	19	54	9	179	292	47

WESTERN CONFERENCE
Central Division

Team		GP	W	L	T	GF	GA	PTS
Detroit	(3)	82	43	32	7	245	202	93
St Louis	(5)	82	37	32	13	237	209	87
Chicago		82	29	41	12	202	248	70
Nashville		82	28	47	7	190	261	63

Pacific Division

Team		GP	W	L	T	GF	GA	PTS
*Dallas	(1)	82	51	19	12	236	168	114
Phoenix	(4)	82	39	31	12	205	197	90
Anaheim	(6)	82	35	34	13	215	206	83
San Jose	(7)	82	31	33	18	196	191	80
Los Angeles		82	32	45	5	189	222	69

Northwest Division

Team		GP	W	L	T	GF	GA	PTS
Colorado	(2)	82	44	28	10	239	205	98
Edmonton	(8)	82	33	37	12	230	226	78
Calgary		82	30	40	12	211	234	72
Vancouver		82	23	47	12	192	258	58

Leading Scorers

Player	Team	GP	G	A	PTS	PIM
Jaromir Jagr	Pittsburgh	81	44	83	127	66
Teemu Selanne	Anaheim	75	47	60	107	30
Paul Kariya	Anaheim	82	39	62	101	40
Peter Forsberg	Colorado	78	30	67	97	108
Joe Sakic	Colorado	73	41	55	96	29
Alexei Yashin	Ottawa	82	44	50	94	54
Eric Lindros	Philadelphia	71	40	53	93	120
Theoren Fleury	Cgy., Col.	75	40	53	93	86
John LeClair	Philadelphia	76	43	47	90	30
Pavol Demitra	St Louis	82	37	52	89	16

1999-2000
EASTERN CONFERENCE
Northeast Division

Team		GP	W	L	T	OTL	GF	GA	PTS
Toronto	(3)	82	45	27	7	3	246	222	100
Ottawa	(6)	82	41	28	11	2	244	210	95
Buffalo	(8)	82	35	32	11	4	213	204	85
Montreal		82	35	34	9	4	196	194	83
Boston		82	24	33	19	6	210	248	73

Atlantic Division

Team		GP	W	L	T	OTL	GF	GA	PTS
Philadelphia	(1)	82	45	22	12	3	237	179	105
*New Jersey	(4)	82	45	24	8	5	251	203	103
Pittsburgh	(7)	82	37	31	8	6	241	236	88
NY Rangers		82	29	38	12	3	218	246	73
NY Islanders		82	24	48	9	1	194	275	58

Southeast Division

Team		GP	W	L	T	OTL	GF	GA	PTS
Washington	(2)	82	44	24	12	2	227	194	102
Florida	(5)	82	43	27	6	6	244	209	98
Carolina		82	37	35	10	0	217	216	84
Tampa Bay		82	19	47	9	7	204	310	54
Atlanta		82	14	57	7	4	170	313	39

WESTERN CONFERENCE
Central Division

Team		GP	W	L	T	OTL	GF	GA	PTS
St. Louis	(1)	82	51	19	11	1	248	165	114
Detroit	(4)	82	48	22	10	2	278	210	108
Chicago		82	33	37	10	2	242	245	78
Nashville		82	28	40	7	7	199	240	70

Pacific Division

Team		GP	W	L	T	OTL	GF	GA	PTS
Dallas	(2)	82	43	23	10	6	211	184	102
Los Angeles	(5)	82	39	27	12	4	245	228	94
Phoenix	(6)	82	39	31	8	4	232	228	90
San Jose	(8)	82	35	30	10	7	225	214	87
Anaheim		82	34	33	12	3	217	227	83

Northwest Division

Team		GP	W	L	T	OTL	GF	GA	PTS
Colorado	(3)	82	42	28	11	1	233	201	96
Edmonton	(7)	82	32	26	16	8	226	212	88
Vancouver		82	30	29	15	8	227	237	83
Calgary		82	31	36	10	5	211	256	77

Leading Scorers

Player	Team	GP	G	A	PTS	PIM
Jaromir Jagr	Pittsburgh	63	42	54	96	50
Pavel Bure	Florida	74	58	36	94	16
Mark Recchi	Philadelphia	82	28	63	91	50
Paul Kariya	Anaheim	74	42	44	86	24
Teemu Selanne	Anaheim	79	33	52	85	12
Owen Nolan	San Jose	78	44	40	84	110
Tony Amonte	Chicago	82	43	41	84	48
Mike Modano	Dallas	77	38	43	81	48
Joe Sakic	Colorado	60	28	53	81	28
Steve Yzerman	Detroit	78	35	44	79	34

2000-01
EASTERN CONFERENCE
Northeast Division

Team		GP	W	L	T	OTL	GF	GA	PTS
Ottawa	(2)	82	48	21	9	4	274	205	109
Buffalo	(5)	82	46	30	5	1	218	184	98
Toronto	(7)	82	37	29	11	5	232	207	90
Boston		82	36	30	8	8	227	249	88
Montreal		82	28	40	8	6	206	232	70

Atlantic Division

Team		GP	W	L	T	OTL	GF	GA	PTS
New Jersey	(1)	82	48	19	12	3	295	195	111
Philadelphia	(4)	82	43	25	11	3	240	207	100
Pittsburgh	(6)	82	42	28	9	3	281	256	96
NY Rangers		82	33	43	5	1	250	290	72
NY Islanders		82	21	51	7	3	185	268	52

Southeast Division

Team		GP	W	L	T	OTL	GF	GA	PTS
Washington	(3)	82	41	27	10	4	233	211	96
Carolina	(8)	82	38	32	9	3	212	225	88
Florida		82	22	38	13	9	200	246	66
Atlanta		82	23	45	12	2	211	289	60
Tampa Bay		82	24	47	6	5	201	280	59

WESTERN CONFERENCE
Central Division

Team		GP	W	L	T	OTL	GF	GA	PTS
Detroit	(2)	82	49	20	9	4	253	202	111
St. Louis	(4)	82	43	22	12	5	249	195	103
Nashville		82	34	36	9	3	186	200	80
Chicago		82	29	40	8	5	210	246	71
Columbus		82	28	39	9	6	190	233	71

Pacific Division

Team		GP	W	L	T	OTL	GF	GA	PTS
Dallas	(3)	82	48	24	8	2	241	187	106
San Jose	(5)	82	40	27	12	3	217	192	95
Los Angeles	(7)	82	38	28	13	3	252	228	92
Phoenix		82	35	27	17	3	214	212	90
Anaheim		82	25	41	11	5	188	245	66

Northwest Division

Team		GP	W	L	T	OTL	GF	GA	PTS
*Colorado	(1)	82	52	16	10	4	270	192	118
Edmonton	(6)	82	39	28	12	3	243	222	93
Vancouver	(8)	82	36	28	11	7	239	238	90
Calgary		82	27	36	15	4	197	236	73
Minnesota		82	25	39	13	5	168	210	68

Leading Scorers

Player	Team	GP	G	A	PTS	PIM
Jaromir Jagr	Pittsburgh	81	52	69	121	42
Joe Sakic	Colorado	82	54	64	118	30
Patrik Elias	New Jersey	82	40	56	96	51
Alex Kovalev	Pittsburgh	79	44	51	95	96
Jason Allison	Boston	82	36	59	95	85
Martin Straka	Pittsburgh	82	27	68	95	38
Pavel Bure	Florida	82	59	33	92	58
Doug Weight	Edmonton	82	25	65	90	91
Ziggy Palffy	Los Angeles	73	38	51	89	20
Peter Forsberg	Colorado	73	27	62	89	54

2001-02
EASTERN CONFERENCE
Northeast Division

Team		GP	W	L	T	OTL	GF	GA	PTS
Boston	(1)	82	43	24	6	9	236	201	101
Toronto	(4)	82	43	25	10	4	249	207	100
Ottawa	(7)	82	39	27	9	7	243	208	94
Montreal	(8)	82	36	31	12	3	207	209	87
Buffalo		82	35	35	11	1	213	200	82

Atlantic Division

Team		GP	W	L	T	OTL	GF	GA	PTS
Philadelphia	(2)	82	42	27	10	3	234	192	97
NY Islanders	(5)	82	42	28	8	4	239	220	96
New Jersey	(6)	82	41	28	9	4	205	187	95
NY Rangers		82	36	38	4	4	227	258	80
Pittsburgh		82	28	41	8	5	198	249	69

Southeast Division

Team		GP	W	L	T	OTL	GF	GA	PTS
Carolina	(3)	82	35	26	16	5	217	217	91
Washington		82	36	33	11	2	228	240	85
Tampa Bay		82	27	40	11	4	178	219	69
Florida		82	22	44	10	6	180	250	60
Atlanta		82	19	47	11	5	187	288	54

WESTERN CONFERENCE

Central Division

*Detroit	(1)	82	51	17	10	4	251	187	116
St. Louis	(4)	82	43	27	8	4	227	188	98
Chicago	(5)	82	41	27	13	1	216	207	96
Nashville		82	28	41	13	0	196	230	69
Columbus		82	22	47	8	5	164	255	57

Pacific Division

San Jose	(3)	82	44	27	8	3	248	199	99
Phoenix	(6)	82	40	27	9	6	228	210	95
Los Angeles	(7)	82	40	27	11	4	214	190	95
Dallas		82	36	28	13	5	215	213	90
Anaheim		82	29	42	8	3	175	198	69

Northwest Division

Colorado	(2)	82	45	28	8	1	212	169	99
Vancouver	(8)	82	42	30	7	3	254	211	94
Edmonton		82	38	28	12	4	205	182	92
Calgary		82	32	35	12	3	201	220	79
Minnesota		82	26	35	12	9	195	238	73

Leading Scorers

Player	Team	GP	G	A	PTS	PIM
Jarome Iginla	Calgary	82	52	44	96	77
Markus Naslund	Vancouver	81	40	50	90	50
Todd Bertuzzi	Vancouver	72	36	49	85	110
Mats Sundin	Toronto	82	41	39	80	94
Jaromir Jagr	Washington	69	31	48	79	30
Joe Sakic	Colorado	82	26	53	79	18
Pavol Demitra	St. Louis	82	35	43	78	46
Adam Oates	Wsh., Phi.	80	14	64	78	28
Mike Modano	Dallas	78	34	43	77	38
Ron Francis	Carolina	80	27	50	77	18

2002-03

EASTERN CONFERENCE

Northeast Division

Team		GP	W	L	T	OTL	GF	GA	PTS
Ottawa	(1)	82	52	21	8	1	263	182	113
Toronto	(5)	82	44	28	7	3	236	208	98
Boston	(7)	82	36	31	11	4	245	237	87
Montreal		82	30	35	8	9	206	234	77
Buffalo		82	27	37	10	8	190	219	72

Atlantic Division

Team		GP	W	L	T	OTL	GF	GA	PTS
*New Jersey	(2)	82	46	20	10	6	216	166	108
Philadelphia	(4)	82	45	20	13	4	211	166	107
NY Islanders	(8)	82	35	34	11	2	224	231	83
NY Rangers		82	32	36	10	4	210	231	78
Pittsburgh		82	27	44	6	5	189	255	65

Southeast Division

Team		GP	W	L	T	OTL	GF	GA	PTS
Tampa Bay	(3)	82	36	25	16	5	219	210	93
Washington	(6)	82	39	29	8	6	224	220	92
Atlanta		82	31	39	7	5	226	284	74
Florida		82	24	36	13	9	176	237	70
Carolina		82	22	43	11	6	171	240	61

WESTERN CONFERENCE

Central Division

Team		GP	W	L	T	OTL	GF	GA	PTS
Detroit	(2)	82	48	20	10	4	269	203	110
St. Louis	(5)	82	41	24	11	6	253	222	99
Chicago		82	30	33	13	6	207	226	79
Nashville		82	27	35	13	7	183	206	74
Columbus		82	29	42	8	3	213	263	69

Pacific Division

Team		GP	W	L	T	OTL	GF	GA	PTS
Dallas	(1)	82	46	17	15	4	245	169	111
Anaheim	(7)	82	40	27	9	6	203	193	95
Los Angeles		82	33	37	6	6	203	221	78
Phoenix		82	31	35	11	5	204	230	78
San Jose		82	28	37	9	8	214	239	73

Northwest Division

Team		GP	W	L	T	OTL	GF	GA	PTS
Colorado	(3)	82	42	19	13	8	251	194	105
Vancouver	(4)	82	45	23	13	1	264	208	104
Minnesota	(6)	82	42	29	10	1	198	178	95
Edmonton	(8)	82	36	26	11	9	231	230	92
Calgary		82	29	36	13	4	186	228	75

Leading Scorers

Player	Team	GP	G	A	PTS	PIM
Peter Forsberg	Colorado	75	29	77	106	70
Markus Naslund	Vancouver	82	48	56	104	52
Joe Thornton	Boston	77	36	65	101	109
Milan Hejduk	Colorado	82	50	48	98	52
Todd Bertuzzi	Vancouver	82	46	51	97	144
Pavol Demitra	St. Louis	78	36	57	93	32
Glen Murray	Boston	82	44	48	92	64
Mario Lemieux	Pittsburgh	67	28	63	91	43
Dany Heatley	Atlanta	77	41	48	89	58
Ziggy Palffy	Los Angeles	76	37	48	85	47
Mike Modano	Dallas	79	28	57	85	30

2003-04

EASTERN CONFERENCE

Northeast Division

Team		GP	W	L	T	OTL	GF	GA	PTS
Boston	(2)	82	41	19	15	7	209	188	104
Toronto	(4)	82	45	24	10	3	242	204	103
Ottawa	(5)	82	43	23	10	6	262	189	102
Montreal	(7)	82	41	30	7	4	208	192	93
Buffalo		82	37	34	7	4	220	221	85

Atlantic Division

Team		GP	W	L	T	OTL	GF	GA	PTS
Philadelphia	(3)	82	40	21	15	6	229	186	101
New Jersey	(6)	82	43	25	12	2	213	164	100
NY Islanders	(8)	82	38	29	11	4	237	210	91
NY Rangers		82	27	40	7	8	206	250	69
Pittsburgh		82	23	47	8	4	190	303	58

Southeast Division

Team		GP	W	L	T	OTL	GF	GA	PTS
*Tampa Bay	(1)	82	46	22	8	6	245	192	106
Atlanta		82	33	37	8	4	214	243	78
Carolina		82	28	34	14	6	172	209	76
Florida		82	28	35	15	4	188	221	75
Washington		82	23	46	10	3	186	253	59

WESTERN CONFERENCE

Central Division

Team		GP	W	L	T	OTL	GF	GA	PTS
Detroit	(1)	82	48	21	11	2	255	189	109
St. Louis	(7)	82	39	30	11	2	191	198	91
Nashville	(8)	82	38	29	11	4	216	217	91
Columbus		82	25	45	8	4	177	238	62
Chicago		82	20	43	11	8	188	259	59

Pacific Division

Team		GP	W	L	T	OTL	GF	GA	PTS
San Jose	(2)	82	43	21	12	6	219	183	104
Dallas	(5)	82	41	26	13	2	194	175	97
Los Angeles		82	28	29	16	9	205	217	81
Anaheim		82	29	35	10	8	184	213	76
Phoenix		82	22	36	18	6	188	245	68

Northwest Division

Team		GP	W	L	T	OTL	GF	GA	PTS
Vancouver	(3)	82	43	24	10	5	235	194	101
Colorado	(4)	82	40	22	13	7	236	198	100
Calgary	(6)	82	42	30	7	3	200	176	94
Edmonton		82	36	29	12	5	221	208	89
Minnesota		82	30	29	20	3	188	183	83

Leading Scorers

Player	Team	GP	G	A	PTS	PIM
Martin St. Louis	Tampa Bay	82	38	56	94	24
Ilya Kovalchuk	Atlanta	81	41	46	87	63
Joe Sakic	Colorado	81	33	54	87	42
Markus Naslund	Vancouver	78	35	49	84	58
Marian Hossa	Ottawa	81	36	46	82	46
Patrik Elias	New Jersey	82	38	43	81	44
Daniel Alfredsson	Ottawa	77	32	48	80	24
Cory Stillman	Tampa Bay	81	25	55	80	36
Robert Lang	Wsh., Det.	69	30	49	79	24
Brad Richards	Tampa Bay	82	26	53	79	12
Alex Tanguay	Colorado	69	25	54	79	42

2004-05

SEASON CANCELLED

2005-06

EASTERN CONFERENCE

Northeast Division

Team		GP	W	L	OL	GF	GA	PTS
Ottawa	(1)	82	52	21	9	314	211	113
Buffalo	(4)	82	52	24	6	281	239	110
Montreal	(7)	82	42	31	9	243	247	93
Toronto		82	41	33	8	257	270	90
Boston		82	29	37	16	230	266	74

Atlantic Division

Team		GP	W	L	OL	GF	GA	PTS
New Jersey	(3)	82	46	27	9	242	229	101
Philadelphia	(5)	82	45	26	11	267	259	101
NY Rangers	(6)	82	44	26	12	257	215	100
NY Islanders		82	36	40	6	230	278	78
Pittsburgh		82	22	46	14	244	316	58

Southeast Division

Team		GP	W	L	OL	GF	GA	PTS
*Carolina	(2)	82	52	22	8	294	260	112
Tampa Bay	(8)	82	43	33	6	252	260	92
Atlanta		82	41	33	8	281	275	90
Florida		82	37	34	11	240	257	85
Washington		82	29	41	12	237	306	70

WESTERN CONFERENCE

Central Division

Team		GP	W	L	OL	GF	GA	PTS
Detroit	(1)	82	58	16	8	305	209	124
Nashville	(4)	82	49	25	8	259	227	106
Columbus		82	35	43	4	223	279	74
Chicago		82	26	43	13	211	285	65
St. Louis		82	21	46	15	197	292	57

Pacific Division

Team		GP	W	L	OL	GF	GA	PTS
Dallas	(2)	82	53	23	6	265	218	112
San Jose	(5)	82	44	27	11	266	242	99
Anaheim	(6)	82	43	27	12	254	229	98
Los Angeles		82	42	35	5	249	270	89
Phoenix		82	38	39	5	246	271	81

Northwest Division

Team		GP	W	L	OL	GF	GA	PTS
Calgary	(3)	82	46	25	11	218	200	103
Colorado	(7)	82	43	30	9	283	257	95
Edmonton	(8)	82	41	28	13	256	251	95
Vancouver		82	42	32	8	256	255	92
Minnesota		82	38	36	8	231	215	84

Leading Scorers

Player	Team	GP	G	A	PTS	PIM
Joe Thornton	Bos., S.J.	81	29	96	125	61
Jaromir Jagr	NY Rangers	82	54	69	123	72
Alex Ovechkin	Washington	81	52	54	106	52
Dany Heatley	Ottawa	82	50	53	103	86
Daniel Alfredsson	Ottawa	77	43	60	103	50
Sidney Crosby	Pittsburgh	81	39	63	102	110
Eric Staal	Carolina	82	45	55	100	81
Ilya Kovalchuk	Atlanta	78	52	46	98	68
Marc Savard	Atlanta	82	28	69	97	100
Jonathan Cheechoo	San Jose	82	56	37	93	58

2006-07

EASTERN CONFERENCE

Northeast Division

Team		GP	W	L	OL	GF	GA	PTS
Buffalo	(1)	82	53	22	7	308	242	113
Ottawa	(4)	82	48	25	9	288	222	105
Toronto		82	40	31	11	258	269	91
Montreal		82	42	34	6	245	256	90
Boston		82	35	41	6	219	289	76

Atlantic Division

Team		GP	W	L	OL	GF	GA	PTS
New Jersey	(2)	82	49	24	9	216	201	107
Pittsburgh	(5)	82	47	24	11	277	246	105
NY Rangers	(6)	82	42	30	10	242	216	94
NY Islanders	(8)	82	40	30	12	248	240	92
Philadelphia		82	22	48	12	214	303	56

Southeast Division

Team		GP	W	L	OL	GF	GA	PTS
Atlanta	(3)	82	43	28	11	246	245	97
Tampa Bay	(7)	82	44	33	5	253	261	93
Carolina		82	40	34	8	241	253	88
Florida		82	35	31	16	247	257	86
Washington		82	28	40	14	235	286	70

WESTERN CONFERENCE

Central Division

Team		GP	W	L	OL	GF	GA	PTS
Detroit	(1)	82	50	19	13	254	199	113
Nashville	(4)	82	51	23	8	272	212	110
St. Louis		82	34	35	13	214	254	81
Columbus		82	33	42	7	201	249	73
Chicago		82	31	42	9	201	258	71

Pacific Division

Team		GP	W	L	OL	GF	GA	PTS
*Anaheim	(2)	82	48	20	14	258	208	110
San Jose	(5)	82	51	26	5	258	199	107
Dallas	(6)	82	50	25	7	226	197	107
Los Angeles		82	27	41	14	227	283	68
Phoenix		82	31	46	5	216	284	67

Northwest Division

Team		GP	W	L	OL	GF	GA	PTS
Vancouver	(3)	82	49	26	7	222	201	105
Minnesota	(7)	82	48	26	8	235	191	104
Calgary	(8)	82	43	29	10	258	226	96
Colorado		82	44	31	7	272	251	95
Edmonton		82	32	43	7	195	248	71

Leading Scorers

Player	Team	GP	G	A	PTS	PIM
Sidney Crosby	Pittsburgh	79	36	84	120	60
Joe Thornton	San Jose	82	22	92	114	44
Vincent Lecavalier	Tampa Bay	82	52	56	108	44
Dany Heatley	Ottawa	82	50	55	105	74
Martin St. Louis	Tampa Bay	82	43	59	102	28
Marian Hossa	Atlanta	82	43	57	100	49
Joe Sakic	Colorado	82	36	64	100	46
Jaromir Jagr	NY Rangers	82	30	66	96	78
Marc Savard	Boston	82	22	74	96	96
Daniel Briere	Buffalo	81	32	63	95	89

2007-08

EASTERN CONFERENCE

Northeast Division

Team		GP	W	L	OL	GF	GA	PTS
Montreal	(1)	82	47	25	10	262	222	104
Ottawa	(7)	82	43	31	8	261	247	94
Boston	(8)	82	41	29	12	212	222	94
Buffalo		82	39	31	12	255	242	90
Toronto		82	36	35	11	231	260	83

Atlantic Division

Pittsburgh	(2)	82	47	27	8	247	216	102
New Jersey	(4)	82	46	29	7	206	197	99
NY Rangers	(5)	82	42	27	13	213	199	97
Philadelphia	(6)	82	42	29	11	248	233	95
NY Islanders		82	35	38	9	194	243	79

Southeast Division

Washington	(3)	82	43	31	8	242	231	94
Carolina		82	43	33	6	252	249	92
Florida		82	38	35	9	216	226	85
Atlanta		82	34	40	8	216	272	76
Tampa Bay		82	31	42	9	223	267	71

WESTERN CONFERENCE

Central Division

*Detroit	(1)	82	54	21	7	257	184	115
Nashville	(8)	82	41	32	9	230	229	91
Chicago		82	40	34	8	239	235	88
Columbus		82	34	36	12	193	218	80
St. Louis		82	33	36	13	205	237	79

Pacific Division

San Jose	(2)	82	49	23	10	222	193	108
Anaheim	(4)	82	47	27	8	205	191	102
Dallas	(5)	82	45	30	7	242	207	97
Phoenix		82	38	37	7	214	231	83
Los Angeles		82	32	43	7	231	266	71

Northwest Division

Minnesota	(3)	82	44	28	10	223	218	98
Colorado	(6)	82	44	31	7	231	219	95
Calgary	(7)	82	42	30	10	229	227	94
Edmonton		82	41	35	6	235	251	88
Vancouver		82	39	33	10	213	215	88

Leading Scorers

Player	Team	GP	G	A	PTS	PIM
Alex Ovechkin	Washington	82	65	47	112	40
Evgeni Malkin	Pittsburgh	82	47	59	106	78
Jarome Iginla	Calgary	82	50	48	98	83
Pavel Datsyuk	Detroit	82	31	66	97	20
Joe Thornton	San Jose	82	29	67	96	59
Henrik Zetterberg	Detroit	75	43	49	92	34
Vincent Lecavalier	Tampa Bay	81	40	52	92	89
Jason Spezza	Ottawa	76	34	58	92	66
Daniel Alfredsson	Ottawa	70	40	49	89	34
Ilya Kovalchuk	Atlanta	79	52	35	87	52

2008-09

EASTERN CONFERENCE

Northeast Division

Team		GP	W	L	OL	GF	GA	PTS
Boston	(1)	82	53	19	10	274	196	116
Montreal	(8)	82	41	30	11	249	247	93
Buffalo		82	41	32	9	250	234	91
Ottawa		82	36	35	11	217	237	83
Toronto		82	34	35	13	250	293	81

Atlantic Division

New Jersey	(3)	82	51	27	4	244	209	106
*Pittsburgh	(4)	82	45	28	9	264	239	99
Philadelphia	(5)	82	44	27	11	264	238	99
NY Rangers	(7)	82	43	30	9	210	218	95
NY Islanders		82	26	47	9	201	279	61

Southeast Division

Washington	(2)	82	50	24	8	272	245	108
Carolina	(6)	82	45	30	7	239	226	97
Florida		82	41	30	11	234	231	93
Atlanta		82	35	41	6	257	280	76
Tampa Bay		82	24	40	18	210	279	66

WESTERN CONFERENCE

Central Division

Detroit	(2)	82	51	21	10	295	244	112
Chicago	(4)	82	46	24	12	264	216	104
St. Louis	(6)	82	41	31	10	233	233	92
Columbus	(7)	82	41	31	10	226	230	92
Nashville		82	40	34	8	213	233	88

Pacific Division

San Jose	(1)	82	53	18	11	257	204	117
Anaheim	(8)	82	42	33	7	245	238	91
Dallas		82	36	35	11	230	257	83
Phoenix		82	36	39	7	208	252	79
Los Angeles		82	34	37	11	207	234	79

Northwest Division

Vancouver	(3)	82	45	27	10	246	220	100
Calgary	(5)	82	46	30	6	254	248	98
Minnesota		82	40	33	9	219	200	89
Edmonton		82	38	35	9	234	248	85
Colorado		82	32	45	5	199	257	69

Leading Scorers

Player	Team	GP	G	A	PTS	PIM
Evgeni Malkin	Pittsburgh	82	35	78	113	80
Alex Ovechkin	Washington	79	56	54	110	72
Sidney Crosby	Pittsburgh	77	33	70	103	76
Pavel Datsyuk	Detroit	81	32	65	97	34
Zach Parise	New Jersey	82	45	49	94	24
Ilya Kovalchuk	Atlanta	79	43	48	91	50
Ryan Getzlaf	Anaheim	81	25	66	91	121
Jarome Iginla	Calgary	82	35	54	89	37
Marc Savard	Boston	82	25	63	88	70
Nicklas Backstrom	Washington	82	22	66	88	46

2009-10

EASTERN CONFERENCE

Northeast Division

Team		GP	W	L	OL	GF	GA	PTS
Buffalo	(3)	82	45	27	10	235	207	100
Ottawa	(5)	82	44	32	6	225	238	94
Boston	(6)	82	39	30	13	206	200	91
Montreal	(8)	82	39	33	10	217	223	88
Toronto		82	30	38	14	214	267	74

Atlantic Division

New Jersey	(2)	82	48	27	7	222	191	103
Pittsburgh	(4)	82	47	28	7	257	237	101
Philadelphia	(7)	82	41	35	6	236	225	88
NY Rangers		82	38	33	11	222	218	87
NY Islanders		82	34	37	11	222	264	79

Southeast Division

Washington	(1)	82	54	15	13	318	233	121
Atlanta		82	35	34	13	234	256	83
Carolina		82	35	37	10	230	256	80
Tampa Bay		82	34	36	12	217	260	80
Florida		82	32	37	13	208	244	77

WESTERN CONFERENCE

Central Division

*Chicago	(2)	82	52	22	8	271	209	112
Detroit	(5)	82	44	24	14	229	216	102
Nashville	(7)	82	47	29	6	225	225	100
St. Louis		82	40	32	10	225	223	90
Columbus		82	32	35	15	216	259	79

Pacific Division

San Jose	(1)	82	51	20	11	264	215	113
Phoenix	(4)	82	50	25	7	225	202	107
Los Angeles	(6)	82	46	27	9	241	219	101
Anaheim		82	39	32	11	238	251	89
Dallas		82	37	31	14	237	254	88

Northwest Division

Vancouver	(3)	82	49	28	5	272	222	103
Colorado	(8)	82	43	30	9	244	233	95
Calgary		82	40	32	10	204	210	90
Minnesota		82	38	36	8	219	246	84
Edmonton		82	27	47	8	214	284	62

Leading Scorers

Player	Team	GP	G	A	PTS	PIM
Henrik Sedin	Vancouver	82	29	83	112	48
Sidney Crosby	Pittsburgh	81	51	58	109	71
Alex Ovechkin	Washington	72	50	59	109	89
Nicklas Backstrom	Washington	82	33	68	101	50
Steven Stamkos	Tampa Bay	82	51	44	95	38
Martin St. Louis	Tampa Bay	82	29	65	94	12
Brad Richards	Dallas	80	24	67	91	14
Joe Thornton	San Jose	79	20	69	89	54
Patrick Kane	Chicago	82	30	58	88	20
Marian Gaborik	NY Rangers	76	42	44	86	37

2010-11

EASTERN CONFERENCE

Northeast Division

Team		GP	W	L	OT	GF	GA	PTS
*Boston	(3)	82	46	25	11	246	195	103
Montreal	(6)	82	44	30	8	216	209	96
Buffalo	(7)	82	43	29	10	245	229	96
Toronto		82	37	34	11	218	251	85
Ottawa		82	32	40	10	192	250	74

Atlantic Division

Philadelphia	(2)	82	47	23	12	259	223	106
Pittsburgh	(4)	82	49	25	8	238	199	106
NY Rangers	(8)	82	44	33	5	233	198	93
New Jersey		82	38	39	5	174	209	81
NY Islanders		82	30	39	13	229	264	73

Southeast Division

Washington	(1)	82	48	23	11	224	197	107
Tampa Bay	(5)	82	46	25	11	247	240	103
Carolina		82	40	31	11	236	239	91
Atlanta		82	34	36	12	223	269	80
Florida		82	30	40	12	195	229	72

WESTERN CONFERENCE

Central Division

Detroit	(3)	82	47	25	10	261	241	104
Nashville	(5)	82	44	27	11	219	194	99
Chicago	(8)	82	44	29	9	258	225	97
St. Louis		82	38	33	11	240	234	87
Columbus		82	34	35	13	215	258	81

Pacific Division

San Jose	(2)	82	48	25	9	248	213	105
Anaheim	(4)	82	47	30	5	239	235	99
Phoenix	(6)	82	43	26	13	231	226	99
Los Angeles	(7)	82	46	30	6	219	198	98
Dallas		82	42	29	11	227	233	95

Northwest Division

Vancouver	(1)	82	54	19	9	262	185	117
Calgary		82	41	29	12	250	237	94
Minnesota		82	39	35	8	206	233	86
Colorado		82	30	44	8	227	288	68
Edmonton		82	25	45	12	193	269	62

Leading Scorers

Player	Team	GP	G	A	PTS	PIM
Daniel Sedin	Vancouver	82	41	63	104	32
Martin St. Louis	Tampa Bay	82	31	68	99	12
Corey Perry	Anaheim	82	50	48	98	104
Henrik Sedin	Vancouver	82	19	75	94	40
Steven Stamkos	Tampa Bay	82	45	46	91	74
Jarome Iginla	Calgary	82	43	43	86	40
Alex Ovechkin	Washington	79	32	53	85	41
Teemu Selanne	Anaheim	73	31	49	80	49
Henrik Zetterberg	Detroit	80	24	56	80	40
Brad Richards	Dallas	72	28	49	77	24

2011-12

EASTERN CONFERENCE

Northeast Division

		GP	W	L	OT	GF	GA	PTS
Boston	(2)	82	49	29	4	269	202	102
Ottawa	(8)	82	41	31	10	249	240	92
Buffalo		82	39	32	11	218	230	89
Toronto		82	35	37	10	231	264	80
Montreal		82	31	35	16	212	226	78

Atlantic Division

NY Rangers	(1)	82	51	24	7	226	187	109
Pittsburgh	(4)	82	51	25	6	282	221	108
Philadelphia	(5)	82	47	26	9	264	232	103
New Jersey	(6)	82	48	28	6	228	209	102
NY Islanders		82	34	37	11	203	255	79

Southeast Division

Florida	(3)	82	38	26	18	203	227	94
Washington	(7)	82	42	32	8	222	230	92
Tampa Bay		82	38	36	8	235	281	84
Winnipeg		82	37	35	10	225	246	84
Carolina		82	33	33	16	213	243	82

WESTERN CONFERENCE

Central Division

St. Louis	(2)	82	49	22	11	210	165	109
Nashville	(4)	82	48	26	8	237	210	104
Detroit	(5)	82	48	28	6	248	203	102
Chicago	(6)	82	45	26	11	248	238	101
Columbus		82	29	46	7	202	262	65

Pacific Division

Phoenix	(3)	82	42	27	13	216	204	97
San Jose	(7)	82	43	29	10	228	210	96
*Los Angeles	(8)	82	40	27	15	194	179	95
Dallas		82	42	35	5	211	222	89
Anaheim		82	34	36	12	204	231	80

Northwest Division

Vancouver	(1)	82	51	22	9	249	198	111
Calgary		82	37	29	16	202	226	90
Colorado		82	41	35	6	208	220	88
Minnesota		82	35	36	11	177	226	81
Edmonton		82	32	40	10	212	239	74

Leading Scorers

Player	Team	GP	G	A	PTS	PIM
Evgeni Malkin	Pittsburgh	75	50	59	109	70
Steven Stamkos	Tampa Bay	82	60	37	97	66
Claude Giroux	Philadelphia	77	28	65	93	29
Jason Spezza	Ottawa	80	34	50	84	36
Ilya Kovalchuk	New Jersey	77	37	46	83	33
Phil Kessel	Toronto	82	37	45	82	20
James Neal	Pittsburgh	80	40	41	81	87
John Tavares	NY Islanders	82	31	50	81	26
Henrik Sedin	Vancouver	82	14	67	81	52
Patrik Elias	New Jersey	81	26	52	78	16

2012-13

EASTERN CONFERENCE

Northeast Division

Team		GP	W	L	OT	GF	GA	PTS
Montreal	(2)	48	29	14	5	149	126	63
Boston	(4)	48	28	14	6	131	109	62
Toronto	(5)	48	26	17	5	145	133	57
Ottawa	(7)	48	25	17	6	116	104	56
Buffalo		48	21	21	6	125	143	48

Atlantic Division

Team		GP	W	L	OT	GF	GA	PTS
Pittsburgh	(1)	48	36	12	0	165	119	72
NY Rangers	(6)	48	26	18	4	130	112	56
NY Islanders	(8)	48	24	17	7	139	139	55
Philadelphia		48	23	22	3	133	141	49
New Jersey		48	19	19	10	112	129	48

Southeast Division

Team		GP	W	L	OT	GF	GA	PTS
Washington	(3)	48	27	18	3	149	130	57
Winnipeg		48	24	21	3	128	144	51
Carolina		48	19	25	4	128	160	42
Tampa Bay		48	18	26	4	148	150	40
Florida		48	15	27	6	112	171	36

WESTERN CONFERENCE

Central Division

Team		GP	W	L	OT	GF	GA	PTS
*Chicago	(1)	48	36	7	5	155	102	77
St. Louis	(4)	48	29	17	2	129	115	60
Detroit	(7)	48	24	16	8	124	115	56
Columbus		48	24	17	7	120	119	55
Nashville		48	16	23	9	111	139	41

Pacific Division

Team		GP	W	L	OT	GF	GA	PTS
Anaheim	(2)	48	30	12	6	140	118	66
Los Angeles	(5)	48	27	16	5	133	118	59
San Jose	(6)	48	25	16	7	124	116	57
Phoenix		48	21	18	9	125	131	51
Dallas		48	22	22	4	130	142	48

Northwest Division

Team		GP	W	L	OT	GF	GA	PTS
Vancouver	(3)	48	26	15	7	127	121	59
Minnesota	(8)	48	26	19	3	122	127	55
Edmonton		48	19	22	7	125	134	45
Calgary		48	19	25	4	128	160	42
Colorado		48	16	25	7	116	152	39

Leading Scorers

Player	Team	GP	G	A	PTS	PIM
Martin St. Louis	Tampa Bay	48	17	43	60	14
Steven Stamkos	Tampa Bay	48	29	28	57	32
Alex Ovechkin	Washington	48	32	24	56	36
Sidney Crosby	Pittsburgh	36	15	41	56	16
Patrick Kane	Chicago	47	23	32	55	8
Eric Staal	Carolina	48	18	35	53	54
Chris Kunitz	Pittsburgh	48	22	30	52	39
Phil Kessel	Toronto	48	20	32	52	18
Taylor Hall	Edmonton	45	16	34	50	33
Ryan Getzlaf	Anaheim	44	15	34	49	41

2013-14

EASTERN CONFERENCE

Atlantic Division

Team		GP	W	L	OT	GF	GA	PTS
Boston	(A1)	82	54	19	9	261	177	117
Tampa Bay	(A2)	82	46	27	9	240	215	101
Montreal	(A3)	82	46	28	8	215	204	100
Detroit	(W2)	82	39	28	15	222	230	93
Ottawa		82	37	31	14	236	265	88
Toronto		82	38	36	8	231	256	84
Florida		82	29	45	8	196	268	66
Buffalo		82	21	51	10	157	248	52

Metropolitan Division

Team		GP	W	L	OT	GF	GA	PTS
Pittsburgh	(M1)	82	51	24	7	249	207	109
NY Rangers	(M2)	82	45	31	6	218	193	96
Philadelphia	(M3)	82	42	30	10	236	235	94
Columbus	(W1)	82	43	32	7	231	216	93
Washington		82	38	30	14	235	240	90
New Jersey		82	35	29	18	197	208	88
Carolina		82	36	35	11	207	230	83
NY Islanders		82	34	37	11	225	267	79

WESTERN CONFERENCE

Central Division

Team		GP	W	L	OT	GF	GA	PTS
Colorado	(C1)	82	52	22	8	250	220	112
St. Louis	(C2)	82	52	23	7	248	191	111
Chicago	(C3)	82	46	21	15	267	220	107
Minnesota	(W1)	82	43	27	12	207	206	98
Dallas	(W2)	82	40	31	11	235	228	91
Nashville		82	38	32	12	216	242	88
Winnipeg		82	37	35	10	227	237	84

Pacific Division

Team		GP	W	L	OT	GF	GA	PTS
Anaheim	(P1)	82	54	20	8	266	209	116
San Jose	(P2)	82	51	22	9	249	200	111
*Los Angeles	(P3)	82	46	28	8	206	174	100
Phoenix		82	37	30	15	216	231	89
Vancouver		82	36	35	11	196	223	83
Calgary		82	35	40	7	209	241	77
Edmonton		82	29	44	9	203	270	67

Leading Scorers

Player	Team	GP	G	A	PTS	PIM
Sidney Crosby	Pittsburgh	80	36	68	104	46
Ryan Getzlaf	Anaheim	77	31	56	87	31
Claude Giroux	Philadelphia	82	28	58	86	46
Tyler Seguin	Dallas	80	37	47	84	18
Corey Perry	Anaheim	81	43	39	82	65
Phil Kessel	Toronto	82	37	43	80	27
Taylor Hall	Edmonton	75	27	53	80	44
Alex Ovechkin	Washington	78	51	28	79	48
Joe Pavelski	San Jose	82	41	38	79	32
Jamie Benn	Dallas	81	34	45	79	64
Nicklas Backstrom	Washington	82	18	61	79	54

2014-15

EASTERN CONFERENCE

Atlantic Division

Team		GP	W	L	OT	GF	GA	PTS
Montreal	(A1)	82	50	22	10	221	189	110
Tampa Bay	(A2)	82	50	24	8	262	211	108
Detroit	(A3)	82	43	25	14	235	221	100
Ottawa	(W1)	82	43	26	13	238	215	99
Boston		82	41	27	14	213	211	96
Florida		82	38	29	15	206	223	91
Toronto		82	30	44	8	211	262	68
Buffalo		82	23	51	8	161	274	54

Metropolitan Division

Team		GP	W	L	OT	GF	GA	PTS
NY Rangers	(M1)	82	53	22	7	252	192	113
Washington	(M2)	82	45	26	11	242	203	101
NY Islanders	(M3)	82	47	28	7	252	230	101
Pittsburgh	(W2)	82	43	27	12	221	210	98
Columbus		82	42	35	5	236	250	89
Philadelphia		82	33	31	18	215	234	84
New Jersey		82	32	36	14	181	216	78
Carolina		82	30	41	11	188	226	71

WESTERN CONFERENCE

Central Division

Team		GP	W	L	OT	GF	GA	PTS
St. Louis	(C1)	82	51	24	7	248	201	109
Nashville	(C2)	82	47	25	10	232	208	104
*Chicago	(C3)	82	48	28	6	229	189	102
Minnesota	(W1)	82	46	28	8	231	201	100
Winnipeg	(W2)	82	43	26	13	230	210	99
Dallas		82	41	31	10	261	260	92
Colorado		82	39	31	12	219	227	90

Pacific Division

Team		GP	W	L	OT	GF	GA	PTS
Anaheim	(P1)	82	51	24	7	236	226	109
Vancouver	(P2)	82	48	29	5	242	222	101
Calgary	(P3)	82	45	30	7	241	216	97
Los Angeles		82	40	27	15	220	205	95
San Jose		82	40	33	9	228	232	89
Edmonton		82	24	44	14	198	283	62
Arizona		82	24	50	8	170	272	56

Leading Scorers

Player	Team	GP	G	A	PTS	PIM
Jamie Benn	Dallas	82	35	52	87	64
John Tavares	NY Islanders	82	38	48	86	46
Sidney Crosby	Pittsburgh	77	28	56	84	47
Alex Ovechkin	Washington	81	53	28	81	58
Jakub Voracek	Philadelphia	82	22	59	81	78
Nicklas Backstrom	Washington	82	18	60	78	40
Tyler Seguin	Dallas	71	37	40	77	20
Jiri Hudler	Calgary	78	31	45	76	14
Daniel Sedin	Vancouver	82	20	56	76	18
Vladimir Tarasenko	St. Louis	77	37	36	73	31

2015-16

EASTERN CONFERENCE

Atlantic Division

Team		GP	W	L	OT	GF	GA	PTS
Florida	(A1)	82	47	26	9	239	203	103
Tampa Bay	(A2)	82	46	31	5	227	201	97
Detroit	(A3)	82	41	30	11	211	224	93
Boston		82	42	31	9	240	230	93
Ottawa		82	38	35	9	236	247	85
Montreal		82	38	38	6	221	236	82
Buffalo		82	35	36	11	201	222	81
Toronto		82	29	42	11	198	246	69

Metropolitan Division

Team		GP	W	L	OT	GF	GA	PTS
Washington	(M1)	82	56	18	8	252	193	120
*Pittsburgh	(M2)	82	48	26	8	245	203	104
NY Rangers	(M3)	82	46	27	9	236	217	101
NY Islanders	(W1)	82	45	27	10	232	216	100
Philadelphia	(W2)	82	41	27	14	214	218	96
Carolina		82	35	31	16	198	226	86
New Jersey		82	38	36	8	184	208	84
Columbus		82	34	40	8	219	252	76

WESTERN CONFERENCE

Central Division

Team		GP	W	L	OT	GF	GA	PTS
Dallas	(C1)	82	50	23	9	267	230	109
St. Louis	(C2)	82	49	24	9	224	201	107
Chicago	(C3)	82	47	26	9	235	209	103
Nashville	(W1)	82	41	27	14	228	215	96
Minnesota	(W2)	82	38	33	11	216	206	87
Colorado		82	39	39	4	216	240	82
Winnipeg		82	35	39	8	215	239	78

Pacific Division

Team		GP	W	L	OT	GF	GA	PTS
Anaheim	(P1)	82	46	25	11	218	192	103
Los Angeles	(P2)	82	48	28	6	225	195	102
San Jose	(P3)	82	46	30	6	241	210	98
Arizona		82	35	39	8	209	245	78
Calgary		82	35	40	7	231	260	77
Vancouver		82	31	38	13	191	243	75
Edmonton		82	31	43	8	203	245	70

Leading Scorers

Player	Team	GP	G	A	PTS	PIM
Patrick Kane	Chicago	82	46	60	106	30
Jamie Benn	Dallas	82	41	48	89	64
Sidney Crosby	Pittsburgh	80	36	49	85	42
Joe Thornton	San Jose	82	19	63	82	54
Erik Karlsson	Ottawa	82	16	66	82	50
Joe Pavelski	San Jose	82	38	40	78	30
Johnny Gaudreau	Calgary	79	30	48	78	20
Blake Wheeler	Winnipeg	82	26	52	78	49
Artemi Panarin	Chicago	80	30	47	77	32
Evgeny Kuznetsov	Washington	82	20	57	77	32

2016-17

EASTERN CONFERENCE

Atlantic Division

Team		GP	W	L	OT	GF	GA	PTS
Montreal	(A1)	82	47	26	9	226	200	103
Ottawa	(A2)	82	44	28	10	212	214	98
Boston	(A3)	82	44	31	7	234	212	95
Toronto	(W2)	82	40	27	15	251	242	95
Tampa Bay		82	42	30	10	234	227	94
Florida		82	35	36	11	210	237	81
Detroit		82	33	36	13	207	244	79
Buffalo		82	33	37	12	201	237	78

Metropolitan Division

Team		GP	W	L	OT	GF	GA	PTS
Washington	(M1)	82	55	19	8	263	182	118
*Pittsburgh	(M2)	82	50	21	11	282	234	111
Columbus	(M3)	82	50	24	8	249	195	108
NY Rangers	(W1)	82	48	28	6	256	220	102
NY Islanders		82	41	29	12	241	242	94
Philadelphia		82	39	33	10	219	236	88
Carolina		82	36	31	15	215	236	87
New Jersey		82	28	40	14	183	244	70

WESTERN CONFERENCE

Central Division

Team		GP	W	L	OT	GF	GA	PTS
Chicago	(C1)	82	50	23	9	244	213	109
Minnesota	(C2)	82	49	25	8	266	208	106
St. Louis	(C3)	82	46	29	7	235	218	99
Nashville	(W2)	82	41	29	12	240	224	94
Winnipeg		82	40	35	7	249	256	87
Dallas		82	34	37	11	223	262	79
Colorado		82	22	56	4	166	278	48

Pacific Division

Team		GP	W	L	OT	GF	GA	PTS
Anaheim	(P1)	82	46	23	13	223	200	105
Edmonton	(P2)	82	47	26	9	247	212	103
San Jose	(P3)	82	46	29	7	221	201	99
Calgary	(W1)	82	45	33	4	226	221	94
Los Angeles		82	39	35	8	201	205	86
Arizona		82	30	42	10	197	260	70
Vancouver		82	30	43	9	182	243	69

Leading Scorers

Player	Team	GP	G	A	PTS	PIM
Connor McDavid	Edmonton	82	30	70	100	26
Sidney Crosby	Pittsburgh	75	44	45	89	24
Patrick Kane	Chicago	82	34	55	89	32
Nicklas Backstrom	Washington	82	23	63	86	38
Nikita Kucherov	Tampa Bay	74	40	45	85	38
Brad Marchand	Boston	80	39	46	85	81
Mark Scheifele	Winnipeg	79	32	50	82	38
Leon Draisaitl	Edmonton	82	29	48	77	20
Brent Burns	San Jose	82	29	47	76	40
Vladimir Tarasenko	St. Louis	82	39	36	75	12

Note: Detailed statistics for 2016-17 are listed in the Final Statistics, 2016-17 section of the *NHL Guide & Record Book*. **See page 137.**

Team Records

Regular Season

FINAL STANDINGS

MOST POINTS, ONE SEASON:
- **132 – Montreal Canadiens**, 1976-77. 60w-8L-12T. 80GP
- 131 – Detroit Red Wings, 1995-96. 62w-13L-7T. 82GP
- 129 – Montreal Canadiens, 1977-78. 59w-10L-11T. 80GP

BEST POINTS PERCENTAGE, ONE SEASON:
- **.875 – Boston Bruins**, 1929-30. 38w-5L-1T. 77PTS in 44GP
- .830 – Montreal Canadiens, 1943-44. 38w-5L-7T. 83PTS in 50GP
- .825 – Montreal Canadiens, 1976-77. 60w-8L-12T. 132PTS in 80GP
- .806 – Montreal Canadiens, 1977-78. 59w-10L-11T. 129PTS in 80GP
- .802 – Chicago Blackhawks, 2012-13. 36w-7L-5OTL. 77PTS in 48GP
- .800 – Montreal Canadiens, 1944-45. 38w-8L-4T. 80PTS in 50GP

FEWEST POINTS, ONE SEASON:
- **8 – Quebec Bulldogs**, 1919-20. 4w-20L-0T. 24GP
- 10 – Toronto Arenas, 1918-19. 5w-13L-0T. 18GP
- 12 – Hamilton Tigers, 1920-21. 6w-18L-0T. 24GP
- – Hamilton Tigers, 1922-23. 6w-18L-0T. 24GP
- – Boston Bruins, 1924-25. 6w-24L-0T. 30GP
- – Philadelphia Quakers, 1930-31. 4w-36L-4T. 44GP

FEWEST POINTS, ONE SEASON (MINIMUM 70-GAME SCHEDULE):
- **21 – Washington Capitals**, 1974-75. 8w-67L-5T. 80GP
- 24 – Ottawa Senators, 1992-93. 10w-70L-4T. 84GP
- – San Jose Sharks, 1992-93. 11w-71L-2T. 84GP
- 30 – New York Islanders, 1972-73. 12w-60L-6T. 78GP

WORST POINTS PERCENTAGE, ONE SEASON:
- **.131 – Washington Capitals**, 1974-75. 8w-67L-5T. 21PTS in 80GP
- .136 – Philadelphia Quakers, 1930-31. 4w-36L-4T. 12PTS in 44GP
- .143 – Ottawa Senators, 1992-93. 10w-70L-4T. 24PTS in 84GP
- – San Jose Sharks, 1992-93. 11w-71L-2T. 24PTS in 84GP
- .148 – Pittsburgh Pirates, 1929-30. 5w-36L-3T. 13PTS in 44GP

TEAM WINS

Most Wins

MOST WINS, ONE SEASON:
- **62 – Detroit Red Wings**, 1995-96. 82GP
- 60 – Montreal Canadiens, 1976-77. 80GP
- 59 – Montreal Canadiens, 1977-78. 80GP

MOST HOME WINS, ONE SEASON:
- **36 – Philadelphia Flyers**, 1975-76. 40GP
- **– Detroit Red Wings**, 1995-96. 41GP
- 33 – Boston Bruins, 1970-71. 39GP
- – Boston Bruins, 1973-74. 39GP
- – Montreal Canadiens, 1976-77. 40GP
- – Philadelphia Flyers, 1976-77. 40GP
- – New York Islanders, 1981-82. 40GP
- – Philadelphia Flyers, 1985-86. 40GP

MOST ROAD WINS, ONE SEASON:
- **31 – Detroit Red Wings**, 2005-06. 41GP
- 28 – New Jersey Devils, 1998-99. 41GP
- – New York Rangers, 2014-15. 41GP
- 27 – Montreal Canadiens, 1976-77. 40GP
- – Montreal Canadiens, 1977-78. 40GP
- – St. Louis Blues, 1999-2000. 41GP
- – San Jose Sharks, 2007-08. 41GP
- – Vancouver Canucks, 2010-11. 41GP
- – Washington Capitals, 2015-16. 41GP
- – New York Rangers, 2016-17. 41GP
- 26 – Boston Bruins, 1971-72. 39GP
- – Montreal Canadiens, 1975-76. 40GP
- – Edmonton Oilers, 1983-84. 40GP
- – Detroit Red Wings, 1995-96. 41GP
- – San Jose Sharks, 2006-07. 41GP
- – Detroit Red Wings, 2010-11. 41GP
- – Colorado Avalanche, 2013-14. 41GP

Fewest Wins

FEWEST WINS, ONE SEASON:
- **4 – Quebec Bulldogs**, 1919-20. 24GP
- **– Philadelphia Quakers**, 1930-31. 44GP
- 5 – Toronto Arenas, 1918-19. 18GP
- Pittsburgh Pirates, 1929-30. 44GP

FEWEST WINS, ONE SEASON (MINIMUM 70-GAME SCHEDULE):
- **8 – Washington Capitals**, 1974-75. 80GP
- 9 – Winnipeg Jets, 1980-81. 80GP
- 10 – Ottawa Senators, 1992-93. 84GP

FEWEST HOME WINS, ONE SEASON:
- **2 – Chicago Blackhawks**, 1927-28. 22GP
- 3 – Boston Bruins, 1924-25. 15GP
- – Chicago Blackhawks, 1928-29. 22GP
- – Philadelphia Quakers, 1930-31. 22GP

FEWEST HOME WINS, ONE SEASON (MINIMUM 70-GAME SCHEDULE):
- **6 – Chicago Blackhawks**, 1954-55. 35GP
- **– Washington Capitals**, 1975-76. 40GP
- 7 – Boston Bruins, 1962-63. 35GP
- – Washington Capitals, 1974-75. 40GP
- – Winnipeg Jets, 1980-81. 40GP

- – Pittsburgh Penguins, 1983-84. 40GP

FEWEST ROAD WINS, ONE SEASON:
- **0 – Toronto Arenas**, 1918-19. 9GP
- **– Quebec Bulldogs**, 1919-20. 12GP
- **– Pittsburgh Pirates**, 1929-30. 22GP
- 1 – Hamilton Tigers, 1921-22. 12GP
- – Toronto St. Patricks, 1925-26. 18GP
- – Philadelphia Quakers, 1930-31. 22GP
- – New York Americans, 1940-41. 24GP
- – Washington Capitals, 1974-75. 40GP
- * – Ottawa Senators, 1992-93. 41GP

FEWEST ROAD WINS, ONE SEASON (MINIMUM 70-GAME SCHEDULE):
- **1 – Washington Capitals**, 1974-75. 40GP
- * **– Ottawa Senators**, 1992-93. 41GP
- 2 – Boston Bruins, 1960-61. 35GP
- – Los Angeles Kings, 1969-70. 38GP
- – New York Islanders, 1972-73. 39GP
- – California Golden Seals, 1973-74. 39GP
- – Colorado Rockies, 1977-78. 40GP
- – Winnipeg Jets, 1980-81. 40GP
- – Quebec Nordiques, 1991-92. 40GP

TEAM LOSSES

Fewest Losses

FEWEST LOSSES, ONE SEASON:
- **5 – Ottawa Senators**, 1919-20. 24GP
- **– Boston Bruins**, 1929-30. 44GP
- **– Montreal Canadiens**, 1943-44. 50GP

FEWEST HOME LOSSES, ONE SEASON:
- **0 – Ottawa Senators**, 1922-23. 12GP
- **– Montreal Canadiens**, 1943-44. 25GP
- 1 – Toronto Arenas, 1917-18. 11GP
- – Ottawa Senators, 1918-19. 9GP
- – Ottawa Senators, 1919-20. 12GP
- – Toronto St. Patricks, 1922-23. 12GP
- – Boston Bruins, 1929-30. 22GP
- – Boston Bruins, 1930-31. 22GP
- – Montreal Canadiens, 1976-77. 40GP
- – Quebec Nordiques, 1994-95. 24GP

FEWEST ROAD LOSSES, ONE SEASON:
- **3 – Montreal Canadiens**, 1928-29. 22GP
- 4 – Ottawa Senators, 1919-20. 12GP
- – Montreal Canadiens, 1927-28. 22GP
- – Boston Bruins, 1929-30. 20GP
- – Boston Bruins, 1940-41. 24GP
- – Chicago Blackhawks, 2012-13. 24GP

FEWEST LOSSES, ONE SEASON (MINIMUM 70-GAME SCHEDULE):
- **8 – Montreal Canadiens**, 1976-77. 80GP
- 10 – Montreal Canadiens, 1972-73. 78GP
- – Montreal Canadiens, 1977-78. 80GP
- 11 – Montreal Canadiens, 1975-76. 80GP

FEWEST HOME LOSSES, ONE SEASON (MINIMUM 70-GAME SCHEDULE):
- **1 – Montreal Canadiens**, 1976-77. 40GP
- 2 – Montreal Canadiens, 1961-62. 35GP
- – New York Rangers, 1970-71. 39GP
- – Philadelphia Flyers, 1975-76. 40GP

FEWEST ROAD LOSSES, ONE SEASON (MINIMUM 70-GAME SCHEDULE):
- **6 – Montreal Canadiens**, 1972-73. 39GP
- **– Montreal Canadiens**, 1974-75. 40GP
- **– Montreal Canadiens**, 1977-78. 40GP
- 7 – Detroit Red Wings, 1951-52. 35GP
- – Montreal Canadiens, 1976-77. 40GP
- – Philadelphia Flyers, 1979-80. 40GP
- – Boston Bruins, 2003-04. 41GP
- – Detroit Red Wings, 2005-06. 41GP

Most Losses

MOST LOSSES, ONE SEASON:
- **71 – San Jose Sharks**, 1992-93. 84GP
- 70 – Ottawa Senators, 1992-93. 84GP
- 67 – Washington Capitals, 1974-75. 80GP
- 61 – Quebec Nordiques, 1989-90. 80GP
- – Ottawa Senators, 1993-94. 84GP

MOST HOME LOSSES, ONE SEASON:
- ***32 – San Jose Sharks**, 1992-93. 41GP
- 29 – Pittsburgh Penguins, 1983-84. 40GP
- * – Ottawa Senators, 1993-94. 41GP

MOST ROAD LOSSES, ONE SEASON:
- ***40 – Ottawa Senators**, 1992-93. 41GP
- 39 – Washington Capitals, 1974-75. 40GP
- 37 – California Golden Seals, 1973-74. 39GP
- * – San Jose Sharks, 1992-93. 41GP

* – Does not include neutral site games

TEAM TIES
Most Ties

MOST TIES, ONE SEASON:
24 – Philadelphia Flyers, 1969-70. 76GP
23 – Montreal Canadiens, 1962-63. 70GP
   – Chicago Blackhawks, 1973-74. 78GP

MOST HOME TIES, ONE SEASON:
13 – New York Rangers, 1954-55. 35GP
   – Philadelphia Flyers, 1969-70. 38GP
   – California Golden Seals, 1971-72. 39GP
   – California Golden Seals, 1972-73. 39GP
   – Chicago Blackhawks, 1973-74. 39GP

MOST ROAD TIES, ONE SEASON:
15 – Philadelphia Flyers, 1976-77. 40GP
14 – Montreal Canadiens, 1952-53. 35GP
   – Montreal Canadiens, 1974-75. 40GP
   – Philadelphia Flyers, 1975-76. 40GP

Fewest Ties

FEWEST TIES, ONE SEASON (Since 1926-27):
1 – Boston Bruins, 1929-30. 44GP
2 – Montreal Canadiens, 1926-27. 44GP
   – New York Americans, 1926-27. 44GP
   – Boston Bruins, 1938-39. 48GP
   – New York Rangers, 1941-42. 48GP
   – San Jose Sharks, 1992-93. 84GP

FEWEST TIES, ONE SEASON (MINIMUM 70-GAME SCHEDULE):
2 – San Jose Sharks, 1992-93. 84GP
3 – New Jersey Devils, 1985-86. 80GP
   – Calgary Flames, 1986-87. 80GP
   – Vancouver Canucks, 1993-94. 84GP

WINNING STREAKS

LONGEST WINNING STREAK, ONE SEASON:
17 Games – Pittsburgh Penguins, Mar. 9 – Apr. 10, 1993.
16 Games – Columbus Blue Jackets, Nov. 29, 2016 – Jan. 3, 2017.
15 Games – New York Islanders, Jan. 21 – Feb. 20, 1982.
   – Pittsburgh Penguins, Mar. 2 – 30, 2013.

LONGEST HOME WINNING STREAK, ONE SEASON:
23 Games – Detroit Red Wings, Nov. 5, 2011 – Feb. 19, 2012.
20 Games – Boston Bruins, Dec. 3, 1929 – Mar. 18, 1930.
   – Philadelphia Flyers, Jan. 4 – Apr. 3, 1976.

LONGEST ROAD WINNING STREAK, ONE SEASON:
12 Games – Detroit Red Wings, Mar. 1 – Apr. 15, 2006.
   – Minnesota Wild, Feb. 18 – Apr. 9, 2015.
10 Games – Buffalo Sabres, Dec. 10, 1983 – Jan. 23, 1984.
   – St. Louis Blues, Jan. 21 – Mar. 2, 2000.
   – New Jersey Devils, Feb. 27 – Apr. 7, 2001.
   – Buffalo Sabres, Oct. 4 – Nov. 13, 2006.
   – San Jose Sharks, Nov. 14 – Dec. 31, 2007.

LONGEST WINNING STREAK FROM START OF SEASON:
10 Games – Toronto Maple Leafs, 1993-94.
   – Buffalo Sabres, 2006-07.
9 Games – Montreal Canadiens, 2015-16.
8 Games – Toronto Maple Leafs, 1934-35.
   – Buffalo Sabres, 1975-76.
   – Nashville Predators, 2005-06.
7 Games – Edmonton Oilers, 1983-84.
   – Quebec Nordiques, 1985-86.
   – Pittsburgh Penguins, 1986-87.
   – Pittsburgh Penguins, 1994-95.
   – Washington Capitals, 2011-12
   – San Jose Sharks, 2012-13.

LONGEST HOME WINNING STREAK FROM START OF SEASON:
11 Games – Chicago Blackhawks, 1963-64.
10 Games – Ottawa Senators, 1925-26.
   – Montreal Canadiens, 2016-17.
9 Games – Montreal Canadiens, 1953-54.
   – Chicago Blackhawks, 1971-72.
   – San Jose Sharks, 2008-09.

LONGEST ROAD WINNING STREAK FROM START OF SEASON:
10 Games – Buffalo Sabres, Oct.4 – Nov. 13, 2006.
9 Games – New Jersey Devils, Oct. 8 – Nov. 12, 2009.
7 Games – Toronto Maple Leafs, Nov. 14 – Dec. 15, 1940.
   – Philadelphia Flyers, Oct. 12 – Nov. 16, 1985.
   – Detroit Red Wings, Oct. 6 – Nov. 6, 2005.
   – Pittsburgh Penguins, Oct. 3 – Nov. 3, 2009

LONGEST WINNING STREAK, INCLUDING PLAYOFFS:
15 Games – Detroit Red Wings, Feb. 27 – Apr. 5, 1955.
   (9 regular-season games, 6 playoff games)
   – New Jersey Devils, Mar. 28 – Apr. 29, 2006.
   (11 regular-season games, 4 playoff games)

LONGEST HOME WINNING STREAK, INCLUDING PLAYOFFS:
24 Games – Philadelphia Flyers, Jan. 4 – Apr. 25, 1976.
   (20 regular-season games, 4 playoff games)

LONGEST ROAD WINNING STREAK, INCLUDING PLAYOFFS:
11 Games – New Jersey Devils, Feb. 27 – Apr. 17, 2001.
   (10 regular-season games, 1 playoff game)

UNDEFEATED STREAKS

LONGEST UNDEFEATED STREAK, ONE SEASON:
35 Games – Philadelphia Flyers, Oct. 14, 1979 – Jan. 6, 1980. 25w-10T
28 Games – Montreal Canadiens, Dec. 18, 1977 – Feb. 23, 1978. 23w-5T

LONGEST HOME UNDEFEATED STREAK, ONE SEASON:
34 Games – Montreal Canadiens, Nov. 1, 1976 – Apr. 2, 1977. 28w-6T
27 Games – Boston Bruins, Nov. 22, 1970 – Mar. 20, 1971. 26w-1T

LONGEST ROAD UNDEFEATED STREAK, ONE SEASON:
23 Games – Montreal Canadiens, Nov. 27, 1974 – Mar. 12, 1975. 14w-9T
17 Games – Montreal Canadiens, Dec. 18, 1977 – Mar. 1, 1978. 14w-3T

LONGEST UNDEFEATED STREAK FROM START OF SEASON:
15 Games – Edmonton Oilers, 1984-85. 12w-3T
14 Games – Montreal Canadiens, 1943-44. 11w-3T

LONGEST HOME UNDEFEATED STREAK FROM START OF SEASON:
26 Games – Philadelphia Flyers, Oct. 11, 1979 – Feb. 3, 1980. 19w-7T

LONGEST ROAD UNDEFEATED STREAK FROM START OF SEASON:
15 Games – Detroit Red Wings, Oct. 18 – Dec. 20, 1951. 10w-5T

LONGEST UNDEFEATED STREAK, INCLUDING PLAYOFFS:
24 Games – Montreal Canadiens, Feb. 21 – Apr. 11, 1980.
   15w-6T in regular season and 3w in playoffs.
21 Games – Philadelphia Flyers, Mar. 9 – May 4, 1975.
   13w-1T in regular season and 7w in playoffs.
   – Pittsburgh Penguins, Mar. 9 – Apr. 22, 1993.
   17w-1T in regular season and 3w in playoffs.

LONGEST HOME UNDEFEATED STREAK, INCLUDING PLAYOFFS:
38 Games – Montreal Canadiens, Nov. 1, 1976 – Apr. 26, 1977.
   28w-6T in regular season and 4w in playoffs.

LONGEST ROAD UNDEFEATED STREAK, INCLUDING PLAYOFFS:
13 Games – Philadelphia Flyers, Feb. 26 – Apr. 21, 1977. 6w-4T in
   regular season and 3w in playoffs.
   – Montreal Canadiens, Feb. 26 – Apr. 20, 1980. 6w-4T in
   regular season and 3w in playoffs.
   – New York Islanders, Mar. 16 – May 1, 1980. 3w-3T in regular
   season and 7w in playoffs.

TEAM POINT STREAKS

LONGEST TEAM POINT STREAK, ONE SEASON:
35 Games – Philadelphia Flyers, Oct. 14, 1979 – Jan. 6, 1980. 25w-10T
28 Games – Montreal Canadiens, Dec. 18, 1977 – Feb. 23, 1978. 23w-5T
24 Games – Chicago Blackhawks, Jan. 19 – Mar. 6, 2013. 21w-3OL

LONGEST TEAM POINT STREAK FROM START OF SEASON:
24 Games – Chicago Blackhawks, Jan. 19 – Mar. 6, 2013. 21w-3OL
16 Games – Anaheim Ducks, Oct. 6 – Nov. 9, 2006. 12w-4OL
15 Games – Edmonton Oilers, Oct. 11 – Nov. 9, 1984. 12w-3T
14 Games – Montreal Canadiens, Oct. 30 – Dec. 4, 1943. 11w-3T

LOSING STREAKS

LONGEST LOSING STREAK, ONE SEASON:
17 Games – Washington Capitals, Feb. 18 – Mar. 26, 1975.
   – San Jose Sharks, Jan. 4 – Feb. 12, 1993.
15 Games – Philadelphia Quakers, Nov. 29, 1930 – Jan. 8, 1931.

LONGEST HOME LOSING STREAK, ONE SEASON:
14 Games – Pittsburgh Penguins, Dec. 31, 2003 – Feb. 22, 2004.
11 Games – Boston Bruins, Dec. 8, 1924 – Feb. 17, 1925.
   – Washington Capitals, Feb. 18 – Mar. 30, 1975.
   – Ottawa Senators, Oct. 27 – Dec. 8, 1993.

LONGEST ROAD LOSING STREAK, ONE SEASON:
***38 Games – Ottawa Senators**, Oct. 10, 1992 – Apr. 3, 1993.
37 Games – Washington Capitals, Oct. 9, 1974 – Mar. 26, 1975.

LONGEST LOSING STREAK FROM START OF SEASON:
11 Games – New York Rangers, 1943-44.
8 Games – Columbus Blue Jackets, 2015-16.
7 Games – Montreal Canadiens, 1938-39.
   – Chicago Blackhawks, 1947-48.
   – Washington Capitals, 1983-84.
   – Chicago Blackhawks, 1997-98.

LONGEST HOME LOSING STREAK FROM START OF SEASON:
8 Games – Los Angeles Kings, Oct. 13 – Nov. 6, 1971.

LONGEST ROAD LOSING STREAK FROM START OF SEASON:
***38 Games – Ottawa Senators**, Oct. 10, 1992 – Apr. 3, 1993.

WINLESS STREAKS

LONGEST WINLESS STREAK, ONE SEASON:
30 Games – Winnipeg Jets, Oct. 19 – Dec. 20, 1980. 23L-7T
27 Games – Kansas City Scouts, Feb. 12 – Apr. 4, 1976. 21L-6T
25 Games – Washington Capitals, Nov. 29, 1975 – Jan. 21, 1976. 22L-3T

LONGEST HOME WINLESS STREAK, ONE SEASON:
17 Games – Ottawa Senators, Oct. 28, 1995 – Jan. 27, 1996. 15L-2T
   – Atlanta Thrashers, Jan. 19 – Mar. 29, 2000. 15L-2T
16 Games – Pittsburgh Penguins, Dec. 31, 2003 – Mar. 4, 2004. 15L-1T

LONGEST ROAD WINLESS STREAK, ONE SEASON:
***38 Games – Ottawa Senators**, Oct. 10, 1992 – Apr. 3, 1993. 38L
37 Games – Washington Capitals, Oct. 9, 1974 – Mar. 26, 1975. 37L

LONGEST WINLESS STREAK FROM START OF SEASON:
15 Games – New York Rangers, 1943-44. 14L-1T
11 Games – Pittsburgh Pirates, 1927-28. 8L-3T
   – Minnesota North Stars, 1973-74. 5L-6T
   – San Jose Sharks, 1995-96. 7L-4T

LONGEST HOME WINLESS STREAK FROM START OF SEASON:
11 Games – Pittsburgh Penguins, Oct. 8 – Nov. 19, 1983. 9L-2T

LONGEST ROAD WINLESS STREAK FROM START OF SEASON:
***38 Games – Ottawa Senators**, Oct. 10, 1992 – Apr. 3, 1993. 38L

NON-SHUTOUT STREAKS

LONGEST NON-SHUTOUT STREAK:
264 Games – Calgary Flames, Nov. 12, 1981 – Jan. 9, 1985.
  261 Games – Los Angeles Kings, Mar. 15, 1986 – Oct. 22, 1989.
  244 Games – Washington Capitals, Oct. 31, 1989 – Nov. 11, 1993.
  236 Games – New York Rangers, Dec. 20, 1989 – Dec. 13, 1992.
  230 Games – Quebec Nordiques, Feb. 10, 1980 – Jan. 12, 1983.

LONGEST NON-SHUTOUT STREAK, INCLUDING PLAYOFFS:
264 Games – Los Angeles Kings, Mar. 15, 1986 – Apr. 6, 1989.
        (5 playoff games in 1987; 5 in 1988; 2 in 1989).
  262 Games – Chicago Blackhawks, Mar. 14, 1970 – Feb. 21, 1973.
        (8 playoff games in 1970; 18 in 1971; 8 in 1972).
  251 Games – Quebec Nordiques, Feb. 10, 1980 – Jan. 12, 1983.
        (5 playoff games in 1981; 16 in 1982).
  246 Games – Pittsburgh Penguins, Jan. 7, 1989 – Oct. 26, 1991.
        (11 playoff games in 1989; 24 in 1991).

TEAM GOALS

Most Goals

MOST GOALS, ONE SEASON:
446 – Edmonton Oilers, 1983-84. 80GP
  426 – Edmonton Oilers, 1985-86. 80GP
  424 – Edmonton Oilers, 1982-83. 80GP
  417 – Edmonton Oilers, 1981-82. 80GP
  401 – Edmonton Oilers, 1984-85. 80GP

MOST GOALS, ONE TEAM, ONE GAME:
16 – Montreal Canadiens, Mar. 3, 1920, at Quebec. Montreal won 16-3.

MOST GOALS, BOTH TEAMS, ONE GAME:
21 – Montreal Canadiens (14), Toronto St. Patricks (7), Jan. 10, 1920,
    at Montreal.
   – **Edmonton Oilers (12), Chicago Blackhawks (9)**, Dec. 11, 1985,
    at Chicago.
  20 – Edmonton Oilers (12), Minnesota North Stars (8), Jan. 4, 1984,
    at Edmonton.
   – Toronto Maple Leafs (11), Edmonton Oilers (9), Jan. 8, 1986,
    at Toronto.
  19 – Montreal Wanderers (10), Toronto Arenas (9), Dec. 19, 1917,
    at Montreal.
   – Montreal Canadiens (16), Quebec Bulldogs (3), Mar. 3, 1920,
    at Quebec.
   – Montreal Canadiens (13), Hamilton Tigers (6), Feb. 26, 1921,
    at Montreal.
   – Boston Bruins (10), New York Rangers (9), Mar. 4, 1944, at Boston.
   – Detroit Red Wings (10), Boston Bruins (9), Mar. 16, 1944, at Detroit.
   – Vancouver Canucks (10), Minnesota North Stars (9), Oct. 7, 1983,
    at Vancouver.

MOST GOALS, ONE TEAM, ONE PERIOD:
9 – Buffalo Sabres, Mar. 19, 1981, at Buffalo, second period during
    14-4 win over Toronto.
  8 – Detroit Red Wings, Jan. 23, 1944, at Detroit, third period during
    15-0 win over NY Rangers.
   – Boston Bruins, Mar. 16, 1969, at Boston, second period during
    11-3 win over Toronto.
   – New York Rangers, Nov. 21, 1971, at NY Rangers, third period during
    12-1 win over California.
   – Philadelphia Flyers, Mar. 31, 1973, at Philadelphia, second period
    during 10-2 win over NY Islanders.
   – Buffalo Sabres, Dec. 21, 1975, at Buffalo, third period during
    14-2 win over Washington.
   – Minnesota North Stars, Nov. 11, 1981, at Minnesota, second
    period during 15-2 win over Winnipeg.
   – Pittsburgh Penguins, Dec. 17, 1991, at Pittsburgh, second period
    during 10-2 win over San Jose.
   – Washington Capitals, Feb. 3, 1999, at Washington, second period
    during 10-1 win over Tampa Bay.

MOST GOALS, BOTH TEAMS, ONE PERIOD:
12 – Buffalo Sabres (9), Toronto Maple Leafs (3), Mar. 19, 1981,
    at Buffalo, second period. Buffalo won 14-4.
   – **Edmonton Oilers (6), Chicago Blackhawks (6)**, Dec. 11, 1985,
    at Chicago, second period. Edmonton won 12-9.
  10 – Ottawa Senators (7), Quebec Bulldogs (3), Mar. 8, 1920,
    at Ottawa, third period. Ottawa won 11-6.
   – New York Rangers (7), New York Americans (3), Mar. 16, 1939,
    at NY Americans, third period. NY Rangers won 11-5.
   – Toronto Maple Leafs (6), Detroit Red Wings (4), Mar. 17, 1946,
    at Detroit, third period. Toronto won 11-7.
   – Buffalo Sabres (6), Vancouver Canucks (4), Jan. 8, 1976,
    at Buffalo, third period. Buffalo won 8-5.
   – Buffalo Sabres (5), Montreal Canadiens (5), Oct. 26, 1982,
    at Montreal, first period. Teams tied 7-7.
   – Quebec Nordiques (6), Boston Bruins (4), Dec. 7, 1982,
    at Quebec, second period. Quebec won 10-5.
   – Vancouver Canucks (6), Calgary Flames (4), Jan. 16, 1987,
    at Vancouver, first period. Vancouver won 9-5.
   – Detroit Red Wings (7), Winnipeg Jets (3), Nov. 25, 1987,
    at Detroit, third period. Detroit won 10-8.
   – Chicago Blackhawks (5), St. Louis Blues (5), Mar. 15, 1988,
    at St. Louis, third period. Teams tied 7-7.

MOST CONSECUTIVE GOALS, ONE TEAM, ONE GAME:
15 – Detroit Red Wings, Jan. 23, 1944, at Detroit during 15-0 win over
    NY Rangers.

Fewest Goals

FEWEST GOALS, ONE SEASON:
33 – Chicago Blackhawks, 1928-29. 44GP
  45 – Montreal Maroons, 1924-25. 30GP
  46 – Pittsburgh Pirates, 1928-29. 44GP

FEWEST GOALS, ONE SEASON (MINIMUM 70-GAME SCHEDULE):
133 – Chicago Blackhawks, 1953-54. 70GP
  147 – Toronto Maple Leafs, 1954-55. 70GP
    – Boston Bruins, 1955-56. 70GP
  150 – New York Rangers, 1954-55. 70GP

TEAM POWER-PLAY GOALS

MOST POWER-PLAY GOALS, ONE SEASON:
119 – Pittsburgh Penguins, 1988-89. 80GP
  113 – Detroit Red Wings, 1992-93. 84GP
  111 – New York Rangers, 1987-88. 80GP
  110 – Pittsburgh Penguins, 1987-88. 80GP
    – Winnipeg Jets, 1987-88. 80GP

TEAM SHORTHAND GOALS

MOST SHORTHAND GOALS, ONE SEASON:
36 – Edmonton Oilers, 1983-84. 80GP
  28 – Edmonton Oilers, 1986-87. 80GP
  27 – Edmonton Oilers, 1985-86. 80GP
    – Edmonton Oilers, 1988-89. 80GP

TEAM GOALS-PER-GAME

HIGHEST GOALS-PER-GAME AVERAGE, ONE SEASON:
5.58 – Edmonton Oilers, 1983-84. 446G in 80GP.
  5.38 – Montreal Canadiens, 1919-20. 129G in 24GP.
  5.33 – Edmonton Oilers, 1985-86. 426G in 80GP.
  5.30 – Edmonton Oilers, 1982-83. 424G in 80GP.
  5.23 – Montreal Canadiens, 1917-18. 115G in 22GP.

LOWEST GOALS-PER-GAME AVERAGE, ONE SEASON:
0.75 – Chicago Blackhawks, 1928-29. 33G in 44GP.
  1.05 – Pittsburgh Pirates, 1928-29. 46G in 44GP.
  1.20 – New York Americans, 1928-29. 53G in 44GP.

TEAM ASSISTS

MOST ASSISTS, ONE SEASON:
737 – Edmonton Oilers, 1985-86. 80GP
  736 – Edmonton Oilers, 1983-84. 80GP
  706 – Edmonton Oilers, 1981-82. 80GP

FEWEST ASSISTS, ONE SEASON (Since 1926-27):
45 – New York Rangers, 1926-27. 44GP

FEWEST ASSISTS, ONE SEASON (MINIMUM 70-GAME SCHEDULE):
206 – Chicago Blackhawks, 1953-54. 70GP

TEAM TOTAL POINTS

MOST SCORING POINTS, ONE SEASON:
1,182 – Edmonton Oilers, 1983-84. (446G-736A) 80GP
  1,163 – Edmonton Oilers, 1985-86. (426G-737A) 80GP
  1,123 – Edmonton Oilers, 1981-82. (417G-706A) 80GP

MOST SCORING POINTS, ONE TEAM, ONE GAME:
40 – Buffalo Sabres, Dec. 21, 1975, at Buffalo.
    Buffalo defeated Washington 14-2, and had 26A.
  39 – Minnesota North Stars, Nov. 11, 1981, at Minnesota.
    Minnesota defeated Winnipeg 15-2, and had 24A.
  37 – Detroit Red Wings, Jan. 23, 1944, at Detroit.
    Detroit defeated NY Rangers 15-0, and had 22A.
   – Toronto Maple Leafs, Mar. 16, 1957, at Toronto.
    Toronto defeated NY Rangers 14-1, and had 23A.
   – Buffalo Sabres, Feb. 25, 1978, at Cleveland.
    Buffalo defeated Cleveland 13-3, and had 24A.
   – Calgary Flames, Feb. 10, 1993, at Calgary.
    Calgary defeated San Jose 13-1, and had 24A.

MOST SCORING POINTS, BOTH TEAMS, ONE GAME:
62 – Edmonton Oilers, Chicago Blackhawks, Dec. 11, 1985, at Chicago.
    Edmonton won 12-9. Edmonton had 24A, Chicago, 17A.
  53 – Quebec Nordiques, Washington Capitals, Feb. 22, 1981, at Washington.
    Quebec won 11-7. Quebec had 22A, Washington, 13A.
   – Edmonton Oilers, Minnesota North Stars, Jan. 4, 1984, at Edmonton.
    Edmonton won 12-8. Edmonton had 20A, Minnesota, 13A.
   – Minnesota North Stars, St. Louis Blues, Jan. 27, 1984, at St. Louis.
    Minnesota won 10-8. Minnesota had 19A, St. Louis, 16A.
   – Toronto Maple Leafs, Edmonton Oilers, Jan. 8, 1986, at Toronto.
    Toronto won 11-9. Toronto had 17A, Edmonton, 16A.
  52 – Montreal Maroons, New York Americans, Feb. 18, 1936, at
    NY Americans. Teams tied 8-8. NY Americans had 20A, Montreal, 16A.
    (3A allowed for each goal.)
   – Vancouver Canucks, Minnesota North Stars, Oct. 7, 1983, at Vancouver.
    Vancouver won 10-9. Vancouver had 16A, Minnesota, 17A.

MOST SCORING POINTS, ONE TEAM, ONE PERIOD:
23 – New York Rangers, Nov. 21, 1971, at NY Rangers, third period during
    12-1 win over California. NY Rangers had 8G, 15A.
   – **Buffalo Sabres**, Dec. 21, 1975, at Buffalo, third period during
    14-2 win over Washington. Buffalo had 8G, 15A.
   – **Buffalo Sabres**, Mar. 19, 1981, at Buffalo, second period during
    14-4 win over Toronto. Buffalo had 9G, 14A.

22 – Detroit Red Wings, Jan. 23, 1944, at Detroit, third period during
15-0 win over NY Rangers. Detroit had 8G, 14A.
– Boston Bruins, Mar. 16, 1969, at Boston, second period during
11-3 win over Toronto. Boston had 8G, 14A.
– Minnesota North Stars, Nov. 11, 1981, at Minnesota, second period
during 15-2 win over Winnipeg. Minnesota had 8G, 14A.
– Pittsburgh Penguins, Dec. 17, 1991, at Pittsburgh, second period
during 10-2 win over San Jose. Pittsburgh had 8G, 14A.
– Washington Capitals, Feb. 3, 1999, at Washington, second period
during 10-1 win over Tampa Bay. Washington had 8G, 14A.

MOST SCORING POINTS, BOTH TEAMS, ONE PERIOD:
35 – Edmonton, Oilers, Chicago Blackhawks, Dec. 11, 1985, at Chicago,
second period. Edmonton won 12-9. Edmonton had 6G, 12A; Chicago,
6G, 11A.
31 – Buffalo Sabres, Toronto Maple Leafs, Mar. 19, 1981, at Buffalo,
second period. Buffalo won 14-4. Buffalo had 9G, 14A; Toronto, 3G, 5A.
29 – Winnipeg Jets, Detroit Red Wings, Nov. 25, 1987, at Detroit,
third period. Detroit won 10-8. Detroit had 7G, 13A; Winnipeg, 3G, 6A.
– Chicago Blackhawks, St. Louis Blues, Mar. 15, 1988, at St. Louis,
third period. Teams tied 7-7. St. Louis had 5G, 10A; Chicago, 5G, 9A.

FASTEST GOALS

FASTEST SIX GOALS, BOTH TEAMS:
3:00 – Quebec Nordiques, Washington Capitals, Feb. 22, 1981, at
Washington. Scorers: Peter Stastny, Quebec, 18:51; Pierre Lacroix, Quebec,
19:57 (first period); Anton Stastny, Quebec, 0:34; Jacques Richard, Quebec,
1:07 and 1:37; Rick Green, Washington, 1:51 (second period). Quebec won
11-7.
3:15 – Montreal Canadiens, Toronto Maple Leafs, Jan. 4, 1944, at Montreal, first
period. Scorers: Maurice Richard, Montreal, 14:10; Don Webster, Toronto,
15:13; Fern Majeau, Montreal, 15:41; Phil Watson, Montreal, 15:52; Lorne
Carr, Toronto, 16:55; Butch Bouchard, Montreal, 17:25. Montreal won 6-3.

FASTEST FIVE GOALS, BOTH TEAMS:
1:24 – Chicago Blackhawks, Toronto Maple Leafs, Oct. 15, 1983, at Toronto,
second period. Scorers: Gaston Gingras, Toronto, 16:49; Denis Savard,
Chicago, 17:12; Steve Larmer, Chicago, 17:27; Denis Savard, Chicago,
17:42; John Anderson, Toronto, 18:13. Toronto won 10-8.
1:39 – Detroit Red Wings, Toronto Maple Leafs, Nov. 15, 1944, at Toronto, third
period. Scorers: Ted Kennedy, Toronto, 10:36 and 10:55; Harold Jackson,
Detroit, 11:48; Steve Wojciechowski, Detroit, 12:02; Don Grosso, Detroit,
12:15. Detroit won 8-4.

FASTEST FIVE GOALS, ONE TEAM:
2:07 – Pittsburgh Penguins, Nov. 22, 1972, at Pittsburgh, third period. Scorers:
Bryan Hextall, Jr., 12:00; Jean Pronovost, 12:18; Al McDonough, 13:40;
Ken Schinkel, 13:49; Ron Schock, 14:07. Pittsburgh defeated St. Louis 10-4.
2:37 – New York Islanders, Jan. 26, 1982, at NY Islanders, first period. Scorers:
Duane Sutter, 1:31; John Tonelli, 2:30; Bryan Trottier, 2:46 and 3:31;
Duane Sutter, 4:08. NY Islanders defeated Pittsburgh 9-2.
2:55 – Boston Bruins, Dec. 19, 1974, at Boston. Scorers: Bobby Schmautz, 19:13
(first period); Ken Hodge, 0:18; Phil Esposito, 0:43; Don Marcotte, 0:58;
John Bucyk, 2:08 (second period). Boston defeated NY Rangers 11-3.

FASTEST FOUR GOALS, BOTH TEAMS:
0:49 – St. Louis Blues, Dallas Stars, Apr. 3, 2015, at Dallas. Scorers: Travis
Moen, Dallas, 19:49 (first period); Patrik Berglund, St. Louis, 0:15; Jaden
Schwartz, St. Louis, 0:32; Jamie Benn, Dallas, 0:38 (second period).
St. Louis won 7-5.
0:53 – Chicago Blackhawks, Toronto Maple Leafs, Oct. 15, 1983, at Toronto,
second period. Scorers: Gaston Gingras, Toronto, 16:49; Denis Savard,
Chicago, 17:12; Steve Larmer, Chicago, 17:27; Denis Savard, Chicago,
17:42. Toronto won 10-8.
0:57 – Quebec Nordiques, Detroit Red Wings, Jan. 27, 1990, at Quebec, first
period. Scorers: Paul Gillis, Quebec, 18:01; Claude Loiselle, Quebec, 18:12;
Joe Sakic, Quebec, 18:27; Jimmy Carson, Detroit, 18:58. Detroit won 8-6

FASTEST FOUR GOALS, ONE TEAM:
1:20 – Boston Bruins, Jan. 21, 1945, at Boston, second period. Scorers: Bill
Thoms, 6:34; Frank Mario, 7:08 and 7:27; Ken Smith, 7:54. Boston
defeated NY Rangers 14-3.

FASTEST THREE GOALS, BOTH TEAMS:
0:15 – Minnesota North Stars, New York Rangers, Feb. 10, 1983, at
Minnesota, second period. Scorers: Mark Pavelich, NY Rangers, 19:18; Ron
Greschner, NY Rangers, 19:27; Willi Plett, Minnesota, 19:33. Minnesota
won 7-5.
0:17 – Minnesota Wild, Buffalo Sabres, Nov. 13, 2014, at Minnesota, first period.
Scorers: Ryan Carter, Minnesota, 6:07; Nino Niederreiter, Minnesota, 6:14;
Zemgus Girgensons, Buffalo, 6:24. Minnesota won 6-3.

FASTEST THREE GOALS, ONE TEAM:
0:20 – Boston Bruins, Feb. 25, 1971, at Boston, third period. Scorers: John
Bucyk, 4:50; Ed Westfall, 5:02; Ted Green, 5:10. Boston defeated
Vancouver 8-3.
0:21 – Chicago Blackhawks, Mar. 23, 1952, at NY Rangers, third period. Bill
Mosienko scored all three goals, at 6:09, 6:20 and 6:30. Chicago defeated
NY Rangers 7-6.
– Washington Capitals, Nov. 23, 1990, at Washington, first period. Scorers:
Michal Pivonka, 16:18; Stephen Leach, 16:29 and 16:39. Washington
defeated Pittsburgh 7-3.

FASTEST THREE GOALS FROM START OF PERIOD, BOTH TEAMS:
0:38 – St. Louis Blues, Dallas Stars, Apr. 3, 2015, at Dallas, second period.
Scorers: Patrik Berglund, St. Louis, 0:15; Jaden Schwartz, St. Louis, 0:32;
Jamie Benn, Dallas, 0:38. St. Louis won 7-5.

FASTEST THREE GOALS FROM START OF PERIOD, ONE TEAM:
0:53 – Calgary Flames, Feb. 10, 1993, at Calgary, third period. Scorers: Gary
Suter, 0:17; Chris Lindberg, 0:40; Ron Stern, 0:53. Calgary defeated
San Jose 13-1.

FASTEST TWO GOALS, BOTH TEAMS:
0:02 – St. Louis Blues, Boston Bruins, Dec. 19, 1987, at Boston, third period.
Scorers: Ken Linseman, Boston, 19:50; Doug Gilmour, St. Louis, 19:52.
St. Louis won 7-5.
– **Minnesota Wild, Columbus Blue Jackets**, Jan. 5, 2016, at Columbus,
third period. Scorers: Nick Foligno, Columbus, 19:44; Mikael Granlund,
MInnesota, 19:46. Minnesota won 4-2.
*0:03 – Chicago Blackhawks, Minnesota North Stars, Nov. 5, 1988, at Minnesota,
third period. Scorers: Steve Thomas, Chicago, 6:03; Dave Gagner,
Minnesota, 6:06. Teams tied 5-5.
– Newspaper accounts of this game note that the clock was slow to start after the first goal was scored.
– Washington Capitals, Tampa Bay Lightning, Dec. 9, 2014, at Tampa Bay,
third period. Scorers: Valtteri Filppula, Tampa Bay, 19:56; Alex Ovechkin,
Washington, 19:59. Washington won 5-3.

FASTEST TWO GOALS, ONE TEAM:
0:03 – St. Louis Eagles, Mar. 12, 1935, at St. Louis, third period. Scorers: Frank
Jerwa, 14:50; Joe Lamb, 14:53. St. Louis defeated Detroit 3-2.
– **Minnesota Wild**, Jan. 21, 2004, at Minnesota, third period. Scorers: Jim
Dowd, 19:44; Richard Park, 19:47. Minnesota defeated Chicago 4-2.
– **New York Islanders**, Nov. 30, 2016, at NY Islanders, third period.
Scorers: Anders Lee, 19:33; Nikolay Kulemin, 19:36. NY Islanders defeated
Pittsburgh 5-3.
0:04 – Montreal Maroons, Jan. 3, 1931, at Montreal, third period. Nels Stewart
scored both goals, at 8:24 and 8:28. Mtl. Maroons defeated Boston 5-3.
– Buffalo Sabres, Oct. 17, 1974, at Buffalo, third period. Scorers: Lee
Fogolin, Jr., 14:55; Don Luce, 14:59. Buffalo defeated California 6-1.
– Toronto Maple Leafs, Dec. 29, 1988, at Quebec, third period. Scorers:
Ed Olczyk, 5:24; Gary Leeman, 5:28. Toronto defeated Quebec 6-5.
– Calgary Flames, Oct. 17, 1989, at Quebec, third period. Scorers: Doug
Gilmour, 19:45; Paul Ranheim, 19:49. Teams tied 8-8.
– NY Rangers, Oct. 9, 1991, at NY Rangers, third period. Scorers: Kris King,
19:45; James Patrick, 19:49. NY Rangers defeated NY Islanders 5-3.
– Winnipeg Jets, Dec. 15, 1995, at Winnipeg, second period. Deron Quint
scored both goals, at 7:51 and 7:55. Winnipeg defeated Edmonton 9-4.
– New York Rangers, Oct. 19, 2014, at NY Rangers, second period. Scorers:
Martin St. Louis, 19:16; Rick Nash, 19:20. NY Rangers defeated San Jose 4-0.

FASTEST TWO GOALS FROM START OF GAME, ONE TEAM:
0:24 – Edmonton Oilers, Mar. 28, 1982, at Los Angeles. Scorers: Mark Messier,
0:14; Dave Lumley, 0:24. Edmonton defeated Los Angeles 6-2.
0:27 – Boston Bruins, Feb. 14, 2003, at Florida. Mike Knuble scored both goals,
at 0:10 and 0:27. Boston defeated Florida 6-5.
0:29 – Pittsburgh Penguins, Dec. 6, 1980, at Pittsburgh. Scorers: George
Ferguson, 0:17; Greg Malone, 0:29. Pittsburgh defeated Chicago 6-4.

FASTEST TWO GOALS FROM START OF PERIOD, BOTH TEAMS:
0:14 – New York Rangers, Quebec Nordiques, Nov. 5, 1983, at Quebec, third
period. Scorers: Andre Savard, Quebec, 0:08; Pierre Larouche, NY Rangers,
0:14. Teams tied 4-4.
0:25 – St. Louis Blues, Chicago Blackhawks, Feb. 2, 2006, at St. Louis, second
period. Scorers: Peter Cajanek, St. Louis, 0:10; Tyler Arnason, Chicago,
0:25. St. Louis won 6-5.
0:28 – Boston Bruins, Montreal Canadiens, Oct. 11, 1989, at Montreal, third
period. Scorers: Jim Wiemer, Boston 0:10; Tom Chorske, Montreal 0:28.
Montreal won 4-2.

FASTEST TWO GOALS FROM START OF PERIOD, ONE TEAM:
0:21 – Chicago Blackhawks, Nov. 5, 1983, at Minnesota, second period.
Scorers: Ken Yaremchuk, 0:12; Darryl Sutter, 0:21. Minnesota defeated
Chicago 10-5.
0:24 – Edmonton Oilers, Mar. 28, 1982, at Los Angeles, first period. Scorers: Mark
Messier, 0:14; Dave Lumley, 0:24. Edmonton defeated Los Angeles 6-2.
0:27 – Boston Bruins, Feb. 14, 2003, at Florida. Mike Knuble scored both goals,
at 0:10 and 0:27. Boston defeated Florida 6-5.

50, 40, 30, 20-GOAL SCORERS

MOST 50-OR-MORE GOAL SCORERS, ONE SEASON:
3 – Edmonton Oilers, 1983-84. 80GP. Wayne Gretzky, 87; Glenn Anderson, 54;
Jari Kurri, 52.
– **Edmonton Oilers**, 1985-86. 80GP. Jari Kurri, 68; Glenn Anderson, 54;
Wayne Gretzky, 52.
2 – Boston Bruins, 1970-71. 78GP. Phil Esposito, 76; John Bucyk, 51.
– Boston Bruins, 1973-74. 78GP. Phil Esposito, 68; Ken Hodge, 50.
– Philadelphia Flyers, 1975-76. 80GP. Reggie Leach, 61; Bill Barber, 50.
– Pittsburgh Penguins, 1975-76. 80GP. Pierre Larouche, 53; Jean Pronovost, 52.
– Montreal Canadiens, 1976-77. 80GP. Steve Shutt, 60; Guy Lafleur, 56.
– Los Angeles Kings, 1979-80. 80GP. Charlie Simmer, 56; Marcel Dionne, 53.
– Montreal Canadiens, 1979-80. 80GP. Pierre Larouche, 50; Guy Lafleur, 50.
– Los Angeles Kings, 1980-81. 80GP. Marcel Dionne, 58; Charlie Simmer, 56.
– Edmonton Oilers, 1981-82. 80GP. Wayne Gretzky, 92; Mark Messier, 50.
– New York Islanders, 1981-82. 80GP. Mike Bossy, 64; Bryan Trottier, 50.
– Edmonton Oilers, 1984-85. 80GP. Wayne Gretzky, 73; Jari Kurri, 71.
– Washington Capitals, 1984-85. 80GP. Bob Carpenter, 53; Mike Gartner, 50.
– Edmonton Oilers, 1986-87. 80GP. Wayne Gretzky, 62; Jari Kurri, 54.
– Calgary Flames, 1987-88. 80GP. Joe Nieuwendyk, 51; Hakan Loob, 50.
– Los Angeles Kings, 1987-88. 80GP. Jimmy Carson, 55; Luc Robitaille, 53.
– Calgary Flames, 1988-89. 80GP. Joe Nieuwendyk, 51; Joe Mullen, 51.
– Los Angeles Kings, 1988-89. 80GP. Bernie Nicholls, 70; Wayne Gretzky, 54.
– Buffalo Sabres, 1992-93. 84GP. Alexander Mogilny, 76; Pat LaFontaine, 53.
– Pittsburgh Penguins, 1992-93. 84GP. Mario Lemieux, 69; Kevin Stevens, 55.
– St. Louis Blues, 1992-93. 84GP. Brett Hull, 54; Brendan Shanahan, 51.
– Detroit Red Wings, 1993-94. 84GP. Sergei Fedorov, 56; Ray Sheppard, 52.
– St. Louis Blues, 1993-94. 84GP. Brett Hull, 57; Brendan Shanahan, 52.
– Pittsburgh Penguins, 1995-96. 82GP. Mario Lemieux, 69; Jaromir Jagr, 62.

MOST 40-OR-MORE GOAL SCORERS, ONE SEASON:
4 – **Edmonton Oilers**, 1982-83. 80GP. Wayne Gretzky, 71; Glenn Anderson, 48; Mark Messier, 48; Jari Kurri, 45.
– **Edmonton Oilers**, 1983-84. 80GP. Wayne Gretzky, 87; Glenn Anderson, 54; Jari Kurri, 52; Paul Coffey, 40.
– **Edmonton Oilers**, 1984-85. 80GP. Wayne Gretzky, 73; Jari Kurri, 71; Mike Krushelnyski, 43; Glenn Anderson, 42.
– **Edmonton Oilers**, 1985-86. 80GP. Jari Kurri, 68; Glenn Anderson, 54; Wayne Gretzky, 52; Paul Coffey, 48.
– **Calgary Flames**, 1987-88. 80GP. Joe Nieuwendyk, 51; Hakan Loob, 50; Mike Bullard, 48; Joe Mullen, 40.
3 – Boston Bruins, 1970-71. 78GP. Phil Esposito, 76; John Bucyk, 51; Ken Hodge, 43.
– New York Rangers, 1971-72. 78GP. Vic Hadfield, 50; Jean Ratelle, 46; Rod Gilbert, 43.
– Buffalo Sabres, 1975-76. 80GP. Danny Gare, 50; Rick Martin, 49; Gilbert Perreault, 44.
– Montreal Canadiens, 1979-80. 80GP. Guy Lafleur, 50; Pierre Larouche, 50; Steve Shutt, 47.
– Buffalo Sabres, 1979-80. 80GP. Danny Gare, 56; Rick Martin, 45; Gilbert Perreault, 40.
– Los Angeles Kings, 1980-81. 80GP. Marcel Dionne, 58; Charlie Simmer, 56; Dave Taylor, 47.
– Los Angeles Kings, 1984-85. 80GP. Marcel Dionne, 46; Bernie Nicholls, 46; Dave Taylor, 41.
– New York Islanders, 1984-85. 80GP. Mike Bossy, 58; Brent Sutter, 42; John Tonelli, 42.
– Chicago Blackhawks, 1985-86. 80GP. Denis Savard, 47; Troy Murray, 45; Al Secord, 40.
– Chicago Blackhawks, 1987-88. 80GP. Denis Savard, 44; Rick Vaive, 43; Steve Larmer, 41.
– Edmonton Oilers, 1987-88. 80GP. Craig Simpson, 43; Jari Kurri, 43; Wayne Gretzky, 40.
– Los Angeles Kings, 1988-89. 80GP. Bernie Nicholls, 70; Wayne Gretzky, 54; Luc Robitaille, 46.
– Los Angeles Kings, 1990-91. 80GP. Luc Robitaille, 45; Tomas Sandstrom, 45; Wayne Gretzky, 41.
– Pittsburgh Penguins, 1991-92. 80GP. Kevin Stevens, 54; Mario Lemieux, 44; Joe Mullen, 42.
– Pittsburgh Penguins, 1992-93. 84GP. Mario Lemieux, 69; Kevin Stevens, 55; Rick Tocchet, 48.
– Calgary Flames, 1993-94. 84GP. Gary Roberts, 41; Robert Reichel, 40; Theoren Fleury, 40.
– Pittsburgh Penguins, 1995-96. 82GP. Mario Lemieux, 69; Jaromir Jagr, 62; Petr Nedved, 45.

MOST 30-OR-MORE GOAL SCORERS, ONE SEASON:
6 – **Buffalo Sabres**, 1974-75. 80GP. Rick Martin, 52; Rene Robert, 40; Gilbert Perreault, 39; Don Luce, 33; Rick Dudley, 31; Danny Gare, 31.
– **New York Islanders**, 1977-78. 80GP. Mike Bossy, 53; Bryan Trottier, 46; Clark Gillies, 35; Denis Potvin, 30; Bob Nystrom, 30; Bob Bourne, 30.
– **Winnipeg Jets**, 1984-85. 80GP. Dale Hawerchuk, 53; Paul MacLean, 41; Laurie Boschman, 32; Brian Mullen, 32; Doug Smail, 31; Thomas Steen, 30.
5 – Chicago Blackhawks, 1968-69. 76GP
– Boston Bruins, 1970-71. 78GP
– Montreal Canadiens, 1971-72. 78GP
– Philadelphia Flyers, 1972-73. 78GP
– Boston Bruins, 1973-74. 78GP
– Montreal Canadiens, 1974-75. 80GP
– Montreal Canadiens, 1975-76. 80GP
– Pittsburgh Penguins, 1975-76. 80GP
– New York Islanders, 1978-79. 80GP
– Detroit Red Wings, 1979-80. 80GP
– Philadelphia Flyers, 1979-80. 80GP
– New York Islanders, 1980-81. 80GP
– St. Louis Blues, 1980-81. 80GP
– Chicago Blackhawks, 1981-82. 80GP
– Edmonton Oilers, 1981-82. 80GP
– Montreal Canadiens, 1981-82. 80GP
– Quebec Nordiques, 1981-82. 80GP
– Washington Capitals, 1981-82. 80GP
– Edmonton Oilers, 1982-83. 80GP
– Edmonton Oilers, 1983-84. 80GP
– Edmonton Oilers, 1984-85. 80GP
– Los Angeles Kings, 1984-85. 80GP
– Edmonton Oilers, 1985-86. 80GP
– Edmonton Oilers, 1986-87. 80GP
– Edmonton Oilers, 1987-88. 80GP
– Edmonton Oilers, 1988-89. 80GP
– Detroit Red Wings, 1991-92. 80GP
– New York Rangers, 1991-92. 80GP
– Pittsburgh Penguins, 1991-92. 80GP
– Detroit Red Wings, 1992-93. 84GP
– Pittsburgh Penguins, 1992-93. 84GP

MOST 20-OR-MORE GOAL SCORERS, ONE SEASON:
11 – **Boston Bruins**, 1977-78. 80GP. Peter McNab, 41; Terry O'Reilly, 29; Bobby Schmautz, 27; Stan Jonathan, 27; Jean Ratelle, 25; Rick Middleton, 25; Wayne Cashman, 24; Gregg Sheppard, 23; Brad Park, 22; Don Marcotte, 20; Bob Miller, 20.
10 – Boston Bruins, 1970-71. 78GP
– Montreal Canadiens, 1974-75. 80GP
– St. Louis Blues, 1980-81. 80GP

100-POINT SCORERS

MOST 100-OR-MORE-POINT SCORERS, ONE SEASON:
4 – **Boston Bruins**, 1970-71. 78GP. Phil Esposito, 76G-76A-152PTS; Bobby Orr, 37G-102A-139PTS; John Bucyk, 51G-65A-116PTS; Ken Hodge, 43G-62A-105PTS.

– **Edmonton Oilers**, 1982-83. 80GP. Wayne Gretzky, 71G-125A-196PTS; Mark Messier, 48G-58A-106PTS; Glenn Anderson, 48G-56A-104PTS; Jari Kurri, 45G-59A-104PTS.
– **Edmonton Oilers**, 1983-84. 80GP. Wayne Gretzky, 87G-118A-205PTS; Paul Coffey, 40G-86A-126PTS; Jari Kurri, 52G-61A-113PTS; Mark Messier, 37G-64A-101PTS.
– **Edmonton Oilers**, 1985-86. 80GP. Wayne Gretzky, 52G-163A-215PTS; Paul Coffey, 48G-90A-138PTS; Jari Kurri, 68G-63A-131PTS; Glenn Anderson, 54G-48A-102PTS.
– **Pittsburgh Penguins**, 1992-93. 84GP. Mario Lemieux, 69G-91A-160PTS; Kevin Stevens, 55G-56A-111PTS; Rick Tocchet, 48G-61A-109PTS; Ron Francis, 24G-76A-100PTS.
3 – Boston Bruins, 1973-74. 78GP. Phil Esposito, 68G-77A-145PTS; Bobby Orr, 32G-90A-122PTS; Ken Hodge, 50G-55A-105PTS.
– New York Islanders, 1978-79. 80GP. Bryan Trottier, 47G-87A-134PTS; Mike Bossy, 69G-57A-126PTS; Denis Potvin, 31G-70A-101PTS.
– Los Angeles Kings, 1980-81. 80GP. Marcel Dionne, 58G-77A-135PTS; Dave Taylor, 47G-65A-112PTS; Charlie Simmer, 56G-49A-105PTS.
– Edmonton Oilers, 1984-85. 80GP. Wayne Gretzky, 73G-135A-208PTS; Jari Kurri, 71G-64A-135PTS; Paul Coffey, 37G-84A-121PTS.
– New York Islanders, 1984-85. 80GP. Mike Bossy, 58G-59A-117PTS; Brent Sutter, 42G-60A-102PTS; John Tonelli, 42G-58A-100PTS.
– Edmonton Oilers, 1986-87. 80GP. Wayne Gretzky, 62G-121A-183PTS; Jari Kurri, 54G-54A-108PTS; Mark Messier, 37G-70A-107PTS.
– Pittsburgh Penguins, 1988-89. 80GP. Mario Lemieux, 85G-114A-199PTS; Rob Brown, 49G-66A-115PTS; Paul Coffey, 30G-83A-113PTS.
– Pittsburgh Penguins, 1995-96. 82GP. Mario Lemieux, 69G-92A-161PTS; Jaromir Jagr, 62G-87A-149PTS; Ron Francis, 27G-92A-119PTS.

SHOTS ON GOAL

MOST SHOTS, BOTH TEAMS, ONE GAME:
141 – **New York Americans, Pittsburgh Pirates**, Dec. 26, 1925, at NY Americans. NY Americans won 3-1 with 73 shots; Pittsburgh had 68 shots.

MOST SHOTS, ONE TEAM, ONE GAME:
83 – **Boston Bruins**, Mar. 4, 1941, at Boston. Boston defeated Chicago 3-2.
82 – Toronto St. Patricks, Jan. 10, 1925 at Toronto. Toronto defeated Hamilton 3-1.
81 – Toronto St. Patricks, Feb. 14, 1925 at Toronto. Toronto defeated Hamilton 3-1.
73 – New York Americans, Dec. 26, 1925, at NY Americans. NY Americans defeated Pittsburgh 3-1.
– Boston Bruins, Mar. 21, 1991, at Boston. Boston tied Quebec 3-3.
72 – Boston Bruins, Dec. 10, 1970, at Boston. Boston defeated Buffalo 8-2.

MOST SHOTS, ONE TEAM, ONE PERIOD:
33 – **Boston Bruins**, Mar. 4, 1941, at Boston, second period. Boston defeated Chicago 3-2.

TEAM GOALS AGAINST

Fewest Goals Against

FEWEST GOALS AGAINST, ONE SEASON:
42 – **Ottawa Senators**, 1925-26. 36GP.
43 – Montreal Canadiens, 1928-29. 44GP.
48 – Montreal Canadiens, 1923-24. 24GP.
– Montreal Canadiens, 1927-28. 44GP.

FEWEST GOALS AGAINST, ONE SEASON (MiNIMUM 70-GAME SCHEDULE):
131 – **Toronto Maple Leafs**, 1953-54. 70GP.
– **Montreal Canadiens**, 1955-56. 70GP.
132 – Detroit Red Wings, 1953-54. 70GP.
133 – Detroit Red Wings, 1951-52. 70GP.
– Detroit Red Wings, 1952-53. 70GP.

LOWEST GOALS-AGAINST-PER-GAME AVERAGE, ONE SEASON:
0.98 – **Montreal Canadiens**, 1928-29. 43GA in 44GP.
1.09 – Montreal Canadiens, 1927-28. 48GA in 44GP.
1.17 – Ottawa Senators, 1925-26. 42GA in 36GP.

Most Goals Against

MOST GOALS AGAINST, ONE SEASON:
446 – **Washington Capitals**, 1974-75. 80GP
415 – Detroit Red Wings, 1985-86. 80GP
414 – San Jose Sharks, 1992-93. 84GP
407 – Quebec Nordiques, 1989-90. 80GP
403 – Hartford Whalers, 1982-83. 80GP

HIGHEST GOALS-AGAINST-PER-GAME AVERAGE, ONE SEASON:
7.38 – **Quebec Bulldogs**, 1919-20. 177GA in 24GP.
6.20 – New York Rangers, 1943-44. 310GA in 50GP.
5.58 – Washington Capitals, 1974-75. 446GA in 80GP.

MOST POWER-PLAY GOALS AGAINST, ONE SEASON:
122 – **Chicago Blackhawks**, 1988-89. 80GP
120 – Pittsburgh Penguins, 1987-88. 80GP
116 – Washington Capitals, 2005-06. 82GP
115 – New Jersey Devils, 1988-89. 80GP
– Ottawa Senators, 1992-93. 84GP
114 – Los Angeles Kings, 1992-93. 84GP

MOST SHORTHAND GOALS AGAINST, ONE SEASON:
22 – **Pittsburgh Penguins**, 1984-85. 80GP
– **Minnesota North Stars**, 1991-92. 80GP
– **Colorado Avalanche**, 1995-96. 82GP
21 – Calgary Flames, 1984-85. 80GP
– Pittsburgh Penguins, 1989-90. 80GP

TEAM SHOOTOUT RECORDS

MOST SHOOTOUT GAMES, ONE SEASON:
21 – Washington, 2013-14 (10w, 11L)
20 – Phoenix, 2009-10 (14w, 6L)
– Minnesota, 2011-12 (11w, 9L)

MOST SHOOTOUT GAMES, ALL-TIME:
142 – Florida (61w, 81L)
133 – Buffalo (69w, 64L)
131 – New Jersey (66w, 65L)

MOST SHOOTOUT WINS, ONE SEASON:
15 – Edmonton, 2007-08, 19GP
14 – Phoenix, 2009-10, 20GP
12 – Dallas, 2005-06, 13GP
– New Jersey, 2011-12, 16GP

MOST SHOOTOUT WINS, ALL-TIME:
73 – Pittsburgh, 121GP
71 – NY Islanders, 127GP
69 – Buffalo, 133GP

MOST SHOOTOUT HOME WINS, ONE SEASON:
8 – Edmonton, 2007-08, 9GP
– New Jersey, 2011-12, 12GP
7 – Toronto, 2013-14, 8GP
– NY Rangers, 2008-09, 9GP
– NY Islanders, 2009-10, 9GP
– Anaheim, 2007-08, 10GP
– Minnesota, 2006-07, 11GP

MOST SHOOTOUT HOME WINS, ALL-TIME:
40 – New Jersey, 72GP
35 – Chicago, 64GP
33 – Pittsburgh, 55GP
– Buffalo, 66GP

MOST SHOOTOUT ROAD WINS, ONE SEASON:
8 – Phoenix, 2009-10, 12GP
– Calgary, 2010-11, 12GP
7 – NY Rangers, 2011-12, 7GP
– Dallas, 2005-06, 8GP
– Dallas, 2006-07, 9GP
– Edmonton, 2007-08, 10GP
– Boston, 2009-10, 10GP
– Pittsburgh, 2010-11, 10GP

MOST SHOOTOUT ROAD WINS, ALL-TIME:
40 – Pittsburgh, 66GP
39 – NY Islanders, 69GP
38 – Colorado, 59GP

MOST SHOOTOUT SHOTS TAKEN, ONE SEASON:
90 – Phoenix, 2009-10, 20GP
81 – Florida, 2014-15, 18GP
80 – Washington, 2013-14, 21GP

MOST SHOOTOUT SHOTS TAKEN, ALL-TIME:
505 – Florida, 142GP
483 – Buffalo, 133GP
469 – Los Angeles, 124GP
– Edmonton, 128GP

MOST SHOOTOUT GOALS SCORED, ONE SEASON:
34 – Phoenix, 2009-10, 20GP, 90s
28 – New Jersey, 2011-12, 16GP, 49s
27 – Minnesota, 2006-07, 17GP, 62s
– Los Angeles, 2009-10, 18GP, 74s
– Washington, 2013-14, 21GP, 80s

MOST SHOOTOUT GOALS SCORED, ALL-TIME:
167 – NY Islanders, 127GP
158 – Buffalo, 133GP
155 – Los Angeles, 124GP

BEST SHOOTOUT SCORING PERCENTAGE, ONE SEASON:
.750 – Pittsburgh, 2012-13, 3GP (6G, 8s)
.636 – St. Louis, 2012-13, 6GP (14G, 22s)
.600 – Minnesota, 2012-13, 6GP (9G, 15s)
– Colorado, 2012-13, 4GP (6G, 10s)

BEST SHOOTOUT SCORING PERCENTAGE, ALL-TIME:
.392 – Colorado, 102GP (142G, 362s)
.365 – NY Islanders, 127GP (167G, 458s)
– Minnesota, 123GP (153G, 419s)

FEWEST SHOOTOUT GOALS AGAINST, ONE SEASON:
1 – Colorado, 2015-16, 4GP (12SA)
– Washington, 2012-13, 3GP (9SA)
2 – Colorado, 2010-11, 7GP (27SA)
– Boston, 2015-16, 6GP (19SA)
– San Jose, 2016-17, 3GP (12SA)
– Pittsburgh, 2012-13, 3GP (8SA)
– Colorado, 2015-16, 3GP (6SA)
– Arizona, 2015-16, 2GP (6SA)
– Carolina, 2012-13, 2GP (5SA)

FEWEST SHOOTOUT GOALS AGAINST, ALL-TIME:
102 – Colorado, 105GP (360SA)
103 – Carolina, 90GP (284SA)
108 – Tampa Bay, 106GP (380SA)

BEST SHOOTOUT WINNING PERCENTAGE, ONE SEASON:
1.000 – Detroit, 2016-17, 9GP (9w)
– Colorado, 2015-16, 4GP (4w)
– Pittsburgh, 2012-13, 3GP (3w)
– Washington, 2012-13, 3GP (3w)

BEST SHOOTOUT WINNING PERCENTAGE, ALL-TIME:
.648 – Colorado, 105GP (68w)
.603 – Pittsburgh, 121GP (73w)
.571 – Dallas, 112GP (64w)

SHUTOUTS

MOST SHUTOUTS, ONE SEASON:
22 – Montreal Canadiens, 1928-29. All by George Hainsworth. 44GP
16 – New York Americans, 1928-29. Roy Worters 13, Flat Walsh 3. 44GP
15 – Ottawa Senators, 1925-26. All by Alec Connell. 36GP
– Ottawa Senators, 1927-28. All by Alec Connell. 44GP
– Boston Bruins, 1927-28. All by Hal Winkler. 44GP
– Chicago Blackhawks, 1969-70. All by Tony Esposito. 76GP
– St. Louis Blues, 2011-12. Brian Elliott 9, Jaroslav Halak 6. 82GP

MOST CONSECUTIVE SHUTOUTS, ONE SEASON:
6 – Ottawa Senators, Jan. 31 – Feb. 18, 1928. All by Alec Connell.

MOST CONSECUTIVE SHUTOUTS TO START SEASON:
5 – Toronto Maple Leafs, Nov. 13 – 22, 1930. Lorne Chabot 3, Benny Grant 2.

MOST GAMES SHUTOUT, ONE SEASON:
20 – Chicago Blackhawks, 1928-29. 44GP

MOST CONSECUTIVE GAMES SHUTOUT:
8 – Chicago Blackhawks, Feb. 7 – 28, 1929.

MOST CONSECUTIVE GAMES SHUTOUT TO START SEASON:
3 – Montreal Maroons, Nov. 11 – 18, 1930.

TEAM PENALTIES

MOST PENALTY MINUTES, ONE SEASON:
2,713 – Buffalo Sabres, 1991-92. 80GP
2,670 – Pittsburgh Penguins, 1988-89. 80GP
2,663 – Chicago Blackhawks, 1991-92. 80GP
2,643 – Calgary Flames, 1991-92. 80GP
2,621 – Philadelphia Flyers, 1980-81. 80GP

MOST PENALTIES, BOTH TEAMS, ONE GAME:
85 – Edmonton Oilers (44), Los Angeles Kings (41), Feb. 28, 1990, at Los Angeles. Edmonton received 26 minors, 7 majors, 6 10-minute misconducts, 4 game misconducts and 1 match penalty; Los Angeles received 26 minors, 9 majors, 3 10-minute misconducts and 3 game misconducts.

MOST PENALTY MINUTES, BOTH TEAMS, ONE GAME:
419 – Ottawa Senators (206), Philadelphia Flyers (213), Mar. 5, 2004, at Philadelphia. Ottawa received 8 minors, 10 majors, 4 10-minute misconducts and 10 game misconducts. Philadelphia received 9 minors, 11 majors, 4 10-minute misconducts and 10 game misconducts.

MOST PENALTIES, ONE TEAM, ONE GAME:
44 – Edmonton Oilers, Feb. 28, 1990, at Los Angeles. Edmonton received 26 minors, 7 majors, 6 10-minute misconducts, 4 game misconducts and 1 match penalty.
42 – Minnesota North Stars, Feb. 26, 1981, at Boston. Minnesota received 18 minors, 13 majors, 4 10-minute misconducts and 7 game misconducts.
– Boston Bruins, Feb. 26, 1981, at Boston vs. Minnesota. Boston received 20 minors, 13 majors, 3 10-minute misconducts and 6 game misconducts.

MOST PENALTY MINUTES, ONE TEAM, ONE GAME:
213 – Philadelphia Flyers, Mar. 5, 2004, at Philadelphia. Philadelphia received 9 minors, 11 majors, 4 10-minute misconducts and 10 game misconducts.

MOST PENALTIES, BOTH TEAMS, ONE PERIOD:
67 – Minnesota North Stars (34), Boston Bruins (33), Feb. 26, 1981, at Boston, first period. Minnesota received 15 minors, 8 majors, 4 10-minute misconducts and 7 game misconducts. Boston had 16 minors, 8 majors, 3 10-minute misconducts and 6 game misconducts.

MOST PENALTY MINUTES, BOTH TEAMS, ONE PERIOD:
409 – Ottawa Senators (200), Philadelphia Flyers (209), Mar. 5, 2004, at Philadelphia, third period. Ottawa received 5 minors, 10 majors, 4 10-minute misconducts and 10 game misconducts. Philadelphia received 7 minors, 11 majors, 4 10-minute misconducts and 10 game misconducts.

MOST PENALTIES, ONE TEAM, ONE PERIOD:
34 – Minnesota North Stars, Feb. 26, 1981, at Boston, first period. Minnesota received 15 minors, 8 majors, 4 10-minute misconducts and 7 game misconducts.

MOST PENALTY MINUTES, ONE TEAM, ONE PERIOD:
209 – Philadelphia Flyers, Mar. 5, 2004, at Philadelphia vs. Ottawa, third period. Philadelphia received 7 minors, 11 majors, 4 10-minute misconducts and 10 game misconducts.
200 – Ottawa Senators, Mar. 5, 2004, at Philadelphia, third period. Ottawa received 5 minors, 10 majors, 4 10-minute misconducts and 10 game misconducts.

NHL Individual Scoring Records – History

Six individual scoring records stand as benchmarks in the history of the game: most goals, single-season and career; most assists, single-season and career; and most points, single-season and career. The evolution of these six records is traced here, beginning with 1917-18, the NHL's first season. New research has resulted in changes to scoring records in the NHL's first nine seasons.

MOST GOALS, ONE SEASON

44 —Joe Malone, Montreal, 1917-18.
Scored goal #44 against Toronto's Harry Holmes on March 2, 1918 and finished the season with 44 goals.
50 —Maurice Richard, Montreal, 1944-45.
Scored goal #45 against Toronto's Frank McCool on February 25, 1945 and finished the season with 50 goals.
50 —Bernie Geoffrion, Montreal, 1960-61.
Scored goal #50 against Toronto's Cesare Maniago on March 16, 1961 and finished the season with 50 goals.
50 —Bobby Hull, Chicago, 1961-62.
Scored goal #50 against NY Rangers' Gump Worsley on March 25, 1962 and finished the season with 50 goals.
54 —Bobby Hull, Chicago, 1965-66.
Scored goal #51 against NY Rangers' Cesare Maniago on March 12, 1966 and finished the season with 54 goals.
58 —Bobby Hull, Chicago, 1968-69.
Scored goal #55 against Boston's Gerry Cheevers on March 20, 1969 and finished the season with 58 goals.
76 —Phil Esposito, Boston, 1970-71.
Scored goal #59 against Los Angeles' Denis DeJordy on March 11, 1971 and finished the season with 76 goals.
92 —Wayne Gretzky, Edmonton, 1981-82.
Scored goal #77 against Buffalo's Don Edwards on February 24, 1982 and finished the season with 92 goals.

MOST ASSISTS, ONE SEASON

10 —Cy Denneny, Ottawa, 1917-18.
　 —Reg Noble, Toronto, 1917-18.
　 —Harry Cameron, Toronto, 1917-18.
　 —Newsy Lalonde, Montreal, 1918-19.
15 —Frank Nighbor, Ottawa, 1919-20.
　 —Jack Darragh, Ottawa, 1920-21.
17 —Harry Cameron, Toronto, 1921-22.
18 —Dick Irvin, Chicago, 1926-27.
　 —Howie Morenz, Montreal, 1927-28.
36 —Frank Boucher, NY Rangers, 1929-30.
37 —Joe Primeau, Toronto, 1931-32.
45 —Bill Cowley, Boston, 1940-41.
　 —Bill Cowley, Boston, 1942-43.
49 —Clint Smith, Chicago, 1943-44.
54 —Elmer Lach, Montreal, 1944-45.
55 —Ted Lindsay, Detroit, 1949-50.
56 —Bert Olmstead, Montreal, 1955-56.
58 —Jean Beliveau, Montreal, 1960-61.
　 —Andy Bathgate, NY Rangers/Toronto, 1963-64.
59 —Stan Mikita, Chicago, 1964-65.
62 —Stan Mikita, Chicago, 1966-67.
77 —Phil Esposito, Boston, 1968-69.
87 —Bobby Orr, Boston, 1969-70.
102 —Bobby Orr, Boston, 1970-71.
109 —Wayne Gretzky, Edmonton, 1980-81.
120 —Wayne Gretzky, Edmonton, 1981-82.
125 —Wayne Gretzky, Edmonton, 1982-83.
135 —Wayne Gretzky, Edmonton, 1984-85.
163 —Wayne Gretzky, Edmonton, 1985-86.

MOST POINTS, ONE SEASON

48 —Joe Malone, Montreal, 1917-18.
49 —Joe Malone, Montreal, 1919-20.
51 —Howie Morenz, Montreal, 1927-28.
73 —Cooney Weiland, Boston, 1929-30.
　 —Doug Bentley, Chicago, 1942-43.
82 —Herb Cain, Boston, 1943-44.
86 —Gordie Howe, Detroit, 1950-51.
95 —Gordie Howe, Detroit, 1952-53.
96 —Dickie Moore, Montreal, 1958-59.
97 —Bobby Hull, Chicago, 1965-66.
　 —Stan Mikita, Chicago, 1966-67.
126 —Phil Esposito, Boston, 1968-69.
152 —Phil Esposito, Boston, 1970-71.
164 —Wayne Gretzky, Edmonton, 1980-81.
212 —Wayne Gretzky, Edmonton, 1981-82.
215 —Wayne Gretzky, Edmonton, 1985-86.

MOST REGULAR-SEASON GOALS, CAREER

44 —Joe Malone, Montreal.
Malone led the NHL in goals in the league's first season with 44 goals in 20 games in 1917-18.
54 —Cy Denneny, Ottawa.
Denneny passed Malone during the 1918-19 season, and led the NHL in goals with 54 after two seasons.
143 —Joe Malone, Montreal, Quebec Bulldogs, Hamilton.
Malone passed Denneny during the 1919-20 season and finished his career with 143 goals.
248 —Cy Denneny, Ottawa, Boston.
Denneny passed Malone with goal #144 during the 1922-23 season and finished his career with 248 goals.
271 —Howie Morenz, Montreal, Chicago, NY Rangers.
Morenz passed Denneny with goal #249 during the 1933-34 season and finished his career with 271 goals.
324 —Nels Stewart, Montreal Maroons, Boston, NY Americans.
Stewart passed Morenz with goal #272 during the 1936-37 season and finished his career with 324 goals.
544 —Maurice Richard, Montreal.
Richard passed Stewart with goal #325 on Nov. 8, 1952 and finished his career with 544 goals.
801 —Gordie Howe, Detroit, Hartford.
Howe passed Richard with goal #545 on Nov. 10, 1963 and finished his career with 801 goals.
894 —Wayne Gretzky, Edmonton, Los Angeles, St. Louis, NY Rangers.
Gretzky passed Howe with goal #802 on March 23, 1994 and finished his career with 894 goals.

Gordie Howe flicks the puck past Johnny Bower during a Detroit Red Wings - Toronto Maple Leafs game in the 1960s. Howe set two new single-season points records during the 1950s and surpassed Maurice Richard as the all-time goal-scoring leader on November 10, 1963.

Nels Stewart spent the last three-plus seasons of his 15-year NHL career playing for the New York Americans and was with that team when he surpassed Howie Morenz as the NHL's all-time leader in goals and points. Stewart's 324 goals were a record until being surpassed by Maurice Richard in 1952.

MOST REGULAR-SEASON ASSISTS, CAREER

(minimum 100 assists)

100 — Frank Boucher, Ottawa, NY Rangers.
In 1930-31, Boucher became the first NHL player to reach the 100-assist milestone.

263 — Frank Boucher, Ottawa, NY Rangers.
Boucher retired as the NHL's career assist leader in 1938 with 253. He returned to the NHL in 1943-44 and remained the NHL's career assist leader until he was overtaken by Bill Cowley in 1943-44. He finished his career with 263 assists.

353 — Bill Cowley, St. Louis Eagles, Boston.
Cowley passed Boucher with assist #264 in 1943-44. He retired as the NHL's career assist leader in 1947 with 353.

408 — Elmer Lach, Montreal.
Lach passed Cowley with assist #354 in 1951-52. He retired as the NHL's career assist leader in 1954 with 408.

1,049 — Gordie Howe, Detroit, Hartford.
Howe passed Lach with assist #409 in 1957-58. He retired as the NHL's career assist leader in 1980 with 1,049.

1,963 — Wayne Gretzky, Edmonton, Los Angeles, St. Louis, NY Rangers.
Gretzky passed Howe with assist #1,050 in 1987-88. He retired as the NHL's current career assist leader with 1,963.

MOST REGULAR-SEASON POINTS, CAREER

(minimum 100 points)

100 — Joe Malone, Montreal, Quebec Bulldogs, Hamilton.
In 1919-20, Malone became the first player in NHL history to record 100 points.

200 — Cy Denneny, Ottawa.
In 1923-24, Denneny became the first player in NHL history to record 200 points.

300 — Cy Denneny, Ottawa.
In 1926-27, Denneny became the first player in NHL history to record 300 points.

333 — Cy Denneny, Ottawa, Boston.
Denneny retired as the NHL's career point-scoring leader in 1929 with 333 points.

472 — Howie Morenz, Montreal, Chicago, NY Rangers.
Morenz passed Cy Denneny with point #334 in 1931-32. At the time his career ended in 1937, he was the NHL's career point- scoring leader with 472 points.

515 — Nels Stewart, Montreal Maroons, Boston, NY Americans.
Stewart passed Morenz with point #473 in 1938-39. He retired as the NHL's career point-scoring leader in 1940 with 515 points.

528 — Syd Howe, Ottawa, Philadelphia Quakers, Toronto, St. Louis Eagles, Detroit.
Howe passed Nels Stewart with point #516 on March 8, 1945. He retired as the NHL's career point-scoring leader in 1946 with 528 points.

548 — Bill Cowley, St. Louis Eagles, Boston.
Cowley passed Syd Howe with point #529 on Feb. 12, 1947. He retired as the NHL's career point-scoring leader in 1947 with 548 points.

610 — Elmer Lach, Montreal.
Lach passed Bill Cowley with point #549 on Feb. 23, 1952. He remained the NHL's career point-scoring leader until he was overtaken by Maurice Richard in 1953-54. He finished his career with 623 points.

946 — Maurice Richard, Montreal.
Richard passed teammate Elmer Lach with point #611 on Dec. 12, 1953. He remained the NHL's career point-scoring leader until he was overtaken by Gordie Howe in 1959-60. He finished his career with 965 points.

1,850 — Gordie Howe, Detroit, Hartford.
Howe passed Richard with point #947 on Jan. 16, 1960. He retired as the NHL's career point-scoring leader in 1980 with 1,850 points.

2,857 — Wayne Gretzky, Edmonton, Los Angeles, St. Louis, NY Rangers.
Gretzky passed Howe with point #1,851 on Oct. 15, 1989. He retired as the NHL's current career points leader with 2,857.

Individual Records

Regular Season

SEASONS

MOST SEASONS:
26 – Gordie Howe, Detroit, 1946-47 – 1970-71; Hartford, 1979-80.
 – Chris Chelios, Montreal, Chicago, Detroit, Atlanta
   1983-84 – 2003-04, 2005-06 – 2009-10.
 25 – Mark Messier, Edmonton, NY Rangers, Vancouver,
   1979-80 – 2003-04.
 24 – Alex Delvecchio, Detroit, 1950-51 – 1973-74.
  – Tim Horton, Toronto, NY Rangers, Pittsburgh, Buffalo,
   1949-50, 1951-52 – 1973-74.
 23 – John Bucyk, Detroit, Boston, 1955-56 – 1977-78.
  – Ron Francis, Hartford, Pittsburgh, Carolina, Toronto, 1981-82 – 2003-04.
  – Al MacInnis, Calgary, St. Louis, 1981-82 – 2003-04.
  – Dave Andreychuk, Buffalo, Toronto, New Jersey, Boston,
   Colorado, Tampa Bay, 1982-83 – 2003-04, 2005-06.
  – Jaromir Jagr, Pittsburgh, Washington, NY Rangers, Philadelphia, Dallas,
   Boston, New Jersey, Florida, 1990-91 – 2003-04, 2005-06 – 2007-08,
   2011-12 – 2016-17.

GAMES

MOST GAMES:
1,767 – Gordie Howe, Detroit, 1946-47 – 1970-71; Hartford, 1979-80.
 1,756 – Mark Messier, Edmonton, NY Rangers, Vancouver, 1979-80 – 2003-04.
 1,731 – Ron Francis, Hartford, Pittsburgh, Carolina, Toronto, 1981-82 – 2003-04.
 1,711 – Jaromir Jagr, Pittsburgh, Washington, NY Rangers, Philadelphia, Dallas,
   Boston, New Jersey, Florida, 1990-91 – 2003-04, 2005-06 – 2007-08,
   2011-12 – 2016-17.
 1,652 – Mark Recchi, Pittsburgh, Philadelphia, Montreal, Carolina, Tampa Bay,
   Boston, 1988-89 – 2003-04, 2005-06 – 2010-11.
 1,651 – Chris Chelios, Montreal, Chicago, Detroit, Atlanta, 1983-84 – 2003-04,
   2005-06 – 2009-10.
 1,639 – Dave Andreychuk, Buffalo, Toronto, New Jersey, Boston,
   Colorado, Tampa Bay, 1982-83 – 2003-04, 2005-06.
 1,635 – Scott Stevens, Washington, St. Louis, New Jersey, 1982-83 – 2003-04.

MOST GAMES, INCLUDING PLAYOFFS:
1,992 – Mark Messier, Edmonton, NY Rangers, Vancouver,
   1,756 regular-season games, 236 playoff games.
 1,924 – Gordie Howe, Detroit, Hartford, 1,767 regular-season games,
   157 playoff games.
 1,919 – Jaromir Jagr, Pittsburgh, Washington, NY Rangers, Philadelphia, Dallas,
   Boston, New Jersey, Florida, 1,711 regular-season games, 208 playoff games.
 1,917 – Chris Chelios, Montreal, Chicago, Detroit, Atlanta, 1,651 regular-season
   games, 266 playoff games.
 1,902 – Ron Francis, Hartford, Pittsburgh, Carolina, Toronto, 1,731 regular-season
   games, 171 playoff games.
 1,868 – Scott Stevens, Washington, St. Louis, New Jersey, 1,635 regular-season
   games, 233 playoff games.

MOST CONSECUTIVE GAMES:
964 – Doug Jarvis, Montreal, Washington, Hartford,
   Oct. 8, 1975 – Oct. 10, 1987.
 914 – Garry Unger, Toronto, Detroit, St. Louis, Atlanta,
   Feb. 24, 1968 – Dec. 21, 1979.
 884 – Steve Larmer, Chicago, Oct. 6, 1982 – Apr. 15, 1993.
 786 – Andrew Cogliano, Edmonton, Anaheim, Oct. 4, 2007 to date.
 776 – Craig Ramsay, Buffalo, Mar. 27, 1973 – Feb. 10, 1983.
 737 – Jay Bouwmeester, Florida, Calgary, St. Louis, Mar. 6, 2004 – Nov. 22, 2014.

GOALS

MOST GOALS:
894 – Wayne Gretzky, Edmonton, Los Angeles, St. Louis, NY Rangers,
   in 20 seasons. 1,487GP.
 801 – Gordie Howe, Detroit, Hartford, in 26 seasons. 1,767GP.
 765 – Jaromir Jagr, Pittsburgh, Washington, NY Rangers, Philadelphia, Dallas,
   Boston, New Jersey, Florida, in 23 seasons. 1,711GP.
 741 – Brett Hull, Calgary, St. Louis, Dallas, Detroit, Phoenix,
   in 19 seasons. 1,269GP.
 731 – Marcel Dionne, Detroit, Los Angeles, NY Rangers, in 18 seasons. 1,348GP.
 717 – Phil Esposito, Chicago, Boston, NY Rangers, in 18 seasons. 1,282GP.

MOST GOALS, INCLUDING PLAYOFFS:
1,016 – Wayne Gretzky, Edmonton, Los Angeles, St. Louis, NY Rangers,
   894G in 1,487 regular-season games, 122G in 208 playoff games.
 869 – Gordie Howe, Detroit, Hartford,
   801G in 1,767 regular-season games, 68G in 157 playoff games.
 844 – Brett Hull, Calgary, St. Louis, Dallas, Detroit, Phoenix,
   741G in 1,269 regular-season games, 103G in 202 playoff games.
 843 – Jaromir Jagr, Pittsburgh, Washington, NY Rangers, Philadelphia, Dallas,
   Boston, New Jersey, Florida, 765G in 1,711 regular-season games,
   78G in 208 playoff games.
 803 – Mark Messier, Edmonton, NY Rangers, Vancouver,
   694G in 1,756 regular-season games, 109G in 236 playoff games.
 778 – Phil Esposito, Chicago, Boston, NY Rangers,
   717G in 1,282 regular-season games, 61G in 130 playoff games.

MOST GOALS, ONE SEASON:
92 – Wayne Gretzky, Edmonton, 1981-82. 80GP – 80 game schedule.
 87 – Wayne Gretzky, Edmonton, 1983-84. 74GP – 80 game schedule.
 86 – Brett Hull, St. Louis, 1990-91. 78GP – 80 game schedule.
 85 – Mario Lemieux, Pittsburgh, 1988-89. 76GP – 80 game schedule.
 76 – Phil Esposito, Boston, 1970-71. 78GP – 78 game schedule.
  – Alexander Mogilny, Buffalo, 1992-93. 77GP – 84 game schedule.
  – Teemu Selanne, Winnipeg, 1992-93. 84GP – 84 game schedule.
 73 – Wayne Gretzky, Edmonton, 1984-85. 80GP – 80 game schedule.
 72 – Brett Hull, St. Louis, 1989-90. 80GP – 80 game schedule.
 71 – Wayne Gretzky, Edmonton, 1982-83. 80GP – 80 game schedule.
  – Jari Kurri, Edmonton, 1984-85. 73GP – 80 game schedule.
 70 – Mario Lemieux, Pittsburgh, 1987-88. 77GP – 80 game schedule.
  – Bernie Nicholls, Los Angeles, 1988-89. 79GP – 80 game schedule.
  – Brett Hull, St. Louis, 1991-92. 73GP – 80 game schedule.

MOST GOALS, ONE SEASON, INCLUDING PLAYOFFS:
100 – Wayne Gretzky, Edmonton, 1983-84,
   87G in 74 regular-season games, 13G in 19 playoff games.
 97 – Wayne Gretzky, Edmonton, 1981-82,
   92G in 80 regular-season games, 5G in 5 playoff games.
  – Mario Lemieux, Pittsburgh, 1988-89,
   85G in 76 regular-season games, 12G in 11 playoff games.
  – Brett Hull, St. Louis, 1990-91,
   86G in 78 regular-season games, 11G in 13 playoff games.
 90 – Wayne Gretzky, Edmonton, 1984-85,
   73G in 80 regular-season games, 17G in 18 playoff games.
  – Jari Kurri, Edmonton, 1984-85,
   71G in 80 regular-season games, 19G in 18 playoff games.
 85 – Mike Bossy, NY Islanders, 1980-81,
   68G in 79 regular-season games, 17G in 18 playoff games.
  – Brett Hull, St. Louis, 1989-90,
   72G in 80 regular-season games, 13G in 12 playoff games.
 83 – Wayne Gretzky, Edmonton, 1982-83,
   71G in 73 regular-season games, 12G in 16 playoff games.
  – Alexander Mogilny, Buffalo, 1992-93,
   76G in 77 regular-season games, 7G in 7 playoff games.

MOST GOALS, 50 GAMES FROM START OF SEASON:
61 – Wayne Gretzky, Edmonton, 1981-82.
   Oct. 7, 1981 – Jan. 22, 1982. (80-game schedule)
 – Wayne Gretzky, Edmonton, 1983-84.
   Oct. 5, 1983 – Jan. 25, 1984. (80-game schedule)
 54 – Mario Lemieux, Pittsburgh, 1988-89.
   Oct. 7, 1988 – Jan. 31, 1989. (80-game schedule)
 53 – Wayne Gretzky, Edmonton, 1984-85.
   Oct. 11, 1984 – Jan. 28, 1985. (80-game schedule)
 52 – Brett Hull, St. Louis, 1990-91.
   Oct. 4, 1990 – Jan. 26, 1991. (80-game schedule)
 50 – Maurice Richard, Montreal, 1944-45.
   Oct. 28, 1944 – Mar. 18, 1945. (50-game schedule)
  – Mike Bossy, NY Islanders, 1980-81.
   Oct. 11, 1980 – Jan. 24, 1981. (80-game schedule)
  – Brett Hull, St. Louis, 1991-92.
   Oct. 5, 1991 – Jan. 28, 1992. (80-game schedule)

MOST GOALS, ONE GAME:
7 – Joe Malone, Quebec, Jan. 31, 1920, at Quebec.
   Quebec 10, Toronto 6.
 6 – Newsy Lalonde, Montreal, Jan. 10, 1920, at Montreal.
   Montreal 14, Toronto 7.
  – Joe Malone, Quebec, Mar. 10, 1920, at Quebec.
   Quebec 10, Ottawa 4.
  – Corb Denneny, Toronto, Jan. 26, 1921, at Toronto.
   Toronto 10, Hamilton 3.
  – Cy Denneny, Ottawa, Mar. 7, 1921, at Ottawa.
   Ottawa 12, Hamilton 5.
  – Syd Howe, Detroit, Feb. 3, 1944, at Detroit.
   Detroit 12, NY Rangers 2.
  – Red Berenson, St. Louis, Nov. 7, 1968, at Philadelphia.
   St. Louis 8, Philadelphia 0.
  – Darryl Sittler, Toronto, Feb. 7, 1976, at Toronto.
   Toronto 11, Boston 4.

Darryl Sittler's six-goal game on February 7, 1976, was part of a 10-point night which remains an NHL record to this day. Sittler finished the 1975-76 season with 41 goals and 59 assists and was the first player in Maple Leafs history to reach the 100-point plateau.

Maurice Richard, seen here in action against the Toronto Maple Leafs during the early 1950s, became the first player in NHL history to score 50 goals in a season in 1944-45 when the NHL schedule was just 50 games long. Richard would also become the NHL's first career 500-goal scorer.

MOST GOALS, ONE ROAD GAME:
6 – Red Berenson, St. Louis, Nov. 7, 1968, at Philadelphia. St. Louis 8, Philadelphia 0.
5 – Joe Malone, Montreal, Dec. 19, 1917, at Ottawa. Montreal 7, Ottawa 4.
  – Red Green, Hamilton, Dec. 5, 1924, at Toronto. Hamilton 10, Toronto 3.
  – Babe Dye, Toronto, Dec. 22, 1924, at Boston. Toronto 10, Boston 1.
  – Punch Broadbent, Mtl. Maroons, Jan. 7, 1925, at Hamilton. Mtl. Maroons 6, Hamilton 2.
  – Don Murdoch, NY Rangers, Oct. 12, 1976, at Minnesota. NY Rangers 10, Minnesota 4.
  – Tim Young, Minnesota, Jan. 15, 1979, at NY Rangers. Minnesota 8, NY Rangers 1.
  – Willy Lindstrom, Winnipeg, Mar. 2, 1982, at Philadelphia. Winnipeg 7, Philadelphia 6.
  – Bengt Gustafsson, Washington, Jan. 8, 1984, at Philadelphia. Washington 7, Philadelphia 1.
  – Wayne Gretzky, Edmonton, Dec. 15, 1984, at St. Louis. Edmonton 8, St. Louis 2.
  – Dave Andreychuk, Buffalo, Feb. 6, 1986, at Boston. Buffalo 8, Boston 6.
  – Mats Sundin, Quebec, Mar. 5, 1992, at Hartford. Quebec 10, Hartford 4.
  – Mario Lemieux, Pittsburgh, Apr. 9, 1993, at NY Rangers. Pittsburgh 10, NY Rangers 4.
  – Mike Ricci, Quebec, Feb. 17, 1994, at San Jose. Quebec 8, San Jose 2.
  – Alex Zhamnov, Winnipeg, Apr. 1, 1995, at Los Angeles. Winnipeg 7, Los Angeles 7.
  – Johan Franzem, Detroit, Feb 2, 2011, at Ottawa. Detroit 7, Ottawa 5.

MOST GOALS, ONE PERIOD:
4 – Busher Jackson, Toronto, Nov. 20, 1934, at St. Louis, third period. Toronto 5, St. Louis 2.
  – **Max Bentley**, Chicago, Jan. 28, 1943, at Chicago, third period. Chicago 10, NY Rangers 1.
  – **Clint Smith**, Chicago, Mar. 4, 1945, at Chicago, third period. Chicago 6, Montreal 4.
  – **Red Berenson**, St. Louis, Nov. 7, 1968, at Philadelphia, second period. St. Louis 8, Philadelphia 0.
  – **Wayne Gretzky**, Edmonton, Feb. 18, 1981, at Edmonton, third period. Edmonton 9, St. Louis 2.
  – **Grant Mulvey**, Chicago, Feb. 3, 1982, at Chicago, first period. Chicago 9, St. Louis 5.
  – **Bryan Trottier**, NY Islanders, Feb. 13, 1982, at NY Islanders, second period. NY Islanders 8, Philadelphia 2.
  – **Al Secord**, Chicago, Jan. 7, 1987, at Chicago, second period. Chicago 6, Toronto 4.
  – **Joe Nieuwendyk**, Calgary, Jan. 11, 1989, at Calgary, second period. Calgary 8, Winnipeg 3.
  – **Peter Bondra**, Washington, Feb. 5, 1994, at Washington, first period. Washington 6, Tampa Bay 3.
  – **Mario Lemieux**, Pittsburgh, Jan. 26, 1997, at Montreal, third period. Pittsburgh 5, Montreal 2.
  – **Patrick Marleau**, San Jose, Jan. 23, 2017, at Colorado, third period. San Jose 5, Colorado 2.

ASSISTS

MOST ASSISTS:
1,963 – Wayne Gretzky, Edmonton, Los Angeles, St. Louis, NY Rangers, in 20 seasons. 1,487GP
1,249 – Ron Francis, Hartford, Pittsburgh, Carolina, Toronto, in 23 seasons. 1,731GP
1,193 – Mark Messier, Edmonton, NY Rangers, Vancouver, in 25 seasons. 1,756GP
1,169 – Raymond Bourque, Boston, Colorado, in 22 seasons. 1,612GP
1,149 – Jaromir Jagr, Pittsburgh, Washington, NY Rangers, Philadelphia, Dallas, Boston, New Jersey, Florida, in 23 seasons. 1,711GP
1,135 – Paul Coffey, Edmonton, Pittsburgh, Los Angeles, Detroit, Hartford, Philadelphia, Chicago, Carolina, Boston, in 21 seasons. 1,409GP

MOST ASSISTS, INCLUDING PLAYOFFS:
2,223 – Wayne Gretzky, Edmonton, Los Angeles, St. Louis, NY Rangers, 1,963A in 1,487 regular-season games, 260A in 208 playoff games.
1,379 – Mark Messier, Edmonton, NY Rangers, Vancouver, 1,193A in 1,756 regular-season games, 186A in 236 playoff games.
1,346 – Ron Francis, Hartford, Pittsburgh, Carolina, Toronto, 1,249A in 1,731 regular-season games, 97A in 171 playoff games.
1,308 – Raymond Bourque, Boston, Colorado, 1,169A in 1,612 regular-season games, 139A in 214 playoff games.
1,272 – Paul Coffey, Edmonton, Pittsburgh, Los Angeles, Detroit, Hartford, Philadelphia, Chicago, Carolina, Boston, 1,135A in 1,409 regular-season games, 137A in 194 playoff games.
  – Jaromir Jagr, Pittsburgh, Washington, NY Rangers, Philadelphia, Dallas, Boston, New Jersey, Florida, 1,149A in 1,711 regular-season games, 123A in 208 playoff games.

MOST ASSISTS, ONE SEASON:
163 – Wayne Gretzky, Edmonton, 1985-86. 80GP – 80 game schedule.
135 – Wayne Gretzky, Edmonton, 1984-85. 80GP – 80 game schedule.
125 – Wayne Gretzky, Edmonton, 1982-83. 80GP – 80 game schedule.
122 – Wayne Gretzky, Los Angeles, 1990-91. 78GP – 80 game schedule.
121 – Wayne Gretzky, Edmonton, 1986-87. 79GP – 80 game schedule.
120 – Wayne Gretzky, Edmonton, 1981-82. 80GP – 80 game schedule.
118 – Wayne Gretzky, Edmonton, 1983-84. 74GP – 80 game schedule.
114 – Mario Lemieux, Pittsburgh, 1988-89. 76GP – 80 game schedule.
  – Wayne Gretzky, Los Angeles, 1988-89. 78GP – 80 game schedule.
109 – Wayne Gretzky, Edmonton, 1980-81. 80GP – 80 game schedule.
  – Wayne Gretzky, Edmonton, 1987-88. 64GP – 80 game schedule.
102 – Bobby Orr, Boston, 1970-71. 78GP – 78 game schedule.
  – Wayne Gretzky, Los Angeles, 1989-90. 73GP – 80 game schedule.

MOST ASSISTS, ONE SEASON, INCLUDING PLAYOFFS:
174 – Wayne Gretzky, Edmonton, 1985-86,
  163A in 80 regular-season games, 11A in 10 playoff games.
165 – Wayne Gretzky, Edmonton, 1984-85,
  135A in 80 regular-season games, 30A in 18 playoff games.
151 – Wayne Gretzky, Edmonton, 1982-83,
  125A in 80 regular-season games, 26A in 16 playoff games.
150 – Wayne Gretzky, Edmonton, 1986-87,
  121A in 79 regular-season games, 29A in 21 playoff games.
140 – Wayne Gretzky, Edmonton, 1983-84,
  118A in 74 regular-season games, 22A in 19 playoff games.
  – Wayne Gretzky, Edmonton, 1987-88,
  109A in 64 regular-season games, 31A in 19 playoff games.
133 – Wayne Gretzky, Los Angeles, 1990-91,
  122A in 78 regular-season games, 11A in 12 playoff games.
131 – Wayne Gretzky, Los Angeles, 1988-89,
  114A in 78 regular-season games, 17A in 11 playoff games.
127 – Wayne Gretzky, Edmonton, 1981-82,
  120A in 80 regular-season games, 7A in 5 playoff games.
123 – Wayne Gretzky, Edmonton, 1980-81,
  109A in 80 regular-season games, 14A in 9 playoff games.
121 – Mario Lemieux, Pittsburgh, 1988-89,
  114A in 76 regular-season games, 7A in 11 playoff games.

MOST ASSISTS, ONE GAME:
7 – Billy Taylor, Detroit, Mar. 16, 1947, at Chicago. Detroit 10, Chicago 6.
  – Wayne Gretzky, Edmonton, Feb. 15, 1980, at Edmonton.
  Edmonton 8, Washington 2.
  – Wayne Gretzky, Edmonton, Dec. 11, 1985, at Chicago.
  Edmonton 12, Chicago 9.
  – Wayne Gretzky, Edmonton, Feb. 14, 1986, at Edmonton.
  Edmonton 8, Quebec 2.
6 – Six assists have been recorded in one game on 24 occasions since
  Elmer Lach of Montreal first accomplished the feat vs. Boston on
  Feb. 6, 1943. The most recent player is Eric Lindros of Philadelphia
  on Feb. 26, 1997 at Ottawa.

MOST ASSISTS, ONE ROAD GAME:
7 – Billy Taylor, Detroit, Mar. 16, 1947, at Chicago. Detroit 10, Chicago 6.
  – Wayne Gretzky, Edmonton, Dec. 11, 1985, at Chicago.
  Edmonton 12, Chicago 9.
6 – Bobby Orr, Boston, Jan. 1, 1973, at Vancouver. Boston 8, Vancouver 2.
  – Patrik Sundstrom, Vancouver, Feb. 29, 1984, at Pittsburgh.
  Vancouver 9, Pittsburgh 5.
  – Mario Lemieux, Pittsburgh, Dec. 5, 1992, at San Jose.
  Pittsburgh 9, San Jose 4.
  – Eric Lindros, Philadelphia, Feb. 26, 1997, at Ottawa.
  Philadelphia 8, Ottawa 5.

MOST ASSISTS, ONE PERIOD:
5 – Dale Hawerchuk, Winnipeg, Mar. 6, 1984, at Los Angeles,
  second period. Winnipeg 7, Los Angeles 3.
4 – Four assists have been recorded in one period on 70 occasions since
  Mickey Roach of Hamilton first accomplished the feat vs. Toronto
  on Feb. 23, 1921. The most recent player is Rostislav Klesla of Phoenix
  on Mar. 28, 2013 vs. Nashville.

POINTS

MOST POINTS:
2,857 – Wayne Gretzky, Edmonton, Los Angeles, St. Louis, NY Rangers,
  in 20 seasons. 1,487GP (894G-1,963A)
1,914 – Jaromir Jagr, Pittsburgh, Washington, NY Rangers, Philadelphia, Dallas,
  Boston, New Jersey, Florida, in 23 seasons. 1,711GP (765G-1,149A)
1,887 – Mark Messier, Edmonton, NY Rangers, Vancouver,
  in 25 seasons. 1,756GP (694G-1,193A)
1,850 – Gordie Howe, Detroit, Hartford, in 26 seasons. 1,767GP (801G-1,049A)
1,798 – Ron Francis, Hartford, Pittsburgh, Carolina, Toronto,
  in 23 seasons. 1,731GP (549G-1,249A)
1,771 – Marcel Dionne, Detroit, Los Angeles, NY Rangers,
  in 18 seasons. 1,348GP (731G-1,040A)

MOST POINTS, INCLUDING PLAYOFFS:
3,239 – Wayne Gretzky, Edmonton, Los Angeles, St. Louis, NY Rangers,
  2,857PTS in 1,487 regular-season games, 382PTS in 208 playoff games.
2,182 – Mark Messier, Edmonton, NY Rangers, Vancouver,
  1,887PTS in 1,756 regular-season games, 295PTS in 236 playoff games.
2,115 – Jaromir Jagr, Pittsburgh, Washington, NY Rangers, Philadelphia, Dallas,
  Boston, New Jersey, Florida, 1,914PTS in 1,711 regular-season games,
  201PTS in 208 playoff games.
2,010 – Gordie Howe, Detroit, Hartford,
  1,850PTS in 1,767 regular-season games, 160PTS in 157 playoff games.
1,941 – Ron Francis, Hartford, Pittsburgh, Carolina, Toronto,
  1,798PTS in 1,731 regular-season games, 143PTS in 171 playoff games.
1,940 – Steve Yzerman, Detroit,
  1,755PTS in 1,514 regular-season games, 185PTS in 196 playoff games.

MOST POINTS, ONE SEASON:
215 – Wayne Gretzky, Edmonton, 1985-86. 80GP – 80 game schedule.
212 – Wayne Gretzky, Edmonton, 1981-82. 80GP – 80 game schedule.
208 – Wayne Gretzky, Edmonton, 1984-85. 80GP – 80 game schedule.
205 – Wayne Gretzky, Edmonton, 1983-84. 74GP – 80 game schedule.
199 – Mario Lemieux, Pittsburgh, 1988-89. 76GP – 80 game schedule.
196 – Wayne Gretzky, Edmonton, 1982-83. 80GP – 80 game schedule.
183 – Wayne Gretzky, Edmonton, 1986-87. 79GP – 80 game schedule.
168 – Mario Lemieux, Pittsburgh, 1987-88. 77GP – 80 game schedule.
  – Wayne Gretzky, Los Angeles, 1988-89. 78GP – 80 game schedule.
164 – Wayne Gretzky, Edmonton, 1980-81. 80GP – 80 game schedule.
163 – Wayne Gretzky, Los Angeles, 1990-91. 78GP – 80 game schedule.
161 – Mario Lemieux, Pittsburgh, 1995-96. 70GP – 82 game schedule.
160 – Mario Lemieux, Pittsburgh, 1992-93. 60GP – 84 game schedule.

MOST POINTS, ONE SEASON, INCLUDING PLAYOFFS:
255 – Wayne Gretzky, Edmonton, 1984-85,
  208PTS in 80 regular-season games, 47PTS in 18 playoff games.
240 – Wayne Gretzky, Edmonton, 1983-84,
  205PTS in 74 regular-season games, 35PTS in 19 playoff games.
234 – Wayne Gretzky, Edmonton, 1982-83,
  196PTS in 80 regular-season games, 38PTS in 16 playoff games.
  – Wayne Gretzky, Edmonton, 1985-86,
  215PTS in 80 regular-season games, 19PTS in 10 playoff games.
224 – Wayne Gretzky, Edmonton, 1981-82,
  212PTS in 80 regular-season games, 12PTS in 5 playoff games.
218 – Mario Lemieux, Pittsburgh, 1988-89,
  199PTS in 76 regular-season games, 19PTS in 11 playoff games.
217 – Wayne Gretzky, Edmonton, 1986-87,
  183PTS in 79 regular-season games, 34PTS in 21 playoff games.
192 – Wayne Gretzky, Edmonton, 1987-88,
  149PTS in 64 regular-season games, 43PTS in 19 playoff games.
190 – Wayne Gretzky, Los Angeles, 1988-89,
  168PTS in 78 regular-season games, 22PTS in 11 playoff games.
188 – Mario Lemieux, Pittsburgh, 1995-96,
  161PTS in 70 regular-season games, 27PTS in 18 playoff games.
185 – Wayne Gretzky, Edmonton, 1980-81,
  164PTS in 80 regular-season games, 21PTS in 9 playoff games.

MOST POINTS, ONE GAME:
10 – Darryl Sittler, Toronto, Feb. 7, 1976, at Toronto, 6G-4A.
  Toronto 11, Boston 4.
8 – Maurice Richard, Montreal, Dec. 28, 1944, at Montreal, 5G-3A.
  Montreal 9, Detroit 1.
  – Bert Olmstead, Montreal, Jan. 9, 1954, at Montreal, 4G-4A.
  Montreal 12, Chicago 1.
  – Tom Bladon, Philadelphia, Dec. 11, 1977, at Philadelphia, 4G-4A.
  Philadelphia 11, Cleveland 1.
  – Bryan Trottier, NY Islanders, Dec. 23, 1978, at NY Islanders, 5G-3A.
  NY Islanders 9, NY Rangers 4.
  – Peter Stastny, Quebec, Feb. 22, 1981, at Washington, 4G-4A.
  Quebec 11, Washington 7.
  – Anton Stastny, Quebec, Feb. 22, 1981, at Washington, 3G-5A.
  Quebec 11, Washington 7.
  – Wayne Gretzky, Edmonton, Nov. 19, 1983, at Edmonton, 3G-5A.
  Edmonton 13, New Jersey 4.
  – Wayne Gretzky, Edmonton, Jan. 4, 1984, at Edmonton, 4G-4A.
  Edmonton 12, Minnesota 8.
  – Paul Coffey, Edmonton, Mar. 14, 1986, at Edmonton, 2G-6A.
  Edmonton 12, Detroit 3.
  – Mario Lemieux, Pittsburgh, Oct. 15, 1988, at Pittsburgh, 2G-6A.
  Pittsburgh 9, St. Louis 2.
  – Bernie Nicholls, Los Angeles, Dec. 1, 1988, at Los Angeles, 2G-6A.
  Los Angeles 9, Toronto 3.
  – Mario Lemieux, Pittsburgh, Dec. 31, 1988, at Pittsburgh, 5G-3A.
  Pittsburgh 8, New Jersey 6.
  – Sam Gagner, Edmonton, Feb. 2, 2012, at Edmonton, 4G-4A.
  Edmonton 8, Chicago 4.

MOST POINTS, ONE ROAD GAME:
8 – Peter Stastny, Quebec, Feb. 22, 1981, at Washington. 4G-4A.
  Quebec 11, Washington 7.
  – Anton Stastny, Quebec, Feb. 22, 1981, at Washington. 3G-5A.
  Quebec 11, Washington 7.
7 – Red Green, Hamilton, Dec. 5, 1924, at Toronto. 5G-2A.
  Hamilton 10, Toronto 3.
  – Billy Taylor, Detroit, Mar. 16, 1947, at Chicago. 7A. Detroit 10, Chicago 6.
  – Red Berenson, St. Louis, Nov. 7, 1968, at Philadelphia. 6G-1A.
  St. Louis 8, Philadelphia 0.
  – Gilbert Perreault, Buffalo, Feb. 1, 1976, at California. 2G-5A.
  Buffalo 9, California 5.
  – Peter Stastny, Quebec, Apr. 1, 1982, at Boston. 3G-4A. Quebec 8, Boston 5.
  – Wayne Gretzky, Edmonton, Nov. 6, 1983, at Winnipeg. 4G-3A.
  Edmonton 8, Winnipeg 5.
  – Patrik Sundstrom, Vancouver, Feb. 29, 1984, at Pittsburgh. 1G-6A.
  Vancouver 9, Pittsburgh 5.
  – Wayne Gretzky, Edmonton, Dec. 11, 1985, at Chicago. 7A.
  Edmonton 12, Chicago 9.
  – Cam Neely, Boston, Oct. 16, 1988, at Chicago. 3G-4A.
  Boston 10, Chicago 3.
  – Mario Lemieux, Pittsburgh, Jan. 21, 1989, at Edmonton. 2G-5A.
  Pittsburgh 7, Edmonton 4.
  – Dino Ciccarelli, Washington, Mar. 18, 1989, at Hartford. 4G-3A.
  Washington 8, Hartford 2.
  – Mats Sundin, Quebec, Mar. 5, 1992, at Hartford. 5G-2A.
  Quebec 10, Hartford 4.
  – Mario Lemieux, Pittsburgh, Dec. 5, 1992, at San Jose. 1G-6A.
  Pittsburgh 9, San Jose 4.
  – Eric Lindros, Philadelphia, Feb. 26, 1997, at Ottawa. 1G-6A.
  Philadelphia 8, Ottawa 5.
  – Daniel Alfredsson, Ottawa, Jan. 24, 2008, at Tampa Bay. 3G-4A.
  Ottawa 8, Tampa Bay 4.

MOST POINTS, ONE PERIOD:
   6 – Bryan Trottier, NY Islanders, Dec. 23, 1978, at NY Islanders,
      second period. 3G-3A. NY Islanders 9, NY Rangers 4.
   5 – Bill Cook, NY Rangers, Mar. 12, 1933, at NY Americans,
      third period. 3G-2A. NY Rangers 8, NY Americans 2.
   – Les Cunningham, Chicago, Jan. 28, 1940, at Chicago,
      third period. 2G-3A. Chicago 8, Montreal 1.
   – Max Bentley, Chicago, Jan. 28, 1943, at Chicago,
      third period. 4G-1A. Chicago 10, NY Rangers 1.
   – Leo Labine, Boston, Nov. 28, 1954, at Boston,
      second period. 3G-2A. Boston 6, Detroit 2.
   – Darryl Sittler, Toronto, Feb. 7, 1976, at Toronto,
      second period. 3G-2A. Toronto 11, Boston 4.
   – Grant Mulvey, Chicago, Feb. 3, 1982, at Chicago,
      first period. 4G-1A. Chicago 9, St. Louis 5.
   – Dale Hawerchuk, Winnipeg, Mar. 6, 1984, at Los Angeles,
      second period. 5A. Winnipeg 7, Los Angeles 3.
   – Jari Kurri, Edmonton, Oct. 26, 1984, at Edmonton,
      second period. 2G-3A. Edmonton 8, Los Angeles 2.
   – Pat Elynuik, Winnipeg, Jan. 20, 1989, at Winnipeg,
      second period. 2G-3A. Winnipeg 7, Pittsburgh 3.
   – Ray Ferraro, Hartford, Dec. 9, 1989, at Hartford,
      first period. 3G-2A. Hartford 7, New Jersey 3.
   – Stephane Richer, Montreal, Feb. 14, 1990, at Montreal,
      first period. 2G-3A. Montreal 10, Vancouver 1.
   – Cliff Ronning, Vancouver, Apr. 15, 1993, at Los Angeles,
      third period. 3G-2A. Vancouver 8, Los Angeles 6.
   – Peter Forsberg, Colorado, Mar. 3, 1999, at Florida,
      third period. 2G-3A. Colorado 7, Florida 5.
   – Sam Gagner, Edmonton, Feb. 2, 2012, at Edmonton,
      third period. 3G-2A. Edmonton 8, Chicago 4.

POWER-PLAY AND SHORTHAND GOALS

MOST POWER-PLAY GOALS, CAREER:
   274 – Dave Andreychuk, Buffalo, Toronto, New Jersey, Boston, Colorado,
      Tampa Bay, in 23 seasons. 1,639GP
   265 – Brett Hull, Calgary, St. Louis, Dallas, Detroit, Phoenix,
      in 19 seasons. 1,269GP
   255 – Teemu Selanne, Winnipeg, Anaheim, San Jose, Colorado,
      in 21 seasons. 1,451GP
   249 – Phil Esposito, Chicago, Boston, NY Rangers, in 18 seasons. 1,282GP

MOST POWER-PLAY GOALS, ONE SEASON:
   34 – Tim Kerr, Philadelphia, 1985-86. 76GP – 80 game schedule.
   32 – Dave Andreychuk, Buffalo, Toronto, 1992-93. 83GP – 84 game schedule.
   31 – Joe Nieuwendyk, Calgary, 1987-88. 75GP – 80 game schedule.
   – Mario Lemieux, Pittsburgh, 1988-89. 76GP – 80 game schedule.
   – Mario Lemieux, Pittsburgh, 1995-96. 70GP – 82 game schedule.
   29 – Michel Goulet, Quebec, 1987-88. 80GP – 80 game schedule.
   – Brett Hull, St. Louis, 1990-91. 78GP – 80 game schedule.
   – Brett Hull, St. Louis, 1992-93. 80GP – 84 game schedule.

MOST POWER-PLAY GOALS, ONE GAME
   4 – Camille Henry, NY Rangers, Mar. 13, 1954, at Detroit.
      NY Rangers 5, Detroit 2.
   – **Bernie Geoffrion**, Montreal, Feb. 19, 1955, at Montreal.
      Montreal 10, NY Rangers 2.
   – **Bryan Trottier**, NY Islanders, Feb. 13, 1982, at NY Islanders.
      NY Islanders 8, Philadephia 2.
   – **Chris Valentine**, Washington, Feb. 27, 1982, at Washington.
      Washington 7, Hartford 1.
   – **Dave Andreychuk**, Buffalo, Mar. 19, 1992, at Los Angeles.
      Buffalo 8, Los Angeles 2.
   – **Mario Lemieux**, Pittsburgh, Mar. 20, 1993, at Pittsburgh.
      Pittsburgh 9, Philadephia 3.
   – **Luc Robitaille**, Los Angeles, Nov. 25, 1993, at Quebec.
      Quebec 8, Los Angeles 6.
   – **Scott Mellanby**, St. Louis, Mar. 6, 2003, at St. Louis.
      St. Louis 6, Phoenix 3.

MOST SHORTHAND GOALS, ONE SEASON:
   13 – Mario Lemieux, Pittsburgh, 1988-89. 76GP – 80 game schedule.
   12 – Wayne Gretzky, Edmonton, 1983-84. 74GP – 80 game schedule.
   11 – Wayne Gretzky, Edmonton, 1984-85. 80GP – 80 game schedule.
   10 – Marcel Dionne, Detroit, 1974-75. 80GP – 80 game schedule.
   – Mario Lemieux, Pittsburgh, 1987-88. 77GP – 80 game schedule.
   – Dirk Graham, Chicago, 1988-89. 80GP – 80 game schedule.

MOST SHORTHAND GOALS, ONE GAME:
   3 – Theoren Fleury, Calgary, Mar. 9, 1991, at St. Louis. Calgary 8,
      St. Louis 4.

OVERTIME SCORING

MOST OVERTIME GOALS, CAREER:
   19 – Jaromir Jagr, Pittsburgh, Washington, NY Rangers, Philadelphia,
      Dallas, New Jersey.
   – **Alex Ovechkin**, Washington.
   16 – Patrik Elias, New Jersey.
   15 – Mats Sundin, Quebec, Toronto.
   – Sergei Fedorov, Detroit, Anaheim, Columbus, Washington.
   – Marian Hossa, Ottawa, Atlanta, Pittsburgh, Detroit, Chicago..
   – Daniel Sedin, Vancouver.
   14 – Ilya Kovalchuk, Atlanta, New Jersey.

MOST OVERTIME ASSISTS, CAREER:
   21 – Nicklas Lidstrom, Detroit.
   – **Patrik Elias**, New Jersey.
   – **Henrik Sedin**, Vancouver.
   18 – Mark Messier, Edmonton, NY Rangers, Vancouver.
   – Pavol Demitra, Ottawa, St. Louis, Los Angeles, Minnesota, Vancouver.
   – Tomas Kaberle, Toronto.
   – Joe Thornton, Boston, San Jose.
   – Ryan Getzlaf, Anaheim.

MOST OVERTIME POINTS, CAREER:
   37 – Patrik Elias, New Jersey. 16G-21A
   35 – Jaromir Jagr, Pittsburgh, Washington, NY Rangers, Philadelphia, Dallas.
      New Jersey, Florida. 19G-16A
   31 – Sergei Fedorov, Detroit, Anaheim, Columbus, Washington. 15G-16A
   29 – Ilya Kovalchuk, Atlanta, New Jersey. 14G-15A
   28 – Mats Sundin, Quebec, Toronto. 15G-13A
   27 – Daniel Sedin, Vancouver. 14G-13A
   – Joe Thornton, Boston, San Jose. 9G-18A

MOST OVERTIME GOALS, ONE SEASON:
   5 – Steven Stamkos, Tampa Bay, 2011-12.
   – **Jonathan Toews**, Chicago, 2015-16.
   – **Alex Galchenyuk**, Montreal, 2016-17.
   4 – Howie Morenz, Montreal, 1929-30.
   – Frank Finnigan, Ottawa, 1929-30.
   – Johnny Gagnon, Montreal, 1936-37.
   – Mats Sundin, Toronto, 1999-2000.
   – Scott Niedermayer, New Jersey, 2001-02.
   – Patrik Elias, New Jersey, 2003-04.
   – Markus Naslund, Vancouver, 2003-04.
   – Olli Jokinen, Florida, 2005-06.
   – Daniel Sedin, Vancouver, 2006-07.
   – Ilya Kovalchuk, New Jersey, 2010-11.
   – John Tavares, NY Islanders, 2014-15.
   – Anze Kopitar, Los Angeles, 2015-16.
   – Shayne Gotisbehere, Philadelphia, 2015-16.
   – Jeff Carter, Los Angeles, 2016-17.

SHOOTOUT GOALS

MOST SHOOTOUT GOALS, ONE SEASON:
   11 – Ilya Kovalchuk, New Jersey, 2011-12. 14s
   10 – Wojtek Wolski, Colorado, 2008-09. 12s
   – Jussi Jokinen, Dallas, 2005-06. 13s
   – Alex Tanguay, Calgary, 2010-11. 16s

MOST SHOOTOUT GOALS, ALL-TIME:
   45 – Radim Vrbata, Carolina, Chicago, Phoenix, Tampa Bay,
      Vancouver, Arizona. 104s
   44 – Frans Nielsen, NY Islanders, Detroit. 90s
   42 – Jonathan Toews, Chicago. 87s
   41 – Mikko Koivu, Minnesota. 98s

MOST SHOOTOUT SHOTS TAKEN, ONE SEASON:
   18 – Radim Vrbata, Phoenix, 2009-10. 8G
   17 – Lauri Korpikoski, Phoenix, 2009-10. 7G
   – Nicklas Backstrom, Washington, 2013-14. 7G
   – Jack Johnson, Los Angeles, 2009-10. 6G
   – Sam Gagner, Edmonton, 2007-08. 5G

MOST SHOOTOUT SHOTS TAKEN, ALL-TIME:
   104 – Radim Vrbata, Carolina, Chicago, Phoenix, Tampa Bay,
      Vancouver, Arizona. 45G
   99 – Zach Parise, New Jersey, Minnesota. 40G
   98 – Mikko Koivu, Minnesota. 41G
   – Pavel Datsyuk, Detroit. 40G

BEST SHOOTOUT SCORING PERCENTAGE, ONE SEASON: *(minimum 5 shots)*
   1.000– Thomas Vanek, Florida, Detroit, 2010-11. 5G, 5s
   .900 – Jarret Stoll, Los Angeles, 2010-11. 9G, 10s
   .857 – Petteri Nummelin, Minnesota, 2006-07. 6G, 7s
   – Joffrey Lupul, Toronto, 2013-14. 6G, 7s

BEST SHOOTOUT SCORING PERCENTAGE, CAREER: *(minimum 10 shots)*
   .800 – Petteri Nummelin, Minnesota. 8G, 10s
   .587 – Vyacheslav Kozlov, Atlanta. 27G, 46s
   .583 – Trevor Linden, Vancouver. 7G, 12s
   .571 – Jeff Tambellini, NY Islanders, Los Angeles, Vancouver. 8G, 14s

MOST GAME DECIDING SHOOTOUT GOALS, ONE SEASON:
   7 – Ilya Kovalchuk, New Jersey, 2011-12. 14s
   6 – Adrian Aucoin, Phoenix, 2009-10. 9s
   5 – Miroslav Satan, NY Islanders, 2005-06. 10s
   – Vyacheslav Kozlov, Atlanta, 2006-07. 11s
   – Viktor Kozlov, New Jersey, 2005-06. 12s
   – T.J. Oshie, St.Louis, 2013-14. 12s
   – Phil Kessel, Boston, 2007-08. 13s
   – Ales Kotalik, Buffalo, Edmonton, 2008-09. 13s
   – Anze Kopitar, Los Angeles, 2013-14. 13s

MOST GAME DECIDING SHOOTOUT GOALS, CAREER:
   19 – T.J. Oshie, St. Louis, Washington. 71s
   – **Frans Nielsen**, NY Islanders, Detroit. 90s
   – Patrick Kane, Chicago. 95s
   – Mikko Koivu, Minnesota. 98s

SCORING BY A CENTER

MOST GOALS BY A CENTER, CAREER:
894 – Wayne Gretzky, Edmonton, Los Angeles, St. Louis, NY Rangers, in 20 seasons. 1,487GP
731 – Marcel Dionne, Detroit, Los Angeles, NY Rangers, in 18 seasons. 1,348GP
717 – Phil Esposito, Chicago, Boston, NY Rangers, in 18 seasons. 1,282GP
694 – Mark Messier, Edmonton, NY Rangers, Vancouver, in 25 seasons. 1,756GP
692 – Steve Yzerman, Detroit, in 22 seasons. 1,514GP

MOST GOALS BY A CENTER, ONE SEASON:
92 – Wayne Gretzky, Edmonton, 1981-82. 80GP – 80 game schedule.
87 – Wayne Gretzky, Edmonton, 1983-84. 74GP – 80 game schedule.
85 – Mario Lemieux, Pittsburgh, 1988-89. 76GP – 80 game schedule.
76 – Phil Esposito, Boston, 1970-71. 78GP – 78 game schedule.
73 – Wayne Gretzky, Edmonton, 1984-85. 80GP – 80 game schedule.

MOST ASSISTS BY A CENTER, CAREER:
1,963 – Wayne Gretzky, Edmonton, Los Angeles, St. Louis, NY Rangers, in 20 seasons. 1,487GP
1,249 – Ron Francis, Hartford, Pittsburgh, Carolina, Toronto, in 23 seasons. 1,731GP
1,193 – Mark Messier, Edmonton, NY Rangers, Vancouver, in 25 seasons. 1,756GP
1,079 – Adam Oates, Detroit, St. Louis, Boston, Washington, Philadelphia, Anaheim, Edmonton, in 19 seasons. 1,337GP
1,063 – Steve Yzerman, Detroit, in 22 seasons. 1,514GP

MOST ASSISTS BY A CENTER, ONE SEASON:
163 – Wayne Gretzky, Edmonton, 1985-86. 80GP – 80 game schedule.
135 – Wayne Gretzky, Edmonton, 1984-85. 80GP – 80 game schedule.
125 – Wayne Gretzky, Edmonton, 1982-83. 80GP – 80 game schedule.
122 – Wayne Gretzky, Los Angeles, 1990-91. 78GP – 80 game schedule.
121 – Wayne Gretzky, Edmonton, 1986-87. 79GP – 80 game schedule.

MOST POINTS BY A CENTER, CAREER:
2,857 – Wayne Gretzky, Edmonton, Los Angeles, St. Louis, NY Rangers, in 20 seasons. 1,487GP (894G-1,963A)
1,887 – Mark Messier, Edmonton, NY Rangers, Vancouver, in 25 seasons. 1,756GP (694G-1,193A)
1,798 – Ron Francis, Hartford, Pittsburgh, Carolina, Toronto, in 23 seasons. 1,731GP (549G-1,249A)
1,771 – Marcel Dionne, Detroit, Los Angeles, NY Rangers, in 18 seasons. 1,348GP (731G-1,040A)
1,755 – Steve Yzerman, Detroit, in 22 seasons. 1,514GP (692G-1,063A)

MOST POINTS BY A CENTER, ONE SEASON:
215 – Wayne Gretzky, Edmonton, 1985-86. 80GP – 80 game schedule.
212 – Wayne Gretzky, Edmonton, 1981-82. 80GP – 80 game schedule.
208 – Wayne Gretzky, Edmonton, 1984-85. 80GP – 80 game schedule.
205 – Wayne Gretzky, Edmonton, 1983-84. 74GP – 80 game schedule.
199 – Mario Lemieux, Pittsburgh, 1988-89. 76GP – 80 game schedule.

SCORING BY A LEFT WING

MOST GOALS BY A LEFT WING, CAREER:
668 – Luc Robitaille, Los Angeles, Pittsburgh, NY Rangers, Detroit, in 19 seasons. 1,431GP
656 – Brendan Shanahan, New Jersey, St. Louis, Hartford, Detroit, NY Rangers, in 21 seasons. 1,524GP
640 – Dave Andreychuk, Buffalo, Toronto, New Jersey, Boston, Colorado, Tampa Bay, in 23 seasons. 1,639GP
610 – Bobby Hull, Chicago, Winnipeg, Hartford, in 16 seasons. 1,063GP
558 – Alex Ovechkin, Washington, in 12 seasons. 921GP
556 – John Bucyk, Detroit, Boston, in 23 seasons. 1,540GP

MOST GOALS BY A LEFT WING, ONE SEASON:
65 – Alex Ovechkin, Washington, 2007-08. 82GP – 82 game schedule.
63 – Luc Robitaille, Los Angeles, 1992-93. 84GP – 84 game schedule.
60 – Steve Shutt, Montreal, 1976-77. 80GP – 80 game schedule.
58 – Bobby Hull, Chicago, 1968-69. 74GP – 76 game schedule.
57 – Michel Goulet, Quebec, 1982-83. 80GP – 80 game schedule.

MOST ASSISTS BY A LEFT WING, CAREER:
813 – John Bucyk, Detroit, Boston, in 23 seasons. 1,540GP
726 – Luc Robitaille, Los Angeles, Pittsburgh, NY Rangers, Detroit, in 19 seasons. 1,431GP
698 – Dave Andreychuk, Buffalo, Toronto, New Jersey, Boston, Colorado, Tampa Bay, in 23 seasons. 1,639GP
 – Brendan Shanahan, New Jersey, St. Louis, Hartford, Detroit, NY Rangers, in 21 seasons. 1,524GP
679 – Ray Whitney, San Jose, Edmonton, Florida, Columbus, Detroit, Carolina, Phoenix, Dallas, in 22 seasons. 1,330GP
604 – Michel Goulet, Quebec, Chicago, in 15 seasons. 1,089GP

MOST ASSISTS BY A LEFT WING, ONE SEASON:
70 – Joe Juneau, Boston, 1992-93. 84GP – 84 game schedule.
69 – Kevin Stevens, Pittsburgh, 1991-92. 80GP – 80 game schedule.
67 – Mats Naslund, Montreal, 1985-86. 80GP – 80 game schedule.
65 – John Bucyk, Boston, 1970-71. 78GP – 78 game schedule.
 – Michel Goulet, Quebec, 1983-84. 75GP – 80 game schedule.
64 – Mark Messier, Edmonton, 1983-84. 73GP – 80 game schedule.

MOST POINTS BY A LEFT WING, CAREER:
1,394 – Luc Robitaille, Los Angeles, Pittsburgh, NY Rangers, Detroit, in 19 seasons. 1,431GP (668G-726A)
1,369 – John Bucyk, Detroit, Boston, in 23 seasons. 1,540GP (556G-813A)
1,354 – Brendan Shanahan, New Jersey, St. Louis, Hartford, Detroit, NY Rangers, in 21 seasons. 1,524GP (656G-698A)
1,338 – Dave Andreychuk, Buffalo, Toronto, New Jersey, Boston, Colorado, Tampa Bay, in 23 seasons. 1,639GP (640G-698A)
1,170 – Bobby Hull, Chicago, Winnipeg, Hartford, in 16 seasons. 1,063GP (610G-560A)

MOST POINTS BY A LEFT WING, ONE SEASON:
125 – Luc Robitaille, Los Angeles, 1992-93. 84GP – 84 game schedule.
123 – Kevin Stevens, Pittsburgh, 1991-92. 80GP – 80 game schedule.
121 – Michel Goulet, Quebec, 1983-84. 75GP – 80 game schedule.
116 – John Bucyk, Boston, 1970-71. 78GP – 78 game schedule.
112 – Bill Barber, Philadelphia, 1975-76. 80GP – 80 game schedule.
 – Alex Ovechkin, Washington, 2007-08. 82GP – 82 game schedule.

SCORING BY A RIGHT WING

MOST GOALS BY A RIGHT WING, CAREER:
801 – Gordie Howe, Detroit, Hartford, in 26 seasons. 1,767GP
765 – Jaromir Jagr, Pittsburgh, Washington, NY Rangers, Philadelphia, Dallas, Boston, New Jersey, Florida, in 23 seasons. 1,711GP
741 – Brett Hull, Calgary, St. Louis, Dallas, Detroit, Phoenix, in 19 seasons. 1,269GP
708 – Mike Gartner, Washington, Minnesota, NY Rangers, Toronto, Phoenix, in 19 seasons. 1,432GP
684 – Teemu Selanne, Winnipeg, Anaheim, San Jose, Colorado, in 21 seasons. 1,451GP
625 – Jarome Iginla, Calgary, Pittsburgh, Boston, Colorado, in 20 seasons. 1,554GP
608 – Dino Ciccarelli, Minnesota, Washington, Detroit, Tampa Bay, Florida, in 19 seasons. 1,232GP

MOST GOALS BY A RIGHT WING, ONE SEASON:
86 – Brett Hull, St. Louis, 1990-91. 78GP – 80 game schedule.
76 – Alexander Mogilny, Buffalo, 1992-93. 77GP – 84 game schedule.
 – Teemu Selanne, Winnipeg, 1992-93. 84GP – 84 game schedule.
72 – Brett Hull, St. Louis, 1989-90. 80GP – 80 game schedule.
71 – Jari Kurri, Edmonton, 1984-85. 73GP – 80 game schedule.
70 – Brett Hull, St. Louis, 1991-92. 73GP – 80 game schedule.

MOST ASSISTS BY A RIGHT WING, CAREER:
1,149 – Jaromir Jagr, Pittsburgh, Washington, NY Rangers, Philadelphia, Dallas, Boston, New Jersey, Florida, in 23 seasons. 1,711GP
1,049 – Gordie Howe, Detroit, Hartford, in 26 seasons. 1,767GP
956 – Mark Recchi, Pittsburgh, Philadelphia, Montreal, Carolina, Atlanta, Boston, in 22 seasons. 1,652GP
797 – Jari Kurri, Edmonton, Los Angeles, NY Rangers, Anaheim, Colorado, in 17 seasons. 1,251GP
793 – Guy Lafleur, Montreal, NY Rangers, Quebec, in 17 seasons. 1,126GP

MOST ASSISTS BY A RIGHT WING, ONE SEASON:
87 – Jaromir Jagr, Pittsburgh, 1995-96. 82GP – 82 game schedule.
83 – Mike Bossy, NY Islanders, 1981-82. 80GP – 80 game schedule.
 – Jaromir Jagr, Pittsburgh, 1998-99. 81GP – 82 game schedule.
80 – Guy Lafleur, Montreal, 1976-77. 80GP – 80 game schedule.
77 – Guy Lafleur, Montreal, 1978-79. 80GP – 80 game schedule.

Marcel Dionne scored 731 goals during his 18 seasons in the NHL. He had 50 or more six times in his career, and though he never led the NHL in goals in a season, he finished among the top-10 goal scorers nine times.

MOST POINTS BY A RIGHT WING, CAREER:
1,914 – Jaromir Jagr, Pittsburgh, Washington, NY Rangers, Philadelphia, Dallas, Boston, New Jersey, Florida in 23 seasons. 1,711GP (765G-1,149A)
1,850 – Gordie Howe, Detroit, Hartford, in 26 seasons. 1,767GP (801G-1,049A)
1,533 – Mark Recchi, Pittsburgh, Philadelphia, Montreal, Carolina, Atlanta, Boston, in 22 seasons. 1,652GP (577G-956A)
1,457 – Teemu Selanne, Winnipeg, Anaheim, San Jose, Colorado, in 21 seasons. 1,451GP (684G-773A)
1,398 – Jari Kurri, Edmonton, Los Angeles, NY Rangers, Anaheim, Colorado, in 17 seasons. 1,251GP (601G-797A)
1,391 – Brett Hull, Calgary, St. Louis, Dallas, Detroit, Phoenix, in 19 seasons. 1,269GP (741G-650A)

MOST POINTS BY A RIGHT WING, ONE SEASON:
149 – Jaromir Jagr, Pittsburgh, 1995-96. 82GP – 82 game schedule.
147 – Mike Bossy, NY Islanders, 1981-82. 80GP – 80 game schedule.
136 – Guy Lafleur, Montreal, 1976-77. 80GP – 80 game schedule.
135 – Jari Kurri, Edmonton, 1984-85. 73GP – 80 game schedule.
132 – Guy Lafleur, Montreal, 1977-78. 78GP – 80 game schedule.
 – Teemu Selanne, Winnipeg, 1992-93. 84GP – 84 game schedule.

SCORING BY A DEFENSEMAN

MOST GOALS BY A DEFENSEMAN, CAREER:
410 – Raymond Bourque, Boston, Colorado, in 22 seasons. 1,612GP
396 – Paul Coffey, Edmonton, Pittsburgh, Los Angeles, Detroit, Hartford, Philadelphia, Chicago, Carolina, Boston, in 21 seasons. 1,409GP
340 – Al MacInnis, Calgary, St. Louis, in 23 seasons. 1,416GP
338 – Phil Housley, Buffalo, Winnipeg, St. Louis, Calgary, New Jersey, Washington, Chicago, Toronto, in 21 seasons. 1,495GP
310 – Denis Potvin, NY Islanders, in 15 seasons. 1,060GP

MOST GOALS BY A DEFENSEMAN, ONE SEASON:
48 – Paul Coffey, Edmonton, 1985-86. 79GP – 80 game schedule.
46 – Bobby Orr, Boston, 1974-75. 80GP – 80 game schedule.
40 – Paul Coffey, Edmonton, 1983-84. 80GP – 80 game schedule.
39 – Doug Wilson, Chicago, 1981-82. 76GP – 80 game schedule.
37 – Bobby Orr, Boston, 1970-71. 78GP – 78 game schedule.
 – Bobby Orr, Boston, 1971-72. 76GP – 78 game schedule.
 – Paul Coffey, Edmonton, 1984-85. 80GP – 80 game schedule.

MOST GOALS BY A DEFENSEMAN, ONE GAME:
5 – Ian Turnbull, Toronto, Feb. 2, 1977, at Toronto. Toronto 9, Detroit 1.
4 – Harry Cameron, Toronto, Dec. 26, 1917, at Toronto. Toronto 7, Montreal 5.
 – Harry Cameron, Montreal, Mar. 3, 1920, at Quebec. Montreal 16, Quebec 3.
 – Sprague Cleghorn, Montreal, Jan. 14, 1922, at Montreal. Montreal 10, Hamilton 6.
 – John McKinnon, Pittsburgh, Nov. 19, 1929, at Pittsburgh. Pittsburgh 10, Toronto 5.
 – Hap Day, Toronto, Nov. 19, 1929, at Pittsburgh. Pittsburgh 10, Toronto 5.
 – Tom Bladon, Philadelphia, Dec. 11, 1977, at Philadelphia. Philadelphia 11, Cleveland 1.
 – Ian Turnbull, Los Angeles, Dec. 12, 1981, at Los Angeles. Los Angeles 7, Vancouver 5.
 – Paul Coffey, Edmonton, Dec. 26, 1984, at Calgary. Edmonton 6, Calgary 5.

MOST ASSISTS BY A DEFENSEMAN, CAREER:
1,169 – Raymond Bourque, Boston, Colorado, in 22 seasons. 1,612GP
1,135 – Paul Coffey, Edmonton, Pittsburgh, Los Angeles, Detroit, Hartford, Philadelphia, Chicago, Carolina, Boston, in 21 seasons. 1,409GP
934 – Al MacInnis, Calgary, St. Louis, in 23 seasons. 1,416GP
929 – Larry Murphy, Los Angeles, Washington, Minnesota, Pittsburgh, Toronto, Detroit, in 21 seasons. 1,615GP
894 – Phil Housley, Buffalo, Winnipeg, St. Louis, Calgary, New Jersey, Washington, Chicago, Toronto, in 21 seasons. 1,495GP

MOST ASSISTS BY A DEFENSEMAN, ONE SEASON:
102 – Bobby Orr, Boston, 1970-71. 78GP – 78 game schedule.
90 – Bobby Orr, Boston, 1973-74. 74GP – 78 game schedule.
 – Paul Coffey, Edmonton, 1985-86. 79GP – 80 game schedule.
89 – Bobby Orr, Boston, 1974-75. 80GP – 80 game schedule.
87 – Bobby Orr, Boston, 1969-70. 76GP – 78 game schedule.

MOST ASSISTS BY A DEFENSEMAN, ONE GAME:
6 – Babe Pratt, Toronto, Jan. 8, 1944, at Toronto. Toronto 12, Boston 3.
 – Pat Stapleton, Chicago, Mar. 30, 1969, at Chicago. Chicago 9, Detroit 5.
 – Bobby Orr, Boston, Jan. 1, 1973, at Vancouver. Boston 8, Vancouver 2.
 – Ron Stackhouse, Pittsburgh, Mar. 8, 1975, at Pittsburgh. Pittsburgh 8, Philadelphia 2.
 – Paul Coffey, Edmonton, Mar. 14, 1986, at Edmonton. Edmonton 12, Detroit 3.
 – Gary Suter, Calgary, Apr. 4, 1986, at Calgary. Calgary 9, Edmonton 3.

MOST POINTS BY A DEFENSEMAN, CAREER:
1,579 – Raymond Bourque, Boston, Colorado, in 22 seasons. 1,612GP (410G-1,169A)
1,531 – Paul Coffey, Edmonton, Pittsburgh, Los Angeles, Detroit, Hartford, Philadelphia, Chicago, Carolina, Boston, in 21 seasons. 1,409GP (396G-1,135A)
1,274 – Al MacInnis, Calgary, St. Louis, in 23 seasons. 1,416GP (340G-934A)
1,232 – Phil Housley, Buffalo, Winnipeg, St. Louis, Calgary, New Jersey, Washington, Chicago, Toronto, in 21 seasons. 1,495GP (338G-894A)
1,216 – Larry Murphy, Los Angeles, Washington, Minnesota, Pittsburgh, Toronto, Detroit, in 21 seasons. 1,615GP (287G-929A)

MOST POINTS BY A DEFENSEMAN, ONE SEASON:
139 – Bobby Orr, Boston, 1970-71. 78GP – 78 game schedule.
138 – Paul Coffey, Edmonton, 1985-86. 79GP – 80 game schedule.
135 – Bobby Orr, Boston, 1974-75. 80GP – 80 game schedule.
126 – Paul Coffey, Edmonton, 1983-84. 80GP – 80 game schedule.
122 – Bobby Orr, Boston, 1973-74. 74GP – 78 game schedule.

MOST POINTS BY A DEFENSEMAN, ONE GAME:
8 – Tom Bladon, Philadelphia, Dec. 11, 1977, at Philadelphia. 4G-4A. Philadelphia 11, Cleveland 1.
 – **Paul Coffey**, Edmonton, Mar. 14, 1986, at Edmonton. 2G-6A. Edmonton 12, Detroit 3.
7 – Bobby Orr, Boston, Nov. 15, 1973, at Boston. 3G-4A. Boston 10, NY Rangers 2.

SCORING BY A GOALTENDER

MOST POINTS BY A GOALTENDER, CAREER:
48 – Tom Barrasso, Buffalo, Pittsburgh, Ottawa, Carolina, Toronto, St. Louis, in 19 seasons. 777GP
47 – Martin Brodeur, New Jersey, St. Louis, in 22 seasons. 1,266GP
46 – Grant Fuhr, Edmonton, Toronto, Buffalo, Los Angeles, St. Louis, Calgary, in 19 seasons. 868GP

MOST POINTS BY A GOALTENDER, ONE SEASON:
14 – Grant Fuhr, Edmonton, 1983-84. 45GP – 80 game schedule.
9 – Curtis Joseph, St. Louis, 1991-92. 60GP – 80 game schedule.
8 – Mike Palmateer, Washington, 1980-81. 49GP – 80 game schedule.
 – Grant Fuhr, Edmonton, 1987-88. 75GP – 80 game schedule.
 – Ron Hextall, Philadelphia, 1988-89. 64GP – 80 game schedule.
 – Tom Barrasso, Pittsburgh, 1992-93. 63GP – 84 game schedule.

MOST POINTS BY A GOALTENDER, ONE GAME:
3 – Jeff Reese, Calgary, Feb. 10, 1993, at Calgary. Calgary 13, San Jose 1.

Paul Coffey ranks second all-time behind either Raymond Bourque or Bobby Orr in numerous scoring categories for NHL defensemen. He ranks first all-time in goals scored by a defenseman in one season with 48 for the Edmonton Oilers in 1985-86.

SCORING BY A ROOKIE

MOST GOALS BY A ROOKIE, ONE SEASON:
76 – **Teemu Selanne**, Winnipeg, 1992-93. 84GP – 84 game schedule.
53 – Mike Bossy, NY Islanders, 1977-78. 73GP – 80 game schedule.
52 – Alex Ovechkin, Washington, 2005-06. 81GP – 82 game schedule.
51 – Joe Nieuwendyk, Calgary, 1987-88. 75GP – 80 game schedule.
45 – Dale Hawerchuk, Winnipeg, 1981-82. 80GP – 80 game schedule.
  – Luc Robitaille, Los Angeles, 1986-87. 79GP – 80 game schedule.

MOST GOALS BY A PLAYER IN HIS FIRST NHL SEASON, ONE GAME:
5 – **Joe Malone**, Montreal, Dec. 19, 1917, at Ottawa.
  Montreal 7, Ottawa 4.
  – **Harry Hyland**, Mtl. Wanderers, Dec. 19, 1917, at Montreal.
  Mtl Wanderers 10, Toronto 9.
  – **Joe Malone**, Montreal, Jan. 12, 1918, at Montreal.
  Montreal 9, Ottawa 4.
  – **Joe Malone**, Montreal, Feb. 2, 1918, at Montreal.
  Montreal 11, Toronto 2.
  – **Mickey Roach**, Toronto, Mar. 6, 1920, at Toronto. Toronto 11, Quebec 2.
  – **Howie Meeker**, Toronto, Jan. 8, 1947, at Toronto. Toronto 10, Chicago 4.
  – **Don Murdoch**, NY Rangers, Oct. 12, 1976, at Minnesota.
  NY Rangers 10, Minnesota 5.

MOST GOALS BY A PLAYER IN HIS FIRST NHL GAME:
5 – **Joe Malone**, Montreal, Dec. 19, 1917, at Ottawa. Montreal 7, Ottawa 4.
  – **Harry Hyland**, Mtl. Wanderers, Dec. 19, 1917, at Montreal.
  Mtl Wanderers 10, Toronto 9.
4 – Reg Noble, Toronto, Dec. 19, 1917, at Montreal.
  Mtl Wanderers 10, Toronto 9.
  – Auston Matthews, Toronto, Oct. 12, 2016, at Ottawa. Ottawa 5, Toronto 4.
3 – Cy Denneny, Ottawa, Dec. 19, 1917, at Ottawa. Montreal 7, Ottawa 4.
  – Alex Smart, Montreal, Jan. 14, 1943, at Montreal. Montreal 5, Chicago 1.
  – Real Cloutier, Quebec, Oct. 10, 1979, at Quebec. Atlanta 5, Quebec 3.
  – Fabian Brunnstrom, Dallas, Oct. 15, 2008, at Dallas.
  Dallas 6, Nashville 4.
  – Derek Stepan, NY Rangers, Oct. 9, 2010, at Buffalo.
  NY Rangers 6, Buffalo 3.

MOST ASSISTS BY A ROOKIE, ONE SEASON:
70 – **Peter Stastny**, Quebec, 1980-81. 77GP – 80 game schedule.
  – **Joe Juneau**, Boston, 1992-93. 84GP – 84 game schedule.
63 – Bryan Trottier, NY Islanders, 1975-76. 80GP – 80 game schedule.
  – Sidney Crosby, Pittsburgh, 2005–06. 81GP – 82 game schedule.
62 – Sergei Makarov, Calgary, 1989-90. 80GP – 80 game schedule.
60 – Larry Murphy, Los Angeles, 1980-81. 80GP – 80 game schedule.

MOST ASSISTS BY A PLAYER IN HIS FIRST NHL SEASON, ONE GAME:
7 – **Wayne Gretzky**, Edmonton, Feb. 15, 1980, at Edmonton.
  Edmonton 8, Washington 2.
6 – Gary Suter, Calgary, Apr. 4, 1986, at Calgary. Calgary 9, Edmonton 3.

MOST ASSISTS BY A PLAYER IN HIS FIRST NHL GAME:
4 – **Dutch Reibel**, Detroit, Oct. 8, 1953, at Detroit. Detroit 4, NY Rangers 1.
  – **Roland Eriksson**, Minnesota, Oct. 6, 1976, at NY Rangers.
  NY Rangers 6, Minnesota 5.
3 – Al Hill, Philadelphia, Feb. 14, 1977, at Philadelphia. Philadelphia 6,
  St. Louis 4.
  – Jarno Kultanen, Boston, Oct. 5, 2000, at Boston. Boston 4, Ottawa 4.
  – Stanislav Chistov, Anaheim, Oct. 10, 2002, at St. Louis. Anaheim 4,
  St. Louis 3.
  – Dominic Moore, NY Rangers, Nov. 1, 2003, at Montreal. NY Rangers 5,
  Montreal 1.

MOST POINTS BY A ROOKIE, ONE SEASON:
132 – **Teemu Selanne**, Winnipeg, 1992-93. 84GP – 84 game schedule.
109 – Peter Stastny, Quebec, 1980-81. 77GP – 80 game schedule.
106 – Alex Ovechkin, Washington, 2005-06. 81GP – 82 game schedule.
103 – Dale Hawerchuk, Winnipeg, 1981-82. 80GP – 80 game schedule.
102 – Joe Juneau, Boston, 1992-93. 84GP – 84 game schedule.
  – Sidney Crosby, Pittsburgh, 2005–06. 81GP – 82 game schedule.
100 – Mario Lemieux, Pittsburgh, 1984-85. 73GP – 80 game schedule.

MOST POINTS BY A PLAYER IN HIS FIRST NHL SEASON, ONE GAME:
8 – **Peter Stastny**, Quebec, Feb. 22, 1981, at Washington. 4G-4A.
  Quebec 11, Washington 7.
  – **Anton Stastny**, Quebec, Feb. 22, 1981, at Washington. 3G-5A.
  Quebec 11, Washington 7.
7 – Wayne Gretzky, Edmonton, Feb. 15, 1980, at Edmonton. 7A.
  Edmonton 8, Washington 2.
  – Sergei Makarov, Calgary, Feb. 25, 1990, at Calgary. 2G-5A.
  Calgary 10, Edmonton 4.
6 – Wayne Gretzky, Edmonton, Mar. 29, 1980, at Toronto. 2G-4A.
  Edmonton 8, Toronto 5.
  – Gary Suter, Calgary, Apr. 4, 1986, at Calgary. 6A.
  Calgary 9, Edmonton 3.

MOST POINTS BY A PLAYER IN HIS FIRST NHL GAME:
5 – **Joe Malone**, Montreal, Dec. 19, 1917, at Ottawa. 5G*.
  Montreal 7, Ottawa 4. * – *Official assists not awarded in 1917-18.*
  – **Harry Hyland**, Mtl. Wanderers, Dec. 19, 1917, at Montreal. 5G*.
  Mtl Wanderers 10, Toronto 9.
  – **Al Hill**, Philadelphia, Feb. 14, 1977, at Philadelphia. 2G-3A.
  Philadelphia 6, St. Louis 4.
4 – Reg Noble, Toronto, Dec. 19, 1917, at Montreal. 4G.
  Mtl Wanderers 10, Toronto 9.
  – Alex Smart, Montreal, Jan. 14, 1943, at Montreal. 3G-1A.
  Montreal 5, Chicago 1.
  – Dutch Reibel, Detroit, Oct. 8, 1953, at Detroit. 4A.
  Detroit 4, NY Rangers 1.
  – Roland Eriksson, Minnesota, Oct. 6, 1976, at NY Rangers. 4A.
  NY Rangers 6, Minnesota 5.
  – Stanislav Chistov, Anaheim, Oct. 10, 2002, at St. Louis. 1G-3A.
  Anaheim 4, St. Louis 3.
  – Auston Matthews, Toronto, Oct. 12, 2016, at Ottawa. 4G.
  Ottawa 5, Toronto 4.

SCORING BY A ROOKIE DEFENSEMAN

MOST GOALS BY A ROOKIE DEFENSEMAN, ONE SEASON:
23 – **Brian Leetch**, NY Rangers, 1988-89. 68GP – 80 game schedule.
22 – Barry Beck, Colorado Rockies, 1977-78. 75GP – 80 game schedule.
20 – Dion Phaneuf, Calgary, 2005-06. 82GP – 82 game schedule.

MOST ASSISTS BY A ROOKIE DEFENSEMAN, ONE SEASON:
60 – **Larry Murphy**, Los Angeles, 1980-81. 80GP – 80 game schedule.
55 – Chris Chelios, Montreal, 1984-85. 74GP – 80 game schedule.
50 – Stefan Persson, NY Islanders, 1977-78. 66GP – 80 game schedule.
  – Gary Suter, Calgary, 1985-86. 80GP – 80 game schedule.
49 – Nicklas Lidstrom, Detroit, 1991-92. 80GP – 80 game schedule.

MOST POINTS BY A ROOKIE DEFENSEMAN, ONE SEASON:
76 – **Larry Murphy**, Los Angeles, 1980-81. 80GP – 80 game schedule.
71 – Brian Leetch, NY Rangers, 1988-89. 68GP – 80 game schedule.
68 – Gary Suter, Calgary, 1985-86. 80GP – 80 game schedule.
66 – Phil Housley, Buffalo, 1982-83. 77GP – 80 game schedule.
65 – Raymond Bourque, Boston, 1979-80. 80GP – 80 game schedule.

Off to a flying start: Auston Matthews displays the pucks from his four-goal debut with the Toronto Maple Leafs against the Ottawa Senators on October 12, 2016. It was the biggest goal-scoring display by a player in his first NHL game since the first night of the NHL's inaugural season in 1917-18.

PER-GAME SCORING AVERAGES

HIGHEST GOALS-PER-GAME AVERAGE, CAREER
(AMONG PLAYERS WITH 200-OR-MORE GOALS):
.762 – **Mike Bossy**, NY Islanders, 1977-78 – 1986-87, with 573G in 752GP.
.756 – Cy Denneny, Ottawa, Boston, 1917-18 – 1928-29, with 248G in 328GP.
.754 – Mario Lemieux, Pittsburgh, 1984-85 – 1996-97, 2000-01 – 2003-04, 2005-06, with 690G in 915GP.
.742 – Babe Dye, Toronto, Hamilton, Chicago, NY Americans, 1919-20 – 1930-31, with 201G in 271GP.
.623 – Pavel Bure, Vancouver, Florida, NY Rangers, 1991-92 – 2002-03, with 437G in 702GP.

HIGHEST GOALS-PER-GAME AVERAGE, ONE SEASON
(AMONG PLAYERS WITH 20-OR-MORE GOALS):
2.20 – **Joe Malone**, Montreal, 1917-18, with 44G in 20GP.
1.80 – Cy Denneny, Ottawa, 1917-18, with 36G in 20GP.
1.64 – Newsy Lalonde, Montreal, 1917-18, with 23G in 14GP.
1.63 – Joe Malone, Quebec, 1919-20, with 39G in 24GP.
1.61 – Newsy Lalonde, Montreal, 1919-20, with 37G in 23GP.

HIGHEST GOALS-PER-GAME AVERAGE, ONE SEASON
(AMONG PLAYERS WITH 50-OR-MORE GOALS):
1.18 – **Wayne Gretzky**, Edmonton, 1983-84, with 87G in 74GP.
1.15 – Wayne Gretzky, Edmonton, 1981-82, with 92G in 80GP.
 – Mario Lemieux, Pittsburgh, 1992-93, with 69G in 60GP.
1.12 – Mario Lemieux, Pittsburgh, 1988-89, with 85G in 76GP.
1.10 – Brett Hull, St. Louis, 1990-91, with 86G in 78GP.
1.02 – Cam Neely, Boston, 1993-94, with 50G in 49GP.
1.00 – Maurice Richard, Montreal, 1944-45, with 50G in 50GP.

HIGHEST ASSISTS-PER-GAME AVERAGE, CAREER
(AMONG PLAYERS WITH 300-OR-MORE ASSISTS):
1.320 – **Wayne Gretzky**, Edmonton, Los Angeles, St. Louis, NY Rangers, 1979-80 – 1998-99, with 1,963A in 1,487GP.
1.129 – Mario Lemieux, Pittsburgh, 1984-85 – 1996-97, 2000-01 – 2003-04, 2005-06, with 1,033A in 915GP.
.982 – Bobby Orr, Boston, Chicago, 1966-67 – 1978-79, with 645A in 657GP.
.898 – Peter Forsberg, Quebec, Colorado, Philadelphia, Nashville, 1994-95 – 2000-01, 2002-03, 2003-04, 2005-06 – 2007-08, 2010-11 with 636A in 708GP.
.825 – Sidney Crosby, Pittsburgh, 2005-06 – 2016-17, with 645A in 782GP.

HIGHEST ASSISTS-PER-GAME AVERAGE, ONE SEASON
(AMONG PLAYERS WITH 35-OR-MORE ASSISTS):
2.04 – **Wayne Gretzky, Edmonton**, 1985-86, with 163A in 80GP.
1.70 – Wayne Gretzky, Edmonton, 1987-88, with 109A in 64GP.
1.69 – Wayne Gretzky, Edmonton, 1984-85, with 135A in 80GP.
1.59 – Wayne Gretzky, Edmonton, 1983-84, with 118A in 74GP.
1.56 – Wayne Gretzky, Edmonton, 1982-83, with 125A in 80GP.
 – Wayne Gretzky, Los Angeles, 1990-91, with 122A in 78GP.
1.53 – Wayne Gretzky, Edmonton, 1986-87, with 121A in 79GP.
1.52 – Mario Lemieux, Pittsburgh, 1992-93, with 91A in 60GP.
1.50 – Wayne Gretzky, Edmonton, 1981-82, with 120A in 80GP.
 – Mario Lemieux, Pittsburgh, 1988-89, with 114A in 76GP.

HIGHEST POINTS-PER-GAME AVERAGE, CAREER
(AMONG PLAYERS WITH 500-OR-MORE POINTS):
1.921 – **Wayne Gretzky**, Edmonton, Los Angeles, St. Louis, NY Rangers, 1979-80 – 1998-99, with 2,857PTS (894G-1,963A) in 1,487GP.
1.883 – Mario Lemieux, Pittsburgh, 1984-85 – 1996-97, 2000-01 – 2003-04, 2005-06, with 1,723PTS (690G-1,033A) in 915GP.
1.497 – Mike Bossy, NY Islanders, 1977-78 – 1986-87, with 1,126PTS (573G-553A) in 752GP.
1.393 – Bobby Orr, Boston, Chicago, 1966-67 – 1978-79, with 915PTS (270G-645A) in 657GP.
1.313 – Sidney Crosby, Pittsburgh, 2005-06 – 2016-17, with 1,027PTS (382G-645A) in 782GP.

HIGHEST POINTS-PER-GAME AVERAGE, ONE SEASON
(AMONG PLAYERS WITH 50-OR-MORE POINTS):
2.77 – **Wayne Gretzky**, Edmonton, 1983-84, with 205PTS in 74GP.
2.69 – Wayne Gretzky, Edmonton, 1985-86, with 215PTS in 80GP.
2.67 – Mario Lemieux, Pittsburgh, 1992-93, with 160PTS in 60GP.
2.65 – Wayne Gretzky, Edmonton, 1981-82, with 212PTS in 80GP.
2.62 – Mario Lemieux, Pittsburgh, 1988-89, with 199PTS in 76GP.
2.60 – Wayne Gretzky, Edmonton, 1984-85, with 208PTS in 80GP.
2.45 – Wayne Gretzky, Edmonton, 1982-83, with 196PTS in 80GP.
2.33 – Wayne Gretzky, Edmonton, 1987-88, with 149PTS in 64GP.
2.32 – Wayne Gretzky, Edmonton, 1986-87, with 183PTS in 79GP.
2.30 – Mario Lemieux, Pittsburgh, 1995-96, with 161PTS in 70GP.
2.18 – Mario Lemieux, Pittsburgh, 1987-88, with 168PTS in 77GP.
2.15 – Wayne Gretzky, Los Angeles, 1988-89, with 168PTS in 78GP.
2.09 – Wayne Gretzky, Los Angeles, 1990-91, with 163PTS in 78GP.
2.08 – Mario Lemieux, Pittsburgh, 1989-90, with 123PTS in 59GP.

SCORING PLATEAUS

MOST 20-OR-MORE GOAL SEASONS:
22 – **Gordie Howe**, Detroit, Hartford, in 26 seasons.
20 – Ron Francis, Hartford, Pittsburgh, Carolina, Toronto, in 23 seasons.
19 – Dave Andreychuk, Buffalo, Toronto, New Jersey, Boston, Colorado, Tampa Bay, in 23 seasons.
 – Brendan Shanahan, New Jersey, St. Louis, Hartford, Detroit, NY Rangers, in 21 seasons.
 – Jaromir Jagr, Pittsburgh, Washington, NY Rangers, Philadelphia, Dallas, Boston, New Jersey, Florida, in 23 seasons.
17 – Marcel Dionne, Detroit, Los Angeles, NY Rangers, in 18 seasons.
 – Mike Gartner, Washington, Minnesota, NY Rangers, Toronto, Phoenix, in 19 seasons.
 – Wayne Gretzky, Edmonton, Los Angeles, St. Louis, NY Rangers, in 20 seasons.
 – Mark Messier, Edmonton, NY Rangers, Vancouver, in 25 seasons.
 – Brett Hull, Calgary, St. Louis, Dallas, Detroit, Phoenix, in 19 seasons.
 – Joe Sakic, Quebec, Colorado, in 20 seasons.
 – Mats Sundin, Quebec, Toronto, Vancouver, in 18 seasons.
 – Teemu Selanne, Winnipeg, Anaheim, San Jose, Colorado, in 21 seasons.
 – Jarome Iginla, Calgary, Pittsburgh, Boston, Colorado, in 19 seasons.

MOST CONSECUTIVE 20-OR-MORE GOAL SEASONS:
22 – **Gordie Howe**, Detroit, 1949-50 – 1970-71.
19 – Brendan Shanahan, New Jersey, St. Louis, Hartford, Detroit, NY Rangers, 1988-89 – 2007-08.
17 – Marcel Dionne, Detroit, Los Angeles, NY Rangers, 1971-72 – 1987-88.
 – Brett Hull, Calgary, St. Louis, Dallas, Detroit, 1987-88 – 2003-04.
 – Jaromir Jagr, Pittsburgh, Washington, NY Rangers, 1990-91 – 2007-08.
 – Mats Sundin, Quebec, Toronto, 1990-91 – 2007-08.

Wayne Gretzky celebrates the final point of his NHL career, having set up Rangers teammate Brian Leetch for a goal against the Pittsburgh Penguins on April 18, 1999. Gretzky averaged nearly two points per game throughout his 20-year NHL career.

MOST 30-OR-MORE GOAL SEASONS:
17 – Mike Gartner, Washington, Minnesota, NY Rangers, Toronto, Phoenix, in 19 seasons.
15 – Jaromir Jagr, Pittsburgh, Washington, NY Rangers, Philadelphia, Dallas, Boston, New Jersey, Florida, in 23 seasons.
14 – Gordie Howe, Detroit, Hartford, in 26 seasons.
– Marcel Dionne, Detroit, Los Angeles, NY Rangers, in 18 seasons.
– Wayne Gretzky, Edmonton, Los Angeles, St. Louis, NY Rangers, in 20 seasons.
13 – Bobby Hull, Chicago, Winnipeg, Hartford, in 16 seasons.
– Phil Esposito, Chicago, Boston, NY Rangers, in 18 seasons.
– Brett Hull, Calgary, St. Louis, Dallas, Detroit, Phoenix, in 19 seasons.
– Mats Sundin, Quebec, Toronto, Vancouver, in 18 seasons.

MOST CONSECUTIVE 30-OR-MORE GOAL SEASONS:
15 – Mike Gartner, Washington, Minnesota, NY Rangers, Toronto, 1979-80 – 1993-94.
– **Jaromir Jagr**, Pittsburgh, Washington, NY Rangers, 1991-92 – 2006-07.
13 – Bobby Hull, Chicago, 1959-60 – 1971-72.
– Phil Esposito, Boston, NY Rangers, 1967-68 – 1979-80.
– Wayne Gretzky, Edmonton, Los Angeles, 1979-80 – 1991-92.

MOST 40-OR-MORE GOAL SEASONS:
12 – Wayne Gretzky, Edmonton, Los Angeles, St. Louis, NY Rangers, in 20 seasons.
10 – Marcel Dionne, Detroit, Los Angeles, NY Rangers, in 18 seasons.
– Mario Lemieux, Pittsburgh, in 17 seasons.
9 – Mike Bossy, NY Islanders, in 10 seasons.
– Mike Gartner, Washington, Minnesota, NY Rangers, Toronto, Phoenix, in 19 seasons.

MOST CONSECUTIVE 40-OR-MORE GOAL SEASONS:
12 – Wayne Gretzky, Edmonton, Los Angeles, 1979-80 – 1990-91.
9 – Mike Bossy, NY Islanders, 1977-78 – 1985-86.
8 – Luc Robitaille, Los Angeles, 1986-87 – 1993-94.
7 – Phil Esposito, Boston, 1968-69 – 1974-75.
– Michel Goulet, Quebec, 1981-82 – 1987-88.
– Jari Kurri, Edmonton, 1982-83 – 1988-89.

MOST 50-OR-MORE GOAL SEASONS:
9 – Mike Bossy, NY Islanders, in 10 seasons.
– **Wayne Gretzky**, Edmonton, Los Angeles, St. Louis, NY Rangers, in 20 seasons.
7 – Alex Ovechkin, Washington, in 12 seasons.
6 – Guy Lafleur, Montreal, NY Rangers, Quebec, in 17 seasons.
– Marcel Dionne, Detroit, Los Angeles, NY Rangers, in 18 seasons.
– Mario Lemieux, Pittsburgh, in 17 seasons.
5 – Bobby Hull, Chicago, Winnipeg, Hartford, in 16 seasons.
– Phil Esposito, Chicago, Boston, NY Rangers, in 18 seasons.
– Brett Hull, Calgary, St. Louis, Dallas, Detroit, Phoenix, in 19 seasons.
– Steve Yzerman, Detroit, in 22 seasons.
– Pavel Bure, Vancouver, Florida, NY Rangers, in 12 seasons.

MOST CONSECUTIVE 50-OR-MORE GOAL SEASONS:
9 – Mike Bossy, NY Islanders, 1977-78 – 1985-86.
8 – Wayne Gretzky, Edmonton, 1979-80 – 1986-87.
6 – Guy Lafleur, Montreal, 1974-75 – 1979-80.
5 – Phil Esposito, Boston, 1970-71 – 1974-75.
– Marcel Dionne, Los Angeles, 1978-79 – 1982-83.
– Brett Hull, St. Louis, 1989-90 – 1993-94.

MOST 60-OR-MORE GOAL SEASONS:
5 – Mike Bossy, NY Islanders, in 10 seasons.
– **Wayne Gretzky**, Edmonton, Los Angeles, St. Louis, NY Rangers, in 20 seasons.
4 – Phil Esposito, Chicago, Boston, NY Rangers, in 18 seasons.
– Mario Lemieux, Pittsburgh, in 17 seasons.

MOST CONSECUTIVE 60-OR-MORE GOAL SEASONS:
4 – Wayne Gretzky, Edmonton, 1981-82 – 1984-85.
3 – Mike Bossy, NY Islanders, 1980-81 – 1982-83.
– Brett Hull, St. Louis, 1989-90 – 1991-92.
2 – Phil Esposito, Boston, 1970-71 – 1971-72, 1973-74 – 1974-75.
– Jari Kurri, Edmonton, 1984-85 – 1985-86.
– Mario Lemieux, Pittsburgh, 1987-88 – 1988-89.
– Steve Yzerman, Detroit, 1988-89 – 1989-90.
– Pavel Bure, Vancouver, 1992-93 – 1993-94.

MOST 100-OR-MORE POINT SEASONS:
15 – Wayne Gretzky, Edmonton, Los Angeles, St. Louis, NY Rangers, in 20 seasons.
10 – Mario Lemieux, Pittsburgh, in 17 seasons.
8 – Marcel Dionne, Detroit, Los Angeles, NY Rangers, in 18 seasons.
7 – Mike Bossy, NY Islanders, in 10 seasons.
– Peter Stastny, Quebec, New Jersey, St. Louis, in 15 seasons.

MOST CONSECUTIVE 100-OR-MORE POINT SEASONS:
13 – Wayne Gretzky, Edmonton, Los Angeles, 1979-80 – 1991-92.
6 – Bobby Orr, Boston, 1969-70 – 1974-75.
– Guy Lafleur, Montreal, 1974-75 – 1979-80.
– Mike Bossy, NY Islanders, 1980-81 – 1985-86.
– Peter Stastny, Quebec, 1980-81 – 1985-86.
– Mario Lemieux, Pittsburgh, 1984-85 – 1989-90.
– Steve Yzerman, Detroit, 1987-88 – 1992-93.

THREE-OR-MORE-GOAL GAMES

MOST THREE-OR-MORE GOAL GAMES, CAREER:
50 – Wayne Gretzky, Edmonton, Los Angeles, St. Louis, NY Rangers, in 20 seasons, 37 three-goal games, 9 four-goal games, 4 five-goal games.
40 – Mario Lemieux, Pittsburgh, in 17 seasons, 27 three-goal games, 10 four-goal games, 3 five-goal games.
39 – Mike Bossy, NY Islanders, in 10 seasons, 30 three-goal games, 9 four-goal games.
33 – Brett Hull, Calgary, St. Louis, Dallas, Detroit, Phoenix, in 19 seasons, 30 three-goal games, 3 four-goal games.
32 – Phil Esposito, Chicago, Boston, NY Rangers, in 18 seasons, 27 three-goal games, 5 four-goal games.

MOST THREE-OR-MORE GOAL GAMES, ONE SEASON:
10 – Wayne Gretzky, Edmonton, 1981-82. 6 three-goal games, 3 four-goal games, 1 five-goal game.
– **Wayne Gretzky**, Edmonton, 1983-84. 6 three-goal games, 4 four-goal games.
9 – Mike Bossy, NY Islanders, 1980-81. 6 three-goal games, 3 four-goal games.
– Mario Lemieux, Pittsburgh, 1988-89. 7 three-goal games, 1 four-goal game, 1 five-goal game.
8 – Brett Hull, St. Louis, 1991-92. 8 three-goal games.
7 – Joe Malone, Montreal, 1917-18. 2 three-goal games, 2 four-goal games, 3 five-goal games.
– Phil Esposito, Boston, 1970-71. 7 three-goal games.
– Rick Martin, Buffalo, 1975-76. 6 three-goal games, 1 four-goal game.
– Alexander Mogilny, Buffalo, 1992-93. 5 three-goal games, 2 four-goal games.

SCORING STREAKS

LONGEST CONSECUTIVE GOAL-SCORING STREAK:
16 Games – Punch Broadbent, Ottawa, 1921-22. 27G
14 Games – Joe Malone, Montreal, 1917-18. 35G
13 Games – Newsy Lalonde, Montreal, 1920-21. 24G
– Charlie Simmer, Los Angeles, 1979-80. 17G
12 Games – Cy Denneny, Ottawa, 1917-18. 23G
– Dave Lumley, Edmonton, 1981-82. 15G
– Mario Lemieux, Pittsburgh, 1992-93. 18G

LONGEST CONSECUTIVE ASSIST-SCORING STREAK:
23 Games – Wayne Gretzky, Los Angeles, 1990-91. 48A
18 Games – Adam Oates, Boston, 1992-93. 28A
17 Games – Wayne Gretzky, Edmonton, 1983-84. 38A
– Paul Coffey, Edmonton, 1985-86. 27A
– Wayne Gretzky, Los Angeles, 1989-90. 35A
16 Games – Jaromir Jagr, Pittsburgh, 2000-01. 24A

LONGEST CONSECUTIVE POINT-SCORING STREAK:
51 Games – Wayne Gretzky, Edmonton, 1983-84. 61G-92A-153PTS
46 Games – Mario Lemieux, Pittsburgh, 1989-90. 39G-64A-103PTS
39 Games – Wayne Gretzky, Edmonton, 1985-86. 33G-75A-108PTS
30 Games – Wayne Gretzky, Edmonton, 1982-83. 24G-52A-76PTS
– Mats Sundin, Quebec, 1992-93. 21G-25A-46PTS

LONGEST CONSECUTIVE POINT-SCORING STREAK FROM START OF SEASON:
51 Games – Wayne Gretzky, Edmonton, 1983-84. 61G-92A-153PTS. Streak ended by Los Angeles and goaltender Markus Mattson on Jan. 28, 1984.

LONGEST CONSECUTIVE POINT-SCORING STREAK BY A DEFENSEMAN:
28 Games – Paul Coffey, Edmonton, 1985-86. 16G-39A-55PTS
19 Games – Raymond Bourque, Boston, 1987-88. 6G-21A-27PTS
17 Games – Raymond Bourque, Boston, 1984-85. 4G-24A-28PTS
– Brian Leetch, NY Rangers, 1991-92. 5G-24A-29PTS
16 Games – Gary Suter, Calgary, 1987-88. 8G-17A-25PTS
15 Games – Bobby Orr, Boston, 1970-71. 10G-23A-33PTS
– Bobby Orr, Boston, 1973-74. 8G-15A-23PTS
– Steve Duchesne, Quebec, 1992-93. 4G-17A-21PTS
– Chris Chelios, Chicago, 1995-96. 4G-16A-20PTS
– Shayne Gostisbehere, Philadelphia, 2015-16. 5G-13A-18PTS

LONGEST CONSECUTIVE POINT-SCORING STREAK BY A ROOKIE:
20 Games – Paul Stastny, Colorado, 2006-07. 11G-18A-29PTS
17 Games – Teemu Selanne, Winnipeg, 1992-93. 20G-14A-34PTS
16 Games – Peter Stastny, Quebec, 1980-81
– Joe Nieuwendyk, Calgary, 1987-88
15 Games – Jude Drouin, Minnesota North Stars, 1970-71
– Shayne Gostisbehere, Philadelphia, 2015-16. 5G-13A-18PTS

FASTEST GOALS AND ASSISTS

FASTEST GOAL FROM START OF A GAME:
0:05 – Merlyn Phillips, Montreal Maroons, Dec. 29, 1926, at Chicago. Chicago 5, Mtl. Maroons 4.
– **Doug Smail**, Winnipeg, Dec. 20, 1981, at Winnipeg. Winnipeg 5, St. Louis 4.
– **Bryan Trottier**, NY Islanders, Mar. 22, 1984, at Boston. NY Islanders 3, Boston 3.
– **Alexander Mogilny**, Buffalo, Dec. 21, 1991, at Toronto. Buffalo 4, Toronto 1.
0:06 – Henry Boucha, Detroit, Jan. 28, 1973, at Montreal. Detroit 4, Montreal 2.
– Jean Pronovost, Pittsburgh, Mar. 25, 1976, at St. Louis. St. Louis 5, Pittsburgh 2.
– Alex Burrows, Vancouver, Mar. 16, 2013, at Vancouver. Detroit 5, Vancouver 2.
0:07 – Charlie Conacher, Toronto, Feb. 6, 1932, at Toronto. Toronto 6, Boston 0.
– Danny Gare, Buffalo, Dec. 17, 1978, at Buffalo. Buffalo 6, Vancouver 3.
– Tiger Williams, Los Angeles, Feb. 14, 1987, at Los Angeles. Los Angeles 5, Hartford 2.
– Evgeni Malkin, Pittsburgh, Jan. 5, 2011, at Pittsburgh. Pittsburgh 8, Tampa Bay 1.

FASTEST GOAL FROM START OF A PERIOD:
0:04 – Claude Provost, Montreal, Nov. 9, 1957, at Montreal,
second period. Montreal 4, Boston 2.
– **Denis Savard**, Chicago, Jan. 12, 1986, at Chicago,
third period. Chicago 4, Hartford 2.
– **James van Riemsdyk**, Toronto, Mar. 28, 2014, at Philadelphia,
second period. Toronto 4, Philadelphia 2.

FASTEST GOAL BY A PLAYER IN HIS FIRST NHL GAME:
0:15 – Gus Bodnar, Toronto, Oct. 30, 1943, at Toronto.
Toronto 5, NY Rangers 2.
0:18 – Danny Gare, Buffalo, Oct. 10, 1974, at Buffalo.
Buffalo 9, Boston 5.
0:20 – Alexander Mogilny, Buffalo, Oct. 5, 1989, at Buffalo.
Buffalo 4, Quebec 3.

FASTEST TWO GOALS FROM START OF A GAME:
0:27 – Mike Knuble, Boston, Feb. 14, 2003, at Florida.
0:10 and 0:27. Boston 6, Florida 5.

FASTEST TWO GOALS:
0:04 – Nels Stewart, Mtl. Maroons, Jan. 3, 1931, at Mtl. Maroons.
8:24 and 8:28, third period. Mtl. Maroons 5, Boston 3.
– **Deron Quint**, Winnipeg, Dec. 15, 1995, at Winnipeg.
7:51 and 7:55, second period. Winnipeg 9, Edmonton 4.
0:05 – Pete Mahovlich, Montreal, Feb. 20, 1971, at Montreal.
12:16 and 12:21, third period. Montreal 7, Chicago 1.
– Nathan Gerbe, Buffalo, Jan. 21, 2011at Buffalo.
16:38 and 16:43, third period. NY Islanders 5, Buffalo 2.
0:06 – Jim Pappin, Chicago, Feb. 16, 1972, at Chicago.
2:57 and 3:03, third period. Chicago 3, Philadelphia 3.
– Ralph Backstrom, Los Angeles, Nov. 2, 1972, at Los Angeles.
8:30 and 8:36, third period. Los Angeles 5, Boston 2.
– Lanny McDonald, Calgary, Mar. 22, 1984, at Calgary.
16:23 and 16:29, first period. Detroit 6, Calgary 4.
– Sylvain Turgeon, Hartford, Mar. 28, 1987, at Hartford.
13:59 and 14:05, second period. Hartford 5, Pittsburgh 4.

FASTEST THREE GOALS:
0:21 – Bill Mosienko, Chicago, Mar. 23, 1952, at NY Rangers, against
goaltender Lorne Anderson. Mosienko scored at 6:09, 6:20 and 6:30 of
third period, all with both teams at full strength. Chicago 7, NY Rangers 6.
0:44 – Jean Béliveau, Montreal, Nov. 5, 1955, at Montreal, against goaltender
Terry Sawchuk. Béliveau scored at 0:42, 1:08 and 1:26 of second period,
all with Montreal holding a 6-4 man advantage. Montreal 4, Boston 2.

FASTEST THREE ASSISTS:
0:21 – Gus Bodnar, Chicago, Mar. 23, 1952, at NY Rangers, Bodnar assisted on
Bill Mosienko's three goals at 6:09, 6:20 and 6:30 of third period.
Chicago 7, NY Rangers 6.
0:44 – Bert Olmstead, Montreal, Nov. 5, 1955, at Montreal, Olmstead assisted on
Jean Béliveau's three goals at 0:42, 1:08 and 1:26 of second period.
Montreal 4, Boston 2.

SHOTS ON GOAL

MOST SHOTS ON GOAL, ONE SEASON:
550 – Phil Esposito, Boston, 1970-71. 78GP – 78 game schedule.
528 – Alex Ovechkin, Washington, 2008-09. 79GP – 82 game schedule.
446 – Alex Ovechkin, Washington, 2007-08. 82GP – 82 game schedule.
429 – Paul Kariya, Anaheim, 1998-99. 82GP – 82 game schedule.
426 – Phil Esposito, Boston, 1971-72. 76GP – 78 game schedule.

*Gus Bodnar scored the fastest goal to start an NHL career with
the Toronto Maple Leafs in 1943-44. As a Chicago Black Hawk,
he had assists on all three goals when Bill Mosienko scored
a hat trick in 21 seconds on March 23, 1952.*

PENALTIES

MOST PENALTY MINUTES, CAREER:
3,966 – Tiger Williams, Toronto, Vancouver, Detroit, Los Angeles, Hartford,
in 14 seasons. 962GP.
3,565 – Dale Hunter, Quebec, Washington, Colorado, in 19 seasons. 1,407GP.
3,515 – Tie Domi, Toronto, NY Rangers, Winnipeg, in 16 seasons. 1,020GP.
3,381 – Marty McSorley, Pittsburgh, Edmonton, Los Angeles, NY Rangers, San Jose,
Boston, in 17 seasons. 961GP.
3,300 – Bob Probert, Detroit, Chicago, in 17 seasons. 935GP.

MOST PENALTY MINUTES, CAREER, INCLUDING PLAYOFFS:
4,421 – Tiger Williams, Toronto, Vancouver, Detroit, Los Angeles, Hartford,
3,966 in 962 regular-season games; 455 in 83 playoff games.
4,294 – Dale Hunter, Quebec, Washington, Colorado,
3,565 in 1,407 regular-season games; 729 in 186 playoff games.
3,755 – Marty McSorley, Pittsburgh, Edmonton, Los Angeles, NY Rangers, San Jose,
Boston, 3,381 in 961 regular-season games; 374 in 115 playoff games.
3,753 – Tie Domi, Toronto, NY Rangers, Winnipeg, 3,515 in 1,020 regular-season
games; 238 in 98 playoff games.
3,584 – Chris Nilan, Montreal, NY Rangers, Boston,
3,043 in 688 regular-season games; 541 in 111 playoff games.

MOST PENALTY MINUTES, ONE SEASON:
472 – Dave Schultz, Philadelphia, 1974-75.
409 – Paul Baxter, Pittsburgh, 1981-82.
408 – Mike Peluso, Chicago, 1991-92.
405 – Dave Schultz, Los Angeles, Pittsburgh, 1977-78.

MOST PENALTIES, ONE GAME:
10 – Chris Nilan, Boston, Mar. 31, 1991, at Boston vs. Hartford. 6 minors,
2 majors, 1 10-minute misconduct, 1 game misconduct.
9 – Jim Dorey, Toronto, Oct. 16, 1968, at Toronto vs. Pittsburgh. 4 minors,
2 majors, 2 10-minute misconducts, 1 game misconduct.
– Dave Schultz, Pittsburgh, Apr. 6, 1978, at Detroit. 5 minors, 2 majors,
2 10-minute misconducts.
– Randy Holt, Los Angeles, Mar. 11, 1979, at Philadelphia. 1 minor,
3 majors, 2 10-minute misconducts, 3 game misconducts.
– Russ Anderson, Pittsburgh, Jan. 19, 1980, at Pittsburgh vs. Edmonton.
3 minors, 3 majors, 3 game misconducts.
– Kim Clackson, Quebec, Mar. 8, 1981, at Quebec vs. Chicago. 4 minors,
3 majors, 2 game misconducts.
– Terry O'Reilly, Boston, Dec. 19, 1984, at Hartford. 5 minors, 3 majors,
1 game misconduct.
– Larry Playfair, Los Angeles, Dec. 9, 1986, at NY Islanders. 6 minors,
2 majors, 1 10-minute misconduct.
– Marty McSorley, Los Angeles, Apr. 14, 1992, at Vancouver. 5 minors,
2 majors, 1 10-minute misconduct, 1 game misconduct.
– Reed Low, St. Louis, Dec. 31, 2002, at Detroit. 4 minors,
1 major, 1 10-minute misconduct, 3 game misconducts.

MOST PENALTY MINUTES, ONE GAME:
67 – Randy Holt, Los Angeles, Mar. 11, 1979, at Philadelphia.
1 minor, 3 majors, 2 10-minute misconducts, 3 game misconducts.
57 – Brad Smith, Toronto, Nov. 15, 1986, at Toronto vs. Detroit.
1 minor, 3 majors, 2 10-minute misconducts, 2 game misconducts.
– Reed Low, St. Louis, Feb. 28, 2002, at St. Louis vs. Calgary.
1 minor, 3 majors, 1 10-minute misconduct, 3 game misconducts.

MOST PENALTIES, ONE PERIOD:
9 – Randy Holt, Los Angeles, Mar. 11, 1979, at Philadelphia, first period.
1 minor, 3 majors, 2 10-minute misconducts, 3 game misconducts.

MOST PENALTY MINUTES, ONE PERIOD:
67 – Randy Holt, Los Angeles, Mar. 11, 1979, at Philadelphia, first period.
1 minor, 3 majors, 2 10-minute misconducts, 3 game misconducts.

GOALTENDING

MOST GAMES APPEARED IN BY A GOALTENDER, CAREER:
1,266 – Martin Brodeur, New Jersey, St. Louis, 1991-92 – 2003-04,
2005-06 – 2014-15.
1,029 – Patrick Roy, Montreal, Colorado,1984-85 – 2002-03.
971 – Terry Sawchuk, Detroit, Boston, Toronto, Los Angeles, NY Rangers,
1949-50 – 1969-70.
966 – Roberto Luongo, NY Islanders, Vancouver, Florida, 1999-2000 – 2003-04,
2005-06 – 2016-17.
963 – Ed Belfour, Chicago, San Jose, Dallas, Toronto, Florida,
1988-89 – 2003-04, 2005-06, 2006-07.

MOST CONSECUTIVE COMPLETE GAMES BY A GOALTENDER:
502 – Glenn Hall, Detroit, Chicago. Played 502 games from beginning of
1955-56 season through first 12 games of 1962-63 season. In his 503rd
straight game, Nov. 7, 1962, at Chicago, Hall was removed from the
game against Boston with a back injury in the first period.

MOST GAMES APPEARED IN BY A GOALTENDER, ONE SEASON:
79 – Grant Fuhr, St. Louis, 1995-96.
78 – Martin Brodeur, New Jersey, 2006-07.
77 – Martin Brodeur, New Jersey, 1995-96.
– Bill Ranford, Edmonton, Boston, 1995-96.
– Arturs Irbe, Carolina, 2000-01.
– Marc Denis, Columbus, 2002-03.
– Evgeni Nabokov, San Jose, 2007-08.
– Martin Brodeur, New Jersey, 2007-08.
– Martin Brodeur, New Jersey, 2009-10.

MOST MINUTES PLAYED BY A GOALTENDER, CAREER:
74,439 – Martin Brodeur, New Jersey, St. Louis, 1991-92 – 2003-04,
2005-06 – 2014-15.
60,235 – Patrick Roy, Montreal, Colorado, 1984-85 – 2002-03.
57,194 – Terry Sawchuk, Detroit, Boston, Toronto, Los Angeles,
NY Rangers, 1949-50 – 1969-70.

MOST MINUTES PLAYED BY A GOALTENDER, ONE SEASON:
4,697 – Martin Brodeur, New Jersey, 2006-07.
4,635 – Martin Brodeur, New Jersey, 2007-08.
4,561 – Evgeni Nabokov, San Jose, 2007-08.
4,555 – Martin Brodeur, New Jersey, 2003-04.
4,511 – Marc Denis, Columbus, 2002-03.

MOST SHUTOUTS, CAREER:
125 – Martin Brodeur, New Jersey, St. Louis, in 22 seasons.
(1991-92, 1993-94 – 2003-04, 2005-06 – 2014-15)
103 – Terry Sawchuk, Detroit, Boston, Toronto, Los Angeles, NY Rangers,
in 21 seasons. (1949-50 – 1969-70)
94 – George Hainsworth, Montreal, Toronto, in 11 seasons.
(1926-27 – 1936-37)

MOST SHUTOUTS, ONE SEASON:
22 – George Hainsworth, Montreal, 1928-29. 44GP
15 – Alec Connell, Ottawa, 1925-26. 36GP
  – Alec Connell, Ottawa, 1927-28. 44GP
  – Hal Winkler, Boston, 1927-28. 44GP
  – Tony Esposito, Chicago, 1969-70. 63GP
14 – George Hainsworth, Montreal, 1926-27. 44GP

LONGEST SHUTOUT SEQUENCE BY A GOALTENDER:
460:49 – Alec Connell, Ottawa, 1927-28, six consecutive shutouts.
(Forward passing not permitted in attacking zones in 1927-28.)
343:05 – George Hainsworth, Montreal, 1928-29, four consecutive shutouts.
(Forward passing not permitted in attacking zones in 1928-29.)
332:01 – Brian Boucher, Phoenix, 2003-04, five consecutive shutouts.
324:40 – Roy Worters, NY Americans, 1930-31, four consecutive shutouts.
309:21 – Bill Durnan, Montreal, 1948-49, four consecutive shutouts.

MOST WINS BY A GOALTENDER, CAREER:
691 – Martin Brodeur, New Jersey, St. Louis, in 22 seasons. 1,266GP
551 – Patrick Roy, Montreal, Colorado, in 19 seasons. 1,029GP
484 – Ed Belfour, Chicago, San Jose, Dallas, Toronto, Florida,
in 17 seasons. 963GP
454 – Curtis Joseph, St. Louis, Edmonton, Toronto, Detroit, Phoenix, Calgary,
in 19 seasons. 943GP
453 – Roberto Luongo, NY Islanders, Vancouver, Florida, in 17 seasons. 966GP
447 – Terry Sawchuk, Detroit, Boston, Toronto, Los Angeles, NY Rangers,
in 21 seasons. 971GP

MOST WINS BY A GOALTENDER, ONE SEASON:
48 – Martin Brodeur, New Jersey, 2006-07. 78GP
  – **Braden Holtby**, Washington, 2015-16. 66GP
47 – Bernie Parent, Philadelphia, 1973-74. 73GP
  – Roberto Luongo, Vancouver, 2006-07. 76GP
46 – Evgeni Nabokov, San Jose, 2007-08. 77GP
45 – Miikka Kiprusoff, Calgary, 2008-09. 76GP
  – Martin Brodeur, New Jersey, 2009-10. 77GP

LONGEST WINNING STREAK BY A GOALTENDER, ONE SEASON:
17 – Gilles Gilbert, Boston, 1975-76.
14 – Tiny Thompson, Boston, 1929-30.
  – Ross Brooks, Boston, 1973-74.
  – Don Beaupre, Minnesota, 1985-86.
  – Tom Barrasso, Pittsburgh, 1992-93.
  – Jonas Hiller, Anaheim, 2013-14.

LONGEST UNDEFEATED STREAK BY A GOALTENDER, ONE SEASON:
32 Games – **Gerry Cheevers**, Boston, 1971-72. 24w-8T
31 Games – Pete Peeters, Boston, 1982-83. 26w-5T
27 Games – Pete Peeters, Philadelphia, 1979-80. 22w-5T

LONGEST UNDEFEATED STREAK BY A GOALTENDER IN HIS FIRST NHL SEASON:
23 Games – Grant Fuhr, Edmonton, 1981-82. 15w-8T

LONGEST UNDEFEATED STREAK BY A GOALTENDER FROM START OF CAREER:
16 Games – Patrick Lalime, Pittsburgh, 1996-97. 14w-2T

MOST 30-OR-MORE WIN SEASONS BY A GOALTENDER:
14 – Martin Brodeur, New Jersey, St. Louis, in 22 seasons.
13 – Patrick Roy, Montreal, Colorado, in 19 seasons.
11 – Henrik Lundqvist, NY Rangers, in 12 seasons.
9 – Ed Belfour, Chicago, San Jose, Dallas, Toronto, Florida, in 17 seasons.
8 – Tony Esposito, Montreal, Chicago, in 16 seasons.
  – Roberto Luongo, NY Islanders, Vancouver, Florida, in 17 seasons.
  – Marc-Andre Fleury, Pittsburgh, in 13 seasons.
7 – Jacques Plante, Montreal, NY Rangers, St. Louis, Toronto, Boston,
in 18 seasons.
  – Ken Dryden, Montreal, in 8 seasons.
  – Curtis Joseph, St. Louis, Edmonton, Toronto, Detroit, Phoenix, Calgary,
in 19 seasons.
  – Dominik Hasek, Chicago, Buffalo, Detroit, Ottawa, in 16 seasons.
  – Miikka Kiprusoff, San Jose, Calgary, in 12 seasons.
  – Ryan Miller, Buffalo, St. Louis, Vancouver, in 14 seasons.

MOST CONSECUTIVE 30-OR-MORE WIN SEASONS BY A GOALTENDER:
12 – Martin Brodeur, New Jersey, 1995-96 – 2003-04, 2005-06 – 2007-08.
8 – Patrick Roy, Montreal, Colorado, 1995-96 – 2002-03.
7 – Tony Esposito, Chicago, 1969-70 – 1975-76.
  – Miikka Kiprusoff, Calgary, 2005-06 – 2011-12.
  – Henrik Lundqvist, NY Rangers, 2005-06 – 2011-12.
  – Roberto Luongo, Florida, Vancouver, 2005-06 – 2011-12.
  – Ryan Miller, Buffalo, 2005-06 – 2011-12.
6 – Jacques Plante, Montreal, 1954-55 – 1959-60.
  – Marty Turco, Dallas, 2002-03, 2003-04, 2005-06 – 2008-09.

MOST 40-OR-MORE WIN SEASONS BY A GOALTENDER:
8 – Martin Brodeur, New Jersey, St. Louis, in 22 seasons.
3 – Terry Sawchuk, Detroit, Boston, Toronto, Los Angeles, NY Rangers,
in 21 seasons.
  – Jacques Plante, Montreal, NY Rangers, St. Louis, Toronto, Boston,
in 18 seasons.
  – Miikka Kiprusoff, San Jose, Calgary, in 12 seasons.
  – Evgeni Nabokov, San Jose, NY Islanders, in 13 seasons.
  – Braden Holtby, Washington, in 7 seasons.
2 – Bernie Parent, Boston, Philadelphia, Toronto, in 13 seasons.
  – Ken Dryden, Montreal, in 8 seasons.
  – Ed Belfour, Chicago, San Jose, Dallas, Toronto, Florida, in 17 seasons.
  – Ryan Miller, Buffalo, St. Louis, Vancouver, in 14 seasons.
  – Roberto Luongo, NY islanders, Florida, Vancouver, in 17 seasons.
  – Marc-Andre Fleury, Pittsburgh, in 13 seasons.
  – Pekka Rinne, Nashville, in 11 seasons.

MOST CONSECUTIVE 40-OR-MORE WIN SEASONS BY A GOALTENDER:
3 – Martin Brodeur, New Jersey, 2005-06 – 2007-08.
  – **Evgeni Nabokov**, San Jose, 2007-08 – 2009-10.
  – **Braden Holtby**, Washington, 2014-15 – 2016-17.
2 – Terry Sawchuk, Detroit, 1950-51, 1951-52.
  – Bernie Parent, Philadelphia, 1973-74, 1974-75.
  – Ken Dryden, Montreal, 1975-76, 1976-77.
  – Martin Brodeur, New Jersey, 1999-2000, 2000-01.
  – Miikka Kiprusoff, Calgary, 2005-06, 2006-07.

MOST LOSSES BY A GOALTENDER, CAREER:
397 – Martin Brodeur, New Jersey, St. Louis in 22 seasons. 1,266GP
365 – Roberto Luongo, NY Islanders, Vancouver, Florida, in 17 seasons. 966GP
352 – Gump Worsley, NY Rangers, Montreal, Minnesota, in 21 seasons. 861GP
  – Curtis Joseph, St. Louis, Edmonton, Toronto, Detroit, Phoenix, Calgary,
in 19 seasons. 943GP
351 – Gilles Meloche, Chicago, California, Cleveland, Minnesota, Pittsburgh,
in 18 seasons. 788GP
346 – John Vanbiesbrouck, NY Rangers, Florida, Philadelphia, NY Islanders,
New Jersey, in 20 seasons. 882GP
341 – Sean Burke, New Jersey, Hartford, Carolina, Vancouver, Philadelphia,
Florida, Phoenix, Tampa Bay, Los Angeles, in 18 seasons. 820GP

MOST LOSSES BY A GOALTENDER, ONE SEASON:
48 – Gary Smith, California, 1970-71. 71GP
47 – Al Rollins, Chicago, 1953-54. 66GP
46 – Peter Sidorkiewicz, Ottawa, 1992-93. 64GP

GOALTENDER SHOOTOUT RECORDS

MOST SHOOTOUT WINS, ONE SEASON:
10 – Mathieu Garon, Edmonton, 2007-08. 10GP
  – **Jonathan Quick**, Los Angelesm 2010-11. 10GP
  – **Ryan Miller**, Buffalo, 2006-07. 14GP
  – **Martin Brodeur**, New Jersey, 2006-07. 16GP

MOST SHOOTOUT WINS, CAREER:
57 – Ryan Miller, Buffalo, St. Louis, Vancouver. 91GP
56 – Henrik Lundqvist, NY Rangers. 97GP
53 – Marc-Andre Fleury, Pittsburgh. 82GP
49 – Roberto Luongo, Florida, Vancouver. 104GP

MOST SHOOTOUT SHOTS AGAINST, ONE SEASON:
75 – Roberto Luongo, Florida, 2014-15. 21GA
62 – Ilya Bryzgalov, Phoenix, 2009-10. 17GA
60 – Martin Brodeur, New Jersey, 2006-07. 20GA
54 – Roberto Luongo, Vancouver, 2007-08. 15GA
  – Jimmy Howard, Detroit, 2009-10. 17GA

MOST SHOOTOUT SHOTS AGAINST, CAREER:
384 – Roberto Luongo, Florida, Vancouver. 123GA
359 – Henrik Lundqvist, NY Rangers. 94GA
318 – Ryan Miller, Buffalo, St. Louis, Vancouver. 90GA
269 – Marc-Andre Fleury, Pittsburgh. 70GA

BEST SHOOTOUT SAVE PERCENTAGE, ONE SEASON: *(minimum 20 shots)*
.958 – Jhonas Enroth, Buffalo, Dallas, 2014-15. 24S-1GA
.938 – Mathieu Garon, Edmonton, 2007-08. 32S-2GA
.917 – Semyon Varlamov, Colorado, 2011-12. 24S-2GA
.900 – Marc Denis, Tampa Bay, 2006-07. 20S-2GA

BEST SHOOTOUT SAVE PERCENTAGE, CAREER: *(minimum 40 shots)*
.854 – Marc Denis, Columbus, Tampa Bay, Montreal. 41S-6GA
.795 – Eddie Lack, Vancouver, Carolina. 44S-9GA
.770 – Jake Allen, St. Louis. 61S-14GA
.764 – Brent Johnson, Washington, Pittsburgh. 55S-13GA

Active NHL Players' Three-or-More-Goal Games

Regular Season

Teams named are the ones the players were with at the time of their multiple-scoring games. Players listed alphabetically.

Player	Team(s)	3-Goals	4-Goals	5-Goals
Abdelkader, Justin	Detroit	2	—	—
Aho, Sebastian	Carolina	1	—	—
Arvidsson, Viktor	Nashville	1	—	—
Atkinson, Cam	Columbus	3	—	—
Backes, David	St. Louis	2	1	—
Backlund, Mikkel	Calgary	1	—	—
Backstrom, Nicklas	Washington	1	—	—
Benn, Jamie	Dallas	2	—	—
Bennett, Sam	Calgary	—	1	—
Bergeron, Patrice	Boston	1	—	—
Berglund, Patrik	St. Louis	1	—	—
Boedker, Mikkel	Ari., S.J.	4	—	—
Bonino, Nick	Ana., Pit.	2	—	—
Bourque, Rene	Calgary	3	—	—
Bozak, Tyler	Toronto	2	—	—
Brouwer, Troy	Washington	1	—	—
Brown, Dustin	Los Angeles	3	—	—
Burns, Brent	San Jose	1	—	—
Burrows, Alexandre	Vancouver	3	—	—
Byfuglien, Dustin	Chicago	1	—	—
Callahan, Ryan	NY Rangers	2	—	—
Calvert, Matt	Columbus	1	—	—
Cammalleri, Mike	Cgy., Mtl., N.J.	6	—	—
Carter, Jeff	Phi., CBJ, L.A.	5	—	—
Chara, Zdeno	Boston	1	—	—
Cogliano, Andrew	Anaheim	1	—	—
Colborne, Joe	Colorado	1	—	—
Comeau, Blake	NYI, Pit.	2	—	—
Couture, Logan	San Jose	1	—	—
Cracknell, Adam	Dallas	1	—	—
Crosby, Sidney	Pittsburgh	10	—	—
Doan, Shane	Phx., Ari.	2	—	—
Domi, Max	Arizona	1	—	—
Duchene, Matt	Colorado	1	—	—
Duclair, Anthony	Arizona	1	—	—
Eaves, Patrick	Det., Dal.	2	—	—
Eberle, Jordan	Edmonton	2	—	—
Ehlers, Nikolaj	Winnipeg	1	—	—
Eller, Lars	Montreal	—	1	—
Eriksson, Loui	Dal., Bos.	3	—	—
Fabbri, Robby	St. Louis	1	—	—
Fiddler, Vernon	Phoenix	1	—	—
Foligno, Nick	Columbus	2	—	—
Fontaine, Justin	Minnesota	1	—	—
Forsberg, Filip	Nashville	4	—	—
Franzen, Johan	Detroit	2	—	1
Frolik, Michael	Calgary	2	—	—
Gaborik, Marian	Min., NYR	12	1	1
Gagner, Sam	Edmonton	1	1	—
Galchenyuk, Alex	Montreal	1	—	—
Gaudreau, Johnny	Calgary	3	—	—
Gionta, Brian	New Jersey	1	—	—
Grabner, Michael	Van., NYI, NYR	4	—	—
Grabovski, Mikhail	Washington	1	—	—
Granlund, Mikael	Minnesota	1	—	—
Green, Mike	Detroit	1	—	—
Hagelin, Carl	NY Rangers	1	—	—
Hall, Taylor	Edmonton	4	—	—
Hansen, Jannik	Vancouver	2	—	—
Hanzal, Martin	Phx., Ari.	2	—	—
Hartman, Ryan	Chicago	1	—	—
Hartnell, Scott	Nsh., Phi., CBJ	9	—	—
Hayes, Jimmy	Boston	1	—	—
Helm, Darren	Detroit	1	—	—
Hemsky, Ales	Edmonton	1	—	—
Hertl, Tomas	San Jose	—	1	—
Hoffman, Mike	Ottawa	1	—	—
Hornqvist, Patric	Pittsburgh	1	—	—
Hossa, Marian	Ott., Atl.	6	1	—
Iginla, Jarome	Calgary	11	1	—
Jagr, Jaromir	Pit., NYR, N.J.	14	1	—
Johnson, Tyler	Tampa Bay	2	—	—
Jokinen, Jussi	Dal., Pit.	1	1	—
Jooris, Josh	Calgary	1	—	—
Kadri, Nazim	Toronto	3	—	—
Kane, Patrick	Chicago	4	—	—
Kelly, Chris	Ottawa	1	—	—
Kesler, Ryan	Van., Ana.	4	—	—
Kessel, Phil	Bos., Tor.	5	—	—
King, Dwight	Los Angeles	1	—	—
Kopitar, Anze	Los Angeles	3	—	—
Korpikoski, Lauri	Edmonton	1	—	—
Kreider, Chris	NY Rangers	2	—	—
Krejci, David	Boston	3	—	—
Kucherov, Nikita	Tampa Bay	3	—	—
Kunitz, Chris	Ana., Pit.	3	1	—
Kuznetsov, Evgeny	Washington	1	—	—
Ladd, Andrew	Chicago	1	—	—
Laich, Brooks	Washington	1	—	—
Laine, Patrik	Winnipeg	3	—	—
Lehtera, Jori	St. Louis	1	—	—
Lindholm, Elias	Carolina	1	—	—
Little, Bryan	Atl., Wpg.	2	—	—
Lucic, Milan	Bos., Edm.	3	—	—
Lupul, Joffrey	Phi., Tor.	3	—	—
MacKinnon, Nathan	Colorado	2	—	—
Malkin, Evgeni	Pittsburgh	11	—	—
Marchand, Brad	Boston	2	—	—
Marchessault, Jonathan	Florida	1	—	—
Marleau, Patrick	San Jose	4	1	—
Maroon, Patrick	Edmonton	1	—	—
Matthews, Auston	Toronto	—	1	—
Matthias, Shawn	Vancouver	1	—	—
McClement, Jay	St. Louis	1	—	—
McDavid, Connor	Edmonton	1	—	—
Michalek, Milan	Ottawa	2	—	—
Moulson, Matt	NY Islanders	2	1	—
Mueller, Peter	Phoenix	2	—	—
Namestnikov, Vladislav	Tampa Bay	1	—	—
Nash, Rick	CBJ, NYR	7	—	—
Neal, James	Dal., Pit., Nsh.	6	—	—
Nelson, Brock	NY Islanders	1	—	—
Niederreiter, Nino	Minnesota	1	—	—
Nielsen, Frans	NY Islanders	1	—	—
Nugent-Hopkins, Ryan	Edmonton	2	—	—
Nylander, William	Toronto	1	—	—
Nyquist, Gustav	Detroit	1	—	—
Okposo, Kyle	NY Islanders	1	1	—
Oshie, T.J.	St.L., Wsh.	3	—	—
Ovechkin, Alex	Washington	14	3	—
Pacioretty, Max	Montreal	5	1	—
Palmieri, Kyle	Anaheim	1	—	—
Panarin, Artemi	Chicago	1	—	—
Panik, Richard	Chicago	1	—	—
Paquette, Cedric	Tampa Bay	1	—	—
Parise, Zach	N.J., Min.	5	—	—
Pavelski, Joe	San Jose	4	—	—
Perreault, Mathieu	Wsh., Wpg.	1	1	—
Perron, David	St.L., Edm.	3	—	—
Perry, Corey	Anaheim	9	—	—
Plekanec, Thomas	Montreal	1	—	—
Pominville, Jason	Buffalo	2	—	—
Puempel, Matt	NY Rangers	1	—	—
Purcell, Teddy	Tampa Bay	1	—	—
Rantanen, Mikko	Colorado	1	—	—
Raymond, Mason	Van., Cgy.	3	—	—
Read, Matt	Philadelphia	1	—	—
Reinhart, Sam	Buffalo	1	—	—
Ribeiro, Mike	Dallas	1	—	—
Richardson, Brad	Los Angeles	1	—	—
Ristolainen, Rasmus	Buffalo	1	—	—
Roussel, Antoine	Dallas	1	—	—
Rust, Bryan	Pittsburgh	1	—	—
Ryan, Bobby	Ana., Ott.	4	—	—
Saad, Brandon	Columbus	1	—	—
Sceviour, Colton	Florida	1	—	—
Scheifele, Mark	Winnipeg	1	—	—
Schenn, Brayden	Philadelphia	2	—	—
Schwartz, Jaden	St. Louis	2	—	—
Sedin, Daniel	Vancouver	5	1	—
Sedin, Henrik	Vancouver	1	—	—
Seguin, Tyler	Bos., Dal.	5	1	—
Sharp, Patrick	Chicago	4	—	—
Silfverberg, Jakob	Anaheim	1	—	—
Simmonds, Wayne	Philadelphia	1	—	—
Sissons, Colton	Nashville	1	—	—
Skinner, Jeff	Carolina	4	—	—
Slavin, Jaccob	Carolina	1	—	—
Sobotka, Vladimir	St. Louis	1	—	—
Spezza, Jason	Ott., Dal.	7	—	—
Staal, Eric	Carolina	12	1	—
Staal, Jordan	Pittsburgh	2	—	—
Stafford, Drew	Buffalo	6	—	—
Stalberg, Viktor	Chicago	1	—	—
Stamkos, Steven	Tampa Bay	8	—	—
Stastny, Paul	Colorado	1	—	—
Steen, Alex	Toronto	1	—	—
Stempniak, Lee	Phx., Cgy.	1	—	—
Stepan, Derek	NY Rangers	3	—	—
Stewart, Chris	Col., St.L.	3	—	—
Subban, P.K.	Montreal	1	—	—
Suter, Ryan	Minnesota	1	—	—
Tarasenko, Vladimir	St. Louis	3	—	—
Tatar, Tomas	Detroit	1	—	—
Tavares, John	NY Islanders	6	—	—
Thornton, Joe	Bos., S.J.	4	—	—
Toews, Jonathan	Chicago	4	—	—
Toffoli, Tyler	Los Angeles	2	—	—
Upshall, Scottie	Phoenix	1	—	—
Vanek, Thomas	Buf., Mtl.	8	1	—
van Riemsdyk, James	Phi., Tor.	1	—	—
Vatrano, Frank	Boston	1	—	—
Vermette, Antoine	Ott., Phx.	3	—	—
Versteeg, Kris	Florida	1	—	—
Voracek, Jakub	Philadelphia	1	—	—
Vrbata, Radim	Col., Car., Phx.. Van.	6	—	—
Ward, Joel	Wsh., S.J.	2	—	—
Weber, Shea	Nashville	1	—	—
Weise, Dale	Montreal	1	—	—
Wheeler, Blake	Boston	1	—	—
Williams, Justin	Car., Wsh.	1	—	—
Yakupov, Nail	Edmonton	1	—	—
Zajac, Travis	New Jersey	2	—	—
Zetterberg, Henrik	Detroit	6	—	—
Zibanejad, Mika	Ottawa	1	—	—
Zuccarello, Mats	NY Rangers	1	—	—

Max Pacioretty celebrates his third of four goals during Montreal's 10-1 win over Colorado on December 10, 2016. Pacioretty, Patrick Marleau and Auston Matthews had four-goal games in 2016-17.

Top 100 All-Time Goal-Scoring Leaders

* active player

Player	Goals	Games	Goals per game	Seasons
1. **Wayne Gretzky**, Edm., L.A., St.L., NYR .	894	1487	.601	20
2. **Gordie Howe**, Det., Hfd.	801	1767	.453	26
* 3. **Jaromir Jagr**, Pit., Wsh., NYR, Phi., Dal., Bos., N.J., Fla.	765	1711	.447	23
4. **Brett Hull**, Cgy., St.L., Dal., Det., Phx.	741	1269	.584	20
5. **Marcel Dionne**, Det., L.A., NYR	731	1348	.542	18
6. **Phil Esposito**, Chi., Bos., NYR	717	1282	.559	18
7. **Mike Gartner**, Wsh., Min., NYR, Tor., Phx.	708	1432	.494	19
8. **Mark Messier**, Edm., NYR, Van.	694	1756	.395	25
9. **Steve Yzerman**, Det.	692	1514	.457	22
10. **Mario Lemieux**, Pit.	690	915	.754	18
11. **Teemu Selanne**, Wpg., Ana., S.J., Col. .	684	1451	.471	21
12. **Luc Robitaille**, L.A., Pit., NYR, Det.	668	1431	.467	19
13. **Brendan Shanahan**, N.J., St.L., Hfd., Det., NYR	656	1524	.430	21
14. **Dave Andreychuk**, Buf., Tor., N.J., Bos., Col., T.B.	640	1639	.390	23
15. **Joe Sakic**, Que., Col.	625	1378	.454	20
* 16. **Jarome Iginla**, Cgy., Pit., Bos., Col., L.A.	625	1554	.402	21
17. **Bobby Hull**, Chi., Wpg., Hfd.	610	1063	.574	16
18. **Dino Ciccarelli**, Min., Wsh., Det., T.B., Fla.	608	1232	.494	19
19. **Jari Kurri**, Edm., L.A., NYR, Ana., Col. . .	601	1251	.480	17
20. **Mark Recchi**, Pit., Phi., Mtl., Car., Atl., T.B., Bos.	577	1652	.349	22
21. **Mike Bossy**, NYI	573	752	.762	10
22. **Joe Nieuwendyk**, Cgy., Dal., N.J., Tor., Fla.	564	1257	.449	20
23. **Mats Sundin**, Que., Tor., Van.	564	1346	.419	18
24. **Mike Modano**, Min., Dal., Det.	561	1499	.374	22
25. **Guy Lafleur**, Mtl., NYR, Que.	560	1126	.497	17
* 26. **Alex Ovechkin**, Wsh.	558	921	.606	12
27. **John Bucyk**, Det., Bos.	556	1540	.361	23
28. **Ron Francis**, Hfd., Pit., Car., Tor.	549	1731	.317	23
29. **Michel Goulet**, Que., Chi.	548	1089	.503	15
30. **Maurice Richard**, Mtl.	544	978	.556	18
31. **Stan Mikita**, Chi.	541	1394	.388	22
32. **Keith Tkachuk**, Wpg., Phx., St.L., Atl. . . .	538	1201	.448	18
33. **Frank Mahovlich**, Tor., Det., Mtl.	533	1181	.451	18
* 34. **Marian Hossa**, Ott., Atl., Pit., Det., Chi.	525	1309	.401	19
35. **Bryan Trottier**, NYI, Pit.	524	1279	.410	18
36. **Pat Verbeek**, N.J., Hfd., NYR, Dal., Det.	522	1424	.367	20
37. **Dale Hawerchuk**, Wpg., Buf., St.L., Phi.	518	1188	.436	16
38. **Pierre Turgeon**, Buf., NYI, Mtl., St.L., Dal., Col.	515	1294	.398	19
39. **Jeremy Roenick**, Chi., Phx., Phi., L.A., S.J.	513	1363	.376	20
40. **Gilbert Perreault**, Buf.	512	1191	.430	17
* 41. **Patrick Marleau**, S.J.	508	1493	.340	19
42. **Jean Beliveau**, Mtl.	507	1125	.451	20
43. **Peter Bondra**, Wsh., Ott., Atl., Chi. . . .	503	1081	.465	16
44. **Joe Mullen**, St.L., Cgy., Pit., Bos.	502	1062	.473	17
45. **Lanny McDonald**, Tor., Col., Cgy.	500	1111	.450	16
46. **Glenn Anderson**, Edm., Tor., NYR, St.L.	498	1129	.441	16
47. **Jean Ratelle**, NYR, Bos.	491	1281	.383	21
48. **Norm Ullman**, Det., Tor.	490	1410	.348	20
49. **Brian Bellows**, Min., Mtl., T.B., Ana., Wsh.	485	1188	.408	17
50. **Darryl Sittler**, Tor., Phi., Det.	484	1096	.442	15
51. **Sergei Fedorov**, Det., Ana., CBJ, Wsh. .	483	1248	.387	18
52. **Bernie Nicholls**, L.A., NYR, Edm., N.J., Chi., S.J.	475	1127	.421	18
53. **Alexander Mogilny**, Buf., Van., N.J., Tor.	473	990	.478	16
54. **Denis Savard**, Chi., Mtl., T.B.	473	1196	.395	17
55. **Pat LaFontaine**, NYI, Buf., NYR	468	865	.541	15
56. **Alex Delvecchio**, Det.	456	1549	.294	24
57. **Theoren Fleury**, Cgy., Col., NYR, Chi. . .	455	1084	.420	15
58. **Rod Brind'Amour**, St.L., Phi., Car.	452	1484	.305	21
59. **Peter Stastny**, Que., N.J., St.L.	450	977	.461	15
60. **Doug Gilmour**, St.L., Cgy., Tor., N.J., Chi., Buf., Mtl.	450	1474	.305	20
61. **Rick Middleton**, NYR, Bos.	448	1005	.446	14
62. **Daniel Alfredsson**, Ott., Det.	444	1246	.356	18
63. **Rick Vaive**, Van., Tor., Chi., Buf.	441	876	.503	13
64. **Steve Larmer**, Chi., NYR	441	1006	.438	15
65. **Rick Tocchet**, Phi., Pit., L.A., Bos., Wsh., Phx.	440	1144	.385	18
66. **Gary Roberts**, Cgy., Car., Tor., Fla., Pit., Phi., Chi., Car., Bos.	438	1224	.358	22
67. **Pavel Bure**, Van., Fla., NYR	437	702	.623	12
68. **Vincent Damphousse**, Tor., Edm., Mtl., S.J.	432	1378	.313	18
69. **Dave Taylor**, L.A.	431	1111	.388	17
70. **Alex Kovalev**, NYR, Pit., Mtl., Ott., Fla. .	430	1316	.327	19

Montreal Canadiens legend Jean Beliveau became the fourth player in NHL history to score 500 goals on February 11, 1971. He retired after that season with 507 goals.

Player	Goals	Games	Goals per game	Seasons
71. **Bill Guerin**, N.J., Edm., Bos., Dal., St.L., NYI, Pit.	429	1263	.340	18
72. **Yvan Cournoyer**, Mtl.	428	968	.442	16
73. **Brian Propp**, Phi., Bos., Min., Hfd.	425	1016	.418	15
74. **Steve Shutt**, Mtl., L.A.	424	930	.456	13
75. **Owen Nolan**, Que., Col., S.J., Tor., Phx., Cgy., Min.	422	1200	.352	18
76. **Stephane Richer**, Mtl., N.J., T.B., St.L., Pit.	421	1054	.399	17
77. **Vincent Lecavalier**, T.B., Phi., L.A.	421	1212	.347	17
78. **Steve Thomas**, Tor., Chi., NYI, N.J., Ana., Det.	421	1235	.341	20
79. **Bill Barber**, Phi.	420	903	.465	12
80. **Ilya Kovalchuk**, Atl., N.J.	417	816	.511	11
81. **Jason Arnott**, Edm., N.J., Dal., Nsh., Wsh., St.L.	417	1244	.335	18
* 82. **Rick Nash**, CBJ, NYR	416	989	.421	14
83. **Tony Amonte**, NYR, Chi., Phx., Phi., Cgy.	416	1174	.354	16
84. **Garry Unger**, Tor., Det., St.L., Atl., L.A., Edm.	413	1105	.374	16
85. **John MacLean**, N.J., S.J., NYR, Dal. . . .	413	1194	.346	18
86. **Raymond Bourque**, Bos., Col.	410	1612	.254	22
87. **Patrik Elias**, N.J.	408	1240	.329	20
88. **Ray Ferraro**, Hfd., NYI, NYR, L.A., Atl., St.L.	408	1258	.324	18
89. **John LeClair**, Mtl., Phi., Pit.	406	967	.420	16
90. **Rod Gilbert**, NYR	406	1065	.381	18
91. **John Ogrodnick**, Det., Que., NYR	402	928	.433	14
92. **Paul Kariya**, Ana., Col., Nsh., St.L.	402	989	.406	15
* 93. **Shane Doan**, Wpg., Phx., Ari.	402	1540	.261	21
* 94. **Marian Gaborik**, Min., NYR, CBJ, L.A. . .	396	989	.400	16
95. **Dave Keon**, Tor., Hfd.	396	1296	.306	18
96. **Paul Coffey**, Edm., Pit., L.A., Det., Hfd., Phi., Chi., Car., Bos.	396	1409	.281	21
97. **Cam Neely**, Van., Bos.	395	726	.544	13
98. **Pierre Larouche**, Pit., Mtl., Hfd., NYR . .	395	812	.486	14
99. **Markus Naslund**, Pit., Van., NYR	395	1117	.354	15
100. **Tomas Sandstrom**, NYR, L.A., Pit., Det., Ana.	394	983	.401	15

Top 100 Active Goal-Scoring Leaders

	Player	Goals	Games	Goals per game	Seasons
1.	**Jaromir Jagr**, Pit., Wsh., NYR, Phi., Dal., Bos., N.J., Fla.	**765**	1711	.447	23
2.	**Jarome Iginla**, Cgy., Pit., Bos., Col., L.A.	**625**	1554	.402	21
3.	**Alex Ovechkin**, Wsh.	**558**	921	.606	12
4.	**Marian Hossa**, Ott., Atl., Pit., Det., Chi.	**525**	1309	.401	19
5.	**Patrick Marleau**, S.J.	**508**	1493	.340	19
6.	**Rick Nash**, CBJ, NYR	**416**	989	.421	14
7.	**Shane Doan**, Wpg., Phx., Ari.	**402**	1540	.261	21
8.	**Marian Gaborik**, Min., NYR, CBJ, L.A.	**396**	989	.400	16
9.	**Joe Thornton**, Bos., S.J.	**384**	1446	.266	19
10.	**Sidney Crosby**, Pit.	**382**	782	.488	12
11.	**Daniel Sedin**, Van.	**370**	1225	.302	16
12.	**Eric Staal**, Car., NYR, Min.	**353**	1011	.349	13
13.	**Corey Perry**, Ana.	**349**	886	.394	12
14.	**Jeff Carter**, Phi., CBJ, L.A.	**339**	877	.387	12
15.	**Thomas Vanek**, Buf., NYI, Mtl., Min., Det., Fla.	**333**	885	.376	12
16.	**Evgeni Malkin**, Pit.	**328**	706	.465	11
17.	**Henrik Zetterberg**, Det.	**326**	1000	.326	14
18.	**Steven Stamkos**, T.B.	**321**	586	.548	9
19.	**Zach Parise**, N.J., Min.	**318**	830	.383	12
20.	**Jason Spezza**, Ott., Dal.	**316**	911	.347	14
21.	**Scott Hartnell**, Nsh., Phi., CBJ	**314**	1187	.265	16
22.	**Phil Kessel**, Bos., Tor., Pit.	**296**	832	.356	11
23.	**Joe Pavelski**, S.J.	**295**	806	.366	11
24.	**Brian Gionta**, N.J., Mtl., Buf.	**289**	1006	.287	15
25.	**Michael Cammalleri**, L.A., Cgy., Mtl., N.J.	**287**	840	.342	14
26.	**Patrick Kane**, Chi.	**285**	740	.385	10
27.	**Radim Vrbata**, Col., Car., Chi., Phx., T.B., Van., Ari.	**279**	1015	.275	15
28.	**Patrick Sharp**, Phi., Chi., Dal.	**277**	869	.319	14
29.	**Justin Williams**, Phi., Car., L.A., Wsh.	**273**	1080	.253	16
30.	**Jonathan Toews**, Chi.	**272**	717	.379	10
31.	**Jason Pominville**, Buf., Min.	**261**	905	.288	13
32.	**Patrice Bergeron**, Bos.	**259**	899	.288	13
33.	**Anze Kopitar**, L.A.	**255**	840	.304	11
34.	**Chris Kunitz**, Ana., Atl., Pit.	**250**	884	.283	13
35.	**Ryan Kesler**, Van., Ana.	**245**	897	.273	13
36.	**James Neal**, Dal., Pit., Nsh.	**238**	632	.377	9
37.	**Henrik Sedin**, Van.	**237**	1248	.190	16
38.	**Ryan Getzlaf**, Ana.	**236**	861	.274	12
39.	**John Tavares**, NYI	**235**	587	.400	8
40.	**Andrew Ladd**, Car., Chi., Atl., Wpg., NYI.	**233**	847	.275	12
41.	**Dustin Brown**, L.A.	**232**	964	.241	13
42.	**Mike Ribeiro**, Mtl., Dal., Wsh., Phx., Nsh.	**228**	1074	.212	17
43.	**Tomas Plekanec**, Mtl.	**226**	921	.245	13
44.	**Bobby Ryan**, Ana., Ott.	**223**	669	.333	10
45.	**Loui Eriksson**, Dal., Bos., Van.	**223**	790	.282	11
46.	**David Backes**, St.L., Bos.	**223**	801	.278	11
47.	**Antoine Vermette**, Ott., CBJ, Phx., Ari., Chi., Ana.	**220**	982	.224	13
48.	**Jamie Benn**, Dal.	**218**	585	.373	8
49.	**Alexander Steen**, Tor., St.L.	**213**	822	.259	12
50.	**Max Pacioretty**, Mtl.	**209**	562	.372	9
51.	**Milan Michalek**, S.J., Ott., Tor.	**208**	747	.278	13
52.	**Paul Stastny**, Col., St.L.	**204**	742	.275	11
53.	**Wayne Simmonds**, L.A., Phi.	**202**	687	.294	9
54.	**Lee Stempniak**, St.L., Tor., Phx., Cgy., Pit., NYR, Wpg., N.J., Bos., Car.	**200**	872	.229	12
55.	**Blake Wheeler**, Bos., Atl., Wpg.	**199**	697	.286	9
56.	**Alexandre Burrows**, Van., Ott.	**199**	842	.236	12
57.	**Brad Marchand**, Bos.	**192**	534	.360	8
58.	**Tyler Seguin**, Bos., Dal.	**189**	508	.372	7
59.	**Nicklas Backstrom**, Wsh.	**188**	734	.256	10
60.	**Zdeno Chara**, NYI, Ott., Bos.	**188**	1350	.139	19
61.	**Johan Franzen**, Det.	**187**	602	.311	12
62.	**Jordan Staal**, Pit., Car.	**187**	764	.245	11
63.	**Jussi Jokinen**, Dal., T.B., Car., Pit., Fla.	**186**	891	.209	12
64.	**Bryan Little**, Atl., Wpg.	**184**	672	.274	10
65.	**Drew Stafford**, Buf., Wpg., Bos.	**183**	725	.252	11
66.	**Shea Weber**, Nsh., Mtl.	**183**	841	.218	12
67.	**Jason Chimera**, Edm., CBJ, Wsh., NYI.	**183**	1033	.177	16
68.	**Milan Lucic**, Bos., L.A., Edm.	**182**	729	.250	10
69.	**Jeff Skinner**, Car.	**180**	497	.362	7
70.	**Claude Giroux**, Phi.	**180**	656	.274	10
71.	**Logan Couture**, S.J.	**179**	504	.355	8
72.	**Mikko Koivu**, Min.	**179**	843	.212	12
73.	**Matt Moulson**, L.A., NYI, Buf., Min.	**176**	636	.277	10
74.	**Matt Duchene**, Col.	**174**	572	.304	8
75.	**Patric Hornqvist**, Nsh., Pit.	**174**	579	.301	9
76.	**Ryan Callahan**, NYR, T.B.	**174**	638	.273	11
77.	**Ales Hemsky**, Edm., Ott., Dal.	**174**	838	.208	14
78.	**Brent Burns**, Min., S.J.	**170**	879	.193	13
79.	**T.J. Oshie**, St.L., Wsh.	**169**	591	.286	9
80.	**Jordan Eberle**, Edm.	**165**	507	.325	7

Patrick Marleau became the newest member of the 500-goal club on February 3, 2017. After 19 season in San Jose, Marleau joins the Toronto Maple Leafs in 2017-18.

	Player	Goals	Games	Goals per game	Seasons
81.	**James van Riemsdyk**, Phi., Tor.	**165**	528	.313	8
82.	**Dustin Byfuglien**, Chi., Atl., Wpg.	**165**	758	.218	12
83.	**Jiri Hudler**, Det., Cgy., Fla., Dal.	**164**	708	.232	12
84.	**Troy Brouwer**, Chi., Wsh., St.L., Cgy.	**163**	687	.237	11
85.	**Rene Bourque**, Chi., Cgy., Mtl., Ana., CBJ, Col.	**163**	725	.225	12
86.	**David Perron**, St.L., Edm., Pit., Ana.	**159**	652	.244	10
87.	**Kyle Okposo**, NYI, Buf.	**158**	594	.266	10
88.	**Evander Kane**, Atl., Wpg., Buf.	**157**	496	.317	8
89.	**David Krejci**, Bos.	**157**	705	.223	11
90.	**Valtteri Filppula**, Det., T.B., Phi.	**157**	795	.197	12
91.	**Jakub Voracek**, CBJ, Phi.	**155**	686	.226	9
92.	**Travis Zajac**, N.J.	**155**	779	.199	11
93.	**Nick Foligno**, Ott., CBJ	**154**	696	.221	10
94.	**Taylor Hall**, Edm., N.J.	**152**	453	.336	7
95.	**Patrik Berglund**, St.L.	**151**	637	.237	9
96.	**Chris Stewart**, Col., St.L., Buf., Min., Ana.	**150**	598	.251	9
97.	**Kris Versteeg**, Chi., Tor., Phi., Fla., Car., L.A., Cgy.	**146**	619	.236	10
98.	**Vladimir Tarasenko**, St.L.	**145**	341	.425	5
99.	**Andrew Cogliano**, Edm., Ana.	**144**	786	.183	10
100.	**Sam Gagner**, Edm., Ari., Phi., CBJ	**142**	696	.204	10

Top 100 All-Time Assist Leaders

* active player

Player	Assists	Games	Assists per game	Seasons
1. **Wayne Gretzky**, Edm., L.A., St.L., NYR .	**1963**	1487	1.320	20
2. **Ron Francis**, Hfd., Pit., Car., Tor.	**1249**	1731	.722	23
3. **Mark Messier**, Edm., NYR, Van.	**1193**	1756	.679	25
4. **Raymond Bourque**, Bos., Col.	**1169**	1612	.725	22
* 5. **Jaromir Jagr**, Pit., Wsh., NYR, Phi., Dal., Bos., N.J., Fla.	**1149**	1711	.672	23
6. **Paul Coffey**, Edm., Pit., L.A., Det., Hfd., Phi., Chi., Car., Bos.	**1135**	1409	.806	21
7. **Adam Oates**, Det., St.L., Bos., Wsh., Phi., Ana., Edm.	**1079**	1337	.807	19
8. **Steve Yzerman**, Det.	**1063**	1514	.702	22
9. **Gordie Howe**, Det., Hfd.	**1049**	1767	.594	26
10. **Marcel Dionne**, Det., L.A., NYR	**1040**	1348	.772	18
11. **Mario Lemieux**, Pit.	**1033**	915	1.129	18
12. **Joe Sakic**, Que., Col.	**1016**	1378	.737	20
* 13. **Joe Thornton**, Bos., S.J.	**1007**	1446	.696	19
14. **Doug Gilmour**, St.L., Cgy., Tor., N.J., Chi., Buf., Mtl.	**964**	1474	.654	20
15. **Mark Recchi**, Pit., Phi., Mtl., Car., Atl., T.B., Bos.	**956**	1652	.579	22
16. **Al MacInnis**, Cgy., St.L.	**934**	1416	.660	23
17. **Larry Murphy**, L.A., Wsh., Min., Pit., Tor., Det.	**929**	1615	.575	21
18. **Stan Mikita**, Chi.	**926**	1394	.664	22
19. **Bryan Trottier**, NYI, Pit.	**901**	1279	.704	18
20. **Phil Housley**, Buf., Wpg., St.L., Cgy., N.J., Wsh., Chi., Tor.	**894**	1495	.598	21
21. **Dale Hawerchuk**, Wpg., Buf., St.L., Phi.	**891**	1188	.750	16
22. **Nicklas Lidstrom**, Det.	**878**	1564	.561	20
23. **Phil Esposito**, Chi., Bos., NYR	**873**	1282	.681	18
24. **Denis Savard**, Chi., Mtl., T.B.	**865**	1196	.723	17
25. **Bobby Clarke**, Phi.	**852**	1144	.745	15
26. **Alex Delvecchio**, Det.	**825**	1549	.533	24
27. **Gilbert Perreault**, Buf.	**814**	1191	.683	17
28. **Mike Modano**, Min., Dal., Det.	**813**	1499	.542	22
29. **John Bucyk**, Det., Bos.	**813**	1540	.528	23
30. **Pierre Turgeon**, Buf., NYI, Mtl., St.L., Dal., Col.	**812**	1294	.628	19
31. **Jari Kurri**, Edm., L.A., NYR, Ana., Col. .	**797**	1251	.637	17
32. **Guy Lafleur**, Mtl., NYR, Que.	**793**	1126	.704	17
33. **Peter Stastny**, Que., N.J., St.L.	**789**	977	.808	15
34. **Mats Sundin**, Que., Tor., Van.	**785**	1346	.583	18
* 35. **Henrik Sedin**, Van.	**783**	1248	.627	16
36. **Brian Leetch**, NYR, Tor., Bos.	**781**	1205	.648	18
37. **Jean Ratelle**, NYR, Bos.	**776**	1281	.606	21
38. **Vincent Damphousse**, Tor., Edm., Mtl., S.J.	**773**	1378	.561	18
39. **Teemu Selanne**, Wpg., Ana., S.J., Col. .	**773**	1451	.533	21
40. **Chris Chelios**, Mtl., Chi., Det., Atl. . . .	**763**	1651	.462	26
41. **Bernie Federko**, St.L., Det.	**761**	1000	.761	14
42. **Doug Weight**, NYR, Edm., St.L., Car., Ana., NYI	**755**	1238	.610	20
43. **Larry Robinson**, Mtl., L.A.	**750**	1384	.542	20
44. **Denis Potvin**, NYI	**742**	1060	.700	15
45. **Norm Ullman**, Det., Tor.	**739**	1410	.524	20
46. **Bernie Nicholls**, L.A., NYR, Edm., N.J., Chi., S.J.	**734**	1127	.651	18
47. **Rod Brind'Amour**, St.L., Phi., Car. . . .	**732**	1484	.493	21
48. **Luc Robitaille**, L.A., Pit., NYR, Det. . . .	**726**	1431	.507	19
49. **Daniel Alfredsson**, Ott., Det.	**713**	1246	.572	18
50. **Jean Beliveau**, Mtl.	**712**	1125	.633	20
51. **Scott Stevens**, Wsh., St.L., N.J.	**712**	1635	.435	22
52. **Jeremy Roenick**, Chi., Phx., Phi., L.A., S.J.	**703**	1363	.516	20
53. **Brendan Shanahan**, N.J., St.L., Hfd., Det., NYR	**698**	1524	.458	21
54. **Dave Andreychuk**, Buf., Tor., N.J., Bos., Col., T.B.	**698**	1639	.426	23
55. **Dale Hunter**, Que., Wsh., Col.	**697**	1407	.495	19
56. **Sergei Fedorov**, Det., Ana., CBJ, Wsh. .	**696**	1248	.558	18
57. **Henri Richard**, Mtl.	**688**	1256	.548	20
58. **Brad Park**, NYR, Bos., Det.	**683**	1113	.614	17
59. **Bobby Smith**, Min., Mtl.	**679**	1077	.630	15
60. **Ray Whitney**, S.J., Edm., Fla., CBJ, Det., Car., Phx., Dal.	**679**	1330	.511	22
* 61. **Jarome Iginla**, Cgy., Pit., Bos., Col., L.A.	**675**	1554	.434	21
62. **Brett Hull**, Cgy., St.L., Dal., Det., Phx. . .	**650**	1269	.512	20
63. **Bobby Orr**, Bos., Chi.	**645**	657	.982	12
* 64. **Sidney Crosby**, Pit.	**645**	782	.825	12
65. **Martin St. Louis**, Cgy., T.B., NYR	**642**	1134	.566	16
66. **Gary Suter**, Cgy., Chi., S.J.	**641**	1145	.560	17
67. **Dave Taylor**, L.A.	**638**	1111	.574	17
68. **Darryl Sittler**, Tor., Phi., Det.	**637**	1096	.581	15
69. **Borje Salming**, Tor., Det.	**637**	1148	.555	17
70. **Peter Forsberg**, Que., Col., Phi., Nsh. . .	**636**	708	.898	14
71. **Neal Broten**, Min., Dal., N.J., L.A.	**634**	1099	.577	17

Though injuries limited him to just 657 games in his career, Bobby Orr collected 645 assists. His assists-per-game average of .982 trails only Wayne Gretzky and Mario Lemieux.

Player	Assists	Games	Assists per game	Seasons
72. **Brad Richards**, T.B., Dal., NYR, Chi., Det.	**634**	1126	.563	15
73. **Theoren Fleury**, Cgy., Col., NYR, Chi. . .	**633**	1084	.584	15
74. **Mike Gartner**, Wsh., Min., NYR, Tor., Phx.	**627**	1432	.438	19
75. **Andy Bathgate**, NYR, Tor., Det., Pit. . . .	**624**	1069	.584	17
76. **Sergei Zubov**, NYR, Pit., Dal.	**619**	1068	.580	16
77. **Patrik Elias**, N.J.	**617**	1240	.498	20
* 78. **Daniel Sedin**, Van.	**616**	1225	.503	16
79. **Rod Gilbert**, NYR	**615**	1065	.577	18
* 80. **Marian Hossa**, Ott., Atl., Pit., Det., Chi.	**609**	1309	.465	19
81. **Pavel Datsyuk**, Det.	**604**	953	.634	14
82. **Michel Goulet**, Que., Chi.	**604**	1089	.555	15
83. **Kirk Muller**, N.J., Mtl., NYI, Tor., Fla., Dal.	**602**	1349	.446	19
84. **Glenn Anderson**, Edm., Tor., NYR, St.L.	**601**	1129	.532	16
85. **Alex Kovalev**, NYR, Pit., Mtl., Ott., Fla. .	**599**	1316	.455	19
86. **Dino Ciccarelli**, Min., Wsh., Det., T.B., Fla.	**592**	1232	.481	19
87. **Sergei Gonchar**, Wsh., Bos., Pit., Ott., Dal., Mtl.	**591**	1301	.454	20
88. **Doug Wilson**, Chi., S.J.	**590**	1024	.576	16
89. **Dave Keon**, Tor., Hfd.	**590**	1296	.455	18
90. **Paul Kariya**, Ana., Col., Nsh., St.L. . . .	**587**	989	.594	15
91. **Dave Babych**, Wpg., Hfd., Van., Phi., L.A.	**581**	1195	.486	19
92. **Alex Tanguay**, Col., Cgy., Mtl., T.B., Ari.	**580**	1088	.533	16
93. **Brian Propp**, Phi., Bos., Min., Hfd. . . .	**579**	1016	.570	15
* 94. **Ryan Getzlaf**, Ana.	**578**	861	.671	12
* 95. **Henrik Zetterberg**, Det.	**578**	1000	.578	14
96. **Saku Koivu**, Mtl., Ana.	**577**	1124	.513	18
97. **Scott Gomez**, N.J., NYR, Mtl., S.J., Fla., St.L., Ott.	**575**	1079	.533	16
* 98. **Patrick Marleau**, S.J.	**574**	1493	.384	19
99. **Steve Larmer**, Chi., NYR	**571**	1006	.568	15
100. **Frank Mahovlich**, Tor., Det., Mtl.	**570**	1181	.483	18

Top 100 Active Assist Leaders

Player	Assists	Games	Assists per game	Seasons
1. **Jaromir Jagr**, Pit., Wsh., NYR, Phi., Dal., Bos., N.J., Fla.	1149	1711	.672	23
2. **Joe Thornton**, Bos., S.J.	1007	1446	.696	19
3. **Henrik Sedin**, Van.	783	1248	.627	16
4. **Jarome Iginla**, Cgy., Pit., Bos., Col., L.A.	675	1554	.434	21
5. **Sidney Crosby**, Pit.	645	782	.825	12
6. **Daniel Sedin**, Van.	616	1225	.503	16
7. **Marian Hossa**, Ott., Atl., Pit., Det., Chi.	609	1309	.465	19
8. **Ryan Getzlaf**, Ana.	578	861	.671	12
9. **Henrik Zetterberg**, Det.	578	1000	.578	14
10. **Patrick Marleau**, S.J.	574	1493	.384	19
11. **Shane Doan**, Wpg., Phx., Ari.	570	1540	.370	21
12. **Mike Ribeiro**, Mtl., Dal., Wsh., Phx., Nsh.	565	1074	.526	17
13. **Jason Spezza**, Ott., Dal.	546	911	.599	14
14. **Nicklas Backstrom**, Wsh.	540	734	.736	10
15. **Evgeni Malkin**, Pit.	504	706	.714	11
16. **Eric Staal**, Car., NYR, Min.	493	1011	.488	13
17. **Anze Kopitar**, L.A.	481	840	.573	11
18. **Alex Ovechkin**, Wsh.	477	921	.518	12
19. **Patrick Kane**, Chi.	467	740	.631	10
20. **Mikko Koivu**, Min.	435	843	.516	12
21. **Duncan Keith**, Chi.	421	913	.461	12
22. **Brian Campbell**, Buf., S.J., Chi., Fla.	417	1082	.385	17
23. **Zdeno Chara**, NYI, Ott., Bos.	416	1350	.308	19
24. **Patrice Bergeron**, Bos.	412	899	.458	13
25. **Justin Williams**, Phi., Car., L.A., Wsh.	409	1080	.379	16
26. **Jason Pominville**, Buf., Min.	401	905	.443	13
27. **Ales Hemsky**, Edm., Ott., Dal.	398	838	.475	14
28. **Marian Gaborik**, Min., NYR, CBJ, L.A.	398	989	.402	16
29. **Claude Giroux**, Phi.	395	656	.602	10
30. **Paul Stastny**, Col., St.L.	389	742	.524	11
31. **Ryan Suter**, Nsh., Min.	373	913	.409	12
32. **David Krejci**, Bos.	369	705	.523	11
33. **Scott Hartnell**, Nsh., Phi., CBJ	369	1187	.311	16
34. **Corey Perry**, Ana.	368	886	.415	12
35. **Thomas Vanek**, Buf., NYI, Mtl., Min., Det., Fla.	364	885	.411	12
36. **Jussi Jokinen**, Dal., T.B., Car., Pit., Fla.	360	891	.404	12
37. **Tomas Plekanec**, Mtl.	355	921	.385	13
38. **Rick Nash**, CBJ, NYR	355	989	.359	14
39. **Phil Kessel**, Bos., Tor., Pit.	353	832	.424	11
40. **Jonathan Toews**, Chi.	350	717	.488	10
41. **Zach Parise**, N.J., Min.	343	830	.413	12
42. **Erik Karlsson**, Ott.	339	556	.610	8
43. **Mark Streit**, Mtl., NYI, Phi., Pit.	338	784	.431	11
44. **Joe Pavelski**, S.J.	336	806	.417	11
45. **Jakub Voracek**, CBJ, Phi.	333	686	.485	9
46. **Keith Yandle**, Phx., Ari., NYR, Fla.	333	743	.448	11
47. **Dion Phaneuf**, Cgy., Tor., Ott.	332	902	.368	12
48. **Chris Kunitz**, Ana., Atl., Pit.	330	884	.373	13
49. **Radim Vrbata**, Col., Car., Chi., Phx., T.B., Van., Ari.	330	1015	.325	15
50. **Brent Burns**, Min., S.J.	329	879	.374	13
51. **Michael Cammalleri**, L.A., Cgy., Mtl., N.J.	326	840	.388	14
52. **Alexander Steen**, Tor., St.L.	319	822	.388	12
53. **Brent Seabrook**, Chi.	318	923	.345	12
54. **Blake Wheeler**, Bos., Atl., Wpg.	315	697	.452	9
55. **Jeff Carter**, Phi., CBJ, L.A.	311	877	.355	12
56. **Jay Bouwmeester**, Fla., Cgy., St.L.	309	1071	.289	14
57. **Ryan Kesler**, Van., Ana.	306	897	.341	13
58. **Loui Eriksson**, Dal., Bos., Van.	305	790	.386	11
59. **John Tavares**, NYI	302	587	.514	8
60. **Niklas Kronwall**, Det.	302	795	.380	13
61. **Shea Weber**, Nsh., Mtl.	302	841	.359	12
62. **Jamie Benn**, Dal.	299	585	.511	8
63. **Kris Letang**, Pit.	299	603	.496	11
64. **Brian Gionta**, N.J., Mtl., Buf.	299	1006	.297	15
65. **Mike Green**, Wsh., Det.	297	721	.412	12
66. **Dennis Wideman**, St.L., Bos., Fla., Wsh., Cgy.	288	815	.353	12
67. **Dustin Byfuglien**, Chi., Atl., Wpg.	284	758	.375	12
68. **John-Michael Liles**, Col., Tor., Car., Bos.	283	836	.339	13
69. **Travis Zajac**, N.J.	280	779	.359	11
70. **Antoine Vermette**, Ott., CBJ, Phx., Ari., Chi., Ana.	279	982	.284	13
71. **David Backes**, St.L., Bos.	275	801	.343	11
72. **Dustin Brown**, L.A.	274	964	.284	13
73. **Valtteri Filppula**, Det., T.B., Phi.	273	795	.343	12
74. **Drew Doughty**, L.A.	270	688	.392	9
75. **Paul Martin**, N.J., Pit., S.J.	268	856	.313	13
76. **Brandon Dubinsky**, NYR, CBJ	267	700	.381	11
77. **Milan Lucic**, Bos., L.A., Edm.	265	729	.364	10
78. **Christian Ehrhoff**, S.J., Van., Buf., Pit., L.A., Chi.	265	789	.336	12
79. **Jiri Hudler**, Det., Cgy., Fla., Dal.	264	708	.373	12

Joe Thornton on the night he collected his 1,000th career assist. Thornton drew an assist on Joe Pavelski's empty-net goal that turned out to be the game winner in San Jose's 3-2 victory over Winnipeg on March 6, 2017.

Player	Assists	Games	Assists per game	Seasons
80. **Andrew Ladd**, Car., Chi., Atl., Wpg., NYI	264	847	.312	12
81. **Dan Hamhuis**, Nsh., Van., Dal.	263	951	.277	13
82. **Steven Stamkos**, T.B.	261	586	.445	9
83. **Sam Gagner**, Edm., Ari., Phi., CBJ	260	696	.374	10
84. **Lee Stempniak**, St.L., Tor., Phx., Cgy., Pit., NYR, Wpg., N.J., Bos., Car.	260	872	.298	12
85. **Matt Stajan**, Tor., Cgy.	259	935	.277	14
86. **Kyle Okposo**, NYI, Buf.	256	594	.431	10
87. **Frans Nielsen**, NYI, Det.	254	685	.371	11
88. **Alex Goligoski**, Pit., Dal., Ari.	252	644	.391	10
89. **Bobby Ryan**, Ana., Ott.	249	669	.372	10
90. **Toby Enstrom**, Atl., Wpg.	249	676	.368	10
91. **Jordan Staal**, Pit., Car.	249	764	.326	11
92. **T.J. Oshie**, St.L., Wsh.	248	591	.420	9
93. **Bryan Little**, Atl., Wpg.	248	672	.369	10
94. **P.K. Subban**, Mtl., Nsh.	245	500	.490	8
95. **Matt Duchene**, Col.	244	572	.427	8
96. **Derick Brassard**, CBJ, NYR, Ott.	241	644	.374	10
97. **Mark Giordano**, Cgy.	241	673	.358	11
98. **Michal Rozsival**, Pit., NYR, Phx., Chi.	241	963	.250	16
99. **Tyler Seguin**, Bos., Dal.	238	508	.469	7
100. **Alex Pietrangelo**, St.L.	238	539	.442	9

Top 100 All-Time Point Leaders

* active player

Player	Points	Games	Points per game	Goals	Assists	Seasons
1. **Wayne Gretzky**, Edm., L.A., St.L., NYR	**2857**	1487	1.921	894	1963	20
* 2. **Jaromir Jagr**, Pit., Wsh., NYR, Phi., Dal., Bos., N.J., Fla.	**1914**	1711	1.119	765	1149	23
3. **Mark Messier**, Edm., NYR, Van.	**1887**	1756	1.075	694	1193	25
4. **Gordie Howe**, Det., Hfd.	**1850**	1767	1.047	801	1049	26
5. **Ron Francis**, Hfd., Pit., Car., Tor.	**1798**	1731	1.039	549	1249	23
6. **Marcel Dionne**, Det., L.A., NYR	**1771**	1348	1.314	731	1040	18
7. **Steve Yzerman**, Det.	**1755**	1514	1.159	692	1063	22
8. **Mario Lemieux**, Pit.	**1723**	915	1.883	690	1033	18
9. **Joe Sakic**, Que., Col.	**1641**	1378	1.191	625	1016	20
10. **Phil Esposito**, Chi., Bos., NYR	**1590**	1282	1.240	717	873	18
11. **Raymond Bourque**, Bos., Col.	**1579**	1612	.980	410	1169	22
12. **Mark Recchi**, Pit., Phi., Mtl., Car., Atl., T.B., Bos.	**1533**	1652	.928	577	956	22
13. **Paul Coffey**, Edm., Pit., L.A., Det., Hfd., Phi., Chi., Car., Bos.	**1531**	1409	1.087	396	1135	21
14. **Stan Mikita**, Chi.	**1467**	1394	1.052	541	926	22
15. **Teemu Selanne**, Wpg., Ana., S.J., Col.	**1457**	1451	1.004	684	773	21
16. **Bryan Trottier**, NYI, Pit.	**1425**	1279	1.114	524	901	18
17. **Adam Oates**, Det., St.L., Bos., Wsh., Phi., Ana., Edm.	**1420**	1337	1.062	341	1079	19
18. **Doug Gilmour**, St.L., Cgy., Tor., N.J., Buf., Mtl.	**1414**	1474	.959	450	964	20
19. **Dale Hawerchuk**, Wpg., Buf., St.L., Phi.	**1409**	1188	1.186	518	891	16
20. **Jari Kurri**, Edm., L.A., NYR, Ana., Col.	**1398**	1251	1.118	601	797	17
21. **Luc Robitaille**, L.A., Pit., NYR, Det.	**1394**	1431	.974	668	726	19
22. **Brett Hull**, Cgy., St.L., Dal., Det., Phx.	**1391**	1269	1.096	741	650	20
* 23. **Joe Thornton**, Bos., S.J.	**1391**	1446	.962	384	1007	19
24. **Mike Modano**, Min., Dal., Det.	**1374**	1499	.917	561	813	22
25. **John Bucyk**, Det., Bos.	**1369**	1540	.889	556	813	23
26. **Brendan Shanahan**, N.J., St.L., Hfd., Det., NYR	**1354**	1524	.888	656	698	21
27. **Guy Lafleur**, Mtl., NYR, Que.	**1353**	1126	1.202	560	793	17
28. **Mats Sundin**, Que., Tor., Van.	**1349**	1346	1.002	564	785	18
29. **Denis Savard**, Chi., Mtl., T.B.	**1338**	1196	1.119	473	865	17
30. **Dave Andreychuk**, Buf., Tor., N.J., Bos., Col., T.B.	**1338**	1639	.816	640	698	23
31. **Mike Gartner**, Wsh., Min., NYR, Tor., Phx.	**1335**	1432	.932	708	627	19
32. **Pierre Turgeon**, Buf., NYI, Mtl., St.L., Dal., Col.	**1327**	1294	1.026	515	812	19
33. **Gilbert Perreault**, Buf.	**1326**	1191	1.113	512	814	17
* 34. **Jarome Iginla**, Cgy., Pit., Bos., Col., L.A.	**1300**	1554	.837	625	675	21
35. **Alex Delvecchio**, Det.	**1281**	1549	.827	456	825	24
36. **Al MacInnis**, Cgy., St.L.	**1274**	1416	.900	340	934	23
37. **Jean Ratelle**, NYR, Bos.	**1267**	1281	.989	491	776	21
38. **Peter Stastny**, Que., N.J., St.L.	**1239**	977	1.268	450	789	15
39. **Phil Housley**, Buf., Wpg., St.L., Cgy., N.J., Wsh., Chi., Tor.	**1232**	1495	.824	338	894	21
40. **Norm Ullman**, Det., Tor.	**1229**	1410	.872	490	739	20
41. **Jean Beliveau**, Mtl.	**1219**	1125	1.084	507	712	20
42. **Jeremy Roenick**, Chi., Phx., Phi., L.A., S.J.	**1216**	1363	.892	513	703	20
43. **Larry Murphy**, L.A., Wsh., Min., Pit., Tor., Det.	**1216**	1615	.753	287	929	21
44. **Bobby Clarke**, Phi.	**1210**	1144	1.058	358	852	15
45. **Bernie Nicholls**, L.A., NYR, Edm., N.J., Chi., S.J.	**1209**	1127	1.073	475	734	18
46. **Vincent Damphousse**, Tor., Edm., Mtl., S.J.	**1205**	1378	.874	432	773	18
47. **Dino Ciccarelli**, Min., Wsh., Det., T.B., Fla.	**1200**	1232	.974	608	592	19
48. **Rod Brind'Amour**, St.L., Phi., Car.	**1184**	1484	.798	452	732	21
49. **Sergei Fedorov**, Det., Ana., CBJ, Wsh.	**1179**	1248	.945	483	696	18
50. **Bobby Hull**, Chi., Wpg., Hfd.	**1170**	1063	1.101	610	560	16
51. **Daniel Alfredsson**, Ott., Det.	**1157**	1246	.929	444	713	18
52. **Michel Goulet**, Que., Chi.	**1152**	1089	1.058	548	604	15
53. **Nicklas Lidstrom**, Det.	**1142**	1564	.730	264	878	20
* 54. **Marian Hossa**, Ott., Atl., Pit., Det., Chi.	**1134**	1309	.866	525	609	19
55. **Bernie Federko**, St.L., Det.	**1130**	1000	1.130	369	761	14
56. **Mike Bossy**, NYI	**1126**	752	1.497	573	553	10
57. **Joe Nieuwendyk**, Cgy., Dal., N.J., Tor., Fla.	**1126**	1257	.896	564	562	20

Jaromir Jagr poses with the puck from his 1,887th career point. Jagr tied Mark Messier on the all-time scoring list on December 20, 2016 and moved past him in his next game two nights later.

Player	Points	Games	Points per game	Goals	Assists	Seasons
58. **Darryl Sittler**, Tor., Phi., Det.	1121	1096	1.023	484	637	15
59. **Frank Mahovlich**, Tor., Det., Mtl.	1103	1181	.934	533	570	18
60. **Glenn Anderson**, Edm., Tor., NYR, St.L.	1099	1129	.973	498	601	16
61. **Theoren Fleury**, Cgy., Col., Chi.	1088	1084	1.004	455	633	15
* 62. **Patrick Marleau**, S.J.	1082	1493	.725	508	574	19
63. **Dave Taylor**, L.A.	1069	1111	.962	431	638	17
64. **Keith Tkachuk**, Wpg., Phx., St.L., Atl.	1065	1201	.887	538	527	18
65. **Ray Whitney**, S.J., Edm., Fla., CBJ, Det., Car., Phx., Dal.	1064	1330	.800	385	679	22
66. **Joe Mullen**, St.L., Cgy., Pit., Bos.	1063	1062	1.001	502	561	17
67. **Pat Verbeek**, N.J., Hfd., NYR, Dal., Det.	1063	1424	.746	522	541	20
68. **Denis Potvin**, NYI	1052	1060	.992	310	742	15
69. **Henri Richard**, Mtl.	1046	1256	.833	358	688	20
70. **Bobby Smith**, Min., Mtl.	1036	1077	.962	357	679	15
* 71. **Alex Ovechkin**, Wsh.	1035	921	1.124	558	477	12
72. **Martin St. Louis**, Cgy., T.B., NYR	1033	1134	.911	391	642	16
73. **Doug Weight**, NYR, Edm., St.L., Car., Ana., NYI	1033	1238	.834	278	755	20
74. **Alexander Mogilny**, Buf., Van., N.J., Tor.	1032	990	1.042	473	559	16
75. **Alex Kovalev**, NYR, Pit., Mtl., Ott., Fla.	1029	1316	.782	430	599	19
76. **Brian Leetch**, NYR, Tor., Bos.	1028	1205	.853	247	781	18
* 77. **Sidney Crosby**, Pit.	1027	782	1.313	382	645	12
78. **Patrik Elias**, N.J.	1025	1240	.827	408	617	20
79. **Brian Bellows**, Min., Mtl., T.B., Ana., Wsh.	1022	1188	.860	485	537	17
80. **Rod Gilbert**, NYR	1021	1065	.959	406	615	18
* 81. **Henrik Sedin**, Van.	1020	1248	.817	237	783	16
82. **Dale Hunter**, Que., Wsh., Col.	1020	1407	.725	323	697	19
83. **Pat LaFontaine**, NYI, Buf., NYR	1013	865	1.171	468	545	15
84. **Steve Larmer**, Chi., NYR	1012	1006	1.006	441	571	15
85. **Lanny McDonald**, Tor., Col., Cgy.	1006	1111	.905	500	506	16
86. **Brian Propp**, Phi., Bos., Min., Hfd.	1004	1016	.988	425	579	15
87. **Paul Kariya**, Ana., Col., Nsh., St.L.	989	989	1.000	402	587	15
88. **Rick Middleton**, NYR, Bos.	988	1005	.983	448	540	14
* 89. **Daniel Sedin**, Van.	986	1225	.805	370	616	16
90. **Dave Keon**, Tor., Hfd.	986	1296	.761	396	590	18
91. **Andy Bathgate**, NYR, Tor., Det., Pit.	973	1069	.910	349	624	17
* 92. **Shane Doan**, Wpg., Phx., Ari.	972	1540	.631	402	570	21
93. **Maurice Richard**, Mtl.	965	978	.987	544	421	18
94. **Kirk Muller**, N.J., Mtl., NYI, Tor., Fla., Det.	959	1349	.711	357	602	19
95. **Larry Robinson**, Mtl., L.A.	958	1384	.692	208	750	20
96. **Rick Tocchet**, Phi., Pit., L.A., Bos., Wsh., Phx.	952	1144	.832	440	512	18
97. **Vincent Lecavalier**, T.B., Phi., L.A.	949	1212	.783	421	528	17
98. **Chris Chelios**, Mtl., Chi., Det., Atl.	948	1651	.574	185	763	26
99. **Jason Arnott**, Edm., N.J., Dal., Nsh., Wsh., St.L.	938	1244	.754	417	521	19
100. **Steve Thomas**, Tor., Chi., NYI, N.J., Ana., Det.	933	1235	.755	421	512	20

Top 100 Active Points Leaders

	Player	Points	Games	Points per game	Goals	Assists	Seasons
1.	Jaromir Jagr, Pit., Wsh., NYR, Phi., Dal., Bos., N.J., Fla. . . .	1914	1711	1.119	765	1149	23
2.	Joe Thornton, Bos., S.J.	1391	1446	.962	384	1007	19
3.	Jarome Iginla, Cgy., Pit., Bos., Col., L.A.	1300	1554	.837	625	675	21
4.	Marian Hossa, Ott., Atl., Pit., Det., Chi. . . .	1134	1309	.866	525	609	19
5.	Patrick Marleau, S.J.	1082	1493	.725	508	574	19
6.	Alex Ovechkin, Wsh.	1035	921	1.124	558	477	12
7.	Sidney Crosby, Pit.	1027	782	1.313	382	645	12
8.	Henrik Sedin, Van.	1020	1248	.817	237	783	16
9.	Daniel Sedin, Van.	986	1225	.805	370	616	16
10.	Shane Doan, Wpg., Phx., Ari. . . .	972	1540	.631	402	570	21
11.	Henrik Zetterberg, Det.	904	1000	.904	326	578	14
12.	Jason Spezza, Ott., Dal.	862	911	.946	316	546	14
13.	Eric Staal, Car., NYR, Min. . . .	846	1011	.837	353	493	13
14.	Evgeni Malkin, Pit.	832	706	1.178	328	504	11
15.	Ryan Getzlaf, Ana.	814	861	.945	236	578	12
16.	Marian Gaborik, Min., NYR, CBJ, L.A.	794	989	.803	396	398	16
17.	Mike Ribeiro, Mtl., Dal., Wsh., Phx., Nsh.	793	1074	.738	228	565	17
18.	Rick Nash, CBJ, NYR	771	989	.780	416	355	14
19.	Patrick Kane, Chi.	752	740	1.016	285	467	10
20.	Anze Kopitar, L.A.	736	840	.876	255	481	11
21.	Nicklas Backstrom, Wsh. . . .	728	734	.992	188	540	10
22.	Corey Perry, Ana.	717	886	.809	349	368	12
23.	Thomas Vanek, Buf., NYI, Mtl., Min., Det., Fla.	697	885	.788	333	364	12
24.	Scott Hartnell, Nsh., Phi., CBJ	683	1187	.575	314	369	16
25.	Justin Williams, Phi., Car., L.A., Wsh.	682	1080	.631	273	409	16
26.	Patrice Bergeron, Bos.	671	899	.746	259	412	13
27.	Jason Pominville, Buf., Min. . .	662	905	.731	261	401	13
28.	Zach Parise, N.J., Min.	661	830	.796	318	343	12
29.	Jeff Carter, Phi., CBJ, L.A. . . .	650	877	.741	339	311	12
30.	Phil Kessel, Bos., Tor., Pit. . . .	649	832	.780	296	353	11
31.	Joe Pavelski, S.J.	631	806	.783	295	336	11
32.	Jonathan Toews, Chi.	622	717	.868	272	350	10
33.	Mikko Koivu, Min.	614	843	.728	179	435	12
34.	Michael Cammalleri, L.A., Cgy., Mtl., N.J.	613	840	.730	287	326	14
35.	Radim Vrbata, Col., Car., Chi., Phx., T.B., Van., Ari. . .	609	1015	.600	279	330	15
36.	Zdeno Chara, NYI, Ott., Bos. .	604	1350	.447	188	416	19
37.	Patrick Sharp, Phi., Chi., Dal. .	599	869	.689	277	322	14
38.	Paul Stastny, Col., St.L.	593	742	.799	204	389	11
39.	Brian Gionta, N.J., Mtl., Buf. . .	588	1006	.584	289	299	15
40.	Steven Stamkos, T.B.	582	586	.993	321	261	9
41.	Tomas Plekanec, Mtl.	581	921	.631	226	355	13
42.	Chris Kunitz, Ana., Atl., Pit. . .	580	884	.656	250	330	13
43.	Claude Giroux, Phi.	575	656	.877	180	395	10
44.	Ales Hemsky, Edm., Ott., Dal. .	572	838	.683	174	398	14
45.	Ryan Kesler, Van., Ana.	551	897	.614	245	306	13
46.	Jussi Jokinen, Dal., T.B., Car., Pit., Fla.	546	891	.613	186	360	12
47.	John Tavares, NYI	537	587	.915	235	302	8
48.	Alexander Steen, Tor., St.L. . . .	532	822	.647	213	319	12
49.	Loui Eriksson, Dal., Bos., Van. .	528	790	.668	223	305	11
50.	David Krejci, Bos.	526	705	.746	157	369	11
51.	Jamie Benn, Dal.	517	585	.884	218	299	8
52.	Blake Wheeler, Bos., Atl., Wpg.	514	697	.737	199	315	9
53.	Duncan Keith, Chi.	511	913	.560	90	421	12
54.	Dustin Brown, L.A.	506	964	.525	232	274	13
55.	Brent Burns, Min., S.J.	499	879	.568	170	329	13
56.	Antoine Vermette, Ott., CBJ, Phx., Ari., Chi., Ana.	499	982	.508	220	279	13
57.	David Backes, St.L., Bos.	498	801	.622	223	275	11
58.	Andrew Ladd, Car., Chi., Atl., Wpg., NYI	497	847	.587	233	264	12
59.	Jakub Voracek, CBJ, Phi.	488	686	.711	155	333	9
60.	Shea Weber, Nsh., Mtl.	485	841	.577	183	302	12
61.	Bobby Ryan, Ana., Ott.	472	669	.706	223	249	10
62.	Dion Phaneuf, Cgy., Tor., Ott. .	462	902	.512	130	332	12
63.	Lee Stempniak, St.L., Tor., Phx., Cgy., Pit., NYR, Wpg., N.J., Bos., Car.	460	872	.528	200	260	12
64.	Erik Karlsson, Ott.	456	556	.820	117	339	8
65.	James Neal, Dal., Pit., Nsh. . .	451	632	.714	238	213	9
66.	Dustin Byfuglien, Chi., Atl., Wpg.	449	758	.592	165	284	12
67.	Milan Lucic, Bos., L.A., Edm. .	447	729	.613	182	265	10
68.	Milan Michalek, S.J., Ott., Tor.	446	747	.597	208	238	13
69.	Ryan Suter, Nsh., Min.	442	913	.484	69	373	12
70.	Jordan Staal, Pit., Car.	436	764	.571	187	249	11
71.	Travis Zajac, N.J.	435	779	.558	155	280	11

Henrik Sedin acknowledges the cheers from the hometown crowd in Vancouver after picking up his 1,000th career point on January 20, 2017. Brother Daniel sits just behind him on the active scoring list.

	Player	Points	Games	Points per game	Goals	Assists	Seasons
72.	Mark Streit, Mtl., NYI, Phi., Pit.	434	784	.554	96	338	11
73.	Bryan Little, Atl., Wpg.	432	672	.643	184	248	10
74.	Mike Green, Wsh., Det.	431	721	.598	134	297	12
75.	Valtteri Filppula, Det., T.B., Phi.	430	795	.541	157	273	12
76.	Jiri Hudler, Det., Cgy., Fla., Dal.	428	708	.605	164	264	12
77.	Tyler Seguin, Bos., Dal.	427	508	.841	189	238	7
78.	Matt Duchene, Col.	418	572	.731	174	244	8
79.	T.J. Oshie, St.L., Wsh.	417	591	.706	169	248	9
80.	Kyle Okposo, NYI, Buf.	414	594	.697	158	256	10
81.	Max Pacioretty, Mtl.	411	562	.731	209	202	9
82.	Keith Yandle, Phx., Ari., NYR, Fla.	410	743	.552	77	333	11
83.	Brandon Dubinsky, NYR, CBJ	408	700	.583	141	267	11
84.	Brent Seabrook, Chi.	406	923	.440	88	318	12
85.	Sam Gagner, Edm., Ari., Phi., CBJ.	402	696	.578	142	260	10
86.	Jason Chimera, Edm., CBJ, Wsh., NYI	402	1033	.389	183	219	16
87.	Matt Stajan, Tor., Cgy.	401	935	.429	142	259	14
88.	Drew Stafford, Buf., Wpg., Bos.	400	725	.552	183	217	11
89.	Wayne Simmonds, L.A., Phi. . .	398	687	.579	202	196	9
90.	Alexandre Burrows, Van., Ott.	395	842	.469	199	196	12
91.	Jay Bouwmeester, Fla., Cgy., St.L.	391	1071	.365	82	309	14
92.	Frans Nielsen, NYI, Det.	390	685	.569	136	254	11
93.	Dennis Wideman, St.L., Bos., Fla., Wsh., Cgy.	387	815	.475	99	288	12
94.	Kris Letang, Pit.	386	603	.640	87	299	11
95.	Derick Brassard, CBJ, NYR, Ott.	382	507	.753	165	217	7
96.	Taylor Hall, Edm., N.J.	382	644	.593	141	241	10
97.	David Perron, St.L., Edm., Pit., Ana.	381	453	.841	152	229	7
98.	Niklas Kronwall, Det.	378	652	.580	159	219	10
99.	Logan Couture, S.J.	378	795	.475	76	302	13
100.	Logan Couture, S.J.	376	504	.746	179	197	8

Top 100 All-Time Games Played Leaders

* active player

Player	Games Played	Seasons
1. **Gordie Howe**, Det., Hfd.	1767	26
2. **Mark Messier**, Edm., NYR, Van.	1756	25
3. **Ron Francis**, Hfd., Pit., Car., Tor.	1731	23
* 4. **Jaromir Jagr**, Pit., Wsh., NYR, Phi., Dal., Bos., N.J., Fla.	1711	23
5. **Mark Recchi**, Pit., Phi., Mtl., Car., Atl., T.B., Bos.	1652	22
6. **Chris Chelios**, Mtl., Chi., Det., Atl.	1651	26
7. **Dave Andreychuk**, Buf., Tor., N.J., Bos., Col., T.B.	1639	23
8. **Scott Stevens**, Wsh., St.L., N.J.	1635	22
9. **Larry Murphy**, L.A., Wsh., Min., Pit., Tor., Det.	1615	21
10. **Raymond Bourque**, Bos., Col.	1612	22
11. **Nicklas Lidstrom**, Det.	1564	20
* 12. **Jarome Iginla**, Cgy., Pit., Bos., Col., L.A.	1554	21
13. **Alex Delvecchio**, Det.	1549	24
* 14. **Shane Doan**, Wpg., Phx., Ari.	1540	21
15. **John Bucyk**, Det., Bos.	1540	23
16. **Brendan Shanahan**, N.J., St.L., Hfd., Det., NYR	1524	21
17. **Steve Yzerman**, Det.	1514	22
18. **Mike Modano**, Min., Dal., Det.	1499	22
19. **Phil Housley**, Buf., Wpg., St.L., Cgy., N.J., Wsh., Chi., Tor.	1495	21
* 20. **Patrick Marleau**, S.J.	1493	19
21. **Wayne Gretzky**, Edm., L.A., St.L., NYR	1487	20
22. **Rod Brind'Amour**, St.L., Phi., Car.	1484	21
23. **Doug Gilmour**, St.L., Cgy., Tor., N.J., Chi., Buf., Mtl.	1474	20
24. **Glen Wesley**, Bos., Hfd., Car., Tor.	1457	20
25. **Teemu Selanne**, Wpg., Ana., S.J., Col.	1451	21
* 26. **Joe Thornton**, Bos., S.J.	1446	19
27. **Tim Horton**, Tor., NYR, Pit., Buf.	1446	24
28. **Mike Gartner**, Wsh., Min., NYR, Tor., Phx.	1432	19
29. **Luc Robitaille**, L.A., Pit., NYR, Det.	1431	19
30. **Scott Mellanby**, Phi., Edm., Fla., St.L., Atl.	1431	21
31. **Pat Verbeek**, N.J., Hfd., NYR, Dal., Det.	1424	20
32. **Luke Richardson**, Tor., Edm., Phi., CBJ, T.B., Ott.	1417	21
33. **Al MacInnis**, Cgy., St.L.	1416	23
34. **Harry Howell**, NYR, Oak., Cal., L.A.	1411	21
35. **Norm Ullman**, Det., Tor.	1410	20
36. **Paul Coffey**, Edm., Pit., L.A., Det., Hfd., Phi., Chi., Car., Bos.	1409	21
37. **Dale Hunter**, Que., Wsh., Col.	1407	19
38. **Roman Hamrlik**, T.B., Edm., NYI, Cgy., Mtl., Wsh., NYR	1395	20
39. **Stan Mikita**, Chi.	1394	22
40. **Doug Mohns**, Bos., Chi., Min., Atl., Wsh.	1390	22
41. **Larry Robinson**, Mtl., L.A.	1384	20
42. **Trevor Linden**, Van., NYI, Mtl., Wsh.	1382	19
43. **Vincent Damphousse**, Tor., Edm., Mtl., S.J.	1378	18
44. **Joe Sakic**, Que., Col.	1378	20
45. **Dean Prentice**, NYR, Bos., Det., Pit., Min.	1378	22
46. **Teppo Numminen**, Wpg., Phx., Dal., Buf.	1372	20
47. **Matt Cullen**, Ana., Fla., Car., NYR, Ott., Min., Nsh., Pit.	1366	19
48. **Jeremy Roenick**, Chi., Phx., Phi., L.A., S.J.	1363	20
49. **Ron Stewart**, Tor., Bos., St.L., NYR, Van., NYI	1353	21
* 50. **Zdeno Chara**, NYI, Ott., Bos.	1350	19
51. **Kirk Muller**, N.J., Mtl., NYI, Tor., Fla., Dal.	1349	19
52. **Marcel Dionne**, Det., L.A., NYR	1348	18
53. **Mats Sundin**, Que., Tor., Van.	1346	18
54. **Adam Oates**, Det., St.L., Bos., Wsh., Phi., Ana., Edm.	1337	19
55. **Ray Whitney**, S.J., Edm., Fla., CBJ, Det., Car., Phx., Dal.	1330	22
56. **Guy Carbonneau**, Mtl., St.L., Dal.	1318	19
57. **Alex Kovalev**, NYR, Pit., Mtl., Ott., Fla.	1316	19
58. **Red Kelly**, Det., Tor.	1316	20
59. **Bobby Holik**, Hfd., N.J., NYR, Atl.	1314	18
* 60. **Marian Hossa**, Ott., Atl., Pit., Det., Chi.	1309	19
61. **Sergei Gonchar**, Wsh., Bos., Pit., Ott., Dal., Mtl.	1301	20
62. **Dave Keon**, Tor., Hfd.	1296	18
63. **Pierre Turgeon**, Buf., NYI, Mtl., St.L., Dal., Col.	1294	19
64. **Dainius Zubrus**, Phi., Mtl., Wsh., Buf., N.J., S.J.	1293	19
65. **Darryl Sydor**, L.A., Dal., CBJ, T.B., Pit., St.L.	1291	18
66. **Mathieu Schneider**, Mtl., NYI, Tor., NYR, L.A., Det., Ana., Atl., Van., Phx.	1289	21
67. **Ken Daneyko**, N.J.	1283	20
68. **Phil Esposito**, Chi., Bos., NYR	1282	18
69. **Jean Ratelle**, NYR, Bos.	1281	21
70. **James Patrick**, NYR, Hfd., Cgy., Buf.	1280	21
71. **Bryan Trottier**, NYI, Pit.	1279	18
72. **Martin Gelinas**, Edm., Que., Van., Car., Cgy., Fla., Nsh.	1273	19
73. **Ryan Smyth**, Edm., NYI, Col., L.A.	1270	19
74. **Rob Blake**, L.A., Col., S.J.	1270	20
75. **Brett Hull**, Cgy., St.L., Dal., Det., Phx.	1269	20
76. **Martin Brodeur**, N.J., St.L.	1266	22
77. **Scott Niedermayer**, N.J., Ana.	1263	18
78. **Bill Guerin**, N.J., Edm., Bos., Dal., St.L., S.J., NYI, Pit.	1263	18
79. **Radek Dvorak**, Fla., NYR, Edm., St.L., Atl., Dal., Ana., Car.	1260	18
80. **Ray Ferraro**, Hfd., NYI, NYR, L.A., Atl., St.L.	1258	18

Jeremy Roenick (left), Jarome Iginla (center) and Shane Doan share a laugh during the 2004 NHL All-Star Super Skills Competition. Iginla and Doan both topped 1,500 career games during the 2016-17 season.

Player	Games Played	Seasons
81. **Joe Nieuwendyk**, Cgy., Dal., N.J., Tor., Fla.	1257	20
82. **Brian Rolston**, N.J., Col., Bos., Min., NYI	1256	17
83. **Craig Ludwig**, Mtl., NYI, Min., Dal.	1256	17
84. **Henri Richard**, Mtl.	1256	20
85. **Kevin Lowe**, Edm., NYR	1254	19
86. **Jari Kurri**, Edm., L.A., NYR, Ana., Col.	1251	17
* 87. **Henrik Sedin**, Van.	1248	16
88. **Sergei Fedorov**, Det., Ana., CBJ, Wsh.	1248	18
89. **Bill Gadsby**, Chi., NYR, Det.	1248	20
90. **Daniel Alfredsson**, Ott., Det.	1246	18
91. **Jason Arnott**, Edm., N.J., Dal., Nsh., Wsh., St.L.	1244	18
92. **Allan Stanley**, NYR, Chi., Bos., Tor., Phi.	1244	21
93. **Patrik Elias**, N.J.	1240	20
94. **Doug Weight**, NYR, Edm., St.L., Car., Ana., NYI	1238	20
95. **Steve Thomas**, Tor., Chi., NYI, N.J., Ana., Det.	1235	20
96. **Dino Ciccarelli**, Min., Wsh., Det., T.B., Fla.	1232	19
97. **Olli Jokinen**, L.A., NYI, Fla., Phx., Cgy., NYR, Wpg., Nsh., Tor., St.L.	1231	17
98. **Ed Westfall**, Bos., NYI	1226	18
* 99. **Daniel Sedin**, Van.	1225	16
100. **Sean O'Donnell**, L.A., Min., N.J., Bos., Phx., Ana., Phi., Chi.	1224	17

Top 100 Active Games Played Leaders

Player	Games Played	Seasons
1. **Jaromir Jagr**, Pit., Wsh., NYR, Phi., Dal., Bos., N.J., Fla.	1711	23
2. **Jarome Iginla**, Cgy., Pit., Bos., Col., L.A.	1554	21
3. **Shane Doan**, Wpg., Phx., Ari.	1540	21
4. **Patrick Marleau**, S.J.	1493	19
5. **Joe Thornton**, Bos., S.J.	1446	19
6. **Zdeno Chara**, NYI, Ott., Bos.	1350	19
7. **Marian Hossa**, Ott., Atl., Pit., Det., Chi.	1309	19
8. **Henrik Sedin**, Van.	1248	16
9. **Daniel Sedin**, Van.	1225	16
10. **Scott Hartnell**, Nsh., Phi., CBJ	1187	16
11. **Justin Williams**, Phi., Car., L.A., Wsh.	1080	16
12. **Mike Ribeiro**, Mtl., Dal., Wsh., Phx., Nsh.	1074	17
13. **Jay Bouwmeester**, Fla., Cgy., St.L.	1071	14
14. **Nick Schultz**, Min., Edm., CBJ, Phi.	1069	15
15. **Jason Chimera**, Edm., CBJ, Wsh., NYI	1033	16
16. **Chris Neil**, Ott.	1026	15
17. **Radim Vrbata**, Col., Car., Chi., Phx., T.B., Van., Ari.	1015	15
18. **Eric Staal**, Car., NYR, Min.	1011	13
19. **Brian Gionta**, N.J., Mtl., Buf.	1006	15
20. **Henrik Zetterberg**, Det.	1000	14
21. **Rick Nash**, CBJ, NYR	989	14
22. **Marian Gaborik**, Min., NYR, CBJ, L.A.	989	16
23. **Antoine Vermette**, Ott., CBJ, Phx., Ari., Chi., Ana.	982	13
24. **Roberto Luongo**, NYI, Fla., Van.	966	17
25. **Dustin Brown**, L.A.	964	13
26. **Michal Rozsival**, Pit., NYR, Phx., Chi.	963	16
27. **Dan Hamhuis**, Nsh., Van., Dal.	951	13
28. **Matt Stajan**, Tor., Cgy.	935	14
29. **Brent Seabrook**, Chi.	923	12
30. **Alex Ovechkin**, Wsh.	921	12
31. **Tomas Plekanec**, Mtl.	921	13
32. **Ryan Suter**, Nsh., Min.	913	12
33. **Duncan Keith**, Chi.	913	12
34. **Jason Spezza**, Ott., Dal.	911	14
35. **Ron Hainsey**, Mtl., CBJ, Atl., Wpg., Car., Pit.	907	14
36. **Jay McClement**, St.L., Col., Tor., Car.	906	12
37. **Jason Pominville**, Buf., Min.	905	13
38. **Dion Phaneuf**, Cgy., Tor., Ott.	902	12
39. **Brooks Orpik**, Pit., Wsh.	901	14
40. **Patrice Bergeron**, Bos.	899	13
41. **Ryan Kesler**, Van., Ana.	897	13
42. **Trevor Daley**, Dal., Chi., Pit.	894	13
43. **Jussi Jokinen**, Dal., T.B., Car., Pit., Fla.	891	12
44. **Corey Perry**, Ana.	886	12
45. **Thomas Vanek**, Buf., NYI, Mtl., Min., Det., Fla.	885	12
46. **Chris Kunitz**, Ana., Atl., Pit.	884	13
47. **Brent Burns**, Min., S.J.	879	13
48. **Jeff Carter**, Phi., CBJ, L.A.	877	12
49. **Vernon Fiddler**, Nsh., Phx., Dal., N.J.	877	14
50. **Lee Stempniak**, St.L., Tor., Phx., Cgy., Pit., NYR, Wpg., N.J., Bos., Car.	872	12
51. **Fedor Tyutin**, NYR, CBJ, Col.	872	13
52. **Patrick Sharp**, Phi., Chi., Dal.	869	14
53. **Ryan Getzlaf**, Ana.	861	12
54. **Paul Martin**, N.J., Pit., S.J.	856	13
55. **Dominic Moore**, NYR, Pit., Min., Tor., Buf., Fla., Mtl., T.B., S.J., Bos.	847	12
56. **Andrew Ladd**, Car., Chi., Atl., Wpg., NYI	847	12
57. **Mikko Koivu**, Min.	843	12
58. **Alexandre Burrows**, Van., Ott.	842	12
59. **Shea Weber**, Nsh., Mtl.	841	12
60. **Anze Kopitar**, L.A.	840	11
61. **Michael Cammalleri**, L.A., Cgy., Mtl., N.J.	840	14
62. **Ales Hemsky**, Edm., Ott., Dal.	838	14
63. **Francois Beauchemin**, Mtl., CBJ, Ana., Tor., Col.	836	13
64. **John-Michael Liles**, Col., Tor., Car., Bos.	836	13
65. **Chris Kelly**, Ott., Bos.	833	13
66. **Phil Kessel**, Bos., Tor., Pit.	832	11
67. **Dennis Seidenberg**, Phi., Phx., Car., Fla., Bos., NYI	831	14
68. **Zach Parise**, N.J., Min.	830	12
69. **Alexander Steen**, Tor., St.L.	822	12
70. **Dennis Wideman**, St.L., Bos., Fla., Wsh., Cgy.	815	12
71. **Marc-Edouard Vlasic**, S.J.	812	11
72. **Joe Pavelski**, S.J.	806	11
73. **David Backes**, St.L., Bos.	801	11
74. **Johnny Oduya**, N.J., Atl., Wpg., Chi., Dal.	798	11
75. **Valtteri Filppula**, Det., T.B., Phi.	795	12
76. **Niklas Kronwall**, Det.	795	13
77. **Loui Eriksson**, Dal., Bos., Van.	790	11
78. **Dan Girardi**, NYR.	788	11
79. **Andrew Cogliano**, Edm., Ana.	786	10
80. **Mark Streit**, Mtl., NYI, Phi., Pit.	784	11

Detroit captain Henrik Zetterberg tries to move past Jay Bouwmeester of the St. Louis Blues. Both players played in their 1,000th career game in 2016-17.

Player	Games Played	Seasons
81. **Zbynek Michalek**, Min., Phx., Pit., Ari., St.L.	784	13
82. **Rob Scuderi**, Pit., L.A., Chi.	783	12
83. **Sidney Crosby**, Pit.	782	12
84. **Travis Zajac**, N.J.	779	11
85. **Braydon Coburn**, Atl., Phi., T.B.	778	12
86. **Kyle Brodziak**, Edm., Min., St.L.	766	12
87. **Jordan Staal**, Pit., Car.	764	11
88. **Brooks Laich**, Ott., Wsh., Tor.	764	12
89. **Dustin Byfuglien**, Chi., Atl., Wpg.	758	12
90. **Chris Thorburn**, Buf., Atl., Wpg.	750	12
91. **Josh Gorges**, S.J., Mtl., Buf.	749	12
92. **Kevin Bieksa**, Van., Ana.	749	12
93. **Milan Michalek**, S.J., Ott., Tor.	747	13
94. **Keith Yandle**, Phx., Ari., NYR, Fla.	743	11
95. **Paul Stastny**, Col., St.L.	742	11
96. **Henrik Lundqvist**, NYR	742	12
97. **Patrick Kane**, Chi.	740	10
98. **Nicklas Backstrom**, Wsh.	734	10
99. **Matt Niskanen**, Dal., Pit., Wsh.	733	10
100. **Matt Carle**, S.J., T.B., Phi., Nsh.	730	12

Goaltending Records

All-Time Shutout Leaders (Minimum 54 Shutouts)

	Goaltender	Team	Shutouts	Games	Seasons
1.	**Martin Brodeur** (1991-2015)	New Jersey	124	1,259	21
		St. Louis	1	7	1
		Total	**125**	**1,266**	**22**
2.	**Terry Sawchuk** (1949-1970)	Detroit	85	734	14
		Boston	11	102	2
		Toronto	4	91	3
		Los Angeles	2	36	1
		NY Rangers	1	8	1
		Total	**103**	**971**	**21**
3.	**George Hainsworth** (1926-1937)	Montreal	75	318	7½
		Toronto	19	147	3½
		Total	**94**	**465**	**11**
4.	**Glenn Hall** (1952-1971)	Detroit	17	148	4
		Chicago	51	618	10
		St. Louis	16	140	4
		Total	**84**	**906**	**18**
5.	**Jacques Plante** (1952-1973)	Montreal	58	556	11
		NY Rangers	5	98	2
		St. Louis	10	69	2
		Toronto	7	106	2¾
		Boston	2	8	¼
		Total	**82**	**837**	**18**
6.	**Alec Connell** (1924-1937)	Ottawa	64	293	8
		Detroit	6	48	1
		NY Americans	0	1	1
		Mtl. Maroons	11	75	2
		Total	**81**	**417**	**12**
7.	**Tiny Thompson** (1928-1940)	Boston	74	468	10¼
		Detroit	7	85	1¾
		Total	**81**	**553**	**12**
8.	**Dominik Hasek** (1990-2008)	Chicago	1	25	2
		Buffalo	55	491	9
		Detroit	20	176	4
		Ottawa	5	43	1
		Total	**81**	**735**	**16**
9.	**Tony Esposito** (1968-1984)	Montreal	2	13	1
		Chicago	74	873	15
		Total	**76**	**886**	**16**
10.	**Ed Belfour** (1988-2007)	Chicago	30	415	7⅔
		San Jose	1	13	⅓
		Dallas	27	307	5
		Toronto	17	170	3
		Florida	1	58	1
		Total	**76**	**963**	**17**
11.	***Roberto Luongo** (1999-2017)	NY Islanders	1	24	1
		Florida	34	494	8¼
		Vancouver	38	448	7¾
		Total	**73**	**966**	**17**
12.	**Lorne Chabot** (1926-1937)	NY Rangers	21	80	2
		Toronto	32	214	5
		Montreal	8	47	1
		Chicago	8	48	1
		Mtl. Maroons	2	16	1
		NY Americans	1	6	1
		Total	**72**	**411**	**11**
13.	**Harry Lumley** (1943-1960)	Detroit	26	324	6½
		NY Rangers	0	1	½
		Chicago	5	134	2
		Toronto	34	267	4
		Boston	6	78	3
		Total	**71**	**804**	**16**
14.	**Roy Worters** (1925-1937)	Pittsburgh Pirates	22	123	3
		NY Americans	45	360	9
		**Montreal	0	1	
		Total	**67**	**484**	**12**
15.	**Patrick Roy** (1984-2003)	Montreal	29	551	11½
		Colorado	37	478	7½
		Total	**66**	**1,029**	**19**
16.	**Turk Broda** (1936-1952)	Toronto	62	629	14
17.	***Henrik Lundqvist** (2005-2017)	NY Rangers	**61**	742	12
18.	**Evgeni Nabokov** (1999-2015)	San Jose	50	563	10
		NY Islanders	9	123	3
		Tampa Bay	0	11	1
		Total	**59**	**697**	**14**
19.	**Clint Benedict** (1917-1930)	Ottawa	19	158	7
		Mtl. Maroons	39	204	6
		Total	**58**	**362**	**13**
20.	**John Ross Roach** (1921-1935)	Toronto	13	222	7
		NY Rangers	30	89	4
		Detroit	15	180	3
		Total	**58**	**491**	**14**
21.	**Bernie Parent** (1965-1979)	Boston	1	57	2
		Philadelphia	50	486	9½
		Toronto	3	65	1½
		Total	**54**	**608**	**13**
22.	**Ed Giacomin** (1965-1978)	NY Rangers	49	539	10¼
		Detroit	5	71	2¾
		Total	**54**	**610**	**13**

* Active goalie
** Played 1 game for Montreal in 1929-30.

Ten or More Shutouts, One Season

Number of Shutouts	Goaltender	Team	Season	Length of Schedule
22	George Hainsworth	Montreal	1928-29	44
15	Alec Connell	Ottawa	1925-26	36
	Alec Connell	Ottawa	1927-28	44
	Hal Winkler	Boston	1927-28	44
	Tony Esposito	Chicago	1969-70	76
14	George Hainsworth	Montreal	1926-27	44
13	Clint Benedict	Mtl. Maroons	1926-27	44
	Alec Connell	Ottawa	1926-27	44
	George Hainsworth	Montreal	1927-28	44
	John Ross Roach	NY Rangers	1928-29	44
	Roy Worters	NY Americans	1928-29	44
	Harry Lumley	Toronto	1953-54	70
	Dominik Hasek	Buffalo	1997-98	82
12	Tiny Thompson	Boston	1928-29	44
	Charlie Gardiner	Chicago	1930-31	44
	Terry Sawchuk	Detroit	1951-52	70
	Terry Sawchuk	Detroit	1953-54	70
	Terry Sawchuk	Detroit	1954-55	70
	Glenn Hall	Detroit	1955-56	70
	Bernie Parent	Philadelphia	1973-74	78
	Bernie Parent	Philadelphia	1974-75	80
	Martin Brodeur	New Jersey	2006-07	82
11	Lorne Chabot	NY Rangers	1927-28	44
	Hap Holmes	Detroit	1927-28	44
	Roy Worters	Pittsburgh Pirates	1927-28	44
	Clint Benedict	Mtl. Maroons	1928-29	44
	Joe Miller	Pittsburgh Pirates	1928-29	44
	Tiny Thompson	Boston	1932-33	48
	Terry Sawchuk	Detroit	1950-51	70
	Dominik Hasek	Buffalo	2000-01	82
	Martin Brodeur	New Jersey	2003-04	82
	Henrik Lundqvist	NY Rangers	2010-11	82
10	Lorne Chabot	NY Rangers	1926-27	44
	Lorne Chabot	Toronto	1928-29	44
	Dolly Dolson	Detroit	1928-29	44
	John Ross Roach	Detroit	1932-33	48
	Charlie Gardiner	Chicago	1933-34	48
	Tiny Thompson	Boston	1935-36	48
	Frank Brimsek	Boston	1938-39	48
	Bill Durnan	Montreal	1948-49	60
	Harry Lumley	Toronto	1952-53	70
	Gerry McNeil	Montreal	1952-53	70
	Tony Esposito	Chicago	1973-74	78
	Ken Dryden	Montreal	1976-77	80
	Martin Brodeur	New Jersey	1996-97	82
	Martin Brodeur	New Jersey	1997-98	82
	Byron Dafoe	Boston	1998-99	82
	Roman Cechmanek	Philadelphia	2000-01	82
	Ed Belfour	Toronto	2003-04	82
	Miikka Kiprusoff	Calgary	2005-06	82
	Henrik Lundqvist	NY Rangers	2007-08	82
	Steve Mason	Columbus	2008-09	82
	Jonathan Quick	Los Angeles	2011-12	82
	Marc-Andre Fleury	Pittsburgh	2014-15	82

All-Time Win Leaders

(Minimum 290 Wins)

	Goaltender	Wins	Losses	OT/Ties	Dec.	GP	Seas.
1.	Martin Brodeur	691	397	154	1,242	1,266	22
2.	Patrick Roy	551	315	131	997	1,029	19
3.	Ed Belfour	484	320	125	929	963	18
4.	Curtis Joseph	454	352	96	902	943	19
5.*	Roberto Luongo	453	365	117	935	966	17
6.	Terry Sawchuk	447	330	172	949	971	21
7.	Jacques Plante	437	246	145	828	837	18
8.	Tony Esposito	423	306	151	880	886	16
9.	Glenn Hall	407	326	163	896	906	18
10.*	Henrik Lundqvist	405	249	76	730	742	12
11.	Grant Fuhr	403	295	114	812	868	19
12.	Chris Osgood	401	216	95	712	744	17
13.	Dominik Hasek	389	223	95	707	735	16
14.	Mike Vernon	385	273	92	750	781	19
15.*	Marc-Andre Fleury	375	216	68	659	691	13
16.	John Vanbiesbrouck	374	346	119	839	882	20
17.	Andy Moog	372	209	88	669	713	18
18.	Tom Barrasso	369	277	86	732	777	19
19.*	Ryan Miller	358	262	74	671	709	14
20.	Rogie Vachon	355	291	127	773	795	16
21.	Evgeni Nabokov	353	227	86	666	697	14
22.	Gump Worsley	335	352	150	837	861	21
23.	Nikolai Khabibulin	333	334	97	764	799	18
24.	Harry Lumley	330	329	142	801	803	16
25.	Sean Burke	324	341	110	775	820	18
26.	Miikka Kiprusoff	319	213	71	603	623	12
27.	Billy Smith	305	233	105	643	680	18
28.	Olaf Kolzig	303	297	87	687	719	17
29.	Turk Broda	302	224	101	627	629	14
30.	Mike Richter	301	258	73	632	666	15
31.	Tomas Vokoun	300	288	78	666	700	15
32.	Ron Hextall	296	214	69	579	608	13
33.*	Kari Lehtonen	295	219	64	578	612	13
34.*	Cam Ward	295	230	80	605	625	12
35.	Mike Liut	294	271	74	639	664	13

* active goaltender

Active Win Leaders

(Minimum 220 Wins)

	Goaltender	Teams	Wins	Losses	OT/Ties	Dec.	GP	Seas.
1.	Roberto Luongo	NYI, Fla., Van.	453	365	117	936	966	17
2.	Henrik Lundqvist	NY Rangers	405	249	76	730	742	12
3.	Marc-Andre Fleury	Pittsburgh	375	216	68	659	691	13
4.	Ryan Miller	Buf., St.L., Van.	358	262	74	694	709	14
5.	Kari Lehtonen	Atlanta, Dallas	295	219	64	568	612	13
6.	Cam Ward	Carolina	295	230	80	605	625	12
7.	Carey Price	Montreal	270	175	55	500	509	10
8.	Pekka Rinne	Nashville	269	155	62	486	508	11
9.	Jonathan Quick	Los Angeles	260	167	53	470	492	10
10.	Craig Anderson	Chi., Fla., Col., Ott.	238	182	57	477	506	14
11.	Antti Niemi	Chi., S.J., Dal.	227	125	51	403	423	9

Active Shutout Leaders

(Minimum 30 Shutouts)

	Goaltender	Teams	Shutouts	Games	Seasons
1.	Roberto Luongo	NY Islanders, Florida, Vancouver	73	966	17
2.	Henrik Lundqvist	NY Rangers	61	742	12
3.	Jonathan Quick	Los Angeles	44	492	10
4.	Marc-Andre Fleury	Pittsburgh	44	691	13
5.	Pekka Rinne	Nashville	43	508	11
6.	Jaroslav Halak	Mtl., St.L., Wsh., NYI	41	395	11
7.	Carey Price	Montreal	39	509	10
8.	Ryan Miller	Buffalo, St. Louis, Vancouver	39	709	14
9.	Tuuka Rask	Boston	38	395	10
10.	Craig Anderson	Chi., Fla., Col., Ott.	38	506	14
11.	Kari Lehtonen	Atlanta, Dallas	37	612	13
12.	Antii Niemi	Chicago, San Jose, Dallas	35	423	9
13.	Brian Elliott	Ott., Col., St. L., Cgy.	36	372	10
14.	Steve Mason	Columbus, Philadelphia	33	463	9
15.	Mike Smith	Dal., T.B., Phx., Ari.	33	474	11
16.	Braden Holtby	Washington	32	307	7

Goals-Against Average Leaders (Minimum 25 games played)

(Exceptions: Minimum 13 games played, 1994-95, 2012-13; minimum 26 games played, 1992-93, 1993-94; minimum 15 games played, 1917-18 to 1925-26)

Season	Goaltender, Team	AVG.	GA	Mins.	GP	SO	Season	Goaltender, Team	AVG.	GA	Mins.	GP	SO
2016-17	Sergei Bobrovsky, Columbus	2.06	127	3,707	63	7	1965-66	Johnny Bower, Toronto	2.25	75	1,998	35	3
2015-16	Ben Bishop, Tampa Bay	2.06	123	3,585	61	6	1964-65	Johnny Bower, Toronto	2.38	81	2,040	34	3
2014-15	Carey Price, Montreal	1.96	130	3,977	66	9	1963-64	Johnny Bower, Toronto	2.11	106	3,009	51	5
2013-14	Josh Harding, Minnesota	1.65	46	1,668	29	3	1962-63	Don Simmons, Toronto	2.46	69	1,680	28	1
2012-13	Craig Anderson, Ottawa	1.69	40	1,421	24	3	1961-62	Jacques Plante, Montreal	2.37	166	4,200	70	4
2011-12	Brian Elliott, St. Louis	1.56	58	2,235	38	9	1960-61	Charlie Hodge, Montreal	2.47	74	1,800	30	4
2010-11	Tim Thomas, Boston	2.00	112	3,634	57	9	1959-60	Jacques Plante, Montreal	2.54	175	4,140	69	3
2009-10	Tuukka Rask, Boston	1.97	84	2,562	45	5	1958-59	Jacques Plante, Montreal	2.16	144	4,000	67	9
2008-09	Tim Thomas, Boston	2.10	114	3,259	54	5	1957-58	Jacques Plante, Montreal	2.11	119	3,386	57	9
2007-08	Chris Osgood, Detroit	2.09	84	2,409	43	4	1956-57	Jacques Plante, Montreal	2.00	122	3,660	61	9
2006-07	Niklas Backstrom, Minnesota	1.97	73	2,227	41	5	1955-56	Jacques Plante, Montreal	1.86	119	3,840	64	7
2005-06	Miikka Kiprusoff, Calgary	2.07	151	4,380	74	10	1954-55	Harry Lumley, Toronto	1.94	134	4,140	69	8
2003-04	Miikka Kiprusoff, Calgary	1.69	65	2,301	38	4	1953-54	Harry Lumley, Toronto	1.86	128	4,140	69	13
2002-03	Marty Turco, Dallas	1.72	92	3,203	55	7	1952-53	Terry Sawchuk, Detroit	1.90	120	3,780	63	9
2001-02	Patrick Roy, Colorado	1.94	122	3,773	63	9	1951-52	Terry Sawchuk, Detroit	1.90	133	4,200	70	12
2000-01	Marty Turco, Dallas	1.90	40	1,266	26	3	1950-51	Al Rollins, Toronto	1.77	70	2,367	40	5
99-2000	Brian Boucher, Philadelphia	1.91	65	2,038	35	4	1949-50	Bill Durnan, Montreal	2.20	141	3,840	64	8
1998-99	Ron Tugnutt, Ottawa	1.79	75	2,508	43	3	1948-49	Bill Durnan, Montreal	2.10	126	3,600	60	10
1997-98	Ed Belfour, Dallas	1.88	112	3,581	61	9	1947-48	Turk Broda, Toronto	2.38	143	3,600	60	5
1996-97	Martin Brodeur, New Jersey	1.88	120	3,838	67	10	1946-47	Bill Durnan, Montreal	2.30	138	3,600	60	4
1995-96	Ron Hextall, Philadelphia	2.17	112	3,102	53	4	1945-46	Bill Durnan, Montreal	2.60	104	2,400	40	4
1994-95	Dominik Hasek, Buffalo	2.11	85	2,416	41	5	1944-45	Bill Durnan, Montreal	2.42	121	3,000	50	1
1993-94	Dominik Hasek, Buffalo	1.95	109	3,358	58	7	1943-44	Bill Durnan, Montreal	2.18	109	3,000	50	2
1992-93	Felix Potvin, Toronto	2.50	116	2,781	48	2	1942-43	Johnny Mowers, Detroit	2.47	124	3,010	50	6
1991-92	Patrick Roy, Montreal	2.36	155	3,935	67	5	1941-42	Frank Brimsek, Boston	2.35	115	2,930	47	3
1990-91	Ed Belfour, Chicago	2.47	170	4,127	74	4	1940-41	Turk Broda, Toronto	2.00	99	2,970	48	5
1989-90	Mike Liut, Hartford, Washington	2.53	91	2,161	37	4	1939-40	Dave Kerr, NY Rangers	1.54	77	3,000	48	8
1988-89	Patrick Roy, Montreal	2.47	113	2,744	48	4	1938-39	Frank Brimsek, Boston	1.56	68	2,610	43	10
1987-88	Pete Peeters, Washington	2.78	88	1,896	35	2	1937-38	Tiny Thompson, Boston	1.80	89	2,970	48	7
1986-87	Brian Hayward, Montreal	2.81	102	2,178	37	1	1936-37	Normie Smith, Detroit	2.05	102	2,980	48	6
1985-86	Bob Froese, Philadelphia	2.55	116	2,728	51	5	1935-36	Tiny Thompson, Boston	1.68	82	2,930	48	10
1984-85	Tom Barrasso, Buffalo	2.66	144	3,248	54	5	1934-35	Lorne Chabot, Chicago	1.80	88	2,940	48	8
1983-84	Pat Riggin, Washington	2.66	102	2,299	41	4	1933-34	Wilf Cude, Detroit, Montreal	1.47	47	1,920	30	5
1982-83	Pete Peeters, Boston	2.36	142	3,611	62	8	1932-33	Tiny Thompson, Boston	1.76	88	3,000	48	11
1981-82	Denis Herron, Montreal	2.64	68	1,547	27	3	1931-32	Charlie Gardiner, Chicago	1.85	92	2,989	48	4
1980-81	Richard Sevigny, Montreal	2.40	71	1,777	33	2	1930-31	Roy Worters, NY Americans	1.61	74	2,760	44	8
1979-80	Bob Sauve, Buffalo	2.36	74	1,880	32	4	1929-30	Tiny Thompson, Boston	2.19	98	2,680	44	3
1978-79	Ken Dryden, Montreal	2.30	108	2,814	47	5	1928-29	George Hainsworth, Montreal	0.92	43	2,800	44	22
1977-78	Ken Dryden, Montreal	2.05	105	3,071	52	5	1927-28	George Hainsworth, Montreal	1.05	48	2,730	44	13
1976-77	Michel Larocque, Montreal	2.09	53	1,525	26	4	1926-27	Clint Benedict, Mtl. Maroons	1.42	65	2,748	43	13
1975-76	Ken Dryden, Montreal	2.03	121	3,580	62	8	1925-26	Alec Connell, Ottawa	1.12	42	2,251	36	15
1974-75	Bernie Parent, Philadelphia	2.03	137	4,041	68	12	1924-25	Georges Vezina, Montreal	1.81	56	1,860	30	5
1973-74	Bernie Parent, Philadelphia	1.89	136	4,314	73	12	1923-24	Georges Vezina, Montreal	1.97	48	1,459	24	3
1972-73	Ken Dryden, Montreal	2.26	119	3,165	54	6	1922-23	Clint Benedict, Ottawa	2.18	54	1,478	24	4
1971-72	Tony Esposito, Chicago	1.77	82	2,780	48	9	1921-22	Clint Benedict, Ottawa	3.34	84	1,508	24	2
1970-71	Jacques Plante, Toronto	1.88	73	2,329	40	4	1920-21	Clint Benedict, Ottawa	3.09	75	1,457	24	2
1969-70	Ernie Wakely, St. Louis	2.11	58	1,651	30	4	1919-20	Clint Benedict, Ottawa	2.66	64	1,444	24	5
1968-69	Jacques Plante, St. Louis	1.96	70	2,139	37	5	1918-19	Clint Benedict, Ottawa	2.86	53	1,113	18	2
1967-68	Gump Worsley, Montreal	1.98	73	2,213	40	6	1917-18	Georges Vezina, Montreal	3.93	84	1,282	21	1
1966-67	Glenn Hall, Chicago	2.38	66	1,664	32	2							

All-Time Regular-Season NHL Coaching Register

Regular Season, 1917-2017

Coach	Team	Games Coached	Wins	Losses	O/T	Years	Cup Wins	Career
Abel, Sid	Chicago	140	39	79	22	2		
	Detroit	811	340	339	132	12		
	St. Louis	10	3	6	1	1		
	Kansas City	3	0	3	0	1		
	Totals	964	382	427	155	16		1952-76
Adams, Jack	Detroit	964	413	390	161	20	3	1927-47
Agnew, Gary	Columbus	5	0	4	1	1		2006-07
Allen, Keith	Philadelphia	150	51	67	32	2		1967-69
Allison, Dave	Ottawa	25	2	22	1	1		1995-96
Anderson, Jim	Washington	54	4	45	5	1		1974-75
Anderson, John	Atlanta	164	70	75	19	2		2008-10
Angotti, Lou	St. Louis	32	6	20	6	2		
	Pittsburgh	80	16	58	6	1		
	Totals	112	22	78	12	3		1973-84
Arbour, Al	St. Louis	107	42	40	25	3		
	NY Islanders	1500	740	537	223	20	4	
	Totals	1607	782	577	248	23	4	1970-08
Armstrong, George	Toronto	47	17	26	4	1		1988-89
Arniel, Scott	Columbus	123	45	60	18	2		2010-12
Babcock, Mike	Anaheim	164	69	62	33	3		
	Detroit	786	458	223	105	10	1	
	Toronto	164	69	69	26	2		
	Totals	1114	596	354	164	15	1	2002-17
Barber, Bill	Philadelphia	136	73	40	23	2		2000-02
Barkley, Doug	Detroit	77	20	46	11	3		1970-76
Beaulieu, Andre	Minnesota	32	6	23	3	1		1977-78
Bednar, Jared	Colorado	82	22	56	4	1		2016-17
Belisle, Danny	Washington	96	28	51	17	2		1978-80
Berenson, Red	St. Louis	204	100	72	32	3		1979-82
Bergeron, Michel	Quebec	634	265	283	86	8		
	NY Rangers	158	73	67	18	2		
	Totals	792	338	350	104	10		1980-90
Berry, Bob	Los Angeles	240	107	94	39	3		
	Montreal	223	116	71	36	3		
	Pittsburgh	240	88	127	25	3		
	St. Louis	157	73	63	21	2		
	Totals	860	384	355	121	11		1978-94
Berube, Craig	Philadelphia	161	75	58	28	2		2013-15
Beverley, Nick	Toronto	17	9	6	2	1		1995-96
Blackburn, Don	Hartford	140	42	63	35	2		1979-81
Blair, Wren	Minnesota	147	48	65	34	3		1967-70
Blake, Toe	Montreal	914	500	255	159	13	8	1955-68
Blashill, Jeff	Detroit	164	74	66	24	2		2015-17
Boileau, Marc	Pittsburgh	151	66	61	24	3		1973-76
Boivin, Leo	St. Louis	97	28	53	16	2		1975-78
Boucher, Frank	NY Rangers	527	181	263	83	11	1	1939-54
Boucher, George	Mtl. Maroons	12	6	5	1	1		
	Ottawa	48	13	29	6	1		
	St. Louis	35	9	20	6	1		
	Boston	70	22	32	16	1		
	Totals	165	50	86	29	4		1930-50
Boucher, Guy	Tampa Bay	195	97	78	20	3		
	Ottawa	82	44	28	10	1		
	Totals	277	141	106	30	4		2010-17
Boudreau, Bruce	Washington	329	201	88	40	5		
	Anaheim	352	208	104	40	5		
	Minnesota	82	49	25	8	1		
	Totals	763	458	217	88	10		2007-17
Bowman, Scotty	St. Louis	238	110	83	45	4		
	Montreal	634	419	110	105	8	5	
	Buffalo	404	210	134	60	7		
	Pittsburgh	164	95	53	16	2	1	
	Detroit	701	410	193	98	9	3	
	Totals	2141	1244	573	324	30	9	1967-02
Bowness, Rick	Winnipeg	28	8	17	3	1		
	Boston	80	36	32	12	1		
	Ottawa	235	39	178	18	4		
	NY Islanders	100	38	50	12	2		
	Phoenix	20	2	12	6	2		
	Totals	463	123	289	51	10		1988-05
Brooks, Herb	NY Rangers	285	131	113	41	4		
	Minnesota	80	19	48	13	1		
	New Jersey	84	40	37	7	1		
	Pittsburgh	57	29	21	7	1		
	Totals	506	219	219	68	7		1981-00
Brophy, John	Toronto	193	64	111	18	3		1986-89
Burnett, George	Edmonton	35	12	20	3	1		1994-95
Burns, Charlie	Minnesota	86	22	50	14	2		1969-75
Burns, Pat	Montreal	320	174	104	42	4		
	Toronto	281	133	107	41	4		
	Boston	254	105	97	52	4		
	New Jersey	164	89	45	30	3	1	
	Totals	1019	501	353	165	15	1	1988-05
Bush, Eddie	Kansas City	32	1	23	8	1		1975-76
Bylsma, Dan	Pittsburgh	401	252	117	32	6	1	
	Buffalo	164	68	73	23	2		
	Totals	565	320	190	55	8	1	2008-17
Cameron, Dave	Ottawa	137	70	50	17	2		2014-16
Campbell, Colin	NY Rangers	269	118	108	43	4		1994-98
Capuano, Jack	NY Islanders	483	227	192	64	7		2010-17
Carbonneau, Guy	Montreal	230	124	83	23	3		2006-09

Coach	Team	Games Coached	Wins	Losses	O/T	Years	Cup Wins	Career
Carlyle, Randy	Anaheim	598	319	205	74	8	1	
	Toronto	188	91	78	19	4		
	Totals	786	410	283	93	11	1	2005-17
Carpenter, Doug	New Jersey	290	100	166	24	4		
	Toronto	91	39	47	5	2		
	Totals	381	139	213	29	6		1984-91
Carroll, Dick	Toronto	40	18	22	0	2	1	1917-19
Carroll, Frank	Toronto	24	15	9	0	1		1920-21
Cashman, Wayne	Philadelphia	61	32	20	9	1		1997-98
Cassidy, Bruce	Washington	110	47	47	16	2		
	Boston	27	18	8	1	1		
	Totals	137	65	55	17	3		2002-17
Chambers, Dave	Quebec	98	19	64	15	2		1990-92
Chapman, Art	NY Americans	48	8	29	11	1		
	Brooklyn	48	16	29	3	1		
	Totals	96	24	58	14	2		1940-42
Charron, Guy	Calgary	16	6	7	3	1		
	Anaheim	49	14	26	9	1		
	Totals	65	20	33	12	2		1991-01
Cheevers, Gerry	Boston	376	204	126	46	5		1980-85
Cherry, Don	Boston	400	231	105	64	5		
	Colorado	80	19	48	13	1		
	Totals	480	250	153	77	6		1974-80
Clancy, King	Mtl. Maroons	18	6	11	1	1		
	Toronto	210	80	81	49	3		
	Totals	228	86	92	50	4		1937-56
Clapper, Dit	Boston	230	102	88	40	4		1945-49
Cleghorn, Odie	Pittsburgh	168	62	86	20	4		1925-29
Cleghorn, Sprague	Mtl. Maroons	48	19	22	7	1		1931-32
Clouston, Cory	Ottawa	198	95	83	20	3		2008-11
Colville, Neil	NY Rangers	93	26	41	26	2		1950-52
Conacher, Charlie	Chicago	162	56	84	22	3		1947-50
Conacher, Lionel	NY Americans	44	14	25	5	1		1929-30
Constantine, Kevin	San Jose	157	55	78	24	3		
	Pittsburgh	189	86	64	39	3		
	New Jersey	31	20	8	3	1		
	Totals	377	161	150	66	7		1993-02
Cook, Bill	NY Rangers	117	34	59	24	2		1951-53
Cooper, Jon	Tampa Bay *	343	188	120	35	5		2012-17

* Hired by Tampa Bay on March 25, 2013 but did not appear behind the bench until March 29. Assistant coaches Dan Lacroix, Martin Raymond, and Steve Thomas worked a 3-2 loss at Winnipeg on March 24. Lacroix and Thomas worked a 2-1 win vs. Buffalo on March 26.

Coach	Team	Games Coached	Wins	Losses	O/T	Years	Cup Wins	Career
Crawford, Marc	Quebec	48	30	13	5	1		
	Colorado	246	135	75	36	3	1	
	Vancouver	529	246	189	94	8		
	Los Angeles	164	59	84	21	2		
	Dallas	164	79	60	25	2		
	Totals	1151	549	421	181	16	1	1994-11
Creamer, Pierre	Pittsburgh	80	36	35	9	1		1987-88
Creighton, Fred	Atlanta	348	156	136	56	5		
	Boston	73	40	20	13	1		
	Totals	421	196	156	69	6		1974-80
Crisp, Terry	Calgary	240	144	63	33	3	1	
	Tampa Bay	391	142	204	45	6		
	Totals	631	286	267	78	9	1	1987-98
Crozier, Joe	Buffalo	192	77	80	35	3		
	Toronto	40	13	22	5	1		
	Totals	232	90	102	40	4		1971-81
Crozier, Roger	Washington	1	0	1	0	1		1981-82
Cunneyworth, Randy	Montreal	50	18	23	9	1		2011-12
Cunniff, John	Hartford	13	3	9	1	1		
	New Jersey	133	59	56	18	2		
	Totals	146	62	65	19	3		1982-91
Curry, Alex	Ottawa	36	24	8	4	1		1925-26
Dandurand, Leo	Montreal	163	78	76	9	6	1	1921-35
Day, Hap	Toronto	546	259	206	81	10	5	1940-50
Dea, Billy	Detroit	11	3	8	0	1		1981-82
DeBoer, Peter	Florida	246	103	107	36	3		
	New Jersey	248	114	93	41	4		
	San Jose	164	92	59	13	2		
	Totals	658	309	259	90	9		2008-17
Delvecchio, Alex	Detroit	245	82	131	32	4		1973-77
Demers, Jacques	Quebec	80	25	44	11	1		
	St. Louis	240	106	106	28	3		
	Detroit	320	137	136	47	4		
	Montreal	220	107	86	27	4	1	
	Tampa Bay	147	34	96	17	2		
	Totals	1007	409	468	130	14	1	1979-99
Denneny, Cy	Ottawa	48	11	27	10	1		1932-33
Desjardins, Willie	Vancouver	246	109	110	27	3		2014-17
Dineen, Bill	Philadelphia	140	60	60	20	2		1991-93
Dineen, Kevin	Florida	146	56	62	28	3		2011-14
Dudley, Rick	Buffalo	188	85	72	31	3		
	Florida	40	13	15	12	1		
	Totals	228	98	87	43	4		1989-04
Duff, Dick	Toronto	2	0	2	0	1		1979-80
Dugal, Jules	Montreal	18	9	6	3	1		1938-39
Duncan, Art	Detroit	33	10	21	2	1		
	Toronto	47	21	16	10	2		
	Totals	80	31	37	12	3		1926-32
Dutton, Red	NY Americans	192	66	97	29	4		1936-40
Eakins, Dallas	Edmonton	113	36	63	14	2		2013-15
Eddolls, Frank	Chicago	70	13	40	17	1		1954-55
Esposito, Phil	NY Rangers	45	24	21	0	2		1986-89
Evans, Jack	California	80	27	42	11	1		
	Cleveland	160	47	87	26	2		
	Hartford	374	163	174	37	5		
	Totals	614	237	303	74	8		1975-88

Coach	Team	Games Coached	Wins	Losses	O/T	Years	Cup Wins	Career
Ferguson, John	NY Rangers	121	43	59	19	2		
	Winnipeg	14	7	6	1	1		
	Totals	135	50	65	20	3		1975-86
Filion, Maurice	Quebec	6	1	3	2	1		1980-81
Francis, Bob	Phoenix	390	165	144	81	5		1999-04
Francis, Emile	NY Rangers	654	342	209	103	10		
	St. Louis	124	46	64	14	3		
	Totals	778	388	273	117	13		1965-83
Fraser, Curt	Atlanta	279	64	169	46	4		1999-03
Fredrickson, Frank	Pittsburgh	44	5	36	3	1		1929-30
Ftorek, Robbie	Los Angeles	132	65	56	11	2		
	New Jersey	156	88	44	24	2		
	Boston	155	76	52	27	2		
	Totals	443	229	152	62	6		1987-03
Gadsby, Bill	Detroit	78	35	31	12	2		1968-70
Gainey, Bob	Minnesota	244	95	119	30	3		
	Dallas	171	70	71	30	3		
	Montreal	57	29	21	7	2		
	Totals	472	194	211	67	8		1990-09
Gallant, Gerard	Columbus	142	56	76	10	4		
	Florida	186	96	65	25	3		
	Totals	328	152	141	35	7		2003-17
Gardiner, Herb	Chicago	32	5	23	4	1		1928-29
Gardner, Jimmy	Hamilton	30	19	10	1	1		1924-25
Garvin, Ted	Detroit	11	2	8	1	1		1973-74
Geoffrion, Bernie	NY Rangers	43	22	18	3	1		
	Atlanta	208	77	92	39	3		
	Montreal	30	15	9	6	1		
	Totals	281	114	119	48	5		1968-80
Gerard, Eddie	Ottawa	22	9	13	0	1		
	Mtl. Maroons	294	129	122	43	7	1	
	NY Americans	92	34	40	18	2		
	St. Louis	13	2	11	0	1		
	Totals	421	174	186	61	11	1	1917-35
Gilbert, Greg	Calgary	121	42	56	23	2		2000-03
Gill, David	Ottawa	132	64	41	27	3	1	1926-29
Glover, Fred	Oakland	152	51	76	25	2		
	California	204	45	131	28	4		
	Los Angeles	68	18	42	8	1		
	Totals	424	114	249	61	6		1968-74
Goodfellow, Ebbie	Chicago	140	30	91	19	2		1950-52
Gordon, Jackie	Minnesota	289	116	123	50	5		1970-75
Gordon, Scott	NY Islanders	181	64	94	23	3		2008-11
Goring, Butch	Boston	93	42	38	13	2		
	NY Islanders	147	41	88	18	2		
	Totals	240	83	126	31	4		1985-01
Gorman, Tommy	NY Americans	80	31	33	16	2	1	
	Chicago	73	28	28	17	2	1	
	Mtl. Maroons	174	74	71	29	4	1	
	Totals	327	133	132	62	8	2	1925-38
Gottselig, Johnny	Chicago	146	53	79	14	4		1944-48
Goyette, Phil	NY Islanders	50	6	40	4	1		1972-73
Graham, Dirk	Chicago	59	16	35	8	1		1998-99
Granato, Tony	Colorado	215	104	78	33	3		2002-09
Green, Gary	Washington	157	50	78	29	3		1979-82
Green, Pete	Ottawa	150	94	52	4	6	3	1919-25
Green, Shorty	NY Americans	44	11	27	6	1		1927-28
Green, Ted	Edmonton	188	65	102	21	3		1991-94
Gretzky, Wayne	Phoenix	328	143	161	24	4		2005-09
Guidolin, Aldo	Colorado	59	12	39	8	1		1978-79
Guidolin, Bep	Boston	104	72	23	9	2		
	Kansas City	125	26	84	15	2		
	Totals	229	98	107	24	4		1972-76
Gulutzan, Glen	Dallas	130	64	57	9	2		
	Calgary	82	45	33	4	1		
	Totals	212	109	90	13	3		2011-17
Hakstol, Dave	Philadelphia	164	80	60	24	2		2015-17
Hanlon, Glen	Washington	239	78	122	39	5		2003-08
Harkness, Ned	Detroit	38	12	22	4	1		1970-71
Harris, Ted	Minnesota	179	48	104	27	3		1975-78
Hart, Cecil	Montreal	394	196	125	73	9	2	1926-39
Hartley, Bob	Colorado	359	193	108	58	5	1	
	Atlanta	291	136	118	37	6		
	Calgary	294	134	135	25	4		
	Totals	944	463	361	120	14	1	1998-16
Hartsburg, Craig	Chicago	246	104	102	40	3		
	Anaheim	197	80	82	35	3		
	Ottawa	48	17	24	7	1		
	Totals	491	201	208	82	7		1995-09
Harvey, Doug	NY Rangers	70	26	32	12	1		1961-62
Hay, Don	Phoenix	82	38	37	7	1		
	Calgary	68	23	28	17	1		
	Totals	150	61	65	24	2		1996-01
Heffernan, Frank	Toronto	12	5	7	0	1		1919-20
Helmer, Rosie	NY Americans	48	16	25	7	1		1935-36
Henning, Lorne	Minnesota	158	68	72	18	2		
	NY Islanders	65	19	39	7	2		
	Totals	223	87	111	25	4		1985-01
Hitchcock, Ken	Dallas	503	277	154	72	7	1	
	Philadelphia	254	131	73	50	5		
	Columbus	284	125	123	36	4		
	St. Louis	413	248	124	41	6		
	Totals	1454	781	474	199	21	1	1995-17
Hlinka, Ivan	Pittsburgh	86	42	32	12	2		2000-02
Holmgren, Paul	Philadelphia	264	107	126	31	4		
	Hartford	161	54	93	14	4		
	Totals	425	161	219	45	8		1988-96
Horachek, Peter	Florida	66	26	36	4	1		
	Toronto	42	9	28	5	1		
	Totals	108	35	64	9	2		2013-15
Howell, Harry	Minnesota	11	3	6	2	1		1978-79
Hunter, Dale	Washington	60	30	23	7	1		2011-12
Hynes, John	New Jersey	164	66	76	22	2		2015-17
Imlach, Punch	Toronto	770	370	275	125	12	4	
	Buffalo	119	32	62	25	2		
	Totals	889	402	337	150	14	4	1958-80
Ingarfield, Earl	NY Islanders	28	6	20	2	1		1972-73
Inglis, Bill	Buffalo	56	28	18	10	1		1978-79
Irvin, Dick	Chicago	126	45	62	19	3		
	Toronto	426	215	152	59	9	1	
	Montreal	896	431	313	152	15	3	
	Totals	1448	691	527	230	27	4	1928-56
Ivan, Tommy	Detroit	470	262	118	90	7	3	
	Chicago	103	26	56	21	2		
	Totals	573	288	174	111	9	3	1947-58
Iverson, Emil	Chicago	71	26	28	17	2		1931-33
Johnson, Bob	Calgary	400	193	155	52	5		
	Pittsburgh	80	41	33	6	1	1	
	Totals	480	234	188	58	6	1	1982-91
Johnson, Tom	Boston	208	142	43	23	3	1	1970-73
Johnston, Eddie	Chicago	80	34	27	19	1		
	Pittsburgh	516	232	224	60	7		
	Totals	596	266	251	79	8		1979-97
Johnston, Marshall	California	69	13	45	11	2		
	Colorado	56	15	32	9	1		
	Totals	125	28	77	20	3		1973-82
Johnston, Mike	Pittsburgh	110	58	37	15	2		2014-16
Julien, Claude	Montreal	183	88	69	26	5		
	New Jersey	79	47	24	8	1		
	Boston	759	419	246	94	10	1	
	Totals	1021	554	339	128	15	1	2002-17
Kasper, Steve	Boston	164	66	78	20	2		1995-97
Keats, Duke	Detroit	11	2	7	2	1		1926-27
Keenan, Mike	Philadelphia	320	190	102	28	4		
	Chicago	320	153	126	41	4		
	NY Rangers	84	52	24	8	1	1	
	St. Louis	163	75	66	22	3		
	Vancouver	108	36	54	18	2		
	Boston	74	33	26	15	1		
	Florida	153	45	73	35	3		
	Calgary	164	88	60	16	2		
	Totals	1386	672	531	183	20	1	1984-09
Kehoe, Rick	Pittsburgh	160	55	81	22	2		2001-03
Kelly, Pat	Colorado	101	22	54	25	2		1977-79
Kelly, Red	Los Angeles	150	55	75	20	2		
	Pittsburgh	274	90	132	52	4		
	Toronto	318	133	123	62	4		
	Totals	742	278	330	134	10		1967-77
King, Dave	Calgary	216	109	76	31	3		
	Columbus	204	64	106	34	3		
	Totals	420	173	182	65	6		1992-03
Kingston, George	San Jose	164	28	129	7	2		1991-93
Kish, Larry	Hartford	49	12	32	5	1		1982-83
Kitchen, Mike	St. Louis	131	38	70	23	4		2003-07
Kromm, Bobby	Detroit	231	79	111	41	3		1977-80
Krueger, Ralph	Edmonton	48	19	22	7	1		2012-13
Kurtenbach, Orland	Vancouver	125	36	62	27	2		1976-78
Laflamme, Jerry	Mtl. Maroons	44	23	16	5	1		1929-30
LaForge, Bill	Vancouver	20	4	14	2	1		1984-85
Lalonde, Newsy	Montreal	207	96	97	14	8		
	NY Americans	44	17	25	2	1		
	Ottawa	88	31	45	12	2		
	Totals	339	144	167	28	11		1917-35
Lamoriello, Lou	New Jersey *	53	34	14	5	2		2005-15

* Shared a record of 20-19-7 with co-coaches Adam Oates and Scott Stevens for New Jersey over the final 46 games of the 2014-15 season. Games are not officially attributed to anyone's coaching record.

Coach	Team	Games Coached	Wins	Losses	O/T	Years	Cup Wins	Career
Laperriere, Jacques	Montreal	1	0	1	0	1		1995-96
Lapointe, Ron	Quebec	89	33	50	6	2		1987-89
Laviolette, Peter	NY Islanders	164	77	62	25	2		
	Carolina	323	167	122	34	6	1	
	Philadelphia	272	145	98	29	5		
	Nashville	246	129	81	36	3		
	Totals	1005	518	363	124	16	1	2001-17
Laycoe, Hal	Los Angeles	24	5	18	1	1		
	Vancouver	156	44	96	16	2		
	Totals	180	49	114	17	3		1969-72
Lehman, Hugh	Chicago	21	3	17	1	1		1927-28
Lemaire, Jacques	Montreal	97	48	37	12	2		
	New Jersey	509	276	166	67	7	1	
	Minnesota	656	293	255	108	9		
	Totals	1262	617	458	187	18	1	1983-11
Lepine, Pit	Montreal	48	10	33	5	1		1939-40
LeSueur, Percy	Hamilton	10	3	7	0	1		1923-24
Lewis, Dave	Detroit *	169	100	42	27	4		
	Boston	82	35	41	6	1		
	Totals	251	135	83	33	5		1998-07

* Shared a record of 4-1-0 with co-coach Barry Smith in 1998-99. Games are attributed to both coach's records.

Coach	Team	Games Coached	Wins	Losses	O/T	Years	Cup Wins	Career
Ley, Rick	Hartford	160	69	71	20	2		
	Vancouver	124	47	50	27	2		
	Totals	284	116	121	47	4		1989-96
Lindsay, Ted	Detroit	29	5	21	3	2		1979-81
Long, Barry	Winnipeg	205	87	93	25	3		1983-86
Loughlin, Clem	Chicago	144	61	63	20	3		1934-37
Low, Ron	Edmonton	341	139	162	40	5		
	NY Rangers	164	69	81	14	2		
	Totals	505	208	243	54	7		1994-02
Lowe, Kevin	Edmonton	82	32	26	24	1		1999-00

Coach	Team	Games Coached	Wins	Losses	O/T	Years	Cup Wins	Career
Ludzik, Steve	**Tampa Bay**	121	31	67	23	2		1999-01
MacDonald, Parker	Minnesota	61	20	30	11	1		
	Los Angeles	42	13	24	5	1		
	Totals	103	33	54	16	2		1973-82
MacLean, Doug	Florida	187	83	71	33	3		
	Columbus	79	24	43	12	2		
	Totals	266	107	114	45	5		1995-04
MacLean, John	**New Jersey**	33	9	22	2	1		2010-11
MacLean, Paul	**Ottawa**	239	114	90	35	4		2011-15
MacMillan, Bill	Colorado	80	22	45	13	1		
	New Jersey	100	19	67	14	2		
	Totals	180	41	112	27	3		1980-84
MacNeil, Al	Montreal	55	31	15	9	1	1	
	Atlanta	80	35	32	13	1		
	Calgary	171	72	66	33	3		
	Totals	306	138	113	55	5	1	1970-03
MacTavish, Craig	**Edmonton**	661	301	255	105	10		2000-15
Magnuson, Keith	**Chicago**	132	48	58	26	2		1980-82
Mahoney, Bill	**Minnesota**	93	42	39	12	2		1983-85
Maloney, Dan	Toronto	160	45	100	15	2		
	Winnipeg	212	91	93	28	3		
	Totals	372	136	193	43	5		1984-89
Maloney, Phil	**Vancouver**	232	95	105	32	4		1973-77
Mantha, Sylvio	**Montreal**	48	11	26	11	1		1935-36
Marshall, Bert	**Colorado**	24	3	17	4	1		1981-82
Martin, Jacques	St. Louis	160	66	71	23	2		
	Ottawa	692	341	235	116	9		
	Florida	246	110	100	36	4		
	Montreal	196	96	75	25	3		
	Totals	1294	613	481	200	18		1986-12
Maurice, Paul	Hartford	152	61	72	19	2		
	Carolina	768	323	319	126	11		
	Toronto	164	76	66	22	2		
	Winnipeg	281	136	112	33	4		
	Totals	1365	596	569	200	19		1995-17
Maxner, Wayne	**Detroit**	129	34	68	27	2		1980-82
McCammon, Bob	Philadelphia	218	119	68	31	4		
	Vancouver	294	102	156	36	4		
	Totals	512	221	224	67	8		1978-91
McCreary, Bill	St. Louis	24	6	14	4	1		
	Vancouver	41	9	25	7	1		
	California	32	8	20	4	1		
	Totals	97	23	59	15	3		1971-75
McGuire, Pierre	**Hartford**	67	23	37	7	1		1993-94
McLellan, John	**Toronto**	310	126	139	45	4		1969-73
McLellan, Todd	San Jose	540	311	163	66	7		
	Edmonton	164	78	69	17	2		
	Totals	704	389	232	83	9		2008-17
McVie, Tom	Washington	204	49	122	33	3		
	Winnipeg	105	20	67	18	2		
	New Jersey	153	57	74	22	3		
	Totals	462	126	263	73	8		1975-92
Meeker, Howie	**Toronto**	70	21	34	15	1		1956-57
Melrose, Barry	Los Angeles	209	79	101	29	3		
	Tampa Bay	16	5	7	4	1		
	Totals	225	84	108	33	4		1992-09
Milbury, Mike	Boston	160	90	49	21	2		
	NY Islanders	191	56	111	24	4		
	Totals	351	146	160	45	6		1989-99
Molleken, Lorne	**Chicago**	47	18	19	10	2		1998-00
Muckler, John	Minnesota	35	6	23	6	1		
	Edmonton	160	75	65	20	2	1	
	Buffalo	268	125	109	34	4		
	NY Rangers	185	70	88	27	3		
	Totals	648	276	285	87	10	1	1968-00
Muldoon, Pete	**Chicago**	44	19	22	3	1		1926-27
Muller, Kirk	**Carolina**	187	80	80	27	3		2011-14
Munro, Dunc	**Mtl. Maroons**	32	14	13	5	1		1930-31
Murdoch, Bob	Chicago	80	30	41	9	1		
	Winnipeg	160	63	75	22	2		
	Totals	240	93	116	31	3		1987-91
Murphy, Mike	Los Angeles	65	20	37	8	2		
	Toronto	164	60	87	17	2		
	Totals	229	80	124	25	4		1986-98
Murray, Andy	Los Angeles	480	215	176	89	7		
	St. Louis	258	118	102	38	4		
	Totals	738	333	278	127	11		1999-10
Murray, Bryan	Washington	672	343	246	83	9		
	Detroit	244	124	91	29	3		
	Florida	59	17	31	11	1		
	Anaheim	82	29	42	11	1		
	Ottawa	182	107	55	20	4		
	Totals	1239	620	465	154	18		1981-08
Murray, Terry	Washington	325	163	134	28	5		
	Philadelphia	212	118	64	30	3		
	Florida	200	79	79	42	3		
	Los Angeles	275	139	106	30	4		
	Totals	1012	499	383	130	15		1989-12
Nanne, Lou	**Minnesota**	29	7	18	4	1		1977-78
Neale, Harry	Vancouver	407	142	189	76	6		
	Detroit	35	8	23	4	1		
	Totals	442	150	212	80	7		1978-86

Coach	Team	Games Coached	Wins	Losses	O/T	Years	Cup Wins	Career
Neilson, Roger	Toronto	160	75	62	23	2		
	Buffalo	80	39	20	21	1		
	Vancouver	133	51	61	21	3		
	Los Angeles	28	8	17	3	1		
	NY Rangers	280	141	104	35	4		
	Florida	132	53	56	23	2		
	Philadelphia	185	92	57	36	3		
	Ottawa	2	1	1	0	1		
	Totals	1000	460	378	162	16		1977-02
Nelson, Todd	**Edmonton**	46	17	22	7	1		2014-15
Noel, Claude	Columbus	24	10	8	6	1		
	Winnipeg	177	80	79	18	3		
	Totals	201	90	87	24	4		2009-14
Nolan, Ted	Buffalo	308	113	159	36	4		
	NY Islanders	163	74	68	21	2		
	Totals	471	187	227	57	6		1995-15
Nykoluk, Mike	**Toronto**	280	89	144	47	4		1980-84
Oates, Adam	**Washington**	130	65	48	17	2		
	New Jersey *	....	....	....	....	0		
	Totals	130	65	48	17	3		2012-15

* Shared a record of 20-19-7 with co-coaches Lou Lamoriello and Scott Stevens for New Jersey over the final 46 games of the 2014-15 season. Games are not officially attributed to anyone's coaching record.

Coach	Team	Games Coached	Wins	Losses	O/T	Years	Cup Wins	Career
O'Connell, Mike	**Boston**	9	3	3	3	1		2002-03
O'Donoghue, George	**Toronto**	29	15	13	1	2	1	1921-23
Olczyk, Ed	**Pittsburgh**	113	31	64	18	3		2003-06
Oliver, Murray	**Minnesota**	37	18	12	7	1		1982-83
Olmstead, Bert	**Oakland** *	74	15	42	17	1		1967-68

* Olmstead, who was also GM, turned over bench duties to assistant coach Gord Fashoway for the last 22 games of the season. Fashoway posted a 5-11-6 record. All games are credited to Olmstead's coaching record.

Coach	Team	Games Coached	Wins	Losses	O/T	Years	Cup Wins	Career
O'Reilly, Terry	**Boston**	227	115	86	26	3		1986-89
Paddock, John	Winnipeg	281	106	138	37	4		
	Ottawa	64	36	22	6	1		
	Totals	345	142	160	43	5		1991-08
Page, Pierre	Minnesota	160	63	77	20	2		
	Quebec	230	98	103	29	3		
	Calgary	164	66	78	20	2		
	Anaheim	82	26	43	13	1		
	Totals	636	253	301	82	8		1988-98
Park, Brad	**Detroit**	45	9	34	2	1		1985-86
Paterson, Rick	**Tampa Bay**	6	0	6	0	1		1997-98
Patrick, Craig	NY Rangers	95	37	45	13	2		
	Pittsburgh	74	29	36	9	2		
	Totals	169	66	81	22	4		1980-97
Patrick, Frank	**Boston**	96	48	36	12	2		1934-36
Patrick, Lester	**NY Rangers**	604	281	216	107	13	2	1926-39
Patrick, Lynn	NY Rangers	107	40	51	16	2		
	Boston	310	117	130	63	5		
	St. Louis	26	8	15	3	3		
	Totals	443	165	196	82	10		1948-76
Patrick, Muzz	**NY Rangers**	136	43	66	27	4		1953-63
Payne, Davis	**St. Louis**	137	67	55	15	3		2009-12
Perron, Jean	Montreal	240	126	84	30	3	1	
	Quebec	47	16	26	5	1		
	Totals	287	142	110	35	4	1	1985-89
Perry, Don	**Los Angeles**	168	52	85	31	3		1981-84
Peters, Bill	**Carolina**	246	101	103	42	3		2014-15
Pike, Alf	**NY Rangers**	123	36	66	21	2		1959-61
Pilous, Rudy	**Chicago**	387	162	151	74	6	1	1957-63
Plager, Barclay	**St. Louis**	178	49	96	33	4		1977-83
Plager, Bob	**St. Louis**	11	4	6	1	1		1992-93
Playfair, Jim	**Calgary**	82	43	29	10	1		2006-07
Pleau, Larry	**Hartford**	224	81	117	26	5		1980-89
Polano, Nick	**Detroit**	240	79	127	34	3		1982-85
Popein, Larry	**NY Rangers**	41	18	14	9	1		1973-74
Powers, Eddie	**Toronto**	66	31	32	3	2		1924-26
Primeau, Joe	**Toronto**	210	97	71	42	3	1	1950-53
Pronovost, Marcel	**Buffalo**	104	52	29	23	2		1977-79
Pulford, Bob	Los Angeles	396	178	150	68	5		
	Chicago	433	186	179	68	7		
	Totals	829	364	329	136	12		1972-00
Quenneville, Joel	St. Louis	593	307	191	95	8		
	Colorado	246	131	92	23	4		
	Chicago	700	413	204	83	9	3	
	Totals	1539	851	487	201	21	3	1996-17
Querrie, Charles	**Toronto**	72	29	38	5	3		1922-27
Quinn, Mike	**Quebec**	24	4	20	0	1		1919-20
Quinn, Pat	Philadelphia	262	141	73	48	4		
	Los Angeles	202	75	101	26	3		
	Vancouver	280	141	111	28	5		
	Toronto	574	300	196	78	8		
	Edmonton	82	27	47	8	1		
	Totals	1400	684	528	188	21		1978-10
Raeder, Cap	**San Jose**	1	1	0	0	1		2002-03
Ramsay, Craig	Buffalo	21	4	15	2	1		
	Philadelphia	28	12	12	4	1		
	Atlanta	82	34	36	12	1		
	Totals	131	50	63	18	3		1986-10
Randall, Ken	**Hamilton**	14	6	8	0	1		1923-24
Reay, Billy	Toronto	90	26	50	14	2		
	Chicago	1012	516	335	161	14		
	Totals	1102	542	385	175	16		1957-77
Regan, Larry	**Los Angeles**	88	27	47	14	2		1970-72
Renney, Tom	Vancouver	101	39	53	9	2		
	NY Rangers	327	164	117	46	6		
	Edmonton	164	57	85	22	2		
	Totals	592	260	255	77	10		1996-12

Coach	Team	Games Coached	Wins	Losses	O/T	Years	Cup Wins	Career
Richards, Todd	Minnesota	164	77	71	16	2		
	Columbus	260	127	112	21	5		
	Totals	424	204	183	37	7		2009-16
Risebrough, Doug	Calgary	144	71	56	17	2		1990-92
Roberts, Jim	Buffalo	45	21	16	8	1		
	Hartford	80	26	41	13	1		
	St. Louis	9	3	3	3	1		
	Totals	134	50	60	24	3		1981-97
Robinson, Larry	Los Angeles	328	122	161	45	4		
	New Jersey	173	87	56	30	4	1	
	Totals	501	209	217	75	8	1	1995-06
Rodden, Mike	Toronto	2	0	2	0	1		1926-27
Rolston, Ron	Buffalo	51	19	26	6	2		2012-14
Romeril, Alex	Toronto	13	7	5	1	1		1926-27
Ross, Art	Mtl. Wanderers	6	1	5	0	1		
	Hamilton	24	6	18	0	1		
	Boston	772	387	290	95	17	2	
	Totals	802	394	313	95	19	2	1917-45
Rowe, Tom	Florida	60	24	26	10	1		2016-17
Roy, Patrick	Colorado	246	130	92	24	3		2013-16
Ruel, Claude	Montreal	305	172	82	51	5	1	1968-81
Ruff, Lindy	Buffalo	1165	571	432	162	16		
	Dallas	328	165	122	41	4		
	Totals	1493	736	554	203	20		1997-17
Sacco, Joe	Colorado	294	130	134	30	4		2009-13
Sather, Glen	Edmonton	842	464	268	110	11	4	
	NY Rangers	90	33	39	18	2		
	Totals	932	497	307	128	13	4	1979-04
Sator, Ted	NY Rangers	99	41	48	10	2		
	Buffalo	207	96	89	22	3		
	Totals	306	137	137	32	4		1985-89
Savard, Andre	Quebec	24	10	13	1	1		1987-88
Savard, Denis	Chicago	147	65	66	16	3		2006-09
Schinkel, Ken	Pittsburgh	203	83	92	28	4		1972-77
Schmidt, Milt	Boston	726	245	360	121	11		
	Washington	44	5	34	5	2		
	Totals	770	250	394	126	13		1954-76
Schoenfeld, Jim	Buffalo	43	19	19	5	1		
	New Jersey	124	50	59	15	3		
	Washington	249	113	102	34	4		
	Phoenix	164	74	66	24	2		
	Totals	580	256	246	78	10		1985-99
Shaughnessy, Tom	Chicago	23	12	8	3	1		1929-30
Shaw, Brad	NY Islanders	40	18	18	4	1		2005-06
Shero, Fred	Philadelphia	554	308	151	95	7	2	
	NY Rangers	180	82	74	24	3		
	Totals	734	390	225	119	10	2	1971-81
Simpson, Joe	NY Americans	144	42	72	30	3		1932-35
Simpson, Terry	NY Islanders	187	81	82	24	3		
	Philadelphia	84	35	39	10	1		
	Winnipeg	97	43	47	7	2		
	Totals	368	159	168	41	6		1986-96
Sims, Al	San Jose	82	27	47	8	1		1996-97
Sinden, Harry	Boston	327	153	116	58	6	1	1966-85
Skinner, Jimmy	Detroit	247	123	78	46	4	1	1954-58
Smeaton, Cooper	Philadelphia	44	4	36	4	1		1930-31
Smith, Alf	Ottawa	18	12	6	0	1		1918-19
Smith, Barry	Detroit *	5	4	1	0	1		1998-99

* Results Shared with co-coach Dave Lewis

Coach	Team	Games Coached	Wins	Losses	O/T	Years	Cup Wins	Career
Smith, Floyd	Buffalo	241	143	62	36	4		
	Toronto	68	30	33	5	1		
	Totals	309	173	95	41	5		1971-80
Smith, Mike	Winnipeg	23	2	17	4	1		1980-81
Smith, Ron	NY Rangers	44	15	22	7	1		1992-93
Smythe, Conn	Toronto	135	58	57	20	5		1927-32
Sonmor, Glen	Minnesota	421	177	161	83	7		1978-87
Sproule, Harvey	Toronto	12	7	5	0	1		1919-20
Stanley, Barney	Chicago	23	4	17	2	1		1927-28
Stasiuk, Vic	Philadelphia	154	45	68	41	2		
	California	75	21	38	16	1		
	Vancouver	78	22	47	9	1		
	Totals	307	88	153	66	4		1969-73
Stevens, John	Philadelphia	263	120	109	34	4		
	Los Angeles	4	2	2	0	1		
	Totals	267	122	111	34	5		2006-12
Stewart, Bill	NY Islanders	37	11	19	7	1		1998-99
Stewart, Bill	Chicago	69	22	35	12	2	1	1937-39
Stewart, Ron	NY Rangers	39	15	20	4	1		
	Los Angeles	80	31	34	15	1		
	Totals	119	46	54	19	2		1975-78
Stirling, Steve	NY Islanders	124	56	51	17	3		2003-06
Suhonen, Alpo	Chicago	82	29	41	12	1		2000-01
Sullivan, Mike	Boston	164	70	56	38	3		
	Pittsburgh	136	83	37	16	2	2	
	Totals	300	153	93	54	5	2	2003-17
Sullivan, Red	NY Rangers	196	58	103	35	4		
	Pittsburgh	150	47	79	24	2		
	Washington	18	2	16	0	1		
	Totals	364	107	198	59	7		1962-75
Sutherland, Bill	Winnipeg	32	7	22	3	2		1979-81
Sutter, Brent	New Jersey	164	97	56	11	2		
	Calgary	246	118	90	38	3		
	Totals	410	215	146	49	5		2007-12
Sutter, Brian	St. Louis	320	153	124	43	4		
	Boston	216	120	73	23	3		
	Calgary	246	87	117	42	3		
	Chicago	246	91	103	52	4		
	Totals	1028	451	417	160	14		1988-05
Sutter, Darryl	Chicago	216	110	80	26	3		
	San Jose	434	192	167	75	6		
	Calgary	210	107	73	30	4		
	Los Angeles	425	225	147	53	6	2	
	Totals	1285	634	467	184	18	2	1992-17
Sutter, Duane	Florida	72	22	35	15	2		2000-02
Talbot, Jean-Guy	St. Louis	120	52	53	15	2		
	NY Rangers	80	30	37	13	1		
	Totals	200	82	90	28	3		1972-78
Tessier, Orval	Chicago	213	99	93	21	3		1982-85
Therrien, Michel	Montreal	542	271	198	73	8		
	Pittsburgh	272	135	105	32	4		
	Totals	814	406	303	105	12		2000-17
Thompson, Paul	Chicago	313	113	153	47	7		1938-45
Thompson, Percy	Hamilton	48	13	35	0	2		1920-22
Tippett, Dave	Dallas	492	271	156	65	7		
	Phoenix	376	193	126	57	5		
	Arizona	246	89	131	26	3		
	Totals	1114	553	413	148	15		2002-17
Tobin, Bill	Chicago	21	9	10	2	1		1929-30
Tocchet, Rick	Tampa Bay	148	53	69	26	2		2008-10
Torchetti, John	Florida	27	10	12	5	1		
	Los Angeles	12	5	7	0	1		
	Minnesota	27	15	11	1	1		
	Totals	66	30	30	6	3		2003-16
Tortorella, John	NY Rangers	319	171	118	30	6		
	Tampa Bay	535	239	222	74	8	1	
	Vancouver	82	36	35	11	1		
	Columbus	157	84	57	16	2		
	Totals	1093	530	432	131	17	1	1999-17
Tremblay, Mario	Montreal	159	71	63	25	2		1995-97
Trottier, Bryan	NY Rangers	54	21	26	7	1		2002-03
Trotz, Barry	Nashville	1196	557	479	160	16		
	Washington	246	156	63	27	3		
	Totals	1442	713	542	187	19		1998-17
Ubriaco, Gene	Pittsburgh	106	50	47	9	2		1988-90
Vachon, Rogie	Los Angeles	10	4	3	3	3		1983-95
Vigneault, Alain	Montreal	266	109	118	39	4		
	Vancouver	540	313	170	57	7		
	NY Rangers	328	192	108	28	4		
	Totals	1134	614	396	124	15		1997-17
Waddell, Don	Atlanta	86	38	39	9	2		2002-08
Watson, Bryan	Edmonton	18	4	9	5	1		1980-81
Watson, Phil	NY Rangers	295	119	124	52	5		
	Boston	84	16	55	13	2		
	Totals	379	135	179	65	7		1955-63
Watt, Tom	Winnipeg	181	72	85	24	3		
	Vancouver	160	52	87	21	2		
	Toronto	149	52	80	17	2		
	Totals	490	176	252	62	7		1981-92
Webster, Tom	NY Rangers	18	5	9	4	1		
	Los Angeles	240	115	94	31	3		
	Totals	258	120	103	35	4		1986-92
Weight, Doug	NY Islanders	40	24	12	4	1		2016-17
Weiland, Cooney	Boston	96	58	20	18	2	1	1939-41
White, Bill	Chicago	46	16	24	6	1		1976-77
Wiley, Jim	San Jose	57	17	37	3	1		1995-96
Wilson, Johnny	Los Angeles	52	9	34	9	1		
	Detroit	145	67	56	22	2		
	Colorado	80	20	46	14	1		
	Pittsburgh	240	91	105	44	3		
	Totals	517	187	241	89	7		1969-80
Wilson, Larry	Detroit	36	3	29	4	1		1976-77
Wilson, Rick	Dallas	32	13	11	8	1		2001-02
Wilson, Ron	Anaheim	296	120	145	31	4		
	Washington	410	192	159	59	6		
	San Jose	385	206	122	57	6		
	Toronto	310	130	135	45	4		
	Totals	1401	648	561	192	19		1993-12
Yawney, Trent	Chicago	103	33	55	15	2		2005-07
Yeo, Mike	Minnesota	349	173	132	44	5		
	St. Louis	32	22	8	2	1		
	Totals	381	195	140	46	6		2011-17
Young, Garry	California	12	2	7	3	1		
	St. Louis	98	41	41	16	2		
	Totals	110	43	48	19	3		1972-76

Year-by-Year Individual Regular-Season Leaders

Season	Goals	G	Assists	A	Points	Pts.	Penalty Minutes	PIM
2016-17	Sidney Crosby	44	Connor McDavid	70	Connor McDavid	100	Mark Borowiecki	154
2015-16	Alex Ovechkin	50	Erik Karlsson	66	Patrick Kane	106	Derek Dorsett	177
2014-15	Alex Ovechkin	53	Nicklas Backstrom	60	Jamie Benn	87	Steve Downie	238
2013-14	Alex Ovechkin	51	Sidney Crosby	68	Sidney Crosby	104	Tom Sestito	213
2012-13	Alex Ovechkin	32	Martin St. Louis	43	Martin St. Louis	60	Colton Orr	155
2011-12	Steven Stamkos	60	Henrik Sedin	67	Evgeni Malkin	109	Derek Dorsett	235
2010-11	Corey Perry	50	Henrik Sedin	75	Daniel Sedin	104	Zenon Konopka	307
2009-10	Sidney Crosby, Steven Stamkos	51	Henrik Sedin	83	Henrik Sedin	112	Zenon Konopka	265
2008-09	Alex Ovechkin	56	Evgeni Malkin	78	Evgeni Malkin	113	Daniel Carcillo	254
2007-08	Alex Ovechkin	65	Joe Thornton	67	Alex Ovechkin	112	Daniel Carcillo	324
2006-07	Vincent Lecavalier	52	Joe Thornton	92	Sidney Crosby	120	Ben Eager	233
2005-06	Jonathan Cheechoo	56	Joe Thornton	96	Joe Thornton	125	Sean Avery	257
2004-05	....	....			....	....		....
2003-04	Rick Nash, Jarome Iginla, Ilya Kovalchuk	41	Scott Gomez, Martin St. Louis	56	Martin St. Louis	94	Sean Avery	261
2002-03	Milan Hejduk	50	Peter Forsberg	77	Peter Forsberg	106	Jody Shelley	249
2001-02	Jarome Iginla	52	Adam Oates	64	Jarome Iginla	96	Peter Worell	354
2000-01	Pavel Bure	59	Jaromir Jagr, Adam Oates	69	Jaromir Jagr	121	Matthew Barnaby	265
99-2000	Pavel Bure	58	Mark Recchi	63	Jaromir Jagr	96	Denny Lambert	219
1998-99	Teemu Selanne	47	Jaromir Jagr	83	Jaromir Jagr	127	Rob Ray	261
1997-98	Teemu Selanne, Peter Bondra	52	Jaromir Jagr, Wayne Gretzky	67	Jaromir Jagr	102	Donald Brashear	372
1996-97	Keith Tkachuk	52	Mario Lemieux, Wayne Gretzky	72	Mario Lemieux	122	Gino Odjick	371
1995-96	Mario Lemieux	69	Mario Lemieux, Ron Francis	92	Mario Lemieux	161	Matthew Barnaby	335
1994-95	Peter Bondra	34	Ron Francis	48	Jaromir Jagr, Eric Lindros	70	Enrico Ciccone	225
1993-94	Pavel Bure	60	Wayne Gretzky	92	Wayne Gretzky	130	Tie Domi	347
1992-93	Teemu Selanne, Alexander Mogilny	76	Adam Oates	97	Mario Lemieux	160	Marty McSorley	399
1991-92	Brett Hull	70	Wayne Gretzky	90	Mario Lemieux	131	Mike Peluso	408
1990-91	Brett Hull	86	Wayne Gretzky	122	Wayne Gretzky	163	Rob Ray	350
1989-90	Brett Hull	72	Wayne Gretzky	102	Wayne Gretzky	142	Basil McRae	351
1988-89	Mario Lemieux	85	Mario Lemieux, Wayne Gretzky	114	Mario Lemieux	199	Tim Hunter	375
1987-88	Mario Lemieux	70	Wayne Gretzky	109	Mario Lemieux	168	Bob Probert	398
1986-87	Wayne Gretzky	62	Wayne Gretzky	121	Wayne Gretzky	183	Tim Hunter	361
1985-86	Jari Kurri	68	Wayne Gretzky	163	Wayne Gretzky	215	Joe Kocur	377
1984-85	Wayne Gretzky	73	Wayne Gretzky	135	Wayne Gretzky	208	Chris Nilan	358
1983-84	Wayne Gretzky	87	Wayne Gretzky	118	Wayne Gretzky	205	Chris Nilan	338
1982-83	Wayne Gretzky	71	Wayne Gretzky	125	Wayne Gretzky	196	Randy Holt	275
1981-82	Wayne Gretzky	92	Wayne Gretzky	120	Wayne Gretzky	212	Paul Baxter	409
1980-81	Mike Bossy	68	Wayne Gretzky	109	Wayne Gretzky	164	Tiger Williams	343
1979-80	Charlie Simmer, Danny Gare, Blaine Stoughton	56	Wayne Gretzky	86	Marcel Dionne, Wayne Gretzky	137	Jimmy Mann	287
1978-79	Mike Bossy	69	Bryan Trottier	87	Bryan Trottier	134	Tiger Williams	298
1977-78	Guy Lafleur	60	Bryan Trottier	77	Guy Lafleur	132	Dave Schultz	405
1976-77	Steve Shutt	60	Guy Lafleur	80	Guy Lafleur	136	Tiger Williams	338
1975-76	Reggie Leach	61	Bobby Clarke	89	Guy Lafleur	125	Steve Durbano	370
1974-75	Phil Esposito	61	Bobby Orr, Bobby Clarke	89	Bobby Orr	135	Dave Schultz	472
1973-74	Phil Esposito	68	Bobby Orr	90	Phil Esposito	145	Dave Schultz	348
1972-73	Phil Esposito	55	Phil Esposito	75	Phil Esposito	130	Dave Schultz	259
1971-72	Phil Esposito	66	Bobby Orr	80	Phil Esposito	133	Bryan Watson	212
1970-71	Phil Esposito	76	Bobby Orr	102	Phil Esposito	152	Keith Magnuson	291
1969-70	Phil Esposito	43	Bobby Orr	87	Bobby Orr	120	Keith Magnuson	213
1968-69	Bobby Hull	58	Phil Esposito	77	Phil Esposito	126	Forbes Kennedy	219
1967-68	Bobby Hull	44	Phil Esposito	49	Stan Mikita	87	Barclay Plager	153
1966-67	Bobby Hull	52	Stan Mikita	62	Stan Mikita	97	John Ferguson	177
1965-66	Bobby Hull	54	Stan Mikita, Bobby Rousseau, Jean Beliveau	48	Bobby Hull	97	Reggie Fleming	166
1964-65	Norm Ullman	42	Stan Mikita	59	Stan Mikita	87	Carl Brewer	177
1963-64	Bobby Hull	43	Andy Bathgate	58	Stan Mikita	89	Vic Hadfield	151
1962-63	Gordie Howe	38	Henri Richard	50	Gordie Howe	86	Howie Young	273
1961-62	Bobby Hull	50	Andy Bathgate	56	Bobby Hull, Andy Bathgate	84	Lou Fontinato	167
1960-61	Bernie Geoffrion	50	Jean Beliveau	58	Bernie Geoffrion	95	Pierre Pilote	165
1959-60	Bobby Hull, Bronco Horvath	39	Don McKenney	49	Bobby Hull	81	Carl Brewer	150
1958-59	Jean Beliveau	45	Dickie Moore	55	Dickie Moore	96	Ted Lindsay	184
1957-58	Dickie Moore	36	Henri Richard	52	Dickie Moore	84	Lou Fontinato	152
1956-57	Gordie Howe	44	Ted Lindsay	55	Gordie Howe	89	Gus Mortson	147
1955-56	Jean Beliveau	47	Bert Olmstead	56	Jean Beliveau	88	Lou Fontinato	202
1954-55	Maurice Richard, Bernie Geoffrion	38	Bert Olmstead	48	Bernie Geoffrion	75	Fern Flaman	150
1953-54	Maurice Richard	37	Gordie Howe	48	Gordie Howe	81	Gus Mortson	132
1952-53	Gordie Howe	49	Gordie Howe	46	Gordie Howe	95	Maurice Richard	112
1951-52	Gordie Howe	47	Elmer Lach	50	Gordie Howe	86	Gus Kyle	127
1950-51	Gordie Howe	43	Gordie Howe, Ted Kennedy	43	Gordie Howe	86	Gus Mortson	142
1949-50	Maurice Richard	43	Ted Lindsay	55	Ted Lindsay	78	Bill Ezinicki	144
1948-49	Sid Abel	28	Doug Bentley	43	Roy Conacher	68	Bill Ezinicki	145
1947-48	Ted Lindsay	33	Doug Bentley	37	Elmer Lach	61	Bill Barilko	147
1946-47	Maurice Richard	45	Billy Taylor	46	Max Bentley	72	Gus Mortson	133
1945-46	Gaye Stewart	37	Elmer Lach	34	Max Bentley	61	Jack Stewart	73
1944-45	Maurice Richard	50	Elmer Lach	54	Elmer Lach	80	Pat Egan	86
1943-44	Doug Bentley	38	Clint Smith	49	Herb Cain	82	Mike McMahon	98
1942-43	Doug Bentley	33	Bill Cowley	45	Doug Bentley	73	Jimmy Orlando	89 *
1941-42	Lynn Patrick	32	Phil Watson	37	Bryan Hextall	56	Pat Egan	124
1940-41	Bryan Hextall	26	Bill Cowley	45	Bill Cowley	62	Jimmy Orlando	99
1939-40	Bryan Hextall	24	Milt Schmidt	30	Milt Schmidt	52	Red Horner	87
1938-39	Roy Conacher	26	Bill Cowley	34	Toe Blake	47	Red Horner	85
1937-38	Gordie Drillon	26	Syl Apps	29	Gordie Drillon	52	Art Coulter	90
1936-37	Larry Aurie, Nels Stewart	23	Syl Apps	29	Sweeney Schriner	46	Red Horner	124
1935-36	Charlie Conacher, Bill Thoms	23	Art Chapman	28	Sweeney Schriner	45	Red Horner	167
1934-35	Charlie Conacher	36	Art Chapman	34	Charlie Conacher	57	Red Horner	125
1933-34	Charlie Conacher	32	Joe Primeau	32	Charlie Conacher	52	Red Horner	126 *
1932-33	Bill Cook	28	Frank Boucher	28	Bill Cook	50	Red Horner	144
1931-32	Charlie Conacher, Bill Cook	34	Joe Primeau	37	Busher Jackson	53	Red Dutton	107
1930-31	Charlie Conacher	31	Joe Primeau	32	Howie Morenz	51	Harvey Rockburn	118
1929-30	Cooney Weiland	43	Frank Boucher	36	Cooney Weiland	73	Joe Lamb	119
1928-29	Ace Bailey	22	Frank Boucher	16	Ace Bailey	32	Red Dutton	139
1927-28	Howie Morenz	33	Howie Morenz	18	Howie Morenz	51	Eddie Shore	165
1926-27	Bill Cook	33	Dick Irvin	18	Bill Cook	37	Nels Stewart	133
1925-26	Nels Stewart	34	Frank Nighbor	13	Nels Stewart	42	Bert Corbeau	121
1924-25	Babe Dye	38	Cy Denneny, Red Green	15	Babe Dye	46	George Boucher	95
1923-24	Cy Denneny	22	George Boucher	10	Cy Denneny	24	Reg Noble	79
1922-23	Babe Dye	26	Eddie Gerard	13	Babe Dye	37	George Boucher	58
1921-22	Punch Broadbent	32	Harry Cameron	17	Punch Broadbent	46	Sprague Cleghorn	63
1920-21	Babe Dye	35	Jack Darragh	15	Newsy Lalonde	43	Bert Corbeau	86
1919-20	Joe Malone	39	Frank Nighbor	15	Joe Malone	49	Cully Wilson	86
1918-19	Newsy Lalonde, Odie Cleghorn	22	Newsy Lalonde	10	Newsy Lalonde	32	Joe Hall	135
1917-18	Joe Malone	44	Cy Denneny, Reg Noble, Harry Cameron	10	Joe Malone	48	Joe Hall	100

* Match Misconduct penalty not included in total penalty minutes.
1946-47 was the first season that a Match penalty was automatically written into the player's total penalty minutes as 20 minutes.
Beginning in 1947-48 all penalties, Match, Game Misconduct, and Misconduct, are written as 10 minutes.

One-Season Scoring Records

Goals-Per-Game Leaders, One-Season

(Among players with 20 goals or more in one season)

Player	Team	Season	Goals per game average	Goals	Games
Joe Malone	Montreal	1917-18	**2.20**	44	20
Cy Denneny	Ottawa	1917-18	**1.80**	36	20
Newsy Lalonde	Montreal	1917-18	**1.64**	23	14
Joe Malone	Quebec	1919-20	**1.63**	39	24
Newsy Lalonde	Montreal	1919-20	**1.61**	37	23
Reg Noble	Toronto	1917-18	**1.50**	30	20
Babe Dye	Ham., Tor.	1920-21	**1.46**	35	24
Cy Denneny	Ottawa	1920-21	**1.42**	34	24
Joe Malone	Hamilton	1920-21	**1.40**	28	20
Newsy Lalonde	Montreal	1920-21	**1.38**	33	24
Punch Broadbent	Ottawa	1921-22	**1.33**	32	24
Babe Dye	Toronto	1924-25	**1.31**	38	29
Babe Dye	Toronto	1921-22	**1.29**	31	24
Newsy Lalonde	Montreal	1918-19	**1.29**	22	17
Odie Cleghorn	Montreal	1918-19	**1.29**	22	17
Cy Denneny	Ottawa	1921-22	**1.23**	27	22
Aurel Joliat	Montreal	1924-25	**1.20**	30	25
Wayne Gretzky	Edmonton	1983-84	**1.18**	87	74
Babe Dye	Toronto	1922-23	**1.18**	26	22
Wayne Gretzky	Edmonton	1981-82	**1.15**	92	80
Mario Lemieux	Pittsburgh	1992-93	**1.15**	69	60
Frank Nighbor	Ottawa	1919-20	**1.13**	26	23
Mario Lemieux	Pittsburgh	1988-89	**1.12**	85	76
Brett Hull	St. Louis	1990-91	**1.10**	86	78
Cam Neely	Boston	1993-94	**1.02**	50	49
Maurice Richard	Montreal	1944-45	**1.00**	50	50
Reg Noble	Toronto	1919-20	**1.00**	24	24
Corb Denneny	Toronto	1919-20	**1.00**	24	24
Joe Malone	Hamilton	1921-22	**1.00**	24	24
Billy Boucher	Montreal	1922-23	**1.00**	24	24
Cy Denneny	Ottawa	1923-24	**1.00**	22	22
Alexander Mogilny	Buffalo	1992-93	**0.99**	76	77
Mario Lemieux	Pittsburgh	1995-96	**0.99**	69	70
Cooney Weiland	Boston	1929-30	**0.98**	43	44
Phil Esposito	Boston	1970-71	**0.97**	76	78
Jari Kurri	Edmonton	1984-85	**0.97**	71	73

One hundred years ago, Joe Malone scored 44 goals in just 20 games played during the first season in NHL history. No one has ever matched his goals-per-game average of 2.20 from 1917-18.

Assists-Per-Game Leaders, One-Season

(Among players with 35 assists or more in one-season)

Player	Team	Season	Assists per game average	Assists	Games
Wayne Gretzky	Edmonton	1985-86	**2.04**	163	80
Wayne Gretzky	Edmonton	1987-88	**1.70**	109	64
Wayne Gretzky	Edmonton	1984-85	**1.69**	135	80
Wayne Gretzky	Edmonton	1983-84	**1.59**	118	74
Wayne Gretzky	Edmonton	1982-83	**1.56**	125	80
Wayne Gretzky	Los Angeles	1990-91	**1.56**	122	78
Wayne Gretzky	Edmonton	1986-87	**1.53**	121	79
Mario Lemieux	Pittsburgh	1992-93	**1.52**	91	60
Wayne Gretzky	Edmonton	1981-82	**1.50**	120	80
Mario Lemieux	Pittsburgh	1988-89	**1.50**	114	76
Adam Oates	St. Louis	1990-91	**1.48**	90	61
Mario Lemieux	Los Angeles	1988-89	**1.46**	114	78
Wayne Gretzky	Los Angeles	1989-90	**1.40**	102	73
Wayne Gretzky	Edmonton	1980-81	**1.36**	109	80
Mario Lemieux	Pittsburgh	1991-92	**1.36**	87	64
Mario Lemieux	Pittsburgh	1989-90	**1.32**	78	59
Bobby Orr	Boston	1970-71	**1.31**	102	78
Mario Lemieux	Pittsburgh	1995-96	**1.31**	92	70
Mario Lemieux	Pittsburgh	1987-88	**1.27**	98	77
Bobby Orr	Boston	1973-74	**1.22**	90	74
Wayne Gretzky	Los Angeles	1991-92	**1.22**	90	74
Joe Thornton	Bos., S.J.	2005-06	**1.19**	96	81
Ron Francis	Pittsburgh	1995-96	**1.19**	92	77
Mario Lemieux	Pittsburgh	1985-86	**1.18**	93	79
Bobby Clarke	Philadelphia	1975-76	**1.17**	89	76
Peter Stastny	Quebec	1981-82	**1.16**	93	80
Adam Oates	Boston	1992-93	**1.15**	97	84
Doug Gilmour	Toronto	1992-93	**1.14**	95	83
Wayne Gretzky	Los Angeles	1993-94	**1.14**	92	81
Paul Coffey	Edmonton	1985-86	**1.14**	90	79
Bobby Orr	Boston	1969-70	**1.14**	87	76
Bryan Trottier	NY Islanders	1978-79	**1.14**	87	76
Bobby Orr	Boston	1972-73	**1.14**	72	63
Bill Cowley	Boston	1943-44	**1.14**	41	36
Sidney Crosby	Pittsburgh	2012-13	**1.14**	41	36
Pat LaFontaine	Buffalo	1992-93	**1.13**	95	84
Steve Yzerman	Detroit	1988-89	**1.13**	90	80
Paul Coffey	Pittsburgh	1987-88	**1.13**	52	46
Joe Thornton	San Jose	2006-07	**1.12**	92	82
Bobby Orr	Boston	1974-75	**1.11**	89	80
Bobby Clarke	Philadelphia	1974-75	**1.11**	89	80
Paul Coffey	Pittsburgh	1988-89	**1.11**	83	75
Wayne Gretzky	Los Angeles	1992-93	**1.11**	49	45
Denis Savard	Chicago	1982-83	**1.10**	86	78
Denis Savard	Chicago	1981-82	**1.09**	87	80
Denis Savard	Chicago	1987-88	**1.09**	87	80
Wayne Gretzky	Edmonton	1979-80	**1.09**	86	79
Ron Francis	Pittsburgh	1994-95	**1.09**	48	44
Paul Coffey	Edmonton	1983-84	**1.08**	86	80
Elmer Lach	Montreal	1944-45	**1.08**	54	50
Peter Stastny	Quebec	1985-86	**1.07**	81	76
Jaromir Jagr	Pittsburgh	1995-96	**1.06**	87	82
Mark Messier	Edmonton	1989-90	**1.06**	84	79
Sidney Crosby	Pittsburgh	2006-07	**1.06**	84	79
Peter Forsberg	Colorado	1995-96	**1.05**	86	82
Paul Coffey	Edmonton	1984-85	**1.05**	84	80
Marcel Dionne	Los Angeles	1979-80	**1.05**	84	80
Bobby Orr	Boston	1971-72	**1.05**	80	76
Mike Bossy	NY Islanders	1981-82	**1.04**	83	80
Adam Oates	Boston	1993-94	**1.04**	80	77
Phil Esposito	Boston	1968-69	**1.04**	77	74
Bryan Trottier	NY Islanders	1983-84	**1.04**	71	68
Jason Spezza	Ottawa	2005-06	**1.04**	71	68
Pete Mahovlich	Montreal	1974-75	**1.03**	82	80
Kent Nilsson	Calgary	1980-81	**1.03**	82	80
Peter Stastny	Quebec	1982-83	**1.03**	77	75
Peter Forsberg	Colorado	2002-03	**1.03**	77	75
Denis Savard	Chicago	1988-89	**1.02**	59	58
Jaromir Jagr	Pittsburgh	1998-99	**1.02**	83	81
Doug Gilmour	Toronto	1993-94	**1.01**	84	83
Henrik Sedin	Vancouver	2009-10	**1.01**	83	82
Bernie Nicholls	Los Angeles	1988-89	**1.01**	80	79
Guy Lafleur	Montreal	1979-80	**1.01**	75	74
Guy Lafleur	Montreal	1976-77	**1.00**	80	80
Marcel Dionne	Los Angeles	1984-85	**1.00**	80	80
Brian Leetch	NY Rangers	1991-92	**1.00**	80	80
Bryan Trottier	NY Islanders	1977-78	**1.00**	77	77
Mike Bossy	NY Islanders	1983-84	**1.00**	67	67
Jean Ratelle	NY Rangers	1971-72	**1.00**	63	63
Steve Yzerman	Detroit	1993-94	**1.00**	58	58
Ron Francis	Hartford	1985-86	**1.00**	53	53
Guy Chouinard	Calgary	1980-81	**1.00**	52	52
Elmer Lach	Montreal	1943-44	**1.00**	48	48

Points-Per-Game Leaders, One-Season

(Among players with 50 points or more in one-season)

Player	Team	Season	Points per game average	Points	Games	Player	Team	Season	Points per game average	Points	Games
Wayne Gretzky	Edmonton	1983-84	2.77	205	74	Denis Savard	Chicago	1987-88	1.64	131	80
Wayne Gretzky	Edmonton	1985-86	2.69	215	80	Wayne Gretzky	Los Angeles	1991-92	1.64	121	74
Mario Lemieux	Pittsburgh	1992-93	2.67	160	60	Steve Yzerman	Detroit	1992-93	1.63	137	84
Wayne Gretzky	Edmonton	1981-82	2.65	212	80	Marcel Dionne	Los Angeles	1978-79	1.63	130	80
Mario Lemieux	Pittsburgh	1988-89	2.62	199	76	Dale Hawerchuk	Winnipeg	1984-85	1.63	130	80
Wayne Gretzky	Edmonton	1984-85	2.60	208	80	Mark Messier	Edmonton	1989-90	1.63	129	79
Wayne Gretzky	Edmonton	1982-83	2.45	196	80	Bryan Trottier	NY Islanders	1983-84	1.63	111	68
Wayne Gretzky	Edmonton	1987-88	2.33	149	64	Pat LaFontaine	Buffalo	1991-92	1.63	93	57
Wayne Gretzky	Edmonton	1986-87	2.32	183	79	Charlie Simmer	Los Angeles	1980-81	1.62	105	65
Mario Lemieux	Pittsburgh	1995-96	2.30	161	70	Guy Lafleur	Montreal	1978-79	1.61	129	80
Mario Lemieux	Pittsburgh	1987-88	2.18	168	77	Bryan Trottier	NY Islanders	1981-82	1.61	129	80
Wayne Gretzky	Los Angeles	1988-89	2.15	168	78	Phil Esposito	Boston	1974-75	1.61	127	79
Wayne Gretzky	Los Angeles	1990-91	2.09	163	78	Steve Yzerman	Detroit	1989-90	1.61	127	79
Mario Lemieux	Pittsburgh	1989-90	2.08	123	59	Peter Stastny	Quebec	1985-86	1.61	122	76
Wayne Gretzky	Edmonton	1980-81	2.05	164	80	Mario Lemieux	Pittsburgh	1996-97	1.61	122	76
Mario Lemieux	Pittsburgh	1991-92	2.05	131	64	Michel Goulet	Quebec	1983-84	1.61	121	75
Bill Cowley	Boston	1943-44	1.97	71	36	Sidney Crosby	Pittsburgh	2010-11	1.61	66	41
Phil Esposito	Boston	1970-71	1.95	152	78	Wayne Gretzky	Los Angeles	1993-94	1.60	130	81
Wayne Gretzky	Los Angeles	1989-90	1.95	142	73	Bryan Trottier	NY Islanders	1977-78	1.60	123	77
Steve Yzerman	Detroit	1988-89	1.94	155	80	Bobby Orr	Boston	1972-73	1.60	101	63
Bernie Nicholls	Los Angeles	1988-89	1.90	150	79	Guy Chouinard	Calgary	1980-81	1.60	83	52
Adam Oates	St. Louis	1990-91	1.89	115	61	Elmer Lach	Montreal	1944-45	1.60	80	50
Phil Esposito	Boston	1973-74	1.86	145	78	Pierre Turgeon	NY Islanders	1992-93	1.59	132	83
Jari Kurri	Edmonton	1984-85	1.85	135	73	Steve Yzerman	Detroit	1987-88	1.59	102	64
Mike Bossy	NY Islanders	1981-82	1.84	147	80	Mike Bossy	NY Islanders	1978-79	1.58	126	80
Jaromir Jagr	Pittsburgh	1995-96	1.82	149	82	Paul Coffey	Edmonton	1983-84	1.58	126	80
Mario Lemieux	Pittsburgh	1985-86	1.78	141	79	Marcel Dionne	Los Angeles	1984-85	1.58	126	80
Bobby Orr	Boston	1970-71	1.78	139	78	Bobby Orr	Boston	1969-70	1.58	120	76
Jari Kurri	Edmonton	1983-84	1.77	113	64	Eric Lindros	Philadelphia	1995-96	1.58	115	73
Mario Lemieux	Pittsburgh	2000-01	1.77	76	43	Charlie Simmer	Los Angeles	1979-80	1.58	101	64
Pat LaFontaine	Buffalo	1992-93	1.76	148	84	Teemu Selanne	Winnipeg	1992-93	1.57	132	84
Bryan Trottier	NY Islanders	1978-79	1.76	134	76	Jaromir Jagr	Pittsburgh	1998-99	1.57	127	81
Mike Bossy	NY Islanders	1983-84	1.76	118	67	Bobby Clarke	Philadelphia	1975-76	1.57	119	76
Paul Coffey	Edmonton	1985-86	1.75	138	79	Guy Lafleur	Montreal	1975-76	1.56	125	80
Phil Esposito	Boston	1971-72	1.75	133	76	Dave Taylor	Los Angeles	1980-81	1.56	112	72
Peter Stastny	Quebec	1981-82	1.74	139	80	Sidney Crosby	Pittsburgh	2012-13	1.56	56	36
Wayne Gretzky	Edmonton	1979-80	1.73	137	79	Denis Savard	Chicago	1982-83	1.55	121	78
Jean Ratelle	NY Rangers	1971-72	1.73	109	63	Ron Francis	Pittsburgh	1995-96	1.55	119	77
Marcel Dionne	Los Angeles	1979-80	1.71	137	80	Joe Thornton	Bos., S.J.	2005-06	1.54	125	81
Herb Cain	Boston	1943-44	1.71	82	48	Mike Bossy	NY Islanders	1985-86	1.54	123	80
Guy Lafleur	Montreal	1976-77	1.70	136	80	Kevin Stevens	Pittsburgh	1991-92	1.54	123	80
Dennis Maruk	Washington	1981-82	1.70	136	80	Bobby Orr	Boston	1971-72	1.54	117	76
Phil Esposito	Boston	1968-69	1.70	126	74	Mike Bossy	NY Islanders	1984-85	1.54	117	76
Guy Lafleur	Montreal	1974-75	1.70	119	70	Kevin Stevens	Pittsburgh	1992-93	1.54	111	72
Mario Lemieux	Pittsburgh	1986-87	1.70	107	63	Doug Bentley	Chicago	1943-44	1.54	77	50
Adam Oates	Boston	1992-93	1.69	142	84	Doug Gilmour	Toronto	1992-93	1.53	127	83
Bobby Orr	Boston	1974-75	1.69	135	80	Marcel Dionne	Los Angeles	1976-77	1.53	122	80
Marcel Dionne	Los Angeles	1980-81	1.69	135	80	Sidney Crosby	Pittsburgh	2006-07	1.52	120	79
Guy Lafleur	Montreal	1977-78	1.69	132	78	Jaromir Jagr	Pittsburgh	99-2000	1.52	96	63
Guy Lafleur	Montreal	1979-80	1.69	125	74	Eric Lindros	Philadelphia	1996-97	1.52	79	52
Rob Brown	Pittsburgh	1988-89	1.69	115	68	Eric Lindros	Philadelphia	1994-95	1.52	70	46
Jari Kurri	Edmonton	1985-86	1.68	131	78	Marcel Dionne	Detroit	1974-75	1.51	121	80
Brett Hull	St. Louis	1990-91	1.68	131	78	Mike Bossy	NY Islanders	1980-81	1.51	119	79
Phil Esposito	Boston	1972-73	1.67	130	78	Paul Coffey	Edmonton	1984-85	1.51	121	80
Cooney Weiland	Boston	1929-30	1.66	73	44	Dale Hawerchuk	Winnipeg	1987-88	1.51	121	80
Alexander Mogilny	Buffalo	1992-93	1.65	127	77	Paul Coffey	Pittsburgh	1988-89	1.51	113	75
Peter Stastny	Quebec	1982-83	1.65	124	75	Alex Ovechkin	Washington	2009-10	1.51	109	72
Bobby Orr	Boston	1973-74	1.65	122	74	Jaromir Jagr	Pittsburgh	1996-97	1.51	95	63
Kent Nilsson	Calgary	1980-81	1.64	131	80	Cam Neely	Boston	1993-94	1.51	74	49

Guy Lafleur of the Montreal Canadiens topped 1.55 points-per-game for six consecutive seasons from 1974 through 1980. Lafleur's highest total came in 1976-77 when he had 136 points in 80 games (1.70 points-per-game).

Wendel Clark (left) set a Toronto Maple Leafs rookie scoring record with 34 goals in 1985-86. The record was broken by Auston Matthews in 2016-17. Matthews led all rookies with 40 goals, which tied him for second in the NHL with Tampa Bay's Nikita Kucherov behind Sidney Crosby's 44.

Rookie Scoring Records

All-Time Top 50 Goal-Scoring Rookies

	Rookie	Team	Position	Season	GP	G	A	PTS
1.	* Teemu Selanne	Winnipeg	Right wing	1992-93	84	**76**	56	132
2.	* Mike Bossy	NY Islanders	Right wing	1977-78	73	**53**	38	91
3.	* Alex Ovechkin	Washington	Left wing	2005-06	81	**52**	54	106
4.	* Joe Nieuwendyk	Calgary	Center	1987-88	75	**51**	41	92
5.	* Dale Hawerchuk	Winnipeg	Center	1981-82	80	**45**	58	103
	* Luc Robitaille	Los Angeles	Left wing	1986-87	79	**45**	39	84
7.	Rick Martin	Buffalo	Left wing	1971-72	73	**44**	30	74
	Barry Pederson	Boston	Center	1981-82	80	**44**	48	92
9.	* Steve Larmer	Chicago	Right wing	1982-83	80	**43**	47	90
	* Mario Lemieux	Pittsburgh	Center	1984-85	73	**43**	57	100
11.	Eric Lindros	Philadelphia	Center	1992-93	61	**41**	34	75
12.	Darryl Sutter	Chicago	Left wing	1980-81	76	**40**	22	62
	Sylvain Turgeon	Hartford	Left wing	1983-84	76	**40**	32	72
	Warren Young	Pittsburgh	Left wing	1984-85	80	**40**	32	72
	* Auston Matthews	Toronto	Center	**2016-17**	82	**40**	29	69
16.	* Eric Vail	Atlanta	Left wing	1974-75	72	**39**	21	60
	* Peter Stastny	Quebec	Center	1980-81	77	**39**	70	109
	Anton Stastny	Quebec	Left wing	1980-81	80	**39**	46	85
	Steve Yzerman	Detroit	Center	1983-84	80	**39**	48	87
	Sidney Crosby	Pittsburgh	Center	2005-06	81	**39**	63	102
21.	* Gilbert Perreault	Buffalo	Center	1970-71	78	**38**	34	72
	Neal Broten	Minnesota	Center	1981-82	73	**38**	60	98
	Ray Sheppard	Buffalo	Right wing	1987-88	74	**38**	27	65
	Mikael Renberg	Philadelphia	Left wing	1993-94	83	**38**	44	82
25.	Jorgen Pettersson	St. Louis	Left wing	1980-81	62	**37**	36	73
	Jimmy Carson	Los Angeles	Center	1986-87	80	**37**	42	79
27.	Mike Foligno	Detroit	Right wing	1979-80	80	**36**	35	71
	Paul MacLean	Winnipeg	Right wing	1981-82	74	**36**	25	61
	Mike Bullard	Pittsburgh	Center	1981-82	75	**36**	27	63
	Tony Granato	NY Rangers	Right wing	1988-89	78	**36**	27	63
	Patrick Laine	Winnipeg	Right wing	**2016-17**	73	**36**	28	64
32.	Marian Stastny	Quebec	Right wing	1981-82	74	**35**	54	89
	Brian Bellows	Minnesota	Right wing	1982-83	78	**35**	30	65
	Tony Amonte	NY Rangers	Right wing	1991-92	79	**35**	34	69
35.	Nels Stewart	Mtl. Maroons	Center	1925-26	36	**34**	8	42
	* Danny Grant	Minnesota	Left wing	1968-69	75	**34**	31	65
	Norm Ferguson	Oakland	Right wing	1968-69	76	**34**	20	54
	Brian Propp	Philadelphia	Left wing	1979-80	80	**34**	41	75
	Wendel Clark	Toronto	Left wing	1985-86	66	**34**	11	45
	* Pavel Bure	Vancouver	Right wing	1991-92	65	**34**	26	60
	Michael Grabner	NY Islanders	Right wing	2010-11	76	**34**	18	52
42.	* Willi Plett	Atlanta	Right wing	1976-77	64	**33**	23	56
	Dale McCourt	Detroit	Center	1977-78	76	**33**	39	72
	Steve Bozek	Los Angeles	Center	1981-82	71	**33**	23	56
	Ron Flockhart	Philadelphia	Center	1981-82	72	**33**	39	72
	Mark Pavelich	NY Rangers	Center	1981-82	79	**33**	43	76
	Jason Arnott	Edmonton	Center	1993-94	78	**33**	35	68
	* Evgeni Malkin	Pittsburgh	Center	2006-07	78	**33**	52	85
49.	Bill Mosienko	Chicago	Right wing	1943-44	50	**32**	38	70
	Michel Bergeron	Detroit	Right wing	1975-76	72	**32**	27	59
	* Bryan Trottier	NY Islanders	Center	1975-76	80	**32**	63	95
	Don Murdoch	NY Rangers	Right wing	1976-77	59	**32**	24	56
	Jari Kurri	Edmonton	Left wing	1980-81	75	**32**	43	75
	Bobby Carpenter	Washington	Center	1981-82	80	**32**	35	67
	Petr Klima	Detroit	Left wing	1985-86	74	**32**	24	56
	Kjell Dahlin	Montreal	Right wing	1985-86	73	**32**	39	71
	Darren Turcotte	NY Rangers	Center	1989-90	76	**32**	34	66
	Joe Juneau	Boston	Center	1992-93	84	**32**	70	102
	Marek Svatos	Colorado	Right wing	2005-06	61	**32**	18	50
	Logan Couture	San Jose	Center	2010-11	79	**32**	24	56

* Calder Trophy Winner

All-Time Top 50 Point-Scoring Rookies

	Rookie	Team	Position	Season	GP	G	A	PTS
1.	* Teemu Selanne	Winnipeg	Right wing	1992-93	84	76	56	**132**
2.	* Peter Stastny	Quebec	Center	1980-81	77	39	70	**109**
3.	* Alex Ovechkin	Washington	Left wing	2005-06	81	52	54	**106**
4.	* Dale Hawerchuk	Winnipeg	Center	1981-82	80	45	58	**103**
5.	Joe Juneau	Boston	Center	1992-93	84	32	70	**102**
	Sidney Crosby	Pittsburgh	Center	2005-06	81	39	63	**102**
7.	* Mario Lemieux	Pittsburgh	Center	1984-85	73	43	57	**100**
8.	Neal Broten	Minnesota	Center	1981-82	73	38	60	**98**
9.	* Bryan Trottier	NY Islanders	Center	1975-76	80	32	63	**95**
10.	Barry Pederson	Boston	Center	1981-82	80	44	48	**92**
	Joe Nieuwendyk	Calgary	Center	1987-88	75	51	41	**92**
12.	* Mike Bossy	NY Islanders	Right wing	1977-78	73	53	38	**91**
13.	* Steve Larmer	Chicago	Right wing	1982-83	80	43	47	**90**
14.	Marian Stastny	Quebec	Right wing	1981-82	74	35	54	**89**
15.	Steve Yzerman	Detroit	Center	1983-84	80	39	48	**87**
16.	* Sergei Makarov	Calgary	Right wing	1989-90	80	24	62	**86**
17.	Anton Stastny	Quebec	Left wing	1980-81	80	39	46	**85**
18.	* Evgeni Malkin	Pittsburgh	Center	2006-07	78	33	52	**85**
19.	* Luc Robitaille	Los Angeles	Left wing	1986-87	79	45	39	**84**
20.	Mikael Renberg	Philadelphia	Left wing	1993-94	83	38	44	**82**
21.	Jimmy Carson	Los Angeles	Center	1986-87	80	37	42	**79**
	Sergei Fedorov	Detroit	Center	1990-91	77	31	48	**79**
	Alexei Yashin	Ottawa	Center	1993-94	83	30	49	**79**
24.	Paul Stastny	Colorado	Center	2006-07	82	28	50	**78**
25.	Marcel Dionne	Detroit	Center	1971-72	78	28	49	**77**
	* Artemi Panarin	Chicago	Left wing	2015-16	80	30	47	**77**
27.	Larry Murphy	Los Angeles	Defense	1980-81	80	16	60	**76**
	Mark Pavelich	NY Rangers	Center	1981-82	79	33	43	**76**
	Dave Poulin	Philadelphia	Center	1983-84	73	31	45	**76**
30.	Brian Propp	Philadelphia	Left wing	1979-80	80	34	41	**75**
	Jari Kurri	Edmonton	Left wing	1980-81	75	32	43	**75**
	Denis Savard	Chicago	Center	1980-81	76	28	47	**75**
	Mike Modano	Minnesota	Center	1989-90	80	29	46	**75**
	Eric Lindros	Philadelphia	Center	1992-93	61	41	34	**75**
35.	Rick Martin	Buffalo	Left wing	1971-72	73	44	30	**74**
	* Bobby Smith	Minnesota	Center	1978-79	80	30	44	**74**
37.	Jorgen Pettersson	St. Louis	Left wing	1980-81	62	37	36	**73**
38.	* Gilbert Perreault	Buffalo	Center	1970-71	78	38	34	**72**
	Dale McCourt	Detroit	Center	1977-78	76	33	39	**72**
	Ron Flockhart	Philadelphia	Center	1981-82	72	33	39	**72**
	Sylvain Turgeon	Hartford	Left wing	1983-84	76	40	32	**72**
	Carey Wilson	Calgary	Center	1984-85	74	24	48	**72**
	Warren Young	Pittsburgh	Left wing	1984-85	80	40	32	**72**
	Alex Zhamnov	Winnipeg	Center	1992-93	68	25	47	**72**
	* Patrick Kane	Chicago	Right wing	2007-08	82	21	51	**72**
46.	Mike Foligno	Detroit	Right wing	1979-80	80	36	35	**71**
	Dave Christian	Winnipeg	Center	1980-81	80	28	43	**71**
	Mats Naslund	Montreal	Left wing	1982-83	74	26	45	**71**
	Kjell Dahlin	Montreal	Right wing	1985-86	77	32	39	**71**
	* Brian Leetch	NY Rangers	Defense	1988-89	68	23	48	**71**

* Calder Trophy Winner

50-Goal Seasons

Maurice Richard

Bernie Geoffrion

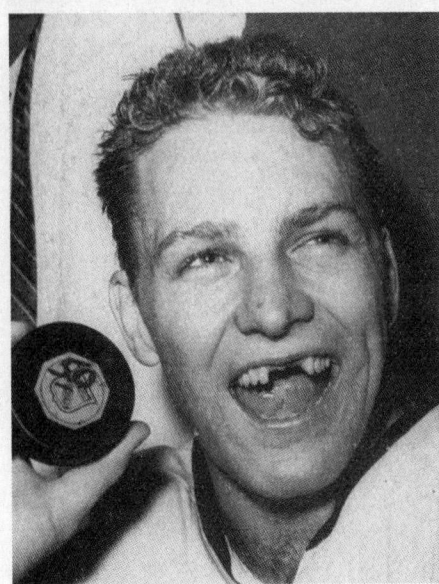

Bobby Hull

Player	Team	Date of 50th Goal	Score			Goaltender	Player's Game No.	Team Game No.	Total Goals	Total Games	Age When First 50th Scored (Yrs. & Mos.)
Maurice Richard	Mtl.	Mar. 18/45	Mtl. 4	at	Bos. 2	Harvey Bennett	50	50	50	50	23.7
Bernie Geoffrion	Mtl.	Mar. 16/61	Tor. 2	at	Mtl. 5	Cesare Maniago	62	68	50	64	30.1
Bobby Hull	Chi.	Mar. 25/62	Chi. 1	at	NYR 4	Gump Worsley	70	70	50	70	23.2
Bobby Hull	Chi.	Mar. 2/66	Det. 4	at	Chi. 5	Hank Bassen	52	57	54	65	
Bobby Hull	Chi.	Mar. 18/67	Chi. 5	at	Tor. 9	Bruce Gamble	63	66	52	66	
Bobby Hull	Chi.	Mar. 5/69	NYR 4	at	Chi. 4	Ed Giacomin	64	66	58	74	
Phil Esposito	Bos.	Feb. 20/71	Bos. 4	at	L.A. 5	Denis DeJordy	58	58	76	78	29.0
John Bucyk	Bos.	Mar. 16/71	Bos. 11	at	Det. 4	Roy Edwards	69	69	51	78	35.10
Phil Esposito	Bos.	Feb. 20/72	Bos. 3	at	Chi. 1	Tony Esposito	60	60	66	76	
Bobby Hull	Chi.	Apr. 2/72	Det. 1	at	Chi. 6	Andy Brown	78	78	50	78	
Vic Hadfield	NYR	Apr. 2/72	Mtl. 6	at	NYR 5	Denis DeJordy	78	78	50	78	31.6
Phil Esposito	Bos.	Mar. 25/73	Buf. 1	at	Bos. 6	Roger Crozier	75	75	55	78	
Mickey Redmond	Det.	Mar. 27/73	Det. 8	at	Tor. 1	Ron Low	73	75	52	76	25.3
Rick MacLeish	Phi.	Apr. 1/73	Phi. 4	at	Pit. 5	Cam Newton	78	78	50	78	23.2
Phil Esposito	Bos.	Feb. 20/74	Bos. 5	at	Min. 5	Cesare Maniago	56	56	68	78	
Mickey Redmond	Det.	Mar. 23/74	NYR 3	at	Det. 5	Ed Giacomin	69	71	51	76	
Ken Hodge	Bos.	Apr. 6/74	Bos. 2	at	Mtl. 6	Michel Larocque	75	77	50	76	29.10
Rick Martin	Buf.	Apr. 7/74	St.L. 2	at	Buf. 5	Wayne Stephenson	78	78	52	78	22.9
Phil Esposito	Bos.	Feb. 8/75	Bos. 8	at	Det. 5	Jim Rutherford	54	54	61	79	
Guy Lafleur	Mtl.	Mar. 29/75	K.C. 1	at	Mtl. 4	Denis Herron	66	76	53	70	23.6
Danny Grant	Det.	Apr. 2/75	Wsh. 3	at	Det. 8	John Adams	78	78	50	80	29.2
Rick Martin	Buf.	Apr. 3/75	Bos. 2	at	Buf. 4	Ken Broderick	67	79	52	68	
Reggie Leach	Phi.	Mar. 14/76	Atl. 1	at	Phi. 6	Dan Bouchard	69	69	61	80	25.11
Jean Pronovost	Pit.	Mar. 24/76	Bos. 5	at	Pit. 5	Gilles Gilbert	74	74	52	80	30.3
Guy Lafleur	Mtl.	Mar. 27/76	K.C. 2	at	Mtl. 8	Denis Herron	76	76	56	80	
Bill Barber	Phi.	Apr. 3/76	Buf. 2	at	Phi. 5	Al Smith	79	79	50	80	23.9
Pierre Larouche	Pit.	Apr. 3/76	Wsh. 5	at	Pit. 4	Ron Low	75	79	53	76	20.5
Danny Gare	Buf.	Apr. 4/76	Tor. 2	at	Buf. 5	Gord McRae	79	80	50	79	21.11
Steve Shutt	Mtl.	Mar. 1/77	Mtl. 5	at	NYI 4	Glenn Resch	65	65	60	80	24.8
Guy Lafleur	Mtl.	Mar. 6/77	Mtl. 1	at	Buf. 4	Don Edwards	68	68	56	80	
Marcel Dionne	L.A.	Apr. 2/77	Min. 2	at	L.A. 7	Pete LoPresti	79	79	53	80	25.8
Guy Lafleur	Mtl.	Mar. 8/78	Wsh. 3	at	Mtl. 4	Jim Bedard	63	65	60	78	
Mike Bossy	NYI	Apr. 1/78	Wsh. 2	at	NYI 3	Bernie Wolfe	69	76	53	73	21.2
Mike Bossy	NYI	Feb. 24/79	Det. 1	at	NYI 3	Rogie Vachon	58	58	69	80	
Marcel Dionne	L.A.	Mar. 11/79	L.A. 3	at	Phi. 6	Wayne Stephenson	68	68	59	80	
Guy Lafleur	Mtl.	Mar. 31/79	Pit. 3	at	Mtl. 5	Denis Herron	76	76	52	80	
Guy Chouinard	Atl.	Apr. 6/79	NYR 2	at	Atl. 9	John Davidson	79	79	50	80	22.5
Marcel Dionne	L.A.	Mar. 12/80	L.A. 2	at	Pit. 4	Nick Ricci	70	70	53	80	
Mike Bossy	NYI	Mar. 16/80	NYI 6	at	Chi. 1	Tony Esposito	68	71	51	75	
Charlie Simmer	L.A.	Mar. 19/80	Det. 3	at	L.A. 4	Jim Rutherford	57	73	56	64	26.0
Pierre Larouche	Mtl.	Mar. 25/80	Chi. 4	at	Mtl. 8	Tony Esposito	72	75	50	73	
Danny Gare	Buf.	Mar. 27/80	Det. 1	at	Buf. 10	Jim Rutherford	71	75	56	76	
Blaine Stoughton	Hfd.	Mar. 28/80	Hfd. 4	at	Van. 4	Glen Hanlon	75	75	56	80	27.0
Guy Lafleur	Mtl.	Apr. 2/80	Mtl. 7	at	Det. 2	Rogie Vachon	72	78	50	74	
Wayne Gretzky	Edm.	Apr. 2/80	Min. 1	at	Edm. 1	Gary Edwards	78	79	51	79	19.2
Reggie Leach	Phi.	Apr. 3/80	Wsh. 2	at	Phi. 4	empty net	75	79	50	76	
Mike Bossy	NYI	Jan. 24/81	Que. 3	at	NYI 7	Ron Grahame	50	50	68	79	
Charlie Simmer	L.A.	Jan. 26/81	L.A. 7	at	Que. 5	Michel Dion	51	51	56	65	
Marcel Dionne	L.A.	Mar. 8/81	L.A. 4	at	Wpg. 1	Markus Mattsson	68	68	58	80	
Wayne Babych	St.L.	Mar. 12/81	St.L. 3	at	Mtl. 4	Richard Sevigny	70	68	54	78	22.9
Wayne Gretzky	Edm.	Mar. 15/81	Edm. 3	at	Cgy. 3	Pat Riggin	69	69	55	80	
Rick Kehoe	Pit.	Mar. 16/81	Pit. 7	at	Edm. 6	Eddie Mio	70	70	55	80	29.7
Jacques Richard	Que.	Mar. 29/81	Mtl. 0	at	Que. 4	Richard Sevigny	76	75	52	78	28.6
Dennis Maruk	Wsh.	Apr. 5/81	Det. 2	at	Wsh. 7	Larry Lozinski	80	80	50	80	25.3
Wayne Gretzky	Edm.	Dec. 30/81	Phi. 5	at	Edm. 7	empty net	39	39	92	80	
Dennis Maruk	Wsh.	Feb. 21/82	Wpg. 3	at	Wsh. 6	Doug Soetaert	61	61	60	80	
Mike Bossy	NYI	Mar. 4/82	Tor. 1	at	NYI 10	Michel Larocque	66	66	64	80	
Dino Ciccarelli	Min.	Mar. 8/82	St.L. 1	at	Min. 8	Mike Liut	67	68	55	76	22.1
Rick Vaive	Tor.	Mar. 24/82	St.L. 3	at	Tor. 4	Mike Liut	72	75	54	77	22.10
Blaine Stoughton	Hfd.	Mar. 28/82	Min. 5	at	Hfd. 2	Gilles Meloche	76	76	52	80	
Rick Middleton	Bos.	Mar. 28/82	Bos. 5	at	Buf. 9	Paul Harrison	72	77	51	75	28.11
Marcel Dionne	L.A.	Mar. 30/82	Cgy. 7	at	L.A. 5	Pat Riggin	75	77	50	78	
Mark Messier	Edm.	Mar. 31/82	L.A. 3	at	Edm. 7	Mario Lessard	78	79	50	78	21.3
Bryan Trottier	NYI	Apr. 3/82	Phi. 3	at	NYI 6	Pete Peeters	79	79	50	80	25.9
Lanny McDonald	Cgy.	Feb. 18/83	Cgy. 1	at	Buf. 5	Bob Sauve	60	60	66	80	30.0
Wayne Gretzky	Edm.	Feb. 19/83	Edm. 10	at	Pit. 7	Nick Ricci	60	60	71	80	
Michel Goulet	Que.	Mar. 5/83	Hfd. 3	at	Que. 10	Mike Veisor	67	67	57	80	22.11
Mike Bossy	NYI	Mar. 12/83	Wsh. 2	at	NYI 6	Al Jensen	70	71	60	79	
Marcel Dionne	L.A.	Mar. 17/83	Que. 3	at	L.A. 4	Dan Bouchard	71	71	56	80	
Al Secord	Chi.	Mar. 20/83	Tor. 3	at	Chi. 7	Mike Palmateer	73	73	54	80	25.0
Rick Vaive	Tor.	Mar. 30/83	Tor. 4	at	Det. 2	Gilles Gilbert	76	78	51	78	
Wayne Gretzky	Edm.	Jan. 7/84	Hfd. 3	at	Edm. 5	Greg Millen	42	42	87	74	
Michel Goulet	Que.	Mar. 8/84	Que. 8	at	Pit. 6	Denis Herron	63	69	56	75	
Rick Vaive	Tor.	Mar. 14/84	Min. 3	at	Tor. 3	Gilles Meloche	69	72	52	76	
Mike Bullard	Pit.	Mar. 14/84	Pit. 6	at	L.A. 7	Markus Mattsson	71	72	51	76	23.0
Jari Kurri	Edm.	Mar. 15/84	Edm. 2	at	Mtl. 3	Rick Wamsley	57	73	52	64	23.10
Glenn Anderson	Edm.	Mar. 21/84	Hfd. 3	at	Edm. 5	Greg Millen	76	76	54	80	23.6
Tim Kerr	Phi.	Mar. 22/84	Pit. 4	at	Phi. 13	Denis Herron	74	75	54	79	24.3

Player	Team	Date of 50th Goal	Score			Goaltender	Player's Game No.	Team Game No.	Total Goals	Total Games	Age When First 50th Scored (Yrs. & Mos.)
Mike Bossy	NYI	Mar. 31/84	NYI 3	at	Wsh. 1	Pat Riggin	67	79	51	67	
Wayne Gretzky	Edm.	Jan. 26/85	Pit. 3	at	Edm. 6	Denis Herron	49	49	73	80	
Jari Kurri	Edm.	Feb. 3/85	Hfd. 3	at	Edm. 6	Greg Millen	50	53	71	73	
Mike Bossy	NYI	Mar. 5/85	Phi. 5	at	NYI 4	Bob Froese	61	65	58	76	
Michel Goulet	Que.	Mar. 6/85	Buf. 3	at	Que. 4	Tom Barrasso	62	73	55	69	
Tim Kerr	Phi.	Mar. 7/85	Wsh. 6	at	Phi. 9	Pat Riggin	63	65	54	74	
John Ogrodnick	Det.	Mar. 13/85	Det. 6	at	Edm. 7	Grant Fuhr	69	69	55	79	25.9
Bob Carpenter	Wsh.	Mar. 21/85	Wsh. 2	at	Mtl. 3	Steve Penney	72	72	53	80	21.9
Dale Hawerchuk	Wpg.	Mar. 29/85	Chi. 5	at	Wpg. 5	W. Skorodenski	77	77	53	80	21.11
Mike Gartner	Wsh.	Apr. 7/85	Pit. 3	at	Wsh. 7	Brian Ford	80	80	50	80	25.5
Jari Kurri	Edm.	Mar. 4/86	Edm. 6	at	Van. 2	Richard Brodeur	63	65	68	78	
Mike Bossy	NYI	Mar. 11/86	Cgy. 4	at	NYI 8	Reggie Lemelin	67	67	61	80	
Glenn Anderson	Edm.	Mar. 14/86	Det. 3	at	Edm. 12	Greg Stefan	63	71	54	72	
Michel Goulet	Que.	Mar. 17/86	Que. 8	at	Mtl. 6	Patrick Roy	67	72	53	75	
Wayne Gretzky	Edm.	Mar. 18/86	Wpg. 2	at	Edm. 6	Brian Hayward	72	72	52	80	
Tim Kerr	Phi.	Mar. 20/86	Pit. 1	at	Phi. 5	Roberto Romano	68	72	58	76	
Wayne Gretzky	Edm.	Feb. 4/87	Edm. 6	at	Min. 5	Don Beaupre	55	55	62	79	
Dino Ciccarelli	Min.	Mar. 7/87	Pit. 7	at	Min. 3	Gilles Meloche	66	66	52	80	
Mario Lemieux	Pit.	Mar. 12/87	Que. 3	at	Pit. 6	Mario Gosselin	53	70	54	63	21.5
Tim Kerr	Phi.	Mar. 17/87	NYR 1	at	Phi. 4	J. Vanbiesbrouck	67	71	58	75	
Jari Kurri	Edm.	Mar. 17/87	N.J. 4	at	Edm. 7	Craig Billington	69	70	54	79	
Mario Lemieux	Pit.	Feb. 2/88	Wsh. 2	at	Pit. 3	Pete Peeters	51	54	70	77	
Steve Yzerman	Det.	Mar. 1/88	Buf. 0	at	Det. 4	Tom Barrasso	64	64	50	64	22.10
Joe Nieuwendyk	Cgy.	Mar. 12/88	Buf. 4	at	Cgy. 10	Tom Barrasso	66	70	51	75	21.5
Craig Simpson	Edm.	Mar. 15/88	Buf. 4	at	Edm. 6	Jacques Cloutier	71	71	56	80	21.1
Jimmy Carson	L.A.	Mar. 26/88	Chi. 5	at	L.A. 9	Darren Pang	77	77	55	88	19.8
Luc Robitaille	L.A.	Apr. 1/88	L.A. 6	at	Cgy. 3	Mike Vernon	79	79	53	80	21.10
Hakan Loob	Cgy.	Apr. 3/88	Min. 1	at	Cgy. 4	Don Beaupre	80	80	50	80	27.9
Stephane Richer	Mtl.	Apr. 3/88	Mtl. 4	at	Buf. 4	Tom Barrasso	72	80	50	72	21.10
Mario Lemieux	Pit.	Jan. 20/89	Pit. 3	at	Wpg. 7	Pokey Reddick	44	46	85	76	
Bernie Nicholls	L.A.	Jan. 28/89	Edm. 7	at	L.A. 6	Grant Fuhr	51	51	70	79	27.7
Steve Yzerman	Det.	Feb. 5/89	Det. 6	at	Wpg. 2	Pokey Reddick	55	55	65	80	
Wayne Gretzky	L.A.	Mar. 4/89	Phi. 2	at	L.A. 6	Ron Hextall	66	67	54	78	
Joe Nieuwendyk	Cgy.	Mar. 21/89	NYI 1	at	Cgy. 4	Mark Fitzpatrick	72	74	51	77	
Joe Mullen	Cgy.	Mar. 31/89	Wpg. 1	at	Cgy. 4	Bob Essensa	78	79	51	79	32.1
Brett Hull	St.L.	Feb. 6/90	Tor. 4	at	St.L. 6	Jeff Reese	54	54	72	80	25.6
Steve Yzerman	Det.	Feb. 24/90	Det. 3	at	NYI 3	Glenn Healy	63	63	62	79	
Cam Neely	Bos.	Mar. 10/90	Bos. 3	at	NYI 3	Mark Fitzpatrick	69	71	55	76	24.9
Brian Bellows	Min.	Mar. 22/90	Min. 5	at	Det. 1	Tim Cheveldae	75	75	55	80	25.6
Pat LaFontaine	NYI	Mar. 24/90	NYI 5	at	Edm. 5	Bill Ranford	71	77	54	74	25.1
Stephane Richer	Mtl.	Mar. 24/90	Mtl. 4	at	Hfd. 7	Peter Sidorkiewicz	75	77	51	75	
Gary Leeman	Tor.	Mar. 28/90	NYI 6	at	Tor. 3	Mark Fitzpatrick	78	78	51	80	26.1
Luc Robitaille	L.A.	Mar. 31/90	L.A. 3	at	Van. 6	Kirk McLean	79	79	52	80	
Brett Hull	St.L.	Jan. 25/91	St.L. 9	at	Det. 4	David Gagnon	49	49	86	78	
Cam Neely	Bos.	Mar. 26/91	Bos. 7	at	Que. 4	empty net	67	78	51	69	
Theoren Fleury	Cgy.	Mar. 26/91	Van. 2	at	Cgy. 7	Bob Mason	77	77	51	79	22.9
Steve Yzerman	Det.	Mar. 30/91	NYR 5	at	Det. 6	Mike Richter	79	79	51	80	
Brett Hull	St.L.	Jan. 28/92	St.L. 3	at	L.A. 3	Kelly Hrudey	50	50	70	73	
Jeremy Roenick	Chi.	Mar. 7/92	Chi. 2	at	Bos. 1	Daniel Berthiaume	67	67	53	80	22.2
Kevin Stevens	Pit.	Mar. 24/92	Pit. 3	at	Det. 4	Tim Cheveldae	74	74	54	80	26.11
Gary Roberts	Cgy.	Mar. 31/92	Edm. 2	at	Cgy. 5	Bill Ranford	73	77	53	76	25.10
Alexander Mogilny	Buf.	Feb. 3/93	Hfd. 2	at	Buf. 3	Sean Burke	46	53	76	77	23.11
Teemu Selanne	Wpg.	Feb. 28/93	Min. 6	at	Wpg. 7	Darcy Wakaluk	63	63	76	84	22.6
Pavel Bure	Van.	Mar. 1/93	Van. 5	at	Buf. 2*	Grant Fuhr	63	63	60	83	21.11
Steve Yzerman	Det.	Mar. 10/93	Det. 6	at	Edm. 3	Bill Ranford	70	70	58	84	
Luc Robitaille	L.A.	Mar. 15/93	L.A. 4	at	Buf. 2	Grant Fuhr	69	69	63	84	
Brett Hull	St.L.	Mar. 20/93	St.L. 2	at	L.A. 3	Robb Stauber	73	73	54	80	
Mario Lemieux	Pit.	Mar. 21/93	Pit. 6	at	Edm. 4**	Ron Tugnutt	48	72	69	60	
Kevin Stevens	Pit.	Mar. 21/93	Pit. 6	at	Edm. 4**	Ron Tugnutt	62	72	55	72	
Dave Andreychuk	Tor.	Mar. 23/93	Tor. 5	at	Wpg. 4	Bob Essensa	72	73	54	83	29.6
Pat LaFontaine	Buf.	Mar. 28/93	Ott. 1	at	Buf. 3	Peter Sidorkiewicz	75	75	53	84	
Pierre Turgeon	NYI	Apr. 2/93	NYI 3	at	NYR 2	Mike Richter	75	76	58	83	23.8
Mark Recchi	Phi.	Apr. 3/93	T.B. 2	at	Phi. 6	J-C Bergeron	77	77	53	84	25.2
Brendan Shanahan	St.L.	Apr. 15/93	T.B. 5	at	St.L. 6	Pat Jablonski	71	84	51	71	24.3
Jeremy Roenick	Chi.	Apr. 15/93	Tor. 2	at	Chi. 3	Felix Potvin	84	84	50	84	
Cam Neely	Bos.	Mar. 7/94	Wsh. 3	at	Bos. 6	Don Beaupre	44	66	50	49	
Sergei Fedorov	Det.	Mar. 15/94	Van. 2	at	Det. 5	Kirk McLean	67	69	56	82	24.3
Pavel Bure	Van.	Mar. 23/94	Van. 6	at	L.A. 3	empty net	65	73	60	76	
Adam Graves	NYR	Mar. 23/94	NYR 5	at	Edm. 3	Bill Ranford	74	74	52	84	25.11
Dave Andreychuk	Tor.	Mar. 24/94	S.J. 2	at	Tor. 1	Arturs Irbe	73	74	53	83	
Brett Hull	St.L.	Mar. 25/94	Dal. 3	at	St.L. 5	Andy Moog	71	74	52	81	
Ray Sheppard	Det.	Mar. 29/94	Hfd. 2	at	Det. 6	Sean Burke	74	76	52	82	27.10
Brendan Shanahan	St.L.	Apr. 12/94	St.L. 5	at	Dal. 9	Andy Moog	80	83	52	81	
Mike Modano	Dal.	Apr. 12/94	St.L. 5	at	Dal. 9	Curtis Joseph	75	83	50	76	23.11
Mario Lemieux	Pit.	Feb. 23/96	Hfd. 4	at	Pit. 5	Sean Burke	50	59	69	70	
Jaromir Jagr	Pit.	Feb. 23/96	Hfd. 4	at	Pit. 5	Sean Burke	59	59	62	82	24.0
Alexander Mogilny	Van.	Feb. 29/96	St.L. 2	at	Van. 2	Grant Fuhr	60	63	55	79	
Peter Bondra	Wsh.	Apr. 3/96	Wsh. 5	at	Buf. 1	Andrei Trefilov	62	77	52	67	28.1
Joe Sakic	Col.	Apr. 7/96	Col. 4	at	Dal. 1	empty net	79	79	51	82	26.7
John LeClair	Phi.	Apr. 10/96	Phi. 5	at	N.J. 1	Corey Schwab	80	80	51	82	26.7
Keith Tkachuk	Wpg.	Apr. 12/96	L.A. 3	at	Wpg. 5	empty net	75	81	50	76	24.0
Paul Kariya	Ana.	Apr. 14/96	Wpg. 2	at	Ana. 5	N. Khabibulin	82	82	50	82	21.5
Keith Tkachuk	Phx.	Apr. 6/97	Phx. 1	at	Col. 2	Patrick Roy	78	79	52	81	
Teemu Selanne	Ana.	Apr. 9/97	L.A. 1	at	Ana. 4	empty net	77	81	51	78	
Mario Lemieux	Pit.	Apr. 11/97	Pit. 2	at	Fla. 4	J. Vanbiesbrouck	75	81	50	76	

Mike Bossy

Wayne Gretzky

Teemu Selanne

Pavel Bure

Phil Esposito

Bobby Clarke

Player	Team	Date of 50th Goal	Score			Goaltender	Player's Game No.	Team Game No.	Total Goals	Total Games	Age When First 50th Scored (Yrs. & Mos.)
John LeClair	Phi.	Apr. 13/97	N.J. 4	at	Phi. 5	Mike Dunham	82	82	50	82	
Teemu Selanne	Ana.	Mar. 25/98	Ana. 3	at	Chi. 2	Jeff Hackett	66	71	52	73	
John LeClair	Phi.	Apr. 13/98	Phi. 1	at	Buf. 2	Dominik Hasek	79	79	51	82	
Pavel Bure	Van.	Apr. 17/98	Cgy. 4	at	Van. 2	Dwayne Roloson	81	81	51	82	
Peter Bondra	Wsh.	Apr. 18/98	Wsh. 4	at	Car. 3	Mike Fountain	75	80	52	76	
Pavel Bure	Fla.	Mar. 18/00	Fla. 4	at	NYI 2	empty net	63	71	58	74	
Pavel Bure	Fla.	Mar. 16/01	Pit. 6	at	Fla. 3	Johan Hedberg	72	72	59	82	
Joe Sakic	Col.	Apr. 4/01	Ana. 1	at	Col. 1	J-S Giguere	80	80	54	82	
Jaromir Jagr	Pit.	Apr. 4/01	T.B. 2	at	Pit. 4	Kevin Weekes	80	80	52	81	
Jarome Iginla	Cgy.	Apr. 7/02	Cgy. 2	at	Chi. 3	Jocelyn Thibault	79	79	52	82	24.9
Milan Hejduk	Col.	Apr. 6/03	St.L. 2	at	Col. 5	Brent Johnson	82	82	50	82	27.1
Jaromir Jagr	NYR	Mar. 24/06	NYR 2	at	Fla. 3	Roberto Luongo	70	70	54	82	
Ilya Kovalchuk	Atl.	Apr. 6/06	Atl. 2	at	T.B. 3	Sean Burke	72	76	52	78	22.11
Jonathan Cheechoo	S.J.	Apr. 10/06	S.J. 3	at	Phx. 2	David LeNeveu	78	78	56	82	25.8
Alex Ovechkin	Wsh.	Apr. 13/06	Wsh. 3	at	Atl. 5	Mike Dunham	78	79	52	81	20.6
Dany Heatley	Ott.	Apr. 18/06	Ott. 5	at	NYR 1	Henrik Lundqvist	82	82	50	82	25.2
Vincent Lecavalier	T.B.	Mar. 30/07	T.B. 4	at	Car. 2	Cam Ward	78	78	52	82	26.11
Dany Heatley	Ott.	Apr. 7/07	Ott. 6	at	Bos. 3	Tim Thomas	82	82	50	82	
Alex Ovechkin	Wsh.	Mar. 3/08	Bos. 2	at	Wsh. 10	Tim Thomas	67	67	65	82	
Ilya Kovalchuk	Atl.	Mar. 18/08	Atl. 2	at	Phi. 3	Antero Niittymaki	72	75	52	79	
Jarome Iginla	Cgy.	Apr. 5/08	Cgy. 7	at	Van. 1	Curtis Sanford	82	82	50	82	
Alex Ovechkin	Wsh.	Mar. 19/09	Wsh. 5	at	T.B. 2	Mike McKenna	70	73	56	79	
Alex Ovechkin	Wsh.	Apr. 9/10	Atl. 2	at	Wsh. 5	Ondrej Pavelec	71	81	50	72	
Steven Stamkos	T.B.	Apr. 10/10	Fla. 3	at	T.B. 4	S. Clemmensen	81	81	51	82	20.2
Sidney Crosby	Pit.	Apr. 11/10	Pit. 6	at	NYI 5	Dwayne Roloson	81	82	51	81	22.8
Corey Perry	Ana.	Apr. 6/11	S.J. 2	at	Ana. 6	Antero Niittymaki	80	80	50	82	25.11
Steven Stamkos	T.B.	Mar. 13/12	Bos. 1	at	T.B. 6	Marty Turco	69	69	60	82	
Evgeni Malkin	Pit.	Apr. 7/12	Phi. 2	at	Pit. 4	Sergei Bobrovsky	75	82	50	82	25.8
Alex Ovechkin	Wsh.	Apr. 8/14	Wsh. 4	at	St.L. 1	Ryan Miller	75	79	51	78	
Alex Ovechkin	Wsh.	Mar. 31/15	Car. 2	at	Wsh. 4	Cam Ward	76	77	53	81	
Alex Ovechkin	Wsh.	Apr. 9/16	Wsh. 5	at	St.L. 1	Anders Nilsson	79	81	50	79	

* neutral site game played at Hamilton; ** neutral site game played at Cleveland

100-Point Seasons

Player	Team	Date of 100th Point	G or A	Score			Player's Game No.	Team Game No.	G - A PTS	Total Games	Age when first 100th point scored (Yrs. & Mos.)
Phil Esposito	Bos.	Mar. 2/69	(G)	Pit. 0	at	Bos. 4	60	62	49-77 — 126	74	27.1
Bobby Hull	Chi.	Mar. 20/69	(G)	Chi. 5	at	Bos. 5	71	71	58-49 — 107	76	30.2
Gordie Howe	Det.	Mar. 30/69	(G)	Det. 5	at	Chi. 9	76	76	44-59 — 103	76	41.0
Bobby Orr	Bos.	Mar. 15/70	(G)	Det. 5	at	Bos. 5	67	67	33-87 — 120	76	22.11
Phil Esposito	Bos.	Feb. 6/71	(A)	Buf. 3	at	Bos. 4	51	51	76-76 — 152	78	
Bobby Orr	Bos.	Feb. 20/71	(A)	Bos. 4	at	L.A. 5	58	58	37-102 — 139	78	
John Bucyk	Bos.	Mar. 13/71	(G)	Bos. 6	at	Van. 3	68	68	51-65 — 116	78	35.10
Ken Hodge	Bos.	Mar. 21/71	(A)	Buf. 7	at	Bos. 5	72	72	43-62 — 105	78	26.9
Jean Ratelle	NYR	Feb. 18/72	(A)	NYR 2	at	Cal. 2	58	58	46-63 — 109	63	31.4
Phil Esposito	Bos.	Feb. 19/72	(A)	Bos. 6	at	Min. 4	59	59	66-67 — 133	76	
Bobby Orr	Bos.	Mar. 2/72	(A)	Van. 3	at	Bos. 7	64	64	37-80 — 117	76	
Vic Hadfield	NYR	Mar. 25/72	(A)	NYR 3	at	Mtl. 3	74	74	50-56 — 106	78	31.5
Phil Esposito	Bos.	Mar. 3/73	(A)	Bos. 1	at	Mtl. 5	64	64	55-75 — 130	78	
Bobby Clarke	Phi.	Mar. 29/73	(G)	Atl. 2	at	Phi. 4	76	76	37-67 — 104	78	23.7
Bobby Orr	Bos.	Mar. 31/73	(G)	Bos. 3	at	Tor. 7	62	77	29-72 — 101	63	
Rick MacLeish	Phi.	Apr. 1/73	(G)	Phi. 4	at	Pit. 5	78	78	50-50 — 100	78	23.3
Phil Esposito	Bos.	Feb. 13/74	(A)	Bos. 9	at	Cal. 6	53	53	68-77 — 145	78	
Bobby Orr	Bos.	Mar. 12/74	(A)	Buf. 0	at	Bos. 4	62	66	32-90 — 122	74	
Ken Hodge	Bos.	Mar. 24/74	(A)	Mtl. 3	at	Bos. 6	72	72	50-55 — 105	76	
Phil Esposito	Bos.	Feb. 8/75	(A)	Bos. 8	at	Det. 5	54	54	61-66 — 127	79	
Bobby Orr	Bos.	Feb. 13/75	(A)	Bos. 1	at	Buf. 3	57	57	46-89 — 135	80	
Guy Lafleur	Mtl.	Mar. 7/75	(G)	Wsh. 4	at	Mtl. 8	56	66	53-66 — 119	70	24.6
Marcel Dionne	Det.	Mar. 9/75	(A)	Det. 5	at	Phi. 8	67	67	47-74 — 121	80	23.7
Pete Mahovlich	Mtl.	Mar. 9/75	(G)	Mtl. 5	at	NYR 3	67	67	35-82 — 117	80	29.5
Bobby Clarke	Phi.	Mar. 22/75	(A)	Min. 0	at	Phi. 4	72	72	27-89 — 116	80	
Rene Robert	Buf.	Apr. 5/75	(A)	Buf. 4	at	Tor. 2	74	80	40-60 — 100	74	26.4
Guy Lafleur	Mtl.	Mar. 10/76	(G)	Mtl. 5	at	Chi. 1	69	69	56-69 — 125	80	
Bobby Clarke	Phi.	Mar. 11/76	(A)	Buf. 1	at	Phi. 6	64	68	30-89 — 119	76	
Bill Barber	Phi.	Mar. 18/76	(A)	Van. 2	at	Phi. 3	71	71	50-62 — 112	80	23.8
Gilbert Perreault	Buf.	Mar. 21/76	(A)	K.C. 1	at	Buf. 3	73	73	44-69 — 113	80	25.4
Pierre Larouche	Pit.	Mar. 24/76	(G)	Bos. 5	at	Pit. 5	70	74	53-58 — 111	76	20.4
Pete Mahovlich	Mtl.	Mar. 28/76	(A)	Mtl. 2	at	Bos. 2	77	77	34-71 — 105	80	
Jean Ratelle	Bos.	Mar. 30/76	(G)	Buf. 4	at	Bos. 4	77	77	36-69 — 105	80	
Jean Pronovost	Pit.	Apr. 3/76	(A)	Wsh. 5	at	Pit. 4	79	79	52-52 — 104	80	30.4
Darryl Sittler	Tor.	Apr. 3/76	(A)	Bos. 4	at	Tor. 2	78	79	41-59 — 100	79	25.7
Guy Lafleur	Mtl.	Feb. 26/77	(A)	Cle. 3	at	Mtl. 5	63	63	56-80 — 136	80	

Player	Team	Date of 100th Point	G or A	Score			Player's Game No.	Team Game No.	G - A PTS	Total Games	Age when first 100th point scored (Yrs. & Mos.)
Marcel Dionne	L.A.	Mar. 5/77	(G)	Pit. 3	at	L.A. 3	67	67	53-69 — 122	80	
Steve Shutt	Mtl.	Mar. 27/77	(A)	Mtl. 6	at	Det. 0	77	77	60-45 — 105	80	24.9
Bryan Trottier	NYI	Feb. 25/78	(A)	Chi. 1	at	NYI 7	59	60	46-77 — 123	77	21.7
Guy Lafleur	Mtl.	Feb. 28/78	(A)	Det. 3	at	Mtl. 9	69	61	60-72 — 132	78	
Darryl Sittler	Tor.	Mar. 12/78	(A)	Tor. 7	at	Pit. 1	67	67	45-72 — 117	80	
Guy Lafleur	Mtl.	Feb. 27/79	(A)	Mtl. 3	at	NYI 7	61	61	52-77 — 129	80	
Bryan Trottier	NYI	Mar. 6/79	(A)	Buf. 3	at	NYI 2	59	63	47-87 — 134	76	
Marcel Dionne	L.A.	Mar. 8/79	(G)	L.A. 4	at	Buf. 6	66	66	59-71 — 130	80	
Mike Bossy	NYI	Mar. 11/79	(G)	NYI 4	at	Bos. 4	66	66	69-57 — 126	80	22.2
Bob MacMillan	Atl.	Mar. 15/79	(A)	Atl. 4	at	Phi. 5	68	69	37-71 — 108	79	26.6
Guy Chouinard	Atl.	Mar. 30/79	(G)	L.A. 3	at	Atl. 5	75	75	50-57 — 107	80	22.5
Denis Potvin	NYI	Apr. 8/79	(A)	NYI 5	at	NYR 2	73	80	31-70 — 101	73	25.5
Marcel Dionne	L.A.	Feb. 6/80	(A)	L.A. 3	at	Hfd. 7	53	53	53-84 — 137	80	
Guy Lafleur	Mtl.	Feb. 10/80	(A)	Mtl. 3	at	Bos. 2	55	55	50-75 — 125	74	
Wayne Gretzky	Edm.	Feb. 24/80	(A)	Bos. 4	at	Edm. 2	61	62	51-86 — 137	79	19.2
Bryan Trottier	NYI	Mar. 30/80	(A)	NYI 9	at	Que. 6	75	77	42-62 — 104	78	
Gilbert Perreault	Buf.	Apr. 1/80	(A)	Buf. 5	at	Atl. 2	77	77	40-66 — 106	80	
Mike Rogers	Hfd.	Apr. 4/80	(A)	Que. 2	at	Hfd. 9	79	79	44-61 — 105	80	25.5
Charlie Simmer	L.A.	Apr. 5/80	(A)	Van. 5	at	L.A. 3	64	80	56-45 — 101	64	26.0
Blaine Stoughton	Hfd.	Apr. 6/80	(A)	Det. 3	at	Hfd. 5	80	80	56-44 — 100	80	27.0
Wayne Gretzky	Edm.	Feb. 6/81	(G)	Wpg. 4	at	Edm. 10	53	53	55-109 — 164	80	
Marcel Dionne	L.A.	Feb. 12/81	(A)	L.A. 5	at	Chi. 5	58	58	58-77 — 135	80	
Charlie Simmer	L.A.	Feb. 14/81	(A)	Bos. 5	at	L.A. 4	59	59	56-49 — 105	65	
Kent Nilsson	Cgy.	Feb. 27/81	(G)	Hfd. 1	at	Cgy. 5	64	64	49-82 — 131	80	24.6
Mike Bossy	NYI	Mar. 3/81	(G)	Edm. 8	at	NYI 8	65	66	68-51 — 119	79	
Dave Taylor	L.A.	Mar. 14/81	(G)	Min. 4	at	L.A. 10	63	70	47-65 — 112	72	25.3
Mike Rogers	Hfd.	Mar. 22/81	(G)	Tor. 3	at	Hfd. 3	74	74	40-65 — 105	80	
Bernie Federko	St.L.	Mar. 28/81	(A)	Buf. 3	at	St.L. 7	74	76	31-73 — 104	78	24.10
Rick Middleton	Bos.	Mar. 28/81	(A)	Chi. 2	at	Bos. 5	76	76	44-59 — 103	80	27.4
Bryan Trottier	NYI	Mar. 29/81	(A)	NYI 5	at	Wsh. 4	69	76	31-72 — 103	73	
Jacques Richard	Que.	Mar. 29/81	(G)	Mtl. 0	at	Que. 4	75	76	52-51 — 103	78	28.6
Peter Stastny	Que.	Mar. 29/81	(A)	Mtl. 0	at	Que. 4	73	76	39-70 — 109	77	24.6
Wayne Gretzky	Edm.	Dec. 27/81	(G)	L.A. 3	at	Edm. 10	38	38	92-120 — 212	80	
Mike Bossy	NYI	Feb. 13/82	(A)	Phi. 2	at	NYI 8	55	55	64-83 — 147	80	
Peter Stastny	Que.	Feb. 16/82	(A)	Wpg. 3	at	Que. 7	60	60	46-93 — 139	80	
Dennis Maruk	Wsh.	Feb. 20/82	(G)	Wsh. 3	at	Min. 7	60	60	60-76 — 136	80	26.3
Bryan Trottier	NYI	Feb. 23/82	(G)	Chi. 1	at	NYI 5	61	61	50-79 — 129	80	
Denis Savard	Chi.	Feb. 27/82	(A)	Chi. 5	at	St.L. 3	64	64	32-87 — 119	80	21.1
Bobby Smith	Min.	Mar. 3/82	(A)	Det. 4	at	Min. 6	66	66	43-71 — 114	80	24.1
Marcel Dionne	L.A.	Mar. 6/82	(G)	L.A. 6	at	Hfd. 7	64	66	50-67 — 117	78	
Dave Taylor	L.A.	Mar. 20/82	(A)	Pit. 5	at	L.A. 7	71	72	39-67 — 106	78	
Dale Hawerchuk	Wpg.	Mar. 24/82	(A)	L.A. 3	at	Wpg. 6	74	74	45-58 — 103	80	18.11
Dino Ciccarelli	Min.	Mar. 27/82	(A)	Min. 6	at	Bos. 5	72	76	55-52 — 107	76	21.8
Glenn Anderson	Edm.	Mar. 28/82	(G)	Edm. 6	at	L.A. 2	78	78	38-67 — 105	80	21.7
Mike Rogers	NYR	Apr. 2/82	(G)	Pit. 7	at	NYR 5	79	79	38-65 — 103	80	
Wayne Gretzky	Edm.	Jan. 5/83	(A)	Edm. 8	at	Wpg. 3	42	42	71-125 — 196	80	
Mike Bossy	NYI	Mar. 3/83	(A)	Tor. 1	at	NYI 5	66	67	60-58 — 118	79	
Peter Stastny	Que.	Mar. 5/83	(A)	Hfd. 3	at	Que. 10	62	67	47-77 — 124	75	
Denis Savard	Chi.	Mar. 6/83	(G)	Mtl. 4	at	Chi. 5	65	67	35-86 — 121	78	
Mark Messier	Edm.	Mar. 23/83	(G)	Edm. 4	at	Wpg. 7	73	76	48-58 — 106	77	22.2
Barry Pederson	Bos.	Mar. 26/83	(A)	Hfd. 4	at	Bos. 7	73	76	46-61 — 107	77	22.0
Marcel Dionne	L.A.	Mar. 26/83	(A)	Edm. 9	at	L.A. 3	75	75	56-51 — 107	80	
Michel Goulet	Que.	Mar. 27/83	(A)	Que. 6	at	Buf. 6	77	77	57-48 — 105	80	22.11
Glenn Anderson	Edm.	Mar. 29/83	(A)	Edm. 7	at	Van. 4	70	78	48-56 — 104	72	
Jari Kurri	Edm.	Mar. 29/83	(A)	Edm. 7	at	Van. 4	78	78	45-59 — 104	80	22.10
Kent Nilsson	Cgy.	Mar. 29/83	(G)	L.A. 3	at	Cgy. 5	78	78	46-58 — 104	80	
Wayne Gretzky	Edm.	Dec. 18/83	(G)	Edm. 7	at	Wpg. 5	34	34	87-118 — 205	74	
Paul Coffey	Edm.	Mar. 4/84	(A)	Mtl. 1	at	Edm. 6	68	68	40-86 — 126	80	22.9
Michel Goulet	Que.	Mar. 4/84	(A)	Que. 1	at	Buf. 1	62	67	56-65 — 121	75	
Jari Kurri	Edm.	Mar. 7/84	(A)	Chi. 4	at	Edm. 7	53	69	52-61 — 113	64	
Peter Stastny	Que.	Mar. 8/84	(A)	Que. 8	at	Pit. 6	69	69	46-73 — 119	80	
Mike Bossy	NYI	Mar. 8/84	(G)	Tor. 5	at	NYI 9	56	68	51-67 — 118	67	
Barry Pederson	Bos.	Mar. 14/84	(A)	Bos. 4	at	Det. 2	71	71	39-77 — 116	80	
Bryan Trottier	NYI	Mar. 18/84	(A)	NYI 4	at	Hfd. 5	62	73	40-71 — 111	68	
Bernie Federko	St.L.	Mar. 20/84	(A)	Wpg. 3	at	St.L. 9	75	76	41-66 — 107	79	
Rick Middleton	Bos.	Mar. 27/84	(G)	Bos. 6	at	Que. 4	77	77	47-58 — 105	80	
Dale Hawerchuk	Wpg.	Mar. 27/84	(G)	Wpg. 3	at	L.A. 3	77	77	37-65 — 102	80	
Mark Messier	Edm.	Mar. 27/84	(G)	Edm. 9	at	Cgy. 2	72	79	37-64 — 101	73	
Wayne Gretzky	Edm.	Dec. 29/84	(A)	Det. 3	at	Edm. 6	35	35	73-135 — 208	80	
Jari Kurri	Edm.	Jan. 29/85	(G)	Edm. 4	at	Cgy. 2	48	51	71-64 — 135	73	
Mike Bossy	NYI	Feb. 23/85	(G)	Bos. 1	at	NYI 7	56	60	58-59 — 117	76	
Dale Hawerchuk	Wpg.	Feb. 25/85	(A)	Wpg. 12	at	NYR 5	64	64	53-77 — 130	80	
Marcel Dionne	L.A.	Mar. 5/85	(A)	Pit. 0	at	L.A. 6	66	66	46-80 — 126	80	
Brent Sutter	NYI	Mar. 12/85	(A)	NYI 6	at	St.L. 5	68	68	42-60 — 102	72	22.10
John Ogrodnick	Det.	Mar. 22/85	(A)	NYR 3	at	Det. 5	73	73	55-50 — 105	79	25.9
Paul Coffey	Edm.	Mar. 26/85	(G)	Edm. 7	at	NYI 5	74	74	37-84 — 121	80	
Denis Savard	Chi.	Mar. 29/85	(A)	Chi. 5	at	Wpg. 5	75	76	38-67 — 105	79	
Peter Stastny	Que.	Apr. 2/85	(A)	Bos. 4	at	Que. 6	74	77	32-68 — 100	75	
Bernie Federko	St.L.	Apr. 4/85	(A)	NYR 5	at	St.L. 4	74	78	30-73 — 103	76	
Paul MacLean	Wpg.	Apr. 6/85	(A)	Wpg. 6	at	Edm. 5	78	79	41-60 — 101	79	27.1
Bernie Nicholls	L.A.	Apr. 6/85	(A)	Van. 4	at	L.A. 4	80	80	46-54 — 100	80	22.9
John Tonelli	NYI	Apr. 6/85	(G)	N.J. 5	at	NYI 5	80	80	42-58 — 100	80	28.1
Mike Gartner	Wsh.	Apr. 7/85	(G)	Pit. 3	at	Wsh. 7	80	80	50-52 — 102	80	25.6
Mario Lemieux	Pit.	Apr. 7/85	(G)	Pit. 3	at	Wsh. 7	73	80	43-57 — 100	73	19.6

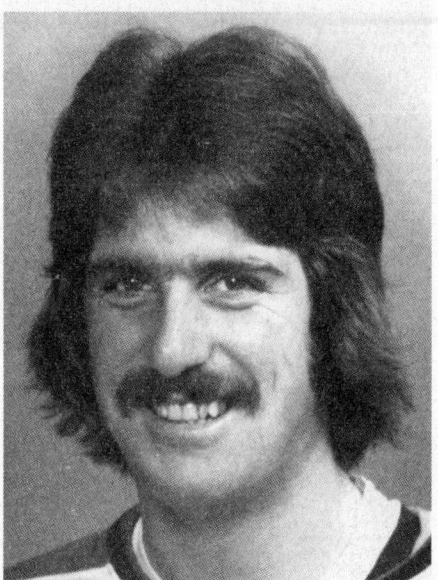

Charlie Simmer

Mark Messier

Mike Gartner

Mario Lemieux

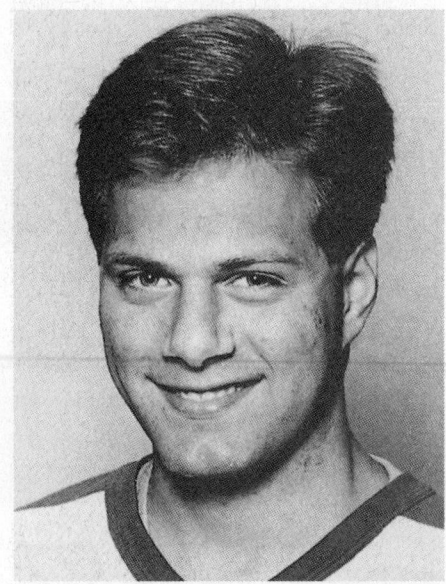

Jimmy Carson

Brett Hull

Player	Team	Date of 100th Point	G or A	Score				Player's Game No.	Team Game No.	G - A	PTS	Total Games	Age when first 100th point scored (Yrs. & Mos.)
Wayne Gretzky	Edm.	Jan. 4/86	(A)	Hfd. 3	at	Edm. 4		39	39	52-163	215	80	
Mario Lemieux	Pit.	Feb. 15/86	(G)	Van. 4	at	Pit. 9		55	56	48-93	141	79	
Paul Coffey	Edm.	Feb. 19/86	(A)	Tor. 5	at	Edm. 9		59	60	48-90	138	79	
Peter Stastny	Que.	Mar. 1/86	(A)	Buf. 8	at	Que. 4		66	68	41-81	122	76	
Jari Kurri	Edm.	Mar. 2/86	(G)	Phi. 1	at	Edm. 2		62	64	68-63	131	78	
Mike Bossy	NYI	Mar. 8/86	(A)	Wsh. 6	at	NYI 2		65	65	61-62	123	80	
Denis Savard	Chi.	Mar. 12/86	(A)	Buf. 7	at	Chi. 6		69	69	47-69	116	80	
Mats Naslund	Mtl.	Mar. 13/86	(A)	Mtl. 2	at	Bos. 3		70	70	43-67	110	80	26.4
Michel Goulet	Que.	Mar. 24/86	(A)	Que. 1	at	Min. 0		70	75	53-50	103	75	
Glenn Anderson	Edm.	Mar. 25/86	(G)	Edm. 7	at	Det. 2		66	74	54-48	102	72	
Neal Broten	Min.	Mar. 26/86	(A)	Min. 6	at	Tor. 1		76	76	29-76	105	80	26.4
Dale Hawerchuk	Wpg.	Mar. 31/86	(A)	Wpg. 5	at	L.A. 2		78	78	46-59	105	80	
Bernie Federko	St.L.	Apr. 5/86	(G)	Chi. 5	at	St.L. 7		79	79	34-68	102	80	
Wayne Gretzky	Edm.	Jan. 11/87	(A)	Cgy. 3	at	Edm. 5		42	42	62-121	183	79	
Jari Kurri	Edm.	Mar. 14/87	(A)	Buf. 3	at	Edm. 5		67	68	54-54	108	79	
Mario Lemieux	Pit.	Mar. 18/87	(A)	St.L. 4	at	Pit. 5		55	72	54-53	107	63	
Mark Messier	Edm.	Mar. 19/87	(A)	Edm. 4	at	Cgy. 5		71	71	37-70	107	77	
Dino Ciccarelli	Min.	Mar. 30/87	(A)	NYR 6	at	Min. 5		78	78	52-51	103	80	
Doug Gilmour	St.L.	Apr. 2/87	(A)	Buf. 3	at	St.L. 5		78	78	42-63	105	80	23.10
Dale Hawerchuk	Wpg.	Apr. 5/87	(A)	Wpg. 3	at	Cgy. 1		80	80	47-53	100	80	
Mario Lemieux	Pit.	Jan. 20/88	(G)	Pit. 8	at	Chi. 3		45	48	70-98	168	77	
Wayne Gretzky	Edm.	Feb. 11/88	(A)	Edm. 7	at	Van. 2		43	56	40-109	149	64	
Denis Savard	Chi.	Feb. 12/88	(A)	St.L. 3	at	Chi. 4		57	57	44-87	131	80	
Dale Hawerchuk	Wpg.	Feb. 23/88	(G)	Wpg. 4	at	Pit. 3		61	61	44-77	121	80	
Steve Yzerman	Det.	Feb. 27/88	(A)	Det. 4	at	Que. 5		63	63	50-52	102	64	22.10
Peter Stastny	Que.	Mar. 8/88	(A)	Hfd. 4	at	Que. 6		63	67	46-65	111	76	
Mark Messier	Edm.	Mar. 15/88	(A)	Buf. 4	at	Edm. 6		68	71	37-74	111	77	
Jimmy Carson	L.A.	Mar. 26/88	(A)	Chi. 5	at	L.A. 9		77	77	55-52	107	80	19.8
Hakan Loob	Cgy.	Mar. 26/88	(G)	Van. 1	at	Cgy. 6		76	76	50-56	106	80	27.9
Mike Bullard	Cgy.	Mar. 26/88	(G)	Van. 1	at	Cgy. 6		76	76	48-55	103	79	27.1
Michel Goulet	Que.	Mar. 27/88	(A)	Pit. 6	at	Que. 3		76	76	48-58	106	80	
Luc Robitaille	L.A.	Mar. 30/88	(G)	Cgy. 7	at	L.A. 9		78	78	53-58	111	80	22.1
Mario Lemieux	Pit.	Dec. 31/88	(A)	N.J. 6	at	Pit. 8		36	38	85-114	199	76	
Wayne Gretzky	L.A.	Jan. 21/89	(A)	L.A. 4	at	Hfd. 5		47	48	54-114	168	78	
Bernie Nicholls	L.A.	Jan. 21/89	(A)	L.A. 4	at	Hfd. 5		48	48	70-80	150	79	
Steve Yzerman	Det.	Jan. 27/89	(G)	Tor. 1	at	Det. 8		50	50	65-90	155	80	
Rob Brown	Pit.	Mar. 16/89	(A)	Pit. 2	at	N.J. 1		60	72	49-66	115	68	20.11
Paul Coffey	Pit.	Mar. 20/89	(A)	Pit. 2	at	Min. 7		69	74	30-83	113	75	
Joe Mullen	Cgy.	Mar. 23/89	(A)	L.A. 2	at	Cgy. 4		74	75	51-59	110	79	32.1
Jari Kurri	Edm.	Mar. 29/89	(A)	Edm. 5	at	Van. 2		75	79	44-58	102	76	
Jimmy Carson	Edm.	Apr. 2/89	(A)	Edm. 2	at	Cgy. 4		80	80	49-51	100	80	
Mario Lemieux	Pit.	Jan. 28/90	(G)	Pit. 2	at	Buf. 7		50	50	45-78	123	59	
Wayne Gretzky	L.A.	Jan. 30/90	(A)	N.J. 2	at	L.A. 5		51	51	40-102	142	73	
Steve Yzerman	Det.	Feb. 19/90	(A)	Mtl. 5	at	Det. 5		61	61	62-65	127	79	
Mark Messier	Edm.	Feb. 20/90	(A)	Edm. 4	at	Van. 2		62	62	45-84	129	79	
Brett Hull	St.L.	Mar. 3/90	(A)	NYI 4	at	St.L. 5		67	67	72-41	113	80	25.7
Bernie Nicholls	NYR	Mar. 12/90	(A)	L.A. 6	at	NYR 2		70	71	39-73	112	79	
Pierre Turgeon	Buf.	Mar. 25/90	(A)	N.J. 4	at	Buf. 3		76	76	40-66	106	80	20.7
Paul Coffey	Pit.	Mar. 25/90	(A)	Pit. 2	at	Hfd. 4		77	77	29-74	103	80	
Pat LaFontaine	NYI	Mar. 27/90	(G)	Cgy. 4	at	NYI 2		72	78	54-51	105	74	25.1
Adam Oates	St.L.	Mar. 29/90	(G)	Pit. 4	at	St.L. 5		79	79	23-79	102	80	27.7
Joe Sakic	Que.	Mar. 31/90	(G)	Hfd. 3	at	Que. 2		79	79	39-63	102	80	20.8
Ron Francis	Hfd.	Mar. 31/90	(G)	Hfd. 3	at	Que. 2		79	79	32-69	101	80	27.0
Luc Robitaille	L.A.	Apr. 1/90	(A)	L.A. 4	at	Cgy. 8		80	80	52-49	101	80	
Wayne Gretzky	L.A.	Jan. 30/91	(A)	N.J. 4	at	L.A. 2		50	51	41-122	163	78	
Brett Hull	St.L.	Feb. 23/91	(G)	Bos. 2	at	St.L. 9		60	62	86-45	131	78	
Mark Recchi	Pit.	Mar. 5/91	(A)	Van. 1	at	Pit. 4		66	67	40-73	113	78	23.1
Steve Yzerman	Det.	Mar. 10/91	(A)	Det. 4	at	St.L. 1		72	72	51-57	108	80	
John Cullen	Hfd.	Mar. 16/91	(G)	N.J. 2	at	Hfd. 6		71	71	39-71	110	78	26.7
Adam Oates	St.L.	Mar. 17/91	(A)	St.L. 4	at	Chi. 6		54	73	25-90	115	61	
Joe Sakic	Que.	Mar. 19/91	(G)	Edm. 7	at	Que. 6		74	74	48-61	109	80	
Steve Larmer	Chi.	Mar. 24/91	(A)	Min. 4	at	Chi. 5		76	76	44-57	101	80	29.9
Theoren Fleury	Cgy.	Mar. 26/91	(G)	Van. 2	at	Cgy. 7		77	77	51-53	104	79	22.9
Al MacInnis	Cgy.	Mar. 28/91	(A)	Edm. 4	at	Cgy. 4		78	78	28-75	103	78	27.8
Brett Hull	St.L.	Mar. 2/92	(G)	St.L. 5	at	Van. 3		66	66	70-39	109	73	
Wayne Gretzky	L.A.	Mar. 3/92	(A)	Phi. 1	at	L.A. 4		60	66	31-90	121	74	
Kevin Stevens	Pit.	Mar. 7/92	(A)	Pit. 3	at	L.A. 5		66	66	54-69	123	80	26.11
Mario Lemieux	Pit.	Mar. 10/92	(A)	Cgy. 2	at	Pit. 5		53	67	44-87	131	64	
Luc Robitaille	L.A.	Mar. 17/92	(A)	Wpg. 4	at	L.A. 5		73	73	44-63	107	80	
Mark Messier	NYR	Mar. 22/92	(A)	N.J. 3	at	NYR 6		74	75	35-72	107	79	
Jeremy Roenick	Chi.	Mar. 29/92	(A)	Tor. 1	at	Chi. 5		77	77	53-50	103	80	22.2
Steve Yzerman	Det.	Apr. 14/92	(G)	Det. 7	at	Min. 4		79	80	45-58	103	79	
Brian Leetch	NYR	Apr. 16/92	(A)	Pit. 1	at	NYR 7		80	80	22-80	102	80	24.1
Mario Lemieux	Pit.	Dec. 31/92	(G)	Tor. 3	at	Pit. 3		38	39	69-91	160	60	
Pat LaFontaine	Buf.	Feb. 10/93	(A)	Buf. 6	at	Wpg. 2		55	55	53-95	148	84	
Adam Oates	Bos.	Feb. 14/93	(A)	Bos. 3	at	T.B. 3		58	58	45-97	142	84	
Steve Yzerman	Det.	Feb. 24/93	(A)	Det. 7	at	Buf. 10		64	64	58-79	137	84	
Pierre Turgeon	NYI	Feb. 28/93	(G)	NYI 7	at	Hfd. 6		62	63	58-74	132	83	
Doug Gilmour	Tor.	Mar. 3/93	(A)	Min. 1	at	Tor. 3		64	64	32-95	127	83	
Alexander Mogilny	Buf.	Mar. 5/93	(A)	Hfd. 4	at	Buf. 2		58	65	76-51	127	77	24.1
Mark Recchi	Phi.	Mar. 7/93	(G)	Phi. 3	at	N.J. 7		66	66	53-70	123	84	
Teemu Selanne	Wpg.	Mar. 9/93	(G)	Wpg. 4	at	T.B. 2		68	68	76-56	132	84	22.7

Player	Team	Date of 100th Point	G or A	Score			Player's Game No.	Team Game No.	G - A PTS	Total Games	Age when first 100th point scored (Yrs. & Mos.)
Luc Robitaille	L.A.	Mar. 15/93	(A)	L.A. 4	at	Buf. 2	69	69	63-62 — 125	84	
Kevin Stevens	Pit.	Mar. 23/93	(A)	S.J. 2	at	Pit. 7	63	73	55-56 — 111	72	
Mats Sundin	Que.	Mar. 27/93	(G)	Phi. 3	at	Que. 8	71	75	47-67 — 114	80	22.1
Pavel Bure	Van.	Apr. 1/93	(A)	Van. 5	at	T.B. 3	77	77	60-50 — 110	83	22.0
Jeremy Roenick	Chi.	Apr. 4/93	(G)	St.L. 4	at	Chi. 5	79	79	50-57 — 107	84	
Craig Janney	St.L.	Apr. 4/93	(G)	St.L. 4	at	Chi. 5	79	79	24-82 — 106	84	25.7
Rick Tocchet	Pit.	Apr. 7/93	(G)	Mtl. 3	at	Pit. 4	77	81	48-61 — 109	80	28.11
Joe Sakic	Que.	Apr. 8/93	(A)	Que. 2	at	Bos. 6	75	81	48-57 — 105	78	
Ron Francis	Pit.	Apr. 9/93	(A)	Pit. 10	at	NYR 4	82	82	24-76 — 100	84	
Brett Hull	St.L.	Apr. 11/93	(G)	Min. 1	at	St.L. 5	78	82	54-47 — 101	80	
Theoren Fleury	Cgy.	Apr. 11/93	(A)	Cgy. 3	at	Van. 6	82	82	34-66 — 100	83	
Joe Juneau	Bos.	Apr. 14/93	(A)	Bos. 4	at	Ott. 2	84	84	32-70 — 102	84	25.3
Wayne Gretzky	L.A.	Feb. 14/94	(A)	Bos. 3	at	L.A. 2	56	56	38-92 — 130	81	
Sergei Fedorov	Det.	Mar. 1/94	(A)	Cgy. 2	at	Det. 5	63	63	56-64 — 120	82	24.2
Doug Gilmour	Tor.	Mar. 23/94	(G)	Tor. 1	at	Fla. 1	74	74	27-84 — 111	83	
Adam Oates	Bos.	Mar. 26/94	(A)	Mtl. 3	at	Bos. 6	68	75	32-80 — 112	77	
Mark Recchi	Phi.	Mar. 27/94	(A)	Ana. 3	at	Phi. 2	76	76	40-67 — 107	84	
Pavel Bure	Van.	Mar. 28/94	(A)	Tor. 2	at	Van. 3	68	76	60-47 — 107	76	
Jeremy Roenick	Chi.	Mar. 31/94	(G)	Chi. 3	at	Wsh. 6	78	78	46-61 — 107	84	
Brendan Shanahan	St.L.	Apr. 12/94	(G)	St.L. 5	at	Dal. 9	80	83	52-50 — 102	81	25.2
Mario Lemieux	Pit.	Jan. 16/96	(G)	Col. 5	at	Pit. 2	38	44	69-92 — 161	70	
Jaromir Jagr	Pit.	Feb. 6/96	(G)	Bos. 5	at	Pit. 6	52	52	62-87 — 149	82	23.11
Ron Francis	Pit.	Mar. 9/96	(A)	N.J. 4	at	Pit. 3	61	66	27-92 — 119	77	
Peter Forsberg	Col.	Mar. 9/96	(A)	Col. 7	at	Van. 5	68	68	30-86 — 116	82	22.7
Joe Sakic	Col.	Mar. 17/96	(A)	Edm. 1	at	Col. 8	70	70	51-69 — 120	82	
Eric Lindros	Phi.	Mar. 25/96	(A)	Hfd. 0	at	Phi. 3	65	73	47-68 — 115	73	23.0
Teemu Selanne	Ana.	Mar. 25/96	(A)	Ana. 1	at	Det. 5	70	73	40-68 — 108	79	
Alexander Mogilny	Van.	Mar. 25/96	(A)	L.A. 1	at	Van. 4	72	75	55-52 — 107	79	
Wayne Gretzky	St.L.	Mar. 28/96	(A)	N.J. 4	at	St.L. 4	76	75	23-79 — 102	80	
Doug Weight	Edm.	Mar. 30/96	(G)	Tor. 4	at	Edm. 3	76	76	25-79 — 104	82	25.3
Sergei Fedorov	Det.	Apr. 2/96	(A)	Det. 3	at	S.J. 6	72	76	39-68 — 107	78	
Paul Kariya	Ana.	Apr. 7/96	(G)	Ana. 5	at	S.J. 3	78	78	50-58 — 108	82	21.5
Mario Lemieux	Pit.	Mar. 8/97	(A)	Phi. 2	at	Pit. 3	61	65	50-72 — 122	76	
Teemu Selanne	Ana.	Apr. 1/97	(A)	Chi. 3	at	Ana. 3	74	78	51-58 — 109	78	
Jaromir Jagr	Pit.	Apr. 15/98	(G)	T.B. 1	at	Pit. 5	76	80	35-67 — 102	77	
Jaromir Jagr	Pit.	Mar. 13/99	(G)	Phi. 0	at	Pit. 4	65	65	44-83 — 127	81	
Teemu Selanne	Ana.	Apr. 5/99	(A)	Ana. 2	at	Det. 3	69	76	47-60 — 107	75	
Paul Kariya	Ana.	Apr. 17/99	(G)	Ana. 3	at	S.J. 3	82	82	39-62 — 101	82	
Jaromir Jagr	Pit.	Mar. 10/01	(G)	Cgy. 3	at	Pit. 6	68	68	52-69 — 121	81	
Joe Sakic	Col.	Mar. 18/01	(G)	Min. 3	at	Col. 4	72	72	54-64 — 118	82	
Markus Naslund	Van.	Mar. 27/03	(A)	Phx. 1	at	Van. 5	78	78	48-56 — 104	82	29.8
Peter Forsberg	Col.	Mar. 31/03	(A)	S.J. 1	at	Col. 3	72	79	29-77 — 106	79	
Joe Thornton	Bos.	Apr. 4/03	(A)	Buf. 5	at	Bos. 8	77	82	36-65 — 101	77	23.9
Jaromir Jagr	NYR	Mar. 18/06	(A)	Tor. 2	at	NYR 5	67	67	54-69 — 123	82	
Joe Thornton	S.J.	Mar. 21/06	(A)	S.J. 6	at	St.L. 0	66	67	29-96 — 125	81	
Alex Ovechkin	Wsh.	Apr. 10/06	(G)	Wsh. 2	at	Bos. 1	77	78	52-54 — 106	81	20.6
Dany Heatley	Ott.	Apr. 13/06	(A)	Fla. 5	at	Ott. 4	80	80	50-53 — 103	82	25.2
Daniel Alfredsson	Ott.	Apr. 15/06	(A)	Ott. 1	at	Tor. 5	76	81	43-60 — 103	77	33.4
Eric Staal	Car.	Apr. 15/06	(A)	Car. 2	at	T.B. 3	81	81	45-55 — 100	82	21.5
Sidney Crosby	Pit.	Apr. 17/06	(A)	NYI 1	at	Pit. 6	80	81	39-63 — 102	81	18.8
Sidney Crosby	Pit.	Mar. 10/07	(G)	NYR 2	at	Pit. 3	65	68	36-84 — 120	79	
Joe Thornton	S.J.	Mar. 22/07	(A)	S.J. 5	at	Atl. 1	75	75	22-92 — 114	82	
Vincent Lecavalier	T.B.	Mar. 24/07	(A)	Ott. 7	at	T.B. 2	76	76	52-56 — 108	82	26.11
Dany Heatley	Ott.	Mar. 31/07	(G)	Ott. 5	at	NYI 2	79	79	50-55 — 105	82	
Martin St. Louis	T.B.	Mar. 31/07	(A)	Wsh. 2	at	T.B. 5	79	79	43-59 — 102	82	31.10
Marian Hossa	Atl.	Apr. 7/07	(A)	T.B. 2	at	Atl. 3	82	82	43-57 — 100	82	28.3
Joe Sakic	Col.	Apr. 8/07	(G)	Cgy. 3	at	Col. 6	82	82	36-64 — 100	82	
Alex Ovechkin	Wsh.	Mar. 18/08	(A)	Wsh. 4	at	Nsh. 2	74	74	65-47 — 112	82	
Evgeni Malkin	Pit.	Mar. 22/08	(G)	N.J. 1	at	Pit. 7	75	75	47-59 — 106	82	21.8
Evgeni Malkin	Pit.	Mar. 17/09	(G)	Atl. 2	at	Pit. 6	72	72	35-78 — 113	82	
Alex Ovechkin	Wsh.	Mar. 27/09	(G)	T.B. 3	at	Wsh. 5	73	76	56-54 — 110	79	
Sidney Crosby	Pit.	Apr. 7/09	(G)	Pit. 6	at	T.B. 4	75	80	33-70 — 103	77	
Henrik Sedin	Van.	Mar. 27/10	(A)	Van. 2	at	S.J. 4	75	75	29-83 — 112	82	29.7
Alex Ovechkin	Wsh.	Mar. 28/10	(A)	Cgy. 5	at	Wsh. 3	65	75	50-59 — 109	72	
Sidney Crosby	Pit.	Apr. 6/10	(A)	Wsh. 6	at	Pit. 3	78	79	51-58 — 109	81	
Nicklas Backstrom	Wsh.	Apr. 9/10	(A)	Atl. 2	at	Wsh. 5	81	81	33-68 — 101	82	22.5
Daniel Sedin	Van.	Mar. 31/11	(A)	L.A. 1	at	Van. 3	78	78	41-63 — 104	82	30.7
Evgeni Malkin	Pit.	Mar. 29/12	(G)	Pit. 3	at	NYI 5	70	77	50-59 — 109	75	
Sidney Crosby	Pit.	Apr. 1/14	(A)	Car. 4	at	Pit. 1	76	76	36-68 — 104	80	
Patrick Kane	Chi.	Apr. 3/16	(G)	Bos. 4	at	Chi. 6	79	79	46-60 — 106	82	27.4
Connor McDavid	Edm.	Apr. 9/17	(A)	Van. 2	at	Edm. 5	82	82	30-70 — 100	82	20.3

Joe Juneau

Peter Forsberg

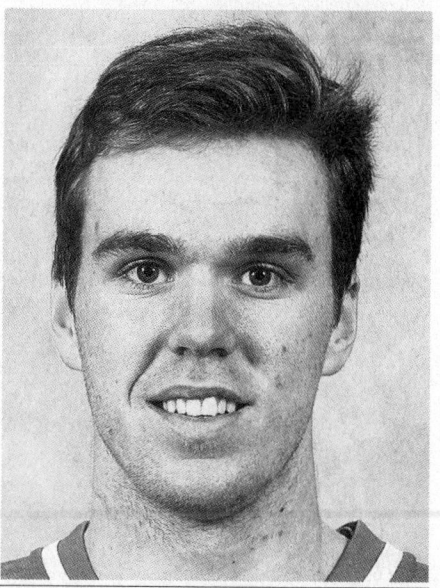

Connor McDavid

Five-or-more-Goal Games

Player	Team	Date	Score				Opposing Goaltender(s)
SEVEN GOALS							
Joe Malone	Quebec Bulldogs	Jan. 31/20	Tor. 6	at	Que. 10		Ivan Mitchell (4) Howard Lockhart (3)
SIX GOALS							
Newsy Lalonde	Montreal	Jan. 10/20	Tor. 7	at	Mtl. 14		Ivan Mitchell (2) Howard Lockhart (4)
Joe Malone	Quebec Bulldogs	Mar. 10/20	Ott. 4	at	Que. 10		Clint Benedict
Corb Denneny	Toronto St. Pats	Jan. 26/21	Ham. 3	at	Tor. 10		Howard Lockhart
Cy Denneny	Ottawa Senators	Mar. 7/21	Ham. 5	at	Ott. 12		Howard Lockhart
Syd Howe	Detroit	Feb. 3/44	NYR 2	at	Det. 12		Ken McAuley
Red Berenson	St. Louis	Nov. 7/68	St.L. 8	at	Phi. 0		Doug Favell
Darryl Sittler	Toronto	Feb. 7/76	Bos. 4	at	Tor. 11		Dave Reece
FIVE GOALS							
Joe Malone	Montreal	Dec. 19/17	Mtl. 7	at	Ott. 4		Clint Benedict
Harry Hyland	Mtl. Wanderers	Dec. 19/17	Tor. 9	at	Mtl. W. 10		Sammy Hebert (3) Art Brooks (2)
Joe Malone	Montreal	Jan. 12/18	Ott. 4	at	Mtl. 9		Clint Benedict
Joe Malone	Montreal	Feb. 2/18	Tor. 2	at	Mtl. 11		Hap Holmes
Mickey Roach	Toronto St. Pats	Mar. 6/20	Que. 2	at	Tor. 11		Howard Lockhart
Newsy Lalonde	Montreal	Feb. 16/21	Ham. 5	at	Mtl. 10		Howard Lockhart
Babe Dye	Toronto St. Pats	Dec. 16/22	Mtl. 2	at	Tor. 7		Georges Vezina
Red Green	Hamilton Tigers	Dec. 5/24	Ham. 10	at	Tor. 3		John Ross Roach
Babe Dye	Toronto St. Pats	Dec. 22/24	Tor. 10	at	Bos. 1		Hec Fowler
Punch Broadbent	Mtl. Maroons	Jan. 7/25	Mtl. 6	at	Ham. 2		George Redding (1) Jake Forbes
Pit Lepine	Montreal	Dec. 14/29	Ott. 4	at	Mtl. 6		Alex Connell
Howie Morenz	Montreal	Mar. 18/30	NYA 3	at	Mtl. 8		Roy Worters
Charlie Conacher	Toronto	Jan. 19/32	NYA 3	at	Tor. 11		Roy Worters (3) Al Shields (2)
Ray Getliffe	Montreal	Feb. 6/43	Bos. 3	at	Mtl. 8		Frank Brimsek
Maurice Richard	Montreal	Dec. 28/44	Det. 1	at	Mtl. 9		Harry Lumley
Howie Meeker	Toronto	Jan. 8/47	Chi. 4	at	Tor. 10		Paul Bibeault
Bernie Geoffrion	Montreal	Feb. 19/55	NYR 2	at	Mtl. 10		Gump Worsley
Bobby Rousseau	Montreal	Feb. 1/64	Det. 3	at	Mtl. 9		Roger Crozier
Yvan Cournoyer	Montreal	Feb. 15/75	Chi. 3	at	Mtl. 12		Mike Veisor
Don Murdoch	NY Rangers	Oct. 12/76	NYR 10	at	Min. 4		Gary Smith
Ian Turnbull	Toronto	Feb. 2/77	Det. 1	at	Tor. 9		Ed Giacomin (2) Jim Rutherford (3)
Bryan Trottier	NY Islanders	Dec. 23/78	NYR 4	at	NYI 9		Wayne Thomas (4) John Davidson (1)
Tim Young	Minnesota	Jan. 15/79	Min. 8	at	NYR 1		Doug Soetaert (3) Wayne Thomas (2)
John Tonelli	NY Islanders	Jan. 6/81	Tor. 3	at	NYI 6		Jiri Crha (4) empty net (1)
Wayne Gretzky	Edmonton	Feb. 18/81	St.L. 2	at	Edm. 9		Mike Liut (3) Ed Staniowski (2)
Wayne Gretzky	Edmonton	Dec. 30/81	Phi. 5	at	Edm. 7		Pete Peeters (4) empty net (1)
Grant Mulvey	Chicago	Feb. 3/82	St.L. 5	at	Chi. 9		Mike Liut (4) Gary Edwards (1)
Bryan Trottier	NY Islanders	Feb. 13/82	Phi. 2	at	NYI 8		Pete Peeters
Willy Lindstrom	Winnipeg	Mar. 2/82	Wpg. 7	at	Phi. 6		Pete Peeters
Mark Pavelich	NY Rangers	Feb. 23/83	Hfd. 3	at	NYR 11		Greg Millen
Jari Kurri	Edmonton	Nov. 19/83	N.J. 4	at	Edm. 13		Glenn Resch (3) Ron Low (2)
Bengt Gustafsson	Washington	Jan. 8/84	Wsh. 7	at	Phi. 1		Pelle Lindbergh
Pat Hughes	Edmonton	Feb. 3/84	Cgy. 5	at	Edm. 10		Don Edwards (3) Reggie Lemelin (2)
Wayne Gretzky	Edmonton	Dec. 15/84	Edm. 8	at	St.L. 2		Rick Wamsley (4) Mike Liut(1)
Dave Andreychuk	Buffalo	Feb. 6/86	Buf. 8	at	Bos. 6		Pat Riggin (1) Doug Keans (4)
Wayne Gretzky	Edmonton	Dec. 6/87	Min. 4	at	Edm. 10		Don Beaupre (4) Kari Takko (1)
Mario Lemieux	Pittsburgh	Dec. 31/88	N.J. 6	at	Pit. 8		Bob Sauve (3) Chris Terreri (1) empty net (1)
Joe Nieuwendyk	Calgary	Jan. 11/89	Wpg. 3	at	Cgy. 8		Daniel Berthiaume (3) Peter Sidorkiewicz (3)
Mats Sundin	Quebec	Mar. 5/92	Que. 10	at	Hfd. 4		Kay Whitmore (2)
Mario Lemieux	Pittsburgh	Apr. 9/93	Pit. 10	at	NYR 4		Corey Hirsch (3) Mike Richter (1)
Peter Bondra	Washington	Feb. 5/94	T.B. 3	at	Wsh. 6		Daren Puppa (4) Pat Jablonski (1)
Mike Ricci	Quebec	Feb. 17/94	Que. 8	at	S.J. 2		Arturs Irbe (3) Jimmy Waite (2)
Alex Zhamnov	Winnipeg	Apr. 1/95	Wpg. 7	at	L.A. 7		Kelly Hrudey (3) Grant Fuhr (2)
Mario Lemieux	Pittsburgh	Mar. 26/96	St.L. 4	at	Pit. 8		Grant Fuhr (1) Jon Casey (4)
Sergei Fedorov	Detroit	Dec. 26/96	Wsh. 4	at	Det. 5		Jim Carey
Marian Gaborik	Minnesota	Dec. 20/07	NYR 3	at	Min. 6		Henrik Lundqvist
Johan Franzen	Detroit	Feb. 2/11	Det. 7	at	Ott. 5		Robin Lehner (2) Brian Elliott (2) empty net (1)

Players' 500th Goals

Regular Season

Player	Team	Date	Game No.	Score			Opposing Goaltender	Total Goals	Total Games
Maurice Richard	Montreal	Oct. 19/57	863	Chi. 1	at	Mtl. 3	Glenn Hall	544	978
Gordie Howe	Detroit	Mar. 14/62	1,045	Det. 2	at	NYR 3	Gump Worsley	801	1,767
Bobby Hull	Chicago	Feb. 21/70	861	NYR. 2	at	Chi. 4	Ed Giacomin	610	1,063
Jean Béliveau	Montreal	Feb. 11/71	1,101	Min. 2	at	Mtl. 6	Gilles Gilbert	507	1,125
Frank Mahovlich	Montreal	Mar. 21/73	1,105	Van. 2	at	Mtl. 3	Dunc Wilson	533	1,181
Phil Esposito	Boston	Dec. 22/74	803	Det. 4	at	Bos. 5	Jim Rutherford	717	1,282
John Bucyk	Boston	Oct. 30/75	1,370	St.L. 2	at	Bos. 3	Yves Bélanger	556	1,540
Stan Mikita	Chicago	Feb. 27/77	1,221	Van. 4	at	Chi. 3	Cesare Maniago	541	1,394
Marcel Dionne	Los Angeles	Dec. 14/82	887	L.A. 2	at	Wsh. 7	Al Jensen	731	1,348
Guy Lafleur	Montreal	Dec. 20/83	918	Mtl. 6	at	N.J. 0	Glenn Resch	560	1,126
Mike Bossy	NY Islanders	Jan. 2/86	647	Bos. 5	at	NYI 7	empty net	573	752
Gilbert Perreault	Buffalo	Mar. 9/86	1,159	N.J. 3	at	Buf. 4	Alain Chevrier	512	1,191
Wayne Gretzky	Edmonton	Nov. 22/86	575	Van. 2	at	Edm. 5	empty net	894	1,487
Lanny McDonald	Calgary	Mar. 21/89	1,107	NYI 1	at	Cgy. 4	Mark Fitzpatrick	500	1,111
Bryan Trottier	NY Islanders	Feb. 13/90	1,104	Cgy. 4	at	NYI 2	Rick Wamsley	524	1,279
Mike Gartner	NY Rangers	Oct. 14/91	936	Wsh. 5	at	NYR 3	Mike Liut	708	1,432
Michel Goulet	Chicago	Feb. 16/92	951	Cgy. 5	at	Chi. 5	Jeff Reese	548	1,089
Jari Kurri	Los Angeles	Oct. 17/92	833	Bos. 6	at	L.A. 8	empty net	601	1,251
Dino Ciccarelli	Detroit	Jan. 8/94	946	Det. 6	at	L.A. 3	Kelly Hrudey	608	1,232
Mario Lemieux	Pittsburgh	Oct. 26/95	605	Pit. 7	at	NYI 5	Tommy Soderstrom	690	915
Mark Messier	NY Rangers	Nov. 6/95	1,141	Cgy. 2	at	NYR 4	Rick Tabaracci	694	1,756
Steve Yzerman	Detroit	Jan. 17/96	906	Col. 2	at	Det. 3	Patrick Roy	692	1,514
Dale Hawerchuk	St. Louis	Jan. 31/96	1,103	St.L. 4	at	Tor. 0	Felix Potvin	518	1,188
Brett Hull	St. Louis	Dec. 22/96	693	L.A. 4	at	St.L. 7	Stephane Fiset	741	1,269
Joe Mullen	Pittsburgh	Mar. 14/97	1,052	Pit. 3	at	Col. 6	Patrick Roy	502	1,062
Dave Andreychuk	New Jersey	Mar. 15/97	1,070	Wsh. 2	at	N.J. 3	Bill Ranford	640	1,639
Luc Robitaille	Los Angeles	Jan. 7/99	928	Buf. 2	at	L.A. 4	Dwayne Roloson	668	1,431
Pat Verbeek	Detroit	Mar. 22/00	1,285	Cgy. 2	at	Det. 2	Fred Brathwaite	522	1,424
Ron Francis	Carolina	Jan. 2/02	1,533	Bos. 6	at	Car. 3	Byron Dafoe	549	1,731
Brendan Shanahan	Detroit	Mar. 23/02	1,100	Det. 2	at	Col. 0	Patrick Roy	656	1,524
Joe Sakic	Colorado	Dec. 11/02	1,044	Col. 1	at	Van. 3	Dan Cloutier	625	1,378
Joe Nieuwendyk	New Jersey	Jan. 17/03	1,094	N.J. 2	at	Car. 1	Kevin Weekes	564	1,257
*Jaromir Jagr	Washington	Feb. 4/03	928	Wsh. 5	at	T.B. 1	John Grahame	765	1,711
Pierre Turgeon	Colorado	Nov. 8/05	1,229	S.J. 2	at	Col. 5	Vesa Toskala	515	1,294
Mats Sundin	Toronto	Oct. 14/06	1,162	Cgy. 4	at	Tor. 5	Miikka Kiprusoff	564	1,346
Teemu Selanne	Anaheim	Nov. 22/06	982	Ana. 2	at	Col. 3	Jose Theodore	684	1,451
Peter Bondra	Chicago	Dec. 22/06	1,050	Tor. 1	at	Chi. 3	J.S. Aubin	503	1,081
Mark Recchi	Pittsburgh	Jan. 26/07	1,303	Pit. 4	at	Dal. 3	Marty Turco	577	1,652
Mike Modano	Dallas	Mar. 13/07	1,225	Phi. 2	at	Dal. 3	Antero Niittymaki	561	1,499
Jeremy Roenick	San Jose	Nov. 10/07	1,267	Phx. 1	at	S.J. 4	Alex Auld	513	1,363
Keith Tkachuk	St. Louis	Apr. 6/08	1,055	St.L. 4	at	CBJ 1	empty net	538	1,201
*Jarome Iginla	Calgary	Jan. 7/12	1,149	Min. 1	at	Cgy. 3	Niklas Backstrom	625	1,554
*Alex Ovechkin	Washington	Jan. 10/16	801	Ott. 1	at	Wsh. 7	Andrew Hammond	558	921
*Marian Hossa	Chicago	Oct. 18/16	1,240	Phi. 4	at	Chi. 7	Michal Neuvirth	525	1,309
*Patrick Marleau	San Jose	Feb. 2/17	1,463	S.J. 4	at	Van. 1	Ryan Miller	508	1,493

*Active

Marian Hossa is congratulated by Jonathan Toews at the Chicago bench after scoring his 500th career goal. Hossa joined Peter Bondra and Stan Mikita (who was raised in Canada) as the only Slovakians to reach the milestone, and all of them did it while playing with the Blackhawks.

Players' 1,000th Points

Regular Season

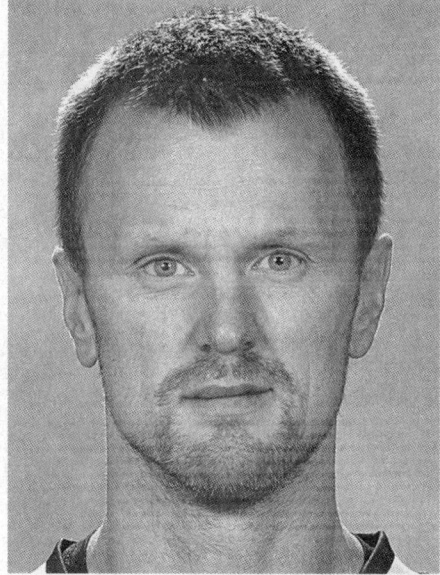

Player	Team	Date	Game No.	G or A	Score				Total Points G A PTS	Total Games
Gordie Howe	Detroit	Nov. 27/60	938	(A)	Tor. 0	at	Det. 2		801-1,049–1,850	1,767
Jean Béliveau	Montreal	Mar. 3/68	911	(G)	Mtl. 2	at	Det. 5		507-712–1,219	1,125
Alex Delvecchio	Detroit	Feb. 16/69	1,143	(A)	L.A. 3	at	Det. 6		456-825–1,281	1,549
Bobby Hull	Chicago	Dec. 13/70	909	(A)	Min. 2	at	Chi. 5		610-560–1,170	1,063
Norm Ullman	Toronto	Oct. 16/71	1,113	(A)	NYR 5	at	Tor. 3		490-739–1,229	1,410
Stan Mikita	Chicago	Oct. 15/72	924	(A)	St.L. 3	at	Chi. 1		541-926–1,467	1,394
John Bucyk	Boston	Nov. 9/72	1,144	(A)	Det. 3	at	Bos. 8		556-813–1,369	1,540
Frank Mahovlich	Montreal	Feb. 17/73	1,090	(A)	Phi. 7	at	Mtl. 6		533-570–1,103	1,181
Henri Richard	Montreal	Dec. 20/73	1,194	(A)	Mtl. 2	at	Buf. 2		358-688–1,046	1,256
Phil Esposito	Boston	Feb. 15/74	745	(A)	Bos. 4	at	Van. 2		717-873–1,590	1,282
Rod Gilbert	NY Rangers	Feb. 19/77	1,027	(G)	NYR 2	at	NYI 5		406-615–1,021	1,065
Jean Ratelle	Boston	Apr. 3/77	1,007	(A)	Tor. 4	at	Bos. 7		491-776–1,267	1,281
Marcel Dionne	Los Angeles	Jan. 7/81	740	(A)	L.A. 5	at	Hfd. 3		731-1,040–1,771	1,348
Guy Lafleur	Montreal	Mar. 4/81	720	(G)	Wpg. 3	at	Mtl. 9		560-793–1,353	1,126
Bobby Clarke	Philadelphia	Mar. 19/81	922	(G)	Bos. 3	at	Phi. 5		358-852–1,210	1,144
Gilbert Perreault	Buffalo	Apr. 3/82	871	(A)	Buf. 5	at	Mtl. 4		512-814–1,326	1,191
Darryl Sittler	Philadelphia	Jan. 20/83	927	(G)	Cgy. 2	at	Phi. 5		484-637–1,121	1,096
Wayne Gretzky	Edmonton	Dec. 19/84	424	(A)	L.A. 3	at	Edm. 7		894-1,963–2,875	1,487
Bryan Trottier	NY Islanders	Jan. 29/85	726	(A)	Min. 4	at	NYI 4		524-901–1,425	1,279
Mike Bossy	NY Islanders	Jan. 24/86	656	(G)	NYI 7	at	Wsh. 5		573-553–1,126	752
Denis Potvin	NY Islanders	Apr. 4/87	987	(G)	Buf. 6	at	NYI 6		310-742–1,052	1,060
Bernie Federko	St. Louis	Mar. 19/88	855	(A)	Hfd. 5	at	St.L. 3		369-761–1,130	1,000
Lanny McDonald	Calgary	Mar. 7/89	1,101	(G)	Wpg. 5	at	Cgy. 9		500-506–1,006	1,111
Peter Stastny	Quebec	Oct. 19/89	682	(G)	Que. 5	at	Chi. 3		450-789–1,239	977
Jari Kurri	Edmonton	Jan. 2/90	716	(A)	Edm. 6	at	St.L. 4		601-797–1,398	1,251
Denis Savard	Chicago	Mar. 11/90	727	(A)	St.L. 6	at	Chi. 4		473-865–1,338	1,196
Paul Coffey	Pittsburgh	Dec. 22/90	770	(A)	Pit. 4	at	NYI 3		396-1,135–1,531	1,409
Mark Messier	Edmonton	Jan. 13/91	822	(A)	Edm. 5	at	Phi. 3		694-1,193–1,887	1,756
Dave Taylor	Los Angeles	Feb. 5/91	930	(A)	L.A. 3	at	Phi. 2		431-638–1,069	1,111
Michel Goulet	Chicago	Feb. 23/91	878	(G)	Chi. 3	at	Min. 3		548-604–1,152	1,089
Dale Hawerchuk	Buffalo	Mar. 8/91	781	(G)	Chi. 5	at	Buf. 3		518-891–1,409	1,188
Bobby Smith	Minnesota	Nov. 30/91	986	(A)	Min. 4	at	Tor. 3		357-679–1,036	1,077
Mike Gartner	NY Rangers	Jan. 4/92	971	(A)	NYR 4	at	N.J. 6		708-627–1,335	1,432
Raymond Bourque	Boston	Feb. 29/92	933	(A)	Wsh. 5	at	Bos. 5		410-1,169–1,579	1,612
Mario Lemieux	Pittsburgh	Mar. 24/92	513	(A)	Pit. 3	at	Det. 4		690-1,033–1,723	915
Glenn Anderson	Toronto	Feb. 22/93	954	(G)	Tor. 8	at	Van. 1		498-601–1,099	1,129
Steve Yzerman	Detroit	Feb. 24/93	737	(A)	Det. 7	at	Buf. 10		692-1,063–1,755	1,514
Ron Francis	Pittsburgh	Oct. 28/93	893	(G)	Que. 7	at	Pit. 3		549-1,249–1,798	1,731
Bernie Nicholls	New Jersey	Feb. 13/94	858	(G)	N.J. 3	at	T.B. 3		475-734–1,209	1,127
Dino Ciccarelli	Detroit	Mar. 9/94	957	(G)	Det. 5	at	Cgy. 1		608-592–1,200	1,232
Brian Propp	Hartford	Mar. 19/94	1,008	(G)	Hfd. 5	at	Phi. 3		425-579–1,004	1,016
Joe Mullen	Pittsburgh	Feb. 7/95	935	(A)	Fla. 3	at	Pit. 7		502-561–1,063	1,062
Steve Larmer	NY Rangers	Mar. 8/95	983	(A)	N.J. 4	at	NYR 6		441-571–1,012	1,006
Doug Gilmour	Toronto	Dec. 23/95	935	(A)	Edm. 1	at	Tor. 6		450-964–1,414	1,474
Larry Murphy	Toronto	Mar. 27/96	1,228	(G)	Tor. 6	at	Van. 2		287-929–1,216	1,615
Dave Andreychuk	New Jersey	Apr. 7/96	998	(G)	NYR 2	at	N.J. 4		640-698–1,338	1,639
Adam Oates	Washington	Oct. 8/97	830	(G)	Wsh. 6	at	NYI 3		341-1,079–1,420	1,337
Phil Housley	Washington	Nov. 8/97	1,081	(A)	Edm. 1	at	Wsh. 2		338-894–1,232	1,495
Dale Hunter	Washington	Jan. 9/98	1,308	(A)	Phi. 1	at	Wsh. 4		323-697–1,020	1,407
Pat LaFontaine	NY Rangers	Jan. 22/98	847	(G)	Phi. 4	at	NYR 3		468-545–1,013	865
Luc Robitaille	Los Angeles	Jan. 29/98	882	(A)	Cgy. 3	at	L.A. 5		668-726–1,394	1,431
Al MacInnis	St. Louis	Apr. 7/98	1,056	(A)	St.L. 3	at	Det. 5		340-934–1,274	1,416
Brett Hull	Dallas	Nov. 14/98	815	(A)	Dal. 3	at	Bos. 1		741-650–1,391	1,269
Brian Bellows	Washington	Jan. 2/99	1,147	(A)	Tor. 2	at	Wsh. 5		485-537–1,022	1,188
Pierre Turgeon	St. Louis	Oct. 9/99	881	(A)	St.L. 4	at	Edm. 3		515-812–1,327	1,294
Joe Sakic	Colorado	Dec. 27/99	810	(A)	St.L. 1	at	Col. 5		625-1,016–1,641	1,378
Pat Verbeek	Detroit	Feb. 27/00	1,275	(A)	T.B. 1	at	Det. 3		522-541–1,063	1,424
V. Damphousse	San Jose	Oct. 14/00	1,090	(A)	Bos. 2	at	S.J. 5		432-773–1,205	1,378
*Jaromir Jagr	Pittsburgh	Dec. 30/00	763	(G)	Ott. 3	at	Pit. 5		765-1,149–1,914	1,711
Mark Recchi	Philadelphia	Mar. 13/01	920	(A)	St.L. 2	at	Phi. 5		577-956–1,533	1,652
Theoren Fleury	NY Rangers	Oct. 29/01	960	(A)	Dal. 2	at	NYR 4		455-633–1,088	1,084
B. Shanahan	Detroit	Jan. 12/02	1,073	(G)	Dal. 2	at	Det. 5		656-698–1,354	1,524
Jeremy Roenick	Philadelphia	Jan. 30/02	961	(G)	Phi. 1	at	Ott. 3		513-703–1,216	1,363
Mike Modano	Dallas	Nov. 15/02	965	(A)	Col. 2	at	Dal. 4		561-813–1,374	1,499
Joe Nieuwendyk	New Jersey	Feb. 23/03	1,094	(G)	N.J. 4	at	Pit. 3		564-562–1,126	1,257
Mats Sundin	Toronto	Mar. 10/03	994	(G)	Tor. 3	at	Edm. 2		564-785–1,349	1,346
Sergei Fedorov	Anaheim	Feb. 14/04	965	(A)	Ana. 2	at	Van. 1		483-696–1,179	1,248
Alexander Mogilny	Toronto	Mar. 15/04	946	(A)	Tor. 6	at	Buf. 5		473-559–1,032	990
Brian Leetch	Boston	Oct. 18/05	1,151	(A)	Bos. 3	at	Mtl. 4		247-781–1,028	1,205
Teemu Selanne	Anaheim	Jan. 30/06	928	(A)	L.A. 3	at	Ana. 4		684-773–1,457	1,451
Rod Brind'Amour	Carolina	Nov. 4/06	1,202	(G)	Car. 3	at	Ott. 2		452-732–1,184	1,484
Keith Tkachuk	St. Louis	Nov. 30/08	1,077	(G)	St.L. 4	at	Atl. 2		538-527–1,065	1,201
Doug Weight	NY Islanders	Jan. 2/09	1,167	(A)	NYI 4	at	Phx. 5		278-755–1,033	1,238
Nicklas Lidstrom	Detroit	Oct. 15/09	1,336	(G)	L.A. 2	at	Det. 5		264-878–1,142	1,564
Daniel Alfredsson	Ottawa	Oct. 22/10	1,009	(G)	Ott. 4	at	Buf. 2		444-713–1,157	1,246
Alex Kovalev	Ottawa	Nov. 22/10	1,249	(G)	L.A. 2	at	Ott. 3		430-599–1,029	1,316
*Jarome Iginla	Calgary	Apr. 1/11	1,103	(G)	Cgy. 3	at	St.L. 2		625-675–1,300	1,554
*Joe Thornton	San Jose	Apr. 8/11	994	(G)	S.J. 3	at	Phx. 4		384-1,007–1,391	1,446
Ray Whitney	Phoenix	Mar. 31/12	1,226	(G)	Ana. 0	at	Phx. 4		385-679–1,064	1,330
*Marian Hossa	Chicago	Oct. 30/14	1,100	(G)	Chi. 5	at	Ott. 4		525-609–1,134	1,309
Martin St. Louis	NY Rangers	Nov. 28/14	1,082	(G)	NYR 3	at	Phi. 0		391-642–1,033	1,134
Patrik Elias	New Jersey	Jan. 6/15	1,187	(G)	Buf. 1	at	N.J. 4		408-617–1,025	1,240
*Patrick Marleau	San Jose	Nov. 21/15	1,349	(A)	S.J. 3	at	Pit. 1		508-574–1,082	1,493
*Alex Ovechkin	Washington	Jan. 11/17	880	(A)	Pit. 2	at	Wsh. 5		558-477–1,035	921
*Henrik Sedin	Vancouver	Jan. 20/17	1,213	(G)	Fla. 1	at	Van. 2		237-783–1,020	1,248
*Sidney Crosby	Pittsburgh	Feb. 16/17	757	(A)	Wpg. 3	at	Pit. 4		382-645–1,027	782

*Active

Alex Ovechkin, Henrik Sedin and Sidney Crosby all reached the 1,000-point plateau in 2016-17. Crosby did it in just 757 games, making him the 12th fastest in NHL history to reach the milestone.

Individual Awards

Hart Memorial Trophy

Art Ross Trophy

Calder Memorial Trophy

James Norris Memorial Trophy

HART MEMORIAL TROPHY

An annual award "to the player adjudged to be the most valuable to his team." Winner selected in a poll by the Professional Hockey Writers' Association in the 30 NHL cities at the end of the regular schedule.

History: The Hart Memorial Trophy was presented by the National Hockey League in 1960 after the original Hart Trophy was retired to the Hockey Hall of Fame. The original Hart Trophy was donated to the NHL in 1924 by Dr. David A. Hart, father of Cecil Hart, former manager-coach of the Montreal Canadiens.

2016-17 Winner: **Connor McDavid, Edmonton Oilers**
Runners-up: Sidney Crosby, Pittsburgh Penguins
Sergei Bobrovsky, Columbus Blue Jackets

Center Connor McDavid is the winner of the Hart Memorial Trophy. McDavid is the first Edmonton Oiler to win the award since Mark Messier in 1990. He was the only player named on each of the 167 ballots cast in 2017 and received 147 first-place votes, 17 second-place votes and three third-place votes for 1,604 points. Pittsburgh Penguins center Sidney Crosby collected 1,104 points and finished second in voting for the second consecutive year. Crosby had 14 first-place tallies, 119 second-place votes, 19 thirds, 11 fourths and three fifth-place votes. Columbus Blue Jackets goaltender Sergei Bobrovsky received four first-place votes and ranked third overall with 469 points. Brent Burns of San Jose (one first-place vote, 273 points), Erik Karlsson of Ottawa (zero, 267), Patrick Kane of Chicago (zero, 212), Boston's Brad Marchand (one, 184), Tampa Bay's Nikita Kucherov (119 points) Washington's Nicklas Backstrom (60) and Braden Holtby of Washington (19) round out the top ten.

McDavid, who also won the Art Ross Trophy and the Ted Lindsay Award, had 30 goals and 70 assists for 100 points, sparking the Oilers (47-26-9) to a berth in the Stanley Cup playoffs for the first time since 2005-06. The team's 103 points were its most in 30 years. McDavid registered at least one point in 59 of his 82 appearances (72 percent), highlighted by a career-high 14-game point streak (seven goals, 18 assists) to close the season - the longest by any NHL player in 2016-17. He also posted a league-best 30 multi-point games. McDavid, who placed third in voting for the Calder Trophy as the NHL's top rookie in 2015-16, becomes the third player in NHL history to win MVP honors before his 21st birthday, joining Sidney Crosby and Wayne Gretzky.

ART ROSS TROPHY

An annual award "to the player who leads the league in scoring points at the end of the regular season."

History: Arthur Howey Ross, former manager-coach of the Boston Bruins, presented the trophy to the National Hockey League in 1948. If two players finish the schedule with the same number of points, the trophy is awarded in the following manner: 1. Player with most goals. 2. Player with fewer games played. 3. Player scoring first goal of the season.

2016-17 Winner: **Connor McDavid, Edmonton Oilers**
Runners-up: Sidney Crosby, Pittsburgh Penguins
Patrick Kane, Chicago Blackhawks

Center Connor McDavid of the Edmonton Oilers won his first career Art Ross Trophy in just his second NHL season. McDavid finished the season with a league-leading 100 points and 70 assists in 82 games, besting Pittsburgh Penguins center Sidney Crosby (44 goals, 45 assists, 89 points in 75 games) and Chicago Blackhawks right winger Patrick Kane (34 goals, 55 assists, 89 points in 82 games). McDavid registered at least one point in 59 of his 82 appearances (72 percent), highlighted by a career-high 14-game point streak to close the season (seven goals, 18 assist, 25 points) which was the longest by any NHL player in 2016-17 and longest by any Oilers player since 1987-88. He also posted a league-best 30 multi-point performances, including his first career hat trick on November 19, 2016 at Dallas. At 20 years, 86 days, McDavid became the third-youngest player to win the Art Ross Trophy, behind only Sidney Crosby (19 years, 244 days in 2006-07) and Wayne Gretzky (20 years, 69 days in 1980-81). He also became the second Oilers player in franchise history to claim the award and first since Gretzky won seven straight from 1980-81 through 1986-87.

CALDER MEMORIAL TROPHY

An annual award "to the player selected as the most proficient in his first year of competition in the National Hockey League." Winner selected in a poll by the Professional Hockey Writers' Association at the end of the regular schedule.

History: From 1936-37 until his death in 1943, Frank Calder, NHL President, bought a trophy each year to be given permanently to the outstanding rookie. After Calder's death, the NHL presented the Calder Memorial Trophy in his memory and the trophy is to be kept in perpetuity. To be eligible for the award, a player cannot have played more than 25 games in any single preceding season nor in six or more games in each of any two preceding seasons in any major professional league. Beginning in 1990-91, to be eligible for this award a player must not have attained his twenty-sixth birthday by September 15th of the season in which he is eligible.

2016-17 Winner: **Auston Matthews, Toronto Maple Leafs**
Runners-up: Patrik Laine, Winnipeg Jets
Zach Werenski, Columbus Blue Jackets

Toronto Maple Leafs center Auston Matthews won the Calder Memorial Trophy. He is the first Toronto player to win the award since Brit Selby in 1966. Matthews was a near-unanimous selection, receiving 164 of 167 first-place votes and three second-place tallies for 1,661 points. Patrik Laine of the Winnipeg Jets, who also was named on all 167 ballots, collected 1,106 voting points to finish in second place. Laine had three first-place votes, 134 second-place votes, 24 third-place votes and six fourth-place votes. Zach Werenski of the Columbus Blue Jackets garnered 711 voting points (0-21-93-28-15) to finish third. Rounding out the top ten were Pittsburgh goalie Matt Murray (346 points), Matthews' Toronto teammates Mitch Marner (273) and William Nylander (143), Calgary's Matthew Tkachuk (72), Carolina's Sebastian Aho (26), Philadelphia's Ivan Provorov (two) and Brayden Point of Tampa Bay and Brady Skjei of the Rangers (one).

The top pick in the 2016 NHL Draft, Matthews paced rookies with 40 goals and 69 points while appearing in all 82 games. His 40 goals also shared second place in the entire league, highlighted by a historic debut in which he became the first player in the NHL's modern era (since 1943-44) to score four times in his first game. The 19-year-old native of Scottsdale, Arizona, set franchise rookie records for goals and points, and also ranked in the top 10 among first-year players in game-winning goals (1st; eight), shots on goal (1st; 279), power-play points (t-2nd; 21), power-play goals (3rd; eight), power-play assists (4th; 13), shooting percentage (7th; 14.3 percent) and assists (7th; 29).

JAMES NORRIS MEMORIAL TROPHY

An annual award "to the defense player who demonstrates throughout the season the greatest all-round ability in the position." Winner selected in a poll by the Professional Hockey Writers' Association at the end of the regular schedule.

History: The James Norris Memorial Trophy was presented in 1953 by the four children of the late James Norris in memory of the former owner-president of the Detroit Red Wings.

2016-17 Winner: **Brent Burns, San Jose Sharks**
Runners-up: Erik Karlsson, Ottawa Senators
Victor Hedman, Tampa Bay Lightning

Brent Burns of the San Jose Sharks won the James Norris Memorial Trophy for the first time in his career. Burns was the only player receiving votes on all 167 ballots and attracted 96 first-place votes, 61 second-place votes and 10 third place votes for 1,437 points. He edged two-time Norris Trophy recipient Erik Karlsson of the Ottawa Senators who had 1,292 points and finished second in the voting for the second consecutive year. Karlsson received 63 first-place votes, 86 second-place votes, nine third-place votes, four fourth-place votes and three fifth-place votes. Victor Hedman of the Tampa Bay Lightning was third (728) in his first year as a finalist. He received three first-place votes. Chicago's Duncan Keith received two first-place votes and finished fourth in balloting with 384 points. Ryan Suter of Minnesota also received two first-place votes and was fifth overall with 175 points. Montreal's Shea Weber earned the final first-place vote and finished sixth with 100 points.

Burns set franchise records for goals and points by a defenseman for the second consecutive season, posting 29 goals and 47 assists for 76 points to top all NHL blueliners in scoring. He became the first defenseman to record back-to-back 75-point seasons since Brian Leetch achieved the feat with the New York Rangers in 1995-96 and 1996-97. Burns' 29 goals were 12 more than any other league defenseman and his 21 even-strength tallies were the most by an NHL defender since the Sharks' Sandis Ozolinsh had 22 in 1993-94. His 320 shots on goal - the most among all skaters - was 33 percent more than the second-ranked blueliner (Winnipeg's Dustin Byfuglien, 241).

Vezina Trophy

Lady Byng Memorial Trophy

Frank J. Selke Trophy

William M. Jennings Trophy

VEZINA TROPHY

An annual award "to the goalkeeper adjudged to be the best at his position" as voted by the general managers of each of the 30 clubs.

History: Leo Dandurand, Louis Letourneau and Joe Cattarinich, former owners of the Montreal Canadiens, presented the trophy to the National Hockey League in 1926-27 in memory of Georges Vezina, outstanding goalkeeper of the Canadiens who collapsed during an NHL game on November 28, 1925, and died of tuberculosis a few months later. Before the 1981-82 season, the goalkeeper(s) of the team allowing the fewest number of goals during the regular season were awarded the Vezina Trophy.

2016-17 Winner: **Sergei Bobrovsky, Columbus Blue Jackets**
Runners-up: **Braden Holtby, Washington Capitals**
Carey Price, Montreal Canadiens

Sergei Bobrovsky of the Columbus Blue Jackets captured the Vezina Trophy for the second time. He won the award previously in 2013. Bobrovsky was a runaway winner this time, garnering 25 first-place votes from the 30 cast by NHL general managers, along with four second-place votes and one third-place vote. His 138 voting points placed him ahead of the 2015-16 Vezina recipient, Braden Holtby of Washington who had 87 points on four first-place ballots, 21 seconds and four thirds. Montreal's Carey Price, who won the Vezina in 2014-15, finished third with 19 points from two second-place votes and 13 third-place votes. Cam Talbot of Edmonton was named first on one-ballot, second on two, and third on six to finish fourth with 17 points. Minnesota's Devan Dubnyk had eight points (0-1-5), while Martin Jones of San Jose (0-0-1) rounded out the voting.

Bobrovsky led the NHL with a 2.06 goals-against average and .931 save percentage to guide the Blue Jackets to their best season in club history. He also ranked in the top five in the league in wins (3rd; 41), shutouts (t-3rd; seven), saves (4th; 1,727) and starts (t-5th; 63). Bobrovsky established a career high and franchise record for victories in one season (41), shattering the mark set by Steve Mason in 2008-09 (33). He also posted career highs and franchise records with a 14-game win streak (November 29 to January 3) and 16-game point streak (15-0-1; November 25 to January 3).

LADY BYNG MEMORIAL TROPHY

An annual award "to the player adjudged to have exhibited the best type of sportsmanship and gentlemanly conduct combined with a high standard of playing ability." Winner selected in a poll by the Professional Hockey Writers' Association at the end of the regular schedule.

History: Lady Byng, wife of Canada's Governor-General at the time, presented the Lady Byng Trophy in the 1924-25 season. After Frank Boucher of the New York Rangers won the award seven times in eight seasons, he was given the trophy to keep and Lady Byng donated another trophy in 1936. After Lady Byng's death in 1949, the National Hockey League presented a new trophy, changing the name to Lady Byng Memorial Trophy.

2016-17 Winner: **Johnny Gaudreau, Calgary Flames**
Runners-up: **Vladimir Tarasenko, St. Louis Blues**
Mikael Granlund, Minnesota Wild

Johnny Gaudreau of the Calgary Flames was the winner of the Lady Byng Memorial Trophy for the first time. The 23-year-old native of Salem, New Jersey, is the second Calgary player to win the Lady Byng Trophy in the past three seasons, following Jiri Hudler in 2014-15. Gaudreau was named on 130 of the 167 ballots, receiving 54 first-place votes, 33 seconds, 15 thirds, 16 fourths and 12 fifths for 906 voting points. Vladimir Tarasenko of the St. Louis Blues was second with 738 points (35-31-25-12-10) and Mikael Granlund of the Minnesota Wild was third with 445 points (12-22-23-16-8). Marian Hossa of Chicago had 17 first-place votes but finished fourth overall with 320 points. Oscar Klefbom of Edmonton had 11 first-place votes and 264 points to finish fifth. In all, first-place votes were spread out among 17 players, including Detroit's Henrik Zetterberg, who had five, and Jason Pominville of Minnesota, who had four, although both finished behind Toronto's Auston Matthews (238 points) and Brandon Saad of Columbus (211) in the overall voting.

Gaudreau (18 goals, 43 assists, 61points, in 72 games) reached the 40-assist and 60-point milestones for the third time in as many NHL seasons to propel the Flames to their second playoff berth in three years. He registered a career-low two minor penalties and four penalty minutes, tied for the fewest among skaters who appeared in at least 41 games. However, Gaudreau's average time on ice (18:29) was four minutes greater than anyone else in that group.

FRANK J. SELKE TROPHY

An annual award "to the forward who best excels in the defensive aspects of the game." Winner selected in a poll by the Professional Hockey Writers' Association at the end of the regular schedule.

History: Presented to the National Hockey League in 1977 by the Board of Governors of the NHL in honor of Frank J. Selke, one of the great architects of Montreal and Toronto championship teams.

2016-17 Winner: **Patrice Bergeron, Boston Bruins**
Runners-up: **Ryan Kesler, Anaheim Ducks**
Mikko Koivu, Minnesota Wild

Center Patrice Bergeron of the Boston Bruins captured the Frank Selke Trophy for the fourth time in his career, tying the mark set by Montreal Canadiens forward Bob Gainey, who took home the prize in each of the first four years it was presented from 1978 through 1981. Bergeron, who won the award previously in 2012, 2014 and 2015, garnered 1,147 voting points, including 71 first-place votes, 39 second-place votes, 24 third-place votes, and 11 fourth- and fifth-place votes. Ryan Kesler of Anaheim, who won the Selke in 2011, had 945 points (45-45-25-15-10), while Minnesota's Mikko Koivu had 752 points (28-34-28-28-10). Mikael Backlund of Calgary was fourth in voting with 310 points, including three first-place ballots. Chicago's Jonathan Toews, the winner in 2013, received five first-place votes but had 273 points overall.

Bergeron was the NHL's busiest player in the face-off circle for the third consecutive season, leading the league with 1,812 draws and 1,089 wins. His face-off win percentage of 60.1 percent ranked third in the NHL. Bergeron also ranked first overall in the team puck possession metric SAT (shot attempts differential), as the Bruins registered 439 more shot attempts than they allowed when Bergeron was on the ice while each team had five skaters per side.

WILLIAM M. JENNINGS TROPHY

An annual award "to the goalkeeper(s) having played a minimum of 25 games (13 games in 2012-13) for the team with the fewest goals scored against it." Winners selected on regular-season play.

History: The Jennings Trophy was presented in 1981-82 by the National Hockey League's Board of Governors to honor the late William M. Jennings, longtime governor and president of the New York Rangers and one of the great builders of hockey in the United States.

2016-17 Winners: **Braden Holtby, Washington Capitals**
Runners-up: **Sergei Bobrovsky, Columbus Blue Jackets**
Carey Price, Montreal Canadiens
John Gibson and Jonathan Bernier, Anaheim Ducks

Braden Holtby of the Washington Capitals won the William M. Jennings Trophy after finishing as runner-up for the award in 2015-16. He claimed his first career Jennings Trophy, as well as the second in franchise history, following the tandem of Al Jensen and Pat Riggin in 1983-84. Holtby saw the most action on a Capitals team that allowed a league-low 182 goals in 2016-17, 13 fewer than the Columbus Blue Jackets. Both the Montreal Canadiens and Anaheim Ducks allowed 200 goals.

Holtby yielded two or fewer goals in 42 of his 63 appearances (66.7 percent) and finished the season tied for the league lead in wins (42), while also ranking in the top five in shutouts (1st; nine), goals-against average (2nd; 2.07) and save percentage (4th; .925). He became the third goaltender in NHL history to post three consecutive 40-win seasons, joining Martin Brodeur (2005 to 2008) and Evgeni Nabokov (2007 to 2010).

Jack Adams Award

Bill Masterton
Memorial Trophy

Lester Patrick Trophy

Conn Smythe Trophy

King Clancy
Memorial Trophy

JACK ADAMS AWARD

An annual award presented by the National Hockey League Broadcasters' Association to "the NHL coach adjudged to have contributed the most to his team's success." Winner selected by a poll among members of the NHL Broadcasters' Association at the end of the regular season.

History: The award was presented by the NHL Broadcasters' Association in 1974 to commemorate the late Jack Adams, coach and general manager of the Detroit Red Wings, whose lifetime dedication to hockey serves as an inspiration to all who aspire to further the game.

2016-17 Winner: **John Tortorella, Columbus Blue Jackets**
Runners-up: **Mike Babcock, Toronto Maple Leafs**
               Todd McLellan, Edmonton Oilers

Columbus Blue Jackets head coach John Tortorella was the winner of the Jack Adams Award. It's the second win for Tortorella, who previously took the award with the Tampa Bay Lightning in 2004. He becomes the first multiple winner of the trophy since Pat Burns won for the third time in 1997-98. Tortorella was named on 73 of 105 ballots cast and received 39 first-place votes, 19 second-place votes and 15 third-place votes in accumulating 267 voting points. Mike Babcock of the Toronto Maple Leafs (182 voting points) narrowly edged Todd McLellan of the Edmonton Oilers (181) for second place. Babcock was named first on 24 ballots, second on 15 and third on 17 while McLellan received 18 first-place votes, 24 seconds and 19 thirds. Joel Quenneville of Chicago was fourth in balloting (12 first-place votes, 103 points), while Washington's Barry Trotz was fifth (six and 63). Mike Sullivan of Pittsburgh received three first-place votes but finished eighth with 25 points behind Glen Gulutzan of Calgary (two, 49) and Ottawa's Guy Boucher (one, 44).

Under Tortorella, the Blue Jackets (50-24-8, 108 points) set franchise records for wins, points, home wins (28) and road points (51). The club posted a 32-point gain over 2015-16, jumping from 29th to second in team defense (3.02 to 2.35 goals against per game). The Blue Jackets reeled off 16 straight victories from November 29 to January 3, the second-longest single-season winning streak in NHL history behind the Pittsburgh Penguins' 17-game run in 1992-93.

BILL MASTERTON MEMORIAL TROPHY

An annual award under the trusteeship of the Professional Hockey Writers' Association to "the National Hockey League player who best exemplifies the qualities of perseverance, sportsmanship and dedication to hockey." Winner selected by a poll among the 30 chapters of the PHWA at the end of the regular season. A $2,500 grant from the PHWA is awarded annually to the Bill Masterton Scholarship Fund, based in Bloomington, MN, in the name of the Masterton Trophy winner.

History: The trophy was presented by the NHL Writers' Association in 1968 to commemorate the late Bill Masterton, a player with the Minnesota North Stars, who exhibited to a high degree the qualities of perseverance, sportsmanship and dedication to hockey, and who died January 15, 1968.

2016-17 Winner: **Craig Anderson, Ottawa Senators**
Runners-up: **Andrew Cogliano, Anaheim Ducks**
              Derek Ryan, Carolina Hurricanes

Ottawa Senators goalie Craig Anderson was the recipient of the Bill Masterton Memorial Trophy. Anderson recorded a successful season for the Senators while supporting his wife, Nicholle, in her fight against a rare form of throat cancer. After leaving the Senators in October to be with Nicholle, Anderson returned to the club at her urging on October 29 when the Senators lost goaltender Andrew Hammond to a groin injury. He left the team in early December to be at Nicholle's side while she underwent treatment and came back after the All-Star break. Anderson backstopped the Senators to a Stanley Cup playoff berth by winning 25 of his 40 starts, surpassed the 500 career game milestone and, on March 11, became the Senators' all-time wins leader (147).

LESTER PATRICK TROPHY

An annual award "for outstanding service to hockey in the United States." Eligible recipients are players, officials, coaches, executives and referees. Winners are selected by an award committee consisting of the commissioner of the NHL, an NHL governor, a representative of the New York Rangers, a member of the Hockey Hall of Fame builder's section, a member of the Hockey Hall of Fame player's section, a member of the U.S. Hockey Hall of Fame, a member of the NHL Broadcasters' Association and a member of the Professional Hockey Writers' Association. Each except the League Commissioner is rotated annually. The winner receives a miniature of the trophy.

History: Presented by the New York Rangers in 1966 to honor the late Lester Patrick, longtime general manager and coach of the New York Rangers, whose teams finished out of the playoffs only once in his first 16 years with the club.

2016 Winner: **Mark Howe**   **2017 Winner:**   *To Be Announced*
                Pat Kelly

Mark Howe was a key member of the 1972 silver medal-winning U.S. Olympic hockey team at Sapporo, Japan as a 16-year-old. He made his professional debut in 1973-74 with the WHA's Houston Aeros, becoming part of hockey history by playing on a line with his legendary father Gordie and brother Marty. Howe joined the NHL with the Hartford Whalers in 1979-80, scoring 80 points in his first NHL season. He joined the Philadelphia Flyers in 1982, and in ten seasons in Philadelphia he became the Flyers' all-time leader among defensemen in goals (138), assists (342) and points (480). He finished his NHL playing career with Detroit and accepted a role in the Red Wings front office upon retirement. His name is engraved four times on the Stanley Cup as a Red Wings' pro scout (1997, 1998, 2002, 2008).

Pat Kelly entered his 64th season in junior and professional hockey in 2016-17 dating back to 1952. He began his coaching career in the Eastern Hockey League, beginning with the Jersey Devils and later with the Clinton (New York) Comets. In addition, Kelly served as head coach and general manager for the Charlotte Checkers in the Southern Hockey League from 1973 to 1976, winning two league titles. He coached the Colorado Rockies in the National Hockey League in 1977-78 and was the only coach in history to lead them into the Stanley Cup playoffs. Named Commissioner Emeritus of the ECHL following the 1995-96 season after serving as Commissioner for the first eight seasons of the ECHL, Kelly was inducted into the ECHL Hall of Fame as part of the inaugural class in 2008.

CONN SMYTHE TROPHY

An annual award "to the most valuable player for his team in the playoffs." Winner selected by the Professional Hockey Writers' Association at the conclusion of the final game in the Stanley Cup Final.

History: Presented by Maple Leaf Gardens Limited in 1964 to honor Conn Smythe, the former coach, manager, president and owner-governor of the Toronto Maple Leafs.

2016-17 Winner: **Sidney Crosby, Pittsburgh Penguins**

Sidney Crosby of the Pittsburgh Penguins was the winner of the Conn Smythe Trophy for the second year in a row after the Penguins became the first team since the Detroit Red Wings in 1997 and 1998 to win back-to-back Stanley Cup championships. Crosby is just the third back-to-back winner of the award, joining Mario Lemieux (1991, 1992) and Bernie Parent (1974, 1975). He is the sixth player to win multiple Conn Smythes, with the others including Lemieux and Parent, Patrick Roy (1986, 1993 and 2001), Bobby Orr (1970 and 1972), and Wayne Gretzky (1985 and 1988). Crosby also joins Jonathan Toews as the only active players to have captained three Stanley Cup-winning teams. Crosby led the 2017 Stanley Cup Final in scoring with seven points (one goal, six assists) and finished second in scoring behind teammate Evgeni Malkin during the 2017 playoffs with 27 points (eight goals, 19 assists).

NHL General Manager
of the Year Award

Maurice "Rocket" Richard Trophy

Ted Lindsay Award

Presidents' Trophy

E.J. McGuire
Award of Excellence

KING CLANCY MEMORIAL TROPHY

An annual award "to the player who best exemplifies leadership qualities on and off the ice and has made a noteworthy humanitarian contribution in his community."

History: The King Clancy Memorial Trophy was presented to the National Hockey League by the Board of Governors in 1988 to honor the late Frank "King" Clancy.

2016-17 Winner: Nick Foligno, Columbus Blue Jackets

Columbus Blue Jackets left winger Nick Foligno was the recipient of the King Clancy Memorial Trophy. Serving his second season as captain, Foligno led Columbus to a 32-point improvement and its best campaign in franchise history. Off the ice, Foligno and his wife, Janelle, committed $1 million split between Nationwide Children's Hospital and Boston Children's Hospital in support of pediatric congenital heart care in honor of their daughter, Milana. The $500,000 donation to Nationwide Children's Hospital benefited the Center for Cardiovascular Research, which houses the newly named Foligno Family Cardiovascular Research Lab. The $500,000 gift to Boston Children's Hospital established funds to support surgical and fetal cardiac research. Additionally, Foligno continued a partnership with Papa John's Pizza, raising money for the Janis Foligno Foundation - created in memory of his late mother, who died from breast cancer in 2009. The 29-year-old Buffalo native also joined his teammates for various community initiatives, including the Blue Jackets' Meals on Wheels campaign during the holiday season.

MAURICE "ROCKET" RICHARD TROPHY

An annual award "presented to the player finishing the regular season as the League's goal-scoring leader."

History: A gift to the NHL from the Montreal Canadiens in 1999, the Maurice "Rocket" Richard Trophy honors one of the game's greatest stars. During his 18-year career with the Canadiens from 1942-43 through 1959-60, Richard was the first player in NHL history to score 50 goals in a season and 500 in his career. He played on eight Stanley Cup champions and led the League in goal scoring five times.

2016-17 Winner: Sidney Crosby, Pittsburgh Penguins
**   Runners-up   Nikita Kucherov, Tampa Bay Lightning**
**   Auston Matthews, Toronto Maple Leafs**

Pittsburgh Penguins center Sidney Crosby claimed the Maurice "Rocket" Richard Trophy for the second time in his career. His previous win came in 2009-10 when he tied Steven Stamkos of Tampa Bay for the league lead with 51 goals. Crosby scored an NHL-best 44 goals in 75 games in 2016-17. Right winger Nikita Kucherov of Tampa Bay scored 40 goals in 74 games, while Toronto center Auston Matthews scored 40 goals in 82 games. Crosby recorded eight multi-goal performances, highlighted by his 10th career hat trick March 19 versus Florida. He became the fifth multiple winner of the Maurice "Rocket" Richard Trophy since it was first handed out in 1998-99, joining Alex Ovechkin (6), Pavel Bure (2), Jarome Iginla (2) and Stamkos (2).

NHL GENERAL MANAGER OF THE YEAR AWARD

An annual award presented to recognize the work of the league's general managers, voting for this award is conducted among the club general managers and a panel of NHL executives, print and broadcast media at the conclusion of the second round of the Stanley Cup Playoffs.

History: This award was first presented in 2010.

2016-17 Winner: David Poile, Nashville Predators
**   Runners-up: Peter Chiarelli, Edmonton Oilers**
**   Pierre Dorion, Ottawa Senators**

David Poile of the Nashville Predators is the winner of the NHL General Manager of the Year Award. Poile captured the award for the first time in his fourth year as a finalist. He received 18 first-place votes, six second-place votes and four third-place votes for a total of 112 points. Peter Chiarelli of Edmonton received six first-place votes and finished second with 52 points. Pierre Dorion of Ottawa was third in voting with two first-place votes and 46 points. Toronto's Lou Lamoriello received five first-place votes but finished fourth with 36 points, while Bob Murray of Anaheim had three first-place votes and also had 36 points. Pittsburgh's Jim Rutherford (two), Jarmo Kekalainen of Columbus (one), Chicago's Stan Bowman (one) and Washington's Brian MacLellan (one) also received first-place votes.

Poile's work helped the Predators earn a postseason berth for the 10th time in 13 seasons and advance to the Stanley Cup Final for the first time. Nashville's leading scorer Viktor Arvidsson, selected 112th overall in 2014, became the latest key player drafted and developed under Poile, joining a list that includes goaltender Pekka Rinne and defensemen Roman Josi, Mattias Ekholm and Ryan Ellis. Poile also added several influential players via trade, with defenseman P.K. Subban (June, 2016) following forwards Ryan Johansen (January, 2016), James Neal (June, 2014), Filip Forsberg (April, 2013) and Mike Fisher (February, 2011).

TED LINDSAY AWARD

The Ted Lindsay Award is presented annually to the "most outstanding player" in the NHL as voted by fellow members of the National Hockey League Players' Association. The winner receives $20,000, and the two finalists receive $10,000 each to donate to the grassroots hockey program of their choice, through the NHLPA's Goals & Dreams Fund.

History: On April 29, 2010, the Ted Lindsay Award was introduced to recognize Lindsay's pioneering efforts in the establishment of the NHL Players' Association. Carrying on the tradition established by the Lester B. Pearson Award, it remains the only award voted on by the players themselves. The award was originally created in 1971 in honor of the late Lester B. Pearson, former Prime Minister of Canada.

2016-17 Winner: Connor McDavid, Edmonton Oilers
**   Runners-up: Sidney Crosby, Pittsburgh Penguins**
**   Brent Burns, San Jose Sharks**

Center Connor McDavid of the Edmonton Oilers is the winner of the Ted Lindsay Award. In his second NHL season, the 20-year-old McDavid joined Sidney Crosby and Mario Lemieux as only the third player in the Award's 46 seasons to be selected by his peers as the most outstanding player before the age of 21.

McDavid, who also won the Art Ross Trophy and the Hart Trophy, scored the most points (100) in the 2016-17 regular season and also led the NHL in assists (70), points per game (1.22), even strength assists (45) and even strength points (71). McDavid finished fourth among forwards in average ice time per game (21:07) and third in power-play assists (24). He captained the Oilers to the fourth-most points in the Western Conference and the club's first playoff berth since 2006.

MARK MESSIER NHL LEADERSHIP AWARD

An annual award presented "to the player who exemplifies great leadership qualitites to his team, on and off the ice during the regular season." Suggestions for nominees are solicited from fans, clubs and NHL personnel, but the selection of the three finalists and the ultimate winner is made by Mark Messier himself.

History: This award was first handed out in 2007.

2016-17 Winner: Nick Foligno, Columbus Blue Jackets
Runners-up: Mark Giordano, Calgary Flames
Ryan Kesler, Anaheim Ducks

Columbus Blue Jackets left winger Nick Foligno is the recipient of the Mark Messier NHL Leadership Award. He is the first player to win the Messier Award and the King Clancy Trophy in the same season. Foligno produced the second highest point total of his career (26 goals, 25 assists, 51 points in 79 games) and led the Blue Jackets to their first 50-win season and third playoff appearance in franchise history. Off the ice, Foligno and his wife, Janelle, donated a total of $1 million to Nationwide Children's Hospital and Boston Children's Hospital to further congenital heart care in honor of the oldest of their three children, Milana. Foligno also continued to be involved in his family's foundation, the Janis Foligno Foundation named for his mother who lost her life to breast cancer. The Jackets' captain has also donated his time to numerous Central Ohio charities with his teammates.

PRESIDENTS' TROPHY

An annual award to the club finishing the regular-season with the best overall record.

History: Presented to the National Hockey League in 1985-86 by the NHL Board of Governors to recognize the team compiling the top regular-season record.

2016-17 Winner: Washington Capitals
Runners-up: Pittsburgh Penguins
Chicago Blackhawks

The Washington Capitals captured the Presidents' Trophy for the second season in a row and the third time in franchise history in 2016-17, leading the NHL with 118 points on a record of 55-19-8. Their 55 wins were one off the club-high 56 wins posted in 2016-17 and their 118 points were three back of the team mark of 121 set when Washington won the Presidents' Trophy for the first time in 2009-10. The Capitals did set a new club record for home victories, posting a 32-7-2 mark at the Verizon Center, and allowed the fewest goals against in the NHL with 182 while ranking third in goals four with 118. The Pittsburgh Penguins finished second to Washington in both the Metropolitan Division and overall NHL standings with 111 points on a record of 50-21-11 and led the NHL with 282 goals scored. Chicago finished first in the Central Division and the Western Conference standings with 109 points on a record of 50-23-9.

NHL FOUNDATION PLAYER AWARD

An annual award presented to "an NHL player who applies the core values of hockey – commitment, perseverance and teamwork – to enrich the lives of people in his community." In recognition of this dedication, the NHL Foundation annually awards $25,000 to a current player's charity.

History: NHL players have a long-standing tradition of supporting charities and other important causes in their communities. NHL member clubs are constant in their quest to help local schools, hospitals and charitable organizations. Clubs submit nominations for the NHL Foundation Player Award and the finalists are selected by a judging panel. This award was first presented in 1998.

2016-17 Winner: Travis Hamonic, New York Islanders
Runner-up: Wayne Simmonds, Philadelphia Flyers

New York Islanders defenseman Travis Hamonic was the recipient of the 2016-17 NHL Foundation Player Award. A reliable defenseman throughout his seven-season NHL career, Hamonic has used his personal experiences to positively impact the community. Through his D-Partner Program, Hamonic has bonded with and directly touched the lives of more than 200 children who, at a young age, have suffered the loss of a parent. The 26-year-old St. Malo, Manitoba, native has spent more than $50,000 hosting D-Partner Program participants at Islanders games, providing VIP treatment as well as special meet-and-greets. Hamonic also has served as an event ambassador for the Children's Wish Foundation and spearheaded numerous Islanders community events, including the team's school and hospital visits.

E.J. McGUIRE AWARD OF EXCELLENCE

An annual award presented to the NHL Draft prospect who best exemplifies commitment to excellence through strength of character, competitiveness and athleticism.

History: First presented in 2015, this award commemorates E.J. McGuire, who joined the NHL's Central Scouting Bureau in 2002 and assumed day-to day responsibility for the department in 2005. McGuire was responsible for several advancements in scouting including the implementation of new technology. He also did much to improve the NHL's annual scouting combine. He passed away in 2011.

2016-17 Winner: Nico Hischier

Nico Hischier was awarded the E.J. McGuire Award of Excellence for 2017. A native of Naters, Switzerland, the 6'1" center became the highest drafted Swiss-born player in NHL Draft history - surpassing Nino Niederreiter (selected fifth overall by New York Islanders in 2010). In 2016-17, Hischier led all QMJHL rookies with 38 goals and 48 assists for 86 points in 57 regular-season games and added three goals and four assists in six playoff contests with the Halifax Mooseheads. He was named the Canadian Hockey League and QMJHL Rookie of the Year and awarded the Mike Bossy Trophy as the QMJHL's Best Professional Prospect. He also represented Switzerland at both the World Junior Championship and the Under-18 World Championship.

NATIONAL HOCKEY LEAGUE INDIVIDUAL AWARD WINNERS

CONN SMYTHE TROPHY

	Winner	
2017	Sidney Crosby	Pittsburgh
2016	Sidney Crosby	Pittsburgh
2015	Duncan Keith	Chicago
2014	Justin Williams	Los Angeles
2013	Patrick Kane	Chicago
2012	Jonathan Quick	Los Angeles
2011	Tim Thomas	Boston
2010	Jonathan Toews	Chicago
2009	Evgeni Malkin	Pittsburgh
2008	Henrik Zetterberg	Detroit
2007	Scott Niedermayer	Anaheim
2006	Cam Ward	Carolina
2005	....	....
2004	Brad Richards	Tampa Bay
2003	Jean-Sebastien Giguere	Anaheim
2002	Nicklas Lidstrom	Detroit
2001	Patrick Roy	Colorado
2000	Scott Stevens	New Jersey
1999	Joe Nieuwendyk	Dallas
1998	Steve Yzerman	Detroit
1997	Mike Vernon	Detroit
1996	Joe Sakic	Colorado
1995	Claude Lemieux	New Jersey
1994	Brian Leetch	NY Rangers
1993	Patrick Roy	Montreal
1992	Mario Lemieux	Pittsburgh
1991	Mario Lemieux	Pittsburgh
1990	Bill Ranford	Edmonton
1989	Al MacInnis	Calgary
1988	Wayne Gretzky	Edmonton
1987	Ron Hextall	Philadelphia
1986	Patrick Roy	Montreal
1985	Wayne Gretzky	Edmonton
1984	Mark Messier	Edmonton
1983	Billy Smith	NY Islanders
1982	Mike Bossy	NY Islanders
1981	Butch Goring	NY Islanders
1980	Bryan Trottier	NY Islanders
1979	Bob Gainey	Montreal
1978	Larry Robinson	Montreal
1977	Guy Lafleur	Montreal
1976	Reggie Leach	Philadelphia
1975	Bernie Parent	Philadelphia
1974	Bernie Parent	Philadelphia
1973	Yvan Cournoyer	Montreal
1972	Bobby Orr	Boston
1971	Ken Dryden	Montreal
1970	Bobby Orr	Boston
1969	Serge Savard	Montreal
1968	Glenn Hall	St. Louis
1967	Dave Keon	Toronto
1966	Roger Crozier	Detroit
1965	Jean Beliveau	Montreal

FRANK J. SELKE TROPHY

	Winner		Runner-up
2017	Patrice Bergeron, Bos.		Ryan Kesler, Ana.
2016	Anze Kopitar, L.A.		Patrice Bergeron, Bos.
2015	Patrice Bergeron, Bos.		Jonathan Toews, Chi.
2014	Patrice Bergeron, Bos.		Anze Kopitar, L.A.
2013	Jonathan Toews, Chi.		Patrice Bergeron, Bos.
2012	Patrice Bergeron, Bos.		David Backes, St.L.
2011	Ryan Kesler, Van.		Jonathan Toews, Chi.
2010	Pavel Datsyuk, Det.		Ryan Kesler, Van.
2009	Pavel Datsyuk, Det.		Mike Richards, Phi.
2008	Pavel Datsyuk, Det.		John Madden, N.J.
2007	Rod Brind'Amour, Car.		Samuel Pahlsson, Ana.
2006	Rod Brind'Amour, Car.		Jere Lehtinen, Dal.
2005	....		....
2004	Kris Draper, Det.		John Madden, N.J.
2003	Jere Lehtinen, Dal.		John Madden, N.J.
2002	Michael Peca, NYI		Craig Conroy, Cgy.
2001	John Madden, N.J.		Joe Sakic, Col.
2000	Steve Yzerman, Det.		Michal Handzus, St.L.
1999	Jere Lehtinen, Dal.		Magnus Arvedson, Ott.
1998	Jere Lehtinen, Dal.		Michael Peca, Buf.
1997	Michael Peca, Buf.		Peter Forsberg, Col.
1996	Sergei Fedorov, Det.		Ron Francis, Pit.
1995	Ron Francis, Pit.		Esa Tikkanen, St.L.
1994	Sergei Fedorov, Det.		Doug Gilmour, Tor.
1993	Doug Gilmour, Tor.		Dave Poulin, Bos.
1992	Guy Carbonneau, Mtl.		Sergei Fedorov, Det.
1991	Dirk Graham, Chi.		Esa Tikkanen, Edm.
1990	Rick Meagher, St.L.		Guy Carbonneau, Mtl.
1989	Guy Carbonneau, Mtl.		Esa Tikkanen, Edm.
1988	Guy Carbonneau, Mtl.		Steve Kasper, Bos.
1987	Dave Poulin, Phi.		Guy Carbonneau, Mtl.
1986	Troy Murray, Chi.		Ron Sutter, Phi.
1985	Craig Ramsay, Buf.		Doug Jarvis, Wsh.
1984	Doug Jarvis, Wsh.		Bryan Trottier, NYI
1983	Bobby Clarke, Phi.		Jari Kurri, Edm.
1982	Steve Kasper, Bos.		Bob Gainey, Mtl.
1981	Bob Gainey, Mtl.		Craig Ramsay, Buf.
1980	Bob Gainey, Mtl.		Craig Ramsay, Buf.
1979	Bob Gainey, Mtl.		Don Marcotte, Bos.
1978	Bob Gainey, Mtl.		Craig Ramsay, Buf.

BILL MASTERTON MEMORIAL TROPHY

	Winner	
2017	Craig Anderson	Ottawa
2016	Jaromir Jagr	Florida
2015	Devan Dubnyk	Minnesota
2014	Dominic Moore	NY Rangers
2013	Josh Harding	Minnesota
2012	Max Pacioretty	Montreal
2011	Ian Laperriere	Philadelphia
2010	Jose Theodore	Washington
2009	Steve Sullivan	Nashville
2008	Jason Blake	Toronto
2007	Phil Kessel	Boston
2006	Teemu Selanne	Anaheim
2005	....	....
2004	Bryan Berard	Chicago
2003	Steve Yzerman	Detroit
2002	Saku Koivu	Montreal
2001	Adam Graves	NY Rangers
2000	Ken Daneyko	New Jersey
1999	John Cullen	Tampa Bay
1998	Jamie McLennan	St. Louis
1997	Tony Granato	San Jose
1996	Gary Roberts	Calgary
1995	Pat LaFontaine	Buffalo
1994	Cam Neely	Boston
1993	Mario Lemieux	Pittsburgh
1992	Mark Fitzpatrick	NY Islanders
1991	Dave Taylor	Los Angeles
1990	Gord Kluzak	Boston
1989	Tim Kerr	Philadelphia
1988	Bob Bourne	Los Angeles
1987	Doug Jarvis	Hartford
1986	Charlie Simmer	Boston
1985	Anders Hedberg	NY Rangers
1984	Brad Park	Detroit
1983	Lanny McDonald	Calgary
1982	Glenn Resch	Colorado
1981	Blake Dunlop	St. Louis
1980	Al MacAdam	Minnesota
1979	Serge Savard	Montreal
1978	Butch Goring	Los Angeles
1977	Ed Westfall	NY Islanders
1976	Rod Gilbert	NY Rangers
1975	Don Luce	Buffalo
1974	Henri Richard	Montreal
1973	Lowell MacDonald	Pittsburgh
1972	Bobby Clarke	Philadelphia
1971	Jean Ratelle	NY Rangers
1970	Pit Martin	Chicago
1969	Ted Hampson	Oakland
1968	Claude Provost	Montreal

ART ROSS TROPHY

	Winner	Runner-up
2017	Connor McDavid, Edm.	Sidney Crosby, Pit.
2016	Patrick Kane, Chi.	Jamie Benn, Dal.
2015	Jamie Benn, Dal.	John Tavares, NYI
2014	Sidney Crosby, Pit.	Ryan Getzlaf, Ana.
2013	Martin St. Louis, T.B.	Steven Stamkos, T.B.
2012	Evgeni Malkin, Pit.	Steven Stamkos, T.B.
2011	Daniel Sedin, Van.	Martin St. Louis, T.B.
2010	Henrik Sedin, Van.	Sidney Crosby, Pit.
2009	Evgeni Malkin, Pit.	Alex Ovechkin, Wsh.
2008	Alex Ovechkin, Wsh.	Evgeni Malkin, Pit.
2007	Sidney Crosby, Pit.	Joe Thornton, S.J.
2006	Joe Thornton, Bos., S.J.	Jaromir Jagr, NYR
2005	....	
2004	Martin St. Louis, T.B.	Ilya Kovalchuk, Atl.
2003	Peter Forsberg, Col.	Markus Naslund, Van.
2002	Jarome Iginla, Cgy.	Markus Naslund, Van.
2001	Jaromir Jagr, Pit.	Joe Sakic, Col.
2000	Jaromir Jagr, Pit.	Pavel Bure, Fla.
1999	Jaromir Jagr, Pit.	Teemu Selanne, Ana.
1998	Jaromir Jagr, Pit.	Peter Forsberg, Col.
1997	Mario Lemieux, Pit.	Teemu Selanne, Ana.
1996	Mario Lemieux, Pit.	Jaromir Jagr, Pit.
1995	Jaromir Jagr, Pit.	Eric Lindros, Phi.
1994	Wayne Gretzky, L.A.	Sergei Fedorov, Det.
1993	Mario Lemieux, Pit.	Pat LaFontaine, Buf.
1992	Mario Lemieux, Pit.	Kevin Stevens, Pit.
1991	Wayne Gretzky, L.A.	Brett Hull, St.L.
1990	Wayne Gretzky, L.A.	Mark Messier, Edm.
1989	Mario Lemieux, Pit.	Wayne Gretzky, L.A.
1988	Mario Lemieux, Pit.	Wayne Gretzky, Edm.
1987	Wayne Gretzky, Edm.	Jari Kurri, Edm.
1986	Wayne Gretzky, Edm.	Mario Lemieux, Pit.
1985	Wayne Gretzky, Edm.	Jari Kurri, Edm.
1984	Wayne Gretzky, Edm.	Paul Coffey, Edm.
1983	Wayne Gretzky, Edm.	Peter Stastny, Que.
1982	Wayne Gretzky, Edm.	Mike Bossy, NYI
1981	Wayne Gretzky, Edm.	Marcel Dionne, L.A.
1980	Marcel Dionne, L.A.	Wayne Gretzky, Edm.
1979	Bryan Trottier, NYI	Marcel Dionne, L.A.
1978	Guy Lafleur, Mtl.	Bryan Trottier, NYI
1977	Guy Lafleur, Mtl.	Marcel Dionne, L.A.
1976	Guy Lafleur, Mtl.	Bobby Clarke, Phi.
1975	Bobby Orr, Bos.	Phil Esposito, Bos.
1974	Phil Esposito, Bos.	Bobby Orr, Bos.
1973	Phil Esposito, Bos.	Bobby Clarke, Phi.
1972	Phil Esposito, Bos.	Bobby Orr, Bos.
1971	Phil Esposito, Bos.	Bobby Orr, Bos.
1970	Bobby Orr, Bos.	Phil Esposito, Bos.
1969	Phil Esposito, Bos.	Bobby Hull, Chi.
1968	Stan Mikita, Chi.	Phil Esposito, Bos.
1967	Stan Mikita, Chi.	Bobby Hull, Chi.
1966	Bobby Hull, Chi.	Stan Mikita, Chi.
1965	Stan Mikita, Chi.	Norm Ullman, Det.
1964	Stan Mikita, Chi.	Bobby Hull, Chi.
1963	Gordie Howe, Det.	Andy Bathgate, NYR
1962	Bobby Hull, Chi.	Andy Bathgate, NYR
1961	Bernie Geoffrion, Mtl.	Jean Beliveau, Mtl.
1960	Bobby Hull, Chi.	Bronco Horvath, Bos.
1959	Dickie Moore, Mtl.	Jean Beliveau, Mtl.
1958	Dickie Moore, Mtl.	Henri Richard, Mtl.
1957	Gordie Howe, Det.	Ted Lindsay, Det.
1956	Jean Beliveau, Mtl.	Gordie Howe, Det.
1955	Bernie Geoffrion, Mtl.	Maurice Richard, Mtl.
1954	Gordie Howe, Det.	Maurice Richard, Mtl.
1953	Gordie Howe, Det.	Ted Lindsay, Det.
1952	Gordie Howe, Det.	Ted Lindsay, Det.
1951	Gordie Howe, Det.	Maurice Richard, Mtl.
1950	Ted Lindsay, Det.	Sid Abel, Det.
1949	Roy Conacher, Chi.	Doug Bentley, Chi.
1948*	Elmer Lach, Mtl.	Buddy O'Connor, NYR
1947	Max Bentley, Chi.	Maurice Richard, Mtl.
1946	Max Bentley, Chi.	Gaye Stewart, Tor.
1945	Elmer Lach, Mtl.	Maurice Richard, Mtl.
1944	Herb Cain, Bos.	Doug Bentley, Chi.
1943	Doug Bentley, Chi.	Bill Cowley, Bos.
1942	Bryan Hextall, NYR	Lynn Patrick, NYR
1941	Bill Cowley, Bos.	Bryan Hextall, NYR
1940	Milt Schmidt, Bos.	Woody Dumart, Bos.
1939	Toe Blake, Mtl.	Sweeney Schriner, NYA
1938	Gordie Drillon, Tor.	Syl Apps, Tor.
1937	Sweeney Schriner, NYA	Syl Apps, Tor.
1936	Sweeney Schriner, NYA	Marty Barry, Det.
1935	Charlie Conacher, Tor.	Syd Howe, St.L., Det.
1934	Charlie Conacher, Tor.	Joe Primeau, Tor
1933	Bill Cook, NYR	Busher Jackson, Tor.
1932	Busher Jackson, Tor.	Joe Primeau, Tor.
1931	Howie Morenz, Mtl.	Ebbie Goodfellow, Det.
1930	Cooney Weiland, Bos.	Frank Boucher, NYR
1929	Ace Bailey, Tor.	Nels Stewart, Mtl.M.
1928	Howie Morenz, Mtl.	Aurel Joliat, Mtl.
1927	Bill Cook, NYR	Dick Irvin, Chi.
1926	Nels Stewart, Mtl.M.	Cy Denneny, Ott.
1925	Babe Dye, Tor.	Cy Denneny, Ott.
1924	Cy Denneny, Ott.	Billy Boucher, Mtl.
1923	Babe Dye, Tor.	Cy Denneny, Ott.
1922	Punch Broadbent, Ott.	Cy Denneny, Ott.
1921	Newsy Lalonde, Mtl.	Babe Dye, Ham., Tor.
1920	Joe Malone, Que.	Newsy Lalonde, Mtl.
1919	Newsy Lalonde, Mtl.	Odie Cleghorn, Mtl.
1918	Joe Malone, Mtl.	Cy Denneny, Ott.

* Trophy first awarded in 1948.
Scoring leaders listed from 1918 to 1947.

HART MEMORIAL TROPHY

	Winner	Runner-up
2017	Connor McDavid, Edm.	Sidney Crosby, Pit.
2016	Patrick Kane, Chi.	Sidney Crosby, Pit.
2015	Carey Price, Mtl.	Alex Ovechkin, Wsh.
2014	Sidney Crosby, Pit.	Ryan Getzlaf, Ana.
2013	Alex Ovechkin, Wsh.	Sidney Crosby, Pit.
2012	Evgeni Malkin, Pit.	Steven Stamkos, T.B.
2011	Corey Perry, Ana.	Daniel Sedin, Van.
2010	Henrik Sedin, Van.	Alex Ovechkin, Wsh.
2009	Alex Ovechkin, Wsh.	Evgeni Malkin, Pit.
2008	Alex Ovechkin, Wsh.	Evgeni Malkin, Pit.
2007	Sidney Crosby, Pit.	Roberto Luongo, Van.
2006	Joe Thornton, Bos., S.J.	Jaromir Jagr, NYR
2005	....	....
2004	Martin St. Louis, T.B.	Jarome Iginla, Cgy.
2003	Peter Forsberg, Col.	Markus Naslund, Van.
2002	Jose Theodore, Mtl.	Jarome Iginla, Cgy.
2001	Joe Sakic, Col.	Mario Lemieux, Pit.
2000	Chris Pronger, St.L.	Jaromir Jagr, Pit.
1999	Jaromir Jagr, Pit.	Alexei Yashin, Ott.
1998	Dominik Hasek, Buf.	Jaromir Jagr, Pit.
1997	Dominik Hasek, Buf.	Paul Kariya, Ana.
1996	Mario Lemieux, Pit.	Mark Messier, NYR
1995	Eric Lindros, Phi.	Jaromir Jagr, Pit.
1994	Sergei Fedorov, Det.	Dominik Hasek, Buf.
1993	Mario Lemieux, Pit.	Doug Gilmour, Tor.
1992	Mark Messier, NYR	Patrick Roy, Mtl.
1991	Brett Hull, St.L.	Wayne Gretzky, L.A.
1990	Mark Messier, Edm.	Raymond Bourque, Bos.
1989	Wayne Gretzky, L.A.	Mario Lemieux, Pit.
1988	Mario Lemieux, Pit.	Grant Fuhr, Edm.
1987	Wayne Gretzky, Edm.	Raymond Bourque, Bos.
1986	Wayne Gretzky, Edm.	Mario Lemieux, Pit.
1985	Wayne Gretzky, Edm.	Dale Hawerchuk, Wpg.
1984	Wayne Gretzky, Edm.	Rod Langway, Wsh.
1983	Wayne Gretzky, Edm.	Pete Peeters, Bos.
1982	Wayne Gretzky, Edm.	Bryan Trottier, NYI
1981	Wayne Gretzky, Edm.	Mike Liut, St.L.
1980	Wayne Gretzky, Edm.	Marcel Dionne, L.A.
1979	Bryan Trottier, NYI	Guy Lafleur, Mtl
1978	Guy Lafleur, Mtl.	Bryan Trottier, NYI
1977	Guy Lafleur, Mtl.	Bobby Clarke, Phi.
1976	Bobby Clarke, Phi.	Denis Potvin, NYI
1975	Bobby Clarke, Phi.	Rogie Vachon, L.A.
1974	Phil Esposito, Bos.	Bernie Parent, Phi.
1973	Bobby Clarke, Phi.	Phil Esposito, Bos.
1972	Bobby Orr, Bos.	Ken Dryden, Mtl.
1971	Bobby Orr, Bos.	Phil Esposito, Bos.
1970	Bobby Orr, Bos.	Tony Esposito, Chi.
1969	Phil Esposito, Bos.	Jean Beliveau, Mtl.
1968	Stan Mikita, Chi.	Jean Beliveau, Mtl.
1967	Stan Mikita, Chi.	Ed Giacomin, NYR
1966	Bobby Hull, Chi.	Jean Beliveau, Mtl.
1965	Bobby Hull, Chi.	Norm Ullman, Det.
1964	Jean Beliveau, Mtl.	Bobby Hull, Chi.
1963	Gordie Howe, Det.	Stan Mikita, Chi.
1962	Jacques Plante, Mtl.	Doug Harvey, NYR
1961	Bernie Geoffrion, Mtl.	Johnny Bower, Tor.
1960	Gordie Howe, Det.	Bobby Hull, Chi.
1959	Andy Bathgate, NYR	Gordie Howe, Det.
1958	Gordie Howe, Det.	Andy Bathgate, NYR
1957	Gordie Howe, Det.	Jean Beliveau, Mtl.
1956	Jean Beliveau, Mtl.	Tod Sloan, Tor.
1955	Ted Kennedy, Tor.	Harry Lumley, Tor.
1954	Al Rollins, Chi.	Red Kelly, Det.
1953	Gordie Howe, Det.	Al Rollins, Chi.
1952	Gordie Howe, Det.	Elmer Lach, Mtl.
1951	Milt Schmidt, Bos.	Maurice Richard, Mtl.
1950	Chuck Rayner, NYR	Ted Kennedy, Tor.
1949	Sid Abel, Det.	Bill Durnan, Mtl.
1948	Buddy O'Connor, NYR	Frank Brimsek, Bos.
1947	Maurice Richard, Mtl.	Milt Schmidt, Bos.
1946	Max Bentley, Chi.	Gaye Stewart, Tor.
1945	Elmer Lach, Mtl.	Maurice Richard, Mtl.
1944	Babe Pratt, Tor.	Bill Cowley, Bos.
1943	Bill Cowley, Bos.	Doug Bentley, Chi.
1942	Tom Anderson, Bro.	Syl Apps, Tor.
1941	Bill Cowley, Bos.	Dit Clapper, Bos.
1940	Ebbie Goodfellow, Det.	Syl Apps, Tor.
1939	Toe Blake, Mtl.	Syl Apps, Tor.
1938	Eddie Shore, Bos.	Paul Thompson, Chi.
1937	Babe Siebert, Mtl.	Lionel Conacher, Mtl.M.
1936	Eddie Shore, Bos.	Hooley Smith, Mtl.M.
1935	Eddie Shore, Bos.	Charlie Conacher, Tor.
1934	Aurel Joliat, Mtl.	Lionel Conacher, Chi.
1933	Eddie Shore, Bos.	Bill Cook, NYR
1932	Howie Morenz, Mtl.	Ching Johnson, NYR
1931	Howie Morenz, Mtl.	Eddie Shore, Bos.
1930	Nels Stewart, Mtl.M.	Lionel Hitchman, Bos.
1929	Roy Worters, NYA	Ace Bailey, Tor.
1928	Howie Morenz, Mtl.	Roy Worters, Pit.
1927	Herb Gardiner, Mtl.	Bill Cook, NYR
1926	Nels Stewart, Mtl.M.	Sprague Cleghorn, Bos.
1925	Billy Burch, Ham.	Howie Morenz, Mtl.
1924	Frank Nighbor, Ott.	Sprague Cleghorn, Mtl.

MARK MESSIER NHL LEADERSHIP AWARD

	Winner	
2017	Nick Foligno	Columbus
2016	Shea Weber	Nashville
2015	Jonathan Toews	Chicago
2014	Dustin Brown	Los Angeles
2013	Daniel Alfredsson	Ottawa
2012	Shane Doan	Phoenix
2011	Zdeno Chara	Boston
2010	Sidney Crosby	Pittsburgh
2009	Jarome Iginla	Calgary
2008	Mats Sundin	Toronto
2007	Chris Chelios	Detroit

WILLIAM M. JENNINGS TROPHY

	Winner	Runner-up
2017	Braden Holtby, Wsh.	Sergei Bobrovsky, CBJ
2016	Frederik Andersen, Ana, John Gibson, Ana.	Braden Holtby, Wsh.
2015	Carey Price, Mtl. (tie) Corey Crawford, Chi. (tie)	Henrik Lundqvist, NYR Cam Talbot, NYR
2014	Jonathan Quick, L.A.	Tuukka Rask, Bos. Chad Johnson, Bos.
2013	Corey Crawford, Chi. Ray Emery, Chi.	Craig Anderson, Ott.
2012	Brian Elliott, St.L. Jaroslav Halak, St.L.	Jonathan Quick, L.A.
2011	Roberto Luongo, Van. Cory Schneider, Van.	Pekka Rinne, Nsh.
2010	Martin Brodeur, N.J.	Tim Thomas, Bos. Tuukka Rask, Bos.
2009	Tim Thomas, Bos. Manny Fernandez, Bos.	Niklas Backstrom, Min.
2008	Chris Osgood, Det. Dominik Hasek, Det.	Jean-Sebastien Giguere, Ana.
2007	Niklas Backstrom, Min. Manny Fernandez, Min.	Dominik Hasek, Det.
2006	Miikka Kiprusoff, Cgy.	Manny Legace, Det. Chris Osgood, Det.
2005	....	....
2004	Martin Brodeur, N.J.	Marty Turco, Dal.
2003	Martin Brodeur, N.J. (tie) Roman Cechmanek, Phi. Robert Esche, Phi. (tie)	Marty Turco, Dal. Ron Tugnutt, Dal.
2002	Patrick Roy, Col.	Tommy Salo, Edm.
2001	Dominik Hasek, Buf.	Ed Belfour, Dal. Marty Turco, Dal.
2000	Roman Turek, St.L.	John Vanbiesbrouck, Phi. Brian Boucher, Phi.
1999	Ed Belfour, Dal. Roman Turek, Dal.	Dominik Hasek, Buf.
1998	Martin Brodeur, N.J.	Ed Belfour, Dal.
1997	Martin Brodeur, N.J. Mike Dunham, N.J.	Chris Osgood, Det. Mike Vernon, Det.
1996	Chris Osgood, Det. Mike Vernon, Det.	Martin Brodeur, N.J.
1995	Ed Belfour, Chi.	Mike Vernon, Det. Chris Osgood, Det.
1994	Dominik Hasek, Buf. Grant Fuhr, Buf.	Martin Brodeur, N.J. Chris Terreri, N.J.
1993	Ed Belfour, Chi.	Felix Potvin, Tor. Grant Fuhr, Tor.
1992	Patrick Roy, Mtl.	Ed Belfour, Chi.
1991	Ed Belfour, Chi.	Patrick Roy, Mtl.
1990	Andy Moog, Bos. Reggie Lemelin, Bos.	Patrick Roy, Mtl. Brian Hayward, Mtl.
1989	Patrick Roy, Mtl. Brian Hayward, Mtl.	Mike Vernon, Cgy. Rick Wamsley, Cgy.
1988	Patrick Roy, Mtl. Brian Hayward, Mtl.	Clint Malarchuk, Wsh. Pete Peeters, Wsh.
1987	Patrick Roy, Mtl. Brian Hayward, Mtl.	Ron Hextall, Phi.
1986	Bob Froese, Phi. Darren Jensen, Phi.	Al Jensen, Wsh. Pete Peeters, Wsh.
1985	Tom Barrasso, Buf. Bob Sauve, Buf.	Pat Riggin, Wsh.
1984	Al Jensen, Wsh. Pat Riggin, Wsh.	Tom Barrasso, Buf. Bob Sauve, Buf.
1983	Roland Melanson, NYI Billy Smith, NYI	Pete Peeters, Bos.
1982	Rick Wamsley, Mtl. Denis Herron, Mtl.	Billy Smith, NYI Roland Melanson, NYI

MAURICE "ROCKET" RICHARD TROPHY

	Winner	
2017	Sidney Crosby	Pittsburgh
2016	Alex Ovechkin	Washington
2015	Alex Ovechkin	Washington
2014	Alex Ovechkin	Washington
2013	Alex Ovechkin	Washington
2012	Steven Stamkos	Tampa Bay
2011	Corey Perry	Anaheim
2010	Sidney Crosby Steven Stamkos	Pittsburgh Tampa Bay
2009	Alex Ovechkin	Washington
2008	Alex Ovechkin	Washington
2007	Vincent Lecavalier	Tampa Bay
2006	Jonathan Cheechoo	San Jose
2005	....	....
2004	Rick Nash Jarome Iginla Ilya Kovalchuk	Columbus Calgary Atlanta
2003	Milan Hejduk	Colorado
2002	Jarome Iginla	Calgary
2001	Pavel Bure	Florida
2000	Pavel Bure	Florida
1999	Teemu Selanne	Anaheim

NHL GENERAL MANAGER OF THE YEAR AWARD

	Winner	
2017	David Poile	Nashville
2016	Jim Rutherford	Pittsburgh
2015	Steve Yzerman	Tampa Bay
2014	Bob Murray	Anaheim
2013	Ray Shero	Pittsburgh
2012	Doug Armstrong	St. Louis
2011	Mike Gillis	Vancouver
2010	Don Maloney	Phoenix

LADY BYNG MEMORIAL TROPHY

	Winner	Runner-up
2017	Johnny Gaudreau, Cgy.	Vladimir Tarasenko, St.L.
2016	Anze Kopitar, L.A.	Aleksander Barkov, Fla.
2015	Jiri Hudler, Cgy.	Pavel Datsyuk, Det.
2014	Ryan O'Reilly, Col.	Martin St. Louis, T.B., NYR
2013	Martin St. Louis, T.B.	Patrick Kane, Chi
2012	Brian Campbell, Fla.	Jordan Eberle, Edm.
2011	Martin St. Louis, T.B.	Nicklas Lidstrom, Det.
2010	Martin St. Louis, T.B.	Brad Richards, Dal.
2009	Pavel Datsyuk, Det.	Martin St. Louis, T.B.
2008	Pavel Datsyuk, Det.	Martin St. Louis, T.B.
2007	Pavel Datsyuk, Det.	Martin St. Louis, T.B.
2006	Pavel Datsyuk, Det.	Brad Richards, T.B.
2005	....	....
2004	Brad Richards, T.B.	Daniel Alfredsson, Ott.
2003	Alexander Mogilny, Tor.	Nicklas Lidstrom, Det.
2002	Ron Francis, Car.	Joe Sakic, Col.
2001	Joe Sakic, Col.	Nicklas Lidstrom, Det.
2000	Pavol Demitra, St.L.	Nicklas Lidstrom, Det.
1999	Wayne Gretzky, NYR.	Nicklas Lidstrom, Det.
1998	Ron Francis, Pit.	Teemu Selanne, Ana.
1997	Paul Kariya, Ana.	Teemu Selanne, Ana.
1996	Paul Kariya, Ana.	Adam Oates, Bos.
1995	Ron Francis, Pit.	Adam Oates, Bos.
1994	Wayne Gretzky, L.A.	Adam Oates, Bos.
1993	Pierre Turgeon, NYI	Adam Oates, Bos.
1992	Wayne Gretzky, L.A.	Joe Sakic, Que.
1991	Wayne Gretzky, L.A.	Brett Hull, St.L.
1990	Brett Hull, St.L.	Wayne Gretzky, L.A.
1989	Joe Mullen, Cgy.	Wayne Gretzky, L.A.
1988	Mats Naslund, Mtl.	Wayne Gretzky, Edm.
1987	Joe Mullen, Cgy.	Wayne Gretzky, Edm.
1986	Mike Bossy, NYI	Jari Kurri, Edm.
1985	Jari Kurri, Edm.	Joe Mullen, St.L.
1984	Mike Bossy, NYI	Rick Middleton, Bos.
1983	Mike Bossy, NYI	Rick Middleton, Bos.
1982	Rick Middleton, Bos.	Mike Bossy, NYI
1981	Rick Kehoe, Pit.	Wayne Gretzky, Edm.
1980	Wayne Gretzky, Edm.	Marcel Dionne, L.A.
1979	Bob MacMillan, Atl.	Marcel Dionne, L.A.
1978	Butch Goring, L.A.	Peter McNab, Bos.
1977	Marcel Dionne, L.A.	Jean Ratelle, Bos.
1976	Jean Ratelle, NYR-Bos.	Jean Pronovost, Pit.
1975	Marcel Dionne, Det.	John Bucyk, Bos.
1974	John Bucyk, Bos.	Lowell MacDonald, Pit.
1973	Gilbert Perreault, Buf.	Jean Ratelle, NYR
1972	Jean Ratelle, NYR	John Bucyk, Bos.
1971	John Bucyk, Bos.	Dave Keon, Tor.
1970	Phil Goyette, St.L.	John Bucyk, Bos.
1969	Alex Delvecchio, Det.	Ted Hampson, Oak.
1968	Stan Mikita, Chi.	John Bucyk, Bos.
1967	Stan Mikita, Chi.	Dave Keon, Tor.
1966	Alex Delvecchio, Det.	Bobby Rousseau, Mtl.
1965	Bobby Hull, Chi.	Alex Delvecchio, Det.
1964	Kenny Wharram, Chi.	Dave Keon, Tor.
1963	Dave Keon, Tor.	Camille Henry, NYR
1962	Dave Keon, Tor.	Claude Provost, Mtl.
1961	Red Kelly, Tor.	Norm Ullman, Det.
1960	Don McKenney, Bos.	Andy Hebenton, NYR
1959	Alex Delvecchio, Det.	Andy Hebenton, NYR
1958	Camille Henry, NYR	Don Marshall, Mtl.
1957	Andy Hebenton, NYR	Dutch Reibel, Det.
1956	Dutch Reibel, Det.	Floyd Curry, Mtl.
1955	Sid Smith, Tor.	Danny Lewicki, NYR
1954	Red Kelly, Det.	Don Raleigh, NYR
1953	Red Kelly, Det.	Wally Hergesheimer, NYR
1952	Sid Smith, Tor.	Red Kelly, Det.
1951	Red Kelly, Det.	Woody Dumart, Bos.
1950	Edgar Laprade, NYR	Red Kelly, Det.
1949	Bill Quackenbush, Det.	Harry Watson, Tor.
1948	Buddy O'Connor, NYR	Syl Apps, Tor.
1947	Bobby Bauer, Bos.	Syl Apps, Tor.
1946	Toe Blake, Mtl.	Clint Smith, Chi.
1945	Bill Mosienko, Chi.	Syd Howe, Det.
1944	Clint Smith, Chi.	Herb Cain, Bos.
1943	Max Bentley, Chi.	Buddy O'Connor, Mtl.
1942	Syl Apps, Tor.	Gordie Drillon, Tor.
1941	Bobby Bauer, Bos.	Gordie Drillon, Tor.
1940	Bobby Bauer, Bos.	Clint Smith, NYR
1939	Clint Smith, NYR	Marty Barry, Det.
1938	Gordie Drillon, Tor.	Clint Smith, NYR
1937	Marty Barry, Det.	Gordie Drillon, Tor.
1936	Doc Romnes, Chi.	Sweeney Schriner, NYA
1935	Frank Boucher, NYR	Russ Blinco, Mtl.M.
1934	Frank Boucher, NYR	Joe Primeau, Tor.
1933	Frank Boucher, NYR	Joe Primeau, Tor.
1932	Joe Primeau, Tor.	Frank Boucher, NYR
1931	Frank Boucher, NYR	Normie Himes, NYA
1930	Frank Boucher, NYR	Normie Himes, NYA
1929	Frank Boucher, NYR	Harold Darragh, Pit.
1928	Frank Boucher, NYR	George Hay, Det.
1927	Billy Burch, NYA	Dick Irvin, Chi.
1926	Frank Nighbor, Ott.	Billy Burch, NYA
1925	Frank Nighbor, Ott.	none

VEZINA TROPHY

	Winner	Runner-up
2017	Sergei Bobrovsky, CBJ	Braden Holtby, Wsh.
2016	Braden Holtby, Wsh.	Ben Bishop, T.B.
2015	Carey Price, Mtl.	Pekka Rinne, Nsh.
2014	Tuukka Rask, Bos.	Semyon Varlamov, Col.
2013	Sergei Bobrovsky, CBJ	Henrik Lundqvist, NYR.
2012	Henrik Lundqvist, NYR	Jonathan Quick, L.A.
2011	Tim Thomas, Bos.	Pekka Rinne, Nsh.
2010	Ryan Miller, Buf.	Ilya Bryzgalov, Phx.
2009	Tim Thomas, Bos.	Steve Mason, CBJ
2008	Martin Brodeur, N.J.	Evgeni Nabokov, S.J.
2007	Martin Brodeur, N.J.	Roberto Luongo, Van.
2006	Miikka Kiprusoff, Cgy.	Martin Brodeur, N.J.
2005	....	....
2004	Martin Brodeur, N.J.	Miikka Kiprusoff, Cgy.
2003	Martin Brodeur, N.J.	Marty Turco, Dal.
2002	Jose Theodore, Mtl.	Patrick Roy, Col.
2001	Dominik Hasek, Buf.	Roman Cechmanek, Phi.
2000	Olaf Kolzig, Wsh.	Roman Turek, St.L.
1999	Dominik Hasek, Buf.	Curtis Joseph, Tor.
1998	Dominik Hasek, Buf.	Martin Brodeur, N.J.
1997	Dominik Hasek, Buf.	Martin Brodeur, N.J.
1996	Jim Carey, Wsh.	Chris Osgood, Det.
1995	Dominik Hasek, Buf.	Ed Belfour, Chi.
1994	Dominik Hasek, Buf.	John Vanbiesbrouck, Fla.
1993	Ed Belfour, Chi.	Tom Barrasso, Pit.
1992	Patrick Roy, Mtl.	Kirk McLean, Van.
1991	Ed Belfour, Chi.	Patrick Roy, Mtl.
1990	Patrick Roy, Mtl.	Daren Puppa, Buf.
1989	Patrick Roy, Mtl.	Mike Vernon, Cgy.
1988	Grant Fuhr, Edm.	Tom Barrasso, Buf.
1987	Ron Hextall, Phi.	Mike Liut, Hfd.
1986	John Vanbiesbrouck, NYR	Bob Froese, Phi.
1985	Pelle Lindbergh, Phi.	Tom Barrasso, Buf.
1984	Tom Barrasso, Buf.	Reggie Lemelin, Cgy.
1983	Pete Peeters, Bos.	Roland Melanson, NYI
1982	Billy Smith, NYI	Grant Fuhr, Edm.
1981	Richard Sevigny, Mtl.	Pete Peeters, Phi.
	Denis Herron, Mtl.	Rick St. Croix, Phi.
	Michel Larocque, Mtl.	
1980	Bob Sauve, Buf.	Gerry Cheevers, Bos.
	Don Edwards, Buf.	Gilles Gilbert, Bos.
1979	Ken Dryden, Mtl.	Glenn Resch, NYI
	Michel Larocque, Mtl.	Billy Smith, NYI
1978	Ken Dryden, Mtl.	Bernie Parent, Phi.
	Michel Larocque, Mtl.	Wayne Stephenson, Phi.
1977	Ken Dryden, Mtl.	Glenn Resch, NYI
	Michel Larocque, Mtl.	Billy Smith, NYI
1976	Ken Dryden, Mtl.	Glenn Resch, NYI
		Billy Smith, NYI
1975	Bernie Parent, Phi.	Rogie Vachon, L.A.
		Gary Edwards, L.A.
1974	Bernie Parent, Phi. (tie)	Gilles Gilbert, Bos.
	Tony Esposito, Chi. (tie)	
1973	Ken Dryden, Mtl.	Ed Giacomin, NYR
		Gilles Villemure, NYR
1972	Tony Esposito, Chi.	Cesare Maniago, Min.
	Gary Smith, Chi.	Gump Worsley, Min.
1971	Ed Giacomin, NYR	Tony Esposito, Chi.
	Gilles Villemure, NYR	
1970	Tony Esposito, Chi.	Jacques Plante, St.L.
		Ernie Wakely, St.L.
1969	Jacques Plante, St.L.	Ed Giacomin, NYR
	Glenn Hall, St.L.	
1968	Gump Worsley, Mtl.	Johnny Bower, Tor.
	Rogie Vachon, Mtl.	Bruce Gamble, Tor.
1967	Glenn Hall, Chi.	Charlie Hodge, Mtl.
	Denis DeJordy, Chi.	
1966	Gump Worsley, Mtl.	Glenn Hall, Chi.
	Charlie Hodge, Mtl.	
1965	Terry Sawchuk, Tor.	Roger Crozier, Det.
	Johnny Bower, Tor.	
1964	Charlie Hodge, Mtl.	Glenn Hall, Chi.
1963	Glenn Hall, Chi.	Johnny Bower, Tor.
		Don Simmons, Tor.
1962	Jacques Plante, Mtl.	Johnny Bower, Tor.
1961	Johnny Bower, Tor.	Glenn Hall, Chi.
1960	Jacques Plante, Mtl.	Glenn Hall, Chi.
1959	Jacques Plante, Mtl.	Johnny Bower, Tor.
		Ed Chadwick, Tor.
1958	Jacques Plante, Mtl.	Gump Worsley, NYR
		Marcel Paille, NYR
1957	Jacques Plante, Mtl.	Glenn Hall, Det.
1956	Jacques Plante, Mtl.	Glenn Hall, Det.
1955	Terry Sawchuk, Det.	Harry Lumley, Tor.
1954	Harry Lumley, Tor.	Terry Sawchuk, Det.
1953	Terry Sawchuk, Det.	Gerry McNeil, Mtl.
1952	Terry Sawchuk, Det.	Al Rollins, Tor.
1951	Al Rollins, Tor.	Terry Sawchuk, Det.
1950	Bill Durnan, Mtl.	Harry Lumley, Det.
1949	Bill Durnan, Mtl.	Harry Lumley, Det.
1948	Turk Broda, Tor.	Harry Lumley, Det.
1947	Bill Durnan, Mtl.	Turk Broda, Tor.
1946	Bill Durnan, Mtl.	Frank Brimsek, Bos.
1945	Bill Durnan, Mtl.	Frank McCool, Tor. (tie)
		Harry Lumley, Det. (tie)
1944	Bill Durnan, Mtl.	Paul Bibeault, Tor.
1943	Johnny Mowers, Det.	Turk Broda, Tor.
1942	Frank Brimsek, Bos.	Turk Broda, Tor.
1941	Turk Broda, Tor.	Frank Brimsek, Bos. (tie)
		Johnny Mowers, Det. (tie)
1940	Dave Kerr, NYR	Frank Brimsek, Bos.
1939	Frank Brimsek, Bos.	Dave Kerr, NYR
1938	Tiny Thompson, Bos.	Dave Kerr, NYR
1937	Normie Smith, Det.	Dave Kerr, NYR
1936	Tiny Thompson, Bos.	Mike Karakas, Chi.
1935	Lorne Chabot, Chi.	Alex Connell, Mtl.M.
1934	Charlie Gardiner, Chi.	Wilf Cude, Det.
1933	Tiny Thompson, Bos.	John Ross Roach, Det.
1932	Charlie Gardiner, Chi.	Alex Connell, Det.
1931	Roy Worters, NYA	Charlie Gardiner, Chi.
1930	Tiny Thompson, Bos.	Charlie Gardiner, Chi.
1929	George Hainsworth, Mtl.	Tiny Thompson, Bos.
1928	George Hainsworth, Mtl.	Alex Connell, Ott.
1927	George Hainsworth, Mtl.	Clint Benedict, Mtl.M.

CALDER MEMORIAL TROPHY

	Winner	Runner-up
2017	Auston Matthews, Tor.	Patrik Laine, Wpg.
2016	Artemi Panarin, Chi.	Shayne Gostisbehere, Phi.
2015	Aaron Ekblad, Fla.	Mark Stone, Ott.
2014	Nathan MacKinnon, Col.	Ondrej Palat, T.B.
2013	Jonathan Huberdeau, Fla.	Brendan Gallagher, Mtl.
2012	Gabriel Landeskog, Col.	Ryan Nugent-Hopkins, Edm.
2011	Jeff Skinner, Car.	Logan Couture, S.J.
2010	Tyler Myers, Buf.	Jimmy Howard, Det.
2009	Steve Mason, CBJ	Bobby Ryan, Ana.
2008	Patrick Kane, Chi.	Nicklas Backstrom, Wsh.
2007	Evgeni Malkin, Pit.	Paul Stastny, Col.
2006	Alex Ovechkin, Wsh.	Sidney Crosby, Pit.
2005	....	....
2004	Andrew Raycroft, Bos.	Michael Ryder, Mtl.
2003	Barret Jackman, St.L.	Henrik Zetterberg, Det.
2002	Dany Heatley, Atl.	Ilya Kovalchuk, Atl.
2001	Evgeni Nabokov, S.J.	Brad Richards, T.B.
2000	Scott Gomez, N.J.	Brad Stuart, S.J.
1999	Chris Drury, Col.	Marian Hossa, Ott.
1998	Sergei Samsonov, Bos.	Mattias Ohlund, Van.
1997	Bryan Berard, NYI	Jarome Iginla, Cgy.
1996	Daniel Alfredsson, Ott.	Eric Daze, Chi.
1995	Peter Forsberg, Que.	Jim Carey, Wsh.
1994	Martin Brodeur, N.J.	Jason Arnott, Edm.
1993	Teemu Selanne, Wpg.	Joe Juneau, Bos.
1992	Pavel Bure, Van.	Nicklas Lidstrom, Det
1991	Ed Belfour, Chi.	Sergei Fedorov, Det.
1990	Sergei Makarov, Cgy.	Mike Modano, Min.
1989	Brian Leetch, NYR	Trevor Linden, Van.
1988	Joe Nieuwendyk, Cgy.	Ray Sheppard, Buf.
1987	Luc Robitaille, L.A.	Ron Hextall, Phi.
1986	Gary Suter, Cgy.	Wendel Clark, Tor.
1985	Mario Lemieux, Pit.	Chris Chelios, Mtl.
1984	Tom Barrasso, Buf.	Steve Yzerman, Det.
1983	Steve Larmer, Chi.	Phil Housley, Buf.
1982	Dale Hawerchuk, Wpg.	Barry Pederson, Bos.
1981	Peter Stastny, Que.	Larry Murphy, L.A.
1980	Raymond Bourque, Bos.	Mike Foligno, Det.
1979	Bobby Smith, Min	Ryan Walter, Wsh.
1978	Mike Bossy, NYI	Barry Beck, Col.
1977	Willi Plett, Atl.	Don Murdoch, NYR
1976	Bryan Trottier, NYI	Glenn Resch, NYI
1975	Eric Vail, Atl.	Pierre Larouche, Pit.
1974	Denis Potvin, NYI	Tom Lysiak, Atl.
1973	Steve Vickers, NYR	Bill Barber, Phi.
1972	Ken Dryden, Mtl.	Rick Martin, Buf.
1971	Gilbert Perreault, Buf.	Jude Drouin, Min.
1970	Tony Esposito, Chi.	Bill Fairbairn, NYR
1969	Danny Grant, Min.	Norm Ferguson, Oak.
1968	Derek Sanderson, Bos.	Jacques Lemaire, Mtl.
1967	Bobby Orr, Bos.	Ed Van Impe, Chi.
1966	Brit Selby, Tor.	Bert Marshall, Det.
1965	Roger Crozier, Det.	Ron Ellis, Tor.
1964	Jacques Laperriere, Mtl.	John Ferguson, Mtl.
1963	Kent Douglas, Tor.	Doug Barkley, Det.
1962	Bobby Rousseau, Mtl.	Cliff Pennington, Bos.
1961	Dave Keon, Tor.	Bob Nevin, Tor.
1960	Bill Hay, Chi.	Murray Oliver, Det.
1959	Ralph Backstrom, Mtl.	Carl Brewer, Tor.
1958	Frank Mahovlich, Tor.	Bobby Hull, Chi.
1957	Larry Regan, Bos.	Ed Chadwick, Tor.
1956	Glenn Hall, Det.	Andy Hebenton, NYR
1955	Ed Litzenberger, Chi.	Don McKenney, Bos.
1954	Camille Henry, NYR	Dutch Reibel, Det.
1953	Gump Worsley, NYR	Gord Hannigan, Tor.
1952	Bernie Geoffrion, Mtl.	Hy Buller, NYR
1951	Terry Sawchuk, Det.	Al Rollins, Tor.
1950	Jack Gelineau, Bos.	Phil Maloney, Bos.
1949	Pentti Lund, NYR	Allan Stanley, NYR
1948	Jim McFadden, Det.	Pete Babando, Bos.
1947	Howie Meeker, Tor.	Jim Conacher, Det.
1946	Edgar Laprade, NYR	George Gee, Chi.
1945	Frank McCool, Tor.	Ken Smith, Bos.
1944	Gus Bodnar, Tor.	Bill Durnan, Mtl.
1943	Gaye Stewart, Tor.	Glen Harmon, Mtl.
1942	Grant Warwick, NYR	Buddy O'Connor, Mtl.
1941	John Quilty, Mtl.	Johnny Mowers, Det.
1940	Kilby MacDonald, NYR	Wally Stanowski, Tor.
1939	Frank Brimsek, Bos.	Roy Conacher, Bos.
1938	Cully Dahlstrom, Chi.	Murph Chamberlain, Tor.
1937	Syl Apps, Tor.	Gordie Drillon, Tor.
1936	Mike Karakas, Chi.	Bucko McDonald, Det.
1935	Sweeney Schriner, NYA	Bert Connelly, NYR
1934	Russ Blinco, Mtl.M.	none
1933	Carl Voss, Det.	none

E.J. MCGUIRE AWARD OF EXCELLENCE

	Winner
2017	Nico Hischier
2016	Neil Doef
2015	Travis Konecny

NHL LIFETIME ACHIEVEMENT AWARD

	Winner
2009	Jean Beliveau
2008	Gordie Howe

JAMES NORRIS MEMORIAL TROPHY

	Winner	Runner-up
2017	Brent Burns, S.J.	Erik Karlsson, Ott.
2016	Drew Doughty, L.A.	Erik Karlsson, Ott.
2015	Erik Karlsson, Ott.	Drew Doughty, L.A.
2014	Duncan Keith, Chi.	Zdeno Chara, Bos.
2013	P.K. Subban, Mtl.	Ryan Suter, Min.
2012	Erik Karlsson, Ott.	Shea Weber, Nsh.
2011	Nicklas Lidstrom, Det.	Shea Weber, Nsh.
2010	Duncan Keith, Chi.	Mike Green, Wsh.
2009	Zdeno Chara, Bos.	Mike Green, Wsh.
2008	Nicklas Lidstrom, Det.	Dion Phaneuf, Cgy.
2007	Nicklas Lidstrom, Det.	Scott Niedermayer, Ana.
2006	Nicklas Lidstrom, Det.	Scott Niedermayer, Ana.
2005	....	....
2004	Scott Niedermayer, N.J.	Zdeno Chara, Ott.
2003	Nicklas Lidstrom, Det.	Al MacInnis, St.L.
2002	Nicklas Lidstrom, Det.	Chris Chelios, Det.
2001	Nicklas Lidstrom, Det.	Raymond Bourque, Col.
2000	Chris Pronger, St.L.	Nicklas Lidstrom, Det.
1999	Al MacInnis, St.L.	Nicklas Lidstrom, Det.
1998	Rob Blake, L.A.	Nicklas Lidstrom, Det.
1997	Brian Leetch, NYR	V. Konstantinov, Det.
1996	Chris Chelios, Chi.	Raymond Bourque, Bos.
1995	Paul Coffey, Det.	Chris Chelios, Chi.
1994	Raymond Bourque, Bos.	Scott Stevens, N.J.
1993	Chris Chelios, Chi.	Raymond Bourque, Bos.
1992	Brian Leetch, NYR	Raymond Bourque, Bos.
1991	Raymond Bourque, Bos.	Al MacInnis, Cgy.
1990	Raymond Bourque, Bos.	Al MacInnis, Cgy.
1989	Chris Chelios, Mtl	Paul Coffey, Pit.
1988	Raymond Bourque, Bos.	Scott Stevens, Wsh.
1987	Raymond Bourque, Bos.	Mark Howe, Phi.
1986	Paul Coffey, Edm.	Mark Howe, Phi.
1985	Paul Coffey, Edm.	Raymond Bourque, Bos.
1984	Rod Langway, Wsh.	Paul Coffey, Edm.
1983	Rod Langway, Wsh.	Mark Howe, Phi.
1982	Doug Wilson, Chi.	Raymond Bourque, Bos.
1981	Randy Carlyle, Pit.	Denis Potvin, NYI
1980	Larry Robinson, Mtl.	Borje Salming, Tor.
1979	Denis Potvin, NYI	Larry Robinson, Mtl.
1978	Denis Potvin, NYI	Brad Park, Bos.
1977	Larry Robinson, Mtl.	Borje Salming, Tor.
1976	Denis Potvin, NYI	Brad Park, NYR-Bos.
1975	Bobby Orr, Bos.	Denis Potvin, NYI
1974	Bobby Orr, Bos.	Brad Park, NYR
1973	Bobby Orr, Bos.	Guy Lapointe, Mtl.
1972	Bobby Orr, Bos.	Brad Park, NYR
1971	Bobby Orr, Bos.	Brad Park, NYR
1970	Bobby Orr, Bos.	Brad Park, NYR
1969	Bobby Orr, Bos.	Tim Horton, Tor.
1968	Bobby Orr, Bos.	J.C. Tremblay, Mtl
1967	Harry Howell, NYR	Pierre Pilote, Chi.
1966	Jacques Laperriere, Mtl.	Pierre Pilote, Chi.
1965	Pierre Pilote, Chi.	Jacques Laperriere, Mtl.
1964	Pierre Pilote, Chi.	Tim Horton, Tor.
1963	Pierre Pilote, Chi.	Carl Brewer, Tor.
1962	Doug Harvey, NYR	Pierre Pilote, Chi.
1961	Doug Harvey, Mtl.	Marcel Pronovost, Det.
1960	Doug Harvey, Mtl.	Allan Stanley, Tor.
1959	Tom Johnson, Mtl.	Bill Gadsby, NYR
1958	Doug Harvey, Mtl.	Bill Gadsby, NYR
1957	Doug Harvey, Mtl.	Red Kelly, Det.
1956	Doug Harvey, Mtl.	Bill Gadsby, NYR
1955	Doug Harvey, Mtl.	Red Kelly, Det.
1954	Red Kelly, Det.	Doug Harvey, Mtl.

JACK ADAMS AWARD

	Winner	Runner-up
2017	John Tortorella, CBJ	Mike Babcock, Tor.
2016	Barry Trotz, Wsh.	Gerard Gallant, Fla.
2015	Bob Hartley, Cgy.	Alain Vigneault, NYR
2014	Patrick Roy, Col.	Mike Babcock, Det.
2013	Paul MacLean, Ott.	Joel Quenneville, Chi.
2012	Ken Hitchcock, St.L.	John Tortorella, NYR
2011	Dan Bylsma, Pit.	Alain Vigneault, Van.
2010	Dave Tippett, Phx.	Barry Trotz, Nsh.
2009	Claude Julien, Bos.	Andy Murray, St.L.
2008	Bruce Boudreau, Wsh.	Guy Carbonneau, Mtl.
2007	Alain Vigneault, Van.	Lindy Ruff, Buf.
2006	Lindy Ruff, Buf.	Peter Laviolette, Car.
2005	....	....
2004	John Tortorella, T.B.	Ron Wilson, S.J.
2003	Jacques Lemaire, Min.	John Tortorella, T.B.
2002	Bob Francis, Phx.	Brian Sutter, Chi.
2001	Bill Barber, Phi.	Scotty Bowman, Det.
2000	Joel Quenneville, St.L.	Alain Vigneault, Mtl.
1999	Jacques Martin, Ott.	Pat Quinn, Tor.
1998	Pat Burns, Bos.	Larry Robinson, L.A.
1997	Ted Nolan, Buf.	Ken Hitchcock, Dal.
1996	Scotty Bowman, Det.	Doug MacLean, Fla.
1995	Marc Crawford, Que.	Scotty Bowman, Det.
1994	Jacques Lemaire, N.J.	Kevin Constantine, S.J.
1993	Pat Burns, Tor.	Brian Sutter, Bos.
1992	Pat Quinn, Van.	Roger Neilson, NYR
1991	Brian Sutter, St.L.	Tom Webster, L.A.
1990	Bob Murdoch, Wpg.	Mike Milbury, Bos.
1989	Pat Burns, Mtl.	Bob McCammon, Van.
1988	Jacques Demers, Det.	Terry Crisp, Cgy.
1987	Jacques Demers, Det.	Jack Evans, Hfd.
1986	Glen Sather, Edm.	Jacques Demers, St.L.
1985	Mike Keenan, Phi.	Barry Long, Wpg.
1984	Bryan Murray, Wsh.	Scotty Bowman, Buf.
1983	Orval Tessier, Chi.	
1982	Tom Watt, Wpg.	
1981	Red Berenson, St.L.	Bob Berry, L.A.
1980	Pat Quinn, Phi.	
1979	Al Arbour, NYI	Fred Shero, NYR
1978	Bobby Kromm, Det.	Don Cherry, Bos.
1977	Scotty Bowman, Mtl.	Tom McVie, Wsh.
1976	Don Cherry, Bos.	
1975	Bob Pulford, L.A.	
1974	Fred Shero, Phi.	

LESTER PATRICK TROPHY

	Winner	
2016	Mark Howe	Pat Kelly
2015	Bob Crocker	Jeremy Jacobs
2014	Bill Daly	Paul Holmgren
2013	Kevin Allen	
2012	Dick Patrick	Bob Chase-Wallestein
2011	Jeff Sauer	Tony Rossi
	Mark Johnson	Bob Pulford
2010	Jerry York	Jack Parker
	Cam Neely	Dave Andrews
2009	Mark Messier	Jim Devellano
	Mike Richter	
2008	Brian Burke	Phil Housley
	Ted Lindsay	Bob Naegele, Jr.
2007	Brian Leetch	Cammi Granato
	Stan Fischler	John Halligan
2006	Red Berenson	Marcel Dionne
	Reed Larson	Glen Sonmor
	Steve Yzerman	
2005	....	
2004	John Davidson	Mike Emrick
	Ray Miron	
2003	Raymond Bourque	Ron DeGregorio
	Willie O'Ree	
2002	Herb Brooks	Larry Pleau
	1960 U.S. Olympic Team	
2001	Gary Bettman	Scotty Bowman
	David Poile	
2000	Mario Lemieux	Craig Patrick
	Lou Vairo	
1999	Harry Sinden	
	1998 U.S. Olympic Women's Team	
1998	Neal Broten	Peter Karmanos
	John Mayasich	Max McNab
1997	Bill Cleary	* Seymour H. Knox III
	Pat LaFontaine	
1996	George Gund	Ken Morrow
	Milt Schmidt	
1995	Bob Fleming	Brian Mullen
	Joe Mullen	
1994	Wayne Gretzky	Robert Ridder
1993	*Frank Boucher	* Mervyn "Red" Dutton
	Bruce McNall	Gil Stein
1992	Al Arbour	Art Berglund
	Lou Lamoriello	
1991	Rod Gilbert	Mike Ilitch
1990	Len Ceglarski	
1989	Dan Kelly	Lou Nanne
	*Lynn Patrick	Bud Poile
1988	Keith Allen	Fred Cusick
	Bob Johnson	
1987	*Hobey Baker	Frank Mathers
1986	John MacInnes	Jack Riley
1985	Jack Butterfield	Arthur M. Wirtz
1984	*Arthur Howey Ross	John A. Ziegler, Jr.
1983	Bill Torrey	
1982	Emile P. Francis	
1981	Charles M. Schulz	
1980	Bobby Clarke	Frederick A. Shero
	Edward M. Snider	1980 U.S. Olympic Team
1979	Bobby Orr	
1978	Phil Esposito	Tom Fitzgerald
	William T. Tutt	William W. Wirtz
1977	Murray A. Armstrong	John P. Bucyk
	John Mariucci	
1976	George A. Leader	Stanley Mikita
	Bruce A. Norris	
1975	William L. Chadwick	Donald M. Clark
	Thomas N. Ivan	
1974	*Weston W. Adams, Sr.	* Charles L. Crovat
	Alex Delvecchio	Murray Murdoch
1973	Walter L. Bush, Jr.	
1972	Clarence S. Campbell	John A. "Snooks" Kelly
	*James D. Norris	Ralph "Cooney" Weiland
1971	William M. Jennings	* Terrance G. Sawchuk
	*John B. Sollenberger	
1970	*James C. V. Hendy	Edward W. Shore
1969	Robert M. Hull	* Edward J. Jeremiah
1968	*Walter A. Brown	* Gen. John R. Kilpatrick
	Thomas F. Lockhart	
1967	*Charles F. Adams	Gordon Howe
	*James Norris, Sr.	
1966	J.J. "Jack" Adams	

* awarded posthumously

NHL FOUNDATION PLAYER AWARD

	Winner	
2017	Travis Hamonic	NY Islanders
2016	Mark Giordano	Calgary
2015	Brent Burns	San Jose
2014	Patrice Bergeron	Boston
2013	Henrik Zetterberg	Detroit
2012	Mike Fisher	Nashville
2011	Dustin Brown	Los Angeles
2010	Ryan Miller	Buffalo
2009	Rick Nash	Columbus
2008	Trevor Linden	Vancouver
	Vincent Lecavalier	Tampa Bay
2007	Joe Sakic	Colorado
2006	Marty Turco	Dallas
2004	Jarome Iginla	Calgary
2003	Darren McCarty	Detroit
2002	Ron Francis	Carolina
2001	Olaf Kolzig	Washington
2000	Adam Graves	NY Rangers
1999	Rob Ray	Buffalo
1998	Kelly Chase	St. Louis

KING CLANCY MEMORIAL TROPHY

	Winner	
2017	Nick Foligno	Columbus
2016	Henrik Sedin	Vancouver
2015	Henrik Zetterberg	Detroit
2014	Andrew Ference	Edmonton
2013	Patrice Bergeron	Boston
2012	Daniel Alfredsson	Ottawa
2011	Doug Weight	NY Islanders
2010	Shane Doan	Phoenix
2009	Ethan Moreau	Edmonton
2008	Vincent Lecavalier	Tampa Bay
2007	Saku Koivu	Montreal
2006	Olaf Kolzig	Washington
2005	....	....
2004	Jarome Iginla	Calgary
2003	Brendan Shanahan	Detroit
2002	Ron Francis	Carolina
2001	Shjon Podein	Colorado
2000	Curtis Joseph	Toronto
1999	Rob Ray	Buffalo
1998	Kelly Chase	St. Louis
1997	Trevor Linden	Vancouver
1996	Kris King	Winnipeg
1995	Joe Nieuwendyk	Calgary
1994	Adam Graves	NY Rangers
1993	Dave Poulin	Boston
1992	Raymond Bourque	Boston
1991	Dave Taylor	Los Angeles
1990	Kevin Lowe	Edmonton
1989	Bryan Trottier	NY Islanders
1988	Lanny McDonald	Calgary

PRESIDENTS' TROPHY

	Winner	Runner-up
2017	Washington Capitals	Pittsburgh Penguins
2016	Washington Capitals	Dallas Stars
2015	New York Rangers	Montreal Canadiens
2014	Boston Bruins	Anaheim Ducks
2013	Chicago Blackhawks	Pittsburgh Penguins
2012	Vancouver Canucks	New York Rangers
2011	Vancouver Canucks	Washington Capitals
2010	Washington Capitals	San Jose Sharks
2009	San Jose Sharks	Boston Bruins
2008	Detroit Red Wings	San Jose Sharks
2007	Buffalo Sabres	Detroit Red Wings
2006	Detroit Red Wings	Ottawa Senators
2005	....	....
2004	Detroit Red Wings	Tampa Bay Lightning
2003	Ottawa Senators	Dallas Stars
2002	Detroit Red Wings	Boston Bruins
2001	Colorado Avalanche	Detroit Red Wings
2000	St. Louis Blues	Detroit Red Wings
1999	Dallas Stars	New Jersey Devils
1998	Dallas Stars	New Jersey Devils
1997	Colorado Avalanche	Dallas Stars
1996	Detroit Red Wings	Colorado Avalanche
1995	Detroit Red Wings	Quebec Nordiques
1994	New York Rangers	New Jersey Devils
1993	Pittsburgh Penguins	Boston Bruins
1992	New York Rangers	Washington Capitals
1991	Chicago Blackhawks	St. Louis Blues
1990	Boston Bruins	Calgary Flames
1989	Calgary Flames	Montreal Canadiens
1988	Calgary Flames	Montreal Canadiens
1987	Edmonton Oilers	Philadelphia Flyers
1986	Edmonton Oilers	Philadelphia Flyers

TED LINDSAY AWARD

	Winner	
2017	Connor McDavid	Edmonton
2016	Patrick Kane	Chicago
2015	Carey Price	Montreal
2014	Sidney Crosby	Pittsburgh
2013	Sidney Crosby	Pittsburgh
2012	Evgeni Malkin	Pittsburgh
2011	Daniel Sedin	Vancouver
2010	Alex Ovechkin	Washington
2009	Alex Ovechkin	Washington
2008	Alex Ovechkin	Washington
2007	Sidney Crosby	Pittsburgh
2006	Jaromir Jagr	NY Rangers
2005	....	....
2004	Martin St. Louis	Tampa Bay
2003	Markus Naslund	Vancouver
2002	Jarome Iginla	Calgary
2001	Joe Sakic	Colorado
2000	Jaromir Jagr	Pittsburgh
1999	Jaromir Jagr	Pittsburgh
1998	Dominik Hasek	Buffalo
1997	Dominik Hasek	Buffalo
1996	Mario Lemieux	Pittsburgh
1995	Eric Lindros	Philadelphia
1994	Sergei Fedorov	Detroit
1993	Mario Lemieux	Pittsburgh
1992	Mark Messier	NY Rangers
1991	Brett Hull	St. Louis
1990	Mark Messier	Edmonton
1989	Steve Yzerman	Detroit
1988	Mario Lemieux	Pittsburgh
1987	Wayne Gretzky	Edmonton
1986	Mario Lemieux	Pittsburgh
1985	Wayne Gretzky	Edmonton
1984	Wayne Gretzky	Edmonton
1983	Wayne Gretzky	Edmonton
1982	Wayne Gretzky	Edmonton
1981	Mike Liut	St. Louis
1980	Marcel Dionne	Los Angeles
1979	Marcel Dionne	Los Angeles
1978	Guy Lafleur	Montreal
1977	Guy Lafleur	Montreal
1976	Guy Lafleur	Montreal
1975	Bobby Orr	Boston
1974	Phil Esposito	Boston
1973	Bobby Clarke	Philadelphia
1972	Jean Ratelle	NY Rangers
1971	Phil Esposito	Boston

NHL Draft

Draft Summary

Following is a summary of the players drafted from the Ontario Hockey League (OHL), Quebec Major Junior Hockey League (QMJHL), Western Hockey League (WHL), United States Hockey League (USHL), United States colleges, United States high schools, European leagues and other North American leagues since 1969. "Other" may include additional Canadian and U.S. junior leagues, minor professional leagues (AHL, IHL), midget and other teams playing in leagues not listed above

	Total	OHL		QMJHL		WHL		USHL		College		Hi School		Int'l		Other	
Year	Picks	Picks	%	Picks	%	Picks	%	Picks	%	Picks	%	Picks	%	Picks	%	Picks	%
Total	**11027**	**2319**	**21.0**	**1144**	**10.4**	**1998**	**18.1**	**433**	**3.9**	**1159**	**10.5**	**869**	**7.9**	**2252**	**20.4**	**853**	**7.7**
2017	217	42	19.4	14	6.5	33	15.2	33	15.2	8	3.7	12	5.5	67	30.9	8	3.7
2016	211	48	22.7	14	6.6	34	16.1	28	13.3	13	6.2	6	2.4	56	26.5	12	5.7
2015	211	31	14.7	30	14.2	34	16.1	30	14.2	9	4.3	12	5.7	55	26.0	10	4.7
2014	210	41	19.5	17	8.1	37	17.7	31	14.8	5	2.4	13	6.2	51	24.3	15	7.1
2013	211	37	17.5	31	14.7	33	15.6	26	12.3	6	2.8	15	7.1	46	21.8	17	8.1
2012	211	48	22.7	19	9.0	32	15.2	24	11.4	9	4.3	19	9.0	43	20.4	17	8.1
2011	210	46	21.9	22	10.4	33	15.7	26	12.4	11	5.2	18	8.6	48	22.9	6	2.9
2010	210	42	20.0	22	10.4	43	20.5	20	9.5	9	4.2	22	10.5	39	18.6	13	6.2
2009	210	45	21.4	23	11.0	31	14.8	16	7.6	7	3.3	19	9.0	41	19.5	28	13.3
2008	211	46	21.8	27	12.8	37	17.5	10	4.7	9	4.2	15	7.1	39	18.5	28	13.3
2007	211	35	16.6	25	11.8	37	17.5	21	10.0	8	3.8	14	6.6	36	17.0	35	16.6
2006	213	29	13.6	25	11.7	24	11.2	9	4.2	18	8.4	19	8.9	63	29.5	26	12.2
2005	230	43	18.7	23	10.0	43	18.7	14	6.1	13	5.6	18	7.8	50	21.7	26	11.3
2004	291	42	14.4	27	9.3	44	15.1	12	4.1	28	9.6	18	6.2	88	30.2	32	11.0
2003	292	44	15.1	38	13.0	41	14.0	16	5.5	23	7.9	10	3.4	93	31.8	27	9.2
2002	290	35	12.1	23	7.9	43	14.8	15	5.2	41	14.1	6	2.1	110	37.9	17	5.9
2001	289	41	14.2	26	9.0	45	15.6	11	3.8	24	8.3	8	2.8	119	41.2	15	5.2
2000	293	39	13.3	21	7.2	41	14.0	13	4.4	35	11.9	7	2.4	123	42.0	14	4.8
1999	272	52	19.1	20	7.4	40	14.7	6	2.2	36	13.2	9	3.3	94	34.6	15	5.5
1998	258	50	19.4	41	15.9	44	17.1	4	1.6	27	10.5	7	2.7	75	29.1	10	3.9
1997	246	52	21.1	19	7.7	63	25.6	11	4.5	26	10.6	4	1.6	63	25.6	8	3.3
1996	241	51	21.2	31	12.9	54	22.4	2	0.8	25	10.4	6	2.5	58	24.1	14	5.8
1995	234	54	23.1	35	15.0	55	23.5	2	0.9	5	2.1	2	0.9	69	29.5	12	5.1
1994	286	45	15.7	28	9.8	66	23.1	9	3.1	6	2.1	28	9.8	80	28.0	24	8.4
1993	286	60	21.0	23	8.0	44	15.4	6	2.1	17	5.9	33	11.5	78	27.3	25	8.7
1992	264	57	21.6	22	8.3	45	17.0	6	2.3	9	3.4	25	9.5	84	31.8	16	6.1
1991	264	43	16.3	25	9.5	40	15.2	8	3.0	43	16.3	37	14.0	55	20.8	13	4.9
1990	250	39	15.6	14	5.6	33	13.2	4	1.6	38	15.2	57	22.8	53	21.2	12	4.8
1989	252	39	15.5	16	6.3	44	17.5	3	1.2	48	19.0	47	18.7	38	15.1	17	6.7
1988	252	32	12.7	22	8.7	30	11.9	5	2.0	48	19.0	56	22.2	39	15.5	20	7.9
1987	252	32	12.7	17	6.7	36	14.3	2	0.8	40	15.9	69	27.4	38	15.1	18	7.1
1986	252	66	26.2	22	8.7	32	12.7	1	0.4	22	8.7	40	15.9	28	11.1	41	16.3
1985	252	59	23.4	15	6.0	48	19.0	1	0.4	20	7.9	48	19.0	31	12.3	30	11.9
1984	250	55	22.0	16	6.4	37	14.8	1	0.4	22	8.8	44	17.6	40	16.0	35	14.0
1983	242	57	23.6	24	9.9	41	16.9	3	1.2	14	5.8	35	14.5	34	14.0	34	14.0
1982	252	60	23.8	17	6.7	55	21.8	3	1.2	20	7.9	47	18.7	35	13.9	15	6.0
1981	211	59	28.0	28	13.3	37	17.5	1	0.5	21	10.0	17	8.1	32	15.2	16	7.6
1980	210	73	34.8	24	11.4	41	19.5	-	-	42	20.0	7	3.3	13	6.2	10	4.8
1979	126	48	38.1	19	15.1	37	29.4	-	-	15	11.9	-	-	6	4.8	1	0.8
1978	234	59	25.2	22	9.4	48	20.5	-	-	73	31.2	-	-	16	6.8	16	6.8
1977	185	42	22.7	40	21.6	44	23.8	-	-	49	26.5	-	-	5	2.7	5	2.7
1976	135	47	34.8	18	13.3	33	24.4	-	-	26	19.3	-	-	8	5.9	3	2.2
1975	217	55	25.3	28	12.9	57	26.3	-	-	59	27.2	-	-	6	2.8	12	5.5
1974	247	69	27.9	40	16.2	66	26.7	-	-	41	16.6	-	-	6	2.4	25	10.1
1973	168	56	33.3	24	14.3	49	29.2	-	-	25	14.9	-	-	-	-	14	8.3
1972	152	46	30.3	30	19.7	44	28.9	-	-	21	13.8	-	-	-	-	11	7.2
1971	117	41	35.0	13	11.1	28	23.9	-	-	22	18.8	-	-	-	-	13	11.1
1970	115	51	44.3	13	11.3	22	19.1	-	-	16	13.9	-	-	-	-	13	11.3
1969	84	36	42.9	11	13.1	20	23.8	-	-	7	8.3	-	-	1	1.2	9	10.7

Total Players Drafted (1969-2017): 11,027

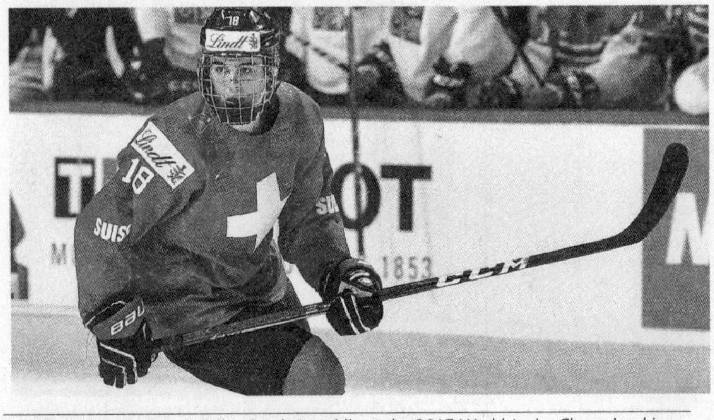

Seen here in action against the Czech Republic at the 2017 World Junior Championships, Nico Hischier became the first player from Switzerland to be chosen first overall when he was selected by the New Jersey Devils at the 2017 NHL Draft.

History

Year	Location	Date	# Drafted
2017	United Center, Chicago	June 23-24	217
2016	First Niagara Center, Buffalo	June 24-25	211
2015	BB&T Center, Florida	June 26-27	211
2014	Wells Fargo Center, Philadelphia	June 27-28	210
2013	Prudential Center, New Jersey	June 30	211
2012	CONSOL Energy Center, Pittsburgh	June 22-23	211
2011	Xcel Energy Center, Minnesota	June 24-25	210
2010	STAPLES Center, Los Angeles	June 25-26	210
2009	Bell Centre, Montreal	June 26-27	210
2008	Scotiabank Place, Ottawa	June 20-21	211
2007	Nationwide Arena, Columbus	June 22-23	211
2006	General Motors Place, Vancouver	June 24	213
2005	Sheraton Hotel and Towers, Ottawa	July 30	230
2004	RBC Center, Carolina	June 26-27	291
2003	Gaylord Entertainment Center, Nashville	June 21-22	292
2002	Air Canada Centre, Toronto	June 22-23	290
2001	National Car Rental Center, Florida	June 23-24	289
2000	Saddledome, Calgary	June 24-25	293
1999	FleetCenter, Boston	June 26	272
1998	Marine Midland Arena, Buffalo	June 27	258
1997	Civic Arena, Pittsburgh	June 21	246
1996	Kiel Center, St. Louis	June 22	241
1995	Edmonton Coliseum	July 8	234
1994	Hartford Civic Center	June 28-29	286
1993	Le Colisée, Quebec	June 26	286
1992	Montreal Forum	June 20	264
1991	Memorial Auditorium, Buffalo	June 22	264
1990	B.C. Place, Vancouver	June 16	250
1989	Met Sports Center, Minnesota	June 17	252
1988	Montreal Forum	June 11	252
1987	Joe Louis Arena, Detroit	June 13	252
1986	Montreal Forum	June 21	252
1985	Toronto Convention Centre	June 15	252
1984	Montreal Forum	June 9	250
1983	Montreal Forum	June 8	242
1982	Montreal Forum	June 9	252
1963–1981	Montreal	—	2323

First Selections

Year	Player	Pos	Team	Drafted From	Age
2017	Nico Hischier	C	New Jersey	Halifax Mooseheads	18.3
2016	Auston Matthews	RW	Toronto	Zurich Lions (Switzerland)	18.9
2015	Connor McDavid	C	Edmonton	Erie Otters	18.5
2014	Aaron Ekblad	D	Florida	Barrie Colts	18.4
2013	Nathan MacKinnon	C	Colorado	Halifax Mooseheads	17.10
2012	Nail Yakupov	RW	Edmonton	Sarnia Sting	18.8
2011	Ryan Nugent-Hopkins	C	Edmonton	Red Deer Rebels	18.2
2010	Taylor Hall	LW	Edmonton	Windsor Spitfires	18.7
2009	John Tavares	C	NY Islanders	London Knights	18.9
2008	Steven Stamkos	C	Tampa Bay	Sarnia Sting	18.4
2007	Patrick Kane	RW	Chicago	London Knights	18.7
2006	Erik Johnson	D	St. Louis	U.S. National U-18	18.3
2005	Sidney Crosby	C	Pittsburgh	Rimouski Oceanic	17.11
2004	Alex Ovechkin	LW	Washington	Dynamo Moscow (Russia)	18.9
2003	Marc-Andre Fleury	G	Pittsburgh	Cape Breton Screaming Eagles	18.0
2002	Rick Nash	LW	Columbus	London Knights	18.0
2001	Ilya Kovalchuk	LW	Atlanta	Spartak (Russia)	18.2
2000	Rick DiPietro	G	NY Islanders	Boston University Terriers	18.9
1999	Patrik Stefan	C	Atlanta	Long Beach Ice Dogs (IHL)	18.9
1998	Vincent Lecavalier	C	Tampa Bay	Rimouski Oceanic	18.2
1997	Joe Thornton	C	Boston	Sault Ste. Marie Greyhounds	17.11
1996	Chris Phillips	D	Ottawa	Prince Albert Raiders	18.3
1995	Bryan Berard	D	Ottawa	Detroit Jr. Red Wings	18.4
1994	Ed Jovanovski	D	Florida	Windsor Spitfires	18.0
1993	Alexandre Daigle	C	Ottawa	Victoriaville Tigres	18.5
1992	Roman Hamrlik	D	Tampa Bay	ZPS Zlin (Czech.)	18.2
1991	Eric Lindros	C	Quebec	Oshawa Generals	18.3
1990	Owen Nolan	RW	Quebec	Cornwall Royals	18.4
1989	Mats Sundin	RW	Quebec	Nacka (Sweden)	18.4
1988	Mike Modano	C	Minnesota	Prince Albert Raiders	18.0
1987	Pierre Turgeon	C	Buffalo	Granby Bisons	17.10
1986	Joe Murphy	C	Detroit	Michigan State Spartans	18.8
1985	Wendel Clark	LW/D	Toronto	Saskatoon Blades	18.7
1984	Mario Lemieux	C	Pittsburgh	Laval Voisins	18.8
1983	Brian Lawton	C	Minnesota	Mount St. Charles HS	18.11
1982	Gord Kluzak	D	Boston	Nanaimo Islanders	18.3
1981	Dale Hawerchuk	C	Winnipeg	Cornwall Royals	18.2
1980	Doug Wickenheiser	C	Montreal	Regina Pats	19.2
1979	Rob Ramage	D	Colorado	London Knights	20.5
1978	Bobby Smith	C	Minnesota	Ottawa 67's	20.4
1977	Dale McCourt	C	Detroit	St. Catharines Fincups	20.4
1976	Rick Green	D	Washington	London Knights	20.3
1975	Mel Bridgman	C	Philadelphia	Victoria Cougars	20.1
1974	Greg Joly	D	Washington	Regina Pats	20.0
1973	Denis Potvin	D	NY Islanders	Ottawa 67's	19.7
1972	Billy Harris	RW	NY Islanders	Toronto Marlboros	20.4
1971	Guy Lafleur	RW	Montreal	Quebec Remparts	19.9
1970	Gilbert Perreault	C	Buffalo	Montreal Jr. Canadiens	19.7
1969	Rejean Houle	LW	Montreal	Montreal Jr. Canadiens	19.8
1968	Michel Plasse	G	Montreal	Drummondville Rangers	20.0
1967	Rick Pagnutti	D	Los Angeles	Garson Native Sons	20.6
1966	Barry Gibbs	D	Boston	Estevan Bruins	17.7
1965	Andre Veilleux	RW	NY Rangers	Montreal Ranger Jr. B	17.5
1964	Claude Gauthier	RW	Detroit	Comite des jeunes (Rosemont)	16.9
1963	Garry Monahan	LW	Montreal	St. Michael's Juveniles	16.7

Ontario Hockey League Draft Selections by Club

Total	Club	'17	'16	'15	'14	'13	'12	'11	'10	'09	'08	'07	'06	'05	'04	'03	'02	'01	'00	'99	'98	'97	'96	'95	'94	'93	'92	'91	'90	'89	'88	'87	'69 to '86
38	Barrie	–	–	4	3	–	1	2	2	2	2	–	1	–	–	1	1	1	3	6	3	4	2	–	–	–	–	–	–	–	–	–	–
39	Erie	1	3	3	1	1	2	–	2	3	1	5	–	2	2	–	2	2	3	2	1	3	–	–	–	–	–	–	–	–	–	–	–
79	Flint/Plymouth	1	2	–	5	1	3	4	3	2	2	3	2	3	3	3	3	3	6	2	2	4	3	6	2	7	2	2	–	–	–	–	–
94	Guelph	4	2	–	1	5	4	2	–	5	3	1	1	2	2	1	2	4	1	3	5	1	6	5	7	2	2	–	–	4	–	2	17
79	Hamilton/Belleville	4	1	–	1	2	4	1	1	1	3	4	2	2	–	–	2	3	1	5	2	5	–	3	3	–	4	1	2	4	–	2	9
113	Kingston	3	1	1	3	2	–	–	2	2	2	–	4	2	–	1	1	2	–	4	1	4	4	3	2	5	3	2	2	–	1	1	55
157	Kitchener	–	3	–	2	2	3	3	1	1	2	4	–	4	2	1	4	1	1	–	5	3	2	4	2	4	1	3	5	7	1	2	84
176	London	4	7	2	2	6	6	2	2	3	1	3	1	3	6	4	2	2	1	4	8	1	4	1	1	4	3	1	3	3	6	2	78
39	Mississauga/St. Mike's	2	5	–	–	1	1	3	3	4	4	–	–	–	4	5	1	5	1	–	–	–	–	–	–	–	–	–	–	–	–	–	–
30	Niagara/Mississauga	2	1	2	4	1	1	3	3	–	1	3	1	1	3	2	–	–	2	–	–	–	–	–	–	–	–	–	–	–	–	–	–
43	North Bay/Brampton	–	3	1	2	1	1	–	2	2	3	–	4	4	2	4	3	3	6	2	–	–	–	–	–	–	–	–	–	–	–	–	–
172	Oshawa	2	1	3	2	2	2	5	2	3	2	2	2	–	3	3	3	1	2	3	4	3	1	10	1	4	4	4	2	4	2	3	87
152	Ottawa	2	2	2	2	1	1	2	4	1	2	1	1	2	3	2	–	3	2	6	2	5	2	1	1	4	6	5	5	–	1	2	79
57	Owen Sound	6	1	2	1	3	5	3	4	3	1	1	2	2	1	1	1	–	1	–	1	2	3	2	3	4	2	1	1	–	–	–	–
181	Peterborough	2	2	2	2	–	2	3	2	2	2	1	1	2	5	5	1	2	1	4	1	5	4	5	2	4	4	3	4	2	2	5	99
87	Saginaw/N. Bay Cents	1	3	1	1	3	3	4	1	3	3	–	2	3	1	2	2	3	2	2	2	1	1	2	7	2	5	2	4	1	3	3	63
48	Sarnia	3	3	2	2	–	2	1	1	–	4	1	1	3	–	5	2	1	3	1	3	2	7	1	–	–	–	–	–	–	–	–	–
136	Sault Ste. Marie	3	3	4	4	3	3	4	2	1	2	3	–	1	3	1	2	1	1	1	4	1	4	3	4	3	7	2	1	3	2	1	59
122	Sudbury	–	2	2	–	2	–	3	1	2	2	1	2	4	–	1	1	2	–	5	5	3	1	2	2	10	2	8	2	1	–	1	52
105	Windsor	2	3	–	3	1	4	1	4	5	4	2	2	3	2	2	2	2	2	2	1	5	1	4	3	–	3	–	1	2	5	–	34

Clubs no longer operating

Total	Club	'17	'16	'15	'14	'13	'12	'11	'10	'09	'08	'07	'06	'05	'04	'03	'02	'01	'00	'99	'98	'97	'96	'95	'94	'93	'92	'91	'90	'89	'88	'87	'69 to '86
27	Brantford	–	–	–	–	–	–	–	–	–	–	–	–	–	–	–	–	–	–	–	–	–	–	–	–	–	–	–	–	–	–	–	27
37	Cornwall	–	–	–	–	–	–	–	–	–	–	–	–	–	–	–	–	–	–	–	–	–	–	–	–	–	5	3	3	2	3	3	18
62	Hamilton	–	–	–	–	–	–	–	–	–	–	–	–	–	–	–	–	–	–	–	–	–	–	–	–	–	–	2	–	–	4	4	52
20	Montreal	–	–	–	–	–	–	–	–	–	–	–	–	–	–	–	–	–	–	–	–	–	–	–	–	–	–	–	–	–	–	–	20
5	Newmarket	–	–	–	–	–	–	–	–	–	–	–	–	–	–	–	–	–	–	–	–	–	–	–	2	3	–	–	–	–	–	–	–
72	Niagara Falls	–	–	–	–	–	–	–	–	–	–	–	–	–	–	–	–	–	–	–	–	–	6	2	3	4	4	4	4	4	–	–	41
52	St. Catharines	–	–	–	–	–	–	–	–	–	–	–	–	–	–	–	–	–	–	–	–	–	–	–	–	–	–	–	–	–	–	–	52
97	Toronto	–	–	–	–	–	–	–	–	–	–	–	–	–	–	–	–	–	–	–	–	–	–	–	–	–	–	–	–	2	2	1	92

Quebec Major Junior Hockey League Draft Selections by Club

Total	Club	'17	'16	'15	'14	'13	'12	'11	'10	'09	'08	'07	'06	'05	'04	'03	'02	'01	'00	'99	'98	'97	'96	'95	'94	'93	'92	'91	'90	'89	'88	'87	'69 to '86
13	Acadie-Bathurst	1	–	1	–	–	1	–	1	–	–	–	2	–	–	3	2	–	–	2	–	–	–	–	–	–	–	–	–	–	–	–	–
31	Baie-Comeau	2	–	1	1	4	1	1	–	1	2	1	3	–	3	2	1	3	2	–	3	–	–	–	–	–	–	–	–	–	–	–	–
14	Blainville-Boisbriand[1]	–	–	1	1	2	1	1	1	1	2	4	–	–	–	–	–	–	–	–	–	–	–	–	–	–	–	–	–	–	–	–	–
26	Cape Breton	2	1	1	3	1	1	1	1	1	1	–	1	–	3	2	2	1	1	–	3	–	–	–	–	–	–	–	–	–	–	–	–
31	Charlottetown[2]	1	–	2	1	3	–	–	1	1	2	2	–	2	8	1	3	1	1	2	–	–	–	–	–	–	–	–	–	–	–	–	–
59	Chicoutimi	–	1	1	–	1	1	1	–	–	3	–	–	4	–	1	3	1	1	–	1	2	–	2	3	1	1	–	1	1	2	2	15
61	Drummondville	1	–	1	–	–	–	2	–	3	–	–	2	2	1	1	–	1	1	–	2	2	3	4	1	2	2	4	–	1	4	2	19
87	Gatineau/Hull	–	2	2	2	2	1	1	3	–	1	1	2	–	4	4	5	2	–	4	3	–	3	3	1	3	3	3	3	2	2	3	22
46	Halifax	3	1	1	1	4	1	2	3	–	–	2	3	1	3	6	–	3	2	–	3	3	1	3	–	–	–	–	–	–	–	–	–
27	Moncton	–	1	1	1	–	1	–	2	2	1	1	3	1	2	3	2	–	–	2	2	1	1	–	–	–	–	–	–	–	–	–	–
34	Quebec	–	–	2	–	3	3	–	1	1	3	2	2	2	1	3	1	3	–	3	4	–	–	–	–	–	–	–	–	–	–	–	–
39	Rimouski	–	–	1	–	4	2	–	2	2	2	4	–	2	3	4	–	4	2	2	5	–	–	–	–	–	–	–	–	–	–	–	–
28	Rouyn-Noranda	1	1	2	2	2	1	–	1	1	2	1	3	1	–	2	–	–	4	1	3	–	–	–	–	–	–	–	–	–	–	–	–
24	Saint John	1	2	7	1	–	–	5	2	2	1	2	1	–	–	–	–	–	–	–	–	–	–	–	–	–	–	–	–	–	–	–	–
92	Shawinigan	–	2	2	–	1	2	3	1	6	–	1	1	1	3	2	2	1	1	1	3	1	4	2	1	1	3	2	–	2	–	1	42
84	Sherbrooke[3]	–	1	2	1	–	–	–	2	1	2	3	2	5	2	1	–	3	–	–	5	1	–	4	2	3	–	–	–	–	–	–	44
35	Val-d'Or	1	1	1	2	2	1	3	1	–	2	–	–	2	1	1	1	2	2	3	–	2	4	2	1	–	–	–	–	–	–	–	–
45	Victoriaville	1	1	1	1	2	1	3	–	1	3	1	–	–	–	–	3	1	3	2	1	2	3	1	1	6	2	–	1	–	4	–	–

Former club names: [1]–Montreal / St. John's, [2]–PEI / Montreal Rocket, [3]–Lewiston / Sherbrooke Castors/Beavers.

Clubs no longer operating

Total	Club	'17	'16	'15	'14	'13	'12	'11	'10	'09	'08	'07	'06	'05	'04	'03	'02	'01	'00	'99	'98	'97	'96	'95	'94	'93	'92	'91	'90	'89	'88	'87	'69 to '86
21	Beauport	–	–	–	–	–	–	–	–	–	–	–	–	–	–	–	–	–	–	–	–	3	3	7	3	1	3	1	–	–	–	–	–
45	Cornwall	–	–	–	–	–	–	–	–	–	–	–	–	–	–	–	–	–	–	–	–	–	–	–	–	–	–	–	–	–	–	–	45
30	Granby	–	–	–	–	–	–	–	–	–	–	–	–	–	–	–	–	–	–	–	–	1	3	2	5	1	–	2	–	2	–	4	7
54	Laval	–	–	–	–	–	–	–	–	–	–	–	–	–	–	–	–	–	–	–	3	1	2	4	5	2	1	4	3	3	1	3	22
12	Longueuil	–	–	–	–	–	–	–	–	–	–	–	–	–	–	–	–	–	–	–	–	–	–	–	–	–	–	3	2	–	–	1	5
32	Montreal Jrs.	–	–	–	–	–	–	–	–	–	–	–	–	–	–	–	–	–	–	–	–	–	–	–	–	–	–	–	–	–	–	–	32
47	Quebec *pre '85*	–	–	–	–	–	–	–	–	–	–	–	–	–	–	–	–	–	–	–	–	–	–	–	–	–	–	–	–	–	–	–	47
15	St. Hyacinthe	–	–	–	–	–	–	–	–	–	–	–	–	–	–	–	–	–	–	–	–	–	4	–	4	1	2	1	3	–	–	–	–
16	St. Jean	–	–	–	–	–	–	–	–	–	–	–	–	–	–	–	–	–	–	–	–	–	–	1	1	2	1	3	–	1	3	–	4
2	St. Jerome	–	–	–	–	–	–	–	–	–	–	–	–	–	–	–	–	–	–	–	–	–	–	–	–	–	–	–	–	–	–	–	2
28	Sorel	–	–	–	–	–	–	–	–	–	–	–	–	–	–	–	–	–	–	–	–	–	–	–	–	–	–	–	–	–	–	–	28
47	Trois Rivieres	–	–	–	–	–	–	–	–	–	–	–	–	–	–	–	–	–	–	–	–	–	–	–	–	–	1	2	1	3	3	1	36
27	Verdun	–	–	–	–	–	–	–	–	–	–	–	–	–	–	–	–	–	–	–	–	–	–	–	–	–	3	–	–	1	3	–	20

United States Hockey League by Club *plus* USA U-18 Team

Total	Club	'17	'16	'15	'14	'13	'12	'11	'10	'09	'08	'07	'06	'05	'04	'03	'02	'01	'00	'99	'98	'97	'96	'95	'94	'93	'92	'91	'90	'89	'88	'87	'69 to '86
3	Bloomington	1	2	–	–	–	–	–	–	–	–	–	–	–	–	–	–	–	–	–	–	–	–	–	–	–	–	–	–	–	–	–	–
18	Cedar Rapids	–	2	2	–	–	–	1	2	2	1	1	–	2	2	–	2	1	–	–	–	–	–	–	–	–	–	–	–	–	–	–	–
16	Chicago	3	1	1	1	–	1	–	1	2	1	–	–	1	1	2	1	–	–	–	–	–	–	–	–	–	–	–	–	–	–	–	–
31	Des Moines	1	–	1	–	1	–	–	2	1	–	3	4	1	–	3	3	2	1	3	1	2	–	1	–	–	–	–	–	–	–	–	1
16	Dubuque	1	–	–	1	2	2	1	–	–	–	–	–	–	–	–	–	–	1	–	–	–	–	–	1	1	1	1	–	–	–	1	3
8	Fargo	2	1	–	–	–	2	1	–	2	–	–	–	–	–	–	–	–	–	–	–	–	–	–	–	–	–	–	–	–	–	–	–
29	Green Bay	2	1	2	1	1	1	4	1	1	–		1	–	3	–	5	–	2	2	–	2	–	–	–	–	–	–	–	–	–	–	–
26	Lincoln	1	2	–	–	1	3	1	–	1	2	3	–	2	–	4	–	2	1	–	1	2	–	–	–	–	–	–	–	–	–	–	–
6	Madison	1	–	1	–	–	–	–	–	–	–	–	–	–	–	–	–	–	–	–	–	–	–	–	1	–	–	–	–	1	1	1	–
9	Muskegon	1	2	2	1	2	1	–	–	–	–	–	–	–	–	–	–	–	–	–	–	–	–	–	–	–	–	–	–	–	–	–	–
33	Omaha	–	–	2	5	1	–	1	–	1	1	4	1	1	–	–	1	1	4	1	–	–	1	1	2	2	1	2	–	–	–	–	–
26	Sioux City	2	–	1	–	2	1	1	1	1	1	2	–	4	2	–	1	2	1	–	–	–	–	–	2	–	–	–	–	–	–	–	2
21	Sioux Falls	2	–	1	2	–	–	1	–	–	–	3	3	2	3	3	–	1	–	–	–	–	–	–	–	–	–	–	–	–	–	–	–
12	Tri-City	2	2	2	1	–	–	–	1	1	–	1	–	–	1	–	–	1	–	–	–	–	–	–	–	–	–	–	–	–	–	–	–
90	USA U-18	10	12	11	12	12	10	11	10	–	–	–	–	–	–	–	–	–	2	–	–	–	–	–	–	–	–	–	–	–	–	–	–
32	Waterloo	3	2	2	2	4	1	–		3	1	3	–	1	–	1	–	1	–	–	–	1	–	–	1	1	2	1	1	–	–	–	1
7	Youngstown	1	1	2	2	–	–	1	–	–	–	–	–	–	–	–	–	–	–	–	–	–	–	–	–	–	–	–	–	–	–	–	–

Clubs no longer operating

Total	Club	'17	'16	'15	'14	'13	'12	'11	'10	'09	'08	'07	'06	'05	'04	'03	'02	'01	'00	'99	'98	'97	'96	'95	'94	'93	'92	'91	'90	'89	'88	'87	'69 to '86
2	Austin	–	–	–	–	–	–	–	–	–	–	–	–	–	–	–	–	–	–	–	–	–	–	–	–	–	–	–	–	–	–	–	2
1	Fargo-Moorhead	–	–	–	–	–	–	–	–	–	–	–	–	–	–	–	–	–	–	–	1	–	–	–	–	–	–	–	–	–	–	–	–
12	Indiana	–	–	–	3	–	2	3	2	1	1	–	–	–	–	–	–	–	–	–	–	–	–	–	–	–	–	–	–	–	–	–	–
4	North Iowa	–	–	–	–	–	–	–	–	–	–	–	–	–	–	–	–	–	–	–	1	3	–	–	–	–	–	–	–	–	–	–	–
3	Ohio	–	–	–	–	–	–	–	–	–	2	1	–	–	–	–	–	–	–	–	–	–	–	–	–	–	–	–	–	–	–	–	–
3	River City	–	–	–	–	–	–	–	–	–	–	–	–	–	–	3	–	–	–	–	–	–	–	–	–	–	–	–	–	–	–	–	–
6	Rochester	–	–	–	–	–	–	–	–	–	–	–	–	–	–	–	–	–	–	–	–	–	–	–	–	–	–	1	3	–	2	–	–
8	Thunder Bay	–	–	–	–	–	–	–	–	–	–	–	–	–	–	–	–	–	1	–	–	–	–	–	2	–	2	1	–	2	–	–	–
2	Topeka	–	–	–	–	–	–	–	–	–	–	–	–	–	–	–	2	–	–	–	–	–	–	–	–	–	–	–	–	–	–	–	–
9	Twin City	–	–	–	–	–	–	–	–	–	–	–	–	–	–	–	–	–	–	–	–	1	1	–	–	2	–	2	–	–	2	–	1

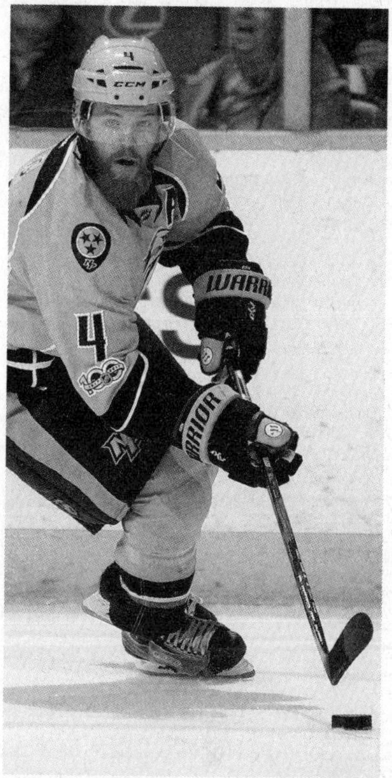

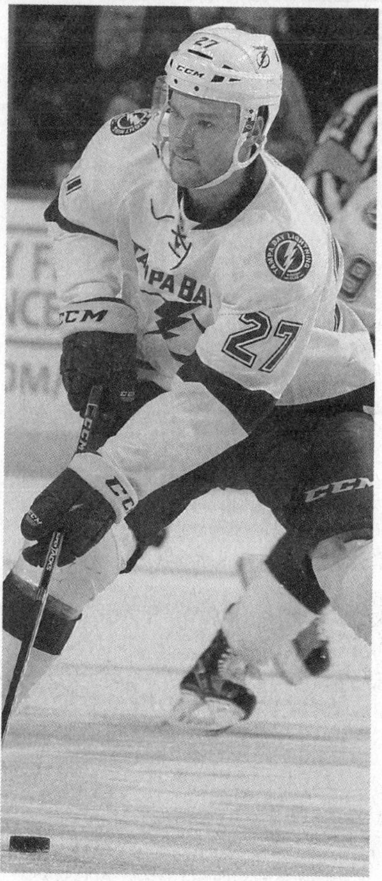

Nashville selected Ryan Ellis (top) from the Windsor Spitfires of the OHL with the 11th pick overall in 2009. Jonathan Drouin, who is now a member of the Montreal Canadiens, was picked third overall by Tampa Bay from Halifax of the QMJHL in 2013.

Western Hockey League Draft Selections by Club

Total	Club	'17	'16	'15	'14	'13	'12	'11	'10	'09	'08	'07	'06	'05	'04	'03	'02	'01	'00	'99	'98	'97	'96	'95	'94	'93	'92	'91	'90	'89	'88	'87	'69 to '86
118	Brandon	3	2	2	3	2	1	1	2	2	2	1	1	2	–	3	4	2	–	–	4	5	2	6	5	2	1	1	1	–	3	3	52
55	Calgary	–	5	1	5	1	3	–	2	2	2	4	1	2	5	3	2	1	4	6	3	–	3	–	–	–	–	–	–	–	–	–	–
16	Edmonton	–	–	–	5	2	3	4	1	1	–	–	–	–	–	–	–	–	–	–	–	–	–	–	–	–	–	–	–	–	–	–	–
19	Everett	–	1	1	–	2	2	–	3	2	1	3	4	–	–	–	–	–	–	–	–	–	–	–	–	–	–	–	–	–	–	–	–
119	Kamloops	1	2	1	1	2	2	–	2	2	–	1	1	2	5	2	5	2	4	4	1	3	4	5	9	2	3	6	4	5	1	3	34
55	Kelowna	2	4	2	2	4	2	1	1	3	4	2	–	2	4	4	1	1	1	2	2	7	4	–	–	–	–	–	–	–	–	–	–
32	Kootenay[1]	2	–	–	4	1	–	1	3	1	–	1	1	3	2	1	3	2	1	2	–	4	–	–	–	–	–	–	–	–	–	–	–
96	Lethbridge	1	–	2	1	–	–	1	–	1	2	2	1	–	2	2	2	1	3	–	1	5	1	3	3	4	3	7	4	3	3	–	38
117	Medicine Hat	2	1	1	–	2	–	1	2	1	2	–	2	4	2	3	3	2	–	1	4	2	7	2	6	1	3	3	1	4	1	5	49
72	Moose Jaw	1	2	–	1	–	2	1	3	–	3	1	1	3	3	3	3	3	5	1	2	4	4	4	3	2	3	2	1	3	–	3	5
137	Portland	4	1	2	4	4	3	4	8	1	–	2	1	3	2	1	2	–	6	1	3	3	1	2	3	4	4	1	1	4	1	3	58
91	Prince Albert	1	1	2	2	1	1	2	–	1	–	–	–	2	4	2	1	4	2	3	3	5	3	4	3	5	2	6	4	3	3	1	20
37	Prince George	1	1	4	–	2	1	–	1	1	–	1	4	1	2	2	–	4	–	2	4	2	2	2	–	–	–	–	–	–	–	–	–
60	Red Deer	1	3	1	3	1	1	2	1	4	1	1	1	1	1	4	4	6	1	1	5	3	4	2	5	3	–	–	–	–	–	–	–
127	Regina	3	2	5	–	2	1	–	2	1	3	3	1	1	–	2	1	2	2	4	2	3	4	2	3	–	4	–	1	5	–	2	66
125	Saskatoon	–	1	–	2	–	3	4	4	3	3	3	–	4	1	–	–	4	1	4	2	2	2	2	4	2	3	2	2	3	4	4	56
104	Seattle	1	–	4	–	1	1	2	1	–	2	1	1	3	2	5	1	5	4	6	2	8	1	5	5	4	2	3	6	2	4	2	20
74	Spokane	3	1	1	–	1	–	3	–	2	3	3	1	4	1	–	3	3	2	1	1	4	5	4	4	4	7	5	1	2	3	1	1
73	Swift Current	2	1	2	3	1	2	3	–	1	4	2	2	1	2	2	4	1	3	1	2	2	1	4	4	5	1	1	2	2	2	5	11
63	Tri-City	4	–	2	–	1	–	1	2	–	2	–	–	2	4	1	3	2	2	1	4	1	6	6	2	2	5	3	3	4	–	–	–
26	Vancouver	–	2	–	–	2	2	2	2	1	3	4	1	3	2	1	1	–	–	–	–	–	–	–	–	–	–	–	–	–	–	–	–
16	Victoria[2]	1	4	1	1	1	2	–	3	1	–	2	–	–	–	–	–	–	–	–	–	–	–	–	–	–	–	–	–	–	–	–	–
	Clubs no longer operating																																
13	Billings	–	–	–	–	–	–	–	–	–	–	–	–	–	–	–	–	–	–	–	–	–	–	–	–	–	–	–	–	–	–	–	13
66	Calgary[3]	–	–	–	–	–	–	–	–	–	–	–	–	–	–	–	–	–	–	–	–	–	–	–	–	–	–	–	–	–	–	2	70
34	Edmonton *pre '78*	–	–	–	–	–	–	–	–	–	–	–	–	–	–	–	–	–	–	–	–	–	–	–	–	–	–	–	–	–	–	–	34
12	Estevan	–	–	–	–	–	–	–	–	–	–	–	–	–	–	–	–	–	–	–	–	–	–	–	–	–	–	–	–	–	–	–	12
39	Flin Flon	–	–	–	–	–	–	–	–	–	–	–	–	–	–	–	–	–	–	–	–	–	–	–	–	–	–	–	–	–	–	–	39
11	Kelowna Wings	–	–	–	–	–	–	–	–	–	–	–	–	–	–	–	–	–	–	–	–	–	–	–	–	–	–	–	–	–	–	–	11
6	Nanaimo	–	–	–	–	–	–	–	–	–	–	–	–	–	–	–	–	–	–	–	–	–	–	–	–	–	–	–	–	–	–	–	6
62	New Westm'r	–	–	–	–	–	–	–	–	–	–	–	–	–	–	–	–	–	–	–	–	–	–	–	–	–	–	–	–	–	1	2	59
12	Tacoma	–	–	–	–	–	–	–	–	–	–	–	–	–	–	–	–	–	–	–	–	–	–	2	5	2	3	–	–	–	–	–	–
2	Vancouver Nats	–	–	–	–	–	–	–	–	–	–	–	–	–	–	–	–	–	–	–	–	–	–	–	–	–	–	–	–	–	–	–	2
79	Victoria	–	–	–	–	–	–	–	–	–	–	–	–	–	–	–	–	–	–	–	–	–	–	–	2	2	1	–	2	4	4	2	62
34	Winnipeg	–	–	–	–	–	–	–	–	–	–	–	–	–	–	–	–	–	–	–	–	–	–	–	–	–	–	–	–	–	–	–	34

Former club names: [1]–Edmonton Ice, [2]–Chilliwack; [3]–Centennials '69-'73, Wranglers '77-'87.

U.S. College Hockey Draft Selections by School

Total	Club	'17	'16	'15	'14	'13	'12	'11	'10	'09	'08	'07	'06	'05	'04	'03	'02	'01	'00	'99	'98	'97	'96	'95	'94	'93	'92	'91	'90	'89	'88	'87	'69 to '86
41	Boston College	–	2	1	1	–	–	–	–	–	1	–	1	1	1	1	3	2	3	–	3	3	2	–	–	–	–	–	–	2	–	2	13
57	Boston U.	1	–	1	–	–	–	3	–	1	1	–	1	–	1	–	3	2	1	3	2	1	1	1	–	1	1	2	2	1	3	2	23
29	Bowling Green	–	1	–	–	–	–	–	–	–	–	–	1	1	–	–	1	1	–	1	1	1	–	–	–	–	1	3	1	2	3	–	11
34	Clarkson	–	–	–	–	–	–	–	1	–	–	–	1	–	–	–	–	–	1	1	3	–	–	–	–	1	1	2	3	1	1	1	17
33	Colorado	–	–	–	–	–	–	–	–	–	–	1	–	1	–	2	1	1	2	1	3	–	–	1	–	–	–	–	2	–	1	–	17
36	Cornell	–	–	–	–	–	2	–	–	–	–	–	–	1	2	2	1	–	2	2	–	1	–	–	–	–	–	–	2	5	2	1	13
48	Denver	–	2	–	–	1	1	1	–	–	–	–	–	2	1	–	1	–	–	1	–	3	–	–	–	–	–	–	–	1	1	4	29
35	Harvard	–	–	1	–	–	–	–	1	–	–	–	–	1	–	–	3	2	2	1	2	1	3	–	1	2	–	–	–	2	1	1	12
25	Lake Superior	–	–	–	–	–	–	–	1	–	–	–	–	–	–	–	1	–	–	1	–	1	1	–	–	1	–	1	3	2	3	–	10
22	Maine	–	–	–	–	–	–	–	–	–	–	–	1	–	1	2	–	–	1	4	1	1	1	–	–	1	–	–	1	2	3	–	3
24	Miami U.	–	–	–	–	–	–	–	–	2	1	1	1	1	2	–	1	1	–	–	1	–	–	–	–	1	1	2	–	2	4	2	1
72	Michigan	1	–	1	1	1	1	–	1	–	–	1	2	1	3	2	3	2	1	2	3	1	3	–	1	1	2	4	5	3	2	1	24
49	Michigan State	–	–	–	–	–	–	–	1	–	–	–	1	–	2	1	4	–	2	2	1	1	1	–	1	1	1	4	5	4	4	1	12
46	Michigan Tech	–	–	1	–	–	–	–	–	–	–	–	–	–	–	–	–	1	–	–	–	–	1	–	2	1	–	2	1	2	1	1	34
69	Minnesota	–	–	–	–	–	–	–	–	1	–	1	1	1	–	2	3	–	3	3	1	2	3	2	–	–	–	–	–	1	1	1	43
32	New Hampshire	–	–	–	–	1	–	–	–	–	–	–	–	–	1	–	1	–	2	1	–	1	–	–	–	–	–	–	–	–	1	–	24
41	North Dakota	–	1	–	–	–	–	1	–	–	–	–	1	–	1	1	1	–	1	1	–	2	–	–	–	–	–	1	1	2	–	–	27
31	Northeastern	–	1	–	–	–	–	1	–	–	–	–	–	–	–	–	–	–	–	1	1	–	–	–	–	–	–	–	1	1	–	–	24
24	Northern Mich.	–	–	–	–	–	–	–	1	–	1	–	–	–	2	2	–	–	1	–	–	–	1	–	–	–	–	1	–	2	1	4	8
35	Notre Dame	–	–	–	–	–	1	1	1	–	–	1	1	–	2	–	2	1	1	2	–	2	1	–	–	–	–	–	–	–	–	–	19
21	Ohio State	–	–	–	–	–	–	–	–	–	–	–	–	1	–	1	2	2	–	1	–	1	1	–	–	1	1	1	1	–	2	2	4
39	Providence	1	1	–	–	1	–	–	–	–	–	–	2	–	–	1	1	–	2	–	2	1	–	–	–	–	–	–	1	–	–	–	26
28	RPI	1	–	–	–	–	–	1	–	–	1	–	–	–	–	–	–	1	2	2	–	1	–	–	–	–	1	3	–	–	2	2	11
23	St. Lawrence	–	–	–	–	–	–	–	–	–	–	–	–	–	–	–	1	–	–	1	–	1	1	–	–	1	–	2	1	1	1	1	12
20	Vermont	–	–	–	–	–	–	–	–	–	–	–	–	1	–	–	–	2	–	–	–	–	1	–	1	–	–	1	–	–	1	–	13
26	W. Michigan	–	–	1	–	–	–	1	–	1	–	–	1	–	–	–	1	–	–	–	1	1	–	–	–	2	–	4	1	1	1	1	10
50	Wisconsin	–	1	–	–	–	2	1	1	–	2	–	–	–	2	–	–	–	3	2	–	–	–	–	–	–	–	1	–	1	–	1	33
16	Yale	–	–	–	–	–	–	–	–	–	–	–	1	–	2	–	3	–	–	–	–	–	–	–	–	1	–	–	–	1	–	2	6

Colleges with fewer than 15 players selected: 14 - Brown; 13 - Colgate, Minn.-Duluth; 12 - St.Cloud State; 11 - Merrimack; 10 - Dartmouth, Ferris State, Princeton; 7 - Mass.-Lowell, Union College; 6 - Illinois-Chicago, St. Louis; 5 - Nebraska-Omaha, Pennsylvania, Mass.-Amherst, Minnesota State (Mankato); 4 - Alaska-Anchorage; 3 - Babson College, Alaska (Fairbanks); 2 - Connecticut, Quinnipiac; 1 - Air Force, American International College, Army, Bemidji State, Greenway, Hamilton, Miami, Penn State, St. Anselm College, St. Thomas, Salem State, San Diego U., Wisconsin-River Falls.

U.S. High and Prep Schools Draft Selections by School (More than 10 players drafted)

Total	School (State)	'17	'16	'15	'14	'13	'12	'11	'10	'09	'08	'07	'06	'05	'04	'03	'02	'01	'00	'99	'98	'97	'96	'95	'94	'93	'92	'91	'90	'89	'88	'80 to '87
16	Avon Old Farms (CT)	–	1	–	–	–	–	1	–	1	1	1	–	–	–	–	–	–	–	–	1	1	–	–	–	–	–	–	3	3	–	3
16	Belmont Hill (MA)	–	–	–	–	–	–	–	–	–	–	–	1	–	–	–	–	–	–	–	–	–	–	–	1	–	2	1	2	3	1	5
11	Canterbury (CT)	–	–	–	–	–	–	–	–	–	–	–	–	–	–	1	–	–	–	–	–	–	–	–	–	1	2	–	2	–	3	2
16	Catholic Memorial (MA)	–	–	–	–	–	–	–	–	–	–	–	–	–	2	–	–	–	–	–	1	–	–	–	2	1	2	–	–	3	1	4
12	Choate-Rosemary (CT)	–	–	–	–	–	–	1	–	–	1	–	–	–	–	–	–	–	1	–	–	–	–	–	–	–	1	1	1	–	3	3
14	Culver Mil. Acad. (IN)	–	1	1	–	–	–	–	–	–	–	–	–	–	–	–	–	–	–	–	–	–	–	–	–	2	2	1	2	2	1	3
24	Cushing Acad. (MA)	–	–	2	–	–	–	–	1	–	–	–	1	1	2	–	–	1	–	–	–	1	1	–	2	2	–	1	3	2	3	1
15	Deerfield (IL)	–	–	–	1	–	–	–	–	–	–	1	–	–	1	1	1	–	2	1	–	–	–	–	–	–	–	1	–	2	1	3
25	Edina (MN)	1	–	–	2	1	1	2	–	2	1	–	–	–	–	–	–	–	–	–	–	–	–	–	–	–	1	–	1	2	2	9
13	Grand Rapids (MN)	–	1	–	–	1	1	–	–	–	–	1	–	–	–	–	–	–	–	1	–	–	–	–	–	–	–	1	2	2	1	2
16	Hill-Murray (MN)	–	1	–	–	–	–	–	–	–	–	–	–	–	–	–	–	–	–	–	–	–	–	–	1	–	–	–	3	2	–	9
15	Hotchkiss (CT)	–	–	–	–	1	–	1	–	1	–	–	–	–	1	–	–	1	–	–	–	–	2	1	3	–	–	–	1	–	1	2
11	Kent School (CT)	–	–	–	–	–	1	–	–	–	2	–	–	–	–	–	–	–	–	–	–	–	–	–	2	–	–	–	–	–	–	6
11	Lawrence Academy (MA)	–	–	1	–	–	–	–	–	–	–	–	–	–	–	–	–	–	–	–	–	–	1	–	1	1	–	1	1	–	2	3
14	Minnetonka (MN)	–	–	–	–	–	–	–	2	1	1	–	–	–	–	–	–	–	–	–	–	–	–	–	–	–	–	1	–	2	–	7
13	Mount St. Charles (RI)	–	–	–	–	–	–	–	–	–	–	–	–	–	–	–	–	–	–	–	–	–	–	–	–	–	–	–	1	1	3	8
11	Nobles (MA)	–	–	1	–	1	3	–	1	1	–	2	–	1	–	–	–	–	–	1	–	–	–	–	–	–	–	–	–	–	–	1
20	Northwood (NY)	1	–	–	–	–	–	–	–	–	1	–	–	–	1	–	–	–	1	–	–	–	–	–	1	1	–	–	3	1	1	7
12	Roseau (MN)	–	–	–	–	–	–	–	–	2	–	–	–	–	–	–	–	–	–	–	–	–	–	–	–	–	–	1	3	1	–	5
11	St. John's Prep (MA)	–	–	–	–	1	1	1	–	–	–	–	–	–	–	–	–	–	–	–	–	–	–	–	1	–	–	–	–	–	2	5
14	St. Sebastian's (MA)	–	–	–	–	–	1	–	–	–	–	–	1	–	–	4	1	1	–	–	1	–	–	–	1	2	2	–	–	–	–	–
21	Shattuck-St. Mary's (MN)	–	–	–	–	1	4	1	3	3	3	1	1	2	–	1	–	–	–	–	–	–	1	–	–	–	–	–	–	–	–	–

Schools with 10 players selected: Burnsville (MN), Duluth East (MN), Hibbing (MN), Matignon (MA), Thayer Academy (MA).

U.S. College and High School Firsts

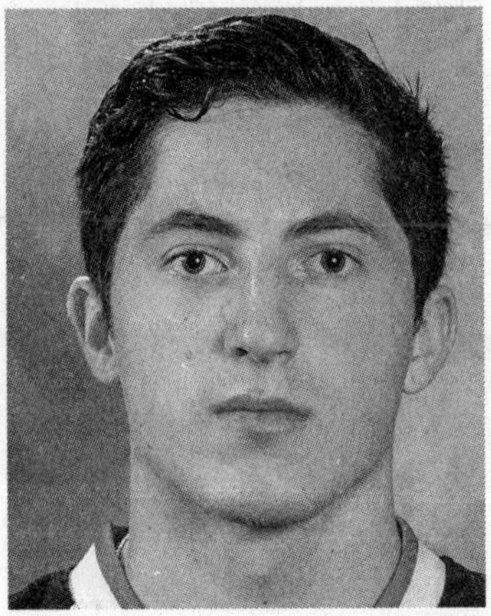

A former member of the USA Hockey National Team Development Program, Columbus chose Zach Werenski from the University of Michigan eighth overall in 2015.

1967 – First U.S. College Player Drafted • Michigan Tech center Al Karlander was selected 17th overall by the Detroit Red Wings.

1979 – First U.S. College First-Round Selection • Minnesota-born defenseman Mike Ramsey was selected 11th overall by the Buffalo Sabres. He was inducted into the U.S. Hockey Hall of Fame in 2001.

1980 – First U.S. High School Player Drafted • Center Jay North of Jefferson H.S. in Bloomington, Minnesota was taken 62nd overall by the Buffalo Sabres in 1980.

1981 – First U.S. High School First-Round Selection • Center Bob Carpenter of St. John's prep school was selected third overall by Washington in 1981.

1983 – First U.S. High School Player Drafted First Overall • Minnesota North Stars selected left winger Brian Lawton from Mount St. Charles H.S. first overall in 1983.

1986 – First U.S. College Player Drafted First Overall • Detroit selected right winger Joe Murphy from Michigan State first overall in 1986.

2003 – Most U.S. College Players Selected in the First Round • The 2003 draft saw seven U.S. college players selected in the first round, the most in Draft history. Six were selected in the first round in 2000 and four in 2001 and 2002. In addition, many players drafted in the first round from the USA U-18 and U-17 teams, high school and prep school programs, U.S. junior and Tier-2 Canadian junior go on to play college hockey.

2013 – Players Born in 22 States Selected • Minnesota, Massachusetts, Michigan and New York led the way, but players born from Alaska to Florida were selected in in 2013.

2014 – 30 USHL Players Selected • 12 of these players were part of the U.S. National Team Development Program's Under-18 squad.

2015 – 31 USHL Players Selected

2015 – Three U.S. College Players selected in top eight of the Draft • Jack Eichel was selected 2nd by Buffalo, Noah Hanifin, 5th by Carolina and Zach Werenski, 8th by Columbus.

European Leagues
Ranked by total number of players drafted

Total	Country	'17	'16	'15	'14	'13	'12	'11	'10	'09	'08	'07	'06	'05	'04	'03	'02	'01	'00	'99	'98	'97	'96	'95	'94	'93	'92	'91	'90	'89	'88	'87	'69 to '86
687	Sweden	32	26	18	30	26	23	25	21	23	19	16	18	15	18	19	24	24	24	19	14	16	8	17	18	11	11	7	9	14	15		113
592	KHL/Russia/CIS/USSR	11	12	12	7	8	7	6	4	6	9	7	16	11	24	32	33	36	44	29	22	16	17	27	35	31	45	25	14	18	11	2	5
441	CzRep/Slovakia	7	2	10	5	–	3	5	1	3	2	4	11	15	24	20	21	28	28	20	17	14	21	18	15	17	9	21	8	5	11	–	56
400	Finland	14	12	12	7	10	8	10	7	8	6	4	13	8	14	12	26	29	19	17	12	11	7	12	8	9	8	6	3	7	6		66
57	Switzerland	2	2	2	2	2	1	1	1	–	1	1	3	–	4	5	4	5	7	3	2	3	1	–	1	2	–	1	–	–	–		1
49	Germany	–	–	–	–	–	–	3	1	1	4	2	1	4	1	7	1	–	–	1	3	1	1	3	2	1	–	2	1				8
10	Norway		–	–	1	–	–	1	–	1	–	–	1	–	–	–	–	1	–	–	–	1	–	1	2	–		2					–
7	Denmark		–	1	–	–	1	–	1			–			2																		1 1
2	Japan		–																														
2	Poland																1																
1	Belarus		–			1																											
1	France	1																															
1	Hungary																	1															
1	Latvia																	1															
1	Scotland			1																													1
1	Austria		1																														

Czech Republic and Slovakia

Total	Club	'17	'16	'15	'14	'13	'12	'11	'10	'09	'08	'07	'06	'05	'04	'03	'02	'01	'00	'99	'98	'97	'96	'95	'94	'93	'92	'91	'90	'89	'88	'87	'69 to '86
10	Brno	1	–	1																1				1			1	2	–				3
35	Ceske Budejovice	2	–	–	–		1	–	1			2	1	2	–		2	3	1	1	2	1	3	2	1			2	1	–	1		4
3	Chomutov	–	1	1											1																		
3	Havirov													2	–				1														
28	Jihlava																	1				2	2	1	1	2	3	1	1	3			10
4	Karlovy Vary												1	1	1	1																	–
24	Kladno	–	1					3	1	1		1	1	2		2		2	1		2	1											5
18	Kosice	–	2						1	1				1		1	1	1	1														6
7	Liberec	1							1		1	1			2																		
35	Litvinov	–	1								3	2		1	1	2	2	2	4	2	3	1	2	2									6
6	Martin												1			1			2				1										–
7	Nitra											1			1	1			1				1										–
8	Olomouc	1																1			2	1		2									–
16	Pardubice	–												3	1			1		1	2		1										4
16	Plzen	–	1		1			1				1			2	1		1	1		1	1											
3	Presov													1			1		1														
31	Slavia Praha	–	–	1	–	1		1	1	2	2	5	3	2	5	4																	1
22	Slovan Bratis.									3	1	2	2	1	1	1		3		1													6
30	Sparta Praha	1				1			1	2	4	1	1	2	1		1	1		1			2	1	2	1							5
31	Trencin								1	1	1	4	3		2	3	2		1	2	1		1	2	2	1	1						1
12	Trinec	–	2				1	1		1	1		1	1	1																		
19	Vitkovice						1	2		2		1	1		1	1	1	3	1														2
14	Vsetin									1	1	3	2	2		1	2																
22	Zlin[1]	1						1	2			2		2		2	2	1		2		2	2										3
8	Zvolen					1						2	2		1	1		1															

Former club names: [1]—Gottwaldov. **Teams with two players selected:** Ingstav Brno, IS Banska Bystrica, Dubnica, Michalovce, Partizan Liptovsky Mikulas, VTJ Pisek, Skalica, Spisska Nova Ves, Topolcany. **Teams with one player selected:** Banik Sokolov, Havlickuv Brod, Hradec Kralove, Ostrava, KC SKP Poprad, Povazska Bystrica, HK Trnava, KHM Zvolen, Slovak U20, Slovak U18.

Finland

Total	Club	'17	'16	'15	'14	'13	'12	'11	'10	'09	'08	'07	'06	'05	'04	'03	'02	'01	'00	'99	'98	'97	'96	'95	'94	'93	'92	'91	'90	'89	'88	'87	'69 to '86
19	Assat	–	–	1	1	–	1	–	–	–	2	–	–	–	1	–	–	1	–	–	1	1	1	–	–	1	–	1	–	1			7
28	Blues Espoo	1	1	1	1	1	1	3	1	–	1	–	–	1	–	–	–	1	2	–	2	1	1	–	1								
45	HIFK Helsinki	1	1	–	1	–	1	1	–	–	4	1	2	–	5	2	2	4	2	1	–	1	–	2	–	–	1	2	–				10
16	HPK	1	1	1		–		–		1	–	–	1	1	3	1	1	1	–	–	2	–	–	1	–								
43	Ilves	1	2	1	–	1	2	1	–	3	3	–	–	2	4	3	1	2	–	2	–	–	1	1	–	1							10
49	Jokerit	2	1	–	1	1	4	3	1	–	–	2	–	1	2	6	4	3	3	1	1	1	–	1	–	3	–	2	–	1	1		4
17	JyP Jyvaskyla	1	–	3	–	–	1	–	1	–	–	–	1	–	2	1	–	3	–	1	2	–											
19	KalPa	–	–	2	2	1	1	1	1	–	–	–	2	–	2	–	1	–	–	2	1	–		1									
33	Karpat	–	2	2	1	1	1	1	1	–	–	2	3	3	3	–	1	1	–	1	1	–	1	–	1					2	5		
3	Kiekoo-67																							3									–
21	Lukko	1	–					1	1	–	1	1	1	3	1	2	–	1	–	–	1												6
10	Pelicans	–	–	1	–	1	–	1	–	1	1	–	1	–	1			–		1	2	–	–										3
7	SaiPa	–	–	1				1	1	–	1	1	–							–	1												7
3	Sport Vaasa	1																															
29	Tappara	1	2	–	1	–	–	2	2	–	1	2	2	2	1	–	2	1	1	–			1				–	1	–	1			7
43	TPS Turku	2	2	1	1	1	–	–	1	1	3	1	3	1	3	3	1	3	2	3	–				–	–	1						9

Teams with two players selected: KooKoo Kouvola, K-Vantaa, Sapko Savonlinna, Sport Vaasa, TuTo. **Teams with one player selected:** Ahmat Hyvinkaa, Hermes Kokkola, Junkkarit Kalajoki, GrIFK Kauniainen, Jokipojat, LeKi, S-Kiekko Seinajoki.

Born in Germany, Leon Draisaitl (top) was chosen third overall by Edmonton from the WHL's Prince Albert Raiders in 2014. Nashville selected Mattias Ekholm of Sweden with the 102nd pick in 2009.

Note: International draft selections played outside North America in their draft year.

European-born players drafted from the OHL, QMJHL, WHL, USHL, U.S. colleges or other North American leagues are not counted as International players.

For analysis by birthplace, see the following page.

2018 NHL Draft
June 22-23, 2018
American Airlines Center
Dallas, Texas

Kontinental Hockey League / Russia / CIS / USSR

Total	Club	'17	'16	'15	'14	'13	'12	'11	'10	'09	'08	'07	'06	'05	'04	'03	'02	'01	'00	'99	'98	'97	'96	'95	'94	'93	'92	'91	'90	'89	'88	'87	'69 to '86
11	Ak Bars Kazan[1]	1	–	1	–	–	–	–	–	–	1	–	–	–	–	2	–	2	1	1	1	–	–	–	1	–	–	–	–	–	–	–	–
18	Atlant Moscow Reg.[2]	–	–	–	1	–	1	–	–	–	–	–	–	–	–	1	1	1	1	–	3	–	–	–	1	–	2	1	3	1	–	–	1
16	Avangard Omsk	–	–	1	–	–	–	–	–	–	–	1	–	–	1	1	1	6	1	–	–	–	1	–	3	–	–	–	–	–	–	–	–
6	Avto. Yekaterinburg[3]	–	1	–	1	–	–	–	–	–	–	–	–	–	–	1	–	–	–	1	1	–	1	–	–	–	–	–	–	–	–	–	–
5	CSK VVS Samara	–	–	–	–	–	–	–	–	–	–	–	–	–	1	1	–	1	–	1	–	–	–	1	–	–	–	–	–	–	–	–	–
83	CSKA Moscow	1	1	–	–	–	2	2	–	–	2	2	3	2	4	5	–	–	–	5	1	2	5	2	5	3	7	4	3	8	5	1	8
70	Dynamo Moscow	4	1	1	–	–	–	–	–	1	–	1	–	–	1	2	–	–	6	2	4	4	1	7	4	3	12	7	4	3	2	–	–
16	Elektrostal	–	–	–	–	–	–	–	–	–	–	–	–	–	–	2	9	1	–	–	1	–	–	–	–	3	–	–	–	–	–	–	–
10	HC CSKA	–	–	–	–	–	–	–	–	–	–	–	–	–	–	–	5	–	5	–	–	–	–	–	–	–	–	–	–	–	–	–	–
4	Kristall Saratov	–	–	–	–	–	–	–	–	–	–	–	–	–	1	–	–	1	–	–	–	–	–	–	–	1	1	–	–	–	–	–	–
37	Krylja Sovetov	–	–	–	–	–	–	–	–	–	–	–	1	1	2	–	4	1	1	2	1	1	2	3	5	2	3	4	2	1	1	–	–
27	Lada Togliatti	–	–	1	–	–	–	–	–	1	–	–	2	1	2	–	2	2	4	4	1	3	1	–	–	2	1	–	–	–	–	–	–
61	Lokomotiv Yaroslavl[4]	–	2	1	1	2	–	1	–	1	2	1	3	2	–	7	3	1	10	1	6	3	3	6	1	–	–	2	1	–	–	–	–
14	Magnitogorsk	1	–	1	1	–	–	1	–	1	1	–	1	–	2	1	1	3	–	–	–	–	–	–	–	–	–	–	–	–	–	–	–
10	Nizhnekamsk	–	–	1	–	1	–	–	–	–	–	–	1	–	1	–	–	3	2	–	–	1	–	–	–	–	–	–	–	–	–	–	–
6	Nizhny Novgorod[5]	–	–	–	–	–	–	–	–	–	–	–	–	–	–	–	2	–	1	–	–	–	–	–	–	2	–	1	–	–	–	–	–
13	Novokuznetsk	–	–	1	1	–	1	–	1	1	–	–	–	–	1	1	–	1	4	1	–	–	–	–	–	–	–	–	–	–	–	–	–
12	Pardaugava Riga[6]	–	–	2	–	–	–	–	–	–	–	–	–	–	–	–	–	–	–	–	–	–	–	–	–	1	4	1	–	2	1	–	1
5	Perm	–	–	–	–	–	–	–	–	–	–	–	–	–	–	–	1	1	1	–	–	–	–	1	1	–	–	–	–	–	–	–	–
4	Russia U18	–	4	–	–	–	–	–	–	–	–	–	–	–	–	–	–	–	–	–	–	–	–	–	–	–	–	–	–	–	–	–	–
20	Severstal Cherepovets[7]	–	–	–	–	1	–	–	1	–	2	–	1	–	–	2	1	–	2	6	–	–	1	1	–	1	1	–	–	–	–	–	–
20	SKA St. Petersburg[8]	3	3	1	1	–	–	–	–	–	–	–	–	–	–	–	–	2	2	2	–	–	–	–	1	–	1	2	–	–	–	–	2
13	Sokol Kiev	–	–	–	–	–	–	–	–	–	–	–	–	–	–	–	–	–	–	–	1	–	–	2	–	1	3	2	1	1	1	–	1
26	Spartak Moscow	–	–	–	1	–	1	–	–	–	–	–	–	–	2	–	–	6	–	1	–	–	–	1	6	–	4	1	–	–	–	1	2
7	THC Tver	–	–	–	–	–	–	–	–	–	–	–	1	–	3	–	–	1	2	–	–	–	–	–	–	–	–	–	–	–	–	–	–
5	Tivali Minsk[9]	–	–	–	–	–	–	–	–	–	–	–	–	–	1	–	–	–	–	–	–	–	–	–	1	2	–	–	–	–	1	–	–
26	Traktor Chelyabinsk	–	–	–	–	1	–	2	1	–	1	1	1	2	–	–	1	–	–	–	1	1	–	1	2	7	2	–	–	2	–	–	–
15	Ufa	1	–	1	–	1	1	–	–	–	–	–	–	1	–	1	–	–	1	–	–	1	2	1	2	2	–	–	–	–	–	–	–
9	Ust-Kamenogorsk	–	–	–	–	–	–	–	–	–	–	–	–	–	–	1	–	–	–	1	2	–	–	1	2	1	1	–	–	–	–	–	–

Former club names: [1]-Ital Kazan, [2]-Khimik Voskresensk, [3]-Dynamo-Erergiya Yekaterinburg, [4]-Torpedo Yaroslavl, [5]-Torpedo Gorky, [6]-Dynamo Riga,HC Riga, [7]-Metallurg Cherepovets, [8]-SKA Leningrad, [9]-Dynamo Minsk.

Teams with two players selected: Dizelist Penza, Mechel Chelyabinsk, Neftyanik Almetjevsk, Vityaz Podolsk, Yunost Minsk.

Teams with one player selected: Amur Khabarovsk, Argus Moscow, HC CSKA Moscow 2, Dynamo Khazov, Dynamo-81 Riga, Gazovik Tyumen, HK Gomel, Izohets St. Petersburg, Kapitan Stupino, Khimik Novopolotsk, Metalurgs Liepaja, Mostovik Kurgan, Omsk 2, Riga Jr., Spartak St. Petersburg, Sibir Novosibirsk, Slovan Bratislava (SVK), Stalkers-Juniors, HK Zelenograd.

Sweden

Total	Club	'17	'16	'15	'14	'13	'12	'11	'10	'09	'08	'07	'06	'05	'04	'03	'02	'01	'00	'99	'98	'97	'96	'95	'94	'93	'92	'91	'90	'89	'88	'87	'69 to '86
35	AIK Solna	–	3	1	–	2	–	1	4	–	–	–	–	–	–	–	1	1	–	3	1	1	–	–	1	–	1	1	1	–	–	–	13
6	Almtuna	2	–	–	–	–	–	1	1	1	–	–	–	–	–	–	–	–	–	–	–	–	–	–	–	–	–	–	–	–	–	–	2
9	Bjorkloven	–	–	–	–	–	–	–	–	–	1	–	2	1	–	–	–	–	–	–	–	–	–	–	–	–	–	–	–	–	1	–	4
3	Boden	–	–	–	–	–	–	–	–	–	–	–	–	–	–	–	–	–	–	–	–	–	–	–	1	–	–	–	–	–	–	–	2
49	Brynas Gavle	2	1	2	3	1	3	1	4	3	4	1	1	–	–	2	–	2	1	1	2	1	1	–	–	1	–	–	–	–	–	4	8
64	Djurgarden	3	3	2	3	4	2	3	2	3	1	–	1	1	2	–	2	1	4	1	–	2	2	3	–	1	1	2	1	1	–	2	11
3	Falun	–	–	–	–	–	–	–	–	–	–	–	–	–	–	–	–	–	–	–	–	–	–	–	–	–	–	1	–	–	1	–	1
46	Farjestad	–	3	2	–	2	2	3	–	1	–	–	1	–	–	–	2	1	–	1	6	3	–	2	–	1	2	1	–	1	–	–	12
74	Frolunda	4	–	2	8	4	3	3	1	3	4	5	3	3	4	2	3	3	4	2	1	–	1	1	3	–	1	–	–	1	1	1	1
3	Grums	–	–	–	–	–	–	–	–	–	–	–	–	–	–	–	–	–	1	1	–	–	–	–	1	–	–	–	–	–	–	–	–
10	Hammarby	–	–	–	–	–	–	–	–	–	–	–	1	–	–	–	3	–	1	–	–	1	–	–	–	1	1	–	–	–	–	–	2
8	Huddinge	–	–	–	–	–	1	–	–	–	–	–	1	–	–	–	1	1	–	1	–	–	2	–	–	–	–	1	–	–	–	–	–
38	HV 71	3	2	3	2	–	–	–	1	1	3	1	–	1	2	1	1	–	1	3	4	1	2	–	2	–	–	–	1	–	1	1	1
36	Leksand	2	–	–	–	1	1	1	–	1	–	–	1	1	–	2	–	–	5	–	2	–	1	–	2	2	–	2	–	1	2	1	8
21	Linkoping	1	1	3	3	3	1	3	–	1	1	1	1	1	1	–	–	–	–	–	–	–	–	–	–	–	–	–	–	–	–	–	–
22	Lulea	1	2	1	1	1	1	–	–	1	–	3	–	–	1	–	–	–	2	–	1	1	–	–	–	–	1	–	–	–	1	1	3
25	Malmo	1	2	–	–	1	–	2	–	1	1	1	1	1	1	1	4	–	1	1	–	–	2	–	1	1	1	–	–	–	1	–	–
53	MODO	2	2	1	3	2	3	1	2	1	–	–	–	1	1	–	3	–	3	7	–	3	3	–	–	5	2	2	–	–	–	1	5
9	Mora	–	–	–	–	–	1	1	–	1	–	–	–	–	–	1	–	1	–	–	–	1	1	–	–	–	–	–	–	–	–	–	2
3	Morrum	–	–	–	–	–	–	–	–	–	–	–	–	–	–	–	2	1	–	–	–	–	–	–	–	–	–	–	–	–	–	–	–
4	Nacka	–	–	–	–	–	–	–	–	–	–	–	–	–	–	–	–	–	–	–	–	–	–	–	–	–	2	–	–	1	–	–	1
7	Orebro	–	1	–	–	–	–	–	–	–	–	–	–	–	1	–	–	–	–	–	–	–	–	–	–	–	–	–	–	–	–	1	4
5	Ostersund	1	–	–	1	–	1	–	–	–	–	–	–	–	–	–	–	–	–	–	–	–	–	–	–	–	–	–	–	–	–	1	1
3	Pitea	–	–	–	–	–	–	–	–	–	–	–	–	–	–	–	–	–	–	–	–	–	–	–	1	–	–	–	1	–	–	–	1
19	Rogle	2	1	1	–	2	2	1	–	–	–	1	–	–	–	–	–	–	–	1	–	–	–	1	2	2	–	–	–	–	2	1	–
27	Skelleftea	2	3	–	5	–	1	1	2	3	–	–	–	–	–	–	–	–	–	–	–	1	–	–	–	1	–	–	–	–	1	–	7
31	Sodertalje	–	–	–	1	1	1	1	2	–	–	1	2	3	1	2	–	1	1	–	1	–	–	–	–	1	–	–	–	2	–	–	10
3	Stocksund	–	–	–	–	–	–	–	–	–	–	–	–	–	2	–	–	–	–	–	–	–	–	–	–	–	–	–	–	–	–	–	1
3	Team Kiruna	–	–	–	–	–	–	–	–	–	–	–	–	–	–	–	–	–	–	–	–	–	–	–	–	1	–	–	–	–	–	–	2
14	Timra	1	1	–	–	1	–	–	1	2	–	–	–	–	–	–	1	–	–	1	–	–	–	–	1	–	–	–	–	–	–	–	5
3	Tingsryd	–	–	–	–	1	–	–	–	–	–	–	1	–	–	–	1	–	–	–	–	–	–	–	–	–	–	–	–	–	–	–	–
4	Troja/Ljungby	–	–	–	–	–	–	–	–	–	–	–	–	–	–	1	–	–	–	1	–	–	–	–	–	–	–	–	–	–	1	–	1
17	Vasteras	–	–	–	–	–	–	1	–	–	1	1	3	–	1	–	1	–	1	–	–	–	–	–	1	1	–	1	1	2	2	–	–
3	Vita Hasten	–	–	–	–	–	–	–	–	–	1	–	–	–	–	–	–	1	–	–	–	–	1	–	–	–	–	–	–	–	–	–	–

Teams with two players selected: Bofors, Skare, Vaxjo. **Teams with one player selected:** Arboga, Arvika, Danderyd Hockey, Fagersta, Jamtland, Karskoga, Karlskrona, Kumla, Oskarshamn, Skovde, S/G Hockey 83 Gavle, Sunne, Talje, Tunabro, Uppsala, Vallentuna, Vasby.

European Draft Firsts

1969 – First European (and Finn) • LW Tommi Salmelainen, 66th overall by St. Louis.

1974 – First Swede • C Per-Arne Alexandersson, 49th overall by Toronto. Four other Swedish-born players were selected that year, including defenseman Stefan Persson who was selected 214th overall by NY Islanders. In 1980 with the Islanders, Persson became the first European-trained player on a Stanley Cup-winning team.

1975 – First Russian • LW Viktor Khatulev, 160th overall by Philadelphia.

1976 – First European in the First Round • Swedish D Bjorn Johansson, 5th overall by California.

1976 – First Swiss • C Jacques Soguel, 121st overall by St. Louis.

1978 – First Czechoslovak • LW Ladislav Svozil, 194th overall by Detroit.

1978 – First Germans • G Bernard Engelbrecht, 196th overall by the Atlanta Flames and C Gerd Truntschka, 200th overall by St. Louis.

1989 – First European (and Swede) Taken First Overall • C Mats Sundin by Quebec.

1992 – First Czechoslovak Taken First Overall • D Roman Hamrlik by Tampa Bay.

2001 – First Russian Taken First Overall • LW Ilya Kovalchuk by Atlanta.

2017 – First Swiss Taken First Overall • C Nico Hischier by New jersey.

2017 Draft Analysis

BY BIRTHPLACE

Country of Origin

Country	Players Drafted
Canada	77
USA	50
Sweden	27
Finland	23
Russia	18
Czech Republic	9
Switzerland	3
Belarus	2
Denmark	2
Slovakia	2
France	1
Germany	1
Norway	1
Slovenia	1
Total	**217**

Canadian-Born Players

Province	Players Drafted
Ontario	37
Alberta	14
Manitoba	8
Quebec	8
British Columbia	6
Nova Scotia	2
Saskatchewan	2
Total	**77**

U.S.-Born Players

State	Players Drafted
Minnesota	17
California	5
Massachusetts	5
Michigan	4
Alaska	2
Connecticut	2
New Jersey	2
North Carolina	2
Pennsylvania	2
Wisconsin	2
Colorado	1
Indiana	1
Missouri	1
New York	1
Ohio	1
Texas	1
Washington	1
Total	**50**

BY BIRTH YEAR

Year	Players Drafted
1999	135
1998	58
1997	19
1996	5

BY POSITION

Position	Players Drafted
Defense	79
Center	60
Right wing	36
Left wing	21
Goaltender	21

Notes on 2017 First-Round Selections

1. NEW JERSEY • **NICO HISCHIER** (*NEE-ko HEE-shuhr*), C. A highly skilled player with excellent hockey sense, Nico Hischier is a complete player who competes hard at both ends of the ice. He has excellent vision and playmaking skills as well as the ability to score goals. Hischier, who represented Switzerland as a 16-year-old at the World Junior Championship in 2016, competed at both the Word Junior and Under-18 World Championship in 2017. He led all rookies in scoring in the Quebec Major Junior Hockey League as a member of the Halifax Moosehead in 2016-17.

2. PHILADELPHIA • **NOLAN PATICK** (*NOH-luhn PA-trihk*), C. A smooth skater who's composed with the puck, Nolan Patrick has excellent hockey sense with very good vision and anticipation. He has the type of leadership qualities that make other players around him better. Nolan was named captain of the Brandon Wheat Kings in 2016-17 and though his season was hampered by injuries he still scored 46 points (20 goals, 26 assists) in just 33 games. Patrick was the Western Hockey League rookie of the year in 2014-15 and the playoff MVP in 2016 when Brandon won its first WHL title in 20 years.

3. DALLAS • **MIRO HEISKANEN** (*MEE-roh HAYZ-kuh-nehn*), D. A smooth skater with great vision, Miro Heiskanen is an excellent two-way player. He played with HIFK in the top professional league in Finland in 2016-17 after winning rookie of the year with the HIFK junior team the year before. Heiskanen was named best defenseman and a tournament all-star at the 2017 Under-18 World Championship and also played at the 2017 World Junior Championship.

4. COLORADO • **CALE MAKAR** (*KAYL mah-KAHR*), D. Able to handle the puck with great vision and good lateral mobility, Cale Makar creates time and space in small areas. He led all Alberta Junior Hockey League defensemen in goals (24), assists (51) and points (75) in 54 games in 2016-17 and was named outstanding defenseman, league MVP and Canadian Junior Hockey League MVP. Makar also captained the Canada West Team at the 2016 World Junior Challenge.

5. VANCOUVER • **ELIAS PETTERSON** (*uh-LIGH-uhs peh-TUHR-suhn*), C. At 6'2" and only 165 pounds, Elias Petterson needs to fill out, but he has excellent speed and offensive instincts. Playing with Timra in the Swedish second division in 2016-17, Petterson averaged nearly a point per game (19 goals, 22 assists in 43 games) as an 18-year-old playing against men. He won a silver medal at the 2016 Under-18 Championship and played at the 2017 World Junior tourney.

6. VEGAS • **CODY GLASS** (*KOH-dee GLAS*), C. A highly skilled player with game-breaking ability, Cody Glass has NHL speed and quickness. He is an excellent playmaker with top-end puck skills. Glass was named co-MVP of the Portland Winterhawks in 2016-17 after leading the team and finishing seventh in the Western Hockey League with 94 points (32 goals, 62 assists). He also played for Canada at the 2017 Under-18 World Championship.

7. NY RANGERS • **LIAS ANDERSSON** (*lee-AHS an-DUHR-suhn*), C. A two-way forward with great moves, Lias Andersson has a good attitude and works hard. His father, Niklas Andersson, was drafted by the Quebec Nordiques in 1989 and played parts of six seasons in the NHL. Andersson led Sweden's junior league in assists (35) and points (59) in 37 games in 2015-16. He won the Swedish title with HV71 in 2016-17 and also played at the World Junior Championship.

8. BUFFALO • **CASEY MITTELSTADT** (*KAY-see MIH-tuhl-stad*), C. A dynamic skater with elite quickness, Casey Mittelstadt shows high-end hockey sense in all areas of the ice and has an NHL shot. He won Minnesota's Mr. Hockey award in 2016-17 as the top senior high school player in the state after splitting his season between Eden Prairie High School and Green Bay of the USHL. He won a bronze medal with Team USA at the 2016 Under-18 World Championship.

9. DETROIT • **MICHAEL RASMUSSEN** (*MIGH-kuhl RAZ-moo-sehn*), C. At nearly 6'6" and 221 pounds, Michael Rasmussen is a solid combination of size and skill. He has a goal-scorers touch, excellent playmaking ability and plays a smart game with and without the puck. Rasmussen led the Tri-City Americans with 15 power-play goals among the 32 he scored in 2016-17. He has represented Canada at the 2015 World Under-17 Challenge and the 2016 Ivan Hlinka tourney.

10. FLORIDA • **OWEN TIPPETT** (*OH-wehn TIH-piht*), RW. The best shooter in the 2017 Draft, Owen Tippett also has exceptional acceleration and separation speed as a skater. He is a dangerous offensive player who ranked fifth in the Ontario Hockey League with 44 goals for the Mississauga Steelheads in 2016-17. Internationally, Tippett was an alternate captain for Canada at the 2016 Ivan Hlinka tourney and played at the 2016 Under-18 World Championship.

11. LOS ANGELES • **GABRIEL VILARDI** (*gay-BREE-uhl vih-LAHR-dee*), C. A high possession, skill player with excellent hockey sense, Gabriel Vilardi is very composed with the puck. His vision and playmaking ability can influence the game in all three zones. Vilardi was one of three members of the Memorial Cup-winning Windsor Spitfires to be named to the tournament all-star team and led the team during the 2016-17 regular season with 29 goals. He won a gold medal with Canada White at the 2015 Under-17 World Challenge.

12. CAROLINA • **MARTIN NECAS** (*MAHR-tihn NEE-chas*), C. A very good skater with acceleration and speed, Martin Necas creates scoring chances with his high-level skill. Necas was the captain and leader when the Czech Under-18 team won the Ivan Hlinka tourney for the first time in 2016. He played a regular role with Brno in the top Czech league in 2016-17 and helped the team win its first championship at that level after winning a championship with Brno's under-18 team in 2015-16. Necas played at the World Junior Championship in 2017.

13. VEGAS • **NICK SUZUKI** (*NIHK suh-ZOO-kee*), C. A smart playmaker with elite hockey sense, Nick Suzuki plays a committed two-way game. He can play all three forward positions and is able to raise the play of those around him. Suzuki was fourth in the Ontario Hockey League in goals (45) and fifth in points (96) with Owen Sound in 2016-17 and won the William Hanley Trophy as the most sportsmanlike player. He won gold with Canada White at the 2015 Under-17 Challenge and played at the 2016 Ivan Hlinka tournament.

14. TAMPA BAY • **CAL FOOTE** (*KAL FUT*), D. The son of long-time Colorado Avalanche defenseman Adam Foote, Cal Foote is a smart, two-way defenseman with good vision. He is an excellent passer and a very good positional defender who uses his size (6'4", 215 pounds) and reach to advantage. Foote led all Kelowna Rockets defensemen in scoring with 57 points (6 goals, 51 assists) in the Western Hockey League in 2016-17. His 51 assists ranked him second on his team.

15. VEGAS • **ERIK BRANNSTROM** (*AIR-ihk BRAN-struhm*), D. A strong skater with good skill, Erik Brannstrom is just 5'9", and 176 pounds but he's a talented defenseman. He was second in the Swedish junior league in assists (14) and points (23) with HV71 in 2016-17 despite playing 25 fewer games than the league leader because he spent most of the season in the Swedish elite league. Brannstrom played at the Under-18 World Championship in 2016 and 2017.

16. CALGARY • **JUUSO VALIMAKI** (*YOO-soh val-ih-MA-kee*), D. A very good skater with speed, quickness and mobility, Juuso Valimaki is a dynamic offensive defenseman. He has excellent on-ice vision and playmaking abilities. Valimaki was a Second-Team All-Star in the Western Hockey League with Tri-City in 2016-17. Internationally, he helped Finland win gold at the 2016 Under-18 World Championship and played at the 2017 World Junior Championship.

17. TORONTO • **TIMOTHY LILJEGREN** (*TIH-moh-thee lihl-YEH-grehn*), D. Smart, skilled and mobile, Timothy Liljegren is a two-way defenseman who missed much of the 2016-17 season with injury and illness. He split his time with Rogle between the junior league and the Swedish elite league and also played at the 2017 Under-18 World Championship. He helped Sweden win a silver medal at that tournament in 2016 after being an all-star at the 2015 Under-17 Challenge.

18. BOSTON • **URHO VAAKANAINEN** (*UHR-hoh va-ka-NIGH-nehn*), D. A very good passer and playmaker with a good understanding of the game, Urho Vaakanainen is a solid and effective defenseman. He was a regular with JYP in the top Finnish league in 2016-17 and represented Finland at both the World Junior Championship and the Under-18 World Championship, where he won a silver medal. Vaakanainen won gold with Finland at the 2016 Under-18 Worlds.

19. SAN JOSE • **JOSHUA NORRIS** (*JAW-shoo-wuh NOHR-ihs*), C. A hard-working player with good hockey sense, Joshua Norris is a smooth skater who can play in all situations. He was the top scorer (27 goals, 33 assists, 60 points in 61 games) with the USA Hockey National Team Development Program in 2016-17 and helped the U.S. win gold at the Under-18 World Championship. Norris has committed to the University of Michigan for 2017-18.

20. ST. LOUIS • **ROBERT THOMAS** (*RAW-buhrt TAW-muhs*), D. A poised playmaker with an excellent hockey IQ, Robert Thomas is a two-way center who is very creative at handling and moving the puck. He is a hard worker who makes players around him better. Thomas won the Memorial Cup as a rookie with the London Knights in 2015-16 and was third on the team in scoring (16 goals, 50 assists, 66 points) in 2016-17. He won gold with Canada White at the 2015 Under-17 Challenge.

21. NY RANGERS • **FILIP CHYTIL** (*FIHL-ihp CHEE-tuhl*), C. A strong, two-way center, Filip Chytil spent most of the 2016-17 season with HC Zlin in the top Czech league. He played two games for Zlin in the junior league and also represented the Czech Republic at the 2017 Under-18 World Championship. In 2016, he helped the Czechs win gold at the Ivan Hlinka Memorial tournament for the first time and in 2015 he played at the World Under-17 Challenge.

22. EDMONTON • **KAILER YAMAMOTO** (*KAY-luhr ya-mah-MOH-toh*), RW. Only 5'8" and 146 pounds, Kailer Yamamoto is a dynamic offensive player with exceptional speed and quickness. He has excellent vision and is able to make plays at top speed. Yamamoto led the Spokane Chiefs, and ranked third in the Western Hockey League, with 99 points (42 goals, 57 assists) in 2016-17. He helped the U.S. win a bronze medal at the 2016 Under-18 World Championship.

23. ARIZONA • **PIERRE-OLIVIER JOSEPH** (*PEE-air-oh-lihv-EE-ay JOH-sehf*), D. A puck-moving defenseman with good quickness and mobility, Pierre-Olivier Joseph will only get better as he adds strength to his 6'2" frame. His older brother Mathieu was selected 120th overall by Tampa Bay in 2015. Joseph has good positioning in the defensive end and competes well. He plays with the Charlottetown Islanders in the Quebec Major Junior Hockey League.

24. WINNIPEG • **KRISTIAN VESALAINEN** (*KRIHS-t'yehn vehs-ah-LIGH-nehn*), LW-RW. At 6'3" and 205 pounds, Kristian Vesalainen is a physical power forward who likes to go straight to the net. He played most of the 2016-17 season with Frolunda in Sweden, where he has helped the team win two straight championships, but also played for HPK in his native Finland and represented Finland at both the World Junior Championship and Under-18 World Championship.

25. MONTREAL • **RYAN POEHLING** (*RIGH-uhn POH-lihng*), C. Standing 6'2", Ryan Poehling has a long stride and a long reach. He has good vision in heavy traffic and is good at protecting the puck. Poehling completed his studies early at Lakeville North High School in Minnesota in order to play with his older twin brothers Jack and Nick at St. Cloud State in 2016-17. Internationally, he won a gold medal with the United States at the 2017 Under-18 World Championship.

26. DALLAS • **JAKE OETTINGER** (*JAYK AW-tihn-juhr*), G. A big goalie who covers a lot of the net, the 6'4", 218-pound Jake Oettinger's positional play is very good and he has great rebound control. Oettinger is a graduate of the USA Hockey National Team Development Program and won bronze at the 2016 Under-18 World Championship. He earned Hockey East All-Rookie honors at Boston University in 2016-17.

27. PHILADELPHIA • **MORGAN FROST** (*MOHR-guhn FRAW-ST*), C. A smart and skilled center with excellent vision and anticipation, Morgan Frost is creative with the puck and generates good scoring chances. His father, Andy, is a popular radio personality in Toronto and former PA announcer at the Air Canada Centre. Frost plays with the Sault Ste. Marie Greyhounds in the Ontario Hockey League.

28. OTTAWA • **SHANE BOWERS** (*SHAYN BOW-uhrz*), C. A hard-working, two-way player, Shane Bowers is a solid skater and good passer with a very good feel for the game. Bowers is a native of Halifax who was drafted by Cape Breton in the Quebec Major Junior Hockey League, but chose Waterloo in the USHL instead. He played for Canada at the 2016 Ivan Hlinka tournament and is committed to Boston College.

29. CHICAGO • **HENRI JOKIHARJU** (*HEHN-ree yoh-kee-HAHR-yoo*), D. An excellent skater with quickness and mobility who is very elusive with the puck, Henri Jokiharju has good offensive instincts and can take away space defensively. The Finnish native played for the Portland Winterhawks in the Western Hockey League in 2016-17. He won a gold medal with Finland at the 2016 Under-18 World Championship.

30. NASHVILLE • **EELI TOLVANEN** (*EH-lee tohl-VA-nehn*), RW. A dynamic player with excellent skill and hockey sense, Eeli Tolvanen is fast and smart and has a strong work ethic. He plays the game at a fast pace and is hard to contain. Tolvanen has starred in the USHL the past two seasons and has represented Finland at the 2016 Under-18 World Championship and the 2017 World Junior Championship.

31. ST. LOUIS • **KLIM KOSTIN** (*KLIHM KAWZ-tihn*), C-LW. A strong, mobile power forward who competes hard, Klim Kostin is 6'3" and 207 pounds and plays a physical game. He is a strong skater with good speed and good hockey sense. Kostin captained Russia's silver medal team at the 2015 Under-17 Challenge and was also captain at the 2016 Ivan Hlinka tournament and Under-18 World Championship.

1: Nico Hischier
C – New Jersey

2: Nolan Patrick
C – Philadelphia

3: Miro Heiskanen
D – Dallas

4: Cale Makar
D – Colorado

5: Elias Pettersson
C – Vancouver

6: Cody Glass
C– Vegas

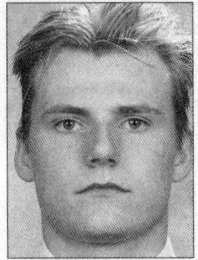
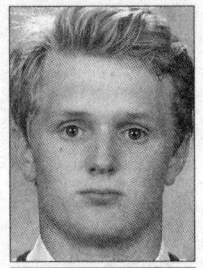

7: Lias Andersson
C – NY Rangers

8: Casey Mittelstadt
C – Buffalo

9: Michael Rasmussen
C – Detroit

10: Owen Tippett
RW – Florida

*Players selected first through tenth
in the 2017 NHL Draft.*

Pick	Claimed by	Amateur Club	Position

2017 NHL DRAFT

FIRST ROUND

Pick	Claimed by		Amateur Club	Position
1	N.J.	Nico Hischier	Halifax	C
2	PHI	Nolan Patrick	Brandon	C
3	DAL	Miro Heiskanen	HIFK	D
4	COL	Cale Makar	Brooks	D
5	VAN	Elias Pettersson	Timra	C
6	VGK	Cody Glass	Portland	C
7	NYR	Lias Andersson	HV 71	C
8	BUF	Casey Mittelstadt	Eden Prairie	C
9	DET	Michael Rasmussen	Tri-City	C
10	FLA	Owen Tippett	Mississauga	RW
11	L.A.	Gabriel Vilardi	Windsor	C
12	CAR	Martin Necas	Brno	C
13	VGK	Nick Suzuki	Owen Sound	C
14	T.B.	Cal Foote	Kelowna	D
15	VGK	Erik Brannstrom	HV 71	D
16	CGY	Juuso Valimaki	Tri-City	D
17	TOR	Timothy Liljegren	Rogle	D
18	BOS	Urho Vaakanainen	JyP	D
19	S.J.	Joshua Norris	USA U-18	C
20	ST.L.	Robert Thomas	London	C
21	NYR	Filip Chytil	Zlin	C
22	EDM	Kailer Yamamoto	Spokane	RW
23	ARI	Pierre-Olivier Joseph	Charlottetown	D
24	WPG	Kristian Vesalainen	Frolunda	RW
25	MTL	Ryan Poehling	St. Cloud State	C
26	DAL	Jake Oettinger	Boston University	G
27	PHI	Morgan Frost	Sault Ste. Marie	C
28	OTT	Shane Bowers	Waterloo	C
29	CHI	Henri Jokiharju	Portland	D
30	NSH	Eeli Tolvanen	Sioux City	RW
31	ST.L.	Klim Kostin	Dynamo Moscow	RW

SECOND ROUNDN

Pick	Claimed by		Amateur Club	Position
32	COL	Conor Timmins	Sault Ste. Marie	D
33	VAN	Kole Lind	Kelowna	RW
34	VGK	Nicolas Hague	Mississauga	D
35	PHI	Isaac Ratcliffe	Guelph	LW
36	N.J.	Jesper Boqvist	Brynas	C
37	BUF	Marcus Davidsson	Djurgarden	C
38	DET	Gustav Lindstrom	Almtuna	D
39	DAL	Jason Robertson	Kingston	LW
40	FLA	Aleksi Heponiemi	Swift Current	C
41	L.A.	Jaret Anderson-Dolan	Spokane	C
42	CAR	Eetu Luostarinen	Kalpa	C
43	WPG	Dylan Samberg	Hermantown	D
44	ARI	Filip Westerlund	Frolunda	D
45	CBJ	Alexandre Texier	Grenoble	C
46	NYI	Robin Salo	Sport	D
47	OTT	Alex Formenton	London	LW
48	T.B.	Alexander Volkov	SKA St. Petersburg 2	RW
49	S.J.	Mario Ferraro	Des Moines	D
50	ANA	Maxime Comtois	Victoriaville	LW
51	PIT	Zachary Lauzon	Rouyn-Noranda	D
52	CAR	Luke Martin	Michigan	D
53	BOS	Jack Studnicka	Oshawa	C
54	BUF	Ukko-Pekka Luukkonen	HPK Jr.	G
55	VAN	Jonah Gadjovich	Owen Sound	LW
56	MTL	Josh Brook	Moose Jaw	D
57	CHI	Ian Mitchell	Spruce Grove	D
58	MTL	Joni Ikonen	Frolunda Jr.	RW
59	TOR	Eemeli Rasanen	Kingston	D
60	ANA	Antoine Morand	Acadie-Bathurst	C
61	NSH	Grant Mismash	USA U-18	LW
62	VGK	Jake Leschyshyn	Regina	C

2017 NHL Draft Order of Selection

The first three picks in the first round of the 2017 NHL Draft were determined by the NHL's annual Draft Lottery. The 14 clubs that did not qualify for the 2017 Stanley Cup Playoffs, or clubs that acquired those clubs' 2017 first-round draft picks, participated in the drawing as did the expansion Vegas Golden Knights.

For 2017, New Jersey moved up from fifth to the top pick, while Philadelphia moved from 13th to second. Dallas moved from eighth to third. As a consequence, Colorado, Vancouver and Vegas picked fourth, fifth and sixth.

(Note that transferred draft choices are indicated as "NYR➡Ari." with the club that selected the player listed at right.)

In the first round of the 2017 NHL Draft, the order of selection was as follows:

a) The winners of the Draft Drawing followed by the remaining non-playoff clubs, in inverse order of points. (Note that the original holder of each selection is listed followed by the club that acquired and used that selection in the first round of the 2017 NHL Draft.) Vegas entered the Draft Lottery with the same odds as the club finishing the regular season in 28th place.

1. New Jersey		9. Detroit	
2. Philadelphia		10. Florida	
3. Dallas		11. Los Angeles	
4. Colorado		12. Carolina	
5. Vancouver		13. Wpg.➡VGK	
6. Vegas		14. Tampa Bay	
7. Ari.➡NYR		15. NYI➡VGK	
8. Buffalo			

b) Clubs eliminated in the first two rounds of the 2017 Stanley Cup Playoffs, regular-season division winners excluded, in inverse order of points;

16. Calgary	20. St. Louis
17. Toronto	21. NY Rangers
18. Boston	22. Edmonton
19. San Jose	23. Min.➡Ari.

c) Regular-season division winning clubs eliminated in the first two rounds of the 2017 Stanley Cup Playoffs, in inverse order of points;

24. CBJ➡VGK➡Wpg.	26. Chi. ➡Dal.
25. Montreal	27. Wsh.➡Phi.

d) Clubs eliminated in the 2017 Conference Finals, in inverse order of points;

28. Ottawa	29. Ana.➡Dal.

e) Loser of Stanley Cup Final

30. Nashville

f) Stanley Cup champion

31. Pit.➡St.L.

In the second and subsequent rounds unless their selections had been traded, the Colorado Avalanche (the club with the fewest regular-season points) picked first.

The Vancouver Canucks (second-fewest regular-season points) picked second.

The expansion Vegas Golden Knights picked third.

The Arizona Coyotes (third-fewest regular-season points) picked fourth.

Pick	Claimed by	Amateur Club	Position

THIRD ROUND

Pick	Claimed by	Amateur Club	Position
63	N.J.	Fabian Zetterlund	Farjestad Jr.	RW
64	VAN	Michael Dipietro	Windsor	G
65	VGK	Jonas Rondbjerg	Vaxjo Jr.	RW
66	FLA	Max Gildon	USA U-18	D
67	CAR	Morgan Geekie	Tri-City	C
68	MTL	Scott Walford	Victoria	D
69	ARI	Mackenzie Entwistle	Hamilton	RW
70	CHI	Andrei Altybarmakyan	LVY St. Petersburg 2	RW
71	DET	Kasper Kotkansalo	Sioux Falls	D
72	L.A.	Matt Villalta	Sault Ste. Marie	G
73	CAR	Stelio Mattheos	Brandon	RW
74	WPG	Johnny Kovacevic	Merrimack	D
75	ARI	Nate Schnarr	Guelph	C
76	T.B.	Alexei Lipanov	Balashikha	C
77	NYI	Ben Mirageas	Chicago	D
78	EDM	Stuart Skinner	Lethbridge	G
79	DAL	Lane Zablocki	Red Deer	RW
80	PHI	Kirill Ustimenko	Dynamo St. Petersburg 2	G
81	N.J.	Reilly Walsh	Proctor Academy	D
82	ARI	Cameron Crotty	Brockville	D
83	DET	Zach Gallant	Peterborough	C
84	EDM	Dmitri Samorukov	Guelph	D
85	MIN	Ivan Lodnia	Erie	RW
86	CBJ	Daniil Tarasov	Ufa 2	G
87	MTL	Cale Fleury	Kootenay	D
88	DET	Keith Petruzzelli	Muskegon	G
89	BUF	Oskari Laaksonen	Ilves Jr.	D
90	CHI	Evan Barratt	USA U-18	C
91	ANA	Jack Badini	Chicago	C
92	NSH	David Farrance	USA U-18	D
93	PIT	Clayton Phillips	Fargo	D

FOURTH ROUND

Pick	Claimed by	Amateur Club	Position
94	COL	Nick Henry	Regina	RW
95	VAN	Jack Rathbone	Dexter School	D
96	VGK	Maxim Zhukov	Green Bay	G
97	MIN	Mason Shaw	Medicine Hat	C
98	N.J.	Nikita Popugayev	Prince George	LW
99	BUF	Jacob Bryson	Providence	D
100	DET	Malte Setkov	Malmo Jr.	D
101	DAL	Liam Hawel	Guelph	C
102	S.J.	Scott Reedy	USA U-18	C
103	L.A.	Michael Anderson	Waterloo	D
104	CAR	Eetu Makiniemi	Jokerit Jr.	G
105	WPG	Santeri Virtanen	TPS Jr.	C
106	PHI	Matthew Strome	Hamilton	LW
107	PHI	Maxim Sushko	Owen Sound	RW
108	ARI	Noel Hoefenmayer	Ottawa	D
109	CGY	Adam Ruzicka	Sarnia	C
110	TOR	Ian Scott	Prince Albert	G
111	BOS	Jeremy Swayman	Sioux Falls	G
112	CHI	Tim Soderlund	Skelleftea	LW
113	ST.L.	Alexei Toropchenko	MVD Balashikha 2	RW
114	COL	Petr Kvaca	C. Budejovice	G
115	EDM	Ostap Safin	Sparta Jr.	RW
116	MIN	Bryce Misley	Oakville	C
117	CBJ	Emil Bemstrom	Leksand Jr.	C
118	L.A.	Markus Phillips	Owen Sound	D
119	CHI	Roope Laavainen	Jokerit Jr.	D
120	WSH	Tobias Geisser	Zug Academy	D
121	OTT	Drake Batherson	Cape Breton	C
122	ANA	Kyle Olson	Tri-City	RW
123	NYR	Brandon Crawley	London	D
124	TOR	Vladislav Kara	Bars Kazan	LW

FIFTH ROUND

Pick	Claimed by	Amateur Club	Position
125	COL	Igor Shvyrev	Magnitogorsk 2	C
126	ARI	Michael Karow	Youngstown	D
127	VGK	Lucas Elvenes	Rogle Jr.	LW
128	ARI	Tyler Steenbergen	Swift Current	C
129	N.J.	Gilles Senn	Davos	G
130	ST.L.	David Noel	Val-D'Or	D
131	DET	Cole Fraser	Peterborough	D
132	DAL	Jacob Peterson	Frolunda Jr.	C
133	FLA	Tyler Inamoto	USA U-18	D
134	L.A.	Cole Hults	Madison	D
135	VAN	Kristoffer Gunnarsson	Frolunda	D
136	WPG	Leon Gawanke	Cape Breton	D
137	PHI	Noah Cates	Stillwater	LW
138	L.A.	Drake Rymsha	Sarnia	C
139	NYI	Sebastian Aho	Skelleftea	D
140	CGY	Zach Fischer	Medicine Hat	RW
141	TOR	Fedor Gordeev	Flint	D
142	VGK	Jonathan Dugan	Northwood School	LW
143	N.J.	Marian Studenic	Hamilton	RW
144	CHI	Parker Foo	Brooks	LW
145	NYR	Calle Sjalin	Ostersund	D
146	EDM	Kirill Maximov	Niagara	RW
147	MIN	Jacob Golden	London	D
148	CBJ	Kale Howarth	Trail	LW
149	MTL	Jarret Tyszka	Seattle	D
150	CHI	Jakub Galvas	Olomouc	D
151	WSH	Sebastian Walfridsson	MODO Jr.	D
152	PIT	Jan Drozg	Leksand U18	LW
153	ANA	Olle Eriksson Ek	Farjestad Jr.	G
154	NSH	Tomas Vomacka	Corpus Christi	G
155	PIT	Linus Olund	Brynas	C

SIXTH ROUND

Pick	Claimed by	Amateur Club	Position
156	COL	Denis Smirnov	Penn State	RW
157	NYR	Dominik Lakatos	Liberec	C
158	VGK	Nick Campoli	North York	C
159	S.J.	Jacob McGrew	Spokane	RW
160	N.J.	Aarne Talvitie	Blues Jr.	C
161	VGK	Jiri Patera	C. Budejovice Jr.	G
162	DET	John Adams	Fargo	RW
163	DAL	Brett Davis	Kootenay	RW
164	DET	Reilly Webb	Hamilton	D
165	NYI	Arnaud Durandeau	Halifax	LW
166	CAR	Brendan De Jong	Portland	D
167	WPG	Arvid Holm	Karlskrona Jr.	G
168	PHI	Olle Lycksell	Linkoping Jr.	RW
169	T.B.	Nicklaus Perbix	Elk River	D
170	CBJ	Jonathan Davidsson	Djurgarden	RW
171	CGY	D'artagnan Joly	Baie-Comeau	RW
172	TOR	Ryan McGregor	Sarnia	C
173	BOS	Cedric Pare	Saint John	C
174	NYR	Morgan Barron	St. Andrews College	C
175	ST.L.	Trenton Bourque	Owen Sound	D
176	NSH	Pavel Koltygin	Drummondville	C
177	EDM	Skyler Brind'Amour	Selects Academy U18	C
178	MIN	Andrei Svetlakov	CSKA	C
179	CBJ	Carson Meyer	Miami	RW
180	T.B.	Cole Guttman	Dubuque	C
181	VAN	Petrus Palmu	Owen Sound	RW
182	WSH	Benton Maass	Elk River	D
183	OTT	Jordan Hollett	Regina	G
184	FLA	Sebastian Repo	Tappara	RW
185	S.J.	Sasha Chmelevski	Ottawa	C
186	PIT	Antti Palojarvi	Lukko Jr.	D

SEVENTH ROUND

Pick	Claimed by	Amateur Club	Position
187	COL	Nick Leivermann	Eden Prairie	D
188	VAN	Matt Brassard	Oshawa	D
189	VGK	Ben Jones	Niagara	C
190	ARI	Erik Walli-Walterholm	Djurgarden U18	RW
191	N.J.	Jocktan Chainey	Halifax	D
192	BUF	Linus Weissbach	Tri-City	LW
193	DET	Brady Gilmour	Saginaw	C
194	DAL	Dylan Ferguson	Kamloops	G
195	BOS	Victor Berglund	MODO Jr.	D
196	PHI	Wyatt Kalynuk	Bloomington	D
197	CAR	Ville Rasanen	Jokipojat	D
198	WPG	Skyler McKenzie	Portland	LW
199	MTL	Cayden Primeau	Lincoln	G
200	T.B.	Samuel Walker	Edina	C
201	NYI	Logan Cockerill	USA U-18	C
202	CGY	Filip Sveningsson	HV 71 Jr.	LW
203	TOR	Ryan O'Connell	St. Andrews College	D
204	BOS	Daniel Bukac	Brandon	D
205	N.J.	Yegor Zaitsev	Balashikha	D
206	ST.L.	Anton Andersson	Lulea Jr.	D
207	NYR	Patrik Virta	TPS	C
208	EDM	Philip Kemp	USA U-18	D
209	MIN	Nick Swaney	Waterloo	RW
210	CBJ	Robbie Stucker	St. Thomas	D
211	WPG	Croix Evingson	Shreveport	D
212	S.J.	Ivan Chekhovich	Baie-Comeau	C
213	WSH	Kris Roykas Marthinsen	Almtuna Jr.	RW
214	N.J.	Matthew Hellickson	Sioux City	D
215	CHI	Josh Ess	Lakeville South	D
216	NSH	Jacob Paquette	Kingston	D
217	PIT	William Reilly	RPI	D

First Two Rounds, 2016–2014

2016

Note: Names in *italics* have not appeared in an NHL regular-season or playoff game.

FIRST ROUND

Pick	Claimed by	Amateur Club	Position
1	TOR	Auston Matthews	Zurich	C
2	WPG	Patrik Laine	Tappara	RW
3	CBJ	*Pierre-Luc Dubois*	*Cape Breton*	*LW*
4	EDM	*Jesse Puljujarvi*	*Karpat*	*RW*
5	VAN	*Olli Juolevi*	*London*	*D*
6	CGY	Matthew Tkachuk	London	LW
7	ARI	Clayton Keller	USA U-18	C
8	BUF	Alexander Nylander	Mississauga	LW
9	MTL	Mikhail Sergachev	Windsor	D
10	COL	Tyson Jost	Penticton	C
11	OTT	*Logan Brown*	*Windsor*	*C*
12	N.J.	Michael McLeod	Mississauga	C
13	CAR	Jake Bean	Calgary	D
14	BOS	Charlie McAvoy	Boston University	D
15	MIN	Luke Kunin	U. of Wisconsin	C
16	ARI	Jakob Chychrun	Sarnia	D
17	NSH	*Dante Fabbro*	*Penticton*	*D*
18	WPG	*Logan Stanley*	*Windsor*	*D*
19	NYI	Kieffer Bellows	USA U-18	LW
20	DET	Dennis Cholowski	Chilliwack	D
21	CAR	*Julien Gauthier*	*Val-D'Or*	*RW*
22	PHI	*German Rubtsov*	*Russia U-18*	*C*
23	FLA	*Henrik Borgstrom*	*HIFK Jr.*	*C*
24	ANA	Max Jones	London	LW
25	DAL	*Riley Tufte*	*Blaine H.S.*	*LW*
26	STL	Tage Thompson	U. of Connecticut	C
27	T.B.	Brett Howden	Moose Jaw	C
28	WSH	*Lucas Johansen*	*Kelowna*	*D*
29	BOS	Trent Frederic	USA U-18	C
30	ANA	Sam Steel	Regina	C

SECOND ROUND

Pick	Claimed by	Amateur Club	Position
31	TOR	*Yegor Korshkov*	*Yaroslavl*	*RW*
32	EDM	*Tyler Benson*	*Vancouver*	*LW*
33	BUF	*Rasmus Asplund*	*Farjestad*	*C*
34	CBJ	*Andrew Peeke*	*Green Bay*	*D*
35	STL	Jordan Kyrou	Sarnia	C
36	PHI	Pascal Laberge	Victoriaville	C
37	T.B.	*Libor Hajek*	*Saskatoon*	*D*
38	FLA	Adam Mascherin	Kitchener	LW
39	CHI	Alexander DeBrincat	Erie	RW
40	COL	Cameron Morrison	Youngstown	LW
41	N.J.	Nathan Bastian	Mississauga	RW
42	OTT	*Jonathan Dahlen*	*Timra*	*C*
43	CAR	*Janne Kuokkanen*	*Karpat Jr.*	*C/LW*
44	T.B.	Boris Katchouk	Sault Ste. Marie	LW
45	CHI	*Chad Krys*	*USA U-18*	*D*
46	DET	Givani Smith	Guelph	RW
47	NSH	*Samuel Girard*	*Shawinigan*	*D*
48	PHI	Carter Hart	Everett	G
49	BOS	Ryan Lindgren	USA U-18	D
50	CAR	*Artur Kayumov*	*Russia U-18*	*LW/RW*
51	L.A.	Kale Clague	Brandon	D
52	PHI	*Wade Allison*	*Tri-City*	*RW*
53	DET	*Filip Hronek*	*Hr. Kralove*	*D*
54	CGY	*Tyler Parsons*	*London*	*G*
55	PIT	Filip Gustavsson	Lulea Jr.	G
56	CGY	Dillon Dube	Kelowna	C
57	TOR	Carl Grundstrom	MODO	RW
58	T.B.	Taylor Raddysh	Erie	RW
59	STL	*Evan Fitzpatrick*	*Sherbrooke*	*G*
60	S.J.	Dylan Gambrell	U. of Denver	C
61	PIT	*Kasper Bjorkqvist*	*Blues Jr.*	*RW*

Matthew Tkachuk, the son of former NHL great Keith Tkachuk, was selected sixth overall in the 2016 NHL Draft. He jumped directly to the NHL with the Calgary Flames in 2016-17, playing 76 games.

Pick	Claimed by	Amateur Club	Position

2015

FIRST ROUND

Pick	Claimed by	Amateur Club	Pos
1	EDM	Connor McDavid	Erie	C
2	BUF	Jack Eichel	Boston University	C
3	ARI	Dylan Strome	Erie	C
4	TOR	Mitch Marner	London	C
5	CAR	Noah Hanifin	Boston College	D
6	N.J.	Pavel Zacha	Sarnia	C
7	PHI	Ivan Provorov	Brandon	D
8	CBJ	Zach Werenski	U. of Michigan	D
9	S.J.	Timo Meier	Halifax	RW
10	COL	Mikko Rantanen	TPS	RW
11	FLA	Lawson Crouse	Kingston	LW
12	DAL	Denis Gurianov	Togliatti Jr.	RW
13	*BOS*	*Jakub Zboril*	*Saint John*	*D*
14	*BOS*	*Jake DeBrusk*	*Swift Current*	*LW*
15	*BOS*	*Zach Senyshyn*	*Sault Ste. Marie*	*RW*
16	NYI	Mathew Barzal	Seattle	C
17	WPG	Kyle Connor	Youngstown	LW
18	OTT	Thomas Chabot	Saint John	D
19	DET	Evgeny Svechnikov	Cape Breton	LW
20	MIN	Joel Eriksson Ek	Farjestad	C
21	OTT	Colin White	USA U-18	C
22	*WSH*	*Ilya Samsonov*	*Magnitogorsk Jr.*	*G*
23	VAN	Brock Boeser	Waterloo	RW
24	PHI	Travis Konecny	Ottawa	C
25	WPG	Jack Roslovic	USA U-18	C
26	*MTL*	*Noah Juulsen*	*Everett*	*D*
27	ANA	Jacob Larsson	Frolunda	D
28	NYI	Anthony Beauvillier	Shawinigan	LW
29	CBJ	Gabriel Carlsson	Linkoping Jr.	D
30	*ARI*	*Nick Merkley*	*Kelowna*	*RW*

SECOND ROUND

Pick	Claimed by	Amateur Club	Pos
31	*S.J.*	*Jeremy Roy*	*Sherbrooke*	*D*
32	ARI	Christian Fischer	USA U-18	RW
33	*T.B.*	*Mitchell Stephens*	*Saginaw*	*C*
34	*TOR*	*Travis Dermott*	*Erie*	*D*
35	CAR	Sebastian Aho	Karpat	LW
36	*OTT*	*Gabriel Gagne*	*Victoriaville*	*RW*
37	BOS	Brandon Carlo	Tri-City	D
38	*CBJ*	*Paul Bittner*	*Portland*	*LW*
39	COL	AJ Greer	Boston University	LW
40	*COL*	*Nicolas Meloche*	*Baie-Comeau*	*D*
41	*NYR*	*Ryan Gropp*	*Seattle*	*LW*
42	*N.J.*	*MacKenzie Blackwood*	*Barrie*	*G*
43	*L.A.*	*Erik Cernak*	*Kosice*	*D*
44	*T.B.*	*Matthew Spencer*	*Peterborough*	*D*
45	BOS	Jakob Forsbacka-Karlsson	Omaha	C
46	PIT	Daniel Sprong	Charlottetown	RW
47	*WPG*	*Jansen Harkins*	*Prince George*	*C*
48	*OTT*	*Filip Chlapik*	*Charlottetown*	*C*
49	*DAL*	*Roope Hintz*	*Ilves*	*LW*
50	*MIN*	*Jordan Greenway*	*USA U-18*	*LW*
51	BUF	Brendan Guhle	Prince Albert	D
52	*BOS*	*Jeremy Lauzon*	*Rouyn-Noranda*	*D*
53	CGY	Rasmus Andersson	Barrie	D
54	*CHI*	*Graham Knott*	*Niagara*	*LW*
55	NSH	Yakov Trenin	Gatineau	C
56	STL	Vince Dunn	Niagara	D
57	*WSH*	*Jonas Siegenthaler*	*Zurich*	*D*
58	*CBJ*	*Kevin Stenlund*	*HV 71 Jr.*	*C*
59	*ANA*	*Julius Nattinen*	*JyP-Akatemia.*	*C*
60	CGY	Oliver Kylington	Farjestad	D
61	*TOR*	*Jeremy Bracco*	*USA U-18*	*RW*

2014

FIRST ROUND

Pick	Claimed by	Amateur Club	Pos
1	FLA	Aaron Ekblad	Barrie	D
2	BUF	Sam Reinhart	Kootenay	C
3	EDM	Leon Draisaitl	Prince Albert	C
4	CGY	Sam Bennett	Kingston	C
5	*NYI*	*Michael Dal Colle*	*Oshawa*	*LW*
6	VAN	Jake Virtanen	Calgary	RW
7	*CAR*	*Haydn Fleury*	*Red Deer*	*D*
8	TOR	William Nylander	MODO Ornskoldsvik	C/RW
9	WPG	Nick Ehlers	Halifax	LW
10	ANA	Nicholas Ritchie	Peterborough	LW
11	NSH	Kevin Fiala	HV 71 Jr.	LW
12	ARI	Brendan Perlini	Niagara	LW
13	WSH	Jakub Vrana	Linkoping	L/RW
14	DAL	Julius Honka	Swift Current	D
15	DET	Dylan Larkin	USA U-18	C
16	CBJ	Sonny Milano	USA U-18	LW
17	*PHI*	*Travis Sanheim*	*Calgary*	*D*
18	MIN	Alex Tuch	USA U-18	RW
19	T.B.	Anthony DeAngelo	Sarnia	D
20	CHI	Nick Schmaltz	Green Bay	C
21	STL	Robby Fabbri	Guelph	C
22	PIT	Kasperi Kapanen	KalPa	RW
23	*COL*	*Conner Bleackley*	*Red Deer*	*C*
24	VAN	Jared McCann	Sault Ste. Marie	C
25	BOS	David Pastrnak	Sodertalje	RW
26	MTL	Nikita Scherbak	Saskatoon	RW
27	S.J.	Nikolay Goldobin	Sarnia	RW
28	NYI	Joshua Ho-Sang	Windsor	C/RW
29	L.A.	Adrian Kempe	MODO Ornskoldsvik	LW
30	N.J.	John Quenneville	Brandon	C

SECOND ROUND

Pick	Claimed by	Amateur Club	Pos
31	*BUF*	*Brendan Lemieux*	*Barrie*	*LW*
32	*FLA*	*Jayce Hawryluk*	*Brandon*	*C*
33	STL	Ivan Barbashev	Moncton	C/LW
34	*CGY*	*Mason McDonald*	*Charlottetown*	*G*
35	*T.B.*	*Dominik Masin*	*Slavia Jr.*	*D*
36	VAN	Thatcher Demko	Boston College	G
37	*CAR*	*Alex Nedeljkovic*	*Plymouth*	*G*
38	*ANA*	*Marcus Pettersson*	*Skelleftea Jr.*	*D*
39	*WSH*	*Vitek Vanecek*	*Liberec Jr.*	*G*
40	*OTT*	*Andreas Englund*	*Djurgarden*	*D*
41	*N.J.*	*Joshua Jacobs*	*Indiana*	*D*
42	NSH	Vladislav Kamenev	Magnitogorsk 2	LW
43	*ARI*	*Ryan MacInnis*	*Kitchener*	*C*
44	*BUF*	*Eric Cornel*	*Peterborough*	*C*
45	*DAL*	*Brett Pollock*	*Edmonton*	*LW*
46	*S.J.*	*Julius Bergman*	*Frolunda Jr.*	*D*
47	*CBJ*	*Ryan Collins*	*USA U-18*	*D*
48	*PHI*	*Nicolas Aube-Kubel*	*Val-d'Or*	*RW*
49	*BUF*	*Vaclav Karabacek*	*Gatineau*	*RW*
50	*L.A.*	*Roland McKeown*	*Kingston*	*D*
51	*NSH*	*Jack Dougherty*	*USA U-18*	*D*
52	*STL*	*Maxim Letunov*	*Youngstown*	*C*
53	*S.J.*	*Noah Rod*	*Geneve Jr.*	*RW*
54	*CGY*	*Hunter Smith*	*Oshawa*	*RW*
55	ANA	Brandon Montour	Waterloo	D
56	*BOS*	*Ryan Donato*	*Dexter School*	*C*
57	*T.B.*	*Johnathan MacLeod*	*USA U-18*	*D*
58	ARI	Christian Dvorak	London	LW
59	*NYR*	*Brandon Halverson*	*Sault Ste. Marie*	*G*
60	*L.A.*	*Alex Lintuniemi*	*Ottawa*	*D*

Note: Names in *italics* are first-round picks who have not appeared in an NHL regular-season or playoff game.

First Round and Other Notable Selections, 2013–1969

2013

FIRST ROUND

Pick	Claimed by	Amateur Club	Pos
1	COL	Nathan MacKinnon	Halifax	C
2	FLA	Aleksander Barkov	Tappara	C
3	T.B.	Jonathan Drouin	Halifax	LW
4	NSH	Seth Jones	Portland	D
5	CAR	Elias Lindholm	Brynas	C
6	CGY	Sean Monahan	Ottawa	C
7	EDM	Darnell Nurse	Sault Ste. Marie	D
8	BUF	Rasmus Ristolainen	TPS Turku	D
9	VAN	Bo Horvat	London	C
10	DAL	Valeri Nichushkin	Chelyabinsk	RW
11	PHI	Samuel Morin	Rimouski	D
12	PHX	Max Domi	London	C/LW
13	WPG	Joshua Morrissey	Prince Albert	D
14	CBJ	Alexander Wennberg	Djurgarden	C
15	NYI	Ryan Pulock	Brandon	D
16	BUF	Nikita Zadorov	London	D
17	OTT	Curtis Lazar	Edmonton	C/RW
18	S.J.	Mirco Mueller	Everett	D
19	CBJ	Kerby Rychel	Windsor	LW
20	DET	Anthony Mantha	Val-d'Or	RW
21	TOR	Frederik Gauthier	Rimouski	C
22	CGY	Emile Poirier	Gatineau	LW
23	WSH	Andre Burakovsky	Malmo	LW
24	VAN	Hunter Shinkaruk	Medicine Hat	C/LW
25	MTL	Michael McCarron	USA U-18	RW
26	ANA	Shea Theodore	Seattle	D
27	CBJ	Marko Dano	Bratislava	C
28	*CGY*	*Morgan Klimchuk*	*Regina*	*LW*
29	DAL	Jason Dickinson	Guelph	C
30	CHI	Ryan Hartman	Plymouth	RW

OTHER NOTABLE SELECTIONS

Pick	Claimed by	Amateur Club	Pos
55	MTL	Artturi Lehkonen	KalPa Kuopio	LW
66	CAR	Brett Pesce	New Hampshire	LW
77	PIT	Jake Guentzel	Nebraska-Omaha	C
80	BUF	Anthony Duclair	Quebec	LW
86	MTL	Sven Andrighetto	Rouyn-Noranda	RW

2012

FIRST ROUND

Pick	Claimed by	Amateur Club	Pos
1	EDM	Nail Yakupov	Sarnia	RW
2	CBJ	Ryan Murray	Everett	D
3	MTL	Alex Galchenyuk	Sarnia	C
4	NYI	Griffin Reinhart	Edmonton	D
5	TOR	Morgan Rielly	Moose Jaw	D
6	ANA	Hampus Lindholm	Rogle Jr.	D
7	MIN	Matt Dumba	Red Deer	D
8	PIT	Derrick Pouliot	Portland	D
9	WPG	Jacob Trouba	USA U-18	D
10	T.B.	Slater Koekkoek	Peterborough	D
11	WSH	Filip Forsberg	Leksand	RW
12	BUF	Mikhail Grigorenko	Quebec	C
13	DAL	Radek Faksa	Kitchener	C
14	BUF	Zemgus Girgensons	Dubuque	C
15	OTT	Cody Ceci	Ottawa	D
16	WSH	Thomas Wilson	Plymouth	RW
17	S.J.	Tomas Hertl	Slavia	C
18	CHI	Teuvo Teravainen	Jokerit	LW
19	T.B.	Andrei Vasilevskiy	Ufa 2	G
20	PHI	Scott Laughton	Oshawa	C
21	CGY	Mark Jankowski	Stanstead College	C
22	PIT	Olli Maatta	London	D
23	FLA	Mike Matheson	Dubuque	D
24	BOS	Malcolm Subban	Belleville	G
25	STL	Jordan Schmaltz	Green Bay	D
26	VAN	Brendan Gaunce	Belleville	C
27	PHX	Henrik Samuelsson	Edmonton	C
28	NYR	Brady Skjei	USA U-18	D
29	N.J.	Stefan Matteau	USA U-18	C
30	L.A.	Tanner Pearson	Barrie	LW

OTHER NOTABLE SELECTIONS

Pick	Claimed by	Amateur Club	Pos
44	BUF	Jake McCabe	U. of Wisconsin	D
55	S.J.	Chris Tierney	London	C
58	PHX	Jordin Martinook	Vancouver	LW
60	N.J.	Damon Severson	Kelowna	D
78	PHI	Shayne Gostisbehere	Union College	D
83	PIT	Matt Murray	Sault. Ste. Marie	G
86	STL	Colton Parayko	Fort McMurray	D
87	ANA	Frederik Andersen	Frolunda	G
101	T.B.	Cedric Paquette	Blainville Boisbrand	C
120	DAL	Jacob Slavin	Chicago	D
137	WSH	Connor Carrick	USA U-18	D
147	VAN	Ben Hutton	Nepean	D

Selected by Washington 11th overall in 2012, Filip Forsberg was dealt to Nashville a year later and has developed into a top scorer with the Predators. He's topped 30 goals in each of the past two seasons.

| Pick | Claimed by | | Amateur Club | Position | | Pick | Claimed by | | Amateur Club | Position | | Pick | Claimed by | | Amateur Club | Position |

2011

FIRST ROUND

1	EDM	Ryan Nugent-Hopkins	Red Deer	C
2	COL	Gabriel Landeskog	Kitchener	LW
3	FLA	Jonathan Huberdeau	Saint John	C
4	N.J.	Adam Larsson	Skelleftea	D
5	NYI	Ryan Strome	Niagara	C
6	OTT	Mika Zibanejad	Djurgarden	C
7	WPG	Mark Scheifele	Barrie	C
8	PHI	Sean Couturier	Drummondville	C
9	BOS	Dougie Hamilton	Niagara	D
10	MIN	Jonas Brodin	Farjestad	D
11	COL	Duncan Siemens	Saskatoon	D
12	CAR	Ryan Murphy	Kitchener	D
13	CGY	Sven Baertschi	Portland	LW
14	DAL	Jamie Oleksiak	Northeastern	D
15	NYR	J.T. Miller	USA U-18	C
16	BUF	Joel Armia	Assat	RW
17	MTL	Nathan Beaulieu	Saint John	D
18	CHI	Mark McNeill	Prince Albert	C
19	EDM	Oscar Klefbom	Farjestad	D
20	PHX	Connor Murphy	USA U-18	D
21	OTT	Stefan Noesen	Plymouth	RW
22	*TOR*	*Tyler Biggs*	*USA U-18*	*RW*
23	PIT	Joe Morrow	Portland	D
24	OTT	Matt Puempel	Peterborough	LW
25	TOR	Stuart Percy	Mississauga St. Michael's	D
26	CHI	Phillip Danault	Victoriaville	C
27	T.B.	Vladislav Namestnikov	London	C
28	*MIN*	*Zack Phillips*	*Saint John*	*C*
29	VAN	Nicklas Jensen	Oshawa	LW/RW
30	ANA	Rickard Rakell	Plymouth	RW

OTHER NOTABLE SELECTIONS

35	DET	Tomas Jurco	Saint John	RW
37	CBJ	Boone Jenner	Oshawa	C
39	ANA	John Gibson	USA U-18	G
43	CHI	Brandon Saad	Saginaw	LW
58	T.B.	Nikita Kucherov	CSKA2	LW
96	OTT	Jean-Gabriel Pageau	Gatineau	C
104	CGY	Johnny Gaudreau	Dubuque	LW
139	CHI	Andrew Shaw	Owen Sound	C
208	T.B.	Ondrej Palat	Drummondville	LW

2010

FIRST ROUND

1	EDM	Taylor Hall	Windsor	LW
2	BOS	Tyler Seguin	Plymouth	C
3	FLA	Erik Gudbranson	Kingston	D
4	CBJ	Ryan Johansen	Portland	C
5	NYI	Nino Niederreiter	Portland	RW
6	T.B.	Brett Connolly	Prince George	RW
7	CAR	Jeff Skinner	Kitchener	C
8	ATL	Alexander Burmistrov	Barrie	C
9	MIN	Mikael Granlund	HIFK Helsinki	C/W
10	NYR	Dylan McIlrath	Moose Jaw	D
11	DAL	Jack Campbell	USA U-18	G
12	ANA	Cam Fowler	Windsor	D
13	PHX	Brandon Gormley	Moncton	D
14	STL	Jaden Schwartz	Tri-City	C
15	L.A.	Derek Forbort	USA U-18	D
16	STL	Vladimir Tarasenko	Novosibirsk	RW
17	COL	Joey Hishon	Owen Sound	C
18	NSH	Austin Watson	Peterborough	LW
19	FLA	Nick Bjugstad	Blaine	C
20	PIT	Beau Bennett	Penticton	RW
21	DET	Riley Sheahan	U. of Notre Dame	C
22	MTL	Jarred Tinordi	USA U-18	D
23	BUF	Mark Pysyk	Edmonton	D
24	CHI	Kevin Hayes	Nobles	RW
25	FLA	Quinton Howden	Moose Jaw	C
26	WSH	Evgeny Kuznetsov	Chelyabinsk	C
27	PHX	Mark Visentin	Niagara	G
28	S.J.	Charlie Coyle	South Shore	C/RW
29	ANA	Emerson Etem	Medicine Hat	RW
30	NYI	Brock Nelson	Warroad	C

OTHER NOTABLE SELECTIONS

37	CAR	Justin Faulk	USA U-18	D
42	ANA	Devante Smith-Pelly	Mississauga	RW
47	L.A.	Tyler Toffoli	Ottawa	C
59	MIN	Jason Zucker	USA U-18	RW
66	T.B.	Radko Gudas	Everett	D
147	MTL	Brendan Gallagher	Vancouver	RW
154	CBJ	Dalton Prout	Barrie	D

Minnesota's first pick, ninth overall, in 2010, Mikael Granlund of Finland emerged as the Wild's top scorer in 2016-17 with 69 points on 26 goals and 43 assists. He also had plus-minus rating of +23.

2009

FIRST ROUND

1	NYI	John Tavares	London	C
2	T.B.	Victor Hedman	MODO Ornskoldsvik	D
3	COL	Matt Duchene	Brampton	C
4	ATL	Evander Kane	Vancouver	C
5	L.A.	Brayden Schenn	Brandon	C
6	PHX	Oliver Ekman-Larsson	Leksand	D
7	TOR	Nazem Kadri	London	C
8	DAL	Scott Glennie	Brandon	RW
9	OTT	Jared Cowen	Spokane	D
10	EDM	Magnus Paajarvi-Svensson	Timra	LW
11	NSH	Ryan Ellis	Windsor	D
12	NYI	Calvin De Haan	Oshawa	D
13	BUF	Zack Kassian	Peterborough	RW
14	FLA	Dmitry Kulikov	Drummondville	D
15	ANA	Peter Holland	Guelph	C
16	MIN	Nick Leddy	Eden Prairie	D
17	STL	David Rundblad	Skelleftea	D
18	MTL	Louis Leblanc	Omaha	C
19	NYR	Chris Kreider	Andover	C
20	N.J.	Jacob Josefson	Djurgarden	C
21	CBJ	John Moore	Chicago Steel	D
22	VAN	Jordan Schroeder	U. of Minnesota	C
23	CGY	Tim Erixon	Skelleftea	D
24	WSH	Marcus Johansson	Farjestad	C
25	BOS	Jordan Caron	Rimouski	RW
26	ANA	Kyle Palmieri	USA U-18	C/RW
27	*CAR*	*Philippe Paradis*	*Shawinigan*	*C*
28	CHI	Dylan Olsen	Camrose	D
29	T.B.	Carter Ashton	Lethbridge	RW
30	PIT	Simon Despres	Saint John	D

OTHER NOTABLE SELECTIONS

33	COL	Ryan O'Reilly	Erie	C
35	L.A.	Kyle Clifford	Barrie	LW
39	OTT	Jakob Silfverberg	Brynas	LW
46	OTT	Robin Lehner	Frolunda Jr.	G
60	DET	Thomas Tatar	Zvolen	LW
85	WSH	Cody Eakin	Swift Current	C
92	NYI	Casey Cizikas	St. Michael's	C
98	NSH	Craig Smith	Waterloo	C
102	NSH	Mattias Ekholm	Mora IK	D
104	BUF	Marcus Foligno	Sudbury	LW
149	CHI	Marcus Kruger	Djurgarden	C
186	L.A.	Jordan Nolan	Sault Ste. Marie	C

2008

FIRST ROUND

1	T.B.	Steven Stamkos	Sarnia	C
2	L.A.	Drew Doughty	Guelph	D
3	ATL	Zach Bogosian	Peterborough	D
4	STL	Alex Pietrangelo	Niagara	D
5	TOR	Luke Schenn	Kelowna	D
6	CBJ	Nikita Filatov	CSKA 2	LW
7	NSH	Colin Wilson	Boston University	C
8	PHX	Mikkel Boedker	Kitchener	LW
9	NYI	Joshua Bailey	Windsor	C
10	VAN	Cody Hodgson	Brampton	C
11	*CHI*	*Kyle Beach*	*Everett*	*C*
12	BUF	Tyler Myers	Kelowna	D
13	L.A.	Colten Teubert	Regina	D
14	CAR	Zach Boychuk	Lethbridge	C
15	OTT	Erik Karlsson	Frolunda Jr.	D
16	BOS	Joe Colborne	Camrose	C
17	ANA	Jake Gardiner	Minnetonka	D
18	*NSH*	*Chet Pickard*	*Tri-City*	*G*
19	PHI	Luca Sbisa	Lethbridge	D
20	NYR	Michael Del Zotto	Oshawa	D
21	*WSH*	*Anton Gustafsson*	*Frolunda Jr.*	*C*
22	EDM	Jordan Eberle	Regina	C
23	MIN	Tyler Cuma	Ottawa	D
24	N.J.	Mattias Tedenby	HV 71 Jonkoping	LW
25	CGY	Greg Nemisz	Windsor	C
26	BUF	Tyler Ennis	Medicine Hat	C
27	WSH	John Carlson	Indiana	D
28	PHX	Viktor Tikhonov	Cherepovets	W
29	*ATL*	*Daultan Leveille*	*St. Catharines*	*C*
30	DET	Tom McCollum	Guelph	G

OTHER NOTABLE SELECTIONS

32	L.A.	Slava Voynov	Chelyabinsk	D
38	NSH	Roman Josi	Bern	D
51	NYR	Derek Stepan	Shattuck-St. Mary's	C
53	NYI	Travis Hamonic	Moose Jaw	D
79	OTT	Zack Smith	Swift Current	C
93	WSH	Braden Holtby	Saskatoon	G
111	NYR	Dale Weise	Swift Current	RW
114	CGY	T.J. Brodie	Saginaw	D
121	Det.	Gustav Nyqvist	Malmo	RW
148	NYI	Matt Martin	Sarnia	LW
156	NYI	Jared Spurgeon	Spokane	D
186	S.J.	Jason Demers	Victoriaville	D

Pick	Claimed by	Amateur Club	Position	Pick	Claimed by	Amateur Club	Position	Pick	Claimed by	Amateur Club	Position

2007

FIRST ROUND

Pick	Claimed by	Amateur Club	Position
1	CHI	Patrick Kane	London	RW
2	PHI	James van Riemsdyk	USA U-18	LW
3	PHX	Kyle Turris	Burnaby	C
4	L.A.	Thomas Hickey	Seattle	D
5	WSH	Karl Alzner	Calgary	D
6	EDM	Sam Gagner	London	C/W
7	CBJ	Jakub Voracek	Halifax	RW
8	BOS	Zach Hamill	Everett	C
9	S.J.	Logan Couture	Ottawa	C
10	FLA	Keaton Ellerby	Kamloops	D
11	CAR	Brandon Sutter	Red Deer	C/RW
12	MTL	Ryan McDonagh	Cretin-Derham	D
13	STL	Lars Eller	Frolunda Jr.	C
14	COL	Kevin Shattenkirk	USA U-18	D
15	EDM	Alex Plante	Calgary	D
16	MIN	Colton Gillies	Saskatoon	C
17	NYR	*Alexei Cherepanov*	*Omsk*	*RW*
18	STL	Ian Cole	USA U-18	D
19	ANA	*Logan MacMillan*	*Halifax*	*C*
20	PIT	*Angelo Esposito*	*Quebec*	*C*
21	EDM	Riley Nash	Salmon Arm	C
22	MTL	Max Pacioretty	Sioux City	LW
23	NSH	Jonathon Blum	Vancouver	D
24	CGY	Mikael Backlund	Vasteras	C
25	VAN	*Patrick White*	*Tri-City*	*C*
26	STL	David Perron	Lewiston	LW
27	DET	Brendan Smith	St. Michael's	D
28	S.J.	Nicholas Petrecki	Omaha	D
29	OTT	Jim O'Brien	U. of Minnesota	C
30	PHX	*Nick Ross*	*Regina*	*D*

OTHER NOTABLE SELECTIONS

Pick	Claimed by	Amateur Club	Position
43	MTL	P.K. Subban	Belleville	D
55	COL	T.J. Galiardi	Dartmouth	LW
58	NSH	Nick Spaling	Kitchener	C
61	L.A.	Wayne Simmonds	Owen Sound	RW
77	T.B.	Alex Killorn	Deerfield	C
95	L.A.	Alec Martinez	Miami University	D
117	N.J.	Matt Halischuk	Kitchener	RW
129	DAL	Jamie Benn	Victoria	LW
168	NYR	Carl Hagelin	Sodertalje Jr	LW
173	S.J.	Nick Bonino	Boston U.	C
194	TOR	Carl Gunnarsson	Linkoping	D
201	S.J.	Justin Braun	UMass-Amherst	D

2006

FIRST ROUND

Pick	Claimed by	Amateur Club	Position
1	STL	Erik Johnson	USA U-18	D
2	PIT	Jordan Staal	Peterborough	C
3	CHI	Jonathan Toews	U. of North Dakota	C
4	WSH	Nicklas Backstrom	Brynas Gavle	C
5	BOS	Phil Kessel	U. of Minnesota	C
6	CBJ	Derick Brassard	Drummondville	C
7	NYI	Kyle Okposo	Des Moines	RW
8	PHX	Peter Mueller	Everett	C
9	MIN	James Sheppard	Cape Breton	C
10	FLA	Michael Frolik	Kladno	C
11	L.A.	Jonathan Bernier	Lewiston	G
12	ATL	Bryan Little	Barrie	C
13	TOR	Jiri Tlusty	Kladno	C
14	VAN	Michael Grabner	Spokane	RW
15	T.B.	Riku Helenius	Ilves Tampere	G
16	S.J.	Ty Wishart	Prince George	D
17	L.A.	Trevor Lewis	Des Moines	C
18	COL	Chris Stewart	Kingston	RW
19	ANA	*Mark Mitera*	*U. of Michigan*	*D*
20	MTL	*David Fischer*	*Apple Valley*	*D*
21	NYR	Bobby Sanguinetti	Owen Sound	D
22	PHI	Claude Giroux	Gatineau	RW
23	WSH	Simeon Varlamov	Yaroslavl 2	G
24	BUF	*Dennis Persson*	*Vasteras*	*D*
25	STL	Patrik Berglund	Vasteras	C
26	CGY	Leland Irving	Everett	G
27	DAL	Ivan Vishnevskiy	Rouyn-Noranda	D
28	OTT	Nick Foligno	Sudbury	LW
29	PHX	Chris Summers	USA U-18	D
30	N.J.	Matthew Corrente	Saginaw	D

OTHER NOTABLE SELECTIONS

Pick	Claimed by	Amateur Club	Position
34	WSH	Michal Neuvirth	Sparta Jr.	G
44	TOR	Nikolai Kulemin	Magnitogorsk	W
46	BUF	Jhonas Enroth	Sodertalje	G
50	BOS	Milan Lucic	Vancouver	LW
54	NYR	Artem Anisimov	Yaroslavl	C
69	CBJ	Steve Mason	London	G
71	BOS	Brad Marchand	Moncton	C
72	MIN	Cal Clutterbuck	Oshawa	RW
99	TOR	James Reimer	Red Deer	G
112	ANA	Matt Beleskey	Belleville	LW
160	NYI	Andrew MacDonald	Moncton	D
161	TOR	Viktor Stalberg	Frolunda	LW
177	WSH	Mathieu Perreault	Acadie-Bathurst	C
189	CBJ	Derek Dorsett	Medicine Hat	RW

Kyle Turris, Patrick Kane and James van Riemsdyk were the top three picks in the 2007 Draft. The selections of Kane and van Riemsdyk marked the first time in NHL history that American-born players were drafted with the first two picks.

2005

FIRST ROUND

Pick	Claimed by	Amateur Club	Position
1	PIT	Sidney Crosby	Rimouski	C
2	ANA	Bobby Ryan	Owen Sound	RW
3	CAR	Jack Johnson	USA U-18	D
4	MIN	Benoit Pouliot	Sudbury	LW
5	MTL	Carey Price	Tri-City	G
6	CBJ	Gilbert Brule	Vancouver	C
7	CHI	Jack Skille	USA U-18	RW
8	S.J.	Devin Setoguchi	Saskatoon	RW
9	OTT	Brian Lee	Moorhead	D
10	VAN	Luc Bourdon	Val d'Or	D
11	L.A.	Anze Kopitar	Sodertalje Jr.	C
12	NYR	Marc Staal	Sudbury	D
13	BUF	*Marek Zagrapan*	*Chicoutimi*	*C*
14	WSH	*Sasha Pokulok*	*Cornell*	*D*
15	NYI	Ryan O'Marra	Erie	C
16	ATL	*Alex Bourret*	*Lewiston*	*RW*
17	PHX	Martin Hanzal	Ceske Budejovice	C
18	NSH	Ryan Parent	Guelph	D
19	DET	Jakub Kindl	Kitchener	D
20	FLA	Kenndal McArdle	Moose Jaw	LW
21	TOR	Tuukka Rask	Ilves Jr.	G
22	BOS	Matt Lashoff	Kitchener	D
23	N.J.	Nicklas Bergfors	Sodertalje	RW
24	STL	T.J. Oshie	Warroad	C
25	EDM	Andrew Cogliano	St. Mike's Jr. A	C
26	CGY	Matt Pelech	Sarnia	D
27	WSH	Joe Finley	Sioux Falls	D
28	DAL	Matt Niskanen	Virginia	D
29	PHI	Steve Downie	Windsor	RW
30	T.B.	Vladimir Mihalik	Presov	D

OTHER NOTABLE SELECTIONS

Pick	Claimed by	Amateur Club	Position
33	DAL	James Neal	Plymouth	LW
35	S.J.	Marc-Edouard Vlasic	Quebec	D
41	ATL	Ondrej Pavelec	Poldi Kladno Jr.	G
42	DET	Justin Abdelkader	Cedar Rapids	LW
44	COL	Paul Stastny	U. of Denver	C
45	MTL	Guillaume Latendresse	Drummondville	RW
51	VAN	Mason Raymond	Camrose	LW
55	CBJ	Adam McQuaid	Sudbury	D
62	PIT	Kris Letang	Val d'Or	D
67	CBJ	Kris Russell	Medicine Hat	D
72	L.A.	Jonathan Quick	Avon Old Farms	G
85	STL	Ben Bishop	Texas	G
105	PHX	Keith Yandle	Cushing Academy	D
108	CHI	Niklas Hjalmarsson	HV 71 Jonkoping	D
230	NSH	Patric Hornqvist	Vasby	RW

2004

FIRST ROUND

Pick	Claimed by	Amateur Club	Position
1	WSH	Alex Ovechkin	Dynamo Moscow	LW
2	PIT	Evgeni Malkin	Magnitogorsk	C
3	CHI	Cam Barker	Medicine Hat	D
4	CAR	Andrew Ladd	Calgary	LW
5	PHX	Blake Wheeler	Breck	RW
6	NYR	Al Montoya	U. of Michigan	G
7	FLA	Rostislav Olesz	Vitkovice	C
8	CBJ	Alexandre Picard	Lewiston	LW
9	ANA	Ladislav Smid	Liberec	D
10	ATL	Boris Valabik	Kitchener	D
11	L.A.	Lauri Tukonen	Blues Espoo	RW
12	MIN	*A.J. Thelen*	*Michigan State*	*D*
13	BUF	Drew Stafford	U. of North Dakota	RW
14	EDM	Devan Dubnyk	Kamloops	G
15	NSH	Alexander Radulov	Tver	LW
16	NYI	Petteri Nokelainen	SaiPa	C
17	STL	Marek Schwarz	Sparta Praha	G
18	MTL	Kyle Chipchura	Prince Albert	C
19	NYR	Lauri Korpikoski	TPS Turku Jr.	LW
20	N.J.	Travis Zajac	Salmon Arm	C
21	COL	Wojtek Wolski	Brampton	LW
22	S.J.	Lukas Kaspar	Litvinov	RW
23	OTT	Andrej Meszaros	Trencin	D
24	CGY	Kris Chucko	Salmon Arm	LW
25	EDM	Rob Schremp	London	C
26	VAN	Cory Schneider	Phillips-Andover	G
27	WSH	Jeff Schultz	Calgary	D
28	DAL	Mark Fistric	Vancouver	D
29	WSH	Mike Green	Saskatoon	D
30	T.B.	*Andy Rogers*	*Calgary*	*D*

OTHER NOTABLE SELECTIONS

Pick	Claimed by	Amateur Club	Position
32	CHI	Dave Bolland	London	C
47	NYI	Blake Comeau	Kelowna	LW
53	FLA	David Booth	Michigan State	LW
56	DAL	Nicklas Grossmann	Sodertalje	D
60	NYR	Brandon Dubinsky	Portland	C
63	BOS	David Krejci	Kladno Jr.	C
70	CGY	Brandon Prust	London	LW
71	BUF	Andrej Sekera	Trencin	D
91	VAN	Alexander Edler	Jamtland	D
97	DET	Johan Franzen	Linkoping	C
127	NYR	Ryan Callahan	Guelph	RW
134	BOS	Kris Versteeg	Lethbridge	RW
150	MTL	Mikhail Grabovski	Nizhnekamsk	C
180	STL	Roman Polak	Vitkovice Jr.	D
214	DET	Troy Brouwer	Moose Jaw	RW
227	NYI	Chris Campoli	Erie	D
258	NSH	Pekka Rinne	Karpat	G
262	MTL	Mark Streit	Zurich	D
265	PHX	Daniel Winnik	New Hampshire	D

Pick	Claimed by	Amateur Club	Position

2003

FIRST ROUND

Pick	Claimed by	Name	Amateur Club	Position
1	PIT	Marc-Andre Fleury	Cape Breton	G
2	CAR	Eric Staal	Peterborough	C
3	FLA	Nathan Horton	Oshawa	C
4	CBJ	Nikolai Zherdev	CSKA Moscow	W
5	BUF	Thomas Vanek	U. of Minnesota	LW
6	S.J.	Milan Michalek	Budejovice	RW
7	NSH	Ryan Suter	USA U-18	D
8	ATL	Braydon Coburn	Portland	D
9	CGY	Dion Phaneuf	Red Deer	D
10	MTL	Andrei Kostitsyn	CSKA 2	RW
11	PHI	Jeff Carter	Sault Ste. Marie	C
12	NYR	Hugh Jessiman	Dartmouth	RW
13	L.A.	Dustin Brown	Guelph	RW
14	CHI	Brent Seabrook	Lethbridge	D
15	NYI	Robert Nilsson	Leksand	C
16	S.J.	Steve Bernier	Moncton	RW
17	N.J.	Zach Parise	North Dakota	C
18	WSH	Eric Fehr	Brandon	RW
19	ANA	Ryan Getzlaf	Calgary	C
20	MIN	Brent Burns	Brampton	RW
21	BOS	Mark Stuart	Colorado College	D
22	EDM	Marc-Antoine Pouliot	Rimouski	C
23	VAN	Ryan Kesler	Ohio State	C
24	PHI	Mike Richards	Kitchener	C
25	FLA	Anthony Stewart	Kingston	C
26	L.A.	Brian Boyle	St. Sebastian's H.S.	C
27	L.A.	Jeff Tambellini	U. of Michigan	LW
28	ANA	Corey Perry	London	RW
29	OTT	Patrick Eaves	Boston College	RW
30	STL	Shawn Belle	Tri-City	D

OTHER NOTABLE SELECTIONS

Pick	Claimed by	Name	Amateur Club	Position
33	DAL	Loui Eriksson	Vastra Frolunda Jr.	LW
37	NSH	Kevin Klein	St. Michael's	D
45	BOS	Patrice Bergeron	Acadie-Bathurst	C
47	S.J.	Matt Carle	River City	D
49	NSH	Shea Weber	Kelowna	D
52	CHI	Corey Crawford	Moncton	G
61	MTL	Maxim Lapierre	Montreal	C
62	STL	David Backes	Lincoln	C
64	DET	Jimmy Howard	U. of Maine	G
205	S.J.	Joe Pavelski	Waterloo Jr. A	C
214	EDM	Kyle Brodziak	Moose Jaw	C
239	ATL	Tobias Enstrom	MODO Ornskolsvik	D
245	CHI	Dustin Byfuglien	Prince George	RW
263	PIT	Matt Moulson	Cornell	C
271	MTL	Jaroslav Halak	Bratislava Jr.	G
291	OTT	Brian Elliott	Ajax	G

2002

FIRST ROUND

Pick	Claimed by	Name	Amateur Club	Position
1	CBJ	Rick Nash	London	LW
2	ATL	Kari Lehtonen	Jokerit	G
3	FLA	Jay Bouwmeester	Medicine Hat	D
4	PHI	Joni Pitkanen	Karpat	D
5	PIT	Ryan Whitney	Boston University	D
6	NSH	Scottie Upshall	Kamloops	RW
7	ANA	Joffrey Lupul	Medicine Hat.	C
8	MIN	Pierre-Marc Bouchard	Chicoutimi	C
9	FLA	Petr Taticek	Sault Ste. Marie	C
10	CGY	Eric Nystrom	U. of Michigan	LW
11	BUF	Keith Ballard	U. of Minnesota	D
12	WSH	Steve Eminger	Kitchener	D
13	WSH	Alexander Semin	Chelyabinsk	LW
14	MTL	Christopher Higgins	Yale	C
15	EDM	*Jesse Niinimaki*	*Ilves Tampere.*	*C*
16	OTT	Jakub Klepis	Portland	C
17	WSH	Boyd Gordon	Red Deer	RW
18	L.A.	Denis Grebeshkov	Yaroslavl	D
19	PHX	*Jakub Koreis*	*Plzen*	*C*
20	BUF	Dan Paille	Guelph	LW
21	CHI	Anton Babchuk	Elektrostal	D
22	NYI	Sean Bergenheim	Jokerit	C
23	PHX	Ben Eager	Oshawa	LW
24	TOR	Alexander Steen	Vastra Frolunda	C
25	CAR	Cam Ward	Red Deer	G
26	DAL	*Martin Vagner*	*Hull*	*D*
27	S.J.	*Mike Morris*	*St. Sebastian's H.S.*	*RW*
28	COL	Jonas Johansson	HV 71 Jonkoping Jr.	RW
29	NSH	Hannu Toivonen	HPK Jr.	G
30	ATL	Jim Slater	Michigan State	C

OTHER NOTABLE SELECTIONS

Pick	Claimed by	Name	Amateur Club	Position
36	EDM	Jarret Stoll	Kootenay	C
38	MIN	Josh Harding	Regina	G
43	DAL	Trevor Daley	Sault Ste. Marie	D
44	EDM	Matt Greene	Green Bay	D
54	CHI	Duncan Keith	Michigan State	D
57	TOR	Matt Stajan	Belleville	C
58	DET	Jiri Hudler	Vsetin	C
63	DET	Tomas Fleischmann	Vitkovice Jr.	LW
67	FLA	Gregory Campbell	Plymouth	LW
90	CGY	Matthew Lombardi	Victoriaville	C
95	DET	Valtteri Filppula	Jokerit Jr.	C
234	PIT	Maxime Talbot	Hull	C
241	BUF	Dennis Wideman	London	D
291	DET	Jonathan Ericsson	Hasten Jr.	D

2001

FIRST ROUND

Pick	Claimed by	Name	Amateur Club	Position
1	ATL	Ilya Kovalchuk	Spartak	LW
2	OTT	Jason Spezza	Windsor	C
3	T.B.	Alexander Svitov	Avangard Omsk	C
4	FLA	Stephen Weiss	Plymouth	C
5	ANA	Stanislav Chistov	Avangard Omsk	LW
6	MIN	Mikko Koivu	TPS Turku	C
7	MTL	Mike Komisarek	U. of Michigan	D
8	CBJ	Pascal Leclaire	Halifax	G
9	CHI	Tuomo Ruutu	Jokerit	C/LW
10	NYR	Dan Blackburn	Kootenay	G
11	PHX	Fredrik Sjostrom	Vastra Frolunda	RW
12	NSH	Dan Hamhuis	Prince George	D
13	EDM	Ales Hemsky	Hull	RW
14	CGY	Chuck Kobasew	Boston College	C
15	CAR	*Igor Knyazev*	*Spartak*	*D*
16	VAN	R.J. Umberger	Ohio State	C
17	TOR	Carlo Colaiacovo	Erie	D
18	L.A.	*Jens Karlsson*	*Vastra Frolunda*	*RW*
19	BOS	Shaone Morrisonn	Kamloops	D
20	S.J.	Marcel Goc	Schwenningen	C
21	PIT	Colby Armstrong	Red Deer	RW
22	BUF	Jiri Novotny	Budejovice	C
23	OTT	Tim Gleason	Windsor	D
24	FLA	Lukas Krajicek	Peterborough	D
25	MTL	Alexander Perezhogin	Avangard Omsk	C
26	DAL	Jason Bacashihua	Chicago Freeze	G
27	PHI	Jeff Woywitka	Red Deer	D
28	N.J.	*Adrian Foster*	*Saskatoon*	*C*
29	CHI	Adam Munro	Erie	G
30	L.A.	Dave Steckel	Ohio State	C

OTHER NOTABLE SELECTIONS

Pick	Claimed by	Name	Amateur Club	Position
33	BUF	Derek Roy	Kitchener	C
40	NYR	Fedor Tyutin	St. Petersburg	D
49	L.A.	Michael Cammalleri	U. of Michigan	C
55	BUF	Jason Pominville	Shawinigan	RW
71	MTL	Tomas Plekanec	Kladno	LW
73	CHI	Craig Anderson	Guelph	G
95	PHI	Patrick Sharp	U. of Vermont	C
98	NSH	Jordin Tootoo	Brandon	RW
99	OTT	Ray Emery	Sault Ste. Marie	G
106	S.J.	Christoph Ehrhoff	Krefeld	D
151	VAN	Kevin Bieksa	Bowling Green	D
161	DAL	Mike Smith	Sudbury	G
172	PHI	Dennis Seidenberg	Mannheim	D
176	NYR	Marek Zidlicky	HIFK Helsinki	D
192	DAL	Jussi Jokinen	Karpat Jr.	F
193	OTT	Brooks Laich	Moose Jaw	C
221	WSH	Johnny Oduya	Victoriaville	D
241	BOS	Milan Jurcina	Halifax	D
264	ANA	P-A Parenteau	Chicoutimi	C

2000

FIRST ROUND

Pick	Claimed by	Name	Amateur Club	Position
1	NYI	Rick DiPietro	Boston University	G
2	ATL	Dany Heatley	U. of Wisconsin	RW
3	MIN	Marian Gaborik	Dukla Trencin	RW
4	CBJ	Rostislav Klesla	Brampton	D
5	NYI	Raffi Torres	Brampton	LW
6	NSH	Scott Hartnell	Prince Albert	LW
7	BOS	Lars Jonsson	Leksand	D
8	T.B.	Nikita Alexeev	Erie	RW
9	CGY	Brent Krahn	Calgary	G
10	CHI	Mikhail Yakubov	Lada Togliatti	C
11	CHI	Pavel Vorobiev	Yaroslavl	RW
12	ANA	Alexei Smirnov	Tver	LW
13	MTL	Ron Hainsey	U. of Mass-Lowell	D
14	COL	Vaclav Nedorost	Budejovice	C
15	BUF	*Artem Kryukov*	*Yaroslavl*	*C*
16	MTL	Marcel Hossa	Portland	LW
17	EDM	Alexei Mikhnov	Yaroslavl	LW
18	PIT	Brooks Orpik	Boston College	D
19	PHX	Krys Kolanos	Boston College	C
20	L.A.	Alexander Frolov	Yaroslavl 2	LW
21	OTT	Anton Volchenkov	HK Moscow	D
22	N.J.	David Hale	Sioux City	D
23	VAN	Nathan Smith	Swift Current	C
24	TOR	Brad Boyes	Erie	C
25	DAL	Steve Ott	Windsor	C
26	WSH	Brian Sutherby	Moose Jaw	C
27	BOS	Martin Samuelsson	MoDo Ornskoldsvik	RW
28	PHI	Justin Williams	Plymouth	RW
29	DET	Niklas Kronwall	Djurgarden	D
30	STL	Jeff Taffe	U. of Minnesota	C

OTHER NOTABLE SELECTIONS

Pick	Claimed by	Name	Amateur Club	Position
33	MIN	Nick Schultz	Prince Albert	D
44	ANA	Ilya Bryzgalov	Lada Togliatti	G
46	CGY	Jarret Stoll	Kootenay	C
55	OTT	Antoine Vermette	Victoriaville	C
60	DAL	Dan Ellis	Omaha	G
62	N.J.	Paul Martin	Elk River H.S.	D
118	L.A.	Lubomir Visnovsky	Bratislava	D
155	CGY	Travis Moen	Kelowna	LW
159	COL	John-Michael Liles	Michigan State	D
205	NYR	Henrik Lundqvist	Vastre Frolunda Jr.	G
215	BUF	Matthew Lombardi	Victoriaville	C

Seen here during the Canadian Hockey League's Top Prospects Game in 2003, Marc-Andre Fleury was the top pick in the 2003 Draft. After 13 seasons with the Pittsburgh Penguins, he was selected by Vegas in the 2017 Expansion Draft.

Pick	Claimed by	Amateur Club	Position

1999

FIRST ROUND

Pick	Claimed by	Amateur Club	Position
1	ATL	Patrik Stefan	Long Beach	C
2	VAN	Daniel Sedin	MoDo Ornskoldsvik	LW
3	VAN	Henrik Sedin	MoDo Ornskoldsvik	C
4	NYR	Pavel Brendl	Calgary	RW
5	NYI	Tim Connolly	Erie	C
6	NSH	Brian Finley	Barrie	G
7	WSH	Kris Beech	Calgary	C
8	NYI	Taylor Pyatt	Sudbury	LW
9	NYR	Jamie Lundmark	Moose Jaw	C
10	NYI	Branislav Mezei	Belleville	D
11	CGY	Oleg Saprykin	Seattle	LW
12	FLA	Denis Shvidki	Barrie	RW
13	EDM	Jani Rita	Jokerit	LW
14	S.J.	Jeff Jillson	U. of Michigan	D
15	*PHX*	*Scott Kelman*	*Seattle*	*C*
16	CAR	David Tanabe	U. of Wisconsin	D
17	STL	Barret Jackman	Regina	D
18	PIT	Konstantin Koltsov	Cherepovets	RW
19	PHX	Kirill Safronov	St. Petersburg	D
20	BUF	Barrett Heisten	U. of Maine	LW
21	BOS	Nick Boynton	Ottawa	D
22	PHI	Maxime Ouellet	Quebec	G
23	CHI	Steve McCarthy	Kootenay	D
24	*TOR*	*Luca Cereda*	*Ambri*	*C*
25	COL	Mikhail Kuleshov	Cherepovets	LW
26	OTT	Martin Havlat	Trinec	LW
27	*N.J.*	*Ari Ahonen*	*JyP HT Jr.*	*G*
28	NYI	Kristian Kudroc	Michalovce	D

OTHER NOTABLE SELECTIONS

Pick	Claimed by	Amateur Club	Position
44	ANA	Jordan Leopold	U. of Minnesota	D
91	EDM	Mike Comrie	U. of Michigan	C
94	OTT	Chris Kelly	London	C
115	PIT	Ryan Malone	Omaha	LW
138	BUF	Ryan Miller	Soo	G
165	CHI	Michael Leighton	Windsor	G
191	NSH	Martin Erat	ZPS Zlin Jr.	LW
210	DET	Henrik Zetterberg	Timra	LW
212	COL	Radim Vrbata	Hull	RW

1998

FIRST ROUND

Pick	Claimed by	Amateur Club	Position
1	T.B.	Vincent Lecavalier	Rimouski	C
2	NSH	David Legwand	Plymouth	C
3	S.J.	Brad Stuart	Regina	D
4	VAN	Bryan Allen	Oshawa	D
5	ANA	Vitaly Vishnevski	Yaroslavl 2	D
6	CGY	Rico Fata	London	RW
7	NYR	Manny Malhotra	Guelph	C
8	CHI	Mark Bell	Ottawa	C
9	NYI	Mike Rupp	Erie	RW
10	TOR	Nik Antropov	Ust-Kamenogorsk	C
11	CAR	Jeff Heerema	Sarnia	RW
12	COL	Alex Tanguay	Halifax	LW
13	*EDM*	*Michael Henrich*	*Barrie*	*RW*
14	PHX	Patrick DesRochers	Sarnia	G
15	OTT	Mathieu Chouinard	Shawinigan	G
16	MTL	Eric Chouinard	Quebec	LW
17	COL	Martin Skoula	Barrie	D
18	BUF	Dmitri Kalinin	Chelyabinsk	D
19	COL	Robyn Regehr	Kamloops	D
20	COL	Scott Parker	Kelowna	RW
21	L.A.	Mathieu Biron	Shawinigan	D
22	PHI	Simon Gagne	Quebec	LW
23	PIT	Milan Kraft	Keramika Plzen Jr.	C
24	STL	Christian Backman	Vastra Frolunda Jr.	D
25	DET	Jiri Fischer	Hull	D
26	N.J.	Mike Van Ryn	U. of Michigan	D
27	N.J.	Scott Gomez	Tri-City	C

OTHER NOTABLE SELECTIONS

Pick	Claimed by	Amateur Club	Position
29	S.J.	Jonathan Cheechoo	Belleville	RW
44	OTT	Mike Fisher	Sudbury	C
45	MTL	Mike Ribeiro	Rouyn-Noranda	C
64	T.B.	Brad Richards	Rimouski	C
68	VAN	Jarkko Ruutu	HIFK Helsinki	RW
71	CAR	Erik Cole	Clarkson	LW
75	MTL	Francois Beauchemin	Laval	D
82	N.J.	Brian Gionta	Boston College	RW
99	EDM	Shawn Horcoff	Michigan State	C
117	FLA	Jaroslav Spacek	Farjestad	D
134	PIT	Rob Scuderi	Boston College	D
145	S.J.	Mikael Samuelsson	Sodertalje	LW
161	OTT	Chris Neil	North Bay	RW
162	MTL	Andrei Markov	Khimik Voskresensk	D
164	BUF	Ales Kotalik	Ceske Budejovice Jr.	RW
171	DET	Pavel Datsyuk	Yekaterinburg	C
216	MTL	Michael Ryder	Hull	RW
230	NSH	Karlis Skrastins	TPS Turku	D

Stanley Cup champions with Tampa Bay and World Cup champions with Canada in 2004, Vincent Lecavalier (left) had been the first pick in the 1998 NHL Draft. The Lightning picked up Brad Richards (center) with the 64th pick that year. Martin St. Louis was never drafted.

1997

FIRST ROUND

Pick	Claimed by	Amateur Club	Position
1	BOS	Joe Thornton	Sault Ste. Marie	C
2	S.J.	Patrick Marleau	Seattle	C
3	L.A.	Olli Jokinen	HIFK Helsinki	C
4	NYI	Roberto Luongo	Val-d'Or	G
5	NYI	Eric Brewer	Prince George	D
6	CGY	Daniel Tkaczuk	Barrie	C
7	T.B.	Paul Mara	Sudbury	D
8	BOS	Sergei Samsonov	Detroit	LW
9	WSH	Nick Boynton	Ottawa	D
10	VAN	Brad Ference	Spokane	D
11	MTL	Jason Ward	Erie	RW
12	OTT	Marian Hossa	Dukla Trencin	RW
13	CHI	Daniel Cleary	Belleville	RW
14	EDM	Michel Riesen	Biel-Bienne	RW
15	*L.A.*	*Matt Zultek*	*Ottawa*	*LW*
16	CHI	Ty Jones	Spokane	RW
17	PIT	Robert Dome	Las Vegas (IHL)	RW
18	ANA	Mikael Holmqvist	Djurgarden	C
19	*NYR*	*Stefan Cherneski*	*Brandon*	*RW*
20	FLA	Mike Brown	Red Deer	LW
21	BUF	Mika Noronen	Tappara Tampere	G
22	CAR	Nikos Tselios	Belleville	D
23	S.J.	Scott Hannan	Kelowna	D
24	N.J.	J-F Damphousse	Moncton	G
25	DAL	Brenden Morrow	Portland	LW
26	*COL*	*Kevin Grimes*	*Kingston*	*D*

OTHER NOTABLE SELECTIONS

Pick	Claimed by	Amateur Club	Position
47	FLA	Kristian Huselius	Farjestad	LW
48	BUF	Henrik Tallinder	AIK Solna	D
69	BUF	Maxim Afinogenov	Dynamo Moscow	RW
78	COL	Ville Nieminen	Tappara Tampere	RW
83	L.A.	Joe Corvo	U. of Western Michigan	D
121	EDM	Jason Chimera	Medicine Hat	LW
144	VAN	Matt Cooke	Windsor	C
156	BUF	Brian Campbell	Ottawa	D
177	STL	Ladislav Nagy	Dragon Presov	LW
190	TOR	Shawn Thornton	Peterborough	RW
208	PIT	Andrew Ference	Portland	D

1996

FIRST ROUND

Pick	Claimed by	Amateur Club	Position
1	OTT	Chris Phillips	Prince Albert	D
2	S.J.	Andrei Zyuzin	Salavat Yulayev Ufa	D
3	NYI	J.P. Dumont	Val-d'Or	RW
4	WSH	Alexandre Volchkov	Barrie	C
5	DAL	Ric Jackman	Sault Ste. Marie	D
6	EDM	Boyd Devereaux	Kitchener	C
7	BUF	Erik Rasmussen	U. of Minnesota	LW/C
8	BOS	Johnathan Aitken	Medicine Hat	D
9	ANA	Ruslan Salei	Las Vegas (IHL)	D
10	N.J.	Lance Ward	Red Deer	D
11	PHX	Dan Focht	Tri-City	D
12	VAN	Josh Holden	Regina	C
13	CGY	Derek Morris	Regina	D
14	STL	Marty Reasoner	Boston College	C
15	PHI	Dainius Zubrus	Pembroke Jr. A	RW
16	T.B.	Mario Larocque	Hull	D
17	WSH	Jaroslav Svejkovsky	Tri-City	RW
18	MTL	Matt Higgins	Moose Jaw	C
19	EDM	Matthieu Descoteaux	Shawinigan	D
20	FLA	Marcus Nilson	Djurgarden	LW
21	S.J.	Marco Sturm	Landshut	LW
22	*NYR*	*Jeff Brown*	*Sarnia*	*D*
23	*PIT*	*Craig Hillier*	*Ottawa*	*G*
24	PHX	Danny Briere	Drummondville	C
25	COL	Peter Ratchuk	Shattuck-St. Mary's	D
26	DET	Jesse Wallin	Red Deer	D

OTHER NOTABLE SELECTIONS

Pick	Claimed by	Amateur Club	Position
27	BUF	Cory Sarich	Saskatoon	D
35	ANA	Matt Cullen	St. Cloud State	C
49	N.J.	Colin White	Hull	D
56	NYI	Zdeno Chara	Dukla Trencin	D
59	EDM	Tom Poti	Cushing Academy	D
79	COL	Mark Parrish	St. Cloud State	RW
89	CGY	Toni Lydman	Reipas Lahti	D
96	L.A.	Eric Belanger	Beauport	C
176	COL	Samuel Pahlsson	MoDo Ornskoldsvik	C
179	T.B.	Pavel Kubina	Vitkovice	D
199	N.J.	Willie Mitchell	Melfort Jr. A	D
204	TOR	Tomas Kaberle	Kladno	D
223	HFD	Craig Adams	Harvard	RW
239	OTT	Sami Salo	TPS Turku	D

Pick	Claimed by	Amateur Club	Position

1995

FIRST ROUND

Pick	Claimed by	Amateur Club	Position
1 OTT	Bryan Berard	Detroit	D
2 NYI	Wade Redden	Brandon	D
3 L.A.	Aki Berg	Kiekko-67 Turku	D
4 ANA	Chad Kilger	Kingston	C
5 T.B.	Daymond Langkow	Tri-City	C
6 EDM	Steve Kelly	Prince Albert	C
7 WPG	Shane Doan	Kamloops	RW
8 MTL	Terry Ryan	Tri-City	LW
9 BOS	Kyle McLaren	Tacoma	D
10 FLA	Radek Dvorak	Ceske Budejovice	RW
11 DAL	Jarome Iginla	Kamloops	RW
12 S.J.	*Teemu Riihijarvi*	*Kiekko-Espoo*	*LW*
13 HFD	Jean-Sebastien Giguere	Halifax	G
14 BUF	Jay McKee	Niagara Falls	D
15 TOR	Jeff Ware	Oshawa	D
16 BUF	Martin Biron	Beauport	G
17 WSH	Brad Church	Prince Albert	LW
18 N.J.	Petr Sykora	Detroit	RW
19 CHI	Dmitri Nabokov	Krylja Sovetov	C/LW
20 CGY	Denis Gauthier	Drummondville	D
21 BOS	Sean Brown	Belleville	D
22 PHI	Brian Boucher	Tri-City	G
23 WSH	Miika Elomo	Kiekko-67 Turku	LW
24 PIT	Aleksey Morozov	Krylja Sovetov	RW
25 COL	Marc Denis	Chicoutimi	G
26 DET	Maxim Kuznetsov	Dynamo Moscow	D

OTHER NOTABLE SELECTIONS

Pick	Claimed by	Amateur Club	Position
31 EDM	Georges Laraque	St-Jean	RW
49 STL	Jochen Hecht	Mannheim	C
67 WPG	Brad Isbister	Portland	LW
79 N.J.	Alyn McCauley	Ottawa	C
87 HFD	Sami Kapanen	HIFK Helsinki	RW
90 S.J.	Vesa Toskala	Ilves Tampere	G
91 NYR	Marc Savard	Oshawa	C
101 STL	Michal Handzus	Banska Bystrica	C
116 S.J.	Miikka Kiprusoff	TPS Turku Jr.	G
122 N.J.	Chris Mason	Prince George	G
144 VAN	Brent Sopel	Swift Current	D
164 MTL	Stephane Robidas	Shawinigan	D
177 BOS	P.J. Axelsson	Vastra Frolunda	LW
192 FLA	Filip Kuba	Vitkovice Jr.	D
223 TOR	Danny Markov	Moscow Spartak	D

1994

FIRST ROUND

Pick	Claimed by	Amateur Club	Position
1 FLA	Ed Jovanovski	Windsor	D
2 ANA	Oleg Tverdovsky	Krylja Sovetov	D
3 OTT	Radek Bonk	Las Vegas (IHL)	C
4 EDM	Jason Bonsignore	Niagara Falls	C
5 HFD	Jeff O'Neill	Guelph	RW
6 EDM	Ryan Smyth	Moose Jaw	LW
7 L.A.	Jamie Storr	Owen Sound	G
8 T.B.	Jason Wiemer	Portland	C
9 NYI	Brett Lindros	Kingston	RW
10 WSH	Nolan Baumgartner	Kamloops	D
11 S.J.	Jeff Friesen	Regina	LW
12 QUE	Wade Belak	Saskatoon	D/RW
13 VAN	Mattias Ohlund	Pitea	D
14 CHI	Ethan Moreau	Niagara Falls	LW
15 WSH	*Alexander Kharlamov*	*CSKA Moscow*	*C*
16 TOR	Eric Fichaud	Chictoutimi	G
17 BUF	Wayne Primeau	Owen Sound	C
18 MTL	Brad Brown	North Bay	D
19 CGY	Chris Dingman	Brandon	LW
20 DAL	Jason Botterill	U. of Michigan	LW
21 BOS	*Evgeni Ryabchikov*	*Molot Perm*	*G*
22 QUE	*Jeffrey Kealty*	*Catholic Memorial H.S.*	*D*
23 DET	Yan Golubovsky	Dynamo 2	D
24 PIT	Chris Wells	Seattle	C
25 N.J.	Vadim Sharifijanov	Salavat Yulayev Ufa	LW
26 NYR	Dan Cloutier	Sault Ste. Marie	G

OTHER NOTABLE SELECTIONS

Pick	Claimed by	Amateur Club	Position
29 OTT	Stan Neckar	Ceske Budejovice	D
44 MTL	Jose Theodore	St-Jean	G
49 DET	Mathieu Dandenault	Sherbrooke	RW/D
50 PIT	Richard Park	Belleville	C
51 N.J.	Patrik Elias	Kladno	C
64 TOR	Fredrik Modin	Timra	LW
71 N.J.	Sheldon Souray	Tri-City	D
72 QUE	Chris Drury	Fairfield Prep	C
87 QUE	Milan Hejduk	Pardubice	RW
90 NYI	Brad Lukowich	Kamloops	D
124 DAL	Marty Turco	Cambridge Jr. A	G
133 OTT	Daniel Alfredsson	Vastra Frolunda	RW
217 QUE	Tim Thomas	U. of Vermont	G
218 PHI	Johan Hedberg	Leksand	G
219 S.J.	Evgeni Nabokov	Ust-Kamenogorsk	G
226 MTL	Tomas Vokoun	Kladno	G
233 N.J.	Steve Sullivan	Sault Ste. Marie	RW
249 WSH	Richard Zednik	Banska Bystricia	LW
257 DET	Tomas Holmstrom	Bodens IK	LW
286 NYR	Kim Johnsson	Malmo	D

1993

FIRST ROUND

Pick	Claimed by	Amateur Club	Position
1 OTT	Alexandre Daigle	Victoriaville	C
2 HFD	Chris Pronger	Peterborough	D
3 T.B.	Chris Gratton	Kingston	C
4 ANA	Paul Kariya	U. of Maine	LW
5 FLA	Rob Niedermayer	Medicine Hat	C
6 S.J.	Viktor Kozlov	Dynamo Moscow	C
7 EDM	Jason Arnott	Oshawa	C
8 NYR	Niklas Sundstrom	MoDo Ornskoldsvik	RW
9 DAL	Todd Harvey	Detroit	RW/C
10 QUE	Jocelyn Thibault	Sherbrooke	G
11 WSH	Brendan Witt	Seattle	D
12 TOR	Kenny Jonsson	Rogle Angelholm	D
13 N.J.	Denis Pederson	Prince Albert	C/RW
14 QUE	Adam Deadmarsh	Portland	RW
15 WPG	Mats Lindgren	Skelleftea	C/LW
16 EDM	Nick Stajduhar	London	D
17 WSH	Jason Allison	London	C
18 CGY	*Jesper Mattsson*	*Malmo*	*C*
19 TOR	Landon Wilson	Dubuque	RW
20 VAN	Mike Wilson	Sudbury	D
21 MTL	Saku Koivu	TPS Turku	C
22 DET	Anders Eriksson	MoDo Ornskoldsvik	D
23 NYI	Todd Bertuzzi	Guelph	RW
24 CHI	*Eric Lecompte*	*Hull*	*LW*
25 BOS	Kevyn Adams	Miami of Ohio	C
26 PIT	Stefan Bergkvist	Leksand	D

OTHER NOTABLE SELECTIONS

Pick	Claimed by	Amateur Club	Position
32 N.J.	Jay Pandolfo	Boston University	LW
35 DAL	Jamie Langenbrunner	Cloquet	C
39 N.J.	Brendan Morrison	Spokane	D
40 NYI	Bryan McCabe	Spokane	D
41 FLA	Kevin Weekes	Owen Sound	G
71 PHI	Vinny Prospal	Ceske Budejovice	C
72 HFD	Marek Malik	Vitkovice	D
89 STL	Jamal Myers	Western Mich.	RW
90 CHI	Eric Daze	Beauport	RW
111 EDM	Miroslav Satan	Dukla Trencin	LW
118 NYI	Tommy Salo	Vasteras	G
124 VAN	Scott Walker	Owen Sound	RW
151 MTL	Darcy Tucker	Kamloops	C
156 PIT	Patrick Lalime	Shawinigan	G
164 NYR	Todd Marchant	Clarkson	C
174 WSH	Andrew Brunette	Owen Sound	LW
188 HFD	Manny Legace	Niagara Falls	G
207 BOS	Hal Gill	Nashoba H.S.	D
219 STL	Mike Grier	St. Sebastian's H.S.	RW
227 OTT	Pavol Demitra	Dukla Trencin	LW
250 L.A.	Kimmo Timonen	KalPa Kuopio	D

1992

FIRST ROUND

Pick	Claimed by	Amateur Club	Position
1 T.B.	Roman Hamrlik	ZPS Zlin	D
2 OTT	Alexei Yashin	Dynamo Moscow	C
3 S.J.	Mike Rathje	Medicine Hat	D
4 QUE	Todd Warriner	Windsor	LW
5 NYI	Darius Kasparaitis	Dynamo Moscow	D
6 CGY	Cory Stillman	Windsor	C
7 PHI	*Ryan Sittler*	*Nichols H.S.*	*LW*
8 TOR	Brandon Convery	Sudbury	C
9 HFD	Robert Petrovicky	Dukla Trencin	C
10 S.J.	Andrei Nazarov	Dynamo Moscow	LW
11 BUF	David Cooper	Medicine Hat	D
12 CHI	Sergei Krivokrasov	CSKA Moscow	RW
13 EDM	Joe Hulbig	St. Sebastian's H.S.	LW
14 WSH	Sergei Gonchar	Traktor Chelyabinsk	D
15 PHI	Jason Bowen	Tri-City	D
16 BOS	Dmitri Kvartalnov	San Diego (IHL)	LW
17 WPG	Sergei Bautin	Dynamo Moscow	D
18 N.J.	Jason Smith	Regina	D
19 PIT	Martin Straka	Skoda Plzen	C
20 MTL	David Wilkie	Kamloops	D
21 VAN	*Libor Polasek*	*Vitkovice*	*C*
22 DET	*Curtis Bowen*	*Ottawa*	*LW*
23 TOR	Grant Marshall	Ottawa	RW
24 NYR	Peter Ferraro	Waterloo Jr. A	LW

OTHER NOTABLE SELECTIONS

Pick	Claimed by	Amateur Club	Position
32 WSH	Jim Carey	Catholic Memorial	G
33 MTL	Valeri Bure	Spokane	RW
38 STL	Igor Korolev	Dynamo Moscow	C
40 VAN	Michael Peca	Ottawa	C
42 N.J.	Sergei Brylin	CSKA Moscow	C
46 DET	Darren McCarty	Belleville	RW
48 NYR	Mattias Norstrom	AIK Solna	D
52 QUE	Manny Fernandez	Laval	G
65 EDM	Kirk Maltby	Owen Sound	RW
68 MTL	Craig Rivet	Kingston	D
88 MIN	Jere Lehtinen	Kiekko-Espoo	RW
117 VAN	Adrian Aucoin	Boston University	D
158 STL	Ian Laperriere	Drummondville	C/RW
186 N.J.	Stephane Yelle	Oshawa	C
204 WPG	Nikolai Khabibulin	CSKA Moscow	G
220 QUE	Anson Carter	Wexford Jr. A	C

1991

FIRST ROUND

Pick	Claimed by	Amateur Club	Position
1 QUE	Eric Lindros	Oshawa	C
2 S.J.	Pat Falloon	Spokane	RW
3 N.J.	Scott Niedermayer	Kamloops	D
4 NYI	Scott Lachance	Boston University	D
5 WPG	Aaron Ward	U. of Michigan	D
6 PHI	Peter Forsberg	MoDo Ornskoldsvik	C
7 VAN	Alek Stojanov	Hamilton	RW
8 MIN	Richard Matvichuk	Saskatoon	D
9 HFD	Patrick Poulin	St-Hyacinthe	C
10 DET	Martin Lapointe	Laval	RW
11 N.J.	Brian Rolston	Det. Compuware Jr. A	C/RW
12 EDM	Tyler Wright	Swift Current	C
13 BUF	Philippe Boucher	Granby	D
14 WSH	Pat Peake	Detroit	C
15 NYR	Alex Kovalev	Dynamo Moscow	RW
16 PIT	Markus Naslund	MoDo Ornskoldsvik	LW
17 MTL	*Brent Bilodeau*	*Seattle*	*D*
18 BOS	Glen Murray	Sudbury	RW
19 CGY	Niklas Sundblad	AIK Solna	RW
20 EDM	Martin Rucinsky	Litvinov	LW
21 WSH	Trevor Halverson	North Bay	LW
22 CHI	Dean McAmmond	Prince Albert	LW

OTHER NOTABLE SELECTIONS

Pick	Claimed by	Amateur Club	Position
23 S.J.	Ray Whitney	Spokane	LW
26 NYI	Ziggy Palffy	AC Nitra	RW
27 STL	Steve Staios	Niagara Falls	D
30 S.J.	Sandis Ozolinsh	Dynamo Riga	D
40 BOS	Jozef Stumpel	AC Nitra	C
47 TOR	Yanic Perreault	Trois-Rivieres	C
54 DET	Chris Osgood	Medicine Hat	G
58 WSH	Steve Konowalchuk	Portland	LW
59 HFD	Michael Nylander	Huddinge	C
76 DET	Mike Knuble	Kalamazoo Jr. A	RW
81 L.A.	Alexei Zhitnik	Sokol Kiev	D
106 BOS	Mariusz Czerkawski	GKS Tychy	RW
122 PHI	Dmitry Yushkevich	Yaroslavl	D
123 BUF	Sean O'Donnell	Sudbury	D
171 MTL	Brian Savage	Miami of Ohio	LW
203 WPG	Igor Ulanov	Khimik Voskresensk	D

Kim Johnsson was the last player selected, 286th overall, in the 1994 NHL Draft. He made his NHL debut with the New York Rangers in 1999 and went on to play 739 games with four teams over 10 seasons.

Pick	Claimed by	Amateur Club	Position

1990

FIRST ROUND

Pick	Claimed by	Amateur Club	Position
1 QUE	Owen Nolan	Cornwall	RW
2 VAN	Petr Nedved	Seattle	C
3 DET	Keith Primeau	Niagara Falls	C
4 PHI	Mike Ricci	Peterborough	C
5 PIT	Jaromir Jagr	Kladno	RW
6 NYI	Scott Scissons	Saskatoon	C
7 L.A.	Darryl Sydor	Kamloops	D
8 MIN	Derian Hatcher	North Bay	D
9 WSH	John Slaney	Cornwall	D
10 TOR	Drake Berehowsky	Kingston	D
11 CGY	Trevor Kidd	Brandon	G
12 MTL	Turner Stevenson	Seattle	RW
13 NYR	*Michael Stewart*	*Michigan State*	*D*
14 BUF	Brad May	Niagara Falls	LW
15 HFD	Mark Greig	Lethbridge	RW
16 CHI	Karl Dykhuis	Hull	D
17 EDM	*Scott Allison*	*Prince Albert*	*C*
18 VAN	Shawn Antoski	North Bay	LW
19 WPG	Keith Tkachuk	Malden Catholic H.S.	LW
20 N.J.	Martin Brodeur	St-Hyacinthe	G
21 BOS	Bryan Smolinski	Michigan State	C

OTHER NOTABLE SELECTIONS

Pick	Claimed by	Amateur Club	Position
25 PHI	Chris Simon	Ottawa	LW
31 TOR	Felix Potvin	Chicoutimi	G
34 NYR	Doug Weight	Lake Superior State	C
36 HFD	Geoff Sanderson	Swift Current	LW
45 DET	Vyacheslav Kozlov	Khimik Voskresensk	RW
77 WPG	Alexei Zhamnov	Dynamo Moscow	C
85 NYR	Sergei Zubov	CSKA Moscow	D
113 MIN	Roman Turek	Plzen	G
123 MTL	Craig Conroy	Northwood Prep	C
133 L.A.	Robert Lang	CHZ Litvinov	C
156 WSH	Peter Bondra	Kosice	RW
158 QUE	Alexander Karpovtsev	VSZ Dynamo	D
177 WSH	Ken Klee	Bowling Green	D
244 NYR	Sergei Nemchinov	Krylja Sovetov	LW

1989

FIRST ROUND

Pick	Claimed by	Amateur Club	Position
1 QUE	Mats Sundin	Nacka	C
2 NYI	Dave Chyzowski	Kamloops	LW
3 TOR	Scott Thornton	Belleville	LW
4 WPG	Stu Barnes	Tri-City	C
5 N.J.	Bill Guerin	Springfield Jr. B	RW
6 CHI	Adam Bennett	Sudbury	D
7 MIN	Doug Zmolek	John Marshall H.S.	D
8 VAN	Jason Herter	North Dakota	D
9 STL	Jason Marshall	Vernon Jr. A.	D
10 HFD	Bobby Holik	Dukla Jihlava	C
11 DET	Mike Sillinger	Regina	C
12 TOR	Rob Pearson	Belleville	RW
13 MTL	Lindsay Vallis	Seattle	D
14 BUF	Kevin Haller	Regina	D
15 EDM	*Jason Soules*	*Niagara Falls*	*D*
16 PIT	Jamie Heward	Regina	D
17 BOS	Shayne Stevenson	Kitchener	RW
18 N.J.	Jason Miller	Medicine Hat	LW
19 WSH	Olaf Kolzig	Tri-City	G
20 NYR	Steven Rice	Kitchener	RW
21 TOR	Steve Bancroft	Belleville	D

OTHER NOTABLE SELECTIONS

Pick	Claimed by	Amateur Club	Position
22 QUE	Adam Foote	Sault Ste. Marie	D
23 NYI	Travis Green	Spokane	C
30 MTL	Patrice Brisebois	Laval	D
53 DET	Nicklas Lidstrom	Vasteras	D
62 WPG	Kris Draper	Canadian National	C
70 CGY	Robert Reichel	Litvinov	C
74 DET	Sergei Fedorov	CSKA Moscow	C
109 WPG	Dan Bylsma	Bowling Green	RW
113 VAN	Pavel Bure	CSKA Moscow	RW
116 DET	Dallas Drake	Northern Michigan	RW
183 BUF	Donald Audette	Laval	RW
191 NYI	Vladimir Malakhov	CSKA Moscow	D
196 MIN	Arturs Irbe	Dynamo Riga	G
221 DET	Vladimir Konstantinov	CSKA Moscow	D

1988

FIRST ROUND

Pick	Claimed by	Amateur Club	Position
1 MIN	Mike Modano	Prince Albert	C
2 VAN	Trevor Linden	Medicine Hat	RW
3 QUE	Curtis Leschyshyn	Saskatoon	D
4 PIT	Darrin Shannon	Windsor	LW
5 QUE	Daniel Dore	Drummondville	RW
6 TOR	Scott Pearson	Kingston	LW
7 L.A.	Martin Gelinas	Hull	LW
8 CHI	Jeremy Roenick	Thayer Academy	C
9 STL	Rod Brind'Amour	Notre Dame Jr. A.	C
10 WPG	Teemu Selanne	Jokerit	RW
11 HFD	Chris Govedaris	Toronto	LW
12 N.J.	Corey Foster	Peterborough	D
13 BUF	Joel Savage	Victoria	RW

Pick	Claimed by	Amateur Club	Position
14 PHI	Claude Boivin	Drummondville	LW
15 WSH	Reggie Savage	Victoriaville	C
16 NYI	*Kevin Cheveldayoff*	*Brandon*	*D*
17 DET	*Kory Kocur*	*Saskatoon*	*RW*
18 BOS	Rob Cimetta	Toronto	W
19 EDM	Francois Leroux	St-Jean	D
20 EDM	Eric Charron	Trois-Rivieres	D
21 CGY	Jason Muzzatti	Michigan State	G

OTHER NOTABLE SELECTIONS

Pick	Claimed by	Amateur Club	Position
27 TOR	Tie Domi	Peterborough	RW
67 PIT	Mark Recchi	Kamloops	RW
68 NYR	Tony Amonte	Thayer Academy	RW
70 L.A.	Rob Blake	Bowling Green	D
76 BUF	Keith Carney	Mount St. Charles H.S.	D
81 BOS	Joe Juneau	RPI	C
89 BUF	Alexander Mogilny	CSKA Moscow	RW
97 BUF	Rob Ray	Cornwall	RW
120 WSH	Dmitri Khristich	Kiev Sokol	RW
129 QUE	Valeri Kamensky	CSKA Moscow	D
198 STL	Bret Hedican	North St. Paul H.S.	D
234 QUE	Claude Lapointe	Laval	LW/C

1987

FIRST ROUND

Pick	Claimed by	Amateur Club	Position
1 BUF	Pierre Turgeon	Granby	C
2 N.J.	Brendan Shanahan	London	LW
3 BOS	Glen Wesley	Portland	D
4 L.A.	Wayne McBean	Medicine Hat	D
5 PIT	Chris Joseph	Seattle	D
6 MIN	Dave Archibald	Portland	C/LW
7 TOR	Luke Richardson	Peterborough	D
8 CHI	Jimmy Waite	Chicoutimi	G
9 QUE	Bryan Fogarty	Kingston	D
10 NYR	Jay More	New Westminster	D
11 DET	Yves Racine	Longueuil	D
12 STL	Keith Osborne	North Bay	RW
13 NYI	Dean Chynoweth	Medicine Hat	D
14 BOS	Stephane Quintal	Granby	D
15 QUE	Joe Sakic	Swift Current	C
16 WPG	Bryan Marchment	Belleville	D
17 MTL	Andrew Cassels	Ottawa	C
18 HFD	Jody Hull	Peterborough	RW
19 CGY	*Bryan Deasley*	*U. of Michigan*	*LW*
20 PHI	Darren Rumble	Kitchener	D
21 EDM	*Peter Soberlak*	*Swift Current*	*LW*

OTHER NOTABLE SELECTIONS

Pick	Claimed by	Amateur Club	Position
33 MTL	John LeClair	Bellows Academy	LW
38 MTL	Eric Desjardins	Granby	D
44 MTL	Mathieu Schneider	Cornwall	D
71 TOR	Joe Sacco	Medford H.S.	RW
110 PIT	Shawn McEachern	Matignon H.S.	RW
114 QUE	Garth Snow	Mount St. Charles H.S.	G
118 NYI	Rob DiMaio	Medicine Hat	RW
149 N.J.	Jim Dowd	Brick H.S.	C
166 CGY	Theoren Fleury	Moose Jaw	RW

1986

FIRST ROUND

Pick	Claimed by	Amateur Club	Position
1 DET	Joe Murphy	Michigan State	RW
2 L.A.	Jimmy Carson	Verdun	C
3 N.J.	Neil Brady	Medicine Hat	C
4 PIT	Zarley Zalapski	Canadian National	D
5 BUF	Shawn Anderson	Canadian National	D
6 TOR	Vincent Damphousse	Laval	C
7 VAN	Dan Woodley	Portland	RW
8 WPG	Pat Elynuik	Prince Albert	RW
9 NYR	Brian Leetch	Avon Old Farms H.S.	D
10 STL	Jocelyn Lemieux	Laval	RW
11 HFD	Scott Young	Boston University	RW
12 MIN	Warren Babe	Lethbridge	LW
13 BOS	Craig Janney	Boston College	C
14 CHI	Everett Sanipass	Verdun	LW
15 MTL	Mark Pederson	Medicine Hat	LW
16 CGY	*George Pelawa*	*Bemidji H.S.*	*RW*
17 NYI	Tom Fitzgerald	Austin Prep	RW
18 QUE	Ken McRae	Sudbury	C
19 WSH	Jeff Greenlaw	Canadian National	LW
20 PHI	Kerry Huffman	Guelph	D
21 EDM	Kim Issel	Prince Albert	RW

OTHER NOTABLE SELECTIONS

Pick	Claimed by	Amateur Club	Position
22 DET	Adam Graves	Windsor	LW
29 WPG	Teppo Numminen	Tappara Tampere	D
57 MTL	Jyrki Lumme	Ilves Tampere	D
67 PIT	Rob Brown	Kamloops	RW
72 NYR	Mark Janssens	Regina	C
81 QUE	Ron Tugnutt	Peterborough	G
85 DET	Johan Garpenlov	Nacka	LW
114 NYR	Darren Turcotte	North Bay	C
141 MTL	Lyle Odelein	Moose Jaw	D

1985

FIRST ROUND

Pick	Claimed by	Amateur Club	Position
1 TOR	Wendel Clark	Saskatoon	LW/D
2 PIT	Craig Simpson	Michigan State	LW
3 N.J.	Craig Wolanin	Kitchener	D
4 VAN	Jim Sandlak	London	RW
5 HFD	Dana Murzyn	Calgary	D
6 NYI	Brad Dalgarno	Hamilton	RW
7 NYR	Ulf Dahlen	Ostersund	LW
8 DET	Brent Fedyk	Regina	RW
9 L.A.	Craig Duncanson	Sudbury	LW
10 L.A.	Dan Gratton	Oshawa	C
11 CHI	Dave Manson	Prince Albert	D
12 MTL	Jose Charbonneau	Drummondville	RW
13 NYI	Derek King	Sault Ste. Marie	LW
14 BUF	Calle Johansson	Vastra Frolunda	D
15 QUE	David Latta	Kitchener	LW
16 MTL	Tom Chorske	Minneapolis SW H.S.	LW
17 CGY	*Chris Biotti*	*Belmont Hill H.S.*	*D*
18 WPG	Ryan Stewart	Kamloops	C
19 WSH	Yvon Corriveau	Toronto	LW
20 EDM	Scott Metcalfe	Kingston	LW
21 PHI	Glen Seabrooke	Peterborough	C

OTHER NOTABLE SELECTIONS

Pick	Claimed by	Amateur Club	Position
24 N.J.	Sean Burke	Toronto	G
27 CGY	Joe Nieuwendyk	Cornell	C
28 NYR	Mike Richter	Northwood Prep	G
32 N.J.	Eric Weinrich	North Yarmouth Academy	D
35 BUF	Benoit Hogue	St-Jean	C
50 DET	Steve Chiasson	Guelph	D
52 BOS	Bill Ranford	New Westminster	G
81 WPG	Fredrik Olausson	Farjestad	D
113 DET	Randy McKay	Michigan Tech	RW
157 BOS	Randy Burridge	Peterborough	LW
188 EDM	Kelly Buchberger	Moose Jaw	RW
189 PHI	Gord Murphy	Oshawa	D
214 VAN	Igor Larionov	CSKA Moscow	C

1984

FIRST ROUND

Pick	Claimed by		Amateur Club	Position
1	PIT	Mario Lemieux	Laval	C
2	N.J.	Kirk Muller	Guelph	LW
3	CHI	Eddie Olczyk	Team USA	C
4	TOR	Al Iafrate	Belleville	D
5	MTL	Petr Svoboda	CHZ Litvinov	D
6	L.A.	Craig Redmond	U. of Denver	D
7	DET	Shawn Burr	Kitchener	LW/C
8	MTL	Shayne Corson	Brantford	LW
9	PIT	Doug Bodger	Kamloops	D
10	VAN	J.J. Daigneault	Longueuil	D
11	HFD	Sylvain Cote	Quebec	D
12	CGY	Gary Roberts	Ottawa	LW
13	*MIN*	*David Quinn*	*Kent H.S.*	*D*
14	NYR	Terry Carkner	Peterborough	D
15	QUE	Trevor Stienburg	Guelph	RW
16	PIT	Roger Belanger	Kingston	C
17	WSH	Kevin Hatcher	North Bay	D
18	BUF	Mikael Andersson	Vastra Frolunda	LW
19	BOS	Dave Pasin	Prince Albert	RW
20	*NYI*	*Duncan MacPherson*	*Saskatoon*	*D*
21	EDM	Selmar Odelein	Regina	D

OTHER NOTABLE SELECTIONS

Pick	Claimed by		Amateur Club	Position
25	TOR	Todd Gill	Windsor	D
27	PHI	Scott Mellanby	Henry Carr Jr. B	RW
29	MTL	Stephane Richer	Granby	RW
36	QUE	Jeff Brown	Sudbury	D
51	MTL	Patrick Roy	Granby	G
59	WSH	Michal Pivonka	Czech Nationals	C
80	WSH	Kris King	Peterborough	LW
107	N.J.	Kirk McLean	Oshawa	G
117	CGY	Brett Hull	Penticton Jr. A	RW
119	NYR	Kjell Samuelsson	Leksand	D
166	BOS	Don Sweeney	St. Paul's H.S.	D
171	L.A.	Luc Robitaille	Hull	LW
180	CGY	Gary Suter	U. of Wisconsin	D

1983

FIRST ROUND

Pick	Claimed by		Amateur Club	Position
1	MIN	Brian Lawton	Mount St. Charles H.S.	LW
2	HFD	Sylvain Turgeon	Hull	LW
3	NYI	Pat LaFontaine	Verdun	C
4	DET	Steve Yzerman	Peterborough	C
5	BUF	Tom Barrasso	Acton-Boxborough	G
6	N.J.	John MacLean	Oshawa	RW
7	TOR	Russ Courtnall	Victoria	RW
8	WPG	Andrew McBain	North Bay	RW
9	VAN	Cam Neely	Portland	RW
10	BUF	Normand Lacombe	New Hampshire	RW
11	BUF	Adam Creighton	Ottawa	C
12	NYR	Dave Gagner	Brantford	C
13	CGY	Dan Quinn	Belleville	C
14	WPG	Bobby Dollas	Laval	D
15	PIT	Bob Errey	Peterborough	LW
16	NYI	Gerald Diduck	Lethbridge	D
17	MTL	Alfie Turcotte	Portland	C
18	CHI	Bruce Cassidy	Ottawa	D
19	EDM	Jeff Beukeboom	Sault Ste. Marie	D
20	HFD	David Jensen	Lawrence Academy	C
21	BOS	Nevin Markwart	Regina	LW

OTHER NOTABLE SELECTIONS

Pick	Claimed by		Amateur Club	Position
26	MTL	Claude Lemieux	Trois-Rivieres	RW
27	MTL	Sergio Momesso	Shawinigan	LW
41	PHI	Peter Zezel	Toronto	C
46	DET	Bob Probert	Brantford	LW
59	CHI	Marc Bergevin	Chicoutimi	D
82	EDM	Esa Tikkanen	HIFK Helsinki	LW
88	DET	Petr Klima	Dukla Jihlava	W
112	L.A.	Kevin Stevens	Silver Lake H.S.	LW
125	PHI	Rick Tocchet	Sault Ste. Marie	RW
139	BUF	Christian Ruuttu	Assat Pori	C
150	N.J.	Viacheslav Fetisov	CSKA Moscow	D
207	CHI	Dominik Hasek	Pardubice	G
223	BUF	Uwe Krupp	Koln	D
241	CGY	Sergei Makarov	CSKA Moscow	RW

Bob Probert (opposite) was selected 46th overall in the 1983 NHL Draft while Tie Domi (opposite, above) was picked 27th in 1988. Although not known as goal scorers, Probert recorded a career-high 29 goals in 1987-88 while Domi reached double digits on three occasions.

1982

FIRST ROUND

Pick	Claimed by		Amateur Club	Position
1	BOS	Gord Kluzak	Billings	D
2	MIN	Brian Bellows	Kitchener	LW
3	TOR	Gary Nylund	Portland	D
4	PHI	Ron Sutter	Lethbridge	C
5	WSH	Scott Stevens	Kitchener	D
6	BUF	Phil Housley	South St. Paul H.S.	D
7	CHI	Ken Yaremchuk	Portland	C
8	N.J.	Rocky Trottier	Nanaimo	RW
9	BUF	Paul Cyr	Victoria	LW
10	PIT	Rich Sutter	Lethbridge	RW
11	VAN	Michel Petit	Sherbrooke	D
12	WPG	Jim Kyte	Cornwall	D
13	QUE	David Shaw	Kitchener	D
14	HFD	Paul Lawless	Windsor	LW
15	NYR	Chris Kontos	Toronto	LW/C
16	BUF	Dave Andreychuk	Oshawa	LW
17	DET	Murray Craven	Medicine Hat	LW
18	N.J.	Ken Daneyko	Seattle	D
19	*MTL*	*Alain Heroux*	*Chicoutimi*	*LW*
20	EDM	Jim Playfair	Portland	D
21	NYI	Pat Flatley	U. of Wisconsin	RW

OTHER NOTABLE SELECTIONS

Pick	Claimed by		Amateur Club	Position
36	NYR	Tomas Sandstrom	Farjestad	RW
43	N.J.	Pat Verbeek	Sudbury	RW
45	TOR	Ken Wregget	Lethbridge	G
56	HFD	Kevin Dineen	U. of Denver	RW
67	HFD	Ulf Samuelsson	Leksand	D
75	WPG	Dave Ellett	Ottawa Jr. A.	D
80	MIN	Bob Rouse	Nanaimo	D
88	HFD	Ray Ferraro	Penticton Jr. A	C
119	PHI	Ron Hextall	Brandon	G
120	NYR	Tony Granato	Northwood Prep	RW
134	STL	Doug Gilmour	Cornwall	C
140	PHI	Dave Brown	Saskatoon	RW
183	NYR	Kelly Miller	Michigan State	LW

1981

FIRST ROUND

Pick	Claimed by		Amateur Club	Position
1	WPG	Dale Hawerchuk	Cornwall	C
2	L.A.	Doug Smith	Ottawa	C
3	WSH	Bob Carpenter	St. John's Prep	C
4	HFD	Ron Francis	Sault Ste. Marie	C
5	COL	Joe Cirella	Oshawa	D
6	TOR	Jim Benning	Portland	D
7	MTL	Mark Hunter	Brantford	RW
8	EDM	Grant Fuhr	Victoria	G
9	NYR	James Patrick	Prince Albert	D
10	VAN	Garth Butcher	Regina	D
11	QUE	Randy Moller	Lethbridge	D
12	CHI	Tony Tanti	Oshawa	RW
13	MIN	Ron Meighan	Niagara Falls	D
14	BOS	Normand Leveille	Chicoutimi	LW
15	CGY	Al MacInnis	Kitchener	D
16	PHI	Steve Smith	Sault Ste. Marie	D
17	*BUF*	*Jiri Dudacek*	*Kladno*	*RW*
18	MTL	Gilbert Delorme	Chicoutimi	D
19	*MTL*	*Jan Ingman*	*Farjestad*	*LW*
20	*STL*	*Marty Ruff*	*Lethbridge*	*D*
21	NYI	Paul Boutilier	Sherbrooke	D

OTHER NOTABLE SELECTIONS

Pick	Claimed by		Amateur Club	Position
22	WPG	Scott Arniel	Cornwall	LW
40	MTL	Chris Chelios	Moose Jaw	D
56	CGY	Mike Vernon	Calgary	G
72	NYR	John Vanbiesbrouck	Sault Ste. Marie	G
107	DET	Gerard Gallant	Sherbrooke	LW
108	COL	Bruce Driver	U. of Wisconsin	D
111	EDM	Steve Smith	London	D
145	MTL	Tom Kurvers	Minnesota-Duluth	D
152	WSH	Gaetan Duchesne	Quebec	LW

1980

FIRST ROUND

Pick	Claimed by		Amateur Club	Position
1	MTL	Doug Wickenheiser	Regina	C
2	WPG	Dave Babych	Portland	D
3	CHI	Denis Savard	Montreal	C
4	L.A.	Larry Murphy	Peterborough	D
5	WSH	Darren Veitch	Regina	D
6	EDM	Paul Coffey	Kitchener	D
7	VAN	Rick Lanz	Oshawa	D
8	HFD	Fred Arthur	Cornwall	D
9	PIT	Mike Bullard	Brantford	C
10	L.A.	Jim Fox	Ottawa	RW
11	DET	Mike Blaisdell	Regina	RW
12	STL	Rik Wilson	Kingston	D
13	CGY	Denis Cyr	Montreal	RW
14	*NYR*	*Jim Malone*	*Toronto*	*C*
15	CHI	Jerome Dupont	Toronto	D
16	MIN	Brad Palmer	Victoria	LW
17	NYI	Brent Sutter	Red Deer Jr. A	C
18	BOS	Barry Pederson	Victoria	C
19	COL	Paul Gagne	Windsor	LW
20	BUF	Steve Patrick	Brandon	RW
21	PHI	Mike Stothers	Kingston	D

OTHER NOTABLE SELECTIONS

Pick	Claimed by		Amateur Club	Position
37	MIN	Don Beaupre	Sudbury	G
38	NYI	Kelly Hrudey	Medicine Hat	G
57	CHI	Troy Murray	St. Albert Jr. A	C
61	MTL	Craig Ludwig	North Dakota	D
69	EDM	Jari Kurri	Jokerit	RW
73	L.A.	Bernie Nicholls	Kingston	C
80	NYI	Greg Gilbert	Toronto	LW
81	BOS	Steve Kasper	Verdun	C
106	COL	Aaron Broten	U. of Minnesota	LW/C
120	CHI	Steve Larmer	Niagara Falls	RW
124	MTL	Mike McPhee	RPI	LW
128	WPG	Brian Mullen	U.S. Jr. National	RW
132	EDM	Andy Moog	Billings	G
181	CGY	Hakan Loob	Farjestad	RW

1979

FIRST ROUND

Pick	Claimed by		Amateur Club	Position
1	COL	Rob Ramage	London	D
2	STL	Perry Turnbull	Portland	C
3	DET	Mike Foligno	Sudbury	RW
4	WSH	Mike Gartner	Niagara Falls	RW
5	VAN	Rick Vaive	Sherbrooke	RW
6	MIN	Craig Hartsburg	Sault Ste. Marie	D
7	CHI	Keith Brown	Portland	D
8	BOS	Raymond Bourque	Verdun	D
9	TOR	Laurie Boschman	Brandon	C
10	MIN	Tom McCarthy	Oshawa	LW
11	BUF	Mike Ramsey	U. of Minnesota	D
12	ATL	Paul Reinhart	Kitchener	D
13	NYR	Doug Sulliman	Kitchener	RW
14	PHI	Brian Propp	Brandon	LW
15	BOS	Brad McCrimmon	Brandon	D
16	L.A.	Jay Wells	Kingston	D
17	NYI	Duane Sutter	Lethbridge	RW
18	HFD	Ray Allison	Brandon	RW
19	WPG	Jimmy Mann	Sherbrooke	RW
20	QUE	Michel Goulet	Quebec	LW
21	EDM	Kevin Lowe	Quebec	D

OTHER NOTABLE SELECTIONS

Pick	Claimed by		Amateur Club	Position
32	BUF	Lindy Ruff	Lethbridge	D/LW
37	MTL	Mats Naslund	Brynas Gavle	LW
40	WPG	Dave Christian	North Dakota	RW
41	QUE	Dale Hunter	Sudbury	C
42	MIN	Neal Broten	U. of Minnesota	C
44	MTL	Guy Carbonneau	Chicoutimi	C
48	EDM	Mark Messier	St. Albert Jr. A	C
54	ATL	Tim Hunter	Seattle	RW
57	BOS	Keith Crowder	Peterborough	RW
58	MTL	Rick Wamsley	Brantford	G
66	DET	John Ogrodnick	New Westminster	LW
69	EDM	Glenn Anderson	U. of Denver	RW
75	ATL	Jim Peplinski	Toronto	RW
83	QUE	Anton Stastny	Slovan Bratislava	LW
89	VAN	Dirk Graham	Regina	RW/LW
103	WPG	Thomas Steen	Leksand	C
120	BOS	Mike Krushelnyski	Montreal	LW/C

1978

FIRST ROUND

Pick	Claimed by		Amateur Club	Position
1	MIN	Bobby Smith	Ottawa	C
2	WSH	Ryan Walter	Seattle	C/LW
3	STL	Wayne Babych	Portland	RW
4	VAN	Bill Derlago	Brandon	C
5	COL	Mike Gillis	Kingston	LW
6	PHI	Behn Wilson	Kingston	D
7	PHI	Ken Linseman	Kingston	C
8	MTL	Danny Geoffrion	Cornwall	RW
9	DET	Willie Huber	Hamilton	D
10	CHI	Tim Higgins	Ottawa	RW
11	ATL	Brad Marsh	London	D
12	DET	Brent Peterson	Portland	C
13	BUF	Larry Playfair	Portland	D
14	PHI	Danny Lucas	Sault Ste. Marie	RW
15	NYI	Steve Tambellini	Lethbridge	C
16	BOS	Al Secord	Hamilton	LW
17	MTL	Dave Hunter	Sudbury	LW
18	WSH	Tim Coulis	Hamilton	LW

OTHER NOTABLE SELECTIONS

Pick	Claimed by		Amateur Club	Position
19	MIN	Steve Payne	Ottawa	LW
21	TOR	Joel Quenneville	Windsor	D
22	VAN	Curt Fraser	Victoria	LW
26	NYR	Don Maloney	Kitchener	LW
32	BUF	Tony McKegney	Kingston	LW
35	PHI	Pelle Lindberg	AIK Solna	G
40	VAN	Stan Smyl	New Westminster	RW
54	MIN	Curt Giles	Minnesota-Duluth	D
55	WSH	Bengt Gustafsson	Farjestad	RW
93	NYR	Tom Laidlaw	Northern Michigan	D
103	MTL	Keith Acton	Peterborough	C
109	STL	Paul MacLean	Hull	RW
153	BOS	Craig MacTavish	U. of Mass-Lowell	C
173	STL	Risto Siltanen	Ilves Tampere	D
179	CHI	Darryl Sutter	Lethbridge	LW
231	MTL	Chris Nilan	Northeastern	RW

Pick	Claimed by	Amateur Club	Position

1977

FIRST ROUND

1 DET	Dale McCourt	St. Catharines	C
2 COL	Barry Beck	New Westminster	D
3 WSH	Robert Picard	Montreal	D
4 VAN	Jere Gillis	Sherbrooke	LW
5 Cle.	Mike Crombeen	Kingston	RW
6 CHI	Doug Wilson	Ottawa	D
7 MIN	Brad Maxwell	New Westminster	D
8 NYR	Lucien DeBlois	Sorel	C
9 STL	Scott Campbell	London	D
10 MTL	Mark Napier	Toronto	RW
11 TOR	John Anderson	Toronto	RW
12 TOR	Trevor Johansen	Toronto	D
13 NYR	Ron Duguay	Sudbury	C/RW
14 BUF	Ric Seiling	St. Catharines	RW/C
15 NYI	Mike Bossy	Laval	RW
16 BOS	Dwight Foster	Kitchener	RW
17 PHI	Kevin McCarthy	Winnipeg	D
18 MTL	Norm Dupont	Montreal	LW

OTHER NOTABLE SELECTIONS

25 MIN	Dave Semenko	Brandon	LW
33 NYI	John Tonelli	Toronto	LW
36 MTL	Rod Langway	New Hampshire	D
40 VAN	Glen Hanlon	Brandon	G
54 MTL	Gordie Roberts	Victoria	D
66 PIT	Mark Johnson	U. of Wisconsin	C
102 PIT	Greg Millen	Peterborough	G
135 PHI	Pete Peeters	Medicine Hat	G
162 MTL	Craig Laughlin	Clarkson	RW

1976

FIRST ROUND

1 WSH	Rick Green	London	D
2 PIT	Blair Chapman	Saskatoon	RW
3 MIN	Glen Sharpley	Hull	C
4 DET	Fred Williams	Saskatoon	C
5 CAL	Bjorn Johansson	Orebro	D
6 NYR	Don Murdoch	Medicine Hat	RW
7 STL	Bernie Federko	Saskatoon	C
8 ATL	Dave Shand	Peterborough	D
9 CHI	Real Cloutier	Quebec	RW
10 ATL	Harold Phillipoff	New Westminster	LW
11 K.C.	Paul Gardner	Oshawa	C
12 MTL	Peter Lee	Ottawa	RW
13 MTL	Rod Schutt	Sudbury	LW
14 NYI	Alex McKendry	Sudbury	W
15 WSH	Greg Carroll	Medicine Hat	C
16 BOS	Clayton Pachal	New Westminster	C/LW
17 PHI	Mark Suzor	Kingston	D
18 MTL	*Bruce Baker*	*Ottawa*	*RW*

OTHER NOTABLE SELECTIONS

19 PIT	Greg Malone	Oshawa	C
20 STL	Brian Sutter	Lethbridge	LW
22 DET	Reed Larson	Minnesota-Duluth	D
30 TOR	Randy Carlyle	Sudbury	D
45 CHI	Thomas Gradin	MoDo Ornskoldsvik	C
47 PIT	Morris Lukowich	Medicine Hat	LW
56 STL	Mike Liut	Bowling Green	G
64 ATL	Kent Nilsson	Djurgarden	C
68 NYI	Ken Morrow	Bowling Green	D
133 MTL	Ron Wilson	St. Catharines	C

1975

FIRST ROUND

1 PHI	Mel Bridgman	Victoria	C
2 K.C.	Barry Dean	Medicine Hat	LW
3 CAL	Ralph Klassen	Saskatoon	C
4 MIN	Bryan Maxwell	Medicine Hat	D
5 DET	Rick Lapointe	Victoria	D
6 TOR	Don Ashby	Calgary	C
7 CHI	Greg Vaydik	Medicine Hat	C
8 ATL	Richard Mulhern	Sherbrooke	D
9 MTL	*Robin Sadler*	*Edmonton*	*D*
10 VAN	Rick Blight	Brandon	RW
11 NYI	Pat Price	Saskatoon	D
12 NYR	Wayne Dillon	Toronto	C
13 PIT	Gord Laxton	New Westminster	G
14 BOS	Doug Halward	Peterborough	D
15 MTL	Pierre Mondou	Montreal	C
16 L.A.	Tim Young	Ottawa	C
17 BUF	Bob Sauve	Laval	G
18 WSH	Alex Forsyth	Kingston	C

OTHER NOTABLE SELECTIONS

21 CAL	Dennis Maruk	London	C
22 MTL	Brian Engblom	U. of Wisconsin	D
24 TOR	Doug Jarvis	Peterborough	C
42 TOR	Bruce Boudreau	Toronto	C
43 CHI	Mike O'Connell	Kingston	D
57 CAL	Greg Smith	Colorado College	D
80 ATL	Willi Plett	St. Catharines	RW
108 PHI	Paul Holmgren	U. of Minnesota	RW
210 L.A.	Dave Taylor	Clarkson	RW

1974

FIRST ROUND

1 WSH	Greg Joly	Regina	D
2 K.C.	Wilf Paiement	St. Catharines	RW
3 CAL	Rick Hampton	St. Catharines	LW/D
4 NYI	Clark Gillies	Regina	LW
5 MTL	Cam Connor	Flin Flon	RW
6 MIN	Doug Hicks	Flin Flon	D
7 MTL	Doug Risebrough	Kitchener	C
8 PIT	Pierre Larouche	Sorel	C
9 DET	Bill Lochead	Oshawa	LW
10 MTL	Rick Chartraw	Kitchener	D/RW
11 BUF	Lee Fogolin Jr.	Oshawa	D
12 MTL	Mario Tremblay	Montreal	RW
13 TOR	Jack Valiquette	Sault Ste. Marie	C
14 NYR	Dave Maloney	Kitchener	D
15 MTL	Gord McTavish	Sudbury	C
16 CHI	Grant Mulvey	Calgary	RW
17 CAL	Ron Chipperfield	Brandon	C
18 BOS	*Don Larway*	*Swift Current*	*RW*

OTHER NOTABLE SELECTIONS

22 NYI	Bryan Trottier	Swift Current	C
25 BOS	Mark Howe	Toronto	D
29 BUF	Danny Gare	Calgary	RW
31 TOR	Tiger Williams	Swift Current	LW
32 NYR	Ron Greschner	New Westminster	D
38 K.C.	Bob Bourne	Saskatoon	C
39 CAL	Charlie Simmer	Sault Ste. Marie	LW
52 CHI	Bob Murray	Cornwall	D
70 CHI	Terry Ruskowski	Swift Current	C
77 VAN	Mike Rogers	Calgary	C
85 TOR	Mike Palmateer	Toronto	G
125 PHI	Reggie Lemelin	Sherbrooke	G
199 MTL	Dave Lumley	New Hampshire	RW
214 NYI	Stefan Persson	Brynas Gavle	D

1973

FIRST ROUND

1 NYI	Denis Potvin	Ottawa	D
2 ATL	Tom Lysiak	Medicine Hat	C
3 VAN	Dennis Ververgaert	London	RW
4 TOR	Lanny McDonald	Medicine Hat	RW
5 STL	John Davidson	Calgary	G
6 BOS	Andre Savard	Quebec	C
7 PIT	Blaine Stoughton	Flin Flon	RW
8 MTL	Bob Gainey	Peterborough	LW
9 VAN	Bob Dailey	Toronto	D
10 TOR	Bob Neely	Peterborough	LW
11 DET	Terry Richardson	New Westminster	G
12 BUF	Morris Titanic	Sudbury	LW
13 CHI	Darcy Rota	Edmonton	LW
14 NYR	Rick Middleton	Oshawa	RW
15 TOR	Ian Turnbull	Ottawa	D
16 ATL	Vic Mercredi	New Westminster	C

OTHER NOTABLE SELECTIONS

21 ATL	Eric Vail	Sudbury	LW
27 PIT	Colin Campbell	Peterborough	D
30 NYR	Pat Hickey	Hamilton	LW
33 NYI	Dave Lewis	Saskatoon	D
49 NYI	Andre St. Laurent	Montreal	C
85 NYI	Ken Houston	Chatham Jr. B.	RW
129 NYI	Bob Lorimer	Michigan Tech	D
130 CAL	Larry Patey	Braintree H.S.	C
134 PIT	Gord Lane	New Westminster	D

1972

FIRST ROUND

1 NYI	Billy Harris	Toronto	RW
2 ATL	Jacques Richard	Quebec	LW
3 VAN	Don Lever	Niagara Falls	LW
4 MTL	Steve Shutt	Toronto	LW
5 BUF	Jim Schoenfeld	Niagara Falls	D
6 MTL	Michel Larocque	Ottawa	G
7 PHI	Bill Barber	Kitchener	C
8 MTL	Dave Gardner	Toronto	C
9 STL	Wayne Merrick	Ottawa	C
10 MTL	*Al Blanchard*	*Kitchener*	*LW*
11 TOR	George Ferguson	Toronto	C
12 MIN	Jerry Byers	Kitchener	LW
13 CHI	Phil Russell	Edmonton	D
14 MTL	John Van Boxmeer	Guelph	D
15 NYR	Bob MacMillan	St. Catharines	RW
16 BOS	Mike Bloom	St. Catharines	LW

OTHER NOTABLE SELECTIONS

17 NYI	Lorne Henning	New Westminster	C
23 PHI	Tom Bladon	Edmonton	D
33 NYI	Bob Nystrom	Calgary	RW
39 PHI	Jimmy Watson	Calgary	D
55 PHI	Al MacAdam	U. of PEI	RW
85 BUF	Peter McNab	U. of Denver	C
97 NYI	Richard Brodeur	Cornwall	G
139 TOR	Pat Boutette	Minnesota-Duluth	C/RW
144 NYI	Garry Howatt	Flin Flon	LW

1971

FIRST ROUND

1 MTL	Guy Lafleur	Quebec	RW
2 DET	Marcel Dionne	St. Catharines	C
3 VAN	Jocelyn Guevremont	Montreal	D
4 STL	Gene Carr	Flin Flon	C
5 BUF	Rick Martin	Montreal	LW
6 BOS	Ron Jones	Edmonton	D
7 MTL	Chuck Arnason	Flin Flon	RW
8 PHI	Larry Wright	Regina	C
9 PHI	Pierre Plante	Drummondville	RW
10 NYR	Steve Vickers	Toronto	LW
11 MTL	Murray Wilson	Ottawa	LW
12 CHI	*Dan Spring*	*Edmonton*	*C*
13 NYR	Steve Durbano	Toronto	D
14 BOS	Terry O'Reilly	Oshawa	RW

OTHER NOTABLE SELECTIONS

17 VAN	Bobby Lalonde	Montreal	C
19 BUF	Craig Ramsay	Peterborough	LW
20 MTL	Larry Robinson	Kitchener	D
22 TOR	Rick Kehoe	Hamilton	RW
33 BUF	Bill Hajt	Saskatoon	D
48 L.A.	Neil Komadoski	Winnipeg	D
55 NYR	Jerry Butler	Hamilton	RW

1970

FIRST ROUND

1 BUF	Gilbert Perreault	Montreal	C
2 VAN	Dale Tallon	Toronto	D
3 BOS	Reggie Leach	Flin Flon	RW
4 BOS	Rick MacLeish	Peterborough	C
5 MTL	*Ray Martyniuk*	*Flin Flon*	*G*
6 MTL	Chuck Lefley	Canadian National	LW
7 PIT	Greg Polis	Estevan	LW
8 TOR	Darryl Sittler	London	C
9 BOS	Ron Plumb	Peterborough	D
10 CAL	Chris Oddleifson	Winnipeg	C
11 NYR	Norm Gratton	Montreal	LW
12 DET	Serge Lajeunesse	Montreal	D/RW
13 BOS	Bob Stewart	Oshawa	D
14 CHI	Dan Maloney	London	LW

OTHER NOTABLE SELECTIONS

18 PHI	Bill Clement	Ottawa	C
20 MIN	Fred Barrett	Toronto	D
22 TOR	Errol Thompson	Charlottetown Sr.	LW
25 NYR	Mike Murphy	Toronto	RW
27 BOS	Dan Bouchard	London	G
32 PHI	Bob Kelly	Oshawa	LW
40 DET	Yvon Lambert	Drummondville	LW
59 L.A.	Billy Smith	Cornwall	G
70 CHI	Gilles Meloche	Verdun	G
88 OAK	Terry Murray	Ottawa	D
103 TOR	Ron Low	Dauphin Jr. A.	G

1969

FIRST ROUND

1 MTL	Rejean Houle	Montreal	RW
2 MTL	Marc Tardif	Montreal	LW
3 BOS	Don Tannahill	Niagara Falls	LW
4 BOS	Frank Spring	Edmonton	RW
5 MIN	Dick Redmond	St. Catharines	D
6 PHI	*Bob Currier*	*Cornwall*	*C*
7 OAK	Tony Featherstone	Peterborough	RW
8 NYR	Andre Dupont	Montreal	D
9 TOR	*Ernie Moser*	*Estevan*	*RW*
10 DET	Jim Rutherford	Hamilton	G
11 BOS	Ivan Boldirev	Oshawa	C
12 NYR	Pierre Jarry	Ottawa	LW
13 CHI	J.P. Bordeleau	Montreal	RW

OTHER NOTABLE SELECTIONS

17 PHI	Bobby Clarke	Flin Flon	C
18 OAK	Ron Stackhouse	Peterborough	D
25 MIN	Gilles Gilbert	London	G
26 PIT	Michel Briere	Shawinigan	C
51 PHI	Butch Goring	Dauphin Jr. A.	C
52 PHI	Dave Schultz	Sorel	LW
55 TOR	Brian Spencer	Swift Current	LW
64 PHI	Don Saleski	Regina	RW

NHL All-Stars

Active Players' All-Star Selection Records

	Total	First Team Selections		Second Team Selections
GOALTENDER				
Sergei Bobrovsky	2	(1) 2012-13; 2016-17.	(0)	
Henrik Lundqvist	2	(1) 2011-12.	(1) 2012-13.	
Braden Holtby	2	(1) 2015-16.	(1) 2016-17.	
Roberto Luongo	2	(0)	(2) 2003-04; 2006-07.	
Ryan Miller	1	(1) 2009-10.	(0)	
Tuukka Rask	1	(1) 2013-14.	(0)	
Carey Price	1	(1) 2014-15.	(0)	
Steve Mason	1	(0)	(1) 2008-09.	
Pekka Rinne	1	(0)	(1) 2010-11.	
Jonathan Quick	1	(0)	(1) 2011-12.	
Semyon Varlamov	1	(0)	(1) 2013-14.	
Devan Dubnyk	1	(0)	(1) 2014-15.	
Ben Bishop	1	(0)	(1) 2015-16.	
DEFENSE				
Zdeno Chara	7	(3) 2003-04; 2008-09; 2013-14.	(4) 2005-06; 2007-08; 2010-11; 2011-12.	
Erik Karlsson	4	(4) 2011-12; 2014-15; 2015-16; 2016-17.	(0)	
Shea Weber	4	(2) 2010-11; 2011-12.	(2) 2013-14; 2014-15.	
Duncan Keith	3	(2) 2009-10; 2013-14.	(1) 2016-17.	
Drew Doughty	3	(1) 2015-16.	(2) 2009-10; 2014-15.	
Mike Green	2	(2) 2008-09; 2009-10.	(0)	
P.K. Subban	2	(2) 2012-13; 2014-15.	(0)	
Brent Burns	2	(1) 2016-17.	(1) 2015-16.	
Alex Pietrangelo	2	(0)	(2) 2011-12; 2013-14.	
Kris Letang	2	(0)	(2) 2012-13; 2015-16.	
Dion Phaneuf	1	(1) 2007-08.	(0)	
Ryan Suter	1	(1) 2012-13	(0)	
Lubomir Visnovsky	1	(0)	(1) 2010-11.	
Francois Beauchemin	1	(0)	(1) 2012-13.	
Victor Hedman	1	(0)	(1) 2016-17.	
CENTER				
Sidney Crosby	7	(4) 2006-07; 2012-13, 2013-14; 2015-16.	(3) 2009-10; 2014-15; 2016-17.	
Joe Thornton	4	(1) 2005-06.	(3) 2002-03; 2007-08; 2015-16.	
Evgeni Malkin	3	(3) 2007-08; 2008-09; 2011-12.	(0)	
Henrik Sedin	2	(2) 2009-10; 2010-11.	(0)	
Steven Stamkos	2	(0)	(2) 2010-11; 2011-12.	
John Tavares	1	(1) 2014-15.	(0)	
Connor McDavid	1	(1) 2016-17.	(0)	
Eric Staal	1	(0)	(1) 2005-06.	
Jonathan Toews	1	(0)	(1) 2012-13.	
Ryan Getzlaf	1	(0)	(1) 2013-14.	
RIGHT WING				
Jaromir Jagr	8	(7) 1994-95; 1995-96; 1997-98 1998-99; 1999-00; 2000-01; 2005-06.	(1) 1996-97.	
Jarome Iginla	4	(3) 2001-02; 2007-08; 2008-09.	(1) 2003-04.	
Patrick Kane	3	(3) 2009-10; 2015-16; 2016-17.	(0)	
Corey Perry	2	(2) 2010-11; 2013-14.	(0)	
Alex Ovechkin	2	(1) 2012-13.	(1) 2013-14.	
Vladimir Tarasenko	2	(0)	(2) 2014-15; 2015-16.	
James Neal	1	(1) 2011-12.	(0)	
Jakub Voracek	1	(1) 2014-15.	(0)	
Marian Hossa	1	(0)	(1) 2008-09.	
Marian Gaborik	1	(0)	(1) 2011-12.	
Nikita Kucherov	1	(0)	(1) 2016-17.	
LEFT WING				
Alex Ovechkin	9	(6) 2005-06; 2006-07; 2007-08; 2008-09; 2009-10; 2014-15.	(3) 2010-11; 2012-13; 2015-16	
Jamie Benn	3	(2) 2013-14; 2015-16.	(1) 2014-15	
Daniel Sedin	2	(1) 2010-11	(1) 2009-10.	
Chris Kunitz	1	(1) 2012-13.	(0)	
Brad Marchand	1	(1) 2016-17.	(0)	
Thomas Vanek	1	(0)	(1) 2006-07.	
Henrik Zetterberg	1	(0)	(1) 2007-08.	
Zach Parise	1	(0)	(1) 2008-09.	
Joe Pavelski	1	(0)	(1) 2013-14.	
Artemi Panarin	1	(0)	(1) 2016-17.	

Leading NHL All-Stars 1930-31 to 2016-17

Player	Pos.	Team(s)	Total Selections	First Team Selections	Second Team Selections	NHL Seasons
Gordie Howe	RW	Detroit	21	12	9	26
Raymond Bourque	D	Bos., Col.	19	13	6	22
Wayne Gretzky	C	Edm., L.A., NYR	15	8	7	20
Maurice Richard	RW	Montreal	14	8	6	18
Bobby Hull	LW	Chicago	12	10	2	16
Nicklas Lidstrom	D	Detroit	12	10	2	20
Doug Harvey	D	Mtl., NYR	11	10	1	19
Glenn Hall	G	Det., Chi., St.L.	11	7	4	18
* Alex Ovechkin	LW/RW	Washington	11	7	4	12
Jean Beliveau	C	Montreal	10	6	4	20
Earl Seibert	D	NYR, Chi.	10	4	6	15
Bobby Orr	D	Boston	9	8	1	12
Ted Lindsay	LW	Detroit	9	8	1	17
Mario Lemieux	C	Pittsburgh	9	5	4	17
Frank Mahovlich	LW	Tor., Det., Mtl.	9	3	6	18
Eddie Shore	D	Boston	8	7	1	14
* Jaromir Jagr	RW	Pit., NYR	8	7	1	23
Phil Esposito	C	Boston	8	6	2	18
Red Kelly	D	Detroit	8	6	2	20
Stan Mikita	C	Chicago	8	6	2	22
Mike Bossy	RW	NY Islanders	8	5	3	10
Pierre Pilote	D	Chicago	8	5	3	14
Luc Robitaille	LW	Los Angeles	8	5	3	19
Paul Coffey	D	Edm., Pit., Det.	8	4	4	21
Frank Brimsek	G	Boston	8	2	6	10
Denis Potvin	D	NY Islanders	7	5	2	15
Brad Park	D	NYR, Bos.	7	5	2	17
Chris Chelios	D	Mtl., Chi., Det.	7	5	2	25
Al MacInnis	D	Cgy., St.L.	7	4	3	23
* Sidney Crosby	C	Pittsburgh	7	4	3	12
* Zdeno Chara	D	Ott., Bos.	7	3	4	19
Jacques Plante	G	Mtl., Tor.	7	3	4	18
Bill Gadsby	D	Chi., NYR, Det.	7	3	4	20
Martin Brodeur	G	New Jersey	7	3	4	22
Terry Sawchuk	G	Detroit	7	3	4	21
Bill Durnan	G	Montreal	6	6	0	7
Dominik Hasek	G	Buffalo	6	6	0	15
Guy Lafleur	RW	Montreal	6	6	0	17
Ken Dryden	G	Montreal	6	5	1	8
Patrick Roy	G	Mtl., Col.	6	4	2	19
Dit Clapper	RW/D	Boston	6	3	3	20
Larry Robinson	D	Montreal	6	3	3	20
Tim Horton	D	Toronto	6	3	3	24
Borje Salming	D	Toronto	6	1	5	17
Bill Cowley	C	Boston	5	4	1	13
Busher Jackson	LW	Toronto	5	4	1	15
Mark Messier	LW/C	Edm., NYR	5	4	1	25
Charlie Conacher	RW	Toronto	5	3	2	12
Jack Stewart	D	Detroit	5	3	2	12
Toe Blake	LW	Montreal	5	3	2	14
Elmer Lach	C	Montreal	5	3	2	14
Bill Quackenbush	D	Det., Bos.	5	3	2	14
Michel Goulet	LW	Quebec	5	3	2	15
Paul Kariya	LW	Anaheim	5	3	2	15
Tony Esposito	G	Chicago	5	3	2	16
Ken Reardon	D	Montreal	5	2	3	7
Syl Apps	C	Toronto	5	2	3	10
Ed Giacomin	G	NY Rangers	5	2	3	13
John LeClair	LW	Mtl., Phi.	5	2	3	16
Brian Leetch	D	NY Rangers	5	2	3	17
Jari Kurri	RW	Edmonton	5	2	3	17
Scott Stevens	D	Wsh., N.J.	5	2	3	21
Martin St. Louis	RW	Tampa Bay	5	1	4	16

* Active

Position Leaders in All-Star Selections

Position	Player	Total	First Team	Second Team	NHL Seasons	Career
GOALTENDER	Glenn Hall	11	7	4	18	1952-53 to 1970-71
	Frank Brimsek	8	2	6	10	1938-39 to 1949-50
	Jacques Plante	7	3	4	18	1952-53 to 1972-73
	Terry Sawchuk	7	3	4	21	1949-50 to 1969-70
	Martin Brodeur	7	3	4	22	1991-92 to 2014-15
	Bill Durnan	6	6	0	7	1943-44 to 1949-50
	Dominik Hasek	6	6	0	15	1990-91 to 2007-08
	Ken Dryden	6	5	1	8	1970-71 to 1978-79
	Patrick Roy	6	4	2	19	1984-85 to 2002-03
DEFENSE	Raymond Bourque	19	13	6	22	1979-80 to 2000-01
	Nicklas Lidstrom	12	10	2	20	1991-92 to 2011-12
	Doug Harvey	11	10	1	20	1947-48 to 1968-69
	Earl Seibert	10	4	6	15	1931-32 to 1945-46
	Bobby Orr	9	8	1	12	1966-67 to 1978-79
	Eddie Shore	8	7	1	14	1926-27 to 1939-40
	Red Kelly	8	6	2	20	1947-48 to 1966-67
	Pierre Pilote	8	5	3	14	1955-56 to 1968-69
	Paul Coffey	8	4	4	21	1980-81 to 2000-01
CENTER	Wayne Gretzky	15	8	7	20	1979-80 to 1998-99
	Jean Beliveau	10	6	4	20	1950-51 to 1970-71
	Mario Lemieux	9	5	4	18	1984-85 to 2005-06
	Phil Esposito	8	6	2	18	1963-64 to 1980-81
	Stan Mikita	8	6	2	22	1958-59 to 1979-80
RIGHT WING	Gordie Howe	21	12	9	26	1946-47 to 1979-80
	Maurice Richard	14	8	6	18	1942-43 to 1959-60
	* Jaromir Jagr	8	7	1	23	1990-91 to 2016-17
	Mike Bossy	8	5	3	10	1977-78 to 1986-87
	Guy Lafleur	6	6	0	17	1971-72 to 1990-91
LEFT WING	Bobby Hull	12	10	2	16	1957-58 to 1979-80
	Ted Lindsay	9	8	1	17	1944-45 to 1964-65
	* Alex Ovechkin	9	6	3	12	2005-06 to 2016-17
	Frank Mahovlich	9	3	6	18	1956-57 to 1973-74
	Luc Robitaille	8	5	3	19	1986-87 to 2005-06

* active player

All-Star Teams

1930-2017

Voting for the NHL All-Star Team is conducted among the representatives of the Professional Hockey Writers' Association at the end of the season.

Following is a list of the First and Second All-Star Teams since their inception in 1930-31.

2016-17

First Team		Second Team
Sergei Bobrovsky, CBJ	G	Braden Holtby, Wsh.
Brent Burns, S.J.	D	Victor Hedman, T.B.
Erik Karlsson, Ott.	D	Duncan Keith, Chi.
Connor McDavid, Edm.	C	Sidney Crosby, Pit.
Patrick Kane, Chi.	RW	Nikita Kucherov, T.B.
Brad Marchand, Bos.	LW	Artemi Panarin, Chi.

2015-16

First Team		Second Team
Braden Holtby, Wsh.	G	Ben Bishop, T.B.
Drew Doughty, L.A.	D	Brent Burns, S.J.
Erik Karlsson, Ott.	D	Kris Letang, Pit.
Sidney Crosby, Pit.	C	Joe Thornton, S.J.
Patrick Kane, Chi.	RW	Vladimir Tarasenko, St.L.
Jamie Benn, Dal.	LW	Alex Ovechkin, Wsh.

2014-15

First Team		Second Team
Carey Price, Mtl.	G	Devan Dubnyk, Min.
Erik Karlsson, Ott.	D	Drew Doughty, L.A.
P.K. Subban, Mtl.	D	Shea Weber, Nsh.
John Tavares, NYI	C	Sidney Crosby, Pit.
Jakub Voracek, Phi.	RW	Vladimir Tarasenko, St.L.
Alex Ovechkin, Wsh.	LW	Jamie Benn, Dal.

2013-14

First Team		Second Team
Tuukka Rask, Bos.	G	Semyon Varlamov, Col.
Duncan Keith, Chi.	D	Shea Weber, Nsh.
Zdeno Chara, Bos.	D	Alex Pietrangelo, St.L.
Sidney Crosby, Pit.	C	Ryan Getzlaf, Ana.
Corey Perry, Ana.	RW	Alex Ovechkin, Wsh.
Jamie Benn, Dal.	LW	Joe Pavelski, S.J.

2012-13

First Team		Second Team
Sergei Bobrovsky, CBJ	G	Henrik Lundqvist, NYR
P.K. Subban, Mtl.	D	Kris Letang, Pit.
Ryan Suter, Min.	D	Francois Beauchemin, Ana.
Sidney Crosby, Pit.	C	Jonathan Toews, Chi.
Alex Ovechkin, Wsh.	RW	Martin St. Louis, T.B.
Chris Kunitz, Pit.	LW	Alex Ovechkin, Wsh.

2011-12

First Team		Second Team
Henrik Lundqvist, NYR	G	Jonathan Quick, L.A.
Erik Karlsson, Ott.	D	Zdeno Chara, Bos.
Shea Weber, Nsh.	D	Alex Pietrangelo, St. L.
Evgeni Malkin, Pit.	C	Steven Stamkos, T.B.
James Neal, Pit.	RW	Marian Gaborik, NYR
Ilya Kovalchuk, N.J.	LW	Ray Whitney, Phx.

2010-11

First Team		Second Team
Tim Thomas, Bos.	G	Pekka Rinne, Nsh.
Nicklas Lidstrom, Det.	D	Zdeno Chara, Bos.
Shea Weber, Nsh.	D	Lubomir Visnovsky, Ana.
Henrik Sedin, Van.	C	Steven Stamkos, T.B.
Corey Perry, Ana.	RW	Martin St. Louis, T.B.
Daniel Sedin, Van.	LW	Alex Ovechkin, Wsh.

2009-10

First Team		Second Team
Ryan Miller, Buf.	G	Ilya Bryzgalov, Phx.
Duncan Keith, Chi.	D	Drew Doughty, L.A..
Mike Green, Wsh.	D	Nicklas Lidstrom, Det.
Henrik Sedin, Van.	C	Sidney Crosby, Pit.
Patrick Kane, Chi.	RW	Martin St. Louis, T.B.
Alex Ovechkin, Wsh.	LW	Daniel Sedin, Van.

2008-09

First Team		Second Team
Tim Thomas, Bos.	G	Steve Mason, CBJ
Zdeno Chara, Bos	D	Nicklas Lidstrom, Det.
Mike Green, Wsh.	D	Dan Boyle, S.J.
Evgeni Malkin, Pit.	C	Pavel Datsyuk, Det.
Jarome Iginla, Cgy.	RW	Marian Hossa, Det.
Alex Ovechkin, Wsh.	LW	Zach Parise, N.J.

2007-08

First Team		Second Team
Evgeni Nabokov, S.J.	G	Martin Brodeur, N.J.
Nicklas Lidstrom, Det.	D	Brian Campbell, Buf., S.J.
Dion Phaneuf, Cgy.	D	Zdeno Chara, Bos.
Evgeni Malkin, Pit.	C	Joe Thornton, S.J.
Jarome Iginla, Cgy.	RW	Alex Kovalev, Mtl.
Alex Ovechkin, Wsh.	LW	Henrik Zetterberg, Det.

2006-07

First Team		Second Team
Martin Brodeur, N.J.	G	Roberto Luongo, Van.
Nicklas Lidstrom, Det.	D	Chris Pronger, Ana.
Scott Niedermayer, Ana.	D	Dan Boyle, T.B.
Sidney Crosby, Pit.	C	Vincent Lecavalier, T.B.
Dany Heatley, Ott.	RW	Martin St. Louis, T.B.
Alex Ovechkin, Wsh.	LW	Thomas Vanek, Buf.

2005-06

First Team		Second Team
Miikka Kiprusoff, Cgy.	G	Martin Brodeur, N.J.
Nicklas Lidstrom, Det.	D	Zdeno Chara, Ott.
Scott Niedermayer, Ana.	D	Sergei Zubov, Dal.
Joe Thornton, Bos., S.J.	C	Eric Staal, Car.
Jaromir Jagr, NYR	RW	Daniel Alfredsson, Ott.
Alex Ovechkin, Wsh.	LW	Dany Heatley, Ott.

2004-05

Season Cancelled

2003-04

First Team		Second Team
Martin Brodeur, N.J.	G	Roberto Luongo, Fla.
Scott Niedermayer, N.J.	D	Chris Pronger, St.L.
Zdeno Chara, Ott.	D	Bryan McCabe, Tor.
Joe Sakic, Col.	C	Mats Sundin, Tor.
Martin St. Louis, T.B.	RW	Jarome Iginla, Cgy.
Markus Naslund, Van.	LW	Ilya Kovalchuk, Atl.

2002-03

First Team		Second Team
Martin Brodeur, N.J.	G	Marty Turco, Dal.
Al MacInnis, St.L.	D	Sergei Gonchar, Wsh.
Nicklas Lidstrom, Det.	D	Derian Hatcher, Dal.
Peter Forsberg, Col.	C	Joe Thornton, Bos.
Todd Bertuzzi, Van.	RW	Milan Hejduk, Col.
Markus Naslund, Van.	LW	Paul Kariya, Ana.

2001-02

First Team		Second Team
Patrick Roy, Col.	G	Jose Theodore, Mtl.
Nicklas Lidstrom, Det.	D	Rob Blake, Col.
Chris Chelios, Det.	D	Sergei Gonchar, Wsh.
Joe Sakic, Col.	C	Mats Sundin, Tor.
Jarome Iginla, Cgy.	RW	Bill Guerin, Bos.
Markus Naslund, Van.	LW	Brendan Shanahan, Det.

2000-01

First Team		Second Team
Dominik Hasek, Buf.	G	Roman Cechmanek, Phi.
Nicklas Lidstrom, Det.	D	Rob Blake, L.A., Col.
Raymond Bourque, Col.	D	Scott Stevens, N.J.
Joe Sakic, Col.	C	Mario Lemieux, Pit.
Jaromir Jagr, Pit.	RW	Pavel Bure, Fla.
Patrik Elias, N.J.	LW	Luc Robitaille, L.A.

1999-2000

First Team		Second Team
Olaf Kolzig, Wsh.	G	Roman Turek, St.L.
Chris Pronger, St.L.	D	Rob Blake, L.A.
Nicklas Lidstrom, Det.	D	Eric Desjardins, Phi.
Steve Yzerman, Det.	C	Mike Modano, Dal.
Jaromir Jagr, Pit.	RW	Pavel Bure, Fla.
Brendan Shanahan, Det.	LW	Paul Kariya, Ana.

1998-99

First Team		Second Team
Dominik Hasek, Buf.	G	Byron Dafoe, Bos.
Al MacInnis, St.L.	D	Raymond Bourque, Bos.
Nicklas Lidstrom, Det.	D	Eric Desjardins, Phi.
Peter Forsberg, Col.	C	Alexei Yashin, Ott.
Jaromir Jagr, Pit.	RW	Teemu Selanne, Ana.
Paul Kariya, Ana.	LW	John LeClair, Phi.

1997-98

First Team		Second Team
Dominik Hasek, Buf.	G	Martin Brodeur, N.J.
Nicklas Lidstrom, Det.	D	Chris Pronger, St.L.
Rob Blake, L.A.	D	Scott Niedermayer, N.J.
Peter Forsberg, Col.	C	Wayne Gretzky, NYR
Jaromir Jagr, Pit.	RW	Teemu Selanne, Ana.
John LeClair, Phi.	LW	Keith Tkachuk, Phx.

1996-97

First Team		Second Team
Dominik Hasek, Buf.	G	Martin Brodeur, N.J.
Brian Leetch, NYR	D	Chris Chelios, Chi.
Sandis Ozolinsh, Col.	D	Scott Stevens, N.J.
Mario Lemieux, Pit.	C	Wayne Gretzky, NYR
Teemu Selanne, Ana.	RW	Jaromir Jagr, Pit.
Paul Kariya, Ana.	LW	John LeClair, Phi.

1995-96

First Team		Second Team
Jim Carey, Wsh.	G	Chris Osgood, Det.
Chris Chelios, Chi.	D	V. Konstantinov, Det.
Raymond Bourque, Bos.	D	Brian Leetch, NYR
Mario Lemieux, Pit.	C	Eric Lindros, Phi.
Jaromir Jagr, Pit.	RW	Alexander Mogilny, Van.
Paul Kariya, Ana.	LW	John LeClair, Phi.

1994-95

First Team		Second Team
Dominik Hasek, Buf.	G	Ed Belfour, Chi.
Paul Coffey, Det.	D	Raymond Bourque, Bos.
Chris Chelios, Chi.	D	Larry Murphy, Pit.
Eric Lindros, Phi.	C	Alexei Zhamnov, Wpg.
Jaromir Jagr, Pit.	RW	Theoren Fleury, Cgy.
John LeClair, Mtl., Phi.	LW	Keith Tkachuk, Wpg.

1993-94

First Team		Second Team
Dominik Hasek, Buf.	G	John Vanbiesbrouck, Fla.
Raymond Bourque, Bos.	D	Al MacInnis, Cgy.
Scott Stevens, N.J.	D	Brian Leetch, NYR
Sergei Fedorov, Det.	C	Wayne Gretzky, L.A.
Pavel Bure, Van.	RW	Cam Neely, Bos.
Brendan Shanahan, St.L.	LW	Adam Graves, NYR

1992-93

First Team		Second Team
Ed Belfour, Chi.	G	Tom Barrasso, Pit.
Chris Chelios, Chi.	D	Larry Murphy, Pit.
Raymond Bourque, Bos.	D	Al Iafrate, Wsh.
Mario Lemieux, Pit.	C	Pat LaFontaine, Buf.
Teemu Selanne, Wpg.	RW	Alexander Mogilny, Buf.
Luc Robitaille, L.A.	LW	Kevin Stevens, Pit.

1991-92

First Team		Second Team
Patrick Roy, Mtl.	G	Kirk McLean, Van.
Brian Leetch, NYR	D	Phil Housley, Wpg.
Raymond Bourque, Bos.	D	Scott Stevens, N.J.
Mark Messier, NYR	C	Mario Lemieux, Pit.
Brett Hull, St.L.	RW	Mark Recchi, Pit., Phi.
Kevin Stevens, Pit.	LW	Luc Robitaille, L.A.

1990-91

First Team		Second Team
Ed Belfour, Chi.	G	Patrick Roy, Mtl.
Raymond Bourque, Bos.	D	Chris Chelios, Chi.
Al MacInnis, Cgy.	D	Brian Leetch, NYR
Wayne Gretzky, L.A.	C	Adam Oates, St.L.
Brett Hull, St.L.	RW	Cam Neely, Bos.
Luc Robitaille, L.A.	LW	Kevin Stevens, Pit.

1989-90

First Team	Pos	Second Team
Patrick Roy, Mtl.	G	Daren Puppa, Buf.
Raymond Bourque, Bos.	D	Paul Coffey, Pit.
Al MacInnis, Cgy.	D	Doug Wilson, Chi.
Mark Messier, Edm.	C	Wayne Gretzky, L.A.
Brett Hull, St.L.	RW	Cam Neely, Bos.
Luc Robitaille, L.A.	LW	Brian Bellows, Min.

1988-89

First Team	Pos	Second Team
Patrick Roy, Mtl.	G	Mike Vernon, Cgy.
Chris Chelios, Mtl.	D	Al MacInnis, Cgy.
Paul Coffey, Pit.	D	Raymond Bourque, Bos.
Mario Lemieux, Pit.	C	Wayne Gretzky, L.A.
Joe Mullen, Cgy.	RW	Jari Kurri, Edm.
Luc Robitaille, L.A.	LW	Gerard Gallant, Det.

1987-88

First Team	Pos	Second Team
Grant Fuhr, Edm.	G	Patrick Roy, Mtl.
Raymond Bourque, Bos.	D	Gary Suter, Cgy.
Scott Stevens, Wsh.	D	Brad McCrimmon, Cgy.
Mario Lemieux, Pit.	C	Wayne Gretzky, Edm.
Hakan Loob, Cgy.	RW	Cam Neely, Bos.
Luc Robitaille, L.A.	LW	Michel Goulet, Que.

1986-87

First Team	Pos	Second Team
Ron Hextall, Phi.	G	Mike Liut, Hfd.
Raymond Bourque, Bos.	D	Larry Murphy, Wsh.
Mark Howe, Phi.	D	Al MacInnis, Cgy.
Wayne Gretzky, Edm.	C	Mario Lemieux, Pit.
Jari Kurri, Edm.	RW	Tim Kerr, Phi.
Michel Goulet, Que.	LW	Luc Robitaille, L.A.

1985-86

First Team	Pos	Second Team
John Vanbiesbrouck, NYR	G	Bob Froese, Phi.
Paul Coffey, Edm.	D	Larry Robinson, Mtl.
Mark Howe, Phi.	D	Raymond Bourque, Bos.
Wayne Gretzky, Edm.	C	Mario Lemieux, Pit.
Mike Bossy, NYI	RW	Jari Kurri, Edm.
Michel Goulet, Que.	LW	Mats Naslund, Mtl.

1984-85

First Team	Pos	Second Team
Pelle Lindbergh, Phi.	G	Tom Barrasso, Buf.
Paul Coffey, Edm.	D	Rod Langway, Wsh.
Raymond Bourque, Bos.	D	Doug Wilson, Chi.
Wayne Gretzky, Edm.	C	Dale Hawerchuk, Wpg.
Jari Kurri, Edm.	RW	Mike Bossy, NYI
John Ogrodnick, Det.	LW	John Tonelli, NYI

1983-84

First Team	Pos	Second Team
Tom Barrasso, Buf.	G	Pat Riggin, Wsh.
Rod Langway, Wsh.	D	Paul Coffey, Edm.
Raymond Bourque, Bos.	D	Denis Potvin, NYI
Wayne Gretzky, Edm.	C	Bryan Trottier, NYI
Mike Bossy, NYI	RW	Jari Kurri, Edm.
Michel Goulet, Que.	LW	Mark Messier, Edm.

1982-83

First Team	Pos	Second Team
Pete Peeters, Bos.	G	Roland Melanson, NYI
Mark Howe, Phi.	D	Raymond Bourque, Bos.
Rod Langway, Wsh.	D	Paul Coffey, Edm.
Wayne Gretzky, Edm.	C	Denis Savard, Chi.
Mike Bossy, NYI	RW	Lanny McDonald, Cgy.
Mark Messier, Edm.	LW	Michel Goulet, Que.

1981-82

First Team	Pos	Second Team
Billy Smith, NYI	G	Grant Fuhr, Edm.
Doug Wilson, Chi.	D	Paul Coffey, Edm.
Raymond Bourque, Bos.	D	Brian Engblom, Mtl.
Wayne Gretzky, Edm.	C	Bryan Trottier, NYI
Mike Bossy, NYI	RW	Rick Middleton, Bos.
Mark Messier, Edm.	LW	John Tonelli, NYI

1980-81

First Team	Pos	Second Team
Mike Liut, St.L.	G	Mario Lessard, L.A.
Denis Potvin, NYI	D	Larry Robinson, Mtl.
Randy Carlyle, Pit.	D	Raymond Bourque, Bos.
Wayne Gretzky, Edm.	C	Marcel Dionne, L.A.
Mike Bossy, NYI	RW	Dave Taylor, L.A.
Charlie Simmer, L.A.	LW	Bill Barber, Phi.

1979-80

First Team	Pos	Second Team
Tony Esposito, Chi.	G	Don Edwards, Buf.
Larry Robinson, Mtl.	D	Borje Salming, Tor.
Raymond Bourque, Bos.	D	Jim Schoenfeld, Buf.
Marcel Dionne, L.A.	C	Wayne Gretzky, Edm.
Guy Lafleur, Mtl.	RW	Danny Gare, Buf.
Charlie Simmer, L.A.	LW	Steve Shutt, Mtl.

1978-79

First Team	Pos	Second Team
Ken Dryden, Mtl.	G	Glenn Resch, NYI
Denis Potvin, NYI	D	Borje Salming, Tor.
Larry Robinson, Mtl.	D	Serge Savard, Mtl.
Bryan Trottier, NYI	C	Marcel Dionne, L.A.
Guy Lafleur, Mtl.	RW	Mike Bossy, NYI
Clark Gillies, NYI	LW	Bill Barber, Phi.

1977-78

First Team	Pos	Second Team
Ken Dryden, Mtl.	G	Don Edwards, Buf.
Denis Potvin, NYI	D	Larry Robinson, Mtl.
Brad Park, Bos.	D	Borje Salming, Tor.
Bryan Trottier, NYI	C	Darryl Sittler, Tor.
Guy Lafleur, Mtl.	RW	Mike Bossy, NYI
Clark Gillies, NYI	LW	Steve Shutt, Mtl.

1976-77

First Team	Pos	Second Team
Ken Dryden, Mtl.	G	Rogie Vachon, L.A.
Larry Robinson, Mtl.	D	Denis Potvin, NYI
Borje Salming, Tor.	D	Guy Lapointe, Mtl.
Marcel Dionne, L.A.	C	Gilbert Perreault, Buf.
Guy Lafleur, Mtl.	RW	Lanny McDonald, Tor.
Steve Shutt, Mtl.	LW	Rick Martin, Buf.

1975-76

First Team	Pos	Second Team
Ken Dryden, Mtl.	G	Glenn Resch, NYI
Denis Potvin, NYI	D	Borje Salming, Tor.
Brad Park, Bos.	D	Guy Lapointe, Mtl.
Bobby Clarke, Phi.	C	Gilbert Perreault, Buf.
Guy Lafleur, Mtl.	RW	Reggie Leach, Phi.
Bill Barber, Phi.	LW	Rick Martin, Buf.

1974-75

First Team	Pos	Second Team
Bernie Parent, Phi.	G	Rogie Vachon, L.A.
Bobby Orr, Bos.	D	Guy Lapointe, Mtl.
Denis Potvin, NYI	D	Borje Salming, Tor.
Bobby Clarke, Phi.	C	Phil Esposito, Bos.
Guy Lafleur, Mtl.	RW	René Robert, Buf.
Rick Martin, Buf.	LW	Steve Vickers, NYR

1973-74

First Team	Pos	Second Team
Bernie Parent, Phi.	G	Tony Esposito, Chi.
Bobby Orr, Bos.	D	Bill White, Chi.
Brad Park, NYR	D	Barry Ashbee, Phi.
Phil Esposito, Bos.	C	Bobby Clarke, Phi.
Ken Hodge, Bos.	RW	Mickey Redmond, Det.
Rick Martin, Buf.	LW	Wayne Cashman, Bos.

1972-73

First Team	Pos	Second Team
Ken Dryden, Mtl.	G	Tony Esposito, Chi.
Bobby Orr, Bos.	D	Brad Park, NYR
Guy Lapointe, Mtl.	D	Bill White, Chi.
Phil Esposito, Bos.	C	Bobby Clarke, Phi.
Mickey Redmond, Det.	RW	Yvan Cournoyer, Mtl.
Frank Mahovlich, Mtl.	LW	Dennis Hull, Chi.

1971-72

First Team	Pos	Second Team
Tony Esposito, Chi.	G	Ken Dryden, Mtl.
Bobby Orr, Bos.	D	Bill White, Chi.
Brad Park, NYR	D	Pat Stapleton, Chi.
Phil Esposito, Bos.	C	Jean Ratelle, NYR
Rod Gilbert, NYR	RW	Yvan Cournoyer, Mtl.
Bobby Hull, Chi.	LW	Vic Hadfield, NYR

1970-71

First Team	Pos	Second Team
Ed Giacomin, NYR	G	Jacques Plante, Tor.
Bobby Orr, Bos.	D	Brad Park, NYR
J.C. Tremblay, Mtl.	D	Pat Stapleton, Chi.
Phil Esposito, Bos.	C	Dave Keon, Tor.
Ken Hodge, Bos.	RW	Yvan Cournoyer, Mtl.
John Bucyk, Bos.	LW	Bobby Hull, Chi.

1969-70

First Team	Pos	Second Team
Tony Esposito, Chi.	G	Ed Giacomin, NYR
Bobby Orr, Bos.	D	Carl Brewer, Det.
Brad Park, NYR	D	Jacques Laperriere, Mtl.
Phil Esposito, Bos.	C	Stan Mikita, Chi.
Gordie Howe, Det.	RW	John McKenzie, Bos.
Bobby Hull, Chi.	LW	Frank Mahovlich, Det.

1968-69

First Team	Pos	Second Team
Glenn Hall, St.L.	G	Ed Giacomin, NYR
Bobby Orr, Bos.	D	Ted Green, Bos.
Tim Horton, Tor.	D	Ted Harris, Mtl.
Phil Esposito, Bos.	C	Jean Béliveau, Mtl.
Gordie Howe, Det.	RW	Yvan Cournoyer, Mtl.
Bobby Hull, Chi.	LW	Frank Mahovlich, Det.

1967-68

First Team	Pos	Second Team
Gump Worsley, Mtl.	G	Ed Giacomin, NYR
Bobby Orr, Bos.	D	J.C. Tremblay, Mtl.
Tim Horton, Tor.	D	Jim Neilson, NYR
Stan Mikita, Chi.	C	Phil Esposito, Bos.
Gordie Howe, Det.	RW	Rod Gilbert, NYR
Bobby Hull, Chi.	LW	John Bucyk, Bos.

1966-67

First Team	Pos	Second Team
Ed Giacomin, NYR	G	Glenn Hall, Chi.
Pierre Pilote, Chi.	D	Tim Horton, Tor.
Harry Howell, NYR	D	Bobby Orr, Bos.
Stan Mikita, Chi.	C	Norm Ullman, Det.
Kenny Wharram, Chi.	RW	Gordie Howe, Det.
Bobby Hull, Chi.	LW	Don Marshall, NYR

1965-66

First Team	Pos	Second Team
Glenn Hall, Chi.	G	Gump Worsley, Mtl.
Jacques Laperriere, Mtl.	D	Allan Stanley, Tor.
Pierre Pilote, Chi.	D	Pat Stapleton, Chi.
Stan Mikita, Chi.	C	Jean Béliveau, Mtl.
Gordie Howe, Det.	RW	Bobby Rousseau, Mtl.
Bobby Hull, Chi.	LW	Frank Mahovlich, Tor.

1964-65

First Team	Pos	Second Team
Roger Crozier, Det.	G	Charlie Hodge, Mtl.
Pierre Pilote, Chi.	D	Bill Gadsby, Det.
Jacques Laperriere, Mtl.	D	Carl Brewer, Tor.
Norm Ullman, Det.	C	Stan Mikita, Chi.
Claude Provost, Mtl.	RW	Gordie Howe, Det.
Bobby Hull, Chi.	LW	Frank Mahovlich, Tor.

1963-64

First Team	Pos	Second Team
Glenn Hall, Chi.	G	Charlie Hodge, Mtl.
Pierre Pilote, Chi.	D	Moose Vasko, Chi.
Tim Horton, Tor.	D	Jacques Laperriere, Mtl.
Stan Mikita, Chi.	C	Jean Béliveau, Mtl.
Kenny Wharram, Chi.	RW	Gordie Howe, Det.
Bobby Hull, Chi.	LW	Frank Mahovlich, Tor.

1962-63

First Team	Pos	Second Team
Glenn Hall, Chi.	G	Terry Sawchuk, Det.
Pierre Pilote, Chi.	D	Tim Horton, Tor.
Carl Brewer, Tor.	D	Moose Vasko, Chi.
Stan Mikita, Chi.	C	Henri Richard, Mtl.
Gordie Howe, Det.	RW	Andy Bathgate, NYR
Frank Mahovlich, Tor.	LW	Bobby Hull, Chi.

1961-62

First Team	Pos	Second Team
Jacques Plante, Mtl.	G	Glenn Hall, Chi.
Doug Harvey, NYR	D	Carl Brewer, Tor.
Jean-Guy Talbot, Mtl.	D	Pierre Pilote, Chi.
Stan Mikita, Chi.	C	Dave Keon, Tor.
Andy Bathgate, NYR	RW	Gordie Howe, Det.
Bobby Hull, Chi.	LW	Frank Mahovlich, Tor.

1960-61

First Team	Pos	Second Team
Johnny Bower, Tor.	G	Glenn Hall, Chi.
Doug Harvey, Mtl.	D	Allan Stanley, Tor.
Marcel Pronovost, Det.	D	Pierre Pilote, Chi.
Jean Béliveau, Mtl.	C	Henri Richard, Mtl.
Bernie Geoffrion, Mtl.	RW	Gordie Howe, Det.
Frank Mahovlich, Tor.	LW	Dickie Moore, Mtl.

1959-60

First Team	Pos	Second Team
Glenn Hall, Chi.	G	Jacques Plante, Mtl.
Doug Harvey, Mtl.	D	Allan Stanley, Tor.
Marcel Pronovost, Det.	D	Pierre Pilote, Chi.
Jean Béliveau, Mtl.	C	Bronco Horvath, Bos.
Gordie Howe, Det.	RW	Bernie Geoffrion, Mtl.
Bobby Hull, Chi.	LW	Dean Prentice, NYR

1958-59

First Team	Pos	Second Team
Jacques Plante, Mtl.	G	Terry Sawchuk, Det.
Tom Johnson, Mtl.	D	Marcel Pronovost, Det.
Bill Gadsby, NYR	D	Doug Harvey, Mtl.
Jean Béliveau, Mtl.	C	Henri Richard, Mtl.
Andy Bathgate, NYR	RW	Gordie Howe, Det.
Dickie Moore, Mtl.	LW	Alex Delvecchio, Det.

1957-58

First Team	Pos	Second Team
Glenn Hall, Chi.	G	Jacques Plante, Mtl.
Doug Harvey, Mtl.	D	Fern Flaman, Bos.
Bill Gadsby, NYR	D	Marcel Pronovost, Det.
Henri Richard, Mtl.	C	Jean Béliveau, Mtl.
Gordie Howe, Det.	RW	Andy Bathgate, NYR
Dickie Moore, Mtl.	LW	Camille Henry, NYR

1956-57

First Team	Pos	Second Team
Glenn Hall, Det.	G	Jacques Plante, Mtl.
Doug Harvey, Mtl.	D	Fern Flaman, Bos.
Red Kelly, Det.	D	Bill Gadsby, NYR
Jean Béliveau, Mtl.	C	Ed Litzenberger, Chi.
Gordie Howe, Det.	RW	Maurice Richard, Mtl.
Ted Lindsay, Det.	LW	Real Chevrefils, Bos.

1955-56

First Team	Pos	Second Team
Jacques Plante, Mtl.	G	Glenn Hall, Det.
Doug Harvey, Mtl.	D	Red Kelly, Det.
Bill Gadsby, NYR	D	Tom Johnson, Mtl.
Jean Béliveau, Mtl.	C	Tod Sloan, Tor.
Maurice Richard, Mtl.	RW	Gordie Howe, Det.
Ted Lindsay, Det.	LW	Bert Olmstead, Mtl.

1954-55

First Team	Pos	Second Team
Harry Lumley, Tor.	G	Terry Sawchuk, Det.
Doug Harvey, Mtl.	D	Bob Goldham, Det.
Red Kelly, Det.	D	Fern Flaman, Bos.
Jean Béliveau, Mtl.	C	Ken Mosdell, Mtl.
Maurice Richard, Mtl.	RW	Bernie Geoffrion, Mtl.
Sid Smith, Tor.	LW	Danny Lewicki, NYR

1953-54

First Team	Pos	Second Team
Harry Lumley, Tor.	G	Terry Sawchuk, Det.
Red Kelly, Det.	D	Bill Gadsby, Chi.
Doug Harvey, Mtl.	D	Tim Horton, Tor.
Ken Mosdell, Mtl.	C	Ted Kennedy, Tor.
Gordie Howe, Det.	RW	Maurice Richard, Mtl.
Ted Lindsay, Det.	LW	Ed Sandford, Bos.

1952-53

First Team	Pos	Second Team
Terry Sawchuk, Det.	G	Gerry McNeil, Mtl.
Red Kelly, Det.	D	Bill Quackenbush, Bos.
Doug Harvey, Mtl.	D	Bill Gadsby, Chi.
Fleming MacKell, Bos.	C	Alex Delvecchio, Det.
Gordie Howe, Det.	RW	Maurice Richard, Mtl.
Ted Lindsay, Det.	LW	Bert Olmstead, Mtl.

1951-52

First Team	Pos	Second Team
Terry Sawchuk, Det.	G	Jim Henry, Bos.
Red Kelly, Det.	D	Hy Buller, NYR
Doug Harvey, Mtl.	D	Jimmy Thomson, Tor.
Elmer Lach, Mtl.	C	Milt Schmidt, Bos.
Gordie Howe, Det.	RW	Maurice Richard, Mtl.
Ted Lindsay, Det.	LW	Sid Smith, Tor.

1950-51

First Team	Pos	Second Team
Terry Sawchuk, Det.	G	Chuck Rayner, NYR
Red Kelly, Det.	D	Jimmy Thomson, Tor.
Bill Quackenbush, Bos.	D	Leo Reise Jr., Det.
Milt Schmidt, Bos.	C	Sid Abel, Det.
		Ted Kennedy, Tor. (tied)
Gordie Howe, Det.	RW	Maurice Richard, Mtl.
Ted Lindsay, Det.	LW	Sid Smith, Tor.

1949-50

First Team	Pos	Second Team
Bill Durnan, Mtl.	G	Chuck Rayner, NYR
Gus Mortson, Tor.	D	Leo Reise Jr., Det.
Ken Reardon, Mtl.	D	Red Kelly, Det.
Sid Abel, Det.	C	Ted Kennedy, Tor.
Maurice Richard, Mtl.	RW	Gordie Howe, Det.
Ted Lindsay, Det.	LW	Tony Leswick, NYR

1948-49

First Team	Pos	Second Team
Bill Durnan, Mtl.	G	Chuck Rayner, NYR
Bill Quackenbush, Det.	D	Glen Harmon, Mtl.
Jack Stewart, Det.	D	Ken Reardon, Mtl.
Sid Abel, Det.	C	Doug Bentley, Chi.
Maurice Richard, Mtl.	RW	Gordie Howe, Det.
Roy Conacher, Chi.	LW	Ted Lindsay, Det.

1947-48

First Team	Pos	Second Team
Turk Broda, Tor.	G	Frank Brimsek, Bos.
Bill Quackenbush, Det.	D	Ken Reardon, Mtl.
Jack Stewart, Det.	D	Neil Colville, NYR
Elmer Lach, Mtl.	C	Buddy O'Connor, NYR
Maurice Richard, Mtl.	RW	Bud Poile, Chi.
Ted Lindsay, Det.	LW	Gaye Stewart, Chi.

1946-47

First Team	Pos	Second Team
Bill Durnan, Mtl.	G	Frank Brimsek, Bos.
Ken Reardon, Mtl.	D	Jack Stewart, Det.
Butch Bouchard, Mtl.	D	Bill Quackenbush, Det.
Milt Schmidt, Bos.	C	Max Bentley, Chi.
Maurice Richard, Mtl.	RW	Bobby Bauer, Bos.
Doug Bentley, Chi.	LW	Woody Dumart, Bos.

1945-46

First Team	Pos	Second Team
Bill Durnan, Mtl.	G	Frank Brimsek, Bos.
Jack Crawford, Bos.	D	Ken Reardon, Mtl.
Butch Bouchard, Mtl.	D	Jack Stewart, Det.
Max Bentley, Chi.	C	Elmer Lach, Mtl.
Maurice Richard, Mtl.	RW	Bill Mosienko, Chi.
Gaye Stewart, Tor.	LW	Toe Blake, Mtl.
Dick Irvin, Mtl.	Coach	Johnny Gottselig, Chi.

1944-45

First Team	Pos	Second Team
Bill Durnan, Mtl.	G	Mike Karakas, Chi.
Butch Bouchard, Mtl.	D	Glen Harmon, Mtl.
Flash Hollett, Det.	D	Babe Pratt, Tor.
Elmer Lach, Mtl.	C	Bill Cowley, Bos.
Maurice Richard, Mtl.	RW	Bill Mosienko, Chi.
Toe Blake, Mtl.	LW	Syd Howe, Det.
Dick Irvin, Mtl.	Coach	Jack Adams, Det.

1943-44

First Team	Pos	Second Team
Bill Durnan, Mtl.	G	Paul Bibeault, Tor.
Earl Seibert, Chi.	D	Butch Bouchard, Mtl.
Babe Pratt, Tor.	D	Dit Clapper, Bos.
Bill Cowley, Bos.	C	Elmer Lach, Mtl.
Lorne Carr, Tor.	RW	Maurice Richard, Mtl.
Doug Bentley, Chi.	LW	Herb Cain, Bos.
Dick Irvin, Mtl.	Coach	Hap Day, Tor.

1942-43

First Team	Pos	Second Team
Johnny Mowers, Det.	G	Frank Brimsek, Bos.
Earl Seibert, Chi.	D	Jack Crawford, Bos.
Jack Stewart, Det.	D	Flash Hollett, Bos.
Bill Cowley, Bos.	C	Syl Apps, Tor.
Lorne Carr, Tor.	RW	Bryan Hextall, NYR
Doug Bentley, Chi.	LW	Lynn Patrick, NYR
Jack Adams, Det.	Coach	Art Ross, Bos.

1941-42

First Team	Pos	Second Team
Frank Brimsek, Bos.	G	Turk Broda, Tor.
Earl Seibert, Chi.	D	Pat Egan, Bro.
Tom Anderson, Bro.	D	Bucko McDonald, Tor.
Syl Apps, Tor.	C	Phil Watson, NYR
Bryan Hextall, NYR	RW	Gordie Drillon, Tor.
Lynn Patrick, NYR	LW	Sid Abel, Det.
Frank Boucher, NYR	Coach	Paul Thompson, Chi.

1940-41

First Team	Pos	Second Team
Turk Broda, Tor.	G	Frank Brimsek, Bos.
Dit Clapper, Bos.	D	Earl Seibert, Chi.
Wally Stanowski, Tor.	D	Ott Heller, NYR
Bill Cowley, Bos.	C	Syl Apps, Tor.
Bryan Hextall, NYR	RW	Bobby Bauer, Bos.
Sweeney Schriner, Tor.	LW	Woody Dumart, Bos.
Cooney Weiland, Bos.	Coach	Dick Irvin, Mtl.

1939-40

First Team	Pos	Second Team
Dave Kerr, NYR	G	Frank Brimsek, Bos.
Dit Clapper, Bos.	D	Art Coulter, NYR
Ebbie Goodfellow, Det.	D	Earl Seibert, Chi.
Milt Schmidt, Bos.	C	Neil Colville, NYR
Bryan Hextall, NYR	RW	Bobby Bauer, Bos.
Toe Blake, Mtl.	LW	Woody Dumart, Bos.
Paul Thompson, Chi.	Coach	Frank Boucher, NYR

1938-39

First Team	Pos	Second Team
Frank Brimsek, Bos.	G	Earl Robertson, NYA
Eddie Shore, Bos.	D	Earl Seibert, Chi.
Dit Clapper, Bos.	D	Art Coulter, NYR
Syl Apps, Tor.	C	Neil Colville, NYR
Gordie Drillon, Tor.	RW	Bobby Bauer, Bos.
Toe Blake, Mtl.	LW	Johnny Gottselig, Chi.
Art Ross, Bos.	Coach	Red Dutton, NYA

1937-38

First Team	Pos	Second Team
Tiny Thompson, Bos.	G	Dave Kerr, NYR
Eddie Shore, Bos.	D	Art Coulter, NYR
Babe Siebert, Mtl.	D	Earl Seibert, Chi.
Bill Cowley, Bos.	C	Syl Apps, Tor.
Cecil Dillon, NYR	RW	
Gordie Drillon, Tor. *(tied)*	RW	
Paul Thompson, Chi.	LW	Toe Blake, Mtl.
Lester Patrick, NYR	Coach	Art Ross, Bos.

1936-37

First Team	Pos	Second Team
Normie Smith, Det.	G	Wilf Cude, Mtl.
Babe Siebert, Mtl.	D	Earl Seibert, Chi.
Ebbie Goodfellow, Det.	D	Lionel Conacher, Mtl. M.
Marty Barry, Det.	C	Art Chapman, NYA
Larry Aurie, Det.	RW	Cecil Dillon, NYR
Busher Jackson, Tor.	LW	Sweeney Schriner, NYA
Jack Adams, Det.	Coach	Cecil Hart, Mtl.

1935-36

First Team	Pos	Second Team
Tiny Thompson, Bos.	G	Wilf Cude, Mtl.
Eddie Shore, Bos.	D	Earl Seibert, Chi.
Babe Siebert, Bos.	D	Ebbie Goodfellow, Det.
Hooley Smith, Mtl. M.	C	Bill Thoms, Tor.
Charlie Conacher, Tor.	RW	Cecil Dillon, NYR
Sweeney Schriner, NYA	LW	Paul Thompson, Chi.
Lester Patrick, NYR	Coach	Tommy Gorman, Mtl. M.

1934-35

First Team	Pos	Second Team
Lorne Chabot, Chi.	G	Tiny Thompson, Bos.
Eddie Shore, Bos.	D	Cy Wentworth, Mtl. M.
Earl Seibert, NYR	D	Art Coulter, Chi.
Frank Boucher, NYR	C	Cooney Weiland, Det.
Charlie Conacher, Tor.	RW	Dit Clapper, Bos.
Busher Jackson, Tor.	LW	Aurel Joliat, Mtl.
Lester Patrick, NYR	Coach	Dick Irvin, Tor.

1933-34

First Team	Pos	Second Team
Charlie Gardiner, Chi.	G	Roy Worters, NYA
King Clancy, Tor.	D	Eddie Shore, Bos.
Lionel Conacher, Chi.	D	Ching Johnson, NYR
Frank Boucher, NYR	C	Joe Primeau, Tor.
Charlie Conacher, Tor.	RW	Bill Cook, NYR
Busher Jackson, Tor.	LW	Aurel Joliat, Mtl.
Lester Patrick, NYR	Coach	Dick Irvin, Tor.

1932-33

First Team	Pos	Second Team
John Ross Roach, Det.	G	Charlie Gardiner, Chi.
Eddie Shore, Bos.	D	King Clancy, Tor.
Ching Johnson, NYR	D	Lionel Conacher, Mtl. M.
Frank Boucher, NYR	C	Howie Morenz, Mtl.
Bill Cook, NYR	RW	Charlie Conacher, Tor.
Baldy Northcott, Mtl. M.	LW	Busher Jackson, Tor.
Lester Patrick, NYR	Coach	Dick Irvin, Tor.

1931-32

First Team	Pos	Second Team
Charlie Gardiner, Chi.	G	Roy Worters, NYA
Eddie Shore, Bos.	D	Sylvio Mantha, Mtl.
Ching Johnson, NYR	D	King Clancy, Tor.
Howie Morenz, Mtl.	C	Hooley Smith, Mtl. M.
Bill Cook, NYR	RW	Charlie Conacher, Tor.
Busher Jackson, Tor.	LW	Aurel Joliat, Mtl.
Lester Patrick, NYR	Coach	Dick Irvin, Tor.

1930-31

First Team	Pos	Second Team
Charlie Gardiner, Chi.	G	Tiny Thompson, Bos.
Eddie Shore, Bos.	D	Sylvio Mantha, Mtl.
King Clancy, Tor.	D	Ching Johnson, NYR
Howie Morenz, Mtl.	C	Frank Boucher, NYR
Bill Cook, NYR	RW	Dit Clapper, Bos.
Aurel Joliat, Mtl.	LW	Bun Cook, NYR
Lester Patrick, NYR	Coach	Dick Irvin, Chi.

NHL ALL-ROOKIE TEAM

Voting for the NHL All-Rookie Team is conducted among the representatives of the Professional Hockey Writers' Association at the end of the season. The rookie all-star team was first selected for the 1982-83 season.

2016-17
Goal	Matt Murray, Pittsburgh
Defense	Brady Skjei, NY Rangers
Defense	Zach Werenski, Columbus
Forward	Patrik Laine, Winnipeg
Forward	Mitch Marner, Toronto
Forward	Auston Matthews, Toronto

2015-16
Goal	John Gibson, Anaheim
Defense	Shayne Gostisbehere, Philadelphia
Defense	Colton Parayko, St. Louis
Forward	Jack Eichel, Buffalo
Forward	Connor McDavid, Edmonton
Forward	Artemi Panarin, Chicago

2014-15
Goal	Jake Allen, St. Louis
Defense	Aaron Ekblad, Florida
Defense	John Klingberg, Dallas
Forward	Filip Forsberg, Nashville
Forward	Johnny Gaudreau, Calgary
Forward	Mark Stone, Ottawa

2013-14
Goal	Frederik Andersen, Anaheim
Defense	Torey Krug, Boston
Defense	Hampus Lindholm, Anaheim
Forward	Tyler Johnson, Tampa Bay
Forward	Nathan MacKinnon, Colorado
Forward	Ondrej Palat, Tampa Bay

2012-13
Goal	Jake Allen, St. Louis
Defense	Jonas Brodin, Minnesota
Defense	Justin Schultz, Edmonton
Forward	Brendan Gallagher, Montreal
Forward	Jonathan Huberdeau, Florida
Forward	Brandon Saad, Chicago

2011-12
Goal	Jhonas Enroth, Buffalo
Defense	Justin Faulk, Carolina
Defense	Jake Gardiner, Toronto
Forward	Adam Henrique, New Jersey
Forward	Gabriel Landeskog, Colorado
Forward	Ryan Nugent-Hopkins, Edmonton

2010-11
Goal	Corey Crawford, Chicago
Defense	John Carlson, Washington
Defense	P.K. Subban, Montreal
Forward	Logan Couture, San Jose
Forward	Michael Grabner, NY Islanders
Forward	Jeff Skinner, Carolina

2009-10
Goal	Jimmy Howard, Detroit
Defense	Tyler Myers, Buffalo
Defense	Michael Del Zotto, NY Rangers
Forward	John Tavares, NY Islanders
Forward	Matt Duchene, Colorado
Forward	Niclas Bergfors, N.J., Atl.

2008-09
Goal	Steve Mason, Columbus
Defense	Drew Doughty, Los Angeles
Defense	Luke Schenn, Toronto
Forward	Patrik Berglund, St. Louis
Forward	Bobby Ryan, Anaheim
Forward	Kris Versteeg, Chicago

2007-08
Goal	Carey Price, Montreal
Defense	Tobias Enstrom, Atlanta
Defense	Tom Gilbert, Edmonton
Forward	Nicklas Backstrom, Washington
Forward	Patrick Kane, Chicago
Forward	Jonathan Toews, Chicago

2006-07
Goal	Mike Smith, Dallas
Defense	Matt Carle, San Jose
Defense	Marc-Edouard Vlasic, San Jose
Forward	Evgeni Malkin, Pittsburgh
Forward	Jordan Staal, Pittsburgh
Forward	Paul Stastny, Colorado

2005-06
Goal	Henrik Lundqvist, NY Rangers
Defense	Andrej Meszaros, Ottawa
Defense	Dion Phaneuf, Calgary
Forward	Brad Boyes, Boston
Forward	Sidney Crosby, Pittsburgh
Forward	Alex Ovechkin, Washington

2004-05
Season Cancelled

2003-04
Goal	Andrew Raycroft, Boston
Defense	John-Michael Liles, Colorado
Defense	Joni Pitkanen, Philadelphia
Forward	Trent Hunter, NY Islanders
Forward	Ryan Malone, Pittsburgh
Forward	Michael Ryder, Montreal

2002-03
Goal	Sebastien Caron, Pittsburgh
Defense	Jay Bouwmeester, Florida
Defense	Barret Jackman, St. Louis
Forward	Tyler Arnason, Chicago
Forward	Rick Nash, Columbus
Forward	Henrik Zetterberg, Detroit

2001-02
Goal	Dan Blackburn, NY Rangers
Defense	Nick Boynton, Boston
Defense	Rostislav Klesla, Columbus
Forward	Dany Heatley, Atlanta
Forward	Ilya Kovalchuk, Atlanta
Forward	Kristian Huselius, Florida

2000-01
Goal	Evgeni Nabokov, San Jose
Defense	Lubomir Visnovsky, Los Angeles
Defense	Colin White, New Jersey
Forward	Martin Havlat, Ottawa
Forward	Brad Richards, Tampa Bay
Forward	Shane Willis, Carolina

1999-2000
Goal	Brian Boucher, Philadelphia
Defense	Brian Rafalski, New Jersey
Defense	Brad Stuart, San Jose
Forward	Simon Gagne, Philadelphia
Forward	Scott Gomez, New Jersey
Forward	Michael York, NY Rangers

1998-99
Goal	Jamie Storr, Los Angeles
Defense	Tom Poti, Edmonton
Defense	Sami Salo, Ottawa
Forward	Chris Drury, Colorado
Forward	Milan Hejduk, Colorado
Forward	Marian Hossa, Ottawa

1997-98
Goal	Jamie Storr, Los Angeles
Defense	Mattias Ohlund, Vancouver
Defense	Derek Morris, Calgary
Forward	Sergei Samsonov, Boston
Forward	Patrick Elias, New Jersey
Forward	Mike Johnson, Toronto

1996-97
Goal	Patrick Lalime, Pittsburgh
Defense	Bryan Berard, NY Islanders
Defense	Janne Niinimaa, Philadelphia
Forward	Jarome Iginla, Calgary
Forward	Jim Campbell, St. Louis
Forward	Sergei Berezin, Toronto

1995-96
Goal	Corey Hirsch, Vancouver
Defense	Ed Jovanovski, Florida
Defense	Kyle McLaren, Boston
Forward	Daniel Alfredsson, Ottawa
Forward	Eric Daze, Chicago
Forward	Petr Sykora, New Jersey

1994-95
Goal	Jim Carey, Washington
Defense	Chris Therien, Philadelphia
Defense	Kenny Jonsson, Toronto
Forward	Peter Forsberg, Quebec
Forward	Jeff Friesen, San Jose
Forward	Paul Kariya, Anaheim

1993-94
Goal	Martin Brodeur, New Jersey
Defense	Chris Pronger, Hartford
Defense	Boris Mironov, Wpg./Edm.
Forward	Jason Arnott, Edmonton
Forward	Mikael Renberg, Philadelphia
Forward	Oleg Petrov, Montreal

1992-93
Goal	Felix Potvin, Toronto
Defense	Vladimir Malakhov, NY Islanders
Defense	Scott Niedermayer, New Jersey
Forward	Eric Lindros, Philadelphia
Forward	Teemu Selanne, Winnipeg
Forward	Joe Juneau, Boston

1991-92
Goal	Dominik Hasek, Chicago
Defense	Nicklas Lidstrom, Detroit
Defense	Vladimir Konstantinov, Detroit
Forward	Kevin Todd, New Jersey
Forward	Tony Amonte, NY Rangers
Forward	Gilbert Dionne, Montreal

1990-91
Goal	Ed Belfour, Chicago
Defense	Eric Weinrich, New Jersey
Defense	Rob Blake, Los Angeles
Forward	Sergei Fedorov, Detroit
Forward	Ken Hodge, Boston
Forward	Jaromir Jagr, Pittsburgh

1989-90
Goal	Bob Essensa, Winnipeg
Defense	Brad Shaw, Hartford
Defense	Geoff Smith, Edmonton
Forward	Mike Modano, Minnesota
Forward	Sergei Makarov, Calgary
Forward	Rod Brind'Amour, St. Louis

1988-89
Goal	Peter Sidorkiewicz, Hartford
Defense	Brian Leetch, NY Rangers
Defense	Zarley Zalapski, Pittsburgh
Forward	Trevor Linden, Vancouver
Forward	Tony Granato, NY Rangers
Forward	David Volek, NY Islanders

1987-88
Goal	Darren Pang, Chicago
Defense	Glen Wesley, Boston
Defense	Calle Johansson, Buffalo
Forward	Joe Nieuwendyk, Calgary
Forward	Ray Sheppard, Buffalo
Forward	Iain Duncan, Winnipeg

1986-87
Goal	Ron Hextall, Philadelphia
Defense	Steve Duchesne, Los Angeles
Defense	Brian Benning, St. Louis
Forward	Jimmy Carson, Los Angeles
Forward	Jim Sandlak, Vancouver
Forward	Luc Robitaille, Los Angeles

1985-86
Goal	Patrick Roy, Montreal
Defense	Gary Suter, Calgary
Defense	Dana Murzyn, Hartford
Forward	Mike Ridley, NY Rangers
Forward	Kjell Dahlin, Montreal
Forward	Wendel Clark, Toronto

1984-85
Goal	Steve Penney, Montreal
Defense	Chris Chelios, Montreal
Defense	Bruce Bell, Quebec
Forward	Mario Lemieux, Pittsburgh
Forward	Tomas Sandstrom, NY Rangers
Forward	Warren Young, Pittsburgh

1983-84
Goal	Tom Barrasso, Buffalo
Defense	Thomas Eriksson, Philadelphia
Defense	Jamie Macoun, Calgary
Forward	Steve Yzerman, Detroit
Forward	Hakan Loob, Calgary
Forward	Sylvain Turgeon, Hartford

1982-83
Goal	Pelle Lindbergh, Philadelphia
Defense	Scott Stevens, Washington
Defense	Phil Housley, Buffalo
Forward	Dan Daoust, Mtl./Tor.
Forward	Steve Larmer, Chicago
Forward	Mats Naslund, Montreal

2017 All-Star Game Summary
JANUARY 29, 2017 at Los Angeles

PLAYERS ON ICE: **Team Atlantic** – Carey Price, Tuukka Rask, Shea Weber, Kyle Okposo, Vincent Trocheck, Auston Matthews, Frans Nielsen, Brad Marchand, Erik Karlsson, Victor Hedman, Nikita Kucherov.
Team Central – Devan Dubnyk, Corey Crawford, Duncan Keith, Jonathan Toews, Ryan Suter, Patrik Laine, Nathan MacKinnon, P.K. Subban, Patrick Kane, Tyler Seguin, Vladimir Tarasenko.
Team Metropolitan – Braden Holtby, Sergei Bobrovsky, Seth Jones, Alex Ovechkin, Taylor Hall, Cam Atkinson, Wayne Simmonds, Justin Faulk, Ryan McDonagh, Sidney Crosby, John Tavares.
Team Pacific – Martin Jones, Mike Smith, Cam Fowler, Drew Doughty, Joe Pavelski, Johnny Gaudreau, Ryan Kesler, Bo Horvat, Jeff Carter, Brent Burns, Connor McDavid.

SUMMARY Game 1 • Pacific 10, Central 3
First Period
1. Pacific Fowler (Gaudreau, Horvat) 2:57
2. Pacific Carter (Doughty) 3:39
3. Central Toews (unassisted) 7:07
4. Pacific McDavid (Kesler) 7:13
5. Pacific Burns (McDavid) 8:00
6. Pacific Doughty (Pavelski, Carter) 9:49
PENALTIES: None

Second Period
7. Central Subban (Seguin) 2:14
8. Pacific Gaudreau (Horvat, Fowler) 2:33
9. Pacific Pavelski (Carter, Doughty) 4:15
10. Central Tarasenko (Seguin) 4:39
11. Pacific Kesler (Burns, McDavid) 5:43
12. Pacific Horvat (Fowler) 6:29
13. Pacific Gaudreau (Fowler, Jones) 6:42
PENALTIES: None

SHOTS ON GOAL BY: Pacific 11-11-22, Central 3-9-12

Team	Goaltenders	Time	SA	GA	Dec.
Pacific	Smith	10:00	3	1	W
Pacific	Jones	10:00	9	2	
Central	Crawford	10:00	11	5	L
Central	Dubnyk	10:00	11	5	

SUMMARY Game 2 • Metropolitan 10, Atlantic 6
First Period
1. Metropolitan Simmonds (unassisted) 2:12
2. Atlantic Kucherov (Trocheck, Hedman) 4:06
3. Metropolitan Simmonds (unassisted) 4:49
4. Atlantic Hedman (Kucherov, Trocheck) 6:30
5. Atlantic Karlsson (Okposo) 7:13
6. Metropolitan Tavares (Atkinson) 8:45
PENALTIES: None

Second Period
7. Atlantic Matthews (Marchand, Weber) 0:50
8. Metropolitan Tavares (Atkinson, Faulk) 1:31
9. Metropolitan Jones (Hall) 1:45
10. Metropolitan Hall (unassisted) 1:50
11. Atlantic Kucherov (Trocheck) 3:15
12. Metropoltan Crosby (Faulk, Ovechkin) 6:26
13. Metropolitan Atkinson (Tavares) 6:35
14. Metropolitan Atkinson (Tavares) 7:45
15. Metropolitan Trocheck (Kucherov) 8:54
16. Metropolitan Ovechkin (Crosby, Faulk) 9:59
PENALTIES: None

SHOTS ON GOAL BY: Metropolitan 6-15-21, Atlantic 10-15-25

Team	Goaltenders	Time	SA	GA	Dec.
Metropolitan	Bobrovsky	10:00	10	3	
Metropolitan	Holtby	10:00	15	3	W
Atlantic	Price	10:00	6	3	
Atlantic	Rask	9:17	14	6	L
Atlantic	empty net	0:43	1	1	

SUMMARY Game 3 • Metropolitan 4, Pacific 3
First Period
1. Pacific Pavelski (Doughty, Carter) 0:22
2. Metropolitan Jones (Hall, Faulk) 1:25
3. Metropolitan Faulk (Tavares) 4:09
4. Pacific McDavid (Kesler) 4:40
5. Pacific Horvat (Gaudreau) 7:52
PENALTIES: None

Second Period
6. Metropolitan Atkinson (unassisted) 4:57
7. Metropolitan Simmonds (Hall) 5:02
PENALTIES: None

SHOTS ON GOAL BY: Metropolitan 7-11-18, Pacific 12- 5-17

Team	Goaltenders	Time	SA	GA	Dec.
Metropolitan	Bobrovsky	10:00	12	3	
Metropolitan	Holtby	10:00	5	0	W
Pacific	Jones	10:00	7	2	
Pacific	Smith	9:06	11	2	L
Pacific	empty net	0:54	0	0	

PP Conversions: (all games) All Teams 0/0.

Referees: Kelly Sutherland, Mike Leggo
Linesmen: Davd Brisebois, Steve Barton
Attendance : 18,665

NHL ALL-STAR GAME MVP
2017   Wayne Simmonds, Phi.

2017 NHL All-Star Game Format

For 2017, the NHL All-Star Game again featured a three-game, 3-on-3 tournament. An 11-man roster was selected from each of the League's four divisions and each game was 20 minutes in length.

Statistics from these games have not been applied to the NHL All-Star Game Records that follow. Game summaries are found on page 235.

All-Star Game Results

Year	Venue	Score	Coaches	Attendance
2015	Columbus	Team Toews 17, Team Foligno 12	Peter Laviolette, Darryl Sutter	18,901
2012	Ottawa	Team Chara 12, Team Alfredsson 9	Claude Julien, Tortorella/MacLellan	20,510
2011	Carolina	Team Lidstrom 11, Team Staal 10	Joel Quenneville, Peter Laviolette	18,680
2009	Montreal	East 12, West 11	Claude Julien, Todd McLellan	21,273
2008	Atlanta	East 8, West 7	John Paddock, Mike Babcock	18,644
2007	Dallas	West 12, East 9	Lindy Ruff, Randy Carlyle	18,532
2004	Minnesota	East 6, West 4	Pat Quinn, Dave Lewis	19,434
2003	Florida	West 6, East 5	Marc Crawford, Jacques Martin	19,250
2002	Los Angeles	World 8, North America 5	Scotty Bowman, Pat Quinn	18,118
2001	Colorado	North America 14, World 12	Joel Quenneville, Jacques Martin	18,646
2000	Toronto	World 9, North America 4	Scotty Bowman, Pat Quinn	19,300
1999	Tampa Bay	North America 8, World 6	Lindy Ruff, Ken Hitchcock	19,758
1998	Vancouver	North America 8, World 7	Jacques Lemaire, Ken Hitchcock	18,422
1997	San Jose	East 11, West 7	Doug MacLean, Ken Hitchcock	17,422
1996	Boston	East 5, West 4	Doug MacLean, Scotty Bowman	17,565
1994	NY Rangers	East 9, West 8	Jacques Demers, Barry Melrose	18,200
1993	Montreal	Wales 16, Campbell 6	Scotty Bowman, Mike Keenan	17,137
1992	Philadelphia	Campbell 10, Wales 6	Bob Gainey, Scotty Bowman	17,380
1991	Chicago	Campbell 11, Wales 5	John Muckler, Mike Milbury	18,472
1990	Pittsburgh	Wales 12, Campbell 7	Pat Burns, Terry Crisp	16,236
1989	Edmonton	Campbell 9, Wales 5	Glen Sather, Terry O'Reilly	17,503
1988	St. Louis	Wales 6, Campbell 5 OT	Mike Keenan, Glen Sather	17,878
1986	Hartford	Wales 4, Campbell 3 OT	Mike Keenan, Glen Sather	15,100
1985	Calgary	Wales 6, Campbell 4	Al Arbour, Glen Sather	16,825
1984	New Jersey	Wales 7, Campbell 6	Al Arbour, Glen Sather	18,939
1983	NY Islanders	Campbell 9, Wales 3	Roger Neilson, Al Arbour	15,230
1982	Washington	Wales 4, Campbell 2	Al Arbour, Glen Sonmor	18,130
1981	Los Angeles	Campbell 4, Wales 1	Pat Quinn, Scotty Bowman	15,761
1980	Detroit	Wales 6, Campbell 3	Scotty Bowman, Al Arbour	21,002
1978	Buffalo	Wales 3, Campbell 2 OT	Scotty Bowman, Fred Shero	16,433
1977	Vancouver	Wales 4, Campbell 3	Scotty Bowman, Fred Shero	15,607
1976	Philadelphia	Wales 7, Campbell 5	Floyd Smith, Fred Shero	16,436
1975	Montreal	Wales 7, Campbell 1	Bep Guidolin, Fred Shero	16,080
1974	Chicago	West 6, East 4	Billy Reay, Scotty Bowman	16,426
1973	NY Rangers	East 5, West 4	Tom Johnson, Billy Reay	16,986
1972	Minnesota	East 3, West 2	Al MacNeil, Billy Reay	15,423
1971	Boston	West 2, East 1	Scotty Bowman, Harry Sinden	14,790
1970	St. Louis	East 4, West 1	Claude Ruel, Scotty Bowman	16,587
1969	Montreal	East 3, West 3	Toe Blake, Scotty Bowman	16,260
1968	Toronto	Toronto 4, All-Stars 3	Punch Imlach, Toe Blake	15,753
1967	Montreal	Montreal 3, All-Stars 0	Toe Blake, Sid Abel	14,284
1965	Montreal	All-Stars 5, Montreal 2	Billy Reay, Toe Blake	13,529
1964	Toronto	All-Stars 3, Toronto 2	Sid Abel, Punch Imlach	14,232
1963	Toronto	All-Stars 3, Toronto 3	Sid Abel, Punch Imlach	14,034
1962	Toronto	Toronto 4, All-Stars 1	Punch Imlach, Rudy Pilous	14,236
1961	Chicago	All-Stars 3, Chicago 1	Sid Abel, Rudy Pilous	14,534
1960	Montreal	All-Stars 2, Montreal 1	Punch Imlach, Toe Blake	13,949
1959	Montreal	Montreal 6, All-Stars 1	Toe Blake, Punch Imlach	13,818
1958	Montreal	Montreal 6, All-Stars 3	Toe Blake, Milt Schmidt	13,989
1957	Montreal	All-Stars 5, Montreal 3	Milt Schmidt, Toe Blake	13,003
1956	Montreal	All-Stars 1, Montreal 1	Jim Skinner, Toe Blake	13,095
1955	Detroit	Detroit 3, All-Stars 1	Jim Skinner, Dick Irvin	10,111
1954	Detroit	All-Stars 2, Detroit 2	King Clancy, Jim Skinner	10,689
1953	Montreal	All-Stars 3, Montreal 1	Lynn Patrick, Dick Irvin	14,153
1952	Detroit	1st Team 1, 2nd Team 1	Tommy Ivan, Dick Irvin	10,680
1951	Toronto	1st Team 2, 2nd Team 2	Joe Primeau, Dick Irvin	11,469
1950	Detroit	Detroit 7, All-Stars 1	Tommy Ivan, Lynn Patrick	9,166
1949	Toronto	All-Stars 3, Toronto 1	Tommy Ivan, Hap Day	13,541
1948	Chicago	All-Stars 3, Toronto 1	Tommy Ivan, Hap Day	12,794
1947	Toronto	All-Stars 4, Toronto 3	Dick Irvin, Hap Day	14,169

There was no All-Star contest during the calendar year of 1966 because the game was moved from the start of season to mid-season. In 1979, the Challenge Cup series between the Soviet Union and Team NHL replaced the All-Star Game. In 1987, Rendez-Vous '87, two games between the Soviet Union and Team NHL replaced the All-Star Game. In 1995, 2005 and 2013 the All-Star Game was not played due to a labour disruption affecting the NHL. In 2006, 2010 and 2014 the All-Star Game was not played because of NHL players' participation in the Olympics.

NHL ALL-STAR GAME MVP

2017	Wayne Simmonds, Phi.	1996	Raymond Bourque, Bos.	1977	Rick Martin, Buf.
2016	John Scott, Mtl.	1994	Mike Richter, NYR	1976	Pete Mahovlich, Mtl.
2015	Ryan Johansen, CBJ	1993	Mike Gartner, NYR	1975	Syl Apps Jr., Pit.
2012	Marian Gaborik, NYR	1992	Brett Hull, St.L.	1974	Garry Unger, St.L.
2011	Patrick Sharp, Chi.	1991	Vincent Damphousse, Tor.	1973	Greg Polis, Pit.
2009	Alex Kovalev, Mtl.	1990	Mario Lemieux, Pit.	1972	Bobby Orr, Bos.
2008	Eric Staal, Car.	1989	Wayne Gretzky, L.A.	1971	Bobby Hull, Chi.
2007	Daniel Briere, Buf.	1988	Mario Lemieux, Pit.	1970	Bobby Hull, Chi.
2004	Joe Sakic, Col..	1986	Grant Fuhr, Edm.	1969	Frank Mahovlich, Det.
2003	Dany Heatley, Chi.	1985	Mario Lemieux, Pit.	1968	Bruce Gamble, Tor.
2002	Eric Daze, Chi.	1984	Don Maloney, NYR	1967	Henri Richard, Mtl.
2001	Bill Guerin, Bos.	1983	Wayne Gretzky, Edm.	1965	Gordie Howe, Det.
2000	Pavel Bure, Fla.	1982	Mike Bossy, NYI	1964	Jean Beliveau, Mtl.
1999	Wayne Gretzky, NYR	1981	Mike Liut, St.L.	1963	Frank Mahovlich, Tor.
1998	Teemu Selanne, Ana.	1980	Reggie Leach, Phi.	1962	Eddie Shack, Tor.
1997	Mark Recchi, Mtl.	1978	Billy Smith, NYI		

All-Star Game Records 1947 through 2015

TEAM RECORDS

MOST GOALS, BOTH TEAMS, ONE GAME:
29 — Team Toews 17, Team Foligno 12, 2015 at Columbus
26 — North America 14, World 12, 2001 at Colorado
23 — East 12, West 11, 2009 at Montreal
22 — Wales 16, Campbell 6, 1993 at Montreal
21 — West 12, East 9, 2007 at Dallas
   — Team Lidstrom 11, Team Staal 10, 2011 at Carolina
   — Team Chara 12, Team Alfredsson 9, 2012 at Ottawa

FEWEST GOALS, BOTH TEAMS, ONE GAME:
2 — First Team All-Stars 1, Second Team All-Stars 1, 1952 at Detroit
   — NHL All-Stars 1, Montreal Canadiens 1, 1956 at Montreal
3 — NHL All-Stars 2, Montreal Canadiens 1, 1960 at Montreal
   — Montreal Canadiens 3, NHL All-Stars 0, 1967 at Montreal
   — West 2, East 1, 1971 at Boston

MOST GOALS, ONE TEAM, ONE GAME:
17 — Team Toews 17, Team Foligno 12, 2015 at Columbus
16 — Wales 16, Campbell 6, 1993 at Montreal
14 — North America 14, World 12, 2001 at Colorado
12 — Wales 12, Campbell 7, 1990 at Pittsburgh
   — World 12, North America 14, 2001 at Colorado
   — West 12, East 9, 2007 at Dallas
   — East 12, West 11, 2009 at Montreal
   — Team Chara 12, Team Alfredsson 9, 2012 at Ottawa
   — Team Foligno 12, Team Toews 17, 2015 at Columbus

FEWEST GOALS, ONE TEAM, ONE GAME:
0 — NHL All-Stars 0, Montreal Canadiens 3, 1967 at Montreal
1 — 17 times (1981, 1975, 1971, 1970, 1962, 1961, 1960, 1959, both teams 1956, 1955, 1953, both teams 1952, 1950, 1949, 1948)

MOST SHOTS, BOTH TEAMS, ONE GAME (SINCE 1955):
102 — 1994 at NY Rangers - East 9 (56 shots), West 8 (46 shots)
   — 2009 at Montreal - East 12 (48 shots), West 11 (54 shots)
98 — 2001 at Colorado - North America 14 (53 shots), World 12 (45 shots)
94 — 2012 at Ottawa - Team Chara 12 (44 shots), Team Alfredsson 9 (50 shots)

FEWEST SHOTS, BOTH TEAMS, ONE GAME (SINCE 1955):
52 — 1978 at Buffalo - Campbell 2 (12 shots), Wales 3 (40 shots)
53 — 1960 at Montreal - NHL All-Stars 2 (27 shots), Montreal Canadiens 1 (26 shots)
55 — 1956 at Montreal - NHL All-Stars 1 (28 shots), Montreal Canadiens 1 (27 shots)
   — 1971 at Boston - West 2 (28 shots), East 1 (27 shots)

MOST SHOTS, ONE TEAM, ONE GAME (SINCE 1955):
56 — 1994 at NY Rangers - East (9-8 vs. West)
54 — 2009 at Montreal - East (12-11 vs. West)
53 — 2001 at Colorado - North America (14-12 vs. World)
51 — 2008 at Atlanta - West (7-8 vs. East)

FEWEST SHOTS, ONE TEAM, ONE GAME (SINCE 1955):
12 — 1978 at Buffalo - Campbell (2-3 vs. Wales)
17 — 1970 at St. Louis - West (1-4 vs. East)
23 — 1961 at Chicago - Chicago Black Hawks (1-3 vs. NHL All-Stars)
24 — 1976 at Philadelphia - Campbell (5-7 vs. Wales)

MOST POWER-PLAY GOALS, BOTH TEAMS, ONE GAME (SINCE 1950):
3 — 1953 at Montreal - NHL All-Stars 3 (2 power-play goals), Montreal Canadiens 1 (1 power-play goal)
   — 1954 at Detroit - NHL All-Stars 2 (1 power-play goal), Detroit Red Wings 2 (2 power-play goals)
   — 1958 at Montreal - NHL All-Stars 3 (1 power-play goal), Montreal Canadiens 6 (2 power-play goals)

FEWEST POWER-PLAY GOALS, BOTH TEAMS, ONE GAME (SINCE 1950):
0 — 28 times (1952, 1959, 1960, 1967, 1968, 1969, 1972, 1973, 1976, 1980, 1981, 1984, 1985, 1992, 1994, 1996, 1999, 2000, 2001, 2002, 2003, 2004, 2007, 2008, 2009, 2011, 2012, 2015)

FASTEST TWO GOALS, BOTH TEAMS, FROM START OF GAME:
0:37 — 1970 at St. Louis — Jacques Laperriere of East scored at 0:20 and Dean Prentice of West scored at 0:37. Final score: East 4, West 1.
1:20 — 2008 at Atlanta — Rick Nash of West scored at 0:12 and Eric Staal of East scored at 1:20. Final score: East 8, West 7.
2:15 — 1998 at Vancouver — Teemu Selanne scored at 0:53 and Jaromir Jagr scored at 2:15 for World. Final score: North America 8, World 7.

FASTEST TWO GOALS, BOTH TEAMS:
0:08 — 1997 at San Jose — Owen Nolan scored at 18:54 and 19:02 of second period for West. Final score: East 11, West 7.
   — 2015 at Columbus — Ryan Suter scored at 0:24 of second period for Team Toews and Claude Giroux scored at 0:32 for Team Foligno. Final score: Team Toews 17, Team Foligno 12.
0:10 — 1976 at Philadelphia — Dennis Ververgaert scored at 4:33 and at 4:43 of third period for Campbell. Final score: Wales 7, Campbell 5.

FASTEST THREE GOALS, BOTH TEAMS:

0:48 — 2007 at Dallas — Martin Havlat scored at 19:00 of third period for West; Sheldon Souray scored at 19:25 for East; Dion Phaneuf scored at 19:48 for West. Final score: West 12, East 9.

0:58 — 2015 at Columbus — Ryan Suter scored at 0:24 of second period for Team Toews; Claude Giroux scored at 0:32 for Team Foligno; Tyler Seguin scored at 1:22 for Team Toews. Final score: Team Toews 17, Team Foligno 12.

1:08 — 1993 at Montreal — all by Wales — Mike Gartner scored at 3:15 and at 3:37 of first period; Peter Bondra scored at 4:23. Final score: Wales 16, Campbell 6.

FASTEST FOUR GOALS, BOTH TEAMS:

2:03 — 2015 at Columbus — Ryan Suter scored at 0:24 of second period for Team Toews; Claude Giroux scored at 0:32 for Team Foligno; Tyler Seguin scored at 1:22 for Team Toews; Steven Stamkos scored at 2:27 for Team Foligno. Final score: Team Toews 17, Team Foligno 12.

2:16 — 2012 at Ottawa — Marian Hossa scored at 12:04 of third period for Team Chara; Zdeno Chara scored at 12:20 of third period for Team Chara; Corey Perry scored at 13:26 of third period for Team Chara; Daniel Sedin scored at 14:20 of third period for Team Alfredsson. Final score: Team Chara 12, Team Alfredsson 9.

2:24 — 1997 at San Jose — Brendan Shanahan scored at 16:38 of second period for West; Dale Hawerchuk scored at 17:28 for East; Owen Nolan scored at 18:54 and 19:02 for West. Final score: East 11, West 7.

FASTEST TWO GOALS, ONE TEAM, FROM START OF GAME:

2:15 — 1998 at Vancouver — World — Teemu Selanne scored at 0:53 and Jaromir Jagr scored at 2:15. Final score: North America 8, World 7.

2:48 — 2011 at Carolina — Team Staal — Alex Ovechkin scored at 0:50 and Paul Stastny scored at 2:48. Final score: Team Lidstrom 11, Team Staal 10.

3:37 — 1993 at Montreal — Wales — Mike Gartner scored at 3:15 and at 3:37. Final score: Wales 16, Campbell 6.

FASTEST TWO GOALS, ONE TEAM:

0:08 — 1997 at San Jose — West — Owen Nolan scored at 18:54 and at 19:02 of second period. Final score: East 11, West 7.

0:10 — 1976 at Philadelphia — Campbell — Dennis Ververgaert scored at 4:33 and at 4:43 of third period. Final score: Wales 7, Campbell 5.

0:14 — 1989 at Edmonton — Campbell — Steve Yzerman and Gary Leeman scored at 17:21 and 17:35 of second period. Final score: Campbell 9, Wales 5.

FASTEST THREE GOALS, ONE TEAM:

1:08 — 1993 at Montreal — Wales — Mike Gartner scored at 3:15 and 3:37 of first period; Peter Bondra scored at 4:23. Final score: Wales 16, Campbell 6.

1:22 — 2012 at Ottawa — Team Chara — Marian Hossa scored at 12:04 of third period; Zdeno Chara scored at 12:20; Corey Perry scored at 13:26. Final score: Team Chara 12, Team Alfredsson 9.

1:32 — 1980 at Detroit — Wales — Ron Stackhouse scored at 11:40 of third period; Craig Hartsburg scored at 12:40; Reed Larson scored at 13:12. Final score: Wales 6, Campbell 3.

FASTEST FOUR GOALS, ONE TEAM:

2:57 — 2002 at Los Angeles — World — Sergei Fedorov scored at 16:59 of third period; Markus Naslund scored at 18:17; Alex Zhamnov scored at 19:12; Sami Kapanen scored at 19:56. Final score: World 8, North America 5.

3:29 — 2012 at Ottawa — Team Chara — Marian Hossa scored at 12:04 of third period; Zdeno Chara scored at 12:20; Corey Perry scored at 13:26; Joffrey Lupul scored at 15:33. Final score: Team Chara 12, Team Alfredsson 9.

4:17 — 2007 at Dallas — Brian Rolston scored at 8:30 of second period; Rick Nash scored at 10:40; Martin Havlat scored at 11:34; Yanic Perreault scored at 12:47. Final score: West 12, East 9.

MOST GOALS, BOTH TEAMS, ONE PERIOD:

11 — 2015 at Columbus — Third Period — Team Toews (7), Team Foligno (4), Final score: Team Toews 17, Team Foligno 12.

10 — 1997 at San Jose — Second period — East (6), West (4). Final score: East 11, West 7.

— 2001 at Colorado — Second period — North America (6), World (4). Final score: North America 14, World 12.

— 2001 at Colorado — Third period — North America (5), World (5). Final score: North America 14, World 12.

— 2009 at Montreal — Second period — West (6), East (4). Final score: East 12, West 11.

MOST GOALS, ONE TEAM, ONE PERIOD:

7 — 1990 at Pittsburgh — First period — Wales. Final score: Wales 12, Campbell 7.

— 2015 at Columbus — Second period — Team Toews. Final score: Team Toews 17, Team Foligno 12.

6 — 1983 at NY Islanders — Third period — Campbell. Final score: Campbell 9, Wales 3.

— 1992 at Philadelphia — Second period — Campbell. Final score: Campbell 10, Wales 6.

— 1993 at Montreal — First period — Wales. Final score: Wales 16, Campbell 6.

— 1993 at Montreal — Second period — Wales. Final score: Wales 16, Campbell 6.

— 1997 at San Jose — Second period — East. Final score: East 11, West 7.

— 2001 at Colorado — Second period — North America. Final score: North America 14, World 12.

— 2007 at Dallas — Second period — West. Final score: West 12, East 9.

— 2009 at Montreal — Second period — West. Final score: East 12, West 11.

— 2012 at Ottawa — Third period — Team Chara. Final score: Team Chara 12, Team Alfredsson 9.

— 2015 at Columbus — Third period — Team Toews. Final score: Team Toews 17, Team Foligno 12.

MOST SHOTS, BOTH TEAMS, ONE PERIOD:

42 — 2009 at Montreal — Second period — West (21), East (21). Final score: East 12, West 11.

40 — 2012 at Ottawa — Third period — Team Alfredsson (21), Team Chara (19). Final score: Team Chara 12, Team Alfredsson 9.

39 — 1994 at NY Rangers — Second period — West (21), East (18). Final score: East 9, West 8.

— 2001 at Colorado — Third period — World (23), North America (16). Final score: North America 14, World 12.

36 — 1990 at Pittsburgh — Third period — Campbell (22), Wales (14). Final score: Wales 12, Campbell 7.

— 1994 at NY Rangers — First period — East (19), West (17). Final score: East 9, West 8.

— 2002 at Los Angeles — Third period — North America (20), World (16). Final score: World 8, North America 5.

MOST SHOTS, ONE TEAM, ONE PERIOD:

23 — 2001 at Colorado — Third period — World. Final score: North America 14, World 12.

22 — 1990 at Pittsburgh — Third period — Campbell. Final score: Wales 12, Campbell 7.

— 1991 at Chicago — Third period — Wales. Final score: Campbell 11, Wales 5.

— 1993 at Montreal — First period — Wales. Final score: Wales 16, Campbell 6.

FEWEST SHOTS, BOTH TEAMS, ONE PERIOD:

9 — 1971 at Boston — Third period — East (2), West (7). Final score: West 2, East 1.

— 1980 at Detroit — Second period — Campbell (4), Wales (5). Final score: Wales 6, Campbell 3.

13 — 1982 at Washington — Third period — Campbell (6), Wales (7). Final score: Wales 4, Campbell 2.

14 — 1978 at Buffalo — First period — Campbell (7), Wales (7). Final score: Wales 3, Campbell 2.

— 1986 at Hartford — First period — Campbell (6), Wales (8). Final score: Wales 4, Campbell 3.

FEWEST SHOTS, ONE TEAM, ONE PERIOD:

2 — 1971 at Boston — Third period — East. Final score: West 2, East 1.

— 1978 at Buffalo — Second period — Campbell. Final score: Wales 3, Campbell 2.

3 — 1978 at Buffalo — Third period — Campbell. Final score: Wales 3, Campbell 2.

4 — 1955 at Detroit — First period — NHL All-Stars. Final score: Detroit Red Wings 3, NHL All-Stars 1.

— 1980 at Detroit — Second period — Campbell. Final score: Wales 6, Campbell 3.

Sidney Crosby and Connor McDavid shake hands after Crosby's Metropolitan Division team beat McDavid's Pacific Division team in the 2017 All-Star Final.

INDIVIDUAL RECORDS

Games

MOST GAMES PLAYED:
23 — Gordie Howe, 1948 through 1980
19 — Raymond Bourque, 1981 through 2001
18 — Wayne Gretzky, 1980 through 1999
15 — Frank Mahovlich, 1959 through 1974
— Mark Messier, 1982 through 2004

Goals

MOST GOALS, CAREER:
13 — Wayne Gretzky in 18GP
— **Mario Lemieux** in 10GP
10 — Gordie Howe in 23GP
9 — Teemu Selanne in 10GP
— Rick Nash in 6GP

MOST GOALS, ONE GAME:
4 — Wayne Gretzky, Campbell, 1983
— **Mario Lemieux**, Wales, 1990
— **Vince Damphousse**, Campbell, 1991
— **Mike Gartner**, Wales, 1993
— **Dany Heatley**, East, 2003
— **John Tavares**, Team Toews, 2015
3 — Ted Lindsay, Detroit, 1950
— Mario Lemieux, Wales, 1988
— Pierre Turgeon, Wales, 1993
— Mark Recchi, East, 1997
— Owen Nolan, West, 1997
— Teemu Selanne, World, 1998
— Pavel Bure, World, 2000
— Bill Guerin, North America, 2001
— Joe Sakic, West, 2004
— Rick Nash, West, 2008
— Marian Gaborik, Team Chara, 2012
— Jakub Voracek, Team Toews, 2015

MOST GOALS, ONE PERIOD:
4 — Wayne Gretzky, Campbell, Third period, 1983
3 — Mario Lemieux, Wales, First period, 1990
— Vincent Damphousse, Campbell, Third period, 1991
— Mike Gartner, Wales, First period, 1993

Assists

MOST ASSISTS, CAREER:
16 — Joe Sakic in 12GP
14 — Mark Messier in 15GP
13 — Raymond Bourque in 19GP

MOST ASSISTS, ONE GAME:
5 — Mats Naslund, Wales, 1988
4 — Raymond Bourque, Wales, 1985
— Adam Oates, Campbell, 1991
— Adam Oates, Wales, 1993
— Mark Recchi, Wales, 1993
— Pierre Turgeon, East, 1994
— Fredrik Modin, World, 2001
— Joe Sakic, West, 2007
— Daniel Briere, East, 2007
— Marian Hossa, East, 2007
— Shea Weber, Team Lidstrom, 2011
— Aaron Ekblad, Team Toews, 2015
— Jonathan Toews, Team Toews, 2015
— Patrice Bergeron, Team Toews, 2015
— Vladimir Tarasenko, Team Toews, 2015

MOST ASSISTS, ONE PERIOD:
4 — Adam Oates, Wales, First period, 1993
3 — Mark Messier, Campbell, Third period, 1983
3 — Marian Hossa, East, Third period, 2007

Points

MOST POINTS, CAREER:
25 — Wayne Gretzky (13G-12A in 18GP)
23 — Mario Lemieux (13G-10A in 10GP)
22 — Joe Sakic (6G-16A in 12GP)
20 — Mark Messier (6G-14A in 15GP)
19 — Gordie Howe (10G-9A in 23GP)

MOST POINTS, ONE GAME:
6 — Mario Lemieux, Wales, 1988 (3G-3A)
— **Jakub Voracek**, Team Toews, 2015 (3G-3A)
5 — Mats Naslund, Wales, 1988 (5A)
— Adam Oates, Campbell, 1991 (1G-4A)
— Mike Gartner, Wales, 1993 (4G-1A)
— Mark Recchi, Wales, 1993 (1G-4A)
— Pierre Turgeon, Wales, 1993 (3G-2A)
— Bill Guerin, North America, 2001 (3G-2A)
— Dany Heatley, East, 2003 (4G-1A)
— Daniel Briere, East, 2007 (1G-4A)
— Patrice Bergeron, Team Toews, 2015 (1G-4A)
— Jonathan Toews, Team Toews, 2015 (1G-4A)

MOST POINTS, ONE PERIOD:
4 — Wayne Gretzky, Campbell, Third period, 1983 (4G)
— **Mike Gartner**, Wales, First period, 1993 (3G-1A)
— **Adam Oates**, Wales, First period, 1993 (4A)
3 — Gordie Howe, NHL All-Stars, Second period, 1965 (1G-2A)
— Pete Mahovlich, Wales, First period, 1976 (1G-2A)
— Mark Messier, Campbell, Third period, 1983 (3A)
— Mario Lemieux, Wales, Second period, 1988 (1G-2A)
— Mario Lemieux, Wales, First period, 1990 (3G)
— Vince Damphousse, Campbell, Third period, 1991 (3G)
— Mark Recchi, Wales, Second period, 1993 (1G-2A)
— Tony Amonte, North America, Second period, 2001 (2G-1A)
— Daniel Alfredsson, East, Second period, 2004 (2G-1A)
— Marian Hossa, East, Third period, 2007 (3A)
— Jakub Voracek, Team Toews, Third period, 2015 (1G-2A)

Power-Play Goals

MOST POWER-PLAY GOALS, CAREER:
6 — Gordie Howe in 23GP
3 — Bobby Hull in 12GP
— Maurice Richard in 13GP

Fastest Goals

FASTEST GOAL FROM START OF GAME:
0:12 — Rick Nash, West, 2008
0:19 — Ted Lindsay, Detroit, 1950
0:20 — Jacques Laperriere, East, 1970
0:21 — Mario Lemieux, Wales, 1990
0:35 — Vincent Damphousse, North America, 2002

FASTEST GOAL FROM START OF A PERIOD:
0:12 — Rick Nash, West, 2008 (first period)
0:17 — Raymond Bourque, North America, 1999 (second period)
0:19 — Ted Lindsay, Detroit, 1950 (first period)
— Rick Tocchet, Wales, 1993 (second period)
0:20 — Jacques Laperriere, East, 1970 (first period)

FASTEST TWO GOALS, ONE PLAYER, FROM START OF GAME:
3:37 — Mike Gartner, Wales, 1993, at 3:15 and 3:37.
4:00 — Teemu Selanne, World, 1998, at 0:53 and 4:00
5:25 — Wally Hergesheimer, NHL All-Stars, 1953, at 4:06 and 5:25.

FASTEST TWO GOALS, ONE PLAYER, FROM START OF A PERIOD:
3:37 — Mike Gartner, Wales, 1993, at 3:15 and 3:37 of first period.
4:00 — Teemu Selanne, World, 1998, at 0:53 and 4:00 of first period.
4:43 — Dennis Ververgaert, Campbell, 1976, at 4:33 and 4:43 of third period.

FASTEST TWO GOALS, ONE PLAYER:
0:08 — Owen Nolan, West, 1997, at 18:54 and 19:02 of second period.
0:10 — Dennis Ververgaert, Campbell, 1976, at 4:33 and 4:43 of third period.
0:22 — Mike Gartner, Wales, 1993, at 3:15 and 3:37 of first period.

Penalties

MOST PENALTY MINUTES:
25 — Gordie Howe in 23GP
21 — Gus Mortson in 9GP
16 — Harry Howell in 7GP

Goaltenders

MOST GAMES PLAYED:
13 — Glenn Hall from 1955 through 1969
11 — Terry Sawchuk from 1950 through 1968
— Patrick Roy from 1988 through 2003
9 — Martin Brodeur from 1996 through 2007
8 — Jacques Plante from 1956 through 1970

MOST MINUTES PLAYED:
540 — Glenn Hall in 13GP
467 — Terry Sawchuk in 11GP
370 — Jacques Plante in 8GP
250 — Patrick Roy in 11GP
209 — Turk Broda in 4GP

MOST GOALS AGAINST:
31 — Patrick Roy in 11GP
22 — Martin Brodeur in 9GP
— Glenn Hall in 13GP
21 — Mike Vernon in 5GP
19 — Terry Sawchuk in 11GP

BEST GOALS-AGAINST-AVERAGE AMONG THOSE WITH AT LEAST TWO GAMES PLAYED:
0.68 — Gilles Villemure in 3GP
1.49 — Gerry McNeil in 3GP
1.50 — Johnny Bower in 4GP
1.51 — Frank Brimsek in 3GP
1.64 — Gump Worsley in 4GP

Hockey Hall of Fame

(Year of induction is listed after each Honoured Members name)

Location: Brookfield Place, at the corner of Front and Yonge Streets in the heart of downtown Toronto. Easy access from all major highways running into Toronto. Close to TTC subway and Union Station.

Telephone: administration (416) 360-7735; information (416) 360-7765.

Public Hours of Operation: Open every day except Christmas Day, New Year's Day and Induction Day (November 13, 2017). Please call our information number (above) or visit our website (below) for times.

The Hockey Hall of Fame can be booked for private functions after hours.

Website address: www.hhof.com

History: The Hockey Hall of Fame was established in 1943. Members were first honoured in 1945. On August 26, 1961, the Hockey Hall of Fame opened its doors to the public in a building located on the grounds of the Canadian National Exhibition in Toronto. The Hockey Hall of Fame relocated to its current location and welcomed the hockey world on June 18, 1993.

Honour Roll: There are 399 Honoured Members in the Hockey Hall of Fame. 276 have been inducted as players including five women, 107 as builders and 16 as Referees/Linesmen. In addition, there are 98 media honourees.

Founding/Premier Sponsors: Cisco Systems, Imperial Oil, International Ice Hockey Federation, National Hockey League, National Hockey League Players' Association, PepsiCo Canada, Scotiabank, The Toronto Sun, Tim Hortons, The Sports Network (TSN/RDS).

Paul Kariya (left) and Teemu Selanne formed a dynamic duo in the early days of the Anaheim Ducks (then known as the Mighty Ducks of Anaheim). They go into the Hockey Hall of Fame together in 2017.

PLAYERS

* Abel, Sidney Gerald 1969
* Adams, John James "Jack" 1959
  Anderson, Glenn 2008
  Andreychuk, Dave 2017
* Apps, Charles Joseph Sylvanus "Syl" 1961
  Armstrong, George Edward 1975
* Bailey, Irvine Wallace "Ace" 1975
* Bain, Donald H. "Dan" 1949
* Baker, Hobart "Hobey" 1945
  Barber, William Charles "Bill" 1990
* Barry, Martin J. "Marty" 1965
* Bathgate, Andrew James "Andy" 1978
* Bauer, Robert Theodore "Bobby" 1996
  Belfour, Ed 2011
* Béliveau, Jean Arthur 1972
* Benedict, Clinton S. 1965
* Bentley, Douglas Wagner 1964
* Bentley, Maxwell H. L. 1966
* Blake, Hector "Toe" 1966
  Blake, Rob 2014
  Boivin, Leo Joseph 1986
* Boon, Richard R. "Dickie" 1952
  Bossy, Michael 1991
* Bouchard, Emile Joseph "Butch" 1966
* Boucher, Frank 1958
* Boucher, George "Buck" 1960
  Bourque, Raymond 2004
  Bower, John William 1976
* Bowie, Russell 1947
* Brimsek, Francis Charles 1966
* Broadbent, Harry L. "Punch" 1962
* Broda, Walter Edward "Turk" 1967
  Bucyk, John Paul 1981
* Burch, Billy 1974
  Bure, Pavel 2012
* Cameron, Harold Hugh "Harry" 1962
  Cheevers, Gerald Michael "Gerry" 1985
  Chelios, Chris 2013
  Ciccarelli, Dino 2010
* Clancy, Francis Michael "King" 1958
* Clapper, Aubrey "Dit" 1947
  Clarke, Robert "Bobby" 1987
* Cleghorn, Sprague 1958
  Coffey, Paul 2004
* Colville, Neil MacNeil 1967
* Conacher, Charles W. 1961
* Conacher, Lionel Pretoria 1994
* Conacher, Roy Gordon 1998
* Connell, Alex 1958
* Cook, Fred "Bun" 1995
* Cook, William Osser 1952
* Coulter, Arthur Edmund 1974
  Cournoyer, Yvan Serge 1982
* Cowley, William Mailes 1968

* Crawford, Samuel Russell "Rusty" 1962
* Darragh, John Proctor "Jack" 1962
* Davidson, Allan M. "Scotty" 1950
* Day, Clarence Henry "Hap" 1961
  Delvecchio, Alex 1977
* Denneny, Cyril "Cy" 1959
  Dionne, Marcel 1992
* Drillon, Gordon Arthur 1975
* Drinkwater, Charles Graham 1950
  Dryden, Kenneth Wayne 1983
  Duff, Dick 2006
* Dumart, Woodrow "Woody" 1992
* Dunderdale, Thomas 1974
* Durnan, William Ronald 1964
* Dutton, Mervyn A. "Red" 1958
* Dye, Cecil Henry "Babe" 1970
  Esposito, Anthony James "Tony" 1988
  Esposito, Philip Anthony 1984
* Farrell, Arthur F. 1965
  Federko, Bernie 2002
  Fedorov, Sergei 2015
  Fetisov, Viacheslav 2001
* Flaman, Ferdinand Charles "Fern" 1990
  Forsberg, Peter 2014
* Foyston, Frank 1958
  Francis, Ron 2007
* Fredrickson, Frank 1958
  Fuhr, Grant 2003
* Gadsby, William Alexander 1970
  Gainey, Bob 1992
* Gardiner, Charles Robert "Chuck" 1945
* Gardiner, Herbert Martin "Herb" 1958
* Gardner, James Henry "Jimmy" 1962
  Gartner, Michael Alfred 2001
* Geoffrion, Jos. A. Bernard "Boom Boom" 1972
* Gerard, Eddie 1945
  Giacomin, Edward "Eddie" 1987
  Gilbert, Rodrigue Gabriel "Rod" 1982
  Gillies, Clark 2002
  Gilmour, Doug 2011
* Gilmour, Hamilton Livingstone "Billy" 1962
* Goheen, Frank Xavier "Moose" 1952
* Goodfellow, Ebenezer R. "Ebbie" 1963
  Goulet, Michel 1998
  Goyette, Danielle 2017
  Granato, Cammi 2010
* Grant, Michael "Mike" 1950
* Green, Wilfred "Shorty" 1962
  Gretzky, Wayne Douglas 1999
* Griffis, Silas Seth "Si" 1950
* Hainsworth, George 1961
  Hall, Glenn Henry 1975

* Hall, Joseph Henry 1961
* Harvey, Douglas Norman 1973
  Hasek, Dominik 2014
  Hawerchuk, Dale Martin 2001
* Hay, George 1958
  Heaney, Geraldine 2013
* Hern, William Milton "Riley" 1962
* Hextall, Bryan Aldwyn 1969
* Holmes, Harry "Hap" 1972
* Hooper, Charles Thomas "Tom" 1962
* Horner, George Reginald "Red" 1965
* Horton, Miles Gilbert "Tim" 1977
  Housley, Phil 2015
* Howe, Gordon 1972
  Howe, Mark 2011
* Howe, Sydney Harris 1965
  Howell, Henry Vernon "Harry" 1979
  Hull, Brett 2009
* Hull, Robert Marvin 1983
* Hutton, John Bower "Bouse" 1962
* Hyland, Harry M. 1962
* Irvin, James Dickenson "Dick" 1958
* Jackson, Harvey "Busher" 1971
  James, Angela 2010
* Johnson, Ernest "Moose" 1952
* Johnson, Ivan "Ching" 1958
* Johnson, Thomas Christian 1970
* Joliat, Aurel 1947
  Kariya, Paul 2017
* Keats, Gordon "Duke" 1958
  Kelly, Leonard Patrick "Red" 1969
* Kennedy, Theodore Samuel "Teeder" 1966
  Keon, David Michael 1986
* Kharlamov, Valeri 2005
  Kurri, Jari 2001
* Lach, Elmer James 1966
  Lafleur, Guy Damien 1988
  LaFontaine, Pat 2003
* Lalonde, Edouard Charles "Newsy" 1950
  Langway, Rod Corry 2002
  Laperriere, Jacques 1987
  Lapointe, Guy 1993
  Laprade, Edgar 1993
  Larionov, Igor 2008
* Laviolette, Jean Baptiste "Jack" 1962
* Lehman, Hugh 1958
  Lemaire, Jacques Gerard 1984
  Lemieux, Mario 1997
* LeSueur, Percy 1961
  Leetch, Brian 2009
* Lewis, Herbert A. 1989
  Lidstrom, Nicklas 2015
  Lindros, Eric 2016
  Lindsay, Robert Blake Theodore "Ted" 1966

* Lumley, Harry 1980
  MacInnis, Al 2007
* MacKay, Duncan "Mickey" 1952
  Mahovlich, Frank William 1981
  Makarov, Sergei 2016
* Malone, Joseph "Joe" 1950
* Mantha, Sylvio 1960
* Marshall, John "Jack" 1965
  Maxwell, Fred G. "Steamer" 1962
  McDonald, Lanny 1992
* McGee, Frank 1945
* McGimsie, William George "Billy" 1962
* McNamara, George 1958
  Messier, Mark 2007
  Mikita, Stanley 1983
  Modano, Mike 2014
* Moore, Richard Winston "Dickie" 1974
* Moran, Patrick Joseph "Paddy" 1958
* Morenz, Howie 1945
* Mosienko, William "Billy" 1965
  Mullen, Joseph P. 2000
  Murphy, Larry 2004
  Neely, Cam 2005
  Niedermayer, Scott 2013
  Nieuwendyk, Joe 2011
* Nighbor, Frank 1947
* Noble, Edward Reginald "Reg" 1962
  Oates, Adam 2012
* O'Connor, Herbert William "Buddy" 1988
* Oliver, Harry 1967
* Olmstead, Murray Bert "Bert" 1985
  Orr, Robert Gordon 1979
  Parent, Bernard Marcel 1984
* Park, Douglas Bradford "Brad" 1988
* Patrick, Joseph Lynn 1980
* Patrick, Lester 1947
  Perreault, Gilbert 1990
* Phillips, Tommy 1945
  Pilote, Joseph Albert Pierre Paul 1975
* Pitre, Didier "Pit" 1962
* Plante, Joseph Jacques Omer 1978
  Potvin, Denis 1991
* Pratt, Walter "Babe" 1966
  Primeau, A. Joseph 1963
  Pronger, Chris 2015
* Pronovost, Joseph René Marcel 1978
  Pulford, Bob 1991
* Pulford, Harvey 1945
* Quackenbush, Hubert George "Bill" 1976
* Rankin, Frank 1961
  Ratelle, Joseph Gilbert Yvan Jean "Jean" 1985
* Rayner, Claude Earl "Chuck" 1973

* Reardon, Kenneth Joseph 1966
Recchi, Mark 2017
Richard, Joseph Henri 1979
* Richard, Joseph Henri Maurice
  "Rocket" 1961
* Richardson, George Taylor 1950
* Roberts, Gordon 1971
Robinson, Larry 1995
Robitaille, Luc 2009
* Ross, Arthur Howey 1949
Roy, Patrick 2006
Ruggiero, Angela 2015
* Russell, Blair 1965
* Russell, Ernest 1965
* Ruttan, J.D. "Jack" 1962
Sakic, Joe 2012
Salming, Borje Anders 1996
Savard, Denis Joseph 2000
Savard, Serge 1986
* Sawchuk, Terrance Gordon "Terry"
  1971
* Scanlan, Fred 1965
* Schmidt, Milton Conrad "Milt" 1961
* Schriner, David "Sweeney" 1962
* Seibert, Earl Walter 1963
* Seibert, Oliver Levi 1961
Selanne, Teemu 2017
Shanahan, Brendan 2013
* Shore, Edward W. "Eddie" 1947
Shutt, Stephen 1993
* Siebert, Albert C. "Babe" 1964
* Simpson, Harold Edward "Bullet Joe"
  1962
Sittler, Darryl Glen 1989
* Smith, Alfred E. 1962
Smith, Clint 1991
* Smith, Reginald "Hooley" 1972
* Smith, Thomas James 1973
Smith, William John "Billy" 1993
* Stanley, Allan Herbert 1981
* Stanley, Russell "Barney" 1962
Stastny, Peter 1998
Stevens, Scott 2007
* Stewart, John Sherratt "Black Jack"
  1964
* Stewart, Nelson "Nels" 1952
* Stuart, Bruce 1961
* Stuart, Hod 1945
Sundin, Mats 2012
* Taylor, Frederick "Cyclone" (O.B.E.)
  1947

*Deceased

* Thompson, Cecil R. "Tiny" 1959
Tretiak, Vladislav 1989
* Trihey, Col. Harry J. 1950
Trottier, Bryan 1997
Ullman, Norman V. Alexander "Norm"
  1982
Vachon, Rogatien, 2016
* Vezina, Georges 1945
* Walker, John Phillip "Jack" 1960
* Walsh, Martin "Marty" 1962
* Watson, Harry E. 1962
* Watson, Harry 1994
* Weiland, Ralph "Cooney" 1971
* Westwick, Harry 1962
* Whitcroft, Fred 1962
* Wilson, Gordon Allan "Phat" 1962
* Worsley, Lorne John "Gump" 1980
* Worters, Roy 1969
Yzerman, Steve 2009

BUILDERS

* Adams, Charles 1960
* Adams, Weston W. 1972
* Ahearn, Thomas Franklin "Frank"
  1962
* Ahearne, John Francis "Bunny" 1977
* Allan, Sir Montagu (C.V.O.) 1945
* Allen, Keith 1992
* Arbour, Alger Joseph "Al" 1996
* Ballard, Harold Edwin 1977
* Bauer, Father David 1989
* Bickell, John Paris 1978
Bowman, Scotty 1991
* Brooks, Herb 2006
* Brown, George V. 1961
* Brown, Walter A. 1962
* Buckland, Frank 1975
* Burns, Pat 2014
* Bush, Walter 2000
* Butterfield, Jack Arlington 1980
* Calder, Frank 1947
* Campbell, Angus D. 1964
* Campbell, Clarence Sutherland 1966
* Cattarinich, Joseph 1977
* Chynoweth, Ed 2008
Costello, Murray 2005
* Dandurand, Joseph Viateur "Leo"
  1963
Devellano, Jim 2010
* Dilio, Francis Paul 1964

Drake, Clare 2017
* Dudley, George S. 1958
* Dunn, James A. 1968
Fletcher, Cliff 2004
Francis, Emile 1982
* Gibson, Dr. John L. "Jack" 1976
* Gorman, Thomas Patrick "Tommy"
  1963
Gregory, Jim 2007
* Griffiths, Frank A. 1993
* Hanley, William 1986
* Hay, Charles 1974
Hay, William "Bill", 2015
* Hendy, James C. 1968
* Hewitt, Foster 1965
* Hewitt, William Abraham 1947
* Hotchkiss, Harley 2006
* Hume, Fred J. 1962
* Illitch, Mike 2003
* Imlach, George "Punch" 1984
* Ivan, Thomas N. 1974
Jacobs, Jeremy 2017
* Jennings, William M. 1975
* Johnson, Bob 1992
* Juckes, Gordon W. 1979
Karmanos, Jr., Peter 2015
* Kilpatrick, Gen. John Reed 1960
Kilrea, Brian Blair 2003
* Knox, Seymour H. III 1993
Lamoriello, Lou 2009
* Leader, George Alfred 1969
* LeBel, Robert 1970
* Lockhart, Thomas F. 1965
* Loicq, Paul 1961
* Mariucci, John 1985
* Mathers, Frank 1992
* McLaughlin, Major Frederic 1963
* Milford, John "Jake" 1984
* Molson, Hon. Hartland de Montarville
  1973
Morrison, Ian "Scotty" 1999
* Murray, Monsignor Athol 1998
* Neilson, Roger 2002
* Nelson, Francis 1947
* Norris, Bruce A. 1969
* Norris, Sr., James 1958
* Norris, James Dougan 1962
* Northey, William M. 1947
* O'Brien, John Ambrose 1962
O'Neill, Brian 1994
* Page, Fred 1993

Patrick, Craig 2001
* Patrick, Frank 1950
* Pickard, Allan W. 1958
* Pilous, Rudy 1985
* Poile, Norman "Bud" 1990
* Pollock, Samuel Patterson Smyth 1978
* Quinn, Pat, 2016
* Raymond, Sen. Donat 1958
* Robertson, John Ross 1947
* Robinson, Claude C. 1947
* Ross, Philip D. 1976
* Sabetzki, Dr. Gunther 1995
Sather, Glen 1997
* Seaman, Daryl "Doc" 2010
* Selke, Frank J. 1960
* Shero, Fred 2013
Sinden, Harry James 1983
* Smith, Frank D. 1962
* Smythe, Conn 1958
* Snider, Edward M. 1988
* Stanley of Preston, Lord (G.C.B.) 1945
* Sutherland, Cap. James T. 1947
* Tarasov, Anatoli V. 1974
Torrey, Bill 1995
* Turner, Lloyd 1958
* Tutt, William Thayer 1978
* Voss, Carl Potter 1974
* Waghorne, Fred 1961
* Wirtz, Arthur Michael 1971
* Wirtz, William W. "Bill" 1976
Ziegler, John A. Jr. 1987

REFEREES/LINESMEN

Armstrong, Neil 1991
* Ashley, John George 1981
* Chadwick, William L. 1964
* D'Amico, John 1993
* Elliott, Chaucer 1961
* Hayes, George William 1988
* Hewitson, Robert W. 1963
* Ion, Fred J. "Mickey" 1961
McCreary, Bill 2014
Pavelich, Matt 1987
* Rodden, Michael J. "Mike" 1962
Scapinello, Ray 2008
* Smeaton, J. Cooper 1961
* Storey, Roy Alvin "Red" 1967
* Udvari, Frank Joseph 1973
Van Hellemond, Andy 1999

Dave Andreychuk (left) and Mark Recchi (center) are two of just 10 players to date who have topped 1,600 games in the NHL. Andreychuk scored 640 goals and Recchi scored 577. Danielle Goyette is the fifth woman to be inducted. She won eight World Championships and two Olympic gold medals playing for Team Canada from the age of 26 to 41.

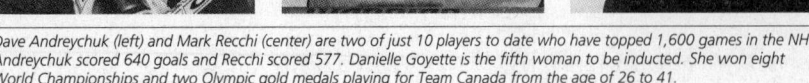

Foster Hewitt Memorial Award Winners

In recognition of members of the radio and television industry who made outstanding contributions to their profession and the game during their career in hockey broadcasting. Selected by the NHL Broadcasters' Association.

Cole, Bob, Hockey Night in Canada 1996
* Cusick, Fred, Boston 1984
* Darling, Ted, Buffalo 1994
Davidson, John, MSG Network/HNIC 2009
Emrick, Mike, New Jersey, U.S. networks, 2008
Foley, Pat, Chicago 2014
* Gallivan, Danny, Montreal 1984
* Garneau, Richard, Montreal 1999
* Hart, Gene, Philadelphia 1997
* Hewitt, Bill, Hockey Night in Canada 2007
* Hewitt, Foster, Toronto 1984
Irvin, Dick, Montreal 1988
Jeanneret, Rick, Buffalo 2012
Kaiton, Chuck, Hartford/Carolina 2004
* Kelly, Dan, St. Louis 1989
Lange, Mike, Pittsburgh 2001
* Lecavalier, René, Montreal 1984
* Lynch, Budd, Detroit 1985
Maher, Peter, Calgary 2006
Martyn, Bruce, Detroit 1991
McDonald, Jiggs, Los Angeles, Atlanta,
  NY Islanders 1990
McFarlane, Brian, Hockey Night in Canada 1995
* McKnight, Wes, Toronto 1986
Meeker, Howie, Hockey Night in Canada 1998
Messina, Sal, New York 2005
Miller, Bob, Los Angeles 2000
Neale, Harry, Hockey Night in Canada,
  Buffalo 2013
Nickson, Nick, Los Angeles 2015
* Pettit, Lloyd, Chicago 1986
Phillips, Rod, Edmonton 2003
Redmond, Mickey, Detroit 2011
Robson, Jim, Vancouver 1992
Rosen, Sam, New York Rangers, 2016
Shaver, Al, Minnesota 1993
* Smith, Doug, Montreal 1985
Strader, Dave, ESPN/ABC/NBC/Dallas, 2017
* Tremblay, Gilles, La Soirée du Hockey 2002
* Weber, Ron, Washington 2010
Wilson, Bob, Boston 1987

Elmer Ferguson
Memorial Award Winners

In recognition of distinguished members of the hockey-writing profession whose words have brought honor to journalism and to hockey. Selected by the Professional Hockey Writers' Association.

Allen, Kevin, USA Today 2014
* Barton, Charlie, Buffalo-Courier Express 1985
* Beauchamp, Jacques, Montreal Matin/Journal de Montréal 1984
* Brennan, Bill, Detroit News 1987
* Burchard, Jim, New York World Telegram 1984
* Burnett, Red, Toronto Star 1984
* Carroll, Dink, Montreal Gazette 1984
Cole, Cam, Edmonton Journal/National Post/Vancouver Sun 2017
* Coleman, Jim, Southam Newspapers 1984
Conway, Russ, Eagle-Tribune 1999
* Damata, Ted, Chicago Tribune 1984
de Foy, Marc, Le Journal de Montreal/ruefrontenac.com 2010
* Delano, Hugh, New York Post 1991
* Desjardins, Marcel, Montréal La Presse 1984
Duhatschek, Eric, Calgary Herald/Globe and Mail 2001
* Dulmage, Jack, Windsor Star 1984
* Dunnell, Milt, Toronto Star 1984
Dupont, Kevin Paul, Boston Globe 2002
Elliott, Helene, Los Angeles Times 2005
Farber, Michael, Montreal Gazette/Sports Illustrated 2003
* Fay, Dave, Washington Times 2007
* Ferguson, Elmer, Montreal Herald/Star 1984
* Fitzgerald, Tom, Boston Globe 1984
* Frayne, Trent, Toronto Telegram/Globe and Mail/Sun 1984
* Gatecliff, Jack, St. Catharines Standard 1995
Greenberg, Jay, Kansas City Star/Philadelphia Daily News/Sports Illustrated 2013
* Gross, George, Toronto Telegram/Sun 1985
* Johnston, Dick, Buffalo News 1986
Jones, Terry, Edmonton Sun 2011
* Kelley, Jim, Buffalo News 2004
* Laney, Al, New York Herald-Tribune 1984
* Larochelle, Claude, Le Soleil 1989
* L'Esperance, Zotique, Journal de Montréal/ le Petit Journal 1985
MacGregor, Roy, Globe and Mail 2012
* MacLeod, Rex, Toronto Globe and Mail/Star 1987
Matheson, Jim, Edmonton Journal 2000
* Mayer, Charles, Journal de Montréal/la Patrie 1985
McKenzie, Bob, The Hockey News/Toronto Star/TSN 2015
* McKenzie, Ken, The Hockey News 1997
Molinari, Dave, Pittsburgh Post-Gazette 2009
* Monahan, Leo, Boston Daily Record/Record-American/Herald American 1986
* Moriarty, Tim, UPI/Newsday 1986
Morrison, Scott, Toronto Sun/Rogers Sportsnet 2006
* Nichols, Joe, New York Times 1984
* O'Brien, Andy, Weekend Magazine 1985
Olan, Ben, New York Associated Press 1987
Orr, Frank, Toronto Star 1989
* O'Meara, Basil, Montreal Star 1984
Pedneault, Yvon, La Presse/Journal de Montréal 1998
* Proudfoot, Jim, Toronto Star 1988
Raymond, Bertrand, Journal de Montréal 1990
* Rosa, Fran, Boston Globe 1987
Stevens, Neil, Canadian Press 2008
Strachan, Al, Globe and Mail/Toronto Sun 1993
Verdi, Bob, Chicago Tribune/Blackhawks 2016
* Vipond, Jim, Toronto Globe and Mail 1984
* Walter, Lewis, Detroit Times 1984
* Young, Scott, Toronto Globe and Mail/Telegram 1988

United States Hockey Hall of Fame

On May 11, 2007, the U.S. Hockey Hall of Fame and USA Hockey came to a historic agreement that transferred rights to the selection process and induction event associated with the Hall, including the Wayne Gretzky International Award, to USA Hockey. As part of the agreement, the U.S. Hockey Hall of Fame Museum, located in Eveleth, Minnesota, formed a separate Board of Directors to govern the national shrine for American Hockey.

There are 177 enshrined members in the U.S. Hockey Hall of Fame (www.ushockeyhalloffame.com). New members are inducted annually and must have made extraordinary contributions to hockey in the United States during the course of their career. A special Wayne Gretzky International Award pays tribute to international individuals who have made major contributions to hockey in the USA.

The United States Hockey Hall of Fame Museum was opened on June 21, 1973. It is dedicated to honoring the sport of ice hockey in the United States by preserving those previous memories and legends of the game. It is located in Eveleth, Minnesota, 60 miles north of Duluth on Highway 53. For further information, call 800-443-7825 or 218-744-5167, or visit www.ushockeyhall.com.

INDIVIDUALS

Players

* Abel, Clarence "Taffy" 1973
Amonte, Tony 2009
* Baker, Hobey 1973
Barrasso, Tom 2009
* Bartholome, Earl 1977
* Bessone, Peter 1978
* Blake, Bob 1985
Boucha, Henry 1995
* Brimsek, Frank 1973
* Brink, Milton "Curly" 2006
Broten, Aaron 2007
Broten, Neal 2000
Bye Dietz, Karyn 2014
Carpenter, Bobby 2007
Cavanagh, Joe 1994
* Chaisson, Ray 1974
* Chase, John P. 1973
Chelios, Chris 2011
Christian, David 2001
* Christian, Roger 1989
Christian, William "Bill" 1984
Christiansen, Keith "Huffer" 2005
* Cleary, Bill 1976
* Cleary, Bob 1981
* Conroy, Tony 1975
Coppo, Paul 2004
Curley, Cindy 2013
Curran, Mike 1998
* Dahlstrom, Carl "Cully" 1973
* Desjardins, Vic 1974
* Desmond, Dick 1988
* Dill, Bob 1979
* Dougherty, Richard "Dick" 2003
Drury, Chris 2015
* Everett, Doug 1974
Fusco, Mark 2002
Fusco, Scott 2002
Ftorek, Robbie 1991
Gambucci, Gary 2006
* Garrison, John 1973
* Garrity, Jack 1986
* Goheen, Frank "Moose" 1973
Granato, Cammi 2008
* Grant, Wally 1994
Guerin, Bill 2012
* Harding, Francis "Austie" 1975
Hatcher, Derian 2010
Hatcher, Kevin 2010
Housley, Phil 2004
Howe, Mark 2003
Hull, Brett 2008
* Iglehart, Stewart 1975
Janney, Craig 2016
Johnson, Mark 2004
Johnson, Paul 2001
* Johnson, Virgil 1974
* Kahler, Nick 1980
* Karakas, Mike 1973
* Kirrane, Jack 1987
LaFontaine, Pat 2003
* Lane, Myles 1973
Langevin, Dave 1993
Langway, Rod 1999
Larson, Reed 1996
LeClair, John 2009
Leetch, Brian 2008
* Linder, Joe 1975
* LoPresti, Sam 1973
MacDonald, Lane 2005

* Mariucci, John 1973
* Matchefts, John 1991
* Mather, Bruce 1998
Mayasich, John 1976
McCartan, Jack 1983
Modano, Mike 2012
* Moe, Bill 1974
Morrow, Ken 1995
* Moseley, Fred 1975
Mullen, Joe 1998
* Murray, Sr. Hugh "Muzz" 1987
* Nelson, Hubert "Hub" 1978
* Nyrop, Bill 1997
Olczyk, Eddie 2012
* Olson, Eddie 1977
* Owen, Jr. George 1973
Palazzari, Doug 2000
* Palmer, Winthrop "Ding" 1973
Paradise, Bob 1989
* Purpur, Clifford "Fido" 1974
Rafalski, Brian 2014
Ramsey, Mike 2001
Richter, Mike 2008
* Riley, Joe 2002
* Riley, Bill 1977
Roberts, Gordie 1999
* Roberts, Moe 2005
Roenick, Jeremy 2010
* Romnes, Elwin "Doc" 1973
* Rondeau, Dick 1985
Ruggiero, Angela 2015
Schneider, Mathieu 2015
Sheehy, Tim 1997
Suter, Gary 2011
Tkachuk, Keith 2011
Vanbiesbrouck, John 2007
* Watson, Sid 1999
Weight, Doug 2013
* Williams, Tommy 1981
* Winters, Frank "Coddy" 1973
* Yakel, Ken 1986
Young, Scott 2017

Coaches
* Almquist, Oscar 1983
Belisle, Bill 2016
* Bessone, Amo 1992
* Brooks, Herb 1990
Ceglarski, Len 1992
* Cunniff, John 2003
* Fullerton, Jim 1992
* Gambucci, Sergio 1996
* Gordon, Malcom K. 1973
* Harkness, Ned 1994
* Heyliger, Vic 1974
* Holt, Jr. Charlie 1997
Ikola, Willard 1990
* Jeremiah, Eddie 1973
* Johnson, Bob 1991
* Kelly, John "Snooks" 1974
Kelley, John "Jack" 1993
* MacInnes, John 2007
* Marvin, Cal 1982
Mason, Ron 2013
Parker, Jack 2017
* Pleban, Connie 1990
* Riley, Jack 1979
* Ross, Larry 1988
* Sauer, Jeff 2014
Smith, Ben 2017

* Stewart, Bill 1982
* Thompson, Cliff 1973
Vairo, Lou 2014
Williamson, Murray 2005
Wilson, Ron 2017
* Winsor, Alfred "Ralph" 1973
Woog, Doug 2002

Administrators
Berglund, Art 2010
* Brown, George 1973
* Brown, Walter 1973
* Bush, Walter 1980
* Clark, Don 1978
* Claypool, Jim 1995
DeGregorio, Ron 2015
* Gibson, John "Doc" 1973
* Ilitch, Mike 2004
* Jennings, William M. "Bill" 1981
Karmanos, Peter 2013
Lamoriello, Lou 2012
* Lockhart, Tom 1973
Patrick, Craig 1996
Pleau, Larry 2000
* Ridder, Bob 1976
* Snider, Ed 2011
* Trumble, Hal 1985
* Tutt, Thayer 1973
* Wirtz, Bill 1984
* Wright, Lyle 1973

Player/Administrators
Milbury, Mike 2006
Nanne, Lou 1998

Referees
* Chadwick, Bill 1974
Collins, Kevin 2017

Support Personnel
Emrick, Mike "Doc" 2011
Nagobads, Dr. V. George 2010
* Schulz, Charles M. 1993
* Zamboni, Frank 2009

TEAMS
1960 Olympic Team (Men's) 2000
1980 Olympic Team (Men's) 2003
1996 World Cup of Hockey Team 2016
1998 Olympic Team (Women's) 2009

WAYNE GRETZKY INTERNATIONAL AWARD
Wayne Gretzky 1999
The Howe Family 2000
Scotty Morrison 2001
Scotty Bowman 2002
Bobby Hull 2003
* Herb Brooks 2004
* Anatoli Tarasov 2008
Murray Costello 2012
Emile Francis 2015

* Deceased

Scott Young won the Stanley Cup twice (1991, 1996) during a 17-year NHL career that saw him amass 342 goals and 415 assists in 1,181 regular-season games. He also represented the United States at many international events.

International Ice Hockey Federation Hall of Fame

The IIHF Hall of Fame was founded in 1997. It now boasts 235 greats from 24 countries.

Candidates for election as Honoured Members in the player category shall be chosen on the basis of their playing ability, sportsmanship, character and their contribution to their team or teams and to the game of ice hockey in general.

Candidates for election as Honoured Members in the builder category shall be chosen on the basis of their coaching, managerial or executive ability, where applicable, their sportsmanship and character, and their contribution to their organization or organizations and to the game of ice hockey in general.

Candidates for election as Honoured Members in the referee or linesman category shall be chosen on the basis of their officiating ability, sportsmanship, character and their contribution to the game of ice hockey in general. The Paul Loicq Award, named for the longtime former IIHF president, is presented to honor a person for his service to the international hockey community.

Inductees' names are followed by their country and year of induction.

PLAYERS

Alexandrov, Veniamin, RUS, 2007
Balderis, Helmut, LAT, 1998
Ball, Rudi, GER, 2004
Bergqvist, Sven, SWE, 1999
Bjorn, Lars, SWE, 1998
Bobrov, Vsevolod, RUS, 1997
Bondra, Peter, SVK, 2016
Bourbonnais, Roger, CAN, 1999
Bouzek, Vladimir, CZE, 2007
Bozon, Phillippe, FRA, 2008
Bubnik, Vlastimil, CZE, 1997
Bure, Pavel, RUS, 2012
Bye, Karyn, USA, 2011
Bykov, Vyacheslav, RUS, 2014
Cattini, Ferdinand, SUI, 1998
Cattini, Hans, SUI, 1998
Cerny, Josef, CZE, 2007
Christian, Bill, USA, 1998
Cleary, Bill, USA, 1997
Cosby, Gerry, USA, 1997
Craig, Jim, USA, 1999
Curran, Mike, USA, 1999
Davydov, Vitaly, RUS, 2004
Drobny, Jaroslav, CZE, 1997
Dzurilla, Vladimir, SVK, 1998
Erhardt, Carl, G.B., 1998
Fedorov, Sergei, RUS, 2016
Fetisov, Viacheslav, RUS, 2005
Firsov, Anatoli, RUS, 1998
Forsberg, Peter, SWE, 2013
Golonka, Josef, SVK, 1998
Goyette, Danielle, CAN, 2013
Granato, Cammi, USA, 2008
Gretzky, Wayne, CAN, 2000
Gruth, Henryk, POL, 2006
Gustafsson, Bengt-Ake, SWE, 2003
Gut, Karel, CZE, 1998
Hasek, Dominik, CZE, 2015
Heaney, Geraldine, CAN, 2008
Hedberg, Anders, SWE, 1997
Hegen, Dieter, GER, 2010
Helminen, Raimo, FIN, 2012
Henderson, Paul, CAN, 2013
Hiti, Rudi, SLO, 2009
Hlinka, Ivan, CZE, 2002
Holecek, Jiri, CZE, 1998
Holik, Jiri, CZE, 1999
Holmqvist, Leif, SWE, 1999
Housley, Phil, USA 2012
Huck, Fran, CAN, 1999
Irbe, Arturs, LAT 2010
Jaenecke, Gustav, GER, 1998
James, Angela, CAN 2008
Johnson, Mark, USA, 1999
Johnston, Marshall, CAN, 1998
Jonsson, Tomas, SWE, 2000
Jutila, Timo, FIN, 2003
Kamensky, Valeri, RUS, 2016
Kasatonov, Alexei, RUS, 2009
Keinonen, Matti, FIN, 2002
Kharlamov, Valeri, RUS, 1998
Khomutov, Andrei, RUS, 2014
Kiessling, Udo, GER, 2000
Koivu, Saku, FIN, 2017
Kolliker, Jakob, SUI, 2007
Konovalenko, Viktor, RUS, 2007
Krupp, Uwe, GER, 2017
Krutov, Vladimir, RUS, 2010
Kuhnhackl, Erich, GER, 1997
Kurri, Jari, FIN, 2000
Kuzkin, Viktor, RUS, 2005
Lacarriere, Jacques, FRA, 1998
Larionov, Igor, RUS, 2008
Lemieux, Mario, CAN, 2008
Lidstrom, Nicklas, SWE, 2014
Loktev, Konstantin, RUS, 2007

Loob, Hakan, SWE, 1998
Lundquist, Vic, CAN, 1997
Lundstrom, Tord, SWE, 2011
Machac, Oldrich, CZE, 1999
MacKenzie, Barry, CAN, 1999
Makarov, Sergei, RUS, 2001
Malecek, Josef, CZE, 2003
Maltsev, Alexander, RUS, 1999
Marjamaki, Pekka, FIN, 1998
Martin, Seth, CAN, 1997
Martinec, Vladimir, CZE, 2001
Mayasich, John, USA, 1997
Mayorov, Boris, RUS, 1999
McCartan, Jack, USA, 1998
McLeod, Jackie, CAN, 1999
Mikhailov, Boris, RUS, 2000
Modry, Bohumil, CZE, 2011
Nanne, Lou, USA, 2004
Naslund, Mats, SWE, 2005
Nedomansky, Vaclav, CZE, 1997
Niedermayer, Scott, CAN, 2015
Nieminen-Valila, Riika, FIN, 2010
Nilsson, Kent, SWE, 2006
Nilsson, Nisse, SWE, 2002
Novy, Milan, CZE, 2012
Numminen, Teppo, FIN, 2013
O'Malley, Terry, CAN, 1998
Oksanen, Lasse, FIN, 1999
Pana, Eduard, ROU, 1998
Patton, Peter, G.B., 2002
Peltonen, Ville, FIN, 2016
Peltonen, Esa, FIN, 2007
Petrov, Vladimir, RUS, 2006
Pettersson, Ronald, SWE, 2004
Pospisil, Frantisek, CZE, 1999
Puschnig, Josef, AUT, 1999
Ragulin, Alexander, RUS, 1997
Rampf, Hans, GER, 2001
Reichel, Robert, CZE, 2015
Rooth, Maria, SWE, 2015
Ruggiero, Angela, USA, 2017
Rundqvist, Thomas, SWE, 2007
Salei, Ruslan, BLR, 2014
Salming, Borje, SWE, 1998
Sakic, Joe, CAN, 2017
Schloder, Alois, GER, 2005
Selanne, Teemu, FIN, 2017
Sinden, Harry, CAN, 1997
Sologubov, Nikolai, RUS, 2004
Starshinov, Vyacheslav, RUS, 2007
Stastny, Peter, SVK, 2000
Sterner, Ulf, SWE, 2001
Stoltz, Roland, SWE, 1999
Suchy, Jan, CZE, 2009
Sundin, Mats, SWE, 2013
Tikal, Frantisek, CZE, 2004
Torriani, Bibi, SUI, 1997
Tretiak, Vladislav, RUS, 1997
Trojak, Ladislav, SVK, 1997
Tumba (Johansson), Sven, SWE, 1997
Tureanu, Doru, ROU, 2011
Valtonen, Jorma, FIN, 1999
Vasiliev, Valeri, RUS, 1998
Wahlsten, Vladimir, FIN, 2006
Watson, Harry, CAN, 1998
Yakushev, Alexander, RUS, 2003
Ylonen, Urpo, FIN, 1997
Yzerman, Steve, CAN, 2014
Zabrodsky, Vladimir, CZE, 1997
Ziesche, Joachim, GER, 1999

BUILDERS

Ahearne, Bunny, G.B., 1997
Aljancic Sr., Ernest, SLO, 2002
Bauer, Father David, CAN, 1997
Berglund, Art, USA 2008
Berglund, Curt, SWE, 2003
Bokac, Ludek, CZE, 2007
Brooks, Herb, USA, 1999
Brown, Walter, USA, 1997
Buckna, Mike, CAN, 2004
Bush, Walter Jr., USA, 2009
Calcaterra, Enrico, ITA, 1999
Chernyshev, Arkady, RUS, 1999
Costello, Murray, CAN, 2014
Dimitriev, Igor, RUS, 2007
Dobida, Hans, AUT, 2007
Edvinsson, Jan-Ake, SWE, 2013
Eklow, Rudolf, SWE, 1999
Fagerlund, Rickard, SWE, 2010
Grunander, Arne, SWE, 1997
Henschel, Heinz, GER, 2003
Hewitt, William, CAN, 1998
Holmes, Derek, CAN, 1999
Horsky, Ladislav, SVK, 2004
Hviid, Jorgen, DEN, 2005
Johannessen, Tore, NOR, 1999
Juckes, Gordon, CAN, 1997
Kalt, Dieter, AUT, 2017
Kawabuchi, Tsutomu, JPN, 2004
Khorozov, Anatoli, UKR, 2006
King, Dave, CAN, 2001
Kostka, Vladimir, CZE, 1997
LeBel, Bob, CAN, 1997
Lindblad, Harry, FIN, 1999
Loicq, Paul, BEL, 1997
Luhti, Cesar W., SUI, 1998
Magnus, Louis, FRA, 1997
Murray, Andy, CAN, 2012
Numminen, Kalevi, FIN, 2011
Pasztor, Gyorgy, HUN, 2001
Quinn, Pat, CAN, 2016
Renwick, Gordon, CAN, 2002
Ridder, Bob, USA, 1998
Rider, Fran, CAN, 2015
Riley, Jack, USA, 1998
Sabetzki, Dr. Gunther, GER, 1997
Smith, Ben, USA, 2016
Starovoitov, Andrei, RUS, 1997
Starsi, Jan, SVK, 1999
Stromberg, Arne, SWE, 1998
Stubb, Goran, FIN, 2000
Subrt, Miroslav, CZE, 2004
Tarasov, Anatoli, RUS, 1997
Tikhonov, Viktor, RUS, 1998
Tomita, Shoichi, JPN, 2006
Trumble, Hal, USA, 1999
Tsutsumi, Yoshiaki, JPN, 1999
Tutt, Thayer, USA, 2002
Unsinn, Xaver, GER, 1998
Wasservogel, Walter, AUT, 1997
Yurzinov, Vladimir, RUS, 2002

REFEREES

Adamec, Quido, CZE, 2005
Dahlberg, Ove, SWE, 2004
Karandin, Yuri, RUS, 2004
Kompalla, Josef, GER, 2003
Schell, Laszlo, HUN, 2009
Wiitala, Unto, FIN, 2003

RICHARD "BIBI" TORRIANI AWARD

Topatigh, Lucio, ITA, 2015
Ocskay, Gabor, HUN, 2016
Hand, Tony, G.B., 2017

PAUL LOICQ AWARD

Montag, Wolf-Dieter, GER, 1998
Neumayer, Roman, GER, 1999
Kukushkin, Vsevolod, RUS, 2000
Kataoka, Isao, JPN, 2001
Marsh, Pat, G.B., 2002
Nagobads, George, USA, 2003
Kukulowicz, Aggie, CAN, 2004
Hrabcek, Rita, AUS, 2005
Tovland, Bo, SWE, 2006
Nadin, Bob, CAN, 2007
Okolicany, Juraj, SVK, 2008
Griebel, Harald, GER, 2009
Vairo, Lou, USA, 2010
Korolev, Yuri, RUS, 2011
Angus, Kent, CAN, 2012
Miller, Gord, CAN, 2013
Aubry, Mark, CAN, 2014
Scheier-Schneider, Monique, LUX, 2015
Ozerov, Nikolai, RUS, 2016
Francheterre, Patrick, FRA, 2017

CENTENNIAL ALL-STAR TEAM (1908-2008)

Goaltender: Vladislav Tretiak, RUS
Defenseman: Viacheslav Fetisov, RUS
Defenseman: Borje Salming, SWE
Winger: Valeri Kharlamov, RUS
Winger: Sergei Makarov, RUS
Center: Wayne Gretzky, CAN

TRIPLE GOLD CLUB

(Olympics, World Championship, Stanley Cup)

Tomas Jonsson, SWE
Mats Naslund, SWE
Hakan Loob, SWE
Valeri Kamensky, RUS
Alexei Gusarov, RUS
Peter Forsberg, SWE
Vyacheslav Fetisov, RUS
Igor Larionov, RUS
Alexander Mogilny, RUS
Vladimir Malakhov, RUS
Rob Blake, CAN
Joe Sakic, CAN
Brendan Shanahan, CAN
Scott Niedermayer, CAN
Jaromir Jagr, CZE
Jiri Slegr, CZE
Nicklas Lidstrom, SWE
Fredrik Modin, SWE
Chris Pronger, CAN
Niklas Kronwall, SWE
Henrik Zetterberg, SWE
Mikael Samuelsson, SWE
Eric Staal, CAN
Jonathan Toews, CAN
Mike Babcock (coach), CAN
Patrice Bergeron, CAN
Sidney Crosby, CAN
Corey Perry, CAN

MILESTONE TROPHY

1954 Soviet Union World Championship team, 2013

Results

2017

Stanley Cup Playoffs

NOTE: *A1, C2, M3 etc. indicate a team's regular-season finish in its division (Atlantic and Metropolitan in the Eastern Conference, Central and Pacific in the Western Conference). W1 and W2 indicate wildcard playoff qualifiers. Regular-season standings are found on page 135.*

FIRST ROUND (FR)
(Best-of-seven series)

Eastern Conference

Series 'A' – A1 vs. W1

Wed. Apr. 12	NY Rangers	2	at	Montreal	0
Fri. Apr. 14	NY Rangers	3	at	Montreal	4 *
Sun. Apr. 16	Montreal	3	at	NY Rangers	1
Tue. Apr. 18	Montreal	1	at	NY Rangers	2
Thu. Apr. 20	NY Rangers	3	at	Montreal	2 **
Sat. Apr. 22	Montreal	1	at	NY Rangers	3

   * Alexander Radulov scored at 18:34 of overtime
   ** Mika Zibanejad scored at 14:22 of overtime
(NY Rangers won Series 4-2)

Series 'B' – A2 vs. A3

Wed. Apr. 12	Boston	2	at	Ottawa	1
Sat. Apr. 15	Boston	3	at	Ottawa	4 *
Mon. Apr. 17	Ottawa	4	at	Boston	3 **
Wed. Apr. 19	Ottawa	1	at	Boston	0
Fri. Apr. 21	Boston	3	at	Ottawa	2 ***
Sun. Apr. 23	Ottawa	3	at	Boston	2 ****

   * Dion Phaneuf scored at 1:59 of overtime
   ** Bobby Ryan scored at 5:43 of overtime
   *** Sean Kuraly scored at 30:19 of overtime
   **** Clarke Macarthur scored at 6:30 of overtime
(Ottawa won Series 4-2)

Series 'C' – M1 vs. W2

Thu. Apr. 13	Toronto	2	at	Washington	3 *
Sat. Apr. 15	Toronto	4	at	Washington	3 **
Mon. Apr. 17	Washington	3	at	Toronto	4 ***
Wed. Apr. 19	Washington	5	at	Toronto	4
Fri. Apr. 21	Toronto	1	at	Washington	2 ****
Sun. Apr. 23	Washington	2	at	Toronto	1 *****

   * Tom Wilson scored at 5:15 of overtime
   ** Kasperi Kapanen scored at 31:53 of overtime
   *** Tyler Bozak scored at 1:37 of overtime
   **** Justin Williams scored at 1:04 of overtime
   ***** Marcus Johansson scored at 6:31 of overtime
(Washington won Series 4-2)

Series 'D' – M2 vs. M3

Wed. Apr. 12	Columbus	1	at	Pittsburgh	3
Fri. Apr. 14	Columbus	1	at	Pittsburgh	4
Sun.apr 16	Pittsburgh	5	at	Columbus	4 *
Tue. Apr. 18	Pittsburgh	4	at	Columbus	5
Thu. Apr. 20	Columbus	2	at	Pittsburgh	5

   * Jake Guentzel scored at 13:10 of overtime
(Pittsburgh won Series 4-1)

Western Conference

Series 'E' – C1 vs. W1

Thu. Apr. 13	Nashville	1	at	Chicago	0
Sat. Apr. 15	Nashville	5	at	Chicago	0
Mon. Apr. 17	Chicago	2	at	Nashville	3 *
Thu. Apr. 20	Chicago	1	at	Nashville	4

   * Kevin Fiala scored at 16:44 of overtime
(Nashville won Series 4-0)

Series 'F' – C2 vs. C3

Wed. Apr. 12	St. Louis	2	at	Minnesota	1 *
Fri. Apr. 14	St. Louis	2	at	Minnesota	1
Sun. Apr. 16	Minnesota	1	at	St. Louis	3
Wed. Apr. 19	Minnesota	2	at	St. Louis	0
Sat. Apr. 22	St. Louis	4	at	Minnesota	3 **

   *Joel Edmundson scored at 17:48 of overtime
   **Magnus Paajarvi scored at 9:42 of overtime
(St. Louis won Series 4-3)

Series 'G' – P1 vs. W2

Thu. Apr. 13	Calgary	2	at	Anaheim	3
Sat. Apr. 15	Calgary	2	at	Anaheim	3
Mon. Apr. 17	Anaheim	5	at	Calgary	4 *
Wed. Apr. 19	Anaheim	3	at	Calgary	1

   *Corey Perry scored at 1:30 of overtime
(Anaheim won Series 4-0)

Series 'H' – P2 vs. P3

Wed. Apr. 12	San Jose	3	at	Edmonton	2 *
Fri. Apr. 14	San Jose	0	at	Edmonton	2
Sun. Apr. 16	Edmonton	1	at	San Jose	0
Tue. Apr. 18	Edmonton	0	at	San Jose	7
Thu. Apr. 20	San Jose	3	at	Edmonton	4 **
Sat. Apr. 22	Edmonton	3	at	San Jose	1

   * Melker Karlsson scored at 3:22 of overtime
   ** David Desharnais scored at 18:15 of overtime
(Edmonton won Series 4-2)

SECOND ROUND (SR)
(Best-of-seven series)

Eastern Conference

Series 'I' – A1 vs. A2

Thu. Apr. 27	NY Rangers	1	at	Ottawa	2
Sat. Apr. 29	NY Rangers	5	at	Ottawa	6 *
Tue. May 2	Ottawa	1	at	NY Rangers	4
Thu. May 4	Ottawa	1	at	NY Rangers	4
Sat. May 6	NY Rangers	4	at	Ottawa	5 **
Tue. May 9	Ottawa	4	at	NY Rangers	2

   * Jean-Gabriel Pageau scored at 22:54 of overtime
   ** Kyle Turris scored at 6:28 of overtime
(Ottawa won Series 4-2)

Series 'J' – M1 vs. M2

Thu. Apr. 27	Pittsburgh	3	at	Washington	2
Sat. Apr. 29	Pittsburgh	6	at	Washington	2
Mon. May 1	Washington	3	at	Pittsburgh	2 *
Wed. May 3	Washington	2	at	Pittsburgh	3
Sat. May 6	Pittsburgh	2	at	Washington	4
Mon. May 8	Washington	5	at	Pittsburgh	2
Wed. May 10	Pittsburgh	2	at	Washington	0

   * Kevin Shattenkirk scored at 3:13 of overtime
(Pittsburgh won Series 4-3)

Western Conference

Series 'K' – C3 vs. W1

Wed. Apr. 26	Nashville	4	at	St. Louis	3
Fri. Apr. 28	Nashville	2	at	St. Louis	3
Sun. Apr. 30	St. Louis	1	at	Nashville	3
Tue. May 2	St. Louis	1	at	Nashville	2
Fri. May 5	Nashville	1	at	St. Louis	2
Sun. May 7	St. Louis	1	at	Nashville	3

(Nashville won Series 4-2)

Series 'L' – P1 vs. P3

Wed. Apr. 26	Edmonton	5	at	Anaheim	3
Fri. Apr. 28	Edmonton	2	at	Anaheim	1
Sun. Apr. 30	Anaheim	6	at	Edmonton	3
Wed. May 3	Anaheim	4	at	Edmonton	3 *
Fri. May 5	Edmonton	3	at	Anaheim	4 **
Sun. May 7	Anaheim	1	at	Edmonton	7
Wed. May 10	Edmonton	1	at	Anaheim	2

   * Jakob Silfverberg scored at 0:45 of overtime
   ** Corey Perry scored at 26:57 of overtime
(Anaheim won Series 4-3)

CONFERENCE FINALS (CF)
(Best-of-seven series)

Eastern Conference

Series 'M' – A2 vs. M1

Sat. May 13	Ottawa	2	at	Pittsburgh	1 *
Mon. May 15	Ottawa	0	at	Pittsburgh	1
Wed. May 17	Pittsburgh	3	at	Ottawa	5
Fri. May 19	Pittsburgh	3	at	Ottawa	2
Sun. May 21	Ottawa	0	at	Pittsburgh	7
Tue. May 23	Pittsburgh	1	at	Ottawa	2
Thu. May 25	Ottawa	2	at	Pittsburgh	3 **

   * Bobby Ryan scored at 4:59 of overtime
   ** Chris Kunitz scored at 25:09 of overtime
(Pittsburgh won Series 4-3)

Western Conference

Series 'N' – C3 vs. P1

Fri. May 12	Nashville	3	at	Anaheim	2 *
Sun. May 14	Nashville	3	at	Anaheim	5
Tue. May 16	Anaheim	1	at	Nashville	2
Thu. May 18	Anaheim	3	at	Nashville	2 **
Sat. May 20	Nashville	3	at	Anaheim	1
Mon. May 22	Anaheim	3	at	Nashville	6

   * James Neal scored at 9:24 of overtime
   ** Corey Perry scored at 10:25 of overtime
(Nashville won Series 4-2)

STANLEY CUP FINAL (F)
(Best-of-seven series)

Series 'O' – A2 vs. C3

Mon. May 29	Nashville	3	at	Pittsburgh	5
Wed. May 31	Nashville	1	at	Pittsburgh	4
Sat. June 3	Pittsburgh	1	at	Nashville	5
Mon. June 5	Pittsburgh	1	at	Nashville	4
Thu. June 8	Nashville	0	at	Pittsburgh	6
Sun. June11	Pittsburgh	2	at	Nashville	0

(Pittsburgh won Series 4-2)

Team Playoff Records

	GP	W	L	GF	GA	%
Pittsburgh	25	16	9	77	57	.640
Nashville	22	14	8	60	48	.636
Ottawa	19	11	8	47	50	.579
Anaheim	17	10	7	50	52	.588
Edmonton	13	7	6	36	35	.538
Washington	13	7	6	36	36	.538
St. Louis	11	6	5	22	23	.545
NY Rangers	12	6	6	34	30	.500
San Jose	6	2	4	14	12	.333
Toronto	6	2	4	16	18	.333
Boston	6	2	4	13	15	.333
Montreal	6	2	4	11	14	.333
Minnesota	5	1	4	8	11	.200
Columbus	5	1	4	13	21	.200
Calgary	4	0	4	9	14	.000
Chicago	4	0	4	3	13	.000

Individual Leaders

Abbreviations: GP – games played; **G** – goals; **A** – assists; **PTS** – points; **+/–** – difference between Goals For (**GF**) scored when a player is on the ice with his team at even strength or shorthanded and Goals Against (**GA**) scored when the same player is on the ice with his team at even strength or on a power play; **PIM** – penalties in minutes; **PP** – power play goals; **SH** – shorthanded goals; **GW** – game-winning goals; **OT** – overtime goals; **S** – shots on goal; **S%** – percentage of shots resulting in goals; **Mins** – minutes played; **GA** – goals against; **Avg.** – goals against average; **W** – wins; **L** – losses; **SA** – shots against; **Sv%** – save percentage; **SO** – shutouts.

Playoff Scoring Leaders

Player	Team	GP	G	A	PTS	+/-	PIM	PP	SH	GW	OT	S	S%
Evgeni Malkin	Pittsburgh	25	10	18	28	9	53	1	0	0	0	60	16.7
Sidney Crosby	Pittsburgh	24	8	19	27	4	10	4	0	0	0	63	12.7
Phil Kessel	Pittsburgh	25	8	15	23	12	2	5	0	2	0	68	11.8
*Jake Guentzel	Pittsburgh	25	13	8	21	1	10	1	1	5	1	52	25.0
Ryan Getzlaf	Anaheim	17	8	11	19	7	8	3	0	1	0	53	15.1
Erik Karlsson	Ottawa	19	2	16	18	13	10	0	0	2	0	53	3.8
Filip Forsberg	Nashville	22	9	7	16	14	14	1	0	0	0	71	12.7
Leon Draisaitl	Edmonton	13	6	10	16	8	19	1	0	1	0	22	27.3
Bobby Ryan	Ottawa	19	6	9	15	1	14	3	0	3	2	42	14.3
Jakob Silfverberg	Anaheim	17	9	5	14	-4	6	2	0	2	1	61	14.8
Roman Josi	Nashville	22	6	8	14	2	12	2	0	1	0	76	7.9
Rickard Rakell	Anaheim	15	7	6	13	13	0	0	0	0	0	48	14.6
Nicklas Backstrom	Washington	13	6	7	13	0	2	1	0	1	0	26	23.1
Ryan Ellis	Nashville	22	5	8	13	4	12	2	0	1	0	48	10.4
Justin Schultz	Pittsburgh	21	4	9	13	3	4	3	0	2	0	26	15.4
Ryan Johansen	Nashville	14	3	10	13	12	12	0	0	1	0	15	20.0
Viktor Arvidsson	Nashville	22	3	10	13	3	19	0	0	1	0	49	6.1
Colton Sissons	Nashville	22	6	6	12	7	16	1	0	2	0	28	21.4
T.J. Oshie	Washington	13	4	8	12	2	4	2	0	1	0	27	14.8
P.K. Subban	Nashville	22	2	10	12	5	29	0	0	0	0	39	5.1

Playoff Defensemen Scoring Leaders

Player	Team	GP	G	A	PTS	+/-	PIM	PP	SH	GW	OT	S	S%
Erik Karlsson	Ottawa	19	2	16	18	13	10	0	0	2	0	53	3.8
Roman Josi	Nashville	22	6	8	14	2	12	2	0	1	0	76	7.9
Ryan Ellis	Nashville	22	5	8	13	4	12	2	0	1	0	48	10.4
Justin Schultz	Pittsburgh	21	4	9	13	3	4	3	0	2	0	26	15.4
P.K. Subban	Nashville	22	2	10	12	5	29	0	0	0	0	39	5.1
Mattias Ekholm	Nashville	22	1	10	11	6	38	1	0	0	0	33	3.0
Cam Fowler	Anaheim	13	2	7	9	-6	2	0	0	0	0	26	7.7
Ian Cole	Pittsburgh	25	0	9	9	2	22	0	0	0	0	23	.0
*Shea Theodore	Anaheim	14	2	6	8	1	4	0	0	0	0	24	8.3
Ron Hainsey	Pittsburgh	25	2	6	8	5	6	0	0	0	0	29	6.9
Olli Maatta	Pittsburgh	25	2	6	8	8	12	0	0	1	0	35	5.7
Ryan McDonagh	NY Rangers	12	2	5	7	0	12	1	0	0	0	26	7.7
*Brandon Montour	Anaheim	17	0	7	7	12	4	0	0	0	0	37	.0
Joel Edmundson	St. Louis	11	3	3	6	12	14	0	0	1	1	9	33.3
Adam Larsson	Edmonton	13	2	4	6	-4	4	0	0	1	0	15	13.3
Sami Vatanen	Anaheim	12	1	5	6	-5	4	1	0	0	0	22	4.5
Kevin Shattenkirk	Washington	13	1	5	6	-4	6	1	0	1	1	36	2.8
Brian Dumoulin	Pittsburgh	25	1	5	6	9	6	0	0	1	0	25	4.0

GOALTENDING LEADERS

(Minimum 7 games played)

Goals Against Average

Goaltender	Team	GP	Mins	GA	Avg.
*Matt Murray	Pittsburgh	11	669	19	**1.70**
Pekka Rinne	Nashville	22	1289	42	**1.96**
Jake Allen	St. Louis	11	675	22	**1.96**
Henrik Lundqvist	NY Rangers	12	775	29	**2.25**
Craig Anderson	Ottawa	19	1178	46	**2.34**

Wins

Goaltender	Team	GP	Mins	W	L
Pekka Rinne	Nashville	22	1289	**14**	8
Craig Anderson	Ottawa	19	1178	**11**	8
Marc-Andre Fleury	Pittsburgh	15	867	**9**	6
John Gibson	Anaheim	16	879	**9**	5
*Matt Murray	Pittsburgh	11	669	**7**	3
Cam Talbot	Edmonton	13	799	**7**	6
Braden Holtby	Washington	13	803	**7**	6

Save Percentage

Goaltender	Team	GP	Mins	GA	SA	Sv%	W	L
*Matt Murray	Pittsburgh	11	669	19	303	**.937**	7	3
Jake Allen	St. Louis	11	675	22	336	**.935**	6	5
Pekka Rinne	Nashville	22	1289	42	599	**.930**	14	8
Henrik Lundqvist	NY Rangers	12	775	29	395	**.927**	6	6
Marc-Andre Fleury	Pittsburgh	15	867	37	490	**.924**	9	6
Cam Talbot	Edmonton	13	799	33	437	**.924**	7	6

Shutouts

Goaltender	Team	GP	Mins	SO	W	L
*Matt Murray	Pittsburgh	11	669	**3**	7	3
Cam Talbot	Edmonton	13	799	**2**	7	6
Marc-Andre Fleury	Pittsburgh	15	867	**2**	9	6
Pekka Rinne	Nashville	22	1289	**2**	14	8

Goals

Player	Team	GP	G
*Jake Guentzel	Pittsburgh	25	13
Evgeni Malkin	Pittsburgh	25	10
Jakob Silfverberg	Anaheim	17	9
Filip Forsberg	Nashville	22	9
Ryan Getzlaf	Anaheim	17	8
Jean-Gabriel Pageau	Ottawa	19	8
Sidney Crosby	Pittsburgh	24	8
Phil Kessel	Pittsburgh	25	8
Rickard Rakell	Anaheim	15	7
Bryan Rust	Pittsburgh	23	7

Assists

Player	Team	GP	A
Sidney Crosby	Pittsburgh	24	19
Evgeni Malkin	Pittsburgh	25	18
Erik Karlsson	Ottawa	19	16
Phil Kessel	Pittsburgh	25	15
Ryan Getzlaf	Anaheim	17	11
Leon Draisaitl	Edmonton	13	10
Ryan Johansen	Nashville	14	10
P.K. Subban	Nashville	22	10
Mattias Ekholm	Nashville	22	10
Viktor Arvidsson	Nashville	22	10

Power-Play Goals

Player	Team	GP	PP
Phil Kessel	Pittsburgh	25	5
Sean Monahan	Calgary	4	4
Mark Letestu	Edmonton	13	4
Sidney Crosby	Pittsburgh	24	4
Ryan Getzlaf	Anaheim	17	3
Bobby Ryan	Ottawa	19	3
Justin Schultz	Pittsburgh	21	3

Shorthanded Goals

Player	Team	GP	SH
Matt Cullen	Pittsburgh	25	1
Michael Grabner	NY Rangers	12	1
Mikael Backlund	Calgary	4	1
Derek Stepan	NY Rangers	12	1
Zack Kassian	Edmonton	13	1
Tim Schaller	Boston	6	1
*Jake Guentzel	Pittsburgh	25	1
Connor McDavid	Edmonton	13	1
Jesper Fast	NY Rangers	12	1

Overtime Goals

Player	Team	GP	OT
Corey Perry	Anaheim	17	3
Bobby Ryan	Ottawa	19	2

Game-Winning Goals

Player	Team	GP	GW
*Jake Guentzel	Pittsburgh	25	5
Jaden Schwartz	St. Louis	11	3
Corey Perry	Anaheim	17	3
Bobby Ryan	Ottawa	19	3
10 players tied with			2

Shots

Player	Team	GP	S
Roman Josi	Nashville	22	76
Filip Forsberg	Nashville	22	71
Phil Kessel	Pittsburgh	25	68
James Neal	Nashville	22	67
Sidney Crosby	Pittsburgh	24	63

Plus/Minus

Player	Team	GP	+/-
Filip Forsberg	Nashville	22	14
Rickard Rakell	Anaheim	15	13
Erik Karlsson	Ottawa	19	13
Joel Edmundson	St. Louis	11	12
Ryan Johansen	Nashville	14	12
*Brandon Montour	Anaheim	17	12
Phil Kessel	Pittsburgh	25	12

* — rookie

TEAMS' PLAYOFF HOME/ROAD RECORD

Team	GP	W	L	HOME GF	GA	Win %	GP	W	L	ROAD GF	GA	Win %
Pittsburgh	13	10	3	46	22	.769	12	6	6	31	35	.500
Nashville	11	9	2	34	17	.818	11	5	6	26	31	.455
Ottawa	9	6	3	29	23	.667	10	5	5	18	27	.500
Anaheim	9	5	4	24	24	.556	8	5	3	26	28	.625
Edmonton	6	3	3	21	17	.500	7	4	3	15	18	.571
Washington	7	3	4	16	20	.429	6	4	2	20	16	.667
St. Louis	5	3	2	11	10	.600	6	3	3	11	13	.500
NY Rangers	6	4	2	16	11	.667	6	2	4	18	19	.333
San Jose	3	1	2	8	4	.333	3	1	2	6	8	.333
Toronto	3	1	2	9	10	.333	3	1	2	7	8	.333
Boston	3	0	3	5	8	.000	3	2	1	8	7	.667
Montreal	3	1	2	6	8	.333	3	1	2	5	6	.333
Minnesota	3	0	3	5	8	.000	2	1	1	3	3	.500
Columbus	2	1	1	9	9	.500	3	0	3	4	12	.000
Calgary	2	0	2	5	8	.000	2	0	2	4	6	.000
Chicago	2	0	2	0	6	.000	2	0	2	3	7	.000
Totals	**87**	**47**	**40**	**244**	**205**	**.540**	**87**	**40**	**47**	**205**	**244**	**.460**

TEAMS' POWER-PLAY RECORD

Abbreviations: ADV-total advantages; **PPGF**-power play goals for; **%** arrived by dividing number of power-play goals by total advantages.

	Team	GP	OVERALL ADV	PPGF	%	Team	GP	HOME ADV	PPGF	%	Team	GP	ROAD ADV	PPGF	%
1	CGY	4	16	6	37.5	CGY	2	8	4	50.0	CHI	2	5	2	40.0
2	WSH	13	40	10	25.0	BOS	3	6	2	33.3	WSH	6	19	5	26.3
3	CHI	4	9	2	22.2	S.J.	3	13	4	30.8	CGY	2	8	2	25.0
4	EDM	13	42	9	21.4	TOR	3	8	2	25.0	NSH	11	29	7	24.1
5	PIT	25	78	16	20.5	MIN	3	12	3	25.0	MTL	3	9	2	22.2
6	S.J.	6	26	5	19.2	WSH	7	21	5	23.8	EDM	7	19	4	21.1
7	BOS	6	16	3	18.8	EDM	6	23	5	21.7	PIT	12	30	6	20.0
8	NSH	22	65	11	16.9	PIT	13	48	10	20.8	CBJ	3	7	1	14.3
9	CBJ	5	12	2	16.7	CBJ	2	5	1	20.0	OTT	10	28	4	14.3
10	MIN	5	18	3	16.7	ANA	9	33	6	18.2	BOS	3	10	1	10.0
11	TOR	6	18	3	16.7	ST.L.	5	16	2	12.5	TOR	3	10	1	10.0
12	MTL	6	20	3	15.0	NSH	11	36	4	11.1	S.J.	3	13	1	7.7
13	ANA	17	54	7	13.0	NYR	6	19	2	10.5	NYR	6	20	1	5.0
14	OTT	19	61	7	11.5	MTL	3	11	1	9.1	ANA	8	21	1	4.8
15	NYR	12	39	3	7.7	OTT	9	33	3	9.1	MIN	2	6	0	.0
16	ST.L.	11	30	2	6.7	CHI	2	4	0	.0	ST.L.	6	14	0	.0
	Totals	**544**	**92**	**16.9**	**87**		**296**	**54**	**18.2**	**87**		**248**	**38**	**15.3**	**87**

TEAMS' PENALTY KILLING RECORD

Abbreviations: TSH – Total times shorthanded; **PPGA** – power-play goals against; **%** arrived by dividing times shorthanded minus power-play goals against by times shorthanded.

	Team	GP	OVERALL TSH	PPGA	%	Team	GP	HOME TSH	PPGA	%	Team	GP	ROAD TSH	PPGA	%
1	MIN	5	15	1	93.3	CGY	2	2	0	100.0	CHI	2	4	0	100.0
2	MTL	6	15	1	93.3	MTL	3	9	0	100.0	BOS	3	11	1	90.9
3	NYR	12	38	4	89.5	MIN	3	10	0	100.0	NYR	6	22	2	90.9
4	NSH	22	64	7	89.1	S.J.	3	6	0	100.0	NSH	11	41	4	90.2
5	CHI	4	8	1	87.5	EDM	6	24	1	95.8	WSH	6	21	3	85.7
6	S.J.	6	16	2	87.5	NYR	6	16	2	87.5	PIT	12	35	5	85.7
7	EDM	13	49	7	85.7	NSH	11	23	3	87.0	MTL	3	6	1	83.3
8	WSH	13	40	6	85.0	OTT	9	30	4	86.7	ST.L.	6	23	4	82.6
9	PIT	25	73	12	83.6	WSH	7	19	3	84.2	MIN	2	5	1	80.0
10	OTT	19	59	11	81.4	TOR	3	6	1	83.3	S.J.	3	10	2	80.0
11	ST.L.	11	35	7	80.0	PIT	13	38	7	81.6	EDM	7	25	6	76.0
12	BOS	6	23	5	78.3	ANA	9	31	7	77.4	OTT	10	29	7	75.9
13	CGY	4	13	3	76.9	CHI	2	4	1	75.0	ANA	8	33	8	75.8
14	ANA	17	64	15	76.6	ST.L.	5	12	3	75.0	CGY	2	11	3	72.7
15	TOR	6	17	5	70.6	CBJ	2	6	2	66.7	CBJ	3	9	3	66.7
16	CBJ	5	15	5	66.7	BOS	3	12	4	66.7	TOR	3	11	4	63.6
	Totals	**87**	**544**	**92**	**83.1**		**87**	**248**	**38**	**84.7**		**87**	**296**	**54**	**81.8**

SHORTHAND GOALS

Team	GOALS FOR GP	GF	Team	GOALS AGAINST GP	GA
NYR	12	3	PIT	25	0
EDM	13	2	NSH	22	0
PIT	25	2	EDM	13	0
CGY	4	1	NYR	12	0
BOS	6	1	STL	11	0
CHI	4	0	BOS	6	0
CBJ	5	0	TOR	6	0
MIN	5	0	MIN	5	0
MTL	6	0	CHI	4	0
TOR	6	0	CGY	4	0
S.J	6	0	ANA	17	1
STL	11	0	WSH	13	1
WSH	13	0	MTL	6	1
ANA	17	0	CBJ	5	1
OTT	19	0	S.J	6	2
NSH	22	0	OTT	19	3
Totals	**67**	**9**		**87**	**9**

TEAM PENALTIES

Abbreviations: GP – games played; **PEN** – total penalty minutes, including bench penalties; **BMI** – total bench minor minutes; **AVG** – average penalty minutes/game arrived by dividing total penalty minutes less bench minor minutes by games played

Team	GP	PEN	BMI	AVG
San Jose	6	34	0	5.7
Chicago	4	30	0	7.5
Minnesota	5	38	0	7.6
Toronto	6	48	2	8.0
St. Louis	11	94	2	8.5
Boston	6	56	4	9.3
Calgary	4	37	0	9.3
Washington	13	130	0	10.0
Montreal	6	61	0	10.2
Columbus	5	54	2	10.8
NY Rangers	12	137	2	11.4
Ottawa	19	218	8	11.5
Pittsburgh	25	288	10	11.5
Nashville	22	271	4	12.3
Edmonton	13	173	6	13.3
Anaheim	17	257	2	15.1
Totals	**87**	**1926**	**42**	**22.1**

Jake Guentzel led the NHL playoffs with 13 goals in 25 games as Pittsburgh became the first repeat champions since the Detroit Red Wings in 1997 and 1998. Guentzel was just one goal short of the playoff rookie record of 14 set by Dino Ciccarelli in 1981.

Stanley Cup Record Book

History: The Stanley Cup, the oldest trophy competed for by professional athletes in North America, was donated by Frederick Arthur, Lord Stanley of Preston and son of the Earl of Derby, in 1893. Lord Stanley purchased the trophy for 10 guineas ($50 at that time) for presentation to the amateur hockey champions of Canada. Since 1906, when Canadian teams began to pay their players openly, the Stanley Cup has been the symbol of professional hockey supremacy. It has been contested only by NHL teams since 1926-27 and has been under the exclusive control of the NHL since 1947.

Stanley Cup Standings

1918-2017

(ranked by Cup wins)

Teams	Cup Wins	Yrs.	Series	Wins	Losses	Games	Wins	Losses	Ties	Goals For	Goals Against	Winning %
Montreal[1,2]	24	83	152	92	59	749	429	312	8	2248	1908	.573
Toronto	13	66	111	58	53	537	256	277	4	1384	1467	.477
Detroit	11	64	121	68	53	622	325	296	1	1748	1575	.523
Boston	6	70	121	57	64	615	301	308	6	1777	1751	.489
Chicago	6	62	112	56	56	539	264	270	5	1539	1639	.490
Edmonton	5	21	51	35	16	264	159	105	0	974	798	.602
Pittsburgh	5	32	66	39	27	365	200	165	0	1118	1052	.548
NY Rangers	4	59	108	53	55	515	244	263	8	1397	1434	.474
NY Islanders	4	24	51	31	20	264	144	120	0	850	787	.545
New Jersey[3]	3	22	44	25	19	254	136	118	0	688	622	.535
Philadelphia	2	38	79	43	36	427	219	208	0	1282	1264	.513
Los Angeles	2	29	48	21	27	251	111	140	0	742	844	.442
Colorado4	2	22	45	25	20	256	135	121	0	746	725	.527
Dallas[5]	1	31	61	29	32	337	166	171	0	981	1008	.493
Calgary[6]	1	28	43	16	27	223	99	124	0	684	748	.444
Carolina[7]	1	13	22	10	12	127	59	68	0	323	368	.465
Anaheim	1	12	28	16	12	158	89	69	0	429	405	.563
Tampa Bay	1	9	20	12	8	116	62	54	0	304	303	.534
St. Louis	0	41	68	27	41	365	164	201	0	999	1105	.449
Buffalo	0	29	50	21	29	256	124	132	0	763	765	.484
Vancouver	0	27	43	16	27	229	101	128	0	634	735	.441
Washington	0	27	43	16	27	251	116	135	0	707	715	.462
Arizona[8]	0	19	23	4	19	119	41	78	0	310	422	.345
San Jose	0	18	36	17	19	211	103	108	0	543	599	.488
Ottawa[9]	0	16	27	11	16	151	72	79	0	357	372	.477
Nashville	0	10	16	6	10	92	42	50	0	227	244	.457
Minnesota	0	7	12	4	8	68	25	43	0	155	183	.368
Florida	0	5	8	3	5	44	18	26	0	108	115	.409
Columbus	0	3	3	0	3	15	3	12	0	38	60	.200
Winnipeg[10]	0	2	2	0	2	8	0	8	0	15	33	.000

1 Includes Stanley Cup championship won in 1916 prior to the formation of the NHL.
2 1919 final incomplete due to influenza epidemic.
3 Includes totals of Colorado Rockies 1976-82.
4 Includes totals of Quebec Nordiques 1979-95.
5 Includes totals of Minnesota North Stars 1967-93.
6 Includes totals of Atlanta Flames 1972-80.
7 Includes totals of Hartford Whalers 1979-97.
8 Includes totals of Phoenix Coyotes, 1997-2014 and Winnipeg Jets, 1979-96
9 Modern Ottawa Senators franchise only, 1992 to date.
10 Includes totals of Atlanta Thrashers 1999-2011.

Stanley Cup Winners Prior to Formation of NHL in 1917

Season	Champions	Manager	Coach
1916-17	Seattle Metropolitans	Pete Muldoon	Pete Muldoon
1915-16	Montreal Canadiens	George Kennedy	George Kennedy
1914-15	Vancouver Millionaires	Frank Patrick	Frank Patrick
1913-14	Toronto Blueshirts	Jack Marshall	Scotty Davidson*
1912-13**	Quebec Bulldogs	M.J. Quinn	Joe Malone*
1911-12	Quebec Bulldogs	M.J. Quinn	Charley Nolan
1910-11	Ottawa Senators		Percy LeSueur
1909-10	Montreal Wanderers (Mar. 1910)	Dickie Boon	Pud Glass*
1909-10	Ottawa Senators (Jan. 1910)		Bruce Stuart*
1908-09	Ottawa Senators		Bruce Stuart*
1907-08	Montreal Wanderers	Dickie Boon	Cecil Blachford*
1906-07	Montreal Wanderers (Mar. 25, 1907)	Dickie Boon	Lester Patrick*
1906-07	Kenora Thistles (Jan./Mar. 18, 1907)	F.A. Hudson	Tom Phillips*
1905-06	Montreal Wanderers (Mar. 1906)	Cecil Blachford*	
1905-06	Ottawa Silver Seven (Feb. 1906)		Alf Smith
1904-05	Ottawa Silver Seven		Alf Smith
1903-04	Ottawa Silver Seven		Alf Smith
1902-03	Ottawa Silver Seven (Mar. 1903)		Alf Smith
1902-03	Montreal A.A.A. (Feb. 1903)		Clare McKerrow
1901-02	Montreal A.A.A. (Mar. 1902)		Clare McKerrow
1901-02	Winnipeg Victorias (Jan. 1902)		
1900-01	Winnipeg Victorias		Dan Bain*
1899-1900	Montreal Shamrocks		Harry Trihey*
1898-99	Montreal Shamrocks (Mar. 1899)		Harry Trihey*
1898-99	Montreal Victorias (Feb. 1899)		Graham Drinkwater*
1897-98	Montreal Victorias		Frank Richardson*
1896-97	Montreal Victorias		Mike Grant*
1895-96	Montreal Victorias (Dec. 1896)		Mike Grant*
1895-96	Winnipeg Victorias (Feb. 1896)		Jack Armytage*
1894-95	Montreal Victorias		Mike Grant*
1893-94	Montreal A.A.A.		
1892-93	Montreal A.A.A.		

* In the early years the teams were frequently run by the Captain. *Indicates Captain
** Victoria defeated Quebec in challenge series. No official recognition.

Stanley Cup Winners

Year	W-L-T in Finals	Winner	Coach	Finalist	Coach
2017	4-2	Pittsburgh	Mike Sullivan	Nashville	Peter Laviolette
2016	4-2	Pittsburgh	Mike Sullivan	San Jose	Peter DeBoer
2015	4-2	Chicago	Joel Quenneville	Tampa Bay	Jon Cooper
2014	4-1	Los Angeles	Darryl Sutter	NY Rangers	Alain Vigneault
2013	4-2	Chicago	Joel Quenneville	Boston	Claude Julien
2012	4-2	Los Angeles	Darryl Sutter	New Jersey	Peter DeBoer
2011	4-3	Boston	Claude Julien	Vancouver	Alain Vigneault
2010	4-2	Chicago	Joel Quenneville	Philadelphia	Peter Laviolette
2009	4-3	Pittsburgh	Dan Bylsma	Detroit	Mike Babcock
2008	4-2	Detroit	Mike Babcock	Pittsburgh	Michel Therrien
2007	4-1	Anaheim	Randy Carlyle	Ottawa	Bryan Murray
2006	4-3	Carolina	Peter Laviolette	Edmonton	Craig MacTavish
2005	....	....		....	....
2004	4-3	Tampa Bay	John Tortorella	Calgary	Darryl Sutter
2003	4-3	New Jersey	Pat Burns	Anaheim	Mike Babcock
2002	4-1	Detroit	Scotty Bowman	Carolina	Paul Maurice
2001	4-3	Colorado	Bob Hartley	New Jersey	Larry Robinson
2000	4-2	New Jersey	Larry Robinson	Dallas	Ken Hitchcock
1999	4-2	Dallas	Ken Hitchcock	Buffalo	Lindy Ruff
1998	4-0	Detroit	Scotty Bowman	Washington	Ron Wilson
1997	4-0	Detroit	Scotty Bowman	Philadelphia	Terry Murray
1996	4-0	Colorado	Marc Crawford	Florida	Doug MacLean
1995	4-0	New Jersey	Jacques Lemaire	Detroit	Scotty Bowman
1994	4-3	NY Rangers	Mike Keenan	Vancouver	Pat Quinn
1993	4-1	Montreal	Jacques Demers	Los Angeles	Barry Melrose
1992	4-0	Pittsburgh	Scotty Bowman	Chicago	Mike Keenan
1991	4-2	Pittsburgh	Bob Johnson	Minnesota	Bob Gainey
1990	4-1	Edmonton	John Muckler	Boston	Mike Milbury
1989	4-2	Calgary	Terry Crisp	Montreal	Pat Burns
1988	4-0	Edmonton	Glen Sather	Boston	Terry O'Reilly
1987	4-3	Edmonton	Glen Sather	Philadelphia	Mike Keenan
1986	4-1	Montreal	Jean Perron	Calgary	Bob Johnson
1985	4-1	Edmonton	Glen Sather	Philadelphia	Mike Keenan
1984	4-1	Edmonton	Glen Sather	NY Islanders	Al Arbour
1983	4-0	NY Islanders	Al Arbour	Edmonton	Glen Sather
1982	4-0	NY Islanders	Al Arbour	Vancouver	Roger Neilson
1981	4-1	NY Islanders	Al Arbour	Minnesota	Glen Sonmor
1980	4-2	NY Islanders	Al Arbour	Philadelphia	Pat Quinn
1979	4-1	Montreal	Scotty Bowman	NY Rangers	Fred Shero
1978	4-2	Montreal	Scotty Bowman	Boston	Don Cherry
1977	4-0	Montreal	Scotty Bowman	Boston	Don Cherry
1976	4-0	Montreal	Scotty Bowman	Philadelphia	Fred Shero
1975	4-2	Philadelphia	Fred Shero	Buffalo	Floyd Smith
1974	4-2	Philadelphia	Fred Shero	Boston	Bep Guidolin
1973	4-2	Montreal	Scotty Bowman	Chicago	Billy Reay
1972	4-2	Boston	Tom Johnson	NY Rangers	Emile Francis
1971	4-3	Montreal	Al MacNeil	Chicago	Billy Reay
1970	4-0	Boston	Harry Sinden	St. Louis	Scotty Bowman
1969	4-0	Montreal	Claude Ruel	St. Louis	Scotty Bowman
1968	4-0	Montreal	Toe Blake	St. Louis	Scotty Bowman
1967	4-2	Toronto	Punch Imlach	Montreal	Toe Blake
1966	4-2	Montreal	Toe Blake	Detroit	Sid Abel
1965	4-3	Montreal	Toe Blake	Chicago	Billy Reay
1964	4-3	Toronto	Punch Imlach	Detroit	Sid Abel
1963	4-1	Toronto	Punch Imlach	Detroit	Sid Abel
1962	4-2	Toronto	Punch Imlach	Chicago	Rudy Pilous
1961	4-2	Chicago	Rudy Pilous	Detroit	Sid Abel
1960	4-0	Montreal	Toe Blake	Toronto	Punch Imlach
1959	4-1	Montreal	Toe Blake	Toronto	Punch Imlach
1958	4-2	Montreal	Toe Blake	Boston	Milt Schmidt
1957	4-1	Montreal	Toe Blake	Boston	Milt Schmidt
1956	4-1	Montreal	Toe Blake	Detroit	Jimmy Skinner
1955	4-3	Detroit	Jimmy Skinner	Montreal	Dick Irvin
1954	4-3	Detroit	Tommy Ivan	Montreal	Dick Irvin
1953	4-1	Montreal	Dick Irvin	Boston	Lynn Patrick
1952	4-0	Detroit	Tommy Ivan	Montreal	Dick Irvin
1951	4-1	Toronto	Joe Primeau	Montreal	Dick Irvin
1950	4-3	Detroit	Tommy Ivan	NY Rangers	Lynn Patrick
1949	4-0	Toronto	Hap Day	Detroit	Tommy Ivan
1948	4-0	Toronto	Hap Day	Detroit	Tommy Ivan
1947	4-2	Toronto	Hap Day	Montreal	Dick Irvin
1946	4-1	Montreal	Dick Irvin	Boston	Dit Clapper
1945	4-3	Toronto	Hap Day	Detroit	Jack Adams
1944	4-0	Montreal	Dick Irvin	Chicago	Paul Thompson
1943	4-0	Detroit	Jack Adams	Boston	Art Ross
1942	4-3	Toronto	Hap Day	Detroit	Jack Adams
1941	4-0	Boston	Cooney Weiland	Detroit	Ebbie Goodfellow
1940	4-2	NY Rangers	Frank Boucher	Toronto	Dick Irvin
1939	4-1	Boston	Art Ross	Toronto	Dick Irvin
1938	3-1	Chicago	Bill Stewart	Toronto	Dick Irvin
1937	3-2	Detroit	Jack Adams	NY Rangers	Lester Patrick
1936	3-1	Detroit	Jack Adams	Toronto	Dick Irvin
1935	3-0	Mtl. Maroons	Tommy Gorman	Toronto	Dick Irvin
1934	3-1	Chicago	Tommy Gorman	Detroit	Herbie Lewis
1933	3-1	NY Rangers	Lester Patrick	Toronto	Dick Irvin
1932	3-0	Toronto	Dick Irvin	NY Rangers	Lester Patrick
1931	3-2	Montreal	Cecil Hart	Chicago	Dick Irvin
1930	2-0	Montreal	Cecil Hart	Boston	Art Ross
1929	2-0	Boston	Art Ross	NY Rangers	Lester Patrick
1928	3-2	NY Rangers	Lester Patrick	Mtl. Maroons	Eddie Gerard
1927	2-0-2	Ottawa	Dave Gill	Boston	Art Ross
		The National Hockey League assumed control of Stanley Cup competition after 1926			
1926	3-1	Mtl. Maroons	Eddie Gerard	Victoria	Lester Patrick
1925	3-1	Victoria	Lester Patrick	Montreal	Leo Dandurand
1924	2-0	Montreal	Leo Dandurand	Cgy. Tigers	Eddie Oatman
1923	2-0	Ottawa	Pete Green	Edm. Eskimos	Ken McKenzie
1922	3-2	Tor. St. Pats	George O'Donoghue	Van. Millionaires	Lloyd Cook/Frank Patrick
1921	3-2	Ottawa	Pete Green	Van. Millionaires	Lloyd Cook/Frank Patrick
1920	3-2	Ottawa	Pete Green	Seattle	Pete Muldoon
1919	2-2-1	No decision - series between Montreal and Seattle cancelled due to influenza epidemic			
1918	3-2	Tor. Arenas	Dick Carroll	Van. Millionaires	Frank Patrick

Championship Trophies

PRINCE OF WALES TROPHY

Beginning with the 1993-94 season, the club which advances to the Stanley Cup Final as the winner of the Eastern Conference Championship is presented with the Prince of Wales Trophy.

History: His Royal Highness, the Prince of Wales, donated the trophy to the National Hockey League in 1925. It was originally awarded to the winner of the first game played in Madison Square Garden, December 15, 1925 (Montreal Canadiens 3 at NY Americans 1). It was then awarded to the NHL playoff champion in 1925-26 and 1926-27. From 1927-28 through 1937-38, the award was presented to the regular-season champion of the American Division of the NHL. (The team finishing first in the Canadian Division received the O'Brien Trophy during these years.) From 1938-39, when the NHL reverted to one section, to 1966-67, it was presented to the team winning the NHL regular-season championship. With expansion in 1967-68, it again became a divisional trophy, awarded to the regular-season champions of the East Division through to the end of the 1973-74 season. Beginning in 1974-75, it was awarded to the regular-season winner of the conference bearing the name of the trophy. From 1981-82 to 1992-93 the trophy was presented to the playoff champion in the Wales Conference. Since 1993-94, the trophy has been presented to the playoff champion in the Eastern Conference.

2016-17 Winner: Pittsburgh Penguins

The Pittsburgh Penguins won the Prince of Wales Trophy on May 25, 2017 after defeating the Ottawa Senators 3-2 in game 7 of the Eastern Conference Finals. Before defeating the Senators, Pittsburgh had series wins over the Columbus Blue Jackets and the Washington Capitals.

PRINCE OF WALES TROPHY WINNERS

2016-17	Pittsburgh	1984-85	Philadelphia	1953-54	Detroit
2015-16	Pittsburgh	1983-84	NY Islanders	1952-53	Detroit
2014-15	Tampa Bay	1982-83	NY Islanders	1951-52	Detroit
2013-14	NY Rangers	1981-82	NY Islanders	1950-51	Detroit
2012-13	Boston	1980-81	Montreal	1949-50	Detroit
2011-12	New Jersey	1979-80	Buffalo	1948-49	Detroit
2010-11	Boston	1978-79	Montreal	1947-48	Toronto
2009-10	Philadelphia	1977-78	Montreal	1946-47	Montreal
2008-09	Pittsburgh	1976-77	Montreal	1945-46	Montreal
2007-08	Pittsburgh	1975-76	Montreal	1944-45	Montreal
2006-07	Ottawa	1974-75	Buffalo	1943-44	Montreal
2005-06	Carolina	1973-74	Boston	1942-43	Detroit
2003-04	Tampa Bay	1972-73	Montreal	1941-42	NY Rangers
2002-03	New Jersey	1971-72	Boston	1940-41	Boston
2001-02	Carolina	1970-71	Boston	1939-40	Boston
2000-01	New Jersey	1969-70	Chicago	1938-39	Boston
99-2000	New Jersey	1968-69	Montreal	1937-38	Boston
1998-99	Buffalo	1967-68	Montreal	1936-37	Detroit
1997-98	Washington	1966-67	Chicago	1935-36	Detroit
1996-97	Philadelphia	1965-66	Montreal	1934-35	Boston
1995-96	Florida	1964-65	Detroit	1933-34	Detroit
1994-95	New Jersey	1963-64	Montreal	1932-33	Boston
1993-94	NY Rangers	1962-63	Toronto	1931-32	NY Rangers
1992-93	Montreal	1961-62	Montreal	1930-31	Boston
1991-92	Pittsburgh	1960-61	Montreal	1929-30	Boston
1990-91	Pittsburgh	1959-60	Montreal	1928-29	Boston
1989-90	Boston	1958-59	Montreal	1927-28	Boston
1988-89	Montreal	1957-58	Montreal	1926-27	Ottawa
1987-88	Boston	1956-57	Detroit	1925-26	Mtl. Maroons
1986-87	Philadelphia	1955-56	Montreal	Dec. 15/25	Montreal
1985-86	Montreal	1954-55	Detroit	1923-24	Montreal*

* Engraved by Montreal Canadiens in 1925-26.

CLARENCE S. CAMPBELL BOWL

Beginning with the 1993-94 season, the club which advances to the Stanley Cup Final as the winner of the Western Conference Championship is presented with the Clarence S. Campbell Bowl.

History: Presented by the member clubs in 1968 for perpetual competition by the National Hockey League in recognition of the services of Clarence S. Campbell, President of the NHL from 1946 to 1977. From 1967-68 through 1973-74, the trophy was awarded to the regular-season champions of the West Division. Beginning in 1974-75, it was awarded to the regular-season winner of the conference bearing the name of the trophy. From 1981-82 to 1992-93 the trophy was presented to the playoff champion in the Campbell Conference. Since 1993-94, the trophy has been presented to the playoff champion in the Western Conference. The trophy itself is a hallmark piece made of sterling silver and was crafted by a British silversmith in 1878.

2016-17 Winner: Nashville Predators

The Nashville Predators won the Clarence S. Campbell Bowl on May 22, 2017 after defeating the Anaheim Ducks 6-3 in game 6 of the Western Conference Finals. Before defeating the Ducks, Nashville had series wins over the Chicago Blackhawks and the St. Louis Blues.

CLARENCE S. CAMPBELL BOWL WINNERS

2016-17	Nashville	1998-99	Dallas	1981-82	Vancouver
2015-16	San Jose	1997-98	Detroit	1980-81	NY Islanders
2014-15	Chicago	1996-97	Detroit	1979-80	Philadelphia
2013-14	Los Angeles	1995-96	Colorado	1978-79	NY Islanders
2012-13	Chicago	1994-95	Detroit	1977-78	NY Islanders
2011-12	Los Angeles	1993-94	Vancouver	1976-77	Philadelphia
2010-11	Vancouver	1992-93	Los Angeles	1975-76	Philadelphia
2009-10	Chicago	1991-92	Chicago	1974-75	Philadelphia
2008-09	Detroit	1990-91	Minnesota	1973-74	Philadelphia
2007-08	Detroit	1989-90	Edmonton	1972-73	Chicago
2006-07	Anaheim	1988-89	Calgary	1971-72	Chicago
2005-06	Edmonton	1987-88	Edmonton	1970-71	Chicago
2003-04	Calgary	1986-87	Edmonton	1969-70	St. Louis
2002-03	Anaheim	1985-86	Calgary	1968-69	St. Louis
2001-02	Detroit	1984-85	Edmonton	1967-68	Philadelphia
2000-01	Colorado	1983-84	Edmonton		
99-2000	Dallas	1982-83	Edmonton		

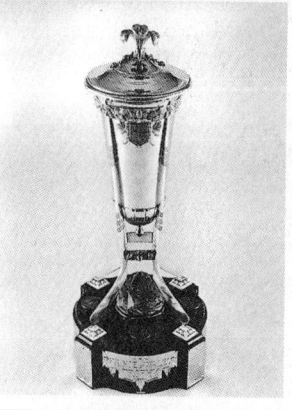

Prince of Wales Trophy

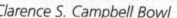

Clarence S. Campbell Bowl

Stanley Cup

Stanley Cup Winners

Rosters and Final Series Scores

2016-17 — Pittsburgh Penguins — Sidney Crosby (Captain), Josh Archibald, Nick Bonino, Ian Cole, Matt Cullen, Trevor Daley, Brian Dumoulin, Marc-Andre Fleury, Jake Guentzel, Carl Hagelin, Ron Hainsey, Patric Hornqvist, Phil Kessel, Tom Kuhnhackl, Chris Kunitz, Kristopher Letang, Olli Maatta, Evgeni Malkin, Matt Murray, Carter Rowney, Bryan Rust, Justin Schultz, Conor Sheary, Mark Streit, Scott Wilson, Mario Lemieux (Co-Owner, Chairman), Ron Burkle, William Kassling (Co-Owners), David Morehouse (CEO/President), Travis Williams (COO/General Counsel), Jim Rutherford (Executive Vice President, General Manager), Jason Botterill (Associate General Manager), Bill Guerin (Assistant General Manager), Jason Karmanos (Vice President, Hockey Operations), Mark Recchi (Development Coach), Mike Sullivan (Head Coach), Rick Tocchet, Jacques Martin (Assistant Coaches), Mike Bales (Goaltending Coach), Andy Saucier (Video Coach), Sergei Gonchar (Development Coach), Dr. Dharmesh Vyas (Team Physician), Chris Stewart (Head Athletic Trainer), Curtis Bell, Patrick Steidle (Assistant Trainers), Andy O'Brien (Director, Sport Science), Dana Heinze (Head Equipment Manager), JC Ihrig, Jon Taglianetti (Assistant Equipment Managers), Jim Britt (Manager, Team Services), Randy Sexton (Director, Amateur Scouting), Derek Clancey (Director, Pro Scouting).

Scores: May 29, at Pittsburgh — Pittsburgh 5, Nashville 3; May 31, at Pittsburgh — Pittsburgh 4, Nashville 1; June 3, at Nashville — Nashville 5, Pittsburgh 1; June 5, at Nashville — Nashville 4, Pittsburgh 1; June 8, at Pittsburgh — Pittsburgh 6, Nashville 0; June 11, at Nashville — Pittsburgh 2, Nashville 0.

2015-16 — Pittsburgh Penguins — Sidney Crosby (Captain), Nick Bonino, Ian Cole, Matt Cullen, Trevor Daley, Brian Dumoulin, Pascal Dupuis, Eric Fehr, Marc-Andre Fleury, Carl Hagelin, Patric Hornqvist, Phil Kessel, Tom Kuhnhackl, Chris Kunitz, Kristopher Letang, Ben Lovejoy, Olli Maatta, Evgeni Malkin, Matt Murray, Kevin Porter, Bryan Rust, Justin Schultz, Conor Sheary, Jeff Zatkoff, Mario Lemieux (Co-Owner/Chairman), Ron Burkle, William Kassling (Co-Owners), David Morehouse (CEO/President), Travis Williams (COO/General Counsel), Jim Rutherford (Executive Vice President/General Manager), Jason Botterill (Associate General Manager), Bill Guerin (Assistant General Manager), Jason Karmanos (Vice President, Hockey Operations), Mark Recchi (Development Coach), Mike Sullivan (Head Coach), Jacques Martin (Special Assistant), Rick Tocchet (Assistant Coach), Mike Bales (Goaltending Coach), Andy Saucier (Video Coach), Dr. Dharmesh Vyas (Team Physician), Chris Stewart (Head Athletic Trainer), Curtis Bell, Patrick Steidle (Assistant Trainers), Andy O'Brien (Director, Sport Science), Alex Trinca (Strength &?Conditioning Coach), Dana Heinze (Equipment Manager), Ted Richards, Jon Taglianetti (Assistant Equipment Managers), Jim Britt (Manager, Team Services), Dan MacKinnon (Director, Player Personnel), Randy Sexton (Director, Amateur Scouting), Derek Clancey (Director, Pro Scouting).

Scores: May 30, at Pittsburgh — Pittsburgh 3, San Jose 2; June 1, at Pittsburgh — Pittsburgh 2, San Jose 1; June 4, at San Jose — San Jose 3, Pittsburgh 2; June 6, at San Jose — Pittsburgh 3, San Jose 1; June 9, at Pittsburgh — San Jose 4, Pittsburgh 2; June 12, at San Jose — Pittsburgh 3, San Jose 1.

2014-15 — Chicago Blackhawks — Jonathan Toews (Captain), Bryan Bickell, Daniel Carcillo, Corey Crawford, Kyle Cumiskey, Scott Darling, Andrew Desjardins, Niklas Hjalmarsson, Marian Hossa, Patrick Kane, Duncan Keith, Marcus Kruger, Joakim Nordstrom, Johnny Oduya, Brad Richards, Michal Rozsival, David Rundblad, Brandon Saad, Brent Seabrook, Patrick Sharp, Andrew Shaw, Teuvo Teravainen, Kimmo Timonen, Trevor van Riemsdyk, Antoine Vermette, Kris Versteeg, W. Rockwell Wirtz (Chairman), John McDonough (President/CEO), Jay Blunk (Executive Vice President), Stan Bowman (Vice President/General Manager), Al MacIsaac (Vice President, Hockey Operations), Norm Maciver (Assistant General Manager), Scotty Bowman (Senior Advisor), Joel Quenneville (Head Coach), Mike Kitchen, Kevin Dineen (Assistant Coaches), Jimmy Waite (Goaltending Coach), Mike Gapski (Head Athletic Trainer), Troy Parchman (Equipment Manager), Jeff Thomas (Assistant Athletic Trainer), Pawel Prylinski (Massage Therapist), Jim Heintzelman (Equipment Assistant), Paul Goodman (Strength and Conditioning Coach), Matt Meacham (Video Coach), Pierre Gauthier (Director, Player Personnel), Mark Kelley (Senior Director, Amateur Scouting), Barry Smith (Director, Player Development), Ryan Stewart (Director, Pro Scouting), Ron Anderson (Director, Player Recruitment), Tony Ommen (Senior Director, Team Services), Mark Bernard (General Manager, Minor League Affiliates), Dr. Michael Terry (Head Team Physician).

***Scores:** June 3, at Tampa Bay — Chicago 2, Tampa Bay 1; June 6, at Tampa Bay — Tampa Bay 4, Chicago 3; June 8, at Chicago — Tampa Bay 3, Chicago 2; June 10, at Chicago — Chicago 2, Tampa Bay 1; June 13, at Tampa Bay — Chicago 2, Tampa Bay 1; June 15, at Chicago —Chicago 2, Tampa Bay 0.*

2013-14 — Los Angeles Kings — Dustin Brown (Captain), Jeff Carter, Kyle Clifford, Drew Doughty, Marian Gaborik, Matt Greene, Martin Jones, Dwight King, Anze Kopitar, Trevor Lewis, Alec Martinez, Willie Mitchell, Jake Muzzin, Jordan Nolan, Tanner Pearson, Jonathan Quick, Robyn Regehr, Mike Richards, Jeff Schultz, Jarret Stoll, Tyler Toffoli, Slava Voynov, Justin Williams, Philip Anschutz (Owner), Nancy Anschutz (Owner), Daniel Beckerman (Alternate Governor), Dean Lombardi (President/General Manager), Luc Robitaille (President, Business Operations), Robert Blake (Assistant General Manager), Jeffrey Solomon (Vice President/Hockey Operations and Legal Affairs), Michael Futa (Director of Amateur Scouting), Darryl Sutter (Head Coach), John Stevens (Assistant Coach), Davis Payne (Assistant Coach), Bill Ranford (Goaltending Coach), Kelly Cheeseman (Chief Operating Officer), Michael Altieri (Vice President, Communications and Broadcasting), Jack Ferreira (Special Assistant to the General Manager), Mike O'Connell (Development Coach), Nelson Emerson (Player Development), Alyn McCauley (Pro Scout), Mark Yannetti (Director of Amateur Scouting), Lee Callans (Scouting Operations Coordinator), Brent McEwen, Tony Gasparini (Amateur Scouts), Mike Donnelly (Collegiate Scout), Marshall Dickerson (Director of Team Operations), Zach Ziegler (Video Coordinator), Darren Granger (Head Equipment Manager), Chris Kingsley (Head Athletic Trainer), Dana C. Bryson (Assistant Equipment Manager), Myles Hirayama (Assistant Athletic Trainer).

***Scores:** June 4, at Los Angeles — Los Angeles 3, NY Rangers 2; June 7, at Los Angeles — Los Angeles 5. NY Rangers 4; June 9, at New York — Los Angeles 3, NY Rangers 0; June 11, at New York — NY Rangers 2, Los Angeles 1; June 13, at Los Angeles — Los Angeles 3, NY Rangers 2.*

2012-13 — Chicago Blackhawks — Jonathan Toews (Captain), Bryan Bickell, Dave Bolland, Brandon Bollig, Sheldon Brookbank, Daniel Carcillo, Corey Crawford, Ray Emery, Michael Frolik, Michal Handzus, Niklas Hjalmarsson, Marian Hossa, Patrick Kane, Duncan Keith, Marcus Kruger, Nick Leddy, Jamal Mayers, Johnny Oduya, Michal Rozsival, Brandon Saad, Brent Seabrook, Patrick Sharp, Andrew Shaw, Ben Smith, Viktor Stalberg, W. Rockwell Wirtz (Chairman), John McDonough (President/CEO),
Jay Blunk (Executive Vice President), Stan Bowman (Vice President/General Manager), Al MacIsaac (Vice President/Assistant to the President), Norm Maciver (Assistant General Manager), Scotty Bowman (Senior Advisor), Joel Quenneville (Head Coach), Mike Kitchen, Jamie Kompon (Assistant Coaches), Stephane Waite (Goaltending Coach), Mike Gapski (Head Athletic Trainer), Troy Parchman (Equipment Manager), Jeff Thomas (Assistant Athletic Trainer), Clint Reif (Assistant Equipment Manager), Pawel Prylinski (Massage Therapist), Jim Heintzelman (Equipment Assistant), Paul Goodman (Strength and Conditioning Coach), Tim Campbell (Video Coach), Pierre Gauthier (Director, Player Personnel), Mark Kelley (Director, Amateur Scouting), Barry Smith (Director, Player Development), Ryan Stewart (Director, Pro Scouting), Ron Anderson (Director, Player Recruitment), Tony Ommen (Senior Director, Team Services), Mark Bernard (General Manager, Minor League Affiliates), Dr. Michael Terry (Head Team Physician).

***Scores:** June 12, at Chicago — Chicago 4, Boston 3; June 15, at Chicago — Boston 2, Chicago 1; June 17, at Boston — Boston 2, Chicago 0; June 19, at Boston — Chicago 6, Boston 5; June 22, at Chicago — Chicago 3, Boston 1; June 24, at Boston — Chicago 3, Boston 2.*

2011-12 — Los Angeles Kings — Dustin Brown (Captain), Jonathan Bernier, Jeff Carter, Kyle Clifford, Drew Doughty, Davis Drewiske, Colin Fraser, Simon Gagne, Matt Greene, Dwight King, Anze Kopitar, Trevor Lewis, Alec Martinez, Willie Mitchell, Jordan Nolan, Dustin Penner, Jonathan Quick, Mike Richards, Brad Richardson, Robert Scuderi, Jarret Stoll, Slava Voynov, Kevin Westgarth, Justin Williams, Philip Anschutz (Owner), Nancy Anschutz (Owner), Timothy Leiweke (Governor), Daniel Beckerman (Chief Financial Officer), Ted Fikre (Chief Legal Officer), Dean Lombardi (President/General Manager), Luc Robitaille (President, Business Operations), Ron Hextall (Vice President/Assistant General Manager), Jeffrey Solomon (Vice President/Hockey Operations and Legal Affairs), Darryl Sutter (Head Coach), John Stevens (Assistant Coach), Jamie Kompon (Assistant Coach), Bill Ranford (Goaltending Coach), Chris McGowan (Chief Operating Officer), Michael Altieri (Vice President, Communications and Content), Jack Ferreira (Special Assistant to the General Manager), Mike O'Connell (Player Development), Nelson Emerson (Player Development), Rob Laird (Senior Pro Scout), Michael Futa (Director of Amateur Scouting), Mark Yannetti (Director of Amateur Scouting), Lee Callans (Scouting Operations Coordinator), Marshall Dickerson (Director of Team Operations), Ryan Colville (Video Coordinator), Darren Granger (Head Equipment Manager), Chris Kingsley (Head Athletic Trainer), Dana C. Bryson (Assistant Equipment Manager), Myles Hirayama (Assistant Athletic Trainer).

***Scores:** May 30, at New Jersey — Los Angeles 2, New Jersey 1; June 2, at New Jersey — Los Angeles 2, New Jersey 1; June 4, at Los Angeles — Los Angeles 4, New Jersey 0; June 5, at Los Angeles — New Jersey 3, Los Angeles 1; June 9, at New Jersey — New Jersey 2, Los Angeles 1; June 11, at Los Angeles — Los Angeles 6, New Jersey 1.*

2010-11 — Boston Bruins — Zdeno Chara (Captain), Patrice Bergeron, Johnny Boychuk, Gregory Campbell, Andrew Ference, Nathan Horton, Tomas Kaberle, Chris Kelly, David Krejci, Milan Lucic, Brad Marchand, Adam McQuaid, Daniel Paille, Rich Peverley, Tuukka Rask, Mark Recchi, Michael Ryder, Marc Savard, Tyler Seguin, Dennis Seidenberg, Tim Thomas, Shawn Thornton, Jeremy and Margaret Jacobs, Charlie Jacobs, Louis Jacobs, Jerry Jacobs Jr. (Ownership), Cam Neely (President), Peter Chiarelli (General Manager), Jim Benning, Don Sweeney (Assistant General Managers), Claude Julien (Head Coach), Doug Jarvis, Geoff Ward, Doug Houda (Assistant Coaches), Bob Essensa (Goaltending Coach), Harry Sinden (Senior Advisor), John Bucyk (Team Road Service Coordinator), Scott Bradley (Director of Player Personnel), Wayne Smith (Director of Amateur Scouting), John Weisbrod (Director of Collegiate Scouting), Adam Creighton, Tom McVie (Scouts), Dale Hamilton-Powers (Director of Administration), Matt Chmura (Director of Communications), Ryan Nadeau (Manager of Hockey Administration), Don DelNegro (Athletic Trainer), John Whitesides (Strength and Conditioning Coach), Keith Robinson (Equipment Manager), Derek Repucci (Assistant Trainer and Massage Therapist), Jim "Beets" Johnson (Assistant Equipment Manager), Scott Waugh (Physical Therapist).

***Scores:** June 1, at Vancouver — Vancouver 1, Boston 0; June 4, at Vancouver — Vancouver 3, Boston 2; June 6, at Boston — Boston 8, Vancouver 1; June 8, at Boston — Boston 4, Vancouver 0; June 10, at Vancouver — Vancouver 1, Boston 0; June 13, at Boston — Boston 5, Vancouver 2; June 15, at Vancouver — Boston 4, Vancouver 0.*

2009-10 — Chicago Blackhawks — Jonathan Toews (Captain), Dave Bolland, Nick Boynton, Troy Brouwer, Adam Burish, Dustin Byfuglien, Brian Campbell, Ben Eager, Colin Fraser, Jordan Hendry, Niklas Hjalmarsson, Marian Hossa, Cristobal Huet, Patrick Kane, Duncan Keith, Tomas Kopecky, Andrew Ladd, John Madden, Antti Niemi, Brent Seabrook, Patrick Sharp, Brent Sopel, Kris Versteeg, W. Rockwell Wirtz (Chairman), John McDonough (President), Jay Blunk (Senior VP, Business Operations), Stan Bowman (General Manager), Kevin Cheveldayoff (Assistant General Manager), Al MacIsaac (Senior Director, Hockey Administration/Assistant to the President), Scotty Bowman, Dale Tallon (Senior Advisors, Hockey Operations), Joel Quenneville (Head Coach), John Torchetti, Mike Haviland (Assistant Coaches), Stephane Waite (Goaltending Coach), Paul Goodman (Strength and Conditioning Coach), Brad Aldrich (Video Coach), Paul Vincent (Skating Coach), Marc Bergevin (Director, Player Personnel), Mark Bernard (G.M., Minor League Affiliations), Norm Maciver (Director, Player Development), Mark Kelley (Director, Amateur Scouting), Ron Anderson (Director, Player Recruitment), Michel Dumas (Chief Amateur Scout), Tony Ommen (Director Team Services), Dr. Michael Terry (Head Team Physician), Mike Gapski (Head Athletic Trainer), Troy Parchman (Equipment Manager), Pawel Prylinski (Massage Therapist), Jeff Thomas (Assistant Athletic Trainer), Clint Reif (Assistant Equipment Manager), Jim Heintzelman (Equipment Assistant).

***Scores:** May 29, at Chicago — Chicago 6, Philadelphia 5; May 31, at Chicago — Chicago 2, Philadelphia 1; June 2 at Philadelphia — Philadelphia 4, Chicago 3; June 4 at Philadelphia — Philadelphia 5, Chicago 3; June 6, at Chicago — Chicago 7, Philadelphia 4; June 9 at Philadelphia — Chicago 4, Philadelphia 3.*

2008-09 — Pittsburgh Penguins — Sidney Crosby (Captain), Craig Adams, Philippe Boucher, Matt Cooke, Pascal Dupuis, Mark Eaton, Ruslan Fedotenko, Marc-Andre Fleury, Mathieu Garon, Hal Gill, Eric Godard, Alex Goligoski, Sergei Gonchar, Bill Guerin, Tyler Kennedy, Chris Kunitz, Kris Letang, Evgeni Malkin, Brooks Orpik, Miroslav Satan, Rob Scuderi, Jordan Staal, Petr Sykora, Maxime Talbot, Mike Zigomanis, Mario Lemieux (Co-owner/Chairman), Ron Burkle (Co-owner), Bill Kassling, Tom Grealish, Tony Liberati (Directors), Ken Sawyer (Chief Executive Officer), David Morehouse (President), Ray Shero (Executive Vice President amd General Manager), Chuck Fletcher (Assistant General Manager), Ed Johnston (Senior Advisor, Hockey Operations), Jason Botterill (Director of Hockey Administration), Dan Bylsma (Head Coach), Mike Yeo (Assistant Coach), Tom Fitzgerald (Director of Player Development), GIlles Meloche (Goaltending Coach), Mike Kadar (Strength and Conditioning Coach), Travis Ramsay (Video Coordinator), Chris Stewart (Head Athletic Trainer), Scott Adams (Assistant Athletic Trainer), Mark Mortland (Physical Therapist), Dana Heinze (Equipment Manager), Paul DeFazio, Danny Kroll (Assistant Equipment Managers), Frank Buonomo (Senior Director of Team Services and Communications), Tom McMillan (Vice President, Communications), Dan MacKinnon (Director of Professional Scouting), Jay Heinbuck (Director of Amateur Scouting).

***Scores:** May 30, at Detroit — Detroit 3, Pittsburgh 1; May 31 at Detroit — Detroit 3, Pittsburgh 1; June 2, at Pittsburgh — Pittsburgh 4, Detroit 2; June 4, at Pittsburgh — Pittsburgh 4, Detroit 2; June 6 at Detroit — Detroit 5, Pittsburgh 0; June 9, at Pittsburgh — Pittsburgh 2, Detroit 1; June 12, at Detroit — Pittsburgh 2, Detroit 1.*

2007-08 — Detroit Red Wings — Nicklas Lidstrom (Captain), Chris Chelios, Daniel Cleary, Pavel Datsyuk, Aaron Downey, Dallas Drake, Kris Draper, Valtteri Filppula, Johan Franzen, Dominik Hasek, Darren Helm, Tomas Holmstrom, Jiri Hudler, Tomas Kopecky, Niklas Kronwall, Brett Lebda, Andreas Lilja, Kirk Maltby, Darren McCarty, Derek Meech, Chris Osgood, Brian Rafalski, Mikael Samuelsson, Brad Stuart, Henrik Zetterberg, Michael Ilitch (Owner/Governor), Marian Ilitch (Owner/Secretary-Treasurer), Christopher Ilitch (Vice President/Alternate Governor), Denise Ilitch, Ronald Ilitch, Michael Ilitch Jr., Lisa Ilitch Murray, Atanas Ilitch, Carole Ilitch. Jim Devellano (Senior Vice President/Alternate Governor), Ken Holland (General Manager/Alternate Governor), Steve Yzerman (Vice President/Alternate Governor), Jim Nill (Assistant General Manager), Ryan Martin (Director, Hockey Operations), Scotty Bowman (Consultant), Mike Babcock (Head Coach), Todd McLellan (Associate Coach), Paul MacLean (Assistant Coach), Jim Bedard (Goaltending Consultant), Jay Woodcroft (Video Coordinator), Mark Howe (Director, Pro Scouting), Joe McDonnell (Director, Amateur Scouting), Hakan Andersson (Director, Amateur Scouting Europe), Piet Van Zant (Athletic Trainer), Paul Boyer (Equipment Manager), Russ Baumann, Christopher Scoppetto (Assistant Athletic Trainers).

***Scores:** May 24, at Detroit — Detroit 4, Pittsburgh 0; May 26, at Detroit — Detroit 3, Pittsburgh 0; May 28, at Pittsburgh — Pittsburgh 3, Detroit 2; May 31, at Pittsburgh — Detroit 2, Pittsburgh 1; June 2, at Detroit — Pittsburgh 4, Detroit 3; June 4, at Pittsburgh — Detroit 3, Pittsburgh 2.*

2006-07 — Anaheim Ducks — Scott Niedermayer (Captain), Rob Niedermayer, Chris Pronger, Teemu Selanne, Sean O'Donnell, Brad May, Todd Marchant, Jean-Sebastien Giguere, Andy McDonald, Samuel Pahlsson, Shawn Thornton, Ric Jackman, Joe DiPenta, Kent Huskins, Chris Kunitz, George Parros, Joe Motzko, Ilya Bryzgalov, Francois Beauchemin, Travis Moen, Ryan Carter, Drew Miller, Ryan Shannon, Dustin Penner, Ryan Getzlaf, Corey Perry; Henry Samueli, Susan Samueli (Owners), Michael Schulman (CEO), Brian Burke (Executive Vice President/General Manager), Tim Ryan (Executive Vice President/COO), Bob Wagner (Senior Vice President/Chief Marketing Officer), Bob Murray (Senior Vice President-Hockey Operations), David McNab (Assistant General Manager), Al Coates (Senior Advisor to GM), Randy Carlyle (Head Coach), Dave Farrish, Newell Brown (Assistant Coaches), Francois Allaire (Goaltending Consultant), Sean Skahan (Strength and Conditioning Coach), Joe Trotta (Video Coordinator), Tim Clark (Head Trainer), Mark O'Neill (Equipment Manager), John Allaway (Assistant Equipment Manager), James Partida (Massage Therapist), Rick Paterson (Director of Professional Scouting), Alain Chainey (Director of Amateur Scouting).

***Scores:** May 28, at Anaheim - Anaheim 3, Ottawa 2; May 30, at Anaheim - Anaheim 1, Ottawa 0; June 2, at Ottawa - Ottawa 5, Anaheim 3; June 4, at Ottawa - Anaheim 3, Ottawa 2; June 6, at Anaheim - Anaheim 6, Ottawa 2.*

2005-06 — Carolina Hurricanes — Rod Brind'Amour (Captain), Glen Wesley, Cory Stillman, Kevyn Adams, Craig Adams, Anton Babchuk, Erik Cole, Mike Commodore, Matt Cullen, Martin Gerber, Bret Hedican, Andrew Hutchinson, Frantisek Kaberle, Andrew Ladd, Chad LaRose, Mark Recchi, Eric Staal, Oleg Tverdovsky, Josef Vasicek, Niclas Wallin, Aaron Ward, Cam Ward, Doug Weight, Ray Whitney, Justin Williams; Peter Karmanos Jr., Thomas Thewes (Owners), Jim Rutherford (President/General

Manager), Jason Karmanos (Vice President/Assistant General Manager), Mike Amendola (Chief Financial Officer), Peter Laviolette (Head Coach), Kevin McCarthy, Jeff Daniels (Assistant Coaches), Greg Stefan (Goaltending Coach), Chris Huffine (Video Coordinator), Skip Cunningham, Wally Tatomir, Bob Gorman (Equipment Managers), Peter Friesen (Head Athletic Therapist/Strength and Conditioning Coach), Chris Stewart (Associate Athletic Trainer), Brian Tatum (Team Services Manager), Kelly Kirwin (Event Coordinator-Hockey Operations), Mike Sundheim (Director of Media Relations), Kyle Hanlin (Manager of Media Relations), Sheldon Ferguson (Director of Amateur Scouting), Marshall Johnston (Director of Professional Scouting), Claude Larose, Ron Smith (Professional Scouts), Bert Marshall, Tony MacDonald, Martin Madden (Amateur Scouts), Tom Rowe (Lowell (AHL) - Coach).

Scores: *June 5, at Carolina - Carolina 5, Edmonton 4; June 7, at Carolina - Carolina 5, Edmonton 0; June 10, at Edmonton - Edmonton 2, Carolina 1; June 12, at Edmonton - Carolina 2, Edmonton 1; June 14, at Carolina - Edmonton 4, Carolina 3; June 17, at Edmonton - Edmonton 4, Carolina 0; June 19, at Carolina - Carolina 3, Edmonton 1.*

2003-04 — Tampa Bay Lightning — Dave Andreychuk (Captain), Fredrik Modin, Vincent Lecavalier, Martin St. Louis, Brad Richards, Nikolai Khabibulin, Pavel Kubina, Dan Boyle, Ruslan Fedotenko, Darryl Sydor, Cory Sarich, Tim Taylor, Cory Stillman, Jassen Cullimore, John Grahame, Chris Dingman, Nolan Pratt, Brad Lukowich, Andre Roy, Dmitry Afanasenkov, Martin Cibak, Ben Clymer, Darren Rumble, Stan Neckar, Eric Perrin; William Davidson (Owner), Tom Wilson (Governor), Ron Campbell (President), Jay Feaster (General Manager), John Tortorella (Head Coach), Craig Ramsay (Associate Coach), Jeff Reese (Assistant Coach), Nigel Kirwan (Video Coach), Eric Lawson (Strength and Conditioning Coach), Tom Mulligan (Trainer), Adam Rambo (Assistant Trainer), Ray Thill (Equipment Manager), Dana Heinze, Jim Pickard (Assistant Equipment Managers), Mike Griebel (Massage Therapist), Bill Barber (Director of Player Personnel), Jake Goertzen (Head Scout), Phil Thibodeau (Director of Team Services), Ryan Belec (Assistant to the GM), Rick Paterson (Chief Pro Scout), Kari Kettunen, Glen Zacharias, Steve Baker, Dave Heitz, Yuri Yanchenkov, (Scouts), Bill Wickett (Senior Vice President - Communications), Sean Henry (Executive Vice President/COO).

Scores: *May 25, at Tampa Bay - Calgary 4, Tampa Bay 1; May 27, at Tampa Bay - Tampa Bay 4, Calgary 1; May 29, at Calgary - Calgary 3, Tampa Bay 0; May 31, at Calgary - Tampa Bay 1, Calgary 0; June 3, at Tampa Bay - Calgary 3, Tampa Bay 2; June 5, at Calgary - Tampa Bay 3, Calgary 2; June 7, at Tampa Bay - Tampa Bay 2, Calgary 1.*

2002-03 — New Jersey Devils — Tommy Albelin, Jiri Bicek, Martin Brodeur, Sergei Brylin, Ken Daneyko, Patrik Elias, Jeff Friesen, Brian Gionta, Scott Gomez, Jamie Langenbrunner, John Madden, Grant Marshall, Jim McKenzie, Scott Niedermayer, Joe Nieuwendyk, Jay Pandolfo, Brian Rafalski, Pascal Rheaume, Mike Rupp, Corey Schwab, Richard Smehlik, Scott Stevens (Captain), Turner Stevenson, Oleg Tverdovsky, Colin White; Raymond Chambers, Lewis Catz (Owners), Peter Simon (Chairman), Lou Lamoriello (CEO/President/General Manager), Pat Burns (Head Coach), Bob Carpenter, John MacLean (Assistant Coaches), Jacques Caron (Goaltending Coach), Larry Robinson (Special Assignment Coach), David Conte (Director - Scouting), Claude Carrier (Assistant Director - Scouting), Chris Lamoriello (Scout/Albany (AHL) - General Manager), Milt Fisher, Dan Labraaten, Marcel Pronovost (Scouts), Bob Hoffmeyer, Jan Ludvig (Pro Scouts), Dr. Barry Fisher (Orthopedist), Chris Modrzynski (Executive Vice President), Terry Farmer (Vice President - Ticket Operations), Vladimir Bure (Fitness Consultant), Taran Singleton (Hockey Operations), Bill Murray (Medical Trainer), Michael Vasalani (Strength and Conditioning Coordinator), Rick Matthews (Equipment Manager), Juergen Merz (Massage Therapist), Alex Abasto (Assistant Equipment Manager).

Scores: *May 27, at New Jersey - New Jersey 3, Anaheim 0; May 29, at New Jersey - New Jersey 3, Anaheim 0; May 31, at Anaheim - Anaheim 3, New Jersey 2; June 2, at Anaheim - Anaheim 1, New Jersey 0; June 5, at New Jersey - New Jersey 6, Anaheim 3; June 7, at Anaheim - Anaheim 5, New Jersey 2; June 9, at New Jersey - New Jersey 3, Anaheim 0.*

2001-02 — Detroit Red Wings — Steve Yzerman (Captain), Dominik Hasek, Manny Legace, Chris Chelios, Mathieu Dandenault, Steve Duchesne, Jiri Fischer, Nicklas Lidstrom, Fredrik Olausson, Jiri Slegr, Pavel Datsyuk, Boyd Devereaux, Kris Draper, Sergei Fedorov, Tomas Holmstrom, Brett Hull, Igor Larionov, Kirk Maltby, Darren McCarty, Luc Robitaille, Brendan Shanahan, Jason Williams; Michael Ilitch (Owner/Governor), Marian Ilitch (Owner/Secretary Treasurer), Christoper Ilitch (Vice President), Denise Ilitch (Alternate Governor), Ronald Ilitch, Michael Ilitch Jr., Lisa Ilitch Murray, Atanas Ilitch, Carole Ilitch, Jim Devellano (Senior Vice President), Ken Holland (General Manager), Jim Nill (Assistant General Manager), Scotty Bowman (Head Coach), Dave Lewis, Barry Smith (Associate Coaches), Jim Bedard (Goaltending Consultant), Joe Kocur (Video Coordinator), John Wharton (Athletic Trainer), Piet Van Zant (Assistant Athletic Trainer), Paul Boyer (Equipment Manager), Paul MacDonald (Senior Director of Finance), Nancy Beard (Executive Assistant), Dan Belisle, Mark Howe, Bob McCammon (Pro Scouts), Hakan Andersson (Director of European Scouting), Bruce Haralson, Mark Leach, Joe McDonnell, Glenn Merkosky (Scouts).

Scores: *June 4, at Detroit - Carolina 3, Detroit 2; June 6, at Detroit - Detroit 3, Carolina 1; June 8, at Carolina - Detroit 3, Carolina 2; June 10, at Carolina - Detroit 3, Carolina 0; June 13, at Detroit - Detroit 3, Carolina 1.*

2000-01 — Colorado Avalanche — David Aebischer, Rob Blake, Raymond Bourque, Greg de Vries, Chris Dingman, Chris Drury, Adam Foote, Peter Forsberg, Milan Hejduk, Dan Hinote, Jon Klemm, Eric Messier, Bryan Muir, Ville Nieminen, Scott Parker, Shjon Podein, Nolan Pratt, Dave Reid, Steve Reinprecht, Patrick Roy, Joe Sakic (Captain), Martin Skoula, Alex Tanguay, Stephane Yelle; E. Stanley Kroenke (Owner/Governor), Pierre Lacroix (President/ General Manager), Bob Hartley (Head Coach), Jacques Cloutier, Bryan Trottier (Assistant Coaches), Paul Fixter (Video Coach), Francois Giguere (Vice President - Hockey Operations), Brian MacDonald (Assistant General Manager), Michel Goulet (Vice President - Player Personnel), Jean Martineau (Vice President - Communications and Team Services), Pat Karns (Head Athletic Trainer), Matthew Sokolowski (Assistant Athletic Trainer), Wayne Flemming, Mark Miller (Equipment Managers), Dave Randolph (Assistant Equipment Manager), Paul Goldberg (Strength and Conditioning Coach), Gregorio Pradera (Massage Therapist), Brad Smith (Pro Scout), Jim Hammett (Chief Scout), Garth Joy, Steve Lyons, Joni Lehto, Orval Tessier (Scouts), Charlotte Grahame (Director of Hockey Administration).

Scores: *May 26, at Colorado - Colorado 5, New Jersey 0; May 29, at Colorado - New Jersey 2, Colorado 1; May 31, at New Jersey - Colorado 3, New Jersey 1; June 2, at New Jersey - New Jersey 3, Colorado 2; June 4, at Colorado - New Jersey 4, Colorado 1; June 7, at New Jersey - Colorado 4, New Jersey 0; June 9, at Colorado - Colorado 3, New Jersey 1.*

1999-2000 — New Jersey Devils — Jason Arnott, Brad Bombardir, Martin Brodeur, Steve Brule, Sergei Brylin, Ken Daneyko, Patrik Elias, Scott Gomez, Bobby Holik, Steve Kelly, Claude Lemieux, John Madden, Vladimir Malakhov, Randy McKay, Alexander Mogilny, Sergei Nemchinov, Scott Niedermayer, Krzysztof Oliwa, Jay Pandolfo, Brian Rafalski, Ken Sutton, Scott Stevens (Captain), Petr Sykora, Chris Terreri, Colin White; Dr. John J. McMullen (Owner/Chairman), Peter S. McMullen (Owner), Lou Lamoriello (President/General Manager), Larry Robinson (Head Coach), Viacheslav Fetisov (Assistant Coach), Jacques Caron (Goaltending Coach), Bob Carpenter (Assistant Coach), John Cuniff (Albany (AHL) - Coach), David Conte (Director of Scouting), Claude Carrier (Assistant Director of Scouting), Milt Fisher, Dan Labraaten, Marcel Pronovost (Scouts), Bob Hoffmeyer (Pro Scout), Dr. Barry Fisher (Orthopedist), Dennis Gendron (Albany (AHL) - Assistant Coach), Robbie Ftorek (Coach), Vladimir Bure (Consultant), Taran Singleton, Marie Carnevale, Callie Smith (Hockey Operations), Bill Murray (Medical Trainer), Michael Vasalani (Strength and Conditioning Coordinator), Dana McGuane (Equipment Manager), Juergen Merz (Massage Therapist), Harry Bricker, Lou Centanni Jr. (Assistant Equipment Managers).

Scores: *May 30, at New Jersey - New Jersey 7, Dallas 3; June 1, at New Jersey - Dallas 2, New Jersey 1; June 3, at Dallas - New Jersey 2, Dallas 1; June 5, at Dallas - New Jersey 3, Dallas 1; June 8, at New Jersey - Dallas 1, New Jersey 0; June 10, at Dallas, New Jersey 2 - Dallas 1.*

1998-99 — Dallas Stars — Derian Hatcher (Captain), Mike Modano, Joe Nieuwendyk, Craig Ludwig, Sergei Zubov, Ed Belfour, Guy Carbonneau, Shawn Chambers, Benoit Hogue, Tony Hrkac, Brett Hull, Mike Keane, Jamie Langenbrunner, Jere Lehtinen, Grant Marshall, Richard Matvichuk, Derek Plante, Dave Reid, Brent Severyn, Jon Sim, Brian Skrudland, Blake Sloan, Darryl Sydor, Roman Turek, Pat Verbeek; Thomas Hicks (Chairman/Owner), Jim Lites (President), Bob Gainey (Vice President - Hockey Operations/General Manager), Doug Armstrong (Assistant General Manager), Craig Button (Director of Player Personnel), Ken Hitchcock (Head Coach), Doug Jarvis, Rick Wilson (Assistant Coaches), Rick McLaughlin (Vice President/Chief Financial Officer), Jeff Cogen (Vice President - Marketing and Promotion), Bill Strong (Vice President - Marketing and Broadcasting), Tim Bernhardt (Director of Amateur Scouting), Doug Overton (Director of Pro Scouting), Bob Gernander (Chief Scout), Stu MacGregor (Western Scout), Dave Suprenant (Medical Trainer), Dave Smith, Rich Matthews (Equipment Managers), J.J. McQueen (Strength and Conditioning Coach), Rick St. Croix (Goaltending Consultant), Dan Stuchal (Director of Team Services), Larry Kelly (Director of Public Relations).

Scores: *June 8, at Dallas - Buffalo 3, Dallas 2; June 10, at Dallas - Dallas 4, Buffalo 2; June 12, at Buffalo - Dallas 2, Buffalo 1; June 15, at Buffalo - Buffalo 2, Dallas 1; June 17, at Dallas - Dallas 2, Buffalo 0; June 19, at Buffalo - Dallas 2, Buffalo 1.*

1997-98 — Detroit Red Wings — Steve Yzerman (Captain), Doug Brown, Mathieu Dandenault, Kris Draper, Anders Eriksson, Sergei Fedorov, Viacheslav Fetisov, Brent Gilchrist, Kevin Hodson, Tomas Holmstrom, Mike Knuble, Joe Kocur, Vladimir Konstantinov, Vyacheslav Kozlov, Martin Lapointe, Igor Larionov, Nicklas Lidstrom, Jamie Macoun, Kirk Maltby, Darren McCarty, Dmitri Mironov, Larry Murphy, Chris Osgood, Bob Rouse, Brendan Shanahan, Aaron Ward; Mike Ilitch, (Owner/Chairman), Marian Ilitch (Owner), Atanas Ilitch, Christopher Ilitch (Vice Presidents), Denise Ilitch, Ronald Ilitch, Michael Ilitch Jr., Lisa Ilitch Murray, Carole Ilitch Trepeck, Jim Devellano (Senior Vice President), Ken Holland (General Manager), Don Waddell (Assistant General Manager), Scotty Bowman (Head Coach), Barry Smith, Dave Lewis (Associate Coaches), Jim Nill (Director of Player Development), Dan Belisle, Mark Howe (Pro Scouts), Jim Bedard (Goaltending Consultant), Hakan Andersson (Director of European Scouting), Mark Leach (USA Scout), Joe McDonnell (Eastern Scout), Bruce Haralson (Western Scout), John Wharton (Athletic Trainer), Paul Boyer (Equipment Manager), Tim Abbott (Assistant Equipment Manager), Bob Huddleston (Masseur), Sergei Mnatsakanov, Wally Crossman (Dressing Room Assistant).

Scores: *June 9, at Detroit — Detroit 2, Washington 1; June 11, at Detroit — Detroit 5, Washington 4; June 13, at Washington — Detroit 2, Washington 1; June 16, at Washington — Detroit 4, Washington 1.*

1996-97 — Detroit Red Wings — Steve Yzerman (Captain), Doug Brown, Mathieu Dandenault, Kris Draper, Sergei Fedorov, Viacheslav Fetisov, Kevin Hodson, Tomas Holmstrom, Joe Kocur, Vladimir Konstantinov, Vyacheslav Kozlov, Martin Lapointe, Igor Larionov, Nicklas Lidstrom, Kirk Maltby, Darren McCarty, Larry Murphy, Chris Osgood, Jamie Pushor, Bob Rouse, Tomas Sandstrom, Brendan Shanahan, Tim Taylor, Mike Vernon, Aaron Ward; Mike Ilitch (Owner/Chairman), Marian Ilitch (Owner), Atanas Ilitch, Christopher Ilitch (Vice Presidents), Denise Ilitch Lites, Ronald Ilitch, Michael Ilitch Jr., Lisa Ilitch Murray, Carole Ilitch Trepeck, Jim Devellano (Senior Vice President), Scotty Bowman (Head Coach/Director of Player Personnel), Ken Holland (Assistant General Manager), Barry Smith, Dave Lewis (Associate Coaches), Mike Krushelnyski (Assistant Coach), Jim Nill (Director of Player Development), Dan Belisle, Bruce Haralson, Mark Howe (Scouts), Hakan Andersson (Director of European Scouting), John Wharton (Athletic Trainer), Wally Crossman (Dressing Room Assistant), Mark Leach (Scout), Paul Boyer (Equipment Manager), Tim Abbott (Assistant Equipment Manager), Sergei Mnatsakanov (Masseur), Joe McDonnell (Scout).

Scores: *May 31, at Philadelphia — Detroit 4, Philadelphia 2; June 3, at Philadelphia — Detroit 4, Philadelphia 2; June 5, at Detroit — Detroit 6, Philadelphia 1; June 7, at Detroit — Detroit 2, Philadelphia 1.*

1995-96 — Colorado Avalanche — Rene Corbet, Adam Deadmarsh, Stephane Fiset, Adam Foote, Peter Forsberg, Alexei Gusarov, Dave Hannan, Valeri Kamensky, Mike Keane, Jon Klemm, Uwe Krupp, Sylvain Lefebvre, Claude Lemieux, Curtis Leschyshyn, Troy Murray, Sandis Ozolinsh, Mike Ricci, Patrick Roy, Warren Rychel, Joe Sakic (Captain), Chris Simon, Craig Wolanin, Stephane Yelle, Scott Young; Charlie Lyons (Chairman/CEO), Pierre Lacroix (Executive Vice President/General Manager), Marc Crawford (Head Coach), Joel Quenneville, Jacques Cloutier (Assistant Coaches), Francois Giguere (Assistant General Manager), Michel Goulet (Director of Player Personnel), Dave Draper (Chief Scout), Jean Martineau (Director of Public Relations), Pat Karns (Trainer), Matthew Sokolowski (Assistant Trainer), Rob McLean (Equipment Manager), Mike Kramer, Brock Gibbins (Assistant Equipment Managers), Skip Allen (Strength and Conditioning Coach), Paul Fixter (Video Coordinator), Leo Vyssokov (Massage Therapist).

Scores: *June 4, at Colorado — Colorado 3, Florida 1; June 6, at Colorado — Colorado 8, Florida 1; June 8, at Florida — Colorado 3, Florida 2; June 10, at Florida — Colorado 1, Florida 0.*

1994-95 — New Jersey Devils — Tommy Albelin, Martin Brodeur, Neal Broten, Sergei Brylin, Bob Carpenter, Shawn Chambers, Tom Chorske, Danton Cole, Ken Daneyko, Kevin Dean, Jim Dowd, Bruce Driver, Bill Guerin, Bobby Holik, Claude Lemieux, John MacLean, Chris McAlpine, Randy McKay, Scott Niedermayer, Mike Peluso, Stephane Richer, Brian Rolston, Scott Stevens (Captain), Chris Terreri, Valeri Zelepukin; Dr. John J. McMullen (Owner/Chairman), Peter S. McMullen (Owner), Lou Lamoriello (President/General Manager), Jacques Lemaire (Head Coach), Jacques Caron (Goaltender Coach), Dennis Gendron, Larry Robinson (Assistant Coaches), Robbie Ftorek (Albany (AHL) - Coach), Alex Abasto (Assistant Equipment Manager), Bob Huddleston (Massage Therapist), David Nichols (Equipment Manager), Ted Schuch (Medical Trainer), Michael Vasalani (Strength and Conditioning Coach), David Conte (Director of Scouting), Milt Fisher, Claude Carrier, Dan Labraaten, Marcel Pronovost (Scouts).

Scores: *June 17, at Detroit — New Jersey 2, Detroit 1; June 20, at Detroit — New Jersey 4, Detroit 2; June 22, at New Jersey — New Jersey 5, Detroit 2; June 24, at New Jersey — New Jersey 5, Detroit 2.*

1993-94 — New York Rangers — Mark Messier (Captain), Brian Leetch, Kevin Lowe, Adam Graves, Steve Larmer, Glenn Anderson, Jeff Beukeboom, Greg Gilbert, Glenn Healy, Mike Hudson, Alexander Karpovtsev, Joe Kocur, Alex Kovalev, Nick Kypreos, Doug Lidster, Stephane Matteau, Craig MacTavish, Sergei Nemchinov, Brian Noonan, Esa Tikkanen, Mike Richter, Jay Wells, Sergei Zubov, Ed Olczyk, Mike Hartman; Neil Smith (President/General Manager/Governor), Robert Gutkowski, Stanley Jaffe, Kenneth Munoz (Governors), Larry Pleau (Assistant General Manager), Mike Keenan (Head Coach), Colin Campbell (Associate Coach), Dick Todd (Assistant Coach), Matthew Loughren (Manager - Team Operations), Barry Watkins (Director - Communications), Christer Rockstrom, Tony Feltrin, Martin Madden, Herb Hammond, Darwin Bennett (Scouts), Dave Smith, Joe Murphy, Mike Folga, Bruce Lifrieri (Trainers).

Scores: *May 31, at New York — Vancouver 3, NY Rangers 2; June 2, at New York — NY Rangers 3, Vancouver 1; June 4, at Vancouver — NY Rangers 5, Vancouver 1; June 7, at Vancouver — NY Rangers 4, Vancouver 2; June 9, at New York — Vancouver 6, at NY Rangers 3; June 11, at Vancouver — Vancouver 4, NY Rangers 1; June 14, at New York — NY Rangers 3, Vancouver 2.*

1992-93 — Montreal Canadiens — Guy Carbonneau (Captain), Patrick Roy, Andre Racicot, Rob Ramage, Kirk Muller, Mike Keane, Kevin Haller, Paul DiPietro, John LeClair, Denis Savard, Benoit Brunet, Brian Bellows, Lyle Odelein, Vincent Damphousse, Gary Leeman, Mathieu Schneider, Eric Desjardins, Jesse Belanger, Ed Ronan, Mario Roberge, Donald Dufresne, Todd Ewen, Sean Hill, Patrice Brisebois, Gilbert Dionne, Stephan Lebeau, J.J. Daigneault; Ronald Corey (President), Serge Savard (Managing Director/Vice President - Hockey), Jacques Demers (Head Coach), Jacques Laperriere, Charles Thiffault (Assistant Coaches), Francois Allaire (Goaltending Instructor), Jean Béliveau (Senior Vice President - Corporate Affairs), Jacques Lemaire (Assistant to the Managing Director), André Boudrias (Assistant to the Managing Director/Director of Scouting), Gaeten Lefebvre (Athletic Trainer), John Shipman (Assistant to the Athletic Trainer), Eddy Palchak (Equipment Manager), Pierre Gervais, Robert Boulanger (Assistants to the Equipment Manager).

Scores: *June 1, at Montreal — Los Angeles 4, Montreal 1; June 3, at Montreal — Montreal 3, Los Angeles 2; June 5, at Los Angeles — Montreal 4, Los Angeles 3; June 7, at Los Angeles — Montreal 3, Los Angeles 2; June 9, at Montreal — Montreal 4, Los Angeles 1.*

1991-92 — Pittsburgh Penguins — Mario Lemieux (Captain), Ron Francis, Bryan Trottier, Kevin Stevens, Bob Errey, Phil Bourque, Troy Loney, Rick Tocchet, Joe Mullen, Jaromir Jagr, Jiri Hrdina, Shawn McEachern, Ulf Samuelsson, Kjell Samuelsson, Larry Murphy, Gordie Roberts, Jim Paek, Paul Stanton, Tom Barrasso, Ken Wregget, Jay Caufield, Jamie Leach, Wendell Young, Grant Jennings, Peter Taglianetti, Jock Callander, Dave Michayluk, Mike Needham, Jeff Chychrun, Ken Priestlay, Jeff Daniels; Morris Belzberg, Howard Baldwin, Thomas Ruta (Owners), Donn Patton (Executive Vice President/Chief Financial Officer), Paul Martha (Executive Vice President/General Counsel), Craig Patrick (Executive Vice President/General Manager), Bob Johnson (Head Coach), Scotty Bowman (Director of Player Development/Coach), Barry Smith, Rick Kehoe, Pierre McGuire, Gilles Meloche, Rick Paterson (Assistant Coaches), Steve Latin (Equipment Manager), Skip Thayer (Trainer), John Welday (Strength and Conditioning Coach), Greg Malone, Les Binkley, Charlie Hodge, John Gill, Ralph Cox (Scouts).

Scores: *May 26, at Pittsburgh — Pittsburgh 5, Chicago 4; May 28, at Pittsburgh — Pittsburgh 3, Chicago 1; May 30, at Chicago — Pittsburgh 1, Chicago 0; June 1, at Chicago — Pittsburgh 6, Chicago 5.*

1990-91 — Pittsburgh Penguins — Mario Lemieux (Captain), Paul Coffey, Randy Hillier, Bob Errey, Tom Barrasso, Phil Bourque, Jay Caufield, Ron Francis, Randy Gilhen, Jiri Hrdina, Jaromir Jagr, Grant Jennings, Troy Loney, Joe Mullen, Larry Murphy, Jim Paek, Frank Pietrangelo, Barry Pederson, Mark Recchi, Gordie Roberts, Ulf Samuelsson, Paul Stanton, Kevin Stevens, Peter Taglianetti, Bryan Trottier, Scott Young, Wendell Young; Edward J. DeBartolo Sr. (Owner), Marie D. DeBartolo York (President), Paul Martha (Vice President/General Counsel), Craig Patrick (General Manager), Scotty Bowman (Director of Player Development and Recruitment), Bob Johnson (Head Coach), Rick Kehoe, Rick Paterson, Barry Smith (Assistant Coaches), Gilles Meloche (Goaltending Coach/Scout), Steve Latin (Equipment Manager), Skip Thayer (Trainer), John Welday (Strength and Conditioning Coach), Greg Malone (Scout).

Scores: *May 15, at Pittsburgh — Minnesota 5, Pittsburgh 4; May 17, at Pittsburgh — Pittsburgh 4, Minnesota 1; May 19, at Minnesota — Minnesota 3, Pittsburgh 1; May 21, at Minnesota — Pittsburgh 5, Minnesota 3; May 23, at Pittsburgh — Pittsburgh 6, Minnesota 4; May 25, at Minnesota — Pittsburgh 8, Minnesota 0.*

1989-90 — Edmonton Oilers — Mark Messier (Captain), Jari Kurri, Kevin Lowe, Steve Smith, Jeff Beukeboom, Mark Lamb, Joe Murphy, Glenn Anderson, Adam Graves, Craig MacTavish, Kelly Buchberger, Craig Simpson, Martin Gelinas, Randy Gregg, Charlie Huddy, Geoff Smith, Reijo Ruotsalainen, Craig Muni, Bill Ranford, Dave Brown, Pokey Reddick, Petr Klima, Esa Tikkanen, Grant Fuhr; Peter Pocklington (Owner), Glen Sather (President/General Manager), John Muckler (Head Coach), Ted Green (Co-Coach), Ron Low (Assistant Coach), Bruce MacGregor (Assistant General Manager), Barry Fraser (Director of Player Personnel), Bill Tuele (Director of Public Relations), Werner Baum (Vice President), Dr. Gordon Cameron (Medical Chief of Staff), Dr. David Reid (Team Physician), Ken Lowe (Athletic Therapist), Barrie Stafford (Athletic Trainer), Stuart Poirier (Massage Therapist), Lyle Kulchisky (Assistant Trainer), John Blackwell (Cape Breton (AHL) - Director of Operations), Ace Bailey, Ed Chadwick, Lorne Davis, Harry Howell, Albert Reeves, Matti Vaisanen (Scouts).

Scores: *May 15, at Boston — Edmonton 3, Boston 2; May 18, at Boston — Edmonton 7, Boston 2; May 20, at Edmonton — Boston 2, Edmonton 1; May 22, at Edmonton — Edmonton 5, Boston 1; May 24, at Boston — Edmonton 4, Boston 1.*

1988-89 — Calgary Flames — Lanny McDonald (Co- Captain), Jim Peplinski (Co-Captain), Tim Hunter, Mike Vernon, Rick Wamsley, Al MacInnis, Brad McCrimmon, Dana Murzyn, Ric Nattress, Joe Mullen, Gary Roberts, Colin Patterson, Hakan Loob, Theoren Fleury, Jiri Hrdina, Gary Suter, Mark Hunter, Joe Nieuwendyk, Brian MacLellan, Joel Otto, Jamie Macoun, Doug Gilmour, Rob Ramage; Norman Green, Harley Hotchkiss, Norman Kwong, Sonia Scurfield, B.J. Seaman, D.K. Seaman (Owners), Cliff Fletcher (President/General Manager), Al MacNeil (Assistant General Manager), Al Coates (Assistant to the President), Terry Crisp (Head Coach), Doug Risebrough, Tom Watt (Assistant Coaches), Glenn Hall (Goaltending Consultant), Jim Murray (Trainer), Al Murray (Assistant Trainer), Bob Stewart (Equipment Manager).

Scores: *May 14, at Calgary — Calgary 3, Montreal 2; May 17, at Calgary— Montreal 4, Calgary 2; May 19, at Montreal — Montreal 4, Calgary 3; May 21, at Montreal — Calgary 4, Montreal 2; May 23, at Calgary — Calgary 3, Montreal 2; May 25, at Montreal — Calgary 4, Montreal 2.*

1987-88 — Edmonton Oilers — Wayne Gretzky (Captain), Keith Acton, Glenn Anderson, Jeff Beukeboom, Geoff Courtnall, Grant Fuhr, Randy Gregg, Dave Hannan, Charlie Huddy, Mike Krushelnyski, Jari Kurri, Normand Lacombe, Kevin Lowe, Craig MacTavish, Kevin McClelland, Marty McSorley, Mark Messier, Craig Muni, Bill Ranford, Craig Simpson, Steve Smith, Esa Tikkanen; Peter Pocklington (Owner), Glen Sather (General Manager/Coach), John Muckler (Co-Coach), Ted Green (Assistant Coach), Bruce MacGregor (Assistant General Manager), Barry Fraser (Director of Player Personnel), Bill Tuele (Director of Public Relations), Dr. Gordon Cameron (Team Doctor), Peter Millar (Athletic Therapist), Juergen Merz (Massage Therapist), Barrie Stafford (Trainer), Lyle Kulchisky (Assistant Trainer).

Scores: *May 18, at Edmonton — Edmonton 2, Boston 1; May 20, at Edmonton — Edmonton 4, Boston 2; May 22, at Boston — Edmonton 6, Boston 3; May 24, at Boston — Boston 3, Edmonton 3 (suspended due to power failure); May 26, at Edmonton — Edmonton 6, Boston 3.*

1986-87 — Edmonton Oilers — Wayne Gretzky (Captain), Glenn Anderson, Jeff Beukeboom, Kelly Buchberger, Paul Coffey, Grant Fuhr, Randy Gregg, Charlie Huddy, Dave Hunter, Mike Krushelnyski, Jari Kurri, Moe Lemay, Kevin Lowe, Craig MacTavish, Kevin McClelland, Marty McSorley, Mark Messier, Andy Moog, Craig Muni, Kent Nilsson, Jaroslav Pouzar, Reijo Ruotsalainen, Steve Smith, Esa Tikkanen; Peter Pocklington (Owner), Glen Sather (General Manager/Coach), Bruce MacGregor (Assistant General Manager), John Muckler (Co-Coach), Ted Green, Ron Low (Assistant Coaches), Barry Fraser (Director of Player Personnel), Garnet Bailey, Ed Chadwick, Lorne Davis, Matti Vaisanen (Scouts), Peter Millar (Athletic Therapist), Juergen Merz (Massage Therapist), Dr. Gordon Cameron (Team Doctor), Barrie Stafford (Trainer), Lyle Kulchisky (Assistant Trainer).

Scores: *May 17, at Edmonton — Edmonton 4, Philadelphia 2; May 20, at Edmonton — Edmonton 3, Philadelphia 2; May 22, at Philadelphia — Philadelphia 5, Edmonton 3; May 24, at Philadelphia — Edmonton 4, Philadelphia 1; May 26, at Edmonton — Philadelphia 4, Edmonton 3; May 28, at Philadelphia — Philadelphia 3, Edmonton 2; May 31, at Edmonton — Edmonton 3, Philadelphia 1.*

1985-86 — Montreal Canadiens — Bob Gainey (Captain), Doug Soetaert, Patrick Roy, Rick Green, David Maley, Ryan Walter, Serge Boisvert, Mario Tremblay, Bobby Smith, Craig Ludwig, Tom Kurvers, Kjell Dahlin, Larry Robinson, Guy Carbonneau, Chris Chelios, Petr Svoboda, Mats Naslund, Lucien DeBlois, Steve Rooney, Gaston Gingras, Mike Lalor, Chris Nilan, John Kordic, Claude Lemieux, Mike McPhee, Brian Skrudland, Stephane Richer; Ronald Corey (President), Serge Savard (General Manager), Jean Perron (Coach), Jacques Laperrière (Assistant Coach), Jean Béliveau, Francois-Xavier Seigneur, Fred Steer (Vice Presidents), Jacques Lemaire, André Boudrias (Assistant General Managers), Claude Ruel (Player Development), Yves Belanger (Athletic Therapist), Gaetan Lefebvre (Assistant Athletic Therapist), Eddy Palchak (Trainer), Sylvain Toupin (Assistant Trainer).

Scores: *May 16, at Calgary — Calgary 5, Montreal 2; May 18, at Calgary — Montreal 3, Calgary 2; May 20, at Montreal — Montreal 5, Calgary 3; May 22, at Montreal — Montreal 1, Calgary 0; May 24, at Calgary — Montreal 4, Calgary 3.*

1984-85 — Edmonton Oilers — Wayne Gretzky (Captain), Glenn Anderson, Billy Carroll, Paul Coffey, Lee Fogolin Jr., Grant Fuhr, Randy Gregg, Charlie Huddy, Pat Hughes, Dave Hunter, Don Jackson, Mike Krushelnyski, Jari Kurri, Willy Lindstrom, Kevin Lowe, Dave Lumley, Kevin McClelland, Larry Melnyk, Mark Messier, Andy Moog, Mark Napier, Jaroslav Pouzar, Dave Semenko, Esa Tikkanen; Peter Pocklington (Owner), Glen Sather (General Manager/Coach), Bruce MacGregor (Assistant General Manager), John Muckler, Ted Green (Assistant Coaches), Barry Fraser (Director of Player Personnel/Chief Scout), Garnet Bailey, Ed Chadwick, Lorne Davis, Matti Vaisanen (Scouts), Peter Millar (Athletic Therapist), Dr. Gordon Cameron (Team Doctor), Barrie Stafford (Trainer), Lyle Kulchisky (Assistant Trainer).

Scores: *May 21, at Philadelphia — Philadelphia 4, Edmonton 1; May 23, at Philadelphia — Edmonton 3, Philadelphia 1; May 25, at Edmonton — Edmonton 4, Philadelphia 3; May 28, at Edmonton — Edmonton 5, Philadelphia 3; May 30, at Edmonton — Edmonton 8, Philadelphia 3.*

1983-84 — Edmonton Oilers — Wayne Gretzky (Captain), Glenn Anderson, Paul Coffey, Pat Conacher, Lee Fogolin Jr., Grant Fuhr, Randy Gregg, Charlie Huddy, Pat Hughes, Dave Hunter, Don Jackson, Jari Kurri, Willy Lindstrom, Ken Linseman, Kevin Lowe, Dave Lumley, Kevin McClelland, Mark Messier, Andy Moog, Jaroslav Pouzar, Dave Semenko; Peter Pocklington (Owner), Glen Sather (General Manager/Coach), Bruce MacGregor (Assistant General Manager), John Muckler, Ted Green (Assistant Coaches), Barry Fraser (Director of Player Personnel/Chief Scout), Pete Millar (Athletic Therapist), Barrie Stafford (Trainer), Lyle Kulchisky (Assistant Trainer).

Scores: *May 10, at New York — Edmonton 1, NY Islanders 0; May 12, at New York — NY Islanders 6, Edmonton 1; May 15, at Edmonton — Edmonton 7, NY Islanders 2; May 17, at Edmonton — Edmonton 7, NY Islanders 2; May 19, at Edmonton — Edmonton 5, NY Islanders 2.*

1982-83 — New York Islanders — Denis Potvin (Captain), Mike Bossy, Bob Bourne, Paul Boutilier, Billy Carroll, Greg Gilbert, Clark Gillies, Butch Goring, Mats Hallin, Tomas Jonsson, Anders Kallur, Gord Lane, Dave Langevin, Mike McEwen, Roland Melanson, Wayne Merrick, Ken Morrow, Bob Nystrom, Stefan Persson, Billy Smith, Brent Sutter, Duane Sutter, John Tonelli, Bryan Trottier; Bill Torrey (President/General Manager), John Pickett Jr. (Chairman), Gerry Ehman (Assistant General Manager/Director of Scouting), Al Arbour (Coach), Lorne Henning (Assistant Coach), Ron Waske (Trainer), Jim Pickard (Assistant Trainer).

Scores: *May 10, at Edmonton — NY Islanders 2, Edmonton 0; May 12, at Edmonton — NY Islanders 6, Edmonton 3; May 14, at New York — NY Islanders 5, Edmonton 1; May 17, at New York — NY Islanders 4, Edmonton 2*

1981-82 — New York Islanders — Denis Potvin (Captain), Mike Bossy, Bob Bourne, Billy Carroll, Greg Gilbert, Clark Gillies, Butch Goring, Tomas Jonsson, Anders Kallur, Gord Lane, Dave Langevin, Hector Marini, Mike McEwen, Roland Melanson, Wayne Merrick, Ken Morrow, Bob Nystrom, Stefan Persson, Billy Smith, Brent Sutter, Duane Sutter, John Tonelli, Bryan Trottier; Bill Torrey (President/General Manager), John Pickett Jr. (Chairman), Jim Devellano (Assistant General Manager/Director of Scouting), Al Arbour (Coach), Lorne Henning (Assistant Coach), Gerry Ehman (Head Scout), Ron Waske (Trainer), Jim Pickard (Assistant Trainer).

Scores: *May 8, at New York — NY Islanders 6, Vancouver 5; May 11, at New York — NY Islanders 6, Vancouver 4; May 13, at Vancouver — NY Islanders 3, Vancouver 0; May 16, at Vancouver — NY Islanders 3, Vancouver 1*

1980-81 — New York Islanders — Denis Potvin (Captain), Mike Bossy, Bob Bourne, Billy Carroll, Clark Gillies, Butch Goring, Garry Howatt, Anders Kallur, Gord Lane, Dave Langevin, Bob Lorimer, Hector Marini, Mike McEwen, Roland Melanson, Wayne Merrick, Ken Morrow, Bob Nystrom, Stefan Persson, Jean Potvin, Billy Smith, Duane Sutter, John Tonelli, Bryan Trottier; Bill Torrey (President/General Manager), John Pickett Jr. (Chairman), Al Arbour (Coach), Lorne Henning (Player/Assistant Coach), Jim Devellano (Chief Scout), Gerry Ehman, Mario Saraceno, Harry Boyd (Scouts), Ron Waske (Trainer), Jim Pickard (Assistant Trainer).

Scores: *May 12, at New York — NY Islanders 6, Minnesota 3; May 14, at New York — NY Islanders 6, Minnesota 3; May 17, at Minnesota — NY Islanders 7, Minnesota 5; May 19, at Minnesota— Minnesota 4, NY Islanders 2; May 21, at New York — NY Islanders 5, Minnesota 1.*

1979-80 — New York Islanders — Denis Potvin (Captain), Mike Bossy, Bob Bourne, Clark Gillies, Butch Goring, Lorne Henning, Garry Howatt, Anders Kallur, Gord Lane, Dave Langevin, Bob Lorimer, Alex McKendry, Wayne Merrick, Ken Morrow, Bob Nystrom, Stefan Persson, Jean Potvin, Glenn Resch, Billy Smith, Duane Sutter, Steve Tambellini, John Tonelli, Bryan Trottier; Bill Torrey (President/General Manager), John Pickett Jr. (Chairman), Al Arbour (Coach), Billy MacMillan (Assistant Coach), Jim Devellano (Chief Scout), Gerry Ehman, Mario Saraceno, Harry Boyd (Scouts), Ron Waske (Trainer), Jim Pickard (Assistant Trainer).

Scores: *May 13, at Philadelphia — NY Islanders 4, Philadelphia 3; May 15, at Philadelphia — Philadelphia 8, NY Islanders 3; May 17, at New York — NY Islanders 6, Philadelphia 2; May 19, at New York — NY Islanders 5, Philadelphia 2; May 22, at Philadelphia — Philadelphia 6, NY Islanders 3; May 24, at New York — NY Islanders 5, Philadelphia 4.*

1978-79 — Montreal Canadiens — Yvan Cournoyer (Captain), Guy Lafleur, Ken Dryden, Rick Chartraw, Brian Engblom, Bob Gainey, Mario Tremblay, Guy Lapointe, Doug Risebrough, Réjean Houle, Pat Hughes, Michel Larocque, Doug Jarvis, Yvon Lambert, Pierre Larouche, Gilles Lupien, Rod Langway, Jacques Lemaire, Pierre Mondou, Larry Robinson, Mark Napier, Serge Savard, Steve Shutt, Cam Connor, Richard Sévigny; Jacques Courtois (President), Sam Pollock (Director), Irving Grundman (Vice President/Managing Director), Jean Beliveau (Vice President - Corporate Affairs), Scotty Bowman (Coach), Claude Ruel (Director of Player Development), Al MacNeil (Director of Player Personnel), Morgan McCammon (Director), Ron Caron (Director of Recruitment), Eddy Palchak (Trainer), Pierre Meilleur (Assistant Trainer).

Scores: *May 13, at Montreal — NY Rangers 4, Montreal 1; May 15, at Montreal — Montreal 6, NY Rangers 2; May 17, at New York — Montreal 4, NY Rangers 1; May 19, at New York — Montreal 4, NY Rangers 3; May 21, at Montreal — Montreal 4, NY Rangers 1.*

1977-78 — Montreal Canadiens — Yvan Cournoyer (Captain), Guy Lafleur, Ken Dryden, Michel Larocque, Rick Chartraw, Réjean Houle, Pierre Larouche, Brian Engblom, Yvon Lambert, Jacques Lemaire, Bob Gainey, Guy Lapointe, Doug Jarvis, Gilles Lupien, Pierre Mondou, Larry Robinson, Bill Nyrop, Murray Wilson, Serge Savard, Steve Shutt, Mario Tremblay, Pierre Bouchard, Doug Risebrough; Jacques Courtois (President), Sam Pollock (Vice President/General Manager), Jean Beliveau (Vice President/Director of Corporate Relations), Scotty Bowman (Coach), Peter Bronfman, Edward Bronfman (Directors), Al MacNeil (Director of Player Development), Eddy Palchak (Trainer), Pierre Meilleur (Assistant Trainer), Claude Ruel (Director of Player Development), Floyd Curry, Ron Caron (Assistant General Managers).

Scores: *May 13, at Montreal — Montreal 4, Boston 1; May 16, at Montreal — Montreal 3, Boston 2; May 18, at Boston — Boston 4, Montreal 0; May 21, at Boston — Boston 4, Montreal 3; May 23, at Montreal — Montreal 4, Boston 1; May 25, at Boston — Montreal 4, Boston 1.*

1976-77 — Montreal Canadiens — Yvan Cournoyer (Captain), Larry Robinson, Guy Lafleur, Pierre Bouchard, Rejean Houle, Yvon Lambert, Bob Gainey, Jacques Lemaire, Guy Lapointe, Ken Dryden, Rick Chartraw, Bill Nyrop, Michel Larocque, Pierre Mondou, Serge Savard, Steve Shutt, Mario Tremblay, Murray Wilson, Doug Jarvis, Mike Polich, Jimmy Roberts, Pete Mahovlich, Doug Risebrough, Jacques Courtois (President), Sam Pollock (Vice President/General Manager), Jean Beliveau (Vice President/Director of Corporate Relations), Scotty Bowman (Coach), Peter Bronfman, Edward Bronfman (Directors), Claude Ruel (Director of Player Development), Floyd Curry, Ron Caron (Assistant General Managers), Pierre Meilleur (Assistant Trainer), Eddy Palchak (Trainer).

Scores: *May 7, at Montreal — Montreal 7, Boston 3; May 10, at Montreal — Montreal 3, Boston 0; May 12, at Boston — Montreal 4, Boston 2; May 14, at Boston — Montreal 2, Boston 1.*

1975-76 — Montreal Canadiens — Yvan Cournoyer (Captain), Bob Gainey, Larry Robinson, Pierre Bouchard, Rick Chartraw, Ken Dryden, Pete Mahovlich, Guy Lafleur, Yvon Lambert, Michel Larocque, Serge Savard, Doug Jarvis, Jacques Lemaire, Guy Lapointe, Jimmy Roberts, Doug Risebrough, Steve Shutt, Murray Wilson, Mario Tremblay, Bill Nyrop, Don Awrey, John Van Boxmeer; Jacques Courtois (President), Jean Beliveau (Vice President), Peter Bronfman (Chairman), Edward Bronfman (Director), Sam Pollock (Vice President/General Manager), Scotty Bowman (Coach), Eddy Palchak (Trainer), Pierre Meilleur (Assistant Trainer), Claude Ruel (Director of Player Development).

Scores: *May 9, at Montreal — Montreal 4, Philadelphia 3; May 11, at Montreal — Montreal 2, Philadelphia 1; May 13, at Philadelphia — Montreal 3, Philadelphia 2; May 16, at Philadelphia — Montreal 5, Philadelphia 3.*

1974-75 — Philadelphia Flyers — Bobby Clarke (Captain), Bernie Parent, Bobby Taylor, Wayne Stephenson, Ed Van Impe, Don Saleski, Tom Bladon, Larry Goodenough, Bill Barber, Gary Dornhoefer, Dave Schultz, Joe Watson, Ross Lonsberry, André Dupont, Terry Crisp, Orest Kindrachuk, Bill Clement, Bob Kelly, Rick MacLeish, Jimmy Watson, Reggie Leach, Ted Harris; Ed Snider (Chairman), Joe Scott (President), Eugene Dixon Jr. (Vice Chairman), Fred Shero (Coach), Keith Allen (Vice President/General Manager), Lou Scheinfeld (Vice President), Mike Nykoluk (Assistant Coach), Marcel Pelletier (Player Personnel Director), Barry Ashbee (Assistant Coach), Frank Lewis (Trainer), Jim McKenzie (Assistant Trainer).

Scores: *May 15, at Philadelphia — Philadelphia 4, Buffalo 1; May 18, at Philadelphia — Philadelphia 2, Buffalo 1; May 20, at Buffalo — Buffalo 5, Philadelphia 4; May 22, at Buffalo — Buffalo 4, Philadelphia 2; May 25, at Philadelphia — Philadelphia 5, Buffalo 1; May 27, at Buffalo — Philadelphia 2, Buffalo 0.*

1973-74 — Philadelphia Flyers — Bobby Clarke (Captain), Bernie Parent, Bobby Taylor, Bill Clement, Ross Lonsberry, Bill Barber, Orest Kindrachuk, Ed Van Impe, Don Saleski, Gary Dornhoefer, Barry Ashbee, Jimmy Watson, Dave Schultz, André Dupont, Bruce Cowick, Rick MacLeish, Terry Crisp, Bill Flett, Simon Nolet, Joe Watson, Bob Kelly, Tom Bladon; Ed Snider (Chairman), Joe Scott (President), Eugene Dixon Jr. (Vice Chairman), Fred Shero (Coach), Keith Allen (Vice President/General Manager), Mike Nykoluk (Assistant Coach), Marcel Pelletier (Player Personnel Director), Frank Lewis (Trainer), Jim McKenzie (Assistant Trainer).

Scores: *May 7, at Boston — Boston 3, Philadelphia 2; May 9, at Boston — Philadelphia 3, Boston 2; May 12, at Philadelphia — Philadelphia 4, Boston 1; May 14, at Philadelphia — Philadelphia 4, Boston 2; May 16, at Boston — Boston 5, Philadelphia 1; May 19, at Philadelphia — Philadelphia 1, Boston 0.*

1972-73 — Montreal Canadiens — Henri Richard (Captain), Jacques Laperrière, Ken Dryden, Yvan Cournoyer, Jacques Lemaire, Marc Tardif, Serge Savard, Pete Mahovlich, Guy Lapointe, Réjean Houle, Claude Larose, Pierre Bouchard, Frank Mahovlich, Jimmy Roberts, Chuck Lefley, Guy Lafleur, Bob Murdoch, Michel Plasse, Murray Wilson, Larry Robinson, Steve Shutt; Jacques Courtois (President), Jean Beliveau (Vice President), Peter Bronfman (Chairman), Sam Pollock (Vice President/General Manager), Edward Bronfman (Executive Director), Scotty Bowman (Coach), Bob Williams (Trainer).

Scores: *April 29, at Montreal — Montreal 8, Chicago 3; May 1, at Montreal — Montreal 4, Chicago 1; May 3, at Chicago — Chicago 7, Montreal 4; May 6, at Chicago — Montreal 4, Chicago 0; May 8, at Montreal — Chicago 8, Montreal 7; May 10, at Chicago — Montreal 6, Chicago 4.*

1971-72 — Boston Bruins — Bobby Orr, Gerry Cheevers, Eddie Johnston, Dallas Smith, Derek Sanderson, Carol Vadnais, Phil Esposito, Fred Stanfield, Don Awrey, Ted Green, Ken Hodge, John Bucyk, Wayne Cashman, John McKenzie, Ed Westfall, Mike Walton, Garnet Bailey, Don Marcotte; Weston Adams (Chairman), Weston Adams Jr. (President), Shelby Davis (Vice President), Charles Mulcahy (Junior Vice President/General Counsel), Eddie Powers (Vice President/Treasurer), Milt Schmidt (General Manager), Tom Johnson (Coach), Dan Canney (Trainer), John Forristall (Assistant Trainer).

Scores: *April 30, at Boston — Boston 6, NY Rangers 5; May 2, at Boston — Boston 2, NY Rangers 1; May 4, at New York — NY Rangers 5, Boston 2; May 7, at New York — Boston 3, NY Rangers 2; May 9, at Boston — NY Rangers 3, Boston 2; May 11, at New York — Boston 3, NY Rangers 0.*

1970-71 — Montreal Canadiens — Jean Béliveau (Captain), Pierre Bouchard, Yvan Cournoyer, John Ferguson, Jacques Laperrière, Terry Harper, Réjean Houle, Guy Lapointe, Claude Larose, Marc Tardif, Chuck Lefley, Jacques Lemaire, Frank Mahovlich, Henri Richard, Phil Roberto, Pete Mahovlich, Bob Murdoch, Serge Savard, Bobby Sheehan, Leon Rochefort, J.C. Tremblay, Ken Dryden, Rogie Vachon; David Molson (President), William Molson, Peter Molson (Vice Presidents), Sam Pollock (Vice President/General Manager), Ron Caron (Assistant General Manager), Al MacNeil (Coach), Yves Belanger (Trainer), Phil Langlois, Eddie Palchak (Assistant Trainers).

Scores: *May 4, at Chicago — Chicago 2, Montreal 1; May 6, at Chicago — Chicago 5, Montreal 3; May 9, at Montreal — Montreal 4, Chicago 2; May 11, at Montreal — Montreal 5, Chicago 2; May 13, at Chicago — Chicago 2, Montreal 0; May 16, at Montreal — Montreal 4, Chicago 3; May 18, at Chicago — Montreal 3, Chicago 2.*

1969-70 — Boston Bruins — Don Awrey, John Bucyk, Garnet Bailey, Wayne Carleton, Wayne Cashman, Gary Doak, Phil Esposito, Ted Green, Ken Hodge, Bobby Orr, Don Marcotte, John McKenzie, Derek Sanderson, Dallas Smith, Rick Smith, Bill Speer, Fred Stanfield, Ed Westfall, Gerry Cheevers, Eddie Johnston, John Adams, Jim Lorentz, Ron Murphy, Bill Lesuk, Ivan Boldirev, Danny Schock; Weston Adams Sr. (Chairman), Weston Adams Jr. (President), Charles Mulcahy, Eddie Powers, Shelby Davis (Vice Presidents), Harry Sinden (Coach), Milt Schmidt (General Manager), Tom Johnson (Assistant General Manager), Dan Canney (Trainer), John Forristall (Assistant Trainer).

Scores: *May 3, at St. Louis — Boston 6, St. Louis 1; May 5, at St. Louis — Boston 6, St. Louis 2; May 7, at Boston — Boston 4, St. Louis 1; May 10, at Boston — Boston 4, St. Louis 3.*

1968-69 — Montreal Canadiens — Jean Béliveau (Captain), Ralph Backstrom, Jacques Lemaire, Dick Duff, Christian Bordeleau, Mickey Redmond, Yvan Cournoyer, Henri Richard, Bobby Rousseau, John Ferguson, Serge Savard, Terry Harper, Gilles Tremblay, Ted Harris, J.C. Tremblay, Larry Hillman, Jacques Laperrière, Claude Provost, Tony Esposito, Rogie Vachon, Gump Worsley; David Molson (President), William Molson, Peter Molson (Vice Presidents), Sam Pollock (Vice President/General Manager), Claude Ruel (Coach), Larry Aubut (Trainer), Eddie Palchak (Assistant Trainer).

Scores: *April 27, at Montreal — Montreal 3, St. Louis 1; April 29, at Montreal — Montreal 3, St. Louis 1; May 1, at St. Louis — Montreal 4, St. Louis 0; May 4, at St. Louis — Montreal 2, St. Louis 1.*

1967-68 — Montreal Canadiens — Jean Béliveau (Captain), Ralph Backstrom, Yvan Cournoyer, Dick Duff, John Ferguson, Danny Grant, Terry Harper, Ted Harris, Serge Savard, Jacques Laperrière, Claude Larose, Jacques Lemaire, Claude Provost, Mickey Redmond, Henri Richard, Bobby Rousseau, Gilles Tremblay, J.C. Tremblay, Carol Vadnais, Rogie Vachon, Ernie Wakely, Gump Worsley; Hartland Molson (Chairman), David Molson (President), Sam Pollock (Vice President/General Manager), Toe Blake (Coach), Larry Aubut (Trainer), Eddie Palchak (Assistant Trainer).

Scores: *May 5, at St. Louis — Montreal 3, St. Louis 2; May 7, at St. Louis — Montreal 1, St. Louis 0; May 9, at Montreal — Montreal 4, St. Louis 3; May 11, at Montreal — Montreal 3, St. Louis 2.*

1966-67 — Toronto Maple Leafs — George Armstrong (Captain), Bob Baun, Johnny Bower, John Brenneman, Brian Conacher, Ron Ellis, Aut Erickson, Larry Hillman, Tim Horton, Red Kelly, Larry Jeffrey, Dave Keon, Frank Mahovlich, Milan Marcetta, Jim Pappin, Marcel Pronovost, Bob Pulford, Terry Sawchuk, Eddie Shack, Allan Stanley, Pete Stemkowski, Mike Walton; Stafford Smythe (President), Harold Ballard (Executive Vice President), John Bassett (Chairman), Punch Imlach (General Manager/Coach), King Clancy (Assistant Coach/Assistant General Manager), Bob Davidson (Chief Scout), John Anderson (Business Manager), Bob Haggert (Trainer), Tom Nayler (Assistant Trainer), Karl Elieff (Physiotherapist), Richard Smythe (Mascot).

Scores: *April 20, at Montreal — Toronto 2, Montreal 6; April 22, at Montreal — Toronto 3, Montreal 0; April 25, at Toronto — Toronto 3, Montreal 2; April 27, at Toronto — Toronto 2, Montreal 6; April 29, at Montreal — Toronto 4, Montreal 1; May 2, at Toronto — Toronto 3, Montreal 1.*

1965-66 — Montreal Canadiens — Jean Béliveau (Captain), Ralph Backstrom, Dave Balon, Yvan Cournoyer, Bobby Rousseau, Dick Duff, John Ferguson, Terry Harper, Ted Harris, Charlie Hodge, Jacques Laperrière, Claude Larose, Noel Price, Claude Provost, Henri Richard, Jimmy Roberts, Leon Rochefort, Jean-Guy Talbot, Gilles Tremblay, J.C. Tremblay, Gump Worsley; Hartland Molson (Chairman), David Molson (President), Sam Pollock (General Manager), Toe Blake (Coach), Andy Galley (Trainer), Larry Aubut (Assistant Trainer).

Scores: *April 24, at Montreal — Detroit 3, Montreal 2; April 26, at Montreal — Detroit 5, Montreal 2; April 28, at Detroit — Montreal 4, Detroit 2; May 1, at Detroit — Montreal 2, Detroit 1; May 3, at Montreal — Montreal 5, Detroit 1; May 5, at Detroit — Montreal 3, Detroit 2.*

1964-65 — Montreal Canadiens — Jean Béliveau (Captain), Ralph Backstrom, Dave Balon, Red Berenson, Yvan Cournoyer, Dick Duff, John Ferguson, Jean Gauthier, Charlie Hodge, Terry Harper, Ted Harris, Jacques Laperrière, Claude Larose, Garry Peters, Noel Picard, Claude Provost, Henri Richard, Jimmy Roberts, Bobby Rousseau, Jean-Guy Talbot, Gilles Tremblay, J.C. Tremblay, Ernie Wakely, Bryan Watson, Gump Worsley; Hartland Molson (Chairman), David Molson (President), Maurice Richard (Assistant to the President), Sam Pollock (General Manager), Toe Blake (Coach), Andy Galley (Trainer), Larry Aubut (Assistant Trainer).

Scores: *April 17, at Montreal — Montreal 3, Chicago 2; April 20, at Montreal — Montreal 2, Chicago 0; April 22, at Chicago — Montreal 1, Chicago 3; April 25, at Chicago — Montreal 1, Chicago 5; April 7, at Montreal — Montreal 6, Chicago 0; April 29, at Chicago — Montreal 1, Chicago 2; May 1, at Montreal — Montreal 4, Chicago 0.*

1963-64 — Toronto Maple Leafs — George Armstrong (Captain), Andy Bathgate, Bob Baun, Johnny Bower, Carl Brewer, Kent Douglas, Gerry Ehman, Billy Harris, Larry Hillman, Dave Keon, Tim Horton, Red Kelly, Frank Mahovlich, Don McKenney, Jim Pappin, Bob Pulford, Eddie Shack, Don Simmons, Allan Stanley, Ron Stewart, Al Arbour, Ed Litzenberger; Stafford Smythe (President), Harold Ballard (Executive Vice President), John Bassett (Chairman), Punch Imlach (Coach/General Manager), King Clancy (Assistant Coach/Assistant General Manager), Bob Haggert (Trainer), Tom Nayler (Assistant Trainer), Hugh Hoult (Stick Boy).

Scores *April 11, at Toronto — Toronto 3, Detroit 2; April 14, at Toronto — Toronto 3, Detroit 4; April 16, at Detroit — Toronto 3, Detroit 4; April 18, at Detroit — Toronto 4, Detroit 2; April 21, at Toronto — Toronto 1, Detroit 2; April 23, at Detroit — Toronto 4, Detroit 3; April 25, at Toronto — Toronto 4, Detroit 0.*

1962-63 — Toronto Maple Leafs — George Armstrong (Captain), Bob Baun, Johnny Bower, Carl Brewer, Kent Douglas, Dick Duff, Billy Harris, Larry Hillman, Tim Horton, Red Kelly, Dave Keon, Ed Litzenberger, John MacMillan, Frank Mahovlich, Bob Nevin, Bob Pulford, Eddie Shack, Don Simmons, Allan Stanley, Ron Stewart; Stafford Smythe (President), Harold Ballard (Executive Vice President), John Bassett (Chairman), Punch Imlach (Coach/General Manager), King Clancy (Assistant Coach/Assistant General Manager), Bob Haggert (Trainer), Tom Nayler (Assistant Trainer), Hugh Hoult (Stick Boy).

Scores: April 9, at Toronto — Toronto 4, Detroit 2; April 11, at Toronto — Toronto 4, Detroit 2; April 14, at Detroit — Toronto 2, Detroit 3; April 16, at Detroit — Toronto 4, Detroit 2; April 18, at Toronto — Toronto 3, Detroit 1.

1961-62 — Toronto Maple Leafs — George Armstrong (Captain), Al Arbour, Bob Baun, Johnny Bower, Carl Brewer, Dick Duff, Billy Harris, Larry Hillman, Dave Keon, Tim Horton, Red Kelly, Ed Litzenberger, John MacMillan, Frank Mahovlich, Bob Nevin, Bert Olmstead, Bob Pulford, Eddie Shack, Allan Stanley, Don Simmons, Ron Stewart; Stafford Smythe (President), Harold Ballard (Executive Vice President), John Bassett (Vice President), Conn Smythe (Chairman), Punch Imlach (Coach/General Manager), King Clancy (Assistant Coach), Bob Davidson (Chief Scout), Bob Haggert (Trainer), Tom Nayler (Assistant Trainer), Hugh Hoult (Stick Boy).

Scores: April 10, at Toronto — Toronto 4, Chicago 1; April 12, at Toronto — Toronto 3, Chicago 2; April 15, at Chicago — Toronto 0, Chicago 3; April 17, at Chicago — Toronto 1, Chicago 4; April 19, at Toronto —Toronto 8, Chicago 4; April 22, at Chicago — Toronto 2, Chicago 1.

1960-61 — Chicago Black Hawks — Ed Litzenberger (Captain), Al Arbour, Earl Balfour, Murray Balfour, Glenn Hall, Jack Evans, Roy Edwards, Denis DeJordy, Bill Hay, Wayne Hicks, Reggie Fleming, Wayne Hillman, Bobby Hull, Chico Maki, Ab McDonald, Moose Vasko, Stan Mikita, Ron Murphy, Eric Nesterenko, Pierre Pilote, Tod Sloan, Dollard St. Laurent, Kenny Wharram; Arthur Wirtz (President), Arthur Wirtz Jr. (Vice President), James Norris (Chairman), Tommy Ivan (General Manager), Rudy Pilous (Coach), Nick Garen, Walter Humeniuk (Trainers).

Scores: April 6, at Chicago — Chicago 3, Detroit 2; April 8, at Detroit — Detroit 3, Chicago 1; April 10, at Chicago — Chicago 3, Detroit 1; April 12, at Detroit — Detroit 2, Chicago 1; April 14, at Chicago — Chicago 6, Detroit 3; April 16, at Detroit — Chicago 5, Detroit 1.

1959-60 — Montreal Canadiens — Maurice Richard (Captain), Ralph Backstrom, Marcel Bonin, Jean Béliveau, Bernie Geoffrion, Phil Goyette, Doug Harvey, Bill Hicke, Charlie Hodge, Tom Johnson, Albert Langlois, Don Marshall, Dickie Moore, Ab McDonald, Jacques Plante, Henri Richard, André Pronovost, Claude Provost, Bob Turner, Jean-Guy Talbot; Senator Hartland Molson (President), Frank Selke (Managing Director), Ken Reardon (Vice President), Sam Pollock (Personnel Director), Toe Blake (Coach), Hector Dubois, Larry Aubut (Trainers).

Scores: April 7, at Montreal — Montreal 4, Toronto 2; April 9, at Montreal — Montreal 2, Toronto 1; April 12, at Toronto — Montreal 5, Toronto 2; April 14, at Toronto — Montreal 4, Toronto 0.

1958-59 — Montreal Canadiens — Maurice Richard (Captain), Ralph Backstrom, Marcel Bonin, Jean Béliveau, Ian Cushenan, Bernie Geoffrion, Charlie Hodge, Phil Goyette, Doug Harvey, Bill Hicke, Tom Johnson, Albert Langlois, Don Marshall, Ab McDonald, Dickie Moore, Jacques Plante, Ken Mosdell, André Pronovost, Claude Provost, Henri Richard, Jean-Guy Talbot, Bob Turner; Senator Hartland Molson (President), Frank Selke (Managing Director), Ken Reardon (Vice President), Sam Pollock (Personnel Director), Toe Blake (Coach), Hector Dubois, Larry Aubut (Trainers).

Scores: April 9, at Montreal — Montreal 5, Toronto 3; April 11, at Montreal — Montreal 3, Toronto 1; April 14, at Toronto — Toronto 3, Montreal 2; April 16, at Toronto — Montreal 3, Toronto 2; April 18, at Montreal — Montreal 5, Toronto 3.

1957-58 — Montreal Canadiens — Maurice Richard (Captain), Jean Béliveau, Marcel Bonin, Floyd Curry, Connie Broden, Bernie Geoffrion, Phil Goyette, Doug Harvey, Charlie Hodge, Tom Johnson, Albert Langlois, Don Marshall, Ab McDonald, Gerry McNeil, Dickie Moore, Bert Olmstead, Jacques Plante, André Pronovost, Henri Richard, Claude Provost, Dollard St. Laurent, Jean-Guy Talbot, Bob Turner; Senator Hartland Molson (President), Frank Selke (Managing Director), Ken Reardon (Vice President), Toe Blake (Coach), Hector Dubois, Larry Aubut (Trainers).

Scores: April 8, at Montreal —Montreal 2, Boston 1; April 10, at Montreal — Boston 5, Montreal 2; April 13, at Boston — Montreal 3, Boston 0; April 15, at Boston — Boston 3, Montreal 1; April 17, at Montreal — Montreal 3, Boston 2; April 20, at Boston — Montreal 5, Boston 3.

1956-57 — Montreal Canadiens — Maurice Richard (Captain), Jean Béliveau, Connie Broden, Floyd Curry, Bernie Geoffrion, Phil Goyette, Doug Harvey, Tom Johnson, Jackie LeClair, Don Marshall, Gerry McNeil, Dickie Moore, Bert Olmstead, Jacques Plante, André Pronovost, Claude Provost, Henri Richard, Dollard St. Laurent, Jean-Guy Talbot, Bob Turner; William Northey (President), Donat Raymond (Chairman), Ken Reardon (Vice President), Frank Selke (Managing Director), Toe Blake (Coach), Hector Dubois, Larry Aubut (Trainers).

Scores: April 6, at Montreal — Montreal 5, Boston 1; April 9, at Montreal — Montreal 1, Boston 0; April 11, at Boston — Montreal 4, Boston 2; April 14, at Boston — Boston 2, Montreal 0; April 16, at Montreal — Montreal 5, Boston 1.

1955-56 — Montreal Canadiens — Butch Bouchard (Captain), Bob Turner, Jean Béliveau, Bert Olmstead, Floyd Curry, Bernie Geoffrion, Jacques Plante, Doug Harvey, Claude Provost, Charlie Hodge, Henri Richard, Tom Johnson, Maurice Richard, Jackie LeClair, Dollard St. Laurent, Don Marshall, Jean-Guy Talbot, Dickie Moore, Ken Mosdell; Donat Raymond (President), Frank Selke (Managing Director), D'Alton Coleman, William Northey (Vice Presidents), Ken Reardon (Assistant Manager), Toe Blake (Coach), Hector Dubois, Gaston Bettez (Trainers).

Scores: March 31, at Montreal — Montreal 6, Detroit 4; April 3, at Montreal — Montreal 5, Detroit 1; April 5, at Detroit — Detroit 3, Montreal 1; April 8, at Detroit — Montreal 3, Detroit 0; April 10, at Montreal — Montreal 3, Detroit 1.

1954-55 — Detroit Red Wings — Dutch Reibel, Terry Sawchuk, Jim Hay, Vic Stasiuk, Johnny Wilson, Gordie Howe, Red Kelly, Tony Leswick, Ted Lindsay (Captain), Marty Pavelich, Marcel Pronovost, Marcel Bonin, Alex Delvecchio, Bill Dineen, Bob Goldham, Benny Woit, Larry Hillman, Glen Skov; Bruce Norris (President), Marguerite Norris (President), Jack Adams (Manager), Jimmy Skinner (Coach), John Mitchell (Chief Scout), Fred Huber (Publicity Director), Carl Mattson, Lefty Wilson (Trainers).

Scores: April 3, at Detroit — Detroit 4, Montreal 2; April 5, at Detroit — Detroit 7, Montreal 1; April 7, at Montreal — Montreal 4, Detroit 2; April 9, at Montreal — Montreal 5, Detroit 3; April 10, at Detroit — Detroit 5, Montreal 1; April 12, at Montreal — Montreal 6, Detroit 3; April 14, at Detroit — Detroit 3, Montreal 1.

1953-54 — Detroit Red Wings — Marty Pavelich, Jimmy Peters, Marcel Pronovost, Metro Prystai, Dutch Reibel, Terry Sawchuk, Bob Goldham, Gordie Howe, Earl Johnson, Red Kelly, Tony Leswick, Ted Lindsay (Captain), Keith Allen, Al Arbour, Alex Delvecchio, Bill Dineen, Gilles Dube, Dave Gatherum, Glen Skov, Vic Stasiuk, Johnny Wilson, Benny Woit; Bruce Norris (Owner), Marguerite Norris (President), Jack Adams (Manager), Tommy Ivan (Coach), John Mitchell (Chief Scout), Fred Huber (Publicity Director), Carl Mattson, Lefty Wilson (Trainers), Wally Crossman (Assistant Trainer).

Scores: April 4, at Detroit — Detroit 3, Montreal 1; April 6, at Detroit — Montreal 3, Detroit 1; April 8, at Montreal — Detroit 5, Montreal 2; April 10, at Montreal — Detroit 2, Montreal 0; April 11, at Detroit — Montreal 1, Detroit 0; April 13, at Montreal — Montreal 4, Detroit 1; April 16, at Detroit — Detroit 2, Montreal 1.

1952-53 — Montreal Canadiens — Floyd Curry, Bernie Geoffrion, Bert Olmstead, Paul Meger, Dick Gamble, Dickie Moore, Tom Johnson, Bud MacPherson, Billy Reay, Ken Mosdell, Paul Masnick, John McCormack, Butch Bouchard (Captain), Maurice Richard, Elmer Lach, Gerry McNeil, Doug Harvey, Dollard St. Laurent, Jacques Plante, Lorne Davis, Calum MacKay, Eddie Mazur, Donat Raymond (President), Dalton Coleman (Director), William Northey (Special Advisor), Frank Selke (Manager), Dick Irvin (Coach), Hector Dubois, Gaston Bettez (Trainers).

Scores: April 9, at Montreal — Montreal 4, Boston 2; April 11, at Montreal — Boston 4, Montreal 1; April 12, at Boston — Montreal 3, Boston 0; April 14, at Boston — Montreal 7, Boston 3; April 16, at Montreal — Montreal 1, Boston 0.

1951-52 — Detroit Red Wings — Metro Prystai, Leo Reise Jr., Terry Sawchuk, Enio Sclisizzi, Glen Skov, Vic Stasiuk, Gordie Howe, Red Kelly, Tony Leswick, Ted Lindsay, Marty Pavelich, Marcel Pronovost, Sid Abel (Captain), Alex Delvecchio, Fred Glover, Bob Goldham, Glenn Hall, Benny Woit, Johnny Wilson, Larry Zeidel; James Norris (President), Bruce Norris (Owner), Jack Adams (Manager), Tommy Ivan (Coach), Fred Huber (Publicity Director), Carson Cooper (Scout), Carl Mattson, Lefty Wilson (Trainers), Wally Crossman (Assistant Trainer).

Scores: April 10, at Montreal — Detroit 3, Montreal 1; April 12, at Montreal — Detroit 2, Montreal 1; April 13, at Detroit — Detroit 3, Montreal 0; April 15, at Detroit — Detroit 3, Montreal 0.

1950-51 — Toronto Maple Leafs — Bill Barilko, Max Bentley, Hugh Bolton, Turk Broda, Fern Flaman, Cal Gardner, Bob Hassard, Bill Juzda, Ted Kennedy (Captain), Joe Klukay, Danny Lewicki, Fleming MacKell, Howie Meeker, Gus Mortson, John McCormack, Al Rollins, Tod Sloan, Sid Smith, Jimmy Thomson, Ray Timgren, Harry Watson; Joe Primeau (Coach), Bill MacBrien (Chairman), Conn Smythe (President/Manager), Hap Day (Assistant Manager), George McCullagh, J.Y. Murdoch (Vice Presidents), J.P. Bickell, Ed Bickle (Directors), Tim Daly (Trainer), Archie Campbell, Tommy Naylor (Assistant Trainers), Dr. Norman Delarue, Dr. James Murray, Dr. Horace MacIntyre (Club Doctors), Ed Fitkin (Publicity Director), Squib Walker (Chief Scout).

Scores: April 11, at Toronto — Toronto 3, Montreal 2; April 14, at Toronto — Montreal 3, Toronto 2; April 17, at Montreal — Toronto 2, Montreal 1; April 19, at Montreal — Toronto 3, Montreal 2; April 21, at Toronto — Toronto 3, Montreal 2.

1949-50 — Detroit Red Wings — Sid Abel (Captain), Pete Babando, Steve Black, Joe Carveth, Gerry Couture, Al Dewsbury, Lee Fogolin, George Gee, Gordie Howe, Red Kelly, Ted Lindsay, Harry Lumley, Clare Martin, Jim McFadden, Max McNab, Marty Pavelich, Jimmy Peters, Marcel Pronovost, Leo Reise Jr., Jack Stewart, Johnny Wilson, Larry Wilson, Doug McKay; James Norris (President), James Norris Jr. (Vice President), Arthur Wirtz (Secretary Treasurer), Jack Adams (Manager), Tommy Ivan (Coach), Fred Huber Jr. (Publicity Director), Carson Cooper (Head Scout), Carl Mattson (Trainer), Walter Humeniuk (Assistant Trainer).

Scores: April 11, at Detroit — Detroit 4, NY Rangers 1; April 13, at Toronto — NY Rangers 3, Detroit 1; April 15, at Toronto* — Detroit 4, NY Rangers 0; April 18, at Detroit — NY Rangers 4, Detroit 3; April 20, at Detroit — NY Rangers 2, Detroit 1; April 22, at Detroit — Detroit 5, NY Rangers 4; April 23, at Detroit — Detroit 4, NY Rangers 3.*
**Ice was unavailable in Madison Square Garden and NY Rangers elected to play second and third games on Toronto ice.*

1948-49 — Toronto Maple Leafs — Bill Barilko, Max Bentley, Garth Boesch, Turk Broda, Bob Dawes, Bill Ezinicki, Cal Gardner, Bill Juzda, Ted Kennedy (Captain), Joe Klukay, Vic Lynn, Howie Meeker, Don Metz, Fleming MacKell, Gus Mortson, Sid Smith, Harry Taylor, Ray Timgren, Jimmy Thomson, Harry Watson; Hap Day (Coach), Bill MacBrien (Chairman), Conn Smythe (President/Manager), George McCullagh, J.Y. Murdoch (Vice Presidents), J.P. Bickell, Ed Bickle (Directors), Tim Daly (Trainer), Archie Campbell (Assistant Trainer), Dr. Norman Delarue, Dr. James Murray, Dr. Horace MacIntyre (Club Doctors), Ed Fitkin (Publicity Director), Squib Walker (Chief Scout), Kerry Day (Mascot).

Scores: April 8, at Detroit — Toronto 3, Detroit 2; April 10, at Detroit — Toronto 3, Detroit 1; April 13, at Toronto — Toronto 3, Detroit 1; April 16, at Toronto — Toronto 3, Detroit 1.

1947-48 — Toronto Maple Leafs — Syl Apps (Captain), Bill Barilko, Max Bentley, Garth Boesch, Turk Broda, Les Costello, Bill Ezinicki, Ted Kennedy, Joe Klukay, Vic Lynn, Howie Meeker, Nick Metz, Don Metz, Gus Mortson, Phil Samis, Sid Smith, Wally Stanowski, Jimmy Thomson, Harry Watson; Hap Day (Coach), Conn Smythe (Manager), Tim Daly (Trainer).

Scores: April 7, at Toronto — Toronto 5, Detroit 3; April 10, at Toronto — Toronto 4, Detroit 2; April 11, at Detroit — Toronto 2, Detroit 0; April 14, at Detroit — Toronto 7, Detroit 2.

1946-47 — Toronto Maple Leafs — Turk Broda, Garth Boesch, Gus Mortson, Jimmy Thomson, Wally Stanowski, Bill Barilko, Harry Watson, Bud Poile, Ted Kennedy, Syl Apps (Captain), Don Metz, Nick Metz, Bill Ezinicki, Vic Lynn, Howie Meeker, Gaye Stewart, Joe Klukay, Gus Bodnar, Bob Goldham; Conn Smythe (Manager), Hap Day (Coach), Tim Daly (Trainer).

Scores: April 8, at Montreal — Montreal 6, Toronto 0; April 10, at Montreal — Toronto 4, Montreal 0; April 12, at Toronto — Toronto 4, Montreal 2; April 15, at Toronto — Toronto 2, Montreal 1; April 17, at Montreal — Montreal 3, Toronto 1; April 19, at Toronto — Toronto 2, Montreal 1.

1945-46 — Montreal Canadiens — Elmer Lach, Toe Blake (Captain), Maurice Richard, Bob Fillion, Dutch Hiller, Murph Chamberlain, Ken Mosdell, Buddy O'Connor, Glen Harmon, Jimmy Peters, Butch Bouchard, Billy Reay, Ken Reardon, Leo Lamoureux, Frank Eddolls, Gerry Plamondon, Joe Benoit, Bill Durnan; Tommy Gorman (Manager), Dick Irvin (Coach), Ernie Cook (Trainer).

Scores: March 30, at Montreal — Montreal 4, Boston 3; April 2, at Montreal — Montreal 3, Boston 2; April 4, at Boston — Montreal 4, Boston 2; April 7, at Boston — Boston 3, Montreal 2; April 9, at Montreal — Montreal 6, Boston 3.

1944-45 — Toronto Maple Leafs — Don Metz, Frank McCool, Wally Stanowski, Reg Hamilton, Moe Morris, John McCreedy, Tom O'Neill, Ted Kennedy, Babe Pratt, Gus Bodnar, Art Jackson, Jack McLean, Mel Hill, Nick Metz, Bob Davidson (Captain), Sweeney Schriner, Lorne Carr, Pete Backor, Ross Johnstone; Conn Smythe (Manager), Frank Selke (Business Manager), Hap Day (Coach), Tim Daly (Trainer).

Scores: April 6, at Detroit — Toronto 1, Detroit 0; April 8, at Detroit — Toronto 2, Detroit 0; April 12, at Toronto — Toronto 1, Detroit 0; April 14, at Toronto — Detroit 5, Toronto 3; April 19, at Detroit — Detroit 2, Toronto 0; April 21, at Toronto — Detroit 1, Toronto 0; April 22, at Detroit — Toronto 2, Detroit 1.

1943-44 — Montreal Canadiens — Toe Blake (Captain), Maurice Richard, Elmer Lach, Ray Getliffe, Murph Chamberlain, Phil Watson, Butch Bouchard, Glen Harmon, Buddy O'Connor, Gerry Heffernan, Mike McMahon, Leo Lamoureux, Fern Majeau, Bob Fillion, Bill Durnan; Tommy Gorman (Manager), Dick Irvin (Coach), Ernie Cook (Trainer).

Scores: April 4, at Montreal — Montreal 5, Chicago 1; April 6, at Chicago — Montreal 3, Chicago 1; April 9, at Chicago — Montreal 3, Chicago 2; April 13, at Montreal — Montreal 5, Chicago 4.

1942-43 — Detroit Red Wings — Jack Stewart, Jimmy Orlando, Sid Abel (captain), Alex Motter, Harry Watson, Joe Carveth, Mud Bruneteau, Eddie Wares, Johnny Mowers, Cully Simon, Don Grosso, Carl Liscombe, Connie Brown, Syd Howe, Les Douglas, Harold Jackson, Joe Fisher, Adam Brown; Jack Adams (Manager), Ebbie Goodfellow (Playing Coach), Honey Walker (Trainer).

Scores: April 1, at Detroit — Detroit 6, Boston 2; April 4, at Detroit — Detroit 4, Boston 3; April 7, at Boston — Detroit 4, Boston 0; April 8, at Boston — Detroit 2, Boston 0.

1941-42 — Toronto Maple Leafs — Wally Stanowski, Syl Apps (Captain), Bob Goldham, Gordie Drillon, Hank Goldup, Ernie Dickens, Sweeney Schriner, Bucko McDonald, Bob Davidson, Nick Metz, Bingo Kampman, Don Metz, Gaye Stewart, Turk Broda, John McCreedy, Lorne Carr, Pete Langelle, Billy Taylor, Reg Hamilton; Conn Smythe (Manager), Hap Day (Coach), Frank Selke (Business Manager), Tim Daly (Trainer).

Scores: *April 4, at Toronto — Detroit 3, Toronto 2; April 7, at Toronto — Detroit 4, Toronto 2; April 9, at Detroit — Detroit 5, Toronto 2; April 12, at Detroit — Toronto 4, Detroit 3; April 14, at Toronto — Toronto 9, Detroit 3; April 16, at Detroit — Toronto 3, Detroit 0; April 18, at Toronto — Toronto 3, Detroit 1.*

1940-41 — Boston Bruins — Bill Cowley, Des Smith, Dit Clapper (Captain), Frank Brimsek, Flash Hollett, Jack Crawford, Bobby Bauer, Pat McReavy, Herb Cain, Mel Hill, Milt Schmidt, Woody Dumart, Roy Conacher, Terry Reardon, Art Jackson, Eddie Wiseman, Jack Shewchuck; Art Ross (Manager), Cooney Weiland (Coach), Win Green (Trainer).

Scores: *April 6, at Boston — Detroit 2, Boston 3; April 8, at Boston — Detroit 1, Boston 2; April 10, at Detroit — Boston 4, Detroit 2; April 12, at Detroit — Boston 3, Detroit 1.*

1939-40 — New York Rangers — Dave Kerr, Art Coulter (Captain), Ott Heller, Alex Shibicky, Mac Colville, Neil Colville, Phil Watson, Lynn Patrick, Clint Smith, Muzz Patrick, Babe Pratt, Bryan Hextall, Kilby MacDonald, Dutch Hiller, Alf Pike, Stan Smith; Lester Patrick (Manager), Frank Boucher (Coach), Harry Westerby (Trainer).

Scores: *April 2, at New York — NY Rangers 2, Toronto 1; April 3, at New York — NY Rangers 6, Toronto 2; April 6, at Toronto — NY Rangers 1, Toronto 2; April 9, at Toronto — NY Rangers 0, Toronto 3; April 11, at Toronto — NY Rangers 2, Toronto 1; April 13, at Toronto — NY Rangers 3, Toronto 2.*

1938-39 — Boston Bruins — Bobby Bauer, Mel Hill, Flash Hollett, Roy Conacher, Gord Pettinger, Charlie Sands, Milt Schmidt, Woody Dumart, Jack Crawford, Ray Getliffe, Frank Brimsek, Eddie Shore, Dit Clapper, Bill Cowley, Jack Portland, Red Hamill, Harry Frost, Cooney Weiland (Captain); Art Ross (Manager/Coach), Win Green (Trainer).

Scores: *April 6, at Boston — Toronto 1, Boston 2; April 9, at Boston — Toronto 3, Boston 2; April 11, at Toronto — Toronto 1, Boston 3; April 13, at Toronto — Toronto 0, Boston 2; April 16, at Boston — Toronto 1, Boston 3.*

1937-38 — Chicago Black Hawks — Art Wiebe, Carl Voss, Harold Jackson, Mike Karakas, Mush March, Jack Shill, Earl Seibert, Cully Dahlstrom, Alex Levinsky, Johnny Gottselig (Captain), Lou Trudel, Pete Palangio, Bill MacKenzie, Doc Romnes, Paul Thompson, Roger Jenkins, Alfie Moore, Bert Connelly, Virgil Johnson, Paul Goodman; Bill Tobin (Vice President), Bill Stewart (Coach), Eddie Froelich (Trainer).

Scores: *April 5, at Toronto — Chicago 3, Toronto 1; April 7, at Toronto — Chicago 1, Toronto 5; April 10, at Chicago — Chicago 2, Toronto 1; April 12, at Chicago — Chicago 4, Toronto 1.*

1936-37 — Detroit Red Wings — Normie Smith, Pete Kelly, Larry Aurie, Herbie Lewis, Hec Kilrea, Mud Bruneteau, Syd Howe, Wally Kilrea, Jimmy Franks, Bucko McDonald, Gord Pettinger, Ebbie Goodfellow, John Gallagher, Ralph Bowman, John Sorrell, Marty Barry, Earl Robertson, John Sherf, Howie Mackie, Rolly Roulston, Doug Young (Captain); Jack Adams (Manager/Coach), Honey Walker (Trainer).

Scores: *April 6, at New York — Detroit 1, NY Rangers 5; April 8, at Detroit — Detroit 4, NY Rangers 2; April 11, at Detroit — Detroit 0, NY Rangers 1; April 13, at Detroit — Detroit 1, NY Rangers 0; April 15, at Detroit — Detroit 3, NY Rangers 0.*

1935-36 — Detroit Red Wings — John Sorrell, Syd Howe, Marty Barry, Herbie Lewis, Mud Bruneteau, Wally Kilrea, Hec Kilrea, Gord Pettinger, Bucko McDonald, Ralph Bowman, Pete Kelly, Doug Young (Captain), Ebbie Goodfellow, Normie Smith, Larry Aurie; Jack Adams (Manager/Coach), Honey Walker (Trainer).

Scores: *April 5, at Detroit — Detroit 3, Toronto 1; April 7, at Detroit — Detroit 9, Toronto 4; April 9, at Toronto — Detroit 3, Toronto 4; April 11, at Toronto — Detroit 3, Toronto 2.*

1934-35 — Montreal Maroons — Lionel Conacher, Cy Wentworth, Alec Connell, Toe Blake, Stewart Evans, Earl Robinson, Bill Miller, Dave Trottier, Jimmy Ward, Baldy Northcott, Hooley Smith (Captain), Russ Blinco, Al Shields, Sammy McManus, Gus Marker, Bob Gracie, Herb Cain, Dutch Gainor; Tommy Gorman (Manager/Coach), Bill O'Brien (Trainer).

Scores: *April 4, at Toronto — Mtl. Maroons 3, Toronto 2; April 6, at Toronto — Mtl. Maroons 3, Toronto 1; April 9, at Montreal — Mtl. Maroons 4, Toronto 1.*

1933-34 — Chicago Black Hawks — Clarence Abel, Rosie Couture, Lou Trudel, Lionel Conacher, Paul Thompson, Leroy Goldsworthy, Art Coulter, Roger Jenkins, Don McFadyen, Tom Cook, Doc Romnes, Johnny Gottselig, Mush March, Johnny Sheppard, Charlie Gardiner (Captain), Bill Kendall, Jack Leswick; Tommy Gorman (Manager/Coach), Eddie Froelich (Trainer).

Scores: *April 3, at Detroit — Chicago 2, Detroit 1; April 5, at Detroit — Chicago 4, Detroit 1; April 8, at Chicago — Detroit 5, Chicago 2; April 10, at Chicago — Chicago 1, Detroit 0.*

1932-33 — New York Rangers — Ching Johnson, Butch Keeling, Frank Boucher, Art Somers, Babe Siebert, Bun Cook, Andy Aitkenhead, Ott Heller, Oscar Asmundson, Gord Pettinger, Doug Brennan, Cecil Dillon, Bill Cook (Captain), Murray Murdoch, Earl Seibert; Lester Patrick (Manager/Coach), Harry Westerby (Trainer).

Scores: *April 4, at New York — NY Rangers 5, Toronto 1; April 8, at Toronto — NY Rangers 3, Toronto 1; April 11, at Toronto — Toronto 3, NY Rangers 2; April 13, at Toronto — NY Rangers 1, Toronto 0.*

1931-32 — Toronto Maple Leafs — Charlie Conacher, Busher Jackson, King Clancy, Andy Blair, Red Horner, Lorne Chabot, Alex Levinsky, Joe Primeau, Harold Darragh, Baldy Cotton, Frank Finnigan, Hap Day (Captain), Ace Bailey, Bob Gracie, Fred Robertson, Earl Miller; Conn Smythe (Manager), Dick Irvin (Coach), Tim Daly (Trainer).

Scores: *April 5, at New York — Toronto 6, NY Rangers 4; April 7, at Boston* — Toronto 6, NY Rangers 2; April 9, at Toronto — Toronto 6, NY Rangers 4.*

1930-31 — Montreal Canadiens — George Hainsworth, Wildor Larochelle, Marty Burke, Sylvio Mantha (Captain), Howie Morenz, Johnny Gagnon, Aurel Joliat, Armand Mondou, Pit Lepine, Albert Leduc, Georges Mantha, Art Lesieur, Nick Wasnie, Gus Rivers, Jean Pusie; Léo Dandurand (Manager), Cecil Hart (Coach), Ed Dufour (Trainer).

Scores: *April 3, at Chicago — Montreal 2, Chicago 1; April 5, at Chicago — Chicago 2, Montreal 1; April 9, at Montreal — Chicago 3, Montreal 2; April 11, at Montreal — Montreal 4, Chicago 2; April 14, at Montreal — Montreal 2, Chicago 0.*

1929-30 — Montreal Canadiens — George Hainsworth, Marty Burke, Sylvio Mantha (Captain), Howie Morenz, Bert McCaffrey, Aurel Joliat, Albert Leduc, Pit Lepine, Wildor Larochelle, Nick Wasnie, Gerry Carson, Armand Mondou, Georges Mantha, Gus Rivers; Léo Dandurand (Manager), Cecil Hart (Coach), Ed Dufour (Trainer).

Scores: *April 1, at Boston — Montreal 3, Boston 0; April 3, at Montreal — Montreal 4, Boston 3.*

1928-29 — Boston Bruins — Tiny Thompson, Eddie Shore, Lionel Hitchman (Captain), Percy Galbraith, Mickey MacKay, Red Green, Dutch Gainor, Harry Oliver, Eddie Rodden, Dit Clapper, Cooney Weiland, Lloyd Klein, Cy Denneny, Bill Carson, George Owen, Myles Lane; Art Ross (Manager/Coach), Win Green (Trainer).

Scores: *March 28, at Boston — Boston 2, NY Rangers 0; March 29, at New York — Boston 2, NY Rangers 1.*

1927-28 — New York Rangers — Lorne Chabot, Clarence Abel, Leo Bourgeault, Ching Johnson, Bill Cook (Captain), Bun Cook, Frank Boucher, Bill Boyd, Murray Murdoch, Paul Thompson, Alex Gray, Joe Miller, Patsy Callighen; Lester Patrick (Manager/Coach), Harry Westerby (Trainer).

Scores: *April 5, at Montreal — Mtl. Maroons 2, NY Rangers 0; April 7, at Montreal — NY Rangers 2, Mtl. Maroons 1; April 10, at Montreal — Mtl. Maroons 2, NY Rangers 0; April 12, at Montreal — NY Rangers 1, Mtl. Maroons 0; April 14, at Montreal — NY Rangers 2, Mtl. Maroons 1.*

1926-27 — Ottawa Senators — Alec Connell, King Clancy, George Boucher (Captain), Ed Gorman, Frank Finnigan, Alex Smith, Hec Kilrea, Hooley Smith, Cy Denneny, Frank Nighbor, Jack Adams, Milt Halliday; Dave Gill (Manager/Coach).

Scores: *April 7, at Boston — Ottawa 0, Boston 0; April 9, at Boston — Ottawa 3, Boston 1; April 11, at Ottawa — Boston 1, Ottawa 1; April 13, at Ottawa — Ottawa 3, Boston 1.*

1925-26 — Montreal Maroons — Clint Benedict, Reg Noble, Frank Carson, Dunc Munro (Captain), Nels Stewart, Punch Broadbent, Babe Siebert, Chuck Dinsmore, Merlyn Phillips, Hobie Kitchen, Sam Rothschild, Albert Holway, George Horne, Bernie Brophy; Eddie Gerard (Manager/Coach), Bill O'Brien (Trainer).

Scores: *March 30, at Montreal — Mtl. Maroons 3, Victoria 0; April 1, at Montreal — Mtl. Maroons 3, Victoria 0; April 3, at Montreal — Victoria 3, Mtl. Maroons 2; April 6, at Montreal — Mtl. Maroons 2, Victoria 0.*

The series in the spring of 1926 ended the annual playoffs between the champions of the East and the champions of the West. Since 1926-27 the annual playoffs in the National Hockey League have decided the Stanley Cup champions.

1924-25 — Victoria Cougars — Hap Holmes, Clem Loughlin (Captain), Gord Fraser, Frank Fredrickson, Jack Walker, Gizzy Hart, Harold Halderson, Frank Foyston, Wally Elmer, Harry Meeking, Jocko Anderson; Lester Patrick (Manager/Coach).

Scores: *March 21, at Victoria — Victoria 5, Montreal 2; March 23, at Vancouver — Victoria 3, Montreal 1; March 27, at Victoria — Montreal 4, Victoria 2; March 30, at Victoria — Victoria 6, Montreal 1.*

1923-24 — Montreal Canadiens — Georges Vezina, Sprague Cleghorn (Captain), Billy Coutu, Howie Morenz, Aurel Joliat, Billy Boucher, Odie Cleghorn, Sylvio Mantha, Bobby Boucher, Billy Bell, Billy Cameron, Joe Malone, Charles Fortier; Leo Dandurand (Manager/Coach).

Scores: *March 22, at Montreal — Montreal 6, Cgy. Tigers 1; March 25, at Ottawa* — Montreal 3, Cgy. Tigers 0.*

** Game transferred to Ottawa to benefit from artificial ice surface.*

1922-23 — Ottawa Senators — George Boucher, Lionel Hitchman, Frank Nighbor, King Clancy, Harry Helman, Clint Benedict, Jack Darragh, Eddie Gerard (Captain), Cy Denneny, Punch Broadbent; Tommy Gorman (Manager), Pete Green (Coach), F. Dolan (Trainer).

Scores: *March 29, at Vancouver — Ottawa 2, Edm. Eskimos 1; March 31, at Vancouver — Ottawa 1, Edm. Eskimos 0.*

1921-22 — Toronto St. Patricks — Ted Stackhouse, Corb Denneny, Rod Smylie, Lloyd Andrews, John Ross Roach, Harry Cameron, Billy Stuart, Babe Dye, Ken Randall, Reg Noble (Captain), Eddie Gerard (borrowed for one game from Ottawa), Stan Jackson, Ivan Mitchell; Charlie Querrie (Manager), George O'Donoghue (Coach).

Scores: *March 17, at Toronto — Van. Millionaires 4, Toronto 3; March 21, at Toronto — Toronto 2, Van. Millionaires 1; March 23, at Toronto — Van. Millionaires 3, Toronto 0; March 25, at Toronto — Toronto 6, Van. Millionaires 0; March 28, at Toronto — Toronto 5, Van. Millionaires 1.*

1920-21 — Ottawa Senators — Jack MacKell, Jack Darragh, Morley Bruce, George Boucher, Eddie Gerard (Captain), Clint Benedict, Sprague Cleghorn, Frank Nighbor, Punch Broadbent, Cy Denneny, Leth Graham; Tommy Gorman (Manager), Pete Green (Coach), F. Dolan (Trainer).

Scores: *March 21, at Vancouver — Van. Millionaires 2, Ottawa 1; March 24, at Vancouver — Ottawa 4, Van. Millionaires 3; March 28, at Vancouver — Ottawa 3, Van. Millionaires 2; March 31, at Vancouver — Van. Millionaires 3, Ottawa 2; April 4, at Vancouver — Ottawa 2, Van. Millionaires 1*

1919-20 — Ottawa Senators — Jack MacKell, Jack Darragh, Morley Bruce, Horace Merrill, George Boucher, Eddie Gerard (Captain), Clint Benedict, Sprague Cleghorn, Frank Nighbor, Punch Broadbent, Cy Denneny, Tommy Gorman (Manager), Pete Green (Coach).

Scores: *March 22, at Ottawa — Ottawa 3, Seattle 2; March 24, at Ottawa — Ottawa 3, Seattle 0; March 27, at Ottawa — Seattle 3, Ottawa 1; March 30, at Toronto* — Seattle 5, Ottawa 2; April 1, at Toronto* — Ottawa 6, Seattle 1.*

** Games transferred to Toronto to benefit from artificial ice surface.*

1918-19 — No decision, Series halted by Spanish influenza epidemic, illness of several players and death of Joe Hall of the Montreal Canadiens from the flu. Five games had been played when the series was halted, each team having won two and tied one. Final scores are listed below.

Scores: *March 19, at Seattle — Seattle 7, Montreal 0; March 22, at Seattle — Montreal 4, Seattle 2; March 24, at Seattle — Seattle 7, Montreal 2; March 26, at Seattle — Montreal 0, Seattle 0; March 30, at Seattle — Montreal 4, Seattle 3.*

1917-18 — Toronto Arenas — Rusty Crawford, Harry Meeking, Ken Randall (Captain), Corb Denneny, Harry Cameron, Jack Adams, Alf Skinner, Harry Mummery, Hap Holmes, Reg Noble, Sammy Hebert, Jack Marks, Jack Coughlin; Charlie Querrie (Manager), Dick Carroll (Coach), Frank Carroll (Trainer).

Scores: *March 20, at Toronto — Toronto 5, Van. Millionaires 3; March 23, at Toronto — Van. Millionaires 6, Toronto 4; March 26, at Toronto — Toronto 6, Van. Millionaires 3; March 28, at Toronto — Van. Millionaires 8, Toronto 1; March 30, at Toronto — Toronto 2, Van. Millionaires 1.*

1916-17 — Seattle Metropolitans — Hap Holmes, Ed Carpenter, Cully Wilson, Jack Walker, Bernie Morris, Frank Foyston, Roy Rickey, Jim Riley, Bobby Rowe (Captain); Peter Muldoon (Manager).

Scores: *March 17, at Seattle — Montreal 8, Seattle 4; March 20, at Seattle — Seattle 6, Montreal 1; March 23, at Seattle — Seattle 4, Montreal 1; March 26, at Seattle — Seattle 9, Montreal 1.*

1915-16 — Montreal Canadiens — Georges Vezina, Bert Corbeau, Jack Laviolette, Newsy Lalonde, Louis Berlinquette, Goldie Prodger, Howard McNamara (Captain), Didier Pitre, Skene Ronan, Amos Arbour, Skinner Poulin, Jack Fournier; George Kennedy (Manager).

Scores: *March 20, at Montreal — Portland 2, Montreal 0; March 22, at Montreal — Montreal 2, Portland 1; March 25, at Montreal — Montreal 6, Portland 3; March 28, at Montreal — Portland 6, Montreal 5; March 30, at Montreal — Montreal 2, Portland 1.*

1914-15 — Vancouver Millionaires — Ken Mallen, Frank Nighbor, Cyclone Taylor, Hugh Lehman, Lloyd Cook, Mickey MacKay, Barney Stanley, Jim Seaborn, Si Griffis (Captain), Johnny Matz; Frank Patrick (Playing Manager).

Scores: *March 22, at Vancouver — Van. Millionaires 6, Ottawa 2; March 24, at Vancouver — Van. Millionaires 8, Ottawa 3; March 26, at Vancouver — Van. Millionaires 12, Ottawa 3.*

1913-14 — Toronto Blueshirts — Con Corbeau, Roy McGiffin, Jack Walker, George McNamara, Cully Wilson, Frank Foyston, Harry Cameron, Hap Holmes, Scotty Davidson (Captain), Harriston; Jack Marshall (Playing Manager), Frank Carroll, Dick Carroll (Trainers).

Scores: *March 14, at Toronto — Toronto 5, Victoria 2; March 17, at Toronto — Toronto 6, Victoria 5; March 19, at Toronto — Toronto 2, Victoria 1.*

Prior to 1914, teams could challenge the Stanley Cup champions for the title, thus there was more than one Championship Series played in most of the seasons between 1894 and 1913.

1912-13 — Quebec Bulldogs — Joe Malone (Captain), Joe Hall, Paddy Moran, Harry Mummery, Tommy Smith, Jack Marks, Rusty Crawford, Billy Creighton, Jeff Malone, Rocket Power; M.J. Quinn (Manager), D. Beland (Trainer).

Scores: *March 8, at Quebec — Que. Bulldogs 14, Sydney 3; March 10, at Quebec — Que. Bulldogs 6, Sydney 2.*

Victoria challenged Quebec but the Bulldogs refused to put the Stanley Cup in competition so the two teams played an exhibition series with Victoria winning two games to one by scores of 7-5, 3-6, 6-1. It was the first meeting between the Eastern champions and the Western champions. The following year, and until the Western Hockey League disbanded after the 1926 playoffs, the Cup went to the winner of the series between East and West.

1911-12 — Quebec Bulldogs — Goldie Prodger, Joe Hall, Walter Rooney, Paddy Moran, Jack Marks, Jack McDonald, Eddie Oatman, George Leonard, Joe Malone (Captain); Charley Nolan (Coach), M.J. Quinn (Manager), D. Beland (Trainer).

Scores: *March 11, at Quebec — Que. Bulldogs 9, Moncton 3; March 13, at Quebec — Que. Bulldogs 8, Moncton 0.*

1910-11 — Ottawa Senators — Hamby Shore, Percy LeSueur (Captain), Jack Darragh, Bruce Stuart, Marty Walsh, Bruce Ridpath, Fred Lake, Dubbie Kerr, Alex Currie, Horace Gaul.

Scores: *March 13, at Ottawa — Ottawa 7, Galt 4; March 16, at Ottawa — Ottawa 13, Port Arthur 4.*

1909-10 — (March) **— Montreal Wanderers —** Cecil Blachford, Moose Johnson, Ernie Russell, Riley Hern, Harry Hyland, Jack Marshall, Pud Glass (Captain), Jimmy Gardner; Dickie Boon (Manager).

Scores: *March 12, at Montreal — Mtl. Wanderers 7, Berlin (Kitchener) 3.*

By winning the 1910 NHA title, the Montreal Wanderers took possession of the Stanley Cup from Ottawa and accepted a challenge from Berlin, 1910 champions of the OPHL

1909-10 — (January) **— Ottawa Senators —** Dubbie Kerr, Fred Lake, Percy LeSueur, Ken Mallen, Bruce Ridpath, Gord Roberts, Hamby Shore, Bruce Stuart (Captain), Marty Walsh.

The Senators accepted two challenges as defending Cup champions. The first was against Galt in a 2-game, total-goals series, and the second was against Edmonton, also a 2-game, total-goals series.

Scores: *January 5, at Ottawa — Ottawa 12, Galt 3; January 7, at Ottawa — Ottawa 3, Galt 1; January 18, at Ottawa — Ottawa 8, Edm. Eskimos 4; January 20, at Ottawa — Ottawa 13, Edm. Eskimos 7.*

1908-09 — Ottawa Senators — Fred Lake, Percy LeSueur, Cyclone Taylor, Billy Gilmour, Dubbie Kerr, Edgar Dey, Marty Walsh, Bruce Stuart (Captain).

Ottawa, as champions of the Eastern Canada Hockey Association took over the Stanley Cup in 1909 and, although a challenge was accepted by the Cup trustees from Winnipeg Shamrocks, games could not be arranged because of the lateness of the season. No other challenges were made in 1909.

1907-08 — Montreal Wanderers — Riley Hern, Art Ross, Walter Smaill, Pud Glass, Bruce Stuart, Ernie Russell, Moose Johnson, Cecil Blachford (Captain), Tom Hooper, Larry Gilmour, Ernie Liffiton; Dickie Boon (Manager).

Scores: *Wanderers accepted four challenges for the Cup: January 9, at Montreal — Mtl. Wanderers 9, Ott. Victorias 3; January 13, at Montreal — Mtl. Wanderers 13, Ott. Victorias 1; March 10, at Montreal — Mtl. Wanderers 11, Wpg. Maple Leafs 5; March 12, at Montreal — Mtl. Wanderers 9, Wpg. Maple Leafs 3; March 14, at Montreal — Mtl. Wanderers 6, Toronto (OPHL) 4. At start of following season, 1908-09, Wanderers were challenged by Edmonton. Results: December 28, at Montreal — Mtl. Wanderers 7, Edm. Eskimos 3; December 30, at Montreal — Edm. Eskimos 7, Mtl. Wanderers 6. Total goals: Mtl. Wanderers 13, Edm. Eskimos 10.*

1906-07 — (March 25) **— Montreal Wanderers —** Billy Strachan, Riley Hern, Lester Patrick (Captain), Hod Stuart, Pud Glass, Ernie Russell, Cecil Blachford, Moose Johnson, Rod Kennedy, Jack Marshall; Dickie Boon (Manager).

1906-07 — (March 18) **— Kenora Thistles —** Eddie Giroux, Si Griffis, Tom Hooper, Fred Whitcroft, Alf Smith, Harry Westwick, Roxy Beaudro, Tommy Phillips (Captain), Russell Phillips.

Scores: *March 16, at Winnipeg — Kenora 8, Brandon 6; March 18, at Winnipeg — Kenora 4, Brandon 1; March 23, at Winnipeg — Mtl. Wanderers 7, Kenora 2; March 25, at Winnipeg — Kenora 6, Mtl. Wanderers 5. Total goals: Mtl. Wanderers 12, Kenora 8.*

1906-07 — (January) **— Kenora Thistles —** Eddie Giroux, Art Ross, Si Griffis, Tom Hooper, Billy McGimsie, Roxy Beaudro, Tommy Phillips (Captain), Joe Hall, Russell Phillips.

Scores: *January 17, at Montreal — Kenora 4, Mtl. Wanderers 2; Jan. 21, at Montreal — Kenora 8, Mtl. Wanderers 6.*

1906-07 — (December) **— Montreal Wanderers —** Riley Hern, Billy Strachan, Rod Kennedy, Lester Patrick (Captain), Pud Glass, Ernie Russell, Moose Johnson, Cecil Blachford, Dickie Boon (Manager).

1905-06 — (March) **— Montreal Wanderers —** Henri Menard, Billy Strachan, Rod Kennedy, Lester Patrick, Pud Glass, Ernie Russell, Moose Johnson, Cecil Blachford (Captain), Josh Arnold; Dickie Boon (Manager).

Scores: *March 14, at Montreal — Mtl. Wanderers 9, Ottawa 1; March 17, at Ottawa — Ottawa 9, Mtl. Wanderers 3. Total goals: Mtl. Wanderers 12, Ottawa 10. Wanderers accepted a challenge from New Glasgow, N.S., prior to the start of the 1906-07 season. Results: December 27, at Montreal — Mtl. Wanderers 10, New Glasgow 3; December 29, at Montreal — Mtl. Wanderers 7, New Glasgow 2.*

1905-06 — (February) **— Ottawa Silver Seven —** Harvey Pulford (Captain), Arthur Moore, Harry Westwick, Frank McGee, Alf Smith (Playing Coach), Billy Gilmour, Billy Hague, Harry Smith, Tommy Smith, Coo Dion, Jack Ebbs.

Scores: *February 27, at Ottawa — Ottawa 16, Queen's University 7; February 28, at Ottawa — Ottawa 12, Queen's University 7; March 6, at Ottawa — Ottawa 6, Smiths Falls 5; March 8, at Ottawa — Ottawa 8, Smiths Falls 2.*

1904-05 — Ottawa Silver Seven — Dave Finnie, Harvey Pulford (Captain), Arthur Moore, Harry Westwick, Frank McGee, Alf Smith (Playing Coach), Billy Gilmour, Frank White, Horace Gaul, Hamby Shore, Bones Allen.

Scores: *January 13, at Ottawa — Ottawa 9, Dawson City 2; January 16, at Ottawa — Ottawa 23, Dawson City 2; March 7, at Ottawa — Rat Portage 9, Ottawa 3; March 9, at Ottawa — Ottawa 4, Rat Portage 2; March 11, at Ottawa — Ottawa 5, Rat Portage 4.*

1903-04 — Ottawa Silver Seven — Suddy Gilmour, Arthur Moore, Frank McGee, Bouse Hutton, Billy Gilmour, Jim McGee, Harry Westwick, Harvey Pulford (Captain), Scott, Alf Smith (Playing Coach).

Scores: *December 30, at Ottawa — Ottawa 9, Wpg. Rowing Club 1; January 1, at Ottawa — Wpg. Rowing Club 6, Ottawa 2; January 4, at Ottawa — Ottawa 2, Wpg. Rowing Club 0. February 23, at Ottawa — Ottawa 6, Tor. Marlboros 3; February 25, at Ottawa — Ottawa 11, Tor. Marlboros 2; March 2, at Montreal — Ottawa 5, Mtl. Wanderers 5. Following the tie game, a new two-game series was ordered to be played in Ottawa but the Wanderers refused unless the tie game was replayed in Montreal. When no settlement could be reached, the series was abandoned and Ottawa retained the Cup and accepted a two-game challenge from Brandon. Results: (both games at Ottawa), March 9, Ottawa 6, Brandon 3; March 11, Ottawa 9, Brandon 3.*

1902-03 — (March) — Ottawa Silver Seven — Suddy Gilmour, Percy Sims, Bouse Hutton, Dave Gilmour, Billy Gilmour, Harry Westwick, Frank McGee, F.H. Wood, A.A. Fraser, Charles Spittal, Harvey Pulford (Captain), Arthur Moore; Alf Smith (Coach).

Scores: *March 7, at Montreal — Ottawa 1, Mtl. Victorias 1; March 10, at Ottawa — Ottawa 8, Mtl. Victorias 0. Total goals: Ottawa 9, Mtl. Victorias 1; March 12, at Ottawa — Ottawa 6, Rat Portage 2; March 14, at Ottawa — Ottawa 4, Rat Portage 2.*

1902-03 — (February) — Montreal AAA — Tom Hodge, Dickie Boon, Billy Nicholson, Tommy Phillips, Art Hooper, Billy Bellingham, Jack Marshall, Jimmy Gardner, Cecil Blachford, George Smith.

Scores: *January 29, at Montreal — Mtl. AAA 8, Wpg. Victorias 1; January 31, at Montreal — Wpg. Victorias 2, Mtl. AAA 2; February 2, at Montreal — Wpg. Victorias 4, Mtl. AAA 2; February 4, at Montreal — Mtl. AAA 5, Wpg. Victorias 1.*

1901-02 — (March) — Montreal AAA — Tom Hodge, Dickie Boon, Billy Nicholson, Art Hooper, Billy Bellingham, Jack Marshall, Roland Elliot, Jimmy Gardner.

Scores: *March 13, at Winnipeg — Wpg. Victorias 1, Mtl. AAA 0; March 15, at Winnipeg — Mtl. AAA 5, Wpg. Victorias 0; March 17, at Winnipeg — Mtl. AAA 2, Wpg. Victorias 1.*

1901-02 — (January) — Winnipeg Victorias — Burke Wood, Tony Gingras, Charles Johnstone, Rod Flett, Magnus Flett, Dan Bain (Captain), Fred Scanlon, F. Cadham, Art Brown.

Scores: *January 21, at Winnipeg — Wpg. Victorias 5, Tor Wellingtons 3; January 23, at Winnipeg — Wpg. Victorias 5, Tor. Wellingtons 3.*

1900-01 — Winnipeg Victorias — Burke Wood, Jack Marshall, Tony Gingras, Charles Johnstone, Rod Flett, Magnus Flett, Dan Bain (Captain), Art Brown, George Carruthers.

Scores: *January 29, at Montreal — Wpg. Victorias 4, Mtl. Shamrocks 3; January 31, at Montreal — Wpg. Victorias 2, Mtl. Shamrocks 1.*

1899-1900 — Montreal Shamrocks — oe McKenna, Frank Tansey, Frank Wall, Art Farrell, Fred Scanlon, Harry Trihey (Captain), Jack Brannen.

Scores: *February 12, at Montreal — Mtl. Shamrocks 4, Wpg. Victorias 3; February 14, at Montreal — Wpg. Victorias 3, Mtl. Shamrocks 2; February 16, at Montreal — Mtl. Shamrocks 5, Wpg. Victorias 4; March 5, at Montreal — Mtl. Shamrocks 10, Halifax 2; March 7, at Montreal — Mtl. Shamrocks 11, Halifax 0.*

1898-99 — (March) — Montreal Shamrocks — Joe McKenna, Frank Tansey, Frank Wall, Harry Trihey (Captain), Art Farrell, Fred Scanlon, Jack Brannen, John Dobby, Charles Hoerner.

Scores: *March 14, at Montreal — Mtl. Shamrocks 6, Queen's University 2.*

1898-99 — (February) — Montreal Victorias — Gordon Lewis, Mike Grant, Graham Drinkwater (Captain), Cam Davidson, Bob McDougall, Ernie McLea, Frank Richardson, Jack Ewing, Russell Bowie, Douglas Acer, Fred McRobie.

Scores: *February 15, at Montreal — Mtl. Victorias 2, Wpg. Victorias 1; February 18, at Montreal — Mtl. Victorias 3, Wpg. Victorias 2.*

1897-98 — Montreal Victorias — Gordon Lewis, Hartland McDougall, Mike Grant, Graham Drinkwater, Cam Davidson, Bob McDougall, Ernie McLea, Frank Richardson (Captain), Jack Ewing.

1896-97 — Montreal Victorias — Gordon Lewis, Harold Henderson, Mike Grant (Captain), Cam Davidson, Graham Drinkwater, Bob McDougall, Ernie McLea, Shirley Davidson, Hartland McDougall, Jack Ewing, Percy Molson, David Gillilan, Harry Massey.

Scores: *December 27, at Montreal — Mtl. Victorias 15, Ott. Capitals 2.*

1895-96 — (December) — Montreal Victorias — Harold Henderson, Mike Grant (Captain), Bob McDougall, Graham Drinkwater, Shirley Davidson, Hartland McDougall, Ernie McLea, Cam Davidson, David Gillilan, Stanley Willett, Gordon Lewis, W. Wallace.

Scores: *December 30, at Winnipeg — Mtl. Victorias 6, Wpg. Victorias 5.*

1895-96 — (February) — Winnipeg Victorias — Whitey Merritt, Rod Flett, Fred Higginbotham, Jack Armytage (Captain), Tote Campbell, Dan Bain, Charles Johnstone, Attie Howard.

Scores: *February 14, at Montreal — Wpg. Victorias 2, Mtl. Victorias 0.*

1894-95 — Montreal Victorias — Robert Jones, Harold Henderson, Mike Grant (Captain), Shirley Davidson, Hartland McDougall, Bob McDougall, Norman Rankin, Graham Drinkwater, Roland Elliot, William Pullan, Arthur Fenwick, A. McDougall.

1893-94 — Montreal AAA — Herb Collins, Allan Cameron, George James, Billy Barlow, Clare Mussen, Archie Hodgson, Haviland Routh, Alex Irving, James Stewart, E. O'Brien, Toad Wand, Alex Kingan.

Scores: *March 17, at Mtl. Victorias — Mtl. AAA 3, Mtl. Victorias 2; March 22, at Montreal — Mtl. AAA 3, Ott. Capitals 1.*

1892-93 — Montreal AAA — Tom Paton, James Stewart, Allan Cameron, Haviland Routh, Archie Hodgson, Billy Barlow, Alex Irving, Alex Kingan, G.S. Low.

All-Time NHL Playoff Formats

1917-18 — The regular-season was split into two halves. The winners of both halves faced each other in a two-game, total-goals series for the NHL championship and the right to meet the PCHA champion in the best-of-five Stanley Cup Final.

1918-19 — Same as 1917-18, except that the NHL championship was a best-of-seven series.

1919-20 — Same as 1917-1918, except that Ottawa won both halves of the split regular-season schedule to earn an automatic berth into the best-of-five Stanley Cup Final against the PCHA champions.

1921-22 — The top two teams at the conclusion of the regular-season faced each other in a two-game, total-goals series for the NHL championship. The NHL champion then moved on to play the winner of the PCHA-WCHL playoff series in the best-of-five Stanley Cup Final.

1922-23 — The top two teams at the conclusion of the regular-season faced each other in a two-game, total-goals series for the NHL championship. The NHL champion then moved on to play the PCHA champion in the best-of-three Stanley Cup Semi-Finals, and the winner of the Semi-Finals played the WCHL champion, which had been given a bye, in the best-of-three Stanley Cup Final.

1923-24 — The top two teams at the conclusion of the regular-season faced each other in a two-game, total-goals series for the NHL championship. The NHL champion then moved on to play the loser of the PCHA-WCHL playoff (the winner of the PCHA-WCHL playoff earned a bye into the Stanley Cup Final) in the best-of-three Stanley Cup Semi-Finals. The winner of this series met the PCHA-WCHL playoff winner in the best-of-three Stanley Cup Final.

1924-25 — The first place team (Hamilton) at the conclusion of the regular-season was supposed to play the winner of a two-game, total-goals series between the second (Toronto) and third (Montreal) place clubs. However, Hamilton refused to abide by this new format, demanding greater compensation than offered by the League. Thus, Toronto and Montreal played their two-game, total-goals series, and the winner (Montreal) earned the NHL title and then played the WCHL champion (Victoria) in the best-of-five Stanley Cup Final.

1925-26 — The format which was intended for 1924-25 went into effect. The winner of the two-game, total-goals series between the second and third place teams squared off against the first place team in the two-game, total-goals NHL championship series. The NHL champion then moved on to play the WHL champion in the best-of-five Stanley Cup Final.

After the 1925-26 season, the NHL was the only major professional hockey league still in existence and consequently took over sole control of the Stanley Cup competition.

1926-27 — The 10-team league was divided into two divisions — Canadian and American — of five teams apiece. In each division, the winner of the two-game, total-goals series between the second and third place teams faced the first place team in a two-game, total-goals series for the division title. The two division title winners then met in the best-of-five Stanley Cup Final.

1928-29 — Both first place teams in the two divisions played each other in a best-of-five series. Both second place teams in the two divisions played each other in a two-game, total-goals series as did the two third place teams. The winners of these latter two series then played each other in a best-of-three series for the right to meet the winner of the series between the two first place clubs. This Stanley Cup Final was a best-of-three.

- Series A: First in Canadian Division vs. first in American (best-of-five)
- Series B: Second in Canadian Division vs. second in American (two-game, total-goals)
- Series C: Third in Canadian Division vs. third in American (two-game, total-goals)
- Series D: Winner of Series B vs. winner of Series C (best-of-three)
- Series E: Winner of Series A vs. winner of Series D (best-of-three) for Stanley Cup

1930-31 — Same as 1928-29, except that Series D was changed to a two-game, total-goals format and Series E was changed to best-of-five.

1936-37 — Same as 1930-31, except that Series B, C and D were each best-of-three.

1938-39 — With the NHL reduced to seven teams, the two-division system was replaced by one seven-team league. Based on final regular-season standings, the following playoff format was adopted:

- Series A: First vs. Second (best-of-seven)
- Series B: Third vs. Fourth (best-of-three)
- Series C: Fifth vs. Sixth (best-of-three)
- Series D: Winner of Series B vs. winner of Series C (best-of-three)
- Series E: Winner of Series A vs. winner of Series D (best-of-seven)

1942-43 — With the NHL reduced to six teams (the "original six"), only the top four finishers qualified for playoff action. The best-of-seven Semi-Finals pitted Team #1 vs. Team #3 and Team #2 vs. Team #4. The winners of each Semi-Final series met in the best-of-seven Stanley Cup Final.

1967-68 — When it doubled in size from 6 to 12 teams, the NHL once again was divided into two divisions — East and West — of six teams apiece. The top four clubs in each division qualified for the playoffs (all series were best-of-seven):

- Series A: Team #1 (East) vs. Team #3 (East)
- Series B: Team #2 (East) vs. Team #4 (East)
- Series C: Team #1 (West) vs. Team #3 (West)
- Series D: Team #2 (West) vs. Team #4 (West)
- Series E: Winner of Series A vs. winner of Series B
- Series F: Winner of Series C vs. winner of Series D
- Series G: Winner of Series E vs. Winner of Series F

1970-71 — Same as 1967-68 except that Series E matched the winners of Series A and D, and Series F matched the winners of Series B and C.

1971-72 — Same as 1970-71, except that Series A and C matched Team #1 vs. Team #4, and Series B and D matched Team #2 vs. Team #3.

1974-75 — With the League now expanded to 18 teams in four divisions, a completely new playoff format was introduced. First, the #2 and #3 teams in each of the four divisions were pooled together in the Preliminary round. These eight (#2 and #3) clubs were ranked #1 to #8 based on regular-season record:

- Series A: Team #1 vs. Team #8 (best-of-three)
- Series B: Team #2 vs. Team #7 (best-of-three)
- Series C: Team #3 vs. Team #6 (best-of-three)
- Series D: Team #4 vs. Team #5 (best-of-three)

The winners of this Preliminary round then pooled together with the four division winners, which had received byes into this Quarter-Final round. These eight teams were again ranked #1 to #8 based on regular-season record:

- Series E: Team #1 vs. Team #8 (best-of-seven)
- Series F: Team #2 vs. Team #7 (best-of-seven)
- Series G: Team #3 vs. Team #6 (best-of-seven)
- Series H: Team #4 vs. Team #5 (best-of-seven)

The four Quarter-Finals winners, which moved on to the Semi-Finals, were then ranked #1 to #4 based on regular season record:

- Series I: Team #1 vs. Team #4 (best-of-seven)
- Series J: Team #2 vs. Team #3 (best-of-seven)
- Series K: Winner of Series I vs. winner of Series J (best-of-seven)

1977-78 — Same as 1974-75, except that the Preliminary round consisted of the #2 teams in the four divisions and the next four teams based on regular-season record (not their standings within their divisions).

1979-80 — With the addition of four WHA franchises, the League expanded its playoff structure to include 16 of its 21 teams. The four first place teams in the four divisions automatically earned playoff berths. Among the 17 other clubs, the top 12, according to regular-season record, also earned berths. All 16 teams were then pooled together and ranked #1 to #16 based on regular-season record:

- Series A: Team #1 vs. Team #16 (best-of-five)
- Series B: Team #2 vs. Team #15 (best-of-five)
- Series C: Team #3 vs. Team #14 (best-of-five)
- Series D: Team #4 vs. Team #13 (best-of-five)
- Series E: Team #5 vs. Team #12 (best-of-five)
- Series F: Team #6 vs. Team #11 (best-of-five)
- Series G: Team #7 vs. Team #10 (best-of-five)
- Series H: Team #8 vs. Team # 9 (best-of-five)

The eight Preliminary round winners, ranked #1 to #8 based on regular-season record, moved on to the Quarter-Finals:

- Series I: Team #1 vs. Team #8 (best-of-seven)
- Series J: Team #2 vs. Team #7 (best-of-seven)
- Series K: Team #3 vs. Team #6 (best-of-seven)
- Series L: Team #4 vs. Team #5 (best-of-seven)

The four Quarter-Finals winners, ranked #1 to #4 based on regular-season record, moved on to the semi-finals:

- Series M: Team #1 vs. Team #4 (best-of-seven)
- Series N: Team #2 vs. Team #3 (best-of-seven)
- Series O: Winner of Series M vs. winner of Series N (best-of-seven)

1981-82 — The first four teams in each division earned playoff berths. In each division, the first-place team opposed the fourth-place team and the second-place team opposed the third-place team in a best-of-five Division Semi-Final series (DSF). In each division, the two winners of the DSF met in a best-of-seven Division Final series (DF). The two DF winners in each conference met in a best-of-seven Conference Final series (CF). In the Prince of Wales Conference, the Adams Division winner opposed the Patrick Division winner; in the Clarence Campbell Conference, the Smythe Division winner opposed the Norris Division winner. The two CF winners met in a best-of-seven Stanley Cup Final (F) series.

1986-87 — Division Semi-Final series changed from best-of-five to best-of-seven.

1993-94 — The NHL's playoff draw is conference-based rather than division-based. At the conclusion of the regular season, the top eight teams in each of the Eastern and Western Conferences qualify for the playoffs. The teams that finish in first place in each of the League's divisions are seeded first and second in each conference's playoff draw and are assured of home ice advantage in the first two playoff rounds. The remaining teams are seeded based on their regular-season point totals. In each conference, the team seeded #1 plays #8; #2 vs. #7; #3 vs. #6; and #4 vs. #5. All series are best-of-seven with home ice rotating on a 2-2-1-1-1 basis, with the exception of matchups between Central and Pacific Division teams. These matchups will be played on a 2-3-2 basis to reduce travel. In a 2-3-2 series, the team with the most points will have its choice to start the series at home or on the road. The Eastern Conference champion will face the Western Conference champion in the Stanley Cup Final.

1994-95 — Same as 1993-94, except that in first, second or third-round playoff series involving Central and Pacific Division teams, the team with the better record has the choice of using either a 2-3-2 or a 2-2-1-1-1 format. When a 2-3-2 format is selected, the higher-ranked team also has the choice of playing games 1, 2, 6 and 7 at home or playing games 3, 4 and 5 at home. The format for the Stanley Cup Final remains 2-2-1-1-1.

1998-99 — The NHL's clubs are re-aligned into two conferences each consisting of three divisions. The number of teams qualifying for the Stanley Cup Playoffs remains unchanged at 16.

First-round playoff berths will be awarded to the first-place team in each division as well as to the next five best teams based on regular-season point totals in each conference. The three division winners in each conference will be seeded first through third, in order of points, for the playoffs and the next five best teams, in order of points, will be seeded fourth through eighth. In each conference, the team seeded #1 will play #8; #2 vs. #7; #3 vs. #6; and #4 vs. #5 in the quarterfinal round. Home-ice in the Conference Quarter-Finals is granted to those teams seeded first through fourth in each conference.

In the Conference Semi-Finals and Conference Finals, teams will be re-seeded according to the same criteria as the Conference Quarter-Finals. Higher seeded teams will have home-ice advantage.

Home ice advantage for the Stanley Cup Final is awarded to the team with the higher number of points in the regular season.

All series remain best-of-seven.

2013-14 — The NHL club's are realigned into two conferences each comprised of two divisions. The number of teams qualifying for the Stanley Cup Playoffs remains unchanged at 16. These 16 playoff teams are seeded and placed in four divisional brackets. Eastern and Western Conference teams are on opposite sides of the draw and do not cross over until the Stanley Cup Final.

Twelve of the 16 berths in the first round of the playoffs are awarded to the top three finishers in each of the four divisions. These clubs are ranked as the first three "seeds" in each divisional bracket. Four additional "wild card" berths are awarded to the next two highest-placed finishers in each conference regardless of division. Each divisional bracket is comprised of the top three finishers in one division plus a wild card team. Wild cards are seeded fourth in their respective divisional brackets.

In each conference, the wild card team with fewer regular-season points is placed in the bracket that includes the first-place finisher with the most regular-season points. The wild card team with more regular-season points is placed in the bracket that includes the first-place finisher with the second-highest number of regular-season points.

In the first round of the playoffs in each bracket, the team seeded #1 plays #4 and the team seeded #2 plays #3. In the second round, the winners of these two first-round series meet.

The two advancing teams in the East and the two advancing teams in the West meet in the Conference Finals.

The Eastern and Western Conference champions meet in the Stanley Cup Final.

Home ice advantage for the Stanley Cup Final is awarded to the team with the higher number of points in the regular season.

All series remain best-of-seven.

The Pittsburgh Penguins relax and celebrate after their second straight Stanley Cup victory in 2017. No team in hockey history has played as many playoff games (49) over two championship seasons as the Penguins.

Team Records

1918-2017

GAMES PLAYED

MOST GAMES PLAYED BY ALL TEAMS, ONE PLAYOFF YEAR:
93 — 2014. There were 48 FR, 27 SR, 13 CF and 5 F Games.
92 — 1991. There were 51 DSF, 24 DF, 11 CF and 6 F games.
91 — 2016. There were 47 FR, 25 SR, 13 CF and 6 F games.
90 — 1994. There were 48 CQF, 23 CSF, 12 CF and 7 F games.
  — 2002. There were 47 CQF, 25 CSF, 13 CF and 5 F games.

MOST GAMES PLAYED, ONE TEAM, ONE PLAYOFF YEAR:
26 — Philadelphia Flyers, 1987. Won DSF 4-2 vs. NY Rangers, DF 4-3 vs. NY Islanders, CF 4-2 vs. Montreal, and lost F 4-3 vs. Edmonton.
  — **Calgary Flames,** 2004. Won DSF 4-3 vs. Vancouver, DF 4-2 vs. Detroit, CF 4-2 vs. San Jose, and lost F 4-3 vs. Tampa Bay.
  — **Los Angeles Kings,** 2014. Won FR 4-3 vs. San Jose, SR 4-3 vs. Anaheim, CF 4-3 vs. Chicago, and won F 4-1 vs. NY Rangers.
  — **Tampa Bay Lightning,** 2015. Won FR 4-3 vs. Detroit, SR 4-2 vs. Montreal, CF 4-3 vs. NY Rangers, and lost F 4-2 vs. Chicago.
25 — New Jersey Devils, 2001. Won CQF 4-2 vs. Carolina, CSF 4-3 vs. Toronto, CF 4-1 vs. Pittsburgh, and lost F 4-3 vs. Colorado.
  — Carolina Hurricanes, 2006. Won CQF 4-2 vs. Montreal, CSF 4-1 vs. New Jersey, CF 4-3 vs. Buffalo, and F 4-3 vs. Edmonton
  — Boston Bruins, 2011. Won CQF 4-3 vs. Montreal, CSF 4-0 vs. Philadelphia, CF 4-3 vs. Tampa Bay, and F 4-3 vs. Vancouver.
  — Vancouver Canucks, 2011. Won CQF 4-3 vs. Chicago, CSF 4-2 vs. Nashville, CF 4-1 vs. San Jose, and lost F 4-3 vs. Boston.
  — New York Rangers, 2014. Won FR 4-3 vs. Philadelphia, SR 4-3 vs. Pittsburgh, CF 4-2 vs. Montreal, and lost F 4-1 vs. Los Angeles.
  — Pittsburgh Penguins, 2017. Won FR 4-1 vs. Columbus, SR 4-3 vs. Washington, CF 4-3 vs. Ottawa, and F 4-2 vs. Nashville.

PLAYOFF APPEARANCES

MOST STANLEY CUP CHAMPIONSHIPS (since 1893):
24 — Montreal Canadiens
  (1916-24-30-31-44-46-53-56-57-58-59-60-65-66-68-69-71-73-76-77-78-79-86-93)
14 — Toronto Maple Leafs (1914-18-22-32-42-45-47-48-49-51-62-63-64-67)
11 — Detroit Red Wings (1936-37-43-50-52-54-55-97-98-2002-08)

MOST CONSECUTIVE STANLEY CUP CHAMPIONSHIPS:
5 — Montreal Canadiens (1956-57-58-59-60)
4 — Montreal Canadiens (1976-77-78-79)
  — New York Islanders (1980-81-82-83)

MOST FINAL SERIES APPEARANCES:
33 — Montreal Canadiens in 100-year history.
24 — Detroit Red Wings in 91-year history.
21 — Toronto Maple Leafs in 100-year history.

MOST CONSECUTIVE FINAL SERIES APPEARANCES:
10 — Montreal Canadiens (1951-60, inclusive)
5 — Montreal Canadiens (1965-69, inclusive)
  — New York Islanders (1980-84, inclusive)

MOST YEARS IN PLAYOFFS:
83 — Montreal Canadiens in 100-year history.
70 — Boston Bruins in 93-year history.
66 — Toronto Maple Leafs in 100-year history.

MOST CONSECUTIVE PLAYOFF APPEARANCES:
29 — Boston Bruins (1968-96, inclusive)
28 — Chicago Blackhawks (1970-97, inclusive)
25 — St. Louis Blues (1980-2004, inclusive)
  — Detroit Red Wings (1991-2016, inclusive)
24 — Montreal Canadiens (1971-94, inclusive)

TEAM WINS

MOST HOME WINS, ONE TEAM, ONE PLAYOFF YEAR:
12 — New Jersey Devils, 2003 in 13 home games.
11 — Edmonton Oilers, 1988 in 11 home games.
  — Detroit Red Wings, 2009 in 13 home games.
  — Chicago Blackhawks, 2013 in 13 home games.
10 — Edmonton Oilers, 1985 in 10 home games.
  — Montreal Canadiens, 1986 in 11 home games.
  — Montreal Canadiens, 1993 in 11 home games.
  — Carolina Hurricanes, 2006 in 14 home games.
  — Anaheim Ducks, 2007 in 12 home games.
  — Boston Bruins, 2011 in 13 home games.
  — Vancouver Canucks, 2011 in 14 home games.
  — Pittsburgh Penguins, 2017 in 13 home games.

MOST HOME WINS, ALL TEAMS, ONE PLAYOFF YEAR:
59 — 2013. Of 86 games played, home teams won 59 (30 CQF, 20 CSF, 6 CF and 3 in F).
57 — 1991. Of 92 games played, home teams won 57 (29 DSF, 17 DF, 8 CF and 3 in F).

MOST ROAD WINS, ONE TEAM, ONE PLAYOFF YEAR:
10 — New Jersey Devils, 1995. Won three at Boston in CQF; two at Pittsburgh in CSF; three at Philadelphia in CF; and two at Detroit in F.
  — **New Jersey Devils,** 2000. Won two at Florida in CQF; two at Toronto in CSF; three at Philadelphia in CF; and three at Dallas in F.
  — **Calgary Flames,** 2004. Won three at Vancouver in DSF; two at Detroit in DF; three at San Jose in CF; and two at Tampa Bay in F.
  — **Los Angeles Kings,** 2012. Won three at Vancouver in CQF; two at St. Louis in CSF; three at Phoenix in CF; and two at New Jersey in F.
8 — New York Islanders, 1980. Won two at Los Angeles in PR; three at Boston in QF; two at Buffalo in SF; and one at Philadelphia in F.
  — Philadelphia Flyers, 1987. Won two at NY Rangers in DSF; two at NY Islanders in DF; three at Montreal in CF; and one at Edmonton in F.
  — Edmonton Oilers, 1990. Won one at Winnipeg in DSF; two at Los Angeles in DF; two at Chicago in CF and three at Boston in F.
  — Pittsburgh Penguins, 1992. Won two at Washington in DSF; two at NY Rangers in DF; two at Boston in CF; and two at Chicago in F.
  — Vancouver Canucks, 1994. Won three at Calgary in CQF; two at Dallas in CSF; one at Toronto in CF; and two at NY Rangers in F.
  — Colorado Avalanche, 1996. Won two at Vancouver in CQF; two at Chicago in CSF; two at Detroit in CF; and two at Florida in F.
  — Detroit Red Wings, 1998. Won two at Phoenix in CQF; three at St. Louis in CSF; one at Dallas in CF; and two at Washington in F.
  — Colorado Avalanche, 1999. Won three at San Jose in CQF; three at Detroit in CSF; and two at Dallas in CF.
  — New Jersey Devils, 2001. Won two at Carolina in CQF; two at Toronto in CSF; two at Pittsburgh in CF; and two at Colorado in F.
  — Detroit Red Wings, 2002. Won three at Vancouver in CQF; one at St. Louis in CSF; two at Colorado in CF; and two at Carolina in F.
  — Chicago Blackhawks, 2010. Won two at Nashville in CQF; three at Vancouver in CSF; two at San Jose in CF; and one at Philadelphia in F.
  — Los Angeles Kings, 2014. Won two at San Jose in FR; three at Anaheim in SR; two at Chicago in CF; and one at NY Rangers in F.
  — Tampa Bay Lightning, 2015. Won two at Detroit in FR; two at Montreal in SR; three at NY Rangers in CF; and one at Chicago in F.

MOST ROAD WINS, ALL TEAMS, ONE PLAYOFF YEAR:
47 — **2012.** Of 86 games played, road teams won 47 (30 CQF, 7 CSF, 7 CF, 3 F).

MOST OVERTIME WINS, ONE TEAM, ONE PLAYOFF YEAR:
10 — **Montreal Canadiens, 1979.** Won two vs. Quebec in DSF; three vs. Buffalo in DF; two vs. NY Islanders in CF; and three vs. Los Angeles in F.
7 — **Carolina Hurricanes, 2002.** Won two vs. New Jersey in CQF; one vs. Montreal in CSF; three vs. Toronto in CF; and one vs. Detroit in F.
— **Anaheim Mighty Ducks, 2003.** Won two vs. Detroit in CQF; two vs. Dallas in CSF; one vs. Minnestoa in CF; and two vs. New Jersey in F.

MOST OVERTIME WINS AT HOME, ONE TEAM, ONE PLAYOFF YEAR:
4 — **St. Louis Blues, 1968.** Won one vs. Philadelphia in QF; three vs. Minnesota in SF.
— **Montreal Canadiens, 1993.** Won one vs. Quebec in DSF; one vs. Buffalo in DF, one vs. NY Islanders in CF; one vs. Los Angeles in F.
— **Chicago Blackhawks, 2013.** Won one vs. Minnesota in CQF; one vs. Detroit in CSF; one vs. Los Angeles in CF; one vs. Boston in F.
— **Pittsburgh Penguins, 2016.** Won two vs. Washington in SR; one vs. Tampa Bay in CF; one vs. San Jose in F.

MOST OVERTIME WINS ON THE ROAD, ONE TEAM, ONE PLAYOFF YEAR:
6 — **Montreal Canadiens, 1993.** Won one vs. Quebec in DSF; two vs. Buffalo in DF; one vs. NY Islanders in CF; two vs. Los Angeles in F.

TEAM LOSSES

MOST LOSSES, ONE TEAM, ONE PLAYOFF YEAR:
12 — **New York Rangers, 2014.** Lost three vs. Philadelphia in FR; three vs. Pittsburgh in SR; two vs. Montreal in CF; four vs. Los Angeles in F.
— **Tampa Bay Lightning, 2015.** Lost three vs. Detroit in FR; two vs. Montreal in SR; three vs. NY Rangers in CF; four vs. Chicago in F.
11 — **Philadelphia Flyers, 1987.** Lost two vs. NY Rangers in DSF; three vs. NY Islanders in DF; two vs. Montreal in CF; four vs. Edmonton in F.
— **Calgary Flames, 2004.** Lost three vs. Vancouver in CQF; two vs. Detroit in CSF; two vs. San Jose in CF; four vs. Tampa Bay in F.

MOST HOME LOSSES, ONE TEAM, ONE PLAYOFF YEAR:
7 — **Calgary Flames, 2004.** Lost two vs. Vancouver in CQF; one vs. Detroit in CSF; two vs. San Jose in CF; two vs. Tampa Bay in F.
— **Tampa Bay Lightning, 2015.** Lost two vs. Detroit in FR; one vs. Montreal in SR; two vs. NY Rangers in CF; two vs. Chicago in F.
6 — **Philadelphia Flyers, 1987.** Lost one vs. NY Rangers in DSF; two vs. NY Islanders in DF; two vs. Montreal in CF; one vs. Edmonton in F.
— **Washington Capitals, 1998.** Lost two vs. Boston in CQF; two vs. Buffalo in CF; two vs. Detroit in F.
— **Colorado Avalanche, 1999.** Lost two vs. San Jose in CQF; two vs. Detroit in CSF; two vs. Dallas in CF.
— **New Jersey Devils, 2001.** Lost one vs. Carolina in CQF; two vs. Toronto in CSF; one vs. Pittsburgh in CF; two vs Colorado in F.
— **Minnesota Wild, 2003.** Lost two vs. Colorado in CQF; two vs. Vancouver in CSF; two vs. Anaheim in CF.
— **St. Louis Blues, 2016.** Lost two vs. Chicago in FR; two vs. Dallas in SR; two vs. San Jose in CF.

MOST ROAD LOSSES, ONE TEAM, ONE PLAYOFF YEAR:
8 — **Los Angeles Kings, 2013.** Lost two at St. Louis in CQF; three at San Jose in CSF; three at Chicago in CF.
7 — **New Jersey Devils, 2003.** Lost one at Boston in CQF; one at Tampa Bay in CSF; two at Ottawa in CF; three at Anaheim in F.
— **Philadelphia Flyers, 2010.** Lost one at New Jersey in CQF; two at Boston in CSF; one at Montreal in CF; three at Chicago in F.
— **New York Rangers, 2014.** Lost two at Philadelphia in FR; one at Pittsburgh in SR; one at Montreal in CF; three at Los Angeles in F.

Bill Barilko (who would die that summer in a plane crash while on a fishing trip) scores the Stanley Cup winner for Toronto against Montreal's Gerry McNeil in 1951. All five games in that year's Final went into overtime.

MOST OVERTIME LOSSES, ONE TEAM, ONE PLAYOFF YEAR:
4 — **Montreal Canadiens, 1951.** Lost four vs. Toronto in F.
— **St. Louis Blues, 1968.** Lost one vs. Philadelphia in QF; one vs. Minnesota in SF; two vs. Montreal in F.
— **New York Rangers, 1979.** Lost one vs. Philadelphia in QF; two vs. NY Islanders in SF; one vs. Montreal in F.
— **Los Angeles Kings, 1991.** Lost one vs. Vancouver in DSF; three vs. Edmonton in DF.
— **Los Angeles Kings, 1993.** Lost one vs. Toronto in CF; three vs. Montreal in F.
— **New Jersey Devils, 1994.** Lost one vs. Buffalo in CQF; one vs. Boston in CSF; two vs. NY Rangers in CF.
— **Chicago Blackhawks, 1995.** Lost one vs. Toronto in CQF; three vs. Detroit in CF.
— **Philadelphia Flyers, 1996.** Lost two vs. Tampa Bay in CQF; two vs. Florida in CSF.
— **Dallas Stars, 1999.** Lost two vs. St. Louis in CSF; one vs. Colorado in CF; one vs. Buffalo in F.
— **Detroit Red Wings, 2002.** Lost one vs. Vancouver in CQF; two vs. Colorado in CF; one vs. Carolina in F.
— **New Jersey Devils, 2003.** Lost two vs. Ottawa in CF; two vs. Anaheim in F.
— **Washington Capitals, 2012.** Lost two vs. Boston in CQF; two vs. NY Rangers in CSF.
— **New York Rangers, 2014.** Lost one vs. Montreal in CF; three vs. Los Angeles in F.
— **San Jose Sharks, 2016.** Lost one vs. Los Angeles in FR; two vs. Nashville in SR; one vs. Pittsburgh in F.

MOST OVERTIME LOSSES AT HOME, ONE TEAM, ONE PLAYOFF YEAR:
4 — **Detroit Red Wings, 2002.** Lost one vs. Vancouver in CQF; two vs. Colorado in CF; one vs. Carolina in F.

MOST OVERTIME LOSSES ON THE ROAD, ONE TEAM, ONE PLAYOFF YEAR:
3 — **Los Angeles Kings, 1991.** Lost one at Vancouver in DSF; two at Edmonton in DF.
— **Chicago Blackhawks, 1995.** Lost one at Toronto in CQF; two at Detroit in CF.
— **St. Louis Blues, 1996.** Lost two at Toronto in CQF; one at Detroit in CSF.
— **Dallas Stars, 1999.** Lost two at St. Louis in CSF; one at Colorado in CF.
— **New Jersey Devils, 2003.** Lost one at Ottawa in CF; two at Anaheim in F.
— **Los Angeles Kings, 2013.** Lost two at St. Louis in CQF; one at Chicago in CF.
— **New York Rangers, 2013.** Lost two at Washington in CQF; one at Boston in CSF.
— **New York Rangers, 2014.** Lost three at Los Angeles in F.
— **Washington Capitals, 2015.** Lost one at NY Islanders in FR; two at NY Rangers in SR.
— **San Jose Sharks, 2016.** Lost two at Nashville in SR; one at Pittsburgh in F.
— **New York Rangers, 2017.** Lost one at Montreal in FR; two at Ottawa in SR.

PLAYOFF WINNING STREAKS

LONGEST PLAYOFF WINNING STREAK:
14 — **Pittsburgh Penguins.** Streak started May 9, 1992 as Pittsburgh won the first of three straight games in DF vs. NY Rangers. Continued with four wins vs. Boston in 1992 CF and four wins vs. Chicago in 1992 F. Pittsburgh then won the first three games of 1993 DSF vs. New Jersey. New Jersey ended the streak April 25, 1993, at New Jersey with a 4-1 win vs. Pittsburgh in the fourth game of 1993 DSF.
12 — Edmonton Oilers. Streak started May 15, 1984 as Edmonton won the first of three straight games in F vs. NY Islanders. Continued with three wins vs. Los Angeles in 1985 DSF and four wins vs. Winnipeg in 1985 DF. Edmonton then won the first two games of 1985 CF vs. Chicago. Chicago ended the streak May 9, 1985, at Chicago with a 5-2 win vs. Edmonton in the third game of 1985 CF.

MOST CONSECUTIVE WINS, ONE TEAM, ONE PLAYOFF YEAR:
11 — **Chicago Blackhawks** in 1992. Chicago won last three games of DSF vs. St. Louis to win series 4-2, defeated Detroit 4-0 in DF and Edmonton 4-0 in CF.
— **Pittsburgh Penguins** in 1992. Pittsburgh won last three games of DF vs. NY Rangers to win series 4-2, defeated Boston 4-0 in CF and Chicago 4-0 in F.
— **Montreal Canadiens** in 1993. Montreal won last four games of DSF vs. Quebec to win series 4-2, defeated Buffalo 4-0 in DF and won first three games of CF vs. NY Islanders.

PLAYOFF LOSING STREAKS

LONGEST PLAYOFF LOSING STREAK:
16 — **Chicago Black Hawks.** Streak started April 20, 1975 at Chicago with a 6-2 loss in fourth game of QF vs. Buffalo, won by Buffalo 4-1. Continued with four consecutive losses vs. Montreal, in 1976 QF and two straight losses vs. NY Islanders in 1977 best-of-three PR. Chicago then lost four games vs. Boston in 1978 QF and four games vs. NY Islanders in 1979 QF. Chicago ended the streak April 8, 1980, at Chicago with a 3-2 win vs. St. Louis in the opening game of 1980 PR.
14 — Los Angeles Kings. Streak started June 3, 1993 at Montreal with a 3-2 loss in second game of F vs. Montreal, won by Montreal 4-1. Los Angeles failed to qualify for the playoffs for the next four years. Then Los Angeles lost four games vs. St. Louis in 1998 CQF; missed the 1999 playoffs and lost four games vs. Detroit in 2000 CQF. Los Angeles then lost the first two games of 2001 CQF vs. Detroit. Los Angeles ended the streak April 15, 2001, at Los Angeles with a 2-1 win vs. Detroit in the third game of 2001 CQF.

MOST GOALS IN A SERIES, ONE TEAM

MOST GOALS, ONE TEAM, ONE PLAYOFF SERIES:
44 — **Edmonton Oilers** in 1985. Edmonton won best-of-seven CF 4-2, outscoring Chicago 44-25.
35 — Edmonton Oilers in 1983. Edmonton won best-of-seven DF 4-1, outscoring Calgary 35-13.
— Calgary Flames in 1995. Calgary lost best-of-seven CQF 4-3, outscoring San Jose 35-26.

MOST GOALS, ONE TEAM, TWO-GAME SERIES:
11 — **Buffalo Sabres** in 1977. Buffalo won best-of-three PR 2-0, outscoring Minnesota 11-3.
— **Toronto Maple Leafs** in 1978. Toronto won best-of-three PR 2-0, outscoring Los Angeles 11-3.

MOST GOALS, ONE TEAM, THREE-GAME SERIES:
23 — **Chicago Blackhawks** in 1985. Chicago won best-of-five DSF 3-0, outscoring Detroit 23-8.
20 — Minnesota North Stars in 1981. Minnesota won best-of-five PR 3-0, outscoring Boston 20-13.
— NY Islanders in 1981. NY Islanders won best-of-five PR 3-0, outscoring Toronto 20-4.

MOST GOALS, ONE TEAM, FOUR-GAME SERIES:
28 — **Boston Bruins** in 1972. Boston won best-of-seven SF 4-0, outscoring St. Louis 28-8.

MOST GOALS, ONE TEAM, FIVE-GAME SERIES:
35 — **Edmonton Oilers** in 1983. Edmonton won best-of-seven DF 4-1, outscoring Calgary 35-13.
32 — Edmonton Oilers in 1987. Edmonton won best-of-seven DSF 4-1, outscoring Los Angeles 32-20.
30 — Calgary Flames in 1988. Calgary won best-of-seven DSF 4-1, outscoring Los Angeles 30-18.

MOST GOALS, ONE TEAM, SIX-GAME SERIES:
44 — **Edmonton Oilers** in 1985. Edmonton won best-of-seven CF 4-2, outscoring Chicago 44-25.
33 — Montreal Canadiens in 1973. Montreal won best-of-seven F 4-2, outscoring Chicago 33-23.
— Chicago Blackhawks in 1985. Chicago won best-of-seven DF 4-2, outscoring Minnesota 33-29.
— Los Angeles Kings in 1993. Los Angeles won best-of-seven DSF 4-2, outscoring Calgary 33-28.

MOST GOALS, ONE TEAM, SEVEN-GAME SERIES:
35 — **Calgary Flames** in 1995. Calgary lost best-of-seven CQF 4-3, outscoring San Jose 35-26.
33 — Philadelphia Flyers in 1976. Philadelphia won best-of-seven QF 4-3, outscoring Toronto 33-23.
— Boston Bruins in 1983. Boston won best-of-seven DF 4-3, outscoring Buffalo 33-23.
— Edmonton Oilers in 1984. Edmonton won best-of-seven DF 4-3, outscoring Calgary 33-27.

FEWEST GOALS IN A SERIES, ONE TEAM

FEWEST GOALS, ONE TEAM, TWO-GAME SERIES:
0 — **Toronto St. Patricks** in 1921. Toronto lost two-game, total-goals NHL F 7-0 vs. Ottawa.
— **New York Americans** in 1929. NY Americans lost two-game, total-goals QF 1-0 vs. NY Rangers.
— **New York Rangers** in 1931. NY Rangers lost two-game, total-goals SF 3-0 vs. Chicago.
— **Chicago Black Hawks** in 1935. Chicago lost two-game, total-goals SF 1-0 vs. Mtl. Maroons.
— **Montreal Maroons** in 1937. Mtl. Maroons lost best-of-three SF 2-0, outscored by NY Rangers 5-0.
— **New York Americans** in 1939. NY Americans lost best-of-three QF 2-0, outscored by Toronto 5-0.

FEWEST GOALS, ONE TEAM, THREE-GAME SERIES:
1 — **Montreal Maroons** in 1936. Mtl. Maroons lost best-of-five SF 3-0, outscored by Detroit 6-1.

FEWEST GOALS, ONE TEAM, FOUR-GAME SERIES:
1 — **Minnesota Wild** in 2003. Minnesota lost best-of-seven CF 4-0, outscored by Anaheim 9-1.

FEWEST GOALS, ONE TEAM, FIVE-GAME SERIES:
2 — **Philadelphia Flyers** in 2002. Philadelphia lost best-of-seven CQF 4-1, outscored by Ottawa 11-2.

FEWEST GOALS, ONE TEAM, SIX-GAME SERIES:
5 — **Boston Bruins** in 1951. Boston lost best-of-seven SF 4-1 with 1 tie, outscored by Toronto 17-5.

FEWEST GOALS, ONE TEAM, SEVEN-GAME SERIES:
8 — **Vancouver Canucks,** in 2011. Vancouver lost best-of-seven F 4-3; outscored by Boston 23-8.
9 — Detroit Red Wings, in 1945. Detroit lost best-of-seven F 4-3; tied with Toronto in scoring 9-9.
— Toronto Maple Leafs, in 1945. Toronto won best-of-seven F 4-3; tied with Detroit in scoring 9-9.

Wayne Gretzky and Jari Kurri led a record-setting offense during the 1985 playoffs as the Edmonton Oilers won their second of five Stanley Cup titles during a seven-year span.

MOST GOALS IN A SERIES, BOTH TEAMS

MOST GOALS, BOTH TEAMS, ONE PLAYOFF SERIES:
69 — **Edmonton Oilers (44), Chicago Black Hawks (25)** in 1985. Edmonton won best-of-seven CF 4-2.
62 — Chicago Black Hawks (33), Minnesota North Stars (29) in 1985. Chicago won best-of-seven DF 4-2.
61 — Los Angeles Kings (33), Calgary Flames (28) in 1993. Los Angeles won best-of-seven DSF 4-2.
— Calgary Flames (35), San Jose Sharks (26) in 1995. San Jose won best-of-seven CQF 4-3.

MOST GOALS, BOTH TEAMS, TWO-GAME SERIES:
17 — **Toronto Arenas (10), Montreal Canadiens (7)** in 1918. Toronto won two-game total-goals NHL F.
15 — Boston Bruins (10), Chicago Black Hawks (5) in 1927. Boston won two-game total-goals QF.
— Pittsburgh Penguins (9), St. Louis Blues (6) in 1975. Pittsburgh won best-of-three PR 2-0.

MOST GOALS, BOTH TEAMS, THREE-GAME SERIES:
33 — **Minnesota North Stars (20), Boston Bruins (13)** in 1981. Minnesota won best-of-five PR 3-0.
31 — Chicago Black Hawks (23), Detroit Red Wings (8) in 1985. Chicago won best-of-five DSF 3-0.
28 — Toronto Maple Leafs (18), New York Rangers (10) in 1932. Toronto won best-of-five F 3-0.

MOST GOALS, BOTH TEAMS, FOUR-GAME SERIES:
36 — **Boston Bruins (28), St. Louis Blues (8)** in 1972. Boston won best-of-seven SF 4-0.
— **Minnesota North Stars (18), Toronto Maple Leafs (18)** in 1983. Minnesota won best-of-five PR 3-1.
— **Edmonton Oilers (25), Chicago Black Hawks (11)** in 1983. Edmonton won best-of-seven CF 4-0.
35 — New York Rangers (23), Los Angeles Kings (12) in 1981. NY Rangers won best-of-five PR 3-1.

MOST GOALS, BOTH TEAMS, FIVE-GAME SERIES:
 52 — Edmonton Oilers (32), Los Angeles Kings (20) in 1987. Edmonton won
  best-of-seven DSF 4-1.
 50 — Los Angeles Kings (27), Edmonton Oilers (23) in 1982. Los Angeles won
  best-of-five DSF 3-2.
 48 — Edmonton Oilers (35), Calgary Flames (13) in 1983. Edmonton won
  best-of-seven DF 4-1.
  — Calgary Flames (30), Los Angeles Kings (18) in 1988. Calgary won
  best-of-seven DSF 4-1.

MOST GOALS, BOTH TEAMS, SIX-GAME SERIES:
 69 — Edmonton Oilers (44), Chicago Black Hawks (25) in 1985. Edmonton won
  best-of-seven CF 4-2.
 62 — Chicago Black Hawks (33), Minnesota North Stars (29) in 1985. Chicago won
  best-of-seven DF 4-2.
 61 — Los Angeles Kings (33), Calgary Flames (28) in 1993. Los Angeles won
  best-of-seven DSF 4-2.

MOST GOALS, BOTH TEAMS, SEVEN-GAME SERIES:
 61 — Calgary Flames (35), San Jose Sharks (26) in 1995. San Jose won
  best-of-seven CQF 4-3.
 60 — Edmonton Oilers (33), Calgary Flames (27) in 1984. Edmonton won
  best-of-seven DF 4-3.

FEWEST GOALS IN A SERIES, BOTH TEAMS

FEWEST GOALS, BOTH TEAMS, TWO-GAME SERIES:
 1 — New York Rangers (1), New York Americans (0) in 1929. NY Rangers won
  two-game total-goals QF.
  — **Montreal Maroons (1), Chicago Black Hawks (0)** in 1935. Mtl. Maroons
  won two-game total-goals SF.

FEWEST GOALS, BOTH TEAMS, THREE-GAME SERIES:
 7 — Boston Bruins (5), Montreal Canadiens (2) in 1929. Boston won
  best-of-five SF 3-0.
  — **Detroit Red Wings (6), Montreal Maroons (1)** in 1936. Detroit won
  best-of-five SF 3-0.

FEWEST GOALS, BOTH TEAMS, FOUR-GAME SERIES:
 9 — Toronto Maple Leafs (7), Boston Bruins (2) in 1935. Toronto won
  best-of-five SF 3-1.

FEWEST GOALS, BOTH TEAMS, FIVE-GAME SERIES:
 11 — Montreal Maroons (6), New York Rangers (5) in 1928. NY Rangers won
  best-of-five F 3-2.

FEWEST GOALS, BOTH TEAMS, SIX-GAME SERIES:
 16 — Carolina Hurricanes (10), Toronto Maple Leafs (6) in 2002. Carolina won
  best-of-seven CF 4-2.

FEWEST GOALS, BOTH TEAMS, SEVEN-GAME SERIES:
 18 — Toronto Maple Leafs (9), Detroit Red Wings (9) in 1945. Toronto won
  best-of-seven F 4-3.

MOST GOALS IN A GAME OR PERIOD

MOST GOALS, ONE TEAM, ONE GAME:
 13 — Edmonton Oilers April 9, 1987, vs. Los Angeles at Edmonton. Edmonton
  won 13-3.
 12 — Los Angeles Kings, April 10, 1990, vs. Calgary at Los Angeles. Los Angeles
  won 12-4.
 11 — Montreal Canadiens, March 30, 1944, vs. Toronto at Montreal. Montreal
  won 11-0.
  — Edmonton Oilers, May 4, 1985, vs. Chicago at Edmonton. Edmonton won
  11-2.

MOST GOALS, ONE TEAM, ONE PERIOD:
 7 — Montreal Canadiens, March 30, 1944, vs. Toronto at Montreal, third
  period. Montreal won 11-0.

MOST GOALS, BOTH TEAMS, ONE GAME:
 18 — Los Angeles Kings (10), Edmonton Oilers (8), April 7, 1982, at Edmonton.
  Los Angeles won best-of-five DSF 3-2.
 17 — Pittsburgh Penguins (10), Philadelphia Flyers (7), April 25, 1989, at Pittsburgh.
  Pittsburgh won best-of-seven DF 4-3.
 16 — Edmonton Oilers (13), Los Angeles Kings (3), April 9, 1987, at Edmonton.
  Edmonton won best-of-seven DSF 4-1.
  — Los Angeles Kings (12), Calgary Flames (4), April 10, 1990, at Los Angeles.
  Los Angeles won best-of-seven DF 4-2.

MOST GOALS, BOTH TEAMS, ONE PERIOD:
 9 — New York Rangers (6), Philadelphia Flyers (3), April 24, 1979, third
  period, at Philadelphia. NY Rangers won 8-3.
  — **Los Angeles Kings (5), Calgary Flames (4)**, April 10, 1990, second period,
  at Los Angeles. Los Angeles won 12-4.
 8 — Chicago Black Hawks (5), Montreal Canadiens (3), May 8, 1973, second
  period, at Montreal. Chicago won 8-7.
  — Chicago Black Hawks (5), Edmonton Oilers (3), May 12, 1985, first period, at
  Chicago. Chicago won 8-6.
  — Edmonton Oilers (6), Winnipeg Jets (2), April 6, 1988, third period, at
  Edmonton. Edmonton won 7-4.
  — Hartford Whalers (5), Montreal Canadiens (3), April 10, 1988, third period, at
  Montreal. Hartford won 7-5.
  — Vancouver Canucks (5), New York Rangers (3), June 9, 1994, third period, at
  NY Rangers. Vancouver won 6-3.
  — Pittsburgh Penguins (5), Ottawa Senators (3), April 20, 2010, second period,
  at Ottawa. Pittsburgh won 7-4.

TEAM POWER-PLAY GOALS

MOST POWER-PLAY GOALS BY ALL TEAMS, ONE PLAYOFF YEAR:
 199 — 1988 in 83 games.

MOST POWER-PLAY GOALS, ONE TEAM, ONE PLAYOFF YEAR:
 35 — Minnesota North Stars, 1991 in 23 games.
 32 — Edmonton Oilers, 1988 in 18 games.
 31 — New York Islanders, 1981 in 18 games.

MOST POWER-PLAY GOALS, ONE TEAM, ONE SERIES:
 15 — New York Islanders in 1980 F vs. Philadelphia. NY Islanders won series 4-2.
  — **Minnesota North Stars** in 1991 DSF vs. Chicago. Minnesota won series 4-2.
 13 — New York Islanders in 1981 QF vs. Edmonton. NY Islanders won series 4-2.
  — Calgary Flames in 1986 CF vs. St. Louis. Calgary won series 4-3.
 12 — Toronto Maple Leafs in 1976 QF vs. Philadelphia. Philadelphia won series 4-3.
  — Quebec Nordiques in 1987 CQF vs. Hartford. Quebec won series 4-3.
  — Colorado Avalanche in 1997 CQF vs. Chicago. Colorado won series 4-2.
  — Philadelphia Flyers in 2012 CQF vs. Pittsburgh. Philadelphia won series 4-2.

MOST POWER-PLAY GOALS, BOTH TEAMS, ONE SERIES:
 21 — New York Islanders (15), Philadelphia Flyers (6) in 1980 best-of-seven F
  won by NY Islanders 4-2.
  — **New York Islanders (13), Edmonton Oilers (8)** in 1981 best-of-seven QF
  won by NY Islanders 4-2.
  — **Philadelphia Flyers (11), Pittsburgh Penguins (10)** in 1989 best-of-seven
  DF won by Philadelphia 4-3.
  — **Minnesota North Stars (15), Chicago Black Hawks (6)** in 1991
  best-of-seven DSF won by Minnesota 4-2.
  — **Philadelphia Flyers (12), Pittsburgh Penguins (9)** in 2012 best-of-seven
  CQF won by Philadelphia 4-2.
 20 — Toronto Maple Leafs (12), Philadelphia Flyers (8) in 1976 best-of-seven QF
  won by Philadelphia 4-3.

MOST POWER-PLAY GOALS, ONE TEAM, ONE GAME:
 6 — Boston Bruins, April 2, 1969, at Boston vs. Toronto. Boston won 10-0.

MOST POWER-PLAY GOALS, BOTH TEAMS, ONE GAME:
 8 — Minnesota North Stars (4), St. Louis Blues (4), April 24, 1991, at
  Minnesota. Minnesota won 8-4.
 7 — Minnesota North Stars (4), Edmonton Oilers (3), April 28, 1984, at Minnesota.
  Edmonton won 8-5.
  — Philadelphia Flyers (4), New York Rangers (3), April 13, 1985, at NY Rangers.
  Philadelphia won 6-5.
  — Chicago Black Hawks (5), Edmonton Oilers (2), May 14, 1985, at Edmonton.
  Edmonton won 10-5.
  — Edmonton Oilers (5), Los Angeles Kings (2), April 9, 1987, at Edmonton.
  Edmonton won 13-3.
  — Vancouver Canucks (4), Calgary Flames (3), April 9, 1989, at Vancouver.
  Vancouver won 5-3.
  — Pittsburgh Penguins (4), Philadelphia Flyers (3), April 18, 2012, at
  Philadelphia. Pittsburgh won 10-5.

MOST POWER-PLAY GOALS, ONE TEAM, ONE PERIOD:
 4 — Toronto Maple Leafs, March 26, 1936, second period vs. Boston at
  Toronto. Toronto won 8-3.
  — **Minnesota North Stars,** April 28, 1984, second period vs. Edmonton at
  Minnesota. Edmonton won 8-5.
  — **Boston Bruins,** April 11, 1991, third period vs. Hartford at Boston. Boston
  won 6-1.
  — **Minnesota North Stars,** April 24, 1991, second period vs. St. Louis at
  Minnesota. Minnesota won 8-4.
  — **St. Louis Blues,** April 27, 1998, third period at Los Angeles. St. Louis won
  4-3.
  — **Washington Capitals,** April 18, 2016, third period at Philadelphia.
  Washington won 6-1.

MOST POWER-PLAY GOALS, BOTH TEAMS, ONE PERIOD:
 5 — Minnesota North Stars (4), Edmonton Oilers (1), April 28, 1984, at
  Minnesota. Edmonton won 8-5.
  — **Vancouver Canucks (3), Calgary Flames (2),** April 9, 1989, at Vancouver.
  Vancouver won 5-3.
  — **Minnesota North Stars (4), St. Louis Blues (1),** April 24, 1991, at
  Minnesota. Minnesota won 8-4.

TEAM SHORTHAND GOALS

MOST SHORTHAND GOALS BY ALL TEAMS, ONE PLAYOFF YEAR:
 33 — 1988, in 83 games.

MOST SHORTHAND GOALS, ONE TEAM, ONE PLAYOFF YEAR:
 10 — Edmonton Oilers, 1983, in 16 games.
 9 — New York Islanders, 1981, in 19 games.
 8 — Philadelphia Flyers, 1989, in 19 games.

MOST SHORTHAND GOALS, ONE TEAM, ONE SERIES:
 6 — Calgary Flames in 1995 vs. San Jose in best-of-seven CQF won by San Jose
  4-3.
  — **Vancouver Canucks** in 1995 vs. St. Louis in best-of-seven CQF won by
  Vancouver 4-3.
 5 — New York Rangers in 1979 vs. Philadelphia in best-of-seven QF won by
  NY Rangers 4-1.
  — Edmonton Oilers in 1983 vs. Calgary in best-of-seven DF won by Edmonton
  4-1.

MOST SHORTHAND GOALS, BOTH TEAMS, ONE SERIES:
 7 — Boston Bruins (4), New York Rangers (3), in 1958 SF won by Boston 4-2.
  — **Edmonton Oilers (5), Calgary Flames (2),** in 1983 DF won by Edmonton
  4-1.
  — **Vancouver Canucks (6), St. Louis Blues (1),** in 1995 CQF won by
  Vancouver 4-3.

MOST SHORTHAND GOALS, ONE TEAM, ONE GAME:
3 — Boston Bruins, April 11, 1981, at Minnesota North Stars. Minnesota won 6-3.
— **New York Islanders,** April 17, 1983, at NY Rangers. NY Rangers won 7-6.
— **Edmonton Oilers,** April 17, 1983, at Calgary Flames. Edmonton won 10-2.

MOST SHORTHAND GOALS, BOTH TEAMS, ONE GAME:
4 — Boston Bruins (3), Minnesota North Stars (1), April 11, 1981, at Minnesota. Minnesota won 6-3.
— **New York Islanders (3), New York Rangers (1),** April 17, 1983, at NY Rangers. NY Rangers won 7-6.
3 — Toronto Maple Leafs (2), Detroit Red Wings (1), April 5, 1947, at Toronto. Toronto won 6-1.
— New York Rangers (2), Boston Bruins (1), April 1, 1958, at Boston. NY Rangers won 5-2.
— Minnesota North Stars (2), Philadelphia Flyers (1), May 4, 1980, at Minnesota. Philadelphia won 5-3.
— Winnipeg Jets (2), Edmonton Oilers (1), April 9, 1988, at Winnipeg. Winnipeg won 6-4.
— New York Islanders (2), New Jersey Devils (1), April 14, 1988, at New Jersey. New Jersey won 6-5.
— Toronto Maple Leafs (2), San Jose Sharks (1), May 8, 1994, at San Jose. Toronto won 8-3.
— Montreal Canadiens (2), New Jersey Devils (1), April 17, 1997, at New Jersey. New Jersey won 5-2.
— Dallas Stars (2), San Jose Sharks (1), May 5, 2000, at San Jose. Dallas won 5-4.
— Detroit Red Wings (2), Calgary Flames (1), April 21, 2007, at Detroit. Detroit won 5-1.

MOST SHORTHAND GOALS, ONE TEAM, ONE PERIOD:
2 — Toronto Maple Leafs, April 5, 1947, first period vs. Detroit at Toronto. Toronto won 6-1.
— **Toronto Maple Leafs,** April 13, 1965, first period vs. Montreal at Toronto. Montreal won 4-3.
— **Boston Bruins,** April 20, 1969, first period vs. Montreal at Boston. Boston won 3-2.
— **Boston Bruins,** April 8, 1970, second period vs. NY Rangers at Boston. Boston won 8-2.
— **Boston Bruins,** April 30, 1972, first period vs. NY Rangers at Boston. Boston won 6-5.
— **Chicago Black Hawks,** May 3, 1973, first period vs. Montreal at Chicago. Chicago won 7-4.
— **Montreal Canadiens,** April 23, 1978, first period at Detroit. Montreal won 8-0.
— **New York Islanders,** April 8, 1980, second period vs. Los Angeles at NY Islanders. NY Islanders won 8-1.
— **Los Angeles Kings,** April 9, 1980, first period at NY Islanders. Los Angeles won 6-3.
— **Boston Bruins,** April 13, 1980, second period at Pittsburgh. Boston won 8-3.
— **Minnesota North Stars,** May 4, 1980, second period vs. Philadelphia at Minnesota. Philadelphia won 5-3.
— **Boston Bruins,** April 11, 1981, third period at Minnesota North Stars. Minnesota won 6-3.
— **New York Islanders,** May 12, 1981, first period vs. Minnesota North Stars at NY Islanders. NY Islanders won 6-3.
— **Montreal Canadiens,** April 7, 1982, third period vs. Quebec at Montreal. Montreal won 5-1.
— **New York Islanders,** April 17, 1983, third period vs NY Rangers. NY Rangers won 7-6.
— **Edmonton Oilers,** April 24, 1983, third period vs. Chicago at Edmonton. Edmonton won 8-4.
— **Winnipeg Jets,** April 14, 1985, second period at Calgary. Winnipeg won 5-3.
— **Boston Bruins,** April 6, 1988, first period vs. Buffalo at Boston. Boston won 7-3.
— **New York Islanders,** April 14, 1988, third period at New Jersey. New Jersey won 6-5.
— **Detroit Red Wings,** April 29, 1993, second period at Toronto. Detroit won 7-3.
— **Toronto Maple Leafs,** May 8, 1994, third period at San Jose. Toronto won 8-3.
— **Calgary Flames,** May 11, 1995, first period at San Jose. Calgary won 9-2.
— **Vancouver Canucks,** May 15, 1995, second period at St. Louis. Vancouver won 6-5.
— **Montreal Canadiens,** April 17, 1997, second period at New Jersey. New Jersey won 5-2.
— **Philadelphia Flyers,** April 26, 1997, first period vs. Pittsburgh at Philadelphia. Philadelphia won 6-3.
— **Phoenix Coyotes,** April 24, 1998, second period at Detroit. Phoenix won 7-4.
— **Buffalo Sabres,** April 27, 1998, second period vs. Philadelphia at Buffalo. Buffalo won 6-5.
— **San Jose Sharks,** April 30, 1999, third period at Colorado. San Jose won 7-3.
— **Detroit Red Wings,** April 27, 2002, second period at Vancouver. Detroit won 6-4.
— **Detroit Red Wings,** April 21, 2007, second period at Detroit. Detroit won 5-1.

MOST SHORTHAND GOALS, BOTH TEAMS, ONE PERIOD:
3 — Toronto Maple Leafs (2), Detroit Red Wings (1), April 5, 1947, first period at Toronto. Toronto won 6-1.
— **Toronto Maple Leafs (2), San Jose Sharks (1),** May 8, 1994, third period at San Jose. Toronto won 8-3.

FASTEST GOALS

FASTEST FIVE GOALS, BOTH TEAMS:
3:06 — Minnesota North Stars, Chicago Black Hawks, April 21, 1985, at Chicago. Keith Brown scored for Chicago at 1:12 of the second period; Ken Yaremchuk, Chicago, 1:27; Dino Ciccarelli, Minnesota, 2:48; Tony McKegney, Minnesota, 4:07; and Curt Fraser, Chicago, 4:18. Chicago won 6-2 and won best-of-seven DF 4-2.
3:20 — Minnesota North Stars, Philadelphia Flyers, April 29, 1980, at Philadelphia. Paul Shmyr scored for Minnesota at 13:20 of the first period; Steve Christoff, Minnesota, 13:59; Ken Linseman, Philadelphia, 14:54; Tom Gorence, Philadelphia, 15:36; and Ken Linseman, Philadelphia, 16:40. Minnesota won 6-5. Philadelphia won best-of-seven SF 4-1.
3:58 — Detroit Red Wings, Phoenix Coyotes, April 16, 2010, at Phoenix. Henrik Zetterberg scored for Detroit at 6:27 of the second period; Wojtek Wolski, Phoenix, 7:05; Pavel Datsyuk, Detroit, 8:20; Matthew Lombardi, Phoenix, 9:09; Valtteri Filppula, Detroit, 10:25. Detroit won 7-4 and won best-of-seven CQF 4-3.

FASTEST FIVE GOALS, ONE TEAM:
3:36 — Montreal Canadiens, March 30, 1944, at Montreal vs. Toronto. Toe Blake scored at 7:58 and 8:37 of the third period; Maurice Richard, 9:17; Ray Getliffe, 10:33; and Buddy O'Connor, 11:34. Canadiens won 11-0 and won best-of-seven SF 4-1.

FASTEST FOUR GOALS, BOTH TEAMS:
1:33 — Toronto Maple Leafs, Philadelphia Flyers, April 20, 1976, at Philadelphia. Don Saleski scored for Philadelphia at 10:04 of the second period; Bob Neely, Toronto, 10:42; Gary Dornhoefer, Philadelphia, 11:24; and Don Saleski, Philadelphia, 11:37. Philadelphia won 7-1 and won best-of-seven SF 4-3.
1:34 — Calgary Flames, Montreal Canadiens, May 20, 1986, at Montreal. Joel Otto scored for Calgary at 17:59 of the first period; Bobby Smith, Montreal, 18:25; Mats Naslund, Montreal, 19:17; and Bob Gainey, Montreal, 19:33. Montreal won 5-3 and won best-of-seven F 4-1.
1:38 — Boston Bruins, Philadelphia Flyers, April 26, 1977, at Philadelphia. Gregg Sheppard scored for Boston at 14:01 of the second period; Mike Milbury, Boston, 15:01; Gary Dornhoefer, Philadelphia, 15:16; and Jean Ratelle, Boston, 15:39. Boston won 5-4 and won best-of-seven SF 4-0.

FASTEST FOUR GOALS, ONE TEAM:
2:35 — Montreal Canadiens, March 30, 1944, at Montreal. Toe Blake scored at 7:58 and 8:37 of the third period; Maurice Richard, 9:17; and Ray Getliffe, 10:33. Montreal won 11-0 and won best-of-seven SF 4-1.

FASTEST THREE GOALS, BOTH TEAMS:
0:21 — Chicago Black Hawks, Edmonton Oilers, May 7, 1985, at Edmonton. Behn Wilson scored for Chicago at 19:22 of the third period; Jari Kurri, Edmonton, 19:36; and Glenn Anderson, Edmonton, 19:43. Edmonton won 7-3 and won best-of-seven CF 4-2.
0:27 — Phoenix Coyotes, Detroit Red Wings, April 24, 1998, at Detroit. Jeremy Roenick scored for Phoenix at 13:24 of the second period; Mathieu Dandenault, Detroit, 13:32; and Keith Tkachuk, Phoenix, 13:51. Phoenix won 7-4. Detroit won best-of-seven CQF 4-2.
0:30 — Pittsburgh Penguins, Chicago Blackhawks, June 1, 1992, at Chicago. Dirk Graham scored for Chicago at 6:21 of the first period; Kevin Stevens, Pittsburgh, 6:33; and Dirk Graham, Chicago, 6:51. Pittsburgh won 6-5 and won best-of-seven F 4-0.

FASTEST THREE GOALS, ONE TEAM:
0:23 — Toronto Maple Leafs, April 12, 1979, at Toronto vs. Atlanta Flames. Darryl Sittler scored at 4:04 and 4:16 of the first period; and Ron Ellis, 4:27. Toronto won 7-4 and won best-of-three PR 2-0.
0:37 — Anaheim Ducks, May 23, 2015, at Chicago. Ryan Kesler scored at 8:42 of the third period; Matt Belesky, 9:05; and Corey Perry, 9:19. Chicago won 5-4 and won best-of-seven CF 4-3.
0:38 — New York Rangers, April 12, 1986, at NY Rangers vs. Philadelphia. Jim Weimer scored at 12:29 of the third period; Bob Brooke, 12:43; and Ron Greschner, 13:07. NY Rangers won 5-2 and won best-of-five DSF 3-2.
— Colorado Avalanche, April 18, 2001, at Vancouver. Peter Forsberg scored at 9:11 of the third period; Joe Sakic, 9:28; and Eric Messier, 9:49. Colorado won 5-1 and won best-of-seven CQF 4-0.

FASTEST TWO GOALS, BOTH TEAMS:
0:05 — Pittsburgh Penguins, Buffalo Sabres, April 14, 1979, at Buffalo. Gilbert Perreault scored for Buffalo at 12:59 of the first period; and Jim Hamilton, Pittsburgh, 13:04. Pittsburgh won 4-3 and won best-of-three PR 2-1.
0:06 — Philadelphia Flyers, Pittsburgh Penguins, April 13, 2012 at Pittsburgh. Claude Giroux scored for Philadelphia at 11:04 of the second period; and Chris Kunitz, Pittsburgh, 11:10. Philadelphia won 8-5. Philadelphia won best-of-seven CQF 4-2.
0:08 — St. Louis Blues, Minnesota North Stars, April 9, 1989, at Minnesota. Bernie Federko scored for St. Louis at 2:28 of the third period; and Perry Berezan, Minnesota, 2:36. Minnesota won 5-4. St. Louis won best-of-seven DSF 4-1.
— Phoenix Coyotes, Detroit Red Wings, April 24, 1998, at Detroit. Jeremy Roenick scored for Phoenix at 13:24 of the second period; and Mathieu Dandenault, Detroit, 13:32. Phoenix won 7-4. Detroit won best-of-seven CQF 4-2.

FASTEST TWO GOALS, ONE TEAM:
0:05 — Detroit Red Wings, April 11, 1965, at Detroit vs. Chicago. Norm Ullman scored at 17:35 and 17:40 of the second period. Detroit won 4-2. Chicago won best-of-seven SF 4-3.

Ottawa's Jean-Gabriel Pageau celebrates his fourth goal of the game to defeat the New York Rangers in overtime on April 29, 2017.

OVERTIME

SHORTEST OVERTIME:
0:09 — Montreal Canadiens, Calgary Flames, May 18, 1986, at Calgary. Montreal won 3-2 on Brian Skrudland's goal at 0:09 of the first overtime period. Montreal won best-of-seven F 4-1.
0:11 — New York Islanders, New York Rangers, April 11, 1975, at NY Rangers. NY Islanders won 4-3 on J.P. Parise's goal at 0:11 of the first overtime period. NY Islanders won best-of-three PR 2-1.
— Vancouver Canucks, Boston Bruins, June 4, 2011, at Vancouver. Vancouver won 3-2 on Alexandre Burrows' goal at 0:11 of the first overtime period. Boston won best-of-seven F 4-3.

LONGEST OVERTIME:
116:30 — Detroit Red Wings, Montreal Maroons, March 24, 1936, at Montreal. Mtl. Maroons won 1-0 on Mud Bruneteau's goal at 16:30 of the sixth overtime period. Detroit won best-of-five SF 3-0.

MOST OVERTIME GAMES, ONE PLAYOFF YEAR:
28 — 1993. Of 85 games played, 28 went into overtime.
27 — 2013. Of 86 games played, 27 went into overtime.
— 2017. Of 87 games played, 27 went into overtime.
26 — 2001. Of 86 games played, 26 went into overtime.
— 2014. Of 93 games played, 26 went into overtime.

FEWEST OVERTIME GAMES, ONE PLAYOFF YEAR:
0 — 1963. None of the 16 games went into overtime, the only year since 1926 that no overtime was required in any playoff series.

MOST OVERTIME GAMES, ONE SERIES:
5 — Toronto Maple Leafs, Montreal Canadiens in 1951. Toronto won best-of-seven F 4-1.
— **Phoenix Coyotes, Chicago Blackhawks** in 2012. Phoenix won best-of-seven CQF 4-2.
— **Washington Capitals, Toronto Maple Leafs** in 2017. Washington won best-of-seven FR 4-2.
4 — Toronto Maple Leafs, Boston Bruins in 1933. Toronto won best-of-five SF 3-2.
— Boston Bruins, New York Rangers in 1939. Boston won best-of-seven SF 4-3.
— St. Louis Blues, Minnesota North Stars in 1968. St. Louis won best-of-seven SF 4-3.
— Dallas Stars, St. Louis Blues in 1999. Dallas won best-of-seven CSF 4-2.
— Dallas Stars, Edmonton Oilers in 2001. Dallas won best-of-seven CQF 4-2.
— Dallas Stars, San Jose Sharks in 2008. Dallas won best-of-seven CSF 4-2
— Washington Capitals, Boston Bruins in 2012. Washington won best-of-seven CQF 4-3
— Detroit Red Wings, Anaheim Ducks in 2013. Detroit won best-of-seven CQF 4-3
— Minnesota Wild, Colorado Avalanche in 2014. Minnesota won best-of-seven FR 4-3
— Chicago Blackhawks, St. Louis Blues in 2014. Chicago won best-of-seven FR 4-2
— Ottawa Senators, Boston Bruins in 2017. Ottawa won best-of-seven FR 4-2

TEAM HAT-TRICKS

MOST HAT-TRICKS, BY ALL TEAMS, ONE PLAYOFF YEAR:
12 — 1983 in 66 games.
— **1988** in 83 games.
11 — 1985 in 70 games.
— 1992 in 86 games.

MOST HAT-TRICKS, ONE TEAM, ONE PLAYOFF YEAR:
6 — Edmonton Oilers in 16 games, 1983.
— **Edmonton Oilers** in 18 games, 1985.

SHUTOUTS

MOST SHUTOUTS, ONE PLAYOFF YEAR, ALL TEAMS:
25 — 2002. Of 90 games played, Detroit had 6; Ottawa had 4; Carolina, Colorado, St. Louis and Toronto had 3 each; while Los Angeles, New Jersey and Philadelphia had 1 each.
23 — 2004. Of 89 games played, Tampa Bay and Calgary had 5 each; Toronto and San Jose had 3 each; while Boston, Colorado, Detroit, Montreal, Nashville, NY Islanders and Philadelphia had 1 each.
19 — 2001. Of 86 games played, Colorado and New Jersey had 4 each, Toronto had 3, Pittsburgh and Los Angeles had 2 each, while Buffalo, Washington, Detroit and San Jose had 1 each.

FEWEST SHUTOUTS, ONE PLAYOFF YEAR, ALL TEAMS:
0 — 1959. 18 games played.

MOST SHUTOUTS, BOTH TEAMS, ONE SERIES:
5 — Toronto Maple Leafs (3), Detroit Red Wings (2), in 1945. Toronto won best-of-seven F 4-3.
— **Toronto Maple Leafs (3), Detroit Red Wings (2),** in 1950. Detroit won best-of-seven SF 4-3.

TEAM PENALTIES

FEWEST PENALTIES, BOTH TEAMS, BEST-OF-SEVEN SERIES:
19 — Detroit Red Wings, Toronto Maple Leafs in 1945. Detroit received 10 minors, Toronto received 9 minors. Toronto won best-of-seven F 4-3.

FEWEST PENALTIES, ONE TEAM, BEST-OF-SEVEN SERIES:
9 — Toronto Maple Leafs in 1945 vs. Detroit. Toronto received 9 minors. Toronto won best-of-seven F 4-3.

MOST PENALTIES, BOTH TEAMS, ONE SERIES:
218 — New Jersey Devils, Washington Capitals in 1988. New Jersey received 97 minors, 11 majors, 9 misconducts and 1 match penalty. Washington received 80 minors, 11 majors, 8 misconducts and 1 match penalty. New Jersey won best-of-seven DF 4-3.

MOST PENALTY MINUTES, BOTH TEAMS, ONE SERIES:
654 — New Jersey Devils (349), Washington Capitals (305) in 1988. New Jersey won best-of-seven DF 4-3.

MOST PENALTIES, ONE TEAM, ONE SERIES:
118 — New Jersey Devils in 1988 vs. Washington. New Jersey received 97 minors, 11 majors, 9 misconducts and 1 match penalty. New Jersey won best-of-seven DF 4-3.

MOST PENALTY MINUTES, ONE TEAM, ONE SERIES:
349 — New Jersey Devils in 1988 vs. Washington. New Jersey won best-of-seven DF 4-3.

MOST PENALTIES, BOTH TEAMS, ONE GAME:
66 — Detroit Red Wings (33), St. Louis Blues (33), April 12, 1991, at St. Louis. St. Louis won 6-1.
63 — Minnesota North Stars (34), Chicago Blackhawks (29), April 6, 1990, at Chicago. Chicago won 5-3.
62 — New Jersey Devils (32), Washington Capitals (30), April 22, 1988, at New Jersey. New Jersey won 10-4.

MOST PENALTY MINUTES, BOTH TEAMS, ONE GAME:
298 — Detroit Red Wings (152), St. Louis Blues (146), April 12, 1991, at St. Louis. Detroit received 33 penalties; St. Louis received 33 penalties. St. Louis won 6-1.
267 — New York Rangers (142), Los Angeles Kings (125), April 9, 1981, at Los Angeles. NY Rangers received 31 penalties; Los Angeles received 28 penalties. Los Angeles won 5-4.

MOST PENALTIES, ONE TEAM, ONE GAME:
34 — Minnesota North Stars, April 6, 1990, at Chicago. Chicago won 5-3.
33 — Detroit Red Wings, April 12, 1991, at St. Louis. St. Louis won 6-1.
— St. Louis Blues, April 12, 1991, at St. Louis vs. Detroit. St. Louis won 6-1.

MOST PENALTY MINUTES, ONE TEAM, ONE GAME:
152 — Detroit Red Wings, April 12, 1991, at St. Louis. St. Louis won 6-1.
146 — St. Louis Blues, April 12, 1991, at St. Louis vs. Detroit. St. Louis won 6-1.
142 — New York Rangers, April 9, 1981, at Los Angeles. Los Angeles won 5-4.

MOST PENALTIES, BOTH TEAMS, ONE PERIOD:
43 — New York Rangers (24), Los Angeles Kings (19), April 9, 1981, first period at Los Angeles. Los Angeles won 5-4.

MOST PENALTY MINUTES, BOTH TEAMS, ONE PERIOD:
248 — New York Islanders (124), Boston Bruins (124), April 17, 1980, first period at Boston. NY Islanders won 5-4.

MOST PENALTIES, ONE TEAM, ONE PERIOD:
24 — New York Rangers, April 9, 1981, first period at Los Angeles. Los Angeles won 5-4.
— **Montreal Canadiens,** May 5, 2013, third period at Ottawa. Ottawa won 6-1.

MOST PENALTY MINUTES, ONE TEAM, ONE PERIOD:
125 — New York Rangers, April 9, 1981, first period at Los Angeles. Los Angeles won 5-4.

Individual Records

GAMES PLAYED

MOST YEARS IN PLAYOFFS:
24 — Chris Chelios, Montreal, Chicago, Detroit (1984-97 inclusive; 1999-2004 inclusive, 2006-2009 inclusive)
21 — Raymond Bourque, Boston, Colorado (1980-96 inclusive; 98-2001 inclusive)
20 — Gordie Howe, Detroit, Hartford
— Larry Robinson, Montreal, Los Angeles
— Larry Murphy, Los Angeles, Washington, Minnesota, Pittsburgh, Toronto, Detroit
— Scott Stevens, Washington, St. Louis, New Jersey
— Steve Yzerman, Detroit
— Nicklas Lidstrom, Detroit

MOST CONSECUTIVE YEARS IN PLAYOFFS:
20 — Larry Robinson, Montreal, Los Angeles (1973-92, inclusive).
— Nicklas Lidstrom, Detroit (1992-2004 inclusive; 2006-2012 inclusive)
19 — Brett Hull, Calgary, St. Louis, Dallas, Detroit (1986-2004, inclusive).
18 — Larry Murphy, Los Angeles, Washington, Minnesota, Pittsburgh, Toronto, Detroit (1984-2001, inclusive).
17 — Brad Park, NY Rangers, Boston, Detroit (1969-85, inclusive).
— Raymond Bourque, Boston (1980-96, inclusive).
— Kris Draper, Detroit (1994-2004 inclusive; 2006-2011 inclusive)

MOST PLAYOFF GAMES:
266 — Chris Chelios, Montreal, Chicago, Detroit
263 — Nicklas Lidstrom, Detroit
247 — Patrick Roy, Montreal, Colorado
236 — Mark Messier, Edmonton, NY Rangers
234 — Claude Lemieux, Montreal, New Jersey, Colorado, Phoenix, Dallas, San Jose

GOALS

MOST GOALS IN PLAYOFFS, CAREER:
122 — Wayne Gretzky, Edmonton, Los Angeles, St. Louis, NY Rangers
109 — Mark Messier, Edmonton, NY Rangers
106 — Jari Kurri, Edmonton, Los Angeles, NY Rangers, Anaheim
103 — Brett Hull, Calgary, St. Louis, Dallas, Detroit
93 — Glenn Anderson, Edmonton, Toronto, NY Rangers, St. Louis

MOST GOALS, ONE PLAYOFF YEAR:
19 — Reggie Leach, Philadelphia, 1976. 16 games.
— Jari Kurri, Edmonton, 1985. 18 games.
18 — Joe Sakic, Colorado, 1996. 22 games.
17 — Newsy Lalonde, Montreal, 1919. 10 games.
— Mike Bossy, NY Islanders, 1981. 18 games.
— Steve Payne, Minnesota, 1981. 19 games.
— Mike Bossy, NY Islanders, 1982. 19 games.
— Mike Bossy, NY Islanders, 1983. 19 games
— Wayne Gretzky, Edmonton, 1985. 18 games.
— Kevin Stevens, Pittsburgh, 1991. 24 games.

MOST GOALS IN ONE SERIES (OTHER THAN FINAL):
12 — Jari Kurri, Edmonton, in 1985 CF, 6 games vs. Chicago.
11 — Newsy Lalonde, Montreal, in 1919 NHL F, 5 games vs. Ottawa.
10 — Tim Kerr, Philadelphia, in 1989 DF, 7 games vs. Pittsburgh.
9 — Reggie Leach, Philadelphia, in 1976 SF, 5 games vs. Boston.
— Bill Barber, Philadelphia, in 1980 SF, 5 games vs. Minnesota.
— Mike Bossy, NY Islanders, in 1983 CF, 6 games vs. Boston.
— Mario Lemieux, Pittsburgh, in 1989 DF, 7 games vs. Philadelphia.
— John Druce, Washington, in 1990 DF, 5 games vs. NY Rangers.
— Johan Franzen, Detroit, in 2008 CSF, 4 games vs. Colorado.

MOST GOALS IN FINAL SERIES (NHL PLAYERS ONLY):
9 — Babe Dye, Toronto, in 1922, 5 games vs. Van. Millionaires.
8 — Alf Skinner, Toronto, in 1918, 5 games vs. Van. Millionaires.
7 — Jean Beliveau, Montreal, in 1956, 5 games vs. Detroit.
— Mike Bossy, NY Islanders, in 1982, 4 games vs. Vancouver.
— Wayne Gretzky, Edmonton, in 1985, 5 games vs. Philadelphia.

MOST GOALS, ONE GAME:
5 — Newsy Lalonde, Montreal, March 1, 1919, at Montreal. Final score: Montreal 6, Ottawa 3.
— Maurice Richard, Montreal, March 23, 1944, at Montreal. Final score: Montreal 5, Toronto 1.
— Darryl Sittler, Toronto, April 22, 1976, at Toronto. Final score: Toronto 8, Philadelphia 5.
— Reggie Leach, Philadelphia, May 6, 1976, at Philadelphia. Final score: Philadelphia 6, Boston 3.
— Mario Lemieux, Pittsburgh, April 25, 1989, at Pittsburgh. Final score: Pittsburgh 10, Philadelphia 7.

MOST GOALS, ONE PERIOD:
4 — Tim Kerr, Philadelphia, April 13, 1985, at NY Rangers, second period. Final score: Philadelphia 6, NY Rangers 5.
— Mario Lemieux, Pittsburgh, April 25, 1989, at Pittsburgh vs. Philadelphia, first period. Final score: Pittsburgh 10, Philadelphia 7.

ASSISTS

MOST ASSISTS IN PLAYOFFS, CAREER:
260 — Wayne Gretzky, Edmonton, Los Angeles, St. Louis, NY Rangers
186 — Mark Messier, Edmonton, NY Rangers
139 — Raymond Bourque, Boston, Colorado
137 — Paul Coffey, Edmonton, Pittsburgh, Los Angeles, Detroit, Philadelphia, Carolina
129 — Nicklas Lidstrom, Detroit

MOST ASSISTS, ONE PLAYOFF YEAR:
31 — Wayne Gretzky, Edmonton, 1988. 19 games.
30 — Wayne Gretzky, Edmonton, 1985. 18 games.
29 — Wayne Gretzky, Edmonton, 1987. 21 games.
28 — Mario Lemieux, Pittsburgh, 1991. 23 games.
26 — Wayne Gretzky, Edmonton, 1983. 16 games.

MOST ASSISTS IN ONE SERIES (OTHER THAN FINAL):
14 — Rick Middleton, Boston, in 1983 DF, 7 games vs. Buffalo.
— Wayne Gretzky, Edmonton, in 1985 CF, 6 games vs. Chicago.
13 — Wayne Gretzky, Edmonton, in 1987 DSF, 5 games vs. Los Angeles.
— Doug Gilmour, Toronto, in 1994 CSF, 7 games vs. San Jose.
11 — Al MacInnis, Calgary, in 1984 DF, 7 games vs. Edmonton.
— Mark Messier, Edmonton, in 1989 DF, 7 games vs. Los Angeles.
— Mike Ridley, Washington, in 1992 DSF, 7 games vs. Pittsburgh.
— Ron Francis, Pittsburgh, in 1995 CQF, 7 games vs. Washington.
— Henrik Sedin, Vancouver, in 2011 CF, 5 games vs. San Jose.

MOST ASSISTS IN FINAL SERIES:
10 — Wayne Gretzky, Edmonton, in 1988, 4 games plus suspended game vs. Boston.
9 — Jacques Lemaire, Montreal, in 1973, 6 games vs. Chicago.
— Wayne Gretzky, Edmonton, in 1987, 7 games vs. Philadelphia.
— Larry Murphy, Pittsburgh, in 1991, 6 games vs. Minnesota.
— Daniel Briere, Philadelphia, in 2010, 6 games vs. Chicago.

MOST ASSISTS, ONE GAME:
6 — Mikko Leinonen, NY Rangers, April 8, 1982, at NY Rangers. Final score: NY Rangers 7, Philadelphia 3.
— Wayne Gretzky, Edmonton, April 9, 1987, at Edmonton. Final score: Edmonton 13, Los Angeles 3.
5 — Toe Blake, Montreal, March 23, 1944, at Montreal. Final score: Montreal 5, Toronto 1.
— Maurice Richard, Montreal, March 27, 1956, at Montreal. Final score: Montreal 7, NY Rangers 0.
— Bert Olmstead, Montreal, March 30, 1957, at Montreal. Final score: Montreal 8, NY Rangers 3.
— Don McKenney, Boston, April 5, 1958, at Boston. Final score: Boston 8, NY Rangers 2.
— Stan Mikita, Chicago, April 4, 1973, at Chicago. Final score: Chicago 7, St. Louis 1.
— Wayne Gretzky, Edmonton, April 8, 1981, at Montreal. Final score: Edmonton 6, Montreal 3.
— Paul Coffey, Edmonton, May 14, 1985, at Edmonton. Final score: Edmonton 10, Chicago 5.
— Doug Gilmour, St. Louis, April 15, 1986, at Minnesota. Final score: St. Louis 6, Minnesota 3.
— Risto Siltanen, Quebec, April 14, 1987, at Hartford. Final score: Quebec 7, Hartford 5.
— Patrik Sundstrom, New Jersey, April 22, 1988, at New Jersey. Final score: New Jersey 10, Washington 4.
— Geoff Courtnall, St. Louis, April 23, 1998, at St. Louis. Final score: St. Louis 8, Los Angeles 3.

MOST ASSISTS, ONE PERIOD:
3 — Three assists by one player in one period of a playoff game has been recorded on 88 occasions. J.T. Miller of the New York Rangers is the most recent to equal this mark with 3 assists in the second period at Pittsburgh, April 16, 2016. Final score: NY Rangers 4, Pittsburgh 2.
— Wayne Gretzky has had 3 assists in one period 5 times; Raymond Bourque, 3 times; Toe Blake, Jean Beliveau, Doug Harvey and Bobby Orr, twice each. Joe Primeau of Toronto was the first player to be credited with 3 assists in one period of a playoff game; third period at Boston vs. NY Rangers, April 7, 1932. Final score: Toronto 6, NY Rangers 2.

POINTS

MOST POINTS IN PLAYOFFS, CAREER:
382 — Wayne Gretzky, Edmonton, Los Angeles, St. Louis, NY Rangers, 122G, 260A
295 — Mark Messier, Edmonton, NY Rangers, 109G, 186A
233 — Jari Kurri, Edmonton, Los Angeles, NY Rangers, Anaheim, 106G, 127A
214 — Glenn Anderson, Edmonton, Toronto, NY Rangers, St. Louis, 93G, 121A
201 — Jaromir Jagr, Pittsburgh, Washington, NY Rangers, Philadelphia, Boston, Florida, 78G, 123A

MOST POINTS, ONE PLAYOFF YEAR:
47 — Wayne Gretzky, Edmonton, in 1985. 17 goals, 30 assists in 18 games.
44 — Mario Lemieux, Pittsburgh, in 1991. 16 goals, 28 assists in 23 games.
43 — Wayne Gretzky, Edmonton, in 1988. 12 goals, 31 assists in 19 games.
40 — Wayne Gretzky, Los Angeles, in 1993. 15 goals, 25 assists in 24 games.
38 — Wayne Gretzky, Edmonton, in 1983. 12 goals, 26 assists in 16 games.

MOST POINTS IN ONE SERIES (OTHER THAN FINAL):
19 — Rick Middleton, Boston, in 1983 DF, 7 games vs. Buffalo. 5 goals, 14 assists.
18 — Wayne Gretzky, Edmonton, in 1985 CF, 6 games vs. Chicago. 4 goals, 14 assists.
17 — Mario Lemieux, Pittsburgh, in 1992 DSF, 6 games vs. Washington. 7 goals, 10 assists.
16 — Barry Pederson, Boston, in 1983 DF, 7 games vs. Buffalo. 7 goals, 9 assists.
— Doug Gilmour, Toronto, in 1994 CSF, 7 games vs. San Jose. 3 goals, 13 assists.
15 — Jari Kurri, Edmonton, in 1985 CF, 6 games vs. Chicago. 12 goals, 3 assists.
— Wayne Gretzky, Edmonton, in 1987 DSF, 5 games vs. Los Angeles. 2 goals, 13 assists.
— Tim Kerr, Philadelphia, in 1989 DF, 7 games vs. Pittsburgh. 10 goals, 5 assists.
— Mario Lemieux, Pittsburgh, in 1991 CF, 6 games vs. Boston. 6 goals, 9 assists.

MOST POINTS IN FINAL SERIES:
13 — Wayne Gretzky, Edmonton, in 1988, 4 games plus suspended game vs. Boston. 3 goals, 10 assists.
12 — Gordie Howe, Detroit, in 1955, 7 games vs. Montreal. 5 goals, 7 assists.
— Yvan Cournoyer, Montreal, in 1973, 6 games vs. Chicago. 6 goals, 6 assists.
— Jacques Lemaire, Montreal, in 1973, 6 games vs. Chicago. 3 goals, 9 assists.
— Mario Lemieux, Pittsburgh, in 1991, 5 games vs. Minnesota. 5 goals, 7 assists.
— Daniel Briere, Philadelphia, in 2010, 6 games vs. Chicago. 3 goals, 9 assists.

MOST POINTS, ONE GAME:
8 — Patrik Sundstrom, New Jersey, April 22, 1988, at New Jersey in 10-4 win over Washington. Sundstrom had 3 goals, 5 assists.
— **Mario Lemieux, Pittsburgh,** April 25, 1989, at Pittsburgh in 10-7 win over Philadelphia. Lemieux had 5 goals, 3 assists.
7 — Wayne Gretzky, Edmonton, April 17, 1983, at Calgary in 10-2 win. Gretzky had 4 goals, 3 assists.
— Wayne Gretzky, Edmonton, April 25,1985, at Winnipeg in 8-3 win. Gretzky had 3 goals, 4 assists.
— Wayne Gretzky, Edmonton, April 9, 1987, at Edmonton in 13-3 win over Los Angeles. Gretzky had 1 goal, 6 assists.
6 — Dickie Moore, Montreal, March 25, 1954, at Montreal in 8-1 win over Boston. Moore had 2 goals, 4 assists.
— Phil Esposito, Boston, April 2, 1969, at Boston in 10-0 win over Toronto. Esposito had 4 goals, 2 assists.
— Darryl Sittler, Toronto, April 22, 1976, at Toronto in 8-5 win over Philadelphia. Sittler had 5 goals, 1 assist.
— Guy Lafleur, Montreal, April 11, 1977, at Montreal in 7-2 win over St. Louis. Lafleur had 3 goals, 3 assists.
— Mikko Leinonen, NY Rangers, April 8, 1982, at NY Rangers in 7-3 win over Philadelphia. Leinonen had 6 assists.
— Paul Coffey, Edmonton, May 14, 1985, at Edmonton in 10-5 win over Chicago. Coffey had 1 goal, 5 assists.
— John Anderson, Hartford, April 12, 1986, at Hartford in 9-4 win over Quebec. Anderson had 2 goals, 4 assists.
— Mario Lemieux, Pittsburgh, April 23, 1992, at Pittsburgh in 6-4 win over Washington. Lemieux had 3 goals, 3 assists.
— Geoff Courtnall, St. Louis, April 23, 1998, at St. Louis in 8-3 win over Los Angeles. Courtnall had 1 goal, 5 assists.
— Patrick Elias, New Jersey, April 22, 2006, at New Jersey in 6-1 win over NY Rangers. Elias had 2 goals, 4 assists.
— Johan Franzen, Detroit, May 6, 2010, at Detroit in 7-1 win over San Jose. Franzen had 4 goals, 2 assists.
— Claude Giroux, Philadelphia, April 13, 2012, at Pittsburgh in 8-5 win. Giroux had 3 goals, 3 assists.

MOST POINTS, ONE PERIOD:
4 — Maurice Richard, Montreal, March 29, 1945, at Montreal, third period, in 10-3 win vs. Toronto. 3 goals, 1 assist.
— **Dickie Moore,** Montreal, March 25, 1954, at Montreal, first period, in 8-1 win vs. Boston. 2 goals, 2 assists.
— **Barry Pederson,** Boston, April 8, 1982, at Boston, second period, in 7-3 win vs. Buffalo. 3 goals, 1 assist.
— **Peter McNab,** Boston, April 11, 1982, at Buffalo, second period, in 5-2 win vs. Buffalo. 1 goal, 3 assists.
— **Tim Kerr,** Philadelphia, April 13, 1985, at NY Rangers, second period, in 6-5 win vs. NY Rangers. 4 goals.
— **Ken Linseman,** Boston, April 14, 1985, at Boston, second period, in 7-6 win vs. Montreal. 2 goals, 2 assists.
— **Wayne Gretzky,** Edmonton, April 12, 1987, at Los Angeles, third period, in 6-3 win vs. Los Angeles. 1 goal, 3 assists.
— **Glenn Anderson,** Edmonton, April 6, 1988, at Edmonton, third period, in 7-4 win vs. Winnipeg. 3 goals, 1 assist.
— **Mario Lemieux,** Pittsburgh, April 25, 1989, at Pittsburgh, first period, in 10-7 win vs. Philadelphia. 4 goals.
— **Dave Gagner,** Minnesota North Stars, April 8, 1991, at Minnesota, first period, in 6-5 loss vs. Chicago. 2 goals, 2 assists.
— **Mario Lemieux,** Pittsburgh, April 23, 1992, at Pittsburgh, second period, in 6-4 win vs. Washington. 2 goals, 2 assists.
— **Alexander Mogilny,** New Jersey, April 28, 2001, at New Jersey, second period, in 6-5 win vs. Toronto. 1 goal, 3 assists.
— **Brad Richards,** Dallas, April 27, 2008, at San Jose, third period, in 5-2 win vs. San Jose. 1 goal, 3 assists.
— **Johan Franzen,** Detroit, May 6, 2010, at Detroit, first period, in 7-1 win over San Jose. 3 goals, 1 assist.
— **Tyler Seguin,** Boston, May 17, 2011, at Boston, second period, in 6-5 win over Tampa Bay. 2 goals, 2 assists.
— **Jeff Carter,** Los Angeles, May 21, 2014, at Chicago, third period, in 6-2 win over Chicago. 3 goals, 1 assist.

POWER-PLAY GOALS

MOST POWER-PLAY GOALS IN PLAYOFFS, CAREER:
38 — Brett Hull, St. Louis, Dallas, Detroit
35 — Mike Bossy, NY Islanders
— Wayne Gretzky, Edmonton, Los Angeles, St. Louis, NY Rangers
34 — Dino Ciccarelli, Minnesota, Washington, Detroit
30 — Nicklas Lidstrom, Detroit

MOST POWER-PLAY GOALS, ONE PLAYOFF YEAR:
9 — Mike Bossy, NY Islanders, 1981. 18 games vs. Toronto, Edmonton, NY Rangers and Minnesota.
— **Cam Neely, Boston,** 1991. 19 games vs. Hartford, Montreal and Pittsburgh.
8 — Tim Kerr, Philadelphia, 1989. 19 games.
— John Druce, Washington, 1990. 15 games.
— Brian Propp, Minnesota, 1991. 23 games.
— Mario Lemieux, Pittsburgh, 1992. 15 games.

MOST POWER-PLAY GOALS, ONE PLAYOFF SERIES:
6 — Chris Kontos, Los Angeles, 1989 DSF vs. Edmonton, won by Los Angeles 4-3.
5 — Andy Bathgate, Detroit, 1966 SF vs. Chicago, won by Detroit 4-2.
— Denis Potvin, NY Islanders, 1981 QF vs. Edmonton, won by NY Islanders 4-2.
— Ken Houston, Calgary, 1981 QF vs. Philadelphia, won by Calgary 4-3.
— Rick Vaive, Chicago, 1988 DSF vs. St. Louis, won by St. Louis 4-1.
— Tim Kerr, Philadelphia, 1989 DF vs. Pittsburgh, won by Philadelphia 4-3.
— Mario Lemieux, Pittsburgh, 1989 DF vs. Philadelphia, won by Philadelphia 4-3.
— John Druce, Washington, 1990 DF vs. NY Rangers, won by Washington 4-1.
— Pat LaFontaine, Buffalo, 1992 DSF vs. Boston, won by Boston 4-3.
— Adam Graves, NY Rangers, 1996 CQF vs Montreal, won by NY Rangers 4-2.

MOST POWER-PLAY GOALS, ONE GAME:
3 — Syd Howe, Detroit, March 23, 1939, at Detroit vs. Montreal. Detroit won 7-3.
— **Sid Smith, Toronto,** April 10, 1949, at Detroit. Toronto won 3-1.
— **Phil Esposito, Boston,** April 2, 1969, at Boston vs. Toronto. Boston won 10-0.
— **John Bucyk, Boston,** April 21, 1974, at Boston vs. Chicago. Boston won 8-6.
— **Denis Potvin, NY Islanders,** April 17, 1981, at NY Islanders vs. Edmonton. NY Islanders won 6-3.
— **Tim Kerr, Philadelphia,** April 13, 1985, at NY Rangers. Philadelphia won 6-5.
— **Jari Kurri, Edmonton,** April 9, 1987, at Edmonton vs. Los Angeles. Edmonton won 13-3.
— **Mark Johnson, New Jersey,** April 22, 1988, at New Jersey vs. Washington. New Jersey won 10-4.
— **Dino Ciccarelli, Detroit,** April 29, 1993, at Toronto. Detroit won 7-3.
— **Dino Ciccarelli, Detroit,** May 11, 1995, at Dallas. Detroit won 5-1.
— **Valeri Kamensky, Colorado,** April 24, 1997, at Colorado vs. Chicago. Colorado won 7-0.
— **Jonathan Toews, Chicago** May 7, 2010, at Vancouver. Chicago won 7-4.

MOST POWER-PLAY GOALS, ONE PERIOD:
3 — Tim Kerr, Philadelphia, April 13, 1985, at NY Rangers, second period in 6-5 win.
2 — Two power-play goals have been scored by one player in one period on 64 occasions. Charlie Conacher of Toronto was the first to score two power-play goals in one period, setting the mark with two power-play goals in the second period at Toronto vs. Boston, March 26, 1936. Final score: Toronto 8, Boston 3. Jared Spurgeon of the Minnesota Wild is the most recent to equal this mark with two power-play goals in the third period vs. Dallas, April 24, 2016. Final score: Dallas 5, Minnesota 4.

SHORTHAND GOALS

MOST SHORTHAND GOALS IN PLAYOFFS, CAREER:
14 — Mark Messier, Edmonton, NY Rangers
12 — Wayne Gretzky, Edmonton, Los Angeles, St. Louis
10 — Jari Kurri, Edmonton, Los Angeles, NY Rangers
8 — Ed Westfall, Boston, NY Islanders
— Hakan Loob, Calgary

MOST SHORTHAND GOALS, ONE PLAYOFF YEAR:
3 — Derek Sanderson, Boston, 1969. 1 vs. Toronto in QF, won by Boston 4-0; 2 vs. Montreal in SF, won by Montreal, 4-2.
— **Bill Barber, Philadelphia,** 1980. All vs. Minnesota in SF, won by Philadelphia 4-1.
— **Lorne Henning, NY Islanders,** 1980. 1 vs. Boston in QF, won by NY Islanders 4-2; 1 vs. Buffalo in SF, won by NY Islanders 4-2, 1 vs. Philadelphia in F, won by NY Islanders 4-2.
— **Wayne Gretzky, Edmonton,** 1983. 2 vs. Winnipeg in DSF, won by Edmonton 3-0; 1 vs. Calgary in DF, won by Edmonton 4-1.
— **Wayne Presley, Chicago,** 1989. All vs. Detroit in DSF, won by Chicago 4-2.
— **Todd Marchant, Edmonton,** 1997. 1 vs. Dallas in CQF, won by Edmonton 4-3; 2 vs. Colorado in CSF, won by Colorado 4-1.

Phil Kessel scored five of his eight playoff goals in 2017 when Pittsburgh had a man advantage, giving him the most power-play goals in the postseason after tying Joe Pavelski for the lead with five in 2016.

MOST SHORTHAND GOALS, ONE PLAYOFF SERIES:

3 — **Bill Barber, Philadelphia,** 1980 SF vs. Minnesota, won by Philadelphia 4-1.
— **Wayne Presley, Chicago,** 1989 DSF vs. Detroit, won by Chicago 4-2.
2 — Mac Colville, NY Rangers, 1940 SF vs. Boston, won by NY Rangers 4-2.
— Jerry Toppazzini, Boston, 1958 SF vs. NY Rangers, won by Boston 4-2.
— Dave Keon, Toronto, 1963 F vs. Detroit, won by Toronto 4-1.
— Bob Pulford, Toronto, 1964 F vs. Detroit, won by Toronto 4-3.
— Serge Savard, Montreal, 1968 F vs. St. Louis, won by Montreal 4-0.
— Derek Sanderson, Boston, 1969 SF vs. Montreal, won by Montreal 4-2.
— Bryan Trottier, NY Islanders, 1980 PR vs. Los Angeles, won by NY Islanders 3-1.
— Bobby Lalonde, Boston, 1981 PR vs. Minnesota, won by Minnesota 3-0.
— Butch Goring, NY Islanders, 1981 SF vs. NY Rangers, won by NY Islanders 4-0.
— Wayne Gretzky, Edmonton, 1983 DSF vs. Winnipeg, won by Edmonton 3-0.
— Mark Messier, Edmonton, 1983 DF vs. Calgary, won by Edmonton 4-1.
— Jari Kurri, Edmonton, 1983 CF vs. Chicago, won by Edmonton 4-0.
— Wayne Gretzky, Edmonton, 1985 DF vs. Winnipeg, won by Edmonton 4-0.
— Kevin Lowe, Edmonton, 1987 F vs. Philadelphia, won by Edmonton 4-3.
— Bob Gould, Washington, 1988 DSF vs. Philadelphia, won by Washington 4-3.
— Dave Poulin, Philadelphia, 1989 DF vs. Pittsburgh, won by Philadelphia 4-3.
— Russ Courtnall, Montreal, 1991 DF vs. Boston, won by Boston 4-3.
— Sergei Fedorov, Detroit, 1992 DSF vs. Minnesota, won by Detroit 4-3.
— Mark Messier, NY Rangers, 1992 DSF vs. New Jersey, won by NY Rangers 4-3.
— Tom Fitzgerald, NY Islanders, 1993 DF vs. Pittsburgh, won by NY Islanders 4-3.
— Mark Osborne, Toronto, 1994 CSF vs. San Jose, won by Toronto 4-3.
— Tony Amonte, Chicago, 1997 CQF vs. Colorado, won by Colorado 4-2.
— Brian Rolston, New Jersey, 1997 CQF vs. Montreal, won by New Jersey 4-1.
— Rod Brind'Amour, Philadelphia, 1997 CQF vs. Pittsburgh, won by Philadelphia 4-1.
— Todd Marchant, Edmonton, 1997 CSF vs. Colorado, won by Colorado 4-1.
— Jeremy Roenick, Phoenix, 1998 CQF vs. Detroit, won by Detroit 4-2.
— Vincent Damphousse, San Jose, 1999 CQF vs. Colorado, won by Colorado 4-2.
— Dixon Ward, Buffalo, 1999 CF vs. Toronto, won by Buffalo 4-1.
— Curtis Brown, Buffalo, 2001 CSF vs. Pittsburgh, won by Pittsburgh 4-3.
— John Madden, New Jersey, 2006 CQF vs. NY Rangers, won by New Jersey 4-0.
— David Legwand, Nashville, 2011 CSF vs. Vancouver, won by Vancouver 4-2.
— Maxime Talbot, Philadelphia, 2012 CQF vs. Pittsburgh, won by Philadelphia 4-2.
— Dustin Brown, Los Angeles, 2012 CQF vs. Vancouver, won by Los Angeles 4-1.
— Pascal Dupuis, Pittsburgh, 2013 CSF vs. Ottawa, won by Pittsburgh 4-1.

MOST SHORTHAND GOALS, ONE GAME:

2 — **Dave Keon, Toronto,** April 18, 1963, at Toronto, in 3-1 win vs. Detroit.
— **Bryan Trottier, NY Islanders,** April 8, 1980, at NY Islanders, in 8-1 win vs. Los Angeles.
— **Bobby Lalonde, Boston,** April 11, 1981, at Minnesota, in 6-3 loss vs. Minnesota.
— **Wayne Gretzky, Edmonton,** April 6, 1983, at Edmonton, in 6-3 win vs. Winnipeg.
— **Jari Kurri, Edmonton,** April 24, 1983, at Edmonton, in 8-3 win vs. Chicago.
— **Wayne Gretzky, Edmonton,** April 25, 1985, at Winnipeg, in 8-3 win by Edmonton.
— **Mark Messier, NY Rangers,** April 21, 1992, at NY Rangers, in 7-3 loss vs. New Jersey.
— **Tom Fitzgerald, NY Islanders,** May 8, 1993, at NY Islanders, in 6-5 win vs. Pittsburgh.
— **Rod Brind'Amour, Philadelphia,** April 26, 1997, at Philadelphia, in 6-3 win vs. Pittsburgh.
— **Jeremy Roenick, Phoenix,** April 24, 1998, at Detroit, in 7-4 win by Phoenix.
— **Vincent Damphousse, San Jose,** April 30, 1999, at Colorado, in 7-3 win by San Jose.
— **John Madden, New Jersey,** April 24, 2006, at New Jersey, in 4-1 win vs. NY Rangers.
— **Dustin Brown, Los Angeles,** April 13, 2012, at Vancouver, in 4-2 win vs. Vancouver.

MOST SHORTHAND GOALS, ONE PERIOD:

2 — **Bryan Trottier, NY Islanders,** April 8, 1980, second period, at NY Islanders, in 8-1 win vs. Los Angeles.
— **Bobby Lalonde, Boston,** April 11, 1981, third period, at Minnesota, in 6-3 loss vs. Minnesota.
— **Jari Kurri, Edmonton,** April 24, 1983, third period, at Edmonton, in 8-4 win vs. Chicago.
— **Rod Brind'Amour, Philadelphia,** April 26, 1997, first period, at Philadelphia, in 6-3 win vs. Pittsburgh.
— **Jeremy Roenick, Phoenix,** April 24, 1998, second period, at Detroit, in 7-4 win by Phoenix.
— **Vincent Damphousse, San Jose,** April 30, 1999, third period, at Colorado, in 7-3 win vs. Colorado.

GAME-WINNING GOALS

MOST GAME-WINNING GOALS IN PLAYOFFS, CAREER:

24 — **Wayne Gretzky, Edmonton, Los Angeles, St. Louis, NY Rangers**
— **Brett Hull, St. Louis, Dallas, Detroit**
19 — Claude Lemieux, Montreal, New Jersey, Colorado
— Joe Sakic, Colorado
18 — Maurice Richard, Montreal

MOST GAME-WINNING GOALS, ONE PLAYOFF YEAR:

7 — **Brad Richards, Tampa Bay,** 2004. 23 games.
6 — Joe Sakic, Colorado, 1996. 22 games.
— Joe Nieuwendyk, Dallas, 1999. 23 games.
5 — Mike Bossy, NY Islanders, 1983. 19 games.
— Jari Kurri, Edmonton, 1987. 21 games.
— Bobby Smith, Minnesota, 1991. 23 games.
— Mario Lemieux, Pittsburgh, 1992. 15 games.
— Fernando Pisani, Edmonton, 2006. 24 games.
— Johan Franzen, Detroit, 2008. 16 games.
— Dustin Byfuglien, Chicago, 2010. 22 games.
— Jake Guentzel, Pittsburgh, 2017. 25 games.

MOST GAME-WINNING GOALS, ONE PLAYOFF SERIES:

4 — **Mike Bossy, NY Islanders,** 1983 CF vs. Boston, won by NY Islanders 4-2.

OVERTIME GOALS

MOST OVERTIME GOALS IN PLAYOFFS, CAREER:

8 — **Joe Sakic, Colorado** (2 in 1996; 1 in 1998; 1 in 2001; 2 in 2004; 1 in 2006; 1 in 2008)
6 — Maurice Richard, Montreal
5 — Glenn Anderson, Edmonton, Toronto, St. Louis
— Patrick Kane, Chicago
4 — Bob Nystrom, NY Islanders
— Dale Hunter, Quebec, Washington
— Wayne Gretzky, Edmonton, Los Angeles
— Stephane Richer, Montreal, New Jersey
— Joe Murphy, Edmonton, Chicago
— Esa Tikkanen, Edmonton, NY Rangers
— Jaromir Jagr, Pittsburgh
— Kirk Muller, Montreal, Dallas
— Jeremy Roenick, Chicago, Philadelphia
— Chris Drury, Colorado, Buffalo
— Jamie Langenbrunner, Dallas, New Jersey
— Patrick Marleau, San Jose
— Martin St. Louis, Tampa Bay, NY Rangers
— Corey Perry, Anaheim

MOST OVERTIME GOALS, ONE PLAYOFF YEAR:

3 — **Mel Hill, Boston,** 1939. All vs. NY Rangers in best-of-seven SF, won by Boston 4-3.
— **Maurice Richard, Montreal,** 1951. 2 vs. Detroit in best-of-seven SF, won by Montreal 4-2; 1 vs. Toronto in best-of-seven F, won by Toronto 4-1.
— **Corey Perry, Anaheim,** 2017. 1 vs. Calgary in best-of-seven FR, won by Anaheim 4-0; 1 vs. Edmonton in best-of-seven SR, won by Anaheim 4-3; 1 vs. Nashville in best-of-seven CF, won by Nashville 4-2.

MOST OVERTIME GOALS, ONE PLAYOFF SERIES:

3 — **Mel Hill, Boston,** 1939, SF vs. NY Rangers, won by Boston 4-3. Hill scored at 59:25 of overtime March 21 for a 2-1 win; at 8:24 of overtime, March 23 for a 3-2 win; and at 48:00 of overtime, April 2 for a 2-1 win.

SCORING BY A DEFENSEMAN

MOST GOALS BY A DEFENSEMAN, ONE PLAYOFF YEAR:

12 — **Paul Coffey, Edmonton,** 1985. 18 games.
11 — Brian Leetch, NY Rangers, 1994. 23 games.
9 — Bobby Orr, Boston, 1970. 14 games.
— Brad Park, Boston, 1978. 15 games.
8 — Denis Potvin, NY Islanders, 1981. 18 games.
— Raymond Bourque, Boston, 1983. 17 games.
— Denis Potvin, NY Islanders, 1983. 20 games.
— Paul Coffey, Edmonton, 1984. 19 games.

MOST GOALS BY A DEFENSEMAN, ONE GAME:

3 — **Bobby Orr, Boston,** April 11, 1971, at Montreal. Final score: Boston 5, Montreal 2.
— **Dick Redmond, Chicago,** April 4, 1973, at Chicago. Final score: Chicago 7, St. Louis 1.
— **Denis Potvin, NY Islanders,** April 17, 1981, at NY Islanders. Final score: NY Islanders 6, Edmonton 3.
— **Paul Reinhart, Calgary,** April 14, 1983, at Edmonton. Final score: Edmonton 6, Calgary 3.
— **Doug Halward, Vancouver,** April 7, 1984, at Vancouver. Final score: Vancouver 7, Calgary 0.
— **Paul Reinhart, Calgary,** April 8, 1984, at Vancouver. Final score: Calgary 5, Vancouver 1.
— **Al Iafrate, Washington,** April 26, 1993, at Washington. Final score: Washington 6, NY Islanders 4.
— **Eric Desjardins, Montreal,** June 3, 1993, at Montreal. Final score: Montreal 3, Los Angeles 2.
— **Gary Suter, Chicago,** April 24, 1994, at Chicago. Final score: Chicago 4, Toronto 3.
— **Brian Leetch, NY Rangers,** May 22, 1995, at Philadelphia. Final score: Philadelphia 4, NY Rangers 3.
— **Andy Delmore, Philadelphia,** May 7, 2000, at Philadelphia. Final score: Philadelphia 6, Pittsburgh 3.

MOST ASSISTS BY A DEFENSEMAN, ONE PLAYOFF YEAR:

25 — **Paul Coffey, Edmonton,** 1985. 18 games.
24 — Al MacInnis, Calgary, 1989. 22 games.
23 — Brian Leetch, NY Rangers, 1994. 23 games.
19 — Bobby Orr, Boston, 1972. 15 games.
18 — Raymond Bourque, Boston, 1988. 23 games.
— Raymond Bourque, Boston, 1991. 19 games.
— Larry Murphy, Pittsburgh, 1991. 23 games.
— Chris Pronger, Philadelphia, 2010. 23 games.
— Duncan Keith, Chicago, 2015. 23 games.

MOST ASSISTS BY A DEFENSEMAN, ONE GAME:
5 — Paul Coffey, Edmonton, May 14, 1985, at Edmonton vs. Chicago. Edmonton won 10-5.
— **Risto Siltanen, Quebec,** April 14, 1987, at Hartford. Quebec won 7-5.

MOST POINTS BY A DEFENSEMAN, ONE PLAYOFF YEAR:
37 — Paul Coffey, Edmonton, 1985. 12 goals, 25 assists in 18 games.
34 — Brian Leetch, NY Rangers, 1994. 11 goals, 23 assists in 23 games.
31 — Al MacInnis, Calgary, 1989. 7 goals, 24 assists in 22 games.
25 — Denis Potvin, NY Islanders, 1981. 8 goals, 17 assists in 18 games.
— Raymond Bourque, Boston, 1991. 7 goals, 18 assists in 19 games.

MOST POINTS BY A DEFENSEMAN, ONE GAME:
6 — Paul Coffey, Edmonton, May 14, 1985, at Edmonton vs. Chicago. 1 goal, 5 assists. Edmonton won 10-5.
5 — Eddie Bush, Detroit, April 9, 1942, at Detroit vs. Toronto. 1 goal, 4 assists. Detroit won 5-2.
— Bob Dailey, Philadelphia, May 1, 1980, at Philadelphia vs. Minnesota. 1 goal, 4 assists. Philadelphia won 7-0.
— Denis Potvin, NY Islanders, April 17, 1981, at NY Islanders vs. Edmonton. 3 goals, 2 assists. NY Islanders won 6-3.
— Risto Siltanen, Quebec, April 14, 1987, at Hartford. 5 assists. Quebec won 7-5.

SCORING BY A ROOKIE

MOST GOALS BY A ROOKIE, ONE PLAYOFF YEAR:
14 — Dino Ciccarelli, Minnesota, 1981. 19 games.
13 — Jake Guentzel, Pittsburgh, 2017. 25 games.
11 — Jeremy Roenick, Chicago, 1990. 20 games.
— Brad Marchand, Boston, 2011. 25 games.
10 — Claude Lemieux, Montreal, 1986. 20 games.

MOST ASSISTS BY A ROOKIE, ONE PLAYOFF YEAR:
14 — Ville Leino, Philadelphia, 2010. 19 games.
13 — Don Maloney, NY Rangers, 1979. 18 games.

MOST POINTS BY A ROOKIE, ONE PLAYOFF YEAR:
21 — Dino Ciccarelli, Minnesota, 1981. 14 goals, 7 assists in 19 games.
— **Ville Leino, Philadelphia,** 2010. 7 goals, 14 assists in 19 games.
— **Jake Guentzel, Pittsburgh,** 2017. 13 goals, 8 assists in 25 games.
20 — Don Maloney, NY Rangers, 1979. 7 goals, 13 assists in 18 games.

THREE-OR-MORE-GOAL GAMES

MOST THREE-OR-MORE-GOAL GAMES IN PLAYOFFS, CAREER:
10 — Wayne Gretzky, Edmonton, Los Angeles, NY Rangers. Eight three-goal games; two four-goal games.
7 — Maurice Richard, Montreal. Four three-goal games; two four-goal games; one five-goal game.
— Jari Kurri, Edmonton. Six three-goal games; one four-goal game.
6 — Dino Ciccarelli, Minnesota, Washington, Detroit. Five three-goal games; one four-goal game.
5 — Mike Bossy, NY Islanders. Four three-goal games; one four-goal game.

MOST THREE-OR-MORE-GOAL GAMES, ONE PLAYOFF YEAR:
4 — Jari Kurri, Edmonton, 1985. 1 four-goal game, 3 three-goal games.
3 — Mark Messier, Edmonton, 1983. 3 three-goal games.
— Mike Bossy, NY Islanders, 1983. 1 four-goal game, 2 three-goal games
2 — Newsy Lalonde, Montreal, 1919. 1 five-goal game, 1 four-goal game.
— Maurice Richard, Montreal, 1944. 1 five-goal game; 1 three-goal game.
— Doug Bentley, Chicago, 1944. 2 three-goal games.
— Norm Ullman, Detroit, 1964. 2 three-goal games.
— Phil Esposito, Boston, 1970. 2 three-goal games.
— Pit Martin, Chicago, 1973. 2 three-goal games.
— Rick MacLeish, Philadelphia, 1975. 2 three-goal games.
— Lanny McDonald, Toronto, 1977. 1 four-goal game; 1 three-goal game.
— Wayne Gretzky, Edmonton, 1981. 2 three-goal games.
— Wayne Gretzky, Edmonton, 1983. 2 four-goal games.
— Wayne Gretzky, Edmonton, 1985. 2 three-goal games.
— Petr Klima, Detroit, 1988. 2 three-goal games.
— Cam Neely, Boston, 1991. 2 three-goal games.
— Wayne Gretzky, NY Rangers, 1997. 2 three-goal games.
— Daniel Alfredsson, Ottawa, 1998. 2 three-goal games.
— Patrick Marleau, San Jose, 2004. 2 three-goal games.
— Johan Franzen, Detroit, 2008. 2 three-goal games.

MOST THREE-OR-MORE-GOAL GAMES, ONE PLAYOFF SERIES:
3 — Jari Kurri, Edmonton, 1985 CF vs. Chicago, won by Edmonton 4-2. Kurri scored 3 goals May 7 at Edmonton in 7-3 win, 3 goals May 14 at Edmonton in 10-5 win and 4 goals May 16 at Chicago in 8-2 win.
2 — Doug Bentley, Chicago, 1944 SF vs. Detroit, won by Chicago 4-1. Bentley scored 3 goals March 28 at Chicago in 7-1 win and 3 goals March 30 at Detroit in 5-2 win.
— Norm Ullman, Detroit, 1964 SF vs. Chicago, won by Detroit 4-3. Ullman scored 3 goals March 29 at Chicago in 5-4 win and 3 goals April 7 at Detroit in 7-2 win.
— Mark Messier, Edmonton, 1983 DF vs. Calgary, won by Edmonton 4-1. Messier scored 4 goals April 14 at Edmonton in 6-3 win and 3 goals April 17 at Calgary in 10-2 win.
— Mike Bossy, NY Islanders, 1983 CF vs. Boston, won by NY Islanders 4-2. Bossy scored 3 goals May 3 at NY Islanders in 8-3 win and 4 goals May 7 at New York in 8-4 win.
— Johan Franzen, Detroit, 2008 CSF vs. Colorado, won by Detroit 4-0. Franzen scored 3 goals Apr. 26 at Detroit in 5-1 win and 3 goals May 1 at Colorado in 8-2 win.

SCORING STREAKS

LONGEST CONSECUTIVE GOAL-SCORING STREAK, ONE PLAYOFF YEAR:
10 Games — Reggie Leach, Philadelphia, 1976. Streak started April 17 at Toronto and ended May 9 at Montreal. He scored one goal in each of eight games; two in one game; and five in another; a total of 15 goals.

LONGEST CONSECUTIVE POINT-SCORING STREAK, ONE PLAYOFF YEAR:
18 games — Bryan Trottier, NY Islanders, 1981. 11 goals, 18 assists, 29 points.
17 games — Wayne Gretzky, Edmonton, 1988. 12 goals, 29 assists, 41 points.
— Al MacInnis, Calgary, 1989. 7 goals, 19 assists, 26 points.

LONGEST CONSECUTIVE POINT-SCORING STREAK, MORE THAN ONE PLAYOFF YEAR:
27 games — Bryan Trottier, NY Islanders, 1980, 1981 and 1982. 7 games in 1980 (3 goals, 5 assists, 8 points), 18 games in 1981 (11 goals, 18 assists, 29 points), and two games in 1982 (2 goals, 3 assists, 5 points). Total points, 42.
19 games — Wayne Gretzky, Edmonton, Los Angeles, 1988 and 1989. 17 games in 1988 (12 goals, 29 assists, 41 points with Edmonton), 2 games in 1989 (1 goal, 2 assists, 3 points with Los Angeles). Total points, 44.
— Al MacInnis, Calgary, 1989 and 1990. 17 games in 1989 (7 goals, 19 assists, 26 points), and two games in 1990 (2 goals, 1 assist, 3 points). Total points, 29.

FASTEST GOALS

FASTEST GOAL FROM START OF GAME:
0:06 — Don Kozak, Los Angeles, April 17, 1977, at Los Angeles vs. Boston and goaltender Gerry Cheevers. Los Angeles won 7-4.
0:07 — Bob Gainey, Montreal, May 5, 1977, at NY Islanders vs. goaltender Glenn Resch. Montreal won 2-1.
— Terry Murray, Philadelphia, April 12, 1981, at Quebec vs. goaltender Dan Bouchard. Quebec won 4-3 in overtime.

FASTEST GOAL FROM START OF PERIOD (OTHER THAN FIRST):
0:06 — Pelle Eklund, Philadelphia, April 25, 1989, at Pittsburgh vs. goaltender Tom Barrasso, second period. Pittsburgh won 10-7.
0:08 — Tomas Jurco, Detroit, April 16, 2015, at Tampa Bay vs. goaltender Ben Bishop, second period. Detroit won 3-2.
0:09 — Bill Collins, Minnesota, April 9, 1968, at Minnesota vs. Los Angeles and goaltender Wayne Rutledge, third period. Minnesota won 7-5.
— Dave Balon, Minnesota, April 25, 1968, at St. Louis vs. goaltender Glenn Hall, third period. Minnesota won 5-1.
— Murray Oliver, Minnesota, April 8, 1971, at St. Louis vs. goaltender Ernie Wakely, third period. St. Louis won 4-2.
— Clark Gillies, NY Islanders, April 15, 1977, at Buffalo vs. goaltender Don Edwards, third period. NY Islanders won 4-3.
— Eric Vail, Atlanta, April 11, 1978, at Atlanta vs. Detroit and goaltender Ron Low, third period. Detroit won 5-3.
— Stan Smyl, Vancouver, April 10, 1979, at Philadelphia vs. goaltender Wayne Stephenson, third period. Vancouver won 3-2.
— Wayne Gretzky, Edmonton, April 6, 1983, at Edmonton vs. Winnipeg and goaltender Brian Hayward, second period. Edmonton won 6-3.
— Mark Messier, Edmonton, April 16, 1984, at Calgary vs. goaltender Don Edwards, third period. Edmonton won 5-3.
— Brian Skrudland, Montreal, May 18, 1986, at Calgary vs. goaltender Mike Vernon, first overtime period. Montreal won 3-2.

FASTEST TWO GOALS:
0:05 — Norm Ullman, Detroit, April 11, 1965, at Detroit vs. Chicago and goaltender Glenn Hall. Ullman scored at 17:35 and 17:40 of second period. Detroit won 4-2.

FASTEST TWO GOALS FROM START OF A GAME:
1:08 — Dick Duff, Toronto, April 9, 1963, at Toronto vs. Detroit and goaltender Terry Sawchuk. Duff scored at 0:49 and 1:08. Toronto won 4-2.

FASTEST TWO GOALS FROM START OF A PERIOD:
0:35 — Pat LaFontaine, NY Islanders, May 19, 1984, at Edmonton vs. goaltender Andy Moog. LaFontaine scored at 0:13 and 0:35 of third period. Edmonton won 5-2.

PENALTIES

MOST PENALTY MINUTES IN PLAYOFFS, CAREER:
731 — Dale Hunter, Quebec, Washington, Colorado
541 — Chris Nilan, Montreal, NY Rangers, Boston
529 — Claude Lemieux, Montreal, New Jersey, Colorado, Phoenix, Dallas
471 — Rick Tocchet, Philadelphia, Pittsburgh, Boston, Phoenix
466 — Willi Plett, Atlanta, Calgary, Minnesota, Boston

MOST PENALTIES, ONE GAME:
8 — Forbes Kennedy, Toronto, April 2, 1969, at Boston. Kennedy was assessed 4 minors, 2 majors, 1 10-minute misconduct, and 1 game misconduct. Boston won 10-0.
— **Kim Clackson, Pittsburgh,** April 14, 1980, at Boston. Clackson was assessed 5 minors, 2 majors, and 1 10-minute misconduct. Boston won 6-2.

MOST PENALTY MINUTES, ONE GAME:
42 — Dave Schultz, Philadelphia, April 22, 1976, at Toronto. Schultz was assessed 1 minor, 2 majors, 1 10-minute misconduct, and 2 game-misconducts. Toronto won 8-5.
— **Derek Engelland, Calgary,** April 17, 2015, at Vancouver. Engelland was assessed 1 minor, 2 majors, and 3 game-misconducts. Vancouver won 4-1.

MOST PENALTIES, ONE PERIOD:
6 — **Ed Hospodar, NY Rangers,** April 9, 1981, at Los Angeles, first period. Hospodar was assessed 2 minors, 1 major, 1 10-minute misconduct, and 2 game misconducts. Los Angeles won 5-4.
— **Deryk Engelland, Calgary,** April 17, 2015, at Vancouver, third period. Engelland was assessed 1 minor, 2 majors, and 3 game misconducts. Vancouver won 4-1.

MOST PENALTY MINUTES, ONE PERIOD:
42 — **Deryk Engelland, Calgary,** April 17, 2015, at Vancouver, third period. Engelland was assessed 1 minor, 2 majors, and 3 game misconducts. Vancouver won 4-1.

39 — Ed Hospodar, NY Rangers, April 9, 1981, at Los Angeles, first period. Hospodar was assessed 2 minors, 1 major, 1 10-minute misconduct, and 2 game misconducts. Los Angeles won 5-4.

GOALTENDING

MOST PLAYOFF GAMES APPEARED IN BY A GOALTENDER, CAREER:
247 — **Patrick Roy, Montreal, Colorado**
205 — Martin Brodeur, New Jersey
161 — Ed Belfour, Chicago, Dallas, Toronto
150 — Grant Fuhr, Edmonton, Buffalo, St. Louis
138 — Mike Vernon, Calgary, Detroit, San Jose, Florida

MOST MINUTES PLAYED BY A GOALTENDER, CAREER:
15,209 — **Patrick Roy, Montreal, Colorado**
12,719 — Martin Brodeur, New Jersey
9,945 — Ed Belfour, Chicago, Dallas, Toronto
8,834 — Grant Fuhr, Edmonton, Buffalo, St. Louis
8,214 — Mike Vernon, Calgary, Detroit, San Jose, Florida

MOST MINUTES PLAYED BY A GOALTENDER, ONE PLAYOFF YEAR:
1,655 — **Miikka Kiprusoff, Calgary,** 2004. 26 games.
1,605 — Jonathan Quick, Los Angeles, 2014. 26 games.
1,544 — Kirk McLean, Vancouver, 1994. 24 games.
— Ed Belfour, Dallas, 1999. 23 games.
1,542 — Tim Thomas, Boston, 2011. 25 games.

MOST SHUTOUTS IN PLAYOFFS, CAREER:
24 — **Martin Brodeur, New Jersey**
23 — Patrick Roy, Montreal, Colorado
16 — Curtis Joseph, St. Louis, Edmonton, Toronto, Detroit

MOST SHUTOUTS, ONE PLAYOFF YEAR:
7 — **Martin Brodeur, New Jersey,** 2003. 24 games.
6 — Dominik Hasek, Detroit, 2002. 23 games.
5 — Jean-Sebastien Giguere, Anaheim, 2003. 21 games.
— Nikolai Khabibulin, Tampa Bay, 2004. 23 games.
— Miikka Kiprusoff, Calgary, 2004. 26 games.

MOST SHUTOUTS, ONE PLAYOFF SERIES:
3 — **Clint Benedict, Mtl. Maroons,** 1926 F vs. Victoria. 4 games.
— **Dave Kerr, NY Rangers,** 1940 SF vs. Boston. 6 games.
— **Frank McCool, Toronto,** 1945 F vs. Detroit. 7 games.
— **Turk Broda, Toronto,** 1950 SF vs. Detroit. 7 games.
— **Felix Potvin, Toronto,** 1994 CQF vs. Chicago. 6 games.
— **Martin Brodeur, New Jersey,** 1995 CQF vs. Boston. 5 games.
— **Brent Johnson, St. Louis,** 2002 CQF vs. Chicago. 5 games.
— **Patrick Lalime, Ottawa,** 2002 CQF vs. Philadelphia. 5 games.
— **Jean-Sebastien Giguere, Anaheim,** 2003 CF vs. Minnesota. 4 games.
— **Martin Brodeur, New Jersey,** 2003 F vs. Anaheim. 7 games.
— **Ed Belfour, Toronto,** 2004 CQF vs. Ottawa. 7 games.
— **Nikolai Khabibulin, Tampa Bay,** 2004 CQF vs. NY Islanders. 5 games.
— **Marty Turco, Dallas,** 2007 CQF vs. Vancouver. 7 games.
— **Michael Leighton, Philadelphia,** 2010 CF vs. Montreal. 5 games.

MOST WINS BY A GOALTENDER, CAREER:
151 — **Patrick Roy, Montreal, Colorado**
113 — Martin Brodeur, New Jersey
92 — Grant Fuhr, Edmonton, Buffalo, St. Louis
88 — Billy Smith, NY Islanders
— Ed Belfour, Chicago, Dallas, Toronto

MOST WINS BY A GOALTENDER, ONE PLAYOFF YEAR:
16 — **Sixteen wins** by a goaltender in one playoff year has been recorded on 22 occasions. Jonathan Quick of the Los Angeles Kings is the most recent to equal this mark, posting a record of 16 wins and 10 losses in 2014. It was first accomplished by Grant Fuhr in 1988.

MOST CONSECUTIVE WINS BY A GOALTENDER,
MORE THAN ONE PLAYOFF YEAR:
14 — **Tom Barrasso, Pittsburgh,** 1992, 1993; 3 wins vs. NY Rangers in 1992 DF, won by Pittsburgh 4-2; 4 wins vs. Boston in 1992 CF, won by Pittsburgh 4-0; 4 wins vs. Chicago in 1992 F, won by Pittsburgh 4-0; 3 wins vs. New Jersey in 1993 DSF, won by Pittsburgh 4-1.

MOST CONSECUTIVE WINS BY A GOALTENDER, ONE PLAYOFF YEAR:
11 — **Ed Belfour, Chicago,** 1992. 3 wins vs. St. Louis in DSF, won by Chicago 4-2; 4 wins vs. Detroit in DF, won by Chicago 4-0; and 4 wins vs. Edmonton in CF, won by Chicago 4-0.
— **Tom Barrasso, Pittsburgh,** 1992. 3 wins vs. NY Rangers in DF, won by Pittsburgh 4-2; 4 wins vs. Boston in CF, won by Pittsburgh 4-0; and 4 wins vs. Chicago in F, won by Pittsburgh 4-0.
— **Patrick Roy, Montreal,** 1993. 4 wins vs. Quebec in DSF, won by Montreal 4-2; 4 wins vs. Buffalo in DF, won by Montreal 4-0; and 3 wins vs. NY Islanders in CF, won by Montreal 4-1.

LONGEST SHUTOUT SEQUENCE:
270:08 — **George Hainsworth,** Montreal, 1930. Hainsworth's shutout streak began after Murray Murdoch scored a goal for the NY Rangers at 15:34 of the first period in the first game of a SF series on March 28, 1930. Hainsworth did not allow another goal in the final 113:18 of that game, won by Montreal 2-1 at 8:52 of the fourth overtime period. Hainsworth then shutout the NY Rangers in the next and final game of the series on March 30, 1930, won by Montreal 2-0. The streak continued with a 3-0 win over Boston in the opening game of the F series on April 1, 1930. His streak ended on April 3, 1930 when Boston's Eddie Shore scored at 16:50 of the second period in the second game of the F series.

MOST CONSECUTIVE SHUTOUTS:
3 — **Clint Benedict, Mtl. Maroons,** 1926. Benedict shut out Ottawa 1-0, March 27; he then shut out Victoria twice, 3-0, March 30; 3-0, April 1. Mtl. Maroons won NHL F vs. Ottawa 2 goals to 1 and won the best-of-five F vs. Victoria 3-1.
— **John Ross Roach, NY Rangers,** 1929. Roach shut out NY Americans twice, 0-0, March 19; 1-0, March 21; he then shut out Toronto 1-0, March 24. NY Rangers won QF vs. NY Americans 1 goal to 0 and won the best-of-three SF vs. Toronto 2-0.
— **Frank McCool, Toronto,** 1945. McCool shut out Detroit three times, 1-0, April 6; 2-0, April 8; 1-0, April 12. Toronto won the best-of-seven F 4-3.
— **Brent Johnson, St. Louis,** 2002. Johnson shut out Chicago three times; 2-0, April 20; 4-0, April 21; 1-0, April 23. St. Louis won the best-of-seven CQF 4-1.
— **Patrick Lalime, Ottawa,** 2002. Lalime shut out Philadelphia three times; 3-0, April 20; 3-0, April 22; 3-0, April 24. Ottawa won the best-of-seven CQF 4-1.
— **Jean-Sebastien Giguere, Anaheim,** 2003. Giguere shut out Minnesota three times, 1-0, May 10; 2-0, May 12; 4-0, May 14. Anaheim won the best-of-seven CF 4-0.
— **Ilya Bryzgalov, Anaheim,** 2006. Bryzgalov shut out Calgary, 3-0, May 3; he then shut out Colorado 5-0, May 5; and 3-0, May 7. Anaheim won best-of-seven CQF vs. Calgary 4-3 and won best-of-seven CSF vs. Colorado 4-0.

Early Playoff Records

1893-1918
Team Records

MOST GOALS, BOTH TEAMS, ONE GAME:
25 — **Ottawa Silver Seven, Dawson City** at Ottawa, Jan. 16, 1905. Ottawa 23, Dawson City 2. Ottawa won best-of-three series 2-0.

MOST GOALS, ONE TEAM, ONE GAME:
23 — **Ottawa Silver Seven** at Ottawa, Jan. 16, 1905. Ottawa defeated Dawson City 23-2.

MOST GOALS, BOTH TEAMS, BEST-OF-THREE SERIES:
42 — **Ottawa Silver Seven, Queen's University** at Ottawa, 1906. Ottawa defeated Queen's 16-7, Feb. 27, and 12-7, Feb. 28.

MOST GOALS, ONE TEAM, BEST-OF-THREE SERIES:
32 — **Ottawa Silver Seven** in 1905 at Ottawa. Defeated Dawson City 9-2, Jan. 13, and 23-2, Jan. 16.

MOST GOALS, BOTH TEAMS, BEST-OF-FIVE SERIES:
39 — **Toronto Arenas, Vancouver Millionaires** at Toronto, 1918. Toronto won 5-3, Mar. 20; 6-3, Mar. 26; 2-1, Mar. 30. Vancouver won 6-4, Mar. 23, and 8-1, Mar. 28. Toronto scored 18 goals; Vancouver 21.

MOST GOALS, ONE TEAM, BEST-OF-FIVE SERIES:
26 — **Vancouver Millionaires** in 1915 at Vancouver. Defeated Ottawa Senators 6-2, Mar. 22; 8-3, Mar. 24; and 12-3, Mar. 26.

Individual Records

MOST GOALS IN PLAYOFFS:
63 — **Frank McGee, Ottawa Silver Seven,** in 22 playoff games. Seven goals in four games, 1903; 21 goals in eight games, 1904; 18 goals in four games, 1905; 17 goals in six games, 1906.

MOST GOALS, ONE PLAYOFF SERIES:
15 — **Frank McGee, Ottawa Silver Seven,** in two games in 1905 at Ottawa. Scored one goal, Jan. 13, in 9-2 victory over Dawson City and 14 goals, Jan. 16, in 23-2 victory.

MOST GOALS, ONE PLAYOFF GAME:
14 — **Frank McGee, Ottawa Silver Seven,** at Ottawa, Jan. 16, 1905, in 23-2 victory over Dawson City.

FASTEST THREE GOALS:
0:40 — **Marty Walsh, Ottawa Senators,** at Ottawa, March 16, 1911, at 3:00, 3:10, and 3:40 of third period. Ottawa defeated Port Arthur 13-4.

All-Time Playoff Goal Leaders since 1918

(45 or more goals)

Player	Teams	G	GP	Yrs.
Wayne Gretzky	Edm., L.A., St.L., NYR	**122**	208	16
Mark Messier	Edm., NYR, Van.	**109**	236	17
Jari Kurri	Edm., L.A., NYR, Ana., Col.	**106**	200	15
Brett Hull	Cgy., St.L., Dal., Det., Phx.	**103**	202	19
Glenn Anderson	Edm., Tor., NYR, St.L.	**93**	225	15
Mike Bossy	NYI	**85**	129	10
Joe Sakic	Que., Col.	**84**	172	13
Maurice Richard	Mtl.	**82**	133	15
Claude Lemieux	Mtl., N.J., Col., Phx., Dal., S.J.	**80**	234	18
Jean Beliveau	Mtl.	**79**	162	17
* Jaromir Jagr	Pit., Wsh., NYR, Phi., Dal., Bos., N.J., Fla.	**78**	208	18
Mario Lemieux	Pit.	**76**	107	8
Dino Ciccarelli	Min., Wsh., Det., T.B., Fla.	**73**	141	14
Esa Tikkanen	Edm., NYR, St.L., N.J., Van., Fla., Wsh.	**72**	186	13
Bryan Trottier	NYI, Pit.	**71**	221	17
Steve Yzerman	Det.	**70**	196	20
Gordie Howe	Det., Hfd.	**68**	157	20
* Patrick Marleau	S.J.	**68**	177	16
Joe Nieuwendyk	Cgy., Dal., N.J., Tor., Fla.	**66**	158	16
Denis Savard	Chi., Mtl., T.B.	**66**	169	16
Yvan Cournoyer	Mtl.	**64**	147	12
Peter Forsberg	Que., Col., Phi., Nsh.	**64**	151	13
Brian Propp	Phi., Bos., Min., Hfd.	**64**	160	13
Bobby Smith	Min., Mtl.	**64**	184	13
Bobby Hull	Chi., Wpg., Hfd.	**62**	119	14
Phil Esposito	Chi., Bos., NYR	**61**	130	15
Jacques Lemaire	Mtl.	**61**	145	11
Mark Recchi	Pit., Phi., Mtl., Car., Atl., T.B., Bos.	**61**	189	14
Joe Mullen	St.L., Cgy., Pit., Bos.	**60**	143	15
Doug Gilmour	St.L., Cgy., Tor., N.J., Chi., Buf., Mtl.	**60**	182	17
Brendan Shanahan	N.J., St.L., Hfd., Det., NYR	**60**	184	19
Stan Mikita	Chi.	**59**	155	18
Paul Coffey	Edm., Pit., L.A., Det., Hfd., Phi., Chi., Car., Bos.	**59**	194	16
Guy Lafleur	Mtl., NYR, Que.	**58**	128	14
Bernie Geoffrion	Mtl., NYR	**58**	132	16
* Evgeni Malkin	Pit.	**58**	149	9
Luc Robitaille	L.A., Pit., NYR, Det.	**58**	159	15
Mike Modano	Min., Dal., Det.	**58**	176	16
Cam Neely	Van., Bos.	**57**	93	9
* Henrik Zetterberg	Det.	**57**	137	12
* Sidney Crosby	Pit.	**57**	148	9
Steve Larmer	Chi., NYR	**56**	140	13
Denis Potvin	NYI	**56**	185	14
Rick MacLeish	Phi., Hfd., Pit., Det.	**54**	114	11
Steve Thomas	Tor., Chi., NYI, N.J., Ana., Det.	**54**	174	16
Nicklas Lidstrom	Det.	**54**	263	19
Daniel Briere	Phx., Buf., Phi., Mtl., Col.	**53**	124	9
Bill Barber	Phi.	**53**	129	11
Stephane Richer	Mtl., N.J., T.B., St.L., Pit.	**53**	134	13
Jeremy Roenick	Chi., Phx., Phi., L.A., S.J.	**53**	154	17
Rick Tocchet	Phi., Pit., L.A., Bos., Wsh., Phx.	**52**	145	13
Sergei Fedorov	Det., Ana., CBJ, Wsh.	**52**	183	15
* Marian Hossa	Ott., Atl., Pit., Det., Chi.	**52**	205	16
Daniel Alfredsson	Ott., Det.	**51**	124	14
Frank Mahovlich	Tor., Det., Mtl.	**51**	137	14
Brian Bellows	Min., Mtl., T.B., Ana., Wsh.	**51**	143	13
Rod Brind'Amour	St.L., Phi., Car.	**51**	159	12
Steve Shutt	Mtl., L.A.	**50**	99	12
* Patrick Kane	Chi.	**50**	127	8
Henri Richard	Mtl.	**49**	180	18
Reggie Leach	Bos., Cal., Phi., Det.	**47**	94	8
Ted Lindsay	Det., Chi.	**47**	133	16
Chris Drury	Col., Cgy., Buf., NYR	**47**	135	9
* Patrick Sharp	Phi., Chi., Dal.	**47**	142	8
Clark Gillies	NYI, Buf.	**47**	164	13
* Alex Ovechkin	Wsh.	**46**	97	8
Kevin Stevens	Pit., Bos., L.A., NYR, Phi.	**46**	103	7
Dickie Moore	Mtl., Tor., St.L.	**46**	135	14
Ron Francis	Hfd., Pit., Car., Tor.	**46**	171	17
Tomas Holmstrom	Det.	**46**	180	14
Rick Middleton	NYR, Bos.	**45**	114	12
Alex Kovalev	NYR, Pit., Mtl., Ott., Fla.	**45**	123	11
Patrik Elias	N.J.	**45**	162	13

* Active

All-Time Playoff Assist Leaders since 1918

(65 or more assists)

Player	Teams	A	GP	Yrs.
Wayne Gretzky	Edm., L.A., St.L., NYR	**260**	208	16
Mark Messier	Edm., NYR, Van.	**186**	236	17
Raymond Bourque	Bos., Col.	**139**	214	21
Paul Coffey	Edm., Pit., L.A., Det., Hfd., Phi., Chi., Car., Bos.	**137**	194	16
Nicklas Lidstrom	Det.	**129**	263	19
Doug Gilmour	St.L., Cgy., Tor., N.J., Chi., Buf., Mtl.	**128**	182	17
Jari Kurri	Edm., L.A., NYR, Ana., Col.	**127**	200	15
Sergei Fedorov	Det., Ana., CBJ, Wsh.	**124**	183	15
* Jaromir Jagr	Pit., Wsh., NYR, Phi., Dal., Bos., N.J., Fla.	**123**	208	18
Al MacInnis	Cgy., St.L.	**121**	177	19
Glenn Anderson	Edm., Tor., NYR, St.L.	**121**	225	15
Larry Robinson	Mtl., L.A.	**116**	227	20
Steve Yzerman	Det.	**115**	196	20
Larry Murphy	L.A., Wsh., Min., Pit., Tor., Det.	**115**	215	20
Adam Oates	Det., St.L., Bos., Wsh., Phi., Ana., Edm.	**114**	163	15
Bryan Trottier	NYI, Pit.	**113**	221	17
Chris Chelios	Mtl., Chi., Det., Atl.	**113**	266	24
Denis Savard	Chi., Mtl., T.B.	**109**	169	16
Denis Potvin	NYI	**108**	185	14
* Sidney Crosby	Pit.	**107**	148	9
Peter Forsberg	Que., Col., Phi., Nsh.	**107**	151	13
Joe Sakic	Que., Col.	**104**	172	13
* Evgeni Malkin	Pit.	**99**	149	9
Jean Beliveau	Mtl.	**97**	162	17
Ron Francis	Hfd., Pit., Car., Tor.	**97**	171	17
* Marian Hossa	Ott., Atl., Pit., Det., Chi.	**97**	205	16
Mario Lemieux	Pit.	**96**	107	8
* Joe Thornton	Bos., S.J.	**96**	160	15
Bobby Smith	Min., Mtl.	**96**	184	13
Chris Pronger	Hfd., St.L., Edm., Ana., Phi.	**95**	173	14
Sergei Zubov	NYR, Pit., Dal.	**93**	164	13
Gordie Howe	Det., Hfd.	**92**	157	20
Scott Stevens	Wsh., St.L., N.J.	**92**	233	20
Stan Mikita	Chi.	**91**	155	18
Brad Park	NYR, Bos., Det.	**90**	161	17
Mike Modano	Min., Dal., Det.	**88**	176	16
Brett Hull	Cgy., St.L., Dal., Det., Phx.	**87**	202	19
Craig Janney	Bos., St.L., S.J., Wpg., Phx., T.B., NYI	**86**	120	11
Mark Recchi	Pit., Phi., Mtl., Car., Atl., T.B., Bos.	**86**	189	14
Brian Propp	Phi., Bos., Min., Hfd.	**84**	160	13
* Ryan Getzlaf	Ana.	**81**	121	10
Patrik Elias	N.J.	**80**	162	13
Henri Richard	Mtl.	**80**	180	18
Jacques Lemaire	Mtl.	**78**	145	11
Claude Lemieux	Mtl., N.J., Col., Phx., Dal., S.J.	**78**	234	18
Ken Linseman	Phi., Edm., Bos., Tor.	**77**	113	11
Bobby Clarke	Phi.	**77**	136	13
Guy Lafleur	Mtl., NYR, Que.	**76**	128	14
Phil Esposito	Chi., Bos., NYR	**76**	130	15
Dale Hunter	Que., Wsh., Col.	**76**	186	18
Mike Bossy	NYI	**75**	129	10
Steve Larmer	Chi., NYR	**75**	140	13
John Tonelli	NYI, Cgy., L.A., Chi., Que.	**75**	172	13
Brendan Shanahan	N.J., St.L., Hfd., Det., NYR	**74**	184	19
* Patrick Kane	Chi.	**73**	127	8
Scott Niedermayer	N.J., Ana.	**73**	202	15
Peter Stastny	Que., N.J., St.L.	**72**	93	12
Bernie Nicholls	L.A., NYR, Edm., N.J., Chi., S.J.	**72**	118	13
Scott Gomez	N.J., NYR, Mtl., S.J., Fla., St.L., Ott.	**72**	149	10
Brian Bellows	Min., Mtl., T.B., Ana., Wsh.	**71**	143	13
Pavel Datsyuk	Det.	**71**	157	13
Brian Rafalski	N.J., Det.	**71**	165	10
Gilbert Perreault	Buf.	**70**	90	11
* Jonathan Toews	Chi.	**70**	128	8
Geoff Courtnall	Bos., Edm., Wsh., St.L., Van.	**70**	156	15
Brian Leetch	NYR, Tor., Bos.	**69**	95	8
Dale Hawerchuk	Wpg., Buf., St.L., Phi.	**69**	97	15
Alex Delvecchio	Det.	**69**	121	14
Jeremy Roenick	Chi., Phx., Phi., L.A., S.J.	**69**	154	17
Luc Robitaille	L.A., Pit., NYR, Det.	**69**	159	15
Sergei Gonchar	Wsh., Bos., Pit., Ott., Dal., Mtl.	**68**	141	13
Brad Richards	T.B., Dal., NYR, Chi., Det.	**68**	146	10
Bobby Hull	Chi., Wpg., Hfd.	**67**	119	14
Sandis Ozolinsh	S.J., Col., Car., Fla., Ana., NYR	**67**	137	10
Frank Mahovlich	Tor., Det., Mtl.	**67**	137	14
Igor Larionov	Van., S.J., Det., Fla., N.J.	**67**	150	13
Bobby Orr	Bos., Chi.	**66**	74	8
Bernie Federko	St.L., Det.	**66**	91	11
Jean Ratelle	NYR, Bos.	**66**	123	15
Charlie Huddy	Edm., L.A., Buf., St.L.	**66**	183	14
Trevor Linden	Van., NYI, Mtl., Wsh.	**65**	124	12
* Chris Kunitz	Ana., Atl., Pit.	**65**	161	11

All-Time Playoff Point Leaders since 1918

(120 or more points)

Player	Teams	Pts.	GP	G	A	Yrs.
Wayne Gretzky	Edm., L.A., St.L., NYR	**382**	208	122	260	16
Mark Messier	Edm., NYR, Van.	**295**	236	109	186	17
Jari Kurri	Edm., L.A., NYR, Ana., Col.	**233**	200	106	127	15
Glenn Anderson	Edm., Tor., NYR, St.L.	**214**	225	93	121	15
* Jaromir Jagr	Pit., Wsh., NYR, Phi., Dal., Bos., N.J., Fla.	**201**	208	78	123	18
Paul Coffey	Edm., Pit., L.A., Det., Hfd., Phi., Chi., Car., Bos.	**196**	194	59	137	16
Brett Hull	Cgy., St.L., Dal., Det., Phx.	**190**	202	103	87	19
Joe Sakic	Que., Col.	**188**	172	84	104	13
Doug Gilmour	St.L., Cgy., Tor., N.J., Chi., Buf., Mtl.	**188**	182	60	128	17
Steve Yzerman	Det.	**185**	196	70	115	20
Bryan Trottier	NYI, Pit.	**184**	221	71	113	17
Nicklas Lidstrom	Det.	**183**	263	54	129	19
Raymond Bourque	Bos., Col.	**180**	214	41	139	21
Jean Beliveau	Mtl.	**176**	162	79	97	17
Sergei Fedorov	Det., Ana., CBJ, Wsh.	**176**	183	52	124	15
Denis Savard	Chi., Mtl., T.B.	**175**	169	66	109	16
Mario Lemieux	Pit.	**172**	107	76	96	8
Peter Forsberg	Que., Col., Phi., Nsh.	**171**	151	64	107	13
* Sidney Crosby	Pit.	**164**	148	57	107	9
Denis Potvin	NYI	**164**	185	56	108	14
Mike Bossy	NYI	**160**	129	85	75	10
Gordie Howe	Det., Hfd.	**160**	157	68	92	20
Al MacInnis	Cgy., St.L.	**160**	177	39	121	19
Bobby Smith	Min., Mtl.	**160**	184	64	96	13
Claude Lemieux	Mtl., N.J., Col., Phx., Dal., S.J.	**158**	234	80	78	18
* Evgeni Malkin	Pit.	**157**	149	58	99	9
Adam Oates	Det., St.L., Bos., Wsh., Phi., Ana., Edm.	**156**	163	42	114	15
Larry Murphy	L.A., Wsh., Min., Pit., Tor., Det.	**152**	215	37	115	20
Stan Mikita	Chi.	**150**	155	59	91	18
* Marian Hossa	Ott., Atl., Pit., Det., Chi.	**149**	205	52	97	16
Brian Propp	Phi., Bos., Min., Hfd.	**148**	160	64	84	13
Mark Recchi	Pit., Phi., Mtl., Car., Atl., T.B., Bos.	**147**	189	61	86	14
Mike Modano	Min., Dal., Det.	**146**	176	58	88	16
Larry Robinson	Mtl., L.A.	**144**	227	28	116	20
Chris Chelios	Mtl., Chi., Det., Atl.	**144**	266	31	113	24
Ron Francis	Hfd., Pit., Car., Tor.	**143**	171	46	97	17
Jacques Lemaire	Mtl.	**139**	145	61	78	11
Phil Esposito	Chi., Bos., NYR	**137**	130	61	76	15
Guy Lafleur	Mtl., NYR, Que.	**134**	128	58	76	14
Brendan Shanahan	N.J., St.L., Hfd., Det., NYR	**134**	184	60	74	19
Esa Tikkanen	Edm., NYR, St.L., N.J., Van., Fla., Wsh.	**132**	186	72	60	13
Steve Larmer	Chi., NYR	**131**	140	56	75	13
Bobby Hull	Chi., Wpg., Hfd.	**129**	119	62	67	14
Henri Richard	Mtl.	**129**	180	49	80	18
Yvan Cournoyer	Mtl.	**127**	147	64	63	12
Luc Robitaille	L.A., Pit., NYR, Det.	**127**	159	58	69	15
Maurice Richard	Mtl.	**126**	133	82	44	15
Brad Park	NYR, Bos., Det.	**125**	161	35	90	17
Patrik Elias	N.J.	**125**	162	45	80	13
* Patrick Kane	Chi.	**123**	127	50	73	8
* Joe Thornton	Bos., S.J.	**123**	160	27	96	15
Brian Bellows	Min., Mtl., T.B., Ana., Wsh.	**122**	143	51	71	13
Jeremy Roenick	Chi., Phx., Phi., L.A., S.J.	**122**	154	53	69	17
Chris Pronger	Hfd., St.L., Edm., Ana., Phi.	**121**	173	26	95	14
Ken Linseman	Phi., Edm., Bos., Tor.	**120**	113	43	77	11
* Henrik Zetterberg	Det.	**120**	137	57	63	12
* Patrick Marleau	S.J.	**120**	177	68	52	16

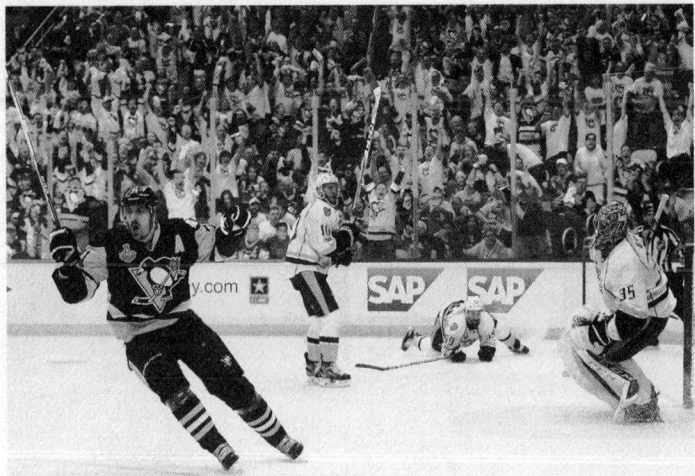

Evgeni Malkin celebrates a goal in game two of the 2017 Stanley Cup Final versus Nashville. Malkin led the playoffs in scoring again, as he did when Pittsburgh won the Stanley Cup in 2009.

Leading Playoff Scorers, 1918–2017

Season	Player, Team	Games Played	Goals	Assists	Points	Season	Player, Team	Games Played	Goals	Assists	Points
2016-17	Evgeni Malkin, Pittsburgh	25	10	18	28	1962-63	Gordie Howe, Detroit	11	7	9	16
2015-16	Logan Couture, San Jose	24	10	20	30		Norm Ullman, Detroit	11	4	12	16
2014-15	Tyler Johnson, Tampa Bay	26	13	10	23	1961-62	Stan Mikita, Chicago	12	6	15	21
	Patrick Kane, Chicago	23	11	12	23	1960-61	Gordie Howe, Detroit	11	4	11	15
2013-14	Anze Kopitar, Los Angeles	26	5	21	26		Pierre Pilote, Chicago	12	3	12	15
2012-13	David Krejci, Boston	22	9	17	26	1959-60	Henri Richard, Montreal	8	3	9	12
2011-12	Dustin Brown, Los Angeles	20	8	12	20		Bernie Geoffrion, Montreal	8	2	10	12
	Anze Kopitar, Los Angeles	20	8	12	20	1958-59	Dickie Moore, Detroit	11	5	12	17
2010-11	David Krejci, Boston	25	12	11	23	1957-58	Fleming MackCell, Boston	12	5	14	19
2009-10	Daniel Briere, Philadelphia	23	12	18	30	1956-57	Bernie Geoffrion, Montreal	10	11	7	18
2008-09	Evgeni Malkin, Pittsburgh	24	14	22	36	1955-56	Jean Béliveau, Montreal	10	12	7	19
2007-08	Henrik Zetterberg, Detroit	22	13	14	27	1954-55	Gordie Howe, Detroit	11	9	11	20
	Sidney Crosby, Pittsburgh	20	6	21	27	1953-54	Dickie Moore, Montreal	11	5	8	13
2006-07	Daniel Alfredsson, Ottawa	20	14	8	22	1952-53	Ed Sandford, Boston	11	8	3	11
	Dany Heatley, Ottawa	20	7	15	22	1951-52	Ted Lindsay, Detroit	8	5	2	7
	Jason Spezza, Ottawa	20	7	15	22		Floyd Curry, Montreal	11	4	3	7
2005-06	Eric Staal, Carolina	25	9	19	28		Metro Prystai, Detroit	8	2	5	7
2004-05	*Season Cancelled*						Gordie Howe, Detroit	8	2	5	7
2003-04	Brad Richards, Tampa Bay	23	12	14	26	1950-51	Maurice Richard, Montreal	11	9	4	13
2002-03	Jamie Langenbrunner, New Jersey	24	11	7	18		Max Bentley, Toronto	11	2	11	13
	Scott Niedermayer, New Jersey	24	2	16	18	1949-50	Pentti Lund, NY Rangers	12	6	5	11
2001-02	Peter Forsberg, Colorado	20	9	18	27	1948-49	Gordie Howe, Detroit	11	8	3	11
2000-01	Joe Sakic, Colorado	21	13	13	26	1947-48	Ted Kennedy, Toronto	9	8	6	14
99-2000	Brett Hull, Dallas	23	11	13	24	1946-47	Maurice Richard, Montreal	10	6	5	11
1998-99	Peter Forsberg, Colorado	19	8	16	24	1945-46	Elmer Lach, Montreal	9	5	12	17
1997-98	Steve Yzerman, Detroit	22	6	18	24	1944-45	Joe Carveth, Detroit	14	5	6	11
1996-97	Eric Lindros, Philadelphia	19	12	14	26	1943-44	Toe Blake, Montreal	9	7	11	18
1995-96	Joe Sakic, Colorado	22	18	16	34	1942-43	Carl Liscombe, Detroit	10	6	8	14
1994-95	Sergei Fedorov, Detroit	17	7	17	24	1941-42	Don Grosso, Detroit	12	8	6	14
1993-94	Brian Leetch, NY Rangers	23	11	23	34		Syl Apps, Toronto	13	5	9	14
1992-93	Wayne Gretzky, Los Angeles	24	15	25	40	1940-41	Milt Schmidt, Boston	11	5	6	11
1991-92	Mario Lemieux, Pittsburgh	15	16	18	34	1939-40	Phil Watson, NY Rangers	12	3	6	9
1990-91	Mario Lemieux, Pittsburgh	23	16	28	44		Neil Colville, NY Rangers	12	2	7	9
1989-90	Craig Simpson, Edmonton	22	16	15	31	1938-39	Bill Cowley, Boston	12	3	11	14
	Mark Messier, Edmonton	22	9	22	31	1937-38	Johnny Gottselig, Chicago	10	5	3	8
1988-89	Al MacInnis, Calgary	22	7	24	31		Gordie Drillon, Toronto	7	7	1	8
1987-88	Wayne Gretzky, Edmonton	19	12	31	43	1936-37	Marty Barry, Detroit	10	4	7	11
1986-87	Wayne Gretzky, Edmonton	21	5	29	34	1935-36	Frank Boll, Toronto	9	7	3	10
1985-86	Doug Gilmour, St. Louis	19	9	12	21	1934-35	Baldy Northcott, Mtl. Maroons	7	4	1	5
	Bernie Federko, St. Louis	19	7	14	21		Busher Jackson, Toronto	7	3	2	5
1984-85	Wayne Gretzky, Edmonton	18	17	30	47		Cy Wentworth, Mtl. Maroons	7	3	2	5
1983-84	Wayne Gretzky, Edmonton	19	13	22	35		Charlie Conacher, Toronto	7	1	4	5
1982-83	Wayne Gretzky, Edmonton	16	12	26	38	1933-34	Larry Aurie, Detroit	9	3	7	10
1981-82	Bryan Trottier, NY Islanders	19	6	23	29	1932-33	Cecil Dillon, NY Rangers	8	8	2	10
1980-81	Mike Bossy, NY Islanders	18	17	18	35	1931-32	Frank Boucher, NY Rangers	7	3	6	9
1979-80	Bryan Trottier, NY Islanders	21	12	17	29	1930-31	Cooney Weiland, Boston	5	6	3	9
1978-79	Jacques Lemaire, Montreal	16	11	12	23	1929-30	Marty Barry, Boston	6	3	3	6
	Guy Lafleur, Montreal	16	10	13	23		Cooney Weiland, Boston	6	1	5	6
1977-78	Guy Lafleur, Montreal	15	10	11	21	1928-29	Andy Blair, Toronto	4	3	0	3
	Larry Robinson, Montreal	15	4	17	21		Butch Keeling, NY Rangers	6	3	0	3
1976-77	Guy Lafleur, Montreal	14	9	17	26		Ace Bailey, Toronto	4	1	2	3
1975-76	Reggie Leach, Philadelphia	16	19	5	24	1927-28	Frank Boucher, NY Rangers	9	7	3	10
1974-75	Rick MacLeish, Philadelphia	17	11	9	20	1926-27	Harry Oliver, Boston	8	4	2	6
1973-74	Rick MacLeish, Philadelphia	17	13	9	22		Percy Galbraith, Boston	8	3	3	6
1972-73	Yvan Cournoyer, Montreal	17	15	10	25	1925-26	Nels Stewart, Mtl. Maroons	8	6	3	9
1971-72	Phil Esposito, Boston	15	9	15	24	1924-25	Howie Morenz, Montreal	6	7	1	8
	Bobby Orr, Boston	15	5	19	24	1923-24	Howie Morenz, Montreal	6	7	3	10
1970-71	Frank Mahovlich, Montreal	20	14	13	27	1922-23	Punch Broadbent, Ottawa	8	6	1	7
1969-70	Phil Esposito, Boston	14	13	14	27	1921-22	Babe Dye, Toronto	7	11	1	12
1968-69	Phil Esposito, Boston	10	8	10	18	1920-21	Cy Denneny, Ottawa	7	4	2	6
1967-68	Bill Goldsworthy, Min. North Stars	14	8	7	15	1919-20	Frank Nighbor, Ottawa	5	6	1	7
1966-67	Jim Pappin, Toronto	12	7	8	15		Jack Darragh, Ottawa	5	5	2	7
1965-66	Norm Ullman, Detroit	12	6	9	15	1918-19	Newsy Lalonde, Montreal	10	17	2	19
1964-65	Bobby Hull, Chicago	14	10	7	17	1917-18	Alf Skinner, Toronto	7	8	3	11
1963-64	Gordie Howe, Detroit	14	9	10	19						

Three-or-more-Goal Games, Playoffs 1918–2017

Player	Team	Date	City	Total Goals	Opposing Goaltender	Score
Wayne Gretzky (10)	Edm.	Apr. 11/81	Edm.	3	Richard Sevigny	Edm. 6 Mtl. 2
		Apr. 19/81	Edm.	3	Billy Smith	Edm. 5 NYI 2
		Apr. 6/83	Edm.	4	Brian Hayward	Edm. 6 Wpg. 3
		Apr. 17/83	Cgy.	4	Reggie Lemelin	Edm. 10 Cgy. 2
		Apr. 25/85	Wpg.	3	Brian Hayward (1) / Marc Behrend (1)	Edm. 8 Wpg. 3
		May 25/85	Edm.	3	Pelle Lindbergh	Edm. 4 Phi. 3
		Apr. 24/86	Cgy.	3	Mike Vernon	Edm. 7 Cgy. 4
	L.A.	May 29/93	Tor.	3	Felix Potvin	L.A. 5 Tor. 4
	NYR	Apr. 23/97	NYR	3	John Vanbiesbrouck	NYR 3 Fla. 2
		May 18/97	Phi.	3	Garth Snow	NYR 5 Phi. 4
Maurice Richard (7)	Mtl.	Mar. 23/44	Mtl.	5	Paul Bibeault	Mtl. 5 Tor. 1
		Apr. 6/44	Chi.	3	Mike Karakas	Mtl. 3 Chi. 1
		Mar. 29/45	Mtl.	4	Frank McCool	Mtl. 10 Tor. 3
		Apr. 14/53	Bos.	3	Gord Henry	Mtl. 7 Bos. 3
		Mar. 20/56	Mtl.	3	Gump Worsley	Mtl. 7 NYR 1
		Apr. 6/57	Mtl.	4	Don Simmons	Mtl. 5 Bos. 1
		Apr. 1/58	Det.	3	Terry Sawchuk	Mtl. 4 Det. 3
Jari Kurri (7)	Edm.	Apr. 4/84	Edm.	3	Doug Soetaert (1) / Mike Veisor (2)	Edm. 9 Wpg. 2
		Apr. 25/85	Wpg.	3	Brian Hayward (2) / Marc Behrend (1)	Edm. 8 Wpg. 3
		May 7/85	Edm.	3	Murray Bannerman	Edm. 7 Chi. 3
		May 14/85	Edm.	3	Murray Bannerman	Edm. 10 Chi. 5
		May 16/85	Chi.	4	Murray Bannerman	Edm. 8 Chi. 2
		Apr. 9/87	Edm.	4	Rollie Melanson (2) / Darren Eliot (2)	Edm. 13 L.A. 3
		May 18/90	Bos.	3	Andy Moog (2) / Reggie Lemelin (1)	Edm. 7 Bos. 2
Dino Ciccarelli (6)	Min.	May 5/81	Min.	3	Pat Riggin	Min. 7 Cgy. 4
		Apr. 10/82	Min.	3	Murray Bannerman	Min. 7 Chi. 1
	Wsh.	Apr. 5/90	N.J.	3	Sean Burke	Wsh. 5 N.J. 4
		Apr. 25/92	Pit.	4	Tom Barrasso (1) / Ken Wregget (3)	Wsh. 7 Pit. 2
	Det.	Apr. 29/93	Tor.	3	Felix Potvin (2) / Daren Puppa (1)	Det. 7 Tor. 3
		May 11/95	Dal.	3	Andy Moog (2) / Darcy Wakaluk (1)	Det. 5 Dal. 1
Mike Bossy (5)	NYI	Apr. 16/79	NYI	3	Tony Esposito	NYI 6 Chi. 2
		May 8/82	NYI	3	Richard Brodeur	NYI 6 Van. 5
		Apr. 10/83	Wsh.	3	Al Jensen	NYI 6 Wsh. 3
		May 3/83	NYI	3	Pete Peeters	NYI 8 Bos. 3
		May 7/83	NYI	4	Pete Peeters	NYI 8 Bos. 4
Phil Esposito (4)	Bos.	Apr. 2/69	Bos.	4	Bruce Gamble	Bos. 10 Tor. 0
		Apr. 8/70	Bos.	3	Ed Giacomin	Bos. 8 NYR 2
		Apr. 19/70	Chi.	3	Tony Esposito	Bos. 6 Chi. 3
		Apr. 8/75	Bos.	3	Tony Esposito (2) / Michel Dumas (1)	Bos. 8 Chi. 2
Mark Messier (4)	Edm.	Apr. 14/83	Edm.	4	Reggie Lemelin	Edm. 6 Cgy. 3
		Apr. 17/83	Cgy.	3	Reggie Lemelin (1) / Don Edwards (2)	Edm. 10 Cgy. 3
		Apr. 26/83	Edm.	3	Murray Bannerman	Edm. 8 Chi. 2
	NYR	May 25/94	N.J.	3	Martin Brodeur (2) / ENG (1)	NYR 4 N.J. 2
Steve Yzerman (4)	Det.	Apr. 6/89	Det.	3	Alain Chevrier	Chi. 5 Det. 4
		Apr. 4/91	St.L.	3	Vincent Riendeau (2) / Pat Jablonski (1)	Det. 6 St.L. 3
		May 8/96	St.L.	3	Jon Casey	St.L. 5 Det. 4
		Apr. 21/99	Det.	3	Guy Hebert (2) / Pat Jablonski (1)	Det. 5 Ana. 3
Bernie Geoffrion (3)	Mtl.	Mar. 27/52	Mtl.	3	Jim Henry	Mtl. 4 Bos. 0
		Apr. 7/55	Mtl.	3	Terry Sawchuk	Mtl. 4 Det. 2
		Mar. 30/57	Mtl.	3	Gump Worsley	Mtl. 8 NYR 3
Norm Ullman (3)	Det.	Mar. 29/64	Chi.	3	Glenn Hall	Det. 5 Chi. 4
		Apr. 7/64	Det.	3	Glenn Hall (2) / Denis DeJordy (1)	Det. 7 Chi. 2
		Apr. 11/65	Det.	3	Glenn Hall	Det. 4 Chi. 2
John Bucyk (3)	Bos.	May 3/70	St.L.	3	Jacques Plante (1) / Ernie Wakely (2)	Bos. 6 St.L. 1
		Apr. 20/72	Bos.	3	Jacques Caron (1) / Ernie Wakely (2)	Bos. 10 St.L. 2
		Apr. 21/74	Bos.	3	Tony Esposito	Bos. 8 Chi. 6
Rick MacLeish (3)	Phi.	Apr. 11/74	Phi.	3	Phil Myre	Phi. 5 Atl. 1
		Apr. 13/75	Phi.	3	Gord McRae	Phi. 6 Tor. 3
		May 13/75	Phi.	3	Glenn Resch	Phi. 4 NYI 1
Denis Savard (3)	Chi.	Apr. 19/82	Chi.	3	Mike Liut	Chi. 7 StL. 4
		Apr. 10/86	Chi.	4	Ken Wregget	Tor. 6 Chi. 4
		Apr. 18/88	St.L.	3	Greg Millen	Chi. 6 St.L. 3
Tim Kerr (3)	Phi.	Apr. 13/85	NYR	4	Glen Hanlon	Phi. 6 NYR 5
		Apr. 20/87	Phi.	3	Kelly Hrudey	Phi. 4 NYI 2
		Apr. 19/89	Pit.	3	Tom Barrasso	Phi. 4 Pit. 2
Cam Neely (3)	Bos.	Apr. 9/87	Mtl.	3	Patrick Roy	Mtl. 4 Bos. 3
		Apr. 5/91	Bos.	3	Peter Sidorkiewicz	Bos. 4 Hfd. 1
		Apr. 25/91	Bos.	3	Patrick Roy	Bos. 4 Mtl. 1
Petr Klima (3)	Det.	Apr. 7/88	Tor.	3	Allan Bester (2) / Ken Wregett (1)	Det. 6 Tor. 2
		Apr. 21/88	St.L.	3	Greg Millen	Det. 6 St.L. 0
	Edm.	May 4/91	Edm.	3	Jon Casey	Edm. 7 Min. 2
Esa Tikkanen (3)	Edm.	May 22/88	Edm.	3	Reggie Lemelin	Edm. 6 Bos. 3
		Apr. 16/91	Cgy.	3	Mike Vernon	Edm. 5 Cgy. 4
		Apr. 26/92	L.A.	3	Kelly Hrudey (2) / Tom Askey (1)	Edm. 5 L.A. 2
Mike Gartner (3)	NYR	Apr. 13/90	NYR	3	Mark Fitzpatrick (2) / Glenn Healy (1)	NYR 6 NYI 5
		Apr. 27/92	NYR	3	Chris Terreri	NYR 8 N.J. 5
	Tor.	Apr. 25/96	Tor.	3	Jon Casey	Tor. 5 St.L. 4
Mario Lemieux (3)	Pit.	Apr. 25/89	Pit.	5	Ron Hextall	Pit. 10 Phi. 7
		Apr. 23/92	Pit.	3	Don Beaupre	Pit. 6 Wsh. 4
		May 11/96	Pit.	3	Mike Richter	Pit. 7 NYR 3
Patrick Marleau (3)	S.J.	Apr. 10/04	S.J.	3	Chris Osgood	S.J. 3 St.L. 1
		Apr. 22/04	S.J.	3	David Aebischer	S.J. 5 Col. 2
		Apr. 27/06	S.J.	3	Chris Mason	Nsh. 4 S.J. 5
Johan Franzen (3)	Det.	Apr. 26/08	Det.	3	Jose Theodore (2) / Peter Budaj (1)	Det. 5 Col. 1
		May 1/08	Col.	3	Jose Theodore (1) / Peter Budaj (2)	Det. 8 Col. 2
		May 6/10	Det.	4	Evgeni Nabokov (3) / Thomas Greiss (1)	Det. 7 S.J. 1
Newsy Lalonde (2)	Mtl.	Mar. 1/19	Mtl.	5	Clint Benedict	Mtl. 6 Ott. 3
		Mar. 22/19	Sea.	4	Hap Holmes	Mtl. 4 Sea. 2
Howie Morenz (2)	Mtl.	Mar. 22/24	Mtl.	3	Charles Reid	Mtl. 6 Cgy.T. 1
		Mar. 27/25	Mtl.	3	Hap Holmes	Mtl. 4 Vic. 2
Doug Bentley (2)	Chi.	Mar. 28/44	Chi.	3	Connie Dion	Chi. 7 Det. 1
		Mar. 30/44	Det.	3	Connie Dion	Chi. 5 Det. 2
Toe Blake (2)	Mtl.	Mar. 22/38	Mtl.	3	Mike Karakas	Mtl. 6 Chi. 4
		Mar. 26/46	Chi.	3	Mike Karakas	Mtl. 7 Chi. 2
Ted Kennedy (2)	Tor.	Apr. 14/45	Tor.	3	Harry Lumley	Det. 5 Tor. 3
		Mar. 27/48	Tor.	3	Frank Brimsek	Tor. 5 Bos. 3
F. St. Marseille (2)	St.L.	Apr. 28/70	St.L.	3	Al Smith	St.L. 5 Pit. 0
		Apr. 6/72	Min.	3	Cesare Maniago	Min. 6 St.L. 5
Bobby Hull (2)	Chi.	Apr. 7/63	Chi.	3	Terry Sawchuk	Det. 7 Chi. 4
		Apr. 9/72	Pit.	3	Jim Rutherford	Chi. 6 Pit. 5
Pit Martin (2)	Chi.	Apr. 4/73	Chi.	3	Wayne Stephenson	Chi. 7 St.L. 1
		May 10/73	Chi.	3	Ken Dryden	Mtl. 8 Chi. 4
Yvan Cournoyer (2)	Mtl.	May 7/73	Mtl.	3	Dave Dryden	Mtl. 7 Buf. 3
		Apr. 11/74	Mtl.	3	Ed Giacomin	Mtl. 4 NYR 1
Guy Lafleur (2)	Mtl.	May 1/75		3	Roger Crozier (1) / Gerry Desjardins (2)	Mtl. 7 Buf. 4
		Apr. 11/77	Mtl.	3	Ed Staniowski	Mtl. 7 St.L. 2
Lanny McDonald (2)	Tor.	Apr. 9/77	Pit.	3	Denis Herron	Tor. 5 Pit. 2
		Apr. 17/77	Tor.	3	Wayne Stephenson	Phi. 6 Tor. 5
Bill Barber (2)	Phi.	May 4/80	Min.	4	Gilles Meloche	Phi. 5 Min. 3
		Apr. 9/81	Phi.	3	Dan Bouchard	Phi. 8 Que. 5
Bryan Trottier (2)	NYI	Apr. 8/80	NYI	3	Doug Keans	NYI 8 L.A. 1
		Apr. 9/81	NYI	3	Michel Larocque	NYI 5 Tor. 1
Butch Goring (2)	L.A.	Apr. 9/77	L.A.	3	Phil Myre	L.A. 4 Atl. 2
	NYI	May 17/81	Min.	3	Gilles Meloche	NYI 7 Min. 5
Paul Reinhart (2)	Cgy.	Apr. 14/83	Edm.	3	Andy Moog	Edm. 6 Cgy. 3
		Apr. 8/84	Van	3	Richard Brodeur	Cgy. 5 Van. 1
Brian Propp (2)	Phi.	Apr. 22/81	Phi.	3	Pat Riggin	Phi. 9 Cgy. 4
		Apr. 21/85	Phi.	3	Billy Smith	Phi. 5 NYI 2
Peter Stastny (2)	Que.	Apr. 5/83	Bos.	3	Pete Peeters	Bos. 4 Que. 3
		Apr. 11/87	Que.	3	Mike Liut (2) / Steve Weeks (1)	Que. 5 Hfd. 1
Michel Goulet (2)	Que.	Apr. 23/85	Que.	3	Steve Penney	Que. 7 Mtl. 6
		Apr. 12/87	Que.	3	Mike Liut	Que. 4 Hfd. 1
Glenn Anderson (2)	Edm.	Apr. 26/83	Edm.	4	Murray Bannerman	Edm. 8 Chi. 2
		Apr. 6/88	Wpg.	3	Daniel Berthiaume	Edm. 7 Wpg. 4
Peter Zezel (2)	Phi.	Apr. 13/86	NYR	3	John Vanbiesbrouck	Phi. 7 NYR 1
	St.L.	Apr. 11/89	St.L.	3	Jon Casey (1) / Kari Takko (1)	St.L. 6 Min. 1
Geoff Courtnall (2)	Van.	Apr. 4/91	L.A.	3	Kelly Hrudey	Van. 6 L.A. 4
		Apr. 30/92	Van.	3	Rick Tabaracci	Van. 5 Win. 0
Joe Sakic (2)	Que.	Jun. 6/95	Que.	3	Mike Richter	Que. 5 NYR 4
	Col.	Apr. 25/96	Col.	3	Corey Hirsch	Col. 5 Van. 4
Daniel Alfredsson (2)	Ott.	Apr. 28/98	Ott.	3	Martin Brodeur	Ott. 4 N.J. 3
		May 11/98	Ott.	3	Olaf Kolzig	Ott. 4 Wsh. 3
David Krejci (2)	Bos.	May 25/11	T.B.	3	Dwayne Roloson	T.B. 5 Bos. 4
	Bos.	May 8/13	Tor.	3	James Reimer	Bos. 4 Tor. 3
Sidney Crosby (2)	Pit.	May 4/09	Wsh.	3	Semyon Varlamov	Wsh. 4 Pit. 3
	Pit.	Apr. 24/13	Pit.	3	Craig Anderson	Pit. 6 Ott. 2
Patrick Kane (2)	Chi.	May 11/09	Chi.	3	Roberto Luongo	Chi. 7 Van. 5
	Chi.	Jun. 8/13	Chi.	3	Jonathan Quick	Chi. 4 L.A. 2
Evgeni Malkin (2)	Pit.	May 21/09	Pit.	3	Cam Ward	Pit. 7 Car. 4
	Pit.	Apr. 28/14	CBJ	3	Sergei Bobrovsky	Pit. 4 CBJ 3
Jeff Carter (2)	L.A.	May 15/12	Phx.	3	Mike Smith	L.A. 4 Phx. 0
	L.A.	Apr. 21/14	L.A.	3	Corey Crawford	L.A. 6 Chi.2
Jean-Gabriel Pageau (2)	Ott.	May 5/13	Ott.	3	Carey Price	Ott. 6 Mtl. 1
	Ott.	Apr. 29/17	Ott.	4	Henrik Lundqvist	Ott. 6 NYR 5
Harry Meeking	Tor.	Mar. 11/18	Tor.	3	Georges Vezina	Tor. 7 Mtl. 3
Alf Skinner	Tor.	Mar. 23/18	Tor.	3	Hugh Lehman	Van.M. 6 Tor. 4
Joe Malone	Mtl.	Feb. 27/19	Mtl.	3	Clint Benedict	Mtl. 8 Ott. 4
Odie Cleghorn	Mtl.	Feb. 27/19	Mtl.	3	Clint Benedict	Mtl. 5 Ott. 3
Jack Darragh	Ott.	Mar. 1/20	Ott.	3	Hap Holmes	Ott. 6 Sea. 1
George Boucher	Ott.	Mar. 10/21	Ott.	3	Jake Forbes	Ott. 5 Tor. 0
Babe Dye	Tor.	Mar. 28/22	Tor.	4	Hugh Lehman	Van.M. 1 Tor. 4
Percy Galbraith	Bos.	Mar. 31/27	Bos.	3	Hugh Lehman	Bos. 4 Chi. 4
Busher Jackson	Tor.	Apr. 5/32	NYR	3	John Ross Roach	Tor. 6 NYR 4
Frank Boucher	NYR					
Charlie Conacher	Tor.	Mar. 26/36		3	Tiny Thompson	Tor. 8 Bos. 3
Syd Howe	Det.	Mar. 23/39	Det.	3	Claude Bourque	Det. 7 Mtl. 3

Three-or-more-Goal Games, Playoffs — *continued*

Player	Team	Date	City	Total Goals	Opposing Goaltender	Score	
Bryan Hextall	NYR	Apr. 3/40	NYR	3	Turk Broda	NYR 6	Tor. 2
Joe Benoit	Mtl.	Mar. 22/41	Mtl.	3	Sam LoPresti	Mtl. 4	Chi. 3
Syl Apps	Tor.	Mar. 25/41	Tor.	3	Frank Brimsek	Tor. 7	Bos. 2
Jack McGill	Bos.	Mar. 29/42	Bos.	3	Johnny Mowers	Det. 6	Bos. 4
Don Metz	Tor.	Apr. 14/42	Tor.	3	Johnny Mowers	Tor. 9	Det. 3
Mud Bruneteau	Det.	Apr. 1/43	Det.	3	Frank Brimsek	Det. 6	Bos. 2
Don Grosso	Det.	Apr. 7/43	Bos.	3	Frank Brimsek	Det. 4	Bos. 0
Carl Liscombe	Det.	Apr. 3/45	Bos.	4	Paul Bibeault	Det. 5	Bos. 3
Billy Reay	Mtl.	Apr. 1/47	Bos.	4	Frank Brimsek	Mtl. 5	Bos. 1
Gerry Plamondon	Mtl.	Mar. 24/49	Det.	3	Harry Lumley	Mtl. 4	Det. 3
Sid Smith	Tor.	Apr. 10/49	Det.	3	Harry Lumley	Tor. 3	Det. 1
Pentti Lund	NYR	Apr. 2/50	NYR	3	Bill Durnan	NYR 4	Mtl. 1
Ted Lindsay	Det.	Apr. 5/55	Det.	4	Charlie Hodge (1)		
					Jacques Plante (3)	Det. 7	Mtl. 1
Gordie Howe	Det.	Apr. 10/55	Det.	3	Jacques Plante	Det. 5	Mtl. 1
Phil Goyette	Mtl.	Mar. 25/58	Mtl.	3	Terry Sawchuk	Mtl. 8	Det. 1
Jerry Toppazzini	Bos.	Apr. 5/58	Bos.	3	Gump Worsley	Bos. 8	NYR 2
Bob Pulford	Tor.	Apr. 19/62	Tor.	3	Glenn Hall	Tor. 8	Chi. 4
Dave Keon	Tor.	Apr. 9/64	Mtl.	3	Charlie Hodge (2)	Tor. 3	Mtl. 1
					ENG (1)		
Henri Richard	Mtl.	Apr. 20/67	Mtl.	3	Terry Sawchuk (2)		
					Johnny Bower (1)	Mtl. 6	Tor. 2
Rosaire Paiement	Phi.	Apr. 13/68	Phi.	3	Glenn Hall (1)		
					Seth Martin (2)	Phi. 6	St.L. 1
Jean Beliveau	Mtl.	Apr. 20/68	Mtl.	3	Denis DeJordy	Mtl. 4	Chi. 1
Red Berenson	St.L.	Apr. 15/69	St.L.	3	Gerry Desjardins	St.L. 4	L.A. 0
Ken Schinkel	Pit.	Apr. 11/70	Oak.	3	Gary Smith	Pit. 5	Oak. 2
Jim Pappin	Chi.	Apr. 11/71	Phi.	3	Bruce Gamble	Chi. 6	Phi. 2
Bobby Orr	Bos.	Apr. 11/71	Mtl.	3	Ken Dryden	Bos. 5	Mtl. 2
Jacques Lemaire	Mtl.	Apr. 20/71	Mtl.	3	Gump Worsley	Mtl. 7	Min. 2
Vic Hadfield	NYR	Apr. 22/71	NYR	3	Tony Esposito	NYR 4	Chi. 1
Fred Stanfield	Bos.	Apr. 18/72	Bos.	3	Jacques Caron	Bos. 6	St.L. 1
Ken Hodge	Bos.	Apr. 30/72	Bos.	3	Ed Giacomin	Bos. 6	NYR 5
Dick Redmond	Chi.	Apr. 4/73	Chi.	3	Wayne Stephenson	Chi. 7	St.L. 1
Steve Vickers	NYR	Apr. 10/73	Bos.	3	Ross Brooks (2)		
					Eddie Johnston (1)	NYR 6	Bos. 3
Tom Williams	L.A.	Apr. 14/74	L.A.	3	Mike Veisor	L.A. 5	Chi. 1
Marcel Dionne	L.A.	Apr. 15/76	L.A.	3	Gilles Gilbert	L.A. 6	Bos. 4
Don Saleski	Phi.	Apr. 20/76	Phi.	3	Wayne Thomas	Phi. 7	Tor. 1
Darryl Sittler	Tor.	Apr. 22/76	Tor.	5	Bernie Parent	Tor. 8	Phi. 5
Reggie Leach	Phi.	May 6/76	Phi.	5	Gilles Gilbert	Phi. 6	Bos. 3
Jim Lorentz	Buf.	Apr. 7/77	Min.	3	Pete LoPresti (2)		
					Gary Smith (1)	Buf. 7	Min. 1
Bobby Schmautz	Bos.	Apr. 11/77	Bos.	3	Rogie Vachon	Bos. 8	L.A. 3
Billy Harris	NYI	Apr. 23/77	Mtl.	3	Ken Dryden	Mtl. 4	NYI 3
George Ferguson	Tor.	Apr. 11/78	Tor.	3	Rogie Vachon	Tor. 7	L.A. 3
Jean Ratelle	Bos.	May 3/79	Bos.	3	Ken Dryden	Bos. 4	Mtl. 3
Stan Jonathan	Bos.	May 8/79	Bos.	3	Ken Dryden	Bos. 5	Mtl. 2
Ron Duguay	NYR	Apr. 20/80	NYR	3	Pete Peeters	NYR 4	Phi. 2
Steve Shutt	Mtl.	Apr. 22/80	Mtl.	3	Gilles Meloche	Mtl. 6	Min. 2
Gilbert Perreault	Buf.	May 6/80	NYI	3	Billy Smith (2)		
					ENG (1)	Buf. 7	NYI 4
Paul Holmgren	Phi.	May 15/80	Phi.	3	Billy Smith	Phi. 8	NYI 3
Steve Payne	Min.	Apr. 8/81	Bos.	3	Rogie Vachon	Min. 5	Bos. 4
Denis Potvin	NYI	Apr. 17/81	NYI	3	Andy Moog	NYI 6	Edm. 3
Barry Pederson	Bos.	Apr. 8/82	Bos.	3	Don Edwards	Bos. 7	Buf. 3
Duane Sutter	NYI	Apr. 15/83	NYI	3	Glen Hanlon	NYI 5	NYR 0
Doug Halward	Van.	Apr. 7/84	Van.	3	Reggie Lemelin (2)		
					Don Edwards (1)	Van. 7	Cgy. 0
Jorgen Pettersson	St.L.	Apr. 8/84	Det.	3	Eddie Mio	St.L. 3	Det. 2
Clark Gillies	NYI	May 12/84	NYI	3	Grant Fuhr	NYI 6	Edm. 1
Ken Linseman	Bos.	Apr. 14/85	Bos.	3	Steve Penney	Bos. 7	Mtl. 6
Dave Andreychuk	Buf.	Apr. 14/85	Buf.	3	Dan Bouchard	Buf. 7	Que. 4
Greg Paslawski	St.L.	Apr. 15/86	Min.	3	Don Beaupre	St.L. 6	Min. 3
Doug Risebrough	Cgy.	May 4/86	Cgy.	3	Rick Wamsley	Cgy. 8	St.L. 2
Mike McPhee	Mtl.	Apr. 11/87	Bos.	3	Doug Keans	Mtl. 5	Bos. 4
John Ogrodnick	Que.	Apr. 14/87	Hfd.	3	Mike Liut	Que. 7	Hfd. 5
Pelle Eklund	Phi.	May 10/87	Mtl.	3	Patrick Roy (1)		
					Brian Hayward (2)	Phi. 6	Mtl. 3
John Tucker	Buf.	Apr. 9/88	Bos.	4	Andy Moog	Buf. 6	Bos. 2
Tony Hrkac	St.L.	Apr. 10/88	St.L.	4	Darren Pang	St.L. 6	Chi. 5
Hakan Loob	Cgy.	Apr. 10/88	Cgy.	3	Glenn Healy	Cgy. 7	L.A. 3
Ed Olczyk	Tor.	Apr. 12/88	Tor.	3	Greg Stefan (2)		
					Glen Hanlon (1)	Tor. 6	Det. 5
Aaron Broten	N.J.	Apr. 20/88	N.J.	3	Pete Peeters	N.J. 5	Wsh. 2
Mark Johnson	N.J.	Apr. 22/88	Wsh.	4	Pete Peeters	N.J. 10	Wsh. 4
Patrik Sundstrom	N.J.	Apr. 22/88	Wsh.	3	Pete Peeters (2)		
					Clint Malarchuk (1)	N.J. 10	Wsh. 4
Bob Brooke	Min.	Apr. 5/89	St.L.	3	Greg Millen	St.L. 4	Min. 3
Chris Kontos	L.A.	Apr. 6/89	L.A.	3	Grant Fuhr	L.A. 5	Edm. 2
Wayne Presley	Chi.	Apr. 13/89	Chi.	3	Greg Stefan (1)		
					Glen Hanlon (2)	Chi. 7	Det. 1
Tony Granato	L.A.	Apr. 10/90	L.A.	3	Mike Vernon (1)		
					Rick Wamsley (2)	L.A. 12	Cgy. 4
Tomas Sandstrom	L.A.	Apr. 10/90	L.A.	3	Mike Vernon (1)		
					Rick Wamsley (2)	L.A. 12	Cgy. 4
Dave Taylor	L.A.	Apr. 10/90	L.A.	3	Mike Vernon (1)		
					Rick Wamsley (2)	L.A. 12	Cgy. 4
Bernie Nicholls	NYR	Apr. 19/90	NYR	3	Mike Liut	NYR 7	Wsh. 3
John Druce	Wsh.	Apr. 21/90	NYR	3	John Vanbiesbrouck	Wsh. 6	NYR 3
Adam Oates	St.L.	Apr. 12/91	St.L.	3	Tim Chevaldae	St.L. 6	Det. 1
Luc Robitaille	L.A.	Apr. 26/91	L.A.	3	Grant Fuhr	L.A. 5	Edm. 2
Ray Sheppard	Det.	Apr. 24/92	Min.	3	Jon Casey	Min. 5	Det. 2
Pavel Bure	Van.	Apr. 28/92	Wpg.	3	Rick Tabaracci	Van. 8	Wpg. 3
Joe Murphy	Edm.	May 6/92	Edm.	3	Kirk McLean	Edm. 5	Van. 2
Ron Francis	Pit.	May 9/92	Pit.	3	Mike Richter (2)		
					John V'brouck (1)	Pit. 5	NYR. 4
Kevin Stevens	Pit.	May 21/92	Bos.	4	Andy Moog	Pit. 5	Bos. 2
Dirk Graham	Chi.	Jun. 1/92	Chi.	3	Tom Barrasso	Pit. 6	Chi. 5
Brian Noonan	Chi.	Apr. 18/93	Chi.	3	Curtis Joseph	St.L. 4	Chi. 3
Dale Hunter	Wsh.	Apr. 20/93	Wsh.	3	Glenn Healy	NYI 5	Wsh. 4
Teemu Selanne	Wpg.	Apr. 23/93	Wpg.	3	Kirk McLean	Wpg. 5	Van. 4
Ray Ferraro	NYI	Apr. 26/93	Wsh.	4	Don Beaupre	Wsh. 6	NYI 4
Al Iafrate	Wsh.	Apr. 26/93	Wsh.	3	Glenn Healy (2)		
					Mark Fitzpatrick (1)	Wsh. 6	NYI 4
Paul DiPietro	Mtl.	Apr. 28/93	Mtl.	3	Ron Hextall	Mtl. 6	Que. 2
Wendel Clark	Tor.	May 27/93	L.A.	3	Kelly Hrudey	L.A. 5	Tor. 4
Eric Desjardins	Mtl.	Jun. 3/93	Mtl.	3	Kelly Hrudey	Mtl. 3	L.A. 2
Tony Amonte	Chi.	Apr. 23/94	Chi.	4	Felix Potvin	Chi. 5	Tor. 4
Gary Suter	Chi.	Apr. 24/94	Chi.	3	Felix Potvin	Chi. 4	Tor. 3
Ulf Dahlen	S.J.	May 6/94	S.J.	3	Felix Potvin	S.J. 5	Tor. 2
Mike Sullivan	Cgy.	May 11/95	S.J.	3	Arturs Irbe (2)		
					Wade Flaherty (1)	Cgy. 9	S.J. 2
Theoren Fleury	Cgy.	May 13/95	S.J.	4	Arturs Irbe (3)		
					ENG (1)	Cgy. 6	S.J. 4
Brendan Shanahan	St.L.	May 13/95	Van.	3	Kirk McLean	St.L. 5	Van. 2
John LeClair	Phi.	May 21/95	Phi.	3	Mike Richter	Phi. 5	NYR 4
Brian Leetch	NYR	May 22/95	Phi.	3	Ron Hextall	Phi. 4	NYR 3
Trevor Linden	Van.	Apr. 25/96	Col.	3	Patrick Roy	Col. 5	Van. 4
Jaromir Jagr	Pit.	May 11/96	Pit.	3	Mike Richter	Pit. 7	NYR 3
Peter Forsberg	Col.	Jun. 6/96	Col.	3	John Vanbiesbrouck	Col. 8	Fla. 1
Valeri Zelepukin	N.J.	Apr. 22/97	Mtl.	3	Jocelyn Thibault	N.J. 6	Mtl. 4
Valeri Kamensky	Col.	Apr. 24/97	Col.	3	Jeff Hackett (2)		
					Chris Terreri (1)	Col. 7	Chi. 0
Eric Lindros	Phi.	May 20/97	NYR	3	Mike Richter	Phi. 6	NYR 3
Matthew Barnaby	Buf.	May 10/98	Buf.	3	Andy Moog (2)	Buf. 6	Mtl. 3
					ENG (1)		
Martin Straka	Pit.	Apr. 25/99	Pit.	3	Martin Brodeur	Pit. 4	N.J. 2
Martin Lapointe	Det.	Apr. 15/00	Det.	3	Stephane Fiset (2)	Det. 8	L.A. 5
					Jamie Storr (1)		
Doug Weight	Edm.	Apr. 16/00	Edm.	3	Ed Belfour	Edm. 5	Dal. 2
Bill Guerin	Edm.	Apr. 18/00	Edm.	3	Ed Belfour	Dal. 4	Edm. 3
Scott Young	St.L.	Apr. 23/00	S.J.	3	Steve Shields	St.L. 6	S.J. 2
Andy Delmore	Phi.	May 7/00	Phi.	3	Ron Tugnutt (2)	Phi. 6	Pit. 3
					Peter Skudra (1)		
Brett Hull	Det.	Apr. 27/02	Van.	3	Peter Skudra	Det. 6	Van. 4
Keith Tkachuk	St.L.	May 7/02	St.L.	3	Dominik Hasek	St.L. 6	Det. 1
Darren McCarty	Det.	May 18/02	Det.	3	Patrick Roy	Det. 5	Col. 3
Alexander Mogilny	Tor.	Apr. 9/03	Phi.	3	Roman Cechmanek (2)	Tor. 5	Phi. 3
					ENG (1)		
Mike Sillinger	St.L.	Apr. 12/04	St.L.	3	Evgeni Nabokov (2)	St.L. 4	S.J. 1
					ENG (1)		
Keith Primeau	Phi.	May 2/04	Phi.	3	Ed Belfour (2)	Phi. 7	Tor. 2
					Trevor Kidd (1)		
J.P. Dumont	Buf.	Apr. 24/06	Buf.	3	Antero Niittymaki (1)	Phi. 2	Buf. 8
					Robert Esche (2)		
John Madden	N.J.	Apr. 24/06	N.J.	3	Kevin Weekes	NYR 1	N.J. 4
Jason Pominville	Buf.	Apr. 24/06	Buf.	3	Antero Niittymaki (2)	Phi. 2	Buf. 8
					Robert Esche (1)		
Joffrey Lupul	Ana.	May 9/06	Col.	4	Jose Theodore	Ana. 4	Col. 3
Michael Nylander	NYR	Apr. 17/07	NYR	3	Kari Lehtonen	NYR 7	Atl. 0
Andy McDonald	Ana.	Apr. 25/07	Ana.	3	Dany Sabourin (1)	Ana. 5	Van. 1
					Roberto Luongo (2)		
Pavel Datsyuk	Det.	May 12/08	Dal.	3	Marty Turco	Det. 5	Dal. 2
Alex Ovechkin	Wsh.	May 4/09	Wsh.	3	Marc-Andre Fleury	Wsh. 4	Pit. 3
Henrik Zetterberg	Det.	Apr. 16/10	Phx.	3	Ilya Bryzgalov	Det. 7	Phx. 4
Andrei Kostitsyn	Mtl.	Apr. 17/10	Wsh.	3	Jose Theodore (1)	Wsh. 6	Mtl. 5
					Semyon Varlamov (2)		
Nicklas Backstrom	Wsh.	Apr. 17/10	Wsh.	3	Jaroslav Halak	Wsh. 6	Mtl. 5
Dustin Byfuglien	Chi.	May 5/10	Van.	3	Roberto Luongo	Chi. 5	Van. 2
Jonathan Toews	Chi.	May 7/10	Van.	3	Roberto Luongo	Chi. 7	Van. 4
Devin Setoguchi	S.J.	May 4/11	Det.	3	Jimmy Howard	S.J. 4	Det. 3
Sean Couturier	Phi.	Apr. 13/12	Pit.	3	Marc-Andre Fleury	Phi. 8	Pit. 5
Claude Giroux	Phi.	Apr. 13/12	Pit.	3	Marc-Andre Fleury	Phi. 8	Pit. 5
Jordan Staal	Pit.	Apr. 18/12	Phi.	3	Ilya Bryzgalov (1)	Pit. 10	Phi. 3
					Sergei Bobrovsky (2)		
James Neal	Pit.	May 24/13	Pit.	3	Craig Anderson	Pit. 6	Ott. 2
Wayne Simmonds	Phi.	Apr. 29/14	Phi.	3	Henrik Lundqvist	Phi. 5	NYR 2
Rene Bourque	Mtl.	May 27/14	Mtl.	3	Henrik Lundqvist (1)	Mtl. 7	NYR 4
					Cam Talbot (2)		
Vladimir Tarasenko	St.L.	Apr. 18/15	St.L.	3	Devan Dubnyk (2)	St.L. 4	Min. 1
					ENG (1)		
Filip Forsberg	Nsh.	Apr. 23/15	Nsh.	3	Scott Darling (2)	Nsh. 5	Chi. 2
					ENG (1)		
Tyler Johnson	T.B.	May 18/15	NYR	3	Henrik Lundqvist	T.B. 6	NYR 2
Derick Brassard	NYR	May 26/15	T.B.	3	Ben Bishop (2)	NYR 7	T.B. 3
					ENG (1)		
Patric Hornqvist	Pit.	Apr. 13/16	Pit.	3	Henrik Lundqvist (1)	Pit. 5	NYR 2
					Antti Raanta (1)		
					ENG (1)		
T.J. Oshie	Wsh.	Apr. 28/16	Wsh.	3	Matt Murray	Wsh. 4	Pit. 3
Jake Guentzel	Pit.	Apr. 16/17	CBJ	3	Sergei Bobrovsky	Pit. 5	CBJ 4
Colton Sissons	Nsh.	May 22/17	Nsh.	3	Jonathan Bernier	Nsh. 6	Ana. 3

Overtime Games since 1918

Abbreviations: Teams/Cities: — **Ana.** - Anaheim; **Atl.** - Atlanta; **Bos.** - Boston; **Buf.** - Buffalo; **Cgy.** - Calgary; **Cgy. T.** - Calgary Tigers (Western Canada Hockey League); **Car.** - Carolina; **Chi.** - Chicago; **Col.** - Colorado; **CBJ** - Columbus; **Dal.** - Dallas; **Det.** - Detroit; **Edm.** - Edmonton; **Edm. E.** - Edmonton Eskimos (WCHL); **Fla.** - Florida; **Hfd.** - Hartford; **L.A.** - Los Angeles; **Min.** - Minnesota; **Mtl.** - Montreal; **Mtl. M.** - Montreal Maroons; **Nsh.** - Nashville; **N.J.** - New Jersey; **NYA** - NY Americans; **NYI** - New York Islanders; **NYR** - New York Rangers; **Oak.** - Oakland; **Ott.** - Ottawa; **Phi.** - Philadelphia; **Phx.** - Phoenix; **Pit.** - Pittsburgh; **Que.** - Quebec; **St.L.** - St. Louis; **Sea.** - Seattle Metropolitans (Pacific Coast Hockey Association); **S.J.** - San Jose; **T.B.** - Tampa Bay; **Tor.** - Toronto; **Van.** - Vancouver; **Van. M.** - Vancouver Millionaires (PCHA); **Vic.** - Victoria Cougars (WCHL); **Wpg.** - Winnipeg; **Wsh.** - Washington.

SERIES — **CF** - conference final; **CQF** - conference quarter-final; **CSF** - conference semi-final; **DF** - division final; **DSF** - division semi-final; **F** - final; **FR** - first round; **PR** - preliminary round; **QF** - quarter-final; **SF** - semi-final; **SR** - second round.

Date	City	Series	Score		Scorer	Overtime	Series Winner
Mar. 26/19	Sea.	F	Mtl. 0	Sea. 0	no scorer	20:00	....
Mar. 29/19	Sea.	F	Mtl. 4	Sea. 3	Jack McDonald	15:57	....
Mar. 21/22	Tor.	F	Tor. 2	Van. M. 1	Babe Dye	4:50	Tor.
Mar. 29/23	Van.	F	Ott. 2	Edm. E. 1	Cy Denneny	2:08	Ott.
Mar. 31/27	Mtl.	QF	Mtl. 1	Mtl. M. 0	Howie Morenz	12:05	Mtl.
Apr. 7/27	Bos.	F	Ott. 0	Bos. 0	no scorer	20:00	Ott.
Apr. 11/27	Ott.	F	Bos. 1	Ott. 1	no scorer	20:00	Ott.
Apr. 3/28	Mtl.	QF	Mtl. M. 1	Mtl. 0	Russell Oatman	8:20	Mtl. M.
Apr. 7/28	Mtl.	F	NYR 2	Mtl. M. 1	Frank Boucher	7:05	NYR
Mar. 21/29	NYR	QF	NYR 1	NYA 0	Butch Keeling	29:50	NYR
Mar. 26/29	Tor.	SF	NYR 2	Tor. 1	Frank Boucher	2:03	NYR
Mar. 20/30	Mtl.	SF	Bos. 2	Mtl. M. 1	Harry Oliver	45:35	Bos.
Mar. 25/30	Bos.	SF	Mtl. M. 1	Bos. 0	Archie Wilcox	26:27	Bos.
Mar. 26/30	Mtl.	QF	Chi. 2	Mtl. 2	Howie Morenz (Mtl.)	51:43	Mtl.
Mar. 28/30	Mtl.	SF	Mtl. 2	NYR 1	Gus Rivers	68:52	Mtl.
Mar. 24/31	Bos.	SF	Bos. 5	Mtl. 4	Cooney Weiland	18:56	Mtl.
Mar. 26/31	Chi.	QF	Chi. 2	Tor. 1	Stew Adams	19:20	Chi.
Mar. 28/31	Mtl.	SF	Mtl. 4	Bos. 3	Georges Mantha	5:10	Mtl.
Apr. 1/31	Mtl.	SF	Mtl. 3	Bos. 2	Wildor Larochelle	19:00	Mtl.
Apr. 5/31	Chi.	F	Chi. 2	Mtl. 1	Johnny Gottselig	24:50	Mtl.
Apr. 9/31	Mtl.	F	Chi. 3	Mtl. 2	Cy Wentworth	53:50	Mtl.
Mar. 26/32	Mtl.	SF	NYR 4	Mtl. 3	Fred Cook	59:32	NYR
Apr. 2/32	Tor.	SF	Tor. 3	Mtl. M. 2	Bob Gracie	17:59	Tor.
Mar. 25/33	Bos.	SF	Bos. 2	Tor. 1	Marty Barry	14:14	Tor.
Mar. 28/33	Bos.	SF	Tor. 1	Bos. 0	Busher Jackson	15:03	Tor.
Mar. 30/33	Tor.	SF	Bos. 2	Tor. 1	Eddie Shore	4:23	Tor.
Apr. 3/33	Tor.	SF	Tor. 1	Bos. 0	Ken Doraty	104:46	Tor.
Apr. 13/33	Tor.	F	NYR 1	Tor. 0	Bill Cook	7:33	NYR
Mar. 22/34	Tor.	SF	Det. 2	Tor. 1	Herbie Lewis	1:33	Det.
Mar. 25/34	Chi.	QF	Chi. 1	Mtl. 1	Mush March (Chi.)	11:05	Chi.
Apr. 3/34	Det.	F	Chi. 2	Det. 1	Paul Thompson	21:10	Chi.
Apr. 10/34	Chi.	F	Chi. 1	Det. 0	Mush March	30:05	Chi.
Mar. 23/35	Bos.	SF	Bos. 1	Tor. 0	Dit Clapper	33:26	Tor.
Mar. 26/35	Chi.	QF	Mtl. M. 1	Chi. 0	Baldy Northcott	4:02	Mtl. M.
Mar. 30/35	Tor.	SF	Tor. 2	Bos. 1	Pep Kelly	1:36	Tor.
Apr. 4/35	Tor.	F	Mtl. M. 3	Tor. 2	Dave Trottier	5:28	Mtl. M.
Mar. 24/36	Mtl.	SF	Det. 1	Mtl. M. 0	Mud Bruneteau	116:30	Det.
Apr. 9/36	Tor.	F	Tor. 4	Det. 3	Buzz Boll	0:31	Det.
Mar. 25/37	NYR	QF	NYR 2	Tor. 1	Babe Pratt	13:05	NYR
Apr. 1/37	Mtl.	SF	Det. 2	Mtl. 1	Hec Kilrea	51:49	Det.
Mar. 22/38	NYR	QF	NYA 2	NYR 1	John Sorrell	21:25	NYA
Mar. 24/38	Tor.	SF	Tor. 1	Bos. 0	George Parsons	21:31	Tor.
Mar. 26/38	Mtl.	QF	Chi. 3	Mtl. 2	Paul Thompson	11:49	Chi.
Mar. 27/38	NYR	QF	NYA 3	NYR 2	Lorne Carr	60:40	NYA
Mar. 29/38	Bos.	SF	Tor. 3	Bos. 2	Gordie Drillon	10:04	Tor.
Mar. 31/38	Chi.	SF	Chi. 1	NYA 0	Cully Dahlstrom	33:01	Chi.
Mar. 21/39	NYR	SF	Bos. 2	NYR 1	Mel Hill	59:25	Bos.
Mar. 23/39	Bos.	SF	Bos. 3	NYR 2	Mel Hill	8:24	Bos.
Mar. 26/39	Det.	QF	Det. 1	Mtl. 0	Marty Barry	7:47	Det.
Mar. 30/39	Bos.	SF	NYR 2	Bos. 1	Clint Smith	17:19	Bos.
Apr. 1/39	Tor.	SF	Tor. 5	Det. 4	Gordie Drillon	5:42	Tor.
Apr. 2/39	Bos.	SF	Bos. 2	NYR 1	Mel Hill	48:00	Bos.
Apr. 9/39	Bos.	F	Tor. 3	Bos. 2	Doc Romnes	10:38	Bos.
Mar. 19/40	Det.	QF	Det. 2	NYA 1	Syd Howe	0:25	Det.
Mar. 19/40	Tor.	QF	Tor. 3	Chi. 2	Syl Apps	6:35	Tor.
Apr. 2/40	NYR	F	NYR 2	Tor. 1	Alf Pike	15:30	NYR
Apr. 11/40	Tor.	F	NYR 2	Tor. 1	Muzz Patrick	31:43	NYR
Apr. 13/40	Tor.	F	NYR 3	Tor. 2	Bryan Hextall	2:07	NYR
Mar. 20/41	Det.	QF	Det. 2	NYR 1	Syd Howe	12:01	Det.
Mar. 22/41	Mtl.	QF	Mtl. 4	Chi. 3	Charlie Sands	34:04	Chi.
Mar. 29/41	Bos.	SF	Tor. 2	Bos. 1	Pete Langelle	17:31	Bos.
Mar. 30/41	Chi.	SF	Det. 2	Chi. 1	Gus Giesebrecht	9:15	Det.
Mar. 22/42	Chi.	QF	Bos. 2	Chi. 1	Des Smith	6:51	Bos.
Mar. 21/43	Bos.	SF	Bos. 5	Mtl. 4	Don Gallinger	12:30	Bos.
Mar. 23/43	Det.	SF	Tor. 3	Det. 2	Jack McLean	70:18	Det.
Mar. 25/43	Mtl.	SF	Bos. 3	Mtl. 2	Busher Jackson	3:20	Bos.
Mar. 30/43	Tor.	SF	Det. 3	Tor. 2	Adam Brown	9:21	Det.
Mar. 30/43	Bos.	SF	Bos. 5	Mtl. 4	Ab DeMarco	3:41	Bos.
Apr. 13/44	Mtl.	F	Mtl. 5	Chi. 4	Toe Blake	9:12	Mtl.
Mar. 27/45	Tor.	SF	Tor. 4	Mtl. 3	Gus Bodnar	12:36	Tor.
Mar. 29/45	Det.	SF	Det. 3	Bos. 2	Mud Bruneteau	17:12	Det.
Apr. 21/45	Tor.	F	Det. 1	Tor. 0	Eddie Bruneteau	14:16	Tor.
Mar. 28/46	Bos.	SF	Bos. 4	Det. 3	Don Gallinger	9:51	Bos.
Mar. 30/46	Mtl.	F	Mtl. 4	Bos. 3	Maurice Richard	9:08	Mtl.
Apr. 2/46	Mtl.	F	Mtl. 3	Bos. 2	Jimmy Peters	16:55	Mtl.
Apr. 7/46	Bos.	F	Bos. 3	Mtl. 2	Terry Reardon	15:13	Mtl.
Mar. 26/47	Tor.	SF	Tor. 3	Det. 2	Howie Meeker	3:05	Tor.
Mar. 27/47	Mtl.	SF	Mtl. 2	Bos. 1	Ken Mosdell	5:38	Mtl.
Apr. 3/47	Mtl.	SF	Mtl. 4	Bos. 3	John Quilty	36:40	Mtl.
Apr. 15/47	Tor.	F	Tor. 2	Mtl. 1	Syl Apps	16:36	Tor.
Mar. 24/48	Tor.	SF	Tor. 5	Bos. 4	Nick Metz	17:03	Tor.
Mar. 22/49	Det.	SF	Det. 2	Mtl. 1	Max McNab	44:52	Det.
Mar. 24/49	Det.	SF	Mtl. 4	Det. 3	Gerry Plamondon	2:59	Det.
Mar. 26/49	Tor.	SF	Bos. 5	Tor. 4	Woody Dumart	16:14	Tor.
Apr. 8/49	Det.	F	Tor. 3	Det. 2	Joe Klukay	17:31	Tor.
Apr. 4/50	Tor.	SF	Det. 2	Tor. 1	Leo Reise Jr.	20:38	Det.
Apr. 4/50	Mtl.	SF	Mtl. 3	NYR 2	Elmer Lach	15:19	NYR
Apr. 9/50	Det.	SF	Det. 1	Tor. 0	Leo Reise Jr.	8:39	Det.
Apr. 18/50	Det.	F	NYR 4	Det. 3	Don Raleigh	8:34	Det.
Apr. 20/50	Det.	F	NYR 2	Det. 1	Don Raleigh	1:38	Det.

Date	City	Series	Score		Scorer	Overtime	Series Winner
Apr. 23/50	Det.	F	Det. 4	NYR 3	Pete Babando	28:31	Det.
Mar. 27/51	Det.	SF	Mtl. 3	Det. 2	Maurice Richard	61:09	Mtl.
Mar. 29/51	Det.	SF	Mtl. 1	Det. 0	Maurice Richard	42:20	Mtl.
Mar. 31/51	Tor.	SF	Bos. 1	Tor. 1	no scorer	20:00	Tor.
Apr. 11/51	Tor.	F	Tor. 3	Mtl. 2	Sid Smith	5:51	Tor.
Apr. 14/51	Tor.	F	Mtl. 3	Tor. 2	Maurice Richard	2:55	Tor.
Apr. 17/51	Mtl.	F	Tor. 2	Mtl. 1	Ted Kennedy	4:47	Tor.
Apr. 19/51	Mtl.	F	Tor. 3	Mtl. 2	Harry Watson	5:15	Tor.
Apr. 21/51	Tor.	F	Tor. 3	Mtl. 2	Bill Barilko	2:53	Tor.
Apr. 6/52	Bos.	SF	Mtl. 3	Bos. 2	Paul Masnick	27:49	Mtl.
Mar. 29/53	Bos.	SF	Bos. 2	Det. 1	Jack McIntyre	12:29	Bos.
Mar. 29/53	Chi.	SF	Chi. 2	Mtl. 1	Al Dewsbury	5:18	Mtl.
Apr. 16/53	Mtl.	F	Mtl. 1	Bos. 0	Elmer Lach	1:22	Mtl.
Apr. 1/54	Det.	SF	Det. 4	Tor. 3	Ted Lindsay	21:01	Det.
Apr. 11/54	Det.	F	Mtl. 1	Det. 0	Ken Mosdell	5:45	Det.
Apr. 16/54	Det.	F	Det. 2	Mtl. 1	Tony Leswick	4:29	Det.
Mar. 29/55	Bos.	SF	Mtl. 4	Bos. 3	Don Marshall	3:05	Mtl.
Mar. 24/56	Tor.	SF	Det. 5	Tor. 4	Ted Lindsay	4:22	Det.
Mar. 28/57	NYR	SF	NYR 4	Mtl. 3	Andy Hebenton	13:38	Mtl.
Apr. 4/57	Mtl.	SF	Mtl. 4	NYR 3	Maurice Richard	1:11	Mtl.
Mar. 27/58	NYR	SF	Bos. 4	NYR 3	Jerry Toppazzini	4:46	Bos.
Mar. 30/58	Det.	SF	Mtl. 2	Det. 1	André Pronovost	11:52	Mtl.
Apr. 17/58	Mtl.	F	Mtl. 3	Bos. 2	Maurice Richard	5:45	Mtl.
Mar. 28/59	Tor.	SF	Tor. 3	Bos. 2	Gerry Ehman	5:02	Tor.
Mar. 31/59	Tor.	SF	Tor. 3	Bos. 2	Frank Mahovlich	11:21	Tor.
Apr. 14/59	Tor.	F	Tor. 3	Mtl. 2	Dick Duff	10:06	Mtl.
Mar. 26/60	Mtl.	SF	Mtl. 4	Chi. 3	Doug Harvey	8:38	Mtl.
Mar. 27/60	Det.	SF	Tor. 5	Det. 4	Frank Mahovlich	43:00	Tor.
Mar. 29/60	Det.	SF	Det. 2	Tor. 1	Gerry Melnyk	1:54	Tor.
Mar. 22/61	Tor.	SF	Tor. 3	Det. 2	George Armstrong	24:51	Det.
Mar. 26/61	Chi.	SF	Chi. 2	Mtl. 1	Murray Balfour	52:12	Chi.
Apr. 5/62	Tor.	SF	Tor. 3	NYR 2	Red Kelly	24:23	Tor.
Apr. 2/64	Det.	SF	Chi. 3	Det. 2	Murray Balfour	8:21	Det.
Apr. 14/64	Tor.	F	Det. 4	Tor. 3	Larry Jeffrey	7:52	Tor.
Apr. 23/64	Det.	F	Tor. 4	Det. 3	Bob Baun	1:43	Tor.
Apr. 6/65	Tor.	SF	Tor. 3	Mtl. 2	Dave Keon	4:17	Mtl.
Apr. 13/65	Tor.	SF	Mtl. 4	Tor. 3	Claude Provost	16:33	Mtl.
May 5/66	Det.	F	Mtl. 3	Det. 2	Henri Richard	2:20	Mtl.
Apr. 13/67	NYR	SF	Mtl. 2	NYR 1	John Ferguson	6:28	Mtl.
Apr. 25/67	Tor.	F	Tor. 3	Mtl. 2	Bob Pulford	28:26	Tor.
Apr. 10/68	St.L.	QF	St.L. 3	Phi. 2	Larry Keenan	24:10	St.L.
Apr. 16/68	St.L.	QF	Phi. 2	St.L. 1	Don Blackburn	31:18	St.L.
Apr. 16/68	Min.	QF	Min. 4	L.A. 3	Milan Marcetta	9:11	Min.
Apr. 22/68	Min.	SF	Min. 3	St.L. 2	Parker MacDonald	3:41	St.L.
Apr. 27/68	St.L.	SF	St.L. 4	Min. 3	Gary Sabourin	1:32	St.L.
Apr. 28/68	Mtl.	SF	Mtl. 4	Chi. 3	Jacques Lemaire	2:14	Mtl.
Apr. 29/68	St.L.	SF	St.L. 3	Min. 2	Bill McCreary	17:27	St.L.
May 3/68	St.L.	SF	St.L. 2	Min. 1	Ron Schock	22:50	St.L.
May 5/68	St.L.	F	Mtl. 3	St.L. 2	Jacques Lemaire	1:41	Mtl.
May 9/68	Mtl.	F	Mtl. 4	St.L. 3	Bobby Rousseau	1:13	Mtl.
Apr. 2/69	Oak.	QF	L.A. 5	Oak. 4	Ted Irvine	0:19	L.A.
Apr. 10/69	Mtl.	SF	Mtl. 3	Bos. 2	Ralph Backstrom	0:42	Mtl.
Apr. 13/69	Mtl.	SF	Mtl. 4	Bos. 3	Mickey Redmond	4:55	Mtl.
Apr. 24/69	Bos.	SF	Mtl. 2	Bos. 1	Jean Béliveau	31:28	Mtl.
Apr. 12/70	Oak.	QF	Pit. 3	Oak. 2	Michel Briere	8:28	Pit.
May 10/70	Bos.	F	Bos. 4	St.L. 3	Bobby Orr	0:40	Bos.
Apr. 15/71	Tor.	QF	NYR 2	Tor. 1	Bob Nevin	9:07	NYR
Apr. 18/71	Chi.	SF	NYR 2	Chi. 1	Pete Stemkowski	1:37	Chi.
Apr. 27/71	Chi.	SF	Chi. 3	NYR 2	Bobby Hull	6:35	Chi.
Apr. 29/71	NYR	SF	NYR 3	Chi. 2	Pete Stemkowski	41:29	Chi.
May 4/71	Chi.	F	Chi. 2	Mtl. 1	Jim Pappin	21:11	Mtl.
Apr. 6/72	Bos.	QF	Tor. 4	Bos. 3	Jim Harrison	2:58	Bos.
Apr. 6/72	Min.	QF	Min. 6	St.L. 5	Bill Goldsworthy	1:36	St.L.
Apr. 9/72	Pit.	QF	Chi. 6	Pit. 5	Pit Martin	0:12	Chi.
Apr. 16/72	Min.	QF	St.L. 2	Min. 1	Kevin O'Shea	10:07	St.L.
Apr. 1/73	Mtl.	QF	Buf. 3	Mtl. 2	René Robert	9:18	Mtl.
Apr. 10/73	Phi.	QF	Phi. 3	Min. 2	Gary Dornhoefer	8:35	Phi.
Apr. 14/73	Mtl.	SF	Phi. 5	Mtl. 4	Rick MacLeish	2:56	Mtl.
Apr. 17/73	Mtl.	SF	Mtl. 4	Phi. 3	Larry Robinson	6:45	Mtl.
Apr. 14/74	Tor.	QF	Bos. 4	Tor. 3	Ken Hodge	1:27	Bos.
Apr. 14/74	Atl.	QF	Phi. 4	Atl. 3	Dave Schultz	5:40	Phi.
Apr. 16/74	Mtl.	QF	NYR 3	Mtl. 2	Ron Harris	4:07	NYR
Apr. 23/74	Chi.	SF	Chi. 4	Bos. 3	Jim Pappin	3:48	Bos.
Apr. 28/74	NYR	SF	NYR 2	Phi. 1	Rod Gilbert	4:20	Phi.
May 9/74	Bos.	F	Phi. 3	Bos. 2	Bobby Clarke	12:01	Phi.
Apr. 8/75	L.A.	PR	L.A. 3	Tor. 2	Mike Murphy	8:53	Tor.
Apr. 10/75	Tor.	PR	Tor. 3	L.A. 2	Blaine Stoughton	10:19	Tor.
Apr. 10/75	Chi.	PR	Chi. 4	Bos. 3	Ivan Boldirev	7:33	Chi.
Apr. 11/75	NYR	PR	NYI 4	NYR 3	J.P. Parise	0:11	NYI
Apr. 17/75	Chi.	QF	Chi. 5	Buf. 4	Stan Mikita	2:31	Buf.
Apr. 19/75	Tor.	QF	Phi. 4	Tor. 3	André Dupont	1:45	Phi.
Apr. 22/75	Mtl.	QF	Mtl. 5	Van. 4	Guy Lafleur	17:06	Mtl.
Apr. 27/75	Buf.	SF	Buf. 6	Mtl. 5	Danny Gare	4:42	Buf.
May 1/75	Phi.	SF	Phi. 5	NYI 4	Bobby Clarke	2:56	Phi.
May 6/75	Buf.	SF	Buf. 5	Mtl. 4	René Robert	5:56	Buf.
May 7/75	NYI	SF	NYI 4	Phi. 3	Jude Drouin	1:53	Phi.
May 20/75	Buf.	F	Buf. 5	Phi. 4	René Robert	18:29	Phi.
Apr. 8/76	Buf.	PR	Buf. 3	St.L. 2	Danny Gare	11:43	Buf.
Apr. 9/76	Buf.	PR	Buf. 2	St.L. 1	Don Luce	14:27	Buf.
Apr. 13/76	Bos.	QF	L.A. 3	Bos. 2	Butch Goring	0:27	Bos.
Apr. 13/76	Buf.	QF	Buf. 3	NYI 2	Danny Gare	14:04	NYI
Apr. 22/76	L.A.	QF	L.A. 4	Bos. 3	Butch Goring	18:28	Bos.
Apr. 29/76	Phi.	SF	Phi. 2	Bos. 1	Reggie Leach	13:38	Phi.
Apr. 15/77	Tor.	QF	Phi. 4	Tor. 3	Rick MacLeish	2:55	Phi.
Apr. 17/77	Tor.	QF	Phi. 6	Tor. 5	Reggie Leach	19:10	Phi.
Apr. 24/77	Phi.	SF	Bos. 4	Phi. 3	Rick Middleton	2:57	Bos.
Apr. 26/77	Phi.	SF	Bos. 5	Phi. 4	Terry O'Reilly	30:07	Bos.
May 3/77	Mtl.	SF	NYI 4	Mtl. 3	Billy Harris	3:58	Mtl.
May 14/77	Bos.	F	Mtl. 2	Bos. 1	Jacques Lemaire	4:32	Mtl.
Apr. 11/78	Phi.	PR	Phi. 3	Col. 2	Mel Bridgman	0:23	Phi.
Apr. 13/78	NYR	PR	NYR 4	Buf. 3	Don Murdoch	1:37	Buf.
Apr. 19/78	Bos.	QF	Bos. 4	Chi. 3	Terry O'Reilly	1:50	Bos.
Apr. 19/78	NYI	QF	NYI 3	Tor. 2	Mike Bossy	2:50	Tor.
Apr. 21/78	Chi.	QF	Bos. 4	Chi. 3	Peter McNab	10:17	Bos.
Apr. 25/78	NYI	QF	NYI 2	Tor. 1	Bob Nystrom	8:02	Tor.
Apr. 29/78	NYI	QF	Tor. 2	NYI 1	Lanny McDonald	4:13	Tor.
May 2/78	Bos.	SF	Bos. 3	Phi. 2	Rick Middleton	1:43	Bos.

Overtime Games since 1918 *— continued*

Date	City	Series	Score		Scorer	Overtime	Series Winner
May 16/78	Mtl.	F	Mtl. 3	Bos. 2	Guy Lafleur	13:09	Mtl.
May 21/78	Bos.	F	Bos. 4	Mtl. 3	Bobby Schmautz	6:22	Mtl.
Apr. 12/79	L.A.	PR	NYR 2	L.A. 1	Phil Esposito	6:11	NYR
Apr. 14/79	Buf.	PR	Pit. 4	Buf. 3	George Ferguson	0:47	Pit.
Apr. 16/79	Phi.	QF	Phi. 3	NYR 2	Ken Linseman	0:44	NYR
Apr. 18/79	NYI	QF	NYI 1	Chi. 0	Mike Bossy	2:31	NYI
Apr. 21/79	Tor.	QF	Mtl. 4	Tor. 3	Cam Connor	25:25	Mtl.
Apr. 22/79	Tor.	QF	Mtl. 5	Tor. 4	Larry Robinson	4:14	Mtl.
Apr. 28/79	NYI	SF	NYI 4	NYR 3	Denis Potvin	8:02	NYR
May 3/79	NYR	SF	NYI 3	NYR 2	Bob Nystrom	3:40	NYR
May 3/79	Bos.	SF	Bos. 4	Mtl. 3	Jean Ratelle	3:46	Mtl.
May 10/79	Mtl.	SF	Mtl. 5	Bos. 4	Yvon Lambert	9:33	Mtl.
May 19/79	NYR	F	Mtl. 4	NYR 3	Serge Savard	7:25	Mtl.
Apr. 8/80	NYR	PR	NYR 2	Atl. 1	Steve Vickers	0:33	NYR
Apr. 8/80	Phi.	PR	Phi. 4	Edm. 3	Bobby Clarke	8:06	Phi.
Apr. 8/80	Chi.	PR	Chi. 3	St.L. 2	Doug Lecuyer	12:34	Chi.
Apr. 11/80	Hfd.	PR	Mtl. 4	Hfd. 3	Yvon Lambert	0:29	Mtl.
Apr. 11/80	Tor.	PR	Min. 4	Tor. 3	Al MacAdam	0:32	Min.
Apr. 11/80	L.A.	PR	NYI 4	L.A. 3	Ken Morrow	6:55	NYI
Apr. 11/80	Edm.	PR	Phi. 3	Edm. 2	Ken Linseman	23:56	Phi.
Apr. 16/80	Bos.	QF	NYI 2	Bos. 1	Clark Gillies	1:02	NYI
Apr. 17/80	Bos.	QF	NYI 5	Bos. 4	Bob Bourne	1:24	NYI
Apr. 21/80	NYI	QF	Bos. 4	NYI 3	Terry O'Reilly	17:13	NYI
May 1/80	Buf.	SF	NYI 2	Buf. 1	Bob Nystrom	21:20	NYI
May 13/80	Phi.	F	NYI 4	Phi. 3	Denis Potvin	4:07	NYI
May 24/80	NYI	F	NYI 5	Phi. 4	Bob Nystrom	7:11	NYI
Apr. 8/81	Buf.	PR	Buf. 3	Van. 2	Alan Haworth	5:00	Buf.
Apr. 8/81	Bos.	PR	Min. 5	Bos. 4	Steve Payne	3:34	Min.
Apr. 11/81	Chi.	PR	Cgy. 5	Chi. 4	Willi Plett	35:17	Cgy.
Apr. 12/81	Que.	PR	Que. 4	Phi. 3	Dale Hunter	0:37	Phi.
Apr. 14/81	St.L.	PR	St.L. 4	Pit. 3	Mike Crombeen	25:16	St.L.
Apr. 16/81	Buf.	QF	Min. 4	Buf. 3	Steve Payne	0:22	Min.
Apr. 20/81	Min.	QF	Buf. 5	Min. 4	Craig Ramsay	16:32	Min.
Apr. 20/81	Edm.	QF	NYI 5	Edm. 4	Ken Morrow	5:41	NYI
Apr. 7/82	Min.	DSF	Chi. 3	Min. 2	Greg Fox	3:34	Chi.
Apr. 8/82	Edm.	DSF	Edm. 3	L.A. 2	Wayne Gretzky	6:20	L.A.
Apr. 8/82	Van.	DSF	Van. 2	Cgy. 1	Tiger Williams	14:20	Van.
Apr. 10/82	Pit.	DSF	Pit. 2	NYI 1	Rick Kehoe	4:14	NYI
Apr. 10/82	L.A.	DSF	L.A. 6	Edm. 5	Daryl Evans	2:35	L.A.
Apr. 13/82	Mtl.	DSF	Que. 3	Mtl. 2	Dale Hunter	0:22	Que.
Apr. 13/82	NYI	DSF	NYI 4	Pit. 3	John Tonelli	6:19	NYI
Apr. 16/82	Van.	DF	L.A. 3	Van. 2	Steve Bozek	4:33	Van.
Apr. 18/82	Que.	DF	Que. 3	Bos. 2	Wilf Paiement	11:44	Que.
Apr. 18/82	NYR	DF	NYI 4	NYR 3	Bryan Trottier	3:00	NYI
Apr. 18/82	L.A.	DF	Van. 4	L.A. 3	Colin Campbell	1:23	Van.
Apr. 21/82	St.L.	DF	St.L. 3	Chi. 2	Bernie Federko	3:28	Chi.
Apr. 23/82	Que.	DF	Bos. 6	Que. 5	Peter McNab	10:54	Que.
Apr. 27/82	Chi.	CF	Van. 2	Chi. 1	Jim Nill	28:58	Van.
May 1/82	Que.	CF	NYI 5	Que. 4	Wayne Merrick	16:52	NYI
May 8/82	NYI	F	NYI 6	Van. 5	Mike Bossy	19:58	NYI
Apr. 5/83	Bos.	DSF	Bos. 4	Que. 3	Barry Pederson	1:46	Bos.
Apr. 6/83	Cgy.	DSF	Cgy. 4	Van. 3	Eddy Beers	12:27	Cgy.
Apr. 7/83	Min.	DSF	Min. 5	Tor. 4	Bobby Smith	5:03	Min.
Apr. 10/83	Tor.	DSF	Min. 5	Tor. 4	Dino Ciccarelli	8:05	Min.
Apr. 10/83	Van.	DSF	Cgy. 4	Van. 3	Greg Meredith	1:06	Cgy.
Apr. 18/83	Min.	DF	Chi. 4	Min. 3	Rich Preston	10:34	Chi.
Apr. 24/83	Bos.	DF	Bos. 3	Buf. 2	Brad Park	1:52	Bos.
Apr. 5/84	Edm.	DSF	Edm. 5	Wpg. 4	Randy Gregg	0:21	Edm.
Apr. 7/84	Det.	DSF	St.L. 4	Det. 3	Mark Reeds	37:07	St.L.
Apr. 8/84	Det.	DSF	St.L. 3	Det. 2	Jorgen Pettersson	2:42	St.L.
Apr. 10/84	NYI	DSF	NYI 3	NYR 2	Ken Morrow	8:56	NYI
Apr. 13/84	Min.	DF	St.L. 4	Min. 3	Doug Gilmour	16:16	Min.
Apr. 13/84	Edm.	DF	Cgy. 6	Edm. 5	Carey Wilson	3:42	Edm.
Apr. 13/84	NYI	DF	NYI 5	Wsh. 4	Anders Kallur	7:35	NYI
Apr. 16/84	Mtl.	DF	Que. 4	Mtl. 3	Bo Berglund	3:00	Mtl.
Apr. 20/84	Cgy.	DF	Cgy. 5	Edm. 4	Lanny McDonald	1:04	Edm.
Apr. 22/84	Min.	DF	Min. 4	St.L. 3	Steve Payne	6:00	Min.
Apr. 10/85	Phi.	DSF	Phi. 5	NYR 4	Mark Howe	8:01	Phi.
Apr. 10/85	Wsh.	DSF	Wsh. 4	NYI 3	Alan Haworth	2:28	NYI
Apr. 10/85	Edm.	DSF	Edm. 3	L.A. 2	Lee Fogolin	3:01	Edm.
Apr. 10/85	Wpg.	DSF	Wpg. 5	Cgy. 4	Brian Mullen	7:56	Wpg.
Apr. 11/85	Wsh.	DSF	Wsh. 2	NYI 1	Mike Gartner	21:23	NYI
Apr. 13/85	L.A.	DSF	Edm. 4	L.A. 3	Glenn Anderson	0:46	Edm.
Apr. 18/85	Mtl.	DF	Que. 2	Mtl. 1	Mark Kumpel	12:23	Que.
Apr. 23/85	Que.	DF	Que. 7	Mtl. 6	Dale Hunter	18:36	Que.
Apr. 25/85	Min.	DF	Chi. 7	Min. 6	Darryl Sutter	21:57	Chi.
Apr. 28/85	Chi.	DF	Min. 5	Chi. 4	Dennis Maruk	1:14	Chi.
Apr. 30/85	Min.	DF	Chi. 6	Min. 5	Darryl Sutter	15:41	Chi.
May 2/85	Mtl.	DF	Que. 3	Mtl. 2	Peter Stastny	2:22	Que.
May 5/85	Que.	CF	Que. 2	Phi. 1	Peter Stastny	6:20	Phi.
Apr. 9/86	Que.	DSF	Hfd. 3	Que. 2	Sylvain Turgeon	2:36	Hfd.
Apr. 12/86	Wpg.	DSF	Cgy. 4	Wpg. 3	Lanny McDonald	8:25	Cgy.
Apr. 17/86	Wsh.	DF	NYR 4	Wsh. 3	Brian MacLellan	1:16	NYR
Apr. 20/86	Edm.	DF	Edm. 6	Cgy. 5	Glenn Anderson	1:04	Cgy.
Apr. 23/86	Hfd.	DF	Hfd. 2	Mtl. 1	Kevin Dineen	1:07	Mtl.
Apr. 23/86	NYR	DF	NYR 6	Wsh. 5	Bob Brooke	2:40	NYR
Apr. 26/86	St L.	DF	St L. 4	Tor. 3	Mark Reeds	7:11	St L.
Apr. 29/86	Mtl.	DF	Mtl. 2	Hfd. 1	Claude Lemieux	5:55	Mtl.
May 5/86	NYR	CF	Mtl. 4	NYR 3	Claude Lemieux	9:41	Mtl.
May 12/86	St L.	CF	St L. 6	Cgy. 5	Doug Wickenheiser	7:30	Cgy.
May 18/86	Cgy.	F	Mtl. 3	Cgy. 2	Brian Skrudland	0:09	Mtl.
Apr. 8/87	Hfd.	DSF	Hfd. 3	Que. 2	Paul MacDermid	2:20	Que.
Apr. 9/87	Mtl.	DSF	Mtl. 4	Bos. 3	Mats Naslund	2:38	Mtl.
Apr. 9/87	St.L.	DSF	Tor. 3	St.L. 2	Rick Lanz	10:17	Tor.
Apr. 11/87	Wpg.	DSF	Cgy. 3	Wpg. 2	Mike Bullard	3:53	Wpg.
Apr. 11/87	Chi.	DSF	Det. 4	Chi. 3	Shawn Burr	4:51	Det.
Apr. 16/87	Que.	DSF	Que. 5	Hfd. 4	Peter Stastny	6:05	Que.
Apr. 18/87	Wsh.	DSF	NYI 3	Wsh. 2	Pat LaFontaine	68:47	NYI
Apr. 21/87	Edm.	DF	Edm. 3	Wpg. 2	Glenn Anderson	0:36	Edm.
Apr. 26/87	Que.	DF	Mtl. 3	Que. 2	Mats Naslund	5:30	Mtl.
Apr. 27/87	Tor.	DF	Tor. 3	Det. 2	Mike Allison	9:31	Det.
May 4/87	Phi.	CF	Phi. 4	Mtl. 3	Ilkka Sinislao	9:11	Phi.
May 20/87	Edm.	F	Edm. 3	Phi. 2	Jari Kurri	6:50	Edm.
Apr. 6/88	NYI	DSF	NYI 4	N.J. 3	Pat LaFontaine	6:11	N.J.
Apr. 10/88	Phi.	DSF	Phi. 5	Wsh. 4	Murray Craven	1:18	Wsh.
Apr. 10/88	N.J.	DSF	NYI 5	N.J. 4	Brent Sutter	15:07	N.J.
Apr. 10/88	Buf.	DSF	Buf. 6	Bos. 5	John Tucker	5:32	Bos.
Apr. 12/88	Det.	DSF	Tor. 6	Det. 5	Ed Olczyk	0:34	Det.
Apr. 16/88	Wsh.	DSF	Wsh. 5	Phi. 4	Dale Hunter	5:57	Wsh.
Apr. 21/88	Cgy.	DF	Edm. 5	Cgy. 4	Wayne Gretzky	7:54	Edm.
May 4/88	Bos.	CF	N.J. 3	Bos. 2	Doug Brown	17:46	Bos.
May 9/88	Det.	CF	Edm. 4	Det. 3	Jari Kurri	11:02	Edm.
Apr. 5/89	St.L.	DSF	St.L. 4	Min. 3	Brett Hull	11:55	St.L.
Apr. 5/89	Cgy.	DSF	Van. 4	Cgy. 3	Paul Reinhart	2:47	Cgy.
Apr. 6/89	St.L.	DSF	St.L. 4	Min. 3	Rick Meagher	5:30	St.L.
Apr. 6/89	Det.	DSF	Chi. 5	Det. 4	Duane Sutter	14:36	Chi.
Apr. 8/89	Hfd.	DSF	Mtl. 5	Hfd. 4	Stephane Richer	5:01	Mtl.
Apr. 8/89	Phi.	DSF	Wsh. 4	Phi. 3	Kelly Miller	0:51	Phi.
Apr. 9/89	Hfd.	DSF	Mtl. 4	Hfd. 3	Russ Courtnall	15:12	Mtl.
Apr. 15/89	Cgy.	DSF	Cgy. 4	Van. 3	Joel Otto	19:21	Cgy.
Apr. 18/89	Cgy.	DF	Cgy. 4	L.A. 3	Doug Gilmour	7:47	Cgy.
Apr. 19/89	Mtl.	DF	Mtl. 3	Bos. 2	Bobby Smith	12:24	Mtl.
Apr. 20/89	St.L.	DF	St.L. 5	Chi. 4	Tony Hrkac	33:49	Chi.
Apr. 21/89	Phi.	DF	Pit. 4	Phi. 3	Phil Bourque	12:08	Phi.
May 8/89	Chi.	CF	Cgy. 2	Chi. 1	Al MacInnis	15:05	Cgy.
May 9/89	Mtl.	CF	Phi. 2	Mtl. 1	Dave Poulin	5:02	Mtl.
May 19/89	Mtl.	F	Mtl. 4	Cgy. 3	Ryan Walter	38:08	Cgy.
Apr. 5/90	N.J.	DSF	Wsh. 5	N.J. 4	Dino Ciccarelli	5:34	Wsh.
Apr. 6/90	Edm.	DSF	Edm. 3	Wpg. 2	Mark Lamb	4:21	Edm.
Apr. 8/90	Tor.	DSF	St.L. 6	Tor. 5	Sergio Momesso	6:04	St.L.
Apr. 8/90	L.A.	DSF	L.A. 2	Cgy. 1	Tony Granato	8:37	L.A.
Apr. 9/90	Mtl.	DSF	Mtl. 2	Buf. 1	Brian Skrudland	12:35	Mtl.
Apr. 9/90	NYI	DSF	NYI 4	NYR 3	Brent Sutter	20:59	NYR
Apr. 10/90	Wpg.	DSF	Wpg. 4	Edm. 3	Dave Ellett	21:08	Edm.
Apr. 14/90	L.A.	DSF	L.A. 4	Cgy. 3	Mike Krushelnyski	23:14	L.A.
Apr. 15/90	Hfd.	DSF	Hfd. 3	Bos. 2	Kevin Dineen	12:30	Bos.
Apr. 21/90	Bos.	DF	Bos. 5	Mtl. 4	Garry Galley	3:42	Bos.
Apr. 24/90	L.A.	DF	Edm. 6	L.A. 5	Joe Murphy	4:42	Edm.
Apr. 25/90	Wsh.	DF	Wsh. 4	NYR 3	Rod Langway	0:34	Wsh.
Apr. 27/90	NYR	DF	Wsh. 2	NYR 1	John Druce	6:48	Wsh.
May 15/90	Bos.	F	Edm. 3	Bos. 2	Petr Klima	55:13	Edm.
Apr. 4/91	Chi.	DSF	Min. 4	Chi. 3	Brian Propp	4:14	Min.
Apr. 5/91	Pit.	DSF	Pit. 5	N.J. 4	Jaromir Jagr	8:52	Pit.
Apr. 6/91	L.A.	DSF	L.A. 3	Van. 2	Wayne Gretzky	11:08	L.A.
Apr. 8/91	Van.	DSF	Van. 2	L.A. 1	Cliff Ronning	3:12	L.A.
Apr. 11/91	NYR	DSF	Wsh. 5	NYR 4	Dino Ciccarelli	6:44	Wsh.
Apr. 11/91	Mtl.	DSF	Mtl. 4	Buf. 3	Russ Courtnall	5:56	Mtl.
Apr. 14/91	Edm.	DSF	Cgy. 2	Edm. 1	Theoren Fleury	4:40	Edm.
Apr. 16/91	Cgy.	DSF	Edm. 5	Cgy. 4	Esa Tikkanen	6:58	Edm.
Apr. 18/91	L.A.	DF	L.A. 4	Edm. 3	Luc Robitaille	2:13	Edm.
Apr. 19/91	Bos.	DF	Mtl. 4	Bos. 3	Stephane Richer	0:27	Bos.
Apr. 19/91	Pit.	DF	Pit. 7	Wsh. 6	Kevin Stevens	8:10	Pit.
Apr. 20/91	L.A.	DF	Edm. 4	L.A. 3	Petr Klima	24:48	Edm.
Apr. 22/91	Edm.	DF	Edm. 4	L.A. 3	Esa Tikkanen	20:48	Edm.
Apr. 27/91	Mtl.	DF	Mtl. 3	Bos. 2	Shayne Corson	17:47	Bos.
Apr. 28/91	Edm.	DF	Edm. 4	L.A. 3	Craig MacTavish	16:57	Edm.
May 3/91	Bos.	CF	Bos. 5	Pit. 4	Vladimir Ruzicka	8:14	Pit.
Apr. 21/92	Bos.	DSF	Bos. 3	Buf. 2	Adam Oates	11:14	Bos.
Apr. 22/92	Min.	DSF	Det. 5	Min. 4	Yves Racine	1:15	Det.
Apr. 22/92	St.L.	DSF	St.L. 5	Chi. 4	Brett Hull	23:33	Chi.
Apr. 25/92	Buf.	DSF	Bos. 5	Buf. 4	Ted Donato	2:08	Bos.
Apr. 28/92	Min.	DSF	Det. 1	Min. 0	Sergei Fedorov	16:13	Det.
Apr. 29/92	Hfd.	DSF	Hfd. 2	Mtl. 1	Yvon Corriveau	0:24	Mtl.
May 1/92	Mtl.	DSF	Mtl. 3	Hfd. 2	Russ Courtnall	25:26	Mtl.
May 3/92	Van.	DF	Edm. 4	Van. 3	Joe Murphy	8:36	Edm.
May 5/92	Mtl.	DF	Bos. 3	Mtl. 2	Peter Douris	3:12	Bos.
May 7/92	Pit.	DF	NYR 6	Pit. 5	Kris King	1:29	Pit.
May 9/92	Pit.	DF	Pit. 5	NYR 4	Ron Francis	2:47	Pit.
May 17/92	Pit.	CF	Pit. 4	Bos. 3	Jaromir Jagr	9:44	Pit.
May 20/92	Edm.	CF	Chi. 4	Edm. 3	Jeremy Roenick	2:45	Chi.
Apr. 18/93	Bos.	DSF	Buf. 5	Bos. 4	Bob Sweeney	11:03	Buf.
Apr. 18/93	Que.	DSF	Que. 3	Mtl. 2	Scott Young	16:49	Mtl.
Apr. 20/93	Wsh.	DSF	NYI 5	Wsh. 4	Brian Mullen	34:50	NYI
Apr. 22/93	Mtl.	DSF	Mtl. 2	Que. 1	Vincent Damphousse	10:30	Mtl.
Apr. 22/93	Buf.	DSF	Buf. 4	Bos. 3	Yuri Khmylev	1:05	Buf.
Apr. 22/93	NYI	DSF	NYI 4	Wsh. 3	Ray Ferraro	4:46	NYI
Apr. 24/93	Buf.	DSF	Buf. 6	Bos. 5	Brad May	4:48	Buf.
Apr. 24/93	NYI	DSF	NYI 4	Wsh. 3	Ray Ferraro	25:40	NYI
Apr. 25/93	St.L.	DSF	St.L. 4	Chi. 3	Craig Janney	10:43	St.L.
Apr. 26/93	Que.	DSF	Mtl. 5	Que. 4	Kirk Muller	8:17	Mtl.
Apr. 27/93	Det.	DSF	Tor. 5	Det. 4	Mike Foligno	2:05	Tor.
Apr. 27/93	Van.	DSF	Wpg. 4	Van. 3	Teemu Selanne	6:18	Van.
Apr. 29/93	Wpg.	DSF	Van. 4	Wpg. 3	Greg Adams	4:30	Van.
May 1/93	Det.	DSF	Tor. 4	Det. 3	Nikolai Borschevsky	2:35	Tor.
May 3/93	Tor.	DF	Tor. 2	St.L. 1	Doug Gilmour	23:16	Tor.
May 4/93	Mtl.	DF	Mtl. 4	Buf. 3	Guy Carbonneau	2:50	Mtl.
May 5/93	Tor.	DF	St.L. 2	Tor. 1	Jeff Brown	23:03	Tor.
May 6/93	Buf.	DF	Mtl. 4	Buf. 3	Gilbert Dionne	8:28	Mtl.
May 8/93	Buf.	DF	Mtl. 4	Buf. 3	Kirk Muller	11:37	Mtl.
May 11/93	Van.	DF	L.A. 4	Van. 3	Gary Shuchuk	26:31	L.A.
May 14/93	Pit.	DF	NYI 4	Pit. 3	Dave Volek	5:16	NYI
May 18/93	Mtl.	CF	Mtl. 4	NYI 3	Stephan Lebeau	26:21	Mtl.
May 20/93	NYI	CF	Mtl. 2	NYI 1	Guy Carbonneau	12:34	Mtl.
May 25/93	Tor.	CF	Tor. 3	L.A. 2	Glenn Anderson	19:20	L.A.
May 27/93	L.A.	CF	L.A. 5	Tor. 4	Wayne Gretzky	1:41	L.A.
Jun. 3/93	Mtl.	F	Mtl. 3	L.A. 2	Eric Desjardins	0:51	Mtl.
Jun. 5/93	L.A.	F	Mtl. 4	L.A. 3	John LeClair	0:34	Mtl.
Jun. 7/93	L.A.	F	Mtl. 3	L.A. 2	John LeClair	14:37	Mtl.
Apr. 20/94	Tor.	CQF	Tor. 1	Chi. 0	Todd Gill	2:15	Tor.
Apr. 22/94	St.L.	CQF	Dal. 5	St.L. 4	Paul Cavallini	8:34	Dal.
Apr. 24/94	Chi.	CQF	Chi. 4	Tor. 3	Jeremy Roenick	1:23	Tor.
Apr. 25/94	Bos.	CQF	Mtl. 2	Bos. 1	Kirk Muller	17:18	Bos.
Apr. 26/94	Cgy.	CQF	Van. 2	Cgy. 1	Geoff Courtnall	7:15	Van.
Apr. 27/94	Buf.	CQF	Buf. 1	N.J. 0	Dave Hannan	65:43	N.J.
Apr. 28/94	Van.	CQF	Van. 3	Cgy. 2	Trevor Linden	16:43	Van.
Apr. 30/94	Cgy.	CQF	Van. 4	Cgy. 3	Pavel Bure	22:20	Van.
May 3/94	N.J.	CSF	Bos. 6	N.J. 5	Don Sweeney	9:08	N.J.
May 7/94	Bos.	CSF	N.J. 5	Bos. 4	Stephane Richer	14:19	N.J.
May 8/94	Van.	CSF	Van. 2	Dal. 1	Sergio Momesso	11:01	Van.
May 12/94	Tor.	CSF	Tor. 3	S.J. 2	Mike Gartner	8:53	Tor.
May 15/94	NYR	CF	N.J. 4	NYR 3	Stephane Richer	35:23	NYR
May 16/94	Tor.	CF	Tor. 3	Van. 2	Peter Zezel	16:55	Van.

Date	City	Series	Score		Scorer	Overtime	Series Winner
May 19/94	N.J.	CF	NYR 3	N.J. 2	Stephane Matteau	26:13	NYR
May 24/94	Van.	CF	Van. 4	Tor. 3	Greg Adams	20:14	Van.
May 27/94	NYR	CF	NYR 2	N.J. 1	Stephane Matteau	24:24	NYR
May 31/94	NYR	F	Van. 3	NYR 2	Greg Adams	19:26	NYR
May 7/95	Phi.	CQF	Phi. 4	Buf. 3	Karl Dykhuis	10:06	Phi.
May 9/95	Cgy.	CQF	S.J. 5	Cgy. 4	Ulf Dahlen	12:21	S.J.
May 12/95	NYR	CQF	NYR 3	Que. 2	Steve Larmer	8:09	NYR
May 12/95	N.J.	CQF	N.J. 1	Bos. 0	Randy McKay	8:51	N.J.
May 14/95	Pit.	CQF	Pit. 6	Wsh. 5	Luc Robitaille	4:30	Pit.
May 15/95	St.L.	CQF	Van. 6	St.L. 5	Cliff Ronning	1:48	Van.
May 17/95	Tor.	CQF	Tor. 5	Chi. 4	Randy Wood	10:00	Chi.
May 19/95	Cgy.	CQF	S.J. 5	Cgy. 4	Ray Whitney	21:54	S.J.
May 21/95	Phi.	CSF	Phi. 5	NYR 4	Eric Desjardins	7:03	Phi.
May 21/95	Chi.	CSF	Chi. 2	Van. 1	Joe Murphy	9:04	Chi.
May 22/95	Phi.	CSF	Phi. 4	NYR 3	Kevin Haller	0:25	Phi.
May 25/95	Van.	CSF	Chi. 3	Van. 2	Chris Chelios	6:22	Chi.
May 26/95	N.J.	CSF	N.J. 2	Pit. 1	Neal Broten	18:36	N.J.
May 27/95	Van.	CSF	Chi. 4	Van. 3	Chris Chelios	5:35	Chi.
Jun. 1/95	Det.	CF	Det. 2	Chi. 1	Nicklas Lidstrom	1:01	Det.
Jun. 6/95	Chi.	CF	Det. 4	Chi. 3	Vladimir Konstantinov	29:25	Det.
Jun. 7/95	N.J.	CF	Phi. 3	N.J. 2	Eric Lindros	4:19	N.J.
Jun. 11/95	Det.	CF	Det. 2	Chi. 1	Vyacheslav Kozlov	22:25	Det.
Apr. 16/96	NYR	CQF	Mtl. 3	NYR 2	Vincent Damphousse	5:04	NYR
Apr. 18/96	Tor.	CQF	Tor. 5	St.L. 4	Mats Sundin	4:02	St.L.
Apr. 18/96	Phi.	CQF	T.B. 2	Phi. 1	Brian Bellows	9:05	Phi.
Apr. 21/96	St.L.	CQF	St.L. 3	Tor. 2	Glenn Anderson	1:24	St.L.
Apr. 21/96	T.B.	CQF	T.B. 5	Phi. 4	Alexander Selivanov	2:04	Phi.
Apr. 23/96	Cgy.	CQF	Chi. 2	Cgy. 1	Joe Murphy	50:02	Chi.
Apr. 24/96	Wsh.	CQF	Pit. 3	Wsh. 2	Petr Nedved	79:15	Pit.
Apr. 25/96	Col.	CQF	Col. 5	Van. 4	Joe Sakic	0:51	Col.
Apr. 25/96	Tor.	CQF	Tor. 5	St.L. 4	Mike Gartner	7:31	St.L.
May 2/96	Col.	CSF	Chi. 3	Col. 2	Jeremy Roenick	6:29	Col.
May 6/96	Chi.	CSF	Chi. 4	Col. 3	Sergei Krivokrasov	0:46	Col.
May 8/96	St.L.	CSF	St.L. 5	Det. 4	Igor Kravchuk	3:23	Det.
May 8/96	Chi.	CSF	Col. 3	Chi. 2	Joe Sakic	44:33	Col.
May 9/96	Fla.	CSF	Fla. 4	Phi. 3	Dave Lowry	4:06	Fla.
May 12/96	Phi.	CSF	Fla. 2	Phi. 1	Mike Hough	28:05	Fla.
May 13/96	Chi.	CSF	Col. 4	Chi. 3	Sandis Ozolinsh	25:18	Col.
May 16/96	Det.	CSF	Det. 1	St.L. 0	Steve Yzerman	21:15	Det.
May 19/96	Det.	CF	Col. 3	Det. 2	Mike Keane	17:31	Col.
Jun. 10/96	Fla.	F	Col. 1	Fla. 0	Uwe Krupp	44:31	Col.
Apr. 20/97	Chi.	CQF	Chi. 4	Col. 3	Sergei Krivokrasov	31:03	Col.
Apr. 20/97	Edm.	CQF	Edm. 4	Dal. 3	Kelly Buchberger	9:15	Edm.
Apr. 22/97	NYR	CQF	NYR 4	Fla. 3	Esa Tikkanen	16:29	NYR
Apr. 23/97	Ott.	CQF	Ott. 1	Buf. 0	Daniel Alfredsson	2:34	Buf.
Apr. 24/97	Mtl.	CQF	Mtl. 4	N.J. 3	Patrice Brisebois	47:37	N.J.
Apr. 25/97	Fla.	CQF	NYR 3	Fla. 2	Esa Tikkanen	12:02	NYR
Apr. 25/97	Dal.	CQF	Edm. 1	Dal. 0	Ryan Smyth	20:22	Edm.
Apr. 27/97	Phx.	CQF	Ana. 3	Phx. 2	Paul Kariya	7:29	Ana.
Apr. 29/97	Buf.	CQF	Buf. 3	Ott. 2	Derek Plante	5:24	Buf.
Apr. 29/97	Dal.	CQF	Edm. 4	Dal. 3	Todd Marchant	12:26	Edm.
May 2/97	Det.	CSF	Det. 2	Ana. 1	Martin Lapointe	0:59	Det.
May 4/97	Det.	CSF	Det. 3	Ana. 2	Vyacheslav Kozlov	41:31	Det.
May 8/97	Ana.	CSF	Det. 3	Ana. 2	Brendan Shanahan	37:03	Det.
May 9/97	Phi.	CSF	Buf. 5	Phi. 4	Ed Ronan	6:24	Phi.
May 9/97	Edm.	CSF	Col. 3	Edm. 2	Claude Lemieux	8:35	Col.
May 11/97	N.J.	CSF	NYR 2	N.J. 1	Adam Graves	14:08	NYR
Apr. 22/98	N.J.	CQF	Ott. 2	N.J. 1	Bruce Gardiner	5:58	Ott.
Apr. 23/98	Pit.	CQF	Mtl. 3	Pit. 2	Benoit Brunet	18:43	Mtl.
Apr. 24/98	Wsh.	CQF	Bos. 4	Wsh. 3	Darren Van Impe	20:54	Wsh.
Apr. 26/98	Ott.	CQF	Ott. 2	N.J. 1	Alexei Yashin	2:47	Ott.
Apr. 26/98	Bos.	CQF	Wsh. 3	Bos. 2	Joe Juneau	26:31	Wsh.
Apr. 26/98	Edm.	CQF	Col. 5	Edm. 4	Joe Sakic	15:25	Edm.
Apr. 28/98	S.J.	CQF	S.J. 1	Dal. 0	Andrei Zyuzin	6:31	Dal.
May 1/98	Phi.	CQF	Buf. 3	Phi. 2	Michal Grosek	5:40	Buf.
May 2/98	S.J.	CQF	Dal. 3	S.J. 2	Mike Keane	3:43	Dal.
May 3/98	Bos.	CQF	Wsh. 3	Bos. 2	Brian Bellows	15:24	Wsh.
May 3/98	Buf.	CSF	Buf. 3	Mtl. 2	Geoff Sanderson	2:37	Buf.
May 11/98	Edm.	CSF	Dal. 1	Edm. 0	Benoit Hogue	13:07	Dal.
May 12/98	Mtl.	CSF	Buf. 5	Mtl. 4	Michael Peca	21:24	Buf.
May 12/98	St.L.	CSF	Det. 3	St.L. 2	Brendan Shanahan	31:12	Det.
May 25/98	Wsh.	CF	Wsh. 3	Buf. 2	Todd Krygier	3:01	Wsh.
May 28/98	Buf.	CF	Wsh. 4	Buf. 3	Peter Bondra	9:37	Wsh.
Jun. 3/98	Dal.	CF	Dal. 3	Det. 2	Jamie Langenbrunner	0:46	Det.
Jun. 4/98	Buf.	CF	Wsh. 3	Buf. 2	Joe Juneau	6:24	Wsh.
Jun. 11/98	Det.	F	Det. 5	Wsh. 4	Kris Draper	15:24	Det.
Apr. 23/99	Ott.	CQF	Buf. 3	Ott. 2	Miroslav Satan	30:35	Buf.
Apr. 24/99	Car.	CQF	Car. 3	Bos. 2	Ray Sheppard	17:05	Bos.
Apr. 24/99	Phx.	CQF	Phx. 4	St.L. 3	Shane Doan	8:58	St.L.
Apr. 26/99	S.J.	CQF	Col. 2	S.J. 1	Milan Hejduk	7:53	Col.
Apr. 27/99	Edm.	CQF	Dal. 3	Edm. 2	Joe Nieuwendyk	57:34	Dal.
Apr. 30/99	Tor.	CQF	Tor. 2	Phi. 1	Yanic Perreault	11:51	Tor.
Apr. 30/99	Car.	CQF	Bos. 4	Car. 3	Anson Carter	34:45	Bos.
Apr. 30/99	Phx.	CQF	St.L. 2	Phx. 1	Scott Young	5:43	St.L.
May 2/99	Pit.	CQF	Pit. 3	N.J. 2	Jaromir Jagr	8:59	Pit.
May 3/99	S.J.	CQF	Col. 3	S.J. 2	Milan Hejduk	13:12	Col.
May 4/99	Phx.	CQF	St.L. 1	Phx. 0	Pierre Turgeon	17:59	St.L.
May 7/99	Col.	CSF	Det. 3	Col. 2	Kirk Maltby	4:18	Col.
May 8/99	Dal.	CSF	Dal. 5	St.L. 4	Joe Nieuwendyk	8:22	Dal.
May 10/99	St.L.	CSF	St.L. 3	Dal. 2	Pavol Demitra	2:43	Dal.
May 12/99	St.L.	CSF	St.L. 3	Dal. 2	Pierre Turgeon	5:52	Dal.
May 13/99	Pit.	CSF	Tor. 3	Pit. 2	Sergei Berezin	2:18	Tor.
May 17/99	Pit.	CSF	Tor. 4	Pit. 3	Garry Valk	1:57	Tor.
May 17/99	St.L.	CSF	Dal. 2	St.L. 1	Mike Modano	2:21	Dal.
May 28/99	Col.	CF	Col. 3	Dal. 2	Chris Drury	19:29	Dal.
Jun. 8/99	Dal.	F	Buf. 3	Dal. 2	Jason Woolley	15:30	Dal.
Jun. 19/99	Buf.	F	Dal. 2	Buf. 1	Brett Hull	54:51	Dal.
Apr. 15/00	Pit.	CQF	Pit. 2	Wsh. 1	Jaromir Jagr	5:49	Pit.
Apr. 18/00	Buf.	CQF	Buf. 3	Phi. 2	Stu Barnes	4:42	Phi.
Apr. 22/00	Tor.	CQF	Tor. 2	Ott. 1	Steve Thomas	14:47	Tor.
May 2/00	Pit.	CSF	Phi. 4	Pit. 3	Andy Delmore	11:01	Phi.
May 3/00	Det.	CSF	Col. 3	Det. 2	Chris Drury	10:21	Col.
May 4/00	Pit.	CSF	Phi. 2	Pit. 1	Keith Primeau	92:01	Phi.
May 23/00	Dal.	CF	Dal. 3	Col. 2	Joe Nieuwendyk	12:10	Dal.
Jun. 8/00	N.J.	F	Dal. 1	N.J. 0	Mike Modano	46:21	N.J.
Jun. 10/00	Dal.	F	N.J. 2	Dal. 1	Jason Arnott	28:20	N.J.
Apr. 11/01	Dal.	CQF	Dal. 2	Edm. 1	Jamie Langenbrunner	2:08	Dal.
Apr. 13/01	Ott.	CQF	Tor. 1	Ott. 0	Mats Sundin	10:49	Tor.

Date	City	Series	Score		Scorer	Overtime	Series Winner
Apr. 14/01	Phi.	CQF	Buf. 4	Phi. 3	Jay McKee	18:02	Buf.
Apr. 15/01	Edm.	CQF	Dal. 3	Edm. 2	Benoit Hogue	19:48	Dal.
Apr. 16/01	Tor.	CQF	Tor. 3	Ott. 2	Cory Cross	2:16	Tor.
Apr. 16/01	Van.	CQF	Col. 4	Van. 3	Peter Forsberg	2:50	Col.
Apr. 17/01	Buf.	CQF	Buf. 4	Phi. 3	Curtis Brown	6:13	Buf.
Apr. 17/01	Edm.	CQF	Edm. 2	Dal. 1	Mike Comrie	17:19	Dal.
Apr. 18/01	Car.	CQF	Car. 3	N.J. 2	Rod Brind'Amour	:46	N.J.
Apr. 18/01	Pit.	CQF	Wsh. 4	Pit. 3	Jeff Halpern	4:01	Pit.
Apr. 18/01	L.A.	CQF	L.A. 4	Det. 3	Eric Belanger	2:36	L.A.
Apr. 19/01	Dal.	CQF	Dal. 4	Edm. 3	Kirk Muller	8:01	Dal.
Apr. 19/01	St.L.	CQF	St.L. 3	S.J. 2	Bryce Salvador	9:54	St.L.
Apr. 23/01	Pit.	CQF	Pit. 4	Wsh. 3	Martin Straka	13:04	Pit.
Apr. 23/01	L.A.	CQF	L.A. 3	Det. 2	Adam Deadmarsh	4:48	L.A.
Apr. 26/01	Col.	CSF	L.A. 4	Col. 3	Jaroslav Modry	14:23	Col.
Apr. 28/01	N.J.	CSF	N.J. 6	Tor. 5	Randy McKay	5:31	N.J.
May 1/01	Tor.	CSF	N.J. 3	Tor. 2	Brian Rafalski	7:00	N.J.
May 1/01	St.L.	CSF	St.L. 3	Dal. 2	Cory Stillman	29:26	St.L.
May 5/01	Buf.	CSF	Buf. 3	Pit. 2	Stu Barnes	8:34	Pit.
May 6/01	L.A.	CSF	L.A. 1	Col. 0	Glen Murray	22:41	Col.
May 8/01	Pit.	CSF	Pit. 3	Buf. 2	Martin Straka	11:29	Pit.
May 10/01	Buf.	CSF	Pit. 3	Buf. 2	Darius Kasparaitis	13:01	Pit.
May 16/01	St.L.	CF	St.L. 4	Col. 3	Scott Young	30:27	Col.
May 18/01	St.L.	CF	Col. 4	St.L. 3	Stephane Yelle	4:23	Col.
May 21/01	Col.	CF	Col. 2	St.L. 1	Joe Sakic	:24	Col.
Apr. 17/02	Phi.	CQF	Phi. 1	Ott. 0	Ruslan Fedotenko	7:47	Ott.
Apr. 17/02	Det.	CQF	Van. 4	Det. 3	Henrik Sedin	13:59	Det.
Apr. 19/02	Car.	CQF	Car. 2	N.J. 1	Bates Battaglia	15:26	Car.
Apr. 24/02	Car.	CQF	Car. 3	N.J. 2	Josef Vasicek	8:16	Car.
Apr. 25/02	Col.	CQF	L.A. 1	Col. 0	Craig Johnson	2:19	Col.
Apr. 26/02	Phi.	CQF	Ott. 2	Phi. 1	Martin Havlat	7:33	Ott.
May 4/02	Tor.	CSF	Tor. 3	Ott. 2	Gary Roberts	44:30	Tor.
May 7/02	Mtl.	CSF	Mtl. 2	Car. 1	Donald Audette	2:26	Car.
May 9/02	Mtl.	CSF	Car. 4	Mtl. 3	Niclas Wallin	3:14	Car.
May 13/02	S.J.	CSF	Col. 2	S.J. 1	Peter Forsberg	2:47	Col.
May 19/02	Car.	CF	Car. 2	Tor. 1	Niclas Wallin	13:42	Car.
May 20/02	Det.	CF	Col. 4	Det. 3	Chris Drury	2:17	Det.
May 21/02	Tor.	CF	Car. 2	Tor. 1	Jeff O'Neill	6:01	Car.
May 22/02	Col.	CF	Det. 2	Col. 1	Fredrik Olausson	12:44	Det.
May 27/02	Det.	CF	Col. 2	Det. 1	Peter Forsberg	6:24	Det.
May 28/02	Tor.	CF	Car. 2	Tor. 1	Martin Gelinas	8:05	Car.
Jun. 4/02	Det.	F	Car. 3	Det. 2	Ron Francis	:58	Det.
Jun. 8/02	Car.	F	Det. 3	Car. 2	Igor Larionov	54:47	Det.
Apr. 10/03	Det.	CQF	Ana. 2	Det. 1	Paul Kariya	43:18	Ana.
Apr. 14/03	NYI	CQF	Ott. 3	NYI 2	Todd White	22:25	Ott.
Apr. 14/03	Tor.	CQF	Tor. 4	Phi. 3	Tomas Kaberle	27:20	Phi.
Apr. 15/03	Wsh.	CQF	T.B. 4	Wsh. 3	Vincent Lecavalier	2:29	T.B.
Apr. 16/03	Tor.	CQF	Phi. 3	Tor. 2	Mark Recchi	53:54	Phi.
Apr. 16/03	Ana.	CQF	Ana. 3	Det. 2	Steve Rucchin	6:53	Ana.
Apr. 20/03	Wsh.	CQF	T.B. 2	Wsh. 1	Martin St. Louis	44:03	T.B.
Apr. 21/03	Tor.	CQF	Tor. 2	Phi. 1	Travis Green	30:51	Phi.
Apr. 21/03	Min.	CQF	Min. 3	Col. 2	Richard Park	4:22	Min.
Apr. 22/03	Col.	CQF	Min. 3	Col. 2	Andrew Brunette	3:25	Min.
Apr. 24/03	Dal.	CSF	Ana. 4	Dal. 3	Petr Sykora	80:48	Ana.
Apr. 25/03	Van.	CSF	Van. 4	Min. 3	Trent Klatt	3:42	Min.
Apr. 26/03	N.J.	CSF	N.J. 3	T.B. 2	Jamie Langenbrunner	2:09	N.J.
Apr. 26/03	Dal.	CSF	Ana. 3	Dal. 2	Mike Leclerc	1:44	Ana.
Apr. 29/03	Phi.	CSF	Ott. 3	Phi. 2	Wade Redden	6:43	Ott.
May 2/03	Min.	CSF	Van. 3	Min. 2	Brent Sopel	15:52	Min.
May 2/03	N.J.	CSF	N.J. 2	T.B. 1	Grant Marshall	51:12	N.J.
May 10/03	Min.	CF	Ana. 1	Min. 0	Petr Sykora	28:06	Ana.
May 10/03	Ott.	CF	Ott. 3	N.J. 2	Shaun Van Allen	3:08	N.J.
May 21/03	N.J.	CF	Ott. 2	N.J. 1	Chris Phillips	15:51	N.J.
May 31/03	Ana.	F	Ana. 3	N.J. 2	Ruslan Salei	6:59	N.J.
Jun. 2/03	Ana.	F	Ana. 1	N.J. 0	Steve Thomas	0:39	N.J.
Apr. 8/04	S.J.	CQF	S.J. 1	St.L. 0	Niko Dimitrakos	9:16	S.J.
Apr. 9/04	Bos.	CQF	Bos. 2	Mtl. 1	Patrice Bergeron	1:26	Mtl.
Apr. 12/04	Dal.	CQF	Dal. 4	Col. 3	Steve Ott	2:11	Col.
Apr. 13/04	Mtl.	CQF	Bos. 4	Mtl. 3	Glen Murray	29:27	Mtl.
Apr. 14/04	Dal.	CQF	Col. 3	Dal. 2	Marek Svatos	25:21	Col.
Apr. 16/04	T.B.	CQF	T.B. 3	NYI 2	Martin St. Louis	4:07	T.B.
Apr. 17/04	Cgy.	CQF	Van. 5	Cgy. 4	Brendan Morrison	42:28	Cgy.
Apr. 18/04	Ott.	CQF	Ott. 2	Tor. 1	Mike Fisher	21:47	Tor.
Apr. 19/04	Van.	CQF	Cgy. 3	Van. 2	Martin Gelinas	1:25	Cgy.
Apr. 22/04	Det.	CSF	Cgy. 2	Det. 1	Marcus Nilson	2:39	Cgy.
Apr. 27/04	Mtl.	CSF	T.B. 4	Mtl 3	Brad Richards	1:05	T.B.
Apr. 28/04	Col	CSF	Col. 1	S.J. 0	Joe Sakic	5:15	S.J.
May 1/04	S.J.	CSF	Col. 2	S.J. 1	Joe Sakic	1:54	S.J.
May 3/04	Cgy	CSF	Cgy. 1	Det. 0	Martin Gelinas	19:13	Cgy.
May 4/04	Phi.	CSF	Phi. 3	Tor. 2	Jeremy Roenick	7:39	Phi.
May 9/04	S.J.	CF	Cgy. 4	S.J. 3	Steve Montador	18:43	Cgy.
May 20/04	Phi.	CF	Phi. 5	T.B. 4	Simon Gagne	18:18	T.B.
Jun. 3/04	T.B.	F	Cgy. 3	T.B. 2	Oleg Saprykin	14:40	T.B.
Jun. 5/04	Cgy.	F	T.B. 3	Cgy. 2	Martin St. Louis	20:33	T.B.
Apr. 21/06	Det.	CQF	Det. 3	Edm. 2	Kirk Maltby	22:39	Edm.
Apr. 21/06	Cgy.	CQF	Cgy. 2	Ana. 1	Darren McCarty	9:45	Ana.
Apr. 22/06	Buf.	CQF	Buf. 3	Phi. 2	Daniel Briere	27:31	Buf.
Apr. 24/06	Car.	CQF	Mtl. 6	Car. 5	Michael Ryder	22:32	Car.
Apr. 24/06	Dal.	CQF	Col. 5	Dal. 4	Joe Sakic	4:36	Col.
Apr. 25/06	Edm.	CQF	Edm. 4	Det. 3	Jarret Stoll	28:44	Edm.
Apr. 26/06	Mtl.	CQF	Car. 2	Mtl. 1	Eric Staal	3:38	Car.
Apr. 26/06	Col.	CQF	Col. 4	Dal. 3	Alex Tanguay	1:09	Col.
Apr. 27/06	Ana.	CQF	Ana. 3	Cgy. 2	Sean O'Donnell	1:36	Ana.
Apr. 30/06	Dal.	CQF	Col. 3	Dal. 2	Andrew Brunette	13:55	Col.
May 2/06	Mtl.	CQF	Car. 2	Mtl. 1	Cory Stillman	1:19	Car.
May 5/06	Ott.	CSF	Buf. 7	Ott. 6	Chris Drury	0:18	Buf.
May 8/06	Car.	CSF	Car. 3	N.J. 2	Niclas Wallin	3:09	Car.
May 9/06	Col.	CSF	Ana. 4	Col. 3	Joffrey Lupul	16:30	Ana.
May 10/06	Buf.	CSF	Buf. 3	Ott. 2	J.P. Dumont	5:05	Buf.
May 10/06	Edm.	CSF	Edm. 3	S.J. 2	Shawn Horcoff	42:24	Edm.
May 13/06	Ott.	CSF	Buf. 3	Ott. 2	Jason Pominville	2:26	Buf.
May 28/06	Car.	CF	Car. 4	Buf. 3	Cory Stillman	8:46	Car.
May 30/06	Buf.	CF	Buf. 2	Car. 1	Daniel Briere	4:22	Car.
June 14/06	Car.	F	Edm. 4	Car. 3	Fernando Pisani	3:31	Car.
Apr. 11/07	Nsh.	CQF	S.J. 5	Nsh. 4	Patrick Rissmiller	28:14	S.J.
Apr. 11/07	Van.	CQF	Van. 5	Dal. 4	Henrik Sedin	78:06	Van.
Apr. 15/07	Dal.	CQF	Van. 2	Dal. 1	Taylor Pyatt	7:47	Van.
Apr. 18/07	T.B.	CQF	N.J. 4	T.B. 3	Scott Gomez	12:54	N.J.

Overtime Games since 1918 — *continued*

Date	City	Series	Score		Scorer	Overtime	Series Winner
Apr. 19/07	Van.	CQF	Dal. 1	Van. 0	Brenden Morrow	6:22	Van.
Apr. 22/07	Cgy.	CQF	Det. 2	Cgy. 1	Johan Franzen	24:23	Det.
Apr. 27/07	Ana.	CSF	Van. 2	Ana. 1	Jeff Cowan	27:49	Ana.
Apr. 28/07	N.J.	CSF	N.J. 3	Ott. 2	Jamie Langenbrunner	21:55	Ott.
Apr. 29/07	NYR	CSF	NYR 2	Buf. 1	Michal Rozsival	36:43	Buf.
May 1/07	Van.	CSF	Ana. 3	Van. 2	Travis Moen	2:07	Ana.
May 2/07	S.J.	CSF	Det. 3	S.J. 2	Mathieu Schnieder	16:04	Det.
May 3/07	Ana.	CSF	Ana. 2	Van. 1	Scott Niedermayer	24:30	Ana.
May 4/07	Buf.	CSF	Buf. 2	NYR 1	Maxim Afinogenov	4:39	Buf.
May 12/07	Buf.	CF	Ott. 4	Buf. 3	Joe Corvo	24:58	Ott.
May 13/07	Det.	CF	Ana. 4	Det. 3	Scott Niedermayer	14:17	Ana.
May 19/07	Buf.	CF	Ott. 3	Buf. 2	Daniel Alfredsson	9:32	Ott.
May 20/07	Det.	CF	Ana. 2	Det. 1	Teemu Selanne	11:57	Ana.
Apr. 9/08	Min.	CQF	Col. 3	Min. 2	Joe Sakic	11:11	Col.
Apr. 11/08	Min.	CQF	Min. 3	Col. 2	Keith Carney	1:14	Col.
Apr. 12/08	Mtl.	CQF	Mtl. 3	Bos. 2	Alex Kovalev	2:30	Mtl.
Apr. 13/08	Mtl.	CQF	Bos. 2	Mtl. 1	Marc Savard	9:25	Mtl.
Apr. 13/08	NYR	CQF	N.J. 4	NYR 3	John Madden	6:01	NYR
Apr. 14/08	Col.	CQF	Min. 3	Col. 2	Pierre-Marc Bouchard	11:58	Col.
Apr. 17/08	Phi.	CQF	Phi. 4	Wsh. 3	Mike Knuble	26:40	Phi.
Apr. 18/08	Det.	CQF	Det. 2	Nsh. 1	Johan Franzen	1:48	Det.
Apr. 22/08	Wsh.	CQF	Phi. 3	Wsh. 2	Joffrey Lupul	6:06	Phi.
Apr. 24/08	Mtl.	CSF	Mtl. 4	Phi. 3	Tom Kostopoulos	0:48	Phi.
Apr. 25/08	S.J.	CSF	Dal. 3	S.J. 2	Brenden Morrow	4:39	Dal.
Apr. 29/08	Dal.	CSF	Dal. 2	S.J. 1	Mattias Norstrom	4:37	Dal.
May 2/08	S.J.	CSF	S.J. 3	Dal. 2	Joe Pavelski	1:05	Dal.
May 4/08	Pit.	CSF	Pit. 3	NYR 2	Marian Hossa	7:10	Pit.
May 4/08	Dal.	CSF	Dal. 2	S.J. 1	Brenden Morrow	69:03	Dal.
June 2/08	Det.	F	Pit. 3	Det. 2	Petr Sykora	49:57	Det.
Apr. 16/09	Chi.	CQF	Chi. 3	Cgy. 2	Martin Havlat	0:12	Chi.
Apr. 17/09	Pit.	CQF	Pit. 3	Phi. 2	Bill Guerin	18:29	Pit.
Apr. 17/09	N.J.	CQF	Car. 2	N.J. 1	Tim Gleason	2:40	Car.
Apr. 19/09	Car.	CQF	N.J. 3	Car. 2	Travis Zajac	4:58	Car.
Apr. 21/09	St.L.	CQF	Van. 3	St.L. 2	Alex Burrows	19:41	Van.
Apr. 25/09	S.J.	CQF	S.J. 3	Ana. 2	Patrick Marleau	6:02	Ana.
May 3/09	Det.	CSF	Ana. 4	Det. 3	Todd Marchant	41:15	Det.
May 6/09	Pit.	CSF	Pit. 3	Wsh. 2	Kris Letang	11:23	Pit.
May 6/09	Car.	CSF	Car. 3	Bos. 2	Jussi Jokinen	2:48	Car.
May 7/09	Chi.	CSF	Chi. 2	Van. 1	Andrew Ladd	2:52	Chi.
May 9/09	Wsh.	CSF	Pit. 4	Wsh. 3	Evgeni Malkin	3:28	Pit.
May 11/09	Pit.	CSF	Wsh. 5	Pit. 4	David Steckel	6:22	Pit.
May 14/09	Bos.	CSF	Car. 3	Bos. 2	Scott Walker	18:46	Car.
May 19/09	Det.	CF	Det. 3	Chi. 2	Mikael Samuelsson	5:14	Det.
May 22/09	Chi.	CF	Chi. 4	Det. 3	Patrick Sharp	1:52	Det.
May 27/09	Det.	CF	Det. 2	Chi. 1	Darren Helm	3:58	Det.
Apr. 15/10	Wsh.	CQF	Mtl. 3	Wsh. 2	Tomas Plekanec	13:19	Mtl.
Apr. 15/10	Van.	CQF	Van. 3	L.A. 2	Mikael Samuelsson	8:52	Van.
Apr. 16/10	S.J.	CQF	S.J. 6	Col. 5	Devin Setoguchi	5:22	S.J.
Apr. 17/10	Wsh.	CQF	Wsh. 6	Mtl. 5	Nicklas Backstrom	0:31	Mtl.
Apr. 17/10	Van.	CQF	L.A. 3	Van. 2	Anze Kopitar	7:28	Van.
Apr. 18/10	Phi.	CQF	Phi. 3	N.J. 2	Daniel Carcillo	3:35	Phi.
Apr. 18/10	Col.	CQF	Col. 1	S.J. 0	Ryan O'Reilly	0:51	S.J.
Apr. 20/10	Col.	CQF	S.J. 2	Col. 1	Joe Pavelski	10:24	S.J.
Apr. 21/10	Bos.	CQF	Bos. 3	Buf. 2	Miroslav Satan	27:41	Bos.
Apr. 22/10	Pit.	CQF	Ott. 4	Pit. 3	Matt Carkner	47:06	Pit.
Apr. 24/10	Chi.	CQF	Chi. 5	Nsh. 4	Marian Hossa	4:07	Chi.
Apr. 24/10	Ott.	CQF	Pit. 4	Ott. 3	Pascal Dupuis	9:56	Pit.
May 1/10	Bos.	CSF	Bos. 5	Phi. 4	Marc Savard	13:52	Phi.
May 4/10	Det.	CSF	S.J. 4	Det. 3	Patrick Marleau	7:07	S.J.
May 7/10	Phi.	CSF	Phi. 5	Bos. 4	Simon Gagne	14:40	Phi.
May 21/10	Chi.	CF	Chi. 3	S.J. 2	Dustin Byfuglien	12:24	Chi.
June 2/10	Phi.	F	Phi. 4	Chi. 3	Claude Giroux	5:59	Chi.
June 9/10	Phi.	F	Chi. 4	Phi. 3	Patrick Kane	4:06	Chi.
Apr. 13/11	Wsh.	CQF	Wsh. 2	NYR 1	Alexander Semin	18:24	Wsh.
Apr. 14/11	S.J.	CQF	S.J. 3	L.A. 2	Joe Pavelski	14:44	S.J.
Apr. 19/11	L.A.	CQF	S.J. 6	L.A. 5	Devin Setoguchi	3:09	S.J.
Apr. 20/11	NYR	CQF	Wsh. 4	NYR 3	Jason Chimera	32:36	Wsh.
Apr. 20/11	T.B.	CQF	Pit. 3	T.B. 2	James Neal	23:38	T.B.
Apr. 21/11	Mtl.	CQF	Bos. 5	Mtl. 4	Michael Ryder	1:59	Bos.
Apr. 22/11	Phi.	CQF	Buf. 4	Phi. 3	Tyler Ennis	5:31	Phi.
Apr. 22/11	Ana.	CQF	Nsh. 4	Ana. 3	Jerred Smithson	1:57	Nsh.
Apr. 23/11	Bos.	CQF	Bos. 2	Mtl. 1	Nathan Horton	29:03	Bos.
Apr. 24/11	Buf.	CQF	Phi. 5	Buf. 4	Ville Leino	4:43	Phi.
Apr. 24/11	Chi.	CQF	Chi. 4	Van. 3	Ben Smith	15:30	Van.
Apr. 25/11	L.A.	CQF	S.J. 4	L.A. 3	Joe Thornton	2:22	S.J.
Apr. 26/11	Van.	CQF	Van. 2	Chi. 1	Alexandre Burrows	5:22	Van.
Apr. 27/11	Bos.	CQF	Bos. 4	Mtl. 3	Nathan Horton	5:43	Bos.
Apr. 29/11	S.J.	CSF	S.J. 2	Det. 1	Benn Ferriero	7:03	S.J.
Apr. 30/11	Van.	CSF	Nsh. 2	Van. 1	Matt Halischuk	34:51	Van.
May 1/11	Wsh.	CSF	T.B. 3	Wsh. 2	Vincent Lecavalier	6:19	T.B.
May 2/11	Phi.	CSF	Bos. 3	Phi. 2	David Krejci	14:00	Bos.
May 3/11	Nsh.	CSF	Van. 3	Nsh. 2	Ryan Kesler	10:49	Van.
May 4/11	Det.	CSF	S.J. 4	Det. 3	Devin Setoguchi	9:21	S.J.
May 24/11	Van.	CF	Van. 3	S.J. 2	Kevin Bieksa	30:18	Van.
June 4/11	Van.	F	Van. 3	Bos. 2	Alexandre Burrows	0:11	Bos.
Apr. 11/12	Pit.	CQF	Phi. 4	Pit. 3	Jakub Voracek	2:23	Phi.
Apr. 12/12	Bos.	CQF	Bos. 1	Wsh. 0	Chris Kelly	1:18	Wsh.
Apr. 12/12	St. L.	CQF	S.J. 3	St. L. 2	Martin Havlat	23:34	St. L.
Apr. 12/12	Phx.	CQF	Phx. 3	Chi. 2	Martin Hanzal	9:29	Phx.
Apr. 14/12	Bos.	CQF	Wsh. 2	Bos. 1	Nicklas Backstrom	22:56	Wsh.
Apr. 14/12	NYR	CQF	Ott. 3	NYR 2	Chris Neil	1:17	NYR
Apr. 14/12	Phx.	CQF	Chi. 4	Phx. 3	Bryan Bickell	10:36	Phx.
Apr. 17/12	Chi.	CQF	Phx. 3	Chi. 2	Mikkel Boedker	13:15	Phx.
Apr. 18/12	Ott.	CQF	Ott. 3	NYR 2	Kyle Turris	2:42	NYR
Apr. 19/12	Chi.	CQF	Phx. 3	Chi. 2	Mikkel Boedker	2:15	Phx.
Apr. 21/12	Phx.	CQF	Chi. 2	Phx. 1	Jonathan Toews	2:44	Phx.
Apr. 22/12	Wsh.	CQF	Bos. 4	Wsh. 3	Tyler Seguin	3:17	Wsh.
Apr. 22/12	Van.	CQF	L.A. 2	Van. 1	Jarret Stoll	4:27	L.A.
Apr. 24/12	N.J.	CQF	N.J. 3	Fla. 2	Travis Zajac	5:39	N.J.
Apr. 25/12	Bos.	CQF	Wsh. 2	Bos. 1	Joel Ward	2:57	Wsh.
Apr. 26/12	Fla.	CQF	N.J. 3	Fla. 2	Adam Henrique	23:47	N.J.
Apr. 27/12	Phx.	CSF	Phx. 4	Nsh. 2	Ray Whitney	14:04	Phx.
Apr. 29/12	Phi.	CSF	Phi. 4	N.J. 3	Daniel Briere	4:36	N.J.
May 2/12	Wsh.	CSF	NYR 2	Wsh. 1	Marian Gaborik	54:41	NYR
May 3/12	N.J.	CSF	N.J. 4	Phi. 3	Alexei Ponikarovsky	17:21	N.J.
May 7/12	NYR	CSF	NYR 3	Wsh. 2	Marc Staal	1:35	NYR
May 22/12	Phx.	CF	L.A. 4	Phx. 3	Dustin Penner	17:42	L.A.
May 25/12	N.J.	CF	N.J. 2	NYR 1	Adam Henrique	1:03	N.J.
May 30/12	N.J.	F	L.A. 2	N.J. 1	Anze Kopitar	8:13	L.A.
June 2/12	N.J.	F	L.A. 2	N.J. 1	Jeff Carter	13:42	L.A.
Apr. 30/13	Chi.	CQF	Chi. 2	Min. 1	Bryan Bickell	16:35	Chi.
Apr. 30/13	St.L.	CQF	St.L. 2	L.A. 1	Alex Steen	13:26	L.A.
May 2/13	Ana.	CQF	Det. 5	Ana. 4	Gustav Nyquist	1:21	Det.
May 3/13	Van.	CQF	S.J. 3	Van. 2	RaffiTorres	5:31	S.J.
May 4/13	Wsh.	CQF	Wsh. 1	NYR 0	Mike Green	8:00	NYR
May 5/13	NYI	CQF	Pit. 5	NYI 4	Chris Kunitz	8:44	Pit.
May 5/13	Min.	CQF	Min. 3	Chi.2	Jason Zucker	2:15	Chi.
May 6/13	Det.	CQF	Det. 3	Ana. 2	Damien Brunner	15:10	Det.
May 7/13	Ott.	CQF	Ott. 3	Mtl. 2	Kyle Turris	2:32	Ott.
May 7/13	S.J.	CQF	S.J. 4	Van. 3	Patrick Marleau	13:18	S.J.
May 8/13	Tor.	CQF	Bos. 4	Tor. 3	David Krejci	13:06	Bos.
May 8/13	Ana.	CQF	Ana. 3	Det. 2	Nick Bonino	1:54	Det.
May 8/13	St.L.	CQF	L.A. 3	St.L. 2	Slava Voynov	8:00	L.A.
May 10/13	Wsh.	CQF	Wsh. 2	NYR 1	Mike Ribeiro	9:24	NYR
May 10/13	Det.	CQF	Det. 4	Ana. 3	Henrik Zetterberg	1:04	Det.
May 11/13	NYI	CQF	Pit. 4	NYI 3	Brooks Orpik	7:49	Pit.
May 13/13	Bos.	CQF	Bos. 5	Tor. 4	Patrice Bergeron	6:05	Bos.
May 16/13	Bos.	CSF	Bos. 3	NYR 2	Brad Marchand	15:40	Bos.
May 18/13	S.J.	CSF	S.J. 2	L.A. 1	Logan Couture	1:29	L.A.
May 19/13	Ott.	CSF	Ott. 2	Pit. 1	Colin Greening	27:39	Pit.
May 23/13	NYR	CSF	NYR 4	Bos. 3	Chris Kreider	7:03	Bos.
May 29/13	Chi.	CSF	Chi. 2	Det. 1	Brent Seabrook	3:35	Chi.
June 5/13	Bos.	CF	Bos.2	Pit. 1	Patrice Bergeron	35:19	Bos.
June 8/13	Chi.	CF	Chi. 4	L.A. 3	Patrick Kane	31:40	Chi.
June 12/13	Chi.	F	Chi. 4	Bos. 3	Andrew Shaw	52:08	Chi.
June 15/13	Chi.	F	Bos.2	Chi. 1	Daniel Paille	13:48	Chi.
June 19/13	Bos.	F	Chi. 6	Bos. 5	Brent Seabrook	9:51	Chi.
Apr. 16/14	T.B.	FR	Mtl. 5	T.B. 4	Dale Weise	18:08	Mtl.
Apr. 17/14	St.L.	FR	St.L. 4	Chi. 3	Alexander Steen	40:26	Chi.
Apr. 17/14	Col,	FR	Col. 5	Min. 4	Paul Stastny	7:27	Min.
Apr. 19/14	Pit.	FR	CBJ 4	Pit. 3	Matt Calvert	21:10	Pit.
Apr. 19/14	St.L.	FR	St.L. 4	Chi. 3	Barret Jackman	5:50	Chi.
Apr. 21/14	Min.	FR	Min. 1	Col. 0	Mikael Granlund	5:08	Min.
Apr. 22/14	L.A.	FR	S.J. 4	L.A. 3	Patrick Marleau	6:20	L.A.
Apr. 23/14	CBJ	FR	CBJ 4	Pit. 3	Nick Foligno	2:49	Pit.
Apr. 23/14	Chi.	FR	Chi. 4	St.L. 3	Patrick Kane	11:17	Chi.
Apr. 24/14	Det.	FR	Bos. 3	Det. 2	Jarome Iginla	13:32	Bos.
Apr. 25/14	St.L.	FR	Chi. 3	St.L. 2	Jonathan Toews	7:36	Chi.
Apr. 26/14	Col.	FR	Col. 4	Min. 3	Nathan MacKinnon	3:27	Min.
Apr. 27/14	Dal.	FR	Ana. 5	Dal. 4	Nick Bonino	2:47	Ana.
Apr. 30/14	Col.	FR	Min. 5	Col. 4	Nino Niederreiter	5:02	Min.
May 1/14	Bos.	SR	Mtl. 4	Bos. 3	P.K. Subban	24:17	Mtl.
May 2/14	Pit.	SR	NYR 3	Pit. 2	Derick Brassard	3:06	NYR
May 3/14	Ana.	SR	L.A. 3	Ana. 2	Marian Gaborik	12:07	L.A.
May 8/14	Mtl.	SR	Bos.1	Mtl. 0	Matt Fraser	1:19	Mtl.
May 13/14	Min.	SR	Chi. 2	Min. 1	Patrick Kane	9:42	Chi.
May 22/14	NYR	CF	Mtl. 3	NYR 2	Alex Galchenyuk	1:12	NYR
May 25/14	NYR	CF	NYR 3	Mtl. 2	Martin St. Louis	6:02	NYR
May 28/14	Chi.	CF	Chi. 3	L.A. 2	Michal Handzus	22:04	L.A.
June 1/14	Chi.	CF	L.A. 5	Chi. 4	Alec Martinez	5:47	L.A.
June 4/14	L.A.	F	L.A. 3	NYR 2	Justin Williams	4:36	L.A.
June 7/14	L.A.	F	L.A. 5	NYR 4	Dustin Brown	30:26	L.A.
June 13/14	L.A.	F	L.A. 3	NYR 2	Alec Martinez	34:43	L.A.
Apr. 15/15	Nsh.	FR	Chi. 4	Nsh. 3	Duncan Keith	27:49	Chi.
Apr. 17/15	Mtl.	FR	Mtl. 3	Ott. 2	Alex Galchenyuk	3:40	Mtl.
Apr. 19/15	NYI	FR	NYI 2	Wsh. 1	John Tavares	0:15	Wsh.
Apr. 19/15	Ott.	FR	Mtl. 2	Ott. 1	Dale Weise	8:47	Mtl.
Apr. 20/15	Wpg.	FR	Ana. 5	Wpg. 4	Rickard Rakell	5:12	Ana.
Apr. 21/15	NYI	FR	Wsh. 2	NYI 1	Nicklas Backstrom	11:09	Wsh.
Apr. 21/15	Chi.	FR	Chi. 3	Nsh. 2	Brent Seabrook	41:00	Chi.
Apr. 22/15	Pit.	FR	NYR 2	Pit. 1	Kevin Hayes	3:14	NYR
Apr. 23/15	Det.	FR	T.B. 3	Det. 2	Tyler Johnson	2:25	T.B.
Apr. 24/15	NYR	FR	NYR 2	Pit. 1	Carl Hagelin	10:52	NYR
May 1/15	Mtl.	SR	T.B. 2	Mtl. 1	Nikita Kucherov	22.06	T.B.
May 5/15	Cgy.	SR	Cgy. 4	Ana. 3	Mikael Backlund	4:24	Ana.
May 8/15	NYR	SR	NYR 2	Wsh. 1	Ryan McDonagh	9:37	NYR
May 10/15	Ana.	SR	Ana. 3	Cgy. 2	Corey Perry	2:26	Ana.
May 13/15	NYR	SR	NYR 2	Wsh. 1	Derek Stepan	11:24	NYR
May 19/15	Ana.	CF	Chi. 3	Ana. 2	Marcus Kruger	56:12	Chi.
May 20/15	T.B.	CF	T.B. 6	NYR 5	Nikita Kucherov	3:33	T.B.
May 23/15	Chi.	CF	Chi. 5	Ana. 4	Antoine Vermette	25:37	Chi.
May 25/15	Ana.	CF	Ana. 5	Chi. 4	Matt Beleskey	0:45	Chi.
Apr. 13/16	St. L.	FR	St.L. 1	Chi. 0	David Backes	9:04	St.L.
Apr. 17/16	NYI	FR	NYI 4	Fla. 3	Thomas Hickey	12:31	NYI
Apr. 18/16	S.J.	FR	L.A. 2	S.J. 1	Tanner Pearson	3:47	S.J.
Apr. 21/16	St.L.	FR	Chi. 4	St.L.3	Patrick Kane	23:07	St.L.
Apr. 22/16	Fla.	FR	NYI 2	Fla. 1	Alan Quine	36:00	NYI
Apr. 22/16	Dal.	FR	Min. 5	Dal. 4	Mikko Koivu	4:55	Dal.
Apr. 24/16	NYI	FR	NYI 2	Fla. 1	John Tavares	30:41	NYI
Apr. 28/16	Wsh.	SR	Wsh. 4	Pit. 3	T.J. Oshie	9:33	Pit.
May 1/16	Dal.	SR	St.L. 4	Dal. 3	David Backes	10:58	St.L.
May 3/16	NYI	SR	T.B. 5	NYI 4	Brian Boyle	2:48	T.B.
May 4/16	Pit.	SR	Pit. 3	Wsh. 2	Patric Hornqvist	2:34	Pit.
May 5/16	St.L.	SR	Dal. 3	St.L. 2	Cody Eakin	2:58	St.L.
May 5/16	Nsh.	SR	Nsh. 4	S.J. 3	Mike Fisher	51:12	S.J.
May 6/16	NYI	SR	T.B. 2	NYI 1	Jason Garrison	1:34	T.B.
May 9/16	Nsh.	SR	Nsh. 4	S.J. 3	Viktor Arvidsson	2:03	S.J.
May 10/16	Pit.	SR	Pit. 4	Wsh. 3	Nick Bonino	6:32	Pit.
May 16/16	Pit.	CF	Pit. 3	T.B. 2	Sidney Crosby	0:40	Pit.
May 22/16	Pit.	CF	T.B. 4	Pit. 3	Tyler Johnson	0:53	Pit.
June 1/16	Pit.	F	Pit. 2	S.J. 1	Conor Sheary	2:35	Pit.
June 4/16	S.J.	F	S.J. 3	Pit. 2	Joonas Donskoi	12:18	Pit.
Apr. 12/17	Min.	FR	St.L. 2	Min. 1	Joel Edmundson	17:48	St.L.
Apr. 12/17	Edm.	FR	S.J. 3	Edm. 2	Melker Karlsson	3:22	Edm.
Apr. 13/17	Wsh.	FR	Wsh. 3	Tor. 2	Tom Wilson	5:15	Wsh.
Apr. 14/17	Mtl.	FR	Mtl. 4	NYR 3	Alexander Radulov	18:34	NYR
Apr. 15/17	Ott.	FR	Ott. 4	Bos. 3	Dion Phaneuf	1:59	Ott.
Apr. 15/17	Wsh.	FR	Tor. 4	Wsh. 3	Kasperi Kapanen	31:53	Wsh.
Apr. 16/17	CBJ	FR	Pit. 5	CBJ 4	Jake Guentzel	13:10	Pit.
Apr. 17/17	Bos.	FR	Ott. 4	Bos. 3	Bobby Ryan	5:43	Ott.
Apr. 17/17	Tor.	FR	Tor. 4	Wsh. 3	Tyler Bozak	1:37	Wsh.

Date	City	Series	Score		Scorer	Overtime	Series Winner
Apr. 17/17	Nsh.	FR	Nsh. 3	Chi. 2	Kevin Fiala	16:44	Nsh.
Apr. 17/17	Cgy.	FR	Ana. 5	Cgy. 4	Corey Perry	1:30	Cgy.
Apr. 20/17	Mtl.	FR	NYR 3	Mtl. 2	Mika Zibanejad	14:22	NYR
Apr. 20/17	Edm.	FR	Edm. 4	S.J. 3	David Desharnais	18:15	Edm.
Apr. 21/17	Wsh.	FR	Wsh. 2	Tor. 1	Justin Williams	1:04	Wsh.
Apr. 21/17	Ott.	FR	Bos. 3	Ott. 2	Sean Kuraly	30:19	Ott.
Apr. 22/17	Min.	FR	St.L. 4	Min. 3	Magnus Paajarvi	9:42	St.L.
Apr. 23/17	Bos.	FR	Ott. 3	Bos. 2	Clarke MacArthur	6:30	Ott.
Apr. 23/17	Tor.	FR	Wsh. 2	Tor. 1	Marcus Johansson	6:31	Wsh.
Apr. 29/17	Ott.	SR	Ott. 6	NYR 5	Jean-Gabriel Pageau	22:54	Ott.
May 1/17	Pit.	SR	Wsh. 3	Pit. 2	Kevin Shattenkirk	3:13	Pit.
May 3/17	Edm.	SR	Ana. 4	Edm. 3	Jakob Silverberg	0:45	Ana.
May 5/17	Ana.	SR	Ana. 4	Edm. 3	Corey Perry	26:57	Ana.
May 6/17	Ott.	SR	Ott. 5	NYR 4	Kyle Turris	6:28	Ott.
May 12/17	Ana.	CF	Nsh. 3	Ana. 2	James Neal	9:24	Nsh.
May 13/17	Pit.	CF	Ott. 2	Pit. 1	Bobby Ryan	4:59	Pit.
May 18/17	Nsh.	CF	Ana. 3	Nsh. 2	Corey Perry	10:25	Nsh.
May 25/17	Pit.	CF	Pit. 3	Ott. 2	Chris Kunitz	5:09	Pit.

Overtime Record of Current Teams

(Listed by number of OT games played)

	Overall				Home					Road				
Team	GP	W	L	T	GP	W	L	T	Last OT Game	GP	W	L	T	Last OT Game
Montreal	149	81	65	3	70	41	28	1	Apr. 21/17	79	40	37	2	Apr. 19/15
Boston	132	57	72	3	62	30	31	1	Apr. 23/17	70	27	41	2	Apr. 21/17
Toronto	115	58	56	1	72	38	33	1	Apr. 23/17	43	20	23	0	Apr. 21/17
Chicago	101	54	45	2	49	30	18	1	May 23/15	52	24	27	1	Apr. 17/17
Detroit	99	43	56	0	59	22	37	0	Apr. 23/15	40	21	19	0	May 29/13
NY Rangers	93	41	52	0	38	19	19	0	May 13/15	55	22	33	0	May 6/17
Philadelphia	74	36	38	0	34	19	15	0	Apr. 29/12	40	17	23	0	May 3/12
Dallas[1]	69	30	39	0	35	13	22	0	May 1/16	34	17	17	0	May 5/16
Colorado[2]	66	37	29	0	29	14	15	0	Apr. 30/14	37	23	14	0	Apr. 21/14
St. Louis	66	35	31	0	38	24	14	0	May 5/16	28	11	17	0	Apr. 22/17
Washington	62	28	34	0	26	12	14	0	Apr. 21/17	36	16	20	0	May 1/17
Buffalo	59	32	27	0	33	20	13	0	Apr. 24/11	26	12	14	0	Apr. 22/11
Pittsburgh	59	30	29	0	36	18	18	0	May 25/17	23	12	11	0	Apr. 16/17
Los Angeles	56	29	27	0	25	14	11	0	June 13/14	31	15	16	0	Apr. 18/16
Vancouver	54	26	28	0	25	11	14	0	May 3/13	29	15	14	0	May 7/13
NY Islanders	49	33	16	0	26	17	9	0	May 6/16	23	16	7	0	Apr. 22/16
New Jersey[3]	47	18	29	0	21	9	12	0	June 2/12	26	9	17	0	Apr. 29/12
Edmonton	46	25	21	0	26	14	12	0	May 3/17	20	11	9	0	May 5/17
San Jose	44	22	22	0	19	10	9	0	June 4/16	25	12	13	0	Apr. 20/17
Calgary[4]	44	18	26	0	21	7	14	0	Apr. 17//17	23	11	12	0	May 10/15
Anaheim	39	24	15	0	16	9	7	0	May 12/17	23	15	8	0	May 18/17
Carolina[5]	34	21	13	0	20	12	8	0	May 6/09	14	9	5	0	May 14/09
Ottawa	38	22	16	0	18	10	8	0	May 6/17	20	12	8	0	May 25/17
Tampa Bay	22	14	8	0	7	3	4	0	May 20/15	15	11	4	0	May 22/16
Arizona[6]	20	8	12	0	14	5	9	0	May 22/12	6	3	3	0	Apr. 19/12
Minnesota	18	8	10	0	10	4	6	0	Apr. 22/17	8	4	4	0	Apr. 22/16
Nashville	14	6	8	0	7	3	4	0	May 18/17	7	3	4	0	May 12/17
Florida	10	2	8	0	5	1	4	0	Apr. 22/16	5	1	4	0	Apr. 24/16
Columbus	3	2	1	0	2	1	1	0	Apr. 16/17	1	1	0	0	Apr. 19/14
Winnipeg[7]	1	0	1	0	1	0	1	0	Apr. 20/15	0	0	0	0	

[1]Totals include those of Minnesota North Stars 1967-93. [2]Totals include those of Quebec Nordiques 1979-95. [3]Totals include those of Kansas City Scouts 1974-76 and Colorado Rockies 1977-82. [4]Totals include those of Atlanta Flames 1972-80. [5]Totals include those of Hartford Whalers 1979-97. [6]Totals include those of Winnipeg Jets 1979-96 and Phoenix Coyotes 1997-2014. [7]Totals include those of Atlanta Thrashers 1999-2011.

Ten Longest Overtime Games

Date	City	Series	Score		Scorer	Overtime	Series Winner
Mar. 24/36	Mtl.	SF	Det. 1	Mtl. M. 0	Mud Bruneteau	116:30	Det.
Apr. 3/33	Tor.	SF	Tor. 1	Bos. 0	Ken Doraty	104:46	Tor.
May 4/00	Pit.	CSF	Phi. 2	Pit. 1	Keith Primeau	92:01	Phi.
Apr. 24/03	Dal.	CSF	Ana. 4	Dal. 3	Petr Sykora	80:48	Ana.
Apr. 24/96	Wsh.	CQF	Pit. 3	Wsh. 2	Petr Nedved	79:15	Pit.
Apr. 11/07	Van.	CQF	Van. 5	Dal. 4	Henrik Sedin	78:06	Van.
Mar. 23/43	Det.	SF	Tor. 3	Det. 2	Jack McLean	70:18	Det.
May 4/08	Dal.	CSF	Dal. 2	S.J. 1	Brenden Morrow	69:03	Dal.
Mar. 28/30	Mtl.	SF	Mtl. 2	NYR 1	Gus Rivers	68:52	Mtl.
Apr. 18/87	Wsh.	DSF	NYI 3	Wsh. 2	Pat LaFontaine	68:47	NYI

Detroit's Ted Lindsay kisses the Stanley Cup after the Red Wings won it in overtime of the seventh game against the Montreal Canadiens in 1954.

Penalty Shots in Stanley Cup Playoff Games

Date	Player, Team	Goaltender, Team	Scored	Final Score				Series
Mar. 21/22	Babe Dye, Toronto	Hugh Lehman, Vancouver	No	Van.	1	at Tor.	2*	F
Mar. 25/37	Lionel Conacher, Mtl. Maroons	Tiny Thompson, Boston	No	Mtl. M.	0	at Bos.	4	QF
Apr. 15/37	Alex Shibicky, NY Rangers	Earl Robertson, Detroit	No	NYR	0	at Det.	3	F
Mar. 24/38	Mush March, Chicago	Wilf Cude, Montreal	No	Mtl.	0	at Chi.	4	QF
Mar. 29/38	Lorne Carr, NY Americans	Mike Karakas, Chicago	No	Chi.	1	at NYA	3	SF
Apr. 10/38	Art Wiebe, Chicago	Turk Broda, Toronto	No	Tor.	1	at Chi.	2	F
Mar. 24/42	Charlie Sands, Montreal	Johnny Mowers, Detroit	No	Det.	0	at Mtl.	5	QF
Apr. 13/44	Virgil Johnson, Chicago	Bill Durnan, Montreal	No	Chi.	4	at Mtl.	5*	F
Apr. 9/68	Wayne Connelly, Minnesota	Terry Sawchuk, Los Angeles	Yes	L.A.	5	at Min.	7	QF
Apr. 27/68	Jim Roberts, St. Louis	Cesare Maniago, Minnesota	No	St.L.	4	at Min.	3	SF
May 16/71	Frank Mahovlich, Montreal	Tony Esposito, Chicago	No	Chi.	3	at Mtl.	4	F
May 7/75	Bill Barber, Philadelphia	Glenn Resch, NY Islanders	No	Phi.	3	at NYI	4*	SF
Apr. 20/79	Mike Walton, Chicago	Glenn Resch, NY Islanders	No	NYI	4	at Chi.	0	QF
Apr. 9/81	Peter McNab, Boston	Don Beaupre, Minnesota	No	Min.	5	at Bos.	4*	PR
Apr. 17/81	Anders Hedberg, NY Rangers	Mike Liut, St. Louis	Yes	NYR	6	at St.L.	4	QF
Apr. 9/83	Denis Potvin, NY Islanders	Pat Riggin, Washington	No	NYI	6	at Wsh.	2	DSF
Apr. 28/84	Wayne Gretzky, Edmonton	Don Beaupre, Minnesota	Yes	Edm.	8	at Min.	5	CF
May 1/84	Mats Naslund, Montreal	Billy Smith, NY Islanders	No	Mtl.	1	at NYI	3	CF
Apr. 14/85	Bob Carpenter, Washington	Billy Smith, NY Islanders	No	Wsh.	4	at NYI.	6	DF
May 28/85	Ron Sutter, Philadelphia	Grant Fuhr, Edmonton	No	Phi.	3	at Edm.	5	F
May 30/85	Dave Poulin, Philadelphia	Grant Fuhr, Edmonton	No	Phi.	3	at Edm.	8	F
Apr. 9/88	John Tucker, Buffalo	Andy Moog, Boston	Yes	Bos.	2	at Buf.	6	DSF
Apr. 9/88	Petr Klima, Detroit	Allan Bester, Toronto	Yes	Det.	6	at Tor.	3	DSF
Apr. 8/89	Neal Broten, Minnesota	Greg Millen, St. Louis	Yes	St.L.	5	at Min.	3	DSF
Apr. 4/90	Al MacInnis, Calgary	Kelly Hrudey, Los Angeles	Yes	L.A.	5	at Cgy.	3	DSF
Apr. 5/90	Randy Wood, NY Islanders	Mike Richter, NY Rangers	No	NYI	1	at NYR	2	DSF
May 3/90	Kelly Miller, Washington	Andy Moog, Boston	No	Wsh.	3	at Bos.	5	CF
May 18/90	Petr Klima, Edmonton	Reggie Lemelin, Boston	No	Edm.	7	at Bos.	2	F
Apr. 6/91	Basil McRae, Minnesota	Ed Belfour, Chicago	Yes	Min.	2	at Chi.	5	DSF
Apr. 10/91	Steve Duchesne, Los Angeles	Kirk McLean, Vancouver	Yes	L.A.	6	at Van.	1	DSF
May 11/92	Jaromir Jagr, Pittsburgh	John Vanbiesbrouck, NYR	Yes	Pit.	3	at NYR	2	DF
May 13/92	Shawn McEachern, Pittsburgh	John Vanbiesbrouck, NYR	No	NYR	1	at Pit.	5	DF
June 7/94	Pavel Bure, Vancouver	Mike Richter, NYR	No	NYR	4	at Van.	2	F
May 9/95	Patrick Poulin, Chicago	Felix Potvin, Toronto	No	Tor.	3	at Chi.	0	CQF
May 10/95	Michal Pivonka, Washington	Tom Barrasso, Pittsburgh	No	Pit.	2	at Wsh.	6	CQF
Apr. 24/96	Joe Juneau, Washington	Ken Wregget, Pittsburgh	No	Pit.	3	at Wsh.	2**	CQF
May 11/97	Eric Lindros, Philadelphia	Steve Shields, Buffalo	Yes	Phi.	6	at Buf.	3	CSF
Apr. 23/98	Aleksey Morozov, Pittsburgh	Andy Moog, Montreal	No	Mtl.	3	at Pit.	2**	CQF
Apr. 22/99	Mats Sundin, Toronto	John Vanbiesbrouck, Phi.	No	Phi.	3	at Tor.	0	CQF
May 29/99	Mats Sundin, Toronto	Dominik Hasek, Buffalo	Yes	Tor.	2	at Buf.	5	CF
Apr. 16/00	Eric Desjardins, Philadelphia	Dominik Hasek, Buffalo	No	Phi.	2	at Buf.	0	CQF
Apr. 11/01	Mark Recchi, Philadelphia	Dominik Hasek, Buffalo	No	Buf.	2	at Phi.	1	CQF
May 2/01	Martin Straka, Pittsburgh	Dominik Hasek, Buffalo	No	Buf.	5	at Pit.	2	CSF
May 12/01	Joe Sakic, Colorado	Roman Turek, St. Louis	Yes	St.L.	1	at Col.	4	CF
Apr. 21/02	Todd Bertuzzi, Vancouver	Dominik Hasek, Detroit	No	Det.	3	at Van.	1	CQF
Apr. 24/02	Shawn Bates, NY Islanders	Curtis Joseph, Toronto	Yes	Tor.	3	at NYI	4	CQF
Apr. 26/02	Mike Johnson, Phoenix	Evgeni Nabokov, San Jose	Yes	Phx.	1	at S.J.	4	CQF
Apr. 15/03	Dainius Zubrus, Washington	Nikolai Khabibulin, Tampa Bay	No	T.B.	4	at Wsh.	3	CQF
Apr. 21/03	Robert Reichel, Toronto	Roman Cechmanek, Philadelphia	No	Phi.	1	at Tor.	2	CQF
Apr. 7/04	Steve Sullivan, Nashville	Manny Legace, Detroit	No	Nsh.	1	at Det.	3	CQF
Apr. 28/06	Derek Roy, Buffalo	Robert Esche, Philadelphia	No	Buf.	4	at Phi.	5	CQF
June 5/06	Chris Pronger, Edmonton***	Cam Ward, Carolina	Yes	Edm.	4	at Car.	5	F
Apr. 21/07	Daniel Cleary, Detroit	Miikka Kiprusoff, Calgary	Yes	Cgy.	1	at Det.	5	CQF
June 6/07	Antoine Vermette, Ottawa	J.S. Giguere, Anaheim	No	Ott.	2	at Ana.	6	F
Apr. 9/08	Ryan Smyth, Colorado	Niklas Backstrom, Minnesota	No	Col.	3	at Min.	2	CQF
Apr. 15/08	Mike Richards, Philadelphia	Cristobal Huet, Washington	Yes	Wsh.	3	at Phi.	6	CQF
Apr. 18/08	John Madden, New Jersey	Henrik Lundqvist, NY Rangers	No	NYR	5	at N.J.	3	CQF
Apr. 24/08	Andrei Kostitsyn, Montreal	Martin Biron, Philadelphia	No	Phi.	3	at Mtl.	4	CSF
Apr. 29/08	Niklas Hagman, Dallas	Evgeni Nabokov, San Jose	No	S.J.	1	at Dal.	2	CSF
May 1/08	Evgeni Malkin, Pittsburgh	Henrik Lundqvist, NY Rangers	No	Pit.	0	at NYR	3	CSF
Apr. 20/10	Martin Erat, Nashville	Antti Niemi, Chicago	Yes	Chi.	1	at Nsh.	4	CQF
May 4/10	Henrik Zetterberg, Detroit	Evgeni Nabokov, San Jose	No	S.J.	4	at Det.	3	CSF
May 8/10	Joe Pavelski, San Jose	Jimmy Howard, Detroit	No	S.J.	2	at Det.	1	CSF
May 12/10	Ville Leino, Philadelphia	Tuukka Rask, Boston	No	Phi.	2	at Bos.	1	CSF
Apr. 24/11	Michael Frolik, Chicago	Cory Schneider, Vancouver	Yes	Van.	3	at Chi.	4	CQF
Apr. 25/11	Chris Connor, Pittsburgh	Dwayne Roloson, Tampa Bay	No	Pit.	3	at T.B.	4	CQF
Apr. 26/11	Alexandre Burrows, Vancouver	Corey Crawford, Chicago	No	Chi.	1	at Van.	2	CQF
Apr. 18/12	Dustin Brown, Los Angeles	Cory Schneider, Vancouver	No	Van.	3	at L.A.	1	CQF
May 27/13	Michael Frolik, Chicago	Jimmy Howard, Detroit	Yes	Chi.	4	at Det.	3	CSF
May 16/14	Corey Perry, Anaheim	Jonathan Quick, Los Angeles	No	L.A.	6	at Ana.	2	SR
May 6/15	Carl Hagelin, NY Rangers	Braden Holtby, Washington	No	NYR	1	at Wsh	2	FR
Apr. 22/16	Aleksander Barkov, Florida	Thomas Greiss, NY Islanders	No	NYI	2	at Fla.	1**	FR
May 5/17	Ryan Getzlaf, Anaheim	Cam Talbot, Edmonton	No	Edm.	3	at Ana.	4	SR

* Game was decided in overtime, but shot taken during regulation time.
** Shot taken in overtime.
*** First penalty shot scored in Stanley Cup Final history

All-Time Playoff NHL Coaching Register

Playoffs, 1917-2017

Coach	Team	Games Coached	Wins	Losses	Ties	Years	Cup Wins	Career
Abel, Sid	Chicago	7	3	4		1		
	Detroit	69	29	40		8		
	Totals	76	32	44		9		1952-76
Adams, Jack	Detroit	105	52	52	1	15	3	1927-47
Allen, Keith	Philadelphia	11	3	8		2		1967-69
Arbour, Al	St. Louis	11	4	7		1		
	NY Islanders	198	119	79		15	4	
	Totals	209	123	86		16	4	1970-08
Babcock, Mike	Anaheim	21	15	6		1		
	Detroit	123	67	56		10	1	
	Toronto	6	2	4		1		
	Totals	150	84	66		12	1	2002-17
Barber, Bill	Philadelphia	11	3	8		2		2000-02
Berenson, Red	St. Louis	14	5	9		2		1979-82
Bergeron, Michel	Quebec	68	31	37		7		1980-90
Berry, Bob	Los Angeles	10	2	8		3		
	Montreal	8	2	6		2		
	St. Louis	15	7	8		2		
	Totals	33	11	22		7		1978-94
Berube, Craig	Philadelphia	7	3	4		1		2013-15
Beverley, Nick	Toronto	6	2	4		1		1995-96
Blackburn, Don	Hartford	3	0	3		1		1979-81
Blair, Wren	Minnesota	14	7	7		1		1967-70
Blake, Toe	Montreal	119	82	37		13	8	1955-68
Blashill, Jeff	Detroit	5	1	4		1		2015-17
Boileau, Marc	Pittsburgh	9	5	4		1		1973-76
Boivin, Leo	St. Louis	3	1	2		1		1975-78
Boucher, Frank	NY Rangers	27	13	14		4	1	1939-54
Boucher, George	Mtl. Maroons	2	0	2	0	1		1930-50
Boucher, Guy	Tampa Bay	18	11	7		1		
	Ottawa	19	11	8	0	1		
	Totals	37	22	15	0	2		2010-17
Boudreau, Bruce	Washington	37	17	20		4		
	Anaheim	43	24	19		4		
	Minnesota	5	1	4		1		
	Totals	85	42	43		9		2007-17
Bowman, Scotty	St. Louis	52	26	26		4		
	Montreal	98	70	28		8	5	
	Buffalo	36	18	18		5		
	Pittsburgh	33	23	10		2	1	
	Detroit	134	86	48		9	3	
	Totals	353	223	130		28	9	1967-02
Bowness, Rick	Boston	15	8	7		1		1988-05
Brooks, Herb	NY Rangers	24	12	12		3		
	New Jersey	5	1	4		1		
	Pittsburgh	11	6	5		1		
	Totals	40	19	21		5		1981-00
Brophy, John	Toronto	19	9	10		2		1986-89
Burns, Charlie	Minnesota	6	2	4		1		1969-75
Burns, Pat	Montreal	56	30	26		4		
	Toronto	46	23	23		3		
	Boston	18	8	10		2		
	New Jersey	29	17	12		2	1	
	Totals	149	78	71		11	1	1988-05
Bylsma, Dan	Pittsburgh	78	43	35		6	1	2008-17
Cameron, Dave	Ottawa	6	2	4		1		2014-16
Campbell, Colin	NY Rangers	36	18	18		3		1994-98
Capuano, Jack	NY Islanders	24	10	14		3		2010-17
Carbonneau, Guy	Montreal	12	5	7		1		2006-09
Carlyle, Randy	Anaheim	79	46	33		6	1	
	Toronto	7	3	4		1		
	Totals	86	49	37		7	1	2005-17
Carpenter, Doug	Toronto	5	1	4		1		1984-91
Carroll, Dick	Toronto	2	1	1	0	1	1	1917-19
Carroll, Frank	Toronto	2	0	2	0	1		1920-21
Cassidy, Bruce	Washington	6	2	4		1		
	Boston	6	2	4		1		
	Totals	12	4	8		2		2002-17
Cheevers, Gerry	Boston	34	15	19		4		1980-85
Cherry, Don	Boston	55	31	24		5		1974-80
Clancy, King	Toronto	14	2	12		3		1937-56
Clapper, Dit	Boston	25	8	17		4		1945-49
Cleghorn, Odie	Pittsburgh	4	1	2	1	2		1925-29
Cleghorn, Sprague	Mtl. Maroons	4	1	1	2	1		1931-32
Clouston, Cory	Ottawa	6	2	4		1		2008-11
Constantine, Kevin	San Jose	25	11	14		2		
	Pittsburgh	19	8	11		2		
	New Jersey	6	2	4		1		
	Totals	50	21	29		5		1993-02
Cooper, Jon	Tampa Bay	47	25	22		3		2012-17
Crawford, Marc	Quebec	6	2	4		1		
	Colorado	46	29	17		3	1	
	Vancouver	27	12	15		3		
	Totals	79	43	36		7	1	1994-11
Creighton, Fred	Atlanta	9	2	7		4		1974-80
Crisp, Terry	Calgary	37	22	15		3	1	
	Tampa Bay	6	2	4		1		
	Totals	43	24	19		4	1	1987-98
Crozier, Joe	Buffalo	6	2	4		1		1971-81
Cunniff, John	New Jersey	6	2	4		1		1982-91
Curry, Alex	Ottawa	2	0	1	1	1		1925-26
Dandurand, Leo	Montreal	8	5	3	0	4	1	1921-35
Day, Hap	Toronto	80	49	31		9	5	1940-50
DeBoer, Peter	New Jersey	24	14	10		1		
	San Jose	30	16	14		2		
	Totals	54	30	24		3		2008-17
Demers, Jacques	St. Louis	33	16	17		3		
	Detroit	38	20	18		3		
	Montreal	27	19	8		2	1	
	Totals	98	55	43		8	1	1979-99
Desjardins, Willie	Vancouver	6	2	4		1		2014-17
Dineen, Kevin	Florida	7	3	4		1		2011-14
Dudley, Rick	Buffalo	12	4	8		2		1989-04
Dugal, Jules	Montreal	3	1	2		1		1938-39
Duncan, Art	Toronto	2	0	1	1	1		1926-32
Dutton, Red	NY Americans	11	4	7		3		1936-40
Esposito, Phil	NY Rangers	10	2	8		2		1986-89
Evans, Jack	Hartford	16	8	8		2		1975-88
Ferguson, John	Winnipeg	3	0	3		1		1975-86
Francis, Bob	Phoenix	10	2	8		2		1999-04
Francis, Emile	NY Rangers	75	34	41		9		
	St. Louis	14	5	9		2		
	Totals	89	39	50		11		1965-83
Ftorek, Robbie	Los Angeles	16	5	11		1		
	New Jersey	7	3	4		1		
	Boston	6	2	4		1		
	Totals	29	10	19		4		1987-03
Gainey, Bob	Minnesota	30	17	13		2		
	Dallas	14	6	8		2		
	Montreal	10	2	8		2		
	Totals	54	25	29		6		1990-09
Gallant, Gerard	Florida	6	2	4		1		2003-15
Geoffrion, Bernie	Atlanta	4	0	4		1		1968-80
Gerard, Eddie	Mtl. Maroons	21	8	8	5	5	1	1917-35
Gill, David	Ottawa	8	3	2	3	2	1	1926-29
Glover, Fred	Oakland	11	3	8		1		1968-74
Gordon, Jackie	Minnesota	25	11	14		3		1970-75
Goring, Butch	Boston	3	0	3		1		1985-01
Gorman, Tommy	NY Americans	2	0	1	1	1		
	Chicago	8	6	1	1	1	1	
	Mtl. Maroons	15	7	6	2	3	1	
	Totals	25	13	8	4	5	2	1925-38
Gottselig, Johnny	Chicago	4	0	4		1		1944-48
Granato, Tony	Colorado	18	9	9		2		2002-09
Green, Pete	Ottawa	8	3	4	1	4	3	1919-25
Green, Ted	Edmonton	16	8	8		1		1991-94
Guidolin, Bep	Boston	21	11	10		2		1972-76
Gulutzan, Glen	Calgary	4	0	4		1		2011-17
Hakstol, Dave	Philadelphia	6	2	4		1		2015-17
Harris, Ted	Minnesota	2	0	2		1		1975-78
Hart, Cecil	Montreal	37	16	17	4	8	2	1926-39
Hartley, Bob	Colorado	80	49	31		4	1	
	Atlanta	4	0	4		1		
	Calgary	11	5	6		1		
	Totals	95	54	41		6	1	1998-16
Hartsburg, Craig	Chicago	16	8	8		2		
	Anaheim	4	0	4		1		
	Totals	20	8	12		3		1995-09
Harvey, Doug	NY Rangers	6	2	4		1		1961-62
Hay, Don	Phoenix	7	3	4		1		1996-01
Helmer, Rosie	NY Americans	5	2	3	0	1		1935-36
Henning, Lorne	Minnesota	5	2	3		1		1985-01
Hitchcock, Ken	Dallas	80	47	33		5	1	
	Philadelphia	37	19	18		3		
	Columbus	4	0	4		1		
	St. Louis	47	20	27		5		
	Totals	168	86	82		14	1	1995-17
Hlinka, Ivan	Pittsburgh	18	9	9		1		2000-02
Holmgren, Paul	Philadelphia	19	10	9		1		1988-96
Hunter, Dale	Washington	14	7	7		1		2011-12
Imlach, Punch	Toronto	92	44	48		11	4	1958-80
Inglis, Bill	Buffalo	3	1	2		1		1978-79
Irvin, Dick	Chicago	9	5	3	1	1		
	Toronto	66	33	32	1	9	1	
	Montreal	115	62	53		14	3	
	Totals	190	100	88	2	24	4	1928-56
Ivan, Tommy	Detroit	67	36	31		7	3	1947-58
Iverson, Emil	Chicago	2	1	1		1		1931-33
Johnson, Bob	Calgary	52	25	27		5		
	Pittsburgh	24	16	8		1	1	
	Totals	76	41	35		6	1	1982-91
Johnson, Tom	Boston	22	15	7		2	1	1970-73
Johnston, Eddie	Chicago	7	3	4		1		
	Pittsburgh	46	22	24		5		
	Totals	53	25	28		6		1979-97
Johnston, Mike	Pittsburgh	5	1	4		1		2014-16
Julien, Claude	Montreal	17	6	11		2		
	Boston	97	57	40		7	1	
	Totals	114	63	51		9	1	2002-17
Kasper, Steve	Boston	5	1	4		1		1995-97
Keenan, Mike	Philadelphia	57	32	25		4		
	Chicago	60	33	27		4		
	NY Rangers	23	16	7		1	1	
	St. Louis	20	10	10		2		
	Calgary	13	5	8		2		
	Totals	173	96	77		13	1	1984-09
Kelly, Pat	Colorado	2	0	2		1		1977-79
Kelly, Red	Los Angeles	18	7	11		2		
	Pittsburgh	14	6	8		2		
	Toronto	30	11	19		4		
	Totals	62	24	38		8		1967-77
King, Dave	Calgary	20	8	12		3		1992-03
Kitchen, Mike	St. Louis	5	1	4		1		2003-07
Kromm, Bobby	Detroit	7	3	4		1		1977-80
Laflamme, Jerry	Mtl. Maroons	4	1	3	0	1		1929-30

Coach	Team	Games Coached	Wins	Losses	Ties	Years	Cup Wins	Career
Lalonde, Newsy	Montreal	11	5	4	2	4		
	Ottawa	2	0	1	1	1		
	Totals	13	5	5	3	5		1917-35
Lamoriello, Lou	New Jersey	20	10	10		2		2005-15
Laviolette, Peter	NY Islanders	12	4	8		2		
	Carolina	25	16	9		1	1	
	Philadelphia	45	23	22		3		
	Nashville	42	23	19		3		
	Totals	124	66	58		9	1	2001-17
Lemaire, Jacques	Montreal	27	15	12		2		
	New Jersey	61	35	26		5	1	
	Minnesota	29	11	18		3		
	Totals	117	61	56		10	1	1983-11
Lewis, Dave	Detroit	16	6	10		2		1998-07
Ley, Rick	Hartford	13	5	8		2		
	Vancouver	11	4	7		1		
	Totals	24	9	15		3		1989-96
Long, Barry	Winnipeg	11	3	8		2		1983-86
Loughlin, Clem	Chicago	4	1	2	1	2		1934-37
Low, Ron	Edmonton	28	10	18		3		1994-02
Lowe, Kevin	Edmonton	5	1	4		1		1999-00
MacLean, Doug	Florida	27	13	14		2		1995-04
MacLean, Paul	Ottawa	17	8	9		2		2011-15
MacNeil, Al	Montreal	20	12	8		1	1	
	Atlanta	4	1	3		1		
	Calgary	19	9	10		2		
	Totals	43	22	21		4	1	1970-03
MacTavish, Craig	Edmonton	36	19	17		3		2000-15
Magnuson, Keith	Chicago	3	0	3	1	1		1980-82
Mahoney, Bill	Minnesota	16	7	9		2		1983-85
Maloney, Dan	Toronto	10	6	4		1		
	Winnipeg	15	5	10		2		
	Totals	25	11	14		3		1984-89
Maloney, Phil	Vancouver	7	1	6		2		1973-77
Martin, Jacques	St. Louis	16	7	9		2		
	Ottawa	69	31	38		8		
	Montreal	26	12	14		2		
	Totals	111	50	61		12		1986-12
Maurice, Paul	Carolina	53	25	28		4		
	Winnipeg	4	0	4		1		
	Totals	57	25	32		5		1995-17
McCammon, Bob	Philadelphia	10	1	9		3		
	Vancouver	7	3	4		1		
	Totals	17	4	13		4		1978-91
McLellan, John	Toronto	11	3	8		2		1969-73
McLellan, Todd	San Jose	62	30	32		6		
	Edmonton	13	7	6		1		
	Totals	75	37	38		7		2008-17
McVie, Tom	New Jersey	14	6	8		2		1975-92
Melrose, Barry	Los Angeles	24	13	11		1		1992-09
Milbury, Mike	Boston	40	23	17		2		1989-99
Muckler, John	Edmonton	40	25	15		2	1	
	Buffalo	27	11	16		4		
	Totals	67	36	31		6	1	1968-00
Muldoon, Pete	Chicago	2	0	1	1	1		1926-27
Murdoch, Bob	Chicago	5	1	4		1		
	Winnipeg	7	3	4		1		
	Totals	12	4	8		2		1987-91
Murphy, Mike	Los Angeles	5	1	4		1		1986-98
Murray, Andy	Los Angeles	24	10	14		3		
	St. Louis	4	0	4		1		
	Totals	28	10	18		4		1999-10
Murray, Bryan	Washington	53	24	29		7		
	Detroit	25	10	15		3		
	Ottawa	34	18	16		3		
	Totals	112	52	60		13		1981-08
Murray, Terry	Washington	39	18	21		4		
	Philadelphia	46	28	18		3		
	Florida	4	0	4		1		
	Los Angeles	12	4	8		2		
	Totals	101	50	51		10		1989-12
Neale, Harry	Vancouver	14	3	11		4		1978-86
Neilson, Roger	Toronto	19	8	11		2		
	Buffalo	8	4	4		1		
	Vancouver	21	12	9		2		
	NY Rangers	29	13	16		3		
	Philadelphia	29	14	15		3		
	Totals	106	51	55		11		1977-02
Nolan, Ted	Buffalo	12	5	7		1		
	NY Islanders	5	1	4		1		
	Totals	17	6	11		2		1995-15
Nykoluk, Mike	Toronto	7	1	6		2		1980-84
Oates, Adam	Washington	7	3	4		1		2012-15
O'Connell, Mike	Boston	5	1	4		1		2002-03
O'Donoghue, George	Toronto	2	1	0	1	1	1	1921-23
Oliver, Murray	Minnesota	9	4	5		1		1982-83
O'Reilly, Terry	Boston *	37	17	19	1	3		1986-89

* Playoff game May 24, 1988 suspended due to power failure. Score tied.

Coach	Team	Games Coached	Wins	Losses	Ties	Years	Cup Wins	Career
Paddock, John	Winnipeg	13	5	8		2		1991-08
Page, Pierre	Minnesota	12	4	8		2		
	Quebec	6	2	4		1		
	Calgary	4	0	4		1		
	Totals	22	6	16		4		1988-98
Patrick, Craig	NY Rangers	17	7	10		2		
	Pittsburgh	5	1	4		1		
	Totals	22	8	14		3		1980-97
Patrick, Frank	Boston	6	2	4	0	2		1934-36
Patrick, Lester	NY Rangers	65	32	26	7	12	2	1926-39

Coach	Team	Games Coached	Wins	Losses	Ties	Years	Cup Wins	Career
Patrick, Lynn	NY Rangers	12	7	5		1		
	Boston *	28	9	18	1	4		
	Totals	40	16	23	1	5		1948-76

* Playoff game March 31, 1951 suspended due to Toronto city curfew. Score tied.

Coach	Team	Games Coached	Wins	Losses	Ties	Years	Cup Wins	Career
Perron, Jean	Montreal	48	30	18		3	1	1985-89
Perry, Don	Los Angeles	10	4	6		1		1981-84
Pilous, Rudy	Chicago	41	19	22		5	1	1957-63
Plager, Barclay	St. Louis	4	1	3		1		1977-83
Playfair, Jim	Calgary	6	2	4		1		2006-07
Pleau, Larry	Hartford	10	2	8		2		1980-89
Polano, Nick	Detroit	7	1	6		2		1982-85
Powers, Eddie	Toronto	2	0	2	0	1		1924-26
Primeau, Joe	Toronto *	15	8	6	1	2	1	1950-53

* Playoff game March 31, 1951 suspended due to Toronto city curfew. Score tied.

Coach	Team	Games Coached	Wins	Losses	Ties	Years	Cup Wins	Career
Pronovost, Marcel	Buffalo	8	3	5		1		1977-79
Pulford, Bob	Los Angeles	26	10	16		4		
	Chicago	45	17	28		6		
	Totals	71	27	44		10		1972-00
Quenneville, Joel	St. Louis	68	34	34		7		
	Colorado	19	8	11		2		
	Chicago	128	76	52		9	3	
	Totals	215	118	97		18	3	1996-17
Quinn, Pat	Philadelphia	39	22	17		3		
	Los Angeles	3	0	3		1		
	Vancouver	61	31	30		5		
	Toronto	80	41	39		6		
	Totals	183	94	89		15		1978-10
Reay, Billy	Chicago	116	56	60		12		1957-77
Renney, Tom	NY Rangers	24	11	13		3		1996-12
Richards, Todd	Columbus	6	2	4		1		2009-16
Risebrough, Doug	Calgary	7	3	4		1		1990-92
Roberts, Jim	Hartford	7	3	4		1		1981-97
Robinson, Larry	Los Angeles	4	0	4		1		
	New Jersey	48	31	17		2	1	
	Totals	52	31	21		3	1	1995-06
Ross, Art	Boston	70	32	33	5	12	2	1917-45
Roy, Patrick	Colorado	7	3	4		1		2013-16
Ruel, Claude	Montreal	27	18	9		3	1	1968-81
Ruff, Lindy	Buffalo	101	57	44		8		
	Dallas	19	9	10		2		
	Totals	120	66	54		10		1997-17
Sacco, Joe	Colorado	6	2	4		1		2009-13
Sather, Glen	Edmonton *	127	89	37	1	10	4	1979-04

* Playoff game May 24, 1988 suspended due to power failure. Score tied.

Coach	Team	Games Coached	Wins	Losses	Ties	Years	Cup Wins	Career
Sator, Ted	NY Rangers	16	8	8		1		
	Buffalo	11	3	8		2		
	Totals	27	11	16		3		1985-89
Schinkel, Ken	Pittsburgh	6	2	4		2		1972-77
Schmidt, Milt	Boston	34	15	19		4		1954-76
Schoenfeld, Jim	New Jersey	20	11	9		1		
	Washington	24	10	14		3		
	Phoenix	13	5	8		2		
	Totals	57	26	31		6		1985-99
Shero, Fred	Philadelphia	83	48	35		6	2	
	NY Rangers	27	15	12		2		
	Totals	110	63	47		8	2	1971-81
Simpson, Terry	NY Islanders	20	9	11		2		
	Winnipeg	6	2	4		1		
	Totals	26	11	15		3		1986-96
Sinden, Harry	Boston	43	24	19		5	1	1966-85
Skinner, Jimmy	Detroit	26	14	12		3	1	1954-58
Smith, Alf	Ottawa	5	1	4	0	1		1918-19
Smith, Floyd	Buffalo	32	16	16		3		1971-80
Smythe, Conn	Toronto	4	2	2	0	1		1927-32
Sonmor, Glen	Minnesota	47	26	21		4		1978-87
Stasiuk, Vic	Philadelphia	4	0	4		1		1969-73
Stevens, John	Philadelphia	23	11	12		2		2006-12
Stewart, Bill	Chicago	10	7	3		1	1	1937-39
Stewart, Ron	Los Angeles	2	0	2		1		1975-78
Stirling, Steve	NY Islanders	5	1	4		1		2003-06
Sullivan, Mike	Boston	7	3	4		1		
	Pittsburgh	49	32	17		2	2	
	Totals	56	35	21		3	2	2003-17
Sutter, Brent	New Jersey	12	4	8		2		2007-12
Sutter, Brian	St. Louis	41	20	21		4		
	Boston	22	7	15		3		
	Chicago	5	1	4		1		
	Totals	68	28	40		8		1988-05
Sutter, Darryl	Chicago	26	11	15		3		
	San Jose	42	18	24		5		
	Calgary	33	18	15		2		
	Los Angeles	69	42	27		4	2	
	Totals	170	89	81		14	2	1992-17
Talbot, Jean-Guy	St. Louis	5	1	4		1		
	NY Rangers	3	1	2		1		
	Totals	8	2	6		2		1972-78
Tessier, Orval	Chicago	18	9	9		3		1982-85
Therrien, Michel	Montreal	47	24	23		4		
	Pittsburgh	25	15	10		2		
	Totals	72	39	33		6		2000-17
Thompson, Paul	Chicago	19	7	12		4		1938-45
Tippett, Dave	Dallas	47	21	26		5		
	Phoenix	27	12	15		3		
	Totals	74	33	41		8		2002-17
Tobin, Bill	Chicago	2	0	1	1	1		1929-30
Torchetti, John	Minnesota	6	2	4		1		2003-16

Coach	Team	Games Coached	Wins	Losses	Ties	Years	Cup Wins	Career
Tortorella, John	NY Rangers	44	19	25		4		
	Tampa Bay	45	24	21		4	1	
	Columbus	5	1	4		1		
	Totals	94	44	50		9	1	1999-17
Tremblay, Mario	Montreal	11	3	8		2		1995-97
Trotz, Barry	Nashville	50	19	31		7		
	Washington	39	20	19		3		
	Totals	89	39	50		10		1998-17
Ubriaco, Gene	Pittsburgh	11	7	4		1		1988-90
Vigneault, Alain	Montreal	10	4	6		1		
	Vancouver	68	33	35		6		
	NY Rangers	61	31	30		4		
	Totals	139	68	71		11		1997-17
Watson, Phil	NY Rangers	16	4	12		3		1955-63
Watt, Tom	Winnipeg	7	1	6		2		
	Vancouver	3	0	3		1		
	Totals	10	1	9		3		1981-92

Coach	Team	Games Coached	Wins	Losses	Ties	Years	Cup Wins	Career
Webster, Tom	Los Angeles	28	12	16		3		1986-92
Weiland, Cooney	Boston	17	10	7		2	1	1939-41
White, Bill	Chicago	2	0	2		1		1976-77
Wilson, Johnny	Pittsburgh	12	4	8		2		1969-80
Wilson, Ron	Anaheim	11	4	7		1		
	Washington	32	15	17		3		
	San Jose	52	28	24		4		
	Totals	95	47	48		8		1993-12
Yeo, Mike	Minnesota	28	11	17		3		
	St. Louis	11	6	5		1		
	Totals	39	17	22		4		2011-17
Young, Garry	St. Louis	2	0	2		1		1972-76

How to Use the Prospect, NHL Player and Goaltender Registers

Demographics: Position, shooting side (catching hand for goaltenders), height, weight, place and date of birth as well as NHL Draft information, if any, is located on this line.

Minor/youth/high school hockey, junior, NCAA, minor pro, European and NHL clubs form a permanent part of each player's data panel. If a player sees action with more than one club in any of the above categories, a separate line is included for each one.

Olympic Team statistics are also listed.

Asterisks (*) indicates league leader in individual statistical categories.

Players' NHL organization as of August 14, 2017. This includes players under contract, unsigned draft choices and other players on reserve lists. Free agents as of this date show a blank here. The complete career data panels of players with NHL experience who announced their retirement before the start of the 2017-18 season are included in the Player Register and Goaltender Register. These newly-retired players also show a blank here. Each NHL club's minor-pro affiliates are listed on page 14.

SAAD, Brandon   (SAHD, BRAN-duhn)   CHI

Left wing. Shoots left. 6'1", 206 lbs.   Born, Pittsburgh, PA, October 27, 1992. Chicago's 4th pick, 43rd overall, in 2011 NHL Draft.

Season	Team	League	GP	G	A	Pts	PIM	PP	SH	GW	S	%	+/-	TF	F%	Min	GP	G	A	Pts	PIM	PP	SH	GW	Min
2007-08	Pittsburgh	MWEHL	26	11	19	30	16																		
2008-09	Mahoning Valley	NAHL	47	29	18	47	48										7	5	1	6	0				
	USAHNTDP	U-17	7	6	5	11	2																		
2009-10	USAHNTDP	USHL	24	12	14	26	18																		
	USAHNTDP	U-18	39	17	15	32	16																		
2010-11	Saginaw Spirit	OHL	59	27	28	55	47										12	3	9	12	1				
2011-12	Saginaw Spirit	OHL	44	34	42	76	38										12	8	9	17					
	Chicago	NHL	2	0	0	0	0	0	0	0	3	0.0	0	0	0.0	14:01	2	0	1	1		0	0	0	12:21
2012-13	Rockford IceHogs	AHL	31	8	12	20	10																		
	♦ Chicago	NHL	46	10	17	27	12	0	1	2	98	10.2	17	46	37.0	16:28	23	1	5	6	4	0	0	0	16:24
2013-14	Chicago	NHL	78	19	28	47	20	3	0	2	159	11.9	20	122	41.0	16:17	19	6	10	16	6	1	0	1	17:31
2014-15	♦ Chicago	NHL	82	23	29	52	12	2	0	6	203	11.3	7	88	43.2	17:15	23	8	3	11	6	0	1	2	20:16
2015-16	Columbus	NHL	78	31	22	53	14	6	0	7	233	13.3	1	34	55.9	17:13									
2016-17	Columbus	NHL	82	24	29	53	8	1	0	4	210	11.4	23	9	44.4	17:02	5	1	2	3	0	0	0	0	15:58
	NHL Totals		368	107	125	232	66	12	1	21	906	11.8		299	42.8	16:53	72	16	21	37	16	1	1	3	17:47

OHL First All-Star Team (2012) • NHL All-Rookie Team (2013)

Played in NHL All-Star Game (2016)

Traded to **Columbus** by **Chicago** with Michael Paliotta and Alex Broadhurst for Artem Anisimov, Jeremy Morin, Corey Tropp, Marko Dano and Columbus' 4th round pick (later traded to NY Islanders – NY Islanders selected Anatoli Golyshev) in 2016 NHL Draft, June 30, 2015. Traded to **Chicago** by **Columbus** with Anton Forsberg and Columbus' 5th round pick in 2018 NHL Draft for Artemi Panarin, Tyler Motte and NY Islanders' 6th round pick (previously acquired, Columbus selected Jonathan Davidsson) in 2017 NHL Draft, June 23, 2017.

Diamond (♦) indicates member of Stanley Cup-winning team.

"Did not play" Indicates that a player did not participate in a pro, junior or college league for an entire season.

Unless requested by the player, birthplace reflects country and city names in use when the player was born. The Czech Republic and Slovakia became independent on January 1, 1993. Previously, players were born in Czechoslovakia. The Russian Republic was established on January 1, 1992. Previously, players were born in the USSR. Germany was unified on October 3, 1990. Previously, players were born in either East or West Germany. Former Soviet Republics (Belarus, Estonia, Kazakhstan, Latvia, Lithuania, Ukraine) achieved independence between August 20 and December 25, 1991.

Pronunciation of Player Names

United Press International phonetic style.

AY	long A as in mate; French long E with acute accent as in Pathe
AI	nasal A as on air A short A as in cat
AW	broad A as in talk; broad O as in fought
AH	short A as in father; short O as in hot
EH	short E as in get
IH	middle E as in pretty; short I as in pity
IGH	long I as in time
EE	long E as in meat; French long I as in machine
OH	long O as in note
OI	OI dipthong as in noise
OO	long double OO as in fool; long U as in rule
U	short double O as in foot; middle U as in put
OW	OW dipthong as in how
EW	long U as in mule; dipthong as in few
UH	short U as in shut or hurt; hollow E as in the
K	hard C as in cat S soft C as in cease
SH	soft CH as in machine
CH	hard CH or TCH as in catch
Z	hard S as in bells S soft S as in sun
G	hard G as in gang J soft G as in general
ZH	soft J as in French version of Joliet
KH	gutteral CH as in Scottish version of Loch

All trades, free agent signings and other transactions involving NHL clubs are listed here and are presented in chronological order. First draft selection for players who re-enter the NHL Draft is noted here as well. Also listed are other special notes. These are highlighted with a bullet (•).

Dates for trades or free agent signings often differ depending upon source. Signings can be reported based on when contracts are filed with NHL Central Registry or on the date a club announces that it has made a trade or come to terms with a free agent.

All-Star Team selections and awards are listed below player's year-by-year data.

NHL All-Star Game appearances are listed above trade notes.

THIS 86TH EDITION OF THE *NHL Official Guide & Record Book* includes additional statistical categories for forwards and defensemen in the National Hockey League. These categories are, from left to right in the sample panel above, power-play goals (PP), shorthand goals (SH), game-winning goals (GW), shots on goal (S), percentage of shots that score (%), plus-minus rating (+/–), total faceoffs taken (TF), faceoff winning percentage (F%), and average time-on-ice per game played (Min).

To integrate this data, the Player Register is split into two sections. The Prospect Register presents data on players who have yet to play in the NHL. The NHL Player Register, containing more information and a photo of each player, lists all active players who have appeared in an NHL regular-season or playoff game at any time.

Goaltenders, whether prospects or active NHLers, are included in one register. With the addition of the shootout to NHL regular-season play, the column formerly used to record tie games for goaltenders has been renamed "O/T." For NHL goaltenders beginning in 2005-06, it lists overtime losses and shootout losses; previous to 2005-06, it lists tie games.

Some information is unavailable at press time. Readers are encouraged to contribute. See page 5 for contact names and addresses.

Registers (with their starting page) are presented in the following order: Prospects (279), NHL Players (351), Goaltenders (589), Retired Players (616) and Retired Goaltenders (665). League abbreviations, page 678. Late additions to the Registers, page 671.

2017-18 Prospect Register

Note: The 2017-18 Prospect Register lists forwards and defensemen only. Goaltenders are listed separately. The Prospect Register lists every player drafted in the 2017 NHL Draft, players on NHL Reserve Lists and other players who have not yet played in the NHL. Trades and roster changes are current as of August 14, 2017.

Abbreviations: GP – games played; **G** – goals; **A** – assists; **Pts** – points; **PIM** – penalties in minutes; ***** – league-leading total.

NHL Player Register begins on page 351.
Goaltender Register begins on page 589.
Retired Player Index begins on page 616.
Retired Goaltender Index begins on page 665.
League Abbreviations are listed on page 678.

AALTONEN, Miro
(AHL-tuh-nehn, MEE-roh) **TOR**
Center. Shoots left. 5'11", 176 lbs.   Born, Joensuu, Finland, June 7, 1993.
(Anaheim's 5th pick, 177th overall, in 2013 NHL Draft).

			Regular Season					Playoffs			
Season	Club	League	GP	G	A	Pts	PIM	GP	G	A	Pts	PIM
2008-09	Jokipojat U18	Fin-U18	1	3	1	4	0	....				
2009-10	Blues Espoo U18	Fin-U18	8	4	12	16	8	11	6	8	14	6
	Blues Espoo Jr.	Fin-Jr.	40	12	15	27	18	....				
2010-11	Blues Espoo U18	Fin-U18	2	0	3	3	2	2	3	1	4	2
	Blues Espoo Jr.	Fin-Jr.	12	3	5	8	6	13	5	6	11	2
2011-12	Blues Espoo Jr.	Fin-Jr.	14	10	17	27	14	4	2	3	5	2
	Jokipojat Joensuu	Finland-2	4	2	3	5	0	....				
	Blues Espoo	Finland	26	1	1	2	2	10	1	1	2	2
2012-13	Blues Espoo	Finland	32	11	5	16	22	....				
	Blues Espoo Jr.	Fin-Jr.	....					8	4	9	13	4
2013-14	Blues Espoo	Finland	60	13	16	29	12	7	3	4	7	0
2014-15	Blues Espoo	Finland	57	16	21	37	14	4	1	1	2	0
2015-16	Karpat Oulu	Finland	58	15	20	35	51	8	0	3	3	0
2016-17	Podolsk	KHL	59	19	25	44	38	4	0	0	0	7

Signed as a free agent by **Toronto**, March 17, 2017.

ABRAMOV, Vitaly
(ah-BRAHM-awf, vih-TAL-ee) **CBJ**
Right wing. Shoots left. 5'10", 181 lbs.   Born, Chelyabinsk, Russia, May 8, 1998.
(Columbus' 3rd pick, 65th overall, in 2016 NHL Draft).

			Regular Season					Playoffs			
Season	Club	League	GP	G	A	Pts	PIM	GP	G	A	Pts	PIM
2014-15	Chelyabinsk Jr.	Russia-Jr.	20	8	6	14	8	2	0	0	0	4
2015-16	Gatineau	QMJHL	63	38	55	93	36	10	7	6	13	8
2016-17	Gatineau	QMJHL	66	46	58	*104	76	7	1	6	7	12
	Cleveland	AHL	4	1	3	4	2	....				

QMJHL Rookie of the Year (2016) • QMJHL First All-Star Team (2017) • QMJHL Player of the Year (2017)

ACOLATSE, Sena
(ah-koh-LAWT-say, SEH-na)
Defense. Shoots right. 6', 210 lbs.   Born, Hayward, CA, November 28, 1990.

			Regular Season					Playoffs			
Season	Club	League	GP	G	A	Pts	PIM	GP	G	A	Pts	PIM
2006-07	Seattle	WHL	45	0	4	4	61	11	0	0	0	8
2007-08	Seattle	WHL	71	7	24	31	107	12	1	2	3	12
2008-09	Seattle	WHL	70	7	14	21	143	5	1	1	2	0
2009-10	Seattle	WHL	39	13	9	22	35	....				
	Saskatoon Blades	WHL	30	3	10	13	25	7	1	1	2	17
2010-11	Saskatoon Blades	WHL	1	0	0	0	2	....				
	Prince George	WHL	66	15	48	63	128	4	3	4	7	4
	Worcester Sharks	AHL	1	0	0	0	0	....				
2011-12	Worcester Sharks	AHL	65	8	13	21	89	....				
2012-13	Worcester Sharks	AHL	50	4	17	21	62	....				
2013-14	Worcester Sharks	AHL	41	5	12	17	66	....				
2014-15	Adirondack Flames	AHL	38	6	13	19	68	....				
2015-16	Portland Pirates	AHL	62	8	5	13	138	3	1	0	1	4
2016-17	Springfield	AHL	68	6	17	23	147	....				

Signed as a free agent by **San Jose**, March 4, 2011. Signed as a free agent by **Calgary**, July 3, 2014. Signed as a free agent by **Florida**, July 1, 2015.

ADAMS, Collin
(A-duhmz, KAW-lihn) **NYI**
Left wing. Shoots left. 5'9", 175 lbs.   Born, Farmington Hills, MI, April 24, 1998.
(NY Islanders' 4th pick, 170th overall, in 2016 NHL Draft).

			Regular Season					Playoffs			
Season	Club	League	GP	G	A	Pts	PIM	GP	G	A	Pts	PIM
2013-14	Det. L.C. U16	HPHL	22	10	7	17	12	....				
2014-15	Det. H-Baked U16	HPHL	25	26	9	35	22	....				
	Muskegon	USHL	3	0	0	0	0	....				
	USAHNTDP	USHL	1	0	0	0	0	....				
	USAHNTDP	U-17	2	2	0	2	0	....				
2015-16	Muskegon	USHL	59	27	34	61	30	....				
2016-17	Muskegon	USHL	57	24	27	51	72	4	3	1	4	2

USHL All-Rookie Team (2016)
• Signed Letter of Intent to attend **University of North Dakota** (NCHC) in fall of 2017.

ADAMS, Jack
(A-duhmz, JAK) **DET**
Right wing. Shoots right. 6'5", 204 lbs.   Born, Boston, MA, May 2, 1997.
(Detroit's 8th pick, 162nd overall, in 2017 NHL Draft).

			Regular Season					Playoffs			
Season	Club	League	GP	G	A	Pts	PIM	GP	G	A	Pts	PIM
2012-13	Malden Catholic	High-MA	....	1	1	2	....	....				
2013-14	Malden Catholic	High-MA	....	7	12	19	....	....				
2014-15	Malden Catholic	High-MA	....	12	7	19	....	....				
2015-16	Fargo Force	USHL	54	8	16	24	42	....				
2016-17	Fargo Force	USHL	56	*37	23	60	55	3	0	0	0	4

• Signed Letter of Intent to attend **Union College** (ECAC) in fall of 2017.

ADDISON, Jeremiah
(A-dih-suhn, jair-ih-MY-uh) **MTL**
Left wing. Shoots left. 6', 178 lbs.   Born, Brampton, ON, October 21, 1996.
(Montreal's 5th pick, 207th overall, in 2015 NHL Draft).

			Regular Season					Playoffs			
Season	Club	League	GP	G	A	Pts	PIM	GP	G	A	Pts	PIM
2011-12	Toronto Marlboros	GTHL	....	28	18	46	37	....				
	Brampton Capitals	ON-Jr.A	1	1	0	1	0	....				
2012-13	Saginaw Spirit	OHL	68	6	10	16	42	4	0	0	0	0
2013-14	Saginaw Spirit	OHL	61	7	10	17	52	5	0	0	0	0
2014-15	Ottawa 67's	OHL	63	19	28	47	49	6	4	6	10	7
2015-16	Ottawa 67's	OHL	66	27	29	56	74	4	1	2	3	8
	St. John's IceCaps	AHL	4	0	1	1	2	....				
2016-17	Windsor Spitfires	OHL	51	24	19	43	62	5	5	0	5	9

AHL, Filip
(AHL, FIHL-ihp) **OTT**
Left wing. Shoots left. 6'4", 218 lbs.   Born, Jonkoping, Sweden, June 12, 1997.
(Ottawa's 6th pick, 109th overall, in 2015 NHL Draft).

			Regular Season					Playoffs			
Season	Club	League	GP	G	A	Pts	PIM	GP	G	A	Pts	PIM
2011-12	HV 71 U18	Swe-U18	6	0	1	1	0	....				
2012-13	HV 71 U18	Swe-U18	33	10	16	26	45	....				
	HV 71 Jr.	Swe-Jr.	1	1	0	1	2	....				
2013-14	HV 71 Jonkoping	Sweden	1	0	0	0	0	2	0	0	0	0
	HV 71 U18	Swe-U18	9	9	6	15	6	....				
	HV 71 Jr.	Swe-Jr.	24	10	9	19	10	5	2	2	4	2
	HV 71 Jonkoping	Sweden	1	0	0	0	0	2	0	0	0	0
2014-15	HV 71 U18	Swe-U18	1	0	1	1	0	4	5	4	9	0
	HV 71 Jr.	Swe-Jr.	34	20	22	42	53	6	3	2	5	4
	HV 71 Jonkoping	Sweden	15	0	2	2	2	....				
2015-16	HV 71 Jr.	Swe-Jr.	18	18	13	31	14	....				
	Dalen	Sweden-3	1	1	0	1	0	....				
	Asploven	Sweden-2	3	0	0	0	2	....				
	Sundsvall	Sweden-2	26	7	4	11	10	....				
	HV 71 Jonkoping	Sweden	17	0	0	0	0	....				
2016-17	Regina Pats	WHL	54	28	20	48	26	20	5	13	18	26

AHO, Sebastian
(AH-hoh, seh-BAS-t'yehn) **NYI**
Defense. Shoots left. 5'10", 176 lbs.   Born, Umea, Sweden, February 17, 1996.
(NY Islanders' 3rd pick, 139th overall, in 2017 NHL Draft).

			Regular Season					Playoffs			
Season	Club	League	GP	G	A	Pts	PIM	GP	G	A	Pts	PIM
2010-11	Bjorkloven U18	Swe-U18	27	3	6	9	16	....				
2011-12	Skelleftea AIK U18	Swe-U18	33	4	14	18	12	7	0	2	2	2
2012-13	Skelleftea AIK U18	Swe-U18	2	0	2	2	0	3	0	1	1	2
	Skelleftea AIK Jr.	Swe-Jr.	38	1	11	12	14	4	0	0	0	0
	Skelleftea AIK	Sweden	1	0	0	0	0	....				
2013-14	Skelleftea AIK Jr.	Swe-Jr.	27	7	16	23	18	13	0	0	0	0
	Skelleftea AIK	Sweden	21	1	4	5	2	13	1	3	4	8
2014-15	Skelleftea AIK Jr.	Swe-Jr.	4	0	2	2	4	....				
	Skelleftea AIK	Sweden	41	1	8	9	14	13	1	3	4	8
2015-16	Skelleftea AIK	Sweden	39	3	13	16	12	16	3	4	7	6
2016-17	Skelleftea AIK	Sweden	50	10	20	30	10	7	0	2	2	0

ALLARD, Frederic (ah-LAHRD, FREHD-uh-rihk) NSH

Defense. Shoots right. 6'1", 183 lbs. Born, Saint-Sauveur, QC, December 27, 1997.
(Nashville's 4th pick, 78th overall, in 2016 NHL Draft).

			Regular Season					Playoffs				
Season	Club	League	GP	G	A	Pts	PIM	GP	G	A	Pts	PIM
2012-13	Sem. St-Francois	QAAA	42	3	19	22	20	16	0	5	5	10
2013-14	Chicoutimi	QMJHL	61	4	19	23	26	3	0	1	1	2
2014-15	Chicoutimi	QMJHL	62	2	28	30	24	5	0	1	1	0
2015-16	Chicoutimi	QMJHL	64	14	45	59	34	6	1	2	3	0
2016-17	Chicoutimi	QMJHL	63	14	51	65	42	17	4	10	14	14

ALLISON, Wade (al-IH-suhn, WAYD) PHI

Right wing. Shoots right. 6'1", 204 lbs. Born, Carman, MB, October 14, 1997.
(Philadelphia's 4th pick, 52nd overall, in 2016 NHL Draft).

			Regular Season					Playoffs				
Season	Club	League	GP	G	A	Pts	PIM	GP	G	A	Pts	PIM
2012-13	Pembina Valley	MMHL	35	15	22	37	16	5	4	3	7	2
2013-14	Om. Lancers U16	Minor-NE	48	49	62	111	....	....	....	....	....	....
	Om. Lancers U16	NAPHL	15	19	9	28	10	5	3	6	9	2
	Om. Lancers U16	Other	....	....	....	....	....	5	4	0	4	0
2014-15	Tri-City Storm	USHL	35	6	7	13	8	7	0	2	2	0
2015-16	Tri-City Storm	USHL	56	25	22	47	46	11	*9	7	16	4
2016-17	Western Mich.	NCHC	36	12	17	29	53	....	....	....	....	....

ALMARI, Niclas (al-MAHR-ee, NIHK-luhs) PIT

Defense. Shoots left. 6'1", 167 lbs. Born, Espoo, Finland, May 11, 1998.
(Pittsburgh's 5th pick, 151st overall, in 2016 NHL Draft).

			Regular Season					Playoffs				
Season	Club	League	GP	G	A	Pts	PIM	GP	G	A	Pts	PIM
2013-14	Blues Espoo U18	Fin-U18	6	0	1	1	2	6	0	3	3	0
2014-15	Blues Espoo U18	Fin-U18	17	2	4	6	10	9	2	3	5	2
	Blues Espoo Jr.	Fin-Jr.	26	4	4	8	16	....	....	....	....	....
2015-16	Blues Espoo U18	Fin-U18	5	2	3	5	0	....	....	....	....	....
	Blues Espoo Jr.	Fin-Jr.	12	0	0	0	4	....	....	....	....	....
	Jokerit Helsinki Jr.	Fin-Jr.	27	2	5	7	10	2	0	1	1	4
2016-17	HPK Jr.	Fin-Jr.	10	1	4	5	0	10	1	10	11	0
	HPK Hameenlinna	Finland	24	3	2	5	10	....	....	....	....	....
	LeKi Lempaala	Finland-2	23	1	6	7	8	....	....	....	....	....

ALTYBARMAKYAN, Andrei (ahl-tee-BAHR-MAHK-yehn, AWN-dray) CHI

Right wing. Shoots left. 5'11", 183 lbs. Born, St. Petersburg, Russia, April 8, 1998.
(Chicago's 3rd pick, 70th overall, in 2017 NHL Draft).

			Regular Season					Playoffs				
Season	Club	League	GP	G	A	Pts	PIM	GP	G	A	Pts	PIM
2014-15	Ser. Ljvy Jr.	Russia-Jr.	2	0	0	0	0	....	....	....	....	....
2015-16	Ser. Ljvy Jr.	Russia-Jr.	42	8	22	30	30	....	....	....	....	....
2016-17	Ser. Ljvy Jr.	Russia-Jr.	31	20	25	45	77	....	....	....	....	....
	SKA-Neva	Russia-2	27	5	4	9	10	11	0	0	0	4

AMADIO, Mike (uh-MA-dee-oh, MIGHK) L.A.

Center. Shoots right. 6'1", 190 lbs. Born, Sault Ste. Marie, ON, May 13, 1996.
(Los Angeles' 4th pick, 90th overall, in 2014 NHL Draft).

			Regular Season					Playoffs				
Season	Club	League	GP	G	A	Pts	PIM	GP	G	A	Pts	PIM
2010-11	Soo Greyhounds	Minor-ON	39	60	*74	*134	16	6	10	*9	19	2
2011-12	Soo North Stars	Minor-ON	29	32	30	62	12	11	5	9	14	6
2012-13	Brampton	OHL	63	6	13	19	8	5	0	0	0	0
2013-14	North Bay	OHL	64	12	26	38	14	22	4	5	9	2
2014-15	North Bay	OHL	68	24	47	71	18	15	6	9	15	4
2015-16	North Bay	OHL	68	50	48	98	40	11	12	6	18	10
	Ontario Reign	AHL	....	....	....	....	....	11	1	4	5	0
2016-17	Ontario Reign	AHL	68	16	25	41	4	5	2	0	2	0

OHL Second All-Star Team (2016)

AMOROSA, Terrance (a-moh-ROH-suh, TAIR-uhns) PHI

Defense. Shoots left. 6'1", 204 lbs. Born, Kirkland, QC, November 13, 1994.
(Philadelphia's 4th pick, 132nd overall, in 2013 NHL Draft).

			Regular Season					Playoffs				
Season	Club	League	GP	G	A	Pts	PIM	GP	G	A	Pts	PIM
2010-11	West Island Royals	Minor-QC	31	5	15	20	6	....	....	....	....	....
2011-12	Holderness School	High-NH	29	6	9	15	....	....	....	....	....	....
2012-13	Holderness School	High-NH	27	9	13	22	....	....	....	....	....	....
2013-14	Sioux City	USHL	50	2	13	15	10	6	0	0	0	2
2014-15	Clarkson Knights	ECAC	18	1	4	5	10	....	....	....	....	....
2015-16	Clarkson Knights	ECAC	27	4	12	16	14	....	....	....	....	....
2016-17	Clarkson Knights	ECAC	30	3	13	16	24	....	....	....	....	....

ANAS, Sam (A-nihs, SAM) MIN

Right wing. Shoots right. 5'8", 163 lbs. Born, Potomac, MD, June 1, 1993.

			Regular Season					Playoffs				
Season	Club	League	GP	G	A	Pts	PIM	GP	G	A	Pts	PIM
2009-10	Team Maryland	AYHL	31	16	17	33	10	....	....	....	....	....
2010-11	Wsh Little Caps	MtJHL	19	20	21	41	4	....	....	....	....	....
	DC Capitals	NAPHL	25	18	23	41	4	5	3	3	6	0
2011-12	Youngstown	USHL	51	17	17	34	14	6	0	4	4	4
2012-13	Youngstown	USHL	64	37	26	63	18	9	3	9	12	6
2013-14	Quinnipiac	ECAC	40	22	21	43	14	....	....	....	....	....
2014-15	Quinnipiac	ECAC	38	23	16	39	20	....	....	....	....	....
2015-16	Quinnipiac	ECAC	43	*24	26	*50	18	....	....	....	....	....
2016-17	Iowa Wild	AHL	66	12	16	28	6	....	....	....	....	....

ECAC Second All-Star Team (2015) • NCAA East Second All-American Team (2015) • ECAC First All-Star Team (2016) • NCAA East First All-American Team (2016)

Signed as a free agent by **Minnesota**, April 15, 2016.

ANDERSON, Joey (AN-duhr-suhn, JOH-ee) N.J.

Right wing. Shoots right. 6', 195 lbs. Born, Roseville, MN, June 19, 1998.
(New Jersey's 3rd pick, 73rd overall, in 2016 NHL Draft).

			Regular Season					Playoffs				
Season	Club	League	GP	G	A	Pts	PIM	GP	G	A	Pts	PIM
2012-13	Hill-Murray	High-MN	12	14	9	23	....	3	1	3	4	0
2013-14	Team Northeast	UMHSEL	20	13	10	23	6	3	2	2	4	2
	Hill-Murray	High-MN	25	21	29	50	16	3	4	2	6	2
2014-15	USAHNTDP	USHL	35	14	10	24	6	....	....	....	....	....
	USAHNTDP	U-17	20	7	11	18	2	....	....	....	....	....
2015-16	USAHNTDP	USHL	25	10	10	20	14	....	....	....	....	....
	USAHNTDP	U-18	39	17	20	37	6	....	....	....	....	....
2016-17	U. Minn-Duluth	NCHC	39	12	25	37	8	....	....	....	....	....

NCHC All-Rookie Team (2017)

ANDERSON, Josh (AN-duhr-suhn, JAWSH) COL

Defense. Shoots left. 6'2", 225 lbs. Born, Nanaimo, BC, August 29, 1998.
(Colorado's 3rd pick, 71st overall, in 2016 NHL Draft).

			Regular Season					Playoffs				
Season	Club	League	GP	G	A	Pts	PIM	GP	G	A	Pts	PIM
2012-13	Cowichan Valley	Minor-BC	52	18	34	52	80	....	....	....	....	....
2013-14	South Island	BCMML	34	1	13	14	72	2	0	0	0	8
	Prince George	WHL	2	0	0	0	2	....	....	....	....	....
2014-15	Prince George	WHL	42	2	2	4	52	2	0	0	0	0
2015-16	Prince George	WHL	39	1	5	6	86	....	....	....	....	....
2016-17	Prince George	WHL	69	3	8	11	75	6	0	0	0	12

• Missed majority of 2015-16 due to back injury at Vancouver (WHL), January 16, 2016.

ANDERSON, Michael (AN-duhr-suhn, MIGH-kuhl) L.A.

Defense. Shoots left. 5'11", 197 lbs. Born, Fridley, MN, May 25, 1999.
(Los Angeles' 4th pick, 103rd overall, in 2017 NHL Draft).

			Regular Season					Playoffs				
Season	Club	League	GP	G	A	Pts	PIM	GP	G	A	Pts	PIM
2013-14	Hill-Murray	High-MN	25	1	5	6	10	3	1	0	1	2
2014-15	Team Northeast	UMHSEL	19	4	8	12	28	3	1	0	1	2
	Hill-Murray	High-MN	25	6	5	11	23	5	2	2	4	2
2015-16	Waterloo	USHL	57	1	15	16	30	9	3	2	5	4
2016-17	Waterloo	USHL	54	5	29	34	52	8	2	1	3	10

• Signed Letter of Intent to attend **University of Minnesota-Duluth** (NCHC) in fall of 2018.

ANDERSON-DOLAN, Jaret (AN-duhr-suhn-DOH-luhn, JAIR-iht) L.A.

Center. Shoots left. 5'11", 191 lbs. Born, Calgary, AB, December 9, 1999.
(Los Angeles' 2nd pick, 41st overall, in 2017 NHL Draft).

			Regular Season					Playoffs				
Season	Club	League	GP	G	A	Pts	PIM	GP	G	A	Pts	PIM
2014-15	Edge School Prep	CSSHL	25	13	17	30	8	3	1	2	3	2
	Edge School Prep	MPHL	16	7	6	13	8	....	....	....	....	....
	Spokane Chiefs	WHL	5	0	0	0	0	1	0	0	0	0
2015-16	Spokane Chiefs	WHL	65	14	12	26	21	6	1	2	3	2
2016-17	Spokane Chiefs	WHL	72	39	37	76	22	....	....	....	....	....

ANDERSSON, Anton (an-DUHR-suhn, AN-tawn) ST.L.

Defense. Shoots left. 6'3", 216 lbs. Born, Boden, , June 1, 1999.
(St. Louis' 6th pick, 206th overall, in 2017 NHL Draft).

			Regular Season					Playoffs				
Season	Club	League	GP	G	A	Pts	PIM	GP	G	A	Pts	PIM
2014-15	Lulea HF U18	Swe-U18	22	4	6	10	12	....	....	....	....	....
2015-16	Lulea HF U18	Swe-U18	24	4	8	12	8	....	....	....	....	....
2016-17	Lulea HF U18	Swe-U18	19	9	12	21	41	5	3	2	5	2
	Lulea HF Jr.	Swe-Jr.	13	2	1	3	2	....	....	....	....	....

ANDERSSON, Lias (an-DUHR-suhn, lee-AHS) NYR

Center. Shoots left. 6', 200 lbs. Born, Smogen, Sweden, October 13, 1998.
(NY Rangers' 1st pick, 7th overall, in 2017 NHL Draft).

			Regular Season					Playoffs				
Season	Club	League	GP	G	A	Pts	PIM	GP	G	A	Pts	PIM
2012-13	Kungalvs IK U18	Swe-U18	27	5	1	6	4	....	....	....	....	....
2013-14	Kungalvs IK 2 U18	Swe-U18	3	4	4	8	2	....	....	....	....	....
	Kungalvs IK U18	Swe-U18	32	18	19	37	76	....	....	....	....	....
	Kungalvs IK Jr.	Swe-Jr.	3	0	0	0	0	....	....	....	....	....
2014-15	HV 71 U18	Swe-U18	13	6	13	19	20	4	2	2	4	2
	HV 71 Jr.	Swe-Jr.	25	6	3	9	16	6	0	2	2	0
2015-16	HV 71 U18	Swe-U18	2	1	5	6	0	....	....	....	....	....
	HV 71 Jr.	Swe-Jr.	37	24	35	59	91	1	2	0	2	2
	HV 71 Jonkoping	Sweden	22	0	0	0	6	4	0	0	0	0
2016-17	HV 71 Jr.	Swe-Jr.	3	2	0	2	2	....	....	....	....	....
	HV 71 Jonkoping	Sweden	42	9	10	19	18	16	4	1	5	18

ANG, Jonathan (ANG, JAWN-ah-thuhn) FLA

Center. Shoots right. 5'11", 165 lbs. Born, Markham, ON, January 31, 1998.
(Florida's 4th pick, 94th overall, in 2016 NHL Draft).

			Regular Season					Playoffs				
Season	Club	League	GP	G	A	Pts	PIM	GP	G	A	Pts	PIM
2013-14	Mark. Waxers MM	Minor-ON	33	28	14	42	34	2	1	2	3	2
	Mark. Waxers Mid.	Minor-ON	....	....	....	....	....	5	4	2	6	0
	Whitby Fury	ON-Jr.A	1	0	0	0	0	....	....	....	....	....
2014-15	Peterborough	OHL	59	10	10	20	18	5	0	1	1	4
2015-16	Peterborough	OHL	68	21	28	49	44	7	3	6	9	2
2016-17	Peterborough	OHL	67	27	32	59	75	12	7	4	11	6

ANGELLO, Anthony (AN-gehl-oh, an-THUH-nee) PIT

Center. Shoots right. 6'4", 197 lbs. Born, Albany, NY, March 6, 1996.
(Pittsburgh's 3rd pick, 145th overall, in 2014 NHL Draft).

			Regular Season					Playoffs				
Season	Club	League	GP	G	A	Pts	PIM	GP	G	A	Pts	PIM
2011-12	Syracuse Jr. Stars	EmJHL	36	11	21	32	18	4	0	1	1	4
	Fayette.-Manlius	High-NY	18	32	31	63	....	1	1	2	3	....
2012-13	Syracuse Jr. Stars	EmJHL	40	31	29	60	60	3	1	3	4	2
	Fayette.-Manlius	High-NY	16	34	32	65	....	....	....	....	....	....
2013-14	Omaha Lancers	USHL	58	11	10	21	85	4	0	1	1	4
2014-15	Omaha Lancers	USHL	56	19	16	35	90	3	1	1	2	4
2015-16	Cornell Big Red	ECAC	34	11	13	24	26	....	....	....	....	....
2016-17	Cornell Big Red	ECAC	35	12	8	20	51	....	....	....	....	....

ANTIPIN, Victor (an-TEE-pihn, VIHK-tohr) **BUF**

Defense. Shoots left. 5'11", 179 lbs. Born, Ust-Kamenogorsk, Kazakhstan, December 6, 1992.

			Regular Season					Playoffs				
Season	**Club**	**League**	**GP**	**G**	**A**	**Pts**	**PIM**	**GP**	**G**	**A**	**Pts**	**PIM**
2009-10	Magnitogorsk Jr.	Russia-Jr.	39	2	9	11	22	5	0	0	0	2
2010-11	Magnitogorsk Jr.	Russia-Jr.	44	4	10	14	68	17	4	2	6	8
	Magnitogorsk	KHL	2	0	0	0	0	....	....	....	....	....
2011-12	Magnitogorsk Jr.	Russia-Jr.	40	6	19	25	18	11	2	4	6	0
2012-13	Magnitogorsk	KHL	50	10	11	21	8	7	1	2	3	0
2013-14	Magnitogorsk	KHL	45	9	8	17	16	21	4	5	9	25
2014-15	Magnitogorsk	KHL	54	5	16	21	4	10	2	5	7	0
2015-16	Magnitogorsk	KHL	56	6	9	15	8	23	3	4	7	8
2016-17	Magnitogorsk	KHL	59	6	18	24	8	18	7	4	11	2

Signed as a free agent by **Buffalo**, May 25, 2017.

APPLETON, Mason (A-puhl-tuhn, MAY-suhn) **WPG**

Center. Shoots right. 6'2", 197 lbs. Born, Green Bay, WI, January 15, 1996.
(Winnipeg's 6th pick, 168th overall, in 2015 NHL Draft).

			Regular Season					Playoffs				
Season	**Club**	**League**	**GP**	**G**	**A**	**Pts**	**PIM**	**GP**	**G**	**A**	**Pts**	**PIM**
2010-11	Ashwaubenon	High-WI	23	15	23	38	12	3	2	5	7	0
2011-12	Notre Dame Acad.	High-WI	24	10	32	42	15	6	2	3	5	0
2012-13	Notre Dame Acad.	High-WI	23	15	21	36	19	5	5	4	9	0
2013-14	Team Wisconsin	UMHSEL	21	1	9	10	16	3	1	0	1	0
	Notre Dame Acad.	High-WI	23	26	34	60	6	5	4	6	10	14
2014-15	Tri-City Storm	USHL	54	12	28	40	84	7	4	4	8	12
2015-16	Michigan State	Big Ten	37	5	17	22	32	....	....	....	....	....
2016-17	Michigan State	Big Ten	35	12	19	31	37	....	....	....	....	....

ARNESSON, Linus (AHR-neh-suhn, LEE-nuhs) **BOS**

Defense. Shoots left. 6'1", 188 lbs. Born, Stockholm, Sweden, September 21, 1994.
(Boston's 1st pick, 60th overall, in 2013 NHL Draft).

			Regular Season					Playoffs				
Season	**Club**	**League**	**GP**	**G**	**A**	**Pts**	**PIM**	**GP**	**G**	**A**	**Pts**	**PIM**
2009-10	Djurgarden U18	Swe-U18	22	2	6	8	14	....	....	....	....	....
2010-11	Djurgarden U18	Swe-U18	21	2	6	8	12	5	1	1	2	0
	Djurgarden Jr.	Swe-Jr.	8	0	0	0	2	....	....	....	....	....
2011-12	Djurgarden U18	Swe-U18	9	0	3	3	8	4	0	2	2	2
	Djurgarden Jr.	Swe-Jr.	40	2	13	15	20	3	0	1	1	2
	Djurgarden	Sweden	3	0	0	0	0	....	....	....	....	....
2012-13	Djurgarden Jr.	Swe-Jr.	13	1	3	4	22	1	0	0	0	0
	Djurgarden	Sweden-2	35	0	1	1	8	....	....	....	....	....
2013-14	Djurgarden	Sweden-2	50	1	5	6	38	....	....	....	....	....
2014-15	Djurgarden	Sweden	41	0	5	5	28	2	0	0	0	0
	Providence Bruins	AHL	11	1	3	4	6	....	....	....	....	....
2015-16	Providence Bruins	AHL	48	0	5	5	8	....	....	....	....	....
2016-17	Providence Bruins	AHL	20	0	1	1	8	13	0	1	1	2

• Missed majority of 2016-17 due to achilles injury at Springfield (AHL), December 3, 2016.

ASPLUND, Rasmus (as-PLUHND, RAZ-muhs) **BUF**

Center. Shoots left. 5'11", 179 lbs. Born, Filipstad, Sweden, December 3, 1997.
(Buffalo's 2nd pick, 33rd overall, in 2016 NHL Draft).

			Regular Season					Playoffs				
Season	**Club**	**League**	**GP**	**G**	**A**	**Pts**	**PIM**	**GP**	**G**	**A**	**Pts**	**PIM**
2012-13	Farjestad U18	Swe-U18	31	10	15	25	20	2	0	0	0	0
2013-14	Farjestad U18	Swe-U18	17	12	15	27	41	4	7	2	9	2
	Farjestad Jr.	Swe-Jr.	38	7	7	14	12	4	1	0	1	0
2014-15	Farjestad Jr.	Swe-Jr.	19	8	17	25	14	6	3	4	7	0
	Farjestad	Sweden	35	2	1	3	4	3	0	0	0	0
2015-16	Farjestad	Sweden	46	4	8	12	16	3	0	0	0	0
2016-17	Farjestad	Sweden	39	6	13	19	10	5	0	3	3	0

ASTON-REESE, Zach (A-stuhn REES, ZAK) **PIT**

Right wing. Shoots left. 6', 190 lbs. Born, Staten Island, NY, August 10, 1994.

			Regular Season					Playoffs				
Season	**Club**	**League**	**GP**	**G**	**A**	**Pts**	**PIM**	**GP**	**G**	**A**	**Pts**	**PIM**
2009-10	N.J. Rockets	MtJHL	36	13	20	33	31	4	3	0	3	12
2010-11	N.J. Rockets	AtJHL	25	9	20	29	65	....	....	....	....	....
	Des Moines	USHL	2	0	0	0	2	....	....	....	....	....
	Lincoln Stars	USHL	25	2	3	5	4	1	0	0	0	5
2011-12	Lincoln Stars	USHL	53	5	10	15	69	8	1	2	3	8
2012-13	Lincoln Stars	USHL	60	9	21	30	113	5	3	2	5	4
2013-14	Northeastern	H-East	35	8	11	19	22	....	....	....	....	....
2014-15	Northeastern	H-East	31	13	10	23	60	....	....	....	....	....
2015-16	Northeastern	H-East	41	14	29	43	28	....	....	....	....	....
2016-17	Northeastern	H-East	38	*31	32	*63	72	....	....	....	....	....
	Wilkes-Barre	AHL	10	3	5	8	7	....	....	....	....	....

Hockey East Second All-Star Team (2016) • Hockey East First All-Star Team (2017) • NCAA East First All-American Team (2017)

Signed as a free agent by **Pittsburgh**, March 14, 2017.

AUBE-KUBEL, Nicolas (oh-BAY-koo-BEHL, NIH-koh-las) **PHI**

Right wing. Shoots right. 5'11", 196 lbs. Born, Slave Lake, AB, May 10, 1996.
(Philadelphia's 2nd pick, 48th overall, in 2014 NHL Draft).

			Regular Season					Playoffs				
Season	**Club**	**League**	**GP**	**G**	**A**	**Pts**	**PIM**	**GP**	**G**	**A**	**Pts**	**PIM**
2009-10	Mortagne	Minor-QC	34	12	20	32	12	....	....	....	....	....
2010-11	Mortagne	Minor-QC	22	10	3	13	6	....	....	....	....	....
2011-12	Antoine-Girouard	QAAA	41	11	13	24	36	11	7	9	16	12
2012-13	Val-d'Or Foreurs	QMJHL	64	10	17	27	26	10	1	0	1	8
2013-14	Val-d'Or Foreurs	QMJHL	65	22	31	53	61	24	4	9	13	20
2014-15	Val-d'Or Foreurs	QMJHL	61	38	42	80	81	17	5	10	15	22
2015-16	Val-d'Or Foreurs	QMJHL	61	38	46	84	71	6	3	0	3	12
	Lehigh Valley	AHL	6	2	1	3	6	....	....	....	....	....
2016-17	Lehigh Valley	AHL	71	9	9	18	55	4	0	0	0	0

AUDETTE, Daniel (AW-deht, DAN-yehl) **MTL**

Center. Shoots left. 5'9", 171 lbs. Born, Buffalo, NY, May 6, 1996.
(Montreal's 4th pick, 147th overall, in 2014 NHL Draft).

			Regular Season					Playoffs				
Season	**Club**	**League**	**GP**	**G**	**A**	**Pts**	**PIM**	**GP**	**G**	**A**	**Pts**	**PIM**
2009-10	Laurentides	Minor-QC	28	19	30	49	20	6	4	2	6	6
2010-11	Laurentides	Minor-QC	21	18	14	32	34	....	....	....	....	....
	Esther-Blondin	QAAA	4	0	0	0	6	2	0	0	0	0
2011-12	Esther-Blondin	QAAA	39	25	35	60	57	13	7	16	23	20
2012-13	Sherbrooke	QMJHL	54	10	19	29	65	4	0	2	2	6
2013-14	Sherbrooke	QMJHL	68	21	55	76	79	....	....	....	....	....
2014-15	Sherbrooke	QMJHL	60	29	44	73	64	6	2	4	6	0
2015-16	Sherbrooke	QMJHL	52	22	37	59	53	5	1	5	6	2
	St. John's IceCaps	AHL	4	0	0	0	0	....	....	....	....	....
2016-17	St. John's IceCaps	AHL	75	10	20	30	37	4	0	1	1	0

AUGER, Justin (AW-guhr, JUHS-tihn) **L.A.**

Right wing. Shoots right. 6'7", 229 lbs. Born, Kitchener, ON, May 14, 1994.
(Los Angeles' 2nd pick, 103rd overall, in 2013 NHL Draft).

			Regular Season					Playoffs				
Season	**Club**	**League**	**GP**	**G**	**A**	**Pts**	**PIM**	**GP**	**G**	**A**	**Pts**	**PIM**
2009-10	Waterloo Wolves	Minor-ON	30	20	11	31	16	14	5	6	11	6
	Waterloo Wolves	Other	20	10	11	21	6	....	....	....	....	....
2010-11	Waterloo Siskins	ON-Jr.B	42	22	15	37	57	4	2	5	7	2
2011-12	Guelph Storm	OHL	58	7	7	14	39	6	0	0	0	0
2012-13	Guelph Storm	OHL	68	16	17	33	39	5	0	0	0	0
2013-14	Guelph Storm	OHL	53	11	12	23	61	20	2	5	7	15
2014-15	Manchester	AHL	70	13	16	29	59	19	1	1	2	8
2015-16	Ontario Reign	AHL	68	19	17	36	57	13	3	2	5	6
2016-17	Ontario Reign	AHL	61	11	9	20	58	5	2	1	3	6

BACHMAN, Karch (BAHK-muhn, KAHRCH) **FLA**

Left wing. Shoots left. 5'11", 175 lbs. Born, Fort Wayne, IN, March 10, 1997.
(Florida's 5th pick, 132nd overall, in 2015 NHL Draft).

			Regular Season					Playoffs				
Season	**Club**	**League**	**GP**	**G**	**A**	**Pts**	**PIM**	**GP**	**G**	**A**	**Pts**	**PIM**
2012-13	Culver Academy	High-IN	25	14	14	28	10	....	....	....	....	....
2013-14	Culver Academy	High-IN	41	36	15	51	28	....	....	....	....	....
	Tri-City Storm	USHL	2	0	0	0	0	....	....	....	....	....
2014-15	Culver Academy	High-IN	32	19	24	43	10	....	....	....	....	....
	USAHNTDP	U-18	2	0	0	0	0	....	....	....	....	....
2015-16	Green Bay	USHL	5	1	1	2	0	....	....	....	....	....
	Chicago Steel	USHL	24	11	4	15	8	....	....	....	....	....
	Cedar Rapids	USHL	6	2	3	5	2	....	....	....	....	....
2016-17	Miami U.	NCHC	34	2	4	6	14	....	....	....	....	....

BACKMAN, Mattias (BAK-man, mah-TIGH-uhs) **DAL**

Defense. Shoots left. 6'2", 180 lbs. Born, Linkoping, Sweden, October 3, 1992.
(Detroit's 7th pick, 146th overall, in 2011 NHL Draft).

			Regular Season					Playoffs				
Season	**Club**	**League**	**GP**	**G**	**A**	**Pts**	**PIM**	**GP**	**G**	**A**	**Pts**	**PIM**
2007-08	Linkopings HC U18	Swe-U18	21	0	2	2	14	....	....	....	....	....
2008-09	Linkopings HC U18	Swe-U18	30	5	8	13	16	1	0	1	1	0
	Linkopings HC Jr.	Swe-Jr.	2	0	0	0	2	....	....	....	....	....
2009-10	Linkopings HC U18	Swe-U18	2	2	1	3	4	3	0	0	0	2
	Linkopings HC	Sweden	5	0	0	0	2	....	....	....	....	....
	Linkopings HC Jr.	Swe-Jr.	33	4	5	9	38	6	1	0	1	10
	Linkopings HC	Sweden	5	0	0	0	2	....	....	....	....	....
2010-11	Linkopings HC Jr.	Swe-Jr.	27	2	18	20	34	3	0	2	2	4
	Linkopings HC	Sweden	6	0	0	0	4	....	....	....	....	....
	Mjolby HC	Sweden-3	2	1	2	3	2	....	....	....	....	....
2011-12	Linkopings HC	Sweden	42	1	7	8	14	....	....	....	....	....
	Linkopings HC Jr.	Swe-Jr.	6	1	1	2	0	6	2	6	8	4
2012-13	Linkopings HC	Sweden	52	2	24	26	34	10	2	4	6	4
2013-14	Linkopings HC	Sweden	54	6	15	21	16	13	0	7	7	6
	Grand Rapids	AHL	2	0	0	0	0	10	1	5	6	2
2014-15	Grand Rapids	AHL	18	0	4	4	6	....	....	....	....	....
	Linkopings HC	Sweden	25	4	13	17	4	9	0	3	3	6
	Texas Stars	AHL	1	0	0	0	0	2	0	1	1	0
2015-16	Texas Stars	AHL	69	8	24	32	34	4	0	2	2	4
2016-17	Texas Stars	AHL	41	3	8	11	24	....	....	....	....	....
	Hershey Bears	AHL	5	1	1	2	2	....	....	....	....	....

Signed as a free agent by **Linkoping** (Sweden), December 24, 2014. Traded to **Dallas** by **Detroit** with Mattias Janmark and Detroit's 2nd round pick (Roope Hintz) in 2015 NHL Draft for Erik Cole and Dallas' 3rd round pick (Vili Saarijarvi) in 2015 NHL Draft, March 1, 2015.

BACKMAN, Sean (BAK-man, SHAWN)

Right wing. Shoots right. 5'9", 170 lbs. Born, Cos Cob, CT, April 29, 1986.

			Regular Season					Playoffs				
Season	**Club**	**League**	**GP**	**G**	**A**	**Pts**	**PIM**	**GP**	**G**	**A**	**Pts**	**PIM**
2002-03	Avon Old Farms	High-CT	25	9	14	23	....	....	....	....	....	....
2003-04	Avon Old Farms	High-CT	28	15	14	29	....	....	....	....	....	....
2004-05	Avon Old Farms	High-CT	27	15	10	25	....	....	....	....	....	....
2005-06	Green Bay	USHL	57	29	27	56	30	....	....	....	....	....
2006-07	Yale	ECAC	29	18	13	31	38	....	....	....	....	....
2007-08	Yale	ECAC	32	18	9	27	16	....	....	....	....	....
2008-09	Yale	ECAC	32	20	13	33	44	....	....	....	....	....
2009-10	Yale	ECAC	29	21	14	35	12	....	....	....	....	....
2010-11	Texas Stars	AHL	67	7	16	23	20	6	0	0	0	6
	Idaho Steelheads	ECHL	5	2	2	4	4	....	....	....	....	....
2011-12	Bridgeport	AHL	66	7	11	18	20	3	0	0	0	0
2012-13	Bridgeport	AHL	67	11	10	21	40	....	....	....	....	....
2013-14	Manchester	AHL	71	10	16	26	24	4	1	0	1	0
2014-15	Manchester	AHL	76	19	25	44	34	19	5	12	17	8
2015-16	Ontario Reign	AHL	68	21	34	55	36	13	1	3	4	8
2016-17	Ontario Reign	AHL	67	12	22	34	24	5	0	1	1	0

ECAC Second All-Star Team (2009) • ECAC First All-Star Team (2010) • NCAA East Second All-American Team (2010)

Signed as a free agent by **Dallas**, March 30, 2010. Signed as a free agent by **NY Islanders**, August 8, 2011. Signed as a free agent by **Manchester** (AHL), August 21, 2013. Signed as a free agent by **Ontario** (AHL), July 27, 2015. Signed as a free agent by **Berlin** (Germany), May 28, 2017.

BADDOCK, Brandon (BA-dawk, BRAN-duhn) N.J.

Left wing. Shoots left. 6'4", 215 lbs. Born, Vermilion, AB, March 29, 1995.
(New Jersey's 6th pick, 161st overall, in 2014 NHL Draft).

			Regular Season					Playoffs				
Season	Club	League	GP	G	A	Pts	PIM	GP	G	A	Pts	PIM
2008-09	Wainwright	Minor-AB	27	16	11	27	18	....	....	....	....	....
2009-10	Lloydminster Heat	AMBHL	33	11	10	21	42	....	....	....	....	....
2010-11	Lloydminster Rage	Minor-AB	38	27	23	50	116	....	....	....	....	....
2011-12	Lloydminster	AJHL	41	2	1	3	91	1	0	0	0	0
	Edmonton	WHL	1	0	0	0	0					
2012-13	Edmonton	WHL	59	7	4	11	73	22	0	1	1	12
2013-14	Edmonton	WHL	56	6	11	17	128	13	1	0	1	6
2014-15	Edmonton	WHL	71	19	21	40	136	5	1	0	1	10
2015-16	Edmonton	WHL	68	22	13	35	143	6	2	0	2	14
2016-17	Adirondack	ECHL	21	0	4	4	15	4	0	1	1	2

BADINI, Jack (bah-DEE-nee, JAK) ANA

Center. Shoots left. 6', 203 lbs. Born, Greenwich, CT, January 19, 1998.
(Anaheim's 3rd pick, 91st overall, in 2017 NHL Draft).

			Regular Season					Playoffs				
Season	Club	League	GP	G	A	Pts	PIM	GP	G	A	Pts	PIM
2012-13	CT Oilers U16	Minor-CT	54	28	23	51	26	....	....	....	....	....
	CT Oilers U18	EJEPL	20	11	12	23	22	5	3	3	6	4
2013-14	Long Island U16	AYHL	25	15	20	35	42	2	0	2	2	2
2014-15	NJ Avalanche U18	AYHL	13	2	6	8	14	....	....	....	....	....
	Lincoln Stars	USHL	28	2	1	3	12	....	....	....	....	....
2015-16	Lincoln Stars	USHL	56	4	7	11	55	4	0	1	1	6
2016-17	Chicago Steel	USHL	59	28	14	42	38	14	7	10	*17	2

• Signed Letter of Intent to attend **Harvard University** (ECAC) in fall of 2017.

BAILEY, Matt (BAY-lee, MAT)

Right wing. Shoots left. 6'1", 197 lbs. Born, Winnipeg, MB, April 5, 1991.

			Regular Season					Playoffs				
Season	Club	League	GP	G	A	Pts	PIM	GP	G	A	Pts	PIM
2006-07	Eastman Selects	MMHL	32	8	9	17	26	....	....	....	....	....
2007-08	Neepawa Natives	MJHL	56	13	15	28	63	....	....	....	....	....
2008-09	Tri-City Storm	USHL	58	10	14	24	49	....	....	....	....	....
2009-10	Sioux Falls	USHL	59	14	33	47	69	3	2	0	2	2
2010-11	Alaska-Anchorage	WCHA	30	10	10	20	23	....	....	....	....	....
2011-12	Alaska-Anchorage	WCHA	34	10	7	17	30	....	....	....	....	....
2012-13	Alaska-Anchorage	WCHA	36	7	12	19	65	....	....	....	....	....
2013-14	Alaska-Anchorage	WCHA	38	20	18	38	49	....	....	....	....	....
	Norfolk Admirals	AHL	11	2	1	3	8	10	0	2	2	10
2014-15	Norfolk Admirals	AHL	56	6	4	10	31	....	....	....	....	....
2015-16	San Diego Gulls	AHL	51	6	13	19	34	8	1	2	3	8
2016-17	Stockton Heat	AHL	17	2	5	7	22	....	....	....	....	....
	Adirondack	ECHL	6	3	6	9	4	....	....	....	....	....

WCHA First All-Star Team (2014)

Signed as a free agent by **Anaheim**, March 25, 2014.

BAILLARGEON, Robert (ba-LAIR-zhee-awn, RAW-buhrt) OTT

Center. Shoots right. 6', 165 lbs. Born, Springfield, MA, November 26, 1993.
(Ottawa's 5th pick, 136th overall, in 2012 NHL Draft).

			Regular Season					Playoffs				
Season	Club	League	GP	G	A	Pts	PIM	GP	G	A	Pts	PIM
2009-10	Cushing	High-MA	32	15	30	45	....	....	....	....	....	....
2010-11	Cushing	High-MA	32	30	34	64	....	....	....	....	....	....
2011-12	Indiana Ice	USHL	54	14	34	48	36	6	4	2	6	2
2012-13	Indiana Ice	USHL	25	6	9	15	30	....	....	....	....	....
	Omaha Lancers	USHL	30	12	14	26	18	....	....	....	....	....
2013-14	Boston University	H-East	35	10	17	27	20	....	....	....	....	....
2014-15	Boston University	H-East	30	3	13	16	14	....	....	....	....	....
2015-16	Boston University	H-East	36	6	6	12	4	....	....	....	....	....
2016-17	Arizona State	NCAA	28	9	12	21	34	....	....	....	....	....

BALCERS, Rudolfs (BAHL-suhrs, ROO-dawlfs) S.J.

Left wing. Shoots left. 5'11", 170 lbs. Born, Liepaja, Latvia, April 8, 1997.
(San Jose's 6th pick, 142nd overall, in 2015 NHL Draft).

			Regular Season					Playoffs				
Season	Club	League	GP	G	A	Pts	PIM	GP	G	A	Pts	PIM
2012-13	Lorenskog IK U18	Nor-U18	26	20	17	37	26	2	3	1	4	2
	Lorenskog IK Jr.	Norway-Jr.	2	1	1	2	0	4	0	1	1	0
2013-14	Viking U18	Nor-U18	22	35	23	58	20	3	3	2	5	0
	Viking	Norway-2	10	6	3	9	4	....	....	....	....	....
	Stavanger Oilers	Norway	2	0	1	1	0	....	....	....	....	....
2014-15	Stavanger Jr.	Norway-Jr.	7	6	3	9	2	12	14	9	23	14
	Stavanger Oilers	Norway	36	8	13	21	8	....	....	....	....	....
	Stavanger U18	Nor-U18	....	....	....	....	....	1	0	0	0	0
2015-16	Stavanger Jr.	Norway-Jr.	2	0	1	1	0	....	....	....	....	....
	Stavanger Oilers	Norway	43	15	9	24	16	17	6	4	10	4
2016-17	Kamloops Blazers	WHL	66	40	37	77	16	6	2	1	3	0

BALISY, Chase (BAL-ih-see, CHAYS) FLA

Center. Shoots left. 5'11", 179 lbs. Born, Fullerton, CA, February 2, 1992.
(Nashville's 6th pick, 170th overall, in 2011 NHL Draft).

			Regular Season					Playoffs				
Season	Club	League	GP	G	A	Pts	PIM	GP	G	A	Pts	PIM
2007-08	Tor. Jr. Canadiens	GTHL	80	40	110	150	....	....	....	....	....	....
2008-09	USAHNTDP	NAHL	42	8	14	22	8	9	0	3	3	0
	USAHNTDP	U-17	16	4	10	14	6	....	....	....	....	....
2009-10	USAHNTDP	U-17	2	0	1	1	2	....	....	....	....	....
	USAHNTDP	USHL	28	5	6	11	8	....	....	....	....	....
	USAHNTDP	U-18	35	4	10	14	6	....	....	....	....	....
2010-11	Western Mich.	CCHA	42	12	18	30	12	....	....	....	....	....
2011-12	Western Mich.	CCHA	41	13	24	37	35	....	....	....	....	....
2012-13	Western Mich.	CCHA	38	11	14	25	12	....	....	....	....	....
2013-14	Western Mich.	NCHC	40	13	24	37	14	....	....	....	....	....
2014-15	St. John's IceCaps	AHL	73	21	23	44	30	....	....	....	....	....
2015-16	Portland Pirates	AHL	69	9	17	26	12	2	0	1	1	0
2016-17	Springfield	AHL	76	17	28	45	26	....	....	....	....	....

CCHA All-Rookie Team (2011) • NCHC Second All-Star Team (2014)

Signed as a free agent by **Florida**, June 1, 2015.

BARDREAU, Cole (BAHR-droh, KOHL) PHI

Forward. Shoots right. 5'10", 193 lbs. Born, Fairport, NY, July 22, 1993.

			Regular Season					Playoffs				
Season	Club	League	GP	G	A	Pts	PIM	GP	G	A	Pts	PIM
2008-09	Rochester Alliance	Minor-NY	35	28	48	76	....	....	....	....	....	....
	Fairport	High-NY	16	16	16	32	....	....	....	....	....	....
2009-10	USAHNTDP	USHL	35	4	8	12	25	....	....	....	....	....
	USAHNTDP	U-17	18	4	0	4	36	....	....	....	....	....
2010-11	USAHNTDP	USHL	24	4	7	11	23	....	....	....	....	....
	USAHNTDP	U-18	36	7	8	15	22	....	....	....	....	....
2011-12	Cornell Big Red	ECAC	34	4	4	8	18	....	....	....	....	....
2012-13	Cornell Big Red	ECAC	13	2	5	7	12	....	....	....	....	....
2013-14	Cornell Big Red	ECAC	26	7	9	16	14	....	....	....	....	....
2014-15	Cornell Big Red	ECAC	30	5	17	22	38	....	....	....	....	....
	Lehigh Valley	AHL	15	1	1	2	2	....	....	....	....	....
2015-16	Lehigh Valley	AHL	54	13	17	30	54	....	....	....	....	....
2016-17	Lehigh Valley	AHL	72	9	15	24	85	5	0	0	0	4

Signed as a free agent by **Philadelphia**, March 12, 2015.

BARRATT, Evan (BAIR-uht, EH-vuhn) CHI

Center. Shoots left. 5'11", 182 lbs. Born, Bristol, PA, February 18, 1999.
(Chicago's 4th pick, 90th overall, in 2017 NHL Draft).

			Regular Season					Playoffs				
Season	Club	League	GP	G	A	Pts	PIM	GP	G	A	Pts	PIM
2014-15	Comcast U16	AYHL	18	19	26	45	18	....	....	....	....	....
	Comcast U16	USPHL	21	24	39	63	20	4	4	4	8	2
2015-16	USAHNTDP	USHL	35	7	10	17	46	....	....	....	....	....
	USAHNTDP	U-17	23	8	15	23	18	....	....	....	....	....
2016-17	USAHNTDP	USHL	26	9	15	24	28	....	....	....	....	....
	USAHNTDP	U-18	37	9	23	32	48	....	....	....	....	....

• Signed Letter of Intent to attend **Penn State University** (Big Ten) in fall of 2017.

BARRON, Morgan (BAIR-uhn, MOHR-guhn) NYR

Center. Shoots left. 6'2", 200 lbs. Born, Halifax, NS, February 12, 1998.
(NY Rangers' 6th pick, 174th overall, in 2017 NHL Draft).

			Regular Season					Playoffs				
Season	Club	League	GP	G	A	Pts	PIM	GP	G	A	Pts	PIM
2013-14	Dartmouth	NSMHL	32	13	6	19	6	17	5	5	10	2
2014-15	Dartmouth	NSMHL	34	17	25	42	14	16	8	16	24	8
2015-16	St. Andrew's	CISAA	15	14	11	25	8	4	1	3	4	0
	St. Andrew's	High-ON	58	40	32	72	22	....	....	....	....	....
2016-17	St. Andrew's	CISAA	11	6	4	10	7	4	4	3	7	0
	St. Andrew's	High-ON	46	28	22	50	15	....	....	....	....	....
	Sioux City	USHL	5	0	0	0	2	....	....	....	....	....

• Signed Letter of Intent to attend **Cornell University** (ECAC) in fall of 2017.

BARRON, Travis (BAIR-uhn, TRA-vihs) COL

Left wing. Shoots left. 6'1", 200 lbs. Born, Brampton, ON, August 17, 1998.
(Colorado's 6th pick, 191st overall, in 2016 NHL Draft).

			Regular Season					Playoffs				
Season	Club	League	GP	G	A	Pts	PIM	GP	G	A	Pts	PIM
2013-14	Tor. Jr. Can. MM	GTHL	30	23	18	41	27	7	4	2	6	6
	Aurora Tigers	ON-Jr.A	5	0	1	1	6	11	1	2	3	2
2014-15	Ottawa 67's	OHL	64	12	9	21	22	6	1	1	2	4
2015-16	Ottawa 67's	OHL	60	13	24	37	26	5	2	4	6	11
2016-17	Ottawa 67's	OHL	59	13	21	34	62	4	1	0	1	16

BASTIAN, Nathan (bash-T'YEHN, NAY-thuhn) N.J.

Right wing. Shoots right. 6'4", 205 lbs. Born, Kitchener, ON, December 6, 1997.
(New Jersey's 2nd pick, 41st overall, in 2016 NHL Draft).

			Regular Season					Playoffs				
Season	Club	League	GP	G	A	Pts	PIM	GP	G	A	Pts	PIM
2012-13	Kit. Jr. Rangers	Minor-ON	30	11	13	24	8	11	5	7	12	0
2013-14	Brantford 99ers	ON-Jr.B	48	17	29	46	24	....	....	....	....	....
	Mississauga	OHL	21	2	1	3	6	4	0	0	0	2
2014-15	Mississauga	OHL	68	17	12	29	22	....	....	....	....	....
2015-16	Mississauga	OHL	64	19	40	59	50	5	0	4	4	0
2016-17	Mississauga	OHL	58	16	29	45	43	20	7	7	14	16

BATHERSON, Drake (BATH-uhr-suhn, DRAYK) OTT

Center. Shoots right. 6'2", 181 lbs. Born, Fort Wayne, IN, April 27, 1998.
(Ottawa's 3rd pick, 121st overall, in 2017 NHL Draft).

			Regular Season					Playoffs				
Season	Club	League	GP	G	A	Pts	PIM	GP	G	A	Pts	PIM
2013-14	OHA Mavs MM	Minor-ON	18	7	10	17	18	....	....	....	....	....
	OHA Gold Mavs	Minor-ON	3	0	2	2	0	....	....	....	....	....
	Valley Wildcats	NSMHL	6	3	2	5	2	5	1	2	3	4
2014-15	Valley Wildcats	NSMHL	34	20	26	46	44	6	5	3	8	10
	Valley Wildcats	MJrHL	4	2	0	2	0	1	0	0	0	0
2015-16	Valley Wildcats	MJrHL	28	4	15	19	18	6	1	2	3	8
	Cape Breton	QMJHL	10	0	2	2	2	....	....	....	....	....
2016-17	Cape Breton	QMJHL	61	22	36	58	70	11	7	5	12	14

BAYREUTHER, Gavin (BAY-roo-thuhr, GA-vihn) DAL

Defense. Shoots left. 6'1", 194 lbs. Born, Canaan, NH, May 12, 1994.

			Regular Season					Playoffs				
Season	Club	League	GP	G	A	Pts	PIM	GP	G	A	Pts	PIM
2009-10	Holderness School	High-NH	26	3	4	7	....	....	....	....	....	....
2010-11	Holderness School	High-NH	24	7	6	13	....	....	....	....	....	....
2011-12	Holderness School	High-NH	29	14	20	34	36	....	....	....	....	....
2012-13	Cedar Rapids	USHL	19	4	8	12	15	....	....	....	....	....
	Fargo Force	USHL	41	5	16	21	28	13	2	1	3	14
2013-14	St. Lawrence	ECAC	38	9	27	36	20	....	....	....	....	....
2014-15	St. Lawrence	ECAC	37	6	11	17	22	....	....	....	....	....
2015-16	St. Lawrence	ECAC	37	12	17	29	26	....	....	....	....	....
2016-17	St. Lawrence	ECAC	30	8	21	29	24	....	....	....	....	....
	Texas Stars	AHL	15	2	3	5	6	....	....	....	....	....

ECAC First All-Team (2017) • NCAA East Second All-American Team (2016, 2017)

Signed as a free agent by **Dallas**, March 15, 2017.

BEAN, Jake (BEEN, JAYK) CAR

Defense. Shoots left. 6'1", 173 lbs. Born, Calgary, AB, June 9, 1998.
(Carolina's 1st pick, 13th overall, in 2016 NHL Draft).

			Regular Season					Playoffs				
Season	**Club**	**League**	**GP**	**G**	**A**	**Pts**	**PIM**	**GP**	**G**	**A**	**Pts**	**PIM**
2012-13	Edge Bantam	Minor-AB	44	19	34	53	24	....	....	....	....	....
2013-14	Edge Elite 15s	CSSHL	24	7	16	23	12	2	1	2	3	2
	Edge Maroon	CSSHL	2	1	0	1	0	....	....	....	....	....
	Edge School	Other	29	18	24	42	12	....	....	....	....	....
2014-15	Calgary Hitmen	WHL	51	5	34	39	2	7	2	4	6	0
2015-16	Calgary Hitmen	WHL	68	24	40	64	28	5	0	2	2	2
2016-17	Calgary Hitmen	WHL	43	8	37	45	14	4	0	2	2	0

WHL East Second All-Star Team (2016, 2017)

BEAR, Ethan (BAIR, EE-thuhn) EDM

Defense. Shoots right. 5'11", 198 lbs. Born, Regina, SK, June 26, 1997.
(Edmonton's 3rd pick, 124th overall, in 2015 NHL Draft).

			Regular Season					Playoffs				
Season	**Club**	**League**	**GP**	**G**	**A**	**Pts**	**PIM**	**GP**	**G**	**A**	**Pts**	**PIM**
2012-13	Yorkton Harvest	SMHL	38	7	28	35	30	5	1	1	2	0
	Seattle	WHL	1	0	0	0	0	....	....	....	....	....
2013-14	Seattle	WHL	58	6	13	19	18	9	2	2	4	6
2014-15	Seattle	WHL	69	13	25	38	23	6	1	2	3	0
2015-16	Seattle	WHL	69	19	46	65	33	18	8	14	22	8
2016-17	Seattle	WHL	67	28	42	70	21	17	6	*20	26	12

WHL West First All-Star Team (2016, 2017)

BEAUDIN, J.C. (boh-DEHN, JAY-CEE) COL

Center. Shoots right. 6'1", 185 lbs. Born, Longueuil, QC, March 25, 1997.
(Colorado's 4th pick, 71st overall, in 2015 NHL Draft).

			Regular Season					Playoffs				
Season	**Club**	**League**	**GP**	**G**	**A**	**Pts**	**PIM**	**GP**	**G**	**A**	**Pts**	**PIM**
2012-13	Antoine-Girouard	QAAA	26	3	8	11	8	13	1	1	2	8
2013-14	Antoine-Girouard	QAAA	40	19	28	47	42	3	0	0	0	0
	Rouyn-Noranda	QMJHL	4	0	0	0	0	2	0	0	0	0
2014-15	Rouyn-Noranda	QMJHL	68	14	39	53	29	6	1	4	5	4
2015-16	Rouyn-Noranda	QMJHL	58	33	49	82	34	17	7	12	19	8
2016-17	Rouyn-Noranda	QMJHL	65	30	50	80	33	13	8	12	20	2

BECKER, Jack (BEH-kuhr, JAK) BOS

Center. Shoots right. 6'3", 199 lbs. Born, Duluth, MN, June 24, 1997.
(Boston's 10th pick, 195th overall, in 2015 NHL Draft).

			Regular Season					Playoffs				
Season	**Club**	**League**	**GP**	**G**	**A**	**Pts**	**PIM**	**GP**	**G**	**A**	**Pts**	**PIM**
2012-13	Mahtomedi	High-MN	25	10	17	27	20	2	1	0	1	2
2013-14	Mahtomedi	High-MN	25	23	13	36	20	3	2	3	5	0
2014-15	Team Northeast	UMHSEL	17	9	4	13	10	3	0	0	0	0
	Mahtomedi	High-MN	23	22	25	47	16	6	8	9	17	4
	Sioux Falls	USHL	2	0	1	1	0	....	....	....	....	....
2015-16	Sioux Falls	USHL	58	8	14	22	20	3	1	0	1	0
2016-17	Sioux Falls	USHL	49	16	12	28	38	....	....	....	....	....

• Signed Letter of Intent to attend **Michigan Tech University** (WCHA) in fall of 2017.

BELLOWS, Kieffer (BEH-lohz, KEE-fuhr) NYI

Left wing. Shoots left. 6'1", 197 lbs. Born, Edina, MN, June 10, 1998.
(NY Islanders' 1st pick, 19th overall, in 2016 NHL Draft).

			Regular Season					Playoffs				
Season	**Club**	**League**	**GP**	**G**	**A**	**Pts**	**PIM**	**GP**	**G**	**A**	**Pts**	**PIM**
2013-14	Team Southwest	UMHSEL	7	1	2	3	10	....	....	....	....	....
	Metro Southwest	MEPDL	3	6	2	8	....	....	....	....	....	....
	Edina Hornets	High-MN	25	10	17	27	45	5	3	4	7	2
2014-15	Sioux Falls	USHL	58	33	19	52	78	12	9	3	12	12
2015-16	USAHNTDP	USHL	23	16	16	32	41	....	....	....	....	....
	USAHNTDP	U-18	39	34	15	49	60	....	....	....	....	....
2016-17	Boston University	H-East	34	7	7	14	40	....	....	....	....	....

USHL All-Rookie Team (2015) • USHL Rookie of the Year (2015)

BELPEDIO, Louis (BEHL-pee-dee-oh, LOO-ee) MIN

Defense. Shoots right. 5'11", 193 lbs. Born, Skokie, IL, May 14, 1996.
(Minnesota's 2nd pick, 80th overall, in 2014 NHL Draft).

			Regular Season					Playoffs				
Season	**Club**	**League**	**GP**	**G**	**A**	**Pts**	**PIM**	**GP**	**G**	**A**	**Pts**	**PIM**
2011-12	Culver Academy	High-IN	36	3	13	16	20	....	....	....	....	....
2012-13	USAHNTDP	USHL	38	0	4	4	23	....	....	....	....	....
	USAHNTDP	U-17	18	1	7	8	10	....	....	....	....	....
2013-14	USAHNTDP	USHL	26	5	10	15	24	....	....	....	....	....
	USAHNTDP	U-18	34	2	6	8	22	....	....	....	....	....
2014-15	Miami U.	NCHC	40	6	13	19	28	....	....	....	....	....
2015-16	Miami U.	NCHC	34	4	13	17	30	....	....	....	....	....
2016-17	Miami U.	NCHC	24	6	11	17	39	....	....	....	....	....

NCHC All-Rookie Team (2015)

BEMSTROM, Emil (BEHM-struhm, eh-MIHL) CBJ

Center. Shoots right. 5'11", 177 lbs. Born, Nykoping, Sweden, January 6, 1999.
(Columbus' 3rd pick, 117th overall, in 2017 NHL Draft).

			Regular Season					Playoffs				
Season	**Club**	**League**	**GP**	**G**	**A**	**Pts**	**PIM**	**GP**	**G**	**A**	**Pts**	**PIM**
2015-16	Leksands IF U18	Swe-U18	35	18	22	40	8	5	1	3	4	0
	Leksands IF Jr.	Swe-Jr.	5	0	0	0	2	....	....	....	....	....
2016-17	Leksands IF Jr.	Swe-Jr.	28	21	12	33	35	3	0	0	0	0
	Leksands IF	Sweden	5	0	0	0	0	....	....	....	....	....
	Leksands IF U18	Swe-U18	....	....	....	....	....	1	1	0	1	0

BENGTSSON, Lukas (BENG-t'suhn, LOO-kuhs) PIT

Defense. Shoots right. 5'11", 172 lbs. Born, Stockholm, Sweden, April 14, 1994.

			Regular Season					Playoffs				
Season	**Club**	**League**	**GP**	**G**	**A**	**Pts**	**PIM**	**GP**	**G**	**A**	**Pts**	**PIM**
2011-12	Mora IK	Sweden-2	3	0	0	0	0	....	....	....	....	....
	Mora IK Jr.	Swe-Jr.	25	3	5	8	37	....	....	....	....	....
2012-13	Mora IK	Sweden-2	22	1	3	4	0	....	....	....	....	....
	Mora IK Jr.	Swe-Jr.	32	4	14	18	18	2	0	2	2	0
2013-14	Mora IK	Sweden-2	45	13	20	33	10	5	2	3	5	0
	Mora IK Jr.	Swe-Jr.	2	2	2	4	4	2	0	0	0	4
2014-15	Mora IK	Sweden-2	43	8	23	31	10	5	0	2	2	2
	Frolunda	Sweden	....	....	....	....	....	9	1	3	4	2
2015-16	Frolunda	Sweden	30	7	7	14	12	12	2	5	7	0
2016-17	Wilkes-Barre	AHL	16	1	5	6	6	....	....	....	....	....

Signed as a free agent by **Pittsburgh**, April 27, 2016.

BENSON, Tyler (BEHN-suhn, TIGH-luhr) EDM

Left wing. Shoots left. 6', 197 lbs. Born, Edmonton, AB, March 15, 1998.
(Edmonton's 2nd pick, 32nd overall, in 2016 NHL Draft).

			Regular Season					Playoffs				
Season	**Club**	**League**	**GP**	**G**	**A**	**Pts**	**PIM**	**GP**	**G**	**A**	**Pts**	**PIM**
2011-12	SSAC Lions	AMBHL	33	34	50	84	44	11	12	*19	*31	4
2012-13	SSAC Lions	AMBHL	33	57	*89	*146	52	11	*15	*22	*37	16
	SSAC Bulldogs	Minor-AB	1	1	1	2	0	....	....	....	....	....
2013-14	PoE Acad. Prep	CSSHL	15	15	20	35	40	3	2	2	4	6
	PoE Acad. U18	NAPHL	21	14	26	40	48	4	3	4	7	28
	PoE Acad. U18	Other	6	3	6	9	6	....	....	....	....	....
	Vancouver Giants	WHL	7	0	0	0	0	....	....	....	....	....
2014-15	Vancouver Giants	WHL	62	14	31	45	55	....	....	....	....	....
2015-16	Vancouver Giants	WHL	30	9	19	28	46	....	....	....	....	....
2016-17	Vancouver Giants	WHL	33	11	31	42	31	....	....	....	....	....

BEREGLAZOV, Alexei (beh-reh-GLAZ-awv, a-LEHX-ay) NYR

Defense. Shoots left. 6'4", 205 lbs. Born, Magnitogorsk, Russia, April 20, 1994.

			Regular Season					Playoffs				
Season	**Club**	**League**	**GP**	**G**	**A**	**Pts**	**PIM**	**GP**	**G**	**A**	**Pts**	**PIM**
2011-12	Magnitogorsk Jr.	Russia-Jr.	38	3	3	6	43	3	0	1	1	2
2012-13	Magnitogorsk Jr.	Russia-Jr.	60	2	14	16	40	3	0	0	0	0
2013-14	Magnitogorsk	KHL	6	0	0	0	2	....	....	....	....	....
	Yuzhny Ural Orsk	Russia-2	10	1	0	1	2	....	....	....	....	....
	Magnitogorsk Jr.	Russia-Jr.	8	0	3	3	0	4	1	2	3	0
2014-15	Yuzhny Ural Orsk	Russia-2	2	0	1	1	0	....	....	....	....	....
	Magnitogorsk	KHL	38	1	5	6	14	10	0	0	0	2
2015-16	Magnitogorsk	KHL	58	3	5	8	37	22	2	6	8	4
2016-17	Magnitogorsk	KHL	60	1	18	19	20	13	0	6	6	2

Signed as a free agent by **NY Rangers**, April 21, 2017.

BERGLUND, Filip (BUHRG-luhnd, FIHL-ihp) EDM

Defense. Shoots right. 6'3", 209 lbs. Born, Skelleftea, Sweden, May 10, 1997.
(Edmonton's 5th pick, 91st overall, in 2016 NHL Draft).

			Regular Season					Playoffs				
Season	**Club**	**League**	**GP**	**G**	**A**	**Pts**	**PIM**	**GP**	**G**	**A**	**Pts**	**PIM**
2012-13	Skelleftea AIK U18	Swe-U18	20	2	13	15	10	9	0	1	1	4
2013-14	Skelleftea AIK U18	Swe-U18	15	4	5	9	2	....	....	....	....	....
	Skelleftea AIK Jr.	Swe-Jr.	5	0	0	0	2	....	....	....	....	....
2014-15	Skelleftea AIK U18	Swe-U18	10	5	8	13	8	1	0	1	1	0
	Skelleftea AIK Jr.	Swe-Jr.	37	1	10	11	12	5	0	1	1	2
2015-16	Skelleftea AIK Jr.	Swe-Jr.	43	19	22	41	6	5	1	3	4	8
	Skelleftea AIK	Sweden	5	0	0	0	0	2	0	0	0	0
2016-17	Skelleftea AIK Jr.	Swe-Jr.	10	3	4	7	2	....	....	....	....	....
	Skelleftea AIK	Sweden	47	0	9	9	10	7	0	0	0	0

BERGLUND, Victor (BUHRG-luhnd, VIHK-tohr) BOS

Defense. Shoots right. 6', 165 lbs. Born, Ornskoldsvik, Sweden, February 8, 1999.
(Boston's 5th pick, 195th overall, in 2017 NHL Draft).

			Regular Season					Playoffs				
Season	**Club**	**League**	**GP**	**G**	**A**	**Pts**	**PIM**	**GP**	**G**	**A**	**Pts**	**PIM**
2014-15	MODO U18	Swe-U18	3	1	0	1	0	....	....	....	....	....
2015-16	MODO U18	Swe-U18	36	5	12	19	43	4	0	0	0	0
	MODO Jr.	Swe-Jr.	2	1	0	1	0	....	....	....	....	....
2016-17	MODO U18	Swe-U18	3	0	2	2	2	4	1	1	2	2
	MODO Jr.	Swe-Jr.	37	5	10	15	16	6	0	0	0	0
	MODO	Sweden-2	12	0	1	1	4	....	....	....	....	....

BERGMAN, Julius (BUHRG-muhn, YOO-lee-uhs) S.J.

Defense. Shoots right. 6'1", 205 lbs. Born, Stockholm, Sweden, November 2, 1995.
(San Jose's 2nd pick, 46th overall, in 2014 NHL Draft).

			Regular Season					Playoffs				
Season	**Club**	**League**	**GP**	**G**	**A**	**Pts**	**PIM**	**GP**	**G**	**A**	**Pts**	**PIM**
2010-11	Karlskrona HK Jr.	Swe-Jr.	14	5	4	9	6	1	0	1	1	0
	Karlskrona HK	Sweden-3	5	0	0	0	0	4	0	0	0	0
2011-12	Karlskrona HK	Sweden-3	36	3	6	9	47	10	1	0	1	12
2012-13	Karlskrona HK U18	Swe-U18	1	1	0	1	16	....	....	....	....	....
	Karlskrona HK Jr.	Swe-Jr.	1	0	0	0	0	....	....	....	....	....
	Karlskrona HK	Sweden-2	23	0	0	0	16	....	....	....	....	....
	Frolunda U18	Swe-U18	2	1	1	2	2	3	0	3	3	6
	Frolunda Jr.	Swe-Jr.	15	1	5	6	6	6	1	2	3	8
2013-14	Frolunda Jr.	Swe-Jr.	45	13	21	34	54	3	0	1	1	8
	Frolunda	Sweden	1	0	0	0	4	....	....	....	....	....
2014-15	London Knights	OHL	60	13	29	42	78	10	4	2	6	6
	Worcester Sharks	AHL	1	0	0	0	2	....	....	....	....	....
2015-16	San Jose Barracuda	AHL	60	3	8	11	40	4	0	0	0	4
2016-17	San Jose Barracuda	AHL	64	3	27	30	40	15	1	7	8	8

BERKOVITZ, Matthew   (BUHR-koh-vihts, MA-thew)   **ANA**

Defense. Shoots left. 6'1", 180 lbs.   Born, Green Bay, WI, February 16, 1996.
(Anaheim's 4th pick, 123rd overall, in 2014 NHL Draft).

			Regular Season					Playoffs			
Season	Club	League	GP	G	A	Pts	PIM	GP	G	A	Pts	PIM
2010-11	Ashwaubenon	High-WI	23	7	22	29	10	3	2	2	4	0
2011-12	Ashwaubenon	High-WI	23	8	13	21	6	1	3	1	4	0
2012-13	Ashwaubenon	High-WI	23	11	14	25	14	....				
2013-14	Team Wisconsin	UMHSEL	21	3	10	13	0	3	0	0	0	2
	Ashwaubenon	High-WI	24	11	26	37	12	3	0	4	4	0
2014-15	Sioux City	USHL	20	0	0	0	12	....				
	Green Bay	USHL	23	0	4	4	6	....				
2015-16	Green Bay	USHL	52	2	8	10	20	3	0	0	0	0
2016-17	Green Bay	USHL	53	2	23	25	20	....				

• Signed Letter of Intent to attend **Army West Point** (NCAA) in fall of 2017.

BERNHARDT, Daniel   (buhrn-HAHRT, DAN-yuhl)   **NYR**

Right wing. Shoots left. 6'3", 194 lbs.   Born, Stockholm, Sweden, April 11, 1996.
(NY Rangers' 6th pick, 119th overall, in 2015 NHL Draft).

			Regular Season					Playoffs			
Season	Club	League	GP	G	A	Pts	PIM	GP	G	A	Pts	PIM
2011-12	Nacka HK U18	Swe-U18	16	4	4	8	2	....				
2012-13	Djurgarden U18	Swe-U18	35	16	9	25	6	9	2	2	4	0
2013-14	Djurgarden U18	Swe-U18	38	25	38	63	28	4	1	2	3	4
	Djurgarden Jr.	Swe-Jr.	11	0	0	0	2	1	0	0	0	0
2014-15	Djurgarden Jr.	Swe-Jr.	44	26	35	61	22	7	2	2	4	0
	Djurgarden	Sweden	2	0	0	0	0	....				
2015-16	Djurgarden Jr.	Swe-Jr.	2	1	0	1	2	....				
	Almtuna	Sweden-2	13	1	3	4	4	....				
	Djurgarden	Sweden	10	1	0	1	0	....				
	London Knights	OHL	29	3	8	11	0	14	2	1	3	0
2016-17	Djurgarden	Sweden	4	0	1	1	0	....				
	VIK Vasteras HK	Sweden-2	38	5	2	7	4	....				

BERNHARDT, David   (BUHRN-hahrt, DAY-vihd)   **PHI**

Defense. Shoots left. 6'3", 203 lbs.   Born, Huddinge, Sweden, December 1, 1997.
(Philadelphia's 10th pick, 199th overall, in 2016 NHL Draft).

			Regular Season					Playoffs			
Season	Club	League	GP	G	A	Pts	PIM	GP	G	A	Pts	PIM
2012-13	Djurgarden U18	Swe-U18	8	0	1	1	2	....				
2013-14	Djurgarden U18	Swe-U18	37	8	16	24	53	4	0	2	2	0
	Djurgarden Jr.	Swe-Jr.	6	0	0	0	2	2	0	0	0	0
2014-15	Djurgarden U18	Swe-U18	11	3	12	15	45	5	0	5	5	8
	Djurgarden Jr.	Swe-Jr.	38	6	9	15	10	7	0	1	1	4
2015-16	Djurgarden Jr.	Swe-Jr.	45	10	28	38	30	7	3	3	6	2
2016-17	Djurgarden Jr.	Swe-Jr.	21	9	12	21	28	2	0	1	1	0
	Djurgarden	Sweden	27	2	5	7	4	....				

BESSE, Grant   (BEH-see, GRANT)   **ANA**

Right wing. Shoots left. 5'10", 175 lbs.   Born, Edina, MN, July 14, 1994.
(Anaheim's 4th pick, 147th overall, in 2013 NHL Draft).

			Regular Season					Playoffs			
Season	Club	League	GP	G	A	Pts	PIM	GP	G	A	Pts	PIM
2009-10	Benilde	High-MN	25	27	19	46	12	2	3	1	4	0
2010-11	Team Northwest	UMHSEL	21	9	11	20	16	3	1	1	2	0
	Benilde	High-MN	25	29	19	48	16	2	4	1	5	2
2011-12	Team Northwest	UMHSEL	21	15	17	32	16	6	3	3	6	4
	Benilde	High-MN	25	40	35	75	20	6	12	6	18	2
2012-13	Team Northwest	UMHSEL	4	2	0	2	0	....				
	Benilde	High-MN	25	44	25	69	16	3	4	3	7	2
	Omaha Lancers	USHL	7	4	0	4	0	....				
2013-14	U. of Wisconsin	Big Ten	36	8	6	14	12	....				
2014-15	U. of Wisconsin	Big Ten	32	11	11	22	6	....				
2015-16	U. of Wisconsin	Big Ten	35	11	22	33	10	....				
2016-17	U. of Wisconsin	Big Ten	35	9	19	28	8	....				

BETKER, Ben   (BEHT-kuhr, BEHN)   **EDM**

Defense. Shoots left. 6'6", 223 lbs.   Born, Cranbrook, BC, September 29, 1994.
(Edmonton's 9th pick, 158th overall, in 2013 NHL Draft).

			Regular Season					Playoffs			
Season	Club	League	GP	G	A	Pts	PIM	GP	G	A	Pts	PIM
2010-11	Kootenay Ice	BCMML	38	1	12	13	56	....				
2011-12	Westside Warriors	BCHL	59	5	13	18	52	....				
	Portland	WHL	1	0	0	0	0	....				
2012-13	Everett Silvertips	WHL	68	1	5	6	100	6	0	1	1	8
2013-14	Everett Silvertips	WHL	68	7	14	21	102	5	0	1	1	8
2014-15	Everett Silvertips	WHL	64	6	25	31	63	9	1	2	3	16
2015-16	Bakersfield	AHL	14	0	2	2	9	....				
	Norfolk Admirals	ECHL	49	3	14	17	53	....				
2016-17	Bakersfield	AHL	30	1	5	6	18	....				
	Norfolk Admirals	ECHL	5	3	2	5	2	....				

BINDULIS, Kris   (BIHN-DUH-lihs, KRIHS)   **WSH**

Defense. Shoots left. 6'3", 181 lbs.   Born, Riga, Latvia, September 17, 1995.

			Regular Season					Playoffs			
Season	Club	League	GP	G	A	Pts	PIM	GP	G	A	Pts	PIM
2011-12	SK Riga U17	Latvia	35	2	11	13	16	3	0	0	0	0
2012-13	Juniors Riga Jr.	Latvia	17	2	6	8	20	....				
	Juniors Riga Jr.	Rus.-Jr. B	34	4	6	10	62	3	0	0	0	2
2013-14	Soo Eagles	NAHL	52	0	11	11	64	....				
2014-15	Soo Eagles	NAHL	28	1	5	6	29	....				
	Des Moines	USHL	30	1	1	2	6	....				
2015-16	Aston Rebels	NAHL	57	10	36	46	75	8	3	2	5	4
2016-17	Lake Superior	WCHA	28	1	11	12	20	....				

Signed as a free agent by **Washington**, March 7, 2017.

BIRD, Tyler   (BUHRD, TIGH-luhr)   **CBJ**

Right wing. Shoots right. 6'1", 192 lbs.   Born, Boston, MA, August 14, 1996.
(Columbus' 6th pick, 137th overall, in 2014 NHL Draft).

			Regular Season					Playoffs			
Season	Club	League	GP	G	A	Pts	PIM	GP	G	A	Pts	PIM
2010-11	St. John's Prep	High-MA	25	3	4	7	....					
2011-12	St. John's Prep	High-MA	24	8	12	20	....					
	Valley Jr. Warriors	EmJHL	17	5	3	8	8	....				
2012-13	St. John's Prep	High-MA	24	12	15	27	....					
2013-14	Kimball Union	High-NH	37	33	27	60	....					
2014-15	Brown U.	ECAC	27	2	2	4	4	....				
2015-16	Brown U.	ECAC	31	6	2	8	6	....				
2016-17	Brown U.	ECAC	31	7	5	12	22	....				

BIRKS, Dane   (BURKS, DAYN)   **PIT**

Defense. Shoots right. 6'3", 183 lbs.   Born, Merritt, BC, August 29, 1995.
(Pittsburgh's 4th pick, 164th overall, in 2013 NHL Draft).

			Regular Season					Playoffs			
Season	Club	League	GP	G	A	Pts	PIM	GP	G	A	Pts	PIM
2010-11	Williams Lake	Minor-BC	STATISTICS NOT AVAILABLE									
2011-12	Creston Valley	KIJHL	47	3	21	24	72	6	0	1	1	20
	Trail Smoke Eaters	BCHL	10	0	0	0	12	....				
2012-13	Merritt	BCHL	52	5	15	20	28	5	0	1	1	6
2013-14	Merritt	BCHL	50	4	17	21	57	1	0	0	0	0
2014-15	Michigan Tech	WCHA	DID NOT PLAY – FRESHMAN									
2015-16	Michigan Tech	WCHA	31	0	3	3	16	....				
2016-17	Michigan Tech	WCHA	42	2	7	9	26	....				

BISCHOFF, Jake   (BIHSH-awf, JAYK)   **VGK**

Defense. Shoots left. 6', 197 lbs.   Born, Cambridge, MN, July 25, 1994.
(NY Islanders' 7th pick, 185th overall, in 2012 NHL Draft).

			Regular Season					Playoffs			
Season	Club	League	GP	G	A	Pts	PIM	GP	G	A	Pts	PIM
2010-11	Grand Rapids	High-MN	24	5	18	23	12	3	0	6	6	2
2011-12	Team North	UMHSEL	24	5	8	13	4	....				
	Grand Rapids	High-MN	24	11	27	38	17	1	0	2	2	0
	Omaha Lancers	USHL	10	0	1	1	2	....				
2012-13	Grand Rapids	High-MN	16	7	11	18	4	3	1	6	7	4
	Omaha Lancers	USHL	12	0	2	2	0	....				
2013-14	U. of Minnesota	Big Ten	28	3	4	7	8	....				
2014-15	U. of Minnesota	Big Ten	36	3	8	11	0	....				
2015-16	U. of Minnesota	Big Ten	37	6	12	18	14	....				
2016-17	U. of Minnesota	Big Ten	38	5	27	32	16	....				
	Bridgeport	AHL	6	2	1	3	2	....				

Traded to **Vegas** by **NY Islanders** with Mikhail Grabovski, NY Islanders' 1st round pick (Erik Brannstrom) in 2017 NHL Draft and NY Islanders' 2nd round pick in 2019 NHL Draft for Expansion Draft considerations, June 21, 2017.

BISHOP, Clark   (BIH-shuhp, KLAHRK)   **CAR**

Center. Shoots left. 6', 194 lbs.   Born, St. John's, NL, March 29, 1996.
(Carolina's 6th pick, 127th overall, in 2014 NHL Draft).

			Regular Season					Playoffs			
Season	Club	League	GP	G	A	Pts	PIM	GP	G	A	Pts	PIM
2011-12	St. John's Priv.	Minor-NF	23	18	20	38	45	....				
2012-13	Cape Breton	QMJHL	58	8	14	22	33	....				
2013-14	Cape Breton	QMJHL	56	14	19	33	54	4	1	0	1	8
2014-15	Cape Breton	QMJHL	38	19	16	35	54	7	5	3	8	4
2015-16	Cape Breton	QMJHL	50	16	23	39	86	3	1	2	3	0
2016-17	Charlotte	AHL	42	2	4	6	11	....				
	Florida Everblades	ECHL	21	3	8	11	16	....				

BITTEN, Will   (BIH-tihn, WIHL)   **MTL**

Center. Shoots right. 5'10", 176 lbs.   Born, Ottawa, ON, July 10, 1998.
(Montreal's 2nd pick, 70th overall, in 2016 NHL Draft).

			Regular Season					Playoffs			
Season	Club	League	GP	G	A	Pts	PIM	GP	G	A	Pts	PIM
2013-14	Ott. Jr. 67's MM	Minor-ON	29	36	42	78	18	11	5	9	14	8
	Ottawa Jr. Sens	ON-Jr.A	1	0	1	1	0	....				
2014-15	Plymouth Whalers	OHL	63	15	16	31	16	....				
2015-16	Flint Firebirds	OHL	67	30	35	65	32	....				
2016-17	Hamilton Bulldogs	OHL	65	23	34	57	36	7	3	0	3	8

BITTNER, Paul   (BIHT-nuhr, PAWL)   **CBJ**

Left wing. Shoots left. 6'4", 216 lbs.   Born, Crookston, MN, November 4, 1996.
(Columbus' 3rd pick, 38th overall, in 2015 NHL Draft).

			Regular Season					Playoffs			
Season	Club	League	GP	G	A	Pts	PIM	GP	G	A	Pts	PIM
2011-12	Team Northeast	MEPDL	16	6	3	9	0	2	2	1	3	0
	Crookston Pirates	High-MN	25	15	6	21	10	1	0	0	0	0
2013-14	Portland	WHL	63	22	27	49	27	21	6	6	12	11
2014-15	Portland	WHL	66	34	37	71	52	17	4	8	12	6
2015-16	Portland	WHL	25	10	11	21	21	....				
	Lake Erie Monsters	AHL	2	0	0	0	0	....				
2016-17	Cleveland	AHL	31	0	3	3	10	....				

BJORK, Anders   (B'YOHRK, AN-duhrz)   **BOS**

Left wing. Shoots left. 6', 186 lbs.   Born, Mequon, WI, August 5, 1996.
(Boston's 4th pick, 146th overall, in 2014 NHL Draft).

			Regular Season					Playoffs			
Season	Club	League	GP	G	A	Pts	PIM	GP	G	A	Pts	PIM
2011-12	Chicago Mission	HPHL	29	14	9	23	8	....				
2012-13	USAHNTDP	U-17	18	4	5	9	20	....				
	USAHNTDP	USHL	38	8	7	15	28	....				
2013-14	USAHNTDP	USHL	26	9	12	21	0	....				
	USAHNTDP	U-18	35	12	9	21	10	....				
2014-15	U. of Notre Dame	H-East	41	7	15	22	14	....				
2015-16	U. of Notre Dame	H-East	35	12	23	35	8	....				
2016-17	U. of Notre Dame	H-East	39	21	31	52	16	....				

Hockey East Second All-Star Team (2016) • Hockey East First All-Star Team (2017) • NCAA East Second All-American Team (2017)

BJORKQVIST, Kasper (B'YOHR-k'vihst, KAHS-puhr) PIT

Right wing. Shoots left. 6'1", 198 lbs. Born, Espoo, Finland, July 10, 1997.
(Pittsburgh's 2nd pick, 61st overall, in 2016 NHL Draft).

			Regular Season					Playoffs				
Season	**Club**	**League**	**GP**	**G**	**A**	**Pts**	**PIM**	**GP**	**G**	**A**	**Pts**	**PIM**
2012-13	Blues Espoo U18	Fin-U18	22	5	9	14	6	5	3	0	3	0
	Blues Ak U18	Fin-U18	3	1	0	1	0	....	....	....	....	....
2013-14	Blues Espoo U18	Fin-U18	21	9	12	21	12	11	5	2	7	16
	Blues Ak U18	Fin-U18	3	5	3	8	0	....	....	....	....	....
	Blues Espoo Jr.	Fin-Jr.	17	3	4	7	8	....	....	....	....	....
2014-15	Blues Espoo Jr.	Fin-Jr.	34	19	11	30	82	8	0	2	2	2
2015-16	Blues Espoo Jr.	Fin-Jr.	45	28	38	66	32	2	1	1	2	2
2016-17	Providence College	H-East	30	3	6	9	8	....	....	....	....	....

BJORKSTRAND, Patrick (bih-YOHRK-strand, PAT-rihk)

Left wing. Shoots left. 6', 192 lbs. Born, Herning, Denmark, July 1, 1992.

			Regular Season					Playoffs				
Season	**Club**	**League**	**GP**	**G**	**A**	**Pts**	**PIM**	**GP**	**G**	**A**	**Pts**	**PIM**
2009-10	Herning Blue Fox	Denmark	32	4	5	9	20	....	....	....	....	....
2010-11	Herning Blue Fox	Denmark	38	3	17	20	16	....	....	....	....	....
2011-12	Herning Blue Fox	Denmark	36	9	25	34	30	....	....	....	....	....
2012-13	Mora IK	Sweden-2	51	6	7	13	12	....	....	....	....	....
2013-14	Medvescak Zagreb	KHL	54	4	9	13	14	4	0	0	0	0
2014-15	Zagreb	KHL	55	7	8	15	2	....	....	....	....	....
	SaiPa	Finland	11	2	0	2	0	7	1	2	3	2
2015-16	Zagreb	KHL	57	13	9	22	12	....	....	....	....	....
2016-17	Ontario Reign	AHL	42	8	4	12	10	2	0	0	0	0

Signed as a free agent by **Los Angeles**, July 13, 2016.

BLACK, Graham (BLAK, GRAY-uhm)

Center. Shoots left. 6', 185 lbs. Born, Regina, SK, January 13, 1993.
(New Jersey's 5th pick, 135th overall, in 2012 NHL Draft).

			Regular Season					Playoffs				
Season	**Club**	**League**	**GP**	**G**	**A**	**Pts**	**PIM**	**GP**	**G**	**A**	**Pts**	**PIM**
2009-10	Reg. Pat Cdns.	SMHL	42	22	27	49	40	....	....	....	....	....
2010-11	Reg. Pat Cdns.	SMHL	43	*47	29	*76	48	5	7	3	10	20
	Swift Current	WHL	6	1	1	2	0	....	....	....	....	....
2011-12	Swift Current	WHL	71	17	33	50	49	....	....	....	....	....
2012-13	Swift Current	WHL	68	24	26	50	33	5	1	3	4	2
2013-14	Swift Current	WHL	69	34	63	97	43	6	2	2	4	6
	Albany Devils	AHL	2	0	0	0	0	....	....	....	....	....
2014-15	Albany Devils	AHL	46	7	7	14	16	....	....	....	....	....
2015-16	Albany Devils	AHL	50	7	2	9	20	5	2	2	4	2
2016-17	Springfield	AHL	33	4	4	8	16	....	....	....	....	....

Traded to **Florida** by **New Jersey** with Paul Thompson for Marc Savard and Florida's 2nd round pick in 2018 NHL Draft, June 10, 2016.

BLACKWELL, Colin (BLAK-wehll, KAWL-ihn)

Center. Shoots right. 5'9", 190 lbs. Born, Lawrence, MA, March 28, 1993.
(San Jose's 6th pick, 194th overall, in 2011 NHL Draft).

			Regular Season					Playoffs				
Season	**Club**	**League**	**GP**	**G**	**A**	**Pts**	**PIM**	**GP**	**G**	**A**	**Pts**	**PIM**
2007-08	St. John's Prep	High-MA	....	2	0	2	....	....	....	....	....	....
2008-09	St. John's Prep	High-MA	....	18	10	28	....	....	....	....	....	....
2009-10	St. John's Prep	High-MA	....	17	19	36	....	....	....	....	....	....
2010-11	St. John's Prep	High-MA	25	33	33	66	....	....	....	....	....	....
2011-12	Harvard Crimson	ECAC	34	5	14	19	46	....	....	....	....	....
2012-13	Harvard Crimson	ECAC	21	3	11	14	10	....	....	....	....	....
2013-14	Harvard Crimson	ECAC		DID NOT PLAY – INJURED								
2014-15	Harvard Crimson	ECAC	11	5	1	6	6	....	....	....	....	....
2015-16	Harvard Crimson	ECAC	28	6	13	19	12	....	....	....	....	....
2016-17	San Jose Barracuda	AHL	57	4	7	11	24	15	3	0	3	8

• Missed 2013-14 and majority of 2014-15 due to post-concussion syndrome.

BLAIS, Samuel (BLAY, SAM-yewl) ST.L.

Left wing. Shoots left. 5'10", 164 lbs. Born, Montmagny, QC, June 17, 1996.
(St. Louis' 9th pick, 176th overall, in 2014 NHL Draft).

			Regular Season					Playoffs				
Season	**Club**	**League**	**GP**	**G**	**A**	**Pts**	**PIM**	**GP**	**G**	**A**	**Pts**	**PIM**
2010-11	Rive-Sud Bantam	Minor-QC	29	20	18	38	....	....	....	....	....	....
	Rive-Sud Express	Minor-QC	3	1	1	2	....	....	....	....	....	....
2011-12	Rive-Sud Express	Minor-QC	23	10	16	26	18	7	2	6	8	4
2012-13	Trois-Rivieres	QAAA	42	16	24	40	18	10	8	4	12	4
2013-14	Levis	QAAA	21	12	23	35	12	....	....	....	....	....
	Victoriaville Tigres	QMJHL	25	4	10	14	0	4	0	1	1	0
2014-15	Victoriaville Tigres	QMJHL	61	34	48	82	50	4	2	3	5	4
2015-16	Victoriaville Tigres	QMJHL	30	17	23	40	19	....	....	....	....	....
	Charlottetown	QMJHL	33	16	26	42	14	12	4	15	19	14
2016-17	Chicago Wolves	AHL	75	26	17	43	58	10	3	5	8	18

BLEACKLEY, Conner (BLEEK-lee, KAW-nuhr) ST.L.

Center. Shoots right. 6', 192 lbs. Born, High River, AB, February 7, 1996.
(St. Louis' 6th pick, 144th overall, in 2016 NHL Draft).

			Regular Season					Playoffs				
Season	**Club**	**League**	**GP**	**G**	**A**	**Pts**	**PIM**	**GP**	**G**	**A**	**Pts**	**PIM**
2010-11	Okotoks Oilers	AMBHL	29	36	32	68	62	....	....	....	....	....
	Keystone Raiders	Minor-AB	5	7	2	9	4	....	....	....	....	....
2011-12	UFA Bisons	AMHL	26	13	17	30	41	2	0	0	0	0
	Red Deer Rebels	WHL	16	2	0	2	6	....	....	....	....	....
2012-13	Red Deer Rebels	WHL	66	9	9	18	28	9	2	1	3	0
2013-14	Red Deer Rebels	WHL	71	29	39	68	48	....	....	....	....	....
	Red Deer Rebels	WHL	71	29	39	68	48	....	....	....	....	....
2014-15	Red Deer Rebels	WHL	51	27	22	49	49	5	1	1	2	4
	Red Deer Rebels	WHL	51	27	22	49	49	5	1	1	2	4
2015-16	Red Deer Rebels	WHL	55	13	33	46	49	....	....	....	....	....
2016-17	Chicago Wolves	AHL	45	2	8	10	8	2	0	0	0	5
	Missouri Mavericks	ECHL	14	7	10	17	14	....	....	....	....	....

• Re-entered NHL Entry Draft. Originally Colorado's 1st pick, 23rd overall, in 2014 NHL Draft.

Traded to **Arizona** by **Colorado** with Alex Tanguay and Kyle Wood for Mikkel Boedker, February 29, 2016.

BLICHFELD, Joachim (BLIHKH-fehld, yoh-AH-kihm) S.J.

Center. Shoots right. 6'2", 180 lbs. Born, Frederikshavn, Denmark, July 17, 1998.
(San Jose's 5th pick, 210th overall, in 2016 NHL Draft).

			Regular Season					Playoffs				
Season	**Club**	**League**	**GP**	**G**	**A**	**Pts**	**PIM**	**GP**	**G**	**A**	**Pts**	**PIM**
2012-13	Frederikshavn U17	Den-U17	16	16	12	28	39	6	6	3	9	8
2013-14	Frederikshavn U17	Den-U17	20	27	25	52	44	6	3	7	10	12
	Frederikshavn Jr.	Den-Jr.	22	24	14	38	18	3	4	0	4	14
	Frederikshavn IK	Den-2	13	4	4	8	2	....	....	....	....	....
2014-15	Malmo U18	Swe-U18	37	20	15	35	20	2	0	1	1	0
	Malmo Jr.	Swe-Jr.	2	0	0	0	0	2	0	0	0	2
2015-16	Malmo U18	Swe-U18	3	0	0	0	2	5	5	3	8	2
	Malmo Jr.	Swe-Jr.	45	15	13	28	10	3	2	0	2	0
2016-17	Portland	WHL	63	28	30	58	34	11	5	5	10	8

BLUEGER, Teddy (BLEW-guhr, TEH-dee) PIT

Center. Shoots left. 6', 185 lbs. Born, Riga, Latvia, August 15, 1994.
(Pittsburgh's 3rd pick, 52nd overall, in 2012 NHL Draft).

			Regular Season					Playoffs				
Season	**Club**	**League**	**GP**	**G**	**A**	**Pts**	**PIM**	**GP**	**G**	**A**	**Pts**	**PIM**
2009-10	Shattuck Midget	High-MN	53	20	40	60	84	....	....	....	....	....
2010-11	Shattuck Midget	High-MN	54	24	42	66	32	....	....	....	....	....
2011-12	Shattuck	High-MN	51	24	64	88	63	....	....	....	....	....
2012-13	Minnesota State	WCHA	37	6	13	19	40	....	....	....	....	....
2013-14	Minnesota State	WCHA	40	4	22	26	55	....	....	....	....	....
2014-15	Minnesota State	WCHA	37	10	18	28	26	....	....	....	....	....
2015-16	Minnesota State	WCHA	41	11	24	35	29	....	....	....	....	....
	Wilkes-Barre	AHL	10	0	0	0	2	10	0	1	1	4
2016-17	Wilkes-Barre	AHL	54	7	24	31	20	5	1	0	1	2

WCHA First All-Star Team (2016)

BLUJUS, Dylan (BLOO-juhs, DIH-luhn)

Defense. Shoots right. 6'3", 191 lbs. Born, Buffalo, NY, January 22, 1994.
(Tampa Bay's 3rd pick, 40th overall, in 2012 NHL Draft).

			Regular Season					Playoffs				
Season	**Club**	**League**	**GP**	**G**	**A**	**Pts**	**PIM**	**GP**	**G**	**A**	**Pts**	**PIM**
2009-10	Buffalo Regals	Minor-NY	47	5	17	22	36	....	....	....	....	....
2010-11	Brampton	OHL	67	4	22	26	26	4	0	0	0	0
2011-12	Brampton	OHL	66	7	27	34	38	8	1	4	5	4
2012-13	Brampton	OHL	68	2	27	29	57	5	2	2	4	2
2013-14	North Bay	OHL	55	4	26	30	56	22	4	6	10	20
2014-15	Syracuse Crunch	AHL	67	4	18	22	18	3	0	0	0	4
2015-16	Syracuse Crunch	AHL	61	6	13	19	33	....	....	....	....	....
2016-17	Syracuse Crunch	AHL	23	1	7	8	16	1	0	0	0	2

BOBYLEV, Vladimir (boh-BUH-lehv, vla-DIH-meer) TOR

Center. Shoots left. 6'2", 202 lbs. Born, Lipetsk, Russia, April 18, 1997.
(Toronto's 8th pick, 122nd overall, in 2016 NHL Draft).

			Regular Season					Playoffs				
Season	**Club**	**League**	**GP**	**G**	**A**	**Pts**	**PIM**	**GP**	**G**	**A**	**Pts**	**PIM**
2013-14	Mytischi Jr.	Russia-Jr.	35	4	4	8	36	3	0	0	0	4
2014-15	Vancouver Giants	WHL	52	3	6	9	39	....	....	....	....	....
2015-16	Victoria Royals	WHL	72	28	39	67	60	5	0	7	7	2
2016-17	Spartak Moscow	KHL	20	1	2	3	10	....	....	....	....	....
	Victoria Royals	WHL	38	9	27	36	53	6	1	2	3	10

BODIE, Mat (BOH-dee, MAT) T.B.

Defense. Shoots left. 6', 175 lbs. Born, East St. Paul, MB, March 7, 1990.

			Regular Season					Playoffs				
Season	**Club**	**League**	**GP**	**G**	**A**	**Pts**	**PIM**	**GP**	**G**	**A**	**Pts**	**PIM**
2006-07	Wpg. Thrashers	MMHL	36	4	38	42	64	....	....	....	....	....
2007-08	Wpg. Thrashers	MMHL	34	11	28	39	42	....	....	....	....	....
2008-09	Powell River Kings	BCHL	53	1	41	42	41	18	2	12	14	20
2009-10	Powell River Kings	BCHL	51	8	34	42	37	23	9	22	31	23
2010-11	Union College	ECAC	40	6	26	32	18	....	....	....	....	....
2011-12	Union College	ECAC	39	8	21	29	32	....	....	....	....	....
2012-13	Union College	ECAC	35	6	18	24	32	....	....	....	....	....
2013-14	Union College	ECAC	40	8	31	39	57	....	....	....	....	....
2014-15	Hartford Wolf Pack	AHL	75	5	27	32	42	15	3	4	7	6
2015-16	Hartford Wolf Pack	AHL	76	7	29	36	38	....	....	....	....	....
2016-17	Hartford Wolf Pack	AHL	45	8	22	30	47	....	....	....	....	....
	Rochester	AHL	17	2	7	9	8	....	....	....	....	....

ECAC All-Rookie Team (2011) • ECAC First All-Star Team (2012, 2014) • NCAA East Second All-American Team (2012) • NCAA East First All-American Team (2014) • NCAA Championship All-Tournament Team (2014)

Signed as a free agent by **NY Rangers**, April 15, 2014. Traded to **Buffalo** by **NY Rangers** for Daniel Catenacci, February 28, 2017. Signed as a free agent by **Tampa Bay**, July 1, 2017.

BOIKOV, Sergei (boi-KAWV, sair-GAY) COL

Defense. Shoots left. 6'2", 200 lbs. Born, Khabarovsk, Russia, January 24, 1996.
(Colorado's 6th pick, 161st overall, in 2015 NHL Draft).

			Regular Season					Playoffs				
Season	**Club**	**League**	**GP**	**G**	**A**	**Pts**	**PIM**	**GP**	**G**	**A**	**Pts**	**PIM**
2012-13	Novokuznetsk Jr.	Russia-Jr.	3	0	0	0	6	....	....	....	....	....
2013-14	Drummondville	QMJHL	68	2	10	12	89	11	0	1	1	8
2014-15	Drummondville	QMJHL	64	3	18	21	64	....	....	....	....	....
2015-16	Drummondville	QMJHL	52	6	20	26	73	4	0	0	0	6
	San Antonio	AHL	4	0	0	0	0	....	....	....	....	....
2016-17	San Antonio	AHL	63	3	13	16	69	....	....	....	....	....
	Colorado Eagles	ECHL	7	1	1	2	2	18	3	7	10	12

BOKA, Nicholas (BOH-kah, NIH-koh-las) MIN

Defense. Shoots right. 6'1", 210 lbs. Born, Commerce, MI, September 8, 1997.
(Minnesota's 5th pick, 171st overall, in 2015 NHL Draft).

			Regular Season					Playoffs				
Season	**Club**	**League**	**GP**	**G**	**A**	**Pts**	**PIM**	**GP**	**G**	**A**	**Pts**	**PIM**
2012-13	Det. Comp. U18	HPHL	24	5	13	18	70	....	....	....	....	....
	Det. Comp. U18	Other	23	6	4	10	....	3	1	1	2	4
2013-14	USAHNTDP	USHL	32	4	7	11	104	....	....	....	....	....
	USAHNTDP	U-17	20	2	6	8	36	....	....	....	....	....
2014-15	USAHNTDP	USHL	20	3	1	4	68	....	....	....	....	....
	USAHNTDP	U-18	34	2	5	7	28	....	....	....	....	....
2015-16	U. of Michigan	Big Ten	38	0	10	10	19	....	....	....	....	....
2016-17	U. of Michigan	Big Ten	34	2	2	4	54	....	....	....	....	....

BONDRA, Radovan (BAWN-druh, RA-doh-van) **CHI**

Left wing. Shoots left. 6'5", 220 lbs. Born, Trebisov, Slovakia, January 27, 1997.
(Chicago's 4th pick, 151st overall, in 2015 NHL Draft).

			Regular Season					Playoffs				
Season	Club	League	GP	G	A	Pts	PIM	GP	G	A	Pts	PIM
2010-11	HK Trebisov U18	Svk-U18	20	8	6	14	10	....	....	....	....	....
2011-12	HC Kosice U18	Svk-U18	41	14	10	24	12	....	....	....	....	....
2012-13	Slovakia U20 B	Slovak-2	8	0	1	1	0	....	....	....	....	....
	HC Kosice U18	Svk-U18	38	37	25	62	26	2	0	0	0	4
	HC Kosice Jr.	Slovak-Jr.	....	....	....	....	....	1	0	0	0	0
2013-14	Slovakia U18	Slovak-2	35	5	4	9	20	....	....	....	....	....
	HC Kosice U18	Svk-U18	7	5	5	10	0	....	....	....	....	....
	HC Kosice Jr.	Slovak-Jr.	8	3	2	5	2	4	0	1	1	0
2014-15	HK VSR SR 20	Slovakia	4	0	0	0	2	....	....	....	....	....
	SR 18	Slovak-2	17	6	6	12	47	....	....	....	....	....
	HC Kosice	Slovakia	15	2	2	4	6	15	1	2	3	4
2015-16	Vancouver Giants	WHL	58	15	15	30	28	....	....	....	....	....
2016-17	Vancouver Giants	WHL	32	19	12	31	14	....	....	....	....	....
	Prince George	WHL	30	13	19	32	26	6	2	3	5	2
	Rockford IceHogs	AHL	5	0	0	0	2	....	....	....	....	....

BOQVIST, Jesper (BOH-kvihst, YES-puhr) **N.J.**

Center. Shoots left. 6', 180 lbs. Born, Falun, Sweden, October 30, 1998.
(New Jersey's 2nd pick, 36th overall, in 2017 NHL Draft).

			Regular Season					Playoffs				
Season	Club	League	GP	G	A	Pts	PIM	GP	G	A	Pts	PIM
2013-14	Hedemora SK U18	Swe-U18	11	12	9	21	4	....	....	....	....	....
	Hedemora SK Jr.	Swe-Jr.	3	0	1	1	0	....	....	....	....	....
	Hedemora SK	Sweden-3	2	0	0	0	0	....	....	....	....	....
2014-15	Brynas U18	Swe-U18	37	31	37	68	18	4	0	2	2	0
	Brynas IF Gavle Jr.	Swe-Jr.	7	1	1	2	0	1	0	0	0	0
2015-16	Brynas IF Gavle	Sweden	8	0	1	1	2	2	0	0	0	0
	Brynas IF Gavle Jr.	Swe-Jr.	38	23	35	58	8	3	0	1	1	0
	Brynas IF Gavle	Sweden	8	0	1	1	2	2	0	0	0	0
2016-17	Brynas IF Gavle Jr.	Swe-Jr.	15	10	5	15	6	....	....	....	....	....
	Brynas IF Gavle	Sweden	16	0	6	6	2	10	1	0	1	0
	Timra IK	Sweden-2	19	3	9	12	0	....	....	....	....	....

BORGEN, William (BOHR-guhn, WIHL-yuhm) **BUF**

Defense. Shoots right. 6'2", 190 lbs. Born, Moorhead, MN, December 19, 1996.
(Buffalo's 3rd pick, 92nd overall, in 2015 NHL Draft).

			Regular Season					Playoffs				
Season	Club	League	GP	G	A	Pts	PIM	GP	G	A	Pts	PIM
2012-13	Moorhead Spuds	High-MN	24	3	16	19	22	6	1	3	4	2
2013-14	Team Great Plains	UMHSEL	13	4	3	7	8	3	0	1	1	2
	Moorhead Spuds	High-MN	24	6	10	16	35	3	2	3	5	2
2014-15	Team Great Plains	UMHSEL	17	1	6	7	41	3	0	2	2	2
	Moorhead Spuds	High-MN	24	5	21	26	64	3	1	1	2	6
	Omaha Lancers	USHL	18	1	7	8	0	3	0	0	0	0
2015-16	St. Cloud State	NCHC	37	1	13	14	36	....	....	....	....	....
2016-17	St. Cloud State	NCHC	33	2	10	12	60	....	....	....	....	....

NCHC All-Rookie Team (2016)

BORGMAN, Andreas (BOHRG-mahn, an-DRAY-uhs) **TOR**

Defense. Shoots left. 6', 205 lbs. Born, Stockholm, Sweden, June 18, 1995.

			Regular Season					Playoffs				
Season	Club	League	GP	G	A	Pts	PIM	GP	G	A	Pts	PIM
2013-14	Timra IK	Sweden-2	18	0	0	0	2	....	....	....	....	....
2014-15	Timra IK	Sweden-2	46	2	4	6	45	....	....	....	....	....
2015-16	VIK Vasteras HK	Sweden-2	52	5	11	16	44	....	....	....	....	....
2016-17	HV 71 Jonkoping	Sweden	45	5	10	15	26	14	2	8	10	6

Signed as a free agent by **Toronto**, May 16, 2017.

BORGSTROM, Henrik (BOHTG-struhm, HEHN-rihk) **FLA**

Center. Shoots left. 6'3", 185 lbs. Born, Helsinki, Finland, August 6, 1997.
(Florida's 1st pick, 23rd overall, in 2016 NHL Draft).

			Regular Season					Playoffs				
Season	Club	League	GP	G	A	Pts	PIM	GP	G	A	Pts	PIM
2013-14	HIFK Helsinki U18	Fin-U18	30	8	12	20	6	5	1	0	1	0
	HJK Helsinki U18	Fin-U18	1	0	0	0	0	....	....	....	....	....
2014-15	HIFK Helsinki U18	Fin-U18	21	12	25	37	4	12	7	8	15	2
2015-16	HIFK Helsinki Jr.	Fin-Jr.	40	29	26	55	20	4	4	2	6	0
2016-17	U. of Denver	NCHC	37	*22	21	43	16	....	....	....	....	....

NCHC All-Rookie Team (2017) • NCHC Second All-Star Team (2017) • NCAA West First All-American Team (2017)

BOURAMMAN, Gustav (BOO-ruh-muhn, GUHS-tav) **MIN**

Defense. Shoots right. 6', 189 lbs. Born, Stockholm, Sweden, January 24, 1997.
(Minnesota's 6th pick, 201st overall, in 2015 NHL Draft).

			Regular Season					Playoffs				
Season	Club	League	GP	G	A	Pts	PIM	GP	G	A	Pts	PIM
2011-12	Nacka HK U18	Swe-U18	7	0	4	4	2	....	....	....	....	....
2012-13	Nacka HK U18 1	Swe-U18	1	0	0	0	0	1	2	2	4	2
	Nacka HK	Sweden-3	1	0	0	0	0	....	....	....	....	....
2013-14	Lulea HF U18	Swe-U18	16	8	17	25	12	5	0	3	3	2
	Lulea HF Jr.	Swe-Jr.	16	2	1	3	12	....	....	....	....	....
2014-15	Sault Ste. Marie	OHL	67	5	39	44	14	11	1	3	4	4
2015-16	Sault Ste. Marie	OHL	68	6	40	46	43	12	1	8	9	12
2016-17	Sault Ste. Marie	OHL	66	2	34	36	44	11	2	1	3	8

OHL All-Rookie Team (2015)

BOURKE, Troy (BOHRK, TROI)

Center. Shoots left. 5'10", 170 lbs. Born, Edmonton, AB, March 30, 1994.
(Colorado's 2nd pick, 72nd overall, in 2012 NHL Draft).

			Regular Season					Playoffs				
Season	Club	League	GP	G	A	Pts	PIM	GP	G	A	Pts	PIM
2007-08	PAC T'Wolves	AMBHL	33	13	15	28	26	2	0	0	0	0
2008-09	PAC T'Wolves	AMBHL	33	*45	38	*83	38	7	5	6	11	10
2009-10	St. Albert Raiders	AMHL	34	27	26	53	24	5	2	0	2	4
	Prince George	WHL	5	3	0	3	4	....	....	....	....	....
2010-11	Prince George	WHL	68	19	23	42	20	4	0	1	1	0
2011-12	Prince George	WHL	71	18	38	56	56	....	....	....	....	....
2012-13	Prince George	WHL	63	15	35	50	37	....	....	....	....	....
2013-14	Prince George	WHL	69	29	56	85	62	....	....	....	....	....
	Lake Erie Monsters	AHL	15	3	4	7	6	....	....	....	....	....
2014-15	Lake Erie Monsters	AHL	61	9	13	22	22	....	....	....	....	....
2015-16	San Antonio	AHL	56	2	7	9	30	....	....	....	....	....
	Fort Wayne	ECHL	9	5	6	11	6	16	7	9	16	6
2016-17	San Antonio	AHL	74	9	15	24	20	....	....	....	....	....

BOURQUE, Simon (BOHRK, SIGH-muhn) **MTL**

Defense. Shoots left. 6'1", 190 lbs. Born, Longueuil, QC, January 12, 1997.
(Montreal's 4th pick, 177th overall, in 2015 NHL Draft).

			Regular Season					Playoffs				
Season	Club	League	GP	G	A	Pts	PIM	GP	G	A	Pts	PIM
2012-13	C.C. Lemoyne	QAAA	42	5	13	18	24	9	1	2	3	6
2013-14	Rimouski Oceanic	QMJHL	55	3	6	9	26	11	0	2	2	2
2014-15	Rimouski Oceanic	QMJHL	68	10	28	38	69	17	1	4	5	18
2015-16	Rimouski Oceanic	QMJHL	66	12	34	46	50	6	0	5	5	2
	St. John's IceCaps	AHL	3	0	1	1	0	....	....	....	....	....
2016-17	Rimouski Oceanic	QMJHL	29	8	20	28	32	....	....	....	....	....
	Saint John	QMJHL	30	7	21	28	26	18	4	9	13	10

QMJHL Second All-Star Team (2017)

BOURQUE, Trenton (BORK, TREHN-tuhn) **ST.L.**

Defense. Shoots left. 6'2", 200 lbs. Born, Burlington, ON, November 6, 1998.
(St. Louis' 5th pick, 175th overall, in 2017 NHL Draft).

			Regular Season					Playoffs				
Season	Club	League	GP	G	A	Pts	PIM	GP	G	A	Pts	PIM
2013-14	Ham. Bulldogs MM	Minor-ON	40	2	19	21	44	9	2	5	7	18
2014-15	Sudbury Wolves	OHL	34	0	1	1	10	....	....	....	....	....
2015-16	Sudbury Wolves	OHL	24	0	2	2	20	....	....	....	....	....
	Owen Sound	OHL	28	0	6	6	12	1	0	0	0	0
2016-17	Owen Sound	OHL	67	0	11	11	36	17	0	2	2	10

BOWERS, Shane (BOW-uhrz, SHAYN) **OTT**

Center. Shoots left. 6'2", 176 lbs. Born, Halifax, NS, July 30, 1999.
(Ottawa's 1st pick, 28th overall, in 2017 NHL Draft).

			Regular Season					Playoffs				
Season	Club	League	GP	G	A	Pts	PIM	GP	G	A	Pts	PIM
2014-15	Halifax McDonalds	NSMHL	34	*23	29	*52	24	17	*15	*18	*33	14
2015-16	Waterloo	USHL	56	15	18	33	16	9	0	2	2	0
2016-17	Waterloo	USHL	60	22	29	51	20	6	2	1	3	2

• Signed Letter of Intent to attend **Boston University** (Hockey East) in fall of 2017.

BOWEY, Madison (BOW-ee, MA-dih-suhn) **WSH**

Defense. Shoots right. 6'1", 195 lbs. Born, Winnipeg, MB, April 22, 1995.
(Washington's 2nd pick, 53rd overall, in 2013 NHL Draft).

			Regular Season					Playoffs				
Season	Club	League	GP	G	A	Pts	PIM	GP	G	A	Pts	PIM
2010-11	Winnipeg Wild	MMHL	41	16	22	38	35	6	2	0	2	10
	Kelowna Rockets	WHL	3	0	1	1	4	1	0	0	0	0
2011-12	Kelowna Rockets	WHL	57	8	13	21	39	4	1	0	1	4
2012-13	Kelowna Rockets	WHL	69	12	18	30	75	11	0	4	4	14
2013-14	Kelowna Rockets	WHL	72	21	39	60	93	14	5	9	14	14
2014-15	Kelowna Rockets	WHL	58	17	43	60	66	19	7	12	19	24
2015-16	Hershey Bears	AHL	70	4	25	29	58	21	0	6	6	35
2016-17	Hershey Bears	AHL	34	3	11	14	28	10	2	2	4	6

WHL West Second All-Star Team (2014) • WHL West First All-Star Team (2015)

BOYD, Travis (BOID, TRA-vihs) **WSH**

Center. Shoots right. 5'10", 185 lbs. Born, Hopkins, MN, September 14, 1993.
(Washington's 3rd pick, 177th overall, in 2011 NHL Draft).

			Regular Season					Playoffs				
Season	Club	League	GP	G	A	Pts	PIM	GP	G	A	Pts	PIM
2008-09	Hopkins Royals	High-MN	26	26	25	51	....	....	....	....	....	....
2009-10	USAHNTDP	USHL	35	8	10	18	18	....	....	....	....	....
	USAHNTDP	U-17	17	2	4	6	4	....	....	....	....	....
	USAHNTDP	U-18	1	0	0	0	0	....	....	....	....	....
2010-11	USAHNTDP	USHL	24	5	13	18	10	....	....	....	....	....
	USAHNTDP	U-18	36	8	12	20	6	....	....	....	....	....
2011-12	U. of Minnesota	WCHA	35	1	8	9	4	....	....	....	....	....
2012-13	U. of Minnesota	WCHA	40	3	11	14	8	....	....	....	....	....
2013-14	U. of Minnesota	Big Ten	41	9	23	32	18	....	....	....	....	....
2014-15	U. of Minnesota	Big Ten	32	19	22	41	10	....	....	....	....	....
	Hershey Bears	AHL	2	1	1	2	0	....	....	....	....	....
2015-16	Hershey Bears	AHL	76	21	32	53	24	21	2	7	9	4
2016-17	Hershey Bears	AHL	76	16	47	63	16	12	1	7	8	2

AHL Second All-Star Team (2017)

BOYLE, Tim (BOIL, TIHM) **OTT**

Defense. Shoots right. 6'2", 185 lbs. Born, Hingham, MA, March 21, 1993.
(Ottawa's 4th pick, 106th overall, in 2012 NHL Draft).

			Regular Season					Playoffs				
Season	Club	League	GP	G	A	Pts	PIM	GP	G	A	Pts	PIM
2010-11	Nobles	High-MA	27	3	25	28	20	....	....	....	....	....
2011-12	Cape Cod Whalers	Minor-MA	33	5	15	20	....	....	....	....	....	....
	Nobles	High-MA	24	6	12	18	10	....	....	....	....	....
2012-13	Union College	ECAC	15	0	2	2	25	....	....	....	....	....
2013-14	South Shore Kings	USPHL	37	5	16	21	87	....	....	....	....	....
2014-15	Endicott College	NCAA-3	18	3	8	11	24	....	....	....	....	....
2015-16	Mississippi	SPHL	42	3	3	6	50	4	1	2	3	4
2016-17	Norfolk Admirals	ECHL	8	0	0	0	2	....	....	....	....	....
	Greenville	ECHL	1	0	0	0	2	....	....	....	....	....
	Wheeling Nailers	ECHL	10	0	7	7	5	....	....	....	....	....

BOZON, Tim (boh-ZAWN, TIHM)

Left wing. Shoots left. 6'1", 201 lbs. Born, St. Louis, MO, March 24, 1994.
(Montreal's 4th pick, 64th overall, in 2012 NHL Draft).

			Regular Season					Playoffs				
Season	**Club**	**League**	**GP**	**G**	**A**	**Pts**	**PIM**	**GP**	**G**	**A**	**Pts**	**PIM**
2007-08	Geneve U17	Swiss-U17	4	4	2	6	0	....	....	....	....	....
2008-09	Geneve U17	Swiss-U17	29	15	8	23	18	....	....	....	....	....
2009-10	Kloten Flyers U17	Swiss-U17	30	26	29	55	22	10	2	4	6	10
	Kloten Flyers Jr.	Swiss-Jr.	3	2	0	2	4	....	....	....	....	....
2010-11	Kloten Flyers Jr.	Swiss-Jr.	3	1	0	1	0	....	....	....	....	....
	HC Lugano U17	Swiss-U17	8	8	9	17	18	5	2	1	3	22
	HC Lugano Jr.	Swiss-Jr.	27	16	13	29	24	3	1	1	2	2
2011-12	Kamloops Blazers	WHL	71	36	35	71	40	11	5	0	5	11
2012-13	Kamloops Blazers	WHL	69	36	55	91	58	8	4	2	6	10
2013-14	Kamloops Blazers	WHL	13	3	4	7	13	....	....	....	....	....
	Kootenay Ice	WHL	50	30	32	62	34	....	....	....	....	....
2014-15	Kootenay Ice	WHL	57	35	28	63	19	7	3	6	9	6
	Hamilton Bulldogs	AHL	1	0	0	0	0	....	....	....	....	....
2015-16	St. John's IceCaps	AHL	41	5	3	8	14	....	....	....	....	....
	Brampton Beast	ECHL	15	3	6	9	2	....	....	....	....	....
2016-17	Springfield	AHL	43	8	7	15	24	....	....	....	....	....
	Manchester	ECHL	14	3	3	6	0	....	....	....	....	....

Traded to **Florida** by **Montreal** for Jonathan Racine. October 8, 2016.

BRACCO, Jeremy (BRA-koh, JAIR-ih-mee) **TOR**

Right wing. Shoots right. 5'10", 190 lbs. Born, Manhasset, NY, March 17, 1997.
(Toronto's 3rd pick, 61st overall, in 2015 NHL Draft).

			Regular Season					Playoffs				
Season	**Club**	**League**	**GP**	**G**	**A**	**Pts**	**PIM**	**GP**	**G**	**A**	**Pts**	**PIM**
2012-13	N.J. Rockets	MtJHL	10	9	15	24	....	....	....	....	....	....
	N.J. Rockets	AtJHL	30	16	34	50	24	4	2	4	6	0
2013-14	USAHNTDP	USHL	34	9	28	37	10	....	....	....	....	....
	USAHNTDP	U-17	20	7	30	37	10	....	....	....	....	....
2014-15	USAHNTDP	USHL	24	14	18	32	6	....	....	....	....	....
	USAHNTDP	U-18	41	16	46	62	4	....	....	....	....	....
2015-16	Boston College	H-East	5	0	3	3	4	....	....	....	....	....
	Kitchener Rangers	OHL	49	21	43	64	19	9	3	11	14	0
2016-17	Kitchener Rangers	OHL	27	17	34	51	4	....	....	....	....	....
	Windsor Spitfires	OHL	30	8	24	32	2	7	2	3	5	0

BRADLEY, Matthew (BRAD-lee, MA-thew)

Center. Shoots right. 6', 194 lbs. Born, Surrey, BC, January 22, 1997.
(Montreal's 3rd pick, 131st overall, in 2015 NHL Draft).

			Regular Season					Playoffs				
Season	**Club**	**League**	**GP**	**G**	**A**	**Pts**	**PIM**	**GP**	**G**	**A**	**Pts**	**PIM**
2012-13	Valley West Hawks	BCMML	25	10	18	28	28	3	1	5	6	0
2013-14	Valley West Hawks	BCMML	37	39	32	71	94	5	7	6	13	10
	Surrey Eagles	BCHL	8	0	0	0	0	....	....	....	....	....
	Medicine Hat	WHL	....	....	....	....	....	17	0	0	0	0
2014-15	Medicine Hat	WHL	71	17	23	40	24	10	0	2	2	2
2015-16	Medicine Hat	WHL	68	23	28	51	35	....	....	....	....	....
2016-17	Medicine Hat	WHL	70	34	43	77	85	11	4	5	9	4

BRANNSTROM, Erik (BRAN-struhm, AIR-ihk) **VGK**

Defense. Shoots left. 5'9", 176 lbs. Born, Eksjo, Sweden, February 9, 1999.
(Las Vegas' 3rd pick, 15th overall, in 2017 NHL Draft).

			Regular Season					Playoffs				
Season	**Club**	**League**	**GP**	**G**	**A**	**Pts**	**PIM**	**GP**	**G**	**A**	**Pts**	**PIM**
2013-14	HV 71 U18	Swe-U18	1	0	0	0	0	....	....	....	....	....
2014-15	HV 71 U18	Swe-U18	33	8	20	28	14	7	2	3	5	4
	HV 71 Jr.	Swe-Jr.	1	0	0	0	2	....	....	....	....	....
2015-16	HV 71 U18	Swe-U18	7	3	4	7	4	....	....	....	....	....
	HV 71 Jr.	Swe-Jr.	41	8	22	30	26	3	0	0	0	0
	HV 71 Jonkoping	Sweden	3	0	0	0	0	....	....	....	....	....
2016-17	HV 71 Jr.	Swe-Jr.	19	9	14	23	18	7	3	4	7	4
	HV 71 Jonkoping	Sweden	35	1	5	6	2	....	....	....	....	....

BRASSARD, Matt (bra-SAHRD, MAT) **VAN**

Defense. Shoots right. 6'2", 197 lbs. Born, Barrie, ON, August 8, 1998.
(Vancouver's 8th pick, 188th overall, in 2017 NHL Draft).

			Regular Season					Playoffs				
Season	**Club**	**League**	**GP**	**G**	**A**	**Pts**	**PIM**	**GP**	**G**	**A**	**Pts**	**PIM**
2013-14	Barrie Colts MM	Minor-ON	30	11	16	27	38	....	....	....	....	....
2014-15	Barrie Colts Mid.	Minor-ON	50	16	25	41	172	....	....	....	....	....
	Stouffville Spirit	ON-Jr.A	5	0	1	1	0	....	....	....	....	....
2015-16	Barrie Colts	OHL	28	1	3	4	13	....	....	....	....	....
2016-17	Barrie Colts	OHL	29	5	9	14	31	....	....	....	....	....
	Oshawa Generals	OHL	33	7	11	18	50	11	1	3	4	20

BRASSART, Brady (BRAS-uhrt, BRAY-dee) **MIN**

Right wing. Shoots right. 6'1", 207 lbs. Born, Vernon, BC, June 15, 1993.

			Regular Season					Playoffs				
Season	**Club**	**League**	**GP**	**G**	**A**	**Pts**	**PIM**	**GP**	**G**	**A**	**Pts**	**PIM**
2008-09	Van. NW Giants	BCMML	40	24	31	55	60	5	4	3	7	2
2009-10	Spokane Chiefs	WHL	53	9	6	15	16	7	0	1	1	4
2010-11	Spokane Chiefs	WHL	65	8	24	32	70	9	1	2	3	10
2011-12	Calgary Hitmen	WHL	70	25	34	59	106	5	0	0	0	8
2012-13	Calgary Hitmen	WHL	65	35	43	78	88	17	9	1	10	22
2013-14	Calgary Hitmen	WHL	70	35	50	85	94	6	3	6	9	8
	Iowa Wild	AHL	9	1	0	1	4	....	....	....	....	....
2014-15	Iowa Wild	AHL	72	8	13	21	22	....	....	....	....	....
2015-16	Iowa Wild	AHL	39	4	3	7	12	....	....	....	....	....
	Quad City	ECHL	28	6	11	17	14	4	0	1	1	14
2016-17	Quad City	ECHL	65	14	29	43	81	5	0	5	5	2

Signed as a free agent by **Minnesota**, March 1, 2014.

BRATT, Jesper (BRAHT, YEHS-puhr) **N.J.**

Left wing. Shoots left. 5'10", 175 lbs. Born, Stockholm, Sweden, July 30, 1998.
(New Jersey's 8th pick, 162nd overall, in 2016 NHL Draft).

			Regular Season					Playoffs				
Season	**Club**	**League**	**GP**	**G**	**A**	**Pts**	**PIM**	**GP**	**G**	**A**	**Pts**	**PIM**
2010-11	Trangsunds IF U18	Swe-U18	3	0	0	0	0	....	....	....	....	....
2011-12	Trangsunds IF U18	Swe-U18	3	1	0	1	0	....	....	....	....	....
2012-13	Trangsunds IF U18	Swe-U18	29	9	15	24	8	....	....	....	....	....
	Trangsunds IF Jr.	Swe-Jr.	2	0	1	1	0	6	1	1	2	2
	Trangsunds IF	Sweden-4	3	0	0	0	0	....	....	....	....	....
2013-14	AIK Solna U18	Swe-U18	38	10	24	34	24	....	....	....	....	....
2014-15	AIK Solna U18	Swe-U18	6	2	7	9	8	2	0	1	1	0
	AIK Solna Jr.	Swe-Jr.	39	17	23	40	20	1	0	0	0	0
	AIK Solna	Sweden-2	5	0	1	1	2	....	....	....	....	....
2015-16	AIK Solna Jr.	Swe-Jr.	2	1	1	2	2	....	....	....	....	....
	AIK Solna	Sweden-2	48	8	9	17	6	10	0	0	0	4
2016-17	AIK Solna Jr.	Swe-Jr.	1	0	1	1	0	2	0	0	0	2
	AIK Solna	Sweden-2	51	6	17	23	6	3	1	0	1	0

BRIND'AMOUR, Skyler (BRIHND-A-moor, SKIGH-luhr) **EDM**

Center. Shoots left. 6'2", 170 lbs. Born, Raleigh, NC, July 27, 1999.
(Edmonton's 6th pick, 177th overall, in 2017 NHL Draft).

			Regular Season					Playoffs				
Season	**Club**	**League**	**GP**	**G**	**A**	**Pts**	**PIM**	**GP**	**G**	**A**	**Pts**	**PIM**
2014-15	Car. Jr. Hurricanes	Minor-NC	62	10	25	35	14	....	....	....	....	....
2015-16	Car. Jr. Hurricanes	Minor-NC	55	16	49	65	22	....	....	....	....	....
2016-17	Selects Acad. U18	Minor-CT	41	16	24	40	....	....	....	....	....	....
	Selects Acad. U18	USPHL	6	3	6	9	2	1	0	1	1	2
	USAHNTDP	USHL	8	1	0	1	0	....	....	....	....	....

• Signed Letter of Intent to attend **Michigan State University** (Big Ten) in fall of 2019.

BRISEBOIS, Guillaume (BREEZ-b'wah, GEE-OHM) **VAN**

Defense. Shoots left. 6'2", 175 lbs. Born, St. Hillaire, QC, July 21, 1997.
(Vancouver's 2nd pick, 66th overall, in 2015 NHL Draft).

			Regular Season					Playoffs				
Season	**Club**	**League**	**GP**	**G**	**A**	**Pts**	**PIM**	**GP**	**G**	**A**	**Pts**	**PIM**
2012-13	Antoine-Girouard	QAAA	40	5	17	22	10	11	1	4	5	4
2013-14	Acadie-Bathurst	QMJHL	60	3	16	19	26	4	1	2	3	2
2014-15	Acadie-Bathurst	QMJHL	63	4	24	28	34	....	....	....	....	....
2015-16	Acadie-Bathurst	QMJHL	52	10	16	26	28	5	0	2	2	2
2016-17	Charlottetown	QMJHL	61	10	37	47	34	13	0	4	4	10

QMJHL Second All-Star Team (2017)

BROADHURST, Alex (BRAWD-hurst, AL-ehx) **CBJ**

Center. Shoots left. 6', 193 lbs. Born, Orland Park, IL, March 7, 1993.
(Chicago's 10th pick, 199th overall, in 2011 NHL Draft).

			Regular Season					Playoffs				
Season	**Club**	**League**	**GP**	**G**	**A**	**Pts**	**PIM**	**GP**	**G**	**A**	**Pts**	**PIM**
2006-07	Chicago Mission	MWEHL	31	20	29	49	10	....	....	....	....	....
2007-08	Chicago Fury	MWEHL	31	4	4	8	6	....	....	....	....	....
2008-09	Team Illinois	T1EHL	31	8	18	26	22	....	....	....	....	....
2009-10	Chicago Mission	T1EHL	48	16	29	45	26	....	....	....	....	....
2010-11	Green Bay	USHL	55	13	20	33	22	11	3	6	9	4
2011-12	Green Bay	USHL	53	26	47	73	40	7	7	6	13	4
2012-13	London Knights	OHL	65	23	40	63	36	21	10	18	28	22
2013-14	Rockford IceHogs	AHL	75	16	29	45	32	....	....	....	....	....
2014-15	Rockford IceHogs	AHL	29	6	8	14	4	7	0	1	1	2
2015-16	Lake Erie Monsters	AHL	60	10	26	36	14	17	3	9	12	6
2016-17	Cleveland	AHL	52	11	14	25	23	....	....	....	....	....

USHL First All-Star Team (2012)

Traded to **Columbus** by **Chicago** with Brandon Saad and Michael Paliotta for Artem Anisimov, Jeremy Morin, Corey Tropp, Marko Dano and Columbus' 4th round pick (later traded to NY Islanders – NY Islanders selected Anatoli Golyshev) in 2016 NHL Draft, June 30, 2015.

BRODZINSKI, Michael (brawd-ZIHN-skee, MIGH-kuhl) **S.J.**

Defense. Shoots right. 5'11", 195 lbs. Born, Ham Lake, MN, May 28, 1995.
(San Jose's 4th pick, 141st overall, in 2013 NHL Draft).

			Regular Season					Playoffs				
Season	**Club**	**League**	**GP**	**G**	**A**	**Pts**	**PIM**	**GP**	**G**	**A**	**Pts**	**PIM**
2009-10	Blaine Bengals	High-MN	24	2	3	5	12	5	1	0	1	0
2010-11	Team Northeast	UMHSEL	21	3	8	11	20	2	0	1	1	2
	Blaine Bengals	High-MN	25	9	14	23	22	5	5	3	8	0
2011-12	Team Northwest	UMHSEL	20	4	10	14	51	3	1	1	2	0
	Blaine Bengals	High-MN	25	13	20	33	26	3	3	0	3	17
	Muskegon	USHL	3	0	1	1	0	....	....	....	....	....
2012-13	Muskegon	USHL	61	16	17	33	47	3	0	1	1	0
2013-14	U. of Minnesota	Big Ten	26	6	7	13	12	....	....	....	....	....
2014-15	U. of Minnesota	Big Ten	36	4	10	14	16	....	....	....	....	....
2015-16	U. of Minnesota	Big Ten	37	8	13	21	34	....	....	....	....	....
	San Jose Barracuda	AHL	6	0	0	0	6	1	0	0	0	2
2016-17	San Jose Barracuda	AHL	9	0	3	3	6	....	....	....	....	....
	Allen Americans	ECHL	23	3	7	10	14	6	0	3	3	4

Big Ten Second All-Star Team (2016)

BROOK, Josh (BRUK, JAWSH) **MTL**

Defense. Shoots right. 6'1", 188 lbs. Born, Yorktown, SK, June 17, 1999.
(Montreal's 2nd pick, 56th overall, in 2017 NHL Draft).

			Regular Season					Playoffs				
Season	**Club**	**League**	**GP**	**G**	**A**	**Pts**	**PIM**	**GP**	**G**	**A**	**Pts**	**PIM**
2013-14	Notre Dame Btm.	Minor-SK	32	6	20	26	50	3	0	1	1	4
	Notre Dame	SMHL	4	0	0	0	2	....	....	....	....	....
2014-15	Notre Dame	SMHL	32	9	27	36	52	6	0	2	2	14
	Moose Jaw	WHL	1	0	0	0	2	....	....	....	....	....
2015-16	Moose Jaw	WHL	30	4	6	10	18	10	1	4	5	6
2016-17	Moose Jaw	WHL	69	8	32	40	61	7	2	5	7	10

BROOKS, Adam (BRUKS, A-duhm) TOR

Center. Shoots left. 5'10", 175 lbs. Born, Winnipeg, MB, May 6, 1996.
(Toronto's 6th pick, 92nd overall, in 2016 NHL Draft).

			Regular Season					Playoffs				
Season	Club	League	GP	G	A	Pts	PIM	GP	G	A	Pts	PIM
2010-11	Winnipeg Hawks	Minor-MB	40	64	47	111	14	....	....	....	....	....
2011-12	Wpg. Thrashers	MMHL	37	17	24	41	6	7	1	3	4	0
2012-13	Regina Pats	WHL	55	4	8	12	13	....	....	....	....	....
2013-14	Regina Pats	WHL	60	4	7	11	24	4	0	1	1	0
2014-15	Regina Pats	WHL	64	30	32	62	18	9	4	3	7	6
2015-16	Regina Pats	WHL	72	38	*82	*120	30	12	7	16	23	6
2016-17	Regina Pats	WHL	66	43	*87	130	61	17	5	13	18	12

WHL East First All-Star Team (2017)

BROWN, Christopher (BROWN, KRIHS-tuh-fuhr) BUF

Center. Shoots right. 6', 183 lbs. Born, Pontiac, MI, February 22, 1996.
(Buffalo's 8th pick, 151st overall, in 2014 NHL Draft).

			Regular Season					Playoffs				
Season	Club	League	GP	G	A	Pts	PIM	GP	G	A	Pts	PIM
2010-11	Cranbrook Cranes	High-MI	25	3	7	10	6	....	....	....	....	....
2011-12	Cranbrook Cranes	High-MI	26	17	17	34	2	....	....	....	....	....
2012-13	Michigan White	Other	16	5	9	14	0	....	....	....	....	....
	Cranbrook Cranes	High-MI	31	23	27	50	6	....	....	....	....	....
2013-14	Michigan Orange	Other	11	*11	6	*17	0	....	....	....	....	....
	Cranbrook Cranes	High-MI	28	26	*58	*84	21	....	....	....	....	....
	Green Bay	USHL	2	0	0	0	0	....	....	....	....	....
2014-15	Green Bay	USHL	43	13	19	32	22	....	....	....	....	....
	Tri-City Storm	USHL	15	0	5	5	2	6	0	0	0	0
2015-16	Boston College	H-East	41	2	9	11	8	....	....	....	....	....
2016-17	Boston College	H-East	34	9	17	26	12	....	....	....	....	....

BROWN, Josh (BROWN, JAWSH) FLA

Defense. Shoots right. 6'5", 225 lbs. Born, London, ON, January 21, 1994.
(Florida's 7th pick, 152nd overall, in 2013 NHL Draft).

			Regular Season					Playoffs				
Season	Club	League	GP	G	A	Pts	PIM	GP	G	A	Pts	PIM
2010-11	Whitby Fury	ON-Jr.A	35	6	4	10	59	....	....	....	....	....
2011-12	Oshawa Generals	OHL	46	0	4	4	49	2	0	0	0	0
2012-13	Oshawa Generals	OHL	68	0	16	16	79	9	1	4	5	11
2013-14	Oshawa Generals	OHL	56	2	10	12	83	9	0	0	0	18
2014-15	Oshawa Generals	OHL	60	4	17	21	92	21	2	2	4	30
2015-16	Portland Pirates	AHL	10	0	1	1	7	....	....	....	....	....
	Manchester	ECHL	54	1	11	12	80	5	0	0	0	4
2016-17	Springfield	AHL	72	3	10	13	96	....	....	....	....	....

BROWN, Logan (BROWN, LOH-guhn) OTT

Center. Shoots left. 6'6", 216 lbs. Born, Raleigh, NC, March 5, 1998.
(Ottawa's 1st pick, 11th overall, in 2016 NHL Draft).

			Regular Season					Playoffs				
Season	Club	League	GP	G	A	Pts	PIM	GP	G	A	Pts	PIM
2013-14	Indiana Jr. Ice U16	Minor-IN	14	18	10	28	10	....	....	....	....	....
	Indiana Jr. Ice U16	HPHL	5	1	2	3	2	....	....	....	....	....
2014-15	Windsor Spitfires	OHL	56	17	26	43	20	....	....	....	....	....
2015-16	Windsor Spitfires	OHL	59	21	53	74	40	5	0	6	6	6
2016-17	Windsor Spitfires	OHL	35	14	26	40	27	7	0	4	4	6

BRYSON, Jacob (BRIGH-suhn, JAY-kuhb) BUF

Defense. Shoots left. 5'9", 178 lbs. Born, London, ON, November 18, 1997.
(Buffalo's 5th pick, 99th overall, in 2017 NHL Draft).

			Regular Season					Playoffs				
Season	Club	League	GP	G	A	Pts	PIM	GP	G	A	Pts	PIM
2012-13	Lon. Knights MM	Minor-ON	29	3	17	20	4	16	1	4	5	4
2013-14	Lon. Knights Mid.	Minor-ON	32	3	19	22	2	16	1	3	4	6
	Lon. Knights Mid.	Other	34	1	16	17	2	....	....	....	....	....
2014-15	Neponset Val. U18	Minor-MA	14	3	9	12	2	....	....	....	....	....
	Loomis Chaffee	High-CT	27	5	10	15	....	....	....	....	....	....
2015-16	Omaha Lancers	USHL	56	3	28	31	36	....	....	....	....	....
2016-17	Providence College	H-East	39	3	17	20	12	....	....	....	....	....

BUCKLES, Matt (BUH-kuhlz, MAT)

Center. Shoots right. 6'3", 218 lbs. Born, Toronto, ON, May 5, 1995.
(Florida's 5th pick, 98th overall, in 2013 NHL Draft).

			Regular Season					Playoffs				
Season	Club	League	GP	G	A	Pts	PIM	GP	G	A	Pts	PIM
2010-11	Don Mills Flyers	GTHL	39	16	15	31	66	....	....	....	....	....
2011-12	Tor. Patriots	ON-Jr.A	46	15	21	36	76	21	5	6	11	20
2012-13	St. Michael's	ON-Jr.A	50	40	31	71	107	17	7	10	17	54
2013-14	Cornell Big Red	ECAC	29	4	0	4	39	....	....	....	....	....
2014-15	Cornell Big Red	ECAC	29	8	3	11	33	....	....	....	....	....
2015-16	Cornell Big Red	ECAC	31	8	3	11	4	....	....	....	....	....
2016-17	Cornell Big Red	ECAC	29	9	9	18	22	....	....	....	....	....
	Springfield	AHL	9	3	4	7	0	....	....	....	....	....

BUDIK, Vojtech (BOO-dihk, VOY-tehk) BUF

Defense. Shoots left. 6'1", 198 lbs. Born, Holice, Czech Rep., January 29, 1998.
(Buffalo's 7th pick, 130th overall, in 2016 NHL Draft).

			Regular Season					Playoffs				
Season	Club	League	GP	G	A	Pts	PIM	GP	G	A	Pts	PIM
2012-13	HC Pardubice U18	CzR-U18	38	3	7	10	8	2	0	0	0	0
2013-14	HC Pardubice U18	CzR-U18	30	2	7	9	8	....	....	....	....	....
	HC Pardubice Jr.	CzRep-Jr.	4	0	0	0	4	....	....	....	....	....
2014-15	HC Pardubice U18	CzR-U18	12	3	9	12	2	8	1	4	5	29
	HC Pardubice Jr.	CzRep-Jr.	19	0	5	5	8	....	....	....	....	....
2015-16	Prince Albert	WHL	70	3	13	16	20	5	1	0	1	2
2016-17	Prince Albert	WHL	56	1	25	26	20	....	....	....	....	....

BUKAC, Daniel (boo-KACH, DAN-yehl) BOS

Defense. Shoots right. 6'5", 197 lbs. Born, Most, Czech Rep., April 29, 1999.
(Boston's 6th pick, 204th overall, in 2017 NHL Draft).

			Regular Season					Playoffs				
Season	Club	League	GP	G	A	Pts	PIM	GP	G	A	Pts	PIM
2014-15	Chomutov U18	CzR-U18	12	0	1	1	0	....	....	....	....	....
2015-16	Chomutov U18	CzR-U18	38	3	12	15	42	2	0	0	0	4
2016-17	Brandon	WHL	72	2	15	17	38	2	0	0	0	0

BUNNAMAN, Connor (BUHN-ah-muhn, KAW-nuhr) PHI

Center. Shoots left. 6'1", 208 lbs. Born, Guelph, ON, April 16, 1998.
(Philadelphia's 6th pick, 109th overall, in 2016 NHL Draft).

			Regular Season					Playoffs				
Season	Club	League	GP	G	A	Pts	PIM	GP	G	A	Pts	PIM
2013-14	Guelph Gryphons	Minor-ON	37	18	17	35	39	9	3	4	7	4
2014-15	Kitchener Rangers	OHL	67	10	5	15	18	6	1	1	2	0
2015-16	Kitchener Rangers	OHL	68	16	22	38	14	9	2	2	4	0
2016-17	Kitchener Rangers	OHL	64	37	15	52	30	3	4	0	4	7

BUNTING, Michael (BUHN-tihng, MIGH-kuhl) ARI

Left wing. Shoots left. 6'1", 191 lbs. Born, Scarborough, ON, September 17, 1995.
(Arizona's 5th pick, 117th overall, in 2014 NHL Draft).

			Regular Season					Playoffs				
Season	Club	League	GP	G	A	Pts	PIM	GP	G	A	Pts	PIM
2012-13	Don Mills Flyers	GTHL	28	27	12	39	44	....	....	....	....	....
2013-14	Sault Ste. Marie	OHL	48	15	27	42	34	9	5	1	6	4
2014-15	Sault Ste. Marie	OHL	57	37	37	74	39	14	9	5	14	10
2015-16	Springfield Falcons	AHL	63	11	14	25	41	....	....	....	....	....
	Rapid City Rush	ECHL	7	2	0	2	4	....	....	....	....	....
2016-17	Tucson	AHL	67	13	15	28	52	....	....	....	....	....

BURGESS, Todd (BUHR-jehs, TAWD) OTT

Right wing. Shoots right. 6'2", 175 lbs. Born, Peoria, AZ, April 3, 1996.
(Ottawa's 3rd pick, 103rd overall, in 2016 NHL Draft).

			Regular Season					Playoffs				
Season	Club	League	GP	G	A	Pts	PIM	GP	G	A	Pts	PIM
2011-12	Phoenix U16	T1EHL	21	4	2	6	4	....	....	....	....	....
2012-13	Phoenix U16	T1EHL	40	17	16	33	51	4	1	2	3	12
	Phoenix U18	T1EHL	5	1	1	2	0	....	....	....	....	....
2013-14	Fairbanks Ice Dogs	NAHL	39	5	11	16	16	13	1	3	4	6
2014-15	Fairbanks Ice Dogs	NAHL	46	15	21	36	48	6	2	2	4	4
2015-16	Fairbanks Ice Dogs	NAHL	60	*38	*57	*95	42	12	5	9	14	6
2016-17			DID NOT PLAY – INJURED									

NAHL First All-Star Team (2016) • NAHL Player of the Year (2016)

• Missed 2016-17 due to recurring knee injury and resulting surgery.

BURLON, Brandon (BUHR-lohn, BRAN-duhn)

Defense. Shoots left. 6', 190 lbs. Born, Nobleton, ON, March 5, 1990.
(New Jersey's 2nd pick, 52nd overall, in 2008 NHL Draft).

			Regular Season					Playoffs				
Season	Club	League	GP	G	A	Pts	PIM	GP	G	A	Pts	PIM
2005-06	Vaughan Kings	GTHL	55	19	29	48	38	....	....	....	....	....
2006-07	St. Michael's	ON-Jr.A	45	4	19	23	46	4	0	1	1	4
2007-08	St. Michael's	ON-Jr.A	32	7	17	24	41	10	2	4	6	8
2008-09	U. of Michigan	CCHA	33	5	10	15	14	....	....	....	....	....
2009-10	U. of Michigan	CCHA	45	3	11	14	24	....	....	....	....	....
2010-11	U. of Michigan	CCHA	38	5	13	18	28	....	....	....	....	....
2011-12	Albany Devils	AHL	57	1	8	9	21	....	....	....	....	....
2012-13	Albany Devils	AHL	53	1	16	17	25	....	....	....	....	....
2013-14	Albany Devils	AHL	54	5	6	11	39	....	....	....	....	....
2014-15	Albany Devils	AHL	72	8	28	36	93	....	....	....	....	....
2015-16	Albany Devils	AHL	56	4	17	21	56	....	....	....	....	....
2016-17	Tucson	AHL	33	3	8	11	39	....	....	....	....	....

CCHA All-Rookie Team (2009)

Signed as a free agent by **Tucson** (AHL), August 3, 2016. Signed as a free agent by **Dusseldorf** (Germany), May 2, 2017.

BURROUGHS, Kyle (BUHR-ohz, KIGHL) NYI

Defense. Shoots right. 6', 198 lbs. Born, Vancouver, BC, July 12, 1995.
(NY Islanders' 7th pick, 196th overall, in 2013 NHL Draft).

			Regular Season					Playoffs				
Season	Club	League	GP	G	A	Pts	PIM	GP	G	A	Pts	PIM
2010-11	Valley West Hawks	BCMML	36	11	25	36	58	4	0	4	4	2
	Aldergrove	PIJHL	4	0	1	1	18	....	....	....	....	....
	Regina Pats	WHL	1	0	0	0	0	....	....	....	....	....
2011-12	Regina Pats	WHL	55	2	6	8	54	5	1	1	2	0
2012-13	Regina Pats	WHL	70	5	28	33	91	....	....	....	....	....
2013-14	Regina Pats	WHL	58	8	32	40	72	4	0	1	1	8
	Bridgeport	AHL	9	0	0	0	2	....	....	....	....	....
2014-15	Regina Pats	WHL	36	5	17	22	47	....	....	....	....	....
	Medicine Hat	WHL	30	2	15	17	38	10	0	3	3	6
2015-16	Bridgeport	AHL	31	2	8	10	30	2	1	1	2	4
	Missouri Mavericks	ECHL	18	1	6	7	17	....	....	....	....	....
2016-17	Bridgeport	AHL	71	3	21	24	116	....	....	....	....	....

BUTCHER, Will (BUH-chuhr, WIHL) COL

Defense. Shoots left. 5'10", 190 lbs. Born, Madison, WI, January 6, 1995.
(Colorado's 5th pick, 123rd overall, in 2013 NHL Draft).

			Regular Season					Playoffs				
Season	Club	League	GP	G	A	Pts	PIM	GP	G	A	Pts	PIM
2010-11	Madison Capitols	T1EHL	34	10	20	30	2	....	....	....	....	....
	Dubuque	USHL	2	0	2	2	0	....	....	....	....	....
2011-12	USAHNTDP	USHL	31	2	8	10	4	....	....	....	....	....
	USAHNTDP	U-17	17	6	17	23	4	....	....	....	....	....
	USAHNTDP	U-18	8	0	0	0	2	....	....	....	....	....
2012-13	USAHNTDP	USHL	26	3	10	13	2	....	....	....	....	....
	USAHNTDP	U-18	41	8	16	24	6	....	....	....	....	....
2013-14	U. of Denver	NCHC	38	8	8	16	8	....	....	....	....	....
2014-15	U. of Denver	NCHC	38	4	14	18	8	....	....	....	....	....
2015-16	U. of Denver	NCHC	39	9	23	32	19	....	....	....	....	....
2016-17	U. of Denver	NCHC	43	7	30	37	18	....	....	....	....	....

NCHC First All-Star Team (2016, 2017) • NCAA West Second All-American Team (2016) • NCAA West First All-American Team (2017) • Hobey Baker Memorial Award (Top U.S. Collegiate Player) (2017)

BYRON, Blaine (BIGH-ruhn, BLAYN)

Center. Shoots left. 6', 172 lbs. Born, Ottawa, ON, February 21, 1995.
(Pittsburgh's 5th pick, 179th overall, in 2013 NHL Draft).

			Regular Season					Playoffs				
Season	Club	League	GP	G	A	Pts	PIM	GP	G	A	Pts	PIM
2009-10	U.C. Cyclones	Minor-ON	28	16	23	39	14	12	6	11	17	8
2010-11	U.C. Cyclones MM	Minor-ON	30	18	30	48	12	....	....	....	....	....
	U.C. Cyclones Mid.	Minor-ON	6	2	1	3	2	....	....	....	....	....
	Kemptville 73's	ON-Jr.A	9	1	1	2	2	....	....	....	....	....
2011-12	Kemptville 73's	ON-Jr.A	42	12	27	39	20	....	....	....	....	....
2012-13	Kemptville 73's	ON-Jr.A	24	7	16	23	8	....	....	....	....	....
	Smiths Falls Bears	ON-Jr.A	27	5	24	29	16	5	0	1	1	0
2013-14	U. of Maine	H-East	32	8	8	16	4	....	....	....	....	....
2014-15	U. of Maine	H-East	39	12	15	27	6	....	....	....	....	....
2015-16	U. of Maine	H-East	38	8	16	24	8	....	....	....	....	....
2016-17	U. of Maine	H-East	36	18	23	41	22	....	....	....	....	....

BYSTROM, Ludwig (B'YEW-struhm, LOOD-wihg) **DAL**

Defense. Shoots left. 6'1", 175 lbs. Born, Ornskoldsvik, Sweden, July 20, 1994.
(Dallas' 2nd pick, 43rd overall, in 2012 NHL Draft).

			Regular Season					Playoffs				
Season	Club	League	GP	G	A	Pts	PIM	GP	G	A	Pts	PIM
2009-10	MODO U18	Swe-U18	24	4	0	4	10	5	0	1	1	0
2010-11	MODO U18	Swe-U18	9	1	5	6	10	3	0	0	0	10
	MODO Jr.	Swe-Jr.	37	1	10	11	28	6	1	2	3	6
	MODO	Sweden	1	0	0	0	0	....	....	....	....	....
2011-12	MODO U18	Swe-U18	1	1	0	1	2	1	0	0	0	10
	MODO Jr.	Swe-Jr.	34	7	22	29	101	8	1	3	4	4
	MODO	Sweden	20	0	1	1	8	1	0	0	0	0
2012-13	MODO	Sweden	30	3	3	6	2	....	....	....	....	....
	Orebro HK	Sweden-2	9	0	0	0	2	....	....	....	....	....
	MODO Jr.	Swe-Jr.	8	1	2	3	4	7	1	5	6	4
2013-14	Farjestad	Sweden	51	3	8	11	24	10	0	0	0	2
2014-15	Texas Stars	AHL	12	0	3	3	4	....	....	....	....	....
	Farjestad Jr.	Swe-Jr.	1	0	0	0	0	....	....	....	....	....
	Timra IK	Sweden-2	5	0	1	1	6	....	....	....	....	....
	Farjestad	Sweden	38	1	4	5	18	3	0	0	0	4
2015-16	Texas Stars	AHL	65	2	14	16	20	4	0	0	0	0
2016-17	Texas Stars	AHL	55	2	14	16	20	....	....	....	....	....

CAAMANO, Nicholas (ka-MAN-oh, nih-KOH-luhs) **DAL**

Right wing. Shoots left. 6'1", 185 lbs. Born, Hamilton, ON, September 7, 1998.
(Dallas' 5th pick, 146th overall, in 2016 NHL Draft).

			Regular Season					Playoffs				
Season	Club	League	GP	G	A	Pts	PIM	GP	G	A	Pts	PIM
2013-14	Ham. Bulldogs MM	Minor-ON	40	22	22	44	54	10	6	7	13	6
	Ancaster	ON-Jr.B	3	1	4	5	0	....	....	....	....	....
2014-15	Plymouth Whalers	OHL	64	3	6	9	29	....	....	....	....	....
2015-16	Flint Firebirds	OHL	64	20	17	37	40	....	....	....	....	....
2016-17	Flint Firebirds	OHL	67	35	29	64	63	5	0	3	3	8
	Texas Stars	AHL	6	0	3	3	2	....	....	....	....	....

CAIRNS, Matthew (KAIRNZ, MA-thew) **EDM**

Defense. Shoots left. 6'2", 200 lbs. Born, Mississauga, ON, April 27, 1998.
(Edmonton's 4th pick, 84th overall, in 2016 NHL Draft).

			Regular Season					Playoffs				
Season	Club	League	GP	G	A	Pts	PIM	GP	G	A	Pts	PIM
2013-14	Toronto Marlboros	GTHL	33	8	9	17	32	16	5	4	9	26
	Toronto Marlboros	Other	....	....	....	....	....	7	1	4	5	4
2014-15	Toronto Patriots	ON-Jr.A	53	1	9	10	54	22	1	3	4	18
2015-16	Georgetown	ON-Jr.A	46	9	24	33	42	22	3	16	19	30
2016-17	Fargo Force	USHL	17	0	4	4	12	....	....	....	....	....
	Powell River Kings	BCHL	18	2	14	16	26	11	0	2	2	10

• Signed Letter of Intent to attend **Cornell University** (ECAC) in fall of 2017.

CALNAN, Chris (KAL-nan, KRIHS) **CHI**

Right wing. Shoots right. 6'2", 203 lbs. Born, Boston, MA, May 5, 1994.
(Chicago's 3rd pick, 79th overall, in 2012 NHL Draft).

			Regular Season					Playoffs				
Season	Club	League	GP	G	A	Pts	PIM	GP	G	A	Pts	PIM
2010-11	Neponset Valley	Minor-MA	11	7	11	18	28	....	....	....	....	....
	Nobles	High-MA	27	14	11	25	8	....	....	....	....	....
2011-12	Cape Cod Whalers	Minor-MA	32	21	28	49	....	....	....	....	....	....
	Nobles	High-MA	27	28	27	55	13	....	....	....	....	....
2012-13	South Shore Kings	EJHL	31	27	22	49	35	2	2	0	2	2
2013-14	Boston College	H-East	37	4	9	13	23	....	....	....	....	....
2014-15	Boston College	H-East	37	11	5	16	8	....	....	....	....	....
2015-16	Boston College	H-East	29	3	8	11	16	....	....	....	....	....
2016-17	Boston College	H-East	39	6	10	16	45	....	....	....	....	....

CAMARA, Anthony (kuh-MAR-uh, an-THUH-nee)

Left wing. Shoots left. 6', 192 lbs. Born, Toronto, ON, September 4, 1993.
(Boston's 3rd pick, 81st overall, in 2011 NHL Draft).

			Regular Season					Playoffs				
Season	Club	League	GP	G	A	Pts	PIM	GP	G	A	Pts	PIM
2008-09	Miss. Senators	GTHL	50	31	25	56	94	....	....	....	....	....
2009-10	Saginaw Spirit	OHL	65	6	6	12	96	6	1	1	2	5
2010-11	Saginaw Spirit	OHL	64	8	9	17	132	12	0	1	1	25
2011-12	Saginaw Spirit	OHL	35	7	12	19	76	....	....	....	....	....
	Barrie Colts	OHL	31	9	5	14	59	13	2	3	5	22
2012-13	Barrie Colts	OHL	50	36	24	60	91	16	9	7	16	*42
2013-14	Providence Bruins	AHL	58	9	13	22	50	....	....	....	....	....
2014-15	Providence Bruins	AHL	59	3	5	8	32	....	....	....	....	....
2015-16	Providence Bruins	AHL	33	0	5	5	54	....	....	....	....	....
	Charlotte	AHL	15	3	5	8	17	....	....	....	....	....
2016-17	Kalamazoo Wings	ECHL	25	9	8	17	50	....	....	....	....	....
	St. John's IceCaps	AHL	23	3	5	8	8	3	0	0	0	4

Traded to **Carolina** by **Boston** with Boston's 3rd round pick (Jack LaFontaine) in 2016 NHL Draft and Boston's 5th round pick (later traded to Vegas – Vegas selected Jack Dugan) in 2017 NHL Draft for John-Michael Liles, February 29, 2016.

CAMERANESI, Tony (kam-uhr-ihn-EHS-ee, TOH-nee) **TOR**

Center. Shoots right. 5'9", 162 lbs. Born, Maple Grove, MN, August 12, 1993.
(Toronto's 5th pick, 130th overall, in 2011 NHL Draft).

			Regular Season					Playoffs				
Season	Club	League	GP	G	A	Pts	PIM	GP	G	A	Pts	PIM
2009-10	Wayzata	High-MN	25	16	29	45	6	2	2	1	3	0
2010-11	Team Northwest	UMHSEL	21	16	17	33	18	3	2	4	6	2
	Wayzata	High-MN	25	15	39	54	26	3	2	7	9	4
2011-12	Waterloo	USHL	55	18	24	42	47	10	1	5	6	4
2012-13	U. Minn-Duluth	WCHA	38	14	20	34	28	....	....	....	....	....
2013-14	U. Minn-Duluth	NCHC	36	7	14	21	19	....	....	....	....	....
2014-15	U. Minn-Duluth	NCHC	40	9	21	30	16	....	....	....	....	....
2015-16	U. Minn-Duluth	NCHC	38	11	28	39	14	....	....	....	....	....
	Toronto Marlies	AHL	6	2	0	2	0	....	....	....	....	....
2016-17	Toronto Marlies	AHL	31	4	3	7	8	1	0	0	0	0
	Orlando	ECHL	43	15	13	28	18	....	....	....	....	....

WCHA All-Rookie Team (2013)

CAMPBELL, Colin (KAM-buhl, KAWL-lihn)

Right wing. Shoots right. 6'1", 207 lbs. Born, Pickering, ON, April 17, 1991.

			Regular Season					Playoffs				
Season	Club	League	GP	G	A	Pts	PIM	GP	G	A	Pts	PIM
2006-07	Tor. Red Wings	GTHL	42	9	12	21	38	....	....	....	....	....
2007-08	Tor. Red Wings	GTHL	30	10	15	25	10	....	....	....	....	....
	Pickering Panthers	ON-Jr.A	1	0	0	0	2	....	....	....	....	....
2008-09	Vaughan Vipers	ON-Jr.A	47	24	42	66	39	9	7	2	9	0
2009-10	Vaughan Vipers	ON-Jr.A	46	32	44	76	55	5	3	2	5	6
2010-11	Lake Superior	CCHA	37	4	3	7	12	....	....	....	....	....
2011-12	Lake Superior	CCHA	37	9	16	25	22	....	....	....	....	....
2012-13	Lake Superior	CCHA	9	0	3	3	4	....	....	....	....	....
2013-14	Lake Superior	WCHA	36	14	15	29	26	....	....	....	....	....
	Grand Rapids	AHL	13	1	0	1	5	3	0	0	0	2
2014-15	Grand Rapids	AHL	44	2	3	5	29	7	0	1	1	2
2015-16	Grand Rapids	AHL	70	10	8	18	58	9	1	1	2	7
2016-17	Grand Rapids	AHL	57	9	11	20	35	17	0	4	4	15

Signed as a free agent by **Detroit**, March 17, 2014.

CAMPBELL, Evan (KAM-buhl, EH-vuhn) **EDM**

Left wing. Shoots left. 6'1", 205 lbs. Born, Port Coquitlam, BC, March 1, 1993.
(Edmonton's 8th pick, 128th overall, in 2013 NHL Draft).

			Regular Season					Playoffs				
Season	Club	League	GP	G	A	Pts	PIM	GP	G	A	Pts	PIM
2009-10	Van. NE Chiefs	BCMML	39	14	14	28	64	4	1	1	2	2
2010-11	Kerry Park	VIJHL	41	14	22	36	28	5	2	1	3	4
	Cowichan Valley	BCHL	1	0	0	0	0	....	....	....	....	....
2011-12	Coquitlam Express	BCHL	17	1	1	2	17	....	....	....	....	....
	Langley Rivermen	BCHL	31	11	8	19	18	....	....	....	....	....
2012-13	Langley Rivermen	BCHL	51	20	46	66	46	4	2	0	2	6
2013-14	U. Mass Lowell	H-East	33	9	2	11	18	....	....	....	....	....
2014-15	U. Mass Lowell	H-East	34	12	15	27	29	....	....	....	....	....
2015-16	U. Mass Lowell	H-East	28	5	7	12	16	....	....	....	....	....
2016-17	U. Mass Lowell	H-East	33	1	4	5	43	....	....	....	....	....
	Bakersfield	AHL	1	0	0	0	0	....	....	....	....	....

CAMPOLI, Nick (kam-POH-lee, NIHK) **VGK**

Center. Shoots left. 5'11", 187 lbs. Born, Toronto, ON, February 16, 1999.
(Las Vegas' 10th pick, 158th overall, in 2017 NHL Draft).

			Regular Season					Playoffs				
Season	Club	League	GP	G	A	Pts	PIM	GP	G	A	Pts	PIM
2014-15	Tor. Jr. Can. MM	GTHL	28	15	14	29	0	....	....	....	....	....
2015-16	North York	ON-Jr.A	37	12	22	34	8	10	3	5	8	6
2016-17	North York	ON-Jr.A	20	9	23	32	18	5	2	2	4	12

• Signed Letter of Intent to attend **Clarkson University** (ECAC) in fall of 2017.

CANDELLA, Cole (kan-DEH-luh, KOHL) **VAN**

Defense. Shoots left. 6'1", 189 lbs. Born, Mississauga, ON, February 13, 1998.
(Vancouver's 3rd pick, 140th overall, in 2016 NHL Draft).

			Regular Season					Playoffs				
Season	Club	League	GP	G	A	Pts	PIM	GP	G	A	Pts	PIM
2013-14	Vaughan M.M.	GTHL	33	6	14	20	10	10	1	3	4	12
	Vaughan M.M.	Other	22	5	26	31	....	5	0	3	3	2
	Vaughan Midget	GTHL	2	0	0	0	0	4	0	1	1	2
	Milton Icehawks	ON-Jr.A	3	0	0	0	0	1	0	0	0	0
2014-15	Belleville Bulls	OHL	60	0	6	6	12	1	0	0	0	0
2015-16	Hamilton Bulldogs	OHL	37	4	16	20	12	....	....	....	....	....
2016-17	Hamilton Bulldogs	OHL	65	3	17	20	32	7	0	0	0	2

CAPOBIANCO, Kyle (ka-poh-bee-AHN-koh, KIGH-uhl) **ARI**

Defense. Shoots left. 6'2", 194 lbs. Born, Mississauga, ON, August 13, 1997.
(Arizona's 4th pick, 63rd overall, in 2015 NHL Draft).

			Regular Season					Playoffs				
Season	Club	League	GP	G	A	Pts	PIM	GP	G	A	Pts	PIM
2012-13	Oak. Rangers MM	Minor-ON	40	7	24	31	38	....	....	....	....	....
	Oakville Rangers	Other	31	7	18	25	36	....	....	....	....	....
	Oakville Blades	ON-Jr.A	3	0	1	1	12	....	....	....	....	....
2013-14	Sudbury Wolves	OHL	53	0	11	11	18	5	0	0	0	0
2014-15	Sudbury Wolves	OHL	68	10	30	40	54	....	....	....	....	....
2015-16	Sudbury Wolves	OHL	68	7	36	43	58	....	....	....	....	....
2016-17	Sudbury Wolves	OHL	65	10	37	47	66	6	0	3	3	10
	Tucson	AHL	4	0	0	0	0	....	....	....	....	....

CARCONE, Michael (kahr-KOH-nay, MIGH-kuhl) **VAN**

Left wing. Shoots left. 5'10", 170 lbs. Born, Ajax, ON, May 19, 1996.

			Regular Season					Playoffs				
Season	Club	League	GP	G	A	Pts	PIM	GP	G	A	Pts	PIM
2013-14	Stouffville Spirit	ON-Jr.A	49	12	25	37	44	....	....	....	....	....
2014-15	Drummondville	QMJHL	50	12	29	41	32	3	0	0	0	12
2015-16	Drummondville	QMJHL	66	47	42	89	80	....	....	....	....	....
2016-17	Utica Comets	AHL	61	5	13	18	31	....	....	....	....	....

Signed as a free agent by **Vancouver**, July 15, 2016.

CAREY, Greg (KAIR-ee, GREHG) **PHI**

Left wing. Shoots left. 6', 195 lbs. Born, Hamilton, ON, April 5, 1990.

			Regular Season					Playoffs				
Season	Club	League	GP	G	A	Pts	PIM	GP	G	A	Pts	PIM
2005-06	Ham. Bulldogs	Minor-ON	58	66	35	101	14	....	....	....	....	....
2006-07	Glanbrook	ON-Jr.C	35	17	16	33	24	6	0	1	1	4
2007-08	Burlington	ON-Jr.A	46	10	12	22	16	3	0	0	0	0
2008-09	Burlington	ON-Jr.A	45	31	34	65	24	8	5	5	10	22
2009-10	Burlington	ON-Jr.A	48	*72	42	114	46	10	7	4	11	13
2010-11	St. Lawrence	ECAC	40	23	17	40	24	....	....	....	....	....
2011-12	St. Lawrence	ECAC	36	15	22	37	22	....	....	....	....	....
2012-13	St. Lawrence	ECAC	38	*28	23	*51	38	....	....	....	....	....
2013-14	St. Lawrence	ECAC	38	18	*39	*57	39	....	....	....	....	....
	Portland Pirates	AHL	13	1	1	2	4	....	....	....	....	....
2014-15	Portland Pirates	AHL	29	2	4	6	18	....	....	....	....	....
	Gwinnett	ECHL	30	15	12	27	6	....	....	....	....	....
2015-16	Springfield Falcons	AHL	64	26	17	43	20	....	....	....	....	....
2016-17	Lehigh Valley	AHL	74	28	23	51	17	5	2	1	3	4

ECAC All-Rookie Team (2011) • ECAC First All-Star Team (2013, 2014) • NCAA East Second All-American Team (2013) • NCAA East First All-American Team (2014)

Signed as a free agent by **Phoenix**, March 20, 2014. Signed as a free agent by **Philadelphia**, July 1, 2016.

CARLSSON, Lucas (KAHRL-suhn, LOO-kuhs) **CHI**

Defense. Shoots left. 6', 187 lbs. Born, Gavle, Sweden, July 5, 1997.
(Chicago's 5th pick, 110th overall, in 2016 NHL Draft).

			Regular Season					Playoffs				
Season	Club	League	GP	G	A	Pts	PIM	GP	G	A	Pts	PIM
2012-13	Brynas U18	Swe-U18	34	4	13	17	50	3	0	0	0	0
2013-14	Brynas U18	Swe-U18	34	14	18	32	96	5	0	5	5	2
	Brynas IF Gavle Jr.	Swe-Jr.	5	1	1	2	10	....	....	....	....	....
2014-15	Brynas U18	Swe-U18	9	8	6	14	33	4	4	2	6	2
	Brynas IF Gavle Jr.	Swe-Jr.	42	6	12	18	60	2	0	1	1	4
	Brynas IF Gavle	Sweden	16	0	1	1	2	1	0	0	0	0
2015-16	Brynas IF Gavle Jr.	Swe-Jr.	15	1	10	11	53	1	0	0	0	25
	Brynas IF Gavle	Sweden	35	4	5	9	8	3	0	2	2	0
2016-17	Brynas IF Gavle	Sweden	41	3	8	11	16	20	0	4	4	4

CARROLL, Austin (KAIR-uhl, AW-stuhn) **CGY**

Right wing. Shoots right. 6'3", 212 lbs. Born, Calgary, AB, March 26, 1994.
(Calgary's 6th pick, 184th overall, in 2014 NHL Draft).

			Regular Season					Playoffs				
Season	Club	League	GP	G	A	Pts	PIM	GP	G	A	Pts	PIM
2009-10	P.F. Chang's U16	T1EHL	12	3	0	3	30	....	....	....	....	....
2010-11	Coquitlam Express	BCHL	42	6	5	11	28	4	0	0	0	4
2011-12	Victoria Royals	WHL	62	8	12	20	80	4	2	0	2	6
2012-13	Victoria Royals	WHL	67	15	27	42	152	4	1	1	2	2
2013-14	Victoria Royals	WHL	70	34	23	57	114	9	5	3	8	16
2014-15	Victoria Royals	WHL	69	38	39	77	124	10	1	8	9	8
2015-16	Stockton Heat	AHL	53	6	7	13	74	....	....	....	....	....
2016-17	Stockton Heat	AHL	46	7	8	15	40	5	1	0	1	2

CARROLL, Noah (KAIR-uhl, NOH-uh) **CAR**

Defense. Shoots left. 6'1", 188 lbs. Born, Strathroy, ON, December 2, 1997.
(Carolina's 9th pick, 164th overall, in 2016 NHL Draft).

			Regular Season					Playoffs				
Season	Club	League	GP	G	A	Pts	PIM	GP	G	A	Pts	PIM
2012-13	Elgin-Mid. Chiefs	Minor-ON	28	4	11	15	16	11	1	6	7	10
2013-14	Guelph Hurricanes	ON-Jr.B	13	0	2	2	24	3	0	0	0	2
2014-15	Guelph Storm	OHL	62	2	14	16	46	8	0	0	0	2
2015-16	Guelph Storm	OHL	67	3	11	14	46	....	....	....	....	....
2016-17	Guelph Storm	OHL	32	2	11	13	31	....	....	....	....	....
	Sault Ste. Marie	OHL	30	3	9	12	12	11	0	2	2	16

• Missed majority of 2013-14 with an undisclosed injury.

CASSELS, Cole (KA-suhlz, KOHL) **VAN**

Center. Shoots right. 6', 178 lbs. Born, Columbus, OH, May 4, 1995.
(Vancouver's 3rd pick, 85th overall, in 2013 NHL Draft).

			Regular Season					Playoffs				
Season	Club	League	GP	G	A	Pts	PIM	GP	G	A	Pts	PIM
2009-10	Cleveland Barons	T1EHL	31	6	22	28	46	....	....	....	....	....
2010-11	Ohio Blue Jackets	T1EHL	37	11	23	34	61	....	....	....	....	....
	Ohio Blue Jackets	Minor-OH	11	11	21	32	....	....	....	....	....	....
2011-12	Oshawa Generals	OHL	64	3	8	11	31	6	1	0	1	6
2012-13	Oshawa Generals	OHL	64	15	28	43	61	9	1	0	1	14
2013-14	Oshawa Generals	OHL	61	24	49	73	90	12	6	11	17	16
2014-15	Oshawa Generals	OHL	54	30	51	81	100	21	10	21	31	14
2015-16	Utica Comets	AHL	67	2	5	7	24	4	1	0	1	0
2016-17	Utica Comets	AHL	66	6	5	11	33	....	....	....	....	....

CASTO, Chris (KAS-toh, KRIHS) **VGK**

Defense. Shoots right. 6'1", 200 lbs. Born, St. Paul, MN, December 27, 1991.

			Regular Season					Playoffs				
Season	Club	League	GP	G	A	Pts	PIM	GP	G	A	Pts	PIM
2010-11	Lincoln Stars	USHL	58	6	19	25	40	2	0	0	0	0
2011-12	U. Minn-Duluth	WCHA	41	2	11	13	14	....	....	....	....	....
2012-13	U. Minn-Duluth	WCHA	36	3	6	9	16	....	....	....	....	....
	Providence Bruins	AHL	4	0	0	0	0	12	0	2	2	13
2013-14	Providence Bruins	AHL	52	3	8	11	23	12	0	2	2	13
	South Carolina	ECHL	1	0	0	0	0	....	....	....	....	....
2014-15	Providence Bruins	AHL	62	1	11	12	35	5	0	0	0	2
2015-16	Providence Bruins	AHL	68	7	16	23	47	3	0	1	1	5
2016-17	Providence Bruins	AHL	59	1	11	12	40	16	1	4	5	16

Signed as a free agent by **Boston**, March 26, 2013. Signed as a free agent by **Vegas**, July 1, 2017.

CATES, Noah (KAYTS, NOH-uh) **PHI**

Left wing. Shoots left. 6'1", 165 lbs. Born, Stillwater, MN, May 2, 1999.
(Philadelphia's 7th pick, 137th overall, in 2017 NHL Draft).

			Regular Season					Playoffs				
Season	Club	League	GP	G	A	Pts	PIM	GP	G	A	Pts	PIM
2014-15	Team Southwest	UMHSEL	5	0	1	1	0	....	....	....	....	....
	Stillwater Ponies	High-MN	25	13	17	30	10	3	0	0	0	0
2015-16	Team Northeast	UMHSEL	20	3	12	15	6	3	0	4	4	0
	Stillwater Ponies	High-MN	25	20	34	54	6	6	5	5	10	2
	Omaha Lancers	USHL	2	1	0	1	2	....	....	....	....	....
2016-17	Team Northeast	UMHSEL	21	9	15	24	10	3	1	1	2	4
	Stillwater Ponies	High-MN	25	20	45	65	10	3	3	2	5	2
	Omaha Lancers	USHL	11	2	5	7	6	....	....	....	....	....

• Signed Letter of Intent to attend **University of Minnesota-Duluth** (NCHC) in fall of 2018.

CAVE, Colby (KOHL-bee, KAYV) **BOS**

Center. Shoots left. 6'1", 200 lbs. Born, Battleford, SK, December 26, 1994.

			Regular Season					Playoffs				
Season	Club	League	GP	G	A	Pts	PIM	GP	G	A	Pts	PIM
2009-10	Battlefords Stars	SMHL	42	15	21	36	40	....	....	....	....	....
2010-11	Battlefords Stars	SMHL	44	14	22	36	28	....	....	....	....	....
	Battlefords	SJHL	3	0	1	1	0	....	....	....	....	....
	Swift Current	WHL	1	0	0	0	0	....	....	....	....	....
2011-12	Swift Current	WHL	70	6	10	16	36	....	....	....	....	....
2012-13	Swift Current	WHL	72	21	20	41	39	5	2	2	4	8
2013-14	Swift Current	WHL	72	33	37	70	30	6	0	2	2	0
2014-15	Swift Current	WHL	72	35	40	75	52	4	2	0	2	2
	Providence Bruins	AHL	1	0	0	0	0	....	....	....	....	....
2015-16	Providence Bruins	AHL	75	13	16	29	27	3	2	1	3	5
2016-17	Providence Bruins	AHL	76	13	22	35	52	17	1	5	6	18

Signed as a free agent by **Boston**, April 7, 2015.

CECCONI, Joseph (seh-KOH-nee, JOH-sehf) **DAL**

Defense. Shoots right. 6'2", 210 lbs. Born, Youngstown, NY, May 23, 1997.
(Dallas' 4th pick, 133rd overall, in 2015 NHL Draft).

			Regular Season					Playoffs				
Season	Club	League	GP	G	A	Pts	PIM	GP	G	A	Pts	PIM
2012-13	Buf. Jr. Sabres U16	T1EHL	40	1	8	9	14	4	1	0	1	0
	Buf. Jr. Sabres U18	T1EHL	4	0	0	0	2	3	0	0	0	2
2013-14	Buf. Jr. Sabres U16	T1EHL	34	10	9	19	31	....	....	....	....	....
	Muskegon	USHL	28	2	4	6	8	....	....	....	....	....
2014-15	Muskegon	USHL	60	3	14	17	35	12	0	2	2	8
2015-16	U. of Michigan	Big Ten	38	0	7	7	16	....	....	....	....	....
2016-17	U. of Michigan	Big Ten	33	1	7	8	18	....	....	....	....	....

CEDERHOLM, Anton (SEH-duhr-holm, an-TAWN) **VAN**

Defense. Shoots left. 6'2", 204 lbs. Born, Helsingborg, Sweden, February 21, 1995.
(Vancouver's 5th pick, 145th overall, in 2013 NHL Draft).

			Regular Season					Playoffs				
Season	Club	League	GP	G	A	Pts	PIM	GP	G	A	Pts	PIM
2009-10	Jonstorps IF U18	Swe-U18	12	1	3	4	14	....	....	....	....	....
	Jonstorps IF Jr.	Swe-Jr.	3	0	0	0	4	....	....	....	....	....
2010-11	Rogle U18	Swe-U18	31	4	8	12	18	4	0	1	1	2
	Rogle Jr.	Swe-Jr.	2	0	0	0	0	....	....	....	....	....
2011-12	Rogle U18	Swe-U18	8	1	3	4	45	....	....	....	....	....
	Rogle Jr.	Swe-Jr.	41	3	5	8	71	....	....	....	....	....
2012-13	Rogle U18	Swe-U18	8	0	1	1	10	3	0	1	1	6
	Rogle Jr.	Swe-Jr.	36	5	8	13	64	2	0	0	0	0
	Rogle	Sweden	12	0	0	0	6	....	....	....	....	....
2013-14	Portland	WHL	71	4	12	16	95	21	2	3	5	16
2014-15	Portland	WHL	68	9	10	19	84	17	1	1	2	6
2015-16	Kalamazoo Wings	ECHL	69	3	14	17	65	4	0	0	0	0
2016-17	Rogle	Sweden	8	0	0	0	4	....	....	....	....	....
	AIK Solna	Sweden-2	38	2	8	10	53	3	0	0	0	6

CEDERHOLM, Jacob (seh-DUUR-hohlm, YAY-kuhb) **WPG**

Defense. Shoots right. 6'4", 204 lbs. Born, Helsingborg, Sweden, January 30, 1998.
(Winnipeg's 4th pick, 97th overall, in 2016 NHL Draft).

			Regular Season					Playoffs				
Season	Club	League	GP	G	A	Pts	PIM	GP	G	A	Pts	PIM
2011-12	Jonstorps IF U18	Swe-U18	16	0	0	0	6	....	....	....	....	....
2012-13	Jonstorps IF U18	Swe-U18	15	1	3	4	4	....	....	....	....	....
	Jonstorps IF Jr.	Swe-Jr.	9	0	5	5	4	4	0	1	1	0
2013-14	Jonstorps IF U18	Swe-U18	17	6	7	13	29	....	....	....	....	....
	Jonstorps IF Jr.	Swe-Jr.	12	3	3	6	4	....	....	....	....	....
2014-15	HV 71 U18	Swe-U18	25	2	8	10	22	6	0	1	1	4
	HV 71 Jr.	Swe-Jr.	16	1	0	1	8	3	0	0	0	0
	HV 71 Jonkoping	Sweden	3	0	0	0	0	....	....	....	....	....
2015-16	HV 71 U18	Swe-U18	7	1	6	7	6	....	....	....	....	....
	HV 71 Jr.	Swe-Jr.	35	1	4	5	28	3	2	0	2	2
	HV 71 Jonkoping	Sweden	9	0	0	0	0	....	....	....	....	....
2016-17	HV 71 Jr.	Swe-Jr.	8	0	2	2	12	6	0	2	2	2
	HV 71 Jonkoping	Sweden	5	0	0	0	0	....	....	....	....	....
	IK Pantern Malmo	Sweden-2	38	1	6	7	20	....	....	....	....	....

CERNAK, Erik (CHAIR-nak, AIR-ihk) **T.B.**

Defense. Shoots right. 6'3", 203 lbs. Born, Kosice, Slovakia, May 28, 1997.
(Los Angeles' 1st pick, 43rd overall, in 2015 NHL Draft).

			Regular Season					Playoffs				
Season	Club	League	GP	G	A	Pts	PIM	GP	G	A	Pts	PIM
2011-12	HC Kosice U18	Svk-U18	37	5	4	9	61	....	....	....	....	....
2012-13	Slovakia U20 B	Slovak-2	8	2	0	2	18	....	....	....	....	....
	Bratislava U18	Svk-U18	....	....	....	....	....	1	0	2	2	0
	Bratislava Jr.	Slovak-Jr.	30	4	6	10	18	12	0	1	1	8
2013-14	Slovakia U20	Slovakia	20	2	1	3	2	....	....	....	....	....
	HC Kosice Jr.	Slovak-Jr.	8	1	3	4	16	....	....	....	....	....
	HC Kosice	Slovakia	13	0	0	0	0	7	0	0	0	2
2014-15	HC Kosice	Slovakia	43	5	8	13	16	7	0	1	1	6
2015-16	Erie Otters	OHL	41	4	11	15	35	13	0	6	6	10
2016-17	Erie Otters	OHL	50	3	18	21	53	22	1	8	9	10

Traded to **Tampa Bay** by **Los Angeles** with Peter Budaj and Los Angeles' 7th round pick (later traded to Philadelphia – Philadelphia selected Wyatt Kalynuk) in 2017 NHL Draft for Ben Bishop and Tampa Bay's 5th round pick (Drake Rymsha) in 2017 NHL Draft, February 26, 2017.

CHAINEY, Jocktan (CHAY-nee, JAWK-tuhn) N.J.

Defense. Shoots left. 6', 200 lbs. Born, Asbestos, QC, September 8, 1999.
(New Jersey's 9th pick, 191st overall, in 2017 NHL Draft).

			Regular Season					Playoffs				
Season	Club	League	GP	G	A	Pts	PIM	GP	G	A	Pts	PIM
2014-15	Trois-Rivieres	QAAA	36	3	10	13	36	6	2	3	5	4
2015-16	Shawinigan	QMJHL	14	1	6	7	6	....	....	....	....	....
	Halifax	QMJHL	32	4	7	11	8	....	....	....	....	....
2016-17	Halifax	QMJHL	55	4	20	24	44	6	0	3	3	0

CHAPIE, Adam (CHA-pee, A-duhm) NYR

Right wing. Shoots right. 6'1", 186 lbs. Born, Oxford, MI, July 6, 1991.

			Regular Season					Playoffs				
Season	Club	League	GP	G	A	Pts	PIM	GP	G	A	Pts	PIM
2009-10	Cle. L'jacks	CSHL	48	30	39	69	38	6	0	5	5	2
2010-11	New Mexico	NAHL	58	15	19	34	56	....	....	....	....	....
2011-12	New Mexico	NAHL	60	31	26	57	63	....	....	....	....	....
2012-13	U. Mass Lowell	H-East	35	6	0	6	12	....	....	....	....	....
2013-14	U. Mass Lowell	H-East	38	12	11	23	14	....	....	....	....	....
2014-15	U. Mass Lowell	H-East	36	12	19	31	22	....	....	....	....	....
2015-16	U. Mass Lowell	H-East	39	16	19	35	57	....	....	....	....	....
2016-17	Hartford Wolf Pack	AHL	24	0	4	4	6	....	....	....	....	....
	Greenville	ECHL	24	4	8	12	16	3	0	2	2	4

Signed as a free agent by **NY Rangers**, April 1, 2016.

CHARTIER, Rourke (SHAHR-t'yay, ROHRK) S.J.

Center. Shoots left. 5'11", 190 lbs. Born, Saskatoon, SK, April 3, 1996.
(San Jose's 7th pick, 149th overall, in 2014 NHL Draft).

			Regular Season					Playoffs				
Season	Club	League	GP	G	A	Pts	PIM	GP	G	A	Pts	PIM
2009-10	Sask. Outlaws	Minor-SK	51	86	45	131	....	....	....	....	....	....
2010-11	Sask. Stallions	Minor-SK	STATISTICS NOT AVAILABLE									
	Sask. Contacts	SMHL	7	2	0	2	4	1	1	1	2	0
2011-12	Sask. Contacts	SMHL	42	23	34	57	14	13	*8	5	13	2
2012-13	Kelowna Rockets	WHL	58	13	17	30	16	3	0	0	0	0
2013-14	Kelowna Rockets	WHL	72	24	34	58	8	14	6	6	12	2
2014-15	Kelowna Rockets	WHL	58	48	34	82	18	16	13	7	20	2
2015-16	Kelowna Rockets	WHL	42	25	21	46	16	18	7	6	13	7
	San Jose Barracuda	AHL	....	....	....	....	....	1	0	0	0	0
2016-17	San Jose Barracuda	AHL	67	17	18	35	10	7	0	6	6	4

WHL West First All-Star Team (2015)

CHASE, Gregory (CHAYS, GREH-goh-ree) EDM

Center/Right wing. Shoots right. 6', 190 lbs. Born, Sherwood Park, AB, January 1, 1995.
(Edmonton's 10th pick, 188th overall, in 2013 NHL Draft).

			Regular Season					Playoffs				
Season	Club	League	GP	G	A	Pts	PIM	GP	G	A	Pts	PIM
2010-11	Sherwood Park	AMHL	30	24	15	39	64	12	7	3	10	36
	Calgary Hitmen	WHL	5	0	0	0	6	....	....	....	....	....
2011-12	Calgary Hitmen	WHL	60	6	22	28	41	5	1	1	2	11
2012-13	Calgary Hitmen	WHL	69	17	32	49	58	17	3	7	10	24
2013-14	Calgary Hitmen	WHL	70	35	50	85	83	6	4	5	9	2
	Oklahoma City	AHL	5	1	0	1	4	....	....	....	....	....
2014-15	Calgary Hitmen	WHL	15	2	13	15	20	....	....	....	....	....
	Victoria Royals	WHL	46	18	26	44	39	10	7	4	11	6
	Oklahoma City	AHL	....	....	....	....	....	4	0	1	1	2
2015-16	Bakersfield	AHL	19	1	6	7	25	....	....	....	....	....
	Norfolk Admirals	ECHL	43	18	19	37	46	....	....	....	....	....
2016-17	Bakersfield	AHL	48	3	11	14	12	....	....	....	....	....

CHATFIELD, Jalen (CHAT-feeld, JAY-lehn) VAN

Defense. Shoots right. 6'1", 188 lbs. Born, Ypsilanti, MI, May 15, 1996.

			Regular Season					Playoffs				
Season	Club	League	GP	G	A	Pts	PIM	GP	G	A	Pts	PIM
2011-12	Oak. Grizzlies U16	T1EHL	39	1	8	9	41	3	1	1	2	4
2012-13	Det. B. Tire U18	T1EHL	40	3	18	21	18	3	0	1	1	4
2013-14	Det. B. Tire U18	T1EHL	37	11	15	26	40	5	0	3	3	2
2014-15	Windsor Spitfires	OHL	60	1	20	21	35	....	....	....	....	....
2015-16	Windsor Spitfires	OHL	68	10	27	37	45	5	2	0	2	0
2016-17	Windsor Spitfires	OHL	61	8	20	28	56	7	0	2	2	4

Signed as a free agent by **Vancouver**, March 13, 2017.

CHEBYKIN, Nikolai (cheh-BEE-kihn, nih-KOH-ligh) TOR

Left wing. Shoots left. 6'3", 209 lbs. Born, Chita, Russia, August 1, 1997.
(Toronto's 11th pick, 182nd overall, in 2016 NHL Draft).

			Regular Season					Playoffs				
Season	Club	League	GP	G	A	Pts	PIM	GP	G	A	Pts	PIM
2014-15	Dyn'o Moscow Jr.	Russia-Jr.	32	2	4	6	55	6	0	0	0	2
2015-16	Dyn'o Moscow Jr.	Russia-Jr.	39	13	22	35	59	....	....	....	....	....
2016-17	Dynamo Moscow	KHL	8	1	0	1	0	1	0	0	0	0
	Dyn'o Balashikha	Russia-2	24	5	3	8	22	15	3	6	9	41
	Dyn'o Moscow Jr.	Russia-Jr.	17	17	10	27	42	....	....	....	....	....

CHEKHOVICH, Ivan (CHEH-koh-vihch, IGH-vuhn) S.J.

Center. Shoots left. 5'10", 180 lbs. Born, Yekaterinburg, Russia, April 1, 1999.
(San Jose's 6th pick, 212th overall, in 2017 NHL Draft).

			Regular Season					Playoffs				
Season	Club	League	GP	G	A	Pts	PIM	GP	G	A	Pts	PIM
2015-16	Dyn'o Moscow Jr.	Russia-Jr.	19	3	4	7	4	....	....	....	....	....
2016-17	Baie-Comeau	QMJHL	60	26	33	59	14	4	1	2	3	2

CHELIOS, Jake (CHEL-EE-ohs, JAYK)

Defense. Shoots left. 6'2", 185 lbs. Born, Bloomfield Hills, MI, March 8, 1991.

			Regular Season					Playoffs				
Season	Club	League	GP	G	A	Pts	PIM	GP	G	A	Pts	PIM
2007-08	Det. Caesars	MWEHL	28	7	18	25	16	....	....	....	....	....
2008-09	Det. Lit. Caesars	T1EHL	46	14	28	42	32	7	5	3	8	2
2009-10	Chicago Steel	USHL	52	12	22	34	45	....	....	....	....	....
2010-11	Michigan State	CCHA	37	8	6	14	34	....	....	....	....	....
2011-12	Michigan State	CCHA	39	2	7	9	44	....	....	....	....	....
2012-13	Michigan State	CCHA	42	5	5	10	79	....	....	....	....	....
2013-14	Michigan State	Big Ten	36	2	19	21	38	....	....	....	....	....
	Toledo Walleye	ECHL	7	1	1	2	2	....	....	....	....	....
	Chicago Wolves	AHL	4	0	1	1	4	....	....	....	....	....
2014-15	Chicago Wolves	AHL	41	1	14	15	32	....	....	....	....	....
	Kalamazoo Wings	ECHL	8	1	2	3	2	4	1	1	2	2
2015-16	Charlotte	AHL	73	7	24	31	44	....	....	....	....	....
2016-17	Charlotte	AHL	76	4	28	32	54	5	0	1	1	6

Signed as a free agent by **Carolina**, April 22, 2016.

CHIZEN, Braydyn (CHIH-ZIHN, BRAY-duhn) MIN

Defense. Shoots right. 6'9", 195 lbs. Born, St. Albert, AB, May 9, 1998.
(Minnesota's 4th pick, 204th overall, in 2016 NHL Draft).

			Regular Season					Playoffs				
Season	Club	League	GP	G	A	Pts	PIM	GP	G	A	Pts	PIM
2012-13	PAC Saints	AMBHL	33	0	11	11	18	....	....	....	....	....
2013-14	St. Albert Flyers	Minor-AB	36	1	5	6	42	....	....	....	....	....
2014-15	Leduc Oil Kings	AMHL	31	2	7	9	56	....	....	....	....	....
	Kelowna Rockets	WHL	2	0	0	0	0	....	....	....	....	....
2015-16	Kelowna Rockets	WHL	45	1	1	2	40	3	0	0	0	2
2016-17	Kelowna Rockets	WHL	65	3	7	10	82	9	0	0	0	2

CHLAPIK, Filip (KHLA-pihk, FIHL-ihp) OTT

Center. Shoots left. 6'2", 204 lbs. Born, Prague, Czech Rep., June 3, 1997.
(Ottawa's 4th pick, 48th overall, in 2015 NHL Draft).

			Regular Season					Playoffs				
Season	Club	League	GP	G	A	Pts	PIM	GP	G	A	Pts	PIM
2011-12	HC Liberec U18	CzR-U18	8	1	4	5	2	....	....	....	....	....
2012-13	HC Liberec U18	CzR-U18	43	19	31	50	12	5	3	1	4	2
2013-14	Sparta U18	CzR-U18	5	1	7	8	2	3	2	1	3	2
	Litomerice	CzRep-2	1	0	0	0	0	....	....	....	....	....
	Sparta Jr.	CzRep-Jr.	38	16	19	35	22	7	3	3	6	6
2014-15	Charlottetown	QMJHL	64	33	42	75	42	9	1	8	9	10
2015-16	Charlottetown	QMJHL	52	12	42	54	50	5	1	1	2	0
2016-17	Charlottetown	QMJHL	57	34	57	91	98	13	5	14	19	27

QMJHL Second All-Star Team (2017)

CHMELEVSKI, Sasha (ch'mehl-EV-skee, SA-shuh) S.J.

Center. Shoots right. 5'11", 179 lbs. Born, Newport Beach, CA, September 6, 1999.
(San Jose's 5th pick, 185th overall, in 2017 NHL Draft).

			Regular Season					Playoffs				
Season	Club	League	GP	G	A	Pts	PIM	GP	G	A	Pts	PIM
2014-15	Det. H-Baked U16	HPHL	25	10	14	24	4	....	....	....	....	....
	Det. H-Baked U18	HPHL	1	0	0	0	0	....	....	....	....	....
2015-16	Sarnia Sting	OHL	29	9	8	17	2	....	....	....	....	....
	Ottawa 67's	OHL	5	2	0	2	2	....	....	....	....	....
	USAHNTDP	U-17	6	2	3	5	0	....	....	....	....	....
2016-17	Ottawa 67's	OHL	58	21	22	43	20	6	2	2	4	2
	USAHNTDP	U-18	2	0	1	1	2	....	....	....	....	....

CHOLOWSKI, Dennis (chuh-LOW-skee, DEH-nihs) DET

Defense. Shoots left. 6'1", 195 lbs. Born, Langley, BC, February 15, 1998.
(Detroit's 1st pick, 20th overall, in 2016 NHL Draft).

			Regular Season					Playoffs				
Season	Club	League	GP	G	A	Pts	PIM	GP	G	A	Pts	PIM
2013-14	Yale Academy	CSSHL	17	1	15	16	8	2	0	5	5	0
	Yale Academy	Other	12	5	20	25	4	....	....	....	....	....
	Chilliwack Chiefs	BCHL	1	0	0	0	0	....	....	....	....	....
2014-15	Chilliwack Chiefs	BCHL	55	4	23	27	4	12	0	7	7	0
2015-16	Chilliwack Chiefs	BCHL	50	12	28	40	16	20	4	11	15	4
2016-17	St. Cloud State	NCHC	36	1	11	12	14	....	....	....	....	....
	Grand Rapids	AHL	1	0	0	0	0	....	....	....	....	....

CHRISTOFFER, Braden (KRIHS-toh-fuhr, BRAY-duhn) EDM

Left wing. Shoots left. 5'10", 190 lbs. Born, Sherwood Park, AB, August 2, 1994.

			Regular Season					Playoffs				
Season	Club	League	GP	G	A	Pts	PIM	GP	G	A	Pts	PIM
2011-12	Sherwood Park	AJHL	47	10	14	24	143	2	0	0	0	4
2012-13	Regina Pats	WHL	69	11	9	20	91	....	....	....	....	....
2013-14	Regina Pats	WHL	61	13	22	35	130	4	0	1	1	14
2014-15	Regina Pats	WHL	72	26	33	59	147	9	2	6	8	12
2015-16	Bakersfield	AHL	33	1	4	5	57	....	....	....	....	....
	Norfolk Admirals	ECHL	24	13	5	18	34	....	....	....	....	....
2016-17	Bakersfield	AHL	49	5	3	8	45	....	....	....	....	....

Signed as a free agent by **Edmonton**, October 6, 2015.

CHUDINOV, Maxim (choo-DEE-nawf, max-EEM) BOS

Defense. Shoots right. 5'11", 187 lbs. Born, Cherepovets, USSR, March 25, 1990.
(Boston's 7th pick, 195th overall, in 2010 NHL Draft).

			Regular Season					Playoffs				
Season	Club	League	GP	G	A	Pts	PIM	GP	G	A	Pts	PIM
2006-07	Cherepovets	Russia	2	0	0	0	0	3	0	0	0	2
2007-08	Cherepovets 2	Russia-3	STATISTICS NOT AVAILABLE									
	Cherepovets	Russia	18	0	0	0	10	1	0	0	0	0
2008-09	Cherepovets	KHL	26	0	0	0	14	....	....	....	....	....
2009-10	Cherepovets Jr.	Russia-Jr.	4	1	0	1	12	2	0	1	1	4
	Cherepovets	KHL	47	6	8	14	30	....	....	....	....	....
2010-11	Cherepovets	KHL	52	8	15	23	30	6	0	2	2	4
	Cherepovets Jr.	Russia-Jr.	....	....	....	....	....	5	2	2	4	8
2011-12	Cherepovets	KHL	52	9	26	35	62	6	0	2	2	10
	Cherepovets Jr.	Russia-Jr.	....	....	....	....	....	5	0	0	0	8
2012-13	SKA St. Petersburg	KHL	47	2	8	10	46	12	1	1	2	6
2013-14	SKA St. Petersburg	KHL	50	7	11	18	44	10	0	1	1	11
2014-15	SKA St. Petersburg	KHL	51	5	12	17	56	21	1	8	9	20
2015-16	SKA St. Petersburg	KHL	56	8	10	18	87	15	1	4	5	6
2016-17	SKA St. Petersburg	KHL	42	4	10	14	26	1	0	1	1	0

CHUKAROV, Ivan (choo-KAH-rawf, IGH-vuhn) BUF

Defense. Shoots left. 6'2", 203 lbs. Born, Des Plaines, IL, April 3, 1995.
(Buffalo's 6th pick, 182nd overall, in 2015 NHL Draft).

			Regular Season					Playoffs				
Season	Club	League	GP	G	A	Pts	PIM	GP	G	A	Pts	PIM
2011-12	Chi. Mission U18	HPHL	26	2	8	10	10	....	....	....	....	....
2012-13	Chi. Mission U18	HPHL	30	0	13	13	10	....	....	....	....	....
2013-14	Min. Wilderness	NAHL	44	4	8	12	28	5	1	2	3	0
2014-15	Min. Wilderness	NAHL	55	12	31	43	63	12	0	6	6	6
2015-16	Massachusetts	H-East	36	3	5	8	10	....	....	....	....	....
2016-17	Massachusetts	H-East	36	2	6	8	40	....	....	....	....	....

CHYTIL, Filip (CHEE-tuhl, FIHL-ihp) NYR

Center. Shoots left. 6'2", 192 lbs. Born, Kromeriz, Czech Rep., May 9, 1999.
(NY Rangers' 2nd pick, 21st overall, in 2017 NHL Draft).

			Regular Season					Playoffs				
Season	Club	League	GP	G	A	Pts	PIM	GP	G	A	Pts	PIM
2014-15	PSG Zlin U18	CzR-U18	19	6	3	9	10	....	....	....	....	....
2015-16	PSG Zlin U18	CzR-U18	30	28	22	50	8	....	....	....	....	....
2016-17	PSG Zlin Jr.	CzRep-Jr.	2	0	0	0	0	1	0	0	0	0
	PSG Zlin	CzRep	40	5	5	10	16	....	....	....	....	....

CIRELLI, Anthony (suh-REH-lee, AN-thuh-nee) T.B.

Center. Shoots left. 6', 171 lbs. Born, Etobicoke, ON, July 15, 1997.
(Tampa Bay's 4th pick, 72nd overall, in 2015 NHL Draft).

			Regular Season					Playoffs				
Season	Club	League	GP	G	A	Pts	PIM	GP	G	A	Pts	PIM
2012-13	Miss. Reps MM	GTHL	33	9	7	16	6	....	....	....	....	....
2013-14	Miss. Reps Midget	GTHL	31	10	18	28	6	....	....	....	....	....
	Mississauga	ON-Jr.A	1	0	0	0	0	1	0	0	0	0
2014-15	Oshawa Generals	OHL	68	13	23	36	22	21	2	8	10	4
2015-16	Oshawa Generals	OHL	62	21	38	59	27	5	2	3	5	0
	Syracuse Crunch	AHL	3	0	0	0	0	....	....	....	....	....
2016-17	Oshawa Generals	OHL	26	13	21	34	8	....	....	....	....	....
	Erie Otters	OHL	25	12	18	30	4	22	*15	16	31	4
	Syracuse Crunch	AHL	....	....	....	....	....	6	0	0	0	6

CLAGUE, Kale (KLAYG, KAYL) L.A.

Defense. Shoots left. 6', 184 lbs. Born, Regina, SK, June 5, 1998.
(Los Angeles' 1st pick, 51st overall, in 2016 NHL Draft).

			Regular Season					Playoffs				
Season	Club	League	GP	G	A	Pts	PIM	GP	G	A	Pts	PIM
2012-13	Lloydminster Heat	AMBHL	33	35	42	77	44	8	4	5	9	20
	Lloydminster	AMHL	1	0	1	1	0	1	0	0	0	0
2013-14	Lloydminster	AMHL	31	11	22	33	34	12	2	*11	13	2
	Brandon	WHL	2	0	0	0	0	3	0	0	0	2
2014-15	Brandon	WHL	20	4	9	13	6	12	1	2	3	4
2015-16	Brandon	WHL	71	6	37	43	54	21	6	8	14	8
2016-17	Brandon	WHL	48	5	35	40	41	4	1	3	4	6

WHL East First All-Star Team (2017)

CLARKE, Cameron (KLAHRK, KAM-ruhn) BOS

Defense. Shoots right. 6'1", 185 lbs. Born, Tecumseh, MI, May 15, 1996.
(Boston's 5th pick, 136th overall, in 2016 NHL Draft).

			Regular Season					Playoffs				
Season	Club	League	GP	G	A	Pts	PIM	GP	G	A	Pts	PIM
2013-14	West Mich. U18	NAPHL	24	7	15	22	10	4	0	0	0	0
2014-15	Sarnia	ON-Jr.B	49	10	25	35	26	12	2	3	5	18
2015-16	Lone Star Brahmas	NAHL	59	9	41	50	29	4	0	1	1	2
2016-17	Ferris State	WCHA	35	1	10	11	26	....	....	....	....	....

NAHL First All-Star Team (2016) • NAHL Defenseman of the Year (2016)

CLIFTON, Connor (KLIHF-tuhn, KAW-nuhr) ARI

Defense. Shoots right. 6', 195 lbs. Born, Matawan, NJ, April 28, 1995.
(Phoenix's 4th pick, 133rd overall, in 2013 NHL Draft).

			Regular Season					Playoffs				
Season	Club	League	GP	G	A	Pts	PIM	GP	G	A	Pts	PIM
2010-11	Jersey Hitmen	EmJHL	36	4	14	18	95	7	2	2	4	10
2011-12	Jersey Hitmen	EmJHL	4	0	1	1	26	....	....	....	....	....
	Jersey Hitmen	EJHL	28	1	11	12	46	6	0	3	3	15
	USAHNTDP	USHL	8	1	0	1	16	....	....	....	....	....
	USAHNTDP	U-17	4	0	1	1	8	....	....	....	....	....
2012-13	USAHNTDP	USHL	25	3	6	9	90	....	....	....	....	....
	USAHNTDP	U-18	41	5	9	14	24	....	....	....	....	....
2013-14	Quinnipiac	ECAC	36	5	4	9	106	....	....	....	....	....
2014-15	Quinnipiac	ECAC	38	0	5	5	54	....	....	....	....	....
2015-16	Quinnipiac	ECAC	43	7	21	28	42	....	....	....	....	....
2016-17	Quinnipiac	ECAC	39	7	7	14	*82	....	....	....	....	....

NCAA Championship All-Tournament Team (2016)

CLIFTON, Tim (KLIHF-tuhn, TIHM) S.J.

Center. Shoots right. 6'1", 195 lbs. Born, Matawan, NJ, May 22, 1992.

			Regular Season					Playoffs				
Season	Club	League	GP	G	A	Pts	PIM	GP	G	A	Pts	PIM
2007-08	Jr. Titans	Minor-NJ	29	10	4	14	28	....	....	....	....	....
2008-09	N.J. Jr. Titans	MtJHL	38	24	23	47	27	8	5	3	8	0
2009-10	Jersey Hitmen	EmJHL	36	25	45	70	38	4	4	0	4	18
	Jersey Hitmen	EJHL	2	3	0	3	6	....	....	....	....	....
2010-11	Jersey Hitmen	EJHL	38	25	24	49	16	8	3	4	7	4
2011-12	Jersey Hitmen	EJHL	39	14	30	44	37	6	3	6	9	4
2012-13	Jersey Hitmen	EJHL	40	30	32	62	32	3	2	2	4	2
2013-14	Quinnipiac	ECAC	40	3	7	10	35	....	....	....	....	....
2014-15	Quinnipiac	ECAC	37	9	8	17	45	....	....	....	....	....
2015-16	Quinnipiac	ECAC	39	19	24	43	*56	....	....	....	....	....
2016-17	Quinnipiac	ECAC	39	13	12	25	44	....	....	....	....	....
	San Jose Barracuda	AHL	8	0	0	0	0	....	....	....	....	....

ECAC Second All-Star Team (2016)

Signed as a free agent by **San Jose**, March 17, 2017.

CLURMAN, Nate (KLUHR-muhn, NAYT) COL

Defense. Shoots right. 6'2", 195 lbs. Born, Boulder, CO, May 8, 1998.
(Colorado's 5th pick, 161st overall, in 2016 NHL Draft).

			Regular Season					Playoffs				
Season	Club	League	GP	G	A	Pts	PIM	GP	G	A	Pts	PIM
2013-14	Culver Acad. U16	High-IN	42	1	9	10	18	....	....	....	....	....
2014-15	Culver Acad. U16	High-IN	39	2	16	18	12	....	....	....	....	....
2015-16	Culver Academy	High-IN	48	9	34	43	49	....	....	....	....	....
2016-17	Culver Academy	High-IN	36	8	24	32	6	....	....	....	....	....
	Tri-City Storm	USHL	2	0	0	0	2	....	....	....	....	....

• Signed Letter of Intent to attend **University of Notre Dame** (Hockey East) in fall of 2017.

COCKERILL, Logan (KAWK-rihl, LOH-guhn) NYI

Left wing. Shoots left. 5'9", 165 lbs. Born, Detroit, MI, March 3, 1999.
(NY Islanders' 5th pick, 201st overall, in 2017 NHL Draft).

			Regular Season					Playoffs				
Season	Club	League	GP	G	A	Pts	PIM	GP	G	A	Pts	PIM
2014-15	Det. B. Tire U16	T1EHL	30	6	13	19	22	3	1	2	2	0
	Det. B. Tire U16	Minor-MI	31	21	17	38	16	....	....	....	....	....
2015-16	USAHNTDP	USHL	29	5	10	15	10	....	....	....	....	....
	USAHNTDP	U-17	18	1	5	6	6	....	....	....	....	....
2016-17	USAHNTDP	USHL	16	4	6	10	0	....	....	....	....	....
	USAHNTDP	U-18	36	10	7	17	12	....	....	....	....	....

• Signed Letter of Intent to attend **Boston University** (Hockey East) in fall of 2017.

COLLINS, Ryan (KAWL-ihnz, RIGH-uhn) CBJ

Defense. Shoots right. 6'5", 216 lbs. Born, Bloomington, MN, May 6, 1996.
(Columbus' 2nd pick, 47th overall, in 2014 NHL Draft).

			Regular Season					Playoffs				
Season	Club	League	GP	G	A	Pts	PIM	GP	G	A	Pts	PIM
2011-12	Benilde	High-MN	23	1	3	4	6	6	0	1	1	2
2012-13	USAHNTDP	USHL	38	0	4	4	12	....	....	....	....	....
	USAHNTDP	U-17	18	2	3	5	8	....	....	....	....	....
2013-14	USAHNTDP	USHL	26	0	2	2	10	....	....	....	....	....
	USAHNTDP	U-18	33	1	4	5	16	....	....	....	....	....
2014-15	U. of Minnesota	Big Ten	32	1	8	9	14	....	....	....	....	....
2015-16	U. of Minnesota	Big Ten	29	0	4	4	35	....	....	....	....	....
2016-17	U. of Minnesota	Big Ten	37	3	6	9	28	....	....	....	....	....
	Cleveland	AHL	5	0	1	1	2	....	....	....	....	....

COLTON, Ross (KOHL-tuhn, RAWS) T.B.

Center. Shoots left. 6', 190 lbs. Born, Robbinsville, NJ, September 11, 1996.
(Tampa Bay's 6th pick, 118th overall, in 2016 NHL Draft).

			Regular Season					Playoffs				
Season	Club	League	GP	G	A	Pts	PIM	GP	G	A	Pts	PIM
2011-12	Mercer Chiefs U16	AYHL	19	19	5	24	12	....	....	....	....	....
2012-13	N.J. Rockets U16	AYHL	23	22	19	41	14	....	....	....	....	....
2013-14	Taft Rhinos	High-CT	24	25	18	43	....	....	....	....	....	....
2014-15	Cedar Rapids	USHL	58	18	15	33	22	3	0	0	0	0
2015-16	Cedar Rapids	USHL	55	35	31	66	79	5	1	0	1	2
2016-17	U. of Vermont	H-East	33	12	15	27	22	....	....	....	....	....

USHL First All-Star Team (2016) • Hockey East All-Rookie Team (2017)

COMRIE, Adam (KAWM-ree, A-duhm)

Defense. Shoots left. 6'4", 226 lbs. Born, Kanata, ON, July 31, 1990.
(Florida's 3rd pick, 80th overall, in 2008 NHL Draft).

			Regular Season					Playoffs				
Season	Club	League	GP	G	A	Pts	PIM	GP	G	A	Pts	PIM
2006-07	Ohio	USHL	19	6	4	10	28	....	....	....	....	....
	Omaha Lancers	USHL	38	1	6	7	27	5	0	0	0	4
2007-08	Saginaw Spirit	OHL	58	10	18	28	90	4	0	0	0	4
2008-09	Saginaw Spirit	OHL	52	9	21	30	70	8	0	2	2	8
2009-10	Guelph Storm	OHL	68	14	26	40	79	5	1	2	3	4
2010-11	Rochester	AHL	44	0	5	5	18	....	....	....	....	....
	Cincinnati	ECHL	13	4	4	8	18	2	1	0	1	2
2011-12	Cincinnati	ECHL	4	3	3	6	2	....	....	....	....	....
	Greenville	ECHL	3	1	0	1	2	1	0	0	0	2
2012-13	Reading Royals	ECHL	45	17	16	33	106	....	....	....	....	....
	Worcester Sharks	AHL	24	3	12	15	24	....	....	....	....	....
2013-14	Worcester Sharks	AHL	56	3	16	19	38	....	....	....	....	....
2014-15	Reading Royals	ECHL	21	7	7	14	28	7	2	2	4	10
	Lehigh Valley	AHL	40	5	13	18	50	....	....	....	....	....
2015-16	Lehigh Valley	AHL	32	9	6	15	11	....	....	....	....	....
	Reading Royals	ECHL	39	15	19	34	57	10	1	4	5	14
2016-17	Syracuse Crunch	AHL	55	8	11	19	33	....	....	....	....	....
	Kalamazoo Wings	ECHL	4	0	1	1	11	....	....	....	....	....

Signed as a free agent by **Greenville** (ECHL), March 19, 2012. Signed as a free agent by **Reading** (ECHL), August 3, 2012. Signed as a free agent by **Worcester** (AHL), February 8, 2013. Signed as a free agent by **San Jose**, July 10, 2013. Signed as a free agent by **Reading** (ECHL), October 6, 2014. • Re-assigned to **Lehigh Valley** (AHL) by **San Jose**, December 27, 2014. Signed as a free agent by **Syracuse** (AHL), July 26, 2016.

COMTOIS, Maxime (KAWM-twah, max-EEM) ANA

Left wing. Shoots left. 6'2", 207 lbs. Born, Longueuil, QC, August 1, 1999.
(Anaheim's 1st pick, 50th overall, in 2017 NHL Draft).

			Regular Season					Playoffs				
Season	Club	League	GP	G	A	Pts	PIM	GP	G	A	Pts	PIM
2014-15	Chateauguay	QAAA	41	23	33	56	50	16	12	19	31	26
2015-16	Victoriaville Tigres	QMJHL	62	26	34	60	68	5	1	5	6	4
2016-17	Victoriaville Tigres	QMJHL	64	22	29	51	88	4	1	0	1	8

COOPER, Brian (KOO-puhr, BRIGH-uhn) ANA

Defense. Shoots left. 5'10", 197 lbs. Born, Anchorage, AK, November 1, 1993.
(Anaheim's 6th pick, 127th overall, in 2012 NHL Draft).

			Regular Season					Playoffs				
Season	Club	League	GP	G	A	Pts	PIM	GP	G	A	Pts	PIM
2009-10	Fargo Force	USHL	55	3	10	13	69	13	0	4	4	22
2010-11	Fargo Force	USHL	51	11	22	33	132	5	2	0	2	18
2011-12	Fargo Force	USHL	55	6	18	24	92	6	1	2	3	8
2012-13	Nebraska-Omaha	WCHA	32	0	2	2	45	....	....	....	....	....
2013-14	Nebraska-Omaha	NCHC	37	2	7	9	30	....	....	....	....	....
2014-15	Nebraska-Omaha	NCHC	39	5	11	16	55	....	....	....	....	....
2015-16	Nebraska-Omaha	NCHC	35	5	11	16	51	....	....	....	....	....
	San Diego Gulls	AHL	5	0	1	1	4	8	0	1	1	4
2016-17	Utah Grizzlies	ECHL	1	0	1	1	0	....	....	....	....	....
	San Diego Gulls	AHL	37	4	6	10	10	10	0	2	2	0

USHL Second All-Star Team (2011, 2012)

CORNEL, Eric (kohr-NEHL, AIR-ihk) BUF

Center. Shoots right. 6'2", 192 lbs. Born, Peterborough, ON, April 11, 1996.
(Buffalo's 3rd pick, 44th overall, in 2014 NHL Draft).

			Regular Season					Playoffs				
Season	Club	League	GP	G	A	Pts	PIM	GP	G	A	Pts	PIM
2009-10	U.C. Cyclones MB	Minor-ON	27	29	18	47	10	11	10	15	25	4
	U.C. Cyclones Bant.	Minor-ON	1	2	1	3	0	2	1	1	2	0
2010-11	U.C. Cyclones Bant.	Minor-ON	30	21	40	61	16	....	....	....	....	....
	U.C. Cyclones MM	Minor-ON	4	1	3	4	0	....	....	....	....	....
2011-12	U.C. Cyclones MM	Minor-ON	26	18	32	50	14	5	0	5	5	4
	Kemptville 73's	ON-Jr.A	8	1	3	4	0	....	....	....	....	....
2012-13	Peterborough	OHL	63	4	12	16	13	....	....	....	....	....
2013-14	Peterborough	OHL	68	25	37	62	25	11	4	3	7	4
2014-15	Peterborough	OHL	66	14	38	52	35	5	0	1	1	2
	Rochester	AHL	6	0	1	1	0	....	....	....	....	....
2015-16	Peterborough	OHL	68	27	56	83	18	7	1	4	5	4
	Rochester	AHL	6	0	1	1	2	....	....	....	....	....
2016-17	Rochester	AHL	67	5	9	14	29	....	....	....	....	....

COTTON, David (KAW-tuhn, DAY-vihd) CAR

Center. Shoots left. 6'2", 200 lbs. Born, Parker, TX, July 9, 1997.
(Carolina's 8th pick, 169th overall, in 2015 NHL Draft).

			Regular Season					Playoffs				
Season	Club	League	GP	G	A	Pts	PIM	GP	G	A	Pts	PIM
2012-13	Col. Rampage U16	T1EHL	4	2	1	3	2	....	....	....	....	....
	Col. T-birds U16	T1EHL	37	7	10	17	16	4	0	0	0	0
2013-14	Boston Jr. Bruins	Minor-MA	12	8	3	11	2	....	....	....	....	....
	Cushing	High-MA	32	19	32	51	....	....	....	....	....	....
2014-15	Boston Jr. Bruins	Minor-MA	13	15	9	24	4	....	....	....	....	....
	Cushing	High-MA	33	27	42	69	....	....	....	....	....	....
2015-16	Waterloo	USHL	48	15	15	30	34	9	0	2	2	8
2016-17	Boston College	H-East	40	10	14	24	16	....	....	....	....	....

COUGHLIN, Liam (KAWF-lihn, LEE-uhm) CHI

Center/Left wing. Shoots left. 6'2", 202 lbs. Born, South Boston, MA , September 19, 1994.
(Edmonton's 4th pick, 130th overall, in 2014 NHL Draft).

			Regular Season					Playoffs				
Season	Club	League	GP	G	A	Pts	PIM	GP	G	A	Pts	PIM
2009-10	Walpole Express	MtJHL	29	3	5	8	....	....	....	....	....	....
2010-11	Catholic Memorial	High-MA	....	10	11	21	....	....	....	....	....	....
	S. Bos. Shamrocks	Minor-MA	STATISTICS NOT AVAILABLE									
2011-12	Catholic Memorial	High-MA	....	5	5	10	....	....	....	....	....	....
2012-13	Catholic Memorial	High-MA	....	28	20	48	....	....	....	....	....	....
2013-14	Vernon Vipers	BCHL	53	18	27	45	70	....	....	....	....	....
2014-15	Vernon Vipers	BCHL	54	20	40	60	31	11	3	7	10	2
2015-16	U. of Vermont	H-East	35	3	9	12	43	....	....	....	....	....
2016-17	U. of Vermont	H-East	31	3	8	11	8	....	....	....	....	....

Traded to **Chicago** by **Edmonton** for Anders Nilsson, July 6, 2015.

CRAWLEY, Brandon (KRAW-lee, BRAN-duhn) NYR

Defense. Shoots left. 6'1", 205 lbs. Born, Glen Rock, NJ, February 2, 1997.
(NY Rangers' 3rd pick, 123rd overall, in 2017 NHL Draft).

			Regular Season					Playoffs				
Season	Club	League	GP	G	A	Pts	PIM	GP	G	A	Pts	PIM
2013-14	Selects Acad. U18	Minor-CT	36	5	12	17	18	....	....	....	....	....
	Selects Acad. U18	USPHL	27	5	6	11	20	3	0	1	1	2
2014-15	London Knights	OHL	64	3	13	16	86	10	0	3	3	11
2015-16	London Knights	OHL	62	6	12	18	99	17	0	3	3	18
2016-17	London Knights	OHL	61	7	20	27	114	14	0	4	4	10

CRESCENZI, Andrew (kruh-SEHN-zee, AN-droo) L.A.

Center. Shoots left. 6'5", 209 lbs. Born, Thornhill, ON, July 29, 1992.

			Regular Season					Playoffs				
Season	Club	League	GP	G	A	Pts	PIM	GP	G	A	Pts	PIM
2008-09	Villanova Knights	ON-Jr.A	45	6	17	23	40	....	....	....	....	....
2009-10	Kitchener Rangers	OHL	68	8	4	12	42	20	1	2	3	11
2010-11	Kitchener Rangers	OHL	55	12	11	23	74	7	1	1	2	6
	Toronto Marlies	AHL	2	0	1	1	0	....	....	....	....	....
2011-12	Kitchener Rangers	OHL	52	24	23	47	74	15	4	7	11	20
2012-13	Toronto Marlies	AHL	15	1	1	2	17	....	....	....	....	....
	San Francisco Bulls	ECHL	23	3	11	14	28	....	....	....	....	....
2013-14	Toronto Marlies	AHL	32	1	1	2	33	....	....	....	....	....
	Manchester	AHL	14	1	1	2	8	....	....	....	....	....
2014-15	Manchester	AHL	54	7	8	15	60	18	0	3	3	19
2015-16	Ontario Reign	AHL	67	5	16	21	56	12	1	2	3	2
2016-17	Ontario Reign	AHL	56	7	8	15	57	....	....	....	....	....

Signed as a free agent by **Toronto**, September 24, 2010. Traded to **Los Angeles** by **Toronto** for Brandon Kozun, January 22, 2014.

CRISCUOLO, Kyle (krihs-KOH-loh, KIGHL) BUF

Center. Shoots right. 5'8", 170 lbs. Born, Southampton, NJ, May 5, 1992.

			Regular Season					Playoffs				
Season	Club	League	GP	G	A	Pts	PIM	GP	G	A	Pts	PIM
2006-07	St. Joseph's Prep	High-PA	23	8	11	19	8	....	....	....	....	....
2007-08	St. Joseph's Prep	High-PA	26	20	30	50	29	....	....	....	....	....
	Comcast U16	AYHL	32	32	34	66	18	....	....	....	....	....
2008-09	St. Joseph's Prep	High-PA	22	26	32	58	18	....	....	....	....	....
	Team Comcast	AYHL	21	31	24	55	8	....	....	....	....	....
2009-10	Choate-Rosemary	High-CT	28	19	22	41	....	....	....	....	....	....
	New York Bobcats	AtJHL	9	3	3	6	4	2	0	1	1	0
2010-11	Choate-Rosemary	High-CT	24	15	27	42	....	....	....	....	....	....
2011-12	Sioux City	USHL	59	21	23	44	24	1	0	1	1	0
2012-13	Harvard Crimson	ECAC	22	6	7	13	4	....	....	....	....	....
2013-14	Harvard Crimson	ECAC	31	11	9	20	22	....	....	....	....	....
2014-15	Harvard Crimson	ECAC	37	17	*31	48	12	....	....	....	....	....
2015-16	Harvard Crimson	ECAC	34	19	13	32	8	....	....	....	....	....
	Grand Rapids	AHL	4	0	0	0	0	....	....	....	....	....
2016-17	Grand Rapids	AHL	76	17	24	41	14	19	5	4	9	14

ECAC Second All-Star Team (2015)

Signed as a free agent by **Buffalo**, July 1, 2017.

CROTTY, Cameron (KRAW-tee, KAM-ih-RUHN) ARI

Defense. Shoots right. 6'2", 186 lbs. Born, Ottawa, ON, May 5, 1999.
(Arizona's 5th pick, 82nd overall, in 2017 NHL Draft).

			Regular Season					Playoffs				
Season	Club	League	GP	G	A	Pts	PIM	GP	G	A	Pts	PIM
2014-15	U.C. Cyclones MM	Minor-ON	29	2	9	11	22	....	....	....	....	....
2015-16	Brockville Braves	ON-Jr.A	57	3	15	18	38	6	1	6	7	0
2016-17	Brockville Braves	ON-Jr.A	41	4	9	13	32	5	1	0	1	2

• Signed Letter of Intent to attend **Boston University** (Hockey East) in fall of 2017.

CUKSTE, Karlis (CHUHK-steh, KAHR-lihs) S.J.

Defense. Shoots left. 6'1", 205 lbs. Born, Riga, Latvia, June 17, 1997.
(San Jose's 5th pick, 130th overall, in 2015 NHL Draft).

			Regular Season					Playoffs				
Season	Club	League	GP	G	A	Pts	PIM	GP	G	A	Pts	PIM
2013-14	SK Riga U18	Latvia-Jr.	22	9	14	23	16	....	....	....	....	....
2014-15	HS Prizma U18	LatviaU18	3	2	2	4	0	....	....	....	....	....
	HK Riga Jr.	Russia-Jr.	56	7	8	15	40	3	0	0	0	0
2015-16	Chicago Steel	USHL	44	4	11	15	10	....	....	....	....	....
2016-17	Quinnipiac	ECAC	38	5	10	15	47	....	....	....	....	....

DAHLEN, Jonathan (DAH-lihn, JAWN-ah-thuhn) VAN

Left wing. Shoots left. 5'11", 178 lbs. Born, Husqvarna, Sweden, December 20, 1997.
(Ottawa's 2nd pick, 42nd overall, in 2016 NHL Draft).

			Regular Season					Playoffs				
Season	Club	League	GP	G	A	Pts	PIM	GP	G	A	Pts	PIM
2012-13	HV 71 U18	Swe-U18	13	1	1	2	2	....	....	....	....	....
2013-14	HV 71 U18	Swe-U18	38	22	26	48	4	....	....	....	....	....
	HV 71 Jr.	Swe-Jr.	6	1	1	2	0	3	1	1	2	0
2014-15	Timra IK U18	Swe-U18	8	8	6	14	4	8	8	3	11	4
	Timra IK Jr.	Swe-Jr.	40	25	25	50	14	2	1	1	2	0
	Timra IK	Sweden-2	5	0	0	0	0	....	....	....	....	....
2015-16	Timra IK Jr.	Swe-Jr.	3	2	1	3	0	2	2	3	5	0
	Timra IK	Sweden-2	56	21	15	36	10	....	....	....	....	....
2016-17	Timra IK	Sweden-2	49	29	21	50	18	....	....	....	....	....
	Timra IK Jr.	Swe-Jr.	....	....	....	....	....	4	5	2	7	6

Traded to **Vancouver** by **Ottawa** for Alexandre Burrows, February 27, 2017.

DAHLSTROM, Carl (DAL-struhm, KAHRL) CHI

Defense. Shoots left. 6'4", 231 lbs. Born, Stockholm, Sweden, January 28, 1995.
(Chicago's 2nd pick, 51st overall, in 2013 NHL Draft).

			Regular Season					Playoffs				
Season	Club	League	GP	G	A	Pts	PIM	GP	G	A	Pts	PIM
2010-11	Djurgarden U18	Swe-U18	1	0	0	0	0	....	....	....	....	....
2011-12	Djurgarden U18	Swe-U18	37	2	13	15	4	4	0	3	3	0
2012-13	Linkopings HC U18	Swe-U18	3	2	2	4	2	2	0	0	0	2
	Linkopings HC Jr.	Swe-Jr.	37	5	8	13	12	5	1	1	2	4
2013-14	Linkopings HC Jr.	Swe-Jr.	23	2	12	14	6	....	....	....	....	....
	Linkopings HC	Sweden	12	0	1	1	0	14	1	2	3	2
2014-15	Linkopings HC	Sweden	55	3	3	6	12	11	0	1	1	4
2015-16	Linkopings HC	Sweden	50	1	7	8	14	6	0	1	1	4
	Rockford IceHogs	AHL	4	0	0	0	6	3	0	1	1	2
2016-17	Rockford IceHogs	AHL	70	6	5	11	16	....	....	....	....	....

DAHLSTROM, John (DAL-struhm, JAWN) CHI

Left wing. Shoots left. 6'1", 187 lbs. Born, Kungsbacka, Sweden, January 22, 1997.
(Chicago's 7th pick, 211th overall, in 2015 NHL Draft).

			Regular Season					Playoffs				
Season	Club	League	GP	G	A	Pts	PIM	GP	G	A	Pts	PIM
2012-13	Frolunda U18	Swe-U18	3	0	1	1	0	....	....	....	....	....
2013-14	Frolunda U18	Swe-U18	39	16	24	40	8	5	0	3	3	2
2014-15	Frolunda U18	Swe-U18	14	14	5	19	6	2	0	1	1	0
	Frolunda Jr.	Swe-Jr.	28	20	15	35	2	8	5	0	5	0
	Frolunda	Sweden	2	0	0	0	0	....	....	....	....	....
2015-16	Frolunda	Sweden	13	0	1	1	0	....	....	....	....	....
	Vita Hasten	Sweden-2	2	0	0	0	0	....	....	....	....	....
	Frolunda Jr.	Swe-Jr.	38	21	14	35	8	4	4	1	5	0
2016-17	Medicine Hat	WHL	63	30	29	59	12	11	6	7	13	4

DAL COLLE, Michael (DAL-KOHL, MIGH-kuhl) NYI

Left wing. Shoots left. 6'3", 198 lbs. Born, Richmond Hill, ON, June 20, 1996.
(NY Islanders' 1st pick, 5th overall, in 2014 NHL Draft).

			Regular Season					Playoffs				
Season	Club	League	GP	G	A	Pts	PIM	GP	G	A	Pts	PIM
2011-12	Vaughan Kings	GTHL	42	44	34	78	....	....	....	....	....	....
	Vaughan Kings	Other	5	4	7	11	0	....	....	....	....	....
	St. Michael's	ON-Jr.A	4	0	0	0	0	1	0	0	0	0
	The Hill Academy	High-ON	STATISTICS NOT AVAILABLE									
2012-13	Oshawa Generals	OHL	63	15	33	48	18	9	2	3	5	6
2013-14	Oshawa Generals	OHL	67	39	56	95	34	12	8	12	20	0
2014-15	Oshawa Generals	OHL	56	42	51	93	18	21	8	23	31	2
2015-16	Oshawa Generals	OHL	30	8	17	25	10	....	....	....	....	....
	Kingston	OHL	30	27	28	55	16	9	6	12	18	2
	Bridgeport	AHL	3	0	0	0	0	3	0	1	1	0
2016-17	Bridgeport	AHL	75	15	26	41	37	....	....	....	....	....

OHL All-Rookie Team (2013) • OHL Second All-Star Team (2014)

DARCY, Cameron (DAHR-see, KAM-ruhn) T.B.

Center. Shoots right. 6', 190 lbs. Born, South Boston, MA, March 2, 1994.
(Tampa Bay's 7th pick, 185th overall, in 2014 NHL Draft).

			Regular Season					Playoffs				
Season	Club	League	GP	G	A	Pts	PIM	GP	G	A	Pts	PIM
2007-08	Dexter School	High-MA	16	3	6	9	....	....	....	....	....	....
2008-09	Dexter School	High-MA	26	16	16	32	....	....	....	....	....	....
2009-10	Dexter School	High-MA	27	21	25	46	....	....	....	....	....	....
2010-11	USAHNTDP	USHL	37	9	4	13	20	2	0	0	0	2
	USAHNTDP	U-17	14	5	3	8	8	....	....	....	....	....
2011-12	USAHNTDP	USHL	24	4	2	6	8	....	....	....	....	....
	USAHNTDP	U-18	36	1	4	5	8	....	....	....	....	....
2012-13	Northeastern	H-East	9	0	2	2	8	....	....	....	....	....
	Muskegon	USHL	45	12	19	31	40	3	1	0	1	4
2013-14	Cape Breton	QMJHL	65	35	47	82	51	4	1	2	3	2
2014-15	Cape Breton	QMJHL	19	1	13	14	14	....	....	....	....	....
	Sherbrooke	QMJHL	37	20	25	45	34	6	5	4	9	8
2015-16	Syracuse Crunch	AHL	56	4	8	12	44	....	....	....	....	....
2016-17	Syracuse Crunch	AHL	34	3	4	7	14	....	....	....	....	....
	Kalamazoo Wings	ECHL	20	5	20	25	10	7	3	7	10	2

QMJHL Second All-Star Team (2014)

DAVIDSSON, Jonathan (DAY-vihd-suhn, JAWN-ah-thuhn) CBJ

Right wing. Shoots right. 5'11", 185 lbs. Born, Tyreso, Sweden, December 3, 1997.
(Columbus' 5th pick, 170th overall, in 2017 NHL Draft).

			Regular Season					Playoffs				
Season	Club	League	GP	G	A	Pts	PIM	GP	G	A	Pts	PIM
2012-13	Djurgarden U18	Swe-U18	36	10	10	20	4	9	2	1	3	0
	Djurgarden Jr.	Swe-Jr.	1	0	0	0	0	....	....	....	....	....
2013-14	Djurgarden U18	Swe-U18	35	22	40	62	34	4	1	3	4	4
	Djurgarden Jr.	Swe-Jr.	11	1	0	1	12	....	....	....	....	....
2014-15	Djurgarden U18	Swe-U18	10	9	6	15	6	5	2	4	6	8
	Djurgarden Jr.	Swe-Jr.	39	17	28	45	18	5	0	2	2	0
2015-16	Djurgarden Jr.	Swe-Jr.	27	9	28	37	34	7	4	5	9	0
	Djurgarden	Sweden	12	0	0	0	2	....	....	....	....	....
	Asploven	Sweden-2	9	0	0	0	2	....	....	....	....	....
2016-17	Djurgarden Jr.	Swe-Jr.	11	5	7	12	0	1	1	0	1	2
	Djurgarden	Sweden	44	3	9	12	16	2	0	0	0	0

DAVIDSSON, Marcus (DAY-vihd-suhn, MAHR-kuhs) BUF

Center. Shoots left. 6', 191 lbs. Born, Tyreso, Sweden, November 18, 1998.
(Buffalo's 2nd pick, 37th overall, in 2017 NHL Draft).

			Regular Season					Playoffs				
Season	Club	League	GP	G	A	Pts	PIM	GP	G	A	Pts	PIM
2013-14	Djurgarden U18	Swe-U18	31	5	15	20	16	4	0	1	1	0
2014-15	Djurgarden U18	Swe-U18	35	17	18	35	10	5	3	3	6	2
	Djurgarden Jr.	Swe-Jr.	2	0	0	0	0	....	....	....	....	....
2015-16	Djurgarden U18	Swe-U18	1	0	0	0	0	5	2	0	2	2
	Djurgarden Jr.	Swe-Jr.	45	17	23	40	24	6	3	3	6	0
	Djurgarden	Sweden	1	1	0	1	0	1	0	0	0	0
2016-17	Djurgarden Jr.	Swe-Jr.	9	6	4	10	2	1	0	0	0	0
	Djurgarden	Sweden	45	5	4	9	6	3	0	0	0	2

DAVIES, Jeremy (DAY-veez, JAIR-eh-mee) N.J.

Defense. Shoots left. 5'11", 180 lbs. Born, Ste-Ann-de-Bellevue, QC, December 4, 1996.
(New Jersey's 9th pick, 192nd overall, in 2016 NHL Draft).

			Regular Season					Playoffs				
Season	Club	League	GP	G	A	Pts	PIM	GP	G	A	Pts	PIM
2011-12	Lac St-LouisTigres	Minor-QC	29	3	9	12	24	3	0	0	0	0
2012-13	Lac St-Louis Lions	QAAA	42	5	27	32	12	5	1	1	2	0
2013-14	Lac St-Louis Lions	QAAA	42	7	26	33	74	16	4	15	19	28
2014-15	Waterloo	USHL	11	1	3	4	6	....	....	....	....	....
	Bloomington	USHL	43	3	17	20	70	....	....	....	....	....
2015-16	Bloomington	USHL	60	13	36	49	48	8	0	6	6	6
2016-17	Northeastern	H-East	38	8	15	23	38	....	....	....	....	....

USHL First All-Star Team (2016)

DAVIS, Brett (DAY-vihs, BREHT) DAL

Right wing. Shoots left. 6'1", 178 lbs. Born, Oakbank, MB, January 6, 1999.
(Dallas' 7th pick, 163rd overall, in 2017 NHL Draft).

			Regular Season					Playoffs				
Season	Club	League	GP	G	A	Pts	PIM	GP	G	A	Pts	PIM
2013-14	Notre Dame Btm.	Minor-SK	36	26	23	49	34	3	3	0	3	2
	Notre Dame	SMHL	2	1	1	2	0	....	....	....	....	....
2014-15	Eastman Selects	MMHL	42	21	26	47	22	4	6	2	8	0
	Lethbridge	WHL	3	0	1	1	0	....	....	....	....	....
2015-16	Lethbridge	WHL	53	5	4	9	17	5	0	0	0	2
2016-17	Lethbridge	WHL	29	7	4	11	4	....	....	....	....	....
	Kootenay Ice	WHL	30	11	11	22	14	....	....	....	....	....

DAY, Sean (DAY, SHAWN) NYR

Defense. Shoots left. 6'2", 231 lbs. Born, Leuven, Belgium, January 9, 1998.
(NY Rangers' 1st pick, 81st overall, in 2016 NHL Draft).

			Regular Season					Playoffs				
Season	Club	League	GP	G	A	Pts	PIM	GP	G	A	Pts	PIM
2012-13	Det. Comp. U16	HPHL	25	3	8	11	22	....	....	....	....	....
	Det. Comp. U16	Other	38	8	16	24	....	....	....	....	....	....
2013-14	Mississauga	OHL	60	6	10	16	34	4	0	1	1	4
2014-15	Mississauga	OHL	61	10	26	36	62	....	....	....	....	....
2015-16	Mississauga	OHL	57	6	16	22	27	7	1	2	3	4
2016-17	Mississauga	OHL	5	3	2	5	4	....	....	....	....	....
	Windsor Spitfires	OHL	58	12	20	32	20	7	0	5	5	0

DE JONG, Brendan (duh-JAWNG, BREHN-duhn) CAR

Defense. Shoots left. 6'5", 201 lbs. Born, Victoria, BC, March 23, 1998.
(Carolina's 7th pick, 166th overall, in 2017 NHL Draft).

			Regular Season					Playoffs				
Season	Club	League	GP	G	A	Pts	PIM	GP	G	A	Pts	PIM
2013-14	PCHA Elite 15	High-BC	32	4	9	13	32	....	....	....	....	....
	Saanich Braves	VIJHL	5	0	1	1	2	....	....	....	....	....
2014-15	Portland	WHL	54	2	3	5	10	1	0	0	0	0
2015-16	Portland	WHL	72	1	7	8	18	4	0	0	0	0
2016-17	Portland	WHL	72	8	15	23	72	11	1	2	3	8

DE JONG, Nolan (deh JAWNG, NOH-luhn) MIN

Defense. Shoots left. 6'2", 199 lbs. Born, Victoria, BC, April 25, 1995.
(Minnesota's 6th pick, 197th overall, in 2013 NHL Draft).

			Regular Season					Playoffs				
Season	Club	League	GP	G	A	Pts	PIM	GP	G	A	Pts	PIM
2009-10	Saanich Braves	Minor-BC	STATISTICS NOT AVAILABLE									
	South Island	BCMML	5	0	0	0	2	....	....	....	....	....
2010-11	South Island	BCMML	35	3	7	10	69	3	0	2	2	4
2011-12	Victoria Grizzlies	BCHL	56	2	15	17	20	....	....	....	....	....
2012-13	Victoria Grizzlies	BCHL	51	5	19	24	16	10	2	2	4	6
2013-14	U. of Michigan	Big Ten	29	0	5	5	12	....	....	....	....	....
2014-15	U. of Michigan	Big Ten	23	0	9	9	14	....	....	....	....	....
2015-16	U. of Michigan	Big Ten	38	0	11	11	14	....	....	....	....	....
2016-17	U. of Michigan	Big Ten	34	4	10	14	37	....	....	....	....	....

DeBRINCAT, Alex (deh-BRIHN-kiht, AL-ehx) CHI

Right wing. Shoots right. 5'7", 165 lbs. Born, Farmington Hills, MI, December 18, 1997.
(Chicago's 1st pick, 39th overall, in 2016 NHL Draft).

			Regular Season					Playoffs				
Season	Club	League	GP	G	A	Pts	PIM	GP	G	A	Pts	PIM
2012-13	Det. V Honda U16	T1EHL	40	25	26	51	28	4	0	2	2	4
	Det. V. Honda U18	T1EHL	2	1	0	1	0	....	....	....	....	....
2013-14	Lake Forest	MPHL	13	16	12	28	16	3	4	2	6	0
	Lake Forest	High-IL	34	34	43	77	....	....	....	....	....	....
2014-15	Erie Otters	OHL	68	51	53	104	73	20	9	7	16	26
2015-16	Erie Otters	OHL	60	51	50	101	28	13	8	11	19	13
2016-17	Erie Otters	OHL	63	*65	62	*127	49	22	13	*25	*38	10

OHL All-Rookie Team (2015) • OHL Rookie of the Year (2015) • OHL First All-Star Team (2017)

DeBRUSK, Jake (duh-BRUHSK, JAYK) BOS

Left wing. Shoots left. 6', 183 lbs. Born, Edmonton, AB, October 17, 1996.
(Boston's 2nd pick, 14th overall, in 2015 NHL Draft).

			Regular Season					Playoffs				
Season	Club	League	GP	G	A	Pts	PIM	GP	G	A	Pts	PIM
2011-12	SSAC Bulldogs	Minor-AB	26	13	20	33	24	5	2	4	6	10
2012-13	SSAC Athletics	AMHL	34	25	27	52	26	14	7	2	9	10
2013-14	Swift Current	WHL	72	15	24	39	21	6	3	1	4	0
2014-15	Swift Current	WHL	72	42	39	81	40	3	0	0	0	10
2015-16	Swift Current	WHL	24	9	17	26	15	....	....	....	....	....
	Red Deer Rebels	WHL	37	12	27	39	32	17	8	9	17	20
2016-17	Providence Bruins	AHL	74	19	30	49	30	17	6	3	9	4

DELNOV, Alexander (dehl-NAWV, al-ehx-AN-duhr) FLA

Left wing. Shoots left. 6', 189 lbs. Born, Moscow, Russia, January 14, 1994.
(Florida's 3rd pick, 114th overall, in 2012 NHL Draft).

			Regular Season					Playoffs				
Season	Club	League	GP	G	A	Pts	PIM	GP	G	A	Pts	PIM
2011-12	Mytischi Jr.	Russia-Jr.	47	11	11	22	16	5	0	0	0	2
2012-13	Seattle	WHL	69	20	29	49	33	7	2	2	4	0
	San Antonio	AHL	6	0	0	0	0	....	....	....	....	....
2013-14	Seattle	WHL	71	29	34	63	42	9	4	0	4	8
2014-15	Khanty-Mansiisk	KHL	2	0	0	0	2	....	....	....	....	....
	Khanty-Mansiisk Jr.	Russia-Jr.	42	15	33	48	39	9	6	7	13	2
2015-16	Amur Khabarovsk	KHL	8	0	0	0	6	....	....	....	....	....
	Dizel Penza	Russia-2	20	10	4	14	2	....	....	....	....	....
	Zvezda-VDV Dm.	Russia-2	4	0	1	1	2	....	....	....	....	....
2016-17	HK Sochi	KHL	20	1	1	2	6	....	....	....	....	....

DERGACHYOV, Alexander (duhr-GAH-chy'awv, al-ehx-AN-duhr) L.A.

Center. Shoots left. 6'4", 200 lbs. Born, Langepas, Russia, September 27, 1996.
(Los Angeles' 2nd pick, 74th overall, in 2015 NHL Draft).

			Regular Season					Playoffs				
Season	Club	League	GP	G	A	Pts	PIM	GP	G	A	Pts	PIM
2012-13	Almetjevsk Jr.	Rus.-Jr. B	12	1	1	2	24	7	0	2	2	4
2013-14	St. Petersburg Jr.	Russia-Jr.	46	12	9	21	30	10	1	1	2	2
2014-15	St. Petersburg Jr.	Russia-Jr.	45	10	29	39	52	19	11	7	18	10
2015-16	St. Petersburg Jr.	Russia-Jr.	1	1	0	1	0	....	....	....	....	....
	SKA-Neva	Russia-2	2	0	0	0	0	....	....	....	....	....
	SKA St. Petersburg	KHL	33	2	0	2	4	15	0	1	1	4
2016-17	SKA St. Petersburg	KHL	31	0	3	3	24	9	0	0	0	27
	SKA-Neva	Russia-2	3	2	0	2	4	8	1	2	3	4

DERMOTT, Travis (DUHR-mawt, TRA-vihs) TOR

Defense. Shoots left. 5'11", 215 lbs. Born, Newmarket, ON, December 22, 1996.
(Toronto's 2nd pick, 34th overall, in 2015 NHL Draft).

			Regular Season					Playoffs				
Season	Club	League	GP	G	A	Pts	PIM	GP	G	A	Pts	PIM
2011-12	York Simcoe	Minor-ON	17	2	6	8	12	....	....	....	....	....
	York Simcoe	Other	2	0	1	1	0	....	....	....	....	....
2012-13	Newmarket	ON-Jr.A	53	1	14	15	24	24	4	11	15	14
2013-14	Erie Otters	OHL	67	3	25	28	45	14	0	5	5	8
2014-15	Erie Otters	OHL	61	8	37	45	53	20	5	12	17	22
2015-16	Erie Otters	OHL	51	6	37	43	65	13	3	11	14	14
	Toronto Marlies	AHL	....	....	....	....	....	1	0	0	0	0
2016-17	Toronto Marlies	AHL	59	5	19	24	60	11	1	4	5	2

OHL All-Rookie Team (2014) • OHL Second All-Star Team (2016)

DESHARNAIS, Vincent (day-hahr-NAY, VIHN-sehnt) EDM

Defense. Shoots right. 6'5", 207 lbs. Born, Laval, QC, May 29, 1996.
(Edmonton's 9th pick, 183rd overall, in 2016 NHL Draft).

			Regular Season					Playoffs				
Season	Club	League	GP	G	A	Pts	PIM	GP	G	A	Pts	PIM
2011-12	Ulysse Prep	High-QC	56	1	6	7	....	....	....	....	....	....
2012-13	Ulysse Prep	High-QC	56	4	12	16	....	....	....	....	....	....
2013-14	Northwood	High-NY	37	5	16	21	....	....	....	....	....	....
2014-15	Chilliwack Chiefs	BCHL	54	1	4	5	52	12	1	7	8	0
2015-16	Providence College	H-East	19	1	1	2	8	....	....	....	....	....
2016-17	Providence College	H-East	32	2	1	3	22	....	....	....	....	....

DeSIMONE, Nick (DEE-sihr-mohn, NIHK) S.J.

Defense. Shoots right. 6'2", 195 lbs. Born, East Amherst, NY, November 21, 1994.

			Regular Season					Playoffs				
Season	Club	League	GP	G	A	Pts	PIM	GP	G	A	Pts	PIM
2011-12	Oak. Grizzlies U18	T1EHL	39	1	12	13	48	....	....	....	....	....
2012-13	Connecticut Oilers	EJHL	37	5	10	15	24	2	1	0	1	2
	Connecticut Oilers	EmJHL	4	3	1	4	2	....	....	....	....	....
2013-14	Buffalo Jr. Sabres	ON-Jr.A	52	13	38	51	30	11	4	2	6	8
2014-15	Union College	ECAC	35	2	9	11	10	....	....	....	....	....
2015-16	Union College	ECAC	36	4	14	18	16	....	....	....	....	....
2016-17	Union College	ECAC	38	9	10	19	16	....	....	....	....	....
	San Jose Barracuda	AHL	4	1	0	1	0	13	1	5	6	0

Signed as a free agent by **San Jose**, March 30, 2017.

DESROCHER, Stephen (duh-ROH-shay, STEE-vehn)

Defense. Shoots left. 6'4", 198 lbs. Born, Toronto, ON, January 26, 1996.
(Toronto's 8th pick, 155th overall, in 2015 NHL Draft).

			Regular Season					Playoffs				
Season	Club	League	GP	G	A	Pts	PIM	GP	G	A	Pts	PIM
2011-12	Mississauga Rebels	GTHL	64	4	22	26	30	....	....	....	....	....
2012-13	Vaughan Midget	GTHL	30	8	16	24	30	....	....	....	....	....
	Oakville Blades	ON-Jr.A	7	0	1	1	4	....	....	....	....	....
2013-14	Oshawa Generals	OHL	43	4	4	8	6	12	1	2	3	6
2014-15	Oshawa Generals	OHL	66	10	13	23	41	21	4	8	12	14
2015-16	Oshawa Generals	OHL	17	5	6	11	6	....	....	....	....	....
	Kingston	OHL	52	6	29	35	33	9	1	5	6	4
2016-17	Kingston	OHL	65	12	39	51	30	11	2	3	5	10

DI PAULI, Thomas (DEE-paw-LEE, TAW-muhs) PIT

Center. Shoots left. 5'11", 188 lbs. Born, Woodbridge, IL, April 29, 1994.
(Washington's 4th pick, 100th overall, in 2012 NHL Draft).

			Regular Season					Playoffs				
Season	Club	League	GP	G	A	Pts	PIM	GP	G	A	Pts	PIM
2009-10	Chicago Mission	T1EHL	30	18	15	33	10	....	....	....	....	....
	Chicago Mission	Other	19	11	26	37	....	....	....	....	....	....
2010-11	USAHNTDP	USHL	32	4	11	15	16	2	0	1	1	0
	USAHNTDP	U-17	17	4	9	12	10	....	....	....	....	....
2011-12	USAHNTDP	USHL	21	6	5	11	6	....	....	....	....	....
	USAHNTDP	U-18	34	5	5	10	16	....	....	....	....	....
2012-13	U. of Notre Dame	CCHA	41	5	7	12	31	....	....	....	....	....
2013-14	U. of Notre Dame	H-East	26	3	2	5	12	....	....	....	....	....
2014-15	U. of Notre Dame	H-East	41	8	21	29	24	....	....	....	....	....
2015-16	U. of Notre Dame	H-East	37	14	18	32	16	....	....	....	....	....
2016-17	Wilkes-Barre	AHL	21	2	0	2	20	....	....	....	....	....

Signed as a free agent by **Pittsburgh**, August 19, 2016.

DIDIER, Josiah (DIH-dee-ay, joh-SIGH-uh)

Defense. Shoots right. 6'2", 202 lbs. Born, Littleton, CO, April 8, 1993.
(Montreal's 2nd pick, 97th overall, in 2011 NHL Draft).

			Regular Season					Playoffs				
Season	Club	League	GP	G	A	Pts	PIM	GP	G	A	Pts	PIM
2009-10	Colorado T-birds	Minor-CO	19	3	15	18	12	....	....	....	....	....
	Colorado T-birds	Other	9	5	2	7	12	....	....	....	....	....
2010-11	Cedar Rapids	USHL	58	8	13	21	81	8	0	2	2	7
2011-12	U. of Denver	WCHA	41	0	3	3	36	....	....	....	....	....
2012-13	U. of Denver	WCHA	31	0	7	7	48	....	....	....	....	....
2013-14	U. of Denver	NCHC	36	1	7	8	61	....	....	....	....	....
2014-15	U. of Denver	NCHC	40	3	8	11	58	....	....	....	....	....
	Hamilton Bulldogs	AHL	8	0	1	1	5	....	....	....	....	....
2015-16	St. John's IceCaps	AHL	53	0	5	5	58	....	....	....	....	....
	Brampton Beast	ECHL	4	1	0	1	4	....	....	....	....	....
2016-17	St. John's IceCaps	AHL	39	2	6	8	25	4	0	0	0	0
	Brampton Beast	ECHL	1	0	1	1	0	....	....	....	....	....

Signed as a free agent by **St. John's** (AHL), June 8, 2015.

DINEEN, Cam (dih-NEEN, KAM) ARI

Defense. Shoots left. 5'11", 187 lbs. Born, Toms River, NJ, June 19, 1998.
(Arizona's 3rd pick, 68th overall, in 2016 NHL Draft).

			Regular Season					Playoffs				
Season	Club	League	GP	G	A	Pts	PIM	GP	G	A	Pts	PIM
2013-14	N.J. Rockets U19	Other	60	6	30	36	8	....	....	....	....	....
2014-15	N.J. Rockets	EHL	39	10	31	41	8	2	0	0	0	0
	N.J. Rockets U19	Other	8	1	1	2	0	....	....	....	....	....
	Tri-City Storm	USHL	3	0	0	0	0	....	....	....	....	....
2015-16	North Bay	OHL	68	13	46	59	18	11	0	8	8	0
2016-17	North Bay	OHL	29	6	8	14	8	....	....	....	....	....

OHL All-Rookie Team (2016)

DJOOS, Christian (YEW-uhs, KRIHS-t'yehn) WSH

Defense. Shoots left. 5'11", 158 lbs. Born, Gothenburg, Sweden, August 6, 1994.
(Washington's 8th pick, 195th overall, in 2012 NHL Draft).

			Regular Season					Playoffs				
Season	Club	League	GP	G	A	Pts	PIM	GP	G	A	Pts	PIM
2009-10	Brynas U18	Swe-U18	35	4	12	16	66	4	1	1	2	4
2010-11	Brynas U18	Swe-U18	38	11	34	45	34	5	0	5	5	4
	Brynas IF Gavle Jr.	Swe-Jr.	11	0	1	1	0	....	....	....	....	....
2011-12	Brynas U18	Swe-U18	7	5	8	13	4	5	1	0	1	2
	Brynas IF Gavle Jr.	Swe-Jr.	40	3	21	24	22	2	0	0	0	0
	Brynas IF Gavle	Sweden	1	0	0	0	0	....	....	....	....	....
2012-13	Brynas IF Gavle Jr.	Swe-Jr.	2	0	2	2	2	....	....	....	....	....
	Brynas IF Gavle	Sweden	47	2	6	8	38	4	0	0	0	0
2013-14	Brynas IF Gavle Jr.	Swe-Jr.	1	0	1	1	0	1	0	0	0	0
	Brynas IF Gavle	Sweden	47	1	12	13	4	5	1	2	3	0
2014-15	Brynas IF Gavle	Sweden	50	5	12	17	22	7	1	1	2	8
	Hershey Bears	AHL	1	0	1	1	0	....	....	....	....	....
2015-16	Hershey Bears	AHL	62	8	14	22	8	21	2	7	9	8
2016-17	Hershey Bears	AHL	66	13	45	58	34	12	2	6	8	2

DONAGHEY, Cody (duhn-a-HEE, KOH-dee) OTT

Defense. Shoots right. 6'1", 193 lbs. Born, Toronto, ON, May 10, 1996.

			Regular Season					Playoffs				
Season	Club	League	GP	G	A	Pts	PIM	GP	G	A	Pts	PIM
2012-13	Rouyn-Noranda	QMJHL	24	3	3	6	4	....	....	....	....	....
	Quebec Remparts	QMJHL	14	0	1	1	4	....	....	....	....	....
2013-14	Quebec Remparts	QMJHL	67	9	29	38	24	....	....	....	....	....
2014-15	Quebec Remparts	QMJHL	27	4	11	15	24	....	....	....	....	....
2015-16	Halifax	QMJHL	21	4	7	11	33	....	....	....	....	....
	Moncton Wildcats	QMJHL	30	7	19	26	30	17	1	7	8	16
2016-17	Charlottetown	QMJHL	37	10	25	35	26	....	....	....	....	....
	Sherbrooke	QMJHL	15	1	4	5	13	....	....	....	....	....

Signed as a free agent by **Toronto**, September 20, 2014. Traded to **Ottawa** by **Toronto** with Dion Phaneuf, Matt Frattin, Casey Bailey and Ryan Rupert for Jared Cowen, Colin Greening, Milan Michalek, Tobias Lindberg and Ottawa's 2nd round pick (Eemeli Rasanen) in 2017 NHL Draft, February 9, 2016.

DONATO, Ryan (duh-NAT-toh, RIGH-uhn) BOS

Center. Shoots left. 6', 188 lbs. Born, Boston, MA, April 9, 1996.
(Boston's 2nd pick, 56th overall, in 2014 NHL Draft).

			Regular Season					Playoffs				
Season	Club	League	GP	G	A	Pts	PIM	GP	G	A	Pts	PIM
2011-12	Cape Cod U16	Minor-MA	12	6	2	8	4	....	....	....	....	....
	Dexter School	High-MA	26	14	22	36	....	....	....	....	....	....
2012-13	Cape Cod U16	Minor-MA	12	*18	14	*32	6	....	....	....	....	....
	Dexter School	High-MA	28	29	31	60	....	....	....	....	....	....
2013-14	Cape Cod Whalers	Minor-MA	9	8	9	17	33	....	....	....	....	....
	Dexter School	High-MA	30	37	41	78	....	....	....	....	....	....
	USAHNTDP	U-18	4	1	0	1	0	....	....	....	....	....
2014-15	Omaha Lancers	USHL	8	5	5	10	4	3	1	0	1	15
	South Shore Kings	USPHL	13	5	5	10	4	....	....	....	....	....
2015-16	Harvard Crimson	ECAC	32	13	8	21	26	....	....	....	....	....
2016-17	Harvard Crimson	ECAC	36	21	19	40	25	....	....	....	....	....

ECAC Second All-Team (2017)

DONNAY, Troy (duh-NAY, TROI) NYR

Defense. Shoots right. 6'7", 205 lbs. Born, Flint, MI, February 18, 1994.

			Regular Season					Playoffs				
Season	Club	League	GP	G	A	Pts	PIM	GP	G	A	Pts	PIM
2009-10	Detroit Belle Tire	T1EHL	37	1	10	11	69	....	....	....	....	....
2010-11	London Knights	OHL	25	0	1	1	12	....	....	....	....	....
2011-12	London Knights	OHL	23	0	3	3	16	....	....	....	....	....
	Erie Otters	OHL	27	1	4	5	28	....	....	....	....	....
2012-13	Erie Otters	OHL	68	1	7	8	48	....	....	....	....	....
2013-14	Erie Otters	OHL	66	2	17	19	92	14	1	1	2	12
2014-15	Erie Otters	OHL	45	4	19	23	53	19	0	5	5	21
2015-16	Hartford Wolf Pack	AHL	1	0	0	0	0	....	....	....	....	....
	Greenville	ECHL	61	2	9	11	48	....	....	....	....	....
2016-17	Greenville	ECHL	61	3	14	17	72	....	....	....	....	....

Signed as a free agent by **NY Rangers**, July 31, 2013.

DOSTIE, Alex (dohs-TEE, AL-ehx) ANA

Center. Shoots left. 5'10", 165 lbs. Born, Drummondville, QC, April 13, 1997.
(Anaheim's 5th pick, 115th overall, in 2016 NHL Draft).

			Regular Season					Playoffs				
Season	Club	League	GP	G	A	Pts	PIM	GP	G	A	Pts	PIM
2012-13	Magog	QAAA	42	13	21	34	12	....	....	....	....	....
2013-14	Gatineau	QMJHL	48	9	16	25	18	....	....	....	....	....
2014-15	Gatineau	QMJHL	68	22	32	54	16	11	0	2	2	6
2015-16	Gatineau	QMJHL	54	25	48	73	10	10	6	4	10	4
2016-17	Gatineau	QMJHL	32	15	21	36	12	....	....	....	....	....
	Charlottetown	QMJHL	31	15	20	35	2	13	8	8	16	13
	San Diego Gulls	AHL	....	....	....	....	....	1	0	0	0	0

DOUGHERTY, Jack (DAWR-ih-tee, JAK) NSH

Defense. Shoots right. 6'1", 186 lbs. Born, St. Paul, MN, May 25, 1996.
(Nashville's 3rd pick, 51st overall, in 2014 NHL Draft).

			Regular Season					Playoffs				
Season	Club	League	GP	G	A	Pts	PIM	GP	G	A	Pts	PIM
2011-12	St. Thomas Acad.	High-MN	24	0	9	9	8	6	1	0	1	0
2012-13	Team Southeast	UMHSEL	19	2	9	11	30	3	0	2	2	4
	St. Thomas Acad.	High-MN	25	3	21	24	16	6	2	9	11	2
2013-14	USAHNTDP	USHL	23	4	8	12	34	....	....	....	....	....
	USAHNTDP	U-18	32	3	9	12	31	....	....	....	....	....
2014-15	U. of Wisconsin	Big Ten	33	2	7	9	29	....	....	....	....	....
2015-16	Portland	WHL	68	11	41	52	71	4	0	2	2	6
	Milwaukee	AHL	3	0	1	1	2	....	....	....	....	....
2016-17	Milwaukee	AHL	75	2	11	13	32	3	0	0	0	4

DOWNING, Grayson (DOW-nihng, GRAY-suhn) EDM

Center. Shoots left. 6', 192 lbs. Born, Abbotsford, BC, April 18, 1992.

			Regular Season					Playoffs				
Season	Club	League	GP	G	A	Pts	PIM	GP	G	A	Pts	PIM
2007-08	Fraser Valley	BCMML	32	15	25	40	32	2	1	1	2	2
2008-09	Westside Warriors	BCHL	37	13	10	23	21	6	0	0	0	0
2009-10	Westside Warriors	BCHL	43	18	18	36	28	11	6	4	10	8
2010-11	Westside Warriors	BCHL	52	24	36	70	30	9	2	7	9	4
2011-12	New Hampshire	H-East	34	10	13	23	12	....	....	....	....	....
2012-13	New Hampshire	H-East	38	15	16	31	44	....	....	....	....	....
2013-14	New Hampshire	H-East	34	10	12	22	46	....	....	....	....	....
2014-15	New Hampshire	H-East	38	21	15	36	18	....	....	....	....	....
	Iowa Wild	AHL	5	0	4	4	4	....	....	....	....	....
2015-16	Iowa Wild	AHL	56	19	21	40	24	....	....	....	....	....
2016-17	Iowa Wild	AHL	47	7	15	22	11	....	....	....	....	....
	Tucson	AHL	12	2	2	4	4	....	....	....	....	....

Signed as a free agent by **Minnesota**, March 24, 2015. Traded to **Arizona** by **Minnesota** with Minnesota's 1st round pick (Pierre-Olivier Joseph) in 2017 NHL Draft, Minnesota's 2nd round pick in 2018 NHL Draft and Minnesota's 4th round pick in 2019 NHL Draft for Martin Hanzal, Ryan White and Arizona's 4th round pick (Mason Shaw) in 2017 NHL Draft, February 26, 2017. Signed as a free agent by **Edmonton**, July 1, 2017.

DOWNING, Michael (DOW-nihng, MIGH-kuhl) FLA

Defense. Shoots left. 6'3", 204 lbs. Born, Canton, MI, May 19, 1995.
(Florida's 4th pick, 97th overall, in 2013 NHL Draft).

			Regular Season					Playoffs				
Season	Club	League	GP	G	A	Pts	PIM	GP	G	A	Pts	PIM
2009-10	Det. Vic. Honda	T1EHL	30	4	6	10	36	....	....	....	....	....
2010-11	Catholic Central	High-MI	26	7	16	23	18	....	....	....	....	....
2011-12	USAHNTDP	U-17	7	0	1	1	0	....	....	....	....	....
	Dubuque	USHL	54	4	10	14	68	5	1	1	2	4
2012-13	Dubuque	USHL	52	3	20	23	107	11	0	3	3	6
2013-14	U. of Michigan	Big Ten	34	2	10	12	60	....	....	....	....	....
2014-15	U. of Michigan	Big Ten	36	6	16	22	*76	....	....	....	....	....
2015-16	U. of Michigan	Big Ten	35	3	17	20	66	....	....	....	....	....
2016-17	Springfield	AHL	67	2	11	13	65	....	....	....	....	....

Big Ten All-Rookie Team (2014)

DRAKE, David (DRAYK, DAY-vihd) PHI

Defense. Shoots left. 6'3", 185 lbs. Born, Naperville, IL, January 7, 1995.
(Philadelphia's 6th pick, 192nd overall, in 2013 NHL Draft).

			Regular Season					Playoffs				
Season	Club	League	GP	G	A	Pts	PIM	GP	G	A	Pts	PIM
2011-12	Indiana Jr. Ice	NAPHL	18	1	4	5	22	5	1	3	4	0
	Indiana Jr. Ice	HPHL	6	2	0	2	2	....	....	....	....	....
2012-13	Chicago Fury	T1EHL	40	2	4	6	16	2	0	0	0	0
	Des Moines	USHL	12	1	0	1	6	....	....	....	....	....
2013-14	Des Moines	USHL	51	0	5	5	26	....	....	....	....	....
2014-15	U. of Connecticut	H-East	32	1	4	5	14	....	....	....	....	....
2015-16	U. of Connecticut	H-East	25	0	5	5	10	....	....	....	....	....
2016-17	U. of Connecticut	H-East	31	3	4	7	20	....	....	....	....	....

DROZG, Jan (DROHZG, YAHN) PIT

Left wing. Shoots right. 6', 174 lbs. Born, Maribor, Slovenia, January 4, 1999.
(Pittsburgh's 3rd pick, 152nd overall, in 2017 NHL Draft).

			Regular Season					Playoffs				
Season	Club	League	GP	G	A	Pts	PIM	GP	G	A	Pts	PIM
2013-14	HK Maribor U18	Austria-U18	25	20	11	31	46	....	....	....	....	....
	HK Maribor U18	Slovenia-U18	....	....	....	....	....	6	5	0	5	10
2014-15	HK Maribor	Slovenia	11	4	3	7	6	....	....	....	....	....
	HK Celje U18	Slovenia-U18	....	....	....	....	....	5	10	9	19	6
	HK Celje U18	Austria-U18	25	47	31	78	37	3	3	2	5	0
2015-16	Leksands IF U18	Swe-U18	38	26	25	51	26	5	0	1	1	0
	Leksands IF Jr.	Swe-Jr.	1	0	0	0	2	....	....	....	....	....
2016-17	Leksands IF U18	Swe-U18	35	19	30	49	18	4	1	2	3	8
	Leksands IF Jr.	Swe-Jr.	4	3	2	5	0	2	1	0	1	0

DUBE, Dillon (doo-BAY, DIH-luhn) CGY

Center. Shoots left. 5'11", 183 lbs. Born, Golden, AB, July 20, 1998.
(Calgary's 3rd pick, 56th overall, in 2016 NHL Draft).

			Regular Season					Playoffs				
Season	Club	League	GP	G	A	Pts	PIM	GP	G	A	Pts	PIM
2011-12	Airdrie Xtreme	AMBHL	21	7	11	18	4	4	2	2	4	0
2012-13	N. Dame Hounds	Minor-SK	26	24	20	44	43	5	6	5	11	8
	Notre Dame Argos	SMHL	4	2	0	2	0	3	0	1	1	14
2013-14	Notre Dame Argos	SMHL	44	21	42	63	65	12	5	8	13	14
	Kelowna Rockets	WHL	....	....	....	....	....	1	0	0	0	0
2014-15	Kelowna Rockets	WHL	45	17	10	27	12	18	5	6	11	8
2015-16	Kelowna Rockets	WHL	65	26	40	66	50	18	2	5	7	16
2016-17	Kelowna Rockets	WHL	40	20	35	55	40	17	7	14	21	18
	Stockton Heat	AHL	....	....	....	....	....	1	0	0	0	0

DUBOIS, Pierre-Luc (doo-BWAH, PEE-aihr-LEWK) CBJ

Left wing. Shoots left. 6'3", 215 lbs. Born, Ste-Agathe-des-Monts, QC, June 24, 1998.
(Columbus' 1st pick, 3rd overall, in 2016 NHL Draft).

			Regular Season					Playoffs				
Season	Club	League	GP	G	A	Pts	PIM	GP	G	A	Pts	PIM
2013-14	Col Notre Dame	QAAA	40	17	21	38	92	3	0	0	0	6
2014-15	Cape Breton	QMJHL	54	10	35	45	58	7	2	3	5	6
2015-16	Cape Breton	QMJHL	62	42	57	99	112	12	7	5	12	14
2016-17	Cape Breton	QMJHL	20	6	12	18	33	....	....	....	....	....
	Blainville-Bois.	QMJHL	28	15	22	37	45	19	9	13	22	26

QMJHL Second All-Star Team (2016)

DUDEK, J.D. (DOO-dehk, JAY-DEE) N.J.

Center. Shoots right. 5'11", 185 lbs. Born, Derry, NH, January 29, 1996.
(New Jersey's 5th pick, 152nd overall, in 2014 NHL Draft).

			Regular Season					Playoffs				
Season	Club	League	GP	G	A	Pts	PIM	GP	G	A	Pts	PIM
2010-11	Pinkerton	High-NH	....	14	25	39	8	....	....	....	....	....
2011-12	Pinkerton	High-NH	....	20	34	54	48	....	....	....	....	....
2012-13	Kimball Union	High-NH	30	17	25	42	....	....	....	....	....	....
2013-14	Kimball Union	High-NH	25	9	35	44	....	....	....	....	....	....
	Islanders H.C.	USPHL	2	0	0	0	12	....	....	....	....	....
2014-15	Dubuque	USHL	41	6	6	12	66	....	....	....	....	....
	Chicago Steel	USHL	13	4	2	6	6	....	....	....	....	....
2015-16	Boston College	H-East	34	1	2	3	6	....	....	....	....	....
2016-17	Boston College	H-East	40	13	9	22	28	....	....	....	....	....

DUGAN, Jack (DUH-guhn, JAK) VGK

Left wing. Shoots right. 6'1", 190 lbs. Born, Pittsburgh, PA, March 24, 1998.
(Las Vegas' 9th pick, 142nd overall, in 2017 NHL Draft).

			Regular Season					Playoffs				
Season	Club	League	GP	G	A	Pts	PIM	GP	G	A	Pts	PIM
2011-12	McQuaid Jesuit	High-NY	15	0	0	0	0	....	....	....	....	....
2012-13	McQuaid Jesuit	High-NY	19	2	11	13	8	3	0	0	0	0
2013-14	McQuaid Jesuit	High-NY	15	10	13	23	12	2	2	1	3	0
	Roch. Mon. U16	Minor-NY	41	15	22	37	....	....	....	....	....	....
2014-15	McQuaid Jesuit	High-NY	18	*19	34	53	*51	6	5	5	10	0
	Roch. Mon. U16	Minor-NY	40	43	36	79	....	....	....	....	....	....
2015-16	Northwood	High-NY	49	24	29	53	....	....	....	....	....	....
2016-17	Northwood	High-NY	47	32	61	93	....	....	....	....	....	....

• Signed Letter of Intent to attend **Providence College** (Hockey East) in fall of 2018.

DUHAIME, Brandon (doo-HAYM, BRAN-duhn) MIN

Right wing. Shoots left. 6'1", 200 lbs. Born, Parkland, FL, May 22, 1997.
(Minnesota's 2nd pick, 106th overall, in 2016 NHL Draft).

			Regular Season					Playoffs				
Season	Club	League	GP	G	A	Pts	PIM	GP	G	A	Pts	PIM
2012-13	PoE Acad. Prep	CSSHL	12	4	3	7	16	2	0	0	0	4
	PoE Acad. U18	NAPHL	22	4	13	17	22	4	2	3	5	0
2013-14	PoE Acad. Prep	CSSHL	25	9	16	25	38	3	2	1	3	2
	PoE Acad. U18	NAPHL	24	9	16	25	18	3	1	0	1	15
	PoE Acad. U18	Other	9	2	6	8	4	....	....	....	....	....
	West Kelowna	BCHL	3	0	0	0	0	....	....	....	....	....
2014-15	Merritt	BCHL	53	6	19	25	43	4	0	0	0	2
2015-16	Chicago Steel	USHL	39	10	22	32	97	....	....	....	....	....
	Tri-City Storm	USHL	18	5	5	10	46	11	4	4	8	24
2016-17	Providence College	H-East	35	4	8	12	45	....	....	....	....	....

DUKE, Reid (DOOK, REED) VGK

Center. Shoots right. 6', 196 lbs. Born, Calgary, AB, January 28, 1996.
(Minnesota's 7th pick, 169th overall, in 2014 NHL Draft).

			Regular Season					Playoffs				
Season	Club	League	GP	G	A	Pts	PIM	GP	G	A	Pts	PIM
2009-10	Calgary Royals	AMBHL	33	10	13	23	50	....	....	....	....	....
2010-11	Calgary Royals	AMBHL	30	28	36	64	79	....	....	....	....	....
	Cgy Royals Gold	Minor-AB	6	5	4	9	4	....	....	....	....	....
2011-12	Calgary Royals	AMHL	29	13	16	29	24	2	0	0	0	0
	Lethbridge	WHL	12	2	4	6	8	....	....	....	....	....
2012-13	Lethbridge	WHL	57	8	16	24	30	....	....	....	....	....
2013-14	Lethbridge	WHL	62	15	25	40	91	....	....	....	....	....
2014-15	Lethbridge	WHL	1	0	0	0	0	....	....	....	....	....
	Brandon	WHL	52	20	31	51	66	6	0	1	1	4
2015-16	Brandon	WHL	68	33	29	62	53	21	8	16	24	24
2016-17	Brandon	WHL	59	37	34	71	81	4	3	0	3	8

Signed as a free agent by **Vegas**, March 6, 2017.

DUNN, Vince (DUHN-duh, VIHNS) ST.L.

Defense. Shoots left. 5'11", 190 lbs. Born, Lindsay, ON, October 29, 1996.
(St. Louis' 1st pick, 56th overall, in 2015 NHL Draft).

			Regular Season					Playoffs				
Season	Club	League	GP	G	A	Pts	PIM	GP	G	A	Pts	PIM
2011-12	Peter. Petes MM	Minor-ON	26	0	14	14	8	....	....	....	....	....
2012-13	Thorold	ON-Jr.B	48	5	23	28	35	13	3	5	8	10
2013-14	Niagara Ice Dogs	OHL	63	5	28	33	45	7	0	1	1	2
2014-15	Niagara Ice Dogs	OHL	68	18	38	56	59	8	6	4	10	22
2015-16	Niagara Ice Dogs	OHL	52	12	31	43	52	12	5	7	12	10
2016-17	Chicago Wolves	AHL	72	13	32	45	71	10	1	5	6	20

DUNN, Vincent (DUHN, VIHN-sehnt) OTT

Center. Shoots left. 6', 187 lbs. Born, Hull, QC, September 14, 1995.
(Ottawa's 5th pick, 138th overall, in 2013 NHL Draft).

			Regular Season					Playoffs				
Season	Club	League	GP	G	A	Pts	PIM	GP	G	A	Pts	PIM
2010-11	Gatineau Intrepide	QAAA	41	22	26	48	122	3	1	1	2	6
2011-12	Val-d'Or Foreurs	QMJHL	56	5	8	13	94	3	1	0	1	5
2012-13	Val-d'Or Foreurs	QMJHL	53	25	27	52	98	10	0	3	3	19
2013-14	Gatineau	QMJHL	50	31	20	51	156	9	3	6	9	26
	Binghamton	AHL	1	0	0	0	0	....	....	....	....	....
2014-15	Rimouski Oceanic	QMJHL	46	19	13	32	153	....	....	....	....	....
2015-16	Binghamton	AHL	3	0	0	0	4	....	....	....	....	....
	Evansville IceMen	ECHL	55	13	14	27	154	....	....	....	....	....
2016-17	Binghamton	AHL	8	0	2	2	9	....	....	....	....	....
	Wichita Thunder	ECHL	47	4	8	12	86	....	....	....	....	....

DUPUY, Jean (doo-PWEE, ZHAWN)

Left wing. Shoots left. 6'3", 206 lbs. Born, Orleans, ON, October 6, 1994.

			Regular Season					Playoffs				
Season	Club	League	GP	G	A	Pts	PIM	GP	G	A	Pts	PIM
2011-12	Kingston	OHL	50	3	5	8	25	....	....	....	....	....
2012-13	Kingston	OHL	42	4	3	7	79	4	0	0	0	9
2013-14	Kingston	OHL	3	1	0	1	5	....	....	....	....	....
	Sault Ste. Marie	OHL	45	9	8	17	41	9	3	1	4	2
2014-15	Sault Ste. Marie	OHL	54	18	28	46	52	10	4	2	6	9
2015-16	Rochester	AHL	74	8	13	21	63	....	....	....	....	....
2016-17	Rochester	AHL	46	3	9	12	46	....	....	....	....	....

Signed as a free agent by **Buffalo**, November 28, 2014.

DURANDEAU, Arnaud (duh-RAN-doh, AHR-NOH) NYI

Left wing. Shoots left. 5'11", 183 lbs. Born, Montreal, QC, January 14, 1999.
(NY Islanders' 4th pick, 165th overall, in 2017 NHL Draft).

			Regular Season					Playoffs				
Season	**Club**	**League**	**GP**	**G**	**A**	**Pts**	**PIM**	**GP**	**G**	**A**	**Pts**	**PIM**
2014-15	Lac St-Louis Lions	QAAA	42	25	26	51	28	16	8	11	19	12
2015-16	Halifax	QMJHL	63	12	17	29	20	....	....	....	....	....
2016-17	Halifax	QMJHL	64	15	26	41	70	6	2	3	5	6

DYBLENKO, Yaroslav (dih-BLEHN-koh, ta-ROH-slahv) N.J.

Defense. Shoots left. 6'2", 195 lbs. Born, Surgut, Russia, December 28, 1993.

			Regular Season					Playoffs				
Season	**Club**	**League**	**GP**	**G**	**A**	**Pts**	**PIM**	**GP**	**G**	**A**	**Pts**	**PIM**
2012-13	Mytischi Jr.	Russia-Jr.	39	7	12	19	28	8	1	5	6	12
	Mytischi	KHL	11	1	2	3	8	5	0	0	0	2
2013-14	Mytischi Jr.	Russia-Jr.	1	0	1	1	0	....	....	....	....	....
	Mytischi	KHL	38	2	4	6	14	....	....	....	....	....
2014-15	Mytischi	KHL	29	3	9	12	32	....	....	....	....	....
2015-16	Spartak Moscow	KHL	51	2	5	7	45	....	....	....	....	....
2016-17	Spartak Moscow	KHL	51	4	7	11	51	....	....	....	....	....

Signed as a free agent by **New Jersey**, April 20, 2017.

DZIERKALS, Martins (d'zee-KAHLZ, MAHR-tihnsh) TOR

Left wing. Shoots left. 5'11", 169 lbs. Born, Riga, Latvia, April 4, 1997.
(Toronto's 5th pick, 68th overall, in 2015 NHL Draft).

			Regular Season					Playoffs				
Season	**Club**	**League**	**GP**	**G**	**A**	**Pts**	**PIM**	**GP**	**G**	**A**	**Pts**	**PIM**
2012-13	SK Saga U18	LatviaU18	20	28	31	59	16	....	....	....	....	....
2013-14	SK Saga U18	Latvia-Jr.	23	35	33	68	43	....	....	....	....	....
2014-15	Ogre/Saga U18	Latvia	6	5	5	10	12	....	....	....	....	....
	HK Riga Jr.	Russia-Jr.	32	10	18	28	49	3	1	0	1	2
2015-16	Rouyn-Noranda	QMJHL	59	24	43	67	42	20	7	10	17	12
2016-17	Rouyn-Noranda	QMJHL	47	21	28	49	44	6	0	2	2	10

EBERT, Nick (EE-buhrt, NIHK) DAL

Defense. Shoots right. 6', 203 lbs. Born, Livingston, NJ, May 11, 1994.
(Los Angeles' 6th pick, 211th overall, in 2012 NHL Draft).

			Regular Season					Playoffs				
Season	**Club**	**League**	**GP**	**G**	**A**	**Pts**	**PIM**	**GP**	**G**	**A**	**Pts**	**PIM**
2007-08	N. Jersey Bant.	AYHL	25	9	9	18	24	....	....	....	....	....
2008-09	N. Jersey Bant.	AYHL	2	0	0	0	0	....	....	....	....	....
	N. Jersey Mid.	AYHL	26	10	15	25	23	....	....	....	....	....
2009-10	Waterloo	USHL	53	6	12	18	26	3	1	0	1	0
2010-11	Windsor Spitfires	OHL	64	11	30	41	44	18	1	2	3	6
2011-12	Windsor Spitfires	OHL	66	6	33	39	58	4	0	2	2	8
2012-13	Windsor Spitfires	OHL	68	11	27	38	58	....	....	....	....	....
	Ontario Reign	ECHL	4	0	3	3	2	10	2	5	7	0
2013-14	Windsor Spitfires	OHL	27	4	16	20	18	....	....	....	....	....
	Guelph Storm	OHL	38	9	25	34	31	20	5	11	16	8
2014-15	Manchester	AHL	45	8	6	14	18	2	0	0	0	0
2015-16	Ontario Reign	AHL	44	2	10	12	28	4	0	0	0	2
2016-17	Texas Stars	AHL	68	9	16	25	40	....	....	....	....	....

OHL All-Rookie Team (2011)

Traded to **Dallas** by **Los Angeles** for Jack Campbell, June 25, 2016.

EHN, Christoffer (EHN, KRIHS-toh-fuhr) DET

Center. Shoots left. 6'3", 181 lbs. Born, Linkoping, Sweden, April 5, 1996.
(Detroit's 3rd pick, 106th overall, in 2014 NHL Draft).

			Regular Season					Playoffs				
Season	**Club**	**League**	**GP**	**G**	**A**	**Pts**	**PIM**	**GP**	**G**	**A**	**Pts**	**PIM**
2010-11	Skara IK U18	Swe-U18	13	9	11	20	0	3	2	1	3	2
2011-12	Skovde IK U18	Swe-U18	25	7	4	11	16	....	....	....	....	....
	Skovde IK Jr.	Swe-Jr.	14	4	0	4	4	....	....	....	....	....
2012-13	Frolunda U18	Swe-U18	33	9	22	1	16	3	1	0	1	2
2013-14	Frolunda U18	Swe-U18	15	8	10	18	4	5	1	3	4	0
	Frolunda	Sweden	2	0	0	0	0	....	....	....	....	....
	Frolunda Jr.	Swe-Jr.	45	4	7	11	14	3	3	0	3	0
2014-15	Frolunda Jr.	Swe-Jr.	40	12	24	36	61	....	....	....	....	....
	IK Oskarshamn	Sweden-2	4	0	0	0	0	....	....	....	....	....
	Frolunda	Sweden	6	0	0	0	2	10	0	0	0	2
2015-16	Frolunda Jr.	Swe-Jr.	14	9	7	16	0	1	2	0	2	0
	Bofors	Sweden-2	13	2	3	5	8	....	....	....	....	....
	Frolunda	Sweden	37	0	2	2	2	16	0	1	1	0
2016-17	Frolunda	Sweden	52	4	9	13	10	14	1	1	2	4

EISENSCHMID, Markus (IGH-zehn-shmiht, MAHR-kuhs) MTL

Center. Shoots right. 6', 180 lbs. Born, Marktoberdorf, Germany, January 22, 1995.

			Regular Season					Playoffs				
Season	**Club**	**League**	**GP**	**G**	**A**	**Pts**	**PIM**	**GP**	**G**	**A**	**Pts**	**PIM**
2013-14	Medicine Hat	WHL	56	7	16	23	20	18	0	5	5	0
2014-15	Medicine Hat	WHL	50	19	25	44	14	10	2	3	5	8
2015-16	St. John's IceCaps	AHL	28	1	4	5	0	....	....	....	....	....
2016-17	St. John's IceCaps	AHL	39	6	4	10	12	....	....	....	....	....

Signed as a free agent by **Montreal**, January 7, 2017.

EISERMAN, Shane (IGH-zuhr-muhn, SHAYN) OTT

Center/Left wing. Shoots left. 6'2", 224 lbs. Born, Beverly, MA, October 10, 1995.
(Ottawa's 3rd pick, 100th overall, in 2014 NHL Draft).

			Regular Season					Playoffs				
Season	**Club**	**League**	**GP**	**G**	**A**	**Pts**	**PIM**	**GP**	**G**	**A**	**Pts**	**PIM**
2010-11	St. John's Prep	High-MA	25	24	28	52	....	....	....	....	....	....
	Valley Jr. Warriors	Minor-MA	10	9	5	14	6	....	....	....	....	....
2011-12	Cushing	High-MA	30	18	26	44	....	....	....	....	....	....
2012-13	USAHNTDP	USHL	22	4	3	7	29	....	....	....	....	....
	USAHNTDP	U-18	39	7	8	15	18	....	....	....	....	....
2013-14	Dubuque	USHL	53	16	24	40	71	7	0	2	2	10
2014-15	New Hampshire	H-East	35	4	11	15	28	....	....	....	....	....
2015-16	New Hampshire	H-East	33	3	10	13	42	....	....	....	....	....
2016-17	New Hampshire	H-East	27	5	8	13	22	....	....	....	....	....

EJDSELL, Victor (EHJ-suhl, VIHK-tohr) NSH

Right wing. Shoots left. 6'5", 214 lbs. Born, Karlstad, Sweden, June 6, 1995.

			Regular Season					Playoffs				
Season	**Club**	**League**	**GP**	**G**	**A**	**Pts**	**PIM**	**GP**	**G**	**A**	**Pts**	**PIM**
2012-13	Viking HC Hagfors	Sweden-5	13	17	17	34	8	....	....	....	....	....
	Sunne IK	Sweden-4	32	23	36	59	18	2	1	2	3	4
2013-14	Farjestad Jr.	Swe-Jr.	37	17	11	28	36	6	2	2	4	2
2014-15	Farjestad Jr.	Swe-Jr.	37	18	21	39	30	6	2	3	5	8
	Farjestad	Sweden	12	1	0	1	0	....	....	....	....	....
2015-16	Farjestad Jr.	Swe-Jr.	8	5	9	14	4	....	....	....	....	....
	Farjestad	Sweden	9	1	0	1	0	2	0	0	0	0
	Timra IK	Sweden-2	25	4	9	13	12	....	....	....	....	....
2016-17	Bofors	Sweden-2	50	25	32	57	34	10	4	3	7	8

Signed as a free agent by **Nashville**, May 15, 2017.

ELFSTROM, Mattias (EHLF-struhm, muh-TIGH-uhs) DET

Center. Shoots left. 6'3", 194 lbs. Born, Stockholm, Sweden, January 8, 1997.
(Detroit's 7th pick, 197th overall, in 2016 NHL Draft).

			Regular Season					Playoffs				
Season	**Club**	**League**	**GP**	**G**	**A**	**Pts**	**PIM**	**GP**	**G**	**A**	**Pts**	**PIM**
2012-13	Boras HC U18	Swe-U18	31	7	11	18	12	....	....	....	....	....
2013-14	Malmo U18	Swe-U18	36	10	15	25	12	....	....	....	....	....
	Malmo Jr.	Swe-Jr.	....	....	....	....	....	1	0	0	0	0
2014-15	Malmo U18	Swe-U18	20	8	5	13	4	1	0	0	0	0
	Malmo Jr.	Swe-Jr.	32	3	2	5	4	1	0	0	0	0
2015-16	Malmo Jr.	Swe-Jr.	43	11	20	31	16	3	1	3	4	0
	Malmo	Sweden	5	0	0	0	2	....	....	....	....	....
	Tyringe SoSS	Sweden-3	2	1	1	2	0	....	....	....	....	....
2016-17	Malmo Jr.	Swe-Jr.	36	18	25	43	16	2	0	1	1	0
	Malmo	Sweden	4	0	0	0	0	....	....	....	....	....
	IK Pantern Malmo	Sweden-2	22	1	3	4	6	....	....	....	....	....

ELGESTAL, Kevin (EHL-geh-stohl, KEH-vuhn) WSH

Right wing. Shoots right. 6'1", 176 lbs. Born, Gothenburg, Sweden, May 29, 1996.
(Washington's 6th pick, 194th overall, in 2014 NHL Draft).

			Regular Season					Playoffs				
Season	**Club**	**League**	**GP**	**G**	**A**	**Pts**	**PIM**	**GP**	**G**	**A**	**Pts**	**PIM**
2011-12	Frolunda U18	Swe-U18	28	7	3	10	4	....	....	....	....	....
2012-13	Frolunda U18	Swe-U18	35	19	20	39	56	3	0	0	0	14
	Frolunda Jr.	Swe-Jr.	5	1	0	1	2	....	....	....	....	....
2013-14	Frolunda U18	Swe-U18	5	4	5	9	8	5	2	1	3	6
	Frolunda	Sweden	2	0	1	1	0	....	....	....	....	....
	Frolunda Jr.	Swe-Jr.	44	13	22	35	34	3	1	0	1	2
2014-15	Frolunda Jr.	Swe-Jr.	33	10	16	26	65	6	2	5	7	29
2015-16	Frolunda Jr.	Swe-Jr.	16	6	6	12	28	....	....	....	....	....
	Vita Hasten	Sweden-2	27	3	2	5	10	....	....	....	....	....
2016-17	Vita Hasten	Sweden-2	30	4	1	5	29	....	....	....	....	....

ELVENES, Lucas (ehl-VAY-nuhs, LOO-kuhs) VGK

Left wing. Shoots left. 6', 175 lbs. Born, Angelholm, Sweden, August 18, 1999.
(Las Vegas' 8th pick, 127th overall, in 2017 NHL Draft).

			Regular Season					Playoffs				
Season	**Club**	**League**	**GP**	**G**	**A**	**Pts**	**PIM**	**GP**	**G**	**A**	**Pts**	**PIM**
2014-15	Rogle U18	Swe-U18	30	6	14	20	20	....	....	....	....	....
2015-16	Rogle U18	Swe-U18	27	20	23	43	16	....	....	....	....	....
	Rogle Jr.	Swe-Jr.	21	4	10	14	14	7	2	3	5	0
2016-17	Rogle U18	Swe-U18	1	0	0	0	0	3	1	1	2	2
	Rogle Jr.	Swe-Jr.	41	15	30	45	22	3	1	1	2	2
	Rogle	Sweden	12	0	0	0	0	....	....	....	....	....

ELYNUIK, Hudson (ehl-IH-nuhk, HUHD-suhn) CAR

Center. Shoots left. 6'5", 194 lbs. Born, Saskatoon, SK, October 12, 1997.
(Carolina's 5th pick, 74th overall, in 2016 NHL Draft).

			Regular Season					Playoffs				
Season	**Club**	**League**	**GP**	**G**	**A**	**Pts**	**PIM**	**GP**	**G**	**A**	**Pts**	**PIM**
2011-12	Calgary Bronks	AMBHL	30	18	24	42	119	3	1	4	5	6
2012-13	Calgary Flames	AMHL	28	11	14	25	82	2	0	1	1	4
	Camrose Kodiaks	AJHL	2	1	0	1	0	....	....	....	....	....
	Kootenay Ice	WHL	4	0	1	1	4	5	0	0	0	0
2013-14	Kootenay Ice	WHL	31	1	1	2	16	....	....	....	....	....
	Spokane Chiefs	WHL	27	2	7	9	39	4	0	0	0	0
2014-15	Spokane Chiefs	WHL	27	2	6	8	16	6	0	0	0	0
2015-16	Spokane Chiefs	WHL	56	19	25	44	46	6	3	0	3	4
2016-17	Spokane Chiefs	WHL	64	29	44	73	70	....	....	....	....	....

ENGVALL, Pierre (EHNG-vuhl, pee-AIHR) TOR

Left wing. Shoots left. 6'4", 196 lbs. Born, Ljungby, Sweden, May 31, 1996.
(Toronto's 6th pick, 188th overall, in 2014 NHL Draft).

			Regular Season					Playoffs				
Season	**Club**	**League**	**GP**	**G**	**A**	**Pts**	**PIM**	**GP**	**G**	**A**	**Pts**	**PIM**
2011-12	Troja U18	Swe-U18	25	9	4	13	10	....	....	....	....	....
2012-13	Frolunda U18	Swe-U18	30	18	16	34	22	3	0	1	1	2
	Frolunda Jr.	Swe-Jr.	4	2	0	2	0	....	....	....	....	....
2013-14	Frolunda U18	Swe-U18	16	11	25	36	8	5	1	0	1	6
	IF Troja-Ljungby	Sweden-2	1	0	0	0	0	....	....	....	....	....
	Frolunda Jr.	Swe-Jr.	39	17	18	35	42	3	0	1	1	0
2014-15	Frolunda Jr.	Swe-Jr.	38	17	34	51	50	8	5	1	6	10
	IK Oskarshamn	Sweden-2	10	0	0	0	0	....	....	....	....	....
	Frolunda	Sweden	2	0	0	0	0	....	....	....	....	....
2015-16	Mora IK	Sweden-2	55	13	12	25	14	....	....	....	....	....
2016-17	Mora IK	Sweden-2	50	21	19	40	20	9	5	5	10	6
	Toronto Marlies	AHL	....	....	....	....	....	1	0	0	0	0

ENTWISTLE, Mackenzie (EHN-twih-suhl, muh-KEH-zee) ARI

Right wing. Shoots right. 6'3", 174 lbs. Born, Georgetown, ON, July 14, 1999.
(Arizona's 3rd pick, 69th overall, in 2017 NHL Draft).

			Regular Season					Playoffs				
Season	**Club**	**League**	**GP**	**G**	**A**	**Pts**	**PIM**	**GP**	**G**	**A**	**Pts**	**PIM**
2014-15	Tor. Marlboros MM	GTHL	66	22	27	49	24	....	....	....	....	....
2015-16	Hamilton Bulldogs	OHL	60	6	8	14	17	....	....	....	....	....
2016-17	Hamilton Bulldogs	OHL	54	12	13	25	25	7	1	1	2	0

ERKAMPS, Macoy (UHR-kamps, MAH-koi) OTT

Defense. Shoots right. 6', 193 lbs. Born, Delta, BC, February 2, 1995.

			Regular Season					Playoffs				
Season	Club	League	GP	G	A	Pts	PIM	GP	G	A	Pts	PIM
2009-10	South Delta Storm	Minor-BC	STATISTICS NOT AVAILABLE									
	Greater Van.	BCMML	3	0	1	1	0	5	0	0	0	0
2010-11	Greater Van.	BCMML	32	4	15	19	49	6	1	3	4	2
2011-12	Lethbridge	WHL	63	4	16	20	62	....	....	....	....	....
2012-13	Lethbridge	WHL	72	5	30	35	65	....	....	....	....	....
2013-14	Lethbridge	WHL	66	5	26	31	83	....	....	....	....	....
2014-15	Brandon	WHL	68	3	28	31	60	19	2	3	5	21
2015-16	Brandon	WHL	72	13	58	71	64	21	4	10	14	18
2016-17	Binghamton	AHL	11	0	2	2	6	....	....	....	....	....
	Wichita Thunder	ECHL	58	6	19	25	50	....	....	....	....	....

Signed as a free agent by **Ottawa**, April 1, 2016.

ESS, Josh (EHS, JAWSH) CHI

Defense. Shoots left. 5'11", 180 lbs. Born, Burnsville, MN, March 4, 1999.
(Chicago's 9th pick, 215th overall, in 2017 NHL Draft).

			Regular Season					Playoffs				
Season	Club	League	GP	G	A	Pts	PIM	GP	G	A	Pts	PIM
2014-15	Lakeville South	High-MN	24	7	13	20	14	2	0	3	3	2
2015-16	Team Southeast	UMHSEL	21	1	9	10	10	....	....	....	....	....
	Lakeville South	High-MN	25	8	18	26	19	2	1	2	3	4
2016-17	Team Southeast	UMHSEL	18	2	11	13	12	3	0	1	1	4
	Lakeville South	High-MN	23	8	20	28	12	6	5	3	8	6
	Cedar Rapids	USHL	2	0	1	1	4	....	....	....	....	....

• Signed Letter of Intent to attend **University of Wisconsin** (Big Ten) in fall of 2019.

ESTEPHAN, Giorgio (EHS-teh-fan, JOHR-jee-oh)

Center. Shoots right. 6', 197 lbs. Born, Edmonton, AB, February 3, 1997.
(Buffalo's 5th pick, 152nd overall, in 2015 NHL Draft).

			Regular Season					Playoffs				
Season	Club	League	GP	G	A	Pts	PIM	GP	G	A	Pts	PIM
2012-13	SSAC Athletics	AMHL	32	17	30	47	12	14	5	6	11	6
	Lethbridge	WHL	3	1	0	1	0	....	....	....	....	....
2013-14	Lethbridge	WHL	64	12	12	24	18	....	....	....	....	....
2014-15	Lethbridge	WHL	64	23	28	51	18	....	....	....	....	....
2015-16	Lethbridge	WHL	59	30	44	74	12	5	2	2	4	4
	Rochester	AHL	6	1	0	1	0	....	....	....	....	....
2016-17	Lethbridge	WHL	68	35	54	89	39	18	11	13	24	8

EVANS, Jake (EN-vuhnz, JAYK) MTL

Center/Right wing. Shoots right. 6'1", 188 lbs. Born, Toronto, ON, June 2, 1996.
(Montreal's 6th pick, 207th overall, in 2014 NHL Draft).

			Regular Season					Playoffs				
Season	Club	League	GP	G	A	Pts	PIM	GP	G	A	Pts	PIM
2011-12	Mississauga Rebels	GTHL	77	34	55	89	38	....	....	....	....	....
	St. Michael's	ON-Jr.A	5	2	2	4	0	....	....	....	....	....
2012-13	St. Michael's	ON-Jr.A	50	12	32	44	45	24	8	9	17	14
2013-14	St. Michael's	ON-Jr.A	49	16	47	63	79	5	0	5	5	8
2014-15	U. of Notre Dame	H-East	41	7	10	17	22	....	....	....	....	....
2015-16	U. of Notre Dame	H-East	37	8	25	33	29	....	....	....	....	....
2016-17	U. of Notre Dame	H-East	40	13	29	42	47	....	....	....	....	....

EVINGSON, Croix (EE-vihng-suhn, KROY) WPG

Defense. Shoots left. 6'6", 217 lbs. Born, Anchorage, AK, August 28, 1997.
(Winnipeg's 8th pick, 211th overall, in 2017 NHL Draft).

			Regular Season					Playoffs				
Season	Club	League	GP	G	A	Pts	PIM	GP	G	A	Pts	PIM
2012-13	S. Anchorage	High-AK	26	3	6	9	6	....	....	....	....	....
	Alaska All-Stars	Minor-AK	32	5	10	15	16	....	....	....	....	....
2013-14	S. Anchorage	High-AK	24	11	16	27	14	....	....	....	....	....
	Alaska Jr. Aces	Minor-AK	19	3	5	8	31	....	....	....	....	....
	Alaska U16	HPHL	4	0	1	1	4	....	....	....	....	....
2014-15	Cle. Barons U18	T1EHL	32	2	11	13	18	4	1	2	3	16
2015-16	Kenai River	NAHL	38	1	3	4	18	....	....	....	....	....
	Chicago Steel	USHL	16	1	0	1	14	....	....	....	....	....
2016-17	Shreveport	NAHL	59	12	40	52	125	3	1	0	1	0

• Signed Letter of Intent to attend **Union College** (ECAC) in fall of 2017.

EYSSIMONT, Michael (ay-SEE-mawnt, MIGH-kuhl) L.A.

Center. Shoots left. 6', 180 lbs. Born, Littleton, CO, September 9, 1996.
(Los Angeles' 3rd pick, 142nd overall, in 2016 NHL Draft).

			Regular Season					Playoffs				
Season	Club	League	GP	G	A	Pts	PIM	GP	G	A	Pts	PIM
2011-12	Col. T-birds U16	T1EHL	36	10	18	28	26	....	....	....	....	....
2012-13	Col. T-birds U16	T1EHL	40	*48	43	*91	66	4	3	2	5	6
	Fargo Force	USHL	4	0	0	0	0	....	....	....	....	....
2013-14	Fargo Force	USHL	58	14	16	30	64	....	....	....	....	....
2014-15	Fargo Force	USHL	46	17	19	36	46	....	....	....	....	....
	Sioux Falls	USHL	14	5	8	13	16	12	7	9	*16	20
2015-16	St. Cloud State	NCHC	40	14	19	33	20	....	....	....	....	....
2016-17	St. Cloud State	NCHC	36	14	16	30	20	....	....	....	....	....

FABBRO, Dante (FAB-roh, dan-TAY) NSH

Defense. Shoots right. 6', 192 lbs. Born, Coquitlam, BC, June 20, 1998.
(Nashville's 1st pick, 17th overall, in 2016 NHL Draft).

			Regular Season					Playoffs				
Season	Club	League	GP	G	A	Pts	PIM	GP	G	A	Pts	PIM
2012-13	Burnaby W.C.	Minor-BC	58	25	53	78	48	....	....	....	....	....
2013-14	Van. NW Giants	BCMML	38	22	39	61	44	6	2	8	10	12
	Langley Rivermen	BCHL	2	0	0	0	0	....	....	....	....	....
2014-15	Penticton Vees	BCHL	44	4	29	33	16	21	4	11	15	10
2015-16	Penticton Vees	BCHL	45	14	53	67	30	11	0	8	8	2
2016-17	Boston University	H-East	36	6	12	18	16	....	....	....	....	....

FALKOVSKY, Stepan (fal-KAWV-skee, STEH-pan) L.A.

Defense. Shoots left. 6'7", 224 lbs. Born, Minsk, Belarus, December 18, 1996.
(Calgary's 9th pick, 186th overall, in 2016 NHL Draft).

			Regular Season					Playoffs				
Season	Club	League	GP	G	A	Pts	PIM	GP	G	A	Pts	PIM
2013-14	Yunost Minsk Jr.	Russia-Jr.	33	0	3	3	18	....	....	....	....	....
	Yunior Minsk	Belarus-2	13	3	3	6	18	17	4	3	7	22
2014-15	Yunost Minsk	Belarus	1	0	0	0	0	....	....	....	....	....
	Yunost Minsk Jr.	Russia-Jr.	22	4	7	11	2	5	0	1	1	8
	Yunior Minsk	Belarus-2	9	4	4	8	14	....	....	....	....	....
2015-16	Ottawa 67's	OHL	58	9	23	32	35	5	1	2	3	4
2016-17	Adirondack	ECHL	54	21	11	32	37	4	0	2	2	0

Signed as a free agent by **Los Angeles**, July 1, 2017.

FANTENBERG, Oscar (FAN-tehn-nuhrg, AWZ-kuhr) L.A.

Defense. Shoots left. 6', 203 lbs. Born, Ljunby, Sweden, October 7, 1991.

			Regular Season					Playoffs				
Season	Club	League	GP	G	A	Pts	PIM	GP	G	A	Pts	PIM
2009-10	HV 71 Jr.	Swe-Jr.	36	7	13	20	28	2	1	0	1	2
	HV 71 Jonkoping	Sweden	3	0	1	1	0	....	....	....	....	....
	IK Oskarshamn	Sweden-2	4	1	0	1	0	....	....	....	....	....
2010-11	HV 71 Jr.	Swe-Jr.	25	8	7	15	12	5	1	3	4	6
	IF Troja-Ljungby	Sweden-2	8	2	1	3	8	....	....	....	....	....
	HV 71 Jonkoping	Sweden	8	0	0	0	0	2	0	0	0	0
2011-12	HV 71 Jr.	Swe-Jr.	9	1	6	7	8	....	....	....	....	....
	IF Troja-Ljungby	Sweden-2	13	1	3	4	2	....	....	....	....	....
	HV 71 Jonkoping	Sweden	37	3	4	7	6	....	....	....	....	....
2012-13	HV 71 Jonkoping	Sweden	28	3	11	14	12	....	....	....	....	....
2013-14	HV 71 Jonkoping	Sweden	47	2	11	13	14	8	0	2	2	22
2014-15	Frolunda	Sweden	50	2	7	9	38	13	0	5	5	0
2015-16	Frolunda	Sweden	43	4	13	17	14	16	2	8	10	6
2016-17	HK Sochi	KHL	44	3	10	23	22	....	....	....	....	....

Signed as a free agent by **Los Angeles**, May 3, 2017.

FARRANCE, David (FAIR-ehnts, DAY-vihd) NSH

Defense. Shoots left. 5'11", 195 lbs. Born, Rochester, NY, June 23, 1999.
(Nashville's 3rd pick, 92nd overall, in 2017 NHL Draft).

			Regular Season					Playoffs				
Season	Club	League	GP	G	A	Pts	PIM	GP	G	A	Pts	PIM
2013-14	Syracuse Stars U16	USPHL	28	20	12	32	50	....	....	....	....	....
	Victor Blue Devils	High-NY	17	31	11	42	12	4	2	2	2	4
2014-15	Syracuse Stars U16	USPHL	29	27	25	52	28	3	2	0	2	4
	Victor Blue Devils	High-NY	14	24	15	39	9	4	4	3	7	2
2015-16	USAHNTDP	USHL	31	4	9	13	14	....	....	....	....	....
	USAHNTDP	U-17	21	4	6	10	10	....	....	....	....	....
2016-17	USAHNTDP	USHL	25	1	16	17	22	....	....	....	....	....
	USAHNTDP	U-18	39	6	14	20	16	....	....	....	....	....

• Signed Letter of Intent to attend **Boston University** (Hockey East) in fall of 2017.

FAZLEEV, Radel (faz-L'YAY-ehv, rah-DEHL) PHI

Left wing. Shoots left. 6'1", 192 lbs. Born, Kazan, Russia, January 7, 1996.
(Philadelphia's 5th pick, 168th overall, in 2014 NHL Draft).

			Regular Season					Playoffs				
Season	Club	League	GP	G	A	Pts	PIM	GP	G	A	Pts	PIM
2012-13	Bars Kazan Jr.	Russia-Jr.	9	0	0	0	0	....	....	....	....	....
	Irbis Kazan Jr.	Rus.-Jr. B	23	7	10	17	8	5	1	2	3	4
2013-14	Calgary Hitmen	WHL	38	5	20	25	12	6	3	4	7	0
2014-15	Calgary Hitmen	WHL	71	18	33	51	36	17	4	10	14	6
2015-16	Calgary Hitmen	WHL	59	19	52	71	46	5	0	0	0	6
2016-17	Lehigh Valley	AHL	65	6	10	16	26	....	....	....	....	....
	Reading Royals	ECHL	1	0	0	0	0	....	....	....	....	....

FERRARO, Mario (fuh-RAHR-oh, ma-REE-oh) S.J.

Defense. Shoots left. 5'11", 185 lbs. Born, Toronto, ON, September 17, 1998.
(San Jose's 2nd pick, 49th overall, in 2017 NHL Draft).

			Regular Season					Playoffs				
Season	Club	League	GP	G	A	Pts	PIM	GP	G	A	Pts	PIM
2013-14	Don Mills MM	GTHL	33	6	5	11	8	2	0	0	0	0
	Don Mills Midget	GTHL	1	0	0	0	0	....	....	....	....	....
2014-15	Toronto Patriots	ON-Jr.A	43	1	11	12	28	22	1	3	4	16
2015-16	Toronto Patriots	ON-Jr.A	51	6	34	40	46	....	....	....	....	....
2016-17	Des Moines	USHL	60	8	33	41	42	3	0	0	0	0

• Signed Letter of Intent to attend **University of Massachusetts-Lowell** (Hockey East) in fall of 2017.

FIDLER, Miguel (FIHD-luhr, mi-G'WEHL) FLA

Left wing. Shoots left. 6'1", 200 lbs. Born, Edina, MN, March 17, 1996.
(Florida's 5th pick, 143rd overall, in 2014 NHL Draft).

			Regular Season					Playoffs				
Season	Club	League	GP	G	A	Pts	PIM	GP	G	A	Pts	PIM
2011-12	Edina Hornets	High-MN	25	2	9	11	42	5	4	3	7	0
2012-13	Metro Southwest	MEPDL	....	4	5	9	....	....	....	....	....	....
	Edina Hornets	High-MN	23	5	6	11	28	6	3	1	4	4
2013-14	Team Southwest	UMHSEL	20	5	4	9	32	3	3	4	7	10
	Edina Hornets	High-MN	25	16	25	41	24	5	4	5	9	4
2014-15	Lincoln Stars	USHL	45	5	16	21	55	....	....	....	....	....
	Madison Capitols	USHL	15	2	4	6	8	....	....	....	....	....
2015-16	Ohio State	Big Ten	20	3	4	7	14	....	....	....	....	....
2016-17	Ohio State	Big Ten	34	4	6	10	26	....	....	....	....	....

FIEGL, Jared (FEE-guhl, JAIR-uhd) ARI

Left wing. Shoots left. 6'1", 217 lbs. Born, Parker, CO, January 23, 1996.
(Arizona's 8th pick, 191st overall, in 2014 NHL Draft).

			Regular Season					Playoffs				
Season	Club	League	GP	G	A	Pts	PIM	GP	G	A	Pts	PIM
2010-11	Col. Rampage	T1EHL	36	6	0	6	14	....	....	....	....	....
2011-12	Col. Rampage	T1EHL	30	11	11	22	28	....	....	....	....	....
	U.S. Youth Oly.	Other	6	1	1	2	8	....	....	....	....	....
2012-13	USAHNTDP	USHL	38	4	4	8	29	....	....	....	....	....
	USAHNTDP	U-17	18	3	5	8	8	....	....	....	....	....
2013-14	USAHNTDP	USHL	16	0	0	0	10	....	....	....	....	....
	USAHNTDP	U-18	29	2	4	6	16	....	....	....	....	....
2014-15	Cornell Big Red	ECAC	26	1	0	1	39	....	....	....	....	....
2015-16	Cornell Big Red	ECAC	30	1	1	2	18	....	....	....	....	....
2016-17	Cornell Big Red	ECAC	35	2	4	6	32	....	....	....	....	....

FILIPE, Matt (feh-LEE-pay, MAT) CAR

Left wing. Shoots left. 6'2", 198 lbs. Born, Newton, MA, December 31, 1997.
(Carolina's 4th pick, 67th overall, in 2016 NHL Draft).

			Regular Season					Playoffs				
Season	Club	League	GP	G	A	Pts	PIM	GP	G	A	Pts	PIM
2012-13	Malden Catholic	High-MA	....	4	11	15	....	....	....	....	....	....
2013-14	Malden Catholic	High-MA	....	18	13	31	....	....	....	....	....	....
2014-15	Malden Catholic	High-MA	....	14	10	24	....	....	....	....	....	....
2015-16	Cedar Rapids	USHL	56	19	17	36	99	5	1	2	3	15
2016-17	Northeastern	H-East	38	9	12	21	36	....	....	....	....	....

FINKELSTEIN, Ben (fihn-KEHL-stighn, BEHN) FLA

Defense. Shoots right. 5'9", 180 lbs. Born, Burlington, VT, October 1, 1997.
(Florida's 7th pick, 195th overall, in 2016 NHL Draft).

			Regular Season					Playoffs				
Season	Club	League	GP	G	A	Pts	PIM	GP	G	A	Pts	PIM
2013-14	Bruins Selects U18	Minor-MA	8	1	3	4	0	....	....	....	....	....
	Kimball Union	High-NH	37	7	18	25	....	....	....	....	....	....
2014-15	Kimball Union	High-NH	28	7	19	26	....	....	....	....	....	....
2015-16	Bruins Selects U18	Minor-MA	11	8	*16	24	2	....	....	....	....	....
	Kimball Union	High-NH	35	24	46	70	....	....	....	....	....	....
2016-17	St. Lawrence	ECAC	37	5	18	23	14	....	....	....	....	....

FIORE, Giovanni (FEE-ohr-ay, GEE-oh-VAHN-ee) ANA

Left wing. Shoots left. 6'1", 195 lbs. Born, Laval, QC, August 13, 1996.

			Regular Season					Playoffs				
Season	Club	League	GP	G	A	Pts	PIM	GP	G	A	Pts	PIM
2011-12	Laval Midget	Minor-QC	29	22	28	50	46	2	1	0	1	2
	Laval-Montreal	QAAA	12	3	3	6	4	....	....	....	....	....
2012-13	Laval-Montreal	QAAA	30	18	18	36	14	....	....	....	....	....
	Acadie-Bathurst	QMJHL	3	0	1	1	0	....	....	....	....	....
	Drummondville	QMJHL	26	1	1	2	6	3	0	0	0	0
2013-14	Drummondville	QMJHL	34	4	8	12	19	....	....	....	....	....
	Shawinigan	QMJHL	27	6	7	13	4	4	0	0	0	2
2014-15	Shawinigan	QMJHL	65	23	21	44	46	7	2	3	5	4
2015-16	Shawinigan	QMJHL	39	13	17	30	28	....	....	....	....	....
	Cape Breton	QMJHL	26	15	17	32	8	13	8	7	15	8
2016-17	Cape Breton	QMJHL	61	*52	38	90	42	11	8	4	12	10

QMJHL First All-Star Team (2017)

Signed as a free agent by **Anaheim**, April 18, 2017.

FISCHER, Zach (FIH-shuhr, ZAK) CGY

Right wing. Shoots right. 6'1", 196 lbs. Born, Lloydminster, AB, July 19, 1997.
(Calgary's 3rd pick, 140th overall, in 2017 NHL Draft).

			Regular Season					Playoffs				
Season	Club	League	GP	G	A	Pts	PIM	GP	G	A	Pts	PIM
2012-13	Lloydminster MM	Minor-AB	32	19	15	34	46	....	....	....	....	....
2013-14	Lloydminster	AMHL	34	14	28	42	32	12	6	8	14	6
2014-15	Medicine Hat	WHL	54	4	6	10	23	....	....	....	....	....
2015-16	Medicine Hat	WHL	35	8	5	13	15	....	....	....	....	....
2016-17	Medicine Hat	WHL	62	34	29	63	145	11	7	3	10	24

FITZGERALD, Casey (fihtz-JAIR-uhld, KAY-see) BUF

Defense. Shoots right. 5'11", 177 lbs. Born, Boca Raton, FL, February 25, 1997.
(Buffalo's 4th pick, 86th overall, in 2016 NHL Draft).

			Regular Season					Playoffs				
Season	Club	League	GP	G	A	Pts	PIM	GP	G	A	Pts	PIM
2011-12	Malden Catholic	High-MA	21	2	16	18	....	....	....	....	....	....
2012-13	Valley Jr. U16	Minor-MA	12	4	5	9	0	....	....	....	....	....
	Malden Catholic	High-MA	25	6	17	23	12	....	....	....	....	....
2013-14	USAHNTDP	USHL	33	2	1	3	18	....	....	....	....	....
	USAHNTDP	U-17	19	1	7	8	25	....	....	....	....	....
2014-15	USAHNTDP	USHL	22	3	5	8	53	....	....	....	....	....
	USAHNTDP	U-18	35	6	11	17	14	....	....	....	....	....
2015-16	Boston College	H-East	39	4	23	27	46	....	....	....	....	....
2016-17	Boston College	H-East	37	5	17	22	46	....	....	....	....	....

Hockey East All-Rookie Team (2016)

FITZGERALD, Cavan (fihtz-JAIR-uhld, KA-vahn) S.J.

Defense. Shoots left. 6'1", 186 lbs. Born, Boston, MA, August 23, 1996.

			Regular Season					Playoffs				
Season	Club	League	GP	G	A	Pts	PIM	GP	G	A	Pts	PIM
2011-12	Cape Breton	NSMHL	35	5	12	17	24	3	1	1	2	4
2012-13	Cape Breton	NSMHL	35	4	21	25	30	5	0	3	3	4
2013-14	Summerside	MJrHL	47	9	24	33	46	5	3	4	7	15
	Halifax	QMJHL	3	1	0	1	0	4	0	0	0	0
2014-15	Halifax	QMJHL	40	4	27	31	17	14	0	10	10	2
2015-16	Halifax	QMJHL	32	10	16	26	25	....	....	....	....	....
	Shawinigan	QMJHL	28	5	14	19	21	21	3	17	20	8
2016-17	Shawinigan	QMJHL	47	15	25	40	20	....	....	....	....	....

Signed as a free agent by **San Jose**, October 7, 2015.

FITZGERALD, Ryan (fihtz-JAIR-uhld, RIGH-uhn) BOS

Center. Shoots right. 5'9", 172 lbs. Born, Boca Raton, FL, October 19, 1994.
(Boston's 3rd pick, 120th overall, in 2013 NHL Draft).

			Regular Season					Playoffs				
Season	Club	League	GP	G	A	Pts	PIM	GP	G	A	Pts	PIM
2009-10	Malden Catholic	High-MA	24	17	30	47	....	....	....	....	....	....
2010-11	Malden Catholic	High-MA	24	28	44	72	....	....	....	....	....	....
2011-12	Malden Catholic	High-MA	19	31	20	51	....	....	....	....	....	....
2012-13	Valley Junior	EJHL	26	14	16	30	50	6	3	3	6	8
	USAHNTDP	U-18	5	1	0	1	8	....	....	....	....	....
2013-14	Boston College	H-East	40	13	16	29	22	....	....	....	....	....
2014-15	Boston College	H-East	38	17	8	25	54	....	....	....	....	....
2015-16	Boston College	H-East	40	*24	23	47	47	....	....	....	....	....
2016-17	Boston College	H-East	34	12	19	31	56	....	....	....	....	....
	Providence Bruins	AHL	8	0	2	2	2	13	1	4	5	6

Hockey East First All-Star Team (2016) • NCAA East Second All-American Team (2016)

FLEURY, Cale (fluh-REE, KAYL) MTL

Defense. Shoots right. 6'2", 202 lbs. Born, Regina, SK, November 19, 1998.
(Montreal's 5th pick, 87th overall, in 2017 NHL Draft).

			Regular Season					Playoffs				
Season	Club	League	GP	G	A	Pts	PIM	GP	G	A	Pts	PIM
2013-14	Notre Dame	SMHL	44	7	22	29	50	....	....	....	....	....
2014-15	Kootenay Ice	WHL	70	1	12	13	8	7	0	1	1	0
2015-16	Kootenay Ice	WHL	61	8	17	25	45	....	....	....	....	....
2016-17	Kootenay Ice	WHL	70	11	27	38	67	....	....	....	....	....

FLEURY, Haydn (FLUH-ree, HAY-duhn) CAR

Defense. Shoots left. 6'3", 221 lbs. Born, Carlyle, SK, July 8, 1996.
(Carolina's 1st pick, 7th overall, in 2014 NHL Draft).

			Regular Season					Playoffs				
Season	Club	League	GP	G	A	Pts	PIM	GP	G	A	Pts	PIM
2009-10	Cam. Red Wings	AMBHL	33	1	8	9	36	....	....	....	....	....
2010-11	Notre Dame	SMBHL	21	7	19	26	30	....	....	....	....	....
	Notre Dame Argos	SMHL	3	0	1	1	0	....	....	....	....	....
2011-12	Notre Dame Argos	SMHL	39	6	15	21	60	8	1	4	5	8
	Red Deer Rebels	WHL	4	0	0	0	0	....	....	....	....	....
2012-13	Red Deer Rebels	WHL	66	4	15	19	21	9	0	2	2	4
2013-14	Red Deer Rebels	WHL	70	8	38	46	46	....	....	....	....	....
2014-15	Red Deer Rebels	WHL	63	6	22	28	63	5	1	1	2	2
	Charlotte	AHL	1	1	0	1	0	....	....	....	....	....
2015-16	Red Deer Rebels	WHL	56	12	29	41	50	17	4	5	9	20
2016-17	Charlotte	AHL	69	7	19	26	8	5	0	0	0	0

FLORENTINO, Anthony (flohr-ehn-TEE-noh, AN-thuh-nee)

Defense. Shoots right. 6'1", 216 lbs. Born, Boston, MA, January 30, 1995.
(Buffalo's 9th pick, 143rd overall, in 2013 NHL Draft).

			Regular Season					Playoffs				
Season	Club	League	GP	G	A	Pts	PIM	GP	G	A	Pts	PIM
2010-11	South Shore Kings	EmJHL	7	0	1	1	26	....	....	....	....	....
	South Kent School	High-CT	24	5	10	15	....	....	....	....	....	....
2011-12	South Kent School	High-CT	36	5	14	19	....	....	....	....	....	....
	USAHNTDP	U-17	3	0	2	2	4	....	....	....	....	....
2012-13	Selects Academy	Minor-CT	62	21	32	53	68	....	....	....	....	....
2013-14	Providence College	H-East	30	5	6	11	16	....	....	....	....	....
2014-15	Providence College	H-East	40	3	12	15	25	....	....	....	....	....
2015-16	Providence College	H-East	31	5	7	12	37	....	....	....	....	....
2016-17	Providence College	H-East	30	9	7	16	20	....	....	....	....	....
	Rochester	AHL	5	0	0	0	0	....	....	....	....	....

NCAA Championship All-Tournament Team (2015)

FOEGELE, Warren (FOH-GEHL, WAHR-ihn) CAR

Left wing. Shoots left. 6'2", 192 lbs. Born, Markham, ON, April 1, 1996.
(Carolina's 3rd pick, 67th overall, in 2014 NHL Draft).

			Regular Season					Playoffs				
Season	Club	League	GP	G	A	Pts	PIM	GP	G	A	Pts	PIM
2011-12	Markham Waxers	Minor-ON	28	10	8	18	38	....	....	....	....	....
	St. Andrew's	MPHL	5	0	1	1	0	2	0	0	0	0
	St. Andrew's	CISAA	1	0	0	0	0	....	....	....	....	....
2012-13	St. Andrew's	MPHL	13	7	10	*17	12	3	2	*5	*7	2
	St. Andrew's	CISAA	15	9	10	19	20	5	3	2	5	6
	St. Andrew's	High-ON	22	16	9	25	8	....	....	....	....	....
2013-14	St. Andrew's	MPHL	13	12	*17	*29	14	3	*6	5	*11	2
	St. Andrew's	CISAA	14	17	6	23	15	5	5	4	9	10
	St. Andrew's	High-ON	17	18	17	35	26	....	....	....	....	....
2014-15	New Hampshire	H-East	34	5	11	16	26	....	....	....	....	....
2015-16	New Hampshire	H-East	5	0	1	1	4	....	....	....	....	....
	Kingston	OHL	52	13	35	48	44	9	8	2	10	12
2016-17	Kingston	OHL	28	11	20	31	20	....	....	....	....	....
	Erie Otters	OHL	33	16	16	32	20	22	13	13	26	25

FOGARTY, Steven (FOH-guhr-tee, STEE-vehn) NYR

Center. Shoots right. 6'3", 206 lbs. Born, Chambersburg, PA, April 19, 1993.
(NY Rangers' 2nd pick, 72nd overall, in 2011 NHL Draft).

			Regular Season					Playoffs				
Season	Club	League	GP	G	A	Pts	PIM	GP	G	A	Pts	PIM
2009-10	Edina Hornets	High-MN	25	18	12	30	4	6	3	7	10	2
2010-11	Team Southwest	UMHSEL	19	10	4	14	10	3	2	5	7	4
	Edina Hornets	High-MN	24	23	17	40	12	6	3	8	11	0
	Chicago Steel	USHL	6	2	0	2	2	....	....	....	....	....
2011-12	Penticton Vees	BCHL	60	33	48	81	32	15	4	4	8	12
2012-13	U. of Notre Dame	CCHA	41	5	5	10	4	....	....	....	....	....
2013-14	U. of Notre Dame	H-East	33	3	8	11	10	....	....	....	....	....
2014-15	U. of Notre Dame	H-East	39	9	12	21	6	....	....	....	....	....
2015-16	U. of Notre Dame	H-East	37	10	13	23	26	....	....	....	....	....
	Hartford Wolf Pack	AHL	3	0	1	1	0	....	....	....	....	....
2016-17	Hartford Wolf Pack	AHL	66	7	13	20	21	....	....	....	....	....

FOLEY, Erik (FOH-lee, AIR-ihk) WPG

Left wing. Shoots left. 6', 195 lbs. Born, Mansfield, MA, June 30, 1997.
(Winnipeg's 4th pick, 78th overall, in 2015 NHL Draft).

			Regular Season					Playoffs				
Season	Club	League	GP	G	A	Pts	PIM	GP	G	A	Pts	PIM
2012-13	Neponset Valley	Minor-MA	12	4	10	14	2	....	....	....	....	....
	Tabor Academy	High-MA	27	9	19	28	....	....	....	....	....	....
2013-14	Cape Cod Whalers	Minor-MA	10	8	4	12	2	....	....	....	....	....
	Tabor Academy	High-MA	28	17	20	37	....	....	....	....	....	....
	Cedar Rapids	USHL	1	0	0	0	2	2	0	0	0	0
2014-15	Cedar Rapids	USHL	55	27	27	54	80	3	1	0	1	6
2015-16	Providence College	H-East	36	7	12	19	20	....	....	....	....	....
2016-17	Providence College	H-East	36	15	19	34	26	....	....	....	....	....

USHL All-Rookie Team (2015)

FONTAINE, Gabriel (fawn-TAYN, gab-REE-ehl) NYR

Center. Shoots left. 6'1", 191 lbs. Born, Sherbrooke, QC, April 30, 1997.
(NY Rangers' 4th pick, 171st overall, in 2016 NHL Draft).

			Regular Season					Playoffs				
Season	Club	League	GP	G	A	Pts	PIM	GP	G	A	Pts	PIM
2012-13	Magog	QAAA	37	10	21	31	14	....	....	....	....	....
2013-14	Magog	QAAA	22	7	16	23	10	11	4	6	10	12
	Sherbrooke	QMJHL	17	0	1	1	6	....	....	....	....	....
2014-15	Sherbrooke	QMJHL	55	4	15	19	32	6	0	0	0	4
2015-16	Rouyn-Noranda	QMJHL	63	20	25	45	43	20	5	11	16	24
2016-17	Rouyn-Noranda	QMJHL	59	23	29	52	37	13	6	5	11	8

FOO, Parker (FOO, PAHR-kuhr) CHI

Left wing. Shoots left. 6'1", 170 lbs. Born, Edmonton, AB, December 9, 1998.
(Chicago's 7th pick, 144th overall, in 2017 NHL Draft).

			Regular Season					Playoffs				
Season	Club	League	GP	G	A	Pts	PIM	GP	G	A	Pts	PIM
2013-14	CAC Minor Midget	Minor-AB	28	18	16	34	6	5	3	3	6	0
	CAC Canadians	AMHL	3	1	2	3	0	....	....	....	....	....
2014-15	CAC Canadians	AMHL	34	15	15	30	18	12	4	4	8	10
	Bonnyville Pontiacs	AJHL	1	0	0	0	0	....	....	....	....	....
2015-16	Bonnyville Pontiacs	AJHL	5	0	1	1	0	....	....	....	....	....
	Brooks Bandits	AJHL	44	8	19	27	56	13	4	2	6	14
2016-17	Brooks Bandits	AJHL	60	34	32	66	58	13	10	10	20	4

• Signed Letter of Intent to attend **Union College** (ECAC) in fall of 2017.

FOO, Spencer (FOO, SPEHN-suhr) CGY

Right wing. Shoots right. 6', 185 lbs. Born, Edmonton, AB, January 1, 1994.

			Regular Season					Playoffs				
Season	Club	League	GP	G	A	Pts	PIM	GP	G	A	Pts	PIM
2009-10	CAC Canadians	AMMHL	30	17	26	43	41	....	....	....	....	....
	CAC Midget-AA	Minor-AB	2	0	1	1	0	....	....	....	....	....
2010-11	CAC Canadians	AMHL	34	6	21	27	30	....	....	....	....	....
2011-12	CAC Canadians	AMHL	34	10	15	25	34	....	....	....	....	....
2012-13	Bonnyville Pontiacs	AJHL	55	13	17	30	59	9	1	1	2	2
2013-14	Bonnyville Pontiacs	AJHL	60	40	27	67	67	3	4	1	5	2
2014-15	Union College	ECAC	39	11	14	25	24	....	....	....	....	....
2015-16	Union College	ECAC	36	12	13	25	14	....	....	....	....	....
2016-17	Union College	ECAC	38	26	*36	62	24	....	....	....	....	....

ECAC All-Rookie Team (2015) • ECAC First All-Team (2017) • NCAA East First All-American Team (2017)

Signed as a free agent by **Calgary**, June 27, 2017.

FOOTE, Cal (FUT, KAL) T.B.

Defense. Shoots right. 6'4", 215 lbs. Born, Denver, CO, December 13, 1998.
(Tampa Bay's 1st pick, 14th overall, in 2017 NHL Draft).

			Regular Season					Playoffs				
Season	Club	League	GP	G	A	Pts	PIM	GP	G	A	Pts	PIM
2013-14	Col. T-birds U16	T1EHL	33	2	12	14	19	....	....	....	....	....
2014-15	Col. T-birds U16	T1EHL	23	4	11	15	42	4	3	2	5	2
	Omaha Lancers	USHL	2	0	1	1	0	....	....	....	....	....
2015-16	Kelowna Rockets	WHL	71	8	28	36	36	18	1	8	9	12
2016-17	Kelowna Rockets	WHL	71	6	51	57	41	14	1	6	7	24

FORMENTON, Alex (fohr-MEHN-tuhn, AL-ehx) OTT

Left wing. Shoots left. 6'2", 165 lbs. Born, Barrie, ON, September 13, 1999.
(Ottawa's 2nd pick, 47th overall, in 2017 NHL Draft).

			Regular Season					Playoffs				
Season	Club	League	GP	G	A	Pts	PIM	GP	G	A	Pts	PIM
2014-15	Miss. Rebels MM	GTHL	65	27	28	55	92	....	....	....	....	....
2015-16	Aurora Tigers	ON-Jr.A	54	13	13	26	66	5	2	0	2	0
2016-17	London Knights	OHL	65	16	18	34	50	14	0	0	0	6

FORTIN, Alexandre (for-TAYN, al-ehx-AHN-druh) CHI

Left wing. Shoots left. 6', 180 lbs. Born, Laval, QC, February 25, 1997.

			Regular Season					Playoffs				
Season	Club	League	GP	G	A	Pts	PIM	GP	G	A	Pts	PIM
2012-13	Esther-Blondin	QAAA	41	10	14	24	8	3	0	0	0	4
2013-14	Esther-Blondin	QAAA	28	20	17	37	20	19	*14	21	35	2
2014-15	Rouyn-Noranda	QMJHL	67	11	29	40	10	6	4	1	5	0
2015-16	Rouyn-Noranda	QMJHL	54	19	24	43	17	20	4	3	7	2
2016-17	Rouyn-Noranda	QMJHL	52	22	30	52	14	13	6	10	16	4

Signed as a free agent by **Chicago**, September 25, 2016.

FOURNIER, Stefan (FOHR-n'yay, STEH-fan)

Right wing. Shoots right. 6'3", 224 lbs. Born, Dorval, QC, April 30, 1992.

			Regular Season					Playoffs				
Season	Club	League	GP	G	A	Pts	PIM	GP	G	A	Pts	PIM
2007-08	Lac St-Louis Lions	QAAA	19	10	17	27	18	....	....	....	....	....
2008-09	Acadie-Bathurst	QMJHL	40	2	1	3	18	....	....	....	....	....
2009-10	Lewiston	QMJHL	52	12	13	25	54	4	1	2	3	2
2010-11	Lewiston	QMJHL	67	20	27	47	69	15	4	6	10	22
2011-12	Victoriaville Tigres	QMJHL	64	32	33	65	96	4	1	1	2	2
2012-13	Halifax	QMJHL	66	35	37	72	100	17	*16	13	29	31
2013-14	Hamilton Bulldogs	AHL	40	2	5	7	86	....	....	....	....	....
	Wheeling Nailers	ECHL	1	0	0	0	0	....	....	....	....	....
2014-15	Hamilton Bulldogs	AHL	14	0	1	1	14	....	....	....	....	....
	Wheeling Nailers	ECHL	12	0	5	5	22	....	....	....	....	....
2015-16	St. John's IceCaps	AHL	24	5	2	7	65	....	....	....	....	....
	Brampton Beast	ECHL	5	0	1	1	19	....	....	....	....	....
	Springfield Falcons	AHL	32	2	2	4	78	....	....	....	....	....
2016-17	Tucson	AHL	29	2	2	4	95	....	....	....	....	....
	Syracuse Crunch	AHL	3	0	0	0	2	....	....	....	....	....
	Kalamazoo Wings	ECHL	2	1	0	1	0	....	....	....	....	....

Signed as a free agent by **Montreal**, July 6, 2013. Traded to **Arizona** by **Montreal** with Jarred Tinordi for Victor Bartley and John Scott, January 15, 2016. Traded to **Tampa Bay** by **Arizona** for Jeremy Morin, February 25, 2017.

FOX, Adam (FAWX, A-duhm) CGY

Defense. Shoots right. 5'11", 181 lbs. Born, Jericho, NY, February 17, 1998.
(Calgary's 4th pick, 66th overall, in 2016 NHL Draft).

			Regular Season					Playoffs				
Season	Club	League	GP	G	A	Pts	PIM	GP	G	A	Pts	PIM
2013-14	Long Island U16	AYHL	22	14	37	51	38	2	1	4	0	....
2014-15	USAHNTDP	USHL	34	3	14	17	26	....	....	....	....	....
	USAHNTDP	U-17	20	1	9	10	14	....	....	....	....	....
2015-16	USAHNTDP	USHL	25	5	17	22	2	....	....	....	....	....
	USAHNTDP	U-18	39	4	33	37	10	....	....	....	....	....
2016-17	Harvard Crimson	ECAC	35	6	34	40	6	....	....	....	....	....

ECAC All-Rookie Team (2017) • ECAC First All-Team (2017) • NCAA East First All-American Team (2017)

FRANKLIN, C.J. (FRANK-lihn, SEE-JAY) WPG

Left wing. Shoots left. 5'11", 190 lbs. Born, Forest Lake, MN, March 17, 1994.
(Winnipeg's 5th pick, 129th overall, in 2014 NHL Draft).

			Regular Season					Playoffs				
Season	Club	League	GP	G	A	Pts	PIM	GP	G	A	Pts	PIM
2009-10	Forest Lake	High-MN	25	18	19	37	18	2	1	2	3	0
2010-11	Forest Lake	High-MN	25	23	10	33	22	1	0	0	0	0
2011-12	Team Northeast	UMHSEL	20	7	5	12	22	3	2	3	5	0
	Forest Lake	High-MN	25	15	23	38	26	2	0	4	4	2
2012-13	Sioux Falls	USHL	62	32	28	60	60	10	1	3	4	7
2013-14	Sioux Falls	USHL	53	22	29	51	43	3	2	1	3	4
2014-15	Minnesota State	WCHA	37	9	19	28	21	....	....	....	....	....
2015-16	Minnesota State	WCHA	41	14	11	25	43	....	....	....	....	....
2016-17	Minnesota State	WCHA	39	12	19	31	38	....	....	....	....	....

WCHA All-Rookie Team (2015) • WCHA Second All-Star Team (2017)

FRASER, Cole (FRAY-zuhr, KOHL) DET

Defense. Shoots right. 6'2", 195 lbs. Born, Ottawa, ON, August 23, 1999.
(Detroit's 7th pick, 131st overall, in 2017 NHL Draft).

			Regular Season					Playoffs				
Season	Club	League	GP	G	A	Pts	PIM	GP	G	A	Pts	PIM
2014-15	Ott. V. Titans MM	Minor-ON	29	7	11	18	62	10	4	6	10	22
	Ott. V. Titans Mid.	Minor-ON	2	1	0	1	8	3	1	0	1	8
2015-16	Peterborough	OHL	50	0	3	3	51	....	....	....	....	....
2016-17	Peterborough	OHL	61	6	13	19	82	12	0	0	0	20

FREDERIC, Trent (FREHD-rihk, TREHNT) BOS

Center. Shoots left. 6'3", 211 lbs. Born, St.Louis, MO, February 11, 1998.
(Boston's 2nd pick, 29th overall, in 2016 NHL Draft).

			Regular Season					Playoffs				
Season	Club	League	GP	G	A	Pts	PIM	GP	G	A	Pts	PIM
2013-14	St.L. AAA Blues	T1EHL	37	11	19	30	30	....	....	....	....	....
2014-15	USAHNTDP	USHL	35	3	2	5	30	....	....	....	....	....
	USAHNTDP	U-17	20	2	7	9	12	....	....	....	....	....
2015-16	USAHNTDP	USHL	23	4	10	14	23	....	....	....	....	....
	USAHNTDP	U-18	38	16	10	26	38	....	....	....	....	....
2016-17	U. of Wisconsin	Big Ten	30	15	18	33	32	....	....	....	....	....

FRIEDMAN, Mark (FREED-muhn, MAHRK) PHI

Defense. Shoots right. 5'11", 194 lbs. Born, Toronto, ON, December 25, 1995.
(Philadelphia's 3rd pick, 86th overall, in 2014 NHL Draft).

			Regular Season					Playoffs				
Season	Club	League	GP	G	A	Pts	PIM	GP	G	A	Pts	PIM
2010-11	Don Mills Flyers	GTHL	37	7	5	12	40	....	....	....	....	....
	North York	ON-Jr.A	2	0	0	0	0	....	....	....	....	....
2011-12	North York	ON-Jr.A	48	9	18	27	44	4	1	3	4	0
2012-13	Waterloo	USHL	64	8	27	35	44	5	2	3	5	2
2013-14	Waterloo	USHL	51	10	30	40	30	12	0	7	7	4
2014-15	Bowling Green	WCHA	39	2	17	19	75	....	....	....	....	....
2015-16	Bowling Green	WCHA	42	6	17	23	40	....	....	....	....	....
2016-17	Bowling Green	WCHA	40	8	18	26	28	....	....	....	....	....
	Lehigh Valley	AHL	1	0	1	1	0	....	....	....	....	....

USHL Second All-Star Team (2014) • WCHA All-Rookie Team (2015) • WCHA First All-Star Team (2016)

FRIEND, Jacob (FREHND, JAY-kuhb) L.A.

Defense. Shoots left. 6'1", 182 lbs. Born, Bowmanville, ON, July 28, 1997.
(Los Angeles' 4th pick, 202nd overall, in 2016 NHL Draft).

			Regular Season					Playoffs				
Season	Club	League	GP	G	A	Pts	PIM	GP	G	A	Pts	PIM
2012-13	Clarington Toros	Minor-ON	32	2	2	4	36	....	....	....	....	....
2013-14	Ajax-Pick. Midget	Minor-ON	30	1	7	8	28	6	0	1	1	0
2014-15	Cobourg Cougars	ON-Jr.A	47	1	6	7	55	10	0	0	0	6
	Owen Sound	OHL	8	0	0	0	6	....	....	....	....	....
2015-16	Owen Sound	OHL	54	4	17	21	106	6	0	0	0	13
2016-17	Owen Sound	OHL	43	2	10	12	65	16	2	5	7	14

FRITZ, Tanner (FRIHTZ, TA-nuhr) NYI

Right wing. Shoots right. 5'11", 192 lbs. Born, Grande Prairie, AB, August 20, 1991.

			Regular Season					Playoffs				
Season	Club	League	GP	G	A	Pts	PIM	GP	G	A	Pts	PIM
2006-07	Grand Prairie Mgt	Minor-AB	36	23	30	53	20	....	....	....	....	....
2007-08	Grande Prairie	AJHL	28	4	4	8	14	12	0	1	1	4
2008-09	Grande Prairie	AJHL	57	19	24	43	30	19	4	8	12	4
2009-10	Grande Prairie	AJHL	54	27	27	54	62	9	1	5	6	2
2010-11	Grande Prairie	AJHL	60	31	43	74	29	5	3	3	6	4
2011-12	Ohio State	CCHA	34	6	8	14	21	....	....	....	....	....
2012-13	Ohio State	CCHA	40	11	*26	37	12	....	....	....	....	....
2013-14	Ohio State	Big Ten	32	8	24	32	8	....	....	....	....	....
2014-15	Ohio State	Big Ten	36	11	16	27	6	....	....	....	....	....
2015-16	Missouri Mavericks	ECHL	43	10	23	33	10	....	....	....	....	....
	Bridgeport	AHL	19	2	10	12	0	3	0	2	2	0
2016-17	Bridgeport	AHL	63	19	23	42	30	....	....	....	....	....

CCHA Second All-Star Team (2013)

Signed as a free agent by **Missouri** (ECHL), June 24, 2015. Signed to a PTO (professional tryout) contract by **Bridgeport** (AHL), February 18, 2016. Signed as a free agent by **NY Islanders**, March 29, 2017.

FROM, Mathias (FROOM, muh-TIGH-uhs) **CHI**

Left wing. Shoots right. 6'1", 161 lbs. Born, Frederikshavn, Denmark, December 16, 1997.
(Chicago's 7th pick, 143rd overall, in 2016 NHL Draft).

			Regular Season					Playoffs				
Season	**Club**	**League**	**GP**	**G**	**A**	**Pts**	**PIM**	**GP**	**G**	**A**	**Pts**	**PIM**
2012-13	Frederikshavn U17	Den-U17	20	17	16	33	34	6	3	2	5	18
	Frederikshavn Jr.	Den-Jr.	6	5	6	11	0	2	1	0	1	0
	Frederikshavn IK	Den-2	1	0	2	2	0	....	....	....	....	....
2013-14	Frederikshavn U17	Den-U17	16	27	28	55	47	6	1	9	10	20
	Frederikshavn Jr.	Den-Jr.	19	15	21	36	39	3	1	3	4	2
	Frederikshavn IK	Den-2	15	5	6	11	4	....	....	....	....	....
2014-15	Rogle U18	Swe-U18	35	18	28	46	28	....	....	....	....	....
	Rogle Jr.	Swe-Jr.	....	....	....	....	....	4	0	0	0	2
2015-16	Rogle Jr.	Swe-Jr.	36	6	15	21	42	7	2	2	4	0
	Rogle	Sweden	16	2	2	4	0	....	....	....	....	....
2016-17	Rogle Jr.	Swe-Jr.	13	9	9	18	8	3	2	0	2	0
	Rogle	Sweden	33	3	1	4	12	....	....	....	....	....
	Rogle	Sweden-Q	....	....	....	....	....	4	0	0	0	0

FROST, Morgan (FRAWST, MOHR-guhn) **PHI**

Center. Shoots left. 5'11", 173 lbs. Born, Aurora, ON, May 14, 1999.
(Philadelphia's 2nd pick, 27th overall, in 2017 NHL Draft).

			Regular Season					Playoffs				
Season	**Club**	**League**	**GP**	**G**	**A**	**Pts**	**PIM**	**GP**	**G**	**A**	**Pts**	**PIM**
2014-15	Barrie Colts MM	Minor-ON	32	30	25	55	34	....	....	....	....	....
	Barrie Colts MM	Other	36	23	28	51	34	....	....	....	....	....
2015-16	Sault Ste. Marie	OHL	65	7	20	27	12	12	1	2	3	0
2016-17	Sault Ste. Marie	OHL	67	20	42	62	36	11	2	6	8	4

GABRIELLE, Jesse (GAY-bree-ehl, JEH-see) **BOS**

Left wing. Shoots left. 6', 196 lbs. Born, Edmonton, AB, June 17, 1997.
(Boston's 8th pick, 105th overall, in 2015 NHL Draft).

			Regular Season					Playoffs				
Season	**Club**	**League**	**GP**	**G**	**A**	**Pts**	**PIM**	**GP**	**G**	**A**	**Pts**	**PIM**
2012-13	Team Southeast	UMHSEL	3	0	0	0	0	....	....	....	....	....
	Team Southeast	MEPDL	13	6	5	11	....	....	....	....	....	....
	Eagan Wildcats	High-MN	25	15	28	43	22	3	0	4	4	0
	Brandon	WHL	2	0	0	0	7	....	....	....	....	....
2013-14	Brandon	WHL	49	12	14	26	68	9	3	3	6	22
2014-15	Brandon	WHL	33	13	12	25	69	....	....	....	....	....
	Regina Pats	WHL	33	10	9	19	43	9	1	3	4	8
2015-16	Prince George	WHL	72	40	35	75	101	3	1	1	2	5
	Providence Bruins	AHL	3	0	0	0	2	....	....	....	....	....
2016-17	Prince George	WHL	61	35	29	64	88	6	1	2	3	8
	Providence Bruins	AHL	1	0	0	0	0	....	....	....	....	....

GADJOVICH, Jonah (GAD-JOH-vihk, JOH-nuh) **VAN**

Left wing. Shoots left. 6'1", 199 lbs. Born, Whitby, ON, December 10, 1998.
(Vancouver's 3rd pick, 55th overall, in 2017 NHL Draft).

			Regular Season					Playoffs				
Season	**Club**	**League**	**GP**	**G**	**A**	**Pts**	**PIM**	**GP**	**G**	**A**	**Pts**	**PIM**
2013-14	Whitby Min. Mid.	Minor-ON	23	15	15	30	20	....	....	....	....	....
2014-15	Owen Sound	OHL	60	4	5	9	59	3	0	0	0	0
2015-16	Owen Sound	OHL	66	14	10	24	42	6	1	1	2	6
2016-17	Owen Sound	OHL	60	46	28	74	32	17	5	3	8	8

OHL Second All-Star Team (2017)

GAGNE, Gabriel (GAH-n'yay, gah-BREE-ehl) **OTT**

Right wing. Shoots right. 6'5", 194 lbs. Born, Laval, QC, November 11, 1996.
(Ottawa's 3rd pick, 36th overall, in 2015 NHL Draft).

			Regular Season					Playoffs				
Season	**Club**	**League**	**GP**	**G**	**A**	**Pts**	**PIM**	**GP**	**G**	**A**	**Pts**	**PIM**
2011-12	Nord Selects	Minor-QC		STATISTICS NOT AVAILABLE								
	Saint-Eustache	QAAA	3	0	0	0	0	....	....	....	....	....
2012-13	Saint-Eustache	QAAA	41	15	11	26	38	4	1	2	3	4
	Victoriaville Tigres	QMJHL	1	0	0	0	0	1	0	0	0	0
2013-14	Victoriaville Tigres	QMJHL	67	16	21	37	14	5	0	2	2	4
2014-15	Victoriaville Tigres	QMJHL	67	35	24	59	39	4	2	1	3	4
2015-16	Victoriaville Tigres	QMJHL	8	5	3	8	6	....	....	....	....	....
	Shawinigan	QMJHL	34	12	16	28	14	21	11	11	22	22
2016-17	Binghamton	AHL	41	2	4	6	9	....	....	....	....	....
	Wichita Thunder	ECHL	19	6	5	11	6	....	....	....	....	....

GALIMOV, Emil (ga-LEE-mawv, eh-MIHL) **S.J.**

Left wing. Shoots left. 6'1", 175 lbs. Born, Nizhnekamsk, Russia, May 9, 1992.
(San Jose's 7th pick, 207th overall, in 2013 NHL Draft).

			Regular Season					Playoffs				
Season	**Club**	**League**	**GP**	**G**	**A**	**Pts**	**PIM**	**GP**	**G**	**A**	**Pts**	**PIM**
2009-10	Nizhnekamsk Jr.	Russia-Jr.	32	6	4	10	69	1	0	1	1	0
2010-11	Nizhnekamsk Jr.	Russia-Jr.	27	11	7	18	34	5	3	0	3	27
	Nizhnekamsk	KHL	18	1	1	2	4	....	....	....	....	....
2011-12	Nizhnekamsk Jr.	Russia-Jr.	9	5	4	9	33	....	....	....	....	....
	Nizhnekamsk	KHL	8	0	0	0	2	....	....	....	....	....
	Loko Yaroslavl Jr.	Russia-Jr.	8	4	5	9	2	....	....	....	....	....
	Yaroslavl	Russia-2	17	9	4	13	12	10	2	3	5	10
2012-13	Loko Yaroslavl Jr.	Russia-Jr.	2	1	1	2	2	....	....	....	....	....
	Yaroslavl-VHL	Russia-2	5	4	1	5	4	....	....	....	....	....
	Yaroslavl	KHL	33	7	13	20	10	6	0	2	2	6
2013-14	Yaroslavl	KHL	43	7	5	12	24	18	1	3	4	8
2014-15	Yaroslavl	KHL	54	9	9	18	28	6	0	2	2	8
2015-16	Yaroslavl	KHL	49	9	14	23	52	5	0	1	1	2
2016-17	Yaroslavl	KHL	42	5	4	9	24	4	0	1	1	6

GALLANT, Alex (ga-LAWNT, AL-ehx) **T.B.**

Left wing. Shoots left. 6', 185 lbs. Born, Summerside, PE, December 8, 1992.

			Regular Season					Playoffs				
Season	**Club**	**League**	**GP**	**G**	**A**	**Pts**	**PIM**	**GP**	**G**	**A**	**Pts**	**PIM**
2008-09	Charlottetown	NBPEI	26	2	5	7	24	4	0	1	1	2
2009-10	Charlottetown	NBPEI	24	0	5	5	94	4	1	1	2	6
	Summerside	MJrHL	5	1	0	1	5	....	....	....	....	....
2010-11	Summerside	MJrHL	45	4	10	14	154	15	0	1	1	4
2011-12	P.E.I. Rocket	QMJHL	32	0	0	0	133	....	....	....	....	....
2012-13	Summerside	MJrHL	29	3	6	9	106	12	4	5	9	36
2013-14	Columbus	SPHL	43	1	3	4	251	6	0	2	2	37
2014-15	Orlando	ECHL	1	0	0	0	7	....	....	....	....	....
	Utah Grizzlies	ECHL	22	1	1	2	99	6	0	0	0	10
2015-16	San Jose Barracuda	AHL	27	1	0	1	122	1	0	0	0	5
	Utah Grizzlies	ECHL	11	0	1	1	37	....	....	....	....	....
2016-17	San Jose Barracuda	AHL	29	0	2	2	126	1	0	0	0	0

Signed as a free agent by **Tampa Bay**, July 1, 2017.

GALLANT, Zach (ga-LAWNT, ZAK) **DET**

Center. Shoots left. 6'1", 198 lbs. Born, London, ON, June 3, 1999.
(Detroit's 4th pick, 83rd overall, in 2017 NHL Draft).

			Regular Season					Playoffs				
Season	**Club**	**League**	**GP**	**G**	**A**	**Pts**	**PIM**	**GP**	**G**	**A**	**Pts**	**PIM**
2014-15	Miss. Rebels MM	GTHL	62	24	34	58	95	....	....	....	....	....
	Oakville Blades	ON-Jr.A	3	2	1	3	2	....	....	....	....	....
2015-16	Peterborough	OHL	51	0	4	4	23	7	0	0	0	9
2016-17	Peterborough	OHL	60	21	26	47	74	12	0	9	9	11

GALVAS, Jakub (gahl-VAS, YAH-kuhb) **CHI**

Defense. Shoots left. 5'11", 162 lbs. Born, Ostrava, Czech Rep., June 15, 1999.
(Chicago's 8th pick, 150th overall, in 2017 NHL Draft).

			Regular Season					Playoffs				
Season	**Club**	**League**	**GP**	**G**	**A**	**Pts**	**PIM**	**GP**	**G**	**A**	**Pts**	**PIM**
2014-15	HC Olomouc U18	CzR-U18	19	3	6	9	6	8	1	0	1	0
2015-16	HC Olomouc U18	CzR-U18	12	3	7	10	4	....	....	....	....	....
	HC Olomouc Jr.	CzRep-Jr.	22	1	11	12	10	....	....	....	....	....
2016-17	HC Olomouc U18	CzR-U18	3	1	4	5	0	....	....	....	....	....
	HC Olomouc Jr.	CzRep-Jr.	5	1	4	5	0	....	....	....	....	....
	HC Olomouc	CzRep	36	1	5	6	14	....	....	....	....	....
	HC Dukla Jihlava	CzRep-2	....	....	....	....	....	1	0	1	1	0

GAMBARDELLA, Joseph (GAM-bar-DEH-la, JOH-sehf) **EDM**

Center. Shoots left. 5'10", 201 lbs. Born, Staten Island, NY, December 1, 1993.

			Regular Season					Playoffs				
Season	**Club**	**League**	**GP**	**G**	**A**	**Pts**	**PIM**	**GP**	**G**	**A**	**Pts**	**PIM**
2010-11	N.J. Rockets	MtJHL	37	33	36	69	19	2	1	0	1	2
	N.J. Rockets	AtJHL	3	0	1	1	0	....	....	....	....	....
2011-12	N.J. Rockets	AtJHL	24	21	7	28	25	....	....	....	....	....
	Des Moines	USHL	31	4	5	9	2	....	....	....	....	....
2012-13	Des Moines	USHL	48	15	21	36	26	....	....	....	....	....
2013-14	U. Mass Lowell	H-East	31	5	5	10	8	....	....	....	....	....
2014-15	U. Mass Lowell	H-East	38	14	16	30	6	....	....	....	....	....
2015-16	U. Mass Lowell	H-East	40	10	27	37	2	....	....	....	....	....
2016-17	U. Mass Lowell	H-East	41	18	34	52	22	....	....	....	....	....

Hockey East Second All-Star Team (2017)

Signed as a free agent by **Edmonton**, March 28, 2017.

GAMBRELL, Dylan (gam-BREHL, DIH-luhn) **S.J.**

Center. Shoots right. 6', 185 lbs. Born, Bonney Lake, WA, August 26, 1996.
(San Jose's 1st pick, 60th overall, in 2016 NHL Draft).

			Regular Season					Playoffs				
Season	**Club**	**League**	**GP**	**G**	**A**	**Pts**	**PIM**	**GP**	**G**	**A**	**Pts**	**PIM**
2011-12	Col. T-birds U16	T1EHL	40	21	21	42	12	....	....	....	....	....
2012-13	Col. T-birds U16	T1EHL	4	4	8	12	10	....	....	....	....	....
	Dubuque	USHL	58	9	18	27	14	9	0	2	2	0
2013-14	Dubuque	USHL	60	14	29	43	29	7	0	0	0	0
2014-15	Dubuque	USHL	54	16	22	38	74	8	3	4	7	2
2015-16	U. of Denver	NCHC	41	17	30	47	19	....	....	....	....	....
2016-17	U. of Denver	NCHC	38	13	29	42	21	....	....	....	....	....

NCHC All-Rookie Team (2016) • NCHC Second All-Star Team (2017)

GANLY, Tyler (GAN-lee, TIGH-luhr) **CAR**

Defense. Shoots right. 6'2", 204 lbs. Born, Mississauga, ON, March 22, 1995.
(Carolina's 4th pick, 156th overall, in 2013 NHL Draft).

			Regular Season					Playoffs				
Season	**Club**	**League**	**GP**	**G**	**A**	**Pts**	**PIM**	**GP**	**G**	**A**	**Pts**	**PIM**
2010-11	Tor. Jr. Canadiens	GTHL	84	14	30	44	44	....	....	....	....	....
	Tor. Canadiens	ON-Jr.A	2	0	1	1	0	....	....	....	....	....
2011-12	Tor. Jr. Canadiens	GTHL	39	9	15	24	60	10	2	4	6	4
	Tor. Jr. Canadiens	Other	24	3	10	13	18	....	....	....	....	....
	Brampton Capitals	ON-Jr.A	7	0	1	1	0	....	....	....	....	....
2012-13	Sault Ste. Marie	OHL	62	0	17	17	64	6	0	0	0	0
2013-14	Sault Ste. Marie	OHL	67	3	18	21	62	9	0	2	2	8
2014-15	Sault Ste. Marie	OHL	38	2	14	16	33	14	2	7	9	4
2015-16	Charlotte	AHL	26	0	2	2	23	....	....	....	....	....
	Florida Everblades	ECHL	15	0	1	1	2	....	....	....	....	....
2016-17	Charlotte	AHL	2	0	0	0	0	....	....	....	....	....
	Florida Everblades	ECHL	11	0	1	1	0	....	....	....	....	....

• Missed majority of 2016-17 due to shoulder injury during Charlotte (AHL) training camp and resulting surgery.

GARDNER, Rhett (GAHRD-nuhr, REHT) **DAL**

Center/Left wing. Shoots left. 6'2", 200 lbs. Born, Moose Jaw, SK, February 28, 1996.
(Dallas' 3rd pick, 116th overall, in 2016 NHL Draft).

			Regular Season					Playoffs				
Season	**Club**	**League**	**GP**	**G**	**A**	**Pts**	**PIM**	**GP**	**G**	**A**	**Pts**	**PIM**
2010-11	Moose Jaw	Minor-SK	22	27	14	41	84	4	1	3	4	24
	Moose Jaw	SMHL	10	2	3	5	12	2	0	0	0	0
2011-12	Moose Jaw	SMHL	41	19	11	30	53	9	4	2	6	2
2012-13	Moose Jaw	SMHL	35	27	21	48	24	2	1	0	1	2
	Green Bay	USHL	1	0	0	0	0	....	....	....	....	....
2013-14	Okotoks Oilers	AJHL	52	13	24	37	82	5	1	1	2	6
2014-15	Okotoks Oilers	AJHL	54	24	30	54	119	7	1	5	6	14
2015-16	North Dakota	NCHC	41	11	7	18	52	....	....	....	....	....
2016-17	North Dakota	NCHC	38	8	13	21	69	....	....	....	....	....

GARLAND, Conor (GAHR-luhnd, KAW-nuhr) **ARI**

Right wing. Shoots right. 5'8", 166 lbs. Born, Scituate, MA, March 11, 1996.
(Arizona's 8th pick, 123rd overall, in 2015 NHL Draft).

			Regular Season					Playoffs				
Season	**Club**	**League**	**GP**	**G**	**A**	**Pts**	**PIM**	**GP**	**G**	**A**	**Pts**	**PIM**
2011-12	Bos. Jr. Bruins	EmJHL	40	42	52	94	53	5	3	6	9	14
	Boston Jr. Bruins	Other	2	1	5	6	0	....	....	....	....	....
2012-13	Muskegon	USHL	6	1	2	3	2	....	....	....	....	....
	Moncton Wildcats	QMJHL	26	6	11	17	16	5	0	0	0	0
2013-14	Moncton Wildcats	QMJHL	51	24	30	54	39	6	2	3	5	2
2014-15	Moncton Wildcats	QMJHL	67	35	*94	*129	66	16	3	22	25	17
2015-16	Moncton Wildcats	QMJHL	62	39	*89	*128	97	17	5	10	15	18
2016-17	Tucson	AHL	55	5	9	14	37	....	....	....	....	....

QMJHL First All-Star Team (2015, 2016) • QMJHL Player of the Year (2015)

GATES, Brent (GAYTZ, BREHNT) **ANA**

Center. Shoots left. 6'2", 196 lbs. Born, Seattle, WA, August 12, 1997.
(Anaheim's 3rd pick, 80th overall, in 2015 NHL Draft).

			Regular Season					Playoffs				
Season	**Club**	**League**	**GP**	**G**	**A**	**Pts**	**PIM**	**GP**	**G**	**A**	**Pts**	**PIM**
2012-13	Det. Comp. U16	HPHL	26	10	9	19	10	....	....	....	....	....
2013-14	Green Bay	USHL	50	11	4	15	16	2	0	0	0	2
2014-15	Green Bay	USHL	33	10	17	27	18	....	....	....	....	....
2015-16	U. of Minnesota	Big Ten	35	3	4	7	6	....	....	....	....	....
2016-17	U. of Minnesota	Big Ten	37	14	7	21	33	....	....	....	....	....

GAUDETTE, Adam (gaw-DEHT, A-duhm) **VAN**

Center. Shoots right. 6'1", 170 lbs. Born, Braintree, MA, October 3, 1996.
(Vancouver's 5th pick, 149th overall, in 2015 NHL Draft).

			Regular Season					Playoffs				
Season	**Club**	**League**	**GP**	**G**	**A**	**Pts**	**PIM**	**GP**	**G**	**A**	**Pts**	**PIM**
2012-13	Bos. Adv. U16	T1EHL	6	2	2	4	2	....	....	....	....	....
	Thayer Academy	High-MA	11	2	3	5	....	....	....	....	....	....
2013-14	Thayer Academy	High-MA	27	29	38	67	....	....	....	....	....	....
2014-15	Cedar Rapids	USHL	50	13	17	30	55	3	0	0	0	4
2015-16	Northeastern	H-East	41	12	18	30	20	....	....	....	....	....
2016-17	Northeastern	H-East	37	26	26	52	20	....	....	....	....	....

GAUTHIER, Julien (goh-T'YAY, joo-LEE-uhn) **CAR**

Right wing. Shoots right. 6'4", 230 lbs. Born, Pointe-aux-Trembles, QC, October 15, 1997.
(Carolina's 2nd pick, 21st overall, in 2016 NHL Draft).

			Regular Season					Playoffs				
Season	**Club**	**League**	**GP**	**G**	**A**	**Pts**	**PIM**	**GP**	**G**	**A**	**Pts**	**PIM**
2012-13	Laval-Montreal	QAAA	42	12	20	32	30	17	3	8	11	6
2013-14	Val-d'Or Foreurs	QMJHL	62	9	21	30	19	24	0	7	7	2
2014-15	Val-d'Or Foreurs	QMJHL	68	38	35	73	46	17	5	5	10	6
2015-16	Val-d'Or Foreurs	QMJHL	54	41	16	57	24	6	2	3	5	8
2016-17	Val-d'Or Foreurs	QMJHL	23	7	20	27	22	....	....	....	....	....
	Saint John	QMJHL	20	10	14	24	18	16	11	6	17	13

GAVRIKOV, Vladislav (GAV-rih-kawv, vla-dih-SLAV) **CBJ**

Defense. Shoots left. 6'3", 205 lbs. Born, Yaroslavl, Russia, November 21, 1995.
(Columbus' 8th pick, 159th overall, in 2015 NHL Draft).

			Regular Season					Playoffs				
Season	**Club**	**League**	**GP**	**G**	**A**	**Pts**	**PIM**	**GP**	**G**	**A**	**Pts**	**PIM**
2011-12	Loko Yaroslavl Jr.	Russia-Jr.	8	1	1	2	4	2	0	0	0	0
2012-13	Loko Yaroslavl Jr.	Russia-Jr.	47	3	3	6	18	....	....	....	....	....
2013-14	Loko Yaroslavl Jr.	Russia-Jr.	45	3	9	12	28	7	0	2	2	4
2014-15	Loko Yaroslavl Jr.	Russia-Jr.	16	1	6	7	16	5	0	0	0	2
	HK Ryazan	Russia-2	11	1	2	3	4	....	....	....	....	....
	Yaroslavl	KHL	16	0	1	1	4	4	0	0	0	0
2015-16	Yaroslavl	KHL	42	3	4	7	18	5	1	0	1	2
2016-17	Yaroslavl	KHL	54	3	4	7	38	15	1	4	5	14

GAVRUS, Artur (GAV-ruhs, ahr-TUHR) **N.J.**

Center/Left wing. Shoots left. 5'10", 185 lbs. Born, Ratichi, Belarus, January 3, 1994.
(New Jersey's 7th pick, 180th overall, in 2012 NHL Draft).

			Regular Season					Playoffs				
Season	**Club**	**League**	**GP**	**G**	**A**	**Pts**	**PIM**	**GP**	**G**	**A**	**Pts**	**PIM**
2009-10	Neman Grodno 2	Belarus-2	41	14	12	26	22	....	....	....	....	....
2010-11	Neman Grodno 2	Belarus-2	19	4	4	8	18	....	....	....	....	....
2011-12	Owen Sound	OHL	45	15	22	37	18	1	0	0	0	0
2012-13	Neman Grodno	Belarus	15	5	7	12	0	....	....	....	....	....
	Neman Grodno 2	Belarus-2	2	0	3	3	0	....	....	....	....	....
	Owen Sound	OHL	21	8	6	14	11	12	3	5	8	2
2013-14	Dynamo Minsk	KHL	30	1	3	4	8	....	....	....	....	....
2014-15	Dynamo Minsk	KHL	36	5	4	9	12	....	....	....	....	....
	Molodechno	Belarus	4	2	4	6	2	....	....	....	....	....
	Bobruisk Jr.	Russia-Jr.	....	....	....	....	....	3	1	1	2	12
2015-16	Dynamo Minsk	KHL	19	3	7	10	0	....	....	....	....	....
2016-17	Dynamo Minsk	KHL	38	5	4	9	6	3	0	1	1	0

GAWANKE, Leon (gah-VEHN-kay, LEE-awn) **WPG**

Defense. Shoots right. 6'1", 190 lbs. Born, Berlin, Germany, May 31, 1999.
(Winnipeg's 5th pick, 136th overall, in 2017 NHL Draft).

			Regular Season					Playoffs				
Season	**Club**	**League**	**GP**	**G**	**A**	**Pts**	**PIM**	**GP**	**G**	**A**	**Pts**	**PIM**
2014-15	Eisb. Jrs. Berl. Jr.	Ger-Jr.	8	0	0	0	2	....	....	....	....	....
2015-16	Eisb. Jrs. Berl. Jr.	Ger-Jr.	45	12	28	40	18	2	1	3	4	0
2016-17	Cape Breton	QMJHL	54	8	24	32	26	11	1	3	4	4

GAWDIN, Glenn (GAW-dihn, GLEHN)

Center. Shoots right. 6'1", 191 lbs. Born, Richmond, BC, March 25, 1997.
(St. Louis' 3rd pick, 116th overall, in 2015 NHL Draft).

			Regular Season					Playoffs				
Season	**Club**	**League**	**GP**	**G**	**A**	**Pts**	**PIM**	**GP**	**G**	**A**	**Pts**	**PIM**
2011-12	Seafair Islanders	Minor-BC	43	58	32	90	34	....	....	....	....	....
	Greater Van.	BCMML	....	....	....	....	....	4	1	0	1	0
2012-13	Greater Van.	BCMML	37	17	29	46	49	6	7	4	11	14
	Swift Current	WHL	2	0	0	0	0	....	....	....	....	....
2013-14	Swift Current	WHL	66	10	12	22	34	6	0	0	0	2
2014-15	Swift Current	WHL	72	15	39	54	59	4	1	1	2	0
2015-16	Swift Current	WHL	53	19	34	53	63	....	....	....	....	....
2016-17	Swift Current	WHL	52	26	33	59	80	14	6	5	11	18

GEEKIE, Morgan (GEE-kee, MOHR-guhn) **CAR**

Center. Shoots right. 6'3", 193 lbs. Born, Strathclair, MB, July 20, 1998.
(Carolina's 4th pick, 67th overall, in 2017 NHL Draft).

			Regular Season					Playoffs				
Season	**Club**	**League**	**GP**	**G**	**A**	**Pts**	**PIM**	**GP**	**G**	**A**	**Pts**	**PIM**
2013-14	Yellowhead Chiefs	MMHL	44	25	28	53	14	3	5	3	8	0
	Tri-City Americans	WHL	1	1	0	1	0	....	....	....	....	....
2014-15	Yellowhead Chiefs	MMHL	44	27	36	63	38	....	....	....	....	....
	Neepawa Natives	MJHL	2	1	1	2	0	....	....	....	....	....
	Tri-City Americans	WHL	9	0	2	2	0	2	0	0	0	0
2015-16	Tri-City Americans	WHL	66	12	13	25	10	....	....	....	....	....
2016-17	Tri-City Americans	WHL	72	35	55	90	40	4	1	0	1	4

WHL West Second All-Star Team (2017)

GEERTSEN, Mason (GEERT-suhn, MAY-suhn) **COL**

Defense. Shoots left. 6'4", 215 lbs. Born, Drayton Valley, AB, April 19, 1995.
(Colorado's 4th pick, 93rd overall, in 2013 NHL Draft).

			Regular Season					Playoffs				
Season	**Club**	**League**	**GP**	**G**	**A**	**Pts**	**PIM**	**GP**	**G**	**A**	**Pts**	**PIM**
2010-11	Sherwood Park	AMHL	31	3	7	10	84	10	1	2	3	24
	Edmonton	WHL	3	0	0	0	4	....	....	....	....	....
2011-12	Edmonton	WHL	34	0	3	3	70	....	....	....	....	....
2012-13	Edmonton	WHL	15	0	4	4	32	....	....	....	....	....
	Vancouver Giants	WHL	58	2	8	10	98	....	....	....	....	....
2013-14	Vancouver Giants	WHL	66	4	19	23	126	4	0	0	0	14
2014-15	Vancouver Giants	WHL	69	13	25	38	107	....	....	....	....	....
	Lake Erie Monsters	AHL	9	0	0	0	2	....	....	....	....	....
2015-16	San Antonio	AHL	42	0	8	8	62	....	....	....	....	....
	Fort Wayne	ECHL	21	1	3	4	18	14	0	3	3	15
2016-17	San Antonio	AHL	36	0	4	4	52	....	....	....	....	....
	Colorado Eagles	ECHL	9	0	5	5	14	19	1	3	4	42

GEISSER, Tobias (GIGH-suhr, toh-BEE-uhs) **WSH**

Defense. Shoots left. 6'4", 200 lbs. Born, Stans, Switz., February 13, 1999.
(Washington's 1st pick, 120th overall, in 2017 NHL Draft).

			Regular Season					Playoffs				
Season	**Club**	**League**	**GP**	**G**	**A**	**Pts**	**PIM**	**GP**	**G**	**A**	**Pts**	**PIM**
2011-12	Engelberg U17	Swiss-U17	2	2	0	2	0	....	....	....	....	....
2013-14	EV Zug U17	Swiss-U17	2	0	0	0	0	2	0	0	0	0
	Argovia Stars U17	Swiss-U17	9	11	1	12	2	....	....	....	....	....
2014-15	EV Zug U17	Swiss-U17	30	20	15	35	6	12	2	5	7	2
	EV Zug Jr.	Swiss-Jr.	8	1	1	2	4	....	....	....	....	....
2015-16	EV Zug U17	Swiss-U17	10	5	5	10	2	....	....	....	....	....
	EV Zug Jr.	Swiss-Jr.	35	1	2	3	2	9	3	1	4	2
2016-17	EV Zug Jr.	Swiss-Jr.	3	1	2	3	0	10	5	4	9	4
	EV Zug	Swiss	14	0	1	1	0	....	....	....	....	....
	EVZ Academy Zug	Swiss-2	34	3	7	10	14	....	....	....	....	....

GELINAS, Guillaume (ZHEHL-ih-nuh, GEE-AWM) **MIN**

Defense. Shoots left. 5'10", 197 lbs. Born, Quebec, QC, June 14, 1993.

			Regular Season					Playoffs				
Season	**Club**	**League**	**GP**	**G**	**A**	**Pts**	**PIM**	**GP**	**G**	**A**	**Pts**	**PIM**
2008-09	St-Francois	QAAA	45	4	10	14	42	3	0	0	0	18
2009-10	St-Francois	QAAA	34	10	22	32	44	4	0	2	2	2
	Val-d'Or Foreurs	QMJHL	16	0	1	1	6	....	....	....	....	....
2010-11	Val-d'Or Foreurs	QMJHL	60	4	17	21	53	4	0	0	0	6
2011-12	Val-d'Or Foreurs	QMJHL	64	10	24	34	43	4	1	0	1	6
2012-13	Val-d'Or Foreurs	QMJHL	68	6	39	45	111	6	1	2	3	2
2013-14	Val-d'Or Foreurs	QMJHL	67	23	69	92	81	24	11	23	34	20
2014-15	Iowa Wild	AHL	37	2	2	4	22	....	....	....	....	....
2015-16	Iowa Wild	AHL	25	2	3	5	6	....	....	....	....	....
	Quad City	ECHL	43	9	18	27	10	2	0	0	0	0
2016-17	Iowa Wild	AHL	1	0	0	0	0	....	....	....	....	....
	Quad City	ECHL	61	9	22	31	33	4	0	0	0	0

QMJHL First All-Star Team (2014)

Signed as a free agent by **Minnesota**, July 1, 2014.

GENDRON, Miles (GEHN-druhn, MIGH-uhlz) **OTT**

Defense. Shoots left. 6'3", 190 lbs. Born, Oakville, ON, June 28, 1996.
(Ottawa's 2nd pick, 70th overall, in 2014 NHL Draft).

			Regular Season					Playoffs				
Season	**Club**	**League**	**GP**	**G**	**A**	**Pts**	**PIM**	**GP**	**G**	**A**	**Pts**	**PIM**
2010-11	The Rivers School	High-MA	24	2	6	8	....	....	....	....	....	....
2011-12	The Rivers School	High-MA	24	7	9	16	....	....	....	....	....	....
2012-13	The Rivers School	High-MA	29	12	18	30	....	....	....	....	....	....
2013-14	Neponset Valley	Minor-MA	11	1	8	9	4	....	....	....	....	....
	The Rivers School	High-MA	22	6	13	19	....	....	....	....	....	....
2014-15	Penticton Vees	BCHL	54	5	12	17	42	22	0	12	12	4
2015-16	U. of Connecticut	H-East	27	2	4	6	16	....	....	....	....	....
2016-17	U. of Connecticut	H-East	36	4	7	11	22	....	....	....	....	....

GENNARO, Matteo (jeh-NAIR-oh, muh-TAY-oh)

Center. Shoots left. 6'2", 198 lbs. Born, St. Albert, AB, March 30, 1997.
(Winnipeg's 8th pick, 203rd overall, in 2015 NHL Draft).

			Regular Season					Playoffs				
Season	**Club**	**League**	**GP**	**G**	**A**	**Pts**	**PIM**	**GP**	**G**	**A**	**Pts**	**PIM**
2012-13	St. Albert Raiders	AMHL	30	9	12	21	32	4	0	2	2	2
2013-14	Prince Albert	WHL	60	5	10	15	14	3	0	0	0	0
2014-15	Prince Albert	WHL	72	16	15	31	44	....	....	....	....	....
2015-16	Prince Albert	WHL	42	12	12	24	28	....	....	....	....	....
	Calgary Hitmen	WHL	28	6	13	19	8	5	0	0	0	2
2016-17	Calgary Hitmen	WHL	69	43	37	80	65	4	1	0	1	4

GERNAT, Martin (GAIR-naht, MAR-tihn) ANA

Defense. Shoots left. 6'4", 202 lbs. Born, Presov, Slovakia, April 11, 1993.
(Edmonton's 8th pick, 122nd overall, in 2011 NHL Draft).

			Regular Season					Playoffs				
Season	Club	League	GP	G	A	Pts	PIM	GP	G	A	Pts	PIM
2008-09	P.H.K. Presov U18	Svk-U18	41	6	28	34	36	....	....	....	....	....
2009-10	HC Kosice U18	Svk-U18	36	4	21	25	20	5	0	3	3	2
	HC Kosice Jr.	Slovak-Jr.	....	....	....	....	....	2	0	0	0	2
2010-11	HC Kosice U18	Svk-U18	8	3	4	7	22	1	0	0	0	2
	HC Kosice Jr.	Slovak-Jr.	28	3	15	18	20	12	3	3	6	10
2011-12	Edmonton	WHL	60	9	46	55	46	20	7	6	13	8
2012-13	Edmonton	WHL	23	3	10	13	14	22	6	11	17	6
2013-14	Bakersfield	ECHL	3	0	1	1	6	....	....	....	....	....
	Oklahoma City	AHL	57	4	17	21	26	1	0	0	0	0
2014-15	Oklahoma City	AHL	54	1	8	9	32	....	....	....	....	....
2015-16	Bakersfield	AHL	22	0	3	3	14	....	....	....	....	....
	San Diego Gulls	AHL	5	0	0	0	2	....	....	....	....	....
2016-17	HC Sparta Praha	CzRep	41	3	9	12	28	4	1	1	2	0

Traded to **Anaheim** by **Edmonton** with Edmonton's 4th round pick (Jack Kopacka) in 2016 NHL Draft for Patrick Maroon, February 29, 2016. Signed as a free agent by **Sparta Praha** (CzRep), May 25, 2016.

GERSICH, Shane (GUHR-sihch, SHAYN) WSH

Center/Left wing. Shoots left. 5'11", 175 lbs. Born, Chaska, MN, July 10, 1996.
(Washington's 4th pick, 134th overall, in 2014 NHL Draft).

			Regular Season					Playoffs				
Season	Club	League	GP	G	A	Pts	PIM	GP	G	A	Pts	PIM
2011-12	Holy Family Cath.	High-MN	20	30	30	60	21	1	0	0	0	0
	U.S. Youth Oly.	Other	6	3	1	4	6	....	....	....	....	....
2012-13	Holy Family Cath.	High-MN	24	28	34	62	35	1	0	0	0	2
	Omaha Lancers	USHL	6	1	0	1	19	....	....	....	....	....
2013-14	USAHNTDP	USHL	26	8	8	16	4	....	....	....	....	....
	USAHNTDP	U-18	35	8	8	16	14	....	....	....	....	....
2014-15	Omaha Lancers	USHL	52	27	23	50	32	3	1	1	2	0
2015-16	North Dakota	NCHC	37	9	2	11	16	....	....	....	....	....
2016-17	North Dakota	NCHC	40	21	16	37	20	....	....	....	....	....

GETTINGER, Tim (Geh-TIHN-juhr, TIHM) NYR

Left wing. Shoots left. 6'6", 217 lbs. Born, Cleveland, OH, April 14, 1998.
(NY Rangers' 3rd pick, 141st overall, in 2016 NHL Draft).

			Regular Season					Playoffs				
Season	Club	League	GP	G	A	Pts	PIM	GP	G	A	Pts	PIM
2013-14	Cle. Barons U16	T1EHL	36	24	8	32	44	....	....	....	....	....
2014-15	Sault Ste. Marie	OHL	54	10	15	25	13	6	1	1	2	2
	USAHNTDP	U-17	4	2	0	2	6	....	....	....	....	....
2015-16	Sault Ste. Marie	OHL	60	17	22	39	32	12	1	3	4	0
2016-17	Sault Ste. Marie	OHL	62	31	23	54	27	11	4	3	7	0

OHL All-Rookie Team (2015)

GIGNAC, Brandon (zhihg-NAK, BRAN-duhn) N.J.

Center. Shoots left. 5'11", 180 lbs. Born, Repentigny, QC, November 7, 1997.
(New Jersey's 4th pick, 80th overall, in 2016 NHL Draft).

			Regular Season					Playoffs				
Season	Club	League	GP	G	A	Pts	PIM	GP	G	A	Pts	PIM
2012-13	Esther-Blondin	QAAA	42	20	17	37	46	3	0	1	1	4
2013-14	Shawinigan	QMJHL	53	5	9	14	18	4	0	1	1	6
2014-15	Shawinigan	QMJHL	63	9	31	40	18	7	2	1	3	4
2015-16	Shawinigan	QMJHL	67	24	37	61	41	20	7	9	16	8
2016-17	Shawinigan	QMJHL	59	23	39	62	30	6	0	4	4	2
	Albany Devils	AHL	2	0	0	0	2	....	....	....	....	....

GILBERT, Dennis (GIHL-buhrt, DEH-nihs) CHI

Defense. Shoots left. 6'1", 195 lbs. Born, Buffalo, NY, October 30, 1996.
(Chicago's 2nd pick, 91st overall, in 2015 NHL Draft).

			Regular Season					Playoffs				
Season	Club	League	GP	G	A	Pts	PIM	GP	G	A	Pts	PIM
2011-12	St. Joseph's	High-NY	27	4	5	9	1.5	....	....	....	....	....
2012-13	St. Joseph's	High-NY	28	12	8	20	21	....	....	....	....	....
2013-14	Buffalo Jr. Sabres	ON-Jr.A	35	4	13	17	36	10	0	3	3	8
2014-15	Chicago Steel	USHL	59	4	23	27	89	....	....	....	....	....
2015-16	U. of Notre Dame	H-East	37	2	8	10	34	....	....	....	....	....
2016-17	U. of Notre Dame	H-East	40	0	22	22	22	....	....	....	....	....

USHL All-Rookie Team (2015)

GILDON, Max (gihl-DAWN, MAX) FLA

Defense. Shoots left. 6'3", 192 lbs. Born, Houston, TX, May 17, 1999.
(Florida's 3rd pick, 66th overall, in 2017 NHL Draft).

			Regular Season					Playoffs				
Season	Club	League	GP	G	A	Pts	PIM	GP	G	A	Pts	PIM
2013-14	Dallas Stars U16	T1EHL	31	6	13	19	22	....	....	....	....	....
2014-15	Dallas Stars U16	T1EHL	24	7	8	15	32	4	2	1	3	4
2015-16	USAHNTDP	USHL	35	0	7	7	34	....	....	....	....	....
	USAHNTDP	U-17	23	1	11	12	18	....	....	....	....	....
2016-17	USAHNTDP	USHL	26	5	9	14	28	....	....	....	....	....
	USAHNTDP	U-18	37	6	13	19	28	....	....	....	....	....

• Signed Letter of Intent to attend **University of New Hampshire** (Hockey East) in fall of 2017.

GILMOUR, Adam (GIHL-mohr, A-duhm) MIN

Center. Shoots right. 6'4", 192 lbs. Born, Albany, NY, January 29, 1994.
(Minnesota's 4th pick, 98th overall, in 2012 NHL Draft).

			Regular Season					Playoffs				
Season	Club	League	GP	G	A	Pts	PIM	GP	G	A	Pts	PIM
2010-11	Nobles	High-MA	27	11	16	27	8	....	....	....	....	....
2011-12	Cape Cod Whalers	Minor-MA	30	19	26	45	....	....	....	....	....	....
	Nobles	High-MA	26	26	30	56	28	....	....	....	....	....
2012-13	Muskegon	USHL	64	19	28	47	12	3	1	0	1	10
2013-14	Boston College	H-East	40	7	13	20	10	....	....	....	....	....
2014-15	Boston College	H-East	38	9	18	27	22	....	....	....	....	....
2015-16	Boston College	H-East	41	12	14	26	16	....	....	....	....	....
	Iowa Wild	AHL	2	0	0	0	0	....	....	....	....	....
2016-17	Iowa Wild	AHL	52	4	6	10	12	....	....	....	....	....
	Quad City	ECHL	11	3	5	8	4	....	....	....	....	....

GILMOUR, Brady (GIHL-mohr, BRAY-dee) DET

Center. Shoots left. 5'10", 170 lbs. Born, Cobourg, ON, April 18, 1999.
(Detroit's 10th pick, 193rd overall, in 2017 NHL Draft).

			Regular Season					Playoffs				
Season	Club	League	GP	G	A	Pts	PIM	GP	G	A	Pts	PIM
2014-15	Quinte Min. Mid.	Minor-ON	36	28	33	61	....	....	....	....	....	....
	Cobourg Cougars	ON-Jr.A	1	0	0	0	0	....	....	....	....	....
2015-16	Saginaw Spirit	OHL	61	7	16	23	6	4	1	2	3	0
2016-17	Saginaw Spirit	OHL	65	26	21	47	4	....	....	....	....	....

GILMOUR, John (GIHL-mohr, JAWN) NYR

Defense. Shoots left. 5'11", 180 lbs. Born, Montreal, QC, May 17, 1993.
(Calgary's 8th pick, 198th overall, in 2013 NHL Draft).

			Regular Season					Playoffs				
Season	Club	League	GP	G	A	Pts	PIM	GP	G	A	Pts	PIM
2010-11	Gilmour Acad.	MPHL	13	4	7	11	8	3	0	2	2	0
	Gilmour Acad.	High-OH	46	....	....	31	....	....	....	....	....	....
2011-12	Cedar Rapids	USHL	58	10	14	24	14	2	0	1	1	0
2012-13	Providence College	H-East	38	4	9	13	35	....	....	....	....	....
2013-14	Providence College	H-East	39	5	13	18	22	....	....	....	....	....
2014-15	Providence College	H-East	30	4	7	11	10	....	....	....	....	....
2015-16	Providence College	H-East	34	9	14	23	18	....	....	....	....	....
2016-17	Hartford Wolf Pack	AHL	76	6	19	25	18	....	....	....	....	....

Signed as a free agent by **NY Rangers**, August 18, 2016.

GIMAYEV, Sergei (gih-MIGH-ehv, SAIR-gay) OTT

Defense. Shoots left. 6'1", 183 lbs. Born, Moscow, USSR, February 16, 1984.
(Ottawa's 6th pick, 166th overall, in 2003 NHL Draft).

			Regular Season					Playoffs				
Season	Club	League	GP	G	A	Pts	PIM	GP	G	A	Pts	PIM
2001-02	CSKA Moscow 2	Russia-3	36	0	10	10	50	....	....	....	....	....
2002-03	Cherepovets	Russia	11	0	0	0	4	....	....	....	....	....
2003-04	Cherepovets	Russia	50	1	3	4	32	....	....	....	....	....
2004-05	Cherepovets	Russia	5	0	1	1	2	....	....	....	....	....
	Sibir Novosibirsk	Russia	31	1	6	7	34	....	....	....	....	....
2005-06	Dynamo Moscow	Russia	46	1	3	4	36	2	0	0	0	0
2006-07	Dynamo Moscow	Russia	23	0	2	2	28	2	0	0	0	6
2007-08	Cherepovets	Russia	39	1	0	1	30	8	1	1	2	4
2008-09	Barys Astana	KHL	45	0	2	2	79	....	....	....	....	....
2009-10	Barys Astana	KHL	54	6	6	12	73	3	0	0	0	8
2010-11	Barys Astana	KHL	52	5	3	8	44	4	0	0	0	4
2011-12	Ufa	KHL	43	1	4	5	27	3	0	0	0	0
2012-13	CSKA Moscow	KHL	43	1	0	1	22	2	0	0	0	2
2013-14	CSKA Moscow	KHL	33	0	3	3	12	4	0	0	0	2
2014-15	Novosibirsk	KHL	53	0	4	4	55	16	0	3	3	6
2015-16	Novosibirsk	KHL	58	0	12	12	47	10	1	0	1	22
2016-17	Podolsk	KHL	57	0	4	4	36	3	0	0	0	0

GIRARD, Felix (zhih-RAHRD, FEE-lihx) COL

Center. Shoots right. 5'10", 197 lbs. Born, Levis, QC, May 9, 1994.
(Nashville's 3rd pick, 95th overall, in 2013 NHL Draft).

			Regular Season					Playoffs				
Season	Club	League	GP	G	A	Pts	PIM	GP	G	A	Pts	PIM
2009-10	St-Francois	QAAA	41	7	11	18	68	3	1	1	2	15
2010-11	Baie-Comeau	QMJHL	64	5	12	17	37	....	....	....	....	....
2011-12	Baie-Comeau	QMJHL	60	6	15	21	63	8	2	1	3	14
2012-13	Baie-Comeau	QMJHL	58	23	38	61	58	19	4	11	15	42
2013-14	Baie-Comeau	QMJHL	58	11	32	43	130	21	4	8	12	43
2014-15	Milwaukee	AHL	61	4	5	9	54	....	....	....	....	....
2015-16	Milwaukee	AHL	76	5	16	21	62	3	0	0	0	2
2016-17	Milwaukee	AHL	35	3	5	8	29	....	....	....	....	....
	San Antonio	AHL	38	7	13	20	76	....	....	....	....	....

Traded to **Colorado** by **Nashville** for Cody McLeod, January 13, 2017.

GIRARD, Samuel (zhih-RAHRD, sam-YUHL) NSH

Defense. Shoots left. 5'9", 166 lbs. Born, Roberval, QC, May 12, 1998.
(Nashville's 2nd pick, 47th overall, in 2016 NHL Draft).

			Regular Season					Playoffs				
Season	Club	League	GP	G	A	Pts	PIM	GP	G	A	Pts	PIM
2013-14	Jonquiere Elites	QAAA	42	7	29	36	16	....	....	....	....	....
2014-15	Shawinigan	QMJHL	64	5	38	43	8	7	0	2	2	2
2015-16	Shawinigan	QMJHL	67	10	64	74	10	21	2	20	22	4
2016-17	Shawinigan	QMJHL	59	9	*66	75	29	5	1	8	9	4
	Milwaukee	AHL	6	1	0	1	0	2	0	0	0	2

QMJHL First All-Star Team (2016, 2017)

GLASS, Cody (GLAS, KOH-dee) VGK

Center. Shoots right. 6'2", 178 lbs. Born, Winnipeg, MB, January 4, 1999.
(Las Vegas' 1st pick, 6th overall, in 2017 NHL Draft).

			Regular Season					Playoffs				
Season	Club	League	GP	G	A	Pts	PIM	GP	G	A	Pts	PIM
2014-15	Wpg. Thrashers	MMHL	40	23	32	55	26	8	2	2	4	6
	Portland	WHL	3	0	0	0	0	....	....	....	....	....
2015-16	Portland	WHL	65	10	17	27	20	4	1	2	3	0
2016-17	Portland	WHL	69	32	62	94	36	11	4	5	9	10

WHL West First All-Star Team (2017)

GLOTOV, Vasili (GLOH-tawv, va-SIHL-ee) BUF

Left wing. Shoots left. 5'10", 158 lbs. Born, Barnaul, Russia, September 4, 1997.
(Buffalo's 10th pick, 190th overall, in 2016 NHL Draft).

			Regular Season					Playoffs				
Season	Club	League	GP	G	A	Pts	PIM	GP	G	A	Pts	PIM
2014-15	Ser. Ljvy Jr.	Russia-Jr.	53	8	6	14	14	4	0	1	1	4
2015-16	Ser. Ljvy Jr.	Russia-Jr.	42	23	32	55	34	....	....	....	....	....
2016-17	Cape Breton	QMJHL	64	15	35	50	14	11	0	4	4	2

GLOVER, Jack (GLUH-vuhr, JAK) WPG

Defense. Shoots right. 6'3", 198 lbs. Born, Golden Valley, MN, May 17, 1996.
(Winnipeg's 2nd pick, 69th overall, in 2014 NHL Draft).

			Regular Season					Playoffs				
Season	Club	League	GP	G	A	Pts	PIM	GP	G	A	Pts	PIM
2011-12	Benilde	High-MN	22	2	14	16	2	5	0	2	2	2
	U.S. Youth Oly.	Other	6	1	1	2	2	....	....	....	....	....
2012-13	USAHNTDP	USHL	37	1	5	6	24	....	....	....	....	....
	USAHNTDP	U-17	19	5	9	14	8	....	....	....	....	....
2013-14	USAHNTDP	USHL	24	1	9	10	12	....	....	....	....	....
	USAHNTDP	U-18	33	1	17	18	18	....	....	....	....	....
2014-15	U. of Minnesota	Big Ten	22	0	3	3	6	....	....	....	....	....
2015-16	U. of Minnesota	Big Ten	36	3	8	11	24	....	....	....	....	....
2016-17	U. of Minnesota	Big Ten	13	0	2	2	6	....	....	....	....	....

GOLDEN, Jacob (GOHL-duhn, JAY-kuhb) MIN

Defense. Shoots left. 5'11", 163 lbs. Born, Toronto, ON, March 20, 1999.
(Minnesota's 4th pick, 147th overall, in 2017 NHL Draft).

			Regular Season					Playoffs				
Season	Club	League	GP	G	A	Pts	PIM	GP	G	A	Pts	PIM
2014-15	Miss. Rebels MM	GTHL	57	7	20	27	18	....	....	....	....	....
2015-16	Upper Canada	High-ON	44	16	15	31	....	....	....	....	....	....
	Upper Canada	CISAA	11	6	4	10	2	2	1	0	1	0
2016-17	London Knights	OHL	38	0	2	2	0	....	....	....	....	....

GOLYSHEV, Anatoli (GOH-LIH-shehv, ANA-toh-lee) NYI

Left wing. Shoots left. 5'8", 178 lbs. Born, Perm, Russia, February 14, 1995.
(NY Islanders' 2nd pick, 95th overall, in 2016 NHL Draft).

			Regular Season					Playoffs				
Season	Club	League	GP	G	A	Pts	PIM	GP	G	A	Pts	PIM
2012-13	Avtomobilist Jr.	Russia-Jr.	54	23	40	63	24	8	1	5	6	2
2013-14	Avtomobilist Jr.	Russia-Jr.	20	12	10	22	8	1	1	1	2	0
	Avtomobilist	KHL	32	2	3	5	4	4	0	0	0	0
2014-15	Avtomobilist	KHL	44	9	10	19	43	5	1	1	2	6
	Avtomobilist Jr.	Russia-Jr.	....	....	....	....	....	1	0	0	0	0
2015-16	Avtomobilist	KHL	56	25	19	44	26	6	1	0	1	10
2016-17	Avtomobilist	KHL	49	7	10	17	59	....	....	....	....	....
	Nizhny Tagil	Russia-2	4	1	0	1	0	....	....	....	....	....

GORDEEV, Fedor (GOHR-DEE-ehv, FAY-dohr) TOR

Defense. Shoots left. 6'6", 211 lbs. Born, Omsk, Russia, January 27, 1999.
(Toronto's 5th pick, 141st overall, in 2017 NHL Draft).

			Regular Season					Playoffs				
Season	Club	League	GP	G	A	Pts	PIM	GP	G	A	Pts	PIM
2014-15	Tor. R. Wings MM	GTHL	56	9	16	25	....	....	....	....	....	....
	Milton Icehawks	ON-Jr.A	9	0	1	1	4	....	....	....	....	....
2015-16	Ancaster	ON-Jr.B	44	6	20	26	36	10	0	1	1	6
	Hamilton Bulldogs	OHL	8	0	2	2	2	....	....	....	....	....
2016-17	Hamilton Bulldogs	OHL	2	1	0	1	2	....	....	....	....	....
	Flint Firebirds	OHL	62	3	10	13	43	5	0	1	1	2

GORTZ, Max (GUHRTS, MAX) ANA

Right wing. Shoots right. 6'3", 202 lbs. Born, Hoor, Sweden, January 28, 1993.
(Nashville's 8th pick, 172nd overall, in 2012 NHL Draft).

			Regular Season					Playoffs				
Season	Club	League	GP	G	A	Pts	PIM	GP	G	A	Pts	PIM
2008-09	Malmo U18	Swe-U18	10	2	0	2	2	....	....	....	....	....
2009-10	Malmo U18	Swe-U18	23	8	23	31	2	....	....	....	....	....
	Malmo Jr.	Swe-Jr.	26	1	3	4	6	....	....	....	....	....
2010-11	Malmo U18	Swe-U18	8	2	1	3	6	....	....	....	....	....
	Malmo Jr.	Swe-Jr.	40	9	9	18	14	5	2	0	2	2
2011-12	Farjestad Jr.	Swe-Jr.	28	17	18	35	6	6	4	3	7	0
	Farjestad	Sweden	18	2	3	5	0	2	0	0	0	2
2012-13	Farjestad Jr.	Swe-Jr.	8	7	1	8	0	4	2	3	5	0
	Farjestad	Sweden	50	9	6	15	4	9	0	2	2	0
2013-14	Farjestad Jr.	Swe-Jr.	4	3	2	5	2	....	....	....	....	....
	Farjestad	Sweden	22	2	2	4	2	....	....	....	....	....
	Frolunda	Sweden	18	6	0	6	2	7	3	2	5	0
2014-15	Frolunda	Sweden	53	14	14	28	6	12	3	1	4	0
2015-16	Milwaukee	AHL	72	18	29	47	18	3	0	1	1	0
	Cincinnati	ECHL	1	0	0	0	0	....	....	....	....	....
2016-17	Milwaukee	AHL	30	1	3	4	2	....	....	....	....	....
	San Diego Gulls	AHL	28	4	15	19	21	8	0	2	2	0

Traded to **Anaheim** by **Nashville** for Andrew O'Brien, January 19, 2017. Signed as a free agent by **Malmo** (Sweden), May 26, 2017.

GOULBOURNE, Tyrell (GOHL-buhrn, tigh-REHL) PHI

Left wing. Shoots left. 6', 200 lbs. Born, Edmonton, AB, January 26, 1994.
(Philadelphia's 3rd pick, 72nd overall, in 2013 NHL Draft).

			Regular Season					Playoffs				
Season	Club	League	GP	G	A	Pts	PIM	GP	G	A	Pts	PIM
2009-10	CAC Canadians	AMHL	31	13	13	26	85	2	0	0	0	2
	Kelowna Rockets	WHL	5	0	1	1	0	....	....	....	....	....
2010-11	CAC Canadians	AMHL	26	10	16	26	69	....	....	....	....	....
	Kelowna Rockets	WHL	13	1	0	1	27	6	0	0	0	6
2011-12	Kelowna Rockets	WHL	63	6	8	14	109	4	0	0	0	2
2012-13	Kelowna Rockets	WHL	64	14	13	27	135	11	1	2	3	15
2013-14	Kelowna Rockets	WHL	68	17	20	37	114	14	2	3	5	23
2014-15	Kelowna Rockets	WHL	62	22	23	45	76	12	1	1	2	23
2015-16	Lehigh Valley	AHL	73	7	10	17	75	....	....	....	....	....
2016-17	Lehigh Valley	AHL	24	1	0	1	24	1	0	0	0	7
	Reading Royals	ECHL	36	8	11	19	35	....	....	....	....	....

GRAHAM, Jesse (GRAY-uhm, JEH-see) COL

Defense. Shoots right. 6', 184 lbs. Born, Oshawa, ON, May 13, 1994.
(NY Islanders' 6th pick, 155th overall, in 2012 NHL Draft).

			Regular Season					Playoffs				
Season	Club	League	GP	G	A	Pts	PIM	GP	G	A	Pts	PIM
2009-10	Tor. Young Nats	GTHL	84	14	74	88	38	....	....	....	....	....
2010-11	Niagara Ice Dogs	OHL	63	1	17	18	22	14	1	8	9	8
2011-12	Niagara Ice Dogs	OHL	68	4	37	41	36	20	1	9	10	20
2012-13	Niagara Ice Dogs	OHL	68	4	35	39	48	5	0	3	3	6
2013-14	Niagara Ice Dogs	OHL	24	6	11	17	21	....	....	....	....	....
	Saginaw Spirit	OHL	42	5	32	37	22	5	0	3	3	2
	Bridgeport	AHL	7	1	3	4	2	....	....	....	....	....
2014-15	Bridgeport	AHL	39	3	16	19	20	....	....	....	....	....
	Florida Everblades	ECHL	23	1	13	14	10	12	1	5	6	4
2015-16	Bridgeport	AHL	52	5	12	17	34	....	....	....	....	....
	Missouri Mavericks	ECHL	11	0	9	9	2	9	0	5	5	14
2016-17	Bridgeport	AHL	19	2	7	9	6	....	....	....	....	....
	Missouri Mavericks	ECHL	24	6	19	25	26	....	....	....	....	....

OHL All-Rookie Team (2011)

Signed as a free agent by **Colorado**, July 25, 2017.

GRAVES, Jacob (GRAYVZ, JAY-kuhb) CBJ

Defense. Shoots right. 6'2", 194 lbs. Born, Barrie, ON, March 28, 1995.

			Regular Season					Playoffs				
Season	Club	League	GP	G	A	Pts	PIM	GP	G	A	Pts	PIM
2011-12	Mississauga	ON-Jr.A	29	0	10	10	95	....	....	....	....	....
	St. Michael's	OHL	34	0	2	2	22	....	....	....	....	....
2012-13	Mississauga	OHL	54	0	1	1	78	6	0	0	0	11
2013-14	Mississauga	OHL	62	2	9	11	130	4	0	0	0	13
2014-15	Kingston	OHL	62	0	7	7	118	4	0	0	0	0
2015-16	Oshawa Generals	OHL	38	0	15	15	59	....	....	....	....	....
	London Knights	OHL	31	1	5	6	45	18	0	10	10	29
2016-17	Cleveland	AHL	19	1	1	2	29	....	....	....	....	....
	Cincinnati	ECHL	9	0	1	1	9	....	....	....	....	....

Signed as a free agent by **Columbus**, July 5, 2016.

GRAVES, Ryan (GRAVZ, RIGH-uhn) NYR

Defense. Shoots left. 6'5", 216 lbs. Born, Yarmouth, NS, May 21, 1995.
(NY Rangers' 4th pick, 110th overall, in 2013 NHL Draft).

			Regular Season					Playoffs				
Season	Club	League	GP	G	A	Pts	PIM	GP	G	A	Pts	PIM
2010-11	South Shore	NSMHL	32	5	7	12	58	5	0	6	6	8
	Yarmouth	MJrHL	1	0	0	0	2	3	0	0	0	2
2011-12	P.E.I. Rocket	QMJHL	62	2	7	9	34	....	....	....	....	....
2012-13	P.E.I. Rocket	QMJHL	68	3	13	16	90	6	0	0	0	6
2013-14	Charlottetown	QMJHL	39	3	9	12	52	....	....	....	....	....
	Val-d'Or Foreurs	QMJHL	26	2	8	10	16	24	1	7	8	24
2014-15	Quebec Remparts	QMJHL	50	15	24	39	49	21	5	6	11	25
2015-16	Hartford Wolf Pack	AHL	74	9	12	21	53	....	....	....	....	....
2016-17	Hartford Wolf Pack	AHL	76	8	22	30	69	....	....	....	....	....

GREEN, Luke (GREEN, LEWK) WPG

Defense. Shoots right. 6', 186 lbs. Born, Bedford, NS, January 12, 1998.
(Winnipeg's 3rd pick, 79th overall, in 2016 NHL Draft).

			Regular Season					Playoffs				
Season	Club	League	GP	G	A	Pts	PIM	GP	G	A	Pts	PIM
2013-14	Dartmouth	NSMHL	34	17	20	37	22	16	7	11	18	39
2014-15	Saint John	QMJHL	60	6	30	36	23	5	1	2	3	2
2015-16	Saint John	QMJHL	61	10	25	35	29	13	1	2	3	14
2016-17	Saint John	QMJHL	27	2	13	15	22	....	....	....	....	....
	Sherbrooke	QMJHL	33	3	19	22	34	....	....	....	....	....
	Manitoba Moose	AHL	4	0	1	1	0	....	....	....	....	....

GREENWAY, J.D. (GREEN-way, JAY-DEE) TOR

Defense. Shoots left. 6'5", 204 lbs. Born, Potsdam, NY, April 27, 1998.
(Toronto's 5th pick, 72nd overall, in 2016 NHL Draft).

			Regular Season					Playoffs				
Season	Club	League	GP	G	A	Pts	PIM	GP	G	A	Pts	PIM
2013-14	Shattuck U16	High-MN	51	6	17	23	88	....	....	....	....	....
2014-15	USAHNTDP	USHL	33	1	1	2	77	....	....	....	....	....
	USAHNTDP	U-17	20	0	4	4	32	....	....	....	....	....
2015-16	USAHNTDP	USHL	25	2	8	10	8	....	....	....	....	....
	USAHNTDP	U-18	39	3	15	18	54	....	....	....	....	....
2016-17	U. of Wisconsin	Big Ten	34	1	6	7	*87	....	....	....	....	....

GREENWAY, Jordan (GREEN-way, JOHR-duhn) MIN

Left wing. Shoots left. 6'6", 226 lbs. Born, Canton, NY, February 16, 1997.
(Minnesota's 2nd pick, 50th overall, in 2015 NHL Draft).

			Regular Season					Playoffs				
Season	Club	League	GP	G	A	Pts	PIM	GP	G	A	Pts	PIM
2012-13	Shattuck U16	High-MN	46	23	39	62	96	....	....	....	....	....
2013-14	USAHNTDP	USHL	33	10	16	26	61	....	....	....	....	....
	USAHNTDP	U-17	19	6	9	15	55	....	....	....	....	....
2014-15	USAHNTDP	USHL	22	5	15	20	16	....	....	....	....	....
	USAHNTDP	U-18	31	4	19	23	34	....	....	....	....	....
2015-16	Boston University	H-East	39	5	21	26	58	....	....	....	....	....
2016-17	Boston University	H-East	37	10	21	31	*82	....	....	....	....	....

GREGOIRE, Jeremy (greh-G'WAHR, JAIR-ih-mee) MTL

Center. Shoots right. 6', 188 lbs. Born, Sherbrooke, QC, September 5, 1995.
(Montreal's 8th pick, 176th overall, in 2013 NHL Draft).

			Regular Season					Playoffs				
Season	Club	League	GP	G	A	Pts	PIM	GP	G	A	Pts	PIM
2009-10	Magog	QAAA	28	4	8	12	22	10	3	1	4	6
2010-11	Magog	QAAA	38	28	25	53	42	13	8	8	16	10
2011-12	Chicoutimi	QMJHL	61	15	15	30	59	18	2	4	6	14
2012-13	Chicoutimi	QMJHL	35	7	8	15	71	....	....	....	....	....
	Baie-Comeau	QMJHL	27	12	5	17	29	18	9	7	16	27
2013-14	Baie-Comeau	QMJHL	65	35	34	69	84	22	9	14	23	35
2014-15	Baie-Comeau	QMJHL	32	20	21	41	59	....	....	....	....	....
2015-16	St. John's IceCaps	AHL	62	6	5	11	70	....	....	....	....	....
2016-17	St. John's IceCaps	AHL	56	9	3	12	78	....	....	....	....	....

GREGOR, Noah (GREH-gohr, NOH-uh) S.J.

Center. Shoots left. 5'11", 177 lbs. Born, Beaumont, AB, July 28, 1998.
(San Jose's 2nd pick, 111th overall, in 2016 NHL Draft).

			Regular Season					Playoffs				
Season	Club	League	GP	G	A	Pts	PIM	GP	G	A	Pts	PIM
2012-13	Leduc Oil Kings	AMBHL	30	43	25	68	64	6	4	5	9	14
2013-14	Leduc Oil Kings	AMHL	35	21	30	*51	26	4	1	1	2	0
2014-15	Moose Jaw	WHL	10	2	4	6	0	....	....	....	....	....
2015-16	Moose Jaw	WHL	72	28	45	73	33	10	3	6	9	4
2016-17	Moose Jaw	WHL	52	27	34	61	29	7	2	0	2	0

GROPP, Ryan (GRAWP, RIGH-uhn) NYR

Left wing. Shoots left. 6'2", 190 lbs. Born, Kamloops, BC, September 16, 1996.
(NY Rangers' 1st pick, 41st overall, in 2015 NHL Draft).

			Regular Season					Playoffs				
Season	Club	League	GP	G	A	Pts	PIM	GP	G	A	Pts	PIM
2011-12	Okanagan H.A.	High-BC	41	21	30	51	60	1	0	1	1	0
	St. Andrew's	CISAA	8	3	5	8	20	2	1	1	2	0
	Penticton Vees	BCHL	2	1	0	1	0	....	....	....	....	....
2012-13	Penticton Vees	BCHL	50	12	19	31	26	15	4	5	9	4
2013-14	Penticton Vees	BCHL	10	3	5	8	2	....	....	....	....	....
	Seattle	WHL	59	18	24	42	22	9	1	3	4	0
2014-15	Seattle	WHL	67	30	28	58	44	6	1	7	8	8
2015-16	Seattle	WHL	66	34	36	70	40	11	6	3	9	4
2016-17	Seattle	WHL	66	35	49	84	26	16	7	12	19	6

GRUNDSTROM, Carl (GRUHND-struhm, KAHRL) TOR

Right wing. Shoots left. 6', 194 lbs. Born, Umea, Sweden, December 1, 1997.
(Toronto's 3rd pick, 57th overall, in 2016 NHL Draft).

			Regular Season					Playoffs				
Season	Club	League	GP	G	A	Pts	PIM	GP	G	A	Pts	PIM
2011-12	Bjorkloven U18	Swe-U18	5	0	1	1	2	....	....	....	....	....
2012-13	Bjorkloven U18	Swe-U18	33	13	10	23	42	....	....	....	....	....
2013-14	MODO U18	Swe-U18	18	19	12	31	47	5	2	2	4	29
	MODO Jr.	Swe-Jr.	31	6	4	10	6	1	0	0	0	0
2014-15	MODO U18	Swe-U18	4	3	3	6	2	3	2	2	4	0
	MODO	Sweden	24	2	3	5	8	....	....	....	....	....
	MODO Jr.	Swe-Jr.	27	21	15	36	53	4	4	2	6	2
	MODO	Sweden	24	2	3	5	8	....	....	....	....	....
2015-16	MODO Jr.	Swe-Jr.	1	0	0	0	0	....	....	....	....	....
	MODO	Sweden	49	7	9	16	53	....	....	....	....	....
	MODO	Sweden-Q	....	....	....	....	....	7	1	3	4	6
2016-17	Frolunda	Sweden	45	14	6	20	6	14	1	1	2	4
	Toronto Marlies	AHL	....	....	....	....	....	6	3	1	4	2

GUDBRANSON, Alex (guhd-BRAN-suhn, AL-ehx) MIN

Defense. Shoots right. 6'2", 229 lbs. Born, Orleans, ON, September 3, 1994.

			Regular Season					Playoffs				
Season	Club	League	GP	G	A	Pts	PIM	GP	G	A	Pts	PIM
2010-11	Kingston	OHL	62	3	11	14	37	5	0	1	1	0
2011-12	Kingston	OHL	50	2	7	9	52	....	....	....	....	....
2012-13	Sault Ste. Marie	OHL	65	3	11	14	62	6	0	0	0	15
2013-14	Sault Ste. Marie	OHL	66	7	8	15	76	9	1	3	4	18
2014-15	Iowa Wild	AHL	46	1	3	4	17	....	....	....	....	....
2015-16	Quad City	ECHL	72	5	17	22	58	4	0	0	0	4
2016-17	Toronto Marlies	AHL	4	0	0	0	2	....	....	....	....	....
	Quad City	ECHL	45	4	11	15	46	....	....	....	....	....

Signed as a free agent by **Minnesota**, September 23, 2014.

GUNNARSSON, Kristoffer (GU-nuhr-suhn, krihs-TAW-fuhr) VAN

Defense. Shoots left. 6'1", 205 lbs. Born, Molndal, Sweden, February 26, 1997.
(Vancouver's 6th pick, 135th overall, in 2017 NHL Draft).

			Regular Season					Playoffs				
Season	Club	League	GP	G	A	Pts	PIM	GP	G	A	Pts	PIM
2012-13	Frolunda U18	Swe-U18	3	0	0	0	0	....	....	....	....	....
2013-14	Frolunda U18	Swe-U18	40	4	9	13	24	5	1	0	1	2
2014-15	Frolunda U18	Swe-U18	20	0	3	3	18	3	0	0	0	2
	Frolunda Jr.	Swe-Jr.	38	0	0	0	16	7	0	0	0	0
2015-16	Frolunda Jr.	Swe-Jr.	36	7	7	14	88	3	0	0	0	4
	Frolunda	Sweden	13	0	0	0	0	....	....	....	....	....
	IK Oskarshamn	Sweden-2	5	0	0	0	2	....	....	....	....	....
2016-17	Frolunda Jr.	Swe-Jr.	4	0	0	0	0	4	0	0	0	6
	Frolunda	Sweden	10	0	0	0	29	8	0	0	0	6
	IK Oskarshamn	Sweden-2	29	1	1	2	8	....	....	....	....	....

GUSEV, Nikita (GOO-sehv, nih-KEE-tuh) VGK

Left wing. Shoots right. 5'9", 163 lbs. Born, Moscow, Russia, July 8, 1992.
(Tampa Bay's 8th pick, 202nd overall, in 2012 NHL Draft).

			Regular Season					Playoffs				
Season	Club	League	GP	G	A	Pts	PIM	GP	G	A	Pts	PIM
2009-10	CSKA Jr.	Russia-Jr.	48	17	40	57	14	5	1	2	3	0
2010-11	CSKA Jr.	Russia-Jr.	38	22	37	59	14	16	17	10	27	6
	CSKA Moscow	KHL	18	1	0	1	2	....	....	....	....	....
2011-12	CSKA Jr.	Russia-Jr.	34	30	46	76	26	19	16	17	33	0
	CSKA Moscow	KHL	15	2	1	3	0	1	0	0	0	0
2012-13	CSKA Moscow	KHL	6	0	1	1	0	....	....	....	....	....
	THK Tver	Russia-2	15	7	6	13	2	....	....	....	....	....
	Amur Khabarovsk	KHL	24	4	8	12	6	12	1	4	5	6
2013-14	Khanty-Mansiisk	KHL	44	8	6	14	10	6	3	3	6	0
2014-15	Khanty-Mansiisk	KHL	55	21	16	37	12	....	....	....	....	....
2015-16	Khanty-Mansiisk	KHL	23	7	7	14	4	....	....	....	....	....
	SKA St. Petersburg	KHL	33	13	22	35	10	15	5	9	14	0
2016-17	SKA St. Petersburg	KHL	57	24	47	71	8	18	7	16	23	2

Traded to **Vegas** by **Tampa Bay** with Tampa Bay's 2nd round pick (later traded to Columbus – Columbus selected Alexandre Texier) in 2017 NHL Draft and Pittsburgh's 4th round pick (prevously acquired) in 2018 NHL Draft for Expansion Draft considerations, June 21, 2017.

GUSTAFSSON, Hampus (GOOS-tahf-suhn, ham-PUHS) WSH

Left wing. Shoots left. 6'4", 205 lbs. Born, Ljungby, Sweden, October 26, 1993.

			Regular Season					Playoffs				
Season	Club	League	GP	G	A	Pts	PIM	GP	G	A	Pts	PIM
2012-13	Amarillo Bulls	NAHL	35	10	17	27	21	7	4	2	6	6
2013-14	Merrimack College	H-East	33	4	6	10	12	....	....	....	....	....
2014-15	Merrimack College	H-East	38	11	14	25	41	....	....	....	....	....
2015-16	Merrimack College	H-East	39	8	18	26	24	....	....	....	....	....
2016-17	Merrimack College	H-East	36	15	11	26	43	....	....	....	....	....
	Hershey Bears	AHL	10	0	2	2	13	4	0	0	0	0

Signed as a free agent by **Washington**, March 7, 2017.

GUTTMAN, Cole (GUHT-muhn, KOHL) T.B.

Center. Shoots right. 5'9", 167 lbs. Born, Northridge, CA, June 4, 1999.
(Tampa Bay's 4th pick, 180th overall, in 2017 NHL Draft).

			Regular Season					Playoffs				
Season	Club	League	GP	G	A	Pts	PIM	GP	G	A	Pts	PIM
2014-15	L.A. Jr. Kings U16	T1EHL	24	9	16	25	16	4	0	3	3	14
2015-16	L.A. Jr. Kings U16	T1EHL	30	24	*24	*48	34	4	3	2	5	6
	USAHNTDP	USHL	3	0	0	0	0	....	....	....	....	....
	Dubuque	USHL	2	0	1	1	0	8	0	0	0	0
2016-17	Dubuque	USHL	53	27	27	54	18	6	1	3	4	2

• Signed Letter of Intent to attend **St. Cloud State University** (NCHC) in fall of 2018.

HAAPALA, Henrik (HAH-PAH-LAH, HEHN-rihk) FLA

Left wing. Shoots left. 5'9", 165 lbs. Born, Lempaala, Finland, February 28, 1994.

			Regular Season					Playoffs				
Season	Club	League	GP	G	A	Pts	PIM	GP	G	A	Pts	PIM
2010-11	Tappara U18	Fin-U17	1	1	0	1	0	4	2	4	6	0
	Tappara U18	Fin-U18	24	8	13	21	18	2	0	2	2	0
	Tappara Jr.	Fin-Jr.	18	2	3	5	6	....	....	....	....	....
2011-12	Tappara U18	Fin-U18	4	1	6	7	0	3	1	4	5	0
	Tappara Jr.	Fin-Jr.	46	16	29	45	18	....	....	....	....	....
	Tappara Tampere	Finland	1	0	0	0	0	....	....	....	....	....
2012-13	Tappara Jr.	Fin-Jr.	7	2	5	7	0	8	3	4	7	4
	Tappara Tampere	Finland	32	3	10	13	12	....	....	....	....	....
	LeKi Lempaala	Finland-2	4	0	1	1	2	....	....	....	....	....
2013-14	Tappara Jr.	Fin-Jr.	2	0	1	1	0	2	0	1	1	0
	Tappara Tampere	Finland	36	1	3	4	2	15	2	1	3	4
2014-15	Tappara Tampere	Finland	25	4	6	10	14	20	3	7	10	8
2015-16	Tappara Tampere	Finland	47	12	18	30	20	18	3	3	6	10
2016-17	Tappara Tampere	Finland	51	15	*45	*60	18	16	2	7	9	6

Signed as a free agent by **Florida**, May 31, 2017.

HACHE, Justin (ha-SHAY, JUHS-tihn) DAL

Defense. Shoots left. 6'2", 202 lbs. Born, Petit-Rocher, NB, January 10, 1994.
(Phoenix's 8th pick, 208th overall, in 2012 NHL Draft).

			Regular Season					Playoffs				
Season	Club	League	GP	G	A	Pts	PIM	GP	G	A	Pts	PIM
2008-09	Miramichi	NBPEI	33	0	4	4	8	3	0	1	1	0
2009-10	Miramichi	NBPEI	31	6	16	22	31	9	0	5	5	4
2010-11	Shawinigan	QMJHL	37	3	12	15	17	10	0	2	2	4
2011-12	Shawinigan	QMJHL	60	2	16	18	46	11	1	0	1	2
2012-13	Cape Breton	QMJHL	68	7	26	33	61	....	....	....	....	....
2013-14	Cape Breton	QMJHL	57	5	41	46	53	3	0	1	1	0
	Portland Pirates	AHL	6	0	0	0	2	....	....	....	....	....
2014-15	Portland Pirates	AHL	60	0	6	6	18	....	....	....	....	....
2015-16	Springfield Falcons	AHL	67	2	12	14	34	....	....	....	....	....
2016-17	Tucson	AHL	5	0	1	1	9	....	....	....	....	....
	Rapid City Rush	ECHL	21	2	7	9	22	....	....	....	....	....
	Texas Stars	AHL	12	0	1	1	19	....	....	....	....	....
	Idaho Steelheads	ECHL	8	0	2	2	4	5	1	0	1	4

QMJHL Second All-Star Team (2014)

Traded to **Dallas** by **Arizona** with Justin Peters for Brendan Ranford and Branden Troock, February 1, 2017.

HAGEL, Brandon (HAY-guhl, BRAN-duhn) BUF

Left wing. Shoots left. 6'1", 157 lbs. Born, Saskatoon, SK, August 27, 1998.
(Buffalo's 8th pick, 159th overall, in 2016 NHL Draft).

			Regular Season					Playoffs				
Season	Club	League	GP	G	A	Pts	PIM	GP	G	A	Pts	PIM
2012-13	Ft. Saskatchewan	AMBHL	33	22	19	41	34	....	....	....	....	....
2013-14	Ft. Saskatchewan	Minor-AB	37	32	26	58	62	....	....	....	....	....
	Ft. Saskatchewan	AMHL	2	0	0	0	0	....	....	....	....	....
2014-15	Ft. Saskatchewan	AMHL	34	23	28	51	42	....	....	....	....	....
	Whitecourt	AJHL	6	1	1	2	0	4	0	1	1	0
2015-16	Whitecourt	AJHL	3	1	2	3	2	....	....	....	....	....
	Red Deer Rebels	WHL	72	13	34	47	46	17	1	9	10	18
2016-17	Red Deer Rebels	WHL	65	31	40	71	85	7	7	1	8	10

HAGEL, Marc (HAY-guhl, MAHRK)

Right wing. Shoots right. 6', 195 lbs. Born, Hamilton, ON, September 12, 1988.

			Regular Season					Playoffs				
Season	Club	League	GP	G	A	Pts	PIM	GP	G	A	Pts	PIM
2008-09	Princeton	ECAC	26	3	2	5	14	....	....	....	....	....
2009-10	Princeton	ECAC	31	7	4	11	8	....	....	....	....	....
2010-11	Princeton	ECAC	4	0	0	0	0	....	....	....	....	....
2011-12	Princeton	ECAC	32	7	12	19	33	....	....	....	....	....
2012-13	Miami U.	CCHA	42	6	13	19	37	....	....	....	....	....
	Lake Erie Monsters	AHL	6	0	2	2	0	....	....	....	....	....
2013-14	Iowa Wild	AHL	46	8	7	15	35	....	....	....	....	....
	South Carolina	ECHL	21	9	8	17	11	2	0	0	0	4
2014-15	Iowa Wild	AHL	67	12	21	33	36	....	....	....	....	....
2015-16	Iowa Wild	AHL	53	4	15	19	43	....	....	....	....	....
2016-17	Iowa Wild	AHL	26	2	5	7	12	....	....	....	....	....
	Binghamton	AHL	27	0	3	3	27	....	....	....	....	....

• Missed majority of 2010-11 due to various injuries. Signed as a free agent by **Minnesota**, July 1, 2015. Traded to **Ottawa** by **Minnesota** for future considerations, February 1, 2017.

HAGGERTY, Ryan (HA-guhr-tee, RIGH-uhn)

Right wing. Shoots right. 5'11", 191 lbs. Born, Stamford, CT, March 4, 1993.

			Regular Season					Playoffs				
Season	Club	League	GP	G	A	Pts	PIM	GP	G	A	Pts	PIM
2008-09	Trinity Cath.	High-CT	25	27	31	58	....	....	....	....	....	....
	Seacoast Kings	Minor-CT	23	17	21	38	....	....	....	....	....	....
2009-10	USAHNTDP	USHL	37	5	6	11	38	....	....	....	....	....
	USAHNTDP	U-17	15	5	3	8	6	....	....	....	....	....
	USAHNTDP	U-18	2	0	0	0	0	....	....	....	....	....
2010-11	USAHNTDP	USHL	23	7	8	15	9	....	....	....	....	....
	USAHNTDP	U-18	31	4	10	14	13	....	....	....	....	....
2011-12	RPI Engineers	ECAC	35	7	8	15	30	....	....	....	....	....
2012-13	RPI Engineers	ECAC	36	12	14	26	30	....	....	....	....	....
2013-14	RPI Engineers	ECAC	35	*28	15	43	42	....	....	....	....	....
2014-15	Hartford Wolf Pack	AHL	76	15	18	33	34	14	2	4	6	4
2015-16	Rockford IceHogs	AHL	36	9	4	13	17	1	0	0	0	0
2016-17	Wilkes-Barre	AHL	58	11	12	23	46	4	0	0	0	2

ECAC First All-Star Team (2014) • NCAA East Second All-American Team (2014)

Signed as a free agent by **NY Rangers**, March 12, 2014. Traded to **Chicago** by **NY Rangers** for Antti Raanta, June 27, 2015.

HAGUE, Nicolas (HAYG, NIH-koh-luhs) VGK

Defense. Shoots left. 6'6", 216 lbs. Born, Kitchener, ON, May 12, 1998.
(Las Vegas' 4th pick, 34th overall, in 2017 NHL Draft).

			Regular Season					Playoffs				
Season	Club	League	GP	G	A	Pts	PIM	GP	G	A	Pts	PIM
2013-14	Kitchener R. MM	Minor-ON	31	3	13	16	44	18	4	13	17	24
	Kitchener R. Mid.	Minor-ON	3	1	1	2	0	....	....	....	....	....
2014-15	Kitchener	ON-Jr.B	43	3	8	11	70	10	3	9	12	20
2015-16	Mississauga	OHL	66	14	10	24	84	7	0	2	2	13
2016-17	Mississauga	OHL	65	18	28	46	107	18	1	11	12	19

HAJEK, Libor (HIGH-ak, LEE-bohr) T.B.

Defense. Shoots left. 6'2", 205 lbs. Born, Smrcek, Czech Rep., February 4, 1998.
(Tampa Bay's 2nd pick, 37th overall, in 2016 NHL Draft).

			Regular Season					Playoffs				
Season	Club	League	GP	G	A	Pts	PIM	GP	G	A	Pts	PIM
2011-12	Brno U18	CzR-U18	2	0	0	0	0	....	....	....	....	....
2012-13	Brno U18	CzR-U18	43	1	3	4	57	3	0	1	1	0
2013-14	Brno U18	CzR-U18	32	4	14	18	24	10	0	7	7	8
	Brno Jr.	CzRep-Jr.	13	0	1	1	10	....	....	....	....	....
2014-15	Brno U18	CzR-U18	2	1	2	3	4	....	....	....	....	....
	Brno Jr.	CzRep-Jr.	44	1	9	10	62	1	0	0	0	0
	HC Kometa Brno	CzRep	17	0	1	1	2	7	0	0	0	0
2015-16	Saskatoon Blades	WHL	69	3	23	26	76	....	....	....	....	....
2016-17	Saskatoon Blades	WHL	65	4	22	26	81	....	....	....	....	....
	Syracuse Crunch	AHL	8	1	0	1	4	....	....	....	....	....

HAKANPAA, Jani (HAHK-an-pah, YAH-nee) ST.L.

Defense. Shoots right. 6'5", 218 lbs. Born, Kirkkonummi, Finland, March 31, 1992.
(St. Louis' 5th pick, 104th overall, in 2010 NHL Draft).

			Regular Season					Playoffs				
Season	Club	League	GP	G	A	Pts	PIM	GP	G	A	Pts	PIM
2007-08	K-Vantaa U18	Fin-U18	2	0	1	1	2	2	0	0	0	0
2008-09	K-Vantaa U18	Fin-U18	10	3	4	7	14	....	....	....	....	....
2009-10	K-Vantaa U18	Fin-U18	32	3	16	19	69	6	0	2	2	6
2010-11	Suomi U20	Finland-2	8	1	2	3	31	....	....	....	....	....
	Blues Espoo Jr.	Fin-Jr.	36	3	20	23	61	12	3	2	5	10
2011-12	Blues Espoo Jr.	Fin-Jr.	5	0	4	4	0	....	....	....	....	....
	Blues Espoo	Finland	41	5	7	12	30	....	....	....	....	....
2012-13	Peoria Rivermen	AHL	14	1	3	4	6	....	....	....	....	....
	Blues Espoo	Finland	34	2	3	5	34	....	....	....	....	....
2013-14	Chicago Wolves	AHL	54	4	4	8	33	3	0	1	1	0
2014-15	Chicago Wolves	AHL	64	1	7	8	47	4	0	1	1	6
	Quad City	ECHL	2	1	0	1	0	....	....	....	....	....
2015-16	Karpat Oulu	Finland	60	1	11	12	40	14	1	5	6	8
2016-17	Karpat Oulu	Finland	53	0	5	5	61	2	0	1	1	2

HALL, Connor (HAWL, KAW-nuhr) PIT

Defense. Shoots right. 6'2", 190 lbs. Born, Cambridge, ON, February 21, 1998.
(Pittsburgh's 3rd pick, 77th overall, in 2016 NHL Draft).

			Regular Season					Playoffs				
Season	Club	League	GP	G	A	Pts	PIM	GP	G	A	Pts	PIM
2013-14	Camb. Hawks MM	Minor-ON	30	6	10	16	91	10	2	3	5	28
2014-15	Elmira Sugar Kings	ON-Jr.B	37	2	3	5	111	11	0	2	2	16
	Kitchener Rangers	OHL	8	0	0	0	11	....	....	....	....	....
2015-16	Elmira Sugar Kings	ON-Jr.B	3	1	0	1	6	....	....	....	....	....
	Kitchener Rangers	OHL	39	2	7	9	49	9	1	4	5	19
2016-17	Kitchener Rangers	OHL	17	1	2	3	35	....	....	....	....	....

• Missed majority of 2016-17 due to shoulder injury vs. Sarnia (OHL), November 23, 2016.

HAMAN AKTELL, Hardy (HAH-MAN AHK-tehl, HAHR-dee) NSH

Defense. Shoots right. 6'3", 198 lbs. Born, Skelleftea, Sweden, July 4, 1998.
(Nashville's 5th pick, 108th overall, in 2016 NHL Draft).

			Regular Season					Playoffs				
Season	Club	League	GP	G	A	Pts	PIM	GP	G	A	Pts	PIM
2013-14	Skelleftea AIK U18	Swe-U18	1	0	0	0	0	....	....	....	....	....
2014-15	Skelleftea AIK U18	Swe-U18	8	0	0	0	2	6	0	2	2	0
2015-16	Skelleftea AIK U18	Swe-U18	26	6	23	29	8	2	0	0	0	0
	Skelleftea AIK Jr.	Swe-Jr.	2	1	0	1	2	1	0	0	0	0
2016-17	Skelleftea AIK Jr.	Swe-Jr.	3	1	2	3	6	....	....	....	....	....

HAMILTON, Wacey (HAM-ihl-tuhn, WAY-see)

Center. Shoots left. 5'11", 185 lbs. Born, Calgary, AB, September 10, 1990.

			Regular Season					Playoffs				
Season	Club	League	GP	G	A	Pts	PIM	GP	G	A	Pts	PIM
2006-07	Camrose Kodiaks	AJHL	49	11	6	17	38	5	1	1	2	8
2007-08	Medicine Hat	WHL	63	13	19	32	95	5	1	0	1	6
2008-09	Medicine Hat	WHL	37	4	13	17	64	11	1	3	4	24
2009-10	Medicine Hat	WHL	67	24	47	71	100	12	3	5	8	23
2010-11	Medicine Hat	WHL	67	20	53	73	113	15	4	8	12	20
2011-12	Binghamton	AHL	74	5	6	11	46	....	....	....	....	....
	Elmira Jackals	ECHL	2	0	2	2	2	....	....	....	....	....
2012-13	Binghamton	AHL	38	4	4	8	17	3	0	0	0	4
2013-14	Binghamton	AHL	63	4	16	20	73	4	0	1	1	0
2014-15	Utica Comets	AHL	41	5	10	15	27	22	2	2	4	25
2015-16	Utica Comets	AHL	53	8	7	15	61	....	....	....	....	....
2016-17	Utica Comets	AHL	67	9	10	19	93	....	....	....	....	....

Signed as a free agent by **Ottawa**, March 8, 2011. Signed as a free agent by **Utica** (AHL), November 18, 2014.

HANSSON, Niklas (HAN-suhn, NIHK-luhs) DAL

Defense. Shoots right. 6'1", 180 lbs. Born, Helsingborg, Sweden, January 8, 1995.
(Dallas' 5th pick, 68th overall, in 2013 NHL Draft).

			Regular Season					Playoffs				
Season	Club	League	GP	G	A	Pts	PIM	GP	G	A	Pts	PIM
2010-11	Jonstorps IF U18	Swe-U18	2	0	0	0	0	....	....	....	....	....
	Jonstorps IF Jr.	Swe-Jr.	1	0	0	0	0	....	....	....	....	....
	Jonstorps IF	Sweden-4	18	0	2	2	2	....	....	....	....	....
	Rogle U18	Swe-U18	5	0	0	0	0	....	....	....	....	....
2011-12	Rogle U18	Swe-U18	33	3	28	31	14	5	1	3	4	0
	Rogle Jr.	Swe-Jr.	18	2	1	3	6	7	0	2	2	0
2012-13	Rogle U18	Swe-U18	7	3	3	6	4	3	0	1	1	0
	Rogle Jr.	Swe-Jr.	39	3	20	23	47	2	0	0	0	0
	Rogle	Sweden	9	0	0	0	4	....	....	....	....	....
	Rogle	Sweden-Q	6	0	1	1	0	....	....	....	....	....
2013-14	Rogle Jr.	Swe-Jr.	12	4	8	12	2	....	....	....	....	....
	Rogle	Sweden-2	63	3	20	23	22	....	....	....	....	....
2014-15	Rogle	Sweden-2	52	2	21	23	12	5	1	1	2	2
	Rogle Jr.	Swe-Jr.	....	....	....	....	....	1	2	0	2	2
2015-16	HV 71 Jonkoping	Sweden	44	7	15	22	14	6	0	0	0	0
	Texas Stars	AHL	6	0	1	1	0	4	0	0	0	2
2016-17	HV 71 Jonkoping	Sweden	46	1	10	11	12	2	0	0	0	0

HANSSON, Petter (HAN-suhn, PEH-tuhr) NYI

Defense. Shoots left. 6'2", 187 lbs. Born, Gislaved, Sweden, May 16, 1996.
(NY Islanders' 7th pick, 202nd overall, in 2015 NHL Draft).

			Regular Season					Playoffs				
Season	Club	League	GP	G	A	Pts	PIM	GP	G	A	Pts	PIM
2011-12	Gislaveds SK U18	Swe-U18	9	2	3	5	0	....	....	....	....	....
	Gislaveds SK Jr.	Swe-Jr.	6	0	3	3	0	....	....	....	....	....
	Gislaveds SK	Sweden-3	22	0	0	0	0	....	....	....	....	....
2012-13	Linkopings HC U18	Swe-U18	40	1	12	13	16	2	0	0	0	0
	Linkopings HC Jr.	Swe-Jr.	1	0	0	0	0	....	....	....	....	....
2013-14	Linkopings HC U18	Swe-U18	26	1	15	16	8	5	4	0	4	2
	Linkopings HC Jr.	Swe-Jr.	19	1	3	4	6	1	0	1	1	0
2014-15	Linkopings HC Jr.	Swe-Jr.	38	15	19	34	32	1	0	0	0	0
	Linkopings HC	Sweden	15	0	1	1	2	1	0	0	0	0
2015-16	Linkopings HC	Sweden	8	0	0	0	0	....	....	....	....	....
	VIK Vasteras HK	Sweden-2	2	0	0	0	0	....	....	....	....	....
	IK Oskarshamn	Sweden-2	7	0	0	0	0	....	....	....	....	....
	Linkopings HC Jr.	Swe-Jr.	12	1	3	4	12	4	0	1	1	0
2016-17	Linkopings HC Jr.	Swe-Jr.	1	0	0	0	0	....	....	....	....	....
	Linkopings HC	Sweden	22	0	1	1	2	....	....	....	....	....
	Vasterviks IK	Sweden-2	33	1	10	11	14	....	....	....	....	....

HARGROVE, Colton (HAHR-grohv, KOHL-tuhn)

Left wing. Shoots left. 6'1", 212 lbs. Born, Dallas, TX, June 25, 1992.
(Boston's 6th pick, 205th overall, in 2012 NHL Draft).

			Regular Season					Playoffs				
Season	Club	League	GP	G	A	Pts	PIM	GP	G	A	Pts	PIM
2009-10	Dallas Stars	T1EHL	16	5	6	11	16	....	....	....	....	....
	St. Louis Blues	T1EHL	30	14	10	24	72	....	....	....	....	....
2010-11	Fargo Force	USHL	56	13	14	27	109	5	0	3	3	2
2011-12	Fargo Force	USHL	54	16	22	38	140	6	0	0	0	10
2012-13	Western Mich.	CCHA	32	9	1	10	29	....	....	....	....	....
2013-14	Western Mich.	NCHC	39	11	13	24	38	....	....	....	....	....
2014-15	Western Mich.	NCHC	34	14	14	28	80	....	....	....	....	....
2015-16	Providence Bruins	AHL	66	14	16	30	71	3	0	0	0	0
2016-17	Providence Bruins	AHL	67	8	16	24	55	14	2	1	3	14

HARKINS, Jansen (HAHR-kihnz, YAN-suhn) WPG

Center. Shoots left. 6'1", 194 lbs. Born, Cleveland, OH, May 23, 1997.
(Winnipeg's 3rd pick, 47th overall, in 2015 NHL Draft).

			Regular Season					Playoffs				
Season	Club	League	GP	G	A	Pts	PIM	GP	G	A	Pts	PIM
2011-12	North Shore W.C.	Minor-BC	74	83	70	153	....	....	....	....	....	....
	Van. NW Giants	BCMML	6	2	5	7	0	3	0	0	0	0
2012-13	Van. NW Giants	BCMML	37	14	45	59	14	8	1	*9	10	14
	Prince George	WHL	5	0	0	0	2	....	....	....	....	....
2013-14	Prince George	WHL	67	10	24	34	18	....	....	....	....	....
2014-15	Prince George	WHL	70	20	59	79	45	5	0	4	4	2
2015-16	Prince George	WHL	69	24	33	57	51	4	2	3	5	4
	Manitoba Moose	AHL	6	1	2	3	2	....	....	....	....	....
2016-17	Prince George	WHL	64	21	51	72	48	6	2	5	7	10
	Manitoba Moose	AHL	4	2	2	4	4	....	....	....	....	....

HARPER, Patrick (HAHR-puhr, pa-TRIHK) **NSH**

Center. Shoots left. 5'7", 150 lbs. Born, New York, NY, July 29, 1998.
(Nashville's 6th pick, 138th overall, in 2016 NHL Draft).

			Regular Season					Playoffs				
Season	Club	League	GP	G	A	Pts	PIM	GP	G	A	Pts	PIM
2012-13	Connecticut Oilers	EJEPL	20	12	14	26	12	5	6	4	10	2
	CT Oilers U16	Other	49	28	20	48	16	....	....	....	....	....
2013-14	CT Oilers U16	EJEPL	17	1	2	3	2	5	1	2	3	0
	N.J. Rockets U19	Other	24	13	16	29	2	....	....	....	....	....
2014-15	Neponset Val. U18	Minor-MA	14	14	16	30	2	....	....	....	....	....
	Avon Old Farms	High-CT	22	20	27	47	....	....	....	....	....	....
	USAHNTDP	U-17	4	0	1	1	2	....	....	....	....	....
2015-16	Neponset Val. U18	Minor-MA	13	19	13	*32	4	....	....	....	....	....
	Avon Old Farms	High-CT	27	20	39	59	....	....	....	....	....	....
	Omaha Lancers	USHL	9	1	3	4	2	....	....	....	....	....
2016-17	Boston University	H-East	38	13	24	37	8	....	....	....	....	....

Hockey East All-Rookie Team (2017)

HART, Brian (HAHRT, BRIGH-uhn) **T.B.**

Right wing. Shoots right. 6'3", 222 lbs. Born, Cumberland, ME, November 25, 1993.
(Tampa Bay's 4th pick, 53rd overall, in 2012 NHL Draft).

			Regular Season					Playoffs				
Season	Club	League	GP	G	A	Pts	PIM	GP	G	A	Pts	PIM
2008-09	Greely Rangers	High-ME	20	28	21	39	....	....	....	....	....	....
2009-10	Brewster Academy	High-NH	28	27	24	51	....	....	....	....	....	....
2010-11	Exeter	High-NH	27	29	32	61	12	....	....	....	....	....
2011-12	Exeter	High-NH	29	31	34	65	20	....	....	....	....	....
2012-13	Harvard Crimson	ECAC	30	5	13	18	10	....	....	....	....	....
2013-14	Harvard Crimson	ECAC	31	6	9	15	22	....	....	....	....	....
2014-15	Harvard Crimson	ECAC	37	7	10	17	21	....	....	....	....	....
2015-16	Syracuse Crunch	AHL	25	2	0	2	14	....	....	....	....	....
	Greenville	ECHL	36	11	4	15	4	....	....	....	....	....
2016-17	Syracuse Crunch	AHL	33	3	4	7	26	....	....	....	....	....
	Kalamazoo Wings	ECHL	33	6	5	11	6	7	4	1	5	7

HAWEL, Liam (HIGH-uhl, LEE-uhm) **DAL**

Center. Shoots right. 6'4", 175 lbs. Born, Kanata, ON, April 18, 1999.
(Dallas' 5th pick, 101st overall, in 2017 NHL Draft).

			Regular Season					Playoffs				
Season	Club	League	GP	G	A	Pts	PIM	GP	G	A	Pts	PIM
2014-15	Ott. V. Titans MM	Minor-ON	25	18	31	49	36	10	5	9	14	8
2015-16	Sault Ste. Marie	OHL	65	4	11	15	12	12	0	2	2	2
2016-17	Sault Ste. Marie	OHL	38	6	8	14	18	....	....	....	....	....
	Guelph Storm	OHL	28	3	11	14	22	....	....	....	....	....

HAWRYLUK, Jayce (HAW-rih-luhk, JAYS) **FLA**

Center. Shoots right. 5'11", 185 lbs. Born, Yorkton, SK, January 1, 1996.
(Florida's 2nd pick, 32nd overall, in 2014 NHL Draft).

			Regular Season					Playoffs				
Season	Club	League	GP	G	A	Pts	PIM	GP	G	A	Pts	PIM
2010-11	Russell Rams	Minor-MB	54	138	126	264	....	....	....	....	....	....
2011-12	Parkland Rangers	MMHL	40	31	36	67	138	....	....	....	....	....
2012-13	Brandon	WHL	61	18	25	43	46	....	....	....	....	....
2013-14	Brandon	WHL	59	24	40	64	44	8	5	7	12	14
2014-15	Brandon	WHL	54	30	35	65	69	16	10	9	19	24
2015-16	Brandon	WHL	58	47	59	106	101	21	7	*23	*30	29
2016-17	Springfield	AHL	47	9	17	26	47	....	....	....	....	....

WHL East Second All-Star Team (2016)

HEALEY, Josh (HEE-lee, JAWSH) **CGY**

Defense. Shoots left. 6', 205 lbs. Born, Edmonton, AB, July 12, 1994.

			Regular Season					Playoffs				
Season	Club	League	GP	G	A	Pts	PIM	GP	G	A	Pts	PIM
2009-10	SSAC Bulldogs	Minor-AB	31	4	12	16	22	6	1	3	4	12
2010-11	SSAC Athletics	AMHL	32	2	11	13	34	5	0	2	2	4
	Sherwood Park	AJHL	1	0	0	0	2	....	....	....	....	....
2011-12	Sherwood Park	AJHL	48	2	10	12	61	9	0	2	2	2
2012-13	Sherwood Park	AJHL	53	10	13	23	126	10	1	3	4	11
2013-14	Ohio State	Big Ten	33	1	4	5	18	....	....	....	....	....
2014-15	Ohio State	Big Ten	32	2	7	9	58	....	....	....	....	....
2015-16	Ohio State	Big Ten	33	5	16	21	66	....	....	....	....	....
2016-17	Ohio State	Big Ten	35	4	21	25	70	....	....	....	....	....
	Stockton Heat	AHL	2	0	0	0	0	....	....	....	....	....

Big Ten First All-Star Team (2016)

Signed as a free agent by **Calgary**, March 25, 2017.

HEATHERINGTON, Dillon (HEH-thuhr-ihng-tuhn, DIH-luhn) **DAL**

Defense. Shoots left. 6'2", 220 lbs. Born, Calgary, AB, May 9, 1995.
(Columbus' 4th pick, 50th overall, in 2013 NHL Draft).

			Regular Season					Playoffs				
Season	Club	League	GP	G	A	Pts	PIM	GP	G	A	Pts	PIM
2010-11	Calgary Flames	AMHL	31	0	11	11	44	4	0	0	0	2
	Swift Current	WHL	1	0	0	0	0	....	....	....	....	....
2011-12	Swift Current	WHL	57	2	8	10	63	....	....	....	....	....
2012-13	Swift Current	WHL	71	4	23	27	80	5	0	3	3	0
2013-14	Swift Current	WHL	70	6	29	35	63	6	0	1	1	8
2014-15	Swift Current	WHL	48	1	14	15	48	4	0	0	0	4
	Springfield Falcons	AHL	3	0	1	1	0	....	....	....	....	....
2015-16	Lake Erie Monsters	AHL	63	3	16	19	50	15	0	3	3	6
2016-17	Cleveland	AHL	38	1	5	6	30	....	....	....	....	....
	Texas Stars	AHL	22	2	6	8	21	....	....	....	....	....

Traded to **Dallas** by **Columbus** for Lauri Korpikoski, March 1, 2017.

HEISKANEN, Miro (HAYZ-kuh-nehn, MEE-roh) **DAL**

Defense. Shoots left. 6'1", 172 lbs. Born, Espoo, Finland, July 18, 1999.
(Dallas' 1st pick, 3rd overall, in 2017 NHL Draft).

			Regular Season					Playoffs				
Season	Club	League	GP	G	A	Pts	PIM	GP	G	A	Pts	PIM
2014-15	HIFK Helsinki U18	Fin-U18	35	7	13	20	8	12	0	2	2	2
2015-16	HIFK Helsinki U18	Fin-U18	7	0	7	7	0	2	0	0	0	2
	HIFK Helsinki Jr.	Fin-Jr.	30	3	11	14	6	....	....	....	....	....
2016-17	HIFK Helsinki	Finland	37	5	5	10	4	8	0	3	3	0

HELEWKA, Adam (huh-LOO-kuh, A-duhm) **S.J.**

Left wing. Shoots left. 6'2", 205 lbs. Born, Burnaby, BC, July 21, 1995.
(San Jose's 4th pick, 106th overall, in 2015 NHL Draft).

			Regular Season					Playoffs				
Season	Club	League	GP	G	A	Pts	PIM	GP	G	A	Pts	PIM
2011-12	Van. NW Giants	BCMML	40	24	29	53	74	5	5	4	9	0
2012-13	Spokane Chiefs	WHL	60	10	17	27	12	9	1	2	3	2
2013-14	Spokane Chiefs	WHL	62	23	27	50	32	4	0	0	0	4
2014-15	Spokane Chiefs	WHL	69	44	43	87	59	6	3	2	5	12
2015-16	Spokane Chiefs	WHL	19	16	13	29	23	....	....	....	....	....
	Red Deer Rebels	WHL	34	26	19	45	34	17	9	9	18	18
	San Jose Barracuda	AHL	3	0	1	1	0	....	....	....	....	....
2016-17	San Jose Barracuda	AHL	58	14	15	29	28	12	3	0	3	6
	Allen Americans	ECHL	2	0	0	0	0	....	....	....	....	....

WHL West Second All-Star Team (2015)

HELLICKSON, Matthew (hehl-IHK-suhn, MA-thew) **N.J.**

Defense. Shoots left. 6', 185 lbs. Born, St. Louis Park, MN, March 21, 1998.
(New Jersey's 11th pick, 214th overall, in 2017 NHL Draft).

			Regular Season					Playoffs				
Season	Club	League	GP	G	A	Pts	PIM	GP	G	A	Pts	PIM
2012-13	Rogers Royals	High-MN	25	4	7	11	23	2	0	0	0	0
2013-14	Rogers Royals	High-MN	24	4	23	27	16	1	1	0	1	0
2014-15	USAHNTDP	USHL	30	0	1	1	14	....	....	....	....	....
	USAHNTDP	U-17	19	1	2	3	6	....	....	....	....	....
2015-16	USAHNTDP	USHL	25	0	5	5	8	....	....	....	....	....
	USAHNTDP	U-18	39	0	11	11	6	....	....	....	....	....
2016-17	Sioux City	USHL	52	6	22	28	30	13	1	0	1	6

• Signed Letter of Intent to attend **University of Notre Dame** (Hockey East) in fall of 2017.

HELT, Filip (HEHLT, FIHL-ihp) **ST.L.**

Left wing. Shoots left. 6'1", 176 lbs. Born, Most, Czech Rep., April 9, 1998.
(St. Louis' 8th pick, 211th overall, in 2016 NHL Draft).

			Regular Season					Playoffs				
Season	Club	League	GP	G	A	Pts	PIM	GP	G	A	Pts	PIM
2013-14	HC Litvinov U18	CzR-U18	9	2	0	2	4	....	....	....	....	....
2014-15	HC Litvinov U18	CzR-U18	28	3	9	12	12	2	0	0	0	2
2015-16	HC Litvinov U18	CzR-U18	42	20	26	46	48	....	....	....	....	....
	HC Litvinov Jr.	CzRep-Jr.	7	0	3	3	2	....	....	....	....	....
2016-17	Sarnia Sting	OHL	53	4	12	16	16	4	0	0	0	0

HENRIKSON, Arvid (HEHN-rihk-suhn, AR-vihd) **MTL**

Defense. Shoots right. 6'5", 217 lbs. Born, Stockholm, Sweden, February 23, 1998.
(Montreal's 6th pick, 187th overall, in 2016 NHL Draft).

			Regular Season					Playoffs				
Season	Club	League	GP	G	A	Pts	PIM	GP	G	A	Pts	PIM
2014-15	AIK Solna U18	Swe-U18	33	2	3	5	18	....	....	....	....	....
2015-16	AIK Solna U18	Swe-U18	36	6	24	30	69	....	....	....	....	....
	AIK Solna Jr.	Swe-Jr.	6	0	0	0	6	....	....	....	....	....
	AIK Solna	Sweden-2	1	0	0	0	0	....	....	....	....	....
2016-17	AIK Solna Jr.	Swe-Jr.	37	2	4	6	26	7	0	2	2	8
	AIK Solna	Sweden-2	2	0	0	0	2	....	....	....	....	....

HENRY, Nick (HEHN-ree, NIHK) **COL**

Right wing. Shoots right. 5'11", 191 lbs. Born, Portage, MB, July 4, 1999.
(Colorado's 3rd pick, 94th overall, in 2017 NHL Draft).

			Regular Season					Playoffs				
Season	Club	League	GP	G	A	Pts	PIM	GP	G	A	Pts	PIM
2014-15	Central Plains	MMHL	26	10	19	29	48	....	....	....	....	....
2015-16	Portage Terriers	MJHL	50	26	35	61	38	12	8	6	14	12
2016-17	Regina Pats	WHL	72	35	46	81	49	22	4	8	12	12

HEPONIEMI, Aleksi (heh-poh-NEE-eh-mee, al-EHX-ay) **FLA**

Center. Shoots left. 5'11", 149 lbs. Born, Tampere, Finland, September 1, 1999.
(Florida's 2nd pick, 40th overall, in 2017 NHL Draft).

			Regular Season					Playoffs				
Season	Club	League	GP	G	A	Pts	PIM	GP	G	A	Pts	PIM
2015-16	Ilves Tampere U18	Fin-U18	39	25	40	65	24	5	2	4	6	2
	Ilves Tampere Jr.	Fin-Jr.	7	2	2	4	2	3	0	2	2	0
2016-17	Swift Current	WHL	72	28	58	86	18	14	0	8	8	8

HERBERT, Caleb (HUHR-buhrt, KAY-lehb)

Center. Shoots right. 5'11", 185 lbs. Born, St. Paul, MN, October 12, 1991.
(Washington's 4th pick, 142nd overall, in 2010 NHL Draft).

			Regular Season					Playoffs				
Season	Club	League	GP	G	A	Pts	PIM	GP	G	A	Pts	PIM
2007-08	Bloomington-Jeff.	High-MN	6	4	3	7	6	....	....	....	....	....
2008-09	Bloomington-Jeff.	High-MN	27	29	24	53	36	....	....	....	....	....
2009-10	Team Southeast	UMHSEL	24	14	8	22	....	....	....	....	....	....
	Bloomington-Jeff.	High-MN	25	26	28	54	42	3	4	4	8	2
2010-11	Sioux City	USHL	51	23	27	50	61	3	0	0	0	4
2011-12	U. Minn-Duluth	WCHA	41	14	19	33	30	....	....	....	....	....
2012-13	U. Minn-Duluth	WCHA	35	6	19	25	53	....	....	....	....	....
2013-14	U. Minn-Duluth	NCHC	36	12	19	31	85	....	....	....	....	....
	Hershey Bears	AHL	7	2	1	3	4	....	....	....	....	....
2014-15	Hershey Bears	AHL	12	0	2	2	4	....	....	....	....	....
	South Carolina	ECHL	42	19	9	28	84	27	3	11	14	26
2015-16	Hershey Bears	AHL	26	0	2	2	12	....	....	....	....	....
	South Carolina	ECHL	15	10	4	14	23	19	10	6	16	22
2016-17	Texas Stars	AHL	35	8	5	13	27	....	....	....	....	....
	Idaho Steelheads	ECHL	13	4	4	8	27	....	....	....	....	....

HERZOG, Fabrice (HUHR-tsawg, fah-BREES) TOR

Right wing. Shoots left. 6'2", 176 lbs. Born, Frauenfeld, Switz., December 9, 1994.
(Toronto's 3rd pick, 142nd overall, in 2013 NHL Draft).

			Regular Season					Playoffs				
Season	Club	League	GP	G	A	Pts	PIM	GP	G	A	Pts	PIM
2007-08	Oberthurgau II U17	Swiss-U17	8	6	3	9	4	....	....	....	....	....
2008-09	Oberthurgau U17	Swiss-U17	17	1	1	2	0	2	0	0	0	0
	SC Herisau U17	Swiss-U17	5	0	0	0	2	....	....	....	....	....
2009-10	Oberthurgau U17	Swiss-U17	32	6	7	13	12	6	6	0	6	6
2010-11	Oberthurgau U17	Swiss-U17	27	22	14	36	14	6	6	3	9	0
	Oberthurgau	Swiss-3	2	0	0	0	0	....	....	....	....	....
	Oberthurgau II U17	Swiss-5	1	0	1	1	2	....	....	....	....	....
2011-12	EV Zug Jr.	Swiss-Jr.	35	18	14	32	45	10	6	2	8	6
2012-13	EV Zug Jr.	Swiss-Jr.	32	28	17	45	26	4	3	2	5	2
	EV Zug	Swiss	20	2	2	4	6	....	....	....	....	....
2013-14	Quebec Remparts	QMJHL	61	32	26	58	34	5	3	2	5	4
	Toronto Marlies	AHL	5	0	0	0	0	....	....	....	....	....
2014-15	EV Zug	Swiss	43	6	3	9	16	6	0	3	3	0
2015-16	ZSC Lions Zurich	Swiss	34	9	13	22	57	4	2	0	2	0
2016-17	ZSC Lions Zurich	Swiss	44	9	11	20	14	6	2	1	3	4

HICKETTS, Joe (HIH-kehts, JOH) DET

Defense. Shoots left. 5'8", 175 lbs. Born, Kamloops, BC, May 4, 1996.

			Regular Season					Playoffs				
Season	Club	League	GP	G	A	Pts	PIM	GP	G	A	Pts	PIM
2012-13	Victoria Royals	WHL	67	6	18	24	45	6	0	1	1	2
2013-14	Victoria Royals	WHL	36	6	18	24	12	9	0	2	2	9
2014-15	Victoria Royals	WHL	62	12	52	64	48	10	0	5	5	10
2015-16	Victoria Royals	WHL	59	8	53	61	44	6	1	6	7	8
2016-17	Grand Rapids	AHL	73	7	27	34	40	19	1	7	8	8

WHL West Second All-Star Team (2015) • WHL West First All-Star Team (2016)

Signed as a free agent by **Detroit**, September 24, 2014.

HICKEY, Brandon (HIH-kee, BRAN-duhn) ARI

Defense. Shoots left. 6'2", 190 lbs. Born, Edmonton, AB, April 13, 1996.
(Calgary's 4th pick, 64th overall, in 2014 NHL Draft).

			Regular Season					Playoffs				
Season	Club	League	GP	G	A	Pts	PIM	GP	G	A	Pts	PIM
2009-10	Leduc Roughnecks	Minor-AB	31	6	13	19	44	....	....	....	....	....
2010-11	Leduc Oil Kings	AMBHL	28	6	12	18	52	2	0	1	1	0
	Leduc Oil Kings	Minor-AB	1	0	0	0	0	....	....	....	....	....
2011-12	Leduc Oil Kings	AMHL	19	4	7	11	12	9	0	1	1	0
	Spruce Grove	AJHL	2	0	0	0	2	....	....	....	....	....
2012-13	Spruce Grove	AJHL	55	1	6	7	11	16	0	0	0	12
2013-14	Spruce Grove	AJHL	49	4	18	22	29	13	0	5	5	4
2014-15	Boston University	H-East	41	6	11	17	18	....	....	....	....	....
2015-16	Boston University	H-East	36	5	3	8	28	....	....	....	....	....
2016-17	Boston University	H-East	35	4	11	15	41	....	....	....	....	....

Traded to **Arizona** by **Calgary** wiith Chad Johnson and a conditional 3rd round pick in 2018 NHL Draft for Mike Smith, June 17, 2017.

HICKMAN, Justin (HIHK-muhn, JUHS-tihn) BOS

Right wing. Shoots right. 6'2", 224 lbs. Born, Kelowna, BC, March 18, 1994.

			Regular Season					Playoffs				
Season	Club	League	GP	G	A	Pts	PIM	GP	G	A	Pts	PIM
2009-10	Okanagan Rockets	BCMML	38	13	12	25	58	1	0	0	0	23
2010-11	Seattle	WHL	46	0	2	2	51	....	....	....	....	....
2011-12	Seattle	WHL	71	12	10	22	106	....	....	....	....	....
2012-13	Seattle	WHL	70	12	22	34	115	6	0	1	1	11
2013-14	Seattle	WHL	67	22	24	46	154	9	2	1	3	12
	Bridgeport	AHL	5	1	0	1	4	....	....	....	....	....
2014-15	Seattle	WHL	31	9	19	28	40	....	....	....	....	....
2015-16	Providence Bruins	AHL	66	5	3	8	65	1	0	0	0	0
2016-17	Providence Bruins	AHL	25	2	1	3	19	....	....	....	....	....
	Atlanta Gladiators	ECHL	4	0	0	0	10	....	....	....	....	....

Signed to ATO (amateur tryout) contract by **Bridgeport** (AHL), April 11, 2014. Signed as a free agent by **Boston**, March 4, 2015.

HIGHMORE, Matthew (HIGH-more, MA-thew) CHI

Center. Shoots left. 5'10", 186 lbs. Born, Halifax, NS, February 27, 1996.

			Regular Season					Playoffs				
Season	Club	League	GP	G	A	Pts	PIM	GP	G	A	Pts	PIM
2010-11	Dartmouth	NSMHL	35	13	14	27	14	9	1	4	5	4
2011-12	Dartmouth	NSMHL	25	13	13	26	42	16	3	8	11	18
2012-13	Saint John	QMJHL	30	4	5	9	26	4	0	0	0	8
2013-14	Saint John	QMJHL	68	19	31	50	62	....	....	....	....	....
2014-15	Saint John	QMJHL	62	11	13	24	60	5	0	1	1	6
2015-16	Saint John	QMJHL	65	22	53	75	38	17	9	11	20	12
2016-17	Saint John	QMJHL	64	34	55	89	46	18	6	18	24	14

Signed as a free agent by **Chicago**, March 2, 2017.

HILLMAN, Blake (HIHL-muhn, BLAYK) CHI

Defense. Shoots left. 6'1", 180 lbs. Born, Elk River, MN, January 26, 1996.
(Chicago's 8th pick, 173rd overall, in 2016 NHL Draft).

			Regular Season					Playoffs				
Season	Club	League	GP	G	A	Pts	PIM	GP	G	A	Pts	PIM
2011-12	Elk River Elks	High-MN	25	2	4	6	4	2	0	0	0	0
2012-13	Elk River Elks	High-MN	24	2	12	14	8	2	0	2	2	2
2013-14	Dubuque	USHL	57	3	10	13	24	7	0	0	0	0
2014-15	Dubuque	USHL	42	3	8	11	12	....	....	....	....	....
	Waterloo	USHL	13	0	7	7	6	....	....	....	....	....
2015-16	U. of Denver	NCHC	39	3	8	11	14	....	....	....	....	....
2016-17	U. of Denver	NCHC	43	1	7	8	18	....	....	....	....	....

HINTZ, Roope (HIHNTZ, ROO-peh) DAL

Left wing. Shoots left. 6'3", 185 lbs. Born, Tampere, Finland, November 17, 1996.
(Dallas' 2nd pick, 49th overall, in 2015 NHL Draft).

			Regular Season					Playoffs				
Season	Club	League	GP	G	A	Pts	PIM	GP	G	A	Pts	PIM
2011-12	Ilves Tampere U18	Fin-U18	18	3	6	9	2	....	....	....	....	....
2012-13	Tampa Bay Juniors	EmJHL	20	20	15	35	0	....	....	....	....	....
	Bismarck Bobcats	NAHL	2	0	0	0	0	....	....	....	....	....
	Ilves Tampere U18	Fin-U18	9	4	9	13	0	....	....	....	....	....
2013-14	Ilves Tampere U18	Fin-U18	1	2	0	2	0	7	3	6	9	4
	Ilves Tampere Jr.	Fin-Jr.	29	18	20	38	16	5	0	0	0	2
	Ilves Tampere	Finland	7	0	0	0	2	....	....	....	....	....
2014-15	Ilves Tampere	Finland	42	5	12	17	10	2	0	0	0	0
	Ilves Tampere Jr.	Fin-Jr.	....	....	....	....	....	6	1	1	2	0
2015-16	HIFK Helsinki	Finland	33	8	12	20	4	18	2	4	6	2
2016-17	HIFK Helsinki	Finland	44	19	11	30	18	14	3	*11	*14	4

HISCHIER, Nico (HEE-shuhr, NEE-ko) N.J.

Center. Shoots left. 6'1", 175 lbs. Born, Brig, Switz., April 1, 1999.
(New Jersey's 1st pick, 1st overall, in 2017 NHL Draft).

			Regular Season					Playoffs				
Season	Club	League	GP	G	A	Pts	PIM	GP	G	A	Pts	PIM
2012-13	EHC Visp U17	Swiss-U17	14	12	11	23	0	....	....	....	....	....
2013-14	EHC Visp U17	Swiss-U17	22	32	45	77	4	....	....	....	....	....
	SC Bern U17	Swiss-U17	2	1	2	3	0	2	0	1	1	2
2014-15	SC Bern U17	Swiss-U17	22	28	33	61	2	3	4	5	9	0
	SC Bern Future Jr.	Swiss-Jr.	11	1	1	2	2	10	3	3	6	0
2015-16	SC Bern Future Jr.	Swiss-Jr.	18	11	17	28	6	9	1	8	9	2
	SC Bern	Swiss	15	1	0	1	2	....	....	....	....	....
	EHC Visp	Swiss-2	7	1	1	2	0	6	2	0	2	8
2016-17	Halifax	QMJHL	57	38	48	86	24	6	3	4	7	0

QMJHL All-Rookie Team (2017)

HOBBS, Connor (HAWBZ, KAW-nuhr) WSH

Defense. Shoots right. 6'1", 187 lbs. Born, Regina, SK, January 4, 1997.
(Washington's 3rd pick, 143rd overall, in 2015 NHL Draft).

			Regular Season					Playoffs				
Season	Club	League	GP	G	A	Pts	PIM	GP	G	A	Pts	PIM
2012-13	Saskatoon Blazers	SMHL	38	6	10	16	68	7	1	3	4	14
2013-14	Saskatoon Blazers	SMHL	33	11	12	23	84	....	....	....	....	....
	Medicine Hat	WHL	10	1	2	3	4	....	....	....	....	....
2014-15	Medicine Hat	WHL	12	1	1	2	15	....	....	....	....	....
	Nipawin Hawks	SJHL	4	0	0	0	4	....	....	....	....	....
	Regina Pats	WHL	33	1	15	16	21	8	2	0	2	7
2015-16	Regina Pats	WHL	58	19	22	41	106	12	4	6	10	6
2016-17	Regina Pats	WHL	67	31	54	85	92	23	6	18	24	22

WHL East First All-Star Team (2017)

HOEFENMAYER, Noel (HAWF-ehn-MIGH-uhr, NOH-uhl) ARI

Defense. Shoots left. 6'1", 196 lbs. Born, North York, ON, January 6, 1999.
(Arizona's 6th pick, 108th overall, in 2017 NHL Draft).

			Regular Season					Playoffs				
Season	Club	League	GP	G	A	Pts	PIM	GP	G	A	Pts	PIM
2014-15	Don Mills MM	GTHL	62	10	23	33	28	....	....	....	....	....
2015-16	Ottawa 67's	OHL	45	2	3	5	18	4	0	0	0	0
2016-17	Ottawa 67's	OHL	62	14	26	40	36	6	2	5	7	6

HOFMANN, Gregory (HAWF-muhn, GREH-goh-ree) CAR

Center. Shoots left. 6', 200 lbs. Born, Tramelan, Switz., November 13, 1992.
(Carolina's 4th pick, 103rd overall, in 2011 NHL Draft).

			Regular Season					Playoffs				
Season	Club	League	GP	G	A	Pts	PIM	GP	G	A	Pts	PIM
2006-07	Chaux-de-Fonds Jr.	Swiss-Jr.	2	0	0	0	0	....	....	....	....	....
2007-08	HC Luzern U17	Swiss-U17	6	2	5	7	14	....	....	....	....	....
	Ambri U17	Swiss-U17	22	14	11	25	64	5	4	3	7	20
	Ambri Jr.	Swiss-Jr.	11	4	1	5	6	8	0	0	0	2
2008-09	Ambri U17	Swiss-U17	20	9	16	25	42	....	....	....	....	....
	Ambri Jr.	Swiss-Jr.	22	10	7	17	26	2	0	0	0	2
2009-10	Ambri Jr.	Swiss-Jr.	34	25	30	55	20	3	1	2	3	6
	HC Ambri-Piotta	Swiss	1	0	0	0	0	1	0	0	0	0
2010-11	Ambri Jr.	Swiss-Jr.	2	2	0	2	2	....	....	....	....	....
	HC Ambri-Piotta	Swiss	41	3	9	12	2	12	0	2	2	2
	HC Ambri-Piotta	Swiss-Q	....	....	....	....	....	5	1	2	3	2
2011-12	HC Ambri-Piotta	Swiss	34	5	1	6	6	8	1	0	1	0
	HC Ambri-Piotta	Swiss-Q	....	....	....	....	....	4	1	1	2	2
	Ambri Jr.	Swiss-Jr.	7	3	1	4	2	2	2	0	2	0
2012-13	HC Davos	Swiss	49	16	11	27	20	7	0	2	2	0
2013-14	HC Davos	Swiss	41	7	10	17	30	....	....	....	....	....
2014-15	HC Davos	Swiss	47	11	14	25	18	13	3	2	5	2
2015-16	HC Lugano	Swiss	46	17	14	31	47	13	4	3	7	6
2016-17	HC Lugano	Swiss	45	12	16	28	26	11	1	1	2	2

HOGBERG, Linus (HOHG-buhrg, LEE-nuhs) PHI

Defense. Shoots left. 6'1", 176 lbs. Born, Stockholm, Sweden, September 4, 1998.
(Philadelphia's 7th pick, 139th overall, in 2016 NHL Draft).

			Regular Season					Playoffs				
Season	Club	League	GP	G	A	Pts	PIM	GP	G	A	Pts	PIM
2013-14	Huddinge IK U18	Swe-U18	29	1	6	7	6	....	....	....	....	....
	Huddinge IK Jr.	Swe-Jr.	2	0	2	2	0	....	....	....	....	....
2014-15	Vaxjo U18	Swe-U18	13	2	3	5	6	3	0	1	1	0
	Vaxjo Jr.	Swe-Jr.	40	2	1	3	8	....	....	....	....	....
2015-16	Vaxjo U18	Swe-U18	13	3	9	12	6	....	....	....	....	....
	Vaxjo Jr.	Swe-Jr.	39	7	18	25	14	2	0	0	0	0
	Vaxjo Lakers HC	Sweden	2	0	0	0	0	1	0	0	0	0
2016-17	Vaxjo Jr.	Swe-Jr.	11	1	8	9	4	3	0	0	0	0
	Vaxjo Lakers HC	Sweden	35	0	4	4	6	....	....	....	....	....
	IF Bjorkloven Umea	Sweden-2	3	0	0	0	0	....	....	....	....	....

HOLL, Justin (HOHL, JUHS-tihn) TOR

Defense. Shoots right. 6'3", 199 lbs. Born, Tonka Bay, MN, January 30, 1992.
(Chicago's 3rd pick, 54th overall, in 2010 NHL Draft).

			Regular Season					Playoffs				
Season	Club	League	GP	G	A	Pts	PIM	GP	G	A	Pts	PIM
2007-08	Minnetonka	High-MN	24	0	1	1	0	....	....	....	....	....
2008-09	Minnetonka	High-MN	28	1	6	7	4	....	....	....	....	....
2009-10	Team Southwest	UMHSEL	STATISTICS NOT AVAILABLE									
	Minnetonka	High-MN	25	17	14	31	8	6	3	3	6	0
2010-11	U. of Minnesota	WCHA	25	1	6	7	12	....	....	....	....	....
2011-12	U. of Minnesota	WCHA	43	3	8	11	34	....	....	....	....	....
2012-13	U. of Minnesota	WCHA	35	3	4	7	10	....	....	....	....	....
2013-14	U. of Minnesota	Big Ten	39	1	12	13	20	....	....	....	....	....
2014-15	Rockford IceHogs	AHL	2	0	0	0	0	....	....	....	....	....
	Indy Fuel	ECHL	66	7	27	34	39	....	....	....	....	....
2015-16	Toronto Marlies	AHL	60	5	16	21	15	15	0	4	4	2
2016-17	Toronto Marlies	AHL	72	8	11	19	30	11	1	6	7	2

Signed as a free agent by **Toronto**, July 2, 2016.

HOLM, Philip (HOHLM, FIHL-ihp) VAN

Defense. Shoots left. 6'1", 196 lbs. Born, Stockholm, Sweden, December 8, 1991.

			Regular Season					Playoffs				
Season	Club	League	GP	G	A	Pts	PIM	GP	G	A	Pts	PIM
2010-11	Djurgarden Jr.	Swe-Jr.	41	7	10	17	43	5	1	2	3	0
	Djurgarden	Sweden	1	0	0	0	0	....	....	....	....	....
2011-12	Djurgarden Jr.	Swe-Jr.	4	1	0	1	4	....	....	....	....	....
	Djurgarden	Sweden	50	2	2	4	18	....	....	....	....	....
	Djurgarden	Sweden-Q	10	0	2	2	2	....	....	....	....	....
2012-13	Djurgarden	Sweden-2	52	6	11	17	34	....	....	....	....	....
2013-14	Djurgarden	Sweden-2	44	1	6	7	54	....	....	....	....	....
2014-15	Djurgarden	Sweden	51	2	7	9	20	2	0	0	0	4
2015-16	Djurgarden	Sweden	43	2	5	7	51	8	1	1	2	10
2016-17	Vaxjo Lakers HC	Sweden	52	4	17	21	30	6	0	0	0	0

Signed as a free agent by **Vancouver**, May 26, 2017.

HOLMSTROM, Axel (HOHLM-struhm, AX-uhl) DET

Center. Shoots left. 6'1", 219 lbs. Born, Arvidsjaur, Sweden, June 29, 1996.
(Detroit's 6th pick, 196th overall, in 2014 NHL Draft).

			Regular Season					Playoffs				
Season	Club	League	GP	G	A	Pts	PIM	GP	G	A	Pts	PIM
2011-12	Skelleftea AIK U18	Swe-U18	1	0	2	2	0	4	1	1	2	0
2012-13	Skelleftea AIK U18	Swe-U18	31	16	48	64	6	8	3	8	11	4
	Skelleftea AIK Jr.	Swe-Jr.	10	2	1	3	0	4	0	1	1	0
2013-14	Skelleftea AIK Jr.	Swe-Jr.	33	15	23	38	12	2	0	0	0	0
	Skelleftea AIK	Sweden	4	0	0	0	0	....	....	....	....	....
	Skelleftea AIK U18	Swe-U18	....	....	....	....	....	3	1	3	4	0
2014-15	Skelleftea AIK Jr.	Swe-Jr.	3	0	4	4	0	....	....	....	....	....
	Skelleftea AIK	Sweden	44	10	10	20	4	15	7	*11	*18	0
2015-16	Skelleftea AIK	Sweden	48	8	15	23	20	10	2	4	6	2
2016-17	Skelleftea AIK Jr.	Swe-Jr.	2	0	1	1	0	....	....	....	....	....
	Skelleftea AIK	Sweden	16	1	1	2	0	7	3	4	7	0
	Grand Rapids	AHL	7	1	1	2	2	4	1	0	1	0

HOLWAY, Patrick (HAWL-way, PA-trihk) DET

Defense. Shoots right. 6'4", 200 lbs. Born, Cohasset, MA, October 1, 1996.
(Detroit's 5th pick, 170th overall, in 2015 NHL Draft).

			Regular Season					Playoffs				
Season	Club	League	GP	G	A	Pts	PIM	GP	G	A	Pts	PIM
2011-12	Bos. Adv. U16	T1EHL	40	2	6	8	18	....	....	....	....	....
2012-13	Bos. Adv. U16	T1EHL	41	4	15	19	43	4	0	3	3	2
	Bos. Adv. U18	T1EHL	1	0	0	0	0	....	....	....	....	....
2013-14	Bos. Adv. U18	T1EHL	34	8	11	19	51	....	....	....	....	....
2014-15	Bos. Adv. U18	T1EHL	28	8	17	25	34	....	....	....	....	....
2015-16	Sioux City	USHL	7	0	1	1	35	....	....	....	....	....
	Dubuque	USHL	37	1	6	7	32	....	....	....	....	....
2016-17	U. of Maine	H-East	33	4	9	13	16	....	....	....	....	....

HOWARTH, Kale (HOW-uhrth, KAIL) CBJ

Left wing. Shoots left. 6'5", 208 lbs. Born, Red Deer, AB, October 6, 1997.
(Columbus' 4th pick, 148th overall, in 2017 NHL Draft).

			Regular Season					Playoffs				
Season	Club	League	GP	G	A	Pts	PIM	GP	G	A	Pts	PIM
2012-13	Red Deer Min. Mid.	Minor-AB	24	5	2	7	20	....	....	....	....	....
2013-14	Red Deer Mid. AA	Minor-AB	STATISTICS NOT AVAILABLE									
2014-15	Red Deer Chiefs	AMHL	33	5	6	11	48	....	....	....	....	....
2015-16	Trail Smoke Eaters	BCHL	53	12	15	27	62	....	....	....	....	....
2016-17	Trail Smoke Eaters	BCHL	51	30	29	59	46	9	1	1	2	10

• Signed Letter of Intent to attend **University of Connecticut** (Hockey East) in fall of 2017.

HOWDEN, Brett (HOW-dehn, BREHT) T.B.

Center. Shoots left. 6'2", 190 lbs. Born, Calgary, AB, March 29, 1998.
(Tampa Bay's 1st pick, 27th overall, in 2016 NHL Draft).

			Regular Season					Playoffs				
Season	Club	League	GP	G	A	Pts	PIM	GP	G	A	Pts	PIM
2012-13	Eastman Selects	MMHL	30	11	13	24	16	....	....	....	....	....
2013-14	Eastman Selects	MMHL	38	24	34	58	38	12	5	9	14	20
	Moose Jaw	WHL	5	1	0	1	2	....	....	....	....	....
2014-15	Moose Jaw	WHL	68	22	24	46	24	....	....	....	....	....
2015-16	Moose Jaw	WHL	68	24	40	64	61	10	4	11	15	4
2016-17	Moose Jaw	WHL	58	38	43	81	73	7	2	1	3	12
	Syracuse Crunch	AHL	5	3	1	4	2	3	0	2	2	0

HRONEK, Filip (KH'RAWN-ehk, FIHL-ihp) DET

Defense. Shoots right. 6', 163 lbs. Born, Hradec Kralove, Czech Rep., November 2, 1997.
(Detroit's 3rd pick, 53rd overall, in 2016 NHL Draft).

			Regular Season					Playoffs				
Season	Club	League	GP	G	A	Pts	PIM	GP	G	A	Pts	PIM
2013-14	Hr. Kralove U18	CzR-U18	43	8	7	15	56	4	0	1	1	2
2014-15	Hr. Kralove U18	CzR-U18	33	5	19	24	108	9	4	5	9	35
	Hr. Kralove Jr.	CzRep-Jr.	23	4	13	17	26	1	0	0	0	0
	Hr. Kralove	CzRep	1	0	0	0	2	....	....	....	....	....
2015-16	Hr. Kralove Jr.	CzRep-Jr.	13	4	12	16	12	10	4	5	9	28
	Hr. Kralove	CzRep	40	0	4	4	22	....	....	....	....	....
	Litomerice	CzRep-2	12	2	2	4	18	....	....	....	....	....
2016-17	Saginaw Spirit	OHL	59	14	47	61	60	....	....	....	....	....
	Grand Rapids	AHL	10	1	1	2	4	2	0	0	0	6

HUGHES, Cameron (HEWZ, KAM-ruhn) BOS

Center. Shoots left. 6', 176 lbs. Born, Edmonton, AB, October 9, 1996.
(Boston's 9th pick, 165th overall, in 2015 NHL Draft).

			Regular Season					Playoffs				
Season	Club	League	GP	G	A	Pts	PIM	GP	G	A	Pts	PIM
2011-12	CAC Canadians	AMHL	32	8	23	31	24	....	....	....	....	....
2012-13	Spruce Grove	AJHL	60	11	20	31	42	14	3	6	9	11
2013-14	Spruce Grove	AJHL	52	21	36	57	58	18	1	16	17	2
2014-15	U. of Wisconsin	Big Ten	34	3	10	13	35	....	....	....	....	....
2015-16	U. of Wisconsin	Big Ten	32	5	20	25	12	....	....	....	....	....
2016-17	U. of Wisconsin	Big Ten	36	7	25	32	16	....	....	....	....	....

HULTS, Cole (HUHLTZ, KOHL) L.A.

Defense. Shoots left. 6', 189 lbs. Born, Madison, WI, May 22, 1998.
(Los Angeles' 6th pick, 134th overall, in 2017 NHL Draft).

			Regular Season					Playoffs				
Season	Club	League	GP	G	A	Pts	PIM	GP	G	A	Pts	PIM
2013-14	Madison Caps U18	Minor-WI	42	5	20	25	45	....	....	....	....	....
	Madison Caps U18	Other	17	2	11	13	29	3	0	2	2	0
2014-15	Madison Caps U18	Minor-WI	36	5	11	16	42	....	....	....	....	....
	Madison Caps U18	NAPHL	24	4	13	17	34	4	0	1	1	2
	Madison Capitols	USHL	9	0	2	2	29	....	....	....	....	....
2015-16	Madison Capitols	USHL	54	0	8	8	65	....	....	....	....	....
2016-17	Madison Capitols	USHL	59	6	26	32	112	....	....	....	....	....

• Signed Letter of Intent to attend **Penn State University** (Big Ten) in fall of 2017.

HULTS, Mitch (HULTS, MIHTCH) ANA

Center. Shoots left. 6'2", 210 lbs. Born, Madison, WI, November 13, 1994.

			Regular Season					Playoffs				
Season	Club	League	GP	G	A	Pts	PIM	GP	G	A	Pts	PIM
2009-10	Madison	T1EHL	38	4	3	7	6	....	....	....	....	....
2010-11	Madison U16	T1EHL	36	2	11	13	40	....	....	....	....	....
	Madison U18	T1EHL	10	0	0	0	0	....	....	....	....	....
2011-12	Team Illinois U18	HPHL	26	7	9	16	12	....	....	....	....	....
	Janesville Jets	NAHL	3	0	0	0	0	....	....	....	....	....
2012-13	Team Illinois U18	HPHL	20	10	13	23	24	....	....	....	....	....
	Indiana Ice	USHL	28	5	8	13	8	....	....	....	....	....
2013-14	Indiana Ice	USHL	36	5	6	11	14	8	5	0	5	2
2014-15	Madison Capitols	USHL	55	13	21	34	90	....	....	....	....	....
2015-16	Lake Superior	WCHA	40	9	11	20	56	....	....	....	....	....
2016-17	Lake Superior	WCHA	36	11	*23	34	42	....	....	....	....	....
	San Diego Gulls	AHL	6	1	3	4	0	2	1	0	1	0

WCHA Second All-Star Team (2017)

Signed as a free agent by **Anaheim**, March 20, 2017.

HULTSTROM, Linus (HUHLT-struhm, LEE-nuhs) FLA

Defense. Shoots right. 5'11", 194 lbs. Born, Vimmerby, Sweden, December 9, 1992.

			Regular Season					Playoffs				
Season	Club	League	GP	G	A	Pts	PIM	GP	G	A	Pts	PIM
2012-13	Linkopings HC	Sweden	55	5	3	8	32	10	0	2	2	2
2013-14	Linkopings HC	Sweden	31	1	1	2	8	11	0	3	3	4
2014-15	Linkopings HC	Sweden	5	0	0	0	0	....	....	....	....	....
	Leksands IF	Sweden	48	10	23	33	20	....	....	....	....	....
2015-16	Djurgarden	Sweden	52	12	19	31	16	8	3	9	12	6
2016-17	Djurgarden	Sweden	44	7	13	20	24	3	0	1	1	2

Signed as a free agent by **Florida**, May 3, 2016,

HUNT, Dryden (HUHNT, DRY-dehn) FLA

Left wing. Shoots left. 6', 197 lbs. Born, Nelson, BC, November 24, 1995.

			Regular Season					Playoffs				
Season	Club	League	GP	G	A	Pts	PIM	GP	G	A	Pts	PIM
2009-10	N. Dame Bantam	Minor-SK	25	30	27	57	41	7	6	10	16	20
	Notre Dame Argos	SMHL	4	0	1	1	2	....	....	....	....	....
2010-11	Kootenay Ice	BCMML	40	19	28	47	84	....	....	....	....	....
	Trail Smoke Eaters	BCHL	4	0	0	0	0	....	....	....	....	....
2011-12	Regina Pats	WHL	62	5	5	10	28	3	0	0	0	0
2012-13	Regina Pats	WHL	2	0	0	0	0	....	....	....	....	....
2013-14	Regina Pats	WHL	62	21	19	40	64	....	....	....	....	....
2014-15	Regina Pats	WHL	37	14	33	47	32	....	....	....	....	....
	Medicine Hat	WHL	34	19	17	36	18	10	5	2	7	6
2015-16	Moose Jaw	WHL	72	*58	58	116	48	10	7	9	16	8
2016-17	Springfield	AHL	70	13	18	31	65	....	....	....	....	....
	Manchester	ECHL	2	2	0	2	0	....	....	....	....	....

HURLEY, Connor (HUHR-lee, KAW-nuhr) BUF

Center. Shoots left. 6'2", 185 lbs. Born, Eagan, MN, September 15, 1995.
(Buffalo's 4th pick, 38th overall, in 2013 NHL Draft).

			Regular Season					Playoffs				
Season	Club	League	GP	G	A	Pts	PIM	GP	G	A	Pts	PIM
2009-10	Shattuck Bantam	High-MN	58	20	39	59	14	....	....	....	....	....
2010-11	Hastings Raiders	High-MN	26	10	26	36	24	....	....	....	....	....
2011-12	Edina Hornets	High-MN	25	22	26	48	10	5	4	6	10	2
2012-13	Edina Hornets	High-MN	25	15	28	43	8	6	5	4	9	2
	Team Southwest	UMHSEL	11	3	13	16	12	....	....	....	....	....
	Muskegon	USHL	11	1	7	8	4	3	0	1	1	4
	USAHNTDP	U-18	10	1	1	2	4	....	....	....	....	....
2013-14	Muskegon	USHL	21	3	11	14	14	....	....	....	....	....
	Green Bay	USHL	35	10	26	36	18	4	2	2	4	2
2014-15	U. of Notre Dame	H-East	41	4	10	14	6	....	....	....	....	....
2015-16	U. of Notre Dame	H-East	36	6	12	18	10	....	....	....	....	....
2016-17	U. of Notre Dame	H-East	21	4	12	16	22	....	....	....	....	....

HYKA, Tomas (HEE-kuh, TAW-muhsh) VGK

Right wing. Shoots right. 5'11", 168 lbs. Born, Mlada Boleslav, Czech Rep., March 23, 1993.
(Los Angeles' 4th pick, 171st overall, in 2012 NHL Draft).

			Regular Season					Playoffs				
Season	Club	League	GP	G	A	Pts	PIM	GP	G	A	Pts	PIM
2007-08	Ml. Boleslav U17	CzR-U17	20	0	2	2	2	1	0	0	0	0
2008-09	Ml. Boleslav U17	CzR-U17	42	28	21	49	18	2	1	0	1	2
2009-10	Ml. Boleslav U18	CzR-U18	46	34	24	58	46	2	1	1	2	0
	Ml. Boleslav Jr.	CzRep-Jr.	2	0	1	1	0	....	....	....	....	....
2010-11	Ml. Boleslav U18	CzR-U18	8	3	9	12	6	....	....	....	....	....
	Ml. Boleslav Jr.	CzRep-Jr.	38	14	17	31	10	....	....	....	....	....
	BK Mlada Boleslav	CzRep	14	1	0	1	6	....	....	....	....	....
2011-12	Gatineau	QMJHL	50	20	44	64	30	4	1	1	2	0
2012-13	Gatineau	QMJHL	49	20	34	54	24	10	2	2	4	8
2013-14	Farjestad	Sweden	40	4	5	9	6	....	....	....	....	....
2014-15	BK Mlada Boleslav	CzRep	22	7	3	10	10	9	2	1	3	4
2015-16	BK Mlada Boleslav	CzRep	47	12	18	30	22	10	3	1	4	2
2016-17	BK Mlada Boleslav	CzRep	48	17	21	38	18	5	4	1	5	6

Signed as a free agent by **Vegas**, June 1, 2017.

IACOPELLI, Matt (YA-koh-peh-lee, MAT) CHI

Right wing. Shoots left. 6'3", 206 lbs. Born, Woodhaven, MI, May 15, 1994.
(Chicago's 2nd pick, 83rd overall, in 2014 NHL Draft).

			Regular Season					Playoffs				
Season	Club	League	GP	G	A	Pts	PIM	GP	G	A	Pts	PIM
2011-12	Det. L.C.	HPHL	17	5	5	10	6	....	....	....	....	....
	Texas Tornado	NAHL	1	0	0	0	0	....	....	....	....	....
2012-13	Det. B. Tire U18	T1EHL	39	26	20	46	65	5	0	2	2	6
	Springfield-IL	NAHL	4	3	1	4	0	....	....	....	....	....
2013-14	Muskegon	USHL	58	*41	22	63	47	....	....	....	....	....
2014-15	Muskegon	USHL	56	23	14	37	38	11	5	2	7	10
2015-16	Western Mich.	NCHC	27	1	6	7	6	....	....	....	....	....
2016-17	Western Mich.	NCHC	40	20	16	36	20	....	....	....	....	....

USHL First All-Star Team (2014)

IAFALLO, Alex (IGH-A-faw-LOW, AL-ehx) L.A.

Center. Shoots left. 6', 185 lbs. Born, Eden, NY, December 21, 1993.

			Regular Season					Playoffs				
Season	Club	League	GP	G	A	Pts	PIM	GP	G	A	Pts	PIM
2010-11	Buffalo Regals	T1EHL	39	15	21	36	27	....	....	....	....	....
2011-12	Fargo Force	USHL	58	17	15	32	8	6	2	2	4	2
2012-13	Fargo Force	USHL	50	20	23	43	15	13	6	10	*16	4
2013-14	U. Minn-Duluth	NCHC	36	11	11	22	10	....	....	....	....	....
2014-15	U. Minn-Duluth	NCHC	34	8	17	25	12	....	....	....	....	....
2015-16	U. Minn-Duluth	NCHC	40	8	15	23	8	....	....	....	....	....
2016-17	U. Minn-Duluth	NCHC	42	21	*30	*51	22	....	....	....	....	....

NCHC All-Rookie Team (2014) • NCHC First All-Star Team (2017) • NCAA West First All-American Team (2017)

Signed as a free agent by **Los Angeles**, April 18, 2017.

IKONEN, Henri (EEH-koh-nehn, AWN-ree)

Left wing. Shoots left. 6', 182 lbs. Born, Savonlinna, Finland, April 17, 1994.
(Tampa Bay's 4th pick, 154th overall, in 2013 NHL Draft).

			Regular Season					Playoffs				
Season	Club	League	GP	G	A	Pts	PIM	GP	G	A	Pts	PIM
2008-09	SaPKo U18	Fin-U18	3	1	2	3	0	....	....	....	....	....
2009-10	SaPKo U18	Fin-U18	5	6	4	10	12	....	....	....	....	....
	SapKo Jr.	Fin-Jr.	14	13	8	21	8	4	3	0	3	4
2010-11	KalPa Kuopio U18	Fin-U18	10	5	6	11	28	4	1	3	4	0
	KalPa Kuopio Jr.	Fin-Jr.	33	9	13	22	10	....	....	....	....	....
2011-12	KalPa Kuopio U18	Fin-U18	6	6	9	15	2	....	....	....	....	....
	KalPa Kuopio Jr.	Fin-Jr.	37	17	28	45	18	9	8	6	14	2
	KalPa Kuopio	Finland	8	0	1	1	4	....	....	....	....	....
2012-13	Kingston	OHL	61	22	29	51	30	4	1	0	1	4
2013-14	Kingston	OHL	54	25	45	70	49	7	1	5	6	8
	Syracuse Crunch	AHL	6	0	2	2	2	....	....	....	....	....
2014-15	Syracuse Crunch	AHL	59	5	8	13	43	3	0	0	0	0
2015-16	Syracuse Crunch	AHL	61	3	8	11	31	....	....	....	....	....
	Greenville	ECHL	3	1	0	1	0	....	....	....	....	....
2016-17	Syracuse Crunch	AHL	54	6	11	17	27	1	0	1	1	0

IKONEN, Joni (IH-koh-nehn, YOH-nee) MTL

Right wing. Shoots right. 5'11", 182 lbs. Born, Espoo, Finland, April 14, 1999.
(Montreal's 3rd pick, 58th overall, in 2017 NHL Draft).

			Regular Season					Playoffs				
Season	Club	League	GP	G	A	Pts	PIM	GP	G	A	Pts	PIM
2014-15	Blues Espoo U18	Fin-U18	45	20	38	58	24	9	4	4	8	4
2015-16	Frolunda U18	Swe-U18	39	31	21	52	43	4	1	0	1	0
2016-17	Frolunda U18	Swe-U18	4	2	3	5	0	7	6	6	12	4
	Frolunda Jr.	Swe-Jr.	40	22	19	41	42	5	3	0	3	2
	Frolunda	Sweden	10	0	0	0	0	....	....	....	....	....

IMAMA, Boko (ih-MA-ma, BOH-KOH) L.A.

Left wing. Shoots left. 6'1", 214 lbs. Born, Montreal, QC, August 3, 1996.
(Tampa Bay's 9th pick, 180th overall, in 2015 NHL Draft).

			Regular Season					Playoffs				
Season	Club	League	GP	G	A	Pts	PIM	GP	G	A	Pts	PIM
2011-12	Laval-Montreal	QAAA	43	7	9	16	30	....	....	....	....	....
2012-13	Baie-Comeau	QMJHL	44	3	3	6	34	5	0	0	0	9
2013-14	Baie-Comeau	QMJHL	59	7	8	15	101	14	0	4	4	14
2014-15	Baie-Comeau	QMJHL	36	10	9	19	89	....	....	....	....	....
	Saint John	QMJHL	23	3	6	9	48	5	0	1	1	6
2015-16	Saint John	QMJHL	48	7	12	19	86	10	1	3	4	15
2016-17	Saint John	QMJHL	66	41	14	55	105	18	8	7	15	22

Traded to **Los Angeles** by **Tampa Bay** for Los Angeles' 7th round pick in 2018 NHL Draft, May 31, 2017.

INAMOTO, Tyler (ihn-a-MOH-toh, TIGH-luhr) FLA

Defense. Shoots left. 6'1", 192 lbs. Born, Flemington, NJ, June 5, 1999.
(Florida's 4th pick, 133rd overall, in 2017 NHL Draft).

			Regular Season					Playoffs				
Season	Club	League	GP	G	A	Pts	PIM	GP	G	A	Pts	PIM
2014-15	Shattuck U16	High-MN	49	2	21	23	69	....	....	....	....	....
2015-16	USAHNTDP	USHL	14	0	1	1	37	....	....	....	....	....
	USAHNTDP	U-17	13	0	2	2	8	....	....	....	....	....
2016-17	USAHNTDP	USHL	17	2	5	7	49	....	....	....	....	....
	USAHNTDP	U-18	34	0	6	6	59	....	....	....	....	....

• Signed Letter of Intent to attend **University of Wisconsin** (Big Ten) in fall of 2017.

JACKSON, Jacob (JAK-suhn, JAY-kuhb) S.J.

Center. Shoots left. 5'11", 190 lbs. Born, Maplewood, MN, December 5, 1994.
(San Jose's 6th pick, 201st overall, in 2013 NHL Draft).

			Regular Season					Playoffs				
Season	Club	League	GP	G	A	Pts	PIM	GP	G	A	Pts	PIM
2010-11	Tartan School	High-MN	25	15	10	25	18	1	1	0	1	0
2011-12	Tartan School	High-MN	25	24	19	43	28	2	1	0	1	2
2012-13	Tartan School	High-MN	25	29	27	56	10	1	3	0	3	0
	Team Northeast	UMHSEL	21	10	4	14	10	....	....	....	....	....
	Waterloo	USHL	2	1	0	1	0	....	....	....	....	....
2013-14	Des Moines	USHL	42	2	6	8	20	....	....	....	....	....
2014-15	Michigan Tech	WCHA	DID NOT PLAY – FRESHMAN									
2015-16	Michigan Tech	WCHA	11	1	0	1	17	....	....	....	....	....
2016-17	Michigan Tech	WCHA	41	10	6	16	20	....	....	....	....	....

JACOBS, Joshua (JAY-kuhbz, JAW-shoo-wah) N.J.

Defense. Shoots right. 6'2", 200 lbs. Born, Shelby Township, MI, February 15, 1996.
(New Jersey's 2nd pick, 41st overall, in 2014 NHL Draft).

			Regular Season					Playoffs				
Season	Club	League	GP	G	A	Pts	PIM	GP	G	A	Pts	PIM
2010-11	Detroit Belle Tire	T1EHL	31	9	19	28	24	....	....	....	....	....
2011-12	Det. Honeybaked	HPHL	24	3	14	17	20	....	....	....	....	....
	Det. Honeybaked	Minor-MI	....	....	....	....	....	7	0	3	3	0
2012-13	Indiana Ice	USHL	48	2	13	15	52	....	....	....	....	....
2013-14	Indiana Ice	USHL	56	5	18	23	46	12	3	2	5	2
2014-15	Michigan State	Big Ten	35	0	9	9	26	....	....	....	....	....
2015-16	Sarnia Sting	OHL	67	4	20	24	38	7	0	5	5	6
	Albany Devils	AHL	1	0	0	0	0	....	....	....	....	....
2016-17	Albany Devils	AHL	49	0	9	9	32	4	0	0	0	0
	Adirondack	ECHL	1	0	0	0	0	....	....	....	....	....

JAROS, Christian (YA-ruhsh, KRIHS-ch'yehn) OTT

Defense. Shoots right. 6'3", 226 lbs. Born, Kosice, Slovakia, April 2, 1996.
(Ottawa's 7th pick, 139th overall, in 2015 NHL Draft).

			Regular Season					Playoffs				
Season	Club	League	GP	G	A	Pts	PIM	GP	G	A	Pts	PIM
2010-11	HC Kosice U18	Svk-U18	2	0	0	0	0	....	....	....	....	....
	HK Trebisov U18	Svk-U18	5	0	0	0	0	....	....	....	....	....
2011-12	HC Kosice U18	Svk-U18	38	4	10	14	26	....	....	....	....	....
2012-13	HC Kosice U18	Svk-U18	15	3	17	20	16	2	0	0	0	0
2013-14	Lulea HF U18	Swe-U18	34	11	14	25	44	5	0	2	2	6
	Lulea HF Jr.	Swe-Jr.	3	1	3	4	0	....	....	....	....	....
2014-15	Lulea HF Jr.	Swe-Jr.	23	4	8	12	74	3	0	1	1	6
	Asploven	Sweden-2	6	0	1	1	0	....	....	....	....	....
	Lulea HF	Sweden	25	0	1	1	6	....	....	....	....	....
2015-16	Asploven	Sweden-2	22	2	3	5	53	....	....	....	....	....
	Lulea HF	Sweden	25	0	5	5	45	10	0	3	3	20
2016-17	Lulea HF	Sweden	36	5	8	13	22	....	....	....	....	....

JASEK, Lukas (YAH-shehk, LOO-kuhs) VAN

Right wing. Shoots right. 6'1", 165 lbs. Born, Trinec, Czech Rep., August 28, 1997.
(Vancouver's 6th pick, 174th overall, in 2015 NHL Draft).

			Regular Season					Playoffs				
Season	Club	League	GP	G	A	Pts	PIM	GP	G	A	Pts	PIM
2011-12	HC Trinec U18	CzR-U18	9	2	4	6	2	....	....	....	....	....
2012-13	HC Trinec U18	CzR-U18	38	21	29	50	4	9	2	7	9	0
	HC Trinec Jr.	CzRep-Jr.	2	0	0	0	0	....	....	....	....	....
2013-14	Sodertalje SK U18	Swe-U18	15	5	7	12	4	....	....	....	....	....
	Sodertalje SK Jr.	Swe-Jr.	25	2	2	4	10	....	....	....	....	....
2014-15	HC Trinec Jr.	CzRep-Jr.	24	10	17	27	6	....	....	....	....	....
	HC Ocelari Trinec	CzRep	27	0	2	2	4	1	0	0	0	0
	HC Trinec U18	CzR-U18	....	....	....	....	....	2	1	1	2	6
2015-16	HC Trinec Jr.	CzRep-Jr.	17	19	19	38	45	7	5	10	15	6
	HC Frydek-Mistek	CzRep-3	2	1	0	1	2	....	....	....	....	....
	Havirov	CzRep-2	2	0	0	0	2	....	....	....	....	....
	HC Ocelari Trinec	CzRep	25	2	1	3	18	1	0	0	0	0
2016-17	HC Trinec Jr.	CzRep-Jr.	2	0	3	3	0	6	4	10	14	0
	HC Ocelari Trinec	CzRep	16	0	0	0	2	4	0	1	1	2
	HC Frydek-Mistek	CzRep-2	30	9	19	28	16	8	3	3	6	54

JENYS, Pavel (YEH-nihsh, PAH-vehl) MIN

Center. Shoots left. 6'3", 202 lbs. Born, Brno, Czech Rep., April 2, 1996.
(Minnesota's 8th pick, 199th overall, in 2014 NHL Draft).

			Regular Season					Playoffs				
Season	Club	League	GP	G	A	Pts	PIM	GP	G	A	Pts	PIM
2010-11	Brno U18	CzR-U18	3	1	0	1	0	....	....	....	....	....
2011-12	Brno U18	CzR-U18	33	8	9	17	18	2	0	0	0	2
2012-13	Brno U18	CzR-U18	9	6	9	15	6	3	0	2	2	2
	Brno Jr.	CzRep-Jr.	29	7	8	15	12	....	....	....	....	....
	HC Kometa Brno	CzRep	1	0	0	0	0	....	....	....	....	....
2013-14	Brno Jr.	CzRep-Jr.	26	13	6	19	35	....	....	....	....	....
	HC Kometa Brno	CzRep	29	2	0	2	4	....	....	....	....	....
	Brno U18	CzR-U18	....	....	....	....	....	10	10	3	13	6
2014-15	Sudbury Wolves	OHL	63	15	30	45	45	....	....	....	....	....
	Iowa Wild	AHL	8	0	3	3	0	....	....	....	....	....
2015-16	Sudbury Wolves	OHL	24	4	8	12	16	....	....	....	....	....
	Niagara Ice Dogs	OHL	42	11	14	25	20	17	8	9	17	4
2016-17	Quad City	ECHL	46	12	4	16	8	1	0	0	0	0

JERABEK, Jakub (yair-A-behk, ya-KUHB) MTL

Defense. Shoots left. 5'11", 190 lbs. Born, Plzen, Czech Rep., May 12, 1991.

			Regular Season					Playoffs				
Season	Club	League	GP	G	A	Pts	PIM	GP	G	A	Pts	PIM
2008-09	HC Plzen Jr.	CzRep-Jr.	40	8	20	28	32	5	0	3	3	8
	Plzen	CzRep	2	0	0	0	2	....	....	....	....	....
	Beroun	CzRep-2	4	0	1	1	6	1	0	0	0	0
2009-10	HC Plzen Jr.	CzRep-Jr.	12	4	12	16	6	4	1	2	3	8
	HC Plzen 1929	CzRep	37	0	2	2	22	2	0	0	0	2
2010-11	HC Plzen Jr.	CzRep-Jr.	3	0	2	2	0	....	....	....	....	....
	HC Plzen 1929	CzRep	41	1	6	7	20	4	0	1	1	2
	Usti nad Labem	CzRep-2	....	....	....	....	....	8	1	2	3	6
2011-12	Pirati Chomutov	CzRep-2	4	0	0	0	2	....	....	....	....	....
	HC Plzen 1929	CzRep	32	1	3	4	22	10	0	2	2	6
	SK Kadan	CzRep-2	12	1	4	5	8	....	....	....	....	....
2012-13	HC Skoda Plzen	CzRep	49	2	6	8	44	17	1	3	4	12
2013-14	HC Skoda Plzen	CzRep	47	1	12	13	24	6	0	1	1	12
2014-15	HC Skoda Plzen	CzRep	48	7	25	32	40	4	0	3	3	8
2015-16	HC Skoda Plzen	CzRep	52	4	29	33	56	11	0	5	5	20
2016-17	Podolsk	KHL	59	5	29	34	56	4	1	1	2	8

Signed as a free agent by **Montreal**, April 28, 2017.

JEVPALOVS, Nikita (yehv-PAH-lahf, nih-KEE-tuh)

Right wing. Shoots right. 6'1", 210 lbs. Born, Riga, Latvia, September 9, 1994.

			Regular Season					Playoffs				
Season	Club	League	GP	G	A	Pts	PIM	GP	G	A	Pts	PIM
2012-13	Blainville-Bois.	QMJHL	60	18	21	39	36	15	3	5	8	2
2013-14	Blainville-Bois.	QMJHL	61	28	26	54	32	20	10	6	16	8
2014-15	Blainville-Bois.	QMJHL	64	49	51	100	30	5	1	5	6	4
2015-16	San Jose Barracuda	AHL	60	5	9	14	12	3	1	0	1	0
	Allen Americans	ECHL	5	1	5	6	2	15	2	6	8	10
2016-17	San Jose Barracuda	AHL	65	13	8	21	41	11	0	0	0	6

QMJHL Second All-Star Team (2015)

Signed as a free agent by **San Jose**, January 26, 2015.

JOHANSEN, Lucas (joh-HAHN-suhn, LOO-kuhs) WSH

Defense. Shoots left. 6'1", 175 lbs. Born, Vancouver, BC, November 16, 1997.
(Washington's 1st pick, 28th overall, in 2016 NHL Draft).

			Regular Season					Playoffs				
Season	Club	League	GP	G	A	Pts	PIM	GP	G	A	Pts	PIM
2012-13	Van. NE Chiefs	BCMML	40	3	7	10	8	3	0	1	1	0
2013-14	Van. NE Chiefs	BCMML	40	7	17	24	26	3	0	1	1	4
2014-15	Kelowna Rockets	WHL	65	1	7	8	16	19	1	4	5	6
2015-16	Kelowna Rockets	WHL	69	10	39	49	20	18	2	6	8	8
2016-17	Kelowna Rockets	WHL	68	6	35	41	39	17	0	8	8	6

JOHANSSON, Emil (yoh-HAHN-suhn, eh-MIHL) BOS

Defense. Shoots left. 6', 189 lbs. Born, Vaxjo, Sweden, May 6, 1996.
(Boston's 5th pick, 206th overall, in 2014 NHL Draft).

			Regular Season					Playoffs				
Season	Club	League	GP	G	A	Pts	PIM	GP	G	A	Pts	PIM
2010-11	Aseda IF Jr.	Swe-Jr.	....	0	3	3	22	....	....	....	....	....
	Aseda IF	Sweden-4	31	1	2	3	12	....	....	....	....	....
2011-12	Aseda IF	Sweden-4	14	4	0	4	14	....	....	....	....	....
2012-13	HV 71 U18	Swe-U18	32	5	12	17	14	....	....	....	....	....
	HV 71 Jr.	Swe-Jr.	1	1	1	2	0	....	....	....	....	....
2013-14	HV 71 U18	Swe-U18	6	2	3	5	20	....	....	....	....	....
	HV 71 Jr.	Swe-Jr.	42	2	7	9	28	....	....	....	....	....
2014-15	HV 71 Jr.	Swe-Jr.	11	0	2	2	10	3	0	0	0	2
	HV 71 Jonkoping	Sweden	35	0	1	1	12	6	0	0	0	4
2015-16	HV 71 Jr.	Swe-Jr.	2	1	2	3	4	....	....	....	....	....
	HV 71 Jonkoping	Sweden	50	2	8	10	12	6	3	2	5	0
2016-17	Djurgarden	Sweden	49	7	10	17	26	3	0	0	0	4
	Providence Bruins	AHL	6	0	1	1	4	1	0	0	0	0

JOHNSON, Adam (JAWN-suhn, A-duhm) PIT

Left wing. Shoots left. 6', 175 lbs. Born, Hibbing, MN, June 22, 1994.

			Regular Season					Playoffs				
Season	Club	League	GP	G	A	Pts	PIM	GP	G	A	Pts	PIM
2009-10	Hibbing/Chis.	High-MN	24	8	15	23	8	3	1	1	2	0
2010-11	Hibbing/Chis.	High-MN	25	34	36	70	8	6	8	7	15	0
2011-12	Team North	UMHSEL	21	9	8	17	8	3	0	0	0	0
	Hibbing/Chis.	High-MN	20	24	28	52	14	3	4	3	7	6
2012-13	Team North	UMHSEL	21	6	8	14	14	3	1	0	1	2
	Hibbing/Chis.	High-MN	24	16	27	43	70	2	4	0	4	0
2013-14	Sioux City	USHL	56	15	31	46	25	8	4	3	7	6
2014-15	Sioux City	USHL	59	31	40	71	24	5	1	2	3	2
2015-16	U. Minn-Duluth	NCHC	39	6	12	18	8	....	....	....	....	....
2016-17	U. Minn-Duluth	NCHC	42	18	19	37	18	....	....	....	....	....

Signed as a free agent by **Pittsburgh**, July 6, 2017.

JOHNSON, Luke (JAWN-suhn, LOOK) CHI

Center. Shoots right. 6', 194 lbs. Born, Grand Forks, ND, September 19, 1994.
(Chicago's 6th pick, 134th overall, in 2013 NHL Draft).

			Regular Season					Playoffs				
Season	Club	League	GP	G	A	Pts	PIM	GP	G	A	Pts	PIM
2008-09	Gr. Forks R.R.R.	High-ND	27	9	17	26	....	....	....	....	....	....
2009-10	Grand Forks C.K.	High-ND	27	17	29	46	....	....	....	....	....	....
2010-11	Team Great Plains	UMHSEL	20	9	12	21	26	3	0	1	1	0
	Grand Forks C.K.	High-ND	25	17	25	42	....	....	....	....	....	....
2011-12	Lincoln Stars	USHL	55	20	35	55	52	8	1	1	2	2
2012-13	Lincoln Stars	USHL	57	19	27	46	32	5	0	0	0	0
2013-14	North Dakota	NCHC	42	8	13	21	26	....	....	....	....	....
2014-15	North Dakota	NCHC	42	11	13	24	54	....	....	....	....	....
2015-16	North Dakota	NCHC	43	11	10	21	45	....	....	....	....	....
2016-17	Rockford IceHogs	AHL	73	8	9	17	31	....	....	....	....	....

JOHNSON, Steven (JAWN-suhn, STEE-vehn) L.A.

Defense. Shoots left. 6', 185 lbs. Born, Excelsior, MN, June 27, 1994.
(Los Angeles' 5th pick, 120th overall, in 2014 NHL Draft).

			Regular Season					Playoffs				
Season	Club	League	GP	G	A	Pts	PIM	GP	G	A	Pts	PIM
2010-11	Minnetonka	High-MN	25	0	8	8	0	2	0	0	0	0
2011-12	Minnetonka	High-MN	25	2	2	4	0	3	2	0	2	2
2012-13	Aberdeen Wings	NAHL	59	6	7	13	32	....	....	....	....	....
2013-14	USAHNTDP	USHL	56	5	26	31	6	4	0	2	2	0
2014-15	U. of Minnesota	Big Ten	11	0	1	1	4	....	....	....	....	....
2015-16	U. of Minnesota	Big Ten	33	3	7	10	6	....	....	....	....	....
2016-17	U. of Minnesota	Big Ten	37	0	14	14	8	....	....	....	....	....

JOHNSSON, Andreas (JAWN-suhn, ahn-DRAY-uhs) TOR

Left wing. Shoots left. 5'10", 184 lbs. Born, Gavle, Sweden, November 21, 1994.
(Toronto's 5th pick, 202nd overall, in 2013 NHL Draft).

			Regular Season					Playoffs				
Season	Club	League	GP	G	A	Pts	PIM	GP	G	A	Pts	PIM
2009-10	Frolunda U18	Swe-U18	5	1	1	2	0	....	....	....	....	....
2010-11	Frolunda U18	Swe-U18	27	23	22	45	26	5	3	1	4	2
	Frolunda Jr.	Swe-Jr.	30	9	5	14	4	3	0	1	1	0
2011-12	Frolunda U18	Swe-U18	6	9	5	14	4	4	2	4	6	4
	Frolunda Jr.	Swe-Jr.	42	19	13	32	75	2	0	0	0	0
2012-13	Frolunda Jr.	Swe-Jr.	42	23	31	54	54	4	1	1	2	12
	Frolunda	Sweden	7	1	0	1	0	5	0	0	0	0
2013-14	Frolunda Jr.	Swe-Jr.	4	1	4	5	0	....	....	....	....	....
	Frolunda	Sweden	44	15	9	24	2	7	1	0	1	4
2014-15	Frolunda	Sweden	55	22	13	35	34	8	2	2	4	4
2015-16	Frolunda	Sweden	52	19	25	44	20	16	2	2	4	8
	Toronto Marlies	AHL	....	....	....	....	....	2	0	0	0	0
2016-17	Toronto Marlies	AHL	75	20	27	47	42	11	6	0	6	13

JOKIHARJU, Henri (yoh-kee-HAHR-yoo, HEHN-ree) CHI

Defense. Shoots right. 6', 188 lbs. Born, Oulu, Finland, June 17, 1999.
(Chicago's 1st pick, 29th overall, in 2017 NHL Draft).

			Regular Season					Playoffs				
Season	Club	League	GP	G	A	Pts	PIM	GP	G	A	Pts	PIM
2014-15	Jokerit U18	Fin-U18	37	8	22	30	6	10	4	2	6	2
2015-16	Tappara U18	Fin-U18	....	....	....	....	....	3	0	2	2	10
	Tappara Jr.	Fin-Jr.	47	9	20	29	20	3	1	2	3	4
2016-17	Portland	WHL	71	9	39	48	38	11	0	3	3	4

JOLY, D'artagnan (ZHOH-lee, DAHR-tan-YUHN) CGY

Right wing. Shoots left. 6'3", 175 lbs. Born, Gatineau, QC, July 4, 1999.
(Calgary's 4th pick, 171st overall, in 2017 NHL Draft).

			Regular Season					Playoffs				
Season	Club	League	GP	G	A	Pts	PIM	GP	G	A	Pts	PIM
2014-15	Gatineau Intrepide	QAAA	41	8	7	15	20	3	0	0	0	2
2015-16	Gatineau Intrepide	QAAA	33	23	20	43	28	....	....	....	....	....
	Gatineau	QMJHL	3	0	0	0	0	....	....	....	....	....
	Baie-Comeau	QMJHL	35	1	7	8	10	....	....	....	....	....
2016-17	Baie-Comeau	QMJHL	66	16	32	48	35	4	1	0	1	9

JONES, Ben (JOHNZ, BEHN) VGK

Center. Shoots left. 5'11", 187 lbs. Born, Waterloo, ON, February 26, 1999.
(Las Vegas' 12th pick, 189th overall, in 2017 NHL Draft).

			Regular Season					Playoffs				
Season	Club	League	GP	G	A	Pts	PIM	GP	G	A	Pts	PIM
2014-15	Tor. Marlboros MM	GTHL	74	27	42	69	50	....	....	....	....	....
	Stouffville Spirit	ON-Jr.A	1	1	1	2	0	....	....	....	....	....
2015-16	Niagara Ice Dogs	OHL	61	5	4	9	16	6	0	0	0	4
2016-17	Niagara Ice Dogs	OHL	63	13	37	50	56	4	0	1	1	6

JONES, Caleb (JOHNZ, KA-lehb) EDM

Defense. Shoots left. 6'1", 192 lbs. Born, Arlington, TX, June 6, 1997.
(Edmonton's 2nd pick, 117th overall, in 2015 NHL Draft).

			Regular Season					Playoffs				
Season	Club	League	GP	G	A	Pts	PIM	GP	G	A	Pts	PIM
2012-13	Dal. Stars MM	T1EHL	40	2	17	19	36	4	0	1	1	2
2013-14	USAHNTDP	USHL	33	0	7	7	57	....	....	....	....	....
	USAHNTDP	U-17	19	1	7	8	33	....	....	....	....	....
2014-15	USAHNTDP	USHL	25	2	6	8	28	....	....	....	....	....
	USAHNTDP	U-18	40	4	13	17	22	....	....	....	....	....
2015-16	Portland	WHL	72	10	45	55	64	4	0	2	2	6
	Bakersfield	AHL	3	0	0	0	2	....	....	....	....	....
2016-17	Portland	WHL	63	9	53	62	54	11	2	8	10	28

JONES, Kellen (JOHNZ, KEHL-ehn)

Left wing. Shoots left. 5'9", 164 lbs. Born, Montrose, BC, August 16, 1990.
(Edmonton's 11th pick, 202nd overall, in 2010 NHL Draft).

			Regular Season					Playoffs				
Season	Club	League	GP	G	A	Pts	PIM	GP	G	A	Pts	PIM
2006-07	Beaver Valley	KIJHL	50	32	35	67	48	13	8	4	12	6
	Vernon Vipers	BCHL	2	0	1	1	0	16	3	5	8	8
2007-08	Vernon Vipers	BCHL	60	12	55	67	30	10	7	4	11	8
2008-09	Vernon Vipers	BCHL	51	15	37	52	16	17	6	12	18	8
2009-10	Vernon Vipers	BCHL	41	12	41	53	18	19	5	14	19	14
2010-11	Quinnipiac	ECAC	38	8	14	22	33	....	....	....	....	....
2011-12	Quinnipiac	ECAC	36	14	22	36	39	....	....	....	....	....
2012-13	Quinnipiac	ECAC	43	13	14	27	24	....	....	....	....	....
2013-14	Quinnipiac	ECAC	40	18	24	42	27	....	....	....	....	....
	Oklahoma City	AHL	5	0	1	1	0	....	....	....	....	....
2014-15	Oklahoma City	AHL	49	5	10	15	10	10	2	1	3	0
	Bakersfield	ECHL	27	7	18	25	12	....	....	....	....	....
2015-16	Missouri Mavericks	ECHL	23	6	19	25	10	6	0	0	0	4
	Bakersfield	AHL	12	1	2	3	6					
	Utica Comets	AHL	21	3	2	5	2	4	0	0	0	2
2016-17	Bridgeport	AHL	58	6	9	15	48	....	....	....	....	....

ECAC Second All-Star Team (2014)

Signed as a free agent by **Oklahoma City** (AHL), April 3, 2014. Signed as a free agent by **Missouri** (ECHL), September 25, 2015. Signed to a PTO (professional tryout) contract by **Bakersfield** (AHL), November 23, 2015. Signed to a PTO (professional tryout) contract by **Utica** (AHL, March 3, 2016. Signed as a free agent by **Bridgeport** (AHL), July 5, 2016.

JONES, Max (JOHNZ, MAX) ANA

Left wing. Shoots left. 6'2", 206 lbs. Born, Rochester, MI, February 17, 1998.
(Anaheim's 1st pick, 24th overall, in 2016 NHL Draft).

			Regular Season					Playoffs				
Season	Club	League	GP	G	A	Pts	PIM	GP	G	A	Pts	PIM
2012-13	Det. Comp. U16	HPHL	20	5	8	13	34	....	....	....	....	....
2013-14	Det. H-Baked U18	HPHL	25	9	13	22	123	....	....	....	....	....
2014-15	USAHNTDP	USHL	24	5	5	10	116	....	....	....	....	....
	USAHNTDP	U-17	16	13	5	18	73	....	....	....	....	....
2015-16	London Knights	OHL	63	28	24	52	106	6	1	1	2	23
2016-17	London Knights	OHL	33	17	19	36	65	14	7	5	12	24
	San Diego Gulls	AHL	....	....	....	....	....	9	1	1	2	6

JONES, Ryan (JOHNZ, RIGH-uhn) PIT

Defense. Shoots left. 6'1", 186 lbs. Born, Munster, IN, May 26, 1996.
(Pittsburgh's 4th pick, 121st overall, in 2016 NHL Draft).

			Regular Season					Playoffs				
Season	Club	League	GP	G	A	Pts	PIM	GP	G	A	Pts	PIM
2012-13	Indiana Jr. Ice U16	Minor-IN	30	0	8	8	38	....	....	....	....	....
	Indiana Jr. Ice U16	HPHL	8	0	1	1	4	....	....	....	....	....
	Indiana Jr. Ice U16	NAPHL	18	1	2	3	32	5	2	1	3	8
2013-14	Indiana Jr. Ice U18	Minor-IN	44	9	12	21	56	....	....	....	....	....
	Indiana Jr. Ice U18	HPHL	10	2	2	4	10	....	....	....	....	....
	Min. Wilderness	NAHL	1	0	0	0	0	....	....	....	....	....
2014-15	Lincoln Stars	USHL	60	4	9	13	69	....	....	....	....	....
2015-16	Lincoln Stars	USHL	60	3	27	30	112	4	0	1	1	16
2016-17	Nebraska-Omaha	NCHC	35	1	5	6	52	....	....	....	....	....

JONSSON-FJALLBY, Axel (YAWN-suhn-FAWL-BEE, AX-uhl) WSH

Left wing. Shoots left. 6', 170 lbs. Born, Stockholm, Sweden, February 10, 1998.
(Washington's 5th pick, 147th overall, in 2016 NHL Draft).

			Regular Season					Playoffs				
Season	Club	League	GP	G	A	Pts	PIM	GP	G	A	Pts	PIM
2012-13	Varmdo HC U18	Swe-U18	4	0	2	2	4	....	....	....	....	....
2013-14	Djurgarden U18	Swe-U18	8	0	1	1	0	1	0	0	0	0
2014-15	Djurgarden U18	Swe-U18	38	11	18	29	6	5	2	1	3	2
2015-16	Djurgarden U18	Swe-U18	6	2	1	3	4	5	1	3	4	2
	Djurgarden Jr.	Swe-Jr.	39	13	16	29	8	7	4	4	8	4
2016-17	Djurgarden Jr.	Swe-Jr.	32	17	20	37	14	1	0	0	0	0
	Djurgarden	Sweden	24	0	1	1	0	2	0	1	1	0

JORG, Mauro (YOHRG, MAHW-roh) N.J.

Right wing. Shoots left. 6', 200 lbs. Born, Chur, Switz., April 29, 1990.
(New Jersey's 5th pick, 204th overall, in 2010 NHL Draft).

			Regular Season					Playoffs				
Season	Club	League	GP	G	A	Pts	PIM	GP	G	A	Pts	PIM
2006-07	HC Lugano Jr.	Swiss-Jr.	4	2	3	5	6	....	....	....	....	....
	EHC Arosa	Swiss-3	7	4	1	5	8	1	0	0	0	2
	EHC Chur	Swiss-2	20	1	1	2	0	....	....	....	....	....
2007-08	Switzerland U20	Swiss-2	1	0	0	0	0	....	....	....	....	....
	EHC Chur Jr.	Swiss-Jr.	4	4	1	5	18	....	....	....	....	....
	EHC Chur	Swiss-2	40	11	9	20	33	....	....	....	....	....
	HC Lugano Jr.	Swiss-Jr.	8	5	2	7	12	....	....	....	....	....
	HC Lugano	Swiss	....	....	....	....	....	1	0	0	0	0
2008-09	Switzerland U20	Swiss-2	5	0	0	0	0	....	....	....	....	....
	HC Lugano	Swiss	47	3	3	6	6	7	0	0	0	0
	HC Ceresio Lugano	Swiss-3	1	0	0	0	0	....	....	....	....	....
	HC Lugano Jr.	Swiss-Jr.	3	0	3	3	0	2	0	3	3	4
2009-10	HC Lugano	Swiss	44	1	7	8	14	4	0	0	0	0
	HC Lugano Jr.	Swiss-Jr.	1	0	0	0	0	....	....	....	....	....
	EHC Visp	Swiss-2	....	....	....	....	....	7	0	1	1	0
2010-11	HC Lugano	Swiss	50	3	9	12	26	4	0	0	0	2
2011-12	HC Lugano	Swiss	48	4	3	7	8	6	0	2	2	0
	Sierre	Swiss-2	2	3	1	4	2	....	....	....	....	....
2012-13	Rapperswil	Swiss	48	4	6	10	10	12	0	4	4	4
2013-14	Rapperswil	Swiss	52	6	11	17	31	6	2	0	2	0
2014-15	HC Davos	Swiss	49	14	8	22	14	14	2	2	4	2
2015-16	HC Davos	Swiss	47	11	18	29	4	9	2	1	3	0
2016-17	HC Davos	Swiss	32	7	7	14	4	10	2	1	3	2

JOSEPH, Mathieu (JOH-seph, MA-tyew) T.B.

Right wing. Shoots right. 6'1", 172 lbs. Born, Laval, QC, February 9, 1997.
(Tampa Bay's 6th pick, 120th overall, in 2015 NHL Draft).

			Regular Season					Playoffs				
Season	Club	League	GP	G	A	Pts	PIM	GP	G	A	Pts	PIM
2012-13	Antoine-Girouard	Minor-QC	34	26	23	49	61	....	....	....	....	....
	Antoine-Girouard	QAAA	3	0	1	1	2	2	0	1	1	0
2013-14	Antoine-Girouard	QAAA	32	11	25	36	68	....	....	....	....	....
	Saint John	QMJHL	30	1	10	11	10	....	....	....	....	....
2014-15	Saint John	QMJHL	59	21	21	42	46	5	1	2	3	4
2015-16	Saint John	QMJHL	58	33	40	73	57	5	5	2	7	8
2016-17	Saint John	QMJHL	54	36	44	80	57	18	13	*19	*32	14

QMJHL Second All-Star Team (2017)

JOSEPH, Pierre-Olivier (JOH-sehf, PEE-air-oh-lihv-EE-ay) ARI

Defense. Shoots left. 6'2", 160 lbs. Born, Laval, QC, July 1, 1999.
(Arizona's 1st pick, 23rd overall, in 2017 NHL Draft).

			Regular Season					Playoffs				
Season	Club	League	GP	G	A	Pts	PIM	GP	G	A	Pts	PIM
2014-15	Antoine-Girouard	QAAA	42	3	8	11	18	....	....	....	....	....
2015-16	Antoine-Girouard	QAAA	19	1	9	10	12	....	....	....	....	....
	Charlottetown	QMJHL	48	1	7	8	30	12	1	2	3	6
2016-17	Charlottetown	QMJHL	62	6	33	39	54	13	1	5	6	12

JOSEPHS, Troy (JOH-sehfs, TROI) PIT

Center. Shoots left. 6'1", 184 lbs. Born, Whitby, ON, May 9, 1994.
(Pittsburgh's 6th pick, 209th overall, in 2013 NHL Draft).

			Regular Season					Playoffs				
Season	Club	League	GP	G	A	Pts	PIM	GP	G	A	Pts	PIM
2009-10	Whitby Wildcats	Minor-ON	70	27	25	52	52	4	0	0	0	6
2010-11	PEAC Panthers	High-ON	52	29	38	67	38	....	....	....	....	....
	Pickering Panthers	ON-Jr.A	7	4	1	5	4	....	....	....	....	....
2011-12	St. Michael's	ON-Jr.A	41	11	13	24	10	5	0	0	0	2
2012-13	St. Michael's	ON-Jr.A	42	17	20	37	64	24	7	13	20	38
2013-14	Clarkson Knights	ECAC	33	2	3	5	60	....	....	....	....	....
2014-15	Clarkson Knights	ECAC	36	3	14	17	14	....	....	....	....	....
2015-16	Clarkson Knights	ECAC	28	5	7	12	35	....	....	....	....	....
2016-17	Clarkson Knights	ECAC	37	20	13	33	42	....	....	....	....	....
	Wilkes-Barre	AHL	13	1	1	2	10	1	0	0	0	0

JOSHUA, Dakota (JAW-shoo-wuh, duh-KOH-tuh) TOR

Center. Shoots left. 6'2", 182 lbs. Born, Dearborn, MI, May 15, 1996.
(Toronto's 4th pick, 128th overall, in 2014 NHL Draft).

			Regular Season					Playoffs				
Season	Club	League	GP	G	A	Pts	PIM	GP	G	A	Pts	PIM
2012-13	Det. H-Baked U16	HPHL	18	12	10	22	18	....	....	....	....	....
	Det. H-Baked U18	HPHL	11	0	0	0	0	....	....	....	....	....
	USAHNTDP	USHL	6	2	0	2	2	....	....	....	....	....
	Sioux Falls	USHL	1	0	1	1	0	....	....	....	....	....
2013-14	Sioux Falls	USHL	55	17	21	38	58	3	0	0	0	8
2014-15	Sioux Falls	USHL	52	20	24	44	74	11	4	9	13	38
2015-16	Ohio State	Big Ten	29	5	12	17	50	....	....	....	....	....
2016-17	Ohio State	Big Ten	33	12	23	35	58	....	....	....	....	....

JUOLEVI, Olli (EW-oh-LEH-vee, oh-LEE) VAN

Defense. Shoots left. 6'2", 188 lbs. Born, Helsinki, Finland, May 5, 1998.
(Vancouver's 1st pick, 5th overall, in 2016 NHL Draft).

			Regular Season					Playoffs				
Season	Club	League	GP	G	A	Pts	PIM	GP	G	A	Pts	PIM
2013-14	Jokerit U18	Fin-U18	33	7	22	29	63	12	1	8	9	16
	Jokerit Helsinki Jr.	Fin-Jr.	11	1	3	4	6	....	....	....	....	....
2014-15	Jokerit Helsinki Jr.	Fin-Jr.	44	6	26	32	28	5	1	2	3	2
2015-16	London Knights	OHL	57	9	33	42	16	18	3	11	14	4
2016-17	London Knights	OHL	58	10	33	43	36	14	3	5	8	8

Memorial Cup All-Star Team (2016)

JUULSEN, Noah (JOOL-suhn, NOH-uh) MTL

Defense. Shoots right. 6'2", 191 lbs. Born, Surrey, BC, April 2, 1997.
(Montreal's 1st pick, 26th overall, in 2015 NHL Draft).

			Regular Season					Playoffs				
Season	Club	League	GP	G	A	Pts	PIM	GP	G	A	Pts	PIM
2012-13	Fraser Valley	BCMML	35	6	19	25	24	....	....	....	....	....
	Everett Silvertips	WHL	1	0	0	0	0	....	....	....	....	....
2013-14	Everett Silvertips	WHL	59	2	8	10	32	3	0	0	0	2
2014-15	Everett Silvertips	WHL	68	9	43	52	42	6	0	1	1	8
2015-16	Everett Silvertips	WHL	63	7	21	28	37	6	0	2	2	10
2016-17	Everett Silvertips	WHL	49	12	22	34	38	10	0	2	2	10
	St. John's IceCaps	AHL	....	....	....	....	....	2	0	0	0	0

WHL West Second All-Star Team (2016) • WHL West First All-Star Team (2017)

KADEYKIN, Alexander (ka-DAY-kihn, al-ehx-AN-duhr) DET

Center. Shoots left. 6'3", 213 lbs. Born, Elektrostal, Russia, October 4, 1993.
(Detroit's 7th pick, 201st overall, in 2014 NHL Draft).

			Regular Season					Playoffs				
Season	Club	League	GP	G	A	Pts	PIM	GP	G	A	Pts	PIM
2008-09	Elektrostal 2	Russia-4	12	2	4	6	0	....	....	....	....	....
2010-11	Mytischi Jr.	Russia-Jr.	48	10	19	29	42	6	1	1	2	2
2011-12	Mytischi Jr.	Russia-Jr.	60	22	36	58	20	12	7	9	16	22
2012-13	Mytischi Jr.	Russia-Jr.	26	14	29	43	4	8	4	7	11	6
	Mytischi	KHL	2	0	0	0	0	2	0	0	0	0
2013-14	Mytischi Jr.	Russia-Jr.	1	1	0	1	2	3	0	3	3	2
	Mytischi	KHL	54	8	15	23	24	3	0	0	0	0
2014-15	Mytischi	KHL	9	0	1	1	2	....	....	....	....	....
	SKA St. Petersburg	KHL	20	4	4	8	2	....	....	....	....	....
2015-16	SKA St. Petersburg	KHL	48	5	6	11	14	4	0	0	0	0
2016-17	Yaroslavl	KHL	41	7	8	15	19	15	2	2	4	10

KALYNUK, Wyatt (KAL-ih-nuhk, WIGH-uht) PHI

Defense. Shoots left. 6'1", 180 lbs. Born, Brandon, MB, April 14, 1997.
(Philadelphia's 9th pick, 196th overall, in 2017 NHL Draft).

			Regular Season					Playoffs				
Season	Club	League	GP	G	A	Pts	PIM	GP	G	A	Pts	PIM
2012-13	Southwest	MMHL	43	1	16	17	34	5	0	2	2	4
2013-14	Virden Oil Capitals	MJHL	56	1	12	13	8	10	1	2	3	6
2014-15	Lincoln Stars	USHL	55	0	15	15	16	....	....	....	....	....
2015-16	Bloomington	USHL	59	3	21	24	16	10	0	2	2	8
2016-17	Bloomington	USHL	60	6	25	31	82	....	....	....	....	....

• Signed Letter of Intent to attend **University of Wisconsin** (Big Ten) in fall of 2017.

KAMPF, David (KAWMPF, DAY-vihd) CHI

Right wing. Shoots left. 6'2", 192 lbs. Born, Jirkov, Czech Rep., January 12, 1995.

			Regular Season					Playoffs				
Season	Club	League	GP	G	A	Pts	PIM	GP	G	A	Pts	PIM
2011-12	Chomutov U18	CzR-U18	42	17	29	46	2	2	2	0	2	2
2012-13	Chomutov U18	CzR-U18	14	13	13	26	8	....	....	....	....	....
	KLH Chomutov Jr.	CzRep-Jr.	24	8	7	15	16	3	0	0	0	0
	Pirati Chomutov	CzRep	2	0	0	0	0	....	....	....	....	....
	SK Kadan	CzRep-2	6	0	3	3	0	2	0	0	0	0
2013-14	KLH Chomutov Jr.	CzRep-Jr.	8	5	10	15	6	1	1	0	1	2
	Pirati Chomutov	CzRep	51	1	3	4	14	....	....	....	....	....
	SK Kadan	CzRep-2	5	0	2	2	2	....	....	....	....	....
	Pirati Chomutov	CzRep-Q	12	1	0	1	0	....	....	....	....	....
2014-15	KLH Chomutov Jr.	CzRep-Jr.	3	0	6	6	6	....	....	....	....	....
	Pirati Chomutov	CzRep-2	53	12	13	25	16	11	2	5	7	6
2015-16	Pirati Chomutov	CzRep	42	9	4	13	22	8	0	1	1	0
	KLH Chomutov Jr.	CzRep-Jr.	....	....	....	....	....	1	2	0	2	2
2016-17	Pirati Chomutov	CzRep	52	15	16	31	16	15	3	7	10	6

Signed as a free agent by **Chicago**, May 1, 2017.

KANZIG, Keegan (KAN-zihg, KEE-guhn) **CAR**

Defense. Shoots left. 6'7", 247 lbs. Born, Athabasca, AB, February 26, 1995.
(Calgary's 4th pick, 67th overall, in 2013 NHL Draft).

			Regular Season					Playoffs				
Season	Club	League	GP	G	A	Pts	PIM	GP	G	A	Pts	PIM
2010-11	Ft. Saskatchewan	AMHL	31	4	8	12	82	3	0	0	0	18
2011-12	Victoria Royals	WHL	63	0	2	2	66	4	0	0	0	8
2012-13	Victoria Royals	WHL	70	0	7	7	159	6	1	0	1	10
2014-15	Victoria Royals	WHL	21	0	6	6	51	....	....	....	....	....
	Calgary Hitmen	WHL	49	3	13	16	*115	17	0	3	3	31
2015-16	Calgary Hitmen	WHL	53	13	7	20	75	5	1	0	1	4
	Stockton Heat	AHL	3	0	0	0	2	....	....	....	....	....
2016-17	Stockton Heat	AHL	6	0	2	2	19	....	....	....	....	....
	Adirondack	ECHL	40	1	4	5	65	6	0	1	1	21

Traded to **Carolina** by **Calgary** with Calgary's 6th round pick in 2019 NHL Draft for Eddie Lack, Ryan Murphy and Carolina's 7th round pick in 2019 NHL Draft, June 29, 2017.

KAPRIZOV, Kirill (kah-PREE-zawf, kih-REEL) **MIN**

Left wing. Shoots left. 5'9", 185 lbs. Born, Novokuznetsk, Russia, April 26, 1997.
(Minnesota's 4th pick, 135th overall, in 2015 NHL Draft).

			Regular Season					Playoffs				
Season	Club	League	GP	G	A	Pts	PIM	GP	G	A	Pts	PIM
2013-14	Novokuznetsk Jr.	Russia-Jr.	52	18	16	34	30	8	1	2	3	2
2014-15	Novokuznetsk	KHL	31	4	4	8	6	....	....	....	....	....
	Novokuznetsk Jr.	Russia-Jr.	3	0	2	2	2	3	0	0	0	2
2015-16	Novokuznetsk Jr.	Russia-Jr.	4	7	3	10	0	4	1	2	3	0
	Novokuznetsk	KHL	53	11	16	27	10	....	....	....	....	....
2016-17	Ufa	KHL	49	20	22	42	66	5	3	0	3	0

KARA, Vladislav (KAH-RAH, vla-dih-SLAHV) **TOR**

Left wing. Shoots left. 6'2", 187 lbs. Born, Salekhard, Russia, April 20, 1998.
(Toronto's 4th pick, 124th overall, in 2017 NHL Draft).

			Regular Season					Playoffs				
Season	Club	League	GP	G	A	Pts	PIM	GP	G	A	Pts	PIM
2014-15	Mozhaisk Jr.	Russia-Jr. B	40	21	27	48	109	....	....	....	....	....
	HK Trnava U18	Svk-U18	3	2	8	10	4	10	13	14	27	36
2015-16	Irbis Kazan Jr.	Russia-Jr.	41	4	9	13	22	....	....	....	....	....
2016-17	Bars Kazan	Russia-2	34	3	5	8	4	....	....	....	....	....
	Irbis Kazan Jr.	Russia-Jr.	31	11	9	20	10	7	4	1	5	4

KARABACEK, Vaclav (kahr-ah-BAH-chehk, VATS-lav) **BUF**

Right wing. Shoots right. 6', 196 lbs. Born, Brandys nad Labem, Czech Rep., May 2, 1996.
(Buffalo's 4th pick, 49th overall, in 2014 NHL Draft).

			Regular Season					Playoffs				
Season	Club	League	GP	G	A	Pts	PIM	GP	G	A	Pts	PIM
2011-12	HC Letnany U18	CzR-U18	25	15	14	29	18	....	....	....	....	....
2012-13	EC Salzburg U18	Aust-U18	21	26	19	45	55	....	....	....	....	....
	EC Salzburg Jr. II	Austria-Jr.	5	2	1	3	2	....	....	....	....	....
2013-14	Gatineau	QMJHL	65	21	26	47	40	9	6	6	12	10
2014-15	Gatineau	QMJHL	31	11	14	25	44	....	....	....	....	....
	Baie-Comeau	QMJHL	28	6	9	15	18	....	....	....	....	....
2015-16	Baie-Comeau	QMJHL	23	8	8	16	30	....	....	....	....	....
	Moncton Wildcats	QMJHL	24	10	4	14	26	17	6	3	9	14
2016-17	Rochester	AHL	23	3	5	8	4	....	....	....	....	....
	Elmira Jackals	ECHL	9	5	6	11	10	....	....	....	....	....

KARJALAINEN, Miro (kah-ree-uh-LIGH-nuhn, MEE-roh) **DAL**

Defense. Shoots right. 6'5", 200 lbs. Born, Espoo, Finland, May 23, 1996.
(Dallas' 6th pick, 135th overall, in 2014 NHL Draft).

			Regular Season					Playoffs				
Season	Club	League	GP	G	A	Pts	PIM	GP	G	A	Pts	PIM
2012-13	K-Vantaa U18	Fin-U18	2	0	0	0	0	....	....	....	....	....
	EKS Espoo U17	Fin-U17	1	0	0	0	25	....	....	....	....	....
	EKS Espoo U18	Fin-U18	4	4	2	6	2	....	....	....	....	....
	EKS Espoo	Finland-5	2	0	0	0	0	....	....	....	....	....
2013-14	K-Vantaa U18	Fin-U18	1	0	0	0	0	....	....	....	....	....
	Jokerit U18	Fin-U18	38	1	7	8	57	11	2	3	5	6
2014-15	HIFK Helsinki Jr.	Fin-Jr.	10	0	1	1	8	3	2	0	2	0
2015-16	HIFK Helsinki Jr.	Fin-Jr.	17	1	6	7	105	....	....	....	....	....
	HIFK Helsinki	Finland	2	0	0	0	0	....	....	....	....	....
	Kiekko-Vantaa	Finland-2	7	0	0	0	25	7	0	2	2	4
2016-17	HIFK Helsinki	Finland	4	1	0	1	0	....	....	....	....	....
	Idaho Steelheads	ECHL	24	1	2	3	21	....	....	....	....	....

KARLSSON, Anton (KAHRL-suhn, AN-tawn) **ARI**

Left wing. Shoots left. 6'1", 188 lbs. Born, Lerum, Sweden, August 3, 1996.
(Arizona's 4th pick, 87th overall, in 2014 NHL Draft).

			Regular Season					Playoffs				
Season	Club	League	GP	G	A	Pts	PIM	GP	G	A	Pts	PIM
2010-11	Frolunda U18	Swe-U18	4	0	1	1	0	....	....	....	....	....
2011-12	Frolunda U18	Swe-U18	28	12	19	31	32	....	....	....	....	....
2012-13	Frolunda U18	Swe-U18	23	20	19	39	64	3	1	3	4	0
	Frolunda Jr.	Swe-Jr.	17	4	4	8	4	3	1	1	2	0
2013-14	Frolunda U18	Swe-U18	5	2	5	7	10	5	3	3	6	2
	Mora IK	Sweden-2	9	0	0	0	2	....	....	....	....	....
	Frolunda Jr.	Swe-Jr.	28	12	10	22	88	3	0	2	2	2
2014-15	Skelleftea AIK	Sweden	6	0	1	1	0	....	....	....	....	....
	Skelleftea AIK Jr.	Swe-Jr.	16	8	6	14	37	....	....	....	....	....
	Frolunda	Sweden	9	0	1	1	2	....	....	....	....	....
	Frolunda Jr.	Swe-Jr.	16	6	9	15	4	8	3	7	10	6
2015-16	Frolunda Jr.	Swe-Jr.	8	1	2	3	2	....	....	....	....	....
	Frolunda	Sweden	19	0	2	2	2	....	....	....	....	....
	Bofors	Sweden-2	3	1	1	2	0	....	....	....	....	....
	Leksands IF	Sweden-2	26	2	7	9	8	7	0	1	1	0
2016-17	Frolunda	Sweden	6	0	0	0	0	....	....	....	....	....
	IK Oskarshamn	Sweden-2	48	6	4	10	16	....	....	....	....	....

KARLSTROM, Fredrik (KAHRL-struhm, FREHD-rihk) **DAL**

Center. Shoots left. 6', 169 lbs. Born, Huddinge, Sweden, January 12, 1998.
(Dallas' 2nd pick, 90th overall, in 2016 NHL Draft).

			Regular Season					Playoffs				
Season	Club	League	GP	G	A	Pts	PIM	GP	G	A	Pts	PIM
2012-13	Trangsunds IF U18	Swe-U18	30	15	21	36	12	....	....	....	....	....
	Trangsunds IF Jr.	Swe-Jr.	1	0	0	0	0	6	1	1	2	0
	Trangsunds IF	Sweden-4	2	0	0	0	0	....	....	....	....	....
2013-14	IFK Taby HC U18	Swe-U18	13	2	9	11	0	....	....	....	....	....
2014-15	AIK Solna U18	Swe-U18	40	20	41	61	12	2	1	0	1	0
	AIK Solna Jr.	Swe-Jr.	....	....	....	....	....	1	0	0	0	2
2015-16	AIK Solna U18	Swe-U18	9	11	12	23	6	....	....	....	....	....
	AIK Solna Jr.	Swe-Jr.	44	13	20	33	16	6	5	6	11	4
	AIK Solna	Sweden-2	2	0	0	0	2	....	....	....	....	....
2016-17	AIK Solna Jr.	Swe-Jr.	1	0	0	0	0	5	3	4	7	0
	AIK Solna	Sweden-2	50	10	15	25	4	2	0	0	0	0

KARNAUKHOV, Pavel (kahr-nuh-OO-kawf, PAH-vehl) **CGY**

Center. Shoots left. 6'3", 206 lbs. Born, Minsk, Belarus, March 15, 1997.
(Calgary's 3rd pick, 136th overall, in 2015 NHL Draft).

			Regular Season					Playoffs				
Season	Club	League	GP	G	A	Pts	PIM	GP	G	A	Pts	PIM
2013-14	CSKA Jr.	Russia-Jr.	48	13	16	29	56	11	3	2	5	4
2014-15	Calgary Hitmen	WHL	69	20	22	42	51	17	6	5	11	10
2015-16	Calgary Hitmen	WHL	49	12	19	31	52	5	2	1	3	4
2016-17	CSKA Moscow	KHL	11	0	1	1	12	8	0	0	0	5
	Zvezda Chekhov	Russia-2	24	7	11	18	10	3	0	0	0	2
	CSKA Jr.	Russia-Jr.	2	0	0	0	4	11	5	5	10	4

KAROW, Michael (KAIR-oh, MIGH-kuhl) **ARI**

Defense. Shoots left. 6'2", 197 lbs. Born, Green Bay, WI, December 18, 1998.
(Arizona's 7th pick, 126th overall, in 2017 NHL Draft).

			Regular Season					Playoffs				
Season	Club	League	GP	G	A	Pts	PIM	GP	G	A	Pts	PIM
2013-14	Green Bay	High-WI	24	7	12	19	20	1	0	1	1	0
2014-15	Notre Dame Acad.	High-WI	22	6	6	12	8	2	0	1	1	0
2015-16	Team Wisconsin	UMHSEL	20	3	10	13	18	3	0	0	0	0
	Notre Dame Acad.	High-WI	24	3	14	17	18	1	1	2	3	0
2016-17	Youngstown	USHL	58	4	17	21	39	5	1	2	3	6

• Signed Letter of Intent to attend **Boston College** (Hockey East) in fall of 2017.

KASE, David (kah-SHEH, DAY-vihd) **PHI**

Right wing. Shoots left. 5'11", 164 lbs. Born, Kadan, Czech Rep., January 28, 1997.
(Philadelphia's 7th pick, 128th overall, in 2015 NHL Draft).

			Regular Season					Playoffs				
Season	Club	League	GP	G	A	Pts	PIM	GP	G	A	Pts	PIM
2011-12	Chomutov U18	CzR-U18	13	3	2	5	2	1	0	0	0	0
2012-13	Chomutov U18	CzR-U18	25	5	21	26	8	....	....	....	....	....
	KLH Chomutov Jr.	CzRep-Jr.	4	0	1	1	0	....	....	....	....	....
2013-14	Chomutov U18	CzR-U18	14	9	22	31	4	3	1	2	3	0
	KLH Chomutov Jr.	CzRep-Jr.	35	11	19	30	10	11	2	1	3	8
2014-15	KLH Chomutov Jr.	CzRep-Jr.	8	7	8	15	2	9	5	7	12	12
	Pirati Chomutov	CzRep-2	30	7	7	14	10	1	0	0	0	0
2015-16	SK Kadan	CzRep-2	16	6	8	14	6	....	....	....	....	....
	KLH Chomutov Jr.	CzRep-Jr.	1	0	1	1	0	2	1	3	4	2
	Pirati Chomutov	CzRep	30	1	0	1	2	8	1	1	2	2
2016-17	SK Trhaci Kadan	CzRep-2	8	4	3	7	0	....	....	....	....	....
	Pirati Chomutov	CzRep	32	3	6	9	8	15	2	4	6	4

KASPICK, Tanner (KAZ-pihk, TA-nuhr) **ST.L.**

Center. Shoots left. 6', 203 lbs. Born, Brandon, MB, January 28, 1998.
(St. Louis' 4th pick, 119th overall, in 2016 NHL Draft).

			Regular Season					Playoffs				
Season	Club	League	GP	G	A	Pts	PIM	GP	G	A	Pts	PIM
2012-13	Brandon	MMHL	42	8	30	38	30	7	3	4	7	4
2013-14	Brandon	MMHL	40	28	35	63	42	7	1	10	11	10
	Brandon	WHL	1	1	0	1	0	....	....	....	....	....
2014-15	Brandon	WHL	53	1	17	18	15	13	1	2	3	4
2015-16	Brandon	WHL	53	13	18	31	37	21	5	5	10	28
2016-17	Brandon	WHL	49	19	26	45	75	3	0	2	2	8

KATCHOUK, Boris (kuh-CHOOK, BOHR-ihs) **T.B.**

Left wing. Shoots left. 6'1", 190 lbs. Born, Waterloo, ON, June 18, 1998.
(Tampa Bay's 3rd pick, 44th overall, in 2016 NHL Draft).

			Regular Season					Playoffs				
Season	Club	League	GP	G	A	Pts	PIM	GP	G	A	Pts	PIM
2013-14	Wat. Wolves MM	Minor-ON	29	25	33	58	35	10	3	9	12	8
2014-15	Soo Thunderbirds	NOJHL	29	18	27	45	18	11	4	11	15	0
	Sault Ste. Marie	OHL	12	0	2	2	17	....	....	....	....	....
2015-16	Sault Ste. Marie	OHL	63	24	27	51	61	12	6	4	10	4
2016-17	Sault Ste. Marie	OHL	66	35	29	64	46	11	8	5	13	12

KAYUMOV, Artur (kigh-YOO-mawv, ahr-TUHR) **CHI**

Left wing. Shoots left. 5'11", 176 lbs. Born, Podgorny, Russia, February 14, 1998.
(Chicago's 3rd pick, 50th overall, in 2016 NHL Draft).

			Regular Season					Playoffs				
Season	Club	League	GP	G	A	Pts	PIM	GP	G	A	Pts	PIM
2014-15	Loko Yaroslavl Jr.	Russia-Jr.	14	1	4	5	25	2	0	0	0	2
	Loko-Yunior Jr.	Rus-Jr. B	32	16	18	34	4	8	1	2	3	2
2015-16	Russia U18	Russia-Jr.	39	12	19	31	12	3	0	1	1	25
2016-17	Yaroslavl	KHL	4	0	0	0	0	....	....	....	....	....
	HK Ryazan	Russia-2	12	1	6	7	8	4	0	0	0	4
	Loko Yaroslavl Jr.	Russia-Jr.	33	8	11	19	43	3	1	1	2	4
	Loko-Yunior Jr.	Russia-Jr. B	....	....	....	....	....	1	1	0	1	0

KEA, Justin (KEE-uh, JUHS-tihn)

Center. Shoots left. 6'4", 223 lbs. Born, Woodville, ON, February 7, 1994.
(Buffalo's 4th pick, 73rd overall, in 2012 NHL Draft).

			Regular Season					Playoffs				
Season	Club	League	GP	G	A	Pts	PIM	GP	G	A	Pts	PIM
2009-10	Cent. Ont. Wolves	Minor-ON	51	22	22	44	44	....	....	....	....	....
2010-11	Saginaw Spirit	OHL	62	4	2	6	49	10	0	1	1	0
2011-12	Saginaw Spirit	OHL	65	3	11	14	76	12	1	4	5	2
2012-13	Saginaw Spirit	OHL	68	22	26	48	102	4	1	0	1	7
2013-14	Saginaw Spirit	OHL	58	22	27	49	97	5	1	3	4	0
	Rochester	AHL	1	0	0	0	0	....	....	....	....	....
2014-15	Rochester	AHL	26	2	0	2	56	....	....	....	....	....
	Elmira Jackals	ECHL	35	5	7	12	65	....	....	....	....	....
2015-16	Rochester	AHL	32	0	1	1	53	....	....	....	....	....
	Elmira Jackals	ECHL	17	4	2	6	9	....	....	....	....	....
2016-17	Rochester	AHL	12	2	2	4	18	....	....	....	....	....
	Elmira Jackals	ECHL	33	9	7	16	73	....	....	....	....	....

KELLY, Dan (KEHL-lee, DAN)

Defense. Shoots left. 6'1", 210 lbs. Born, Morrisonville, NY, May 17, 1989.

			Regular Season					Playoffs				
Season	Club	League	GP	G	A	Pts	PIM	GP	G	A	Pts	PIM
2003-04	Beekmantown	High-NY	STATISTICS NOT AVAILABLE									
2004-05	Pembroke	ON-Jr.A	50	2	12	14	80	11	0	1	1	2
2005-06	Pembroke	ON-Jr.A	46	2	15	17	95	11	0	3	3	18
	Kitchener Rangers	OHL	9	0	3	3	8	....	....	....	....	....
2006-07	Kitchener Rangers	OHL	59	0	19	19	79	9	1	1	2	10
2007-08	Kitchener Rangers	OHL	65	1	17	18	61	8	0	2	2	4
2008-09	Kitchener Rangers	OHL	44	4	11	15	30	....	....	....	....	....
2009-10	Kitchener Rangers	OHL	58	6	21	27	99	20	4	9	13	23
2010-11	Albany Devils	AHL	61	2	5	7	71	....	....	....	....	....
2011-12	Albany Devils	AHL	54	2	4	6	93	....	....	....	....	....
2012-13	Albany Devils	AHL	47	2	6	8	62	....	....	....	....	....
2013-14	Albany Devils	AHL	71	3	14	17	86	1	0	0	0	2
2014-15	Albany Devils	AHL	64	1	10	11	130	....	....	....	....	....
2015-16	Albany Devils	AHL	55	4	11	15	93	8	1	2	3	21
2016-17	San Jose Barracuda	AHL	53	1	6	7	116	6	0	1	1	7

Signed as a free agent by **New Jersey**, May 19, 2010. Signed as a free agent by **San Jose**, July 11, 2016.

KEMP, Philip (KEHMP, FIHL-ihp) EDM

Defense. Shoots right. 6'3", 202 lbs. Born, Greenwich, CT, December 2, 1999.
(Edmonton's 7th pick, 208th overall, in 2017 NHL Draft).

			Regular Season					Playoffs				
Season	Club	League	GP	G	A	Pts	PIM	GP	G	A	Pts	PIM
2013-14	Brunswick Bruins	High-CT	23	2	5	7	....	....	....	....	....	....
2014-15	Brunswick Bruins	High-CT	32	4	12	16	....	....	....	....	....	....
2015-16	USAHNTDP	USHL	35	1	3	4	2	....	....	....	....	....
	USAHNTDP	U-17	23	0	8	8	12	....	....	....	....	....
2016-17	USAHNTDP	USHL	25	2	2	4	8	....	....	....	....	....
	USAHNTDP	U-18	39	3	6	9	14	....	....	....	....	....

• Signed Letter of Intent to attend **Yale University** (ECAC) in fall of 2017.

KEMPE, Mario (KEHM-peh, MAHR-ee-oh) ARI

Center. Shoots left. 6', 185 lbs. Born, Kramfors, Sweden, September 19, 1988.
(Philadelphia's 4th pick, 122nd overall, in 2007 NHL Draft).

			Regular Season					Playoffs				
Season	Club	League	GP	G	A	Pts	PIM	GP	G	A	Pts	PIM
2003-04	Hoga Kusten	Sweden-4	STATISTICS NOT AVAILABLE									
2004-05	MODO U18	Swe-U18	14	5	7	12	40	4	1	1	2	4
2005-06	MODO U18	Swe-U18	6	4	2	6	29	2	0	2	2	0
	MODO Jr.	Swe-Jr.	36	20	12	32	16	2	0	0	0	10
2006-07	St. John's	QMJHL	62	23	19	42	51	4	0	0	0	2
2007-08	St. John's	QMJHL	48	25	24	49	36	6	4	3	7	8
2008-09	Rogle	Sweden	30	2	8	10	8	....	....	....	....	....
	Philadelphia	AHL	5	0	0	0	2	3	0	0	0	2
2009-10	Rogle	Sweden	51	7	11	18	14	....	....	....	....	....
	Rogle	Sweden-Q	10	7	2	9	4	....	....	....	....	....
2010-11	Djurgarden	Sweden	54	10	7	17	6	7	0	0	0	0
2011-12	Djurgarden	Sweden	52	8	7	15	14	....	....	....	....	....
	Djurgarden	Sweden-Q	10	2	5	7	4	....	....	....	....	....
2012-13	MODO	Sweden	53	15	12	27	12	5	0	0	0	0
2013-14	MODO	Sweden	54	9	8	17	18	2	0	0	0	0
2014-15	Podolsk	KHL	54	13	19	32	52	....	....	....	....	....
2015-16	Podolsk	KHL	56	12	5	17	64	....	....	....	....	....
2016-17	Podolsk	KHL	56	14	20	34	28	4	0	1	1	0

Signed as a free agent by **Arizona**, May 16, 2017.

KERFOOT, Alexander (KUHR-fut, al-ehx-AN-duhr) N.J.

Center. Shoots left. 5'10", 175 lbs. Born, Vancouver, BC, August 11, 1994.
(New Jersey's 6th pick, 150th overall, in 2012 NHL Draft).

			Regular Season					Playoffs				
Season	Club	League	GP	G	A	Pts	PIM	GP	G	A	Pts	PIM
2009-10	Van. NW Giants	BCMML	26	7	14	21	4	....	....	....	....	....
2010-11	Van. NW Giants	BCMML	38	36	*72	*108	58	5	6	6	*12	6
	Coquitlam Express	BCHL	5	0	0	0	0	1	0	0	0	0
2011-12	Coquitlam Express	BCHL	51	25	44	69	24	6	4	0	4	6
2012-13	Coquitlam Express	BCHL	16	8	11	19	16	....	....	....	....	....
2013-14	Harvard Crimson	ECAC	25	8	6	14	8	....	....	....	....	....
2014-15	Harvard Crimson	ECAC	27	8	22	30	12	....	....	....	....	....
2015-16	Harvard Crimson	ECAC	33	4	*30	34	16	....	....	....	....	....
2016-17	Harvard Crimson	ECAC	36	16	29	45	18	....	....	....	....	....

ECAC First All-Team (2017) • NCAA East Second All-American Team (2017)

KESSY, Kale (KEH-see, KAYL)

Left wing. Shoots left. 6'3", 212 lbs. Born, Shaunavon, SK, December 4, 1992.
(Phoenix's 5th pick, 111th overall, in 2011 NHL Draft).

			Regular Season					Playoffs				
Season	Club	League	GP	G	A	Pts	PIM	GP	G	A	Pts	PIM
2008-09	Medicine Hat	AMHL	33	17	12	29	42	....	....	....	....	....
	Medicine Hat	WHL	9	0	0	0	2	....	....	....	....	....
2009-10	Medicine Hat	WHL	70	11	18	29	123	12	1	3	4	10
2010-11	Medicine Hat	WHL	65	10	14	24	129	14	3	3	6	37
2011-12	Medicine Hat	WHL	49	4	12	16	151	2	0	1	1	2
2012-13	Medicine Hat	WHL	2	2	0	2	17	....	....	....	....	....
	Vancouver Giants	WHL	27	7	9	16	45	....	....	....	....	....
	Kamloops Blazers	WHL	31	12	13	25	44	15	11	3	14	21
2013-14	Oklahoma City	AHL	54	2	4	6	88	....	....	....	....	....
	Bakersfield	ECHL	3	1	0	1	0	....	....	....	....	....
2014-15	Oklahoma City	AHL	17	3	3	6	61	....	....	....	....	....
2015-16	Bakersfield	AHL	56	7	5	12	79	....	....	....	....	....
2016-17	Tulsa Oilers	ECHL	32	11	12	23	72	....	....	....	....	....
	Manitoba Moose	AHL	16	0	1	1	16	....	....	....	....	....

Traded to **Edmonton** by **Phoenix** for Tobias Rieder, March 30, 2013. • Missed majority of 2014-15 due to knee injury vs. Utica (AHL), December 2, 2014. Signed as a free agent by **Tulsa** (ECHL), October 2, 2016. • Loaned to **Manitoba** (AHL) by **Tulsa** (ECHL), November 19, 2016.

KICHTON, Brenden (KIHCH-tuhn, BREHN-duhn) CAR

Defense. Shoots right. 6', 190 lbs. Born, Edmonton, AB, June 18, 1992.
(Winnipeg's 9th pick, 190th overall, in 2013 NHL Draft).

			Regular Season					Playoffs				
Season	Club	League	GP	G	A	Pts	PIM	GP	G	A	Pts	PIM
2007-08	St. Albert	AMHL	35	10	16	26	14	1	0	0	0	2
2008-09	Spokane Chiefs	WHL	57	1	8	9	12	8	0	0	0	0
2009-10	Spokane Chiefs	WHL	70	4	15	19	21	7	0	0	0	4
2010-11	Spokane Chiefs	WHL	64	23	58	81	31	17	1	10	11	2
2011-12	Spokane Chiefs	WHL	71	17	57	74	49	1	0	1	1	0
2012-13	Spokane Chiefs	WHL	71	22	63	85	30	9	2	5	7	6
2013-14	St. John's IceCaps	AHL	76	10	38	48	14	21	2	5	7	2
2014-15	St. John's IceCaps	AHL	65	8	21	29	32	....	....	....	....	....
2015-16	Manitoba Moose	AHL	68	11	30	41	36	....	....	....	....	....
2016-17	Manitoba Moose	AHL	63	1	22	23	52	....	....	....	....	....

• Re-entered NHL Entry Draft. Originally NY Islanders' 7th pick, 127th overall, in 2011 NHL Draft.

WHL West Second All-Star Team (2011) • WHL West First All-Star Team (2012, 2013) • AHL All-Rookie Team (2014)

Signed as a free agent by **Carolina**, July 1, 2017.

KIRKLAND, Justin (KUHRK-luhnd, JUHS-tihn) NSH

Left wing. Shoots left. 6'3", 183 lbs. Born, Winnipeg, MB, August 2, 1996.
(Nashville's 4th pick, 62nd overall, in 2014 NHL Draft).

			Regular Season					Playoffs				
Season	Club	League	GP	G	A	Pts	PIM	GP	G	A	Pts	PIM
2009-10	Cam. Red Wings	AMBHL	32	5	2	7	42	....	....	....	....	....
2010-11	Cam. Red Wings	AMBHL	33	18	22	40	46	....	....	....	....	....
2011-12	Notre Dame Argos	SMHL	43	13	22	35	26	8	5	4	9	8
	Kelowna Rockets	WHL	6	0	1	1	0	....	....	....	....	....
2012-13	Notre Dame Argos	SMHL	44	25	24	49	42	3	0	2	2	2
	Notre Dame	SJHL	1	0	0	0	0	....	....	....	....	....
	Kelowna Rockets	WHL	6	2	0	2	6	6	0	1	1	0
2013-14	Kelowna Rockets	WHL	68	17	31	48	40	14	5	5	10	20
2014-15	Kelowna Rockets	WHL	50	21	30	51	25	9	3	2	5	0
2015-16	Kelowna Rockets	WHL	69	31	36	67	69	18	11	4	15	15
2016-17	Milwaukee	AHL	56	9	12	21	34	3	0	2	2	4
	Cincinnati	ECHL	4	1	1	2	2	....	....	....	....	....

KLIMCHUK, Morgan (KLIHM-chuhk, MOHR-guhn) CGY

Left wing. Shoots left. 6', 185 lbs. Born, Regina, SK, March 2, 1995.
(Calgary's 3rd pick, 28th overall, in 2013 NHL Draft).

			Regular Season					Playoffs				
Season	Club	League	GP	G	A	Pts	PIM	GP	G	A	Pts	PIM
2010-11	Calgary Buffaloes	AMHL	32	27	23	50	12	2	0	0	0	0
	Regina Pats	WHL	5	0	1	1	0	....	....	....	....	....
2011-12	Regina Pats	WHL	67	18	18	36	27	5	0	1	1	2
2012-13	Regina Pats	WHL	72	36	40	76	20	....	....	....	....	....
2013-14	Abbotsford Heat	AHL	4	0	0	0	4	....	....	....	....	....
	Regina Pats	WHL	57	30	44	74	27	4	3	2	5	2
2014-15	Regina Pats	WHL	27	14	16	30	12	....	....	....	....	....
	Brandon	WHL	33	20	30	50	12	13	3	10	13	2
2015-16	Stockton Heat	AHL	55	3	6	9	10	....	....	....	....	....
2016-17	Stockton Heat	AHL	66	19	24	43	36	2	0	0	0	0

KLOOS, Justin (KLOOS, JUHS-tihn) MIN

Right wing. Shoots right. 5'9", 178 lbs. Born, Lakeville, MN, November 30, 1993.

			Regular Season					Playoffs				
Season	Club	League	GP	G	A	Pts	PIM	GP	G	A	Pts	PIM
2009-10	Lakeville South	High-MN	18	21	17	38	2	3	4	3	7	0
2010-11	Team Southwest	UMHSEL	20	9	16	25	10	2	2	3	5	2
	Lakeville South	High-MN	24	35	44	79	8	3	6	5	11	0
	Waterloo	USHL	10	3	2	5	2	2	0	0	0	0
2011-12	Team Southwest	UMHSEL	21	17	30	47	2	3	1	2	3	0
	Lakeville South	High-MN	25	34	47	81	4	6	7	15	22	0
	Waterloo	USHL	2	2	2	4	0	....	....	....	....	....
2012-13	Waterloo	USHL	54	29	*58	87	22	5	0	4	4	2
2013-14	U. of Minnesota	Big Ten	41	16	16	32	16	....	....	....	....	....
2014-15	U. of Minnesota	Big Ten	39	13	19	32	26	....	....	....	....	....
2015-16	U. of Minnesota	Big Ten	37	16	27	43	26	....	....	....	....	....
2016-17	U. of Minnesota	Big Ten	38	18	25	43	28	....	....	....	....	....
	Iowa Wild	AHL	9	1	0	1	4	....	....	....	....	....

Big Ten Second All-Star Team (2016)

Signed as a free agent by **Minnesota**, March 29, 2017.

KNOTT, Graham (NAWT, GRAY-uhm) CHI

Left wing. Shoots left. 6'4", 195 lbs. Born, Etobicoke, ON, January 13, 1997.
(Chicago's 1st pick, 54th overall, in 2015 NHL Draft).

			Regular Season					Playoffs				
Season	Club	League	GP	G	A	Pts	PIM	GP	G	A	Pts	PIM
2012-13	York Simcoe	Minor-ON	25	8	8	16	22	....	....	....	....	....
	Aurora Tigers	ON-Jr.A	1	0	0	0	0	....	....	....	....	....
2013-14	Niagara Ice Dogs	OHL	64	8	14	22	18	7	0	1	1	0
2014-15	Niagara Ice Dogs	OHL	59	25	18	43	33	11	2	2	4	2
2015-16	Niagara Ice Dogs	OHL	68	12	30	42	67	17	2	3	5	24
2016-17	Niagara Ice Dogs	OHL	14	4	13	17	22	....	....	....	....	....
	Windsor Spitfires	OHL	45	11	24	35	39	7	2	2	4	8

KOBERSTEIN, Nikolas (KOH-burh-steen, NIH-koh-las) MTL

Defense. Shoots right. 6'2", 202 lbs. Born, Ponoka, AB, January 19, 1996.
(Montreal's 3rd pick, 125th overall, in 2014 NHL Draft).

			Regular Season					Playoffs				
Season	Club	League	GP	G	A	Pts	PIM	GP	G	A	Pts	PIM
2009-10	PAC Saints	AMBHL	33	0	11	11	8	....	....	....	....	....
2010-11	PAC Saints	AMBHL	28	4	19	23	24	....	....	....	....	....
	PAC Saints	Minor-AB	1	0	0	0	0	....	....	....	....	....
2011-12	PAC Saints	Minor-AB	37	9	23	32	71	....	....	....	....	....
	St. Albert Raiders	AMHL	6	0	3	3	2	....	....	....	....	....
2012-13	St. Albert Raiders	AMHL	34	1	11	12	34	4	0	0	0	4
2013-14	Olds Grizzlys	AJHL	51	5	13	18	153	9	0	2	2	24
2014-15	Sioux Falls	USHL	30	1	0	1	75	....	....	....	....	....
	Bloomington	USHL	31	3	8	11	63	....	....	....	....	....
2015-16	Alaska	WCHA	23	1	1	2	8	....	....	....	....	....
2016-17	Alaska	WCHA	31	2	4	6	33	....	....	....	....	....

KOIVULA, Otto (KOI-voo-lah, AW-toh) NYI

Right wing. Shoots left. 6'4", 220 lbs. Born, Nokia, Finland, September 1, 1998.
(NY Islanders' 3rd pick, 120th overall, in 2016 NHL Draft).

			Regular Season					Playoffs				
Season	Club	League	GP	G	A	Pts	PIM	GP	G	A	Pts	PIM
2013-14	Ilves Tampere U18	Fin-U18	5	4	2	6	0	5	0	1	1	0
2014-15	Ilves Tampere U18	Fin-U18	21	22	32	54	10	3	1	0	1	2
	Ilves Tampere Jr.	Fin-Jr.	22	4	6	10	12	....	....	....	....	....
2015-16	Ilves Tampere Jr.	Fin-Jr.	49	26	32	58	18	7	5	7	12	4
	Ilves Tampere	Finland	1	0	0	0	0	....	....	....	....	....
2016-17	Ilves Tampere	Finland	50	10	20	30	6	10	2	3	5	2

KOLESAR, Keegan (KOHL-uh-sahr, KEE-guhn) VGK

Right wing. Shoots right. 6'2", 216 lbs. Born, Brandon, MB, April 8, 1997.
(Columbus' 5th pick, 69th overall, in 2015 NHL Draft).

			Regular Season					Playoffs				
Season	Club	League	GP	G	A	Pts	PIM	GP	G	A	Pts	PIM
2012-13	Wpg. Thrashers	MMHL	41	21	17	38	26	11	3	4	7	4
	Seattle	WHL	1	0	0	0	0	2	0	0	0	0
2013-14	Seattle	WHL	60	2	6	8	45	9	0	2	2	2
2014-15	Seattle	WHL	64	19	19	38	85	....	....	....	....	....
2015-16	Seattle	WHL	64	30	31	61	107	16	7	8	15	8
2016-17	Seattle	WHL	54	26	34	60	101	19	12	19	*31	*37

Traded to **Vegas** by **Columbus** for Tampa Bay's 2nd round pick (previously acquired, Columbus selected Alexandre Texier) in 2017 NHL Draft, June 24, 2017.

KOLTYGIN, Pavel (kohl-TEE-gihn, pah-VEHL) NSH

Center. Shoots left. 6', 189 lbs. Born, Moscow, Russia, February 17, 1999.
(Nashville's 5th pick, 176th overall, in 2017 NHL Draft).

			Regular Season					Playoffs				
Season	Club	League	GP	G	A	Pts	PIM	GP	G	A	Pts	PIM
2015-16	Russia U18	Russia-Jr.	17	1	4	5	8	3	0	0	0	2
2016-17	Drummondville	QMJHL	65	22	25	47	44	4	1	0	1	6

KOPACKA, Jack (koh-PA-kuh, JAK) ANA

Left wing. Shoots left. 6'1", 191 lbs. Born, Lapeer, MI, March 5, 1998.
(Anaheim's 4th pick, 93rd overall, in 2016 NHL Draft).

			Regular Season					Playoffs				
Season	Club	League	GP	G	A	Pts	PIM	GP	G	A	Pts	PIM
2013-14	Det. Comp. U16	HPHL	22	7	17	24	0	....	....	....	....	....
	Det. Comp. U16	Other	29	6	11	17	0	....	....	....	....	....
2014-15	Det. Comp. U18	HPHL	21	8	10	18	0	....	....	....	....	....
	Sault Ste. Marie	OHL	4	0	1	1	0	....	....	....	....	....
2015-16	Sault Ste. Marie	OHL	67	20	23	43	12	12	2	2	4	2
2016-17	Sault Ste. Marie	OHL	65	30	19	49	16	11	5	6	11	2
	San Diego Gulls	AHL	....	....	....	....	....	3	0	0	0	0

KOPPANEN, Joona (koh-PAH-nehen, YOH-nuh) BOS

Center. Shoots left. 6'5", 197 lbs. Born, Tampere, Finland, February 25, 1998.
(Boston's 4th pick, 135th overall, in 2016 NHL Draft).

			Regular Season					Playoffs				
Season	Club	League	GP	G	A	Pts	PIM	GP	G	A	Pts	PIM
2013-14	Ilves Tampere U18	Fin-U18	11	4	4	8	0	4	0	2	2	0
2014-15	Ilves Tampere U18	Fin-U18	38	25	32	57	20	3	0	3	3	14
2015-16	Ilves Tampere Jr.	Fin-Jr.	40	9	17	26	14	7	0	2	2	2
2016-17	Ilves Tampere Jr.	Fin-Jr.	38	23	31	54	18	6	2	4	6	2

KORSHKOV, Yegor (kohrsh-KAWV, YEE-gohr) TOR

Right wing. Shoots left. 6'4", 180 lbs. Born, Novosibirsk, Russia, July 10, 1996.
(Toronto's 2nd pick, 31st overall, in 2016 NHL Draft).

			Regular Season					Playoffs				
Season	Club	League	GP	G	A	Pts	PIM	GP	G	A	Pts	PIM
2011-12	Barys Astana 2	Kazakhstan	32	6	10	16	22	....	....	....	....	....
2012-13	Yaroslavl U17	Rus-U17	6	3	3	6	4	....	....	....	....	....
2013-14	Loko Yaroslavl Jr.	Russia-Jr.	43	12	10	22	22	7	0	1	1	6
2014-15	Yaroslavl	KHL	24	1	2	3	4	....	....	....	....	....
	Loko Yaroslavl Jr.	Russia-Jr.	23	13	15	28	18	14	5	8	13	10
2015-16	Yaroslavl	KHL	41	6	6	12	23	4	0	0	0	0
	Loko Yaroslavl Jr.	Russia-Jr.	4	2	4	6	6	15	9	10	19	10
2016-17	Yaroslavl	KHL	36	6	13	19	24	15	1	2	3	10
	Loko Yaroslavl Jr.	Russia-Jr.	2	0	0	0	4	....	....	....	....	....

KOSOV, Yaroslav (KAW-sawf, YAHR-oh-slahv) FLA

Center. Shoots left. 6'3", 220 lbs. Born, Magnitogorsk, Russia, July 5, 1993.
(Florida's 8th pick, 124th overall, in 2011 NHL Draft).

			Regular Season					Playoffs				
Season	Club	League	GP	G	A	Pts	PIM	GP	G	A	Pts	PIM
2010-11	Magnitogorsk Jr.	Russia-Jr.	42	11	10	21	22	17	6	1	7	0
2011-12	Magnitogorsk Jr.	Russia-Jr.	12	6	4	10	6	6	0	0	0	0
	Magnitogorsk	KHL	27	4	5	9	6	7	0	0	0	0
2012-13	Magnitogorsk	KHL	40	4	3	7	10	5	0	0	0	0
	Magnitogorsk Jr.	Russia-Jr.	....	....	....	....	....	3	0	1	1	0
2013-14	Magnitogorsk Jr.	Russia-Jr.	2	1	2	3	0	....	....	....	....	....
	Yuzhny Ural Orsk	Russia-2	2	1	1	2	2	....	....	....	....	....
	Magnitogorsk	KHL	32	2	2	4	0	21	2	1	3	0
2014-15	Magnitogorsk	KHL	52	4	5	9	14	5	0	0	0	4
2015-16	Magnitogorsk	KHL	53	4	1	5	28	23	4	3	7	6
2016-17	Magnitogorsk	KHL	41	3	2	5	27	18	4	2	6	8

KOSTALEK, Jan (kawsh-TAH-lehk, YAHN) WPG

Defense. Shoots right. 6'1", 196 lbs. Born, Prague, Czech Rep., February 17, 1995.
(Winnipeg's 7th pick, 114th overall, in 2013 NHL Draft).

			Regular Season					Playoffs				
Season	Club	League	GP	G	A	Pts	PIM	GP	G	A	Pts	PIM
2010-11	Sparta U18	CzR-U18	39	2	9	11	34	5	0	0	0	8
	Sparta Jr.	CzRep-Jr.	1	0	0	0	0	....	....	....	....	....
2011-12	Sparta U18	CzR-U18	7	0	13	13	12	3	1	3	4	2
	Sparta Jr.	CzRep-Jr.	32	3	4	7	30	4	0	0	0	2
	HC Sparta Praha	CzRep	10	0	0	0	4	....	....	....	....	....
2012-13	Rimouski Oceanic	QMJHL	48	5	13	18	53	6	0	1	1	2
2013-14	Rimouski Oceanic	QMJHL	55	5	22	27	40	6	0	3	3	4
2014-15	Rimouski Oceanic	QMJHL	57	7	36	43	35	20	8	13	21	10
2015-16	Manitoba Moose	AHL	52	1	8	9	20	....	....	....	....	....
2016-17	Manitoba Moose	AHL	60	2	5	7	20	....	....	....	....	....

QMJHL All-Rookie Team (2013) • QMJHL First All-Star Team (2015)

KOSTIN, Klim (KAWZ-tihn, KLIHM) ST.L.

Right wing. Shoots left. 6'3", 207 lbs. Born, Penza, Russia, May 5, 1999.
(St. Louis' 2nd pick, 31st overall, in 2017 NHL Draft).

			Regular Season					Playoffs				
Season	Club	League	GP	G	A	Pts	PIM	GP	G	A	Pts	PIM
2015-16	Dyn'o Moscow Jr.	Russia-Jr.	30	8	13	21	74	....	....	....	....	....
2016-17	Dynamo Moscow	KHL	8	0	0	0	27	....	....	....	....	....
	Dyn'o Balashikha	Russia-2	9	1	0	1	4	....	....	....	....	....
	Dyn'o Moscow Jr.	Russia-Jr.	1	0	1	1	2	....	....	....	....	....

KOTKANSALO, Kasper (KAWT-kan-SA-loh, KA-spuhr) DET

Defense. Shoots left. 6'3", 196 lbs. Born, Helsinki, Finland, November 16, 1998.
(Detroit's 3rd pick, 71st overall, in 2017 NHL Draft).

			Regular Season					Playoffs				
Season	Club	League	GP	G	A	Pts	PIM	GP	G	A	Pts	PIM
2013-14	Blues Ak U18	Fin-U18	4	1	1	2	0	....	....	....	....	....
	Blues Espoo U18	Fin-U18	....	....	....	....	....	2	0	0	0	0
2014-15	Blues Espoo U18	Fin-U18	17	4	10	14	10	9	0	4	4	6
2015-16	Blues Espoo Jr.	Fin-Jr.	48	4	15	19	36	6	0	3	3	4
2016-17	Sioux Falls	USHL	47	1	11	12	43	....	....	....	....	....

• Signed Letter of Intent to attend **Boston University** (Hockey East) in fall of 2017.

KOVACEVIC, Johnny (KOH-va-SEH-vihch, JAW-nee) WPG

Defense. Shoots right. 6'5", 210 lbs. Born, Grimsby, ON, July 12, 1997.
(Winnipeg's 3rd pick, 74th overall, in 2017 NHL Draft).

			Regular Season					Playoffs				
Season	Club	League	GP	G	A	Pts	PIM	GP	G	A	Pts	PIM
2012-13	N.F. Rivermen	Minor-ON	38	2	11	13	22	....	....	....	....	....
2013-14	Hill Academy	High-ON	66	5	23	28	....	....	....	....	....	....
2014-15	Ottawa Jr. Sens	ON-Jr.A	52	5	14	19	20	10	0	3	3	6
2015-16	Ottawa Jr. Sens	ON-Jr.A	21	2	8	10	6	....	....	....	....	....
	Hawkesbury	ON-Jr.A	30	6	20	26	21	10	0	7	7	10
2016-17	Merrimack College	H-East	36	3	16	19	30	....	....	....	....	....

KOVACS, Robin (KOH-vach, RAW-bihn) NYR

Right wing. Shoots left. 6', 186 lbs. Born, Stockholm, Sweden, November 16, 1996.
(NY Rangers' 2nd pick, 62nd overall, in 2015 NHL Draft).

			Regular Season					Playoffs				
Season	Club	League	GP	G	A	Pts	PIM	GP	G	A	Pts	PIM
2010-11	Flem'sberg U18 2	Swe-U18	7	6	8	14	24	....	....	....	....	....
	Flem'sberg U18 1	Swe-U18	13	6	5	11	10	....	....	....	....	....
2011-12	AIK Solna U18	Swe-U18	35	12	16	28	61	....	....	....	....	....
2012-13	AIK Solna U18	Swe-U18	36	32	32	64	83	5	4	4	8	8
	AIK Solna Jr.	Swe-Jr.	6	2	2	4	4	1	0	0	0	0
	AIK Solna	Sweden	1	0	0	0	0	....	....	....	....	....
2013-14	AIK Solna U18	Swe-U18	7	2	5	7	51	....	....	....	....	....
	AIK Solna Jr.	Swe-Jr.	40	15	13	28	87	2	1	1	2	6
	AIK Solna	Sweden	3	0	0	0	0	....	....	....	....	....
2014-15	AIK Solna Jr.	Swe-Jr.	9	5	5	10	8	....	....	....	....	....
	AIK Solna	Sweden-2	62	19	16	35	67	....	....	....	....	....
2015-16	Rogle	Sweden	4	0	1	1	0	....	....	....	....	....
	AIK Solna	Sweden-2	44	21	13	34	54	7	1	3	4	29
2016-17	Hartford Wolf Pack	AHL	72	2	10	12	20	....	....	....	....	....

KRAG CHRISTENSEN, Nikolaj (KRAG krihs-T'YEHN-sehn, nih-KOH-ligh) **ST.L.**

Center. Shoots left. 5'11", 176 lbs. Born, Rodovre, Denmark, August 12, 1998.
(St. Louis' 7th pick, 209th overall, in 2016 NHL Draft).

			Regular Season					Playoffs				
Season	Club	League	GP	G	A	Pts	PIM	GP	G	A	Pts	PIM
2011-12	Rodovre SIK U17	Den-U17	4	1	0	1	0	....	....	....	....	....
2012-13	Rodovre SIK U17	Den-U17	15	17	6	23	4	4	1	1	2	4
2013-14	Rodovre SIK U17	Den-U17	10	10	4	14	0	6	5	2	7	14
	Rodovre SIK U18	Den-U18	6	10	5	15	6	....	....	....	....	....
	Rodovre SIK Jr.	Den Jr.	12	10	16	26	4	3	2	3	5	0
	Rodovre SIK	Den-2	13	4	8	12	6	3	1	0	1	4
2014-15	Rodovre SIK U17	Den-U17	3	5	8	13	0	1	2	1	3	4
	Rodovre SIK Jr.	Den Jr.	3	3	4	7	0	3	1	2	3	2
	Rodovre SIK	Den-2	26	14	11	25	22	9	7	9	16	2
	Rodovre	Denmark	9	1	1	2	0	....	....	....	....	....
2015-16	Rodovre SIK	Den-2	9	5	8	13	2	....	....	....	....	....
	Rodovre	Denmark	30	2	2	4	10	....	....	....	....	....
2016-17	Rogle Jr.	Swe-Jr.	43	12	12	24	28	3	0	2	2	0
	Rogle	Sweden	5	0	0	0	0	....	....	....	....	....

KRAMER, Darren (KRAY-muhr, DAIR-uhn)

Center. Shoots left. 6'1", 210 lbs. Born, Peace River, AB, November 19, 1991.
(Ottawa's 7th pick, 156th overall, in 2011 NHL Draft).

			Regular Season					Playoffs				
Season	Club	League	GP	G	A	Pts	PIM	GP	G	A	Pts	PIM
2007-08	Peace River Royals	Minor-AB	30	26	22	48	58	9	9	8	17	18
	Peace River	NWJHL	1	0	0	0	0	....	....	....	....	....
2008-09	Grande Prairie	AJHL	38	4	0	4	220	14	1	0	1	45
2009-10	Grande Prairie	AJHL	58	19	11	30	*311	9	2	2	4	23
2010-11	Grande Prairie	AJHL	10	4	1	5	28	....	....	....	....	....
	Spokane Chiefs	WHL	68	7	7	14	*306	17	5	3	8	21
2011-12	Spokane Chiefs	WHL	71	22	18	40	200	12	3	3	6	20
2012-13	Binghamton	AHL	21	1	0	1	83	....	....	....	....	....
	Elmira Jackals	ECHL	19	3	7	10	127	....	....	....	....	....
2013-14	Binghamton	AHL	45	2	2	4	178	3	0	0	0	2
2014-15	Binghamton	AHL	70	5	12	17	*284	....	....	....	....	....
2015-16	Manitoba Moose	AHL	61	7	5	12	138	....	....	....	....	....
2016-17	Manitoba Moose	AHL	42	3	1	4	89	....	....	....	....	....

Signed as a free agent by **Manitoba** (AHL), July 1, 2015.

KRASKOVSKY, Pavel (kras-KOHV-skee, PAH-vehl) **WPG**

Center. Shoots left. 6'4", 187 lbs. Born, Yaroslavl, Russia, September 11, 1996.
(Winnipeg's 6th pick, 164th overall, in 2014 NHL Draft).

			Regular Season					Playoffs				
Season	Club	League	GP	G	A	Pts	PIM	GP	G	A	Pts	PIM
2012-13	Loko Yaroslavl Jr.	Russia-Jr.	19	2	3	5	0	....	....	....	....	....
2013-14	Loko Yaroslavl Jr.	Russia-Jr.	39	10	17	27	16	7	0	0	0	2
	Yaroslavl	KHL	8	1	0	1	14	....	....	....	....	....
2014-15	Yaroslavl	KHL	3	0	0	0	0	....	....	....	....	....
	Loko Yaroslavl Jr.	Russia-Jr.	38	11	19	30	56	15	4	9	13	8
2015-16	Loko Yaroslavl Jr.	Russia-Jr.	4	4	2	6	0	14	6	4	10	24
	Yaroslavl	KHL	40	2	3	5	14	5	0	0	0	4
2016-17	Yaroslavl	KHL	58	8	10	18	18	15	3	1	4	13

KRISTO, Danny (KRIHS-toh, DAN-ee)

Right wing. Shoots right. 6', 195 lbs. Born, Edina, MN, June 18, 1990.
(Montreal's 1st pick, 56th overall, in 2008 NHL Draft).

			Regular Season					Playoffs				
Season	Club	League	GP	G	A	Pts	PIM	GP	G	A	Pts	PIM
2006-07	USAHNTDP	U-17	14	4	5	9	0	....	....	....	....	....
	USAHNTDP	NAHL	39	8	10	18	34	6	0	1	1	2
2007-08	USAHNTDP	U-18	43	18	14	32	18	....	....	....	....	....
	USAHNTDP	NAHL	14	4	4	8	6	....	....	....	....	....
2008-09	Omaha Lancers	USHL	50	22	35	57	18	3	3	0	3	2
2009-10	North Dakota	WCHA	41	15	21	36	8	....	....	....	....	....
2010-11	North Dakota	WCHA	34	8	20	28	18	....	....	....	....	....
2011-12	North Dakota	WCHA	42	19	26	45	33	....	....	....	....	....
2012-13	North Dakota	WCHA	40	*26	26	52	24	....	....	....	....	....
	Hamilton Bulldogs	AHL	9	0	3	3	2	....	....	....	....	....
2013-14	Hartford Wolf Pack	AHL	65	25	18	43	18	....	....	....	....	....
2014-15	Hartford Wolf Pack	AHL	72	22	24	46	35	15	3	3	6	2
2015-16	Chicago Wolves	AHL	71	25	23	48	29	....	....	....	....	....
2016-17	Chicago Wolves	AHL	8	0	2	2	2	....	....	....	....	....
	Wilkes-Barre	AHL	32	6	5	11	10	....	....	....	....	....
	Charlotte	AHL	14	4	6	10	4	5	0	1	1	0

WCHA All-Rookie Team (2010) • WCHA Rookie of the Year (2010) • WCHA First All-Star Team (2013) • NCAA West First All-American Team (2013)

Traded to **NY Rangers** by **Montreal** for Christian Thomas, July 2, 2013. Signed as a free agent by **St. Louis**, July 2, 2015. Traded to **Pittsburgh** by **St. Louis** for Reid McNeill, November 19, 2016. Traded to **Carolina** by **Pittsburgh** with Pittsburgh's 2nd round pick (later traded to Vegas – Vegas selected Jake Leschyshyn) in 2017 NHL Draft for Ron Hainsey, February 23, 2017.

KRYS, Chad (KRIHS, CHAD) **CHI**

Defense. Shoots left. 5'11", 185 lbs. Born, Philadelphia, PA, April 10, 1998.
(Chicago's 2nd pick, 45th overall, in 2016 NHL Draft).

			Regular Season					Playoffs				
Season	Club	League	GP	G	A	Pts	PIM	GP	G	A	Pts	PIM
2012-13	Connecticut Oilers	EJEPL	18	2	25	27	8	5	0	4	4	6
	CT Oilers U16	Other	49	20	51	71	18	....	....	....	....	....
2013-14	N.J. Rockets U19	Other	41	10	35	45	22	....	....	....	....	....
	N.J. Rockets	EHL	1	1	0	1	2	....	....	....	....	....
2014-15	USAHNTDP	USHL	35	4	22	26	16	....	....	....	....	....
	USAHNTDP	U-17	19	1	15	16	8	....	....	....	....	....
	USAHNTDP	U-18	8	1	6	7	4	....	....	....	....	....
2015-16	USAHNTDP	USHL	18	2	11	13	19	....	....	....	....	....
	USAHNTDP	U-18	35	1	15	16	59	....	....	....	....	....
2016-17	Boston University	H-East	39	5	6	11	10	....	....	....	....	....

KUDLA, Patrick (KUHD-LA, pa-TRIHK) **ARI**

Defense. Shoots left. 6'2", 178 lbs. Born, Guelph, ON, April 2, 1996.
(Arizona's 4th pick, 158th overall, in 2016 NHL Draft).

			Regular Season					Playoffs				
Season	Club	League	GP	G	A	Pts	PIM	GP	G	A	Pts	PIM
2011-12	Guelph Jr. Storm	Minor-ON	36	15	30	45	68	5	0	4	4	0
	Guelph Jr. Storm	Other	17	5	11	16	34	....	....	....	....	....
2012-13	Guelph Hurricanes	ON-Jr.B	48	4	13	17	86	....	....	....	....	....
2013-14	Guelph Hurricanes	ON-Jr.B	27	2	11	13	14	5	1	2	3	6
	Wellington Dukes	ON-Jr.A	10	1	1	2	4	....	....	....	....	....
2014-15	Guelph Hurricanes	ON-Jr.B	48	15	46	61	56	4	1	6	7	8
2015-16	Oakville Blades	ON-Jr.A	50	13	53	66	86	11	1	7	8	18
2016-17	Dubuque	USHL	58	8	30	38	71	8	3	6	9	2

• Signed Letter of Intent to attend **Arizona State University** (NCAA) in fall of 2017.

KUJAWINSKI, Ryan (koo-juh-WIHN-skee, RIGH-uhn) **N.J.**

Center. Shoots left. 6'2", 205 lbs. Born, Kirkland Lake, ON, March 30, 1995.
(New Jersey's 2nd pick, 73rd overall, in 2013 NHL Draft).

			Regular Season					Playoffs				
Season	Club	League	GP	G	A	Pts	PIM	GP	G	A	Pts	PIM
2010-11	Sud. Wolves MM	Minor-ON	24	35	21	56	24	....	....	....	....	....
	Sud. Wolves Mid.	Minor-ON	2	1	1	2	0	3	4	6	10	4
2011-12	Sarnia Sting	OHL	29	1	5	6	2	....	....	....	....	....
	Kingston	OHL	30	15	15	30	15	....	....	....	....	....
2012-13	Kingston	OHL	66	17	31	48	40	4	2	0	2	2
2013-14	Kingston	OHL	45	23	18	41	39	7	1	1	2	2
2014-15	Kingston	OHL	27	13	10	23	18	....	....	....	....	....
	North Bay	OHL	34	21	15	36	12	15	6	3	9	11
2015-16	Albany Devils	AHL	59	6	15	21	34	7	0	1	1	2
2016-17	Albany Devils	AHL	32	6	6	12	24	....	....	....	....	....

KUNIN, Luke (KUH-nihn, LEWK) **MIN**

Center. Shoots right. 6', 191 lbs. Born, Chesterfield, MO, December 4, 1997.
(Minnesota's 1st pick, 15th overall, in 2016 NHL Draft).

			Regular Season					Playoffs				
Season	Club	League	GP	G	A	Pts	PIM	GP	G	A	Pts	PIM
2012-13	St.L. AAA Blues	T1EHL	34	30	38	68	18	5	2	4	6	0
2013-14	USAHNTDP	USHL	32	11	12	23	27	....	....	....	....	....
	USAHNTDP	U-17	20	9	7	16	8	....	....	....	....	....
2014-15	USAHNTDP	USHL	20	10	4	14	12	....	....	....	....	....
	USAHNTDP	U-18	41	17	11	28	22	....	....	....	....	....
2015-16	U. of Wisconsin	Big Ten	34	19	13	32	34	....	....	....	....	....
2016-17	U. of Wisconsin	Big Ten	35	22	16	38	30	....	....	....	....	....
	Iowa Wild	AHL	12	5	3	8	16	....	....	....	....	....

Big Ten All-Rookie Team (2016) • NCAA West Second All-American Team (2017)

KUOKKANEN, Janne (koo-OH-kuh-nehn, YAH-neh) **CAR**

Left wing. Shoots left. 6'1", 195 lbs. Born, Oulunsalo, Finland, May 25, 1998.
(Carolina's 3rd pick, 43rd overall, in 2016 NHL Draft).

			Regular Season					Playoffs				
Season	Club	League	GP	G	A	Pts	PIM	GP	G	A	Pts	PIM
2013-14	Karpat Oulu U18	Fin-U18	44	26	27	53	32	5	5	2	7	0
2014-15	Karpat Oulu U18	Fin-U18	3	1	4	5	4	9	3	4	7	0
	Karpat Oulu Jr.	Fin-Jr.	35	3	12	15	16	....	....	....	....	....
2015-16	Karpat Oulu Jr.	Fin-Jr.	47	22	31	53	53	3	0	1	1	2
	Karpat Oulu	Finland	1	2	0	2	0	....	....	....	....	....
	Hokki Kajaani	Finland-2	1	1	1	2	2	....	....	....	....	....
	Karpat Oulu U18	Fin-U18	....	....	....	....	....	5	1	4	5	0
2016-17	London Knights	OHL	60	26	36	62	14	14	10	6	16	2
	Charlotte	AHL	....	....	....	....	....	1	0	0	0	0

KURKER, Sam (KUHR-kuhr, SAM) **ST.L.**

Right wing. Shoots right. 6'2", 202 lbs. Born, Boston, MA, April 8, 1994.
(St. Louis' 2nd pick, 56th overall, in 2012 NHL Draft).

			Regular Season					Playoffs				
Season	Club	League	GP	G	A	Pts	PIM	GP	G	A	Pts	PIM
2010-11	Bos. Little Bruins	Minor-MA	STATISTICS NOT AVAILABLE									
	St. John's Prep	High-MA	25	20	17	37	24	....	....	....	....	....
2011-12	Bos. Little Bruins	Minor-MA	STATISTICS NOT AVAILABLE									
	St. John's Prep	High-MA	24	32	28	60	23	....	....	....	....	....
	USAHNTDP	U-18	2	0	0	0	2	....	....	....	....	....
2012-13	Boston University	H-East	35	3	2	5	61	....	....	....	....	....
2013-14	Boston University	H-East	12	1	0	1	14	....	....	....	....	....
	Indiana Ice	USHL	24	6	8	14	45	12	3	3	6	6
2014-15	Sioux City	USHL	56	24	25	49	86	5	0	2	2	18
2015-16	Northeastern	H-East	41	6	12	18	50	....	....	....	....	....
2016-17	Northeastern	H-East	28	3	3	6	38	....	....	....	....	....
	Albany Devils	AHL	1	0	0	0	0	....	....	....	....	....

KYROU, Jordan (KIGH-ROO, JOHR-duhn) **ST.L.**

Center. Shoots right. 6', 169 lbs. Born, Toronto, ON, May 5, 1998.
(St. Louis' 2nd pick, 35th overall, in 2016 NHL Draft).

			Regular Season					Playoffs				
Season	Club	League	GP	G	A	Pts	PIM	GP	G	A	Pts	PIM
2013-14	Miss. Senators	GTHL	33	19	21	40	38	5	0	0	0	0
2014-15	Sarnia Sting	OHL	63	13	23	36	12	5	1	5	6	0
2015-16	Sarnia Sting	OHL	65	17	34	51	14	7	1	6	7	2
2016-17	Sarnia Sting	OHL	66	30	64	94	36	4	1	2	3	0
	Chicago Wolves	AHL	1	0	0	0	0	....	....	....	....	....

LAAKSONEN, Oskari (lahk-SOH-nehn, aws-KAH-ree) **BUF**

Defense. Shoots right. 6'2", 165 lbs. Born, Tampere, , February 7, 1999.
(Buffalo's 4th pick, 89th overall, in 2017 NHL Draft).

			Regular Season					Playoffs				
Season	Club	League	GP	G	A	Pts	PIM	GP	G	A	Pts	PIM
2015-16	Ilves Tampere U18	Fin-U18	48	7	18	25	16	4	1	3	4	29
2016-17	Ilves Tampere U18	Fin-U18	10	0	10	10	12	4	2	2	4	4
	Ilves Tampere Jr.	Fin-Jr.	27	6	3	9	14	6	1	1	2	4

LAAVAINEN, Roope (lah-VIGH-nihn, ROO-PAY) CHI

Defense. Shoots right. 6'1", 187 lbs. Born, Vantaa, Finland, August 23, 1998.
(Chicago's 6th pick, 119th overall, in 2017 NHL Draft).

			Regular Season					Playoffs				
Season	**Club**	**League**	**GP**	**G**	**A**	**Pts**	**PIM**	**GP**	**G**	**A**	**Pts**	**PIM**
2014-15	Jokerit U18	Fin-U18	46	11	15	26	32	10	0	1	1	18
2015-16	Jokerit U18	Fin-U18	26	5	17	22	68	....	....	....	....	....
2016-17	Jokerit Helsinki Jr.	Fin-Jr.	48	5	16	21	42	....	....	....	....	....

LABBE, Dylan (la-BAY, DIH-luhn) MIN

Defense. Shoots left. 6'2", 205 lbs. Born, St. Benjamin, QC, January 9, 1995.
(Minnesota's 3rd pick, 107th overall, in 2013 NHL Draft).

			Regular Season					Playoffs				
Season	**Club**	**League**	**GP**	**G**	**A**	**Pts**	**PIM**	**GP**	**G**	**A**	**Pts**	**PIM**
2011-12	Levis	QAAA	38	13	11	24	30	4	0	1	1	0
	Shawinigan	QMJHL	6	0	0	0	7	4	0	1	1	0
2012-13	Shawinigan	QMJHL	61	7	21	28	57	....	....	....	....	....
2013-14	Shawinigan	QMJHL	63	9	18	27	20	3	0	0	0	2
	Iowa Wild	AHL	11	1	2	3	4	....	....	....	....	....
2014-15	Shawinigan	QMJHL	63	15	36	51	43	7	1	7	8	15
	Iowa Wild	AHL	3	0	0	0	0	....	....	....	....	....
2015-16	Iowa Wild	AHL	54	4	2	6	50	....	....	....	....	....
2016-17	Iowa Wild	AHL	16	0	2	2	11	....	....	....	....	....
	Quad City	ECHL	17	3	3	6	21	3	1	0	1	2

LABERGE, Pascal (luh-BAIRJ, pas-KAL) PHI

Center. Shoots right. 6'1", 174 lbs. Born, Chateauguay, QC, April 9, 1998.
(Philadelphia's 2nd pick, 36th overall, in 2016 NHL Draft).

			Regular Season					Playoffs				
Season	**Club**	**League**	**GP**	**G**	**A**	**Pts**	**PIM**	**GP**	**G**	**A**	**Pts**	**PIM**
2013-14	Chateauguay	QAAA	40	20	23	43	52	21	11	13	24	26
2014-15	Gatineau	QMJHL	27	4	6	10	4	....	....	....	....	....
	Victoriaville Tigres	QMJHL	31	6	15	21	24	2	0	0	0	4
2015-16	Victoriaville Tigres	QMJHL	56	23	45	68	64	5	3	2	5	6
2016-17	Victoriaville Tigres	QMJHL	46	12	20	32	35	4	2	0	2	4

LABRIE, Hubert (la-BREE, hew-BAIR)

Defense. Shoots left. 5'11", 190 lbs. Born, Victoriaville, QC, July 12, 1991.

			Regular Season					Playoffs				
Season	**Club**	**League**	**GP**	**G**	**A**	**Pts**	**PIM**	**GP**	**G**	**A**	**Pts**	**PIM**
2006-07	Trois-Rivieres	QAAA	34	3	9	12	96	8	1	1	2	18
2007-08	Gatineau	QMJHL	61	2	15	17	79	19	1	3	4	26
2008-09	Gatineau	QMJHL	55	1	3	4	82	5	0	0	0	14
2009-10	Gatineau	QMJHL	67	4	16	20	99	11	3	4	7	20
2010-11	Gatineau	QMJHL	9	3	4	7	8	24	4	8	12	30
2011-12	Texas Stars	AHL	33	2	1	3	18	....	....	....	....	....
	Idaho Steelheads	ECHL	8	1	4	5	0	6	0	0	0	4
2012-13	Texas Stars	AHL	27	0	3	3	45	....	....	....	....	....
	Idaho Steelheads	ECHL	22	2	3	5	46	17	0	1	1	21
2013-14	Texas Stars	AHL	40	2	5	7	49	4	0	0	0	6
	Idaho Steelheads	ECHL	4	0	0	0	7	....	....	....	....	....
2014-15	Springfield Falcons	AHL	46	1	8	9	65	....	....	....	....	....
2015-16	San Antonio	AHL	50	0	7	7	61	....	....	....	....	....
	Chicago Wolves	AHL	15	2	2	4	20	....	....	....	....	....
2016-17	Hershey Bears	AHL	70	3	8	11	66	12	0	4	4	4

Signed as a free agent by **Dallas**, September 18, 2009. Signed as a free agent by **Springfield** (AHL), July 25, 2014. Signed as a free agent by **San Antonio** (AHL), July 30, 2015. • Re-assigned to **Chicago** (AHL) by **San Antonio** (AHL), March 5, 2016. Signed as a free agent by **Hershey** (AHL), July 7, 2016.

LACZYNSKI, Tanner (luh-SIHN-skee, TA-nuhr) PHI

Center. Shoots right. 6', 190 lbs. Born, Minooka, IL, June 1, 1997.
(Philadelphia's 8th pick, 169th overall, in 2016 NHL Draft).

			Regular Season					Playoffs				
Season	**Club**	**League**	**GP**	**G**	**A**	**Pts**	**PIM**	**GP**	**G**	**A**	**Pts**	**PIM**
2012-13	Chi. Mission U16	HPHL	25	12	11	23	14	....	....	....	....	....
2013-14	Chi. Mission U16	HPHL	25	20	18	38	18	....	....	....	....	....
	Chi. Mission U18	HPHL	3	0	6	6	0	....	....	....	....	....
	Chicago Steel	USHL	2	0	0	0	0	....	....	....	....	....
2014-15	Chicago Steel	USHL	57	18	28	46	10	....	....	....	....	....
2015-16	Chicago Steel	USHL	33	13	27	40	20	....	....	....	....	....
	Lincoln Stars	USHL	19	11	12	33	18	4	1	2	3	0
2016-17	Ohio State	Big Ten	34	10	22	32	22	....	....	....	....	....

USHL Second All-Star Team (2016)

LAFFERTY, Sam (LAF-fuhr-tee, SAM) PIT

Center/Left wing. Shoots right. 6'1", 184 lbs. Born, Hollidaysburg, PA, March 6, 1995.
(Pittsburgh's 2nd pick, 113th overall, in 2014 NHL Draft).

			Regular Season					Playoffs				
Season	**Club**	**League**	**GP**	**G**	**A**	**Pts**	**PIM**	**GP**	**G**	**A**	**Pts**	**PIM**
2011-12	Deerfield Academy	High-MA	25	8	8	16	....	....	....	....	....	....
2012-13	Deerfield Academy	High-MA	24	9	15	24	....	....	....	....	....	....
2013-14	Boston Jr. Bruins	Minor-MA	11	2	9	11	2	....	....	....	....	....
	Deerfield Academy	High-MA	25	21	34	55	....	....	....	....	....	....
2014-15	Brown U.	ECAC	31	4	8	12	16	....	....	....	....	....
2015-16	Brown U.	ECAC	31	4	6	10	4	....	....	....	....	....
2016-17	Brown U.	ECAC	31	13	22	35	32	....	....	....	....	....

LAFRANCHISE, Kane (lah-FRAN-chighz, KAYN) NYI

Defense. Shoots left. 6'1", 196 lbs. Born, Edmonton, AB, May 27, 1988.

			Regular Season					Playoffs				
Season	**Club**	**League**	**GP**	**G**	**A**	**Pts**	**PIM**	**GP**	**G**	**A**	**Pts**	**PIM**
2003-04	CAC Canadians	AMHL	35	6	9	15	12	....	....	....	....	....
2004-05	CAC Canadians	AMHL	31	6	14	20	50	....	....	....	....	....
	Spruce Grove	AJHL	1	0	0	0	0	....	....	....	....	....
2005-06	Spruce Grove	AJHL	60	7	13	20	16	13	1	6	7	8
2006-07	Spruce Grove	AJHL	58	12	23	35	55	10	1	3	4	4
2007-08	Alaska-Anchorage	WCHA	33	3	5	8	8	....	....	....	....	....
2008-09	Alaska-Anchorage	WCHA	31	3	7	10	25	....	....	....	....	....
2009-10	Alaska-Anchorage	WCHA	33	3	12	15	30	....	....	....	....	....
2010-11	Alaska Aces	ECHL	22	0	5	5	6	....	....	....	....	....
2011-12	Alaska Aces	ECHL	69	3	31	34	20	10	1	4	5	4
2012-13	Alaska Aces	ECHL	52	5	28	33	18	11	0	6	6	2
	Oklahoma City	AHL	9	0	0	0	0	....	....	....	....	....
	Houston Aeros	AHL	1	0	0	0	0	....	....	....	....	....
2013-14	Abbotsford Heat	AHL	34	0	13	13	2	4	1	0	1	2
	Alaska Aces	ECHL	14	3	3	6	6	15	1	10	11	4
2014-15	Utica Comets	AHL	27	2	8	10	4	....	....	....	....	....
	Kalamazoo Wings	ECHL	24	0	16	16	0	4	0	2	2	0
2015-16	Bridgeport	AHL	33	1	14	15	6	3	0	1	1	2
	Kalamazoo Wings	ECHL	37	4	13	17	12	....	....	....	....	....
2016-17	Bridgeport	AHL	67	5	16	21	28	....	....	....	....	....

Signed as a free agent by **NY Islanders**, July 5, 2017.

LAGANIERE, Antoine (LA-GAH-n'yay, an-TWAHN)

Center. Shoots left. 6'4", 196 lbs. Born, L'Ile-Cadieux, QC, July 5, 1990.

			Regular Season					Playoffs				
Season	**Club**	**League**	**GP**	**G**	**A**	**Pts**	**PIM**	**GP**	**G**	**A**	**Pts**	**PIM**
2005-06	Chateauguay	QAAA	44	14	12	26	8	19	11	10	21	14
2006-07	Chateauguay	QAAA	44	20	23	43	30	3	2	2	4	2
2007-08	Deerfield Academy	High-MA	25	8	30	38	14	....	....	....	....	....
2008-09	Deerfield Academy	High-MA	....	12	16	28	....	....	....	....	....	....
2009-10	Yale	ECAC	25	7	3	10	18	....	....	....	....	....
2010-11	Yale	ECAC	25	5	8	13	14	....	....	....	....	....
2011-12	Yale	ECAC	35	19	14	33	45	....	....	....	....	....
2012-13	Yale	ECAC	37	15	14	29	58	....	....	....	....	....
2013-14	Norfolk Admirals	AHL	72	10	8	18	36	4	0	0	0	2
2014-15	Norfolk Admirals	AHL	73	14	7	21	42	....	....	....	....	....
2015-16	San Diego Gulls	AHL	57	16	16	32	36	9	2	2	4	4
2016-17	San Diego Gulls	AHL	64	21	16	37	30	10	1	2	3	2

Signed as a free agent by **Anaheim**, April 16, 2013. Signed as a free agent by **San Diego** (AHL), July 8, 2015.

LAGESSON, William (lah-GUH-suhn, WIHL-yuhm) EDM

Defense. Shoots left. 6'3", 197 lbs. Born, Gothenburg, Sweden, February 22, 1996.
(Edmonton's 2nd pick, 91st overall, in 2014 NHL Draft).

			Regular Season					Playoffs				
Season	**Club**	**League**	**GP**	**G**	**A**	**Pts**	**PIM**	**GP**	**G**	**A**	**Pts**	**PIM**
2011-12	Frolunda U18	Swe-U18	25	0	3	3	2	2	0	0	0	0
2012-13	Frolunda U18	Swe-U18	32	4	15	19	74	3	1	2	3	4
	Frolunda Jr.	Swe-Jr.	6	0	0	0	0	2	0	0	0	0
2013-14	Frolunda U18	Swe-U18	4	0	1	1	0	5	2	2	4	10
	Frolunda Jr.	Swe-Jr.	44	8	12	20	30	3	0	1	1	2
2014-15	Dubuque	USHL	52	2	14	16	79	8	1	1	2	4
2015-16	Massachusetts	H-East	27	2	5	7	26	....	....	....	....	....
2016-17	Massachusetts	H-East	36	2	6	8	28	....	....	....	....	....

LAJOIE, Maxime (luh-ZHWUH, max-EEM) OTT

Defense. Shoots left. 6'1", 185 lbs. Born, Quebec, QC, November 5, 1997.
(Ottawa's 4th pick, 133rd overall, in 2016 NHL Draft).

			Regular Season					Playoffs				
Season	**Club**	**League**	**GP**	**G**	**A**	**Pts**	**PIM**	**GP**	**G**	**A**	**Pts**	**PIM**
2011-12	Calgary Royals	AMBHL	33	3	9	12	18	....	....	....	....	....
2012-13	Calgary Royals	AMHL	28	1	10	11	12	5	1	2	3	0
2013-14	Calgary Royals	AMHL	32	7	10	17	10	3	0	0	0	0
	Swift Current	WHL	1	0	0	0	0	....	....	....	....	....
2014-15	Swift Current	WHL	72	7	34	41	22	4	1	2	3	0
2015-16	Swift Current	WHL	62	8	29	37	28	....	....	....	....	....
2016-17	Swift Current	WHL	68	7	35	42	26	14	1	8	9	10

LAKATOS, Dominik (la-KA-tohsh, DOHM-ihn-ihk) NYR

Center. Shoots left. 6'1", 200 lbs. Born, Liberec, Czech Rep., August 4, 1997.
(NY Rangers' 5th pick, 157th overall, in 2017 NHL Draft).

			Regular Season					Playoffs				
Season	**Club**	**League**	**GP**	**G**	**A**	**Pts**	**PIM**	**GP**	**G**	**A**	**Pts**	**PIM**
2012-13	HC Liberec U18	CzR-U18	35	10	7	17	38	5	0	0	0	18
2013-14	HC Liberec U18	CzR-U18	41	17	28	45	60	10	5	8	13	10
	HC Liberec Jr.	CzRep-Jr.	1	0	0	0	2	....	....	....	....	....
2014-15	HC Liberec U18	CzR-U18	29	20	23	43	56	3	4	1	5	10
	HC Liberec Jr.	CzRep-Jr.	19	3	10	13	22	6	2	1	3	6
	Liberec	CzRep	1	0	0	0	4	....	....	....	....	....
2015-16	HC Liberec Jr.	CzRep-Jr.	....	....	....	....	....	2	2	2	4	25
	Bili Tygri Liberec	CzRep	36	7	4	11	20	12	1	4	5	10
	Benatky	CzRep-2	19	6	15	21	14	....	....	....	....	....
2016-17	Benatky	CzRep-2	7	2	5	7	4	....	....	....	....	....
	Bili Tygri Liberec	CzRep	41	10	12	22	80	16	8	5	13	8

LALEGGIA, Joey (lah-lehj-EE-a, JOH-ee) EDM

Defense. Shoots left. 5'9", 182 lbs. Born, Burnaby, BC, June 24, 1992.
(Edmonton's 6th pick, 123rd overall, in 2012 NHL Draft).

			Regular Season					Playoffs				
Season	Club	League	GP	G	A	Pts	PIM	GP	G	A	Pts	PIM
2006-07	Burnaby W.C.	Minor-BC	65	7	37	44	58	....	....	....	....	....
2007-08	Van. NW Giants	BCMML	40	7	34	41	32	2	0	1	1	0
2008-09	Van. NW Giants	BCMML	40	15	39	54	67	5	2	4	6	0
	Penticton Vees	BCHL	2	0	0	0	0	....	....	....	....	....
2009-10	Penticton Vees	BCHL	54	13	52	65	19	16	2	10	12	8
2010-11	Penticton Vees	BCHL	58	20	62	82	47	9	1	9	10	12
2011-12	U. of Denver	WCHA	43	11	27	38	35	....	....	....	....	....
2012-13	U. of Denver	WCHA	39	11	18	29	31	....	....	....	....	....
2013-14	U. of Denver	NCHC	37	12	13	25	36	....	....	....	....	....
2014-15	Oklahoma City	AHL	5	1	1	2	2	2	0	0	0	0
	U. of Denver	NCHC	37	15	25	40	56	....	....	....	....	....
2015-16	Bakersfield	AHL	63	8	19	27	38	....	....	....	....	....
2016-17	Bakersfield	AHL	67	20	18	38	30	....	....	....	....	....

WCHA All-Rookie Team (2012) • WCHA Rookie of the Year (2012) • WCHA Second All-Star Team (2013) • NCHC First All-Star Team (2014, 2015) • NCAA West Second All-American Team (2014) • NCHC Player of the Year (2015) • NCAA West First All-American Team (2015)

LAMMIKKO, Juho (lah-MIH-koh, YOO-hoh) FLA

Left wing. Shoots left. 6'2", 207 lbs. Born, Noormarkku, Finland, January 29, 1996.
(Florida's 3rd pick, 65th overall, in 2014 NHL Draft).

			Regular Season					Playoffs				
Season	Club	League	GP	G	A	Pts	PIM	GP	G	A	Pts	PIM
2011-12	Assat Pori U18	Fin-U18	2	0	1	1	0	....	....	....	....	....
	Assat Pori Jr.	Fin-Jr.	2	0	1	1	0	....	....	....	....	....
2012-13	Assat Pori U18	Fin-U18	31	21	32	53	22	9	5	6	11	12
	Assat Pori Jr.	Fin-Jr.	15	0	1	1	10	....	....	....	....	....
2013-14	Assat Pori Jr.	Fin-Jr.	37	17	25	42	32	11	3	5	8	28
	Assat Pori	Finland	20	0	1	1	0	....	....	....	....	....
2014-15	Kingston	OHL	64	18	26	44	36	4	1	1	2	8
2015-16	Assat Pori	Finland	5	2	0	2	4	....	....	....	....	....
	Kingston	OHL	59	22	33	55	51	9	3	4	7	6
	Portland Pirates	AHL	1	0	0	0	2	....	....	....	....	....
2016-17	Springfield	AHL	47	6	5	11	24	....	....	....	....	....

LANDRY, Jon (LAN-dree, JAWN)

Defense. Shoots left. 6'2", 212 lbs. Born, Montreal, QC, May 1, 1983.

			Regular Season					Playoffs				
Season	Club	League	GP	G	A	Pts	PIM	GP	G	A	Pts	PIM
99-2000	Lac St-Louis Lions	QAAA	42	17	27	44	32	7	2	5	7	10
2000-01	St. Paul's School	High-NH	26	10	23	33		....	....	....	....	....
2001-02	St. Paul's School	High-NH	STATISTICS NOT AVAILABLE									
2002-03	Bowdoin College	NCAA-3	23	11	14	25	14	....	....	....	....	....
2003-04	Bowdoin College	NCAA-3	24	13	20	33	20	....	....	....	....	....
2004-05	Bowdoin College	NCAA-3	24	11	14	25	16	....	....	....	....	....
2005-06	Bowdoin College	NCAA-3	27	16	22	38	37	....	....	....	....	....
	Portland Pirates	AHL	2	0	0	0	2	....	....	....	....	....
2006-07	Augusta Lynx	ECHL	2	1	0	1	2	....	....	....	....	....
	Arizona Sundogs	CHL	41	7	7	14	41	14	0	0	0	4
2007-08	Arizona Sundogs	CHL	60	9	33	42	70	17	3	6	9	14
2008-09	Arizona Sundogs	CHL	64	11	31	42	63	....	....	....	....	....
2009-10	Arizona Sundogs	CHL	38	9	22	31	54	....	....	....	....	....
	Kolner Haie	Germany	9	0	2	2	20	....	....	....	....	....
2010-11	Braehead Clan	Britain	54	18	40	58	67	....	....	....	....	....
2011-12	Colorado Eagles	ECHL	35	12	18	30	44	....	....	....	....	....
	Bridgeport	AHL	34	2	18	20	27	2	0	0	0	0
2012-13	Bridgeport	AHL	72	8	25	33	57	....	....	....	....	....
2013-14	Iowa Wild	AHL	50	0	18	18	32	....	....	....	....	....
2014-15	Hershey Bears	AHL	64	3	11	14	38	5	1	0	1	0
2015-16	Utica Comets	AHL	47	7	19	26	38	2	0	2	2	10
2016-17	Bridgeport	AHL	53	4	14	18	28	....	....	....	....	....

Signed as a free agent by **Koln** (Germany), January 29, 2010. Signed as a free agent by **Braehead** (Britain), July 13, 2010. Signed as a free agent by **Colorado** (ECHL), September 21, 2011. Signed as a free agent by **Bridgeport** (AHL), February 24, 2012. Signed as a free agent by **NY Islanders**, July 1, 2012. Signed as a free agent by **Minnesota**, July 9, 2013. Signed as a free agent by **Washington**, July 1, 2014.

LANG, Chase (LANG, CHAYS) MIN

Center. Shoots left. 6'1", 191 lbs. Born, Nanaimo, BC, September 13, 1996.
(Minnesota's 6th pick, 167th overall, in 2014 NHL Draft).

			Regular Season					Playoffs				
Season	Club	League	GP	G	A	Pts	PIM	GP	G	A	Pts	PIM
2010-11	PoE Academy	High-BC	53	32	48	80	50	....	....	....	....	....
2011-12	North Island	BCMML	40	29	32	61	52	....	....	....	....	....
	Alberni Valley	BCHL	5	0	0	0	2	....	....	....	....	....
2012-13	Calgary Hitmen	WHL	44	4	7	11	10	5	0	0	0	0
2013-14	Calgary Hitmen	WHL	68	10	15	25	52	6	0	3	3	13
2014-15	Calgary Hitmen	WHL	63	25	31	56	61	10	4	3	7	10
2015-16	Calgary Hitmen	WHL	14	2	5	7	20	....	....	....	....	....
	Vancouver Giants	WHL	55	25	31	56	56	....	....	....	....	....
	Iowa Wild	AHL	11	2	1	3	4	....	....	....	....	....
2016-17	Iowa Wild	AHL	1	0	0	0	0	....	....	....	....	....
	Quad City	ECHL	12	4	2	6	4	....	....	....	....	....

• Missed majority of 2016-17 due to pre-season back injury.

LANGLOIS, Jeremy (LANG-LOYS, JAIR-ih-mee)

Right wing. Shoots right. 6', 175 lbs. Born, Tempe, AZ, June 2, 1990.

			Regular Season					Playoffs				
Season	Club	League	GP	G	A	Pts	PIM	GP	G	A	Pts	PIM
2006-07	Phoenix	WSHL	45	32	41	73	51	6	2	2	4	6
2007-08	Phoenix	WSHL	47	30	54	84	47	6	4	10	14	2
2008-09	Jersey Hitmen	EJHL	45	35	47	*82	16	7	*6	*5	*11	4
2009-10	Quinnipiac	ECAC	40	8	12	20	18	....	....	....	....	....
2010-11	Quinnipiac	ECAC	39	18	5	23	16	....	....	....	....	....
2011-12	Quinnipiac	ECAC	35	17	9	26	18	....	....	....	....	....
2012-13	Quinnipiac	ECAC	42	13	18	31	32	....	....	....	....	....
2013-14	Springfield Falcons	AHL	5	0	0	0	0	....	....	....	....	....
	Evansville IceMen	ECHL	49	16	36	52	15	....	....	....	....	....
	Bridgeport	AHL	7	2	2	4	2	....	....	....	....	....
	Stockton Thunder	ECHL	7	3	5	8	0	3	4	5	9	0
2014-15	Worcester Sharks	AHL	42	16	10	26	8	4	0	1	1	15
2015-16	San Jose Barracuda	AHL	68	12	22	34	26	4	1	1	2	0
2016-17	Rockford IceHogs	AHL	66	8	6	14	13	....	....	....	....	....

Signed as a free agent by **Springfield** (AHL), July 2, 2013. Signed as a free agent by **Worcester** (AHL), August 28, 2014. Signed as a free agent by **San Jose**, June 27, 2015. Signed as a free agent by **Rockford** (AHL), July 2, 2016.

LAUZON, Jeremy (LOH-zawn, JAIR-ih-mee) BOS

Defense. Shoots left. 6'2", 197 lbs. Born, Val d'Or, QC, April 28, 1997.
(Boston's 6th pick, 52nd overall, in 2015 NHL Draft).

			Regular Season					Playoffs				
Season	Club	League	GP	G	A	Pts	PIM	GP	G	A	Pts	PIM
2012-13	Amos Forestiers	QAAA	41	4	11	15	52	....	....	....	....	....
2013-14	Rouyn-Noranda	QMJHL	55	5	11	16	64	9	2	2	4	4
2014-15	Rouyn-Noranda	QMJHL	60	15	21	36	88	....	....	....	....	....
2015-16	Rouyn-Noranda	QMJHL	46	10	40	50	80	9	1	7	8	8
2016-17	Rouyn-Noranda	QMJHL	39	5	23	28	50	13	5	9	14	22

QMJHL Second All-Star Team (2016)

LAUZON, Zachary (LOH-zawn, za-KAH-ree) PIT

Defense. Shoots left. 6'1", 187 lbs. Born, Val-d'Or, QC, October 10, 1998.
(Pittsburgh's 1st pick, 51st overall, in 2017 NHL Draft).

			Regular Season					Playoffs				
Season	Club	League	GP	G	A	Pts	PIM	GP	G	A	Pts	PIM
2013-14	Amos Forestiers	QAAA	42	6	10	16	40	5	0	0	0	2
2014-15	Amos Forestiers	QAAA	35	4	10	14	94	4	0	2	2	2
	Rouyn-Noranda	QMJHL	11	0	1	1	6	1	0	0	0	0
2015-16	Rouyn-Noranda	QMJHL	61	1	11	12	77	17	2	4	6	13
2016-17	Rouyn-Noranda	QMJHL	63	3	18	21	90	11	1	1	2	0

LEBLANC, Chris (luh-BLAWNK, KRIHS) OTT

Right wing. Shoots right. 6'4", 207 lbs. Born, Winthrop, MA , September 12, 1993.
(Ottawa's 6th pick, 161st overall, in 2013 NHL Draft).

			Regular Season					Playoffs				
Season	Club	League	GP	G	A	Pts	PIM	GP	G	A	Pts	PIM
2008-09	Winthrop Vikings	High-MA	20	6	10	16	18	....	....	....	....	....
2009-10	Winthrop Vikings	High-MA	20	13	18	31	32	3	3	3	6	6
2010-11	Winthrop Vikings	High-MA	....	21	25	46	....	....	....	....	....	....
2011-12	Winthrop Vikings	High-MA	....	24	22	46	....	....	....	....	....	....
2012-13	South Shore Kings	EJHL	44	13	20	33	38	2	1	0	1	0
2013-14	Merrimack College	H-East	23	6	6	12	8	....	....	....	....	....
2014-15	Merrimack College	H-East	28	5	4	9	18	....	....	....	....	....
2015-16	Merrimack College	H-East	35	6	6	12	22	....	....	....	....	....
2016-17	Merrimack College	H-East	27	5	10	15	17	....	....	....	....	....
	Binghamton	AHL	6	0	0	0	0	....	....	....	....	....
	Wichita Thunder	ECHL	7	0	5	5	2	....	....	....	....	....

LEDUC, Loic (luh-DOOK, LOYK)

Defense. Shoots right. 6'6", 229 lbs. Born, Mercier, QC, June 14, 1994.
(NY Islanders' 4th pick, 103rd overall, in 2012 NHL Draft).

			Regular Season					Playoffs				
Season	Club	League	GP	G	A	Pts	PIM	GP	G	A	Pts	PIM
2009-10	Lac St-L. Patriotes	Minor-QC	STATISTICS NOT AVAILABLE									
	Chateauguay	QAAA	1	0	0	0	0	....	....	....	....	....
2010-11	Cape Breton	QMJHL	36	1	3	4	27	2	0	0	0	0
2011-12	Cape Breton	QMJHL	65	2	8	10	99	4	0	1	1	4
2012-13	Cape Breton	QMJHL	38	0	2	2	50	....	....	....	....	....
2013-14	Cape Breton	QMJHL	37	3	5	8	58	....	....	....	....	....
	Rimouski Oceanic	QMJHL	26	3	4	7	44	11	0	2	2	27
2014-15	Stockton Thunder	ECHL	44	3	2	5	85	....	....	....	....	....
	Colorado Eagles	ECHL	11	1	1	2	10	4	0	0	0	2
2015-16	Bridgeport	AHL	20	0	1	1	40	....	....	....	....	....
	Missouri Mavericks	ECHL	21	1	1	2	25	....	....	....	....	....
2016-17	Bridgeport	AHL	33	1	2	3	36	....	....	....	....	....

LEEDAHL, Dawson (LEE-dahl, DAH-suhn) NYR

Left wing. Shoots left. 6'2", 195 lbs. Born, Saskatoon, SK, March 19, 1996.

			Regular Season					Playoffs				
Season	Club	League	GP	G	A	Pts	PIM	GP	G	A	Pts	PIM
2011-12	Sask. Contacts	SMHL	42	11	21	32	64	13	4	9	13	24
2012-13	Everett Silvertips	WHL	56	3	6	9	34	6	2	1	3	4
2013-14	Everett Silvertips	WHL	70	8	24	32	66	5	0	2	2	8
2014-15	Everett Silvertips	WHL	52	14	19	33	68	4	0	2	2	11
2015-16	Everett Silvertips	WHL	48	12	15	27	78	8	3	2	5	*27
2016-17	Regina Pats	WHL	71	35	54	89	121	23	12	13	25	34

Signed as a free agent by **NY Rangers**, May 8, 2017.

LEIVERMANN, Nick (LEE-vuhr-mahn, NIHK) COL

Defense. Shoots left. 5'11", 194 lbs. Born, Edina, MN, September 14, 1998.
(Colorado's 7th pick, 187th overall, in 2017 NHL Draft).

			Regular Season					Playoffs				
Season	Club	League	GP	G	A	Pts	PIM	GP	G	A	Pts	PIM
2014-15	Team Southwest	UMHSEL	2	0	0	0	0	....	....	....	....	....
	Eden Prairie Eagles	High-MN	25	6	13	19	24	5	1	1	2	4
2015-16	Team Northwest	UMHSEL	20	5	3	8	4	....	....	....	....	....
	Eden Prairie Eagles	High-MN	25	10	22	32	16	6	3	7	10	4
	Bloomington	USHL	1	0	0	0	0	....	....	....	....	....
2016-17	Team Northwest	UMHSEL	19	5	11	16	12	....	....	....	....	....
	Eden Prairie Eagles	High-MN	21	10	24	34	16	5	2	4	6	6
	Bloomington	USHL	8	1	0	1	0	....	....	....	....	....

• Signed Letter of Intent to attend **University of Notre Dame** (Hockey East) in fall of 2017.

LEMIEUX, Brendan (luh-M'YEW, BREHN-duhn) **WPG**

Left wing. Shoots left. 6'1", 212 lbs. Born, Denver, CO, March 15, 1996.
(Buffalo's 2nd pick, 31st overall, in 2014 NHL Draft).

			Regular Season					Playoffs				
Season	**Club**	**League**	**GP**	**G**	**A**	**Pts**	**PIM**	**GP**	**G**	**A**	**Pts**	**PIM**
2011-12	Tor. Red Wings	GTHL	26	9	23	32	....	....	....	....	....	....
	The Hill Academy	High-ON	STATISTICS NOT AVAILABLE									
2012-13	Green Bay	USHL	11	1	1	2	34	....	....	....	....	....
	Barrie Colts	OHL	42	6	8	14	52	21	2	0	2	35
2013-14	Barrie Colts	OHL	65	27	26	53	145	11	7	3	10	16
2014-15	Barrie Colts	OHL	57	41	19	60	145	5	1	2	3	12
2015-16	Barrie Colts	OHL	11	9	5	14	28	....	....	....	....	....
	Windsor Spitfires	OHL	34	23	25	48	37	3	4	1	5	13
	Manitoba Moose	AHL	5	2	1	3	6	....	....	....	....	....
2016-17	Manitoba Moose	AHL	61	12	7	19	130	....	....	....	....	....

Traded to **Winnipeg** by **Buffalo** with Tyler Myers, Drew Stafford, Joel Armia and St. Louis' 1st round pick (previously acquired, Winnipeg selected Jack Roslovic) in 2015 NHL Draft for Evander Kane, Zach Bogosian and Jason Kasdorf, February 11, 2015.

LESCHYSHYN, Jake (lehs-CHIH-shihn, JAYK) **VGK**

Center. Shoots left. 5'10", 185 lbs. Born, Raleigh, NC, October 3, 1999.
(Las Vegas' 5th pick, 62nd overall, in 2017 NHL Draft).

			Regular Season					Playoffs				
Season	**Club**	**League**	**GP**	**G**	**A**	**Pts**	**PIM**	**GP**	**G**	**A**	**Pts**	**PIM**
2014-15	Saskatoon Blazers	SMHL	38	15	20	35	30	....	....	....	....	....
	Regina Pats	WHL	12	3	0	3	0	9	1	0	1	0
2015-16	Regina Pats	WHL	66	7	9	16	38	12	1	3	4	8
2016-17	Regina Pats	WHL	47	17	23	40	22	....	....	....	....	....

LESLIE, Zachary (LEHS-lee, za-KAH-ree) **L.A.**

Defense. Shoots left. 6', 175 lbs. Born, Ottawa, ON, January 31, 1994.
(Los Angeles' 6th pick, 178th overall, in 2013 NHL Draft).

			Regular Season					Playoffs				
Season	**Club**	**League**	**GP**	**G**	**A**	**Pts**	**PIM**	**GP**	**G**	**A**	**Pts**	**PIM**
2009-10	Ott. Jr. 67's MM	Minor-ON	29	10	24	34	36	11	2	6	8	12
	Ott. Jr. 67's Mid.	Minor-ON	5	1	1	2	2	3	0	2	2	4
	Gloucester	ON-Jr.A	1	0	0	0	0	....	....	....	....	....
2010-11	Gloucester	ON-Jr.A	56	13	22	35	26	9	1	3	4	4
2011-12	Guelph Storm	OHL	65	2	15	17	54	5	0	0	0	4
2012-13	Guelph Storm	OHL	68	12	28	40	58	5	0	1	1	4
2013-14	Guelph Storm	OHL	60	14	36	50	39	20	1	9	10	22
2014-15	Guelph Storm	OHL	57	11	37	48	57	....	....	....	....	....
2015-16	Ontario Reign	AHL	30	0	5	5	13	3	0	1	1	2
	Manchester	ECHL	5	1	0	1	2	....	....	....	....	....
2016-17	Ontario Reign	AHL	65	5	18	23	29	5	0	0	0	6

LETTIERI, Vinni (luh-TAYR-ee, VIH-nee) **NYR**

Right wing. Shoots right. 5'11", 195 lbs. Born, Excelsior, MN, February 6, 1995.

			Regular Season					Playoffs				
Season	**Club**	**League**	**GP**	**G**	**A**	**Pts**	**PIM**	**GP**	**G**	**A**	**Pts**	**PIM**
2010-11	Minnetonka	High-MN	25	15	22	37	12	2	2	1	3	2
2011-12	Team Southwest	UMHSEL	21	14	13	27	11	3	2	0	2	2
	Minnetonka	High-MN	25	22	36	58	24	3	1	1	2	0
	Lincoln Stars	USHL	15	4	4	8	14	7	0	1	1	0
2012-13	Lincoln Stars	USHL	61	28	28	56	35	5	1	2	3	0
2013-14	U. of Minnesota	Big Ten	37	2	6	8	8	....	....	....	....	....
2014-15	U. of Minnesota	Big Ten	37	9	3	12	14	....	....	....	....	....
2015-16	U. of Minnesota	Big Ten	37	7	19	26	18	....	....	....	....	....
2016-17	U. of Minnesota	Big Ten	38	19	18	37	36	....	....	....	....	....
	Hartford Wolf Pack	AHL	9	0	1	1	4	....	....	....	....	....

USHL All-Rookie Team (2013)

Signed as a free agent by **NY Rangers**, March 27, 2017.

LETUNOV, Maxim (leh-too-NAWV, max-EEM) **S.J.**

Center. Shoots left. 6'4", 180 lbs. Born, Moscow, Russia, February 20, 1996.
(St. Louis' 3rd pick, 52nd overall, in 2014 NHL Draft).

			Regular Season					Playoffs				
Season	**Club**	**League**	**GP**	**G**	**A**	**Pts**	**PIM**	**GP**	**G**	**A**	**Pts**	**PIM**
2012-13	Dallas Midget	EHL Midget	40	29	37	66	6	4	2	2	4	6
2013-14	Youngstown	USHL	60	19	24	43	42	....	....	....	....	....
2014-15	Youngstown	USHL	58	25	39	64	18	4	0	1	1	0
2015-16	U. of Connecticut	H-East	36	16	24	40	2	....	....	....	....	....
2016-17	U. of Connecticut	H-East	33	7	20	27	25	....	....	....	....	....

Hockey East All-Rookie Team (2016) • Hockey East Second All-Star Team (2016)

Traded to **Arizona** by **St. Louis** for Zbynek Michalek and future considerations, March 2, 2015. Traded to **San Jose** by **Arizona** with Arizona's 6th round pick (Jacob McGrew) in 2017 NHL Draft for San Jose's 4th round pick (later traded to NY Islanders – NY Islanders selected Otto Koivula) in 2016 NHL Draft and Detroit's 3rd round pick (previously acquired, Arizona selected Mackenzie Entwistle) in 2017 NHL Draft, June 20, 2016.

LEWINGTON, Tyler (LOO-ihng-tuhn, TIGH-luhr) **WSH**

Defense. Shoots right. 6'1", 189 lbs. Born, Edmonton, AB, December 5, 1994.
(Washington's 6th pick, 204th overall, in 2013 NHL Draft).

			Regular Season					Playoffs				
Season	**Club**	**League**	**GP**	**G**	**A**	**Pts**	**PIM**	**GP**	**G**	**A**	**Pts**	**PIM**
2010-11	Sherwood Park	AMHL	34	4	22	26	46	13	1	8	9	4
2011-12	Medicine Hat	WHL	44	0	3	3	46	8	0	1	1	2
2012-13	Medicine Hat	WHL	69	2	24	26	131	8	1	0	1	14
2013-14	Medicine Hat	WHL	68	7	31	38	121	18	0	3	3	26
2014-15	Medicine Hat	WHL	69	9	36	45	113	9	1	1	2	10
2015-16	Hershey Bears	AHL	32	3	3	6	89	21	4	1	5	19
	South Carolina	ECHL	14	1	5	6	20	....	....	....	....	....
2016-17	Hershey Bears	AHL	72	4	13	17	142	12	1	3	4	17

LILJEGREN, Timothy (lihl-YEH-grehn, TIH-moh-thee) **TOR**

Defense. Shoots right. 6', 191 lbs. Born, Kristianstad, Sweden, April 30, 1999.
(Toronto's 1st pick, 17th overall, in 2017 NHL Draft).

			Regular Season					Playoffs				
Season	**Club**	**League**	**GP**	**G**	**A**	**Pts**	**PIM**	**GP**	**G**	**A**	**Pts**	**PIM**
2012-13	Kristian./Osby U18	Swe-U18	4	0	3	3	4	....	....	....	....	....
	Kristian./Osby Jr.	Swe-Jr.	16	1	3	4	2	....	....	....	....	....
2014-15	Rogle U18	Swe-U18	28	7	13	20	8	....	....	....	....	....
2015-16	Rogle U18	Swe-U18	2	0	0	0	0	....	....	....	....	....
	Rogle Jr.	Swe-Jr.	29	7	15	22	26	3	1	2	3	0
	Rogle	Sweden	19	1	4	5	4	....	....	....	....	....
2016-17	Rogle Jr.	Swe-Jr.	12	5	2	7	8	3	1	4	5	0
	Rogle	Sweden	19	1	4	5	4	....	....	....	....	....
	Timra IK	Sweden-2	5	0	1	1	4	....	....	....	....	....
	Rogle U18	Swe-U18	....	....	....	....	....	1	0	0	0	0

LIND, Kole (LIHND, KOHL) **VAN**

Right wing. Shoots right. 6'1", 185 lbs. Born, Swift Current, SK, October 16, 1998.
(Vancouver's 2nd pick, 33rd overall, in 2017 NHL Draft).

			Regular Season					Playoffs				
Season	**Club**	**League**	**GP**	**G**	**A**	**Pts**	**PIM**	**GP**	**G**	**A**	**Pts**	**PIM**
2013-14	Sask. Contacts	SMHL	44	21	16	37	38	3	0	2	2	2
2014-15	Sask. Contacts	SMHL	44	45	34	79	54	4	4	2	6	14
	Kelowna Rockets	WHL	6	0	1	1	4	7	0	3	3	4
2015-16	Kelowna Rockets	WHL	70	14	27	41	54	16	0	0	0	12
2016-17	Kelowna Rockets	WHL	70	30	57	87	79	17	6	6	12	10

WHL West Second All-Star Team (2017)

LINDBLOM, Oskar (LIHND-blawm, AWS-kuhr) **PHI**

Left wing. Shoots left. 6'1", 193 lbs. Born, Gavle, Sweden, August 15, 1996.
(Philadelphia's 4th pick, 138th overall, in 2014 NHL Draft).

			Regular Season					Playoffs				
Season	**Club**	**League**	**GP**	**G**	**A**	**Pts**	**PIM**	**GP**	**G**	**A**	**Pts**	**PIM**
2011-12	Brynas U18	Swe-U18	30	12	14	26	8	1	0	1	1	0
2012-13	Brynas U18	Swe-U18	33	31	28	59	14	8	4	5	9	2
	Brynas IF Gavle Jr.	Swe-Jr.	3	1	0	1	0	....	....	....	....	....
2013-14	Brynas U18	Swe-U18	6	8	5	13	0	....	....	....	....	....
	Brynas IF Gavle	Sweden	4	0	0	0	0	....	....	....	....	....
	Brynas IF Gavle Jr.	Swe-Jr.	43	13	20	33	28	7	6	1	7	6
2014-15	Brynas IF Gavle	Sweden	37	8	7	15	16	7	1	1	2	0
2015-16	Lehigh Valley	AHL	8	2	5	7	0	....	....	....	....	....
	Brynas IF Gavle	Sweden	48	8	17	25	14	3	1	2	3	6
	Brynas IF Gavle Jr.	Swe-Jr.	....	....	....	....	....	2	1	0	1	2
2016-17	Brynas IF Gavle	Sweden	52	22	25	47	18	20	4	*10	14	10

LINDGREN, Jesper (LIHND-gruhn, YEHS-puhr) **TOR**

Defense. Shoots right. 6', 161 lbs. Born, Umea, Sweden, May 19, 1997.
(Toronto's 6th pick, 95th overall, in 2015 NHL Draft).

			Regular Season					Playoffs				
Season	**Club**	**League**	**GP**	**G**	**A**	**Pts**	**PIM**	**GP**	**G**	**A**	**Pts**	**PIM**
2012-13	Bjorkloven U18	Swe-U18	35	1	15	16	8	....	....	....	....	....
2013-14	MODO U18	Swe-U18	35	7	25	32	34	5	0	0	0	0
	MODO Jr.	Swe-Jr.	8	1	3	4	2	....	....	....	....	....
2014-15	MODO U18	Swe-U18	6	0	9	9	8	3	1	1	2	0
	MODO Jr.	Swe-Jr.	39	6	27	33	39	4	0	1	1	2
	MODO	Sweden	4	0	1	1	0	....	....	....	....	....
2015-16	MODO Jr.	Swe-Jr.	20	4	10	14	22	2	0	0	0	0
	IF Bjorkloven Umea	Sweden-2	4	0	2	2	0	....	....	....	....	....
	MODO	Sweden	26	2	1	3	4	....	....	....	....	....
2016-17	MODO Jr.	Swe-Jr.	7	1	9	10	6	6	1	3	4	2
	MODO	Sweden-2	50	3	21	24	12	....	....	....	....	....

LINDGREN, Ryan (LIHND-grehn, RIGH-uhn) **BOS**

Defense. Shoots left. 5'11", 208 lbs. Born, Burnsville, MN, February 11, 1998.
(Boston's 3rd pick, 49th overall, in 2016 NHL Draft).

			Regular Season					Playoffs				
Season	**Club**	**League**	**GP**	**G**	**A**	**Pts**	**PIM**	**GP**	**G**	**A**	**Pts**	**PIM**
2013-14	Shattuck	High-MN	51	3	12	15	80	....	....	....	....	....
2014-15	USAHNTDP	USHL	35	3	10	13	65	....	....	....	....	....
	USAHNTDP	U-17	20	0	6	6	20	....	....	....	....	....
2015-16	USAHNTDP	USHL	25	4	8	12	16	....	....	....	....	....
	USAHNTDP	U-18	36	6	19	25	60	....	....	....	....	....
2016-17	U. of Minnesota	Big Ten	32	1	6	7	65	....	....	....	....	....

LINDSTROM, Gustav (lihnd-STRUHM, GOO-stahv) **DET**

Defense. Shoots right. 6'2", 187 lbs. Born, Ostervala, Sweden, October 20, 1998.
(Detroit's 2nd pick, 38th overall, in 2017 NHL Draft).

			Regular Season					Playoffs				
Season	**Club**	**League**	**GP**	**G**	**A**	**Pts**	**PIM**	**GP**	**G**	**A**	**Pts**	**PIM**
2012-13	Ostervala IF Jr.	Swe-Jr.	5	3	3	6	4	....	....	....	....	....
	Ostervala IF	Sweden-6	13	5	4	9	2	6	0	1	1	2
2013-14	Ostervala IF	Sweden-6	21	9	9	18	46	8	2	5	7	0
2014-15	Almtuna U18	Swe-U18	39	7	21	28	50	....	....	....	....	....
	Almtuna Jr.	Swe-Jr.	....	....	....	....	....	4	1	1	2	6
2015-16	Almtuna U18	Swe-U18	20	13	10	23	18	3	0	3	3	4
	Almtuna Jr.	Swe-Jr.	3	0	4	4	2	1	0	0	0	0
2016-17	Almtuna Jr.	Swe-Jr.	6	6	4	10	10	....	....	....	....	....
	Almtuna	Sweden-2	48	2	7	9	26	....	....	....	....	....

LINDSTROM, Linus (LIHND-struhm, LEE-nuhs) **CGY**

Center. Shoots left. 6', 165 lbs. Born, Skelleftea, Sweden, January 8, 1998.
(Calgary's 5th pick, 96th overall, in 2016 NHL Draft).

			Regular Season					Playoffs				
Season	**Club**	**League**	**GP**	**G**	**A**	**Pts**	**PIM**	**GP**	**G**	**A**	**Pts**	**PIM**
2013-14	Skelleftea AIK U18	Swe-U18	33	6	23	29	8	2	0	0	0	0
2014-15	Skelleftea AIK U18	Swe-U18	22	16	19	35	18	....	....	....	....	....
	Skelleftea AIK Jr.	Swe-Jr.	23	11	7	18	4	....	....	....	....	....
2015-16	Skelleftea AIK U18	Swe-U18	2	1	4	5	0	1	0	0	0	0
	Skelleftea AIK Jr.	Swe-Jr.	40	14	30	44	28	6	5	5	10	0
	Skelleftea AIK	Sweden	4	1	0	1	0	....	....	....	....	....
2016-17	Skelleftea AIK Jr.	Swe-Jr.	6	4	4	8	2	2	0	1	1	0
	Skelleftea AIK	Sweden	50	2	4	6	8	....	....	....	....	....

LINTUNIEMI, Alex (LIHN-too-nee-EH-mee, AL-ehx) L.A.

Defense. Shoots left. 6'3", 231 lbs. Born, Helsinki, Finland, September 23, 1995.
(Los Angeles' 3rd pick, 60th overall, in 2014 NHL Draft).

			Regular Season					Playoffs				
Season	Club	League	GP	G	A	Pts	PIM	GP	G	A	Pts	PIM
2010-11	HIFK Helsinki U18	Fin-U18	24	3	11	14	6	3	0	1	1	2
2011-12	Jokerit U18	Fin-U18	37	4	17	21	24	11	2	5	7	8
	Jokerit Helsinki Jr.	Fin-Jr.	3	0	1	1	0	....	....	....	....	....
2012-13	Jokerit Helsinki Jr.	Fin-Jr.	38	4	10	14	76	....	....	....	....	....
	Kiekko-Vantaa	Finland-2	11	1	2	3	6	....	....	....	....	....
	Jokerit U18	Fin-U18	....	....	....	....	....	10	4	4	8	6
2013-14	Ottawa 67's	OHL	68	4	17	21	26	....	....	....	....	....
2014-15	Ottawa 67's	OHL	58	7	29	36	22	6	1	2	3	2
	Manchester	AHL	4	0	1	1	0	....	....	....	....	....
2015-16	Manchester	ECHL	38	1	17	18	8	5	0	0	0	0
2016-17	Ontario Reign	AHL	41	2	8	10	6	5	0	0	0	0

LIPANOV, Alexei (LIH-pa-nawv, al-EHX-ay) T.B.

Center. Shoots left. 6', 169 lbs. Born, Moscow, Russia, August 17, 1999.
(Tampa Bay's 2nd pick, 76th overall, in 2017 NHL Draft).

			Regular Season					Playoffs				
Season	Club	League	GP	G	A	Pts	PIM	GP	G	A	Pts	PIM
2015-16	Dyn'o Moscow Jr.	Russia-Jr.	32	3	5	8	16	....	....	....	....	....
2016-17	Dyn'o Moscow Jr.	Russia-Jr.	11	0	3	3	6	....	....	....	....	....
	Dyn'o Balashikha	Russia-2	21	3	5	8	8	6	0	3	3	6

LOCKWOOD, William (LAWK-wud, WIHL-yuhm) VAN

Right wing. Shoots right. 6', 171 lbs. Born, Bloomfield Hills, MI, June 20, 1998.
(Vancouver's 2nd pick, 64th overall, in 2016 NHL Draft).

			Regular Season					Playoffs				
Season	Club	League	GP	G	A	Pts	PIM	GP	G	A	Pts	PIM
2013-14	Oak. Grizzlies U16	T1EHL	31	19	19	38	41	....	....	....	....	....
	Oak. Grizzlies	Minor-MI	....	....	....	....	....	4	1	2	3	10
2014-15	USAHNTDP	USHL	35	8	5	13	10	....	....	....	....	....
	USAHNTDP	U-17	18	6	2	8	6	....	....	....	....	....
2015-16	USAHNTDP	USHL	20	3	3	6	27	....	....	....	....	....
	USAHNTDP	U-18	39	10	17	27	8	....	....	....	....	....
2016-17	U. of Michigan	Big Ten	30	8	12	20	33	....	....	....	....	....

LODGE, Jimmy (LAWDG, JIHM-ee) WPG

Center. Shoots right. 6'1", 174 lbs. Born, Downington, PA, March 5, 1995.
(Winnipeg's 4th pick, 84th overall, in 2013 NHL Draft).

			Regular Season					Playoffs				
Season	Club	League	GP	G	A	Pts	PIM	GP	G	A	Pts	PIM
2010-11	Toronto Titans	GTHL	29	18	25	43	44	....	....	....	....	....
2011-12	Saginaw Spirit	OHL	45	8	4	12	10	11	0	0	0	0
2012-13	Saginaw Spirit	OHL	64	28	39	67	28	4	1	2	3	7
2013-14	Saginaw Spirit	OHL	59	19	27	46	49	5	2	2	4	2
2014-15	Saginaw Spirit	OHL	18	10	8	18	8	....	....	....	....	....
	Mississauga	OHL	40	18	27	45	45	....	....	....	....	....
	St. John's IceCaps	AHL	1	0	0	0	0	....	....	....	....	....
2015-16	Manitoba Moose	AHL	44	3	3	6	10	....	....	....	....	....
	Tulsa Oilers	ECHL	13	1	7	8	12	....	....	....	....	....
2016-17	Manitoba Moose	AHL	63	8	10	18	34	....	....	....	....	....

LODNIA, Ivan (LAWD-nee-uh, IGH-vuhn) MIN

Right wing. Shoots right. 5'11", 176 lbs. Born, Los Angeles, CA, August 31, 1999.
(Minnesota's 1st pick, 85th overall, in 2017 NHL Draft).

			Regular Season					Playoffs				
Season	Club	League	GP	G	A	Pts	PIM	GP	G	A	Pts	PIM
2014-15	Det. H-Baked U16	HPHL	26	15	14	29	14	....	....	....	....	....
	Det. H-Baked U18	HPHL	2	0	0	0	0	....	....	....	....	....
2015-16	Erie Otters	OHL	62	16	23	39	14	13	0	4	4	2
	USAHNTDP	U-17	5	2	0	2	0	....	....	....	....	....
2016-17	Erie Otters	OHL	66	24	33	57	24	22	2	0	2	8

LOHIN, Ryan (LOW-IHN, RIGH-uhn) T.B.

Center. Shoots left. 6', 193 lbs. Born, Chester, PA, June 26, 1996.
(Tampa Bay's 10th pick, 208th overall, in 2016 NHL Draft).

			Regular Season					Playoffs				
Season	Club	League	GP	G	A	Pts	PIM	GP	G	A	Pts	PIM
2011-12	Phi. L. Flyers U16	AYHL	21	11	14	25	6	....	....	....	....	....
2012-13	Phi. L. Flyers U16	AYHL	17	12	24	36	20	....	....	....	....	....
	Phi. L. Flyers	AtJHL	19	7	15	22	10	....	....	....	....	....
2013-14	Comcast U18	AYHL	20	17	14	31	18	....	....	....	....	....
	Comcast U18	T1EHL	36	30	38	68	30	....	....	....	....	....
2014-15	Madison Capitols	USHL	60	10	16	26	49	....	....	....	....	....
2015-16	Madison Capitols	USHL	48	16	23	39	50	....	....	....	....	....
	Waterloo	USHL	14	7	11	18	4	9	1	4	5	16
2016-17	U. Mass Lowell	H-East	41	12	17	29	18	....	....	....	....	....

LOMBERG, Ryan (LOM-burg, RIGH-uhn) CGY

Center. Shoots left. 5'9", 187 lbs. Born, Richmond Hill, ON, September 12, 1994.

			Regular Season					Playoffs				
Season	Club	League	GP	G	A	Pts	PIM	GP	G	A	Pts	PIM
2009-10	Mississauga Reps	GTHL	64	52	39	91	....	....	....	....	....	....
	North York	ON-Jr.A	4	0	0	0	0	....	....	....	....	....
2010-11	The Hill Academy	High-ON	57	52	47	99	64	....	....	....	....	....
	Upper Canada	ON-Jr.A	1	0	0	0	0	4	0	0	0	0
2011-12	Muskegon	USHL	52	22	18	40	154	....	....	....	....	....
2012-13	U. of Maine	H-East	32	7	7	14	42	....	....	....	....	....
2013-14	U. of Maine	H-East	34	11	7	18	40	....	....	....	....	....
2014-15	Youngstown	USHL	56	24	19	43	146	4	1	1	2	6
2015-16	Adirondack	ECHL	43	18	17	35	48	12	3	3	6	27
	Stockton Heat	AHL	15	0	3	3	42	....	....	....	....	....
2016-17	Stockton Heat	AHL	68	13	16	29	127	1	0	0	0	0

Signed as a free agent by **Stockton** (AHL), September 4, 2015. Signed as a free agent by **Calgary**, March 19, 2017.

LOOKE, Jens (LOH-keh, YEHNZ) ARI

Right wing. Shoots right. 6', 188 lbs. Born, Gavle, Sweden, April 11, 1997.
(Arizona's 7th pick, 83rd overall, in 2015 NHL Draft).

			Regular Season					Playoffs				
Season	Club	League	GP	G	A	Pts	PIM	GP	G	A	Pts	PIM
2011-12	Brynas U18	Swe-U18	1	0	0	0	0	....	....	....	....	....
2012-13	Brynas U18	Swe-U18	34	16	14	30	2	8	2	6	8	2
2013-14	Brynas U18	Swe-U18	32	15	25	40	14	5	3	4	7	2
	Brynas IF Gavle Jr.	Swe-Jr.	7	2	0	2	0	2	0	1	1	0
2014-15	Brynas U18	Swe-U18	1	1	4	5	0	4	3	3	6	0
	Brynas IF Gavle Jr.	Swe-Jr.	18	10	8	18	4	2	1	1	2	2
	Brynas IF Gavle	Sweden	43	2	4	6	2	7	0	0	0	0
2015-16	Brynas IF Gavle Jr.	Swe-Jr.	10	6	8	14	4	4	0	2	2	0
	Brynas IF Gavle	Sweden	5	0	0	0	2	....	....	....	....	....
	Almtuna	Sweden-2	34	4	9	13	2	....	....	....	....	....
2016-17	Timra IK	Sweden-2	49	9	10	19	10	....	....	....	....	....

LORENTZ, Steven (LAWR-ehntz, STEE-vehn) CAR

Center/Left wing. Shoots left. 6'4", 202 lbs. Born, Kitchener, ON, April 13, 1996.
(Carolina's 9th pick, 186th overall, in 2015 NHL Draft).

			Regular Season					Playoffs				
Season	Club	League	GP	G	A	Pts	PIM	GP	G	A	Pts	PIM
2011-12	Wat. Wolves MM	Minor-ON	56	19	28	47	24	....	....	....	....	....
2012-13	Wat. Wolves Mid.	Minor-ON	31	17	17	34	24	16	8	15	23	10
	Waterloo Siskins	ON-Jr.B	3	0	0	0	2	....	....	....	....	....
2013-14	Peterborough	OHL	64	7	11	18	18	11	2	0	2	0
2014-15	Peterborough	OHL	59	16	21	37	15	5	0	1	1	2
2015-16	Peterborough	OHL	58	23	25	48	27	7	2	3	5	0
2016-17	Peterborough	OHL	66	29	32	61	37	12	9	7	16	0

LOUIS, Anthony (LOO-ihs, AN-thuh-nee) CHI

Center. Shoots left. 5'8", 158 lbs. Born, Wheaton, IL, February 10, 1995.
(Chicago's 7th pick, 181st overall, in 2013 NHL Draft).

			Regular Season					Playoffs				
Season	Club	League	GP	G	A	Pts	PIM	GP	G	A	Pts	PIM
2010-11	Team Illinois	T1EHL	35	33	27	60	18	....	....	....	....	....
2011-12	USAHNTDP	USHL	32	16	6	22	12	....	....	....	....	....
	USAHNTDP	U-17	17	12	8	20	6	....	....	....	....	....
	USAHNTDP	U-18	7	0	1	1	2	....	....	....	....	....
2012-13	USAHNTDP	USHL	24	10	15	25	10	....	....	....	....	....
	USAHNTDP	U-18	38	12	14	26	10	....	....	....	....	....
2013-14	Miami U.	NCHC	36	12	13	25	10	....	....	....	....	....
2014-15	Miami U.	NCHC	37	9	27	36	8	....	....	....	....	....
2015-16	Miami U.	NCHC	36	11	15	26	27	....	....	....	....	....
2016-17	Miami U.	NCHC	36	14	25	39	20	....	....	....	....	....
	Rockford IceHogs	AHL	13	1	2	3	4	....	....	....	....	....

NCHC First All-Star Team (2017)

LOVERDE, Vincent (LOH-vuhr-dee, VIHN-sehnt) TOR

Defense. Shoots right. 5'11", 205 lbs. Born, Chicago, IL, April 14, 1989.

			Regular Season					Playoffs				
Season	Club	League	GP	G	A	Pts	PIM	GP	G	A	Pts	PIM
2004-05	Chicago Y.A.	MWEHL	28	3	12	15	38	....	....	....	....	....
2005-06	Waterloo	USHL	53	5	6	11	78	....	....	....	....	....
2006-07	Waterloo	USHL	46	4	17	21	96	9	1	2	3	31
2007-08	Miami U.	CCHA	42	0	8	8	20	....	....	....	....	....
2008-09	Miami U.	CCHA	38	1	7	8	40	....	....	....	....	....
2009-10	Miami U.	CCHA	40	3	8	11	48	....	....	....	....	....
2010-11	Miami U.	CCHA	39	2	7	9	28	....	....	....	....	....
2011-12	Ontario Reign	ECHL	64	5	19	24	54	5	0	1	1	0
2012-13	Ontario Reign	ECHL	27	7	10	17	15	....	....	....	....	....
	Manchester	AHL	51	2	11	13	30	4	0	0	0	2
2013-14	Manchester	AHL	70	2	18	20	46	4	0	0	0	0
2014-15	Manchester	AHL	63	9	11	20	63	19	2	8	10	27
2015-16	Ontario Reign	AHL	56	11	21	32	54	13	1	2	3	10
2016-17	Ontario Reign	AHL	61	9	26	35	68	5	0	0	0	6

Signed as a free agent by **Ontario** (ECHL), October 21, 2011. Signed to a PTO (professional tryout) contract by **Manchester** (AHL), November 9, 2012. Signed as a free agent by **Los Angeles**, May 15, 2014. Signed as a free agent by **Toronto**, July 1, 2017.

LOWRY, Joel (LOW-ree, JOHL)

Left wing. Shoots left. 6'2", 185 lbs. Born, Calgary, AB, November 15, 1991.
(Los Angeles' 5th pick, 140th overall, in 2011 NHL Draft).

			Regular Season					Playoffs				
Season	Club	League	GP	G	A	Pts	PIM	GP	G	A	Pts	PIM
2008-09	Calgary Buffaloes	AMHL	32	14	16	30	32	15	5	6	11	20
	Okotoks Oilers	AJHL	3	0	0	0	0	....	....	....	....	....
2009-10	Victoria Grizzlies	BCHL	57	15	29	44	55	6	1	4	5	2
2010-11	Victoria Grizzlies	BCHL	42	24	43	67	35	12	5	12	17	6
2011-12	Cornell Big Red	ECAC	35	6	16	22	47	....	....	....	....	....
2012-13	Cornell Big Red	ECAC	33	12	11	23	55	....	....	....	....	....
2013-14	Cornell Big Red	ECAC	32	7	17	24	39	....	....	....	....	....
2014-15	Cornell Big Red	ECAC	11	4	4	8	14	....	....	....	....	....
2015-16	Ontario Reign	AHL	41	5	6	11	32	12	4	2	6	4
	Manchester	ECHL	3	0	1	1	2	....	....	....	....	....
2016-17	Ontario Reign	AHL	40	1	7	8	64	4	0	0	0	0

LUCIA, Mario (LOO-chee-a, MAR-ee-oh) MIN

Left wing. Shoots left. 6'3", 200 lbs. Born, Fairbanks, AK, August 25, 1993.
(Minnesota's 3rd pick, 60th overall, in 2011 NHL Draft).

			Regular Season					Playoffs				
Season	Club	League	GP	G	A	Pts	PIM	GP	G	A	Pts	PIM
2009-10	Wayzata	High-MN	25	15	25	40	6	2	0	2	2	0
2010-11	Team Northwest	UMHSEL	10	6	6	12	4	1	0	0	0	0
	Wayzata	High-MN	24	25	22	47	14	3	5	2	7	2
	USAHNTDP	USHL	6	3	0	3	0	....	....	....	....	....
	USAHNTDP	U-18	9	1	1	2	0	....	....	....	....	....
2011-12	Penticton Vees	BCHL	56	42	51	93	42	15	6	10	16	2
2012-13	U. of Notre Dame	CCHA	32	12	11	23	18	....	....	....	....	....
2013-14	U. of Notre Dame	H-East	40	16	15	31	12	....	....	....	....	....
2014-15	U. of Notre Dame	H-East	42	21	11	32	22	....	....	....	....	....
2015-16	U. of Notre Dame	H-East	37	12	12	24	12	....	....	....	....	....
	Iowa Wild	AHL	9	2	2	4	2	....	....	....	....	....
2016-17	Iowa Wild	AHL	44	9	13	22	18	....	....	....	....	....

CCHA All-Rookie Team (2013)

LUFF, Matt (LUHF, MAT) **L.A.**

Right wing. Shoots right. 6'2", 190 lbs. Born, Oakville, ON, May 5, 1997.

			Regular Season					Playoffs				
Season	**Club**	**League**	**GP**	**G**	**A**	**Pts**	**PIM**	**GP**	**G**	**A**	**Pts**	**PIM**
2012-13	Oak. Rangers MM	Minor-ON	71	20	41	61	26	....	....	....	....	....
2013-14	Oak. Rangers Mid.	Minor-ON	66	56	42	98	....	....	....	....	....	....
	Oakville Blades	ON-Jr.A	10	3	3	6	6	....	....	....	....	....
2014-15	Belleville Bulls	OHL	64	9	22	31	20	4	1	1	2	4
2015-16	Hamilton Bulldogs	OHL	61	27	30	57	43	....	....	....	....	....
2016-17	Hamilton Bulldogs	OHL	45	25	24	49	33	7	4	5	9	4
	Ontario Reign	AHL	2	0	1	1	0	....	....	....	....	....

Signed as a free agent by **Los Angeles**, September 22, 2016.

LUOSTARINEN, Eetu (loo-oh-STAR-ih-nehn, AY-too) **CAR**

Center. Shoots left. 6'3", 184 lbs. Born, Siilinjarvi, Finland, February 9, 1998.
(Carolina's 2nd pick, 42nd overall, in 2017 NHL Draft).

			Regular Season					Playoffs				
Season	**Club**	**League**	**GP**	**G**	**A**	**Pts**	**PIM**	**GP**	**G**	**A**	**Pts**	**PIM**
2014-15	KalPa Kuopio U18	Fin-U18	18	7	4	11	4	....	....	....	....	....
2015-16	KalPa Kuopio U18	Fin-U18	46	11	23	34	58	2	2	0	2	12
2016-17	KalPa Kuopio Jr.	Fin-Jr.	23	11	8	19	49	....	....	....	....	....
	KalPa Kuopio	Finland	32	3	4	7	14	17	1	2	3	14

LYAMIN, Kirill (L'YAH-mihn, kih-RIHL) **OTT**

Defense. Shoots left. 6'2", 211 lbs. Born, Moscow, USSR, January 13, 1986.
(Ottawa's 2nd pick, 58th overall, in 2004 NHL Draft).

			Regular Season					Playoffs				
Season	**Club**	**League**	**GP**	**G**	**A**	**Pts**	**PIM**	**GP**	**G**	**A**	**Pts**	**PIM**
2001-02	Moscow 18	Exhib.	5	0	3	3	4	....	....	....	....	....
2002-03	CSKA Moscow 2	Russia-3	5	0	0	0	10	....	....	....	....	....
	Moscow 18	Exhib.	5	0	0	0	6	....	....	....	....	....
2003-04	CSKA Moscow 2	Russia-3	STATISTICS NOT AVAILABLE									
	CSKA Moscow	Russia	28	0	3	3	12	....	....	....	....	....
2004-05	CSKA Moscow 2	Russia-3	STATISTICS NOT AVAILABLE									
2005-06	CSKA Moscow	Russia	25	0	1	1	28	2	0	0	0	0
2006-07	CSKA Moscow	Russia	47	1	7	8	48	12	1	0	1	8
2007-08	Mytischi	Russia	40	1	6	7	77	3	0	0	0	0
2008-09	Spartak Moscow	KHL	54	1	7	8	82	6	0	0	0	4
2009-10	Spartak Moscow	KHL	48	3	9	12	52	9	0	1	1	8
2010-11	Cherepovets	KHL	49	3	9	12	66	6	1	2	3	8
2011-12	Omsk	KHL	49	1	4	5	53	19	0	5	5	12
2012-13	Omsk	KHL	37	3	1	4	32	12	1	0	1	6
2013-14	Omsk	KHL	52	3	11	14	22	11	1	3	4	4
2014-15	Omsk	KHL	57	2	8	10	28	12	0	2	2	2
2015-16	Nizhnekamsk	KHL	56	5	8	13	30	2	0	1	1	2
2016-17	Nizhnekamsk	KHL	44	2	12	14	22	....	....	....	....	....

LYCKSELL, Olle (LIHK-sehl, OH-leh) **PHI**

Right wing. Shoots left. 5'10", 163 lbs. Born, Oskarshamn, , August 24, 1999.
(Philadelphia's 8th pick, 168th overall, in 2017 NHL Draft).

			Regular Season					Playoffs				
Season	**Club**	**League**	**GP**	**G**	**A**	**Pts**	**PIM**	**GP**	**G**	**A**	**Pts**	**PIM**
2015-16	Oskarshamn U18	Swe-U18	34	8	31	39	8	....	....	....	....	....
	IK Oskarshamn	Sweden-2	1	0	0	0	0	....	....	....	....	....
2016-17	Linkopings HC U18	Swe-U18	22	19	17	36	35	6	2	6	8	0
	Linkopings HC Jr.	Swe-Jr.	29	4	5	9	2	2	1	0	1	2

LYYTINEN, Joonas (LEE'YOO-tih-nehn, YOH-nuhs) **NSH**

Defense. Shoots left. 6', 154 lbs. Born, Espoo, Finland, April 4, 1995.
(Nashville's 6th pick, 132nd overall, in 2014 NHL Draft).

			Regular Season					Playoffs				
Season	**Club**	**League**	**GP**	**G**	**A**	**Pts**	**PIM**	**GP**	**G**	**A**	**Pts**	**PIM**
2010-11	KalPa Kuopio U18	Fin-U18	7	1	1	2	6	1	0	1	1	0
2011-12	KalPa Kuopio U18	Fin-U18	32	8	10	18	40	3	0	0	0	2
	KalPa Kuopio Jr.	Fin-Jr.	5	1	3	4	6	....	....	....	....	....
2012-13	KalPa Kuopio U18	Fin-U18	3	0	2	2	4	....	....	....	....	....
	KalPa Kuopio Jr.	Fin-Jr.	31	4	9	13	30	3	0	0	0	4
2013-14	KalPa Kuopio Jr.	Fin-Jr.	24	7	17	24	32	....	....	....	....	....
	KalPa Kuopio	Finland	30	3	6	9	24	....	....	....	....	....
2014-15	KalPa Kuopio	Finland	52	8	9	17	34	6	0	0	0	6
2015-16	KalPa Kuopio	Finland	47	2	7	9	22	3	0	0	0	0
	KalPa Kuopio Jr.	Fin-Jr.	....	....	....	....	....	8	2	4	6	10
2016-17	KalPa Kuopio	Finland	54	8	16	24	34	18	2	5	7	16

MAASS, Benton (MAWS, BEHN-TUHN) **WSH**

Defense. Shoots right. 6'1", 185 lbs. Born, Elk River, MN, November 25, 1998.
(Washington's 3rd pick, 182nd overall, in 2017 NHL Draft).

			Regular Season					Playoffs				
Season	**Club**	**League**	**GP**	**G**	**A**	**Pts**	**PIM**	**GP**	**G**	**A**	**Pts**	**PIM**
2014-15	Elk River Elks	High-MN	25	5	9	14	18	3	1	2	3	0
2015-16	Elk River Elks	High-MN	25	6	16	22	6	2	1	0	1	4
2016-17	Elk River Elks	High-MN	25	6	23	29	6	2	2	2	4	0
	Fairbanks Ice Dogs	NAHL	26	7	9	16	12	7	2	2	4	0

• Signed Letter of Intent to attend **University of New Hampshire** (Hockey East) in fall of 2018.

MacDERMID, Kurtis (MAK-DUHR-mihd, KUHR-this) **L.A.**

Defense. Shoots left. 6'5", 208 lbs. Born, Sauble Beach, ON, March 25, 1994.

			Regular Season					Playoffs				
Season	**Club**	**League**	**GP**	**G**	**A**	**Pts**	**PIM**	**GP**	**G**	**A**	**Pts**	**PIM**
2010-11	Owen Sound	ON-Jr.B	51	6	16	22	124	....	....	....	....	....
2011-12	Owen Sound	ON-Jr.B	20	3	6	9	80	....	....	....	....	....
	Owen Sound	OHL	9	0	2	2	7	....	....	....	....	....
2012-13	Owen Sound	OHL	65	1	7	8	110	12	0	3	3	11
2013-14	Owen Sound	OHL	38	5	12	17	*90	....	....	....	....	....
	Erie Otters	OHL	28	2	1	3	*75	12	0	3	3	29
2014-15	Erie Otters	OHL	61	8	32	40	129	12	0	5	5	23
2015-16	Ontario Reign	AHL	56	4	12	16	121	13	2	1	3	12
2016-17	Ontario Reign	AHL	58	6	14	20	135	5	0	0	0	4

Signed as a free agent by **Los Angeles**, September 12, 2012.

MacEACHERN, Mackenzie (MAK-EHK-uhrn, muh-KEHN-zee) **ST.L.**

Left wing. Shoots left. 6'2", 190 lbs. Born, Royal Oak, MI, March 9, 1994.
(St. Louis' 3rd pick, 67th overall, in 2012 NHL Draft).

			Regular Season					Playoffs				
Season	**Club**	**League**	**GP**	**G**	**A**	**Pts**	**PIM**	**GP**	**G**	**A**	**Pts**	**PIM**
2010-11	Brother Rice	High-MI	30	23	41	64	12	....	....	....	....	....
2011-12	Brother Rice	High-MI	29	42	48	90	16	....	....	....	....	....
	Michigan D.H.L.	Other	18	7	8	15	8	....	....	....	....	....
2012-13	Chicago Steel	USHL	50	8	13	21	35	....	....	....	....	....
2013-14	Michigan State	Big Ten	36	8	4	12	14	....	....	....	....	....
2014-15	Michigan State	Big Ten	35	11	15	26	10	....	....	....	....	....
2015-16	Michigan State	Big Ten	37	14	16	30	20	....	....	....	....	....
2016-17	Chicago Wolves	AHL	55	5	6	11	8	10	2	1	3	4

MacEWEN, Zack (ma-KEW-ehn, ZAK) **VAN**

Right wing. Shoots right. 6'4", 212 lbs. Born, Charlottetown, PE, July 8, 1996.

			Regular Season					Playoffs				
Season	**Club**	**League**	**GP**	**G**	**A**	**Pts**	**PIM**	**GP**	**G**	**A**	**Pts**	**PIM**
2012-13	Chalottetown	NBPEI	35	11	19	30	24	7	1	5	6	6
2013-14	Amherst Ramblers	MJrHL	50	9	5	14	35	7	0	1	1	0
2014-15	Amherst Ramblers	MJrHL	46	29	23	52	103	....	....	....	....	....
	Moncton Wildcats	QMJHL	9	1	1	2	6	9	2	2	4	10
2015-16	Moncton Wildcats	QMJHL	66	10	30	40	56	17	4	4	8	14
2016-17	Gatineau	QMJHL	66	31	43	74	90	7	6	3	9	2

Signed as a free agent by **Vancouver**, March 3, 2017.

MacINNIS, Ryan (muh-KIH-nihs, RIGH-uhn) **ARI**

Center. Shoots left. 6'4", 191 lbs. Born, St. Louis, MO, February 14, 1996.
(Arizona's 2nd pick, 43rd overall, in 2014 NHL Draft).

			Regular Season					Playoffs				
Season	**Club**	**League**	**GP**	**G**	**A**	**Pts**	**PIM**	**GP**	**G**	**A**	**Pts**	**PIM**
2011-12	St. Louis Blues	T1EHL	34	27	20	47	18	....	....	....	....	....
	U.S. Youth Oly.	Other	6	4	2	6	4	....	....	....	....	....
2012-13	USAHNTDP	USHL	41	8	6	14	6	....	....	....	....	....
	USAHNTDP	U-17	11	7	4	11	0	....	....	....	....	....
2013-14	Kitchener Rangers	OHL	66	16	21	37	18	....	....	....	....	....
2014-15	Kitchener Rangers	OHL	67	25	37	62	28	6	3	5	8	6
2015-16	Kitchener Rangers	OHL	59	38	43	81	49	9	5	8	13	8
	Springfield Falcons	AHL	2	0	0	0	0	....	....	....	....	....
2016-17	Tucson	AHL	68	8	9	17	50	....	....	....	....	....

MacLEOD, Johnathan (muh-KLOWD, JAWN-ah-thuhn) **T.B.**

Defense. Shoots right. 6'2", 200 lbs. Born, Lowell, MA, June 2, 1996.
(Tampa Bay's 3rd pick, 57th overall, in 2014 NHL Draft).

			Regular Season					Playoffs				
Season	**Club**	**League**	**GP**	**G**	**A**	**Pts**	**PIM**	**GP**	**G**	**A**	**Pts**	**PIM**
2011-12	Kimball Union	High-NH	31	0	13	13	22	....	....	....	....	....
2012-13	USAHNTDP	USHL	33	0	2	2	71	....	....	....	....	....
	USAHNTDP	U-17	13	0	3	3	22	....	....	....	....	....
2013-14	USAHNTDP	USHL	19	1	4	5	36	....	....	....	....	....
	USAHNTDP	U-18	32	4	3	7	38	....	....	....	....	....
2014-15	Boston University	H-East	37	2	7	9	58	....	....	....	....	....
2015-16	Boston University	H-East	26	1	1	2	26	....	....	....	....	....
2016-17	Boston University	H-East	33	2	6	8	30	....	....	....	....	....

MacMILLAN, Mark (muhk-MIHL-uhn, MAHRK)

Center. Shoots left. 6', 182 lbs. Born, Penticton, BC, January 23, 1992.
(Montreal's 2nd pick, 113th overall, in 2010 NHL Draft).

			Regular Season					Playoffs				
Season	**Club**	**League**	**GP**	**G**	**A**	**Pts**	**PIM**	**GP**	**G**	**A**	**Pts**	**PIM**
2008-09	Okanagan Prep	Minor-BC	50	16	21	37	34	....	....	....	....	....
2009-10	Alberni Valley	BCHL	59	26	54	80	44	13	5	9	14	16
2010-11	Penticton Vees	BCHL	40	21	36	57	43	3	0	5	5	6
2011-12	North Dakota	WCHA	42	7	16	23	26	....	....	....	....	....
2012-13	North Dakota	WCHA	42	13	12	25	28	....	....	....	....	....
2013-14	North Dakota	NCHC	38	10	16	26	26	....	....	....	....	....
2014-15	North Dakota	NCHC	29	16	9	25	27	....	....	....	....	....
2015-16	St. John's IceCaps	AHL	62	6	11	17	41	....	....	....	....	....
	Brampton Beast	ECHL	6	2	3	5	2	....	....	....	....	....
2016-17	St. John's IceCaps	AHL	58	6	7	13	12	3	0	0	0	2

NCHC First All-Star Team (2015)

MAHURA, Joshua (ma-HOO-ruh, jaw-SHOO-uh) **ANA**

Defense. Shoots left. 6', 184 lbs. Born, St. Albert, AB, May 5, 1998.
(Anaheim's 3rd pick, 85th overall, in 2016 NHL Draft).

			Regular Season					Playoffs				
Season	**Club**	**League**	**GP**	**G**	**A**	**Pts**	**PIM**	**GP**	**G**	**A**	**Pts**	**PIM**
2012-13	St. Albert Sabres	AMBHL	25	9	13	22	51	....	....	....	....	....
	St. Albert Flyers	Minor-AB	9	1	2	3	6	....	....	....	....	....
2013-14	Okan. HA Midget	Minor-BC	37	14	26	40	42	....	....	....	....	....
	Okanagan Prep	CSSHL	21	11	15	26	26	3	1	1	2	2
2014-15	Red Deer Rebels	WHL	51	2	6	8	20	5	0	1	1	2
2015-16	Red Deer Rebels	WHL	2	0	1	1	0	17	2	2	4	2
2016-17	Red Deer Rebels	WHL	39	9	24	33	35	....	....	....	....	....
	Regina Pats	WHL	34	8	12	20	22	23	8	13	21	16

• Missed majority of 2015-16 due to knee injury vs. Edmonton (WHL), September 26, 2015.

MAKAR, Cale (mah-KAHR, KAYL) **COL**

Defense. Shoots right. 5'11", 180 lbs. Born, Calgary, AB, October 30, 1998.
(Colorado's 1st pick, 4th overall, in 2017 NHL Draft).

			Regular Season					Playoffs				
Season	**Club**	**League**	**GP**	**G**	**A**	**Pts**	**PIM**	**GP**	**G**	**A**	**Pts**	**PIM**
2013-14	NWCAA Min. Mid.	Minor-AB	36	9	19	28	35	....	....	....	....	....
	Calgary Flames	AMHL	6	0	1	1	4	1	0	0	0	0
2014-15	Calgary Flames	AMHL	34	7	16	23	14	2	0	0	0	0
	Brooks Bandits	AJHL	3	1	4	5	4	20	1	6	7	4
2015-16	Brooks Bandits	AJHL	54	10	45	55	28	13	3	11	14	0
2016-17	Brooks Bandits	AJHL	54	24	51	75	18	13	5	13	18	4

• Signed Letter of Intent to attend **University of Massachusetts** (Hockey East) in fall of 2017.

MAKELA, Aleksi (ma-KIH-luh, A-LEHK-see) DAL

Defense. Shoots left. 6'2", 200 lbs. Born, Tampere, Finland, February 8, 1995.
(Dallas' 9th pick, 182nd overall, in 2013 NHL Draft).

			Regular Season					Playoffs				
Season	Club	League	GP	G	A	Pts	PIM	GP	G	A	Pts	PIM
2011-12	Ilves Tampere U17	Fin-U17	2	0	2	2	2	9	4	6	10	10
	Ilves Tampere U18	Fin-U18	35	4	10	14	10	3	1	0	1	2
	Ilves Tampere Jr.	Fin-Jr.	4	0	0	0	2	....	....	....	....	....
2012-13	Ilves Tampere U18	Fin-U18	8	0	9	9	4	....	....	....	....	....
	Ilves Tampere Jr.	Fin-Jr.	37	8	9	17	42	....	....	....	....	....
	Ilves Tampere	Finland	7	1	1	2	4	....	....	....	....	....
	Ilves Tampere	Finland-Q	....	....	....	....	....	3	0	1	1	0
2013-14	Ilves Tampere	Finland	9	0	0	0	4	....	....	....	....	....
	LeKi Lempaala	Finland-2	3	0	0	0	2	....	....	....	....	....
	Ilves Tampere Jr.	Fin-Jr.	25	3	11	14	16	2	0	0	0	2
2014-15	Ilves Tampere	Finland	30	0	6	6	22	....	....	....	....	....
	LeKi Lempaala	Finland-2	7	0	0	0	4	....	....	....	....	....
2015-16	Ilves Tampere Jr.	Fin-Jr.	1	0	0	0	2	7	1	0	1	2
	LeKi Lempaala	Finland-2	12	0	2	2	10	....	....	....	....	....
	Ilves Tampere	Finland	42	0	2	2	20	....	....	....	....	....
2016-17	Assat Pori	Finland	48	0	2	2	26	3	0	0	0	0

MALENSTYN, Beck (MAL-ehn-STIGHN, BEK) WSH

Left wing. Shoots left. 6'1", 190 lbs. Born, Delta, BC, February 4, 1998.
(Washington's 4th pick, 145th overall, in 2016 NHL Draft).

			Regular Season					Playoffs				
Season	Club	League	GP	G	A	Pts	PIM	GP	G	A	Pts	PIM
2012-13	Okan. HA Bantam	Minor-BC	57	62	57	119	108	....	....	....	....	....
	Okanagan Red	CSSHL	9	3	3	6	0	....	....	....	....	....
2013-14	Okan. HA Midget	Minor-BC	45	33	26	59	44	....	....	....	....	....
	Okanagan H.A.	CSSHL	21	15	11	26	18	3	3	1	4	4
	Campbell River	VIJHL	2	0	2	2	0	....	....	....	....	....
	Calgary Hitmen	WHL	5	0	3	3	4	....	....	....	....	....
2014-15	Calgary Hitmen	WHL	51	8	4	12	25	11	1	1	2	4
2015-16	Calgary Hitmen	WHL	70	8	17	25	47	5	2	1	3	2
2016-17	Calgary Hitmen	WHL	70	32	24	56	60	4	0	0	0	2

MALETTA, Jordan (ma-LEH-tah, JOHR-duhn) CBJ

Center. Shoots right. 6'3", 215 lbs. Born, St. Catharines, ON, April 30, 1995.

			Regular Season					Playoffs				
Season	Club	League	GP	G	A	Pts	PIM	GP	G	A	Pts	PIM
2010-11	St. Cath. Falcons	Minor-ON	48	33	26	59	38	....	....	....	....	....
	St. Catharines	ON-Jr.B	1	0	0	0	0	3	0	0	0	0
2011-12	Windsor Spitfires	OHL	57	5	15	20	59	4	1	1	2	6
2012-13	Windsor Spitfires	OHL	36	4	8	12	38	....	....	....	....	....
	Niagara Ice Dogs	OHL	26	3	5	8	27	5	1	0	1	0
2013-14	Niagara Ice Dogs	OHL	59	12	28	40	58	7	2	1	3	4
2014-15	Niagara Ice Dogs	OHL	68	24	28	52	41	11	6	3	9	2
2015-16	Niagara Ice Dogs	OHL	68	34	25	59	55	17	2	9	11	15
2016-17	Cleveland	AHL	76	12	11	23	69	....	....	....	....	....

Signed as a free agent by **Columbus**, March 21, 2016.

MALMSTROM, Alfons (MAHLM-struhm, AL-FAWNZ) DET

Defense. Shoots right. 6'2", 185 lbs. Born, Lulea, Sweden, June 12, 1998.
(Detroit's 4th pick, 107th overall, in 2016 NHL Draft).

			Regular Season					Playoffs				
Season	Club	League	GP	G	A	Pts	PIM	GP	G	A	Pts	PIM
2012-13	Overtornea HF	Sweden-4	11	0	2	2	2	....	....	....	....	....
2013-14	Lulea HF U18	Swe-U18	32	3	14	17	8	....	....	....	....	....
2014-15	Lulea HF U18	Swe-U18	35	3	15	18	8	....	....	....	....	....
	Lulea HF Jr.	Swe-Jr.	2	0	0	0	0	....	....	....	....	....
2015-16	Orebro HK U18	Swe-U18	6	3	1	4	10	2	1	0	1	2
	Orebro HK Jr.	Swe-Jr.	41	2	6	8	36	....	....	....	....	....
2016-17	Orebro HK Jr.	Swe-Jr.	38	2	3	5	18	5	0	2	2	0

MALTSEV, Mikhail (MAHL-tsehv, mih-KIGH-ehl) N.J.

Left wing. Shoots left. 6'3", 200 lbs. Born, St. Petersburg, Russia, March 12, 1998.
(New Jersey's 5th pick, 102nd overall, in 2016 NHL Draft).

			Regular Season					Playoffs				
Season	Club	League	GP	G	A	Pts	PIM	GP	G	A	Pts	PIM
2015-16	Russia U18	Russia-Jr.	29	11	12	23	20	3	0	2	2	0
2016-17	SKA-Neva	Russia-2	34	2	13	15	21	11	3	2	5	4
	St. Petersburg Jr.	Russia-Jr.	14	5	9	14	2	3	1	1	2	2

MAMIN, Maxim (MA-MIHN, max-EEM) FLA

Right wing. Shoots left. 6'2", 191 lbs. Born, Moscow, Russia, January 13, 1995.
(Florida's 6th pick, 175th overall, in 2016 NHL Draft).

			Regular Season					Playoffs				
Season	Club	League	GP	G	A	Pts	PIM	GP	G	A	Pts	PIM
2011-12	CSKA Jr.	Russia-Jr.	38	1	4	5	12	5	1	0	1	4
2012-13	CSKA Jr.	Russia-Jr.	61	14	15	29	45	....	....	....	....	....
2013-14	Vityaz Podolsk	KHL	32	1	2	3	18	2	1	0	1	2
	CSKA Jr.	Russia-Jr.	49	11	24	35	14	20	5	16	21	0
2014-15	CSKA Jr.	Russia-Jr.	4	1	4	5	2	4	3	4	7	8
	Podolsk	KHL	26	5	1	6	21	....	....	....	....	....
	CSKA Moscow	KHL	39	5	5	10	10	14	0	0	0	27
2015-16	CSKA Moscow	KHL	48	4	3	7	67	19	1	1	2	14
	Zvezda Chekhov	Russia-2	5	0	1	1	2	....	....	....	....	....
2016-17	CSKA Moscow	KHL	42	12	13	25	15	9	2	1	3	2
	Zvezda Chekhov	Russia-2	4	2	3	5	0	....	....	....	....	....

MANGIAPANE, Andrew (MAN-gee-AH-pah-nee, an-DROO) CGY

Left wing. Shoots left. 5'10", 184 lbs. Born, Bolton, ON, April 4, 1996.
(Calgary's 4th pick, 166th overall, in 2015 NHL Draft).

			Regular Season					Playoffs				
Season	Club	League	GP	G	A	Pts	PIM	GP	G	A	Pts	PIM
2011-12	Miss. Senators	GTHL	46	22	17	39	44	....	....	....	....	....
2012-13	Tor. Jr. Can. Midg.	GTHL	32	14	22	36	22	7	5	2	7	8
	Tor. Canadiens	ON-Jr.A	4	0	0	0	2	....	....	....	....	....
2013-14	Barrie Colts	OHL	68	24	27	51	28	11	2	5	7	8
2014-15	Barrie Colts	OHL	68	43	61	104	54	9	6	4	10	12
2015-16	Barrie Colts	OHL	59	51	55	106	50	15	10	11	21	14
2016-17	Stockton Heat	AHL	66	20	21	41	64	5	1	2	3	2

OHL All-Rookie Team (2014) • OHL Second All-Star Team (2016)

MANTHA, Ryan (MAN-thuh, RIGH-uhn) EDM

Defense. Shoots right. 6'5", 225 lbs. Born, Clarkston, MI, June 18, 1996.
(NY Rangers' 3rd pick, 104th overall, in 2014 NHL Draft).

			Regular Season					Playoffs				
Season	Club	League	GP	G	A	Pts	PIM	GP	G	A	Pts	PIM
2010-11	Det. L.C. Bant.	T1EHL	28	4	10	14	29	....	....	....	....	....
	Det. L.C. U16	T1EHL	4	0	0	0	2	....	....	....	....	....
2011-12	Detroit Belle Tire	T1EHL	38	8	14	22	41	6	0	1	1	19
2012-13	Sioux City	USHL	52	1	6	7	48	....	....	....	....	....
2013-14	Sioux City	USHL	29	1	5	6	51	....	....	....	....	....
	Indiana Ice	USHL	24	2	7	9	20	10	0	3	3	11
2014-15	Niagara Ice Dogs	OHL	52	10	15	25	45	11	1	5	6	6
2015-16	Niagara Ice Dogs	OHL	65	5	20	25	62	17	3	7	10	14
2016-17	Niagara Ice Dogs	OHL	65	17	41	58	70	4	2	2	4	8
	Bakersfield	AHL	2	0	0	0	0	....	....	....	....	....

OHL Second All-Star Team (2017)

Signed as a free agent by **Edmonton**, March 1, 2017.

MARINO, John (muh-REE-noh, JAWN) EDM

Defense. Shoots right. 6'2", 190 lbs. Born, Brockton, MA, May 21, 1997.
(Edmonton's 4th pick, 154th overall, in 2015 NHL Draft).

			Regular Season					Playoffs				
Season	Club	League	GP	G	A	Pts	PIM	GP	G	A	Pts	PIM
2012-13	South Shore Kings	EJHL	37	3	31	34	12	6	0	3	3	6
2013-14	South Shore U18	USPHL	12	1	4	5	12	....	....	....	....	....
	South Shore Kings	USPHL	34	6	11	17	16	5	0	2	2	2
2014-15	South Shore Kings	USPHL	49	4	24	28	42	5	0	2	2	6
2015-16	Tri-City Storm	USHL	56	5	25	30	43	11	0	2	2	6
2016-17	Harvard Crimson	ECAC	35	2	13	15	24	....	....	....	....	....

MARODY, Cooper (mah-ROH-dee, KOO-puhr) PHI

Center. Shoots right. 6', 177 lbs. Born, Brighton, MI, December 20, 1996.
(Philadelphia's 8th pick, 158th overall, in 2015 NHL Draft).

			Regular Season					Playoffs				
Season	Club	League	GP	G	A	Pts	PIM	GP	G	A	Pts	PIM
2011-12	St. Mary's Prep	High-MI	7	1	3	4	2	....	....	....	....	....
2012-13	St. Mary's Prep	High-MI	26	19	23	42	20	....	....	....	....	....
	St. Mary's Prep	Other	2	1	2	3	0	....	....	....	....	....
2013-14	Muskegon	USHL	58	9	21	30	36	....	....	....	....	....
2014-15	Muskegon	USHL	14	2	7	9	4	....	....	....	....	....
	Sioux Falls	USHL	38	20	29	49	28	12	1	*11	12	10
2015-16	U. of Michigan	Big Ten	32	10	14	24	20	....	....	....	....	....
2016-17	U. of Michigan	Big Ten	18	5	10	15	8	....	....	....	....	....

MARTEL, Danick (MAHR-tehl, dah-NEEK) PHI

Center. Shoots left. 5'8", 166 lbs. Born, Drummondville, QC, December 12, 1994.

			Regular Season					Playoffs				
Season	Club	League	GP	G	A	Pts	PIM	GP	G	A	Pts	PIM
2010-11	Magog	QAAA	41	10	8	18	60	13	7	4	11	8
2011-12	Magog	QAAA	41	23	29	52	83	7	6	3	9	10
	Blainville-Bois.	QMJHL	1	0	0	0	0	....	....	....	....	....
2012-13	Blainville-Bois.	QMJHL	68	19	22	41	50	15	3	4	7	16
2013-14	Blainville-Bois.	QMJHL	63	32	28	60	42	11	8	1	9	8
2014-15	Blainville-Bois.	QMJHL	64	48	54	102	85	6	4	3	7	8
	Lehigh Valley	AHL	5	1	2	3	4	....	....	....	....	....
2015-16	Lehigh Valley	AHL	67	22	15	37	68	....	....	....	....	....
2016-17	Lehigh Valley	AHL	68	20	20	40	67	5	1	0	1	4

QMJHL First All-Star Team (2015)

Signed as a free agent by **Philadelphia**, March 10, 2015.

MARTENET, Chris (MAHR-tih-neht, KRIHS) DAL

Defense. Shoots left. 6'7", 200 lbs. Born, Waukesha, WI, September 25, 1996.
(Dallas' 3rd pick, 103rd overall, in 2015 NHL Draft).

			Regular Season					Playoffs				
Season	Club	League	GP	G	A	Pts	PIM	GP	G	A	Pts	PIM
2011-12	Shattuck Midget	High-MN	37	1	16	17	34	....	....	....	....	....
2012-13	Shattuck Midget	High-MN	43	8	22	30	20	....	....	....	....	....
2013-14	Indiana Ice	USHL	35	0	5	5	20	2	0	0	0	0
2014-15	London Knights	OHL	64	7	9	16	49	10	0	0	0	2
2015-16	London Knights	OHL	67	3	9	12	85	18	0	0	0	6
2016-17	London Knights	OHL	27	1	5	6	10	....	....	....	....	....
	Ottawa 67's	OHL	28	4	6	10	28	6	0	1	1	2
	Texas Stars	AHL	3	0	0	0	2	....	....	....	....	....

MARTIN, Brycen (MAHR-tihn, BRIGH-suhn) BUF

Defense. Shoots left. 6'2", 206 lbs. Born, Calgary, AB, May 9, 1996.
(Buffalo's 6th pick, 74th overall, in 2014 NHL Draft).

			Regular Season					Playoffs				
Season	Club	League	GP	G	A	Pts	PIM	GP	G	A	Pts	PIM
2009-10	Calgary Bisons	AMBHL	33	2	22	24	18	13	0	6	6	4
2010-11	Calgary Bisons	AMBHL	31	6	36	42	60	....	....	....	....	....
	CBHA Rangers	Minor-AB	1	0	0	0	0	....	....	....	....	....
2011-12	Calgary Buffaloes	AMHL	25	6	11	17	65	5	0	2	2	8
	Swift Current	WHL	3	0	0	0	0	....	....	....	....	....
2012-13	Swift Current	WHL	67	2	17	19	32	5	0	0	0	0
2013-14	Swift Current	WHL	72	6	31	37	42	6	0	2	2	4
2014-15	Swift Current	WHL	39	2	14	16	22	....	....	....	....	....
	Saskatoon Blades	WHL	30	5	17	22	19	....	....	....	....	....
	Rochester	AHL	2	0	0	0	0	....	....	....	....	....
2015-16	Saskatoon Blades	WHL	25	3	21	24	18	....	....	....	....	....
	Everett Silvertips	WHL	41	3	10	13	21	9	1	1	2	4
2016-17	Rochester	AHL	18	0	0	0	12	....	....	....	....	....
	Elmira Jackals	ECHL	34	2	5	7	10	....	....	....	....	....

MARTIN, Jonathon (MAHR-tihn, JAWN-ah-thuhn) **S.J.**

Right wing. Shoots right. 6'2", 215 lbs. Born, Winnipeg, MB, August 23, 1995.

			Regular Season					Playoffs				
Season	Club	League	GP	G	A	Pts	PIM	GP	G	A	Pts	PIM
2010-11	Wpg. Monarchs	Minor-MB	29	24	13	37	84	....	....	....	....	....
	Winnipeg Wild	MMHL	3	0	0	0	4	....	....	....	....	....
2011-12	Kootenay Ice	WHL	59	6	4	10	52	2	0	0	0	0
2012-13	Kootenay Ice	WHL	68	9	7	16	97	5	0	0	0	10
2013-14	Kootenay Ice	WHL	63	10	8	18	105	13	2	1	3	8
2014-15	Kootenay Ice	WHL	56	7	17	24	86	6	0	2	2	2
2015-16	Kootenay Ice	WHL	4	3	1	4	6	....	....	....	....	....
	Swift Current	WHL	66	38	31	69	74	....	....	....	....	....
	San Jose Barracuda	AHL	8	0	0	0	2	3	0	0	0	0
2016-17	San Jose Barracuda	AHL	26	2	3	5	23	....	....	....	....	....
	Allen Americans	ECHL	7	2	2	4	12	....	....	....	....	....

Signed as a free agent by **San Jose**, March 1, 2016.

MARTIN, Luke (MAHR-tihn, LEWK) **CAR**

Defense. Shoots right. 6'2", 219 lbs. Born, St. Louis, MO, September 20, 1998.
(Carolina's 3rd pick, 52nd overall, in 2017 NHL Draft).

			Regular Season					Playoffs				
Season	Club	League	GP	G	A	Pts	PIM	GP	G	A	Pts	PIM
2013-14	St.L. AAA Blues	T1EHL	35	4	14	18	43	....	....	....	....	....
2014-15	USAHNTDP	USHL	34	1	6	7	28	....	....	....	....	....
	USAHNTDP	U-17	18	1	5	6	10	....	....	....	....	....
2015-16	USAHNTDP	USHL	25	3	4	7	20	....	....	....	....	....
	USAHNTDP	U-18	38	1	12	13	12	....	....	....	....	....
2016-17	U. of Michigan	Big Ten	35	1	6	7	12	....	....	....	....	....

MASCHERIN, Adam (mas-KUHR-ihn, A-duhm) **FLA**

Left wing. Shoots left. 5'10", 193 lbs. Born, Maple, ON, June 6, 1998.
(Florida's 2nd pick, 38th overall, in 2016 NHL Draft).

			Regular Season					Playoffs				
Season	Club	League	GP	G	A	Pts	PIM	GP	G	A	Pts	PIM
2013-14	Vaughan M.M.	GTHL	33	40	30	70	26	11	4	12	16	20
	Vaughan M.M.	Other	23	23	39	52	....	5	4	3	7	10
	Vaughan Midget	GTHL	4	3	2	5	0	3	4	1	5	0
	Georgetown	ON-Jr.A	5	5	7	12	0	11	6	2	8	0
2014-15	Kitchener Rangers	OHL	62	12	17	29	18	6	1	1	2	4
2015-16	Kitchener Rangers	OHL	65	35	46	81	16	9	6	6	12	0
2016-17	Kitchener Rangers	OHL	65	35	65	100	20	5	1	3	4	2

OHL First All-Star Team (2017)

MASIN, Dominik (MAH-shihn, DOHM-ihn-ihk) **T.B.**

Defense. Shoots left. 6'2", 189 lbs. Born, Mestec Kralove, Czech Rep., February 1, 1996.
(Tampa Bay's 2nd pick, 35th overall, in 2014 NHL Draft).

			Regular Season					Playoffs				
Season	Club	League	GP	G	A	Pts	PIM	GP	G	A	Pts	PIM
2010-11	Slavia U18	CzR-U18	16	1	2	3	18	3	0	1	1	2
2011-12	Slavia U18	CzR-U18	34	0	3	3	26	....	....	....	....	....
2012-13	Slavia U18	CzR-U18	12	3	3	6	41	2	0	0	0	4
	HC Slavia Praha Jr.	CzRep-Jr.	25	1	2	3	16	....	....	....	....	....
2013-14	HC Slavia Praha Jr.	CzRep-Jr.	39	2	19	21	102	5	1	1	2	33
	Slavia U18	CzR-U18	....	....	....	....	....	2	1	0	1	2
2014-15	Peterborough	OHL	48	7	19	26	70	....	....	....	....	....
2015-16	Peterborough	OHL	57	8	32	40	50	7	0	3	3	12
	Syracuse Crunch	AHL	4	0	0	0	0	....	....	....	....	....
2016-17	Syracuse Crunch	AHL	69	3	3	6	73	22	0	2	2	16

MASONIUS, Joe (mah-SOH-nihs, JOH) **PIT**

Defense. Shoots left. 6', 190 lbs. Born, Long Branch, NJ, February 17, 1997.
(Pittsburgh's 6th pick, 181st overall, in 2016 NHL Draft).

			Regular Season					Playoffs				
Season	Club	League	GP	G	A	Pts	PIM	GP	G	A	Pts	PIM
2012-13	Jersey Hitmen	EmJHL	17	5	12	17	24	....	....	....	....	....
	Jersey Hitmen	EJHL	10	1	2	3	35	4	0	0	0	0
2013-14	USAHNTDP	USHL	22	0	2	2	32	....	....	....	....	....
	USAHNTDP	U-17	17	0	6	6	22	....	....	....	....	....
2014-15	USAHNTDP	USHL	24	0	10	10	45	....	....	....	....	....
	USAHNTDP	U-18	41	6	13	19	42	....	....	....	....	....
2015-16	U. of Connecticut	H-East	34	6	15	21	40	....	....	....	....	....
2016-17	U. of Connecticut	H-East	34	2	11	13	47	....	....	....	....	....

MASSIE, Jake (MA-see, JAYK) **CHI**

Defense. Shoots left. 6'1", 177 lbs. Born, Montreal, QC, January 21, 1997.
(Carolina's 7th pick, 156th overall, in 2015 NHL Draft).

			Regular Season					Playoffs				
Season	Club	League	GP	G	A	Pts	PIM	GP	G	A	Pts	PIM
2012-13	John Rennie	High-QC	24	1	4	5	....	....	....	....	....	....
2013-14	John Rennie	High-QC	30	9	14	23	....	....	....	....	....	....
2014-15	Boston Jr. Bruins	Minor-MA	14	6	5	11	20	....	....	....	....	....
	Kimball Union	High-NH	34	5	15	20	....	....	....	....	....	....
2015-16	Omaha Lancers	USHL	44	4	6	10	43	....	....	....	....	....
2016-17	U. of Vermont	H-East	29	0	7	7	14	....	....	....	....	....

Traded to **Chicago** by **Carolina** with Dennis Robertson and Carolina's 5th round pick (later traded to Vancouver – Vancouver selected Kristoffer Gunnarsson) in 2017 NHL Draft for Kris Versteeg, Joakim Nordstrom and Chicago's 3rd round pick (later traded back to Chicago, later traded to Detroit – Detroit selected Keith Petruzzelli) in 2017 NHL Draft, September 11, 2015.

MATTHEOS, Stelio (ma-THAY-ohs, STEHL-ee-oh) **CAR**

Right wing. Shoots right. 6'1", 191 lbs. Born, Winnipeg, MB, June 14, 1999.
(Carolina's 5th pick, 73rd overall, in 2017 NHL Draft).

			Regular Season					Playoffs				
Season	Club	League	GP	G	A	Pts	PIM	GP	G	A	Pts	PIM
2014-15	Winnipeg Wild	MMHL	27	14	11	25	18	....	....	....	....	....
	Brandon	WHL	1	1	0	1	0	9	1	0	1	0
2015-16	Brandon	WHL	50	13	17	30	10	21	4	3	7	10
2016-17	Brandon	WHL	69	26	35	61	59	4	1	4	5	8

MATTINEN, Nicolas (MA-tih-nehn, nih-KOH-luhs) **TOR**

Defense. Shoots right. 6'4", 220 lbs. Born, Orleans, ON, March 5, 1998.
(Toronto's 10th pick, 179th overall, in 2016 NHL Draft).

			Regular Season					Playoffs				
Season	Club	League	GP	G	A	Pts	PIM	GP	G	A	Pts	PIM
2013-14	E. Ont. Wild MM	Minor-ON	30	6	14	20	24	5	1	0	1	8
	E. Ont. Wild Mid.	Minor-ON	2	0	2	2	4	3	1	1	2	2
	Cumberland	ON-Jr.A	2	0	0	0	0	....	....	....	....	....
2014-15	Cumberland	ON-Jr.A	52	4	10	14	48	....	....	....	....	....
2015-16	London Knights	OHL	39	4	6	10	24	5	1	0	1	2
2016-17	London Knights	OHL	66	2	6	8	75	14	0	1	1	4

MATTSON, Mitchell (MAT-suhn, MIH-chuhl) **CGY**

Center. Shoots left. 6'4", 191 lbs. Born, Grand Rapids, MN, January 2, 1998.
(Calgary's 6th pick, 126th overall, in 2016 NHL Draft).

			Regular Season					Playoffs				
Season	Club	League	GP	G	A	Pts	PIM	GP	G	A	Pts	PIM
2013-14	Grand Rapids	High-MN	25	11	26	37	18	2	0	2	2	0
2014-15	Team North	UMHSEL	21	8	7	15	12	3	2	4	6	2
	Grand Rapids	High-MN	25	22	26	48	6	2	1	2	3	6
	Bloomington	USHL	13	2	5	7	2	....	....	....	....	....
2015-16	Grand Rapids	High-MN	25	17	29	46	22	6	4	10	14	2
	Bloomington	USHL	21	2	0	2	8	10	1	0	1	0
2016-17	Bloomington	USHL	55	12	16	28	44	....	....	....	....	....

• Signed Letter of Intent to attend **University of North Dakota** (NCHC) in fall of 2017.

MAXIMOV, Kirill (mak-SIH-mawv, kih-RIHL) **EDM**

Right wing. Shoots right. 6'2", 192 lbs. Born, Moscow, Russia, January 6, 1999.
(Edmonton's 5th pick, 146th overall, in 2017 NHL Draft).

			Regular Season					Playoffs				
Season	Club	League	GP	G	A	Pts	PIM	GP	G	A	Pts	PIM
2014-15	Tor. Jr. Can. MM	GTHL	28	16	17	33	12	....	....	....	....	....
2015-16	Saginaw Spirit	OHL	54	6	15	21	18	4	1	2	3	2
2016-17	Saginaw Spirit	OHL	37	6	10	16	26	....	....	....	....	....
	Niagara Ice Dogs	OHL	29	15	7	22	15	4	4	0	4	6

MAYO, Dysin (MAY-oh, DIGH-sihn) **ARI**

Defense. Shoots right. 6'1", 194 lbs. Born, Victoria, BC, August 17, 1996.
(Arizona's 6th pick, 133rd overall, in 2014 NHL Draft).

			Regular Season					Playoffs				
Season	Club	League	GP	G	A	Pts	PIM	GP	G	A	Pts	PIM
2010-11	PoE Academy	High-BC	51	8	33	41	30	....	....	....	....	....
	PoE Academy	CSSHL	....	....	....	....	....	4	0	2	2	0
2011-12	PoE Academy	NAPHL	17	3	1	4	12	5	0	1	1	6
	Victoria Cougars	VIJHL	1	0	1	1	0	....	....	....	....	....
2012-13	Edmonton	WHL	42	1	4	5	12	19	0	4	4	2
2013-14	Edmonton	WHL	63	7	28	35	50	21	3	12	15	10
2014-15	Edmonton	WHL	72	14	37	51	75	5	0	2	2	2
2015-16	Edmonton	WHL	71	6	37	43	86	6	0	0	0	8
	Springfield Falcons	AHL	5	0	1	1	2	....	....	....	....	....
2016-17	Tucson	AHL	25	1	2	3	0	....	....	....	....	....
	Rapid City Rush	ECHL	25	1	15	16	4	....	....	....	....	....

McGAULEY, Tim (mihk-GAW-lee, TIHM) **WSH**

Center. Shoots left. 6', 175 lbs. Born, Nelson, BC, July 23, 1995.

			Regular Season					Playoffs				
Season	Club	League	GP	G	A	Pts	PIM	GP	G	A	Pts	PIM
2010-11	Reg. Pat Cdns.	SMHL	38	12	9	21	10	4	1	0	1	0
	Saskatoon Blades	WHL	5	0	0	0	2	....	....	....	....	....
2011-12	Notre Dame	SMHL	41	29	24	53	51	....	....	....	....	....
	Notre Dame	SJHL	1	0	0	0	0	....	....	....	....	....
	Brandon	WHL	14	0	0	0	0	1	0	0	0	0
2012-13	Brandon	WHL	66	17	28	45	6	....	....	....	....	....
2013-14	Brandon	WHL	68	21	39	60	21	9	3	2	5	2
2014-15	Brandon	WHL	72	42	63	105	24	19	8	11	19	2
2015-16	Brandon	WHL	51	22	27	49	24	21	8	18	26	8
2016-17	South Carolina	ECHL	39	4	13	17	8	....	....	....	....	....

Signed as a free agent by **Washington**, October 5, 2015.

McGREGOR, Ryan (muhk-GREG-uhr, RIGH-uhn) **TOR**

Center. Shoots left. 6', 157 lbs. Born, Burlington, ON, January 29, 1999.
(Toronto's 6th pick, 172nd overall, in 2017 NHL Draft).

			Regular Season					Playoffs				
Season	Club	League	GP	G	A	Pts	PIM	GP	G	A	Pts	PIM
2014-15	Burlington MM	Minor-ON	32	17	20	27	16	....	....	....	....	....
	Appleby College	CISSA	15	2	3	5	0	2	0	0	0	0
2015-16	Sarnia Sting	OHL	58	11	13	24	4	7	1	0	1	0
2016-17	Sarnia Sting	OHL	65	14	13	27	16	4	1	1	2	0

McGREW, Jacob (muh-GROO, JAY-kuhb) **S.J.**

Right wing. Shoots right. 5'10", 205 lbs. Born, Orange, CA, February 25, 1999.
(San Jose's 4th pick, 159th overall, in 2017 NHL Draft).

			Regular Season					Playoffs				
Season	Club	League	GP	G	A	Pts	PIM	GP	G	A	Pts	PIM
2014-15	L.A. Jr. Kings U16	T1EHL	24	6	5	11	18	4	0	0	0	4
2015-16	L.A. Jr. Kings U16	T1EHL	32	*29	18	47	28	3	0	0	0	0
2016-17	Spokane Chiefs	WHL	DID NOT PLAY – INJURED									

• Missed 2016-17 due to knee injury in Spokane (WHL) training camp, September, 2016.

McKENZIE, Brett (muh-KEHN-zee, BREHT) **VAN**

Center. Shoots left. 6'1", 190 lbs. Born, Vars, ON, March 12, 1997.
(Vancouver's 6th pick, 194th overall, in 2016 NHL Draft).

			Regular Season					Playoffs				
Season	Club	League	GP	G	A	Pts	PIM	GP	G	A	Pts	PIM
2011-12	E. Ont. Wild Btm.	Minor-ON	28	17	36	53	50	13	8	15	23	12
	E. Ont. Wild MM	Minor-ON	3	0	0	0	0	....	....	....	....	....
2012-13	Oak. Rangers MM	Minor-ON	40	22	41	63	18	....	....	....	....	....
	Oakville Rangers	Other	16	14	20	34	8	7	2	3	5	2
2013-14	North Bay	OHL	63	13	10	23	25	22	2	4	6	11
2014-15	North Bay	OHL	68	11	21	32	38	15	0	7	7	8
2015-16	North Bay	OHL	66	26	27	53	43	11	2	3	5	12
2016-17	North Bay	OHL	67	29	38	67	60	....	....	....	....	....

McKENZIE, Skyler   (muhk-KEHN-zee, SKIGH-luhr)   **WPG**

Left wing. Shoots left. 5'8", 158 lbs.   Born, Sherwood Park, AB, January 20, 1998.
(Winnipeg's 7th pick, 198th overall, in 2017 NHL Draft).

			Regular Season						Playoffs			
Season	Club	League	GP	G	A	Pts	PIM	GP	G	A	Pts	PIM
2013-14	Sherwood Park	AMHL	29	17	11	28	32	3	1	1	2	2
	Portland	WHL	5	0	0	0	0	....	....	....	....	....
2014-15	Portland	WHL	65	4	12	16	48	17	0	3	3	8
2015-16	Portland	WHL	68	8	17	25	48	4	0	1	1	0
2016-17	Portland	WHL	72	42	42	84	60	9	4	2	6	0

McKEOWN, Roland   (muh-KOW-uhn, ROH-luhnd)   **CAR**

Defense. Shoots right. 6'1", 195 lbs.   Born, Listowel, ON, January 20, 1996.
(Los Angeles' 2nd pick, 50th overall, in 2014 NHL Draft).

			Regular Season						Playoffs			
Season	Club	League	GP	G	A	Pts	PIM	GP	G	A	Pts	PIM
2011-12	Toronto Marlboros	GTHL	28	10	25	35	30	....	....	....	....	....
2012-13	Kingston	OHL	61	7	22	29	33	4	0	0	0	4
2013-14	Kingston	OHL	62	11	32	43	61	7	1	3	4	8
2014-15	Kingston	OHL	65	7	25	32	57	4	0	1	1	9
	Charlotte	AHL	4	0	1	1	0	....	....	....	....	....
2015-16	Kingston	OHL	59	7	35	42	49	9	3	9	12	6
2016-17	Charlotte	AHL	71	1	10	11	16	5	0	3	3	5

OHL All-Rookie Team (2013)
Traded to **Carolina** by **Los Angeles** with Los Angeles' 1st round pick (Julien Gauthier) in 2016 NHL Draft for Andrej Sekera, February 25, 2015.

McLEOD, Michael   (muh-KLOWD, MIGH-kuhl)   **N.J.**

Center. Shoots right. 6'2", 195 lbs.   Born, Mississauga, ON, February 3, 1998.
(New Jersey's 1st pick, 12th overall, in 2016 NHL Draft).

			Regular Season						Playoffs			
Season	Club	League	GP	G	A	Pts	PIM	GP	G	A	Pts	PIM
2013-14	Toronto Marlboros	GTHL	33	21	36	57	20	16	10	5	15	24
2014-15	Mississauga	OHL	63	12	17	29	33	....	....	....	....	....
2015-16	Mississauga	OHL	57	21	40	61	71	7	3	6	9	6
2016-17	Mississauga	OHL	57	27	46	73	49	20	11	16	27	19

McNALLY, Patrick   (muhk-NAL-ee, PAT-rihk)

Defense. Shoots left. 6'2", 205 lbs.   Born, Glen Head, NY, December 4, 1991.
(Vancouver's 1st pick, 115th overall, in 2010 NHL Draft).

			Regular Season						Playoffs			
Season	Club	League	GP	G	A	Pts	PIM	GP	G	A	Pts	PIM
2008-09	Suffolk PAL S.S.	MtJHL	52	25	41	66	72	....	....	....	....	....
2009-10	Milton Academy	High-MA	28	14	21	35		....	....	....	....	....
2010-11	Milton Academy	High-MA	28	22	29	51		....	....	....	....	....
2011-12	Harvard Crimson	ECAC	34	6	22	28	40	....	....	....	....	....
2012-13	Harvard Crimson	ECAC	7	1	2	3	6	....	....	....	....	....
2013-14	Harvard Crimson	ECAC	20	1	7	8	12	....	....	....	....	....
2014-15	Harvard Crimson	ECAC	21	6	15	21	10	....	....	....	....	....
2015-16	San Jose Barracuda	AHL	35	1	2	3	17	2	0	0	0	0
2016-17	San Jose Barracuda	AHL	59	3	12	15	30	1	0	0	0	0

ECAC All-Rookie Team (2012) • ECAC First All-Star Team (2015)
• Left Harvard University (ECAC) for academic reasons, December 12, 2012. Traded to **San Jose** by **Vancouver** for Tampa Bay's 7th round pick (previously acquired, Vancouver selected Tate Olson) in 2015 NHL Draft, June 27, 2015.

McNEILL, Reid   (muhk-NEEL, REED)

Defense. Shoots left. 6'4", 215 lbs.   Born, London, ON, April 29, 1992.
(Pittsburgh's 6th pick, 170th overall, in 2010 NHL Draft).

			Regular Season						Playoffs			
Season	Club	League	GP	G	A	Pts	PIM	GP	G	A	Pts	PIM
2008-09	Lambeth Lancers	ON-Jr.D	16	0	4	4	12	....	....	....	....	....
	Lucas High School	High-ON				STATISTICS NOT AVAILABLE						
2009-10	London Nationals	ON-Jr.B	20	0	7	7	6	....	....	....	....	....
	London Knights	OHL	53	2	3	5	32	12	0	1	1	0
2010-11	London Knights	OHL	62	2	4	6	70	6	0	0	0	4
2011-12	Barrie Colts	OHL	51	3	9	12	60	13	0	0	0	22
2012-13	Wilkes-Barre	AHL	3	0	0	0	0	12	0	1	1	12
	Wheeling Nailers	ECHL	44	2	4	6	90	....	....	....	....	....
2013-14	Wilkes-Barre	AHL	55	1	4	5	119	10	1	2	3	14
2014-15	Wilkes-Barre	AHL	54	2	5	7	121	8	0	1	1	11
2015-16	Wilkes-Barre	AHL	64	0	11	11	58	1	0	0	0	0
2016-17	Wilkes-Barre	AHL	14	1	1	2	21	....	....	....	....	....
	Chicago Wolves	AHL	47	2	6	8	46	....	....	....	....	....

Traded to **St. Louis** by **Pittsburgh** for Danny Kristo, November 19, 2016.

McPHEE, Graham   (mihk-FEE, GRAY-uhm)   **EDM**

Left wing. Shoots left. 6', 173 lbs.   Born, Bethesda, MD, July 24, 1998.
(Edmonton's 7th pick, 149th overall, in 2016 NHL Draft).

			Regular Season						Playoffs			
Season	Club	League	GP	G	A	Pts	PIM	GP	G	A	Pts	PIM
2013-14	Shattuck U16	High-MN	58	28	30	58	97	....	....	....	....	....
2014-15	USAHNTDP	USHL	31	2	10	12	42	....	....	....	....	....
	USAHNTDP	U-17	12	2	5	7	10	....	....	....	....	....
2015-16	USAHNTDP	USHL	20	5	0	5	16	....	....	....	....	....
	USAHNTDP	U-18	38	5	8	13	35	....	....	....	....	....
2016-17	Boston College	H-East	39	2	8	10	42	....	....	....	....	....

MEGALINSKY, Dmitri   (meh-gahl-IHN-skee, dih-MEE-tree)   **OTT**

Defense. Shoots left. 6'2", 212 lbs.   Born, Perm, USSR, April 15, 1985.
(Ottawa's 7th pick, 186th overall, in 2005 NHL Draft).

			Regular Season						Playoffs			
Season	Club	League	GP	G	A	Pts	PIM	GP	G	A	Pts	PIM
2003-04	HK Voronezh	Russia-2	42	4	8	12	159	....	....	....	....	....
	Yaroslavl	Russia	1	0	0	0	0	....	....	....	....	....
	Yaroslavl 2	Russia-3	11	0	4	4	16	....	....	....	....	....
2004-05	Yaroslavl	Russia	1	0	0	0	2	....	....	....	....	....
	Yaroslavl 2	Russia-3	30	6	12	18	82	....	....	....	....	....
2005-06	Yaroslavl 2	Russia-3	12	4	10	14	6	....	....	....	....	....
	Yaroslavl	Russia	20	0	1	1	8	8	0	0	0	6
2006-07	Khimik	Russia-2	33	4	7	11	34	7	0	1	1	16
2007-08	Vityaz Chekhov	Russia	25	2	7	9	20	....	....	....	....	....
2008-09	Vityaz Chekhov	KHL	52	2	5	7	72	....	....	....	....	....
2009-10	Vityaz Chekhov	KHL	52	4	16	20	98	....	....	....	....	....
2010-11	Vityaz Chekhov	KHL	27	0	3	3	18	....	....	....	....	....
2011-12	Novokuznetsk	KHL	46	2	11	13	34	....	....	....	....	....
2012-13	Novokuznetsk	KHL	38	5	9	14	18	....	....	....	....	....
2013-14	Spartak Moscow	KHL	19	0	0	0	6	....	....	....	....	....
	Avtomobilist	KHL	28	4	6	10	22	4	1	0	1	0
2014-15	Avtomobilist	KHL	40	3	6	9	22	5	0	1	1	4
2015-16	Avtomobilist	KHL	45	5	11	16	18	6	0	1	1	2
2016-17	Avtomobilist	KHL	52	5	4	9	63	....	....	....	....	....

MELOCHE, Nicolas   (meh-LAWSH, NIH-koh-las)   **COL**

Defense. Shoots right. 6'3", 204 lbs.   Born, LaSalle, QC, July 18, 1997.
(Colorado's 3rd pick, 40th overall, in 2015 NHL Draft).

			Regular Season						Playoffs			
Season	Club	League	GP	G	A	Pts	PIM	GP	G	A	Pts	PIM
2012-13	Saint-Eustache	QAAA	38	9	17	26	58	1	0	1	1	0
2013-14	Baie-Comeau	QMJHL	54	6	19	25	47	22	0	8	8	8
2014-15	Baie-Comeau	QMJHL	44	10	24	34	99	12	4	6	10	22
2015-16	Baie-Comeau	QMJHL	25	8	8	16	54	....	....	....	....	....
	Gatineau	QMJHL	28	5	12	17	38	9	1	2	3	10
2016-17	Gatineau	QMJHL	26	7	14	21	38	....	....	....	....	....
	Charlottetown	QMJHL	35	9	17	26	35	13	3	4	7	30

QMJHL All-Rookie Team (2014)

MERKLEY, Nick   (MUHR-klee, NIHK)   **ARI**

Right wing. Shoots right. 5'10", 189 lbs.   Born, Calgary, AB, May 23, 1997.
(Arizona's 2nd pick, 30th overall, in 2015 NHL Draft).

			Regular Season						Playoffs			
Season	Club	League	GP	G	A	Pts	PIM	GP	G	A	Pts	PIM
2011-12	Calgary Bisons	AMBHL	32	41	32	73	42	9	9	4	13	14
2012-13	Calgary Buffaloes	AMHL	30	14	19	33	95	11	4	6	10	16
	Kelowna Rockets	WHL	1	0	0	0	0	7	0	3	3	0
2013-14	Kelowna Rockets	WHL	66	25	33	58	46	14	4	13	17	12
2014-15	Kelowna Rockets	WHL	72	20	70	90	79	19	5	22	27	18
2015-16	Kelowna Rockets	WHL	43	17	31	48	44	....	....	....	....	....
2016-17	Kelowna Rockets	WHL	63	23	40	63	73	17	6	13	19	22

WHL West Second All-Star Team (2015)

MERMIS, Dakota   (MUHR-mihs, da-KOH-tah)   **ARI**

Defense. Shoots left. 6', 187 lbs.   Born, Alton, IL, January 5, 1994.

			Regular Season						Playoffs			
Season	Club	League	GP	G	A	Pts	PIM	GP	G	A	Pts	PIM
2009-10	St.L. Blues U18	T1EHL	48	11	26	37	76	....	....	....	....	....
	Lincoln Stars	USHL	2	0	1	1	0	....	....	....	....	....
2010-11	USAHNTDP	USHL	36	4	4	8	53	2	0	0	0	0
	USAHNTDP	U-17	17	1	4	5	20	....	....	....	....	....
2011-12	Green Bay	USHL	60	5	22	27	98	12	0	1	1	20
2012-13	U. of Denver	WCHA	19	1	3	4	14	....	....	....	....	....
	London Knights	OHL	27	2	9	11	34	21	1	3	4	21
2013-14	London Knights	OHL	66	5	20	25	76	9	1	3	4	12
2014-15	London Knights	OHL	36	1	10	11	36	....	....	....	....	....
	Oshawa Generals	OHL	30	5	14	19	50	21	1	14	15	14
2015-16	Springfield Falcons	AHL	63	3	10	13	58	....	....	....	....	....
	Rapid City Rush	ECHL	5	1	2	3	6	....	....	....	....	....
2016-17	Tucson	AHL	67	2	10	12	75	....	....	....	....	....

Signed as a free agent by **Arizona**, July 1, 2015.

METE, Victor   (MEH-TAY, VIHK-ohr)   **MTL**

Defense. Shoots left. 5'9", 181 lbs.   Born, Toronto, ON, June 7, 1998.
(Montreal's 3rd pick, 100th overall, in 2016 NHL Draft).

			Regular Season						Playoffs			
Season	Club	League	GP	G	A	Pts	PIM	GP	G	A	Pts	PIM
2013-14	Tor. Jr. Can. MM	GTHL	33	12	18	30	10	14	3	3	6	2
	Tor. Jr. Can. Midg	GTHL	1	0	0	0	0	....	....	....	....	....
2014-15	London Knights	OHL	58	7	16	23	14	10	1	7	8	2
2015-16	London Knights	OHL	68	8	30	38	18	18	4	7	11	0
2016-17	London Knights	OHL	50	15	29	44	14	14	1	6	7	4

MEYER, Carson   (MIGH-uhr, KAR-suhn)   **CBJ**

Right wing. Shoots right. 5'11", 180 lbs.   Born, Powell, OH, August 18, 1997.
(Columbus' 6th pick, 179th overall, in 2017 NHL Draft).

			Regular Season						Playoffs			
Season	Club	League	GP	G	A	Pts	PIM	GP	G	A	Pts	PIM
2012-13	Ohio B-Jack. U16	T1EHL	40	10	10	20	4	4	2	1	3	2
2013-14	Ohio B-Jack. U16	T1EHL	36	14	19	33	18	....	....	....	....	....
2014-15	Ohio B-Jack. U16	T1EHL	32	21	30	51	43	4	2	7	9	0
	Tri-City Storm	USHL	2	0	1	1	0	....	....	....	....	....
2015-16	Tri-City Storm	USHL	56	32	19	51	47	11	5	6	11	4
2016-17	Miami U.	NCHC	32	10	16	26	14	....	....	....	....	....

MIDDLETON, Jacob (MIH-duhl-tuhn, JAY-kuhb)

Defense. Shoots left. 6'3", 210 lbs. Born, Stratford, ON, January 2, 1996.
(Los Angeles' 10th pick, 210th overall, in 2014 NHL Draft).

			Regular Season					Playoffs				
Season	Club	League	GP	G	A	Pts	PIM	GP	G	A	Pts	PIM
2011-12	Huron-Perth MM	Minor-ON	25	7	16	23	26	8	1	7	8	16
	Huron-Perth Mid.	Minor-ON	2	1	0	1	4	....	....	....	....	....
	Stratford Cullitons	ON-Jr.B	4	0	3	3	0	....	....	....	....	....
2012-13	Owen Sound	OHL	14	0	1	1	7	....	....	....	....	....
	Ottawa 67's	OHL	15	1	3	4	18	....	....	....	....	....
2013-14	Ottawa 67's	OHL	65	2	21	23	64	....	....	....	....	....
2014-15	Ottawa 67's	OHL	64	4	23	27	62	6	1	1	2	4
2015-16	Ottawa 67's	OHL	68	7	24	31	68	5	0	2	2	2
	Manchester	ECHL	2	0	1	1	0	5	0	0	0	0
2016-17	San Jose Barracuda	AHL	50	1	8	9	56	13	0	4	4	10

Signed as a free agent by **San Jose** (AHL), September 20, 2016.

MIDDLETON, Keaton (MIH-duhl-tuhn, KEE-tuhn) TOR

Defense. Shoots left. 6'5", 235 lbs. Born, Stratford, ON, February 10, 1998.
(Toronto's 7th pick, 101st overall, in 2016 NHL Draft).

			Regular Season					Playoffs				
Season	Club	League	GP	G	A	Pts	PIM	GP	G	A	Pts	PIM
2013-14	Huron-Perth MM	Minor-ON	31	3	20	23	24	15	1	7	8	8
	Stratford Cullitons	ON-Jr.B	3	0	0	0	0	4	0	0	0	0
2014-15	Saginaw Spirit	OHL	61	2	7	9	58	4	0	1	1	0
2015-16	Saginaw Spirit	OHL	66	1	6	7	66	4	0	1	1	0
2016-17	Saginaw Spirit	OHL	64	4	14	18	48	....	....	....	....	....

MIKKOLA, Niko (mih-KOH-luh, NEE-koh) ST.L.

Defense. Shoots left. 6'4", 185 lbs. Born, Kiiminki, Finland, April 27, 1996.
(St. Louis' 4th pick, 127th overall, in 2015 NHL Draft).

			Regular Season					Playoffs				
Season	Club	League	GP	G	A	Pts	PIM	GP	G	A	Pts	PIM
2012-13	KalPa Kuopio U18	Fin-U18	12	0	0	0	6	....	....	....	....	....
2013-14	KalPa Kuopio U18	Fin-U18	46	4	13	17	103	8	0	2	2	6
2014-15	KalPa Kuopio Jr.	Fin-Jr.	37	9	14	23	80	....	....	....	....	....
	KalPa Kuopio	Finland	10	0	1	1	4	....	....	....	....	....
	Hokki Kajaani	Finland-2	5	1	0	1	8	7	0	1	1	2
2015-16	KalPa Kuopio	Finland	55	3	6	9	22	3	0	1	1	4
2016-17	KalPa Kuopio	Finland	56	4	11	15	89	10	1	2	3	4

MIRAGEAS, Ben (mihr-A-juhz, BEHN) NYI

Defense. Shoots left. 6'1", 171 lbs. Born, Newburyport, MA, August 5, 1999.
(NY Islanders' 2nd pick, 77th overall, in 2017 NHL Draft).

			Regular Season					Playoffs				
Season	Club	League	GP	G	A	Pts	PIM	GP	G	A	Pts	PIM
2013-14	Newburyport	High-MA	....	7	11	18	....	....	....	....	....	....
2014-15	Springfield U16	Minor-MA	13	3	3	6	2	....	....	....	....	....
	Avon Old Farms	High-CT	24	1	6	7	....	....	....	....	....	....
2015-16	Neponset Val. U18	Minor-MA	12	1	6	7	6	....	....	....	....	....
	Avon Old Farms	High-CT	24	6	16	22	....	....	....	....	....	....
	Bloomington	USHL	4	0	0	0	4	....	....	....	....	....
2016-17	Bloomington	USHL	45	1	9	10	18	....	....	....	....	....
	Chicago Steel	USHL	14	1	8	9	4	14	0	10	10	6

• Signed Letter of Intent to attend **Providence College** (Hockey East) in fall of 2017.

MIRNOV, Igor (mihr-NAWF, EE-gohr) OTT

Left wing. Shoots left. 6', 187 lbs. Born, Chita, USSR, September 19, 1984.
(Ottawa's 2nd pick, 67th overall, in 2003 NHL Draft).

			Regular Season					Playoffs				
Season	Club	League	GP	G	A	Pts	PIM	GP	G	A	Pts	PIM
2001-02	Dyn'o Moscow 2	Russia-3	30	33	17	50	34	....	....	....	....	....
	Dynamo Moscow	Russia	6	0	0	0	0	....	....	....	....	....
2002-03	Dynamo Moscow	Russia	50	3	7	10	49	5	0	0	0	2
2003-04	Dynamo Moscow	Russia	53	11	10	21	26	3	0	0	0	2
2004-05	Dynamo Moscow	Russia	55	13	13	26	50	9	2	4	6	0
2005-06	Dynamo Moscow	Russia	32	8	10	18	36	4	0	2	2	4
2006-07	Dynamo Moscow	Russia	49	21	25	46	54	3	2	1	3	4
2007-08	Dynamo Moscow	Russia	24	3	3	6	16	....	....	....	....	....
	Magnitogorsk	Russia	23	9	6	15	20	13	3	1	4	4
2008-09	Magnitogorsk	KHL	39	11	8	19	24	11	2	7	9	8
2009-10	Mytischi	KHL	20	2	4	6	0	....	....	....	....	....
	MVD	KHL	10	1	3	4	4	....	....	....	....	....
	Sibir Novosibirsk	KHL	12	7	5	12	8	....	....	....	....	....
2010-11	Sibir Novosibirsk	KHL	53	16	25	41	30	4	0	2	2	2
2011-12	Ufa	KHL	50	14	10	24	14	5	0	1	1	6
2012-13	Ufa	KHL	49	21	16	37	32	14	2	3	5	2
2013-14	Ufa	KHL	48	18	13	31	14	18	8	2	10	0
2014-15	Ak Bars Kazan	KHL	57	10	20	30	14	20	2	6	8	10
2015-16	Ak Bars Kazan	KHL	37	7	7	14	16	1	0	0	0	0
2016-17	Chelyabinsk	KHL	17	1	4	5	2	....	....	....	....	....
	Spartak Moscow	KHL	35	8	6	14	14	....	....	....	....	....

MIRONOV, Andrei (mih-RAW-nawv, AWN-dray) COL

Defense. Shoots left. 6'3", 194 lbs. Born, Moscow, Russia, July 29, 1994.
(Colorado's 5th pick, 101st overall, in 2015 NHL Draft).

			Regular Season					Playoffs				
Season	Club	League	GP	G	A	Pts	PIM	GP	G	A	Pts	PIM
2011-12	Dyn'o Moscow Jr.	Russia-Jr.	59	1	8	9	87	2	0	0	0	0
2012-13	Dynamo Moscow	KHL	40	0	5	5	26	18	1	2	3	8
	Dyn'o Moscow Jr.	Russia-Jr.	6	0	1	1	0	1	0	0	0	4
2013-14	Dynamo Moscow	KHL	46	3	7	10	16	7	0	1	1	6
	Dyn'o Moscow Jr.	Russia-Jr.	3	0	1	1	2	....	....	....	....	....
2014-15	Dynamo Moscow	KHL	52	5	3	8	20	11	0	1	1	6
	Dyn'o Balashikha	Russia-2	1	0	0	0	2	....	....	....	....	....
2015-16	Dynamo Moscow	KHL	40	3	10	13	21	9	1	1	2	6
2016-17	Dynamo Moscow	KHL	18	1	3	4	10	9	0	3	3	4

MISLEY, Bryce (MIHZ-lee, BRIGHS) MIN

Center. Shoots left. 6'1", 185 lbs. Born, Calgary, AB, May 9, 1999.
(Minnesota's 3rd pick, 116th overall, in 2017 NHL Draft).

			Regular Season					Playoffs				
Season	Club	League	GP	G	A	Pts	PIM	GP	G	A	Pts	PIM
2014-15	Don Mills Flyers	GTHL	61	22	30	52	16	....	....	....	....	....
2015-16	Oakville Blades	ON-Jr.A	53	19	20	39	23	13	7	4	11	20
2016-17	Oakville Blades	ON-Jr.A	46	26	36	62	14	16	5	9	14	14

• Signed Letter of Intent to attend **University of Vermont** (Hockey East) in fall of 2018.

MISMASH, Grant (MIHS-MASH, GRANT) NSH

Left wing. Shoots left. 6', 181 lbs. Born, Brooklyn Park, MN, February 19, 1999.
(Nashville's 2nd pick, 61st overall, in 2017 NHL Draft).

			Regular Season					Playoffs				
Season	Club	League	GP	G	A	Pts	PIM	GP	G	A	Pts	PIM
2014-15	Shattuck	High-MN	52	31	31	62	64	....	....	....	....	....
2015-16	USAHNTDP	USHL	35	14	9	23	54	....	....	....	....	....
	USAHNTDP	U-17	23	9	12	21	34	....	....	....	....	....
2016-17	USAHNTDP	USHL	26	8	16	24	44	....	....	....	....	....
	USAHNTDP	U-18	39	18	19	37	62	....	....	....	....	....

• Signed Letter of Intent to attend **University of North Dakota** (NCHC) in fall of 2018.

MITCHELL, Ian (MIH-chuhl, EE-uhn) CHI

Defense. Shoots right. 5'11", 173 lbs. Born, St. Albert, AB, January 18, 1999.
(Chicago's 2nd pick, 57th overall, in 2017 NHL Draft).

			Regular Season					Playoffs				
Season	Club	League	GP	G	A	Pts	PIM	GP	G	A	Pts	PIM
2014-15	St. Albert Raiders	AMHL	27	1	10	11	6	1	0	0	0	0
	Spruce Grove	AJHL	2	0	0	0	0	....	....	....	....	....
2015-16	Spruce Grove	AJHL	54	6	21	27	8	14	1	4	5	6
2016-17	Spruce Grove	AJHL	53	8	29	37	34	10	1	3	4	0

• Signed Letter of Intent to attend **University of Denver** (NCHC) in fall of 2017.

MITCHELL, Mason (MIH-chuhl, MAY-suhn) WSH

Left wing. Shoots left. 6'2", 209 lbs. Born, Edmonton, AB, June 13, 1994.

			Regular Season					Playoffs				
Season	Club	League	GP	G	A	Pts	PIM	GP	G	A	Pts	PIM
2011-12	Calgary Northstars	AMHL	32	7	5	12	176	6	0	2	2	34
2012-13	Nanaimo Clippers	BCHL	43	14	6	20	89	1	0	0	0	2
2013-14	Nanaimo Clippers	BCHL	39	9	10	19	115	5	1	0	1	8
2014-15	Calgary Mustangs	AJHL	39	19	15	34	217	2	0	1	1	19
2015-16	Alaska-Anchorage	WCHA	19	3	9	12	47	....	....	....	....	....
2016-17	Alaska-Anchorage	WCHA	31	12	2	14	73	....	....	....	....	....

Signed as a free agent by **Washington**, March 2, 2017.

MITTELSTADT, Casey (MIH-tuhl-stad, KAY-see) BUF

Center. Shoots left. 5'11", 199 lbs. Born, Edina, MN, November 22, 1998.
(Buffalo's 1st pick, 8th overall, in 2017 NHL Draft).

			Regular Season					Playoffs				
Season	Club	League	GP	G	A	Pts	PIM	GP	G	A	Pts	PIM
2014-15	Team Southeast	UMHSEL	20	14	14	28	8	3	2	2	4	0
	Eden Prairie Eagles	High-MN	25	22	25	47	4	5	4	1	5	2
2015-16	Team Southeast	UMHSEL	19	14	27	41	24	....	....	....	....	....
	Eden Prairie Eagles	High-MN	25	22	37	59	16	6	11	10	21	0
	USAHNTDP	USHL	2	2	0	2	2	....	....	....	....	....
	USAHNTDP	U-18	11	5	6	11	4	....	....	....	....	....
2016-17	Eden Prairie Eagles	High-MN	25	21	43	64	8	5	2	6	8	2
	Green Bay	USHL	24	13	17	30	2	....	....	....	....	....

• Signed Letter of Intent to attend **University of Minnesota** (Big Ten) in fall of 2017.

MOORE, Trevor (MOOR, TREH-vuhr) TOR

Left wing. Shoots left. 5'10", 183 lbs. Born, Thousand Oaks, CA, March 31, 1995.

			Regular Season					Playoffs				
Season	Club	League	GP	G	A	Pts	PIM	GP	G	A	Pts	PIM
2010-11	L.A. Selects	T1EHL	35	19	22	41	47	....	....	....	....	....
2011-12	Tri-City Storm	USHL	49	12	20	32	6	2	0	2	2	0
2012-13	Tri-City Storm	USHL	62	20	43	63	26	....	....	....	....	....
2013-14	U. of Denver	NCHC	42	14	18	32	14	....	....	....	....	....
2014-15	U. of Denver	NCHC	39	*22	22	44	7	....	....	....	....	....
2015-16	U. of Denver	NCHC	40	11	33	44	8	....	....	....	....	....
2016-17	Toronto Marlies	AHL	57	13	20	33	18	11	2	2	4	4

NCHC All-Rookie Team (2014) • NCHC First All-Star Team (2015) • NCAA West Second All-American Team (2015)

Signed as a free agent by **Toronto**, July 26, 2016.

MORAND, Antoine (mohr-AN, an-TWAHN) ANA

Center. Shoots left. 5'10", 175 lbs. Born, Chateauguay, QC, February 18, 1999.
(Anaheim's 2nd pick, 60th overall, in 2017 NHL Draft).

			Regular Season					Playoffs				
Season	Club	League	GP	G	A	Pts	PIM	GP	G	A	Pts	PIM
2014-15	Chateauguay	QAAA	42	18	37	55	34	16	12	18	30	16
2015-16	Acadie-Bathurst	QMJHL	48	14	36	50	37	5	0	3	3	0
2016-17	Acadie-Bathurst	QMJHL	67	28	46	74	52	11	2	10	12	8

MOROZ, Mitchell (maw-RAWZ, MIH-chuhl)

Left wing. Shoots left. 6'2", 214 lbs. Born, Edmonton, AB, May 3, 1994.
(Edmonton's 2nd pick, 32nd overall, in 2012 NHL Draft).

			Regular Season					Playoffs				
Season	Club	League	GP	G	A	Pts	PIM	GP	G	A	Pts	PIM
2007-08	Cgy. N. Sabres	AMBHL	31	5	7	12	40	2	0	2	2	12
2008-09	Cgy. N. Sabres	AMBHL	31	20	16	36	50	....	....	....	....	....
2009-10	Edge School	High-AB	43	20	23	43	80	....	....	....	....	....
	Edmonton	WHL	7	0	1	1	2	....	....	....	....	....
2010-11	Calgary Northstars	AMHL	22	10	4	14	34	2	0	0	0	0
	Edmonton	WHL	1	0	0	0	0	....	....	....	....	....
2011-12	Edmonton	WHL	66	16	9	25	131	20	4	4	8	24
2012-13	Edmonton	WHL	69	13	21	34	140	22	2	5	7	41
2013-14	Edmonton	WHL	70	35	28	63	156	21	6	13	19	40
2014-15	Oklahoma City	AHL	66	5	4	9	169	6	0	1	1	6
2015-16	Bakersfield	AHL	40	5	5	10	99	....	....	....	....	....
2016-17	Bakersfield	AHL	17	1	2	3	14	....	....	....	....	....
	Tucson	AHL	24	3	3	6	32	....	....	....	....	....

Traded to **Arizona** by **Edmonton** for Henrik Samuelsson, February 1, 2017.

MORRISON, Cam (MOHR-ih-suhn, KAM) COL

Left wing. Shoots left. 6'2", 200 lbs. Born, Aurora, ON, August 27, 1998.
(Colorado's 2nd pick, 40th overall, in 2016 NHL Draft).

			Regular Season					Playoffs				
Season	Club	League	GP	G	A	Pts	PIM	GP	G	A	Pts	PIM
2013-14	York Simcoe	Minor-ON	32	17	26	43	14	5	1	3	4	2
	Aurora Tigers	ON-Jr.A	3	0	0	0	10	....	....	....	....	....
2014-15	Aurora Tigers	ON-Jr.A	49	31	22	53	8	12	6	5	11	0
2015-16	Youngstown	USHL	60	34	32	66	42	....	....	....	....	....
2016-17	U. of Notre Dame	H-East	40	12	12	24	12	....	....	....	....	....

USHL All-Rookie Team (2016) • USHL First All-Star Team (2016)

MORRISON, Kenney (MOHR-ih-suhn, KEHN-nee)

Defense. Shoots right. 6'2", 208 lbs. Born, Lloydminster, AB, February 13, 1992.

			Regular Season					Playoffs				
Season	Club	League	GP	G	A	Pts	PIM	GP	G	A	Pts	PIM
2008-09	Lloydminster	AMHL	34	0	7	7	14	....	....	....	....	....
2009-10	Lloydminster	AMHL	35	7	18	25	52	10	2	7	9	10
	Lloydminster	AJHL	1	0	0	0	2	....	....	....	....	....
2010-11	Alberni Valley	BCHL	55	8	27	35	26	4	0	2	2	2
2011-12	Omaha Lancers	USHL	57	15	20	35	44	3	0	0	0	0
2012-13	Western Mich.	CCHA	38	7	13	20	32	....	....	....	....	....
2013-14	Western Mich.	NCHC	40	4	15	19	83	....	....	....	....	....
2014-15	Western Mich.	NCHC	37	5	10	15	36	....	....	....	....	....
	Adirondack Flames	AHL	10	2	4	6	4	....	....	....	....	....
2015-16	Stockton Heat	AHL	44	3	10	13	30	....	....	....	....	....
2016-17	Stockton Heat	AHL	51	4	8	12	36	....	....	....	....	....

Signed as a free agent by **Calgary**, March 19, 2015.

MOUTREY, Nick (MOO-tree, NIHK) CBJ

Center/Left wing. Shoots left. 6'3", 215 lbs. Born, Toronto, ON, June 24, 1995.
(Columbus' 6th pick, 105th overall, in 2013 NHL Draft).

			Regular Season					Playoffs				
Season	Club	League	GP	G	A	Pts	PIM	GP	G	A	Pts	PIM
2010-11	York Simcoe	Minor-ON	69	43	46	89	46	....	....	....	....	....
2011-12	Saginaw Spirit	OHL	66	2	7	9	46	12	0	0	0	4
2012-13	Saginaw Spirit	OHL	65	16	27	43	44	4	0	0	0	12
2013-14	Saginaw Spirit	OHL	68	15	26	41	82	5	0	3	3	2
2014-15	Saginaw Spirit	OHL	36	15	26	41	40	....	....	....	....	....
	North Bay	OHL	26	10	12	22	14	15	7	6	13	12
2015-16	Lake Erie Monsters	AHL	53	6	5	11	39	2	0	0	0	2
2016-17	Cleveland	AHL	61	8	9	17	42	....	....	....	....	....

MOVERARE, Jacob (moh-VEH-ruh-ruh, YAH-kuhb) L.A.

Defense. Shoots left. 6'2", 198 lbs. Born, Ostersund, Sweden, August 31, 1998.
(Los Angeles' 2nd pick, 112th overall, in 2016 NHL Draft).

			Regular Season					Playoffs				
Season	Club	League	GP	G	A	Pts	PIM	GP	G	A	Pts	PIM
2012-13	Skelleftea AIK U18	Swe-U18	20	0	1	1	2	....	....	....	....	....
2013-14	Skelleftea AIK U18	Swe-U18	34	1	7	8	22	2	0	1	1	2
2014-15	HV 71 U18	Swe-U18	4	1	1	2	2	3	1	1	2	0
	HV 71 Jr.	Swe-Jr.	42	1	9	10	6	6	0	0	0	2
2015-16	HV 71 U18	Swe-U18	5	1	1	2	31	....	....	....	....	....
	HV 71 Jr.	Swe-Jr.	41	5	16	21	22	3	0	1	1	4
	HV 71 Jonkoping	Sweden	4	0	0	0	0	....	....	....	....	....
2016-17	Mississauga	OHL	63	2	30	32	20	20	2	5	7	10

MOY, Tyler (MOY, TIGH-luhr) NSH

Center. Shoots right. 6'1", 195 lbs. Born, La Jolla, CA, July 18, 1995.
(Nashville's 6th pick, 175th overall, in 2015 NHL Draft).

			Regular Season					Playoffs				
Season	Club	League	GP	G	A	Pts	PIM	GP	G	A	Pts	PIM
2010-11	Cal. Titans U16	NAPHL	20	12	17	29	18	5	2	5	7	4
2011-12	Chicago Fury U18	T1EHL	40	18	27	45	6	....	....	....	....	....
2012-13	Omaha Lancers	USHL	64	4	19	23	22	....	....	....	....	....
2013-14	Harvard Crimson	ECAC	27	4	6	10	2	....	....	....	....	....
2014-15	Harvard Crimson	ECAC	37	12	15	27	16	....	....	....	....	....
2015-16	Harvard Crimson	ECAC	31	7	12	19	26	....	....	....	....	....
2016-17	Harvard Crimson	ECAC	36	22	23	45	20	....	....	....	....	....
	Milwaukee	AHL	3	1	3	4	2	2	0	0	0	0

MUIR, Aidan (MEWR, AY-duhn) EDM

Left wing. Shoots right. 6'3", 182 lbs. Born, Brampton, ON, August 21, 1995.
(Edmonton's 7th pick, 113th overall, in 2013 NHL Draft).

			Regular Season					Playoffs				
Season	Club	League	GP	G	A	Pts	PIM	GP	G	A	Pts	PIM
2011-12	Det. Vic. Honda	T1EHL	40	13	7	20	8	4	3	4	7	8
2012-13	Det. Vic. Honda	T1EHL	37	17	23	40	41	3	0	1	1	0
2013-14	Indiana Ice	USHL	54	14	27	41	60	10	1	1	2	2
2014-15	Western Mich.	NCHC	36	6	9	15	4	....	....	....	....	....
2015-16	Western Mich.	NCHC	35	2	6	8	20	....	....	....	....	....
2016-17	Western Mich.	NCHC	20	2	9	11	8	....	....	....	....	....

MULLEN, Patrick (MUHL-uhn, PA-trihk)

Defense. Shoots right. 5'11", 185 lbs. Born, Pittsburgh, PA, May 6, 1986.

			Regular Season					Playoffs				
Season	Club	League	GP	G	A	Pts	PIM	GP	G	A	Pts	PIM
2004-05	Sioux City	USHL	60	14	23	37	8	....	....	....	....	....
2005-06	U. of Denver	WCHA	37	7	10	17	24	....	....	....	....	....
2006-07	U. of Denver	WCHA	37	5	12	17	20	....	....	....	....	....
2007-08	U. of Denver	WCHA	40	4	18	22	65	....	....	....	....	....
2008-09	U. of Denver	WCHA	38	4	21	25	39	....	....	....	....	....
2009-10	Manchester	AHL	44	4	6	10	16	2	0	0	0	2
	Ontario Reign	ECHL	1	0	0	0	0	....	....	....	....	....
2010-11	Manchester	AHL	67	3	17	20	32	7	0	1	1	4
2011-12	Manchester	AHL	69	13	28	41	45	4	1	2	3	8
2012-13	Chicago Wolves	AHL	2	0	0	0	0	....	....	....	....	....
2013-14	Utica Comets	AHL	46	7	13	20	23	....	....	....	....	....
	Binghamton	AHL	20	1	11	12	12	4	0	2	2	6
2014-15	Binghamton	AHL	54	5	24	29	32	....	....	....	....	....
2015-16	Binghamton	AHL	36	1	15	16	18	....	....	....	....	....
	Milwaukee	AHL	29	2	12	14	19	3	0	1	1	2
2016-17	Dynamo Riga (LAT)	KHL	39	4	8	12	26	....	....	....	....	....
	Rochester	AHL	27	4	10	14	22	....	....	....	....	....

Signed as a free agent by **Los Angeles**, April 3, 2009. Signed as a free agent by **Vancouver**, July 5, 2012. Traded to **Ottawa** by **Vancouver** for Jeff Costello, March 4, 2014. Traded to **Nashville** by **Ottawa** for Conor Allen, January 14, 2016. Signed as a free agent by **Riga** (KHL), July 28, 2016. Signed as a free agent by **Rochester** (AHL), February 2, 2017. Signed as a free agent by **Linkoping** (Sweden(, July 10, 2017.

MURPHY, Trevor (MUHR-fee, TRE-vuhr) NSH

Defense. Shoots left. 5'10", 180 lbs. Born, Windsor, ON, July 17, 1995.

			Regular Season					Playoffs				
Season	Club	League	GP	G	A	Pts	PIM	GP	G	A	Pts	PIM
2011-12	Peterborough	OHL	60	1	19	20	52	....	....	....	....	....
2012-13	Peterborough	OHL	23	2	2	4	23	....	....	....	....	....
	Windsor Spitfires	OHL	42	7	17	24	60	....	....	....	....	....
2013-14	Windsor Spitfires	OHL	51	8	21	29	57	....	....	....	....	....
2014-15	Windsor Spitfires	OHL	59	24	39	63	104	....	....	....	....	....
2015-16	Milwaukee	AHL	59	11	21	32	37	3	1	0	1	2
2016-17	Milwaukee	AHL	75	12	21	33	92	3	2	0	2	4

Signed as a free agent by **Nashville**, September 17, 2015.

MURRAY, Brett (MUHR-ee, BREHT) BUF

Left wing. Shoots left. 6'5", 214 lbs. Born, Bolton, ON, July 20, 1998.
(Buffalo's 5th pick, 99th overall, in 2016 NHL Draft).

			Regular Season					Playoffs				
Season	Club	League	GP	G	A	Pts	PIM	GP	G	A	Pts	PIM
2013-14	Brampton 45s	Minor-ON	40	12	15	27	18	5	0	1	1	6
2014-15	The Hill Academy	High-ON	66	40	47	87	....	....	....	....	....	....
2015-16	Carleton Place	ON-Jr.A	48	14	32	46	16	16	5	8	13	4
2016-17	Penn State	Big Ten	12	0	1	1	4	....	....	....	....	....
	Youngstown	USHL	27	7	13	20	22	....	....	....	....	....

MUSIL, Adam (mew-SEEL, A-duhm) ST.L.

Center. Shoots right. 6'3", 202 lbs. Born, Ottawa, ON, March 26, 1997.
(St. Louis' 2nd pick, 94th overall, in 2015 NHL Draft).

			Regular Season					Playoffs				
Season	Club	League	GP	G	A	Pts	PIM	GP	G	A	Pts	PIM
2012-13	Greater Van.	BCMML	32	16	28	44	30	6	1	2	3	6
	Red Deer Rebels	WHL	3	0	0	0	0	3	0	0	0	2
2013-14	Red Deer Rebels	WHL	60	11	18	29	36	....	....	....	....	....
2014-15	Red Deer Rebels	WHL	66	15	24	39	71	....	....	....	....	....
2015-16	Red Deer Rebels	WHL	66	19	24	43	46	17	3	7	10	19
2016-17	Red Deer Rebels	WHL	56	20	31	51	74	5	0	4	4	0
	Chicago Wolves	AHL	2	0	0	0	0	6	3	2	5	2

MYERS, Philippe (MIGH-uhrz, FIHL-ihp) PHI

Defense. Shoots right. 6'5", 196 lbs. Born, Moncton, NB, January 25, 1997.

			Regular Season					Playoffs				
Season	Club	League	GP	G	A	Pts	PIM	GP	G	A	Pts	PIM
2013-14	Rouyn-Noranda	QMJHL	46	0	4	4	11	9	0	3	3	2
2014-15	Rouyn-Noranda	QMJHL	60	2	6	8	55	6	0	2	2	15
2015-16	Rouyn-Noranda	QMJHL	63	17	28	45	44	20	4	12	16	18
2016-17	Rouyn-Noranda	QMJHL	34	10	25	35	46	13	3	6	9	14

QMJHL First All-Star Team (2016)

Signed as a free agent by **Philadelphia**, September 21, 2015.

NANNE, Louis (NA-nee, LOO-ee) MIN

Left wing. Shoots left. 5'10", 178 lbs. Born, Edina, MN, June 18, 1994.
(Minnesota's 7th pick, 188th overall, in 2012 NHL Draft).

			Regular Season					Playoffs				
Season	Club	League	GP	G	A	Pts	PIM	GP	G	A	Pts	PIM
2009-10	Edina Hornets	High-MN	20	3	0	3	4	6	1	1	2	2
2010-11	Edina Hornets	High-MN	21	11	12	23	10	6	2	4	6	2
2011-12	Team Southwest	UMHSEL	23	7	13	20	12	....	....	....	....	....
	Edina Hornets	High-MN	24	12	8	20	30	4	3	4	7	4
2012-13	Penticton Vees	BCHL	45	19	22	41	16	15	6	6	12	4
2013-14	Sioux Falls	USHL	37	4	5	9	12	3	1	0	1	0
2014-15	RPI Engineers	ECAC	31	5	5	10	12	....	....	....	....	....
2015-16	RPI Engineers	ECAC	40	6	17	23	19	....	....	....	....	....
2016-17	RPI Engineers	ECAC	35	3	8	11	4	....	....	....	....	....

NANNE, Tyler (NA-nee, TIGH-luhr) NYR

Defense. Shoots right. 5'10", 192 lbs. Born, Edina, MN, March 17, 1996.
(NY Rangers' 7th pick, 142nd overall, in 2014 NHL Draft).

			Regular Season					Playoffs				
Season	Club	League	GP	G	A	Pts	PIM	GP	G	A	Pts	PIM
2011-12	Edina Hornets	High-MN	25	5	10	15	10	5	2	5	7	4
2012-13	Edina Hornets	High-MN	25	9	10	19	6	6	1	3	4	4
	Lincoln Stars	USHL	2	0	0	0	0	....	....	....	....	....
2013-14	Team Southwest	UMHSEL	20	2	6	8	18	3	0	3	3	4
	Edina Hornets	High-MN	25	7	20	27	41	5	5	6	11	11
	Sioux Falls	USHL	4	0	2	2	4	3	0	0	0	0
	USAHNTDP	U-18	1	0	0	0	2	....	....	....	....	....
2014-15	Sioux Falls	USHL	14	1	2	3	14	....	....	....	....	....
	Madison Capitols	USHL	29	7	6	13	32	....	....	....	....	....
2015-16	Ohio State	Big Ten	DID NOT PLAY – FRESHMAN									
2016-17	U. of Minnesota	Big Ten	DID NOT PLAY – TRANSFERRED COLLEGES									

NANTEL, Julien (nan-TEHL, JOO-lee-ehn) COL

Center. Shoots left. 6', 193 lbs. Born, Laval, QC, September 6, 1996.
(Colorado's 7th pick, 204th overall, in 2014 NHL Draft).

			Regular Season					Playoffs				
Season	Club	League	GP	G	A	Pts	PIM	GP	G	A	Pts	PIM
2011-12	Laval-Montreal	QAAA	40	11	17	28	8	....	....	....	....	....
2012-13	Laval-Montreal	QAAA	36	19	21	40	18	17	6	11	17	6
	Rouyn-Noranda	QMJHL	4	1	0	1	0	....	....	....	....	....
2013-14	Rouyn-Noranda	QMJHL	68	14	20	34	18	9	0	4	4	2
2014-15	Rouyn-Noranda	QMJHL	64	26	35	61	34	6	3	1	4	2
2015-16	Rouyn-Noranda	QMJHL	52	22	24	46	28	20	4	4	8	12
2016-17	San Antonio	AHL	59	5	3	8	10	....	....	....	....	....
	Colorado Eagles	ECHL	5	2	0	2	0	20	8	8	16	6

NASSEN, Linus (nahs-EE-ehn, LEE-nuhs) FLA

Defense. Shoots left. 6', 162 lbs. Born, Norrtalje, Sweden, May 10, 1998.
(Florida's 3rd pick, 89th overall, in 2016 NHL Draft).

			Regular Season					Playoffs				
Season	Club	League	GP	G	A	Pts	PIM	GP	G	A	Pts	PIM
2013-14	SDE U18	Swe-U18	29	6	7	13	8	6	1	1	2	2
2014-15	Lulea HF U18	Swe-U18	39	8	19	27	32	....	....	....	....	....
	Lulea HF Jr.	Swe-Jr.	5	0	0	0	0	....	....	....	....	....
2015-16	Lulea HF U18	Swe-U18	3	2	6	8	4	....	....	....	....	....
	Lulea HF Jr.	Swe-Jr.	42	5	16	21	22	2	0	0	0	2
	Lulea HF	Sweden	10	0	0	0	0	....	....	....	....	....
2016-17	Lulea HF Jr.	Swe-Jr.	25	3	13	16	37	3	1	0	1	0
	Lulea HF	Sweden	21	1	1	2	2	....	....	....	....	....
	AIK Solna	Sweden-2	4	0	0	0	2	....	....	....	....	....

NASTASIUK, Zach (nas-TAYZ-ee-uhk, ZAK) DET

Right wing. Shoots right. 6'2", 202 lbs. Born, Barrie, ON, March 30, 1995.
(Detroit's 2nd pick, 48th overall, in 2013 NHL Draft).

			Regular Season					Playoffs				
Season	Club	League	GP	G	A	Pts	PIM	GP	G	A	Pts	PIM
2010-11	Barrie Colts	Minor-ON	41	17	23	40	38	....	....	....	....	....
	Orangeville Flyers	ON-Jr.A	1	0	0	0	0	....	....	....	....	....
2011-12	Owen Sound	OHL	68	11	8	19	15	5	1	0	1	0
2012-13	Owen Sound	OHL	62	20	20	40	32	12	4	7	11	0
2013-14	Owen Sound	OHL	62	24	27	51	26	5	3	1	4	2
	Grand Rapids	AHL	5	0	0	0	0	7	0	1	1	0
2014-15	Owen Sound	OHL	64	35	42	77	34	5	1	0	1	4
	Grand Rapids	AHL	6	0	0	0	0	4	0	0	0	0
2015-16	Grand Rapids	AHL	27	3	5	8	4	....	....	....	....	....
	Toledo Walleye	ECHL	25	10	10	20	10	....	....	....	....	....
2016-17	Grand Rapids	AHL	7	0	1	1	0	....	....	....	....	....
	Toledo Walleye	ECHL	47	13	21	34	8	13	4	3	7	4

NATTINEN, Julius (na-TIH-nehn, YOO-lee-uhs) ANA

Center. Shoots left. 6'2", 191 lbs. Born, Jyvaskyla, Finland, January 14, 1997.
(Anaheim's 2nd pick, 59th overall, in 2015 NHL Draft).

			Regular Season					Playoffs				
Season	Club	League	GP	G	A	Pts	PIM	GP	G	A	Pts	PIM
2011-12	JyP Jyvaskyla U18	Fin-U18	9	3	2	5	2	....	....	....	....	....
2012-13	JyP Jyvaskyla U18	Fin-U18	20	16	11	27	8	....	....	....	....	....
	JyP Jyvaskyla Jr.	Fin-Jr.	24	5	10	15	6	5	1	0	1	2
2013-14	JyP Jyvaskyla U18	Fin-U18	4	1	7	8	2	....	....	....	....	....
	JyP Jyvaskyla Jr.	Fin-Jr.	32	5	22	27	14	....	....	....	....	....
	JYP Jyvaskyla	Finland	1	0	0	0	2	....	....	....	....	....
	JYP-Akatemia	Finland-2	5	0	0	0	0	....	....	....	....	....
2014-15	JYP Jyvaskyla	Finland	9	0	3	3	0	....	....	....	....	....
	JYP-Akatemia	Finland-2	39	11	18	29	8	6	0	0	0	2
2015-16	Barrie Colts	OHL	52	22	49	71	18	12	2	6	8	0
2016-17	Windsor Spitfires	OHL	51	13	25	38	16	7	1	3	4	4

NECAS, Martin (NEE-chas, MAHR-tihn) CAR

Center. Shoots right. 6'2", 179 lbs. Born, Nove Mesto na Morave, Cz. Rep., January 15, 1999.
(Carolina's 1st pick, 12th overall, in 2017 NHL Draft).

			Regular Season					Playoffs				
Season	Club	League	GP	G	A	Pts	PIM	GP	G	A	Pts	PIM
2014-15	Brno U18	CzR-U18	4	1	2	3	0	....	....	....	....	....
2015-16	Brno U18	CzR-U18	18	9	21	30	14	10	4	11	15	6
2016-17	Brno Jr.	CzRep-Jr.	1	1	2	3	4	....	....	....	....	....
	HC Kometa Brno	CzRep	41	7	8	15	6	10	4	0	4	8
	Trebic	CzRep-2	....	....	....	....	....	1	0	0	0	0

NEHRING, Chad (NAIR-ihng, CHAD)

Center. Shoots right. 5'11", 200 lbs. Born, Springside, SK, June 14, 1987.

			Regular Season					Playoffs				
Season	Club	League	GP	G	A	Pts	PIM	GP	G	A	Pts	PIM
2004-05	Yorkton Terriers	SJHL	45	6	5	11	61	....	....	....	....	....
2005-06	Yorkton Terriers	SJHL	55	28	29	57	102	....	....	....	....	....
2006-07	Yorkton Terriers	SJHL	51	25	36	61	61	....	....	....	....	....
2007-08	Lake Superior	CCHA	37	4	9	13	18	....	....	....	....	....
2008-09	Lake Superior	CCHA	37	6	5	11	20	....	....	....	....	....
2009-10	Lake Superior	CCHA	36	12	5	17	12	....	....	....	....	....
2010-11	Lake Superior	CCHA	37	8	4	12	18	....	....	....	....	....
	Idaho Steelheads	ECHL	5	1	2	3	0	10	3	4	7	2
2011-12	Idaho Steelheads	ECHL	59	17	15	32	52	10	3	4	7	2
2012-13	Arizona Sundogs	CHL	66	33	24	57	55	4	2	1	3	6
2013-14	Las Vegas	ECHL	49	22	20	42	59	4	0	2	2	4
2014-15	Greenville	ECHL	17	5	7	12	13	....	....	....	....	....
	Hartford Wolf Pack	AHL	53	4	8	12	50	15	2	1	3	4
2015-16	Hartford Wolf Pack	AHL	76	22	26	48	42	....	....	....	....	....
2016-17	Binghamton	AHL	50	5	13	18	16	....	....	....	....	....

Signed as a free agent by **Ottawa**, July 1, 2016.

NIELSEN, Andrew (NEEL-sehn, an-DROO) TOR

Defense. Shoots right. 6'3", 220 lbs. Born, Red Deer, AB, November 13, 1996.
(Toronto's 4th pick, 65th overall, in 2015 NHL Draft).

			Regular Season					Playoffs				
Season	Club	League	GP	G	A	Pts	PIM	GP	G	A	Pts	PIM
2012-13	Red Deer Elks	Minor-AB	33	8	17	25	124	5	0	4	4	16
2013-14	Red Deer Chiefs	AMHL	35	3	15	18	34	11	0	5	5	8
	Lethbridge	WHL	1	0	0	0	0	....	....	....	....	....
2014-15	Lethbridge	WHL	59	7	17	24	101	....	....	....	....	....
2015-16	Lethbridge	WHL	71	18	52	70	122	5	1	2	3	6
	Toronto Marlies	AHL	5	0	2	2	0	....	....	....	....	....
2016-17	Toronto Marlies	AHL	74	14	25	39	82	11	1	3	4	24

WHL East First All-Star Team (2016)

NIEMELAINEN, Markus (nee-meh-LIGH-nehn, MAHR-kuhs) EDM

Defense. Shoots left. 6'6", 205 lbs. Born, Kuopio, Finland, June 8, 1998.
(Edmonton's 3rd pick, 63rd overall, in 2016 NHL Draft).

			Regular Season					Playoffs				
Season	Club	League	GP	G	A	Pts	PIM	GP	G	A	Pts	PIM
2012-13	HPK U18	Fin-U18	....	....	....	....	....	3	0	1	1	2
2013-14	Tappara U18	Fin-U18	40	3	11	14	14	3	0	0	0	0
2014-15	HPK U18	Fin-U18	4	0	2	2	0	....	....	....	....	....
	HPK Jr.	Fin-Jr.	39	2	14	16	28	12	0	5	5	4
2015-16	Saginaw Spirit	OHL	65	1	26	27	28	4	0	0	0	0
2016-17	Saginaw Spirit	OHL	59	3	6	9	40	....	....	....	....	....

NIKU, Sami (NEE-koo, SA-mee) WPG

Defense. Shoots left. 6'1", 194 lbs. Born, Haapavesi, Finland, October 10, 1996.
(Winnipeg's 7th pick, 198th overall, in 2015 NHL Draft).

			Regular Season					Playoffs				
Season	Club	League	GP	G	A	Pts	PIM	GP	G	A	Pts	PIM
2011-12	JyP Jyvaskyla U18	Fin-U18	17	1	1	2	0	....	....	....	....	....
2012-13	JyP Jyvaskyla U18	Fin-U18	3	2	1	3	0	....	....	....	....	....
	JyP Jyvaskyla Jr.	Fin-Jr.	30	0	8	8	22	6	0	0	0	2
2013-14	JyP Jyvaskyla U18	Fin-U18	1	0	3	3	0	....	....	....	....	....
	JyP Jyvaskyla Jr.	Fin-Jr.	20	4	10	14	20	....	....	....	....	....
	JYP-Akatemia	Finland-2	30	0	3	3	16	....	....	....	....	....
2014-15	JYP Jyvaskyla	Finland	12	0	1	1	6	....	....	....	....	....
	JYP-Akatemia	Finland-2	39	3	22	25	24	6	0	5	5	4
2015-16	JYP-Akatemia	Finland-2	7	0	2	2	4	....	....	....	....	....
	JYP Jyvaskyla	Finland	38	4	7	11	2	....	....	....	....	....
2016-17	JYP Jyvaskyla	Finland	59	5	22	27	26	15	1	5	6	2

NOEL, David (NOH-ehl, DAY-vihd) ST.L.

Defense. Shoots left. 6'1", 175 lbs. Born, Quebec City, QC, October 4, 1999.
(St. Louis' 4th pick, 130th overall, in 2017 NHL Draft).

			Regular Season					Playoffs				
Season	Club	League	GP	G	A	Pts	PIM	GP	G	A	Pts	PIM
2014-15	Sem. St-Francois	QAAA	42	3	7	10	20	....	....	....	....	....
2015-16	Sem. St-Francois	QAAA	45	18	16	34	10	5	0	0	0	2
	Chicoutimi	QMJHL	2	0	0	0	0	....	....	....	....	....
2016-17	Chicoutimi	QMJHL	36	3	11	14	23	....	....	....	....	....
	Val-d'Or Foreurs	QMJHL	29	8	10	18	6	10	2	6	8	2

NOEL, Nathan (noh-EHL, NAY-thuhn) CHI

Center. Shoots right. 5'10", 179 lbs. Born, St. John's, NL, June 21, 1997.
(Chicago's 6th pick, 113th overall, in 2016 NHL Draft).

			Regular Season					Playoffs				
Season	Club	League	GP	G	A	Pts	PIM	GP	G	A	Pts	PIM
2011-12	Shattuck Bantam	High-MN	56	45	59	104	44	....	....	....	....	....
2012-13	Shattuck	High-MN	52	10	30	40	41	....	....	....	....	....
2013-14	Saint John	QMJHL	63	16	23	39	31	....	....	....	....	....
2014-15	Saint John	QMJHL	66	24	38	62	61	5	5	2	7	6
2015-16	Saint John	QMJHL	61	21	36	57	94	16	3	10	13	30
2016-17	Saint John	QMJHL	52	24	26	50	82	18	2	7	9	*31

NORELL, Robin (NOH-REHL, RAW-bihn) CHI

Defense. Shoots left. 6'3", 205 lbs. Born, Stockholm, Sweden, February 18, 1995.
(Chicago's 4th pick, 111th overall, in 2013 NHL Draft).

			Regular Season					Playoffs				
Season	Club	League	GP	G	A	Pts	PIM	GP	G	A	Pts	PIM
2010-11	Djurgarden U18	Swe-U18	4	0	0	0	0	....	....	....	....	....
2011-12	Djurgarden U18	Swe-U18	37	2	9	11	24	4	0	0	0	2
	Djurgarden Jr.	Swe-Jr.	....	....	....	....	....	1	0	0	0	0
2012-13	Djurgarden U18	Swe-U18	30	10	7	17	16	9	2	1	3	6
	Djurgarden Jr.	Swe-Jr.	33	1	4	5	4	2	0	0	0	2
2013-14	Djurgarden Jr.	Swe-Jr.	1	0	0	0	0	....	....	....	....	....
	Djurgarden	Sweden-2	32	0	6	6	10	....	....	....	....	....
2014-15	Djurgarden	Sweden	48	3	6	9	12	2	0	0	0	0
	Rockford IceHogs	AHL	....	....	....	....	....	3	0	0	0	2
2015-16	Djurgarden	Sweden	51	2	6	8	16	7	0	0	0	2
	Rockford IceHogs	AHL	8	0	2	2	2	2	0	0	0	2
2016-17	Rockford IceHogs	AHL	65	1	8	9	18	....	....	....	....	....

NORRIS, Joshua (NOHR-ihs, JAW-shoo-wuh) S.J.

Center. Shoots left. 6'1", 190 lbs. Born, Oxford, MI, May 5, 1999.
(San Jose's 1st pick, 19th overall, in 2017 NHL Draft).

			Regular Season					Playoffs				
Season	Club	League	GP	G	A	Pts	PIM	GP	G	A	Pts	PIM
2014-15	Oak. Grizzlies U16	T1EHL	7	3	5	8	2	2	0	0	0	0
	Oak. Grizzlies U16	Minor-MI	12	7	13	20	12	....	....	....	....	....
2015-16	USAHNTDP	USHL	24	2	5	7	16	....	....	....	....	....
	USAHNTDP	U-17	20	12	8	20	18	....	....	....	....	....
2016-17	USAHNTDP	USHL	25	12	14	26	18	....	....	....	....	....
	USAHNTDP	U-18	36	12	16	28	12	....	....	....	....	....

• Signed Letter of Intent to attend **University of Michigan** (Big Ten) in fall of 2017.

NOVAK, Thomas (NOH-vak, TAW-muhs) NSH

Center. Shoots left. 6'1", 179 lbs. Born, St. Paul, MN, April 28, 1997.
(Nashville's 2nd pick, 85th overall, in 2015 NHL Draft).

			Regular Season					Playoffs				
Season	Club	League	GP	G	A	Pts	PIM	GP	G	A	Pts	PIM
2011-12	St. Thomas Acad.	High-MN	25	14	20	34	0	6	4	5	9	2
2012-13	St. Thomas Acad.	High-MN	25	25	22	47	6	6	3	7	10	0
2013-14	Team Southeast	UMHSEL	19	11	22	33	8	3	0	2	2	0
	St. Thomas Acad.	High-MN	25	26	44	70	8	3	4	4	8	2
	USAHNTDP	USHL	2	0	0	0	0	....	....	....	....	....
2014-15	Waterloo	USHL	46	14	34	48	12	....	....	....	....	....
2015-16	U. of Minnesota	Big Ten	37	6	21	27	4	....	....	....	....	....
2016-17	U. of Minnesota	Big Ten	20	5	9	14	10	....	....	....	....	....

NURMI, Markus (NUHR-mee, MAHR-kuhs) OTT

Right wing. Shoots right. 6'5", 180 lbs. Born, Turku, Finland, June 29, 1998.
(Ottawa's 5th pick, 163rd overall, in 2016 NHL Draft).

			Regular Season					Playoffs				
Season	Club	League	GP	G	A	Pts	PIM	GP	G	A	Pts	PIM
2012-13	TPS Turku U18	Fin-U18	9	5	4	9	4	3	0	0	0	2
2013-14	TPS Turku U18	Fin-U18	44	13	11	24	26	....	....	....	....	....
	TPS Turku Jr.	Fin-Jr.	1	0	0	0	0	....	....	....	....	....
2014-15	TPS Turku U18	Fin-U18	9	6	7	13	4	....	....	....	....	....
	TPS Turku Jr.	Fin-Jr.	20	2	4	6	12	....	....	....	....	....
2015-16	TPS Turku Jr.	Fin-Jr.	49	19	17	36	34	2	0	0	0	2
	TPS Turku	Finland	2	0	0	0	0	....	....	....	....	....
	TPS Turku U18	Fin-U18	....	....	....	....	....	3	2	0	2	0
2016-17	TPS Turku Jr.	Fin-Jr.	27	12	16	28	58	1	1	0	1	2
	TPS Turku	Finland	5	0	0	0	2	....	....	....	....	....
	TuTo Turku	Finland-2	11	2	0	2	2	6	0	1	1	4

NYBERG, John (NIGH-buhrg, JAWN) DAL

Defense. Shoots left. 6'2", 190 lbs. Born, Harryda, Sweden, July 14, 1996.
(Dallas' 8th pick, 165th overall, in 2014 NHL Draft).

			Regular Season					Playoffs				
Season	Club	League	GP	G	A	Pts	PIM	GP	G	A	Pts	PIM
2011-12	Frolunda U18	Swe-U18	12	0	0	0	0	....	....	....	....	....
2012-13	Frolunda U18	Swe-U18	40	4	10	14	36	3	0	0	0	2
2013-14	Frolunda U18	Swe-U18	33	11	27	38	22	5	2	0	2	12
	Frolunda Jr.	Swe-Jr.	19	1	3	4	0	....	....	....	....	....
2014-15	Mora IK	Sweden-2	4	0	0	0	0	....	....	....	....	....
	IK Oskarshamn	Sweden-2	9	0	1	1	2	....	....	....	....	....
	Frolunda Jr.	Swe-Jr.	25	7	10	17	26	8	1	1	2	16
	Frolunda	Sweden	17	0	1	1	2	....	....	....	....	....
2015-16	Frolunda Jr.	Swe-Jr.	3	1	2	3	0	3	0	3	3	6
	Frolunda	Sweden	6	0	0	0	2	....	....	....	....	....
	IK Oskarshamn	Sweden-2	51	1	8	9	36	....	....	....	....	....
2016-17	Frolunda	Sweden	49	7	8	15	32	14	1	0	1	10

NYBERG, Philip (NIGH-buhrg, FIHL-ihp) BUF

Defense. Shoots right. 6'4", 189 lbs. Born, Karlskrona, Sweden, April 27, 1997.
(Buffalo's 6th pick, 129th overall, in 2016 NHL Draft).

			Regular Season					Playoffs				
Season	Club	League	GP	G	A	Pts	PIM	GP	G	A	Pts	PIM
2012-13	Linkopings HC U18	Swe-U18	4	0	0	0	2	....	....	....	....	....
2013-14	Linkopings HC U18	Swe-U18	33	4	9	13	28	5	0	0	0	0
	Linkopings HC Jr.	Swe-Jr.	1	0	0	0	0	....	....	....	....	....
2014-15	Linkopings HC U18	Swe-U18	29	3	11	14	24	5	1	1	2	4
	Linkopings HC Jr.	Swe-Jr.	3	0	0	0	2	2	0	0	0	0
2015-16	Linkopings HC Jr.	Swe-Jr.	45	4	14	18	51	4	1	0	1	2
2016-17	U. of Connecticut	H-East	16	1	5	6	14	....	....	....	....	....

NYGREN, Magnus (NEW-grihn, MAG-nuhs) MTL

Defense. Shoots right. 6'1", 193 lbs. Born, Karlstad, Sweden, June 7, 1990.
(Montreal's 3rd pick, 113th overall, in 2011 NHL Draft).

			Regular Season					Playoffs				
Season	Club	League	GP	G	A	Pts	PIM	GP	G	A	Pts	PIM
2006-07	Farjestad U18	Swe-U18	7	0	4	4	4	8	1	2	3	6
2007-08	Farjestad U18	Swe-U18	31	9	19	28	61	8	2	6	8	12
2008-09	Skare Jr.	Swe-Jr.	2	2	3	5	0	....	....	....	....	....
	Skare BK Karlstad	Sweden-3	41	7	21	28	32	3	1	0	1	2
2009-10	Skare BK	Sweden-3	24	9	18	27	10	....	....	....	....	....
	Farjestad	Sweden	9	0	0	0	4	....	....	....	....	....
	Mora IK	Sweden-2	21	2	5	7	10	2	0	1	1	2
2010-11	Bofors	Sweden-2	35	5	6	11	10	....	....	....	....	....
	Farjestad	Sweden	22	4	11	15	4	14	3	7	10	6
2011-12	Farjestad Jr.	Swe-Jr.	1	1	0	1	2	....	....	....	....	....
	Bofors	Sweden-2	3	1	1	2	4	....	....	....	....	....
	Farjestad	Sweden	50	7	11	18	6	10	2	0	2	0
2012-13	Farjestad	Sweden	51	13	19	32	49	10	1	3	4	10
2013-14	Hamilton Bulldogs	AHL	16	1	7	8	14	....	....	....	....	....
	Farjestad	Sweden	25	12	8	20	8	15	2	3	5	6
2014-15	Hamilton Bulldogs	AHL	15	4	6	10	2	....	....	....	....	....
2015-16	Farjestad	Sweden	47	8	18	26	24	5	1	1	2	4
2016-17	Farjestad	Sweden	49	11	20	31	26	7	2	3	5	2

• Missed majority of 2014-15 due to head injury vs. Lake Erie (AHL), November 29, 2014. Signed as a free agent by **Farjestad** (Sweden), May 8, 2015.

O'BRIEN, Andrew (oh-BRIGH-uhn, an-DROO) NSH

Defense. Shoots left. 6'4", 208 lbs. Born, Hamilton, ON, November 21, 1992.
(Anaheim's 5th pick, 108th overall, in 2012 NHL Draft).

			Regular Season					Playoffs				
Season	Club	League	GP	G	A	Pts	PIM	GP	G	A	Pts	PIM
2008-09	Humber Valley	Minor-ON	STATISTICS NOT AVAILABLE									
	Milton Icehawks	ON-Jr.A	2	0	0	0	0	....	....	....	....	....
2009-10	Dixie Beehives	ON-Jr.A	44	3	4	7	45	....	....	....	....	....
2010-11	Chicoutimi	QMJHL	55	1	9	10	33	4	1	1	2	6
2011-12	Chicoutimi	QMJHL	68	8	21	29	95	18	1	9	10	31
2012-13	Rouyn-Noranda	QMJHL	67	2	16	18	113	14	0	4	4	22
2013-14	Norfolk Admirals	AHL	4	0	0	0	4	....	....	....	....	....
	Utah Grizzlies	ECHL	24	2	3	5	70	3	0	0	0	0
2014-15	Norfolk Admirals	AHL	62	4	10	14	118	....	....	....	....	....
2015-16	San Diego Gulls	AHL	59	6	8	14	54	2	0	0	0	0
	Utah Grizzlies	ECHL	1	1	0	1	2	....	....	....	....	....
2016-17	San Diego Gulls	AHL	10	0	2	2	4	....	....	....	....	....
	Milwaukee	AHL	32	2	8	10	36	1	0	0	0	0

Traded to **Nashville** by **Anaheim** for Max Gortz, January 19, 2017.

O'CONNELL, Ryan (OH-CAW-nuhl, RIGH-uhn) TOR

Defense. Shoots left. 6'1", 170 lbs. Born, Ottawa, ON, April 25, 1999.
(Toronto's 7th pick, 203rd overall, in 2017 NHL Draft).

			Regular Season					Playoffs				
Season	Club	League	GP	G	A	Pts	PIM	GP	G	A	Pts	PIM
2014-15	Ott. Jr. 67's MM	Minor-ON	21	2	16	18	8	10	2	6	8	0
2015-16	St. Andrew's	CISAA	14	1	7	8	4	4	0	3	3	0
	St. Andrew's	High-ON	55	4	27	31	14	....	....	....	....	....
2016-17	St. Andrew's	CISAA	7	0	4	4	5	5	1	4	5	2
	St. Andrew's	High-ON	47	6	27	33	18	....	....	....	....	....

• Signed Letter of Intent to attend **Boston University** (Hockey East) in fall of 2018.

OLHAVER, Gustav (OH-luh-vuhr, GUHS-tav) COL

Center. Shoots left. 6'6", 225 lbs. Born, Angelholm, Sweden, July 3, 1997.
(Colorado's 7th pick, 191st overall, in 2015 NHL Draft).

			Regular Season					Playoffs				
Season	Club	League	GP	G	A	Pts	PIM	GP	G	A	Pts	PIM
2012-13	Rogle U18	Swe-U18	4	0	1	1	0	....	....	....	....	....
2013-14	Rogle U18	Swe-U18	37	19	8	27	16	....	....	....	....	....
	Rogle Jr.	Swe-Jr.	5	1	0	1	2	....	....	....	....	....
2014-15	Rogle U18	Swe-U18	18	14	11	25	8	....	....	....	....	....
	Rogle Jr.	Swe-Jr.	41	6	6	12	10	6	0	0	0	2
2015-16	Seattle	WHL	31	2	3	5	17	....	....	....	....	....
	Swift Current	WHL	20	1	2	3	2	....	....	....	....	....
2016-17	Rogle Jr.	Swe-Jr.	36	15	23	38	41	3	1	0	1	0
	Rogle	Sweden	10	0	1	1	0	....	....	....	....	....
	Helsingborgs HC	Sweden-2	1	0	0	0	0	....	....	....	....	....

OLLAS MATTSSON, Adam (OH-luhs MAT-suhn, A-duhm) CGY

Defense. Shoots left. 6'5", 216 lbs. Born, Stockholm, Sweden, July 30, 1996.
(Calgary's 5th pick, 175th overall, in 2014 NHL Draft).

			Regular Season					Playoffs				
Season	Club	League	GP	G	A	Pts	PIM	GP	G	A	Pts	PIM
2010-11	Varmdo Jr.	Swe-Jr.	1	0	0	0	0	....	....	....	....	....
2011-12	Djurgarden U18	Swe-U18	1	0	0	0	0	....	....	....	....	....
2012-13	Djurgarden U18	Swe-U18	32	0	8	8	44	8	0	1	1	6
2013-14	Djurgarden U18	Swe-U18	3	0	1	1	0	3	1	0	1	2
	Djurgarden	Sweden-2	6	0	2	2	4	....	....	....	....	....
	Djurgarden Jr.	Swe-Jr.	33	1	8	9	42	4	0	2	2	2
2014-15	Djurgarden Jr.	Swe-Jr.	19	1	6	7	42	7	0	2	2	29
	Djurgarden	Sweden	34	0	2	2	4	1	0	0	0	0
2015-16	Djurgarden	Sweden	22	1	3	4	2	1	0	0	0	0
	Djurgarden Jr.	Swe-Jr.	....	....	....	....	....	3	0	3	3	0
2016-17	Djurgarden	Sweden	52	1	3	4	29	3	0	0	0	0
	Stockton Heat	AHL	9	1	1	2	6	....	....	....	....	....

OLOFSSON, Fredrik (OH-lawf-suhn, FREHD-rihk) CHI

Left wing. Shoots left. 6'2", 200 lbs. Born, Helsingborg, Sweden, May 27, 1996.
(Chicago's 4th pick, 98th overall, in 2014 NHL Draft).

			Regular Season					Playoffs				
Season	Club	League	GP	G	A	Pts	PIM	GP	G	A	Pts	PIM
2011-12	Col. T-birds Ban.	T1EHL	56	28	37	65	26	....	....	....	....	....
	Col. T-birds U16	T1EHL	4	2	1	3	4	....	....	....	....	....
2012-13	Col. T-birds U16	T1EHL	31	26	43	69	8	4	1	4	5	2
	Green Bay	USHL	8	0	0	0	0	....	....	....	....	....
2013-14	Green Bay	USHL	28	2	4	6	21	....	....	....	....	....
	Chicago Steel	USHL	24	4	11	15	24	....	....	....	....	....
2014-15	Chicago Steel	USHL	57	27	33	60	14	....	....	....	....	....
2015-16	Nebraska-Omaha	NCHC	34	8	9	17	14	....	....	....	....	....
2016-17	Nebraska-Omaha	NCHC	34	11	13	24	21	....	....	....	....	....

OLOFSSON, Victor (OH-lawf-suhn, VIHK-tuhr) BUF

Right wing. Shoots left. 5'11", 179 lbs. Born, Ornskoldsvik, Sweden, July 18, 1995.
(Buffalo's 9th pick, 181st overall, in 2014 NHL Draft).

			Regular Season					Playoffs				
Season	Club	League	GP	G	A	Pts	PIM	GP	G	A	Pts	PIM
2010-11	MODO U18	Swe-U18	3	1	0	1	0	....	....	....	....	....
2011-12	MODO U18	Swe-U18	39	19	15	34	4	2	1	0	1	0
2012-13	MODO U18	Swe-U18	37	31	24	55	6	4	1	2	3	0
	MODO Jr.	Swe-Jr.	7	2	3	5	0	6	0	1	1	0
2013-14	MODO Jr.	Swe-Jr.	44	32	21	53	16	5	4	5	9	2
	MODO	Sweden	11	0	0	0	0	....	....	....	....	....
2014-15	MODO Jr.	Swe-Jr.	6	1	3	4	0	5	3	5	8	0
	MODO	Sweden	39	10	8	18	4	....	....	....	....	....
	Timra IK	Sweden-2	8	2	0	2	0	....	....	....	....	....
2015-16	MODO	Sweden	49	14	15	29	6	....	....	....	....	....
	MODO	Sweden-Q	....	....	....	....	....	7	6	2	8	2
2016-17	Frolunda	Sweden	51	9	18	27	2	14	4	8	12	0

OLSEN, Ryan (OHL-suhn, RIGH-uhn)

Center. Shoots right. 6'1", 187 lbs. Born, Delta, BC, March 25, 1994.
(Winnipeg's 5th pick, 160th overall, in 2012 NHL Draft).

			Regular Season					Playoffs				
Season	Club	League	GP	G	A	Pts	PIM	GP	G	A	Pts	PIM
2008-09	South Delta Storm	Minor-BC	60	65	67	132		....	....	....	....	....
2009-10	Greater Van.	BCMML	38	24	23	47	32	5	2	1	3	20
	Saskatoon Blades	WHL	5	0	0	0	2	....	....	....	....	....
2010-11	Saskatoon Blades	WHL	63	7	7	14	39	3	0	0	0	4
2011-12	Saskatoon Blades	WHL	67	15	17	32	64	4	0	0	0	4
2012-13	Kelowna Rockets	WHL	69	32	24	56	87	11	1	5	6	14
2013-14	Kelowna Rockets	WHL	71	30	34	64	73	14	4	3	7	8
2014-15	St. John's IceCaps	AHL	60	4	5	9	47	....	....	....	....	....
2015-16	Manitoba Moose	AHL	65	6	7	13	90	....	....	....	....	....
2016-17	Manitoba Moose	AHL	56	7	4	11	54	....	....	....	....	....
	Tulsa Oilers	ECHL	3	0	1	1	0	....	....	....	....	....

OLSON, Kyle (OHL-suhn, KIGHL) ANA

Right wing. Shoots right. 5'11", 161 lbs. Born, Calgary, AB, March 22, 1999.
(Anaheim's 4th pick, 122nd overall, in 2017 NHL Draft).

			Regular Season					Playoffs				
Season	Club	League	GP	G	A	Pts	PIM	GP	G	A	Pts	PIM
2014-15	Calgary Buffaloes	AMHL	32	16	20	36	79	4	0	1	1	8
	Okotoks Oilers	AJHL	3	1	2	3	2	1	0	0	0	0
2015-16	Tri-City Americans	WHL	19	3	7	10	20	....	....	....	....	....
2016-17	Tri-City Americans	WHL	72	20	37	57	52	4	1	0	1	4

OLUND, Linus (OH-luhnd, LEE-nuhs) **PIT**

Center. Shoots left. 5'11", 185 lbs. Born, Gavle, Sweden, May 6, 1997.
(Pittsburgh's 4th pick, 155th overall, in 2017 NHL Draft).

			Regular Season					Playoffs				
Season	Club	League	GP	G	A	Pts	PIM	GP	G	A	Pts	PIM
2012-13	Brynas U18	Swe-U18	19	2	2	4	2	....	....	....	....	....
2013-14	Brynas U18	Swe-U18	36	30	30	60	20	5	2	1	3	2
	Brynas IF Gavle Jr.	Swe-Jr.	10	1	3	4	2	....	....	....	....	....
2014-15	Brynas U18	Swe-U18	10	7	6	13	4	4	3	2	5	0
	Brynas IF Gavle Jr.	Swe-Jr.	41	15	11	26	10	2	1	1	2	0
	Brynas IF Gavle	Sweden	3	0	0	0	0	....	....	....	....	....
2015-16	Brynas IF Gavle Jr.	Swe-Jr.	27	18	16	34	4	4	1	3	4	2
	Brynas IF Gavle	Sweden	23	0	1	1	0	1	0	0	0	0
2016-17	Brynas IF Gavle Jr.	Swe-Jr.	12	8	9	17	12	....	....	....	....	....
	Brynas IF Gavle	Sweden	39	8	7	15	2	20	6	4	10	2
	AIK Solna	Sweden-2	2	0	0	0	0	....	....	....	....	....

O'NEILL, Will (oh-NEEL, WIHL) **PHI**

Defense. Shoots left. 6'1", 190 lbs. Born, Boston, MA, April 28, 1988.
(Atlanta's 8th pick, 210th overall, in 2006 NHL Draft).

			Regular Season					Playoffs				
Season	Club	League	GP	G	A	Pts	PIM	GP	G	A	Pts	PIM
2004-05	Tabor	High-MA		1	16	17	....	....	....	....	....	....
2005-06	Tabor	High-MA	28	5	25	30	38	....	....	....	....	....
2006-07	Omaha Lancers	USHL	57	4	9	13	73	5	0	0	0	8
2007-08	Omaha Lancers	USHL	58	5	19	24	95	14	1	6	7	38
2008-09	U. of Maine	H-East	34	4	12	16	82	....	....	....	....	....
2009-10	U. of Maine	H-East	39	8	23	31	69	....	....	....	....	....
2010-11	U. of Maine	H-East	28	4	17	21	44	....	....	....	....	....
2011-12	U. of Maine	H-East	40	3	30	33	68	....	....	....	....	....
	St. John's IceCaps	AHL	7	1	2	3	9	....	....	....	....	....
2012-13	St. John's IceCaps	AHL	59	3	18	21	32	....	....	....	....	....
2013-14	St. John's IceCaps	AHL	68	9	26	35	80	18	3	*13	16	27
2014-15	St. John's IceCaps	AHL	72	10	38	48	74	....	....	....	....	....
2015-16	Wilkes-Barre	AHL	74	8	42	50	78	9	1	3	4	12
2016-17	Lehigh Valley	AHL	57	3	28	31	44	....	....	....	....	....

AHL Second All-Star Team (2016)

• Transferred to **Winnipeg** after **Atlanta** franchise relocated, June 21, 2011. Signed as a free agent by **Pittsburgh**, July 2, 2015. Signed as a free agent by **Philadelphia**, July 1, 2016.

OSMANSKI, Austin (ohz-MAN-skee, AW-stuhn) **BUF**

Defense. Shoots left. 6'4", 202 lbs. Born, East Aurora, NY, April 30, 1998.
(Buffalo's 9th pick, 189th overall, in 2016 NHL Draft).

			Regular Season					Playoffs				
Season	Club	League	GP	G	A	Pts	PIM	GP	G	A	Pts	PIM
2013-14	Buffalo Regals	Minor-ON	40	2	12	14	38	4	0	0	0	4
2014-15	Buf. Jr. Sabres U16	T1EHL	23	5	2	7	59	4	0	1	1	0
	Buf. Jr. Sabres U18	T1EHL	6	0	4	4	4	....	....	....	....	....
2015-16	Mississauga	OHL	65	2	8	10	53	7	0	1	1	8
2016-17	Mississauga	OHL	55	2	6	8	74	20	0	0	0	20

PAIGIN, Ziyat (pigh-GEEN, zee-YAT) **EDM**

Defense. Shoots left. 6'6", 209 lbs. Born, Penza, Russia, February 8, 1995.
(Edmonton's 6th pick, 209th overall, in 2015 NHL Draft).

			Regular Season					Playoffs				
Season	Club	League	GP	G	A	Pts	PIM	GP	G	A	Pts	PIM
2011-12	Irbis Kazan Jr.	Rus.-Jr. B	35	6	12	18	38	4	0	0	0	0
2012-13	Bars Kazan Jr.	Russia-Jr.	46	3	9	12	16	4	0	0	0	2
	Irbis Kazan Jr.	Rus.-Jr. B	8	1	1	2	6	....	....	....	....	....
2013-14	Bars Kazan Jr.	Russia-Jr.	47	3	8	11	14	12	0	1	1	2
2014-15	Bars Kazan	Russia-2	3	0	1	1	4	....	....	....	....	....
	Ak Bars Kazan	KHL	33	1	1	2	2	2	0	0	0	0
2015-16	Bars Kazan	Russia-2	10	1	4	5	2	....	....	....	....	....
	Ak Bars Kazan	KHL	8	0	1	1	2	....	....	....	....	....
	HK Sochi	KHL	37	9	18	27	8	4	0	0	0	2
2016-17	Ak Bars Kazan	KHL	17	1	3	4	4	....	....	....	....	....
	Bars Kazan	Russia-2	17	5	2	7	24	....	....	....	....	....
	Bakersfield	AHL	5	0	0	0	2	....	....	....	....	....

PALMQUIST, Zach (PAHM-kwihst, ZAK) **MIN**

Defense. Shoots left. 6', 187 lbs. Born, South St. Paul, MN, December 9, 1990.

			Regular Season					Playoffs				
Season	Club	League	GP	G	A	Pts	PIM	GP	G	A	Pts	PIM
2008-09	South St. Paul	High-MN	25	14	24	38	32	....	....	....	....	....
	Waterloo	USHL	12	0	3	3	18	2	0	0	0	2
2009-10	Waterloo	USHL	53	9	27	36	60	3	0	0	0	0
2010-11	Waterloo	USHL	59	4	14	18	67	2	0	1	1	0
2011-12	Minnesota State	WCHA	38	6	13	19	31	....	....	....	....	....
2012-13	Minnesota State	WCHA	41	7	18	25	20	....	....	....	....	....
2013-14	Minnesota State	WCHA	41	4	19	23	36	....	....	....	....	....
2014-15	Minnesota State	WCHA	40	8	21	29	20	....	....	....	....	....
	Iowa Wild	AHL	8	0	3	3	4	....	....	....	....	....
2015-16	Iowa Wild	AHL	69	4	7	11	26	....	....	....	....	....
2016-17	Iowa Wild	AHL	72	2	19	21	20	....	....	....	....	....

WCHA First All-Star Team (2014, 2015) • NCAA West Second All-American Team (2015)

Signed as a free agent by **Minnesota**, March 30, 2015.

PALMU, Petrus (PAHL-ih-moo, PAY-truhs) **VAN**

Right wing. Shoots left. 5'6", 175 lbs. Born, Joensuu, Finland, July 16, 1997.
(Vancouver's 7th pick, 181st overall, in 2017 NHL Draft).

			Regular Season					Playoffs				
Season	Club	League	GP	G	A	Pts	PIM	GP	G	A	Pts	PIM
2011-12	Jokipojat U18	Fin-U18	6	4	4	8	0	....	....	....	....	....
2012-13	Jokerit U18	Fin-U18	27	9	10	19	32	....	....	....	....	....
2013-14	Jokerit U18	Fin-U18	31	25	29	54	28	12	7	5	12	4
	Jokerit Helsinki Jr.	Fin-Jr.	10	1	2	3	6	....	....	....	....	....
2014-15	Owen Sound	OHL	62	22	20	42	20	5	1	0	1	0
2015-16	Owen Sound	OHL	52	23	26	49	30	6	3	3	6	8
2016-17	Owen Sound	OHL	62	40	58	98	34	17	13	8	21	6

OHL Second All-Star Team (2017)

PALOJARVI, Antti (pah-LOH-YAHR-vee, AN-tee) **PIT**

Defense. Shoots left. 6'1", 176 lbs. Born, Kouvola, Finland, January 18, 1999.
(Pittsburgh's 5th pick, 186th overall, in 2017 NHL Draft).

			Regular Season					Playoffs				
Season	Club	League	GP	G	A	Pts	PIM	GP	G	A	Pts	PIM
2013-14	KooKoo U18	Fin-U18	1	0	0	0	2	....	....	....	....	....
2014-15	KooKoo U18	Fin-U18	42	3	7	10	32	....	....	....	....	....
2015-16	KooKoo U18	Fin-U18	45	10	16	26	102	....	....	....	....	....
	KooKoo Jr.	Fin-Jr.	1	0	0	0	0	....	....	....	....	....
2016-17	Lukko Rauma U18	Fin-U18	5	0	3	3	0	....	....	....	....	....
	KeuPa HT Keuruu	Finland-2	1	0	0	0	0	....	....	....	....	....
	Lukko Rauma Jr.	Fin-Jr.	47	1	10	11	14	8	1	1	2	0

PAQUETTE, Chris (pah-KEHT, KRIHS) **T.B.**

Center. Shoots right. 6'1", 207 lbs. Born, Victoria, BC, March 27, 1998.
(Tampa Bay's 7th pick, 148th overall, in 2016 NHL Draft).

			Regular Season					Playoffs				
Season	Club	League	GP	G	A	Pts	PIM	GP	G	A	Pts	PIM
2013-14	Kingston Front.	Minor-ON	36	23	29	52	14	3	0	2	2	0
2014-15	Niagara Ice Dogs	OHL	54	7	7	14	10	10	0	2	2	0
2015-16	Niagara Ice Dogs	OHL	57	5	11	16	18	15	2	2	4	2
2016-17	Niagara Ice Dogs	OHL	37	12	17	29	14	....	....	....	....	....
	Peterborough	OHL	29	7	12	19	14	12	3	3	6	15

PAQUETTE, Jacob (pah-KEHT, JAY-kuhb) **NSH**

Defense. Shoots left. 6'3", 204 lbs. Born, Ottawa, ON, May 26, 1999.
(Nashville's 6th pick, 216th overall, in 2017 NHL Draft).

			Regular Season					Playoffs				
Season	Club	League	GP	G	A	Pts	PIM	GP	G	A	Pts	PIM
2014-15	Ott. Jr. 67's MM	Minor-ON	26	5	7	12	38	9	3	2	5	6
2015-16	Kingston	OHL	56	3	10	13	24	9	0	2	2	4
2016-17	Kingston	OHL	59	1	9	10	36	11	0	3	3	11

PARE, Cedric (pah-RAY, SEH-drihk) **BOS**

Center. Shoots left. 6'3", 215 lbs. Born, Levis, QC, January 24, 1999.
(Boston's 4th pick, 173rd overall, in 2017 NHL Draft).

			Regular Season					Playoffs				
Season	Club	League	GP	G	A	Pts	PIM	GP	G	A	Pts	PIM
2014-15	Levis	QAAA	41	6	7	13	14	10	0	3	3	12
2015-16	Levis	QAAA	43	16	28	44	52	3	0	0	0	8
	Saint John	QMJHL	5	0	1	1	2	3	0	0	0	0
2016-17	Saint John	QMJHL	64	5	11	16	26	18	1	2	3	0

PARISI, Tom (pah-REE-see, TAWM) **MTL**

Defense. Shoots left. 5'11", 185 lbs. Born, Commack, NY, July 15, 1993.

			Regular Season					Playoffs				
Season	Club	League	GP	G	A	Pts	PIM	GP	G	A	Pts	PIM
2008-09	Long Island Gulls	AYHL	20	3	7	10	14	....	....	....	....	....
2009-10	New York Bobcats	AtJHL	38	5	18	23	38	3	0	2	2	2
2010-11	New York Bobcats	AtJHL	37	7	21	28	45	3	3	2	5	2
2011-12	N.H. Jr. Monarchs	EJHL	37	12	19	31	30	7	0	2	2	6
	USAHNTDP	USHL	4	0	0	0	0	....	....	....	....	....
	USAHNTDP	U-18	2	0	0	0	2	....	....	....	....	....
2012-13	Providence College	H-East	31	5	4	9	16	....	....	....	....	....
2013-14	Providence College	H-East	36	1	10	11	28	....	....	....	....	....
2014-15	Providence College	H-East	39	5	14	19	28	....	....	....	....	....
2015-16	Providence College	H-East	38	1	15	16	24	....	....	....	....	....
	St. John's IceCaps	AHL	5	0	1	1	4	....	....	....	....	....
2016-17	St. John's IceCaps	AHL	45	1	8	9	10	....	....	....	....	....

Signed as a free agent by **Montreal**, March 26, 2016.

PASHNIN, Mikhail (pahsh-NIHN, mih-KHIGH-eel) **NYR**

Defense. Shoots left. 6'1", 191 lbs. Born, Chelyabinsk, USSR, May 11, 1989.
(NY Rangers' 7th pick, 200th overall, in 2009 NHL Draft).

			Regular Season					Playoffs				
Season	Club	League	GP	G	A	Pts	PIM	GP	G	A	Pts	PIM
2005-06	Mechel 2	Russia-3	25	0	5	5	30	....	....	....	....	....
2006-07	Mechel 2	Russia-3	12	1	3	4	26	....	....	....	....	....
	Mechel	Russia-2	41	0	2	2	40	4	0	0	0	8
2007-08	Mechel 2	Russia-3	8	4	1	5	12	....	....	....	....	....
	Mechel	Russia-2	49	2	5	7	58	....	....	....	....	....
2008-09	Mechel 2	Russia-3	3	0	1	1	4	....	....	....	....	....
	Mechel	Russia-2	35	2	4	6	40	7	0	2	2	8
2009-10	CSKA Moscow	KHL	44	1	4	5	52	1	0	0	0	0
	CSKA Jr.	Russia-Jr.	4	0	3	3	2	4	1	1	2	20
2010-11	CSKA Moscow	KHL	42	2	2	4	38	....	....	....	....	....
	CSKA Jr.	Russia-Jr.	10	2	2	4	14	16	1	4	5	60
2011-12	CSKA Moscow	KHL	50	3	2	5	68	5	0	1	1	20
2012-13	Yaroslavl	KHL	32	1	1	2	75	6	0	0	0	6
2013-14	Yaroslavl	KHL	32	0	3	3	114	16	0	1	1	14
2014-15	Yaroslavl	KHL	32	0	2	2	22	5	0	0	0	29
2015-16	Yaroslavl	KHL	39	3	5	8	42	3	0	0	0	14
2016-17	Yaroslavl	KHL	58	0	11	11	78	15	0	0	0	14

PASTUJOV, Nick (PAS-TOO-jawv, NIHK) **NYI**

Left wing. Shoots left. 6', 202 lbs. Born, Bradenton, FL, January 21, 1998.
(NY Islanders' 5th pick, 193rd overall, in 2016 NHL Draft).

			Regular Season					Playoffs				
Season	Club	League	GP	G	A	Pts	PIM	GP	G	A	Pts	PIM
2013-14	Det. H-Baked U16	HPHL	15	6	13	19	26	....	....	....	....	....
2014-15	USAHNTDP	USHL	28	3	8	11	43	....	....	....	....	....
	USAHNTDP	U-17	17	10	9	19	10	....	....	....	....	....
2015-16	USAHNTDP	USHL	21	3	5	8	22	....	....	....	....	....
	USAHNTDP	U-18	39	10	3	13	46	....	....	....	....	....
2016-17	U. of Michigan	Big Ten	28	1	2	3	14	....	....	....	....	....

PATRICK, Nolan (PA-trihk, NOH-luhn) **PHI**

Center. Shoots right. 6'2", 199 lbs. Born, Winnipeg, MB, September 19, 1998.
(Philadelphia's 1st pick, 2nd overall, in 2017 NHL Draft).

			Regular Season					Playoffs				
Season	**Club**	**League**	**GP**	**G**	**A**	**Pts**	**PIM**	**GP**	**G**	**A**	**Pts**	**PIM**
2013-14	Wpg. Thrashers	MMHL	39	33	30	63	42	8	3	7	10	6
2014-15	Brandon	WHL	55	30	26	56	19	19	8	7	15	14
2015-16	Brandon	WHL	72	41	61	102	41	21	13	17	*30	16
2016-17	Brandon	WHL	33	20	26	46	36	....	....	....	....	....

• Missed majority of 2016-17 due to upper-body injury and sports hernia surgery.

PAULOVIC, Matej (PAWL-oh-vihch, mah-TAY) **DAL**

Left wing. Shoots right. 6'3", 195 lbs. Born, Topolcany, Slovakia, January 13, 1995.
(Dallas' 8th pick, 149th overall, in 2013 NHL Draft).

			Regular Season					Playoffs				
Season	**Club**	**League**	**GP**	**G**	**A**	**Pts**	**PIM**	**GP**	**G**	**A**	**Pts**	**PIM**
2009-10	HC Topolcany U18	Svk-U18	39	17	16	33	26	....	....	....	....	....
2010-11	HC Topolcany U18	Svk-U18	42	33	29	62	34	....	....	....	....	....
	HK Nitra Jr.	Slovak-Jr.	2	0	0	0	0	....	....	....	....	....
2011-12	Farjestad U18	Swe-U18	33	17	23	40	51	6	2	1	3	2
	Farjestad Jr.	Swe-Jr.	12	2	1	3	6	....	....	....	....	....
2012-13	Farjestad U18	Swe-U18	8	3	4	7	8	....	....	....	....	....
	Farjestad Jr.	Swe-Jr.	34	5	12	17	6	7	1	1	2	6
2013-14	Peterborough	OHL	18	2	2	4	4	....	....	....	....	....
	Muskegon	USHL	29	6	10	16	39	....	....	....	....	....
2014-15	Muskegon	USHL	51	17	33	50	79	12	3	5	8	12
2015-16	Muskegon	USHL	49	20	33	53	50	....	....	....	....	....
2016-17	HC Nove Zamky	Slovakia	56	12	12	24	8	5	3	0	3	2

Signed as a free agent by **Zarnsky** (Slovakia), August 8, 2016. Signd as a free agent by **Nitra**, (Slovakia), May 17, 2017.

PAVLYCHEV, Nikita (pav-LIH-chehv, nih-KEE-ta) **PIT**

Center. Shoots left. 6'7", 211 lbs. Born, Yaroslavl, Russia, March 23, 1997.
(Pittsburgh's 4th pick, 197th overall, in 2015 NHL Draft).

			Regular Season					Playoffs				
Season	**Club**	**League**	**GP**	**G**	**A**	**Pts**	**PIM**	**GP**	**G**	**A**	**Pts**	**PIM**
2012-13	Wilkes Barre U16	AYHL	21	10	16	26	47	2	0	3	3	10
2013-14	Wilkes Barre U18	AYHL	22	9	14	23	65	....	....	....	....	....
	Des Moines	USHL	4	0	1	1	0	....	....	....	....	....
2014-15	Des Moines	USHL	42	6	10	16	80	....	....	....	....	....
2015-16	Des Moines	USHL	58	9	13	22	161	....	....	....	....	....
2016-17	Penn State	Big Ten	36	6	7	13	46	....	....	....	....	....

PEARSON, Chase (PEER-suhn, CHAYS) **DET**

Center. Shoots left. 6'3", 186 lbs. Born, Cornwall, ON, August 23, 1997.
(Detroit's 4th pick, 140th overall, in 2015 NHL Draft).

			Regular Season					Playoffs				
Season	**Club**	**League**	**GP**	**G**	**A**	**Pts**	**PIM**	**GP**	**G**	**A**	**Pts**	**PIM**
2012-13	Atlanta Fire U16	NAPHL	22	11	13	24	50	4	4	6	10	10
2013-14	Cornwall Colts	ON-Jr.A	39	8	15	23	18	5	0	1	1	2
	Youngstown	USHL	2	0	0	0	0	....	....	....	....	....
2014-15	Youngstown	USHL	57	12	14	26	96	4	0	2	2	0
2015-16	Youngstown	USHL	55	12	38	50	61	....	....	....	....	....
2016-17	U. of Maine	H-East	36	14	8	22	56	....	....	....	....	....

PEDERSON, Lane (PEE-duhr-suhn, LAYN) **ARI**

Center. Shoots right. 6'1", 200 lbs. Born, Saskatoon, SK, August 4, 1997.

			Regular Season					Playoffs				
Season	**Club**	**League**	**GP**	**G**	**A**	**Pts**	**PIM**	**GP**	**G**	**A**	**Pts**	**PIM**
2012-13	Saskatoon Blazers	SMHL	38	14	21	35	20	7	3	4	7	0
2013-14	Saskatoon Blazers	SMHL	37	21	20	41	16	....	....	....	....	....
	Seattle	WHL	2	0	0	0	0	3	0	0	0	0
2014-15	Seattle	WHL	63	8	12	20	17	....	....	....	....	....
2015-16	Red Deer Rebels	WHL	35	6	15	21	19	6	0	0	0	0
	Swift Current	WHL	37	14	20	34	29	....	....	....	....	....
2016-17	Swift Current	WHL	62	25	40	65	39	12	3	4	7	0

Signed as a free agent by **Arizona**, October 13, 2016.

PEDRIE, Vince (PEE-dree, VIHNS) **NYR**

Defense. Shoots left. 6', 195 lbs. Born, Rochester, MN, January 17, 1994.

			Regular Season					Playoffs				
Season	**Club**	**League**	**GP**	**G**	**A**	**Pts**	**PIM**	**GP**	**G**	**A**	**Pts**	**PIM**
2009-10	Apple Valley	High-MN	21	5	12	17	12	6	0	2	2	4
2010-11	Apple Valley	High-MN	25	8	26	34	34	3	0	1	1	2
2011-12	Omaha Lancers	USHL	40	0	5	5	40	4	0	0	0	0
2012-13	Omaha Lancers	USHL	11	0	3	3	6	....	....	....	....	....
	Indiana Ice	USHL	45	3	12	15	35	....	....	....	....	....
2013-14	Indiana Ice	USHL	36	5	9	14	46	....	....	....	....	....
2014-15	Bloomington	USHL	39	9	13	22	49	....	....	....	....	....
	Tri-City Storm	USHL	23	4	3	7	21	5	1	1	2	12
2015-16	Penn State	Big Ten	32	8	14	22	32	....	....	....	....	....
2016-17	Penn State	Big Ten	39	8	22	30	24	....	....	....	....	....
	Hartford Wolf Pack	AHL	9	0	5	5	8	....	....	....	....	....

Big Ten All-Rookie Team (2016) • Big Ten Second All-Star Team (2016)

Signed as a free agent by **NY Rangers**, March 28, 2017.

PEEKE, Andrew (PEEK, AN-droo) **CBJ**

Defense. Shoots right. 6'3", 198 lbs. Born, Parkland, FL, March 17, 1998.
(Columbus' 2nd pick, 34th overall, in 2016 NHL Draft).

			Regular Season					Playoffs				
Season	**Club**	**League**	**GP**	**G**	**A**	**Pts**	**PIM**	**GP**	**G**	**A**	**Pts**	**PIM**
2013-14	Selects Acad. U16	USPHL	28	1	9	10	16	3	0	0	0	....
	Selects Academy	Minor-CT	43	3	6	9	....	....	....	....	....	....
2014-15	Selects Acad. U18	USPHL	28	8	12	20	8	4	1	1	2	2
	Selects Academy	Minor-CT	37	7	17	24	17	....	....	....	....	....
2015-16	Green Bay	USHL	56	4	26	30	30	4	1	1	2	2
2016-17	U. of Notre Dame	H-East	40	4	10	14	16	....	....	....	....	....

USHL All-Rookie Team (2016) • Hockey East All-Rookie Team (2017)

PERBIX, Nicklaus (PUHR-bihx, NIHK-luhs) **T.B.**

Defense. Shoots right. 6'2", 191 lbs. Born, Minneapolis, MN, June 15, 1998.
(Tampa Bay's 3rd pick, 169th overall, in 2017 NHL Draft).

			Regular Season					Playoffs				
Season	**Club**	**League**	**GP**	**G**	**A**	**Pts**	**PIM**	**GP**	**G**	**A**	**Pts**	**PIM**
2013-14	Elk River Elks	High-MN	23	0	3	3	2	3	0	0	0	0
2014-15	Elk River Elks	High-MN	23	0	3	3	0	3	0	2	2	0
2015-16	Elk River Elks	High-MN	25	5	17	22	10	2	1	3	4	2
2016-17	Team Northwest	UMHSEL	21	3	10	13	6	....	....	....	....	....
	Elk River Elks	High-MN	25	10	30	40	6	2	2	5	7	0

• Signed Letter of Intent to attend **St. Cloud State University** (NCHC) in fall of 2017.

PERRON, Francis (pair-AWN, FRAN-sihs) **OTT**

Left wing. Shoots left. 6', 176 lbs. Born, Laval, QC, April 18, 1996.
(Ottawa's 5th pick, 190th overall, in 2014 NHL Draft).

			Regular Season					Playoffs				
Season	**Club**	**League**	**GP**	**G**	**A**	**Pts**	**PIM**	**GP**	**G**	**A**	**Pts**	**PIM**
2011-12	Saint-Eustache	QAAA	14	5	13	18	14	....	....	....	....	....
2012-13	Rouyn-Noranda	QMJHL	57	7	11	18	28	5	1	1	2	7
2013-14	Rouyn-Noranda	QMJHL	68	16	39	55	32	9	1	7	8	4
2014-15	Rouyn-Noranda	QMJHL	64	29	47	76	39	6	3	4	7	14
2015-16	Rouyn-Noranda	QMJHL	62	41	67	108	38	18	12	*21	*33	11
2016-17	Binghamton	AHL	68	6	20	26	14	....	....	....	....	....

QMJHL First All-Star Team (2016) • QMJHL Player of the Year (2016)

PETERSON, Avery (PEE-tuhr-suhn, AY-vuhr-ee) **MIN**

Center. Shoots left. 6'3", 209 lbs. Born, Grand Rapids, MN, June 20, 1995.
(Minnesota's 5th pick, 167th overall, in 2013 NHL Draft).

			Regular Season					Playoffs				
Season	**Club**	**League**	**GP**	**G**	**A**	**Pts**	**PIM**	**GP**	**G**	**A**	**Pts**	**PIM**
2010-11	Grand Rapids	High-MN	28	8	18	26	28	3	1	3	4	8
2011-12	Grand Rapids	High-MN	25	14	32	46	46	1	0	2	2	0
2012-13	Grand Rapids	High-MN	23	23	31	54	2	3	4	4	8	0
	Team North	UMHSEL	21	5	10	15	19	....	....	....	....	....
	Sioux City	USHL	8	1	3	4	7	....	....	....	....	....
2013-14	Sioux City	USHL	27	6	15	21	16	....	....	....	....	....
2014-15	Nebraska-Omaha	NCHC	39	11	10	21	18	....	....	....	....	....
2015-16	Nebraska-Omaha	NCHC	14	0	1	1	6	....	....	....	....	....
2016-17	U. Minn-Duluth	NCHC	25	7	8	15	27	....	....	....	....	....

PETERSON, Jacob (pee-TUHR-suhn, JAY-kuhb) **DAL**

Center. Shoots left. 6', 165 lbs. Born, Lidkoping, Sweden, July 19, 1999.
(Dallas' 6th pick, 132nd overall, in 2017 NHL Draft).

			Regular Season					Playoffs				
Season	**Club**	**League**	**GP**	**G**	**A**	**Pts**	**PIM**	**GP**	**G**	**A**	**Pts**	**PIM**
2014-15	HC Lidkoping U18	Swe-U18	17	22	19	41	14	....	....	....	....	....
	HC Lidkoping	Sweden-5	13	9	12	21	6	....	....	....	....	....
2015-16	Frolunda U18	Swe-U18	33	13	13	26	20	6	0	1	1	4
2016-17	Frolunda U18	Swe-U18	10	13	7	20	10	7	4	4	8	6
	Frolunda Jr.	Swe-Jr.	44	15	12	27	8	5	0	0	0	0

PETERSON, Judd (PEE-tuhr-suhn, JUHD) **BUF**

Center/Right wing. Shoots right. 6', 191 lbs. Born, Duluth, MN, September 27, 1993.
(Buffalo's 8th pick, 204th overall, in 2012 NHL Draft).

			Regular Season					Playoffs				
Season	**Club**	**League**	**GP**	**G**	**A**	**Pts**	**PIM**	**GP**	**G**	**A**	**Pts**	**PIM**
2009-10	Duluth Marshall	High-MN	23	15	14	29	24	2	1	0	1	0
2010-11	Team North	UMHSEL	24	8	3	11	22	....	....	....	....	....
	Duluth Marshall	High-MN	25	24	19	43	40	2	1	2	3	0
2011-12	Team North	UMHSEL	16	4	2	6	22	....	....	....	....	....
	Duluth Marshall	High-MN	25	41	33	74	30	5	6	3	9	2
2012-13	Cedar Rapids	USHL	46	11	15	26	38	....	....	....	....	....
2013-14	Cedar Rapids	USHL	47	16	15	31	43	2	0	0	0	0
2014-15	St. Cloud State	NCHC	37	4	3	7	20	....	....	....	....	....
2015-16	St. Cloud State	NCHC	38	16	7	23	14	....	....	....	....	....
2016-17	St. Cloud State	NCHC	36	11	6	17	8	....	....	....	....	....

PETRYK, Reid (PEH-TRIHK, REED) **COL**

Center. Shoots right. 6'1", 205 lbs. Born, Edmonton, AB, February 2, 1993.

			Regular Season					Playoffs				
Season	**Club**	**League**	**GP**	**G**	**A**	**Pts**	**PIM**	**GP**	**G**	**A**	**Pts**	**PIM**
2009-10	Medicine Hat	WHL	45	1	6	7	4	....	....	....	....	....
2010-11	Medicine Hat	WHL	68	13	5	18	34	15	1	3	4	8
2011-12	Medicine Hat	WHL	43	7	12	19	56	....	....	....	....	....
	Everett Silvertips	WHL	32	11	9	20	34	4	0	1	1	0
2012-13	Everett Silvertips	WHL	70	16	24	40	61	6	3	2	5	4
	Lake Erie Monsters	AHL	2	0	0	0	2	....	....	....	....	....
2013-14	Everett Silvertips	WHL	1	0	0	0	5	....	....	....	....	....
	Edmonton	WHL	62	17	39	56	51	17	2	7	9	16
2014-15	Lake Erie Monsters	AHL	35	4	9	13	13	....	....	....	....	....
	Fort Wayne	ECHL	26	0	5	5	6	....	....	....	....	....
2015-16	San Antonio	AHL	72	15	22	37	34	....	....	....	....	....
2016-17	San Antonio	AHL	45	10	5	15	15	....	....	....	....	....

Signed as a free agent by **Colorado**, July 1, 2016.

PETTERSSON, Elias (peh-TUHR-suhn, uh-LIGH-uhs) **VAN**

Center. Shoots left. 6'2", 165 lbs. Born, Sundsvall, Sweden, December 11, 1998.
(Vancouver's 1st pick, 5th overall, in 2017 NHL Draft).

			Regular Season					Playoffs				
Season	**Club**	**League**	**GP**	**G**	**A**	**Pts**	**PIM**	**GP**	**G**	**A**	**Pts**	**PIM**
2013-14	Timra IK U18	Swe-U18	2	0	0	0	0	....	....	....	....	....
2014-15	Timra IK U18	Swe-U18	40	31	34	65	8	8	5	9	14	4
	Timra IK Jr.	Swe-Jr.	6	4	9	13	2	1	1	1	2	0
2015-16	Timra IK U18	Swe-U18	2	3	1	4	2	1	0	1	1	0
	Timra IK Jr.	Swe-Jr.	22	6	8	14	20	2	3	4	7	0
	Timra IK	Sweden-2	30	3	10	13	2	....	....	....	....	....
2016-17	Timra IK	Sweden-2	43	19	22	41	14	3	2	4	6	0
	Timra IK Jr.	Swe-Jr.	....	....	....	....	....	2	0	1	1	2

PETTERSSON, Emil (PEH-tuhr-suhn, eh-MIHL) NSH

Center. Shoots left. 6'2", 164 lbs. Born, Sundsvall, Sweden, January 14, 1994.
(Nashville's 7th pick, 155th overall, in 2013 NHL Draft).

			Regular Season					Playoffs				
Season	Club	League	GP	G	A	Pts	PIM	GP	G	A	Pts	PIM
2010-11	Timra IK U18	Swe-U18	34	10	16	26	26	5	0	1	1	0
2011-12	Timra IK U18	Swe-U18	31	19	22	41	94	3	1	4	5	10
	Timra IK Jr.	Swe-Jr.	17	4	2	6	10	3	1	1	2	2
2012-13	Timra IK Jr.	Swe-Jr.	44	13	31	44	38	2	0	0	0	2
	Timra IK	Sweden	2	0	0	0	0	....	....	....	....	....
	Timra IK	Sweden-Q	2	1	0	1	0	....	....	....	....	....
2013-14	Timra IK	Sweden-2	44	6	8	14	12	....	....	....	....	....
	Timra IK Jr.	Swe-Jr.	12	10	9	19	12	2	2	0	2	4
2014-15	Timra IK	Sweden-2	52	12	23	35	16	....	....	....	....	....
	MODO	Sweden	2	1	0	1	2	....	....	....	....	....
	MODO	Sweden-Q	....	....	....	....	....	4	1	3	4	0
2015-16	MODO	Sweden	52	12	14	26	28	....	....	....	....	....
	MODO	Sweden-Q	....	....	....	....	....	7	3	2	5	2
2016-17	Skelleftea AIK	Sweden	24	6	6	12	4	....	....	....	....	....
	Vaxjo Lakers HC	Sweden	27	9	17	26	8	6	4	3	7	4

PETTERSSON, Marcus (PEH-tuhr-suhn, MAHR-kuhs) ANA

Defense. Shoots left. 6'4", 167 lbs. Born, Skelleftea, Sweden, May 8, 1996.
(Anaheim's 2nd pick, 38th overall, in 2014 NHL Draft).

			Regular Season					Playoffs				
Season	Club	League	GP	G	A	Pts	PIM	GP	G	A	Pts	PIM
2010-11	Skelleftea AIK U18	Swe-U18	2	0	0	0	0	....	....	....	....	....
2011-12	Skelleftea AIK U18	Swe-U18	33	5	7	12	12	7	1	3	4	14
2012-13	Skelleftea AIK U18	Swe-U18	2	0	0	0	0	9	2	7	9	4
	Skelleftea AIK Jr.	Swe-Jr.	37	4	8	12	16	2	0	0	0	0
2013-14	Skelleftea AIK Jr.	Swe-Jr.	38	4	14	18	38	2	0	0	0	2
	Skelleftea AIK	Sweden	10	0	0	0	2	....	....	....	....	....
	Skelleftea AIK U18	Swe-U18	....	....	....	....	....	3	0	1	1	4
2014-15	Vita Hasten	Sweden-2	15	3	3	6	22	4	0	1	1	2
	Skelleftea AIK Jr.	Swe-Jr.	20	2	8	10	20	1	0	0	0	2
	Skelleftea AIK	Sweden	14	0	0	0	0	....	....	....	....	....
2015-16	Skelleftea AIK Jr.	Swe-Jr.	3	1	3	4	4	2	0	0	0	8
	Skelleftea AIK	Sweden	46	2	5	7	10	8	0	0	0	0
2016-17	Skelleftea AIK	Sweden	41	2	7	9	49	....	....	....	....	....

PEZZETTA, Michael (puh-ZEH-tuh, MIGH-kuhl) MTL

Center. Shoots left. 6'1", 212 lbs. Born, Toronto, ON, March 13, 1998.
(Montreal's 5th pick, 160th overall, in 2016 NHL Draft).

			Regular Season					Playoffs				
Season	Club	League	GP	G	A	Pts	PIM	GP	G	A	Pts	PIM
2013-14	Miss. Senators	GTHL	29	11	15	26	10	10	4	7	11	18
2014-15	Sudbury Wolves	OHL	61	5	7	12	56	....	....	....	....	....
2015-16	Sudbury Wolves	OHL	64	10	18	28	98	....	....	....	....	....
2016-17	Sudbury Wolves	OHL	54	10	9	19	88	5	2	0	2	17

PHILLIPS, Clayton (FIH-lihps, KLAY-tuhn) PIT

Defense. Shoots left. 5'11", 180 lbs. Born, Edina, MN, September 9, 1999.
(Pittsburgh's 2nd pick, 93rd overall, in 2017 NHL Draft).

			Regular Season					Playoffs				
Season	Club	League	GP	G	A	Pts	PIM	GP	G	A	Pts	PIM
2014-15	Edina Hornets	High-MN	25	4	8	12	6	5	1	5	6	0
2015-16	Team Southwest	UMHSEL	9	2	3	5	6	....	....	....	....	....
	Fargo Force	USHL	3	0	0	0	0	....	....	....	....	....
	Edina Hornets	High-MN	25	2	13	15	20	2	3	1	4	2
2016-17	Fargo Force	USHL	56	7	13	20	35	3	0	0	0	2

• Signed Letter of Intent to attend **University of Minnesota** (Big Ten) in fall of 2018.

PHILLIPS, Markus (FIH-lihps, MAHR-kuhs) L.A.

Defense. Shoots left. 6', 202 lbs. Born, Markham, ON, March 21, 1999.
(Los Angeles' 5th pick, 118th overall, in 2017 NHL Draft).

			Regular Season					Playoffs				
Season	Club	League	GP	G	A	Pts	PIM	GP	G	A	Pts	PIM
2014-15	Tor. Titans MM	GTHL	24	4	17	21	....	....	....	....	....	....
	Tor. Titans Mid.	GTHL	1	0	0	0	0	....	....	....	....	....
	Newmarket	ON-Jr.A	2	0	1	1	4	....	....	....	....	....
2015-16	Owen Sound	OHL	63	3	9	12	22	6	0	0	0	2
2016-17	Owen Sound	OHL	66	13	30	43	44	17	0	5	5	10

PHILLIPS, Matthew (FIH-lihps, MA-thew) CGY

Center. Shoots right. 5'7", 140 lbs. Born, Calgary, AB, April 6, 1998.
(Calgary's 8th pick, 166th overall, in 2016 NHL Draft).

			Regular Season					Playoffs				
Season	Club	League	GP	G	A	Pts	PIM	GP	G	A	Pts	PIM
2012-13	Calgary Bisons	AMBHL	33	40	37	77	8	5	4	4	8	0
	CBHA Blackhawks	Minor-AB	4	4	4	8	2	....	....	....	....	....
2013-14	Calgary Buffaloes	AMHL	33	15	20	35	22	8	3	2	5	4
2014-15	Calgary Buffaloes	AMHL	34	33	40	73	30	6	5	3	8	6
	Victoria Royals	WHL	2	1	2	3	0	....	....	....	....	....
2015-16	Victoria Royals	WHL	72	37	39	76	16	13	5	3	8	2
2016-17	Victoria Royals	WHL	70	50	40	90	50	6	1	2	3	2
	Stockton Heat	AHL	1	0	1	1	0	2	0	0	0	2

WHL West First All-Star Team (2017)

PICCINICH, J.J. (pih-SIH-nihch, JAY-JAY) TOR

Right wing. Shoots right. 6', 190 lbs. Born, Paramus, NJ, June 12, 1996.
(Toronto's 3rd pick, 103rd overall, in 2014 NHL Draft).

			Regular Season					Playoffs				
Season	Club	League	GP	G	A	Pts	PIM	GP	G	A	Pts	PIM
2011-12	N.J. Avalanche	AYHL	22	*23	19	*42	16	....	....	....	....	....
2012-13	Youngstown	USHL	63	3	12	15	4	9	1	1	2	0
2013-14	Youngstown	USHL	60	27	31	58	31	....	....	....	....	....
	USAHNTDP	U-18	1	0	0	0	0	....	....	....	....	....
2014-15	Boston University	H-East	25	1	3	4	2	....	....	....	....	....
2015-16	London Knights	OHL	66	30	36	66	19	18	2	10	12	4
2016-17	London Knights	OHL	66	26	46	72	24	14	1	2	3	12

PILON, Garrett (PEE-lawn, GAIR-eht) WSH

Center. Shoots right. 5'10", 175 lbs. Born, Kindersley, SK, April 13, 1998.
(Washington's 2nd pick, 87th overall, in 2016 NHL Draft).

			Regular Season					Playoffs				
Season	Club	League	GP	G	A	Pts	PIM	GP	G	A	Pts	PIM
2012-13	West Central	SBHL	27	24	28	52	16	3	1	4	5	0
2013-14	Sask. Contacts	SMHL	43	10	19	29	10	3	2	0	2	0
2014-15	Sask. Contacts	SMHL	44	30	*57	*87	40	4	1	4	5	2
2015-16	Kamloops Blazers	WHL	71	15	32	47	24	7	2	1	3	0
2016-17	Kamloops Blazers	WHL	67	20	45	65	20	6	1	3	4	6
	Hershey Bears	AHL	....	....	....	....	....	1	0	0	0	0

PINHO, Brian (PIHN-oh, BRIGH-uhn) WSH

Center. Shoots right. 6', 173 lbs. Born, Beverly, MA, May 11, 1995.
(Washington's 5th pick, 174th overall, in 2013 NHL Draft).

			Regular Season					Playoffs				
Season	Club	League	GP	G	A	Pts	PIM	GP	G	A	Pts	PIM
2010-11	Valley Jr. Warriors	Minor-MA	10	4	4	8	8	....	....	....	....	....
	Valley Jr. Warriors	EmJHL	6	4	1	5	2	....	....	....	....	....
2011-12	St. John's Prep	High-MA	24	20	37	57	....	....	....	....	....	....
	Valley Jr. Warriors	Minor-MA	10	0	10	10	2	....	....	....	....	....
2012-13	St. John's Prep	High-MA	24	15	27	42	....	....	....	....	....	....
2013-14	Indiana Ice	USHL	59	28	28	56	21	12	2	4	6	0
2014-15	Providence College	H-East	39	6	12	18	6	....	....	....	....	....
2015-16	Providence College	H-East	38	9	16	25	16	....	....	....	....	....
2016-17	Providence College	H-East	39	12	28	40	24	....	....	....	....	....

PIONK, Neal (PEE-ohnk, NEEL) NYR

Defense. Shoots right. 6', 190 lbs. Born, Hermantown, MN, July 29, 1995.

			Regular Season					Playoffs				
Season	Club	League	GP	G	A	Pts	PIM	GP	G	A	Pts	PIM
2011-12	Hermantown	High-MN	25	7	6	13	12	6	1	3	4	6
2012-13	Team North	UMHSEL	20	1	10	11	32	3	1	0	1	0
	Hermantown	High-MN	25	14	15	29	25	6	2	8	10	4
	Sioux City	USHL	12	1	5	6	2	....	....	....	....	....
2013-14	Sioux City	USHL	54	2	21	23	93	7	0	1	1	10
2014-15	Sioux City	USHL	53	7	41	48	104	5	0	1	1	10
2015-16	U. Minn-Duluth	NCHC	40	4	13	17	44	....	....	....	....	....
2016-17	U. Minn-Duluth	NCHC	42	7	27	34	25	....	....	....	....	....

USHL First All-Star Team (2015) • NCHC Second All-Star Team (2017)

Signed as a free agent by **NY Rangers**, May 1, 2017.

PITLICK, Rem (PIHT-lihk, REHM) NSH

Center. Shoots left. 5'9", 196 lbs. Born, Ottawa, ON, April 2, 1997.
(Nashville's 3rd pick, 76th overall, in 2016 NHL Draft).

			Regular Season					Playoffs				
Season	Club	League	GP	G	A	Pts	PIM	GP	G	A	Pts	PIM
2012-13	Shattuck U16	High-MN	53	15	37	52	28	....	....	....	....	....
2013-14	Shattuck	High-MN	53	9	25	34	32	....	....	....	....	....
2014-15	Waterloo	USHL	47	7	9	16	29	....	....	....	....	....
2015-16	Muskegon	USHL	56	*46	*43	*89	74	....	....	....	....	....
2016-17	U. of Minnesota	Big Ten	36	14	18	32	22	....	....	....	....	....

USHL First All-Star Team (2016) • USHL Player of the Year (2016)

PLATZER, Kyle (PLAT-zuhr, KIGHL) EDM

Center. Shoots right. 6', 172 lbs. Born, Waterloo, ON, March 4, 1995.
(Edmonton's 6th pick, 96th overall, in 2013 NHL Draft).

			Regular Season					Playoffs				
Season	Club	League	GP	G	A	Pts	PIM	GP	G	A	Pts	PIM
2010-11	Wat. Wolves MM	Minor-ON	30	20	22	42	20	13	6	7	13	16
	Wat. Wolves Mid.	Minor-ON	8	2	2	4	8	....	....	....	....	....
	Waterloo Siskins	ON-Jr.B	2	0	0	0	0	....	....	....	....	....
2011-12	Waterloo Siskins	ON-Jr.B	50	31	24	55	70	6	4	6	10	6
	London Knights	OHL	4	0	1	1	0	....	....	....	....	....
2012-13	London Knights	OHL	65	5	17	22	15	21	2	4	6	8
2013-14	London Knights	OHL	39	9	8	17	14	....	....	....	....	....
	Owen Sound	OHL	27	13	6	19	12	5	1	2	3	6
2014-15	Owen Sound	OHL	68	34	47	81	46	5	1	4	5	4
	Oklahoma City	AHL	4	2	1	3	0	3	0	0	0	0
2015-16	Bakersfield	AHL	48	6	11	17	24	....	....	....	....	....
2016-17	Bakersfield	AHL	51	1	7	8	14	....	....	....	....	....

POCHIRO, Zach (puh-CHUHR-oh, ZAK) EDM

Left wing. Shoots right. 6'1", 155 lbs. Born, St. Louis, MO, March 6, 1994.
(St. Louis' 3rd pick, 112th overall, in 2013 NHL Draft).

			Regular Season					Playoffs				
Season	Club	League	GP	G	A	Pts	PIM	GP	G	A	Pts	PIM
2010-11	L.A. Jr. Kings	T1EHL	31	22	12	34	128	....	....	....	....	....
2011-12	Wichita Falls	NAHL	52	18	16	34	154	....	....	....	....	....
2012-13	Prince George	WHL	65	15	24	39	105	....	....	....	....	....
2013-14	Prince George	WHL	63	27	39	66	123	....	....	....	....	....
	Kalamazoo Wings	ECHL	9	0	2	2	0	....	....	....	....	....
2014-15	Prince George	WHL	41	19	23	42	69	5	4	2	6	6
	Alaska Aces	ECHL	8	0	2	2	13	....	....	....	....	....
2015-16	Quad City	ECHL	44	9	17	26	69	....	....	....	....	....
	Chicago Wolves	AHL	1	0	0	0	0	....	....	....	....	....
2016-17	Bakersfield	AHL	4	0	2	2	0	....	....	....	....	....
	Norfolk Admirals	ECHL	42	3	24	27	66	....	....	....	....	....

• Re-assigned to **Quad City** (ECHL) by **St. Louis**, October 21, 2015. Traded to **Edmonton** by **St. Louis** with St. Louis' 3rd round pick (later traded to Arizona – Arizona selected Cameron Crotty) in 2017 NHL Draft for Nail Yakupov, October 7, 2016.

POEHLING, Ryan (POH-lihng, RIGH-uhn) MTL

Center. Shoots left. 6'2", 189 lbs. Born, Lakeville, MN, March 1, 1999.
(Montreal's 1st pick, 25th overall, in 2017 NHL Draft).

			Regular Season					Playoffs				
Season	Club	League	GP	G	A	Pts	PIM	GP	G	A	Pts	PIM
2013-14	Lakeville North	High-MN	24	11	16	27	21	6	0	8	8	0
2014-15	Team Southeast	UMHSEL	20	3	2	5	20	3	1	1	2	0
	Lakeville North	High-MN	25	14	24	38	12	6	2	9	11	14
2015-16	Team Southeast	UMHSEL	20	6	14	20	12	....	....	....	....	....
	Lakeville North	High-MN	25	20	34	54	10	3	1	7	8	2
	Lincoln Stars	USHL	9	2	2	4	0	....	....	....	....	....
2016-17	St. Cloud State	NCHC	35	7	6	13	12	....	....	....	....	....
	USAHNTDP	U-18	9	4	2	6	4	....	....	....	....	....

POGANSKI, Austin (POH-gan-skee, AW-stuhn) **ST.L.**

Right wing. Shoots right. 6'1", 198 lbs. Born, St. Cloud, MN, February 16, 1996.
(St. Louis' 6th pick, 110th overall, in 2014 NHL Draft).

			Regular Season					Playoffs				
Season	Club	League	GP	G	A	Pts	PIM	GP	G	A	Pts	PIM
2010-11	St. Cloud Cath.	High-MN	25	22	13	35	6	2	0	3	3	0
2011-12	St. Cloud Cath.	High-MN	25	22	27	49	6	2	2	1	3	0
2012-13	Team Great Plains	UMHSEL	19	8	12	20	6	3	2	2	4	0
	St. Cloud Cath.	High-MN	23	25	22	47	14	3	10	9	19	2
	USAHNTDP	U-17	11	7	0	7	2	....	....	....	....	....
	Tri-City Storm	USHL	2	1	1	2	0	....	....	....	....	....
2013-14	Tri-City Storm	USHL	55	19	12	31	57	....	....	....	....	....
2014-15	North Dakota	NCHC	38	4	10	14	19	....	....	....	....	....
2015-16	North Dakota	NCHC	44	10	15	25	18	....	....	....	....	....
2016-17	North Dakota	NCHC	40	12	13	25	45	....	....	....	....	....

POKKA, Ville (POH-ka, VIHL-ee) **CHI**

Defense. Shoots right. 6', 214 lbs. Born, Tornio, Finland, June 3, 1994.
(NY Islanders' 2nd pick, 34th overall, in 2012 NHL Draft).

			Regular Season					Playoffs				
Season	Club	League	GP	G	A	Pts	PIM	GP	G	A	Pts	PIM
2009-10	Karpat Oulu U18	Fin-U18	25	0	7	7	10	5	0	0	0	4
2010-11	Karpat Oulu Jr.	Fin-Jr.	33	6	16	22	18	....	....	....	....	....
	Karpat Oulu	Finland	2	0	0	0	2	....	....	....	....	....
	Kiekko-Laser Oulu	Finland-2	3	0	3	3	0	....	....	....	....	....
	Karpat Oulu U18	Fin-U18	3	0	2	2	0	9	0	7	7	8
2011-12	Karpat Oulu Jr.	Fin-Jr.	4	3	4	7	2	....	....	....	....	....
	Karpat Oulu	Finland	35	0	3	3	12	9	0	3	3	2
2012-13	Karpat Oulu Jr.	Fin-Jr.	3	0	0	0	4	....	....	....	....	....
	Karpat Oulu	Finland	47	6	6	12	8	3	0	2	2	0
2013-14	Karpat Oulu	Finland	54	6	21	27	16	16	2	9	11	10
2014-15	Rockford IceHogs	AHL	68	8	22	30	16	8	0	3	3	0
2015-16	Rockford IceHogs	AHL	76	10	35	45	24	3	0	1	1	0
2016-17	Rockford IceHogs	AHL	76	6	24	30	35	....	....	....	....	....

AHL All-Rookie Team (2015)

Traded to **Chicago** by **NY Islanders** with T.J. Brennan and Anders Nilsson for Nick Leddy and Kent Simpson, October 4, 2014.

POLLOCK, Brett (PAW-luhk, BREHT) **CGY**

Left wing. Shoots left. 6'3", 195 lbs. Born, Regina, SK, March 17, 1996.
(Dallas' 2nd pick, 45th overall, in 2014 NHL Draft).

			Regular Season					Playoffs				
Season	Club	League	GP	G	A	Pts	PIM	GP	G	A	Pts	PIM
2009-10	Sherwood Park	Minor-AB	31	13	17	30	26	....	....	....	....	....
	Sherwood Park	AMBHL	1	0	0	0	0	....	....	....	....	....
2010-11	Sherwood Park	AMBHL	33	20	17	37	46	....	....	....	....	....
	Sherwood Park	Minor-AB	3	1	1	2	2	....	....	....	....	....
2011-12	Sherwood Park	AMHL	34	8	17	25	54	1	0	0	0	19
2012-13	Edmonton	WHL	40	2	2	4	2	....	....	....	....	....
2013-14	Edmonton	WHL	71	25	30	55	36	21	11	8	19	10
2014-15	Edmonton	WHL	70	32	30	62	88	5	3	2	5	4
2015-16	Edmonton	WHL	72	30	48	78	76	6	2	2	4	12
	Stockton Heat	AHL	3	1	0	1	2	....	....	....	....	....
2016-17	Adirondack	ECHL	61	15	16	31	14	6	0	4	4	2

Traded to **Calgary** by **Dallas** with Jyrki Jokipakka and Dallas' 2nd round pick (Dillon Dube) in 2016 NHL Draft for Kris Russell, February 29, 2016.

POOLMAN, Tucker (POOL-MAN, TUH-kuhr) **WPG**

Defense. Shoots right. 6'3", 214 lbs. Born, East Grand Forks, MN, June 8, 1993.
(Winnipeg's 8th pick, 127th overall, in 2013 NHL Draft).

			Regular Season					Playoffs				
Season	Club	League	GP	G	A	Pts	PIM	GP	G	A	Pts	PIM
2008-09	E. Grand Forks	High-MN	25	3	4	7	2	....	....	....	....	....
2009-10	E. Grand Forks	High-MN	25	3	7	10	10	2	0	2	2	0
2010-11	Team Great Plains	UMHSEL	16	2	3	5	4	3	0	2	2	0
	E. Grand Forks	High-MN	23	5	17	22	13	2	0	0	0	0
2011-12	Wichita Falls	NAHL	59	7	22	29	29	....	....	....	....	....
2012-13	Omaha Lancers	USHL	64	14	14	28	49	....	....	....	....	....
2013-14	Omaha Lancers	USHL	58	15	26	41	23	4	1	3	4	4
2014-15	North Dakota	NCHC	40	8	10	18	16	....	....	....	....	....
2015-16	North Dakota	NCHC	40	5	19	24	4	....	....	....	....	....
2016-17	North Dakota	NCHC	38	7	23	30	14	....	....	....	....	....

USHL First All-Star Team (2014) • NCHC First All-Star Team (2017) • NCAA West First All-American Team (2017)

POPE, David (POHP, DAY-vihd) **DET**

Left wing. Shoots left. 6'3", 195 lbs. Born, Edmonton, AB, September 27, 1994.
(Detroit's 5th pick, 109th overall, in 2013 NHL Draft).

			Regular Season					Playoffs				
Season	Club	League	GP	G	A	Pts	PIM	GP	G	A	Pts	PIM
2007-08	Calgary Bisons	AMBHL	27	3	13	16	10	....	....	....	....	....
2008-09	Notre Dame	Minor-SK	26	28	22	50	12	5	5	3	8	0
2009-10	K of C Pats	AMHL	27	2	8	10	12	....	....	....	....	....
2010-11	PoE Academy	High-BC	STATISTICS NOT AVAILABLE									
	PoE Academy	CSSHL	10	8	8	16	2	5	4	4	8	2
2011-12	Cowichan Valley	BCHL	24	2	5	7	12	....	....	....	....	....
	Westside Warriors	BCHL	20	6	12	18	19	....	....	....	....	....
2012-13	West Kelowna	BCHL	42	17	22	39	20	7	4	1	5	2
2013-14	West Kelowna	BCHL	45	27	23	50	20	6	2	4	6	2
2014-15	Nebraska-Omaha	NCHC	33	8	6	14	6	....	....	....	....	....
2015-16	Nebraska-Omaha	NCHC	31	4	4	8	8	....	....	....	....	....
2016-17	Nebraska-Omaha	NCHC	34	13	18	31	14	....	....	....	....	....

POPUGAEV, Nikita (pawp-uh-GIGH-ehv, nih-KEE-tuh) **N.J.**

Left wing. Shoots right. 6'6", 205 lbs. Born, Moscow, Russia, November 20, 1998.
(New Jersey's 5th pick, 98th overall, in 2017 NHL Draft).

			Regular Season					Playoffs				
Season	Club	League	GP	G	A	Pts	PIM	GP	G	A	Pts	PIM
2014-15	CSKA Jr.	Russia-Jr.	28	2	2	4	4	12	0	0	0	6
2015-16	Moose Jaw	WHL	70	16	31	47	28	6	2	2	4	0
2016-17	Moose Jaw	WHL	40	22	29	51	14	....	....	....	....	....
	Prince George	WHL	31	7	11	18	15	6	1	2	3	2

PRAPAVESSIS, Michael (pra-PA-veh-sihs, MIGH-kuhl) **DAL**

Defense. Shoots left. 6'1", 180 lbs. Born, Mississauga, ON, January 7, 1996.
(Dallas' 4th pick, 105th overall, in 2014 NHL Draft).

			Regular Season					Playoffs				
Season	Club	League	GP	G	A	Pts	PIM	GP	G	A	Pts	PIM
2011-12	Mississauga Rebels	GTHL	63	7	20	27	20	....	....	....	....	....
2012-13	Mississauga Rebels	GTHL	26	3	6	9	4	....	....	....	....	....
	Tor. Patriots	ON-Jr.A	25	2	9	11	2	6	0	3	3	2
2013-14	Tor. Patriots	ON-Jr.A	47	5	50	55	2	19	2	13	15	4
2014-15	RPI Engineers	ECAC	41	1	7	8	12	....	....	....	....	....
2015-16	RPI Engineers	ECAC	40	4	15	19	16	....	....	....	....	....
2016-17	RPI Engineers	ECAC	36	2	14	16	34	....	....	....	....	....

PRIBYL, Daniel (PRIH-buhl, DAN-yehl) **CGY**

Center. Shoots right. 6'3", 207 lbs. Born, Pisek, Czech., December 18, 1992.
(Montreal's 5th pick, 168th overall, in 2011 NHL Draft).

			Regular Season					Playoffs				
Season	Club	League	GP	G	A	Pts	PIM	GP	G	A	Pts	PIM
2008-09	IHC Pisek U17	CzR-U17	44	30	17	47	88	....	....	....	....	....
2009-10	Sparta U18	CzR-U18	38	19	18	37	30	3	2	1	3	0
	Sparta Jr.	CzRep-Jr.	7	1	1	2	10	1	0	0	0	0
2010-11	Sparta Jr.	CzRep-Jr.	41	27	31	58	22	4	4	1	5	2
	Beroun	CzRep-2	1	0	0	0	0	....	....	....	....	....
	HC Sparta Praha	CzRep	7	2	1	3	0	....	....	....	....	....
2011-12	HC Sparta Praha	CzRep	17	2	0	2	6	....	....	....	....	....
	Beroun	CzRep-2	22	9	4	13	4	....	....	....	....	....
	Sparta Jr.	CzRep-Jr.	5	4	2	6	4	4	5	2	7	2
2012-13	Litomerice	CzRep-2	1	1	0	1	0	....	....	....	....	....
	HC Sparta Praha	CzRep	42	12	10	22	10	6	0	0	0	4
2013-14	HC Sparta Praha	CzRep	46	9	16	25	18	12	5	3	8	4
2014-15	HC Sparta Praha	CzRep	21	8	7	15	14	10	1	4	5	8
2015-16	HC Sparta Praha	CzRep	45	16	29	45	16	9	5	6	11	2
2016-17	Stockton Heat	AHL	33	5	10	15	4	....	....	....	....	....

Signed as a free agent by **Calgary**, April 29, 2016.

PRISKIE, Chase (PRIHS-KEE, CHAYS) **WSH**

Defense. Shoots right. 6', 185 lbs. Born, Pembroke Pines, FL, March 19, 1996.
(Washington's 6th pick, 177th overall, in 2016 NHL Draft).

			Regular Season					Playoffs				
Season	Club	League	GP	G	A	Pts	PIM	GP	G	A	Pts	PIM
2011-12	Selects Acad. U16	Minor-CT	47	15	27	42	....	....	....	....	....	....
2012-13	Selects Acad. U16	Minor-CT	59	18	36	54	....	....	....	....	....	....
2013-14	Selects Acad. U18	USPHL	24	8	18	26	18	3	2	1	3	0
	Selects Academy	Minor-CT	37	17	19	36	19	....	....	....	....	....
	Fargo Force	USHL	3	0	1	1	0	....	....	....	....	....
2014-15	Salmon Arm	BCHL	57	6	14	20	18	....	....	....	....	....
2015-16	Quinnipiac	ECAC	43	4	22	26	2	....	....	....	....	....
2016-17	Quinnipiac	ECAC	38	7	19	26	16	....	....	....	....	....

ECAC All-Rookie Team (2016)

PROW, Ethan (PROW, EE-thuhn) **PIT**

Defense. Shoots right. 6', 185 lbs. Born, Sauk Rapids, MN, November 17, 1992.

			Regular Season					Playoffs				
Season	Club	League	GP	G	A	Pts	PIM	GP	G	A	Pts	PIM
2007-08	Sauk Rapids	High-MN	25	2	23	25	4	2	0	2	2	0
2008-09	Sauk Rapids	High-MN	24	7	25	32	2	2	0	4	4	0
2009-10	Team North	UMHSEL	23	0	6	6	6	....	....	....	....	....
	Sauk Rapids	High-MN	24	20	18	38	31	2	0	4	4	0
2010-11	Des Moines	USHL	59	8	14	22	28	....	....	....	....	....
2011-12	Des Moines	USHL	56	2	22	24	22	....	....	....	....	....
2012-13	St. Cloud State	WCHA	39	3	12	15	2	....	....	....	....	....
2013-14	St. Cloud State	NCHC	38	4	19	23	14	....	....	....	....	....
2014-15	St. Cloud State	NCHC	35	4	19	23	6	....	....	....	....	....
2015-16	St. Cloud State	NCHC	37	8	30	38	2	....	....	....	....	....
	Wilkes-Barre	AHL	5	0	1	1	6	2	0	0	0	0
2016-17	Wilkes-Barre	AHL	59	1	15	16	24	5	1	0	1	0
	Wheeling Nailers	ECHL	1	0	2	2	0	....	....	....	....	....

NCHC First All-Star Team (2016) • NCHC Player of the Year (2016) • NCAA West First All-American Team (2016)

Signed as a free agent by **Pittsburgh**, March 29, 2016.

PU, Cliff (POO, KLIHF) **BUF**

Right wing. Shoots right. 6'2", 191 lbs. Born, Richmond Hill, ON, June 3, 1998.
(Buffalo's 3rd pick, 69th overall, in 2016 NHL Draft).

			Regular Season					Playoffs				
Season	Club	League	GP	G	A	Pts	PIM	GP	G	A	Pts	PIM
2013-14	Toronto Marlboros	GTHL	33	23	24	47	10	16	4	13	17	4
2014-15	Oshawa Generals	OHL	17	2	1	3	2	....	....	....	....	....
	London Knights	OHL	24	2	4	6	2	4	0	0	0	0
2015-16	London Knights	OHL	63	12	19	31	24	18	8	5	13	6
2016-17	London Knights	OHL	63	35	51	86	36	14	2	5	7	8

QUENNEVILLE, David (KWEHN-vihl, DAY-vihd) **NYI**

Defense. Shoots right. 5'8", 182 lbs. Born, Edmonton, AB, March 13, 1998.
(NY Islanders' 6th pick, 200th overall, in 2016 NHL Draft).

			Regular Season					Playoffs				
Season	Club	League	GP	G	A	Pts	PIM	GP	G	A	Pts	PIM
2011-12	SSAC Lions	AMBHL	32	16	28	44	16	11	6	15	21	18
	SSAC Bulldogs	Minor-AB	2	1	1	2	0	....	....	....	....	....
2012-13	SSAC Lions	AMBHL	32	34	38	72	28	11	8	20	28	12
2013-14	SSAC Athletics	AMHL	32	11	16	27	40	3	2	3	5	2
	Medicine Hat	WHL	1	0	0	0	0	....	....	....	....	....
2014-15	Medicine Hat	WHL	66	6	14	20	47	1	0	0	0	0
2015-16	Medicine Hat	WHL	64	14	41	55	30	....	....	....	....	....
2016-17	Medicine Hat	WHL	49	23	36	59	37	11	4	9	13	6

QUENNEVILLE, Peter (KWEHN-vihl, PEE-tuhr) CBJ

Center/Right wing. Shoots right. 5'11", 191 lbs. Born, Edmonton, AB, March 9, 1994.
(Columbus' 8th pick, 195th overall, in 2013 NHL Draft).

			Regular Season					Playoffs				
Season	Club	League	GP	G	A	Pts	PIM	GP	G	A	Pts	PIM
2009-10	Edmonton MLAC	AMHL	33	13	11	24	10	....	....	....	....	....
2010-11	Sherwood Park	AJHL	54	6	16	22	8	3	0	0	0	0
2011-12	Sherwood Park	AJHL	53	31	50	81	22	10	4	4	8	10
2012-13	Dubuque	USHL	63	33	37	70	18	9	6	3	9	2
2013-14	Quinnipiac	ECAC	5	0	4	4	2	....	....	....	....	....
	Brandon	WHL	44	21	31	52	10	8	1	3	4	4
2014-15	Brandon	WHL	72	27	48	75	20	19	10	10	20	4
2015-16	Cincinnati	ECHL	58	11	15	26	34	....	....	....	....	....
	Lake Erie Monsters	AHL	1	0	0	0	0	....	....	....	....	....
2016-17	Aalborg	Denmark	45	30	10	49	26	7	1	2	3	27

USHL Second All-Star Team (2013)

• Re-assigned to **Cincinnati** (ECHL) by **Columbus**, October 7, 2015. Signed as a free agent by **Aalborg** (Denmark), July 14, 2016. Signed as a free agent by **Pardubice** (CzRep), July 8, 2017.

RADDYSH, Taylor (RA-DIHSH, TAY-luhr) T.B.

Right wing. Shoots right. 6'1", 203 lbs. Born, Caledon, ON, February 18, 1998.
(Tampa Bay's 4th pick, 58th overall, in 2016 NHL Draft).

			Regular Season					Playoffs				
Season	Club	League	GP	G	A	Pts	PIM	GP	G	A	Pts	PIM
2013-14	Toronto Marlboros	GTHL	31	25	27	52	28	14	3	4	7	10
2014-15	Erie Otters	OHL	58	21	6	27	13	20	3	3	6	8
2015-16	Erie Otters	OHL	67	24	49	73	18	12	4	6	10	2
2016-17	Erie Otters	OHL	58	42	*67	109	37	22	12	19	31	18

RAMSEY, Jack (RAM-zee, JAK) CHI

Right wing. Shoots right. 6'3", 191 lbs. Born, Farmington, MI, November 2, 1995.
(Chicago's 9th pick, 208th overall, in 2014 NHL Draft).

			Regular Season					Playoffs				
Season	Club	League	GP	G	A	Pts	PIM	GP	G	A	Pts	PIM
2011-12	Metro Northwest	MEPDL	13	5	5	10	0	....	....	....	....	....
	Team Southeast	UMHSEL	4	0	1	1	0	....	....	....	....	....
	Team Northeast	UMHSEL	1	0	1	1	0	1	0	0	0	0
2012-13	Minnetonka	High-MN	22	8	18	26	2	2	1	0	1	4
2013-14	Penticton Vees	BCHL	57	9	16	25	27	11	1	7	8	0
2014-15	Penticton Vees	BCHL	54	17	21	38	24	22	3	6	9	4
2015-16	U. of Minnesota	Big Ten	31	0	5	5	2	....	....	....	....	....
2016-17	U. of Minnesota	Big Ten	36	1	4	5	4	....	....	....	....	....

RASANEN, Aapeli (RAH-sah-nehn, a-ah-PUHL-ee) EDM

Center. Shoots right. 6', 196 lbs. Born, Tampere, Finland, June 1, 1998.
(Edmonton's 8th pick, 153rd overall, in 2016 NHL Draft).

			Regular Season					Playoffs				
Season	Club	League	GP	G	A	Pts	PIM	GP	G	A	Pts	PIM
2012-13	Tappara U18	Fin-U18	17	4	3	7	8	3	1	0	1	0
2013-14	Tappara U18	Fin-U18	36	16	21	37	54	3	1	1	2	4
2014-15	Tappara Jr.	Fin-Jr.	41	5	7	12	22	....	....	....	....	....
2015-16	Tappara Jr.	Fin-Jr.	50	19	19	38	26	3	1	0	1	0
	Tappara U18	Fin-U18	....	....	....	....	....	3	3	0	3	2
2016-17	Sioux City	USHL	38	7	18	25	30	13	2	2	4	12

• Signed Letter of Intent to attend **Boston College** (Hockey East) in fall of 2017.

RASANEN, Eemeli (RA-sah-nihn, eh-MEH-lee) TOR

Defense. Shoots right. 6'7", 214 lbs. Born, Joensuu, Finland, June 3, 1999.
(Toronto's 2nd pick, 59th overall, in 2017 NHL Draft).

			Regular Season					Playoffs				
Season	Club	League	GP	G	A	Pts	PIM	GP	G	A	Pts	PIM
2013-14	Jokipojat U18	Fin-U18	4	0	1	1	0	....	....	....	....	....
2014-15	Jokipojat U18	Fin-U18	22	8	8	16	16	1	0	0	0	0
	Jokipojat Jr.	Fin-Jr.	15	1	3	4	10	3	0	2	2	0
2015-16	Assat Pori U18	Fin-U18	28	2	19	21	12	....	....	....	....	....
	Assat Pori Jr.	Fin-Jr.	4	0	0	0	4	....	....	....	....	....
2016-17	Kingston	OHL	66	6	33	39	41	11	1	4	5	4

RASANEN, Ville (RA-sah-nihn, VIHL-ee) CAR

Defense. Shoots left. 6'2", 177 lbs. Born, Joensuu, Finland, August 10, 1998.
(Carolina's 8th pick, 197th overall, in 2017 NHL Draft).

			Regular Season					Playoffs				
Season	Club	League	GP	G	A	Pts	PIM	GP	G	A	Pts	PIM
2014-15	Jokipojat U18	Fin-U18	44	6	14	20	28	....	....	....	....	....
2015-16	Jokipojat U18	Fin-U18	26	10	20	30	20	....	....	....	....	....
	Jokipojat Jr.	Fin-Jr.	18	3	8	11	8	....	....	....	....	....
2016-17	Jokipojat Jr.	Fin-Jr.	22	9	9	18	10	1	0	0	0	0
	Jokipojat Joensuu	Finland-2	21	1	5	6	6	3	0	1	1	0

RASMUSSEN, Michael (RAZ-moo-sehn, MIGH-kuhl) DET

Center. Shoots left. 6'6", 221 lbs. Born, Vancouver, BC, April 17, 1999.
(Detroit's 1st pick, 9th overall, in 2017 NHL Draft).

			Regular Season					Playoffs				
Season	Club	League	GP	G	A	Pts	PIM	GP	G	A	Pts	PIM
2014-15	Okan. H.A. White	CSSHL	28	27	23	50	36	3	3	5	8	4
	Penticton Vees	BCHL	1	0	0	0	0	....	....	....	....	....
	Tri-City Americans	WHL	1	0	0	0	2	3	0	0	0	0
2015-16	Tri-City Americans	WHL	63	18	25	43	37	....	....	....	....	....
2016-17	Tri-City Americans	WHL	50	32	23	55	50	....	....	....	....	....

RATCLIFFE, Isaac (RAT-klihf, IGH-zuhk) PHI

Left wing. Shoots left. 6'6", 200 lbs. Born, London, ON, February 15, 1999.
(Philadelphia's 3rd pick, 35th overall, in 2017 NHL Draft).

			Regular Season					Playoffs				
Season	Club	League	GP	G	A	Pts	PIM	GP	G	A	Pts	PIM
2014-15	Lon. Knights MM	Minor-ON	32	22	27	49	16	13	6	1	7	12
2015-16	Guelph Storm	OHL	46	5	8	13	24	....	....	....	....	....
2016-17	Guelph Storm	OHL	67	28	26	54	65	....	....	....	....	....

RATHBONE, Jack (RATH-BOWN, JAK) VAN

Defense. Shoots left. 5'11", 172 lbs. Born, Boston, MA, May 20, 1999.
(Vancouver's 5th pick, 95th overall, in 2017 NHL Draft).

			Regular Season					Playoffs				
Season	Club	League	GP	G	A	Pts	PIM	GP	G	A	Pts	PIM
2014-15	Cape Cod U16	Minor-MA	15	5	8	13	12	....	....	....	....	....
	Dexter School	High-MA	31	3	4	7	....	....	....	....	....	....
2015-16	Cape Cod U16	Minor-MA	12	5	8	13	18	....	....	....	....	....
	Dexter School	High-MA	29	11	15	26	....	....	....	....	....	....
2016-17	Cape Cod U18	Minor-MA	14	4	8	12	8	....	....	....	....	....
	Cape Cod U18	Other	9	4	2	6	....	....	....	....	....	....
	Dexter School	High-MA	22	16	19	35	....	....	....	....	....	....
	Youngstown	USHL	4	0	1	1	0	....	....	....	....	....

• Signed Letter of Intent to attend **Harvard University** (ECAC) in fall of 2018.

REDDEKOPP, Chaz (REH-deh-kawp, CHAZ) L.A.

Defense. Shoots left. 6'3", 219 lbs. Born, Abbotsford, BC, January 1, 1997.
(Los Angeles' 5th pick, 187th overall, in 2015 NHL Draft).

			Regular Season					Playoffs				
Season	Club	League	GP	G	A	Pts	PIM	GP	G	A	Pts	PIM
2012-13	PoE Academy	CSSHL	10	3	10	13	22	2	1	1	2	0
	PoE Academy	NAPHL	21	3	10	13	15	4	1	3	4	4
	Victoria Royals	WHL	1	0	0	0	0	....	....	....	....	....
2013-14	Victoria Royals	WHL	40	1	8	9	33	2	0	0	0	0
2014-15	Victoria Royals	WHL	72	5	16	21	53	10	0	2	2	12
2015-16	Victoria Royals	WHL	70	4	26	30	102	13	0	5	5	4
2016-17	Victoria Royals	WHL	51	10	33	43	63	6	0	2	2	14
	Ontario Reign	AHL	3	0	0	0	4	....	....	....	....	....

REEDY, Scott (REE-dee, SKAWT) S.J.

Center. Shoots right. 6'2", 205 lbs. Born, Prior Lake, MN, April 4, 1999.
(San Jose's 3rd pick, 102nd overall, in 2017 NHL Draft).

			Regular Season					Playoffs				
Season	Club	League	GP	G	A	Pts	PIM	GP	G	A	Pts	PIM
2014-15	Shattuck	High-MN	54	23	32	55	24	....	....	....	....	....
2015-16	USAHNTDP	USHL	33	9	19	28	10	....	....	....	....	....
	USAHNTDP	U-17	23	11	15	26	16	....	....	....	....	....
2016-17	USAHNTDP	USHL	21	10	4	14	39	....	....	....	....	....
	USAHNTDP	U-18	39	12	16	28	12	....	....	....	....	....

• Signed Letter of Intent to attend **University of Minnesota** (Big Ten) in fall of 2017.

REILLY, William (RIGH-lee, WIHL-y'uhm) PIT

Defense. Shoots right. 6'2", 197 lbs. Born, Toronto, ON, July 23, 1997.
(Pittsburgh's 6th pick, 217th overall, in 2017 NHL Draft).

			Regular Season					Playoffs				
Season	Club	League	GP	G	A	Pts	PIM	GP	G	A	Pts	PIM
2012-13	Tor. R. Wings MM	GTHL	33	2	5	7	6	....	....	....	....	....
	Upper Canada	CISAA	8	1	1	2	0	....	....	....	....	....
2013-14	Upper Canada	CISAA	15	1	6	7	18	6	0	3	3	16
	Oakville Blades	ON-Jr.A	1	0	0	0	0	....	....	....	....	....
2014-15	North York	ON-Jr.A	47	17	18	35	96	6	0	1	1	8
2015-16	Nanaimo Clippers	BCHL	52	9	23	32	75	14	2	1	3	16
2016-17	RPI Engineers	ECAC	35	2	13	15	68	....	....	....	....	....

REPO, Sebastian (REH-poh, seh-BAS-t'yehn) FLA

Right wing. Shoots right. 6'3", 189 lbs. Born, Lahti, Finland, June 23, 1996.
(Florida's 5th pick, 184th overall, in 2017 NHL Draft).

			Regular Season					Playoffs				
Season	Club	League	GP	G	A	Pts	PIM	GP	G	A	Pts	PIM
2011-12	Pelicans Lahti U18	Fin-U18	1	0	0	0	0	....	....	....	....	....
2012-13	Pelicans Lahti U17	Fin-U17	2	2	3	5	10	2	2	2	4	0
	Pelicans Lahti U18	Fin-U18	39	16	28	44	26	....	....	....	....	....
2013-14	Pelicans Lahti U18	Fin-U18	7	8	6	14	10	2	0	1	1	0
	Pelicans Lahti Jr.	Fin-Jr.	45	14	22	36	32	11	0	3	3	10
2014-15	Pelicans Lahti Jr.	Fin-Jr.	19	7	8	15	67	....	....	....	....	....
	Pelicans Lahti	Finland	10	0	0	0	2	....	....	....	....	....
	Peliitat Heinola	Finland-2	4	0	0	0	2	....	....	....	....	....
	Sioux City	USHL	25	6	9	15	20	5	0	0	0	2
2015-16	Pelicans Lahti Jr.	Fin-Jr.	2	3	3	6	0	....	....	....	....	....
	Peliitat Heinola	Finland-2	1	1	2	3	0	....	....	....	....	....
	Pelicans Lahti	Finland	50	15	13	28	14	6	0	2	2	4
2016-17	Peliitat Heinola	Finland-2	4	2	2	4	4	....	....	....	....	....
	Pelicans Lahti	Finland	8	0	3	3	2	....	....	....	....	....
	Tappara Tampere	Finland	46	11	21	32	78	18	*6	1	7	16

REUNANEN, Tarmo (ray-OO-na-nehn, TAHR-moh) NYR

Defense. Shoots left. 6', 178 lbs. Born, Aanekoski, Finland, March 1, 1998.
(NY Rangers' 2nd pick, 98th overall, in 2016 NHL Draft).

			Regular Season					Playoffs				
Season	Club	League	GP	G	A	Pts	PIM	GP	G	A	Pts	PIM
2012-13	TPS Turku U18	Fin-U18	12	0	1	1	6	....	....	....	....	....
2013-14	TPS Turku U18	Fin-U18	42	10	10	20	26	....	....	....	....	....
2014-15	TPS Turku Jr.	Fin-Jr.	42	8	22	30	24	12	1	1	2	0
2015-16	TPS Turku Jr.	Fin-Jr.	11	2	4	6	14	2	0	0	0	2
	TPS Turku U18	Fin-U18	....	....	....	....	....	3	0	3	3	2
2016-17	TPS Turku Jr.	Fin-Jr.	4	1	2	3	6	3	1	1	2	2
	TPS Turku	Finland	2	0	0	0	0	....	....	....	....	....
	TuTo Turku	Finland-2	42	0	9	9	54	....	....	....	....	....

REWAY, Martin (rih-VIGH, MAR-tihn) MTL

Left wing. Shoots left. 5'8", 171 lbs. Born, Prague, Czech Rep., January 24, 1995.
(Montreal's 7th pick, 116th overall, in 2013 NHL Draft).

			Regular Season					Playoffs				
Season	Club	League	GP	G	A	Pts	PIM	GP	G	A	Pts	PIM
2008-09	Dolny Kubin U18	Svk-U18	13	8	12	20	10	....	....	....	....	....
	MHC Martin U18	Svk-U18	2	0	0	0	0	....	....	....	....	....
2009-10	Dolny Kubin U18	Svk-U18	26	32	38	70	24	....	....	....	....	....
2010-11	MHC Martin U18	Svk-U18	20	13	22	35	65	....	....	....	....	....
	MHC Martin Jr.	Slovak-Jr.	10	5	5	10	0	....	....	....	....	....
2011-12	Sparta U18	CzR-U18	25	21	39	60	42	9	8	16	24	12
	Sparta Jr.	CzRep-Jr.	5	2	4	6	2	....	....	....	....	....
2012-13	Gatineau	QMJHL	47	22	28	50	56	10	1	11	12	20
2013-14	Gatineau	QMJHL	43	20	42	62	48	9	5	10	15	16
2014-15	HC Sparta Praha	CzRep	34	9	28	37	54	8	1	6	7	20
2015-16	HC Sparta Praha	CzRep	14	5	10	15	6	....	....	....	....	....
	Fribourg	Swiss	19	8	13	21	14	....	....	....	....	....
2016-17			DID NOT PLAY – INJURED									

• Missed 2016-17 due to heart inflammation and a serious infection.

RIAT, Damien (ree-AT, DAY-mee-uhn) WSH

Center. Shoots right. 6', 172 lbs. Born, Geneva, Switzerland, February 26, 1997.
(Washington's 3rd pick, 117th overall, in 2016 NHL Draft).

			Regular Season					Playoffs				
Season	Club	League	GP	G	A	Pts	PIM	GP	G	A	Pts	PIM
2011-12	Geneve U17	Swiss-U17	18	3	4	7	52	5	1	1	2	2
	HC Geneve U17 II	Swiss-U17	1	1	0	1	2	....	....	....	....	....
2012-13	Notre Dame Argos	SMHL	36	4	9	13	58	3	0	0	0	2
2013-14	Notre Dame Argos	SMHL	44	18	38	56	56	12	5	7	12	28
2014-15	Malmo U18	Swe-U18	1	0	0	0	0	....	....	....	....	....
	Malmo Jr.	Swe-Jr.	40	7	7	14	70	....	....	....	....	....
	Malmo	Sweden-2	3	0	0	0	0	....	....	....	....	....
2015-16	Geneve Jr.	Swiss-Jr.	4	3	5	8	10	....	....	....	....	....
	Geneve	Swiss	45	9	12	21	34	4	1	2	3	10
2016-17	Geneve	Swiss	46	7	7	14	36	4	0	0	0	4

RICHARD, Anthony (rih-SHAHRD, AN-thuh-nee) NSH

Center. Shoots left. 5'10", 163 lbs. Born, Trois-Rivieres, QC, December 20, 1996.
(Nashville's 3rd pick, 100th overall, in 2015 NHL Draft).

			Regular Season					Playoffs				
Season	Club	League	GP	G	A	Pts	PIM	GP	G	A	Pts	PIM
2011-12	Trois-Rivieres	QAAA	41	11	17	28	50	8	3	5	8	14
2012-13	Trois-Rivieres	QAAA	12	9	6	15	8	....	....	....	....	....
	Val-d'Or Foreurs	QMJHL	42	6	2	8	15	9	0	1	1	5
2013-14	Val-d'Or Foreurs	QMJHL	66	25	27	52	49	24	10	7	17	12
2014-15	Val-d'Or Foreurs	QMJHL	66	43	48	91	78	17	12	10	22	10
2015-16	Val-d'Or Foreurs	QMJHL	58	37	50	87	37	3	2	1	3	2
	Milwaukee	AHL	....	....	....	....	....	3	0	0	0	0
2016-17	Milwaukee	AHL	55	4	12	16	23	3	0	1	1	4
	Cincinnati	ECHL	5	1	1	2	0	....	....	....	....	....

ROBERTSON, Dennis (RAW-buhrt-suhn, DEH-nihs) CAR

Defense. Shoots left. 6'1", 215 lbs. Born, Fort St. John, BC, May 24, 1991.
(Toronto's 7th pick, 173rd overall, in 2011 NHL Draft).

			Regular Season					Playoffs				
Season	Club	League	GP	G	A	Pts	PIM	GP	G	A	Pts	PIM
2006-07	Okanagan Prep	Minor-BC	62	15	15	30	78	....	....	....	....	....
2007-08	Summerland Sting	KIJHL	50	9	18	27	66	4	2	1	3	12
2008-09	Langley Chiefs	BCHL	55	1	11	12	64	4	0	1	1	4
2009-10	Langley Chiefs	BCHL	53	9	25	34	83	10	2	2	4	14
2010-11	Brown U.	ECAC	30	6	11	17	48	....	....	....	....	....
2011-12	Brown U.	ECAC	32	2	14	16	72	....	....	....	....	....
2012-13	Brown U.	ECAC	36	3	17	20	69	....	....	....	....	....
2013-14	Brown U.	ECAC	30	6	11	17	78	....	....	....	....	....
	Charlotte	AHL	1	0	0	0	0	....	....	....	....	....
2014-15	Charlotte	AHL	57	3	14	17	70	....	....	....	....	....
2015-16	Rockford IceHogs	AHL	37	2	4	6	30	....	....	....	....	....
	Charlotte	AHL	21	0	3	3	4	....	....	....	....	....
2016-17	Charlotte	AHL	65	6	10	16	52	5	1	2	3	6

ECAC All-Rookie Team (2011)

Traded to **Carolina** by **Toronto** with John-Michael Liles for Tim Gleason, January 1, 2014. Traded to **Chicago** by **Carolina** with Jake Massie and Carolina's 5th round pick (later traded to Vancouver –Vancouver selected Kristoffer Gunnarsson) in 2017 NHL Draft for Kris Versteeg, Joakim Nordstrom and Chicago's 3rd round pick (later traded back to Chicago, later traded to Detroit – Detroit selected Keith Petruzzelli) in 2017 NHL Draft, September 11, 2015. Traded to **Carolina** by **Chicago** for Drew MacIntyre, February 29, 2016.

ROBERTSON, Jason (raw-BUHRT-suhn, JAY-suhn) DAL

Left wing. Shoots left. 6'2", 196 lbs. Born, Arcadia, CA, July 22, 1999.
(Dallas' 3rd pick, 39th overall, in 2017 NHL Draft).

			Regular Season					Playoffs				
Season	Club	League	GP	G	A	Pts	PIM	GP	G	A	Pts	PIM
2013-14	Detroit Kings 15U	Minor-MI	51	40	47	87	6	....	....	....	....	....
2014-15	Don Mills MM	GTHL	62	28	33	61	14	....	....	....	....	....
2015-16	Kingston	OHL	54	18	14	32	6	4	1	1	2	2
2016-17	Kingston	OHL	68	42	39	81	29	11	5	13	18	0

ROD, Noah (RAWD, NOH-uh) S.J.

Right wing. Shoots left. 6', 195 lbs. Born, La Chaux-de-Fonds, Switz., June 7, 1996.
(San Jose's 3rd pick, 53rd overall, in 2014 NHL Draft).

			Regular Season					Playoffs				
Season	Club	League	GP	G	A	Pts	PIM	GP	G	A	Pts	PIM
2009-10	Lausanne U17 II	Swiss-U17	2	1	0	1	2	....	....	....	....	....
2010-11	Lausanne HC U17	Swiss-U17	7	0	0	0	2	....	....	....	....	....
	Lausanne U17 II	Swiss-U17	3	1	3	4	2	....	....	....	....	....
2011-12	Geneve U17	Swiss-U17	26	11	24	35	46	6	2	4	6	8
	Geneve U17 II	Swiss-U17	1	1	0	1	0	....	....	....	....	....
	Geneve Jr.	Swiss-Jr.	18	0	2	2	16	....	....	....	....	....
2012-13	Geneve U17	Swiss-U17	6	3	7	10	10	5	4	1	5	4
	Geneve Jr.	Swiss-Jr.	39	19	19	38	96	....	....	....	....	....
2013-14	Geneve Jr.	Swiss-Jr.	31	16	21	37	58	2	0	1	1	29
	Geneve	Swiss	28	1	2	3	8	12	1	3	4	4
2014-15	Geneve	Swiss	38	1	3	4	22	10	2	1	3	6
2015-16	Geneve Jr.	Swiss-Jr.	3	1	6	7	4	....	....	....	....	....
	Geneve	Swiss	44	7	9	16	12	6	2	2	4	4
2016-17	Geneve	Swiss	27	5	9	14	22	4	0	0	0	2
	San Jose Barracuda	AHL	2	0	1	1	0	5	0	0	0	0

RONDBJERG, Jonas (RAWND-buhrg, YOH-nuhs) VGK

Right wing. Shoots left. 6'1", 197 lbs. Born, Horsholm, Denmark, March 31, 1999.
(Las Vegas' 6th pick, 65th overall, in 2017 NHL Draft).

			Regular Season					Playoffs				
Season	Club	League	GP	G	A	Pts	PIM	GP	G	A	Pts	PIM
2012-13	Rungsted U17	Den-U17	14	9	9	18	2	4	2	1	3	2
	Rungsted Jr.	Den-Jr.	....	....	....	....	....	1	0	0	0	0
2013-14	Rungsted U17	Den-U17	19	29	24	53	6	3	6	3	9	0
	Gladsaxe Bears Jr.	Den-Jr.	7	3	4	7	2	....	....	....	....	....
2014-15	Rubgsted IK U17	Den-U17	6	16	19	35	0	3	1	2	3	2
	Rungsted IK 2	Den-2	11	6	8	14	4	....	....	....	....	....
	Rungsted IK	Denmark	30	3	1	4	0	7	0	1	1	0
2015-16	Rungsted	Denmark	35	10	4	14	6	4	1	1	2	2
2016-17	Vaxjo Lakers HC	Sweden	5	0	0	0	0	....	....	....	....	....
	Vaxjo U18	Swe-U18	1	1	0	1	0	....	....	....	....	....
	Vaxjo Jr.	Swe-Jr.	42	9	22	31	4	7	2	3	5	0

RONNING, Ty (RAW-nihng, TIGH) NYR

Right wing. Shoots right. 5'9", 167 lbs. Born, Burnaby, BC, October 20, 1997.
(NY Rangers' 6th pick, 201st overall, in 2016 NHL Draft).

			Regular Season					Playoffs				
Season	Club	League	GP	G	A	Pts	PIM	GP	G	A	Pts	PIM
2011-12	Burnaby W.C.	Minor-BC	72	77	76	153	....	....	....	....	....	....
2012-13	Delta Academy	Minor-BC	12	14	11	25	6	....	....	....	....	....
2013-14	Vancouver Giants	WHL	56	9	11	20	4	2	0	0	0	0
2014-15	Vancouver Giants	WHL	24	1	1	2	8	....	....	....	....	....
2015-16	Vancouver Giants	WHL	67	31	28	59	18	....	....	....	....	....
2016-17	Vancouver Giants	WHL	68	25	28	53	35	....	....	....	....	....
	Hartford Wolf Pack	AHL	12	2	3	5	6	....	....	....	....	....

• Missed majority of 2012-13 due to wrist injury at Vancouver (WHL) training camp.

ROSEN, Calle TOR

Defense. Shoots left. 6', 175 lbs. Born, Vaxjo, Sweden, February 2, 1994.

			Regular Season					Playoffs				
Season	Club	League	GP	G	A	Pts	PIM	GP	G	A	Pts	PIM
2012-13	Karlskrona HK	Sweden-2	12	1	2	3	0	....	....	....	....	....
2013-14	Karlskrona HK	Sweden-2	52	7	7	14	18	....	....	....	....	....
2014-15	Vaxjo Lakers HC	Sweden	3	0	0	0	2	....	....	....	....	....
	Rogle	Sweden-2	42	10	13	23	8	....	....	....	....	....
2015-16	Vaxjo Lakers HC	Sweden	52	3	11	14	4	13	1	4	5	0
2016-17	Vaxjo Lakers HC	Sweden	41	6	13	19	10	6	0	0	0	2

Signed as a free agent by **Toronto**, May 16, 2017.

ROY, Jeremy (WAH, JAIR-ih-mee) S.J.

Defense. Shoots right. 6', 185 lbs. Born, Longueuil, QC, May 14, 1997.
(San Jose's 2nd pick, 31st overall, in 2015 NHL Draft).

			Regular Season					Playoffs				
Season	Club	League	GP	G	A	Pts	PIM	GP	G	A	Pts	PIM
2011-12	Antoine-Girouard	QAAA	41	7	25	32	22	11	1	2	3	2
2012-13	Antoine-Girouard	QAAA	42	12	42	54	18	13	4	11	15	6
2013-14	Sherbrooke	QMJHL	64	14	30	44	23	....	....	....	....	....
2014-15	Sherbrooke	QMJHL	46	5	38	43	37	6	1	4	5	0
2015-16	Sherbrooke	QMJHL	45	6	28	34	27	....	....	....	....	....
2016-17	Blainville-Bois.	QMJHL	10	2	1	3	9	....	....	....	....	....

QMJHL All-Rookie Team (2014)

ROY, Kevin (ROY, KEH-vihn) ANA

Center. Shoots left. 5'9", 174 lbs. Born, Greenfield Park, QC, May 20, 1993.
(Anaheim's 4th pick, 97th overall, in 2012 NHL Draft).

			Regular Season					Playoffs				
Season	Club	League	GP	G	A	Pts	PIM	GP	G	A	Pts	PIM
2009-10	Deerfield Academy	High-MA	27	12	16	28	....	....	....	....	....	....
2010-11	Deerfield Academy	High-MA	18	19	15	34	6	....	....	....	....	....
2011-12	Lincoln Stars	USHL	59	54	50	104	50	8	7	3	10	4
2012-13	Northeastern	H-East	29	17	17	34	24	....	....	....	....	....
2013-14	Northeastern	H-East	37	19	27	46	30	....	....	....	....	....
2014-15	Northeastern	H-East	35	19	25	44	28	....	....	....	....	....
2015-16	Northeastern	H-East	29	10	16	26	10	....	....	....	....	....
	San Diego Gulls	AHL	2	0	0	0	0	....	....	....	....	....
2016-17	San Diego Gulls	AHL	67	16	30	46	16	10	2	3	5	0

USHL All-Rookie Team (2012) • USHL First All-Star Team (2012) • USHL Player of the Year (2012) • Hockey East All-Rookie Team (2013) • Hockey East Second All-Star Team (2014) • Hockey East First All-Star Team (2015) • NCAA East Second All-American Team (2015)

ROY, Matt (ROI, MAT) L.A.

Defense. Shoots right. 6', 200 lbs. Born, Canton, MI, March 1, 1995.
(Los Angeles' 6th pick, 194th overall, in 2015 NHL Draft).

			Regular Season					Playoffs				
Season	Club	League	GP	G	A	Pts	PIM	GP	G	A	Pts	PIM
2010-11	Det. V. Honda U16	T1EHL	35	3	10	13	24	....	....	....	....	....
	Det. V. Honda U16	Other	11	2	2	4	14	....	....	....	....	....
2011-12	Det. V. Honda U18	T1EHL	37	1	8	9	28	7	2	0	2	5
2012-13	Det. V. Honda U18	T1EHL	41	12	21	33	62	4	0	2	2	4
	Indiana Ice	USHL	10	1	2	3	4	....	....	....	....	....
2013-14	Indiana Ice	USHL	24	4	5	9	21	12	2	4	6	4
2014-15	Michigan Tech	WCHA	36	0	9	9	22	....	....	....	....	....
2015-16	Michigan Tech	WCHA	37	7	13	20	27	....	....	....	....	....
2016-17	Michigan Tech	WCHA	42	5	21	26	74	....	....	....	....	....
	Ontario Reign	AHL	8	0	1	1	7	2	0	0	0	2

WCHA Second All-Star Team (2016) • WCHA First All-Star Team (2017)

ROY, Nicolas (WAH, NIH-koh-las) CAR

Center. Shoots right. 6'4", 209 lbs. Born, Amos, QC, February 5, 1997.
(Carolina's 4th pick, 96th overall, in 2015 NHL Draft).

			Regular Season					Playoffs				
Season	Club	League	GP	G	A	Pts	PIM	GP	G	A	Pts	PIM
2011-12	Amos Forestiers	QAAA	43	13	18	31	30	....	....	....	....	....
2012-13	Amos Forestiers	QAAA	27	15	18	33	24	....	....	....	....	....
2013-14	Chicoutimi	QMJHL	63	16	25	41	19	4	0	2	2	8
2014-15	Chicoutimi	QMJHL	68	16	34	50	40	5	2	3	5	8
2015-16	Chicoutimi	QMJHL	63	*48	42	90	71	6	3	4	7	16
	Charlotte	AHL	2	0	0	0	4	....	....	....	....	....
2016-17	Chicoutimi	QMJHL	53	36	44	80	46	17	8	13	21	14

QMJHL First All-Star Team (2016, 2017)

ROYKAS MARTHINSEN, Kristian (roy-KUHS-mahr-TIHN-sihn, K.) WSH

Right wing. Shoots left. 6', 185 lbs. Born, Oslo, , August 28, 1999.
(Washington's 4th pick, 213th overall, in 2017 NHL Draft).

			Regular Season					Playoffs				
Season	Club	League	GP	G	A	Pts	PIM	GP	G	A	Pts	PIM
2013-14	Lorenskog IK U18	Nor-U18	7	3	1	4	0	....	....	....	....	....
2014-15	Lorenskog IK U18	Nor-U18	29	24	18	42	67	8	2	6	8	2
	Lorenskog Jr.	Norway-Jr.	6	1	2	3	2	....	....	....	....	....
2015-16	Almtuna U18	Swe-U18	37	18	15	33	57	4	0	0	0	2
	Almtuna Jr.	Swe-Jr.	3	4	1	5	0	....	....	....	....	....
2016-17	Almtuna U18	Swe-U18	28	10	7	17	66	5	5	1	6	8
	Almtuna Jr.	Swe-Jr.	19	13	5	18	24	2	1	0	1	0
	Almtuna	Sweden-2	1	1	0	1	0	1	0	0	0	0

RUBTSOV, German (ROOB-sawv, GAIR-muhn) PHI

Center. Shoots left. 6'1", 190 lbs. Born, Chekhov, Russia, June 27, 1998.
(Philadelphia's 1st pick, 22nd overall, in 2016 NHL Draft).

			Regular Season					Playoffs				
Season	Club	League	GP	G	A	Pts	PIM	GP	G	A	Pts	PIM
2014-15	Chekhov Jr.	Russia-Jr.	11	1	4	5	4	1	0	0	0	0
2015-16	Russia U18	Russia-Jr.	28	12	14	26	10	3	0	1	1	0
2016-17	Podolsk	KHL	15	0	0	0	6	....	....	....	....	....
	Chicoutimi	QMJHL	16	9	13	22	4	....	....	....	....	....

RUGGIERO, Steven (roo-zhee-AIR-oh, STEE-vehn) ANA

Defense. Shoots left. 6'3", 200 lbs. Born, Kings Park, NY, January 1, 1997.
(Anaheim's 6th pick, 178th overall, in 2015 NHL Draft).

			Regular Season					Playoffs				
Season	Club	League	GP	G	A	Pts	PIM	GP	G	A	Pts	PIM
2012-13	NY Metro F.M.	MtJHL	20	2	7	9	16	4	0	0	0	4
	Long Island Gulls	AYHL	1	0	0	0	0	....	....	....	....	....
2013-14	Long Island Gulls	AYHL	2	0	0	0	0	....	....	....	....	....
	Youngstown	USHL	41	1	4	5	22	....	....	....	....	....
2014-15	USAHNTDP	USHL	25	0	7	7	16	....	....	....	....	....
	USAHNTDP	U-18	41	1	7	8	28	....	....	....	....	....
2015-16	Providence College	H-East	10	0	1	1	19	....	....	....	....	....
2016-17	Providence College	H-East	6	0	1	1	10	....	....	....	....	....
	Youngstown	USHL	29	0	5	5	72	5	0	0	0	2

• Signed Letter of Intent to attend **Lake Superior State** (WCHA) in fall of 2017.

RUOPP, Sam (ROO-awp, SAM)

Defense. Shoots left. 6'3", 195 lbs. Born, Regina, SK, June 3, 1996.
(Columbus' 6th pick, 129th overall, in 2015 NHL Draft).

			Regular Season					Playoffs				
Season	Club	League	GP	G	A	Pts	PIM	GP	G	A	Pts	PIM
2011-12	Reg. Pat Cdns.	SMHL	41	0	10	10	44	....	....	....	....	....
2012-13	Reg. Pat Cdns.	SMHL	37	3	11	14	34	8	0	2	2	4
	Prince George	WHL	6	0	0	0	0	....	....	....	....	....
2013-14	Prince George	WHL	64	5	11	16	55	....	....	....	....	....
2014-15	Prince George	WHL	64	3	23	26	140	5	1	2	3	4
2015-16	Prince George	WHL	69	4	21	25	100	3	0	0	0	2
2016-17	Prince George	WHL	55	4	20	24	51	6	0	1	1	2

RUPERT, Ryan (ROO-puhrt, RIGH-uhn)

Center. Shoots left. 5'8", 194 lbs. Born, Grand Bend, ON, June 2, 1994.
(Toronto's 5th pick, 157th overall, in 2012 NHL Draft).

			Regular Season					Playoffs				
Season	Club	League	GP	G	A	Pts	PIM	GP	G	A	Pts	PIM
2008-09	Lambton Jr. Sting	Minor-ON	27	21	20	41	53	11	3	3	6	14
2009-10	Elgin-Mid. Chiefs	Minor-ON	30	22	27	49	40	15	11	10	21	22
	Elgin-Mid. Chiefs	Other	11	3	11	14	38	....	....	....	....	....
	Lambton Shores	ON-Jr.B	4	0	2	2	12	....	....	....	....	....
2010-11	Lambton Shores	ON-Jr.B	25	15	21	36	107	....	....	....	....	....
	London Knights	OHL	39	9	18	27	30	6	2	1	3	6
2011-12	London Knights	OHL	63	17	31	48	120	19	9	6	15	31
2012-13	London Knights	OHL	54	11	35	46	75	21	11	9	20	12
2013-14	London Knights	OHL	68	21	52	73	54	9	3	7	10	10
2014-15	Toronto Marlies	AHL	57	15	12	27	39	5	0	1	1	2
	Orlando	ECHL	17	5	9	14	28	....	....	....	....	....
2015-16	Toronto Marlies	AHL	29	6	6	12	14	....	....	....	....	....
	Orlando	ECHL	7	3	2	5	5	....	....	....	....	....
	Binghamton	AHL	30	7	6	13	35	....	....	....	....	....
2016-17	Binghamton	AHL	33	3	3	6	25	....	....	....	....	....
	Wichita Thunder	ECHL	29	9	12	21	12	....	....	....	....	....

Traded to **Ottawa** by **Toronto** with Dion Phaneuf, Matt Frattin, Casey Bailey and Cody Donaghey for Jared Cowen, Colin Greening, Milan Michalek, Tobias Lindberg and Ottawa's 2nd round pick (Eemeli Rasanen) iin 2017 NHL Draft, February 9, 2016.

RUSSELL, Patrick (RUH-sehl, PA-trihk) EDM

Right wing. Shoots right. 6'1", 205 lbs. Born, Birkerod, Denmark, January 4, 1993.

			Regular Season					Playoffs				
Season	Club	League	GP	G	A	Pts	PIM	GP	G	A	Pts	PIM
2008-09	IC Gentofte U17	Den-U17	8	15	10	25	10	....	....	....	....	....
	IC Gentofte Jr.	Den-Jr.	27	31	15	46	28	3	1	2	3	0
	Gentofte Stars	Den-2	13	5	2	7	4	6	0	1	1	2
2009-10	Linkopings HC U18	Swe-U18	30	16	11	27	10	3	0	0	0	2
2010-11	Linkopings HC U18	Swe-U18	33	19	19	38	16	3	1	0	1	0
	Linkopings HC Jr.	Swe-Jr.	4	0	0	0	2	....	....	....	....	....
2011-12	Linkopings HC Jr.	Swe-Jr.	1	0	0	0	0	1	0	0	0	0
2012-13	Linkopings HC Jr.	Swe-Jr.	37	18	18	36	6	5	0	3	3	4
2013-14	Waterloo	USHL	55	29	20	49	40	12	5	3	8	6
2014-15	St. Cloud State	NCHC	40	10	15	25	12	....	....	....	....	....
2015-16	St. Cloud State	NCHC	41	20	21	41	14	....	....	....	....	....
2016-17	Bakersfield	AHL	68	8	9	17	22	....	....	....	....	....

NCHC All-Rookie Team (2015)

Signed as a free agent by **Edmonton**, May 9, 2016.

RUTTA, Jan (ROO-tuh, YAN) CHI

Defense. Shoots right. 6'3", 200 lbs. Born, Pisek, Czech., July 29, 1990.

			Regular Season					Playoffs				
Season	Club	League	GP	G	A	Pts	PIM	GP	G	A	Pts	PIM
2010-11	KLH Chomutov Jr.	CzRep-Jr.	44	14	21	35	40	....	....	....	....	....
	KLH Chomutov	CzRep-2	24	0	0	0	10	....	....	....	....	....
2011-12	Pirati Chomutov	CzRep-2	48	2	6	8	16	12	1	4	5	6
	KLH Chomutov Jr.	CzRep-Jr.	....	....	....	....	....	2	0	1	1	4
2012-13	Pirati Chomutov	CzRep	43	2	8	10	20	....	....	....	....	....
	Pirati Chomutov	CzRep-Q	8	0	0	0	6	....	....	....	....	....
	SK Kadan	CzRep-2	7	0	3	3	0	....	....	....	....	....
2013-14	Pirati Chomutov	CzRep	19	1	2	3	6	....	....	....	....	....
	Pirati Chomutov	CzRep-Q	9	1	2	3	0	....	....	....	....	....
	SK Kadan	CzRep-2	18	1	3	4	8	....	....	....	....	....
2014-15	Pirati Chomutov	CzRep-2	61	12	20	32	50	11	4	3	7	24
2015-16	Pirati Chomutov	CzRep	44	10	11	21	22	7	1	2	3	8
2016-17	Pirati Chomutov	CzRep	46	8	24	32	30	17	2	*11	13	8

Signed as a free agent by **Chicago**, June 7, 2017.

RUZICKA, Adam (roo-SEECH-kah, a-DUHM) CGY

Center. Shoots left. 6'4", 209 lbs. Born, Bratislava, Slovakia, November 5, 1999.
(Calgary's 2nd pick, 109th overall, in 2017 NHL Draft).

			Regular Season					Playoffs				
Season	Club	League	GP	G	A	Pts	PIM	GP	G	A	Pts	PIM
2012-13	Ruzinov U18	Svk-U18	7	9	2	11	0	....	....	....	....	....
2013-14	Ruzinov U18	Svk-U18	16	8	4	12	6	....	....	....	....	....
	Bratislava U18	Svk-U18	7	5	5	10	0	8	1	1	2	0
2014-15	HC Pardubice U18	CzR-U18	22	10	12	22	4	4	4	1	5	4
	HC Pardubice Jr.	CzRep-Jr.	11	3	3	6	0	....	....	....	....	....
2015-16	HC Pardubice U18	CzR-U18	3	5	3	8	2	4	2	2	4	4
	HC Pardubice Jr.	CzRep-Jr.	30	14	16	30	39	....	....	....	....	....
	SR 18	Slovak-Jr.	4	3	2	5	2	....	....	....	....	....
2016-17	Sarnia Sting	OHL	61	25	21	46	30	4	0	2	2	0

RYAN, Joakim (RIGHN, YOH-ah-kihm) S.J.

Defense. Shoots left. 5'11", 185 lbs. Born, Rumson, NJ, June 17, 1993.
(San Jose's 6th pick, 198th overall, in 2012 NHL Draft).

			Regular Season					Playoffs				
Season	Club	League	GP	G	A	Pts	PIM	GP	G	A	Pts	PIM
2009-10	N.J. Devils Youth	AYHL	32	13	23	36	34	....	....	....	....	....
2010-11	Dubuque	USHL	53	3	29	32	26	11	2	3	5	2
2011-12	Cornell Big Red	ECAC	34	7	10	17	20	....	....	....	....	....
2012-13	Cornell Big Red	ECAC	34	3	20	23	12	....	....	....	....	....
2013-14	Cornell Big Red	ECAC	32	8	16	24	27	....	....	....	....	....
2014-15	Cornell Big Red	ECAC	23	1	13	14	27	....	....	....	....	....
	Worcester Sharks	AHL	7	0	2	2	2	....	....	....	....	....
2015-16	San Jose Barracuda	AHL	66	2	26	28	26	4	0	3	3	0
2016-17	San Jose Barracuda	AHL	65	10	39	49	41	15	4	7	11	4

ECAC Second All-Star Team (2014) • ECAC First All-Star Team (2015)

RYCZEK, Jake (RIGH-zihk, JAYK) CHI

Defense. Shoots right. 5'10", 181 lbs. Born, Springfield, MA, March 19, 1998.
(Chicago's 9th pick, 203rd overall, in 2016 NHL Draft).

			Regular Season					Playoffs				
Season	Club	League	GP	G	A	Pts	PIM	GP	G	A	Pts	PIM
2013-14	Selects Acad. U16	USPHL	26	7	10	17	6	3	1	0	1	4
	Selects Academy	Minor-CT	36	9	15	24	....	....	....	....	....	....
2014-15	Sioux City	USHL	55	6	12	18	26	....	....	....	....	....
2015-16	Sioux City	USHL	29	3	11	14	8	....	....	....	....	....
	Waterloo	USHL	18	4	16	20	4	9	0	4	4	2

• Signed Letter of Intent to attend **Providence College** (Hockey East) in fall of 2017.

RYKOV, Yegor (RIGH-kawv, YEE-gohr) N.J.

Defense. Shoots left. 6'2", 205 lbs. Born, Vidnoe, Russia, April 14, 1997.
(New Jersey's 7th pick, 132nd overall, in 2016 NHL Draft).

			Regular Season					Playoffs				
Season	Club	League	GP	G	A	Pts	PIM	GP	G	A	Pts	PIM
2013-14	St. Petersburg Jr.	Russia-Jr.	37	1	6	7	20	4	0	0	0	2
2014-15	St. Petersburg Jr.	Russia-Jr.	42	5	16	21	8	7	1	1	2	0
2015-16	St. Petersburg Jr.	Russia-Jr.	20	3	7	10	10	2	0	0	0	0
	SKA-Neva	Russia-2	10	0	2	2	8	5	1	0	1	0
	SKA St. Petersburg	KHL	10	0	1	1	0	2	0	0	0	2
2016-17	SKA St. Petersburg	KHL	47	0	9	9	8	15	0	0	0	7

RYMSHA, Drake (RIHM-SHAH, DRAYK) L.A.

Center. Shoots right. 6', 187 lbs. Born, Huntington Woods, MI, June 8, 1998.
(Los Angeles' 7th pick, 138th overall, in 2017 NHL Draft).

			Regular Season					Playoffs				
Season	Club	League	GP	G	A	Pts	PIM	GP	G	A	Pts	PIM
2013-14	Tor. Jr. Can. MM	GTHL	33	15	26	41	26	13	3	5	8	18
2014-15	London Knights	OHL	62	5	7	12	51	10	0	0	0	8
2015-16	London Knights	OHL	4	0	0	0	4	....	....	....	....	....
	Ottawa 67's	OHL	28	3	6	9	24	5	0	0	0	6
2016-17	Ottawa 67's	OHL	37	15	14	29	41	....	....	....	....	....
	Sarnia Sting	OHL	28	20	13	33	39	4	1	2	3	17

SAARELA, Aleksi (sah'ah-REH-lah, al-EHX-ay) CAR

Center. Shoots left. 5'11", 200 lbs. Born, Helsinki, Finland, January 7, 1997.
(NY Rangers' 4th pick, 89th overall, in 2015 NHL Draft).

			Regular Season					Playoffs				
Season	Club	League	GP	G	A	Pts	PIM	GP	G	A	Pts	PIM
2012-13	Lukko Rauma U18	Fin-U18	16	17	19	36	14	....	....	....	....	....
	Lukko Rauma Jr.	Fin-Jr.	22	8	10	18	6	10	2	6	8	2
	Lukko Rauma	Finland	3	1	1	2	0	....	....	....	....	....
2013-14	Lukko Rauma Jr.	Fin-Jr.	17	6	16	22	8	....	....	....	....	....
	Lukko Rauma	Finland	12	0	2	2	2	....	....	....	....	....
2014-15	Assat Pori	Finland	51	6	6	12	18	2	0	1	1	0
2015-16	Assat Pori Jr.	Fin-Jr.	2	0	2	2	0	3	1	2	3	0
	Assat Pori	Finland	51	20	13	33	14	....	....	....	....	....
2016-17	Lukko Rauma	Finland	49	15	13	28	10	....	....	....	....	....
	Charlotte	AHL	9	6	4	10	2	5	0	0	0	2

Traded to **Carolina** by **NY Rangers** with NY Rangers' 2nd round pick (later traded to Chicago – Chicago selected Artur Kayumov) in 2016 NHL Draft and NY Rangers' 2nd round pick (Luke Martin) in 2017 NHL Draft for Eric Staal, February 27, 2016.

SAARIJARVI, Vili (sah'ah-rih-YAHR-vee, VIH-lee) DET

Defense. Shoots right. 5'10", 172 lbs. Born, Rovaniemi, Finland, May 15, 1997.
(Detroit's 2nd pick, 73rd overall, in 2015 NHL Draft).

			Regular Season					Playoffs				
Season	Club	League	GP	G	A	Pts	PIM	GP	G	A	Pts	PIM
2012-13	Karpat Oulu U18	Fin-U18	38	5	25	30	24	3	0	1	1	2
	Karpat Oulu Jr.	Fin-Jr.	3	0	1	1	0	2	0	0	0	4
2013-14	Karpat Oulu U18	Fin-U18	8	3	7	10	2	....	....	....	....	....
	Karpat Oulu Jr.	Fin-Jr.	40	7	21	28	10	12	1	0	1	6
2014-15	Green Bay	USHL	57	6	17	23	14	....	....	....	....	....
2015-16	Flint Firebirds	OHL	59	12	31	43	32	....	....	....	....	....
	Toledo Walleye	ECHL	5	1	3	4	0	....	....	....	....	....
2016-17	Mississauga	OHL	34	11	20	31	14	20	5	10	15	8

SABOURIN, Scott (SA-boo-rihn, SKAWT) ANA

Right wing. Shoots right. 6'3", 206 lbs. Born, Orleans, ON, July 30, 1992.

			Regular Season					Playoffs				
Season	Club	League	GP	G	A	Pts	PIM	GP	G	A	Pts	PIM
2007-08	Ottawa Jr. 67's	Minor-ON	25	12	3	15	39	8	1	3	4	14
2008-09	Brockville Braves	ON-Jr.A	57	9	8	17	64	9	1	2	3	4
2009-10	Kanata Stallions	ON-Jr.A	43	4	2	6	64	....	....	....	....	....
	Oshawa Generals	OHL	4	0	1	1	2	....	....	....	....	....
2010-11	Oshawa Generals	OHL	42	6	4	10	75	10	1	2	3	15
2011-12	Oshawa Generals	OHL	55	10	9	19	111	6	0	0	0	10
2012-13	Oshawa Generals	OHL	65	30	20	50	142	9	4	3	7	12
	Manchester	AHL	5	0	1	1	4	3	0	0	0	7
2013-14	Manchester	AHL	69	12	14	26	115	4	0	0	0	0
2014-15	Manchester	AHL	51	5	6	11	138	....	....	....	....	....
2015-16	Ontario Reign	AHL	28	3	2	5	56	....	....	....	....	....
	Manchester	ECHL	3	0	0	0	2	....	....	....	....	....
	Iowa Wild	AHL	14	1	1	2	34	....	....	....	....	....
2016-17	San Diego Gulls	AHL	54	8	9	17	147	8	0	0	0	10

Signed as a free agent by **Manchester** (AHL), April 10, 2013. Signed as a free agent by **Los Angeles**, October 7, 2013. Traded to **Minnesota** by **Los Angeles** for Brett Sutter, February 29, 2016. Signed as a free agent by **San Diego** (AHL), September 8, 2016. Signed as a free agent by **Anaheim**, July 2, 2017.

SADEK, Jack (SAY-dehk, JAK) MIN

Defense. Shoots right. 6'2", 197 lbs. Born, Lakeville, MN, April 19, 1997.
(Minnesota's 7th pick, 204th overall, in 2015 NHL Draft).

			Regular Season					Playoffs				
Season	Club	League	GP	G	A	Pts	PIM	GP	G	A	Pts	PIM
2012-13	Lakeville North	High-MN	25	2	1	3	18	5	0	3	3	4
2013-14	Lakeville North	High-MN	25	4	9	13	16	6	2	2	4	6
2014-15	Team Southeast	UMHSEL	21	3	6	9	48	3	1	1	2	16
	Lakeville North	High-MN	25	5	20	25	36	6	2	6	8	2
2015-16	U. of Minnesota	Big Ten	15	0	5	5	12	....	....	....	....	....
2016-17	U. of Minnesota	Big Ten	34	4	7	11	12	....	....	....	....	....

SADOWY, Dylan (sa-DOH-way, DIH-luhn) DET

Left wing. Shoots left. 6'1", 195 lbs. Born, Brampton, ON, April 2, 1996.
(San Jose's 5th pick, 81st overall, in 2014 NHL Draft).

			Regular Season					Playoffs				
Season	Club	League	GP	G	A	Pts	PIM	GP	G	A	Pts	PIM
2011-12	Vaughan Kings	GTHL	53	33	45	78	....	....	....	....	....	....
2012-13	Saginaw Spirit	OHL	61	2	6	8	45	3	0	1	1	7
2013-14	Saginaw Spirit	OHL	68	27	9	36	69	5	4	0	4	2
2014-15	Saginaw Spirit	OHL	65	42	32	74	66	4	0	0	0	4
2015-16	Saginaw Spirit	OHL	36	20	14	34	31	....	....	....	....	....
	Barrie Colts	OHL	28	25	11	36	34	8	2	3	5	11
2016-17	Grand Rapids	AHL	38	4	2	6	18	....	....	....	....	....
	Toledo Walleye	ECHL	6	1	3	4	14	....	....	....	....	....

Traded to **Detroit** by **San Jose** for Detroit's 3rd round pick (later traded to Arizona – Arizona selected Mackenzie Entwistle) in 2017 NHL Draft, May 26, 2016.

SAFIN, Ostap (SA-fihn, AWZ-TAP) EDM

Right wing. Shoots left. 6'5", 192 lbs. Born, Prague, Czech Rep., November 2, 1999.
(Edmonton's 4th pick, 115th overall, in 2017 NHL Draft).

			Regular Season					Playoffs				
Season	Club	League	GP	G	A	Pts	PIM	GP	G	A	Pts	PIM
2014-15	Sparta U18	CzR-U18	4	2	2	4	0	1	0	0	0	0
2015-16	Sparta U18	CzR-U18	38	28	19	47	26	10	3	8	11	4
	Sparta Jr.	CzRep-Jr.	2	0	0	0	2	....	....	....	....	....
	HC Sparta Praha	CzRep	1	0	0	0	0	....	....	....	....	....
2016-17	Sparta U18	CzR-U18	1	0	0	0	0	2	1	1	2	2
	HC Sparta Praha	CzRep	8	1	1	2	2	....	....	....	....	....
	Litomerice	CzRep-2	3	0	0	0	0	....	....	....	....	....
	Sparta Jr.	CzRep-Jr.	24	6	12	18	66	6	4	5	9	2

SALINITRI, Anthony (sal-ihn-EE-tree, AN-thuh-nee) PHI

Center. Shoots left. 5'10", 168 lbs. Born, Windsor, ON, March 5, 1998.
(Philadelphia's 9th pick, 172nd overall, in 2016 NHL Draft).

			Regular Season					Playoffs				
Season	Club	League	GP	G	A	Pts	PIM	GP	G	A	Pts	PIM
2013-14	W. Jr. Spitfires MM	Minor-ON	32	23	17	40	38	9	2	3	5	18
	W. Jr. Spitfires Mid.	Minor-ON	....	....	....	....	....	3	1	2	3	2
	Leamington Flyers	ON-Jr.B	1	1	0	1	0	1	0	0	0	0
2014-15	Sault Ste. Marie	OHL	21	1	6	7	0	....	....	....	....	....
	Sarnia Sting	OHL	29	7	5	12	8	5	0	2	2	0
2015-16	Sarnia Sting	OHL	62	17	13	30	29	7	2	0	2	8
2016-17	Sarnia Sting	OHL	66	28	30	58	33	4	0	1	1	6

SALITURO, Dante (sal-IH-tuhr-oh, DAHN-tay) MIN

Center. Shoots right. 5'8", 178 lbs. Born, Willowdale, ON, November 15, 1996.

			Regular Season					Playoffs				
Season	Club	League	GP	G	A	Pts	PIM	GP	G	A	Pts	PIM
2012-13	Ottawa 67's	OHL	64	14	26	40	56	....	....	....	....	....
2013-14	Ottawa 67's	OHL	68	22	37	59	76	....	....	....	....	....
2014-15	Ottawa 67's	OHL	68	37	41	78	38	6	5	5	10	2
2015-16	Ottawa 67's	OHL	65	38	45	83	55	5	2	2	4	6
2016-17	London Knights	OHL	30	11	11	22	18	14	0	2	2	8
	Cleveland	AHL	5	1	0	1	2	....	....	....	....	....
	Cincinnati	ECHL	2	0	0	0	0	....	....	....	....	....
	Norfolk Admirals	ECHL	5	1	1	2	2	....	....	....	....	....

Signed as a free agent by **Columbus**, July 1, 2016. Traded to **Minnesota** by **Columbus** for Jordan Schroeder, June 23, 2017. • Re-assigned to **Cincnnati** (AHL) by **Columbus**, December 8, 2016. • Loaned to **Norfolk** (AHL) by **Columbus**, December 19, 2016.

SALLINEN, Jere (sa-LIGH-nehn, YAIR-ray) EDM

Right wing. Shoots left. 6', 198 lbs. Born, Espoo, Finland, October 26, 1990.
(Minnesota's 6th pick, 163rd overall, in 2009 NHL Draft).

			Regular Season					Playoffs				
Season	Club	League	GP	G	A	Pts	PIM	GP	G	A	Pts	PIM
2006-07	Blues Espoo U18	Fin-U18	26	9	3	12	44	7	2	2	4	16
2007-08	Blues Espoo U18	Fin-U18	13	8	10	18	16	4	1	5	6	12
	Blues Espoo Jr.	Fin-Jr.	36	11	19	30	94	3	0	2	2	8
	Blues Espoo	Finland	6	0	0	0	2	....	....	....	....	....
2008-09	Blues Espoo Jr.	Fin-Jr.	9	1	2	3	31	....	....	....	....	....
2009-10	Suomi U20	Finland-2	3	0	0	0	2	....	....	....	....	....
	Blues Espoo	Finland	38	5	6	11	18	3	0	2	2	2
	Blues Espoo Jr.	Fin-Jr.	6	5	3	8	10	....	....	....	....	....
2010-11	Blues Espoo	Finland	55	6	8	14	28	11	1	0	1	10
	Blues Espoo Jr.	Fin-Jr.	....	....	....	....	....	3	5	0	5	4
2011-12	Blues Espoo	Finland	21	1	2	3	39	....	....	....	....	....
	HPK Hameenlinna	Finland	11	1	2	3	2	....	....	....	....	....
2012-13	HPK Hameenlinna	Finland	57	15	27	42	30	5	1	1	2	6
2013-14	Orebro HK	Sweden	6	2	1	3	0	....	....	....	....	....
	HPK Hameenlinna	Finland	51	5	14	19	88	....	....	....	....	....
	Orebro HK	Sweden-Q	10	4	3	7	8	....	....	....	....	....
2014-15	Jokerit	KHL	48	8	7	15	28	10	1	3	4	6
2015-16	Jokerit	KHL	50	8	11	19	79	6	0	0	0	8
2016-17	Bakersfield	AHL	53	4	6	10	20	....	....	....	....	....

Signed as a free agent by **Edmonton**, March 13, 2016. Signed as a free agent by **Orebro** (Sweden), May 13, 2017.

SALO, Robin (SA-loh, RAW-bihn) NYI

Defense. Shoots left. 6'1", 189 lbs. Born, Espoo, Finland, October 13, 1998.
(NY Islanders' 1st pick, 46th overall, in 2017 NHL Draft).

			Regular Season					Playoffs				
Season	Club	League	GP	G	A	Pts	PIM	GP	G	A	Pts	PIM
2013-14	Sport Vaasa U17	Fin-U17	3	2	2	4	2	....	....	....	....	....
	Sport Vaasa U18	Fin-U18	43	8	8	16	16	....	....	....	....	....
2014-15	Sport Vaasa Jr.	Fin-Jr.	45	10	16	26	32	....	....	....	....	....
	Sport Vaasa	Finland	4	0	0	0	0	....	....	....	....	....
2015-16	Sport Vaasa	Finland	16	0	0	0	0	....	....	....	....	....
	Sport Vaasa Jr.	Fin-Jr.	27	10	7	17	8	....	....	....	....	....
	Sport Vaasa	Finland	16	0	0	0	0	....	....	....	....	....
	Hermes Kokkola	Finland-2	7	1	0	1	18	....	....	....	....	....
2016-17	Sport Vaasa	Finland	54	1	15	16	14	....	....	....	....	....

SAMBERG, Dylan (SAM-buhrg, DIH-luhn) WPG

Defense. Shoots left. 6'4", 208 lbs. Born, Hermantown, MN, January 24, 1999.
(Winnipeg's 2nd pick, 43rd overall, in 2017 NHL Draft).

			Regular Season					Playoffs				
Season	Club	League	GP	G	A	Pts	PIM	GP	G	A	Pts	PIM
2014-15	Hermantown	High-MN	11	1	0	1	0	6	0	0	0	0
2015-16	Team North	UMHSEL	10	0	2	2	2	....	....	....	....	....
	Hermantown	High-MN	23	5	13	18	6	6	2	2	4	2
2016-17	Team North	UMHSEL	18	5	7	12	14	3	1	1	2	4
	Hermantown	High-MN	25	10	18	28	43	6	1	5	6	2
	Waterloo	USHL	6	1	1	2	0	8	1	2	3	8

• Signed Letter of Intent to attend **University of Minnesota-Duluth** (NCHC) in fall of 2017.

SAMBROOK, Jordan (SAM-brook, JOHR-duhn) DET

Defense. Shoots right. 6'2", 187 lbs. Born, Markham, ON, April 11, 1998.
(Detroit's 5th pick, 137th overall, in 2016 NHL Draft).

			Regular Season					Playoffs				
Season	Club	League	GP	G	A	Pts	PIM	GP	G	A	Pts	PIM
2013-14	South Central	Minor-ON	34	5	13	18	40	7	0	6	6	4
2014-15	Tor. Nationals	GTHL	32	13	11	24	32	11	2	4	6	10
	Aurora Tigers	ON-Jr.A	7	0	0	0	0	1	0	0	0	0
2015-16	Erie Otters	OHL	67	9	18	27	40	13	0	4	4	14
2016-17	Erie Otters	OHL	61	15	25	40	61	22	5	5	10	26

SAMORUKOV, Dmitri (sa-moh-ROO-kawv, dih-MEE-tree) EDM

Defense. Shoots left. 6'2", 185 lbs. Born, Volgograd, Russia, June 16, 1999.
(Edmonton's 3rd pick, 84th overall, in 2017 NHL Draft).

			Regular Season					Playoffs				
Season	Club	League	GP	G	A	Pts	PIM	GP	G	A	Pts	PIM
2015-16	CSKA Jr.	Russia-Jr.	3	0	1	1	0	....	....	....	....	....
2016-17	Guelph Storm	OHL	67	4	16	20	41	....	....	....	....	....

SANDBERG, Filip (SAND-buhrg, FIH-lihp) S.J.

Right wing. Shoots right. 5'8", 190 lbs. Born, Jarfalla, Sweden, July 23, 1994.

			Regular Season					Playoffs				
Season	Club	League	GP	G	A	Pts	PIM	GP	G	A	Pts	PIM
2012-13	HV 71 Jr.	Swe-Jr.	33	24	29	53	20	7	3	5	8	4
	HV 71 Jonkoping	Sweden	15	1	1	2	0	....	....	....	....	....
2013-14	HV 71 Jr.	Swe-Jr.	14	8	11	19	8	4	4	4	8	0
	VIK Vasteras HK	Sweden-2	10	1	2	3	2	....	....	....	....	....
	HV 71 Jonkoping	Sweden	30	1	4	5	8	8	0	0	0	0
2014-15	HV 71 Jonkoping	Sweden	55	6	12	18	8	6	0	1	1	0
2015-16	HV 71 Jonkoping	Sweden	52	9	12	21	14	6	1	2	3	2
2016-17	HV 71 Jonkoping	Sweden	52	8	17	25	16	16	6	8	14	4

Signed as a free agent by **San Jose**, May 23, 2017.

SANHEIM, Travis (SAN-highm, TRA-vihs) **PHI**

Defense. Shoots left. 6'4", 199 lbs. Born, Elkhorn, MB, March 29, 1996.
(Philadelphia's 1st pick, 17th overall, in 2014 NHL Draft).

			Regular Season					Playoffs				
Season	Club	League	GP	G	A	Pts	PIM	GP	G	A	Pts	PIM
2010-11	Elkhorn Bm AA	Minor-MB	STATISTICS NOT AVAILABLE									
2011-12	Yellowhead Chiefs	MMHL	44	15	24	39	14	2	0	1	1	2
2012-13	Yellowhead Chiefs	MMHL	43	12	23	35	44	4	2	3	5	2
	Winkler Flyers	MJHL	....	....	....	....	....	6	0	1	1	2
2013-14	Calgary Hitmen	WHL	67	5	24	29	14	6	1	1	2	6
2014-15	Calgary Hitmen	WHL	67	15	50	65	52	17	5	13	18	10
2015-16	Calgary Hitmen	WHL	52	15	53	68	66	5	1	5	6	8
	Lehigh Valley	AHL	4	1	2	3	0	....	....	....	....	....
2016-17	Lehigh Valley	AHL	76	10	27	37	46	5	0	3	3	2

WHL East First All-Star Team (2015) • WHL East Second All-Star Team (2016)

SAUTNER, Ashton (SAWT-nuhr, ASH-tuhn) **VAN**

Defense. Shoots left. 6'1", 195 lbs. Born, Flaxcombe, SK, May 27, 1994.

			Regular Season					Playoffs				
Season	Club	League	GP	G	A	Pts	PIM	GP	G	A	Pts	PIM
2009-10	Moose Jaw	SMHL	42	1	10	11	24	4	0	2	2	6
2010-11	Moose Jaw	SMHL	42	12	23	35	43	6	1	2	3	12
2011-12	Edmonton	WHL	59	2	10	12	38	19	0	2	2	10
2012-13	Edmonton	WHL	62	2	10	12	28	14	3	2	5	10
2013-14	Edmonton	WHL	72	8	34	42	26	20	3	9	12	8
2014-15	Edmonton	WHL	72	12	39	51	38	5	0	1	1	6
2015-16	Utica Comets	AHL	50	4	7	11	12	2	0	0	0	0
2016-17	Utica Comets	AHL	47	0	5	5	30	....	....	....	....	....

Signed as a free agent by **Vancouver**, March 14, 2015.

SCARLETT, Reece (SKAR-leht, REES) **FLA**

Defense. Shoots right. 6'1", 175 lbs. Born, Edmonton, AB, March 31, 1993.
(New Jersey's 6th pick, 159th overall, in 2011 NHL Draft).

			Regular Season					Playoffs				
Season	Club	League	GP	G	A	Pts	PIM	GP	G	A	Pts	PIM
2007-08	Sherwood Park	AMBHL	33	14	16	30	48	12	4	5	9	26
	Sherwood Park	Minor-AB	3	1	0	1	4	....	....	....	....	....
2008-09	Sherwood Park	AMHL	34	4	13	17	60	11	2	6	8	4
	Swift Current	WHL	1	0	0	0	0	....	....	....	....	....
2009-10	Swift Current	WHL	65	1	9	10	49	4	0	2	2	4
2010-11	Swift Current	WHL	72	6	18	24	59	....	....	....	....	....
2011-12	Swift Current	WHL	71	9	40	49	74	....	....	....	....	....
2012-13	Swift Current	WHL	67	9	40	49	66	5	0	3	3	10
2013-14	Albany Devils	AHL	48	6	14	20	18	....	....	....	....	....
2014-15	Albany Devils	AHL	57	2	23	25	27	....	....	....	....	....
2015-16	Albany Devils	AHL	60	4	22	26	64	10	0	0	0	0
2016-17	Albany Devils	AHL	50	4	17	21	53	....	....	....	....	....
	Springfield	AHL	1	1	0	1	0	....	....	....	....	....

Traded to **Florida** by **New Jersey** for Shane Harper, March 1, 2017.

SCHEMITSCH, Thomas (SHEHM-ihtch, TAW-muhs) **FLA**

Defense. Shoots right. 6'4", 200 lbs. Born, Thornhill, ON, October 26, 1996.
(Florida's 3rd pick, 88th overall, in 2015 NHL Draft).

			Regular Season					Playoffs				
Season	Club	League	GP	G	A	Pts	PIM	GP	G	A	Pts	PIM
2011-12	Miss. Senators	GTHL	33	6	11	17	18	....	....	....	....	....
2012-13	Tor. Titans Midg.	GTHL	30	12	15	27	....	....	....	....	....	....
	Tor. Patriots	ON-Jr.A	4	0	0	0	0	1	0	0	0	0
2013-14	Owen Sound	OHL	63	6	11	17	26	5	1	0	1	2
2014-15	Owen Sound	OHL	68	14	35	49	36	5	0	2	2	2
2015-16	Owen Sound	OHL	51	9	22	31	22	6	0	4	4	2
2016-17	Springfield	AHL	37	1	3	4	4	....	....	....	....	....
	Manchester	ECHL	17	1	7	8	6	16	0	6	6	8

SCHEMPP, Kyle (SHEHMP, KIGHL) **NYI**

Center. Shoots left. 6', 190 lbs. Born, Saginaw, MI, January 13, 1994.
(NY Islanders' 6th pick, 155th overall, in 2014 NHL Draft).

			Regular Season					Playoffs				
Season	Club	League	GP	G	A	Pts	PIM	GP	G	A	Pts	PIM
2009-10	Det. Comp. U16	T1EHL	35	5	16	21	32	....	....	....	....	....
	Det. Comp. U16	Other	6	3	3	6	2	....	....	....	....	....
2010-11	Det. Comp. U18	T1EHL	40	21	9	30	16	....	....	....	....	....
	Det. Comp. U18	Other	13	4	4	8	17	....	....	....	....	....
2011-12	Traverse City	NAHL	59	13	22	35	29	4	0	1	1	0
2012-13	Sioux Falls	USHL	64	14	27	41	28	10	0	5	5	2
2013-14	Ferris State	WCHA	43	10	15	25	12	....	....	....	....	....
2014-15	Ferris State	WCHA	37	10	6	16	22	....	....	....	....	....
2015-16	Ferris State	WCHA	41	9	16	25	28	....	....	....	....	....
	Bridgeport	AHL	2	0	2	2	2	....	....	....	....	....
2016-17	Bridgeport	AHL	11	0	1	1	2	....	....	....	....	....
	Missouri Mavericks	ECHL	43	9	12	21	30	....	....	....	....	....

WCHA All-Rookie Team (2014)

SCHNARR, Nate (SHNAHR, NAYT) **ARI**

Center. Shoots right. 6'3", 180 lbs. Born, Waterloo, ON, February 25, 1999.
(Arizona's 4th pick, 75th overall, in 2017 NHL Draft).

			Regular Season					Playoffs				
Season	Club	League	GP	G	A	Pts	PIM	GP	G	A	Pts	PIM
2014-15	Wat. Wolves MM	Minor-ON	26	16	24	40	14	13	6	7	13	2
	Wat. Wolves MM	Other	16	13	14	27	10	5	0	3	3	0
2015-16	Waterloo Siskins	ON-Jr.B	45	26	28	54	40	15	7	10	17	6
	Guelph Storm	OHL	6	1	3	4	0	....	....	....	....	....
2016-17	Guelph Storm	OHL	54	18	18	36	27	....	....	....	....	....

SCHOENBORN, Alex (SHAYN-bohrn, AL-ehx) **S.J.**

Right wing. Shoots right. 6'1", 200 lbs. Born, Minot, ND, December 12, 1995.
(San Jose's 4th pick, 72nd overall, in 2014 NHL Draft).

			Regular Season					Playoffs				
Season	Club	League	GP	G	A	Pts	PIM	GP	G	A	Pts	PIM
2010-11	Minot Magicians	High-ND	27	23	22	45	48	....	....	....	....	....
2011-12	Om. Lancers U16	NAPHL	17	10	24	34	47	4	6	4	10	8
	Om. Lancers U16	Other	42	29	44	73	99	....	....	....	....	....
	Lincoln Stars	USHL	3	0	0	0	2	....	....	....	....	....
2012-13	Portland	WHL	20	1	1	2	22	....	....	....	....	....
	Wenatchee Wild	NAHL	10	0	1	1	34	....	....	....	....	....
2013-14	Portland	WHL	72	18	18	36	121	21	3	2	5	41
2014-15	Portland	WHL	49	15	18	33	66	17	3	1	4	18
2015-16	Portland	WHL	67	27	30	57	80	4	1	0	1	8
	San Jose Barracuda	AHL	1	0	0	0	0	....	....	....	....	....
	Allen Americans	ECHL	2	0	1	1	0	....	....	....	....	....
2016-17	San Jose Barracuda	AHL	29	1	3	4	25	....	....	....	....	....
	Allen Americans	ECHL	6	2	0	2	7	....	....	....	....	....

SCOTT, Justin (SKAWT, JUHS-tihn) **CBJ**

Center. Shoots left. 6'1", 206 lbs. Born, Burlington, ON, August 13, 1995.

			Regular Season					Playoffs				
Season	Club	League	GP	G	A	Pts	PIM	GP	G	A	Pts	PIM
2010-11	Burlington Eagles	Minor-ON	55	26	32	58	28	....	....	....	....	....
2011-12	Burlington	ON-Jr.A	47	14	21	35	22	6	1	2	3	7
2012-13	Barrie Colts	OHL	55	4	5	9	24	7	0	0	0	0
2013-14	Barrie Colts	OHL	61	7	13	20	29	11	2	1	3	4
2014-15	Barrie Colts	OHL	68	30	23	53	39	9	1	6	7	10
2015-16	Barrie Colts	OHL	67	28	37	65	60	15	17	3	20	8
2016-17	Cleveland	AHL	58	13	10	23	55	....	....	....	....	....

Signed as a free agent by **Columbus**, April 15, 2016.

SELMAN, Justin (SEHL-muhn, JUHS-tihn) **ST.L.**

Left wing. Shoots left. 5'11", 188 lbs. Born, Upper Saddle River, NJ, October 2, 1993.

			Regular Season					Playoffs				
Season	Club	League	GP	G	A	Pts	PIM	GP	G	A	Pts	PIM
2008-09	N. Jersey Mid.	AYHL	29	21	20	41	36	....	....	....	....	....
	N. Jersey Mid.	MtJHL	1	0	0	0	0	....	....	....	....	....
	N. Jersey Mid.	Exhib	47	23	32	55	2	....	....	....	....	....
2009-10	N. Jersey Mid.	AYHL	34	25	36	61	81	....	....	....	....	....
2010-11	Des Moines	USHL	52	8	14	22	46	....	....	....	....	....
2011-12	Sioux Falls	USHL	59	11	23	34	91	....	....	....	....	....
2012-13	U. of Michigan	CCHA	30	4	6	10	8	....	....	....	....	....
2013-14	U. of Michigan	Big Ten	19	1	2	3	8	....	....	....	....	....
2014-15	U. of Michigan	Big Ten	26	11	12	23	10	....	....	....	....	....
2015-16	U. of Michigan	Big Ten	38	13	18	31	24	....	....	....	....	....
	Chicago Wolves	AHL	7	1	1	2	2	....	....	....	....	....
2016-17	Chicago Wolves	AHL	17	1	1	2	6	....	....	....	....	....
	Missouri Mavericks	ECHL	17	3	3	6	12	....	....	....	....	....

Signed as a free agent by **St. Louis**, March 28, 2016.

SENEY, Brett (SEE-nee, BREHT) **N.J.**

Left wing. Shoots left. 5'9", 170 lbs. Born, London, ON, February 28, 1996.
(New Jersey's 5th pick, 157th overall, in 2015 NHL Draft).

			Regular Season					Playoffs				
Season	Club	League	GP	G	A	Pts	PIM	GP	G	A	Pts	PIM
2011-12	Lon. Knights MM	Minor-ON	29	20	26	46	20	11	6	13	19	6
	Lon. Knights Mid.	Minor-ON	1	1	1	2	2	1	0	0	0	2
2012-13	Kingston	ON-Jr.A	49	3	7	10	18	15	2	0	2	8
2013-14	Kingston	ON-Jr.A	49	26	43	69	67	11	5	7	12	12
2014-15	Merrimack College	H-East	34	11	15	26	55	....	....	....	....	....
2015-16	Merrimack College	H-East	32	8	18	26	34	....	....	....	....	....
2016-17	Merrimack College	H-East	36	10	21	31	38	....	....	....	....	....

SENYSHYN, Zach (SEH-nih-shihn, ZAK) **BOS**

Right wing. Shoots right. 6'1", 199 lbs. Born, Ottawa, ON, March 30, 1997.
(Boston's 3rd pick, 15th overall, in 2015 NHL Draft).

			Regular Season					Playoffs				
Season	Club	League	GP	G	A	Pts	PIM	GP	G	A	Pts	PIM
2012-13	Ott. Senators MM	Minor-ON	27	22	11	33	21	11	6	6	12	0
2013-14	Smiths Falls Bears	ON-Jr.A	57	22	10	32	8	16	4	6	10	0
	Sault Ste. Marie	OHL	4	1	1	2	0	....	....	....	....	....
2014-15	Sault Ste. Marie	OHL	66	26	19	45	17	14	4	3	7	2
2015-16	Sault Ste. Marie	OHL	66	45	20	65	20	12	2	7	9	6
2016-17	Sault Ste. Marie	OHL	59	42	23	65	31	11	4	1	5	8
	Providence Bruins	AHL	....	....	....	....	....	4	0	0	0	2

SERGEEV, Dmitrii (sair-GAY-ehf, dih-MEE-tree) **ST.L.**

Defense. Shoots right. 6'3", 200 lbs. Born, Chelyabinsk, Russia, March 26, 1996.

			Regular Season					Playoffs				
Season	Club	League	GP	G	A	Pts	PIM	GP	G	A	Pts	PIM
2013-14	Kitchener Rangers	OHL	49	2	7	9	22	....	....	....	....	....
2014-15	Kitchener Rangers	OHL	54	5	23	28	44	6	0	2	2	8
2015-16	Kitchener Rangers	OHL	35	2	14	16	26	4	0	2	2	5
2016-17	Missouri Mavericks	ECHL	14	0	1	1	2	....	....	....	....	....
	Norfolk Admirals	ECHL	22	1	3	4	6	....	....	....	....	....

Signed as a free agent by **St. Louis**, September 28, 2014. • Re-assigned to **Missouri** (ECHL) by **St. Louis**, October 13, 2016. • Re-assigned to **Norfolk** (ECHL) by **St. Louis**, December 15, 2016.

SETKOV, Malte (SEHT-kawv, MAL-tay) **DET**

Defense. Shoots left. 6'6", 192 lbs. Born, Rodovre, Denmark, January 14, 1999.
(Detroit's 6th pick, 100th overall, in 2017 NHL Draft).

			Regular Season					Playoffs				
Season	Club	League	GP	G	A	Pts	PIM	GP	G	A	Pts	PIM
2013-14	Rodovre U17	Den-U17	12	0	1	1	6	8	0	0	0	2
	Rodovre U18	Den-U18	9	1	1	2	10	....	....	....	....	....
2014-15	Malmo U18	Swe-U18	2	0	0	0	2	....	....	....	....	....
2015-16	Malmo U18	Swe-U18	32	1	8	9	10	....	....	....	....	....
	Malmo Jr.	Swe-Jr.	2	0	0	0	0	....	....	....	....	....
2016-17	Malmo U18	Swe-U18	10	4	5	9	10	4	0	0	0	2
	Malmo Jr.	Swe-Jr.	38	2	10	12	18	2	0	0	0	0

SEXTON, Ben (SEHKS-tuhn, BEHN) OTT

Center. Shoots right. 5'11", 196 lbs. Born, Ottawa, ON, June 6, 1991.
(Boston's 5th pick, 206th overall, in 2009 NHL Draft).

			Regular Season					Playoffs				
Season	**Club**	**League**	**GP**	**G**	**A**	**Pts**	**PIM**	**GP**	**G**	**A**	**Pts**	**PIM**
2007-08	Nepean Raiders	ON-Jr.A	48	15	15	30	71	6	1	5	6	4
2008-09	Nepean Raiders	ON-Jr.A	38	14	21	35	54	11	3	9	12	22
2009-10	Penticton Vees	BCHL	50	13	29	42	83	5	1	2	3	4
2010-11	Clarkson Knights	ECAC	12	5	3	8	12	....	....	....	....	....
2011-12	Clarkson Knights	ECAC	27	8	21	29	44	....	....	....	....	....
2012-13	Clarkson Knights	ECAC	28	5	15	20	70	....	....	....	....	....
2013-14	Clarkson Knights	ECAC	35	6	22	28	88	....	....	....	....	....
	Providence Bruins	AHL	9	1	1	2	9	....	....	....	....	....
2014-15	Providence Bruins	AHL	35	3	9	12	57	5	0	0	0	2
2015-16	Providence Bruins	AHL	29	4	1	5	45	1	0	0	0	2
2016-17	Albany Devils	AHL	54	19	12	31	60	4	0	2	2	0

• Missed majority of 2010-11 due to arm injury vs. Colgate (ECAC), November 5, 2010. Signed as a free agent by **Ottawa**, July 1, 2017.

SHARIPZIANOV, Damir (sha-rihp-ZEE-a-nawv, da-MIHR) L.A.

Defense. Shoots left. 6'2", 203 lbs. Born, Nizhnekamsk, Russia, February 17, 1996.

			Regular Season					Playoffs				
Season	**Club**	**League**	**GP**	**G**	**A**	**Pts**	**PIM**	**GP**	**G**	**A**	**Pts**	**PIM**
2013-14	Owen Sound	OHL	67	5	11	16	65	5	0	1	1	0
2014-15	Owen Sound	OHL	66	9	25	34	59	5	1	2	3	6
2015-16	Owen Sound	OHL	46	5	16	21	34	6	1	3	4	4
	Ontario Reign	AHL	1	0	0	0	0	....	....	....	....	....
2016-17	Ontario Reign	AHL	38	0	3	3	57	....	....	....	....	....

Signed as a free agent by **Los Angeles**, August 27, 2015.

SHAW, Mason (SHAW, MAY-suhn) MIN

Center. Shoots left. 5'9", 173 lbs. Born, Lloydminster, AB, March 11, 1998.
(Minnesota's 2nd pick, 97th overall, in 2017 NHL Draft).

			Regular Season					Playoffs				
Season	**Club**	**League**	**GP**	**G**	**A**	**Pts**	**PIM**	**GP**	**G**	**A**	**Pts**	**PIM**
2013-14	Lloydminster	AMHL	31	17	33	50	42	11	8	11	19	12
2014-15	Medicine Hat	WHL	23	3	6	9	13	....	....	....	....	....
2015-16	Medicine Hat	WHL	67	17	43	60	72	....	....	....	....	....
2016-17	Medicine Hat	WHL	71	27	67	94	57	11	0	12	12	16

SHEA, Patrick (SHAY, PA-trihk) FLA

Center. Shoots right. 5'11", 193 lbs. Born, Marshfield, MA, March 25, 1997.
(Florida's 7th pick, 192nd overall, in 2015 NHL Draft).

			Regular Season					Playoffs				
Season	**Club**	**League**	**GP**	**G**	**A**	**Pts**	**PIM**	**GP**	**G**	**A**	**Pts**	**PIM**
2011-12	Marshfield Rams	High-MA	12	2	14	16	....	....	....	....	....	....
2012-13	Marshfield Rams	High-MA	16	8	20	28	....	....	....	....	....	....
2013-14	Cape Cod U16	Minor-MA	11	6	8	14	2	....	....	....	....	....
	Marshfield Rams	High-MA	21	19	36	55	....	....	....	....	....	....
2014-15	Boston Jr. Bruins	Minor-MA	11	5	7	12	20	....	....	....	....	....
	Kimball Union	High-NH	33	19	20	39	....	....	....	....	....	....
2015-16	Bruins Selects U18	Minor-MA	11	6	9	15	50	....	....	....	....	....
	Kimball Union	High-NH	35	26	45	71	....	....	....	....	....	....
2016-17	U. of Maine	H-East	33	5	11	16	12	....	....	....	....	....

SHEA, Ryan (SHAY, RIGH-uhn) CHI

Defense. Shoots left. 6', 175 lbs. Born, Milton, MA, February 11, 1997.
(Chicago's 3rd pick, 121st overall, in 2015 NHL Draft).

			Regular Season					Playoffs				
Season	**Club**	**League**	**GP**	**G**	**A**	**Pts**	**PIM**	**GP**	**G**	**A**	**Pts**	**PIM**
2012-13	Bos. College High	High-MA	23	3	9	12	....	....	....	....	....	....
2013-14	Cape Cod U16	Minor-MA	12	1	7	8	4	....	....	....	....	....
	Bos. College High	High-MA	19	5	16	21	....	....	....	....	....	....
2014-15	Cape Cod U18	Minor-MA	14	3	6	9	0	....	....	....	....	....
	Bos. College High	High-MA	22	6	29	35	....	....	....	....	....	....
	Youngstown	USHL	2	0	0	0	0	....	....	....	....	....
2015-16	Youngstown	USHL	28	2	5	7	32	....	....	....	....	....
2016-17	Northeastern	H-East	38	1	13	14	8	....	....	....	....	....

SHERMAN, Wiley (SHUHR-man, WIGH-lee) BOS

Defense. Shoots left. 6'6", 215 lbs. Born, Greenwich, CT, May 24, 1995.
(Boston's 4th pick, 150th overall, in 2013 NHL Draft).

			Regular Season					Playoffs				
Season	**Club**	**League**	**GP**	**G**	**A**	**Pts**	**PIM**	**GP**	**G**	**A**	**Pts**	**PIM**
2010-11	Hotchkiss School	High-CT	23	0	4	4	....	....	....	....	....	....
2011-12	Hotchkiss School	High-CT	24	2	5	7	....	....	....	....	....	....
2012-13	Hotchkiss School	High-CT	26	4	6	10	32	....	....	....	....	....
	Mid Fairfield Blues	Minor-CT	20	2	5	7	....	....	....	....	....	....
2013-14	Hotchkiss School	High-CT	26	5	12	17	40	....	....	....	....	....
	Mid Fairfield Blues	Minor-CT	STATISTICS NOT AVAILABLE									
2014-15	Harvard Crimson	ECAC	37	0	3	3	4	....	....	....	....	....
2015-16	Harvard Crimson	ECAC	31	4	6	10	10	....	....	....	....	....
2016-17	Harvard Crimson	ECAC	36	0	13	13	24	....	....	....	....	....

SHERWOOD, Kole (SHUHR-wud, KOHL) CBJ

Right wing. Shoots right. 6'1", 201 lbs. Born, Columbus, OH, January 22, 1997.

			Regular Season					Playoffs				
Season	**Club**	**League**	**GP**	**G**	**A**	**Pts**	**PIM**	**GP**	**G**	**A**	**Pts**	**PIM**
2012-13	Ohio B-Jack. U16	T1EHL	40	13	11	24	19	4	1	3	4	2
2013-14	Ohio B-Jack. U16	T1EHL	34	24	18	42	17	....	....	....	....	....
2014-15	Ohio B-Jack. U16	T1EHL	31	22	26	48	29	4	1	3	4	16
	Youngstown	USHL	3	1	1	2	0	....	....	....	....	....
2015-16	London Knights	OHL	63	12	22	34	53	7	0	0	0	0
2016-17	Flint Firebirds	OHL	60	33	52	85	60	5	4	1	5	10
	Cleveland	AHL	2	0	0	0	2	....	....	....	....	....

Signed as a free agent by **Columbus**, July 7, 2015.

SHIELDS, David (SHEELDZ, DAY-vihd)

Defense. Shoots right. 6'3", 204 lbs. Born, Buffalo, NY, January 27, 1991.
(St. Louis' 5th pick, 168th overall, in 2009 NHL Draft).

			Regular Season					Playoffs				
Season	**Club**	**League**	**GP**	**G**	**A**	**Pts**	**PIM**	**GP**	**G**	**A**	**Pts**	**PIM**
2006-07	Maksymum	Minor-NY	37	4	16	20	60	....	....	....	....	....
2007-08	Erie Otters	OHL	60	1	3	4	31	....	....	....	....	....
2008-09	Erie Otters	OHL	61	1	16	17	28	5	0	0	0	5
2009-10	Erie Otters	OHL	68	7	12	19	42	4	0	0	0	12
2010-11	Erie Otters	OHL	61	6	21	27	48	7	1	4	5	4
2011-12	Peoria Rivermen	AHL	48	0	4	4	10	....	....	....	....	....
	Alaska Aces	ECHL	12	1	5	6	2	3	0	2	2	0
2012-13	Peoria Rivermen	AHL	59	0	5	5	41	....	....	....	....	....
2013-14	Chicago Wolves	AHL	55	5	10	15	21	3	0	0	0	2
2014-15	Chicago Wolves	AHL	42	0	6	6	10	....	....	....	....	....
2015-16	Utica Comets	AHL	32	3	7	10	8	3	0	1	1	0
	Adirondack	ECHL	15	2	7	9	9	....	....	....	....	....
2016-17	Utica Comets	AHL	48	0	10	10	8	....	....	....	....	....

SHIPACHEV, Vadim (SHIHP-a-chehv, vah-DEEM) VGK

Center. Shoots left. 6'1", 190 lbs. Born, Cherepovets, USSR, March 12, 1987.

			Regular Season					Playoffs				
Season	**Club**	**League**	**GP**	**G**	**A**	**Pts**	**PIM**	**GP**	**G**	**A**	**Pts**	**PIM**
2009-10	Cherepovets	KHL	55	14	30	44	30	....	....	....	....	....
2010-11	Cherepovets	KHL	51	13	25	38	22	6	2	1	3	8
2011-12	Cherepovets	KHL	54	22	37	59	26	6	1	2	3	4
2012-13	Cherepovets	KHL	51	17	24	41	12	6	1	5	6	14
2013-14	SKA St. Petersburg	KHL	52	12	20	32	10	10	1	0	1	2
2014-15	SKA St. Petersburg	KHL	49	12	42	54	20	22	6	15	21	2
2015-16	SKA St. Petersburg	KHL	54	17	43	60	63	15	7	9	16	12
2016-17	SKA St. Petersburg	KHL	50	26	50	76	22	17	4	16	20	8

Signed as a free agent by **Vegas**, May 4, 2017.

SHOEMAKER, Mark (SHOO-MAY-kuhr, MAHRK) S.J.

Defense. Shoots right. 6'3", 211 lbs. Born, Mississauga, ON, September 28, 1997.
(San Jose's 4th pick, 180th overall, in 2016 NHL Draft).

			Regular Season					Playoffs				
Season	**Club**	**League**	**GP**	**G**	**A**	**Pts**	**PIM**	**GP**	**G**	**A**	**Pts**	**PIM**
2012-13	Miss. Reps MM	GTHL	33	1	8	9	4	....	....	....	....	....
2013-14	Brampton	ON-Jr.B	46	2	10	12	27	5	0	1	1	0
2014-15	North Bay	OHL	39	1	4	5	0	....	....	....	....	....
2015-16	North Bay	OHL	67	4	9	13	16	11	0	3	3	0
2016-17	North Bay	OHL	68	0	16	16	22	....	....	....	....	....

SHVYREV, Igor (SHVIH-rehv, EE-gohr) COL

Center. Shoots left. 6'1", 191 lbs. Born, Magnitogorsk, Russia, July 10, 1998.
(Colorado's 5th pick, 125th overall, in 2017 NHL Draft).

			Regular Season					Playoffs				
Season	**Club**	**League**	**GP**	**G**	**A**	**Pts**	**PIM**	**GP**	**G**	**A**	**Pts**	**PIM**
2014-15	Magnitogorsk Jr.	Russia-Jr.	19	1	7	8	2	5	0	1	1	0
2015-16	Magnitogorsk	KHL	1	0	0	0	0	....	....	....	....	....
	Magnitogorsk Jr.	Russia-Jr.	44	12	26	38	40	8	1	4	5	4
2016-17	Magnitogorsk	KHL	10	0	0	0	2	....	....	....	....	....
	Magnitogorsk Jr.	Russia-Jr.	40	21	49	70	26	5	2	1	3	4

SIDEROFF, Deven (SIH-duhr-awf, DEH-vuhn) ANA

Right wing. Shoots right. 5'11", 171 lbs. Born, Kamloops, BC, April 14, 1997.
(Anaheim's 4th pick, 84th overall, in 2015 NHL Draft).

			Regular Season					Playoffs				
Season	**Club**	**League**	**GP**	**G**	**A**	**Pts**	**PIM**	**GP**	**G**	**A**	**Pts**	**PIM**
2012-13	Okanagan H.A.	High-BC	STATISTICS NOT AVAILABLE									
	Okanagan H.A.	CSSHL	12	4	8	12	22	1	0	0	0	0
	Kamloops Blazers	WHL	2	1	1	2	0	....	....	....	....	....
2013-14	Okanagan H.A.	High-BC	15	12	13	25	26	....	....	....	....	....
	Okanagan H.A.	CSSHL	24	18	23	41	40	3	2	6	8	6
	Kamloops Blazers	WHL	12	2	4	6	6	....	....	....	....	....
2014-15	Kamloops Blazers	WHL	64	17	25	42	25	....	....	....	....	....
2015-16	Kamloops Blazers	WHL	63	19	40	59	28	7	0	3	3	4
	San Diego Gulls	AHL	1	0	0	0	0	....	....	....	....	....
2016-17	Kamloops Blazers	WHL	67	36	42	78	49	6	0	1	1	2
	San Diego Gulls	AHL	3	0	1	1	4	....	....	....	....	....

SIEBENALER, Blake (SEE-beh-nay-luhr, BLAYK) CBJ

Defense. Shoots right. 6'1", 201 lbs. Born, Toledo, OH, February 27, 1996.
(Columbus' 4th pick, 77th overall, in 2014 NHL Draft).

			Regular Season					Playoffs				
Season	**Club**	**League**	**GP**	**G**	**A**	**Pts**	**PIM**	**GP**	**G**	**A**	**Pts**	**PIM**
2010-11	Ft. Wayne Car.	High-IN	14	15	11	26	0	4	3	3	6	0
	Ft. Wayne Car.	Other	15	10	6	16	10	....	....	....	....	....
2011-12	Cle. Barons U16	T1EHL	40	5	7	12	6	....	....	....	....	....
2012-13	Det. B. Tire U16	T1EHL	39	9	9	18	22	4	2	1	3	0
	Belle Tire U16	Minor-MI	....	....	....	....	....	7	2	2	4	0
	USAHNTDP	U-17	4	0	0	0	0	....	....	....	....	....
	Indiana Ice	USHL	11	1	2	3	8	....	....	....	....	....
2013-14	Niagara Ice Dogs	OHL	68	6	24	30	24	7	1	3	4	2
2014-15	Niagara Ice Dogs	OHL	66	12	25	37	30	11	0	1	1	8
2015-16	Niagara Ice Dogs	OHL	65	7	22	29	15	17	1	5	6	2
2016-17	Cleveland	AHL	43	3	3	6	10	....	....	....	....	....

SIEGENTHALER, Jonas (zee-GEHN-tahl-uhr, YOH-nuhs) WSH

Defense. Shoots left. 6'3", 220 lbs. Born, Zurich, Switzerland, May 6, 1997.
(Washington's 2nd pick, 57th overall, in 2015 NHL Draft).

			Regular Season					Playoffs				
Season	Club	League	GP	G	A	Pts	PIM	GP	G	A	Pts	PIM
2010-11	Zurich U17 II	Swiss-U17	17	6	4	10	24	....	....	....	....	....
	ZSC Zurich U17	Swiss-U17	2	0	0	0	0	5	0	0	0	4
2011-12	ZSC Zurich U17	Swiss-U17	29	3	9	12	103	8	0	2	2	50
	ZSC Zurich Jr.	Swiss-Jr.	2	0	0	0	0	....	....	....	....	....
	GCK Zurich Jr.	Swiss-Jr.	7	0	2	2	4	....	....	....	....	....
2012-13	Zurich U17	Swiss-U17	5	1	7	8	20	5	0	2	2	31
	GCK Zurich Jr.	Swiss-Jr.	34	2	12	14	54	7	0	1	1	8
2013-14	GCK Zurich Jr.	Swiss-Jr.	....	....	....	....	....	7	0	0	0	2
	GCK Lions Zurich	Swiss-2	40	2	6	8	24	....	....	....	....	....
	ZSC Lions Zurich	Swiss	6	0	0	0	2	....	....	....	....	....
2014-15	GCK Lions Zurich	Swiss-2	10	1	7	8	10	....	....	....	....	....
	ZSC Lions Zurich	Swiss	41	0	3	3	39	18	0	2	2	4
2015-16	ZSC Lions Zurich	Swiss	40	3	5	8	28	4	0	0	0	2
	GCK Zurich Jr.	Swiss-Jr.	....	....	....	....	....	1	1	0	1	2
	Hershey Bears	AHL	6	0	1	1	8	....	....	....	....	....
2016-17	ZSC Lions Zurich	Swiss	28	1	6	7	16	6	0	0	0	8
	Hershey Bears	AHL	7	0	0	0	2	5	0	0	0	2

SIKURA, Dylan (SIH-koo-ruh, DIH-luhn) CHI

Center. Shoots left. 5'11", 160 lbs. Born, Aurora, ON, June 1, 1995.
(Chicago's 7th pick, 178th overall, in 2014 NHL Draft).

			Regular Season					Playoffs				
Season	Club	League	GP	G	A	Pts	PIM	GP	G	A	Pts	PIM
2011-12	Aurora Tigers	ON-Jr.A	44	6	12	18	2	9	2	0	2	0
2012-13	Aurora Tigers	ON-Jr.A	46	8	20	28	28	6	0	1	1	0
2013-14	Aurora Tigers	ON-Jr.A	41	17	47	64	16	21	10	11	21	28
2014-15	Northeastern	H-East	25	5	2	7	0	....	....	....	....	....
2015-16	Northeastern	H-East	39	10	18	28	2	....	....	....	....	....
2016-17	Northeastern	H-East	38	21	36	57	12	....	....	....	....	....

Hockey East Second All-Star Team (2017)

SIMEK, Radim (SHIH-mehk, ra-DIHM) S.J.

Defense. Shoots left. 5'11", 200 lbs. Born, Mlada Boleslav, Czech., September 20, 1992.

			Regular Season					Playoffs				
Season	Club	League	GP	G	A	Pts	PIM	GP	G	A	Pts	PIM
2010-11	HC Liberec Jr.	CzRep-Jr.	36	1	9	10	16	....	....	....	....	....
2011-12	HC Liberec Jr.	CzRep-Jr.	32	6	4	10	14	....	....	....	....	....
	Benatky	CzRep-2	9	0	0	0	8	7	0	0	0	2
2012-13	Benatky	CzRep-2	37	0	5	5	41	....	....	....	....	....
	Liberec	CzRep	13	0	0	0	6	....	....	....	....	....
	Liberec	CzRep-Q	9	0	1	1	4	....	....	....	....	....
2013-14	Liberec	CzRep	24	0	0	0	4	....	....	....	....	....
	Benatky	CzRep-2	19	1	1	2	20	2	0	0	0	0
2014-15	Benatky	CzRep-2	2	1	0	1	0	....	....	....	....	....
	Liberec	CzRep	47	10	13	23	24	4	2	3	5	4
2015-16	Bili Tygri Liberec	CzRep	51	9	12	21	28	14	3	7	10	8
2016-17	Bili Tygri Liberec	CzRep	42	11	13	24	30	16	2	6	8	6

Signed as a free agent by **San Jose**, May 23, 2017.

SIMPSON, Wayne (SIHMP-suhn, WAYN) WSH

Right wing. Shoots right. 5'11", 195 lbs. Born, Fort Gordon, GA, November 19, 1989.

			Regular Season					Playoffs				
Season	Club	League	GP	G	A	Pts	PIM	GP	G	A	Pts	PIM
2006-07	Lawrence	High-MA	29	9	17	26	....	....	....	....	....	....
2007-08	Lawrence	High-MA	30	18	30	48	....	....	....	....	....	....
2008-09	Lawrence	High-MA	30	31	29	60	....	....	....	....	....	....
2009-10	Union College	ECAC	39	6	12	18	8	....	....	....	....	....
2010-11	Union College	ECAC	40	16	14	30	18	....	....	....	....	....
2011-12	Union College	ECAC	41	18	13	31	12	....	....	....	....	....
2012-13	Union College	ECAC	39	16	20	36	10	....	....	....	....	....
2013-14	South Carolina	ECHL	66	22	19	41	6	4	0	1	1	2
2014-15	South Carolina	ECHL	65	16	39	55	23	27	13	25	38	8
	Providence Bruins	AHL	4	1	0	1	0	....	....	....	....	....
2015-16	Portland Pirates	AHL	68	8	28	36	6	3	1	0	1	0
2016-17	Providence Bruins	AHL	76	16	33	49	10	17	4	10	14	4

Signed as a free agent by **Washington**, July 11, 2017.

SISSONS, Colby (SIH-suhnz, KOHL_bee) N.J.

Defense. Shoots left. 6'2", 190 lbs. Born, Edmonton, AB, January 15, 1998.

			Regular Season					Playoffs				
Season	Club	League	GP	G	A	Pts	PIM	GP	G	A	Pts	PIM
2013-14	SSAC Bulldogs	Minor-AB	37	9	22	31	28	5	1	4	5	4
	SSAC Athletics	AMHL	1	0	0	0	0	....	....	....	....	....
2014-15	SSAC Athletics	AMHL	33	7	10	17	26	7	1	1	2	6
	Swift Current	WHL	2	0	0	0	0	....	....	....	....	....
2015-16	Swift Current	WHL	71	3	19	22	26	....	....	....	....	....
2016-17	Swift Current	WHL	63	6	22	28	30	14	4	2	6	6

Signed as a free agent by **New Jersey**, October 3, 2016.

SJALIN, Calle (SHAW-lihn, KAHL-leh) NYR

Defense. Shoots left. 6'1", 179 lbs. Born, Ostersund, Sweden, February 9, 1999.
(NY Rangers' 4th pick, 145th overall, in 2017 NHL Draft).

			Regular Season					Playoffs				
Season	Club	League	GP	G	A	Pts	PIM	GP	G	A	Pts	PIM
2014-15	Ostersunds IK U18	Swe-U18	27	9	11	20	22	....	....	....	....	....
2015-16				STATISTICS NOT AVAILABLE								
2016-17	Ostersunds IK	Sweden-3	34	5	10	15	26	....	....	....	....	....
	Timra IK Jr.	Swe-Jr.	1	0	1	1	0	4	0	0	0	2
	Timra IK	Sweden-2	2	0	0	0	0	4	1	0	1	0

SJALIN, Pontus (SHA-lihn, PAWN-tuhs) MIN

Defense. Shoots left. 6', 170 lbs. Born, Ostersund, Sweden, June 12, 1996.
(Minnesota's 5th pick, 160th overall, in 2014 NHL Draft).

			Regular Season					Playoffs				
Season	Club	League	GP	G	A	Pts	PIM	GP	G	A	Pts	PIM
2011-12	Ostersunds IK U18	Swe-U18	19	2	5	7	8	....	....	....	....	....
2012-13	Ostersunds IK U18	Swe-U18	24	8	5	13	22	....	....	....	....	....
	Ostersunds IK Jr.	Swe-Jr.	4	2	4	6	2	....	....	....	....	....
	Ostersunds IK	Sweden-3	1	1	0	1	0	....	....	....	....	....
2013-14	Ostersunds IK U18	Swe-U18	6	1	2	3	0	....	....	....	....	....
	Ostersunds IK Jr.	Swe-Jr.	8	1	3	4	4	....	....	....	....	....
	Ostersunds IK	Sweden-3	21	3	1	4	8	4	0	0	0	0
2014-15	Leksands IF Jr.	Swe-Jr.	37	3	16	19	18	3	0	3	3	6
	Ostersunds IK	Sweden-3	1	0	0	0	0	....	....	....	....	....
	Leksands IF	Sweden	2	0	0	0	0	....	....	....	....	....
2015-16	Lulea HF Jr.	Swe-Jr.	7	2	1	3	4	....	....	....	....	....
	Asploven	Sweden-2	31	1	4	5	6	....	....	....	....	....
	Lulea HF	Sweden	25	0	0	0	2	1	0	0	0	0
2016-17	Lulea HF Jr.	Swe-Jr.	1	0	0	0	0	....	....	....	....	....
	Lulea HF	Sweden	35	1	0	1	4	2	0	0	0	0
	IF Bjorkloven Umea	Sweden-2	2	0	0	0	0	....	....	....	....	....

SMALLMAN, Spencer (SMAWL-muhn, SPEHN-suhr) CAR

Right wing. Shoots right. 6'1", 201 lbs. Born, Summerside, PE, September 9, 1996.
(Carolina's 6th pick, 138th overall, in 2015 NHL Draft).

			Regular Season					Playoffs				
Season	Club	League	GP	G	A	Pts	PIM	GP	G	A	Pts	PIM
2011-12	Fredericton	NBPEI	34	16	25	41	4	10	4	*13	17	2
2012-13	Saint John	QMJHL	42	2	4	6	14	4	0	0	0	0
2013-14	Saint John	QMJHL	66	12	23	35	42	....	....	....	....	....
2014-15	Saint John	QMJHL	66	23	33	56	73	5	1	3	4	4
2015-16	Saint John	QMJHL	59	19	28	47	59	17	3	16	19	12
2016-17	Saint John	QMJHL	60	30	49	79	35	18	11	11	22	2

SMERECK, Jalen (SMAIR-ihk, JAY-lehn) ARI

Defense. Shoots left. 6', 184 lbs. Born, Detroit, MI, January 15, 1997.

			Regular Season					Playoffs				
Season	Club	League	GP	G	A	Pts	PIM	GP	G	A	Pts	PIM
2012-13	Oak. Grizzlies U16	T1EHL	41	6	5	11	55	4	0	1	1	0
2013-14	Oak. Grizzlies U18	T1EHL	36	2	21	23	69	4	1	0	1	0
	Odessa Jackalopes	NAHL	2	0	1	1	4	....	....	....	....	....
2014-15	Bloomington	USHL	51	3	15	18	18	....	....	....	....	....
2015-16	Oshawa Generals	OHL	63	5	20	25	65	5	1	4	5	8
2016-17	Flint Firebirds	OHL	60	9	36	45	62	5	1	2	3	6
	Tucson	AHL	2	1	1	2	0	....	....	....	....	....

Signed as a free agent by **Arizona**, October 6, 2016.

SMIRNOV, Denis (SMIHR-nawv, DEH-nihs) COL

Right wing. Shoots left. 5'8", 185 lbs. Born, Moscow, Russia, August 12, 1997.
(Colorado's 6th pick, 156th overall, in 2017 NHL Draft).

			Regular Season					Playoffs				
Season	Club	League	GP	G	A	Pts	PIM	GP	G	A	Pts	PIM
2012-13	Wilkes Barre U16	AYHL	21	23	21	44	24	....	....	....	....	....
2013-14	Indiana Ice	USHL	47	15	26	41	22	12	3	2	5	2
2014-15	Fargo Force	USHL	53	18	22	40	28	....	....	....	....	....
2015-16	Fargo Force	USHL	60	29	32	61	37	....	....	....	....	....
2016-17	Penn State	Big Ten	39	19	28	47	18	....	....	....	....	....

SMITH, Adam (SMIHTH, A-duhm) NSH

Defense. Shoots left. 6'1", 195 lbs. Born, Sharon, ON, November 6, 1996.
(Nashville's 8th pick, 198th overall, in 2016 NHL Draft).

			Regular Season					Playoffs				
Season	Club	League	GP	G	A	Pts	PIM	GP	G	A	Pts	PIM
2012-13	York Simcoe	Minor-ON	28	5	6	11	8	....	....	....	....	....
2013-14	Newmarket	ON-Jr.A	50	3	12	15	46	4	0	0	0	0
2014-15	Newmarket	ON-Jr.A	30	2	7	9	16	5	0	1	1	2
2015-16	Newmarket	ON-Jr.A	32	5	9	14	38	....	....	....	....	....
	Bowling Green	WCHA	22	1	2	3	8	....	....	....	....	....
2016-17	Bowling Green	WCHA	28	1	4	5	26	....	....	....	....	....

SMITH, Givani (SMIHTH, jih-VAH-nee) DET

Right wing. Shoots left. 6'1", 205 lbs. Born, Thornhill, ON, February 28, 1998.
(Detroit's 2nd pick, 46th overall, in 2016 NHL Draft).

			Regular Season					Playoffs				
Season	Club	League	GP	G	A	Pts	PIM	GP	G	A	Pts	PIM
2013-14	Miss. Senators	GTHL	26	9	8	17	71	7	4	4	8	4
2014-15	Barrie Colts	OHL	31	0	4	4	20	....	....	....	....	....
	Guelph Storm	OHL	30	7	8	15	56	9	2	3	5	18
2015-16	Guelph Storm	OHL	65	23	19	42	*146	....	....	....	....	....
2016-17	Guelph Storm	OHL	64	26	18	44	*139	....	....	....	....	....
	Grand Rapids	AHL	3	0	0	0	2	....	....	....	....	....

SMITH, Hunter (SMIHTH, HUHN-tuhr) CGY

Right wing. Shoots right. 6'7", 231 lbs. Born, Windsor, ON, September 11, 1995.
(Calgary's 3rd pick, 54th overall, in 2014 NHL Draft).

			Regular Season					Playoffs				
Season	Club	League	GP	G	A	Pts	PIM	GP	G	A	Pts	PIM
2010-11	Wind. Jr. Spitfires	Minor-ON	30	15	15	30	64	9	8	0	8	18
	Wind. Jr. Spitfires	Other	10	8	6	14	10	....	....	....	....	....
2011-12	LaSalle Vipers	ON-Jr.B	41	5	9	14	109	4	1	2	3	2
	Windsor Spitfires	OHL	15	1	0	1	19	2	0	0	0	0
2012-13	Oshawa Generals	OHL	30	0	1	1	22	3	0	0	0	0
2013-14	Oshawa Generals	OHL	64	16	24	40	100	12	3	8	11	25
2014-15	Oshawa Generals	OHL	57	23	26	49	122	21	9	9	18	38
2015-16	Stockton Heat	AHL	54	2	6	8	90	....	....	....	....	....
2016-17	Stockton Heat	AHL	34	3	8	11	34	....	....	....	....	....

SNUGGERUD, Luc (snuh-GUH-rood, LEWK) CHI

Defense. Shoots left. 6', 187 lbs. Born, Edina, MN, September 18, 1995.
(Chicago's 5th pick, 141st overall, in 2014 NHL Draft).

			Regular Season					Playoffs				
Season	Club	League	GP	G	A	Pts	PIM	GP	G	A	Pts	PIM
2011-12	Team Southwest	UMHSEL	19	1	12	13	8	3	0	1	1	0
	Eden Prairie Eagles	High-MN	25	5	15	20	14	1	0	0	0	0
2012-13	Team Southeast	UMHSEL	21	1	8	9	14	3	1	2	3	0
	Eden Prairie Eagles	High-MN	25	5	33	38	24	2	0	4	4	2
2013-14	Team Southeast	UMHSEL	19	5	16	21	8	3	0	2	2	2
	Eden Prairie Eagles	High-MN	25	8	30	38	19	6	1	9	10	2
	Muskegon	USHL	3	1	2	3	0	....	....	....	....	....
	Omaha Lancers	USHL	4	0	2	2	6	4	0	1	1	4
2014-15	Nebraska-Omaha	NCHC	39	2	14	16	18	....	....	....	....	....
2015-16	Nebraska-Omaha	NCHC	35	4	14	18	22	....	....	....	....	....
2016-17	Nebraska-Omaha	NCHC	39	11	20	31	36	....	....	....	....	....
	Rockford IceHogs	AHL	13	1	4	5	2	....	....	....	....	....

NCHC All-Rookie Team (2015) • NCHC Second All-Star Team (2017) • NCAA West Second All-American Team (2017)

SODERBERG, Andreas (SOH-duhr-buhrg, ahn-DRAY-uhs) CHI

Defense. Shoots left. 6'4", 200 lbs. Born, Skelleftea, Sweden, June 16, 1996.
(Chicago's 6th pick, 148th overall, in 2014 NHL Draft).

			Regular Season					Playoffs				
Season	Club	League	GP	G	A	Pts	PIM	GP	G	A	Pts	PIM
2011-12	Skelleftea AIK U18	Swe-U18	10	0	2	2	0	....	....	....	....	....
2012-13	Skelleftea AIK U18	Swe-U18	39	7	18	25	24	9	0	3	3	2
2013-14	Skelleftea AIK U18	Swe-U18	12	1	2	3	20	3	1	0	1	0
	Skelleftea AIK Jr.	Swe-Jr.	36	1	5	6	14	2	1	0	1	0
2014-15	Skelleftea AIK Jr.	Swe-Jr.	44	1	6	7	34	5	0	0	0	6
2015-16	Skelleftea AIK Jr.	Swe-Jr.	9	0	1	1	6	6	0	2	2	4
	Vita Hasten	Sweden-2	45	0	1	1	8	....	....	....	....	....
2016-17	IK Pantern Malmo	Sweden-2	57	3	7	10	22	....	....	....	....	....

SODERLUND, Tim (soh-DUHR-luhnd, TIHM) CHI

Left wing. Shoots left. 5'9", 163 lbs. Born, Skelleftea, Sweden, January 23, 1998.
(Chicago's 5th pick, 112th overall, in 2017 NHL Draft).

			Regular Season					Playoffs				
Season	Club	League	GP	G	A	Pts	PIM	GP	G	A	Pts	PIM
2012-13	Clemensnas U18	Swe-U18	19	3	8	11	8	1	0	0	0	2
2013-14	Lulea HF U18	Swe-U18	28	9	19	28	71	3	1	2	3	0
	Lulea HF Jr.	Swe-Jr.	2	0	0	0	0	....	....	....	....	....
2014-15	Lulea HF U18	Swe-U18	5	2	1	3	0	....	....	....	....	....
	Lulea HF Jr.	Swe-Jr.	30	8	15	23	24	3	0	0	0	0
2015-16	Skelleftea AIK U18	Swe-U18	1	0	1	1	0	1	0	0	0	2
	Skelleftea AIK Jr.	Swe-Jr.	42	21	18	39	26	6	1	2	3	0
	Skelleftea AIK	Sweden	8	0	0	0	2	....	....	....	....	....
2016-17	Skelleftea AIK	Sweden	39	3	4	7	8	1	0	0	0	0
	Skelleftea AIK Jr.	Swe-Jr.	6	2	3	5	4	2	0	1	1	14

SOKOLOV, Dmitri (SAW-koh-lawf, dih-MEE-tree) MIN

Center. Shoots left. 6', 220 lbs. Born, Omsk, Russia, April 14, 1998.
(Minnesota's 3rd pick, 196th overall, in 2016 NHL Draft).

			Regular Season					Playoffs				
Season	Club	League	GP	G	A	Pts	PIM	GP	G	A	Pts	PIM
2014-15	Omsk Jr.	Russia-Jr.	29	13	3	16	4	6	0	1	1	0
2015-16	Sudbury Wolves	OHL	68	30	22	52	13	....	....	....	....	....
2016-17	Sudbury Wolves	OHL	64	48	24	72	8	6	6	3	9	0
	Iowa Wild	AHL	2	1	0	1	0	....	....	....	....	....

SOLEWAY, Jedd (SOHL-way, JEHD) ARI

Center. Shoots right. 6'3", 220 lbs. Born, Vernon, BC, May 12, 1994.
(Phoenix's 6th pick, 193rd overall, in 2013 NHL Draft).

			Regular Season					Playoffs				
Season	Club	League	GP	G	A	Pts	PIM	GP	G	A	Pts	PIM
2010-11	Okanagan Rockets	BCMML	40	16	17	33	97	....	....	....	....	....
2011-12	Vernon Vipers	BCHL	58	13	12	25	50	....	....	....	....	....
2012-13	Vernon Vipers	BCHL	26	5	12	17	29	....	....	....	....	....
	Penticton Vees	BCHL	22	14	15	29	33	15	5	6	11	6
2013-14	U. of Wisconsin	Big Ten	35	1	7	8	28	....	....	....	....	....
2014-15	U. of Wisconsin	Big Ten	35	7	2	9	48	....	....	....	....	....
2015-16	U. of Wisconsin	Big Ten	32	6	4	10	*78	....	....	....	....	....
2016-17	U. of Wisconsin	Big Ten	9	0	1	1	2	....	....	....	....	....

• Missed majority of 2016-17 due to a recurring shoulder injury.

SOMPPI, Otto (SAWM-pee, AW-toh) T.B.

Center. Shoots left. 6'1", 189 lbs. Born, Helsinki, Finland, January 12, 1998.
(Tampa Bay's 9th pick, 206th overall, in 2016 NHL Draft).

			Regular Season					Playoffs				
Season	Club	League	GP	G	A	Pts	PIM	GP	G	A	Pts	PIM
2012-13	Jokerit U18	Fin-U18	2	0	1	1	0	....	....	....	....	....
2013-14	Jokerit U18	Fin-U18	45	23	23	46	28	9	1	6	7	2
2014-15	Jokerit U18	Fin-U18	3	4	8	12	0	10	3	7	10	2
	Jokerit Helsinki Jr.	Fin-Jr.	38	6	7	13	10	2	0	0	0	0
2015-16	Halifax	QMJHL	59	13	33	46	25	....	....	....	....	....
2016-17	Halifax	QMJHL	60	17	24	41	30	4	0	1	1	2

SONG, Andong (SAWNG, AN-dawng) NYI

Defense. Shoots left. 6', 180 lbs. Born, Beijing, China, January 31, 1997.
(NY Islanders' 6th pick, 172nd overall, in 2015 NHL Draft).

			Regular Season					Playoffs				
Season	Club	League	GP	G	A	Pts	PIM	GP	G	A	Pts	PIM
2012-13	Lawrenceville	High-NJ	24	3	5	8	....	....	....	....	....	....
2013-14	Lawrenceville	High-NJ	17	0	7	7	....	....	....	....	....	....
2014-15	Lawrenceville	High-NJ	26	3	7	10	....	....	....	....	....	....
2015-16	Andover	High-MA	27	1	7	8	....	....	....	....	....	....
2016-17	Madison Capitols	USHL	52	0	2	2	8	....	....	....	....	....

SOSUNOV, Oleg (soh-soo-NAWV, OH-lehg) T.B.

Defense. Shoots left. 6'8", 243 lbs. Born, Moscow, Russia, April 13, 1998.
(Tampa Bay's 8th pick, 178th overall, in 2016 NHL Draft).

			Regular Season					Playoffs				
Season	Club	League	GP	G	A	Pts	PIM	GP	G	A	Pts	PIM
2014-15	Molniya Ryazan Jr.	Rus-Jr. B	49	6	3	9	50	....	....	....	....	....
2015-16	Loko Yaroslavl Jr.	Russia-Jr.	3	0	0	0	0	....	....	....	....	....
	Loko-Yunior Jr.	Rus-Jr.B	39	4	8	12	66	12	0	2	2	10
2016-17	Loko Yaroslavl Jr.	Russia-Jr.	32	0	0	0	79	1	0	0	0	2
	Loko-Yunior Jr.	Russia-Jr. B	8	0	0	0	12	5	0	3	3	6

SOUCY, Carson (SOO-SEE, KAR-suhn) MIN

Defense. Shoots left. 6'4", 212 lbs. Born, Viking, AB, July 27, 1994.
(Minnesota's 4th pick, 137th overall, in 2013 NHL Draft).

			Regular Season					Playoffs				
Season	Club	League	GP	G	A	Pts	PIM	GP	G	A	Pts	PIM
2009-10	Lloydminster	Minor-AB	34	1	7	8	58	....	....	....	....	....
2010-11	Lloydminster	AMHL	34	3	8	11	20	2	0	0	0	2
2011-12	Lloydminster	AMHL	30	9	20	29	100	3	0	4	4	10
	Spruce Grove	AJHL	7	0	0	0	4	....	....	....	....	....
2012-13	Spruce Grove	AJHL	35	5	10	15	71	16	1	1	2	30
2013-14	U. Minn-Duluth	NCHC	34	0	6	6	60	....	....	....	....	....
2014-15	U. Minn-Duluth	NCHC	40	6	8	14	40	....	....	....	....	....
2015-16	U. Minn-Duluth	NCHC	38	3	9	12	*61	....	....	....	....	....
2016-17	U. Minn-Duluth	NCHC	35	3	12	15	55	....	....	....	....	....
	Iowa Wild	AHL	3	0	0	0	2	....	....	....	....	....

SOY, Tyler (SOI, TIGH-luhr) ANA

Center. Shoots left. 6', 174 lbs. Born, Richmond, BC, February 10, 1997.
(Anaheim's 6th pick, 205th overall, in 2016 NHL Draft).

			Regular Season					Playoffs				
Season	Club	League	GP	G	A	Pts	PIM	GP	G	A	Pts	PIM
2011-12	Cloverdale Colts	Minor-BC	20	24	41	65	....	....	....	....	....	....
	Cloverdale Colts	Other	31	37	80	117	....	....	....	....	....	....
2012-13	Okan. HA Midget	Minor-BC	52	38	61	99	16	....	....	....	....	....
	Okanagan Prep	CSSHL	12	10	9	19	6	2	1	1	2	2
	Victoria Royals	WHL	7	1	1	2	0	6	1	1	2	0
2013-14	Victoria Royals	WHL	65	15	15	30	15	9	2	1	3	2
2014-15	Victoria Royals	WHL	69	28	35	63	29	10	2	5	7	4
2015-16	Victoria Royals	WHL	72	46	39	85	27	13	7	5	12	10
2016-17	Victoria Royals	WHL	44	25	30	55	15	6	2	2	4	0
	San Diego Gulls	AHL	2	0	0	0	0	....	....	....	....	....

WHL West Second All-Star Team (2016)

SPACEK, Michael (SHPAH-chehk, MIGH-kuhl) WPG

Right wing. Shoots right. 5'11", 195 lbs. Born, Pardubice, Czech Rep., April 9, 1997.
(Winnipeg's 5th pick, 108th overall, in 2015 NHL Draft).

			Regular Season					Playoffs				
Season	Club	League	GP	G	A	Pts	PIM	GP	G	A	Pts	PIM
2011-12	HC Pardubice U18	CzR-U18	7	4	1	5	6	....	....	....	....	....
2012-13	HC Pardubice U18	CzR-U18	39	28	22	50	69	2	0	0	0	2
2013-14	HC Pardubice U18	CzR-U18	6	4	5	9	8	....	....	....	....	....
	HC Pardubice Jr.	CzRep-Jr.	31	15	13	28	56	....	....	....	....	....
	Pardubice	CzRep	4	0	0	0	0	....	....	....	....	....
2014-15	HC Pardubice Jr.	CzRep-Jr.	5	2	5	7	38	....	....	....	....	....
	Pardubice	CzRep	40	5	7	12	12	4	0	0	0	0
	HC Pardubice U18	CzR-U18	....	....	....	....	....	4	3	3	6	12
2015-16	Red Deer Rebels	WHL	61	18	36	54	18	17	3	10	13	2
2016-17	Red Deer Rebels	WHL	59	30	55	85	34	7	4	8	12	6
	Manitoba Moose	AHL	4	0	1	1	8	....	....	....	....	....

SPENCER, Matthew (SPEHN-suhr, MA-thew) T.B.

Defense. Shoots right. 6'2", 203 lbs. Born, Guelph, ON, March 24, 1997.
(Tampa Bay's 2nd pick, 44th overall, in 2015 NHL Draft).

			Regular Season					Playoffs				
Season	Club	League	GP	G	A	Pts	PIM	GP	G	A	Pts	PIM
2012-13	Oak. Rangers MM	Minor-ON	40	9	27	36	34	....	....	....	....	....
	Oakville Rangers	Other	31	8	12	20	42	....	....	....	....	....
	Oakville Blades	ON-Jr.A	3	0	0	0	2	1	0	0	0	0
2013-14	Peterborough	OHL	64	1	14	15	33	11	0	4	4	19
2014-15	Peterborough	OHL	67	6	24	30	64	5	1	0	1	2
2015-16	Peterborough	OHL	60	5	19	24	46	7	0	1	1	13
	Syracuse Crunch	AHL	1	0	0	0	0	....	....	....	....	....
2016-17	Peterborough	OHL	60	7	22	29	60	12	1	6	7	6

SPINNER, Steven (SPIH-nuhr, STEE-vehn) WSH

Right wing. Shoots right. 6', 196 lbs. Born, Eden Prairie, MN, December 15, 1995.
(Washington's 5th pick, 159th overall, in 2014 NHL Draft).

			Regular Season					Playoffs				
Season	Club	League	GP	G	A	Pts	PIM	GP	G	A	Pts	PIM
2011-12	Eden Prairie Eagles	High-MN	24	20	10	30	21	1	0	0	0	0
2012-13	Team Southeast	UMHSEL	20	10	11	21	28	3	1	4	5	0
	Eden Prairie Eagles	High-MN	23	15	26	41	29	2	4	1	5	4
2013-14	Team Southeast	UMHSEL	20	7	13	20	24	3	3	3	6	4
	Eden Prairie Eagles	High-MN	25	17	22	39	42	6	6	5	11	4
	Muskegon	USHL	3	2	1	3	0	....	....	....	....	....
	Omaha Lancers	USHL	8	0	2	2	14	4	0	0	0	0
2014-15	Omaha Lancers	USHL	56	22	20	42	28	3	0	1	1	6
2015-16	Nebraska-Omaha	NCHC	33	5	6	11	10	....	....	....	....	....
2016-17	Nebraska-Omaha	NCHC	39	8	13	21	26	....	....	....	....	....

STALLARD, Jordy (STAL-uhrd, JOHR-dee) WPG

Center. Shoots left. 6'2", 179 lbs. Born, Brandon, MB, September 18, 1997.
(Winnipeg's 5th pick, 127th overall, in 2016 NHL Draft).

			Regular Season					Playoffs				
Season	Club	League	GP	G	A	Pts	PIM	GP	G	A	Pts	PIM
2011-12	Brandon Bantam	Minor-MB	30	10	27	37	14	....	....	....	....	....
2012-13	Brandon	MMHL	38	8	9	17	10	7	2	2	4	2
2013-14	Brandon	MMHL	44	28	48	76	22	8	4	9	13	4
2014-15	Calgary Hitmen	WHL	58	6	20	26	12	17	3	5	8	4
2015-16	Calgary Hitmen	WHL	68	21	28	49	20	5	2	0	2	5
2016-17	Calgary Hitmen	WHL	32	8	19	27	17	....	....	....	....	....
	Prince Albert	WHL	8	6	4	10	2	....	....	....	....	....

STANLEY, Logan (STAN-lee, LOH-guhn) **WPG**

Defense. Shoots left. 6'7", 239 lbs. Born, Waterloo, ON, May 26, 1998.
(Winnipeg's 2nd pick, 18th overall, in 2016 NHL Draft).

			Regular Season					Playoffs				
Season	**Club**	**League**	**GP**	**G**	**A**	**Pts**	**PIM**	**GP**	**G**	**A**	**Pts**	**PIM**
2013-14	Wat. Wolves MM	Minor-ON	28	8	20	28	95	9	0	5	5	35
	Waterloo Siskins	ON-Jr.B	....	....	....	....	....	2	1	0	1	0
2014-15	Windsor Spitfires	OHL	59	0	4	4	60	....	....	....	....	....
2015-16	Windsor Spitfires	OHL	64	5	12	17	103	5	1	0	1	16
2016-17	Windsor Spitfires	OHL	35	4	13	17	62	....	....	....	....	....

STARRETT, Beau (STAIR-eht, BOH) **CHI**

Center. Shoots left. 6'5", 223 lbs. Born, Framingham, MA, November 1, 1995.
(Chicago's 3rd pick, 88th overall, in 2014 NHL Draft).

			Regular Season					Playoffs				
Season	**Club**	**League**	**GP**	**G**	**A**	**Pts**	**PIM**	**GP**	**G**	**A**	**Pts**	**PIM**
2011-12	Catholic Memorial	High-MA	....	2	5	7	....	....	....	....	....	....
2012-13	South Shore Kings	EmJHL	18	11	11	22	20	....	....	....	....	....
	Catholic Memorial	High-MA	....	9	9	18	....	....	....	....	....	....
2013-14	South Shore Kings	USPHL	48	11	36	47	94	....	....	....	....	....
	South Shore Kings	Other	3	0	3	3	2	....	....	....	....	....
2014-15	South Shore Kings	USPHL	7	2	3	5	6	....	....	....	....	....
2015-16	Cornell Big Red	ECAC	15	1	0	1	2	....	....	....	....	....
2016-17	Cornell Big Red	ECAC	35	4	10	14	26	....	....	....	....	....

• Missed majority of 2014-15 due to recurring shoulder injury.

STAUM, Casey (STAWM, KAY-see) **MTL**

Defense. Shoots left. 6', 178 lbs. Born, Minneapolis, MN, January 8, 1998.
(Montreal's 4th pick, 124th overall, in 2016 NHL Draft).

			Regular Season					Playoffs				
Season	**Club**	**League**	**GP**	**G**	**A**	**Pts**	**PIM**	**GP**	**G**	**A**	**Pts**	**PIM**
2013-14	Hill-Murray	High-MN	23	3	6	9	8	3	0	0	0	2
2014-15	Hill-Murray	High-MN	24	0	7	7	2	5	0	0	0	0
2015-16	Team Southwest	UMHSEL	17	2	10	12	8	3	0	0	0	0
	Hill-Murray	High-MN	12	3	4	7	4	3	0	1	1	0
2016-17	Dubuque	USHL	55	0	16	16	18	8	0	1	1	0

• Signed Letter of Intent to attend **University of Nebraska-Omaha** (NCHC) in fall of 2017.

STEEL, Sam (STEEL, SAM) **ANA**

Center. Shoots left. 5'11", 178 lbs. Born, Ardrossan, AB, February 3, 1998.
(Anaheim's 2nd pick, 30th overall, in 2016 NHL Draft).

			Regular Season					Playoffs				
Season	**Club**	**League**	**GP**	**G**	**A**	**Pts**	**PIM**	**GP**	**G**	**A**	**Pts**	**PIM**
2012-13	Sherwood Park	AMBHL	31	52	52	104	16	5	3	8	11	0
	Sherwood Park	Minor-SK	3	5	3	8	0	5	3	4	7	0
2013-14	Sherwood Park	AMHL	14	7	16	23	8	3	2	1	3	0
	Sherwood Park	AJHL	1	0	0	0	0	....	....	....	....	....
	Regina Pats	WHL	5	0	0	0	0	2	0	0	0	0
2014-15	Regina Pats	WHL	61	17	37	54	16	....	....	....	....	....
2015-16	Regina Pats	WHL	72	23	47	70	24	12	6	10	16	4
2016-17	Regina Pats	WHL	66	50	81	*131	40	23	11	19	30	8

WHL East First All-Star Team (2017)

STEEN, Oskar (STEEN, AWS-kuhr) **BOS**

Center. Shoots right. 5'9", 178 lbs. Born, Karlstad, Sweden, March 9, 1998.
(Boston's 6th pick, 165th overall, in 2016 NHL Draft).

			Regular Season					Playoffs				
Season	**Club**	**League**	**GP**	**G**	**A**	**Pts**	**PIM**	**GP**	**G**	**A**	**Pts**	**PIM**
2013-14	Farjestad U18	Swe-U18	25	9	5	14	6	1	0	0	0	0
2014-15	Farjestad U18	Swe-U18	8	6	11	17	2	2	0	0	0	2
	Farjestad Jr.	Swe-Jr.	36	7	6	13	16	6	2	2	4	4
2015-16	Farjestad Jr.	Swe-Jr.	33	8	24	32	37	....	....	....	....	....
	Farjestad	Sweden	17	0	6	6	4	5	0	0	0	2
2016-17	Farjestad Jr.	Swe-Jr.	8	5	6	11	8	....	....	....	....	....
	Forshaga IF	Sweden-3	1	1	1	2	0	....	....	....	....	....
	MODO	Sweden-2	4	0	0	0	2	....	....	....	....	....
	Farjestad	Sweden	47	1	2	3	8	7	0	0	0	0

STEENBERGEN, Tyler (STEEN-BUHR-gehn, TIGH-luhr) **ARI**

Center. Shoots left. 5'10", 180 lbs. Born, Sylvan Lake, AB, January 7, 1998.
(Arizona's 8th pick, 128th overall, in 2017 NHL Draft).

			Regular Season					Playoffs				
Season	**Club**	**League**	**GP**	**G**	**A**	**Pts**	**PIM**	**GP**	**G**	**A**	**Pts**	**PIM**
2013-14	Red Deer Chiefs	AMHL	32	14	17	31	16	11	6	5	11	4
2014-15	Swift Current	WHL	72	5	6	11	13	4	1	0	1	0
2015-16	Swift Current	WHL	67	20	26	46	18	....	....	....	....	....
2016-17	Swift Current	WHL	72	*51	39	90	22	14	8	6	14	8

WHL East Second All-Star Team (2017)

STENLUND, Kevin (STEHN-luhnd, KEH-vihn) **CBJ**

Center. Shoots right. 6'4", 210 lbs. Born, Huddinge, Sweden, September 20, 1996.
(Columbus' 4th pick, 58th overall, in 2015 NHL Draft).

			Regular Season					Playoffs				
Season	**Club**	**League**	**GP**	**G**	**A**	**Pts**	**PIM**	**GP**	**G**	**A**	**Pts**	**PIM**
2011-12	Botkyrka U18	Swe-U18	16	24	15	39	44	5	4	4	8	20
	Botkyrka Jr.	Swe-Jr.	2	0	0	0	0	5	3	0	3	4
	Botkyrka	Sweden-4	1	0	0	0	0	....	....	....	....	....
2012-13	HV 71 U18	Swe-U18	5	1	2	3	0	....	....	....	....	....
2013-14	HV 71 U18	Swe-U18	9	8	3	11	4	....	....	....	....	....
	HV 71 Jr.	Swe-Jr.	29	4	5	9	16	7	1	1	2	0
2014-15	HV 71 Jr.	Swe-Jr.	36	14	22	36	16	6	1	3	4	4
	HV 71 Jonkoping	Sweden	17	1	0	1	2	....	....	....	....	....
2015-16	HV 71 Jr.	Swe-Jr.	17	5	19	24	31	....	....	....	....	....
	Vita Hasten	Sweden-2	1	0	0	0	0	....	....	....	....	....
	HV 71 Jonkoping	Sweden	43	1	1	2	20	6	1	0	1	2
2016-17	HV 71 Jr.	Swe-Jr.	3	2	1	3	12	....	....	....	....	....
	Vasterviks IK	Sweden-2	2	1	3	4	2	....	....	....	....	....
	HV 71 Jonkoping	Sweden	48	13	7	20	16	16	4	6	10	6

STENQVIST, Jakob (STEHN-kvihst, JAY-kuhb) **DAL**

Defense. Shoots right. 6'2", 163 lbs. Born, Mora, Sweden, March 17, 1998.
(Dallas' 6th pick, 176th overall, in 2016 NHL Draft).

			Regular Season					Playoffs				
Season	**Club**	**League**	**GP**	**G**	**A**	**Pts**	**PIM**	**GP**	**G**	**A**	**Pts**	**PIM**
2012-13	Orsa IK U18	Swe-U18	7	0	2	2	4	....	....	....	....	....
2013-14	Mora IK U18	Swe-U18	14	4	5	9	4	....	....	....	....	....
	Orsa IK U18	Swe-U18	2	1	3	4	4	....	....	....	....	....
2014-15	MODO U18	Swe-U18	38	2	17	19	14	2	0	0	0	0
	MODO Jr.	Swe-Jr.	5	1	1	2	4	1	0	0	0	0
2015-16	MODO U18	Swe-U18	17	10	19	29	14	4	2	2	4	2
	MODO Jr.	Swe-Jr.	36	3	4	7	14	2	0	1	1	0
2016-17	MODO Jr.	Swe-Jr.	17	3	14	17	10	6	1	2	3	2
	MODO	Sweden-2	41	2	4	6	22	....	....	....	....	....

STEPHENS, Devante (STEE-vehnz, duh-VAHN-tay) **BUF**

Defense. Shoots left. 6'2", 184 lbs. Born, Surrey, BC, January 2, 1997.
(Buffalo's 4th pick, 122nd overall, in 2015 NHL Draft).

			Regular Season					Playoffs				
Season	**Club**	**League**	**GP**	**G**	**A**	**Pts**	**PIM**	**GP**	**G**	**A**	**Pts**	**PIM**
2013-14	Valley West Hawks	BCMML	22	6	14	20	32	5	0	2	2	10
2014-15	Kelowna Rockets	WHL	64	4	7	11	33	17	0	4	4	8
2015-16	Kelowna Rockets	WHL	72	2	9	11	58	18	0	1	1	12
2016-17	Kelowna Rockets	WHL	67	13	22	35	75	17	0	7	7	16

STEPHENS, Mitchell (STEE-vehnz, mih-CHUHL) **T.B.**

Center. Shoots right. 5'11", 188 lbs. Born, Peterborough, ON, February 5, 1997.
(Tampa Bay's 1st pick, 33rd overall, in 2015 NHL Draft).

			Regular Season					Playoffs				
Season	**Club**	**League**	**GP**	**G**	**A**	**Pts**	**PIM**	**GP**	**G**	**A**	**Pts**	**PIM**
2012-13	Toronto Marlboros	GTHL	58	44	40	84	12	....	....	....	....	....
2013-14	Saginaw Spirit	OHL	57	9	12	21	8	5	0	2	2	2
2014-15	Saginaw Spirit	OHL	62	22	26	48	44	4	0	0	0	0
2015-16	Saginaw Spirit	OHL	39	20	18	38	14	4	2	1	3	0
	Syracuse Crunch	AHL	5	1	0	1	0	....	....	....	....	....
2016-17	Saginaw Spirit	OHL	22	11	17	28	14	....	....	....	....	....
	London Knights	OHL	29	11	14	25	12	14	7	3	10	2
	Syracuse Crunch	AHL	....	....	....	....	....	3	0	0	0	0

STEVENS, John (STEE-vehns, JAWN) **NYI**

Center. Shoots left. 6'2", 184 lbs. Born, Springfield, MA, April 17, 1994.

			Regular Season					Playoffs				
Season	**Club**	**League**	**GP**	**G**	**A**	**Pts**	**PIM**	**GP**	**G**	**A**	**Pts**	**PIM**
2009-10	Comcast U16	AYHL	34	11	18	29	29	....	....	....	....	....
2010-11	Salisbury School	High-CT	27	11	11	22	....	....	....	....	....	....
2011-12	Salisbury School	High-CT	28	7	21	28	16	....	....	....	....	....
	Dubuque	USHL	2	0	0	0	0	....	....	....	....	....
2012-13	Dubuque	USHL	59	13	35	48	14	9	1	1	2	6
2013-14	Northeastern	H-East	37	7	15	22	20	....	....	....	....	....
2014-15	Northeastern	H-East	36	4	17	21	16	....	....	....	....	....
2015-16	Northeastern	H-East	40	10	25	35	45	....	....	....	....	....
2016-17	Northeastern	H-East	25	5	23	28	20	....	....	....	....	....
	Bridgeport	AHL	8	0	1	1	0	....	....	....	....	....

Signed as a free agent by **NY Islanders**, March 27, 2017.

STEVENS, Luke (STEE-vehnz, LOOK) **CAR**

Left wing. Shoots left. 6'5", 208 lbs. Born, Bellair, CA, February 11, 1997.
(Carolina's 5th pick, 126th overall, in 2015 NHL Draft).

			Regular Season					Playoffs				
Season	**Club**	**League**	**GP**	**G**	**A**	**Pts**	**PIM**	**GP**	**G**	**A**	**Pts**	**PIM**
2012-13	Duxbury	High-MA	....	16	10	26	....	....	....	....	....	....
	Bos. Adv. U16	T1EHL	4	1	0	1	0	....	....	....	....	....
2013-14	Cape Cod U16	Minor-MA	11	5	5	10	2	....	....	....	....	....
	Nobles	High-MA	28	15	7	22	....	....	....	....	....	....
2014-15	Cape Cod U18	Minor-MA	14	5	12	17	0	....	....	....	....	....
	Nobles	High-MA	23	11	18	29	....	....	....	....	....	....
2015-16	Cape Cod U16	Minor-MA	13	5	9	14	4	....	....	....	....	....
	Nobles	High-MA	28	24	31	55	....	....	....	....	....	....
2016-17	Yale	ECAC	17	2	3	5	4	....	....	....	....	....

STEVENS, Nolan (STEE-vuhnz, NOH-luhn) **ST.L.**

Center. Shoots left. 6'2", 183 lbs. Born, Brantford, ON, July 22, 1996.
(St. Louis' 5th pick, 125th overall, in 2016 NHL Draft).

			Regular Season					Playoffs				
Season	**Club**	**League**	**GP**	**G**	**A**	**Pts**	**PIM**	**GP**	**G**	**A**	**Pts**	**PIM**
2011-12	L.A. Jr. Kings	T1EHL	24	17	15	32	23	....	....	....	....	....
2012-13	USAHNTDP	USHL	21	3	2	5	6	....	....	....	....	....
	USAHNTDP	U-17	4	0	3	3	0	....	....	....	....	....
	USAHNTDP	U-18	1	0	0	0	0	....	....	....	....	....
2013-14	USAHNTDP	USHL	25	3	6	9	6	....	....	....	....	....
	USAHNTDP	U-18	35	1	3	4	4	....	....	....	....	....
2014-15	Northeastern	H-East	36	3	9	12	8	....	....	....	....	....
2015-16	Northeastern	H-East	41	20	22	42	10	....	....	....	....	....
2016-17	Northeastern	H-East	17	10	12	22	12	....	....	....	....	....

• Missed majority of 2016-17 due to an injury suffered in practice, November 2, 2016.

STEVENSON, Dustin (STEE-vehn-suhn, DUHS-tihn) **DAL**

Defense. Shoots left. 6'5", 215 lbs. Born, Gull Lake, SK, August 12, 1989.

			Regular Season					Playoffs				
Season	**Club**	**League**	**GP**	**G**	**A**	**Pts**	**PIM**	**GP**	**G**	**A**	**Pts**	**PIM**
2006-07	Swift Current	SMHL	STATISTICS NOT AVAILABLE									
	La Ronge	SJHL	1	0	0	0	2	....	....	....	....	....
2007-08	La Ronge	SJHL	53	2	11	13	63	6	0	2	2	2
2008-09	La Ronge	SJHL	53	15	24	39	124	....	....	....	....	....
2009-10	La Ronge	SJHL	56	11	36	47	134	....	....	....	....	....
2010-11	South Carolina	ECHL	63	3	9	12	44	....	....	....	....	....
2011-12	South Carolina	ECHL	72	0	7	7	113	9	1	2	3	6
2012-13	Reading Royals	ECHL	65	0	10	10	103	22	1	8	9	14
2013-14	Wilkes-Barre	AHL	7	0	0	0	7	....	....	....	....	....
	Wheeling Nailers	ECHL	57	5	21	26	115	10	1	3	4	12
2014-15	Adirondack Flames	AHL	45	3	8	11	94	....	....	....	....	....
2015-16	Stockton Heat	AHL	45	2	6	8	104	....	....	....	....	....
2016-17	Texas Stars	AHL	59	2	4	6	119	....	....	....	....	....

Signed as a free agent by **Washington**, April 5, 2010. Signed as a free agent by **Wilkes-Barre** (AHL), August 8, 2013. Signed as a free agent by **Adirondack** (AHL), October 9, 2014. Signed as a free agent by **Stockton** (AHL), July 15, 2015. Signed as a free agent by **Dallas**, July 1, 2016.

STEWART, Dean (STEW-uhrt, DEEN) **ARI**

Defense. Shoots right. 6'2", 188 lbs. Born, Portage, MB, June 12, 1998.
(Arizona's 5th pick, 188th overall, in 2016 NHL Draft).

			Regular Season					Playoffs				
Season	Club	League	GP	G	A	Pts	PIM	GP	G	A	Pts	PIM
2012-13	Central Plains Bant.	Minor-MB	28	0	8	8	18	....	....	....	....	....
	Central Plains Mid	Minor-MB	1	0	0	0	0	....	....	....	....	....
2013-14	Central Plains	MMHL	23	1	10	11	6	....	....	....	....	....
2014-15	Central Plains	MMHL	21	2	4	6	52	....	....	....	....	....
	Portage Terriers	MJHL	33	1	5	6	2	1	0	0	0	2
2015-16	Portage Terriers	MJHL	42	8	14	22	28	13	3	10	13	8
2016-17	Nebraska-Omaha	NCHC	29	0	7	7	14	....	....	....	....	....

STEWART, Mackenze (STEW-uhrt, muh-KEHN-zee) **VAN**

Defense. Shoots left. 6'3", 240 lbs. Born, Calgary, AB, August 10, 1995.
(Vancouver's 7th pick, 186th overall, in 2014 NHL Draft).

			Regular Season					Playoffs				
Season	Club	League	GP	G	A	Pts	PIM	GP	G	A	Pts	PIM
2009-10	Calgary Blazers	Minor-AB	STATISTICS NOT AVAILABLE									
	Calgary Northstars	AMBHL	1	0	0	0	0	....	....	....	....	....
2010-11	Edge Maroon	Minor-AB	12	0	5	5	0	....	....	....	....	....
	Edge Maroon	CSSHL	24	3	10	13	8	6	0	1	1	2
	Edge School	MPHL	1	1	0	1	0	....	....	....	....	....
2011-12	High River Flyers	HJHL	13	1	1	2	8	....	....	....	....	....
	Okotoks Bisons	HJHL	12	3	6	9	12	....	....	....	....	....
	Calgary Blazers	CgJHL	STATISTICS NOT AVAILABLE									
2012-13	Prince Albert	WHL	6	0	0	0	2	....	....	....	....	....
	Calgary Mustangs	AJHL	33	1	4	5	65	3	0	0	0	17
2013-14	Prince Albert	WHL	55	5	4	9	69	4	0	1	1	2
2014-15	Prince Albert	WHL	66	5	6	11	114	....	....	....	....	....
2015-16	Tri-City Americans	WHL	36	5	6	11	47	....	....	....	....	....
	Utica Comets	AHL	4	0	0	0	17	....	....	....	....	....
	Kalamazoo Wings	ECHL	6	0	0	0	5	....	....	....	....	....
2016-17	Alaska Aces	ECHL	70	6	7	13	117	....	....	....	....	....

STILLMAN, Riley (STIHL-muhn, RIGH-lee) **FLA**

Defense. Shoots left. 6'1", 190 lbs. Born, Peterborough, ON, March 9, 1998.
(Florida's 5th pick, 114th overall, in 2016 NHL Draft).

			Regular Season					Playoffs				
Season	Club	League	GP	G	A	Pts	PIM	GP	G	A	Pts	PIM
2013-14	Peter. Petes MM	Minor-ON	36	7	23	30	42	8	2	3	5	2
2014-15	Cobourg Cougars	ON-Jr.A	46	5	19	24	53	9	1	1	2	16
	Oshawa Generals	OHL	9	0	0	0	5	....	....	....	....	....
2015-16	Oshawa Generals	OHL	62	6	15	21	69	5	0	0	0	2
2016-17	Oshawa Generals	OHL	62	11	22	33	76	11	1	8	9	8

STORM, Ben (STOHRM, BEHN) **COL**

Left wing. Shoots left. 6'6", 220 lbs. Born, Laurium, MI, March 30, 1994.
(Colorado's 6th pick, 153rd overall, in 2013 NHL Draft).

			Regular Season					Playoffs				
Season	Club	League	GP	G	A	Pts	PIM	GP	G	A	Pts	PIM
2009-10	Calumet High	High-MI	29	13	14	27	35	....	....	....	....	....
2010-11	Calumet High	High-MI	30	11	19	30	34	....	....	....	....	....
2011-12	Calumet High	High-MI	26	15	20	35	24	....	....	....	....	....
2012-13	Muskegon	USHL	52	2	10	12	82	3	0	0	0	2
2013-14	St. Cloud State	NCHC	30	0	1	1	14	....	....	....	....	....
2014-15	St. Cloud State	NCHC	33	2	3	5	14	....	....	....	....	....
2015-16	St. Cloud State	NCHC	29	2	5	7	15	....	....	....	....	....
2016-17	St. Cloud State	NCHC	29	0	4	4	29	....	....	....	....	....
	San Antonio	AHL	7	0	0	0	0	....	....	....	....	....

STOYKEWYCH, Peter (STOY-kuh-wihch, PEE-tuhr)

Defense. Shoots left. 6'2", 190 lbs. Born, Winnipeg, MB, July 14, 1992.
(Atlanta's 9th pick, 199th overall, in 2010 NHL Draft).

			Regular Season					Playoffs				
Season	Club	League	GP	G	A	Pts	PIM	GP	G	A	Pts	PIM
2007-08	Winnipeg Wild	MMHL	39	1	21	22	22	....	....	....	....	....
2008-09	Wpg. South Blues	MJHL	28	2	7	9	....	....	....	....	....	....
2009-10	Wpg. South Blues	MJHL	56	6	25	31	63	4	1	0	1	16
2010-11	Des Moines	USHL	58	5	10	15	77	....	....	....	....	....
2011-12	Colorado College	WCHA	26	0	3	3	14	....	....	....	....	....
2012-13	Colorado College	WCHA	42	2	9	11	20	....	....	....	....	....
2013-14	Colorado College	NCHC	37	1	8	9	46	....	....	....	....	....
2014-15	Colorado College	NCHC	34	3	8	11	42	....	....	....	....	....
	St. John's IceCaps	AHL	6	0	1	1	11	....	....	....	....	....
2015-16	Manitoba Moose	AHL	47	0	7	7	38	....	....	....	....	....
2016-17	Manitoba Moose	AHL	72	5	15	20	47	....	....	....	....	....

• Transferred to **Winnipeg** after **Atlanta** franchise relocated, June 21, 2011.

STRANSKY, Matej (STRAHN-skee, MAH-tay) **DAL**

Right wing. Shoots right. 6'3", 210 lbs. Born, Ostrava, Czech Rep., July 11, 1993.
(Dallas' 5th pick, 165th overall, in 2011 NHL Draft).

			Regular Season					Playoffs				
Season	Club	League	GP	G	A	Pts	PIM	GP	G	A	Pts	PIM
2006-07	HC Vitkovice U17	CzR-U17	1	0	0	0	0	....	....	....	....	....
2007-08	HC Vitkovice U17	CzR-U17	43	5	14	19	22	3	1	1	2	2
2008-09	HC Vitkovice U17	CzR-U17	46	40	23	63	68	7	5	5	10	6
2009-10	HC Vitkovice U18	CzR-U18	43	17	33	50	112	2	1	2	3	4
	HC Vitkovice Jr.	CzRep-Jr.	11	2	1	3	4	....	....	....	....	....
2010-11	Saskatoon Blades	WHL	71	14	12	26	53	10	3	6	9	8
2011-12	Saskatoon Blades	WHL	70	39	42	81	75	4	1	1	2	2
2012-13	Saskatoon Blades	WHL	72	40	45	85	88	4	0	0	0	4
2013-14	Texas Stars	AHL	65	9	14	23	53	21	1	4	5	10
2014-15	Texas Stars	AHL	70	7	12	19	60	2	0	0	0	0
2015-16	Texas Stars	AHL	74	23	16	39	63	4	0	1	1	4
2016-17	Texas Stars	AHL	76	27	20	47	60	....	....	....	....	....

STROME, Matthew (STROHM, MA-thew) **PHI**

Left wing. Shoots left. 6'4", 207 lbs. Born, Mississauga, ON, June 1, 1999.
(Philadelphia's 5th pick, 106th overall, in 2017 NHL Draft).

			Regular Season					Playoffs				
Season	Club	League	GP	G	A	Pts	PIM	GP	G	A	Pts	PIM
2014-15	Tor. Marlboros MM	GTHL	64	23	37	60	36	....	....	....	....	....
2015-16	Hamilton Bulldogs	OHL	61	16	22	38	29	....	....	....	....	....
2016-17	Hamilton Bulldogs	OHL	66	34	28	62	62	7	1	7	8	4

STROMWALL, Malte (STRAWM-WAHL, MAHL-teh) **NYR**

Left wing. Shoots right. 6', 191 lbs. Born, Lulea, Sweden, August 24, 1994.

			Regular Season					Playoffs				
Season	Club	League	GP	G	A	Pts	PIM	GP	G	A	Pts	PIM
2010-11	Linkopings HC Jr.	Swe-Jr.	21	12	6	18	14	....	....	....	....	....
2011-12	Tri-City Americans	WHL	64	11	16	27	33	15	3	4	7	6
2012-13	Tri-City Americans	WHL	66	21	45	66	36	5	1	4	5	2
2013-14	Vaxjo Lakers HC	Sweden	40	3	4	7	6	6	1	0	1	0
	IF Troja-Ljungby	Sweden-2	2	1	2	3	2	....	....	....	....	....
2014-15	Lulea HF	Sweden	14	1	1	2	2	....	....	....	....	....
	Vaxjo Lakers HC	Sweden	21	2	0	2	41	....	....	....	....	....
	Asploven	Sweden-2	4	1	0	1	41	....	....	....	....	....
	HV 71 Jonkoping	Sweden	12	3	0	3	4	6	0	1	1	0
2015-16	AIK Solna	Sweden-2	49	25	17	42	26	10	1	0	1	2
2016-17	Hartford Wolf Pack	AHL	44	2	4	6	20	....	....	....	....	....

Signed as a free agent by **NY Rangers**, April 12, 2016.

STUCKER, Robbie (STUH-kuhr, RAW-bee) **CBJ**

Defense. Shoots right. 6'3", 178 lbs. Born, St. Paul, MN, September 30, 1998.
(Columbus' 7th pick, 210th overall, in 2017 NHL Draft).

			Regular Season					Playoffs				
Season	Club	League	GP	G	A	Pts	PIM	GP	G	A	Pts	PIM
2013-14	St. Thomas Acad.	High-MN	12	0	1	1	0	....	....	....	....	....
2014-15	St. Thomas Acad.	High-MN	25	6	12	18	10	6	0	1	1	2
2015-16	Team Southeast	UMHSEL	21	0	8	8	30	....	....	....	....	....
	St. Thomas Acad.	High-MN	25	3	18	21	26	3	1	3	4	0
2016-17	Team Southeast	UMHSEL	19	0	13	13	40	3	1	3	4	4
	St. Thomas Acad.	High-MN	25	8	32	40	20	6	3	8	11	2

• Signed Letter of Intent to attend **Colorado College** (NCHC) in fall of 2018.

STUDENIC, Marian (Stoo-deh-NEESH, Ma-REE-uhn) **N.J.**

Right wing. Shoots left. 6', 165 lbs. Born, Holic, Slovakia, October 28, 1998.
(New Jersey's 7th pick, 143rd overall, in 2017 NHL Draft).

			Regular Season					Playoffs				
Season	Club	League	GP	G	A	Pts	PIM	GP	G	A	Pts	PIM
2013-14	HK 36 Skalica U18	Svk-U18	14	4	7	11	6	....	....	....	....	....
2014-15	HK 36 Skalica Jr.	Slovak-Jr.	14	6	6	12	2	....	....	....	....	....
	HK 36 Skalica U18	Svk-U18	30	39	25	64	16	4	1	3	4	6
	HK 36 Skalica	Slovakia	1	0	0	0	0	....	....	....	....	....
2015-16	MHKM Skalica Jr.	Slovak-Jr.	3	0	2	2	2	....	....	....	....	....
	HK 36 Skalica	Slovakia	35	8	8	16	20	....	....	....	....	....
	SR 18	Slovak-Jr.	3	1	4	5	2	....	....	....	....	....
	HK VSR SR 20	Slovakia	2	0	1	1	1	....	....	....	....	....
	HK Dukla Trencin	Slovakia	2	0	0	0	0	....	....	....	....	....
	Trencin Jr.	Slovak-Jr.	....	....	....	....	....	8	2	5	7	6
2016-17	Hamilton Bulldogs	OHL	58	18	12	30	23	7	2	2	4	4

STUDNICKA, Jack (stuhd-NEE-ka, JAK) **BOS**

Center. Shoots right. 6'1", 171 lbs. Born, Windsor, ON, February 18, 1999.
(Boston's 2nd pick, 53rd overall, in 2017 NHL Draft).

			Regular Season					Playoffs				
Season	Club	League	GP	G	A	Pts	PIM	GP	G	A	Pts	PIM
2014-15	Det. B. Tire U16	T1EHL	32	9	*32	41	24	4	1	0	1	7
	Det. B. Tire U16	Minor-MI	35	21	26	47	18	....	....	....	....	....
2015-16	Oshawa Generals	OHL	62	4	22	26	25	5	0	0	0	2
2016-17	Oshawa Generals	OHL	64	18	34	52	36	11	5	12	17	6

STUKEL, Jakob (STOO-kuhl, JAY-kuhb) **VAN**

Left wing. Shoots left. 6', 182 lbs. Born, Surrey, BC, March 6, 1997.
(Vancouver's 4th pick, 154th overall, in 2016 NHL Draft).

			Regular Season					Playoffs				
Season	Club	League	GP	G	A	Pts	PIM	GP	G	A	Pts	PIM
2011-12	Cloverdale Colts	Minor-BC	20	25	37	62	....	....	....	....	....	....
	Cloverdale Colts	Other	31	34	24	58	....	....	....	....	....	....
2012-13	Valley West Hawks	BCMML	38	30	13	43	14	3	4	0	4	0
	Vancouver Giants	WHL	6	2	2	4	2	....	....	....	....	....
2013-14	Vancouver Giants	WHL	DID NOT PLAY – INJURED									
2014-15	Vancouver Giants	WHL	49	5	11	16	10	....	....	....	....	....
2015-16	Vancouver Giants	WHL	12	2	2	4	4	....	....	....	....	....
	Calgary Hitmen	WHL	57	34	22	56	8	5	2	1	3	0
2016-17	Calgary Hitmen	WHL	70	23	30	53	36	4	0	1	1	0

• Missed 2013-14 due to knee injury in summer training.

SUBBAN, Jordan (soo-BAN, JOHR-duhn) **VAN**

Defense. Shoots right. 5'9", 175 lbs. Born, Rexdale, ON, March 3, 1995.
(Vancouver's 4th pick, 115th overall, in 2013 NHL Draft).

			Regular Season					Playoffs				
Season	Club	League	GP	G	A	Pts	PIM	GP	G	A	Pts	PIM
2010-11	Toronto Marlboros	GTHL	68	21	43	64	64	....	....	....	....	....
2011-12	Belleville Bulls	OHL	56	5	15	20	31	5	0	0	0	4
2012-13	Belleville Bulls	OHL	68	15	36	51	47	17	2	3	5	20
2013-14	Belleville Bulls	OHL	66	12	30	42	63	....	....	....	....	....
2014-15	Belleville Bulls	OHL	63	25	27	52	62	4	3	0	3	2
2015-16	Utica Comets	AHL	67	11	25	36	38	4	2	1	3	2
2016-17	Utica Comets	AHL	65	16	20	36	36	....	....	....	....	....

SULAK, Libor (SHOO-lahk, LIH-bohr) **DET**

Defense. Shoots left. 6'2", 190 lbs. Born, Pelhrimov, Czech Rep., March 4, 1994.

			Regular Season					Playoffs				
Season	Club	League	GP	G	A	Pts	PIM	GP	G	A	Pts	PIM
2015-16	HC Orli Znojmo	Austria	52	6	12	18	14	18	2	4	6	16
2016-17	HC Orli Znojmo	Austria	54	10	18	28	41	4	3	0	3	2

Signed as a free agent by **Detroit**, May 24, 2017.

SUMMERS, Kelly (SUH-muhrz, KEH-lee) OTT

Defense. Shoots right. 6'2", 198 lbs. Born, Renfrew, ON, April 29, 1996.
(Ottawa's 4th pick, 189th overall, in 2014 NHL Draft).

			Regular Season					Playoffs				
Season	Club	League	GP	G	A	Pts	PIM	GP	G	A	Pts	PIM
2011-12	Ott. Valley Titans	Minor-ON	30	9	22	31	20	8	3	6	9	....
	Carleton Place	ON-Jr.A	2	0	0	0	0	....	....	....	....	....
2012-13	Carleton Place	ON-Jr.A	59	13	20	33	14	12	1	1	2	4
2013-14	Carleton Place	ON-Jr.A	56	17	43	60	12	16	5	8	13	4
2014-15	Clarkson Knights	ECAC	33	6	4	10	4	....	....	....	....	....
2015-16	Clarkson Knights	ECAC	37	3	11	14	20	....	....	....	....	....
2016-17	Clarkson Knights	ECAC	39	3	14	17	30	....	....	....	....	....

ECAC All-Rookie Team (2015)

SUSHKO, Maxim (SOOSH-koh, MAK-sihm) PHI

Right wing. Shoots left. 6', 181 lbs. Born, Drogichin, Belarus, October 2, 1999.
(Philadelphia's 6th pick, 107th overall, in 2017 NHL Draft).

			Regular Season					Playoffs				
Season	Club	League	GP	G	A	Pts	PIM	GP	G	A	Pts	PIM
2013-14	Brest U18	Belarus-U18	3	1	1	2	8	....	....	....	....	....
2014-15	Soligorsk U18	Belarus-U18	17	37	29	66	28	....	....	....	....	....
	Soligorsk 2	Belarus-2	20	14	16	30	28	8	3	10	13	14
2015-16	Dynamo-Raubichi	Belarus-2	8	3	7	10	8	....	....	....	....	....
	Soligorsk 2	Belarus-2	21	9	21	30	44	16	3	10	13	18
2016-17	Owen Sound	OHL	54	17	15	32	24	17	3	8	11	10

SUZUKI, Nick (suh-ZOO-kee, NIHK) VGK

Center. Shoots right. 5'11", 183 lbs. Born, London, ON, October 8, 1999.
(Las Vegas' 2nd pick, 13th overall, in 2017 NHL Draft).

			Regular Season					Playoffs				
Season	Club	League	GP	G	A	Pts	PIM	GP	G	A	Pts	PIM
2014-15	Lon. Knights MM	Minor-ON	31	34	34	68	16	13	4	5	9	10
	London Nationals	ON-Jr.B	1	0	1	1	0	....	....	....	....	....
2015-16	Owen Sound	OHL	63	20	18	38	4	6	2	0	2	0
2016-17	Owen Sound	OHL	65	45	51	96	10	17	8	14	22	10

OHL Second All-Star Team (2017)

SVENINGSSON, Filip (sveh-NIHNG-suhn, FIHL-ihp) CGY

Left wing. Shoots left. 6', 180 lbs. Born, Gislaved, Sweden, March 7, 1999.
(Calgary's 5th pick, 202nd overall, in 2017 NHL Draft).

			Regular Season					Playoffs				
Season	Club	League	GP	G	A	Pts	PIM	GP	G	A	Pts	PIM
2012-13	Gislaveds SK U18	Swe-U18	4	1	2	3	0	....	....	....	....	....
2013-14	Gislaveds SK Jr.	Swe-Jr.	10	5	1	6	10	....	....	....	....	....
2014-15	HV 71 U18	Swe-U18	23	4	3	7	6	7	2	3	5	6
2015-16	HV 71 U18	Swe-U18	34	26	25	51	46	....	....	....	....	....
	HV 71 Jr.	Swe-Jr.	11	1	2	3	10	3	0	1	1	4
2016-17	HV 71 U18	Swe-U18	1	1	0	1	4	2	0	0	0	2
	HV 71 Jonkoping	Sweden	2	0	0	0	0	....	....	....	....	....
	HV 71 Jr.	Swe-Jr.	37	15	14	29	59	7	4	4	8	2

SVETLAKOV, Andrei (sveht-LAH-kawv, AWN-dray) MIN

Center. Shoots left. 6', 202 lbs. Born, Moscow, Russia, June 4, 1996.
(Minnesota's 5th pick, 178th overall, in 2017 NHL Draft).

			Regular Season					Playoffs				
Season	Club	League	GP	G	A	Pts	PIM	GP	G	A	Pts	PIM
2012-13	CSKA Jr.	Russia-Jr.	33	1	3	4	10	....	....	....	....	....
2013-14	CSKA Jr.	Russia-Jr.	35	4	4	8	18	8	0	0	0	2
2014-15	CSKA Jr.	Russia-Jr.	49	18	34	52	92	10	5	6	11	10
2015-16	CSKA Jr.	Russia-Jr.	1	0	0	0	2	....	....	....	....	....
	CSKA Moscow	KHL	30	7	3	10	14	8	0	2	2	6
	Zvezda Chekhov	Russia-2	5	1	1	2	8	....	....	....	....	....
2016-17	Zvezda Chekhov	Russia-2	2	1	1	2	6	....	....	....	....	....
	CSKA Moscow	KHL	37	4	12	16	42	10	3	0	3	18

SWANEY, Nick (SWAY-nee, NIHK) MIN

Right wing. Shoots right. 5'10", 175 lbs. Born, Burnsville, MN, September 9, 1997.
(Minnesota's 6th pick, 209th overall, in 2017 NHL Draft).

			Regular Season					Playoffs				
Season	Club	League	GP	G	A	Pts	PIM	GP	G	A	Pts	PIM
2012-13	Lakeville South	High-MN	25	12	13	25	7	3	1	2	3	0
2013-14	Lakeville South	High-MN	24	13	31	44	14	2	2	4	6	2
	Waterloo	USHL	4	1	0	1	2	....	....	....	....	....
2014-15	Team Southeast	UMHSEL	20	9	18	27	27	3	2	4	6	2
	Lakeville South	High-MN	24	25	32	57	0	2	4	0	4	0
	Waterloo	USHL	15	9	4	13	0	....	....	....	....	....
2015-16	Waterloo	USHL	54	30	20	50	26	9	5	4	9	2
2016-17	Waterloo	USHL	47	26	25	51	12	8	1	1	2	6

• Signed Letter of Intent to attend **University of Minnesota-Duluth** (NCHC) in fall of 2017.

TALVITIE, Aarne (TAL-VIH-tay, AHR-neh) N.J.

Center. Shoots left. 5'11", 200 lbs. Born, Espoo, Finland, November 2, 1999.
(New Jersey's 8th pick, 160th overall, in 2017 NHL Draft).

			Regular Season					Playoffs				
Season	Club	League	GP	G	A	Pts	PIM	GP	G	A	Pts	PIM
2014-15	Blues Espoo U18	Fin-U18	9	4	3	7	2	....	....	....	....	....
2015-16	Blues Espoo U18	Fin-U18	38	14	16	30	26	4	1	0	1	0
	Blues Espoo Jr.	Fin-Jr.	6	0	1	1	0	....	....	....	....	....
2016-17	Blues Espoo Jr.	Fin-Jr.	46	13	24	37	36	4	3	1	4	2
	Blues Espoo U18	Fin-U18	....	....	....	....	....	4	2	1	3	0

TAMBELLINI, Adam (tam-buh-LEE-nee, A-duhm) NYR

Center. Shoots left. 6'4", 195 lbs. Born, Port Moody, BC, November 1, 1994.
(NY Rangers' 1st pick, 65th overall, in 2013 NHL Draft).

			Regular Season					Playoffs				
Season	Club	League	GP	G	A	Pts	PIM	GP	G	A	Pts	PIM
2008-09	Southgate	AMBHL	33	6	13	19	4	11	1	3	4	2
2009-10	SSAC Bulldogs	Minor-AB	34	27	24	51	20	6	6	4	10	10
2010-11	SSAC Athletics	AMHL	33	22	25	47	4	5	4	2	6	0
	Sherwood Park	AJHL	3	1	0	1	0	....	....	....	....	....
2011-12	Vernon Vipers	BCHL	55	27	29	56	28	....	....	....	....	....
2012-13	Vernon Vipers	BCHL	36	22	17	39	18	....	....	....	....	....
	Surrey Eagles	BCHL	16	14	12	26	8	17	*10	8	*18	6
2013-14	North Dakota	NCHC	16	2	2	4	31	....	....	....	....	....
	Calgary Hitmen	WHL	31	17	22	39	10	6	5	4	9	2
2014-15	Calgary Hitmen	WHL	71	47	39	86	30	16	13	13	26	10
2015-16	Hartford Wolf Pack	AHL	74	17	15	32	24	....	....	....	....	....
2016-17	Hartford Wolf Pack	AHL	68	13	22	35	22	....	....	....	....	....

WHL East Second All-Star Team (2015)

TAMMELA, Jonne (tah-MEH-lah, YOH-nay) T.B.

Right wing. Shoots left. 5'11", 185 lbs. Born, Ylivieska, Finland, August 5, 1997.
(Tampa Bay's 5th pick, 118th overall, in 2015 NHL Draft).

			Regular Season					Playoffs				
Season	Club	League	GP	G	A	Pts	PIM	GP	G	A	Pts	PIM
2012-13	JyP Jyvaskyla U18	Fin-U18	21	12	10	22	16	....	....	....	....	....
	JyP Jyvaskyla Jr.	Fin-Jr.	10	1	2	3	18	3	1	0	1	0
2013-14	KalPa Kuopio U18	Fin-U18	3	2	3	5	2	8	6	4	10	0
	KalPa Kuopio Jr.	Fin-Jr.	24	5	11	16	12	....	....	....	....	....
2014-15	KalPa Kuopio Jr.	Fin-Jr.	26	11	16	27	26	....	....	....	....	....
	KalPa Kuopio	Finland	32	4	0	4	6	4	0	0	0	4
2015-16	KalPa Kuopio	Finland	37	5	8	13	16	3	0	0	0	2
	KalPa Kuopio Jr.	Fin-Jr.	....	....	....	....	....	8	2	3	5	6
	Syracuse Crunch	AHL	3	0	1	1	0	....	....	....	....	....
2016-17	Peterborough	OHL	2	1	0	1	0	....	....	....	....	....

• Missed majority of 2016-17 due to recurring knee injury and resulting surgery.

TAYLOR, Jeff (TAY-luhr, JEHF) PIT

Defense. Shoots left. 5'11", 181 lbs. Born, Albany, NY, April 13, 1994.
(Pittsburgh's 5th pick, 203rd overall, in 2014 NHL Draft).

			Regular Season					Playoffs				
Season	Club	League	GP	G	A	Pts	PIM	GP	G	A	Pts	PIM
2010-11	Albany	High-NY	36	7	28	35	....	....	....	....	....	....
2011-12	Albany	High-NY	26	10	28	38	....	....	....	....	....	....
2012-13	Dubuque	USHL	57	5	22	27	16	11	0	5	5	4
2013-14	Union College	ECAC	41	3	13	16	18	....	....	....	....	....
2014-15	Union College	ECAC	34	4	27	31	28	....	....	....	....	....
2015-16	Union College	ECAC	36	2	10	12	37	....	....	....	....	....
2016-17	Union College	ECAC	38	9	24	33	24	....	....	....	....	....
	Wilkes-Barre	AHL	6	0	0	0	0	....	....	....	....	....

ECAC Second All-Team (2017)

TERRY, Troy (TAIR-ee, TROY) ANA

Center/Right wing. Shoots right. 5'11", 160 lbs. Born, Denver, CO, September 10, 1997.
(Anaheim's 5th pick, 148th overall, in 2015 NHL Draft).

			Regular Season					Playoffs				
Season	Club	League	GP	G	A	Pts	PIM	GP	G	A	Pts	PIM
2012-13	Col. T-birds U16	T1EHL	41	14	35	49	6	2	0	0	0	0
2013-14	Col. T-birds U16	T1EHL	31	16	25	41	0	....	....	....	....	....
	Indiana Ice	USHL	1	0	0	0	0	....	....	....	....	....
2014-15	USAHNTDP	USHL	25	6	8	14	4	....	....	....	....	....
	USAHNTDP	U-18	41	13	17	30	4	....	....	....	....	....
2015-16	U. of Denver	NCHC	41	9	13	22	8	....	....	....	....	....
2016-17	U. of Denver	NCHC	35	*22	23	45	22	....	....	....	....	....

TEXIER, Alexandre (tehx-EE-ay, Al-ehx-AHN-druh) CBJ

Center. Shoots left. 6', 187 lbs. Born, Grenoble, France, September 13, 1999.
(Columbus' 1st pick, 45th overall, in 2017 NHL Draft).

			Regular Season					Playoffs				
Season	Club	League	GP	G	A	Pts	PIM	GP	G	A	Pts	PIM
2013-14	Grenoble U18	France-U18	8	7	4	11	4	....	....	....	....	....
2014-15	Grenoble U18	France-U18	17	16	18	34	32	6	6	6	12	6
2015-16	Grenoble U18	France-U18	17	40	30	70	26	6	9	12	21	10
	Grenoble U22	France-U22	11	9	8	17	14	6	7	4	11	8
2016-17	Grenoble	France	40	10	9	19	69	12	5	5	10	12

THOMAS, Ben (TAW-muhs, BEHN) T.B.

Defense. Shoots right. 6'1", 190 lbs. Born, Calgary, AB, May 28, 1996.
(Tampa Bay's 5th pick, 119th overall, in 2014 NHL Draft).

			Regular Season					Playoffs				
Season	Club	League	GP	G	A	Pts	PIM	GP	G	A	Pts	PIM
2009-10	CNHA Blazers	Minor-AB	28	1	3	4	20	2	0	1	1	0
	Calgary Northstars	AMBHL	1	0	0	0	0	....	....	....	....	....
2010-11	Calgary Northstars	AMBHL	32	1	10	11	46	....	....	....	....	....
2011-12	Calgary Northstars	AMHL	34	2	15	17	46	6	0	0	0	8
2012-13	Calgary Mustangs	AJHL	12	1	0	1	4	....	....	....	....	....
	Calgary Canucks	AJHL	31	4	3	7	33	....	....	....	....	....
	Calgary Hitmen	WHL	7	0	0	0	0	1	0	0	0	0
2013-14	Calgary Hitmen	WHL	72	7	24	31	39	6	1	5	6	13
2014-15	Calgary Hitmen	WHL	60	7	24	31	28	17	0	4	4	2
2015-16	Calgary Hitmen	WHL	14	0	3	3	10	....	....	....	....	....
	Vancouver Giants	WHL	60	8	17	25	40	....	....	....	....	....
	Syracuse Crunch	AHL	8	1	3	4	0	....	....	....	....	....
2016-17	Syracuse Crunch	AHL	71	3	18	21	30	22	5	8	13	12

THOMAS, Robert (TAW-muhs, RAW-buhrt) ST.L.

Center. Shoots right. 6', 193 lbs. Born, Aurora, ON, February 7, 1999.
(St. Louis' 1st pick, 20th overall, in 2017 NHL Draft).

			Regular Season					Playoffs				
Season	Club	League	GP	G	A	Pts	PIM	GP	G	A	Pts	PIM
2014-15	York Simcoe MM	Minor-ON	34	18	27	45	22	....	....	....	....	....
	St. Andrew's	High-ON	1	0	0	0	0	....	....	....	....	....
2015-16	London Knights	OHL	40	3	12	15	0	15	1	4	5	2
2016-17	London Knights	OHL	66	16	50	66	26	14	3	9	12	6

THOMPSON, Keaton (TAWM-suhn, KEE-tuhn) ANA

Defense. Shoots left. 6', 182 lbs. Born, Edina, MN, September 14, 1995.
(Anaheim's 3rd pick, 87th overall, in 2013 NHL Draft).

			Regular Season					Playoffs				
Season	Club	League	GP	G	A	Pts	PIM	GP	G	A	Pts	PIM
2010-11	Team Great Plains	UMHSEL	16	0	1	1	12	3	0	2	2	4
	Fargo Force	USHL	13	0	0	0	4	2	0	0	0	5
2011-12	USAHNTDP	USHL	35	4	9	13	17	2	0	0	0	2
	USAHNTDP	U-17	17	1	8	9	14	....	....	....	....	....
2012-13	USAHNTDP	USHL	26	3	6	9	18	....	....	....	....	....
	USAHNTDP	U-18	41	1	12	13	22	....	....	....	....	....
2013-14	North Dakota	NCHC	26	3	5	8	12	....	....	....	....	....
2014-15	North Dakota	NCHC	36	3	8	11	14	....	....	....	....	....
2015-16	North Dakota	NCHC	43	2	15	17	36	....	....	....	....	....
2016-17	San Diego Gulls	AHL	52	4	12	16	29	10	2	1	3	4
	Utah Grizzlies	ECHL	4	0	0	0	0	....	....	....	....	....

THOMPSON, Tage (TAWM-suhn, TAYJ) ST.L.

Center. Shoots right. 6'5", 195 lbs. Born, Phoenix, AZ, October 30, 1997.
(St. Louis' 1st pick, 26th overall, in 2016 NHL Draft).

			Regular Season					Playoffs				
Season	Club	League	GP	G	A	Pts	PIM	GP	G	A	Pts	PIM
2012-13	Long Island U16	AYHL	16	14	14	28	19	....	....	....	....	....
2013-14	PAL Islanders	USPHL	16	17	14	31	8	....	....	....	....	....
2014-15	USAHNTDP	USHL	25	7	7	14	20	....	....	....	....	....
	USAHNTDP	U-18	39	5	7	12	12	....	....	....	....	....
2015-16	U. of Connecticut	H-East	36	14	18	32	12	....	....	....	....	....
2016-17	U. of Connecticut	H-East	34	19	13	32	24	....	....	....	....	....
	Chicago Wolves	AHL	16	1	1	2	2	10	2	1	3	4

THURKAUF, Calvin (TUHR-KAWF, KAL-vihn) CBJ

Left wing. Shoots left. 6'1", 206 lbs. Born, Zug, Switzerland, June 27, 1997.
(Columbus' 5th pick, 185th overall, in 2016 NHL Draft).

			Regular Season					Playoffs				
Season	Club	League	GP	G	A	Pts	PIM	GP	G	A	Pts	PIM
2010-11	EV Zug U17 II	Swiss-U17	2	2	2	4	2	....	....	....	....	....
2011-12	EV Zug U17	Swiss-U17	1	0	0	0	0	....	....	....	....	....
	EV Zug U17 II	Swiss-U17	1	2	1	3	2	....	....	....	....	....
2012-13	EV Zug U17	Swiss-U17	27	21	17	38	70	10	8	5	13	10
	EV Zug Jr.	Swiss-Jr.	4	1	0	1	2	2	0	0	0	0
2013-14	EV Zug U17	Swiss-U17	4	3	4	7	16	4	1	3	4	35
	EV Zug Jr.	Swiss-Jr.	8	1	1	2	6	2	0	0	0	4
2014-15	EV Zug Jr.	Swiss-Jr.	38	11	10	21	54	12	1	1	2	20
	SC Langenthal	Swiss-2	....	....	....	....	....	1	0	0	0	4
2015-16	Kelowna Rockets	WHL	61	18	27	45	54	18	2	6	8	16
2016-17	Kelowna Rockets	WHL	60	33	37	70	87	17	8	13	21	24

TIFFELS, Frederik (TIH-fuhlz, FREHD-uhr-ihk) PIT

Left wing. Shoots left. 6', 192 lbs. Born, Cologne, Germany, May 20, 1995.
(Pittsburgh's 3rd pick, 167th overall, in 2015 NHL Draft).

			Regular Season					Playoffs				
Season	Club	League	GP	G	A	Pts	PIM	GP	G	A	Pts	PIM
2010-11	Heil./Mann. Jr.	Ger-Jr.	36	9	23	32	12	4	0	0	0	2
2011-12	Heil./Mann. Jr.	Ger-Jr.	36	6	22	28	6	8	3	5	8	0
2012-13	Muskegon	USHL	50	3	22	25	10	3	1	0	1	0
2013-14	Muskegon	USHL	13	3	2	5	4	....	....	....	....	....
	Fargo Force	USHL	12	1	4	5	2	....	....	....	....	....
	Cedar Rapids	USHL	31	9	18	27	4	4	1	0	1	2
2014-15	Western Mich.	NCHC	32	11	10	21	14	....	....	....	....	....
2015-16	Western Mich.	NCHC	36	7	10	17	25	....	....	....	....	....
2016-17	Western Mich.	NCHC	37	9	12	21	12	....	....	....	....	....

TIMASHOV, Dmytro (tihm-ah-SHAWV, dih-mih-TROH) TOR

Left wing. Shoots left. 5'10", 194 lbs. Born, Kirovograd, Ukraine, October 1, 1996.
(Toronto's 7th pick, 125th overall, in 2015 NHL Draft).

			Regular Season					Playoffs				
Season	Club	League	GP	G	A	Pts	PIM	GP	G	A	Pts	PIM
2011-12	SDE U18	Swe-U18	17	10	13	23	37	....	....	....	....	....
	Djurgarden U18	Swe-U18	17	2	4	6	4	4	0	0	0	0
2012-13	Djurgarden U18	Swe-U18	11	4	5	9	8	....	....	....	....	....
	Djurgarden Jr.	Swe-Jr.	22	4	6	10	8	....	....	....	....	....
	MODO U18	Swe-U18	2	2	1	3	0	2	0	1	1	0
	MODO Jr.	Swe-Jr.	16	5	7	12	4	7	0	1	1	0
2013-14	MODO Jr.	Swe-Jr.	40	12	29	41	18	6	0	1	1	8
	MODO	Sweden	3	0	1	1	0	....	....	....	....	....
	Mora IK	Sweden-2	6	0	1	1	2	....	....	....	....	....
	IF Bjorkloven Umea	Sweden-2	4	0	0	0	25	....	....	....	....	....
	MODO U18	Swe-U18	....	....	....	....	....	4	2	5	7	2
2014-15	Quebec Remparts	QMJHL	66	19	71	90	54	22	3	15	18	18
2015-16	Quebec Remparts	QMJHL	29	18	35	53	51	....	....	....	....	....
	Shawinigan	QMJHL	28	4	28	32	28	21	13	15	28	*40
2016-17	Toronto Marlies	AHL	63	11	13	24	32	6	0	0	0	2

QMJHL All-Rookie Team (2015) • QMJHL Rookie of the Year (2015)

TIMMINS, Conor (TIH-mihnz, KOH-nuhr) COL

Defense. Shoots right. 6'1", 185 lbs. Born, St. Catharines, ON, September 18, 1998.
(Colorado's 2nd pick, 32nd overall, in 2017 NHL Draft).

			Regular Season					Playoffs				
Season	Club	League	GP	G	A	Pts	PIM	GP	G	A	Pts	PIM
2013-14	Southern Tier	Minor-ON	38	4	18	22	39	10	2	2	4	6
2014-15	Thorold	ON-Jr.B	15	2	8	10	28	....	....	....	....	....
	St. Catharines	ON-Jr.B	15	5	3	8	13	13	3	5	8	6
2015-16	Sault Ste. Marie	OHL	60	4	9	13	20	12	0	1	1	6
2016-17	Sault Ste. Marie	OHL	67	7	54	61	69	11	1	7	8	10

TIPPETT, Owen (TIH-piht, OH-wehn) FLA

Right wing. Shoots right. 6'1", 203 lbs. Born, Peterborough, ON, February 16, 1999.
(Florida's 1st pick, 10th overall, in 2017 NHL Draft).

			Regular Season					Playoffs				
Season	Club	League	GP	G	A	Pts	PIM	GP	G	A	Pts	PIM
2013-14	Tor. R. Wings MM	GTHL	31	15	6	21	8	....	....	....	....	....
2014-15	Tor. R. Wings MM	GTHL	50	52	35	87	....	....	....	....	....	....
	Tor. R. Wings Mid.	GTHL	....	....	....	....	....	1	0	0	0	0
	Tor. Canadiens	ON-Jr.A	6	2	1	3	2	....	....	....	....	....
2015-16	Mississauga	OHL	48	15	5	20	10	7	1	2	3	4
2016-17	Mississauga	OHL	60	44	31	75	36	20	10	9	19	14

TOEWS, Devon (TAYVZ, deh-VAWN) NYI

Defense. Shoots left. 6'1", 181 lbs. Born, Abbotsford, BC, February 21, 1994.
(NY Islanders' 5th pick, 108th overall, in 2014 NHL Draft).

			Regular Season					Playoffs				
Season	Club	League	GP	G	A	Pts	PIM	GP	G	A	Pts	PIM
2008-09	Abbotsford Hawks	Minor-BC	61	8	56	64	60	....	....	....	....	....
2009-10	Fraser Valley	BCMML	39	2	5	7	60	....	....	....	....	....
	Yale Lions	High-BC	3	2	9	11	0	3	3	8	11	2
2010-11	Fraser Valley	BCMML	39	12	25	37	62	....	....	....	....	....
	Yale Lions	High-BC	4	6	8	14	0	....	....	....	....	....
	Abbotsford Pilots	PIJHL	5	1	1	2	0	13	1	5	6	2
2011-12	Surrey Eagles	BCHL	54	7	22	29	42	12	5	7	12	15
2012-13	Surrey Eagles	BCHL	48	10	37	47	55	17	0	9	9	10
2013-14	Quinnipiac	ECAC	37	1	16	17	10	....	....	....	....	....
2014-15	Quinnipiac	ECAC	31	4	16	20	16	....	....	....	....	....
2015-16	Quinnipiac	ECAC	40	7	23	30	26	....	....	....	....	....
2016-17	Bridgeport	AHL	76	5	40	45	18	....	....	....	....	....

ECAC Second All-Star Team (2016) • AHL All-Rookie Team (2017)

TOLVANEN, Eeli (tohl-VA-nehn, EH-lee) NSH

Right wing. Shoots left. 5'11", 189 lbs. Born, Vihti, Finland, April 22, 1999.
(Nashville's 1st pick, 30th overall, in 2017 NHL Draft).

			Regular Season					Playoffs				
Season	Club	League	GP	G	A	Pts	PIM	GP	G	A	Pts	PIM
2013-14	Blues Espoo U18	Fin-U18	10	2	4	6	0	1	0	0	0	0
2014-15	Blues Espoo U18	Fin-U18	41	39	45	84	24	9	1	3	4	14
	Blues Espoo Jr.	Fin-Jr.	7	2	3	5	2	....	....	....	....	....
2015-16	Sioux City	USHL	49	17	21	38	12	....	....	....	....	....
2016-17	Sioux City	USHL	52	30	24	54	26	13	5	5	10	6

• Signed Letter of Intent to attend **Boston College** (Hockey East) in fall of 2017.

TONINATO, Dominic (toh-nee-NAH-toh, DOHM-ihn-ihk) TOR

Center. Shoots left. 6'1", 165 lbs. Born, Duluth, MN, March 9, 1994.
(Toronto's 3rd pick, 126th overall, in 2012 NHL Draft).

			Regular Season					Playoffs				
Season	Club	League	GP	G	A	Pts	PIM	GP	G	A	Pts	PIM
2009-10	Duluth East	High-MN	25	4	7	11	6	6	4	4	8	6
2010-11	Team North	UMHSEL	24	11	8	19	12	....	....	....	....	....
	Duluth East	High-MN	23	24	27	51	12	6	6	4	10	0
2011-12	Team North	UMHSEL	24	10	15	25	30	....	....	....	....	....
	Duluth East	High-MN	25	27	34	61	28	6	6	6	12	4
	Fargo Force	USHL	4	1	0	1	2	....	....	....	....	....
2012-13	Fargo Force	USHL	64	29	41	70	50	12	3	3	6	6
2013-14	U. Minn-Duluth	NCHC	35	7	8	15	51	....	....	....	....	....
2014-15	U. Minn-Duluth	NCHC	34	16	10	26	58	....	....	....	....	....
2015-16	U. Minn-Duluth	NCHC	40	15	6	21	36	....	....	....	....	....
2016-17	U. Minn-Duluth	NCHC	42	16	13	29	30	....	....	....	....	....

USHL Second All-Star Team (2013)

TOROPCHENKO, Alexei (toh-rohp-CHEHN-koh, al-EHX-ay) ST.L.

Right wing. Shoots left. 6'3", 187 lbs. Born, Moscow, Russia, June 25, 1999.
(St. Louis' 3rd pick, 113th overall, in 2017 NHL Draft).

			Regular Season					Playoffs				
Season	Club	League	GP	G	A	Pts	PIM	GP	G	A	Pts	PIM
2015-16	Dyn'o Moscow Jr.	Russia-Jr.	21	1	2	3	2	....	....	....	....	....
2016-17	Dyn'o Balashikha	Russia-2	1	0	0	0	0	....	....	....	....	....
	Dyn'o Moscow Jr.	Russia-Jr.	45	19	12	31	50	....	....	....	....	....

TRENIN, Yakov (TREH-nihn, YA-kawv) NSH

Left wing. Shoots left. 6'2", 201 lbs. Born, Chelyabinsk, Russia, January 13, 1997.
(Nashville's 1st pick, 55th overall, in 2015 NHL Draft).

			Regular Season					Playoffs				
Season	Club	League	GP	G	A	Pts	PIM	GP	G	A	Pts	PIM
2013-14	Chelyabinsk Jr.	Russia-Jr.	22	7	7	14	12	4	0	1	1	2
2014-15	Gatineau	QMJHL	58	18	49	67	34	11	3	8	11	10
2015-16	Gatineau	QMJHL	57	26	35	61	56	5	0	2	2	4
	Milwaukee	AHL	....	....	....	....	....	2	0	1	1	2
2016-17	Gatineau	QMJHL	54	30	37	67	84	7	3	7	10	24
	Milwaukee	AHL	5	1	2	3	2	1	0	0	0	0

TROOCK, Branden (TROOK, BRAN-duhn)

Right wing. Shoots right. 6'2", 220 lbs. Born, Edmonton, AB, March 20, 1994.
(Dallas' 7th pick, 134th overall, in 2012 NHL Draft).

			Regular Season					Playoffs				
Season	Club	League	GP	G	A	Pts	PIM	GP	G	A	Pts	PIM
2008-09	CAC Lehigh	AMBHL	32	21	28	49	82	....	....	....	....	....
2009-10	CAC Canadians	AMHL	27	19	18	37	38	2	0	3	3	2
	Seattle	WHL	9	2	4	6	4	....	....	....	....	....
2010-11			DID NOT PLAY – INJURED									
2011-12	Seattle	WHL	58	14	12	26	83	....	....	....	....	....
2012-13	Seattle	WHL	19	5	6	11	19	....	....	....	....	....
2013-14	Seattle	WHL	58	24	34	58	69	9	4	3	7	8
	Texas Stars	AHL	1	0	0	0	0	1	0	0	0	0
2014-15	Texas Stars	AHL	49	6	9	15	27	....	....	....	....	....
	Idaho Steelheads	ECHL	5	1	1	2	2	....	....	....	....	....
2015-16	Texas Stars	AHL	38	3	8	11	38	....	....	....	....	....
	Idaho Steelheads	ECHL	8	2	3	5	8	....	....	....	....	....
2016-17	Texas Stars	AHL	10	0	4	4	4	....	....	....	....	....
	Idaho Steelheads	ECHL	15	7	2	9	4	....	....	....	....	....
	Tucson	AHL	20	4	3	7	11	....	....	....	....	....

• Missed remainder of 2009-10 and all of 2010-11 due to head injury, playing for Team Alberta, in Western Canada Under-16 Challenge Tournament, October 31, 2009. • Missed majority of 2012-13 due to shoulder injury vs. Lethbridge (WHL), January 20, 2013. Traded to **Arizona** by **Dallas** with Brendan Ranford for Justin Peters and Justin Hache, February 1, 2017.

TSCHANTZ, Dwyer (SHAHNTZ, DWIGH-uhr) **ST.L.**

Right wing. Shoots right. 6'5", 209 lbs. Born, Wilmington, DE, March 22, 1995.
(St. Louis' 10th pick, 202nd overall, in 2014 NHL Draft).

			Regular Season					Playoffs				
Season	Club	League	GP	G	A	Pts	PIM	GP	G	A	Pts	PIM
2010-11	Phi. Jr. Flyers	T1EHL	36	9	11	20	22	....	....	....	....	....
2011-12	Comcast U18	T1EHL	37	17	15	32	28	....	....	....	....	....
2012-13	Comcast U18	T1EHL	40	20	32	52	28	4	0	0	0	22
	USAHNTDP	USHL	1	0	0	0	0	....	....	....	....	....
2013-14	Indiana Ice	USHL	52	24	20	44	58	8	0	3	3	7
2014-15	Cornell Big Red	ECAC	19	2	3	5	14	....	....	....	....	....
2015-16	Cornell Big Red	ECAC	20	2	3	5	12	....	....	....	....	....
2016-17	Cornell Big Red	ECAC	15	1	5	6	4	....	....	....	....	....

TUFTE, Riley (TUHF-TEE, RIGH-lee) **DAL**

Left wing. Shoots left. 6'5", 211 lbs. Born, Coon Rapids, MN, April 10, 1998.
(Dallas' 1st pick, 25th overall, in 2016 NHL Draft).

			Regular Season					Playoffs				
Season	Club	League	GP	G	A	Pts	PIM	GP	G	A	Pts	PIM
2012-13	Blaine JV	High-MN	1	1	0	1	2	....	....	....	....	....
	Blaine Bengals	High-MN	24	2	1	3	4	2	0	0	0	0
2013-14	Blaine Bengals	High-MN	25	17	18	35	26	3	0	2	2	0
2014-15	Team Northeast	UMHSEL	21	12	9	21	33	3	0	2	2	2
	Blaine Bengals	High-MN	24	23	28	51	30	6	6	6	12	2
	Fargo Force	USHL	7	1	4	5	2	....	....	....	....	....
	USAHNTDP	U-17	7	0	1	1	6	....	....	....	....	....
2015-16	Blaine Bengals	High-MN	25	*47	31	78	53	2	2	5	7	0
	Fargo Force	USHL	27	10	4	14	30	....	....	....	....	....
2016-17	U. Minn-Duluth	NCHC	37	9	7	16	26	....	....	....	....	....

TURGEON, Dominic (TUHR-zhawn, DOHM-ihn-ihk) **DET**

Center. Shoots left. 6'2", 203 lbs. Born, Pointe-Claire, QC, February 25, 1996.
(Detroit's 2nd pick, 63rd overall, in 2014 NHL Draft).

			Regular Season					Playoffs				
Season	Club	League	GP	G	A	Pts	PIM	GP	G	A	Pts	PIM
2010-11	Col. T-Birds U14	Minor-CO	76	44	72	116	12	....	....	....	....	....
2011-12	Col. T-Birds U16	T1EHL	40	25	15	40	4	....	....	....	....	....
	Col. T-Birds U16	Minor-CO	22	9	17	26	4	....	....	....	....	....
	Portland	WHL	1	0	0	0	0	....	....	....	....	....
2012-13	Portland	WHL	54	3	5	8	2	5	0	0	0	0
	USAHNTDP	U-17	7	0	3	3	0	....	....	....	....	....
2013-14	Portland	WHL	65	10	21	31	31	21	2	6	8	18
2014-15	Portland	WHL	67	18	25	43	36	17	8	1	9	0
2015-16	Portland	WHL	72	36	34	70	22	2	0	1	1	0
2016-17	Grand Rapids	AHL	71	6	12	18	6	19	1	1	2	2

TUULOLA, Eetu (too-LOH-la, EE-TOO) **CGY**

Left wing. Shoots right. 6'3", 224 lbs. Born, Hameenlinna, Finland, March 17, 1998.
(Calgary's 7th pick, 156th overall, in 2016 NHL Draft).

			Regular Season					Playoffs				
Season	Club	League	GP	G	A	Pts	PIM	GP	G	A	Pts	PIM
2012-13	HPK U18	Fin-U18	2	0	0	0	4	....	....	....	....	....
2013-14	HPK U18	Fin-U18	18	9	6	15	20	3	1	0	1	0
2014-15	HPK U18	Fin-U18	5	0	2	2	6	1	0	0	0	0
	HPK Jr.	Fin-Jr.	33	21	7	28	30	11	2	7	9	14
2015-16	HPK Jr.	Fin-Jr.	29	9	5	14	22	6	0	1	1	27
	HPK Hameenlinna	Finland	10	0	1	1	0	....	....	....	....	....
2016-17	Everett Silvertips	WHL	62	18	13	31	34	10	6	1	7	4

TUULOLA, Joni (TOO'oo-oh-luh, YOH-nee) **CHI**

Defense. Shoots left. 6'2", 180 lbs. Born, Hameenlinna, Finland, January 1, 1996.
(Chicago's 6th pick, 181st overall, in 2015 NHL Draft).

			Regular Season					Playoffs				
Season	Club	League	GP	G	A	Pts	PIM	GP	G	A	Pts	PIM
2010-11	HPK U18	Fin-U18	3	0	1	1	2	....	....	....	....	....
2011-12	HPK U18	Fin-U18	24	1	7	8	28	....	....	....	....	....
2012-13	HPK U18	Fin-U18	41	10	21	31	26	7	0	1	1	25
	HPK Jr.	Fin-Jr.	6	1	0	1	4	....	....	....	....	....
2013-14	HPK U18	Fin-U18	10	3	9	12	2	1	0	0	0	2
	HPK Jr.	Fin-Jr.	47	8	16	24	34	3	0	0	0	0
	HPK Hameenlinna	Finland	2	1	0	1	0	2	0	0	0	0
2014-15	HPK Jr.	Fin-Jr.	6	0	4	4	2	....	....	....	....	....
	HPK Hameenlinna	Finland	32	5	5	10	8	....	....	....	....	....
2015-16	HPK Jr.	Fin-Jr.	4	0	4	4	2	8	0	2	2	10
	HPK Hameenlinna	Finland	53	2	12	14	18	....	....	....	....	....
2016-17	HPK Hameenlinna	Finland	54	2	6	8	12	7	0	1	1	12

TWARYNSKI, Carsen (t'wawr-IHN-skee, KAHR-suhn) **PHI**

Left wing. Shoots left. 6'2", 196 lbs. Born, St.Albert, AB, November 24, 1997.
(Philadelphia's 5th pick, 82nd overall, in 2016 NHL Draft).

			Regular Season					Playoffs				
Season	Club	League	GP	G	A	Pts	PIM	GP	G	A	Pts	PIM
2011-12	Calgary Bisons	AMBHL	27	2	7	9	24	....	....	....	....	....
2012-13	CBHA Rangers	Minor-AB	32	11	23	34	16	....	....	....	....	....
2013-14	Calgary Buffaloes	AMHL	32	13	16	29	31	8	5	4	9	0
	Okotoks Oilers	AJHL	2	0	0	0	0	....	....	....	....	....
2014-15	Calgary Hitmen	WHL	58	6	16	22	22	16	1	4	5	14
2015-16	Calgary Hitmen	WHL	67	20	25	45	42	5	0	1	1	0
2016-17	Calgary Hitmen	WHL	36	10	11	21	42	....	....	....	....	....
	Kelowna Rockets	WHL	28	7	15	22	18	16	3	2	5	17

TYSZKA, Jarret (TIHSH-ka, JAIR-iht) **MTL**

Defense. Shoots left. 6'2", 188 lbs. Born, Langley, BC, March 15, 1999.
(Montreal's 6th pick, 149th overall, in 2017 NHL Draft).

			Regular Season					Playoffs				
Season	Club	League	GP	G	A	Pts	PIM	GP	G	A	Pts	PIM
2014-15	Yale Acad. Prep	CSSHL	25	3	7	10	37	3	0	0	0	2
	Chilliwack Chiefs	BCHL	4	0	0	0	0	....	....	....	....	....
2015-16	Seattle	WHL	48	3	3	6	14	18	0	1	1	6
2016-17	Seattle	WHL	54	6	19	25	28	20	2	5	7	6

ULLY, Cole (YEW-lee, KOHL) **DAL**

Left wing. Shoots left. 6', 170 lbs. Born, Calgary, AB, February 20, 1995.
(Dallas' 7th pick, 131st overall, in 2013 NHL Draft).

			Regular Season					Playoffs				
Season	Club	League	GP	G	A	Pts	PIM	GP	G	A	Pts	PIM
2010-11	Calgary Flames	AMHL	32	17	17	34	20	2	0	0	0	0
	Kamloops Blazers	WHL	1	0	1	1	0	....	....	....	....	....
2011-12	Kamloops Blazers	WHL	55	9	11	20	2	6	1	1	2	2
2012-13	Kamloops Blazers	WHL	62	22	28	50	37	15	1	7	8	4
2013-14	Kamloops Blazers	WHL	69	30	42	72	34	....	....	....	....	....
2014-15	Kamloops Blazers	WHL	69	34	60	94	32	....	....	....	....	....
	Texas Stars	AHL	2	0	1	1	0	....	....	....	....	....
2015-16	Texas Stars	AHL	42	7	11	18	18	....	....	....	....	....
	Idaho Steelheads	ECHL	6	1	5	6	0	....	....	....	....	....
2016-17	Texas Stars	AHL	61	13	11	24	29	....	....	....	....	....

WHL West First All-Star Team (2015)

USTASKI, Matt (YEW-staz-kee, MAT) **WPG**

Center. Shoots left. 6'6", 228 lbs. Born, Glenview, IL, May 27, 1994.
(Winnipeg's 7th pick, 192nd overall, in 2014 NHL Draft).

			Regular Season					Playoffs				
Season	Club	League	GP	G	A	Pts	PIM	GP	G	A	Pts	PIM
2011-12	Lake Forest	MPHL	13	3	6	9	2	3	1	0	1	17
	Lake Forest	High-IL	....	10	12	22	....	....	....	....	....	....
2012-13	Langley Rivermen	BCHL	55	11	16	27	38	....	....	....	....	....
2013-14	Langley Rivermen	BCHL	54	29	20	49	30	....	....	....	....	....
2014-15	U. of Wisconsin	Big Ten	24	4	4	8	20	....	....	....	....	....
2015-16	U. of Wisconsin	Big Ten	25	2	0	2	12	....	....	....	....	....
2016-17	U. of Wisconsin	Big Ten	27	6	2	8	8	....	....	....	....	....

VAAKANAINEN, Urho (va-ka-NIGH-nehn, UHR-hoh) **BOS**

Defense. Shoots left. 6', 188 lbs. Born, Joensuu, Finland, January 1, 1999.
(Boston's 1st pick, 18th overall, in 2017 NHL Draft).

			Regular Season					Playoffs				
Season	Club	League	GP	G	A	Pts	PIM	GP	G	A	Pts	PIM
2012-13	Jokipojat U18	Fin-U18	22	4	13	17	56	....	....	....	....	....
2013-14	Blues Espoo U18	Fin-U18	41	8	25	33	48	5	0	3	3	2
2014-15	Blues Espoo U18	Fin-U18	....	....	....	....	....	1	0	0	0	0
	Blues Espoo Jr.	Fin-Jr.	30	4	8	12	34	9	2	0	2	0
2015-16	Blues Espoo Jr.	Fin-Jr.	18	2	11	13	8	2	0	0	0	2
	Blues Espoo	Finland	25	1	5	6	8	....	....	....	....	....
2016-17	JyP Jyvaskyla Jr.	Fin-Jr.	1	0	0	0	0	....	....	....	....	....
	JYP-Akatemia	Finland-2	3	0	1	1	29	....	....	....	....	....
	JYP Jyvaskyla	Finland	41	2	4	6	12	14	0	3	3	2

VAHATALO, Julius (vah-hah-TAL-oh, YOO-lee-uhs) **DET**

Center. Shoots left. 6'5", 191 lbs. Born, Vahto, Finland, March 23, 1995.
(Detroit's 5th pick, 166th overall, in 2014 NHL Draft).

			Regular Season					Playoffs				
Season	Club	League	GP	G	A	Pts	PIM	GP	G	A	Pts	PIM
2010-11	TuTo Turku U18	Fin-U18	27	4	9	13	35	....	....	....	....	....
2011-12	TuTo Turku U17	Fin-U17	5	1	0	1	4	....	....	....	....	....
	TuTo Turku U18	Fin-U18	6	3	3	6	2	....	....	....	....	....
	TPS Turku U18	Fin-U18	17	5	12	17	14	6	2	4	6	0
	TPS Turku Jr.	Fin-Jr.	8	1	1	2	0	....	....	....	....	....
2012-13	TPS Turku U18	Fin-U18	13	11	13	24	8	1	0	2	2	0
	TPS Turku Jr.	Fin-Jr.	8	0	4	4	2	....	....	....	....	....
2013-14	TPS Turku Jr.	Fin-Jr.	33	18	21	39	6	3	0	0	0	0
	TPS Turku	Finland	18	3	0	3	0	....	....	....	....	....
2014-15	TPS Turku Jr.	Fin-Jr.	12	7	9	16	6	12	7	6	13	0
	TPS Turku	Finland	36	1	1	2	8	....	....	....	....	....
2015-16	TPS Turku Jr.	Fin-Jr.	3	1	5	6	0	....	....	....	....	....
	TPS Turku	Finland	49	9	4	13	6	6	0	0	0	0
2016-17	TPS Turku Jr.	Fin-Jr.	7	0	4	4	0	....	....	....	....	....
	TuTo Turku	Finland-2	2	2	1	3	0	....	....	....	....	....
	TPS Turku	Finland	45	3	4	7	8	4	0	0	0	12

VAINIO, Veeti (VIGH-n'yoh, vee-eh-TAY) **CBJ**

Defense. Shoots right. 6'2", 184 lbs. Born, Espoo, Finland, June 16, 1997.
(Columbus' 7th pick, 141st overall, in 2015 NHL Draft).

			Regular Season					Playoffs				
Season	Club	League	GP	G	A	Pts	PIM	GP	G	A	Pts	PIM
2012-13	Blues Espoo U18	Fin-U18	27	2	9	11	30	....	....	....	....	....
2013-14	Blues Espoo U18	Fin-U18	4	1	3	4	10	2	1	1	2	4
	Blues Ak U18	Fin-U18	1	1	2	3	0	....	....	....	....	....
	Blues Espoo Jr.	Fin-Jr.	35	9	14	23	46	11	5	5	10	2
2014-15	Blues Espoo	Finland	2	0	1	1	0	1	0	0	0	0
	Blues Espoo Jr.	Fin-Jr.	42	13	31	44	42	5	2	5	7	4
2015-16	Blues Espoo Jr.	Fin-Jr.	1	0	0	0	0	2	2	0	2	2
	KeuPa HT Keuruu	Finland-2	6	1	4	5	18	....	....	....	....	....
	Blues Espoo	Finland	30	0	4	4	47	....	....	....	....	....
2016-17	KooKoo Kouvola	Finland	7	0	1	1	4	....	....	....	....	....
	Peliitat Heinola	Finland-2	2	1	1	2	2	....	....	....	....	....

VALA, Ondrej (VAH-LAH, AWN-dray) **DAL**

Defense. Shoots left. 6'4", 210 lbs. Born, Kolin, Czech Rep., April 13, 1998.

			Regular Season					Playoffs				
Season	Club	League	GP	G	A	Pts	PIM	GP	G	A	Pts	PIM
2014-15	HC Pardubice U18	CzR-U18	14	5	8	13	18	5	1	1	2	4
	HC Pardubice Jr.	CzRep-Jr.	29	9	2	11	20	....	....	....	....	....
2015-16	Kamloops Blazers	WHL	72	4	17	21	52	7	0	1	1	4
2016-17	Kamloops Blazers	WHL	60	10	15	25	89	6	1	0	1	6
	Texas Stars	AHL	3	0	1	1	0	....	....	....	....	....

Signed as a free agent by **Dallas**, September 29, 2016.

VALENTINE, Scott
(VAL-ehn-tighn, SKAWT) **NSH**

Defense. Shoots left. 6'2", 201 lbs. Born, Ottawa, ON, May 2, 1991.
(Anaheim's 7th pick, 166th overall, in 2009 NHL Draft).

			Regular Season					Playoffs				
Season	Club	League	GP	G	A	Pts	PIM	GP	G	A	Pts	PIM
2007-08	Hawkesbury	ON-Jr.A	51	2	15	17	81	11	3	4	7	18
	London Knights	OHL	3	0	0	0	2	....	....	....	....	....
2008-09	London Knights	OHL	17	0	0	0	20	....	....	....	....	....
	Oshawa Generals	OHL	26	1	8	9	51	....	....	....	....	....
2009-10	Oshawa Generals	OHL	63	5	14	19	82	....	....	....	....	....
2010-11	Oshawa Generals	OHL	62	4	32	36	106	9	1	1	2	28
2011-12	Milwaukee	AHL	63	2	10	12	69	2	0	0	0	0
2012-13	Milwaukee	AHL	64	6	4	10	74	2	0	0	0	2
2013-14	Milwaukee	AHL	65	2	9	11	59	....	....	....	....	....
2014-15	Idaho Steelheads	ECHL	12	0	6	6	20	....	....	....	....	....
	Texas Stars	AHL	48	3	7	10	77	....	....	....	....	....
2015-16	Krefeld Pinguine	Germany	43	5	5	10	126	....	....	....	....	....
2016-17	Augsburg	Germany	48	2	10	12	71	7	1	0	1	2

Signed as a free agent by **Nashville**, September 30. 2011. • Re-assigned to **Idaho** (ECHL by **Nashville**, October 19, 2015. Signed as a free agent by **Texas** (AHL), November 19, 2014. Signed as a free agent by **Krefeld** (Germany), October 4, 2015. Signed as a free agent by **Augsburg** (Germany), May 13, 2016.

VALIMAKI, Juuso
(val-ih-MA-kee, YOO-soh) **CGY**

Defense. Shoots left. 6'2", 204 lbs. Born, Nokia, Finland, June 10, 1998.
(Calgary's 1st pick, 16th overall, in 2017 NHL Draft).

			Regular Season					Playoffs				
Season	Club	League	GP	G	A	Pts	PIM	GP	G	A	Pts	PIM
2013-14	Ilves Tampere U18	Fin-U18	44	7	26	33	22	10	2	4	6	4
2014-15	Ilves Tampere Jr.	Fin-Jr.	44	5	15	20	20	10	1	3	4	6
2015-16	Tri-City Americans	WHL	56	7	25	32	24	....	....	....	....	....
2016-17	Tri-City Americans	WHL	60	19	42	61	34	4	0	1	1	8

WHL West Second All-Star Team (2017)

VALK, Curtis
(VAWLK, KUHR-this) **FLA**

Center. Shoots left. 5'9", 170 lbs. Born, Medicine Hat, AB, February 8, 1993.

			Regular Season					Playoffs				
Season	Club	League	GP	G	A	Pts	PIM	GP	G	A	Pts	PIM
2008-09	Med. Hat MM AA	Minor-AB	32	37	28	65	....	....	....	....	....	....
	Medicine Hat	AMHL	4	0	0	0	0	....	....	....	....	....
2009-10	Medicine Hat	AMHL	31	17	23	40	34	....	....	....	....	....
	Brooks Bandits	AJHL	2	0	0	0	0	....	....	....	....	....
	Medicine Hat	WHL	4	0	0	0	2	....	....	....	....	....
2010-11	Medicine Hat	WHL	56	8	9	17	19	15	1	4	5	6
2011-12	Medicine Hat	WHL	67	24	31	55	35	8	6	4	10	4
2012-13	Medicine Hat	WHL	71	46	45	91	54	8	3	2	5	4
2013-14	Medicine Hat	WHL	72	47	45	92	36	18	12	9	21	10
2014-15	Kalamazoo Wings	ECHL	31	11	19	30	12	....	....	....	....	....
	Utica Comets	AHL	1	0	0	0	0	....	....	....	....	....
2015-16	Utica Comets	AHL	12	2	4	6	2	....	....	....	....	....
	Kalamazoo Wings	ECHL	30	16	17	33	14	....	....	....	....	....
2016-17	Utica Comets	AHL	75	16	30	46	49	....	....	....	....	....

WHL East First All-Star Team (2013) • WHL East Second All-Star Team (2014)

Signed as a free agent by **Florida**, July 1, 2017.

VALLEAU, Nolan
(VAH-loh, NOH-luhn)

Defense. Shoots left. 6'1", 180 lbs. Born, Novi, MI, November 15, 1992.

			Regular Season					Playoffs				
Season	Club	League	GP	G	A	Pts	PIM	GP	G	A	Pts	PIM
2011-12	New Mexico	NAHL	11	2	5	7	6	....	....	....	....	....
	Port Huron	NAHL	42	4	20	24	46	8	1	0	1	0
2012-13	Des Moines	USHL	37	5	13	18	24	....	....	....	....	....
	Chicago Steel	USHL	27	3	5	8	14	....	....	....	....	....
2013-14	Bowling Green	WCHA	DID NOT PLAY – FRESHMAN									
2014-15	Bowling Green	WCHA	39	2	17	19	35	....	....	....	....	....
2015-16	Rockford IceHogs	AHL	62	1	11	12	20	....	....	....	....	....
2016-17	Rockford IceHogs	AHL	46	3	5	8	14	....	....	....	....	....

• Four season totals with Novi Wildcats (High-MI) from 2007-08 through 2010-11 are 115 games, 72 goals, 114 asssists, 186 points. Signed as a free agent by **Chicago**, August 18, 2015.

VANDE SOMPEL, Mitchell
(VAN-duh SUHM-puhl, mih-CHUHL) **NYI**

Defense. Shoots left. 6', 192 lbs. Born, London, ON, February 11, 1997.
(NY Islanders' 3rd pick, 82nd overall, in 2015 NHL Draft).

			Regular Season					Playoffs				
Season	Club	League	GP	G	A	Pts	PIM	GP	G	A	Pts	PIM
2012-13	Lon. Knights MM	Minor-ON	23	9	23	32	16	14	8	10	18	4
	Lon. Knights Mid.	Minor-ON	....	....	....	....	....	1	0	0	0	0
	St. Thomas Stars	ON-Jr.B	2	0	1	1	0	....	....	....	....	....
2013-14	Oshawa Generals	OHL	47	5	15	20	18	12	1	2	3	0
2014-15	Oshawa Generals	OHL	58	12	51	63	38	21	5	9	14	4
2015-16	Oshawa Generals	OHL	46	10	28	38	36	5	1	3	4	8
2016-17	Oshawa Generals	OHL	37	17	20	37	35	....	....	....	....	....
	London Knights	OHL	30	3	13	16	0	14	1	5	6	2

OHL All-Rookie Team (2014)

VANNELLI, Thomas
(vuh-NEHL-ee, TAW-muhs) **ST.L.**

Defense. Shoots right. 6'2", 165 lbs. Born, Minneapolis, MN, January 26, 1995.
(St. Louis' 1st pick, 47th overall, in 2013 NHL Draft).

			Regular Season					Playoffs				
Season	Club	League	GP	G	A	Pts	PIM	GP	G	A	Pts	PIM
2011-12	Minnetonka	High-MN	25	6	14	20	8	3	1	4	5	0
2012-13	Team Northwest	UMHSEL	20	4	10	14	16	3	0	0	0	0
	Minnetonka	High-MN	25	8	23	31	14	2	2	2	4	0
	USAHNTDP	USHL	11	1	1	2	4	....	....	....	....	....
	USAHNTDP	U-18	9	2	1	3	0	....	....	....	....	....
2013-14	Medicine Hat	WHL	60	14	27	41	34	18	2	6	8	10
2014-15	Medicine Hat	WHL	44	12	23	35	52	10	0	4	4	2
2015-16	Chicago Wolves	AHL	7	0	1	1	8	....	....	....	....	....
2016-17	Missouri Mavericks	ECHL	11	0	2	2	2	....	....	....	....	....
	Atlanta Gladiators	ECHL	35	1	16	17	19	....	....	....	....	....

• Re-assigned to **Missouri** by **St.Lous**, December 6, 2016. • Re-assigned to **Atlanta** (ECHL) by **St. Louis**, January 13, 2017.

VEILLEUX, Yannick
(VAY-yew, YA-nihk)

Left wing. Shoots left. 6'2", 206 lbs. Born, Saint-Hippolyte, QC, February 22, 1993.
(St. Louis' 5th pick, 102nd overall, in 2011 NHL Draft).

			Regular Season					Playoffs				
Season	Club	League	GP	G	A	Pts	PIM	GP	G	A	Pts	PIM
2008-09	Saint-Eustache	QAAA	43	21	13	34	44	5	1	4	5	23
2009-10	Shawinigan	QMJHL	55	3	6	9	17	6	0	0	0	6
2010-11	Shawinigan	QMJHL	68	19	29	48	40	12	2	5	7	14
2011-12	Shawinigan	QMJHL	59	27	31	58	69	11	5	6	11	17
2012-13	Moncton Wildcats	QMJHL	65	34	39	73	102	4	2	0	2	10
	Peoria Rivermen	AHL	8	2	1	3	0	....	....	....	....	....
2013-14	Kalamazoo Wings	ECHL	62	16	23	39	65	6	3	0	3	4
	Chicago Wolves	AHL	4	0	1	1	5	....	....	....	....	....
2014-15	Chicago Wolves	AHL	64	9	4	13	83	5	0	0	0	2
2015-16	Chicago Wolves	AHL	72	8	15	23	79	....	....	....	....	....
2016-17	St. John's IceCaps	AHL	53	6	10	16	59	4	0	0	0	4
	Brampton Beast	ECHL	11	3	8	11	31	....	....	....	....	....

VEJDEMO, Lukas
(vay-DEH-moh, LOO-kuhs) **MTL**

Center. Shoots left. 6'2", 193 lbs. Born, Stockholm, Sweden, January 25, 1996.
(Montreal's 2nd pick, 87th overall, in 2015 NHL Draft).

			Regular Season					Playoffs				
Season	Club	League	GP	G	A	Pts	PIM	GP	G	A	Pts	PIM
2011-12	SDE U18	Swe-U18	32	9	10	19	8	2	0	0	0	0
2012-13	Djurgarden U18	Swe-U18	39	12	30	42	10	9	2	3	5	2
	Djurgarden Jr.	Swe-Jr.	5	0	0	0	0	1	0	0	0	0
2013-14	Djurgarden U18	Swe-U18	20	11	20	31	34	4	1	1	2	4
	Djurgarden Jr.	Swe-Jr.	3	1	0	1	2	1	0	0	0	0
2014-15	Djurgarden Jr.	Swe-Jr.	34	23	25	48	51	7	4	2	6	4
	Djurgarden	Sweden	3	0	0	0	0	....	....	....	....	....
2015-16	Djurgarden	Sweden	52	5	12	17	12	8	1	0	1	0
	Djurgarden Jr.	Swe-Jr.	....	....	....	....	....	2	0	1	1	2
2016-17	Djurgarden	Sweden	48	4	4	8	8	3	0	1	1	2

VELA, Marcus
(VEH-lah, MAHR-kuhs) **S.J.**

Center. Shoots right. 6'2", 200 lbs. Born, Burnaby, BC, March 3, 1997.
(San Jose's 8th pick, 190th overall, in 2015 NHL Draft).

			Regular Season					Playoffs				
Season	Club	League	GP	G	A	Pts	PIM	GP	G	A	Pts	PIM
2012-13	Burnaby Bulldogs	Minor-BC	30	25	55	80	....	....	....	....	....	....
2013-14	Langley Rivermen	BCHL	54	11	11	22	41	12	1	4	5	6
2014-15	Langley Rivermen	BCHL	50	20	26	46	57	3	0	1	1	4
2015-16	New Hampshire	H-East	37	7	9	16	24	....	....	....	....	....
2016-17	New Hampshire	H-East	29	4	5	9	16	....	....	....	....	....

VERHAEGHE, Carter
(vuhr-HAY-GEE, KAR-tuhr) **T.B.**

Center. Shoots left. 6'2", 190 lbs. Born, Waterdown, ON, August 14, 1995.
(Toronto's 2nd pick, 82nd overall, in 2013 NHL Draft).

			Regular Season					Playoffs				
Season	Club	League	GP	G	A	Pts	PIM	GP	G	A	Pts	PIM
2010-11	Ham. Bulldogs	Minor-ON	45	34	30	64	28	....	....	....	....	....
2011-12	Niagara Ice Dogs	OHL	62	4	12	16	10	19	1	2	3	2
2012-13	Niagara Ice Dogs	OHL	67	18	26	44	22	5	2	2	4	6
2013-14	Niagara Ice Dogs	OHL	65	28	54	82	60	6	2	2	4	6
	Toronto Marlies	AHL	2	0	1	1	0	....	....	....	....	....
2014-15	Niagara Ice Dogs	OHL	68	33	49	82	38	11	6	8	14	4
2015-16	Bridgeport	AHL	30	6	9	15	6	....	....	....	....	....
	Missouri Mavericks	ECHL	20	8	17	25	2	10	2	9	11	2
2016-17	Bridgeport	AHL	45	16	13	29	20	....	....	....	....	....
	Missouri Mavericks	ECHL	16	12	20	32	4	....	....	....	....	....

Traded to **NY Islanders** by **Toronto** with Christopher Gibson, Tom Nilsson, Taylor Beck and Matt Finn for Michael Grabner, September 17, 2015. Traded to **Tampa Bay** by **NY Islanders** for Kristers Gudlevskis, July 1, 2017.

VESALAINEN, Kristian
(vehs-ah-LIGH-nehn, KRIHS-t'yehn) **WPG**

Right wing. Shoots left. 6'3", 205 lbs. Born, Helsinki, Finland, June 1, 1999.
(Winnipeg's 1st pick, 24th overall, in 2017 NHL Draft).

			Regular Season					Playoffs				
Season	Club	League	GP	G	A	Pts	PIM	GP	G	A	Pts	PIM
2013-14	HIFK Helsinki U18	Fin-U18	9	1	1	2	0	....	....	....	....	....
	HJK Helsinki U18	Fin-U18	3	2	3	5	2	....	....	....	....	....
2014-15	HIFK Helsinki U18	Fin-U18	18	10	5	15	29	12	5	3	8	4
	HIFK Helsinki Jr.	Fin-Jr.	17	1	1	2	0	1	0	0	0	0
2015-16	Frolunda U18	Swe-U18	....	....	....	....	....	2	1	0	1	0
	Frolunda Jr.	Swe-Jr.	37	15	19	34	0	1	0	1	1	0
	Frolunda	Sweden	19	1	1	2	0	5	0	0	0	2
2016-17	Frolunda Jr.	Swe-Jr.	10	4	0	4	14	5	2	1	3	0
	Frolunda	Sweden	26	1	5	6	2	1	0	0	0	0
	HPK Hameenlinna	Finland	9	1	0	1	0	....	....	....	....	....

VESEL, Tyler
(VEH-suhl, TIGH-luhr) **EDM**

Center. Shoots right. 5'11", 182 lbs. Born, Duluth, MN, April 14, 1994.
(Edmonton's 5th pick, 153rd overall, in 2014 NHL Draft).

			Regular Season					Playoffs				
Season	Club	League	GP	G	A	Pts	PIM	GP	G	A	Pts	PIM
2011-12	Shat.-St. Mary's	UMHSEL	15	4	7	11	2	....	....	....	....	....
	Shattuck	High-MN	57	29	45	74	4	....	....	....	....	....
2012-13	Shat.-St. Mary's	UMHSEL	15	11	6	17	6	....	....	....	....	....
	Shattuck	High-MN	55	32	45	77	16	....	....	....	....	....
2013-14	Omaha Lancers	USHL	49	33	38	71	22	4	3	1	4	0
2014-15	Nebraska-Omaha	NCHC	39	8	15	23	2	....	....	....	....	....
2015-16	Nebraska-Omaha	NCHC	35	6	12	18	2	....	....	....	....	....
2016-17	Nebraska-Omaha	NCHC	39	14	21	35	6	....	....	....	....	....

USHL Second All-Star Team (2014)

VESEY, Nolan
(VEE-see, NOH-luhn) **TOR**

Left wing. Shoots left. 6'1", 195 lbs. Born, North Reading, MA, March 28, 1995.
(Toronto's 5th pick, 158th overall, in 2014 NHL Draft).

			Regular Season					Playoffs				
Season	Club	League	GP	G	A	Pts	PIM	GP	G	A	Pts	PIM
2012-13	Austin Prep	High-MA	24	21	13	34	....	....	....	....	....	....
2013-14	South Shore Kings	USPHL	48	26	40	66	30	5	0	2	2	2
	South Shore U18	USPHL	1	2	1	3	0	....	....	....	....	....
2014-15	U. of Maine	H-East	36	10	13	23	37	....	....	....	....	....
2015-16	U. of Maine	H-East	36	5	6	11	41	....	....	....	....	....
2016-17	U. of Maine	H-East	36	10	13	23	36	....	....	....	....	....

VIGNEAULT, Sam (VEEN-yoh, SAM) CBJ

Center. Shoots left. 6'5", 203 lbs. Born, Baie-Comeau, QC, September 7, 1995.

			Regular Season					Playoffs				
Season	Club	League	GP	G	A	Pts	PIM	GP	G	A	Pts	PIM
2011-12	Jonquiere Elites	QAAA	43	5	9	14	20	4	0	1	1	4
2012-13	Baie-Comeau	Minor-QC	23	19	38	57	26	4	3	10	13	8
	La Tuque Loups	QJHL	5	0	1	1	10	....	....	....	....	....
2013-14	Andre-Lauren.	QCHL	37	28	32	60	70	10	4	9	13	10
2014-15	Clarkson Knights	ECAC	31	6	7	13	18	....	....	....	....	....
2015-16	Clarkson Knights	ECAC	36	12	14	26	20	....	....	....	....	....
2016-17	Clarkson Knights	ECAC	39	12	24	36	41	....	....	....	....	....
	Cleveland	AHL	16	1	4	5	8	....	....	....	....	....

Signed as a free agent by **Columbus**, March 16, 2017.

VILARDI, Gabriel (vih-LAHR-dee, gay-BREE-uhl) L.A.

Center. Shoots right. 6'3", 203 lbs. Born, Kingston, ON, August 16, 1999.
(Los Angeles' 1st pick, 11th overall, in 2017 NHL Draft).

			Regular Season					Playoffs				
Season	Club	League	GP	G	A	Pts	PIM	GP	G	A	Pts	PIM
2014-15	CIHA V'geurs MM	Minor-ON	21	18	21	39	12	....	....	....	....	....
	CIHA V'geurs Mid.	Minor-ON	3	4	4	8	6	8	3	7	10	10
2015-16	Windsor Spitfires	OHL	62	17	21	38	14	5	1	3	4	2
2016-17	Windsor Spitfires	OHL	49	29	32	61	12	7	2	4	6	4

VIRTA, Patrik (VIHR-tah, PA-trihk) NYR

Center. Shoots right. 5'11", 180 lbs. Born, Hameenlinna, Finland, June 3, 1996.
(NY Rangers' 7th pick, 207th overall, in 2017 NHL Draft).

			Regular Season					Playoffs				
Season	Club	League	GP	G	A	Pts	PIM	GP	G	A	Pts	PIM
2012-13	HPK U17	Fin-U17	1	0	2	2	0	9	9	2	11	4
	HPK U18	Fin-U18	46	18	28	46	43	6	5	2	7	2
2013-14	HPK U18	Fin-U18	5	7	4	11	0	1	1	0	1	0
	HPK Jr.	Fin-Jr.	32	15	14	29	8	3	0	0	0	2
2014-15	HPK Jr.	Fin-Jr.	43	29	46	75	55	12	10	5	15	10
	HPK Hameenlinna	Finland	5	2	0	2	2	....	....	....	....	....
2015-16	TPS Turku	Finland	33	2	2	4	8	1	0	0	0	0
	HPK Jr.	Fin-Jr.	2	0	1	1	2	....	....	....	....	....
	TuTo Turku	Finland-2	4	1	1	2	4	....	....	....	....	....
	SaPKo Savonlinna	Finland-2	7	2	2	4	2	5	2	2	4	0
2016-17	TPS Turku	Finland	49	14	12	26	22	6	5	1	6	4

VIRTANEN, Santeri (vihr-TA-nehn, SAHN-tehr-ee) WPG

Center. Shoots left. 6'2", 202 lbs. Born, Kirkkonummi, Finland, May 11, 1999.
(Winnipeg's 4th pick, 105th overall, in 2017 NHL Draft).

			Regular Season					Playoffs				
Season	Club	League	GP	G	A	Pts	PIM	GP	G	A	Pts	PIM
2013-14	TuTo Turku U18	Fin-U18	1	1	0	1	0	....	....	....	....	....
2014-15	TPS Turku U18	Fin-U18	35	9	17	26	6	2	0	0	0	0
	TPS Turku Jr.	Fin-Jr.	4	0	0	0	0	....	....	....	....	....
2015-16	TPS Turku U18	Fin-U18	35	14	31	45	10	4	0	1	1	0
	TPS Turku Jr.	Fin-Jr.	8	0	0	0	2	....	....	....	....	....
2016-17	TPS Turku Jr.	Fin-Jr.	5	2	4	6	0	3	2	0	2	2
	TPS Turku U18	Fin-U18	....	....	....	....	....	5	0	5	5	12

VOGELHUBER, Trent (VOH-guhl-hew-buhr, TREHNT) COL

Right wing. Shoots right. 6'2", 185 lbs. Born, Dublin, OH, July 13, 1988.
(Columbus' 7th pick, 211th overall, in 2007 NHL Draft).

			Regular Season					Playoffs				
Season	Club	League	GP	G	A	Pts	PIM	GP	G	A	Pts	PIM
2004-05	Ohio AAA	Ind.	67	32	30	62	77	....	....	....	....	....
2005-06	Ohio AAA	GLHL	44	27	52	79	28	....	....	....	....	....
2006-07	St. Louis Bandits	NAHL	31	10	16	26	24	....	....	....	....	....
2007-08	Des Moines	USHL	2	0	1	1	0	....	....	....	....	....
2008-09	Miami U.	CCHA	29	2	2	4	22	....	....	....	....	....
2009-10	Miami U.	CCHA	42	8	4	12	30	....	....	....	....	....
2010-11	Miami U.	CCHA	39	7	14	21	16	....	....	....	....	....
2011-12	Miami U.	CCHA	39	4	10	14	55	....	....	....	....	....
	Springfield Falcons	AHL	2	0	0	0	4	....	....	....	....	....
2012-13	Springfield Falcons	AHL	27	4	3	7	14	8	2	0	2	0
	Evansville IceMen	ECHL	34	6	10	16	20	....	....	....	....	....
2013-14	Springfield Falcons	AHL	30	1	8	9	19	1	0	1	1	0
2014-15	Springfield Falcons	AHL	64	8	8	16	55	....	....	....	....	....
2015-16	Lake Erie Monsters	AHL	70	11	16	27	65	17	2	5	7	8
2016-17	San Antonio	AHL	15	0	2	2	8	....	....	....	....	....

• Missed majority of 2007-08 due to recurring knee injury. Signed as a free agent by **Springfield** (AHL), June 10, 2014. Signed as a free agent by **Lake Erie** (AHL), June 29, 2015. Signed as a free agent by **Colorado**, July 1, 2016.

VOLKOV, Alexander (VOHL-kawv, al-EHX-AN-duhr) T.B.

Right wing. Shoots left. 6'1", 191 lbs. Born, Moscow, Russia, February 8, 1997.
(Tampa Bay's 6th pick, 48th overall, in 2017 NHL Draft).

			Regular Season					Playoffs				
Season	Club	League	GP	G	A	Pts	PIM	GP	G	A	Pts	PIM
2013-14	St. Petersburg Jr.	Russia-Jr.	16	2	2	4	6	5	0	0	0	0
2014-15	St. Petersburg Jr.	Russia-Jr.	54	11	8	19	36	16	1	1	2	4
	SKA-Varyagi Jr.	Russia-Jr. B	2	2	2	4	0	....	....	....	....	....
2015-16	St. Petersburg Jr.	Russia-Jr.	42	16	11	27	34	3	0	0	0	0
2016-17	SKA-Neva	Russia-2	15	3	0	3	4	8	1	2	3	6
	St. Petersburg Jr.	Russia-Jr.	16	6	5	11	12	4	2	2	4	2

VOROBYEV, Mikhail (voh-roh-bee-AWV, mih-KIGH-ehl) PHI

Center. Shoots left. 6'2", 194 lbs. Born, Ufa, Russia, January 5, 1997.
(Philadelphia's 6th pick, 104th overall, in 2015 NHL Draft).

			Regular Season					Playoffs				
Season	Club	League	GP	G	A	Pts	PIM	GP	G	A	Pts	PIM
2013-14	Tolpar Ufa Jr.	Russia-Jr.	4	0	3	3	0	....	....	....	....	....
2014-15	Tolpar Ufa Jr.	Russia-Jr.	39	8	12	20	40	8	3	0	3	2
2015-16	Tolpar Ufa Jr.	Russia-Jr.	21	6	17	23	28	....	....	....	....	....
	Ufa	KHL	28	2	1	3	14	1	0	0	0	0
2016-17	Ufa	KHL	44	3	8	11	18	5	0	0	0	4

WAGNER, Austin (WAG-nuhr, AW-stuhn) L.A.

Left wing. Shoots left. 6'1", 178 lbs. Born, Calgary, AB, June 23, 1997.
(Los Angeles' 3rd pick, 99th overall, in 2015 NHL Draft).

			Regular Season					Playoffs				
Season	Club	League	GP	G	A	Pts	PIM	GP	G	A	Pts	PIM
2012-13	Calgary Northstars	AMHL	28	7	3	10	30	2	0	0	0	15
	Regina Pats	WHL	1	0	0	0	0	....	....	....	....	....
2013-14	Regina Pats	WHL	42	1	1	2	18	2	0	0	0	0
2014-15	Regina Pats	WHL	61	20	19	39	53	9	1	2	3	8
2015-16	Regina Pats	WHL	70	28	34	62	84	12	3	6	9	12
2016-17	Regina Pats	WHL	64	30	36	66	94	22	*16	5	21	29

WAKED, Antoine (WIH-kehd, an-TWAHN) MTL

Right wing. Shoots right. 6'1", 194 lbs. Born, St. Bruno-de-Montarv, QC, May 17, 1996.

			Regular Season					Playoffs				
Season	Club	League	GP	G	A	Pts	PIM	GP	G	A	Pts	PIM
2011-12	Mortagne	Minor-QC	31	9	30	39	12	....	....	....	....	....
	Antoine-Girouard	QAAA	1	0	0	0	0	....	....	....	....	....
2012-13	Antoine-Girouard	QAAA	37	6	20	26	35	13	4	6	10	12
2013-14	Rouyn-Noranda	QMJHL	48	3	5	8	33	7	0	0	0	4
2014-15	Rouyn-Noranda	QMJHL	61	15	16	31	68	....	....	....	....	....
2015-16	Rouyn-Noranda	QMJHL	48	11	27	38	47	19	4	2	6	21
2016-17	Rouyn-Noranda	QMJHL	67	39	41	80	67	1	0	0	0	0

Signed as a free agent by **Montreal**, April 28, 2017.

WALCOTT, Daniel (WAWL-kawt, DAN-yehl) T.B.

Defense. Shoots left. 5'11", 165 lbs. Born, Ile Perrot, QC, February 19, 1994.
(NY Rangers' 6th pick, 140th overall, in 2014 NHL Draft).

			Regular Season					Playoffs				
Season	Club	League	GP	G	A	Pts	PIM	GP	G	A	Pts	PIM
2011-12	New Trier Trevians	High-IL	STATISTICS NOT AVAILABLE									
2012-13	Lindenwood Lions	NCAA-2	33	4	9	13	30	....	....	....	....	....
2013-14	Blainville-Bois.	QMJHL	67	10	29	39	71	19	4	6	10	18
2014-15	Blainville-Bois.	QMJHL	54	7	34	41	40	6	1	3	4	4
	Hartford Wolf Pack	AHL	1	0	0	0	0	....	....	....	....	....
2015-16	Syracuse Crunch	AHL	62	2	11	13	54	....	....	....	....	....
	Greenville	ECHL	3	0	0	0	10	....	....	....	....	....
2016-17	Syracuse Crunch	AHL	55	4	11	15	68	13	0	4	4	12

QMJHL First All-Star Team (2015)

Traded to **Tampa Bay** by **NY Rangers** for NY Rangers' 7th round pick (previously acquired, later traded to Edmonton – Edmonton selected Ziyat Paigin) in 2015 NHL Draft, June 1, 2015. • Re-assigned to **Greenville** (ECHL) by **Tampa Bay**, November 11, 2015.

WALFORD, Scott (WAHL-fohrd, SKAWT) MTL

Defense. Shoots left. 6'1", 187 lbs. Born, New Westminster, BC, December 1, 1999.
(Montreal's 4th pick, 68th overall, in 2017 NHL Draft).

			Regular Season					Playoffs				
Season	Club	League	GP	G	A	Pts	PIM	GP	G	A	Pts	PIM
2014-15	Okan. H.A. White	CSSHL	28	6	15	21	20	3	1	2	3	0
	Victoria Royals	WHL	2	0	0	0	0	....	....	....	....	....
2015-16	Victoria Royals	WHL	36	1	10	11	12	13	2	4	6	6
2016-17	Victoria Royals	WHL	60	6	24	30	36	1	0	0	0	0

WALFRIDSSON, Sebastian (WAWL-frihd-suhn, seh-BAS-t'yehn) WSH

Defense. Shoots left. 6'1", 194 lbs. Born, Ingaro, Sweden, March 19, 1999.
(Washington's 2nd pick, 151st overall, in 2017 NHL Draft).

			Regular Season					Playoffs				
Season	Club	League	GP	G	A	Pts	PIM	GP	G	A	Pts	PIM
2012-13	Varmdo HC U18	Swe-U18	8	1	3	4	2	2	1	0	1	0
	Varmdo UC	Sweden-4	1	0	0	0	0	....	....	....	....	....
2013-14	Varmdo HC U18	Swe-U18	16	15	5	20	44	....	....	....	....	....
	Varmdo HC Jr.	Swe-Jr.	5	1	1	2	0	....	....	....	....	....
2014-15	Varmdo HC U18	Swe-U18	1	1	1	2	0	....	....	....	....	....
	Varmdo HC Jr.	Swe-Jr.	10	0	5	5	14	....	....	....	....	....
	Varmdo UC	Sweden-3	2	0	0	0	0	....	....	....	....	....
	MODO U18	Swe-U18	17	1	3	4	6	1	0	0	0	0
	MODO Jr.	Swe-Jr.	....	....	....	....	....	1	0	0	0	2
2015-16	MODO U18	Swe-U18	....	....	....	....	....	4	1	1	2	4
	MODO Jr.	Swe-Jr.	41	3	4	7	20	2	0	0	0	4
2016-17	MODO U18	Swe-U18	2	0	3	3	6	3	0	1	1	2
	MODO Jr.	Swe-Jr.	38	2	5	7	36	6	0	2	2	4
	MODO	Sweden-2	3	0	0	0	0	....	....	....	....	....

WALKER, Jack (WAW-kuhr, JAK) TOR

Left wing. Shoots left. 5'10", 179 lbs. Born, Fargo, ND, July 30, 1996.
(Toronto's 9th pick, 152nd overall, in 2016 NHL Draft).

			Regular Season					Playoffs				
Season	Club	League	GP	G	A	Pts	PIM	GP	G	A	Pts	PIM
2011-12	Edina Lakers	MNJHL	4	1	0	1	2	....	....	....	....	....
	Edina Hornets	High-MN	24	1	9	10	18	5	1	3	4	4
2012-13	Victoria Royals	WHL	58	9	13	22	21	6	0	0	0	6
2013-14	Victoria Royals	WHL	48	7	8	15	23	7	0	0	0	2
2014-15	Victoria Royals	WHL	70	18	37	55	65	10	4	7	11	12
2015-16	Victoria Royals	WHL	72	36	48	84	85	13	8	8	16	20
2016-17	Victoria Royals	WHL	70	31	41	72	65	2	2	2	4	0

WALKER, Nathan (WAW-kuhr, NAY-thuhn) WSH

Left wing. Shoots left. 5'8", 179 lbs. Born, Cardiff, Wales, February 7, 1994.
(Washington's 3rd pick, 89th overall, in 2014 NHL Draft).

			Regular Season					Playoffs				
Season	Club	League	GP	G	A	Pts	PIM	GP	G	A	Pts	PIM
2007-08	HC Vitkovice U17	CzR-U17	1	0	0	0	2	....	....	....	....	....
2008-09	HC Vitkovice U17	CzR-U17	33	6	9	15	12	5	1	0	1	4
2009-10	HC Vitkovice U18	CzR-U18	28	22	20	42	47	2	2	2	4	4
	HC Vitkovice Jr.	CzRep-Jr.	23	5	5	10	16	1	0	0	0	0
	Sydney Ice Dogs	Australia	4	0	1	1	0	....	....	....	....	....
2010-11	HC Vitkovice U18	CzR-U18	10	4	10	14	22	....	....	....	....	....
	HC Vitkovice Jr.	CzRep-Jr.	37	20	22	42	20	....	....	....	....	....
	Sydney Ice Dogs	Australia	3	1	1	2	6	....	....	....	....	....
2011-12	HC Vitkovice Jr.	CzRep-Jr.	14	14	6	20	16	3	0	1	1	0
	HC Vitkovice Steel	CzRep	34	4	5	9	8	1	0	0	0	2
	HC Olomouc	CzRep-2	2	0	1	1	4	5	0	0	0	6
	HC Vitkovice U18	CzR-U18	....	....	....	....	....	3	4	1	5	14
2012-13	HC Vitkovice Jr.	CzRep-Jr.	13	12	12	24	42	....	....	....	....	....
	Youngstown	USHL	29	7	20	27	63	....	....	....	....	....
	HC Vitkovice Steel	CzRep	20	0	1	1	27	....	....	....	....	....
	Salith Sumperk	CzRep-2	3	0	1	1	2	....	....	....	....	....
2013-14	Hershey Bears	AHL	43	5	6	11	40	....	....	....	....	....
2014-15	Hershey Bears	AHL	28	1	3	4	30	....	....	....	....	....
	South Carolina	ECHL	6	2	2	4	0	....	....	....	....	....
2015-16	Hershey Bears	AHL	73	17	24	41	41	20	2	3	5	11
2016-17	Hershey Bears	AHL	58	11	12	23	33	12	2	4	6	0

WALKER, Samuel (WAW-kuhr, SAM-yewl) T.B.

Center. Shoots right. 5'10", 142 lbs. Born, Edina, MN, July 6, 1999.
(Tampa Bay's 5th pick, 200th overall, in 2017 NHL Draft).

			Regular Season					Playoffs				
Season	Club	League	GP	G	A	Pts	PIM	GP	G	A	Pts	PIM
2014-15	Edina Hornets	High-MN	25	3	3	6	6	5	2	1	3	2
2015-16	Team Southwest	UMHSEL	21	10	4	14	20	....	....	....	....	....
	Edina Hornets	High-MN	25	19	18	37	14	2	0	1	1	0
2016-17	Team Southwest	UMHSEL	20	9	16	25	18	....	....	....	....	....
	Edina Hornets	High-MN	25	22	24	46	6	3	2	4	6	0
	Lincoln Stars	USHL	4	0	0	0	6	....	....	....	....	....

• Signed Letter of Intent to attend **University of Minnesota** (Big Ten) in fall of 2018.

WALLI-WALTERHOLM, Erik (VAH-LEE-vahl-TUHR-hohlm, AIR-ihk) ARI

Right wing. Shoots right. 6'2", 185 lbs. Born, Sollentuna, Sweden, February 27, 1999.
(Arizona's 9th pick, 190th overall, in 2017 NHL Draft).

			Regular Season					Playoffs				
Season	Club	League	GP	G	A	Pts	PIM	GP	G	A	Pts	PIM
2014-15	SDE U18	Swe-U18	18	3	5	8	22	5	2	3	5	6
	SDE Jr.	Swe-Jr.	1	0	0	0	0	....	....	....	....	....
2015-16	SDE U18	Swe-U18	31	8	12	20	59	....	....	....	....	....
	SDE Jr.	Swe-Jr.	4	2	1	3	4	....	....	....	....	....
2016-17	SDE U18	Swe-U18	20	19	13	32	26	....	....	....	....	....
	Djurgarden U18	Swe-U18	14	8	6	14	16	4	3	1	4	4
	Djurgarden Jr.	Swe-Jr.	11	1	0	1	10	1	0	0	0	2

WALMAN, Jake (WAWL-muhn, JAYK) ST.L.

Defense. Shoots left. 6'1", 170 lbs. Born, Toronto, ON, February 20, 1996.
(St. Louis' 4th pick, 82nd overall, in 2014 NHL Draft).

			Regular Season					Playoffs				
Season	Club	League	GP	G	A	Pts	PIM	GP	G	A	Pts	PIM
2011-12	North York	GTHL	33	10	12	22	18	....	....	....	....	....
2012-13	Tor. Jr. Canadiens	GTHL	30	6	12	18	8	7	1	1	2	16
2013-14	Tor. Canadiens	ON-Jr.A	43	7	26	33	87	....	....	....	....	....
2014-15	Providence College	H-East	41	1	15	16	44	....	....	....	....	....
2015-16	Providence College	H-East	27	13	15	28	20	....	....	....	....	....
2016-17	Providence College	H-East	39	7	18	25	42	....	....	....	....	....
	Chicago Wolves	AHL	7	2	1	3	2	8	2	1	3	2

Hockey East First All-Star Team (2016, 2017) • NCAA East First All-American Team (2016) • NCAA East Second All-American Team (2017)

WALSH, Reilly (WAWLSH, RIGH-lee) N.J.

Defense. Shoots right. 6', 185 lbs. Born, Andover, NH, April 21, 1999.
(New Jersey's 4th pick, 81st overall, in 2017 NHL Draft).

			Regular Season					Playoffs				
Season	Club	League	GP	G	A	Pts	PIM	GP	G	A	Pts	PIM
2013-14	Proctor Academy	High-NH	31	7	20	27	18	....	....	....	....	....
2014-15	Proctor Academy	High-NH	35	13	32	45	38	....	....	....	....	....
2015-16	Proctor Academy	High-NH	26	14	26	40	....	....	....	....	....	....
	Tri-City Storm	USHL	2	1	1	2	0	....	....	....	....	....
	USAHNTDP	U-17	9	3	3	6	4	....	....	....	....	....
2016-17	Proctor Academy	High-NH	30	30	39	69	....	....	....	....	....	....
	Chicago Steel	USHL	24	2	8	10	12	....	....	....	....	....

• Signed Letter of Intent to attend **Harvard University** (ECAC) in fall of 2017.

WARNER, Hunter (WAHR-nuhr, HUHN-tuhr) MIN

Defense. Shoots right. 6'4", 221 lbs. Born, Eden Prairie, MN, September 21, 1995.

			Regular Season					Playoffs				
Season	Club	League	GP	G	A	Pts	PIM	GP	G	A	Pts	PIM
2011-12	Eden Prairie Eagles	High-MN	25	1	8	9	37	1	0	1	1	0
2012-13	Eden Prairie Eagles	High-MN	23	3	7	10	58	2	0	1	1	4
	Waterloo	USHL	6	0	1	1	7	....	....	....	....	....
2013-14	Waterloo	USHL	7	0	0	0	2	....	....	....	....	....
	Fargo Force	USHL	43	2	10	12	125	....	....	....	....	....
2014-15	Prince Albert	WHL	24	0	3	3	25	....	....	....	....	....
2015-16	Prince Albert	WHL	72	3	18	21	78	4	0	0	0	11
	Iowa Wild	AHL	3	0	1	1	2	....	....	....	....	....
2016-17	Iowa Wild	AHL	52	2	5	7	57	....	....	....	....	....

Signed as a free agent by **Minnesota**, September 23, 2014.

WARREN, Brendan (WAW-rehn, BREHN-duhn) PHI

Left wing. Shoots left. 6'2", 191 lbs. Born, Carleton, MI, May 7, 1997.
(Arizona's 6th pick, 81st overall, in 2015 NHL Draft).

			Regular Season					Playoffs				
Season	Club	League	GP	G	A	Pts	PIM	GP	G	A	Pts	PIM
2012-13	Det. Comp. U18	HPHL	26	10	14	24	13	....	....	....	....	....
	Det. Comp. U18	Other	....	....	....	....	....	3	0	1	1	2
2013-14	USAHNTDP	USHL	33	6	13	19	41	....	....	....	....	....
	USAHNTDP	U-17	20	8	13	21	24	....	....	....	....	....
2014-15	USAHNTDP	USHL	20	7	6	13	33	....	....	....	....	....
	USAHNTDP	U-18	41	12	13	25	16	....	....	....	....	....
2015-16	U. of Michigan	Big Ten	38	5	12	17	18	....	....	....	....	....
2016-17	U. of Michigan	Big Ten	35	3	7	10	16	....	....	....	....	....

Traded to **Philadelphia** by **Arizona** with Arizona's 5th round pick in 2018 NHL Draft for Nick Cousins and Merrick Madsen, June 16, 2017.

WATSON, Spencer (WAWT-suhn, SPEHN-suhr) L.A.

Right wing. Shoots right. 5'10", 170 lbs. Born, London, ON, April 25, 1996.
(Los Angeles' 9th pick, 209th overall, in 2014 NHL Draft).

			Regular Season					Playoffs				
Season	Club	League	GP	G	A	Pts	PIM	GP	G	A	Pts	PIM
2011-12	Lon. Knights MM	Minor-ON	30	43	24	67	26	11	12	6	18	10
	Lon. Knights Mid.	Minor-ON	2	3	0	3	0	....	....	....	....	....
	London Nationals	ON-Jr.B	2	0	0	0	0	7	3	1	4	2
2012-13	Kingston	OHL	63	23	20	43	18	2	1	1	2	0
2013-14	Kingston	OHL	65	33	35	68	16	7	1	4	5	0
2014-15	Kingston	OHL	41	20	28	48	10	4	0	1	1	0
2015-16	Kingston	OHL	64	43	46	89	32	9	3	14	17	2
2016-17	Mississauga	OHL	41	28	25	53	12	20	15	10	25	14

OHL All-Rookie Team (2013)

WEBB, Reilly (WEHB, RIGH-lee) DET

Defense. Shoots right. 6'4", 195 lbs. Born, Stoney Creek, ON, April 5, 1999.
(Detroit's 9th pick, 164th overall, in 2017 NHL Draft).

			Regular Season					Playoffs				
Season	Club	League	GP	G	A	Pts	PIM	GP	G	A	Pts	PIM
2014-15	Tor. Titans MM	GTHL	32	9	11	20	....	....	....	....	....	....
2015-16	Hamilton Bulldogs	OHL	8	0	0	0	4	....	....	....	....	....
	Ancaster	ON-Jr.B	9	1	3	4	6	10	0	3	3	20
2016-17	Hamilton Bulldogs	OHL	12	0	1	1	5	7	0	0	0	7

• Missed majority of 2015-16 and 2016-17 due to recurring shoulder and ankle injuries.

WEGWERTH, Joe (WEHG-wuhrth, JOH) FLA

Right wing. Shoots left. 6'3", 230 lbs. Born, Burnsville, MN, June 16, 1996.
(Florida's 4th pick, 92nd overall, in 2014 NHL Draft).

			Regular Season					Playoffs				
Season	Club	League	GP	G	A	Pts	PIM	GP	G	A	Pts	PIM
2011-12	Brewster Bulldogs	EmJHL	34	17	35	52	52	....	....	....	....	....
	U.S. Youth Oly.	Other	6	2	2	4	18	....	....	....	....	....
2012-13	USAHNTDP	USHL	16	3	1	4	32	....	....	....	....	....
	USAHNTDP	U-17	11	4	5	9	2	....	....	....	....	....
2013-14	USAHNTDP	USHL	25	2	1	3	78	....	....	....	....	....
	USAHNTDP	U-18	35	1	5	6	49	....	....	....	....	....
2014-15	Green Bay	USHL	35	5	16	21	59	....	....	....	....	....
	Cedar Rapids	USHL	24	4	5	9	38	3	1	2	3	4
2015-16	U. of Notre Dame	H-East	30	1	3	4	18	....	....	....	....	....
2016-17	U. of Notre Dame	H-East	33	7	4	11	14	....	....	....	....	....

WEISSBACH, Linus (WIGHS-bak, LEE-nuhs) BUF

Left wing. Shoots left. 5'8", 161 lbs. Born, Gothenburg, Sweden, April 19, 1998.
(Buffalo's 6th pick, 192nd overall, in 2017 NHL Draft).

			Regular Season					Playoffs				
Season	Club	League	GP	G	A	Pts	PIM	GP	G	A	Pts	PIM
2013-14	Frolunda U18	Swe-U18	24	7	11	18	4	5	0	0	0	0
2014-15	Frolunda U18	Swe-U18	22	18	19	37	6	4	2	1	3	2
	Frolunda Jr.	Swe-Jr.	16	2	4	6	6	....	....	....	....	....
2015-16	Frolunda Jr.	Swe-Jr.	44	17	31	48	34	3	1	1	2	0
	Frolunda U18	Swe-U18	....	....	....	....	....	4	1	1	2	0
	Frolunda	Sweden	1	0	0	0	0	....	....	....	....	....
2016-17	Tri-City Storm	USHL	49	19	28	47	4	....	....	....	....	....

• Signed Letter of Intent to attend **University of Wisconsin** (Big Ten) in fall of 2017.

WELINSKI, Andy (wehl-IHN-skee, AN-dee) ANA

Defense. Shoots right. 6'1", 196 lbs. Born, Duluth, MN, April 27, 1993.
(Anaheim's 5th pick, 83rd overall, in 2011 NHL Draft).

			Regular Season					Playoffs				
Season	Club	League	GP	G	A	Pts	PIM	GP	G	A	Pts	PIM
2009-10	Duluth East	High-MN	19	3	12	15	16	6	2	7	9	2
2010-11	Green Bay	USHL	51	6	8	14	14	11	2	0	2	4
2011-12	Green Bay	USHL	54	15	22	37	37	7	1	1	2	4
2012-13	U. Minn-Duluth	WCHA	38	4	14	18	24	....	....	....	....	....
2013-14	U. Minn-Duluth	NCHC	36	5	14	19	51	....	....	....	....	....
2014-15	U. Minn-Duluth	NCHC	40	9	12	21	24	....	....	....	....	....
2015-16	U. Minn-Duluth	NCHC	40	6	13	19	45	....	....	....	....	....
	San Diego Gulls	AHL	5	0	1	1	2	8	0	2	2	4
2016-17	San Diego Gulls	AHL	63	6	23	29	16	10	0	3	3	0

USHL First All-Star Team (2012) • WCHA All-Rookie Team (2013) • NCHC Second All-Star Team (2015, 2016)

WESLEY, Josh (WEHZ-lee, JAWSH) CAR

Defense. Shoots right. 6'3", 200 lbs. Born, Hartford, CT, April 9, 1996.
(Carolina's 4th pick, 96th overall, in 2014 NHL Draft).

			Regular Season					Playoffs				
Season	Club	League	GP	G	A	Pts	PIM	GP	G	A	Pts	PIM
2011-12	Car. Jr. Hurricanes	NAPHL	18	7	6	13	10	5	1	6	7	14
2012-13	USAHNTDP	USHL	38	0	1	1	14	....	....	....	....	....
	USAHNTDP	U-17	18	0	6	6	6	....	....	....	....	....
2013-14	Plymouth Whalers	OHL	68	1	8	9	62	5	0	1	1	2
2014-15	Plymouth Whalers	OHL	63	5	5	10	67	....	....	....	....	....
	Charlotte	AHL	1	0	0	0	0	....	....	....	....	....
2015-16	Flint Firebirds	OHL	24	2	10	12	21	....	....	....	....	....
	Niagara Ice Dogs	OHL	33	3	3	6	14	17	2	2	4	12
2016-17	Charlotte	AHL	9	1	0	1	0	....	....	....	....	....
	Florida Everblades	ECHL	48	9	20	29	27	12	0	1	1	4

WESTERLUND, Filip (WEHS-tuhr-luhnd, FIHL-ihp) ARI

Defense. Shoots right. 5'11", 172 lbs. Born, Harnosand, Sweden, April 17, 1999.
(Arizona's 2nd pick, 44th overall, in 2017 NHL Draft).

			Regular Season					Playoffs				
Season	**Club**	**League**	**GP**	**G**	**A**	**Pts**	**PIM**	**GP**	**G**	**A**	**Pts**	**PIM**
2013-14	Harnosand U18	Swe-U18	34	1	6	7	4	....	....	....	....	....
2014-15	Harnosand U18	Swe-U18	33	11	16	27	12	....	....	....	....	....
2015-16	Frolunda U18	Swe-U18	39	4	12	16	20	6	0	1	1	4
	Frolunda Jr.	Swe-Jr.	3	0	0	0	2	....	....	....	....	....
2016-17	Frolunda Jr.	Swe-Jr.	23	1	6	7	8	5	0	1	1	6
	Frolunda	Sweden	33	0	4	4	6	....	....	....	....	....
	Frolunda U18	Swe-U18	....	....	....	....	....	3	0	1	1	0

WESTLUND, David (WEHST-luhnd, DAY-vihd) ARI

Defense. Shoots left. 6'3", 220 lbs. Born, Ostersund, Sweden, February 5, 1995.
(Arizona's 7th pick, 163rd overall, in 2014 NHL Draft).

			Regular Season					Playoffs				
Season	**Club**	**League**	**GP**	**G**	**A**	**Pts**	**PIM**	**GP**	**G**	**A**	**Pts**	**PIM**
2010-11	Brynas U18	Swe-U18	8	0	0	0	4	....	....	....	....	....
2011-12	Brynas U18	Swe-U18	37	5	12	17	63	6	0	0	0	6
2012-13	Brynas U18	Swe-U18	19	3	5	8	63	7	1	2	3	6
	Brynas IF Gavle Jr.	Swe-Jr.	32	1	5	6	59	2	0	0	0	4
2013-14	Brynas IF Gavle Jr.	Swe-Jr.	33	5	5	10	61	7	0	2	2	10
	Brynas IF Gavle	Sweden	21	0	1	1	0	....	....	....	....	....
2014-15	Brynas IF Gavle Jr.	Swe-Jr.	12	4	4	8	41	3	1	3	4	4
	Brynas IF Gavle	Sweden	53	0	2	2	8	3	0	0	0	0
2015-16	Karlskrona HK Jr.	Swe-Jr.	5	1	0	1	2	....	....	....	....	....
	Karlskrona HK	Sweden	9	1	0	1	4	....	....	....	....	....
	Karlskrona HK	Sweden-Q	....	....	....	....	....	1	0	0	0	0
2016-17	Timra IK	Sweden-2	11	0	1	1	8	....	....	....	....	....

WHITE, Colton (WIGHT, KOHL-tuhn) N.J.

Defense. Shoots left. 6'1", 195 lbs. Born, London, ON, May 3, 1997.
(New Jersey's 4th pick, 97th overall, in 2015 NHL Draft).

			Regular Season					Playoffs				
Season	**Club**	**League**	**GP**	**G**	**A**	**Pts**	**PIM**	**GP**	**G**	**A**	**Pts**	**PIM**
2011-12	Lon. Knights Bant.	Minor-ON	STATISTICS NOT AVAILABLE									
	Lon. Knights MM	Minor-ON	6	0	1	1	4	4	0	0	0	0
2012-13	Lon. Knights MM	Minor-ON	27	7	13	20	22	16	3	4	7	6
2013-14	Sault Ste. Marie	OHL	57	0	5	5	2	9	0	1	1	0
2014-15	Sault Ste. Marie	OHL	67	6	16	22	30	14	0	2	2	0
2015-16	Sault Ste. Marie	OHL	68	9	26	35	13	12	1	2	3	4
2016-17	Sault Ste. Marie	OHL	64	6	25	31	41	11	0	3	3	8

WIEDERER, Manuel (wee-DUHR-ruhr, MAN-wehl) S.J.

Center. Shoots right. 6'1", 175 lbs. Born, Deggendorf, Germany, November 21, 1996.
(San Jose's 3rd pick, 150th overall, in 2016 NHL Draft).

			Regular Season					Playoffs				
Season	**Club**	**League**	**GP**	**G**	**A**	**Pts**	**PIM**	**GP**	**G**	**A**	**Pts**	**PIM**
2011-12	Deggendorf U18	Ger-U18	15	20	26	46	24	....	....	....	....	....
2012-13	Deggendorf U18	Ger-U18	22	69	52	121	72	....	....	....	....	....
	Deggendorf Jr.	Ger-Jr.	17	36	40	76	34	....	....	....	....	....
	Deggendorf Fire	German-3	15	1	1	2	2	8	2	2	4	0
2013-14	Deggendorf U18	Ger-U18	22	51	75	126	66	3	4	11	15	4
	Deggendorf Jr.	Ger-Jr.	4	15	6	21	6	....	....	....	....	....
	Deggendorf Fire	German-3	40	12	12	24	16	4	4	1	5	2
2014-15	Straubing Tigers	Germany	29	1	1	2	31	....	....	....	....	....
	Kaufbeuren Jr.	Ger-Jr.	5	7	7	14	10	....	....	....	....	....
	ESV Kaufbeuren	German-2	15	2	4	6	10	....	....	....	....	....
2015-16	Moncton Wildcats	QMJHL	54	29	35	64	41	17	12	4	16	12
2016-17	Moncton Wildcats	QMJHL	30	15	15	30	23	....	....	....	....	....
	Rouyn-Noranda	QMJHL	30	14	9	23	6	12	4	6	10	16

WIKSTRAND, Mikael (VIHK-strand, mih-kigh-EHL) OTT

Defense. Shoots left. 6'1", 212 lbs. Born, Karlstad, Sweden, November 5, 1993.
(Ottawa's 7th pick, 196th overall, in 2012 NHL Draft).

			Regular Season					Playoffs				
Season	**Club**	**League**	**GP**	**G**	**A**	**Pts**	**PIM**	**GP**	**G**	**A**	**Pts**	**PIM**
2007-08	Ore U18	Swe-U18	14	0	4	4	6	....	....	....	....	....
2008-09	Ore U18	Swe-U18	9	0	2	2	31	1	1	1	2	....
	IFK Ore Furudal	Sweden-5	3	0	0	0	....	....	....	....	....	....
2009-10	Mora IK U18	Swe-U18	23	10	11	21	26	....	....	....	....	....
	Mora IK Jr.	Swe-Jr.	14	1	2	3	8	....	....	....	....	....
2010-11	Mora IK U18	Swe-U18	4	1	2	3	6	3	1	3	4	4
	Mora IK Jr.	Swe-Jr.	16	3	5	8	6	....	....	....	....	....
	Mora IK	Sweden-2	37	0	1	1	8	....	....	....	....	....
2011-12	Mora IK Jr.	Swe-Jr.	11	3	4	7	2	2	1	3	4	2
	Mora IK	Sweden-2	47	2	1	3	14	....	....	....	....	....
2012-13	Mora IK Jr.	Swe-Jr.	2	0	1	1	0	....	....	....	....	....
	Mora IK	Sweden-2	45	11	14	25	35	....	....	....	....	....
2013-14	Mora IK	Sweden-2	27	4	16	20	14	....	....	....	....	....
	Frolunda	Sweden	19	4	7	11	4	7	1	1	2	0
2014-15	Frolunda	Sweden	46	5	15	20	10	13	0	5	5	8
2015-16	Farjestad	Sweden	17	1	8	9	6	5	0	3	3	0
2016-17	Farjestad	Sweden	48	4	15	19	12	7	2	3	5	2

• Loaned to **Farjestad** (Sweden) by **Ottawa**, January 20, 2016.

WILKIE, Chris (WIHL-kee, KRIHS) FLA

Right wing. Shoots right. 6', 190 lbs. Born, Omaha, NE, July 10, 1996.
(Florida's 6th pick, 162nd overall, in 2015 NHL Draft).

			Regular Season					Playoffs				
Season	**Club**	**League**	**GP**	**G**	**A**	**Pts**	**PIM**	**GP**	**G**	**A**	**Pts**	**PIM**
2010-11	Om. Lancers U16	NAPHL	20	3	5	8	0	4	0	0	0	2
2011-12	Om. Lancers U16	NAPHL	18	22	26	48	8	4	3	10	13	6
	Lincoln Stars	USHL	1	0	0	0	0	....	....	....	....	....
2012-13	USAHNTDP	USHL	38	7	7	14	38	....	....	....	....	....
	USAHNTDP	U-17	18	6	11	17	2	....	....	....	....	....
2013-14	Tri-City Storm	USHL	57	17	19	36	39	....	....	....	....	....
2014-15	Tri-City Storm	USHL	59	*35	20	55	66	7	3	3	6	22
2015-16	North Dakota	NCHC	32	5	4	9	14	....	....	....	....	....
2016-17	North Dakota	NCHC	30	1	9	10	18	....	....	....	....	....

USHL Second All-Star Team (2015)

WILLCOX, Reece (WIHL-cawx, REES) PHI

Defense. Shoots right. 6'4", 208 lbs. Born, Surrey, BC, March 20, 1994.
(Philadelphia's 6th pick, 141st overall, in 2012 NHL Draft).

			Regular Season					Playoffs				
Season	**Club**	**League**	**GP**	**G**	**A**	**Pts**	**PIM**	**GP**	**G**	**A**	**Pts**	**PIM**
2009-10	Surrey Thunder	Minor-BC	STATISTICS NOT AVAILABLE									
	West Valley Hawks	BCMML	9	1	3	4	0	....	....	....	....	....
2010-11	Merritt	BCHL	53	5	9	14	16	4	1	2	3	0
2011-12	Merritt	BCHL	52	5	18	23	26	9	2	2	4	6
2012-13	Cornell Big Red	ECAC	34	0	5	5	8	....	....	....	....	....
2013-14	Cornell Big Red	ECAC	32	2	5	7	10	....	....	....	....	....
2014-15	Cornell Big Red	ECAC	21	1	3	4	10	....	....	....	....	....
2015-16	Cornell Big Red	ECAC	33	2	11	13	2	....	....	....	....	....
	Lehigh Valley	AHL	6	1	2	3	8	....	....	....	....	....
2016-17	Lehigh Valley	AHL	48	3	4	7	12	....	....	....	....	....
	Reading Royals	ECHL	5	1	1	2	0	1	0	0	0	0

WILLIAMS, Colby (WIHL-yuhmz, KOHL-bee) WSH

Defense. Shoots right. 6', 195 lbs. Born, Regina, SK, January 26, 1995.
(Washington's 4th pick, 173rd overall, in 2015 NHL Draft).

			Regular Season					Playoffs				
Season	**Club**	**League**	**GP**	**G**	**A**	**Pts**	**PIM**	**GP**	**G**	**A**	**Pts**	**PIM**
2010-11	Reg. Pat Cdns.	SMHL	35	4	14	18	54	....	....	....	....	....
	Regina Pats	WHL	2	0	0	0	0	....	....	....	....	....
2011-12	Reg. Pat Cdns.	SMHL	43	7	24	31	144	....	....	....	....	....
	Melville	SJHL	....	....	....	....	....	6	0	0	0	0
	Regina Pats	WHL	1	0	0	0	2	....	....	....	....	....
2012-13	Regina Pats	WHL	59	0	19	19	70	....	....	....	....	....
2013-14	Regina Pats	WHL	66	9	23	32	82	4	0	0	0	8
2014-15	Regina Pats	WHL	64	11	30	41	95	9	3	5	8	12
2015-16	Regina Pats	WHL	19	5	7	12	20	12	2	7	9	14
2016-17	Hershey Bears	AHL	60	4	12	16	40	3	1	0	1	4

WHL East Second All-Star Team (2015)

WILLMAN, Max (WIHL-muhn, MAX) BUF

Center. Shoots left. 6', 187 lbs. Born, Barnstable, MA, February 13, 1995.
(Buffalo's 7th pick, 121st overall, in 2014 NHL Draft).

			Regular Season					Playoffs				
Season	**Club**	**League**	**GP**	**G**	**A**	**Pts**	**PIM**	**GP**	**G**	**A**	**Pts**	**PIM**
2009-10	Barnstable	High-MA	....	4	3	7	....	....	....	....	....	....
2010-11	Barnstable	High-MA	....	13	9	22	....	....	....	....	....	....
2011-12	Barnstable	High-MA	....	19	16	35	....	....	....	....	....	....
2012-13	Barnstable	High-MA	....	19	13	32	....	....	....	....	....	....
2013-14	Springfield Rifles	Minor-MA	11	5	13	18	6	....	....	....	....	....
	Williston North.	High-MA	25	21	23	44	....	....	....	....	....	....
2014-15	Brown U.	ECAC	30	1	2	3	12	....	....	....	....	....
2015-16	Brown U.	ECAC	29	3	8	11	10	....	....	....	....	....
2016-17	Brown U.	ECAC	31	11	15	26	10	....	....	....	....	....

WOLANIN, Christian (woh-LA-nihn, KRIHS-ch'yehn) OTT

Defense. Shoots left. 6'1", 185 lbs. Born, Quebec City, QC, March 17, 1995.
(Ottawa's 5th pick, 107th overall, in 2015 NHL Draft).

			Regular Season					Playoffs				
Season	**Club**	**League**	**GP**	**G**	**A**	**Pts**	**PIM**	**GP**	**G**	**A**	**Pts**	**PIM**
2010-11	Det. L.C. U16	T1EHL	34	13	13	26	30	....	....	....	....	....
	Det. L.C. U16	Other	14	3	6	9	35	....	....	....	....	....
2011-12	Det. L.C. U18	HPHL	22	3	10	13	28	....	....	....	....	....
	Det. L.C. U18	Other	....	....	....	....	....	7	1	3	4	2
2012-13	Green Bay	USHL	54	0	8	8	70	4	1	0	1	2
2013-14	Green Bay	USHL	23	1	4	5	30	....	....	....	....	....
	Muskegon	USHL	32	5	16	21	44	....	....	....	....	....
2014-15	Muskegon	USHL	56	14	27	41	107	12	3	5	8	20
2015-16	North Dakota	NCHC	32	4	11	15	20	....	....	....	....	....
2016-17	North Dakota	NCHC	37	6	16	22	37	....	....	....	....	....

USHL Second All-Star Team (2015)

WOOD, Kyle (WUD, KIGHL) ARI

Defense. Shoots right. 6'5", 235 lbs. Born, Waterloo, ON, May 4, 1996.
(Colorado's 2nd pick, 84th overall, in 2014 NHL Draft).

			Regular Season					Playoffs				
Season	**Club**	**League**	**GP**	**G**	**A**	**Pts**	**PIM**	**GP**	**G**	**A**	**Pts**	**PIM**
2011-12	Wat. Wolves MM	Minor-ON	30	9	11	20	54	14	3	13	16	6
	Waterloo Siskins	ON-Jr.B	2	0	0	0	0	5	0	2	2	4
2012-13	Orangeville Flyers	ON-Jr.A	46	6	11	17	10	....	....	....	....	....
	Brampton	OHL	16	1	1	2	8	5	0	0	0	2
2013-14	North Bay	OHL	33	2	10	12	21	22	2	8	10	6
2014-15	North Bay	OHL	67	16	24	40	18	15	1	10	11	2
2015-16	North Bay	OHL	49	8	31	39	18	11	2	11	13	2
	Springfield Falcons	AHL	2	0	0	0	2	....	....	....	....	....
2016-17	Tucson	AHL	68	14	29	43	16	....	....	....	....	....

AHL All-Rookie Team (2017)

Traded to **Arizona** by **Colorado** with Alex Tanguay and Connor Bleackley for Mikkel Boedker, February 29, 2016.

WOTHERSPOON, Parker (WAW-thuhr-spoon, PAHR-kuhr) NYI

Defense. Shoots left. 6', 180 lbs. Born, Surrey, BC, August 24, 1997.
(NY Islanders' 4th pick, 112th overall, in 2015 NHL Draft).

			Regular Season					Playoffs				
Season	**Club**	**League**	**GP**	**G**	**A**	**Pts**	**PIM**	**GP**	**G**	**A**	**Pts**	**PIM**
2011-12	Cloverdale Colts	Minor-BC	45	15	34	49	....	8	1	4	5	....
2012-13	Valley West Hawks	BCMML	37	7	19	22	118	....	....	....	....	....
	Tri-City Americans	WHL	5	0	0	0	4	2	0	0	0	0
2013-14	Tri-City Americans	WHL	62	2	16	18	74	5	0	2	2	2
2014-15	Tri-City Americans	WHL	72	9	33	42	93	4	0	1	1	4
2015-16	Tri-City Americans	WHL	71	11	45	56	78	....	....	....	....	....
	Bridgeport	AHL	6	0	1	1	15	2	0	1	1	0
2016-17	Tri-City Americans	WHL	69	10	55	65	99	4	0	1	1	8
	Bridgeport	AHL	4	0	0	0	4	....	....	....	....	....

WHL West Second All-Star Team (2017)

YAMAMOTO, Kailer (ya-mah-MOH-toh, KAY-luhr) **EDM**

Right wing. Shoots right. 5'8", 146 lbs.   Born, Spokane, WA, September 29, 1998.
(Edmonton's 1st pick, 22nd overall, in 2017 NHL Draft).

Season	Club	League	GP	G	A	Pts	PIM	GP	G	A	Pts	PIM
2013-14	L.A. Jr. Kings U16	T1EHL	34	17	23	40	14	....	....	....	....	....
2014-15	Spokane Chiefs	WHL	68	23	34	57	50	6	2	3	5	6
	USAHNTDP	U-17	7	3	4	7	2	....	....	....	....	....
2015-16	Spokane Chiefs	WHL	57	19	52	71	34	6	1	4	5	10
	USAHNTDP	U-17	9	7	7	14	12	....	....	....	....	....
2016-17	Spokane Chiefs	WHL	65	42	57	99	46	....	....	....	....	....

YAN, Dennis (YAN, DEH-nihs) **T.B.**

Left wing. Shoots left. 6'1", 184 lbs.   Born, Portland, OR, April 14, 1997.
(Tampa Bay's 3rd pick, 64th overall, in 2015 NHL Draft).

Season	Club	League	GP	G	A	Pts	PIM	GP	G	A	Pts	PIM
2011-12	Lambton Jr. Sting	Minor-ON	30	22	11	33	26	12	10	7	17	24
2012-13	Det. B. Tire U18	T1EHL	40	30	15	45	47	5	5	1	6	6
	USAHNTDP	U-17	18	6	11	17	10	....	....	....	....	....
2013-14	USAHNTDP	USHL	30	6	5	11	49	....	....	....	....	....
2014-15	Shawinigan	QMJHL	59	33	31	64	71	7	7	1	8	6
2015-16	Shawinigan	QMJHL	62	32	37	69	86	20	10	5	15	32
2016-17	Shawinigan	QMJHL	64	46	29	75	52	6	3	2	5	8
	Syracuse Crunch	AHL	3	0	0	0	2	....	....	....	....	....

ZAAR, Daniel (ZAHR, DAN-yehl) **CBJ**

Right wing. Shoots right. 5'11", 175 lbs.   Born, Helsingborg, Sweden, April 24, 1994.
(Columbus' 5th pick, 152nd overall, in 2012 NHL Draft).

Season	Club	League	GP	G	A	Pts	PIM	GP	G	A	Pts	PIM
2009-10	Jonstorps IF U18	Swe-U18	17	12	11	23	10	....	....	....	....	....
	Jonstorps IF Jr.	Swe-Jr.	4	3	3	6	4	....	....	....	....	....
	Jonstorps IF	Sweden-4						4	1	1	2	0
2010-11	Rogle U18	Swe-U18	23	16	18	34	4	4	0	4	4	4
	Rogle Jr.	Swe-Jr.	26	3	3	6	14	3	0	0	0	0
2011-12	Rogle U18	Swe-U18	7	6	6	12	0	5	5	4	9	6
	Rogle Jr.	Swe-Jr.	44	14	24	38	28	7	5	3	8	8
2012-13	Rogle Jr.	Swe-Jr.	17	11	8	19	6	1	0	0	0	2
	Bofors	Sweden-2	21	2	8	10	4	....	....	....	....	....
	Rogle	Sweden	25	2	1	3	0	....	....	....	....	....
	Rogle	Sweden-Q	7	1	0	1	2	....	....	....	....	....
2013-14	Rogle	Sweden-2	68	22	36	58	44	....	....	....	....	....
2014-15	Lulea HF	Sweden	55	9	18	27	18	9	2	2	4	6
2015-16	Lake Erie Monsters	AHL	71	21	22	43	22	17	7	5	12	4
2016-17	Cleveland	AHL	55	8	22	30	24	....	....	....	....	....

ZABLOCKI, Lane (zuh-BLAW-kee, LAYN) **DAL**

Right wing. Shoots right. 5'11", 179 lbs.   Born, Peace River, AB, December 27, 1998.
(Dallas' 4th pick, 79th overall, in 2017 NHL Draft).

Season	Club	League	GP	G	A	Pts	PIM	GP	G	A	Pts	PIM
2013-14	Leduc Min. Mid.	Minor-AB	37	*45	36	*81	54	....	....	....	....	....
	Leduc Oil Kings	AMHL	6	3	2	5	6	....	....	....	....	....
2014-15	Sherwood Park	AJHL	55	15	10	25	114	2	1	0	1	0
2015-16	Regina Pats	WHL	72	18	19	37	95	12	7	2	9	19
2016-17	Regina Pats	WHL	33	9	16	25	48	....	....	....	....	....
	Red Deer Rebels	WHL	31	19	10	29	49	6	6	2	8	20

ZAITSEV, Dmitri (ZIGHT-sehv, dih-MEE-tree) **WSH**

Defense. Shoots left. 6'1", 185 lbs.   Born, Togliatti, Russia, January 18, 1998.
(Washington's 7th pick, 207th overall, in 2016 NHL Draft).

Season	Club	League	GP	G	A	Pts	PIM	GP	G	A	Pts	PIM
2014-15	Magnitogorsk Jr.	Russia-Jr.	11	1	0	1	8	5	0	0	0	2
2015-16	W-Barre/Scranton	NAHL	53	7	15	22	74	....	....	....	....	....
2016-17	Moose Jaw	WHL	70	2	18	20	55	7	0	0	0	2

ZAITSEV, Yegor (ZIGHT-sehv, EE-gohr) **N.J.**

Defense. Shoots left. 6', 180 lbs.   Born, Moscow, Russia, March 5, 1998.
(New Jersey's 10th pick, 205th overall, in 2017 NHL Draft).

Season	Club	League	GP	G	A	Pts	PIM	GP	G	A	Pts	PIM
2014-15	Dyn'o Moscow Jr.	Russia-Jr.	27	2	2	4	14	2	0	0	0	0
2015-16	Dyn'o Moscow Jr.	Russia-Jr.	11	1	5	6	12	....	....	....	....	....
	Dyn'o Balashikha	Russia-2	16	0	1	1	2	8	0	0	0	10
2016-17	Dyn'o Moscow Jr.	Russia-Jr.	2	0	1	1	4	....	....	....	....	....
	Dyn'o Balashikha	Russia-2	24	2	4	6	44	5	0	1	1	15
	Dynamo Moscow	KHL	19	0	1	1	10	2	0	0	0	0

ZBORIL, Jakub (zuh-BAW-rihl, YA-kuhb) **BOS**

Defense. Shoots left. 6'1", 196 lbs.   Born, Brno, Czech Rep., February 21, 1997.
(Boston's 1st pick, 13th overall, in 2015 NHL Draft).

Season	Club	League	GP	G	A	Pts	PIM	GP	G	A	Pts	PIM
2010-11	Brno U18	CzR-U18	2	0	0	0	0	....	....	....	....	....
2011-12	Brno U18	CzR-U18	35	2	4	6	69	2	0	0	0	0
2012-13	Brno U18	CzR-U18	27	4	5	9	70	3	0	2	2	8
2013-14	Brno U18	CzR-U18	2	1	1	2	0	10	3	5	8	14
	Brno Jr.	CzRep-Jr.	36	5	16	21	57	....	....	....	....	....
2014-15	Saint John	QMJHL	44	13	20	33	73	5	1	2	3	18
2015-16	Saint John	QMJHL	50	6	14	20	57	17	2	8	10	6
2016-17	Saint John	QMJHL	50	9	32	41	44	16	3	4	7	12

ZBOROVSKIY, Sergey (z'bohr-AWV-skee, SAIR-gay) **NYR**

Defense. Shoots right. 6'4", 200 lbs.   Born, Moscow, Russia, February 21, 1997.
(NY Rangers' 3rd pick, 79th overall, in 2015 NHL Draft).

Season	Club	League	GP	G	A	Pts	PIM	GP	G	A	Pts	PIM
2013-14	Dyn'o Moscow Jr.	Russia-Jr.	4	0	0	0	2	....	....	....	....	....
2014-15	Regina Pats	WHL	71	3	16	19	70	6	0	1	1	13
2015-16	Regina Pats	WHL	64	8	17	25	61	12	0	5	5	2
2016-17	Regina Pats	WHL	63	7	33	40	64	23	0	8	8	14

WHL East Second All-Star Team (2017)

ZETTERLUND, Fabian (SEH-tuhr-luhnd, fay-BEE-uhn) **N.J.**

Right wing. Shoots right. 5'11", 195 lbs.   Born, Karlstad, Sweden, August 25, 1999.
(New Jersey's 3rd pick, 63rd overall, in 2017 NHL Draft).

Season	Club	League	GP	G	A	Pts	PIM	GP	G	A	Pts	PIM
2013-14	Farjestad U18	Swe-U18	4	2	0	2	2	....	....	....	....	....
2014-15	Farjestad U18	Swe-U18	30	15	17	32	18	1	0	0	0	0
2015-16	Farjestad	Sweden	1	0	0	0	0	....	....	....	....	....
	Farjestad U18	Swe-U18	25	13	17	30	18	....	....	....	....	....
	Farjestad Jr.	Swe-Jr.	18	0	9	9	16	4	1	0	1	0
	Farjestad	Sweden	10	0	0	0	0	....	....	....	....	....
2016-17	Farjestad Jr.	Swe-Jr.	40	16	20	36	18	2	0	1	1	0
	Farjestad	Sweden	14	0	0	0	2	....	....	....	....	....
	Farjestad U18	Swe-U18						2	0	1	1	2

ZIMMER, Max (ZIH-muhr, MAX) **CAR**

Left wing. Shoots left. 6', 202 lbs.   Born, Plymouth, MN, October 29, 1997.
(Carolina's 7th pick, 104th overall, in 2016 NHL Draft).

Season	Club	League	GP	G	A	Pts	PIM	GP	G	A	Pts	PIM
2012-13	Wayzata	High-MN	25	14	9	23	6	6	1	4	5	2
2013-14	Team Northwest	UMHSEL	21	5	6	11	8	1	0	0	0	0
	Wayzata	High-MN	25	10	21	31	10	2	0	3	3	0
	Sioux City	USHL	2	0	0	0	0	....	....	....	....	....
2014-15	Wayzata	High-MN	23	8	20	28	4	2	1	2	3	0
	Chicago Steel	USHL	8	1	0	1	2	....	....	....	....	....
2015-16	Chicago Steel	USHL	55	16	21	37	14	....	....	....	....	....
2016-17	U. of Wisconsin	Big Ten	35	3	6	9	8	....	....	....	....	....

ZUHLSDORF, Ryan (ZOHLZ-dohrf, RIGH-uhn) **T.B.**

Defense. Shoots left. 6', 188 lbs.   Born, Edina, MN, July 1, 1997.
(Tampa Bay's 7th pick, 150th overall, in 2015 NHL Draft).

Season	Club	League	GP	G	A	Pts	PIM	GP	G	A	Pts	PIM
2013-14	Team Southwest	UMHSEL	2	0	0	0	0	....	....	....	....	....
	Team Northeast	UMHSEL	2	0	1	1	0	....	....	....	....	....
	Team Southeast	UMHSEL	12	2	3	5	10	5	0	1	1	2
	Edina Hornets	High-MN	25	1	11	12	6	5	0	4	4	0
2014-15	Sioux City	USHL	56	3	19	22	58	5	0	2	2	0
2015-16	Sioux City	USHL	30	0	23	23	51	....	....	....	....	....
	Dubuque	USHL	16	0	5	5	8	12	0	4	4	12
2016-17	U. of Minnesota	Big Ten	37	2	3	5	35	....	....	....	....	....

USHL All-Rookie Team (2015)

2017-18 NHL Player Register

Note: The 2017-18 NHL Player Register lists forwards and defensemen only. Goaltenders are listed separately. The NHL Player Register lists every active skater who played in the NHL in 2016-17 plus additional players with NHL experience. Trades and roster changes are current as of August 14, 2017.

Abbreviations: GP – games played; **G** – goals; **A** – assists; **Pts** – points; **PIM** – penalties in minutes; **PP** – power-play goals; **SH** – shorthanded goals; **GW** – game-winning goals; **S** – shots; **S%** – shooting percentage; **+/–** – plus/minus; **TF** – total faceoffs taken; **F%** – faceoff winning percentage; **Min** – average time on ice per game; * – league-leading total ♦ – member of Stanley Cup-winning team.

Prospect Register begins on page 279.
Goaltender Register begins on page 589.
Retired Player Index begins on page 616.
Retired Goaltender Index begins on page 665.
League abbreviations are listed on page 678.

ABBOTT, Spencer
(A-buht, SPEHN-suhr) **ANA**

Right wing. Shoots right. 5'9", 170 lbs. Born, Hamilton, ON, April 30, 1988.

Season	Club	League	GP	G	A	Pts	PIM	PP	SH	GW	S	S%	+/-	TF	F%	Min	Playoffs GP	G	A	Pts	PIM	PP	SH	GW	Min
2005-06	Sherwood Saints	High-ON	STATISTICS NOT AVAILABLE																						
	Hamilton Reps	Minor-ON	STATISTICS NOT AVAILABLE																						
	Hamilton	ON-Jr.A	11	1	0	1	0	....	....	....	....	....	....	....	....	....	1	0	0	0	0	....	....	....	....
2006-07	Hamilton	ON-Jr.A	49	32	43	75	22	....	....	....	....	....	....	....	....	....	19	4	5	9	12	....	....	....	....
2007-08	Hamilton	ON-Jr.A	48	42	41	83	42	....	....	....	....	....	....	....	....	....	5	2	4	6	2	....	....	....	....
2008-09	U. of Maine	H-East	38	7	9	16	8	....	....	....	....	....	....	....	....	....	....	....	....	....	....	....	....	....	....
2009-10	U. of Maine	H-East	38	9	19	28	6	....	....	....	....	....	....	....	....	....	....	....	....	....	....	....	....	....	....
2010-11	U. of Maine	H-East	36	17	23	40	16	....	....	....	....	....	....	....	....	....	....	....	....	....	....	....	....	....	....
2011-12	U. of Maine	H-East	39	21	41	62	34	....	....	....	....	....	....	....	....	....	....	....	....	....	....	....	....	....	....
	Toronto Marlies	AHL	3	0	1	1	0	....	....	....	....	....	....	....	....	....	5	0	0	0	0	....	....	....	....
2012-13	Toronto Marlies	AHL	55	13	20	33	10	....	....	....	....	....	....	....	....	....	5	2	3	5	2	....	....	....	....
2013-14	**Toronto**	**NHL**	**1**	**0**	**0**	**0**	**0**	**0**	**0**	**0**	**2**	**0.0**	**–2**	**0**	**0.0**	**5:16**	....	....	....	....	....	....	....	....	....
	Toronto Marlies	AHL	64	17	52	69	16	....	....	....	....	....	....	....	....	....	11	4	7	11	2	....	....	....	....
2014-15	Toronto Marlies	AHL	46	7	17	24	10	....	....	....	....	....	....	....	....	....	....	....	....	....	....	....	....	....	....
	Rockford IceHogs	AHL	19	12	9	21	6	....	....	....	....	....	....	....	....	....	8	3	3	6	2	....	....	....	....
2015-16	Frolunda	Sweden	42	14	21	35	4	....	....	....	....	....	....	....	....	....	9	0	1	1	0	....	....	....	....
2016-17	**Chicago**	**NHL**	**1**	**0**	**0**	**0**	**0**	**0**	**0**	**0**	**1**	**0.0**	**0**	**0**	**0.0**	**8:34**	....	....	....	....	....	....	....	....	....
	Rockford IceHogs	AHL	53	15	20	35	14	....	....	....	....	....	....	....	....	....	....	....	....	....	....	....	....	....	....
	San Diego Gulls	AHL	16	3	11	14	2	....	....	....	....	....	....	....	....	....	8	1	5	6	0	....	....	....	....
	NHL Totals		**2**	**0**	**0**	**0**	**0**	**0**	**0**	**0**	**3**	**0.0**		**0**	**0.0**	**6:55**	....	....	....	....	....	....	....	....	....

Hockey East First All-Star Team (2012) • NCAA East First All-American Team (2012) • AHL Second All-Star Team (2014)

Signed as a free agent by **Toronto**, March 28, 2012. Traded to **Chicago** by **Toronto** for T.J. Brennan, February 26, 2015. Signed as a free agent by **Frolunda** (Sweden), June 16, 2015. Signed as a free agent by **Chicago**, July 1, 2016. Traded to **Anaheim** by **Chicago** with Sam Carrick for Kenton Hegelsen and Anaheim's 7th round pck in 2019 NHL Draft, March 1, 2017.

ABDELKADER, Justin
(abdehl-KAY-duhr, JUHS-tihn) **DET**

Left wing. Shoots left. 6'2", 218 lbs. Born, Muskegon, MI, February 25, 1987. Detroit's 2nd pick, 42nd overall, in 2005 NHL Draft.

Season	Club	League	GP	G	A	Pts	PIM	PP	SH	GW	S	S%	+/-	TF	F%	Min	Playoffs GP	G	A	Pts	PIM	PP	SH	GW	Min
2003-04	Muskegon M.S.	High-MI	28	37	43	80	....	....	....	....	....	....	....	....	....	....	....	....	....	....	....	....	....	....	....
2004-05	Cedar Rapids	USHL	60	27	25	52	86	....	....	....	....	....	....	....	....	....	11	0	4	4	8	....	....	....	....
2005-06	Michigan State	CCHA	44	10	12	22	83	....	....	....	....	....	....	....	....	....	....	....	....	....	....	....	....	....	....
2006-07	Michigan State	CCHA	38	15	18	33	91	....	....	....	....	....	....	....	....	....	....	....	....	....	....	....	....	....	....
2007-08	Michigan State	CCHA	42	19	21	40	107	....	....	....	....	....	....	....	....	....	....	....	....	....	....	....	....	....	....
	Detroit	**NHL**	**2**	**0**	**0**	**0**	**2**	**0**	**0**	**0**	**6**	**0.0**	**0**	**12**	**41.7**	**12:13**	....	....	....	....	....	....	....	....	....
2008-09	**Detroit**	**NHL**	**2**	**0**	**0**	**0**	**0**	**0**	**0**	**0**	**2**	**0.0**	**0**	**7**	**57.1**	**9:18**	**10**	**2**	**1**	**3**	**0**	**0**	**0**	**0**	**6:58**
	Grand Rapids	AHL	76	24	28	52	102	....	....	....	....	....	....	....	....	....	10	6	2	8	23	....	....	....	....
2009-10	**Detroit**	**NHL**	**50**	**3**	**3**	**6**	**35**	**0**	**0**	**0**	**79**	**3.8**	**–11**	**318**	**46.5**	**10:35**	**11**	**1**	**1**	**2**	***36**	**0**	**0**	**0**	**7:30**
	Grand Rapids	AHL	33	11	13	24	86	....	....	....	....	....	....	....	....	....	....	....	....	....	....	....	....	....	....
2010-11	**Detroit**	**NHL**	**74**	**7**	**12**	**19**	**61**	**0**	**0**	**1**	**129**	**5.4**	**15**	**430**	**52.8**	**12:18**	**11**	**0**	**0**	**0**	**22**	**0**	**0**	**0**	**13:27**
2011-12	**Detroit**	**NHL**	**81**	**8**	**14**	**22**	**62**	**0**	**0**	**1**	**121**	**6.6**	**4**	**452**	**52.9**	**12:19**	**5**	**0**	**0**	**0**	**2**	**0**	**0**	**0**	**12:31**
2012-13	**Detroit**	**NHL**	**48**	**10**	**3**	**13**	**34**	**0**	**0**	**0**	**96**	**10.4**	**6**	**125**	**52.0**	**14:49**	**12**	**2**	**1**	**3**	**33**	**0**	**1**	**0**	**16:57**
2013-14	**Detroit**	**NHL**	**70**	**10**	**18**	**28**	**31**	**1**	**0**	**3**	**147**	**6.8**	**2**	**55**	**41.8**	**15:17**	**5**	**0**	**2**	**2**	**6**	**0**	**0**	**0**	**15:48**
2014-15	**Detroit**	**NHL**	**71**	**23**	**21**	**44**	**72**	**8**	**0**	**5**	**154**	**14.9**	**3**	**15**	**46.7**	**17:55**	**5**	**0**	**2**	**2**	**6**	**0**	**0**	**0**	**16:44**
2015-16	**Detroit**	**NHL**	**82**	**19**	**23**	**42**	**120**	**6**	**0**	**4**	**155**	**12.3**	**–16**	**14**	**35.7**	**18:26**	**5**	**1**	**0**	**1**	**35**	**0**	**0**	**0**	**19:09**
2016-17	**Detroit**	**NHL**	**64**	**7**	**14**	**21**	**50**	**5**	**0**	**1**	**104**	**6.7**	**–20**	**17**	**29.4**	**16:40**	....	....	....	....	....	....	....	....	....
	NHL Totals		**544**	**87**	**108**	**195**	**467**	**20**	**0**	**15**	**993**	**8.8**		**1445**	**50.4**	**14:55**	**64**	**6**	**7**	**13**	**140**	**0**	**1**	**0**	**12:53**

NCAA Championship All-Tournament Team (2007) • NCAA Championship Tournament MVP (2007) • AHL All-Rookie Team (2009)

ABERG, Pontus
(AW-buhrg, PAWN-tuhs) **NSH**

Left wing. Shoots right. 5'11", 196 lbs. Born, Stockholm, Sweden, September 23, 1993. Nashville's 1st pick, 37th overall, in 2012 NHL Draft.

Season	Club	League	GP	G	A	Pts	PIM	PP	SH	GW	S	S%	+/-	TF	F%	Min	Playoffs GP	G	A	Pts	PIM	PP	SH	GW	Min
2008-09	Djurgarden U18	Swe-U18	27	6	3	9	8	....	....	....	....	....	....	....	....	....	....	....	....	....	....	....	....	....	....
2009-10	Djurgarden U18	Swe-U18	36	29	33	62	24	....	....	....	....	....	....	....	....	....	5	4	7	11	4	....	....	....	....
	Djurgarden Jr.	Swe-Jr.	11	0	1	1	4	....	....	....	....	....	....	....	....	....	....	....	....	....	....	....	....	....	....
2010-11	Djurgarden U18	Swe-U18	8	11	7	18	27	....	....	....	....	....	....	....	....	....	3	0	2	2	2	....	....	....	....
	Djurgarden Jr.	Swe-Jr.	41	13	17	30	16	....	....	....	....	....	....	....	....	....	4	2	3	5	2	....	....	....	....
	Djurgarden	Sweden	1	0	0	0	0	....	....	....	....	....	....	....	....	....	....	....	....	....	....	....	....	....	....
2011-12	Djurgarden Jr.	Swe-Jr.	6	4	2	6	0	....	....	....	....	....	....	....	....	....	1	1	0	1	0	....	....	....	....
	Djurgarden	Sweden	47	8	7	15	6	....	....	....	....	....	....	....	....	....	....	....	....	....	....	....	....	....	....
	Djurgarden	Sweden-Q	7	1	0	1	0	....	....	....	....	....	....	....	....	....	....	....	....	....	....	....	....	....	....
2012-13	Djurgarden	Sweden-2	58	15	29	44	8	....	....	....	....	....	....	....	....	....	....	....	....	....	....	....	....	....	....
	Djurgarden Jr.	Swe-Jr.	3	1	3	4	2	....	....	....	....	....	....	....	....	....	....	....	....	....	....	....	....	....	....
2013-14	Farjestad	Sweden	52	15	16	31	41	....	....	....	....	....	....	....	....	....	1	0	0	0	0	....	....	....	....
2014-15	Milwaukee	AHL	69	16	18	34	28	....	....	....	....	....	....	....	....	....	13	2	2	4	4	....	....	....	....
2015-16	Milwaukee	AHL	74	25	15	40	32	....	....	....	....	....	....	....	....	....	....	....	....	....	....	....	....	....	....
																	3	0	0	0	0	....	....	....	....
	Nashville	**NHL**	....	....	....	....	....	....	....	....	....	....	....	....	....	....	**2**	**0**	**0**	**0**	**0**	**0**	**0**	**0**	**6:43**

			Regular Season														Playoffs								
Season	Club	League	GP	G	A	Pts	PIM	PP	SH	GW	S	S%	+/-	TF	F%	Min	GP	G	A	Pts	PIM	PP	SH	GW	Min
2016-17	**Nashville**	**NHL**	**15**	**1**	**1**	**2**	**4**	**0**	**0**	**0**	**12**	**8.3**	**–2**	**1**	**100.0**	**12:20**	**16**	**2**	**3**	**5**	**2**	**0**	**0**	**1**	**12:55**
	Milwaukee	AHL	56	31	21	52	40	....	....	....	....	....	....	....	....	....	....	....	....	....	....	....	....	....	....
	NHL Totals		**15**	**1**	**1**	**2**	**4**	**0**	**0**	**0**	**12**	**8.3**		**1**	**100.0**	**12:20**	**18**	**2**	**3**	**5**	**2**	**0**	**0**	**1**	**12:14**

ACCIARI, Noel

(A-char-ee, NOHL) **BOS**

Center. Shoots right. 5'10", 208 lbs. Born, Johnston, RI, December 1, 1991.

Season	Club	League	GP	G	A	Pts	PIM	PP	SH	GW	S	S%	+/-	TF	F%	Min	GP	G	A	Pts	PIM	PP	SH	GW	Min
2009-10	Kent Prep School	High-CT	26	18	20	38	....	....	....	....	....	....	....	....	....	....	....	....	....	....	....	....	....	....	....
2010-11	Kent Prep School	High-CT	27	31	21	52	....	....	....	....	....	....	....	....	....	....	....	....	....	....	....	....	....	....	....
2011-12	Providence	H-East	DID NOT PLAY – FRESHMAN																						
2012-13	Providence	H-East	33	6	5	11	26	....	....	....	....	....	....	....	....	....	....	....	....	....	....	....	....	....	....
2013-14	Providence	H-East	39	11	11	22	20	....	....	....	....	....	....	....	....	....	....	....	....	....	....	....	....	....	....
2014-15	Providence	H-East	41	15	17	32	26	....	....	....	....	....	....	....	....	....	....	....	....	....	....	....	....	....	....
2015-16	**Boston**	**NHL**	**19**	**0**	**1**	**1**	**8**	**0**	**0**	**0**	**18**	**0.0**	**–4**	**136**	**44.1**	**9:54**	....	....	....	....	....	....	....	....	....
	Providence Bruins	AHL	45	7	12	19	19	....	....	....	....	....	....	....	....	....	3	1	2	3	4	....	....	....	....
2016-17	**Boston**	**NHL**	**29**	**2**	**3**	**5**	**16**	**0**	**0**	**0**	**24**	**8.3**	**3**	**29**	**37.9**	**10:22**	**4**	**1**	**0**	**1**	**2**	**0**	**0**	**0**	**19:03**
	Providence Bruins	AHL	30	6	8	14	11	....	....	....	....	....	....	....	....	....	5	0	4	4	0	....	....	....	....
	NHL Totals		**48**	**2**	**4**	**6**	**24**	**0**	**0**	**0**	**42**	**4.8**		**165**	**43.0**	**10:11**	**4**	**1**	**0**	**1**	**2**	**0**	**0**	**0**	**19:03**

Signed as a free agent by **Boston**, June 3, 2015.

AGOSTINO, Kenny

(a-goh-STEE-noh, KEHN-nee) **BOS**

Left wing. Shoots left. 6', 205 lbs. Born, Morristown, NJ, April 30, 1992. Pittsburgh's 4th pick, 140th overall, in 2010 NHL Draft.

Season	Club	League	GP	G	A	Pts	PIM	PP	SH	GW	S	S%	+/-	TF	F%	Min	GP	G	A	Pts	PIM	PP	SH	GW	Min
2007-08	Delbarton	High-NJ	....	24	48	72	....	....	....	....	....	....	....	....	....	....	....	....	....	....	....	....	....	....	....
2008-09	Delbarton	High-NJ	STATISTICS NOT AVAILABLE																						
2009-10	Delbarton	High-NJ	27	50	33	83	40	....	....	....	....	....	....	....	....	....	....	....	....	....	....	....	....	....	....
	USAHNTDP	U-18	2	0	0	0	2	....	....	....	....	....	....	....	....	....	....	....	....	....	....	....	....	....	....
2010-11	Yale	ECAC	31	11	14	25	30	....	....	....	....	....	....	....	....	....	....	....	....	....	....	....	....	....	....
2011-12	Yale	ECAC	33	14	20	34	32	....	....	....	....	....	....	....	....	....	....	....	....	....	....	....	....	....	....
2012-13	Yale	ECAC	37	17	24	41	32	....	....	....	....	....	....	....	....	....	....	....	....	....	....	....	....	....	....
2013-14	Yale	ECAC	33	14	18	32	46	....	....	....	....	....	....	....	....	....	....	....	....	....	....	....	....	....	....
	Calgary	**NHL**	**8**	**1**	**1**	**2**	**0**	**0**	**0**	**0**	**12**	**8.3**	**–2**	**0**	**0.0**	**11:06**	....	....	....	....	....	....	....	....	....
2014-15	Adirondack	AHL	67	15	28	43	52	....	....	....	....	....	....	....	....	....	....	....	....	....	....	....	....	....	....
2015-16	**Calgary**	**NHL**	**2**	**0**	**0**	**0**	**0**	**0**	**0**	**0**	**3**	**0.0**	**–2**	**0**	**0.0**	**13:33**	....	....	....	....	....	....	....	....	....
	Stockton Heat	AHL	65	23	34	57	18	....	....	....	....	....	....	....	....	....	....	....	....	....	....	....	....	....	....
2016-17	**St. Louis**	**NHL**	**7**	**1**	**2**	**3**	**2**	**0**	**0**	**0**	**17**	**5.9**	**0**	**0**	**0.0**	**12:47**	....	....	....	....	....	....	....	....	....
	Chicago Wolves	AHL	65	24	*59	*83	48	....	....	....	....	....	....	....	....	....	10	5	5	10	8	....	....	....	....
	NHL Totals		**17**	**2**	**3**	**5**	**2**	**0**	**0**	**0**	**32**	**6.3**		**0**	**0.0**	**12:04**	....	....	....	....	....	....	....	....	....

ECAC Second All-Star Team (2013) • AHL First All-Star Team (2017) • John P. Sollenberger Trophy (AHL - Top Scorer) (2017)

Traded to **Calgary** by **Pittsburgh** with Ben Hanowski and Pittsburgh's 1st round pick (Morgan Klimchuk) in 2013 NHL Draft for Jarome Iginla, March 28, 2013. Signed as a free agent by **St. Louis**, July 2, 2016. Signed as a free agent by **Boston**, July 1, 2017.

AGOZZINO, Andrew

(a-guh-ZEEN-oh, AN-droo) **COL**

Left wing. Shoots left. 5'10", 187 lbs. Born, Kleinburg, ON, January 3, 1991.

Season	Club	League	GP	G	A	Pts	PIM	PP	SH	GW	S	S%	+/-	TF	F%	Min	GP	G	A	Pts	PIM	PP	SH	GW	Min
2007-08	Niagara Ice Dogs	OHL	50	12	10	22	47	....	....	....	....	....	....	....	....	....	....	....	....	....	....	....	....	....	....
2008-09	Niagara Ice Dogs	OHL	67	27	29	56	88	....	....	....	....	....	....	....	....	....	12	6	5	11	24	....	....	....	....
2009-10	Niagara Ice Dogs	OHL	66	37	29	66	95	....	....	....	....	....	....	....	....	....	5	3	2	5	15	....	....	....	....
	Peoria Rivermen	AHL	2	0	0	0	0	....	....	....	....	....	....	....	....	....	....	....	....	....	....	....	....	....	....
2010-11	Niagara Ice Dogs	OHL	68	43	31	74	73	....	....	....	....	....	....	....	....	....	14	6	7	13	19	....	....	....	....
2011-12	Niagara Ice Dogs	OHL	67	40	48	88	67	....	....	....	....	....	....	....	....	....	20	11	7	18	16	....	....	....	....
2012-13	Lake Erie	AHL	76	20	32	52	73	....	....	....	....	....	....	....	....	....	....	....	....	....	....	....	....	....	....
2013-14	Lake Erie	AHL	75	17	32	49	73	....	....	....	....	....	....	....	....	....	....	....	....	....	....	....	....	....	....
2014-15	**Colorado**	**NHL**	**1**	**0**	**1**	**1**	**0**	**0**	**0**	**0**	**1**	**0.0**	**1**	**2**	**0.0**	**9:45**	....	....	....	....	....	....	....	....	....
	Lake Erie	AHL	74	30	34	64	55	....	....	....	....	....	....	....	....	....	....	....	....	....	....	....	....	....	....
2015-16	**Colorado**	**NHL**	**9**	**0**	**2**	**2**	**0**	**0**	**0**	**0**	**3**	**0.0**	**–1**	**45**	**53.3**	**8:34**	....	....	....	....	....	....	....	....	....
	San Antonio	AHL	41	12	17	29	32	....	....	....	....	....	....	....	....	....	....	....	....	....	....	....	....	....	....
2016-17	Chicago Wolves	AHL	71	18	36	54	57	....	....	....	....	....	....	....	....	....	10	3	3	6	6	....	....	....	....
	NHL Totals		**10**	**0**	**3**	**3**	**0**	**0**	**0**	**0**	**4**	**0.0**		**47**	**51.1**	**8:41**	....	....	....	....	....	....	....	....	....

Signed to a ATO (amateur tryout) contract by **Peoria** (AHL), April 8, 2010. Signed as a free agent by **Lake Erie** (AHL), August 28, 2012. Signed as a free agent by **Colorado**, March 22, 2013. Signed as a free agent by **St. Louis**, July 1, 2016. Signed as a free agent by **Colorado**, July 1, 2017.

AHO, Sebastian

(AH-hoh, seh-BAS-t'yehn) **CAR**

Left wing. Shoots left. 5'11", 172 lbs. Born, Rauma, Finland, July 26, 1997. Carolina's 2nd pick, 35th overall, in 2015 NHL Draft.

Season	Club	League	GP	G	A	Pts	PIM	PP	SH	GW	S	S%	+/-	TF	F%	Min	GP	G	A	Pts	PIM	PP	SH	GW	Min
2011-12	Karpat Oulu U18	Fin-U18	4	0	2	2	4	....	....	....	....	....	....	....	....	....	....	....	....	....	....	....	....	....	....
2012-13	Karpat Oulu U18	Fin-U18	38	28	32	60	32	....	....	....	....	....	....	....	....	....	....	....	....	....	....	....	....	....	....
	Karpat Oulu Jr.	Fin-Jr.	5	2	2	4	0	....	....	....	....	....	....	....	....	....	5	0	1	1	2	....	....	....	....
2013-14	Karpat Oulu U18	Fin-U18	2	3	3	6	0	....	....	....	....	....	....	....	....	....	....	....	....	....	....	....	....	....	....
	Karpat Oulu Jr.	Fin-Jr.	44	25	34	59	18	....	....	....	....	....	....	....	....	....	12	4	8	12	10	....	....	....	....
	Karpat Oulu	Finland	3	0	1	1	0	....	....	....	....	....	....	....	....	....	....	....	....	....	....	....	....	....	....
2014-15	Karpat Oulu Jr.	Fin-Jr.	10	1	9	10	4	....	....	....	....	....	....	....	....	....	5	1	4	5	2	....	....	....	....
	Assat Pori	Finland	3	0	2	2	0	....	....	....	....	....	....	....	....	....	....	....	....	....	....	....	....	....	....
	Karpat Oulu	Finland	27	4	7	11	8	....	....	....	....	....	....	....	....	....	10	1	2	3	2	....	....	....	....
2015-16	Karpat Oulu	Finland	45	20	25	45	2	....	....	....	....	....	....	....	....	....	14	4	11	15	8	....	....	....	....
2016-17	**Carolina**	**NHL**	**82**	**24**	**25**	**49**	**26**	**6**	**1**	**4**	**214**	**11.2**	**–1**	**35**	**48.6**	**16:47**	....	....	....	....	....	....	....	....	....
	NHL Totals		**82**	**24**	**25**	**49**	**26**	**6**	**1**	**4**	**214**	**11.2**		**35**	**48.6**	**16:47**	....	....	....	....	....	....	....	....	....

AKESON, Jason

(AK-uh-suhn, JAY-suhn)

Right wing. Shoots right. 5'10", 190 lbs. Born, Orleans, ON, June 3, 1990.

Season	Club	League	GP	G	A	Pts	PIM	PP	SH	GW	S	S%	+/-	TF	F%	Min	GP	G	A	Pts	PIM	PP	SH	GW	Min
2006-07	Cumberland	ON-Jr.A	54	17	36	53	40	....	....	....	....	....	....	....	....	....	....	....	....	....	....	....	....	....	....
2007-08	Cumberland	ON-Jr.A	34	18	43	61	14	....	....	....	....	....	....	....	....	....	....	....	....	....	....	....	....	....	....
	Kitchener Rangers	OHL	13	0	2	2	4	....	....	....	....	....	....	....	....	....	16	0	1	1	0	....	....	....	....
2008-09	Kitchener Rangers	OHL	56	20	44	64	16	....	....	....	....	....	....	....	....	....	....	....	....	....	....	....	....	....	....
2009-10	Kitchener Rangers	OHL	65	24	56	80	24	....	....	....	....	....	....	....	....	....	20	8	11	19	14	....	....	....	....
2010-11	Kitchener Rangers	OHL	67	24	*84	*108	23	....	....	....	....	....	....	....	....	....	7	3	6	9	0	....	....	....	....
2011-12	Adirondack	AHL	76	14	41	55	26	....	....	....	....	....	....	....	....	....	....	....	....	....	....	....	....	....	....
2012-13	Adirondack	AHL	62	20	33	53	27	....	....	....	....	....	....	....	....	....	....	....	....	....	....	....	....	....	....
	Trenton Titans	ECHL	14	2	8	10	7	....	....	....	....	....	....	....	....	....	....	....	....	....	....	....	....	....	....
	Philadelphia	**NHL**	**1**	**1**	**0**	**1**	**0**	**0**	**0**	**0**	**2**	**50.0**	**2**	**0**	**0.0**	**12:23**	....	....	....	....	....	....	....	....	....
2013-14	**Philadelphia**	**NHL**	**1**	**0**	**1**	**1**	**0**	**0**	**0**	**0**	**2**	**0.0**	**1**	**0**	**0.0**	**13:22**	**7**	**2**	**1**	**3**	**4**	**1**	**0**	**0**	**13:00**
	Adirondack	AHL	70	24	40	64	42	....	....	....	....	....	....	....	....	....	....	....	....	....	....	....	....	....	....
2014-15	**Philadelphia**	**NHL**	**13**	**0**	**0**	**0**	**8**	**0**	**0**	**0**	**9**	**0.0**	**–1**	**2**	**50.0**	**8:03**	....	....	....	....	....	....	....	....	....
	Lehigh Valley	AHL	57	23	30	53	25	....	....	....	....	....	....	....	....	....	....	....	....	....	....	....	....	....	....
2015-16	Rochester	AHL	52	8	22	30	18	....	....	....	....	....	....	....	....	....	....	....	....	....	....	....	....	....	....
	Binghamton	AHL	21	5	17	22	0	....	....	....	....	....	....	....	....	....	....	....	....	....	....	....	....	....	....
2016-17	Vladivostok	KHL	17	1	4	5	2	....	....	....	....	....	....	....	....	....	....	....	....	....	....	....	....	....	....
	Binghamton	AHL	57	20	31	51	22	....	....	....	....	....	....	....	....	....	....	....	....	....	....	....	....	....	....
	NHL Totals		**15**	**1**	**1**	**2**	**8**	**0**	**0**	**0**	**13**	**7.7**		**2**	**50.0**	**8:42**	**7**	**2**	**1**	**3**	**4**	**1**	**0**	**0**	**13:00**

OHL Second All-Star Team (2011)

Signed as a free agent by **Philadelphia**, March 2, 2011. Signed as a free agent by **Buffalo**, July 1, 2015. Traded to **Ottawa** by **Buffalo** with Phil Varone, Jerome Leduc and future considerations (conditions not met) for Michael Sdao, Eric O'Dell, Cole Schneider and Alexander Guptill, February 27, 2016. Signed as a free agent by **Vladivostok** (KHL), September 20, 2016. Signed as a free agent by **Ottawa**, November 30. 2016.

ALBERT, John

(AL-buhrt, JAWN) **WSH**

Center. Shoots left. 5'11", 190 lbs. Born, Cleveland, OH, January 19, 1989. Atlanta's 3rd pick, 175th overall, in 2007 NHL Draft.

			Regular Season														Playoffs								
Season	Club	League	GP	G	A	Pts	PIM	PP	SH	GW	S	S%	+/-	TF	F%	Min	GP	G	A	Pts	PIM	PP	SH	GW	Min
2004-05	Cleveland Barons	MWEHL	67	34	60	94	....	....	....	....	....	....	....	....	....	....	....	....	....	....	....	....	....	....	....
	Cleveland Barons	NAHL	3	0	0	0	0	....	....	....	....	....	....	....	....	....	....	....	....	....	....	....	....	....	....
2005-06	USAHNTDP	U-17	19	8	15	23	25	....	....	....	....	....	....	....	....	....	....	....	....	....	....	....	....	....	....
	USAHNTDP	NAHL	36	8	15	23	23	....	....	....	....	....	....	....	....	....	....	....	....	....	....	....	....	....	....
2006-07	USAHNTDP	U-18	41	8	16	24	10	....	....	....	....	....	....	....	....	....	....	....	....	....	....	....	....	....	....
	USAHNTDP	NAHL	15	4	9	13	4	....	....	....	....	....	....	....	....	....	....	....	....	....	....	....	....	....	....
2007-08	Ohio State	CCHA	41	4	17	21	10	....	....	....	....	....	....	....	....	....	....	....	....	....	....	....	....	....	....
2008-09	Ohio State	CCHA	42	11	28	39	20	....	....	....	....	....	....	....	....	....	....	....	....	....	....	....	....	....	....
2009-10	Ohio State	CCHA	39	6	24	30	20	....	....	....	....	....	....	....	....	....	....	....	....	....	....	....	....	....	....
2010-11	Ohio State	CCHA	37	12	22	34	18	....	....	....	....	....	....	....	....	....	....	....	....	....	....	....	....	....	....
2011-12	St. John's IceCaps	AHL	64	9	18	27	28	....	....	....	....	....	....	....	....	....	15	3	2	5	8	....	....	....	....
2012-13	St. John's IceCaps	AHL	24	3	2	5	10	....	....	....	....	....	....	....	....	....	....	....	....	....	....	....	....	....	....
2013-14	**Winnipeg**	**NHL**	**9**	**1**	**0**	**1**	**0**	**0**	**0**	**0**	**5**	**20.0**	**–3**	**21**	**42.9**	**5:07**	....	....	....	....	....	....	....	....	....
	St. John's IceCaps	AHL	63	28	17	45	20	....	....	....	....	....	....	....	....	....	21	1	6	7	18	....	....	....	....
2014-15	St. John's IceCaps	AHL	66	16	26	42	26	....	....	....	....	....	....	....	....	....	....	....	....	....	....	....	....	....	....
2015-16	Manitoba Moose	AHL	66	12	24	36	20	....	....	....	....	....	....	....	....	....	....	....	....	....	....	....	....	....	....
2016-17	Karpat Oulu	Finland	42	12	12	24	16	....	....	....	....	....	....	....	....	....	2	1	1	2	0	....	....	....	....
	NHL Totals		**9**	**1**	**0**	**1**	**0**	**0**	**0**	**0**	**5**	**20.0**		**21**	**42.9**	**5:07**	....	....	....	....	....	....	....	....	....

• Transferred to **Winnipeg** after **Atlanta** franchise relocated, June 21, 2011. Signed as a free agent by **Karpat** (Finland), July 4, 2016. Signed as a free agent by **Washington**, July 1, 2017.

ALLEN, Conor

(AL-uhn, KAW-nuhr)

Defense. Shoots left. 6'1", 210 lbs. Born, Chicago, IL, January 31, 1990.

			Regular Season														Playoffs								
Season	Club	League	GP	G	A	Pts	PIM	PP	SH	GW	S	S%	+/-	TF	F%	Min	GP	G	A	Pts	PIM	PP	SH	GW	Min
2008-09	St. Louis Bandits	NAHL	46	5	10	15	48	....	....	....	....	....	....	....	....	....	12	1	4	5	15	....	....	....	....
2009-10	Sioux Falls	USHL	48	7	8	15	69	....	....	....	....	....	....	....	....	....	....	....	....	....	....	....	....	....	....
2010-11	Massachusetts	H-East	31	2	4	6	29	....	....	....	....	....	....	....	....	....	....	....	....	....	....	....	....	....	....
2011-12	Massachusetts	H-East	35	7	7	14	28	....	....	....	....	....	....	....	....	....	....	....	....	....	....	....	....	....	....
2012-13	Massachusetts	H-East	33	5	14	19	53	....	....	....	....	....	....	....	....	....	....	....	....	....	....	....	....	....	....
	Connecticut	AHL	1	0	0	0	0	....	....	....	....	....	....	....	....	....	....	....	....	....	....	....	....	....	....
2013-14	**NY Rangers**	**NHL**	**3**	**0**	**0**	**0**	**0**	**0**	**0**	**0**	**2**	**0.0**	**–1**	**0**	**0.0**	**14:26**	....	....	....	....	....	....	....	....	....
	Hartford	AHL	72	6	25	31	71	....	....	....	....	....	....	....	....	....	....	....	....	....	....	....	....	....	....
2014-15	**NY Rangers**	**NHL**	**4**	**0**	**0**	**0**	**4**	**0**	**0**	**0**	**2**	**0.0**	**–1**	**0**	**0.0**	**12:12**	....	....	....	....	....	....	....	....	....
	Hartford	AHL	72	11	23	34	113	....	....	....	....	....	....	....	....	....	12	1	1	2	10	....	....	....	....
2015-16	Milwaukee	AHL	31	1	5	6	52	....	....	....	....	....	....	....	....	....	....	....	....	....	....	....	....	....	....
	Binghamton	AHL	17	1	4	5	10	....	....	....	....	....	....	....	....	....	....	....	....	....	....	....	....	....	....
	Iowa Wild	AHL	18	1	2	3	6	....	....	....	....	....	....	....	....	....	....	....	....	....	....	....	....	....	....
2016-17	Grand Rapids	AHL	56	1	10	11	49	....	....	....	....	....	....	....	....	....	....	....	....	....	....	....	....	....	....
	NHL Totals		**7**	**0**	**0**	**0**	**4**	**0**	**0**	**0**	**4**	**0.0**		**0**	**0.0**	**13:10**	....	....	....	....	....	....	....	....	....

Signed as a free agent by **NY Rangers**, March 29, 2013. Signed as a free agent by **Nashville**, July 2, 2015. Traded to **Ottawa** by **Nashville** for Patrick Mullen, January 14, 2016. Signed as a free agent by **Tucson** (AHL), August 18, 2016.14, 2016. Traded to **Minnesota** by **Ottawa** for Michael Keranen, February 29, 2016. Signed as a free agent by **Grand Rapids** (AHL), August 18, 2016.

ALT, Mark

(AHLT, MAHRK) **PHI**

Defense. Shoots right. 6'4", 201 lbs. Born, Kansas City, MO, October 18, 1991. Carolina's 3rd pick, 53rd overall, in 2010 NHL Draft.

			Regular Season														Playoffs								
Season	Club	League	GP	G	A	Pts	PIM	PP	SH	GW	S	S%	+/-	TF	F%	Min	GP	G	A	Pts	PIM	PP	SH	GW	Min
2007-08	Cretin-Derham	High-MN	17	1	5	6	4	....	....	....	....	....	....	....	....	....	....	....	....	....	....	....	....	....	....
2008-09	Cretin-Derham	High-MN	26	11	16	27	10	....	....	....	....	....	....	....	....	....	....	....	....	....	....	....	....	....	....
2009-10	Cretin-Derham	High-MN	22	6	9	15	12	....	....	....	....	....	....	....	....	....	2	0	5	5	2	....	....	....	....
	Team Northeast	UMHSEL	24	13	9	22	....	....	....	....	....	....	....	....	....	....	....	....	....	....	....	....	....	....	....
2010-11	U. of Minnesota	WCHA	35	2	8	10	22	....	....	....	....	....	....	....	....	....	....	....	....	....	....	....	....	....	....
2011-12	U. of Minnesota	WCHA	43	5	17	22	43	....	....	....	....	....	....	....	....	....	....	....	....	....	....	....	....	....	....
2012-13	U. of Minnesota	WCHA	39	0	7	7	20	....	....	....	....	....	....	....	....	....	....	....	....	....	....	....	....	....	....
	Adirondack	AHL	6	1	1	2	2	....	....	....	....	....	....	....	....	....	....	....	....	....	....	....	....	....	....
2013-14	Adirondack	AHL	75	4	22	26	31	....	....	....	....	....	....	....	....	....	....	....	....	....	....	....	....	....	....
2014-15	**Philadelphia**	**NHL**	**1**	**0**	**0**	**0**	**0**	**0**	**0**	**0**	**0**	**0.0**	**–1**	**0**	**0.0**	**9:25**	....	....	....	....	....	....	....	....	....
	Lehigh Valley	AHL	44	2	8	10	18	....	....	....	....	....	....	....	....	....	....	....	....	....	....	....	....	....	....
2015-16	Lehigh Valley	AHL	72	4	15	19	46	....	....	....	....	....	....	....	....	....	....	....	....	....	....	....	....	....	....
2016-17	Lehigh Valley	AHL	40	1	10	11	10	....	....	....	....	....	....	....	....	....	5	0	0	0	2	....	....	....	....
	NHL Totals		**1**	**0**	**0**	**0**	**0**	**0**	**0**	**0**	**0**	**0.0**		**0**	**0.0**	**9:25**	....	....	....	....	....	....	....	....	....

Traded to **Philadelphia** by **Carolina** with Brian Boucher for Luke Pither, January 13, 2013.

ALZNER, Karl

(ALZ-nuhr, KARL) **MTL**

Defense. Shoots left. 6'3", 219 lbs. Born, Burnaby, BC, September 24, 1988. Washington's 1st pick, 5th overall, in 2007 NHL Draft.

			Regular Season														Playoffs								
Season	Club	League	GP	G	A	Pts	PIM	PP	SH	GW	S	S%	+/-	TF	F%	Min	GP	G	A	Pts	PIM	PP	SH	GW	Min
2002-03	Burnaby W.C.	Minor-BC	64	17	31	48	24	....	....	....	....	....	....	....	....	....	....	....	....	....	....	....	....	....	....
2003-04	Richmond	PIJHL	41	3	9	12	8	....	....	....	....	....	....	....	....	....	13	0	2	2	0	....	....	....	....
	Calgary Hitmen	WHL	1	0	0	0	0	....	....	....	....	....	....	....	....	....	....	....	....	....	....	....	....	....	....
2004-05	Calgary Hitmen	WHL	66	0	10	10	19	....	....	....	....	....	....	....	....	....	12	0	3	3	9	....	....	....	....
2005-06	Calgary Hitmen	WHL	70	4	20	24	28	....	....	....	....	....	....	....	....	....	13	1	3	4	4	....	....	....	....
2006-07	Calgary Hitmen	WHL	63	8	39	47	32	....	....	....	....	....	....	....	....	....	18	1	12	13	4	....	....	....	....
2007-08	Calgary Hitmen	WHL	60	7	29	36	15	....	....	....	....	....	....	....	....	....	16	6	2	8	4	....	....	....	....
2008-09	**Washington**	**NHL**	**30**	**1**	**4**	**5**	**2**	**0**	**0**	**0**	**31**	**3.2**	**–1**	**0**	**0.0**	**19:25**	....	....	....	....	....	....	....	....	....
	Hershey Bears	AHL	48	4	16	20	10	....	....	....	....	....	....	....	....	....	10	0	2	2	2	....	....	....	....
2009-10	**Washington**	**NHL**	**21**	**0**	**5**	**5**	**8**	**0**	**0**	**0**	**16**	**0.0**	**–2**	**0**	**0.0**	**16:24**	**1**	**0**	**0**	**0**	**0**	**0**	**0**	**0**	**15:09**
	Hershey Bears	AHL	56	3	18	21	10	....	....	....	....	....	....	....	....	....	20	3	7	10	4	....	....	....	....
2010-11	**Washington**	**NHL**	**82**	**2**	**10**	**12**	**24**	**0**	**0**	**0**	**64**	**3.1**	**14**	**0**	**0.0**	**20:01**	**9**	**0**	**1**	**1**	**0**	**0**	**0**	**0**	**22:44**
2011-12	**Washington**	**NHL**	**82**	**1**	**16**	**17**	**29**	**0**	**0**	**0**	**56**	**1.8**	**12**	**0**	**0.0**	**20:52**	**14**	**0**	**2**	**2**	**0**	**0**	**0**	**0**	**24:53**
2012-13	**Washington**	**NHL**	**48**	**1**	**4**	**5**	**14**	**0**	**0**	**0**	**39**	**2.6**	**–6**	**0**	**0.0**	**20:57**	**7**	**1**	**1**	**2**	**2**	**0**	**0**	**0**	**22:18**
2013-14	**Washington**	**NHL**	**82**	**2**	**16**	**18**	**26**	**0**	**0**	**1**	**95**	**2.1**	**–7**	**0**	**0.0**	**20:32**	....	....	....	....	....	....	....	....	....
2014-15	**Washington**	**NHL**	**82**	**5**	**16**	**21**	**20**	**0**	**0**	**0**	**72**	**6.9**	**14**	**0**	**0.0**	**19:26**	**14**	**2**	**2**	**4**	**6**	**0**	**0**	**1**	**20:14**
2015-16	**Washington**	**NHL**	**82**	**4**	**17**	**21**	**26**	**0**	**0**	**1**	**75**	**5.3**	**14**	**0**	**0.0**	**21:23**	**12**	**0**	**2**	**2**	**6**	**0**	**0**	**0**	**21:23**
2016-17	**Washington**	**NHL**	**82**	**3**	**10**	**13**	**28**	**0**	**0**	**0**	**81**	**3.7**	**23**	**0**	**0.0**	**19:47**	**7**	**0**	**0**	**0**	**2**	**0**	**0**	**0**	**15:45**
	NHL Totals		**591**	**19**	**98**	**117**	**177**	**0**	**0**	**2**	**529**	**3.6**		**0**	**0.0**	**20:12**	**64**	**3**	**8**	**11**	**16**	**0**	**0**	**1**	**21:29**

WHL East Second All-Star Team (2007) • Canadian Major Junior Second All-Star Team (2007) • WHL East First All-Star Team (2008) • WHL Defenseman of the Year (2008) • WHL Player of the Year (2008) • Canadian Major Junior First All-Star Team (2008) • Canadian Major Junior Defenseman of the Year (2008)

Signed as a free agent by **Montreal**, July 1, 2017.

ANDERSON, Josh

(AN-duhr-suhn, JAWSH) **CBJ**

Right wing. Shoots right. 6'3", 221 lbs. Born, Burlington, ON, May 7, 1994. Columbus' 4th pick, 95th overall, in 2012 NHL Draft.

			Regular Season														Playoffs								
Season	Club	League	GP	G	A	Pts	PIM	PP	SH	GW	S	S%	+/-	TF	F%	Min	GP	G	A	Pts	PIM	PP	SH	GW	Min
2010-11	Burlington Eagles	Minor-ON	58	41	35	76	....	....	....	....	....	....	....	....	....	....	....	....	....	....	....	....	....	....	....
	Burlington	ON-Jr.A	4	0	2	2	0	....	....	....	....	....	....	....	....	....	1	0	0	0	0	....	....	....	....
2011-12	London Knights	OHL	64	12	10	22	34	....	....	....	....	....	....	....	....	....	19	2	3	5	4	....	....	....	....
2012-13	London Knights	OHL	68	23	26	49	77	....	....	....	....	....	....	....	....	....	19	1	2	3	23	....	....	....	....
2013-14	London Knights	OHL	59	27	25	52	81	....	....	....	....	....	....	....	....	....	9	5	4	9	14	....	....	....	....
2014-15	**Columbus**	**NHL**	**6**	**0**	**1**	**1**	**2**	**0**	**0**	**0**	**10**	**0.0**	**–1**	**0**	**0.0**	**13:27**	....	....	....	....	....	....	....	....	....
	Springfield	AHL	52	7	10	17	76	....	....	....	....	....	....	....	....	....	....	....	....	....	....	....	....	....	....
2015-16	**Columbus**	**NHL**	**12**	**1**	**3**	**4**	**2**	**0**	**0**	**0**	**11**	**9.1**	**0**	**0**	**0.0**	**10:42**	....	....	....	....	....	....	....	....	....
	Lake Erie	AHL	58	18	21	39	108	....	....	....	....	....	....	....	....	....	15	7	5	12	24	....	....	....	....
2016-17	**Columbus**	**NHL**	**78**	**17**	**12**	**29**	**89**	**0**	**0**	**3**	**119**	**14.3**	**12**	**29**	**27.6**	**12:01**	**5**	**1**	**1**	**2**	**2**	**0**	**0**	**0**	**13:43**
	NHL Totals		**96**	**18**	**16**	**34**	**93**	**0**	**0**	**3**	**140**	**12.9**		**29**	**27.6**	**11:57**	**5**	**1**	**1**	**2**	**2**	**0**	**0**	**0**	**13:43**

ANDERSSON, Rasmus
(AN-duhr-suhn, RAZ-muhs) **CGY**

Defense. Shoots right. 6'1", 214 lbs. Born, Malmo, Sweden, October 27, 1996. Calgary's 1st pick, 53rd overall, in 2015 NHL Draft.

			Regular Season														Playoffs								
Season	Club	League	GP	G	A	Pts	PIM	PP	SH	GW	S	S%	+/-	TF	F%	Min	GP	G	A	Pts	PIM	PP	SH	GW	Min
2010-11	Malmo U18	Swe-U18	17	0	1	1	22	....	....	....	....	....	....	....	....	....	....	....	....	....	....	....	....	....	....
2011-12	Malmo U18	Swe-U18	23	6	16	22	47	....	....	....	....	....	....	....	....	....	5	1	1	2	18	....	....	....	....
	Malmo Jr.	Swe-Jr.	13	0	3	3	6	....	....	....	....	....	....	....	....	....	3	0	0	0	0	....	....	....	....
2012-13	Malmo U18	Swe-U18	1	0	2	2	0	....	....	....	....	....	....	....	....	....	2	0	2	2	2	....	....	....	....
	Malmo Jr.	Swe-Jr.	8	5	1	6	48	....	....	....	....	....	....	....	....	....	1	0	0	0	2	....	....	....	....
	Malmo	Sweden-2	38	3	8	11	22	....	....	....	....	....	....	....	....	....	....	....	....	....	....	....	....	....	....
2013-14	Malmo Jr.	Swe-Jr.	8	1	4	5	12	....	....	....	....	....	....	....	....	....	....	....	....	....	....	....	....	....	....
	Malmo	Sweden-2	53	3	10	13	26	....	....	....	....	....	....	....	....	....	....	....	....	....	....	....	....	....	....
2014-15	Barrie Colts	OHL	67	12	52	64	88	....	....	....	....	....	....	....	....	....	9	1	3	4	6	....	....	....	....
2015-16	Barrie Colts	OHL	64	9	51	60	60	....	....	....	....	....	....	....	....	....	15	2	13	15	16	....	....	....	....
2016-17	**Calgary**	**NHL**	**1**	**0**	**0**	**0**	**0**	**0**	**0**	**0**	**0**	**0.0**	**–1**	**0**	**0.0**	**18:33**	....	....	....	....	....	....	....	....	....
	Stockton Heat	AHL	54	3	19	22	38	....	....	....	....	....	....	....	....	....	5	0	0	0	6	....	....	....	....
	NHL Totals		**1**	**0**	**0**	**0**	**0**	**0**	**0**	**0**	**0**	**0.0**		**0**	**0.0**	**18:33**	....	....	....	....	....	....	....	....	....

OHL Second All-Star Team (2015) • OHL First All-Star Team (2016)

ANDREOFF, Andy
(AN-dree-awf, AN-dee) **L.A.**

Left wing. Shoots left. 6'1", 203 lbs. Born, Pickering, ON, May 17, 1991. Los Angeles' 2nd pick, 80th overall, in 2011 NHL Draft.

2006-07	Ajax-Pickering	Minor-ON	48	17	21	38	58	....	....	....	....	....	....	....	....	....	....	....	....	....	....	....	....	....	....
2007-08	Pickering Panthers	ON-Jr.A	40	12	15	27	58	....	....	....	....	....	....	....	....	....	....	....	....	....	....	....	....	....	....
	Oshawa Generals	OHL	25	0	1	1	8	....	....	....	....	....	....	....	....	....	9	0	0	0	2	....	....	....	....
2008-09	Oshawa Generals	OHL	66	11	14	25	37	....	....	....	....	....	....	....	....	....	....	....	....	....	....	....	....	....	....
2009-10	Oshawa Generals	OHL	67	15	33	48	70	....	....	....	....	....	....	....	....	....	....	....	....	....	....	....	....	....	....
2010-11	Oshawa Generals	OHL	66	33	42	75	109	....	....	....	....	....	....	....	....	....	10	3	8	11	16	....	....	....	....
2011-12	Oshawa Generals	OHL	57	22	36	58	88	....	....	....	....	....	....	....	....	....	6	1	3	4	4	....	....	....	....
	Manchester	AHL	5	1	0	1	4	....	....	....	....	....	....	....	....	....	4	2	0	2	2	....	....	....	....
2012-13	Manchester	AHL	69	13	13	26	111	....	....	....	....	....	....	....	....	....	4	0	3	3	0	....	....	....	....
2013-14	Manchester	AHL	76	11	24	35	133	....	....	....	....	....	....	....	....	....	4	1	2	3	2	....	....	....	....
2014-15	**Los Angeles**	**NHL**	**18**	**2**	**1**	**3**	**18**	**0**	**0**	**1**	**14**	**14.3**	**1**	**61**	**52.5**	**8:34**	....	....	....	....	....	....	....	....	....
	Manchester	AHL	7	5	5	10	11	....	....	....	....	....	....	....	....	....	....	....	....	....	....	....	....	....	....
2015-16	**Los Angeles**	**NHL**	**60**	**8**	**2**	**10**	**76**	**0**	**0**	**1**	**46**	**17.4**	**1**	**268**	**50.0**	**8:48**	**1**	**0**	**0**	**0**	**0**	**0**	**0**	**0**	**9:52**
2016-17	**Los Angeles**	**NHL**	**36**	**0**	**2**	**2**	**70**	**0**	**0**	**0**	**38**	**0.0**	**–2**	**69**	**59.4**	**10:36**	....	....	....	....	....	....	....	....	....
	NHL Totals		**114**	**10**	**5**	**15**	**164**	**0**	**0**	**2**	**98**	**10.2**		**398**	**52.0**	**9:20**	**1**	**0**	**0**	**0**	**0**	**0**	**0**	**0**	**9:52**

ANDRIGHETTO, Sven
(an-drih-GEH-toh, SVEHN) **COL**

Right wing. Shoots left. 5'10", 188 lbs. Born, Zurich, Switz., March 21, 1993. Montreal's 6th pick, 86th overall, in 2013 NHL Draft.

2007-08	Zurich II U17	Swiss-U17	17	10	13	23	26	....	....	....	....	....	....	....	....	....	....	....	....	....	....	....	....	....	....
	Zurich U17	Swiss-U17	1	0	0	0	0	....	....	....	....	....	....	....	....	....	....	....	....	....	....	....	....	....	....
2008-09	Zurich U17	Swiss-U17	28	14	11	25	40	....	....	....	....	....	....	....	....	....	10	3	2	5	8	....	....	....	....
	Dubendorf Jr.	Swiss-Jr.	4	1	4	5	0	....	....	....	....	....	....	....	....	....	....	....	....	....	....	....	....	....	....
2009-10	Zurich U17	Swiss-U17	22	24	31	55	14	....	....	....	....	....	....	....	....	....	10	16	8	24	18	....	....	....	....
	GCK Zurich Jr.	Swiss-Jr.	14	3	4	7	4	....	....	....	....	....	....	....	....	....	....	....	....	....	....	....	....	....	....
2010-11	GCK Lions Zurich	Swiss-2	36	11	12	23	20	....	....	....	....	....	....	....	....	....	....	....	....	....	....	....	....	....	....
	EHC Visp	Swiss-2	2	0	0	0	0	....	....	....	....	....	....	....	....	....	17	1	2	3	12	....	....	....	....
2011-12	Rouyn-Noranda	QMJHL	62	36	38	74	50	....	....	....	....	....	....	....	....	....	4	0	2	2	4	....	....	....	....
2012-13	Rouyn-Noranda	QMJHL	53	31	67	98	45	....	....	....	....	....	....	....	....	....	14	8	22	30	14	....	....	....	....
2013-14	Hamilton	AHL	64	17	27	44	40	....	....	....	....	....	....	....	....	....	....	....	....	....	....	....	....	....	....
2014-15	**Montreal**	**NHL**	**12**	**2**	**1**	**3**	**0**	**0**	**0**	**0**	**12**	**16.7**	**0**	**15**	**20.0**	**9:25**	....	....	....	....	....	....	....	....	....
	Hamilton	AHL	60	14	29	43	42	....	....	....	....	....	....	....	....	....	....	....	....	....	....	....	....	....	....
2015-16	**Montreal**	**NHL**	**44**	**7**	**10**	**17**	**6**	**1**	**0**	**0**	**74**	**9.5**	**1**	**7**	**42.9**	**14:07**	....	....	....	....	....	....	....	....	....
	St. John's IceCaps	AHL	26	10	13	23	22	....	....	....	....	....	....	....	....	....	....	....	....	....	....	....	....	....	....
2016-17	**Montreal**	**NHL**	**27**	**2**	**6**	**8**	**4**	**0**	**0**	**0**	**31**	**6.5**	**1**	**0**	**0.0**	**11:29**	....	....	....	....	....	....	....	....	....
	St. John's IceCaps	AHL	20	8	14	22	8	....	....	....	....	....	....	....	....	....	....	....	....	....	....	....	....	....	....
	Colorado	**NHL**	**19**	**5**	**11**	**16**	**8**	**2**	**0**	**0**	**37**	**13.5**	**0**	**10**	**70.0**	**17:30**	....	....	....	....	....	....	....	....	....
	NHL Totals		**102**	**16**	**28**	**44**	**18**	**3**	**0**	**0**	**154**	**10.4**		**32**	**40.6**	**13:30**	....	....	....	....	....	....	....	....	....

Traded to **Colorado** by **Montreal** for Andreas Martinsen, March 1, 2017.

ANGELIDIS, Mike
(AN-gehl-EE-dihs, MIGHK)

Left wing. Shoots left. 6'1", 214 lbs. Born, Woodbridge, ON, June 27, 1985.

2002-03	Owen Sound	OHL	65	7	10	17	81	....	....	....	....	....	....	....	....	....	4	1	1	2	0	....	....	....	....
2003-04	Owen Sound	OHL	66	9	9	18	118	....	....	....	....	....	....	....	....	....	7	4	1	5	4	....	....	....	....
2004-05	Owen Sound	OHL	41	9	10	19	126	....	....	....	....	....	....	....	....	....	8	3	2	5	10	....	....	....	....
2005-06	Owen Sound	OHL	68	53	25	78	167	....	....	....	....	....	....	....	....	....	11	5	9	14	38	....	....	....	....
2006-07	Albany River Rats	AHL	27	4	5	9	44	....	....	....	....	....	....	....	....	....	4	0	0	0	10	....	....	....	....
	Florida Everblades	ECHL	24	10	8	18	54	....	....	....	....	....	....	....	....	....	....	....	....	....	....	....	....	....	....
2007-08	Albany River Rats	AHL	74	11	16	27	151	....	....	....	....	....	....	....	....	....	7	0	2	2	6	....	....	....	....
2008-09	Albany River Rats	AHL	67	15	10	25	142	....	....	....	....	....	....	....	....	....	....	....	....	....	....	....	....	....	....
2009-10	Albany River Rats	AHL	67	12	12	24	119	....	....	....	....	....	....	....	....	....	8	2	4	6	12	....	....	....	....
2010-11	Norfolk Admirals	AHL	80	20	18	38	169	....	....	....	....	....	....	....	....	....	3	0	0	0	2	....	....	....	....
2011-12	**Tampa Bay**	**NHL**	**6**	**1**	**0**	**1**	**5**	**0**	**0**	**0**	**8**	**12.5**	**–1**	**7**	**57.1**	**6:30**	....	....	....	....	....	....	....	....	....
	Norfolk Admirals	AHL	54	14	13	27	135	....	....	....	....	....	....	....	....	....	18	1	5	6	35	....	....	....	....
2012-13	Syracuse Crunch	AHL	71	11	13	24	158	....	....	....	....	....	....	....	....	....	18	2	4	6	49	....	....	....	....
	Tampa Bay	**NHL**	**1**	**0**	**0**	**0**	**0**	**0**	**0**	**0**	**0**	**0.0**	**0**	**7**	**42.9**	**7:22**	....	....	....	....	....	....	....	....	....
2013-14	Syracuse Crunch	AHL	75	12	21	33	161	....	....	....	....	....	....	....	....	....	....	....	....	....	....	....	....	....	....
2014-15	**Tampa Bay**	**NHL**	**3**	**0**	**0**	**0**	**12**	**0**	**0**	**0**	**0**	**0.0**	**0**	**19**	**36.8**	**7:21**	....	....	....	....	....	....	....	....	....
	Syracuse Crunch	AHL	64	20	18	38	138	....	....	....	....	....	....	....	....	....	3	0	1	1	6	....	....	....	....
2015-16	**Tampa Bay**	**NHL**	**4**	**1**	**0**	**1**	**5**	**0**	**0**	**1**	**1**	**100.0**	**2**	**31**	**32.3**	**9:00**	....	....	....	....	....	....	....	....	....
	Syracuse Crunch	AHL	53	7	8	15	75	....	....	....	....	....	....	....	....	....	....	....	....	....	....	....	....	....	....
2016-17	Stockton Heat	AHL	49	7	13	20	97	....	....	....	....	....	....	....	....	....	5	1	2	3	2	....	....	....	....
	NHL Totals		**14**	**2**	**0**	**2**	**22**	**0**	**0**	**1**	**9**	**22.2**		**64**	**37.5**	**7:27**	....	....	....	....	....	....	....	....	....

OHL First All-Star Team (2006) • Canadian Major Junior Humanitarian Player of the Year (2006)

Signed as a free agent by **Carolina**, July 27, 2006. Signed as a free agent by **Tampa Bay**, August 3, 2010. Signed as a free agent by **Stockton** (AHL), August 8, 2016.

ANISIMOV, Artem
(a-NEE-see-mawv, AHR-tehm) **CHI**

Center. Shoots left. 6'4", 198 lbs. Born, Yaroslavl, Russia, May 24, 1988. NY Rangers' 2nd pick, 54th overall, in 2006 NHL Draft.

2004-05	Yaroslavl 2	Russia-3	24	3	5	8	10	....	....	....	....	....	....	....	....	....	....	....	....	....	....	....	....	....	....
2005-06	Yaroslavl 2	Russia-3	32	15	12	27	28	....	....	....	....	....	....	....	....	....	....	....	....	....	....	....	....	....	....
	Yaroslavl	Russia	10	0	1	1	4	....	....	....	....	....	....	....	....	....	....	....	....	....	....	....	....	....	....
2006-07	Yaroslavl 2	Russia-3	2	2	0	2	0	....	....	....	....	....	....	....	....	....	....	....	....	....	....	....	....	....	....
	Yaroslavl	Russia	39	2	8	10	26	....	....	....	....	....	....	....	....	....	7	3	2	5	4	....	....	....	....
2007-08	Hartford	AHL	74	16	27	43	30	....	....	....	....	....	....	....	....	....	5	1	0	1	2	....	....	....	....
2008-09	**NY Rangers**	**NHL**	**1**	**0**	**0**	**0**	**0**	**0**	**0**	**0**	**1**	**0.0**	**0**	**5**	**40.0**	**9:27**	**1**	**0**	**0**	**0**	**0**	**0**	**0**	**0**	**5:35**
	Hartford	AHL	80	37	44	81	50	....	....	....	....	....	....	....	....	....	6	2	0	2	0	....	....	....	....
2009-10	**NY Rangers**	**NHL**	**82**	**12**	**16**	**28**	**32**	**1**	**0**	**2**	**124**	**9.7**	**–2**	**690**	**44.9**	**12:54**	....	....	....	....	....	....	....	....	....
2010-11	**NY Rangers**	**NHL**	**82**	**18**	**26**	**44**	**20**	**3**	**0**	**2**	**190**	**9.5**	**3**	**688**	**44.5**	**16:12**	**5**	**1**	**0**	**1**	**0**	**0**	**0**	**0**	**15:10**
2011-12	**NY Rangers**	**NHL**	**79**	**16**	**20**	**36**	**34**	**4**	**1**	**1**	**132**	**12.1**	**12**	**345**	**46.7**	**15:24**	**20**	**3**	**7**	**10**	**4**	**0**	**0**	**0**	**13:52**
2012-13	Yaroslavl	KHL	36	12	17	29	22	....	....	....	....	....	....	....	....	....	....	....	....	....	....	....	....	....	....
	Columbus	**NHL**	**35**	**11**	**7**	**18**	**12**	**1**	**0**	**3**	**68**	**16.2**	**–6**	**509**	**48.9**	**16:25**	....	....	....	....	....	....	....	....	....
2013-14	**Columbus**	**NHL**	**81**	**22**	**17**	**39**	**20**	**3**	**2**	**5**	**162**	**13.6**	**–2**	**965**	**49.3**	**16:36**	**6**	**1**	**2**	**3**	**4**	**1**	**0**	**0**	**17:28**
	Russia	Olympics	5	0	0	0	2	....	....	....	....	....	....	....	....	....	....	....	....	....	....	....	....	....	....
2014-15	**Columbus**	**NHL**	**52**	**7**	**20**	**27**	**8**	**0**	**0**	**2**	**88**	**8.0**	**–6**	**229**	**44.5**	**16:23**	....	....	....	....	....	....	....	....	....

								Regular Season									Playoffs								
Season	Club	League	GP	G	A	Pts	PIM	PP	SH	GW	S	S%	+/-	TF	F%	Min	GP	G	A	Pts	PIM	PP	SH	GW	Min
2015-16	**Chicago**	**NHL**	**77**	**20**	**22**	**42**	**12**	**5**	**3**	**1**	**121**	**16.5**	**8**	**1148**	**44.2**	**18:05**	**7**	**3**	**0**	**3**	**2**	**1**	**0**	**0**	**17:44**
2016-17	**Chicago**	**NHL**	**64**	**22**	**23**	**45**	**30**	**4**	**0**	**7**	**105**	**21.0**	**9**	**922**	**45.1**	**17:51**	**4**	**0**	**0**	**0**	**0**	**0**	**0**	**0**	**17:22**
	NHL Totals		**553**	**128**	**151**	**279**	**168**	**21**	**6**	**23**	**991**	**12.9**		**5501**	**46.0**	**16:08**	**43**	**8**	**9**	**17**	**10**	**2**	**0**	**0**	**15:17**

Traded to **Columbus** by **NY Rangers** with Brandon Dubinsky, Tim Erixon and NY Rangers' 1st round pick (Kerby Rychel) in 2013 NHL Draft for Rick Nash, Steven Delisle and Columbus' 3rd round pick (Pavel Buchnevich) in 2013 NHL Draft, July 23, 2012. Signed as a free agent by **Yaroslavl** (KHL), September 20, 2012. Traded to **Chicago** by **Columbus** with Jeremy Morin, Corey Tropp, Marko Dano and Columbus' 4th round pick (later traded to NY Islanders – NY Islanders selected Anatoli Golyshev) in 2016 NHL Draft for Brandon Saad, Michael Paliotta and Alex Broadhurst, June 30, 2015.

ARCHIBALD, Darren

(ahr-CHIH-bawld, DAIR-ehn)

Right wing. Shoots left. 6'3", 210 lbs. Born, Newmarket, ON, February 9, 1990.

Season	Club	League	GP	G	A	Pts	PIM	PP	SH	GW	S	S%	+/-	TF	F%	Min	GP	G	A	Pts	PIM	PP	SH	GW	Min
2007-08	Stouffville Spirit	ON-Jr.A	49	21	27	48	46	....	....	....	....	....	....	....	....	....	15	9	9	18	35	....	....	....	....
2008-09	Barrie Colts	OHL	68	25	24	49	35	....	....	....	....	....	....	....	....	....	5	4	3	7	2	....	....	....	....
2009-10	Barrie Colts	OHL	57	26	33	59	62	....	....	....	....	....	....	....	....	....	16	5	5	10	16	....	....	....	....
2010-11	Barrie Colts	OHL	24	18	12	30	21	....	....	....	....	....	....	....	....	....	....	....	....	....	....	....	....	....	....
	Niagara Ice Dogs	OHL	37	23	13	36	30	....	....	....	....	....	....	....	....	....	14	10	4	14	6	....	....	....	....
2011-12	Chicago Wolves	AHL	20	1	0	1	10	....	....	....	....	....	....	....	....	....	....	....	....	....	....	....	....	....	....
	Kalamazoo Wings	ECHL	49	14	31	45	59	....	....	....	....	....	....	....	....	....	14	2	4	6	21	....	....	....	....
2012-13	Chicago Wolves	AHL	55	12	10	22	47	....	....	....	....	....	....	....	....	....	....	....	....	....	....	....	....	....	....
	Kalamazoo Wings	ECHL	18	6	7	13	29	....	....	....	....	....	....	....	....	....	....	....	....	....	....	....	....	....	....
2013-14	**Vancouver**	**NHL**	**16**	**1**	**2**	**3**	**0**	**0**	**0**	**0**	**11**	**9.1**	**1**	**1**	**0.0**	**7:48**	....	....	....	....	....	....	....	....	....
	Utica Comets	AHL	59	10	12	22	102	....	....	....	....	....	....	....	....	....	....	....	....	....	....	....	....	....	....
2014-15	Utica Comets	AHL	70	14	10	24	107	....	....	....	....	....	....	....	....	....	6	1	2	3	2	....	....	....	....
2015-16	Utica Comets	AHL	51	10	9	19	96	....	....	....	....	....	....	....	....	....	1	1	0	1	0	....	....	....	....
	Kalamazoo Wings	ECHL	6	2	0	2	0	....	....	....	....	....	....	....	....	....	....	....	....	....	....	....	....	....	....
2016-17	Utica Comets	AHL	76	23	24	47	58	....	....	....	....	....	....	....	....	....	....	....	....	....	....	....	....	....	....
	NHL Totals		**16**	**1**	**2**	**3**	**0**	**0**	**0**	**0**	**11**	**9.1**		**1**	**0.0**	**7:48**	....	....	....	....	....	....	....	....	....

Signed as a free agent by **Vancouver**, December 13, 2010.

ARCHIBALD, Josh

(AHR-chih-bawld, JAWSH) **PIT**

Wing. Shoots right. 5'10", 176 lbs. Born, Regina, SK, October 6, 1992. Pittsburgh's 4th pick, 174th overall, in 2011 NHL Draft.

Season	Club	League	GP	G	A	Pts	PIM	PP	SH	GW	S	S%	+/-	TF	F%	Min	GP	G	A	Pts	PIM	PP	SH	GW	Min
2009-10	Brainerd	High-MN	25	20	30	50	72	....	....	....	....	....	....	....	....	....	2	2	5	7	2	....	....	....	....
2010-11	Team North	UMHSEL	21	8	7	15	49	....	....	....	....	....	....	....	....	....	3	0	2	2	6	....	....	....	....
	Brainerd	High-MN	25	27	46	73	40	....	....	....	....	....	....	....	....	....	2	3	2	5	0	....	....	....	....
2011-12	Nebraska-Omaha	WCHA	36	10	5	15	33	....	....	....	....	....	....	....	....	....	....	....	....	....	....	....	....	....	....
2012-13	Nebraska-Omaha	WCHA	39	19	17	36	34	....	....	....	....	....	....	....	....	....	....	....	....	....	....	....	....	....	....
2013-14	Nebraska-Omaha	NCHC	37	*29	14	43	62	....	....	....	....	....	....	....	....	....	....	....	....	....	....	....	....	....	....
	Wilkes-Barre	AHL	7	1	0	1	13	....	....	....	....	....	....	....	....	....	2	1	0	1	0	....	....	....	....
2014-15	Wilkes-Barre	AHL	45	5	8	13	24	....	....	....	....	....	....	....	....	....	3	0	1	1	0	....	....	....	....
	Wheeling Nailers	ECHL	9	7	4	11	4	....	....	....	....	....	....	....	....	....	....	....	....	....	....	....	....	....	....
2015-16	**Pittsburgh**	**NHL**	**1**	**0**	**0**	**0**	**0**	**0**	**0**	**0**	**0**	**0.0**	**0**	**0**	**0.0**	**5:02**	....	....	....	....	....	....	....	....	....
	Wilkes-Barre	AHL	69	9	9	18	75	....	....	....	....	....	....	....	....	....	10	1	0	1	10	....	....	....	....
2016-17	**Pittsburgh**	**NHL**	**10**	**3**	**0**	**3**	**4**	**0**	**1**	**0**	**11**	**27.3**	**3**	**1**	**0.0**	**10:52**	**4**	**0**	**0**	**0**	**2**	**0**	**0**	**0**	**7:51**
	Wilkes-Barre	AHL	61	16	13	29	54	....	....	....	....	....	....	....	....	....	5	2	0	2	16	....	....	....	....
	NHL Totals		**11**	**3**	**0**	**3**	**4**	**0**	**1**	**0**	**11**	**27.3**		**1**	**0.0**	**10:20**	**4**	**0**	**0**	**0**	**2**	**0**	**0**	**0**	**7:51**

NCHC First All-Star Team (2014) • NCHC Player of the Year (2014) • NCAA West First All-American Team (2014)

ARCOBELLO, Mark

(ahr-koh-BEHL-oh, MAHRK)

Right wing. Shoots right. 5'8", 174 lbs. Born, Milford, CT, August 12, 1988.

Season	Club	League	GP	G	A	Pts	PIM	PP	SH	GW	S	S%	+/-	TF	F%	Min	GP	G	A	Pts	PIM	PP	SH	GW	Min
2005-06	Salisbury School	High-CT	....	26	21	47	....	....	....	....	....	....	....	....	....	....	....	....	....	....	....	....	....	....	....
2006-07	Yale	ECAC	29	10	14	24	49	....	....	....	....	....	....	....	....	....	....	....	....	....	....	....	....	....	....
2007-08	Yale	ECAC	34	7	14	21	40	....	....	....	....	....	....	....	....	....	....	....	....	....	....	....	....	....	....
2008-09	Yale	ECAC	34	17	18	35	68	....	....	....	....	....	....	....	....	....	....	....	....	....	....	....	....	....	....
2009-10	Yale	ECAC	34	15	21	36	46	....	....	....	....	....	....	....	....	....	....	....	....	....	....	....	....	....	....
2010-11	Stockton Thunder	ECHL	33	7	13	20	10	....	....	....	....	....	....	....	....	....	....	....	....	....	....	....	....	....	....
	Oklahoma City	AHL	26	11	11	22	4	....	....	....	....	....	....	....	....	....	6	1	1	2	0	....	....	....	....
2011-12	Oklahoma City	AHL	73	17	26	43	28	....	....	....	....	....	....	....	....	....	14	5	8	13	6	....	....	....	....
2012-13	Oklahoma City	AHL	74	22	46	68	48	....	....	....	....	....	....	....	....	....	17	12	8	20	14	....	....	....	....
	Edmonton	**NHL**	**1**	**0**	**0**	**0**	**0**	**0**	**0**	**0**	**0**	**0.0**	**0**	**10**	**30.0**	**18:15**	....	....	....	....	....	....	....	....	....
2013-14	**Edmonton**	**NHL**	**41**	**4**	**14**	**18**	**8**	**1**	**0**	**1**	**70**	**5.7**	**–7**	**404**	**51.0**	**15:04**	....	....	....	....	....	....	....	....	....
	Oklahoma City	AHL	15	10	18	28	6	....	....	....	....	....	....	....	....	....	....	....	....	....	....	....	....	....	....
2014-15	**Edmonton**	**NHL**	**36**	**7**	**5**	**12**	**12**	**0**	**0**	**0**	**54**	**13.0**	**–7**	**526**	**47.9**	**15:23**	....	....	....	....	....	....	....	....	....
	Nashville	**NHL**	**4**	**1**	**0**	**1**	**0**	**0**	**0**	**0**	**3**	**33.3**	**0**	**3**	**66.7**	**10:35**	....	....	....	....	....	....	....	....	....
	Pittsburgh	**NHL**	**10**	**0**	**2**	**2**	**2**	**0**	**0**	**0**	**13**	**0.0**	**1**	**7**	**28.6**	**12:05**	....	....	....	....	....	....	....	....	....
	Arizona	**NHL**	**27**	**9**	**7**	**16**	**6**	**1**	**0**	**2**	**59**	**15.3**	**–4**	**403**	**53.4**	**15:41**	....	....	....	....	....	....	....	....	....
2015-16	**Toronto**	**NHL**	**20**	**3**	**1**	**4**	**0**	**0**	**0**	**0**	**43**	**7.0**	**0**	**242**	**54.6**	**12:41**	....	....	....	....	....	....	....	....	....
	Toronto Marlies	AHL	49	25	34	59	22	....	....	....	....	....	....	....	....	....	15	2	9	11	2	....	....	....	....
2016-17	SC Bern	Swiss	50	25	30	55	30	....	....	....	....	....	....	....	....	....	16	8	*12	*20	12	....	....	....	....
	NHL Totals		**139**	**24**	**29**	**53**	**28**	**2**	**0**	**3**	**242**	**9.9**		**1595**	**50.9**	**14:36**	....	....	....	....	....	....	....	....	....

ECAC First All-Star Team (2009) • NCAA East Second All-American Team (2009)

Signed as a free agent by **Oklahoma City** (AHL), September 27, 2010. • Re-assigned to **Stockton** (ECHL) by **Oklahoma City** (AHL), October 13, 2010. Signed as a free agent by **Edmonton**, April 1, 2011. Traded to **Nashville** by **Edmonton** for Derek Roy, December 29, 2014. Claimed on waivers by **Pittsburgh** from **Nashville**, January 14, 2015. Claimed on waivers by **Arizona** from **Pittsburgh**, February 11, 2015. Signed as a free agent by **Toronto**, July 1, 2015. Signed as a free agent by **Bern** (Swiss), May 30, 2016.

ARMIA, Joel

(ahr-MEE-uh, JOHL) **WPG**

Right wing. Shoots right. 6'3", 205 lbs. Born, Pori, Finland, May 31, 1993. Buffalo's 1st pick, 16th overall, in 2011 NHL Draft.

Season	Club	League	GP	G	A	Pts	PIM	PP	SH	GW	S	S%	+/-	TF	F%	Min	GP	G	A	Pts	PIM	PP	SH	GW	Min
2008-09	Assat Pori U18	Fin-U18	8	3	1	4	2	....	....	....	....	....	....	....	....	....	....	....	....	....	....	....	....	....	....
2009-10	Assat Pori U18	Fin-U18	9	7	9	16	31	....	....	....	....	....	....	....	....	....	6	6	3	9	8	....	....	....	....
	Assat Pori Jr.	Fin-Jr.	27	15	6	21	32	....	....	....	....	....	....	....	....	....	5	1	1	2	0	....	....	....	....
2010-11	Suomi U20	Finland-2	4	0	3	3	6	....	....	....	....	....	....	....	....	....	....	....	....	....	....	....	....	....	....
	Assat Pori	Finland	48	18	11	29	24	....	....	....	....	....	....	....	....	....	5	2	0	2	4	....	....	....	....
2011-12	Assat Pori	Finland	54	18	20	38	64	....	....	....	....	....	....	....	....	....	3	0	2	2	0	....	....	....	....
2012-13	Assat Pori	Finland	47	19	14	33	32	....	....	....	....	....	....	....	....	....	16	3	5	8	20	....	....	....	....
2013-14	Rochester	AHL	54	7	20	27	30	....	....	....	....	....	....	....	....	....	5	3	3	6	9	....	....	....	....
2014-15	**Buffalo**	**NHL**	**1**	**0**	**0**	**0**	**0**	**0**	**0**	**0**	**0**	**0.0**	**0**	**0**	**0.0**	**14:47**	....	....	....	....	....	....	....	....	....
	Rochester	AHL	33	10	15	25	39	....	....	....	....	....	....	....	....	....	....	....	....	....	....	....	....	....	....
	St. John's IceCaps	AHL	21	2	6	8	22	....	....	....	....	....	....	....	....	....	....	....	....	....	....	....	....	....	....
2015-16	**Winnipeg**	**NHL**	**43**	**4**	**6**	**10**	**12**	**0**	**0**	**1**	**52**	**7.7**	**2**	**2**	**0.0**	**12:10**	....	....	....	....	....	....	....	....	....
	Manitoba Moose	AHL	18	3	5	8	16	....	....	....	....	....	....	....	....	....	....	....	....	....	....	....	....	....	....
2016-17	**Winnipeg**	**NHL**	**57**	**10**	**9**	**19**	**20**	**0**	**4**	**1**	**111**	**9.0**	**–8**	**7**	**42.9**	**15:08**	....	....	....	....	....	....	....	....	....
	NHL Totals		**101**	**14**	**15**	**29**	**32**	**0**	**4**	**2**	**163**	**8.6**		**9**	**33.3**	**13:52**	....	....	....	....	....	....	....	....	....

Traded to **Winnipeg** by **Buffalo** with Tyler Myers, Drew Stafford, Brendan Lemieux and St. Louis' 1st round pick (previously acquired, Winnipeg selected Jack Roscovic) in 2015 NHL Draft for Evander Kane, Zach Bogosian and Jason Kasdorf, February 11, 2015.

ARVIDSSON, Viktor

(AHR-vihd-suhn, VIHK-tuhr) **NSH**

Right wing. Shoots right. 5'9", 180 lbs. Born, Skelleftea, Sweden, April 8, 1993. Nashville's 5th pick, 112th overall, in 2014 NHL Draft.

Season	Club	League	GP	G	A	Pts	PIM	PP	SH	GW	S	S%	+/-	TF	F%	Min	GP	G	A	Pts	PIM	PP	SH	GW	Min
2008-09	Skelleftea AIK U18	Swe-U18	14	7	7	14	16	....	....	....	....	....	....	....	....	....	5	1	2	3	4	....	....	....	....
2009-10	Skelleftea AIK U18	Swe-U18	40	52	48	100	60	....	....	....	....	....	....	....	....	....	3	1	1	2	0	....	....	....	....
	Skelleftea AIK Jr.	Swe-Jr.	2	0	1	1	2	....	....	....	....	....	....	....	....	....	2	1	0	1	0	....	....	....	....
2010-11	Skelleftea AIK U18	Swe-U18	4	7	7	14	18	....	....	....	....	....	....	....	....	....	7	4	6	10	4	....	....	....	....
	Skelleftea AIK Jr.	Swe-Jr.	40	15	19	34	51	....	....	....	....	....	....	....	....	....	5	3	3	6	4	....	....	....	....
	Skelleftea AIK	Sweden	3	0	0	0	0	....	....	....	....	....	....	....	....	....	....	....	....	....	....	....	....	....	....
2011-12	Skelleftea AIK Jr.	Swe-Jr.	43	25	17	42	18	....	....	....	....	....	....	....	....	....	3	0	0	0	0	....	....	....	....
	Skelleftea AIK	Sweden	4	0	0	0	0	....	....	....	....	....	....	....	....	....	....	....	....	....	....	....	....	....	....

			Regular Season														Playoffs								
Season	Club	League	GP	G	A	Pts	PIM	PP	SH	GW	S	S%	+/-	TF	F%	Min	GP	G	A	Pts	PIM	PP	SH	GW	Min
2012-13	Skelleftea AIK Jr.	Swe-Jr.	4	3	1	4	0	....	....	....	....	....	....	....	....	....	....	....	....	....	....	....	....	....	....
	Skelleftea AIK	Sweden	49	7	5	12	12	....	....	....	....	....	....	....	....	....	13	6	2	8	2	....	....	....	....
2013-14	Skelleftea AIK	Sweden	50	16	24	40	59	....	....	....	....	....	....	....	....	....	14	4	12	16	4	....	....	....	....
2014-15	**Nashville**	**NHL**	**6**	**0**	**0**	**0**	**0**	**0**	**0**	**0**	**9**	**0.0**	**0**	**0**	**0.0**	**10:15**	....	....	....	....	....	....	....	....	....
	Milwaukee	AHL	70	22	33	55	43	....	....	....	....	....	....	....	....	....	....	....	....	....	....	....	....	....	....
2015-16	**Nashville**	**NHL**	**56**	**8**	**8**	**16**	**35**	**1**	**0**	**3**	**139**	**5.8**	**–8**	**0**	**0.0**	**12:24**	**14**	**1**	**1**	**2**	**8**	**0**	**0**	**1**	**13:30**
	Milwaukee	AHL	17	8	10	18	6	....	....	....	....	....	....	....	....	....	....	....	....	....	....	....	....	....	....
2016-17	**Nashville**	**NHL**	**80**	**31**	**30**	**61**	**28**	**4**	***5**	**6**	**246**	**12.6**	**16**	**16**	**25.0**	**17:09**	**22**	**3**	**10**	**13**	**19**	**0**	**0**	**1**	**18:39**
	NHL Totals		**142**	**39**	**38**	**77**	**63**	**5**	**5**	**9**	**394**	**9.9**		**16**	**25.0**	**14:59**	**36**	**4**	**11**	**15**	**27**	**0**	**0**	**2**	**16:39**

AHL All-Rookie Team (2015)

ATHANASIOU, Andreas (ath-ah-nah-SEE-yew, an-DRAY-uhs) DET

Center/Left wing. Shoots left. 6'2", 192 lbs. Born, London, ON, August 6, 1994. Detroit's 3rd pick, 110th overall, in 2012 NHL Draft.

Season	Club	League	GP	G	A	Pts	PIM	PP	SH	GW	S	S%	+/-	TF	F%	Min	GP	G	A	Pts	PIM	PP	SH	GW	Min
2009-10	Toronto Titans	GTHL	56	24	34	58	32	....	....	....	....	....	....	....	....	....	....	....	....	....	....	....	....	....	....
2010-11	London Knights	OHL	57	11	11	22	21	....	....	....	....	....	....	....	....	....	6	0	0	0	0	....	....	....	....
2011-12	London Knights	OHL	63	22	15	37	22	....	....	....	....	....	....	....	....	....	11	1	4	5	0	....	....	....	....
2012-13	Barrie Colts	OHL	66	29	38	67	30	....	....	....	....	....	....	....	....	....	22	12	13	25	11	....	....	....	....
2013-14	Barrie Colts	OHL	66	49	46	95	52	....	....	....	....	....	....	....	....	....	11	3	9	12	2	....	....	....	....
	Grand Rapids	AHL	2	1	2	3	0	....	....	....	....	....	....	....	....	....	6	0	1	1	6	....	....	....	....
2014-15	Grand Rapids	AHL	55	16	16	32	25	....	....	....	....	....	....	....	....	....	16	5	4	9	6	....	....	....	....
2015-16	**Detroit**	**NHL**	**37**	**9**	**5**	**14**	**5**	**0**	**1**	**1**	**53**	**17.0**	**1**	**129**	**41.1**	**9:01**	**5**	**1**	**0**	**1**	**0**	**0**	**0**	**1**	**8:40**
	Grand Rapids	AHL	26	8	8	16	9	....	....	....	....	....	....	....	....	....	6	2	3	5	2	....	....	....	....
2016-17	**Detroit**	**NHL**	**64**	**18**	**11**	**29**	**28**	**1**	**0**	**3**	**120**	**15.0**	**–7**	**83**	**44.6**	**13:28**	....	....	....	....	....	....	....	....	....
	NHL Totals		**101**	**27**	**16**	**43**	**33**	**1**	**1**	**4**	**173**	**15.6**		**212**	**42.5**	**11:50**	**5**	**1**	**0**	**1**	**0**	**0**	**0**	**1**	**8:40**

ATKINSON, Cam (AT-kihn-suhn, KAM) CBJ

Right wing. Shoots right. 5'8", 180 lbs. Born, Riverside, CT, June 5, 1989. Columbus' 8th pick, 157th overall, in 2008 NHL Draft.

Season	Club	League	GP	G	A	Pts	PIM	PP	SH	GW	S	S%	+/-	TF	F%	Min	GP	G	A	Pts	PIM	PP	SH	GW	Min
2005-06	Avon Old Farms	High-CT	25	15	20	35	16	....	....	....	....	....	....	....	....	....	....	....	....	....	....	....	....	....	....
2006-07	Avon Old Farms	High-CT	27	28	24	52	12	....	....	....	....	....	....	....	....	....	....	....	....	....	....	....	....	....	....
2007-08	Avon Old Farms	High-CT	28	26	37	63	10	....	....	....	....	....	....	....	....	....	....	....	....	....	....	....	....	....	....
2008-09	Boston College	H-East	36	7	12	19	28	....	....	....	....	....	....	....	....	....	....	....	....	....	....	....	....	....	....
2009-10	Boston College	H-East	42	*30	23	53	30	....	....	....	....	....	....	....	....	....	....	....	....	....	....	....	....	....	....
2010-11	Boston College	H-East	39	*31	21	*52	28	....	....	....	....	....	....	....	....	....	....	....	....	....	....	....	....	....	....
	Springfield	AHL	5	3	2	5	0	....	....	....	....	....	....	....	....	....	....	....	....	....	....	....	....	....	....
2011-12	**Columbus**	**NHL**	**27**	**7**	**7**	**14**	**14**	**1**	**0**	**0**	**66**	**10.6**	**1**	**1**	**0.0**	**15:23**	....	....	....	....	....	....	....	....	....
	Springfield	AHL	51	29	15	44	31	....	....	....	....	....	....	....	....	....	....	....	....	....	....	....	....	....	....
2012-13	Springfield	AHL	33	17	21	38	14	....	....	....	....	....	....	....	....	....	....	....	....	....	....	....	....	....	....
	Columbus	**NHL**	**35**	**9**	**9**	**18**	**4**	**1**	**0**	**1**	**91**	**9.9**	**9**	**0**	**0.0**	**15:35**	....	....	....	....	....	....	....	....	....
2013-14	**Columbus**	**NHL**	**79**	**21**	**19**	**40**	**18**	**4**	**1**	**5**	**216**	**9.7**	**–4**	**0**	**0.0**	**15:47**	**6**	**1**	**2**	**3**	**0**	**0**	**0**	**0**	**16:45**
2014-15	**Columbus**	**NHL**	**78**	**22**	**18**	**40**	**22**	**7**	**1**	**7**	**212**	**10.4**	**–2**	**9**	**44.4**	**16:59**	....	....	....	....	....	....	....	....	....
2015-16	**Columbus**	**NHL**	**81**	**27**	**26**	**53**	**22**	**4**	**2**	**3**	**226**	**11.9**	**–8**	**4**	**50.0**	**17:48**	....	....	....	....	....	....	....	....	....
2016-17	**Columbus**	**NHL**	**82**	**35**	**27**	**62**	**22**	**10**	**3**	**9**	**240**	**14.6**	**13**	**3**	**66.7**	**18:05**	**5**	**2**	**1**	**3**	**0**	**0**	**0**	**0**	**19:35**
	NHL Totals		**382**	**121**	**106**	**227**	**102**	**27**	**7**	**25**	**1051**	**11.5**		**17**	**47.1**	**16:54**	**11**	**3**	**3**	**6**	**0**	**0**	**0**	**0**	**18:02**

Hockey East Second All-Star Team (2010) • NCAA Championship All-Tournament Team (2010) • Hockey East First All-Star Team (2011) • NCAA East First All-American Team (2011)
Played in NHL All-Star Game (2017)

AULIE, Keith (AW-lee, KEETH)

Defense. Shoots left. 6'6", 228 lbs. Born, Rouleau, SK, June 11, 1989. Calgary's 3rd pick, 116th overall, in 2007 NHL Draft.

Season	Club	League	GP	G	A	Pts	PIM	PP	SH	GW	S	S%	+/-	TF	F%	Min	GP	G	A	Pts	PIM	PP	SH	GW	Min
2004-05	Notre Dame	SMHL	38	2	7	9	53	....	....	....	....	....	....	....	....	....	....	....	....	....	....	....	....	....	....
2005-06	Brandon	WHL	38	0	2	2	32	....	....	....	....	....	....	....	....	....	4	0	0	0	4	....	....	....	....
2006-07	Brandon	WHL	66	1	8	9	82	....	....	....	....	....	....	....	....	....	11	0	2	2	14	....	....	....	....
2007-08	Brandon	WHL	72	5	12	17	81	....	....	....	....	....	....	....	....	....	6	0	3	3	11	....	....	....	....
2008-09	Brandon	WHL	58	6	27	33	83	....	....	....	....	....	....	....	....	....	12	2	7	9	12	....	....	....	....
2009-10	Abbotsford Heat	AHL	43	2	4	6	32	....	....	....	....	....	....	....	....	....	....	....	....	....	....	....	....	....	....
	Toronto Marlies	AHL	5	0	0	0	6	....	....	....	....	....	....	....	....	....	....	....	....	....	....	....	....	....	....
2010-11	**Toronto**	**NHL**	**40**	**2**	**0**	**2**	**32**	**0**	**0**	**0**	**32**	**6.3**	**–1**	**0**	**0.0**	**19:08**	....	....	....	....	....	....	....	....	....
	Toronto Marlies	AHL	36	3	6	9	61	....	....	....	....	....	....	....	....	....	....	....	....	....	....	....	....	....	....
2011-12	**Toronto**	**NHL**	**17**	**0**	**2**	**2**	**16**	**0**	**0**	**0**	**14**	**0.0**	**–2**	**0**	**0.0**	**16:07**	....	....	....	....	....	....	....	....	....
	Toronto Marlies	AHL	23	0	1	1	30	....	....	....	....	....	....	....	....	....	....	....	....	....	....	....	....	....	....
	Tampa Bay	**NHL**	**19**	**0**	**1**	**1**	**13**	**0**	**0**	**0**	**4**	**0.0**	**–5**	**0**	**0.0**	**11:02**	....	....	....	....	....	....	....	....	....
	Norfolk Admirals	AHL	3	0	2	2	0	....	....	....	....	....	....	....	....	....	18	1	5	6	10	....	....	....	....
2012-13	Syracuse Crunch	AHL	20	3	3	6	34	....	....	....	....	....	....	....	....	....	....	....	....	....	....	....	....	....	....
	Tampa Bay	**NHL**	**45**	**2**	**5**	**7**	**60**	**0**	**0**	**0**	**37**	**5.4**	**1**	**0**	**0.0**	**12:49**	....	....	....	....	....	....	....	....	....
2013-14	**Tampa Bay**	**NHL**	**15**	**0**	**1**	**1**	**9**	**0**	**0**	**0**	**6**	**0.0**	**–3**	**0**	**0.0**	**9:49**	**1**	**0**	**0**	**0**	**0**	**0**	**0**	**0**	**12:22**
2014-15	**Edmonton**	**NHL**	**31**	**0**	**1**	**1**	**66**	**0**	**0**	**0**	**25**	**0.0**	**–3**	**0**	**0.0**	**14:18**	....	....	....	....	....	....	....	....	....
	Oklahoma City	AHL	8	0	1	1	0	....	....	....	....	....	....	....	....	....	....	....	....	....	....	....	....	....	....
2015-16	Springfield	AHL	7	1	0	1	11	....	....	....	....	....	....	....	....	....	....	....	....	....	....	....	....	....	....
	HIFK Helsinki	Finland	23	1	4	5	12	....	....	....	....	....	....	....	....	....	17	1	1	2	4	....	....	....	....
2016-17	Cleveland	AHL	3	0	0	0	2	....	....	....	....	....	....	....	....	....	....	....	....	....	....	....	....	....	....
	Stockton Heat	AHL	54	2	5	7	90	....	....	....	....	....	....	....	....	....	2	0	0	0	0	....	....	....	....
	NHL Totals		**167**	**4**	**10**	**14**	**196**	**0**	**0**	**0**	**118**	**3.4**		**0**	**0.0**	**14:28**	**1**	**0**	**0**	**0**	**0**	**0**	**0**	**0**	**12:22**

WHL East First All-Star Team (2009)

Traded to **Toronto** by **Calgary** with Dion Phaneuf and Fredrik Sjostrom for Matt Stajan, Niklas Hagman, Jamal Mayers and Ian White, January 31, 2010. Traded to **Tampa Bay** by **Toronto** for Carter Ashton, February 27, 2012. • Missed majority of 2013-14 due to hand injury vs. Ottawa, December 5, 2013 and as a healthy reserve. Signed as a free agent by **Edmonton**, July 1, 2014. • Missed majority of 2014-15 as a healthy reserve. Signed to a PTO (professional tryout) contact by **Arizona**, September 9, 2015. Signed as a free agent by **HIFK Helsinki** (Finland), January 3, 2016. Signed as a free agent by **Cleveland** (AHL), October 18, 2016. Signed as a free agent by **Stockton** (AHL), November 3, 2016.

AUSTIN, Brady (AWZ-tihn, BRAY-dee)

Defense. Shoots left. 6'3", 227 lbs. Born, Bobcaygeon, ON, June 16, 1993. Buffalo's 7th pick, 193rd overall, in 2012 NHL Draft.

Season	Club	League	GP	G	A	Pts	PIM	PP	SH	GW	S	S%	+/-	TF	F%	Min	GP	G	A	Pts	PIM	PP	SH	GW	Min
2008-09	Cent. Ont. Wolves	Minor-ON	60	25	27	52	72	....	....	....	....	....	....	....	....	....	....	....	....	....	....	....	....	....	....
2009-10	Erie Otters	OHL	64	5	10	15	24	....	....	....	....	....	....	....	....	....	4	0	0	0	0	....	....	....	....
2010-11	Erie Otters	OHL	59	1	12	13	47	....	....	....	....	....	....	....	....	....	7	0	0	0	0	....	....	....	....
2011-12	Belleville Bulls	OHL	68	6	20	26	59	....	....	....	....	....	....	....	....	....	6	1	0	1	0	....	....	....	....
2012-13	Belleville Bulls	OHL	64	8	15	23	22	....	....	....	....	....	....	....	....	....	17	0	5	5	6	....	....	....	....
2013-14	Belleville Bulls	OHL	7	1	4	5	6	....	....	....	....	....	....	....	....	....	....	....	....	....	....	....	....	....	....
	London Knights	OHL	60	8	20	28	36	....	....	....	....	....	....	....	....	....	4	1	2	3	2	....	....	....	....
2014-15	Rochester	AHL	66	1	9	10	31	....	....	....	....	....	....	....	....	....	....	....	....	....	....	....	....	....	....
	Elmira Jackals	ECHL	1	0	0	0	0	....	....	....	....	....	....	....	....	....	....	....	....	....	....	....	....	....	....
2015-16	Rochester	AHL	72	2	9	11	37	....	....	....	....	....	....	....	....	....	....	....	....	....	....	....	....	....	....
2016-17	**Buffalo**	**NHL**	**5**	**0**	**0**	**0**	**4**	**0**	**0**	**0**	**8**	**0.0**	**0**	**0**	**0.0**	**16:05**	....	....	....	....	....	....	....	....	....
	Rochester	AHL	72	4	8	12	59	....	....	....	....	....	....	....	....	....	....	....	....	....	....	....	....	....	....
	NHL Totals		**5**	**0**	**0**	**0**	**4**	**0**	**0**	**0**	**8**	**0.0**		**0**	**0.0**	**16:05**	....	....	....	....	....	....	....	....	....

AUVITU, Yohann (oh-VEE-too, YOH-han) EDM

Defense. Shoots left. 5'11", 191 lbs. Born, Ivry-sur-Seine, France, July 27, 1989.

Season	Club	League	GP	G	A	Pts	PIM	PP	SH	GW	S	S%	+/-	TF	F%	Min	GP	G	A	Pts	PIM	PP	SH	GW	Min
2010-11	JYP Jyvaskyla	Finland	7	0	0	0	0	....	....	....	....	....	....	....	....	....	....	....	....	....	....	....	....	....	....
2011-12	JYP Jyvaskyla	Finland	33	1	1	2	8	....	....	....	....	....	....	....	....	....	11	1	0	1	6	....	....	....	....
2012-13	JYP Jyvaskyla	Finland	44	3	9	12	18	....	....	....	....	....	....	....	....	....	10	1	1	2	8	....	....	....	....
2013-14	JYP Jyvaskyla	Finland	29	1	5	6	8	....	....	....	....	....	....	....	....	....	6	2	1	3	2	....	....	....	....
2014-15	HIFK Helsinki	Finland	55	8	8	16	10	....	....	....	....	....	....	....	....	....	8	3	2	5	2	....	....	....	....
2015-16	HIFK Helsinki	Finland	48	6	15	21	6	....	....	....	....	....	....	....	....	....	18	6	7	13	14	....	....	....	....

			Regular Season														Playoffs								
Season	Club	League	GP	G	A	Pts	PIM	PP	SH	GW	S	S%	+/-	TF	F%	Min	GP	G	A	Pts	PIM	PP	SH	GW	Min
2016-17	**New Jersey**	**NHL**	**25**	**2**	**2**	**4**	**2**	**0**	**0**	**0**	**54**	**3.7**	**1**	**0**	**0.0**	**15:36**	....	....	....	....	....	....	....	....	....
	Albany Devils	AHL	29	5	8	13	2	....	....	....	....	....	....	....	....	....	....	....	....	....	....	....	....	....	....
	NHL Totals		**25**	**2**	**2**	**4**	**2**	**0**	**0**	**0**	**54**	**3.7**		**0**	**0.0**	**15:36**	....	....	....	....	....	....	....	....	....

Signed as a free agent by **New Jersey**, May 27, 2016. Signed as a free agent by **Edmonton**, July 10, 2017.

BACKES, David
(BA-kuhs, DAY-vihd) **BOS**

Center. Shoots right. 6'3", 221 lbs. Born, Blaine, MN, May 1, 1984. St. Louis' 2nd pick, 62nd overall, in 2003 NHL Draft.

Season	Club	League	GP	G	A	Pts	PIM	PP	SH	GW	S	S%	+/-	TF	F%	Min	GP	G	A	Pts	PIM	PP	SH	GW	Min
99-2000	Spring Lake Park	High-MN	24	17	20	37	....	....	....	....	....	....	....	....	....	....	....	....	....	....	....	....	....	....	....
2000-01	Spring Lake Park	High-MN	24	29	46	75	....	....	....	....	....	....	....	....	....	....	....	....	....	....	....	....	....	....	....
2001-02	Spring Lake Park	High-MN	25	31	36	67	....	....	....	....	....	....	....	....	....	....	2	1	1	2	....	....	....	....	....
	Lincoln Stars	USHL	30	11	10	21	54	....	....	....	....	....	....	....	....	....	3	0	0	0	2	....	....	....	....
2002-03	Lincoln Stars	USHL	57	28	41	69	126	....	....	....	....	....	....	....	....	....	7	4	1	5	17	....	....	....	....
2003-04	Minnesota State	WCHA	39	16	21	37	66	....	....	....	....	....	....	....	....	....	....	....	....	....	....	....	....	....	....
2004-05	Minnesota State	WCHA	38	17	23	40	55	....	....	....	....	....	....	....	....	....	....	....	....	....	....	....	....	....	....
2005-06	Minnesota State	WCHA	38	13	29	42	91	....	....	....	....	....	....	....	....	....	....	....	....	....	....	....	....	....	....
	Peoria Rivermen	AHL	12	5	5	10	10	....	....	....	....	....	....	....	....	....	3	1	1	2	8	....	....	....	....
2006-07	**St. Louis**	**NHL**	**49**	**10**	**13**	**23**	**37**	**2**	**0**	**2**	**89**	**11.2**	**6**	**26**	**46.2**	**13:25**	....	....	....	....	....	....	....	....	....
	Peoria Rivermen	AHL	31	10	3	13	47	....	....	....	....	....	....	....	....	....	....	....	....	....	....	....	....	....	....
2007-08	**St. Louis**	**NHL**	**72**	**13**	**18**	**31**	**99**	**3**	**0**	**2**	**129**	**10.1**	**-11**	**67**	**44.8**	**14:41**	....	....	....	....	....	....	....	....	....
2008-09	**St. Louis**	**NHL**	**82**	**31**	**23**	**54**	**165**	**6**	**2**	**1**	**208**	**14.9**	**-3**	**477**	**44.4**	**17:41**	**4**	**1**	**2**	**3**	**10**	**0**	**0**	**0**	**22:56**
2009-10	**St. Louis**	**NHL**	**79**	**17**	**31**	**48**	**106**	**5**	**0**	**3**	**163**	**10.4**	**-4**	**1065**	**47.3**	**18:18**	....	....	....	....	....	....	....	....	....
	United States	Olympics	6	1	2	3	2	....	....	....	....	....	....	....	....	....	....	....	....	....	....	....	....	....	....
2010-11	**St. Louis**	**NHL**	**82**	**31**	**31**	**62**	**93**	**5**	**0**	**2**	**211**	**14.7**	**32**	**1138**	**44.5**	**19:42**	....	....	....	....	....	....	....	....	....
2011-12	**St. Louis**	**NHL**	**82**	**24**	**30**	**54**	**101**	**8**	**2**	**4**	**234**	**10.3**	**15**	**1353**	**48.6**	**20:00**	**9**	**2**	**2**	**4**	**18**	**0**	**0**	**0**	**20:19**
2012-13	**St. Louis**	**NHL**	**48**	**6**	**22**	**28**	**62**	**1**	**0**	**1**	**100**	**6.0**	**5**	**912**	**52.3**	**19:37**	**6**	**1**	**2**	**3**	**0**	**0**	**0**	**0**	**20:32**
2013-14	**St. Louis**	**NHL**	**74**	**27**	**30**	**57**	**119**	**10**	**0**	**5**	**165**	**16.4**	**14**	**1201**	**51.7**	**19:33**	**4**	**0**	**1**	**1**	**2**	**0**	**0**	**0**	**23:26**
	United States	Olympics	6	3	1	4	6	....	....	....	....	....	....	....	....	....	....	....	....	....	....	....	....	....	....
2014-15	**St. Louis**	**NHL**	**80**	**26**	**32**	**58**	**104**	**10**	**0**	**3**	**183**	**14.2**	**7**	**1130**	**54.6**	**18:38**	**6**	**1**	**1**	**2**	**2**	**0**	**0**	**0**	**19:06**
2015-16	**St. Louis**	**NHL**	**79**	**21**	**24**	**45**	**83**	**8**	**0**	**3**	**168**	**12.5**	**4**	**1192**	**52.0**	**19:14**	**20**	**7**	**7**	**14**	**8**	**3**	**0**	**3**	**18:40**
2016-17	**Boston**	**NHL**	**74**	**17**	**21**	**38**	**69**	**2**	**0**	**2**	**175**	**9.7**	**2**	**123**	**48.8**	**17:07**	**6**	**1**	**3**	**4**	**2**	**0**	**0**	**0**	**17:41**
	NHL Totals		**801**	**223**	**275**	**498**	**1038**	**60**	**4**	**28**	**1825**	**12.2**		**8684**	**49.7**	**18:08**	**55**	**13**	**18**	**31**	**42**	**3**	**0**	**3**	**19:44**

USHL First All-Star Team (2003) • WCHA All-Rookie Team (2004) • WCHA Second All-Star Team (2006) • NCAA West Second All-American Team (2006)

Played in NHL All-Star Game (2011)

Signed as a free agent by **Boston**, July 1, 2016.

BACKLUND, Mikael
(BAHK-luhnd, mih-KIGH-ehl) **CGY**

Center. Shoots left. 6'1", 199 lbs. Born, Vasteras, Sweden, March 17, 1989. Calgary's 1st pick, 24th overall, in 2007 NHL Draft.

Season	Club	League	GP	G	A	Pts	PIM	PP	SH	GW	S	S%	+/-	TF	F%	Min	GP	G	A	Pts	PIM	PP	SH	GW	Min
2004-05	Vasteras U18	Swe-U18	14	5	6	11	14	....	....	....	....	....	....	....	....	....	4	2	1	3	2	....	....	....	....
2005-06	Vasteras Jr.	Swe-Jr.	25	15	16	31	30	....	....	....	....	....	....	....	....	....	....	....	....	....	....	....	....	....	....
	VIK Vasteras HK	Sweden-2	12	2	2	4	14	....	....	....	....	....	....	....	....	....	....	....	....	....	....	....	....	....	....
2006-07	Vasteras U18	Swe-U18	2	2	1	3	2	....	....	....	....	....	....	....	....	....	1	0	0	0	10	....	....	....	....
	Vasteras Jr.	Swe-Jr.	7	5	4	9	8	....	....	....	....	....	....	....	....	....	5	1	0	1	4	....	....	....	....
	VIK Vasteras HK	Sweden-2	18	1	2	3	14	....	....	....	....	....	....	....	....	....	....	....	....	....	....	....	....	....	....
2007-08	Vasteras Jr.	Swe-Jr.	9	7	6	13	20	....	....	....	....	....	....	....	....	....	....	....	....	....	....	....	....	....	....
	VIK Vasteras HK	Sweden-2	46	11	4	15	28	....	....	....	....	....	....	....	....	....	5	4	3	7	0	....	....	....	....
2008-09	Vasteras Jr.	Swe-Jr.	2	3	2	5	0	....	....	....	....	....	....	....	....	....	....	....	....	....	....	....	....	....	....
	VIK Vasteras HK	Sweden-2	17	4	4	8	39	....	....	....	....	....	....	....	....	....	....	....	....	....	....	....	....	....	....
	Calgary	**NHL**	**1**	**0**	**0**	**0**	**0**	**0**	**0**	**0**	**1**	**0.0**	**0**	**7**	**28.6**	**10:44**	....	....	....	....	....	....	....	....	....
	Kelowna Rockets	WHL	28	12	18	30	26	....	....	....	....	....	....	....	....	....	19	*13	10	23	26	....	....	....	....
2009-10	**Calgary**	**NHL**	**23**	**1**	**9**	**10**	**6**	**0**	**0**	**0**	**47**	**2.1**	**5**	**191**	**53.4**	**12:36**	....	....	....	....	....	....	....	....	....
	Abbotsford Heat	AHL	54	15	17	32	26	....	....	....	....	....	....	....	....	....	13	1	8	9	14	....	....	....	....
2010-11	**Calgary**	**NHL**	**73**	**10**	**15**	**25**	**18**	**2**	**0**	**1**	**144**	**6.9**	**4**	**664**	**48.0**	**12:05**	....	....	....	....	....	....	....	....	....
	Abbotsford Heat	AHL	1	0	0	0	0	....	....	....	....	....	....	....	....	....	....	....	....	....	....	....	....	....	....
2011-12	**Calgary**	**NHL**	**41**	**4**	**7**	**11**	**16**	**2**	**0**	**2**	**85**	**4.7**	**-13**	**496**	**45.4**	**15:23**	....	....	....	....	....	....	....	....	....
2012-13	VIK Vasteras HK	Sweden-2	23	12	18	30	22	....	....	....	....	....	....	....	....	....	....	....	....	....	....	....	....	....	....
	Calgary	**NHL**	**32**	**8**	**8**	**16**	**29**	**2**	**0**	**1**	**88**	**9.1**	**-6**	**407**	**47.7**	**15:07**	....	....	....	....	....	....	....	....	....
2013-14	**Calgary**	**NHL**	**76**	**18**	**21**	**39**	**32**	**5**	**4**	**3**	**178**	**10.1**	**4**	**1322**	**47.5**	**18:32**	....	....	....	....	....	....	....	....	....
2014-15	**Calgary**	**NHL**	**52**	**10**	**17**	**27**	**14**	**0**	**2**	**2**	**103**	**9.7**	**4**	**875**	**48.3**	**17:45**	**11**	**1**	**1**	**2**	**8**	**0**	**0**	**1**	**18:52**
2015-16	**Calgary**	**NHL**	**82**	**21**	**26**	**47**	**28**	**3**	**3**	**4**	**155**	**13.5**	**10**	**1143**	**47.2**	**16:26**	....	....	....	....	....	....	....	....	....
2016-17	**Calgary**	**NHL**	**81**	**22**	**31**	**53**	**36**	**7**	**0**	**7**	**197**	**11.2**	**9**	**1479**	**48.1**	**17:36**	**4**	**1**	**2**	**3**	**0**	**0**	**1**	**0**	**19:49**
	NHL Totals		**461**	**94**	**134**	**228**	**179**	**21**	**9**	**20**	**998**	**9.4**		**6584**	**47.7**	**16:03**	**15**	**2**	**3**	**5**	**8**	**0**	**1**	**1**	**19:07**

Signed as a free agent by **Vasteras** (Sweden-2), October 4, 2012.

BACKSTROM, Nicklas
(BAK-struhm, NIHK-luhs) **WSH**

Center. Shoots left. 6'1", 213 lbs. Born, Gavle, Sweden, November 23, 1987. Washington's 1st pick, 4th overall, in 2006 NHL Draft.

Season	Club	League	GP	G	A	Pts	PIM	PP	SH	GW	S	S%	+/-	TF	F%	Min	GP	G	A	Pts	PIM	PP	SH	GW	Min
2001-02	Brynas U18	Swe-U18	2	0	0	0	0	....	....	....	....	....	....	....	....	....	....	....	....	....	....	....	....	....	....
2002-03	Brynas U18	Swe-U18	STATISTICS NOT AVAILABLE																						
2003-04	Brynas U18	Swe-U18	6	9	5	14	4	....	....	....	....	....	....	....	....	....	3	0	3	3	0	....	....	....	....
	Brynas IF Gavle Jr.	Swe-Jr.	21	2	6	8	2	....	....	....	....	....	....	....	....	....	5	0	0	0	4	....	....	....	....
2004-05	Brynas IF Gavle Jr.	Swe-Jr.	29	17	17	34	24	....	....	....	....	....	....	....	....	....	....	....	....	....	....	....	....	....	....
	Brynas IF Gavle	Sweden	19	0	0	0	2	....	....	....	....	....	....	....	....	....	....	....	....	....	....	....	....	....	....
2005-06	Brynas IF Gavle	Sweden	46	10	16	26	30	....	....	....	....	....	....	....	....	....	4	1	0	1	2	....	....	....	....
	Brynas IF Gavle Jr.	Swe-Jr.	....	....	....	....	....	....	....	....	....	....	....	....	....	....	1	0	0	0	2	....	....	....	....
2006-07	Brynas IF Gavle	Sweden	45	12	28	40	46	....	....	....	....	....	....	....	....	....	7	3	3	6	6	....	....	....	....
2007-08	**Washington**	**NHL**	**82**	**14**	**55**	**69**	**24**	**3**	**0**	**4**	**153**	**9.2**	**13**	**874**	**46.3**	**19:00**	**7**	**4**	**2**	**6**	**2**	**3**	**0**	**0**	**20:26**
2008-09	**Washington**	**NHL**	**82**	**22**	**66**	**88**	**46**	**14**	**0**	**1**	**174**	**12.6**	**16**	**1171**	**48.7**	**19:57**	**14**	**3**	**12**	**15**	**8**	**2**	**0**	**0**	**21:40**
2009-10	**Washington**	**NHL**	**82**	**33**	**68**	**101**	**50**	**11**	**0**	**4**	**222**	**14.9**	**37**	**1336**	**49.9**	**20:27**	**7**	**5**	**4**	**9**	**4**	**0**	**0**	**1**	**21:03**
	Sweden	Olympics	4	1	5	6	0	....	....	....	....	....	....	....	....	....	....	....	....	....	....	....	....	....	....
2010-11	**Washington**	**NHL**	**77**	**18**	**47**	**65**	**40**	**4**	**1**	**2**	**202**	**8.9**	**24**	**1315**	**52.5**	**20:36**	**9**	**0**	**2**	**2**	**4**	**0**	**0**	**0**	**23:18**
2011-12	**Washington**	**NHL**	**42**	**14**	**30**	**44**	**24**	**3**	**0**	**4**	**95**	**14.7**	**-4**	**691**	**51.1**	**19:10**	**13**	**2**	**6**	**8**	**18**	**0**	**0**	**1**	**21:31**
2012-13	Dynamo Moscow	KHL	19	10	15	25	10	....	....	....	....	....	....	....	....	....	....	....	....	....	....	....	....	....	....
	Washington	**NHL**	**48**	**8**	**40**	**48**	**20**	**3**	**0**	**1**	**82**	**9.8**	**8**	**840**	**51.4**	**19:54**	**7**	**1**	**2**	**3**	**0**	**0**	**0**	**0**	**19:47**
2013-14	**Washington**	**NHL**	**82**	**18**	**61**	**79**	**54**	**6**	**1**	**1**	**196**	**9.2**	**-20**	**1415**	**50.5**	**19:48**	....	....	....	....	....	....	....	....	....
	Sweden	Olympics	5	0	4	4	0	....	....	....	....	....	....	....	....	....	....	....	....	....	....	....	....	....	....
2014-15	**Washington**	**NHL**	**82**	**18**	***60**	**78**	**40**	**3**	**0**	**3**	**153**	**11.8**	**5**	**1609**	**53.6**	**20:32**	**14**	**3**	**5**	**8**	**2**	**1**	**0**	**1**	**21:36**
2015-16	**Washington**	**NHL**	**75**	**20**	**50**	**70**	**36**	**3**	**0**	**4**	**129**	**15.5**	**17**	**1357**	**48.6**	**19:11**	**12**	**2**	**9**	**11**	**8**	**0**	**0**	**1**	**20:02**
2016-17	**Washington**	**NHL**	**82**	**23**	**63**	**86**	**38**	**8**	**0**	**5**	**162**	**14.2**	**17**	**1333**	**51.4**	**18:16**	**13**	**6**	**7**	**13**	**2**	**1**	**0**	**1**	**20:44**
	NHL Totals		**734**	**188**	**540**	**728**	**372**	**58**	**2**	**29**	**1568**	**12.0**		**11941**	**50.6**	**19:42**	**96**	**26**	**49**	**75**	**48**	**7**	**0**	**5**	**21:11**

NHL All-Rookie Team (2008)

Played in NHL All-Star Game (2016)

Signed as a free agent by **Dynamo Moscow** (KHL), October 18, 2012.

BAERTSCHI, Sven
(BEHR-chee, SVEHN) **VAN**

Left wing. Shoots left. 5'11", 190 lbs. Born, Bern, Switzerland, October 5, 1992. Calgary's 1st pick, 13th overall, in 2011 NHL Draft.

Season	Club	League	GP	G	A	Pts	PIM	PP	SH	GW	S	S%	+/-	TF	F%	Min	GP	G	A	Pts	PIM	PP	SH	GW	Min
2006-07	Langenthal U17	Swiss-U17	13	15	23	38	16	....	....	....	....	....	....	....	....	....	....	....	....	....	....	....	....	....	....
2007-08	Langenthal U17	Swiss-U17	17	16	22	38	22	....	....	....	....	....	....	....	....	....	....	....	....	....	....	....	....	....	....
	SC Langenthal Jr.	Swiss-Jr.	18	3	3	6	4	....	....	....	....	....	....	....	....	....	7	1	2	3	4	....	....	....	....
2008-09	Langenthal U17	Swiss-U17	3	4	4	8	0	....	....	....	....	....	....	....	....	....	....	....	....	....	....	....	....	....	....
	SC Langenthal Jr.	Swiss-Jr.	37	21	32	53	40	....	....	....	....	....	....	....	....	....	6	4	3	7	35	....	....	....	....
	SC Langenthal	Swiss-2	2	0	0	0	0	....	....	....	....	....	....	....	....	....	....	....	....	....	....	....	....	....	....
2009-10	SC Langenthal Jr.	Swiss-Jr.	2	3	0	3	2	....	....	....	....	....	....	....	....	....	....	....	....	....	....	....	....	....	....
	EV Zug Jr.	Swiss-Jr.	9	10	13	23	4	....	....	....	....	....	....	....	....	....	2	3	1	4	2	....	....	....	....
	SC Langenthal	Swiss-2	37	6	6	12	8	....	....	....	....	....	....	....	....	....	7	0	3	3	4	....	....	....	....
2010-11	Portland	WHL	66	34	51	85	74	....	....	....	....	....	....	....	....	....	21	10	17	27	16	....	....	....	....

			Regular Season														Playoffs								
Season	Club	League	GP	G	A	Pts	PIM	PP	SH	GW	S	S%	+/-	TF	F%	Min	GP	G	A	Pts	PIM	PP	SH	GW	Min
2011-12	Calgary	NHL	5	3	0	3	4	0	0	0	10	30.0	2	0	0.0	11:08	....	....	....	....	....	....	....	....	....
	Portland	WHL	47	33	61	94	36	....	....	....	....	....	....	....	....	....	22	14	20	34	10	....	....	....	....
2012-13	Calgary	NHL	20	3	7	10	6	0	0	0	28	10.7	0	1	100.0	13:24	....	....	....	....	....	....	....	....	....
	Abbotsford Heat	AHL	32	10	16	26	16	....	....	....	....	....	....	....	....	....	....	....	....	....	....	....	....	....	....
2013-14	Calgary	NHL	26	2	9	11	6	1	0	0	30	6.7	–4	0	0.0	14:07	....	....	....	....	....	....	....	....	....
	Abbotsford Heat	AHL	41	13	16	29	18	....	....	....	....	....	....	....	....	....	4	0	1	1	6	....	....	....	....
2014-15	Calgary	NHL	15	0	4	4	6	0	0	0	11	0.0	–3	0	0.0	9:13	....	....	....	....	....	....	....	....	....
	Adirondack	AHL	36	8	17	25	6	....	....	....	....	....	....	....	....	....	....	....	....	....	....	....	....	....	....
	Vancouver	NHL	3	2	0	2	4	0	0	0	4	50.0	0	0	0.0	12:02	2	0	0	0	0	0	0	0	9:40
	Utica Comets	AHL	15	7	8	15	4	....	....	....	....	....	....	....	....	....	21	8	7	15	6	....	....	....	....
2015-16	Vancouver	NHL	69	15	13	28	14	2	0	1	108	13.9	–14	1	0.0	13:27	....	....	....	....	....	....	....	....	....
2016-17	Vancouver	NHL	68	18	17	35	8	2	0	5	114	15.8	–6	1	100.0	15:53	....	....	....	....	....	....	....	....	....
	NHL Totals		206	43	50	93	48	5	0	6	305	14.1		3	66.7	13:57	2	0	0	0	0	0	0	0	9:40

WHL West Second All-Star Team (2012)

Traded to **Vancouver** by **Calgary** for Vancouver's 2nd round pick (Rasmus Andersson) in 2015 NHL Draft, March 2, 2015.

BAILEY, Casey

(BAY-lee, KAY-see)

Center. Shoots right. 6'3", 195 lbs. Born, Anchorage, AK, October 27, 1991.

2008-09	Anchorage	Minor-AK	16	15	16	31	50	....	....	....	....	....	....	....	....	....	....	....	....	....	....	....	....	....	....
2009-10	Alberni Valley	BCHL	51	13	11	24	43	....	....	....	....	....	....	....	....	....	13	0	2	2	2	....	....	....	....
2010-11	Alberni Valley	BCHL	60	28	30	58	74	....	....	....	....	....	....	....	....	....	4	4	3	7	4	....	....	....	....
2011-12	Omaha Lancers	USHL	60	27	33	60	83	....	....	....	....	....	....	....	....	....	4	2	2	4	6	....	....	....	....
2012-13	Penn State	NCAA	27	14	13	27	34	....	....	....	....	....	....	....	....	....	....	....	....	....	....	....	....	....	....
2013-14	Penn State	Big Ten	32	9	4	13	20	....	....	....	....	....	....	....	....	....	....	....	....	....	....	....	....	....	....
2014-15	Penn State	Big Ten	37	*22	18	40	37	....	....	....	....	....	....	....	....	....	....	....	....	....	....	....	....	....	....
	Toronto	NHL	6	1	0	1	2	0	0	0	9	11.1	1	0	0.0	9:02	....	....	....	....	....	....	....	....	....
2015-16	Toronto Marlies	AHL	38	4	14	18	16	....	....	....	....	....	....	....	....	....	....	....	....	....	....	....	....	....	....
	Binghamton	AHL	30	7	14	21	10	....	....	....	....	....	....	....	....	....	....	....	....	....	....	....	....	....	....
2016-17	Ottawa	NHL	7	0	0	0	0	0	0	0	10	0.0	–1	1	0.0	8:00	....	....	....	....	....	....	....	....	....
	Binghamton	AHL	62	21	16	37	20	....	....	....	....	....	....	....	....	....	....	....	....	....	....	....	....	....	....
	NHL Totals		13	1	0	1	2	0	0	0	19	5.3		1	0.0	8:29	....	....	....	....	....	....	....	....	....

Signed as a free agent by **Toronto**, March 21, 2015. Traded to **Ottawa** by **Toronto** with Dion Phaneuf, Matt Frattin, Ryan Rupert and Cody Donaghey for Jared Cowen, Colin Greening, Milan Michalek, Tobias Lindberg and Ottawa's 2nd round pick (Eemeli Rasanen) iin 2017 NHL Draft, February 9, 2016.

BAILEY, Josh

(BAY-lee, JAWSH) **NYI**

Center. Shoots left. 6'1", 210 lbs. Born, Bowmanville, ON, October 2, 1989. NY Islanders' 1st pick, 9th overall, in 2008 NHL Draft.

2004-05	Clarington Toros	Minor-ON	69	53	59	112	38	....	....	....	....	....	....	....	....	....	....	....	....	....	....	....	....	....	....
2005-06	Owen Sound	OHL	55	7	19	26	8	....	....	....	....	....	....	....	....	....	11	0	0	0	0	....	....	....	....
2006-07	Owen Sound	OHL	27	11	15	26	8	....	....	....	....	....	....	....	....	....	....	....	....	....	....	....	....	....	....
	Windsor Spitfires	OHL	42	11	24	35	16	....	....	....	....	....	....	....	....	....	....	....	....	....	....	....	....	....	....
2007-08	Windsor Spitfires	OHL	67	29	67	96	32	....	....	....	....	....	....	....	....	....	5	1	5	6	2	....	....	....	....
2008-09	NY Islanders	NHL	68	7	18	25	16	3	0	0	74	9.5	–14	807	41.1	15:29	....	....	....	....	....	....	....	....	....
2009-10	NY Islanders	NHL	73	16	19	35	18	3	1	2	112	14.3	5	426	40.1	15:09	....	....	....	....	....	....	....	....	....
2010-11	NY Islanders	NHL	70	11	17	28	37	5	0	2	102	10.8	–13	615	44.4	17:50	....	....	....	....	....	....	....	....	....
	Bridgeport	AHL	11	6	11	17	4	....	....	....	....	....	....	....	....	....	....	....	....	....	....	....	....	....	....
2011-12	NY Islanders	NHL	80	13	19	32	32	1	3	1	104	12.5	–10	736	43.9	15:13	....	....	....	....	....	....	....	....	....
2012-13	Bietigheim	German-2	6	3	8	11	16	....	....	....	....	....	....	....	....	....	....	....	....	....	....	....	....	....	....
	NY Islanders	NHL	38	11	8	19	6	0	0	1	76	14.5	7	75	46.7	16:23	6	0	3	3	0	0	0	0	20:14
2013-14	NY Islanders	NHL	77	8	30	38	26	2	0	1	98	8.2	–8	228	49.6	15:50	....	....	....	....	....	....	....	....	....
2014-15	NY Islanders	NHL	70	15	26	41	12	2	0	1	140	10.7	3	66	45.5	16:47	7	2	3	5	0	0	0	0	17:26
2015-16	NY Islanders	NHL	81	12	20	32	22	4	0	2	105	11.4	–7	34	41.2	15:51	9	2	1	3	2	1	0	0	16:10
2016-17	NY Islanders	NHL	82	13	43	56	12	3	0	1	173	7.5	5	15	53.3	18:22	....	....	....	....	....	....	....	....	....
	NHL Totals		639	106	200	306	181	23	4	11	984	10.8		3002	43.3	16:19	22	4	7	11	2	1	0	0	17:41

Signed as a free agent by **Bietigheim** (German-2), November 9, 2012.

BAILEY, Justin

(BAY-lee, JUHS-tihn) **BUF**

Right wing. Shoots right. 6'3", 208 lbs. Born, Buffalo, NY, July 1, 1995. Buffalo's 5th pick, 52nd overall, in 2013 NHL Draft.

2010-11	Buffalo Regals	T1EHL	12	4	1	5	0	....	....	....	....	....	....	....	....	....	....	....	....	....	....	....	....	....	....
	Buffalo Regals	Minor-NY	10	5	12	17	12	....	....	....	....	....	....	....	....	....	....	....	....	....	....	....	....	....	....
2011-12	Long Island	AYHL	22	21	13	34	52	....	....	....	....	....	....	....	....	....	....	....	....	....	....	....	....	....	....
	Indiana Ice	USHL	2	1	0	1	0	....	....	....	....	....	....	....	....	....	....	....	....	....	....	....	....	....	....
2012-13	Kitchener Rangers	OHL	57	17	19	36	34	....	....	....	....	....	....	....	....	....	10	1	2	3	4	....	....	....	....
2013-14	Kitchener Rangers	OHL	54	25	18	43	20	....	....	....	....	....	....	....	....	....	....	....	....	....	....	....	....	....	....
2014-15	Kitchener Rangers	OHL	35	22	19	41	32	....	....	....	....	....	....	....	....	....	....	....	....	....	....	....	....	....	....
	Sault Ste. Marie	OHL	22	12	16	28	12	....	....	....	....	....	....	....	....	....	14	7	7	14	6	....	....	....	....
2015-16	Buffalo	NHL	8	0	0	0	2	0	0	0	22	0.0	–2	0	0.0	11:36	....	....	....	....	....	....	....	....	....
	Rochester	AHL	70	20	25	45	16	....	....	....	....	....	....	....	....	....	....	....	....	....	....	....	....	....	....
2016-17	Buffalo	NHL	32	2	2	4	4	0	0	1	36	5.6	0	1	0.0	10:38	....	....	....	....	....	....	....	....	....
	Rochester	AHL	52	23	13	36	35	....	....	....	....	....	....	....	....	....	....	....	....	....	....	....	....	....	....
	NHL Totals		40	2	2	4	6	0	0	1	58	3.4		1	0.0	10:50	....	....	....	....	....	....	....	....	....

BANCKS, Carter

(BANKS, KAHR-tuhr)

Left wing. Shoots left. 5'11", 180 lbs. Born, Marysville, BC, August 9, 1989.

2005-06	Kimberley	KIJHL	50	24	49	73	57	....	....	....	....	....	....	....	....	....	13	5	7	12	6	....	....	....	....
	Lethbridge	WHL	2	0	0	0	0	....	....	....	....	....	....	....	....	....	6	0	0	0	4	....	....	....	....
2006-07	Lethbridge	WHL	67	11	20	31	64	....	....	....	....	....	....	....	....	....	....	....	....	....	....	....	....	....	....
2007-08	Lethbridge	WHL	70	15	30	45	56	....	....	....	....	....	....	....	....	....	19	6	4	10	19	....	....	....	....
2008-09	Lethbridge	WHL	53	13	34	47	68	....	....	....	....	....	....	....	....	....	3	0	0	0	4	....	....	....	....
2009-10	Lethbridge	WHL	70	19	36	55	96	....	....	....	....	....	....	....	....	....	....	....	....	....	....	....	....	....	....
	Abbotsford Heat	AHL	9	0	0	0	0	....	....	....	....	....	....	....	....	....	13	0	1	1	7	....	....	....	....
2010-11	Abbotsford Heat	AHL	29	5	14	19	16	....	....	....	....	....	....	....	....	....	....	....	....	....	....	....	....	....	....
2011-12	Abbotsford Heat	AHL	55	2	8	10	57	....	....	....	....	....	....	....	....	....	8	0	0	0	14	....	....	....	....
2012-13	Abbotsford Heat	AHL	59	5	7	12	53	....	....	....	....	....	....	....	....	....	....	....	....	....	....	....	....	....	....
	Calgary	NHL	2	0	0	0	0	0	0	0	0	0.0	0	0	0.0	14:41	....	....	....	....	....	....	....	....	....
2013-14	Abbotsford Heat	AHL	72	3	8	11	53	....	....	....	....	....	....	....	....	....	4	0	0	0	0	....	....	....	....
2014-15	Utica Comets	AHL	57	6	8	14	44	....	....	....	....	....	....	....	....	....	10	0	0	0	4	....	....	....	....
2015-16	Utica Comets	AHL	76	14	25	39	46	....	....	....	....	....	....	....	....	....	4	0	0	0	0	....	....	....	....
2016-17	Utica Comets	AHL	69	10	12	22	27	....	....	....	....	....	....	....	....	....	....	....	....	....	....	....	....	....	....
	NHL Totals		2	0	0	0	0	0	0	0	0	0.0		0	0.0	14:41	....	....	....	....	....	....	....	....	....

Signed to a ATO (amateur tryout) contract by **Abbotsford** (AHL), March 18, 2010. Signed as a free agent by **Calgary**, July 1, 2011. Signed to a PTO (professional tryout) contract by **Utica** (AHL), September 27, 2014.

BAPTISTE, Nicholas

(bap-TEEST, NIH-koh-las) **BUF**

Right wing. Shoots right. 6'1", 206 lbs. Born, Ottawa, ON, August 4, 1995. Buffalo's 6th pick, 69th overall, in 2013 NHL Draft.

2010-11	Ott. Senators MM	Minor-ON	24	22	33	55	26	....	....	....	....	....	....	....	....	....	....	....	....	....	....	....	....	....	....
	Ott. Senators M.M.		Other	18	17	15	32	12	....	....	....	....	....	....	....	....	....	....	....	....	....	....	....	....	....
....																									
	Cumberland	ON-Jr.A	2	1	0	1	0	....	....	....	....	....	....	....	....	....	....	....	....	....	....	....	....	....	....
2011-12	Sudbury Wolves	OHL	64	8	19	27	42	....	....	....	....	....	....	....	....	....	4	0	0	0	2	....	....	....	....
2012-13	Sudbury Wolves	OHL	66	21	27	48	44	....	....	....	....	....	....	....	....	....	9	3	1	4	6	....	....	....	....
2013-14	Sudbury Wolves	OHL	65	45	44	89	59	....	....	....	....	....	....	....	....	....	5	1	4	5	8	....	....	....	....
2014-15	Sudbury Wolves	OHL	12	6	5	11	8	....	....	....	....	....	....	....	....	....	....	....	....	....	....	....	....	....	....
	Erie Otters	OHL	41	26	27	53	18	....	....	....	....	....	....	....	....	....	20	12	11	23	10	....	....	....	....

Season	Club	League	Regular Season GP	G	A	Pts	PIM	PP	SH	GW	S	S%	+/-	TF	F%	Min	Playoffs GP	G	A	Pts	PIM	PP	SH	GW	Min
2015-16	Rochester	AHL	62	13	15	28	30																		
2016-17	**Buffalo**	**NHL**	**14**	**3**	**1**	**4**	**6**	**0**	**0**	**0**	**16**	**18.8**	**1**	**3**	**33.3**	**9:14**									
	Rochester	AHL	59	25	16	41	34																		
	NHL Totals		**14**	**3**	**1**	**4**	**6**	**0**	**0**	**0**	**16**	**18.8**		**3**	**33.3**	**9:14**									

BARBASHEV, Ivan
(bahr-BUH-shawv, ee-VAHN) **ST.L.**

Center. Shoots left. 6', 180 lbs. Born, Moscow, Russia, December 14, 1995. St. Louis' 2nd pick, 33rd overall, in 2014 NHL Draft.

Season	Club	League	GP	G	A	Pts	PIM	PP	SH	GW	S	S%	+/-	TF	F%	Min	GP	G	A	Pts	PIM	PP	SH	GW	Min
2011-12	Dyn'o Moscow Jr.	Russia-Jr.	38	8	2	10	18										4	2	2	4	25				
2012-13	Moncton Wildcats	QMJHL	68	18	44	62	36										5	1	2	3	0				
2013-14	Moncton Wildcats	QMJHL	48	25	43	68	27										6	4	6	10	8				
2014-15	Moncton Wildcats	QMJHL	57	45	50	95	59										16	13	11	24	14				
2015-16	Chicago Wolves	AHL	65	10	18	28	15																		
2016-17	**St. Louis**	**NHL**	**30**	**5**	**7**	**12**	**2**	**0**	**0**	**1**	**20**	**25.0**	**5**	**207**	**40.1**	**11:47**	**6**	**0**	**0**	**0**	**2**	**0**	**0**	**0**	**12:48**
	Chicago Wolves	AHL	46	19	18	37	14										2	0	0	0	0				
	NHL Totals		**30**	**5**	**7**	**12**	**2**	**0**	**0**	**1**	**20**	**25.0**		**207**	**40.1**	**11:47**	**6**	**0**	**0**	**0**	**2**	**0**	**0**	**0**	**12:48**

QMJHL All-Rookie Team (2013)

BARBER, Riley
(BAHR-buhr, RIGH-lee) **WSH**

Right wing. Shoots right. 6', 194 lbs. Born, Livonia, MI, February 7, 1994. Washington's 7th pick, 167th overall, in 2012 NHL Draft.

Season	Club	League	GP	G	A	Pts	PIM	PP	SH	GW	S	S%	+/-	TF	F%	Min	GP	G	A	Pts	PIM	PP	SH	GW	Min
2009-10	Det. Compuware	T1EHL	38	16	22	38	28										5	2	3	5	0				
	Det. Compuware	Other	6	1	4	5	8																		
2010-11	Dubuque	USHL	57	14	14	28	48										11	2	0	2	6				
2011-12	USAHNTDP	USHL	24	5	6	11	59																		
	USAHNTDP	U-18	36	16	9	25	26																		
2012-13	Miami U.	CCHA	40	15	24	39	22																		
2013-14	Miami U.	NCHC	38	19	25	44	28																		
2014-15	Miami U.	NCHC	38	20	20	40	12																		
2015-16	Hershey Bears	AHL	74	26	29	55	34										17	1	3	4	24				
2016-17	**Washington**	**NHL**	**3**	**0**	**0**	**0**	**0**	**0**	**0**	**0**	**2**	**0.0**	**0**	**0**	**0.0**	**8:35**									
	Hershey Bears	AHL	39	13	14	27	12										12	1	4	5	4				
	NHL Totals		**3**	**0**	**0**	**0**	**0**	**0**	**0**	**0**	**2**	**0.0**		**0**	**0.0**	**8:35**									

CCHA All-Rookie Team (2013) • CCHA First All-Star Team (2013) • CCHA Rookie of the Year (2013) • NCHC Second All-Star Team (2014)

BARBERIO, Mark
(bahr-BAIR-ee-oh, MAHRK) **COL**

Defense. Shoots left. 6'1", 207 lbs. Born, Montreal, QC, March 23, 1990. Tampa Bay's 5th pick, 152nd overall, in 2008 NHL Draft.

Season	Club	League	GP	G	A	Pts	PIM	PP	SH	GW	S	S%	+/-	TF	F%	Min	GP	G	A	Pts	PIM	PP	SH	GW	Min
2005-06	Lac St-Louis Lions	QAAA	43	2	12	14	80										10	1	7	8	26				
2006-07	Cape Breton	QMJHL	41	2	8	10	42																		
	Moncton Wildcats	QMJHL	19	1	6	7	21										7	0	2	2	8				
2007-08	Moncton Wildcats	QMJHL	70	11	35	46	75																		
2008-09	Moncton Wildcats	QMJHL	66	15	30	45	42										10	0	4	4	8				
2009-10	Moncton Wildcats	QMJHL	65	17	43	60	72										21	5	17	22	12				
2010-11	Norfolk Admirals	AHL	68	9	22	31	28										6	1	0	1	4				
2011-12	Norfolk Admirals	AHL	74	13	48	61	39										18	2	7	9	12				
2012-13	Syracuse Crunch	AHL	73	8	34	42	44										18	3	12	15	18				
	Tampa Bay	**NHL**	**2**	**0**	**0**	**0**	**0**	**0**	**0**	**0**	**1**	**0.0**	**–2**	**0**	**0.0**	**15:30**									
2013-14	**Tampa Bay**	**NHL**	**49**	**5**	**5**	**10**	**28**	**1**	**0**	**0**	**54**	**9.3**	**10**	**0**	**0.0**	**14:35**	**2**	**0**	**0**	**0**	**6**	**0**	**0**	**0**	**9:04**
2014-15	**Tampa Bay**	**NHL**	**52**	**1**	**6**	**7**	**16**	**0**	**0**	**0**	**53**	**1.9**	**–4**	**0**	**0.0**	**16:47**	**1**	**0**	**0**	**0**	**0**	**0**	**0**	**0**	**8:44**
2015-16	**Montreal**	**NHL**	**30**	**2**	**8**	**10**	**6**	**0**	**0**	**0**	**32**	**6.3**	**0**	**0**	**0.0**	**15:00**									
	St. John's IceCaps	AHL	26	2	18	20	25																		
2016-17	**Montreal**	**NHL**	**26**	**0**	**4**	**4**	**10**	**0**	**0**	**0**	**28**	**0.0**	**1**	**0**	**0.0**	**15:07**									
	St. John's IceCaps	AHL	20	3	15	18	28																		
	Colorado	**NHL**	**34**	**2**	**7**	**9**	**4**	**1**	**0**	**0**	**52**	**3.8**	**–6**	**0**	**0.0**	**20:40**									
	NHL Totals		**193**	**10**	**30**	**40**	**64**	**2**	**0**	**0**	**220**	**4.5**		**0**	**0.0**	**16:23**	**3**	**0**	**0**	**0**	**6**	**0**	**0**	**0**	**8:57**

QMJHL All-Rookie Team (2007) • QMJHL Second All-Star Team (2010) • AHL First All-Star Team (2012) • Eddie Shore Award (AHL - Outstanding Defenseman) (2012) • AHL Second All-Star Team (2013)

Signed as a free agent by **Montreal**, July 1, 2015. Claimed on waivers by **Colorado** from **Montreal**, February 2, 2017.

BARKOV, Aleksander
(bar-KAWV, al-ehx-AN-duhr) **FLA**

Center. Shoots left. 6'3", 213 lbs. Born, Tampere, Finland, September 2, 1995. Florida's 1st pick, 2nd overall, in 2013 NHL Draft.

Season	Club	League	GP	G	A	Pts	PIM	PP	SH	GW	S	S%	+/-	TF	F%	Min	GP	G	A	Pts	PIM	PP	SH	GW	Min
2010-11	Tappara U18	Fin-U18	11	7	8	15	8										2	3	0	3	0				
	Tappara Jr.	Fin-Jr.	25	5	12	17	6																		
2011-12	Tappara Jr.	Fin-Jr.	5	2	3	5	2																		
	Tappara Tampere	Finland	32	7	9	16	4																		
2012-13	Tappara Tampere	Finland	53	21	27	48	8										5	0	5	5	2				
2013-14	**Florida**	**NHL**	**54**	**8**	**16**	**24**	**10**	**3**	**0**	**1**	**87**	**9.2**	**–3**	**819**	**48.8**	**17:06**									
	Finland	Olympics	2	0	1	1	2																		
2014-15	**Florida**	**NHL**	**71**	**16**	**20**	**36**	**16**	**3**	**0**	**3**	**123**	**13.0**	**–4**	**1002**	**46.1**	**17:30**									
2015-16	**Florida**	**NHL**	**66**	**28**	**31**	**59**	**8**	**9**	**1**	**8**	**171**	**16.4**	**18**	**1156**	**49.2**	**19:26**	**6**	**2**	**1**	**3**	**2**	**0**	**0**	**0**	**25:54**
2016-17	**Florida**	**NHL**	**61**	**21**	**31**	**52**	**10**	**3**	**0**	**5**	**142**	**14.8**	**13**	**1023**	**46.5**	**19:24**									
	NHL Totals		**252**	**73**	**98**	**171**	**44**	**18**	**1**	**17**	**523**	**14.0**		**4000**	**47.7**	**18:23**	**6**	**2**	**1**	**3**	**2**	**0**	**0**	**0**	**25:54**

BARRIE, Tyson
(BAIR-ree, TIGH-suhn) **COL**

Defense. Shoots right. 5'10", 190 lbs. Born, Victoria, BC, July 26, 1991. Colorado's 4th pick, 64th overall, in 2009 NHL Draft.

Season	Club	League	GP	G	A	Pts	PIM	PP	SH	GW	S	S%	+/-	TF	F%	Min	GP	G	A	Pts	PIM	PP	SH	GW	Min
2006-07	Juan de Fuca	Minor-BC	72	43	87	130																			
	Kelowna Rockets	WHL	7	0	3	3	2																		
2007-08	Kelowna Rockets	WHL	64	9	34	43	32										7	1	3	4	0				
2008-09	Kelowna Rockets	WHL	68	12	40	52	31										22	4	14	18	12				
2009-10	Kelowna Rockets	WHL	63	19	53	72	31										12	3	8	11	6				
2010-11	Kelowna Rockets	WHL	54	11	47	58	34										10	2	9	11	8				
2011-12	**Colorado**	**NHL**	**10**	**0**	**0**	**0**	**0**	**0**	**0**	**0**	**15**	**0.0**	**–2**	**0**	**0.0**	**17:39**									
	Lake Erie	AHL	49	5	27	32	24																		
2012-13	Lake Erie	AHL	38	7	22	29	7																		
	Colorado	**NHL**	**32**	**2**	**11**	**13**	**10**	**1**	**0**	**1**	**58**	**3.4**	**–11**	**0**	**0.0**	**21:35**									
2013-14	**Colorado**	**NHL**	**64**	**13**	**25**	**38**	**20**	**4**	**0**	**5**	**101**	**12.9**	**17**	**0**	**0.0**	**18:33**	**3**	**0**	**2**	**2**	**0**	**0**	**0**	**0**	**18:17**
	Lake Erie	AHL	6	0	3	3	0																		
2014-15	**Colorado**	**NHL**	**80**	**12**	**41**	**53**	**26**	**2**	**0**	**0**	**139**	**8.6**	**5**	**0**	**0.0**	**21:22**									
2015-16	**Colorado**	**NHL**	**78**	**13**	**36**	**49**	**31**	**3**	**1**	**5**	**172**	**7.6**	**–16**	**0**	**0.0**	**23:12**									
2016-17	**Colorado**	**NHL**	**74**	**7**	**31**	**38**	**18**	**1**	**0**	**2**	**182**	**3.8**	**–34**	**0**	**0.0**	**23:18**									
	NHL Totals		**338**	**47**	**144**	**191**	**105**	**11**	**1**	**13**	**667**	**7.0**		**0**	**0.0**	**21:35**	**3**	**0**	**2**	**2**	**0**	**0**	**0**	**0**	**18:17**

Canadian Major Junior All-Rookie Team (2008) • WHL West First All-Star Team (2010, 2011) • WHL Defenseman of the Year (2010) • Canadian Major Junior Second All-Star Team (2010)

BARTKOWSKI, Matt
(bahrt-KOW-skee, MATT) **CGY**

Defense. Shoots left. 6'1", 196 lbs. Born, Pittsburgh, PA, June 4, 1988. Florida's 5th pick, 190th overall, in 2008 NHL Draft.

Season	Club	League	GP	G	A	Pts	PIM	PP	SH	GW	S	S%	+/-	TF	F%	Min	GP	G	A	Pts	PIM	PP	SH	GW	Min
2005-06	Mt. Lebanon	High-PA	STATISTICS NOT AVAILABLE																						
2006-07	Lincoln Stars	USHL	57	3	6	9	95										3	0	0	0	2				
2007-08	Lincoln Stars	USHL	60	4	37	41	135										8	1	4	5	10				
2008-09	Ohio State	CCHA	41	5	15	20	46																		
2009-10	Ohio State	CCHA	39	6	12	18	*99																		
2010-11	**Boston**	**NHL**	**6**	**0**	**0**	**0**	**4**	**0**	**0**	**0**	**2**	**0.0**	**–1**	**0**	**0.0**	**9:10**									
	Providence Bruins	AHL	69	5	18	23	42																		
2011-12	**Boston**	**NHL**	**3**	**0**	**0**	**0**	**0**	**0**	**0**	**0**	**0**	**0.0**	**–2**	**0**	**0.0**	**6:08**									
	Providence Bruins	AHL	50	3	19	22	38																		

			Regular Season													Playoffs								
Season	Club	League	GP	G	A	Pts	PIM	PP	SH	GW	S	S%	+/-	TF	F%	Min	GP	G	A	Pts	PIM	PP	SH	GW	Min
2012-13	Providence Bruins	AHL	56	3	21	24	56	....	....	....	....	....	....	....	....	....	5	0	5	5	4	....	....	....	....
	Boston	NHL	11	0	2	2	6	0	0	0	9	0.0	0	0	0.0	13:29	7	1	1	2	4	0	0	0	19:47
2013-14	Boston	NHL	64	0	18	18	30	0	0	0	91	0.0	22	0	0.0	19:32	8	0	1	1	10	0	0	0	20:21
2014-15	Boston	NHL	47	0	4	4	37	0	0	0	67	0.0	−6	0	0.0	16:56	....	....	....	....	....	....	....	....	....
2015-16	Vancouver	NHL	80	6	12	18	50	0	0	0	85	7.1	−19	0	0.0	18:37	....	....	....	....	....	....	....	....	....
2016-17	Calgary	NHL	24	1	1	2	26	0	0	0	16	6.3	−4	0	0.0	15:23	4	0	0	0	0	0	0	0	12:45
	Providence Bruins	AHL	34	2	8	10	27	....	....	....	....	....	....	....	....	....	....	....	....	....	....	....	....	....	....
	NHL Totals		235	7	37	44	153	0	0	0	270	2.6		0	0.0	17:34	19	1	2	3	14	0	0	0	18:32

CCHA All-Rookie Team (2009) • USHL First All-Star Team (2008)

Traded to **Boston** by **Florida** with Dennis Seidenberg for Byron Bitz, Craig Weller and Tampa Bay's 2nd round pick (previously acquired, Florida selected Alexander Petrovic) in 2010 NHL Draft, March 3, 2010. Signed as a free agent by **Vancouver**, July 1, 2015. Signed to a PTO (professional tryout) contract by **Providence** (AHL), October 13, 2016. Signed as a free agent by **Calgary**, February 16, 2017.

BARTLEY, Victor

(BAR-tlee, WAYD)

Defense. Shoots left. 6', 215 lbs. Born, Ottawa, ON, February 17, 1988.

Season	Club	League	GP	G	A	Pts	PIM	PP	SH	GW	S	S%	+/-	TF	F%	Min	GP	G	A	Pts	PIM	PP	SH	GW	Min
2003-04	Delta Ice Hawks	PIJHL	42	2	25	27	66	....	....	....	....	....	....	....	....	....	....	....	....	....	....	....	....	....	....
	Kamloops Blazers	WHL	3	0	0	0	0	....	....	....	....	....	....	....	....	....	....	....	....	....	....	....	....	....	....
2004-05	Kamloops Blazers	WHL	68	4	6	10	58	....	....	....	....	....	....	....	....	....	5	0	3	3	4	....	....	....	....
2005-06	Kamloops Blazers	WHL	65	3	24	27	114	....	....	....	....	....	....	....	....	....	....	....	....	....	....	....	....	....	....
2006-07	Kamloops Blazers	WHL	67	4	39	43	104	....	....	....	....	....	....	....	....	....	4	0	2	2	8	....	....	....	....
2007-08	Kamloops Blazers	WHL	36	3	15	18	51	....	....	....	....	....	....	....	....	....	....	....	....	....	....	....	....	....	....
	Regina Pats	WHL	25	7	17	24	42	....	....	....	....	....	....	....	....	....	6	1	3	4	8	....	....	....	....
2008-09	Regina Pats	WHL	72	15	31	46	97	....	....	....	....	....	....	....	....	....	....	....	....	....	....	....	....	....	....
	Providence Bruins	AHL	10	0	0	0	6	....	....	....	....	....	....	....	....	....	....	....	....	....	....	....	....	....	....
2009-10	Bridgeport	AHL	8	2	0	2	6	....	....	....	....	....	....	....	....	....	....	....	....	....	....	....	....	....	....
	Utah Grizzlies	ECHL	21	2	11	13	21	....	....	....	....	....	....	....	....	....	....	....	....	....	....	....	....	....	....
2010-11	Rogle	Sweden-2	52	11	23	34	56	....	....	....	....	....	....	....	....	....	....	....	....	....	....	....	....	....	....
2011-12	Milwaukee	AHL	76	9	30	39	64	....	....	....	....	....	....	....	....	....	1	1	0	1	0	....	....	....	....
2012-13	Milwaukee	AHL	54	7	19	26	35	....	....	....	....	....	....	....	....	....	2	0	1	1	0	....	....	....	....
	Nashville	NHL	24	0	7	7	6	0	0	0	19	0.0	2	0	0.0	19:33	....	....	....	....	....	....	....	....	....
2013-14	Nashville	NHL	50	1	5	6	23	0	0	0	21	4.8	0	0	0.0	15:22	....	....	....	....	....	....	....	....	....
2014-15	Nashville	NHL	37	0	10	10	26	0	0	0	28	0.0	1	0	0.0	13:26	4	0	0	0	2	0	0	0	11:21
2015-16	Nashville	NHL	1	0	0	0	0	0	0	0	0	0.0	−1	0	0.0	13:15	....	....	....	....	....	....	....	....	....
	Milwaukee	AHL	14	0	1	1	10	....	....	....	....	....	....	....	....	....	....	....	....	....	....	....	....	....	....
	Montreal	NHL	9	0	0	0	6	0	0	0	8	0.0	3	0	0.0	13:20	....	....	....	....	....	....	....	....	....
	St. John's IceCaps	AHL	10	1	2	3	6	....	....	....	....	....	....	....	....	....	....	....	....	....	....	....	....	....	....
2016-17	Iowa Wild	AHL	DID NOT PLAY – INJURED																						
	NHL Totals		121	1	22	23	61	0	0	0	76	1.3		0	0.0	15:26	4	0	0	0	2	0	0	0	11:21

Signed as a free agent by **Rogle** (Sweden-2), May 26, 2010. Signed as a free agent by **Nashville**, May 24, 2011. • Missed majority of 2014-15 and 2015-16 as a healthy reserve. Traded to **Arizona** by **Nashville** for Stefan Elliott, January 15, 2016. Traded to **Montreal** by **Arizona** with John Scott for Jarred Tinordi and Stefan Fournier, January 15, 2016. Signed as a free agent by **Minnesota**, July 1, 2016. • Missed 2016-17 due to arm injury vs. Carolina in pre-season game, October 2, 2016.

BARZAL, Mathew

(BAHR-zahl, MA-thew) **NYI**

Center. Shoots right. 6', 182 lbs. Born, Coquitlam, BC, May 26, 1997. NY Islanders' 1st pick, 16th overall, in 2015 NHL Draft.

Season	Club	League	GP	G	A	Pts	PIM	PP	SH	GW	S	S%	+/-	TF	F%	Min	GP	G	A	Pts	PIM	PP	SH	GW	Min
2011-12	Burnaby W.C.	Minor-BC	51	55	98	153	....	....	....	....	....	....	....	....	....	....	....	....	....	....	....	....	....	....	....
2012-13	Van. NE Chiefs	BCMML	34	29	*74	*103	34	....	....	....	....	....	....	....	....	....	3	3	3	6	8	....	....	....	....
2013-14	Seattle	WHL	59	14	40	54	20	....	....	....	....	....	....	....	....	....	9	1	5	6	4	....	....	....	....
2014-15	Seattle	WHL	44	12	45	57	20	....	....	....	....	....	....	....	....	....	6	4	4	8	4	....	....	....	....
2015-16	Seattle	WHL	58	27	61	88	58	....	....	....	....	....	....	....	....	....	18	5	21	26	16	....	....	....	....
2016-17	NY Islanders	NHL	2	0	0	0	6	0	0	0	0	0.0	−2	13	46.2	9:45	....	....	....	....	....	....	....	....	....
	Seattle	WHL	41	10	69	79	20	....	....	....	....	....	....	....	....	....	16	7	18	25	16	....	....	....	....
	NHL Totals		2	0	0	0	6	0	0	0	0	0.0		13	46.2	9:45	....	....	....	....	....	....	....	....	....

WHL West First All-Star Team (2016, 2017)

BASS, Cody

(BAS, KOH-dee) **NSH**

Center. Shoots right. 6', 205 lbs. Born, Owen Sound, ON, January 7, 1987. Ottawa's 3rd pick, 95th overall, in 2005 NHL Draft.

Season	Club	League	GP	G	A	Pts	PIM	PP	SH	GW	S	S%	+/-	TF	F%	Min	GP	G	A	Pts	PIM	PP	SH	GW	Min
2002-03	Guelph	ON-Jr.B	48	3	19	22	70	....	....	....	....	....	....	....	....	....	6	0	0	0	16	....	....	....	....
2003-04	Mississauga	OHL	61	3	7	10	30	....	....	....	....	....	....	....	....	....	24	2	3	5	21	....	....	....	....
2004-05	Mississauga	OHL	66	11	17	28	103	....	....	....	....	....	....	....	....	....	5	1	1	2	8	....	....	....	....
2005-06	Mississauga	OHL	67	16	25	41	152	....	....	....	....	....	....	....	....	....	....	....	....	....	....	....	....	....	....
	Binghamton	AHL	9	1	0	1	2	....	....	....	....	....	....	....	....	....	....	....	....	....	....	....	....	....	....
2006-07	Mississauga	OHL	23	5	11	16	37	....	....	....	....	....	....	....	....	....	....	....	....	....	....	....	....	....	....
	Saginaw Spirit	OHL	30	5	24	29	49	....	....	....	....	....	....	....	....	....	6	1	2	3	10	....	....	....	....
	Binghamton	AHL	5	0	2	2	9	....	....	....	....	....	....	....	....	....	....	....	....	....	....	....	....	....	....
2007-08	Ottawa	NHL	21	2	2	4	19	0	1	1	12	16.7	−1	73	43.8	5:19	4	1	0	1	6	0	0	0	8:21
	Binghamton	AHL	24	3	5	8	44	....	....	....	....	....	....	....	....	....	....	....	....	....	....	....	....	....	....
2008-09	Ottawa	NHL	12	0	0	0	15	0	0	0	5	0.0	−2	50	42.0	5:41	....	....	....	....	....	....	....	....	....
	Binghamton	AHL	18	1	1	2	41	....	....	....	....	....	....	....	....	....	....	....	....	....	....	....	....	....	....
2009-10	Binghamton	AHL	57	5	6	11	109	....	....	....	....	....	....	....	....	....	....	....	....	....	....	....	....	....	....
2010-11	Ottawa	NHL	1	0	0	0	0	0	0	0	0	0.0	0	0	0.0	7:09	....	....	....	....	....	....	....	....	....
	Binghamton	AHL	58	6	9	15	111	....	....	....	....	....	....	....	....	....	18	2	2	4	24	....	....	....	....
2011-12	Columbus	NHL	14	0	1	1	32	0	0	0	13	0.0	0	8	62.5	9:05	....	....	....	....	....	....	....	....	....
	Springfield	AHL	23	5	6	11	43	....	....	....	....	....	....	....	....	....	....	....	....	....	....	....	....	....	....
2012-13	Springfield	AHL	18	2	5	7	54	....	....	....	....	....	....	....	....	....	8	2	2	4	26	....	....	....	....
2013-14	Columbus	NHL	1	0	0	0	5	0	0	0	0	0.0	0	0	0.0	2:43	....	....	....	....	....	....	....	....	....
	Springfield	AHL	58	8	10	18	132	....	....	....	....	....	....	....	....	....	4	0	0	0	4	....	....	....	....
2014-15	Rockford IceHogs	AHL	61	6	8	14	165	....	....	....	....	....	....	....	....	....	8	0	1	1	31	....	....	....	....
2015-16	Nashville	NHL	17	0	0	0	17	0	0	0	11	0.0	−1	21	57.1	7:40	6	0	0	0	2	0	0	0	6:13
	Milwaukee	AHL	39	4	5	9	84	....	....	....	....	....	....	....	....	....	....	....	....	....	....	....	....	....	....
2016-17	Nashville	NHL	9	0	0	0	19	0	0	0	1	0.0	−1	2	0.0	6:46	....	....	....	....	....	....	....	....	....
	Milwaukee	AHL	13	2	2	4	33	....	....	....	....	....	....	....	....	....	....	....	....	....	....	....	....	....	....
	NHL Totals		75	2	3	5	107	0	1	1	42	4.8		154	45.5	6:46	10	1	0	1	8	0	0	0	7:04

Yanick Dupre Memorial Award (AHL - Outstanding Humanitarian Contribution) (2011)

• Missed remainder of 2008-09 due to shoulder injury at Calgary, December 27, 2008. Signed as a free agent by **Columbus**, July 13, 2011. • Missed majority of 2011-12 due to shoulder injury at Springfield (AHL) practice, December 19, 2011. • Missed majority of 2012-13 due to shoulder injury vs. Portland (AHL), October 28, 2012. Signed as a free agent by **Chicago**, July 1, 2014. Signed as a free agent by **Nashville**, July 4, 2015.

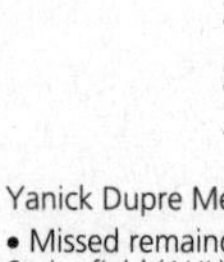

BAUN, Kyle

(BAHN, KIGH-uhl) **CHI**

Right wing. Shoots right. 6'2", 209 lbs. Born, Toronto, ON, May 4, 1992.

Season	Club	League	GP	G	A	Pts	PIM	PP	SH	GW	S	S%	+/-	TF	F%	Min	GP	G	A	Pts	PIM	PP	SH	GW	Min
2008-09	Toronto Titans	GTHL	STATISTICS NOT AVAILABLE																						
	Tor. Canadiens	ON-Jr.A	1	0	1	1	0	....	....	....	....	....	....	....	....	....	....	....	....	....	....	....	....	....	....
2009-10	Tor. Canadiens	ON-Jr.A	45	5	10	15	27	....	....	....	....	....	....	....	....	....	7	0	0	0	6	....	....	....	....
2010-11	Cornwall Colts	ON-Jr.A	56	19	23	42	44	....	....	....	....	....	....	....	....	....	16	7	1	8	26	....	....	....	....
2011-12	Cornwall Colts	ON-Jr.A	42	29	32	61	50	....	....	....	....	....	....	....	....	....	17	8	12	20	16	....	....	....	....
2012-13	Colgate	ECAC	36	14	10	24	30	....	....	....	....	....	....	....	....	....	....	....	....	....	....	....	....	....	....
2013-14	Colgate	ECAC	39	11	15	26	53	....	....	....	....	....	....	....	....	....	....	....	....	....	....	....	....	....	....
2014-15	Colgate	ECAC	38	14	15	29	68	....	....	....	....	....	....	....	....	....	....	....	....	....	....	....	....	....	....
	Chicago	NHL	3	0	0	0	0	0	0	0	4	0.0	−1	0	0.0	12:32	....	....	....	....	....	....	....	....	....
2015-16	Chicago	NHL	2	0	0	0	0	0	0	0	1	0.0	−2	0	0.0	9:03	....	....	....	....	....	....	....	....	....
	Rockford IceHogs	AHL	43	1	8	9	16	....	....	....	....	....	....	....	....	....	3	0	0	0	0	....	....	....	....
2016-17	Rockford IceHogs	AHL	74	14	20	34	42	....	....	....	....	....	....	....	....	....	....	....	....	....	....	....	....	....	....
	NHL Totals		5	0	0	0	0	0	0	0	5	0.0		0	0.0	11:09	....	....	....	....	....	....	....	....	....

ECAC All-Rookie Team (2013)

Signed as a free agent by **Chicago**, March 26, 2015.

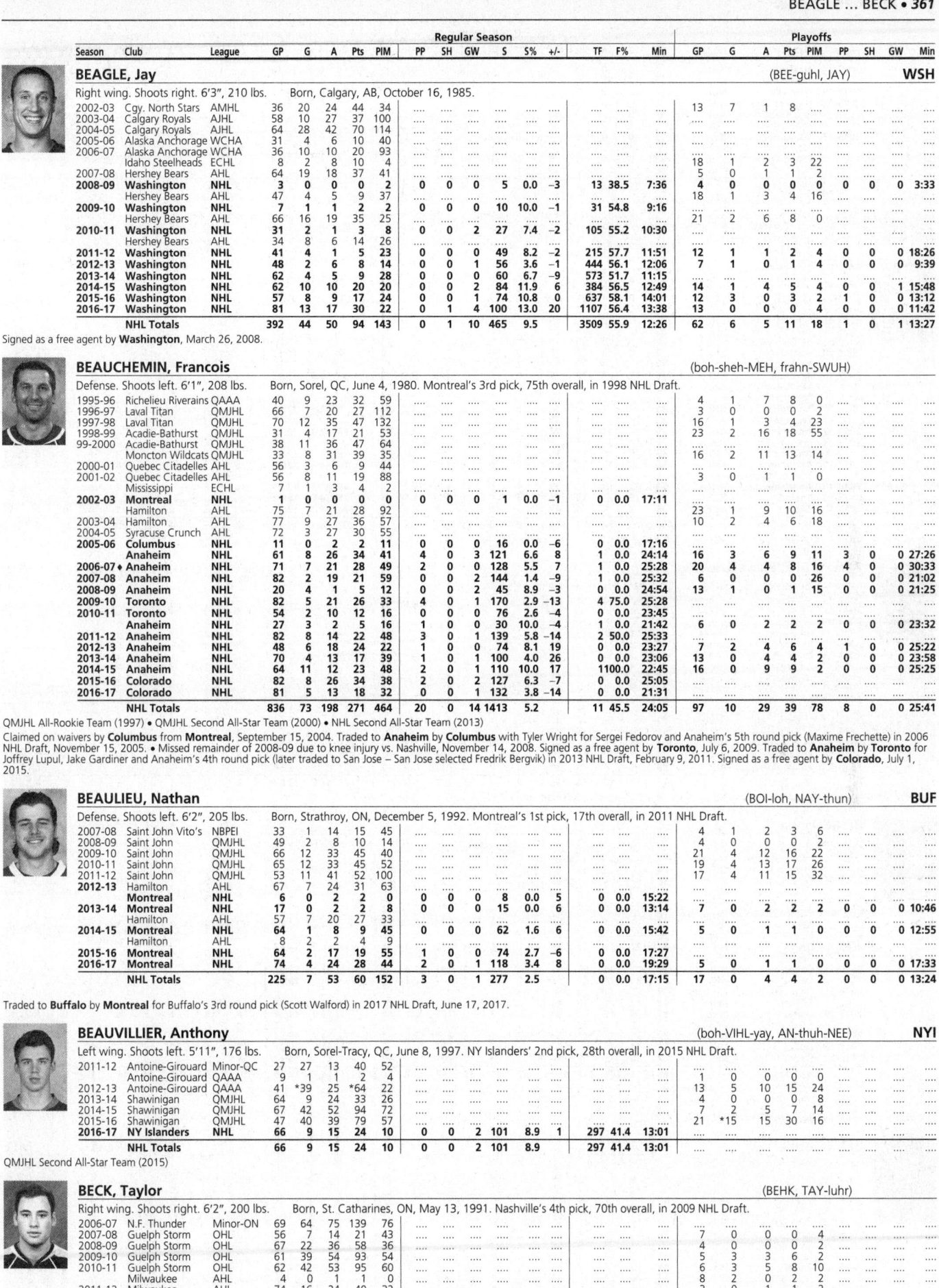

BEAGLE, Jay
(BEE-guhl, JAY) **WSH**

Right wing. Shoots right. 6'3", 210 lbs. Born, Calgary, AB, October 16, 1985.

Season	Club	League	GP	G	A	Pts	PIM	PP	SH	GW	S	S%	+/-	TF	F%	Min	GP	G	A	Pts	PIM	PP	SH	GW	Min
			Regular Season														Playoffs								
2002-03	Cgy. North Stars	AMHL	36	20	24	44	34	....	....	....	....	....	....	....	....	....	13	7	1	8	....	....	....	....	....
2003-04	Calgary Royals	AJHL	58	10	27	37	100	....	....	....	....	....	....	....	....	....	....	....	....	....	....	....	....	....	....
2004-05	Calgary Royals	AJHL	64	28	42	70	114	....	....	....	....	....	....	....	....	....	....	....	....	....	....	....	....	....	....
2005-06	Alaska Anchorage	WCHA	31	4	6	10	40	....	....	....	....	....	....	....	....	....	....	....	....	....	....	....	....	....	....
2006-07	Alaska Anchorage	WCHA	36	10	10	20	93	....	....	....	....	....	....	....	....	....	....	....	....	....	....	....	....	....	....
	Idaho Steelheads	ECHL	8	2	8	10	4	....	....	....	....	....	....	....	....	....	18	1	2	3	22	....	....	....	....
2007-08	Hershey Bears	AHL	64	19	18	37	41	....	....	....	....	....	....	....	....	....	5	0	1	1	2	....	....	....	....
2008-09	**Washington**	**NHL**	**3**	**0**	**0**	**0**	**2**	**0**	**0**	**0**	**5**	**0.0**	**–3**	**13**	**38.5**	**7:36**	**4**	**0**	**0**	**0**	**0**	**0**	**0**	**0**	**3:33**
	Hershey Bears	AHL	47	4	5	9	37	....	....	....	....	....	....	....	....	....	18	1	3	4	16	....	....	....	....
2009-10	**Washington**	**NHL**	**7**	**1**	**1**	**2**	**2**	**0**	**0**	**0**	**10**	**10.0**	**–1**	**31**	**54.8**	**9:16**	....	....	....	....	....	....	....	....	....
	Hershey Bears	AHL	66	16	19	35	25	....	....	....	....	....	....	....	....	....	21	2	6	8	0	....	....	....	....
2010-11	**Washington**	**NHL**	**31**	**2**	**1**	**3**	**8**	**0**	**0**	**2**	**27**	**7.4**	**–2**	**105**	**55.2**	**10:30**	....	....	....	....	....	....	....	....	....
	Hershey Bears	AHL	34	8	6	14	26	....	....	....	....	....	....	....	....	....	....	....	....	....	....	....	....	....	....
2011-12	**Washington**	**NHL**	**41**	**4**	**1**	**5**	**23**	**0**	**0**	**0**	**49**	**8.2**	**–2**	**215**	**57.7**	**11:51**	**12**	**1**	**1**	**2**	**4**	**0**	**0**	**0**	**18:26**
2012-13	**Washington**	**NHL**	**48**	**2**	**6**	**8**	**14**	**0**	**0**	**1**	**56**	**3.6**	**–1**	**444**	**56.1**	**12:06**	**7**	**1**	**0**	**1**	**4**	**0**	**0**	**0**	**9:39**
2013-14	**Washington**	**NHL**	**62**	**4**	**5**	**9**	**28**	**0**	**0**	**0**	**60**	**6.7**	**–9**	**573**	**51.7**	**11:15**	....	....	....	....	....	....	....	....	....
2014-15	**Washington**	**NHL**	**62**	**10**	**10**	**20**	**20**	**0**	**0**	**2**	**84**	**11.9**	**6**	**384**	**56.5**	**12:49**	**14**	**1**	**4**	**5**	**4**	**0**	**0**	**1**	**15:48**
2015-16	**Washington**	**NHL**	**57**	**8**	**9**	**17**	**24**	**0**	**0**	**1**	**74**	**10.8**	**0**	**637**	**58.1**	**14:01**	**12**	**3**	**0**	**3**	**2**	**1**	**0**	**0**	**13:12**
2016-17	**Washington**	**NHL**	**81**	**13**	**17**	**30**	**22**	**0**	**1**	**4**	**100**	**13.0**	**20**	**1107**	**56.4**	**13:38**	**13**	**0**	**0**	**0**	**4**	**0**	**0**	**0**	**11:42**
	NHL Totals		**392**	**44**	**50**	**94**	**143**	**0**	**1**	**10**	**465**	**9.5**		**3509**	**55.9**	**12:26**	**62**	**6**	**5**	**11**	**18**	**1**	**0**	**1**	**13:27**

Signed as a free agent by **Washington**, March 26, 2008.

BEAUCHEMIN, Francois
(boh-sheh-MEH, frahn-SWUH)

Defense. Shoots left. 6'1", 208 lbs. Born, Sorel, QC, June 4, 1980. Montreal's 3rd pick, 75th overall, in 1998 NHL Draft.

Season	Club	League	GP	G	A	Pts	PIM	PP	SH	GW	S	S%	+/-	TF	F%	Min	GP	G	A	Pts	PIM	PP	SH	GW	Min
			Regular Season														Playoffs								
1995-96	Richelieu Riverains	QAAA	40	9	23	32	59	....	....	....	....	....	....	....	....	....	4	1	7	8	0	....	....	....	....
1996-97	Laval Titan	QMJHL	66	7	20	27	112	....	....	....	....	....	....	....	....	....	3	0	0	0	2	....	....	....	....
1997-98	Laval Titan	QMJHL	70	12	35	47	132	....	....	....	....	....	....	....	....	....	16	1	3	4	23	....	....	....	....
1998-99	Acadie-Bathurst	QMJHL	31	4	17	21	53	....	....	....	....	....	....	....	....	....	23	2	16	18	55	....	....	....	....
99-2000	Acadie-Bathurst	QMJHL	38	11	36	47	64	....	....	....	....	....	....	....	....	....	....	....	....	....	....	....	....	....	....
	Moncton Wildcats	QMJHL	33	8	31	39	35	....	....	....	....	....	....	....	....	....	16	2	11	13	14	....	....	....	....
2000-01	Quebec Citadelles	AHL	56	3	6	9	44	....	....	....	....	....	....	....	....	....	....	....	....	....	....	....	....	....	....
2001-02	Quebec Citadelles	AHL	56	8	11	19	88	....	....	....	....	....	....	....	....	....	3	0	1	1	0	....	....	....	....
	Mississippi	ECHL	7	1	3	4	2	....	....	....	....	....	....	....	....	....	....	....	....	....	....	....	....	....	....
2002-03	**Montreal**	**NHL**	**1**	**0**	**0**	**0**	**0**	**0**	**0**	**0**	**1**	**0.0**	**–1**	**0**	**0.0**	**17:11**	....	....	....	....	....	....	....	....	....
	Hamilton	AHL	75	7	21	28	92	....	....	....	....	....	....	....	....	....	23	1	9	10	16	....	....	....	....
2003-04	Hamilton	AHL	77	9	27	36	57	....	....	....	....	....	....	....	....	....	10	2	4	6	18	....	....	....	....
2004-05	Syracuse Crunch	AHL	72	3	27	30	55	....	....	....	....	....	....	....	....	....	....	....	....	....	....	....	....	....	....
2005-06	**Columbus**	**NHL**	**11**	**0**	**2**	**2**	**11**	**0**	**0**	**0**	**16**	**0.0**	**–6**	**0**	**0.0**	**17:16**	....	....	....	....	....	....	....	....	....
	Anaheim	**NHL**	**61**	**8**	**26**	**34**	**41**	**4**	**0**	**3**	**121**	**6.6**	**8**	**1**	**0.0**	**24:14**	**16**	**3**	**6**	**9**	**11**	**3**	**0**	**0**	**27:26**
2006-07 ♦	**Anaheim**	**NHL**	**71**	**7**	**21**	**28**	**49**	**2**	**0**	**0**	**128**	**5.5**	**7**	**1**	**0.0**	**25:28**	**20**	**4**	**4**	**8**	**16**	**4**	**0**	**0**	**30:33**
2007-08	**Anaheim**	**NHL**	**82**	**2**	**19**	**21**	**59**	**0**	**0**	**2**	**144**	**1.4**	**–9**	**1**	**0.0**	**25:32**	**6**	**0**	**0**	**0**	**26**	**0**	**0**	**0**	**21:02**
2008-09	**Anaheim**	**NHL**	**20**	**4**	**1**	**5**	**12**	**0**	**0**	**2**	**45**	**8.9**	**–3**	**0**	**0.0**	**24:54**	**13**	**1**	**0**	**1**	**15**	**0**	**0**	**0**	**21:25**
2009-10	**Toronto**	**NHL**	**82**	**5**	**21**	**26**	**33**	**4**	**0**	**1**	**170**	**2.9**	**–13**	**4**	**75.0**	**25:28**	....	....	....	....	....	....	....	....	....
2010-11	**Toronto**	**NHL**	**54**	**2**	**10**	**12**	**16**	**0**	**0**	**0**	**76**	**2.6**	**–4**	**0**	**0.0**	**23:45**	....	....	....	....	....	....	....	....	....
	Anaheim	**NHL**	**27**	**3**	**2**	**5**	**16**	**1**	**0**	**0**	**30**	**10.0**	**–4**	**1**	**0.0**	**21:42**	**6**	**0**	**2**	**2**	**2**	**0**	**0**	**0**	**23:32**
2011-12	**Anaheim**	**NHL**	**82**	**8**	**14**	**22**	**48**	**3**	**0**	**1**	**139**	**5.8**	**–14**	**2**	**50.0**	**25:33**	....	....	....	....	....	....	....	....	....
2012-13	**Anaheim**	**NHL**	**48**	**6**	**18**	**24**	**22**	**1**	**0**	**0**	**74**	**8.1**	**19**	**0**	**0.0**	**23:27**	**7**	**2**	**4**	**6**	**4**	**1**	**0**	**0**	**25:22**
2013-14	**Anaheim**	**NHL**	**70**	**4**	**13**	**17**	**39**	**1**	**0**	**1**	**100**	**4.0**	**26**	**0**	**0.0**	**23:06**	**13**	**0**	**4**	**4**	**2**	**0**	**0**	**0**	**23:58**
2014-15	**Anaheim**	**NHL**	**64**	**11**	**12**	**23**	**48**	**2**	**0**	**1**	**110**	**10.0**	**17**	**1**	**100.0**	**22:45**	**16**	**0**	**9**	**9**	**2**	**0**	**0**	**0**	**25:25**
2015-16	**Colorado**	**NHL**	**82**	**8**	**26**	**34**	**38**	**2**	**0**	**2**	**127**	**6.3**	**–7**	**0**	**0.0**	**25:05**	....	....	....	....	....	....	....	....	....
2016-17	**Colorado**	**NHL**	**81**	**5**	**13**	**18**	**32**	**0**	**0**	**1**	**132**	**3.8**	**–14**	**0**	**0.0**	**21:31**	....	....	....	....	....	....	....	....	....
	NHL Totals		**836**	**73**	**198**	**271**	**464**	**20**	**0**	**14**	**1413**	**5.2**		**11**	**45.5**	**24:05**	**97**	**10**	**29**	**39**	**78**	**8**	**0**	**0**	**25:41**

QMJHL All-Rookie Team (1997) • QMJHL Second All-Star Team (2000) • NHL Second All-Star Team (2013)

Claimed on waivers by **Columbus** from **Montreal**, September 15, 2004. Traded to **Anaheim** by **Columbus** with Tyler Wright for Sergei Fedorov and Anaheim's 5th round pick (Maxime Frechette) in 2006 NHL Draft, November 15, 2005. • Missed remainder of 2008-09 due to knee injury vs. Nashville, November 14, 2008. Signed as a free agent by **Toronto**, July 6, 2009. Traded to **Anaheim** by **Toronto** for Joffrey Lupul, Jake Gardiner and Anaheim's 4th round pick (later traded to San Jose – San Jose selected Fredrik Bergvik) in 2013 NHL Draft, February 9, 2011. Signed as a free agent by **Colorado**, July 1, 2015.

BEAULIEU, Nathan
(BOI-loh, NAY-thun) **BUF**

Defense. Shoots left. 6'2", 205 lbs. Born, Strathroy, ON, December 5, 1992. Montreal's 1st pick, 17th overall, in 2011 NHL Draft.

Season	Club	League	GP	G	A	Pts	PIM	PP	SH	GW	S	S%	+/-	TF	F%	Min	GP	G	A	Pts	PIM	PP	SH	GW	Min
			Regular Season														Playoffs								
2007-08	Saint John Vito's	NBPEI	33	1	14	15	45	....	....	....	....	....	....	....	....	....	4	1	2	3	6	....	....	....	....
2008-09	Saint John	QMJHL	49	2	8	10	14	....	....	....	....	....	....	....	....	....	4	0	0	0	2	....	....	....	....
2009-10	Saint John	QMJHL	66	12	33	45	40	....	....	....	....	....	....	....	....	....	21	4	12	16	22	....	....	....	....
2010-11	Saint John	QMJHL	65	12	33	45	52	....	....	....	....	....	....	....	....	....	19	4	13	17	26	....	....	....	....
2011-12	Saint John	QMJHL	53	11	41	52	100	....	....	....	....	....	....	....	....	....	17	4	11	15	32	....	....	....	....
2012-13	Hamilton	AHL	67	7	24	31	63	....	....	....	....	....	....	....	....	....	....	....	....	....	....	....	....	....	....
	Montreal	**NHL**	**6**	**0**	**2**	**2**	**0**	**0**	**0**	**0**	**8**	**0.0**	**5**	**0**	**0.0**	**15:22**	....	....	....	....	....	....	....	....	....
2013-14	**Montreal**	**NHL**	**17**	**0**	**2**	**2**	**8**	**0**	**0**	**0**	**15**	**0.0**	**6**	**0**	**0.0**	**13:14**	**7**	**0**	**2**	**2**	**2**	**0**	**0**	**0**	**10:46**
	Hamilton	AHL	57	7	20	27	33	....	....	....	....	....	....	....	....	....	....	....	....	....	....	....	....	....	....
2014-15	**Montreal**	**NHL**	**64**	**1**	**8**	**9**	**45**	**0**	**0**	**0**	**62**	**1.6**	**6**	**0**	**0.0**	**15:42**	**5**	**0**	**1**	**1**	**0**	**0**	**0**	**0**	**12:55**
	Hamilton	AHL	8	2	2	4	9	....	....	....	....	....	....	....	....	....	....	....	....	....	....	....	....	....	....
2015-16	**Montreal**	**NHL**	**64**	**2**	**17**	**19**	**55**	**1**	**0**	**0**	**74**	**2.7**	**–6**	**0**	**0.0**	**17:27**	....	....	....	....	....	....	....	....	....
2016-17	**Montreal**	**NHL**	**74**	**4**	**24**	**28**	**44**	**2**	**0**	**1**	**118**	**3.4**	**8**	**0**	**0.0**	**19:29**	**5**	**0**	**1**	**1**	**0**	**0**	**0**	**0**	**17:33**
	NHL Totals		**225**	**7**	**53**	**60**	**152**	**3**	**0**	**1**	**277**	**2.5**		**0**	**0.0**	**17:15**	**17**	**0**	**4**	**4**	**2**	**0**	**0**	**0**	**13:24**

Traded to **Buffalo** by **Montreal** for Buffalo's 3rd round pick (Scott Walford) in 2017 NHL Draft, June 17, 2017.

BEAUVILLIER, Anthony
(boh-VIHL-yay, AN-thuh-NEE) **NYI**

Left wing. Shoots left. 5'11", 176 lbs. Born, Sorel-Tracy, QC, June 8, 1997. NY Islanders' 2nd pick, 28th overall, in 2015 NHL Draft.

Season	Club	League	GP	G	A	Pts	PIM	PP	SH	GW	S	S%	+/-	TF	F%	Min	GP	G	A	Pts	PIM	PP	SH	GW	Min
			Regular Season														Playoffs								
2011-12	Antoine-Girouard	Minor-QC	27	27	13	40	52	....	....	....	....	....	....	....	....	....	....	....	....	....	....	....	....	....	....
	Antoine-Girouard	QAAA	9	1	1	2	4	....	....	....	....	....	....	....	....	....	1	0	0	0	0	....	....	....	....
2012-13	Antoine-Girouard	QAAA	41	*39	25	*64	22	....	....	....	....	....	....	....	....	....	13	5	10	15	24	....	....	....	....
2013-14	Shawinigan	QMJHL	64	9	24	33	26	....	....	....	....	....	....	....	....	....	4	0	0	0	8	....	....	....	....
2014-15	Shawinigan	QMJHL	67	42	52	94	72	....	....	....	....	....	....	....	....	....	7	2	5	7	14	....	....	....	....
2015-16	Shawinigan	QMJHL	47	40	39	79	57	....	....	....	....	....	....	....	....	....	21	*15	15	30	16	....	....	....	....
2016-17	**NY Islanders**	**NHL**	**66**	**9**	**15**	**24**	**10**	**0**	**0**	**2**	**101**	**8.9**	**1**	**297**	**41.4**	**13:01**	....	....	....	....	....	....	....	....	....
	NHL Totals		**66**	**9**	**15**	**24**	**10**	**0**	**0**	**2**	**101**	**8.9**		**297**	**41.4**	**13:01**	....	....	....	....	....	....	....	....	....

QMJHL Second All-Star Team (2015)

BECK, Taylor
(BEHK, TAY-luhr)

Right wing. Shoots right. 6'2", 200 lbs. Born, St. Catharines, ON, May 13, 1991. Nashville's 4th pick, 70th overall, in 2009 NHL Draft.

Season	Club	League	GP	G	A	Pts	PIM	PP	SH	GW	S	S%	+/-	TF	F%	Min	GP	G	A	Pts	PIM	PP	SH	GW	Min
			Regular Season														Playoffs								
2006-07	N.F. Thunder	Minor-ON	69	64	75	139	76	....	....	....	....	....	....	....	....	....	....	....	....	....	....	....	....	....	....
2007-08	Guelph Storm	OHL	56	7	14	21	43	....	....	....	....	....	....	....	....	....	7	0	0	0	4	....	....	....	....
2008-09	Guelph Storm	OHL	67	22	36	58	36	....	....	....	....	....	....	....	....	....	4	0	0	0	2	....	....	....	....
2009-10	Guelph Storm	OHL	61	39	54	93	54	....	....	....	....	....	....	....	....	....	5	3	3	6	2	....	....	....	....
2010-11	Guelph Storm	OHL	62	42	53	95	60	....	....	....	....	....	....	....	....	....	6	3	5	8	10	....	....	....	....
	Milwaukee	AHL	4	0	1	1	0	....	....	....	....	....	....	....	....	....	8	2	0	2	2	....	....	....	....
2011-12	Milwaukee	AHL	74	16	24	40	32	....	....	....	....	....	....	....	....	....	3	0	1	1	2	....	....	....	....
2012-13	Milwaukee	AHL	50	11	30	41	28	....	....	....	....	....	....	....	....	....	2	0	1	1	2	....	....	....	....
	Nashville	**NHL**	**16**	**3**	**4**	**7**	**2**	**1**	**0**	**0**	**39**	**7.7**	**0**	**9**	**66.7**	**16:06**	....	....	....	....	....	....	....	....	....

			Regular Season														Playoffs								
Season	Club	League	GP	G	A	Pts	PIM	PP	SH	GW	S	S%	+/-	TF	F%	Min	GP	G	A	Pts	PIM	PP	SH	GW	Min
2013-14	**Nashville**	**NHL**	**7**	**0**	**0**	**0**	**6**	**0**	**0**	**0**	**9**	**0.0**	**–2**	**0**	**0.0**	**12:50**	....	....	....	....	....	....	....	....	....
	Milwaukee	AHL	65	17	32	49	38	....	....	....	....	....	....	....	....	....	3	0	0	0	2	....	....	....	....
2014-15	**Nashville**	**NHL**	**62**	**8**	**8**	**16**	**18**	**2**	**0**	**3**	**78**	**10.3**	**–4**	**10**	**50.0**	**11:56**	**5**	**0**	**0**	**0**	**2**	**0**	**0**	**0**	**12:55**
2015-16	**NY Islanders**	**NHL**	**2**	**0**	**0**	**0**	**2**	**0**	**0**	**0**	**0**	**0.0**	**0**	**0**	**0.0**	**8:29**	....	....	....	....	....	....	....	....	....
	Bridgeport	AHL	46	16	17	33	30	....	....	....	....	....	....	....	....	....	....	....	....	....	....	....	....	....	....
	San Antonio	AHL	4	1	0	1	2	....	....	....	....	....	....	....	....	....	....	....	....	....	....	....	....	....	....
2016-17	**Edmonton**	**NHL**	**3**	**0**	**0**	**0**	**4**	**0**	**0**	**0**	**0**	**0.0**	**–1**	**0**	**0.0**	**5:53**	....	....	....	....	....	....	....	....	....
	Bakersfield	AHL	40	13	37	50	18	....	....	....	....	....	....	....	....	....	....	....	....	....	....	....	....	....	....
	NY Rangers	**NHL**	**2**	**0**	**0**	**0**	**0**	**0**	**0**	**0**	**5**	**0.0**	**–2**	**1**	**0.0**	**13:12**	....	....	....	....	....	....	....	....	....
	Hartford	AHL	16	6	10	16	6	....	....	....	....	....	....	....	....	....	....	....	....	....	....	....	....	....	....
	NHL Totals		**92**	**11**	**12**	**23**	**32**	**3**	**0**	**3**	**131**	**8.4**		**20**	**55.0**	**12:29**	**5**	**0**	**0**	**0**	**2**	**0**	**0**	**0**	**12:55**

OHL Second All-Star Team (2010) • AHL First All-Star Team (2017)

Traded to **Toronto** by **Nashville** for Jamie Devane, July 12, 2015. Traded to **NY Islanders** by **Toronto** with Carter Verhaeghe, Christopher Gibson, Tom Nilsson and Matt Finn for Michael Grabner, September 17, 2015. Traded to **Colorado** by **NY Islanders** for Marc-Andre Cliché, February 29, 2016. Signed as a free agent by **Edmonton**, July 3, 2016. Traded to **NY Rangers** by **Edmonton** for Justin Fontaine, March 1, 2017.

BELESKEY, Matt (beh-LEH-skee, MAT) BOS

Left wing. Shoots left. 6', 203 lbs. Born, Windsor, ON, June 7, 1988. Anaheim's 4th pick, 112th overall, in 2006 NHL Draft.

Season	Club	League	GP	G	A	Pts	PIM	PP	SH	GW	S	S%	+/-	TF	F%	Min	GP	G	A	Pts	PIM	PP	SH	GW	Min
2003-04	Collingwood	ON-Jr.A	46	8	13	21	110	....	....	....	....	....	....	....	....	....	8	1	7	8	18	....	....	....	....
2004-05	Belleville Bulls	OHL	68	10	13	23	118	....	....	....	....	....	....	....	....	....	5	0	0	0	18	....	....	....	....
2005-06	Belleville Bulls	OHL	61	20	20	40	119	....	....	....	....	....	....	....	....	....	6	1	2	3	10	....	....	....	....
2006-07	Belleville Bulls	OHL	66	27	41	68	124	....	....	....	....	....	....	....	....	....	15	4	10	14	18	....	....	....	....
2007-08	Belleville Bulls	OHL	62	41	49	90	106	....	....	....	....	....	....	....	....	....	21	12	21	33	23	....	....	....	....
2008-09	**Anaheim**	**NHL**	**2**	**0**	**0**	**0**	**0**	**0**	**0**	**0**	**0**	**0.0**	**0**	**2**	**0.0**	**11:10**	....	....	....	....	....	....	....	....	....
	Iowa Chops	AHL	58	11	24	35	58	....	....	....	....	....	....	....	....	....	....	....	....	....	....	....	....	....	....
2009-10	**Anaheim**	**NHL**	**60**	**11**	**7**	**18**	**35**	**0**	**0**	**3**	**123**	**8.9**	**–10**	**20**	**40.0**	**13:59**	....	....	....	....	....	....	....	....	....
	San Antonio	AHL	12	1	4	5	19	....	....	....	....	....	....	....	....	....	....	....	....	....	....	....	....	....	....
	Toronto Marlies	AHL	3	1	1	2	2	....	....	....	....	....	....	....	....	....	....	....	....	....	....	....	....	....	....
2010-11	**Anaheim**	**NHL**	**35**	**3**	**7**	**10**	**36**	**0**	**0**	**0**	**58**	**5.2**	**–10**	**8**	**37.5**	**12:59**	**6**	**1**	**0**	**1**	**4**	**0**	**0**	**0**	**11:14**
	Syracuse Crunch	AHL	27	11	13	24	39	....	....	....	....	....	....	....	....	....	....	....	....	....	....	....	....	....	....
2011-12	**Anaheim**	**NHL**	**70**	**4**	**11**	**15**	**72**	**0**	**0**	**0**	**75**	**5.3**	**–2**	**26**	**42.3**	**10:16**	....	....	....	....	....	....	....	....	....
2012-13	Coventry Blaze	Britain	26	12	21	33	39	....	....	....	....	....	....	....	....	....	....	....	....	....	....	....	....	....	....
	Anaheim	**NHL**	**42**	**8**	**5**	**13**	**56**	**2**	**0**	**1**	**61**	**13.1**	**2**	**19**	**31.6**	**12:01**	**7**	**2**	**1**	**3**	**2**	**1**	**0**	**0**	**11:01**
2013-14	**Anaheim**	**NHL**	**55**	**9**	**15**	**24**	**64**	**0**	**0**	**2**	**112**	**8.0**	**8**	**18**	**44.4**	**12:26**	**5**	**2**	**2**	**4**	**8**	**1**	**0**	**1**	**14:34**
	Norfolk Admirals	AHL	3	1	0	1	0	....	....	....	....	....	....	....	....	....	....	....	....	....	....	....	....	....	....
2014-15	**Anaheim**	**NHL**	**65**	**22**	**10**	**32**	**39**	**4**	**0**	**8**	**145**	**15.2**	**13**	**19**	**42.1**	**14:29**	**16**	**8**	**1**	**9**	**2**	**3**	**0**	**3**	**16:00**
2015-16	**Boston**	**NHL**	**80**	**15**	**22**	**37**	**65**	**3**	**0**	**1**	**168**	**8.9**	**6**	**25**	**24.0**	**15:51**	....	....	....	....	....	....	....	....	....
2016-17	**Boston**	**NHL**	**49**	**3**	**5**	**8**	**47**	**0**	**0**	**0**	**79**	**3.8**	**–10**	**70**	**41.4**	**13:16**	**3**	**0**	**0**	**0**	**4**	**0**	**0**	**0**	**7:59**
	NHL Totals		**458**	**75**	**82**	**157**	**414**	**9**	**0**	**15**	**821**	**9.1**		**207**	**38.2**	**13:17**	**37**	**13**	**4**	**17**	**20**	**5**	**0**	**4**	**13:26**

Signed as a free agent by **Coventry** (Britain), October 9, 2012. Signed as a free agent by **Boston**, July 1, 2015.

BELLEMARE, Pierre-Edouard (BEHL-mahr, PEE-air-EHD-wawrd) VGK

Left wing. Shoots left. 6', 198 lbs. Born, Paris, France, March 6, 1985.

Season	Club	League	GP	G	A	Pts	PIM	PP	SH	GW	S	S%	+/-	TF	F%	Min	GP	G	A	Pts	PIM	PP	SH	GW	Min
2002-03	HC Rouen	France	11	0	1	1	6	....	....	....	....	....	....	....	....	....	....	....	....	....	....	....	....	....	....
2003-04	HC Rouen	France	22	10	10	20	16	....	....	....	....	....	....	....	....	....	4	1	1	2	4	....	....	....	....
2004-05	HC Rouen	France	28	4	15	19	20	....	....	....	....	....	....	....	....	....	12	7	5	12	6	....	....	....	....
2005-06	HC Rouen	France	26	12	17	29	24	....	....	....	....	....	....	....	....	....	9	2	7	9	6	....	....	....	....
2006-07	Leksands IF	Sweden-2	44	8	11	19	24	....	....	....	....	....	....	....	....	....	10	1	0	1	4	....	....	....	....
2007-08	Leksands IF Jr.	Swe-Jr.	2	1	0	1	14	....	....	....	....	....	....	....	....	....	....	....	....	....	....	....	....	....	....
	Leksands IF	Sweden-2	40	14	15	29	12	....	....	....	....	....	....	....	....	....	10	2	3	5	4	....	....	....	....
2008-09	Leksands IF	Sweden-2	41	31	18	49	113	....	....	....	....	....	....	....	....	....	10	5	5	10	6	....	....	....	....
2009-10	Skelleftea AIK	Sweden	49	9	5	14	16	....	....	....	....	....	....	....	....	....	12	2	7	9	8	....	....	....	....
2010-11	Skelleftea AIK	Sweden	53	10	8	18	20	....	....	....	....	....	....	....	....	....	16	1	4	5	0	....	....	....	....
2011-12	Skelleftea AIK	Sweden	55	19	17	36	40	....	....	....	....	....	....	....	....	....	15	4	8	12	12	....	....	....	....
2012-13	Skelleftea AIK	Sweden	29	6	16	22	47	....	....	....	....	....	....	....	....	....	9	0	1	1	2	....	....	....	....
2013-14	Skelleftea AIK	Sweden	52	20	15	35	32	....	....	....	....	....	....	....	....	....	14	9	5	14	6	....	....	....	....
2014-15	**Philadelphia**	**NHL**	**81**	**6**	**6**	**12**	**18**	**0**	**0**	**1**	**113**	**5.3**	**–3**	**761**	**47.3**	**12:50**	....	....	....	....	....	....	....	....	....
2015-16	**Philadelphia**	**NHL**	**74**	**7**	**7**	**14**	**27**	**0**	**1**	**1**	**102**	**6.9**	**–8**	**579**	**47.0**	**13:34**	**5**	**0**	**1**	**1**	**15**	**0**	**0**	**0**	**14:11**
2016-17	**Philadelphia**	**NHL**	**82**	**4**	**4**	**8**	**20**	**0**	**0**	**0**	**90**	**4.4**	**–1**	**831**	**48.4**	**12:58**	....	....	....	....	....	....	....	....	....
	NHL Totals		**237**	**17**	**17**	**34**	**65**	**0**	**1**	**2**	**305**	**5.6**		**2171**	**47.6**	**13:07**	**5**	**0**	**1**	**1**	**15**	**0**	**0**	**0**	**14:11**

Signed as a free agent by **Philadelphia**, June 11, 2014. Claimed by **Vegas** from **Philadelphia** in Expansion Draft, June 21, 2017.

BENN, Jamie (BEHN, JAY-mee) DAL

Left wing. Shoots left. 6'2", 210 lbs. Born, Victoria, BC, July 18, 1989. Dallas' 5th pick, 129th overall, in 2007 NHL Draft.

Season	Club	League	GP	G	A	Pts	PIM	PP	SH	GW	S	S%	+/-	TF	F%	Min	GP	G	A	Pts	PIM	PP	SH	GW	Min
2004-05	Peninsula Eagles	Minor-BC	STATISTICS NOT AVAILABLE																						
	Peninsula	VIJHL	4	1	2	3	2	....	....	....	....	....	....	....	....	....	2	0	0	0	0	....	....	....	....
2005-06	Peninsula	VIJHL	38	31	24	55	92	....	....	....	....	....	....	....	....	....	7	5	7	10	20	....	....	....	....
	Victoria Salsa	BCHL	6	0	0	0	0	....	....	....	....	....	....	....	....	....	....	....	....	....	....	....	....	....	....
2006-07	Victoria Grizzlies	BCHL	53	42	23	65	78	....	....	....	....	....	....	....	....	....	11	5	4	9	12	....	....	....	....
2007-08	Victoria Grizzlies	BCHL	2	0	0	0	2	....	....	....	....	....	....	....	....	....	....	....	....	....	....	....	....	....	....
	Kelowna Rockets	WHL	51	33	32	65	68	....	....	....	....	....	....	....	....	....	7	3	8	11	4	....	....	....	....
2008-09	Kelowna Rockets	WHL	56	46	36	82	71	....	....	....	....	....	....	....	....	....	19	*13	*20	*33	18	....	....	....	....
2009-10	**Dallas**	**NHL**	**82**	**22**	**19**	**41**	**45**	**2**	**0**	**3**	**182**	**12.1**	**–1**	**236**	**46.2**	**14:42**	....	....	....	....	....	....	....	....	....
	Texas Stars	AHL	....	....	....	....	....	....	....	....	....	....	....	....	....	....	24	*14	12	26	22	....	....	....	....
2010-11	**Dallas**	**NHL**	**69**	**22**	**34**	**56**	**52**	**6**	**4**	**3**	**177**	**12.4**	**–5**	**195**	**43.1**	**18:01**	....	....	....	....	....	....	....	....	....
2011-12	**Dallas**	**NHL**	**71**	**26**	**37**	**63**	**55**	**2**	**1**	**7**	**203**	**12.8**	**15**	**751**	**46.2**	**18:04**	....	....	....	....	....	....	....	....	....
2012-13	Hamburg Freezers	Germany	19	7	13	20	30	....	....	....	....	....	....	....	....	....	....	....	....	....	....	....	....	....	....
	Dallas	**NHL**	**41**	**12**	**21**	**33**	**40**	**3**	**0**	**3**	**110**	**10.9**	**–12**	**709**	**46.1**	**19:55**	....	....	....	....	....	....	....	....	....
2013-14	**Dallas**	**NHL**	**81**	**34**	**45**	**79**	**64**	**5**	**1**	**3**	**279**	**12.2**	**21**	**778**	**52.8**	**19:09**	**6**	**4**	**1**	**5**	**4**	**1**	**1**	**1**	**21:10**
	Canada	Olympics	6	2	0	2	4	....	....	....	....	....	....	....	....	....	....	....	....	....	....	....	....	....	....
2014-15	**Dallas**	**NHL**	**82**	**35**	**52**	***87**	**64**	**10**	**2**	**6**	**253**	**13.8**	**1**	**576**	**51.7**	**19:57**	....	....	....	....	....	....	....	....	....
2015-16	**Dallas**	**NHL**	**82**	**41**	**48**	**89**	**64**	**17**	**2**	**5**	**247**	**16.6**	**7**	**478**	**47.3**	**20:01**	**13**	**5**	**10**	**15**	**10**	**0**	**0**	**1**	**21:22**
2016-17	**Dallas**	**NHL**	**77**	**26**	**43**	**69**	**66**	**12**	**1**	**4**	**201**	**12.9**	**–9**	**412**	**51.5**	**19:22**	....	....	....	....	....	....	....	....	....
	NHL Totals		**585**	**218**	**299**	**517**	**450**	**57**	**11**	**34**	**1652**	**13.2**		**4135**	**48.7**	**18:35**	**19**	**9**	**11**	**20**	**14**	**1**	**1**	**2**	**21:18**

WHL West First All-Star Team (2009) • NHL First All-Star Team (2014, 2016) • NHL Second All-Star Team (2015) • Art Ross Trophy (2015)

Played in NHL All-Star Game (2012, 2016)

Signed as a free agent by **Hamburg** (Germany), October 3, 2012.

BENN, Jordie (BEHN, JOHR-dee) MTL

Defense. Shoots left. 6'2", 200 lbs. Born, Victoria, BC, July 26, 1987.

Season	Club	League	GP	G	A	Pts	PIM	PP	SH	GW	S	S%	+/-	TF	F%	Min	GP	G	A	Pts	PIM	PP	SH	GW	Min
2004-05	Peninsula	VIJHL	45	5	21	26	35	....	....	....	....	....	....	....	....	....	....	....	....	....	....	....	....	....	....
	Victoria Salsa	BCHL	4	0	1	1	6	....	....	....	....	....	....	....	....	....	1	0	0	0	2	....	....	....	....
2005-06	Victoria Salsa	BCHL	55	5	20	25	61	....	....	....	....	....	....	....	....	....	16	1	5	6	6	....	....	....	....
2006-07	Victoria Grizzlies	BCHL	53	4	37	41	62	....	....	....	....	....	....	....	....	....	11	1	7	8	22	....	....	....	....
2007-08	Victoria Grizzlies	BCHL	60	15	32	47	78	....	....	....	....	....	....	....	....	....	11	2	8	10	8	....	....	....	....
2008-09	Victoria	ECHL	55	1	11	12	26	....	....	....	....	....	....	....	....	....	3	0	0	0	0	....	....	....	....
2009-10	Allen Americans	CHL	45	9	9	18	55	....	....	....	....	....	....	....	....	....	20	2	9	11	12	....	....	....	....
2010-11	Texas Stars	AHL	60	2	10	12	39	....	....	....	....	....	....	....	....	....	1	0	0	0	0	....	....	....	....
2011-12	**Dallas**	**NHL**	**3**	**0**	**2**	**2**	**0**	**0**	**0**	**0**	**1**	**0.0**	**1**	**0**	**0.0**	**13:57**	....	....	....	....	....	....	....	....	....
	Texas Stars	AHL	62	9	23	32	33	....	....	....	....	....	....	....	....	....	....	....	....	....	....	....	....	....	....
2012-13	Texas Stars	AHL	43	7	14	21	33	....	....	....	....	....	....	....	....	....	7	0	2	2	10	....	....	....	....
	Dallas	**NHL**	**26**	**1**	**5**	**6**	**10**	**1**	**0**	**0**	**31**	**3.2**	**–4**	**0**	**0.0**	**17:19**	....	....	....	....	....	....	....	....	....
2013-14	**Dallas**	**NHL**	**78**	**3**	**17**	**20**	**30**	**1**	**0**	**0**	**91**	**3.3**	**16**	**1**	**100.0**	**19:09**	**6**	**0**	**3**	**3**	**2**	**0**	**0**	**0**	**21:57**
2014-15	**Dallas**	**NHL**	**73**	**2**	**14**	**16**	**34**	**0**	**0**	**0**	**70**	**2.9**	**–5**	**1**	**0.0**	**18:04**	....	....	....	....	....	....	....	....	....

			Regular Season														Playoffs								
Season	Club	League	GP	G	A	Pts	PIM	PP	SH	GW	S	S%	+/-	TF	F%	Min	GP	G	A	Pts	PIM	PP	SH	GW	Min
2015-16	Dallas	NHL	64	3	9	12	21	1	0	2	58	5.2	2	0	0.0	15:39	1	0	0	0	4	0	0	0	12:21
2016-17	Dallas	NHL	58	2	13	15	24	0	0	0	59	3.4	−3	0	0.0	18:37	....	....	....	....	....	....	....	....	....
	Montreal	NHL	13	2	0	2	4	0	0	1	9	22.2	−1	0	0.0	16:50	6	0	0	0	6	0	0	0	20:20
	NHL Totals		315	13	60	73	123	3	0	3	319	4.1		2	50.0	17:48	13	0	3	3	12	0	0	0	20:28

Signed as a free agent by **Texas** (AHL), October 8, 2010. Signed as a free agent by **Dallas**, July 1, 2011. Traded to **Montreal** by **Dallas** for Greg Pateryn and Montreal's 4th round pick (later traded to Los Angeles – Los Angeles selected Markus Phillips) in 2017 NHL Draft, February 26, 2017.

BENNETT, Beau
(BEH-neht, BOH) **ST.L.**

Right wing. Shoots right. 6'2", 195 lbs. Born, Gardena, CA, November 27, 1991. Pittsburgh's 1st pick, 20th overall, in 2010 NHL Draft.

Season	Club	League	GP	G	A	Pts	PIM	PP	SH	GW	S	S%	+/-	TF	F%	Min	GP	G	A	Pts	PIM	PP	SH	GW	Min
2008-09	L.A. Jr. Kings	T1EHL	46	25	33	58	10	....	....	....	....	....	....	....	....	....	....	....	....	....	....	....	....	....	....
2009-10	Penticton Vees	BCHL	56	41	79	*120	20	....	....	....	....	....	....	....	....	....	15	5	9	14	6	....	....	....	....
2010-11	U. of Denver	WCHA	37	9	16	25	18	....	....	....	....	....	....	....	....	....	....	....	....	....	....	....	....	....	....
2011-12	U. of Denver	WCHA	10	4	9	13	25	....	....	....	....	....	....	....	....	....	....	....	....	....	....	....	....	....	....
2012-13	Wilkes-Barre	AHL	39	7	21	28	18	....	....	....	....	....	....	....	....	....	....	....	....	....	....	....	....	....	....
	Pittsburgh	NHL	26	3	11	14	6	1	0	2	30	10.0	7	4	25.0	12:18	6	1	0	1	0	1	0	1	11:05
2013-14	Pittsburgh	NHL	21	3	4	7	0	0	0	1	27	11.1	−2	2	100.0	13:51	12	1	4	5	8	1	0	0	12:24
	Wilkes-Barre	AHL	3	0	1	1	0	....	....	....	....	....	....	....	....	....	....	....	....	....	....	....	....	....	....
2014-15	Pittsburgh	NHL	49	4	8	12	16	0	0	1	81	4.9	−1	2	0.0	12:29	2	0	0	0	0	0	0	0	8:02
	Wilkes-Barre	AHL	2	0	5	5	0	....	....	....	....	....	....	....	....	....	....	....	....	....	....	....	....	....	....
2015-16	Pittsburgh	NHL	33	6	6	12	10	1	0	0	52	11.5	−1	6	33.3	11:54	1	0	0	0	0	0	0	0	11:18
2016-17	New Jersey	NHL	65	8	11	19	20	1	0	1	101	7.9	−3	16	18.8	13:33	....	....	....	....	....	....	....	....	....
	NHL Totals		194	24	40	64	52	3	0	5	291	8.2		30	26.7	12:52	21	2	4	6	8	2	0	1	11:33

• Missed majority of 2013-14 due to wrist injury vs. Boston, November 22, 2013. • Missed majority of 2015-16 due to recurring upper-body injury and as a healthy reserve. Traded to **New Jersey** by **Pittsburgh** for Detroit's 3rd round pick (previously acquired, Pittsburgh selected Connor Hall) in 2016 NHL Draft, June 25, 2016. Signed as a free agent by **St. Louis**, July 1, 2017.

BENNETT, Sam
(BEH-neht, SAM) **CGY**

Center. Shoots left. 6'1", 186 lbs. Born, Holland Landing, ON, June 20, 1996. Calgary's 1st pick, 4th overall, in 2014 NHL Draft.

Season	Club	League	GP	G	A	Pts	PIM	PP	SH	GW	S	S%	+/-	TF	F%	Min	GP	G	A	Pts	PIM	PP	SH	GW	Min
2011-12	Tor. Marlboros	GTHL	37	33	36	69	34	....	....	....	....	....	....	....	....	....	....	....	....	....	....	....	....	....	....
2012-13	Kingston	OHL	60	18	22	40	87	....	....	....	....	....	....	....	....	....	4	0	3	3	2	....	....	....	....
2013-14	Kingston	OHL	57	36	55	91	118	....	....	....	....	....	....	....	....	....	7	5	4	9	18	....	....	....	....
2014-15	Kingston	OHL	11	11	13	24	14	....	....	....	....	....	....	....	....	....	4	0	3	3	4	....	....	....	....
	Calgary	NHL	1	0	1	1	0	0	0	0	1	0.0	−1	6	16.7	16:00	11	3	1	4	8	0	0	1	14:01
2015-16	Calgary	NHL	77	18	18	36	37	3	0	2	136	13.2	−11	347	46.1	15:09	....	....	....	....	....	....	....	....	....
2016-17	Calgary	NHL	81	13	13	26	75	4	0	0	122	10.7	−16	811	46.1	14:59	4	2	0	2	4	1	0	0	13:40
	NHL Totals		159	31	32	63	112	7	0	2	259	12.0		1164	46.0	15:04	15	5	1	6	12	1	0	1	13:56

• Missed majority of 2014-15 due to recurring shoulder injury.

BENNING, Matt
(BENH-ihng, MAT) **EDM**

Defense. Shoots right. 6'1", 195 lbs. Born, Edmonton, AB, May 25, 1994. Boston's 5th pick, 175th overall, in 2012 NHL Draft.

Season	Club	League	GP	G	A	Pts	PIM	PP	SH	GW	S	S%	+/-	TF	F%	Min	GP	G	A	Pts	PIM	PP	SH	GW	Min
2008-09	St. Albert Sabres	AMBHL	33	2	15	17	44	....	....	....	....	....	....	....	....	....	....	....	....	....	....	....	....	....	....
2009-10	St. Albert Raiders	AMHL	33	7	14	21	32	....	....	....	....	....	....	....	....	....	4	1	0	1	2	....	....	....	....
2010-11	Spruce Grove	AJHL	43	0	7	7	65	....	....	....	....	....	....	....	....	....	13	0	1	1	20	....	....	....	....
2011-12	Spruce Grove	AJHL	44	4	14	18	87	....	....	....	....	....	....	....	....	....	11	2	1	3	16	....	....	....	....
2012-13	Dubuque	USHL	57	10	16	26	73	....	....	....	....	....	....	....	....	....	10	1	1	2	6	....	....	....	....
2013-14	Northeastern	H-East	33	3	10	13	28	....	....	....	....	....	....	....	....	....	....	....	....	....	....	....	....	....	....
2014-15	Northeastern	H-East	36	0	24	24	36	....	....	....	....	....	....	....	....	....	....	....	....	....	....	....	....	....	....
2015-16	Northeastern	H-East	41	6	13	19	37	....	....	....	....	....	....	....	....	....	....	....	....	....	....	....	....	....	....
2016-17	Edmonton	NHL	62	3	12	15	29	1	0	0	69	4.3	8	0	0.0	16:37	12	0	3	3	12	0	0	0	17:08
	NHL Totals		62	3	12	15	29	1	0	0	69	4.3		0	0.0	16:37	12	0	3	3	12	0	0	0	17:08

Signed as a free agent by **Edmonton**, August 27, 2016.

BENOIT, Andre
(behn-WAH, AWN-dray) **CBJ**

Defense. Shoots left. 5'11", 191 lbs. Born, St. Albert, ON, January 6, 1984.

Season	Club	League	GP	G	A	Pts	PIM	PP	SH	GW	S	S%	+/-	TF	F%	Min	GP	G	A	Pts	PIM	PP	SH	GW	Min
2000-01	Kitchener Rangers	OHL	65	16	19	35	37	....	....	....	....	....	....	....	....	....	....	....	....	....	....	....	....	....	....
2001-02	Kitchener Rangers	OHL	62	13	32	45	77	....	....	....	....	....	....	....	....	....	4	1	0	1	8	....	....	....	....
2002-03	Kitchener Rangers	OHL	65	22	45	67	77	....	....	....	....	....	....	....	....	....	21	1	16	17	16	....	....	....	....
2003-04	Kitchener Rangers	OHL	65	24	51	75	67	....	....	....	....	....	....	....	....	....	5	1	1	2	6	....	....	....	....
2004-05	Kitchener Rangers	OHL	67	24	53	77	72	....	....	....	....	....	....	....	....	....	15	5	13	18	6	....	....	....	....
2005-06	Hamilton	AHL	70	7	19	26	60	....	....	....	....	....	....	....	....	....	....	....	....	....	....	....	....	....	....
2006-07	Hamilton	AHL	64	10	21	31	41	....	....	....	....	....	....	....	....	....	22	2	11	13	22	....	....	....	....
2007-08	Tappara Tampere	Finland	54	12	26	38	96	....	....	....	....	....	....	....	....	....	11	2	3	5	10	....	....	....	....
2008-09	Sodertalje SK	Sweden	54	4	16	20	34	....	....	....	....	....	....	....	....	....	....	....	....	....	....	....	....	....	....
	Sodertalje SK	Sweden-Q	10	0	2	'2	10	....	....	....	....	....	....	....	....	....	....	....	....	....	....	....	....	....	....
2009-10	Hamilton	AHL	78	6	30	36	63	....	....	....	....	....	....	....	....	....	19	3	11	14	8	....	....	....	....
2010-11	Ottawa	NHL	8	0	1	1	6	0	0	0	17	0.0	−1	0	0.0	16:50	....	....	....	....	....	....	....	....	....
	Binghamton	AHL	73	11	44	55	53	....	....	....	....	....	....	....	....	....	23	3	*15	18	14	....	....	....	....
2011-12	Spartak Moscow	KHL	53	5	12	17	34	....	....	....	....	....	....	....	....	....	....	....	....	....	....	....	....	....	....
2012-13	Binghamton	AHL	34	9	16	25	28	....	....	....	....	....	....	....	....	....	....	....	....	....	....	....	....	....	....
	Ottawa	NHL	33	3	7	10	8	1	0	2	50	6.0	−3	0	0.0	16:25	5	0	3	3	0	0	0	0	15:28
2013-14	Colorado	NHL	79	7	21	28	26	1	0	2	113	6.2	2	0	0.0	20:13	7	0	1	1	6	0	0	0	21:17
2014-15	Buffalo	NHL	59	1	8	9	20	0	1	0	45	2.2	−19	0	0.0	18:09	....	....	....	....	....	....	....	....	....
2015-16	St. Louis	NHL	2	0	0	0	0	0	0	0	0	0.0	1	0	0.0	13:35	....	....	....	....	....	....	....	....	....
	Chicago Wolves	AHL	72	8	25	33	26	....	....	....	....	....	....	....	....	....	....	....	....	....	....	....	....	....	....
2016-17	Malmo	Sweden	52	6	18	24	22	....	....	....	....	....	....	....	....	....	13	0	2	2	8	....	....	....	....
	NHL Totals		181	11	37	48	60	2	1	4	225	4.9		0	0.0	18:38	12	0	4	4	6	0	0	0	18:52

AHL Second All-Star Team (2011)

Signed as a free agent by **Montreal**, January 9, 2006. Signed as a free agent by **Tappara Tampere** (Finland), June 21, 2007. Signed as a free agent by **Sodertalje** (Sweden), April 7, 2008. Signed as a free agent by **Montreal**, May 13, 2009. Signed as a free agent by **Ottawa**, August 6, 2010. Signed as a free agent by **Spartak Moscow** (KHL), August 11, 2011. Signed as a free agent by **Ottawa**, July 2, 2012. Signed as a free agent by **Colorado**, July 5, 2013. Signed as a free agent by **Buffalo**, July 23, 2014. Signed as a free agent by **St. Louis**, July 6, 2015. Signed as a free agent by **Malmo** (Sweden), July 22, 2016. Signed as a free agent by **Columbus**, July 1, 2017.

BERGERON, Patrice
(BUHR-zhuhr-uhn, pa-TREES) **BOS**

Center. Shoots right. 6'1", 195 lbs. Born, Ancienne-Lorette, QC, July 24, 1985. Boston's 2nd pick, 45th overall, in 2003 NHL Draft.

Season	Club	League	GP	G	A	Pts	PIM	PP	SH	GW	S	S%	+/-	TF	F%	Min	GP	G	A	Pts	PIM	PP	SH	GW	Min
2000-01	Ste-Foy	QAAA	5	1	2	3	0	....	....	....	....	....	....	....	....	....	....	....	....	....	....	....	....	....	....
2001-02	St-Francois	QAAA	38	25	37	62	18	....	....	....	....	....	....	....	....	....	8	6	4	10	10	....	....	....	....
	Acadie-Bathurst	QMJHL	4	0	1	1	0	....	....	....	....	....	....	....	....	....	....	....	....	....	....	....	....	....	....
2002-03	Acadie-Bathurst	QMJHL	70	23	50	73	62	....	....	....	....	....	....	....	....	....	11	6	9	15	6	....	....	....	....
2003-04	Boston	NHL	71	16	23	39	22	7	0	2	133	12.0	5	699	49.4	16:21	7	1	3	4	0	0	0	1	17:13
2004-05	Providence Bruins	AHL	68	21	40	61	59	....	....	....	....	....	....	....	....	....	16	5	7	12	4	....	....	....	....
2005-06	Boston	NHL	81	31	42	73	22	12	1	6	310	10.0	3	1447	54.7	20:36	....	....	....	....	....	....	....	....	....
2006-07	Boston	NHL	77	22	48	70	26	14	0	6	224	9.8	−28	1560	51.2	20:49	....	....	....	....	....	....	....	....	....
2007-08	Boston	NHL	10	3	4	7	2	2	0	0	24	12.5	2	175	50.3	18:10	....	....	....	....	....	....	....	....	....
2008-09	Boston	NHL	64	8	31	39	16	1	1	1	155	5.2	2	1025	54.5	17:59	11	0	5	5	11	0	0	0	17:56
2009-10	Boston	NHL	73	19	33	52	28	0	1	4	184	10.3	6	1342	58.0	18:54	13	4	7	11	2	0	0	1	20:23
	Canada	Olympics	7	0	1	1	2	....	....	....	....	....	....	....	....	....	....	....	....	....	....	....	....	....	....
2010-11 ♦	Boston	NHL	80	22	35	57	26	3	2	4	211	10.4	20	1439	56.6	17:53	23	6	14	20	28	0	*2	1	18:42
2011-12	Boston	NHL	81	22	42	64	20	5	2	3	191	11.5	36	1641	59.3	18:35	7	0	2	2	8	0	0	0	19:38
2012-13	HC Lugano	Swiss	21	11	18	29	8	....	....	....	....	....	....	....	....	....	....	....	....	....	....	....	....	....	....
	Boston	NHL	42	10	22	32	18	2	0	3	125	8.0	24	884	62.1	19:18	22	9	6	15	13	4	0	2	20:44
2013-14	Boston	NHL	80	30	32	62	43	7	1	7	243	12.3	38	1732	58.6	17:59	12	3	6	9	4	0	0	0	19:42
	Canada	Olympics	6	0	2	2	4	....	....	....	....	....	....	....	....	....	....	....	....	....	....	....	....	....	....
2014-15	Boston	NHL	81	23	32	55	44	4	1	4	234	9.8	2	1951	60.2	18:08	....	....	....	....	....	....	....	....	....

			Regular Season														Playoffs								
Season	Club	League	GP	G	A	Pts	PIM	PP	SH	GW	S	S%	+/-	TF	F%	Min	GP	G	A	Pts	PIM	PP	SH	GW	Min
2015-16	Boston	NHL	80	32	36	68	49	12	1	6	282	11.3	12	1978	57.1	19:50	....	....	....	....	....	....	....	....	....
2016-17	Boston	NHL	79	21	32	53	24	8	0	7	302	7.0	12	1812	60.1	19:25	6	2	2	4	2	1	0	0	22:52
	NHL Totals		899	259	412	671	340	77	10	53	2618	9.9		17685	57.1	18:49	101	25	45	70	68	5	2	5	19:36

QAAA Second All-Star Team (2002) • Frank J. Selke Trophy (2012, 2014, 2015, 2017) • King Clancy Memorial Trophy (2013) • NHL Foundation Player Award (2014)
Played in NHL All-Star Game (2015, 2016)
• Missed majority of 2007-08 due to head injury vs. Philadelphia, October 27, 2007. Signed as a free agent by **Lugano** (Swiss), October 2, 2012.

BERGLUND, Patrik

(BUHRG-luhnd, PAT-rihk) **ST.L.**

Center. Shoots left. 6'3", 217 lbs. Born, Vasteras, Sweden, June 2, 1988. St. Louis' 2nd pick, 25th overall, in 2006 NHL Draft.

2002-03	Vasteras U18	Swe-U18	1	0	1	1	0	....	....	....	....	....	....	....	....	....	....	....	....	....	....	....	....	....	....
2003-04	Vasteras U18	Swe-U18	10	4	1	5	18	....	....	....	....	....	....	....	....	....	....	....	....	....	....	....	....	....	....
2004-05	Vasteras U18	Swe-U18	5	2	1	3	4	....	....	....	....	....	....	....	....	....	3	0	1	1	6	....	....	....	....
	Vasteras Jr.	Swe-Jr.	25	5	5	10	14	....	....	....	....	....	....	....	....	....	....	....	....	....	....	....	....	....	....
2005-06	Vasteras Jr.	Swe-Jr.	27	17	12	29	38	....	....	....	....	....	....	....	....	....	....	....	....	....	....	....	....	....	....
	VIK Vasteras HK	Sweden-2	21	3	1	4	4	....	....	....	....	....	....	....	....	....	....	....	....	....	....	....	....	....	....
2006-07	VIK Vasteras HK	Sweden-2	35	21	27	48	30	....	....	....	....	....	....	....	....	....	1	0	0	0	2	....	....	....	....
	Vasteras Jr.	Swe-Jr.	....	....	....	....	....	....	....	....	....	....	....	....	....	....	5	4	5	9	6	....	....	....	....
2007-08	VIK Vasteras HK	Sweden-2	46	22	32	54	26	....	....	....	....	....	....	....	....	....	5	1	2	3	6	....	....	....	....
2008-09	**St. Louis**	**NHL**	**76**	**21**	**26**	**47**	**16**	**7**	**0**	**1**	**143**	**14.7**	**19**	**540**	**39.8**	**14:43**	**4**	**0**	**0**	**0**	**2**	**0**	**0**	**0**	**10:11**
2009-10	**St. Louis**	**NHL**	**71**	**13**	**13**	**26**	**16**	**6**	**0**	**4**	**129**	**10.1**	**–5**	**504**	**43.7**	**13:30**	....	....	....	....	....	....	....	....	....
2010-11	**St. Louis**	**NHL**	**81**	**22**	**30**	**52**	**26**	**8**	**0**	**1**	**175**	**12.6**	**–3**	**974**	**46.2**	**17:11**	....	....	....	....	....	....	....	....	....
2011-12	**St. Louis**	**NHL**	**82**	**19**	**19**	**38**	**30**	**0**	**2**	**3**	**188**	**10.1**	**4**	**1168**	**48.5**	**17:58**	**9**	**3**	**4**	**7**	**6**	**2**	**0**	**0**	**20:08**
2012-13	VIK Vasteras HK	Sweden-2	30	20	12	32	20	....	....	....	....	....	....	....	....	....	....	....	....	....	....	....	....	....	....
	St. Louis	**NHL**	**48**	**17**	**8**	**25**	**12**	**5**	**2**	**3**	**74**	**23.0**	**–2**	**603**	**46.3**	**16:50**	**6**	**1**	**1**	**2**	**2**	**0**	**0**	**0**	**17:46**
2013-14	**St. Louis**	**NHL**	**78**	**14**	**18**	**32**	**38**	**2**	**0**	**2**	**144**	**9.7**	**10**	**783**	**47.6**	**16:10**	**4**	**0**	**0**	**0**	**0**	**0**	**0**	**0**	**15:06**
	Sweden	Olympics	6	2	1	3	4	....	....	....	....	....	....	....	....	....	....	....	....	....	....	....	....	....	....
2014-15	**St. Louis**	**NHL**	**77**	**12**	**15**	**27**	**26**	**0**	**0**	**0**	**145**	**8.3**	**–2**	**329**	**48.6**	**14:35**	**6**	**2**	**2**	**4**	**0**	**0**	**0**	**0**	**13:58**
2015-16	**St. Louis**	**NHL**	**42**	**10**	**5**	**15**	**16**	**4**	**0**	**5**	**80**	**12.5**	**1**	**277**	**50.2**	**15:29**	**20**	**4**	**5**	**9**	**4**	**0**	**0**	**0**	**14:46**
2016-17	**St. Louis**	**NHL**	**82**	**23**	**11**	**34**	**32**	**4**	**0**	**5**	**153**	**15.0**	**–7**	**1169**	**50.0**	**15:59**	**11**	**0**	**4**	**4**	**10**	**0**	**0**	**0**	**16:47**
	NHL Totals		**637**	**151**	**145**	**296**	**212**	**36**	**4**	**24**	**1231**	**12.3**		**6347**	**47.1**	**15:51**	**60**	**10**	**16**	**26**	**24**	**2**	**0**	**0**	**15:53**

NHL All-Rookie Team (2009)
Signed as a free agent by **Vasteras** (Sweden-2), September 18, 2012.

BERNIER, Steve

(BUHRN-yay, STEEV) **NYI**

Right wing. Shoots right. 6'3", 220 lbs. Born, Quebec City, QC, March 31, 1985. San Jose's 2nd pick, 16th overall, in 2003 NHL Draft.

1998-99	Quebec AA Aces	QAHA	28	33	23	56	24	....	....	....	....	....	....	....	....	....	....	....	....	....	....	....	....	....	....
99-2000	Quebec AA Aces	QAHA	26	12	23	35	42	....	....	....	....	....	....	....	....	....	....	....	....	....	....	....	....	....	....
2000-01	Ste-Foy	QAAA	39	17	35	52	48	....	....	....	....	....	....	....	....	....	16	9	17	26	8	....	....	....	....
2001-02	Moncton Wildcats	QMJHL	66	31	28	59	51	....	....	....	....	....	....	....	....	....	....	....	....	....	....	....	....	....	....
2002-03	Moncton Wildcats	QMJHL	71	49	52	101	90	....	....	....	....	....	....	....	....	....	2	1	0	1	2	....	....	....	....
2003-04	Moncton Wildcats	QMJHL	66	36	46	82	80	....	....	....	....	....	....	....	....	....	20	7	10	17	17	....	....	....	....
2004-05	Moncton Wildcats	QMJHL	68	35	36	71	114	....	....	....	....	....	....	....	....	....	12	6	13	19	22	....	....	....	....
2005-06	**San Jose**	**NHL**	**39**	**14**	**13**	**27**	**35**	**2**	**1**	**1**	**75**	**18.7**	**4**	**8**	**62.5**	**14:08**	**11**	**1**	**5**	**6**	**8**	**1**	**0**	**1**	**15:17**
	Cleveland Barons	AHL	49	20	23	43	33	....	....	....	....	....	....	....	....	....	....	....	....	....	....	....	....	....	....
2006-07	**San Jose**	**NHL**	**62**	**15**	**16**	**31**	**29**	**6**	**0**	**4**	**104**	**14.4**	**5**	**18**	**27.8**	**13:35**	**11**	**0**	**1**	**1**	**2**	**0**	**0**	**0**	**10:39**
	Worcester Sharks	AHL	10	3	4	7	2	....	....	....	....	....	....	....	....	....	....	....	....	....	....	....	....	....	....
2007-08	**San Jose**	**NHL**	**59**	**13**	**10**	**23**	**62**	**4**	**0**	**0**	**96**	**13.5**	**–2**	**10**	**50.0**	**13:07**	....	....	....	....	....	....	....	....	....
	Buffalo	**NHL**	**17**	**3**	**6**	**9**	**2**	**0**	**0**	**0**	**35**	**8.6**	**1**	**5**	**20.0**	**14:06**	....	....	....	....	....	....	....	....	....
2008-09	**Vancouver**	**NHL**	**81**	**15**	**17**	**32**	**27**	**2**	**0**	**4**	**137**	**10.9**	**4**	**21**	**23.8**	**13:50**	**10**	**2**	**2**	**4**	**7**	**2**	**0**	**2**	**15:00**
2009-10	**Vancouver**	**NHL**	**59**	**11**	**11**	**22**	**21**	**3**	**0**	**0**	**95**	**11.6**	**0**	**34**	**20.6**	**14:10**	**12**	**4**	**1**	**5**	**0**	**2**	**0**	**0**	**9:59**
2010-11	**Florida**	**NHL**	**68**	**5**	**10**	**15**	**21**	**3**	**0**	**0**	**97**	**5.2**	**–14**	**17**	**23.5**	**13:02**	....	....	....	....	....	....	....	....	....
2011-12	Albany Devils	AHL	17	3	3	6	8	....	....	....	....	....	....	....	....	....	....	....	....	....	....	....	....	....	....
	New Jersey	**NHL**	**32**	**1**	**5**	**6**	**16**	**0**	**0**	**0**	**23**	**4.3**	**6**	**15**	**20.0**	**11:58**	**24**	**2**	**5**	**7**	**27**	**0**	**0**	**0**	**10:21**
2012-13	**New Jersey**	**NHL**	**47**	**8**	**7**	**15**	**17**	**2**	**0**	**1**	**88**	**9.1**	**–7**	**10**	**50.0**	**13:46**	....	....	....	....	....	....	....	....	....
2013-14	**New Jersey**	**NHL**	**78**	**3**	**9**	**12**	**33**	**0**	**0**	**1**	**104**	**2.9**	**–15**	**18**	**33.3**	**12:27**	....	....	....	....	....	....	....	....	....
2014-15	**New Jersey**	**NHL**	**67**	**16**	**16**	**32**	**28**	**4**	**0**	**2**	**107**	**15.0**	**2**	**2**	**50.0**	**12:56**	....	....	....	....	....	....	....	....	....
	Albany Devils	AHL	9	1	4	5	17	....	....	....	....	....	....	....	....	....	....	....	....	....	....	....	....	....	....
2015-16	**NY Islanders**	**NHL**	**24**	**1**	**5**	**6**	**9**	**0**	**0**	**0**	**27**	**3.7**	**3**	**0**	**0.0**	**11:14**	**6**	**0**	**0**	**0**	**0**	**0**	**0**	**0**	**12:45**
2016-17	Bridgeport	AHL	33	16	10	26	26	....	....	....	....	....	....	....	....	....	....	....	....	....	....	....	....	....	....
	NHL Totals		**633**	**105**	**125**	**230**	**300**	**26**	**1**	**13**	**988**	**10.6**		**158**	**29.7**	**13:15**	**74**	**9**	**14**	**23**	**44**	**5**	**0**	**3**	**11:53**

QMJHL All-Rookie Team (2002) • QMJHL Second All-Star Team (2003, 2004) • Canadian Major Junior Second All-Star Team (2003)
Traded to **Buffalo** by **San Jose** with San Jose's 1st round pick (Tyler Ennis) in 2008 NHL Draft for Brian Campbell and Buffalo's 7th round pick (Drew Daniels) in 2008 NHL Draft, February 26, 2008. Traded to **Vancouver** by **Buffalo** for Los Angeles' 3rd round pick (previously acquired, Buffalo selected Brayden McNabb) in 2009 NHL Draft and Vancouver's 2nd round pick (later traded to Columbus – Columbus selected Petr Straka) in 2010 NHL Draft, July 4, 2008. Traded to **Florida** by **Vancouver** with Michael Grabner and Vancouver's 1st round pick (Quinton Howden) in 2010 NHL Draft for Keith Ballard and Victor Oreskovich, June 25, 2010. Signed as a free agent by **Albany** (AHL), October 26, 2011. Signed as a free agent by **New Jersey**, January 30, 2012. Signed as a free agent by **NY Islanders**, September 17, 2015. • Missed majority of 2015-16 and 2016-17 as a healthy reserve.

BERTSCHY, Christoph

(BAIRT-chee, KRIHS-tawf) **MIN**

Center. Shoots right. 5'10", 189 lbs. Born, Fribourg, Switz., April 5, 1994. Minnesota's 6th pick, 158th overall, in 2012 NHL Draft.

2007-08	Fribourg U17	Swiss-U17	3	0	0	0	0	....	....	....	....	....	....	....	....	....	....	....	....	....	....	....	....	....	....
	Ecole U17	Swiss-U17	2	0	0	0	2	....	....	....	....	....	....	....	....	....	....	....	....	....	....	....	....	....	....
2008-09	Fribourg U17	Swiss-U17	34	3	4	7	50	....	....	....	....	....	....	....	....	....	....	....	....	....	....	....	....	....	....
2009-10	SC Bern Future Jr.	Swiss-Jr.	4	0	1	1	0	....	....	....	....	....	....	....	....	....	....	....	....	....	....	....	....	....	....
	SC Bern U17	Swiss-U17	29	25	15	40	46	....	....	....	....	....	....	....	....	....	9	4	7	11	10	....	....	....	....
2010-11	SC Bern Future Jr.	Swiss-Jr.	36	16	16	32	34	....	....	....	....	....	....	....	....	....	1	0	0	0	4	....	....	....	....
	SC Bern U17	Swiss-U17	4	7	4	11	2	....	....	....	....	....	....	....	....	....	9	8	15	23	10	....	....	....	....
2011-12	SC Bern Future Jr.	Swiss-Jr.	13	7	15	22	22	....	....	....	....	....	....	....	....	....	....	....	....	....	....	....	....	....	....
	SC Bern	Swiss	31	8	7	15	8	....	....	....	....	....	....	....	....	....	17	1	1	2	8	....	....	....	....
2012-13	SC Bern Future Jr.	Swiss-Jr.	2	2	1	3	2	....	....	....	....	....	....	....	....	....	....	....	....	....	....	....	....	....	....
	SC Bern	Swiss	41	4	2	6	18	....	....	....	....	....	....	....	....	....	20	2	1	3	2	....	....	....	....
2013-14	SC Bern	Swiss	43	6	10	16	14	....	....	....	....	....	....	....	....	....	....	....	....	....	....	....	....	....	....
2014-15	SC Bern	Swiss	44	14	16	30	26	....	....	....	....	....	....	....	....	....	7	1	2	3	0	....	....	....	....
2015-16	**Minnesota**	**NHL**	**3**	**0**	**0**	**0**	**0**	**0**	**0**	**0**	**3**	**0.0**	**0**	**0**	**0.0**	**6:57**	....	....	....	....	....	....	....	....	....
	Iowa Wild	AHL	72	11	24	35	46	....	....	....	....	....	....	....	....	....	....	....	....	....	....	....	....	....	....
2016-17	**Minnesota**	**NHL**	**5**	**0**	**1**	**1**	**4**	**0**	**0**	**0**	**5**	**0.0**	**0**	**0**	**0.0**	**8:08**	....	....	....	....	....	....	....	....	....
	Iowa Wild	AHL	67	11	13	24	30	....	....	....	....	....	....	....	....	....	....	....	....	....	....	....	....	....	....
	NHL Totals		**8**	**0**	**1**	**1**	**4**	**0**	**0**	**0**	**8**	**0.0**		**0**	**0.0**	**7:41**	....	....	....	....	....	....	....	....	....

BERTUZZI, Tyler

(buhr-TOO-zee, TIGH-luhr) **DET**

Left wing. Shoots left. 6'1", 190 lbs. Born, Sudbury, ON, February 24, 1995. Detroit's 3rd pick, 58th overall, in 2013 NHL Draft.

2010-11	Sud. Wolves MM	Minor-ON	32	20	45	65	58	....	....	....	....	....	....	....	....	....	....	....	....	....	....	....	....	....	....
	Sud. Wolves Mid.	Minor-ON	3	1	1	2	12	....	....	....	....	....	....	....	....	....	2	0	0	0	12	....	....	....	....
2011-12	Guelph Storm	OHL	61	6	11	17	117	....	....	....	....	....	....	....	....	....	6	0	2	2	7	....	....	....	....
2012-13	Guelph Storm	OHL	43	13	9	22	68	....	....	....	....	....	....	....	....	....	5	0	0	0	14	....	....	....	....
2013-14	Guelph Storm	OHL	29	9	26	35	49	....	....	....	....	....	....	....	....	....	18	10	7	17	24	....	....	....	....
2014-15	Guelph Storm	OHL	68	43	55	98	91	....	....	....	....	....	....	....	....	....	9	6	2	8	10	....	....	....	....
	Grand Rapids	AHL	2	1	0	1	0	....	....	....	....	....	....	....	....	....	14	7	5	12	10	....	....	....	....
2015-16	Grand Rapids	AHL	71	12	18	30	133	....	....	....	....	....	....	....	....	....	9	7	1	8	8	....	....	....	....
2016-17	**Detroit**	**NHL**	**7**	**0**	**0**	**0**	**0**	**0**	**0**	**0**	**3**	**0.0**	**–1**	**2**	**50.0**	**9:06**	....	....	....	....	....	....	....	....	....
	Grand Rapids	AHL	48	12	25	37	37	....	....	....	....	....	....	....	....	....	19	9	10	19	*50	....	....	....	....
	NHL Totals		**7**	**0**	**0**	**0**	**0**	**0**	**0**	**0**	**3**	**0.0**		**2**	**50.0**	**9:06**	....	....	....	....	....	....	....	....	....

OHL Second All-Star Team (2015) • Jack A. Butterfield Trophy (AHL – Playoff MVP) (2017)

BICKEL, Stu

(BIH-kuhl, STEW)

Defense. Shoots right. 6'4", 210 lbs. Born, Chanhassen, MN, October 2, 1986.

			Regular Season														Playoffs								
Season	Club	League	GP	G	A	Pts	PIM	PP	SH	GW	S	S%	+/-	TF	F%	Min	GP	G	A	Pts	PIM	PP	SH	GW	Min
2004-05	Green Bay	USHL	13	0	0	0	20	....	....	....	....	....	....	....	....	....	....	....	....	....	....	....	....	....	....
2005-06	Green Bay	USHL	14	0	0	0	25	....	....	....	....	....	....	....	....	....	....	....	....	....	....	....	....	....	....
2006-07	Sioux Falls	USHL	57	2	11	13	*215	....	....	....	....	....	....	....	....	....	8	0	3	3	29	....	....	....	....
2007-08	U. of Minnesota	WCHA	45	1	6	7	*92	....	....	....	....	....	....	....	....	....	....	....	....	....	....	....	....	....	....
2008-09	Iowa Chops	AHL	21	0	1	1	51	....	....	....	....	....	....	....	....	....	....	....	....	....	....	....	....	....	....
2009-10	San Antonio	AHL	36	2	2	4	38	....	....	....	....	....	....	....	....	....	....	....	....	....	....	....	....	....	....
	Bakersfield	ECHL	24	1	12	13	50	....	....	....	....	....	....	....	....	....	9	0	2	2	14	....	....	....	....
2010-11	Syracuse Crunch	AHL	6	0	3	3	14	....	....	....	....	....	....	....	....	....	....	....	....	....	....	....	....	....	....
	Elmira Jackals	ECHL	1	0	0	0	0	....	....	....	....	....	....	....	....	....	....	....	....	....	....	....	....	....	....
	Connecticut	AHL	54	2	7	9	135	....	....	....	....	....	....	....	....	....	6	0	1	1	6	....	....	....	....
2011-12	**NY Rangers**	**NHL**	**51**	**0**	**9**	**9**	**108**	**0**	**0**	**0**	**22**	**0.0**	**2**	**1**	**100.0**	**10:26**	**18**	**0**	**0**	**0**	**16**	**0**	**0**	**0**	**5:10**
	Connecticut	AHL	27	1	3	4	80	....	....	....	....	....	....	....	....	....	....	....	....	....	....	....	....	....	....
2012-13	Connecticut	AHL	10	0	1	1	18	....	....	....	....	....	....	....	....	....	....	....	....	....	....	....	....	....	....
	NY Rangers	**NHL**	**16**	**0**	**0**	**0**	**49**	**0**	**0**	**0**	**2**	**0.0**	**–2**	**0**	**0.0**	**5:31**	....	....	....	....	....	....	....	....	....
2013-14	Hartford	AHL	24	1	7	8	85	....	....	....	....	....	....	....	....	....	....	....	....	....	....	....	....	....	....
2014-15	**Minnesota**	**NHL**	**9**	**0**	**1**	**1**	**46**	**0**	**0**	**0**	**3**	**0.0**	**1**	**0**	**0.0**	**5:26**	....	....	....	....	....	....	....	....	....
	Iowa Wild	AHL	43	3	8	11	93	....	....	....	....	....	....	....	....	....	....	....	....	....	....	....	....	....	....
2015-16	San Diego Gulls	AHL	59	1	6	7	*210	....	....	....	....	....	....	....	....	....	6	0	0	0	6	....	....	....	....
2016-17	San Diego Gulls	AHL	26	2	4	6	148	....	....	....	....	....	....	....	....	....	3	0	1	1	2	....	....	....	....
	NHL Totals		**76**	**0**	**10**	**10**	**203**	**0**	**0**	**0**	**27**	**0.0**		**1**	**100.0**	**8:49**	**18**	**0**	**0**	**0**	**16**	**0**	**0**	**0**	**5:10**

Signed as a free agent by **Anaheim**, July 2, 2008. Traded to **NY Rangers** by **Anaheim** for Nigel Williams, November 23, 2010. • Missed majority of 2012-13, 2013-14 and 2016-17 as a healthy reserve. Signed as a free agent by **Minnesota**, July 1, 2014. Signed as a free agent by **San Diego** (AHL), October 9, 2015.

BICKELL, Bryan

(BIH-kuhl, BRIGH-uhn)

Left wing. Shoots left. 6'4", 223 lbs. Born, Bowmanville, ON, March 9, 1986. Chicago's 3rd pick, 41st overall, in 2004 NHL Draft.

Season	Club	League	GP	G	A	Pts	PIM	PP	SH	GW	S	S%	+/-	TF	F%	Min	GP	G	A	Pts	PIM	PP	SH	GW	Min
2000-01	Tor. Red Wings	GTHL	68	24	26	50	20	....	....	....	....	....	....	....	....	....	5	3	1	4	4	....	....	....	....
2001-02	Tor. Red Wings	GTHL	65	31	41	72	76	....	....	....	....	....	....	....	....	....	2	2	2	4	0	....	....	....	....
2002-03	Ottawa 67's	OHL	50	7	10	17	4	....	....	....	....	....	....	....	....	....	20	5	3	8	12	....	....	....	....
2003-04	Ottawa 67's	OHL	59	20	16	36	76	....	....	....	....	....	....	....	....	....	7	3	0	3	11	....	....	....	....
2004-05	Ottawa 67's	OHL	66	22	32	54	95	....	....	....	....	....	....	....	....	....	21	5	12	17	32	....	....	....	....
2005-06	Ottawa 67's	OHL	41	28	22	50	41	....	....	....	....	....	....	....	....	....	....	....	....	....	....	....	....	....	....
	Windsor Spitfires	OHL	26	17	16	33	19	....	....	....	....	....	....	....	....	....	7	5	5	10	10	....	....	....	....
2006-07	**Chicago**	**NHL**	**3**	**2**	**0**	**2**	**0**	**0**	**0**	**0**	**10**	**20.0**	**1**	**0**	**0.0**	**11:49**	....	....	....	....	....	....	....	....	....
	Norfolk Admirals	AHL	48	10	15	25	66	....	....	....	....	....	....	....	....	....	2	0	0	0	0	....	....	....	....
2007-08	**Chicago**	**NHL**	**4**	**0**	**0**	**0**	**2**	**0**	**0**	**0**	**3**	**0.0**	**–1**	**0**	**0.0**	**9:08**	....	....	....	....	....	....	....	....	....
	Rockford IceHogs	AHL	73	19	20	39	52	....	....	....	....	....	....	....	....	....	12	2	3	5	11	....	....	....	....
2008-09	Rockford IceHogs	AHL	42	6	8	14	60	....	....	....	....	....	....	....	....	....	4	0	2	2	4	....	....	....	....
2009-10	**Chicago**	**NHL**	**16**	**3**	**1**	**4**	**5**	**0**	**0**	**1**	**20**	**15.0**	**4**	**2**	**0.0**	**9:36**	**4**	**0**	**1**	**1**	**2**	**0**	**0**	**0**	**13:14**
	Rockford IceHogs	AHL	65	16	15	31	58	....	....	....	....	....	....	....	....	....	....	....	....	....	....	....	....	....	....
2010-11	**Chicago**	**NHL**	**78**	**17**	**20**	**37**	**40**	**2**	**0**	**2**	**130**	**13.1**	**6**	**12**	**25.0**	**13:50**	**5**	**2**	**2**	**4**	**0**	**0**	**0**	**0**	**13:05**
2011-12	**Chicago**	**NHL**	**71**	**9**	**15**	**24**	**48**	**0**	**0**	**0**	**84**	**10.7**	**–3**	**1**	**0.0**	**12:08**	**6**	**2**	**0**	**2**	**4**	**1**	**0**	**1**	**16:46**
2012-13	Orli Znojmo	Austria	28	9	18	27	14	....	....	....	....	....	....	....	....	....	....	....	....	....	....	....	....	....	....
	♦ **Chicago**	**NHL**	**48**	**9**	**14**	**23**	**25**	**0**	**0**	**2**	**82**	**11.0**	**12**	**6**	**33.3**	**12:48**	**23**	**9**	**8**	**17**	**14**	**1**	**0**	**2**	**15:22**
2013-14	**Chicago**	**NHL**	**59**	**11**	**4**	**15**	**28**	**0**	**0**	**2**	**93**	**11.8**	**–6**	**2**	**50.0**	**11:21**	**19**	**7**	**3**	**10**	**8**	**2**	**0**	**0**	**16:17**
2014-15 ♦	**Chicago**	**NHL**	**80**	**14**	**14**	**28**	**38**	**1**	**0**	**3**	**113**	**12.4**	**5**	**2**	**0.0**	**12:05**	**18**	**0**	**5**	**5**	**14**	**0**	**0**	**0**	**14:33**
2015-16	**Chicago**	**NHL**	**25**	**0**	**2**	**2**	**2**	**0**	**0**	**0**	**21**	**0.0**	**–5**	**2**	**100.0**	**9:47**	....	....	....	....	....	....	....	....	....
	Rockford IceHogs	AHL	47	15	16	31	23	....	....	....	....	....	....	....	....	....	3	0	1	1	2	....	....	....	....
2016-17	**Carolina**	**NHL**	**11**	**1**	**0**	**1**	**4**	**1**	**0**	**1**	**8**	**12.5**	**–4**	**2**	**0.0**	**10:26**	....	....	....	....	....	....	....	....	....
	Charlotte	AHL	10	1	3	4	4	....	....	....	....	....	....	....	....	....	....	....	....	....	....	....	....	....	....
	NHL Totals		**395**	**66**	**70**	**136**	**192**	**4**	**0**	**11**	**564**	**11.7**		**29**	**27.6**	**12:06**	**75**	**20**	**19**	**39**	**42**	**4**	**0**	**3**	**15:15**

Signed as a free agent by **Znojmo** (Austria), October 3, 2012. Traded to **Carolina** by **Chicago** with Teuvo Teravainen for NY Rangers' 2nd round pick (previously acquired, Chicago selected Artur Kayumov) in 2016 NHL Draft and Chicago's 3rd round pick (previously acquired, later traded to Detroit – Detroit selected Keith Petruzzelli) in 2017 NHL Draft, June 15, 2016. • Missed majority of 2016-17 due to treatment for multiple sclerosis. • Officially announced his retirement, April 10, 2017.

BIEGA, Alex

(bee-AY-guh, AL-ehx) **VAN**

Defense. Shoots right. 5'10", 187 lbs. Born, Montreal, QC, April 4, 1988. Buffalo's 5th pick, 147th overall, in 2006 NHL Draft.

Season	Club	League	GP	G	A	Pts	PIM	PP	SH	GW	S	S%	+/-	TF	F%	Min	GP	G	A	Pts	PIM	PP	SH	GW	Min
2003-04	West Island Lions	QAAA	36	7	16	23	56	....	....	....	....	....	....	....	....	....	9	0	9	9	15	....	....	....	....
2004-05	Salisbury School	High-CT	27	9	22	31	45	....	....	....	....	....	....	....	....	....	....	....	....	....	....	....	....	....	....
2005-06	Salisbury School	High-CT	28	10	17	27	51	....	....	....	....	....	....	....	....	....	....	....	....	....	....	....	....	....	....
2006-07	Harvard Crimson	ECAC	33	6	12	18	36	....	....	....	....	....	....	....	....	....	....	....	....	....	....	....	....	....	....
2007-08	Harvard Crimson	ECAC	34	3	19	22	28	....	....	....	....	....	....	....	....	....	....	....	....	....	....	....	....	....	....
2008-09	Harvard Crimson	ECAC	31	4	16	20	46	....	....	....	....	....	....	....	....	....	....	....	....	....	....	....	....	....	....
2009-10	Harvard Crimson	ECAC	33	2	8	10	30	....	....	....	....	....	....	....	....	....	....	....	....	....	....	....	....	....	....
2010-11	Portland Pirates	AHL	61	3	15	18	52	....	....	....	....	....	....	....	....	....	12	1	1	2	6	....	....	....	....
2011-12	Rochester	AHL	65	5	18	23	47	....	....	....	....	....	....	....	....	....	2	0	2	2	6	....	....	....	....
2012-13	Rochester	AHL	72	5	20	25	59	....	....	....	....	....	....	....	....	....	3	0	2	2	2	....	....	....	....
2013-14	Utica Comets	AHL	73	3	19	22	53	....	....	....	....	....	....	....	....	....	....	....	....	....	....	....	....	....	....
2014-15	**Vancouver**	**NHL**	**7**	**1**	**0**	**1**	**0**	**0**	**0**	**1**	**7**	**14.3**	**–2**	**0**	**0.0**	**15:48**	....	....	....	....	....	....	....	....	....
	Utica Comets	AHL	62	3	16	19	24	....	....	....	....	....	....	....	....	....	23	0	4	4	16	....	....	....	....
2015-16	**Vancouver**	**NHL**	**51**	**0**	**7**	**7**	**22**	**0**	**0**	**0**	**61**	**0.0**	**–11**	**0**	**0.0**	**16:46**	....	....	....	....	....	....	....	....	....
	Utica Comets	AHL	14	1	5	6	8	....	....	....	....	....	....	....	....	....	....	....	....	....	....	....	....	....	....
2016-17	**Vancouver**	**NHL**	**36**	**0**	**3**	**3**	**18**	**0**	**0**	**0**	**37**	**0.0**	**–4**	**0**	**0.0**	**13:10**	....	....	....	....	....	....	....	....	....
	Utica Comets	AHL	1	0	0	0	2	....	....	....	....	....	....	....	....	....	....	....	....	....	....	....	....	....	....
	NHL Totals		**94**	**1**	**10**	**11**	**40**	**0**	**0**	**1**	**105**	**1.0**		**0**	**0.0**	**15:19**	....	....	....	....	....	....	....	....	....

ECAC All-Rookie Team (2007)

Signed as a free agent by **Vancouver**, July 6, 2013. • Missed majority of 2016-17 as a healthy reserve.

BIEKSA, Kevin

(BEE-ehks-ah, KEH-vihn) **ANA**

Defense. Shoots right. 6'1", 200 lbs. Born, Grimsby, ON, June 16, 1981. Vancouver's 4th pick, 151st overall, in 2001 NHL Draft.

Season	Club	League	GP	G	A	Pts	PIM	PP	SH	GW	S	S%	+/-	TF	F%	Min	GP	G	A	Pts	PIM	PP	SH	GW	Min
1997-98	Stoney Creek	ON-Jr.B	15	2	9	11	29	....	....	....	....	....	....	....	....	....	....	....	....	....	....	....	....	....	....
	Burlington	ON-Jr.A	27	0	3	3	10	....	....	....	....	....	....	....	....	....	....	....	....	....	....	....	....	....	....
1998-99	Burlington	ON-Jr.A	49	8	29	37	83	....	....	....	....	....	....	....	....	....	....	....	....	....	....	....	....	....	....
99-2000	Burlington	ON-Jr.A	49	6	27	33	139	....	....	....	....	....	....	....	....	....	....	....	....	....	....	....	....	....	....
2000-01	Bowling Green	CCHA	35	4	9	13	90	....	....	....	....	....	....	....	....	....	....	....	....	....	....	....	....	....	....
2001-02	Bowling Green	CCHA	40	5	10	15	68	....	....	....	....	....	....	....	....	....	....	....	....	....	....	....	....	....	....
2002-03	Bowling Green	CCHA	34	8	17	25	92	....	....	....	....	....	....	....	....	....	....	....	....	....	....	....	....	....	....
2003-04	Bowling Green	CCHA	38	7	15	22	66	....	....	....	....	....	....	....	....	....	....	....	....	....	....	....	....	....	....
	Manitoba Moose	AHL	4	0	2	2	2	....	....	....	....	....	....	....	....	....	....	....	....	....	....	....	....	....	....
2004-05	Manitoba Moose	AHL	80	12	27	39	192	....	....	....	....	....	....	....	....	....	14	1	1	2	52	....	....	....	....
2005-06	**Vancouver**	**NHL**	**39**	**0**	**6**	**6**	**77**	**0**	**0**	**0**	**38**	**0.0**	**–1**	**0**	**0.0**	**16:06**	....	....	....	....	....	....	....	....	....
	Manitoba Moose	AHL	23	3	17	20	71	....	....	....	....	....	....	....	....	....	13	0	10	10	38	....	....	....	....
2006-07	**Vancouver**	**NHL**	**81**	**12**	**30**	**42**	**134**	**6**	**0**	**2**	**203**	**5.9**	**1**	**0**	**0.0**	**24:16**	**9**	**0**	**0**	**0**	**20**	**0**	**0**	**0**	**28:01**
2007-08	**Vancouver**	**NHL**	**34**	**2**	**10**	**12**	**90**	**1**	**0**	**1**	**64**	**3.1**	**–11**	**0**	**0.0**	**23:24**	....	....	....	....	....	....	....	....	....
	Manitoba Moose	AHL	1	0	1	1	2	....	....	....	....	....	....	....	....	....	....	....	....	....	....	....	....	....	....
2008-09	**Vancouver**	**NHL**	**72**	**11**	**32**	**43**	**97**	**5**	**0**	**2**	**153**	**7.2**	**–4**	**0**	**0.0**	**23:29**	**10**	**0**	**5**	**5**	**14**	**0**	**0**	**0**	**24:08**
2009-10	**Vancouver**	**NHL**	**55**	**3**	**19**	**22**	**85**	**1**	**0**	**0**	**95**	**3.2**	**–5**	**0**	**0.0**	**21:49**	**12**	**3**	**5**	**8**	**14**	**1**	**0**	**1**	**22:37**
2010-11	**Vancouver**	**NHL**	**66**	**6**	**16**	**22**	**73**	**1**	**0**	**2**	**105**	**5.7**	**32**	**0**	**0.0**	**22:28**	**25**	**5**	**5**	**10**	**51**	**1**	**0**	**1**	**25:40**
2011-12	**Vancouver**	**NHL**	**78**	**8**	**36**	**44**	**94**	**2**	**0**	**2**	**166**	**4.8**	**12**	**1**	**0.0**	**23:38**	**5**	**1**	**0**	**1**	**6**	**0**	**0**	**1**	**24:46**
2012-13	**Vancouver**	**NHL**	**36**	**6**	**6**	**12**	**48**	**2**	**0**	**1**	**77**	**7.8**	**6**	**0**	**0.0**	**21:56**	**4**	**1**	**0**	**1**	**8**	**0**	**0**	**0**	**25:51**
2013-14	**Vancouver**	**NHL**	**76**	**4**	**20**	**24**	**104**	**1**	**0**	**1**	**167**	**2.4**	**–8**	**1**	**100.0**	**22:46**	....	....	....	....	....	....	....	....	....
2014-15	**Vancouver**	**NHL**	**60**	**4**	**10**	**14**	**77**	**0**	**0**	**1**	**99**	**4.0**	**0**	**0**	**0.0**	**20:50**	**6**	**0**	**0**	**0**	**9**	**0**	**0**	**0**	**18:19**

Season	Club	League	GP	G	A	Pts	PIM	PP	SH	GW	S	S%	+/-	TF	F%	Min	GP	G	A	Pts	PIM	PP	SH	GW	Min
		Regular Season															Playoffs								
2015-16	**Anaheim**	**NHL**	**71**	**4**	**11**	**15**	**99**	**2**	**0**	**1**	**109**	**3.7**	**–7**	**0**	**0.0**	**21:01**	**6**	**0**	**1**	**1**	**2**	**0**	**0**	**0**	**19:43**
2016-17	**Anaheim**	**NHL**	**81**	**3**	**11**	**14**	**63**	**1**	**0**	**1**	**94**	**3.2**	**0**	**0**	**0.0**	**18:45**	**8**	**0**	**4**	**4**	**23**	**0**	**0**	**0**	**16:56**
	NHL Totals		**749**	**63**	**207**	**270**	**1041**	**22**	**0**	**14**	**1370**	**4.6**		**2**	**50.0**	**21:53**	**85**	**10**	**20**	**30**	**147**	**2**	**0**	**3**	**23:30**

AHL All-Rookie Team (2005)

Traded to **Anaheim** by **Vancouver** for Anaheim's 2nd round pick (later traded to Pittsburgh – Pittsburgh selected Filip Gustavsson) in 2016 NHL Draft, June 30, 2015.

BIGRAS, Chris (bee-GRAH, KRIHS) COL

Defense. Shoots left. 6'1", 190 lbs. Born, Orillia, ON, February 22, 1995. Colorado's 2nd pick, 32nd overall, in 2013 NHL Draft.

Season	Club	League	GP	G	A	Pts	PIM	PP	SH	GW	S	S%	+/-	TF	F%	Min	GP	G	A	Pts	PIM	PP	SH	GW	Min
2010-11	Barrie Colts	Minor-ON	43	7	25	32	20	....	....	....	....	....	....	....	....	....	....	....	....	....	....	....	....	....	....
2011-12	Owen Sound	OHL	49	3	16	19	33	....	....	....	....	....	....	....	....	....	5	2	3	5	0	....	....	....	....
2012-13	Owen Sound	OHL	68	8	30	38	34	....	....	....	....	....	....	....	....	....	12	0	2	2	8	....	....	....	....
2013-14	Owen Sound	OHL	55	4	23	27	46	....	....	....	....	....	....	....	....	....	5	1	2	3	4	....	....	....	....
2014-15	Owen Sound	OHL	62	20	51	71	52	....	....	....	....	....	....	....	....	....	5	1	2	3	4	....	....	....	....
	Lake Erie	AHL	7	0	4	4	2	....	....	....	....	....	....	....	....	....	....	....	....	....	....	....	....	....	....
2015-16	**Colorado**	**NHL**	**31**	**1**	**2**	**3**	**16**	**0**	**0**	**0**	**21**	**4.8**	**–2**	**0**	**0.0**	**13:21**	....	....	....	....	....	....	....	....	....
	San Antonio	AHL	37	6	13	19	6	....	....	....	....	....	....	....	....	....	....	....	....	....	....	....	....	....	....
2016-17	San Antonio	AHL	45	5	14	19	37	....	....	....	....	....	....	....	....	....	....	....	....	....	....	....	....	....	....
	NHL Totals		**31**	**1**	**2**	**3**	**16**	**0**	**0**	**0**	**21**	**4.8**		**0**	**0.0**	**13:21**	....	....	....	....	....	....	....	....	....

OHL First All-Star Team (2015)

BILLINS, Chad (BIHL-uhns, CHAD)

Defense. Shoots left. 5'10", 175 lbs. Born, Marysville, MI, May 26, 1989.

Season	Club	League	GP	G	A	Pts	PIM	PP	SH	GW	S	S%	+/-	TF	F%	Min	GP	G	A	Pts	PIM	PP	SH	GW	Min
2005-06	Det. Caesers	MWEHL	22	1	4	5	18	....	....	....	....	....	....	....	....	....	3	0	1	1	6	....	....	....	....
	Alpena IceDiggers	NAHL	1	0	0	0	0	....	....	....	....	....	....	....	....	....	....	....	....	....	....	....	....	....	....
2006-07	Alpena IceDiggers	NAHL	61	7	18	25	98	....	....	....	....	....	....	....	....	....	3	0	0	0	0	....	....	....	....
2007-08	Waterloo	USHL	60	10	26	36	81	....	....	....	....	....	....	....	....	....	11	5	4	9	0	....	....	....	....
2008-09	Ferris State	CCHA	27	2	9	11	38	....	....	....	....	....	....	....	....	....	....	....	....	....	....	....	....	....	....
2009-10	Ferris State	CCHA	40	3	8	11	26	....	....	....	....	....	....	....	....	....	....	....	....	....	....	....	....	....	....
2010-11	Ferris State	CCHA	39	5	11	16	20	....	....	....	....	....	....	....	....	....	....	....	....	....	....	....	....	....	....
2011-12	Ferris State	CCHA	43	7	22	29	24	....	....	....	....	....	....	....	....	....	....	....	....	....	....	....	....	....	....
2012-13	Grand Rapids	AHL	76	10	27	37	40	....	....	....	....	....	....	....	....	....	24	2	12	14	12	....	....	....	....
2013-14	**Calgary**	**NHL**	**10**	**0**	**3**	**3**	**0**	**0**	**0**	**0**	**3**	**0.0**	**–3**	**0**	**0.0**	**12:13**	....	....	....	....	....	....	....	....	....
	Abbotsford Heat	AHL	65	10	31	41	40	....	....	....	....	....	....	....	....	....	4	0	2	2	2	....	....	....	....
2014-15	CSKA Moscow	KHL	21	2	4	6	8	....	....	....	....	....	....	....	....	....	....	....	....	....	....	....	....	....	....
	Lulea HF	Sweden	23	1	5	6	4	....	....	....	....	....	....	....	....	....	9	1	1	2	2	....	....	....	....
2015-16	Linkopings HC	Sweden	50	7	24	31	14	....	....	....	....	....	....	....	....	....	6	2	2	4	4	....	....	....	....
2016-17	Utica Comets	AHL	72	3	17	20	16	....	....	....	....	....	....	....	....	....	....	....	....	....	....	....	....	....	....
	NHL Totals		**10**	**0**	**3**	**3**	**0**	**0**	**0**	**0**	**3**	**0.0**		**0**	**0.0**	**12:13**	....	....	....	....	....	....	....	....	....

CCHA First All-Star Team (2012) • NCAA West Second All-American Team (2012)

Signed as a free agent by **Calgary**, July 5, 2013. Signed as a free agent by **CSKA Moscow** (KHL), June 30, 2014. Signed as a free agent by **Lulea** (Sweden), December 20, 2014. Signed as a free agent by **Linkoping** (Sweden), June 12, 2015. Signed as a free agent by **Vancouver**, July 1, 2016.

BITETTO, Anthony (bih-TEH-toh, AN-thuh-nee) NSH

Defense. Shoots left. 6'1", 210 lbs. Born, Island Park, NY, July 15, 1990. Nashville's 4th pick, 168th overall, in 2010 NHL Draft.

Season	Club	League	GP	G	A	Pts	PIM	PP	SH	GW	S	S%	+/-	TF	F%	Min	GP	G	A	Pts	PIM	PP	SH	GW	Min
2007-08	NY Apple Core	EmJHL	12	4	10	14	32	....	....	....	....	....	....	....	....	....	....	....	....	....	....	....	....	....	....
	NY Apple Core	EJHL	17	2	6	8	28	....	....	....	....	....	....	....	....	....	....	....	....	....	....	....	....	....	....
2008-09	NY Apple Core	EJHL	30	2	9	11	50	....	....	....	....	....	....	....	....	....	....	....	....	....	....	....	....	....	....
	Indiana Ice	USHL	24	1	3	4	29	....	....	....	....	....	....	....	....	....	13	0	3	3	6	....	....	....	....
2009-10	Indiana Ice	USHL	58	11	29	40	99	....	....	....	....	....	....	....	....	....	9	2	2	4	19	....	....	....	....
2010-11	Northeastern	H-East	38	3	17	20	66	....	....	....	....	....	....	....	....	....	....	....	....	....	....	....	....	....	....
2011-12	Northeastern	H-East	34	4	11	15	34	....	....	....	....	....	....	....	....	....	....	....	....	....	....	....	....	....	....
	Milwaukee	AHL	....	....	....	....	....	....	....	....	....	....	....	....	....	....	1	0	0	0	0	....	....	....	....
2012-13	Cincinnati	ECHL	23	1	2	3	16	....	....	....	....	....	....	....	....	....	....	....	....	....	....	....	....	....	....
	Milwaukee	AHL	34	1	5	6	35	....	....	....	....	....	....	....	....	....	....	....	....	....	....	....	....	....	....
2013-14	Milwaukee	AHL	73	11	25	36	85	....	....	....	....	....	....	....	....	....	3	0	0	0	8	....	....	....	....
2014-15	**Nashville**	**NHL**	**7**	**0**	**0**	**0**	**7**	**0**	**0**	**0**	**2**	**0.0**	**–1**	**1**	**100.0**	**11:47**	....	....	....	....	....	....	....	....	....
	Milwaukee	AHL	70	4	26	30	96	....	....	....	....	....	....	....	....	....	....	....	....	....	....	....	....	....	....
2015-16	**Nashville**	**NHL**	**28**	**1**	**5**	**6**	**19**	**0**	**0**	**0**	**19**	**5.3**	**0**	**0**	**0.0**	**12:08**	**14**	**0**	**0**	**0**	**6**	**0**	**0**	**0**	**11:30**
	Milwaukee	AHL	6	1	3	4	27	....	....	....	....	....	....	....	....	....	....	....	....	....	....	....	....	....	....
2016-17	**Nashville**	**NHL**	**29**	**0**	**7**	**7**	**25**	**0**	**0**	**0**	**17**	**0.0**	**–1**	**0**	**0.0**	**11:48**	....	....	....	....	....	....	....	....	....
	Milwaukee	AHL	3	1	2	3	0	....	....	....	....	....	....	....	....	....	....	....	....	....	....	....	....	....	....
	NHL Totals		**64**	**1**	**12**	**13**	**51**	**0**	**0**	**0**	**38**	**2.6**		**1**	**100.0**	**11:57**	**14**	**0**	**0**	**0**	**6**	**0**	**0**	**0**	**11:30**

USHL Second All-Star Team (2010) • Hockey East All-Rookie Team (2011)

• Missed majority of 2015-16 and 2016-17 as a healthy reserve.

BJORKSTRAND, Oliver (bih-YOHRK-strand, AWL-ih-vuhr) CBJ

Right wing. Shoots right. 6', 177 lbs. Born, Herning, Denmark, April 10, 1995. Columbus' 5th pick, 89th overall, in 2013 NHL Draft.

Season	Club	League	GP	G	A	Pts	PIM	PP	SH	GW	S	S%	+/-	TF	F%	Min	GP	G	A	Pts	PIM	PP	SH	GW	Min
2009-10	Herning IK U17	Den-U17	10	7	9	16	2	....	....	....	....	....	....	....	....	....	....	....	....	....	....	....	....	....	....
2010-11	Herning IK U17	Den-U17	19	28	26	54	39	....	....	....	....	....	....	....	....	....	....	....	....	....	....	....	....	....	....
	Herning IK Jr.	Den-Jr.	11	13	6	19	2	....	....	....	....	....	....	....	....	....	6	1	7	8	0	....	....	....	....
	Herning IK II	Den-2	....	....	....	....	....	....	....	....	....	....	....	....	....	....	1	0	0	0	0	....	....	....	....
2011-12	Herning IK II	Den-2	5	1	2	3	0	....	....	....	....	....	....	....	....	....	....	....	....	....	....	....	....	....	....
	Herning Blue Fox	Denmark	36	13	13	26	10	....	....	....	....	....	....	....	....	....	10	1	2	3	4	....	....	....	....
2012-13	Portland	WHL	65	31	32	63	10	....	....	....	....	....	....	....	....	....	21	8	11	19	4	....	....	....	....
2013-14	Portland	WHL	69	50	59	109	36	....	....	....	....	....	....	....	....	....	21	*16	17	*33	8	....	....	....	....
2014-15	Portland	WHL	59	*63	55	*118	35	....	....	....	....	....	....	....	....	....	17	13	12	25	10	....	....	....	....
2015-16	**Columbus**	**NHL**	**12**	**4**	**4**	**8**	**0**	**0**	**0**	**1**	**25**	**16.0**	**6**	**0**	**0.0**	**15:59**	....	....	....	....	....	....	....	....	....
	Lake Erie	AHL	51	17	12	29	10	....	....	....	....	....	....	....	....	....	17	*10	6	16	2	....	....	....	....
2016-17	**Columbus**	**NHL**	**26**	**6**	**7**	**13**	**6**	**0**	**0**	**2**	**55**	**10.9**	**4**	**1**	**100.0**	**14:05**	**5**	**0**	**1**	**1**	**0**	**0**	**0**	**0**	**12:51**
	Cleveland	AHL	37	14	12	26	6	....	....	....	....	....	....	....	....	....	....	....	....	....	....	....	....	....	....
	NHL Totals		**38**	**10**	**11**	**21**	**6**	**0**	**0**	**3**	**80**	**12.5**		**1**	**100.0**	**14:41**	**5**	**0**	**1**	**1**	**0**	**0**	**0**	**0**	**12:51**

WHL West First All-Star Team (2014, 2015) • WHL Player of the Year (2015) • Jack A. Butterfield Trophy (AHL - Playoff MVP) (2016)

BJUGSTAD, Nick (BYOOG-stad, NIHK) FLA

Center. Shoots right. 6'6", 218 lbs. Born, Minneapolis, MN, July 17, 1992. Florida's 2nd pick, 19th overall, in 2010 NHL Draft.

Season	Club	League	GP	G	A	Pts	PIM	PP	SH	GW	S	S%	+/-	TF	F%	Min	GP	G	A	Pts	PIM	PP	SH	GW	Min
2007-08	Blaine Bengals	High-MN	24	6	14	20	10	....	....	....	....	....	....	....	....	....	....	....	....	....	....	....	....	....	....
2008-09	Blaine Bengals	High-MN	25	26	25	51	20	....	....	....	....	....	....	....	....	....	....	....	....	....	....	....	....	....	....
2009-10	Team Northwest	UMHSEL	23	13	8	21	18	....	....	....	....	....	....	....	....	....	....	....	....	....	....	....	....	....	....
	Blaine Bengals	High-MN	25	29	31	60	24	....	....	....	....	....	....	....	....	....	5	6	3	9	2	....	....	....	....
	USAHNTDP	U-18	4	0	0	0	0	....	....	....	....	....	....	....	....	....	....	....	....	....	....	....	....	....	....
2010-11	U. of Minnesota	WCHA	29	8	12	20	51	....	....	....	....	....	....	....	....	....	....	....	....	....	....	....	....	....	....
2011-12	U. of Minnesota	WCHA	40	25	17	42	28	....	....	....	....	....	....	....	....	....	....	....	....	....	....	....	....	....	....
2012-13	U. of Minnesota	WCHA	40	21	15	36	28	....	....	....	....	....	....	....	....	....	....	....	....	....	....	....	....	....	....
	Florida	**NHL**	**11**	**1**	**0**	**1**	**2**	**0**	**0**	**0**	**17**	**5.9**	**–8**	**132**	**40.2**	**15:13**	....	....	....	....	....	....	....	....	....
2013-14	**Florida**	**NHL**	**76**	**16**	**22**	**38**	**16**	**0**	**1**	**4**	**185**	**8.6**	**–14**	**1123**	**48.9**	**16:13**	....	....	....	....	....	....	....	....	....
2014-15	**Florida**	**NHL**	**72**	**24**	**19**	**43**	**38**	**7**	**0**	**3**	**207**	**11.6**	**–7**	**994**	**48.9**	**16:35**	....	....	....	....	....	....	....	....	....
2015-16	**Florida**	**NHL**	**67**	**15**	**19**	**34**	**41**	**6**	**0**	**3**	**171**	**8.8**	**–8**	**868**	**51.7**	**15:31**	**5**	**2**	**2**	**4**	**2**	**0**	**0**	**1**	**19:08**
2016-17	**Florida**	**NHL**	**54**	**7**	**7**	**14**	**22**	**1**	**0**	**1**	**91**	**7.7**	**–19**	**391**	**47.6**	**13:09**	....	....	....	....	....	....	....	....	....
	NHL Totals		**280**	**63**	**67**	**130**	**119**	**14**	**1**	**11**	**671**	**9.4**		**3508**	**49.1**	**15:31**	**5**	**2**	**2**	**4**	**2**	**0**	**0**	**1**	**19:08**

WCHA First All-Star Team (2012) • NCAA West Second All-American Team (2012)

			Regular Season														Playoffs								
Season	Club	League	GP	G	A	Pts	PIM	PP	SH	GW	S	S%	+/-	TF	F%	Min	GP	G	A	Pts	PIM	PP	SH	GW	Min

BLANDISI, Joseph — (blan-DEE-zee, JOH-sehf) — **N.J.**

Center/Right wing. Shoots left. 6', 200 lbs.   Born, Markham, ON, July 18, 1994. Colorado's 4th pick, 162nd overall, in 2012 NHL Draft.

Season	Club	League	GP	G	A	Pts	PIM	PP	SH	GW	S	S%	+/-	TF	F%	Min	GP	G	A	Pts	PIM	PP	SH	GW	Min
2010-11	Vaughan Kings	GTHL	41	51	41	92		....	....	....	....	....	....	....	....	....	....	....	....	....	....	....	....	....	....
	Vaughan Vipers	ON-Jr.A	7	2	0	2	14	....	....	....	....	....	....	....	....	....	....	....	....	....	....	....	....	....	....
2011-12	Owen Sound	OHL	68	17	14	31	72	....	....	....	....	....	....	....	....	....	5	0	1	1	8	....	....	....	....
2012-13	Owen Sound	OHL	37	7	18	25	49	....	....	....	....	....	....	....	....	....	....	....	....	....	....	....	....	....	....
	Ottawa 67's	OHL	26	8	18	26	68	....	....	....	....	....	....	....	....	....	....	....	....	....	....	....	....	....	....
2013-14	Ottawa 67's	OHL	37	21	16	37	57	....	....	....	....	....	....	....	....	....	....	....	....	....	....	....	....	....	....
	Barrie Colts	OHL	10	3	10	13	16	....	....	....	....	....	....	....	....	....	....	....	....	....	....	....	....	....	....
2014-15	Barrie Colts	OHL	68	*52	60	112	126	....	....	....	....	....	....	....	....	....	9	6	8	14	22	....	....	....	....
2015-16	**New Jersey**	**NHL**	41	5	12	17	34	4	0	1	43	11.6	−14	33	33.3	15:36	....	....	....	....	....	....	....	....	....
	Albany Devils	AHL	27	9	14	23	49	....	....	....	....	....	....	....	....	....	11	2	1	3	14	....	....	....	....
2016-17	**New Jersey**	**NHL**	27	3	6	9	26	1	0	2	24	12.5	−10	169	45.0	13:22	....	....	....	....	....	....	....	....	....
	Albany Devils	AHL	31	8	17	25	60	....	....	....	....	....	....	....	....	....	2	0	0	0	6	....	....	....	....
	NHL Totals		68	8	18	26	60	5	0	3	67	11.9		202	43.1	14:43	....	....	....	....	....	....	....	....	....

Signed as a free agent by **New Jersey**, January 14, 2015.

BLIDH, Anton — (BLIHD, AN-tawn) — **BOS**

Left wing. Shoots left. 6', 201 lbs.   Born, Molnlycke, Sweden, March 14, 1995. Boston's 5th pick, 180th overall, in 2013 NHL Draft.

Season	Club	League	GP	G	A	Pts	PIM	PP	SH	GW	S	S%	+/-	TF	F%	Min	GP	G	A	Pts	PIM	PP	SH	GW	Min
2010-11	Frolunda U18	Swe-U18	12	2	1	3	8	....	....	....	....	....	....	....	....	....	1	0	0	0	25	....	....	....	....
2011-12	Frolunda U18	Swe-U18	38	13	19	32	28	....	....	....	....	....	....	....	....	....	4	2	0	2	4	....	....	....	....
2012-13	Frolunda U18	Swe-U18	8	5	2	7	14	....	....	....	....	....	....	....	....	....	3	1	3	4	0	....	....	....	....
	Frolunda Jr.	Swe-Jr.	43	17	10	27	80	....	....	....	....	....	....	....	....	....	6	1	2	3	0	....	....	....	....
2013-14	Frolunda Jr.	Swe-Jr.	27	11	14	25	20	....	....	....	....	....	....	....	....	....	....	....	....	....	....	....	....	....	....
	Karlskrona HK	Sweden-2	11	1	1	2	6	....	....	....	....	....	....	....	....	....	....	....	....	....	....	....	....	....	....
	Frolunda	Sweden	24	0	5	5	2	....	....	....	....	....	....	....	....	....	6	1	2	3	0	....	....	....	....
2014-15	Frolunda Jr.	Swe-Jr.	1	1	1	2	2	....	....	....	....	....	....	....	....	....	....	....	....	....	....	....	....	....	....
	Frolunda	Sweden	48	5	0	5	26	....	....	....	....	....	....	....	....	....	13	1	0	1	4	....	....	....	....
2015-16	Providence Bruins	AHL	65	10	4	14	48	....	....	....	....	....	....	....	....	....	....	....	....	....	....	....	....	....	....
2016-17	**Boston**	**NHL**	19	1	1	2	7	0	0	0	26	3.8	−2	0	0.0	8:47	....	....	....	....	....	....	....	....	....
	Providence Bruins	AHL	53	10	6	16	41	....	....	....	....	....	....	....	....	....	17	1	0	1	6	....	....	....	....
	NHL Totals		19	1	1	2	7	0	0	0	26	3.8		0	0.0	8:47	....	....	....	....	....	....	....	....	....

BLUM, Jonathon — (BLUHM, JAWN-ah-thuhn)

Defense. Shoots right. 6'1", 188 lbs.   Born, Long Beach, CA, January 30, 1989. Nashville's 1st pick, 23rd overall, in 2007 NHL Draft.

Season	Club	League	GP	G	A	Pts	PIM	PP	SH	GW	S	S%	+/-	TF	F%	Min	GP	G	A	Pts	PIM	PP	SH	GW	Min
2004-05	California Wave	Minor-CA	55	15	50	65	65	....	....	....	....	....	....	....	....	....	....	....	....	....	....	....	....	....	....
2005-06	Vancouver Giants	WHL	61	7	17	24	25	....	....	....	....	....	....	....	....	....	18	1	7	8	16	....	....	....	....
2006-07	Vancouver Giants	WHL	72	8	43	51	48	....	....	....	....	....	....	....	....	....	22	3	6	9	8	....	....	....	....
2007-08	Vancouver Giants	WHL	64	18	45	63	44	....	....	....	....	....	....	....	....	....	10	3	4	7	10	....	....	....	....
2008-09	Vancouver Giants	WHL	51	16	50	66	30	....	....	....	....	....	....	....	....	....	17	7	11	18	6	....	....	....	....
	Milwaukee	AHL	....	....	....	....	....	....	....	....	....	....	....	....	....	....	5	0	0	0	0	....	....	....	....
2009-10	Milwaukee	AHL	80	11	30	41	32	....	....	....	....	....	....	....	....	....	7	1	7	8	0	....	....	....	....
2010-11	**Nashville**	**NHL**	23	3	5	8	8	1	0	1	18	16.7	8	0	0.0	17:45	12	0	2	2	0	0	0	0	18:51
	Milwaukee	AHL	54	7	27	34	20	....	....	....	....	....	....	....	....	....	1	0	0	0	0	....	....	....	....
2011-12	**Nashville**	**NHL**	33	3	4	7	6	0	0	1	25	12.0	−14	0	0.0	17:56	....	....	....	....	....	....	....	....	....
	Milwaukee	AHL	48	4	22	26	36	....	....	....	....	....	....	....	....	....	3	0	1	1	4	....	....	....	....
2012-13	Milwaukee	AHL	34	1	11	12	16	....	....	....	....	....	....	....	....	....	....	....	....	....	....	....	....	....	....
	Nashville	**NHL**	35	1	6	7	6	0	0	0	26	3.8	−1	0	0.0	14:18	....	....	....	....	....	....	....	....	....
2013-14	**Minnesota**	**NHL**	15	0	1	1	0	0	0	0	11	0.0	−1	0	0.0	11:40	....	....	....	....	....	....	....	....	....
	Iowa Wild	AHL	54	7	22	29	23	....	....	....	....	....	....	....	....	....	....	....	....	....	....	....	....	....	....
2014-15	**Minnesota**	**NHL**	4	0	1	1	2	0	0	0	3	0.0	−3	0	0.0	9:52	....	....	....	....	....	....	....	....	....
	Iowa Wild	AHL	66	12	25	37	18	....	....	....	....	....	....	....	....	....	....	....	....	....	....	....	....	....	....
2015-16	Vladivostok	KHL	55	8	22	30	45	....	....	....	....	....	....	....	....	....	5	0	1	1	4	....	....	....	....
2016-17	Vladivostok	KHL	36	2	19	21	20	....	....	....	....	....	....	....	....	....	4	0	1	1	6	....	....	....	....
	NHL Totals		110	7	17	24	22	1	0	2	83	8.4		0	0.0	15:36	12	0	2	2	0	0	0	0	18:51

WHL West Second All-Star Team (2008) • WHL West First All-Star Team (2009) • WHL Defenseman of the Year (2009) • Canadian Major Junior First All-Star Team (2009) • Canadian Major Junior Defenseman of the Year (2009)

Signed as a free agent by **Minnesota**, July 12, 2013. Signed as a free agent by **Vladivostok** (KHL), August 9, 2015.

BLUNDEN, Mike — (BLUHN-dehn, MIGHK) — **OTT**

Right wing. Shoots right. 6'4", 217 lbs.   Born, Toronto, ON, December 15, 1986. Chicago's 2nd pick, 43rd overall, in 2005 NHL Draft.

Season	Club	League	GP	G	A	Pts	PIM	PP	SH	GW	S	S%	+/-	TF	F%	Min	GP	G	A	Pts	PIM	PP	SH	GW	Min
2001-02	Gloucester	Minor-ON	32	23	12	35	52	....	....	....	....	....	....	....	....	....	....	....	....	....	....	....	....	....	....
	Gloucester	ON-Jr.A	2	0	0	0	2	....	....	....	....	....	....	....	....	....	....	....	....	....	....	....	....	....	....
2002-03	Erie Otters	OHL	63	10	7	17	55	....	....	....	....	....	....	....	....	....	....	....	....	....	....	....	....	....	....
2003-04	Erie Otters	OHL	52	22	17	39	53	....	....	....	....	....	....	....	....	....	3	0	0	0	0	....	....	....	....
2004-05	Erie Otters	OHL	61	22	19	41	75	....	....	....	....	....	....	....	....	....	2	0	0	0	2	....	....	....	....
2005-06	Erie Otters	OHL	60	46	38	84	63	....	....	....	....	....	....	....	....	....	....	....	....	....	....	....	....	....	....
	Norfolk Admirals	AHL	11	1	5	6	2	....	....	....	....	....	....	....	....	....	1	0	0	0	0	....	....	....	....
2006-07	**Chicago**	**NHL**	9	0	0	0	10	0	0	0	10	0.0	−5	1	0.0	11:23	....	....	....	....	....	....	....	....	....
	Norfolk Admirals	AHL	17	4	5	9	15	....	....	....	....	....	....	....	....	....	....	....	....	....	....	....	....	....	....
2007-08	**Chicago**	**NHL**	1	0	0	0	0	0	0	0	1	0.0	−1	0	0.0	7:51	....	....	....	....	....	....	....	....	....
	Rockford IceHogs	AHL	74	16	21	37	83	....	....	....	....	....	....	....	....	....	12	1	3	4	35	....	....	....	....
2008-09	Rockford IceHogs	AHL	37	3	7	10	42	....	....	....	....	....	....	....	....	....	....	....	....	....	....	....	....	....	....
	Syracuse Crunch	AHL	39	9	12	21	68	....	....	....	....	....	....	....	....	....	....	....	....	....	....	....	....	....	....
2009-10	**Columbus**	**NHL**	40	2	2	4	59	0	0	0	40	5.0	3	90	32.2	8:07	....	....	....	....	....	....	....	....	....
	Syracuse Crunch	AHL	25	7	9	16	43	....	....	....	....	....	....	....	....	....	....	....	....	....	....	....	....	....	....
2010-11	**Columbus**	**NHL**	1	0	0	0	0	0	0	0	2	0.0	−1	10	50.0	10:31	....	....	....	....	....	....	....	....	....
	Springfield	AHL	37	12	9	21	41	....	....	....	....	....	....	....	....	....	....	....	....	....	....	....	....	....	....
2011-12	**Montreal**	**NHL**	39	2	2	4	27	0	0	0	34	5.9	−1	5	40.0	9:22	....	....	....	....	....	....	....	....	....
	Hamilton	AHL	17	3	5	8	12	....	....	....	....	....	....	....	....	....	....	....	....	....	....	....	....	....	....
2012-13	Hamilton	AHL	54	10	12	22	76	....	....	....	....	....	....	....	....	....	....	....	....	....	....	....	....	....	....
	Montreal	**NHL**	5	0	0	0	4	0	0	0	5	0.0	−1	0	0.0	8:21	1	0	0	0	10	0	0	0	8:12
2013-14	**Montreal**	**NHL**	7	0	0	0	0	0	0	0	2	0.0	−2	0	0.0	6:08	....	....	....	....	....	....	....	....	....
	Hamilton	AHL	68	18	19	37	79	....	....	....	....	....	....	....	....	....	....	....	....	....	....	....	....	....	....
2014-15	**Tampa Bay**	**NHL**	2	0	0	0	2	0	0	0	0	0.0	−1	0	0.0	9:47	....	....	....	....	....	....	....	....	....
	Syracuse Crunch	AHL	33	13	9	22	28	....	....	....	....	....	....	....	....	....	....	....	....	....	....	....	....	....	....
2015-16	**Tampa Bay**	**NHL**	20	3	2	5	34	0	0	1	14	21.4	3	0	0.0	8:39	7	0	0	0	4	0	0	0	5:49
	Syracuse Crunch	AHL	49	21	17	38	68	....	....	....	....	....	....	....	....	....	....	....	....	....	....	....	....	....	....
2016-17	**Ottawa**	**NHL**	2	0	0	0	4	0	0	0	1	0.0	0	0	0.0	8:07	....	....	....	....	....	....	....	....	....
	Binghamton	AHL	67	14	15	29	57	....	....	....	....	....	....	....	....	....	....	....	....	....	....	....	....	....	....
	NHL Totals		126	7	6	13	145	0	0	1	109	6.4		106	34.0	8:46	8	0	0	0	14	0	0	0	6:07

• Missed majority of 2006-07 due to shoulder injury vs. Hershey (AHL), December 10, 2006. Traded to **Columbus** by **Chicago** for Adam Pineault, January 10, 2008. • Missed majority of 2010-11 due to shoulder injury vs. Worcester (AHL), January 14, 2011. Traded to **Montreal** by **Columbus** for Ryan Russell, July 7, 2011. Signed as a free agent by **Tampa Bay**, July 1, 2014. • Missed majority of 2014-15 due to knee injury vs. Rochester (AHL), January 30, 2015. Signed as a free agent by **Ottawa**, July 1, 2016.

BODNARCHUK, Andrew — (BAWD-nahr-chuhk, AN-droo) — **DAL**

Defense. Shoots left. 5'11", 196 lbs.   Born, Drumheller, AB, July 11, 1988. Boston's 5th pick, 128th overall, in 2006 NHL Draft.

Season	Club	League	GP	G	A	Pts	PIM	PP	SH	GW	S	S%	+/-	TF	F%	Min	GP	G	A	Pts	PIM	PP	SH	GW	Min
2003-04	Dartmouth	NSMHL	58	16	23	39	81	....	....	....	....	....	....	....	....	....	....	....	....	....	....	....	....	....	....
2004-05	St. Paul's School	High-NH	36	3	15	18		....	....	....	....	....	....	....	....	....	....	....	....	....	....	....	....	....	....
2005-06	Halifax	QMJHL	68	6	17	23	136	....	....	....	....	....	....	....	....	....	11	0	2	2	22	....	....	....	....
2006-07	Halifax	QMJHL	63	16	41	57	96	....	....	....	....	....	....	....	....	....	12	1	10	11	25	....	....	....	....
	Providence Bruins	AHL	....	....	....	....	....	....	....	....	....	....	....	....	....	....	1	0	0	0	0	....	....	....	....
2007-08	Halifax	QMJHL	65	10	33	43	89	....	....	....	....	....	....	....	....	....	14	0	9	9	16	....	....	....	....
2008-09	Providence Bruins	AHL	62	1	8	9	33	....	....	....	....	....	....	....	....	....	15	0	2	2	22	....	....	....	....

			Regular Season														Playoffs								
Season	Club	League	GP	G	A	Pts	PIM	PP	SH	GW	S	S%	+/-	TF	F%	Min	GP	G	A	Pts	PIM	PP	SH	GW	Min
2009-10	**Boston**	**NHL**	**5**	**0**	**0**	**0**	**2**	**0**	**0**	**0**	**0**	**0.0**	**–2**	**0**	**0.0**	**7:19**	....	....	....	....	....	....	....	....	....
	Providence Bruins	AHL	70	5	10	15	51	....	....	....	....	....	....	....	....	....	....	....	....	....	....	....	....	....	....
2010-11	Providence Bruins	AHL	75	1	15	16	91	....	....	....	....	....	....	....	....	....	....	....	....	....	....	....	....	....	....
2011-12	Providence Bruins	AHL	63	5	12	17	44	....	....	....	....	....	....	....	....	....	....	....	....	....	....	....	....	....	....
2012-13	Manchester	AHL	69	5	15	20	77	....	....	....	....	....	....	....	....	....	4	0	0	0	0	....	....	....	....
2013-14	Manchester	AHL	73	8	24	32	89	....	....	....	....	....	....	....	....	....	4	0	0	0	0	....	....	....	....
2014-15	Manchester	AHL	61	5	20	25	84	....	....	....	....	....	....	....	....	....	19	0	6	6	14	....	....	....	....
2015-16	**Columbus**	**NHL**	**16**	**0**	**2**	**2**	**8**	**0**	**0**	**0**	**5**	**0.0**	**–6**	**0**	**0.0**	**14:32**	....	....	....	....	....	....	....	....	....
	Lake Erie	AHL	14	2	6	8	10	....	....	....	....	....	....	....	....	....	....	....	....	....	....	....	....	....	....
	Colorado	**NHL**	**21**	**0**	**2**	**2**	**6**	**0**	**0**	**0**	**4**	**0.0**	**–1**	**0**	**0.0**	**10:40**	....	....	....	....	....	....	....	....	....
2016-17	Texas Stars	AHL	69	5	21	26	69	....	....	....	....	....	....	....	....	....	....	....	....	....	....	....	....	....	....
	NHL Totals		**42**	**0**	**4**	**4**	**16**	**0**	**0**	**0**	**9**	**0.0**		**0**	**0.0**	**11:45**	....	....	....	....	....	....	....	....	....

QMJHL All-Rookie Team (2006)

Signed as a free agent by **Los Angeles**, July 6, 2012. Signed as a free agent by **Columbus**, July 2, 2015. Claimed on waivers by **Colorado** from **Columbus**, January 5, 2016. Signed as a free agent by **Dallas**, July 1, 2016.

BOEDKER, Mikkel (BAWD-kuhr, MIH-kehl) S.J.

Left wing. Shoots left. 6', 210 lbs. Born, Brondby, Denmark, December 16, 1989. Phoenix's 1st pick, 8th overall, in 2008 NHL Draft.

Season	Club	League	GP	G	A	Pts	PIM	PP	SH	GW	S	S%	+/-	TF	F%	Min	GP	G	A	Pts	PIM	PP	SH	GW	Min
2004-05	Rodovre IK	Den-2	1	0	1	1	0	....	....	....	....	....	....	....	....	....	....	....	....	....	....	....	....	....	....
2005-06	Frolunda U18	Swe-U18	5	2	0	2	0	....	....	....	....	....	....	....	....	....	2	0	1	1	0	....	....	....	....
	Frolunda Jr.	Swe-Jr.	37	9	8	17	22	....	....	....	....	....	....	....	....	....	2	1	2	3	0	....	....	....	....
2006-07	Frolunda U18	Swe-U18	3	3	2	5	2	....	....	....	....	....	....	....	....	....	6	5	4	9	2	....	....	....	....
	Frolunda Jr.	Swe-Jr.	39	19	30	49	14	....	....	....	....	....	....	....	....	....	8	6	5	11	6	....	....	....	....
	Frolunda	Sweden	2	0	0	0	0	....	....	....	....	....	....	....	....	....	....	....	....	....	....	....	....	....	....
2007-08	Kitchener Rangers	OHL	62	29	44	73	14	....	....	....	....	....	....	....	....	....	20	9	*26	35	2	....	....	....	....
2008-09	**Phoenix**	**NHL**	**78**	**11**	**17**	**28**	**18**	**2**	**0**	**3**	**116**	**9.5**	**–6**	**8**	**12.5**	**15:32**	....	....	....	....	....	....	....	....	....
2009-10	**Phoenix**	**NHL**	**14**	**1**	**2**	**3**	**0**	**0**	**0**	**0**	**7**	**14.3**	**2**	**0**	**0.0**	**8:43**	....	....	....	....	....	....	....	....	....
	San Antonio	AHL	64	11	27	38	4	....	....	....	....	....	....	....	....	....	....	....	....	....	....	....	....	....	....
2010-11	**Phoenix**	**NHL**	**34**	**4**	**10**	**14**	**8**	**0**	**0**	**0**	**39**	**10.3**	**11**	**5**	**60.0**	**10:54**	**4**	**0**	**1**	**1**	**2**	**0**	**0**	**0**	**8:58**
	San Antonio	AHL	36	12	22	34	8	....	....	....	....	....	....	....	....	....	....	....	....	....	....	....	....	....	....
2011-12	**Phoenix**	**NHL**	**82**	**11**	**13**	**24**	**12**	**0**	**0**	**2**	**86**	**12.8**	**–2**	**2**	**50.0**	**13:38**	**16**	**4**	**4**	**8**	**0**	**0**	**0**	**2**	**16:56**
2012-13	Lukko Rauma	Finland	29	21	12	33	10	....	....	....	....	....	....	....	....	....	....	....	....	....	....	....	....	....	....
	Phoenix	**NHL**	**48**	**7**	**19**	**26**	**12**	**3**	**0**	**2**	**83**	**8.4**	**0**	**11**	**9.1**	**18:29**	....	....	....	....	....	....	....	....	....
2013-14	**Phoenix**	**NHL**	**82**	**19**	**32**	**51**	**20**	**5**	**0**	**1**	**166**	**11.4**	**–9**	**7**	**42.9**	**17:25**	....	....	....	....	....	....	....	....	....
2014-15	**Arizona**	**NHL**	**45**	**14**	**14**	**28**	**6**	**3**	**0**	**2**	**79**	**17.7**	**–10**	**2**	**0.0**	**17:29**	....	....	....	....	....	....	....	....	....
2015-16	**Arizona**	**NHL**	**62**	**13**	**26**	**39**	**10**	**3**	**0**	**4**	**144**	**9.0**	**–28**	**1**	**0.0**	**18:39**	....	....	....	....	....	....	....	....	....
	Colorado	**NHL**	**18**	**4**	**8**	**12**	**2**	**0**	**0**	**1**	**22**	**18.2**	**–5**	**2**	**50.0**	**18:07**	....	....	....	....	....	....	....	....	....
2016-17	**San Jose**	**NHL**	**81**	**10**	**16**	**26**	**10**	**0**	**1**	**2**	**122**	**8.2**	**0**	**18**	**27.8**	**14:21**	**4**	**1**	**1**	**2**	**2**	**0**	**0**	**0**	**14:04**
	NHL Totals		**544**	**94**	**157**	**251**	**98**	**16**	**1**	**17**	**864**	**10.9**		**56**	**26.8**	**15:45**	**24**	**5**	**6**	**11**	**4**	**0**	**0**	**2**	**15:07**

Signed as a free agent by **Rauma** (Finland), September 27, 2012. Traded to **Colorado** by **Arizona** for Alex Tanguay, Connor Bleackley and Kyle Wood, February 29, 2016. Signed as a free agent by **San Jose**, July 1, 2016.

BOESER, Brock (BEH-suhr, BRAWK) VAN

Right wing. Shoots right. 6'1", 191 lbs. Born, Burnsville, MN, February 25, 1997. Vancouver's 1st pick, 23rd overall, in 2015 NHL Draft.

Season	Club	League	GP	G	A	Pts	PIM	PP	SH	GW	S	S%	+/-	TF	F%	Min	GP	G	A	Pts	PIM	PP	SH	GW	Min
2012-13	Burnsville Blaze	High-MN	16	12	17	29	4	....	....	....	....	....	....	....	....	....	3	0	5	5	2	....	....	....	....
2013-14	Team Southeast	UMHSEL	14	9	5	14	21	....	....	....	....	....	....	....	....	....	3	3	0	3	0	....	....	....	....
	Burnsville Blaze	High-MN	24	21	25	46	25	....	....	....	....	....	....	....	....	....	2	2	2	4	0	....	....	....	....
	Sioux City	USHL	8	3	2	5	2	....	....	....	....	....	....	....	....	....	8	1	0	1	0	....	....	....	....
2014-15	Waterloo	USHL	57	*35	33	68	30	....	....	....	....	....	....	....	....	....	....	....	....	....	....	....	....	....	....
2015-16	North Dakota	NCHC	42	*27	33	*60	26	....	....	....	....	....	....	....	....	....	....	....	....	....	....	....	....	....	....
2016-17	North Dakota	NCHC	32	16	18	34	24	....	....	....	....	....	....	....	....	....	....	....	....	....	....	....	....	....	....
	Vancouver	**NHL**	**9**	**4**	**1**	**5**	**0**	**2**	**0**	**1**	**25**	**16.0**	**0**	**0**	**0.0**	**16:13**	....	....	....	....	....	....	....	....	....
	NHL Totals		**9**	**4**	**1**	**5**	**0**	**2**	**0**	**1**	**25**	**16.0**		**0**	**0.0**	**16:13**	....	....	....	....	....	....	....	....	....

USHL All-Rookie Team (2015) • USHL First All-Star Team (2015) • NCHC All-Rookie Team (2016) • NCHC First All-Star Team (2016) • NCHC Rookie of the Year (2016) • NCAA West First All-American Team (2016) • NCAA Championship All-Tournament Team (2016)

BOGOSIAN, Zach (buh-GOH-zhuhn, ZAK) BUF

Defense. Shoots right. 6'3", 219 lbs. Born, Massena, NY, July 15, 1990. Atlanta's 1st pick, 3rd overall, in 2008 NHL Draft.

Season	Club	League	GP	G	A	Pts	PIM	PP	SH	GW	S	S%	+/-	TF	F%	Min	GP	G	A	Pts	PIM	PP	SH	GW	Min
2005-06	Cushing	High-MA	36	1	16	17	....	....	....	....	....	....	....	....	....	....	....	....	....	....	....	....	....	....	....
2006-07	Peterborough	OHL	67	7	26	33	63	....	....	....	....	....	....	....	....	....	....	....	....	....	....	....	....	....	....
2007-08	Peterborough	OHL	60	11	50	61	72	....	....	....	....	....	....	....	....	....	5	0	3	3	8	....	....	....	....
2008-09	**Atlanta**	**NHL**	**47**	**9**	**10**	**19**	**47**	**2**	**1**	**1**	**90**	**10.0**	**11**	**0**	**0.0**	**18:06**	....	....	....	....	....	....	....	....	....
	Chicago Wolves	AHL	5	1	0	1	0	....	....	....	....	....	....	....	....	....	....	....	....	....	....	....	....	....	....
2009-10	**Atlanta**	**NHL**	**81**	**10**	**13**	**23**	**61**	**3**	**1**	**0**	**155**	**6.5**	**–18**	**0**	**0.0**	**21:25**	....	....	....	....	....	....	....	....	....
2010-11	**Atlanta**	**NHL**	**71**	**5**	**12**	**17**	**29**	**0**	**0**	**1**	**155**	**3.2**	**–27**	**0**	**0.0**	**22:24**	....	....	....	....	....	....	....	....	....
2011-12	**Winnipeg**	**NHL**	**65**	**5**	**25**	**30**	**71**	**1**	**0**	**0**	**150**	**3.3**	**–3**	**0**	**0.0**	**23:19**	....	....	....	....	....	....	....	....	....
2012-13	**Winnipeg**	**NHL**	**33**	**5**	**9**	**14**	**29**	**0**	**0**	**0**	**85**	**5.9**	**–5**	**0**	**0.0**	**23:07**	....	....	....	....	....	....	....	....	....
2013-14	**Winnipeg**	**NHL**	**55**	**3**	**8**	**11**	**48**	**0**	**0**	**0**	**134**	**2.2**	**3**	**0**	**0.0**	**22:55**	....	....	....	....	....	....	....	....	....
2014-15	**Winnipeg**	**NHL**	**41**	**3**	**10**	**13**	**40**	**0**	**0**	**0**	**74**	**4.1**	**1**	**0**	**0.0**	**22:10**	....	....	....	....	....	....	....	....	....
	Buffalo	**NHL**	**21**	**0**	**7**	**7**	**38**	**0**	**0**	**0**	**51**	**0.0**	**–7**	**0**	**0.0**	**26:34**	....	....	....	....	....	....	....	....	....
2015-16	**Buffalo**	**NHL**	**64**	**7**	**17**	**24**	**68**	**3**	**0**	**1**	**121**	**5.8**	**–11**	**0**	**0.0**	**22:21**	....	....	....	....	....	....	....	....	....
2016-17	**Buffalo**	**NHL**	**56**	**2**	**9**	**11**	**46**	**0**	**0**	**1**	**73**	**2.7**	**–17**	**0**	**0.0**	**20:05**	....	....	....	....	....	....	....	....	....
	NHL Totals		**534**	**49**	**120**	**169**	**477**	**9**	**2**	**4**	**1088**	**4.5**		**0**	**0.0**	**21:59**	....	....	....	....	....	....	....	....	....

OHL First All-Star Team (2008)

• Transferred to **Winnipeg** after **Atlanta** franchise relocated, June 21, 2011. Traded to **Buffalo** by **Winnipeg** with Evander Kane and Jason Kasdorf for Tyler Myers, Drew Stafford, Joel Armia, Brendan Lemieux and St. Louis' 1st round pick (previously acquired, Winnipeg selected Jack Roslovic) in 2015 NHL Draft, February 11, 2015.

BOLL, Jared (BOWL, JAIR-ehd) ANA

Right wing. Shoots right. 6'3", 209 lbs. Born, Charlotte, NC, May 13, 1986. Columbus' 4th pick, 101st overall, in 2005 NHL Draft.

Season	Club	League	GP	G	A	Pts	PIM	PP	SH	GW	S	S%	+/-	TF	F%	Min	GP	G	A	Pts	PIM	PP	SH	GW	Min
2003-04	Lincoln Stars	USHL	57	6	8	14	*176	....	....	....	....	....	....	....	....	....	....	....	....	....	....	....	....	....	....
2004-05	Lincoln Stars	USHL	59	23	24	47	*294	....	....	....	....	....	....	....	....	....	4	1	3	4	25	....	....	....	....
2005-06	Plymouth Whalers	OHL	65	19	22	41	205	....	....	....	....	....	....	....	....	....	13	2	4	6	21	....	....	....	....
2006-07	Plymouth Whalers	OHL	66	28	27	55	198	....	....	....	....	....	....	....	....	....	20	6	4	10	*66	....	....	....	....
2007-08	**Columbus**	**NHL**	**75**	**5**	**5**	**10**	**226**	**0**	**0**	**3**	**63**	**7.9**	**–4**	**6**	**33.3**	**8:01**	....	....	....	....	....	....	....	....	....
2008-09	**Columbus**	**NHL**	**75**	**4**	**10**	**14**	**180**	**1**	**0**	**0**	**73**	**5.5**	**–6**	**4**	**0.0**	**8:54**	**1**	**0**	**0**	**0**	**0**	**0**	**0**	**0**	**5:17**
2009-10	**Columbus**	**NHL**	**68**	**4**	**3**	**7**	**149**	**0**	**0**	**0**	**56**	**7.1**	**–8**	**3**	**0.0**	**7:12**	....	....	....	....	....	....	....	....	....
2010-11	**Columbus**	**NHL**	**73**	**7**	**5**	**12**	**182**	**0**	**0**	**2**	**66**	**10.6**	**–2**	**6**	**0.0**	**7:40**	....	....	....	....	....	....	....	....	....
2011-12	**Columbus**	**NHL**	**54**	**2**	**1**	**3**	**126**	**0**	**0**	**0**	**35**	**5.7**	**–8**	**5**	**60.0**	**8:07**	....	....	....	....	....	....	....	....	....
2012-13	TuTo Turku	Finland-2	5	2	1	3	31	....	....	....	....	....	....	....	....	....	....	....	....	....	....	....	....	....	....
	Columbus	**NHL**	**43**	**2**	**4**	**6**	**100**	**0**	**0**	**0**	**19**	**10.5**	**1**	**9**	**44.4**	**8:05**	....	....	....	....	....	....	....	....	....
2013-14	**Columbus**	**NHL**	**28**	**1**	**1**	**2**	**62**	**0**	**0**	**0**	**12**	**8.3**	**–6**	**1**	**0.0**	**7:38**	**2**	**0**	**0**	**0**	**0**	**0**	**0**	**0**	**6:35**
2014-15	**Columbus**	**NHL**	**72**	**1**	**4**	**5**	**109**	**0**	**0**	**0**	**28**	**3.6**	**–13**	**2**	**0.0**	**7:16**	....	....	....	....	....	....	....	....	....
2015-16	**Columbus**	**NHL**	**30**	**1**	**2**	**3**	**61**	**0**	**0**	**0**	**11**	**9.1**	**–3**	**2**	**100.0**	**6:39**	....	....	....	....	....	....	....	....	....
2016-17	**Anaheim**	**NHL**	**51**	**0**	**3**	**3**	**87**	**0**	**0**	**0**	**13**	**0.0**	**–3**	**1**	**0.0**	**5:49**	**8**	**0**	**0**	**0**	**5**	**0**	**0**	**0**	**4:30**
	NHL Totals		**569**	**27**	**38**	**65**	**1282**	**1**	**0**	**5**	**376**	**7.2**		**39**	**28.2**	**7:37**	**11**	**0**	**0**	**0**	**5**	**0**	**0**	**0**	**4:57**

Signed as a free agent by **TuTo Turku** (Finland-2), November 15, 2012. • Missed majority of 2013-14 due to recurring ankle injury and tendon surgery, November 25, 2013. • Missed majority of 2015-16 due to recurring foot and neck injuries and as a healthy reserve. Signed as a free agent by **Anaheim**, July 5, 2016.

BOLLIG, Brandon
(BOH-lihg, BRAN-duhn) **S.J.**

Left wing. Shoots left. 6'2", 230 lbs. Born, St. Charles, MO, January 31, 1987.

Season	Club	League	GP	G	A	Pts	PIM	PP	SH	GW	S	S%	+/-	TF	F%	Min	Playoffs GP	G	A	Pts	PIM	PP	SH	GW	Min
2005-06	Lincoln Stars	USHL	58	8	8	16	175	....	....	....	....	....	....	....	....	....	9	1	2	3	12	....	....	....	....
2006-07	Lincoln Stars	USHL	57	14	12	26	207	....	....	....	....	....	....	....	....	....	4	0	2	2	2	....	....	....	....
2007-08	Lincoln Stars	USHL	58	15	16	31	211	....	....	....	....	....	....	....	....	....	8	2	4	6	40	....	....	....	....
2008-09	St. Lawrence	ECAC	36	6	7	13	51	....	....	....	....	....	....	....	....	....	....	....	....	....	....	....	....	....	....
2009-10	St. Lawrence	ECAC	42	7	18	25	83	....	....	....	....	....	....	....	....	....	....	....	....	....	....	....	....	....	....
	Rockford IceHogs	AHL	3	1	1	2	7	....	....	....	....	....	....	....	....	....	....	....	....	....	....	....	....	....	....
2010-11	Rockford IceHogs	AHL	55	4	0	4	115	....	....	....	....	....	....	....	....	....	....	....	....	....	....	....	....	....	....
2011-12	**Chicago**	**NHL**	**18**	**0**	**0**	**0**	**58**	**0**	**0**	**0**	**16**	**0.0**	**–2**	**0**	**0.0**	**5:53**	**4**	**1**	**0**	**1**	**19**	**0**	**0**	**0**	**6:01**
	Rockford IceHogs	AHL	53	3	6	9	163	....	....	....	....	....	....	....	....	....	....	....	....	....	....	....	....	....	....
2012-13	Rockford IceHogs	AHL	35	5	4	9	157	....	....	....	....	....	....	....	....	....	....	....	....	....	....	....	....	....	....
	♦ **Chicago**	**NHL**	**25**	**0**	**0**	**0**	**51**	**0**	**0**	**0**	**34**	**0.0**	**–1**	**3**	**0.0**	**8:01**	**5**	**0**	**0**	**0**	**2**	**0**	**0**	**0**	**8:51**
2013-14	**Chicago**	**NHL**	**82**	**7**	**7**	**14**	**92**	**0**	**0**	**1**	**109**	**6.4**	**–1**	**1**	**100.0**	**10:17**	**15**	**0**	**1**	**1**	**16**	**0**	**0**	**0**	**6:24**
2014-15	**Calgary**	**NHL**	**62**	**1**	**4**	**5**	**88**	**0**	**0**	**0**	**67**	**1.5**	**–9**	**5**	**60.0**	**8:36**	**11**	**2**	**0**	**2**	**38**	**0**	**0**	**0**	**6:53**
2015-16	**Calgary**	**NHL**	**54**	**2**	**2**	**4**	**103**	**0**	**0**	**0**	**56**	**3.6**	**–10**	**3**	**66.7**	**9:17**	....	....	....	....	....	....	....	....	....
2016-17	Stockton Heat	AHL	60	11	11	22	136	....	....	....	....	....	....	....	....	....	5	1	0	1	2	....	....	....	....
	NHL Totals		**241**	**10**	**13**	**23**	**392**	**0**	**0**	**1**	**282**	**3.5**		**12**	**50.0**	**9:04**	**35**	**3**	**1**	**4**	**75**	**0**	**0**	**0**	**6:52**

Signed as a free agent by **Chicago**, April 3, 2010. Traded to **Calgary** by **Chicago** for Pittsburgh's 3rd round pick (previously acquired, Chicago selected Matt Iacopelli) in 2014 NHL Draft, June 28, 2014. Signed as a free agent by **San Jose**, July 4, 2017.

BONINO, Nick
(boh-NEE-noh, NIHK) **NSH**

Center. Shoots left. 6'1", 196 lbs. Born, Hartford, CT, April 20, 1988. San Jose's 6th pick, 173rd overall, in 2007 NHL Draft.

Season	Club	League	GP	G	A	Pts	PIM	PP	SH	GW	S	S%	+/-	TF	F%	Min	Playoffs GP	G	A	Pts	PIM	PP	SH	GW	Min
2003-04	Farmington	High-CT	24	44	23	67	10	....	....	....	....	....	....	....	....	....	....	....	....	....	....	....	....	....	....
2004-05	Farmington	High-CT	24	68	23	91	12	....	....	....	....	....	....	....	....	....	....	....	....	....	....	....	....	....	....
2005-06	Avon Old Farms	High-CT	25	26	30	56	10	....	....	....	....	....	....	....	....	....	....	....	....	....	....	....	....	....	....
2006-07	Avon Old Farms	High-CT	26	24	42	66	14	....	....	....	....	....	....	....	....	....	....	....	....	....	....	....	....	....	....
2007-08	Boston University	H-East	39	16	13	29	10	....	....	....	....	....	....	....	....	....	....	....	....	....	....	....	....	....	....
2008-09	Boston University	H-East	44	18	32	50	30	....	....	....	....	....	....	....	....	....	....	....	....	....	....	....	....	....	....
2009-10	Boston University	H-East	33	11	27	38	12	....	....	....	....	....	....	....	....	....	....	....	....	....	....	....	....	....	....
	Anaheim	**NHL**	**9**	**1**	**1**	**2**	**6**	**1**	**0**	**0**	**14**	**7.1**	**0**	**78**	**43.6**	**14:13**	....	....	....	....	....	....	....	....	....
2010-11	**Anaheim**	**NHL**	**26**	**0**	**0**	**0**	**4**	**0**	**0**	**0**	**23**	**0.0**	**–3**	**166**	**47.0**	**9:48**	**4**	**0**	**0**	**0**	**2**	**0**	**0**	**0**	**11:36**
	Syracuse Crunch	AHL	50	12	33	45	32	....	....	....	....	....	....	....	....	....	....	....	....	....	....	....	....	....	....
2011-12	**Anaheim**	**NHL**	**50**	**5**	**13**	**18**	**8**	**0**	**0**	**0**	**63**	**7.9**	**1**	**454**	**43.0**	**12:29**	....	....	....	....	....	....	....	....	....
	Syracuse Crunch	AHL	19	6	16	22	2	....	....	....	....	....	....	....	....	....	....	....	....	....	....	....	....	....	....
2012-13	Neumarkt/Egna	Italy-2	19	26	26	52	14	....	....	....	....	....	....	....	....	....	....	....	....	....	....	....	....	....	....
	Anaheim	**NHL**	**27**	**5**	**8**	**13**	**8**	**1**	**0**	**0**	**37**	**13.5**	**–3**	**295**	**46.8**	**15:53**	**7**	**3**	**1**	**4**	**4**	**2**	**0**	**2**	**16:38**
2013-14	**Anaheim**	**NHL**	**77**	**22**	**27**	**49**	**22**	**7**	**0**	**2**	**159**	**13.8**	**14**	**1194**	**48.8**	**16:14**	**13**	**4**	**4**	**8**	**8**	**1**	**0**	**1**	**17:44**
2014-15	**Vancouver**	**NHL**	**75**	**15**	**24**	**39**	**22**	**1**	**0**	**6**	**149**	**10.1**	**7**	**1245**	**47.4**	**16:55**	**6**	**1**	**2**	**3**	**4**	**0**	**0**	**0**	**16:35**
2015-16 ♦	**Pittsburgh**	**NHL**	**63**	**9**	**20**	**29**	**31**	**2**	**1**	**0**	**97**	**9.3**	**13**	**918**	**50.4**	**15:50**	**24**	**4**	**14**	**18**	**12**	**0**	**0**	**2**	**17:12**
2016-17 ♦	**Pittsburgh**	**NHL**	**80**	**18**	**19**	**37**	**16**	**6**	**1**	**1**	**142**	**12.7**	**–5**	**1213**	**48.0**	**16:39**	**21**	**4**	**3**	**7**	**2**	**0**	**0**	**1**	**16:52**
	NHL Totals		**407**	**75**	**112**	**187**	**117**	**18**	**2**	**9**	**684**	**11.0**		**5563**	**47.9**	**15:26**	**75**	**16**	**24**	**40**	**32**	**3**	**0**	**6**	**16:48**

NCAA Championship All-Tournament Team (2009)

Traded to **Anaheim** by **San Jose** with Timo Pielmeier and San Jose's 4th round pick (Andrew O'Brien) in 2012 NHL Draft for Travis Moen and Kent Huskins, March 4, 2009. Signed as a free agent by **Neumarkt/Egna** (Italy-2), October 16, 2012. Traded to **Vancouver** by **Anaheim** with Luca Sbisa and Anaheim's 1st (Jared McCann) and 3rd (later traded to NY Rangers – NY Rangers selected Keegan Iverson) round picks in 2014 NHL Draft for Ryan Kesler and Vancouver's 3rd round pick (Deven Sideroff) in 2015 NHL Draft, June 27, 2014. Traded to **Pittsburgh** by **Vancouver** with Adam Clendening and Anaheim's 2nd round pick (previously acquired, Pittsburgh selected Filip Gustavsson) in 2016 NHL Draft for Brandon Sutter and Vancouver's 3rd round pick (lpreviously acquired, Vancouver selected William Lockwood) in 2016 NHL Draft, July 28, 2015. Signed as a free agent by **Nashville**, July 1, 2017.

BOROWIECKI, Mark
(BOHR-vee-YHET-skee, MAHRK) **OTT**

Defense. Shoots left. 6'2", 205 lbs. Born, Ottawa, ON, July 12, 1989. Ottawa's 6th pick, 139th overall, in 2008 NHL Draft.

Season	Club	League	GP	G	A	Pts	PIM	PP	SH	GW	S	S%	+/-	TF	F%	Min	Playoffs GP	G	A	Pts	PIM	PP	SH	GW	Min
2006-07	Smiths Falls Bears	ON-Jr.A	53	3	25	28	85	....	....	....	....	....	....	....	....	....	6	0	0	0	10	....	....	....	....
2007-08	Smiths Falls Bears	ON-Jr.A	46	2	24	26	80	....	....	....	....	....	....	....	....	....	15	1	10	11	22	....	....	....	....
2008-09	Clarkson Knights	ECAC	33	1	1	2	24	....	....	....	....	....	....	....	....	....	....	....	....	....	....	....	....	....	....
2009-10	Clarkson Knights	ECAC	35	8	11	19	55	....	....	....	....	....	....	....	....	....	....	....	....	....	....	....	....	....	....
2010-11	Clarkson Knights	ECAC	31	3	8	11	67	....	....	....	....	....	....	....	....	....	....	....	....	....	....	....	....	....	....
	Binghamton	AHL	9	0	0	0	6	....	....	....	....	....	....	....	....	....	21	0	2	2	8	....	....	....	....
2011-12	**Ottawa**	**NHL**	**2**	**0**	**0**	**0**	**2**	**0**	**0**	**0**	**1**	**0.0**	**–1**	**0**	**0.0**	**12:30**	....	....	....	....	....	....	....	....	....
	Binghamton	AHL	73	5	17	22	127	....	....	....	....	....	....	....	....	....	....	....	....	....	....	....	....	....	....
2012-13	Binghamton	AHL	53	4	10	14	157	....	....	....	....	....	....	....	....	....	3	1	0	1	4	....	....	....	....
	Ottawa	**NHL**	**6**	**0**	**0**	**0**	**18**	**0**	**0**	**0**	**1**	**0.0**	**1**	**0**	**0.0**	**13:00**	....	....	....	....	....	....	....	....	....
2013-14	**Ottawa**	**NHL**	**13**	**1**	**0**	**1**	**48**	**0**	**0**	**0**	**6**	**16.7**	**–2**	**0**	**0.0**	**12:35**	....	....	....	....	....	....	....	....	....
	Binghamton	AHL	50	2	6	8	158	....	....	....	....	....	....	....	....	....	4	0	0	0	4	....	....	....	....
2014-15	**Ottawa**	**NHL**	**63**	**1**	**10**	**11**	**107**	**0**	**0**	**0**	**30**	**3.3**	**15**	**0**	**0.0**	**15:55**	**6**	**0**	**0**	**0**	**6**	**0**	**0**	**0**	**16:24**
2015-16	**Ottawa**	**NHL**	**63**	**1**	**1**	**2**	**107**	**0**	**0**	**0**	**27**	**3.7**	**–4**	**1**	**0.0**	**14:38**	....	....	....	....	....	....	....	....	....
2016-17	**Ottawa**	**NHL**	**70**	**1**	**2**	**3**	***154**	**0**	**0**	**0**	**50**	**2.0**	**–3**	**1**	**100.0**	**14:01**	**2**	**0**	**0**	**0**	**2**	**0**	**0**	**0**	**10:25**
	NHL Totals		**217**	**4**	**13**	**17**	**436**	**0**	**0**	**0**	**115**	**3.5**		**2**	**50.0**	**14:37**	**8**	**0**	**0**	**0**	**8**	**0**	**0**	**0**	**14:54**

BORTUZZO, Robert
(bohr-TOOZ-oh, RAW-buhrt) **ST.L.**

Defense. Shoots right. 6'4", 215 lbs. Born, Thunder Bay, ON, March 18, 1989. Pittsburgh's 3rd pick, 78th overall, in 2007 NHL Draft.

Season	Club	League	GP	G	A	Pts	PIM	PP	SH	GW	S	S%	+/-	TF	F%	Min	Playoffs GP	G	A	Pts	PIM	PP	SH	GW	Min
2005-06	F-Wm. North Stars	ON-Jr.A	40	4	18	22	....	....	....	....	....	....	....	....	....	....	....	....	....	....	....	....	....	....	....
2006-07	Kitchener Rangers	OHL	63	2	12	14	67	....	....	....	....	....	....	....	....	....	9	1	2	3	8	....	....	....	....
2007-08	Kitchener Rangers	OHL	52	3	15	18	61	....	....	....	....	....	....	....	....	....	18	0	8	8	14	....	....	....	....
2008-09	Kitchener Rangers	OHL	23	1	16	17	24	....	....	....	....	....	....	....	....	....	....	....	....	....	....	....	....	....	....
2009-10	Wilkes-Barre	AHL	75	2	10	12	109	....	....	....	....	....	....	....	....	....	4	0	0	0	0	....	....	....	....
2010-11	Wilkes-Barre	AHL	79	4	22	26	111	....	....	....	....	....	....	....	....	....	12	0	1	1	6	....	....	....	....
2011-12	**Pittsburgh**	**NHL**	**6**	**0**	**0**	**0**	**2**	**0**	**0**	**0**	**3**	**0.0**	**1**	**0**	**0.0**	**10:54**	....	....	....	....	....	....	....	....	....
	Wilkes-Barre	AHL	51	3	9	12	61	....	....	....	....	....	....	....	....	....	12	0	1	1	13	....	....	....	....
2012-13	Wilkes-Barre	AHL	31	1	3	4	34	....	....	....	....	....	....	....	....	....	....	....	....	....	....	....	....	....	....
	Pittsburgh	**NHL**	**15**	**2**	**2**	**4**	**27**	**0**	**0**	**0**	**10**	**20.0**	**3**	**0**	**0.0**	**13:17**	....	....	....	....	....	....	....	....	....
2013-14	**Pittsburgh**	**NHL**	**54**	**0**	**10**	**10**	**74**	**0**	**0**	**0**	**50**	**0.0**	**–3**	**1**	**0.0**	**15:29**	**8**	**0**	**1**	**1**	**4**	**0**	**0**	**0**	**13:14**
2014-15	**Pittsburgh**	**NHL**	**38**	**2**	**4**	**6**	**68**	**0**	**0**	**0**	**37**	**5.4**	**–6**	**1**	**100.0**	**15:28**	....	....	....	....	....	....	....	....	....
	St. Louis	**NHL**	**13**	**1**	**1**	**2**	**25**	**0**	**0**	**0**	**19**	**5.3**	**–3**	**0**	**0.0**	**14:06**	....	....	....	....	....	....	....	....	....
2015-16	**St. Louis**	**NHL**	**40**	**2**	**1**	**3**	**52**	**0**	**0**	**0**	**47**	**4.3**	**2**	**0**	**0.0**	**13:16**	**5**	**0**	**1**	**1**	**2**	**0**	**0**	**0**	**11:23**
2016-17	**St. Louis**	**NHL**	**38**	**1**	**3**	**4**	**15**	**0**	**0**	**0**	**45**	**2.2**	**11**	**0**	**0.0**	**14:05**	**10**	**0**	**0**	**0**	**4**	**0**	**0**	**0**	**11:31**
	NHL Totals		**204**	**8**	**21**	**29**	**263**	**0**	**0**	**0**	**211**	**3.8**		**2**	**50.0**	**14:24**	**23**	**0**	**2**	**2**	**10**	**0**	**0**	**0**	**12:05**

Traded to **St. Louis** by **Pittsburgh** with Pittsburgh's 7th round pick (Filip Helt) in 2016 NHL Draft for Ian Cole, March 2, 2015. • Missed majority of 2015-16 and 2016-17 as a healthy reserve.

BOUCHER, Reid
(BOO-shay, REED) **VAN**

Left wing. Shoots left. 5'10", 195 lbs. Born, Lansing, MI, September 8, 1993. New Jersey's 4th pick, 99th overall, in 2011 NHL Draft.

Season	Club	League	GP	G	A	Pts	PIM	PP	SH	GW	S	S%	+/-	TF	F%	Min	Playoffs GP	G	A	Pts	PIM	PP	SH	GW	Min
2008-09	Lansing Capitals	Minor-MI	64	79	41	120	119	....	....	....	....	....	....	....	....	....	....	....	....	....	....	....	....	....	....
2009-10	USAHNTDP	USHL	24	10	4	14	22	....	....	....	....	....	....	....	....	....	....	....	....	....	....	....	....	....	....
	USAHNTDP	U-17	17	7	9	16	16	....	....	....	....	....	....	....	....	....	....	....	....	....	....	....	....	....	....
	USAHNTDP	U-18	1	0	0	0	0	....	....	....	....	....	....	....	....	....	....	....	....	....	....	....	....	....	....
2010-11	USAHNTDP	USHL	24	14	6	20	13	....	....	....	....	....	....	....	....	....	....	....	....	....	....	....	....	....	....
	USAHNTDP	U-18	35	12	8	20	20	....	....	....	....	....	....	....	....	....	....	....	....	....	....	....	....	....	....
2011-12	Sarnia Sting	OHL	67	28	22	50	19	....	....	....	....	....	....	....	....	....	6	2	1	3	4	....	....	....	....
	Albany Devils	AHL	1	0	0	0	0	....	....	....	....	....	....	....	....	....	....	....	....	....	....	....	....	....	....
2012-13	Sarnia Sting	OHL	68	*62	33	95	53	....	....	....	....	....	....	....	....	....	4	2	3	5	4	....	....	....	....
	Albany Devils	AHL	11	3	2	5	6	....	....	....	....	....	....	....	....	....	....	....	....	....	....	....	....	....	....
2013-14	**New Jersey**	**NHL**	**23**	**2**	**5**	**7**	**4**	**0**	**0**	**0**	**27**	**7.4**	**2**	**3**	**33.3**	**11:21**	....	....	....	....	....	....	....	....	....
	Albany Devils	AHL	56	22	16	38	10	....	....	....	....	....	....	....	....	....	4	1	0	1	0	....	....	....	....
2014-15	**New Jersey**	**NHL**	**11**	**1**	**0**	**1**	**0**	**0**	**0**	**0**	**20**	**5.0**	**–4**	**0**	**0.0**	**11:08**	....	....	....	....	....	....	....	....	....
	Albany Devils	AHL	62	15	15	30	36	....	....	....	....	....	....	....	....	....	....	....	....	....	....	....	....	....	....

Season	Club	League	GP	G	A	Pts	PIM	PP	SH	GW	S	S%	+/-	TF	F%	Min	GP	G	A	Pts	PIM	PP	SH	GW	Min
			Regular Season														Playoffs								
2015-16	New Jersey	NHL	39	8	11	19	6	2	0	4	74	10.8	-13	3	33.3	14:16									
	Albany Devils	AHL	34	19	13	32	4										11	4	6	10	4				
2016-17	New Jersey	NHL	9	0	2	2	2	0	0	0	12	0.0	0	0	0.0	12:15									
	Nashville	NHL	3	1	0	1	0	0	0	0	3	33.3	1	0	0.0	8:42									
	Milwaukee	AHL	5	4	1	5	0																		
	Vancouver	NHL	27	5	2	7	6	1	0	0	55	9.1	-7	1	0.0	12:11									
	NHL Totals		112	17	20	37	18	3	0	4	191	8.9		7	28.6	12:33									

OHL First All-Star Team (2013)

Claimed on waivers by **Nashville** from **New Jersey**, December 3. 2016. Claimed on waivers by **New Jersey** from **Nashville**, January 2, 2017. Claimed on waivers by **Vancouver** from **New Jersey**, January 4, 2017.

BOUMA, Lance

(BOW-ma, LANTZ) **CHI**

Center. Shoots left. 6'2", 208 lbs. Born, Provost, AB, March 25, 1990. Calgary's 3rd pick, 78th overall, in 2008 NHL Draft.

Season	Club	League	GP	G	A	Pts	PIM	PP	SH	GW	S	S%	+/-	TF	F%	Min	GP	G	A	Pts	PIM	PP	SH	GW	Min
2005-06	Wainwright	RAMHL	37	21	29	50	86										5	1	4	5	6				
	Vancouver Giants	WHL	5	1	3	4	0																		
2006-07	Vancouver Giants	WHL	49	3	5	8	31										22	3	3	6	12				
2007-08	Vancouver Giants	WHL	71	12	23	35	93										10	0	1	1	8				
2008-09	Vancouver Giants	WHL	48	9	16	25	116										17	7	5	12	30				
2009-10	Vancouver Giants	WHL	57	14	29	43	134										16	4	13	17	*47				
	Abbotsford Heat	AHL															5	1	0	1	2				
2010-11	Calgary	NHL	16	0	1	1	2	0	0	0	9	0.0	-1	3	0.0	5:52									
	Abbotsford Heat	AHL	61	12	8	20	53																		
2011-12	Calgary	NHL	27	1	2	3	11	0	0	0	26	3.8	-5	22	50.0	10:10									
	Abbotsford Heat	AHL	31	3	3	6	53																		
2012-13	Abbotsford Heat	AHL	3	1	0	1	2																		
2013-14	Calgary	NHL	78	5	10	15	41	0	1	0	82	6.1	-4	85	25.9	12:36									
2014-15	Calgary	NHL	78	16	18	34	54	0	0	4	104	15.4	10	74	39.2	14:01	2	0	0	0	2	0	0	0	14:16
2015-16	Calgary	NHL	44	2	5	7	31	0	0	0	49	4.1	-6	13	38.5	12:02									
2016-17	Calgary	NHL	61	3	4	7	35	0	0	1	53	5.7	-2	12	33.3	11:21	3	0	0	0	2	0	0	0	10:00
	NHL Totals		304	27	40	67	174	0	1	5	323	8.4		209	34.0	12:04	5	0	0	0	4	0	0	0	11:42

• Missed majority of 2012-13 due to knee injury vs. Chicago (AHL), October 19, 2012. Signed as a free agent by **Chicago**, July 1, 2017.

BOURNIVAL, Michael

(boor-nee-VAHL, MIGH-kuhl) **T.B.**

Left wing. Shoots left. 5'11", 194 lbs. Born, Shawinigan, QC, May 31, 1992. Colorado's 3rd pick, 71st overall, in 2010 NHL Draft.

Season	Club	League	GP	G	A	Pts	PIM	PP	SH	GW	S	S%	+/-	TF	F%	Min	GP	G	A	Pts	PIM	PP	SH	GW	Min
2007-08	Trois-Rivieres	QAAA	52	33	23	56	66										7	3	3	6	10				
2008-09	Shawinigan	QMJHL	46	11	11	22	29										21	1	3	4	12				
2009-10	Shawinigan	QMJHL	58	24	38	62	37										6	2	2	4	6				
2010-11	Shawinigan	QMJHL	56	28	36	64	28										12	5	8	13	10				
2011-12	Shawinigan	QMJHL	41	30	26	56	27										11	1	6	7	12				
2012-13	Hamilton	AHL	69	10	20	30	26																		
2013-14	Montreal	NHL	60	7	7	14	18	1	0	1	78	9.0	-6	61	45.9	10:19	14	0	1	1	0	0	0	0	10:16
	Hamilton	AHL	3	2	1	3	2																		
2014-15	Montreal	NHL	29	3	2	5	4	0	0	1	27	11.1	3	5	80.0	7:53									
	Hamilton	AHL	12	3	6	9	8																		
2015-16	St. John's IceCaps	AHL	20	1	7	8	12																		
2016-17	Tampa Bay	NHL	19	2	1	3	2	0	0	0	25	8.0	-3	3	33.3	10:09									
	Syracuse Crunch	AHL	38	9	10	19	18										22	8	7	15	14				
	NHL Totals		108	12	10	22	24	1	0	2	130	9.2		69	47.8	9:38	14	0	1	1	0	0	0	0	10:16

Traded to **Montreal** by **Colorado** for Ryan O'Byrne, November 11, 2010. • Missed majority of 2014-15 due to shoulder injury at Buffalo, November 5, 2014 and as a healthy reserve. Signed as a free agent by **Tampa Bay**, July 1, 2016. • Missed majority of 2015-16 due to post-concussion syndrome.

BOURQUE, Chris

(BOHRK, KRIHS)

Center. Shoots left. 5'8", 174 lbs. Born, Boston, MA, January 29, 1986. Washington's 4th pick, 33rd overall, in 2004 NHL Draft.

Season	Club	League	GP	G	A	Pts	PIM	PP	SH	GW	S	S%	+/-	TF	F%	Min	GP	G	A	Pts	PIM	PP	SH	GW	Min
2002-03	Cushing	High-MA	28	31	26	57	49																		
2003-04	Cushing	High-MA	31	37	53	90	96																		
2004-05	Boston University	H-East	35	10	13	23	50																		
	Portland Pirates	AHL	6	1	1	2	2																		
2005-06	Hershey Bears	AHL	52	8	28	36	40										1	0	0	0	0				
2006-07	Hershey Bears	AHL	76	25	33	58	49										19	2	6	8	18				
2007-08	Washington	NHL	4	0	0	0	2	0	0	0	4	0.0	0	1	0.0	8:42									
	Hershey Bears	AHL	73	28	35	63	56										5	1	3	4	8				
2008-09	Washington	NHL	8	1	0	1	0	0	0	0	11	9.1	0	0	0.0	9:46									
	Hershey Bears	AHL	69	21	52	73	57										22	5	16	21	30				
2009-10	Pittsburgh	NHL	20	0	3	3	10	0	0	0	20	0.0	-4	0	0.0	9:35									
	Washington	NHL	1	0	0	0	0	0	0	0	1	0.0	-2	0	0.0	9:37									
	Hershey Bears	AHL	49	22	48	70	26										21	7	20	*27	10				
2010-11	Mytischi	KHL	8	1	0	1	0																		
	HC Lugano	Swiss	39	14	19	33	24										2	1	4	5	0				
2011-12	Hershey Bears	AHL	73	27	*66	*93	42										5	1	3	4	0				
2012-13	Providence Bruins	AHL	39	10	28	38	34										12	5	9	14	14				
	Boston	NHL	18	1	3	4	6	0	0	1	24	4.2	-6	1	0.0	12:05									
2013-14	Ak Bars Kazan	KHL	11	2	0	2	6																		
	EHC Biel-Bienne	Swiss	25	7	8	15	14										6	3	2	5	4				
2014-15	Hartford	AHL	73	29	37	66	68										15	4	13	17	12				
2015-16	Hershey Bears	AHL	72	30	50	*80	56										21	4	8	12	20				
2016-17	Hershey Bears	AHL	76	18	42	60	46										12	6	4	10	4				
	NHL Totals		51	2	6	8	18	0	0	1	60	3.3		2	0.0	10:25									

Hockey East All-Rookie Team (2005) • Jack A. Butterfield Trophy (AHL – Playoff MVP) (2010) • AHL First All-Star Team (2012, 2015, 2016) • John P. Sollenberger Trophy (AHL - Top Scorer) (2012, 2016) • Les Cunningham Award (AHL – MVP) (2016)

Claimed on waivers by **Pittsburgh** from **Washington**, September 30, 2009. Claimed on waivers by **Washington** from **Pittsburgh**, December 5, 2009. Signed as a free agent by **Mytischi** (KHL), June 23, 2010. Signed as a free agent by **Lugano** (Swiss), October 4, 2010. Traded to **Boston** by **Washington** for Zach Hamill, May 26, 2012. Signed as a free agent by **Kazan** (KHL), June 18, 2013. Signed as a free agent by **Biel-Bienne** (Swiss), November 29, 2013. Signed as a free agent by **NY Rangers**, July 1, 2014. Signed as a free agent by **Washington**, July 2, 2015.

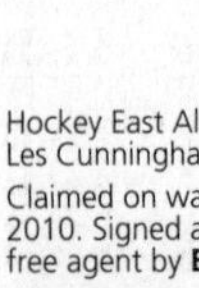

BOURQUE, Gabriel

(BOHRK, gah-BREE-ehl) **COL**

Left wing. Shoots left. 5'10", 206 lbs. Born, Rimouski, QC, September 23, 1990. Nashville's 9th pick, 132nd overall, in 2009 NHL Draft.

Season	Club	League	GP	G	A	Pts	PIM	PP	SH	GW	S	S%	+/-	TF	F%	Min	GP	G	A	Pts	PIM	PP	SH	GW	Min
2006-07	Ecole Notre Dame	QAAA	43	15	35	50	115										13	8	16	24	14				
2007-08	Baie-Comeau	QMJHL	65	10	18	28	38										5	0	0	0	0				
2008-09	Baie-Comeau	QMJHL	60	22	39	61	82										5	0	2	2	16				
2009-10	Baie-Comeau	QMJHL	30	13	25	38	61																		
	Moncton Wildcats	QMJHL	25	3	11	14	37										21	19	10	29	18				
2010-11	Milwaukee	AHL	78	18	18	36	19										13	7	6	13	4				
2011-12	Nashville	NHL	43	7	12	19	6	0	0	1	59	11.9	-2	1	0.0	12:47	10	3	2	5	4	0	0	1	13:00
	Milwaukee	AHL	25	2	14	16	23																		
2012-13	Milwaukee	AHL	15	7	5	12	4																		
	Nashville	NHL	34	11	5	16	4	3	1	2	50	22.0	6	6	66.7	15:50									
2013-14	Nashville	NHL	74	9	17	26	8	0	0	1	108	8.3	-5	1	0.0	13:50									
2014-15	Nashville	NHL	69	3	10	13	10	0	0	0	76	3.9	-13	6	50.0	12:01	5	0	0	0	2	0	0	0	15:26
2015-16	Nashville	NHL	22	1	3	4	18	0	0	0	25	4.0	0	1	0.0	12:22									
	Milwaukee	AHL	4	0	0	0	0																		
2016-17	Colorado	NHL	6	0	0	0	0	0	0	0	4	0.0	0	1	0.0	11:12									
	San Antonio	AHL	61	10	23	33	20																		
	NHL Totals		248	31	47	78	46	3	1	4	322	9.6		16	43.8	13:14	15	3	2	5	6	0	0	1	13:48

• Missed majority of 2015-16 due to upper-body injury vs. Philadelphia, November 27, 2015. Signed as a free agent by **Colorado**, October 10, 2016.

BOURQUE, Rene
(BOHRK, reh-NAY)

Right wing. Shoots left. 6'2", 217 lbs. Born, Lac La Biche, AB, December 10, 1981.

Season	Club	League	GP	G	A	Pts	PIM	PP	SH	GW	S	S%	+/-	TF	F%	Min	GP	G	A	Pts	PIM	PP	SH	GW	Min
			Regular Season														Playoffs								
1998-99	Notre Dame	SMHL	42	22	19	41	84	....	....	....	....	....	....	....	....	....	3	1	0	1	6	....	....	....	....
	Notre Dame	SJHL	5	1	0	0	0	....	....	....	....	....	....	....	....	....	1	0	0	0	0	....	....	....	....
2000-01	U. of Wisconsin	WCHA	32	10	5	15	18	....	....	....	....	....	....	....	....	....	....	....	....	....	....	....	....	....	....
2001-02	U. of Wisconsin	WCHA	38	12	7	19	26	....	....	....	....	....	....	....	....	....	....	....	....	....	....	....	....	....	....
2002-03	U. of Wisconsin	WCHA	40	19	8	27	54	....	....	....	....	....	....	....	....	....	....	....	....	....	....	....	....	....	....
2003-04	U. of Wisconsin	WCHA	42	16	20	36	74	....	....	....	....	....	....	....	....	....	....	....	....	....	....	....	....	....	....
2004-05	Norfolk Admirals	AHL	78	33	27	60	105	....	....	....	....	....	....	....	....	....	6	1	0	1	8	....	....	....	....
2005-06	**Chicago**	**NHL**	**77**	**16**	**18**	**34**	**56**	**4**	**0**	**2**	**180**	**8.9**	**3**	**11**	**36.4**	**15:20**	....	....	....	....	....	....	....	....	....
2006-07	**Chicago**	**NHL**	**44**	**7**	**10**	**17**	**38**	**2**	**1**	**1**	**82**	**8.5**	**-4**	**9**	**22.2**	**16:01**	....	....	....	....	....	....	....	....	....
	Norfolk Admirals	AHL	1	0	0	0	0	....	....	....	....	....	....	....	....	....	....	....	....	....	....	....	....	....	....
2007-08	**Chicago**	**NHL**	**62**	**10**	**14**	**24**	**42**	**0**	**5**	**2**	**103**	**9.7**	**6**	**8**	**25.0**	**15:16**	....	....	....	....	....	....	....	....	....
2008-09	**Calgary**	**NHL**	**58**	**21**	**19**	**40**	**70**	**0**	**1**	**0**	**149**	**14.1**	**18**	**18**	**50.0**	**16:05**	**5**	**1**	**0**	**1**	**22**	**0**	**0**	**0**	**17:06**
2009-10	**Calgary**	**NHL**	**73**	**27**	**31**	**58**	**88**	**6**	**4**	**5**	**215**	**12.6**	**7**	**25**	**32.0**	**18:19**	....	....	....	....	....	....	....	....	....
2010-11	**Calgary**	**NHL**	**80**	**27**	**23**	**50**	**42**	**6**	**1**	**6**	**218**	**12.4**	**-17**	**24**	**29.2**	**17:45**	....	....	....	....	....	....	....	....	....
2011-12	**Calgary**	**NHL**	**38**	**13**	**3**	**16**	**41**	**3**	**0**	**1**	**91**	**14.3**	**-3**	**13**	**69.2**	**17:10**	....	....	....	....	....	....	....	....	....
	Montreal	**NHL**	**38**	**5**	**3**	**8**	**27**	**0**	**1**	**0**	**67**	**7.5**	**-16**	**7**	**42.9**	**18:29**	....	....	....	....	....	....	....	....	....
2012-13	**Montreal**	**NHL**	**27**	**7**	**6**	**13**	**32**	**2**	**0**	**1**	**63**	**11.1**	**-1**	**1**	**0.0**	**16:20**	**5**	**2**	**1**	**3**	**10**	**1**	**0**	**0**	**16:08**
2013-14	**Montreal**	**NHL**	**63**	**9**	**7**	**16**	**32**	**3**	**0**	**2**	**118**	**7.6**	**-1**	**8**	**50.0**	**14:11**	**17**	**8**	**3**	**11**	**27**	**0**	**0**	**2**	**14:40**
2014-15	**Montreal**	**NHL**	**13**	**0**	**2**	**2**	**6**	**0**	**0**	**0**	**18**	**0.0**	**-9**	**5**	**60.0**	**12:21**	....	....	....	....	....	....	....	....	....
	Hamilton	AHL	4	2	2	4	4	....	....	....	....	....	....	....	....	....	....	....	....	....	....	....	....	....	....
	Anaheim	**NHL**	**30**	**2**	**6**	**8**	**12**	**1**	**0**	**0**	**44**	**4.5**	**-4**	**5**	**20.0**	**12:08**	....	....	....	....	....	....	....	....	....
	Columbus	**NHL**	**8**	**4**	**0**	**4**	**4**	**1**	**0**	**1**	**23**	**17.4**	**-2**	**0**	**0.0**	**15:00**	....	....	....	....	....	....	....	....	....
2015-16	**Columbus**	**NHL**	**49**	**3**	**5**	**8**	**38**	**0**	**0**	**0**	**77**	**3.9**	**-9**	**9**	**33.3**	**10:27**	....	....	....	....	....	....	....	....	....
2016-17	**Colorado**	**NHL**	**65**	**12**	**6**	**18**	**56**	**2**	**0**	**2**	**111**	**10.8**	**-19**	**5**	**0.0**	**13:57**	....	....	....	....	....	....	....	....	....
	NHL Totals		**725**	**163**	**153**	**316**	**584**	**30**	**13**	**23**	**1559**	**10.5**		**148**	**37.2**	**15:33**	**27**	**11**	**4**	**15**	**59**	**1**	**0**	**2**	**15:24**

AHL All-Rookie Team (2005) • Dudley "Red" Garrett Memorial Trophy (AHL – Rookie of the Year) (2005)

Signed as a free agent by **Chicago**, July 29, 2004. Traded to **Calgary** by **Chicago** for Calgary's 2nd round pick (later traded to Toronto – Toronto selected Brad Ross) in 2010 NHL Draft, July 1, 2008. Traded to **Montreal** by **Calgary** with Patrick Holland and Calgary's 2nd round pick (Zachary Fucale) in 2013 NHL Draft for Mike Cammalleri, Karri Ramo and Montreal's 5th round pick (Ryan Culkin) in 2012 NHL Draft, January 12, 2012. Traded to **Anaheim** by **Montreal** for Bryan Allen, November 20, 2014. Traded to **Columbus** by **Anaheim** with William Karlsson and Anaheim's 2nd round pick (Kevin Stenlund) in 2015 NHL Draft for James Wisniewski and Detroit's 3rd round pick (previously acquired, Anaheim selected Brent Gates) in 2015 NHL Draft, March 2, 2015. Signed as a free agent by **Colorado**, October 10, 2016.

BOURQUE, Ryan
(BOHRK, RIGH-uhn)

Center. Shoots left. 5'9", 170 lbs. Born, Boxford, MA, January 3, 1991. NY Rangers' 3rd pick, 80th overall, in 2009 NHL Draft.

Season	Club	League	GP	G	A	Pts	PIM	PP	SH	GW	S	S%	+/-	TF	F%	Min	GP	G	A	Pts	PIM	PP	SH	GW	Min
2006-07	Cushing	High-MA	29	19	31	50	....	....	....	....	....	....	....	....	....	....	....	....	....	....	....	....	....	....	....
2007-08	USAHNTDP	NAHL	34	11	9	20	14	....	....	....	....	....	....	....	....	....	....	....	....	....	....	....	....	....	....
	USAHNTDP	U-17	7	4	3	7	10	....	....	....	....	....	....	....	....	....	....	....	....	....	....	....	....	....	....
	USAHNTDP	U-18	27	4	12	16	18	....	....	....	....	....	....	....	....	....	....	....	....	....	....	....	....	....	....
2008-09	USAHNTDP	NAHL	14	7	9	16	10	....	....	....	....	....	....	....	....	....	....	....	....	....	....	....	....	....	....
	USAHNTDP	U-18	43	14	24	38	48	....	....	....	....	....	....	....	....	....	....	....	....	....	....	....	....	....	....
2009-10	Quebec Remparts	QMJHL	44	19	24	43	20	....	....	....	....	....	....	....	....	....	9	3	7	10	6	....	....	....	....
2010-11	Quebec Remparts	QMJHL	49	26	33	59	22	....	....	....	....	....	....	....	....	....	18	5	11	16	8	....	....	....	....
2011-12	Connecticut	AHL	69	6	8	14	10	....	....	....	....	....	....	....	....	....	9	2	1	3	4	....	....	....	....
2012-13	Connecticut	AHL	53	8	7	15	11	....	....	....	....	....	....	....	....	....	....	....	....	....	....	....	....	....	....
2013-14	Hartford	AHL	74	21	16	37	22	....	....	....	....	....	....	....	....	....	....	....	....	....	....	....	....	....	....
2014-15	**NY Rangers**	**NHL**	**1**	**0**	**0**	**0**	**0**	**0**	**0**	**0**	**1**	**0.0**	**-1**	**0**	**0.0**	**11:49**	....	....	....	....	....	....	....	....	....
	Hartford	AHL	73	12	20	32	27	....	....	....	....	....	....	....	....	....	5	0	1	1	2	....	....	....	....
2015-16	Hartford	AHL	56	10	14	24	15	....	....	....	....	....	....	....	....	....	....	....	....	....	....	....	....	....	....
	Hershey Bears	AHL	19	1	4	5	8	....	....	....	....	....	....	....	....	....	21	2	3	5	2	....	....	....	....
2016-17	Hershey Bears	AHL	53	4	10	14	16	....	....	....	....	....	....	....	....	....	12	0	0	0	4	....	....	....	....
	NHL Totals		**1**	**0**	**0**	**0**	**0**	**0**	**0**	**0**	**1**	**0.0**		**0**	**0.0**	**11:49**	....	....	....	....	....	....	....	....	....

Traded to **Washington** by **NY Rangers** for Chris Brown, February 28, 2016. Signed as a free agent by **Hershey** (AHL), July 6, 2016.

BOUWMEESTER, Jay
(BOW-mee-stuhr, JAY) **ST.L.**

Defense. Shoots left. 6'4", 212 lbs. Born, Edmonton, AB, September 27, 1983. Florida's 1st pick, 3rd overall, in 2002 NHL Draft.

Season	Club	League	GP	G	A	Pts	PIM	PP	SH	GW	S	S%	+/-	TF	F%	Min	GP	G	A	Pts	PIM	PP	SH	GW	Min
1998-99	Edmonton SSAC	AMHL	32	14	29	43	36	....	....	....	....	....	....	....	....	....	....	....	....	....	....	....	....	....	....
	Medicine Hat	WHL	8	2	1	3	2	....	....	....	....	....	....	....	....	....	....	....	....	....	....	....	....	....	....
99-2000	Medicine Hat	WHL	64	13	21	34	26	....	....	....	....	....	....	....	....	....	....	....	....	....	....	....	....	....	....
2000-01	Medicine Hat	WHL	61	14	39	53	44	....	....	....	....	....	....	....	....	....	....	....	....	....	....	....	....	....	....
2001-02	Medicine Hat	WHL	61	11	50	61	42	....	....	....	....	....	....	....	....	....	....	....	....	....	....	....	....	....	....
2002-03	**Florida**	**NHL**	**82**	**4**	**12**	**16**	**14**	**2**	**0**	**0**	**110**	**3.6**	**-29**	**0**	**0.0**	**20:09**	....	....	....	....	....	....	....	....	....
2003-04	**Florida**	**NHL**	**61**	**2**	**18**	**20**	**30**	**0**	**0**	**0**	**85**	**2.4**	**-15**	**0**	**0.0**	**23:02**	....	....	....	....	....	....	....	....	....
	San Antonio	AHL	2	0	1	1	2	....	....	....	....	....	....	....	....	....	....	....	....	....	....	....	....	....	....
2004-05	San Antonio	AHL	64	4	13	17	50	....	....	....	....	....	....	....	....	....	....	....	....	....	....	....	....	....	....
	Chicago Wolves	AHL	18	6	3	9	12	....	....	....	....	....	....	....	....	....	18	0	0	0	14	....	....	....	....
2005-06	**Florida**	**NHL**	**82**	**5**	**41**	**46**	**79**	**0**	**0**	**0**	**189**	**2.6**	**1**	**1**	**0.0**	**25:29**	....	....	....	....	....	....	....	....	....
	Canada	Olympics	6	0	0	0	0	....	....	....	....	....	....	....	....	....	....	....	....	....	....	....	....	....	....
2006-07	**Florida**	**NHL**	**82**	**12**	**30**	**42**	**66**	**3**	**0**	**3**	**174**	**6.9**	**23**	**0**	**0.0**	**26:09**	....	....	....	....	....	....	....	....	....
2007-08	**Florida**	**NHL**	**82**	**15**	**22**	**37**	**72**	**4**	**0**	**0**	**182**	**8.2**	**-5**	**0**	**0.0**	**27:28**	....	....	....	....	....	....	....	....	....
2008-09	**Florida**	**NHL**	**82**	**15**	**27**	**42**	**68**	**9**	**0**	**2**	**182**	**8.2**	**-2**	**0**	**0.0**	**26:59**	....	....	....	....	....	....	....	....	....
2009-10	**Calgary**	**NHL**	**82**	**3**	**26**	**29**	**48**	**1**	**0**	**0**	**130**	**2.3**	**-4**	**0**	**0.0**	**25:55**	....	....	....	....	....	....	....	....	....
2010-11	**Calgary**	**NHL**	**82**	**4**	**20**	**24**	**44**	**1**	**0**	**1**	**121**	**3.3**	**-2**	**0**	**0.0**	**25:59**	....	....	....	....	....	....	....	....	....
2011-12	**Calgary**	**NHL**	**82**	**5**	**24**	**29**	**26**	**2**	**0**	**1**	**107**	**4.7**	**-21**	**0**	**0.0**	**25:57**	....	....	....	....	....	....	....	....	....
2012-13	**Calgary**	**NHL**	**33**	**6**	**9**	**15**	**16**	**1**	**0**	**0**	**55**	**10.9**	**-11**	**0**	**0.0**	**25:10**	....	....	....	....	....	....	....	....	....
	St. Louis	**NHL**	**14**	**1**	**6**	**7**	**6**	**0**	**0**	**0**	**24**	**4.2**	**5**	**0**	**0.0**	**23:24**	**6**	**0**	**1**	**1**	**0**	**0**	**0**	**0**	**25:08**
2013-14	**St. Louis**	**NHL**	**82**	**4**	**33**	**37**	**20**	**1**	**0**	**0**	**152**	**2.6**	**26**	**4**	**75.0**	**24:03**	**6**	**0**	**1**	**1**	**2**	**0**	**0**	**0**	**25:52**
	Canada	Olympics	6	0	1	1	0	....	....	....	....	....	....	....	....	....	....	....	....	....	....	....	....	....	....
2014-15	**St. Louis**	**NHL**	**72**	**2**	**11**	**13**	**24**	**0**	**0**	**0**	**92**	**2.2**	**7**	**0**	**0.0**	**22:40**	**6**	**0**	**0**	**0**	**2**	**0**	**0**	**0**	**20:28**
2015-16	**St. Louis**	**NHL**	**72**	**3**	**16**	**19**	**18**	**1**	**0**	**0**	**105**	**2.9**	**-4**	**0**	**0.0**	**23:07**	**20**	**0**	**4**	**4**	**24**	**0**	**0**	**0**	**24:38**
2016-17	**St. Louis**	**NHL**	**81**	**1**	**14**	**15**	**28**	**0**	**0**	**0**	**106**	**0.9**	**6**	**0**	**0.0**	**22:24**	**11**	**0**	**0**	**0**	**4**	**0**	**0**	**0**	**24:15**
	NHL Totals		**1071**	**82**	**309**	**391**	**559**	**25**	**0**	**7**	**1814**	**4.5**		**5**	**60.0**	**24:38**	**49**	**0**	**6**	**6**	**32**	**0**	**0**	**0**	**24:15**

WHL East First All-Star Team (2002) • NHL All-Rookie Team (2003)

Played in NHL All-Star Game (2007, 2009)

• Loaned to **Chicago** (AHL) by **Florida** for cash, March 8, 2005. Traded to **Calgary** by **Florida** for Jordan Leopold and Phoenix's 3rd round pick (previously acquired, Florida selected Josh Birkholz) in 2009 NHL Draft, June 27, 2009. Traded to **St. Louis** by **Calgary** for Mark Cundari, Reto Berra and St. Louis' 1st round pick (Emile Poirier) in 2013 NHL Draft, April 1, 2013.

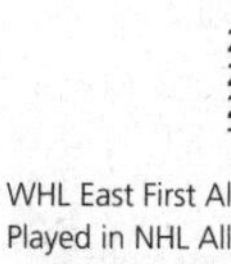

BOYCHUK, Johnny
(BOY-chuhk, JAW-nee) **NYI**

Defense. Shoots right. 6'2", 227 lbs. Born, Edmonton, AB, January 19, 1984. Colorado's 2nd pick, 61st overall, in 2002 NHL Draft.

Season	Club	League	GP	G	A	Pts	PIM	PP	SH	GW	S	S%	+/-	TF	F%	Min	GP	G	A	Pts	PIM	PP	SH	GW	Min
1998-99	Edm. Cycle	AMBHL	36	8	20	28	59	....	....	....	....	....	....	....	....	....	....	....	....	....	....	....	....	....	....
99-2000	Edm. Cycle	AMHL	35	6	17	23	59	....	....	....	....	....	....	....	....	....	....	....	....	....	....	....	....	....	....
	Calgary Hitmen	WHL	1	0	0	0	0	....	....	....	....	....	....	....	....	....	....	....	....	....	....	....	....	....	....
2000-01	Calgary Hitmen	WHL	66	4	8	12	61	....	....	....	....	....	....	....	....	....	12	1	1	2	17	....	....	....	....
2001-02	Calgary Hitmen	WHL	70	8	32	40	85	....	....	....	....	....	....	....	....	....	7	1	1	2	6	....	....	....	....
2002-03	Calgary Hitmen	WHL	40	8	18	26	58	....	....	....	....	....	....	....	....	....	....	....	....	....	....	....	....	....	....
	Moose Jaw	WHL	27	5	17	22	32	....	....	....	....	....	....	....	....	....	13	2	6	8	29	....	....	....	....
2003-04	Moose Jaw	WHL	62	13	20	33	71	....	....	....	....	....	....	....	....	....	10	1	9	10	9	....	....	....	....
2004-05	Hershey Bears	AHL	80	3	12	15	69	....	....	....	....	....	....	....	....	....	....	....	....	....	....	....	....	....	....
2005-06	Lowell	AHL	74	6	26	32	73	....	....	....	....	....	....	....	....	....	....	....	....	....	....	....	....	....	....
2006-07	Albany River Rats	AHL	80	10	18	28	125	....	....	....	....	....	....	....	....	....	5	1	1	2	4	....	....	....	....
2007-08	**Colorado**	**NHL**	**4**	**0**	**0**	**0**	**0**	**0**	**0**	**0**	**3**	**0.0**	**1**	**1**	**0.0**	**8:57**	....	....	....	....	....	....	....	....	....
	Lake Erie	AHL	60	8	18	26	63	....	....	....	....	....	....	....	....	....	....	....	....	....	....	....	....	....	....
2008-09	**Boston**	**NHL**	**1**	**0**	**0**	**0**	**0**	**0**	**0**	**0**	**0**	**0.0**	**0**	**0**	**0.0**	**14:48**	....	....	....	....	....	....	....	....	....
	Providence Bruins	AHL	78	20	46	66	61	....	....	....	....	....	....	....	....	....	16	3	5	8	19	....	....	....	....

			Regular Season														Playoffs								
Season	Club	League	GP	G	A	Pts	PIM	PP	SH	GW	S	S%	+/-	TF	F%	Min	GP	G	A	Pts	PIM	PP	SH	GW	Min
2009-10	**Boston**	**NHL**	**51**	**5**	**10**	**15**	**43**	**0**	**0**	**0**	**96**	**5.2**	**10**	**0**	**0.0**	**17:39**	**13**	**2**	**4**	**6**	**6**	**1**	**0**	**0**	**26:10**
	Providence Bruins	AHL	2	1	0	1	0	....	....	....	....	....	....	....	....	....	....	....	....	....	....	....	....	....	....
2010-11 ♦	**Boston**	**NHL**	**69**	**3**	**13**	**16**	**45**	**1**	**0**	**1**	**154**	**1.9**	**15**	**0**	**0.0**	**20:30**	**25**	**3**	**6**	**9**	**12**	**0**	**0**	**1**	**20:38**
2011-12	**Boston**	**NHL**	**77**	**5**	**10**	**15**	**53**	**0**	**0**	**2**	**171**	**2.9**	**27**	**0**	**0.0**	**20:37**	**7**	**1**	**2**	**3**	**4**	**1**	**0**	**0**	**22:16**
2012-13	Salzburg	Austria	15	2	6	8	2	....	....	....	....	....	....	....	....	....	....	....	....	....	....	....	....	....	....
	Boston	**NHL**	**44**	**1**	**5**	**6**	**12**	**0**	**0**	**0**	**75**	**1.3**	**5**	**0**	**0.0**	**20:24**	**22**	**6**	**1**	**7**	**10**	**0**	**0**	**1**	**23:56**
2013-14	**Boston**	**NHL**	**75**	**5**	**18**	**23**	**45**	**0**	**0**	**1**	**142**	**3.5**	**31**	**0**	**0.0**	**21:12**	**12**	**1**	**1**	**2**	**2**	**0**	**0**	**0**	**22:17**
2014-15	**NY Islanders**	**NHL**	**72**	**9**	**26**	**35**	**14**	**5**	**0**	**1**	**192**	**4.7**	**15**	**2**	**100.0**	**21:41**	**7**	**0**	**2**	**2**	**2**	**0**	**0**	**0**	**26:00**
2015-16	**NY Islanders**	**NHL**	**70**	**9**	**16**	**25**	**31**	**1**	**0**	**1**	**165**	**5.5**	**17**	**0**	**0.0**	**21:22**	**11**	**0**	**0**	**0**	**4**	**0**	**0**	**0**	**21:56**
2016-17	**NY Islanders**	**NHL**	**66**	**6**	**17**	**23**	**19**	**1**	**1**	**2**	**155**	**3.9**	**11**	**1**	**100.0**	**20:44**	....	....	....	....	....	....	....	....	....
	NHL Totals		**529**	**43**	**115**	**158**	**262**	**8**	**1**	**8**	**1153**	**3.7**		**4**	**75.0**	**20:32**	**97**	**13**	**16**	**29**	**40**	**2**	**0**	**2**	**22:59**

AHL First All-Star Team (2009) • Eddie Shore Award (AHL – Outstanding Defenseman) (2009)

Traded to **Boston** by **Colorado** for Matt Hendricks, June 24, 2008. Signed as a free agent by **Salzburg** (Austria), November 16, 2012. Traded to **NY Islanders** by **Boston** for Philadelphia's 2nd round pick (previously acquired, Boston selected Brandon Carlo) in 2015 NHL Draft and NY Islanders' 2nd round pick (Ryan Lindgren) in 2016 NHL Draft, October 4, 2014.

BOYLE, Brian (BOIL, BRIGH-uhn) N.J.

Center. Shoots left. 6'6", 245 lbs. Born, Hingham, MA, December 18, 1984. Los Angeles' 2nd pick, 26th overall, in 2003 NHL Draft.

Season	Club	League	GP	G	A	Pts	PIM	PP	SH	GW	S	S%	+/-	TF	F%	Min	GP	G	A	Pts	PIM	PP	SH	GW	Min
2000-01	St. Sebastian's	High-MA	25	20	19	39	23	....	....	....	....	....	....	....	....	....	....	....	....	....	....	....	....	....	....
2001-02	St. Sebastian's	High-MA	28	21	26	47	22	....	....	....	....	....	....	....	....	....	....	....	....	....	....	....	....	....	....
2002-03	St. Sebastian's	High-MA	31	32	31	62	46	....	....	....	....	....	....	....	....	....	....	....	....	....	....	....	....	....	....
2003-04	Boston College	H-East	35	5	3	8	36	....	....	....	....	....	....	....	....	....	....	....	....	....	....	....	....	....	....
2004-05	Boston College	H-East	40	19	8	27	64	....	....	....	....	....	....	....	....	....	....	....	....	....	....	....	....	....	....
2005-06	Boston College	H-East	42	22	*30	52	90	....	....	....	....	....	....	....	....	....	....	....	....	....	....	....	....	....	....
2006-07	Boston College	H-East	42	19	*34	*53	*104	....	....	....	....	....	....	....	....	....	....	....	....	....	....	....	....	....	....
	Manchester	AHL	2	0	0	0	2	....	....	....	....	....	....	....	....	....	16	3	5	8	13	....	....	....	....
2007-08	**Los Angeles**	**NHL**	**8**	**4**	**1**	**5**	**4**	**0**	**0**	**0**	**19**	**21.1**	**4**	**80**	**46.3**	**13:38**	....	....	....	....	....	....	....	....	....
	Manchester	AHL	70	31	31	62	87	....	....	....	....	....	....	....	....	....	....	....	....	....	....	....	....	....	....
2008-09	**Los Angeles**	**NHL**	**28**	**4**	**1**	**5**	**42**	**0**	**0**	**1**	**36**	**11.1**	**–9**	**225**	**45.3**	**10:08**	....	....	....	....	....	....	....	....	....
	Manchester	AHL	42	10	11	21	73	....	....	....	....	....	....	....	....	....	....	....	....	....	....	....	....	....	....
2009-10	**NY Rangers**	**NHL**	**71**	**4**	**2**	**6**	**47**	**0**	**0**	**1**	**73**	**5.5**	**–6**	**323**	**38.7**	**8:25**	....	....	....	....	....	....	....	....	....
2010-11	**NY Rangers**	**NHL**	**82**	**21**	**14**	**35**	**74**	**4**	**1**	**2**	**218**	**9.6**	**2**	**1101**	**48.5**	**15:44**	**5**	**0**	**0**	**0**	**6**	**0**	**0**	**0**	**21:30**
2011-12	**NY Rangers**	**NHL**	**82**	**11**	**15**	**26**	**59**	**0**	**0**	**2**	**165**	**6.7**	**2**	**1215**	**51.8**	**15:14**	**17**	**3**	**3**	**6**	**15**	**0**	**0**	**2**	**16:44**
2012-13	**NY Rangers**	**NHL**	**38**	**2**	**3**	**5**	**29**	**0**	**0**	**1**	**56**	**3.6**	**–13**	**381**	**56.4**	**14:13**	**11**	**3**	**2**	**5**	**2**	**1**	**0**	**0**	**18:50**
2013-14	**NY Rangers**	**NHL**	**82**	**6**	**12**	**18**	**56**	**1**	**0**	**1**	**137**	**4.4**	**1**	**578**	**52.9**	**12:46**	**25**	**3**	**5**	**8**	**19**	**0**	**1**	**0**	**13:18**
2014-15	**Tampa Bay**	**NHL**	**82**	**15**	**9**	**24**	**54**	**0**	**3**	**5**	**140**	**10.7**	**3**	**905**	**50.8**	**13:00**	**25**	**1**	**1**	**2**	**10**	**0**	**1**	**0**	**13:40**
2015-16	**Tampa Bay**	**NHL**	**76**	**13**	**7**	**20**	**57**	**2**	**2**	**4**	**117**	**11.1**	**–7**	**682**	**50.7**	**12:55**	**17**	**5**	**0**	**5**	**20**	**0**	**0**	**1**	**15:28**
2016-17	**Tampa Bay**	**NHL**	**54**	**13**	**9**	**22**	**48**	**3**	**0**	**2**	**109**	**11.9**	**5**	**330**	**53.0**	**13:42**	....	....	....	....	....	....	....	....	....
	Toronto	**NHL**	**21**	**0**	**3**	**3**	**18**	**0**	**0**	**0**	**22**	**0.0**	**–2**	**251**	**51.0**	**11:19**	**6**	**0**	**2**	**2**	**6**	**0**	**0**	**0**	**12:27**
	NHL Totals		**624**	**93**	**76**	**169**	**488**	**10**	**6**	**19**	**1092**	**8.5**		**6071**	**50.4**	**13:03**	**106**	**15**	**13**	**28**	**78**	**1**	**2**	**3**	**15:12**

Hockey East First All-Star Team (2006, 2007) • NCAA East Second All-American Team (2006) • NCAA East First All-American Team (2007) • NCAA Championship All-Tournament Team (2007) • AHL All-Rookie Team (2008)

Traded to **NY Rangers** by **Los Angeles** for NY Rangers' 3rd round pick (Jordan Weal) in 2010 NHL Draft, June 27, 2009. Signed as a free agent by **Tampa Bay**, July 1, 2014. Traded to **Toronto** by **Tampa Bay** for Byron Froese and Toronto's 2nd round pick (Alexander Volkov) in 2017 NHL Draft, February 27, 2017. Signed as a free agent by **New Jersey**, July 1, 2017.

BOZAK, Tyler (BOH-zak, TIGH-luhr) TOR

Center. Shoots right. 6'1", 196 lbs. Born, Regina, SK, March 19, 1986.

Season	Club	League	GP	G	A	Pts	PIM	PP	SH	GW	S	S%	+/-	TF	F%	Min	GP	G	A	Pts	PIM	PP	SH	GW	Min
2003-04	Reg. Pat Cdns.	SMHL	42	17	19	36	40	....	....	....	....	....	....	....	....	....	....	....	....	....	....	....	....	....	....
2004-05	Victoria Salsa	BCHL	55	15	16	31	24	....	....	....	....	....	....	....	....	....	5	0	2	2	2	....	....	....	....
2005-06	Victoria Salsa	BCHL	56	31	38	69	26	....	....	....	....	....	....	....	....	....	16	8	8	16	14	....	....	....	....
2006-07	Victoria Grizzlies	BCHL	59	45	83	128	45	....	....	....	....	....	....	....	....	....	11	4	9	13	6	....	....	....	....
2007-08	U. of Denver	WCHA	41	18	16	34	22	....	....	....	....	....	....	....	....	....	....	....	....	....	....	....	....	....	....
2008-09	U. of Denver	WCHA	19	8	15	23	10	....	....	....	....	....	....	....	....	....	....	....	....	....	....	....	....	....	....
2009-10	**Toronto**	**NHL**	**37**	**8**	**19**	**27**	**6**	**2**	**0**	**1**	**51**	**15.7**	**–5**	**648**	**55.3**	**19:14**	....	....	....	....	....	....	....	....	....
	Toronto Marlies	AHL	32	4	16	20	6	....	....	....	....	....	....	....	....	....	....	....	....	....	....	....	....	....	....
2010-11	**Toronto**	**NHL**	**82**	**15**	**17**	**32**	**14**	**6**	**1**	**4**	**120**	**12.5**	**–29**	**1441**	**54.6**	**19:17**	....	....	....	....	....	....	....	....	....
2011-12	**Toronto**	**NHL**	**73**	**18**	**29**	**47**	**22**	**4**	**0**	**1**	**109**	**16.5**	**–7**	**1198**	**52.7**	**18:51**	....	....	....	....	....	....	....	....	....
2012-13	**Toronto**	**NHL**	**46**	**12**	**16**	**28**	**6**	**4**	**1**	**3**	**61**	**19.7**	**–1**	**1063**	**52.6**	**20:19**	**5**	**1**	**1**	**2**	**4**	**0**	**1**	**0**	**21:44**
2013-14	**Toronto**	**NHL**	**58**	**19**	**30**	**49**	**14**	**5**	**1**	**1**	**90**	**21.1**	**2**	**1399**	**48.7**	**20:57**	....	....	....	....	....	....	....	....	....
2014-15	**Toronto**	**NHL**	**82**	**23**	**26**	**49**	**44**	**12**	**2**	**3**	**154**	**14.9**	**–34**	**1775**	**53.2**	**19:09**	....	....	....	....	....	....	....	....	....
2015-16	**Toronto**	**NHL**	**57**	**12**	**23**	**35**	**18**	**3**	**0**	**1**	**99**	**12.1**	**–9**	**1059**	**56.4**	**17:20**	....	....	....	....	....	....	....	....	....
2016-17	**Toronto**	**NHL**	**78**	**18**	**37**	**55**	**30**	**7**	**0**	**1**	**145**	**12.4**	**–1**	**1366**	**56.7**	**16:26**	**6**	**2**	**2**	**4**	**4**	**1**	**0**	**1**	**18:45**
	NHL Totals		**513**	**125**	**197**	**322**	**154**	**43**	**5**	**15**	**829**	**15.1**		**9949**	**53.6**	**18:50**	**11**	**3**	**3**	**6**	**8**	**1**	**1**	**1**	**20:06**

WCHA All-Rookie Team (2008)

Signed as a free agent by **Toronto**, April 3, 2009.

BRASSARD, Derick (bruh-SAHRD, DAIR-ihk) OTT

Center. Shoots left. 6'1", 205 lbs. Born, Hull, QC, September 22, 1987. Columbus' 1st pick, 6th overall, in 2006 NHL Draft.

Season	Club	League	GP	G	A	Pts	PIM	PP	SH	GW	S	S%	+/-	TF	F%	Min	GP	G	A	Pts	PIM	PP	SH	GW	Min
2002-03	Gatineau	QAAA	42	7	33	40	38	....	....	....	....	....	....	....	....	....	5	0	1	1	2	....	....	....	....
2003-04	Gatineau	QAAA	29	19	47	66	104	....	....	....	....	....	....	....	....	....	4	3	7	10	6	....	....	....	....
	Drummondville	QMJHL	10	0	1	1	0	....	....	....	....	....	....	....	....	....	7	0	0	0	0	....	....	....	....
2004-05	Drummondville	QMJHL	69	25	51	76	25	....	....	....	....	....	....	....	....	....	6	1	5	6	6	....	....	....	....
2005-06	Drummondville	QMJHL	58	44	72	116	92	....	....	....	....	....	....	....	....	....	7	5	4	9	10	....	....	....	....
2006-07	Drummondville	QMJHL	14	6	19	25	24	....	....	....	....	....	....	....	....	....	12	9	15	24	12	....	....	....	....
2007-08	**Columbus**	**NHL**	**17**	**1**	**1**	**2**	**6**	**0**	**0**	**0**	**13**	**7.7**	**–4**	**80**	**42.5**	**9:03**	....	....	....	....	....	....	....	....	....
	Syracuse Crunch	AHL	42	15	36	51	51	....	....	....	....	....	....	....	....	....	13	4	9	13	10	....	....	....	....
2008-09	**Columbus**	**NHL**	**31**	**10**	**15**	**25**	**17**	**3**	**0**	**1**	**59**	**16.9**	**12**	**332**	**48.5**	**14:25**	....	....	....	....	....	....	....	....	....
2009-10	**Columbus**	**NHL**	**79**	**9**	**27**	**36**	**48**	**4**	**0**	**0**	**125**	**7.2**	**–17**	**503**	**41.8**	**14:57**	....	....	....	....	....	....	....	....	....
2010-11	**Columbus**	**NHL**	**74**	**17**	**30**	**47**	**55**	**6**	**0**	**3**	**183**	**9.3**	**–11**	**888**	**46.6**	**17:02**	....	....	....	....	....	....	....	....	....
2011-12	**Columbus**	**NHL**	**74**	**14**	**27**	**41**	**42**	**5**	**0**	**3**	**125**	**11.2**	**–20**	**617**	**45.1**	**16:20**	....	....	....	....	....	....	....	....	....
2012-13	Salzburg	Austria	6	4	1	5	6	....	....	....	....	....	....	....	....	....	....	....	....	....	....	....	....	....	....
	Columbus	**NHL**	**34**	**7**	**11**	**18**	**16**	**1**	**0**	**1**	**63**	**11.1**	**–2**	**283**	**45.6**	**16:32**	....	....	....	....	....	....	....	....	....
	NY Rangers	**NHL**	**13**	**5**	**6**	**11**	**0**	**2**	**0**	**0**	**25**	**20.0**	**3**	**163**	**52.8**	**16:38**	**12**	**2**	**10**	**12**	**2**	**1**	**0**	**1**	**18:55**
2013-14	**NY Rangers**	**NHL**	**81**	**18**	**27**	**45**	**46**	**7**	**0**	**4**	**159**	**11.3**	**2**	**977**	**48.0**	**15:48**	**23**	**6**	**6**	**12**	**8**	**0**	**0**	**2**	**15:47**
2014-15	**NY Rangers**	**NHL**	**80**	**19**	**41**	**60**	**34**	**6**	**0**	**3**	**168**	**11.3**	**9**	**1376**	**48.8**	**17:24**	**19**	**9**	**7**	**16**	**20**	**2**	**0**	**1**	**17:49**
2015-16	**NY Rangers**	**NHL**	**80**	**27**	**31**	**58**	**30**	**8**	**0**	**5**	**182**	**14.8**	**12**	**1346**	**50.2**	**17:53**	**5**	**1**	**3**	**4**	**0**	**0**	**0**	**0**	**16:47**
2016-17	**Ottawa**	**NHL**	**81**	**14**	**25**	**39**	**24**	**3**	**0**	**3**	**195**	**7.2**	**12**	**1225**	**50.0**	**17:23**	**19**	**4**	**7**	**11**	**8**	**0**	**0**	**0**	**18:11**
	NHL Totals		**644**	**141**	**241**	**382**	**318**	**45**	**0**	**23**	**1297**	**10.9**		**7790**	**48.0**	**16:22**	**78**	**22**	**33**	**55**	**38**	**3**	**0**	**4**	**17:25**

QMJHL First All-Star Team (2006) • Canadian Major Junior Second All-Star Team (2006)

• Missed majority of 2006-07 due to pre-season shoulder injury. • Missed majority of 2008-09 due to shoulder injury at Dallas, December 18, 2008. Signed as a free agent by **Salzburg** (Austria), November 26, 2012. Traded to **NY Rangers** by **Columbus** with Derek Dorsett, John Moore and Columbus' 6th round pick (later traded to Minnesota – Minnesota selected Chase Lang) in 2014 NHL Draft for Marian Gaborik, Blake Parlett and Steven Delisle, April 3, 2013. Traded to **Ottawa** by **NY Rangers** with NY Rangers' 7th round pick in 2018 NHL Draft for Mika Zibanejad and Ottawa's 2nd round pick in 2018 NHL Draft, July 18, 2016.

BRAUN, Justin (BRAWN, JUHS-tihn) S.J.

Defense. Shoots right. 6'2", 205 lbs. Born, St. Paul, MN, February 10, 1987. San Jose's 7th pick, 201st overall, in 2007 NHL Draft.

Season	Club	League	GP	G	A	Pts	PIM	PP	SH	GW	S	S%	+/-	TF	F%	Min	GP	G	A	Pts	PIM	PP	SH	GW	Min
2004-05	White Bear Lake	High-MN	STATISTICS NOT AVAILABLE																						
	Green Bay	USHL	10	0	0	0	2	....	....	....	....	....	....	....	....	....	....	....	....	....	....	....	....	....	....
2005-06	Green Bay	USHL	59	2	11	13	69	....	....	....	....	....	....	....	....	....	3	0	0	0	2	....	....	....	....
2006-07	Massachusetts	H-East	39	4	10	14	20	....	....	....	....	....	....	....	....	....	....	....	....	....	....	....	....	....	....
2007-08	Massachusetts	H-East	36	4	16	20	20	....	....	....	....	....	....	....	....	....	....	....	....	....	....	....	....	....	....
2008-09	Massachusetts	H-East	39	7	16	23	50	....	....	....	....	....	....	....	....	....	....	....	....	....	....	....	....	....	....
2009-10	Massachusetts	H-East	36	8	23	31	30	....	....	....	....	....	....	....	....	....	....	....	....	....	....	....	....	....	....
	Worcester Sharks	AHL	3	0	3	3	0	....	....	....	....	....	....	....	....	....	11	0	3	3	4	....	....	....	....

Season	Club	League	GP	G	A	Pts	PIM	PP	SH	GW	S	S%	+/-	TF	F%	Min	GP	G	A	Pts	PIM	PP	SH	GW	Min
					Regular Season												Playoffs								
2010-11	San Jose	NHL	28	2	9	11	2	2	0	0	44	4.5	–1	0	0.0	16:30	1	0	0	0	0	0	0	0	15:32
	Worcester Sharks	AHL	34	5	18	23	8	....	....	....	....	....	....	....	....	....	....	....	....	....	....	....	....	....	....
2011-12	San Jose	NHL	66	2	9	11	23	1	0	0	113	1.8	–2	0	0.0	16:33	5	0	0	0	15	0	0	0	17:55
	Worcester Sharks	AHL	6	0	3	3	0	....	....	....	....	....	....	....	....	....	....	....	....	....	....	....	....	....	....
2012-13	Tappara Tampere	Finland	6	0	3	3	2	....	....	....	....	....	....	....	....	....	....	....	....	....	....	....	....	....	....
	San Jose	NHL	41	0	7	7	6	0	0	0	48	0.0	–5	0	0.0	18:48	11	0	1	1	0	0	0	0	19:38
2013-14	San Jose	NHL	82	4	13	17	20	1	0	1	121	3.3	19	0	0.0	20:59	7	1	1	2	7	0	0	1	20:24
2014-15	San Jose	NHL	70	1	22	23	48	0	0	0	94	1.1	8	0	0.0	21:02	....	....	....	....	....	....	....	....	....
2015-16	San Jose	NHL	80	4	19	23	36	0	0	0	114	3.5	11	0	0.0	20:34	24	2	5	7	6	0	0	0	21:23
2016-17	San Jose	NHL	81	4	9	13	28	0	0	0	95	4.2	1	0	0.0	20:05	6	0	1	1	0	0	0	0	22:07
	NHL Totals		448	17	88	105	163	4	0	1	629	2.7		0	0.0	19:37	54	3	8	11	28	0	0	1	20:33

Hockey East All-Rookie Team (2007) • Hockey East Second All-Star Team (2009) • Hockey East First All-Star Team (2010) • NCAA East Second All-American Team (2010)

Signed as a free agent by **Tappara Tampere** (Finland), November 23, 2012.

BREEN, Chris
(BREEN, KRIHS)

Defense. Shoots left. 6'7", 226 lbs. Born, Uxbridge, ON, June 29, 1989.

Season	Club	League	GP	G	A	Pts	PIM	PP	SH	GW	S	S%	+/-	TF	F%	Min	GP	G	A	Pts	PIM	PP	SH	GW	Min
2005-06	Mississauga	ON-Jr.A	33	1	6	7	10	....	....	....	....	....	....	....	....	....	....	....	....	....	....	....	....	....	....
	Saginaw Spirit	OHL	25	0	0	0	10	....	....	....	....	....	....	....	....	....	....	....	....	....	....	....	....	....	....
2006-07	Saginaw Spirit	OHL	39	1	2	3	32	....	....	....	....	....	....	....	....	....	2	0	0	0	2	....	....	....	....
2007-08	Saginaw Spirit	OHL	55	0	6	6	67	....	....	....	....	....	....	....	....	....	4	0	1	1	0	....	....	....	....
2008-09	Saginaw Spirit	OHL	6	0	1	1	9	....	....	....	....	....	....	....	....	....	....	....	....	....	....	....	....	....	....
	Erie Otters	OHL	59	0	12	12	31	....	....	....	....	....	....	....	....	....	5	0	1	1	7	....	....	....	....
2009-10	Erie Otters	OHL	12	0	2	2	11	....	....	....	....	....	....	....	....	....	....	....	....	....	....	....	....	....	....
	Peterborough	OHL	53	4	8	12	36	....	....	....	....	....	....	....	....	....	4	1	0	1	5	....	....	....	....
	Abbotsford Heat	AHL	1	0	1	1	4	....	....	....	....	....	....	....	....	....	....	....	....	....	....	....	....	....	....
2010-11	Abbotsford Heat	AHL	73	4	7	11	47	....	....	....	....	....	....	....	....	....	....	....	....	....	....	....	....	....	....
2011-12	Abbotsford Heat	AHL	70	1	6	7	37	....	....	....	....	....	....	....	....	....	8	1	0	1	0	....	....	....	....
2012-13	Abbotsford Heat	AHL	60	3	4	7	55	....	....	....	....	....	....	....	....	....	....	....	....	....	....	....	....	....	....
2013-14	Calgary	NHL	9	0	2	2	5	0	0	0	4	0.0	1	0	0.0	9:23	....	....	....	....	....	....	....	....	....
	Abbotsford Heat	AHL	41	1	3	4	29	....	....	....	....	....	....	....	....	....	4	0	2	2	2	....	....	....	....
2014-15	Providence Bruins	AHL	52	2	8	10	33	....	....	....	....	....	....	....	....	....	5	0	1	1	0	....	....	....	....
2015-16	Providence Bruins	AHL	66	1	11	12	38	....	....	....	....	....	....	....	....	....	3	1	0	1	0	....	....	....	....
2016-17	Providence Bruins	AHL	37	1	2	3	38	....	....	....	....	....	....	....	....	....	17	0	3	3	6	....	....	....	....
	NHL Totals		9	0	2	2	5	0	0	0	4	0.0		0	0.0	9:23	....	....	....	....	....	....	....	....	....

Signed to an ATO (amateur tryout) contract by **Abbotsford** (AHL), March 30, 2010. Signed as a free agent by **Calgary**, May 28, 2010. Signed as a free agent by **Boston**, July 2, 2014.

BRENNAN, T.J.
(BREH-nan, TEE-JAY) **PHI**

Defense. Shoots left. 6'1", 216 lbs. Born, Willingboro, NJ, April 3, 1989. Buffalo's 1st pick, 31st overall, in 2007 NHL Draft.

Season	Club	League	GP	G	A	Pts	PIM	PP	SH	GW	S	S%	+/-	TF	F%	Min	GP	G	A	Pts	PIM	PP	SH	GW	Min
2005-06	Phi. Little Flyers	AtJHL	42	9	23	32	....	....	....	....	....	....	....	....	....	....	....	....	....	....	....	....	....	....	....
2006-07	St. John's	QMJHL	68	16	25	41	79	....	....	....	....	....	....	....	....	....	4	1	1	2	4	....	....	....	....
2007-08	St. John's	QMJHL	65	16	25	41	92	....	....	....	....	....	....	....	....	....	6	2	4	6	12	....	....	....	....
2008-09	Montreal	QMJHL	59	5	29	34	63	....	....	....	....	....	....	....	....	....	10	4	8	12	34	....	....	....	....
2009-10	Portland Pirates	AHL	65	6	17	23	64	....	....	....	....	....	....	....	....	....	4	0	1	1	2	....	....	....	....
2010-11	Portland Pirates	AHL	72	15	24	39	49	....	....	....	....	....	....	....	....	....	4	0	1	1	6	....	....	....	....
2011-12	Buffalo	NHL	11	1	0	1	6	0	0	0	14	7.1	0	0	0.0	14:07	....	....	....	....	....	....	....	....	....
	Rochester	AHL	52	16	14	30	39	....	....	....	....	....	....	....	....	....	3	2	0	2	6	....	....	....	....
2012-13	Rochester	AHL	36	14	21	35	57	....	....	....	....	....	....	....	....	....	....	....	....	....	....	....	....	....	....
	Buffalo	NHL	10	1	0	1	6	1	0	0	18	5.6	–1	0	0.0	14:49	....	....	....	....	....	....	....	....	....
	Florida	NHL	19	2	7	9	2	0	0	0	24	8.3	–8	0	0.0	17:41	....	....	....	....	....	....	....	....	....
2013-14	Toronto Marlies	AHL	76	25	47	72	115	....	....	....	....	....	....	....	....	....	14	6	8	14	10	....	....	....	....
2014-15	Rockford IceHogs	AHL	54	9	27	36	59	....	....	....	....	....	....	....	....	....	....	....	....	....	....	....	....	....	....
	Toronto	NHL	6	0	1	1	9	0	0	0	11	0.0	–7	0	0.0	16:49	....	....	....	....	....	....	....	....	....
	Toronto Marlies	AHL	19	3	13	16	12	....	....	....	....	....	....	....	....	....	5	3	4	7	12	....	....	....	....
2015-16	Toronto	NHL	7	1	0	1	6	0	0	0	11	9.1	–6	0	0.0	15:06	....	....	....	....	....	....	....	....	....
	Toronto Marlies	AHL	69	25	43	68	53	....	....	....	....	....	....	....	....	....	15	5	4	9	14	....	....	....	....
2016-17	Lehigh Valley	AHL	76	21	39	60	101	....	....	....	....	....	....	....	....	....	5	1	3	4	4	....	....	....	....
	NHL Totals		53	5	8	13	29	1	0	0	78	6.4		0	0.0	15:58	....	....	....	....	....	....	....	....	....

AHL First All-Star Team (2014, 2016, 2017) • Eddie Shore Award (AHL – Outstanding Defenseman) (2014, 2016)

Traded to **Florida** by **Buffalo** for New Jersey's 5th round pick (previously acquired, later traded to Buffalo – Buffalo selected Gustav Possler) in 2013 NHL Draft, March 15, 2013. Traded to **Nashville** by **Florida** for Bobby Butler, June 14, 2013. Signed as a free agent by **Toronto**, July 5, 2013. Signed as a free agent by **NY Islanders**, July 1, 2014. Traded to **Chicago** by **NY Islanders** with Ville Pokka and Anders Nilsson for Nick Leddy and Kent Simpson, October 4, 2014. Traded to **Toronto** by **Chicago** for Spencer Abbott, February 26, 2015. Signed as a free agent by **Philadelphia**, July 5, 2016.

BRICKLEY, Connor
(BRIH-klee, KAW-nuhr) **FLA**

Center. Shoots left. 6', 203 lbs. Born, Malden, MA, February 25, 1992. Florida's 6th pick, 50th overall, in 2010 NHL Draft.

Season	Club	League	GP	G	A	Pts	PIM	PP	SH	GW	S	S%	+/-	TF	F%	Min	GP	G	A	Pts	PIM	PP	SH	GW	Min
2008-09	Belmont Hill	High-MA	30	17	18	35	60	....	....	....	....	....	....	....	....	....	....	....	....	....	....	....	....	....	....
2009-10	Des Moines	USHL	52	22	21	43	68	....	....	....	....	....	....	....	....	....	....	....	....	....	....	....	....	....	....
	USAHNTDP	U-18	14	2	5	7	6	....	....	....	....	....	....	....	....	....	....	....	....	....	....	....	....	....	....
2010-11	U. of Vermont	H-East	35	4	9	13	33	....	....	....	....	....	....	....	....	....	....	....	....	....	....	....	....	....	....
2011-12	U. of Vermont	H-East	23	9	3	12	16	....	....	....	....	....	....	....	....	....	....	....	....	....	....	....	....	....	....
2012-13	U. of Vermont	H-East	24	3	5	8	31	....	....	....	....	....	....	....	....	....	....	....	....	....	....	....	....	....	....
2013-14	U. of Vermont	H-East	35	5	10	15	49	....	....	....	....	....	....	....	....	....	....	....	....	....	....	....	....	....	....
	San Antonio	AHL	8	1	1	2	4	....	....	....	....	....	....	....	....	....	....	....	....	....	....	....	....	....	....
2014-15	San Antonio	AHL	73	22	25	47	66	....	....	....	....	....	....	....	....	....	3	1	1	2	0	....	....	....	....
2015-16	Florida	NHL	23	1	4	5	14	0	0	1	13	7.7	1	0	0.0	8:44	....	....	....	....	....	....	....	....	....
	Portland Pirates	AHL	45	12	15	27	26	....	....	....	....	....	....	....	....	....	5	0	1	1	2	....	....	....	....
2016-17	Charlotte	AHL	69	15	11	26	57	....	....	....	....	....	....	....	....	....	5	2	2	4	0	....	....	....	....
	NHL Totals		23	1	4	5	14	0	0	1	13	7.7		0	0.0	8:44	....	....	....	....	....	....	....	....	....

Traded to **Carolina** by **Florida** for Brody Sutter, October 11, 2016. Claimed by **Vegas** from **Carolina** in Expansion Draft, June 21, 2017. Signed as a free agent by **Florida**, July 1, 2017.

BRODIE, T.J.
(BROH-dee, TEE-JAY) **CGY**

Defense. Shoots left. 6'1", 182 lbs. Born, Chatham, ON, June 7, 1990. Calgary's 5th pick, 114th overall, in 2008 NHL Draft.

Season	Club	League	GP	G	A	Pts	PIM	PP	SH	GW	S	S%	+/-	TF	F%	Min	GP	G	A	Pts	PIM	PP	SH	GW	Min
2006-07	Leamington Flyers	ON-Jr.B	43	8	38	46	104	....	....	....	....	....	....	....	....	....	5	1	2	3	12	....	....	....	....
	Saginaw Spirit	OHL	20	0	4	4	23	....	....	....	....	....	....	....	....	....	3	0	1	1	2	....	....	....	....
2007-08	Saginaw Spirit	OHL	68	4	26	30	73	....	....	....	....	....	....	....	....	....	4	0	3	3	2	....	....	....	....
2008-09	Saginaw Spirit	OHL	63	12	38	50	67	....	....	....	....	....	....	....	....	....	8	3	6	9	8	....	....	....	....
2009-10	Saginaw Spirit	OHL	19	4	19	23	20	....	....	....	....	....	....	....	....	....	....	....	....	....	....	....	....	....	....
	Barrie Colts	OHL	46	3	30	33	38	....	....	....	....	....	....	....	....	....	17	1	14	15	14	....	....	....	....
2010-11	Calgary	NHL	3	0	0	0	2	0	0	0	1	0.0	–3	0	0.0	16:00	....	....	....	....	....	....	....	....	....
	Abbotsford Heat	AHL	68	5	29	34	32	....	....	....	....	....	....	....	....	....	....	....	....	....	....	....	....	....	....
2011-12	Calgary	NHL	54	2	12	14	14	1	0	2	44	4.5	3	0	0.0	16:29	....	....	....	....	....	....	....	....	....
	Abbotsford Heat	AHL	12	1	2	3	10	....	....	....	....	....	....	....	....	....	....	....	....	....	....	....	....	....	....
2012-13	Abbotsford Heat	AHL	35	1	19	20	22	....	....	....	....	....	....	....	....	....	....	....	....	....	....	....	....	....	....
	Calgary	NHL	47	2	12	14	8	0	0	0	44	4.5	–9	0	0.0	20:13	....	....	....	....	....	....	....	....	....
2013-14	Calgary	NHL	81	4	27	31	20	1	0	2	104	3.8	0	0	0.0	24:04	....	....	....	....	....	....	....	....	....
2014-15	Calgary	NHL	81	11	30	41	30	3	1	3	133	8.3	15	0	0.0	25:12	11	1	4	5	0	0	0	0	27:07
2015-16	Calgary	NHL	70	6	39	45	18	2	0	1	79	7.6	4	0	0.0	25:16	....	....	....	....	....	....	....	....	....
2016-17	Calgary	NHL	82	6	30	36	24	1	1	2	78	7.7	–16	0	0.0	23:35	4	0	4	4	2	0	0	0	22:20
	NHL Totals		418	31	150	181	116	8	2	10	483	6.4		0	0.0	22:55	15	1	8	9	2	0	0	0	25:50

BRODIN, Jonas

(BROH-deen, JOH-nuhs) **MIN**

Defense. Shoots left. 6'1", 193 lbs. Born, Karlstad, Sweden, July 12, 1993. Minnesota's 1st pick, 10th overall, in 2011 NHL Draft.

			Regular Season														Playoffs								
Season	Club	League	GP	G	A	Pts	PIM	PP	SH	GW	S	S%	+/-	TF	F%	Min	GP	G	A	Pts	PIM	PP	SH	GW	Min
2008-09	Farjestad U18	Swe-U18	22	3	8	11	10	....	....	....	....	....	....	....	....	....	4	1	1	2	4	....	....	....	....
2009-10	Skare BK Jr.	Swe-Jr.	2	0	1	1	2	....	....	....	....	....	....	....	....	....	....	....	....	....	....	....	....	....	....
	Skare BK	Sweden-3	21	1	6	7	10	....	....	....	....	....	....	....	....	....	....	....	....	....	....	....	....	....	....
	Farjestad	Sweden	3	0	0	0	2	....	....	....	....	....	....	....	....	....	....	....	....	....	....	....	....	....	....
	Farjestad U18	Swe-U18	19	6	11	17	6	....	....	....	....	....	....	....	....	....	7	3	8	11	8	....	....	....	....
2010-11	Farjestad U18	Swe-U18	2	0	1	1	2	....	....	....	....	....	....	....	....	....	....	....	....	....	....	....	....	....	....
	Farjestad	Sweden	42	0	4	4	12	....	....	....	....	....	....	....	....	....	14	2	0	2	2	....	....	....	....
2011-12	Farjestad Jr.	Swe-Jr.	1	0	0	0	0	....	....	....	....	....	....	....	....	....	....	....	....	....	....	....	....	....	....
	Farjestad	Sweden	49	0	8	8	14	....	....	....	....	....	....	....	....	....	11	2	0	2	6	....	....	....	....
2012-13	Houston Aeros	AHL	9	2	2	4	4	....	....	....	....	....	....	....	....	....	....	....	....	....	....	....	....	....	....
	Minnesota	**NHL**	**45**	**2**	**9**	**11**	**10**	**1**	**0**	**0**	**51**	**3.9**	**3**	**0**	**0.0**	**23:13**	**5**	**0**	**0**	**0**	**0**	**0**	**0**	**0**	**26:23**
2013-14	**Minnesota**	**NHL**	**79**	**8**	**11**	**19**	**22**	**3**	**0**	**0**	**74**	**10.8**	**0**	**0**	**0.0**	**23:54**	**13**	**0**	**2**	**2**	**12**	**0**	**0**	**0**	**23:38**
2014-15	**Minnesota**	**NHL**	**71**	**3**	**14**	**17**	**8**	**0**	**0**	**1**	**95**	**3.2**	**21**	**0**	**0.0**	**24:10**	**10**	**0**	**0**	**0**	**0**	**0**	**0**	**0**	**21:53**
2015-16	**Minnesota**	**NHL**	**68**	**2**	**5**	**7**	**18**	**0**	**0**	**0**	**58**	**3.4**	**–5**	**0**	**0.0**	**20:25**	**6**	**1**	**2**	**3**	**0**	**0**	**0**	**0**	**20:36**
2016-17	**Minnesota**	**NHL**	**68**	**3**	**22**	**25**	**20**	**2**	**0**	**2**	**85**	**3.5**	**5**	**0**	**0.0**	**19:34**	**5**	**0**	**1**	**1**	**0**	**0**	**0**	**0**	**19:01**
	NHL Totals		**331**	**18**	**61**	**79**	**78**	**6**	**0**	**3**	**363**	**5.0**		**0**	**0.0**	**22:16**	**39**	**1**	**5**	**6**	**12**	**0**	**0**	**0**	**22:28**

NHL All-Rookie Team (2013)

BRODZIAK, Kyle

(brohd-ZEE-ak, KIGHL) **ST.L.**

Center. Shoots right. 6'2", 212 lbs. Born, St. Paul, AB, May 25, 1984. Edmonton's 9th pick, 214th overall, in 2003 NHL Draft.

Season	Club	League	GP	G	A	Pts	PIM	PP	SH	GW	S	S%	+/-	TF	F%	Min	GP	G	A	Pts	PIM	PP	SH	GW	Min
99-2000	Ft. Saskatchewan	AMBHL	36	23	33	56	57	....	....	....	....	....	....	....	....	....	....	....	....	....	....	....	....	....	....
	Moose Jaw	WHL	2	0	0	0	0	....	....	....	....	....	....	....	....	....	....	....	....	....	....	....	....	....	....
2000-01	Moose Jaw	WHL	57	2	8	10	47	....	....	....	....	....	....	....	....	....	3	0	0	0	0	....	....	....	....
2001-02	Moose Jaw	WHL	72	8	12	20	56	....	....	....	....	....	....	....	....	....	12	0	3	3	11	....	....	....	....
2002-03	Moose Jaw	WHL	72	32	30	62	84	....	....	....	....	....	....	....	....	....	13	5	3	8	16	....	....	....	....
2003-04	Moose Jaw	WHL	70	39	54	93	58	....	....	....	....	....	....	....	....	....	10	5	4	9	10	....	....	....	....
2004-05	Edmonton	AHL	56	6	26	32	49	....	....	....	....	....	....	....	....	....	....	....	....	....	....	....	....	....	....
2005-06	**Edmonton**	**NHL**	**10**	**0**	**0**	**0**	**4**	**0**	**0**	**0**	**7**	**0.0**	**–4**	**75**	**52.0**	**11:02**	....	....	....	....	....	....	....	....	....
	Iowa Stars	AHL	55	12	19	31	41	....	....	....	....	....	....	....	....	....	7	1	3	4	2	....	....	....	....
2006-07	**Edmonton**	**NHL**	**6**	**1**	**0**	**1**	**2**	**0**	**0**	**0**	**11**	**9.1**	**0**	**48**	**52.1**	**17:08**	....	....	....	....	....	....	....	....	....
	Wilkes-Barre	AHL	62	24	32	56	44	....	....	....	....	....	....	....	....	....	11	1	5	6	14	....	....	....	....
2007-08	**Edmonton**	**NHL**	**80**	**14**	**17**	**31**	**33**	**0**	**1**	**3**	**125**	**11.2**	**–6**	**297**	**51.5**	**12:55**	....	....	....	....	....	....	....	....	....
2008-09	**Edmonton**	**NHL**	**79**	**11**	**16**	**27**	**21**	**1**	**1**	**3**	**99**	**11.1**	**4**	**947**	**51.6**	**12:43**	....	....	....	....	....	....	....	....	....
2009-10	**Minnesota**	**NHL**	**82**	**9**	**23**	**32**	**22**	**0**	**0**	**3**	**140**	**6.4**	**–3**	**1001**	**48.4**	**15:20**	....	....	....	....	....	....	....	....	....
2010-11	**Minnesota**	**NHL**	**80**	**16**	**21**	**37**	**56**	**2**	**1**	**1**	**126**	**12.7**	**–4**	**1088**	**48.9**	**15:47**	....	....	....	....	....	....	....	....	....
2011-12	**Minnesota**	**NHL**	**82**	**22**	**22**	**44**	**66**	**5**	**0**	**0**	**160**	**13.8**	**–15**	**1429**	**49.5**	**19:04**	....	....	....	....	....	....	....	....	....
2012-13	**Minnesota**	**NHL**	**48**	**8**	**4**	**12**	**20**	**1**	**1**	**1**	**88**	**9.1**	**–18**	**763**	**49.4**	**17:21**	**5**	**0**	**2**	**2**	**4**	**0**	**0**	**0**	**20:41**
2013-14	**Minnesota**	**NHL**	**81**	**8**	**16**	**24**	**61**	**0**	**1**	**1**	**115**	**7.0**	**0**	**1223**	**48.2**	**16:13**	**12**	**3**	**3**	**6**	**2**	**0**	**0**	**0**	**13:15**
2014-15	**Minnesota**	**NHL**	**73**	**9**	**11**	**20**	**47**	**0**	**1**	**0**	**86**	**10.5**	**–6**	**687**	**49.2**	**13:03**	**10**	**0**	**0**	**0**	**2**	**0**	**0**	**0**	**12:30**
2015-16	**St. Louis**	**NHL**	**76**	**7**	**4**	**11**	**37**	**0**	**3**	**4**	**49**	**14.3**	**–1**	**556**	**49.5**	**10:48**	**20**	**2**	**0**	**2**	**6**	**0**	**1**	**1**	**8:38**
2016-17	**St. Louis**	**NHL**	**69**	**8**	**7**	**15**	**27**	**0**	**0**	**2**	**55**	**14.5**	**2**	**653**	**49.5**	**11:12**	**10**	**0**	**2**	**2**	**2**	**0**	**0**	**0**	**12:18**
	NHL Totals		**766**	**113**	**141**	**254**	**396**	**9**	**9**	**18**	**1061**	**10.7**		**8767**	**49.4**	**14:24**	**57**	**5**	**7**	**12**	**16**	**0**	**1**	**1**	**11:59**

WHL East First All-Star Team (2004) • Canadian Major Junior Second All-Star Team (2004)

Traded to **Minnesota** by **Edmonton** with Edmonton's 6th round pick (Darcy Kuemper) in 2009 NHL Draft for Dallas's 4th round pick (previously acquired, Edmonton selected Kyle Bigos) in 2009 NHL Draft and Minnesota's 5th round pick (Olivier Roy) in 2009 NHL Draft, June 27, 2009. Signed as a free agent by **St. Louis**, July 2, 2015.

BRODZINSKI, Jonny

(brawd-ZIHN-skee, JAW-nee) **L.A.**

Center. Shoots right. 6', 202 lbs. Born, Ham Lake, MN, June 19, 1993. Los Angeles' 5th pick, 148th overall, in 2013 NHL Draft.

Season	Club	League	GP	G	A	Pts	PIM	PP	SH	GW	S	S%	+/-	TF	F%	Min	GP	G	A	Pts	PIM	PP	SH	GW	Min
2009-10	Blaine Bengals	High-MN	25	22	20	42	18	....	....	....	....	....	....	....	....	....	5	0	6	6	0	....	....	....	....
2010-11	Team Northwest	UMHSEL	21	11	14	25	10	....	....	....	....	....	....	....	....	....	3	2	3	5	2	....	....	....	....
	Blaine Bengals	High-MN	25	27	25	52	16	....	....	....	....	....	....	....	....	....	5	4	4	8	2	....	....	....	....
	Fargo Force	USHL	10	2	3	5	2	....	....	....	....	....	....	....	....	....	2	0	0	0	0	....	....	....	....
2011-12	Fargo Force	USHL	58	10	12	22	18	....	....	....	....	....	....	....	....	....	6	1	1	2	0	....	....	....	....
2012-13	St. Cloud State	WCHA	42	22	11	33	10	....	....	....	....	....	....	....	....	....	....	....	....	....	....	....	....	....	....
2013-14	St. Cloud State	NCHC	38	21	20	41	16	....	....	....	....	....	....	....	....	....	....	....	....	....	....	....	....	....	....
2014-15	St. Cloud State	NCHC	40	21	17	38	49	....	....	....	....	....	....	....	....	....	....	....	....	....	....	....	....	....	....
2015-16	Ontario Reign	AHL	65	15	13	28	16	....	....	....	....	....	....	....	....	....	4	2	1	3	2	....	....	....	....
2016-17	**Los Angeles**	**NHL**	**6**	**0**	**2**	**2**	**2**	**0**	**0**	**0**	**17**	**0.0**	**2**	**0**	**0.0**	**12:17**	....	....	....	....	....	....	....	....	....
	Ontario Reign	AHL	59	27	22	49	12	....	....	....	....	....	....	....	....	....	5	2	2	4	2	....	....	....	....
	NHL Totals		**6**	**0**	**2**	**2**	**2**	**0**	**0**	**0**	**17**	**0.0**		**0**	**0.0**	**12:17**	....	....	....	....	....	....	....	....	....

NCHC First All-Star Team (2015)

BROLL, David

(BROHL, DAY-vihd)

Left wing. Shoots left. 6'2", 235 lbs. Born, Mississauga, ON, January 4, 1993. Toronto's 6th pick, 152nd overall, in 2011 NHL Draft.

Season	Club	League	GP	G	A	Pts	PIM	PP	SH	GW	S	S%	+/-	TF	F%	Min	GP	G	A	Pts	PIM	PP	SH	GW	Min
2008-09	Tor. Young Nats	GTHL	73	31	26	57	....	....	....	....	....	....	....	....	....	....	....	....	....	....	....	....	....	....	....
2009-10	Erie Otters	OHL	64	9	9	18	42	....	....	....	....	....	....	....	....	....	4	0	0	0	2	....	....	....	....
2010-11	Erie Otters	OHL	41	8	14	22	51	....	....	....	....	....	....	....	....	....	....	....	....	....	....	....	....	....	....
	Sault Ste. Marie	OHL	24	5	7	12	34	....	....	....	....	....	....	....	....	....	....	....	....	....	....	....	....	....	....
2011-12	Sault Ste. Marie	OHL	59	8	25	33	81	....	....	....	....	....	....	....	....	....	....	....	....	....	....	....	....	....	....
	Toronto Marlies	AHL	3	0	0	0	5	....	....	....	....	....	....	....	....	....	2	0	0	0	0	....	....	....	....
2012-13	Sault Ste. Marie	OHL	67	17	37	54	77	....	....	....	....	....	....	....	....	....	6	0	2	2	21	....	....	....	....
	Toronto Marlies	AHL	7	0	0	0	15	....	....	....	....	....	....	....	....	....	3	0	0	0	2	....	....	....	....
2013-14	**Toronto**	**NHL**	**5**	**0**	**1**	**1**	**5**	**0**	**0**	**0**	**3**	**0.0**	**1**	**0**	**0.0**	**8:11**	....	....	....	....	....	....	....	....	....
	Toronto Marlies	AHL	63	3	13	16	120	....	....	....	....	....	....	....	....	....	4	0	0	0	6	....	....	....	....
2014-15	Toronto Marlies	AHL	21	0	0	0	79	....	....	....	....	....	....	....	....	....	....	....	....	....	....	....	....	....	....
	Orlando	ECHL	16	2	7	9	9	....	....	....	....	....	....	....	....	....	....	....	....	....	....	....	....	....	....
	Syracuse Crunch	AHL	20	0	3	3	40	....	....	....	....	....	....	....	....	....	2	0	0	0	2	....	....	....	....
2015-16	Syracuse Crunch	AHL	60	2	6	8	112	....	....	....	....	....	....	....	....	....	....	....	....	....	....	....	....	....	....
2016-17	St. John's IceCaps	AHL	54	5	3	8	115	....	....	....	....	....	....	....	....	....	....	....	....	....	....	....	....	....	....
	NHL Totals		**5**	**0**	**1**	**1**	**5**	**0**	**0**	**0**	**3**	**0.0**		**0**	**0.0**	**8:11**	....	....	....	....	....	....	....	....	....

Traded to **Tampa Bay** by **Toronto** with Carter Ashton for future considerations (conditions not met), February 6, 2015. Signed as a free agent by **St. John's** (AHL), October 11, 2016.

BROUILLETTE, Julien

(BREE-eht, JOO-lee-ehn)

Defense. Shoots left. 5'11", 185 lbs. Born, St. Esprit, QC, December 5, 1986.

Season	Club	League	GP	G	A	Pts	PIM	PP	SH	GW	S	S%	+/-	TF	F%	Min	GP	G	A	Pts	PIM	PP	SH	GW	Min
2002-03	Cap-d-Madeleine	QAAA	41	8	20	28	26	....	....	....	....	....	....	....	....	....	....	....	....	....	....	....	....	....	....
2003-04	Trois-Rivieres	QAAA	13	5	15	20	16	....	....	....	....	....	....	....	....	....	....	....	....	....	....	....	....	....	....
	Chicoutimi	QMJHL	24	0	0	0	7	....	....	....	....	....	....	....	....	....	18	0	4	4	0	....	....	....	....
2004-05	Chicoutimi	QMJHL	65	7	11	18	61	....	....	....	....	....	....	....	....	....	17	4	4	8	23	....	....	....	....
2005-06	Chicoutimi	QMJHL	70	10	42	52	86	....	....	....	....	....	....	....	....	....	9	1	3	4	8	....	....	....	....
2006-07	Chicoutimi	QMJHL	68	10	43	53	52	....	....	....	....	....	....	....	....	....	4	1	2	3	8	....	....	....	....
2007-08	Columbia Inferno	ECHL	67	6	11	17	55	....	....	....	....	....	....	....	....	....	13	0	4	4	6	....	....	....	....
2008-09	Charlotte	ECHL	70	11	18	29	67	....	....	....	....	....	....	....	....	....	6	0	1	1	2	....	....	....	....
2009-10	Charlotte	ECHL	47	13	20	33	23	....	....	....	....	....	....	....	....	....	7	0	5	5	2	....	....	....	....
	Providence Bruins	AHL	3	0	1	1	0	....	....	....	....	....	....	....	....	....	....	....	....	....	....	....	....	....	....
	Hartford	AHL	21	1	3	4	4	....	....	....	....	....	....	....	....	....	....	....	....	....	....	....	....	....	....
2010-11	Greenville	ECHL	25	11	12	23	8	....	....	....	....	....	....	....	....	....	1	0	0	0	0	....	....	....	....
	Charlotte	AHL	1	0	0	0	0	....	....	....	....	....	....	....	....	....	....	....	....	....	....	....	....	....	....
	Lake Erie	AHL	49	2	15	17	20	....	....	....	....	....	....	....	....	....	7	1	1	2	2	....	....	....	....
2011-12	Hershey Bears	AHL	74	7	14	21	24	....	....	....	....	....	....	....	....	....	3	0	1	1	4	....	....	....	....
2012-13	Hershey Bears	AHL	61	2	5	7	35	....	....	....	....	....	....	....	....	....	5	0	3	3	0	....	....	....	....
	Reading Royals	ECHL	1	0	0	0	2	....	....	....	....	....	....	....	....	....	....	....	....	....	....	....	....	....	....

			Regular Season														Playoffs								
Season	Club	League	GP	G	A	Pts	PIM	PP	SH	GW	S	S%	+/-	TF	F%	Min	GP	G	A	Pts	PIM	PP	SH	GW	Min
2013-14	**Washington**	**NHL**	**10**	**1**	**1**	**2**	**0**	**0**	**0**	**1**	**4**	**25.0**	**3**	**0**	**0.0**	**15:33**	....	....	....	....	....	....	....	....	....
	Hershey Bears	AHL	51	10	10	20	22	....	....	....	....	....	....	....	....	....	....	....	....	....	....	....	....	....	....
2014-15	**Winnipeg**	**NHL**	**1**	**0**	**0**	**0**	**0**	**0**	**0**	**0**	**0**	**0.0**	**0**	**0**	**0.0**	**9:33**	....	....	....	....	....	....	....	....	....
	St. John's IceCaps	AHL	49	7	11	18	16	....	....	....	....	....	....	....	....	....	....	....	....	....	....	....	....	....	....
2015-16	Karlskrona HK	Sweden	52	5	12	17	32	....	....	....	....	....	....	....	....	....	....	....	....	....	....	....	....	....	....
	Karlskrona HK	Sweden-Q	....	....	....	....	....	....	....	....	....	....	....	....	....	....	5	0	1	1	2	....	....	....	....
2016-17	St. John's IceCaps	AHL	57	3	10	13	14	....	....	....	....	....	....	....	....	....	4	0	0	0	0	....	....	....	....
	NHL Totals		**11**	**1**	**1**	**2**	**0**	**0**	**0**	**1**	**4**	**25.0**		**0**	**0.0**	**15:00**	....	....	....	....	....	....	....	....	....

Signed as a free agent by **Washington**, April 5, 2013. Signed as a free agent by **Winnipeg**, August 8, 2014. Signed as a free agent by **Karlskrona** (Sweden), June 1, 2015.

BROUWER, Troy

(BROW-uhr, TROI) **CGY**

Right wing. Shoots right. 6'3", 215 lbs. Born, Vancouver, BC, August 17, 1985. Chicago's 13th pick, 214th overall, in 2004 NHL Draft.

Season	Club	League	GP	G	A	Pts	PIM	PP	SH	GW	S	S%	+/-	TF	F%	Min	GP	G	A	Pts	PIM	PP	SH	GW	Min
2001-02	Delta Ice Hawks	PIJHL	30	21	18	39	130	....	....	....	....	....	....	....	....	....	....	....	....	....	....	....	....	....	....
	Moose Jaw	WHL	13	0	0	0	7	....	....	....	....	....	....	....	....	....	....	....	....	....	....	....	....	....	....
2002-03	Moose Jaw	WHL	59	9	12	21	54	....	....	....	....	....	....	....	....	....	13	1	2	3	14	....	....	....	....
2003-04	Moose Jaw	WHL	72	23	26	49	111	....	....	....	....	....	....	....	....	....	10	3	0	3	12	....	....	....	....
2004-05	Moose Jaw	WHL	71	22	25	47	132	....	....	....	....	....	....	....	....	....	5	1	2	3	8	....	....	....	....
2005-06	Moose Jaw	WHL	72	49	53	*102	122	....	....	....	....	....	....	....	....	....	17	10	4	14	34	....	....	....	....
2006-07	**Chicago**	**NHL**	**10**	**0**	**0**	**0**	**7**	**0**	**0**	**0**	**7**	**0.0**	**-7**	**0**	**0.0**	**9:55**	....	....	....	....	....	....	....	....	....
	Norfolk Admirals	AHL	66	41	38	79	70	....	....	....	....	....	....	....	....	....	6	1	0	1	4	....	....	....	....
2007-08	**Chicago**	**NHL**	**2**	**0**	**1**	**1**	**0**	**0**	**0**	**0**	**0**	**0.0**	**1**	**0**	**0.0**	**11:56**	....	....	....	....	....	....	....	....	....
	Rockford IceHogs	AHL	75	35	19	54	154	....	....	....	....	....	....	....	....	....	12	5	4	9	16	....	....	....	....
2008-09	**Chicago**	**NHL**	**69**	**10**	**16**	**26**	**50**	**4**	**1**	**0**	**126**	**7.9**	**7**	**20**	**45.0**	**15:05**	**17**	**0**	**2**	**2**	**12**	**0**	**0**	**0**	**11:51**
	Rockford IceHogs	AHL	5	2	6	8	20	....	....	....	....	....	....	....	....	....	....	....	....	....	....	....	....	....	....
2009-10 ♦	**Chicago**	**NHL**	**78**	**22**	**18**	**40**	**66**	**7**	**1**	**7**	**116**	**19.0**	**9**	**9**	**55.6**	**16:22**	**19**	**4**	**4**	**8**	**8**	**0**	**0**	**0**	**11:01**
2010-11	**Chicago**	**NHL**	**79**	**17**	**19**	**36**	**38**	**7**	**0**	**5**	**122**	**13.9**	**-2**	**25**	**48.0**	**15:06**	**7**	**0**	**0**	**0**	**11**	**0**	**0**	**0**	**14:25**
2011-12	**Washington**	**NHL**	**82**	**18**	**15**	**33**	**61**	**3**	**0**	**5**	**133**	**13.5**	**-15**	**83**	**45.8**	**17:11**	**14**	**2**	**2**	**4**	**8**	**1**	**0**	**1**	**19:01**
2012-13	**Washington**	**NHL**	**47**	**19**	**14**	**33**	**28**	**7**	**1**	**5**	**111**	**17.1**	**-5**	**232**	**47.8**	**18:32**	**7**	**1**	**1**	**2**	**10**	**0**	**0**	**0**	**19:34**
2013-14	**Washington**	**NHL**	**82**	**25**	**18**	**43**	**92**	**12**	**0**	**3**	**161**	**15.5**	**-6**	**436**	**51.2**	**18:51**	....	....	....	....	....	....	....	....	....
2014-15	**Washington**	**NHL**	**82**	**21**	**22**	**43**	**53**	**8**	**2**	**3**	**145**	**14.5**	**11**	**441**	**56.9**	**17:31**	**14**	**0**	**3**	**3**	**10**	**0**	**0**	**0**	**17:59**
2015-16	**St. Louis**	**NHL**	**82**	**18**	**21**	**39**	**62**	**7**	**0**	**4**	**142**	**12.7**	**2**	**114**	**57.0**	**17:00**	**20**	**8**	**5**	**13**	**26**	**3**	**0**	**1**	**18:59**
2016-17	**Calgary**	**NHL**	**74**	**13**	**12**	**25**	**31**	**5**	**1**	**2**	**86**	**15.1**	**-11**	**64**	**31.3**	**16:13**	**4**	**0**	**2**	**2**	**0**	**0**	**0**	**0**	**14:04**
	NHL Totals		**687**	**163**	**156**	**319**	**488**	**60**	**6**	**34**	**1149**	**14.2**		**1424**	**51.5**	**16:44**	**102**	**15**	**19**	**34**	**85**	**4**	**0**	**2**	**15:43**

WHL East First All-Star Team (2006) • Canadian Major Junior Second All-Star Team (2006) • AHL All-Rookie Team (2007) • AHL Second All-Star Team (2007)

Traded to **Washington** by **Chicago** for Washington's 1st round pick (Phillip Danault) in 2011 NHL Draft, June 24, 2011. Traded to **St. Louis** by **Washington** with Pheonix Copley and Washington's 3rd round pick (later traded back to Washington – Washington selected Garrett Pilon) in 2016 NHL Draft for T.J. Oshie, July 2, 2015. Signed as a free agent by **Calgary**, July 1, 2016.

BROWN, Chris

(BROWN, KRIHS)

Center. Shoots right. 6'2", 215 lbs. Born, Flower Mound, TX, February 3, 1991. Phoenix's 2nd pick, 36th overall, in 2009 NHL Draft.

Season	Club	League	GP	G	A	Pts	PIM	PP	SH	GW	S	S%	+/-	TF	F%	Min	GP	G	A	Pts	PIM	PP	SH	GW	Min
2007-08	USAHNTDP	NAHL	43	8	6	14	66	....	....	....	....	....	....	....	....	....	3	0	0	0	0	....	....	....	....
	USAHNTDP	U-17	17	5	1	6	8	....	....	....	....	....	....	....	....	....	....	....	....	....	....	....	....	....	....
2008-09	USAHNTDP	NAHL	15	6	2	8	37	....	....	....	....	....	....	....	....	....	....	....	....	....	....	....	....	....	....
	USAHNTDP	U-18	47	14	16	30	83	....	....	....	....	....	....	....	....	....	....	....	....	....	....	....	....	....	....
2009-10	U. of Michigan	CCHA	45	13	15	28	58	....	....	....	....	....	....	....	....	....	....	....	....	....	....	....	....	....	....
2010-11	U. of Michigan	CCHA	42	9	14	23	59	....	....	....	....	....	....	....	....	....	....	....	....	....	....	....	....	....	....
2011-12	U. of Michigan	CCHA	38	12	17	29	66	....	....	....	....	....	....	....	....	....	....	....	....	....	....	....	....	....	....
2012-13	Portland Pirates	AHL	68	29	18	47	98	....	....	....	....	....	....	....	....	....	3	1	1	2	6	....	....	....	....
	Phoenix	**NHL**	**5**	**0**	**0**	**0**	**2**	**0**	**0**	**0**	**6**	**0.0**	**0**	**0**	**0.0**	**7:38**	....	....	....	....	....	....	....	....	....
2013-14	**Phoenix**	**NHL**	**6**	**0**	**0**	**0**	**17**	**0**	**0**	**0**	**4**	**0.0**	**0**	**2**	**0.0**	**7:41**	....	....	....	....	....	....	....	....	....
	Portland Pirates	AHL	51	14	21	35	68	....	....	....	....	....	....	....	....	....	....	....	....	....	....	....	....	....	....
	Washington	**NHL**	**6**	**1**	**1**	**2**	**0**	**0**	**0**	**0**	**4**	**25.0**	**0**	**38**	**39.5**	**9:42**	....	....	....	....	....	....	....	....	....
	Hershey Bears	AHL	12	2	3	5	2	....	....	....	....	....	....	....	....	....	....	....	....	....	....	....	....	....	....
2014-15	**Washington**	**NHL**	**5**	**1**	**0**	**1**	**2**	**0**	**0**	**0**	**4**	**25.0**	**1**	**3**	**33.3**	**6:28**	....	....	....	....	....	....	....	....	....
	Hershey Bears	AHL	64	17	11	28	70	....	....	....	....	....	....	....	....	....	9	3	2	5	10	....	....	....	....
2015-16	**Washington**	**NHL**	**1**	**0**	**0**	**0**	**0**	**0**	**0**	**0**	**1**	**0.0**	**0**	**0**	**0.0**	**7:41**	....	....	....	....	....	....	....	....	....
	Hershey Bears	AHL	20	3	6	9	20	....	....	....	....	....	....	....	....	....	....	....	....	....	....	....	....	....	....
	Hartford	AHL	20	3	6	9	20	....	....	....	....	....	....	....	....	....	....	....	....	....	....	....	....	....	....
2016-17	Hartford	AHL	64	14	13	27	78	....	....	....	....	....	....	....	....	....	....	....	....	....	....	....	....	....	....
	NHL Totals		**23**	**2**	**1**	**3**	**21**	**0**	**0**	**0**	**19**	**10.5**		**43**	**37.2**	**7:56**	....	....	....	....	....	....	....	....	....

CCHA All-Rookie Team (2010)

Traded to **Washington** by **Phoenix** with Rostislav Klesla and Arizona's 4th round pick (later traded to Carolina – Carolina selected Callum Booth) in 2015 NHL Draft for Martin Erat and John Mitchell, March 4, 2014. Traded to **NY Rangers** by **Washington** for Ryan Bourque, February 28, 2016.

BROWN, Connor

(BROWN, KAW-nuhr) **TOR**

Right wing. Shoots right. 6', 185 lbs. Born, Etobicoke, ON, January 14, 1994. Toronto's 4th pick, 156th overall, in 2012 NHL Draft.

Season	Club	League	GP	G	A	Pts	PIM	PP	SH	GW	S	S%	+/-	TF	F%	Min	GP	G	A	Pts	PIM	PP	SH	GW	Min
2009-10	Tor. Marlboros	GTHL	80	25	44	69	16	....	....	....	....	....	....	....	....	....	....	....	....	....	....	....	....	....	....
2010-11	St. Michael's	ON-Jr.A	49	17	22	39	18	....	....	....	....	....	....	....	....	....	3	0	1	1	0	....	....	....	....
2011-12	Erie Otters	OHL	68	25	28	53	14	....	....	....	....	....	....	....	....	....	....	....	....	....	....	....	....	....	....
2012-13	Erie Otters	OHL	63	28	41	69	39	....	....	....	....	....	....	....	....	....	....	....	....	....	....	....	....	....	....
2013-14	Erie Otters	OHL	68	45	*83	*128	22	....	....	....	....	....	....	....	....	....	14	8	10	18	8	....	....	....	....
2014-15	Toronto Marlies	AHL	76	21	40	61	10	....	....	....	....	....	....	....	....	....	5	1	3	4	2	....	....	....	....
2015-16	**Toronto**	**NHL**	**7**	**1**	**5**	**6**	**0**	**1**	**0**	**0**	**11**	**9.1**	**-2**	**0**	**0.0**	**14:58**	....	....	....	....	....	....	....	....	....
	Toronto Marlies	AHL	34	11	18	29	8	....	....	....	....	....	....	....	....	....	15	7	2	9	6	....	....	....	....
2016-17	**Toronto**	**NHL**	**82**	**20**	**16**	**36**	**10**	**2**	**1**	**4**	**139**	**14.4**	**3**	**8**	**25.0**	**16:12**	**6**	**0**	**1**	**1**	**0**	**0**	**0**	**0**	**18:14**
	NHL Totals		**89**	**21**	**21**	**42**	**10**	**3**	**1**	**4**	**150**	**14.0**		**8**	**25.0**	**16:07**	**6**	**0**	**1**	**1**	**0**	**0**	**0**	**0**	**18:14**

OHL All-Rookie Team (2012) • OHL First All-Star Team (2014) • AHL All-Rookie Team (2015)

BROWN, Dustin

(BROWN, DUHS-tihn) **L.A.**

Right wing. Shoots right. 6', 206 lbs. Born, Ithaca, NY, November 4, 1984. Los Angeles' 1st pick, 13th overall, in 2003 NHL Draft.

Season	Club	League	GP	G	A	Pts	PIM	PP	SH	GW	S	S%	+/-	TF	F%	Min	GP	G	A	Pts	PIM	PP	SH	GW	Min
1998-99	Ithaca	High-NY	18	4	13	17	....	....	....	....	....	....	....	....	....	....	....	....	....	....	....	....	....	....	....
99-2000	Ithaca	High-NY	24	33	21	54	....	....	....	....	....	....	....	....	....	....	....	....	....	....	....	....	....	....	....
2000-01	Guelph Storm	OHL	53	23	22	45	45	....	....	....	....	....	....	....	....	....	4	0	0	0	10	....	....	....	....
2001-02	Guelph Storm	OHL	63	41	32	73	56	....	....	....	....	....	....	....	....	....	9	8	5	13	14	....	....	....	....
2002-03	Guelph Storm	OHL	58	34	42	76	89	....	....	....	....	....	....	....	....	....	11	7	8	15	6	....	....	....	....
2003-04	**Los Angeles**	**NHL**	**31**	**1**	**4**	**5**	**16**	**0**	**0**	**0**	**40**	**2.5**	**0**	**1**	**0.0**	**10:29**	....	....	....	....	....	....	....	....	....
2004-05	Manchester	AHL	79	29	45	74	96	....	....	....	....	....	....	....	....	....	6	5	2	7	10	....	....	....	....
2005-06	**Los Angeles**	**NHL**	**79**	**14**	**14**	**28**	**80**	**6**	**0**	**2**	**159**	**8.8**	**-10**	**15**	**66.7**	**13:59**	....	....	....	....	....	....	....	....	....
2006-07	**Los Angeles**	**NHL**	**81**	**17**	**29**	**46**	**54**	**13**	**0**	**1**	**195**	**8.7**	**-21**	**77**	**49.4**	**18:43**	....	....	....	....	....	....	....	....	....
2007-08	**Los Angeles**	**NHL**	**78**	**33**	**27**	**60**	**55**	**12**	**2**	**4**	**219**	**15.1**	**-13**	**40**	**50.0**	**20:18**	....	....	....	....	....	....	....	....	....
2008-09	**Los Angeles**	**NHL**	**80**	**24**	**29**	**53**	**64**	**7**	**0**	**6**	**292**	**8.2**	**-15**	**54**	**46.3**	**19:24**	....	....	....	....	....	....	....	....	....
2009-10	**Los Angeles**	**NHL**	**82**	**24**	**32**	**56**	**41**	**7**	**0**	**3**	**248**	**9.7**	**-6**	**39**	**43.6**	**19:15**	**6**	**1**	**4**	**5**	**6**	**1**	**0**	**0**	**18:53**
	United States	Olympics	6	0	0	0	0	....	....	....	....	....	....	....	....	....	....	....	....	....	....	....	....	....	....
2010-11	**Los Angeles**	**NHL**	**82**	**28**	**29**	**57**	**67**	**7**	**0**	**2**	**228**	**12.3**	**17**	**37**	**48.7**	**19:22**	**6**	**1**	**1**	**2**	**6**	**1**	**0**	**0**	**20:00**
2011-12 ♦	**Los Angeles**	**NHL**	**82**	**22**	**32**	**54**	**53**	**9**	**1**	**6**	**214**	**10.3**	**18**	**39**	**43.6**	**20:10**	**20**	***8**	***12**	***20**	**34**	**1**	***2**	**3**	**20:44**
2012-13	ZSC Lions Zurich	Swiss	16	8	5	13	26	....	....	....	....	....	....	....	....	....	....	....	....	....	....	....	....	....	....
	Los Angeles	**NHL**	**46**	**18**	**11**	**29**	**22**	**8**	**0**	**1**	**142**	**12.7**	**6**	**41**	**36.6**	**19:30**	**18**	**3**	**1**	**4**	**8**	**2**	**0**	**0**	**18:47**
2013-14 ♦	**Los Angeles**	**NHL**	**79**	**15**	**12**	**27**	**66**	**1**	**0**	**2**	**195**	**7.7**	**7**	**19**	**31.6**	**15:50**	**26**	**6**	**8**	**14**	**22**	**1**	**0**	**2**	**16:57**
	United States	Olympics	6	2	1	3	4	....	....	....	....	....	....	....	....	....	....	....	....	....	....	....	....	....	....
2014-15	**Los Angeles**	**NHL**	**82**	**11**	**16**	**27**	**26**	**1**	**0**	**3**	**189**	**5.8**	**-17**	**35**	**42.9**	**16:31**	....	....	....	....	....	....	....	....	....

			Regular Season														Playoffs								
Season	Club	League	GP	G	A	Pts	PIM	PP	SH	GW	S	S%	+/-	TF	F%	Min	GP	G	A	Pts	PIM	PP	SH	GW	Min
2015-16	**Los Angeles**	**NHL**	**82**	**11**	**17**	**28**	**30**	**2**	**0**	**0**	**218**	**5.0**	**–5**	**17**	**47.1**	**16:10**	**5**	**0**	**1**	**1**	**4**	**0**	**0**	**0**	**16:09**
2016-17	**Los Angeles**	**NHL**	**80**	**14**	**22**	**36**	**22**	**4**	**1**	**1**	**175**	**8.0**	**–4**	**5**	**40.0**	**16:00**	....	....	....	....	....	....	....	....	....
	NHL Totals		**964**	**232**	**274**	**506**	**596**	**77**	**4**	**31**	**2514**	**9.2**		**419**	**45.6**	**17:39**	**81**	**19**	**27**	**46**	**80**	**6**	**2**	**5**	**18:37**

OHL All-Rookie Team (2001) • Canadian Major Junior Scholastic Player of the Year (2003) • NHL Foundation Player Award (2011) • Mark Messier NHL Leadership Award (2014)
Played in NHL All-Star Game (2009)
• Missed majority of 2003-04 due to ankle injury vs. Chicago, November 29, 2003. Signed as a free agent by **Zurich** (Swiss), November 1, 2012.

BROWN, J.T.

(BROWN, JAY-TEE) **T.B.**

Right wing. Shoots right. 5'10", 175 lbs. Born, High Point, NC, July 2, 1990.

Season	Club	League	GP	G	A	Pts	PIM	PP	SH	GW	S	S%	+/-	TF	F%	Min	GP	G	A	Pts	PIM	PP	SH	GW	Min
2008-09	Waterloo	USHL	36	14	22	36	28	....	....	....	....	....	....	....	....	....	3	1	0	1	4	....	....	....	....
2009-10	Waterloo	USHL	60	34	43	77	64	....	....	....	....	....	....	....	....	....	3	1	0	1	0	....	....	....	....
2010-11	U. Minn-Duluth	WCHA	42	16	21	37	50	....	....	....	....	....	....	....	....	....	....	....	....	....	....	....	....	....	....
2011-12	U. Minn-Duluth	WCHA	39	24	23	47	59	....	....	....	....	....	....	....	....	....	....	....	....	....	....	....	....	....	....
	Tampa Bay	**NHL**	**5**	**0**	**1**	**1**	**0**	**0**	**0**	**0**	**13**	**0.0**	**2**	**0**	**0.0**	**13:51**	....	....	....	....	....	....	....	....	....
2012-13	Syracuse Crunch	AHL	51	10	18	28	27	....	....	....	....	....	....	....	....	....	18	4	5	9	18	....	....	....	....
2013-14	**Tampa Bay**	**NHL**	**63**	**4**	**15**	**19**	**6**	**0**	**0**	**0**	**113**	**3.5**	**–9**	**22**	**31.8**	**13:02**	**4**	**0**	**2**	**2**	**0**	**0**	**0**	**0**	**15:00**
	Syracuse Crunch	AHL	13	4	6	10	24	....	....	....	....	....	....	....	....	....	....	....	....	....	....	....	....	....	....
2014-15	**Tampa Bay**	**NHL**	**52**	**3**	**6**	**9**	**30**	**0**	**0**	**0**	**74**	**4.1**	**–2**	**13**	**46.2**	**10:36**	**24**	**1**	**1**	**2**	**0**	**0**	**0**	**0**	**12:21**
2015-16	**Tampa Bay**	**NHL**	**78**	**8**	**14**	**22**	**59**	**0**	**0**	**0**	**140**	**5.7**	**16**	**50**	**46.0**	**13:22**	**9**	**0**	**2**	**2**	**2**	**0**	**0**	**0**	**10:35**
2016-17	**Tampa Bay**	**NHL**	**64**	**3**	**3**	**6**	**73**	**0**	**1**	**1**	**67**	**4.5**	**–7**	**38**	**31.6**	**10:22**	....	....	....	....	....	....	....	....	....
	NHL Totals		**262**	**18**	**39**	**57**	**168**	**0**	**1**	**1**	**407**	**4.4**		**123**	**39.0**	**12:01**	**37**	**1**	**5**	**6**	**2**	**0**	**0**	**0**	**12:12**

USHL Second All-Star Team (2010) • WCHA All-Rookie Team (2011) • NCAA Championship All-Tournament Team (2011) • NCAA Championship Tournament MVP (2011) • WCHA First All-Star Team (2012) • NCAA West Second All-American Team (2012)
Signed as a free agent by **Tampa Bay**, March 28, 2012.

BROWN, Patrick

(BROWN, PAT-rihk) **CAR**

Left wing. Shoots right. 6'1", 210 lbs. Born, Bloomfield Hills, MI, May 29, 1992.

Season	Club	League	GP	G	A	Pts	PIM	PP	SH	GW	S	S%	+/-	TF	F%	Min	GP	G	A	Pts	PIM	PP	SH	GW	Min
2009-10	Cranbrook Cranes	High-MI	30	23	25	48	14	....	....	....	....	....	....	....	....	....	....	....	....	....	....	....	....	....	....
2010-11	Boston College	H-East	29	0	1	1	8	....	....	....	....	....	....	....	....	....	....	....	....	....	....	....	....	....	....
2011-12	Boston College	H-East	13	1	0	1	6	....	....	....	....	....	....	....	....	....	....	....	....	....	....	....	....	....	....
2012-13	Boston College	H-East	38	5	6	11	14	....	....	....	....	....	....	....	....	....	....	....	....	....	....	....	....	....	....
2013-14	Boston College	H-East	40	15	15	30	30	....	....	....	....	....	....	....	....	....	....	....	....	....	....	....	....	....	....
2014-15	**Carolina**	**NHL**	**7**	**0**	**0**	**0**	**4**	**0**	**0**	**0**	**4**	**0.0**	**–4**	**2**	**0.0**	**8:53**	....	....	....	....	....	....	....	....	....
	Charlotte	AHL	60	2	8	10	34	....	....	....	....	....	....	....	....	....	....	....	....	....	....	....	....	....	....
2015-16	**Carolina**	**NHL**	**7**	**1**	**1**	**2**	**4**	**0**	**0**	**0**	**8**	**12.5**	**4**	**0**	**0.0**	**12:36**	....	....	....	....	....	....	....	....	....
	Charlotte	AHL	70	13	12	25	29	....	....	....	....	....	....	....	....	....	....	....	....	....	....	....	....	....	....
2016-17	**Carolina**	**NHL**	**14**	**0**	**0**	**0**	**0**	**0**	**0**	**0**	**12**	**0.0**	**–6**	**15**	**60.0**	**9:43**	....	....	....	....	....	....	....	....	....
	Charlotte	AHL	66	12	16	28	45	....	....	....	....	....	....	....	....	....	5	1	0	1	0	....	....	....	....
	NHL Totals		**28**	**1**	**1**	**2**	**8**	**0**	**0**	**0**	**24**	**4.2**		**17**	**52.9**	**10:14**	....	....	....	....	....	....	....	....	....

Signed as a free agent by **Carolina**, April 14, 2014.

BUCHNEVICH, Pavel

(buhtch-NY'AY-vihch, PAH-vehl) **NYR**

Left wing. Shoots left. 6'2", 193 lbs. Born, Cherepovets, Russia, April 17, 1995. NY Rangers' 2nd pick, 75th overall, in 2013 NHL Draft.

Season	Club	League	GP	G	A	Pts	PIM	PP	SH	GW	S	S%	+/-	TF	F%	Min	GP	G	A	Pts	PIM	PP	SH	GW	Min
2011-12	Cherepovets Jr.	Russia-Jr.	45	15	29	44	55	....	....	....	....	....	....	....	....	....	10	4	3	7	4	....	....	....	....
2012-13	Cherepovets Jr.	Russia-Jr.	24	8	15	23	36	....	....	....	....	....	....	....	....	....	3	1	4	5	12	....	....	....	....
	Cherepovets	KHL	12	1	1	2	0	....	....	....	....	....	....	....	....	....	6	0	0	0	0	....	....	....	....
2013-14	Cherepovets Jr.	Russia-Jr.	2	0	2	2	2	....	....	....	....	....	....	....	....	....	7	4	5	9	12	....	....	....	....
	Cherepovets	KHL	40	7	11	18	12	....	....	....	....	....	....	....	....	....	6	1	1	2	9	....	....	....	....
2014-15	Cherepovets	KHL	48	13	17	30	16	....	....	....	....	....	....	....	....	....	....	....	....	....	....	....	....	....	....
2015-16	Cherepovets	KHL	40	12	17	29	20	....	....	....	....	....	....	....	....	....	....	....	....	....	....	....	....	....	....
	St. Petersburg	KHL	18	4	4	8	4	....	....	....	....	....	....	....	....	....	14	1	2	3	29	....	....	....	....
2016-17	**NY Rangers**	**NHL**	**41**	**8**	**12**	**20**	**13**	**1**	**0**	**0**	**55**	**14.5**	**6**	**7**	**14.3**	**13:16**	**5**	**0**	**1**	**1**	**0**	**0**	**0**	**0**	**12:17**
	Hartford	AHL	4	3	2	5	0	....	....	....	....	....	....	....	....	....	....	....	....	....	....	....	....	....	....
	NHL Totals		**41**	**8**	**12**	**20**	**13**	**1**	**0**	**0**	**55**	**14.5**		**7**	**14.3**	**13:16**	**5**	**0**	**1**	**1**	**0**	**0**	**0**	**0**	**12:17**

BURAKOVSKY, Andre

(buhr-a-KAWV-skee, AHN-DRAY) **WSH**

Left wing. Shoots left. 6'3", 188 lbs. Born, Klagenfurt , Austria, February 9, 1995. Washington's 1st pick, 23rd overall, in 2013 NHL Draft.

Season	Club	League	GP	G	A	Pts	PIM	PP	SH	GW	S	S%	+/-	TF	F%	Min	GP	G	A	Pts	PIM	PP	SH	GW	Min
2010-11	Malmo U18	Swe-U18	27	8	9	17	6	....	....	....	....	....	....	....	....	....	....	....	....	....	....	....	....	....	....
2011-12	Malmo U18	Swe-U18	9	6	8	14	14	....	....	....	....	....	....	....	....	....	4	2	4	6	0	....	....	....	....
	Malmo Jr.	Swe-Jr.	42	17	25	42	43	....	....	....	....	....	....	....	....	....	5	1	4	5	2	....	....	....	....
	Malmo	Sweden-2	10	0	1	1	0	....	....	....	....	....	....	....	....	....	3	0	0	0	0	....	....	....	....
2012-13	Malmo U18	Swe-U18	3	6	4	10	2	....	....	....	....	....	....	....	....	....	4	3	3	6	0	....	....	....	....
	Malmo Jr.	Swe-Jr.	13	3	4	7	8	....	....	....	....	....	....	....	....	....	3	1	2	3	8	....	....	....	....
	Malmo	Sweden-2	43	4	7	11	8	....	....	....	....	....	....	....	....	....	....	....	....	....	....	....	....	....	....
2013-14	Erie Otters	OHL	57	41	46	87	35	....	....	....	....	....	....	....	....	....	14	10	3	13	2	....	....	....	....
2014-15	**Washington**	**NHL**	**53**	**9**	**13**	**22**	**10**	**2**	**0**	**2**	**65**	**13.8**	**12**	**167**	**44.3**	**12:55**	**11**	**2**	**1**	**3**	**0**	**0**	**0**	**1**	**12:25**
	Hershey Bears	AHL	13	3	4	7	6	....	....	....	....	....	....	....	....	....	1	1	0	1	0	....	....	....	....
2015-16	**Washington**	**NHL**	**79**	**17**	**21**	**38**	**12**	**0**	**0**	**1**	**126**	**13.5**	**4**	**37**	**46.0**	**13:01**	**12**	**1**	**0**	**1**	**6**	**0**	**0**	**0**	**12:32**
2016-17	**Washington**	**NHL**	**64**	**12**	**23**	**35**	**14**	**2**	**0**	**1**	**111**	**10.8**	**13**	**7**	**28.6**	**13:16**	**13**	**3**	**3**	**6**	**2**	**0**	**0**	**0**	**14:20**
	NHL Totals		**196**	**38**	**57**	**95**	**36**	**4**	**0**	**4**	**302**	**12.6**		**211**	**44.1**	**13:04**	**36**	**6**	**4**	**10**	**8**	**0**	**0**	**1**	**13:09**

BURGDOERFER, Erik

(BUHRG-dohr-fuhr, AIR-ihk) **OTT**

Defense. Shoots right. 6'2", 210 lbs. Born, East Setauket, NY, December 11, 1988.

Season	Club	League	GP	G	A	Pts	PIM	PP	SH	GW	S	S%	+/-	TF	F%	Min	GP	G	A	Pts	PIM	PP	SH	GW	Min
2005-06	NY Apple Core	EJHL	45	5	10	16	60	....	....	....	....	....	....	....	....	....	....	....	....	....	....	....	....	....	....
2006-07	RPI Engineers	ECAC	23	1	1	2	32	....	....	....	....	....	....	....	....	....	....	....	....	....	....	....	....	....	....
2007-08	RPI Engineers	ECAC	32	2	3	5	47	....	....	....	....	....	....	....	....	....	....	....	....	....	....	....	....	....	....
2008-09	RPI Engineers	ECAC	35	3	2	5	106	....	....	....	....	....	....	....	....	....	....	....	....	....	....	....	....	....	....
2009-10	RPI Engineers	ECAC	39	1	6	7	51	....	....	....	....	....	....	....	....	....	....	....	....	....	....	....	....	....	....
	Bakersfield	ECHL	3	0	0	0	10	....	....	....	....	....	....	....	....	....	....	....	....	....	....	....	....	....	....
2010-11	Bakersfield	ECHL	68	2	14	16	50	....	....	....	....	....	....	....	....	....	4	1	0	1	2	....	....	....	....
2011-12	Bakersfield	ECHL	60	5	11	16	91	....	....	....	....	....	....	....	....	....	....	....	....	....	....	....	....	....	....
2012-13	Bakersfield	ECHL	71	4	17	21	67	....	....	....	....	....	....	....	....	....	....	....	....	....	....	....	....	....	....
2013-14	Bakersfield	ECHL	67	11	11	22	70	....	....	....	....	....	....	....	....	....	16	1	5	6	7	....	....	....	....
	Oklahoma City	AHL	3	0	1	1	4	....	....	....	....	....	....	....	....	....	....	....	....	....	....	....	....	....	....
2014-15	South Carolina	ECHL	3	0	0	0	2	....	....	....	....	....	....	....	....	....	....	....	....	....	....	....	....	....	....
	Hershey Bears	AHL	58	1	6	7	58	....	....	....	....	....	....	....	....	....	10	0	1	1	2	....	....	....	....
2015-16	Hershey Bears	AHL	74	6	14	20	59	....	....	....	....	....	....	....	....	....	21	0	4	4	18	....	....	....	....
2016-17	**Buffalo**	**NHL**	**2**	**0**	**0**	**0**	**0**	**0**	**0**	**0**	**2**	**0.0**	**–1**	**0**	**0.0**	**11:10**	....	....	....	....	....	....	....	....	....
	Rochester	AHL	52	1	16	17	44	....	....	....	....	....	....	....	....	....	....	....	....	....	....	....	....	....	....
	NHL Totals		**2**	**0**	**0**	**0**	**0**	**0**	**0**	**0**	**2**	**0.0**		**0**	**0.0**	**11:10**	....	....	....	....	....	....	....	....	....

Signed as a free agent by **Buffalo**, July 21, 2016. Signed as a free agent by **Ottawa**, July 1, 2017.

BURMISTROV, Alexander

(buhr-MIHS-trawf, al-ehx-AN-duhr) **VAN**

Center. Shoots left. 6'1", 180 lbs. Born, Kazan, Russia, October 21, 1991. Atlanta's 1st pick, 8th overall, in 2010 NHL Draft.

Season	Club	League	GP	G	A	Pts	PIM	PP	SH	GW	S	S%	+/-	TF	F%	Min	GP	G	A	Pts	PIM	PP	SH	GW	Min
2008-09	Ak Bars Kazan 2	Russia-3	34	25	25	50	54	....	....	....	....	....	....	....	....	....	....	....	....	....	....	....	....	....	....
	Ak Bars Kazan	KHL	1	0	0	0	0	....	....	....	....	....	....	....	....	....	....	....	....	....	....	....	....	....	....
2009-10	Barrie Colts	OHL	62	22	43	65	49	....	....	....	....	....	....	....	....	....	17	8	8	16	22	....	....	....	....
2010-11	**Atlanta**	**NHL**	**74**	**6**	**14**	**20**	**27**	**0**	**0**	**2**	**92**	**6.5**	**–12**	**696**	**41.5**	**13:13**	....	....	....	....	....	....	....	....	....
2011-12	**Winnipeg**	**NHL**	**76**	**13**	**15**	**28**	**42**	**1**	**1**	**0**	**123**	**10.6**	**4**	**564**	**44.0**	**16:40**	....	....	....	....	....	....	....	....	....
2012-13	**Winnipeg**	**NHL**	**44**	**4**	**6**	**10**	**14**	**0**	**0**	**0**	**55**	**7.3**	**0**	**301**	**47.2**	**15:38**	....	....	....	....	....	....	....	....	....
2013-14	Ak Bars Kazan	KHL	54	10	28	38	32	....	....	....	....	....	....	....	....	....	6	0	2	2	9	....	....	....	....

			Regular Season														Playoffs								
Season	Club	League	GP	G	A	Pts	PIM	PP	SH	GW	S	S%	+/-	TF	F%	Min	GP	G	A	Pts	PIM	PP	SH	GW	Min
2014-15	Ak Bars Kazan	KHL	53	10	16	26	40	....	....	....	....	....	....	....	....	....	17	1	3	4	8	....	....	....	....
2015-16	Winnipeg	NHL	81	7	14	21	32	0	0	2	102	6.9	-11	512	40.0	16:10	....	....	....	....	....	....	....	....	....
2016-17	Winnipeg	NHL	23	0	2	2	6	0	0	0	13	0.0	-6	147	36.1	11:02	....	....	....	....	....	....	....	....	....
	Arizona	NHL	26	5	9	14	6	4	0	0	32	15.6	-1	290	43.1	15:24	....	....	....	....	....	....	....	....	....
	NHL Totals		324	35	60	95	127	5	1	4	417	8.4		2510	42.3	15:07	....	....	....	....	....	....	....	....	....

• Transferred to **Winnipeg** after **Atlanta** franchise relocated, June 21, 2011. Signed as a free agent by **Kazan** (KHL), July 8, 2013. Signed as a free agent by **Winnipeg**, July 1, 2015. Claimed on waivers by **Arizona** from **Winnipeg**, January 2, 2017. Signed as a free agent by **Vancouver**, July 1, 2017.

BURNS, Brent

(BUHRNZ, BREHNT) **S.J.**

Defense. Shoots right. 6'5", 230 lbs. Born, Ajax, ON, March 9, 1985. Minnesota's 1st pick, 20th overall, in 2003 NHL Draft.

Season	Club	League	GP	G	A	Pts	PIM	PP	SH	GW	S	S%	+/-	TF	F%	Min	GP	G	A	Pts	PIM	PP	SH	GW	Min
2001-02	Couchiching	ON-Jr.A	46	4	7	11	16	....	....	....	....	....	....	....	....	....	....	....	....	....	....	....	....	....	....
2002-03	Brampton	OHL	68	15	25	40	14	....	....	....	....	....	....	....	....	....	11	5	6	11	6	....	....	....	....
2003-04	Minnesota	NHL	36	1	5	6	12	0	0	0	34	2.9	-10	7	28.6	13:29	....	....	....	....	....	....	....	....	....
	Houston Aeros	AHL	1	0	1	1	2	....	....	....	....	....	....	....	....	....	....	....	....	....	....	....	....	....	....
2004-05	Houston Aeros	AHL	73	11	16	27	57	....	....	....	....	....	....	....	....	....	5	0	0	0	4	....	....	....	....
2005-06	Minnesota	NHL	72	4	12	16	32	1	0	1	73	5.5	-7	11	54.6	14:07	....	....	....	....	....	....	....	....	....
2006-07	Minnesota	NHL	77	7	18	25	26	3	0	3	108	6.5	16	4	25.0	15:48	5	0	1	1	14	0	0	0	18:59
2007-08	Minnesota	NHL	82	15	28	43	80	8	0	4	158	9.5	12	1	100.0	23:06	6	0	2	2	6	0	0	0	27:35
2008-09	Minnesota	NHL	59	8	19	27	45	4	0	2	147	5.4	-7	5	60.0	22:25	....	....	....	....	....	....	....	....	....
2009-10	Minnesota	NHL	47	3	17	20	32	2	0	0	104	2.9	-15	0	0.0	22:22	....	....	....	....	....	....	....	....	....
2010-11	Minnesota	NHL	80	17	29	46	98	8	0	3	170	10.0	-10	2	50.0	25:03	....	....	....	....	....	....	....	....	....
2011-12	San Jose	NHL	81	11	26	37	34	5	0	2	201	5.5	8	0	0.0	22:32	5	1	1	2	4	1	0	0	25:07
2012-13	San Jose	NHL	30	9	11	20	20	2	0	0	81	11.1	0	13	30.8	16:17	11	2	2	4	8	0	0	0	17:50
2013-14	San Jose	NHL	69	22	26	48	34	2	0	3	245	9.0	26	131	46.6	16:49	7	2	1	3	23	1	0	0	17:32
2014-15	San Jose	NHL	82	17	43	60	65	7	0	2	245	6.9	-9	0	0.0	23:57	....	....	....	....	....	....	....	....	....
2015-16	San Jose	NHL	82	27	48	75	53	7	1	4	353	7.6	-5	1	100.0	25:52	24	7	17	24	12	4	0	0	25:07
2016-17	San Jose	NHL	82	29	47	76	40	8	0	6	320	9.1	19	0	0.0	24:52	6	0	3	3	6	0	0	0	25:04
	NHL Totals		879	170	329	499	571	57	1	30	2239	7.6		175	45.7	21:09	64	12	27	39	73	6	0	0	22:47

NHL Foundation Player Award (2015) • NHL Second All-Star Team (2016) • NHL First All-Star Team (2017) • James Norris Memorial Trophy (2017)

Played in NHL All-Star Game (2011, 2015, 2016, 2017)

• Missed majority of 2003-04 on assignment to Team Canada and as a healthy reserve. • Missed majority of 2009-10 due to head injury vs. Phoenix, November 18, 2009. Traded to **San Jose** by **Minnesota** with Minnesota's 2nd round pick (later traded to Tampa Bay, later traded to Nashville – Nashville selected Pontius Aberg) in 2012 NHL Draft for Devin Setoguchi, Charlie Coyle and San Jose's 1st round pick (Zack Phillips) in 2011 NHL Draft, June 24, 2011.

BURROWS, Alexandre

(BUHR-ohz, al-ehx-AHN-druh) **OTT**

Left wing. Shoots left. 6'1", 188 lbs. Born, Pincourt, QC, April 11, 1981.

Season	Club	League	GP	G	A	Pts	PIM	PP	SH	GW	S	S%	+/-	TF	F%	Min	GP	G	A	Pts	PIM	PP	SH	GW	Min
99-2000	Kahnawake	QJHL	53	24	45	69	223	....	....	....	....	....	....	....	....	....	....	....	....	....	....	....	....	....	....
2000-01	Shawinigan	QMJHL	63	16	14	30	105	....	....	....	....	....	....	....	....	....	10	2	1	3	8	....	....	....	....
2001-02	Shawinigan	QMJHL	64	35	35	70	184	....	....	....	....	....	....	....	....	....	12	9	11	20	34	....	....	....	....
2002-03	Greenville	ECHL	53	9	17	26	201	....	....	....	....	....	....	....	....	....	....	....	....	....	....	....	....	....	....
	Baton Rouge	ECHL	13	4	2	6	64	....	....	....	....	....	....	....	....	....	....	....	....	....	....	....	....	....	....
2003-04	Manitoba Moose	AHL	2	0	0	0	0	....	....	....	....	....	....	....	....	....	....	....	....	....	....	....	....	....	....
	Columbia Inferno	ECHL	64	29	44	73	194	....	....	....	....	....	....	....	....	....	4	2	0	2	28	....	....	....	....
2004-05	Manitoba Moose	AHL	72	9	17	26	107	....	....	....	....	....	....	....	....	....	14	0	3	3	37	....	....	....	....
	Columbia Inferno	ECHL	4	5	1	6	4	....	....	....	....	....	....	....	....	....	....	....	....	....	....	....	....	....	....
2005-06	Vancouver	NHL	43	7	5	12	61	0	1	1	49	14.3	5	19	47.4	10:24	....	....	....	....	....	....	....	....	....
	Manitoba Moose	AHL	33	12	18	30	57	....	....	....	....	....	....	....	....	....	13	6	7	13	27	....	....	....	....
2006-07	Vancouver	NHL	81	3	6	9	93	0	0	1	70	4.3	-7	16	43.8	11:26	11	1	0	1	14	0	0	0	10:34
2007-08	Vancouver	NHL	82	12	19	31	179	1	3	3	126	9.5	11	37	35.1	15:06	....	....	....	....	....	....	....	....	....
2008-09	Vancouver	NHL	82	28	23	51	150	0	4	3	175	16.0	23	80	46.3	16:51	10	3	1	4	20	0	0	1	18:48
2009-10	Vancouver	NHL	82	35	32	67	121	4	5	3	209	16.7	34	34	41.2	17:52	12	3	3	6	22	0	0	0	18:51
2010-11	Vancouver	NHL	72	26	22	48	77	1	1	4	152	17.1	26	14	42.9	17:02	25	9	8	17	34	1	1	2	20:40
2011-12	Vancouver	NHL	80	28	24	52	90	3	2	7	198	14.1	24	20	35.0	18:28	5	1	0	1	7	0	0	0	18:50
2012-13	Vancouver	NHL	47	13	11	24	54	1	0	2	140	9.3	15	108	44.4	18:54	4	2	1	3	6	1	0	0	20:36
2013-14	Vancouver	NHL	49	5	10	15	71	2	0	0	104	4.8	-9	55	41.8	17:49	....	....	....	....	....	....	....	....	....
2014-15	Vancouver	NHL	70	18	15	33	68	4	1	3	145	12.4	0	14	42.9	15:29	3	0	2	2	21	0	0	0	14:22
2015-16	Vancouver	NHL	79	9	13	22	49	2	0	0	135	6.7	-13	22	45.5	15:10	....	....	....	....	....	....	....	....	....
2016-17	Vancouver	NHL	55	9	11	20	53	0	0	1	114	7.9	-3	6	0.0	14:58	....	....	....	....	....	....	....	....	....
	Ottawa	NHL	20	6	5	11	9	1	0	1	29	20.7	6	8	62.5	13:47	15	0	5	5	18	0	0	0	14:24
	NHL Totals		842	199	196	395	1075	19	17	29	1646	12.1		433	42.7	15:48	85	19	20	39	142	2	1	3	17:27

Signed as a free agent by **Manitoba** (AHL), October 21, 2003. Signed as a free agent by **Vancouver**, November 8, 2005. Traded to **Ottawa** by **Vancouver** for Jonathan Dahlen, February 27, 2017.

BUTLER, Chris

(BUHT-luhr, KRIHS) **ST.L.**

Defense. Shoots left. 6'1", 196 lbs. Born, St. Louis, MO, October 27, 1986. Buffalo's 4th pick, 96th overall, in 2005 NHL Draft.

Season	Club	League	GP	G	A	Pts	PIM	PP	SH	GW	S	S%	+/-	TF	F%	Min	GP	G	A	Pts	PIM	PP	SH	GW	Min
2003-04	Sioux City	USHL	55	3	6	9	37	....	....	....	....	....	....	....	....	....	7	0	1	1	6	....	....	....	....
2004-05	Sioux City	USHL	60	6	22	28	90	....	....	....	....	....	....	....	....	....	13	1	6	7	10	....	....	....	....
2005-06	U. of Denver	WCHA	35	7	15	22	28	....	....	....	....	....	....	....	....	....	....	....	....	....	....	....	....	....	....
2006-07	U. of Denver	WCHA	39	10	17	27	42	....	....	....	....	....	....	....	....	....	....	....	....	....	....	....	....	....	....
2007-08	U. of Denver	WCHA	41	3	14	17	38	....	....	....	....	....	....	....	....	....	....	....	....	....	....	....	....	....	....
2008-09	Buffalo	NHL	47	2	4	6	18	0	0	1	36	5.6	11	0	0.0	16:43	....	....	....	....	....	....	....	....	....
	Portland Pirates	AHL	27	2	10	12	14	....	....	....	....	....	....	....	....	....	4	0	0	0	0	....	....	....	....
2009-10	Buffalo	NHL	59	1	20	21	22	0	0	0	61	1.6	-15	0	0.0	20:01	....	....	....	....	....	....	....	....	....
2010-11	Buffalo	NHL	49	2	7	9	26	0	0	0	52	3.8	8	0	0.0	18:10	7	0	1	1	10	0	0	0	22:59
2011-12	Calgary	NHL	68	2	13	15	34	0	0	0	62	3.2	-9	0	0.0	21:36	....	....	....	....	....	....	....	....	....
2012-13	Karlskrona HK	Sweden-2	5	0	0	0	8	....	....	....	....	....	....	....	....	....	....	....	....	....	....	....	....	....	....
	Calgary	NHL	44	1	7	8	19	0	1	0	40	2.5	-10	0	0.0	17:02	....	....	....	....	....	....	....	....	....
2013-14	Calgary	NHL	82	2	14	16	39	0	0	1	83	2.4	-23	0	0.0	20:16	....	....	....	....	....	....	....	....	....
2014-15	St. Louis	NHL	33	3	6	9	23	0	1	0	54	5.6	8	0	0.0	17:11	....	....	....	....	....	....	....	....	....
	Chicago Wolves	AHL	14	1	8	9	6	....	....	....	....	....	....	....	....	....	....	....	....	....	....	....	....	....	....
2015-16	St. Louis	NHL	5	0	0	0	4	0	0	0	4	0.0	-1	0	0.0	11:30	....	....	....	....	....	....	....	....	....
	Chicago Wolves	AHL	46	4	14	18	39	....	....	....	....	....	....	....	....	....	....	....	....	....	....	....	....	....	....
2016-17	St. Louis	NHL	1	0	0	0	0	0	0	0	1	0.0	0	0	0.0	21:28	....	....	....	....	....	....	....	....	....
	Chicago Wolves	AHL	72	5	21	26	46	....	....	....	....	....	....	....	....	....	9	1	5	6	4	....	....	....	....
	NHL Totals		388	13	71	84	185	0	2	2	393	3.3		0	0.0	19:02	7	0	1	1	10	0	0	0	23:00

USHL First All-Star Team (2005) • WCHA All-Rookie Team (2006) • WCHA Second All-Star Team (2008) • NCAA West Second All-American Team (2008)

Traded to **Calgary** by **Buffalo** with Paul Byron for Robyn Regehr, Ales Kotalik and Calgary's 2nd round pick (Jake McCabe) in 2012 NHL Draft, June 25, 2011. Signed as a free agent by **Karlskrona** (Sweden-2), November 27, 2012. Signed as a free agent by **St. Louis**, July 16, 2014.

BYFUGLIEN, Dustin

(BUHF-lihn, DUHS-tihn) **WPG**

Defense. Shoots right. 6'5", 260 lbs. Born, Roseau, MN, March 27, 1985. Chicago's 8th pick, 245th overall, in 2003 NHL Draft.

Season	Club	League	GP	G	A	Pts	PIM	PP	SH	GW	S	S%	+/-	TF	F%	Min	GP	G	A	Pts	PIM	PP	SH	GW	Min
2001-02	Chicago Mission	MAHL	52	32	30	62	40	....	....	....	....	....	....	....	....	....	....	....	....	....	....	....	....	....	....
	Brandon	WHL	3	0	0	0	0	....	....	....	....	....	....	....	....	....	....	....	....	....	....	....	....	....	....
2002-03	Brandon	WHL	8	1	1	2	4	....	....	....	....	....	....	....	....	....	....	....	....	....	....	....	....	....	....
	Prince George	WHL	48	9	28	37	74	....	....	....	....	....	....	....	....	....	5	1	3	4	12	....	....	....	....
2003-04	Prince George	WHL	66	16	29	45	137	....	....	....	....	....	....	....	....	....	....	....	....	....	....	....	....	....	....
2004-05	Prince George	WHL	64	22	36	58	184	....	....	....	....	....	....	....	....	....	....	....	....	....	....	....	....	....	....
2005-06	Chicago	NHL	25	3	2	5	24	0	0	1	45	6.7	-6	0	0.0	17:19	....	....	....	....	....	....	....	....	....
	Norfolk Admirals	AHL	53	8	15	23	75	....	....	....	....	....	....	....	....	....	4	1	2	3	4	....	....	....	....
2006-07	Chicago	NHL	9	1	2	3	10	0	0	0	18	5.6	-2	0	0.0	17:18	....	....	....	....	....	....	....	....	....
	Norfolk Admirals	AHL	63	16	28	44	146	....	....	....	....	....	....	....	....	....	6	0	2	2	18	....	....	....	....
2007-08	Chicago	NHL	67	19	17	36	59	7	0	4	163	11.7	-7	1	0.0	17:02	....	....	....	....	....	....	....	....	....
	Rockford IceHogs	AHL	8	2	5	7	25	....	....	....	....	....	....	....	....	....	....	....	....	....	....	....	....	....	....
2008-09	Chicago	NHL	77	15	16	31	81	3	0	4	202	7.4	7	11	18.2	14:52	17	3	6	9	26	1	0	0	17:11
2009-10♦	Chicago	NHL	82	17	17	34	94	6	0	3	211	8.1	-7	2	50.0	16:25	22	11	5	16	20	5	0	5	16:16

								Regular Season									Playoffs								
Season	Club	League	GP	G	A	Pts	PIM	PP	SH	GW	S	S%	+/-	TF	F%	Min	GP	G	A	Pts	PIM	PP	SH	GW	Min
2010-11	**Atlanta**	**NHL**	**81**	**20**	**33**	**53**	**93**	**8**	**0**	**6**	**347**	**5.8**	**–2**	**0**	**0.0**	**23:18**	....	....	....	....	....	....	....	....	....
2011-12	**Winnipeg**	**NHL**	**66**	**12**	**41**	**53**	**72**	**4**	**0**	**3**	**223**	**5.4**	**–8**	**0**	**0.0**	**24:07**	....	....	....	....	....	....	....	....	....
2012-13	**Winnipeg**	**NHL**	**43**	**8**	**20**	**28**	**34**	**4**	**0**	**2**	**142**	**5.6**	**–1**	**0**	**0.0**	**24:24**	....	....	....	....	....	....	....	....	....
2013-14	**Winnipeg**	**NHL**	**78**	**20**	**36**	**56**	**86**	**8**	**0**	**1**	**256**	**7.8**	**–20**	**2**	**0.0**	**23:05**	....	....	....	....	....	....	....	....	....
2014-15	**Winnipeg**	**NHL**	**69**	**18**	**27**	**45**	**124**	**5**	**0**	**3**	**209**	**8.6**	**5**	**3**	**0.0**	**22:41**	**4**	**0**	**1**	**1**	**4**	**0**	**0**	**0**	**23:00**
2015-16	**Winnipeg**	**NHL**	**81**	**19**	**34**	**53**	**119**	**3**	**1**	**6**	**247**	**7.7**	**4**	**0**	**0.0**	**25:12**	....	....	....	....	....	....	....	....	....
2016-17	**Winnipeg**	**NHL**	**80**	**13**	**39**	**52**	**117**	**1**	**0**	**1**	**241**	**5.4**	**10**	**0**	**0.0**	**27:27**	....	....	....	....	....	....	....	....	....
	NHL Totals		**758**	**165**	**284**	**449**	**913**	**49**	**1**	**34**	**2304**	**7.2**		**19**	**15.8**	**21:34**	**43**	**14**	**12**	**26**	**50**	**6**	**0**	**5**	**17:15**

AHL Second All-Star Team (2007)

Played in NHL All-Star Game (2011, 2015, 2016)

Traded to **Atlanta** by **Chicago** with Brent Sopel, Ben Eager and Akim Aliu for Marty Reasoner, Joey Crabb, Jeremy Morin and New Jersey's 1st (previously acquired, Chicago selected Kevin Hayes) and 2nd (previously acquired, Chicago selected Justin Holl) round picks in 2010 NHL Draft, June 24, 2010. • Transferred to **Winnipeg** after **Atlanta** franchise relocated, June 21, 2011.

BYRON, Paul (BIGH-ruhn, PAWL) MTL

Center. Shoots left. 5'9", 160 lbs. Born, Ottawa, ON, April 27, 1989. Buffalo's 6th pick, 179th overall, in 2007 NHL Draft.

Season	Club	League	GP	G	A	Pts	PIM	PP	SH	GW	S	S%	+/-	TF	F%	Min	GP	G	A	Pts	PIM	PP	SH	GW	Min
2005-06	Ottawa West	ON-Jr.B	33	20	23	43	33	....	....	....	....	....	....	....	....	....	7	3	8	11	4	....	....	....	....
2006-07	Gatineau	QMJHL	68	21	23	44	46	....	....	....	....	....	....	....	....	....	5	5	1	6	2	....	....	....	....
2007-08	Gatineau	QMJHL	52	37	31	68	25	....	....	....	....	....	....	....	....	....	19	*21	11	32	12	....	....	....	....
2008-09	Gatineau	QMJHL	64	33	66	99	32	....	....	....	....	....	....	....	....	....	10	2	14	16	4	....	....	....	....
2009-10	Portland Pirates	AHL	57	14	19	33	59	....	....	....	....	....	....	....	....	....	4	0	0	0	0	....	....	....	....
2010-11	**Buffalo**	**NHL**	**8**	**1**	**1**	**2**	**2**	**0**	**0**	**0**	**5**	**20.0**	**0**	**71**	**40.9**	**10:57**	....	....	....	....	....	....	....	....	....
	Portland Pirates	AHL	67	26	27	53	52	....	....	....	....	....	....	....	....	....	12	2	5	7	6	....	....	....	....
2011-12	**Calgary**	**NHL**	**22**	**3**	**2**	**5**	**2**	**0**	**0**	**1**	**13**	**23.1**	**3**	**22**	**36.4**	**10:14**	....	....	....	....	....	....	....	....	....
	Abbotsford Heat	AHL	39	7	14	21	40	....	....	....	....	....	....	....	....	....	8	1	3	4	2	....	....	....	....
2012-13	**Calgary**	**NHL**	**4**	**0**	**1**	**1**	**2**	**0**	**0**	**0**	**1**	**0.0**	**–2**	**17**	**41.2**	**10:27**	....	....	....	....	....	....	....	....	....
	Abbotsford Heat	AHL	38	6	9	15	38	....	....	....	....	....	....	....	....	....	....	....	....	....	....	....	....	....	....
2013-14	**Calgary**	**NHL**	**47**	**7**	**14**	**21**	**27**	**2**	**1**	**1**	**46**	**15.2**	**6**	**32**	**21.9**	**14:27**	....	....	....	....	....	....	....	....	....
	Abbotsford Heat	AHL	23	5	13	18	4	....	....	....	....	....	....	....	....	....	....	....	....	....	....	....	....	....	....
2014-15	**Calgary**	**NHL**	**57**	**6**	**13**	**19**	**8**	**1**	**0**	**0**	**62**	**9.7**	**–2**	**97**	**35.1**	**14:28**	....	....	....	....	....	....	....	....	....
2015-16	**Montreal**	**NHL**	**62**	**11**	**7**	**18**	**11**	**0**	**3**	**2**	**50**	**22.0**	**–9**	**5**	**60.0**	**13:46**	....	....	....	....	....	....	....	....	....
2016-17	**Montreal**	**NHL**	**81**	**22**	**21**	**43**	**29**	**0**	**1**	**6**	**96**	**22.9**	**21**	**15**	**66.7**	**15:04**	**6**	**1**	**0**	**1**	**0**	**0**	**0**	**0**	**16:48**
	NHL Totals		**281**	**50**	**59**	**109**	**81**	**3**	**5**	**10**	**273**	**18.3**		**259**	**37.8**	**13:59**	**6**	**1**	**0**	**1**	**0**	**0**	**0**	**0**	**16:48**

QMJHL Second All-Star Team (2009)

Traded to **Calgary** by **Buffalo** with Chris Butler for Robyn Regehr, Ales Kotalik and Calgary's 2nd round pick (Jake McCabe) in 2012 NHL Draft, June 25, 2011. Claimed on waivers by **Montreal** from **Calgary**, October 6, 2015.

CAGGIULA, Drake (CA-zhoo-lah, DRAYK) EDM

Left wing. Shoots left. 5'10", 185 lbs. Born, Pickering, ON, June 20, 1994.

Season	Club	League	GP	G	A	Pts	PIM	PP	SH	GW	S	S%	+/-	TF	F%	Min	GP	G	A	Pts	PIM	PP	SH	GW	Min
2009-10	Ajax-Pickering	Minor-ON	66	56	39	95	140	....	....	....	....	....	....	....	....	....	....	....	....	....	....	....	....	....	....
2010-11	Stouffville Spirit	ON-Jr.A	48	22	23	45	35	....	....	....	....	....	....	....	....	....	8	2	6	8	4	....	....	....	....
2011-12	Des Moines	USHL	4	1	1	2	8	....	....	....	....	....	....	....	....	....	....	....	....	....	....	....	....	....	....
	Stouffville Spirit	ON-Jr.A	25	10	24	34	36	....	....	....	....	....	....	....	....	....	23	17	20	37	38	....	....	....	....
2012-13	North Dakota	WCHA	39	8	8	16	31	....	....	....	....	....	....	....	....	....	....	....	....	....	....	....	....	....	....
2013-14	North Dakota	NCHC	42	11	13	24	52	....	....	....	....	....	....	....	....	....	....	....	....	....	....	....	....	....	....
2014-15	North Dakota	NCHC	42	18	18	36	30	....	....	....	....	....	....	....	....	....	....	....	....	....	....	....	....	....	....
2015-16	North Dakota	NCHC	39	25	26	51	60	....	....	....	....	....	....	....	....	....	....	....	....	....	....	....	....	....	....
2016-17	**Edmonton**	**NHL**	**60**	**7**	**11**	**18**	**16**	**2**	**0**	**2**	**93**	**7.5**	**3**	**284**	**41.2**	**13:14**	**13**	**3**	**0**	**3**	**25**	**0**	**0**	**0**	**15:23**
	NHL Totals		**60**	**7**	**11**	**18**	**16**	**2**	**0**	**2**	**93**	**7.5**		**284**	**41.2**	**13:14**	**13**	**3**	**0**	**3**	**25**	**0**	**0**	**0**	**15:23**

NCHC Second All-Star Team (2015) • NCHC First All-Star Team (2016) • NCAA West Second All-American Team (2016) • NCAA Championship All-Tournament Team (2016) • NCAA Championship Tournament MVP (2016)

Signed as a free agent by **Edmonton**, May 7, 2016.

CALLAHAN, Mitch (kal-AH-han, MIHCH) EDM

Right wing. Shoots right. 6', 196 lbs. Born, Whittier, CA, August 17, 1991. Detroit's 6th pick, 180th overall, in 2009 NHL Draft.

Season	Club	League	GP	G	A	Pts	PIM	PP	SH	GW	S	S%	+/-	TF	F%	Min	GP	G	A	Pts	PIM	PP	SH	GW	Min
2007-08	L.A. Jr. Kings	Minor-CA	52	32	37	69	62	....	....	....	....	....	....	....	....	....	....	....	....	....	....	....	....	....	....
2008-09	Kelowna Rockets	WHL	70	14	13	27	188	....	....	....	....	....	....	....	....	....	22	1	3	4	43	....	....	....	....
2009-10	Kelowna Rockets	WHL	72	20	27	47	165	....	....	....	....	....	....	....	....	....	12	2	4	6	10	....	....	....	....
2010-11	Kelowna Rockets	WHL	62	23	31	54	87	....	....	....	....	....	....	....	....	....	10	5	4	9	17	....	....	....	....
2011-12	Grand Rapids	AHL	48	6	3	9	103	....	....	....	....	....	....	....	....	....	....	....	....	....	....	....	....	....	....
2012-13	Grand Rapids	AHL	71	11	9	20	93	....	....	....	....	....	....	....	....	....	24	6	5	11	33	....	....	....	....
2013-14	**Detroit**	**NHL**	**1**	**0**	**0**	**0**	**0**	**0**	**0**	**0**	**0**	**0.0**	**0**	**0**	**0.0**	**9:01**	....	....	....	....	....	....	....	....	....
	Grand Rapids	AHL	70	26	18	44	51	....	....	....	....	....	....	....	....	....	8	1	4	5	6	....	....	....	....
2014-15	Grand Rapids	AHL	48	16	22	38	24	....	....	....	....	....	....	....	....	....	....	....	....	....	....	....	....	....	....
2015-16	Grand Rapids	AHL	62	19	13	32	94	....	....	....	....	....	....	....	....	....	9	0	2	2	9	....	....	....	....
2016-17	**Detroit**	**NHL**	**4**	**0**	**0**	**0**	**0**	**0**	**0**	**0**	**2**	**0.0**	**0**	**0**	**0.0**	**6:49**	....	....	....	....	....	....	....	....	....
	Grand Rapids	AHL	66	16	27	43	57	....	....	....	....	....	....	....	....	....	19	6	10	16	18	....	....	....	....
	NHL Totals		**5**	**0**	**0**	**0**	**0**	**0**	**0**	**0**	**2**	**0.0**		**0**	**0.0**	**7:15**	....	....	....	....	....	....	....	....	....

Signed as a free agent by **Edmonton**, July 1, 2017.

CALLAHAN, Ryan (kal-AH-han, RIGH-uhn) T.B.

Right wing. Shoots right. 5'10", 186 lbs. Born, Rochester, NY, March 21, 1985. NY Rangers' 9th pick, 127th overall, in 2004 NHL Draft.

Season	Club	League	GP	G	A	Pts	PIM	PP	SH	GW	S	S%	+/-	TF	F%	Min	GP	G	A	Pts	PIM	PP	SH	GW	Min
99-2000	Rochester	EmJHL	21	16	16	32	31	....	....	....	....	....	....	....	....	....	3	4	1	5	28	....	....	....	....
2000-01	Rochester	EmJHL	23	18	16	34	54	....	....	....	....	....	....	....	....	....	3	3	0	3	9	....	....	....	....
	Syracuse	ON-Jr.A	3	4	2	6	0	....	....	....	....	....	....	....	....	....	....	....	....	....	....	....	....	....	....
2001-02	Buffalo Lightning	ON-Jr.A	47	13	23	36	75	....	....	....	....	....	....	....	....	....	....	....	....	....	....	....	....	....	....
2002-03	Guelph Storm	OHL	59	14	17	31	47	....	....	....	....	....	....	....	....	....	11	0	3	3	2	....	....	....	....
2003-04	Guelph Storm	OHL	68	36	32	68	86	....	....	....	....	....	....	....	....	....	22	*13	8	21	20	....	....	....	....
2004-05	Guelph Storm	OHL	60	28	26	54	108	....	....	....	....	....	....	....	....	....	4	1	1	2	6	....	....	....	....
2005-06	Guelph Storm	OHL	62	52	32	84	126	....	....	....	....	....	....	....	....	....	13	7	17	24	20	....	....	....	....
2006-07	**NY Rangers**	**NHL**	**14**	**4**	**2**	**6**	**9**	**0**	**0**	**1**	**40**	**10.0**	**5**	**3**	**66.7**	**10:31**	**10**	**2**	**1**	**3**	**6**	**1**	**0**	**0**	**12:19**
	Hartford	AHL	60	35	20	55	74	....	....	....	....	....	....	....	....	....	....	....	....	....	....	....	....	....	....
2007-08	**NY Rangers**	**NHL**	**52**	**8**	**5**	**13**	**31**	**0**	**1**	**1**	**92**	**8.7**	**7**	**5**	**20.0**	**12:22**	**10**	**2**	**2**	**4**	**10**	**0**	**1**	**1**	**15:55**
	Hartford	AHL	11	7	8	15	27	....	....	....	....	....	....	....	....	....	....	....	....	....	....	....	....	....	....
2008-09	**NY Rangers**	**NHL**	**81**	**22**	**18**	**40**	**45**	**2**	**1**	**1**	**237**	**9.3**	**7**	**10**	**70.0**	**17:04**	**7**	**2**	**0**	**2**	**4**	**1**	**0**	**1**	**19:44**
2009-10	**NY Rangers**	**NHL**	**77**	**19**	**18**	**37**	**48**	**9**	**0**	**3**	**204**	**9.3**	**–12**	**35**	**48.6**	**19:24**	....	....	....	....	....	....	....	....	....
	United States	Olympics	6	0	1	1	2	....	....	....	....	....	....	....	....	....	....	....	....	....	....	....	....	....	....
2010-11	**NY Rangers**	**NHL**	**60**	**23**	**25**	**48**	**46**	**10**	**0**	**5**	**179**	**12.8**	**–7**	**17**	**11.8**	**19:54**	....	....	....	....	....	....	....	....	....
2011-12	**NY Rangers**	**NHL**	**76**	**29**	**25**	**54**	**61**	**13**	**1**	**9**	**235**	**12.3**	**–8**	**20**	**50.0**	**21:02**	**20**	**6**	**4**	**10**	**12**	**2**	**0**	**0**	**23:32**
2012-13	**NY Rangers**	**NHL**	**45**	**16**	**15**	**31**	**12**	**6**	**2**	**4**	**144**	**11.1**	**9**	**30**	**46.7**	**21:31**	**12**	**2**	**3**	**5**	**6**	**0**	**0**	**0**	**23:22**
2013-14	**NY Rangers**	**NHL**	**45**	**11**	**14**	**25**	**16**	**4**	**1**	**2**	**109**	**10.1**	**–3**	**19**	**36.8**	**17:57**	....	....	....	....	....	....	....	....	....
	United States	Olympics	6	0	1	1	0	....	....	....	....	....	....	....	....	....	....	....	....	....	....	....	....	....	....
	Tampa Bay	**NHL**	**20**	**6**	**5**	**11**	**8**	**3**	**0**	**1**	**54**	**11.1**	**4**	**13**	**46.2**	**20:13**	**4**	**0**	**0**	**0**	**0**	**0**	**0**	**0**	**20:42**
2014-15	**Tampa Bay**	**NHL**	**77**	**24**	**30**	**54**	**41**	**10**	**0**	**4**	**191**	**12.6**	**9**	**31**	**48.4**	**17:44**	**25**	**2**	**6**	**8**	**14**	**1**	**0**	**0**	**16:53**
2015-16	**Tampa Bay**	**NHL**	**73**	**10**	**18**	**28**	**45**	**2**	**0**	**1**	**156**	**6.4**	**–5**	**36**	**58.3**	**17:14**	**16**	**2**	**2**	**4**	**29**	**1**	**0**	**0**	**17:32**
2016-17	**Tampa Bay**	**NHL**	**18**	**2**	**2**	**4**	**23**	**0**	**0**	**1**	**22**	**9.1**	**–4**	**9**	**55.6**	**14:09**	....	....	....	....	....	....	....	....	....
	NHL Totals		**638**	**174**	**177**	**351**	**385**	**59**	**6**	**33**	**1663**	**10.5**		**228**	**46.9**	**18:03**	**104**	**18**	**18**	**36**	**81**	**6**	**1**	**2**	**18:49**

OHL Second All-Star Team (2006) • AHL All-Rookie Team (2007)

Traded to **Tampa Bay** by **NY Rangers** with NY Rangers' 1st round pick (later traded to NY Islanders – NY Islanders selected Joshua Ho-Sang) in 2014 NHL Draft and NY Rangers' 1st (later traded to NY Islanders – NY Islanders selected Anthony Beauvillier) and 7th (later traded to Edmonton – Edmonton selected Ziyat Paigin) round picks in 2015 NHL Draft for Martin St. Louis and Tampa Bay's 2nd round pick (later traded to Calgary – Calgary selected Oliver Kylington) in 2015 NHL Draft, March 5, 2014. • Missed majority of 2016-17 due to recurring hip injury and resulting surgery, June 21, 2016.

CALVERT, Matt

(KAL-vuhrt, MAT) **CBJ**

Left wing. Shoots left. 5'11", 188 lbs. Born, Brandon, MB, December 24, 1989. Columbus' 5th pick, 127th overall, in 2008 NHL Draft.

			Regular Season														Playoffs								
Season	Club	League	GP	G	A	Pts	PIM	PP	SH	GW	S	S%	+/-	TF	F%	Min	GP	G	A	Pts	PIM	PP	SH	GW	Min
2005-06	Brandon	MMHL	38	24	30	54	48	....	....	....	....	....	....	....	....	....	6	3	6	9	18	....	....	....	....
2006-07	Brandon	MMHL	30	28	55	83	46	....	....	....	....	....	....	....	....	....	16	5	13	18	16	....	....	....	....
	Winkler Flyers	MJHL	1	0	0	0	15	....	....	....	....	....	....	....	....	....	....	....	....	....	....	....	....	....	....
2007-08	Brandon	WHL	72	24	40	64	53	....	....	....	....	....	....	....	....	....	6	1	2	3	2	....	....	....	....
2008-09	Brandon	WHL	58	28	39	67	58	....	....	....	....	....	....	....	....	....	12	9	8	17	22	....	....	....	....
2009-10	Brandon	WHL	68	47	52	99	70	....	....	....	....	....	....	....	....	....	15	9	7	16	15	....	....	....	....
2010-11	**Columbus**	**NHL**	**42**	**11**	**9**	**20**	**12**	**3**	**0**	**1**	**50**	**22.0**	**3**	**9**	**33.3**	**11:06**	....	....	....	....	....	....	....	....	....
	Springfield	AHL	38	13	12	25	12	....	....	....	....	....	....	....	....	....	....	....	....	....	....	....	....	....	....
2011-12	**Columbus**	**NHL**	**13**	**0**	**3**	**3**	**16**	**0**	**0**	**0**	**4**	**0.0**	**–5**	**0**	**0.0**	**9:08**	....	....	....	....	....	....	....	....	....
	Springfield	AHL	56	17	19	36	52	....	....	....	....	....	....	....	....	....	....	....	....	....	....	....	....	....	....
2012-13	Springfield	AHL	34	10	11	21	39	....	....	....	....	....	....	....	....	....	....	....	....	....	....	....	....	....	....
	Columbus	**NHL**	**42**	**9**	**7**	**16**	**32**	**0**	**1**	**2**	**63**	**14.3**	**–9**	**6**	**33.3**	**14:11**	....	....	....	....	....	....	....	....	....
2013-14	**Columbus**	**NHL**	**56**	**9**	**15**	**24**	**53**	**2**	**0**	**1**	**90**	**10.0**	**–1**	**9**	**33.3**	**16:06**	**6**	**2**	**2**	**4**	**4**	**0**	**1**	**1**	**17:35**
2014-15	**Columbus**	**NHL**	**56**	**13**	**10**	**23**	**28**	**0**	**0**	**3**	**93**	**14.0**	**1**	**10**	**60.0**	**16:00**	....	....	....	....	....	....	....	....	....
2015-16	**Columbus**	**NHL**	**73**	**11**	**13**	**24**	**51**	**1**	**0**	**1**	**114**	**9.6**	**1**	**14**	**50.0**	**15:08**	....	....	....	....	....	....	....	....	....
2016-17	**Columbus**	**NHL**	**65**	**10**	**5**	**15**	**48**	**0**	**3**	**1**	**92**	**10.9**	**–4**	**16**	**12.5**	**13:21**	**4**	**1**	**1**	**2**	**4**	**0**	**0**	**0**	**14:14**
	NHL Totals		**347**	**63**	**62**	**125**	**240**	**6**	**4**	**9**	**506**	**12.5**		**64**	**35.9**	**14:16**	**10**	**3**	**3**	**6**	**8**	**0**	**1**	**1**	**16:15**

WHL East Second All-Star Team (2010)

CAMMALLERI, Michael

(kam-UH-LAIR-ee, MIGH-kuhl) **L.A.**

Left wing. Shoots left. 5'9", 185 lbs. Born, Toronto, ON, June 8, 1982. Los Angeles' 3rd pick, 49th overall, in 2001 NHL Draft.

Season	Club	League	GP	G	A	Pts	PIM	PP	SH	GW	S	S%	+/-	TF	F%	Min	GP	G	A	Pts	PIM	PP	SH	GW	Min
1997-98	Bramalea Blues	ON-Jr.A	46	36	52	88	30	....	....	....	....	....	....	....	....	....	....	....	....	....	....	....	....	....	....
1998-99	Bramalea Blues	ON-Jr.A	41	31	72	103	51	....	....	....	....	....	....	....	....	....	....	....	....	....	....	....	....	....	....
99-2000	U. of Michigan	CCHA	39	13	13	26	32	....	....	....	....	....	....	....	....	....	....	....	....	....	....	....	....	....	....
2000-01	U. of Michigan	CCHA	42	*29	32	61	24	....	....	....	....	....	....	....	....	....	....	....	....	....	....	....	....	....	....
2001-02	U. of Michigan	CCHA	29	23	21	44	28	....	....	....	....	....	....	....	....	....	....	....	....	....	....	....	....	....	....
2002-03	**Los Angeles**	**NHL**	**28**	**5**	**3**	**8**	**22**	**2**	**0**	**2**	**40**	**12.5**	**–4**	**253**	**51.4**	**14:05**	....	....	....	....	....	....	....	....	....
	Manchester	AHL	13	5	15	20	12	....	....	....	....	....	....	....	....	....	....	....	....	....	....	....	....	....	....
2003-04	**Los Angeles**	**NHL**	**31**	**9**	**6**	**15**	**20**	**2**	**0**	**2**	**53**	**17.0**	**1**	**280**	**53.6**	**13:18**	....	....	....	....	....	....	....	....	....
	Manchester	AHL	41	20	19	39	28	....	....	....	....	....	....	....	....	....	1	0	1	1	0	....	....	....	....
2004-05	Manchester	AHL	79	*46	63	109	60	....	....	....	....	....	....	....	....	....	6	1	5	6	0	....	....	....	....
2005-06	**Los Angeles**	**NHL**	**80**	**26**	**29**	**55**	**50**	**15**	**0**	**4**	**206**	**12.6**	**–14**	**578**	**53.5**	**16:45**	....	....	....	....	....	....	....	....	....
2006-07	**Los Angeles**	**NHL**	**81**	**34**	**46**	**80**	**48**	**16**	**0**	**5**	**299**	**11.4**	**5**	**301**	**54.2**	**18:03**	....	....	....	....	....	....	....	....	....
2007-08	**Los Angeles**	**NHL**	**63**	**19**	**28**	**47**	**30**	**10**	**0**	**1**	**210**	**9.0**	**–16**	**380**	**54.2**	**18:35**	....	....	....	....	....	....	....	....	....
2008-09	**Calgary**	**NHL**	**81**	**39**	**43**	**82**	**44**	**19**	**0**	**6**	**255**	**15.3**	**–2**	**368**	**60.3**	**17:33**	**6**	**1**	**2**	**3**	**2**	**0**	**0**	**0**	**18:02**
2009-10	**Montreal**	**NHL**	**65**	**26**	**24**	**50**	**16**	**4**	**0**	**4**	**218**	**11.9**	**7**	**51**	**51.0**	**19:31**	**19**	***13**	**6**	**19**	**6**	**4**	**0**	**3**	**20:40**
2010-11	**Montreal**	**NHL**	**67**	**19**	**28**	**47**	**33**	**7**	**0**	**2**	**193**	**9.8**	**2**	**74**	**44.6**	**18:29**	**7**	**3**	**7**	**10**	**0**	**1**	**0**	**0**	**23:35**
2011-12	**Montreal**	**NHL**	**38**	**9**	**13**	**22**	**10**	**1**	**0**	**2**	**111**	**8.1**	**–6**	**29**	**34.5**	**17:49**	....	....	....	....	....	....	....	....	....
	Calgary	**NHL**	**28**	**11**	**8**	**19**	**16**	**2**	**0**	**2**	**64**	**17.2**	**–4**	**199**	**47.2**	**18:30**	....	....	....	....	....	....	....	....	....
2012-13	**Calgary**	**NHL**	**44**	**13**	**19**	**32**	**25**	**5**	**0**	**3**	**102**	**12.7**	**–15**	**496**	**51.0**	**18:03**	....	....	....	....	....	....	....	....	....
2013-14	**Calgary**	**NHL**	**63**	**26**	**19**	**45**	**26**	**6**	**0**	**8**	**191**	**13.6**	**–13**	**191**	**46.1**	**19:51**	....	....	....	....	....	....	....	....	....
2014-15	**New Jersey**	**NHL**	**68**	**27**	**15**	**42**	**28**	**9**	**2**	**8**	**156**	**17.3**	**2**	**282**	**42.2**	**18:20**	....	....	....	....	....	....	....	....	....
2015-16	**New Jersey**	**NHL**	**42**	**14**	**24**	**38**	**18**	**3**	**0**	**1**	**101**	**13.9**	**15**	**14**	**50.0**	**19:17**	....	....	....	....	....	....	....	....	....
2016-17	**New Jersey**	**NHL**	**61**	**10**	**21**	**31**	**21**	**1**	**0**	**3**	**142**	**7.0**	**–9**	**28**	**60.7**	**17:21**	....	....	....	....	....	....	....	....	....
	NHL Totals		**840**	**287**	**326**	**613**	**407**	**102**	**2**	**53**	**2341**	**12.3**		**3524**	**51.8**	**17:56**	**32**	**17**	**15**	**32**	**8**	**5**	**0**	**3**	**20:49**

CCHA First All-Star Team (2001) • NCAA West Second All-American Team (2001) • CCHA Second All-Star Team (2002) • NCAA West First All-American Team (2002) • AHL Second All-Star Team (2005) • Willie Marshall Award (AHL - Top Goal-scorer) (2005)

• Missed majority of 2002-03 due to head injury vs. San Jose, January 28, 2003. Traded to **Calgary** by **Los Angeles** with Calgary's 2nd round pick (previously acquired, Calgary selected Mitch Wahl) in 2008 NHL Draft for Calgary's 1st round pick (later traded to Anaheim – Anaheim selected Jake Gardiner) in 2008 NHL Draft and Calgary's 2nd round pick (later traded to Carolina – Carolina selected Brian Dumoulin) in 2009 NHL Draft, June 20, 2008. Signed as a free agent by **Montreal**, July 1, 2009. Traded to **Calgary** by **Montreal** with Karri Ramo and Montreal's 5th round pick (Ryan Culkin) in 2012 NHL Draft for Rene Bourque, Patrick Holland and Calgary's 2nd round pick (Zachary Fucale) in 2013 NHL Draft, January 12, 2012. Signed as a free agent by **New Jersey**, July 1, 2014. Signed as a free agent by **Los Angeles**, July 1, 2017.

CAMPBELL, Andrew

(KAM-buhl, AN-droo) **ARI**

Defense. Shoots left. 6'4", 206 lbs. Born, Caledonia, ON, February 4, 1988. Los Angeles' 5th pick, 74th overall, in 2008 NHL Draft.

Season	Club	League	GP	G	A	Pts	PIM	PP	SH	GW	S	S%	+/-	TF	F%	Min	GP	G	A	Pts	PIM	PP	SH	GW	Min
2005-06	Sault Ste. Marie	OHL	31	1	3	4	23	....	....	....	....	....	....	....	....	....	3	0	0	0	4	....	....	....	....
2006-07	Sault Ste. Marie	OHL	63	4	14	18	75	....	....	....	....	....	....	....	....	....	13	0	1	1	6	....	....	....	....
2007-08	Sault Ste. Marie	OHL	68	13	22	35	64	....	....	....	....	....	....	....	....	....	14	2	3	5	13	....	....	....	....
2008-09	Manchester	AHL	72	3	5	8	72	....	....	....	....	....	....	....	....	....	....	....	....	....	....	....	....	....	....
2009-10	Manchester	AHL	74	2	9	11	68	....	....	....	....	....	....	....	....	....	16	1	4	5	6	....	....	....	....
2010-11	Manchester	AHL	76	1	11	12	68	....	....	....	....	....	....	....	....	....	7	0	0	0	0	....	....	....	....
2011-12	Manchester	AHL	76	2	17	19	54	....	....	....	....	....	....	....	....	....	4	0	0	0	9	....	....	....	....
2012-13	Manchester	AHL	47	2	9	11	40	....	....	....	....	....	....	....	....	....	4	0	0	0	2	....	....	....	....
2013-14	**Los Angeles**	**NHL**	**3**	**0**	**0**	**0**	**0**	**0**	**0**	**0**	**4**	**0.0**	**0**	**0**	**0.0**	**12:42**	....	....	....	....	....	....	....	....	....
	Manchester	AHL	69	3	13	16	58	....	....	....	....	....	....	....	....	....	4	1	0	1	0	....	....	....	....
2014-15	**Arizona**	**NHL**	**33**	**0**	**1**	**1**	**10**	**0**	**0**	**0**	**28**	**0.0**	**–13**	**0**	**0.0**	**17:32**	....	....	....	....	....	....	....	....	....
	Portland Pirates	AHL	40	3	9	12	30	....	....	....	....	....	....	....	....	....	....	....	....	....	....	....	....	....	....
2015-16	**Toronto**	**NHL**	**6**	**0**	**1**	**1**	**2**	**0**	**0**	**0**	**1**	**0.0**	**0**	**0**	**0.0**	**11:35**	....	....	....	....	....	....	....	....	....
	Toronto Marlies	AHL	66	9	15	24	72	....	....	....	....	....	....	....	....	....	9	0	2	2	4	....	....	....	....
2016-17	Toronto Marlies	AHL	75	6	16	22	62	....	....	....	....	....	....	....	....	....	11	0	1	1	8	....	....	....	....
	NHL Totals		**42**	**0**	**2**	**2**	**12**	**0**	**0**	**0**	**33**	**0.0**		**0**	**0.0**	**16:20**	....	....	....	....	....	....	....	....	....

Signed as a free agent by **Arizona**, July 1, 2014. Signed as a free agent by **Toronto** (AHL), July 3, 2015. Signed as a free agent by **Toronto**, September 29, 2015. Signed as a free agent by **Arizona**, July 1, 2017.

CAMPBELL, Brian

(KAM-buhl, BRIGH-uhn)

Defense. Shoots left. 5'10", 192 lbs. Born, Strathroy, ON, May 23, 1979. Buffalo's 7th pick, 156th overall, in 1997 NHL Draft.

Season	Club	League	GP	G	A	Pts	PIM	PP	SH	GW	S	S%	+/-	TF	F%	Min	GP	G	A	Pts	PIM	PP	SH	GW	Min
1994-95	Petrolia Oil Barons	ON-Jr.B	49	11	27	38	43	....	....	....	....	....	....	....	....	....	....	....	....	....	....	....	....	....	....
1995-96	Ottawa 67's	OHL	66	5	22	27	23	....	....	....	....	....	....	....	....	....	4	0	1	1	2	....	....	....	....
1996-97	Ottawa 67's	OHL	66	7	36	43	12	....	....	....	....	....	....	....	....	....	24	2	11	13	8	....	....	....	....
1997-98	Ottawa 67's	OHL	66	14	39	53	31	....	....	....	....	....	....	....	....	....	13	1	14	15	0	....	....	....	....
1998-99	Ottawa 67's	OHL	62	12	75	87	27	....	....	....	....	....	....	....	....	....	9	2	10	12	6	....	....	....	....
	Rochester	AHL	....	....	....	....	....	....	....	....	....	....	....	....	....	....	2	0	0	0	0	....	....	....	....
99-2000	**Buffalo**	**NHL**	**12**	**1**	**4**	**5**	**4**	**0**	**0**	**0**	**10**	**10.0**	**–2**	**0**	**0.0**	**15:48**	....	....	....	....	....	....	....	....	....
	Rochester	AHL	67	2	24	26	22	....	....	....	....	....	....	....	....	....	21	0	3	3	0	....	....	....	....
2000-01	**Buffalo**	**NHL**	**8**	**0**	**0**	**0**	**2**	**0**	**0**	**0**	**7**	**0.0**	**–2**	**0**	**0.0**	**15:40**	....	....	....	....	....	....	....	....	....
	Rochester	AHL	65	7	25	32	24	....	....	....	....	....	....	....	....	....	4	0	1	1	0	....	....	....	....
2001-02	**Buffalo**	**NHL**	**29**	**3**	**3**	**6**	**12**	**0**	**0**	**0**	**30**	**10.0**	**0**	**1**	**0.0**	**15:18**	....	....	....	....	....	....	....	....	....
	Rochester	AHL	45	2	35	37	13	....	....	....	....	....	....	....	....	....	....	....	....	....	....	....	....	....	....
2002-03	**Buffalo**	**NHL**	**65**	**2**	**17**	**19**	**20**	**0**	**0**	**1**	**90**	**2.2**	**–8**	**1**	**0.0**	**18:40**	....	....	....	....	....	....	....	....	....
2003-04	**Buffalo**	**NHL**	**53**	**3**	**8**	**11**	**12**	**0**	**0**	**0**	**45**	**6.7**	**–8**	**0**	**0.0**	**16:02**	....	....	....	....	....	....	....	....	....
2004-05	Jokerit Helsinki	Finland	44	12	13	25	12	....	....	....	....	....	....	....	....	....	12	3	4	7	6	....	....	....	....
2005-06	**Buffalo**	**NHL**	**79**	**12**	**32**	**44**	**16**	**5**	**0**	**5**	**105**	**11.4**	**–14**	**0**	**0.0**	**17:43**	**18**	**0**	**6**	**6**	**12**	**0**	**0**	**0**	**20:29**
2006-07	**Buffalo**	**NHL**	**82**	**6**	**42**	**48**	**35**	**1**	**0**	**1**	**92**	**6.5**	**28**	**0**	**0.0**	**21:53**	**16**	**3**	**4**	**7**	**14**	**2**	**0**	**0**	**21:39**
2007-08	**Buffalo**	**NHL**	**63**	**5**	**38**	**43**	**12**	**3**	**0**	**0**	**102**	**4.9**	**–1**	**0**	**0.0**	**25:06**	....	....	....	....	....	....	....	....	....
	San Jose	**NHL**	**20**	**3**	**16**	**19**	**8**	**2**	**0**	**0**	**40**	**7.5**	**9**	**0**	**0.0**	**25:07**	**13**	**1**	**6**	**7**	**4**	**0**	**0**	**0**	**29:19**
2008-09	**Chicago**	**NHL**	**82**	**7**	**45**	**52**	**22**	**4**	**0**	**1**	**108**	**6.5**	**5**	**0**	**0.0**	**22:34**	**17**	**2**	**8**	**10**	**0**	**2**	**0**	**0**	**20:29**
2009-10 •	**Chicago**	**NHL**	**68**	**7**	**31**	**38**	**18**	**3**	**0**	**2**	**131**	**5.3**	**18**	**0**	**0.0**	**23:13**	**19**	**1**	**4**	**5**	**2**	**0**	**0**	**0**	**19:35**
2010-11	**Chicago**	**NHL**	**65**	**5**	**22**	**27**	**6**	**2**	**0**	**1**	**84**	**6.0**	**28**	**0**	**0.0**	**22:59**	**7**	**1**	**2**	**3**	**6**	**0**	**0**	**0**	**26:26**
2011-12	**Florida**	**NHL**	**82**	**4**	**49**	**53**	**6**	**1**	**0**	**0**	**131**	**3.1**	**–9**	**0**	**0.0**	**26:54**	**7**	**1**	**4**	**5**	**2**	**1**	**0**	**1**	**28:00**
2012-13	**Florida**	**NHL**	**48**	**8**	**19**	**27**	**12**	**6**	**0**	**2**	**70**	**11.4**	**–22**	**0**	**0.0**	**26:25**	....	....	....	....	....	....	....	....	....
2013-14	**Florida**	**NHL**	**82**	**7**	**30**	**37**	**20**	**2**	**0**	**2**	**116**	**6.0**	**–6**	**1**	**0.0**	**26:57**	....	....	....	....	....	....	....	....	....
2014-15	**Florida**	**NHL**	**82**	**3**	**24**	**27**	**22**	**1**	**0**	**0**	**118**	**2.5**	**4**	**0**	**0.0**	**23:13**	....	....	....	....	....	....	....	....	....

Season	Club	League	GP	G	A	Pts	PIM	PP	SH	GW	S	S%	+/-	TF	F%	Min	GP	G	A	Pts	PIM	PP	SH	GW	Min
												Regular Season									**Playoffs**				
2015-16	Florida	NHL	82	6	25	31	26	0	1	1	99	6.1	31	0	0.0	22:17	6	0	1	1	0	0	0	0	25:39
2016-17	Chicago	NHL	80	5	12	17	24	2	0	1	74	6.8	12	0	0.0	18:26	4	0	0	0	0	0	0	0	16:10
	NHL Totals		1082	87	417	504	277	32	1	17	1452	6.0		3	0.0	22:06	107	9	35	44	40	5	0	1	22:35

OHL First All-Star Team (1999) • OHL MVP (1999) • Canadian Major Junior First All-Star Team (1999) • Canadian Major Junior Player of the Year (1999) • NHL Second All-Star Team (2008) • Lady Byng Trophy (2012)

Played in NHL All-Star Game (2007, 2008, 2009, 2012)

Signed as a free agent by **Jokerit Helsinki** (Finland), October 19, 2004. Traded to **San Jose** by **Buffalo** with Buffalo's 7th round pick (Drew Daniels) in 2008 NHL Draft for Steve Bernier and San Jose's 1st round pick (Tyler Ennis) in 2008 NHL Draft, February 26, 2008. Signed as a free agent by **Chicago**, July 1, 2008. Traded to **Florida** by **Chicago** for Rostislav Olesz, June 25, 2011. Signed as a free agent by **Chicago**, July 1, 2016.

CAMPER, Carter
(KAM-puhr, KAR-tuhr)

Right wing. Shoots right. 5'9", 175 lbs.   Born, Rocky River, OH, July 6, 1988.

Season	Club	League	GP	G	A	Pts	PIM	PP	SH	GW	S	S%	+/-	TF	F%	Min	GP	G	A	Pts	PIM	PP	SH	GW	Min
2004-05	Cleveland Barons	NAHL	54	14	23	37	12										14	6	15	21	4				
2005-06	Cleveland Barons	NAHL	57	31	51	82	26										4	1	1	2	2				
2006-07	Lincoln Stars	USHL	56	23	48	71	40																		
2007-08	Miami U.	CCHA	33	15	26	41	20																		
2008-09	Miami U.	CCHA	40	20	22	42	24																		
2009-10	Miami U.	CCHA	44	15	28	43	14																		
2010-11	Miami U.	CCHA	39	19	38	57	27																		
	Providence Bruins	AHL	3	1	1	2	2																		
2011-12	**Boston**	**NHL**	3	1	0	1	0	0	0	0	1	100.0	1	14	42.9	6:42									
	Providence Bruins	AHL	69	18	30	48	18																		
2012-13	Providence Bruins	AHL	57	10	37	47	6										12	8	5	13	0				
2013-14	Providence Bruins	AHL	41	8	23	31	16																		
	Springfield	AHL	19	4	16	20	8										5	1	4	5	0				
2014-15	Binghamton	AHL	75	15	37	52	16																		
2015-16	Hershey Bears	AHL	64	9	25	34	16										21	6	11	17	2				
2016-17	Albany Devils	AHL	47	6	29	35	18										4	2	0	2	2				
	NHL Totals		3	1	0	1	0	0	0	0	1	100.0		14	42.9	6:42									

CCHA All-Rookie Team (2008) • CCHA First All-Star Team (2009, 2011) • NCAA West Second All-American Team (2009, 2011)

Signed as a free agent by **Boston**, April 7, 2011. Traded to **Columbus** by **Boston** for Blake Parlett, February 7, 2014. Signed as a free agent by **Ottawa**, July 2, 2014. Signed as a free agent by **Washington**, July 1, 2015. Signed as a free agent by **New Jersey**, July 1, 2016.

CANNONE, Pat
(ka-NOHN, PAT)   **MIN**

Right wing. Shoots right. 5'10", 190 lbs.   Born, Bayport, NY, August 9, 1986.

Season	Club	League	GP	G	A	Pts	PIM	PP	SH	GW	S	S%	+/-	TF	F%	Min	GP	G	A	Pts	PIM	PP	SH	GW	Min
2004-05	N.E. Jr. Falcons	EJHL	49	26	28	54	50																		
2005-06	N.E. Jr. Falcons	EJHL	45	22	31	53	52										3	1	3	4	2				
2006-07	Cedar Rapids	USHL	59	18	37	55	46										6	1	7	8	6				
2007-08	Miami U.	CCHA	42	6	24	30	20																		
2008-09	Miami U.	CCHA	41	11	24	35	16																		
2009-10	Miami U.	CCHA	44	14	17	31	22																		
2010-11	Miami U.	CCHA	39	14	23	37	25																		
	Binghamton	AHL	2	1	1	2	2																		
2011-12	Binghamton	AHL	76	19	24	43	32										3	0	0	0	4				
2012-13	Binghamton	AHL	74	10	15	25	41										9	0	2	2	4				
2013-14	Chicago Wolves	AHL	59	16	18	34	16										5	0	6	6	0				
2014-15	Chicago Wolves	AHL	64	14	33	47	18																		
2015-16	Chicago Wolves	AHL	73	20	32	52	38																		
2016-17	**Minnesota**	**NHL**	3	0	0	0	0	0	0	0	2	0.0	0	21	52.4	7:53									
	Iowa Wild	AHL	73	9	29	38	26																		
	NHL Totals		3	0	0	0	0	0	0	0	2	0.0		21	52.4	7:53									

Signed as a free agent by **Ottawa**, April 8, 2011. Traded to **St. Louis** by **Ottawa** for future considerations, July 8, 2013. Signed as a free agent by **Minnesota**, July 1, 2016.

CAREY, Matt
(KAIR-ee, MAT)

Left wing. Shoots left. 6', 189 lbs.   Born, Hamilton, ON, February 28, 1992.

Season	Club	League	GP	G	A	Pts	PIM	PP	SH	GW	S	S%	+/-	TF	F%	Min	GP	G	A	Pts	PIM	PP	SH	GW	Min
2007-08	Ham. Bulldogs	Minor-ON	48	13	14	27	...										11	8	9	17	22				
2008-09	Hamilton Reps	Minor-ON	36	16	28	44	48																		
2009-10	Burlington	ON-Jr.A	5	0	0	0	0										10	1	2	3	20				
	Hamilton	ON-Jr.A	20	7	6	13	20										7	3	2	5	10				
2010-11	Hamilton	ON-Jr.A	45	25	59	84	40																		
2011-12	Hamilton	ON-Jr.A	23	17	21	38	8										10	9	5	14	18				
	Tor. Canadiens	ON-Jr.A	25	16	15	31	24																		
2012-13	St. Lawrence	ECAC	DID NOT PLAY – FRESHMAN																						
2013-14	St. Lawrence	ECAC	38	18	19	37	47																		
	Chicago	**NHL**	2	1	0	1	2	0	0	0	1	100.0	-1	21	47.6	9:38									
2014-15	Rockford IceHogs	AHL	67	10	11	21	43										2	0	0	0	0				
2015-16	Iowa Wild	AHL	21	2	2	4	14																		
	Quad City	ECHL	49	25	22	47	46										3	2	2	4	2				
2016-17	Hartford	AHL	73	21	8	29	82																		
	NHL Totals		2	1	0	1	2	0	0	0	1	100.0		21	47.6	9:38									

ECAC All-Rookie Team (2014)

Signed as a free agent by **Chicago**, March 20, 2014. Signed as a free agent by **Iowa** (AHL), July 13, 2015. • Re-assigned to **Quad City** (ECHL) by **Iowa** (AHL), December 3, 2015. Signed as a free agent by **Hartford** (AHL), September 7, 2016.

CAREY, Paul
(KAIR-ee, PAWL)   **NYR**

Center. Shoots left. 6'1", 200 lbs.   Born, Boston, MA, September 24, 1988. Colorado's 7th pick, 135th overall, in 2007 NHL Draft.

Season	Club	League	GP	G	A	Pts	PIM	PP	SH	GW	S	S%	+/-	TF	F%	Min	GP	G	A	Pts	PIM	PP	SH	GW	Min
2005-06	Salisbury School	High-CT	27	14	11	25	18																		
2006-07	Salisbury School	High-CT	24	16	11	27	16																		
2007-08	Indiana Ice	USHL	60	34	32	66	32										4	1	2	3	2				
2008-09	Boston College	H-East	24	5	4	9	8																		
2009-10	Boston College	H-East	41	9	12	21	29																		
2010-11	Boston College	H-East	38	13	13	26	18																		
2011-12	Boston College	H-East	44	18	12	30	30																		
	Lake Erie	AHL	2	0	0	0	2																		
2012-13	Lake Erie	AHL	72	19	22	41	29																		
2013-14	**Colorado**	**NHL**	12	0	0	0	0	0	0	0	6	0.0	2	0	0.0	6:26	3	0	0	0	0	0	0	0	3:46
	Lake Erie	AHL	54	8	13	21	42																		
2014-15	**Colorado**	**NHL**	10	0	1	1	0	0	0	0	5	0.0	0	3	0.0	7:53									
	Lake Erie	AHL	43	13	14	27	16										4	1	0	1	4				
	Providence Bruins	AHL	17	2	5	7	10																		
2015-16	**Washington**	**NHL**	4	1	0	1	0	0	0	0	5	20.0	0	0	0.0	9:58									
	Hershey Bears	AHL	44	13	18	31	18																		
2016-17	**Washington**	**NHL**	6	0	0	0	0	0	0	0	8	0.0	-2	0	0.0	10:29	1	0	0	0	0	0	0	0	5:40
	Hershey Bears	AHL	55	24	31	55	29										4	1	1	2	0				
	NHL Totals		32	1	1	2	0	0	0	0	24	4.2		3	0.0	8:05	4	0	0	0	0	0	0	0	4:15

USHL All-Rookie Team (2008) • USHL Second All-Star Team (2008) • NCAA Championship All-Tournament Team (2012)

Traded to **Boston** by **Colorado** with Max Talbot for Jordan Caron and Boston's 6th round pick (later traded back to Boston – Boston selected Oskar Steen) in 2016 NHL Draft, March 2, 2015. Signed as a free agent by **Washington**, July 8, 2015. Signed as a free agent by **NY Rangers**, July 1, 2017.

CARLE, Matt
(KAHRL, MAT)

Defense. Shoots left. 6', 197 lbs. Born, Anchorage, AK, September 25, 1984. San Jose's 4th pick, 47th overall, in 2003 NHL Draft.

			Regular Season														Playoffs								
Season	Club	League	GP	G	A	Pts	PIM	PP	SH	GW	S	S%	+/-	TF	F%	Min	GP	G	A	Pts	PIM	PP	SH	GW	Min
99-2000	Alaska All-Stars	AASHA	42	14	28	42	....	....	....	....	....	....	....	....	....	....	....	....	....	....	....	....	....	....	....
2000-01	USAHNTDP	U-17	13	0	1	1	....	....	....	....	....	....	....	....	....	....	....	....	....	....	....	....	....	....	....
	USAHNTDP	NAHL	55	1	4	5	33	....	....	....	....	....	....	....	....	....	....	....	....	....	....	....	....	....	....
2001-02	USAHNTDP	U-18	45	3	13	16	30	....	....	....	....	....	....	....	....	....	....	....	....	....	....	....	....	....	....
	USAHNTDP	NAHL	7	1	2	3	0	....	....	....	....	....	....	....	....	....	....	....	....	....	....	....	....	....	....
	USAHNTDP	USHL	12	0	0	0	21	....	....	....	....	....	....	....	....	....	....	....	....	....	....	....	....	....	....
2002-03	River City Lancers	USHL	59	12	30	42	98	....	....	....	....	....	....	....	....	....	11	2	2	4	20	....	....	....	....
2003-04	U. of Denver	WCHA	30	5	20	25	33	....	....	....	....	....	....	....	....	....	....	....	....	....	....	....	....	....	....
2004-05	U. of Denver	WCHA	43	13	31	44	68	....	....	....	....	....	....	....	....	....	....	....	....	....	....	....	....	....	....
2005-06	U. of Denver	WCHA	39	11	*42	53	58	....	....	....	....	....	....	....	....	....	....	....	....	....	....	....	....	....	....
	San Jose	NHL	12	3	3	6	14	2	0	1	11	27.3	-2	0	0.0	16:07	11	0	3	3	4	0	0	0	15:17
2006-07	San Jose	NHL	77	11	31	42	30	8	0	1	111	9.9	9	1	0.0	18:08	11	2	3	5	0	1	0	1	14:51
	Worcester Sharks	AHL	3	0	2	2	0	....	....	....	....	....	....	....	....	....	....	....	....	....	....	....	....	....	....
2007-08	San Jose	NHL	62	2	13	15	26	2	0	1	63	3.2	-8	1	100.0	16:33	11	0	1	1	4	0	0	0	13:56
2008-09	Tampa Bay	NHL	12	1	1	2	6	0	0	0	13	7.7	1	0	0.0	21:58	....	....	....	....	....	....	....	....	....
	Philadelphia	NHL	64	4	20	24	16	0	0	2	72	5.6	2	0	0.0	21:17	6	0	3	3	4	0	0	0	22:15
2009-10	Philadelphia	NHL	80	6	29	35	16	2	0	1	137	4.4	19	0	0.0	23:23	23	1	12	13	8	0	0	0	25:54
2010-11	Philadelphia	NHL	82	1	39	40	23	0	0	0	117	0.9	30	0	0.0	21:59	11	0	4	4	2	0	0	0	23:24
2011-12	Philadelphia	NHL	82	4	34	38	36	3	0	0	132	3.0	4	0	0.0	23:01	11	2	4	6	6	1	0	0	25:19
2012-13	Tampa Bay	NHL	48	5	17	22	4	2	0	0	66	7.6	1	0	0.0	23:45	....	....	....	....	....	....	....	....	....
2013-14	Tampa Bay	NHL	82	2	29	31	28	1	0	0	115	1.7	11	1	0.0	22:11	4	1	0	1	0	0	0	0	25:11
2014-15	Tampa Bay	NHL	59	4	14	18	26	1	0	0	73	5.5	12	0	0.0	20:29	25	0	3	3	4	0	0	0	16:30
2015-16	Tampa Bay	NHL	64	2	7	9	26	0	0	1	54	3.7	4	0	0.0	16:47	14	0	5	5	4	0	0	0	15:04
2016-17	Nashville	NHL	6	0	1	1	0	0	0	0	2	0.0	-1	0	0.0	13:09	....	....	....	....	....	....	....	....	....
	NHL Totals		730	45	238	283	251	21	0	7	966	4.7		3	33.3	20:43	127	6	38	44	36	2	0	1	19:29

USHL First All-Star Team (2003) • USHL Defenseman of the Year (2003) • WCHA All-Rookie Team (2004) • WCHA First All-Star Team (2005, 2006) • NCAA West First All-American Team (2005, 2006) • NCAA Championship All-Tournament Team (2005) • WCHA Player of the Year (2006) • Hobey Baker Memorial Award (Top U.S. Collegiate Player) (2006) • NHL All-Rookie Team (2007)

Traded to **Tampa Bay** by **San Jose** with Ty Wishart, San Jose's 1st round pick (later traded to Ottawa, later traded to NY Islanders, later traded to Columbus, later traded to Anaheim – Anaheim selected Kyle Palmieri) in 2009 NHL Draft and San Jose's 4th round pick (James Mullin) in 2010 NHL Draft for Dan Boyle and Brad Lukowich, July 4, 2008. Traded to **Philadelphia** by **Tampa Bay** with San Jose's 3rd round pick (previously acquired, Philadelphia selected Simon Bertilsson) in 2009 NHL Draft for Steve Eminger, Steve Downie and Tampa Bay's 4th round pick (previously acquired, Tampa Bay selected Alex Hutchings) in 2009 NHL Draft, November 7, 2008. Signed as a free agent by **Tampa Bay**, July 4, 2012. Signed as a free agent by **Nashville**, July 27, 2016. • Officially announced his retirement, November 25, 2016.

CARLO, Brandon
(KAHR-loh, BRAN-duhn) **BOS**

Defense. Shoots right. 6'5", 203 lbs. Born, Colorado Springs, CO, November 26, 1996. Boston's 4th pick, 37th overall, in 2015 NHL Draft.

			Regular Season														Playoffs								
Season	Club	League	GP	G	A	Pts	PIM	PP	SH	GW	S	S%	+/-	TF	F%	Min	GP	G	A	Pts	PIM	PP	SH	GW	Min
2011-12	Col. T-birds U16	T1EHL	40	6	11	17	20	....	....	....	....	....	....	....	....	....	....	....	....	....	....	....	....	....	....
2012-13	Col. T-birds U16	T1EHL	41	10	37	47	58	....	....	....	....	....	....	....	....	....	4	1	2	3	6	....	....	....	....
	Tri-City	WHL	....	....	....	....	....	....	....	....	....	....	....	....	....	....	5	1	0	1	8	....	....	....	....
2013-14	Tri-City	WHL	71	3	10	13	66	....	....	....	....	....	....	....	....	....	5	0	1	1	8	....	....	....	....
2014-15	Tri-City	WHL	63	4	21	25	90	....	....	....	....	....	....	....	....	....	4	0	1	1	4	....	....	....	....
2015-16	Tri-City	WHL	52	4	23	27	94	....	....	....	....	....	....	....	....	....	....	....	....	....	....	....	....	....	....
	Providence Bruins	AHL	7	0	1	1	0	....	....	....	....	....	....	....	....	....	1	0	0	0	0	....	....	....	....
2016-17	Boston	NHL	82	6	10	16	59	0	1	0	88	6.8	9	0	0.0	20:49	....	....	....	....	....	....	....	....	....
	NHL Totals		82	6	10	16	59	0	1	0	88	6.8		0	0.0	20:49	....	....	....	....	....	....	....	....	....

CARLSON, John
(KAHRL-suhn, JAWN) **WSH**

Defense. Shoots right. 6'3", 215 lbs. Born, Natick, MA, January 10, 1990. Washington's 2nd pick, 27th overall, in 2008 NHL Draft.

			Regular Season														Playoffs								
Season	Club	League	GP	G	A	Pts	PIM	PP	SH	GW	S	S%	+/-	TF	F%	Min	GP	G	A	Pts	PIM	PP	SH	GW	Min
2005-06	N.J. Rockets	AtJHL	38	2	10	12	42	....	....	....	....	....	....	....	....	....	....	....	....	....	....	....	....	....	....
2006-07	N.J. Rockets	AtJHL	44	12	38	50	96	....	....	....	....	....	....	....	....	....	....	....	....	....	....	....	....	....	....
	Indiana Ice	USHL	2	0	0	0	6	....	....	....	....	....	....	....	....	....	....	....	....	....	....	....	....	....	....
2007-08	Indiana Ice	USHL	59	12	31	43	72	....	....	....	....	....	....	....	....	....	4	1	0	1	0	....	....	....	....
2008-09	London Knights	OHL	59	16	60	76	65	....	....	....	....	....	....	....	....	....	14	7	15	22	16	....	....	....	....
	Hershey Bears	AHL	....	....	....	....	....	....	....	....	....	....	....	....	....	....	16	2	1	3	0	....	....	....	....
2009-10	Washington	NHL	22	1	5	6	8	0	0	0	21	4.8	11	0	0.0	15:15	7	1	3	4	0	0	0	0	20:14
	Hershey Bears	AHL	48	4	35	39	26	....	....	....	....	....	....	....	....	....	13	2	4	6	8	....	....	....	....
2010-11	Washington	NHL	82	7	30	37	44	1	0	3	144	4.9	21	0	0.0	22:39	9	2	1	3	4	0	0	0	24:23
2011-12	Washington	NHL	82	9	23	32	22	4	0	0	152	5.9	-15	1	0.0	21:52	14	2	3	5	8	1	0	0	24:02
2012-13	Washington	NHL	48	6	16	22	18	0	0	0	97	6.2	11	1	100.0	23:01	7	0	1	1	4	0	0	0	22:29
2013-14	Washington	NHL	82	10	27	37	22	5	0	0	208	4.8	-3	1	0.0	24:31	....	....	....	....	....	....	....	....	....
	United States	Olympics	6	1	1	2	0	....	....	....	....	....	....	....	....	....	....	....	....	....	....	....	....	....	....
2014-15	Washington	NHL	82	12	43	55	28	3	1	3	193	6.2	11	0	0.0	23:04	14	1	5	6	4	1	0	0	23:57
2015-16	Washington	NHL	56	8	31	39	14	2	0	4	124	6.5	16	0	0.0	23:42	12	5	7	12	4	4	0	1	26:54
2016-17	Washington	NHL	72	9	28	37	10	3	0	3	180	5.0	7	0	0.0	22:43	13	2	2	4	4	2	0	0	22:24
	NHL Totals		526	62	203	265	166	18	1	13	1119	5.5		3	33.3	22:44	76	13	22	35	28	8	0	1	23:45

USHL All-Rookie Team (2008) • USHL Second All-Star Team (2008) • OHL Second All-Star Team (2009) • Canadian Major Junior All-Rookie Team (2009) • AHL All-Rookie Team (2010) • NHL All-Rookie Team (2011)

CARLSSON, Gabriel
(KAHRL-suhn, GA-bree-ehl) **CBJ**

Defense. Shoots left. 6'4", 191 lbs. Born, Orebro, Sweden, January 2, 1997. Columbus' 2nd pick, 29th overall, in 2015 NHL Draft.

			Regular Season														Playoffs								
Season	Club	League	GP	G	A	Pts	PIM	PP	SH	GW	S	S%	+/-	TF	F%	Min	GP	G	A	Pts	PIM	PP	SH	GW	Min
2012-13	Orebro HK U18	Swe-U18	16	1	5	6	4	....	....	....	....	....	....	....	....	....	....	....	....	....	....	....	....	....	....
	Orebro HUF U18	Swe-U18	2	2	0	2	0	....	....	....	....	....	....	....	....	....	....	....	....	....	....	....	....	....	....
2013-14	Linkoping U18	Swe-U18	40	4	15	19	14	....	....	....	....	....	....	....	....	....	5	0	0	0	4	....	....	....	....
2014-15	Linkoping U18	Swe-U18	7	2	3	5	2	....	....	....	....	....	....	....	....	....	....	....	....	....	....	....	....	....	....
	Linkopings HC Jr.	Swe-Jr.	39	0	7	7	14	....	....	....	....	....	....	....	....	....	3	0	2	2	2	....	....	....	....
	Linkopings HC	Sweden	7	0	2	2	0	....	....	....	....	....	....	....	....	....	10	0	1	1	2	....	....	....	....
2015-16	Linkopings HC Jr.	Swe-Jr.	11	2	6	8	8	....	....	....	....	....	....	....	....	....	1	0	0	0	0	....	....	....	....
	Linkopings HC	Sweden	45	1	8	9	2	....	....	....	....	....	....	....	....	....	6	0	0	0	0	....	....	....	....
2016-17	Linkopings HC	Sweden	40	2	2	4	6	....	....	....	....	....	....	....	....	....	6	0	0	0	0	....	....	....	....
	Columbus	NHL	2	0	1	1	0	0	0	0	3	0.0	-2	0	0.0	17:08	5	0	0	0	0	0	0	0	10:58
	Cleveland	AHL	3	0	1	1	2	....	....	....	....	....	....	....	....	....	....	....	....	....	....	....	....	....	....
	NHL Totals		2	0	1	1	0	0	0	0	3	0.0		0	0.0	17:08	5	0	0	0	0	0	0	0	10:58

CARON, Jordan
(kuh-RAWN, JOHR-dihn)

Right wing. Shoots left. 6'3", 204 lbs. Born, Sayabec, QC, November 2, 1990. Boston's 1st pick, 25th overall, in 2009 NHL Draft.

			Regular Season														Playoffs								
Season	Club	League	GP	G	A	Pts	PIM	PP	SH	GW	S	S%	+/-	TF	F%	Min	GP	G	A	Pts	PIM	PP	SH	GW	Min
2005-06	Notre Dame	SMHL	35	8	16	24	32	....	....	....	....	....	....	....	....	....	....	....	....	....	....	....	....	....	....
2006-07	Rimouski Oceanic	QMJHL	59	18	22	40	41	....	....	....	....	....	....	....	....	....	....	....	....	....	....	....	....	....	....
2007-08	Rimouski Oceanic	QMJHL	46	20	23	43	42	....	....	....	....	....	....	....	....	....	9	3	1	4	18	....	....	....	....
2008-09	Rimouski Oceanic	QMJHL	56	36	31	67	66	....	....	....	....	....	....	....	....	....	13	6	5	11	16	....	....	....	....
2009-10	Rimouski Oceanic	QMJHL	20	9	11	20	8	....	....	....	....	....	....	....	....	....	....	....	....	....	....	....	....	....	....
	Rouyn-Noranda	QMJHL	23	17	16	33	16	....	....	....	....	....	....	....	....	....	11	7	11	18	15	....	....	....	....
2010-11	Boston	NHL	23	3	4	7	6	0	0	1	27	11.1	3	7	14.3	12:40	....	....	....	....	....	....	....	....	....
	Providence Bruins	AHL	47	12	16	28	16	....	....	....	....	....	....	....	....	....	....	....	....	....	....	....	....	....	....
2011-12	Boston	NHL	48	7	8	15	14	0	0	0	57	12.3	0	2	50.0	11:32	2	0	0	0	0	0	0	0	6:41
	Providence Bruins	AHL	17	4	9	13	10	....	....	....	....	....	....	....	....	....	....	....	....	....	....	....	....	....	....
2012-13	Providence Bruins	AHL	47	11	7	18	38	....	....	....	....	....	....	....	....	....	12	2	7	9	10	....	....	....	....
	Boston	NHL	17	1	2	3	4	0	0	0	20	5.0	1	0	0.0	9:24	....	....	....	....	....	....	....	....	....
2013-14	Boston	NHL	35	1	2	3	36	0	0	0	52	1.9	-8	4	25.0	10:55	7	1	0	1	4	0	0	0	7:54
2014-15	Boston	NHL	11	0	0	0	16	0	0	0	4	0.0	-1	1	0.0	7:56	....	....	....	....	....	....	....	....	....
	Providence Bruins	AHL	23	9	10	19	10	....	....	....	....	....	....	....	....	....	....	....	....	....	....	....	....	....	....
	Colorado	NHL	19	0	0	0	2	0	0	0	8	0.0	-1	0	0.0	8:06	....	....	....	....	....	....	....	....	....

			Regular Season														Playoffs								
Season	Club	League	GP	G	A	Pts	PIM	PP	SH	GW	S	S%	+/-	TF	F%	Min	GP	G	A	Pts	PIM	PP	SH	GW	Min
2015-16	**St. Louis**	**NHL**	**4**	**0**	**0**	**0**	**0**	**0**	**0**	**0**	**1**	**0.0**	**–3**	**0**	**0.0**	**8:08**	....	....	....	....	....	....	....	....	....
	Chicago Wolves	AHL	70	17	19	36	115	....	....	....	....	....	....	....	....	....	....	....	....	....	....	....	....	....	....
2016-17	Chicago Wolves	AHL	57	5	20	25	47	....	....	....	....	....	....	....	....	....	9	0	1	1	2	....	....	....	....
	NHL Totals		**157**	**12**	**16**	**28**	**78**	**0**	**0**	**1**	**169**	**7.1**		**14**	**21.4**	**10:35**	**9**	**1**	**0**	**1**	**4**	**0**	**0**	**0**	**7:38**

• Missed majority of 2013-14 as a healthy reserve. Traded to **Colorado** by **Boston** with Boston's 6th round pick (later traded back to Boston – Boston selected Oskar Steen) in 2016 NHL Draft for Max Talbot and Paul Carey, March 2, 2015. Signed as a free agent by **St. Louis**, July 3, 2015.

CARPENTER, Ryan

(KAHR-pehn-tuhr, RIGH-uhn) **S.J.**

Right wing. Shoots right. 6', 195 lbs. Born, Oviedo, FL, January 18, 1991.

Season	Club	League	GP	G	A	Pts	PIM	PP	SH	GW	S	S%	+/-	TF	F%	Min	GP	G	A	Pts	PIM	PP	SH	GW	Min
2007-08	Det. Vic. Honda	MWEHL	31	15	14	29	26	....	....	....	....	....	....	....	....	....	....	....	....	....	....	....	....	....	....
	Det. Vic. Honda	Other	3	0	1	1	0	....	....	....	....	....	....	....	....	....	....	....	....	....	....	....	....	....	....
2008-09	Det. Honeybaked	T1EHL	46	19	13	32	26	....	....	....	....	....	....	....	....	....	4	0	1	1	0	....	....	....	....
2009-10	Sioux City	USHL	58	10	12	22	45	....	....	....	....	....	....	....	....	....	....	....	....	....	....	....	....	....	....
2010-11	Sioux City	USHL	59	13	32	45	30	....	....	....	....	....	....	....	....	....	3	2	1	3	2	....	....	....	....
2011-12	Bowling Green	CCHA	44	11	19	30	31	....	....	....	....	....	....	....	....	....	....	....	....	....	....	....	....	....	....
2012-13	Bowling Green	CCHA	41	18	15	33	20	....	....	....	....	....	....	....	....	....	....	....	....	....	....	....	....	....	....
2013-14	Bowling Green	WCHA	15	8	8	16	0	....	....	....	....	....	....	....	....	....	....	....	....	....	....	....	....	....	....
2014-15	Worcester Sharks	AHL	74	12	22	34	40	....	....	....	....	....	....	....	....	....	4	1	2	3	2	....	....	....	....
2015-16	**San Jose**	**NHL**	**1**	**0**	**0**	**0**	**0**	**0**	**0**	**0**	**0**	**0.0**	**0**	**2**	**0.0**	**7:27**	....	....	....	....	....	....	....	....	....
	San Jose	AHL	66	18	37	55	33	....	....	....	....	....	....	....	....	....	4	1	1	2	2	....	....	....	....
2016-17	**San Jose**	**NHL**	**11**	**2**	**2**	**4**	**4**	**0**	**0**	**0**	**20**	**10.0**	**5**	**75**	**45.3**	**10:23**	....	....	....	....	....	....	....	....	....
	San Jose	AHL	54	14	25	39	24	....	....	....	....	....	....	....	....	....	15	9	8	17	8	....	....	....	....
	NHL Totals		**12**	**2**	**2**	**4**	**4**	**0**	**0**	**0**	**20**	**10.0**		**77**	**44.2**	**10:08**	....	....	....	....	....	....	....	....	....

CCHA Second All-Star Team (2013) • Yanick Dupre Memorial Award (AHL - Outstanding Humanitarian Contribution) (2016)

Signed as a free agent by **San Jose**, March 26, 2014.

CARR, Daniel

(KARR, DAHN-yehl) **MTL**

Left wing. Shoots left. 6', 191 lbs. Born, Sherwood Park, AB, November 1, 1991.

Season	Club	League	GP	G	A	Pts	PIM	PP	SH	GW	S	S%	+/-	TF	F%	Min	GP	G	A	Pts	PIM	PP	SH	GW	Min
2005-06	Leduc Oil Kings	AMBHL	34	29	56	85	34	....	....	....	....	....	....	....	....	....	9	8	8	16	....	....	....	....	....
2006-07	Leduc Oil Kings	Minor-AB	30	17	30	47	42	....	....	....	....	....	....	....	....	....	....	....	....	....	....	....	....	....	....
2007-08	St. Albert Steel	AJHL	62	16	11	27	36	....	....	....	....	....	....	....	....	....	5	0	0	0	0	....	....	....	....
2008-09	St. Albert Steel	AJHL	59	27	28	55	81	....	....	....	....	....	....	....	....	....	4	2	2	4	2	....	....	....	....
2009-10	St. Albert Steel	AJHL	30	24	30	54	15	....	....	....	....	....	....	....	....	....	....	....	....	....	....	....	....	....	....
	Powell River Kings	BCHL	22	10	17	27	14	....	....	....	....	....	....	....	....	....	23	15	11	26	10	....	....	....	....
2010-11	Union College	ECAC	40	20	15	35	28	....	....	....	....	....	....	....	....	....	....	....	....	....	....	....	....	....	....
2011-12	Union College	ECAC	41	20	20	40	30	....	....	....	....	....	....	....	....	....	....	....	....	....	....	....	....	....	....
2012-13	Union College	ECAC	40	16	16	32	26	....	....	....	....	....	....	....	....	....	....	....	....	....	....	....	....	....	....
2013-14	Union College	ECAC	39	22	28	50	28	....	....	....	....	....	....	....	....	....	....	....	....	....	....	....	....	....	....
2014-15	Hamilton	AHL	76	24	15	39	21	....	....	....	....	....	....	....	....	....	....	....	....	....	....	....	....	....	....
2015-16	**Montreal**	**NHL**	**23**	**6**	**3**	**9**	**8**	**1**	**0**	**1**	**39**	**15.4**	**0**	**0**	**0.0**	**12:04**	....	....	....	....	....	....	....	....	....
	St. John's IceCaps	AHL	24	10	11	21	10	....	....	....	....	....	....	....	....	....	....	....	....	....	....	....	....	....	....
2016-17	**Montreal**	**NHL**	**33**	**2**	**7**	**9**	**6**	**0**	**0**	**1**	**44**	**4.5**	**4**	**3**	**66.7**	**10:15**	....	....	....	....	....	....	....	....	....
	St. John's IceCaps	AHL	19	6	5	11	2	....	....	....	....	....	....	....	....	....	....	....	....	....	....	....	....	....	....
	NHL Totals		**56**	**8**	**10**	**18**	**14**	**1**	**0**	**2**	**83**	**9.6**		**3**	**66.7**	**11:00**	....	....	....	....	....	....	....	....	....

ECAC All-Rookie Team (2011) • ECAC First All-Star Team (2014) • NCAA East Second All-American Team (2014)

Signed as a free agent by **Montreal**, April 25, 2014.

CARRICK, Connor

(KAIR-ihk, KAW-nuhr) **TOR**

Defense. Shoots right. 5'11", 193 lbs. Born, Orland Park, IL, April 13, 1994. Washington's 6th pick, 137th overall, in 2012 NHL Draft.

Season	Club	League	GP	G	A	Pts	PIM	PP	SH	GW	S	S%	+/-	TF	F%	Min	GP	G	A	Pts	PIM	PP	SH	GW	Min
2009-10	Chicago Fury U18	T1EHL	22	2	4	6	2	....	....	....	....	....	....	....	....	....	....	....	....	....	....	....	....	....	....
	Chicago Fury	T1EHL	37	7	15	22	48	....	....	....	....	....	....	....	....	....	....	....	....	....	....	....	....	....	....
2010-11	USAHNTDP	USHL	36	1	6	7	42	....	....	....	....	....	....	....	....	....	2	0	0	0	2	....	....	....	....
	USAHNTDP	U-17	17	3	10	13	10	....	....	....	....	....	....	....	....	....	....	....	....	....	....	....	....	....	....
2011-12	USAHNTDP	USHL	21	1	4	5	30	....	....	....	....	....	....	....	....	....	....	....	....	....	....	....	....	....	....
	USAHNTDP	U-18	36	7	9	16	16	....	....	....	....	....	....	....	....	....	....	....	....	....	....	....	....	....	....
2012-13	Plymouth Whalers	OHL	68	12	32	44	79	....	....	....	....	....	....	....	....	....	15	2	16	18	6	....	....	....	....
2013-14	**Washington**	**NHL**	**34**	**1**	**5**	**6**	**23**	**0**	**0**	**0**	**26**	**3.8**	**–9**	**0**	**0.0**	**15:58**	....	....	....	....	....	....	....	....	....
	Hershey Bears	AHL	13	0	4	4	15	....	....	....	....	....	....	....	....	....	....	....	....	....	....	....	....	....	....
2014-15	Hershey Bears	AHL	73	8	34	42	132	....	....	....	....	....	....	....	....	....	10	2	2	4	12	....	....	....	....
2015-16	**Washington**	**NHL**	**3**	**0**	**0**	**0**	**0**	**0**	**0**	**0**	**2**	**0.0**	**–2**	**0**	**0.0**	**10:07**	....	....	....	....	....	....	....	....	....
	Hershey Bears	AHL	47	10	16	26	50	....	....	....	....	....	....	....	....	....	....	....	....	....	....	....	....	....	....
	Toronto	**NHL**	**16**	**2**	**2**	**4**	**15**	**0**	**0**	**1**	**19**	**10.5**	**–3**	**0**	**0.0**	**16:33**	....	....	....	....	....	....	....	....	....
	Toronto Marlies	AHL	5	1	2	3	2	....	....	....	....	....	....	....	....	....	15	7	11	*18	12	....	....	....	....
2016-17	**Toronto**	**NHL**	**67**	**2**	**6**	**8**	**51**	**1**	**0**	**0**	**89**	**2.2**	**8**	**0**	**0.0**	**16:20**	**6**	**0**	**0**	**0**	**4**	**0**	**0**	**0**	**12:16**
	NHL Totals		**120**	**5**	**13**	**18**	**89**	**1**	**0**	**1**	**136**	**3.7**		**0**	**0.0**	**16:06**	**6**	**0**	**0**	**0**	**4**	**0**	**0**	**0**	**12:16**

Traded to **Toronro** by **Washington** with Brooks Laich and Washington's 2nd round pick (Carl Grundstrom) in 2016 NHL Draft for Daniel Winnik and Anaheim's 5th round pick (previously acquired, Washington selected Beck Malenstyn) in 2016 NHL Draft, February 28, 2016.

CARRICK, Sam

(KAIR-ihk, SAM) **ANA**

Center. Shoots right. 6', 207 lbs. Born, Stouffville, ON, February 4, 1992. Toronto's 5th pick, 144th overall, in 2010 NHL Draft.

Season	Club	League	GP	G	A	Pts	PIM	PP	SH	GW	S	S%	+/-	TF	F%	Min	GP	G	A	Pts	PIM	PP	SH	GW	Min
2007-08	Tor. Red Wings	GTHL	55	40	30	70	130	....	....	....	....	....	....	....	....	....	....	....	....	....	....	....	....	....	....
2008-09	Brampton	OHL	61	10	11	21	47	....	....	....	....	....	....	....	....	....	21	1	0	1	16	....	....	....	....
2009-10	Brampton	OHL	66	21	21	42	96	....	....	....	....	....	....	....	....	....	8	2	2	4	8	....	....	....	....
2010-11	Brampton	OHL	59	16	23	39	74	....	....	....	....	....	....	....	....	....	4	0	1	1	4	....	....	....	....
2011-12	Brampton	OHL	68	37	30	67	104	....	....	....	....	....	....	....	....	....	8	4	4	8	16	....	....	....	....
2012-13	Idaho Steelheads	ECHL	50	16	21	37	70	....	....	....	....	....	....	....	....	....	....	....	....	....	....	....	....	....	....
	Toronto Marlies	AHL	19	2	2	4	18	....	....	....	....	....	....	....	....	....	5	0	0	0	0	....	....	....	....
2013-14	Toronto Marlies	AHL	62	14	21	35	115	....	....	....	....	....	....	....	....	....	14	5	4	9	10	....	....	....	....
2014-15	**Toronto**	**NHL**	**16**	**1**	**1**	**2**	**9**	**0**	**0**	**0**	**17**	**5.9**	**1**	**91**	**41.8**	**6:29**	....	....	....	....	....	....	....	....	....
	Toronto Marlies	AHL	59	9	18	27	112	....	....	....	....	....	....	....	....	....	5	1	2	3	4	....	....	....	....
2015-16	**Toronto**	**NHL**	**3**	**0**	**0**	**0**	**4**	**0**	**0**	**0**	**4**	**0.0**	**–2**	**1**	**100.0**	**11:28**	....	....	....	....	....	....	....	....	....
	Toronto Marlies	AHL	52	16	18	34	90	....	....	....	....	....	....	....	....	....	12	0	5	5	19	....	....	....	....
2016-17	Rockford IceHogs	AHL	57	11	17	28	85	....	....	....	....	....	....	....	....	....	....	....	....	....	....	....	....	....	....
	San Diego Gulls	AHL	15	3	8	11	20	....	....	....	....	....	....	....	....	....	10	4	3	7	14	....	....	....	....
	NHL Totals		**19**	**1**	**1**	**2**	**13**	**0**	**0**	**0**	**21**	**4.8**		**92**	**42.4**	**7:16**	....	....	....	....	....	....	....	....	....

Signed as a free agent by **Chicago**, July 1, 2016. Traded to **Anaheim** by **Chicago** with Spencer Abbott for Kenton Hegelsen and Anaheim's 7th round pck in 2019 NHL Draft, March 1, 2017.

CARRICK, Trevor

(KAIR-ihk, TREH-vuhr) **CAR**

Defense. Shoots left. 6'2", 186 lbs. Born, Stouffville, ON, July 4, 1994. Carolina's 5th pick, 115th overall, in 2012 NHL Draft.

Season	Club	League	GP	G	A	Pts	PIM	PP	SH	GW	S	S%	+/-	TF	F%	Min	GP	G	A	Pts	PIM	PP	SH	GW	Min
2009-10	Markham Majors	GTHL	49	6	23	29	48	....	....	....	....	....	....	....	....	....	....	....	....	....	....	....	....	....	....
	Upper Canada	ON-Jr.A	2	0	1	1	2	....	....	....	....	....	....	....	....	....	....	....	....	....	....	....	....	....	....
2010-11	Stouffville Spirit	ON-Jr.A	40	6	13	19	44	....	....	....	....	....	....	....	....	....	19	2	11	13	10	....	....	....	....
2011-12	St. Michael's	OHL	68	6	13	19	64	....	....	....	....	....	....	....	....	....	6	1	0	1	7	....	....	....	....
2012-13	Mississauga	OHL	56	10	21	31	56	....	....	....	....	....	....	....	....	....	6	0	2	2	11	....	....	....	....
2013-14	Mississauga	OHL	41	16	15	31	65	....	....	....	....	....	....	....	....	....	....	....	....	....	....	....	....	....	....
	Sudbury Wolves	OHL	29	6	14	20	52	....	....	....	....	....	....	....	....	....	5	1	2	3	10	....	....	....	....
2014-15	Charlotte	AHL	76	7	25	32	94	....	....	....	....	....	....	....	....	....	....	....	....	....	....	....	....	....	....
2015-16	**Carolina**	**NHL**	**2**	**0**	**0**	**0**	**0**	**0**	**0**	**0**	**3**	**0.0**	**–1**	**0**	**0.0**	**16:40**	....	....	....	....	....	....	....	....	....
	Charlotte	AHL	70	9	33	42	51	....	....	....	....	....	....	....	....	....	....	....	....	....	....	....	....	....	....
2016-17	Charlotte	AHL	57	4	12	16	45	....	....	....	....	....	....	....	....	....	5	0	3	3	0	....	....	....	....
	NHL Totals		**2**	**0**	**0**	**0**	**0**	**0**	**0**	**0**	**3**	**0.0**		**0**	**0.0**	**16:40**	....	....	....	....	....	....	....	....	....

CARRIER, Alexandre

(kair-EE-ay, Al-ehx-AHN-druh) **NSH**

Defense. Shoots right. 5'11", 174 lbs. Born, Quebec City, QC, October 8, 1996. Nashville's 4th pick, 115th overall, in 2015 NHL Draft.

			Regular Season														Playoffs								
Season	Club	League	GP	G	A	Pts	PIM	PP	SH	GW	S	S%	+/-	TF	F%	Min	GP	G	A	Pts	PIM	PP	SH	GW	Min
2011-12	Antoine-Girouard	QAAA	40	5	25	30	30										11	1	1	2	2				
2012-13	Gatineau	QMJHL	50	2	5	7	28										9	1	0	1	6				
2013-14	Gatineau	QMJHL	67	3	25	28	29										9	1	4	5	4				
2014-15	Gatineau	QMJHL	68	12	43	55	64										11	2	3	5	18				
2015-16	Gatineau	QMJHL	57	12	35	47	50										10	0	5	5	4				
2016-17	**Nashville**	**NHL**	**2**	**0**	**0**	**0**	**0**	**0**	**0**	**0**	**1**	**0.0**	**1**	**0**	**0.0**	**10:24**									
	Milwaukee	AHL	72	6	33	39	45										3	0	2	2	0				
	NHL Totals		**2**	**0**	**0**	**0**	**0**	**0**	**0**	**0**	**1**	**0.0**		**0**	**0.0**	**10:24**									

QMJHL Second All-Star Team (2015)

CARRIER, William

(kair-ree-AY, WIHL-yuhm) **VGK**

Left wing. Shoots left. 6'2", 212 lbs. Born, La Salle, QC, December 20, 1994. St. Louis' 2nd pick, 57th overall, in 2013 NHL Draft.

			Regular Season														Playoffs								
Season	Club	League	GP	G	A	Pts	PIM	PP	SH	GW	S	S%	+/-	TF	F%	Min	GP	G	A	Pts	PIM	PP	SH	GW	Min
2009-10	Lac St-L. Royals	Minor-QC	STATISTICS NOT AVAILABLE																						
	Lac St-Louis Lions	QAAA	3	0	0	0	2																		
2010-11	Cape Breton	QMJHL	61	8	4	12	54										4	0	0	0	2				
2011-12	Cape Breton	QMJHL	66	27	43	70	65										4	3	3	6	4				
2012-13	Cape Breton	QMJHL	34	16	26	42	41																		
2013-14	Cape Breton	QMJHL	39	12	29	41	42																		
	Drummondville	QMJHL	27	10	14	24	45										4	1	3	4	6				
2014-15	Rochester	AHL	63	7	14	21	38																		
2015-16	Rochester	AHL	56	13	17	30	48																		
2016-17	**Buffalo**	**NHL**	**41**	**5**	**3**	**8**	**21**	**0**	**0**	**1**	**50**	**10.0**	**–1**	**2**	**50.0**	**9:00**									
	Rochester	AHL	8	3	2	5	6																		
	NHL Totals		**41**	**5**	**3**	**8**	**21**	**0**	**0**	**1**	**50**	**10.0**		**2**	**50.0**	**9:00**									

Traded to **Buffalo** by **St. Louis** with Jaroslav Halak, Chris Stewart, St. Louis' 1st round pick (later traded to Winnipeg – Winnipeg selected Jack Roslovic) in 2015 NHL Draft and St. Louis' 3rd round pick (later traded to Florida – Florida selected Linus Nassen) in 2016 NHL Draft for Ryan Miller and Steve Ott, February 28, 2014. Claimed by **Vegas** from **Buffalo** in Expansion Draft, June 21, 2017.

CARTER, Jeff

(KAHR-tuhr, JEHF) **L.A.**

Center. Shoots right. 6'4", 215 lbs. Born, London, ON, January 1, 1985. Philadelphia's 1st pick, 11th overall, in 2003 NHL Draft.

			Regular Season														Playoffs								
Season	Club	League	GP	G	A	Pts	PIM	PP	SH	GW	S	S%	+/-	TF	F%	Min	GP	G	A	Pts	PIM	PP	SH	GW	Min
2000-01	Strathroy Rockets	ON-Jr.B	49	27	20	47	10																		
2001-02	Sault Ste. Marie	OHL	63	18	17	35	12										4	0	0	0	2				
2002-03	Sault Ste. Marie	OHL	61	35	36	71	55										4	0	2	2	2				
2003-04	Sault Ste. Marie	OHL	57	36	30	66	26																		
	Philadelphia	AHL															12	4	1	5	0				
2004-05	Sault Ste. Marie	OHL	55	34	40	74	40										7	5	5	10	6				
	Philadelphia	AHL	3	0	1	1	4										21	12	11	23	12				
2005-06	**Philadelphia**	**NHL**	**81**	**23**	**19**	**42**	**40**	**6**	**2**	**7**	**189**	**12.2**	**10**	**683**	**48.2**	**12:04**	**6**	**0**	**0**	**0**	**10**	**0**	**0**	**0**	**13:04**
2006-07	**Philadelphia**	**NHL**	**62**	**14**	**23**	**37**	**48**	**3**	**2**	**1**	**215**	**6.5**	**–17**	**1062**	**45.4**	**19:00**									
2007-08	**Philadelphia**	**NHL**	**82**	**29**	**24**	**53**	**55**	**7**	**2**	**5**	**260**	**11.2**	**6**	**1378**	**47.7**	**18:51**	**17**	**6**	**5**	**11**	**12**	**3**	**0**	**1**	**20:08**
2008-09	**Philadelphia**	**NHL**	**82**	**46**	**38**	**84**	**68**	**13**	**4**	***12**	**342**	**13.5**	**23**	**1725**	**48.3**	**20:57**	**6**	**1**	**0**	**1**	**8**	**0**	**0**	**0**	**20:21**
2009-10	**Philadelphia**	**NHL**	**74**	**33**	**28**	**61**	**38**	**11**	**2**	**6**	**319**	**10.3**	**2**	**1314**	**52.4**	**19:18**	**12**	**5**	**2**	**7**	**2**	**2**	**0**	**1**	**17:57**
2010-11	**Philadelphia**	**NHL**	**80**	**36**	**30**	**66**	**39**	**8**	**0**	**7**	**335**	**10.7**	**27**	**605**	**54.7**	**18:15**	**6**	**1**	**1**	**2**	**2**	**1**	**0**	**0**	**15:15**
2011-12	**Columbus**	**NHL**	**39**	**15**	**10**	**25**	**14**	**8**	**0**	**1**	**130**	**11.5**	**–11**	**740**	**51.0**	**19:38**									
	♦ Los Angeles	**NHL**	**16**	**6**	**3**	**9**	**2**	**2**	**0**	**1**	**54**	**11.1**	**–1**	**34**	**47.1**	**18:06**	**20**	***8**	**5**	**13**	**4**	**4**	**0**	***3**	**18:02**
2012-13	**Los Angeles**	**NHL**	**48**	**26**	**7**	**33**	**16**	**8**	**0**	***8**	**133**	**19.5**	**0**	**384**	**52.6**	**17:35**	**18**	**6**	**7**	**13**	**14**	**1**	**0**	**0**	**19:37**
2013-14♦	**Los Angeles**	**NHL**	**72**	**27**	**23**	**50**	**44**	**8**	**1**	**5**	**256**	**10.5**	**8**	**644**	**52.2**	**18:57**	**26**	**10**	**15**	**25**	**4**	***4**	**0**	**1**	**18:16**
	Canada	Olympics	6	3	2	5	2																		
2014-15	**Los Angeles**	**NHL**	**82**	**28**	**34**	**62**	**28**	**10**	**1**	**5**	**218**	**12.8**	**7**	**1193**	**52.6**	**17:58**									
2015-16	**Los Angeles**	**NHL**	**77**	**24**	**38**	**62**	**20**	**4**	**1**	**6**	**242**	**9.9**	**18**	**1228**	**48.7**	**18:23**	**5**	**2**	**0**	**2**	**4**	**1**	**0**	**0**	**18:39**
2016-17	**Los Angeles**	**NHL**	**82**	**32**	**34**	**66**	**41**	**10**	**1**	**9**	**250**	**12.8**	**2**	**1415**	**51.9**	**18:02**									
	NHL Totals		**877**	**339**	**311**	**650**	**453**	**98**	**16**	**73**	**2943**	**11.5**		**12405**	**50.1**	**18:10**	**116**	**39**	**35**	**74**	**60**	**16**	**0**	**6**	**18:22**

OHL Second All-Star Team (2004) • OHL First All-Star Team (2005) • Canadian Major Junior Sportsman of the Year (2005) • Canadian Major Junior First All-Star Team (2005)

Played in NHL All-Star Game (2009, 2017)

Traded to **Columbus** by **Philadelphia** for Jakub Voracek and Columbus' 1st (Sean Couturier) and 3rd (Nick Cousins) round picks in 2011 NHL Draft, June 23, 2011. Traded to **Los Angeles** by **Columbus** for Jack Johnson and Los Angeles' 1st round pick (Marko Dano) in 2013 NHL Draft, February 23, 2012.

CARTER, Ryan

(KAHR-tuhr, RIGH-uhn)

Left wing. Shoots left. 6'1", 202 lbs. Born, White Bear Lake, MN, August 3, 1983.

			Regular Season														Playoffs								
Season	Club	League	GP	G	A	Pts	PIM	PP	SH	GW	S	S%	+/-	TF	F%	Min	GP	G	A	Pts	PIM	PP	SH	GW	Min
2001-02	White Bear Lake	High-MN	STATISTICS NOT AVAILABLE																						
	Green Bay	USHL	1	0	0	0	2																		
2002-03	Green Bay	USHL	55	19	17	36	94																		
2003-04	Green Bay	USHL	59	22	23	45	131																		
2004-05	Minnesota State	WCHA	37	15	8	23	44																		
2005-06	Minnesota State	WCHA	39	19	16	35	71																		
2006-07	Portland Pirates	AHL	76	16	20	36	85																		
	♦ Anaheim	**NHL**															**4**	**0**	**0**	**0**	**0**	**0**	**0**	**0**	**3:12**
2007-08	**Anaheim**	**NHL**	**34**	**4**	**4**	**8**	**36**	**0**	**0**	**1**	**56**	**7.1**	**–2**	**299**	**61.5**	**10:29**	**6**	**0**	**0**	**0**	**6**	**0**	**0**	**0**	**11:03**
	Portland Pirates	AHL	13	3	2	5	38																		
2008-09	**Anaheim**	**NHL**	**48**	**3**	**6**	**9**	**52**	**0**	**0**	**1**	**40**	**7.5**	**3**	**304**	**48.0**	**9:06**	**10**	**2**	**3**	**5**	**0**	**1**	**0**	**0**	**12:14**
2009-10	**Anaheim**	**NHL**	**38**	**4**	**5**	**9**	**31**	**0**	**0**	**1**	**38**	**10.5**	**0**	**221**	**52.5**	**9:51**									
2010-11	**Anaheim**	**NHL**	**18**	**1**	**2**	**3**	**22**	**0**	**0**	**0**	**23**	**4.3**	**–4**	**171**	**50.3**	**10:44**									
	Carolina	**NHL**	**32**	**0**	**3**	**3**	**22**	**0**	**0**	**0**	**26**	**0.0**	**0**	**208**	**50.5**	**8:18**									
	Florida	**NHL**	**12**	**2**	**1**	**3**	**22**	**0**	**0**	**0**	**14**	**14.3**	**3**	**99**	**51.5**	**13:30**									
2011-12	**Florida**	**NHL**	**7**	**0**	**0**	**0**	**6**	**0**	**0**	**0**	**3**	**0.0**	**–1**	**39**	**46.2**	**9:19**									
	New Jersey	**NHL**	**65**	**4**	**4**	**8**	**84**	**0**	**0**	**0**	**47**	**8.5**	**–12**	**393**	**50.1**	**10:28**	**23**	**5**	**2**	**7**	**32**	**0**	**0**	**2**	**8:43**
2012-13	**New Jersey**	**NHL**	**44**	**6**	**9**	**15**	**31**	**0**	**1**	**1**	**63**	**9.5**	**–2**	**83**	**51.8**	**13:03**									
2013-14	**New Jersey**	**NHL**	**62**	**7**	**3**	**10**	**35**	**0**	**0**	**2**	**69**	**10.1**	**–6**	**36**	**44.4**	**11:20**									
2014-15	**Minnesota**	**NHL**	**53**	**3**	**10**	**13**	**55**	**0**	**1**	**0**	**47**	**6.4**	**3**	**70**	**41.4**	**10:05**	**1**	**0**	**0**	**0**	**0**	**0**	**0**	**0**	**6:18**
2015-16	**Minnesota**	**NHL**	**60**	**7**	**5**	**12**	**48**	**0**	**1**	**0**	**62**	**11.3**	**–3**	**39**	**53.9**	**11:08**	**2**	**0**	**0**	**0**	**10**	**0**	**0**	**0**	**10:04**
2016-17	Iowa Wild	AHL	18	1	2	3	25																		
	NHL Totals		**473**	**41**	**52**	**93**	**444**	**0**	**3**	**6**	**488**	**8.4**		**1962**	**51.6**	**10:36**	**46**	**7**	**5**	**12**	**48**	**1**	**0**	**2**	**9:19**

Signed as a free agent by **Anaheim**, July 12, 2006. • Missed majority of 2009-10 due to foot injury in pre-game skate at Columbus, November 13, 2009. Traded to **Carolina** by **Anaheim** for Stefan Chaput and Matt Kennedy, November 23, 2010. Traded to **Florida** by **Carolina** with Carolina's 5th round pick (later traded to Atlanta, later traded to San Jose – San Jose selected Sean Kuraly) in 2011 NHL Draft for Cory Stillman, February 24, 2011. Claimed on waivers by **New Jersey** from **Florida**, October 26, 2011. Signed as a free agent by **Minnesota**, October 7, 2014. Signed to a PTO (professional tryout) contract by **Iowa** (AHL), February 18, 2017.

CATENACCI, Daniel

(ka-tehn-AH-chee, DAN-yehl) **NYR**

Center. Shoots left. 5'10", 196 lbs. Born, Richmond Hill, ON, March 9, 1993. Buffalo's 2nd pick, 77th overall, in 2011 NHL Draft.

			Regular Season														Playoffs								
Season	Club	League	GP	G	A	Pts	PIM	PP	SH	GW	S	S%	+/-	TF	F%	Min	GP	G	A	Pts	PIM	PP	SH	GW	Min
2008-09	York Simcoe	Minor-ON	39	42	45	87	152																		
	Villanova Knights	ON-Jr.A	1	1	0	1	2																		
2009-10	Sault Ste. Marie	OHL	65	10	20	30	68										5	1	1	2	6				
2010-11	Sault Ste. Marie	OHL	67	26	45	71	117																		
2011-12	Owen Sound	OHL	67	33	39	72	114										5	1	3	4	8				
2012-13	Owen Sound	OHL	67	38	41	79	115										12	3	6	9	32				
	Rochester	AHL	2	1	2	3	0																		
2013-14	Rochester	AHL	76	10	10	20	32										2	0	0	0	0				
2014-15	Rochester	AHL	68	15	14	29	60																		
2015-16	**Buffalo**	**NHL**	**11**	**0**	**0**	**0**	**0**	**0**	**0**	**0**	**7**	**0.0**	**–2**	**2**	**100.0**	**8:44**									
	Rochester	AHL	50	12	12	24	39																		

			Regular Season														Playoffs								
Season	Club	League	GP	G	A	Pts	PIM	PP	SH	GW	S	S%	+/-	TF	F%	Min	GP	G	A	Pts	PIM	PP	SH	GW	Min
2016-17	Rochester	AHL	50	5	8	13	44	....	....	....	....	....	....	....	....	....	....	....	....	....	....	....	....	....	....
	Hartford	AHL	19	4	5	9	26	....	....	....	....	....	....	....	....	....	....	....	....	....	....	....	....	....	....
	NHL Totals		**11**	**0**	**0**	**0**	**0**	**0**	**0**	**0**	**7**	**0.0**		**2**	**100.0**	**8:44**	....	....	....	....	....	....	....	....	....

Traded to **NY Rangers** by **Buffalo** for Mat Bodie, February 28, 2017.

CECI, Cody

(SEE-SEE, KOH-dee) **OTT**

Defense. Shoots right. 6'3", 205 lbs. Born, Ottawa, ON, December 21, 1993. Ottawa's 1st pick, 15th overall, in 2012 NHL Draft.

2008-09	Peter. Petes Mid.	Minor-ON	57	24	48	72	26	....	....	....	....	....	....	....	....	....	....	....	....	....	....	....	....	....	....
2009-10	Ottawa 67's	OHL	64	4	8	12	12	....	....	....	....	....	....	....	....	....	12	0	3	3	0	....	....	....	....
2010-11	Ottawa 67's	OHL	68	9	25	34	28	....	....	....	....	....	....	....	....	....	4	0	2	2	4	....	....	....	....
2011-12	Ottawa 67's	OHL	64	17	43	60	14	....	....	....	....	....	....	....	....	....	18	2	13	15	4	....	....	....	....
2012-13	Ottawa 67's	OHL	42	11	29	40	10	....	....	....	....	....	....	....	....	....	....	....	....	....	....	....	....	....	....
	Owen Sound	OHL	27	8	16	24	2	....	....	....	....	....	....	....	....	....	12	1	9	10	0	....	....	....	....
	Binghamton	AHL	3	1	1	2	0	....	....	....	....	....	....	....	....	....	3	0	0	0	0	....	....	....	....
2013-14	**Ottawa**	**NHL**	**49**	**3**	**6**	**9**	**14**	**0**	**0**	**2**	**82**	**3.7**	**–5**	**0**	**0.0**	**17:12**	....	....	....	....	....	....	....	....	....
	Binghamton	AHL	27	2	17	19	10	....	....	....	....	....	....	....	....	....	4	1	1	2	0	....	....	....	....
2014-15	**Ottawa**	**NHL**	**81**	**5**	**16**	**21**	**6**	**1**	**0**	**0**	**130**	**3.8**	**–4**	**0**	**0.0**	**19:17**	**6**	**0**	**2**	**2**	**0**	**0**	**0**	**0**	**18:00**
2015-16	**Ottawa**	**NHL**	**75**	**10**	**16**	**26**	**18**	**0**	**0**	**2**	**116**	**8.6**	**9**	**0**	**0.0**	**19:18**	....	....	....	....	....	....	....	....	....
2016-17	**Ottawa**	**NHL**	**79**	**2**	**15**	**17**	**20**	**0**	**0**	**0**	**143**	**1.4**	**–11**	**1**	**100.0**	**23:12**	**19**	**0**	**1**	**1**	**2**	**0**	**0**	**0**	**23:36**
	NHL Totals		**284**	**20**	**53**	**73**	**58**	**1**	**0**	**4**	**471**	**4.2**		**1**	**100.0**	**20:01**	**25**	**0**	**3**	**3**	**2**	**0**	**0**	**0**	**22:15**

OHL Second All-Star Team (2012, 2013)

CEHLARIK, Peter

(T'SECH-lahr-ihk, PEE-tuhr) **BOS**

Left wing. Shoots left. 6'3", 202 lbs. Born, Zilina, Slovakia, August 2, 1995. Boston's 2nd pick, 90th overall, in 2013 NHL Draft.

2008-09	MsHK Zilina U18	Svk-U18	1	0	0	0	0	....	....	....	....	....	....	....	....	....	....	....	....	....	....	....	....	....	....
2009-10	Zilina U18	Svk-U18	28	4	4	8	4	....	....	....	....	....	....	....	....	....	....	....	....	....	....	....	....	....	....
2010-11	MsHK Zilina U18	Svk-U18	40	15	18	33	8	....	....	....	....	....	....	....	....	....	....	....	....	....	....	....	....	....	....
2011-12	MsHK Zilina U18	Svk-U18	6	6	2	8	16	....	....	....	....	....	....	....	....	....	....	....	....	....	....	....	....	....	....
	MsHK Zilina Jr.	Slovak-Jr.	4	1	2	3	2	....	....	....	....	....	....	....	....	....	....	....	....	....	....	....	....	....	....
	Lulea HF U18	Swe-U18	24	15	15	30	0	....	....	....	....	....	....	....	....	....	4	2	0	2	0	....	....	....	....
	Lulea HF Jr.	Swe-Jr.	8	2	2	4	2	....	....	....	....	....	....	....	....	....	1	3	0	3	0	....	....	....	....
2012-13	Lulea HF U18	Swe-U18	10	8	9	17	0	....	....	....	....	....	....	....	....	....	....	....	....	....	....	....	....	....	....
	Lulea HF Jr.	Swe-Jr.	38	17	20	37	10	....	....	....	....	....	....	....	....	....	3	0	1	1	2	....	....	....	....
	Lulea HF	Sweden	8	3	3	6	0	....	....	....	....	....	....	....	....	....	6	1	0	1	0	....	....	....	....
2013-14	Lulea HF Jr.	Swe-Jr.	4	5	2	7	0	....	....	....	....	....	....	....	....	....	....	....	....	....	....	....	....	....	....
	Lulea HF	Sweden	32	2	2	4	4	....	....	....	....	....	....	....	....	....	2	0	0	0	0	....	....	....	....
	Asploven	Sweden-2	18	5	8	13	6	....	....	....	....	....	....	....	....	....	....	....	....	....	....	....	....	....	....
2014-15	Lulea HF Jr.	Swe-Jr.	1	0	0	0	0	....	....	....	....	....	....	....	....	....	....	....	....	....	....	....	....	....	....
	Lulea HF	Sweden	46	6	13	19	6	....	....	....	....	....	....	....	....	....	8	1	1	2	2	....	....	....	....
2015-16	Lulea HF	Sweden	46	11	9	20	4	....	....	....	....	....	....	....	....	....	11	3	2	5	0	....	....	....	....
2016-17	**Boston**	**NHL**	**11**	**0**	**2**	**2**	**0**	**0**	**0**	**0**	**8**	**0.0**	**0**	**3**	**66.7**	**13:55**	....	....	....	....	....	....	....	....	....
	Providence Bruins	AHL	49	20	18	38	20	....	....	....	....	....	....	....	....	....	2	0	1	1	2	....	....	....	....
	NHL Totals		**11**	**0**	**2**	**2**	**0**	**0**	**0**	**0**	**8**	**0.0**		**3**	**66.7**	**13:55**	....	....	....	....	....	....	....	....	....

CHABOT, Thomas

(shuh-BAWT, TAW-muhs) **OTT**

Defense. Shoots left. 6'2", 190 lbs. Born, Sainte-Marie, QC, January 30, 1997. Ottawa's 1st pick, 18th overall, in 2015 NHL Draft.

2012-13	Levis	QAAA	41	6	20	26	22	....	....	....	....	....	....	....	....	....	4	1	1	2	8	....	....	....	....
2013-14	Saint John	QMJHL	55	1	21	22	36	....	....	....	....	....	....	....	....	....	....	....	....	....	....	....	....	....	....
2014-15	Saint John	QMJHL	66	12	29	41	62	....	....	....	....	....	....	....	....	....	5	0	1	1	6	....	....	....	....
2015-16	Saint John	QMJHL	47	11	34	45	79	....	....	....	....	....	....	....	....	....	17	3	18	21	13	....	....	....	....
2016-17	**Ottawa**	**NHL**	**1**	**0**	**0**	**0**	**0**	**0**	**0**	**0**	**1**	**0.0**	**–2**	**0**	**0.0**	**7:09**	....	....	....	....	....	....	....	....	....
	Saint John	QMJHL	34	10	35	45	43	....	....	....	....	....	....	....	....	....	18	5	18	23	12	....	....	....	....
	NHL Totals		**1**	**0**	**0**	**0**	**0**	**0**	**0**	**0**	**1**	**0.0**		**0**	**0.0**	**7:09**	....	....	....	....	....	....	....	....	....

QMJHL Second All-Star Team (2016) • QMJHL First All-Star Team (2017)

CHAPUT, Michael

(sha-PUT, MIGH-kuhl) **VAN**

Center. Shoots left. 6'2", 204 lbs. Born, Ile Bizard, QC, April 9, 1992. Philadelphia's 1st pick, 89th overall, in 2010 NHL Draft.

2007-08	Lac St-L. Royals	Minor-QC	STATISTICS NOT AVAILABLE																						
	Lac St-Louis Lions	QAAA	4	0	0	0	0	....	....	....	....	....	....	....	....	....	....	....	....	....	....	....	....	....	....
2008-09	Lewiston	QMJHL	29	3	7	10	34	....	....	....	....	....	....	....	....	....	....	....	....	....	....	....	....	....	....
2009-10	Lewiston	QMJHL	68	28	27	55	60	....	....	....	....	....	....	....	....	....	4	0	1	1	2	....	....	....	....
2010-11	Lewiston	QMJHL	62	25	34	59	97	....	....	....	....	....	....	....	....	....	13	7	13	20	11	....	....	....	....
2011-12	Shawinigan	QMJHL	57	21	42	63	47	....	....	....	....	....	....	....	....	....	11	4	8	12	2	....	....	....	....
2012-13	Springfield	AHL	73	13	19	32	57	....	....	....	....	....	....	....	....	....	8	1	1	2	4	....	....	....	....
2013-14	**Columbus**	**NHL**	**17**	**0**	**1**	**1**	**2**	**0**	**0**	**0**	**6**	**0.0**	**0**	**98**	**42.9**	**8:54**	....	....	....	....	....	....	....	....	....
	Springfield	AHL	55	19	26	45	51	....	....	....	....	....	....	....	....	....	5	2	1	3	6	....	....	....	....
2014-15	**Columbus**	**NHL**	**33**	**1**	**4**	**5**	**21**	**0**	**0**	**0**	**23**	**4.3**	**–8**	**294**	**48.6**	**10:12**	....	....	....	....	....	....	....	....	....
	Springfield	AHL	45	10	11	21	22	....	....	....	....	....	....	....	....	....	....	....	....	....	....	....	....	....	....
2015-16	**Columbus**	**NHL**	**8**	**1**	**1**	**2**	**5**	**0**	**0**	**0**	**10**	**10.0**	**3**	**75**	**65.3**	**9:00**	....	....	....	....	....	....	....	....	....
	Lake Erie	AHL	63	16	29	45	31	....	....	....	....	....	....	....	....	....	17	2	6	8	13	....	....	....	....
2016-17	**Vancouver**	**NHL**	**68**	**4**	**5**	**9**	**29**	**0**	**0**	**0**	**64**	**6.3**	**–12**	**385**	**52.7**	**11:01**	....	....	....	....	....	....	....	....	....
	Utica Comets	AHL	10	2	11	13	10	....	....	....	....	....	....	....	....	....	....	....	....	....	....	....	....	....	....
	NHL Totals		**126**	**6**	**11**	**17**	**57**	**0**	**0**	**0**	**103**	**5.8**		**852**	**51.3**	**10:23**	....	....	....	....	....	....	....	....	....

• Missed majority of 2008-09 due to recurring shoulder injury. Traded to **Columbus** by **Philadelphia** with Greg Moore for Tom Sestito, February 28, 2011. Signed as a free agent by **Vancouver**, July 1, 2016.

CHARA, Zdeno

(CHAH-rah, z'DEHN-oh) **BOS**

Defense. Shoots left. 6'9", 250 lbs. Born, Trencin, Czechoslovakia, March 18, 1977. NY Islanders' 3rd pick, 56th overall, in 1996 NHL Draft.

1994-95	Dukla Trencin U18	Svk-U18	30	22	22	44	113	....	....	....	....	....	....	....	....	....	....	....	....	....	....	....	....	....	....
	Dukla Trencin Jr.	Slovak-Jr.	2	0	0	0	0	....	....	....	....	....	....	....	....	....	....	....	....	....	....	....	....	....	....
1995-96	Dukla Trencin Jr.	Slovak-Jr.	22	1	13	14	80	....	....	....	....	....	....	....	....	....	....	....	....	....	....	....	....	....	....
	HK VTJ Piestany	Slovak-2	10	1	3	4	10	....	....	....	....	....	....	....	....	....	....	....	....	....	....	....	....	....	....
	Sparta Jr.	CzRep-Jr.	15	1	2	3	42	....	....	....	....	....	....	....	....	....	....	....	....	....	....	....	....	....	....
	HC Sparta Praha	CzRep	1	0	0	0	0	....	....	....	....	....	....	....	....	....	....	....	....	....	....	....	....	....	....
1996-97	Prince George	WHL	49	3	19	22	120	....	....	....	....	....	....	....	....	....	15	1	7	8	45	....	....	....	....
1997-98	**NY Islanders**	**NHL**	**25**	**0**	**1**	**1**	**50**	**0**	**0**	**0**	**10**	**0.0**	**1**	....	....	....	....	....	....	....	....	....	....	....	....
	Kentucky	AHL	48	4	9	13	125	....	....	....	....	....	....	....	....	....	1	0	0	0	4	....	....	....	....
1998-99	**NY Islanders**	**NHL**	**59**	**2**	**6**	**8**	**83**	**0**	**1**	**0**	**56**	**3.6**	**–8**	**0**	**0.0**	**18:54**	....	....	....	....	....	....	....	....	....
	Lowell	AHL	23	2	2	4	47	....	....	....	....	....	....	....	....	....	....	....	....	....	....	....	....	....	....
99-2000	**NY Islanders**	**NHL**	**65**	**2**	**9**	**11**	**57**	**0**	**0**	**1**	**47**	**4.3**	**–27**	**0**	**0.0**	**22:52**	....	....	....	....	....	....	....	....	....
2000-01	**NY Islanders**	**NHL**	**82**	**2**	**7**	**9**	**157**	**0**	**1**	**0**	**83**	**2.4**	**–27**	**0**	**0.0**	**22:20**	....	....	....	....	....	....	....	....	....
2001-02	Dukla Trencin	Slovakia	8	2	2	4	32	....	....	....	....	....	....	....	....	....	....	....	....	....	....	....	....	....	....
	Ottawa	**NHL**	**75**	**10**	**13**	**23**	**156**	**4**	**1**	**2**	**105**	**9.5**	**30**	**0**	**0.0**	**22:16**	**10**	**0**	**1**	**1**	**12**	**0**	**0**	**0**	**26:07**
2002-03	**Ottawa**	**NHL**	**74**	**9**	**30**	**39**	**116**	**3**	**0**	**2**	**168**	**5.4**	**29**	**0**	**0.0**	**24:57**	**18**	**1**	**6**	**7**	**14**	**0**	**0**	**0**	**25:07**
2003-04	**Ottawa**	**NHL**	**79**	**16**	**25**	**41**	**147**	**7**	**0**	**3**	**185**	**8.6**	**33**	**0**	**0.0**	**24:38**	**7**	**1**	**1**	**2**	**8**	**0**	**0**	**0**	**24:38**
2004-05	Farjestad	Sweden	33	10	15	25	132	....	....	....	....	....	....	....	....	....	13	3	5	8	82	....	....	....	....
2005-06	**Ottawa**	**NHL**	**71**	**16**	**27**	**43**	**135**	**10**	**1**	**3**	**212**	**7.5**	**17**	**24**	**41.7**	**27:11**	**10**	**1**	**3**	**4**	**23**	**1**	**0**	**0**	**27:32**
	Slovakia	Olympics	6	1	1	2	2	....	....	....	....	....	....	....	....	....	....	....	....	....	....	....	....	....	....
2006-07	**Boston**	**NHL**	**80**	**11**	**32**	**43**	**100**	**9**	**0**	**3**	**204**	**5.4**	**–21**	**1**	**0.0**	**27:58**	....	....	....	....	....	....	....	....	....
2007-08	**Boston**	**NHL**	**77**	**17**	**34**	**51**	**114**	**9**	**1**	**0**	**207**	**8.2**	**14**	**0**	**0.0**	**26:50**	**7**	**1**	**1**	**2**	**12**	**1**	**0**	**0**	**25:52**
2008-09	**Boston**	**NHL**	**80**	**19**	**31**	**50**	**95**	**11**	**0**	**3**	**216**	**8.8**	**23**	**4**	**25.0**	**26:04**	**11**	**1**	**3**	**4**	**12**	**1**	**0**	**1**	**25:11**
2009-10	**Boston**	**NHL**	**80**	**7**	**37**	**44**	**87**	**4**	**0**	**1**	**242**	**2.9**	**19**	**2**	**50.0**	**25:22**	**13**	**2**	**5**	**7**	**29**	**0**	**0**	**1**	**28:08**
	Slovakia	Olympics	7	0	3	3	6	....	....	....	....	....	....	....	....	....	....	....	....	....	....	....	....	....	....
2010-11 ♦	**Boston**	**NHL**	**81**	**14**	**30**	**44**	**88**	**8**	**1**	**2**	**264**	**5.3**	***33**	**0**	**0.0**	**25:26**	**24**	**2**	**7**	**9**	**34**	**1**	**0**	**0**	**27:39**

			Regular Season														Playoffs								
Season	Club	League	GP	G	A	Pts	PIM	PP	SH	GW	S	S%	+/-	TF	F%	Min	GP	G	A	Pts	PIM	PP	SH	GW	Min
2011-12	**Boston**	**NHL**	**79**	**12**	**40**	**52**	**86**	**8**	**0**	**0**	**224**	**5.4**	**33**	**1**	**0.0**	**25:00**	**7**	**1**	**2**	**3**	**8**	**0**	**0**	**1**	**27:21**
2012-13	HC Lev Praha	KHL	25	4	6	10	24	....	....	....	....	....	....	....	....	....	....	....	....	....	....	....	....	....	....
	Boston	**NHL**	**48**	**7**	**12**	**19**	**70**	**3**	**0**	**2**	**119**	**5.9**	**14**	**1**	**0.0**	**24:56**	**22**	**3**	**12**	**15**	**20**	**0**	**0**	**0**	**29:32**
2013-14	**Boston**	**NHL**	**77**	**17**	**23**	**40**	**66**	**10**	**0**	**3**	**168**	**10.1**	**25**	**0**	**0.0**	**24:39**	**12**	**2**	**2**	**4**	**14**	**2**	**0**	**0**	**25:20**
	Slovakia	Olympics	4	0	1	1	4	....	....	....	....	....	....	....	....	....	....	....	....	....	....	....	....	....	....
2014-15	**Boston**	**NHL**	**63**	**8**	**12**	**20**	**42**	**4**	**0**	**0**	**138**	**5.8**	**0**	**1**	**100.0**	**23:21**	....	....	....	....	....	....	....	....	....
2015-16	**Boston**	**NHL**	**80**	**9**	**28**	**37**	**71**	**1**	**0**	**3**	**158**	**5.7**	**12**	**1**	**0.0**	**24:06**	....	....	....	....	....	....	....	....	....
2016-17	**Boston**	**NHL**	**75**	**10**	**19**	**29**	**59**	**1**	**2**	**0**	**136**	**7.4**	**18**	**1**	**0.0**	**23:20**	**6**	**0**	**1**	**1**	**2**	**0**	**0**	**0**	**28:46**
	NHL Totals		**1350**	**188**	**416**	**604**	**1779**	**92**	**8**	**28**	**2942**	**6.4**		**36**	**36.1**	**24:33**	**147**	**15**	**44**	**59**	**188**	**6**	**0**	**3**	**26:59**

AHL All-Rookie Team (1998) • NHL First All-Star Team (2004, 2009, 2014) • NHL Second All-Star Team (2006, 2008, 2011, 2012) • James Norris Memorial Trophy (2009) • Mark Messier NHL Leadership Award (2011)

Played in NHL All-Star Game (2003, 2007, 2008, 2009, 2011, 2012)

Traded to **Ottawa** by **NY Islanders** with Bill Muckalt and NY Islanders' 1st round pick (Jason Spezza) in 2001 NHL Draft for Alexei Yashin, June 23, 2001. Signed as a free agent by **Farjestad** (Sweden), September 24, 2004. Signed as a free agent by **Boston**, July 1, 2006. Signed as a free agent by **Lev Praha** (KHL), October 2, 2012.

CHIAROT, Ben

(CHAIR-awt, BEHN) **WPG**

Defense. Shoots left. 6'3", 219 lbs. Born, Hamilton, ON, May 9, 1991. Atlanta's 5th pick, 120th overall, in 2009 NHL Draft.

Season	Club	League	GP	G	A	Pts	PIM	PP	SH	GW	S	S%	+/-	TF	F%	Min	GP	G	A	Pts	PIM	PP	SH	GW	Min
2006-07	Mississauga Reps	GTHL	60	21	42	63	166	....	....	....	....	....	....	....	....	....	....	....	....	....	....	....	....	....	....
2007-08	Guelph Storm	OHL	31	0	0	0	14	....	....	....	....	....	....	....	....	....	....	....	....	....	....	....	....	....	....
2008-09	Guelph Storm	OHL	67	2	10	12	111	....	....	....	....	....	....	....	....	....	4	0	3	3	8	....	....	....	....
2009-10	Guelph Storm	OHL	41	4	9	13	106	....	....	....	....	....	....	....	....	....	....	....	....	....	....	....	....	....	....
	Sudbury Wolves	OHL	26	4	4	8	61	....	....	....	....	....	....	....	....	....	4	1	1	2	6	....	....	....	....
	Chicago Wolves	AHL	1	0	0	0	4	....	....	....	....	....	....	....	....	....	....	....	....	....	....	....	....	....	....
2010-11	Sudbury Wolves	OHL	25	5	8	13	62	....	....	....	....	....	....	....	....	....	....	....	....	....	....	....	....	....	....
	Saginaw Spirit	OHL	39	5	19	24	51	....	....	....	....	....	....	....	....	....	12	1	4	5	21	....	....	....	....
2011-12	St. John's IceCaps	AHL	18	1	1	2	19	....	....	....	....	....	....	....	....	....	....	....	....	....	....	....	....	....	....
	Colorado Eagles	ECHL	24	6	7	13	13	....	....	....	....	....	....	....	....	....	....	....	....	....	....	....	....	....	....
2012-13	St. John's IceCaps	AHL	61	1	11	12	81	....	....	....	....	....	....	....	....	....	....	....	....	....	....	....	....	....	....
2013-14	**Winnipeg**	**NHL**	**1**	**0**	**0**	**0**	**0**	**0**	**0**	**0**	**0**	**0.0**	**–3**	**0**	**0.0**	**10:47**	....	....	....	....	....	....	....	....	....
	St. John's IceCaps	AHL	65	6	14	20	96	....	....	....	....	....	....	....	....	....	21	2	3	5	16	....	....	....	....
2014-15	**Winnipeg**	**NHL**	**40**	**2**	**6**	**8**	**22**	**0**	**0**	**0**	**37**	**5.4**	**5**	**0**	**0.0**	**17:01**	**2**	**0**	**0**	**0**	**2**	**0**	**0**	**0**	**13:42**
	St. John's IceCaps	AHL	24	4	5	9	21	....	....	....	....	....	....	....	....	....	....	....	....	....	....	....	....	....	....
2015-16	**Winnipeg**	**NHL**	**70**	**1**	**9**	**10**	**43**	**0**	**0**	**0**	**74**	**1.4**	**–9**	**0**	**0.0**	**14:27**	....	....	....	....	....	....	....	....	....
2016-17	**Winnipeg**	**NHL**	**59**	**2**	**10**	**12**	**33**	**0**	**0**	**0**	**49**	**4.1**	**2**	**0**	**0.0**	**15:19**	....	....	....	....	....	....	....	....	....
	NHL Totals		**170**	**5**	**25**	**30**	**98**	**0**	**0**	**0**	**160**	**3.1**		**0**	**0.0**	**15:20**	**2**	**0**	**0**	**0**	**2**	**0**	**0**	**0**	**13:42**

• Transferred to **Winnipeg** after **Atlanta** franchise relocated, June 21, 2011.

CHIASSON, Alex

(CHAY-sahn, Al-ehx)

Right wing. Shoots right. 6'4", 208 lbs. Born, Montreal, QC, October 1, 1990. Dallas' 2nd pick, 38th overall, in 2009 NHL Draft.

Season	Club	League	GP	G	A	Pts	PIM	PP	SH	GW	S	S%	+/-	TF	F%	Min	GP	G	A	Pts	PIM	PP	SH	GW	Min
2005-06	Sem. St-Francois	QAAA	13	1	1	2	16	....	....	....	....	....	....	....	....	....	2	1	1	2	0	....	....	....	....
2006-07	Sem. St-Francois	QAAA	43	12	18	30	41	....	....	....	....	....	....	....	....	....	18	4	18	22	18	....	....	....	....
2007-08	Northwood	High-NY	45	35	46	81	....	....	....	....	....	....	....	....	....	....	....	....	....	....	....	....	....	....	....
2008-09	Des Moines	USHL	56	17	33	50	101	....	....	....	....	....	....	....	....	....	....	....	....	....	....	....	....	....	....
2009-10	Boston University	H-East	35	7	12	19	44	....	....	....	....	....	....	....	....	....	....	....	....	....	....	....	....	....	....
2010-11	Boston University	H-East	35	14	20	34	75	....	....	....	....	....	....	....	....	....	....	....	....	....	....	....	....	....	....
2011-12	Boston University	H-East	38	15	31	46	67	....	....	....	....	....	....	....	....	....	....	....	....	....	....	....	....	....	....
	Texas Stars	AHL	9	1	4	5	9	....	....	....	....	....	....	....	....	....	....	....	....	....	....	....	....	....	....
2012-13	Texas Stars	AHL	57	13	22	35	43	....	....	....	....	....	....	....	....	....	7	2	1	3	4	....	....	....	....
	Dallas	**NHL**	**7**	**6**	**1**	**7**	**0**	**1**	**0**	**1**	**13**	**46.2**	**3**	**18**	**27.8**	**14:05**	....	....	....	....	....	....	....	....	....
2013-14	**Dallas**	**NHL**	**79**	**13**	**22**	**35**	**38**	**6**	**0**	**4**	**144**	**9.0**	**–21**	**132**	**48.5**	**15:07**	**6**	**1**	**1**	**2**	**2**	**1**	**0**	**0**	**15:41**
2014-15	**Ottawa**	**NHL**	**76**	**11**	**15**	**26**	**67**	**3**	**0**	**1**	**105**	**10.5**	**–5**	**21**	**14.3**	**13:23**	**4**	**0**	**0**	**0**	**0**	**0**	**0**	**0**	**9:14**
2015-16	**Ottawa**	**NHL**	**77**	**8**	**6**	**14**	**45**	**2**	**1**	**1**	**88**	**9.1**	**2**	**5**	**60.0**	**13:38**	....	....	....	....	....	....	....	....	....
2016-17	**Calgary**	**NHL**	**81**	**12**	**12**	**24**	**46**	**0**	**1**	**1**	**104**	**11.5**	**–6**	**29**	**24.1**	**13:23**	**4**	**0**	**0**	**0**	**2**	**0**	**0**	**0**	**12:49**
	NHL Totals		**320**	**50**	**56**	**106**	**196**	**12**	**2**	**8**	**454**	**11.0**		**205**	**40.0**	**13:53**	**14**	**1**	**1**	**2**	**4**	**1**	**0**	**0**	**13:01**

Traded to **Ottawa** by **Dallas** with Alexander Guptill, Nicholas Paul and Dallas' 2nd round pick (later traded to New Jersey – New Jersey selected Mackenzie Blackwood) in 2015 NHL Draft for Jason Spezza and Ludwig Karlsson, July 1, 2014. Traded to **Calgary** by **Ottawa** for Pat Sieloff, June 27, 2016.

CHIMERA, Jason

(shih-MAIR-uh, JAY-suhn) **NYI**

Left wing. Shoots left. 6'3", 216 lbs. Born, Edmonton, AB, May 2, 1979. Edmonton's 5th pick, 121st overall, in 1997 NHL Draft.

Season	Club	League	GP	G	A	Pts	PIM	PP	SH	GW	S	S%	+/-	TF	F%	Min	GP	G	A	Pts	PIM	PP	SH	GW	Min
1994-95	Edmonton Pats	AMHL	33	27	31	58	42	....	....	....	....	....	....	....	....	....	....	....	....	....	....	....	....	....	....
1995-96	Edmonton Pats	AMHL	34	23	24	47	44	....	....	....	....	....	....	....	....	....	....	....	....	....	....	....	....	....	....
1996-97	Medicine Hat	WHL	71	16	23	39	54	....	....	....	....	....	....	....	....	....	4	0	1	1	4	....	....	....	....
1997-98	Medicine Hat	WHL	72	34	32	66	93	....	....	....	....	....	....	....	....	....	....	....	....	....	....	....	....	....	....
	Hamilton	AHL	4	0	0	0	8	....	....	....	....	....	....	....	....	....	....	....	....	....	....	....	....	....	....
1998-99	Medicine Hat	WHL	37	18	22	40	84	....	....	....	....	....	....	....	....	....	....	....	....	....	....	....	....	....	....
	Brandon	WHL	21	14	12	26	32	....	....	....	....	....	....	....	....	....	5	4	1	5	8	....	....	....	....
99-2000	Hamilton	AHL	78	15	13	28	77	....	....	....	....	....	....	....	....	....	10	0	2	2	12	....	....	....	....
2000-01	**Edmonton**	**NHL**	**1**	**0**	**0**	**0**	**0**	**0**	**0**	**0**	**0**	**0.0**	**0**	**0**	**0.0**	**6:58**	....	....	....	....	....	....	....	....	....
	Hamilton	AHL	78	29	25	54	93	....	....	....	....	....	....	....	....	....	....	....	....	....	....	....	....	....	....
2001-02	**Edmonton**	**NHL**	**3**	**1**	**0**	**1**	**0**	**0**	**0**	**0**	**3**	**33.3**	**–3**	**0**	**0.0**	**12:44**	....	....	....	....	....	....	....	....	....
	Hamilton	AHL	77	26	51	77	158	....	....	....	....	....	....	....	....	....	15	4	6	10	10	....	....	....	....
2002-03	**Edmonton**	**NHL**	**66**	**14**	**9**	**23**	**36**	**0**	**1**	**4**	**90**	**15.6**	**–2**	**11**	**54.6**	**10:46**	**2**	**0**	**2**	**2**	**0**	**0**	**0**	**0**	**10:55**
2003-04	**Edmonton**	**NHL**	**60**	**4**	**8**	**12**	**57**	**0**	**0**	**1**	**79**	**5.1**	**–1**	**22**	**31.8**	**10:07**	....	....	....	....	....	....	....	....	....
2004-05	AS Varese Hockey	Italy	15	7	3	10	34	....	....	....	....	....	....	....	....	....	5	2	1	3	31	....	....	....	....
2005-06	**Columbus**	**NHL**	**80**	**17**	**13**	**30**	**95**	**1**	**1**	**5**	**127**	**13.4**	**–10**	**16**	**50.0**	**12:41**	....	....	....	....	....	....	....	....	....
2006-07	**Columbus**	**NHL**	**82**	**15**	**21**	**36**	**91**	**2**	**2**	**2**	**151**	**9.9**	**2**	**38**	**36.8**	**15:22**	....	....	....	....	....	....	....	....	....
2007-08	**Columbus**	**NHL**	**81**	**14**	**17**	**31**	**98**	**1**	**1**	**3**	**198**	**7.1**	**–5**	**35**	**45.7**	**17:30**	....	....	....	....	....	....	....	....	....
2008-09	**Columbus**	**NHL**	**49**	**8**	**14**	**22**	**41**	**1**	**0**	**1**	**115**	**7.0**	**8**	**42**	**42.9**	**16:15**	**4**	**0**	**1**	**1**	**2**	**0**	**0**	**0**	**13:21**
2009-10	**Columbus**	**NHL**	**39**	**8**	**9**	**17**	**47**	**1**	**0**	**1**	**92**	**8.7**	**–7**	**23**	**65.2**	**14:47**	....	....	....	....	....	....	....	....	....
	Washington	**NHL**	**39**	**7**	**10**	**17**	**51**	**0**	**0**	**0**	**68**	**10.3**	**6**	**17**	**41.2**	**12:36**	**7**	**1**	**2**	**3**	**2**	**0**	**0**	**1**	**11:46**
2010-11	**Washington**	**NHL**	**81**	**10**	**16**	**26**	**64**	**2**	**0**	**1**	**162**	**6.2**	**–10**	**39**	**51.3**	**13:15**	**9**	**2**	**2**	**4**	**2**	**0**	**0**	**2**	**12:53**
2011-12	**Washington**	**NHL**	**82**	**20**	**19**	**39**	**78**	**1**	**2**	**5**	**205**	**9.8**	**4**	**62**	**48.4**	**14:26**	**14**	**4**	**3**	**7**	**6**	**0**	**0**	**1**	**13:42**
2012-13	Pirati Chomutov	CzRep	5	1	0	1	10	....	....	....	....	....	....	....	....	....	....	....	....	....	....	....	....	....	....
	Washington	**NHL**	**47**	**3**	**11**	**14**	**48**	**0**	**0**	**0**	**92**	**3.3**	**–5**	**36**	**58.3**	**12:40**	**7**	**1**	**2**	**3**	**4**	**0**	**0**	**0**	**13:40**
2013-14	**Washington**	**NHL**	**82**	**15**	**27**	**42**	**36**	**1**	**0**	**0**	**167**	**9.0**	**4**	**87**	**43.7**	**15:25**	....	....	....	....	....	....	....	....	....
2014-15	**Washington**	**NHL**	**77**	**7**	**12**	**19**	**51**	**0**	**0**	**2**	**96**	**7.3**	**–1**	**76**	**56.6**	**12:56**	**14**	**3**	**4**	**7**	**4**	**0**	**0**	**1**	**15:36**
2015-16	**Washington**	**NHL**	**82**	**20**	**20**	**40**	**22**	**4**	**2**	**3**	**165**	**12.1**	**0**	**28**	**28.6**	**14:03**	**12**	**1**	**1**	**2**	**12**	**0**	**0**	**1**	**13:00**
2016-17	**NY Islanders**	**NHL**	**82**	**20**	**13**	**33**	**40**	**0**	**1**	**2**	**121**	**16.5**	**1**	**34**	**47.1**	**13:04**	....	....	....	....	....	....	....	....	....
	NHL Totals		**1033**	**183**	**219**	**402**	**855**	**14**	**10**	**30**	**1931**	**9.5**		**566**	**47.2**	**13:48**	**69**	**12**	**17**	**29**	**32**	**0**	**0**	**6**	**13:33**

AHL First All-Star Team (2002)

Traded to **Phoenix** by **Edmonton** with Edmonton's 3rd round pick (later traded to Carolina, later traded to NY Rangers – NY Rangers selected Billy Ryan) in 2004 NHL Draft for New Jersey's 2nd round pick (previously acquired, Edmonton selected Geoff Paukovich) in 2004 NHL Draft and Buffalo's 4th round pick (previously acquired, Edmonton selected Liam Reddox) in 2004 NHL Draft, June 26, 2004. Signed as a free agent by **Varese** (Italy), December 15, 2004. Traded to **Columbus** by **Phoenix** with Cale Hulse and Mike Rupp for Geoff Sanderson and Tim Jackman, October 8, 2005. Traded to **Washington** by **Columbus** for Chris Clark and Milan Jurcina, December 28, 2009. Signed as a free agent by **Chomutov** (CzRep), November 14, 2012. Signed as a free agent by **NY Islanders**, July 1, 2016.

CHORNEY, Taylor

(CHOHR-nee, TAY-luhr) **WSH**

Defense. Shoots left. 6'1", 190 lbs. Born, Thunder Bay, ON, April 27, 1987. Edmonton's 2nd pick, 36th overall, in 2005 NHL Draft.

Season	Club	League	GP	G	A	Pts	PIM	PP	SH	GW	S	S%	+/-	TF	F%	Min	GP	G	A	Pts	PIM	PP	SH	GW	Min
2003-04	Shattuck	High-MN	74	12	44	56	58	....	....	....	....	....	....	....	....	....	....	....	....	....	....	....	....	....	....
2004-05	Shattuck	High-MN	50	4	30	34	52	....	....	....	....	....	....	....	....	....	....	....	....	....	....	....	....	....	....
2005-06	North Dakota	WCHA	44	3	15	18	54	....	....	....	....	....	....	....	....	....	....	....	....	....	....	....	....	....	....
2006-07	North Dakota	WCHA	39	8	23	31	48	....	....	....	....	....	....	....	....	....	....	....	....	....	....	....	....	....	....
2007-08	North Dakota	WCHA	43	3	21	24	24	....	....	....	....	....	....	....	....	....	....	....	....	....	....	....	....	....	....
2008-09	**Edmonton**	**NHL**	**2**	**0**	**0**	**0**	**0**	**0**	**0**	**0**	**0**	**0.0**	**–4**	**0**	**0.0**	**15:43**	....	....	....	....	....	....	....	....	....
	Springfield	AHL	68	5	16	21	22	....	....	....	....	....	....	....	....	....	....	....	....	....	....	....	....	....	....

			Regular Season														Playoffs								
Season	Club	League	GP	G	A	Pts	PIM	PP	SH	GW	S	S%	+/-	TF	F%	Min	GP	G	A	Pts	PIM	PP	SH	GW	Min
2009-10	Edmonton	NHL	42	0	3	3	12	0	0	0	35	0.0	−21	0	0.0	17:24									
	Springfield	AHL	32	4	9	13	14																		
2010-11	Edmonton	NHL	12	1	3	4	4	1	0	1	13	7.7	−5	0	0.0	15:59									
	Oklahoma City	AHL	46	3	13	16	22																		
2011-12	St. Louis	NHL	2	0	0	0	0	0	0	0	1	0.0	0	0	0.0	11:40									
	Edmonton	NHL	3	0	0	0	0	0	0	0	1	0.0	−1	0	0.0	15:48									
	Oklahoma City	AHL	50	6	18	24	29										10	0	1	1	6				
2012-13	Peoria Rivermen	AHL	73	4	20	24	37																		
2013-14	Chicago Wolves	AHL	69	5	20	25	37										9	1	1	2	2				
2014-15	Pittsburgh	NHL	7	0	0	0	0	0	0	0	4	0.0	−1	0	0.0	12:10	5	0	0	0	2	0	0	0	16:35
	Wilkes-Barre	AHL	62	4	15	19	42										6	1	1	2	6				
2015-16	Washington	NHL	55	1	5	6	21	0	0	0	28	3.6	8	0	0.0	13:11	7	0	1	1	4	0	0	0	12:34
2016-17	Washington	NHL	18	1	4	5	11	0	0	1	19	5.3	8	0	0.0	14:16									
	NHL Totals		141	3	15	18	48	1	0	2	101	3.0		0	0.0	14:50	12	0	1	1	6	0	0	0	14:15

WCHA Second All-Star Team (2007) • NCAA West Second All-American Team (2007) • WCHA First All-Star Team (2008)

Claimed on waivers by **St. Louis** from **Edmonton** October 11, 2011. Claimed on waivers by **Edmonton** from **St. Louis** November 10, 2011. Signed as a free agent by **St. Louis**, July 1, 2012. Signed as a free agent by **Pittsburgh**, July 1, 2014. Signed as a free agent by **Washington**, July 1, 2015. • Missed majority of 2016-17 as a healthy reserve.

CHYCHRUN, Jakob (CHIHK-ruhn, JAY-kuhb) ARI

Defense. Shoots left. 6'3", 200 lbs. Born, Boca Raton, FL, March 31, 1998. Arizona's 2nd pick, 16th overall, in 2016 NHL Draft.

Season	Club	League	GP	G	A	Pts	PIM	PP	SH	GW	S	S%	+/-	TF	F%	Min	GP	G	A	Pts	PIM	PP	SH	GW	Min
2012-13	Det. L.C. U16	HPHL	25	11	7	18	43																		
	Det. L.C. U16	Minor-MI															4	2	1	3	2				
2013-14	Tor. Jr. Can. MM	GTHL	29	16	27	43	28										14	5	8	13	16				
2014-15	Sarnia Sting	OHL	42	16	17	33	37																		
2015-16	Sarnia Sting	OHL	62	11	38	49	51										7	2	6	8	8				
2016-17	Arizona	NHL	68	7	13	20	47	1	0	0	86	8.1	−14	0	0.0	16:40									
	NHL Totals		68	7	13	20	47	1	0	0	86	8.1		0	0.0	16:40									

OHL All-Rookie Team (2015) • OHL Second All-Star Team (2016)

CIZIKAS, Casey (sih-ZEE-kuhs, KAY-see) NYI

Center. Shoots left. 5'11", 201 lbs. Born, Toronto, ON, February 27, 1991. NY Islanders' 5th pick, 92nd overall, in 2009 NHL Draft.

Season	Club	League	GP	G	A	Pts	PIM	PP	SH	GW	S	S%	+/-	TF	F%	Min	GP	G	A	Pts	PIM	PP	SH	GW	Min
2006-07	Mississauga Reps	GTHL	77	46	60	106	88																		
2007-08	St. Michael's	OHL	62	18	23	41	41										4	1	2	3	6				
2008-09	St. Michael's	OHL	55	16	20	36	39										11	5	4	9	11				
2009-10	St. Michael's	OHL	68	25	37	62	77										16	7	7	14	16				
2010-11	St. Michael's	OHL	52	29	35	64	40										16	5	14	19	14				
2011-12	NY Islanders	NHL	15	0	4	4	6	0	0	0	12	0.0	1	115	40.9	10:36									
	Bridgeport	AHL	52	15	30	45	30										3	0	0	0	20				
2012-13	Bridgeport	AHL	31	10	11	21	35																		
	NY Islanders	NHL	45	6	9	15	14	0	0	1	45	13.3	0	276	52.2	10:47	6	2	2	4	12	0	0	0	10:46
2013-14	NY Islanders	NHL	80	6	10	16	30	1	0	1	79	7.6	−12	1011	48.4	13:22									
2014-15	NY Islanders	NHL	70	9	9	18	24	0	2	2	90	10.0	−2	855	52.2	12:31	7	1	0	1	0	0	0	0	13:42
2015-16	NY Islanders	NHL	80	8	21	29	31	0	1	4	84	9.5	4	959	48.9	12:41	11	0	3	3	16	0	0	0	14:51
2016-17	NY Islanders	NHL	59	8	17	25	30	0	0	1	82	9.8	9	846	49.7	13:54									
	NHL Totals		349	37	70	107	135	1	3	9	392	9.4		4062	49.6	12:41	24	3	5	8	28	0	0	0	13:29

CLAESSON, Fredrik (KLA-suhn, FREH-drihk) OTT

Defense. Shoots left. 6'1", 205 lbs. Born, Stockholm, Sweden, November 24, 1992. Ottawa's 6th pick, 126th overall, in 2011 NHL Draft.

Season	Club	League	GP	G	A	Pts	PIM	PP	SH	GW	S	S%	+/-	TF	F%	Min	GP	G	A	Pts	PIM	PP	SH	GW	Min
2007-08	Hammarby U18	Swe-U18	15	1	2	3	29																		
	Hammarby	Sweden-2	2	0	0	0	2																		
2008-09	Djurgarden U18	Swe-U18	28	9	8	17	4																		
	Djurgarden Jr.	Swe-Jr.	7	0	0	0	0																		
2009-10	Djurgarden U18	Swe-U18	3	1	1	2	0										5	0	3	3	6				
	Djurgarden Jr.	Swe-Jr.	22	0	4	4	18																		
2010-11	Djurgarden Jr.	Swe-Jr.	18	2	3	5	6										5	0	1	1	0				
	Djurgarden	Sweden	35	2	0	2	6										7	0	1	1	0				
2011-12	Djurgarden Jr.	Swe-Jr.	1	0	0	0	2																		
	Djurgarden	Sweden	47	1	6	7	8																		
	Djurgarden	Sweden-Q	10	1	1	2	0																		
2012-13	Binghamton	AHL	70	3	8	11	51										3	0	1	1	2				
2013-14	Binghamton	AHL	75	3	26	29	39										4	0	0	0	4				
2014-15	Binghamton	AHL	76	4	15	19	42																		
2015-16	Ottawa	NHL	16	0	2	2	2	0	0	0	15	0.0	−6	0	0.0	19:17									
	Binghamton	AHL	55	3	7	10	50																		
2016-17	Ottawa	NHL	33	3	8	11	4	0	0	0	25	12.0	5	0	0.0	13:08	14	0	3	3	4	0	0	0	14:49
	Binghamton	AHL	9	0	1	1	2																		
	NHL Totals		49	3	10	13	6	0	0	0	40	7.5		0	0.0	15:09	14	0	3	3	4	0	0	0	14:49

CLARK, Mat (KLAHRK, MAT)

Defense. Shoots right. 6'3", 225 lbs. Born, Wheat Ridge, CO, October 17, 1990. Anaheim's 3rd pick, 37th overall, in 2009 NHL Draft.

Season	Club	League	GP	G	A	Pts	PIM	PP	SH	GW	S	S%	+/-	TF	F%	Min	GP	G	A	Pts	PIM	PP	SH	GW	Min
2006-07	Brampton	ON-Jr.A	47	2	7	9	50										8	1	1	2	19				
2007-08	Brampton	ON-Jr.A	46	6	11	17	82										8	1	4	5	45				
2008-09	Brampton	OHL	63	3	20	23	91										21	0	5	5	37				
2009-10	Brampton	OHL	66	7	16	23	88										7	2	4	6	9				
	Manitoba Moose	AHL	1	0	0	0	0										6	0	0	0	2				
2010-11	Syracuse Crunch	AHL	80	2	14	16	128																		
2011-12	Anaheim	NHL	2	0	0	0	0	0	0	0	2	0.0	−2	0	0.0	11:02									
	Syracuse Crunch	AHL	62	1	11	12	72										4	1	1	2	11				
2012-13	Norfolk Admirals	AHL	71	1	9	10	79																		
2013-14	Norfolk Admirals	AHL	23	0	2	2	37																		
2014-15	Anaheim	NHL	7	0	1	1	6	0	0	0	2	0.0	2	0	0.0	12:46									
	Norfolk Admirals	AHL	45	1	5	6	60																		
	Lake Erie	AHL	21	0	1	1	11																		
2015-16	San Antonio	AHL	60	1	7	8	36																		
2016-17	San Antonio	AHL	38	1	6	7	29																		
	NHL Totals		9	0	1	1	6	0	0	0	4	0.0		0	0.0	12:23									

• Missed majority of 2013-14 due to shoulder injury at Syracuse (AHL), December 6, 2013. Traded to **Colorado** by **Anaheim** for Michael Sgarbossa, March 2, 2015. • Missed majority of 2016-17 as a healthy reserve.

CLARKSON, David (KLAHRK-suhn, DAYV-ihd) VGK

Right wing. Shoots right. 6', 207 lbs. Born, Toronto, ON, March 31, 1984.

Season	Club	League	GP	G	A	Pts	PIM	PP	SH	GW	S	S%	+/-	TF	F%	Min	GP	G	A	Pts	PIM	PP	SH	GW	Min
2000-01	Port Hope	ON-Jr.A	47	18	14	32	118																		
2001-02	Aurora Tigers	ON-Jr.A	37	26	21	47	141																		
	Belleville Bulls	OHL	22	2	7	9	34										8	1	1	2	6				
2002-03	Belleville Bulls	OHL	3	0	0	0	11																		
	Kitchener Rangers	OHL	54	17	11	28	122										21	4	3	7	23				
2003-04	Kitchener Rangers	OHL	55	22	17	39	173																		
2004-05	Kitchener Rangers	OHL	51	33	21	54	145										15	6	2	8	40				
2005-06	Albany River Rats	AHL	56	13	21	34	233																		
2006-07	New Jersey	NHL	7	3	1	4	6	2	0	1	18	16.7	−1	1	0.0	17:02	3	0	0	0	2	0	0	0	6:42
	Lowell Devils	AHL	67	20	18	38	150																		
2007-08	New Jersey	NHL	81	9	13	22	183	0	0	1	151	6.0	1	15	40.0	12:02	5	0	0	0	4	0	0	0	12:20
2008-09	New Jersey	NHL	82	17	15	32	164	4	0	3	158	10.8	−1	7	28.6	12:03	7	2	0	2	19	1	0	1	8:32
2009-10	New Jersey	NHL	46	11	13	24	85	3	0	2	106	10.4	3	20	30.0	14:27	5	0	0	0	22	0	0	0	12:28

			Regular Season														Playoffs								
Season	Club	League	GP	G	A	Pts	PIM	PP	SH	GW	S	S%	+/-	TF	F%	Min	GP	G	A	Pts	PIM	PP	SH	GW	Min
2010-11	**New Jersey**	**NHL**	**82**	**12**	**6**	**18**	**116**	**1**	**0**	**1**	**192**	**6.3**	**-20**	**45**	**42.2**	**13:37**	....	....	....	....	....	....	....	....	....
2011-12	**New Jersey**	**NHL**	**80**	**30**	**16**	**46**	**138**	**8**	**0**	**7**	**228**	**13.2**	**-8**	**243**	**42.0**	**16:22**	**24**	**3**	**9**	**12**	**32**	**0**	**0**	***3**	**14:52**
2012-13	Salzburg	Austria	5	2	1	3	18	....	....	....	....	....	....	....	....	....	....	....	....	....	....	....	....	....	....
	New Jersey	**NHL**	**48**	**15**	**9**	**24**	**78**	**6**	**0**	**5**	**180**	**8.3**	**-6**	**25**	**24.0**	**17:36**	....	....	....	....	....	....	....	....	....
2013-14	**Toronto**	**NHL**	**60**	**5**	**6**	**11**	**93**	**1**	**0**	**1**	**102**	**4.9**	**-14**	**21**	**38.1**	**15:06**	....	....	....	....	....	....	....	....	....
2014-15	**Toronto**	**NHL**	**58**	**10**	**5**	**15**	**92**	**1**	**0**	**1**	**93**	**10.8**	**-11**	**63**	**31.8**	**13:53**	....	....	....	....	....	....	....	....	....
	Columbus	**NHL**	**3**	**0**	**0**	**0**	**14**	**0**	**0**	**0**	**2**	**0.0**	**-1**	**10**	**50.0**	**12:18**	....	....	....	....	....	....	....	....	....
2015-16	**Columbus**	**NHL**	**23**	**2**	**2**	**4**	**23**	**0**	**0**	**1**	**24**	**8.3**	**-8**	**12**	**16.7**	**9:13**	....	....	....	....	....	....	....	....	....
2016-17	**Columbus**	**NHL**	DID NOT PLAY – INJURED																						
	NHL Totals		**570**	**114**	**86**	**200**	**992**	**26**	**0**	**23**	**1254**	**9.1**		**462**	**38.1**	**14:00**	**44**	**5**	**9**	**14**	**79**	**1**	**0**	**4**	**12:44**

Signed as a free agent by **New Jersey**, August 12, 2005. Signed as a free agent by **Salzburg** (Austria), October 24, 2012. Signed as a free agent by **Toronto**, July 5, 2013. Traded to **Columbus** by **Toronto** for Nathan Horton, February 26, 2015. • Missed majority of 2015-16 and all of 2016-17 due to back injury at San Jose, November 3, 2015. Traded to **Vegas** by **Columbus** with Winnipeg's 1st round pick (previously acquired, Vegas selected Nick Suzuki) in 2017 NHL Draft and Columbus' 2nd round pick in 2019 NHL Draft for Expansion Draft considerations, June 21, 2017.

CLENDENING, Adam
(klehn-DEHN-ihng, A-duhm) **ARI**

Defense. Shoots right. 6', 196 lbs. Born, Niagara Falls, NY, October 26, 1992. Chicago's 3rd pick, 36th overall, in 2011 NHL Draft.

2007-08	Tor. Marlboros	GTHL	60	8	42	50	116	....	....	....	....	....	....	....	....	....	....	....	....	....	....	....	....	....	....
2008-09	USAHNTDP	NAHL	34	0	9	9	38	....	....	....	....	....	....	....	....	....	....	....	....	....	....	....	....	....	....
	USAHNTDP	U-17	15	1	5	6	18	....	....	....	....	....	....	....	....	....	....	....	....	....	....	....	....	....	....
	USAHNTDP	U-18	13	1	5	6	14	....	....	....	....	....	....	....	....	....	....	....	....	....	....	....	....	....	....
2009-10	USAHNTDP	USHL	26	4	13	17	44	....	....	....	....	....	....	....	....	....	....	....	....	....	....	....	....	....	....
	USAHNTDP	U-18	39	10	22	32	76	....	....	....	....	....	....	....	....	....	....	....	....	....	....	....	....	....	....
2010-11	Boston University	H-East	39	5	21	26	80	....	....	....	....	....	....	....	....	....	....	....	....	....	....	....	....	....	....
2011-12	Boston University	H-East	38	4	29	33	64	....	....	....	....	....	....	....	....	....	....	....	....	....	....	....	....	....	....
2012-13	Rockford IceHogs	AHL	73	9	37	46	67	....	....	....	....	....	....	....	....	....	....	....	....	....	....	....	....	....	....
2013-14	Rockford IceHogs	AHL	74	12	47	59	64	....	....	....	....	....	....	....	....	....	....	....	....	....	....	....	....	....	....
2014-15	**Chicago**	**NHL**	**4**	**1**	**1**	**2**	**2**	**1**	**0**	**0**	**2**	**50.0**	**1**	**0**	**0.0**	**13:10**	....	....	....	....	....	....	....	....	....
	Rockford IceHogs	AHL	38	1	12	13	20	....	....	....	....	....	....	....	....	....	....	....	....	....	....	....	....	....	....
	Vancouver	**NHL**	**17**	**0**	**2**	**2**	**8**	**0**	**0**	**0**	**15**	**0.0**	**1**	**0**	**0.0**	**17:27**	....	....	....	....	....	....	....	....	....
	Utica Comets	AHL	11	1	4	5	28	....	....	....	....	....	....	....	....	....	23	3	5	8	26	....	....	....	....
2015-16	**Pittsburgh**	**NHL**	**9**	**0**	**1**	**1**	**10**	**0**	**0**	**0**	**11**	**0.0**	**3**	**0**	**0.0**	**13:08**	....	....	....	....	....	....	....	....	....
	Wilkes-Barre	AHL	6	0	3	3	0	....	....	....	....	....	....	....	....	....	....	....	....	....	....	....	....	....	....
	Edmonton	**NHL**	**20**	**1**	**5**	**6**	**10**	**0**	**0**	**0**	**32**	**3.1**	**3**	**0**	**0.0**	**15:33**	....	....	....	....	....	....	....	....	....
2016-17	**NY Rangers**	**NHL**	**31**	**2**	**9**	**11**	**17**	**1**	**0**	**0**	**38**	**5.3**	**3**	**0**	**0.0**	**15:49**	....	....	....	....	....	....	....	....	....
	NHL Totals		**81**	**4**	**18**	**22**	**47**	**2**	**0**	**0**	**98**	**4.1**		**0**	**0.0**	**15:40**	....	....	....	....	....	....	....	....	....

Hockey East All-Rookie Team (2011) • Hockey East First All-Star Team (2012) • AHL Second All-Star Team (2013) • AHL First All-Star Team (2014)

Traded to **Vancouver** by **Chicago** for Gustav Forsling, January 29, 2015. Traded to **Pittsburgh** by **Vancouver** with Nick Bonino and Anaheim's 2nd round pick (previously acquired, Pittsburgh selected Filip Gustavsson) in 2016 NHL Draft for Brandon Sutter and Vancouver's 3rd round pick (previously acquired, Vancouver selected William Lockwood) in 2016 NHL Draft, July 28, 2015. Traded to **Anaheim** by **Pittsburgh** with David Perron for Carl Hagelin, January 16, 2016. Claimed on waivers by **Edmonton** from **Anaheim**, January 27, 2016. • Missed majority of 2015-16 and 2016-17 as a healthy reserve. Signed as a free agent by **NY Rangers**, July 1, 2016. Signed as a free agent by **Arizona**, July 1, 2017.

CLICHE, Marc-Andre
(KLEESH, MAHRK-AWN-dray)

Center. Shoots right. 6', 202 lbs. Born, Rouyn-Noranda, QC, March 23, 1987. NY Rangers' 3rd pick, 56th overall, in 2005 NHL Draft.

2002-03	Amos Forestiers	QAAA	42	26	16	42	18	....	....	....	....	....	....	....	....	....	15	6	12	18	6	....	....	....	....
2003-04	Lewiston	QMJHL	52	8	10	18	17	....	....	....	....	....	....	....	....	....	7	1	2	3	0	....	....	....	....
2004-05	Lewiston	QMJHL	19	4	4	8	8	....	....	....	....	....	....	....	....	....	....	....	....	....	....	....	....	....	....
2005-06	Lewiston	QMJHL	66	37	45	82	60	....	....	....	....	....	....	....	....	....	6	2	2	4	0	....	....	....	....
2006-07	Lewiston	QMJHL	52	24	30	54	42	....	....	....	....	....	....	....	....	....	16	6	16	22	10	....	....	....	....
2007-08	Manchester	AHL	52	11	10	21	25	....	....	....	....	....	....	....	....	....	4	0	1	1	2	....	....	....	....
2008-09	Manchester	AHL	31	5	4	9	19	....	....	....	....	....	....	....	....	....	....	....	....	....	....	....	....	....	....
2009-10	**Los Angeles**	**NHL**	**1**	**0**	**0**	**0**	**0**	**0**	**0**	**0**	**0**	**0.0**	**1**	**6**	**66.7**	**7:23**	....	....	....	....	....	....	....	....	....
	Manchester	AHL	66	11	14	25	45	....	....	....	....	....	....	....	....	....	12	1	1	2	8	....	....	....	....
2010-11	Manchester	AHL	63	14	21	35	35	....	....	....	....	....	....	....	....	....	....	....	....	....	....	....	....	....	....
2011-12	Manchester	AHL	72	17	24	41	35	....	....	....	....	....	....	....	....	....	4	1	0	1	6	....	....	....	....
2012-13	Manchester	AHL	57	10	10	20	46	....	....	....	....	....	....	....	....	....	3	0	0	0	4	....	....	....	....
2013-14	**Colorado**	**NHL**	**76**	**1**	**6**	**7**	**17**	**0**	**0**	**0**	**69**	**1.4**	**-11**	**719**	**46.0**	**10:34**	**7**	**0**	**0**	**0**	**2**	**0**	**0**	**0**	**14:20**
2014-15	**Colorado**	**NHL**	**74**	**2**	**5**	**7**	**17**	**0**	**0**	**0**	**68**	**2.9**	**-2**	**735**	**51.3**	**10:36**	....	....	....	....	....	....	....	....	....
2015-16	San Antonio	AHL	38	6	13	19	8	....	....	....	....	....	....	....	....	....	....	....	....	....	....	....	....	....	....
	Bridgeport	AHL	6	1	0	1	32	....	....	....	....	....	....	....	....	....	3	2	0	2	0	....	....	....	....
2016-17	Toronto Marlies	AHL	16	1	2	3	6	....	....	....	....	....	....	....	....	....	....	....	....	....	....	....	....	....	....
	NHL Totals		**151**	**3**	**11**	**14**	**34**	**0**	**0**	**0**	**137**	**2.2**		**1460**	**48.8**	**10:34**	**7**	**0**	**0**	**0**	**2**	**0**	**0**	**0**	**14:20**

• Missed majority of 2004-05 due to recurring shoulder injury. Traded to **Los Angeles** by **NY Rangers** with Jason Ward, Jan Marek and NY Rangers' 3rd round pick (later traded to Buffalo - Buffalo selected Corey Fienhage) in 2008 NHL Draft for Sean Avery and John Seymour, February 5, 2007. • Missed majority of 2008-09 due to training camp shoulder injury. Claimed on waivers by **Colorado** from **Los Angeles**, September 22, 2013. Traded to **NY Islanders** by **Colorado** for Taylor Beck, February 29, 2016. Signed as a free agent by **Toronto** (AHL), July 4, 2016. • Missed majority of 2016-17 as a healthy reserve.

CLIFFORD, Kyle
(KLIHF-fuhrd, KIGHL) **L.A.**

Left wing. Shoots left. 6'2", 206 lbs. Born, Ayr, ON, January 13, 1991. Los Angeles' 2nd pick, 35th overall, in 2009 NHL Draft.

2006-07	Cambridge	Minor-ON	70	31	49	80	119	....	....	....	....	....	....	....	....	....	....	....	....	....	....	....	....	....	....
2007-08	Barrie Colts	OHL	66	1	14	15	83	....	....	....	....	....	....	....	....	....	9	0	1	1	4	....	....	....	....
2008-09	Barrie Colts	OHL	60	16	12	28	133	....	....	....	....	....	....	....	....	....	5	0	0	0	13	....	....	....	....
2009-10	Barrie Colts	OHL	58	28	29	57	111	....	....	....	....	....	....	....	....	....	17	5	9	14	28	....	....	....	....
	Manchester	AHL	....	....	....	....	....	....	....	....	....	....	....	....	....	....	7	0	2	2	12	....	....	....	....
2010-11	**Los Angeles**	**NHL**	**76**	**7**	**7**	**14**	**141**	**0**	**0**	**0**	**69**	**10.1**	**-10**	**15**	**53.3**	**9:30**	**6**	**3**	**2**	**5**	**7**	**0**	**0**	**1**	**13:17**
2011-12♦	**Los Angeles**	**NHL**	**81**	**5**	**7**	**12**	**123**	**0**	**0**	**2**	**88**	**5.7**	**-5**	**8**	**12.5**	**9:24**	**3**	**0**	**0**	**0**	**2**	**0**	**0**	**0**	**5:01**
2012-13	Ontario Reign	ECHL	9	4	3	7	2	....	....	....	....	....	....	....	....	....	....	....	....	....	....	....	....	....	....
	Los Angeles	**NHL**	**48**	**7**	**7**	**14**	**51**	**0**	**0**	**1**	**56**	**12.5**	**1**	**9**	**11.1**	**10:36**	**14**	**0**	**2**	**2**	**8**	**0**	**0**	**0**	**10:21**
2013-14♦	**Los Angeles**	**NHL**	**71**	**3**	**5**	**8**	**81**	**0**	**0**	**0**	**74**	**4.1**	**6**	**12**	**50.0**	**10:10**	**24**	**1**	**6**	**7**	***39**	**0**	**0**	**0**	**9:47**
2014-15	**Los Angeles**	**NHL**	**80**	**6**	**9**	**15**	**87**	**0**	**0**	**1**	**117**	**5.1**	**5**	**6**	**33.3**	**10:44**	....	....	....	....	....	....	....	....	....
2015-16	**Los Angeles**	**NHL**	**56**	**3**	**6**	**9**	**55**	**0**	**0**	**0**	**68**	**4.4**	**-1**	**7**	**42.9**	**9:21**	**4**	**0**	**1**	**1**	**0**	**0**	**0**	**0**	**8:31**
	Ontario Reign	AHL	2	0	0	0	2	....	....	....	....	....	....	....	....	....	....	....	....	....	....	....	....	....	....
2016-17	**Los Angeles**	**NHL**	**73**	**6**	**6**	**12**	**92**	**0**	**0**	**0**	**122**	**4.9**	**-2**	**5**	**40.0**	**10:43**	....	....	....	....	....	....	....	....	....
	NHL Totals		**485**	**37**	**47**	**84**	**630**	**0**	**0**	**4**	**594**	**6.2**		**62**	**37.1**	**10:04**	**51**	**4**	**11**	**15**	**56**	**0**	**0**	**1**	**9:58**

Signed as a free agent by **Ontario** (ECHL), November 20, 2012.

CLUNE, Rich
(KLOON, RITCH)

Left wing. Shoots left. 5'10", 207 lbs. Born, Toronto, ON, April 25, 1987. Dallas' 3rd pick, 71st overall, in 2005 NHL Draft.

2002-03	Tor. Marlboros	GTHL	27	23	22	55	128	....	....	....	....	....	....	....	....	....	....	....	....	....	....	....	....	....	....
2003-04	Sarnia Sting	OHL	58	3	13	16	72	....	....	....	....	....	....	....	....	....	5	0	1	1	0	....	....	....	....
2004-05	Sarnia Sting	OHL	68	21	13	34	103	....	....	....	....	....	....	....	....	....	....	....	....	....	....	....	....	....	....
2005-06	Sarnia Sting	OHL	61	20	32	52	126	....	....	....	....	....	....	....	....	....	....	....	....	....	....	....	....	....	....
2006-07	Barrie Colts	OHL	67	32	46	78	151	....	....	....	....	....	....	....	....	....	8	3	4	7	8	....	....	....	....
	Iowa Stars	AHL	1	0	0	0	2	....	....	....	....	....	....	....	....	....	....	....	....	....	....	....	....	....	....
2007-08	Iowa Stars	AHL	38	3	5	8	137	....	....	....	....	....	....	....	....	....	....	....	....	....	....	....	....	....	....
	Idaho Steelheads	ECHL	19	1	9	10	41	....	....	....	....	....	....	....	....	....	....	....	....	....	....	....	....	....	....
2008-09	Manchester	AHL	35	3	6	9	87	....	....	....	....	....	....	....	....	....	....	....	....	....	....	....	....	....	....
2009-10	**Los Angeles**	**NHL**	**14**	**0**	**2**	**2**	**26**	**0**	**0**	**0**	**7**	**0.0**	**1**	**5**	**40.0**	**7:17**	**4**	**0**	**0**	**0**	**5**	**0**	**0**	**0**	**5:12**
	Manchester	AHL	44	4	10	14	126	....	....	....	....	....	....	....	....	....	....	....	....	....	....	....	....	....	....
2010-11	Manchester	AHL	66	8	14	22	222	....	....	....	....	....	....	....	....	....	7	0	3	3	6	....	....	....	....
2011-12	Manchester	AHL	56	6	9	15	253	....	....	....	....	....	....	....	....	....	4	0	0	0	14	....	....	....	....
2012-13	Manchester	AHL	35	2	5	7	98	....	....	....	....	....	....	....	....	....	....	....	....	....	....	....	....	....	....
	Nashville	**NHL**	**47**	**4**	**5**	**9**	**113**	**0**	**0**	**1**	**46**	**8.7**	**3**	**2**	**0.0**	**9:24**	....	....	....	....	....	....	....	....	....
2013-14	**Nashville**	**NHL**	**58**	**3**	**4**	**7**	**166**	**0**	**0**	**1**	**29**	**10.3**	**-7**	**0**	**0.0**	**8:27**	....	....	....	....	....	....	....	....	....
2014-15	**Nashville**	**NHL**	**1**	**0**	**0**	**0**	**0**	**0**	**0**	**0**	**0**	**0.0**	**0**	**0**	**0.0**	**5:30**	....	....	....	....	....	....	....	....	....
	Milwaukee	AHL	62	6	11	17	181	....	....	....	....	....	....	....	....	....	....	....	....	....	....	....	....	....	....

			Regular Season														Playoffs								
Season	Club	League	GP	G	A	Pts	PIM	PP	SH	GW	S	S%	+/-	TF	F%	Min	GP	G	A	Pts	PIM	PP	SH	GW	Min
2015-16	**Toronto**	**NHL**	**19**	**0**	**4**	**4**	**22**	**0**	**0**	**0**	**10**	**0.0**	**1**	**0**	**0.0**	**8:06**	....	....	....	....	....	....	....	....	....
	Toronto Marlies	AHL	49	8	16	24	146	....	....	....	....	....	....	....	....	....	15	1	2	3	34	....	....	....	....
2016-17	Toronto Marlies	AHL	37	3	7	10	87	....	....	....	....	....	....	....	....	....	5	1	1	2	14	....	....	....	....
	NHL Totals		**139**	**7**	**15**	**22**	**327**	**0**	**0**	**2**	**92**	**7.6**		**7**	**28.6**	**8:35**	**4**	**0**	**0**	**0**	**5**	**0**	**0**	**0**	**5:12**

Traded to **Los Angeles** by **Dallas** for Lauri Tukonen, July 21, 2008. Claimed on waivers by **Nashville** from **Los Angeles**, January 15, 2013. Signed as a free agent by **Toronto**, October 29, 2015. Signed as a free agent by **Toronto** (AHL), July 4, 2016. • Missed majority of 2016-17 as a healthy reserve.

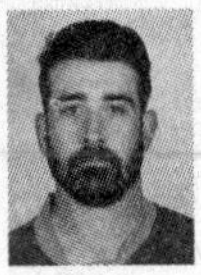

CLUTTERBUCK, Cal

(KLUH-tuhr-buhck, KAL) **NYI**

Right wing. Shoots right. 5'11", 218 lbs. Born, Welland, ON, November 18, 1987. Minnesota's 3rd pick, 72nd overall, in 2006 NHL Draft.

Season	Club	League	GP	G	A	Pts	PIM	PP	SH	GW	S	S%	+/-	TF	F%	Min	GP	G	A	Pts	PIM	PP	SH	GW	Min
2001-02	Welland Tigers	Minor-ON	36	42	38	80	40	....	....	....	....	....	....	....	....	....	....	....	....	....	....	....	....	....	....
2002-03	Welland Cougars	ON-Jr.B	48	24	29	53	26	....	....	....	....	....	....	....	....	....	....	....	....	....	....	....	....	....	....
2003-04	St. Michael's	OHL	60	4	7	11	112	....	....	....	....	....	....	....	....	....	18	3	5	8	20	....	....	....	....
2004-05	St. Michael's	OHL	38	10	6	16	55	....	....	....	....	....	....	....	....	....	....	....	....	....	....	....	....	....	....
	Oshawa Generals	OHL	27	9	9	18	42	....	....	....	....	....	....	....	....	....	....	....	....	....	....	....	....	....	....
2005-06	Oshawa Generals	OHL	66	35	33	68	139	....	....	....	....	....	....	....	....	....	....	....	....	....	....	....	....	....	....
2006-07	Oshawa Generals	OHL	65	35	54	89	153	....	....	....	....	....	....	....	....	....	9	8	5	13	21	....	....	....	....
2007-08	**Minnesota**	**NHL**	**2**	**0**	**0**	**0**	**0**	**0**	**0**	**0**	**0**	**0.0**	**0**	**1**	**100.0**	**7:05**	....	....	....	....	....	....	....	....	....
	Houston Aeros	AHL	73	11	13	24	97	....	....	....	....	....	....	....	....	....	5	0	0	0	14	....	....	....	....
2008-09	**Minnesota**	**NHL**	**78**	**11**	**7**	**18**	**76**	**1**	**0**	**1**	**136**	**8.1**	**-5**	**17**	**11.8**	**13:00**	....	....	....	....	....	....	....	....	....
	Houston Aeros	AHL	2	0	0	0	0	....	....	....	....	....	....	....	....	....	....	....	....	....	....	....	....	....	....
2009-10	**Minnesota**	**NHL**	**74**	**13**	**8**	**21**	**52**	**1**	**2**	**1**	**136**	**9.6**	**-8**	**10**	**30.0**	**14:17**	....	....	....	....	....	....	....	....	....
2010-11	**Minnesota**	**NHL**	**76**	**19**	**15**	**34**	**79**	**4**	**0**	**3**	**191**	**9.9**	**-5**	**11**	**27.3**	**15:51**	....	....	....	....	....	....	....	....	....
2011-12	**Minnesota**	**NHL**	**74**	**15**	**12**	**27**	**103**	**3**	***4**	**2**	**161**	**9.3**	**-4**	**15**	**33.3**	**16:21**	....	....	....	....	....	....	....	....	....
2012-13	**Minnesota**	**NHL**	**42**	**4**	**6**	**10**	**27**	**0**	**0**	**1**	**87**	**4.6**	**-5**	**2**	**50.0**	**13:44**	**5**	**1**	**1**	**2**	**4**	**0**	**0**	**0**	**15:51**
2013-14	**NY Islanders**	**NHL**	**73**	**12**	**7**	**19**	**50**	**0**	**3**	**1**	**172**	**7.0**	**-9**	**16**	**43.8**	**14:20**	....	....	....	....	....	....	....	....	....
2014-15	**NY Islanders**	**NHL**	**76**	**7**	**9**	**16**	**60**	**0**	**2**	**4**	**124**	**5.6**	**1**	**9**	**66.7**	**12:44**	**7**	**2**	**1**	**3**	**26**	**0**	**0**	**0**	**12:50**
2015-16	**NY Islanders**	**NHL**	**77**	**15**	**8**	**23**	**22**	**0**	**2**	**5**	**80**	**18.8**	**7**	**3**	**33.3**	**11:55**	**11**	**2**	**1**	**3**	**12**	**0**	**0**	**0**	**13:35**
2016-17	**NY Islanders**	**NHL**	**66**	**5**	**15**	**20**	**28**	**0**	**0**	**1**	**115**	**4.3**	**2**	**8**	**37.5**	**14:00**	....	....	....	....	....	....	....	....	....
	NHL Totals		**638**	**101**	**87**	**188**	**497**	**9**	**13**	**19**	**1202**	**8.4**		**92**	**34.8**	**14:00**	**23**	**5**	**3**	**8**	**42**	**0**	**0**	**0**	**13:51**

Traded to **NY Islanders** by **Minnesota** with New Jersey's 3rd round pick (previously acquired, NY Islanders selected Eamon McAdam) in 2013 NHL Draft for Nino Niederreiter, June 30, 2013.

COBURN, Braydon

(KOH-buhrn, BRAY-duhn) **T.B.**

Defense. Shoots left. 6'5", 226 lbs. Born, Calgary, AB, February 27, 1985. Atlanta's 1st pick, 8th overall, in 2003 NHL Draft.

Season	Club	League	GP	G	A	Pts	PIM	PP	SH	GW	S	S%	+/-	TF	F%	Min	GP	G	A	Pts	PIM	PP	SH	GW	Min
2000-01	Notre Dame	SMHL	32	3	19	22	70	....	....	....	....	....	....	....	....	....	....	....	....	....	....	....	....	....	....
	Portland	WHL	2	0	1	1	0	....	....	....	....	....	....	....	....	....	14	0	4	4	2	....	....	....	....
2001-02	Portland	WHL	68	4	33	37	100	....	....	....	....	....	....	....	....	....	7	1	1	2	9	....	....	....	....
2002-03	Portland	WHL	53	3	16	19	147	....	....	....	....	....	....	....	....	....	7	0	1	1	8	....	....	....	....
2003-04	Portland	WHL	55	10	20	30	92	....	....	....	....	....	....	....	....	....	5	0	1	1	10	....	....	....	....
2004-05	Portland	WHL	60	12	32	44	144	....	....	....	....	....	....	....	....	....	7	1	5	6	6	....	....	....	....
	Chicago Wolves	AHL	3	0	1	1	5	....	....	....	....	....	....	....	....	....	18	0	1	1	36	....	....	....	....
2005-06	**Atlanta**	**NHL**	**9**	**0**	**1**	**1**	**4**	**0**	**0**	**0**	**4**	**0.0**	**-2**	**0**	**0.0**	**7:43**	....	....	....	....	....	....	....	....	....
	Chicago Wolves	AHL	73	6	20	26	134	....	....	....	....	....	....	....	....	....	....	....	....	....	....	....	....	....	....
2006-07	**Atlanta**	**NHL**	**29**	**0**	**4**	**4**	**30**	**0**	**0**	**0**	**21**	**0.0**	**1**	**0**	**0.0**	**11:41**	....	....	....	....	....	....	....	....	....
	Chicago Wolves	AHL	15	1	10	11	36	....	....	....	....	....	....	....	....	....	....	....	....	....	....	....	....	....	....
	Philadelphia	**NHL**	**20**	**3**	**4**	**7**	**16**	**1**	**0**	**0**	**33**	**9.1**	**-2**	**0**	**0.0**	**20:58**	....	....	....	....	....	....	....	....	....
2007-08	**Philadelphia**	**NHL**	**78**	**9**	**27**	**36**	**74**	**5**	**0**	**2**	**113**	**8.0**	**17**	**0**	**0.0**	**21:14**	**14**	**0**	**6**	**6**	**14**	**0**	**0**	**0**	**22:25**
2008-09	**Philadelphia**	**NHL**	**80**	**7**	**21**	**28**	**97**	**3**	**0**	**0**	**130**	**5.4**	**7**	**0**	**0.0**	**24:37**	**6**	**0**	**3**	**3**	**7**	**0**	**0**	**0**	**26:29**
2009-10	**Philadelphia**	**NHL**	**81**	**5**	**14**	**19**	**54**	**1**	**0**	**0**	**122**	**4.1**	**-6**	**0**	**0.0**	**21:08**	**23**	**1**	**3**	**4**	**22**	**1**	**0**	**1**	**25:09**
2010-11	**Philadelphia**	**NHL**	**82**	**2**	**14**	**16**	**53**	**1**	**0**	**0**	**114**	**1.8**	**15**	**0**	**0.0**	**21:04**	**11**	**1**	**2**	**3**	**6**	**0**	**0**	**0**	**24:07**
2011-12	**Philadelphia**	**NHL**	**81**	**4**	**20**	**24**	**56**	**0**	**0**	**0**	**113**	**3.5**	**10**	**1**	**0.0**	**22:03**	**11**	**0**	**4**	**4**	**8**	**0**	**0**	**0**	**27:10**
2012-13	**Philadelphia**	**NHL**	**33**	**1**	**4**	**5**	**41**	**0**	**0**	**0**	**38**	**2.6**	**-10**	**0**	**0.0**	**22:37**	....	....	....	....	....	....	....	....	....
2013-14	**Philadelphia**	**NHL**	**82**	**5**	**12**	**17**	**63**	**0**	**1**	**2**	**122**	**4.1**	**-6**	**0**	**0.0**	**22:27**	**7**	**0**	**3**	**3**	**4**	**0**	**0**	**0**	**21:11**
2014-15	**Philadelphia**	**NHL**	**39**	**1**	**8**	**9**	**16**	**0**	**0**	**0**	**45**	**2.2**	**-1**	**0**	**0.0**	**20:14**	....	....	....	....	....	....	....	....	....
	Tampa Bay	**NHL**	**4**	**0**	**2**	**2**	**9**	**0**	**0**	**0**	**1**	**0.0**	**3**	**0**	**0.0**	**17:02**	**26**	**1**	**3**	**4**	**21**	**0**	**0**	**1**	**17:00**
2015-16	**Tampa Bay**	**NHL**	**80**	**1**	**9**	**10**	**53**	**0**	**0**	**0**	**92**	**1.1**	**12**	**0**	**0.0**	**16:45**	**17**	**0**	**2**	**2**	**12**	**0**	**0**	**0**	**18:38**
2016-17	**Tampa Bay**	**NHL**	**80**	**5**	**7**	**12**	**50**	**0**	**1**	**0**	**102**	**4.9**	**-1**	**0**	**0.0**	**16:44**	....	....	....	....	....	....	....	....	....
	NHL Totals		**778**	**43**	**147**	**190**	**616**	**10**	**2**	**4**	**1050**	**4.1**		**1**	**0.0**	**20:19**	**115**	**3**	**26**	**29**	**94**	**1**	**0**	**2**	**21:56**

WHL Rookie of the Year (2002) • WHL West First All-Star Team (2004, 2005) • Canadian Major Junior Second All-Star Team (2005)

Traded to **Philadelphia** by **Atlanta** for Alexei Zhitnik, February 24, 2007. Traded to **Tampa Bay** by **Philadelphia** for Radko Gudas and Tampa Bay's 1st (later traded to Columbus – Columbus selected Gabriel Carlsson) and 3rd (Matej Tomek) round picks in 2015 NHL Draft, March 2, 2015.

COGLIANO, Andrew

(kawg-lee-A-noh, AN-droo) **ANA**

Center. Shoots left. 5'10", 184 lbs. Born, Toronto, ON, June 14, 1987. Edmonton's 1st pick, 25th overall, in 2005 NHL Draft.

Season	Club	League	GP	G	A	Pts	PIM	PP	SH	GW	S	S%	+/-	TF	F%	Min	GP	G	A	Pts	PIM	PP	SH	GW	Min
2002-03	Vaughan Kings	GTHL	58	39	54	93	122	....	....	....	....	....	....	....	....	....	....	....	....	....	....	....	....	....	....
2003-04	St. Mike's B's	ON-Jr.A	36	26	47	73	14	....	....	....	....	....	....	....	....	....	24	11	20	31	12	....	....	....	....
2004-05	St. Mike's B's	ON-Jr.A	49	36	*66	*102	33	....	....	....	....	....	....	....	....	....	25	*22	*24	*46	20	....	....	....	....
2005-06	U. of Michigan	CCHA	39	12	16	28	38	....	....	....	....	....	....	....	....	....	....	....	....	....	....	....	....	....	....
2006-07	U. of Michigan	CCHA	38	24	26	50	12	....	....	....	....	....	....	....	....	....	....	....	....	....	....	....	....	....	....
2007-08	**Edmonton**	**NHL**	**82**	**18**	**27**	**45**	**20**	**1**	**2**	**5**	**98**	**18.4**	**1**	**542**	**39.5**	**13:40**	....	....	....	....	....	....	....	....	....
2008-09	**Edmonton**	**NHL**	**82**	**18**	**20**	**38**	**22**	**4**	**0**	**4**	**116**	**15.5**	**-6**	**702**	**37.2**	**14:24**	....	....	....	....	....	....	....	....	....
2009-10	**Edmonton**	**NHL**	**82**	**10**	**18**	**28**	**31**	**1**	**0**	**1**	**139**	**7.2**	**-5**	**379**	**43.0**	**14:11**	....	....	....	....	....	....	....	....	....
2010-11	**Edmonton**	**NHL**	**82**	**11**	**24**	**35**	**64**	**0**	**1**	**3**	**129**	**8.5**	**-12**	**1108**	**41.6**	**17:15**	....	....	....	....	....	....	....	....	....
2011-12	**Anaheim**	**NHL**	**82**	**13**	**13**	**26**	**15**	**2**	**0**	**2**	**115**	**11.3**	**-4**	**386**	**42.0**	**14:42**	....	....	....	....	....	....	....	....	....
2012-13	Klagenfurter AC	Austria	7	2	4	6	2	....	....	....	....	....	....	....	....	....	....	....	....	....	....	....	....	....	....
	Anaheim	**NHL**	**48**	**13**	**10**	**23**	**6**	**0**	**2**	**1**	**79**	**16.5**	**14**	**92**	**34.8**	**15:22**	**7**	**0**	**1**	**1**	**4**	**0**	**0**	**0**	**15:47**
2013-14	**Anaheim**	**NHL**	**82**	**21**	**21**	**42**	**26**	**0**	**3**	**5**	**157**	**13.4**	**13**	**27**	**40.7**	**15:24**	**13**	**1**	**6**	**7**	**8**	**0**	**1**	**1**	**14:54**
2014-15	**Anaheim**	**NHL**	**82**	**15**	**14**	**29**	**14**	**0**	**3**	**2**	**134**	**11.2**	**5**	**49**	**32.7**	**14:36**	**16**	**3**	**6**	**9**	**4**	**0**	**0**	**0**	**16:16**
2015-16	**Anaheim**	**NHL**	**82**	**9**	**23**	**32**	**28**	**0**	**2**	**3**	**131**	**6.9**	**2**	**17**	**35.3**	**14:26**	**7**	**2**	**2**	**4**	**0**	**0**	**0**	**0**	**14:24**
2016-17	**Anaheim**	**NHL**	**82**	**16**	**19**	**35**	**26**	**0**	**3**	**2**	**178**	**9.0**	**11**	**18**	**44.4**	**15:08**	**17**	**1**	**2**	**3**	**9**	**0**	**0**	**0**	**13:49**
	NHL Totals		**786**	**144**	**189**	**333**	**252**	**8**	**16**	**28**	**1276**	**11.3**		**3320**	**40.2**	**14:54**	**60**	**7**	**17**	**24**	**25**	**0**	**1**	**1**	**15:00**

CCHA All-Rookie Team (2006)

Traded to **Anaheim** by **Edmonton** for Anaheim's 2nd round pick (Marc-Olivier Roy) in 2013 NHL Draft, July 12, 2011. Signed as a free agent by **Klagenfurt** (Austria), November 17, 2012.

COLBORNE, Joe

(KOHL-bohrn, JOH) **COL**

Center. Shoots left. 6'5", 221 lbs. Born, Calgary, AB, January 30, 1990. Boston's 1st pick, 16th overall, in 2008 NHL Draft.

Season	Club	League	GP	G	A	Pts	PIM	PP	SH	GW	S	S%	+/-	TF	F%	Min	GP	G	A	Pts	PIM	PP	SH	GW	Min
2004-05	Calgary Titans	Minor-AB	44	13	13	26	28	....	....	....	....	....	....	....	....	....	....	....	....	....	....	....	....	....	....
2005-06	Notre Dame	SMHL	48	13	14	27	26	....	....	....	....	....	....	....	....	....	....	....	....	....	....	....	....	....	....
2006-07	Camrose Kodiaks	AJHL	53	20	28	48	44	....	....	....	....	....	....	....	....	....	16	5	1	6	10	....	....	....	....
2007-08	Camrose Kodiaks	AJHL	55	33	*57	90	48	....	....	....	....	....	....	....	....	....	18	8	8	*16	26	....	....	....	....
2008-09	U. of Denver	WCHA	40	10	21	31	24	....	....	....	....	....	....	....	....	....	....	....	....	....	....	....	....	....	....
2009-10	U. of Denver	WCHA	39	22	19	41	30	....	....	....	....	....	....	....	....	....	....	....	....	....	....	....	....	....	....
	Providence Bruins	AHL	6	0	2	2	2	....	....	....	....	....	....	....	....	....	....	....	....	....	....	....	....	....	....
2010-11	Providence Bruins	AHL	55	12	14	26	35	....	....	....	....	....	....	....	....	....	....	....	....	....	....	....	....	....	....
	Toronto	**NHL**	**1**	**0**	**1**	**1**	**0**	**0**	**0**	**0**	**1**	**0.0**	**1**	**9**	**33.3**	**18:41**	....	....	....	....	....	....	....	....	....
	Toronto Marlies	AHL	20	8	8	16	8	....	....	....	....	....	....	....	....	....	....	....	....	....	....	....	....	....	....
2011-12	**Toronto**	**NHL**	**10**	**1**	**4**	**5**	**4**	**0**	**0**	**0**	**7**	**14.3**	**2**	**78**	**35.9**	**13:41**	....	....	....	....	....	....	....	....	....
	Toronto Marlies	AHL	65	16	23	39	46	....	....	....	....	....	....	....	....	....	15	2	6	8	8	....	....	....	....
2012-13	Toronto Marlies	AHL	65	14	28	42	53	....	....	....	....	....	....	....	....	....	4	0	1	1	2	....	....	....	....
	Toronto	**NHL**	**5**	**0**	**0**	**0**	**2**	**0**	**0**	**0**	**4**	**0.0**	**-1**	**29**	**51.7**	**9:07**	**2**	**0**	**0**	**0**	**0**	**0**	**0**	**0**	**13:28**
2013-14	**Calgary**	**NHL**	**80**	**10**	**18**	**28**	**34**	**1**	**0**	**1**	**80**	**12.5**	**-17**	**441**	**48.5**	**14:16**	....	....	....	....	....	....	....	....	....
2014-15	**Calgary**	**NHL**	**64**	**8**	**20**	**28**	**43**	**1**	**1**	**1**	**67**	**11.9**	**7**	**336**	**52.4**	**15:25**	**11**	**1**	**2**	**3**	**20**	**0**	**1**	**0**	**17:13**

			Regular Season														Playoffs								
Season	Club	League	GP	G	A	Pts	PIM	PP	SH	GW	S	S%	+/-	TF	F%	Min	GP	G	A	Pts	PIM	PP	SH	GW	Min
2015-16	**Calgary**	**NHL**	**73**	**19**	**25**	**44**	**27**	**3**	**0**	**2**	**100**	**19.0**	**-9**	**155**	**54.8**	**15:10**									
2016-17	**Colorado**	**NHL**	**62**	**4**	**4**	**8**	**34**	**2**	**0**	**0**	**48**	**8.3**	**-21**	**117**	**38.5**	**10:42**									
	NHL Totals		**295**	**42**	**72**	**114**	**144**	**7**	**1**	**4**	**307**	**13.7**		**1165**	**48.6**	**13:54**	**13**	**1**	**2**	**3**	**20**	**0**	**1**	**0**	**16:39**

WCHA All-Rookie Team (2009)

Traded to **Toronto** by **Boston** with Boston's 1st round pick (later traded to Anaheim – Anaheim selected Rickard Rakell) in 2011 NHL Draft and Boston's 2nd round pick (later traded to Colorado, later traded to Washington, later traded to Dallas – Dallas selected Mke Winther) in 2012 NHL Draft for Tomas Kaberle, February 18, 2011. Traded to **Calgary** by **Toronto** for Calgary's 4th round pick (later traded to St. Louis – St. Louis selected Ville Husso) in 2014 NHL Draft, September 29, 2013. Signed as a free agent by **Colorado**, July 1, 2016.

COLE, Ian

(KOHL, EE-an) **PIT**

Defense. Shoots left. 6'1", 219 lbs. Born, Ann Arbour, MI, February 21, 1989. St. Louis' 2nd pick, 18th overall, in 2007 NHL Draft.

2004-05	Det. Vic. Honda	MWEHL	60	15	25	40																			
2005-06	USAHNTDP	U-17	18	2	1	3	14																		
	USAHNTDP	NAHL	40	2	8	10	75										12	0	3	3	14				
2006-07	USAHNTDP	U-18	42	6	11	17	36																		
	USAHNTDP	NAHL	16	2	7	9	28																		
2007-08	U. of Notre Dame	CCHA	43	8	12	20	40																		
2008-09	U. of Notre Dame	CCHA	38	6	20	26	58																		
2009-10	U. of Notre Dame	CCHA	30	3	16	19	55																		
	Peoria Rivermen	AHL	9	1	4	5	4																		
2010-11	**St. Louis**	**NHL**	**26**	**1**	**3**	**4**	**35**	**0**	**0**	**0**	**22**	**4.5**	**6**	**0**	**0.0**	**17:36**									
	Peoria Rivermen	AHL	44	5	10	15	63																		
2011-12	**St. Louis**	**NHL**	**26**	**1**	**5**	**6**	**22**	**0**	**0**	**0**	**18**	**5.6**	**7**	**0**	**0.0**	**15:55**	**2**	**0**	**0**	**0**	**0**	**0**	**0**	**0**	**10:26**
	Peoria Rivermen	AHL	22	1	3	4	26																		
2012-13	Peoria Rivermen	AHL	34	3	11	14	43																		
	St. Louis	**NHL**	**15**	**0**	**1**	**1**	**10**	**0**	**0**	**0**	**10**	**0.0**	**-4**	**0**	**0.0**	**17:45**									
2013-14	**St. Louis**	**NHL**	**46**	**3**	**8**	**11**	**31**	**0**	**0**	**0**	**45**	**6.7**	**15**	**0**	**0.0**	**15:05**									
2014-15	**St. Louis**	**NHL**	**54**	**4**	**5**	**9**	**44**	**0**	**0**	**0**	**52**	**7.7**	**16**	**0**	**0.0**	**15:03**									
	Pittsburgh	**NHL**	**20**	**1**	**7**	**8**	**7**	**0**	**0**	**0**	**31**	**3.2**	**-2**	**0**	**0.0**	**18:29**	**5**	**0**	**2**	**2**	**8**	**0**	**0**	**0**	**23:00**
2015-16 ♦	**Pittsburgh**	**NHL**	**70**	**0**	**12**	**12**	**59**	**0**	**0**	**0**	**72**	**0.0**	**-3**	**0**	**0.0**	**17:14**	**24**	**1**	**2**	**3**	**14**	**0**	**0**	**0**	**16:13**
2016-17 ♦	**Pittsburgh**	**NHL**	**81**	**5**	**21**	**26**	**72**	**0**	**0**	**1**	**89**	**5.6**	**26**	**0**	**0.0**	**19:49**	**25**	**0**	**9**	**9**	**22**	**0**	**0**	**0**	**18:50**
	NHL Totals		**338**	**15**	**62**	**77**	**280**	**0**	**0**	**1**	**339**	**4.4**		**0**	**0.0**	**17:14**	**56**	**1**	**13**	**14**	**44**	**0**	**0**	**0**	**17:47**

CCHA First All-Star Team (2009) • NCAA West First All-American Team (2009)

Traded to **Pittsburgh** by **St. Louis** for Robert Bortuzzo and Pittsburgh's 7th round pick (Filip Helt) in 2016 NHL Draft, March 2, 2015.

COLEMAN, Blake

(KOHL-man, BLAYK) **N.J.**

Center. Shoots left. 5'11", 200 lbs. Born, Plano, TX, November 28, 1991. New Jersey's 3rd pick, 75th overall, in 2011 NHL Draft.

2009-10	Tri-City Storm	USHL	22	2	10	12	32																		
	Indiana Ice	USHL	36	8	8	16	24										9	0	2	2	13				
2010-11	Indiana Ice	USHL	59	34	*58	*92	72										5	2	2	4	10				
2011-12	Miami U.	CCHA	39	12	11	23	56																		
2012-13	Miami U.	CCHA	40	9	10	19	56																		
2013-14	Miami U.	NCHC	27	19	9	28	65																		
2014-15	Miami U.	NCHC	37	20	17	37	*99																		
2015-16	Albany Devils	AHL	14	4	3	7	19																		
2016-17	**New Jersey**	**NHL**	**23**	**1**	**1**	**2**	**27**	**0**	**0**	**0**	**29**	**3.4**	**-7**	**226**	**42.5**	**12:51**									
	Albany Devils	AHL	52	19	20	39	56										4	0	1	1	6				
	NHL Totals		**23**	**1**	**1**	**2**	**27**	**0**	**0**	**0**	**29**	**3.4**		**226**	**42.5**	**12:51**									

USHL First All-Star Team (2011) • USHL Player of the Year (2011)

• Missed majority of 2015-16 due to shoulder injury vs. Binghamton (AHL), November 27, 2015.

COMEAU, Blake

(KOH-moh, BLAYK) **COL**

Left wing. Shoots right. 6'1", 202 lbs. Born, Meadow Lake, SK, February 18, 1986. NY Islanders' 2nd pick, 47th overall, in 2004 NHL Draft.

2001-02	Sask. Contacts	SMHL	42	27	33	60	72																		
	Kelowna Rockets	WHL	3	0	0	0	4																		
2002-03	Kelowna Rockets	WHL	54	5	18	23	77										19	2	1	3	20				
2003-04	Kelowna Rockets	WHL	71	10	23	33	123										17	4	2	6	23				
2004-05	Kelowna Rockets	WHL	65	24	23	47	108										24	6	12	18	34				
2005-06	Kelowna Rockets	WHL	60	21	53	74	85										12	4	9	13	22				
	Bridgeport	AHL															7	0	3	3	0				
2006-07	**NY Islanders**	**NHL**	**3**	**0**	**0**	**0**	**0**	**0**	**0**	**0**	**1**	**0.0**	**0**	**0**	**0.0**	**9:25**									
	Bridgeport	AHL	61	12	31	43	46																		
2007-08	**NY Islanders**	**NHL**	**51**	**8**	**7**	**15**	**22**	**1**	**0**	**1**	**67**	**11.9**	**1**	**27**	**29.6**	**11:40**									
	Bridgeport	AHL	31	4	15	19	30																		
2008-09	**NY Islanders**	**NHL**	**53**	**7**	**18**	**25**	**32**	**2**	**0**	**0**	**78**	**9.0**	**-17**	**45**	**31.1**	**16:17**									
	Bridgeport	AHL	19	4	15	19	22										2	0	0	0	0				
2009-10	**NY Islanders**	**NHL**	**61**	**17**	**18**	**35**	**40**	**0**	**1**	**2**	**133**	**12.8**	**-2**	**21**	**47.6**	**15:25**									
2010-11	**NY Islanders**	**NHL**	**77**	**24**	**22**	**46**	**43**	**5**	**1**	**3**	**182**	**13.2**	**-17**	**112**	**31.3**	**18:41**									
2011-12	**NY Islanders**	**NHL**	**16**	**0**	**0**	**0**	**6**	**0**	**0**	**0**	**20**	**0.0**	**-11**	**8**	**25.0**	**13:04**									
	Calgary	**NHL**	**58**	**5**	**10**	**15**	**24**	**0**	**0**	**0**	**117**	**4.3**	**0**	**83**	**32.5**	**16:06**									
2012-13	**Calgary**	**NHL**	**33**	**4**	**3**	**7**	**14**	**0**	**1**	**1**	**44**	**9.1**	**-9**	**81**	**45.7**	**12:17**									
	Columbus	**NHL**	**9**	**2**	**3**	**5**	**6**	**0**	**0**	**0**	**4**	**50.0**	**5**	**5**	**60.0**	**11:41**									
2013-14	**Columbus**	**NHL**	**61**	**5**	**11**	**16**	**36**	**0**	**0**	**0**	**107**	**4.7**	**-2**	**17**	**58.8**	**12:04**	**6**	**0**	**0**	**0**	**10**	**0**	**0**	**0**	**11:51**
2014-15	**Pittsburgh**	**NHL**	**61**	**16**	**15**	**31**	**65**	**0**	**0**	**5**	**147**	**10.9**	**6**	**9**	**77.8**	**15:17**	**5**	**1**	**0**	**1**	**8**	**0**	**0**	**0**	**14:13**
2015-16	**Colorado**	**NHL**	**81**	**12**	**24**	**36**	**58**	**2**	**2**	**3**	**142**	**8.5**	**-9**	**566**	**48.8**	**17:38**									
2016-17	**Colorado**	**NHL**	**77**	**8**	**12**	**20**	**58**	**2**	**1**	**1**	**103**	**7.8**	**-19**	**246**	**46.3**	**14:59**									
	NHL Totals		**641**	**108**	**143**	**251**	**404**	**12**	**6**	**16**	**1145**	**9.4**		**1220**	**44.5**	**15:14**	**11**	**1**	**0**	**1**	**18**	**0**	**0**	**0**	**12:55**

WHL West First All-Star Team (2006)

Claimed on waivers by **Calgary** from **NY Islanders**, November 25, 2011. Traded to **Columbus** by **Calgary** for Columbus' 5th round pick (Eric Roy) in 2013 NHL Draft, April 3, 2013. Signed as a free agent by **Pittsburgh**, July 1, 2014. Signed as a free agent by **Colorado**, July 1, 2015.

COMPHER, J.T.

(KUHM-fuhr, JAY-TEE) **COL**

Left wing. Shoots right. 6', 193 lbs. Born, Northbrook, IL, April 8, 1995. Buffalo's 3rd pick, 35th overall, in 2013 NHL Draft.

2010-11	Team Illinois	T1EHL	34	17	22	39	56																		
2011-12	USAHNTDP	USHL	32	13	14	27	37																		
	USAHNTDP	U-17	17	8	15	23	18																		
	USAHNTDP	U-18	9	4	3	7	4																		
2012-13	USAHNTDP	USHL	21	7	17	24	23																		
	USAHNTDP	U-18	31	11	15	26	18																		
2013-14	U. of Michigan	Big Ten	35	11	20	31	22																		
2014-15	U. of Michigan	Big Ten	34	12	12	24	40																		
2015-16	U. of Michigan	Big Ten	38	16	*47	63	28																		
2016-17	**Colorado**	**NHL**	**21**	**3**	**2**	**5**	**4**	**1**	**0**	**1**	**30**	**10.0**	**0**	**164**	**47.6**	**14:56**									
	San Antonio	AHL	41	13	17	30	22																		
	NHL Totals		**21**	**3**	**2**	**5**	**4**	**1**	**0**	**1**	**30**	**10.0**		**164**	**47.6**	**14:56**									

Big Ten All-Rookie Team (2014) • Big Ten Second All-Star Team (2014) • Big Ten Rookie of the Year (2014) • Big Ten First All-Star Team (2016) • NCAA West Second All-American Team (2016)

Traded to **Colorado** by **Buffalo** with Nikita Zadorov, Mikhail Grigorenko and Buffalo's 2nd round pick (later traded to San Jose – San Jose selected Jeremy Roy) in 2015 NHL Draft for Ryan O'Reilly and Jamie McGinn, June 26, 2015.

CONACHER, Cory

(KAW-nuh-kuhr, KOHR-ee) **T.B.**

Left wing. Shoots left. 5'8", 180 lbs. Born, Burlington, ON, December 14, 1989.

			Regular Season														Playoffs								
Season	Club	League	GP	G	A	Pts	PIM	PP	SH	GW	S	S%	+/-	TF	F%	Min	GP	G	A	Pts	PIM	PP	SH	GW	Min
2006-07	Burlington	ON-Jr.A	48	22	40	62	62	....	....	....	....	....	....	....	....	....	6	3	3	6	8	....	....	....	....
2007-08	Canisius College	AH	20	7	10	17	24	....	....	....	....	....	....	....	....	....	....	....	....	....	....	....	....	....	....
2008-09	Canisius College	AH	37	12	23	35	40	....	....	....	....	....	....	....	....	....	....	....	....	....	....	....	....	....	....
2009-10	Canisius College	AH	35	20	33	53	36	....	....	....	....	....	....	....	....	....	....	....	....	....	....	....	....	....	....
2010-11	Canisius College	AH	37	23	19	42	54	....	....	....	....	....	....	....	....	....	....	....	....	....	....	....	....	....	....
	Rochester	AHL	2	1	0	1	2	....	....	....	....	....	....	....	....	....	....	....	....	....	....	....	....	....	....
	Cincinnati	ECHL	3	5	2	7	0	....	....	....	....	....	....	....	....	....	....	....	....	....	....	....	....	....	....
	Milwaukee	AHL	5	3	2	5	2	....	....	....	....	....	....	....	....	....	7	0	1	1	6	....	....	....	....
2011-12	Norfolk Admirals	AHL	75	*39	41	80	114	....	....	....	....	....	....	....	....	....	18	2	13	15	28	....	....	....	....
2012-13	**Tampa Bay**	**NHL**	**35**	**9**	**15**	**24**	**16**	**1**	**0**	**2**	**53**	**17.0**	**–3**	**3**	**0.0**	**14:22**	....	....	....	....	....	....	....	....	....
	Syracuse Crunch	AHL	36	12	16	28	56	....	....	....	....	....	....	....	....	....	....	....	....	....	....	....	....	....	....
	Ottawa	**NHL**	**12**	**2**	**3**	**5**	**4**	**0**	**0**	**1**	**14**	**14.3**	**6**	**12**	**33.3**	**12:51**	**8**	**3**	**0**	**3**	**31**	**1**	**0**	**1**	**11:57**
2013-14	**Ottawa**	**NHL**	**60**	**4**	**16**	**20**	**34**	**0**	**0**	**1**	**73**	**5.5**	**8**	**13**	**61.5**	**12:18**	....	....	....	....	....	....	....	....	....
	Buffalo	**NHL**	**19**	**3**	**3**	**6**	**16**	**1**	**0**	**1**	**27**	**11.1**	**–7**	**1**	**100.0**	**14:58**	....	....	....	....	....	....	....	....	....
2014-15	**NY Islanders**	**NHL**	**15**	**1**	**2**	**3**	**14**	**0**	**0**	**0**	**23**	**4.3**	**–3**	**3**	**33.3**	**13:29**	....	....	....	....	....	....	....	....	....
	Bridgeport	AHL	28	5	18	23	30	....	....	....	....	....	....	....	....	....	....	....	....	....	....	....	....	....	....
	Utica Comets	AHL	20	7	9	16	22	....	....	....	....	....	....	....	....	....	23	5	3	8	28	....	....	....	....
2015-16	SC Bern	Swiss	48	22	30	52	68	....	....	....	....	....	....	....	....	....	14	5	4	9	20	....	....	....	....
2016-17	**Tampa Bay**	**NHL**	**11**	**1**	**3**	**4**	**4**	**1**	**0**	**0**	**16**	**6.3**	**0**	**2**	**50.0**	**11:34**	....	....	....	....	....	....	....	....	....
	Syracuse Crunch	AHL	56	17	43	60	113	....	....	....	....	....	....	....	....	....	22	*12	16	*28	27	....	....	....	....
	NHL Totals		**152**	**20**	**42**	**62**	**88**	**3**	**0**	**5**	**206**	**9.7**		**34**	**44.1**	**13:13**	**8**	**3**	**0**	**3**	**31**	**1**	**0**	**1**	**11:57**

AHL All-Rookie Team (2012) • AHL Second All-Star Team (2012, 2017) • Dudley "Red" Garrett Memorial Trophy (AHL – Rookie of the Year) (2012) • Willie Marshall Award (AHL - Top Goal-scorer) (2012) • Les Cunningham Award (AHL - MVP) (2012)

Signed to an ATO (amateur tryout) contract by **Rochester** (AHL), March 24, 2011. Signed to an ATO (amateur tryout) contract by **Cincinatti** (ECHL), March 27, 2011. Signed to an ATO (amateur tryout) contract by **Milwaukee** (AHL), April 12, 2011. Signed as a free agent by **Norfolk** (AHL), July 5, 2011. Signed as a free agent by **Tampa Bay**, March 1, 2012. Traded to **Ottawa** by **Tampa Bay** with Philadelphia's 4th round pick (previously acquired, Ottawa selected Tobias Lindberg) in 2013 NHL Draft for Ben Bishop, April 3, 2013. Claimed on waivers by **Buffalo** from **Ottawa**, March 5, 2014. Signed as a free agent by **NY Islanders**, July 1, 2014. Traded to **Vancouver** by **NY Islanders** for Dustin Jeffrey, March 2, 2015. Signed as a free agent by **Bern** (Swiss), July 1, 2015. Signed as a free agent by **Tampa Bay**, July 13, 2016.

CONDRA, Erik

(KAWN-druh, AIR-ihk) **T.B.**

Right wing. Shoots right. 5'11", 183 lbs. Born, Trenton, MI, August 6, 1986. Ottawa's 7th pick, 211th overall, in 2006 NHL Draft.

			Regular Season														Playoffs								
Season	Club	League	GP	G	A	Pts	PIM	PP	SH	GW	S	S%	+/-	TF	F%	Min	GP	G	A	Pts	PIM	PP	SH	GW	Min
2004-05	Lincoln Stars	USHL	60	30	30	60	56	....	....	....	....	....	....	....	....	....	4	0	2	2	4	....	....	....	....
2005-06	U. of Notre Dame	CCHA	36	6	28	34	32	....	....	....	....	....	....	....	....	....	....	....	....	....	....	....	....	....	....
2006-07	U. of Notre Dame	CCHA	42	14	34	48	18	....	....	....	....	....	....	....	....	....	....	....	....	....	....	....	....	....	....
2007-08	U. of Notre Dame	CCHA	41	15	23	38	26	....	....	....	....	....	....	....	....	....	....	....	....	....	....	....	....	....	....
2008-09	U. of Notre Dame	CCHA	40	13	25	38	34	....	....	....	....	....	....	....	....	....	....	....	....	....	....	....	....	....	....
2009-10	Binghamton	AHL	80	11	27	38	61	....	....	....	....	....	....	....	....	....	....	....	....	....	....	....	....	....	....
2010-11	**Ottawa**	**NHL**	**26**	**6**	**5**	**11**	**12**	**1**	**0**	**2**	**48**	**12.5**	**–1**	**4**	**50.0**	**15:52**	....	....	....	....	....	....	....	....	....
	Binghamton	AHL	55	17	30	47	28	....	....	....	....	....	....	....	....	....	23	5	12	17	8	....	....	....	....
2011-12	**Ottawa**	**NHL**	**81**	**8**	**17**	**25**	**30**	**0**	**2**	**1**	**140**	**5.7**	**11**	**27**	**40.7**	**14:10**	**7**	**1**	**0**	**1**	**0**	**0**	**0**	**0**	**11:41**
2012-13	EV Fussen	German-3	7	8	11	19	2	....	....	....	....	....	....	....	....	....	....	....	....	....	....	....	....	....	....
	Riessersee	German-2	10	10	5	15	8	....	....	....	....	....	....	....	....	....	....	....	....	....	....	....	....	....	....
	Ottawa	**NHL**	**48**	**4**	**8**	**12**	**34**	**0**	**0**	**0**	**73**	**5.5**	**3**	**21**	**38.1**	**13:10**	**10**	**1**	**6**	**7**	**2**	**1**	**0**	**0**	**13:36**
2013-14	**Ottawa**	**NHL**	**76**	**6**	**10**	**16**	**30**	**0**	**1**	**0**	**85**	**7.1**	**0**	**15**	**6.7**	**11:39**	....	....	....	....	....	....	....	....	....
2014-15	**Ottawa**	**NHL**	**68**	**9**	**14**	**23**	**30**	**0**	**1**	**1**	**106**	**8.5**	**13**	**9**	**22.2**	**14:27**	**6**	**1**	**0**	**1**	**0**	**0**	**0**	**0**	**17:31**
2015-16	**Tampa Bay**	**NHL**	**54**	**6**	**5**	**11**	**34**	**0**	**0**	**0**	**58**	**10.3**	**–4**	**3**	**33.3**	**10:42**	**3**	**0**	**0**	**0**	**0**	**0**	**0**	**0**	**5:02**
2016-17	**Tampa Bay**	**NHL**	**13**	**0**	**0**	**0**	**4**	**0**	**0**	**0**	**8**	**0.0**	**–4**	**1**	**100.0**	**9:38**	....	....	....	....	....	....	....	....	....
	Syracuse Crunch	AHL	55	15	33	48	37	....	....	....	....	....	....	....	....	....	18	5	11	16	22	....	....	....	....
	NHL Totals		**366**	**39**	**59**	**98**	**174**	**1**	**4**	**4**	**518**	**7.5**		**80**	**32.5**	**13:01**	**26**	**3**	**6**	**9**	**2**	**1**	**0**	**0**	**13:00**

CCHA All-Rookie Team (2006) • CCHA Second All-Star Team (2009) • NCAA West Second All-American Team (2009)

Signed as a free agent by **Fussen** (German-3), October 16, 2012. Signed as a free agent by **Riessersee** (German-2), November 12, 2012. Signed as a free agent by **Tampa Bay**, July 1, 2015.

CONNAUTON, Kevin

(kuh-NAW-tuhn, KEH-vihn) **ARI**

Defense. Shoots left. 6'2", 205 lbs. Born, Edmonton, AB, February 23, 1990. Vancouver's 3rd pick, 83rd overall, in 2009 NHL Draft.

			Regular Season														Playoffs								
Season	Club	League	GP	G	A	Pts	PIM	PP	SH	GW	S	S%	+/-	TF	F%	Min	GP	G	A	Pts	PIM	PP	SH	GW	Min
2007-08	Spruce Grove	AJHL	56	13	32	45	59	....	....	....	....	....	....	....	....	....	15	5	0	5	18	....	....	....	....
2008-09	Western Mich.	CCHA	40	7	11	18	44	....	....	....	....	....	....	....	....	....	....	....	....	....	....	....	....	....	....
2009-10	Vancouver Giants	WHL	69	24	48	72	107	....	....	....	....	....	....	....	....	....	16	3	10	13	21	....	....	....	....
2010-11	Manitoba Moose	AHL	73	11	12	23	51	....	....	....	....	....	....	....	....	....	6	1	0	1	0	....	....	....	....
2011-12	Chicago Wolves	AHL	73	13	20	33	58	....	....	....	....	....	....	....	....	....	5	0	1	1	8	....	....	....	....
2012-13	Chicago Wolves	AHL	60	7	18	25	67	....	....	....	....	....	....	....	....	....	....	....	....	....	....	....	....	....	....
	Texas Stars	AHL	9	2	4	6	6	....	....	....	....	....	....	....	....	....	9	2	3	5	6	....	....	....	....
2013-14	**Dallas**	**NHL**	**36**	**1**	**7**	**8**	**16**	**0**	**0**	**0**	**56**	**1.8**	**–6**	**0**	**0.0**	**15:20**	**4**	**0**	**0**	**0**	**16**	**0**	**0**	**0**	**10:44**
	Texas Stars	AHL	6	0	1	1	23	....	....	....	....	....	....	....	....	....	....	....	....	....	....	....	....	....	....
2014-15	**Dallas**	**NHL**	**8**	**0**	**2**	**2**	**6**	**0**	**0**	**0**	**10**	**0.0**	**4**	**0**	**0.0**	**12:05**	....	....	....	....	....	....	....	....	....
	Columbus	**NHL**	**54**	**9**	**10**	**19**	**29**	**0**	**0**	**4**	**86**	**10.5**	**1**	**0**	**0.0**	**16:50**	....	....	....	....	....	....	....	....	....
2015-16	**Columbus**	**NHL**	**27**	**1**	**7**	**8**	**21**	**0**	**0**	**0**	**44**	**2.3**	**10**	**0**	**0.0**	**15:35**	....	....	....	....	....	....	....	....	....
	Arizona	**NHL**	**38**	**4**	**5**	**9**	**39**	**0**	**0**	**0**	**65**	**6.2**	**–3**	**0**	**0.0**	**17:33**	....	....	....	....	....	....	....	....	....
2016-17	**Arizona**	**NHL**	**24**	**0**	**1**	**1**	**24**	**0**	**0**	**0**	**21**	**0.0**	**–1**	**0**	**0.0**	**13:08**	....	....	....	....	....	....	....	....	....
	Tucson	AHL	2	1	2	3	2	....	....	....	....	....	....	....	....	....	....	....	....	....	....	....	....	....	....
	NHL Totals		**187**	**15**	**32**	**47**	**135**	**0**	**0**	**4**	**282**	**5.3**		**0**	**0.0**	**15:50**	**4**	**0**	**0**	**0**	**16**	**0**	**0**	**0**	**10:44**

WHL West First All-Star Team (2010) • Canadian Major Junior All-Rookie Team (2010)

Traded to **Dallas** by **Vancouver** with Vancouver's 2nd round pick (Philippe Desrosiers) in 2013 NHL Draft for Derek Roy, April 2, 2013. Claimed on waivers by **Columbus** from **Dallas**, November 18, 2014. Claimed on waivers by **Arizona** from **Columbus**, January 13, 2016.

CONNER, Chris

(KAWN-uhr, KRIHS)

Right wing. Shoots left. 5'7", 181 lbs. Born, Westland, MI, December 23, 1983.

			Regular Season														Playoffs								
Season	Club	League	GP	G	A	Pts	PIM	PP	SH	GW	S	S%	+/-	TF	F%	Min	GP	G	A	Pts	PIM	PP	SH	GW	Min
2000-01	Chicago Freeze	NAHL	56	17	28	45	18	....	....	....	....	....	....	....	....	....	3	2	1	3	4	....	....	....	....
2001-02	Chicago Freeze	NAHL	30	18	15	33	30	....	....	....	....	....	....	....	....	....	....	....	....	....	....	....	....	....	....
	Det. Compuware	NAHL	19	4	9	13	23	....	....	....	....	....	....	....	....	....	6	3	1	4	2	....	....	....	....
2002-03	Michigan Tech	WCHA	38	13	24	37	8	....	....	....	....	....	....	....	....	....	....	....	....	....	....	....	....	....	....
2003-04	Michigan Tech	WCHA	38	25	14	39	12	....	....	....	....	....	....	....	....	....	....	....	....	....	....	....	....	....	....
2004-05	Michigan Tech	WCHA	37	14	10	24	6	....	....	....	....	....	....	....	....	....	....	....	....	....	....	....	....	....	....
2005-06	Michigan Tech	WCHA	38	17	12	29	18	....	....	....	....	....	....	....	....	....	....	....	....	....	....	....	....	....	....
	Iowa Stars	AHL	15	2	3	5	0	....	....	....	....	....	....	....	....	....	7	1	1	2	2	....	....	....	....
2006-07	**Dallas**	**NHL**	**11**	**1**	**2**	**3**	**4**	**0**	**0**	**0**	**18**	**5.6**	**–3**	**1**	**100.0**	**11:15**	....	....	....	....	....	....	....	....	....
	Iowa Stars	AHL	48	19	18	37	24	....	....	....	....	....	....	....	....	....	12	2	5	7	2	....	....	....	....
2007-08	**Dallas**	**NHL**	**22**	**3**	**2**	**5**	**6**	**0**	**0**	**0**	**27**	**11.1**	**0**	**1**	**100.0**	**12:00**	**1**	**0**	**0**	**0**	**0**	**0**	**0**	**0**	**4:17**
	Iowa Stars	AHL	55	13	26	39	17	....	....	....	....	....	....	....	....	....	....	....	....	....	....	....	....	....	....
2008-09	**Dallas**	**NHL**	**38**	**3**	**10**	**13**	**10**	**0**	**0**	**1**	**34**	**8.8**	**–5**	**1**	**0.0**	**10:56**	....	....	....	....	....	....	....	....	....
	Peoria Rivermen	AHL	30	16	12	28	10	....	....	....	....	....	....	....	....	....	....	....	....	....	....	....	....	....	....
2009-10	**Pittsburgh**	**NHL**	**8**	**2**	**1**	**3**	**0**	**0**	**0**	**1**	**11**	**18.2**	**–1**	**1**	**0.0**	**9:36**	**1**	**0**	**0**	**0**	**0**	**0**	**0**	**0**	**11:03**
	Wilkes-Barre	AHL	59	19	37	56	21	....	....	....	....	....	....	....	....	....	4	2	2	4	2	....	....	....	....
2010-11	**Pittsburgh**	**NHL**	**60**	**7**	**9**	**16**	**10**	**0**	**0**	**3**	**91**	**7.7**	**5**	**4**	**25.0**	**11:49**	**7**	**1**	**0**	**1**	**0**	**0**	**0**	**0**	**12:22**
	Wilkes-Barre	AHL	11	3	6	9	2	....	....	....	....	....	....	....	....	....	....	....	....	....	....	....	....	....	....
2011-12	**Detroit**	**NHL**	**8**	**1**	**2**	**3**	**0**	**0**	**0**	**0**	**10**	**10.0**	**2**	**0**	**0.0**	**10:34**	....	....	....	....	....	....	....	....	....
	Grand Rapids	AHL	57	16	37	53	22	....	....	....	....	....	....	....	....	....	....	....	....	....	....	....	....	....	....
2012-13	Portland Pirates	AHL	60	13	27	40	28	....	....	....	....	....	....	....	....	....	1	0	1	1	2	....	....	....	....
	Phoenix	**NHL**	**12**	**1**	**1**	**2**	**2**	**0**	**0**	**0**	**15**	**6.7**	**3**	**2**	**0.0**	**11:23**	....	....	....	....	....	....	....	....	....
2013-14	**Pittsburgh**	**NHL**	**19**	**4**	**1**	**5**	**2**	**0**	**0**	**0**	**17**	**23.5**	**–3**	**1**	**0.0**	**11:46**	....	....	....	....	....	....	....	....	....
	Wilkes-Barre	AHL	17	6	5	11	8	....	....	....	....	....	....	....	....	....	....	....	....	....	....	....	....	....	....
2014-15	**Washington**	**NHL**	**2**	**0**	**0**	**0**	**4**	**0**	**0**	**0**	**3**	**0.0**	**1**	**0**	**0.0**	**8:49**	....	....	....	....	....	....	....	....	....
	Hershey Bears	AHL	61	19	33	52	10	....	....	....	....	....	....	....	....	....	10	2	5	7	2	....	....	....	....

Season	Club	League	GP	G	A	Pts	PIM	PP	SH	GW	S	S%	+/-	TF	F%	Min	GP	G	A	Pts	PIM	PP	SH	GW	Min
												Regular Season								**Playoffs**				
2015-16	Lehigh Valley	AHL	58	16	39	55	14	....	....	....	....	....	....	....	....	....									
2016-17	Lehigh Valley	AHL	70	22	34	56	10	....	....	....	....	....	....	....	....	....	5	1	3	4	2				
	NHL Totals		180	22	28	50	38	0	0	5	226	9.7		11	27.3	11:24	9	1	0	1	0	0	0	0	11:20

WCHA Second All-Star Team (2004)

Signed as a free agent by **Dallas**, July 13, 2006. Signed as a free agent by **Pittsburgh**, July 5. 2009. Signed as a free agent by **Detroit**, July 5, 2011. Signed as a free agent by **Phoenix**, July 2, 2012. Signed as a free agent by **Pittsburgh**, July 6, 2013. • Missed majority of 2013-14 due to hand injury at New Jersey, December 31, 2013. Signed as a free agent by **Washington**, July 1, 2014. Signed as a free agent by **Philadelphia**, July 1, 2015.

CONNOLLY, Brett

(KAW-nuh-lee, BREHT)   **WSH**

Right wing. Shoots right. 6'2", 193 lbs.   Born, Prince George, BC, May 2, 1992. Tampa Bay's 1st pick, 6th overall, in 2010 NHL Draft.

Season	Club	League	GP	G	A	Pts	PIM	PP	SH	GW	S	S%	+/-	TF	F%	Min	GP	G	A	Pts	PIM	PP	SH	GW	Min
2007-08	Cariboo Cougars	BCMML	38	16	16	32	80	....	....	....	....	....	....	....	....	....	6	4	1	5	10				
	Prince George	WHL	4	0	0	0	0	....	....	....	....	....	....	....	....	....									
2008-09	Prince George	WHL	65	30	30	60	38	....	....	....	....	....	....	....	....	....	4	0	2	2	6				
2009-10	Prince George	WHL	16	10	9	19	8	....	....	....	....	....	....	....	....	....									
2010-11	Prince George	WHL	59	46	27	73	26	....	....	....	....	....	....	....	....	....	1	0	0	0	0				
2011-12	**Tampa Bay**	**NHL**	68	4	11	15	30	1	0	2	94	4.3	-9	52	38.5	11:28									
2012-13	Syracuse Crunch	AHL	71	31	32	63	53	....	....	....	....	....	....	....	....	....	18	6	5	11	12				
	Tampa Bay	**NHL**	5	1	0	1	0	1	0	0	10	10.0	-3	5	80.0	10:16									
2013-14	**Tampa Bay**	**NHL**	11	1	0	1	4	0	0	1	12	8.3	-5	52	48.1	12:01									
	Syracuse Crunch	AHL	66	21	36	57	50	....	....	....	....	....	....	....	....	....									
2014-15	**Tampa Bay**	**NHL**	50	12	3	15	38	2	0	2	74	16.2	4	42	42.9	11:56									
	Boston	**NHL**	5	0	2	2	10	0	0	0	9	0.0	-1	1	0.0	14:22									
2015-16	**Boston**	**NHL**	71	9	16	25	20	2	0	2	95	9.5	-1	31	45.2	12:58									
2016-17	**Washington**	**NHL**	66	15	8	23	40	1	0	3	81	18.5	20	14	28.6	10:41	7	0	0	0	0	0	0	0	8:34
	NHL Totals		276	42	40	82	142	7	0	10	375	11.2		197	43.1	11:48	7	0	0	0	0	0	0	0	8:34

WHL Rookie of the Year (2009) • Canadian Major Junior All-Rookie Team (2009) • Canadian Major Junior Rookie of the Year (2009) • AHL Second All-Star Team (2013)

• Missed majority of 2009-10 due to pre-season hip injury. Traded to **Boston** by **Tampa Bay** for Boston's 2nd round pick (Matthew Spencer) in 2015 NHL Draft and Boston's 2nd round pick (Boris Katchouk) in 2016 NHL Draft, March 2, 2015. Signed as a free agent by **Washington**, July 1, 2016.

CONNOR, Kyle

(KAW-nuhr, KIGH-uhl)   **WPG**

Left wing. Shoots left. 6'1", 182 lbs.   Born, Shelby Twp., MI, December 9, 1996. Winnipeg's 1st pick, 17th overall, in 2015 NHL Draft.

Season	Club	League	GP	G	A	Pts	PIM	PP	SH	GW	S	S%	+/-	TF	F%	Min	GP	G	A	Pts	PIM	PP	SH	GW	Min
2011-12	Det. B. Tire U16	T1EHL	40	14	39	53	14	....	....	....	....	....	....	....	....	....	7	1	5	6	2				
2012-13	Youngstown	USHL	62	17	24	41	16	....	....	....	....	....	....	....	....	....	9	0	3	3	0				
2013-14	Youngstown	USHL	56	31	43	74	12	....	....	....	....	....	....	....	....	....									
2014-15	Youngstown	USHL	56	34	46	*80	6	....	....	....	....	....	....	....	....	....	4	3	1	4	0				
2015-16	U. of Michigan	Big Ten	38	*35	36	*71	6	....	....	....	....	....	....	....	....	....									
2016-17	**Winnipeg**	**NHL**	20	2	3	5	4	0	0	1	24	8.3	-7	2	50.0	12:13									
	Manitoba Moose	AHL	52	25	19	44	14	....	....	....	....	....	....	....	....	....									
	NHL Totals		20	2	3	5	4	0	0	1	24	8.3		2	50.0	12:13									

USHL First All-Star Team (2014, 2015) • USHL Player of the Year (2015) • Big Ten All-Rookie Team (2016) • Big Ten First All-Star Team (2016) • Big Ten Rookie of the Year (2016) • Big Ten Player of the Year (2016) • NCAA West First All-American Team (2016)

COPP, Andrew

(KAWP, AN-droo)   **WPG**

Center. Shoots left. 6'1", 206 lbs.   Born, Ann Arbor, MI, July 8, 1994. Winnipeg's 6th pick, 104th overall, in 2013 NHL Draft.

Season	Club	League	GP	G	A	Pts	PIM	PP	SH	GW	S	S%	+/-	TF	F%	Min	GP	G	A	Pts	PIM	PP	SH	GW	Min
2009-10	Det. Compuware	T1EHL	38	12	15	27	12	....	....	....	....	....	....	....	....	....									
2010-11	Det. Compuware	T1EHL	17	2	7	9	6	....	....	....	....	....	....	....	....	....									
	USAHNTDP	USHL	22	1	4	5	4	....	....	....	....	....	....	....	....	....	1	0	0	0	0				
	USAHNTDP	U-17	3	1	0	1	0	....	....	....	....	....	....	....	....	....									
	USAHNTDP	U-18	5	0	0	0	0	....	....	....	....	....	....	....	....	....									
2011-12	USAHNTDP	USHL	18	3	7	10	2	....	....	....	....	....	....	....	....	....									
	USAHNTDP	U-17	7	3	3	6		....	....	....	....	....	....	....	....	....									
	USAHNTDP	U-18	7	0	1	1	2	....	....	....	....	....	....	....	....	....									
2012-13	U. of Michigan	CCHA	38	11	10	21	12	....	....	....	....	....	....	....	....	....									
2013-14	U. of Michigan	Big Ten	33	15	14	29	26	....	....	....	....	....	....	....	....	....									
2014-15	U. of Michigan	Big Ten	36	14	17	31	29	....	....	....	....	....	....	....	....	....									
	Winnipeg	**NHL**	1	0	1	1	0	0	0	0	4	0.0	2	9	66.7	13:16									
2015-16	**Winnipeg**	**NHL**	77	7	6	13	6	0	0	0	54	13.0	8	486	46.1	8:00									
2016-17	**Winnipeg**	**NHL**	64	9	8	17	18	0	1	1	77	11.7	8	192	49.5	12:21									
	Manitoba Moose	AHL	8	0	5	5	4	....	....	....	....	....	....	....	....	....									
	NHL Totals		142	16	15	31	24	0	1	1	135	11.9		687	47.3	10:00									

CORMIER, Patrice

(KOHR-mee-ay, pa-TREEZ)

Center. Shoots left. 6'2", 215 lbs.   Born, Moncton, NB, June 14, 1990. New Jersey's 3rd pick, 54th overall, in 2008 NHL Draft.

Season	Club	League	GP	G	A	Pts	PIM	PP	SH	GW	S	S%	+/-	TF	F%	Min	GP	G	A	Pts	PIM	PP	SH	GW	Min
2005-06	Dieppe	MJrHL	43	21	27	48	41	....	....	....	....	....	....	....	....	....	6	2	2	4	6				
2006-07	Rimouski Oceanic	QMJHL	53	11	10	21	73	....	....	....	....	....	....	....	....	....	9	4	5	9	10				
2007-08	Rimouski Oceanic	QMJHL	51	18	23	41	84	....	....	....	....	....	....	....	....	....	9	4	5	9	10				
2008-09	Rimouski Oceanic	QMJHL	54	23	28	51	118	....	....	....	....	....	....	....	....	....	13	4	6	10	30				
2009-10	Rimouski Oceanic	QMJHL	28	11	15	26	57	....	....	....	....	....	....	....	....	....									
	Rouyn-Noranda	QMJHL	3	0	5	5	7	....	....	....	....	....	....	....	....	....									
	Chicago Wolves	AHL						....	....	....	....	....	....	....	....	....	9	0	0	0	8				
2010-11	**Atlanta**	**NHL**	21	1	1	2	4	0	0	0	27	3.7	-5	67	58.2	9:39									
	Chicago Wolves	AHL	11	2	3	5	14	....	....	....	....	....	....	....	....	....									
2011-12	**Winnipeg**	**NHL**	9	0	0	0	0	0	0	0	8	0.0	1	30	73.3	6:22									
	St. John's IceCaps	AHL	56	18	15	33	75	....	....	....	....	....	....	....	....	....	15	3	0	3	12				
2012-13	St. John's IceCaps	AHL	35	7	4	11	69	....	....	....	....	....	....	....	....	....									
	Winnipeg	**NHL**	10	0	0	0	7	0	0	0	4	0.0	-3	6	16.7	3:53									
2013-14	**Winnipeg**	**NHL**	9	0	3	3	7	0	0	0	4	0.0	2	46	56.5	6:58									
	St. John's IceCaps	AHL	61	9	17	26	98	....	....	....	....	....	....	....	....	....	21	2	5	7	22				
2014-15	**Winnipeg**	**NHL**	1	0	0	0	0	0	0	0	0	0.0	0	5	60.0	4:54									
	St. John's IceCaps	AHL	47	12	9	21	74	....	....	....	....	....	....	....	....	....									
2015-16	**Winnipeg**	**NHL**	2	0	0	0	0	0	0	0	1	0.0	0	9	33.3	4:30									
	Manitoba Moose	AHL	65	16	17	32	73	....	....	....	....	....	....	....	....	....									
2016-17	Manitoba Moose	AHL	69	13	16	29	101	....	....	....	....	....	....	....	....	....									
	NHL Totals		52	1	4	5	18	0	0	0	44	2.3		163	57.7	7:13									

Traded to **Atlanta** by **New Jersey** with Johnny Oduya, Niclas Bergfors and New Jersey's 1st (later traded to Chicago - Chicago selected Kevin Hayes) and 2nd (later traded to Chicago - Chicago selected Justin Holl) round picks in 2010 NHL Draft for Ilya Kovalchuk, Anssi Salmela and Atlanta's 2nd round pick (Jonathon Merrill) in 2010 NHL Draft, February 4, 2010. • Missed majority of 2010-11 due to foot injury in training camp and upper-body injury at Phoenix, February 17, 2011. • Transferred to **Winnipeg** after **Atlanta** franchise relocated, June 21, 2011.

CORRADO, Frank

(koh-RA-doh, FRANK)   **PIT**

Defense. Shoots right. 6', 195 lbs.   Born, Woodbridge, ON, March 26, 1993. Vancouver's 6th pick, 150th overall, in 2011 NHL Draft.

Season	Club	League	GP	G	A	Pts	PIM	PP	SH	GW	S	S%	+/-	TF	F%	Min	GP	G	A	Pts	PIM	PP	SH	GW	Min
2008-09	Vaughan Kings	GTHL	62	15	33	48	136	....	....	....	....	....	....	....	....	....									
2009-10	Sudbury Wolves	OHL	63	1	8	9	46	....	....	....	....	....	....	....	....	....	4	0	1	1	0				
2010-11	Sudbury Wolves	OHL	67	4	26	30	94	....	....	....	....	....	....	....	....	....	8	1	4	5	8				
2011-12	Sudbury Wolves	OHL	60	3	23	26	81	....	....	....	....	....	....	....	....	....	4	0	0	0	12				
	Chicago Wolves	AHL	4	0	1	1	0	....	....	....	....	....	....	....	....	....	2	0	0	0	0				
2012-13	Sudbury Wolves	OHL	41	6	21	27	44	....	....	....	....	....	....	....	....	....									
	Kitchener Rangers	OHL	28	1	17	18	45	....	....	....	....	....	....	....	....	....	10	1	1	2	6				
	Chicago Wolves	AHL	3	0	2	2	0	....	....	....	....	....	....	....	....	....									
	Vancouver	**NHL**	3	0	0	0	0	0	0	0	4	0.0	-1	0	0.0	19:24	4	0	0	0	0	0	0	0	12:19
2013-14	**Vancouver**	**NHL**	15	1	0	1	4	0	0	0	20	5.0	-2	0	0.0	12:34									
	Utica Comets	AHL	59	6	11	17	46	....	....	....	....	....	....	....	....	....									
2014-15	**Vancouver**	**NHL**	10	1	0	1	0	0	0	0	8	12.5	-7	0	0.0	15:40									
	Utica Comets	AHL	35	7	9	16	31	....	....	....	....	....	....	....	....	....	18	1	0	1	24				

Season	Club	League	GP	G	A	Pts	PIM	PP	SH	GW	S	S%	+/-	TF	F%	Min	Playoffs GP	G	A	Pts	PIM	PP	SH	GW	Min
			Regular Season														Playoffs								
2015-16	**Toronto**	**NHL**	39	1	5	6	26	0	0	0	46	2.2	-12	0	0.0	14:27	....	....	....	....	....	....	....	....	....
	Toronto Marlies	AHL	7	0	3	3	2	....	....	....	....	....	....	....	....	....	....	....	....	....	....	....	....	....	....
2016-17	**Toronto**	**NHL**	2	0	0	0	6	0	0	0	2	0.0	0	0	0.0	14:00	....	....	....	....	....	....	....	....	....
	Toronto Marlies	AHL	18	1	11	12	14	....	....	....	....	....	....	....	....	....	....	....	....	....	....	....	....	....	....
	Pittsburgh	**NHL**	2	0	0	0	2	0	0	0	1	0.0	-1	0	0.0	7:33	....	....	....	....	....	....	....	....	....
	Wilkes-Barre	AHL	17	1	3	4	6	....	....	....	....	....	....	....	....	....	1	0	0	0	2	....	....	....	....
	NHL Totals		71	3	5	8	38	0	0	0	81	3.7		0	0.0	14:14	4	0	0	0	0	0	0	0	12:19

Claimed on waivers by **Toronto** from **Vancouver**, October 6, 2015. Traded to **Pittsburgh** by **Toronto** for Eric Fehr, Steve Oleksy and Pittsburgh's 4th round pick (Vladislav Kara) in 2017 NHL Draft, March 1, 2017.

COUSINS, Nick

(KUH-zihnz, NIHK) **ARI**

Center. Shoots left. 5'10", 188 lbs. Born, Belleville, ON, July 20, 1993. Philadelphia's 2nd pick, 68th overall, in 2011 NHL Draft.

Season	Club	League	GP	G	A	Pts	PIM	PP	SH	GW	S	S%	+/-	TF	F%	Min	Playoffs GP	G	A	Pts	PIM	PP	SH	GW	Min
2008-09	Quinte Red Devils	Minor-ON	71	72	67	139	....	....	....	....	....	....	....	....	....	....	....	....	....	....	....	....	....	....	....
	Trenton Hercs	ON-Jr.A	5	0	1	1	2	....	....	....	....	....	....	....	....	....	....	....	....	....	....	....	....	....	....
2009-10	Sault Ste. Marie	OHL	67	11	21	32	34	....	....	....	....	....	....	....	....	....	5	0	1	1	2	....	....	....	....
2010-11	Sault Ste. Marie	OHL	68	29	39	68	56	....	....	....	....	....	....	....	....	....	....	....	....	....	....	....	....	....	....
2011-12	Sault Ste. Marie	OHL	65	35	53	88	88	....	....	....	....	....	....	....	....	....	....	....	....	....	....	....	....	....	....
	Adirondack	AHL	1	0	0	0	0	....	....	....	....	....	....	....	....	....	....	....	....	....	....	....	....	....	....
2012-13	Sault Ste. Marie	OHL	64	27	76	103	83	....	....	....	....	....	....	....	....	....	6	3	3	6	12	....	....	....	....
	Adirondack	AHL	7	0	1	1	2	....	....	....	....	....	....	....	....	....	....	....	....	....	....	....	....	....	....
2013-14	Adirondack	AHL	74	11	18	29	47	....	....	....	....	....	....	....	....	....	....	....	....	....	....	....	....	....	....
2014-15	**Philadelphia**	**NHL**	11	0	0	0	2	0	0	0	6	0.0	1	52	44.2	8:49	....	....	....	....	....	....	....	....	....
	Lehigh Valley	AHL	64	22	34	56	73	....	....	....	....	....	....	....	....	....	....	....	....	....	....	....	....	....	....
2015-16	**Philadelphia**	**NHL**	36	6	5	11	4	0	0	1	41	14.6	5	237	46.0	10:44	6	0	0	0	2	0	0	0	10:59
	Lehigh Valley	AHL	38	12	26	38	45	....	....	....	....	....	....	....	....	....	....	....	....	....	....	....	....	....	....
2016-17	**Philadelphia**	**NHL**	60	6	10	16	31	1	0	0	99	6.1	-6	217	41.0	12:00	....	....	....	....	....	....	....	....	....
	NHL Totals		107	12	15	27	37	1	0	1	146	8.2		506	43.7	11:15	6	0	0	0	2	0	0	0	10:59

Traded to **Arizona** by **Philadelphia** with Merrick Madsen for Brendan Warren and Arizona's 5th round pick in 2018 NHL Draft, June 16, 2017.

COUTURE, Logan

(koh-TYOOR, LOH-guhn) **S.J.**

Center. Shoots left. 6'1", 200 lbs. Born, Guelph, ON, March 28, 1989. San Jose's 1st pick, 9th overall, in 2007 NHL Draft.

Season	Club	League	GP	G	A	Pts	PIM	PP	SH	GW	S	S%	+/-	TF	F%	Min	Playoffs GP	G	A	Pts	PIM	PP	SH	GW	Min
2004-05	St. Thomas Stars	ON-Jr.B	48	23	22	45	6	....	....	....	....	....	....	....	....	....	....	....	....	....	....	....	....	....	....
2005-06	Ottawa 67's	OHL	65	25	39	64	52	....	....	....	....	....	....	....	....	....	6	3	4	7	0	....	....	....	....
2006-07	Ottawa 67's	OHL	54	26	52	78	24	....	....	....	....	....	....	....	....	....	5	1	7	8	4	....	....	....	....
2007-08	Ottawa 67's	OHL	51	21	37	58	37	....	....	....	....	....	....	....	....	....	4	2	1	3	0	....	....	....	....
2008-09	Ottawa 67's	OHL	62	39	48	87	46	....	....	....	....	....	....	....	....	....	7	3	7	10	6	....	....	....	....
	Worcester Sharks	AHL	4	0	0	0	7	....	....	....	....	....	....	....	....	....	12	2	1	3	11	....	....	....	....
2009-10	**San Jose**	**NHL**	25	5	4	9	6	1	0	1	42	11.9	4	143	52.5	10:16	15	4	0	4	4	0	0	1	11:23
	Worcester Sharks	AHL	42	20	33	53	12	....	....	....	....	....	....	....	....	....	....	....	....	....	....	....	....	....	....
2010-11	**San Jose**	**NHL**	79	32	24	56	41	10	0	8	253	12.6	18	888	53.4	17:49	18	7	7	14	2	1	0	0	19:23
2011-12	**San Jose**	**NHL**	80	31	34	65	16	11	2	5	245	12.7	2	910	51.4	18:34	5	1	3	4	0	0	0	0	19:54
2012-13	Geneve	Swiss	22	7	16	23	10	....	....	....	....	....	....	....	....	....	....	....	....	....	....	....	....	....	....
	San Jose	**NHL**	48	21	16	37	4	7	0	5	151	13.9	7	489	51.5	18:06	11	5	6	11	0	*5	0	3	20:31
2013-14	**San Jose**	**NHL**	65	23	31	54	20	4	2	6	233	9.9	21	950	50.4	18:56	7	1	2	3	7	0	0	0	18:36
2014-15	**San Jose**	**NHL**	82	27	40	67	12	6	2	4	263	10.3	-6	990	48.2	19:04	....	....	....	....	....	....	....	....	....
2015-16	**San Jose**	**NHL**	52	15	21	36	20	5	0	4	137	10.9	2	576	47.1	17:23	24	10	*20	*30	8	4	0	2	19:21
2016-17	**San Jose**	**NHL**	73	25	27	52	12	11	0	3	174	14.4	11	753	39.4	17:36	6	2	1	3	0	1	0	0	18:19
	NHL Totals		504	179	197	376	131	55	6	36	1498	11.9		5699	49.0	17:52	86	30	39	69	21	11	0	6	18:01

AHL All-Rookie Team (2010) • NHL All-Rookie Team (2011)
Played in NHL All-Star Game (2012)
Signed as a free agent by **Geneve** (Swiss), September 18, 2012.

COUTURIER, Sean

(koo-TOO-ree-ay, SHAWN) **PHI**

Center. Shoots left. 6'3", 211 lbs. Born, Phoenix, AZ, December 7, 1992. Philadelphia's 1st pick, 8th overall, in 2011 NHL Draft.

Season	Club	League	GP	G	A	Pts	PIM	PP	SH	GW	S	S%	+/-	TF	F%	Min	Playoffs GP	G	A	Pts	PIM	PP	SH	GW	Min
2007-08	Notre Dame	SMHL	40	19	37	56	32	....	....	....	....	....	....	....	....	....	10	3	8	11	10	....	....	....	....
2008-09	Drummondville	QMJHL	58	9	22	31	14	....	....	....	....	....	....	....	....	....	19	1	7	8	8	....	....	....	....
2009-10	Drummondville	QMJHL	68	41	55	*96	47	....	....	....	....	....	....	....	....	....	14	10	8	18	18	....	....	....	....
2010-11	Drummondville	QMJHL	58	36	60	96	36	....	....	....	....	....	....	....	....	....	10	6	5	11	14	....	....	....	....
2011-12	**Philadelphia**	**NHL**	77	13	14	27	14	0	2	4	116	11.2	18	804	47.0	14:08	11	3	1	4	2	0	0	0	14:30
2012-13	Adirondack	AHL	31	10	18	28	16	....	....	....	....	....	....	....	....	....	....	....	....	....	....	....	....	....	....
	Philadelphia	**NHL**	46	4	11	15	10	0	0	0	75	5.3	-8	553	43.9	15:53	....	....	....	....	....	....	....	....	....
2013-14	**Philadelphia**	**NHL**	82	13	26	39	45	0	1	2	165	7.9	1	1353	47.8	19:05	7	0	0	0	6	0	0	0	19:35
2014-15	**Philadelphia**	**NHL**	82	15	22	37	28	1	1	0	148	10.1	4	1330	48.4	18:23	....	....	....	....	....	....	....	....	....
2015-16	**Philadelphia**	**NHL**	63	11	28	39	30	2	0	1	119	9.2	8	1105	48.6	18:36	1	0	0	0	0	0	0	0	9:04
2016-17	**Philadelphia**	**NHL**	66	14	20	34	33	0	0	2	120	11.7	12	1066	55.1	18:27	....	....	....	....	....	....	....	....	....
	NHL Totals		416	70	121	191	160	3	4	9	743	9.4		6211	48.8	17:30	19	3	1	4	8	0	0	0	16:05

QMJHL Second All-Star Team (2010) • QMJHL First All-Star Team (2011) • QMJHL Player of the Year (2011)

COWEN, Jared

(KOW-ehn, JAIR-ehd)

Defense. Shoots left. 6'5", 235 lbs. Born, Saskatoon, SK, January 25, 1991. Ottawa's 1st pick, 9th overall, in 2009 NHL Draft.

Season	Club	League	GP	G	A	Pts	PIM	PP	SH	GW	S	S%	+/-	TF	F%	Min	Playoffs GP	G	A	Pts	PIM	PP	SH	GW	Min
2006-07	Sask. Contacts	SMHL	41	6	22	28	103	....	....	....	....	....	....	....	....	....	....	....	....	....	....	....	....	....	....
	Spokane Chiefs	WHL	6	0	2	2	2	....	....	....	....	....	....	....	....	....	6	0	1	1	6	....	....	....	....
2007-08	Spokane Chiefs	WHL	68	4	14	18	62	....	....	....	....	....	....	....	....	....	21	1	3	4	17	....	....	....	....
2008-09	Spokane Chiefs	WHL	48	7	14	21	45	....	....	....	....	....	....	....	....	....	....	....	....	....	....	....	....	....	....
2009-10	Spokane Chiefs	WHL	59	8	22	30	74	....	....	....	....	....	....	....	....	....	7	1	1	2	8	....	....	....	....
	Ottawa	**NHL**	1	0	0	0	2	0	0	0	0	0.0	0	0	0.0	6:46	....	....	....	....	....	....	....	....	....
2010-11	Spokane Chiefs	WHL	58	18	30	48	91	....	....	....	....	....	....	....	....	....	17	2	12	14	16	....	....	....	....
	Binghamton	AHL	....	....	....	....	....	....	....	....	....	....	....	....	....	....	10	0	4	4	0	....	....	....	....
2011-12	**Ottawa**	**NHL**	82	5	12	17	56	0	0	1	58	8.6	-4	0	0.0	18:54	7	0	1	1	4	0	0	0	17:02
2012-13	Binghamton	AHL	3	0	3	3	2	....	....	....	....	....	....	....	....	....	....	....	....	....	....	....	....	....	....
	Ottawa	**NHL**	7	1	0	1	10	0	0	0	8	12.5	1	0	0.0	20:17	10	0	3	3	21	0	0	0	18:34
2013-14	**Ottawa**	**NHL**	68	6	9	15	45	0	0	2	68	8.8	0	0	0.0	20:31	....	....	....	....	....	....	....	....	....
2014-15	**Ottawa**	**NHL**	54	3	6	9	45	0	0	1	47	6.4	-11	0	0.0	18:09	....	....	....	....	....	....	....	....	....
2015-16	**Ottawa**	**NHL**	37	0	4	4	16	0	0	0	23	0.0	7	0	0.0	16:59	....	....	....	....	....	....	....	....	....
2016-17			DID NOT PLAY – INJURED																						
	NHL Totals		249	15	31	46	174	0	0	4	204	7.4		0	0.0	18:53	17	0	4	4	25	0	0	0	17:56

WHL West Second All-Star Team (2010) • WHL West First All-Star Team (2011)
• Missed majority of 2012-13 due to hip injury vs. Albany (AHL), October 6, 2012. Traded to **Toronto** by **Ottawa** with Colin Greening, Milan Michalek, Tobias Lindberg and Ottawa's 2nd round pick (Eemeli Rasanen) in 2017 NHL Draft for Dion Phaneuf, Matt Frattin, Casey Bailey, Ryan Rupert and Cody Donaghey, February 9, 2016. • Missed majority of 2015-16 and all of 2016-17 due to recurring injury to oblique muscle in abdomen.

COYLE, Charlie

(KOYL, CHAR-lee) **MIN**

Center/Right wing. Shoots right. 6'3", 221 lbs. Born, E. Weymouth, MA, March 2, 1992. San Jose's 1st pick, 28th overall, in 2010 NHL Draft.

Season	Club	League	GP	G	A	Pts	PIM	PP	SH	GW	S	S%	+/-	TF	F%	Min	Playoffs GP	G	A	Pts	PIM	PP	SH	GW	Min
2007-08	Thayer Academy	High-MA	....	14	23	37	....	....	....	....	....	....	....	....	....	....	....	....	....	....	....	....	....	....	....
2008-09	Thayer Academy	High-MA	26	20	28	48	4	....	....	....	....	....	....	....	....	....	....	....	....	....	....	....	....	....	....
2009-10	South Shore	EJHL	42	21	42	63	50	....	....	....	....	....	....	....	....	....	4	2	1	3	0	....	....	....	....
	USAHNTDP	U-18	4	1	0	1	2	....	....	....	....	....	....	....	....	....	....	....	....	....	....	....	....	....	....
2010-11	Boston University	H-East	37	7	19	26	34	....	....	....	....	....	....	....	....	....	....	....	....	....	....	....	....	....	....
2011-12	Boston University	H-East	16	3	11	14	20	....	....	....	....	....	....	....	....	....	....	....	....	....	....	....	....	....	....
	Saint John	QMJHL	23	15	23	38	8	....	....	....	....	....	....	....	....	....	17	15	19	34	8	....	....	....	....
2012-13	Houston Aeros	AHL	47	14	11	25	22	....	....	....	....	....	....	....	....	....	....	....	....	....	....	....	....	....	....
	Minnesota	**NHL**	37	8	6	14	28	1	0	2	50	16.0	3	26	34.6	15:04	5	0	2	2	2	0	0	0	18:10

Season	Club	League	GP	G	A	Pts	PIM	PP	SH	GW	S	S%	+/-	TF	F%	Min	GP	G	A	Pts	PIM	PP	SH	GW	Min
			Regular Season														Playoffs								
2013-14	**Minnesota**	**NHL**	**70**	**12**	**18**	**30**	**33**	**2**	**0**	**2**	**135**	**8.9**	**-7**	**458**	**41.9**	**17:05**	**13**	**3**	**4**	**7**	**6**	**1**	**0**	**1**	**17:50**
2014-15	**Minnesota**	**NHL**	**82**	**11**	**24**	**35**	**39**	**1**	**0**	**4**	**120**	**9.2**	**13**	**718**	**46.5**	**14:33**	**10**	**1**	**1**	**2**	**0**	**0**	**0**	**0**	**14:22**
2015-16	**Minnesota**	**NHL**	**82**	**21**	**21**	**42**	**16**	**2**	**0**	**4**	**140**	**15.0**	**1**	**502**	**45.4**	**17:18**	**6**	**1**	**1**	**2**	**6**	**0**	**0**	**0**	**18:50**
2016-17	**Minnesota**	**NHL**	**82**	**18**	**38**	**56**	**36**	**4**	**0**	**5**	**159**	**11.3**	**13**	**248**	**46.0**	**16:42**	**5**	**2**	**0**	**2**	**2**	**0**	**0**	**1**	**17:11**
	NHL Totals		**353**	**70**	**107**	**177**	**152**	**10**	**0**	**17**	**604**	**11.6**		**1952**	**44.9**	**16:15**	**39**	**7**	**8**	**15**	**16**	**1**	**0**	**2**	**17:03**

Hockey East All-Rookie Team (2011) • Hockey East Rookie of the Year (2011)

Traded to **Minnesota** by **San Jose** with Devin Setoguchi and San Jose's 1st round pick (Zack Phillips) in 2011 NHL Draft for Brent Burns and Minnesota's 2nd round pick (later traded to Tampa Bay – later traded to Nashville – Nashville selected Pontus Aberg) in 2012 NHL Draft, June 24, 2011.

CRACKNELL, Adam (krak-NEHL, A-duhm) DAL

Right wing. Shoots right. 6'2", 210 lbs. Born, Prince Albert, SK, July 15, 1985. Calgary's 10th pick, 279th overall, in 2004 NHL Draft.

Season	Club	League	GP	G	A	Pts	PIM	PP	SH	GW	S	S%	+/-	TF	F%	Min	GP	G	A	Pts	PIM	PP	SH	GW	Min
2001-02	Saanich Braves	VIJHL	47	21	30	51	83	....	....	....	....	....	....	....	....	....	....	....	....	....	....	....	....	....	....
2002-03	Kootenay Ice	WHL	67	7	4	11	37	....	....	....	....	....	....	....	....	....	11	0	0	0	2	....	....	....	....
2003-04	Kootenay Ice	WHL	72	26	35	61	63	....	....	....	....	....	....	....	....	....	4	1	1	2	2	....	....	....	....
2004-05	Kootenay Ice	WHL	72	19	29	48	65	....	....	....	....	....	....	....	....	....	16	8	8	16	6	....	....	....	....
2005-06	Kootenay Ice	WHL	72	42	51	93	85	....	....	....	....	....	....	....	....	....	6	1	4	5	6	....	....	....	....
	Omaha	AHL	6	1	2	3	2	....	....	....	....	....	....	....	....	....	....	....	....	....	....	....	....	....	....
2006-07	Las Vegas	ECHL	31	8	14	22	35	....	....	....	....	....	....	....	....	....	8	3	3	6	6	....	....	....	....
2007-08	Quad City Flames	AHL	4	1	0	1	0	....	....	....	....	....	....	....	....	....	....	....	....	....	....	....	....	....	....
	Las Vegas	ECHL	61	29	30	59	47	....	....	....	....	....	....	....	....	....	21	9	13	22	4	....	....	....	....
2008-09	Quad City Flames	AHL	79	10	16	26	36	....	....	....	....	....	....	....	....	....	....	....	....	....	....	....	....	....	....
2009-10	Peoria Rivermen	AHL	76	17	21	38	40	....	....	....	....	....	....	....	....	....	....	....	....	....	....	....	....	....	....
2010-11	**St. Louis**	**NHL**	**24**	**3**	**4**	**7**	**8**	**0**	**0**	**0**	**26**	**11.5**	**1**	**118**	**39.0**	**8:55**	....	....	....	....	....	....	....	....	....
	Peoria Rivermen	AHL	61	6	19	25	54	....	....	....	....	....	....	....	....	....	4	2	0	2	0	....	....	....	....
2011-12	**St. Louis**	**NHL**	**2**	**1**	**0**	**1**	**0**	**0**	**0**	**0**	**1**	**100.0**	**1**	**1**	**0.0**	**7:39**	....	....	....	....	....	....	....	....	....
	Peoria Rivermen	AHL	72	23	26	49	54	....	....	....	....	....	....	....	....	....	....	....	....	....	....	....	....	....	....
2012-13	Peoria Rivermen	AHL	49	17	16	33	26	....	....	....	....	....	....	....	....	....	....	....	....	....	....	....	....	....	....
	St. Louis	**NHL**	**20**	**2**	**4**	**6**	**4**	**0**	**0**	**0**	**21**	**9.5**	**3**	**25**	**24.0**	**8:37**	**5**	**0**	**0**	**0**	**0**	**0**	**0**	**0**	**7:59**
2013-14	**St. Louis**	**NHL**	**19**	**0**	**2**	**2**	**0**	**0**	**0**	**0**	**16**	**0.0**	**0**	**27**	**37.0**	**8:11**	**5**	**1**	**0**	**1**	**2**	**0**	**0**	**0**	**12:43**
	Chicago Wolves	AHL	28	12	13	25	8	....	....	....	....	....	....	....	....	....	7	3	1	4	2	....	....	....	....
2014-15	**Columbus**	**NHL**	**17**	**0**	**1**	**1**	**2**	**0**	**0**	**0**	**17**	**0.0**	**-8**	**58**	**34.5**	**9:57**	....	....	....	....	....	....	....	....	....
	Springfield	AHL	18	3	4	7	2	....	....	....	....	....	....	....	....	....	....	....	....	....	....	....	....	....	....
	Chicago Wolves	AHL	22	7	6	13	8	....	....	....	....	....	....	....	....	....	5	1	0	1	4	....	....	....	....
2015-16	**Vancouver**	**NHL**	**44**	**5**	**5**	**10**	**14**	**0**	**0**	**1**	**55**	**9.1**	**1**	**382**	**39.8**	**12:24**	....	....	....	....	....	....	....	....	....
	Edmonton	**NHL**	**8**	**0**	**0**	**0**	**6**	**0**	**0**	**0**	**13**	**0.0**	**-2**	**13**	**30.8**	**11:18**	....	....	....	....	....	....	....	....	....
2016-17	**Dallas**	**NHL**	**69**	**10**	**6**	**16**	**12**	**0**	**1**	**2**	**87**	**11.5**	**9**	**295**	**45.8**	**10:28**	....	....	....	....	....	....	....	....	....
	NHL Totals		**203**	**21**	**22**	**43**	**46**	**0**	**1**	**3**	**236**	**8.9**		**919**	**40.6**	**10:16**	**10**	**1**	**0**	**1**	**2**	**0**	**0**	**0**	**10:21**

WHL West Second All-Star Team (2006)

Signed as a free agent by **St. Louis**, July 23, 2009. Signed as a free agent by **Los Angeles**, July 1, 2014. Claimed on waivers by **Columbus** from **Los Angeles**, October 7, 2014. Traded to **St. Louis** by **Columbus** for future considerations, February 26, 2015. Signed as a free agent by **Vancouver**, August 25, 2015. Claimed on waivers by **Edmonton** from **Vancouver**, February 29, 2016. Signed as a free agent by **Dallas**, July 3, 2016.

CRAMAROSSA, Joseph (kra-ma-ROH-sa, JOH-sehf)

Center. Shoots left. 6', 192 lbs. Born, Toronto, ON, October 26, 1992. Anaheim's 4th pick, 65th overall, in 2011 NHL Draft.

Season	Club	League	GP	G	A	Pts	PIM	PP	SH	GW	S	S%	+/-	TF	F%	Min	GP	G	A	Pts	PIM	PP	SH	GW	Min
2007-08	Markham Majors	GTHL	70	31	37	68	64	....	....	....	....	....	....	....	....	....	....	....	....	....	....	....	....	....	....
2008-09	Markham Waxers	ON-Jr.A	38	7	3	10	14	....	....	....	....	....	....	....	....	....	12	1	2	3	0	....	....	....	....
2009-10	St. Michael's	OHL	64	6	10	16	60	....	....	....	....	....	....	....	....	....	14	0	2	2	11	....	....	....	....
2010-11	St. Michael's	OHL	59	12	20	32	101	....	....	....	....	....	....	....	....	....	14	2	2	4	6	....	....	....	....
2011-12	St. Michael's	OHL	15	6	5	11	40	....	....	....	....	....	....	....	....	....	....	....	....	....	....	....	....	....	....
	Belleville Bulls	OHL	29	8	8	16	43	....	....	....	....	....	....	....	....	....	6	2	2	4	18	....	....	....	....
2012-13	Belleville Bulls	OHL	68	19	44	63	89	....	....	....	....	....	....	....	....	....	17	5	4	9	35	....	....	....	....
2013-14	Norfolk Admirals	AHL	47	1	3	4	52	....	....	....	....	....	....	....	....	....	2	0	0	0	0	....	....	....	....
	Utah Grizzlies	ECHL	3	0	2	2	7	....	....	....	....	....	....	....	....	....	....	....	....	....	....	....	....	....	....
2014-15	Norfolk Admirals	AHL	54	5	5	10	75	....	....	....	....	....	....	....	....	....	....	....	....	....	....	....	....	....	....
2015-16	San Diego Gulls	AHL	61	11	6	17	68	....	....	....	....	....	....	....	....	....	9	3	0	3	6	....	....	....	....
2016-17	**Anaheim**	**NHL**	**49**	**4**	**6**	**10**	**51**	**0**	**0**	**1**	**26**	**15.4**	**1**	**7**	**85.7**	**9:49**	....	....	....	....	....	....	....	....	....
	San Diego Gulls	AHL	2	0	0	0	8	....	....	....	....	....	....	....	....	....	....	....	....	....	....	....	....	....	....
	Vancouver	**NHL**	**10**	**0**	**0**	**0**	**9**	**0**	**0**	**0**	**10**	**0.0**	**-1**	**0**	**0.0**	**10:35**	....	....	....	....	....	....	....	....	....
	NHL Totals		**59**	**4**	**6**	**10**	**60**	**0**	**0**	**1**	**36**	**11.1**		**7**	**85.7**	**9:57**	....	....	....	....	....	....	....	....	....

Claimed on waivers by **Vancouver** from **Anaheim**, March 1, 2017.

CROSBY, Sidney (KRAWZ-bee, SIHD-nee) PIT

Center. Shoots left. 5'11", 200 lbs. Born, Cole Harbour, NS, August 7, 1987. Pittsburgh's 1st pick, 1st overall, in 2005 NHL Draft.

Season	Club	League	GP	G	A	Pts	PIM	PP	SH	GW	S	S%	+/-	TF	F%	Min	GP	G	A	Pts	PIM	PP	SH	GW	Min
2001-02	Dartmouth	NSMHL	74	95	98	193	114	....	....	....	....	....	....	....	....	....	....	....	....	....	....	....	....	....	....
2002-03	Shattuck	High-MN	57	72	90	162	....	....	....	....	....	....	....	....	....	....	....	....	....	....	....	....	....	....	....
2003-04	Rimouski Oceanic	QMJHL	59	54	*81	*135	74	....	....	....	....	....	....	....	....	....	9	7	9	16	10	....	....	....	....
2004-05	Rimouski Oceanic	QMJHL	62	*66	*102	*168	84	....	....	....	....	....	....	....	....	....	13	*14	*17	*31	16	....	....	....	....
2005-06	**Pittsburgh**	**NHL**	**81**	**39**	**63**	**102**	**110**	**16**	**0**	**5**	**278**	**14.0**	**-1**	**1174**	**45.5**	**20:08**	....	....	....	....	....	....	....	....	....
2006-07	**Pittsburgh**	**NHL**	**79**	**36**	**84**	***120**	**60**	**13**	**0**	**4**	**250**	**14.4**	**10**	**1686**	**49.8**	**20:46**	**5**	**3**	**2**	**5**	**4**	**1**	**0**	**1**	**21:40**
2007-08	**Pittsburgh**	**NHL**	**53**	**24**	**48**	**72**	**39**	**6**	**0**	**4**	**173**	**13.9**	**18**	**1103**	**51.4**	**20:51**	**20**	**6**	***21**	***27**	**12**	**2**	**0**	**1**	**20:42**
2008-09♦	**Pittsburgh**	**NHL**	**77**	**33**	**70**	**103**	**76**	**7**	**0**	**3**	**238**	**13.9**	**3**	**1615**	**51.3**	**21:57**	**24**	***15**	**16**	**31**	**14**	**5**	**0**	**2**	**20:49**
2009-10	**Pittsburgh**	**NHL**	**81**	***51**	**58**	**109**	**71**	**13**	**2**	**6**	**298**	**17.1**	**15**	**1791**	**55.9**	**21:57**	**13**	**6**	**13**	**19**	**6**	**1**	**0**	**1**	**23:32**
	Canada	Olympics	7	4	3	7	4	....	....	....	....	....	....	....	....	....	....	....	....	....	....	....	....	....	....
2010-11	**Pittsburgh**	**NHL**	**41**	**32**	**34**	**66**	**31**	**10**	**1**	**3**	**161**	**19.9**	**20**	**981**	**55.7**	**21:55**	....	....	....	....	....	....	....	....	....
2011-12	**Pittsburgh**	**NHL**	**22**	**8**	**29**	**37**	**14**	**2**	**0**	**3**	**75**	**10.7**	**15**	**453**	**50.1**	**18:28**	**6**	**3**	**5**	**8**	**9**	**0**	**0**	**0**	**20:37**
2012-13	**Pittsburgh**	**NHL**	**36**	**15**	**41**	**56**	**16**	**3**	**0**	**1**	**124**	**12.1**	**26**	**834**	**54.3**	**21:06**	**14**	**7**	**8**	**15**	**8**	**2**	**0**	**0**	**23:05**
2013-14	**Pittsburgh**	**NHL**	**80**	**36**	***68**	***104**	**46**	**11**	**0**	**5**	**259**	**13.9**	**18**	**1887**	**52.5**	**21:58**	**13**	**1**	**8**	**9**	**4**	**0**	**0**	**1**	**21:19**
	Canada	Olympics	6	1	2	3	0	....	....	....	....	....	....	....	....	....	....	....	....	....	....	....	....	....	....
2014-15	**Pittsburgh**	**NHL**	**77**	**28**	**56**	**84**	**47**	**10**	**0**	**3**	**237**	**11.8**	**5**	**1597**	**49.9**	**19:58**	**5**	**2**	**2**	**4**	**0**	**0**	**0**	**0**	**20:09**
2015-16♦	**Pittsburgh**	**NHL**	**80**	**36**	**49**	**85**	**42**	**10**	**0**	**9**	**248**	**14.5**	**19**	**1907**	**51.7**	**20:28**	**24**	**6**	**13**	**19**	**4**	**3**	**0**	**3**	**20:26**
2016-17♦	**Pittsburgh**	**NHL**	**75**	***44**	**45**	**89**	**24**	**14**	**0**	**5**	**255**	**17.3**	**17**	**1748**	**48.2**	**19:53**	**24**	**8**	***19**	**27**	**10**	**4**	**0**	**0**	**19:24**
	NHL Totals		**782**	**382**	**645**	**1027**	**576**	**115**	**3**	**51**	**2596**	**14.7**		**16776**	**51.3**	**20:53**	**148**	**57**	**107**	**164**	**71**	**18**	**0**	**9**	**21:00**

QMJHL All-Rookie Team (2004) • QMJHL First All-Star Team (2004, 2005) • QMJHL Player of the Year (2004, 2005) • Canadian Major Junior First All-Star Team (2004, 2005) • Canadian Major Junior Rookie of the Year (2004) • Canadian Major Junior Player of the Year (2004, 2005) • NHL All-Rookie Team (2006) • NHL First All-Star Team (2007, 2013, 2014, 2016) • Art Ross Trophy (2007, 2014) • Lester B. Pearson Award (2007) • Hart Memorial Trophy (2007, 2014) • NHL Second All-Star Team (2010, 2015, 2017) • Mark Messier NHL Leadership Award (2010) • Maurice "Rocket" Richard Trophy (2010) (tied with Steven Stamkos) • Ted Lindsay Award (2013, 2014) • Conn Smythe Trophy (2016, 2017) • Maurice "Rocket" Richard Trophy (2017)

Played in NHL All-Star Game (2007, 2017)

• Missed majority of 2010-11 and 2011-12 due to post-concussion syndrome.

CROSS, Tommy (KRAWS, TAW-mee) BOS

Defense. Shoots left. 6'3", 205 lbs. Born, Hartford, CT, September 12, 1989. Boston's 2nd pick, 35th overall, in 2007 NHL Draft.

Season	Club	League	GP	G	A	Pts	PIM	PP	SH	GW	S	S%	+/-	TF	F%	Min	GP	G	A	Pts	PIM	PP	SH	GW	Min
2004-05	Simsbury	High-CT	23	5	40	45	18	....	....	....	....	....	....	....	....	....	....	....	....	....	....	....	....	....	....
2005-06	Simsbury	High-CT	22	15	35	50	....	....	....	....	....	....	....	....	....	....	....	....	....	....	....	....	....	....	....
2006-07	Westminster	High-CT	25	8	12	20	20	....	....	....	....	....	....	....	....	....	....	....	....	....	....	....	....	....	....
	USAHNTDP	NAHL	2	0	2	2	0	....	....	....	....	....	....	....	....	....	....	....	....	....	....	....	....	....	....
	USAHNTDP	U-18	11	0	1	1	8	....	....	....	....	....	....	....	....	....	....	....	....	....	....	....	....	....	....
2007-08	Westminster	High-CT	25	9	12	21	....	....	....	....	....	....	....	....	....	....	....	....	....	....	....	....	....	....	....
	Ohio	USHL	9	0	4	4	8	....	....	....	....	....	....	....	....	....	....	....	....	....	....	....	....	....	....
2008-09	Boston College	H-East	24	0	8	8	24	....	....	....	....	....	....	....	....	....	....	....	....	....	....	....	....	....	....
2009-10	Boston College	H-East	38	5	5	10	36	....	....	....	....	....	....	....	....	....	....	....	....	....	....	....	....	....	....
2010-11	Boston College	H-East	28	7	11	18	45	....	....	....	....	....	....	....	....	....	....	....	....	....	....	....	....	....	....
2011-12	Boston College	H-East	44	5	19	24	66	....	....	....	....	....	....	....	....	....	....	....	....	....	....	....	....	....	....
	Providence Bruins	AHL	2	0	0	0	2	....	....	....	....	....	....	....	....	....	....	....	....	....	....	....	....	....	....

			Regular Season														Playoffs								
Season	Club	League	GP	G	A	Pts	PIM	PP	SH	GW	S	S%	+/-	TF	F%	Min	GP	G	A	Pts	PIM	PP	SH	GW	Min
2012-13	Providence Bruins	AHL	42	1	10	11	23	....	....	....	....	....	....	....	....	....	12	0	3	3	8	....	....	....	....
	South Carolina	ECHL	24	6	13	19	23	....	....	....	....	....	....	....	....	....	....	....	....	....	....	....	....	....	....
2013-14	Providence Bruins	AHL	55	3	4	7	54	....	....	....	....	....	....	....	....	....	4	0	1	1	4	....	....	....	....
2014-15	Providence Bruins	AHL	54	4	18	22	85	....	....	....	....	....	....	....	....	....	4	1	0	1	4	....	....	....	....
2015-16	**Boston**	**NHL**	**3**	**0**	**1**	**1**	**0**	**0**	**0**	**0**	**0**	**0.0**	**–1**	**0**	**0.0**	**13:05**	....	....	....	....	....	....	....	....	....
	Providence Bruins	AHL	64	3	20	23	97	....	....	....	....	....	....	....	....	....	3	1	1	2	0	....	....	....	....
2016-17	Providence Bruins	AHL	74	12	23	35	69	....	....	....	....	....	....	....	....	....	16	2	7	9	20	....	....	....	....
	Boston	**NHL**	....	....	....	....	....	....	....	....	....	....	....	....	....	....	**1**	**0**	**1**	**1**	**0**	**0**	**0**	**0**	**13:08**
	NHL Totals		**3**	**0**	**1**	**1**	**0**	**0**	**0**	**0**	**0**	**0.0**		**0**	**0.0**	**13:05**	**1**	**0**	**1**	**1**	**0**	**0**	**0**	**0**	**13:08**

CROUSE, Lawson

(KROWS, LAW-suhn) **ARI**

Left wing. Shoots left. 6'4", 220 lbs. Born, Mt. Brydges, ON, June 23, 1997. Florida's 1st pick, 11th overall, in 2015 NHL Draft.

2012-13	Elgin-Mid. Chiefs	Minor-ON	27	22	28	50	51	....	....	....	....	....	....	....	....	....	7	4	5	9	10	....	....	....	....
	St. Thomas Stars	ON-Jr.B	5	0	1	1	0	....	....	....	....	....	....	....	....	....	....	....	....	....	....	....	....	....	....
2013-14	Kingston	OHL	63	15	12	27	64	....	....	....	....	....	....	....	....	....	7	0	3	3	7	....	....	....	....
2014-15	Kingston	OHL	56	29	22	51	70	....	....	....	....	....	....	....	....	....	4	2	1	3	18	....	....	....	....
2015-16	Kingston	OHL	49	23	39	62	56	....	....	....	....	....	....	....	....	....	9	7	4	11	2	....	....	....	....
	Portland Pirates	AHL	2	0	0	0	0	....	....	....	....	....	....	....	....	....	....	....	....	....	....	....	....	....	....
2016-17	**Arizona**	**NHL**	**72**	**5**	**7**	**12**	**48**	**0**	**1**	**2**	**84**	**6.0**	**–20**	**2**	**50.0**	**11:53**	....	....	....	....	....	....	....	....	....
	NHL Totals		**72**	**5**	**7**	**12**	**48**	**0**	**1**	**2**	**84**	**6.0**		**2**	**50.0**	**11:53**	....	....	....	....	....	....	....	....	....

Traded to **Arizona** by **Florida** with Dave Bolland for Arizona's 3rd round pick (Max Glidon) in 2017 NHL Draft and Arizona's 2nd round pick in 2018 NHL Draft, August 25, 2016.

CULLEN, Matt

(KUH-lehn, MAT)

Center. Shoots left. 6'1", 200 lbs. Born, Virginia, MN, November 2, 1976. Anaheim's 2nd pick, 35th overall, in 1996 NHL Draft.

1993-94	Moorhead Spuds	High-MN	STATISTICS NOT AVAILABLE																						
1994-95	Moorhead Spuds	High-MN	28	47	42	89	78	....	....	....	....	....	....	....	....	....	....	....	....	....	....	....	....	....	....
1995-96	St. Cloud State	WCHA	39	12	29	41	28	....	....	....	....	....	....	....	....	....	....	....	....	....	....	....	....	....	....
1996-97	St. Cloud State	WCHA	36	15	30	45	70	....	....	....	....	....	....	....	....	....	....	....	....	....	....	....	....	....	....
	Baltimore Bandits	AHL	6	3	3	6	7	....	....	....	....	....	....	....	....	....	3	0	2	2	0	....	....	....	....
1997-98	**Anaheim**	**NHL**	**61**	**6**	**21**	**27**	**23**	**2**	**0**	**0**	**75**	**8.0**	**–4**	....	....	....	....	....	....	....	....	....	....	....	....
	Cincinnati	AHL	18	15	12	27	2	....	....	....	....	....	....	....	....	....	....	....	....	....	....	....	....	....	....
1998-99	**Anaheim**	**NHL**	**75**	**11**	**14**	**25**	**47**	**5**	**1**	**1**	**112**	**9.8**	**–12**	**1047**	**47.7**	**15:31**	**4**	**0**	**0**	**0**	**0**	**0**	**0**	**0**	**15:30**
	Cincinnati	AHL	3	1	2	3	8	....	....	....	....	....	....	....	....	....	....	....	....	....	....	....	....	....	....
99-2000	**Anaheim**	**NHL**	**80**	**13**	**26**	**39**	**24**	**1**	**0**	**1**	**137**	**9.5**	**5**	**1247**	**44.6**	**16:54**	....	....	....	....	....	....	....	....	....
2000-01	**Anaheim**	**NHL**	**82**	**10**	**30**	**40**	**38**	**4**	**0**	**1**	**159**	**6.3**	**–23**	**1478**	**48.0**	**18:15**	....	....	....	....	....	....	....	....	....
2001-02	**Anaheim**	**NHL**	**79**	**18**	**30**	**48**	**24**	**3**	**1**	**4**	**164**	**11.0**	**–1**	**1283**	**51.4**	**17:01**	....	....	....	....	....	....	....	....	....
2002-03	**Anaheim**	**NHL**	**50**	**7**	**14**	**21**	**12**	**1**	**0**	**1**	**77**	**9.1**	**–4**	**271**	**50.6**	**14:18**	....	....	....	....	....	....	....	....	....
	Florida	**NHL**	**30**	**6**	**6**	**12**	**22**	**2**	**1**	**1**	**54**	**11.1**	**–4**	**423**	**47.3**	**14:43**	....	....	....	....	....	....	....	....	....
2003-04	**Florida**	**NHL**	**56**	**6**	**13**	**19**	**24**	**1**	**0**	**2**	**75**	**8.0**	**–2**	**735**	**50.6**	**14:12**	....	....	....	....	....	....	....	....	....
2004-05	SG Cortina	Italy	36	*27	33	60	64	....	....	....	....	....	....	....	....	....	18	8	14	22	32	....	....	....	....
2005-06♦	**Carolina**	**NHL**	**78**	**25**	**24**	**49**	**40**	**8**	**0**	**5**	**214**	**11.7**	**4**	**583**	**52.1**	**16:26**	**25**	**4**	**14**	**18**	**12**	**2**	**0**	**1**	**15:37**
2006-07	**NY Rangers**	**NHL**	**80**	**16**	**25**	**41**	**52**	**2**	**3**	**2**	**217**	**7.4**	**0**	**1134**	**54.6**	**17:10**	**10**	**1**	**3**	**4**	**6**	**0**	**0**	**1**	**16:55**
2007-08	**Carolina**	**NHL**	**59**	**13**	**36**	**49**	**32**	**8**	**0**	**1**	**137**	**9.5**	**2**	**649**	**56.1**	**16:52**	....	....	....	....	....	....	....	....	....
2008-09	**Carolina**	**NHL**	**69**	**22**	**21**	**43**	**20**	**4**	**2**	**2**	**139**	**15.8**	**11**	**884**	**51.7**	**16:48**	**18**	**3**	**3**	**6**	**14**	**0**	**1**	**0**	**16:41**
2009-10	**Carolina**	**NHL**	**60**	**12**	**28**	**40**	**26**	**1**	**2**	**1**	**137**	**8.8**	**0**	**898**	**49.1**	**19:02**	....	....	....	....	....	....	....	....	....
	Ottawa	**NHL**	**21**	**4**	**4**	**8**	**8**	**1**	**0**	**1**	**58**	**6.9**	**–7**	**223**	**58.7**	**17:59**	**6**	**3**	**5**	**8**	**0**	**2**	**0**	**0**	**23:14**
2010-11	**Minnesota**	**NHL**	**78**	**12**	**27**	**39**	**34**	**5**	**4**	**2**	**150**	**8.0**	**–14**	**843**	**56.1**	**18:02**	....	....	....	....	....	....	....	....	....
2011-12	**Minnesota**	**NHL**	**73**	**14**	**21**	**35**	**24**	**4**	**0**	**0**	**164**	**8.5**	**–10**	**1178**	**53.2**	**18:56**	....	....	....	....	....	....	....	....	....
2012-13	**Minnesota**	**NHL**	**42**	**7**	**20**	**27**	**10**	**0**	**0**	**0**	**79**	**8.9**	**9**	**448**	**54.7**	**15:53**	**5**	**0**	**3**	**3**	**2**	**0**	**0**	**0**	**19:08**
2013-14	**Nashville**	**NHL**	**77**	**10**	**29**	**39**	**32**	**1**	**0**	**2**	**134**	**7.5**	**4**	**772**	**56.7**	**15:30**	....	....	....	....	....	....	....	....	....
2014-15	**Nashville**	**NHL**	**62**	**7**	**18**	**25**	**16**	**0**	**0**	**1**	**90**	**7.8**	**8**	**287**	**54.0**	**13:01**	**6**	**1**	**1**	**2**	**4**	**0**	**0**	**0**	**17:19**
2015-16♦	**Pittsburgh**	**NHL**	**82**	**16**	**16**	**32**	**20**	**0**	**3**	**4**	**118**	**13.6**	**5**	**1044**	**55.8**	**13:53**	**24**	**4**	**2**	**6**	**8**	**0**	**0**	**2**	**13:50**
2016-17♦	**Pittsburgh**	**NHL**	**72**	**13**	**18**	**31**	**30**	**2**	**2**	**2**	**93**	**14.0**	**4**	**859**	**51.2**	**13:55**	**25**	**2**	**7**	**9**	**24**	**0**	**1**	**0**	**14:19**
	NHL Totals		**1366**	**248**	**441**	**689**	**558**	**55**	**19**	**34**	**2583**	**9.6**		**16286**	**51.6**	**16:16**	**123**	**18**	**38**	**56**	**70**	**4**	**2**	**4**	**15:52**

WCHA Second All-Star Team (1997)

Traded to **Florida** by **Anaheim** with Pavel Trnka and Anaheim's 4th round pick (James Pemberton) in 2003 NHL Draft for Sandis Ozolinsh and Lance Ward, January 30, 2003. Signed as a free agent by **Carolina**, August 5, 2004. Signed as a free agent by **Cortina** (Italy), September 18, 2004. Signed as a free agent by **NY Rangers**, July 1, 2006. Traded to **Carolina** by **NY Rangers** for Andrew Hutchinson, Joe Barnes and Carolina's 3rd round pick (Evgeny Grachev) in 2008 NHL Draft, July 17, 2007. Traded to **Ottawa** by **Carolina** for Alexandre Picard and Ottawa's 2nd round pick (later traded to Edmonton – Edmonton selected Martin Marincin) in 2010 NHL Draft, February 12, 2010. Signed as a free agent by **Minnesota**, July 1, 2010. Signed as a free agent by **Nashville**, July 5, 2013. Signed as a free agent by **Pittsburgh**, August 6, 2015.

CZARNIK, Austin

(ZAHR-nihk, AW-stuhn) **BOS**

Center. Shoots right. 5'9", 167 lbs. Born, Washington, MI, December 12, 1992.

2007-08	Det. Belle Tire U16	MWEHL	31	7	14	21	8	....	....	....	....	....	....	....	....	....	....	....	....	....	....	....	....	....	....
	Det. Belle Tire U16	Other	36	23	31	54	10	....	....	....	....	....	....	....	....	....	....	....	....	....	....	....	....	....	....
2008-09	USAHNTDP	NAHL	42	16	18	34	12	....	....	....	....	....	....	....	....	....	9	4	2	6	10	....	....	....	....
	USAHNTDP	U-17	14	4	12	16	6	....	....	....	....	....	....	....	....	....	....	....	....	....	....	....	....	....	....
2009-10	USAHNTDP	USHL	26	10	18	28	25	....	....	....	....	....	....	....	....	....	....	....	....	....	....	....	....	....	....
	USAHNTDP	U-18	35	12	14	26	2	....	....	....	....	....	....	....	....	....	....	....	....	....	....	....	....	....	....
2010-11	Green Bay	USHL	46	20	14	34	33	....	....	....	....	....	....	....	....	....	11	3	1	4	2	....	....	....	....
2011-12	Miami U.	CCHA	40	10	27	37	31	....	....	....	....	....	....	....	....	....	....	....	....	....	....	....	....	....	....
2012-13	Miami U.	CCHA	42	14	*26	*40	24	....	....	....	....	....	....	....	....	....	....	....	....	....	....	....	....	....	....
2013-14	Miami U.	NCHC	37	13	*34	*47	28	....	....	....	....	....	....	....	....	....	....	....	....	....	....	....	....	....	....
2014-15	Miami U.	NCHC	40	9	*36	*45	36	....	....	....	....	....	....	....	....	....	....	....	....	....	....	....	....	....	....
	Providence Bruins	AHL	3	0	2	2	4	....	....	....	....	....	....	....	....	....	....	....	....	....	....	....	....	....	....
2015-16	Providence Bruins	AHL	68	20	41	61	24	....	....	....	....	....	....	....	....	....	3	2	1	3	2	....	....	....	....
2016-17	**Boston**	**NHL**	**49**	**5**	**8**	**13**	**12**	**0**	**0**	**1**	**66**	**7.6**	**–10**	**133**	**42.9**	**13:01**	....	....	....	....	....	....	....	....	....
	Providence Bruins	AHL	22	6	17	23	4	....	....	....	....	....	....	....	....	....	17	3	4	7	10	....	....	....	....
	NHL Totals		**49**	**5**	**8**	**13**	**12**	**0**	**0**	**1**	**66**	**7.6**		**133**	**42.9**	**13:01**	....	....	....	....	....	....	....	....	....

CCHA All-Rookie Team (2012) • CCHA First All-Star Team (2013) • CCHA Player of the Year (2013) • NCAA West First All-American Team (2013) • NCHC First All-Star Team (2014) • NCHC Second All-Star Team (2015) • NCAA West Second All-American Team (2014, 2015) • AHL All-Rookie Team (2016)

Signed as a free agent by **Boston**, April 1, 2015.

CZUCZMAN, Kevin

(CHUHRCH-muhn, KEH-vihn) **PIT**

Defense. Shoots left. 6'2", 206 lbs. Born, Port Elgin, ON, January 9, 1991.

2006-07	Grey Bruce	Minor-ON	59	2	19	21	50	....	....	....	....	....	....	....	....	....	4	1	0	1	0	....	....	....	....
2007-08	Grey Bruce	Minor-ON	54	6	20	26	76	....	....	....	....	....	....	....	....	....	4	1	2	3	6	....	....	....	....
	Owen Sound	ON-Jr.B	2	0	0	0	0	....	....	....	....	....	....	....	....	....	....	....	....	....	....	....	....	....	....
2008-09	Listowel Cyclones	ON-Jr.B	2	0	0	0	0	....	....	....	....	....	....	....	....	....	....	....	....	....	....	....	....	....	....
	Walkerton Hawks	ON-Jr.C	35	3	20	23	49	....	....	....	....	....	....	....	....	....	10	2	3	5	4	....	....	....	....
2009-10	Waterloo Siskins	ON-Jr.B	51	2	23	25	84	....	....	....	....	....	....	....	....	....	10	1	1	2	15	....	....	....	....
2010-11	Newmarket	ON-Jr.A	47	4	19	23	40	....	....	....	....	....	....	....	....	....	10	1	3	4	13	....	....	....	....
2011-12	Lake Superior	CCHA	40	2	11	13	26	....	....	....	....	....	....	....	....	....	....	....	....	....	....	....	....	....	....
2012-13	Lake Superior	CCHA	38	2	9	11	42	....	....	....	....	....	....	....	....	....	....	....	....	....	....	....	....	....	....
2013-14	Lake Superior	WCHA	36	10	11	21	73	....	....	....	....	....	....	....	....	....	....	....	....	....	....	....	....	....	....
	NY Islanders	**NHL**	**13**	**0**	**2**	**2**	**14**	**0**	**0**	**0**	**24**	**0.0**	**–5**	**1**	**100.0**	**19:33**	....	....	....	....	....	....	....	....	....
2014-15	Bridgeport	AHL	50	1	6	7	56	....	....	....	....	....	....	....	....	....	....	....	....	....	....	....	....	....	....
	Florida Everblades	ECHL	9	1	0	1	4	....	....	....	....	....	....	....	....	....	12	0	0	0	6	....	....	....	....
2015-16	Bridgeport	AHL	74	4	11	15	95	....	....	....	....	....	....	....	....	....	3	0	0	0	0	....	....	....	....
2016-17	Manitoba Moose	AHL	76	9	23	32	48	....	....	....	....	....	....	....	....	....	....	....	....	....	....	....	....	....	....
	NHL Totals		**13**	**0**	**2**	**2**	**14**	**0**	**0**	**0**	**24**	**0.0**		**1**	**100.0**	**19:33**	....	....	....	....	....	....	....	....	....

WCHA Second All-Star Team (2014)

Signed as a free agent by **NY Islanders**, March 11, 2014. Signed as a free agent by **Pittsburgh**, July 3, 2017.

DADONOV, Evgeny
(do-DON-nauv, ehv-GEH-nee) **FLA**

Right wing. Shoots left. 5'11", 184 lbs. Born, Chelyabinsk, USSR, March 12, 1989. Florida's 3rd pick, 71st overall, in 2007 NHL Draft.

			Regular Season														Playoffs								
Season	Club	League	GP	G	A	Pts	PIM	PP	SH	GW	S	S%	+/-	TF	F%	Min	GP	G	A	Pts	PIM	PP	SH	GW	Min
2005-06	Chelyabinsk 2	Russia-3	12	1	4	5	2																		
	Chelyabinsk	Russia-2															1	0	0	0	0				
2006-07	Chelyabinsk 2	Russia-3	4	2	0	2	14																		
	Chelyabinsk	Russia	24	1	1	2	8																		
2007-08	Chelyabinsk 2	Russia-3	12	4	7	11	32																		
	Chelyabinsk	Russia	43	7	13	20	20										2	0	0	0	0				
2008-09	Chelyabinsk	KHL	40	11	4	15	8										3	0	0	0	2				
2009-10	**Florida**	**NHL**	**4**	**0**	**0**	**0**	**0**	**0**	**0**	**0**	**4**	**0.0**	**–1**	**0**	**0.0**	**13:14**									
	Rochester	AHL	76	17	23	40	36										7	0	1	1	0				
2010-11	**Florida**	**NHL**	**36**	**8**	**9**	**17**	**14**	**1**	**0**	**0**	**60**	**13.3**	**0**	**5**	**20.0**	**14:15**									
	Rochester	AHL	24	8	8	16	4																		
2011-12	**Florida**	**NHL**	**15**	**2**	**1**	**3**	**2**	**0**	**0**	**0**	**21**	**9.5**	**–4**	**6**	**0.0**	**10:03**									
	San Antonio	AHL	20	5	4	9	4																		
	Charlotte	AHL	35	3	16	19	6																		
2012-13	Donetsk	KHL	54	14	24	38	12																		
2013-14	Donetsk	KHL	54	15	14	29	24										13	7	5	12	4				
2014-15	St. Petersburg	KHL	53	19	27	46	10										22	*15	5	20	8				
2015-16	St. Petersburg	KHL	59	23	23	46	4										15	3	6	9	2				
2016-17	St. Petersburg	KHL	53	30	36	66	39										18	9	10	19	2				
	NHL Totals		**55**	**10**	**10**	**20**	**16**	**1**	**0**	**0**	**85**	**11.8**		**11**	**9.1**	**13:02**									

Traded to **Carolina** by **Florida** with A.J. Jenks for Jon Matsumoto and Mattias Lindstrom, January 18, 2012. Signed as a free agent by **Donetsk** (KHL), July 4, 2012. Signed as a free agent by **St. Petersburg** (KHL), June 11, 2014. Signed as a free agent by **Florida**, July 1, 2017.

DAHLBECK, Klas
(DAHL-behk, KLAHS) **CAR**

Defense. Shoots left. 6'3", 207 lbs. Born, Katrineholm, Sweden, July 6, 1991. Chicago's 6th pick, 79th overall, in 2011 NHL Draft.

			Regular Season														Playoffs								
Season	Club	League	GP	G	A	Pts	PIM	PP	SH	GW	S	S%	+/-	TF	F%	Min	GP	G	A	Pts	PIM	PP	SH	GW	Min
2007-08	Vaxjo U18	Swe-U18	16	7	10	17	4																		
	Vaxjo Jr.	Swe-Jr.	22	3	4	7	14																		
2008-09	Vaxjo U18	Swe-U18	14	4	5	9	6																		
	Vaxjo Jr.	Swe-Jr.	15	4	6	10	8																		
2009-10	Linkopings HC Jr.	Swe-Jr.	39	4	7	11	8										6	1	1	2	4				
	Mjolby HC	Sweden-3	2	0	0	0	0																		
	Linkopings HC	Sweden	6	0	0	0	0										3	0	0	0	0				
2010-11	Linkopings HC	Sweden	47	0	8	8	12										7	0	0	0	0				
2011-12	Linkopings HC	Sweden	55	2	2	4	20																		
2012-13	Rockford IceHogs	AHL	70	1	5	6	29																		
2013-14	Rockford IceHogs	AHL	75	10	25	35	49																		
2014-15	**Chicago**	**NHL**	**4**	**1**	**0**	**1**	**2**	**0**	**0**	**0**	**4**	**25.0**	**–1**	**0**	**0.0**	**10:24**									
	Rockford IceHogs	AHL	49	4	6	10	35																		
	Arizona	**NHL**	**19**	**0**	**3**	**3**	**6**	**0**	**0**	**0**	**16**	**0.0**	**–7**	**0**	**0.0**	**19:11**									
	Portland Pirates	AHL	3	0	1	1	0										5	0	1	1	4				
2015-16	**Arizona**	**NHL**	**71**	**2**	**6**	**8**	**28**	**0**	**0**	**0**	**64**	**3.1**	**–5**	**0**	**0.0**	**15:44**									
2016-17	**Carolina**	**NHL**	**43**	**2**	**4**	**6**	**30**	**0**	**0**	**0**	**37**	**5.4**	**–12**	**0**	**0.0**	**13:53**									
	Charlotte	AHL	6	0	1	1	0																		
	NHL Totals		**137**	**5**	**13**	**18**	**66**	**0**	**0**	**0**	**121**	**4.1**		**0**	**0.0**	**15:29**									

Traded to **Arizona** by **Chicago** with Chicago's 1st round pick (Nick Merkley) in 2015 NHL Draft for Antoine Vermette, February 28, 2015. Signed as a free agent by **Arizona**, July 1, 2016. Claimed on waivers by **Carolina** from **Arizona**, October 11. 2016.

DALEY, Trevor
(DAY-lee, TREH-vuhr) **DET**

Defense. Shoots left. 5'11", 195 lbs. Born, Toronto, ON, October 9, 1983. Dallas' 5th pick, 43rd overall, in 2002 NHL Draft.

			Regular Season														Playoffs								
Season	Club	League	GP	G	A	Pts	PIM	PP	SH	GW	S	S%	+/-	TF	F%	Min	GP	G	A	Pts	PIM	PP	SH	GW	Min
1998-99	Vaughan Vipers	ON-Jr.A	44	10	36	46	79																		
99-2000	Sault Ste. Marie	OHL	54	16	30	46	77										15	3	7	10	12				
2000-01	Sault Ste. Marie	OHL	58	14	27	41	105																		
2001-02	Sault Ste. Marie	OHL	47	9	39	48	38										6	2	2	4	4				
2002-03	Sault Ste. Marie	OHL	57	20	33	53	128										1	0	0	0	2				
2003-04	**Dallas**	**NHL**	**27**	**1**	**5**	**6**	**14**	**1**	**0**	**0**	**34**	**2.9**	**–6**	**0**	**0.0**	**16:02**	**1**	**0**	**0**	**0**	**0**	**0**	**0**	**0**	**10:21**
	Utah Grizzlies	AHL	40	8	6	14	76																		
2004-05	Hamilton	AHL	78	7	27	34	109										4	0	1	1	2				
2005-06	**Dallas**	**NHL**	**81**	**3**	**11**	**14**	**87**	**0**	**0**	**1**	**91**	**3.3**	**–2**	**0**	**0.0**	**18:40**	**3**	**0**	**0**	**0**	**0**	**0**	**0**	**0**	**11:30**
2006-07	**Dallas**	**NHL**	**74**	**4**	**8**	**12**	**63**	**0**	**0**	**1**	**68**	**5.9**	**2**	**0**	**0.0**	**19:23**	**7**	**1**	**0**	**1**	**4**	**0**	**0**	**0**	**22:26**
2007-08	**Dallas**	**NHL**	**82**	**5**	**19**	**24**	**85**	**0**	**0**	**1**	**87**	**5.7**	**–1**	**1**	**100.0**	**19:48**	**18**	**1**	**0**	**1**	**20**	**0**	**0**	**0**	**18:52**
2008-09	**Dallas**	**NHL**	**75**	**7**	**18**	**25**	**73**	**0**	**0**	**2**	**104**	**6.7**	**2**	**1**	**0.0**	**22:00**									
2009-10	**Dallas**	**NHL**	**77**	**6**	**16**	**22**	**25**	**2**	**0**	**2**	**107**	**5.6**	**3**	**0**	**0.0**	**22:11**									
2010-11	**Dallas**	**NHL**	**82**	**8**	**19**	**27**	**34**	**2**	**0**	**1**	**131**	**6.1**	**7**	**0**	**0.0**	**22:29**									
2011-12	**Dallas**	**NHL**	**79**	**4**	**21**	**25**	**42**	**1**	**0**	**2**	**134**	**3.0**	**3**	**0**	**0.0**	**21:39**									
2012-13	**Dallas**	**NHL**	**44**	**4**	**9**	**13**	**14**	**2**	**0**	**0**	**58**	**6.9**	**1**	**0**	**0.0**	**21:25**									
2013-14	**Dallas**	**NHL**	**67**	**9**	**16**	**25**	**38**	**1**	**0**	**3**	**107**	**8.4**	**10**	**0**	**0.0**	**21:09**	**6**	**2**	**3**	**5**	**16**	**0**	**0**	**0**	**25:48**
2014-15	**Dallas**	**NHL**	**68**	**16**	**22**	**38**	**34**	**6**	**2**	**2**	**113**	**14.2**	**–13**	**0**	**0.0**	**22:53**									
2015-16	**Chicago**	**NHL**	**29**	**0**	**6**	**6**	**8**	**0**	**0**	**0**	**43**	**0.0**	**1**	**1**	**0.0**	**14:46**									
	♦ Pittsburgh	**NHL**	**53**	**6**	**16**	**22**	**26**	**1**	**0**	**0**	**87**	**6.9**	**8**	**0**	**0.0**	**20:27**	**15**	**1**	**5**	**6**	**10**	**0**	**0**	**0**	**22:08**
2016-17	**♦ Pittsburgh**	**NHL**	**56**	**5**	**14**	**19**	**37**	**1**	**0**	**0**	**84**	**6.0**	**7**	**0**	**0.0**	**20:23**	**21**	**1**	**4**	**5**	**24**	**1**	**0**	**0**	**19:07**
	NHL Totals		**894**	**78**	**200**	**278**	**580**	**17**	**2**	**15**	**1248**	**6.3**		**3**	**33.3**	**20:40**	**71**	**6**	**12**	**18**	**74**	**1**	**0**	**0**	**20:08**

Traded to **Chicago** by **Dallas** with Ryan Garbutt for Patrick Sharp and Stephen Johns, July 12, 2015 Traded to **Pittsburgh** by **Chicago** for Rob Scuderi, December 14, 2015. Signed as a free agent by **Detroit**, July 1, 2017.

DALPE, Zac
(DAL-pee, ZAK) **CBJ**

Right wing. Shoots right. 6'2", 200 lbs. Born, Paris, ON, November 1, 1989. Carolina's 2nd pick, 45th overall, in 2008 NHL Draft.

			Regular Season														Playoffs								
Season	Club	League	GP	G	A	Pts	PIM	PP	SH	GW	S	S%	+/-	TF	F%	Min	GP	G	A	Pts	PIM	PP	SH	GW	Min
2006-07	Stratford Cullitons	ON-Jr.B	52	30	43	73	68																		
2007-08	Penticton Vees	BCHL	46	27	36	63	14										15	8	9	17	4				
2008-09	Ohio State	CCHA	37	13	12	25	25																		
2009-10	Ohio State	CCHA	39	*21	24	45	19																		
	Albany River Rats	AHL	9	6	2	8	0										8	3	3	6	0				
2010-11	**Carolina**	**NHL**	**15**	**3**	**1**	**4**	**0**	**0**	**0**	**1**	**16**	**18.8**	**0**	**26**	**26.9**	**7:56**									
	Charlotte	AHL	61	23	34	57	21										16	6	7	13	6				
2011-12	**Carolina**	**NHL**	**16**	**1**	**2**	**3**	**4**	**0**	**0**	**0**	**20**	**5.0**	**–3**	**11**	**45.5**	**9:35**									
	Charlotte	AHL	56	18	14	32	17																		
2012-13	Charlotte	AHL	54	21	21	42	12										5	0	0	0	4				
	Carolina	**NHL**	**10**	**1**	**2**	**3**	**0**	**0**	**0**	**0**	**18**	**5.6**	**–7**	**3**	**33.3**	**12:18**									
2013-14	**Vancouver**	**NHL**	**55**	**4**	**3**	**7**	**6**	**1**	**0**	**0**	**52**	**7.7**	**–7**	**231**	**45.9**	**7:08**									
	Utica Comets	AHL	6	0	3	3	2																		
2014-15	**Buffalo**	**NHL**	**21**	**1**	**2**	**3**	**4**	**0**	**0**	**0**	**29**	**3.4**	**–11**	**33**	**60.6**	**9:17**									
	Rochester	AHL	44	16	12	28	0																		
2015-16	**Minnesota**	**NHL**	**2**	**1**	**0**	**1**	**0**	**0**	**0**	**0**	**3**	**33.3**	**0**	**17**	**64.7**	**10:15**	**3**	**0**	**0**	**0**	**0**	**0**	**0**	**0**	**8:09**
	Iowa Wild	AHL	8	3	1	4	24																		
2016-17	**Minnesota**	**NHL**	**9**	**1**	**2**	**3**	**9**	**0**	**0**	**0**	**8**	**12.5**	**0**	**59**	**45.8**	**8:33**									
	Iowa Wild	AHL	12	2	0	2	0																		
	Cleveland	AHL	20	8	6	14	22																		
	NHL Totals		**128**	**12**	**12**	**24**	**23**	**1**	**0**	**1**	**146**	**8.2**		**380**	**46.6**	**8:26**	**3**	**0**	**0**	**0**	**0**	**0**	**0**	**0**	**8:09**

CCHA All-Rookie Team (2009) • CCHA First All-Star Team (2010) • NCAA West Second All-American Team (2010) • AHL All-Rookie Team (2011)

Traded to **Vancouver** by **Carolina** with Jeremy Welsh for Kellan Tochkin and Vancouver's 4th round pick (Josh Wesley) in 2014 NHL Draft, September 29, 2013. Signed as a free agent by **Buffalo** July 13, 2014. Signed as a free agent by **Minnesota**, July 1, 2015. • Missed majority of 2015-16 and 2016-17 due to recurring knee injuriy and resulting surgery, October 30, 2016. Claimed on waivers by **Columbus** from **Minnesota**, February 27, 2017.

DANAULT, Phillip
(duh-NOH, FIHL-ihp) **MTL**

Center. Shoots left. 6', 193 lbs. Born, Victoriaville, QC, February 24, 1993. Chicago's 2nd pick, 26th overall, in 2011 NHL Draft.

			Regular Season														Playoffs								
Season	Club	League	GP	G	A	Pts	PIM	PP	SH	GW	S	S%	+/-	TF	F%	Min	GP	G	A	Pts	PIM	PP	SH	GW	Min
2008-09	Trois-Rivieres	QAAA	44	8	19	27	39	....	....	....	....	....	....	....	....	....	19	4	11	15	8	....	....	....	....
2009-10	Victoriaville Tigres	QMJHL	61	10	18	28	54	....	....	....	....	....	....	....	....	....	16	0	1	1	8	....	....	....	....
2010-11	Victoriaville Tigres	QMJHL	64	23	44	67	59	....	....	....	....	....	....	....	....	....	9	5	10	15	6	....	....	....	....
2011-12	Victoriaville Tigres	QMJHL	62	18	53	71	61	....	....	....	....	....	....	....	....	....	4	0	3	3	4	....	....	....	....
	Rockford IceHogs	AHL	7	0	2	2	10	....	....	....	....	....	....	....	....	....	....	....	....	....	....	....	....	....	....
2012-13	Victoriaville Tigres	QMJHL	29	14	30	44	28	....	....	....	....	....	....	....	....	....	....	....	....	....	....	....	....	....	....
	Moncton Wildcats	QMJHL	27	9	32	41	22	....	....	....	....	....	....	....	....	....	4	1	3	4	0	....	....	....	....
	Rockford IceHogs	AHL	5	0	0	0	2	....	....	....	....	....	....	....	....	....	....	....	....	....	....	....	....	....	....
2013-14	Rockford IceHogs	AHL	72	6	20	26	40	....	....	....	....	....	....	....	....	....	....	....	....	....	....	....	....	....	....
2014-15	**Chicago**	**NHL**	**2**	**0**	**0**	**0**	**0**	**0**	**0**	**0**	**2**	**0.0**	**0**	**20**	**30.0**	**9:30**	....	....	....	....	....	....	....	....	....
	Rockford IceHogs	AHL	70	13	25	38	38	....	....	....	....	....	....	....	....	....	8	3	2	5	20	....	....	....	....
2015-16	**Chicago**	**NHL**	**30**	**1**	**4**	**5**	**6**	**0**	**0**	**1**	**48**	**2.1**	**–3**	**369**	**44.2**	**12:51**	....	....	....	....	....	....	....	....	....
	Rockford IceHogs	AHL	6	1	1	2	4	....	....	....	....	....	....	....	....	....	....	....	....	....	....	....	....	....	....
	Montreal	**NHL**	**21**	**3**	**2**	**5**	**8**	**0**	**0**	**0**	**24**	**12.5**	**–2**	**150**	**56.0**	**12:38**	....	....	....	....	....	....	....	....	....
2016-17	**Montreal**	**NHL**	**82**	**13**	**27**	**40**	**35**	**0**	**0**	**3**	**133**	**9.8**	**5**	**1031**	**51.7**	**15:35**	**6**	**0**	**2**	**2**	**2**	**0**	**0**	**0**	**16:39**
	NHL Totals		**135**	**17**	**33**	**50**	**49**	**0**	**0**	**4**	**207**	**8.2**		**1570**	**50.1**	**14:25**	**6**	**0**	**2**	**2**	**2**	**0**	**0**	**0**	**16:39**

Traded to **Montreal** by **Chicago** with Chicago's 2nd round pick in 2018 NHL Draft for Tomas Fleischmann and Dale Weise, February 26, 2016.

DANO, Marko
(DA-noh, MAHR-koh) **WPG**

Center. Shoots left. 5'11", 183 lbs. Born, Eisenstadt , Austria, November 30, 1994. Columbus' 3rd pick, 27th overall, in 2013 NHL Draft.

Season	Club	League	GP	G	A	Pts	PIM	PP	SH	GW	S	S%	+/-	TF	F%	Min	GP	G	A	Pts	PIM	PP	SH	GW	Min
2008-09	Dukla Trencin U18	Svk-U18	5	1	0	1	14	....	....	....	....	....	....	....	....	....	....	....	....	....	....	....	....	....	....
2009-10	Dukla Trencin U18	Svk-U18	36	13	12	25	77	....	....	....	....	....	....	....	....	....	....	....	....	....	....	....	....	....	....
2010-11	Dukla Trencin U18	Svk-U18	9	13	4	17	2	....	....	....	....	....	....	....	....	....	4	2	2	4	8	....	....	....	....
	Dukla Trencin Jr.	Slovak-Jr.	28	18	22	40	86	....	....	....	....	....	....	....	....	....	8	4	2	6	14	....	....	....	....
	Dukla Trencin	Slovakia	8	0	1	1	10	....	....	....	....	....	....	....	....	....	3	0	0	0	0	....	....	....	....
2011-12	Dukla Trencin Jr.	Slovak-Jr.	3	3	1	4	18	....	....	....	....	....	....	....	....	....	3	4	2	6	4	....	....	....	....
	Dukla Trencin	Slovakia	32	4	6	10	12	....	....	....	....	....	....	....	....	....	9	0	3	3	18	....	....	....	....
2012-13	Bratislava	KHL	37	3	4	7	26	....	....	....	....	....	....	....	....	....	4	0	0	0	4	....	....	....	....
	Dukla Trencin Jr.	Slovak-Jr.	....	....	....	....	....	....	....	....	....	....	....	....	....	....	2	0	0	0	0	....	....	....	....
2013-14	Bratislava	KHL	41	3	2	5	41	....	....	....	....	....	....	....	....	....	....	....	....	....	....	....	....	....	....
	Springfield	AHL	10	2	4	6	4	....	....	....	....	....	....	....	....	....	5	0	2	2	0	....	....	....	....
2014-15	**Columbus**	**NHL**	**35**	**8**	**13**	**21**	**14**	**0**	**0**	**1**	**84**	**9.5**	**12**	**37**	**43.2**	**13:15**	....	....	....	....	....	....	....	....	....
	Springfield	AHL	39	11	8	19	34	....	....	....	....	....	....	....	....	....	....	....	....	....	....	....	....	....	....
2015-16	**Chicago**	**NHL**	**13**	**1**	**1**	**2**	**2**	**0**	**0**	**0**	**15**	**6.7**	**0**	**4**	**25.0**	**9:41**	....	....	....	....	....	....	....	....	....
	Rockford IceHogs	AHL	34	4	19	23	40	....	....	....	....	....	....	....	....	....	....	....	....	....	....	....	....	....	....
	Winnipeg	**NHL**	**21**	**4**	**4**	**8**	**8**	**0**	**0**	**0**	**39**	**10.3**	**–7**	**2**	**50.0**	**13:50**	....	....	....	....	....	....	....	....	....
2016-17	**Winnipeg**	**NHL**	**38**	**4**	**7**	**11**	**10**	**2**	**0**	**0**	**44**	**9.1**	**0**	**4**	**25.0**	**10:41**	....	....	....	....	....	....	....	....	....
	Manitoba Moose	AHL	6	0	2	2	4	....	....	....	....	....	....	....	....	....	....	....	....	....	....	....	....	....	....
	NHL Totals		**107**	**17**	**25**	**42**	**34**	**2**	**0**	**1**	**182**	**9.3**		**47**	**40.4**	**12:01**	....	....	....	....	....	....	....	....	....

Traded to **Chicago** by **Columbus** with Artem Anisimov, Jeremy Morin, Corey Tropp and Columbus' 4th round pick (later traded to NY Islanders – NY Islanders selected Anatoli Golyshev) in 2016 NHL Draft for Brandon Saad, Michael Paliotta and Alex Broadhurst, June 30, 2015. Traded to **Winnipeg** by **Chicago** with Chicago's 1st round pick (later traded to Philadelphia – Philadelphia selected German Rubtsov) in 2016 NHL Draft for Andrew Ladd, Matt Fraser and Jay Harrison, February 25, 2016.

DAUPHIN, Laurent
(daw-PHEHN, LOHR-awnt) **CHI**

Center. Shoots left. 6'1", 180 lbs. Born, Repentigny, QC, March 27, 1995. Phoenix's 2nd pick, 39th overall, in 2013 NHL Draft.

Season	Club	League	GP	G	A	Pts	PIM	PP	SH	GW	S	S%	+/-	TF	F%	Min	GP	G	A	Pts	PIM	PP	SH	GW	Min
2010-11	Esther-Blondin	QAAA	41	16	25	41	28	....	....	....	....	....	....	....	....	....	3	0	1	1	0	....	....	....	....
2011-12	Esther-Blondin	QAAA	40	17	45	62	48	....	....	....	....	....	....	....	....	....	13	12	14	*26	12	....	....	....	....
2012-13	Chicoutimi	QMJHL	62	25	32	57	50	....	....	....	....	....	....	....	....	....	6	2	2	4	8	....	....	....	....
2013-14	Chicoutimi	QMJHL	52	24	30	54	56	....	....	....	....	....	....	....	....	....	....	....	....	....	....	....	....	....	....
2014-15	Chicoutimi	QMJHL	56	31	44	75	74	....	....	....	....	....	....	....	....	....	5	5	3	8	12	....	....	....	....
	Portland Pirates	AHL	4	1	0	1	2	....	....	....	....	....	....	....	....	....	5	0	2	2	0	....	....	....	....
2015-16	**Arizona**	**NHL**	**8**	**1**	**0**	**1**	**4**	**0**	**0**	**0**	**7**	**14.3**	**0**	**73**	**43.8**	**11:19**	....	....	....	....	....	....	....	....	....
	Springfield	AHL	66	11	13	24	72	....	....	....	....	....	....	....	....	....	....	....	....	....	....	....	....	....	....
2016-17	**Arizona**	**NHL**	**24**	**2**	**1**	**3**	**12**	**0**	**1**	**1**	**32**	**6.3**	**–2**	**82**	**45.1**	**10:55**	....	....	....	....	....	....	....	....	....
	Tucson	AHL	38	17	11	28	44	....	....	....	....	....	....	....	....	....	....	....	....	....	....	....	....	....	....
	NHL Totals		**32**	**3**	**1**	**4**	**16**	**0**	**1**	**1**	**39**	**7.7**		**155**	**44.5**	**11:01**	....	....	....	....	....	....	....	....	....

Traded to **Chicago** by **Arizona** with Connor Murphy for Nklas Hjalmarsson, June 23, 2017.

DAVIDSON, Brandon
(DAY-vihn-suhn, BRAN-duhn) **MTL**

Defense. Shoots left. 6'2", 210 lbs. Born, Lethbridge, AB, August 21, 1991. Edmonton's 8th pick, 162nd overall, in 2010 NHL Draft.

Season	Club	League	GP	G	A	Pts	PIM	PP	SH	GW	S	S%	+/-	TF	F%	Min	GP	G	A	Pts	PIM	PP	SH	GW	Min
2008-09	Lethbridge	AMHL	31	7	14	21	52	....	....	....	....	....	....	....	....	....	7	2	5	7	14	....	....	....	....
2009-10	Regina Pats	WHL	59	1	33	34	37	....	....	....	....	....	....	....	....	....	....	....	....	....	....	....	....	....	....
2010-11	Regina Pats	WHL	72	8	43	51	71	....	....	....	....	....	....	....	....	....	....	....	....	....	....	....	....	....	....
	Oklahoma City	AHL	1	0	0	0	0	....	....	....	....	....	....	....	....	....	1	0	0	0	0	....	....	....	....
2011-12	Regina Pats	WHL	69	13	36	49	83	....	....	....	....	....	....	....	....	....	4	0	1	1	6	....	....	....	....
2012-13	Oklahoma City	AHL	26	2	3	5	14	....	....	....	....	....	....	....	....	....	17	0	6	6	2	....	....	....	....
	Stockton Thunder	ECHL	11	7	5	12	4	....	....	....	....	....	....	....	....	....	....	....	....	....	....	....	....	....	....
2013-14	Oklahoma City	AHL	68	5	8	13	58	....	....	....	....	....	....	....	....	....	3	0	1	1	0	....	....	....	....
2014-15	**Edmonton**	**NHL**	**12**	**1**	**0**	**1**	**0**	**0**	**0**	**0**	**7**	**14.3**	**–5**	**0**	**0.0**	**15:08**	....	....	....	....	....	....	....	....	....
	Oklahoma City	AHL	55	4	6	10	43	....	....	....	....	....	....	....	....	....	10	1	1	2	12	....	....	....	....
2015-16	**Edmonton**	**NHL**	**51**	**4**	**7**	**11**	**20**	**2**	**0**	**0**	**63**	**6.3**	**7**	**0**	**0.0**	**19:12**	....	....	....	....	....	....	....	....	....
2016-17	**Edmonton**	**NHL**	**28**	**0**	**1**	**1**	**16**	**0**	**0**	**0**	**29**	**0.0**	**1**	**0**	**0.0**	**15:24**	....	....	....	....	....	....	....	....	....
	Montreal	**NHL**	**10**	**0**	**2**	**2**	**4**	**0**	**0**	**0**	**13**	**0.0**	**–3**	**0**	**0.0**	**16:38**	**3**	**0**	**0**	**0**	**0**	**0**	**0**	**0**	**12:46**
	NHL Totals		**101**	**5**	**10**	**15**	**40**	**2**	**0**	**0**	**112**	**4.5**		**0**	**0.0**	**17:24**	**3**	**0**	**0**	**0**	**0**	**0**	**0**	**0**	**12:46**

WHL East Second All-Star Team (2012) • Fred T. Hunt Memorial Award (AHL – Sportsmanship) (2013)
Traded to **Montreal** by **Edmonton** for David Desharnais, February 28, 2017.

de HAAN, Calvin
(DUH HAWN, CAL-vihn) **NYI**

Defense. Shoots left. 6'1", 197 lbs. Born, Carp, ON, May 9, 1991. NY Islanders' 2nd pick, 12th overall, in 2009 NHL Draft.

Season	Club	League	GP	G	A	Pts	PIM	PP	SH	GW	S	S%	+/-	TF	F%	Min	GP	G	A	Pts	PIM	PP	SH	GW	Min
2006-07	Ott. Valley Titans	Minor-ON	32	4	22	26	20	....	....	....	....	....	....	....	....	....	....	....	....	....	....	....	....	....	....
2007-08	Kemptville 73's	ON-Jr.A	58	3	39	42	14	....	....	....	....	....	....	....	....	....	....	....	....	....	....	....	....	....	....
2008-09	Oshawa Generals	OHL	68	8	55	63	40	....	....	....	....	....	....	....	....	....	....	....	....	....	....	....	....	....	....
2009-10	Oshawa Generals	OHL	34	5	19	24	14	....	....	....	....	....	....	....	....	....	....	....	....	....	....	....	....	....	....
2010-11	Oshawa Generals	OHL	55	6	42	48	48	....	....	....	....	....	....	....	....	....	10	1	11	12	6	....	....	....	....
2011-12	**NY Islanders**	**NHL**	**1**	**0**	**0**	**0**	**0**	**0**	**0**	**0**	**2**	**0.0**	**1**	**0**	**0.0**	**13:01**	....	....	....	....	....	....	....	....	....
	Bridgeport	AHL	56	2	14	16	24	....	....	....	....	....	....	....	....	....	3	0	2	2	2	....	....	....	....
2012-13	Bridgeport	AHL	3	0	2	2	4	....	....	....	....	....	....	....	....	....	....	....	....	....	....	....	....	....	....
2013-14	**NY Islanders**	**NHL**	**51**	**3**	**13**	**16**	**30**	**1**	**0**	**1**	**71**	**4.2**	**–7**	**0**	**0.0**	**21:01**	....	....	....	....	....	....	....	....	....
	Bridgeport	AHL	17	1	2	3	8	....	....	....	....	....	....	....	....	....	....	....	....	....	....	....	....	....	....
2014-15	**NY Islanders**	**NHL**	**65**	**1**	**11**	**12**	**24**	**0**	**1**	**0**	**92**	**1.1**	**3**	**0**	**0.0**	**19:01**	**5**	**0**	**1**	**1**	**2**	**0**	**0**	**0**	**17:21**
2015-16	**NY Islanders**	**NHL**	**72**	**2**	**14**	**16**	**20**	**0**	**0**	**0**	**102**	**2.0**	**3**	**1**	**0.0**	**20:38**	**11**	**0**	**2**	**2**	**2**	**0**	**0**	**0**	**20:43**
2016-17	**NY Islanders**	**NHL**	**82**	**5**	**20**	**25**	**36**	**1**	**0**	**1**	**116**	**4.3**	**15**	**0**	**0.0**	**19:51**	....	....	....	....	....	....	....	....	....
	NHL Totals		**271**	**11**	**58**	**69**	**110**	**2**	**1**	**2**	**383**	**2.9**		**1**	**0.0**	**20:03**	**16**	**0**	**3**	**3**	**4**	**0**	**0**	**0**	**19:40**

• Missed majority of 2012-13 due to shoulder injury at Wilkes-Barre (AHL), October 20, 2012.

			Regular Season														Playoffs								
Season	Club	League	GP	G	A	Pts	PIM	PP	SH	GW	S	S%	+/-	TF	F%	Min	GP	G	A	Pts	PIM	PP	SH	GW	Min

De LEO, Chase

(duh-LEE-oh, CHAYS) **WPG**

Center. Shoots left. 5'10", 185 lbs. Born, La Mirada, CA, October 25, 1995. Winnipeg's 3rd pick, 99th overall, in 2014 NHL Draft.

Season	Club	League	GP	G	A	Pts	PIM	PP	SH	GW	S	S%	+/-	TF	F%	Min	GP	G	A	Pts	PIM	PP	SH	GW	Min
2009-10	LA Selects U14	Minor-CA	28	27	56	83	....	....	....	....	....	....	....	....	....	....	....	....	....	....	....	....	....	....	....
2010-11	LA Selects U16	Minor-CA	35	20	19	39	28	....	....	....	....	....	....	....	....	....	....	....	....	....	....	....	....	....	....
2011-12	Portland	WHL	69	14	16	30	25	....	....	....	....	....	....	....	....	....	22	0	*1	1	2	....	....	....	....
2012-13	Portland	WHL	71	18	38	56	24	....	....	....	....	....	....	....	....	....	21	5	12	17	15	....	....	....	....
2013-14	Portland	WHL	72	39	42	81	36	....	....	....	....	....	....	....	....	....	21	10	9	19	6	....	....	....	....
2014-15	Portland	WHL	67	39	45	84	30	....	....	....	....	....	....	....	....	....	17	7	12	19	10	....	....	....	....
2015-16	**Winnipeg**	**NHL**	**2**	**0**	**0**	**0**	**0**	**0**	**0**	**0**	**2**	**0.0**	**1**	**1**	**100.0**	**9:25**	....	....	....	....	....	....	....	....	....
	Manitoba Moose	AHL	73	19	21	40	34	....	....	....	....	....	....	....	....	....	....	....	....	....	....	....	....	....	....
2016-17	Manitoba Moose	AHL	69	14	18	32	12	....	....	....	....	....	....	....	....	....	....	....	....	....	....	....	....	....	....
	NHL Totals		**2**	**0**	**0**	**0**	**0**	**0**	**0**	**0**	**2**	**0.0**		**1**	**100.0**	**9:25**	....	....	....	....	....	....	....	....	....

DEA, Jean-Sebastien

(DAY, ZHAWN-suh-BAS-t'yehn) **PIT**

Center. Shoots right. 6'11", 175 lbs. Born, Laval, QC, February 8, 1994.

Season	Club	League	GP	G	A	Pts	PIM	PP	SH	GW	S	S%	+/-	TF	F%	Min	GP	G	A	Pts	PIM	PP	SH	GW	Min
2010-11	C.C. Lemoyne	QAAA	42	26	29	55	26	....	....	....	....	....	....	....	....	....	5	6	3	9	6	....	....	....	....
2011-12	Rouyn-Noranda	QMJHL	50	17	15	32	42	....	....	....	....	....	....	....	....	....	4	1	2	3	0	....	....	....	....
2012-13	Rouyn-Noranda	QMJHL	68	45	40	85	59	....	....	....	....	....	....	....	....	....	14	12	9	21	24	....	....	....	....
2013-14	Rouyn-Noranda	QMJHL	65	49	26	75	53	....	....	....	....	....	....	....	....	....	9	6	3	9	12	....	....	....	....
	Wilkes-Barre	AHL	1	0	0	0	0	....	....	....	....	....	....	....	....	....	....	....	....	....	....	....	....	....	....
2014-15	Wilkes-Barre	AHL	43	10	11	21	16	....	....	....	....	....	....	....	....	....	4	0	0	0	2	....	....	....	....
	Wheeling Nailers	ECHL	14	4	3	7	6	....	....	....	....	....	....	....	....	....	....	....	....	....	....	....	....	....	....
2015-16	Wilkes-Barre	AHL	75	20	16	36	36	....	....	....	....	....	....	....	....	....	10	0	0	0	18	....	....	....	....
2016-17	**Pittsburgh**	**NHL**	**1**	**0**	**0**	**0**	**2**	**0**	**0**	**0**	**1**	**0.0**	**0**	**2**	**50.0**	**11:18**	....	....	....	....	....	....	....	....	....
	Wilkes-Barre	AHL	73	18	16	34	59	....	....	....	....	....	....	....	....	....	5	2	1	3	4	....	....	....	....
	NHL Totals		**1**	**0**	**0**	**0**	**2**	**0**	**0**	**0**	**1**	**0.0**		**2**	**50.0**	**11:18**	....	....	....	....	....	....	....	....	....

Signed as a free agent by **Pittsburgh**, September 17, 2013.

DeANGELO, Tony

(dee-AN-gehl-oh, TOH-nee) **NYR**

Defense. Shoots right. 5'11", 183 lbs. Born, Sewell, NJ, October 24, 1995. Tampa Bay's 1st pick, 19th overall, in 2014 NHL Draft.

Season	Club	League	GP	G	A	Pts	PIM	PP	SH	GW	S	S%	+/-	TF	F%	Min	GP	G	A	Pts	PIM	PP	SH	GW	Min
2008-09	Mercer Chiefs	AYHL	29	31	29	60	176	....	....	....	....	....	....	....	....	....	....	....	....	....	....	....	....	....	....
2009-10	Westchester	Minor-NY	STATISTICS NOT AVAILABLE																						
	Westchester	Other	7	5	2	7	0	....	....	....	....	....	....	....	....	....	....	....	....	....	....	....	....	....	....
2010-11	Cedar Rapids	USHL	28	1	14	15	19	....	....	....	....	....	....	....	....	....	....	....	....	....	....	....	....	....	....
2011-12	Sarnia Sting	OHL	68	6	17	23	46	....	....	....	....	....	....	....	....	....	6	1	0	1	2	....	....	....	....
2012-13	Sarnia Sting	OHL	62	9	49	58	60	....	....	....	....	....	....	....	....	....	4	1	2	3	8	....	....	....	....
2013-14	Sarnia Sting	OHL	51	15	56	71	90	....	....	....	....	....	....	....	....	....	....	....	....	....	....	....	....	....	....
2014-15	Sarnia Sting	OHL	29	10	28	38	64	....	....	....	....	....	....	....	....	....	....	....	....	....	....	....	....	....	....
	Sault Ste. Marie	OHL	26	15	36	51	51	....	....	....	....	....	....	....	....	....	13	0	16	16	18	....	....	....	....
2015-16	Syracuse Crunch	AHL	69	6	37	43	84	....	....	....	....	....	....	....	....	....	....	....	....	....	....	....	....	....	....
2016-17	**Arizona**	**NHL**	**39**	**5**	**9**	**14**	**37**	**2**	**0**	**1**	**60**	**8.3**	**–13**	**0**	**0.0**	**17:06**	....	....	....	....	....	....	....	....	....
	Tucson	AHL	25	3	13	16	31	....	....	....	....	....	....	....	....	....	....	....	....	....	....	....	....	....	....
	NHL Totals		**39**	**5**	**9**	**14**	**37**	**2**	**0**	**1**	**60**	**8.3**		**0**	**0.0**	**17:06**	....	....	....	....	....	....	....	....	....

OHL First All-Star Team (2015)

Traded to **Arizona** by **Tampa Bay** for Arizona's 2nd round pick (Libor Hajek) in 2016 NHL Draft, June 25, 2016. Traded to **NY Rangers** by **Arizona** with Arizona's 1st round pick (Lias Andersson) in 2017 NHL Draft for Derek Stepan and Antti Raanta, June 23, 2017.

DeKEYSER, Danny

(duh-KIGH-zuhr, DAN-ee) **DET**

Defense. Shoots left. 6'3", 191 lbs. Born, Detroit, MI, March 7, 1990.

Season	Club	League	GP	G	A	Pts	PIM	PP	SH	GW	S	S%	+/-	TF	F%	Min	GP	G	A	Pts	PIM	PP	SH	GW	Min
2008-09	Trail	BCHL	58	8	17	25	12	....	....	....	....	....	....	....	....	....	3	1	0	1	4	....	....	....	....
2009-10	Sioux City	USHL	41	1	10	11	12	....	....	....	....	....	....	....	....	....	....	....	....	....	....	....	....	....	....
2010-11	Western Mich.	CCHA	42	5	12	17	43	....	....	....	....	....	....	....	....	....	....	....	....	....	....	....	....	....	....
2011-12	Western Mich.	CCHA	41	5	12	17	42	....	....	....	....	....	....	....	....	....	....	....	....	....	....	....	....	....	....
2012-13	Western Mich.	CCHA	35	2	13	15	22	....	....	....	....	....	....	....	....	....	....	....	....	....	....	....	....	....	....
	Detroit	**NHL**	**11**	**0**	**1**	**1**	**2**	**0**	**0**	**0**	**15**	**0.0**	**4**	**0**	**0.0**	**18:03**	**2**	**0**	**0**	**0**	**0**	**0**	**0**	**0**	**17:53**
	Grand Rapids	AHL	....	....	....	....	....	....	....	....	....	....	....	....	....	....	6	0	1	1	8	....	....	....	....
2013-14	**Detroit**	**NHL**	**65**	**4**	**19**	**23**	**30**	**1**	**1**	**0**	**84**	**4.8**	**10**	**0**	**0.0**	**21:38**	**5**	**0**	**0**	**0**	**6**	**0**	**0**	**0**	**23:11**
2014-15	**Detroit**	**NHL**	**80**	**2**	**29**	**31**	**42**	**0**	**0**	**1**	**89**	**2.2**	**11**	**0**	**0.0**	**20:56**	**7**	**1**	**0**	**1**	**12**	**0**	**0**	**0**	**21:22**
2015-16	**Detroit**	**NHL**	**78**	**8**	**12**	**20**	**44**	**0**	**0**	**3**	**72**	**11.1**	**2**	**0**	**0.0**	**21:48**	**5**	**0**	**1**	**1**	**4**	**0**	**0**	**0**	**21:49**
2016-17	**Detroit**	**NHL**	**82**	**4**	**8**	**12**	**33**	**0**	**0**	**2**	**85**	**4.7**	**–22**	**0**	**0.0**	**21:57**	....	....	....	....	....	....	....	....	....
	NHL Totals		**316**	**18**	**69**	**87**	**151**	**1**	**1**	**6**	**345**	**5.2**		**0**	**0.0**	**21:27**	**19**	**1**	**1**	**2**	**22**	**0**	**0**	**0**	**21:36**

CCHA All-Rookie Team (2011) • CCHA Second All-Star Team (2012) • CCHA First All-Star Team (2013) • NCAA West Second All-American Team (2012, 2013)

Signed as a free agent by **Detroit**, March 29, 2013.

DEL ZOTTO, Michael

(DEHL ZAW-toh, MIGH-kuhl) **VAN**

Defense. Shoots left. 6', 195 lbs. Born, Stouffville, ON, June 24, 1990. NY Rangers' 1st pick, 20th overall, in 2008 NHL Draft.

Season	Club	League	GP	G	A	Pts	PIM	PP	SH	GW	S	S%	+/-	TF	F%	Min	GP	G	A	Pts	PIM	PP	SH	GW	Min
2005-06	Markham Waxers	Minor-ON	73	30	90	120	90	....	....	....	....	....	....	....	....	....	....	....	....	....	....	....	....	....	....
2006-07	Oshawa Generals	OHL	64	10	47	57	78	....	....	....	....	....	....	....	....	....	9	3	9	12	14	....	....	....	....
2007-08	Oshawa Generals	OHL	64	16	47	63	82	....	....	....	....	....	....	....	....	....	15	2	6	8	38	....	....	....	....
2008-09	Oshawa Generals	OHL	34	7	26	33	48	....	....	....	....	....	....	....	....	....	....	....	....	....	....	....	....	....	....
	London Knights	OHL	28	6	24	30	30	....	....	....	....	....	....	....	....	....	14	3	16	19	18	....	....	....	....
2009-10	**NY Rangers**	**NHL**	**80**	**9**	**28**	**37**	**32**	**4**	**0**	**1**	**81**	**11.1**	**–20**	**0**	**0.0**	**18:58**	....	....	....	....	....	....	....	....	....
2010-11	**NY Rangers**	**NHL**	**47**	**2**	**9**	**11**	**20**	**2**	**0**	**0**	**58**	**3.4**	**–5**	**0**	**0.0**	**19:29**	....	....	....	....	....	....	....	....	....
	Connecticut	AHL	11	0	7	7	8	....	....	....	....	....	....	....	....	....	....	....	....	....	....	....	....	....	....
2011-12	**NY Rangers**	**NHL**	**77**	**10**	**31**	**41**	**36**	**1**	**1**	**2**	**113**	**8.8**	**20**	**0**	**0.0**	**22:26**	**20**	**2**	**8**	**10**	**12**	**1**	**0**	**1**	**21:39**
2012-13	Rapperswil	Swiss	9	2	5	7	10	....	....	....	....	....	....	....	....	....	....	....	....	....	....	....	....	....	....
	NY Rangers	**NHL**	**46**	**3**	**18**	**21**	**18**	**0**	**1**	**0**	**81**	**3.7**	**6**	**0**	**0.0**	**23:10**	**12**	**1**	**1**	**2**	**8**	**0**	**0**	**0**	**21:10**
2013-14	**NY Rangers**	**NHL**	**42**	**2**	**9**	**11**	**10**	**1**	**0**	**0**	**64**	**3.1**	**–5**	**0**	**0.0**	**17:45**	....	....	....	....	....	....	....	....	....
	Nashville	**NHL**	**25**	**1**	**4**	**5**	**8**	**0**	**0**	**0**	**26**	**3.8**	**–4**	**1**	**0.0**	**16:18**	....	....	....	....	....	....	....	....	....
2014-15	**Philadelphia**	**NHL**	**64**	**10**	**22**	**32**	**34**	**1**	**1**	**4**	**119**	**8.4**	**–5**	**0**	**0.0**	**21:55**	....	....	....	....	....	....	....	....	....
2015-16	**Philadelphia**	**NHL**	**52**	**4**	**9**	**13**	**16**	**0**	**0**	**1**	**98**	**4.1**	**–8**	**0**	**0.0**	**23:25**	....	....	....	....	....	....	....	....	....
2016-17	**Philadelphia**	**NHL**	**51**	**6**	**12**	**18**	**28**	**0**	**0**	**0**	**92**	**6.5**	**–5**	**1**	**0.0**	**19:30**	....	....	....	....	....	....	....	....	....
	NHL Totals		**484**	**47**	**142**	**189**	**202**	**9**	**3**	**8**	**732**	**6.4**		**2**	**0.0**	**20:39**	**32**	**3**	**9**	**12**	**20**	**1**	**0**	**1**	**21:28**

NHL All-Rookie Team (2010)

Signed as a free agent by **Rapperswil** (Swiss), October 31, 2012. Traded to **Nashville** by **NY Rangers** for Kevin Klein, January 22, 2014. Signed as a free agent by **Philadelphia** August 5, 2014. Signed as a free agent by **Vancouver**, July 1, 2017.

DE LA ROSE, Jacob

(deh la ROHZ, YA-kuhb) **MTL**

Left wing. Shoots left. 6'3", 204 lbs. Born, Arvika, Sweden, May 20, 1995. Montreal's 2nd pick, 34th overall, in 2013 NHL Draft.

Season	Club	League	GP	G	A	Pts	PIM	PP	SH	GW	S	S%	+/-	TF	F%	Min	GP	G	A	Pts	PIM	PP	SH	GW	Min
2008-09	Nor U18	Swe-U18	11	3	14	17	4	....	....	....	....	....	....	....	....	....	....	....	....	....	....	....	....	....	....
2009-10	Farjestad U18	Swe-U18	6	0	0	0	2	....	....	....	....	....	....	....	....	....	7	0	0	0	0	....	....	....	....
2010-11	Leksands IF U18	Swe-U18	30	12	13	25	22	....	....	....	....	....	....	....	....	....	6	0	4	4	4	....	....	....	....
	Leksands IF Jr.	Swe-Jr.	2	1	0	1	0	....	....	....	....	....	....	....	....	....	....	....	....	....	....	....	....	....	....
2011-12	Leksands IF U18	Swe-U18	4	3	3	6	6	....	....	....	....	....	....	....	....	....	....	....	....	....	....	....	....	....	....
	Leksands IF Jr.	Swe-Jr.	28	4	9	13	24	....	....	....	....	....	....	....	....	....	....	....	....	....	....	....	....	....	....
	Leksands IF	Sweden-2	24	4	0	4	12	....	....	....	....	....	....	....	....	....	....	....	....	....	....	....	....	....	....
2012-13	Leksands IF Jr.	Swe-Jr.	4	1	4	5	0	....	....	....	....	....	....	....	....	....	....	....	....	....	....	....	....	....	....
	Leksands IF	Sweden-2	48	6	7	13	33	....	....	....	....	....	....	....	....	....	....	....	....	....	....	....	....	....	....
2013-14	Leksands IF	Sweden	49	7	6	13	18	....	....	....	....	....	....	....	....	....	3	0	0	0	0	....	....	....	....
	Sweden	Olympics	7	3	3	6	6	....	....	....	....	....	....	....	....	....	....	....	....	....	....	....	....	....	....

			Regular Season														Playoffs								
Season	Club	League	GP	G	A	Pts	PIM	PP	SH	GW	S	S%	+/-	TF	F%	Min	GP	G	A	Pts	PIM	PP	SH	GW	Min
2014-15	Montreal	NHL	33	4	2	6	12	0	1	0	38	10.5	–5	160	40.0	13:48	12	0	0	0	4	0	0	0	12:40
	Hamilton	AHL	37	6	5	11	11	....	....	....	....	....	....	....	....	....	....	....	....	....	....	....	....	....	....
2015-16	Montreal	NHL	22	0	1	1	6	0	0	0	20	0.0	–6	130	51.5	12:26	....	....	....	....	....	....	....	....	....
	St. John's IceCaps	AHL	34	7	7	14	18	....	....	....	....	....	....	....	....	....	....	....	....	....	....	....	....	....	....
2016-17	Montreal	NHL	9	0	0	0	4	0	0	0	4	0.0	–3	34	50.0	10:54	....	....	....	....	....	....	....	....	....
	St. John's IceCaps	AHL	62	14	17	31	38	....	....	....	....	....	....	....	....	....	4	1	2	3	6	....	....	....	....
	NHL Totals		64	4	3	7	22	0	1	0	62	6.5		324	45.7	12:55	12	0	0	0	4	0	0	0	12:40

DeMELO, Dylan

(dih-MEH-loh, DIH-luhn) **S.J.**

Defense. Shoots right. 6'1", 195 lbs. Born, London, ON, May 1, 1993. San Jose's 5th pick, 179th overall, in 2011 NHL Draft.

Season	Club	League	GP	G	A	Pts	PIM	PP	SH	GW	S	S%	+/-	TF	F%	Min	GP	G	A	Pts	PIM	PP	SH	GW	Min
2008-09	Lon. Jr. Knights	Minor-ON	74	11	34	45	46	....	....	....	....	....	....	....	....	....	....	....	....	....	....	....	....	....	....
2009-10	Mississauga	ON-Jr.A	36	9	20	29	24	....	....	....	....	....	....	....	....	....	....	....	....	....	....	....	....	....	....
	St. Michael's	OHL	20	0	1	1	12	....	....	....	....	....	....	....	....	....	....	....	....	....	....	....	....	....	....
2010-11	St. Michael's	OHL	67	3	24	27	70	....	....	....	....	....	....	....	....	....	20	1	4	5	15	....	....	....	....
2011-12	St. Michael's	OHL	67	7	40	47	70	....	....	....	....	....	....	....	....	....	6	1	1	2	13	....	....	....	....
	Worcester Sharks	AHL	4	0	1	1	2	....	....	....	....	....	....	....	....	....	....	....	....	....	....	....	....	....	....
2012-13	Mississauga	OHL	64	15	35	50	68	....	....	....	....	....	....	....	....	....	6	1	3	4	6	....	....	....	....
	Worcester Sharks	AHL	10	0	4	4	6	....	....	....	....	....	....	....	....	....	....	....	....	....	....	....	....	....	....
2013-14	Worcester Sharks	AHL	68	2	22	24	51	....	....	....	....	....	....	....	....	....	....	....	....	....	....	....	....	....	....
2014-15	Worcester Sharks	AHL	65	5	17	22	32	....	....	....	....	....	....	....	....	....	4	1	2	3	6	....	....	....	....
2015-16	San Jose	NHL	45	2	2	4	14	2	0	0	42	4.8	0	0	0.0	13:37	....	....	....	....	....	....	....	....	....
	San Jose	AHL	15	0	6	6	2	....	....	....	....	....	....	....	....	....	....	....	....	....	....	....	....	....	....
2016-17	San Jose	NHL	25	1	7	8	14	0	0	0	32	3.1	2	0	0.0	15:54	....	....	....	....	....	....	....	....	....
	NHL Totals		70	3	9	12	28	2	0	0	74	4.1		0	0.0	14:26	....	....	....	....	....	....	....	....	....

• Missed majotity of 2016-17 due to wrist injury at Edmonton, January 10, 2017.

DEMERS, Jason

(duh-MAIRZ, JAY-suhn) **FLA**

Defense. Shoots right. 6'1", 200 lbs. Born, Dorval, QC, June 9, 1988. San Jose's 6th pick, 186th overall, in 2008 NHL Draft.

Season	Club	League	GP	G	A	Pts	PIM	PP	SH	GW	S	S%	+/-	TF	F%	Min	GP	G	A	Pts	PIM	PP	SH	GW	Min
2003-04	Lac St-L. Tigres	Minor-QC	STATISTICS NOT AVAILABLE																						
2004-05	Moncton Wildcats	QMJHL	25	0	1	1	10	....	....	....	....	....	....	....	....	....	....	....	....	....	....	....	....	....	....
2005-06	Moncton Wildcats	QMJHL	21	1	3	4	15	....	....	....	....	....	....	....	....	....	....	....	....	....	....	....	....	....	....
	Victoriaville Tigres	QMJHL	33	2	13	15	58	....	....	....	....	....	....	....	....	....	5	0	2	2	10	....	....	....	....
2006-07	Victoriaville Tigres	QMJHL	69	5	19	24	98	....	....	....	....	....	....	....	....	....	6	0	0	0	2	....	....	....	....
2007-08	Victoriaville Tigres	QMJHL	67	9	55	64	91	....	....	....	....	....	....	....	....	....	6	1	5	6	6	....	....	....	....
2008-09	Worcester Sharks	AHL	78	2	31	33	54	....	....	....	....	....	....	....	....	....	12	0	4	4	6	....	....	....	....
2009-10	San Jose	NHL	51	4	17	21	21	3	0	1	52	7.7	5	0	0.0	15:26	15	1	4	5	8	1	0	0	11:10
	Worcester Sharks	AHL	25	4	13	17	24	....	....	....	....	....	....	....	....	....	....	....	....	....	....	....	....	....	....
2010-11	San Jose	NHL	75	2	22	24	28	0	0	0	105	1.9	19	0	0.0	19:30	13	2	1	3	8	0	0	0	19:56
2011-12	San Jose	NHL	57	4	9	13	22	2	0	1	73	5.5	–8	0	0.0	16:51	3	0	0	0	2	0	0	0	15:28
2012-13	Karpat Oulu	Finland	30	5	16	21	18	....	....	....	....	....	....	....	....	....	....	....	....	....	....	....	....	....	....
	San Jose	NHL	22	1	2	3	10	0	0	0	27	3.7	–4	0	0.0	18:38	1	0	0	0	2	0	0	0	3:47
2013-14	San Jose	NHL	75	5	29	34	30	1	0	0	105	4.8	14	0	0.0	19:29	7	0	1	1	12	0	0	0	19:58
2014-15	San Jose	NHL	20	0	3	3	8	0	0	0	20	0.0	–6	0	0.0	18:11	....	....	....	....	....	....	....	....	....
	Dallas	NHL	61	5	17	22	63	2	0	2	79	6.3	3	0	0.0	19:26	....	....	....	....	....	....	....	....	....
2015-16	Dallas	NHL	62	7	16	23	72	3	1	1	94	7.4	16	0	0.0	20:52	13	0	3	3	8	0	0	0	19:12
2016-17	Florida	NHL	81	9	19	28	53	0	0	2	98	9.2	–14	1	0.0	19:37	....	....	....	....	....	....	....	....	....
	NHL Totals		504	37	134	171	307	11	1	7	653	5.7		1	0.0	18:52	52	3	9	12	40	1	0	0	16:40

Signed as a free agent by **Oulu** (Finland), September 15, 2012. Traded to **Dallas** by **San Jose** with San Jose's 3rd round pick (Fredrik Karlstrom) in 2016 NHL Draft for Brenden Dillon, November 21, 2014. Signed as a free agent by **Anaheim**, July 2, 2016. Signed as a free agent by **Florida**, July 2, 2016.

DESHARNAIS, David

(day-hahr-NAY, DAY-vihd) **NYR**

Center. Shoots left. 5'7", 180 lbs. Born, Laurier-Station, QC, September 14, 1986.

Season	Club	League	GP	G	A	Pts	PIM	PP	SH	GW	S	S%	+/-	TF	F%	Min	GP	G	A	Pts	PIM	PP	SH	GW	Min
2001-02	Rive-Sud Express	Minor-QC	STATISTICS NOT AVAILABLE																						
	Levis	QAAA	2	0	2	2	0	....	....	....	....	....	....	....	....	....	....	....	....	....	....	....	....	....	....
2002-03	Levis	QAAA	42	27	42	69	10	....	....	....	....	....	....	....	....	....	13	6	12	18	8	....	....	....	....
2003-04	Chicoutimi	QMJHL	70	23	28	51	12	....	....	....	....	....	....	....	....	....	18	4	7	11	8	....	....	....	....
2004-05	Chicoutimi	QMJHL	68	32	65	97	39	....	....	....	....	....	....	....	....	....	17	5	10	15	8	....	....	....	....
2005-06	Chicoutimi	QMJHL	63	33	85	118	44	....	....	....	....	....	....	....	....	....	9	2	9	11	4	....	....	....	....
2006-07	Chicoutimi	QMJHL	61	38	70	108	32	....	....	....	....	....	....	....	....	....	4	1	5	6	2	....	....	....	....
	Bridgeport	AHL	7	1	1	2	4	....	....	....	....	....	....	....	....	....	....	....	....	....	....	....	....	....	....
2007-08	Hamilton	AHL	4	0	1	1	6	....	....	....	....	....	....	....	....	....	....	....	....	....	....	....	....	....	....
	Cincinnati	ECHL	68	29	*77	*106	18	....	....	....	....	....	....	....	....	....	22	9	*24	*33	18	....	....	....	....
2008-09	Hamilton	AHL	77	24	34	58	20	....	....	....	....	....	....	....	....	....	6	1	3	4	4	....	....	....	....
2009-10	Montreal	NHL	6	0	1	1	0	0	0	0	2	0.0	–1	28	57.1	8:27	....	....	....	....	....	....	....	....	....
	Hamilton	AHL	60	27	51	78	34	....	....	....	....	....	....	....	....	....	19	10	13	23	16	....	....	....	....
2010-11	Montreal	NHL	43	8	14	22	12	4	0	0	55	14.5	–3	445	49.7	12:52	5	0	1	1	2	0	0	0	11:03
	Hamilton	AHL	35	10	35	45	24	....	....	....	....	....	....	....	....	....	....	....	....	....	....	....	....	....	....
2011-12	Montreal	NHL	81	16	44	60	24	3	0	2	98	16.3	10	1371	49.5	18:24	....	....	....	....	....	....	....	....	....
2012-13	Fribourg	Swiss	16	4	12	16	12	....	....	....	....	....	....	....	....	....	....	....	....	....	....	....	....	....	....
	Montreal	NHL	48	10	18	28	26	2	0	3	66	15.2	–2	764	50.0	16:28	5	0	1	1	2	0	0	0	17:14
2013-14	Montreal	NHL	79	16	36	52	24	3	0	2	96	16.7	11	1202	50.8	17:12	17	2	6	8	6	1	0	0	18:40
2014-15	Montreal	NHL	82	14	34	48	24	2	0	4	90	15.6	22	1189	52.9	17:15	11	1	2	3	4	0	0	1	16:15
2015-16	Montreal	NHL	65	11	18	29	20	3	0	4	90	12.2	–6	803	48.7	16:00	....	....	....	....	....	....	....	....	....
2016-17	Montreal	NHL	31	4	6	10	6	0	0	1	30	13.3	5	159	47.8	13:06	....	....	....	....	....	....	....	....	....
	Edmonton	NHL	18	2	2	4	6	0	0	0	16	12.5	–1	173	54.3	11:21	13	1	3	4	0	0	0	1	9:32
	NHL Totals		453	81	173	254	142	17	0	16	543	14.9		6134	50.5	16:08	51	4	13	17	14	1	0	2	14:56

ECHL Rookie of the Year (2008) • ECHL Leading Scorer (2008) • ECHL MVP (2008)

Signed as a free agent by **Montreal**, November 5, 2008. Signed as a free agent by **Fribourg** (Swiss), November 2, 2012. Traded to **Edmonton** by **Montreal** for Brandon Davidson, February 28, 2017. Signed as a free agent by **NY Rangers**, July 5, 2017.

DESJARDINS, Andrew

(deh-ZHAHR-dehn, AN-droo)

Center. Shoots right. 6'1", 195 lbs. Born, Lively, ON, July 27, 1986.

Season	Club	League	GP	G	A	Pts	PIM	PP	SH	GW	S	S%	+/-	TF	F%	Min	GP	G	A	Pts	PIM	PP	SH	GW	Min
2002-03	Rayside	Minor-ON	STATISTICS NOT AVAILABLE																						
	Espanola	ON-Jr.A	8	1	4	5	14	....	....	....	....	....	....	....	....	....	....	....	....	....	....	....	....	....	....
2003-04	Sault Ste. Marie	OHL	55	3	6	9	41	....	....	....	....	....	....	....	....	....	....	....	....	....	....	....	....	....	....
2004-05	Sault Ste. Marie	OHL	68	17	17	34	49	....	....	....	....	....	....	....	....	....	7	0	0	0	2	....	....	....	....
2005-06	Sault Ste. Marie	OHL	6	12	16	28	78	....	....	....	....	....	....	....	....	....	4	2	3	5	10	....	....	....	....
2006-07	Sault Ste. Marie	OHL	65	16	26	42	96	....	....	....	....	....	....	....	....	....	13	2	5	7	18	....	....	....	....
2007-08	Laredo Bucks	CHL	64	22	37	59	112	....	....	....	....	....	....	....	....	....	11	2	4	6	21	....	....	....	....
2008-09	Phoenix	ECHL	5	2	0	2	6	....	....	....	....	....	....	....	....	....	....	....	....	....	....	....	....	....	....
	Worcester Sharks	AHL	74	8	14	22	99	....	....	....	....	....	....	....	....	....	12	4	2	6	13	....	....	....	....
2009-10	Worcester Sharks	AHL	80	19	27	46	126	....	....	....	....	....	....	....	....	....	11	2	2	4	32	....	....	....	....
2010-11	San Jose	NHL	17	1	2	3	4	0	0	0	12	8.3	–1	56	55.4	7:08	3	1	0	1	4	0	0	0	6:48
	Worcester Sharks	AHL	58	12	17	29	69	....	....	....	....	....	....	....	....	....	....	....	....	....	....	....	....	....	....
2011-12	San Jose	NHL	76	4	13	17	47	0	0	3	80	5.0	4	362	53.0	9:35	5	1	0	1	2	0	0	0	11:32
2012-13	San Jose	NHL	42	2	1	3	61	0	0	0	51	3.9	–6	72	54.2	10:07	11	0	0	0	6	0	0	0	10:58
2013-14	San Jose	NHL	81	3	14	17	86	0	0	1	95	3.2	–8	675	55.0	11:09	7	0	2	2	31	0	0	0	10:14
2014-15	San Jose	NHL	56	5	3	8	50	0	0	1	43	11.6	–2	293	49.8	10:27	....	....	....	....	....	....	....	....	....
	♦ Chicago	NHL	13	0	2	2	7	0	0	0	16	0.0	1	19	63.2	12:00	21	1	3	4	4	0	0	0	13:56
2015-16	Chicago	NHL	77	8	5	13	30	0	0	1	96	8.3	–8	87	49.4	13:23	6	0	0	0	0	0	0	0	8:49
2016-17	Chicago	NHL	46	0	1	1	22	0	0	0	46	0.0	–6	69	56.5	9:24	....	....	....	....	....	....	....	....	....
	NHL Totals		408	23	41	64	307	0	0	6	439	5.2		1633	53.5	10:44	53	3	5	8	47	0	0	0	11:37

Signed as a free agent by **Worcester** (AHL), October, 2008. Signed as a free agent by **San Jose**, June 26, 2010. Traded to **Chicago** by **San Jose** for Ben Smith and Chicago's 7th round pick (Ivan Chekhovich) in 2017 NHL Draft, March 2, 2015.

DESLAURIERS, Nicolas
(duh-LOHR-ree-AY, NIH-koh-las) **BUF**

Left wing. Shoots left. 6'1", 212 lbs. Born, LaSalle, QC, February 22, 1991. Los Angeles' 3rd pick, 84th overall, in 2009 NHL Draft.

			Regular Season														Playoffs								
Season	**Club**	**League**	**GP**	**G**	**A**	**Pts**	**PIM**	**PP**	**SH**	**GW**	**S**	**S%**	**+/-**	**TF**	**F%**	**Min**	**GP**	**G**	**A**	**Pts**	**PIM**	**PP**	**SH**	**GW**	**Min**
2006-07	Chateauguay	QAAA	43	2	10	12	28	....	....	....	....	....	....	....	....	....	3	1	0	1	4	....	....	....	....
2007-08	Rouyn-Noranda	QMJHL	42	2	7	9	38	....	....	....	....	....	....	....	....	....	4	0	0	0	0	....	....	....	....
2008-09	Rouyn-Noranda	QMJHL	68	11	19	30	80	....	....	....	....	....	....	....	....	....	6	2	2	4	8	....	....	....	....
2009-10	Rouyn-Noranda	QMJHL	65	9	36	45	72	....	....	....	....	....	....	....	....	....	11	2	6	8	2	....	....	....	....
2010-11	Gatineau	QMJHL	48	13	30	43	53	....	....	....	....	....	....	....	....	....	24	5	15	20	19	....	....	....	....
2011-12	Manchester	AHL	65	1	13	14	67	....	....	....	....	....	....	....	....	....	4	0	0	0	7	....	....	....	....
2012-13	Manchester	AHL	63	4	19	23	80	....	....	....	....	....	....	....	....	....	4	2	2	4	2	....	....	....	....
2013-14	Manchester	AHL	60	18	21	39	76	....	....	....	....	....	....	....	....	....	....	....	....	....	....	....	....	....	....
	Buffalo	**NHL**	**17**	**1**	**0**	**1**	**18**	**0**	**0**	**0**	**30**	**3.3**	**–10**	**1**	**0.0**	**13:09**	....	....	....	....	....	....	....	....	....
	Rochester	AHL	5	1	2	3	9	....	....	....	....	....	....	....	....	....	5	1	1	2	9	....	....	....	....
2014-15	**Buffalo**	**NHL**	**82**	**5**	**10**	**15**	**71**	**0**	**0**	**1**	**76**	**6.6**	**–24**	**1**	**0.0**	**11:52**	....	....	....	....	....	....	....	....	....
2015-16	**Buffalo**	**NHL**	**70**	**6**	**6**	**12**	**59**	**0**	**0**	**1**	**72**	**8.3**	**–14**	**1**	**0.0**	**10:20**	....	....	....	....	....	....	....	....	....
2016-17	**Buffalo**	**NHL**	**42**	**0**	**2**	**2**	**38**	**0**	**0**	**0**	**26**	**0.0**	**–6**	**3**	**0.0**	**7:25**	....	....	....	....	....	....	....	....	....
	NHL Totals		**211**	**12**	**18**	**30**	**186**	**0**	**0**	**2**	**204**	**5.9**		**6**	**0.0**	**10:34**	....	....	....	....	....	....	....	....	....

Traded to **Buffalo** by **Los Angeles** with Hudson Fasching for Brayden McNabb, Jonathan Parker, Los Angeles' 2nd round pick (previously acquired, Los Angeles selected Alex Lintuniemi) in 2014 NHL Draft and Los Angeles' 2nd round pick (previously acquired, Los Angeles selected Erik Cernak) in 2015 NHL Draft, March 5, 2014.

DESPRES, Simon
(duh-PRAY, see-MOHN)

Defense. Shoots left. 6'4", 218 lbs. Born, Laval, QC, July 27, 1991. Pittsburgh's 1st pick, 30th overall, in 2009 NHL Draft.

2006-07	Laval-Bourassa	QAAA	42	8	31	39	36	....	....	....	....	....	....	....	....	....	5	0	2	2	8	....	....	....	....
2007-08	Saint John	QMJHL	64	1	13	14	30	....	....	....	....	....	....	....	....	....	14	0	4	4	18	....	....	....	....
2008-09	Saint John	QMJHL	66	2	30	32	74	....	....	....	....	....	....	....	....	....	4	0	4	4	2	....	....	....	....
2009-10	Saint John	QMJHL	63	9	38	47	87	....	....	....	....	....	....	....	....	....	21	2	17	19	18	....	....	....	....
2010-11	Saint John	QMJHL	47	13	28	41	54	....	....	....	....	....	....	....	....	....	19	4	8	12	16	....	....	....	....
2011-12	**Pittsburgh**	**NHL**	**18**	**1**	**3**	**4**	**10**	**1**	**0**	**0**	**22**	**4.5**	**5**	**0**	**0.0**	**14:13**	**3**	**0**	**0**	**0**	**2**	**0**	**0**	**0**	**9:18**
	Wilkes-Barre	AHL	44	5	10	15	45	....	....	....	....	....	....	....	....	....	10	1	1	2	2	....	....	....	....
2012-13	Wilkes-Barre	AHL	27	4	3	7	28	....	....	....	....	....	....	....	....	....	....	....	....	....	....	....	....	....	....
	Pittsburgh	**NHL**	**33**	**2**	**5**	**7**	**20**	**0**	**0**	**0**	**33**	**6.1**	**9**	**0**	**0.0**	**15:07**	**3**	**0**	**0**	**0**	**0**	**0**	**0**	**0**	**11:07**
2013-14	**Pittsburgh**	**NHL**	**34**	**0**	**5**	**5**	**26**	**0**	**0**	**0**	**41**	**0.0**	**4**	**0**	**0.0**	**16:45**	....	....	....	....	....	....	....	....	....
	Wilkes-Barre	AHL	36	6	16	22	39	....	....	....	....	....	....	....	....	....	17	2	7	9	32	....	....	....	....
2014-15	**Pittsburgh**	**NHL**	**59**	**2**	**15**	**17**	**64**	**0**	**0**	**1**	**76**	**2.6**	**9**	**1**	**0.0**	**16:23**	....	....	....	....	....	....	....	....	....
	Anaheim	**NHL**	**16**	**1**	**5**	**6**	**22**	**0**	**0**	**0**	**27**	**3.7**	**2**	**0**	**0.0**	**18:40**	**16**	**1**	**6**	**7**	**6**	**0**	**0**	**1**	**20:46**
2015-16	**Anaheim**	**NHL**	**32**	**0**	**4**	**4**	**8**	**0**	**0**	**0**	**32**	**0.0**	**2**	**0**	**0.0**	**19:38**	**7**	**0**	**0**	**0**	**6**	**0**	**0**	**0**	**17:25**
	San Diego Gulls	AHL	4	1	1	2	6	....	....	....	....	....	....	....	....	....	....	....	....	....	....	....	....	....	....
2016-17	**Anaheim**	**NHL**	**1**	**0**	**0**	**0**	**0**	**0**	**0**	**0**	**1**	**0.0**	**0**	**0**	**0.0**	**16:08**	....	....	....	....	....	....	....	....	....
	NHL Totals		**193**	**6**	**37**	**43**	**150**	**1**	**0**	**1**	**232**	**2.6**		**1**	**0.0**	**16:45**	**29**	**1**	**6**	**7**	**14**	**0**	**0**	**1**	**17:46**

QMJHL All-Rookie Team (2008) • QMJHL First All-Star Team (2011) • QMJHL Defenseman of the Year (2011)

Traded to **Anaheim** by **Pittsburgh** for Ben Lovejoy, March 2, 2015. • Missed majority of 2015-16 due to upper-body injury vs. Colorado, November 15, 2015. • Missed majority of 2016-17 due to head injury at Dallas, October 13, 2016.

DEVANE, Jamie
(dah-VAN, JAY-mee)

Left wing. Shoots left. 6'5", 232 lbs. Born, Mississauga, ON, February 20, 1991. Toronto's 4th pick, 68th overall, in 2009 NHL Draft.

2007-08	Vaughan Kings	GTHL	15	4	11	15	24	....	....	....	....	....	....	....	....	....	....	....	....	....	....	....	....	....	....
	Vaughan Vipers	ON-Jr.A	19	2	0	2	17	....	....	....	....	....	....	....	....	....	1	0	0	0	0	....	....	....	....
2008-09	Plymouth Whalers	OHL	64	5	12	17	92	....	....	....	....	....	....	....	....	....	11	0	0	0	17	....	....	....	....
2009-10	Plymouth Whalers	OHL	51	6	8	14	84	....	....	....	....	....	....	....	....	....	9	0	1	1	12	....	....	....	....
	Toronto Marlies	AHL	2	0	0	0	4	....	....	....	....	....	....	....	....	....	....	....	....	....	....	....	....	....	....
2010-11	Plymouth Whalers	OHL	63	18	20	38	131	....	....	....	....	....	....	....	....	....	10	2	3	5	19	....	....	....	....
2011-12	Plymouth Whalers	OHL	59	23	22	45	104	....	....	....	....	....	....	....	....	....	13	2	1	3	19	....	....	....	....
2012-13	Toronto Marlies	AHL	22	2	3	5	41	....	....	....	....	....	....	....	....	....	....	....	....	....	....	....	....	....	....
	San Francisco	ECHL	12	1	0	1	45	....	....	....	....	....	....	....	....	....	....	....	....	....	....	....	....	....	....
2013-14	**Toronto**	**NHL**	**2**	**0**	**0**	**0**	**0**	**0**	**0**	**0**	**1**	**0.0**	**–1**	**0**	**0.0**	**5:52**	....	....	....	....	....	....	....	....	....
	Toronto Marlies	AHL	55	4	4	8	146	....	....	....	....	....	....	....	....	....	2	0	0	0	2	....	....	....	....
2014-15	Toronto Marlies	AHL	39	0	2	2	62	....	....	....	....	....	....	....	....	....	....	....	....	....	....	....	....	....	....
2015-16	Milwaukee	AHL	62	6	5	11	82	....	....	....	....	....	....	....	....	....	3	0	0	0	2	....	....	....	....
2016-17	Stockton Heat	AHL	43	4	9	13	77	....	....	....	....	....	....	....	....	....	5	1	1	2	4	....	....	....	....
	NHL Totals		**2**	**0**	**0**	**0**	**0**	**0**	**0**	**0**	**1**	**0.0**		**0**	**0.0**	**5:52**	....	....	....	....	....	....	....	....	....

• Missed majority of 2014-15 as a healthy reserve. Traded to **Nashville** by **Toronto** for Taylor Beck, July 12, 2015. Signed to a PTO (professional tryout) contract by **Calgary**, August 16, 2016. Signed as a free agent by **Stockton**, September 2, 2016.

Di GIUSEPPE, Phil
(DEE-joo-SEH-pee, FIHL) **CAR**

Left wing. Shoots left. 6', 200 lbs. Born, Toronto, ON, October 9, 1993. Carolina's 1st pick, 38th overall, in 2012 NHL Draft.

2008-09	Vaughan Kings	GTHL	41	16	17	33	19	....	....	....	....	....	....	....	....	....	....	....	....	....	....	....	....	....	....
2009-10	Villanova Knights	ON-Jr.A	56	16	31	47	44	....	....	....	....	....	....	....	....	....	6	1	3	4	0	....	....	....	....
2010-11	Villanova Knights	ON-Jr.A	49	24	39	63	25	....	....	....	....	....	....	....	....	....	10	6	10	16	6	....	....	....	....
2011-12	U. of Michigan	CCHA	40	11	15	26	18	....	....	....	....	....	....	....	....	....	....	....	....	....	....	....	....	....	....
2012-13	U. of Michigan	CCHA	40	9	19	28	32	....	....	....	....	....	....	....	....	....	....	....	....	....	....	....	....	....	....
2013-14	U. of Michigan	Big Ten	35	13	11	24	29	....	....	....	....	....	....	....	....	....	....	....	....	....	....	....	....	....	....
	Charlotte	AHL	3	0	1	1	6	....	....	....	....	....	....	....	....	....	....	....	....	....	....	....	....	....	....
2014-15	Charlotte	AHL	76	11	19	30	20	....	....	....	....	....	....	....	....	....	....	....	....	....	....	....	....	....	....
2015-16	**Carolina**	**NHL**	**41**	**7**	**10**	**17**	**18**	**0**	**0**	**1**	**68**	**10.3**	**0**	**20**	**35.0**	**14:16**	....	....	....	....	....	....	....	....	....
2016-17	**Carolina**	**NHL**	**36**	**1**	**6**	**7**	**15**	**0**	**0**	**1**	**68**	**1.5**	**–12**	**2**	**0.0**	**12:18**	....	....	....	....	....	....	....	....	....
	Charlotte	AHL	40	12	16	28	22	....	....	....	....	....	....	....	....	....	5	1	0	1	4	....	....	....	....
	NHL Totals		**77**	**8**	**16**	**24**	**33**	**0**	**0**	**2**	**136**	**5.9**		**22**	**31.8**	**13:21**	....	....	....	....	....	....	....	....	....

DICKINSON, Jason
(DIH-kihn-suhn, JAY-suhn) **DAL**

Center. Shoots left. 6'2", 200 lbs. Born, Georgetown, ON, July 4, 1995. Dallas' 2nd pick, 29th overall, in 2013 NHL Draft.

2010-11	Halton Hurricanes	Minor-ON	59	45	34	79	22	....	....	....	....	....	....	....	....	....	....	....	....	....	....	....	....	....	....
2011-12	Guelph Storm	OHL	63	13	22	35	24	....	....	....	....	....	....	....	....	....	6	3	2	5	6	....	....	....	....
2012-13	Guelph Storm	OHL	66	18	29	47	31	....	....	....	....	....	....	....	....	....	5	1	1	2	0	....	....	....	....
2013-14	Guelph Storm	OHL	68	26	52	78	42	....	....	....	....	....	....	....	....	....	20	8	16	24	6	....	....	....	....
2014-15	Guelph Storm	OHL	56	27	44	71	32	....	....	....	....	....	....	....	....	....	9	4	4	8	10	....	....	....	....
	Texas Stars	AHL	2	0	3	3	0	....	....	....	....	....	....	....	....	....	3	0	0	0	2	....	....	....	....
2015-16	**Dallas**	**NHL**	**1**	**1**	**0**	**1**	**0**	**0**	**0**	**0**	**2**	**50.0**	**1**	**7**	**14.3**	**11:55**	....	....	....	....	....	....	....	....	....
	Texas Stars	AHL	73	22	31	53	32	....	....	....	....	....	....	....	....	....	4	0	1	1	2	....	....	....	....
2016-17	**Dallas**	**NHL**	**10**	**2**	**0**	**2**	**0**	**0**	**0**	**0**	**9**	**22.2**	**–3**	**13**	**30.8**	**11:47**	....	....	....	....	....	....	....	....	....
	Texas Stars	AHL	58	9	21	30	41	....	....	....	....	....	....	....	....	....	....	....	....	....	....	....	....	....	....
	NHL Totals		**11**	**3**	**0**	**3**	**0**	**0**	**0**	**0**	**11**	**27.3**		**20**	**25.0**	**11:48**	....	....	....	....	....	....	....	....	....

DIDOMENICO, Chris
(dee-DOH-mehn-ih-koh,KRIHS) **OTT**

Center. Shoots right. 5'11", 174 lbs. Born, Toronto, ON, February 20, 1989. Toronto's 5th pick, 164th overall, in 2007 NHL Draft.

2005-06	North York	GTHL	36	28	35	63	....	....	....	....	....	....	....	....	....	....	....	....	....	....	....	....	....	....	....
	North York	ON-Jr.A	2	2	0	2	0	....	....	....	....	....	....	....	....	....	....	....	....	....	....	....	....	....	....
2006-07	Saint John	QMJHL	70	25	50	75	60	....	....	....	....	....	....	....	....	....	....	....	....	....	....	....	....	....	....
2007-08	Saint John	QMJHL	70	39	56	95	103	....	....	....	....	....	....	....	....	....	14	8	11	19	20	....	....	....	....
2008-09	Saint John	QMJHL	26	11	23	34	34	....	....	....	....	....	....	....	....	....	....	....	....	....	....	....	....	....	....
	Drummondville	QMJHL	25	8	17	25	28	....	....	....	....	....	....	....	....	....	15	4	*31	35	24	....	....	....	....
2009-10	Drummondville	QMJHL	12	7	15	22	10	....	....	....	....	....	....	....	....	....	14	7	14	21	18	....	....	....	....
2010-11	Rockford IceHogs	AHL	25	0	4	4	6	....	....	....	....	....	....	....	....	....	....	....	....	....	....	....	....	....	....
	Toledo Walleye	ECHL	37	9	16	25	31	....	....	....	....	....	....	....	....	....	....	....	....	....	....	....	....	....	....

			Regular Season														Playoffs								
Season	Club	League	GP	G	A	Pts	PIM	PP	SH	GW	S	S%	+/-	TF	F%	Min	GP	G	A	Pts	PIM	PP	SH	GW	Min
2011-12	Rockford IceHogs	AHL	49	2	11	13	24	....	....	....	....	....	....	....	....	....	....	....	....	....	....	....	....	....	....
	Toledo Walleye	ECHL	17	4	13	17	14	....	....	....	....	....	....	....	....	....	....	....	....	....	....	....	....	....	....
2012-13	HC Asiago	Italy	37	22	38	60	82	....	....	....	....	....	....	....	....	....	15	11	31	42	34	....	....	....	....
2013-14	HC Asiago	Italy	31	24	48	72	50	....	....	....	....	....	....	....	....	....	....	....	....	....	....	....	....	....	....
	Langnau	Swiss-2	1	0	0	0	0	....	....	....	....	....	....	....	....	....	15	10	12	22	34	....	....	....	....
2014-15	Langnau	Swiss-2	43	25	38	63	75	....	....	....	....	....	....	....	....	....	15	5	21	26	48	....	....	....	....
	Langnau	Swiss-Q	....	....	....	....	....	....	....	....	....	....	....	....	....	....	4	2	7	9	4	....	....	....	....
2015-16	Langnau	Swiss	46	12	26	38	42	....	....	....	....	....	....	....	....	....	10	1	13	14	18	....	....	....	....
2016-17	Langnau	Swiss	40	10	28	38	30	....	....	....	....	....	....	....	....	....	....	....	....	....	....	....	....	....	....
	Ottawa	**NHL**	**3**	**0**	**0**	**0**	**6**	**0**	**0**	**0**	**5**	**0.0**	**0**	**3**	**66.7**	**11:01**	....	....	....	....	....	....	....	....	....
	NHL Totals		**3**	**0**	**0**	**0**	**6**	**0**	**0**	**0**	**5**	**0.0**		**3**	**66.7**	**11:01**	....	....	....	....	....	....	....	....	....

QMJHL All-Rookie Team (2007)

• Missed majority of 2009-10 due to leg injury in playoff game vs. Shawinigan (QMJHL), May 5, 2009. Traded to **Chicago** by **Toronto** with Viktor Stalberg and Phillipe Paradis for Kris Versteeg and Bill Sweatt, June 30, 2010. Signed as a free agent by **Asiago** (Swiss), August 27, 2012. Signed as a free agent by **Langnau** (Swiss), February 12, 2014. Signed as a free agent by **Ottawa**, February 28, 2017.

DIETZ, Darren

(DEETZ, DAIR-uhn)

Defense. Shoots right. 6'1", 201 lbs. Born, Medicine Hat, AB, July 17, 1993. Montreal's 4th pick, 138th overall, in 2011 NHL Draft.

Season	Club	League	GP	G	A	Pts	PIM	PP	SH	GW	S	S%	+/-	TF	F%	Min	GP	G	A	Pts	PIM	PP	SH	GW	Min
2008-09	Medicine Hat	AMHL	34	0	4	4	62	....	....	....	....	....	....	....	....	....	....	....	....	....	....	....	....	....	....
2009-10	Lethbridge	AMHL	33	9	15	24	105	....	....	....	....	....	....	....	....	....	5	4	3	7	14	....	....	....	....
	Saskatoon Blades	WHL	8	1	1	2	4	....	....	....	....	....	....	....	....	....	3	0	0	0	2	....	....	....	....
2010-11	Saskatoon Blades	WHL	68	8	19	27	66	....	....	....	....	....	....	....	....	....	10	1	4	5	15	....	....	....	....
2011-12	Saskatoon Blades	WHL	72	15	29	44	118	....	....	....	....	....	....	....	....	....	3	0	1	1	5	....	....	....	....
2012-13	Saskatoon Blades	WHL	72	24	34	58	100	....	....	....	....	....	....	....	....	....	4	1	1	2	2	....	....	....	....
2013-14	Hamilton	AHL	34	0	5	5	49	....	....	....	....	....	....	....	....	....	....	....	....	....	....	....	....	....	....
2014-15	Hamilton	AHL	71	4	13	17	64	....	....	....	....	....	....	....	....	....	....	....	....	....	....	....	....	....	....
2015-16	**Montreal**	**NHL**	**13**	**1**	**4**	**5**	**13**	**0**	**0**	**0**	**13**	**7.7**	**–1**	**0**	**0.0**	**14:32**	....	....	....	....	....	....	....	....	....
	St. John's IceCaps	AHL	61	4	12	16	61	....	....	....	....	....	....	....	....	....	....	....	....	....	....	....	....	....	....
2016-17	Hershey Bears	AHL	39	6	6	12	53	....	....	....	....	....	....	....	....	....	....	....	....	....	....	....	....	....	....
	Texas Stars	AHL	13	0	2	2	8	....	....	....	....	....	....	....	....	....	....	....	....	....	....	....	....	....	....
	NHL Totals		**13**	**1**	**4**	**5**	**13**	**0**	**0**	**0**	**13**	**7.7**		**0**	**0.0**	**14:32**	....	....	....	....	....	....	....	....	....

WHL East First All-Star Team (2013)

Signed as a free agent by **Washington**, July 1, 2016.

DILLON, Brenden

(DIHL-uhn, BREHN-duhn) **S.J.**

Defense. Shoots left. 6'3", 220 lbs. Born, Surrey, BC, November 13, 1990.

Season	Club	League	GP	G	A	Pts	PIM	PP	SH	GW	S	S%	+/-	TF	F%	Min	GP	G	A	Pts	PIM	PP	SH	GW	Min
2006-07	Hope Icebreakers	PIJHL	45	4	27	31	38	....	....	....	....	....	....	....	....	....	2	0	0	0	0	....	....	....	....
2007-08	Seattle	WHL	71	1	10	11	54	....	....	....	....	....	....	....	....	....	12	0	2	2	21	....	....	....	....
2008-09	Seattle	WHL	70	0	10	10	68	....	....	....	....	....	....	....	....	....	5	0	1	1	6	....	....	....	....
2009-10	Seattle	WHL	67	2	12	14	101	....	....	....	....	....	....	....	....	....	....	....	....	....	....	....	....	....	....
2010-11	Seattle	WHL	72	8	51	59	139	....	....	....	....	....	....	....	....	....	....	....	....	....	....	....	....	....	....
	Texas Stars	AHL	10	0	0	0	8	....	....	....	....	....	....	....	....	....	6	0	2	2	7	....	....	....	....
2011-12	**Dallas**	**NHL**	**1**	**0**	**0**	**0**	**0**	**0**	**0**	**0**	**6**	**0.0**	**0**	**0**	**0.0**	**19:59**	....	....	....	....	....	....	....	....	....
	Texas Stars	AHL	76	6	23	29	97	....	....	....	....	....	....	....	....	....	....	....	....	....	....	....	....	....	....
2012-13	Texas Stars	AHL	37	3	11	14	45	....	....	....	....	....	....	....	....	....	....	....	....	....	....	....	....	....	....
	Dallas	**NHL**	**48**	**3**	**5**	**8**	**65**	**0**	**0**	**1**	**75**	**4.0**	**1**	**0**	**0.0**	**21:23**	....	....	....	....	....	....	....	....	....
2013-14	**Dallas**	**NHL**	**80**	**6**	**11**	**17**	**86**	**0**	**2**	**1**	**97**	**6.2**	**9**	**0**	**0.0**	**21:06**	**2**	**0**	**0**	**0**	**2**	**0**	**0**	**0**	**18:13**
2014-15	**Dallas**	**NHL**	**20**	**0**	**1**	**1**	**23**	**0**	**0**	**0**	**16**	**0.0**	**–2**	**0**	**0.0**	**20:37**	....	....	....	....	....	....	....	....	....
	San Jose	**NHL**	**60**	**2**	**7**	**9**	**54**	**0**	**1**	**1**	**75**	**2.7**	**–11**	**0**	**0.0**	**19:13**	....	....	....	....	....	....	....	....	....
2015-16	**San Jose**	**NHL**	**76**	**2**	**9**	**11**	**61**	**0**	**0**	**1**	**93**	**2.2**	**8**	**0**	**0.0**	**16:41**	**24**	**0**	**2**	**2**	**11**	**0**	**0**	**0**	**15:09**
2016-17	**San Jose**	**NHL**	**81**	**2**	**8**	**10**	**60**	**0**	**0**	**0**	**86**	**2.3**	**–2**	**0**	**0.0**	**16:28**	**6**	**0**	**1**	**1**	**4**	**0**	**0**	**0**	**16:29**
	NHL Totals		**366**	**15**	**41**	**56**	**349**	**0**	**3**	**4**	**448**	**3.3**		**0**	**0.0**	**18:51**	**32**	**0**	**3**	**3**	**17**	**0**	**0**	**0**	**15:36**

Signed as a free agent by **Dallas**, March 1, 2011. Traded to **San Jose** by **Dallas** for Jason Demers and San Jose's 3rd round pick (Fredrik Karlstrom) in 2016 NHL Draft, November 21, 2014.

DOAN, Shane

(DOHN, SHAYN)

Right wing. Shoots right. 6'1", 223 lbs. Born, Halkirk, AB, October 10, 1976. Winnipeg's 1st pick, 7th overall, in 1995 NHL Draft.

Season	Club	League	GP	G	A	Pts	PIM	PP	SH	GW	S	S%	+/-	TF	F%	Min	GP	G	A	Pts	PIM	PP	SH	GW	Min
1991-92	Killam Selects	AAHA	56	80	84	164	74	....	....	....	....	....	....	....	....	....	....	....	....	....	....	....	....	....	....
1992-93	Kamloops Blazers	WHL	51	7	12	19	65	....	....	....	....	....	....	....	....	....	13	0	1	1	8	....	....	....	....
1993-94	Kamloops Blazers	WHL	52	24	24	48	88	....	....	....	....	....	....	....	....	....	....	....	....	....	....	....	....	....	....
1994-95	Kamloops Blazers	WHL	71	37	57	94	106	....	....	....	....	....	....	....	....	....	21	6	10	16	16	....	....	....	....
1995-96	**Winnipeg**	**NHL**	**74**	**7**	**10**	**17**	**101**	**1**	**0**	**3**	**106**	**6.6**	**–9**	....	....	....	**6**	**0**	**0**	**0**	**6**	**0**	**0**	**0**	....
1996-97	**Phoenix**	**NHL**	**63**	**4**	**8**	**12**	**49**	**0**	**0**	**0**	**100**	**4.0**	**–3**	....	....	....	**4**	**0**	**0**	**0**	**2**	**0**	**0**	**0**	....
1997-98	**Phoenix**	**NHL**	**33**	**5**	**6**	**11**	**35**	**0**	**0**	**3**	**42**	**11.9**	**–3**	....	....	....	**6**	**1**	**0**	**1**	**6**	**0**	**0**	**0**	....
	Springfield	AHL	39	21	21	42	64	....	....	....	....	....	....	....	....	....	....	....	....	....	....	....	....	....	....
1998-99	**Phoenix**	**NHL**	**79**	**6**	**16**	**22**	**54**	**0**	**0**	**0**	**156**	**3.8**	**–5**	**6**	**16.7**	**12:42**	**7**	**2**	**2**	**4**	**6**	**0**	**0**	**2**	**17:58**
99-2000	**Phoenix**	**NHL**	**81**	**26**	**25**	**51**	**66**	**1**	**1**	**4**	**221**	**11.8**	**6**	**25**	**36.0**	**16:51**	**4**	**1**	**2**	**3**	**8**	**1**	**0**	**0**	**18:11**
2000-01	**Phoenix**	**NHL**	**76**	**26**	**37**	**63**	**89**	**6**	**1**	**6**	**220**	**11.8**	**0**	**15**	**40.0**	**19:32**	....	....	....	....	....	....	....	....	....
2001-02	**Phoenix**	**NHL**	**81**	**20**	**29**	**49**	**61**	**6**	**0**	**2**	**205**	**9.8**	**11**	**52**	**44.2**	**18:10**	**5**	**2**	**2**	**4**	**6**	**0**	**0**	**0**	**17:21**
2002-03	**Phoenix**	**NHL**	**82**	**21**	**37**	**58**	**86**	**7**	**0**	**2**	**225**	**9.3**	**3**	**623**	**39.8**	**18:47**	....	....	....	....	....	....	....	....	....
2003-04	**Phoenix**	**NHL**	**79**	**27**	**41**	**68**	**47**	**9**	**2**	**1**	**254**	**10.6**	**–11**	**55**	**40.0**	**21:46**	....	....	....	....	....	....	....	....	....
2004-05			DID NOT PLAY																						
2005-06	**Phoenix**	**NHL**	**82**	**30**	**36**	**66**	**123**	**17**	**0**	**7**	**254**	**11.8**	**–9**	**126**	**43.7**	**19:08**	....	....	....	....	....	....	....	....	....
	Canada	Olympics	6	2	1	3	2	....	....	....	....	....	....	....	....	....	....	....	....	....	....	....	....	....	....
2006-07	**Phoenix**	**NHL**	**73**	**27**	**28**	**55**	**73**	**11**	**0**	**7**	**209**	**12.9**	**–14**	**174**	**39.1**	**20:27**	....	....	....	....	....	....	....	....	....
2007-08	**Phoenix**	**NHL**	**80**	**28**	**50**	**78**	**59**	**9**	**2**	**5**	**243**	**11.5**	**4**	**187**	**41.2**	**20:46**	....	....	....	....	....	....	....	....	....
2008-09	**Phoenix**	**NHL**	**82**	**31**	**42**	**73**	**72**	**10**	**0**	**4**	**230**	**13.5**	**5**	**362**	**44.2**	**20:15**	....	....	....	....	....	....	....	....	....
2009-10	**Phoenix**	**NHL**	**82**	**18**	**37**	**55**	**41**	**5**	**0**	**4**	**234**	**7.7**	**3**	**153**	**45.8**	**19:10**	**3**	**1**	**1**	**2**	**4**	**0**	**0**	**0**	**13:22**
2010-11	**Phoenix**	**NHL**	**72**	**20**	**40**	**60**	**67**	**11**	**0**	**6**	**221**	**9.0**	**5**	**159**	**45.9**	**19:17**	**4**	**3**	**2**	**5**	**6**	**2**	**0**	**0**	**21:42**
2011-12	**Phoenix**	**NHL**	**79**	**22**	**28**	**50**	**48**	**5**	**0**	**5**	**226**	**9.7**	**–8**	**59**	**55.9**	**19:36**	**16**	**5**	**4**	**9**	**41**	**1**	**0**	**2**	**20:47**
2012-13	**Phoenix**	**NHL**	**48**	**13**	**14**	**27**	**37**	**0**	**0**	**2**	**129**	**10.1**	**6**	**15**	**26.7**	**18:03**	....	....	....	....	....	....	....	....	....
2013-14	**Phoenix**	**NHL**	**69**	**23**	**24**	**47**	**34**	**10**	**0**	**4**	**167**	**13.8**	**–7**	**12**	**50.0**	**18:56**	....	....	....	....	....	....	....	....	....
2014-15	**Arizona**	**NHL**	**79**	**14**	**22**	**36**	**65**	**5**	**0**	**0**	**189**	**7.4**	**–29**	**11**	**27.3**	**18:53**	....	....	....	....	....	....	....	....	....
2015-16	**Arizona**	**NHL**	**72**	**28**	**19**	**47**	**98**	**12**	**0**	**4**	**170**	**16.5**	**4**	**143**	**51.8**	**17:36**	....	....	....	....	....	....	....	....	....
2016-17	**Arizona**	**NHL**	**74**	**6**	**21**	**27**	**48**	**3**	**0**	**0**	**144**	**4.2**	**–3**	**199**	**47.2**	**15:03**	....	....	....	....	....	....	....	....	....
	NHL Totals		**1540**	**402**	**570**	**972**	**1353**	**128**	**6**	**69**	**3945**	**10.2**		**2376**	**43.2**	**18:38**	**55**	**15**	**13**	**28**	**85**	**4**	**0**	**4**	**19:06**

King Clancy Memorial Trophy (2010) • Mark Messier NHL Leadership Award (2012)

Played in NHL All-Star Game (2004, 2009)

• Transferred to **Phoenix** after **Winnipeg** franchise relocated, July 1, 1996.

DOMI, Max

(DOH-mee, MAX) **ARI**

Left wing. Shoots left. 5'10", 198 lbs. Born, Winnipeg, MB, March 2, 1995. Phoenix's 1st pick, 12th overall, in 2013 NHL Draft.

Season	Club	League	GP	G	A	Pts	PIM	PP	SH	GW	S	S%	+/-	TF	F%	Min	GP	G	A	Pts	PIM	PP	SH	GW	Min
2010-11	Don Mills Flyers	GTHL	30	27	30	57	45	....	....	....	....	....	....	....	....	....	....	....	....	....	....	....	....	....	....
	St. Michael's	ON-Jr.A	2	1	1	2	0	....	....	....	....	....	....	....	....	....	....	....	....	....	....	....	....	....	....
2011-12	London Knights	OHL	62	21	28	49	48	....	....	....	....	....	....	....	....	....	19	4	5	9	10	....	....	....	....
2012-13	London Knights	OHL	64	39	48	87	71	....	....	....	....	....	....	....	....	....	21	11	21	32	26	....	....	....	....
2013-14	London Knights	OHL	61	34	59	93	90	....	....	....	....	....	....	....	....	....	9	4	6	10	8	....	....	....	....
2014-15	London Knights	OHL	57	32	70	102	66	....	....	....	....	....	....	....	....	....	9	5	4	9	16	....	....	....	....
2015-16	**Arizona**	**NHL**	**81**	**18**	**34**	**52**	**72**	**3**	**0**	**0**	**156**	**11.5**	**3**	**55**	**36.4**	**16:22**	....	....	....	....	....	....	....	....	....
2016-17	**Arizona**	**NHL**	**59**	**9**	**29**	**38**	**40**	**1**	**0**	**1**	**108**	**8.3**	**–9**	**10**	**50.0**	**16:59**	....	....	....	....	....	....	....	....	....
	NHL Totals		**140**	**27**	**63**	**90**	**112**	**4**	**0**	**1**	**264**	**10.2**		**65**	**38.5**	**16:38**	....	....	....	....	....	....	....	....	....

OHL First All-Star Team (2015)

DONSKOI, Joonas
(DAWN-skoy, YOH-nuhs) **S.J.**

Right wing. Shoots right. 6', 190 lbs. Born, Raahe, Finland, April 13, 1992. Florida's 10th pick, 99th overall, in 2010 NHL Draft.

Season	Club	League	GP	G	A	Pts	PIM	PP	SH	GW	S	S%	+/-	TF	F%	Min	GP	G	A	Pts	PIM	PP	SH	GW	Min
			Regular Season														Playoffs								
2007-08	Karpat Oulu U18	Fin-U18	30	18	20	38	26	....	....	....	....	....	....	....	....	....	5	3	4	7	0	....	....	....	....
2008-09	Karpat Oulu U18	Fin-U18	4	2	5	7	0	....	....	....	....	....	....	....	....	....	6	6	7	13	0	....	....	....	....
	Karpat Oulu Jr.	Fin-Jr.	32	7	17	24	12	....	....	....	....	....	....	....	....	....	....	....	....	....	....	....	....	....	....
2009-10	Suomi U20	Finland-2	4	1	0	1	0	....	....	....	....	....	....	....	....	....	....	....	....	....	....	....	....	....	....
	Karpat Oulu Jr.	Fin-Jr.	18	14	15	29	2	....	....	....	....	....	....	....	....	....	12	5	10	15	4	....	....	....	....
	Karpat Oulu	Finland	18	2	2	4	4	....	....	....	....	....	....	....	....	....	....	....	....	....	....	....	....	....	....
	Karpat Oulu U18	Fin-U18	....	....	....	....	....	....	....	....	....	....	....	....	....	....	1	1	1	2	0	....	....	....	....
2010-11	Suomi U20	Finland-2	2	1	0	1	0	....	....	....	....	....	....	....	....	....	....	....	....	....	....	....	....	....	....
	Karpat Oulu	Finland	52	16	11	27	10	....	....	....	....	....	....	....	....	....	3	1	0	1	0	....	....	....	....
2011-12	Karpat Oulu	Finland	52	8	17	25	12	....	....	....	....	....	....	....	....	....	6	3	3	6	0	....	....	....	....
2012-13	Karpat Oulu	Finland	31	4	10	14	8	....	....	....	....	....	....	....	....	....	3	0	1	1	2	....	....	....	....
2013-14	Karpat Oulu	Finland	60	11	26	37	10	....	....	....	....	....	....	....	....	....	16	4	2	6	4	....	....	....	....
2014-15	Karpat Oulu	Finland	58	19	30	49	10	....	....	....	....	....	....	....	....	....	19	6	16	22	6	....	....	....	....
2015-16	**San Jose**	**NHL**	**76**	**11**	**25**	**36**	**20**	**3**	**0**	**1**	**107**	**10.3**	**4**	**3**	**66.7**	**14:09**	**24**	**6**	**6**	**12**	**4**	**0**	**0**	**2**	**15:32**
2016-17	**San Jose**	**NHL**	**61**	**6**	**11**	**17**	**10**	**1**	**0**	**0**	**95**	**6.3**	**–5**	**16**	**50.0**	**13:49**	**5**	**0**	**2**	**2**	**0**	**0**	**0**	**0**	**13:06**
	NHL Totals		**137**	**17**	**36**	**53**	**30**	**4**	**0**	**1**	**202**	**8.4**		**19**	**52.6**	**14:00**	**29**	**6**	**8**	**14**	**4**	**0**	**0**	**2**	**15:07**

Signed as a free agent by **San Jose**, May 19, 2015.

DORSETT, Derek
(DOHRS-iht, DAIR-ihk) **VAN**

Right wing. Shoots right. 6', 192 lbs. Born, Kindersley, SK, December 20, 1986. Columbus' 9th pick, 189th overall, in 2006 NHL Draft.

Season	Club	League	GP	G	A	Pts	PIM	PP	SH	GW	S	S%	+/-	TF	F%	Min	GP	G	A	Pts	PIM	PP	SH	GW	Min
			Regular Season														Playoffs								
2003-04	Swift Current	SMHL	42	19	34	53	132	....	....	....	....	....	....	....	....	....	5	2	6	8	8	....	....	....	....
	Kindersley	SJHL	STATISTICS NOT AVAILABLE																						
2004-05	Kindersley	SJHL	25	12	8	20	172	....	....	....	....	....	....	....	....	....	....	....	....	....	....	....	....	....	....
	Medicine Hat	WHL	51	5	11	16	108	....	....	....	....	....	....	....	....	....	13	5	1	6	35	....	....	....	....
2005-06	Medicine Hat	WHL	68	25	23	48	*279	....	....	....	....	....	....	....	....	....	13	8	4	12	53	....	....	....	....
2006-07	Medicine Hat	WHL	61	19	45	64	206	....	....	....	....	....	....	....	....	....	17	8	8	16	56	....	....	....	....
2007-08	Syracuse Crunch	AHL	64	10	8	18	289	....	....	....	....	....	....	....	....	....	12	0	1	1	56	....	....	....	....
2008-09	**Columbus**	**NHL**	**52**	**4**	**1**	**5**	**150**	**0**	**0**	**1**	**59**	**6.8**	**–1**	**9**	**44.4**	**8:53**	**3**	**0**	**0**	**0**	**2**	**0**	**0**	**0**	**9:11**
	Syracuse Crunch	AHL	7	1	5	6	35	....	....	....	....	....	....	....	....	....	....	....	....	....	....	....	....	....	....
2009-10	**Columbus**	**NHL**	**51**	**4**	**10**	**14**	**105**	**0**	**0**	**0**	**57**	**7.0**	**6**	**33**	**27.3**	**10:53**	....	....	....	....	....	....	....	....	....
2010-11	**Columbus**	**NHL**	**76**	**4**	**13**	**17**	**184**	**0**	**0**	**0**	**112**	**3.6**	**–15**	**51**	**37.3**	**13:12**	....	....	....	....	....	....	....	....	....
2011-12	**Columbus**	**NHL**	**77**	**12**	**8**	**20**	***235**	**2**	**1**	**1**	**137**	**8.8**	**–11**	**28**	**50.0**	**14:42**	....	....	....	....	....	....	....	....	....
2012-13	Salzburg	Austria	4	0	1	1	25	....	....	....	....	....	....	....	....	....	....	....	....	....	....	....	....	....	....
	Columbus	**NHL**	**24**	**3**	**6**	**9**	**53**	**0**	**0**	**0**	**38**	**7.9**	**–11**	**23**	**56.5**	**15:59**	....	....	....	....	....	....	....	....	....
	NY Rangers	**NHL**	....	....	....	....	....	....	....	....	....	....	....	....	....	....	**11**	**0**	**1**	**1**	**28**	**0**	**0**	**0**	**10:46**
2013-14	**NY Rangers**	**NHL**	**51**	**4**	**4**	**8**	**128**	**0**	**0**	**0**	**67**	**6.0**	**–1**	**3**	**0.0**	**11:02**	**23**	**0**	**1**	**1**	**19**	**0**	**0**	**0**	**9:29**
2014-15	**Vancouver**	**NHL**	**79**	**7**	**18**	**25**	**175**	**0**	**2**	**3**	**89**	**7.9**	**4**	**16**	**43.8**	**12:03**	**6**	**0**	**0**	**0**	**20**	**0**	**0**	**0**	**12:37**
2015-16	**Vancouver**	**NHL**	**71**	**5**	**11**	**16**	***177**	**0**	**0**	**0**	**91**	**5.5**	**–13**	**10**	**30.0**	**12:35**	....	....	....	....	....	....	....	....	....
2016-17	**Vancouver**	**NHL**	**14**	**1**	**3**	**4**	**33**	**0**	**0**	**0**	**24**	**4.2**	**–6**	**1**	**100.0**	**9:56**	....	....	....	....	....	....	....	....	....
	NHL Totals		**495**	**44**	**74**	**118**	**1240**	**2**	**3**	**5**	**674**	**6.5**		**174**	**40.2**	**12:17**	**43**	**0**	**2**	**2**	**69**	**0**	**0**	**0**	**10:13**

Signed as a free agent by **Salzburg** (Austria), November 26, 2012. Traded to **NY Rangers** by **Columbus** with Derick Brassard, John Moore and Columbus' 6th round pick (later traded to Minnesota – Minnesota selected Chase Lang) in 2014 NHL Draft for Marian Gaborik, Blake Parlett and Steven Delisle, April 3, 2013. Traded to **Vancouver** by **NY Rangers** for Anaheim's 3rd round pick (previously acquired, NY Rangers selected Keegan Iverson) in 2014 NHL Draft, June 27, 2014.

DOTCHIN, Jake
(DAW-CHIHN, JAYK) **T.B.**

Defense. Shoots right. 6'2", 207 lbs. Born, Cambridge, ON, March 24, 1994. Tampa Bay's 7th pick, 161st overall, in 2012 NHL Draft.

Season	Club	League	GP	G	A	Pts	PIM	PP	SH	GW	S	S%	+/-	TF	F%	Min	GP	G	A	Pts	PIM	PP	SH	GW	Min
			Regular Season														Playoffs								
2009-10	Cambridge	Minor-ON	30	8	19	27	60	....	....	....	....	....	....	....	....	....	11	4	6	10	26	....	....	....	....
	Cambridge	Other	11	5	10	15	6	....	....	....	....	....	....	....	....	....	....	....	....	....	....	....	....	....	....
2010-11	Cambridge	ON-Jr.B	41	5	10	15	88	....	....	....	....	....	....	....	....	....	5	1	3	4	8	....	....	....	....
2011-12	Owen Sound	OHL	64	3	16	19	77	....	....	....	....	....	....	....	....	....	5	0	3	3	8	....	....	....	....
2012-13	Owen Sound	OHL	38	2	12	14	39	....	....	....	....	....	....	....	....	....	....	....	....	....	....	....	....	....	....
	Barrie Colts	OHL	28	2	6	8	42	....	....	....	....	....	....	....	....	....	17	1	4	5	25	....	....	....	....
2013-14	Barrie Colts	OHL	63	11	25	36	121	....	....	....	....	....	....	....	....	....	11	3	2	5	13	....	....	....	....
2014-15	Syracuse Crunch	AHL	55	6	14	20	114	....	....	....	....	....	....	....	....	....	3	0	0	0	0	....	....	....	....
2015-16	Syracuse Crunch	AHL	67	1	10	11	120	....	....	....	....	....	....	....	....	....	....	....	....	....	....	....	....	....	....
2016-17	**Tampa Bay**	**NHL**	**35**	**0**	**11**	**11**	**35**	**0**	**0**	**0**	**50**	**0.0**	**10**	**0**	**0.0**	**18:26**	....	....	....	....	....	....	....	....	....
	Syracuse Crunch	AHL	35	4	9	13	105	....	....	....	....	....	....	....	....	....	19	0	6	6	43	....	....	....	....
	NHL Totals		**35**	**0**	**11**	**11**	**35**	**0**	**0**	**0**	**50**	**0.0**		**0**	**0.0**	**18:26**	....	....	....	....	....	....	....	....	....

DOUGHTY, Drew
(DOW-tee, DROO) **L.A.**

Defense. Shoots right. 6'1", 195 lbs. Born, London, ON, December 8, 1989. Los Angeles' 1st pick, 2nd overall, in 2008 NHL Draft.

Season	Club	League	GP	G	A	Pts	PIM	PP	SH	GW	S	S%	+/-	TF	F%	Min	GP	G	A	Pts	PIM	PP	SH	GW	Min
			Regular Season														Playoffs								
2004-05	Lon. Jr. Knights	Minor-ON	55	19	30	49	31	....	....	....	....	....	....	....	....	....	....	....	....	....	....	....	....	....	....
2005-06	Guelph Storm	OHL	65	5	28	33	40	....	....	....	....	....	....	....	....	....	14	0	13	13	18	....	....	....	....
2006-07	Guelph Storm	OHL	67	21	53	74	76	....	....	....	....	....	....	....	....	....	4	2	3	5	8	....	....	....	....
2007-08	Guelph Storm	OHL	58	13	37	50	68	....	....	....	....	....	....	....	....	....	10	3	6	9	14	....	....	....	....
2008-09	**Los Angeles**	**NHL**	**81**	**6**	**21**	**27**	**56**	**3**	**0**	**1**	**126**	**4.8**	**–17**	**0**	**0.0**	**23:50**	....	....	....	....	....	....	....	....	....
2009-10	**Los Angeles**	**NHL**	**82**	**16**	**43**	**59**	**54**	**9**	**0**	**5**	**142**	**11.3**	**20**	**0**	**0.0**	**24:59**	**6**	**3**	**4**	**7**	**4**	**2**	**0**	**0**	**27:26**
	Canada	Olympics	7	0	2	2	2	....	....	....	....	....	....	....	....	....	....	....	....	....	....	....	....	....	....
2010-11	**Los Angeles**	**NHL**	**76**	**11**	**29**	**40**	**68**	**5**	**0**	**3**	**139**	**7.9**	**13**	**0**	**0.0**	**25:39**	**6**	**2**	**2**	**4**	**8**	**1**	**0**	**0**	**27:08**
2011-12♦	**Los Angeles**	**NHL**	**77**	**10**	**26**	**36**	**69**	**3**	**0**	**3**	**168**	**6.0**	**–2**	**0**	**0.0**	**24:54**	**20**	**4**	**12**	**16**	**14**	**1**	**0**	**0**	**26:09**
2012-13	**Los Angeles**	**NHL**	**48**	**6**	**16**	**22**	**36**	**3**	**0**	**0**	**114**	**5.3**	**4**	**0**	**0.0**	**26:24**	**18**	**2**	**3**	**5**	**8**	**1**	**0**	**0**	**27:57**
2013-14♦	**Los Angeles**	**NHL**	**78**	**10**	**27**	**37**	**64**	**6**	**0**	**2**	**177**	**5.6**	**17**	**0**	**0.0**	**25:43**	**26**	**5**	**13**	**18**	**30**	**1**	**0**	**1**	**28:45**
	Canada	Olympics	6	4	2	6	0	....	....	....	....	....	....	....	....	....	....	....	....	....	....	....	....	....	....
2014-15	**Los Angeles**	**NHL**	**82**	**7**	**39**	**46**	**56**	**1**	**0**	**2**	**219**	**3.2**	**3**	**1**	**0.0**	**29:00**	....	....	....	....	....	....	....	....	....
2015-16	**Los Angeles**	**NHL**	**82**	**14**	**37**	**51**	**52**	**9**	**1**	**3**	**197**	**7.1**	**24**	**0**	**0.0**	**28:01**	**5**	**0**	**1**	**1**	**2**	**0**	**0**	**0**	**30:49**
2016-17	**Los Angeles**	**NHL**	**82**	**12**	**32**	**44**	**46**	**5**	**0**	**1**	**181**	**6.6**	**8**	**1**	**100.0**	**27:09**	....	....	....	....	....	....	....	....	....
	NHL Totals		**688**	**92**	**270**	**362**	**501**	**44**	**1**	**20**	**1463**	**6.3**		**2**	**50.0**	**26:11**	**81**	**16**	**35**	**51**	**66**	**6**	**0**	**1**	**27:51**

OHL All-Rookie Team (2006) • OHL First All-Star Team (2007, 2008) • Canadian Major Junior First All-Star Team (2008) • NHL All-Rookie Team (2009) • NHL Second All-Star Team (2010, 2015) • Olympic All-Star Team (2014) • NHL First All-Star Team (2016) • James Norris Memorial Trophy (2016)

Played in NHL All-Star Game (2015, 2016, 2017)

DOWD, Nic
(DOWD, NIHK) **L.A.**

Center. Shoots right. 6'2", 195 lbs. Born, Huntsville, AL, May 27, 1990. Los Angeles' 10th pick, 198th overall, in 2009 NHL Draft.

Season	Club	League	GP	G	A	Pts	PIM	PP	SH	GW	S	S%	+/-	TF	F%	Min	GP	G	A	Pts	PIM	PP	SH	GW	Min
			Regular Season														Playoffs								
2007-08	Culver Academy	High-IN	45	15	31	46	38	....	....	....	....	....	....	....	....	....	....	....	....	....	....	....	....	....	....
2008-09	St. Louis Bandits	NAHL	3	0	0	0	2	....	....	....	....	....	....	....	....	....	....	....	....	....	....	....	....	....	....
	Wenatchee Wild	NAHL	43	16	33	49	71	....	....	....	....	....	....	....	....	....	13	8	*14	*22	34	....	....	....	....
2009-10	Indiana Ice	USHL	46	16	23	39	48	....	....	....	....	....	....	....	....	....	9	2	4	6	2	....	....	....	....
2010-11	St. Cloud State	WCHA	36	5	13	18	34	....	....	....	....	....	....	....	....	....	....	....	....	....	....	....	....	....	....
2011-12	St. Cloud State	WCHA	39	11	13	24	36	....	....	....	....	....	....	....	....	....	....	....	....	....	....	....	....	....	....
2012-13	St. Cloud State	WCHA	42	14	25	39	41	....	....	....	....	....	....	....	....	....	....	....	....	....	....	....	....	....	....
2013-14	St. Cloud State	NCHC	38	22	18	40	32	....	....	....	....	....	....	....	....	....	....	....	....	....	....	....	....	....	....
	Manchester	AHL	7	0	3	3	0	....	....	....	....	....	....	....	....	....	4	1	0	1	0	....	....	....	....
2014-15	Manchester	AHL	75	9	32	41	44	....	....	....	....	....	....	....	....	....	19	7	6	13	10	....	....	....	....
2015-16	**Los Angeles**	**NHL**	**5**	**0**	**0**	**0**	**2**	**0**	**0**	**0**	**3**	**0.0**	**1**	**34**	**52.9**	**10:35**	....	....	....	....	....	....	....	....	....
	Ontario Reign	AHL	58	14	34	48	49	....	....	....	....	....	....	....	....	....	13	4	7	11	14	....	....	....	....
2016-17	**Los Angeles**	**NHL**	**70**	**6**	**16**	**22**	**25**	**1**	**0**	**2**	**78**	**7.7**	**–15**	**707**	**47.8**	**12:27**	....	....	....	....	....	....	....	....	....
	NHL Totals		**75**	**6**	**16**	**22**	**27**	**1**	**0**	**2**	**81**	**7.4**		**741**	**48.0**	**12:20**	....	....	....	....	....	....	....	....	....

NCHC First All-Star Team (2014) • NCAA West First All-American Team (2014)

						Regular Season											Playoffs								
Season	Club	League	GP	G	A	Pts	PIM	PP	SH	GW	S	S%	+/-	TF	F%	Min	GP	G	A	Pts	PIM	PP	SH	GW	Min

DOWELL, Jake (DOW-uhl, JAYK)

Center. Shoots left. 6', 200 lbs. Born, Eau Claire, WI, March 4, 1985. Chicago's 10th pick, 140th overall, in 2004 NHL Draft.

Season	Club	League	GP	G	A	Pts	PIM	PP	SH	GW	S	S%	+/-	TF	F%	Min	GP	G	A	Pts	PIM	PP	SH	GW	Min
2000-01	Eau Claire Mem.	High-WI	24	25	30	55																			
2001-02	USAHNTDP	U-17	11	5	1	6	14																		
	USAHNTDP	NAHL	44	5	12	17	51																		
2002-03	USAHNTDP	U-18	54	8	17	25	54																		
	USAHNTDP	NAHL	9	2	2	4	13																		
2003-04	U. of Wisconsin	WCHA	37	6	13	19	48																		
2004-05	U. of Wisconsin	WCHA	38	12	14	26	74																		
2005-06	U. of Wisconsin	WCHA	43	5	15	20	42																		
2006-07	U. of Wisconsin	WCHA	41	19	6	25	54																		
	Norfolk Admirals	AHL	9	2	3	5	8										6	0	3	3	4				
2007-08	**Chicago**	**NHL**	19	2	1	3	10	0	1	0	19	10.5	1	170	46.5	11:56									
	Rockford IceHogs	AHL	49	7	10	17	64										12	1	1	2	6				
2008-09	**Chicago**	**NHL**	1	0	0	0	2	0	0	0	0	0.0	1	12	66.7	13:37									
	Rockford IceHogs	AHL	75	6	14	20	128										4	0	0	0	4				
2009-10	**Chicago**	**NHL**	3	1	1	2	5	0	0	0	4	25.0	1	4	50.0	6:56									
	Rockford IceHogs	AHL	78	7	16	23	96										4	0	0	0	0				
2010-11	**Chicago**	**NHL**	79	6	15	21	63	0	0	0	74	8.1	5	652	48.9	11:49	2	0	0	0	0	0	0	0	8:23
2011-12	**Dallas**	**NHL**	52	2	5	7	53	0	0	0	39	5.1	-3	197	47.7	7:38									
2012-13	Houston Aeros	AHL	37	4	5	9	34										4	0	1	1	4				
	Minnesota	**NHL**	2	0	0	0	0	0	0	0	3	0.0	0	3	66.7	8:33									
2013-14	**Minnesota**	**NHL**	1	0	0	0	0	0	0	0	1	0.0	-1	4	50.0	7:09									
	Iowa Wild	AHL	57	7	12	19	56																		
2014-15	Hamilton	AHL	76	5	10	15	75																		
2015-16	Rockford IceHogs	AHL	72	11	24	35	99										3	0	0	0	0				
2016-17	Rockford IceHogs	AHL	66	4	11	15	101																		
	NHL Totals		**157**	**11**	**22**	**33**	**133**	**0**	**1**	**0**	**140**	**7.9**		**1042**	**48.6**	**10:17**	**2**	**0**	**0**	**0**	**0**	**0**	**0**	**0**	**8:23**

Fred T. Hunt Memorial Award (AHL – Sportsmanship) (2014)

Signed as a free agent by **Dallas**, July 1, 2011. Signed as a free agent by **Minnesota**, July 4, 2012. Signed as a free agent by **Hamilton** (AHL), July 28, 2014. Signed as a free agent by **Rockford** (AHL), October 22, 2015.

DOWLING, Justin (DOW-lihng, JUHS-tihn) **DAL**

Center. Shoots left. 5'10", 185 lbs. Born, Cochrane, AB, October 1, 1990.

Season	Club	League	GP	G	A	Pts	PIM	PP	SH	GW	S	S%	+/-	TF	F%	Min	GP	G	A	Pts	PIM	PP	SH	GW	Min
2006-07	Swift Current	WHL	3	0	3	3	0										1	0	0	0	0				
2007-08	Swift Current	WHL	71	7	20	27	4										12	4	3	7	2				
2008-09	Swift Current	WHL	71	22	44	66	16										7	2	4	6	0				
2009-10	Swift Current	WHL	72	32	46	78	19										4	2	2	4	2				
2010-11	Swift Current	WHL	63	20	47	67	18																		
	Abbotsford Heat	AHL	8	1	3	4	2																		
2011-12	Utah Grizzlies	ECHL	26	6	18	24	6										3	0	0	0	2				
	Abbotsford Heat	AHL	22	1	1	2	6																		
2012-13	Idaho Steelheads	ECHL	34	13	33	46	16										9	4	3	7	2				
	Texas Stars	AHL	38	16	14	30	4																		
2013-14	Texas Stars	AHL	74	12	35	47	8										14	4	10	14	4				
2014-15	Texas Stars	AHL	65	24	26	50	22										3	0	0	0	0				
2015-16	Texas Stars	AHL	52	11	35	46	10										4	2	1	3	0				
2016-17	**Dallas**	**NHL**	9	0	2	2	2	0	0	0	11	0.0	0	69	55.1	10:28									
	Texas Stars	AHL	49	8	20	28	8																		
	NHL Totals		**9**	**0**	**2**	**2**	**2**	**0**	**0**	**0**	**11**	**0.0**		**69**	**55.1**	**10:28**									

Signed to a ATO (amateur tryout) contract by **Abbotsford** (AHL), March, 2011. Signed as a free agent by **Idaho** (ECHL), September 4, 2012. Signed as a free agent by **Texas** (AHL), January 7, 2013. Signed as a free agent by **Dallas**, March 26, 2014.

DRAISAITL, Leon (DRIGH-zigh-tuhl, LEE-awn) **EDM**

Center. Shoots left. 6'1", 214 lbs. Born, Cologne, Germany, October 27, 1995. Edmonton's 1st pick, 3rd overall, in 2014 NHL Draft.

Season	Club	League	GP	G	A	Pts	PIM	PP	SH	GW	S	S%	+/-	TF	F%	Min	GP	G	A	Pts	PIM	PP	SH	GW	Min
2010-11	Heil./Mann. Jr.	Ger-Jr.	6	0	1	1	2																		
2011-12	Heil./Mann. Jr.	Ger-Jr.	35	21	35	56	39										8	6	6	12	2				
2012-13	Prince Albert	WHL	64	21	37	58	22										4	0	4	4	0				
2013-14	Prince Albert	WHL	64	38	67	105	24										4	1	2	3	4				
2014-15	**Edmonton**	**NHL**	37	2	7	9	4	1	0	1	49	4.1	-17	315	40.6	12:42									
	Kelowna Rockets	WHL	32	19	34	53	25										19	10	18	28	12				
2015-16	**Edmonton**	**NHL**	72	19	32	51	20	5	0	2	133	14.3	-2	1038	48.4	18:04									
	Bakersfield	AHL	6	1	1	2	4																		
2016-17	**Edmonton**	**NHL**	82	29	48	77	20	10	0	5	172	16.9	7	972	49.0	18:53	13	6	10	16	19	1	0	1	19:32
	NHL Totals		**191**	**50**	**87**	**137**	**44**	**16**	**0**	**8**	**354**	**14.1**		**2325**	**47.6**	**17:22**	**13**	**6**	**10**	**16**	**19**	**1**	**0**	**1**	**19:32**

WHL East First All-Star Team (2014)

DROUIN, Jonathan (droo-EHN, JAWN-ah-thuhn) **MTL**

Left wing. Shoots left. 5'11", 188 lbs. Born, Ste-Agathe, QC, March 28, 1995. Tampa Bay's 1st pick, 3rd overall, in 2013 NHL Draft.

Season	Club	League	GP	G	A	Pts	PIM	PP	SH	GW	S	S%	+/-	TF	F%	Min	GP	G	A	Pts	PIM	PP	SH	GW	Min
2010-11	Lac St-Louis Lions	QAAA	38	22	36	58	38										15	11	17	28	18				
2011-12	Lac St-Louis Lions	QAAA	21	21	29	50	35										17	9	17	26	4				
	Halifax	QMJHL	33	7	22	29	12										17	12	*23	*35	14				
2012-13	Halifax	QMJHL	49	41	64	105	32										16	13	*28	*41	18				
2013-14	Halifax	QMJHL	46	29	*79	108	43																		
2014-15	**Tampa Bay**	**NHL**	70	4	28	32	34	3	0	0	76	5.3	3	21	52.4	13:14	6	0	0	0	2	0	0	0	10:02
	Syracuse Crunch	AHL	2	1	2	3	0																		
2015-16	**Tampa Bay**	**NHL**	21	4	6	10	4	0	0	1	25	16.0	1	19	47.4	14:27	17	5	9	14	14	1	0	1	17:02
	Syracuse Crunch	AHL	17	11	2	13	12																		
2016-17	**Tampa Bay**	**NHL**	73	21	32	53	16	9	0	6	183	11.5	-13	220	43.6	17:42									
	NHL Totals		**164**	**29**	**66**	**95**	**54**	**12**	**0**	**7**	**284**	**10.2**		**260**	**44.6**	**15:23**	**23**	**5**	**9**	**14**	**16**	**1**	**0**	**1**	**15:13**

QMJHL First All-Star Team (2013, 2014) • QMJHL Player of the Year (2013) • Canadian Major Junior Player of the Year (2013)

• Suspended by **Tampa Bay** for failing to report to **Syracuse** (AHL), January 20, 2016. • Suspension lifted by **Tampa Bay**, March 7, 2016. Traded to **Montreal** by **Tampa Bay** with a conditional 6th round pick in 2018 NHL Draft for Mikhail Sergachev and a conditional 2nd round pick in 2018 NHL Draft June 15, 2017.

DUBINSKY, Brandon (doo-BIHN-skee, BRAN-duhn) **CBJ**

Center. Shoots left. 6'2", 216 lbs. Born, Anchorage, AK, April 29, 1986. NY Rangers' 6th pick, 60th overall, in 2004 NHL Draft.

Season	Club	League	GP	G	A	Pts	PIM	PP	SH	GW	S	S%	+/-	TF	F%	Min	GP	G	A	Pts	PIM	PP	SH	GW	Min
2001-02	Alaska All-Stars	AASHA	37	14	24	38																				
2002-03	Portland	WHL	44	8	18	26	35										7	2	2	4	10				
2003-04	Portland	WHL	71	30	48	78	137										5	0	2	2	6				
2004-05	Portland	WHL	68	23	36	59	160										7	4	5	9	8				
2005-06	Portland	WHL	51	21	46	67	98										12	5	10	15	24				
	Hartford	AHL															11	5	5	10	14				
2006-07	**NY Rangers**	**NHL**	6	0	0	0	2	0	0	0	9	0.0	0	26	46.2	8:10									
	Hartford	AHL	71	21	22	43	115										7	1	3	4	12				
2007-08	**NY Rangers**	**NHL**	82	14	26	40	79	1	0	0	157	8.9	8	995	51.5	14:30	10	4	4	8	12	2	0	0	18:59
2008-09	**NY Rangers**	**NHL**	82	13	28	41	112	3	1	7	188	6.9	-6	870	53.6	16:38	7	1	3	4	18	0	0	1	18:14
2009-10	**NY Rangers**	**NHL**	69	20	24	44	54	6	2	5	165	12.1	9	675	51.4	19:33									
2010-11	**NY Rangers**	**NHL**	77	24	30	54	100	4	2	2	202	11.9	-3	875	52.5	20:14	5	2	1	3	2	0	0	1	24:56
2011-12	**NY Rangers**	**NHL**	77	10	24	34	110	0	1	1	140	7.1	16	395	51.9	16:16	9	0	2	2	14	0	0	0	14:27
2012-13	Alaska Aces	ECHL	17	9	7	16	22																		
	Columbus	**NHL**	29	2	18	20	76	1	0	0	50	4.0	2	439	58.3	18:24									
2013-14	**Columbus**	**NHL**	76	16	34	50	98	4	2	2	189	8.5	5	1107	52.9	18:47	6	1	5	6	6	0	0	0	20:43
2014-15	**Columbus**	**NHL**	47	13	23	36	43	0	1	1	100	13.0	11	859	50.8	18:04									

Season	Club	League	Regular Season GP	G	A	Pts	PIM	PP	SH	GW	S	S%	+/-	TF	F%	Min	Playoffs GP	G	A	Pts	PIM	PP	SH	GW	Min
2015-16	Columbus	NHL	75	17	31	48	71	5	0	3	158	10.8	–16	1484	52.6	18:46	....	....	....	....	....	....	....	....	....
2016-17	Columbus	NHL	80	12	29	41	91	1	1	5	115	10.4	16	1488	51.8	17:54	5	1	1	2	6	0	0	0	17:57
	NHL Totals		700	141	267	408	836	25	10	26	1473	9.6		9213	52.4	17:44	42	9	16	25	58	2	0	2	18:43

WHL West Second All-Star Team (2004, 2006)

Traded to **Columbus** by **NY Rangers** with Artem Anisimov, Tim Erixon and NY Rangers' 1st round pick (Kerby Rychel) in 2013 NHL Draft for Rick Nash, Steven Delisle and Columbus' 3rd round pick (Pavel Buchnevich) in 2013 NHL Draft, July 23, 2012. Signed as a free agent by **Alaska** (ECHL), October 1, 2012.

DUCHENE, Matt

(DOO-shayn, MAT) **COL**

Center. Shoots left. 5'11", 195 lbs. Born, Haliburton, ON, January 16, 1991. Colorado's 1st pick, 3rd overall, in 2009 NHL Draft.

Season	Club	League	GP	G	A	Pts	PIM	PP	SH	GW	S	S%	+/-	TF	F%	Min	GP	G	A	Pts	PIM	PP	SH	GW	Min
2006-07	Cent. Ont. Wolves	Minor-ON	52	69	37	106	36	....	....	....	....	....	....	....	....	....	....	....	....	....	....	....	....	....	....
2007-08	Brampton	OHL	64	30	20	50	22	....	....	....	....	....	....	....	....	....	5	1	1	2	10	....	....	....	....
2008-09	Brampton	OHL	57	31	48	79	42	....	....	....	....	....	....	....	....	....	21	14	12	26	21	....	....	....	....
2009-10	Colorado	NHL	81	24	31	55	16	10	1	2	180	13.3	1	1088	44.0	17:44	6	0	3	3	0	0	0	0	19:20
2010-11	Colorado	NHL	80	27	40	67	33	3	0	2	202	13.4	–8	1246	50.4	18:57	....	....	....	....	....	....	....	....	....
2011-12	Colorado	NHL	58	14	14	28	8	5	0	2	132	10.6	–11	391	51.2	16:17	....	....	....	....	....	....	....	....	....
2012-13	Frolunda	Sweden	19	4	10	14	12	....	....	....	....	....	....	....	....	....	....	....	....	....	....	....	....	....	....
	HC Ambri-Piotta	Swiss	4	2	3	5	2	....	....	....	....	....	....	....	....	....	....	....	....	....	....	....	....	....	....
	Colorado	NHL	47	17	26	43	12	2	0	3	132	12.9	–12	893	54.7	20:55	....	....	....	....	....	....	....	....	....
2013-14	Colorado	NHL	71	23	47	70	19	5	0	6	217	10.6	8	1058	50.3	18:30	2	0	3	3	2	0	0	0	20:15
	Canada	Olympics	4	0	0	0	0	....	....	....	....	....	....	....	....	....	....	....	....	....	....	....	....	....	....
2014-15	Colorado	NHL	82	21	34	55	16	2	0	4	207	10.1	3	1217	52.2	18:34	....	....	....	....	....	....	....	....	....
2015-16	Colorado	NHL	76	30	29	59	24	8	0	6	200	15.0	–8	739	57.9	18:35	....	....	....	....	....	....	....	....	....
2016-17	Colorado	NHL	77	18	23	41	12	3	1	3	160	11.3	–34	1098	62.6	18:18	....	....	....	....	....	....	....	....	....
	NHL Totals		572	174	244	418	140	38	2	28	1430	12.2		7730	52.7	18:25	8	0	6	6	2	0	0	0	19:33

NHL All-Rookie Team (2010)

Played in NHL All-Star Game (2011, 2016)

Signed as a free agent by **Frolunda** (Sweden), October 2, 2012. Signed as a free agent by **Ambri-Piotta** (Swiss), December 9, 2012.

DUCLAIR, Anthony

(doo-KLAIR, AN-thuh-nee) **ARI**

Left wing. Shoots left. 5'11", 185 lbs. Born, Pointe-Claire, QC, August 26, 1995. NY Rangers' 3rd pick, 80th overall, in 2013 NHL Draft.

Season	Club	League	GP	G	A	Pts	PIM	PP	SH	GW	S	S%	+/-	TF	F%	Min	GP	G	A	Pts	PIM	PP	SH	GW	Min
2009-10	Laurentides	Minor-QC	59	81	47	128	32	....	....	....	....	....	....	....	....	....	....	....	....	....	....	....	....	....	....
2010-11	Lac St-Louis Lions	QAAA	34	25	32	57	36	....	....	....	....	....	....	....	....	....	14	9	14	23	20	....	....	....	....
2011-12	Quebec Remparts	QMJHL	63	31	35	66	50	....	....	....	....	....	....	....	....	....	11	3	5	8	8	....	....	....	....
2012-13	Quebec Remparts	QMJHL	55	20	30	50	22	....	....	....	....	....	....	....	....	....	11	3	5	8	12	....	....	....	....
2013-14	Quebec Remparts	QMJHL	59	50	49	99	56	....	....	....	....	....	....	....	....	....	....	....	....	....	....	....	....	....	....
2014-15	NY Rangers	NHL	18	1	6	7	4	0	0	0	18	5.6	4	0	0.0	12:09	....	....	....	....	....	....	....	....	....
	Quebec Remparts	QMJHL	26	15	19	34	24	....	....	....	....	....	....	....	....	....	22	8	18	26	18	....	....	....	....
2015-16	Arizona	NHL	81	20	24	44	49	8	0	2	105	19.0	12	1	0.0	14:23	....	....	....	....	....	....	....	....	....
2016-17	Arizona	NHL	58	5	10	15	14	0	0	1	76	6.6	–7	8	50.0	13:18	....	....	....	....	....	....	....	....	....
	Tucson	AHL	16	1	7	8	4	....	....	....	....	....	....	....	....	....	....	....	....	....	....	....	....	....	....
	NHL Totals		157	26	40	66	67	8	0	3	199	13.1		9	44.4	13:44	....	....	....	....	....	....	....	....	....

QMJHL First All-Star Team (2014)

Traded to **Arizona** by **NY Rangers** with John Moore, Tampa Bay's 2nd round pick (previously acquired, later traded to Calgary – Calgary selected Oliver Kylington) in 2015 NHL Draft and NY Rangers' 1st round pick (later traded to Detroit – Detroit selected Dennis Cholowski) in 2016 NHL Draft for Keith Yandle, Chris Summers and Arizona's 4th round pick (Tarmo Reunanen) in 2016 NHL Draft, March 1, 2015.

DUMBA, Matt

(DUHM-ba, MAT) **MIN**

Defense. Shoots right. 6', 183 lbs. Born, Regina, SK, July 25, 1994. Minnesota's 1st pick, 7th overall, in 2012 NHL Draft.

Season	Club	League	GP	G	A	Pts	PIM	PP	SH	GW	S	S%	+/-	TF	F%	Min	GP	G	A	Pts	PIM	PP	SH	GW	Min
2007-08	Calgary Bronks	AMBHL	33	3	8	11	26	....	....	....	....	....	....	....	....	....	2	1	1	2	2	....	....	....	....
2008-09	Calgary Bronks	AMBHL	33	20	18	38	96	....	....	....	....	....	....	....	....	....	....	....	....	....	....	....	....	....	....
2009-10	Edge School	High-AB	41	16	28	44	47	....	....	....	....	....	....	....	....	....	....	....	....	....	....	....	....	....	....
	Red Deer Rebels	WHL	6	0	2	2	4	....	....	....	....	....	....	....	....	....	2	0	0	0	4	....	....	....	....
2010-11	Red Deer Rebels	WHL	62	15	11	26	83	....	....	....	....	....	....	....	....	....	9	2	0	2	20	....	....	....	....
2011-12	Red Deer Rebels	WHL	69	20	37	57	67	....	....	....	....	....	....	....	....	....	....	....	....	....	....	....	....	....	....
2012-13	Red Deer Rebels	WHL	62	16	26	42	80	....	....	....	....	....	....	....	....	....	9	2	2	4	14	....	....	....	....
	Houston Aeros	AHL	3	0	0	0	2	....	....	....	....	....	....	....	....	....	5	0	0	0	0	....	....	....	....
2013-14	Minnesota	NHL	13	1	1	2	2	1	0	0	12	8.3	–5	0	0.0	12:27	....	....	....	....	....	....	....	....	....
	Portland	WHL	26	8	16	24	37	....	....	....	....	....	....	....	....	....	21	8	10	18	33	....	....	....	....
2014-15	Minnesota	NHL	58	8	8	16	23	2	0	2	86	9.3	13	0	0.0	15:01	10	2	2	4	2	2	0	0	16:05
	Iowa Wild	AHL	20	5	9	14	6	....	....	....	....	....	....	....	....	....	....	....	....	....	....	....	....	....	....
2015-16	Minnesota	NHL	81	10	16	26	38	6	0	3	152	6.6	1	0	0.0	16:50	6	0	2	2	6	0	0	0	14:31
2016-17	Minnesota	NHL	76	11	23	34	59	6	0	1	131	8.4	15	0	0.0	20:20	5	0	0	0	2	0	0	0	23:54
	NHL Totals		228	30	48	78	122	15	0	6	381	7.9		0	0.0	17:17	21	2	4	6	10	2	0	0	17:30

• Missed majority of 2013-14 as a healthy reserve.

DUMONT, Gabriel

(doo-MAWNT, gah-BREE-ehl) **T.B.**

Center. Shoots right. 5'10", 181 lbs. Born, Ville Degelis, QC, October 6, 1990. Montreal's 5th pick, 139th overall, in 2009 NHL Draft.

Season	Club	League	GP	G	A	Pts	PIM	PP	SH	GW	S	S%	+/-	TF	F%	Min	GP	G	A	Pts	PIM	PP	SH	GW	Min
2005-06	Ecole Notre Dame	QAAA	29	5	16	21	50	....	....	....	....	....	....	....	....	....	9	0	1	1	12	....	....	....	....
2006-07	Ecole Notre Dame	QAAA	39	30	42	72	127	....	....	....	....	....	....	....	....	....	13	11	12	23	20	....	....	....	....
	Drummondville	QMJHL	8	1	1	2	6	....	....	....	....	....	....	....	....	....	6	0	2	2	0	....	....	....	....
2007-08	Drummondville	QMJHL	59	11	14	25	103	....	....	....	....	....	....	....	....	....	....	....	....	....	....	....	....	....	....
2008-09	Drummondville	QMJHL	51	28	21	49	63	....	....	....	....	....	....	....	....	....	19	6	13	19	32	....	....	....	....
2009-10	Drummondville	QMJHL	62	*51	42	93	127	....	....	....	....	....	....	....	....	....	14	*11	10	21	19	....	....	....	....
	Hamilton	AHL	....	....	....	....	....	....	....	....	....	....	....	....	....	....	11	2	0	2	12	....	....	....	....
2010-11	Hamilton	AHL	64	5	13	18	79	....	....	....	....	....	....	....	....	....	20	6	3	9	6	....	....	....	....
2011-12	Montreal	NHL	3	0	0	0	0	0	0	0	1	0.0	–1	18	16.7	8:34	....	....	....	....	....	....	....	....	....
	Hamilton	AHL	59	13	11	24	55	....	....	....	....	....	....	....	....	....	....	....	....	....	....	....	....	....	....
2012-13	Hamilton	AHL	55	16	15	31	83	....	....	....	....	....	....	....	....	....	....	....	....	....	....	....	....	....	....
	Montreal	NHL	10	1	2	3	13	0	0	0	20	5.0	1	46	63.0	9:41	3	0	0	0	12	0	0	0	6:21
2013-14	Montreal	NHL	2	0	0	0	0	0	0	0	1	0.0	0	8	37.5	6:50	....	....	....	....	....	....	....	....	....
	Hamilton	AHL	74	19	17	36	111	....	....	....	....	....	....	....	....	....	....	....	....	....	....	....	....	....	....
2014-15	Montreal	NHL	3	0	0	0	0	0	0	0	4	0.0	–1	13	84.6	9:07	....	....	....	....	....	....	....	....	....
	Hamilton	AHL	66	20	25	45	88	....	....	....	....	....	....	....	....	....	....	....	....	....	....	....	....	....	....
2015-16	St. John's IceCaps	AHL	71	19	30	49	76	....	....	....	....	....	....	....	....	....	....	....	....	....	....	....	....	....	....
2016-17	Tampa Bay	NHL	39	2	2	4	29	0	0	0	34	5.9	1	242	55.0	9:40	....	....	....	....	....	....	....	....	....
	Syracuse Crunch	AHL	20	5	5	10	24	....	....	....	....	....	....	....	....	....	22	5	6	11	12	....	....	....	....
	NHL Totals		57	3	4	7	42	0	0	0	60	5.0		327	54.7	9:29	3	0	0	0	12	0	0	0	6:21

QMJHL First All-Star Team (2010) • Canadian Major Junior Second All-Star Team (2010)

Signed as a free agent by **Tampa Bay**, July 1, 2016.

DUMOULIN, Brian

(DOO-moh-lihn, BRIGH-uhn) **PIT**

Defense. Shoots left. 6'4", 207 lbs. Born, Biddeford, ME, September 6, 1991. Carolina's 2nd pick, 51st overall, in 2009 NHL Draft.

Season	Club	League	GP	G	A	Pts	PIM	PP	SH	GW	S	S%	+/-	TF	F%	Min	GP	G	A	Pts	PIM	PP	SH	GW	Min
2007-08	Biddeford Tigers	High-ME	24	13	48	61	10	....	....	....	....	....	....	....	....	....	....	....	....	....	....	....	....	....	....
2008-09	N.H. Jr. Monarchs	EJHL	41	7	23	30	30	....	....	....	....	....	....	....	....	....	7	0	3	3	2	....	....	....	....
2009-10	Boston College	H-East	42	1	21	22	16	....	....	....	....	....	....	....	....	....	....	....	....	....	....	....	....	....	....
2010-11	Boston College	H-East	37	3	30	33	6	....	....	....	....	....	....	....	....	....	....	....	....	....	....	....	....	....	....
2011-12	Boston College	H-East	44	7	21	28	26	....	....	....	....	....	....	....	....	....	....	....	....	....	....	....	....	....	....
2012-13	Wilkes-Barre	AHL	73	6	18	24	18	....	....	....	....	....	....	....	....	....	15	2	6	8	6	....	....	....	....
2013-14	Pittsburgh	NHL	6	0	1	1	4	0	0	0	3	0.0	1	0	0.0	19:14	....	....	....	....	....	....	....	....	....
	Wilkes-Barre	AHL	53	5	16	21	21	....	....	....	....	....	....	....	....	....	17	3	9	12	22	....	....	....	....

			Regular Season														Playoffs								
Season	Club	League	GP	G	A	Pts	PIM	PP	SH	GW	S	S%	+/-	TF	F%	Min	GP	G	A	Pts	PIM	PP	SH	GW	Min
2014-15	**Pittsburgh**	**NHL**	**8**	**1**	**0**	**1**	**2**	**0**	**0**	**0**	**4**	**25.0**	**0**	**0**	**0.0**	**15:40**	**5**	**0**	**0**	**0**	**0**	**0**	**0**	**0**	**14:06**
	Wilkes-Barre	AHL	62	4	29	33	18	....	....	....	....	....	....	....	....	....	6	0	3	3	0	....	....	....	....
2015-16 ♦	**Pittsburgh**	**NHL**	**79**	**0**	**16**	**16**	**14**	**0**	**0**	**0**	**101**	**0.0**	**11**	**1**	**100.0**	**18:53**	**24**	**2**	**6**	**8**	**2**	**1**	**0**	**0**	**21:31**
2016-17 ♦	**Pittsburgh**	**NHL**	**70**	**1**	**14**	**15**	**14**	**0**	**0**	**0**	**78**	**1.3**	**0**	**0**	**0.0**	**20:33**	**25**	**1**	**5**	**6**	**6**	**0**	**0**	**1**	**21:59**
	NHL Totals		**163**	**2**	**31**	**33**	**34**	**0**	**0**	**0**	**186**	**1.1**		**1**	**100.0**	**19:27**	**54**	**3**	**11**	**14**	**8**	**1**	**0**	**1**	**21:03**

Hockey East All-Rookie Team (2010) • NCAA Championship All-Tournament Team (2010, 2012) • Hockey East First All-Star Team (2011, 2012) • NCAA East First All-American Team (2011, 2012)
Traded to **Pittsburgh** by **Carolina** with Brandon Sutter and Carolina's 1st round pick (Derrick Pouliot) in 2012 NHL Draft for Jordan Staal, June 22, 2012.

DVORAK, Christian

(duh-VOHR-ak, KRIHS-t'yen) **ARI**

Center. Shoots left. 6', 198 lbs. Born, Palos, IL, February 2, 1996. Arizona's 3rd pick, 58th overall, in 2014 NHL Draft.

Season	Club	League	GP	G	A	Pts	PIM	PP	SH	GW	S	S%	+/-	TF	F%	Min	GP	G	A	Pts	PIM	PP	SH	GW	Min
2009-10	Chicago Mission	T1EHL	31	33	17	50	14	....	....	....	....	....	....	....	....	....	....	....	....	....	....	....	....	....	....
2010-11	Chi. Mission Bant.	T1EHL	22	10	14	24	0	....	....	....	....	....	....	....	....	....	....	....	....	....	....	....	....	....	....
2011-12	Chicago Mission	HPHL	29	21	24	45	2	....	....	....	....	....	....	....	....	....	....	....	....	....	....	....	....	....	....
2012-13	Chi. Mission U18	HPHL	31	19	33	52	4	....	....	....	....	....	....	....	....	....	....	....	....	....	....	....	....	....	....
	Chi. Mission U18	Other	27	16	24	40	4	....	....	....	....	....	....	....	....	....	....	....	....	....	....	....	....	....	....
	Chicago Steel	USHL	9	2	3	5	2	....	....	....	....	....	....	....	....	....	....	....	....	....	....	....	....	....	....
2013-14	London Knights	OHL	33	6	8	14	0	....	....	....	....	....	....	....	....	....	....	....	....	....	....	....	....	....	....
2014-15	London Knights	OHL	66	41	68	109	24	....	....	....	....	....	....	....	....	....	10	5	8	13	0	....	....	....	....
	Portland Pirates	AHL	2	1	1	2	4	....	....	....	....	....	....	....	....	....	5	0	1	1	0	....	....	....	....
2015-16	London Knights	OHL	59	*52	69	121	27	....	....	....	....	....	....	....	....	....	18	14	21	35	4	....	....	....	....
2016-17	**Arizona**	**NHL**	**78**	**15**	**18**	**33**	**22**	**2**	**0**	**1**	**88**	**17.0**	**7**	**1006**	**46.8**	**15:37**	....	....	....	....	....	....	....	....	....
	NHL Totals		**78**	**15**	**18**	**33**	**22**	**2**	**0**	**1**	**88**	**17.0**		**1006**	**46.8**	**15:37**	....	....	....	....	....	....	....	....	....

OHL First All-Star Team (2016)

DWYER, Patrick

(DWIGH-uhr, PAT-rihk)

Right wing. Shoots right. 5'11", 175 lbs. Born, Spokane, WA, June 22, 1983. Atlanta's 3rd pick, 116th overall, in 2002 NHL Draft.

Season	Club	League	GP	G	A	Pts	PIM	PP	SH	GW	S	S%	+/-	TF	F%	Min	GP	G	A	Pts	PIM	PP	SH	GW	Min
99-2000	Great Falls	AWHL	38	5	9	14	35	....	....	....	....	....	....	....	....	....	....	....	....	....	....	....	....	....	....
2000-01	Great Falls	AWHL	40	33	57	90	106	....	....	....	....	....	....	....	....	....	12	10	12	22	....	....	....	....	....
2001-02	Western Mich.	CCHA	38	17	17	34	26	....	....	....	....	....	....	....	....	....	....	....	....	....	....	....	....	....	....
2002-03	Western Mich.	CCHA	33	9	10	19	20	....	....	....	....	....	....	....	....	....	....	....	....	....	....	....	....	....	....
2003-04	Western Mich.	CCHA	35	13	13	26	22	....	....	....	....	....	....	....	....	....	....	....	....	....	....	....	....	....	....
2004-05	Western Mich.	CCHA	36	6	16	22	56	....	....	....	....	....	....	....	....	....	....	....	....	....	....	....	....	....	....
2005-06	Chicago Wolves	AHL	73	16	29	45	49	....	....	....	....	....	....	....	....	....	....	....	....	....	....	....	....	....	....
2006-07	Albany River Rats	AHL	79	16	25	41	39	....	....	....	....	....	....	....	....	....	5	0	1	1	5	....	....	....	....
2007-08	Albany River Rats	AHL	59	13	12	25	29	....	....	....	....	....	....	....	....	....	7	0	2	2	0	....	....	....	....
2008-09	**Carolina**	**NHL**	**13**	**1**	**0**	**1**	**0**	**0**	**0**	**0**	**9**	**11.1**	**–2**	**12**	**41.7**	**8:34**	**2**	**0**	**1**	**1**	**0**	**0**	**0**	**0**	**4:48**
	Albany River Rats	AHL	62	24	16	40	29	....	....	....	....	....	....	....	....	....	....	....	....	....	....	....	....	....	....
2009-10	**Carolina**	**NHL**	**58**	**7**	**5**	**12**	**6**	**0**	**0**	**2**	**80**	**8.8**	**–3**	**224**	**34.8**	**12:30**	....	....	....	....	....	....	....	....	....
2010-11	**Carolina**	**NHL**	**80**	**8**	**10**	**18**	**12**	**0**	**1**	**2**	**104**	**7.7**	**–6**	**238**	**33.6**	**12:35**	....	....	....	....	....	....	....	....	....
2011-12	**Carolina**	**NHL**	**73**	**5**	**7**	**12**	**23**	**0**	**2**	**0**	**120**	**4.2**	**0**	**29**	**51.7**	**15:22**	....	....	....	....	....	....	....	....	....
2012-13	**Carolina**	**NHL**	**46**	**8**	**8**	**16**	**12**	**1**	**1**	**0**	**93**	**8.6**	**–7**	**47**	**36.2**	**15:26**	....	....	....	....	....	....	....	....	....
2013-14	**Carolina**	**NHL**	**75**	**8**	**14**	**22**	**14**	**0**	**2**	**2**	**134**	**6.0**	**–2**	**24**	**37.5**	**14:39**	....	....	....	....	....	....	....	....	....
2014-15	**Carolina**	**NHL**	**71**	**5**	**7**	**12**	**10**	**0**	**0**	**0**	**77**	**6.5**	**–12**	**19**	**26.3**	**12:46**	....	....	....	....	....	....	....	....	....
2015-16	MODO	Sweden	33	0	7	7	6	....	....	....	....	....	....	....	....	....	....	....	....	....	....	....	....	....	....
	MODO	Sweden-Q	....	....	....	....	....	....	....	....	....	....	....	....	....	....	6	1	0	1	29	....	....	....	....
2016-17	Charlotte	AHL	58	14	12	26	20	....	....	....	....	....	....	....	....	....	5	0	0	0	0	....	....	....	....
	NHL Totals		**416**	**42**	**51**	**93**	**77**	**1**	**6**	**6**	**617**	**6.8**		**593**	**35.2**	**13:39**	**2**	**0**	**1**	**1**	**0**	**0**	**0**	**0**	**4:48**

CCHA All-Rookie Team (2002) • CCHA Rookie of the Year (2002)
Signed as a free agent by **Carolina**, July 7, 2006. Signed as a free agent by **MODO** (Sweden), October 23, 2015. Signed as a free agent by **Charlotte** (AHL), October 11, 2016.

DZINGEL, Ryan

(ZIHN-guhl, RIGH-uhn) **OTT**

Center. Shoots left. 6', 190 lbs. Born, Wheaton, IL, March 9, 1992. Ottawa's 10th pick, 204th overall, in 2011 NHL Draft.

Season	Club	League	GP	G	A	Pts	PIM	PP	SH	GW	S	S%	+/-	TF	F%	Min	GP	G	A	Pts	PIM	PP	SH	GW	Min
2006-07	Chicago Mission	MWEHL	31	12	8	20	26	....	....	....	....	....	....	....	....	....	....	....	....	....	....	....	....	....	....
2007-08	Team Illinois	MWEHL	31	6	14	20	20	....	....	....	....	....	....	....	....	....	....	....	....	....	....	....	....	....	....
2008-09	Team Illinois	T1EHL	31	18	15	33	30	....	....	....	....	....	....	....	....	....	....	....	....	....	....	....	....	....	....
2009-10	Team Illinois	T1EHL	31	19	27	46	28	....	....	....	....	....	....	....	....	....	....	....	....	....	....	....	....	....	....
	Lincoln Stars	USHL	36	11	15	26	38	....	....	....	....	....	....	....	....	....	....	....	....	....	....	....	....	....	....
2010-11	Lincoln Stars	USHL	54	23	44	67	8	....	....	....	....	....	....	....	....	....	2	1	0	1	2	....	....	....	....
2011-12	Ohio State	CCHA	33	7	17	24	32	....	....	....	....	....	....	....	....	....	....	....	....	....	....	....	....	....	....
2012-13	Ohio State	CCHA	40	16	22	38	22	....	....	....	....	....	....	....	....	....	....	....	....	....	....	....	....	....	....
2013-14	Ohio State	Big Ten	37	*22	24	*46	34	....	....	....	....	....	....	....	....	....	....	....	....	....	....	....	....	....	....
	Binghamton	AHL	9	2	5	7	9	....	....	....	....	....	....	....	....	....	1	0	0	0	0	....	....	....	....
2014-15	Binghamton	AHL	66	17	17	34	50	....	....	....	....	....	....	....	....	....	....	....	....	....	....	....	....	....	....
2015-16	**Ottawa**	**NHL**	**30**	**3**	**6**	**9**	**11**	**0**	**0**	**0**	**23**	**13.0**	**4**	**4**	**50.0**	**10:48**	....	....	....	....	....	....	....	....	....
	Binghamton	AHL	44	12	24	36	22	....	....	....	....	....	....	....	....	....	....	....	....	....	....	....	....	....	....
2016-17	**Ottawa**	**NHL**	**81**	**14**	**18**	**32**	**30**	**1**	**1**	**1**	**123**	**11.4**	**7**	**30**	**30.0**	**14:23**	**15**	**2**	**1**	**3**	**4**	**1**	**0**	**0**	**12:08**
	NHL Totals		**111**	**17**	**24**	**41**	**41**	**1**	**1**	**1**	**146**	**11.6**		**34**	**32.4**	**13:25**	**15**	**2**	**1**	**3**	**4**	**1**	**0**	**0**	**12:08**

Big Ten First All-Star Team (2014) • NCAA West First All-American Team (2014)

EAKIN, Cody

(EE-kihn, KOH-dee) **VGK**

Center. Shoots left. 6', 190 lbs. Born, Winnipeg, MB, May 24, 1991. Washington's 3rd pick, 85th overall, in 2009 NHL Draft.

Season	Club	League	GP	G	A	Pts	PIM	PP	SH	GW	S	S%	+/-	TF	F%	Min	GP	G	A	Pts	PIM	PP	SH	GW	Min
2006-07	Winnipeg Wild	MMHL	38	29	35	64	62	....	....	....	....	....	....	....	....	....	7	5	4	9	10	....	....	....	....
	Swift Current	WHL	3	0	0	0	0	....	....	....	....	....	....	....	....	....	....	....	....	....	....	....	....	....	....
2007-08	Swift Current	WHL	55	11	6	17	52	....	....	....	....	....	....	....	....	....	12	3	4	7	6	....	....	....	....
2008-09	Swift Current	WHL	54	24	24	48	42	....	....	....	....	....	....	....	....	....	7	3	0	3	10	....	....	....	....
2009-10	Swift Current	WHL	70	47	44	91	71	....	....	....	....	....	....	....	....	....	4	1	1	2	2	....	....	....	....
	Hershey Bears	AHL	4	2	0	2	2	....	....	....	....	....	....	....	....	....	5	0	0	0	2	....	....	....	....
2010-11	Swift Current	WHL	30	18	21	39	24	....	....	....	....	....	....	....	....	....	....	....	....	....	....	....	....	....	....
	Kootenay Ice	WHL	26	18	26	44	19	....	....	....	....	....	....	....	....	....	19	11	16	27	14	....	....	....	....
2011-12	**Washington**	**NHL**	**30**	**4**	**4**	**8**	**4**	**0**	**0**	**0**	**31**	**12.9**	**2**	**40**	**52.5**	**9:17**	....	....	....	....	....	....	....	....	....
	Hershey Bears	AHL	43	13	14	27	10	....	....	....	....	....	....	....	....	....	5	0	1	1	0	....	....	....	....
2012-13	Texas Stars	AHL	35	12	12	24	14	....	....	....	....	....	....	....	....	....	....	....	....	....	....	....	....	....	....
	Dallas	**NHL**	**48**	**7**	**17**	**24**	**31**	**3**	**0**	**1**	**67**	**10.4**	**1**	**626**	**48.6**	**15:05**	....	....	....	....	....	....	....	....	....
2013-14	**Dallas**	**NHL**	**81**	**16**	**19**	**35**	**36**	**3**	**1**	**2**	**161**	**9.9**	**–9**	**1223**	**47.8**	**17:20**	**6**	**2**	**3**	**5**	**0**	**1**	**0**	**1**	**18:32**
2014-15	**Dallas**	**NHL**	**78**	**19**	**21**	**40**	**26**	**2**	**2**	**6**	**142**	**13.4**	**–1**	**1292**	**50.8**	**17:12**	....	....	....	....	....	....	....	....	....
2015-16	**Dallas**	**NHL**	**82**	**16**	**19**	**35**	**42**	**2**	**3**	**1**	**132**	**12.1**	**3**	**1188**	**47.7**	**16:22**	**13**	**1**	**7**	**8**	**8**	**0**	**0**	**1**	**18:49**
2016-17	**Dallas**	**NHL**	**60**	**3**	**9**	**12**	**49**	**0**	**0**	**1**	**82**	**3.7**	**–7**	**1001**	**52.4**	**16:49**	....	....	....	....	....	....	....	....	....
	NHL Totals		**379**	**65**	**89**	**154**	**188**	**10**	**6**	**11**	**615**	**10.6**		**5370**	**49.5**	**16:05**	**19**	**3**	**10**	**13**	**8**	**1**	**0**	**2**	**18:44**

WHL East Second All-Star Team (2010, 2011)
Traded to **Dallas** by **Washington** with Boston's 2nd round pick (previously acquired, Dallas selected Mike Winther) in 2012 NHL Draft for Mike Ribeiro. June 22, 2012. Claimed by **Vegas** from **Dallas** in Expansion Draft, June 21, 2017.

EAVES, Patrick

(EEVZ, PAT-rihk) **ANA**

Right wing. Shoots right. 6', 200 lbs. Born, Calgary, AB, May 1, 1984. Ottawa's 1st pick, 29th overall, in 2003 NHL Draft.

Season	Club	League	GP	G	A	Pts	PIM	PP	SH	GW	S	S%	+/-	TF	F%	Min	GP	G	A	Pts	PIM	PP	SH	GW	Min
99-2000	Shattuck	High-MN	50	23	24	47	....	....	....	....	....	....	....	....	....	....	....	....	....	....	....	....	....	....	....
2000-01	USAHNTDP	U-17	13	7	8	15	3	....	....	....	....	....	....	....	....	....	....	....	....	....	....	....	....	....	....
	USAHNTDP	NAHL	34	12	11	23	75	....	....	....	....	....	....	....	....	....	....	....	....	....	....	....	....	....	....
2001-02	USAHNTDP	U-18	32	19	21	40	87	....	....	....	....	....	....	....	....	....	....	....	....	....	....	....	....	....	....
	USAHNTDP	USHL	9	1	4	5	18	....	....	....	....	....	....	....	....	....	....	....	....	....	....	....	....	....	....
	USAHNTDP	NAHL	8	5	3	8	37	....	....	....	....	....	....	....	....	....	....	....	....	....	....	....	....	....	....
2002-03	Boston College	H-East	14	10	8	18	61	....	....	....	....	....	....	....	....	....	....	....	....	....	....	....	....	....	....
2003-04	Boston College	H-East	34	18	23	41	66	....	....	....	....	....	....	....	....	....	....	....	....	....	....	....	....	....	....

Season	Club	League	GP	G	A	Pts	PIM	PP	SH	GW	S	S%	+/-	TF	F%	Min	GP	G	A	Pts	PIM	PP	SH	GW	Min
			Regular Season														Playoffs								
2004-05	Boston College	H-East	36	19	29	48	36	....	....	....	....	....	....	....	....	....	....	....	....	....	....	....	....	....	....
2005-06	**Ottawa**	**NHL**	**58**	**20**	**9**	**29**	**22**	**5**	**1**	**4**	**100**	**20.0**	**7**	**14**	**21.4**	**12:29**	**10**	**1**	**0**	**1**	**10**	**0**	**0**	**0**	**11:40**
	Binghamton	AHL	18	5	8	13	10	....	....	....	....	....	....	....	....	....	....	....	....	....	....	....	....	....	....
2006-07	**Ottawa**	**NHL**	**73**	**14**	**18**	**32**	**36**	**3**	**1**	**1**	**130**	**10.8**	**1**	**9**	**11.1**	**12:13**	**7**	**0**	**2**	**2**	**2**	**0**	**0**	**0**	**7:23**
2007-08	**Ottawa**	**NHL**	**26**	**4**	**6**	**10**	**6**	**1**	**0**	**1**	**59**	**6.8**	**0**	**1**	**100.0**	**12:44**	....	....	....	....	....	....	....	....	....
	Carolina	**NHL**	**11**	**1**	**4**	**5**	**4**	**1**	**0**	**0**	**22**	**4.5**	**–2**	**2**	**0.0**	**12:51**	....	....	....	....	....	....	....	....	....
2008-09	**Carolina**	**NHL**	**74**	**6**	**8**	**14**	**31**	**1**	**1**	**1**	**115**	**5.2**	**7**	**12**	**41.7**	**11:15**	**18**	**1**	**2**	**3**	**13**	**0**	**0**	**0**	**9:29**
2009-10	**Detroit**	**NHL**	**65**	**12**	**10**	**22**	**26**	**0**	**1**	**1**	**120**	**10.0**	**0**	**14**	**28.6**	**13:26**	**8**	**0**	**0**	**0**	**2**	**0**	**0**	**0**	**11:58**
2010-11	**Detroit**	**NHL**	**63**	**13**	**7**	**20**	**14**	**2**	**1**	**1**	**108**	**12.0**	**–2**	**10**	**30.0**	**12:42**	**11**	**3**	**1**	**4**	**6**	**0**	**0**	**0**	**11:24**
2011-12	**Detroit**	**NHL**	**10**	**0**	**1**	**1**	**2**	**0**	**0**	**0**	**24**	**0.0**	**0**	**5**	**40.0**	**11:03**	....	....	....	....	....	....	....	....	....
2012-13	**Detroit**	**NHL**	**34**	**2**	**6**	**8**	**4**	**0**	**0**	**1**	**42**	**4.8**	**–1**	**11**	**63.6**	**10:35**	**13**	**1**	**2**	**3**	**4**	**0**	**0**	**0**	**10:00**
2013-14	**Detroit**	**NHL**	**25**	**2**	**3**	**5**	**2**	**1**	**0**	**0**	**51**	**3.9**	**–4**	**15**	**46.7**	**11:33**	....	....	....	....	....	....	....	....	....
	Grand Rapids	AHL	8	4	2	6	8	....	....	....	....	....	....	....	....	....	....	....	....	....	....	....	....	....	....
	Nashville	**NHL**	**5**	**0**	**0**	**0**	**0**	**0**	**0**	**0**	**2**	**0.0**	**–3**	**0**	**0.0**	**9:46**	....	....	....	....	....	....	....	....	....
2014-15	**Dallas**	**NHL**	**47**	**14**	**13**	**27**	**8**	**6**	**0**	**2**	**91**	**15.4**	**12**	**5**	**40.0**	**13:43**	....	....	....	....	....	....	....	....	....
2015-16	**Dallas**	**NHL**	**54**	**11**	**6**	**17**	**27**	**5**	**0**	**2**	**86**	**12.8**	**–5**	**11**	**27.3**	**12:58**	**9**	**3**	**3**	**6**	**2**	**2**	**0**	**0**	**15:16**
2016-17	**Dallas**	**NHL**	**59**	**21**	**16**	**37**	**16**	**11**	**0**	**1**	**154**	**13.6**	**–10**	**4**	**50.0**	**16:39**	....	....	....	....	....	....	....	....	....
	Anaheim	**NHL**	**20**	**11**	**3**	**14**	**8**	**2**	**0**	**1**	**55**	**20.0**	**8**	**0**	**0.0**	**15:42**	**7**	**2**	**2**	**4**	**6**	**0**	**0**	**0**	**16:53**
	NHL Totals		**624**	**131**	**110**	**241**	**206**	**38**	**5**	**16**	**1159**	**11.3**		**113**	**35.4**	**12:53**	**83**	**11**	**12**	**23**	**45**	**2**	**0**	**0**	**11:24**

Hockey East Second All-Star Team (2004) • NCAA East Second All-American Team (2004) • Hockey East First All-Star Team (2005) • NCAA East First All-American Team (2005)

• Missed majority of 2002-03 due to neck injury vs. University of Maine (Hockey East), December 7, 2002. Traded to **Carolina** by **Ottawa** with Joe Corvo for Cory Stillman and Mike Commodore, February 11, 2008. • Missed majority of 2007-08 due to shoulder injury at Buffalo, November 21, 2007. Traded to **Boston** by **Carolina** with Carolina's 4th round pick (Craig Cunningham) in 2010 NHL Draft for Aaron Ward, July 24, 2009. Signed as a free agent by **Detroit**, August 4, 2009. • Missed majority of 2011-12 due to head injury vs. Nashville, November 26, 2012. Traded to **Nashville** by **Detroit** with Calle Jarnkrok and Detroit's 2nd round pick (later traded to San Jose – San Jose selected Julius Bergman) in 2014 NHL Draft for David Legwand, March 5, 2014. • Missed majority of 2013-14 due to pre-season knee injury and lower-body injury at Vancouver, March 19, 2014. Signed as a free agent by **Dallas**, July 1, 2014. Traded to **Anaheim** by **Dallas** for Anaheim's 1st round pick (later traded to Chicago – Chicago selected Henri Jokiharju) in 2017 NHL Draft February 24, 2017.

EBERLE, Jordan

(EH-buhr-lee, JOHR-dahn) **NYI**

Center. Shoots right. 5'11", 181 lbs. Born, Regina, SK, May 15, 1990. Edmonton's 1st pick, 22nd overall, in 2008 NHL Draft.

Season	Club	League	GP	G	A	Pts	PIM	PP	SH	GW	S	S%	+/-	TF	F%	Min	GP	G	A	Pts	PIM	PP	SH	GW	Min
2005-06	Calgary Buffaloes	AMHL	31	14	20	34	6	....	....	....	....	....	....	....	....	....	11	7	1	8	8	....	....	....	....
2006-07	Regina Pats	WHL	66	28	27	55	32	....	....	....	....	....	....	....	....	....	6	2	5	7	2	....	....	....	....
2007-08	Regina Pats	WHL	70	42	33	75	20	....	....	....	....	....	....	....	....	....	5	2	4	6	7	....	....	....	....
2008-09	Regina Pats	WHL	61	35	39	74	20	....	....	....	....	....	....	....	....	....	....	....	....	....	....	....	....	....	....
	Springfield	AHL	9	3	6	9	4	....	....	....	....	....	....	....	....	....	....	....	....	....	....	....	....	....	....
2009-10	Regina Pats	WHL	57	50	56	106	32	....	....	....	....	....	....	....	....	....	....	....	....	....	....	....	....	....	....
	Springfield	AHL	11	6	8	14	0	....	....	....	....	....	....	....	....	....	....	....	....	....	....	....	....	....	....
2010-11	**Edmonton**	**NHL**	**69**	**18**	**25**	**43**	**22**	**4**	**2**	**5**	**158**	**11.4**	**–12**	**26**	**42.3**	**17:41**	....	....	....	....	....	....	....	....	....
2011-12	**Edmonton**	**NHL**	**78**	**34**	**42**	**76**	**10**	**10**	**0**	**4**	**180**	**18.9**	**4**	**27**	**44.4**	**17:36**	....	....	....	....	....	....	....	....	....
2012-13	Oklahoma City	AHL	34	25	26	51	10	....	....	....	....	....	....	....	....	....	....	....	....	....	....	....	....	....	....
	Edmonton	**NHL**	**48**	**16**	**21**	**37**	**16**	**3**	**0**	**3**	**133**	**12.0**	**–4**	**19**	**42.1**	**19:00**	....	....	....	....	....	....	....	....	....
2013-14	**Edmonton**	**NHL**	**80**	**28**	**37**	**65**	**18**	**7**	**1**	**4**	**200**	**14.0**	**–11**	**21**	**38.1**	**19:33**	....	....	....	....	....	....	....	....	....
2014-15	**Edmonton**	**NHL**	**81**	**24**	**39**	**63**	**24**	**6**	**0**	**2**	**183**	**13.1**	**–16**	**6**	**16.7**	**19:03**	....	....	....	....	....	....	....	....	....
2015-16	**Edmonton**	**NHL**	**69**	**25**	**22**	**47**	**14**	**7**	**0**	**4**	**173**	**14.5**	**–12**	**8**	**62.5**	**17:51**	....	....	....	....	....	....	....	....	....
2016-17	**Edmonton**	**NHL**	**82**	**20**	**31**	**51**	**16**	**4**	**0**	**0**	**208**	**9.6**	**3**	**20**	**50.0**	**16:46**	**13**	**0**	**2**	**2**	**2**	**0**	**0**	**0**	**14:32**
	NHL Totals		**507**	**165**	**217**	**382**	**120**	**41**	**3**	**22**	**1235**	**13.4**		**127**	**43.3**	**18:11**	**13**	**0**	**2**	**2**	**2**	**0**	**0**	**0**	**14:32**

WHL East First All-Star Team (2008, 2010) • WHL Player of the Year (2010) • Canadian Major Junior First All-Star Team (2010) • Canadian Major Junior Player of the Year (2010)

Played in NHL All-Star Game (2012)

Traded to **NY Islanders** by **Edmonton** for Ryan Strome. June 22, 2017.

EDLER, Alexander

(EHD-luhr, al-EHX-AN-duhr) **VAN**

Defense. Shoots left. 6'3", 215 lbs. Born, Ostersund, Sweden, April 21, 1986. Vancouver's 2nd pick, 91st overall, in 2004 NHL Draft.

Season	Club	League	GP	G	A	Pts	PIM	PP	SH	GW	S	S%	+/-	TF	F%	Min	GP	G	A	Pts	PIM	PP	SH	GW	Min
2001-02	Jamtland	Exhib.	8	0	1	1	2	....	....	....	....	....	....	....	....	....	....	....	....	....	....	....	....	....	....
2002-03	Jamtland	Exhib.	8	2	1	3	0	....	....	....	....	....	....	....	....	....	....	....	....	....	....	....	....	....	....
2003-04	Jamtland Jr.	Swe-Jr.	6	0	3	3	6	....	....	....	....	....	....	....	....	....	....	....	....	....	....	....	....	....	....
	Jamtland	Sweden-3	24	3	6	9	20	....	....	....	....	....	....	....	....	....	....	....	....	....	....	....	....	....	....
2004-05	MODO Jr.	Swe-Jr.	33	8	15	23	40	....	....	....	....	....	....	....	....	....	5	1	0	1	6	....	....	....	....
2005-06	Kelowna Rockets	WHL	62	13	40	53	44	....	....	....	....	....	....	....	....	....	12	3	5	8	12	....	....	....	....
2006-07	**Vancouver**	**NHL**	**22**	**1**	**2**	**3**	**6**	**0**	**0**	**0**	**10**	**10.0**	**3**	**0**	**0.0**	**11:27**	**3**	**0**	**0**	**0**	**2**	**0**	**0**	**0**	**11:51**
	Manitoba Moose	AHL	49	5	21	26	28	....	....	....	....	....	....	....	....	....	8	0	0	0	2	....	....	....	....
2007-08	**Vancouver**	**NHL**	**75**	**8**	**12**	**20**	**42**	**4**	**0**	**0**	**124**	**6.5**	**6**	**1**	**100.0**	**21:20**	....	....	....	....	....	....	....	....	....
	Manitoba Moose	AHL	2	0	1	1	0	....	....	....	....	....	....	....	....	....	....	....	....	....	....	....	....	....	....
2008-09	**Vancouver**	**NHL**	**80**	**10**	**27**	**37**	**54**	**5**	**0**	**1**	**145**	**6.9**	**11**	**1**	**100.0**	**21:08**	**10**	**1**	**7**	**8**	**6**	**1**	**0**	**0**	**22:09**
2009-10	**Vancouver**	**NHL**	**76**	**5**	**37**	**42**	**40**	**2**	**0**	**0**	**161**	**3.1**	**0**	**2**	**0.0**	**22:39**	**12**	**2**	**4**	**6**	**10**	**1**	**0**	**0**	**23:07**
2010-11	**Vancouver**	**NHL**	**51**	**8**	**25**	**33**	**24**	**5**	**0**	**1**	**121**	**6.6**	**13**	**2**	**0.0**	**24:17**	**25**	**2**	**9**	**11**	**8**	**0**	**0**	**0**	**24:46**
2011-12	**Vancouver**	**NHL**	**82**	**11**	**38**	**49**	**34**	**5**	**1**	**0**	**228**	**4.8**	**0**	**3**	**0.0**	**23:52**	**5**	**2**	**0**	**2**	**8**	**1**	**0**	**0**	**24:17**
2012-13	**Vancouver**	**NHL**	**45**	**8**	**14**	**22**	**37**	**5**	**0**	**0**	**113**	**7.1**	**–5**	**1**	**100.0**	**23:51**	**4**	**1**	**0**	**1**	**2**	**0**	**0**	**0**	**26:57**
2013-14	**Vancouver**	**NHL**	**63**	**7**	**15**	**22**	**50**	**4**	**0**	**0**	**178**	**3.9**	**–39**	**3**	**66.7**	**23:17**	....	....	....	....	....	....	....	....	....
	Sweden	Olympics	4	1	1	2	0	....	....	....	....	....	....	....	....	....	....	....	....	....	....	....	....	....	....
2014-15	**Vancouver**	**NHL**	**74**	**8**	**23**	**31**	**54**	**5**	**0**	**2**	**175**	**4.6**	**13**	**1**	**0.0**	**23:59**	**6**	**0**	**3**	**3**	**4**	**0**	**0**	**0**	**23:41**
2015-16	**Vancouver**	**NHL**	**52**	**6**	**14**	**20**	**46**	**3**	**0**	**0**	**111**	**5.4**	**–8**	**0**	**0.0**	**24:27**	....	....	....	....	....	....	....	....	....
2016-17	**Vancouver**	**NHL**	**68**	**6**	**15**	**21**	**36**	**2**	**0**	**0**	**138**	**4.3**	**–20**	**3**	**66.7**	**24:19**	....	....	....	....	....	....	....	....	....
	NHL Totals		**688**	**78**	**222**	**300**	**423**	**40**	**1**	**4**	**1504**	**5.2**		**17**	**41.2**	**22:49**	**65**	**8**	**23**	**31**	**40**	**3**	**0**	**0**	**23:28**

Played in NHL All-Star Game (2012)

EDMUNDSON, Joel

(EHD-muhnd-suhn, JOHL) **ST.L.**

Defense. Shoots left. 6'4", 207 lbs. Born, Brandon, MB, June 28, 1993. St. Louis' 3rd pick, 46th overall, in 2011 NHL Draft.

Season	Club	League	GP	G	A	Pts	PIM	PP	SH	GW	S	S%	+/-	TF	F%	Min	GP	G	A	Pts	PIM	PP	SH	GW	Min
2008-09	Brandon	MMHL	41	5	18	23	58	....	....	....	....	....	....	....	....	....	6	2	4	6	4	....	....	....	....
2009-10	Brandon	MMHL	44	10	25	35	54	....	....	....	....	....	....	....	....	....	7	0	5	5	10	....	....	....	....
2010-11	Moose Jaw	WHL	71	2	18	20	95	....	....	....	....	....	....	....	....	....	6	0	0	0	2	....	....	....	....
2011-12	Moose Jaw	WHL	56	4	19	23	91	....	....	....	....	....	....	....	....	....	14	3	2	5	12	....	....	....	....
2012-13	Moose Jaw	WHL	29	2	6	8	70	....	....	....	....	....	....	....	....	....	....	....	....	....	....	....	....	....	....
	Kamloops Blazers	WHL	34	7	10	17	71	....	....	....	....	....	....	....	....	....	15	3	5	8	29	....	....	....	....
2013-14	Chicago Wolves	AHL	64	4	4	8	108	....	....	....	....	....	....	....	....	....	5	0	0	0	16	....	....	....	....
2014-15	Chicago Wolves	AHL	30	4	8	12	49	....	....	....	....	....	....	....	....	....	5	2	0	2	2	....	....	....	....
2015-16	**St. Louis**	**NHL**	**67**	**1**	**8**	**9**	**63**	**0**	**0**	**0**	**90**	**1.1**	**0**	**0**	**0.0**	**14:56**	**16**	**1**	**0**	**1**	**8**	**0**	**0**	**0**	**10:56**
	Chicago Wolves	AHL	6	0	0	0	15	....	....	....	....	....	....	....	....	....	....	....	....	....	....	....	....	....	....
2016-17	**St. Louis**	**NHL**	**69**	**3**	**12**	**15**	**60**	**0**	**0**	**1**	**81**	**3.7**	**11**	**0**	**0.0**	**17:46**	**11**	**3**	**3**	**6**	**14**	**0**	**0**	**1**	**21:06**
	NHL Totals		**136**	**4**	**20**	**24**	**123**	**0**	**0**	**1**	**171**	**2.3**		**0**	**0.0**	**16:22**	**27**	**4**	**3**	**7**	**22**	**0**	**0**	**1**	**15:05**

EHLERS, Nikolaj

(EE-luhrs, NIH-koh-ligh) **WPG**

Left wing. Shoots left. 6', 172 lbs. Born, Aalborg, Denmark, February 14, 1996. Winnipeg's 1st pick, 9th overall, in 2014 NHL Draft.

Season	Club	League	GP	G	A	Pts	PIM	PP	SH	GW	S	S%	+/-	TF	F%	Min	GP	G	A	Pts	PIM	PP	SH	GW	Min
2009-10	Biel U17	Swiss-U17	1	0	0	0	0	....	....	....	....	....	....	....	....	....	1	0	0	0	0	....	....	....	....
2010-11	Biel U17	Swiss-U17	28	19	11	30	8	....	....	....	....	....	....	....	....	....	7	7	9	16	6	....	....	....	....
2011-12	Biel U17	Swiss-U17	7	4	5	9	12	....	....	....	....	....	....	....	....	....	10	5	8	13	6	....	....	....	....
	Biel Jr.	Swiss-Jr.	32	19	19	38	12	....	....	....	....	....	....	....	....	....	....	....	....	....	....	....	....	....	....
2012-13	Biel Jr.	Swiss-Jr.	34	30	23	53	36	....	....	....	....	....	....	....	....	....	....	....	....	....	....	....	....	....	....
	EHC Biel-Bienne	Swiss	11	1	1	2	0	....	....	....	....	....	....	....	....	....	7	0	3	3	0	....	....	....	....
2013-14	Halifax	QMJHL	63	49	55	104	51	....	....	....	....	....	....	....	....	....	16	11	17	28	18	....	....	....	....
2014-15	Halifax	QMJHL	51	37	64	101	67	....	....	....	....	....	....	....	....	....	14	10	21	31	14	....	....	....	....
2015-16	**Winnipeg**	**NHL**	**72**	**15**	**23**	**38**	**21**	**4**	**0**	**0**	**167**	**9.0**	**3**	**2**	**0.0**	**16:06**	....	....	....	....	....	....	....	....	....
2016-17	**Winnipeg**	**NHL**	**82**	**25**	**39**	**64**	**38**	**5**	**0**	**4**	**204**	**12.3**	**1**	**4**	**0.0**	**17:29**	....	....	....	....	....	....	....	....	....
	NHL Totals		**154**	**40**	**62**	**102**	**59**	**9**	**0**	**4**	**371**	**10.8**		**6**	**0.0**	**16:50**	....	....	....	....	....	....	....	....	....

QMJHL All-Rookie Team (2014) • QMJHL Second All-Star Team (2014) • Canadian Major Junior Rookie of the Year (2014) • QMJHL First All-Star Team (2015)

EICHEL, Jack
(IGH-kuhl, JAK) **BUF**

Center. Shoots right. 6'2", 201 lbs. Born, North Chelmsford, MA, October 28, 1996. Buffalo's 1st pick, 2nd overall, in 2015 NHL Draft.

			Regular Season															Playoffs								
Season	Club	League	GP	G	A	Pts	PIM	PP	SH	GW	S	S%	+/-	TF	F%	Min	GP	G	A	Pts	PIM	PP	SH	GW	Min
2010-11	Bos. Jr. Bruins	EmJHL	40	15	21	36	16	....	....	....	....	....	....	....	....	....	7	2	5	7	6	....	....	....	....
2011-12	Bos. Jr. Bruins	EmJHL	36	39	47	86	36	....	....	....	....	....	....	....	....	....	5	3	1	4	0	....	....	....	....
	Bos. Jr. Bruins	EJHL	3	0	0	0	0	....	....	....	....	....	....	....	....	....	....	....	....	....	....	....	....	....	....
2012-13	USAHNTDP	USHL	35	13	14	27	14	....	....	....	....	....	....	....	....	....	....	....	....	....	....	....	....	....	....
	USAHNTDP	U-17	16	15	8	23	10	....	....	....	....	....	....	....	....	....	....	....	....	....	....	....	....	....	....
	USAHNTDP	U-18	7	1	1	2	6	....	....	....	....	....	....	....	....	....	....	....	....	....	....	....	....	....	....
2013-14	USAHNTDP	USHL	24	20	25	45	20	....	....	....	....	....	....	....	....	....	....	....	....	....	....	....	....	....	....
	USAHNTDP	U-18	29	18	24	42	22	....	....	....	....	....	....	....	....	....	....	....	....	....	....	....	....	....	....
2014-15	Boston University	H-East	40	*26	*45	*71	28	....	....	....	....	....	....	....	....	....	....	....	....	....	....	....	....	....	....
2015-16	**Buffalo**	**NHL**	**81**	**24**	**32**	**56**	**22**	**8**	**0**	**5**	**238**	**10.1**	**-16**	**980**	**41.0**	**19:07**	....	....	....	....	....	....	....	....	....
2016-17	**Buffalo**	**NHL**	**61**	**24**	**33**	**57**	**22**	**10**	**0**	**4**	**249**	**9.6**	**-13**	**796**	**38.9**	**19:55**	....	....	....	....	....	....	....	....	....
	NHL Totals		**142**	**48**	**65**	**113**	**44**	**18**	**0**	**9**	**487**	**9.9**		**1776**	**40.1**	**19:28**	....	....	....	....	....	....	....	....	....

Hockey East All-Rookie Team (2015) • Hockey East First All-Star Team (2015) • Hockey East Rookie of the Year (2015) • Hockey East Player of the Year (2015) • NCAA East First All-American Team (2015) • NCAA Championship All-Tournament Team (2015) • Hobey Baker Memorial Award (Top U.S. Collegiate Player) (2015) • NHL All-Rookie Team (2016)

EKBLAD, Aaron
(EHK-blad, AIR-uhn) **FLA**

Defense. Shoots right. 6'4", 216 lbs. Born, Windsor, ON, February 7, 1996. Florida's 1st pick, 1st overall, in 2014 NHL Draft.

Season	Club	League	GP	G	A	Pts	PIM	PP	SH	GW	S	S%	+/-	TF	F%	Min	GP	G	A	Pts	PIM	PP	SH	GW	Min
2010-11	Sun County	Minor-ON	30	4	30	34	34	....	....	....	....	....	....	....	....	....	18	5	16	21	14	....	....	....	....
	Sun County	Other	14	5	7	12	18	....	....	....	....	....	....	....	....	....	....	....	....	....	....	....	....	....	....
2011-12	Barrie Colts	OHL	63	10	19	29	34	....	....	....	....	....	....	....	....	....	13	2	3	5	8	....	....	....	....
2012-13	Barrie Colts	OHL	54	7	27	34	64	....	....	....	....	....	....	....	....	....	22	7	10	17	28	....	....	....	....
2013-14	Barrie Colts	OHL	58	23	30	53	91	....	....	....	....	....	....	....	....	....	9	2	4	6	14	....	....	....	....
2014-15	**Florida**	**NHL**	**81**	**12**	**27**	**39**	**32**	**6**	**0**	**4**	**170**	**7.1**	**12**	**0**	**0.0**	**21:49**	....	....	....	....	....	....	....	....	....
2015-16	**Florida**	**NHL**	**78**	**15**	**21**	**36**	**41**	**3**	**0**	**4**	**182**	**8.2**	**18**	**0**	**0.0**	**21:41**	**6**	**0**	**1**	**1**	**0**	**0**	**0**	**0**	**25:37**
2016-17	**Florida**	**NHL**	**68**	**10**	**11**	**21**	**58**	**4**	**1**	**2**	**225**	**4.4**	**-23**	**0**	**0.0**	**21:28**	....	....	....	....	....	....	....	....	....
	NHL Totals		**227**	**37**	**59**	**96**	**131**	**13**	**1**	**10**	**577**	**6.4**		**0**	**0.0**	**21:40**	**6**	**0**	**1**	**1**	**0**	**0**	**0**	**0**	**25:37**

OHL First All-Star Team (2014) • NHL All-Rookie Team (2015) • Calder Memorial Trophy (2015)
Played in NHL All-Star Game (2015, 2016)

EKHOLM, Mattias
(EHK-hohlm, ma-TEE-uhs) **NSH**

Defense. Shoots left. 6'4", 215 lbs. Born, Borlange, Sweden, May 24, 1990. Nashville's 7th pick, 102nd overall, in 2009 NHL Draft.

Season	Club	League	GP	G	A	Pts	PIM	PP	SH	GW	S	S%	+/-	TF	F%	Min	GP	G	A	Pts	PIM	PP	SH	GW	Min
2006-07	Mora IK U18	Swe-U18	5	2	2	4	6	....	....	....	....	....	....	....	....	....	....	....	....	....	....	....	....	....	....
	Mora IK Jr.	Swe-Jr.	36	0	4	4	28	....	....	....	....	....	....	....	....	....	2	0	0	0	0	....	....	....	....
2007-08	Mora IK U18	Swe-U18	9	4	5	9	12	....	....	....	....	....	....	....	....	....	....	....	....	....	....	....	....	....	....
	Mora IK Jr.	Swe-Jr.	37	5	7	12	54	....	....	....	....	....	....	....	....	....	....	....	....	....	....	....	....	....	....
	Mora IK	Sweden	1	0	0	0	0	....	....	....	....	....	....	....	....	....	....	....	....	....	....	....	....	....	....
	Mora IK	Sweden-Q	6	0	0	0	2	....	....	....	....	....	....	....	....	....	....	....	....	....	....	....	....	....	....
2008-09	Mora IK Jr.	Swe-Jr.	21	3	5	8	32	....	....	....	....	....	....	....	....	....	....	....	....	....	....	....	....	....	....
	Mora IK	Sweden-2	38	2	11	13	12	....	....	....	....	....	....	....	....	....	3	0	0	0	4	....	....	....	....
2009-10	Mora IK	Sweden-2	41	1	21	22	54	....	....	....	....	....	....	....	....	....	2	0	0	0	6	....	....	....	....
2010-11	Brynas IF Gavle	Sweden	55	10	23	33	38	....	....	....	....	....	....	....	....	....	5	0	4	4	10	....	....	....	....
2011-12	**Nashville**	**NHL**	**2**	**0**	**0**	**0**	**0**	**0**	**0**	**0**	**1**	**0.0**	**-1**	**0**	**0.0**	**12:25**	....	....	....	....	....	....	....	....	....
	Brynas IF Gavle	Sweden	41	9	8	17	55	....	....	....	....	....	....	....	....	....	17	1	8	9	12	....	....	....	....
2012-13	Milwaukee	AHL	59	10	22	32	30	....	....	....	....	....	....	....	....	....	4	0	1	1	0	....	....	....	....
	Nashville	**NHL**	**1**	**0**	**0**	**0**	**0**	**0**	**0**	**0**	**0**	**0.0**	**-1**	**0**	**0.0**	**16:05**	....	....	....	....	....	....	....	....	....
2013-14	**Nashville**	**NHL**	**62**	**1**	**8**	**9**	**10**	**0**	**0**	**0**	**58**	**1.7**	**-8**	**0**	**0.0**	**16:49**	....	....	....	....	....	....	....	....	....
2014-15	**Nashville**	**NHL**	**80**	**7**	**11**	**18**	**52**	**1**	**0**	**1**	**86**	**8.1**	**12**	**0**	**0.0**	**19:01**	**6**	**1**	**0**	**1**	**2**	**0**	**0**	**0**	**26:25**
2015-16	**Nashville**	**NHL**	**82**	**8**	**27**	**35**	**44**	**1**	**1**	**3**	**114**	**7.0**	**14**	**0**	**0.0**	**20:15**	**14**	**3**	**4**	**7**	**4**	**0**	**0**	**0**	**23:48**
2016-17	**Nashville**	**NHL**	**82**	**3**	**20**	**23**	**34**	**0**	**0**	**1**	**120**	**2.5**	**4**	**0**	**0.0**	**23:28**	**22**	**1**	**10**	**11**	**38**	**1**	**0**	**0**	**25:20**
	NHL Totals		**309**	**19**	**66**	**85**	**140**	**2**	**1**	**5**	**379**	**5.0**		**0**	**0.0**	**20:01**	**42**	**5**	**14**	**19**	**44**	**1**	**0**	**0**	**24:59**

EKMAN-LARSSON, Oliver
(EHK-man-LAHR-suhn, AW-lih-vuhr) **ARI**

Defense. Shoots left. 6'2", 200 lbs. Born, Karlskrona, Sweden, July 17, 1991. Phoenix's 1st pick, 6th overall, in 2009 NHL Draft.

Season	Club	League	GP	G	A	Pts	PIM	PP	SH	GW	S	S%	+/-	TF	F%	Min	GP	G	A	Pts	PIM	PP	SH	GW	Min
2005-06	Tingsryds AIF Jr.	Swe-Jr.	1	0	0	0	2	....	....	....	....	....	....	....	....	....	....	....	....	....	....	....	....	....	....
2006-07	Tingsryds AIF U18	Swe-U18	23	0	3	3	28	....	....	....	....	....	....	....	....	....	....	....	....	....	....	....	....	....	....
2007-08	Tingsryds AIF U18	Swe-U18	12	2	3	5	57	....	....	....	....	....	....	....	....	....	....	....	....	....	....	....	....	....	....
	Tingsryds AIF Jr.	Swe-Jr.	7	2	4	6	16	....	....	....	....	....	....	....	....	....	....	....	....	....	....	....	....	....	....
	Tingsryds AIF	Sweden-3	27	3	5	8	10	....	....	....	....	....	....	....	....	....	....	....	....	....	....	....	....	....	....
2008-09	Leksands IF	Sweden-2	47	5	16	21	38	....	....	....	....	....	....	....	....	....	....	....	....	....	....	....	....	....	....
2009-10	Leksands IF	Sweden-2	52	11	22	33	106	....	....	....	....	....	....	....	....	....	....	....	....	....	....	....	....	....	....
2010-11	**Phoenix**	**NHL**	**48**	**1**	**10**	**11**	**24**	**0**	**0**	**0**	**50**	**2.0**	**3**	**0**	**0.0**	**15:02**	....	....	....	....	....	....	....	....	....
	San Antonio	AHL	15	3	7	10	16	....	....	....	....	....	....	....	....	....	....	....	....	....	....	....	....	....	....
2011-12	**Phoenix**	**NHL**	**82**	**13**	**19**	**32**	**32**	**2**	**1**	**2**	**147**	**8.8**	**0**	**0**	**0.0**	**22:07**	**16**	**1**	**3**	**4**	**8**	**1**	**0**	**1**	**25:47**
2012-13	Portland Pirates	AHL	20	7	14	21	28	....	....	....	....	....	....	....	....	....	....	....	....	....	....	....	....	....	....
	Phoenix	**NHL**	**48**	**3**	**21**	**24**	**26**	**0**	**0**	**1**	**101**	**3.0**	**5**	**0**	**0.0**	**25:06**	....	....	....	....	....	....	....	....	....
2013-14	**Phoenix**	**NHL**	**80**	**15**	**29**	**44**	**50**	**8**	**0**	**6**	**199**	**7.5**	**-4**	**1**	**0.0**	**25:54**	....	....	....	....	....	....	....	....	....
	Sweden	Olympics	6	0	3	3	2	....	....	....	....	....	....	....	....	....	....	....	....	....	....	....	....	....	....
2014-15	**Arizona**	**NHL**	**82**	**23**	**20**	**43**	**40**	**10**	**1**	**7**	**264**	**8.7**	**-18**	**0**	**0.0**	**25:13**	....	....	....	....	....	....	....	....	....
2015-16	**Arizona**	**NHL**	**75**	**21**	**34**	**55**	**96**	**12**	**0**	**8**	**228**	**9.2**	**-6**	**0**	**0.0**	**24:46**	....	....	....	....	....	....	....	....	....
2016-17	**Arizona**	**NHL**	**79**	**12**	**27**	**39**	**48**	**8**	**0**	**1**	**145**	**8.3**	**-25**	**0**	**0.0**	**24:37**	....	....	....	....	....	....	....	....	....
	NHL Totals		**494**	**88**	**160**	**248**	**316**	**40**	**2**	**25**	**1134**	**7.8**		**1**	**0.0**	**23:39**	**16**	**1**	**3**	**4**	**8**	**1**	**0**	**1**	**25:47**

Played in NHL All-Star Game (2015)

ELIE, Remi
(EH-lee, REH-mee) **DAL**

Left wing. Shoots left. 6'1", 210 lbs. Born, Cornwall, ON, April 16, 1995. Dallas' 3rd pick, 40th overall, in 2013 NHL Draft.

Season	Club	League	GP	G	A	Pts	PIM	PP	SH	GW	S	S%	+/-	TF	F%	Min	GP	G	A	Pts	PIM	PP	SH	GW	Min
2010-11	E. Ont. Wild MM	Minor-ON	29	15	24	39	43	....	....	....	....	....	....	....	....	....	5	3	3	6	6	....	....	....	....
	E. Ont. Wild Mid.	Minor-ON	2	0	2	2	2	....	....	....	....	....	....	....	....	....	1	1	0	1	4	....	....	....	....
2011-12	Hawkesbury	ON-Jr.A	59	21	25	46	39	....	....	....	....	....	....	....	....	....	9	5	4	9	12	....	....	....	....
2012-13	London Knights	OHL	65	7	10	17	34	....	....	....	....	....	....	....	....	....	21	4	4	8	8	....	....	....	....
2013-14	London Knights	OHL	6	1	2	3	4	....	....	....	....	....	....	....	....	....	....	....	....	....	....	....	....	....	....
	Belleville Bulls	OHL	61	28	37	65	44	....	....	....	....	....	....	....	....	....	....	....	....	....	....	....	....	....	....
2014-15	Belleville Bulls	OHL	35	14	20	34	24	....	....	....	....	....	....	....	....	....	....	....	....	....	....	....	....	....	....
	Erie Otters	OHL	28	16	26	42	14	....	....	....	....	....	....	....	....	....	20	4	20	24	20	....	....	....	....
2015-16	Texas Stars	AHL	64	6	11	17	51	....	....	....	....	....	....	....	....	....	4	0	0	0	0	....	....	....	....
2016-17	**Dallas**	**NHL**	**18**	**1**	**6**	**7**	**8**	**0**	**0**	**0**	**15**	**6.7**	**5**	**1**	**100.0**	**15:38**	....	....	....	....	....	....	....	....	....
	Texas Stars	AHL	53	9	19	28	37	....	....	....	....	....	....	....	....	....	....	....	....	....	....	....	....	....	....
	NHL Totals		**18**	**1**	**6**	**7**	**8**	**0**	**0**	**0**	**15**	**6.7**		**1**	**100.0**	**15:38**	....	....	....	....	....	....	....	....	....

ELLER, Lars
(EHL-uhr, LARZ) **WSH**

Center. Shoots left. 6'2", 207 lbs. Born, Rodovre, Denmark, May 8, 1989. St. Louis' 1st pick, 13th overall, in 2007 NHL Draft.

Season	Club	League	GP	G	A	Pts	PIM	PP	SH	GW	S	S%	+/-	TF	F%	Min	GP	G	A	Pts	PIM	PP	SH	GW	Min
2004-05	Rodovre IK Jr.	Den-Jr.	28	21	26	47	20	....	....	....	....	....	....	....	....	....	....	....	....	....	....	....	....	....	....
	Rodovre	Denmark	1	3	1	4	0	....	....	....	....	....	....	....	....	....	....	....	....	....	....	....	....	....	....
2005-06	Frolunda U18	Swe-U18	8	2	4	6	10	....	....	....	....	....	....	....	....	....	2	0	0	0	0	....	....	....	....
	Frolunda Jr.	Swe-Jr.	36	7	7	14	6	....	....	....	....	....	....	....	....	....	2	0	0	0	0	....	....	....	....
2006-07	Frolunda U18	Swe-U18	3	1	4	5	6	....	....	....	....	....	....	....	....	....	6	3	2	5	8	....	....	....	....
	Frolunda Jr.	Swe-Jr.	39	18	37	55	58	....	....	....	....	....	....	....	....	....	8	4	1	5	24	....	....	....	....
2007-08	Boras HC	Sweden-2	19	2	6	8	8	....	....	....	....	....	....	....	....	....	....	....	....	....	....	....	....	....	....
	Frolunda Jr.	Swe-Jr.	9	4	4	8	10	....	....	....	....	....	....	....	....	....	7	5	6	11	14	....	....	....	....
	Frolunda	Sweden	14	0	2	2	4	....	....	....	....	....	....	....	....	....	7	0	1	1	2	....	....	....	....

								Regular Season									Playoffs								
Season	Club	League	GP	G	A	Pts	PIM	PP	SH	GW	S	S%	+/-	TF	F%	Min	GP	G	A	Pts	PIM	PP	SH	GW	Min
2008-09	Frolunda	Sweden	48	12	17	29	28	....	....	....	....	....	....	....	....	....	10	3	1	4	12	....	....	....	....
	Denmark	Oly-Q	3	1	1	2	8	....	....	....	....	....	....	....	....	....	....	....	....	....	....	....	....	....	....
2009-10	**St. Louis**	**NHL**	**7**	**2**	**0**	**2**	**4**	**1**	**0**	**0**	**8**	**25.0**	**2**	**19**	**47.4**	**10:49**	....	....	....	....	....	....	....	....	....
	Peoria Rivermen	AHL	70	18	39	57	84	....	....	....	....	....	....	....	....	....	....	....	....	....	....	....	....	....	....
2010-11	**Montreal**	**NHL**	**77**	**7**	**10**	**17**	**48**	**0**	**0**	**2**	**79**	**8.9**	**–4**	**431**	**42.5**	**11:08**	**7**	**0**	**2**	**2**	**4**	**0**	**0**	**0**	**13:04**
2011-12	**Montreal**	**NHL**	**79**	**16**	**12**	**28**	**66**	**2**	**2**	**2**	**129**	**12.4**	**–5**	**685**	**46.6**	**15:19**	....	....	....	....	....	....	....	....	....
2012-13	JYP Jyvaskyla	Finland	15	5	10	15	18	....	....	....	....	....	....	....	....	....	....	....	....	....	....	....	....	....	....
	Montreal	**NHL**	**46**	**8**	**22**	**30**	**45**	**1**	**0**	**1**	**84**	**9.5**	**8**	**542**	**49.3**	**14:50**	**1**	**0**	**0**	**0**	**0**	**0**	**0**	**0**	**8:43**
2013-14	**Montreal**	**NHL**	**77**	**12**	**14**	**26**	**68**	**2**	**1**	**3**	**137**	**8.8**	**–15**	**979**	**53.2**	**15:58**	**17**	**5**	**8**	**13**	**18**	**0**	**1**	**1**	**16:27**
2014-15	**Montreal**	**NHL**	**77**	**15**	**12**	**27**	**42**	**1**	**0**	**7**	**150**	**10.0**	**–6**	**784**	**51.7**	**15:30**	**12**	**1**	**2**	**3**	**4**	**0**	**1**	**0**	**15:59**
2015-16	**Montreal**	**NHL**	**79**	**13**	**13**	**26**	**28**	**1**	**1**	**2**	**149**	**8.7**	**–13**	**409**	**50.6**	**15:15**	....	....	....	....	....	....	....	....	....
2016-17	**Washington**	**NHL**	**81**	**12**	**13**	**25**	**36**	**0**	**1**	**2**	**115**	**10.4**	**15**	**883**	**47.1**	**13:54**	**13**	**0**	**5**	**5**	**10**	**0**	**0**	**0**	**14:18**
	NHL Totals		**523**	**85**	**96**	**181**	**337**	**8**	**5**	**19**	**851**	**10.0**		**4732**	**49.2**	**14:29**	**50**	**6**	**17**	**23**	**36**	**0**	**2**	**1**	**15:09**

AHL All-Rookie Team (2010)

Traded to **Montreal** by **St. Louis** with Ian Schultz for Jaroslav Halak, June 17, 2010. Signed as a free agent by **Jyvaskyla** (Finland), October 28, 2012. Traded to **Washington** by **Montreal** for Washington's 2nd round pick (Joni Ikonen) in 2017 NHL Draft and Washington's 2nd round pick in 2018 NHL Draft, June 24, 2016.

ELLIOTT, Stefan

(ehl-LEE-awt, STEH-fan)

Defense. Shoots right. 6'1", 190 lbs. Born, Vancouver, BC, January 30, 1991. Colorado's 3rd pick, 49th overall, in 2009 NHL Draft.

2006-07	Van. NW Giants	BCMML	36	12	19	31	18	....	....	....	....	....	....	....	....	....	....	....	....	....	....	....	....	....	....
	Saskatoon Blades	WHL	1	0	0	0	0	....	....	....	....	....	....	....	....	....	....	....	....	....	....	....	....	....	....
2007-08	Saskatoon Blades	WHL	67	9	31	40	17	....	....	....	....	....	....	....	....	....	....	....	....	....	....	....	....	....	....
2008-09	Saskatoon Blades	WHL	71	16	39	55	26	....	....	....	....	....	....	....	....	....	7	1	3	4	4	....	....	....	....
2009-10	Saskatoon Blades	WHL	72	26	39	65	24	....	....	....	....	....	....	....	....	....	10	3	5	8	4	....	....	....	....
2010-11	Saskatoon Blades	WHL	71	31	50	81	14	....	....	....	....	....	....	....	....	....	10	3	5	8	0	....	....	....	....
	Lake Erie	AHL	....	....	....	....	....	....	....	....	....	....	....	....	....	....	5	0	2	2	0	....	....	....	....
2011-12	**Colorado**	**NHL**	**39**	**4**	**9**	**13**	**8**	**0**	**0**	**1**	**84**	**4.8**	**2**	**0**	**0.0**	**17:09**	....	....	....	....	....	....	....	....	....
	Lake Erie	AHL	30	5	9	14	4	....	....	....	....	....	....	....	....	....	....	....	....	....	....	....	....	....	....
2012-13	Lake Erie	AHL	44	5	8	13	6	....	....	....	....	....	....	....	....	....	....	....	....	....	....	....	....	....	....
	Colorado	**NHL**	**18**	**1**	**3**	**4**	**2**	**0**	**0**	**0**	**35**	**2.9**	**–3**	**0**	**0.0**	**17:30**	....	....	....	....	....	....	....	....	....
2013-14	**Colorado**	**NHL**	**1**	**1**	**0**	**1**	**0**	**0**	**0**	**0**	**1**	**100.0**	**0**	**0**	**0.0**	**16:51**	....	....	....	....	....	....	....	....	....
	Lake Erie	AHL	61	14	14	28	14	....	....	....	....	....	....	....	....	....	....	....	....	....	....	....	....	....	....
2014-15	**Colorado**	**NHL**	**5**	**0**	**0**	**0**	**2**	**0**	**0**	**0**	**10**	**0.0**	**–2**	**0**	**0.0**	**13:56**	....	....	....	....	....	....	....	....	....
	Lake Erie	AHL	64	19	21	40	22	....	....	....	....	....	....	....	....	....	....	....	....	....	....	....	....	....	....
2015-16	**Arizona**	**NHL**	**19**	**2**	**4**	**6**	**4**	**0**	**0**	**0**	**35**	**5.7**	**–2**	**0**	**0.0**	**14:14**	....	....	....	....	....	....	....	....	....
	Nashville	**NHL**	**2**	**0**	**0**	**0**	**0**	**0**	**0**	**0**	**2**	**0.0**	**–1**	**0**	**0.0**	**13:31**	....	....	....	....	....	....	....	....	....
	Milwaukee	AHL	35	8	11	19	14	....	....	....	....	....	....	....	....	....	3	0	1	1	2	....	....	....	....
2016-17	Ak Bars Kazan	KHL	31	4	7	11	12	....	....	....	....	....	....	....	....	....	1	0	0	0	0	....	....	....	....
	NHL Totals		**84**	**8**	**16**	**24**	**16**	**0**	**0**	**1**	**167**	**4.8**		**0**	**0.0**	**16:17**	....	....	....	....	....	....	....	....	....

Canadian Major Junior Scholastic Player of the Year (2009) • WHL East First All-Star Team (2011) • WHL Defenseman of the Year (2011)

Traded to **Arizona** by **Colorado** for Brandon Gormley, September 9, 2015. Traded to **Nashville** by **Arizona** for Victor Bartley, January 15, 2016. Signed as a free agent by **Kazan** (KHL), September 29, 2016.

ELLIS, Morgan

(EHL-ihs, MOHR-guhn)

Defense. Shoots right. 6'1", 207 lbs. Born, Summerside, PE, April 30, 1992. Montreal's 3rd pick, 117th overall, in 2010 NHL Draft.

2007-08	Charlottetown	NBPEI	33	3	4	7	28	....	....	....	....	....	....	....	....	....	7	0	2	2	10	....	....	....	....
	Charlottetown	Other	16	2	6	8	16	....	....	....	....	....	....	....	....	....	....	....	....	....	....	....	....	....	....
2008-09	Cape Breton	QMJHL	52	0	6	6	45	....	....	....	....	....	....	....	....	....	10	0	1	1	4	....	....	....	....
2009-10	Cape Breton	QMJHL	60	4	25	29	56	....	....	....	....	....	....	....	....	....	5	1	0	1	10	....	....	....	....
2010-11	Cape Breton	QMJHL	65	8	28	36	65	....	....	....	....	....	....	....	....	....	4	0	0	0	8	....	....	....	....
2011-12	Cape Breton	QMJHL	34	7	18	25	18	....	....	....	....	....	....	....	....	....	....	....	....	....	....	....	....	....	....
	Shawinigan	QMJHL	26	8	19	27	38	....	....	....	....	....	....	....	....	....	11	4	7	11	6	....	....	....	....
2012-13	Hamilton	AHL	71	4	4	8	57	....	....	....	....	....	....	....	....	....	....	....	....	....	....	....	....	....	....
2013-14	Hamilton	AHL	59	3	7	10	36	....	....	....	....	....	....	....	....	....	....	....	....	....	....	....	....	....	....
2014-15	Hamilton	AHL	27	3	6	9	13	....	....	....	....	....	....	....	....	....	....	....	....	....	....	....	....	....	....
	Wheeling Nailers	ECHL	39	13	13	26	22	....	....	....	....	....	....	....	....	....	5	0	2	2	0	....	....	....	....
2015-16	**Montreal**	**NHL**	**3**	**0**	**0**	**0**	**2**	**0**	**0**	**0**	**3**	**0.0**	**0**	**0**	**0.0**	**8:57**	....	....	....	....	....	....	....	....	....
	St. John's IceCaps	AHL	73	16	26	42	51	....	....	....	....	....	....	....	....	....	....	....	....	....	....	....	....	....	....
2016-17	Chicago Wolves	AHL	74	9	21	30	36	....	....	....	....	....	....	....	....	....	10	0	1	1	0	....	....	....	....
	NHL Totals		**3**	**0**	**0**	**0**	**2**	**0**	**0**	**0**	**3**	**0.0**		**0**	**0.0**	**8:57**	....	....	....	....	....	....	....	....	....

QMJHL Second All-Star Team (2012)

Signed as a free agent by **St. Louis**, July 2, 2016.

ELLIS, Ryan

(EHL-ihs, RIGH-uhn) **NSH**

Defense. Shoots right. 5'10", 180 lbs. Born, Hamilton, ON, January 3, 1991. Nashville's 1st pick, 11th overall, in 2009 NHL Draft.

2006-07	Cambridge	Minor-ON	75	37	56	93	151	....	....	....	....	....	....	....	....	....	....	....	....	....	....	....	....	....	....
2007-08	Windsor Spitfires	OHL	63	15	48	63	51	....	....	....	....	....	....	....	....	....	5	2	3	5	2	....	....	....	....
2008-09	Windsor Spitfires	OHL	57	22	*67	89	57	....	....	....	....	....	....	....	....	....	20	8	*23	31	20	....	....	....	....
2009-10	Windsor Spitfires	OHL	48	12	49	61	38	....	....	....	....	....	....	....	....	....	19	3	*30	33	14	....	....	....	....
2010-11	Windsor Spitfires	OHL	58	24	77	101	61	....	....	....	....	....	....	....	....	....	18	6	13	19	12	....	....	....	....
	Milwaukee	AHL	....	....	....	....	....	....	....	....	....	....	....	....	....	....	7	1	1	2	2	....	....	....	....
2011-12	**Nashville**	**NHL**	**32**	**3**	**8**	**11**	**4**	**2**	**0**	**2**	**34**	**8.8**	**5**	**0**	**0.0**	**14:50**	**3**	**0**	**0**	**0**	**0**	**0**	**0**	**0**	**6:54**
	Milwaukee	AHL	29	4	14	18	8	....	....	....	....	....	....	....	....	....	....	....	....	....	....	....	....	....	....
2012-13	Milwaukee	AHL	32	5	9	14	18	....	....	....	....	....	....	....	....	....	4	0	0	0	0	....	....	....	....
	Nashville	**NHL**	**32**	**2**	**4**	**6**	**15**	**2**	**0**	**0**	**48**	**4.2**	**–2**	**0**	**0.0**	**16:23**	....	....	....	....	....	....	....	....	....
2013-14	**Nashville**	**NHL**	**80**	**6**	**21**	**27**	**24**	**0**	**0**	**2**	**123**	**4.9**	**9**	**0**	**0.0**	**16:04**	....	....	....	....	....	....	....	....	....
2014-15	**Nashville**	**NHL**	**58**	**9**	**18**	**27**	**27**	**2**	**0**	**0**	**118**	**7.6**	**8**	**0**	**0.0**	**18:59**	**6**	**0**	**3**	**3**	**2**	**0**	**0**	**0**	**26:24**
2015-16	**Nashville**	**NHL**	**79**	**10**	**22**	**32**	**35**	**3**	**1**	**2**	**152**	**6.6**	**13**	**0**	**0.0**	**20:54**	**14**	**0**	**6**	**6**	**4**	**0**	**0**	**0**	**24:12**
2016-17	**Nashville**	**NHL**	**71**	**16**	**22**	**38**	**29**	**4**	**1**	**3**	**140**	**11.4**	**17**	**0**	**0.0**	**23:57**	**22**	**5**	**8**	**13**	**12**	**2**	**0**	**1**	**23:26**
	NHL Totals		**352**	**46**	**95**	**141**	**134**	**13**	**2**	**9**	**615**	**7.5**		**0**	**0.0**	**19:08**	**45**	**5**	**17**	**22**	**18**	**2**	**0**	**1**	**22:58**

Canadian Major Junior All-Rookie Team (2008) • OHL First All-Star Team (2009, 2011) • Canadian Major Junior First All-Star Team (2009) • OHL Second All-Star Team (2010) • Canadian Major Junior Defenseman of the Year (2011) • Canadian Major Junior Player of the Year (2011)

ELSON, Turner

(EHL-suhn, TUHR-nuhr) **DET**

Center. Shoots left. 6', 195 lbs. Born, New Westminster, BC, September 13, 1992.

2008-09	St. Albert Raiders	AMHL	33	11	12	23	77	....	....	....	....	....	....	....	....	....	2	0	0	0	4	....	....	....	....
2009-10	Red Deer Rebels	WHL	66	9	8	17	94	....	....	....	....	....	....	....	....	....	4	0	0	0	4	....	....	....	....
2010-11	Red Deer Rebels	WHL	68	16	15	31	124	....	....	....	....	....	....	....	....	....	9	0	4	4	23	....	....	....	....
2011-12	Red Deer Rebels	WHL	55	21	25	46	59	....	....	....	....	....	....	....	....	....	....	....	....	....	....	....	....	....	....
	Abbotsford Heat	AHL	1	0	0	0	2	....	....	....	....	....	....	....	....	....	....	....	....	....	....	....	....	....	....
2012-13	Red Deer Rebels	WHL	64	26	31	57	60	....	....	....	....	....	....	....	....	....	9	5	4	9	6	....	....	....	....
	Abbotsford Heat	AHL	2	0	0	0	0	....	....	....	....	....	....	....	....	....	....	....	....	....	....	....	....	....	....
2013-14	Abbotsford Heat	AHL	37	2	1	3	19	....	....	....	....	....	....	....	....	....	....	....	....	....	....	....	....	....	....
	Alaska Aces	ECHL	18	5	10	15	18	....	....	....	....	....	....	....	....	....	21	7	4	11	16	....	....	....	....
2014-15	Adirondack	AHL	59	17	13	30	52	....	....	....	....	....	....	....	....	....	....	....	....	....	....	....	....	....	....
2015-16	**Calgary**	**NHL**	**1**	**0**	**1**	**1**	**0**	**0**	**0**	**0**	**0**	**0.0**	**1**	**0**	**0.0**	**14:54**	....	....	....	....	....	....	....	....	....
	Stockton Heat	AHL	63	14	16	30	59	....	....	....	....	....	....	....	....	....	....	....	....	....	....	....	....	....	....
2016-17	San Antonio	AHL	13	1	2	3	12	....	....	....	....	....	....	....	....	....	....	....	....	....	....	....	....	....	....
	NHL Totals		**1**	**0**	**1**	**1**	**0**	**0**	**0**	**0**	**0**	**0.0**		**0**	**0.0**	**14:54**	....	....	....	....	....	....	....	....	....

Signed as a free agent by **Calgary**, September 22, 2011. Signed as a free agent by **Colorado**, July 1, 2016. Signed as a free agent by **Detroit**, July 1, 2017. • Missed majority of 2016-17 due to lower-body injury vs. Chicago (AHL), October 23, 2016.

EMELIN, Alexei

(YEH-muh-lihn, al-EHX-ay) **NSH**

Defense. Shoots left. 6'2", 216 lbs. Born, Togliatti, USSR, April 25, 1986. Montreal's 2nd pick, 84th overall, in 2004 NHL Draft.

Season	Club	League	Regular Season														Playoffs								
			GP	G	A	Pts	PIM	PP	SH	GW	S	S%	+/-	TF	F%	Min	GP	G	A	Pts	PIM	PP	SH	GW	Min
2002-03	Lada Togliatti 2	Russia-3	31	1	1	2	20	....	....	....	....	....	....	....	....	....	....	....	....	....	....	....	....	....	....
2003-04	Lada Togliatti 2	Russia-3	2	0	0	0	10	....	....	....	....	....	....	....	....	....	....	....	....	....	....	....	....	....	....
	CSK VVS Samara	Russia-2	52	2	4	6	180	....	....	....	....	....	....	....	....	....	1	0	0	0	18	....	....	....	....
2004-05	Lada Togliatti	Russia	12	0	1	1	24	....	....	....	....	....	....	....	....	....	2	0	0	0	2	....	....	....	....
2005-06	Lada Togliatti	Russia	44	6	6	12	131	....	....	....	....	....	....	....	....	....	6	0	1	1	*47	....	....	....	....
2006-07	Lada Togliatti	Russia	43	2	5	7	74	....	....	....	....	....	....	....	....	....	3	0	0	0	4	....	....	....	....
2007-08	Ak Bars Kazan	Russia	56	0	5	5	123	....	....	....	....	....	....	....	....	....	10	0	1	1	10	....	....	....	....
2008-09	Ak Bars Kazan	KHL	51	0	3	3	58	....	....	....	....	....	....	....	....	....	7	1	0	1	20	....	....	....	....
2009-10	Ak Bars Kazan	KHL	46	1	6	7	50	....	....	....	....	....	....	....	....	....	22	5	8	13	24	....	....	....	....
2010-11	Ak Bars Kazan	KHL	52	11	16	27	92	....	....	....	....	....	....	....	....	....	9	0	0	0	4	....	....	....	....
2011-12	**Montreal**	**NHL**	**67**	**3**	**4**	**7**	**30**	**0**	**1**	**0**	**62**	**4.8**	**-18**	**0**	**0.0**	**17:18**	....	....	....	....	....	....	....	....	....
2012-13	Ak Bars Kazan	KHL	24	2	7	9	40	....	....	....	....	....	....	....	....	....	....	....	....	....	....	....	....	....	....
	Montreal	**NHL**	**38**	**3**	**9**	**12**	**33**	**0**	**0**	**0**	**33**	**9.1**	**2**	**0**	**0.0**	**19:40**	....	....	....	....	....	....	....	....	....
2013-14	**Montreal**	**NHL**	**59**	**3**	**14**	**17**	**59**	**1**	**0**	**0**	**58**	**5.2**	**-1**	**0**	**0.0**	**19:15**	**15**	**0**	**2**	**2**	**4**	**0**	**0**	**0**	**22:21**
	Russia	Olympics	5	0	0	0	8	....	....	....	....	....	....	....	....	....	....	....	....	....	....	....	....	....	....
2014-15	**Montreal**	**NHL**	**68**	**3**	**11**	**14**	**59**	**0**	**0**	**0**	**43**	**7.0**	**5**	**0**	**0.0**	**19:49**	**12**	**0**	**2**	**2**	**10**	**0**	**0**	**0**	**21:29**
2015-16	**Montreal**	**NHL**	**72**	**0**	**12**	**12**	**71**	**0**	**0**	**0**	**71**	**0.0**	**-7**	**0**	**0.0**	**20:30**	....	....	....	....	....	....	....	....	....
2016-17	**Montreal**	**NHL**	**76**	**2**	**8**	**10**	**71**	**0**	**0**	**0**	**82**	**2.4**	**1**	**0**	**0.0**	**21:19**	**2**	**1**	**0**	**1**	**2**	**0**	**0**	**0**	**17:55**
	NHL Totals		**380**	**14**	**58**	**72**	**323**	**1**	**1**	**0**	**349**	**4.0**		**0**	**0.0**	**19:42**	**29**	**1**	**4**	**5**	**16**	**0**	**0**	**0**	**21:41**

Signed as a free agent by **Kazan** (KHL), October 13, 2012. Claimed by **Vegas** from **Montreal** in Expansion Draft, June 21, 2017. Traded to **Nashville** by **Vegas** for Nashville's 3rd round pick in 2019 NHL Draft, July 1. 2017.

ENGELLAND, Deryk

(ehn-GUHL-uhnd, DEH-rihk) **VGK**

Defense. Shoots right. 6'2", 214 lbs. Born, Edmonton, AB, April 5, 1982. New Jersey's 11th pick, 194th overall, in 2000 NHL Draft.

Season	Club	League	Regular Season														Playoffs								
			GP	G	A	Pts	PIM	PP	SH	GW	S	S%	+/-	TF	F%	Min	GP	G	A	Pts	PIM	PP	SH	GW	Min
1997-98	Chetwynd Flames	Minor-BC	STATISTICS NOT AVAILABLE																						
1998-99	Sicamous Eagles	KIJHL	51	9	27	36	114	....	....	....	....	....	....	....	....	....	....	....	....	....	....	....	....	....	....
	Moose Jaw	WHL	2	0	0	0	0	....	....	....	....	....	....	....	....	....	....	....	....	....	....	....	....	....	....
99-2000	Moose Jaw	WHL	55	0	5	5	62	....	....	....	....	....	....	....	....	....	4	0	0	0	0	....	....	....	....
2000-01	Moose Jaw	WHL	65	4	11	15	157	....	....	....	....	....	....	....	....	....	4	0	0	0	10	....	....	....	....
2001-02	Moose Jaw	WHL	56	7	10	17	102	....	....	....	....	....	....	....	....	....	12	0	2	2	27	....	....	....	....
2002-03	Moose Jaw	WHL	65	3	8	11	199	....	....	....	....	....	....	....	....	....	13	1	1	2	20	....	....	....	....
2003-04	Lowell	AHL	26	0	0	0	34	....	....	....	....	....	....	....	....	....	....	....	....	....	....	....	....	....	....
	Las Vegas	ECHL	35	2	11	13	63	....	....	....	....	....	....	....	....	....	2	0	0	0	0	....	....	....	....
2004-05	Las Vegas	ECHL	72	5	16	21	138	....	....	....	....	....	....	....	....	....	....	....	....	....	....	....	....	....	....
2005-06	South Carolina	ECHL	35	3	13	16	20	....	....	....	....	....	....	....	....	....	....	....	....	....	....	....	....	....	....
	Hershey Bears	AHL	37	0	4	4	77	....	....	....	....	....	....	....	....	....	1	0	0	0	0	....	....	....	....
2006-07	Hershey Bears	AHL	44	4	6	10	95	....	....	....	....	....	....	....	....	....	14	0	0	0	14	....	....	....	....
	Reading Royals	ECHL	6	0	3	3	8	....	....	....	....	....	....	....	....	....	....	....	....	....	....	....	....	....	....
2007-08	Wilkes-Barre	AHL	80	2	15	17	141	....	....	....	....	....	....	....	....	....	23	1	3	4	14	....	....	....	....
2008-09	Wilkes-Barre	AHL	80	3	11	14	143	....	....	....	....	....	....	....	....	....	12	0	2	2	6	....	....	....	....
2009-10	**Pittsburgh**	**NHL**	**9**	**0**	**2**	**2**	**17**	**0**	**0**	**0**	**4**	**0.0**	**-2**	**0**	**0.0**	**16:08**	....	....	....	....	....	....	....	....	....
	Wilkes-Barre	AHL	71	5	6	11	121	....	....	....	....	....	....	....	....	....	4	0	1	1	7	....	....	....	....
2010-11	**Pittsburgh**	**NHL**	**63**	**3**	**7**	**10**	**123**	**0**	**0**	**0**	**49**	**6.1**	**-5**	**0**	**0.0**	**13:20**	....	....	....	....	....	....	....	....	....
2011-12	**Pittsburgh**	**NHL**	**73**	**4**	**13**	**17**	**56**	**0**	**0**	**1**	**86**	**4.7**	**10**	**0**	**0.0**	**16:09**	**6**	**0**	**1**	**1**	**14**	**0**	**0**	**0**	**11:30**
2012-13	Rosenborg Elite	Norway	15	1	8	9	43	....	....	....	....	....	....	....	....	....	....	....	....	....	....	....	....	....	....
	Pittsburgh	**NHL**	**42**	**0**	**6**	**6**	**54**	**0**	**0**	**0**	**31**	**0.0**	**5**	**0**	**0.0**	**13:55**	**7**	**0**	**0**	**0**	**8**	**0**	**0**	**0**	**15:28**
2013-14	**Pittsburgh**	**NHL**	**56**	**6**	**6**	**12**	**58**	**0**	**0**	**1**	**59**	**10.2**	**-6**	**0**	**0.0**	**13:03**	....	....	....	....	....	....	....	....	....
2014-15	**Calgary**	**NHL**	**76**	**2**	**9**	**11**	**53**	**0**	**0**	**0**	**51**	**3.9**	**-16**	**0**	**0.0**	**14:23**	**11**	**0**	**1**	**1**	**50**	**0**	**0**	**0**	**20:04**
2015-16	**Calgary**	**NHL**	**69**	**3**	**9**	**12**	**54**	**0**	**0**	**0**	**71**	**4.2**	**7**	**0**	**0.0**	**15:14**	....	....	....	....	....	....	....	....	....
2016-17	**Calgary**	**NHL**	**81**	**4**	**12**	**16**	**85**	**0**	**0**	**2**	**107**	**3.7**	**2**	**1**	**100.0**	**18:20**	**4**	**0**	**0**	**0**	**2**	**0**	**0**	**0**	**15:17**
	NHL Totals		**469**	**22**	**64**	**86**	**500**	**0**	**0**	**4**	**458**	**4.8**		**1**	**100.0**	**15:09**	**28**	**0**	**2**	**2**	**74**	**0**	**0**	**0**	**16:24**

Signed as a free agent by **Pittsburgh**, July 16, 2007. Signed as a free agent by **Rosenborg** (Norway), October 12, 2012. Signed as a free agent by **Calgary**, July 1, 2014. Claimed by **Vegas** from **Calgary** in Expansion Draft, June 21, 2017.

ENGLUND, Andreas

(EHNG-luhnd, ahn-DRAY-uhs) **OTT**

Defense. Shoots left. 6'4", 205 lbs. Born, Stockholm, Sweden, January 21, 1996. Ottawa's 1st pick, 40th overall, in 2014 NHL Draft.

Season	Club	League	Regular Season														Playoffs								
			GP	G	A	Pts	PIM	PP	SH	GW	S	S%	+/-	TF	F%	Min	GP	G	A	Pts	PIM	PP	SH	GW	Min
2011-12	Djurgarden U18	Swe-U18	27	0	4	4	6	....	....	....	....	....	....	....	....	....	4	0	0	0	0	....	....	....	....
2012-13	Djurgarden U18	Swe-U18	32	3	5	8	46	....	....	....	....	....	....	....	....	....	9	0	0	0	0	....	....	....	....
	Djurgarden Jr.	Swe-Jr.	2	0	0	0	0	....	....	....	....	....	....	....	....	....	....	....	....	....	....	....	....	....	....
2013-14	Djurgarden U18	Swe-U18	1	1	0	1	0	....	....	....	....	....	....	....	....	....	....	....	....	....	....	....	....	....	....
	Djurgarden Jr.	Swe-Jr.	33	5	5	10	26	....	....	....	....	....	....	....	....	....	....	....	....	....	....	....	....	....	....
	Djurgarden	Sweden-2	29	1	1	2	20	....	....	....	....	....	....	....	....	....	....	....	....	....	....	....	....	....	....
2014-15	Djurgarden	Sweden	49	2	3	5	32	....	....	....	....	....	....	....	....	....	2	0	0	0	0	....	....	....	....
2015-16	Djurgarden	Sweden	46	2	4	6	36	....	....	....	....	....	....	....	....	....	8	0	0	0	4	....	....	....	....
	Djurgarden Jr.	Swe-Jr.	....	....	....	....	....	....	....	....	....	....	....	....	....	....	2	1	0	1	0	....	....	....	....
2016-17	**Ottawa**	**NHL**	**5**	**0**	**0**	**0**	**2**	**0**	**0**	**0**	**3**	**0.0**	**-3**	**0**	**0.0**	**10:38**	....	....	....	....	....	....	....	....	....
	Binghamton	AHL	69	3	7	10	82	....	....	....	....	....	....	....	....	....	....	....	....	....	....	....	....	....	....
	NHL Totals		**5**	**0**	**0**	**0**	**2**	**0**	**0**	**0**	**3**	**0.0**		**0**	**0.0**	**10:38**	....	....	....	....	....	....	....	....	....

ENNIS, Tyler

(EH-nihs, TIGH-luhr) **MIN**

Center. Shoots left. 5'9", 160 lbs. Born, Edmonton, AB, October 6, 1989. Buffalo's 2nd pick, 26th overall, in 2008 NHL Draft.

Season	Club	League	Regular Season														Playoffs								
			GP	G	A	Pts	PIM	PP	SH	GW	S	S%	+/-	TF	F%	Min	GP	G	A	Pts	PIM	PP	SH	GW	Min
2004-05	K of C Pats	AMHL	36	15	17	32	10	....	....	....	....	....	....	....	....	....	....	....	....	....	....	....	....	....	....
2005-06	Medicine Hat	WHL	43	3	7	10	10	....	....	....	....	....	....	....	....	....	7	0	0	0	0	....	....	....	....
2006-07	Medicine Hat	WHL	71	26	24	50	30	....	....	....	....	....	....	....	....	....	22	8	4	12	6	....	....	....	....
2007-08	Medicine Hat	WHL	70	43	48	91	42	....	....	....	....	....	....	....	....	....	5	0	4	4	6	....	....	....	....
2008-09	Medicine Hat	WHL	61	43	42	85	21	....	....	....	....	....	....	....	....	....	11	8	11	19	10	....	....	....	....
2009-10	**Buffalo**	**NHL**	**10**	**3**	**6**	**9**	**6**	**0**	**0**	**0**	**23**	**13.0**	**1**	**31**	**41.9**	**15:20**	**6**	**1**	**3**	**4**	**0**	**0**	**0**	**0**	**17:09**
	Portland Pirates	AHL	69	23	42	65	12	....	....	....	....	....	....	....	....	....	....	....	....	....	....	....	....	....	....
2010-11	**Buffalo**	**NHL**	**82**	**20**	**29**	**49**	**30**	**5**	**0**	**1**	**210**	**9.5**	**0**	**9**	**22.2**	**15:40**	**7**	**2**	**2**	**4**	**4**	**0**	**0**	**1**	**16:38**
2011-12	**Buffalo**	**NHL**	**48**	**15**	**19**	**34**	**14**	**2**	**0**	**1**	**82**	**18.3**	**11**	**316**	**45.9**	**16:10**	....	....	....	....	....	....	....	....	....
2012-13	Langnau	Swiss	9	3	5	8	0	....	....	....	....	....	....	....	....	....	....	....	....	....	....	....	....	....	....
	Buffalo	**NHL**	**47**	**10**	**21**	**31**	**16**	**2**	**0**	**0**	**108**	**9.3**	**-14**	**377**	**41.9**	**17:53**	....	....	....	....	....	....	....	....	....
2013-14	**Buffalo**	**NHL**	**80**	**21**	**22**	**43**	**42**	**6**	**0**	**0**	**210**	**10.0**	**-25**	**625**	**38.7**	**18:51**	....	....	....	....	....	....	....	....	....
2014-15	**Buffalo**	**NHL**	**78**	**20**	**26**	**46**	**37**	**6**	**1**	**2**	**185**	**10.8**	**-19**	**183**	**36.6**	**19:07**	....	....	....	....	....	....	....	....	....
2015-16	**Buffalo**	**NHL**	**23**	**3**	**8**	**11**	**11**	**2**	**0**	**0**	**57**	**5.3**	**-9**	**2**	**100.0**	**18:04**	....	....	....	....	....	....	....	....	....
2016-17	**Buffalo**	**NHL**	**51**	**5**	**8**	**13**	**12**	**0**	**0**	**1**	**89**	**5.6**	**-10**	**16**	**18.8**	**12:50**	....	....	....	....	....	....	....	....	....
	NHL Totals		**419**	**97**	**139**	**236**	**168**	**23**	**1**	**5**	**964**	**10.1**		**1559**	**40.5**	**17:00**	**13**	**3**	**5**	**8**	**4**	**0**	**0**	**1**	**16:52**

WHL East First All-Star Team (2008, 2009) • AHL All-Rookie Team (2010) • Dudley "Red" Garrett Memorial Award (AHL – Rookie of the Year) (2010)

Signed as a free agent by **Langnau** (Swiss), September 21, 2012. • Missed majority of 2015-16 due to recurring upper-body injury. Traded to **Minnesota** by **Buffalo** with Marcus Foligno and Buffalo's 3rd round pick in 2018 NHL Draft for Jason Pominville, Marco Scandella and Minnesota's 4th round pick in 2018 NHL Draft, June 30, 2017.

ENSTROM, Toby

(EHN-struhm, toh-BEE) **WPG**

Defense. Shoots left. 5'10", 180 lbs. Born, Nordingra, Sweden, November 5, 1984. Atlanta's 8th pick, 239th overall, in 2003 NHL Draft.

Season	Club	League	Regular Season														Playoffs								
			GP	G	A	Pts	PIM	PP	SH	GW	S	S%	+/-	TF	F%	Min	GP	G	A	Pts	PIM	PP	SH	GW	Min
99-2000	MoDo U18	Swe-U18	3	0	0	0	0	....	....	....	....	....	....	....	....	....	....	....	....	....	....	....	....	....	....
2000-01	MoDo U18	Swe-U18	16	7	6	13	18	....	....	....	....	....	....	....	....	....	....	....	....	....	....	....	....	....	....
	MoDo Jr.	Swe-Jr.	1	0	0	0	0	....	....	....	....	....	....	....	....	....	....	....	....	....	....	....	....	....	....
2001-02	MODO Jr.	Swe-Jr.	21	1	7	8	10	....	....	....	....	....	....	....	....	....	2	1	1	2	2	....	....	....	....
2002-03	MODO Jr.	Swe-Jr.	7	4	6	10	31	....	....	....	....	....	....	....	....	....	....	....	....	....	....	....	....	....	....
	MODO	Sweden	42	1	5	6	16	....	....	....	....	....	....	....	....	....	6	0	1	1	4	....	....	....	....
2003-04	MODO	Sweden	33	1	4	5	6	....	....	....	....	....	....	....	....	....	6	1	1	2	2	....	....	....	....
2004-05	MODO	Sweden	49	4	10	14	24	....	....	....	....	....	....	....	....	....	2	0	0	0	0	....	....	....	....
2005-06	MODO	Sweden	47	4	7	11	48	....	....	....	....	....	....	....	....	....	4	0	1	1	25	....	....	....	....

			Regular Season														Playoffs								
Season	Club	League	GP	G	A	Pts	PIM	PP	SH	GW	S	S%	+/-	TF	F%	Min	GP	G	A	Pts	PIM	PP	SH	GW	Min
2006-07	MODO	Sweden	55	7	21	28	52										20	1	11	12	37				
2007-08	**Atlanta**	**NHL**	**82**	**5**	**33**	**38**	**42**	**4**	**0**	**0**	**105**	**4.8**	**-5**	**0**	**0.0**	**24:28**									
2008-09	**Atlanta**	**NHL**	**82**	**5**	**27**	**32**	**52**	**2**	**1**	**1**	**86**	**5.8**	**14**	**2**	**50.0**	**23:32**									
2009-10	**Atlanta**	**NHL**	**82**	**6**	**44**	**50**	**30**	**2**	**0**	**0**	**109**	**5.5**	**-5**	**0**	**0.0**	**22:16**									
	Sweden	Olympics	4	0	2	2	4																		
2010-11	**Atlanta**	**NHL**	**72**	**10**	**41**	**51**	**54**	**6**	**0**	**1**	**113**	**8.8**	**-10**	**0**	**0.0**	**23:41**									
2011-12	**Winnipeg**	**NHL**	**62**	**6**	**27**	**33**	**38**	**2**	**0**	**1**	**94**	**6.4**	**6**	**0**	**0.0**	**23:51**									
2012-13	Salzburg	Austria	5	1	0	1	4																		
	Winnipeg	**NHL**	**22**	**4**	**11**	**15**	**8**	**1**	**0**	**2**	**21**	**19.0**	**-8**	**0**	**0.0**	**22:31**									
2013-14	**Winnipeg**	**NHL**	**82**	**10**	**20**	**30**	**56**	**4**	**0**	**3**	**106**	**9.4**	**-9**	**1**	**100.0**	**23:54**									
2014-15	**Winnipeg**	**NHL**	**60**	**4**	**19**	**23**	**36**	**1**	**0**	**0**	**58**	**6.9**	**13**	**0**	**0.0**	**23:34**	**4**	**0**	**1**	**1**	**0**	**0**	**0**	**0**	**20:46**
2015-16	**Winnipeg**	**NHL**	**72**	**2**	**14**	**16**	**44**	**0**	**0**	**0**	**50**	**4.0**	**8**	**0**	**0.0**	**20:51**									
2016-17	**Winnipeg**	**NHL**	**60**	**1**	**13**	**14**	**42**	**0**	**1**	**0**	**46**	**2.2**	**-7**	**0**	**0.0**	**21:54**									
	NHL Totals		**676**	**53**	**249**	**302**	**402**	**22**	**2**	**7**	**788**	**6.7**		**3**	**66.7**	**23:07**	**4**	**0**	**1**	**1**	**0**	**0**	**0**	**0**	**20:46**

NHL All-Rookie Team (2008)

• Transferred to **Winnipeg** after **Atlanta** franchise relocated, June 21, 2011. Signed as a free agent by **Salzburg** (Austria), October 22, 2012. • Missed majority of 2012-13 due to shoulder (February 15, 2013 vs. Pittsburgh) and back (April 9, 2013 vs. Buffalo) injuries.

ERICSSON, Jonathan

(AIR-ihk-suhn, JAWN-ah-thuhn) **DET**

Defense. Shoots left. 6'4", 220 lbs. Born, Karlskrona, Sweden, March 2, 1984. Detroit's 10th pick, 291st overall, in 2002 NHL Draft.

Season	Club	League	GP	G	A	Pts	PIM	PP	SH	GW	S	S%	+/-	TF	F%	Min	GP	G	A	Pts	PIM	PP	SH	GW	Min
2001-02	Hasten Jr.	Swe-Jr.	STATISTICS NOT AVAILABLE																						
2002-03	Vita Hasten	Sweden-3	40	2	4	6	36																		
2003-04	Sodertalje SK	Sweden	42	1	0	1	12																		
2004-05	Sodertalje SK	Sweden	15	0	0	0	4										1	0	0	0	0				
2005-06	Sodertalje SK Jr.	Swe-Jr.	1	0	0	0	2																		
	Almtuna	Sweden-2	19	2	3	5	44																		
	Sodertalje SK	Sweden	24	0	0	0	20																		
	Sodertalje SK	Sweden-Q	7	0	1	1	4																		
2006-07	Grand Rapids	AHL	67	5	24	29	102										7	0	0	0	8				
2007-08	**Detroit**	**NHL**	**8**	**1**	**0**	**1**	**4**	**1**	**0**	**0**	**19**	**5.3**	**-3**	**0**	**0.0**	**15:58**									
	Grand Rapids	AHL	69	10	24	34	83																		
2008-09	**Detroit**	**NHL**	**19**	**1**	**3**	**4**	**15**	**0**	**0**	**0**	**25**	**4.0**	**-1**	**0**	**0.0**	**17:40**	**22**	**4**	**4**	**8**	**25**	**0**	**0**	**1**	**18:44**
	Grand Rapids	AHL	40	2	13	15	48																		
2009-10	**Detroit**	**NHL**	**62**	**4**	**9**	**13**	**44**	**0**	**1**	**1**	**55**	**7.3**	**-15**	**0**	**0.0**	**16:42**	**12**	**0**	**2**	**2**	**8**	**0**	**0**	**0**	**14:17**
2010-11	**Detroit**	**NHL**	**74**	**3**	**12**	**15**	**87**	**1**	**0**	**0**	**89**	**3.4**	**8**	**0**	**0.0**	**18:50**	**11**	**1**	**2**	**3**	**4**	**0**	**0**	**0**	**18:47**
2011-12	**Detroit**	**NHL**	**69**	**1**	**10**	**11**	**47**	**0**	**0**	**0**	**63**	**1.6**	**16**	**0**	**0.0**	**17:05**	**5**	**0**	**0**	**0**	**6**	**0**	**0**	**0**	**19:49**
2012-13	Vita Hasten	Sweden-3	3	0	3	3	4																		
	Sodertalje SK	Sweden-2	4	0	1	1	6																		
	Detroit	**NHL**	**45**	**3**	**10**	**13**	**29**	**0**	**0**	**1**	**34**	**8.8**	**6**	**0**	**0.0**	**21:19**	**14**	**0**	**3**	**3**	**2**	**0**	**0**	**0**	**22:33**
2013-14	**Detroit**	**NHL**	**48**	**1**	**10**	**11**	**34**	**0**	**0**	**0**	**66**	**1.5**	**2**	**0**	**0.0**	**21:15**									
	Sweden	Olympics	6	0	1	1	8																		
2014-15	**Detroit**	**NHL**	**82**	**3**	**12**	**15**	**70**	**0**	**0**	**0**	**82**	**3.7**	**-5**	**0**	**0.0**	**19:35**	**7**	**0**	**4**	**4**	**8**	**0**	**0**	**0**	**19:51**
2015-16	**Detroit**	**NHL**	**71**	**3**	**12**	**15**	**56**	**0**	**0**	**0**	**68**	**4.4**	**2**	**0**	**0.0**	**18:32**	**5**	**0**	**1**	**1**	**2**	**0**	**0**	**0**	**17:17**
2016-17	**Detroit**	**NHL**	**51**	**1**	**8**	**9**	**63**	**0**	**0**	**0**	**43**	**2.3**	**-2**	**0**	**0.0**	**19:13**									
	NHL Totals		**529**	**21**	**86**	**107**	**449**	**2**	**1**	**2**	**544**	**3.9**		**0**	**0.0**	**18:49**	**76**	**5**	**16**	**21**	**55**	**0**	**0**	**1**	**18:49**

Signed as a free agent by **Vita Hasten** (Sweden-3). October 7, 2012. Signed as a free agent by **Sodertalje** (Sweden-2), October 26, 2012.

ERIKSSON, Loui

(AIR-ihk-suhn, LOO-ee) **VAN**

Left wing. Shoots left. 6'2", 183 lbs. Born, Goteborg, Sweden, July 17, 1985. Dallas' 1st pick, 33rd overall, in 2003 NHL Draft.

Season	Club	League	GP	G	A	Pts	PIM	PP	SH	GW	S	S%	+/-	TF	F%	Min	GP	G	A	Pts	PIM	PP	SH	GW	Min
2000-01	V.Frolunda U18	Swe-U18	9	5	3	8	4																		
	V.Frolunda Jr.	Swe-Jr.	1	0	0	0	0																		
2001-02	V.Frolunda U18	Swe-U18	1	1	0	1	0																		
	V.Frolunda Jr.	Swe-Jr.	35	7	15	22	2										8	2	3	5	2				
2002-03	V.Frolunda Jr.	Swe-Jr.	30	16	15	31	10										8	4	6	10	4				
2003-04	V.Frolunda	Sweden	46	8	5	13	4										10	1	5	6	0				
2004-05	Frolunda	Sweden	39	5	9	14	4										12	0	0	0	0				
2005-06	Iowa Stars	AHL	78	31	29	60	27										7	2	5	7	0				
2006-07	**Dallas**	**NHL**	**59**	**6**	**13**	**19**	**18**	**2**	**0**	**0**	**78**	**7.7**	**-3**	**9**	**44.4**	**13:11**	**4**	**0**	**1**	**1**	**0**	**0**	**0**	**0**	**15:47**
	Iowa Stars	AHL	15	5	3	8	13										9	2	5	7	0				
2007-08	**Dallas**	**NHL**	**69**	**14**	**17**	**31**	**28**	**4**	**0**	**0**	**120**	**11.7**	**5**	**13**	**15.4**	**14:02**	**18**	**4**	**4**	**8**	**8**	**1**	**0**	**0**	**18:12**
	Iowa Stars	AHL	2	1	2	3	2																		
2008-09	**Dallas**	**NHL**	**82**	**36**	**27**	**63**	**14**	**7**	**1**	**4**	**178**	**20.2**	**14**	**11**	**18.2**	**19:50**									
2009-10	**Dallas**	**NHL**	**82**	**29**	**42**	**71**	**26**	**6**	**2**	**4**	**214**	**13.6**	**-4**	**11**	**36.4**	**19:46**									
	Sweden	Olympics	4	3	1	4	0																		
2010-11	**Dallas**	**NHL**	**79**	**27**	**46**	**73**	**8**	**10**	**1**	**6**	**179**	**15.1**	**10**	**4**	**25.0**	**20:34**									
2011-12	**Dallas**	**NHL**	**82**	**26**	**45**	**71**	**12**	**5**	**2**	**3**	**187**	**13.9**	**18**	**16**	**43.8**	**19:46**									
2012-13	HC Davos	Swiss	7	3	3	6	0																		
	Dallas	**NHL**	**48**	**12**	**17**	**29**	**8**	**2**	**1**	**3**	**104**	**11.5**	**-9**	**34**	**26.5**	**20:07**									
2013-14	**Boston**	**NHL**	**61**	**10**	**27**	**37**	**6**	**2**	**0**	**2**	**115**	**8.7**	**14**	**0**	**0.0**	**16:32**	**12**	**2**	**3**	**5**	**4**	**1**	**0**	**0**	**17:39**
	Sweden	Olympics	6	2	1	3	0																		
2014-15	**Boston**	**NHL**	**81**	**22**	**25**	**47**	**14**	**6**	**0**	**4**	**169**	**13.0**	**1**	**12**	**33.3**	**18:29**									
2015-16	**Boston**	**NHL**	**82**	**30**	**33**	**63**	**12**	**10**	**2**	**5**	**184**	**16.3**	**13**	**21**	**57.1**	**19:29**									
2016-17	**Vancouver**	**NHL**	**65**	**11**	**13**	**24**	**8**	**5**	**0**	**1**	**132**	**8.3**	**-9**	**1**	**0.0**	**18:41**									
	NHL Totals		**790**	**223**	**305**	**528**	**154**	**59**	**9**	**32**	**1660**	**13.4**		**132**	**34.1**	**18:23**	**34**	**6**	**8**	**14**	**12**	**2**	**0**	**0**	**17:43**

Played in NHL All-Star Game (2011)

Signed as a free agent by **Davos** (Swiss), December 4, 2012. Traded to **Boston** by **Dallas** with Joe Morrow, Reilly Smith and Matt Fraser for Tyler Seguin, Rich Peverley and Ryan Button, July 4, 2013. Signed as a free agent by **Vancouver**, July 1, 2016.

ERIKSSON EK, Joel

(AIR-ihk-suhn EHK, JOHL) **MIN**

Center. Shoots left. 6'2", 198 lbs. Born, Karlstad, Sweden, January 29, 1997. Minnesota's 1st pick, 20th overall, in 2015 NHL Draft.

Season	Club	League	GP	G	A	Pts	PIM	PP	SH	GW	S	S%	+/-	TF	F%	Min	GP	G	A	Pts	PIM	PP	SH	GW	Min
2012-13	Farjestad U18	Swe-U18	26	1	6	7	10																		
2013-14	Farjestad U18	Swe-U18	33	22	18	40	22										5	2	6	8	2				
	Farjestad Jr.	Swe-Jr.	13	2	2	4	4										4	1	1	2	2				
2014-15	Farjestad Jr.	Swe-Jr.	25	21	11	32	20										6	5	5	10	6				
	Farjestad	Sweden	34	4	2	6	4										3	0	0	0	2				
2015-16	Farjestad	Sweden	41	9	6	15	18										4	1	0	1	2				
2016-17	Farjestad	Sweden	26	8	8	16	12										7	3	3	6	0				
	Minnesota	**NHL**	**15**	**3**	**4**	**7**	**4**	**0**	**0**	**1**	**15**	**20.0**	**1**	**109**	**41.3**	**10:37**	**3**	**0**	**0**	**0**	**0**	**0**	**0**	**0**	**7:35**
	Iowa Wild	AHL	1	1	0	1	0																		
	NHL Totals		**15**	**3**	**4**	**7**	**4**	**0**	**0**	**1**	**15**	**20.0**		**109**	**41.3**	**10:37**	**3**	**0**	**0**	**0**	**0**	**0**	**0**	**0**	**7:35**

ERIXON, Tim

(AIR-ihx-uhn, TIHM)

Defense. Shoots left. 6'2", 200 lbs. Born, Port Chester, NY, February 24, 1991. Calgary's 1st pick, 23rd overall, in 2009 NHL Draft.

Season	Club	League	GP	G	A	Pts	PIM	PP	SH	GW	S	S%	+/-	TF	F%	Min	GP	G	A	Pts	PIM	PP	SH	GW	Min
2005-06	Skelleftea U18	Swe-U18	9	0	2	2	4																		
2006-07	Skelleftea U18	Swe-U18	8	2	2	4	20																		
	Skelleftea Jr.	Swe-Jr.	8	0	2	2	2										2	0	0	0	4				
2007-08	Skelleftea U18	Swe-U18	4	0	1	1	10																		
	Skelleftea Jr.	Swe-Jr.	28	3	11	14	78										1	0	1	1	4				
	Skelleftea AIK HK	Sweden	2	0	0	0	0																		
2008-09	Skelleftea AIK U18	Swe-U18	1	0	2	2	10										5	1	5	6	14				
	Skelleftea AIK Jr.	Swe-Jr.	9	2	12	14	10										5	1	2	3	4				
	Malmo	Sweden-2	3	0	2	2	0																		
	Skelleftea AIK	Sweden	45	2	5	7	12										9	0	0	0	4				
2009-10	Skelleftea AIK	Sweden	45	7	6	13	44										12	1	0	1	8				
2010-11	Skelleftea AIK	Sweden	48	5	19	24	40										18	3	5	8	12				

			Regular Season														Playoffs								
Season	Club	League	GP	G	A	Pts	PIM	PP	SH	GW	S	S%	+/-	TF	F%	Min	GP	G	A	Pts	PIM	PP	SH	GW	Min
2011-12	**NY Rangers**	**NHL**	18	0	2	2	8	0	0	0	9	0.0	–2	0	0.0	13:00	....	....	....	....	....	....	....	....	....
	Connecticut	AHL	52	3	30	33	42	....	....	....	....	....	....	....	....	....	9	0	4	4	8	....	....	....	....
2012-13	Springfield	AHL	40	5	24	29	38	....	....	....	....	....	....	....	....	....	....	....	....	....	....	....	....	....	....
	Columbus	**NHL**	31	0	5	5	14	0	0	0	21	0.0	4	0	0.0	15:42	....	....	....	....	....	....	....	....	....
2013-14	**Columbus**	**NHL**	2	0	0	0	2	0	0	0	1	0.0	2	0	0.0	14:21	....	....	....	....	....	....	....	....	....
	Springfield	AHL	40	5	33	38	16	....	....	....	....	....	....	....	....	....	5	1	1	2	4	....	....	....	....
2014-15	**Columbus**	**NHL**	19	1	5	6	4	1	0	0	20	5.0	–3	0	0.0	16:58	....	....	....	....	....	....	....	....	....
	Chicago	**NHL**	8	0	0	0	4	0	0	0	6	0.0	1	0	0.0	9:59	....	....	....	....	....	....	....	....	....
	Toronto	**NHL**	15	1	0	1	6	0	0	0	10	10.0	–5	0	0.0	15:48	....	....	....	....	....	....	....	....	....
2015-16	Wilkes-Barre	AHL	65	3	17	20	44	....	....	....	....	....	....	....	....	....	10	2	4	6	6	....	....	....	....
2016-17	Wilkes-Barre	AHL	54	4	13	17	24	....	....	....	....	....	....	....	....	....	5	1	1	2	4	....	....	....	....
	NHL Totals		93	2	12	14	38	1	0	0	67	3.0		0	0.0	14:56	....	....	....	....	....	....	....	....	....

Traded to **NY Rangers** by **Calgary** with Calgary's 5th round pick (Shane McColgan) in 2011 NHL Draft for Roman Horak, NY Rangers' 2nd round pick (Markus Granlund) in 2011 NHL Draft and Pittsburgh's 2nd round pick (previously acquired, Calgary selected Tyler Wotherspoon) in 2011 NHL Draft, June 1, 2011. Traded to **Columbus** by **NY Rangers** with Brandon Dubinsky, Artem Anisimov and NY Rangers' 1st round pick (Kerby Rychel) in 2013 NHL Draft for Rick Nash, Steven Delisle and Columbus' 3rd round pick (Pavel Buchnevich) in 2013 NHL Draft, July 23, 2012. Traded to **Chicago** by **Columbus** for Jeremy Morin, December 14, 2014. Claimed on waivers by **Toronto** from **Chicago**, March 1, 2015. Traded to **Pittsburgh** by **Toronto** with Phil Kessel, Tyler Biggs and Pittsburgh's 2nd round pick (previously acquired, Pittsburgh selected Kasper Bjorkqvist) in 2016 NHL Draft for Nick Spaling, Kasperi Kapanen, Scott Harrington, Pittsburgh's 1st round pick (later traded to Anaheim – Anaheim selected Sam Steel) in 2016 NHL Draft and New Jersey's 3rd round pick (previously acquired, Toronto selected James Greenway) in 2016 NHL Draft, July 1, 2015.

ERNE, Adam

(UHR-nee, A-duhm) **T.B.**

Left wing. Shoots left. 6'1", 210 lbs. Born, New Haven, CT, April 20, 1995. Tampa Bay's 2nd pick, 33rd overall, in 2013 NHL Draft.

2009-10	L.A. Selects	Minor-CA	STATISTICS NOT AVAILABLE																						
2010-11	Indiana Ice	USHL	45	10	8	18	49	....	....	....	....	....	....	....	....	....	3	0	1	1	0	....	....	....	....
2011-12	Quebec Remparts	QMJHL	64	28	27	55	32	....	....	....	....	....	....	....	....	....	11	2	4	6	10	....	....	....	....
2012-13	Quebec Remparts	QMJHL	68	28	44	72	67	....	....	....	....	....	....	....	....	....	11	5	5	10	19	....	....	....	....
2013-14	Quebec Remparts	QMJHL	48	21	41	62	65	....	....	....	....	....	....	....	....	....	1	1	0	1	2	....	....	....	....
	Syracuse Crunch	AHL	8	1	3	4	2	....	....	....	....	....	....	....	....	....	....	....	....	....	....	....	....	....	....
2014-15	Quebec Remparts	QMJHL	60	41	45	86	102	....	....	....	....	....	....	....	....	....	22	21	9	30	17	....	....	....	....
2015-16	Syracuse Crunch	AHL	59	14	15	29	74	....	....	....	....	....	....	....	....	....	....	....	....	....	....	....	....	....	....
2016-17	**Tampa Bay**	**NHL**	26	3	0	3	11	0	0	0	40	7.5	–9	2	0.0	11:48	....	....	....	....	....	....	....	....	....
	Syracuse Crunch	AHL	42	14	15	29	42	....	....	....	....	....	....	....	....	....	22	3	7	10	8	....	....	....	....
	NHL Totals		26	3	0	3	11	0	0	0	40	7.5		2	0.0	11:48	....	....	....	....	....	....	....	....	....

ETEM, Emerson

(EE-tehm, EHM-ur-suhn) **ARI**

Wing. Shoots left. 6'1", 212 lbs. Born, Long Beach, CA, June 16, 1992. Anaheim's 2nd pick, 29th overall, in 2010 NHL Draft.

2007-08	Shattuck	High-MN	58	13	15	28	20	....	....	....	....	....	....	....	....	....	....	....	....	....	....	....	....	....	....
2008-09	USAHNTDP	NAHL	40	19	14	33	16	....	....	....	....	....	....	....	....	....	9	4	4	8	4	....	....	....	....
	USAHNTDP	U-17	13	6	7	13	0	....	....	....	....	....	....	....	....	....	....	....	....	....	....	....	....	....	....
2009-10	Medicine Hat	WHL	72	37	28	65	26	....	....	....	....	....	....	....	....	....	12	7	3	10	0	....	....	....	....
2010-11	Medicine Hat	WHL	65	45	35	80	24	....	....	....	....	....	....	....	....	....	15	10	11	21	7	....	....	....	....
2011-12	Medicine Hat	WHL	65	*61	46	107	34	....	....	....	....	....	....	....	....	....	7	7	6	13	13	....	....	....	....
	Syracuse Crunch	AHL	2	1	0	1	2	....	....	....	....	....	....	....	....	....	4	2	0	2	0	....	....	....	....
2012-13	Norfolk Admirals	AHL	45	13	3	16	12	....	....	....	....	....	....	....	....	....	....	....	....	....	....	....	....	....	....
	Anaheim	**NHL**	38	3	7	10	9	0	0	0	48	6.3	7	5	40.0	11:28	7	3	2	5	2	0	0	0	12:50
2013-14	**Anaheim**	**NHL**	29	7	4	11	4	1	1	2	44	15.9	3	1	0.0	12:47	4	0	0	0	12	0	0	0	10:22
	Norfolk Admirals	AHL	50	24	30	54	10	....	....	....	....	....	....	....	....	....	4	0	2	2	0	....	....	....	....
2014-15	**Anaheim**	**NHL**	45	5	5	10	4	0	0	0	77	6.5	–6	4	50.0	12:15	12	3	0	3	0	0	0	0	11:42
	Norfolk Admirals	AHL	22	13	8	21	2	....	....	....	....	....	....	....	....	....	....	....	....	....	....	....	....	....	....
2015-16	**NY Rangers**	**NHL**	19	0	3	3	2	0	0	0	23	0.0	–4	2	50.0	11:05	....	....	....	....	....	....	....	....	....
	Vancouver	**NHL**	39	7	5	12	9	0	0	1	77	9.1	–8	2	50.0	14:10	....	....	....	....	....	....	....	....	....
2016-17	**Anaheim**	**NHL**	3	0	0	0	2	0	0	0	0	0.0	1	1	0.0	8:48	....	....	....	....	....	....	....	....	....
	San Diego Gulls	AHL	1	1	0	1	0	....	....	....	....	....	....	....	....	....	....	....	....	....	....	....	....	....	....
	NHL Totals		173	22	24	46	30	1	1	3	269	8.2		15	40.0	12:24	23	6	2	8	14	0	0	0	11:49

WHL East First All-Star Team (2012)

Traded to **NY Rangers** by **Anaheim** with Florida's 2nd round pick (previously acquired, NY Rangers selected Ryan Gropp) in 2015 NHL Draft for Carl Hagelin and NY Rangers' 2nd (Julius Naatinen) and 6th (Garrett Metcalf) round picks in 2015 NHL Draft, June 27, 2015. Traded to **Vancouver** by **NY Rangers** for Nicklas Jensen and Vancouver's 6th round pick (Dominik Lakatos) in 2017 NHL Draft, January 8, 2016. Claimed on waivers by **Anaheim** from **Vancouver**, October 13. 2016. • Missed majority of 2016-17 due to recurring knee injury and resulting surgery, December 2, 2016. Signed as a free agent by **Arizona**, July 5, 2017.

EVERBERG, Dennis

(EH-vuhr-buhrg, DEH-nihs)

Right wing. Shoots left. 6'4", 205 lbs. Born, Vasteras, Sweden, December 31, 1991.

2009-10	Rogle Jr.	Swe-Jr.	36	6	12	18	55	....	....	....	....	....	....	....	....	....	2	1	0	1	2	....	....	....	....
	Rogle	Sweden	12	1	1	2	6	....	....	....	....	....	....	....	....	....	....	....	....	....	....	....	....	....	....
	Rogle	Sweden-Q	8	0	0	0	0	....	....	....	....	....	....	....	....	....	....	....	....	....	....	....	....	....	....
2010-11	Rogle Jr.	Swe-Jr.	18	4	2	6	54	....	....	....	....	....	....	....	....	....	1	1	1	2	2	....	....	....	....
	Rogle	Sweden-2	49	5	7	12	20	....	....	....	....	....	....	....	....	....	....	....	....	....	....	....	....	....	....
2011-12	Rogle Jr.	Swe-Jr.	3	0	4	4	0	....	....	....	....	....	....	....	....	....	....	....	....	....	....	....	....	....	....
	Rogle	Sweden-2	15	2	4	6	0	....	....	....	....	....	....	....	....	....	6	1	0	1	0	....	....	....	....
2012-13	Rogle	Sweden	55	5	3	8	47	....	....	....	....	....	....	....	....	....	....	....	....	....	....	....	....	....	....
	Rogle	Sweden-Q	10	0	1	1	0	....	....	....	....	....	....	....	....	....	....	....	....	....	....	....	....	....	....
2013-14	Rogle	Sweden-2	63	25	20	45	42	....	....	....	....	....	....	....	....	....	....	....	....	....	....	....	....	....	....
2014-15	**Colorado**	**NHL**	55	3	9	12	10	0	0	0	62	4.8	–7	3	0.0	11:48	....	....	....	....	....	....	....	....	....
	Lake Erie	AHL	12	5	2	7	4	....	....	....	....	....	....	....	....	....	....	....	....	....	....	....	....	....	....
2015-16	**Colorado**	**NHL**	15	0	0	0	0	0	0	0	9	0.0	–5	0	0.0	8:57	....	....	....	....	....	....	....	....	....
	San Antonio	AHL	54	15	25	40	42	....	....	....	....	....	....	....	....	....	....	....	....	....	....	....	....	....	....
2016-17	Vaxjo Lakers HC	Sweden	52	18	19	37	53	....	....	....	....	....	....	....	....	....	6	0	3	3	*27	....	....	....	....
	NHL Totals		70	3	9	12	10	0	0	0	71	4.2		3	0.0	11:11	....	....	....	....	....	....	....	....	....

Signed as a free agent by **Colorado**, April 29, 2014. Signed as a free agent by **Vaxjo** (Sweden), May 6, 2016. Signed as a free agent by **Omsk** (KHL), May 18, 2017.

FABBRI, Robby

(FAB-ree, RAW-bee) **ST.L.**

Center. Shoots left. 5'10", 180 lbs. Born, Mississauga, ON, January 22, 1996. St. Louis' 1st pick, 21st overall, in 2014 NHL Draft.

2009-10	Miss. Rebels	GTHL	71	58	45	103	102	....	....	....	....	....	....	....	....	....	....	....	....	....	....	....	....	....	....
2010-11	Miss. Rebels	GTHL	75	66	68	134	68	....	....	....	....	....	....	....	....	....	....	....	....	....	....	....	....	....	....
2011-12	Miss. Rebels	GTHL	69	62	56	118	92	....	....	....	....	....	....	....	....	....	....	....	....	....	....	....	....	....	....
	Tor. Canadiens	ON-Jr.A	1	0	3	3	0	....	....	....	....	....	....	....	....	....	1	0	0	0	0	....	....	....	....
2012-13	Guelph Storm	OHL	59	10	23	33	38	....	....	....	....	....	....	....	....	....	5	0	1	1	4	....	....	....	....
2013-14	Guelph Storm	OHL	58	45	42	87	55	....	....	....	....	....	....	....	....	....	16	13	15	28	12	....	....	....	....
2014-15	Guelph Storm	OHL	30	25	26	51	40	....	....	....	....	....	....	....	....	....	9	1	3	4	17	....	....	....	....
	Chicago Wolves	AHL	3	1	3	4	2	....	....	....	....	....	....	....	....	....	3	0	0	0	0	....	....	....	....
2015-16	**St. Louis**	**NHL**	72	18	19	37	25	2	0	3	114	15.8	–2	15	40.0	13:19	20	4	11	15	6	2	0	0	14:22
2016-17	**St. Louis**	**NHL**	51	11	18	29	27	4	0	0	91	12.1	–16	24	54.2	15:37	....	....	....	....	....	....	....	....	....
	NHL Totals		123	29	37	66	52	6	0	3	205	14.1		39	48.7	14:16	20	4	11	15	6	2	0	0	14:22

OHL Playoff MVP (2014)

FAKSA, Radek

(FAK-suh, RA-dehk) **DAL**

Center. Shoots left. 6'3", 210 lbs. Born, Vitkov, Czech Rep., January 9, 1994. Dallas' 1st pick, 13th overall, in 2012 NHL Draft.

2007-08	HC Trinec U17	CzR-U17	2	0	1	1	0	....	....	....	....	....	....	....	....	....	1	0	0	0	0	....	....	....	....
2008-09	HC Trinec U17	CzR-U17	44	16	21	37	32	....	....	....	....	....	....	....	....	....	9	0	2	2	8	....	....	....	....
2009-10	HC Trinec U18	CzR-U18	36	19	19	38	52	....	....	....	....	....	....	....	....	....	....	....	....	....	....	....	....	....	....
	HC Trinec Jr.	CzRep-Jr.	3	0	0	0	2	....	....	....	....	....	....	....	....	....	....	....	....	....	....	....	....	....	....
2010-11	HC Trinec U18	CzR-U18	28	19	30	49	32	....	....	....	....	....	....	....	....	....	2	1	0	1	10	....	....	....	....
	HC Trinec Jr.	CzRep-Jr.	24	9	6	15	12	....	....	....	....	....	....	....	....	....	2	2	2	4	4	....	....	....	....
2011-12	Kitchener Rangers	OHL	62	29	37	66	47	....	....	....	....	....	....	....	....	....	13	2	4	6	10	....	....	....	....

Season	Club	League	GP	G	A	Pts	PIM	PP	SH	GW	S	S%	+/-	TF	F%	Min	GP	G	A	Pts	PIM	PP	SH	GW	Min
			Regular Season														Playoffs								
2012-13	Kitchener Rangers	OHL	39	9	22	31	26	....	....	....	....	....	....	....	....	....	10	4	2	6	4	....	....	....	....
	Texas Stars	AHL	2	0	1	1	0	....	....	....	....	....	....	....	....	....	....	....	....	....	....	....	....	....	....
2013-14	Kitchener Rangers	OHL	30	16	11	27	22	....	....	....	....	....	....	....	....	....	....	....	....	....	....	....	....	....	....
	Sudbury Wolves	OHL	29	5	16	21	26	....	....	....	....	....	....	....	....	....	5	1	2	3	10	....	....	....	....
	Texas Stars	AHL	6	1	2	3	6	....	....	....	....	....	....	....	....	....	21	4	0	4	8	....	....	....	....
2014-15	Texas Stars	AHL	32	4	6	10	12	....	....	....	....	....	....	....	....	....	....	....	....	....	....	....	....	....	....
2015-16	**Dallas**	**NHL**	**45**	**5**	**7**	**12**	**16**	**0**	**0**	**1**	**67**	**7.5**	**9**	**401**	**49.1**	**12:21**	**13**	**3**	**2**	**5**	**2**	**0**	**0**	**2**	**16:08**
	Texas Stars	AHL	28	15	11	26	22	....	....	....	....	....	....	....	....	....	....	....	....	....	....	....	....	....	....
2016-17	**Dallas**	**NHL**	**80**	**12**	**21**	**33**	**67**	**0**	**0**	**0**	**132**	**9.1**	**-6**	**1222**	**48.3**	**16:10**	....	....	....	....	....	....	....	....	....
	NHL Totals		**125**	**17**	**28**	**45**	**83**	**0**	**0**	**1**	**199**	**8.5**		**1623**	**48.5**	**14:48**	**13**	**3**	**2**	**5**	**2**	**0**	**0**	**2**	**16:08**

OHL All-Rookie Team (2012)

FALK, Justin

(FAWLK, JUHS-tihn) **BUF**

Defense. Shoots left. 6'5", 224 lbs. Born, Snowflake, MB, October 11, 1988. Minnesota's 2nd pick, 110th overall, in 2007 NHL Draft.

Season	Club	League	GP	G	A	Pts	PIM	PP	SH	GW	S	S%	+/-	TF	F%	Min	GP	G	A	Pts	PIM	PP	SH	GW	Min
2004-05	Swan Valley	MJHL	56	0	8	8	46	....	....	....	....	....	....	....	....	....	....	....	....	....	....	....	....	....	....
	Calgary Hitmen	WHL	4	0	0	0	2	....	....	....	....	....	....	....	....	....	5	0	0	0	0	....	....	....	....
2005-06	Calgary Hitmen	WHL	5	0	2	2	0	....	....	....	....	....	....	....	....	....	....	....	....	....	....	....	....	....	....
	Spokane Chiefs	WHL	48	0	8	8	35	....	....	....	....	....	....	....	....	....	....	....	....	....	....	....	....	....	....
2006-07	Spokane Chiefs	WHL	62	3	12	15	88	....	....	....	....	....	....	....	....	....	6	0	0	0	8	....	....	....	....
2007-08	Spokane Chiefs	WHL	72	4	22	26	98	....	....	....	....	....	....	....	....	....	21	1	4	5	12	....	....	....	....
2008-09	Houston Aeros	AHL	65	0	3	3	44	....	....	....	....	....	....	....	....	....	20	0	2	2	4	....	....	....	....
2009-10	**Minnesota**	**NHL**	**3**	**0**	**0**	**0**	**0**	**0**	**0**	**0**	**1**	**0.0**	**-2**	**0**	**0.0**	**7:33**	....	....	....	....	....	....	....	....	....
	Houston Aeros	AHL	69	3	6	9	87	....	....	....	....	....	....	....	....	....	....	....	....	....	....	....	....	....	....
2010-11	**Minnesota**	**NHL**	**22**	**0**	**3**	**3**	**6**	**0**	**0**	**0**	**7**	**0.0**	**-4**	**0**	**0.0**	**14:09**	....	....	....	....	....	....	....	....	....
	Houston Aeros	AHL	55	3	11	14	41	....	....	....	....	....	....	....	....	....	24	0	5	5	33	....	....	....	....
2011-12	**Minnesota**	**NHL**	**47**	**1**	**8**	**9**	**54**	**1**	**0**	**0**	**46**	**2.2**	**-13**	**0**	**0.0**	**19:30**	....	....	....	....	....	....	....	....	....
2012-13	**Minnesota**	**NHL**	**36**	**0**	**3**	**3**	**40**	**0**	**0**	**0**	**27**	**0.0**	**-9**	**0**	**0.0**	**13:13**	**4**	**0**	**0**	**0**	**2**	**0**	**0**	**0**	**11:33**
2013-14	**NY Rangers**	**NHL**	**21**	**0**	**2**	**2**	**20**	**0**	**0**	**0**	**10**	**0.0**	**-5**	**0**	**0.0**	**11:56**	....	....	....	....	....	....	....	....	....
2014-15	**Minnesota**	**NHL**	**13**	**0**	**0**	**0**	**7**	**0**	**0**	**0**	**10**	**0.0**	**-6**	**0**	**0.0**	**9:08**	....	....	....	....	....	....	....	....	....
	Iowa Wild	AHL	39	1	6	7	34	....	....	....	....	....	....	....	....	....	....	....	....	....	....	....	....	....	....
	Columbus	**NHL**	**5**	**1**	**1**	**2**	**7**	**0**	**0**	**0**	**8**	**12.5**	**-3**	**0**	**0.0**	**15:13**	....	....	....	....	....	....	....	....	....
2015-16	**Columbus**	**NHL**	**24**	**0**	**4**	**4**	**17**	**0**	**0**	**0**	**16**	**0.0**	**2**	**0**	**0.0**	**14:14**	....	....	....	....	....	....	....	....	....
	Lake Erie	AHL	32	2	7	9	43	....	....	....	....	....	....	....	....	....	17	0	4	4	8	....	....	....	....
2016-17	**Buffalo**	**NHL**	**52**	**0**	**8**	**8**	**29**	**0**	**0**	**0**	**33**	**0.0**	**-3**	**0**	**0.0**	**13:42**	....	....	....	....	....	....	....	....	....
	Rochester	AHL	10	0	0	0	11	....	....	....	....	....	....	....	....	....	....	....	....	....	....	....	....	....	....
	NHL Totals		**223**	**2**	**29**	**31**	**180**	**1**	**0**	**0**	**158**	**1.3**		**0**	**0.0**	**14:28**	**4**	**0**	**0**	**0**	**2**	**0**	**0**	**0**	**11:33**

Traded to **NY Rangers** by **Minnesota** for Benn Ferriero and Columbus' 6th round pick (previously acquired, Minnesota selected Chase Lang) in 2014 NHL Draft, June 30, 2013. • Missed majority of 2013-14 as a healthy reserve. Signed as a free agent by **Minnesota**, August 1, 2014. Traded to **Columbus** by **Minnesota** with Minnesota's 5th round pick (Veeti Vainio) in 2015 NHL Draft for Jordan Leopold, March 2, 2015. Signed as a free agent by **Buffalo**, July 1, 2016.

FARNHAM, Bobby

(FAHRN-uhm, BAW-bee)

Left wing. Shoots left. 5'10", 190 lbs. Born, North Andover, MA, January 21, 1989.

Season	Club	League	GP	G	A	Pts	PIM	PP	SH	GW	S	S%	+/-	TF	F%	Min	GP	G	A	Pts	PIM	PP	SH	GW	Min
2008-09	Brown U.	ECAC	31	4	3	7	24	....	....	....	....	....	....	....	....	....	....	....	....	....	....	....	....	....	....
2009-10	Brown U.	ECAC	36	3	8	11	14	....	....	....	....	....	....	....	....	....	....	....	....	....	....	....	....	....	....
2010-11	Brown U.	ECAC	31	8	7	15	39	....	....	....	....	....	....	....	....	....	....	....	....	....	....	....	....	....	....
2011-12	Brown U.	ECAC	31	8	13	21	51	....	....	....	....	....	....	....	....	....	....	....	....	....	....	....	....	....	....
	Providence Bruins	AHL	3	0	0	0	4	....	....	....	....	....	....	....	....	....	....	....	....	....	....	....	....	....	....
	Worcester Sharks	AHL	3	0	0	0	2	....	....	....	....	....	....	....	....	....	....	....	....	....	....	....	....	....	....
2012-13	Wheeling Nailers	ECHL	9	3	1	4	46	....	....	....	....	....	....	....	....	....	....	....	....	....	....	....	....	....	....
	Wilkes-Barre	AHL	65	3	8	11	274	....	....	....	....	....	....	....	....	....	6	0	0	0	4	....	....	....	....
2013-14	Wilkes-Barre	AHL	64	7	7	14	166	....	....	....	....	....	....	....	....	....	12	0	0	0	30	....	....	....	....
2014-15	**Pittsburgh**	**NHL**	**11**	**0**	**0**	**0**	**24**	**0**	**0**	**0**	**6**	**0.0**	**0**	**0**	**0.0**	**7:11**	....	....	....	....	....	....	....	....	....
	Wilkes-Barre	AHL	62	7	7	14	226	....	....	....	....	....	....	....	....	....	8	0	0	0	14	....	....	....	....
2015-16	**Pittsburgh**	**NHL**	**3**	**0**	**0**	**0**	**5**	**0**	**0**	**0**	**2**	**0.0**	**0**	**0**	**0.0**	**6:41**	....	....	....	....	....	....	....	....	....
	New Jersey	**NHL**	**50**	**8**	**2**	**10**	**92**	**0**	**0**	**0**	**48**	**16.7**	**-2**	**4**	**50.0**	**9:28**	....	....	....	....	....	....	....	....	....
2016-17	**Montreal**	**NHL**	**3**	**0**	**0**	**0**	**17**	**0**	**0**	**0**	**4**	**0.0**	**0**	**1**	**100.0**	**8:16**	....	....	....	....	....	....	....	....	....
	St. John's IceCaps	AHL	71	11	17	28	137	....	....	....	....	....	....	....	....	....	4	0	0	0	2	....	....	....	....
	NHL Totals		**67**	**8**	**2**	**10**	**138**	**0**	**0**	**0**	**60**	**13.3**		**5**	**60.0**	**8:55**	....	....	....	....	....	....	....	....	....

Signed as a free agent by **Pittsburgh**, July 6, 2013. Claimed on waivers by **New Jersey** from **Pittsburgh**, October 26, 2015. Signed as a free agent by **Montreal**, July 22, 2016.

FASCHING, Hudson

(FA-shihng, HUHD-suhn) **BUF**

Right wing. Shoots right. 6'2", 208 lbs. Born, Milwaukee, WI, July 28, 1995. Los Angeles' 3rd pick, 118th overall, in 2013 NHL Draft.

Season	Club	League	GP	G	A	Pts	PIM	PP	SH	GW	S	S%	+/-	TF	F%	Min	GP	G	A	Pts	PIM	PP	SH	GW	Min
2009-10	Apple Valley	High-MN	25	20	16	36	12	....	....	....	....	....	....	....	....	....	6	4	2	6	0	....	....	....	....
2010-11	Team Southeast	UMHSEL	18	7	8	15	12	....	....	....	....	....	....	....	....	....	3	1	3	4	4	....	....	....	....
	Apple Valley	High-MN	25	16	29	45	14	....	....	....	....	....	....	....	....	....	3	2	3	5	2	....	....	....	....
2011-12	USAHNTDP	USHL	37	7	14	21	38	....	....	....	....	....	....	....	....	....	1	1	1	2	2	....	....	....	....
	USAHNTDP	U-17	16	8	5	13	12	....	....	....	....	....	....	....	....	....	....	....	....	....	....	....	....	....	....
	USAHNTDP	U-18	1	0	0	0	0	....	....	....	....	....	....	....	....	....	....	....	....	....	....	....	....	....	....
2012-13	USAHNTDP	USHL	25	4	7	11	8	....	....	....	....	....	....	....	....	....	....	....	....	....	....	....	....	....	....
	USAHNTDP	U-18	40	7	18	25	50	....	....	....	....	....	....	....	....	....	....	....	....	....	....	....	....	....	....
2013-14	U. of Minnesota	Big Ten	40	14	16	30	22	....	....	....	....	....	....	....	....	....	....	....	....	....	....	....	....	....	....
2014-15	U. of Minnesota	Big Ten	38	12	14	26	24	....	....	....	....	....	....	....	....	....	....	....	....	....	....	....	....	....	....
2015-16	U. of Minnesota	Big Ten	37	20	18	38	16	....	....	....	....	....	....	....	....	....	....	....	....	....	....	....	....	....	....
	Buffalo	**NHL**	**7**	**1**	**1**	**2**	**4**	**0**	**0**	**0**	**9**	**11.1**	**2**	**0**	**0.0**	**11:31**	....	....	....	....	....	....	....	....	....
2016-17	**Buffalo**	**NHL**	**10**	**0**	**1**	**1**	**2**	**0**	**0**	**0**	**6**	**0.0**	**-1**	**0**	**0.0**	**10:25**	....	....	....	....	....	....	....	....	....
	Rochester	AHL	37	8	4	12	8	....	....	....	....	....	....	....	....	....	....	....	....	....	....	....	....	....	....
	NHL Totals		**17**	**1**	**2**	**3**	**6**	**0**	**0**	**0**	**15**	**6.7**		**0**	**0.0**	**10:52**	....	....	....	....	....	....	....	....	....

Big Ten All-Rookie Team (2014) • Big Ten Second All-Star Team (2016)

Traded to **Buffalo** by **Los Angeles** with Nicolas Deslauriers for Brayden McNabb, Jonathan Parker, Los Angeles' 2nd round pick (previously acquired, Los Angeles selected Alex Lintuniemi) in 2014 NHL Draft and Los Angeles' 2nd round pick (previously acquired, Los Angeles selected Erik Cernak) in 2015 NHL Draft, March 5, 2014.

FAST, Jesper

(FAHST, YEHS-puhr) **NYR**

Right wing. Shoots right. 6', 190 lbs. Born, Nassjo, Sweden, December 2, 1991. NY Rangers' 5th pick, 157th overall, in 2010 NHL Draft.

Season	Club	League	GP	G	A	Pts	PIM	PP	SH	GW	S	S%	+/-	TF	F%	Min	GP	G	A	Pts	PIM	PP	SH	GW	Min
2007-08	HV 71 U18	Swe-U18	30	15	11	26	14	....	....	....	....	....	....	....	....	....	....	....	....	....	....	....	....	....	....
	HV 71 Jr.	Swe-Jr.	3	0	0	0	2	....	....	....	....	....	....	....	....	....	....	....	....	....	....	....	....	....	....
2008-09	HV 71 U18	Swe-U18	3	2	2	4	2	....	....	....	....	....	....	....	....	....	....	....	....	....	....	....	....	....	....
	HV 71 Jr.	Swe-Jr.	37	7	7	14	16	....	....	....	....	....	....	....	....	....	7	2	1	3	6	....	....	....	....
2009-10	HV 71 Jr.	Swe-Jr.	37	23	26	49	10	....	....	....	....	....	....	....	....	....	3	0	2	2	0	....	....	....	....
	HV 71 Jonkoping	Sweden	2	0	0	0	0	....	....	....	....	....	....	....	....	....	....	....	....	....	....	....	....	....	....
2010-11	HV 71 Jonkoping	Sweden	36	7	9	16	6	....	....	....	....	....	....	....	....	....	3	0	0	0	0	....	....	....	....
	HV 71 Jr.	Swe-Jr.	6	3	7	10	4	....	....	....	....	....	....	....	....	....	3	2	2	4	2	....	....	....	....
2011-12	HV 71 Jonkoping	Sweden	21	5	11	16	4	....	....	....	....	....	....	....	....	....	5	2	1	3	0	....	....	....	....
2012-13	HV 71 Jonkoping	Sweden	47	18	17	35	4	....	....	....	....	....	....	....	....	....	5	1	4	5	0	....	....	....	....
	Connecticut	AHL	1	1	0	1	2	....	....	....	....	....	....	....	....	....	....	....	....	....	....	....	....	....	....
2013-14	**NY Rangers**	**NHL**	**11**	**0**	**0**	**0**	**2**	**0**	**0**	**0**	**7**	**0.0**	**-5**	**0**	**0.0**	**11:17**	**3**	**0**	**1**	**1**	**0**	**0**	**0**	**0**	**9:40**
	Hartford	AHL	48	17	17	34	30	....	....	....	....	....	....	....	....	....	....	....	....	....	....	....	....	....	....
2014-15	**NY Rangers**	**NHL**	**58**	**6**	**8**	**14**	**8**	**0**	**0**	**0**	**52**	**11.5**	**-1**	**20**	**20.0**	**11:48**	**19**	**3**	**3**	**6**	**2**	**0**	**0**	**0**	**14:50**
	Hartford	AHL	11	1	8	9	2	....	....	....	....	....	....	....	....	....	....	....	....	....	....	....	....	....	....
2015-16	**NY Rangers**	**NHL**	**79**	**10**	**20**	**30**	**18**	**0**	**0**	**3**	**75**	**13.3**	**9**	**6**	**16.7**	**14:56**	**5**	**0**	**1**	**1**	**0**	**0**	**0**	**0**	**14:02**
2016-17	**NY Rangers**	**NHL**	**68**	**6**	**15**	**21**	**16**	**0**	**0**	**1**	**56**	**10.7**	**6**	**44**	**38.6**	**13:48**	**12**	**3**	**3**	**6**	**0**	**0**	**1**	**0**	**14:59**
	NHL Totals		**216**	**22**	**43**	**65**	**44**	**0**	**0**	**4**	**190**	**11.6**		**70**	**31.4**	**13:33**	**39**	**6**	**8**	**14**	**2**	**0**	**1**	**0**	**14:23**

			Regular Season														Playoffs								
Season	Club	League	GP	G	A	Pts	PIM	PP	SH	GW	S	S%	+/-	TF	F%	Min	GP	G	A	Pts	PIM	PP	SH	GW	Min

FAULK, Justin

(FAWLK, JUHS-tihn) **CAR**

Defense. Shoots right. 6', 215 lbs. Born, South St. Paul, MN, March 20, 1992. Carolina's 2nd pick, 37th overall, in 2010 NHL Draft.

Season	Club	League	GP	G	A	Pts	PIM	PP	SH	GW	S	S%	+/-	TF	F%	Min	GP	G	A	Pts	PIM	PP	SH	GW	Min
2007-08	South St. Paul	High-MN	26	6	15	21	32	....	....	....	....	....	....	....	....	....	....	....	....	....	....	....	....	....	....
2008-09	USAHNTDP	NAHL	38	3	9	12	20	....	....	....	....	....	....	....	....	....	9	3	3	6	6	....	....	....	....
	USAHNTDP	U-17	17	7	9	16	35	....	....	....	....	....	....	....	....	....	....	....	....	....	....	....	....	....	....
	USAHNTDP	U-18	1	0	0	0	0	....	....	....	....	....	....	....	....	....	....	....	....	....	....	....	....	....	....
2009-10	USAHNTDP	USHL	21	9	3	12	46	....	....	....	....	....	....	....	....	....	....	....	....	....	....	....	....	....	....
	USAHNTDP	U-18	39	12	9	21	20	....	....	....	....	....	....	....	....	....	....	....	....	....	....	....	....	....	....
2010-11	U. Minn-Duluth	WCHA	39	8	25	33	47	....	....	....	....	....	....	....	....	....	....	....	....	....	....	....	....	....	....
	Charlotte	AHL	....	....	....	....	....	....	....	....	....	....	....	....	....	....	13	0	2	2	2	....	....	....	....
2011-12	**Carolina**	**NHL**	**66**	**8**	**14**	**22**	**29**	**5**	**0**	**2**	**101**	**7.9**	**–16**	**0**	**0.0**	**22:51**	....	....	....	....	....	....	....	....	....
	Charlotte	AHL	12	2	4	6	11	....	....	....	....	....	....	....	....	....	....	....	....	....	....	....	....	....	....
2012-13	Charlotte	AHL	31	5	19	24	16	....	....	....	....	....	....	....	....	....	....	....	....	....	....	....	....	....	....
	Carolina	**NHL**	**38**	**5**	**10**	**15**	**15**	**1**	**1**	**0**	**76**	**6.6**	**1**	**0**	**0.0**	**24:00**	....	....	....	....	....	....	....	....	....
2013-14	**Carolina**	**NHL**	**76**	**5**	**27**	**32**	**37**	**2**	**0**	**1**	**152**	**3.3**	**–9**	**0**	**0.0**	**23:25**	....	....	....	....	....	....	....	....	....
	United States	Olympics	2	0	0	0	0	....	....	....	....	....	....	....	....	....	....	....	....	....	....	....	....	....	....
2014-15	**Carolina**	**NHL**	**82**	**15**	**34**	**49**	**30**	**7**	**2**	**4**	**238**	**6.3**	**–19**	**0**	**0.0**	**24:26**	....	....	....	....	....	....	....	....	....
2015-16	**Carolina**	**NHL**	**64**	**16**	**21**	**37**	**27**	**12**	**0**	**4**	**184**	**8.7**	**–22**	**1**	**0.0**	**24:03**	....	....	....	....	....	....	....	....	....
2016-17	**Carolina**	**NHL**	**75**	**17**	**20**	**37**	**32**	**4**	**0**	**2**	**225**	**7.6**	**–18**	**0**	**0.0**	**23:08**	....	....	....	....	....	....	....	....	....
	NHL Totals		**401**	**66**	**126**	**192**	**170**	**31**	**3**	**13**	**976**	**6.8**		**1**	**0.0**	**23:38**	....	....	....	....	....	....	....	....	....

WCHA All-Rookie Team (2011) • NCAA Championship All-Tournament Team (2011) • NHL All-Rookie Team (2012)
Played in NHL All-Star Game (2015, 2016, 2017)

FAYNE, Mark

(FAYN, MAHRK) **EDM**

Defense. Shoots right. 6'3", 212 lbs. Born, Nashua, NH, May 15, 1987. New Jersey's 5th pick, 155th overall, in 2005 NHL Draft.

Season	Club	League	GP	G	A	Pts	PIM	PP	SH	GW	S	S%	+/-	TF	F%	Min	GP	G	A	Pts	PIM	PP	SH	GW	Min
2003-04	Nobles	High-MA	20	3	5	8	14	....	....	....	....	....	....	....	....	....	....	....	....	....	....	....	....	....	....
2004-05	Nobles	High-MA	24	1	17	18	16	....	....	....	....	....	....	....	....	....	....	....	....	....	....	....	....	....	....
2005-06	Nobles	High-MA	29	10	24	34	....	....	....	....	....	....	....	....	....	....	....	....	....	....	....	....	....	....	....
2006-07	Providence	H-East	36	5	7	12	43	....	....	....	....	....	....	....	....	....	....	....	....	....	....	....	....	....	....
2007-08	Providence	H-East	36	2	4	6	18	....	....	....	....	....	....	....	....	....	....	....	....	....	....	....	....	....	....
2008-09	Providence	H-East	33	4	5	9	30	....	....	....	....	....	....	....	....	....	....	....	....	....	....	....	....	....	....
2009-10	Providence	H-East	34	5	17	22	14	....	....	....	....	....	....	....	....	....	....	....	....	....	....	....	....	....	....
2010-11	**New Jersey**	**NHL**	**57**	**4**	**10**	**14**	**27**	**0**	**0**	**0**	**77**	**5.2**	**10**	**0**	**0.0**	**17:50**	....	....	....	....	....	....	....	....	....
	Albany Devils	AHL	19	1	3	4	6	....	....	....	....	....	....	....	....	....	....	....	....	....	....	....	....	....	....
2011-12	**New Jersey**	**NHL**	**82**	**4**	**13**	**17**	**26**	**0**	**0**	**1**	**94**	**4.3**	**–4**	**0**	**0.0**	**20:11**	**24**	**0**	**3**	**3**	**6**	**0**	**0**	**0**	**20:19**
2012-13	**New Jersey**	**NHL**	**31**	**1**	**5**	**6**	**16**	**0**	**1**	**0**	**34**	**2.9**	**6**	**0**	**0.0**	**18:06**	....	....	....	....	....	....	....	....	....
2013-14	**New Jersey**	**NHL**	**72**	**4**	**7**	**11**	**30**	**0**	**1**	**0**	**88**	**4.5**	**–5**	**0**	**0.0**	**18:19**	....	....	....	....	....	....	....	....	....
2014-15	**Edmonton**	**NHL**	**74**	**2**	**6**	**8**	**14**	**0**	**0**	**0**	**78**	**2.6**	**–21**	**0**	**0.0**	**17:56**	....	....	....	....	....	....	....	....	....
2015-16	**Edmonton**	**NHL**	**69**	**2**	**5**	**7**	**18**	**0**	**0**	**0**	**61**	**3.3**	**–6**	**0**	**0.0**	**16:43**	....	....	....	....	....	....	....	....	....
	Bakersfield	AHL	4	0	1	1	4	....	....	....	....	....	....	....	....	....	....	....	....	....	....	....	....	....	....
2016-17	**Edmonton**	**NHL**	**4**	**0**	**2**	**2**	**0**	**0**	**0**	**0**	**4**	**0.0**	**1**	**0**	**0.0**	**7:55**	....	....	....	....	....	....	....	....	....
	Bakersfield	AHL	39	3	14	17	16	....	....	....	....	....	....	....	....	....	....	....	....	....	....	....	....	....	....
	NHL Totals		**389**	**17**	**48**	**65**	**131**	**0**	**2**	**1**	**436**	**3.9**		**0**	**0.0**	**18:10**	**24**	**0**	**3**	**3**	**6**	**0**	**0**	**0**	**20:19**

Signed as a free agent by **Edmonton**, July 1, 2014.

FEDUN, Taylor

(fuh-DOON, TAY-luhr) **BUF**

Defense. Shoots right. 6', 200 lbs. Born, Edmonton, AB, June 4, 1988.

Season	Club	League	GP	G	A	Pts	PIM	PP	SH	GW	S	S%	+/-	TF	F%	Min	GP	G	A	Pts	PIM	PP	SH	GW	Min
2003-04	SSAC Thunder	Minor-AB	36	8	26	34	24	....	....	....	....	....	....	....	....	....	....	....	....	....	....	....	....	....	....
	SSAC Athletics	AMHL	1	0	0	0	0	....	....	....	....	....	....	....	....	....	....	....	....	....	....	....	....	....	....
2004-05	SSAC Athletics	AMHL	36	7	13	20	68	....	....	....	....	....	....	....	....	....	....	....	....	....	....	....	....	....	....
	Ft. Saskatchewan	AJHL	1	0	1	1	0	....	....	....	....	....	....	....	....	....	....	....	....	....	....	....	....	....	....
2005-06	Ft. Saskatchewan	AJHL	60	13	18	31	72	....	....	....	....	....	....	....	....	....	3	1	1	2	4	....	....	....	....
2006-07	Spruce Grove	AJHL	50	10	33	43	103	....	....	....	....	....	....	....	....	....	10	3	5	8	31	....	....	....	....
2007-08	Princeton	ECAC	32	4	10	14	32	....	....	....	....	....	....	....	....	....	....	....	....	....	....	....	....	....	....
2008-09	Princeton	ECAC	35	3	12	15	50	....	....	....	....	....	....	....	....	....	....	....	....	....	....	....	....	....	....
2009-10	Princeton	ECAC	31	3	14	17	34	....	....	....	....	....	....	....	....	....	....	....	....	....	....	....	....	....	....
2010-11	Princeton	ECAC	29	10	12	22	38	....	....	....	....	....	....	....	....	....	....	....	....	....	....	....	....	....	....
2011-12			DID NOT PLAY – INJURED																						
2012-13	Oklahoma City	AHL	70	8	19	27	30	....	....	....	....	....	....	....	....	....	17	3	3	6	6	....	....	....	....
2013-14	**Edmonton**	**NHL**	**4**	**2**	**0**	**2**	**0**	**0**	**0**	**0**	**6**	**33.3**	**–1**	**0**	**0.0**	**12:13**	....	....	....	....	....	....	....	....	....
	Oklahoma City	AHL	65	10	28	38	51	....	....	....	....	....	....	....	....	....	3	0	1	1	4	....	....	....	....
2014-15	**San Jose**	**NHL**	**7**	**0**	**4**	**4**	**4**	**0**	**0**	**0**	**12**	**0.0**	**0**	**0**	**0.0**	**16:59**	....	....	....	....	....	....	....	....	....
	Worcester Sharks	AHL	65	6	28	34	37	....	....	....	....	....	....	....	....	....	4	1	0	1	6	....	....	....	....
2015-16	**Vancouver**	**NHL**	**1**	**0**	**1**	**1**	**0**	**0**	**0**	**0**	**0**	**0.0**	**1**	**0**	**0.0**	**18:48**	....	....	....	....	....	....	....	....	....
	Utica Comets	AHL	63	8	25	33	48	....	....	....	....	....	....	....	....	....	4	0	0	0	4	....	....	....	....
2016-17	**Buffalo**	**NHL**	**27**	**0**	**7**	**7**	**16**	**0**	**0**	**0**	**24**	**0.0**	**3**	**0**	**0.0**	**13:22**	....	....	....	....	....	....	....	....	....
	Rochester	AHL	29	5	18	23	29	....	....	....	....	....	....	....	....	....	....	....	....	....	....	....	....	....	....
	NHL Totals		**39**	**2**	**12**	**14**	**20**	**0**	**0**	**0**	**42**	**4.8**		**0**	**0.0**	**14:02**	....	....	....	....	....	....	....	....	....

ECAC Second All-Star Team (2010) • ECAC First All-Star Team (2011) • NCAA East Second All-American Team (2011)

Signed as a free agent by **Edmonton**, March 8, 2011. • Missed 2011-12 due to pre-season leg injury vs. Minnesota, September 30, 2011. Signed as a free agent by **San Jose**, July 2, 2014. Signed as a free agent by **Vancouver**, July 1, 2015. Signed as a free agent by **Buffalo**, July 1, 2016.

FEHR, Eric

(FAIR, AIR-ihk) **TOR**

Right wing. Shoots right. 6'4", 212 lbs. Born, Winkler, MB, September 7, 1985. Washington's 1st pick, 18th overall, in 2003 NHL Draft.

Season	Club	League	GP	G	A	Pts	PIM	PP	SH	GW	S	S%	+/-	TF	F%	Min	GP	G	A	Pts	PIM	PP	SH	GW	Min
2000-01	Pembina Valley	MMMHL	36	45	13	58	30	....	....	....	....	....	....	....	....	....	....	....	....	....	....	....	....	....	....
	Brandon	WHL	4	0	0	0	0	....	....	....	....	....	....	....	....	....	....	....	....	....	....	....	....	....	....
2001-02	Brandon	WHL	63	11	16	27	29	....	....	....	....	....	....	....	....	....	12	1	1	2	0	....	....	....	....
2002-03	Brandon	WHL	70	26	29	55	76	....	....	....	....	....	....	....	....	....	17	4	8	12	26	....	....	....	....
2003-04	Brandon	WHL	71	50	34	84	129	....	....	....	....	....	....	....	....	....	7	5	0	5	16	....	....	....	....
2004-05	Brandon	WHL	71	*59	52	*111	91	....	....	....	....	....	....	....	....	....	24	16	16	*32	47	....	....	....	....
2005-06	**Washington**	**NHL**	**11**	**0**	**0**	**0**	**2**	**0**	**0**	**0**	**10**	**0.0**	**0**	**4**	**25.0**	**5:45**	....	....	....	....	....	....	....	....	....
	Hershey Bears	AHL	70	25	28	53	70	....	....	....	....	....	....	....	....	....	19	8	3	11	8	....	....	....	....
2006-07	**Washington**	**NHL**	**14**	**2**	**1**	**3**	**8**	**0**	**0**	**1**	**25**	**8.0**	**3**	**6**	**16.7**	**10:43**	....	....	....	....	....	....	....	....	....
	Hershey Bears	AHL	40	22	19	41	63	....	....	....	....	....	....	....	....	....	....	....	....	....	....	....	....	....	....
2007-08	**Washington**	**NHL**	**23**	**1**	**5**	**6**	**6**	**0**	**0**	**0**	**40**	**2.5**	**4**	**2**	**0.0**	**10:31**	**5**	**1**	**0**	**1**	**0**	**0**	**0**	**0**	**9:41**
	Hershey Bears	AHL	11	3	4	7	4	....	....	....	....	....	....	....	....	....	2	1	3	4	2	....	....	....	....
2008-09	**Washington**	**NHL**	**61**	**12**	**13**	**25**	**22**	**1**	**0**	**2**	**134**	**9.0**	**8**	**3**	**33.3**	**11:15**	**9**	**0**	**0**	**0**	**0**	**0**	**0**	**0**	**7:22**
2009-10	**Washington**	**NHL**	**69**	**21**	**18**	**39**	**24**	**3**	**0**	**3**	**145**	**14.5**	**18**	**2**	**50.0**	**12:08**	**7**	**3**	**1**	**4**	**4**	**0**	**0**	**0**	**11:24**
2010-11	**Washington**	**NHL**	**52**	**10**	**10**	**20**	**16**	**3**	**0**	**1**	**120**	**8.3**	**0**	**1**	**0.0**	**12:35**	**5**	**1**	**0**	**1**	**0**	**0**	**0**	**0**	**13:28**
2011-12	**Winnipeg**	**NHL**	**35**	**2**	**1**	**3**	**12**	**0**	**0**	**1**	**54**	**3.7**	**–6**	**0**	**0.0**	**9:42**	....	....	....	....	....	....	....	....	....
2012-13	HPK Hameenlinna	Finland	21	13	12	25	22	....	....	....	....	....	....	....	....	....	....	....	....	....	....	....	....	....	....
	Washington	**NHL**	**41**	**9**	**8**	**17**	**10**	**2**	**1**	**2**	**72**	**12.5**	**14**	**4**	**0.0**	**13:22**	**7**	**0**	**0**	**0**	**6**	**0**	**0**	**0**	**15:52**
2013-14	**Washington**	**NHL**	**73**	**13**	**18**	**31**	**32**	**0**	**0**	**2**	**137**	**9.5**	**0**	**426**	**46.0**	**14:45**	....	....	....	....	....	....	....	....	....
2014-15	**Washington**	**NHL**	**75**	**19**	**14**	**33**	**20**	**1**	**1**	**4**	**142**	**13.4**	**8**	**863**	**52.0**	**14:51**	**4**	**0**	**0**	**0**	**2**	**0**	**0**	**0**	**9:53**
2015-16 ♦	**Pittsburgh**	**NHL**	**55**	**8**	**6**	**14**	**19**	**0**	**4**	**2**	**74**	**10.8**	**0**	**242**	**44.2**	**13:03**	**23**	**3**	**1**	**4**	**6**	**0**	**0**	**2**	**11:39**
2016-17	**Pittsburgh**	**NHL**	**52**	**6**	**5**	**11**	**14**	**0**	**0**	**3**	**61**	**9.8**	**3**	**150**	**50.0**	**10:56**	....	....	....	....	....	....	....	....	....
	Toronto	**NHL**	**1**	**0**	**0**	**0**	**0**	**0**	**0**	**0**	**1**	**0.0**	**–1**	**4**	**100.0**	**10:44**	....	....	....	....	....	....	....	....	....
	NHL Totals		**562**	**103**	**99**	**202**	**185**	**10**	**6**	**21**	**1015**	**10.1**		**1707**	**48.9**	**12:28**	**60**	**8**	**2**	**10**	**18**	**0**	**0**	**2**	**11:21**

WHL East First All-Star Team (2005) • WHL Player of the Year (2005) • Canadian Major Junior Second All-Star Team (2005)

• Missed majority of 2011-12 due to shoulder surgery and as a healthy reserve. Traded to **Winnipeg** by **Washington** for Danick Paquette and Winnipeg's 4th round pick (Thomas Di Pauli) in 2012 NHL Draft, July 8, 2011. Signed as a free agent by **Hameenlinna** (Finland), October 23, 2012. Signed as a free agent by **Washington**, Janiuary 12, 2013. Signed as a free agent by **Pittsburgh**, July 28, 2015. Traded to **Toronto** by **Pittsburgh** with Steve Oleksy and Pittsburgh's 4th round pick (Vladislav Kara) in 2017 NHL Draft for Frank Corrado, March 1, 2017.

FERLAND, Micheal

(FAIR-land, MIGH-kuhl) **CGY**

Left wing. Shoots left. 6'2", 210 lbs. Born, Swan River, MB, April 20, 1992. Calgary's 5th pick, 133rd overall, in 2010 NHL Draft.

			Regular Season														Playoffs								
Season	Club	League	GP	G	A	Pts	PIM	PP	SH	GW	S	S%	+/-	TF	F%	Min	GP	G	A	Pts	PIM	PP	SH	GW	Min
2007-08	Brandon	MMHL	40	12	8	20	20	....	....	....	....	....	....	....	....	....	6	3	2	5	4	....	....	....	....
2008-09	Brandon	MMHL	44	45	40	85	52	....	....	....	....	....	....	....	....	....	6	4	5	9	8	....	....	....	....
2009-10	Brandon	WHL	61	9	19	28	85	....	....	....	....	....	....	....	....	....	15	3	1	4	8	....	....	....	....
2010-11	Brandon	WHL	56	23	33	56	110	....	....	....	....	....	....	....	....	....	6	4	2	6	4	....	....	....	....
2011-12	Brandon	WHL	68	47	49	96	84	....	....	....	....	....	....	....	....	....	8	3	3	6	6	....	....	....	....
2012-13	Brandon	WHL	4	1	1	2	4	....	....	....	....	....	....	....	....	....	....	....	....	....	....	....	....	....	....
	Saskatoon Blades	WHL	26	8	21	29	18	....	....	....	....	....	....	....	....	....	4	0	0	0	2	....	....	....	....
	Abbotsford Heat	AHL	7	0	0	0	10	....	....	....	....	....	....	....	....	....	....	....	....	....	....	....	....	....	....
	Utah Grizzlies	ECHL	3	0	1	1	5	....	....	....	....	....	....	....	....	....	....	....	....	....	....	....	....	....	....
2013-14	Abbotsford Heat	AHL	25	6	12	18	31	....	....	....	....	....	....	....	....	....	....	....	....	....	....	....	....	....	....
2014-15	**Calgary**	**NHL**	**26**	**2**	**3**	**5**	**16**	**0**	**0**	**1**	**34**	**5.9**	**1**	**0**	**0.0**	**10:31**	**9**	**3**	**2**	**5**	**23**	**0**	**0**	**0**	**12:34**
	Adirondack	AHL	32	7	8	15	30	....	....	....	....	....	....	....	....	....	....	....	....	....	....	....	....	....	....
2015-16	**Calgary**	**NHL**	**71**	**4**	**14**	**18**	**45**	**1**	**0**	**0**	**122**	**3.3**	**–15**	**12**	**58.3**	**12:37**	....	....	....	....	....	....	....	....	....
2016-17	**Calgary**	**NHL**	**76**	**15**	**10**	**25**	**50**	**2**	**0**	**1**	**106**	**14.2**	**–1**	**7**	**42.9**	**11:34**	**4**	**0**	**0**	**0**	**7**	**0**	**0**	**0**	**12:28**
	NHL Totals		**173**	**21**	**27**	**48**	**111**	**3**	**0**	**2**	**262**	**8.0**		**19**	**52.6**	**11:50**	**13**	**3**	**2**	**5**	**30**	**0**	**0**	**0**	**12:32**

WHL East Second All-Star Team (2012)

FERLIN, Brian

(FUHR-lihn, BRIGH-uhn) **EDM**

Right wing. Shoots right. 6'2", 207 lbs. Born, Jacksonville, FL, June 3, 1992. Boston's 4th pick, 121st overall, in 2011 NHL Draft.

Season	Club	League	GP	G	A	Pts	PIM	PP	SH	GW	S	S%	+/-	TF	F%	Min	GP	G	A	Pts	PIM	PP	SH	GW	Min
2009-10	Indiana Ice	USHL	57	6	10	16	36	....	....	....	....	....	....	....	....	....	8	1	2	3	2	....	....	....	....
2010-11	Indiana Ice	USHL	55	25	48	73	26	....	....	....	....	....	....	....	....	....	5	1	4	5	4	....	....	....	....
2011-12	Cornell Big Red	ECAC	26	8	13	21	30	....	....	....	....	....	....	....	....	....	....	....	....	....	....	....	....	....	....
2012-13	Cornell Big Red	ECAC	34	10	14	24	55	....	....	....	....	....	....	....	....	....	....	....	....	....	....	....	....	....	....
2013-14	Cornell Big Red	ECAC	32	13	14	27	26	....	....	....	....	....	....	....	....	....	....	....	....	....	....	....	....	....	....
2014-15	**Boston**	**NHL**	**7**	**0**	**1**	**1**	**0**	**0**	**0**	**0**	**6**	**0.0**	**0**	**1**	**0.0**	**8:48**	....	....	....	....	....	....	....	....	....
	Providence Bruins	AHL	53	11	9	20	40	....	....	....	....	....	....	....	....	....	....	....	....	....	....	....	....	....	....
2015-16	Providence Bruins	AHL	23	6	8	14	27	....	....	....	....	....	....	....	....	....	3	0	1	1	2	....	....	....	....
2016-17	Providence Bruins	AHL	2	0	0	0	2	....	....	....	....	....	....	....	....	....	....	....	....	....	....	....	....	....	....
	NHL Totals		**7**	**0**	**1**	**1**	**0**	**0**	**0**	**0**	**6**	**0.0**		**1**	**0.0**	**8:48**	....	....	....	....	....	....	....	....	....

ECAC All-Rookie Team (2012) • ECAC Rookie of the Year (2012)

• Missed majority of 2015-16 and 2016-17 due to upper-body injury vs. Wilkes-Barre (AHL), October 9, 2015. Signed as a free agent by **Edmonton**, July 1, 2017.

FERRARO, Landon

(fuh-RAHR-oh, LAN-duhn) **MIN**

Center. Shoots right. 6', 186 lbs. Born, Trail, BC, August 8, 1991. Detroit's 1st pick, 32nd overall, in 2009 NHL Draft.

Season	Club	League	GP	G	A	Pts	PIM	PP	SH	GW	S	S%	+/-	TF	F%	Min	GP	G	A	Pts	PIM	PP	SH	GW	Min
2006-07	Van. NW Giants	BCMML	25	21	13	34	77	....	....	....	....	....	....	....	....	....	....	....	....	....	....	....	....	....	....
	Red Deer Rebels	WHL	4	0	0	0	0	....	....	....	....	....	....	....	....	....	1	0	0	0	0	....	....	....	....
2007-08	Red Deer Rebels	WHL	54	13	11	24	65	....	....	....	....	....	....	....	....	....	....	....	....	....	....	....	....	....	....
2008-09	Red Deer Rebels	WHL	68	37	18	55	99	....	....	....	....	....	....	....	....	....	....	....	....	....	....	....	....	....	....
2009-10	Red Deer Rebels	WHL	53	16	30	46	55	....	....	....	....	....	....	....	....	....	3	0	0	0	2	....	....	....	....
	Grand Rapids	AHL	2	0	0	0	0	....	....	....	....	....	....	....	....	....	....	....	....	....	....	....	....	....	....
2010-11	Everett Silvertips	WHL	41	10	17	27	51	....	....	....	....	....	....	....	....	....	4	0	3	3	13	....	....	....	....
2011-12	Grand Rapids	AHL	56	9	11	20	47	....	....	....	....	....	....	....	....	....	....	....	....	....	....	....	....	....	....
2012-13	Grand Rapids	AHL	72	24	23	47	44	....	....	....	....	....	....	....	....	....	24	5	11	16	11	....	....	....	....
2013-14	**Detroit**	**NHL**	**4**	**0**	**0**	**0**	**2**	**0**	**0**	**0**	**2**	**0.0**	**0**	**0**	**0.0**	**8:59**	....	....	....	....	....	....	....	....	....
	Grand Rapids	AHL	70	15	16	31	52	....	....	....	....	....	....	....	....	....	9	1	2	3	2	....	....	....	....
2014-15	**Detroit**	**NHL**	**3**	**1**	**0**	**1**	**0**	**0**	**0**	**1**	**4**	**25.0**	**1**	**0**	**0.0**	**11:59**	**7**	**0**	**0**	**0**	**2**	**0**	**0**	**0**	**10:09**
	Grand Rapids	AHL	70	27	15	42	61	....	....	....	....	....	....	....	....	....	....	....	....	....	....	....	....	....	....
2015-16	**Detroit**	**NHL**	**10**	**0**	**0**	**0**	**7**	**0**	**0**	**0**	**12**	**0.0**	**–3**	**4**	**25.0**	**9:33**	....	....	....	....	....	....	....	....	....
	Boston	**NHL**	**58**	**5**	**5**	**10**	**20**	**0**	**0**	**1**	**65**	**7.7**	**–8**	**82**	**34.2**	**10:48**	....	....	....	....	....	....	....	....	....
2016-17	Chicago Wolves	AHL	22	7	8	15	12	....	....	....	....	....	....	....	....	....	....	....	....	....	....	....	....	....	....
	NHL Totals		**75**	**6**	**5**	**11**	**29**	**0**	**0**	**2**	**83**	**7.2**		**86**	**33.7**	**10:35**	**7**	**0**	**0**	**0**	**2**	**0**	**0**	**0**	**10:09**

Claimed on waivers by **Boston** from **Detroit**, November 22, 2015. Signed as a free agent by **St. Louis**, July 9, 2016. • Missed majority of 2016-17 due to lower-body injury vs. Rockford (AHL), December 1, 2016. Signed as a free agent by **Minnesota**, July 1, 2017.

FIALA, Kevin

(fee-A-lah, KEH-vuhn) **NSH**

Left wing. Shoots left. 5'10", 193 lbs. Born, St. Gallen, Switzerland, July 22, 1996. Nashville's 1st pick, 11th overall, in 2014 NHL Draft.

Season	Club	League	GP	G	A	Pts	PIM	PP	SH	GW	S	S%	+/-	TF	F%	Min	GP	G	A	Pts	PIM	PP	SH	GW	Min
2009-10	EHC Uzwil U17	Swiss-U17	19	19	15	34	10	....	....	....	....	....	....	....	....	....	....	....	....	....	....	....	....	....	....
2010-11	ZSC Zurich U17	Swiss-U17	25	10	10	20	14	....	....	....	....	....	....	....	....	....	7	0	2	2	0	....	....	....	....
2011-12	ZSC Zurich U17	Swiss-U17	28	34	18	52	98	....	....	....	....	....	....	....	....	....	8	6	8	14	24	....	....	....	....
	ZSC Zurich Jr.	Swiss-Jr.	7	1	4	5	8	....	....	....	....	....	....	....	....	....	4	3	2	5	18	....	....	....	....
	GCK Zurich Jr.	Swiss-Jr.	2	0	1	1	0	....	....	....	....	....	....	....	....	....	....	....	....	....	....	....	....	....	....
2012-13	Malmo U18	Swe-U18	9	6	4	10	28	....	....	....	....	....	....	....	....	....	4	4	3	7	4	....	....	....	....
	Malmo Jr.	Swe-Jr.	33	9	19	28	28	....	....	....	....	....	....	....	....	....	3	0	0	0	2	....	....	....	....
2013-14	HV 71 Jr.	Swe-Jr.	27	10	15	25	40	....	....	....	....	....	....	....	....	....	....	....	....	....	....	....	....	....	....
	HV 71 Jonkoping	Sweden	8	3	8	11	10	....	....	....	....	....	....	....	....	....	8	1	5	6	14	....	....	....	....
2014-15	HV 71 Jonkoping	Sweden	20	5	9	14	14	....	....	....	....	....	....	....	....	....	....	....	....	....	....	....	....	....	....
	Nashville	**NHL**	**1**	**0**	**0**	**0**	**0**	**0**	**0**	**0**	**3**	**0.0**	**–1**	**0**	**0.0**	**11:25**	**1**	**0**	**0**	**0**	**0**	**0**	**0**	**0**	**11:05**
	Milwaukee	AHL	33	11	9	20	18	....	....	....	....	....	....	....	....	....	....	....	....	....	....	....	....	....	....
2015-16	**Nashville**	**NHL**	**5**	**1**	**0**	**1**	**0**	**0**	**0**	**0**	**11**	**9.1**	**0**	**0**	**0.0**	**13:09**	....	....	....	....	....	....	....	....	....
	Milwaukee	AHL	66	18	32	50	78	....	....	....	....	....	....	....	....	....	3	0	0	0	2	....	....	....	....
2016-17	**Nashville**	**NHL**	**54**	**11**	**5**	**16**	**18**	**0**	**0**	**1**	**114**	**9.6**	**1**	**0**	**0.0**	**13:31**	**5**	**2**	**0**	**2**	**0**	**1**	**0**	**1**	**13:54**
	Milwaukee	AHL	22	7	12	19	45	....	....	....	....	....	....	....	....	....	....	....	....	....	....	....	....	....	....
	NHL Totals		**60**	**12**	**5**	**17**	**18**	**0**	**0**	**1**	**128**	**9.4**		**0**	**0.0**	**13:27**	**6**	**2**	**0**	**2**	**0**	**1**	**0**	**1**	**13:26**

FIDDLER, Vernon

(FIHD-luhr, VUHR-nuhn)

Center. Shoots left. 5'11", 205 lbs. Born, Edmonton, AB, May 9, 1980.

Season	Club	League	GP	G	A	Pts	PIM	PP	SH	GW	S	S%	+/-	TF	F%	Min	GP	G	A	Pts	PIM	PP	SH	GW	Min
1997-98	Kelowna Rockets	WHL	65	10	11	21	31	....	....	....	....	....	....	....	....	....	7	0	1	1	4	....	....	....	....
1998-99	Kelowna Rockets	WHL	68	22	21	43	82	....	....	....	....	....	....	....	....	....	6	2	0	2	8	....	....	....	....
99-2000	Kelowna Rockets	WHL	64	20	28	48	60	....	....	....	....	....	....	....	....	....	5	1	3	4	4	....	....	....	....
2000-01	Kelowna Rockets	WHL	3	0	2	2	0	....	....	....	....	....	....	....	....	....	....	....	....	....	....	....	....	....	....
	Medicine Hat	WHL	67	33	38	71	100	....	....	....	....	....	....	....	....	....	....	....	....	....	....	....	....	....	....
	Arkansas	ECHL	3	0	1	1	2	....	....	....	....	....	....	....	....	....	5	3	0	3	5	....	....	....	....
2001-02	Roanoke Express	ECHL	44	27	28	55	71	....	....	....	....	....	....	....	....	....	....	....	....	....	....	....	....	....	....
	Norfolk Admirals	AHL	38	8	5	13	28	....	....	....	....	....	....	....	....	....	4	1	3	4	2	....	....	....	....
2002-03	**Nashville**	**NHL**	**19**	**4**	**2**	**6**	**14**	**0**	**0**	**1**	**20**	**20.0**	**2**	**171**	**53.8**	**9:40**	....	....	....	....	....	....	....	....	....
	Milwaukee	AHL	54	8	16	24	70	....	....	....	....	....	....	....	....	....	6	1	2	3	14	....	....	....	....
2003-04	**Nashville**	**NHL**	**17**	**0**	**0**	**0**	**23**	**0**	**0**	**0**	**8**	**0.0**	**–6**	**123**	**49.6**	**8:06**	....	....	....	....	....	....	....	....	....
	Milwaukee	AHL	47	9	15	24	72	....	....	....	....	....	....	....	....	....	22	5	3	8	36	....	....	....	....
2004-05	Milwaukee	AHL	73	20	22	42	70	....	....	....	....	....	....	....	....	....	7	0	0	0	18	....	....	....	....
2005-06	**Nashville**	**NHL**	**40**	**8**	**4**	**12**	**42**	**3**	**0**	**2**	**46**	**17.4**	**–2**	**464**	**52.6**	**13:49**	**2**	**0**	**1**	**1**	**0**	**0**	**0**	**0**	**8:48**
	Milwaukee	AHL	11	1	6	7	20	....	....	....	....	....	....	....	....	....	....	....	....	....	....	....	....	....	....
2006-07	**Nashville**	**NHL**	**72**	**11**	**15**	**26**	**40**	**0**	**1**	**1**	**90**	**12.2**	**11**	**680**	**51.6**	**13:38**	**5**	**1**	**1**	**2**	**4**	**0**	**0**	**0**	**12:21**
2007-08	**Nashville**	**NHL**	**79**	**11**	**21**	**32**	**47**	**2**	**1**	**1**	**97**	**11.3**	**–4**	**384**	**50.3**	**13:56**	**6**	**0**	**0**	**0**	**0**	**0**	**0**	**0**	**16:48**
2008-09	**Nashville**	**NHL**	**78**	**11**	**6**	**17**	**24**	**1**	**2**	**2**	**114**	**9.6**	**–13**	**612**	**54.1**	**13:58**	....	....	....	....	....	....	....	....	....
2009-10	**Phoenix**	**NHL**	**76**	**8**	**22**	**30**	**46**	**0**	**3**	**1**	**119**	**6.7**	**13**	**1121**	**52.5**	**14:21**	**6**	**1**	**1**	**2**	**14**	**0**	**0**	**0**	**14:04**
2010-11	**Phoenix**	**NHL**	**71**	**6**	**16**	**22**	**46**	**0**	**1**	**2**	**97**	**6.2**	**3**	**1224**	**53.9**	**15:33**	**4**	**0**	**0**	**0**	**0**	**0**	**0**	**0**	**9:57**
2011-12	**Dallas**	**NHL**	**82**	**8**	**13**	**21**	**60**	**0**	**0**	**1**	**123**	**6.5**	**–13**	**1049**	**50.9**	**13:59**	....	....	....	....	....	....	....	....	....
2012-13	**Dallas**	**NHL**	**46**	**4**	**13**	**17**	**48**	**1**	**0**	**0**	**56**	**7.1**	**3**	**619**	**51.5**	**12:51**	....	....	....	....	....	....	....	....	....
2013-14	**Dallas**	**NHL**	**76**	**6**	**17**	**23**	**37**	**0**	**0**	**1**	**109**	**5.5**	**3**	**982**	**52.2**	**13:17**	**6**	**1**	**2**	**3**	**24**	**0**	**0**	**0**	**14:26**
2014-15	**Dallas**	**NHL**	**80**	**13**	**16**	**29**	**34**	**3**	**1**	**2**	**132**	**9.8**	**–5**	**1097**	**51.9**	**13:08**	....	....	....	....	....	....	....	....	....
2015-16	**Dallas**	**NHL**	**82**	**12**	**10**	**22**	**31**	**1**	**2**	**0**	**98**	**12.2**	**5**	**897**	**50.7**	**11:38**	**13**	**1**	**2**	**3**	**8**	**0**	**0**	**0**	**8:56**

			Regular Season														Playoffs								
Season	Club	League	GP	G	A	Pts	PIM	PP	SH	GW	S	S%	+/-	TF	F%	Min	GP	G	A	Pts	PIM	PP	SH	GW	Min
2016-17	**New Jersey**	**NHL**	**39**	**1**	**2**	**3**	**29**	**0**	**1**	**0**	**37**	**2.7**	**-11**	**473**	**52.2**	**12:14**	....	....	....	....	....	....	....	....	....
	Nashville	**NHL**	**20**	**1**	**0**	**1**	**37**	**0**	**0**	**0**	**11**	**9.1**	**-4**	**216**	**56.9**	**10:31**	**9**	**1**	**1**	**2**	**25**	**0**	**0**	**1**	**8:02**
	NHL Totals		**877**	**104**	**157**	**261**	**558**	**11**	**12**	**14**	**1157**	**9.0**		**10112**	**52.2**	**13:19**	**51**	**5**	**8**	**13**	**75**	**0**	**0**	**1**	**11:21**

ECHL All-Rookie Team (2002)

Signed as a free agent by **Nashville**, May 6, 2002. Signed as a free agent by **Phoenix**, July 1, 2009. Signed as a free agent by **Dallas**, July 1, 2011. Signed as a free agent by **New Jersey**, July 1, 2016. Traded to **Nashville** by **New Jersey** for Nashville's 4th round pick (later traded to San Jose, later traded to NY Rangers – NY Rangers selected Brandon Crawley) in 2017 NHL Draft, February 4, 2017.

FILPPULA, Valtteri

(FIHL-poo-luh, VAL-tuhr-ee) **PHI**

Center. Shoots left. 6', 196 lbs. Born, Vantaa, Finland, March 20, 1984. Detroit's 3rd pick, 95th overall, in 2002 NHL Draft.

Season	Club	League	GP	G	A	Pts	PIM	PP	SH	GW	S	S%	+/-	TF	F%	Min	GP	G	A	Pts	PIM	PP	SH	GW	Min
2000-01	Jokerit U18	Fin-U18	31	18	29	47	4	....	....	....	....	....	....	....	....	....	6	4	4	8	0	....	....	....	....
	Jokerit Helsinki Jr.	Fin-Jr.	1	0	1	1	0	....	....	....	....	....	....	....	....	....	....	....	....	....	....	....	....	....	....
2001-02	Jokerit U18	Fin-U18	1	0	1	1	0	....	....	....	....	....	....	....	....	....	8	4	9	13	2	....	....	....	....
	Jokerit Helsinki Jr.	Fin-Jr.	40	8	15	23	14	....	....	....	....	....	....	....	....	....	1	0	0	0	0	....	....	....	....
2002-03	Jokerit Helsinki Jr.	Fin-Jr.	35	16	37	53	14	....	....	....	....	....	....	....	....	....	11	4	10	14	4	....	....	....	....
2003-04	Suomi U20	Finland-2	1	0	0	0	2	....	....	....	....	....	....	....	....	....	....	....	....	....	....	....	....	....	....
	Jokerit Helsinki	Finland	49	5	13	18	6	....	....	....	....	....	....	....	....	....	....	....	....	....	....	....	....	....	....
2004-05	Jokerit Helsinki	Finland	55	10	20	30	20	....	....	....	....	....	....	....	....	....	12	5	6	11	2	....	....	....	....
2005-06	**Detroit**	**NHL**	**4**	**0**	**1**	**1**	**2**	**0**	**0**	**0**	**1**	**0.0**	**1**	**21**	**47.6**	**7:19**	....	....	....	....	....	....	....	....	....
	Grand Rapids	AHL	74	20	51	71	30	....	....	....	....	....	....	....	....	....	16	7	9	16	4	....	....	....	....
2006-07	**Detroit**	**NHL**	**73**	**10**	**7**	**17**	**20**	**0**	**0**	**1**	**76**	**13.2**	**8**	**267**	**55.8**	**11:16**	**18**	**3**	**2**	**5**	**2**	**0**	**0**	**0**	**12:12**
	Grand Rapids	AHL	3	2	2	4	2	....	....	....	....	....	....	....	....	....	....	....	....	....	....	....	....	....	....
2007-08 ♦	**Detroit**	**NHL**	**78**	**19**	**17**	**36**	**28**	**3**	**0**	**3**	**122**	**15.6**	**16**	**621**	**50.6**	**16:58**	**22**	**5**	**6**	**11**	**2**	**0**	**0**	**0**	**16:40**
2008-09	**Detroit**	**NHL**	**80**	**12**	**28**	**40**	**42**	**1**	**0**	**1**	**129**	**9.3**	**9**	**785**	**52.1**	**16:06**	**23**	**3**	**13**	**16**	**8**	**1**	**0**	**1**	**17:38**
2009-10	**Detroit**	**NHL**	**55**	**11**	**24**	**35**	**24**	**1**	**1**	**1**	**114**	**9.6**	**-4**	**573**	**51.7**	**18:14**	**12**	**4**	**5**	**9**	**6**	**2**	**0**	**0**	**18:34**
	Finland	Olympics	6	3	0	3	0	....	....	....	....	....	....	....	....	....	....	....	....	....	....	....	....	....	....
2010-11	**Detroit**	**NHL**	**71**	**16**	**23**	**39**	**22**	**4**	**0**	**5**	**115**	**13.9**	**-1**	**928**	**51.5**	**16:43**	**11**	**2**	**6**	**8**	**6**	**0**	**0**	**2**	**17:47**
2011-12	**Detroit**	**NHL**	**81**	**23**	**43**	**66**	**14**	**3**	**1**	**1**	**144**	**16.0**	**18**	**373**	**51.7**	**18:16**	**5**	**0**	**2**	**2**	**2**	**0**	**0**	**0**	**19:20**
2012-13	Jokerit Helsinki	Finland	16	6	9	15	6	....	....	....	....	....	....	....	....	....	....	....	....	....	....	....	....	....	....
	Detroit	**NHL**	**41**	**9**	**8**	**17**	**6**	**3**	**0**	**0**	**78**	**11.5**	**-4**	**323**	**55.4**	**17:47**	**14**	**2**	**4**	**6**	**4**	**0**	**0**	**1**	**16:36**
2013-14	**Tampa Bay**	**NHL**	**75**	**25**	**33**	**58**	**20**	**6**	**0**	**2**	**131**	**19.1**	**5**	**1326**	**52.3**	**19:59**	**4**	**0**	**1**	**1**	**0**	**0**	**0**	**0**	**21:15**
2014-15	**Tampa Bay**	**NHL**	**82**	**12**	**36**	**48**	**24**	**2**	**0**	**0**	**91**	**13.2**	**-14**	**1185**	**52.4**	**19:01**	**26**	**4**	**10**	**14**	**4**	**2**	**0**	**1**	**19:13**
2015-16	**Tampa Bay**	**NHL**	**76**	**8**	**23**	**31**	**46**	**1**	**1**	**2**	**101**	**7.9**	**-6**	**1216**	**52.0**	**18:15**	**17**	**1**	**6**	**7**	**0**	**0**	**0**	**0**	**20:45**
2016-17	**Tampa Bay**	**NHL**	**59**	**7**	**27**	**34**	**24**	**0**	**0**	**1**	**74**	**9.5**	**1**	**924**	**46.5**	**17:30**	....	....	....	....	....	....	....	....	....
	Philadelphia	**NHL**	**20**	**5**	**3**	**8**	**2**	**0**	**0**	**0**	**23**	**21.7**	**-2**	**238**	**52.9**	**17:08**	....	....	....	....	....	....	....	....	....
	NHL Totals		**795**	**157**	**273**	**430**	**274**	**24**	**3**	**17**	**1199**	**13.1**		**8780**	**51.6**	**17:13**	**152**	**24**	**55**	**79**	**34**	**5**	**0**	**5**	**17:37**

Signed as a free agent by **Jokerit Helsinki** (Finland), September 21, 2012. Signed as a free agent by **Tampa Bay**, July 5, 2013. Traded to **Philadelphia** by **Tampa Bay** with Tampa Bay's 4th round pick (Maksim Sushko) in 2017 NHL Draft and Los Angeles' 7th round pick (previously acqured, Philadelphia selected Wyatt Kalynuk) in 2017 NHL Draft for Mark Streit, March 1, 2017.

FISCHER, Christian

(FIH-shuhr, KRIHS-ch'yehn) **ARI**

Right wing. Shoots right. 6'2", 212 lbs. Born, Chicago, IL, April 15, 1997. Arizona's 3rd pick, 32nd overall, in 2015 NHL Draft.

Season	Club	League	GP	G	A	Pts	PIM	PP	SH	GW	S	S%	+/-	TF	F%	Min	GP	G	A	Pts	PIM	PP	SH	GW	Min
2012-13	Chi. Mission U16	HPHL	25	12	14	26	10	....	....	....	....	....	....	....	....	....	....	....	....	....	....	....	....	....	....
2013-14	USAHNTDP	USHL	34	11	12	23	6	....	....	....	....	....	....	....	....	....	....	....	....	....	....	....	....	....	....
	USAHNTDP	U-17	20	8	11	19	19	....	....	....	....	....	....	....	....	....	....	....	....	....	....	....	....	....	....
2014-15	USAHNTDP	USHL	25	15	15	30	10	....	....	....	....	....	....	....	....	....	....	....	....	....	....	....	....	....	....
	USAHNTDP	U-18	41	16	19	35	12	....	....	....	....	....	....	....	....	....	....	....	....	....	....	....	....	....	....
2015-16	Windsor Spitfires	OHL	66	40	50	90	34	....	....	....	....	....	....	....	....	....	5	1	2	3	0	....	....	....	....
	Springfield	AHL	6	2	1	3	0	....	....	....	....	....	....	....	....	....	....	....	....	....	....	....	....	....	....
2016-17	**Arizona**	**NHL**	**7**	**3**	**0**	**3**	**0**	**0**	**0**	**1**	**10**	**30.0**	**0**	**0**	**0.0**	**12:20**	....	....	....	....	....	....	....	....	....
	Tucson	AHL	57	20	27	47	28	....	....	....	....	....	....	....	....	....	....	....	....	....	....	....	....	....	....
	NHL Totals		**7**	**3**	**0**	**3**	**0**	**0**	**0**	**1**	**10**	**30.0**		**0**	**0.0**	**12:20**	....	....	....	....	....	....	....	....	....

FISHER, Mike

(FIH-shuhr, MIGHK)

Center. Shoots right. 6'1", 216 lbs. Born, Peterborough, ON, June 5, 1980. Ottawa's 2nd pick, 44th overall, in 1998 NHL Draft.

Season	Club	League	GP	G	A	Pts	PIM	PP	SH	GW	S	S%	+/-	TF	F%	Min	GP	G	A	Pts	PIM	PP	SH	GW	Min
1996-97	Peterborough	ON-Jr.A	51	26	30	56	35	....	....	....	....	....	....	....	....	....	....	....	....	....	....	....	....	....	....
1997-98	Sudbury Wolves	OHL	66	24	25	49	65	....	....	....	....	....	....	....	....	....	9	2	2	4	13	....	....	....	....
1998-99	Sudbury Wolves	OHL	68	41	65	106	55	....	....	....	....	....	....	....	....	....	4	2	1	3	4	....	....	....	....
99-2000	**Ottawa**	**NHL**	**32**	**4**	**5**	**9**	**15**	**0**	**0**	**1**	**49**	**8.2**	**-6**	**356**	**47.8**	**12:57**	....	....	....	....	....	....	....	....	....
2000-01	**Ottawa**	**NHL**	**60**	**7**	**12**	**19**	**46**	**0**	**0**	**3**	**83**	**8.4**	**-1**	**709**	**50.2**	**11:38**	**4**	**0**	**1**	**1**	**4**	**0**	**0**	**0**	**13:41**
2001-02	**Ottawa**	**NHL**	**58**	**15**	**9**	**24**	**55**	**0**	**3**	**4**	**123**	**12.2**	**8**	**848**	**48.7**	**14:05**	**10**	**2**	**1**	**3**	**0**	**0**	**0**	**0**	**16:17**
2002-03	**Ottawa**	**NHL**	**74**	**18**	**20**	**38**	**54**	**5**	**1**	**3**	**142**	**12.7**	**13**	**1077**	**48.1**	**15:59**	**18**	**2**	**2**	**4**	**16**	**0**	**1**	**1**	**16:58**
2003-04	**Ottawa**	**NHL**	**24**	**4**	**6**	**10**	**39**	**1**	**0**	**0**	**47**	**8.5**	**-3**	**357**	**42.0**	**17:26**	**7**	**1**	**0**	**1**	**4**	**0**	**0**	**1**	**16:11**
2004-05	EV Zug	Swiss	21	9	18	27	34	....	....	....	....	....	....	....	....	....	9	2	3	5	10	....	....	....	....
2005-06	**Ottawa**	**NHL**	**68**	**22**	**22**	**44**	**64**	**2**	**4**	**3**	**150**	**14.7**	**23**	**883**	**50.3**	**17:09**	**10**	**2**	**2**	**4**	**12**	**0**	**1**	**0**	**18:50**
2006-07	**Ottawa**	**NHL**	**68**	**22**	**26**	**48**	**41**	**7**	**2**	**3**	**193**	**11.4**	**15**	**1191**	**52.1**	**18:25**	**20**	**5**	**5**	**10**	**24**	**2**	**1**	**1**	**17:43**
2007-08	**Ottawa**	**NHL**	**79**	**23**	**24**	**47**	**82**	**6**	**2**	**4**	**215**	**10.7**	**-10**	**1230**	**50.2**	**19:46**	....	....	....	....	....	....	....	....	....
2008-09	**Ottawa**	**NHL**	**78**	**13**	**19**	**32**	**66**	**1**	**2**	**3**	**182**	**7.1**	**0**	**1044**	**51.3**	**18:30**	....	....	....	....	....	....	....	....	....
2009-10	**Ottawa**	**NHL**	**79**	**25**	**28**	**53**	**59**	**10**	**0**	**6**	**212**	**11.8**	**1**	**1307**	**52.0**	**18:58**	**6**	**2**	**3**	**5**	**6**	**2**	**0**	**0**	**23:04**
2010-11	**Ottawa**	**NHL**	**55**	**14**	**10**	**24**	**33**	**3**	**0**	**1**	**132**	**10.6**	**-19**	**825**	**48.4**	**18:25**	....	....	....	....	....	....	....	....	....
	Nashville	**NHL**	**27**	**5**	**7**	**12**	**10**	**1**	**0**	**1**	**60**	**8.3**	**2**	**421**	**48.2**	**18:15**	**12**	**3**	**4**	**7**	**11**	**0**	**0**	**1**	**20:43**
2011-12	**Nashville**	**NHL**	**72**	**24**	**27**	**51**	**33**	**5**	**0**	**7**	**157**	**15.3**	**11**	**1217**	**48.3**	**19:18**	**10**	**1**	**3**	**4**	**8**	**0**	**0**	**0**	**20:44**
2012-13	**Nashville**	**NHL**	**38**	**10**	**11**	**21**	**27**	**1**	**0**	**0**	**68**	**14.7**	**6**	**563**	**48.9**	**19:28**	....	....	....	....	....	....	....	....	....
2013-14	**Nashville**	**NHL**	**75**	**20**	**29**	**49**	**60**	**4**	**0**	**4**	**177**	**11.3**	**-4**	**1146**	**52.0**	**19:45**	....	....	....	....	....	....	....	....	....
2014-15	**Nashville**	**NHL**	**59**	**19**	**20**	**39**	**39**	**7**	**1**	**1**	**111**	**17.1**	**4**	**1149**	**52.3**	**18:26**	**3**	**0**	**1**	**1**	**0**	**0**	**0**	**0**	**11:32**
2015-16	**Nashville**	**NHL**	**70**	**13**	**10**	**23**	**29**	**3**	**0**	**2**	**98**	**13.3**	**-14**	**1250**	**53.4**	**17:10**	**14**	**5**	**2**	**7**	**2**	**1**	**0**	**1**	**18:39**
2016-17	**Nashville**	**NHL**	**72**	**18**	**24**	**42**	**55**	**7**	**0**	**3**	**120**	**15.0**	**1**	**1280**	**54.9**	**16:37**	**20**	**0**	**4**	**4**	**2**	**0**	**0**	**0**	**17:17**
	NHL Totals		**1088**	**276**	**309**	**585**	**807**	**63**	**15**	**49**	**2319**	**11.9**		**16853**	**50.6**	**17:31**	**134**	**23**	**28**	**51**	**89**	**5**	**3**	**5**	**18:01**

NHL Foundation Player Award (2012)

• Missed majority of 1999-2000 due to knee injury vs. Boston, December 30, 1999. • Missed majority of 2003-04 due to elbow injury in practice, October 4, 2003. Signed as a free agent by **Zug** (Swiss), November 1, 2004. Traded to **Nashville** by **Ottawa** for Nashville's 1st round pick (Stefan Noesen) in 2011 NHL Draft and Nashville's 3rd round pick (Jarrod Maidens) in 2012 NHL Draft , February 10, 2011. • Officially announced his retirement, August 3, 2017.

FLOREK, Justin

(FLOHR-ehk, JUHS-tihn)

Left wing. Shoots left. 6'4", 205 lbs. Born, Marquette, MI, May 18, 1990. Boston's 5th pick, 135th overall, in 2010 NHL Draft.

Season	Club	League	GP	G	A	Pts	PIM	PP	SH	GW	S	S%	+/-	TF	F%	Min	GP	G	A	Pts	PIM	PP	SH	GW	Min
2006-07	USAHNTDP	NAHL	47	11	10	21	40	....	....	....	....	....	....	....	....	....	6	3	0	3	4	....	....	....	....
	USAHNTDP	U-17	13	6	1	7	8	....	....	....	....	....	....	....	....	....	....	....	....	....	....	....	....	....	....
2007-08	USAHNTDP	NAHL	13	3	3	6	8	....	....	....	....	....	....	....	....	....	....	....	....	....	....	....	....	....	....
	USAHNTDP	U-17	1	0	0	0	2	....	....	....	....	....	....	....	....	....	....	....	....	....	....	....	....	....	....
	USAHNTDP	U-18	41	5	5	10	20	....	....	....	....	....	....	....	....	....	....	....	....	....	....	....	....	....	....
2008-09	Northern Mich.	CCHA	40	9	8	17	6	....	....	....	....	....	....	....	....	....	....	....	....	....	....	....	....	....	....
2009-10	Northern Mich.	CCHA	41	12	23	35	22	....	....	....	....	....	....	....	....	....	....	....	....	....	....	....	....	....	....
2010-11	Northern Mich.	CCHA	39	13	15	28	14	....	....	....	....	....	....	....	....	....	....	....	....	....	....	....	....	....	....
2011-12	Northern Mich.	CCHA	37	19	17	36	18	....	....	....	....	....	....	....	....	....	....	....	....	....	....	....	....	....	....
	Providence Bruins	AHL	8	2	2	4	2	....	....	....	....	....	....	....	....	....	....	....	....	....	....	....	....	....	....
2012-13	Providence Bruins	AHL	71	11	16	27	37	....	....	....	....	....	....	....	....	....	12	1	2	3	4	....	....	....	....
2013-14	**Boston**	**NHL**	**4**	**1**	**1**	**2**	**0**	**0**	**0**	**0**	**5**	**20.0**	**1**	**1**	**0.0**	**11:51**	**6**	**1**	**0**	**1**	**4**	**0**	**0**	**0**	**11:50**
	Providence Bruins	AHL	69	19	19	38	27	....	....	....	....	....	....	....	....	....	4	1	0	1	0	....	....	....	....
2014-15	Providence Bruins	AHL	73	11	24	35	33	....	....	....	....	....	....	....	....	....	5	0	0	0	2	....	....	....	....
2015-16	Bridgeport	AHL	76	7	9	16	31	....	....	....	....	....	....	....	....	....	3	1	0	1	0	....	....	....	....
2016-17	Milwaukee	AHL	75	12	18	30	12	....	....	....	....	....	....	....	....	....	3	0	0	0	2	....	....	....	....
	NHL Totals		**4**	**1**	**1**	**2**	**0**	**0**	**0**	**0**	**5**	**20.0**		**1**	**0.0**	**11:51**	**6**	**1**	**0**	**1**	**4**	**0**	**0**	**0**	**11:50**

CCHA Second All-Star Team (2012)

Signed as a free agent by **NY Islanders**, July 2, 2015.

FLYNN, Brian

(FLIHN, BRIGH-uhn) **DAL**

Right wing. Shoots right. 6'1", 183 lbs. Born, Lynnfield, MA, July 26, 1988.

Season	Club	League	GP	G	A	Pts	PIM	PP	SH	GW	S	S%	+/-	TF	F%	Min	Playoffs GP	G	A	Pts	PIM	PP	SH	GW	Min
2007-08	N.H. Jr. Monarchs	EJHL	41	26	19	45	24										6	1	4	5	10				
2008-09	U. of Maine	H-East	38	12	13	25	10																		
2009-10	U. of Maine	H-East	39	19	28	47	12																		
2010-11	U. of Maine	H-East	36	20	16	36	8																		
2011-12	U. of Maine	H-East	40	18	30	48	37																		
	Rochester	AHL	5	0	1	1	2																		
2012-13	Rochester	AHL	45	16	16	32	18										3	0	0	0	4				
	Buffalo	**NHL**	26	6	5	11	0	0	1	1	49	12.2	6	60	40.0	14:41									
2013-14	**Buffalo**	**NHL**	79	6	7	13	14	0	1	1	102	5.9	−10	389	47.3	14:25									
2014-15	**Buffalo**	**NHL**	54	5	12	17	8	0	0	0	73	6.8	−3	330	47.6	15:53									
	Montreal	**NHL**	9	0	0	0	0	0	0	0	9	0.0	−2	29	51.7	9:04	6	1	2	3	0	0	0	1	11:00
2015-16	**Montreal**	**NHL**	56	4	6	10	6	0	1	0	73	5.5	−3	346	57.8	11:44									
2016-17	**Montreal**	**NHL**	51	6	4	10	4	0	0	0	47	12.8	2	149	46.3	12:04	1	0	0	0	0	0	0	0	15:33
	NHL Totals		275	27	34	61	32	0	3	1	353	7.6		1303	49.8	13:34	7	1	2	3	0	0	0	1	11:39

Hockey East First All-Star Team (2012)

Signed as a free agent by **Buffalo**, March 29, 2012. Traded to **Montreal** by **Buffalo** for Montreal's 5th round pick (Vojtech Budik) in 2016 NHL Draft, March 2, 2015. Signed as a free agent by **Dallas**, July 1, 2017.

FOLIGNO, Marcus

(foh-LEE-noh, MAHR-kuhs) **MIN**

Left wing. Shoots left. 6'3", 228 lbs. Born, Buffalo, NY, August 10, 1991. Buffalo's 3rd pick, 104th overall, in 2009 NHL Draft.

Season	Club	League	GP	G	A	Pts	PIM	PP	SH	GW	S	S%	+/-	TF	F%	Min	Playoffs GP	G	A	Pts	PIM	PP	SH	GW	Min
2006-07	Sud. Nickel Cap's	Minor-ON	30	21	15	36	70																		
2007-08	Sudbury Wolves	OHL	66	5	6	11	38																		
2008-09	Sudbury Wolves	OHL	65	12	18	30	96										6	1	2	3	9				
2009-10	Sudbury Wolves	OHL	67	14	25	39	156										4	1	1	2	6				
2010-11	Sudbury Wolves	OHL	47	23	36	59	92										8	2	1	3	24				
2011-12	**Buffalo**	**NHL**	14	6	7	13	9	2	0	1	23	26.1	6	3	0.0	15:49									
	Rochester	AHL	60	16	23	39	78										3	2	1	3	4				
2012-13	Rochester	AHL	33	10	17	27	38																		
	Buffalo	**NHL**	47	5	13	18	41	1	0	0	55	9.1	−4	75	60.0	13:38									
2013-14	**Buffalo**	**NHL**	74	7	12	19	82	0	1	3	79	8.9	−17	301	48.5	15:04									
2014-15	**Buffalo**	**NHL**	57	8	12	20	50	0	0	0	66	12.1	−5	132	43.2	16:14									
2015-16	**Buffalo**	**NHL**	75	10	13	23	79	0	2	2	81	12.3	4	4	25.0	13:11									
2016-17	**Buffalo**	**NHL**	80	13	10	23	73	0	1	0	97	13.4	−1	5	20.0	15:28									
	NHL Totals		347	49	67	116	334	3	4	6	401	12.2		520	48.1	14:47									

OHL Second All-Star Team (2011)

Traded to **Minnesota** by **Buffalo** with Tyler Ennis and Buffalo's 3rd round pick in 2018 NHL Draft for Jason Pominville, Marco Scandella and Minnesota's 4th round pick in 2018 NHL Draft, June 30, 2017.

FOLIGNO, Nick

(foh-LEE-noh, NIHK) **CBJ**

Left wing. Shoots left. 6', 205 lbs. Born, Buffalo, NY, October 31, 1987. Ottawa's 1st pick, 28th overall, in 2006 NHL Draft.

Season	Club	League	GP	G	A	Pts	PIM	PP	SH	GW	S	S%	+/-	TF	F%	Min	Playoffs GP	G	A	Pts	PIM	PP	SH	GW	Min
2003-04	USAHNTDP	U-17	18	7	9	16	28																		
	USAHNTDP	NAHL	43	8	12	20	44										7	2	1	3	8				
2004-05	USAHNTDP	U-18	4	2	1	3	0																		
	Sudbury Wolves	OHL	65	10	28	38	111										12	5	5	10	16				
2005-06	Sudbury Wolves	OHL	65	24	46	70	146										10	1	3	4	28				
2006-07	Sudbury Wolves	OHL	66	31	57	88	135										21	12	17	29	36				
2007-08	**Ottawa**	**NHL**	45	6	3	9	20	0	0	0	44	13.6	0	49	44.9	9:10	4	1	0	1	2	0	0	0	12:50
	Binghamton	AHL	28	6	13	19	16																		
2008-09	**Ottawa**	**NHL**	81	17	15	32	59	7	0	2	145	11.7	−10	47	44.7	13:41									
2009-10	**Ottawa**	**NHL**	61	9	17	26	53	2	0	2	83	10.8	6	50	34.0	14:19	6	0	1	1	2	0	0	0	17:07
2010-11	**Ottawa**	**NHL**	82	14	20	34	43	5	0	3	149	9.4	−19	138	47.1	15:35									
2011-12	**Ottawa**	**NHL**	82	15	32	47	124	1	0	3	153	9.8	2	149	41.6	14:39	7	1	3	4	8	0	0	0	15:10
2012-13	**Columbus**	**NHL**	45	6	13	19	28	1	0	2	69	8.7	6	9	33.3	16:31									
2013-14	**Columbus**	**NHL**	70	18	21	39	96	3	0	5	111	16.2	5	13	46.2	16:04	4	2	0	2	4	0	0	1	14:56
2014-15	**Columbus**	**NHL**	79	31	42	73	50	11	0	3	182	17.0	16	263	47.5	18:50									
2015-16	**Columbus**	**NHL**	72	12	25	37	53	0	0	2	149	8.1	−14	176	47.2	16:54									
2016-17	**Columbus**	**NHL**	79	26	25	51	55	11	0	5	185	14.1	−4	89	46.1	18:26	4	0	2	2	6	0	0	0	20:25
	NHL Totals		696	154	213	367	581	41	0	27	1270	12.1		983	45.3	15:40	25	4	6	10	22	0	0	1	16:04

Mark Messier NHL Leadership Award (2017) • King Clancy Memorial Trophy (2017)

Played in NHL All-Star Game (2015)

Traded to **Columbus** by **Ottawa** for Marc Methot, July 1, 2012.

FOLIN, Christian

(FOH-lihn, KRIHS-t'yehn) **L.A.**

Defense. Shoots right. 6'4", 219 lbs. Born, Gothenburg, Sweden, February 9, 1991.

Season	Club	League	GP	G	A	Pts	PIM	PP	SH	GW	S	S%	+/-	TF	F%	Min	Playoffs GP	G	A	Pts	PIM	PP	SH	GW	Min
2007-08	Frolunda U18	Swe-U18	28	3	10	13	10										5	0	0	0	2				
2008-09	Frolunda U18	Swe-U18	27	6	17	23	55										7	1	3	4	6				
	Frolunda Jr.	Swe-Jr.	13	2	1	3	4										4	0	0	0	2				
2009-10	Frolunda Jr.	Swe-Jr.	38	3	16	19	22										5	0	3	3	20				
	Hanhals HF	Sweden-4	1	1	1	2	0																		
2010-11	Fargo Force	USHL	12	2	2	4	6																		
	Austin Bruins	NAHL	33	2	9	11	27																		
2011-12	Austin Bruins	NAHL	54	11	20	31	50										2	0	1	1	2				
2012-13	U. Mass Lowell	H-East	38	6	15	21	24																		
2013-14	U. Mass Lowell	H-East	41	6	14	20	31																		
	Minnesota	**NHL**	1	0	1	1	0	0	0	0	0	0.0	3	0	0.0	19:26									
2014-15	**Minnesota**	**NHL**	40	2	8	10	13	0	0	0	39	5.1	3	0	0.0	15:12									
	Iowa Wild	AHL	13	2	2	4	4																		
2015-16	**Minnesota**	**NHL**	26	0	4	4	11	0	0	0	14	0.0	−1	0	0.0	14:35									
	Iowa Wild	AHL	28	4	9	13	8																		
2016-17	**Minnesota**	**NHL**	51	2	6	8	26	0	0	0	39	5.1	10	0	0.0	14:56	2	0	0	0	2	0	0	0	11:24
	NHL Totals		118	4	19	23	50	0	0	0	92	4.3		0	0.0	14:59	2	0	0	0	2	0	0	0	11:24

Signed as a free agent by **Minnesota**, April 2, 2014. Signed as a free agent by **Los Angeles**, July 1, 2017.

FONTAINE, Justin

(fawn-TAYN, JUHS-tihn) **EDM**

Right wing. Shoots right. 5'10", 174 lbs. Born, Bonnyville, AB, November 6, 1987.

Season	Club	League	GP	G	A	Pts	PIM	PP	SH	GW	S	S%	+/-	TF	F%	Min	Playoffs GP	G	A	Pts	PIM	PP	SH	GW	Min
2004-05	N.E. Panthers	Minor-AB	STATISTICS NOT AVAILABLE																						
	Bonnyville	AJHL	12	1	4	5	12																		
2005-06	Bonnyville	AJHL	50	26	55	81	36										9	1	6	7	4				
2006-07	Bonnyville	AJHL	52	30	41	71	60										5	3	5	8	10				
2007-08	U. Minn-Duluth	WCHA	35	4	8	12	8																		
2008-09	U. Minn-Duluth	WCHA	43	15	33	48	18																		
2009-10	U. Minn-Duluth	WCHA	39	21	25	46	22																		
2010-11	U. Minn-Duluth	WCHA	42	22	36	58	42																		
2011-12	Houston Aeros	AHL	73	16	39	55	32										4	0	0	0	0				
2012-13	Houston Aeros	AHL	64	23	33	56	18										5	3	5	8	4				
2013-14	**Minnesota**	**NHL**	66	13	8	21	26	1	0	1	79	16.5	6	2	100.0	12:15	9	1	1	2	2	0	0	0	11:06
2014-15	**Minnesota**	**NHL**	71	9	22	31	12	0	0	2	104	8.7	13	2	50.0	11:57	6	1	1	2	2	0	0	1	10:45
2015-16	**Minnesota**	**NHL**	60	5	11	16	20	0	0	1	54	9.3	3	4	25.0	11:51	4	0	0	0	0	0	0	0	13:21

Season	Club	League	Regular Season GP	G	A	Pts	PIM	PP	SH	GW	S	S%	+/-	TF	F%	Min	Playoffs GP	G	A	Pts	PIM	PP	SH	GW	Min
2016-17	Hartford	AHL	50	9	21	30	20	....	....	....	....	....	....	....	....	....	....	....	....	....	....	....	....	....	....
	Bakersfield	AHL	15	2	9	11	6	....	....	....	....	....	....	....	....	....	....	....	....	....	....	....	....	....	....
	NHL Totals		197	27	41	68	58	1	0	4	237	11.4		8	50.0	12:02	19	2	2	4	4	0	0	1	11:28

WCHA Second All-Star Team (2009, 2010, 2011)

Signed as a free agent by **Minnesota**, April 19, 2011. Signed as a free agent by **NY Rangers**, October 16, 2016. Traded to **Edmonton** by **NY Rangers** for Taylor Beck, March 1, 2017.

FORBORT, Derek

(FOHR-bohrt, DAIR-ihk) **L.A.**

Defense. Shoots left. 6'4", 216 lbs. Born, Duluth, MN, March 4, 1992. Los Angeles' 1st pick, 15th overall, in 2010 NHL Draft.

Season	Club	League	GP	G	A	Pts	PIM	PP	SH	GW	S	S%	+/-	TF	F%	Min	GP	G	A	Pts	PIM	PP	SH	GW	Min
2008-09	Duluth East	High-MN	25	7	21	28	....	....	....	....	....	....	....	....	....	....	....	....	....	....	....	....	....	....	....
	USAHNTDP	NAHL	2	0	1	1	6	....	....	....	....	....	....	....	....	....	....	....	....	....	....	....	....	....	....
	USAHNTDP	U-17	7	1	4	5	4	....	....	....	....	....	....	....	....	....	....	....	....	....	....	....	....	....	....
2009-10	USAHNTDP	USHL	26	4	10	14	26	....	....	....	....	....	....	....	....	....	....	....	....	....	....	....	....	....	....
	USAHNTDP	U-18	39	1	13	14	20	....	....	....	....	....	....	....	....	....	....	....	....	....	....	....	....	....	....
2010-11	North Dakota	WCHA	38	0	15	15	26	....	....	....	....	....	....	....	....	....	....	....	....	....	....	....	....	....	....
2011-12	North Dakota	WCHA	35	2	11	13	28	....	....	....	....	....	....	....	....	....	....	....	....	....	....	....	....	....	....
2012-13	North Dakota	WCHA	42	4	13	17	22	....	....	....	....	....	....	....	....	....	....	....	....	....	....	....	....	....	....
	Manchester	AHL	6	0	1	1	0	....	....	....	....	....	....	....	....	....	4	0	0	0	4	....	....	....	....
2013-14	Manchester	AHL	74	1	16	17	42	....	....	....	....	....	....	....	....	....	3	0	0	0	0	....	....	....	....
2014-15	Manchester	AHL	67	4	11	15	52	....	....	....	....	....	....	....	....	....	19	0	6	6	12	....	....	....	....
2015-16	**Los Angeles**	**NHL**	**14**	**1**	**1**	**2**	**17**	**0**	**0**	**0**	**14**	**7.1**	**-1**	**0**	**0.0**	**11:03**	....	....	....	....	....	....	....	....	....
	Ontario Reign	AHL	40	2	8	10	40	....	....	....	....	....	....	....	....	....	13	0	2	2	0	....	....	....	....
2016-17	**Los Angeles**	**NHL**	**82**	**2**	**16**	**18**	**54**	**0**	**0**	**0**	**100**	**2.0**	**8**	**11**	**100.0**	**20:07**	....	....	....	....	....	....	....	....	....
	NHL Totals		**96**	**3**	**17**	**20**	**71**	**0**	**0**	**0**	**114**	**2.6**		**11**	**100.0**	**18:48**	....	....	....	....	....	....	....	....	....

FORSBACKA KARLSSON, Jakob

(forz-BAH-kuh KAHRL-suhn, YA-kuhb) **BOS**

Center. Shoots right. 6'1", 184 lbs. Born, Stockholm, Sweden, October 31, 1996. Boston's 5th pick, 45th overall, in 2015 NHL Draft.

Season	Club	League	GP	G	A	Pts	PIM	PP	SH	GW	S	S%	+/-	TF	F%	Min	GP	G	A	Pts	PIM	PP	SH	GW	Min
2011-12	Nacka HK U18	Swe-U18	26	13	19	32	16	....	....	....	....	....	....	....	....	....	....	....	....	....	....	....	....	....	....
2012-13	Linkoping U18	Swe-U18	17	15	20	35	16	....	....	....	....	....	....	....	....	....	2	0	0	0	0	....	....	....	....
	Linkopings HC Jr.	Swe-Jr.	31	9	7	16	26	....	....	....	....	....	....	....	....	....	5	0	2	2	4	....	....	....	....
2013-14	Omaha Lancers	USHL	60	11	22	33	26	....	....	....	....	....	....	....	....	....	4	0	1	1	4	....	....	....	....
2014-15	Omaha Lancers	USHL	50	15	38	53	38	....	....	....	....	....	....	....	....	....	....	....	....	....	....	....	....	....	....
2015-16	Boston University	H-East	39	10	20	30	28	....	....	....	....	....	....	....	....	....	....	....	....	....	....	....	....	....	....
2016-17	Boston University	H-East	39	14	19	33	32	....	....	....	....	....	....	....	....	....	....	....	....	....	....	....	....	....	....
	Boston	**NHL**	**1**	**0**	**0**	**0**	**0**	**0**	**0**	**0**	**0**	**0.0**	**0**	**2**	**50.0**	**8:25**	....	....	....	....	....	....	....	....	....
	NHL Totals		**1**	**0**	**0**	**0**	**0**	**0**	**0**	**0**	**0**	**0.0**		**2**	**50.0**	**8:25**	....	....	....	....	....	....	....	....	....

Hockey East All-Rookie Team (2016)

FORSBERG, Filip

(FOHRZ-buhrg, FIH-lihp) **NSH**

Center. Shoots right. 6'1", 205 lbs. Born, Ostervala, Sweden, August 13, 1994. Washington's 1st pick, 11th overall, in 2012 NHL Draft.

Season	Club	League	GP	G	A	Pts	PIM	PP	SH	GW	S	S%	+/-	TF	F%	Min	GP	G	A	Pts	PIM	PP	SH	GW	Min
2008-09	Leksands IF U18 2	Swe-U18	15	12	9	21	14	....	....	....	....	....	....	....	....	....	....	....	....	....	....	....	....	....	....
2009-10	Leksands IF U18	Swe-U18	31	21	16	37	22	....	....	....	....	....	....	....	....	....	4	5	3	8	0	....	....	....	....
	Leksands IF Jr.	Swe-Jr.	....	....	....	....	....	....	....	....	....	....	....	....	....	....	5	0	0	0	0	....	....	....	....
2010-11	Leksands IF U18	Swe-U18	3	1	5	6	4	....	....	....	....	....	....	....	....	....	6	2	2	4	2	....	....	....	....
	Leksands IF Jr.	Swe-Jr.	36	21	19	40	22	....	....	....	....	....	....	....	....	....	....	....	....	....	....	....	....	....	....
	Leksands IF	Sweden-2	16	1	1	2	0	....	....	....	....	....	....	....	....	....	....	....	....	....	....	....	....	....	....
2011-12	Leksands IF U18	Swe-U18	1	0	2	2	0	....	....	....	....	....	....	....	....	....	....	....	....	....	....	....	....	....	....
	Leksands IF Jr.	Swe-Jr.	6	0	1	1	2	....	....	....	....	....	....	....	....	....	....	....	....	....	....	....	....	....	....
	Leksands IF	Sweden-2	53	10	10	20	33	....	....	....	....	....	....	....	....	....	....	....	....	....	....	....	....	....	....
2012-13	Leksands IF	Sweden-2	47	20	22	42	22	....	....	....	....	....	....	....	....	....	....	....	....	....	....	....	....	....	....
	Nashville	**NHL**	**5**	**0**	**1**	**1**	**0**	**0**	**0**	**0**	**14**	**0.0**	**-5**	**1**	**0.0**	**15:29**	....	....	....	....	....	....	....	....	....
2013-14	**Nashville**	**NHL**	**13**	**1**	**4**	**5**	**4**	**1**	**0**	**0**	**20**	**5.0**	**-8**	**0**	**0.0**	**11:24**	....	....	....	....	....	....	....	....	....
	Milwaukee	AHL	47	15	19	34	14	....	....	....	....	....	....	....	....	....	3	1	1	2	0	....	....	....	....
	Sweden	Olympics	7	4	8	12	2	....	....	....	....	....	....	....	....	....	....	....	....	....	....	....	....	....	....
2014-15	**Nashville**	**NHL**	**82**	**26**	**37**	**63**	**24**	**6**	**0**	**6**	**237**	**11.0**	**15**	**7**	**42.9**	**17:20**	**6**	**4**	**2**	**6**	**4**	**1**	**0**	**0**	**20:36**
2015-16	**Nashville**	**NHL**	**82**	**33**	**31**	**64**	**47**	**8**	**1**	**3**	**247**	**13.4**	**1**	**9**	**22.2**	**19:03**	**14**	**2**	**2**	**4**	**2**	**1**	**0**	**1**	**19:58**
2016-17	**Nashville**	**NHL**	**82**	**31**	**27**	**58**	**32**	**3**	**3**	**9**	**234**	**13.2**	**-4**	**18**	**27.8**	**18:31**	**22**	**9**	**7**	**16**	**14**	**1**	**0**	**0**	**20:00**
	NHL Totals		**264**	**91**	**100**	**191**	**107**	**18**	**4**	**18**	**752**	**12.1**		**35**	**28.6**	**17:54**	**42**	**15**	**11**	**26**	**20**	**3**	**0**	**1**	**20:04**

NHL All-Rookie Team (2015)

Played in NHL All-Star Game (2015)

Traded to **Nashville** by **Washington** for Martin Erat and Michael Latta, April 3, 2013.

FORSLING, Gustav

(FOHRZ-lihng, GOO-stahv) **CHI**

Defense. Shoots left. 6', 186 lbs. Born, Linkoping, Sweden, June 12, 1996. Vancouver's 5th pick, 126th overall, in 2014 NHL Draft.

Season	Club	League	GP	G	A	Pts	PIM	PP	SH	GW	S	S%	+/-	TF	F%	Min	GP	G	A	Pts	PIM	PP	SH	GW	Min
2011-12	Linkoping U18	Swe-U18	27	5	3	8	10	....	....	....	....	....	....	....	....	....	3	0	1	1	0	....	....	....	....
2012-13	Linkoping U18	Swe-U18	31	7	8	15	20	....	....	....	....	....	....	....	....	....	2	0	0	0	0	....	....	....	....
	Linkopings HC Jr.	Swe-Jr.	14	0	1	1	8	....	....	....	....	....	....	....	....	....	1	0	0	0	0	....	....	....	....
2013-14	Linkoping U18	Swe-U18	5	3	3	6	2	....	....	....	....	....	....	....	....	....	5	1	0	1	0	....	....	....	....
	Linkopings HC Jr.	Swe-Jr.	44	6	12	18	36	....	....	....	....	....	....	....	....	....	2	1	3	4	2	....	....	....	....
2014-15	Linkopings HC	Sweden	38	3	3	6	8	....	....	....	....	....	....	....	....	....	....	....	....	....	....	....	....	....	....
2015-16	Linkopings HC	Sweden	48	6	15	21	4	....	....	....	....	....	....	....	....	....	6	1	2	3	4	....	....	....	....
2016-17	**Chicago**	**NHL**	**38**	**2**	**3**	**5**	**4**	**0**	**0**	**0**	**48**	**4.2**	**3**	**0**	**0.0**	**14:49**	....	....	....	....	....	....	....	....	....
	Rockford IceHogs	AHL	30	1	7	8	12	....	....	....	....	....	....	....	....	....	....	....	....	....	....	....	....	....	....
	NHL Totals		**38**	**2**	**3**	**5**	**4**	**0**	**0**	**0**	**48**	**4.2**		**0**	**0.0**	**14:49**	....	....	....	....	....	....	....	....	....

Traded to **Chicago** by **Vancouver** for Adam Clendening, January 29, 2015.

FORTUNUS, Maxime

(fohr-TOON-uhs, MAX-eem)

Defense. Shoots right. 6'1", 198 lbs. Born, Longueil, QC, July 28, 1983.

Season	Club	League	GP	G	A	Pts	PIM	PP	SH	GW	S	S%	+/-	TF	F%	Min	GP	G	A	Pts	PIM	PP	SH	GW	Min
1998-99	C.C. Lemoyne	QAAA	39	3	10	13	18	....	....	....	....	....	....	....	....	....	17	0	9	9	8	....	....	....	....
99-2000	Baie-Comeau	QMJHL	68	6	15	21	36	....	....	....	....	....	....	....	....	....	6	0	0	0	2	....	....	....	....
2000-01	Baie-Comeau	QMJHL	71	10	31	41	106	....	....	....	....	....	....	....	....	....	11	2	4	6	6	....	....	....	....
2001-02	Baie-Comeau	QMJHL	72	11	30	41	76	....	....	....	....	....	....	....	....	....	5	0	1	1	2	....	....	....	....
2002-03	Baie-Comeau	QMJHL	69	12	32	44	44	....	....	....	....	....	....	....	....	....	12	2	4	6	6	....	....	....	....
2003-04	Baie-Comeau	QMJHL	5	1	0	1	15	....	....	....	....	....	....	....	....	....	....	....	....	....	....	....	....	....	....
	Houston Aeros	AHL	12	0	2	2	2	....	....	....	....	....	....	....	....	....	1	0	0	0	0	....	....	....	....
	Louisiana	ECHL	64	3	15	18	27	....	....	....	....	....	....	....	....	....	4	1	1	2	0	....	....	....	....
2004-05	Houston Aeros	AHL	13	0	0	0	4	....	....	....	....	....	....	....	....	....	....	....	....	....	....	....	....	....	....
	Louisiana	ECHL	59	8	16	24	26	....	....	....	....	....	....	....	....	....	....	....	....	....	....	....	....	....	....
2005-06	Manitoba Moose	AHL	76	3	10	13	36	....	....	....	....	....	....	....	....	....	13	0	0	0	10	....	....	....	....
2006-07	Manitoba Moose	AHL	72	2	18	20	64	....	....	....	....	....	....	....	....	....	13	1	4	5	10	....	....	....	....
2007-08	Manitoba Moose	AHL	65	8	13	21	28	....	....	....	....	....	....	....	....	....	6	0	1	1	4	....	....	....	....
2008-09	Manitoba Moose	AHL	58	7	12	19	18	....	....	....	....	....	....	....	....	....	22	3	7	10	2	....	....	....	....
2009-10	**Dallas**	**NHL**	**8**	**0**	**0**	**0**	**4**	**0**	**0**	**0**	**5**	**0.0**	**-6**	**0**	**0.0**	**15:09**	....	....	....	....	....	....	....	....	....
	Texas Stars	AHL	72	11	12	23	28	....	....	....	....	....	....	....	....	....	24	2	7	9	14	....	....	....	....
2010-11	Texas Stars	AHL	73	5	29	34	20	....	....	....	....	....	....	....	....	....	6	0	1	1	2	....	....	....	....
2011-12	Texas Stars	AHL	60	6	14	20	18	....	....	....	....	....	....	....	....	....	....	....	....	....	....	....	....	....	....
2012-13	Texas Stars	AHL	67	7	21	28	16	....	....	....	....	....	....	....	....	....	9	0	1	1	2	....	....	....	....
2013-14	**Dallas**	**NHL**	**1**	**0**	**1**	**1**	**0**	**0**	**0**	**0**	**0**	**0.0**	**1**	**0**	**0.0**	**16:17**	....	....	....	....	....	....	....	....	....
	Texas Stars	AHL	65	6	22	28	18	....	....	....	....	....	....	....	....	....	21	0	4	4	8	....	....	....	....
2014-15	Texas Stars	AHL	65	9	25	34	31	....	....	....	....	....	....	....	....	....	3	0	0	0	2	....	....	....	....

			Regular Season														Playoffs								
Season	Club	League	GP	G	A	Pts	PIM	PP	SH	GW	S	S%	+/-	TF	F%	Min	GP	G	A	Pts	PIM	PP	SH	GW	Min
2015-16	Iowa Wild	AHL	66	6	11	17	18	....	....	....	....	....	....	....	....	....	....	....	....	....	....	....	....	....	....
2016-17	Iowa Wild	AHL	64	4	11	15	20	....	....	....	....	....	....	....	....	....	....	....	....	....	....	....	....	....	....
	NHL Totals		**9**	**0**	**1**	**1**	**4**	**0**	**0**	**0**	**5**	**0.0**		**0**	**0.0**	**15:16**	....	....	....	....	....	....	....	....	....

Signed as a free agent by **Dallas**, July 3, 2008.

FOWLER, Cam (FOW-luhr, KAM) ANA

Defense. Shoots left. 6'1", 207 lbs. Born, Windsor, ON, December 5, 1991. Anaheim's 1st pick, 12th overall, in 2010 NHL Draft.

Season	Club	League	GP	G	A	Pts	PIM	PP	SH	GW	S	S%	+/-	TF	F%	Min	GP	G	A	Pts	PIM	PP	SH	GW	Min
2006-07	Det. Honeybaked	MWEHL	21	5	13	18	18	....	....	....	....	....	....	....	....	....	....	....	....	....	....	....	....	....	....
	Det. Honeybaked	Minor-MI	31	3	7	10	....	....	....	....	....	....	....	....	....	....	....	....	....	....	....	....	....	....	....
2007-08	USAHNTDP	NAHL	38	3	10	13	2	....	....	....	....	....	....	....	....	....	3	0	0	0	2	....	....	....	....
	USAHNTDP	U-17	18	0	2	2	8	....	....	....	....	....	....	....	....	....	....	....	....	....	....	....	....	....	....
	USAHNTDP	U-18	1	0	0	0	0	....	....	....	....	....	....	....	....	....	....	....	....	....	....	....	....	....	....
2008-09	USAHNTDP	NAHL	14	2	7	9	12	....	....	....	....	....	....	....	....	....	....	....	....	....	....	....	....	....	....
	USAHNTDP	U-18	33	6	25	31	32	....	....	....	....	....	....	....	....	....	....	....	....	....	....	....	....	....	....
2009-10	Windsor Spitfires	OHL	55	8	47	55	14	....	....	....	....	....	....	....	....	....	19	3	11	14	10	....	....	....	....
2010-11	**Anaheim**	**NHL**	**76**	**10**	**30**	**40**	**20**	**6**	**0**	**3**	**123**	**8.1**	**–25**	**0**	**0.0**	**22:08**	**6**	**1**	**3**	**4**	**2**	**1**	**0**	**0**	**22:13**
2011-12	**Anaheim**	**NHL**	**82**	**5**	**24**	**29**	**18**	**2**	**0**	**0**	**123**	**4.1**	**–28**	**1**	**100.0**	**23:16**	....	....	....	....	....	....	....	....	....
2012-13	Sodertalje SK	Sweden-2	14	2	5	7	14	....	....	....	....	....	....	....	....	....	....	....	....	....	....	....	....	....	....
	Anaheim	**NHL**	**37**	**1**	**10**	**11**	**4**	**1**	**0**	**0**	**50**	**2.0**	**–4**	**0**	**0.0**	**20:26**	**7**	**0**	**3**	**3**	**0**	**0**	**0**	**0**	**22:45**
2013-14	**Anaheim**	**NHL**	**70**	**6**	**30**	**36**	**14**	**4**	**1**	**2**	**100**	**6.0**	**15**	**0**	**0.0**	**23:52**	**13**	**0**	**4**	**4**	**4**	**0**	**0**	**0**	**23:52**
	United States	Olympics	6	1	0	1	0	....	....	....	....	....	....	....	....	....	....	....	....	....	....	....	....	....	....
2014-15	**Anaheim**	**NHL**	**80**	**7**	**27**	**34**	**14**	**1**	**1**	**2**	**87**	**8.0**	**4**	**0**	**0.0**	**21:09**	**16**	**2**	**8**	**10**	**2**	**0**	**0**	**0**	**23:08**
2015-16	**Anaheim**	**NHL**	**69**	**5**	**23**	**28**	**27**	**3**	**0**	**0**	**113**	**4.4**	**–8**	**0**	**0.0**	**22:47**	**7**	**1**	**2**	**3**	**4**	**1**	**0**	**0**	**25:22**
2016-17	**Anaheim**	**NHL**	**80**	**11**	**28**	**39**	**20**	**5**	**1**	**3**	**186**	**5.9**	**7**	**0**	**0.0**	**24:51**	**13**	**2**	**7**	**9**	**2**	**0**	**0**	**0**	**26:30**
	NHL Totals		**494**	**45**	**172**	**217**	**117**	**22**	**3**	**10**	**782**	**5.8**		**1**	**100.0**	**22:48**	**62**	**6**	**27**	**33**	**14**	**2**	**0**	**0**	**24:07**

Played in NHL All-Star Game (2017)

Signed as a free agent by **Sodertalje** (Sweden-2), November 14, 2012.

FRANSON, Cody (FRAN-suhn, KOH-dee)

Defense. Shoots right. 6'5", 234 lbs. Born, Sicamous, BC, August 8, 1987. Nashville's 3rd pick, 79th overall, in 2005 NHL Draft.

Season	Club	League	GP	G	A	Pts	PIM	PP	SH	GW	S	S%	+/-	TF	F%	Min	GP	G	A	Pts	PIM	PP	SH	GW	Min
2002-03	Sicamous	Minor-BC	65	44	82	126	42	....	....	....	....	....	....	....	....	....	....	....	....	....	....	....	....	....	....
	Vancouver Giants	WHL	3	0	0	0	2	....	....	....	....	....	....	....	....	....	....	....	....	....	....	....	....	....	....
2003-04	Beaver Valley	KIJHL	48	10	22	32	70	....	....	....	....	....	....	....	....	....	....	....	....	....	....	....	....	....	....
	Trail	BCHL	2	0	1	1	0	....	....	....	....	....	....	....	....	....	....	....	....	....	....	....	....	....	....
	Vancouver Giants	WHL	2	0	0	0	0	....	....	....	....	....	....	....	....	....	....	....	....	....	....	....	....	....	....
2004-05	Vancouver Giants	WHL	64	2	11	13	44	....	....	....	....	....	....	....	....	....	4	0	1	1	0	....	....	....	....
2005-06	Vancouver Giants	WHL	71	15	40	55	61	....	....	....	....	....	....	....	....	....	18	5	15	20	12	....	....	....	....
2006-07	Vancouver Giants	WHL	59	17	34	51	88	....	....	....	....	....	....	....	....	....	19	3	4	7	10	....	....	....	....
2007-08	Milwaukee	AHL	76	11	25	36	40	....	....	....	....	....	....	....	....	....	6	0	2	2	2	....	....	....	....
2008-09	Milwaukee	AHL	76	11	41	52	47	....	....	....	....	....	....	....	....	....	11	3	5	8	8	....	....	....	....
2009-10	**Nashville**	**NHL**	**61**	**6**	**15**	**21**	**16**	**1**	**0**	**3**	**90**	**6.7**	**15**	**0**	**0.0**	**14:12**	**4**	**0**	**1**	**1**	**2**	**0**	**0**	**0**	**9:02**
	Milwaukee	AHL	6	2	5	7	4	....	....	....	....	....	....	....	....	....	....	....	....	....	....	....	....	....	....
2010-11	**Nashville**	**NHL**	**80**	**8**	**21**	**29**	**30**	**2**	**0**	**2**	**156**	**5.1**	**10**	**0**	**0.0**	**15:10**	**12**	**1**	**5**	**6**	**0**	**0**	**0**	**0**	**15:19**
2011-12	**Toronto**	**NHL**	**57**	**5**	**16**	**21**	**22**	**2**	**0**	**0**	**65**	**7.7**	**–1**	**0**	**0.0**	**16:11**	....	....	....	....	....	....	....	....	....
2012-13	Brynas IF Gavle	Sweden	26	3	4	7	10	....	....	....	....	....	....	....	....	....	....	....	....	....	....	....	....	....	....
	Toronto	**NHL**	**45**	**4**	**25**	**29**	**8**	**3**	**0**	**0**	**70**	**5.7**	**4**	**0**	**0.0**	**18:47**	**7**	**3**	**3**	**6**	**0**	**1**	**0**	**0**	**22:49**
2013-14	**Toronto**	**NHL**	**79**	**5**	**28**	**33**	**30**	**1**	**0**	**0**	**115**	**4.3**	**–20**	**0**	**0.0**	**20:41**	....	....	....	....	....	....	....	....	....
2014-15	**Toronto**	**NHL**	**55**	**6**	**26**	**32**	**26**	**4**	**0**	**0**	**92**	**6.5**	**–7**	**0**	**0.0**	**21:23**	....	....	....	....	....	....	....	....	....
	Nashville	**NHL**	**23**	**1**	**3**	**4**	**2**	**1**	**0**	**0**	**35**	**2.9**	**0**	**0**	**0.0**	**15:25**	**5**	**0**	**2**	**2**	**0**	**0**	**0**	**0**	**14:36**
2015-16	**Buffalo**	**NHL**	**59**	**4**	**13**	**17**	**26**	**1**	**0**	**1**	**92**	**4.3**	**–5**	**0**	**0.0**	**16:50**	....	....	....	....	....	....	....	....	....
2016-17	**Buffalo**	**NHL**	**68**	**3**	**16**	**19**	**34**	**1**	**0**	**0**	**93**	**3.2**	**–5**	**0**	**0.0**	**18:29**	....	....	....	....	....	....	....	....	....
	NHL Totals		**527**	**42**	**163**	**205**	**194**	**16**	**0**	**6**	**808**	**5.2**		**0**	**0.0**	**17:35**	**28**	**4**	**11**	**15**	**2**	**1**	**0**	**0**	**16:10**

WHL West Second All-Star Team (2006) • WHL West First All-Star Team (2007)• AHL All-Rookie Team (2008) • AHL Second All-Star Team (2009)

Traded to **Toronto** by **Nashville** with Matthew Lombardi for Robert Slaney, Brett Lebda and Toronto's 4th round pick (later traded to St. Louis – St. Louis selected Zachary Pochiro) in 2013 NHL Draft, July 3, 2011. Signed as a free agent by **Gavle** (Sweden), October 1, 2012. Traded to **Nashville** by **Toronto** with Mike Santorelli for Olli Jokinen, Brendan Leipsic and Nashville's 1st round pick (later traded to Philadelphia – Philadelphia selected Travis Konecny) in 2015 NHL Draft, February 15, 2015. Signed as a free agent by **Buffalo**, September 11, 2015.

FRANZEN, Johan (FRAN-zehn, YOH-han) DET

Left wing. Shoots left. 6'4", 232 lbs. Born, Landsbro, Sweden, December 23, 1979. Detroit's 1st pick, 97th overall, in 2004 NHL Draft.

Season	Club	League	GP	G	A	Pts	PIM	PP	SH	GW	S	S%	+/-	TF	F%	Min	GP	G	A	Pts	PIM	PP	SH	GW	Min
2001-02	Linkopings HC	Sweden	36	2	6	8	64	....	....	....	....	....	....	....	....	....	....	....	....	....	....	....	....	....	....
2002-03	Linkopings HC	Sweden	37	2	4	6	14	....	....	....	....	....	....	....	....	....	....	....	....	....	....	....	....	....	....
2003-04	Linkopings HC	Sweden	49	12	18	30	26	....	....	....	....	....	....	....	....	....	5	0	1	1	8	....	....	....	....
2004-05	Linkopings HC	Sweden	43	7	7	14	45	....	....	....	....	....	....	....	....	....	6	2	0	2	16	....	....	....	....
2005-06	**Detroit**	**NHL**	**80**	**12**	**4**	**16**	**36**	**0**	**2**	**2**	**119**	**10.1**	**4**	**171**	**41.5**	**12:27**	**6**	**1**	**2**	**3**	**4**	**0**	**0**	**0**	**12:00**
2006-07	**Detroit**	**NHL**	**69**	**10**	**20**	**30**	**37**	**0**	**1**	**2**	**151**	**6.6**	**20**	**45**	**40.0**	**15:35**	**18**	**3**	**4**	**7**	**10**	**0**	**0**	**2**	**16:47**
2007-08♦	**Detroit**	**NHL**	**72**	**27**	**11**	**38**	**51**	**14**	**0**	**8**	**199**	**13.6**	**12**	**390**	**48.5**	**17:44**	**16**	***13**	**5**	**18**	**14**	***6**	***2**	***5**	**18:49**
2008-09	**Detroit**	**NHL**	**71**	**34**	**25**	**59**	**44**	**11**	**1**	**8**	**246**	**13.8**	**21**	**241**	**56.0**	**18:06**	**23**	**12**	**11**	**23**	**12**	**4**	**0**	**3**	**19:41**
2009-10	**Detroit**	**NHL**	**27**	**10**	**11**	**21**	**22**	**6**	**0**	**1**	**91**	**11.0**	**1**	**27**	**55.6**	**18:42**	**12**	**6**	**12**	**18**	**16**	**1**	**0**	**1**	**17:34**
	Sweden	Olympics	4	1	1	2	2	....	....	....	....	....	....	....	....	....	....	....	....	....	....	....	....	....	....
2010-11	**Detroit**	**NHL**	**76**	**28**	**27**	**55**	**58**	**10**	**0**	**5**	**248**	**11.3**	**5**	**147**	**50.3**	**17:26**	**8**	**2**	**1**	**3**	**6**	**0**	**0**	**0**	**15:47**
2011-12	**Detroit**	**NHL**	**77**	**29**	**27**	**56**	**40**	**11**	**0**	**10**	**211**	**13.7**	**23**	**179**	**44.1**	**17:42**	**5**	**1**	**0**	**1**	**8**	**0**	**0**	**1**	**16:07**
2012-13	**Detroit**	**NHL**	**41**	**14**	**17**	**31**	**41**	**6**	**0**	**1**	**116**	**12.1**	**13**	**62**	**48.4**	**18:05**	**14**	**4**	**2**	**6**	**8**	**3**	**0**	**0**	**19:30**
2013-14	**Detroit**	**NHL**	**54**	**16**	**25**	**41**	**40**	**7**	**0**	**4**	**149**	**10.7**	**6**	**225**	**52.9**	**17:39**	**5**	**0**	**2**	**2**	**2**	**0**	**0**	**0**	**18:53**
2014-15	**Detroit**	**NHL**	**33**	**7**	**15**	**22**	**30**	**4**	**0**	**3**	**74**	**9.5**	**–12**	**15**	**33.3**	**16:04**	....	....	....	....	....	....	....	....	....
2015-16	**Detroit**	**NHL**	**2**	**0**	**1**	**1**	**2**	**0**	**0**	**0**	**3**	**0.0**	**0**	**1**	**0.0**	**12:57**	....	....	....	....	....	....	....	....	....
2016-17	**Detroit**	**NHL**	DID NOT PLAY – INJURED																						
	NHL Totals		**602**	**187**	**183**	**370**	**401**	**69**	**4**	**44**	**1607**	**11.6**		**1503**	**48.9**	**16:44**	**107**	**42**	**39**	**81**	**80**	**14**	**2**	**12**	**17:53**

• Missed majority of 2009-10 due to knee injury vs. Chicago, October 8, 2009. • Missed majority of 2014-15 and 2015-16 and all of 2016-17 due to head injury at Edmonton, January 6, 2015.

FRASER, Mark (FRAY-zuhr, MAHRK) EDM

Defense. Shoots left. 6'4", 220 lbs. Born, Ottawa, ON, September 29, 1986. New Jersey's 3rd pick, 84th overall, in 2005 NHL Draft.

Season	Club	League	GP	G	A	Pts	PIM	PP	SH	GW	S	S%	+/-	TF	F%	Min	GP	G	A	Pts	PIM	PP	SH	GW	Min
2002-03	Clarence Beavers	ON-Jr.B	STATISTICS NOT AVAILABLE																						
	Gloucester	ON-Jr.A	5	0	0	0	4	....	....	....	....	....	....	....	....	....	3	0	0	0	0	....	....	....	....
2003-04	Gloucester	ON-Jr.A	52	0	11	11	107	....	....	....	....	....	....	....	....	....	20	0	3	3	32	....	....	....	....
2004-05	Gloucester	ON-Jr.A	11	0	5	5	22	....	....	....	....	....	....	....	....	....	....	....	....	....	....	....	....	....	....
	Kitchener Rangers	OHL	58	0	8	8	96	....	....	....	....	....	....	....	....	....	15	0	3	3	26	....	....	....	....
2005-06	Kitchener Rangers	OHL	59	0	5	5	129	....	....	....	....	....	....	....	....	....	5	0	1	1	4	....	....	....	....
	Albany River Rats	AHL	4	0	0	0	2	....	....	....	....	....	....	....	....	....	....	....	....	....	....	....	....	....	....
2006-07	**New Jersey**	**NHL**	**7**	**0**	**0**	**0**	**7**	**0**	**0**	**0**	**1**	**0.0**	**–1**	**0**	**0.0**	**3:34**	....	....	....	....	....	....	....	....	....
	Lowell Devils	AHL	71	1	8	9	73	....	....	....	....	....	....	....	....	....	....	....	....	....	....	....	....	....	....
2007-08	Lowell Devils	AHL	79	1	17	18	96	....	....	....	....	....	....	....	....	....	....	....	....	....	....	....	....	....	....
2008-09	Lowell Devils	AHL	74	3	14	17	152	....	....	....	....	....	....	....	....	....	....	....	....	....	....	....	....	....	....
2009-10	**New Jersey**	**NHL**	**61**	**3**	**3**	**6**	**36**	**0**	**0**	**0**	**24**	**12.5**	**3**	**0**	**0.0**	**12:23**	**1**	**0**	**0**	**0**	**0**	**0**	**0**	**0**	**5:52**
2010-11	**New Jersey**	**NHL**	**26**	**0**	**2**	**2**	**29**	**0**	**0**	**0**	**16**	**0.0**	**2**	**0**	**0.0**	**13:59**	....	....	....	....	....	....	....	....	....
	Albany Devils	AHL	5	0	1	1	0	....	....	....	....	....	....	....	....	....	....	....	....	....	....	....	....	....	....
2011-12	**New Jersey**	**NHL**	**4**	**0**	**0**	**0**	**14**	**0**	**0**	**0**	**0**	**0.0**	**–2**	**0**	**0.0**	**14:20**	....	....	....	....	....	....	....	....	....
	Syracuse Crunch	AHL	25	0	5	5	35	....	....	....	....	....	....	....	....	....	....	....	....	....	....	....	....	....	....
	Toronto Marlies	AHL	20	0	2	2	32	....	....	....	....	....	....	....	....	....	17	0	3	3	31	....	....	....	....
2012-13	Toronto Marlies	AHL	30	2	3	5	114	....	....	....	....	....	....	....	....	....	....	....	....	....	....	....	....	....	....
	Toronto	**NHL**	**45**	**0**	**8**	**8**	**85**	**0**	**0**	**0**	**33**	**0.0**	**18**	**0**	**0.0**	**16:57**	**4**	**0**	**1**	**1**	**7**	**0**	**0**	**0**	**18:26**
2013-14	**Toronto**	**NHL**	**19**	**0**	**1**	**1**	**33**	**0**	**0**	**0**	**6**	**0.0**	**–8**	**0**	**0.0**	**15:13**	....	....	....	....	....	....	....	....	....
	Edmonton	**NHL**	**23**	**1**	**0**	**1**	**43**	**0**	**0**	**0**	**5**	**20.0**	**–7**	**0**	**0.0**	**15:30**	....	....	....	....	....	....	....	....	....
2014-15	Albany Devils	AHL	18	1	2	3	45	....	....	....	....	....	....	....	....	....	....	....	....	....	....	....	....	....	....
	New Jersey	**NHL**	**34**	**0**	**4**	**4**	**55**	**0**	**0**	**0**	**19**	**0.0**	**2**	**0**	**0.0**	**16:17**	....	....	....	....	....	....	....	....	....

			Regular Season														Playoffs								
Season	Club	League	GP	G	A	Pts	PIM	PP	SH	GW	S	S%	+/-	TF	F%	Min	GP	G	A	Pts	PIM	PP	SH	GW	Min
2015-16	Binghamton	AHL	60	2	5	7	136																		
2016-17	Bakersfield	AHL	65	3	3	6	79																		
	NHL Totals		**219**	**4**	**18**	**22**	**302**	**0**	**0**	**0**	**104**	**3.8**		**0**	**0.0**	**14:27**	**5**	**0**	**1**	**1**	**7**	**0**	**0**	**0**	**15:55**

• Missed majority of 2010-11 due to hand injury at Buffalo, October 13. 2010 and as a healthy reserve. Traded to **Anaheim** by **New Jersey** with Rod Pelley and New Jersey's 7th round pick (Jaycob Megna) in 2012 NHL Draft for Kurtis Foster and Timo Pielmeier, December 12, 2011. Traded to **Toronto** by **Anaheim** for Dale Mitchell, February 27, 2012. Traded to **Edmonton** by **Toronto** for Cameron Abney and Teemu Hartikainen, January 31, 2014. Signed as a free agent by **Albany** (AHL), November 3, 2014. Signed as a free agent by **New Jersey**, December 18, 2014. Signed as a free agent by **Edmonton**, July 1, 2016.

FRATTIN, Matt

(FRA-tihn, MAT)

Right wing. Shoots right. 6', 205 lbs. Born, Edmonton, AB, January 3, 1988. Toronto's 2nd pick, 99th overall, in 2007 NHL Draft.

Season	Club	League	GP	G	A	Pts	PIM	PP	SH	GW	S	S%	+/-	TF	F%	Min	GP	G	A	Pts	PIM	PP	SH	GW	Min
2004-05	CAC Canadians	AMHL	34	12	13	25	14																		
2005-06	CAC Canadians	AMHL	34	20	17	37	48										6	5	1	6	4				
	Ft. Saskatchewan	AJHL	3	2	0	2	0																		
2006-07	Ft. Saskatchewan	AJHL	58	49	34	83	75										15	5	6	11	10				
2007-08	North Dakota	WCHA	43	4	11	15	18																		
2008-09	North Dakota	WCHA	42	13	12	25	48																		
2009-10	North Dakota	WCHA	24	11	8	19	21																		
2010-11	North Dakota	WCHA	44	*36	24	*60	42																		
	Toronto	**NHL**	**1**	**0**	**0**	**0**	**0**	**0**	**0**	**0**	**5**	**0.0**	**–1**	**0**	**0.0**	**15:34**									
2011-12	**Toronto**	**NHL**	**56**	**8**	**7**	**15**	**25**	**0**	**0**	**2**	**92**	**8.7**	**–4**	**8**	**25.0**	**13:10**									
	Toronto Marlies	AHL	23	14	4	18	20										13	10	3	13	6				
2012-13	Toronto Marlies	AHL	21	9	8	17	14																		
	Toronto	**NHL**	**25**	**7**	**6**	**13**	**4**	**0**	**0**	**3**	**42**	**16.7**	**6**	**8**	**62.5**	**13:14**	**6**	**0**	**2**	**2**	**0**	**0**	**0**	**0**	**13:47**
2013-14	**Los Angeles**	**NHL**	**40**	**2**	**4**	**6**	**11**	**1**	**0**	**0**	**60**	**3.3**	**–6**	**4**	**50.0**	**11:59**									
	Columbus	**NHL**	**4**	**0**	**1**	**1**	**0**	**0**	**0**	**0**	**1**	**0.0**	**2**	**0**	**0.0**	**12:22**									
2014-15	**Toronto**	**NHL**	**9**	**0**	**0**	**0**	**4**	**0**	**0**	**0**	**6**	**0.0**	**0**	**1**	**100.0**	**7:03**									
	Toronto Marlies	AHL	59	26	22	48	26										5	3	3	6	14				
2015-16	Toronto Marlies	AHL	71	13	21	34	51										1	0	0	0	0				
2016-17	Stockton Heat	AHL	54	18	18	36	18										3	0	1	1	2				
	NHL Totals		**135**	**17**	**18**	**35**	**44**	**1**	**0**	**5**	**206**	**8.3**		**21**	**47.6**	**12:25**	**6**	**0**	**2**	**2**	**0**	**0**	**0**	**0**	**13:47**

WCHA First All-Star Team (2011) • NCAA West First All-American Team (2011) • WCHA Player of the Year (2011)

Traded to **Los Angeles** by **Toronto** with Ben Scrivens and Toronto's 2nd round pick (later traded to Columbus, later traded back to Toronto – Toronto selected Travis Dermott) in 2015 NHL Draft for Jonathan Bernier, June 23, 2013. Traded to **Columbus** by **Los Angeles** with Los Angeles' 3rd round pick (later traded to Detroit – Detroit selected Dominic Turgeon) in 2014 NHL Draft and Toronto's 2nd round pick (previously acquired, later traded back to Toronto – Toronto selected Travis Dermott) in 2015 NHL Draft for Marian Gaborik, March 5, 2014. Traded to **Toronto** by **Columbus** for Jerry D'Amigo and future considerations, July 1, 2014. Traded to **Ottawa** by **Toronto** with Dion Phaneuf, Casey Bailey, Ryan Rupert and Cody Donaghey for Jared Cowen, Colin Greening, Milan Michalek, Tobias Lindberg and Ottawa's 2nd round pick (Eemeli Rasanen) iin 2017 NHL Draft, February 9, 2016. Signed as a free agent by **Stockton** (AHL), September 3, 2016. Signed as a free agent by **Kunlun** (KHL), July 16, 2017.

FRIBERG, Max

(FREE-buhrg, MAX) **MTL**

Left wing. Shoots right. 5'11", 200 lbs. Born, Skovde, Sweden, November 20, 1992. Anaheim's 6th pick, 143rd overall, in 2011 NHL Draft.

Season	Club	League	GP	G	A	Pts	PIM	PP	SH	GW	S	S%	+/-	TF	F%	Min	GP	G	A	Pts	PIM	PP	SH	GW	Min
2007-08	Skovde IK U18	Swe-U18	24	6	3	9	44																		
	Skovde IK Jr.	Swe-Jr.	12	1	2	3	0																		
2008-09	Skovde IK U18	Swe-U18	10	14	18	32	4																		
	Skovde IK Jr.	Swe-Jr.	17	13	7	20	18																		
	Skovde IK	Sweden-3	24	1	3	4	2																		
2009-10	Skovde IK U18	Swe-U18	5	5	6	11	2																		
	Skovde IK Jr.	Swe-Jr.	1	0	3	3	0																		
	Skovde IK	Sweden-3	36	12	18	30	22																		
2010-11	Skovde IK Jr.	Swe-Jr.	2	1	3	4	2																		
	Skovde IK	Sweden-3	34	13	27	40	6																		
2011-12	Timra IK Jr.	Swe-Jr.	2	2	2	4	0																		
	Sundsvall	Sweden-2	1	0	0	0	0																		
	Timra IK	Sweden	48	5	5	10	8																		
	Timra IK	Sweden-Q	10	3	4	7	4																		
2012-13	Timra IK	Sweden	55	8	8	16	12																		
	Timra IK	Sweden-Q	10	4	2	6	0																		
	Norfolk Admirals	AHL	6	1	0	1	0																		
2013-14	Norfolk Admirals	AHL	74	17	23	40	55										10	3	2	5	2				
2014-15	**Anaheim**	**NHL**	**1**	**0**	**0**	**0**	**0**	**0**	**0**	**0**	**0**	**0.0**	**0**	**0**	**0.0**	**8:47**									
	Norfolk Admirals	AHL	58	15	25	40	46																		
2015-16	**Anaheim**	**NHL**	**5**	**0**	**0**	**0**	**2**	**0**	**0**	**0**	**1**	**0.0**	**–1**	**0**	**0.0**	**8:50**									
	San Diego Gulls	AHL	25	5	12	17	2																		
	St. John's IceCaps	AHL	42	7	12	19	12																		
2016-17	St. John's IceCaps	AHL	71	11	20	31	18										4	0	3	3	2				
	NHL Totals		**6**	**0**	**0**	**0**	**2**	**0**	**0**	**0**	**1**	**0.0**		**0**	**0.0**	**8:50**									

Traded to **Montreal** by **Anaheim** for Dustin Tokarski, January 7, 2016.

FRIESEN, Alex

(FREE-zuhn, AL-ehx)

Center. Shoots left. 5'9", 186 lbs. Born, Niagara-on-the-Lake, ON, January 30, 1991. Vancouver's 3rd pick, 172nd overall, in 2010 NHL Draft.

Season	Club	League	GP	G	A	Pts	PIM	PP	SH	GW	S	S%	+/-	TF	F%	Min	GP	G	A	Pts	PIM	PP	SH	GW	Min
2006-07	N.F. Thunder	Minor-ON	69	45	67	112	66																		
2007-08	Niagara Ice Dogs	OHL	46	5	9	14	26										10	0	2	2	6				
2008-09	Niagara Ice Dogs	OHL	64	11	22	33	94										12	3	7	10	25				
2009-10	Niagara Ice Dogs	OHL	60	23	37	60	94										5	1	6	7	8				
2010-11	Niagara Ice Dogs	OHL	60	26	40	66	61										14	2	8	10	19				
2011-12	Niagara Ice Dogs	OHL	62	26	45	71	106										20	8	14	22	18				
2012-13	Chicago Wolves	AHL	42	1	4	5	22																		
	Kalamazoo Wings	ECHL	10	0	4	4	2																		
2013-14	Utica Comets	AHL	54	6	14	20	32																		
2014-15	Utica Comets	AHL	60	10	20	30	57										23	4	6	10	12				
2015-16	**Vancouver**	**NHL**	**1**	**0**	**0**	**0**	**0**	**0**	**0**	**0**	**1**	**0.0**	**–2**	**1**	**0.0**	**11:43**									
	Utica Comets	AHL	65	14	17	31	75										4	1	1	2	2				
2016-17	Chicago Wolves	AHL	76	3	9	12	47										10	1	3	4	8				
	NHL Totals		**1**	**0**	**0**	**0**	**0**	**0**	**0**	**0**	**1**	**0.0**		**1**	**0.0**	**11:43**									

Signed as a free agent by **St. Louis**, July 2, 2016.

FRK, Martin

(FUHRK, MAHR-tihn) **DET**

Right wing. Shoots right. 6'1", 194 lbs. Born, Pelhrimov, Czech Rep., October 5, 1993. Detroit's 1st pick, 49th overall, in 2012 NHL Draft.

Season	Club	League	GP	G	A	Pts	PIM	PP	SH	GW	S	S%	+/-	TF	F%	Min	GP	G	A	Pts	PIM	PP	SH	GW	Min
2006-07	Karlovy Vary U17	CzR-U17	5	0	1	1	0																		
2007-08	Karlovy Vary U17	CzR-U17	44	25	17	42	56										2	1	0	1	4				
2008-09	Karlovy Vary U17	CzR-U17	22	26	12	38	85																		
	Karlovy Vary Jr.	CzRep-Jr.	16	8	12	20	6																		
2009-10	Karlovy Vary U18	CzR-U18	8	9	4	13	41																		
	Karlovy Vary Jr.	CzRep-Jr.	41	28	30	58	186										6	2	3	5	4				
2010-11	Halifax	QMJHL	62	22	28	50	75										4	0	2	2	8				
2011-12	Halifax	QMJHL	34	16	13	29	41										17	5	6	11	26				
2012-13	Halifax	QMJHL	56	35	49	84	84										17	13	20	33	32				
2013-14	Grand Rapids	AHL	50	3	9	12	22										4	0	0	0	0				
	Toledo Walleye	ECHL	15	5	8	13	10																		
2014-15	Grand Rapids	AHL	32	6	6	12	16										2	0	2	2	0				
	Toledo Walleye	ECHL	29	23	15	38	16										14	9	4	13	10				
2015-16	Grand Rapids	AHL	67	27	17	44	89										4	1	3	4	2				
2016-17	**Carolina**	**NHL**	**2**	**0**	**0**	**0**	**0**	**0**	**0**	**0**	**1**	**0.0**	**–3**	**0**	**0.0**	**8:20**									
	Grand Rapids	AHL	65	27	23	50	58										16	5	10	15	20				
	NHL Totals		**2**	**0**	**0**	**0**	**0**	**0**	**0**	**0**	**1**	**0.0**		**0**	**0.0**	**8:20**									

Claimed on waivers by **Carolina** from **Detroit**, October 9. 2016. Claimed on waivers by **Detroit** from **Carolina**, November 1, 2016.

FROESE, Byron

(FRAYZ, BIGH-ruhn) **MTL**

Center. Shoots right. 6', 201 lbs. Born, Winkler, MB, March 12, 1991. Chicago's 4th pick, 119th overall, in 2009 NHL Draft.

			Regular Season														Playoffs								
Season	Club	League	GP	G	A	Pts	PIM	PP	SH	GW	S	S%	+/-	TF	F%	Min	GP	G	A	Pts	PIM	PP	SH	GW	Min
2007-08	Pembina Valley	MMHL	23	14	20	34	8	....	....	....	....	....	....	....	....	....	11	7	7	14	8	....	....	....	....
2008-09	Everett Silvertips	WHL	72	19	38	57	30	....	....	....	....	....	....	....	....	....	5	0	3	3	4	....	....	....	....
2009-10	Everett Silvertips	WHL	70	29	32	61	37	....	....	....	....	....	....	....	....	....	7	3	2	5	0	....	....	....	....
2010-11	Red Deer Rebels	WHL	70	43	38	81	37	....	....	....	....	....	....	....	....	....	9	5	2	7	4	....	....	....	....
2011-12	Rockford IceHogs	AHL	57	4	6	10	17	....	....	....	....	....	....	....	....	....	....	....	....	....	....	....	....	....	....
	Toledo Walleye	ECHL	3	1	1	2	2	....	....	....	....	....	....	....	....	....	....	....	....	....	....	....	....	....	....
2012-13	Rockford IceHogs	AHL	9	0	2	2	4	....	....	....	....	....	....	....	....	....	....	....	....	....	....	....	....	....	....
	Toledo Walleye	ECHL	38	12	21	33	12	....	....	....	....	....	....	....	....	....	6	2	4	6	6	....	....	....	....
2013-14	Rockford IceHogs	AHL	28	0	5	5	14	....	....	....	....	....	....	....	....	....	....	....	....	....	....	....	....	....	....
	Cincinnati	ECHL	25	11	10	21	20	....	....	....	....	....	....	....	....	....	23	8	17	25	20	....	....	....	....
2014-15	San Antonio	AHL	3	0	0	0	2	....	....	....	....	....	....	....	....	....	....	....	....	....	....	....	....	....	....
	Cincinnati	ECHL	17	8	16	24	14	....	....	....	....	....	....	....	....	....	....	....	....	....	....	....	....	....	....
	Toronto Marlies	AHL	46	18	24	42	26	....	....	....	....	....	....	....	....	....	5	1	3	4	4	....	....	....	....
2015-16	**Toronto**	**NHL**	**56**	**2**	**3**	**5**	**16**	**0**	**0**	**0**	**64**	**3.1**	**–11**	**642**	**48.3**	**12:38**	....	....	....	....	....	....	....	....	....
	Toronto Marlies	AHL	4	3	0	3	0	....	....	....	....	....	....	....	....	....	....	....	....	....	....	....	....	....	....
2016-17	**Toronto**	**NHL**	**2**	**0**	**0**	**0**	**5**	**0**	**0**	**0**	**2**	**0.0**	**0**	**20**	**35.0**	**8:01**	....	....	....	....	....	....	....	....	....
	Toronto Marlies	AHL	48	24	15	39	18	....	....	....	....	....	....	....	....	....	....	....	....	....	....	....	....	....	....
	Tampa Bay	**NHL**	**4**	**0**	**0**	**0**	**0**	**0**	**0**	**0**	**4**	**0.0**	**–3**	**36**	**52.8**	**11:49**	....	....	....	....	....	....	....	....	....
	Syracuse Crunch	AHL	6	3	4	7	4	....	....	....	....	....	....	....	....	....	22	6	7	13	8	....	....	....	....
	NHL Totals		**62**	**2**	**3**	**5**	**21**	**0**	**0**	**0**	**70**	**2.9**		**698**	**48.1**	**12:26**	....	....	....	....	....	....	....	....	....

Signed to a PTO (professional tryout) contract by **San Antonio** (AHL), September 30, 2014. Signed as a free agent by **Toronto** (AHL), January 7, 2015. Signed as a free agent by **Toronto**, July 3, 2015. Traded to **Tampa Bay** by **Toronto** with Toronto's 2nd round pick (Alexander Volkov) in 2017 NHL Draft for Brian Boyle, February 26, 2017. Signed as a free agent by **Montreal**, July 1, 2017.

FROLIK, Michael

(FROH-lihk, MIGH-kuhl) **CGY**

Left wing. Shoots left. 6'1", 194 lbs. Born, Kladno, Czech., February 17, 1988. Florida's 1st pick, 10th overall, in 2006 NHL Draft.

			Regular Season														Playoffs								
Season	Club	League	GP	G	A	Pts	PIM	PP	SH	GW	S	S%	+/-	TF	F%	Min	GP	G	A	Pts	PIM	PP	SH	GW	Min
2002-03	HC Kladno U17	CzR-U17	46	37	21	58	36	....	....	....	....	....	....	....	....	....	9	9	1	10	18	....	....	....	....
	HC Kladno Jr.	CzRep-Jr.	....	....	....	....	....	....	....	....	....	....	....	....	....	....	1	0	0	0	2	....	....	....	....
2003-04	HC Kladno U17	CzR-U17	1	0	1	1	2	....	....	....	....	....	....	....	....	....	....	....	....	....	....	....	....	....	....
	HC Kladno Jr.	CzRep-Jr.	53	21	23	44	22	....	....	....	....	....	....	....	....	....	7	3	1	4	6	....	....	....	....
2004-05	HC Kladno U17	CzR-U17	....	....	....	....	....	....	....	....	....	....	....	....	....	....	1	1	0	1	0	....	....	....	....
	HC Kladno Jr.	CzRep-Jr.	15	9	11	20	18	....	....	....	....	....	....	....	....	....	5	1	0	1	0	....	....	....	....
	HC Rabat Kladno	CzRep	27	3	1	4	6	....	....	....	....	....	....	....	....	....	1	0	0	0	0	....	....	....	....
2005-06	HC Kladno Jr.	CzRep-Jr.	3	1	2	3	0	....	....	....	....	....	....	....	....	....	6	3	9	12	6	....	....	....	....
	HC Rabat Kladno	CzRep	48	2	7	9	32	....	....	....	....	....	....	....	....	....	....	....	....	....	....	....	....	....	....
2006-07	Rimouski Oceanic	QMJHL	52	31	42	73	40	....	....	....	....	....	....	....	....	....	....	....	....	....	....	....	....	....	....
2007-08	Rimouski Oceanic	QMJHL	45	24	41	65	22	....	....	....	....	....	....	....	....	....	9	2	4	6	12	....	....	....	....
2008-09	**Florida**	**NHL**	**79**	**21**	**24**	**45**	**22**	**1**	**0**	**2**	**158**	**13.3**	**10**	**67**	**40.3**	**14:48**	....	....	....	....	....	....	....	....	....
2009-10	**Florida**	**NHL**	**82**	**21**	**22**	**43**	**43**	**5**	**0**	**1**	**219**	**9.6**	**–4**	**35**	**37.1**	**17:29**	....	....	....	....	....	....	....	....	....
2010-11	**Florida**	**NHL**	**52**	**8**	**21**	**29**	**16**	**1**	**0**	**1**	**158**	**5.1**	**2**	**12**	**41.7**	**16:02**	....	....	....	....	....	....	....	....	....
	Chicago	**NHL**	**28**	**3**	**6**	**9**	**14**	**0**	**0**	**0**	**93**	**3.2**	**0**	**107**	**40.2**	**14:46**	**7**	**2**	**3**	**5**	**2**	**0**	**0**	**0**	**17:28**
2011-12	**Chicago**	**NHL**	**63**	**5**	**10**	**15**	**22**	**0**	**0**	**0**	**117**	**4.3**	**–10**	**48**	**33.3**	**12:52**	**4**	**2**	**1**	**3**	**0**	**0**	**0**	**0**	**17:23**
2012-13	Pirati Chomutov	CzRep	32	14	10	24	22	....	....	....	....	....	....	....	....	....	....	....	....	....	....	....	....	....	....
	♦ **Chicago**	**NHL**	**45**	**3**	**7**	**10**	**8**	**0**	**0**	**1**	**98**	**3.1**	**5**	**40**	**37.5**	**12:31**	**23**	**3**	**7**	**10**	**6**	**0**	**1**	**1**	**13:09**
2013-14	**Winnipeg**	**NHL**	**81**	**15**	**27**	**42**	**12**	**1**	**0**	**2**	**189**	**7.9**	**8**	**68**	**63.2**	**16:40**	....	....	....	....	....	....	....	....	....
	Czech Republic	Olympics	5	0	0	0	0	....	....	....	....	....	....	....	....	....	....	....	....	....	....	....	....	....	....
2014-15	**Winnipeg**	**NHL**	**82**	**19**	**23**	**42**	**18**	**3**	**3**	**4**	**206**	**9.2**	**4**	**41**	**34.2**	**17:30**	**4**	**0**	**0**	**0**	**2**	**0**	**0**	**0**	**17:22**
2015-16	**Calgary**	**NHL**	**64**	**15**	**17**	**32**	**24**	**0**	**2**	**4**	**155**	**9.7**	**1**	**10**	**50.0**	**15:49**	....	....	....	....	....	....	....	....	....
2016-17	**Calgary**	**NHL**	**82**	**17**	**27**	**44**	**58**	**3**	**2**	**1**	**202**	**8.4**	**13**	**29**	**44.8**	**17:05**	**4**	**0**	**1**	**1**	**0**	**0**	**0**	**0**	**18:49**
	NHL Totals		**658**	**127**	**184**	**311**	**237**	**14**	**7**	**16**	**1595**	**8.0**		**457**	**42.5**	**15:50**	**42**	**7**	**12**	**19**	**10**	**0**	**1**	**1**	**15:13**

QMJHL All-Rookie Team (2007)

Traded to **Chicago** by **Florida** with Alexander Salak for Jack Skille, Hugh Jessiman and David Pacan, February 9, 2011. Signed as a free agent by **Chomutov** (CzRep), September 22, 2012. Traded to **Winnipeg** by **Chicago** for Winnipeg's 3rd (John Hayden) and 5th (Luke Johnson) round picks in 2013 NHL Draft, June 30, 2013. Signed as a free agent by **Calgary**, July 1, 2015.

GABORIK, Marian

(GAB-uhr-ihk, MAIR-ee-uhn) **L.A.**

Right wing. Shoots left. 6'1", 205 lbs. Born, Trencin, Czech., February 14, 1982. Minnesota's 1st pick, 3rd overall, in 2000 NHL Draft.

			Regular Season														Playoffs								
Season	Club	League	GP	G	A	Pts	PIM	PP	SH	GW	S	S%	+/-	TF	F%	Min	GP	G	A	Pts	PIM	PP	SH	GW	Min
1997-98	Dukla Trencin Jr.	Slovak-Jr.	36	37	22	59	28	....	....	....	....	....	....	....	....	....	....	....	....	....	....	....	....	....	....
	Dukla Trencin	Slovakia	1	1	0	1	0	....	....	....	....	....	....	....	....	....	....	....	....	....	....	....	....	....	....
1998-99	Dukla Trencin	Slovakia	33	11	9	20	6	....	....	....	....	....	....	....	....	....	3	1	0	1	2	....	....	....	....
99-2000	Dukla Trencin	Slovakia	50	25	21	46	34	....	....	....	....	....	....	....	....	....	5	1	2	3	2	....	....	....	....
2000-01	**Minnesota**	**NHL**	**71**	**18**	**18**	**36**	**32**	**6**	**0**	**3**	**179**	**10.1**	**–6**	**3**	**33.3**	**15:26**	....	....	....	....	....	....	....	....	....
2001-02	**Minnesota**	**NHL**	**78**	**30**	**37**	**67**	**34**	**10**	**0**	**4**	**221**	**13.6**	**0**	**4**	**25.0**	**16:47**	....	....	....	....	....	....	....	....	....
2002-03	**Minnesota**	**NHL**	**81**	**30**	**35**	**65**	**46**	**5**	**1**	**8**	**280**	**10.7**	**12**	**16**	**25.0**	**17:24**	**18**	**9**	**8**	**17**	**6**	**4**	**0**	**0**	**18:12**
2003-04	Dukla Trencin	Slovakia	9	10	3	13	10	....	....	....	....	....	....	....	....	....	....	....	....	....	....	....	....	....	....
	Minnesota	**NHL**	**65**	**18**	**22**	**40**	**20**	**3**	**0**	**4**	**220**	**8.2**	**10**	**11**	**45.5**	**18:17**	....	....	....	....	....	....	....	....	....
2004-05	Dukla Trencin	Slovakia	29	25	27	52	46	....	....	....	....	....	....	....	....	....	12	8	9	17	26	....	....	....	....
	Farjestad	Sweden	12	6	4	10	45	....	....	....	....	....	....	....	....	....	....	....	....	....	....	....	....	....	....
2005-06	**Minnesota**	**NHL**	**65**	**38**	**28**	**66**	**64**	**10**	**2**	**7**	**252**	**15.1**	**6**	**11**	**27.3**	**18:26**	....	....	....	....	....	....	....	....	....
	Slovakia	Olympics	6	3	4	7	4	....	....	....	....	....	....	....	....	....	....	....	....	....	....	....	....	....	....
2006-07	**Minnesota**	**NHL**	**48**	**30**	**27**	**57**	**40**	**12**	**1**	**7**	**196**	**15.3**	**12**	**4**	**0.0**	**19:38**	**5**	**3**	**1**	**4**	**8**	**1**	**1**	**1**	**19:32**
2007-08	**Minnesota**	**NHL**	**77**	**42**	**41**	**83**	**63**	**11**	**1**	**8**	**278**	**15.1**	**17**	**21**	**28.6**	**19:36**	**6**	**0**	**1**	**1**	**4**	**0**	**0**	**0**	**21:51**
2008-09	**Minnesota**	**NHL**	**17**	**13**	**10**	**23**	**2**	**2**	**1**	**2**	**68**	**19.1**	**3**	**5**	**0.0**	**20:00**	....	....	....	....	....	....	....	....	....
2009-10	**NY Rangers**	**NHL**	**76**	**42**	**44**	**86**	**37**	**14**	**1**	**4**	**272**	**15.4**	**15**	**7**	**28.6**	**21:15**	....	....	....	....	....	....	....	....	....
	Slovakia	Olympics	7	4	1	5	6	....	....	....	....	....	....	....	....	....	....	....	....	....	....	....	....	....	....
2010-11	**NY Rangers**	**NHL**	**62**	**22**	**26**	**48**	**18**	**7**	**0**	**4**	**192**	**11.5**	**8**	**0**	**0.0**	**18:05**	**5**	**1**	**1**	**2**	**2**	**0**	**0**	**0**	**23:55**
2011-12	**NY Rangers**	**NHL**	**82**	**41**	**35**	**76**	**34**	**10**	**0**	**7**	**276**	**14.9**	**15**	**2**	**0.0**	**19:31**	**20**	**5**	**6**	**11**	**2**	**0**	**0**	**1**	**19:56**
2012-13	**NY Rangers**	**NHL**	**35**	**9**	**10**	**19**	**8**	**1**	**0**	**4**	**113**	**8.0**	**–8**	**2**	**0.0**	**18:40**	....	....	....	....	....	....	....	....	....
	Columbus	**NHL**	**12**	**3**	**5**	**8**	**6**	**0**	**0**	**1**	**38**	**7.9**	**5**	**1**	**100.0**	**18:05**	....	....	....	....	....	....	....	....	....
2013-14	**Columbus**	**NHL**	**22**	**6**	**8**	**14**	**6**	**0**	**0**	**0**	**47**	**12.8**	**0**	**0**	**0.0**	**16:25**	....	....	....	....	....	....	....	....	....
	♦ **Los Angeles**	**NHL**	**19**	**5**	**11**	**16**	**4**	**1**	**0**	**0**	**56**	**8.9**	**7**	**2**	**0.0**	**17:42**	**26**	***14**	**8**	**22**	**6**	**3**	**0**	**1**	**17:46**
2014-15	**Los Angeles**	**NHL**	**69**	**27**	**20**	**47**	**16**	**11**	**0**	**2**	**174**	**15.5**	**7**	**1**	**100.0**	**16:55**	....	....	....	....	....	....	....	....	....
2015-16	**Los Angeles**	**NHL**	**54**	**12**	**10**	**22**	**20**	**1**	**0**	**3**	**142**	**8.5**	**–6**	**3**	**33.3**	**14:57**	**4**	**0**	**1**	**1**	**2**	**0**	**0**	**0**	**15:14**
2016-17	**Los Angeles**	**NHL**	**56**	**10**	**11**	**21**	**18**	**3**	**0**	**3**	**123**	**8.1**	**–4**	**1**	**0.0**	**14:47**	....	....	....	....	....	....	....	....	....
	NHL Totals		**989**	**396**	**398**	**794**	**468**	**107**	**7**	**71**	**3127**	**12.7**		**94**	**26.6**	**17:54**	**84**	**32**	**26**	**58**	**30**	**8**	**1**	**3**	**19:01**

NHL Second All-Star Team (2012)

Played in NHL All-Star Game (2003, 2008, 2012)

Signed as a free agent by **Trencin** (Slovakia), July 5, 2004. Signed as a free agent by **Farjestad** (Sweden), December 21, 2004. • Missed majority of 2008-09 due to hip surgery, January 5, 2009. Signed as a free agent by **NY Rangers**, July 1, 2009. Traded to **Columbus** by **NY Rangers** with Blake Parlett and Steven Delisle for Derek Dorsett, Derick Brassard, John Moore and Columbus' 6th round pick (later traded to Minnesota – Minnesota selected Chase Lang) in 2014 NHL Draft, April 3, 2013. Traded to **Los Angeles** by **Columbus** for Matt Frattin, Los Angeles' 3rd round pick (later traded to Detroit – Detroit selected Dominic Turgeon) in 2014 NHL Draft and Toronto's 2nd round pick (previously acquired, later traded back to Toronto – Toronto selected Travis Dermott) in 2015 NHL Draft, March 5, 2014.

GABRIEL, Kurtis

(GAY-bree-uhl, KUHR-tihs) **MIN**

Right wing. Shoots right. 6'4", 212 lbs. Born, Newmarket, ON, April 20, 1993. Minnesota's 2nd pick, 81st overall, in 2013 NHL Draft.

			Regular Season														Playoffs								
Season	Club	League	GP	G	A	Pts	PIM	PP	SH	GW	S	S%	+/-	TF	F%	Min	GP	G	A	Pts	PIM	PP	SH	GW	Min
2009-10	Markham Waxers	Minor-ON	50	16	23	39	....	....	....	....	....	....	....	....	....	....	....	....	....	....	....	....	....	....	....
2010-11	Owen Sound	OHL	40	1	3	4	20	....	....	....	....	....	....	....	....	....	....	....	....	....	....	....	....	....	....
2011-12	Owen Sound	OHL	65	4	13	17	72	....	....	....	....	....	....	....	....	....	3	0	0	0	0	....	....	....	....
2012-13	Owen Sound	OHL	67	13	15	28	100	....	....	....	....	....	....	....	....	....	12	3	2	5	34	....	....	....	....
2013-14	Owen Sound	OHL	60	15	36	51	99	....	....	....	....	....	....	....	....	....	5	0	1	1	22	....	....	....	....
2014-15	Iowa Wild	AHL	67	7	9	16	125	....	....	....	....	....	....	....	....	....	....	....	....	....	....	....	....	....	....
2015-16	**Minnesota**	**NHL**	**3**	**0**	**0**	**0**	**10**	**0**	**0**	**0**	**1**	**0.0**	**1**	**0**	**0.0**	**4:30**	**4**	**0**	**0**	**0**	**0**	**0**	**0**	**0**	**5:25**
	Iowa Wild	AHL	66	6	4	10	137	....	....	....	....	....	....	....	....	....	....	....	....	....	....	....	....	....	....

			Regular Season														Playoffs								
Season	Club	League	GP	G	A	Pts	PIM	PP	SH	GW	S	S%	+/-	TF	F%	Min	GP	G	A	Pts	PIM	PP	SH	GW	Min
2016-17	**Minnesota**	**NHL**	**13**	**0**	**1**	**1**	**29**	**0**	**0**	**0**	**3**	**0.0**	**0**	**0**	**0.0**	**5:49**	....	....	....	....	....	....	....	....	....
	Iowa Wild	AHL	49	8	2	10	68	....	....	....	....	....	....	....	....	....	....	....	....	....	....	....	....	....	....
	NHL Totals		**16**	**0**	**1**	**1**	**39**	**0**	**0**	**0**	**4**	**0.0**		**0**	**0.0**	**5:34**	**4**	**0**	**0**	**0**	**0**	**0**	**0**	**0**	**5:25**

GAGNER, Sam

(GAH-n'yay, SAM) **VAN**

Center. Shoots right. 5'11", 202 lbs. Born, London, ON, August 10, 1989. Edmonton's 1st pick, 6th overall, in 2007 NHL Draft.

Season	Club	League	GP	G	A	Pts	PIM	PP	SH	GW	S	S%	+/-	TF	F%	Min	GP	G	A	Pts	PIM	PP	SH	GW	Min
2001-02	Tor. Marlboros	GTHL	68	56	61	117	42	....	....	....	....	....	....	....	....	....	....	....	....	....	....	....	....	....	....
2002-03	Tor. Marlboros	GTHL	72	68	86	154	35	....	....	....	....	....	....	....	....	....	....	....	....	....	....	....	....	....	....
2003-04	Tor. Marlboros	GTHL	85	64	108	171	36	....	....	....	....	....	....	....	....	....	....	....	....	....	....	....	....	....	....
2004-05	Tor. Marlboros	GTHL	70	62	118	180	56	....	....	....	....	....	....	....	....	....	....	....	....	....	....	....	....	....	....
	Milton Icehawks	ON-Jr.A	13	5	10	15	10	....	....	....	....	....	....	....	....	....	....	....	....	....	....	....	....	....	....
2005-06	Sioux City	USHL	56	11	35	46	60	....	....	....	....	....	....	....	....	....	....	....	....	....	....	....	....	....	....
2006-07	London Knights	OHL	53	35	83	118	36	....	....	....	....	....	....	....	....	....	16	7	*22	29	22	....	....	....	....
2007-08	**Edmonton**	**NHL**	**79**	**13**	**36**	**49**	**23**	**4**	**0**	**1**	**135**	**9.6**	**-21**	**299**	**41.8**	**15:41**	....	....	....	....	....	....	....	....	....
2008-09	**Edmonton**	**NHL**	**76**	**16**	**25**	**41**	**51**	**6**	**0**	**1**	**156**	**10.3**	**-1**	**690**	**42.0**	**16:46**	....	....	....	....	....	....	....	....	....
2009-10	**Edmonton**	**NHL**	**68**	**15**	**26**	**41**	**33**	**6**	**0**	**1**	**170**	**8.8**	**-8**	**709**	**47.4**	**16:17**	....	....	....	....	....	....	....	....	....
2010-11	**Edmonton**	**NHL**	**68**	**15**	**27**	**42**	**37**	**3**	**1**	**2**	**138**	**10.9**	**-17**	**935**	**43.9**	**17:45**	....	....	....	....	....	....	....	....	....
2011-12	**Edmonton**	**NHL**	**75**	**18**	**29**	**47**	**36**	**6**	**0**	**0**	**149**	**12.1**	**5**	**701**	**47.7**	**17:11**	....	....	....	....	....	....	....	....	....
2012-13	Klagenfurter AC	Austria	21	10	10	20	8	....	....	....	....	....	....	....	....	....	....	....	....	....	....	....	....	....	....
	Edmonton	**NHL**	**48**	**14**	**24**	**38**	**23**	**4**	**0**	**1**	**113**	**12.4**	**-6**	**741**	**43.9**	**19:25**	....	....	....	....	....	....	....	....	....
2013-14	**Edmonton**	**NHL**	**67**	**10**	**27**	**37**	**41**	**1**	**0**	**1**	**143**	**7.0**	**-29**	**963**	**46.8**	**18:23**	....	....	....	....	....	....	....	....	....
2014-15	**Arizona**	**NHL**	**81**	**15**	**26**	**41**	**28**	**6**	**0**	**1**	**183**	**8.2**	**-28**	**771**	**46.8**	**17:15**	....	....	....	....	....	....	....	....	....
2015-16	**Philadelphia**	**NHL**	**53**	**8**	**8**	**16**	**25**	**2**	**0**	**2**	**86**	**9.3**	**4**	**97**	**35.1**	**13:52**	**6**	**0**	**2**	**2**	**8**	**0**	**0**	**0**	**15:37**
	Lehigh Valley	AHL	9	1	5	6	4	....	....	....	....	....	....	....	....	....	....	....	....	....	....	....	....	....	....
2016-17	**Columbus**	**NHL**	**81**	**18**	**32**	**50**	**22**	**8**	**0**	**1**	**178**	**10.1**	**10**	**425**	**47.5**	**13:43**	**5**	**0**	**2**	**2**	**2**	**0**	**0**	**0**	**12:40**
	NHL Totals		**696**	**142**	**260**	**402**	**319**	**46**	**1**	**11**	**1451**	**9.8**		**6331**	**45.3**	**16:33**	**11**	**0**	**4**	**4**	**10**	**0**	**0**	**0**	**14:17**

USHL All-Rookie Team (2006) • OHL All-Rookie Team (2007)

Signed as a free agent by **Klagenfurt** (Austria), October 15, 2012. Traded to **Tampa Bay** by **Edmonton** for Teddy Purcell, June 29, 2014. Traded to **Arizona** by **Tampa Bay** with B.J. Crombeen for Arizona's 6th round pick (Kristian Oldham) in 2015 NHL Draft, June 29, 2014. Traded to **Philadelphia** by **Arizona** with Arizona's 4th round pick (Otto Koivula) in 2016 NHL Draft for Nicklas Grossmann and Chris Pronger, June 27, 2015. Signed as a free agent by **Columbus**, August 1, 2016. Signed as a free agent by **Vancouver**, July 1, 2017.

GALCHENYUK, Alex

(gal-CHEHN-yuhk, AL-ehx) **MTL**

Center. Shoots left. 6'1", 210 lbs. Born, Milwaukee, WI, February 12, 1994. Montreal's 1st pick, 3rd overall, in 2012 NHL Draft.

Season	Club	League	GP	G	A	Pts	PIM	PP	SH	GW	S	S%	+/-	TF	F%	Min	GP	G	A	Pts	PIM	PP	SH	GW	Min
2009-10	Chi. Americans	T1EHL	38	44	43	87	56	....	....	....	....	....	....	....	....	....	....	....	....	....	....	....	....	....	....
2010-11	Sarnia Sting	OHL	68	31	52	83	52	....	....	....	....	....	....	....	....	....	....	....	....	....	....	....	....	....	....
2011-12	Sarnia Sting	OHL	2	0	0	0	0	....	....	....	....	....	....	....	....	....	6	2	2	4	4	....	....	....	....
2012-13	Sarnia Sting	OHL	33	27	34	61	22	....	....	....	....	....	....	....	....	....	....	....	....	....	....	....	....	....	....
	Montreal	**NHL**	**48**	**9**	**18**	**27**	**20**	**0**	**0**	**2**	**79**	**11.4**	**14**	**138**	**42.8**	**12:19**	**5**	**1**	**2**	**3**	**0**	**0**	**0**	**0**	**13:00**
2013-14	**Montreal**	**NHL**	**65**	**13**	**18**	**31**	**26**	**3**	**0**	**2**	**110**	**11.8**	**-12**	**15**	**33.3**	**14:24**	**5**	**2**	**1**	**3**	**2**	**1**	**0**	**1**	**15:01**
2014-15	**Montreal**	**NHL**	**80**	**20**	**26**	**46**	**39**	**3**	**0**	**1**	**163**	**12.3**	**8**	**174**	**47.1**	**16:26**	**12**	**1**	**3**	**4**	**10**	**0**	**0**	**1**	**16:01**
2015-16	**Montreal**	**NHL**	**82**	**30**	**26**	**56**	**20**	**9**	**0**	**4**	**201**	**14.9**	**-8**	**749**	**47.9**	**16:16**	....	....	....	....	....	....	....	....	....
2016-17	**Montreal**	**NHL**	**61**	**17**	**27**	**44**	**24**	**6**	**0**	**6**	**104**	**16.3**	**-5**	**642**	**42.7**	**15:56**	**6**	**0**	**3**	**3**	**4**	**0**	**0**	**0**	**16:36**
	NHL Totals		**336**	**89**	**115**	**204**	**129**	**21**	**0**	**15**	**657**	**13.5**		**1718**	**45.3**	**15:19**	**28**	**4**	**9**	**13**	**16**	**1**	**0**	**2**	**15:25**

OHL All-Rookie Team (2011)

• Missed majority of 2011-12 due to pre-season knee injury vs. Windsor (OHL), September 16, 2011.

GALIEV, Stanislav

(gah-LEE-ehv, stan-ihs-LAHV)

Right wing. Shoots right. 6'1", 187 lbs. Born, Moscow, Russia, January 17, 1992. Washington's 2nd pick, 86th overall, in 2010 NHL Draft.

Season	Club	League	GP	G	A	Pts	PIM	PP	SH	GW	S	S%	+/-	TF	F%	Min	GP	G	A	Pts	PIM	PP	SH	GW	Min
2008-09	Indiana Ice	USHL	60	29	35	64	46	....	....	....	....	....	....	....	....	....	13	5	4	9	8	....	....	....	....
2009-10	Saint John	QMJHL	67	15	45	60	38	....	....	....	....	....	....	....	....	....	21	8	11	19	14	....	....	....	....
2010-11	Saint John	QMJHL	64	37	28	65	40	....	....	....	....	....	....	....	....	....	19	10	17	27	12	....	....	....	....
2011-12	Saint John	QMJHL	20	13	6	19	16	....	....	....	....	....	....	....	....	....	17	16	18	34	6	....	....	....	....
2012-13	Hershey Bears	AHL	17	0	1	1	8	....	....	....	....	....	....	....	....	....	....	....	....	....	....	....	....	....	....
	Reading Royals	ECHL	46	23	24	47	32	....	....	....	....	....	....	....	....	....	10	4	7	11	0	....	....	....	....
2013-14	Hershey Bears	AHL	16	3	3	6	0	....	....	....	....	....	....	....	....	....	....	....	....	....	....	....	....	....	....
	Reading Royals	ECHL	14	5	8	13	6	....	....	....	....	....	....	....	....	....	3	1	1	2	0	....	....	....	....
2014-15	**Washington**	**NHL**	**2**	**1**	**0**	**1**	**0**	**0**	**0**	**0**	**2**	**50.0**	**1**	**0**	**0.0**	**9:23**	....	....	....	....	....	....	....	....	....
	Hershey Bears	AHL	67	25	20	45	24	....	....	....	....	....	....	....	....	....	5	1	0	1	0	....	....	....	....
2015-16	Hershey Bears	AHL	5	3	0	3	2	....	....	....	....	....	....	....	....	....	....	....	....	....	....	....	....	....	....
	Washington	**NHL**	**24**	**0**	**3**	**3**	**4**	**0**	**0**	**0**	**30**	**0.0**	**2**	**0**	**0.0**	**9:07**	....	....	....	....	....	....	....	....	....
2016-17	Hershey Bears	AHL	56	21	19	40	20	....	....	....	....	....	....	....	....	....	12	3	4	7	4	....	....	....	....
	NHL Totals		**26**	**1**	**3**	**4**	**4**	**0**	**0**	**0**	**32**	**3.1**		**0**	**0.0**	**9:08**	....	....	....	....	....	....	....	....	....

QMJHL All-Rookie Team (2010)

• Missed majority of 2015-16 as a healthy reserve,.

GALLAGHER, Brendan

(gal-lah-GUR, BREHN-duhn) **MTL**

Right wing. Shoots right. 5'9", 182 lbs. Born, Edmonton, AB, May 6, 1992. Montreal's 4th pick, 147th overall, in 2010 NHL Draft.

Season	Club	League	GP	G	A	Pts	PIM	PP	SH	GW	S	S%	+/-	TF	F%	Min	GP	G	A	Pts	PIM	PP	SH	GW	Min
2007-08	Greater Van.	BCMML	39	23	33	56	66	....	....	....	....	....	....	....	....	....	2	0	1	1	0	....	....	....	....
2008-09	Vancouver Giants	WHL	52	10	21	31	61	....	....	....	....	....	....	....	....	....	16	1	2	3	10	....	....	....	....
2009-10	Vancouver Giants	WHL	72	41	40	81	111	....	....	....	....	....	....	....	....	....	16	11	10	21	14	....	....	....	....
2010-11	Vancouver Giants	WHL	66	44	47	91	108	....	....	....	....	....	....	....	....	....	4	2	0	2	16	....	....	....	....
2011-12	Vancouver Giants	WHL	54	41	36	77	79	....	....	....	....	....	....	....	....	....	6	5	5	10	16	....	....	....	....
2012-13	Hamilton	AHL	36	10	10	20	61	....	....	....	....	....	....	....	....	....	....	....	....	....	....	....	....	....	....
	Montreal	**NHL**	**44**	**15**	**13**	**28**	**33**	**3**	**0**	**3**	**117**	**12.8**	**10**	**25**	**32.0**	**13:52**	**5**	**2**	**0**	**2**	**5**	**1**	**0**	**1**	**14:26**
2013-14	**Montreal**	**NHL**	**81**	**19**	**22**	**41**	**73**	**8**	**0**	**0**	**211**	**9.0**	**4**	**128**	**36.7**	**15:58**	**17**	**4**	**7**	**11**	**6**	**1**	**0**	**0**	**16:36**
2014-15	**Montreal**	**NHL**	**82**	**24**	**23**	**47**	**31**	**3**	**0**	**6**	**254**	**9.4**	**18**	**99**	**43.4**	**16:35**	**12**	**3**	**2**	**5**	**0**	**0**	**0**	**1**	**18:02**
2015-16	**Montreal**	**NHL**	**53**	**19**	**21**	**40**	**24**	**7**	**0**	**0**	**173**	**11.0**	**13**	**29**	**41.4**	**16:35**	....	....	....	....	....	....	....	....	....
2016-17	**Montreal**	**NHL**	**64**	**10**	**19**	**29**	**39**	**1**	**0**	**2**	**187**	**5.3**	**7**	**74**	**40.5**	**15:06**	**6**	**1**	**2**	**3**	**8**	**1**	**0**	**0**	**17:22**
	NHL Totals		**324**	**87**	**98**	**185**	**200**	**22**	**0**	**11**	**942**	**9.2**		**355**	**39.4**	**15:46**	**40**	**10**	**11**	**21**	**19**	**3**	**0**	**2**	**16:52**

WHL West First All-Star Team (2011, 2012) • NHL All-Rookie Team (2013)

GALLANT, Brett

(guh-LANT, BREHT)

Left wing. Shoots left. 6', 194 lbs. Born, Summerside, PEI, December 28, 1988.

Season	Club	League	GP	G	A	Pts	PIM	PP	SH	GW	S	S%	+/-	TF	F%	Min	GP	G	A	Pts	PIM	PP	SH	GW	Min
2005-06	Saint John	QMJHL	26	0	1	1	72	....	....	....	....	....	....	....	....	....	....	....	....	....	....	....	....	....	....
	Summerside	MJrHL	9	0	2	2	148	....	....	....	....	....	....	....	....	....	....	....	....	....	....	....	....	....	....
2006-07	Saint John	QMJHL	48	5	1	6	192	....	....	....	....	....	....	....	....	....	....	....	....	....	....	....	....	....	....
2007-08	Saint John	QMJHL	57	3	2	5	175	....	....	....	....	....	....	....	....	....	11	1	0	1	15	....	....	....	....
2008-09	Summerside	MJrHL	50	24	49	73	235	....	....	....	....	....	....	....	....	....	....	....	....	....	....	....	....	....	....
2009-10	Elmira Jackals	ECHL	38	1	1	2	185	....	....	....	....	....	....	....	....	....	....	....	....	....	....	....	....	....	....
	Syracuse Crunch	AHL	1	0	0	0	5	....	....	....	....	....	....	....	....	....	....	....	....	....	....	....	....	....	....
2010-11	Elmira Jackals	ECHL	13	0	0	0	80	....	....	....	....	....	....	....	....	....	....	....	....	....	....	....	....	....	....
	Reading Royals	ECHL	12	1	2	3	52	....	....	....	....	....	....	....	....	....	....	....	....	....	....	....	....	....	....
	Bridgeport	AHL	17	1	0	1	73	....	....	....	....	....	....	....	....	....	....	....	....	....	....	....	....	....	....
2011-12	Bridgeport	AHL	25	2	1	3	80	....	....	....	....	....	....	....	....	....	....	....	....	....	....	....	....	....	....
2012-13	Bridgeport	AHL	42	0	0	0	202	....	....	....	....	....	....	....	....	....	....	....	....	....	....	....	....	....	....
2013-14	**NY Islanders**	**NHL**	**4**	**0**	**0**	**0**	**17**	**0**	**0**	**0**	**3**	**0.0**	**0**	**0**	**0.0**	**6:53**	....	....	....	....	....	....	....	....	....
	Bridgeport	AHL	58	1	1	2	255	....	....	....	....	....	....	....	....	....	....	....	....	....	....	....	....	....	....
2014-15	Bridgeport	AHL	45	2	4	6	247	....	....	....	....	....	....	....	....	....	....	....	....	....	....	....	....	....	....
2015-16	Lake Erie	AHL	48	0	1	1	151	....	....	....	....	....	....	....	....	....	1	0	1	1	0	....	....	....	....
2016-17	Cleveland	AHL	50	3	2	5	128	....	....	....	....	....	....	....	....	....	....	....	....	....	....	....	....	....	....
	NHL Totals		**4**	**0**	**0**	**0**	**17**	**0**	**0**	**0**	**3**	**0.0**		**0**	**0.0**	**6:53**	....	....	....	....	....	....	....	....	....

• Missed majority of 2011-12 due to recurring shoulder injury. Signed as a free agent by **NY Islanders**, February 5, 2013. Signed as a free agent by **Columbus**, July 2, 2015.

GARBUTT, Ryan
(GAHR-buht, RIGH-uhn)

Center. Shoots left. 6', 195 lbs. Born, Winnipeg, MB, August 12, 1985.

Season	Club	League	GP	G	A	Pts	PIM	PP	SH	GW	S	S%	+/-	TF	F%	Min	Playoffs GP	G	A	Pts	PIM	PP	SH	GW	Min
2003-04	Wpg. South Blues	MJHL	60	23	25	48	143	....	....	....	....	....	....	....	....	....	7	3	5	8	25	....	....	....	....
2004-05	Wpg. South Blues	MJHL	63	47	34	81	303	....	....	....	....	....	....	....	....	....	12	9	7	16	40	....	....	....	....
2005-06	Brown U.	ECAC	28	2	4	6	61	....	....	....	....	....	....	....	....	....	....	....	....	....	....	....	....	....	....
2006-07	Brown U.	ECAC	29	9	4	13	30	....	....	....	....	....	....	....	....	....	....	....	....	....	....	....	....	....	....
2007-08	Brown U.	ECAC	29	12	11	23	56	....	....	....	....	....	....	....	....	....	....	....	....	....	....	....	....	....	....
2008-09	Brown U.	ECAC	30	6	10	16	56	....	....	....	....	....	....	....	....	....	....	....	....	....	....	....	....	....	....
2009-10	Corpus Christi	CHL	64	22	28	50	204	....	....	....	....	....	....	....	....	....	1	0	0	0	2	....	....	....	....
2010-11	Gwinnett	ECHL	10	10	7	17	24	....	....	....	....	....	....	....	....	....	....	....	....	....	....	....	....	....	....
	Chicago Wolves	AHL	65	19	18	37	118	....	....	....	....	....	....	....	....	....	....	....	....	....	....	....	....	....	....
2011-12	**Dallas**	**NHL**	20	2	1	3	22	0	0	1	28	7.1	-1	27	44.4	8:17	....	....	....	....	....	....	....	....	....
	Texas Stars	AHL	50	16	17	33	96	....	....	....	....	....	....	....	....	....	....	....	....	....	....	....	....	....	....
2012-13	**Dallas**	**NHL**	36	3	7	10	32	0	0	0	59	5.1	1	17	41.2	9:55	....	....	....	....	....	....	....	....	....
2013-14	**Dallas**	**NHL**	75	17	15	32	106	0	2	1	165	10.3	10	10	40.0	13:04	6	3	0	3	25	0	0	0	11:57
2014-15	**Dallas**	**NHL**	67	8	17	25	55	0	1	2	143	5.6	-9	25	64.0	13:34	....	....	....	....	....	....	....	....	....
2015-16	**Chicago**	**NHL**	43	2	4	6	27	0	0	1	83	2.4	-7	2	0.0	10:20	....	....	....	....	....	....	....	....	....
	Anaheim	**NHL**	37	5	3	8	21	0	1	2	52	9.6	-4	6	16.7	11:26	7	1	0	1	6	0	0	0	9:49
2016-17	**Anaheim**	**NHL**	27	2	1	3	20	0	0	1	26	7.7	-3	11	63.6	9:10	....	....	....	....	....	....	....	....	....
	San Diego Gulls	AHL	28	4	6	10	45	....	....	....	....	....	....	....	....	....	....	....	....	....	....	....	....	....	....
	NHL Totals		**305**	**39**	**48**	**87**	**283**	**0**	**4**	**8**	**556**	**7.0**		**98**	**48.0**	**11:34**	**13**	**4**	**0**	**4**	**31**	**0**	**0**	**0**	**10:48**

Signed as a free agent by **Dallas**, July 1, 2011. Traded to **Chicago** by **Dallas** with Trevor Daley for Patrick Sharp and Stephen Johns, July 12, 2015. Traded to **Anaheim** by **Chicago** for Jiri Sekac, January 21, 2016.

GARDINER, Jake
(GAHR-dih-nuhr, JAYK) **TOR**

Defense. Shoots left. 6'2", 197 lbs. Born, Minnetonka, MN, July 4, 1990. Anaheim's 1st pick, 17th overall, in 2008 NHL Draft.

Season	Club	League	GP	G	A	Pts	PIM	PP	SH	GW	S	S%	+/-	TF	F%	Min	Playoffs GP	G	A	Pts	PIM	PP	SH	GW	Min
2005-06	Minnetonka	High-MN	21	2	14	16	6	....	....	....	....	....	....	....	....	....	....	....	....	....	....	....	....	....	....
2006-07	Minnetonka	High-MN	19	10	22	32	20	....	....	....	....	....	....	....	....	....	....	....	....	....	....	....	....	....	....
	Team Southwest	UMWEHL	11	4	3	7	....	....	....	....	....	....	....	....	....	....	....	....	....	....	....	....	....	....	....
2007-08	Minnetonka	High-MN	24	20	28	48	14	....	....	....	....	....	....	....	....	....	....	....	....	....	....	....	....	....	....
	Team Southwest	UMWEHL	11	8	7	15	....	....	....	....	....	....	....	....	....	....	....	....	....	....	....	....	....	....	....
2008-09	U. of Wisconsin	WCHA	39	3	18	21	16	....	....	....	....	....	....	....	....	....	....	....	....	....	....	....	....	....	....
2009-10	U. of Wisconsin	WCHA	41	6	7	13	20	....	....	....	....	....	....	....	....	....	....	....	....	....	....	....	....	....	....
2010-11	U. of Wisconsin	WCHA	41	10	31	41	24	....	....	....	....	....	....	....	....	....	....	....	....	....	....	....	....	....	....
	Toronto Marlies	AHL	10	0	3	3	4	....	....	....	....	....	....	....	....	....	....	....	....	....	....	....	....	....	....
2011-12	**Toronto**	**NHL**	75	7	23	30	18	1	0	0	79	8.9	-2	0	0.0	21:35	....	....	....	....	....	....	....	....	....
	Toronto Marlies	AHL	4	0	2	2	2	....	....	....	....	....	....	....	....	....	17	2	9	11	10	....	....	....	....
2012-13	Toronto Marlies	AHL	43	10	21	31	12	....	....	....	....	....	....	....	....	....	....	....	....	....	....	....	....	....	....
	Toronto	**NHL**	12	0	4	4	0	0	0	0	12	0.0	0	0	0.0	20:29	6	1	4	5	0	1	0	0	23:01
2013-14	**Toronto**	**NHL**	80	10	21	31	19	2	1	1	136	7.4	-3	0	0.0	21:05	....	....	....	....	....	....	....	....	....
2014-15	**Toronto**	**NHL**	79	4	20	24	24	0	0	0	100	4.0	-23	0	0.0	20:58	....	....	....	....	....	....	....	....	....
2015-16	**Toronto**	**NHL**	79	7	24	31	32	1	0	2	122	5.7	-15	2	100.0	20:37	....	....	....	....	....	....	....	....	....
2016-17	**Toronto**	**NHL**	82	9	34	43	34	2	0	2	127	7.1	24	0	0.0	21:32	6	1	2	3	4	0	0	0	28:38
	NHL Totals		**407**	**37**	**126**	**163**	**127**	**6**	**1**	**5**	**576**	**6.4**		**2**	**100.0**	**21:08**	**12**	**2**	**6**	**8**	**4**	**1**	**0**	**0**	**25:50**

WCHA All-Rookie Team (2009) • WCHA Second All-Star Team (2011) • NCAA West Second All-American Team (2011) • NHL All-Rookie Team (2012)

Traded to **Toronto** by **Anaheim** with Joffrey Lupul and Anaheim's 4th round pick (later traded to San Jose – San Jose selected Fredrik Bergvik) in 2013 NHL Draft for Francois Beauchemin, February 9, 2011.

GARRISON, Jason
(GAIR-ih-suhn, JAY-suhn) **VGK**

Defense. Shoots left. 6'2", 223 lbs. Born, White Rock, BC, November 13, 1984.

Season	Club	League	GP	G	A	Pts	PIM	PP	SH	GW	S	S%	+/-	TF	F%	Min	Playoffs GP	G	A	Pts	PIM	PP	SH	GW	Min
2002-03	Richmond	PIJHL	STATISTICS NOT AVAILABLE																						
2003-04	Nanaimo Clippers	BCHL	52	7	20	27	31	....	....	....	....	....	....	....	....	....	24	3	10	13	12	....	....	....	....
2004-05	Nanaimo Clippers	BCHL	57	22	40	62	42	....	....	....	....	....	....	....	....	....	....	....	....	....	....	....	....	....	....
2005-06	U. Minn-Duluth	WCHA	40	3	9	12	26	....	....	....	....	....	....	....	....	....	....	....	....	....	....	....	....	....	....
2006-07	U. Minn-Duluth	WCHA	21	1	2	3	16	....	....	....	....	....	....	....	....	....	....	....	....	....	....	....	....	....	....
2007-08	U. Minn-Duluth	WCHA	26	5	9	14	26	....	....	....	....	....	....	....	....	....	....	....	....	....	....	....	....	....	....
2008-09	**Florida**	**NHL**	1	0	0	0	0	0	0	0	0	0.0	0	0	0.0	11:57	....	....	....	....	....	....	....	....	....
	Rochester	AHL	75	8	27	35	68	....	....	....	....	....	....	....	....	....	....	....	....	....	....	....	....	....	....
2009-10	**Florida**	**NHL**	39	2	6	8	23	0	0	0	24	8.3	5	0	0.0	15:08	....	....	....	....	....	....	....	....	....
	Rochester	AHL	38	3	16	19	33	....	....	....	....	....	....	....	....	....	7	2	7	9	0	....	....	....	....
2010-11	**Florida**	**NHL**	73	5	13	18	26	0	0	3	116	4.3	-2	0	0.0	22:18	....	....	....	....	....	....	....	....	....
2011-12	**Florida**	**NHL**	77	16	17	33	32	9	0	3	168	9.5	6	2	50.0	23:42	4	1	2	3	0	1	0	0	25:11
2012-13	**Vancouver**	**NHL**	47	8	8	16	28	3	0	2	94	8.5	18	0	0.0	21:41	4	0	0	0	2	0	0	0	23:44
2013-14	**Vancouver**	**NHL**	81	7	26	33	57	4	1	1	181	3.9	-5	0	0.0	20:54	....	....	....	....	....	....	....	....	....
2014-15	**Tampa Bay**	**NHL**	70	4	26	30	19	1	0	3	111	3.6	27	0	0.0	20:01	23	2	5	7	8	1	0	1	19:29
2015-16	**Tampa Bay**	**NHL**	72	5	6	11	18	0	0	1	99	5.1	-4	0	0.0	18:28	17	1	6	7	12	0	0	1	19:29
2016-17	**Tampa Bay**	**NHL**	70	1	8	9	14	0	0	0	96	1.0	-8	0	0.0	18:34	....	....	....	....	....	....	....	....	....
	NHL Totals		**530**	**48**	**110**	**158**	**217**	**17**	**1**	**13**	**889**	**5.4**		**2**	**50.0**	**20:22**	**48**	**4**	**13**	**17**	**22**	**2**	**0**	**2**	**20:19**

Signed as a free agent by **Florida**, April 2, 2008. Signed as a free agent by **Vancouver**, July 1, 2012. Traded to **Tampa Bay** by **Vancouver** with Jeff Costello and Vancouver's 7th round pick (later traded to Minnesota – Minnesota selected Jack Sedak) in 2015 NHL Draft for Tampa Bay's 2nd round pick (later traded to Los Angeles – Los Angeles selected Roland McKeown) in 2014 NHL Draft, June 27, 2014. Claimed by **Vegas** from **Tampa Bay** in Expansion Draft, June 21, 2017.

GAUDET, Tyler
(GAH-deht, TIGH-luhr) **ARI**

Center. Shoots left. 6'3", 205 lbs. Born, Hamilton, ON, April 4, 1993.

Season	Club	League	GP	G	A	Pts	PIM	PP	SH	GW	S	S%	+/-	TF	F%	Min	Playoffs GP	G	A	Pts	PIM	PP	SH	GW	Min
2010-11	Hamilton	ON-Jr.A	41	4	15	19	14	....	....	....	....	....	....	....	....	....	7	3	3	6	6	....	....	....	....
2011-12	Gatineau	QMJHL	38	3	2	5	25	....	....	....	....	....	....	....	....	....	....	....	....	....	....	....	....	....	....
	Pembroke	ON-Jr.A	22	4	12	16	6	....	....	....	....	....	....	....	....	....	11	0	3	3	2	....	....	....	....
2012-13	Pembroke	ON-Jr.A	25	10	12	22	6	....	....	....	....	....	....	....	....	....	....	....	....	....	....	....	....	....	....
	Sault Ste. Marie	OHL	34	3	5	8	10	....	....	....	....	....	....	....	....	....	6	1	0	1	10	....	....	....	....
2013-14	Sault Ste. Marie	OHL	65	26	35	61	35	....	....	....	....	....	....	....	....	....	9	2	6	8	0	....	....	....	....
	Portland Pirates	AHL	2	0	0	0	0	....	....	....	....	....	....	....	....	....	....	....	....	....	....	....	....	....	....
2014-15	**Arizona**	**NHL**	2	0	0	0	0	0	0	0	1	0.0	-1	17	52.9	9:35	....	....	....	....	....	....	....	....	....
	Portland Pirates	AHL	71	8	12	20	22	....	....	....	....	....	....	....	....	....	4	1	1	2	0	....	....	....	....
2015-16	**Arizona**	**NHL**	14	1	2	3	0	0	0	0	6	16.7	-2	92	46.7	10:36	....	....	....	....	....	....	....	....	....
	Springfield	AHL	44	4	9	13	23	....	....	....	....	....	....	....	....	....	....	....	....	....	....	....	....	....	....
2016-17	**Arizona**	**NHL**	4	0	1	1	0	0	0	0	3	0.0	0	35	40.0	12:59	....	....	....	....	....	....	....	....	....
	Tucson	AHL	62	6	16	22	36	....	....	....	....	....	....	....	....	....	....	....	....	....	....	....	....	....	....
	NHL Totals		**20**	**1**	**3**	**4**	**0**	**0**	**0**	**0**	**10**	**10.0**		**144**	**45.8**	**10:59**	....	....	....	....	....	....	....	....	....

Signed as a free agent by **Phoenix**, November 4, 2013.

GAUDREAU, Frederick
(goo-DROH, FREHD-uhr-ihk) **NSH**

Center. Shoots right. 6', 192 lbs. Born, Bromont, QC, May 1, 1993.

Season	Club	League	GP	G	A	Pts	PIM	PP	SH	GW	S	S%	+/-	TF	F%	Min	Playoffs GP	G	A	Pts	PIM	PP	SH	GW	Min
2011-12	Shawinigan	QMJHL	64	5	15	20	2	....	....	....	....	....	....	....	....	....	8	1	0	1	0	....	....	....	....
2012-13	Shawinigan	QMJHL	68	13	30	43	22	....	....	....	....	....	....	....	....	....	....	....	....	....	....	....	....	....	....
2013-14	Shawinigan	QMJHL	27	13	18	31	0	....	....	....	....	....	....	....	....	....	....	....	....	....	....	....	....	....	....
	Drummondville	QMJHL	36	19	21	40	2	....	....	....	....	....	....	....	....	....	11	10	4	14	0	....	....	....	....
2014-15	Milwaukee	AHL	43	4	7	11	12	....	....	....	....	....	....	....	....	....	....	....	....	....	....	....	....	....	....
	Cincinnati	ECHL	14	5	2	7	4	....	....	....	....	....	....	....	....	....	....	....	....	....	....	....	....	....	....
2015-16	Milwaukee	AHL	75	15	27	42	31	....	....	....	....	....	....	....	....	....	3	0	1	1	0	....	....	....	....
2016-17	**Nashville**	**NHL**	9	0	1	1	0	0	0	0	8	0.0	1	12	33.3	8:40	8	3	0	3	0	0	0	2	11:29
	Milwaukee	AHL	66	25	23	48	14	....	....	....	....	....	....	....	....	....	3	3	1	4	0	....	....	....	....
	NHL Totals		**9**	**0**	**1**	**1**	**0**	**0**	**0**	**0**	**8**	**0.0**		**12**	**33.3**	**8:40**	**8**	**3**	**0**	**3**	**0**	**0**	**0**	**2**	**11:29**

Signed as a free agent by **Nashville**, January 5, 2016.

			Regular Season														Playoffs								
Season	Club	League	GP	G	A	Pts	PIM	PP	SH	GW	S	S%	+/-	TF	F%	Min	GP	G	A	Pts	PIM	PP	SH	GW	Min

GAUDREAU, Johnny  (gaw-DROH, JAWN-nee)   CGY
Left wing. Shoots left. 5'9", 157 lbs.   Born, Salem, NJ, August 13, 1993. Calgary's 4th pick, 104th overall, in 2011 NHL Draft.

Season	Club	League	GP	G	A	Pts	PIM	PP	SH	GW	S	S%	+/-	TF	F%	Min	GP	G	A	Pts	PIM	PP	SH	GW	Min
2009-10	Gloucester Cath.	High-NJ	14	21	27	48																				
	Team Comcast	T1EHL	48	29	29	58	16																			
2010-11	Dubuque	USHL	60	36	36	72	36											11	5	6	11	6				
2011-12	Boston College	H-East	44	21	23	44	10																			
2012-13	Boston College	H-East	35	21	30	*51	29																			
2013-14	Boston College	H-East	40	*36	*44	*80	14																			
	Calgary	**NHL**	1	1	0	1	0	0	0	0	1	100.0	1	0	0.0	15:11									
2014-15	**Calgary**	**NHL**	80	24	40	64	14	8	0	4	167	14.4	11	8	37.5	17:43	11	4	5	9	6	2	0	0	19:10
2015-16	**Calgary**	**NHL**	79	30	48	78	20	6	0	6	217	13.8	4	5	40.0	19:56									
2016-17	**Calgary**	**NHL**	72	18	43	61	4	4	0	3	182	9.9	-7	0	0.0	18:29	4	0	2	2	0	0	0	0	19:51
	NHL Totals		232	73	131	204	38	18	0	13	567	12.9		13	38.5	18:42	15	4	7	11	6	2	0	0	19:21

USHL All-Rookie Team (2011) • USHL Second All-Star Team (2011) • USHL Rookie of the Year (2011) • Hockey East All-Rookie Team (2012) • Hockey East First All-Star Team (2013, 2014) • Hockey East Player of the Year (2013, 2014) • NCAA East First All-American Team (2013, 2014) • Hobey Baker Memorial Award (Top U.S. Collegiate Player) (2014) • NHL All-Rookie Team (2015) • Lady Byng Memorial Trophy (2017)
Played in NHL All-Star Game (2015, 2016, 2017)

GAUNCE, Brendan  (GAWNS, BREHN-duhn)   VAN
Center. Shoots left. 6'2", 207 lbs.   Born, Markham, ON, March 25, 1994. Vancouver's 1st pick, 26th overall, in 2012 NHL Draft.

Season	Club	League	GP	G	A	Pts	PIM	PP	SH	GW	S	S%	+/-	TF	F%	Min	GP	G	A	Pts	PIM	PP	SH	GW	Min
2009-10	Markham Waxers	Minor-ON	86	55	93	*148	54																		
	Markham Waxers	ON-Jr.A	1	0	0	0	0																		
2010-11	Belleville Bulls	OHL	65	11	25	36	40											4	0	0	0	4				
2011-12	Belleville Bulls	OHL	68	28	40	68	68											6	1	2	3	2				
2012-13	Belleville Bulls	OHL	60	33	27	60	44											17	8	14	22	10				
2013-14	Belleville Bulls	OHL	22	10	16	26	27																			
	Erie Otters	OHL	43	21	25	46	32											14	5	11	16	16				
2014-15	Utica Comets	AHL	74	11	18	29	31											21	4	5	9	12				
2015-16	**Vancouver**	**NHL**	20	1	0	1	2	0	0	0	34	2.9	-9	107	45.8	12:46									
	Utica Comets	AHL	46	17	21	38	16											4	0	0	0	4				
2016-17	**Vancouver**	**NHL**	57	0	5	5	33	0	0	0	51	0.0	-2	164	51.2	9:29									
	Utica Comets	AHL	4	2	1	3	2																			
	NHL Totals		77	1	5	6	35	0	0	0	85	1.2		271	49.1	10:20									

GAUNCE, Cameron  (GAWNS, KAM-ruhn)   CBJ
Defense. Shoots left. 6'1", 210 lbs.   Born, Sudbury, ON, March 19, 1990. Colorado's 1st pick, 50th overall, in 2008 NHL Draft.

Season	Club	League	GP	G	A	Pts	PIM	PP	SH	GW	S	S%	+/-	TF	F%	Min	GP	G	A	Pts	PIM	PP	SH	GW	Min
2005-06	Markham Waxers	Minor-ON	72	11	60	71	122																			
2006-07	Markham Waxers	ON-Jr.A	45	2	12	14	68											11	0	3	3	26				
2007-08	St. Michael's	OHL	63	10	30	40	99											4	0	1	1	6				
2008-09	St. Michael's	OHL	67	17	47	64	110											11	4	6	10	20				
2009-10	St. Michael's	OHL	55	6	31	37	112											16	0	13	13	34				
2010-11	**Colorado**	**NHL**	11	0	1	1	16	0	0	0	4	25.0	-3	0	0.0	12:44									
	Lake Erie	AHL	61	2	20	22	84																			
2011-12	Lake Erie	AHL	75	6	21	27	90																			
2012-13	Lake Erie	AHL	61	1	10	11	98											9	0	0	0	0				
	Texas Stars	AHL	9	1	4	5	0																			
2013-14	**Dallas**	**NHL**	9	0	0	0	7	0	0	0	9	0.0	1	0	0.0	13:50									
	Texas Stars	AHL	65	3	15	18	73											18	0	4	4	12				
2014-15	Texas Stars	AHL	73	4	10	14	113											3	0	0	0	0				
2015-16	Portland Pirates	AHL	75	2	35	37	60											5	0	0	0	4				
2016-17	**Pittsburgh**	**NHL**	12	1	3	4	13	0	0	0	8	12.5	1	0	0.0	12:31									
	Wilkes-Barre	AHL	49	2	11	13	38											4	0	1	1	0				
	NHL Totals		32	2	5	5	36	0	0	0	21	9.5		0	0.0	12:58									

OHL Second All-Star Team (2009, 2010)
Traded to **Dallas** by **Colorado** for Tomas Vincour, April 2, 2013. Signed as a free agent by **Florida**, July 1, 2015. Signed as a free agent by **Pittsburgh**, July 1, 2016. Signed as a free agent by **Columbus**, July 1, 2017.

GAUTHIER, Frederik  (GOH-t'yay, frehd-RIHK)   TOR
Center. Shoots left. 6'5", 232 lbs.   Born, St-Lin, QC, April 26, 1995. Toronto's 1st pick, 21st overall, in 2013 NHL Draft.

Season	Club	League	GP	G	A	Pts	PIM	PP	SH	GW	S	S%	+/-	TF	F%	Min	GP	G	A	Pts	PIM	PP	SH	GW	Min
2010-11	Esther-Blondin	QAAA	37	7	14	21	6											3	0	0	0	0				
2011-12	Esther-Blondin	QAAA	39	26	25	51	28											13	13	11	24	6				
2012-13	Rimouski Oceanic	QMJHL	62	22	38	60	26											6	0	2	2	2				
2013-14	Rimouski Oceanic	QMJHL	54	18	34	52	27											11	3	6	9	6				
2014-15	Rimouski Oceanic	QMJHL	37	16	16	32	21											20	2	14	16	4				
2015-16	**Toronto**	**NHL**	7	0	1	1	0	0	0	0	3	0.0	-5	110	47.3	13:51									
	Toronto Marlies	AHL	56	6	12	18	10											9	0	0	0	4				
2016-17	**Toronto**	**NHL**	21	2	1	3	23	0	0	0	15	13.3	2	235	51.1	9:42									
	Toronto Marlies	AHL	46	4	9	13	14											6	1	3	4	2				
	NHL Totals		28	2	2	4	23	0	0	0	18	11.1		345	49.9	10:44									

QMJHL All-Rookie Team (2013)

GAZDIC, Luke  (GAZ-dihk, LEWK)   CGY
Left wing. Shoots left. 6'4", 225 lbs.   Born, Toronto, ON, July 25, 1989. Dallas' 8th pick, 172nd overall, in 2007 NHL Draft.

Season	Club	League	GP	G	A	Pts	PIM	PP	SH	GW	S	S%	+/-	TF	F%	Min	GP	G	A	Pts	PIM	PP	SH	GW	Min
2004-05	North York	GTHL	38	13	16	29	24																			
2005-06	Wexford Raiders	ON-Jr.A	47	17	16	33	105																			
2006-07	Erie Otters	OHL	58	5	8	13	136																			
2007-08	Erie Otters	OHL	67	17	12	29	144																			
2008-09	Erie Otters	OHL	63	20	10	30	127											5	0	0	0	9				
	Idaho Steelheads	ECHL	2	1	0	1	14											2	0	0	0	0				
2009-10	Texas Stars	AHL	49	3	1	4	155																			
	Idaho Steelheads	ECHL	4	1	1	2	10																			
2010-11	Texas Stars	AHL	72	9	8	17	110											5	0	0	0	2				
2011-12	Texas Stars	AHL	76	11	12	23	102																			
2012-13	Texas Stars	AHL	59	4	7	11	80											8	0	0	0	19				
2013-14	**Edmonton**	**NHL**	67	2	2	4	127	0	0	0	30	6.7	-8	3	100.0	5:48									
2014-15	**Edmonton**	**NHL**	40	2	1	3	43	0	0	0	26	7.7	-4	0	0.0	7:23									
	Oklahoma City	AHL	5	0	2	2	7																			
2015-16	**Edmonton**	**NHL**	29	1	0	1	24	0	0	0	18	5.6	-6	1	0.0	6:12									
	Bakersfield	AHL	11	1	2	3	6																			
2016-17	**New Jersey**	**NHL**	11	0	0	0	12	0	0	0	3	0.0	-2	0	0.0	7:08									
	Albany Devils	AHL	37	1	6	7	63																			
	NHL Totals		147	5	3	8	206	0	0	0	77	6.5		4	75.0	6:25									

Claimed on waivers by **Edmonton** from **Dallas**, September 29, 2013. • Missed majority of 2015-16 as a healthy reserve. Signed as a free agent by **New Jersey**, July 5, 2016. Signed as a free agent by **Calgary**, July 2, 2017.

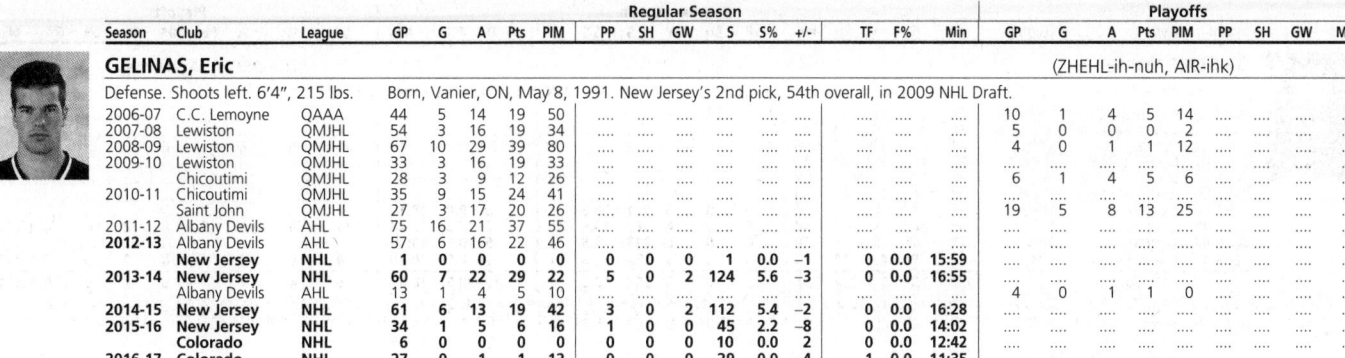

GELINAS, Eric

(ZHEHL-ih-nuh, AIR-ihk)

Defense. Shoots left. 6'4", 215 lbs. Born, Vanier, ON, May 8, 1991. New Jersey's 2nd pick, 54th overall, in 2009 NHL Draft.

			Regular Season														Playoffs								
Season	Club	League	GP	G	A	Pts	PIM	PP	SH	GW	S	S%	+/-	TF	F%	Min	GP	G	A	Pts	PIM	PP	SH	GW	Min
2006-07	C.C. Lemoyne	QAAA	44	5	14	19	50	....	....	....	....	....	....	....	....	....	10	1	4	5	14	....	....	....	....
2007-08	Lewiston	QMJHL	54	3	16	19	34	....	....	....	....	....	....	....	....	....	5	0	0	0	2	....	....	....	....
2008-09	Lewiston	QMJHL	67	10	29	39	80	....	....	....	....	....	....	....	....	....	4	0	1	1	12	....	....	....	....
2009-10	Lewiston	QMJHL	33	3	16	19	33	....	....	....	....	....	....	....	....	....	....	....	....	....	....	....	....	....	....
	Chicoutimi	QMJHL	28	3	9	12	26	....	....	....	....	....	....	....	....	....	6	1	4	5	6	....	....	....	....
2010-11	Chicoutimi	QMJHL	35	9	15	24	41	....	....	....	....	....	....	....	....	....	....	....	....	....	....	....	....	....	....
	Saint John	QMJHL	27	3	17	20	26	....	....	....	....	....	....	....	....	....	19	5	8	13	25	....	....	....	....
2011-12	Albany Devils	AHL	75	16	21	37	55	....	....	....	....	....	....	....	....	....	....	....	....	....	....	....	....	....	....
2012-13	Albany Devils	AHL	57	6	16	22	46	....	....	....	....	....	....	....	....	....	....	....	....	....	....	....	....	....	....
	New Jersey	**NHL**	**1**	**0**	**0**	**0**	**0**	**0**	**0**	**0**	**1**	**0.0**	**–1**	**0**	**0.0**	**15:59**	....	....	....	....	....	....	....	....	....
2013-14	**New Jersey**	**NHL**	**60**	**7**	**22**	**29**	**22**	**5**	**0**	**2**	**124**	**5.6**	**–3**	**0**	**0.0**	**16:55**	....	....	....	....	....	....	....	....	....
	Albany Devils	AHL	13	1	4	5	10	....	....	....	....	....	....	....	....	....	4	0	1	1	0	....	....	....	....
2014-15	**New Jersey**	**NHL**	**61**	**6**	**13**	**19**	**42**	**3**	**0**	**2**	**112**	**5.4**	**–2**	**0**	**0.0**	**16:28**	....	....	....	....	....	....	....	....	....
2015-16	**New Jersey**	**NHL**	**34**	**1**	**5**	**6**	**16**	**1**	**0**	**0**	**45**	**2.2**	**–8**	**0**	**0.0**	**14:02**	....	....	....	....	....	....	....	....	....
	Colorado	**NHL**	**6**	**0**	**0**	**0**	**0**	**0**	**0**	**0**	**10**	**0.0**	**2**	**0**	**0.0**	**12:42**	....	....	....	....	....	....	....	....	....
2016-17	**Colorado**	**NHL**	**27**	**0**	**1**	**1**	**12**	**0**	**0**	**0**	**29**	**0.0**	**–4**	**1**	**0.0**	**11:35**	....	....	....	....	....	....	....	....	....
	San Antonio	AHL	27	3	9	12	14	....	....	....	....	....	....	....	....	....	....	....	....	....	....	....	....	....	....
	NHL Totals		**189**	**14**	**41**	**55**	**92**	**9**	**0**	**4**	**321**	**4.4**		**1**	**0.0**	**15:21**	....	....	....	....	....	....	....	....	....

Traded to **Colorado** by **New Jersey** for Colorado's 3rd round pick (Fabian Zetterlund) in 2017 NHL Draft, February 29, 2016. • Missed majority of 2015-16 due to elbow injury at Calgary, March 15, 2016 and as a healthy reserve.

GERBE, Nathan

(GUHR-bee, NAY-thuhn)

Center. Shoots left. 5'4", 178 lbs. Born, Oxford, MI, July 24, 1987. Buffalo's 5th pick, 142nd overall, in 2005 NHL Draft.

			Regular Season														Playoffs								
Season	Club	League	GP	G	A	Pts	PIM	PP	SH	GW	S	S%	+/-	TF	F%	Min	GP	G	A	Pts	PIM	PP	SH	GW	Min
2002-03	River City Lancers	USHL	25	3	3	6	49	....	....	....	....	....	....	....	....	....	7	1	1	2	2	....	....	....	....
2003-04	USAHNTDP	U-17	32	14	12	26	66	....	....	....	....	....	....	....	....	....	....	....	....	....	....	....	....	....	....
	USAHNTDP	NAHL	26	11	7	18	87	....	....	....	....	....	....	....	....	....	....	....	....	....	....	....	....	....	....
2004-05	USAHNTDP	U-18	26	6	11	17	48	....	....	....	....	....	....	....	....	....	....	....	....	....	....	....	....	....	....
	USAHNTDP	NAHL	12	7	5	12	25	....	....	....	....	....	....	....	....	....	....	....	....	....	....	....	....	....	....
2005-06	Boston College	H-East	39	11	7	18	75	....	....	....	....	....	....	....	....	....	....	....	....	....	....	....	....	....	....
2006-07	Boston College	H-East	41	*25	22	47	76	....	....	....	....	....	....	....	....	....	....	....	....	....	....	....	....	....	....
2007-08	Boston College	H-East	43	*35	33	*68	65	....	....	....	....	....	....	....	....	....	....	....	....	....	....	....	....	....	....
2008-09	**Buffalo**	**NHL**	**10**	**0**	**1**	**1**	**4**	**0**	**0**	**0**	**24**	**0.0**	**3**	**1**	**100.0**	**13:37**	....	....	....	....	....	....	....	....	....
	Portland Pirates	AHL	57	30	26	56	63	....	....	....	....	....	....	....	....	....	5	0	0	0	4	....	....	....	....
2009-10	**Buffalo**	**NHL**	**10**	**2**	**3**	**5**	**4**	**2**	**0**	**1**	**29**	**6.9**	**1**	**3**	**33.3**	**14:39**	**2**	**1**	**1**	**2**	**0**	**0**	**0**	**0**	**14:38**
	Portland Pirates	AHL	44	11	27	38	46	....	....	....	....	....	....	....	....	....	4	1	1	2	4	....	....	....	....
2010-11	**Buffalo**	**NHL**	**64**	**16**	**15**	**31**	**34**	**2**	**0**	**3**	**171**	**9.4**	**11**	**17**	**23.5**	**13:20**	**7**	**2**	**0**	**2**	**18**	**0**	**0**	**0**	**13:20**
2011-12	**Buffalo**	**NHL**	**62**	**6**	**19**	**25**	**32**	**0**	**0**	**2**	**137**	**4.4**	**2**	**19**	**36.8**	**14:12**	....	....	....	....	....	....	....	....	....
2012-13	**Buffalo**	**NHL**	**42**	**5**	**5**	**10**	**14**	**0**	**1**	**0**	**64**	**7.8**	**–3**	**1**	**0.0**	**12:30**	....	....	....	....	....	....	....	....	....
2013-14	**Carolina**	**NHL**	**81**	**16**	**15**	**31**	**36**	**3**	**2**	**1**	**221**	**7.2**	**–6**	**6**	**33.3**	**16:24**	....	....	....	....	....	....	....	....	....
2014-15	**Carolina**	**NHL**	**78**	**10**	**18**	**28**	**34**	**2**	**0**	**2**	**235**	**4.3**	**–14**	**15**	**60.0**	**16:27**	....	....	....	....	....	....	....	....	....
2015-16	**Carolina**	**NHL**	**47**	**3**	**4**	**7**	**14**	**0**	**0**	**0**	**73**	**4.1**	**–15**	**5**	**40.0**	**13:28**	....	....	....	....	....	....	....	....	....
2016-17	Geneve	Swiss	26	11	17	28	22	....	....	....	....	....	....	....	....	....	4	0	2	2	2	....	....	....	....
	NHL Totals		**394**	**58**	**80**	**138**	**172**	**9**	**3**	**9**	**954**	**6.1**		**67**	**38.8**	**14:41**	**9**	**3**	**1**	**4**	**18**	**0**	**0**	**0**	**13:38**

Hockey East Second Alll-Star Team (2007) • NCAA Championship All-Tournament Team (2007, 2008) • Hockey East First All-Star Team (2008) • NCAA East First All-American Team (2008) • NCAA Championship Tournament MVP (2008) • AHL All-Rookie Team (2009) • Dudley "Red" Garrett Memorial Award (AHL – Rookie of the Year) (2009)

Signed as a free agent by **Carolina**, July 26, 2013. Signed as a free agent by **Geneve** (Swiss), October 19, 2016.

GETZLAF, Ryan

(GEHTZ-laf, RIGH-uhn) **ANA**

Center. Shoots right. 6'4", 221 lbs. Born, Regina, SK, May 10, 1985. Anaheim's 1st pick, 19th overall, in 2003 NHL Draft.

			Regular Season														Playoffs								
Season	Club	League	GP	G	A	Pts	PIM	PP	SH	GW	S	S%	+/-	TF	F%	Min	GP	G	A	Pts	PIM	PP	SH	GW	Min
2000-01	Regina Rangers	SBHL	41	33	41	74	189	....	....	....	....	....	....	....	....	....	....	....	....	....	....	....	....	....	....
	Reg. Pat Cdns.	SMHL	8	4	3	7	8	....	....	....	....	....	....	....	....	....	....	....	....	....	....	....	....	....	....
2001-02	Calgary Hitmen	WHL	63	9	9	18	34	....	....	....	....	....	....	....	....	....	7	2	1	3	4	....	....	....	....
2002-03	Calgary Hitmen	WHL	70	29	39	68	121	....	....	....	....	....	....	....	....	....	5	1	1	2	6	....	....	....	....
2003-04	Calgary Hitmen	WHL	49	28	47	75	97	....	....	....	....	....	....	....	....	....	7	5	1	6	12	....	....	....	....
2004-05	Calgary Hitmen	WHL	51	29	25	54	102	....	....	....	....	....	....	....	....	....	12	4	13	17	18	....	....	....	....
	Cincinnati	AHL	....	....	....	....	....	....	....	....	....	....	....	....	....	....	10	1	4	5	4	....	....	....	....
2005-06	**Anaheim**	**NHL**	**57**	**14**	**25**	**39**	**22**	**10**	**0**	**1**	**116**	**12.1**	**6**	**534**	**44.0**	**12:35**	**16**	**3**	**4**	**7**	**13**	**2**	**0**	**1**	**15:49**
	Portland Pirates	AHL	17	8	25	33	36	....	....	....	....	....	....	....	....	....	1	0	0	0	4	....	....	....	....
2006-07♦	**Anaheim**	**NHL**	**82**	**25**	**33**	**58**	**66**	**11**	**1**	**6**	**203**	**12.3**	**17**	**888**	**49.4**	**15:04**	**21**	**7**	**10**	**17**	**32**	**3**	**1**	**3**	**21:43**
2007-08	**Anaheim**	**NHL**	**77**	**24**	**58**	**82**	**94**	**4**	**1**	**2**	**185**	**13.0**	**32**	**1152**	**47.3**	**19:39**	**6**	**2**	**3**	**5**	**6**	**1**	**0**	**0**	**20:29**
2008-09	**Anaheim**	**NHL**	**81**	**25**	**66**	**91**	**121**	**9**	**0**	**2**	**227**	**11.0**	**5**	**1128**	**50.2**	**20:08**	**13**	**4**	**14**	**18**	**25**	**1**	**0**	**0**	**24:08**
2009-10	**Anaheim**	**NHL**	**66**	**19**	**50**	**69**	**79**	**8**	**0**	**5**	**149**	**12.8**	**4**	**1124**	**47.4**	**21:40**	....	....	....	....	....	....	....	....	....
	Canada	Olympics	7	3	4	7	2	....	....	....	....	....	....	....	....	....	....	....	....	....	....	....	....	....	....
2010-11	**Anaheim**	**NHL**	**67**	**19**	**57**	**76**	**35**	**7**	**0**	**4**	**117**	**16.2**	**14**	**1183**	**45.8**	**21:51**	**6**	**2**	**4**	**6**	**9**	**0**	**0**	**1**	**24:01**
2011-12	**Anaheim**	**NHL**	**82**	**11**	**46**	**57**	**75**	**4**	**0**	**4**	**185**	**5.9**	**–11**	**1354**	**47.2**	**21:36**	....	....	....	....	....	....	....	....	....
2012-13	**Anaheim**	**NHL**	**44**	**15**	**34**	**49**	**41**	**4**	**3**	**3**	**99**	**15.2**	**14**	**739**	**48.0**	**20:12**	**7**	**3**	**3**	**6**	**6**	**1**	**1**	**0**	**21:28**
2013-14	**Anaheim**	**NHL**	**77**	**31**	**56**	**87**	**31**	**5**	**0**	**7**	**204**	**15.2**	**28**	**1411**	**49.0**	**21:17**	**12**	**4**	**11**	**15**	**10**	**1**	**0**	**0**	**21:26**
	Canada	Olympics	6	1	2	3	4	....	....	....	....	....	....	....	....	....	....	....	....	....	....	....	....	....	....
2014-15	**Anaheim**	**NHL**	**77**	**25**	**45**	**70**	**62**	**3**	**0**	**6**	**191**	**13.1**	**15**	**1249**	**50.6**	**20:06**	**16**	**2**	**18**	**20**	**6**	**2**	**0**	**0**	**22:25**
2015-16	**Anaheim**	**NHL**	**77**	**13**	**50**	**63**	**55**	**6**	**0**	**5**	**178**	**7.3**	**14**	**1219**	**49.4**	**19:30**	**7**	**2**	**3**	**5**	**4**	**1**	**0**	**0**	**22:06**
2016-17	**Anaheim**	**NHL**	**74**	**15**	**58**	**73**	**49**	**6**	**2**	**3**	**138**	**10.9**	**7**	**1012**	**50.3**	**21:04**	**17**	**8**	**11**	**19**	**8**	**3**	**0**	**1**	**24:10**
	NHL Totals		**861**	**236**	**578**	**814**	**730**	**77**	**7**	**48**	**1992**	**11.8**		**12993**	**48.4**	**19:37**	**121**	**37**	**81**	**118**	**119**	**15**	**2**	**6**	**21:40**

WHL East First All-Star Team (2004) • WHL East Second All-Star Team (2005) • NHL Second All-Star Team (2014)

Played in NHL All-Star Game (2008, 2009, 2015)

GIBBONS, Brian

(GIH-buhnz, BRIGH-uhn) **N.J.**

Center. Shoots left. 5'8", 175 lbs. Born, Braintree, MA, February 26, 1988.

			Regular Season														Playoffs								
Season	Club	League	GP	G	A	Pts	PIM	PP	SH	GW	S	S%	+/-	TF	F%	Min	GP	G	A	Pts	PIM	PP	SH	GW	Min
2006-07	Salisbury School	High-CT	25	8	19	27	....	....	....	....	....	....	....	....	....	....	....	....	....	....	....	....	....	....	....
2007-08	Boston College	H-East	43	13	22	35	32	....	....	....	....	....	....	....	....	....	....	....	....	....	....	....	....	....	....
2008-09	Boston College	H-East	36	9	19	28	52	....	....	....	....	....	....	....	....	....	....	....	....	....	....	....	....	....	....
2009-10	Boston College	H-East	42	16	34	50	78	....	....	....	....	....	....	....	....	....	....	....	....	....	....	....	....	....	....
2010-11	Boston College	H-East	39	18	*33	51	79	....	....	....	....	....	....	....	....	....	....	....	....	....	....	....	....	....	....
2011-12	Wilkes-Barre	AHL	70	11	19	30	26	....	....	....	....	....	....	....	....	....	9	0	0	0	8	....	....	....	....
2012-13	Wilkes-Barre	AHL	70	8	22	30	34	....	....	....	....	....	....	....	....	....	15	3	5	8	22	....	....	....	....
2013-14	**Pittsburgh**	**NHL**	**41**	**5**	**12**	**17**	**6**	**1**	**0**	**0**	**29**	**17.2**	**5**	**22**	**40.9**	**11:57**	**8**	**2**	**1**	**3**	**2**	**0**	**1**	**0**	**10:37**
	Wilkes-Barre	AHL	28	11	19	30	43	....	....	....	....	....	....	....	....	....	10	1	2	3	18	....	....	....	....
2014-15	**Columbus**	**NHL**	**25**	**0**	**5**	**5**	**8**	**0**	**0**	**0**	**21**	**0.0**	**2**	**9**	**44.4**	**13:49**	....	....	....	....	....	....	....	....	....
	Springfield	AHL	26	3	8	11	14	....	....	....	....	....	....	....	....	....	....	....	....	....	....	....	....	....	....
2015-16	Hartford	AHL	63	6	17	23	30	....	....	....	....	....	....	....	....	....	....	....	....	....	....	....	....	....	....
2016-17	Albany Devils	AHL	72	16	20	36	38	....	....	....	....	....	....	....	....	....	4	1	0	1	2	....	....	....	....
	NHL Totals		**66**	**5**	**17**	**22**	**14**	**1**	**0**	**0**	**50**	**10.0**		**31**	**41.9**	**12:39**	**8**	**2**	**1**	**3**	**2**	**0**	**1**	**0**	**10:37**

Hockey East First All-Star Team (2010) • Hockey East Second All-Star Team (2011)

Signed as a free agent by **Pittsburgh**, April 4, 2011. Signed as a free agent by **Columbus**, July 4, 2014. Signed as a free agent by **NY Rangers**, July 1, 2015. Signed as a free agent by **New Jersey**, July 1, 2017.

GILBERT, Tom
(GIHL-buhrt, TAWM)

Defense. Shoots right. 6'2", 202 lbs. Born, Bloomington, MN, January 10, 1983. Colorado's 5th pick, 129th overall, in 2002 NHL Draft.

			Regular Season														Playoffs								
Season	Club	League	GP	G	A	Pts	PIM	PP	SH	GW	S	S%	+/-	TF	F%	Min	GP	G	A	Pts	PIM	PP	SH	GW	Min
99-2000	Bloomington-Jeff.	High-MN	18	7	18	25	....	....	....	....	....	....	....	....	....	....	....	....	....	....	....	....	....	....	....
2000-01	Bloomington-Jeff.	High-MN	23	20	18	38	....	....	....	....	....	....	....	....	....	....	....	....	....	....	....	....	....	....	....
	Chicago Steel	USHL	1	0	0	0	0	....	....	....	....	....	....	....	....	....	....	....	....	....	....	....	....	....	....
2001-02	Chicago Steel	USHL	57	13	15	28	62	....	....	....	....	....	....	....	....	....	4	0	0	0	4	....	....	....	....
2002-03	U. of Wisconsin	WCHA	39	7	13	20	36	....	....	....	....	....	....	....	....	....	....	....	....	....	....	....	....	....	....
2003-04	U. of Wisconsin	WCHA	39	6	15	21	36	....	....	....	....	....	....	....	....	....	....	....	....	....	....	....	....	....	....
2004-05	U. of Wisconsin	WCHA	41	8	9	17	48	....	....	....	....	....	....	....	....	....	....	....	....	....	....	....	....	....	....
2005-06	U. of Wisconsin	WCHA	43	12	19	31	32	....	....	....	....	....	....	....	....	....	....	....	....	....	....	....	....	....	....
2006-07	**Edmonton**	**NHL**	**12**	**1**	**5**	**6**	**0**	**0**	**0**	**0**	**13**	**7.7**	**–1**	**0**	**0.0**	**20:05**	....	....	....	....	....	....	....	....	....
	Wilkes-Barre	AHL	48	4	26	30	32	....	....	....	....	....	....	....	....	....	10	1	7	8	10	....	....	....	....
2007-08	**Edmonton**	**NHL**	**82**	**13**	**20**	**33**	**20**	**3**	**0**	**1**	**98**	**13.3**	**–6**	**0**	**0.0**	**22:12**	....	....	....	....	....	....	....	....	....
2008-09	**Edmonton**	**NHL**	**82**	**5**	**40**	**45**	**26**	**2**	**0**	**1**	**107**	**4.7**	**6**	**0**	**0.0**	**21:58**	....	....	....	....	....	....	....	....	....
2009-10	**Edmonton**	**NHL**	**82**	**5**	**26**	**31**	**16**	**1**	**1**	**0**	**98**	**5.1**	**–10**	**0**	**0.0**	**22:25**	....	....	....	....	....	....	....	....	....
2010-11	**Edmonton**	**NHL**	**79**	**6**	**20**	**26**	**32**	**3**	**0**	**0**	**106**	**5.7**	**–14**	**0**	**0.0**	**24:30**	....	....	....	....	....	....	....	....	....
2011-12	**Edmonton**	**NHL**	**47**	**3**	**14**	**17**	**12**	**2**	**0**	**1**	**50**	**6.0**	**–3**	**0**	**0.0**	**22:49**	....	....	....	....	....	....	....	....	....
	Minnesota	**NHL**	**20**	**0**	**5**	**5**	**8**	**0**	**0**	**0**	**22**	**0.0**	**–5**	**0**	**0.0**	**27:01**	....	....	....	....	....	....	....	....	....
2012-13	**Minnesota**	**NHL**	**43**	**3**	**10**	**13**	**18**	**1**	**0**	**0**	**36**	**8.3**	**–11**	**0**	**0.0**	**19:19**	**5**	**0**	**0**	**0**	**2**	**0**	**0**	**0**	**16:16**
2013-14	**Florida**	**NHL**	**73**	**3**	**25**	**28**	**18**	**2**	**0**	**1**	**93**	**3.2**	**–5**	**0**	**0.0**	**21:20**	....	....	....	....	....	....	....	....	....
2014-15	**Montreal**	**NHL**	**72**	**4**	**8**	**12**	**30**	**0**	**0**	**0**	**70**	**5.7**	**10**	**0**	**0.0**	**19:20**	**12**	**2**	**3**	**5**	**14**	**0**	**0**	**0**	**19:34**
2015-16	**Montreal**	**NHL**	**45**	**1**	**1**	**2**	**12**	**0**	**0**	**0**	**36**	**2.8**	**3**	**0**	**0.0**	**16:52**	....	....	....	....	....	....	....	....	....
2016-17	**Los Angeles**	**NHL**	**18**	**1**	**4**	**5**	**6**	**0**	**0**	**0**	**12**	**8.3**	**–4**	**0**	**0.0**	**15:27**	....	....	....	....	....	....	....	....	....
	Ontario Reign	AHL	5	0	1	1	4	....	....	....	....	....	....	....	....	....	....	....	....	....	....	....	....	....	....
	Hershey Bears	AHL	25	3	10	13	6	....	....	....	....	....	....	....	....	....	9	0	2	2	0	....	....	....	....
	NHL Totals		**655**	**45**	**178**	**223**	**198**	**14**	**1**	**4**	**741**	**6.1**		**0**	**0.0**	**21:29**	**17**	**2**	**3**	**5**	**16**	**0**	**0**	**0**	**18:36**

WCHA First All-Star Team (2006) • NCAA West Second All-American Team (2006) • NCAA Championship All-Tournament Team (2006) • NHL All-Rookie Team (2008)

Traded to **Edmonton** by **Colorado** for Tommy Salo and Edmonton's 6th round pick (Justin Mercier) in 2005 NHL Draft, March 8, 2004. Traded to **Minnesota** by **Edmonton** for Nick Schultz, February 27, 2012. Signed as a free agent by **Florida**, September 28, 2013. Signed as a free agent by **Montreal**, July 1, 2014. Signed as a free agent by **Los Angeles**, July 1, 2016. Traded to **Washington** by **Los Angeles** for future considerations (conditions not met), February 15, 2017.

GIONTA, Brian
(jee-OHN-tuh, BRIGH-uhn)

Right wing. Shoots right. 5'7", 178 lbs. Born, Rochester, NY, January 18, 1979. New Jersey's 4th pick, 82nd overall, in 1998 NHL Draft.

Season	Club	League	GP	G	A	Pts	PIM	PP	SH	GW	S	S%	+/-	TF	F%	Min	GP	G	A	Pts	PIM	PP	SH	GW	Min
1994-95	Rochester	EmJHL	28	*52	37	*89	....	....	....	....	....	....	....	....	....	....	....	....	....	....	....	....	....	....	....
1995-96	Niagara Scenic	ON-Jr.A	51	47	44	91	59	....	....	....	....	....	....	....	....	....	....	....	....	....	....	....	....	....	....
1996-97	Niagara Scenic	ON-Jr.A	50	57	70	127	101	....	....	....	....	....	....	....	....	....	6	6	11	17	21	....	....	....	....
1997-98	Boston College	H-East	40	30	32	62	44	....	....	....	....	....	....	....	....	....	....	....	....	....	....	....	....	....	....
1998-99	Boston College	H-East	39	27	33	60	46	....	....	....	....	....	....	....	....	....	....	....	....	....	....	....	....	....	....
99-2000	Boston College	H-East	42	*33	23	56	66	....	....	....	....	....	....	....	....	....	....	....	....	....	....	....	....	....	....
2000-01	Boston College	H-East	43	*33	21	*54	47	....	....	....	....	....	....	....	....	....	....	....	....	....	....	....	....	....	....
2001-02	**New Jersey**	**NHL**	**33**	**4**	**7**	**11**	**8**	**0**	**0**	**0**	**58**	**6.9**	**10**	**36**	**44.4**	**13:25**	**6**	**2**	**2**	**4**	**0**	**0**	**1**	**2**	**17:08**
	Albany River Rats	AHL	37	9	16	25	18	....	....	....	....	....	....	....	....	....	....	....	....	....	....	....	....	....	....
2002-03 ♦	**New Jersey**	**NHL**	**58**	**12**	**13**	**25**	**23**	**2**	**0**	**3**	**129**	**9.3**	**5**	**14**	**57.1**	**14:48**	**24**	**1**	**8**	**9**	**6**	**0**	**0**	**0**	**14:31**
2003-04	**New Jersey**	**NHL**	**75**	**21**	**8**	**29**	**36**	**0**	**0**	**8**	**174**	**12.1**	**19**	**60**	**58.3**	**14:44**	**5**	**2**	**3**	**5**	**0**	**1**	**0**	**0**	**15:41**
2004-05	Albany River Rats	AHL	15	5	7	12	10	....	....	....	....	....	....	....	....	....	....	....	....	....	....	....	....	....	....
2005-06	**New Jersey**	**NHL**	**82**	**48**	**41**	**89**	**46**	**24**	**1**	**10**	**291**	**16.5**	**18**	**73**	**38.4**	**19:49**	**9**	**3**	**4**	**7**	**2**	**1**	**1**	**2**	**20:06**
	United States	Olympics	6	4	0	4	2	....	....	....	....	....	....	....	....	....	....	....	....	....	....	....	....	....	....
2006-07	**New Jersey**	**NHL**	**62**	**25**	**20**	**45**	**36**	**11**	**0**	**4**	**194**	**12.9**	**–3**	**31**	**38.7**	**18:49**	**11**	**8**	**1**	**9**	**4**	**3**	**0**	**1**	**19:15**
2007-08	**New Jersey**	**NHL**	**82**	**22**	**31**	**53**	**46**	**8**	**1**	**4**	**257**	**8.6**	**1**	**55**	**54.6**	**18:16**	**5**	**1**	**0**	**1**	**2**	**0**	**0**	**0**	**17:52**
2008-09	**New Jersey**	**NHL**	**81**	**20**	**40**	**60**	**32**	**3**	**3**	**1**	**248**	**8.1**	**12**	**132**	**38.6**	**16:58**	**7**	**2**	**3**	**5**	**4**	**0**	**0**	**0**	**17:49**
2009-10	**Montreal**	**NHL**	**61**	**28**	**18**	**46**	**26**	**10**	**0**	**3**	**237**	**11.8**	**3**	**13**	**53.9**	**20:45**	**19**	**9**	**6**	**15**	**14**	**4**	**0**	**1**	**22:11**
2010-11	**Montreal**	**NHL**	**82**	**29**	**17**	**46**	**24**	**7**	**2**	**6**	**298**	**9.7**	**3**	**59**	**32.2**	**19:37**	**7**	**3**	**2**	**5**	**0**	**1**	**0**	**2**	**22:35**
2011-12	**Montreal**	**NHL**	**31**	**8**	**7**	**15**	**16**	**2**	**0**	**0**	**75**	**10.7**	**–7**	**33**	**42.4**	**19:26**	....	....	....	....	....	....	....	....	....
2012-13	**Montreal**	**NHL**	**48**	**14**	**12**	**26**	**8**	**5**	**0**	**3**	**112**	**12.5**	**3**	**42**	**33.3**	**18:07**	**2**	**0**	**1**	**1**	**0**	**0**	**0**	**0**	**17:10**
2013-14	**Montreal**	**NHL**	**81**	**18**	**22**	**40**	**22**	**2**	**0**	**3**	**184**	**9.8**	**1**	**60**	**38.3**	**17:51**	**17**	**1**	**6**	**7**	**2**	**0**	**1**	**0**	**17:49**
2014-15	**Buffalo**	**NHL**	**69**	**13**	**22**	**35**	**18**	**3**	**1**	**2**	**153**	**8.5**	**–13**	**169**	**40.8**	**18:03**	....	....	....	....	....	....	....	....	....
2015-16	**Buffalo**	**NHL**	**79**	**12**	**21**	**33**	**12**	**1**	**0**	**2**	**169**	**7.1**	**–5**	**120**	**45.0**	**17:44**	....	....	....	....	....	....	....	....	....
2016-17	**Buffalo**	**NHL**	**82**	**15**	**20**	**35**	**22**	**3**	**1**	**3**	**149**	**10.1**	**–11**	**106**	**43.4**	**16:36**	....	....	....	....	....	....	....	....	....
	NHL Totals		**1006**	**289**	**299**	**588**	**375**	**81**	**9**	**52**	**2728**	**10.6**		**1003**	**42.5**	**17:46**	**112**	**32**	**36**	**68**	**34**	**10**	**3**	**8**	**18:20**

Hockey East Rookie of the Year (1998) • Hockey East Second All-Star Team (1998) • NCAA East Second All-American Team (1998) • Hockey East First All-Star Team (1999, 2000, 2001) • NCAA East First All-American Team (1999, 2000, 2001) • Hockey East Player of the Year (2001)

Signed as a free agent by **Montreal**, July 1, 2009. • Missed majority of 2011-12 due to arm injury vs. St. Louis, January 10, 2012. Signed as a free agent by **Buffalo**, July 1, 2014.

GIONTA, Stephen
(jee-OHN-tuh, STEE-vehn)

Center. Shoots right. 5'7", 175 lbs. Born, Rochester, NY, October 9, 1983.

Season	Club	League	GP	G	A	Pts	PIM	PP	SH	GW	S	S%	+/-	TF	F%	Min	GP	G	A	Pts	PIM	PP	SH	GW	Min
99-2000	Rochester	NAHL	41	11	15	26	56	....	....	....	....	....	....	....	....	....	....	....	....	....	....	....	....	....	....
2000-01	USAHNTDP	USHL	16	1	2	3	12	....	....	....	....	....	....	....	....	....	....	....	....	....	....	....	....	....	....
	USAHNTDP	NAHL	1	0	0	0	0	....	....	....	....	....	....	....	....	....	....	....	....	....	....	....	....	....	....
2001-02	USAHNTDP	NAHL	22	2	5	7	33	....	....	....	....	....	....	....	....	....	....	....	....	....	....	....	....	....	....
2002-03	Boston College	H-East	33	5	10	15	36	....	....	....	....	....	....	....	....	....	....	....	....	....	....	....	....	....	....
2003-04	Boston College	H-East	41	9	15	24	36	....	....	....	....	....	....	....	....	....	....	....	....	....	....	....	....	....	....
2004-05	Boston College	H-East	38	8	11	19	44	....	....	....	....	....	....	....	....	....	....	....	....	....	....	....	....	....	....
2005-06	Boston College	H-East	37	11	21	32	66	....	....	....	....	....	....	....	....	....	....	....	....	....	....	....	....	....	....
	Albany River Rats	AHL	3	5	1	6	2	....	....	....	....	....	....	....	....	....	....	....	....	....	....	....	....	....	....
2006-07	Lowell Devils	AHL	67	7	8	15	15	....	....	....	....	....	....	....	....	....	....	....	....	....	....	....	....	....	....
2007-08	Lowell Devils	AHL	63	16	13	29	33	....	....	....	....	....	....	....	....	....	....	....	....	....	....	....	....	....	....
2008-09	Lowell Devils	AHL	52	2	9	11	30	....	....	....	....	....	....	....	....	....	....	....	....	....	....	....	....	....	....
2009-10	Lowell Devils	AHL	68	15	19	34	26	....	....	....	....	....	....	....	....	....	5	0	1	1	0	....	....	....	....
2010-11	**New Jersey**	**NHL**	**12**	**0**	**0**	**0**	**6**	**0**	**0**	**0**	**13**	**0.0**	**–3**	**0**	**0.0**	**9:00**	....	....	....	....	....	....	....	....	....
	Albany Devils	AHL	54	10	20	30	21	....	....	....	....	....	....	....	....	....	....	....	....	....	....	....	....	....	....
2011-12	**New Jersey**	**NHL**	**1**	**1**	**0**	**1**	**0**	**0**	**0**	**1**	**2**	**50.0**	**1**	**8**	**62.5**	**10:37**	**24**	**3**	**4**	**7**	**4**	**0**	**0**	**0**	**9:14**
	Albany Devils	AHL	56	6	10	16	40	....	....	....	....	....	....	....	....	....	....	....	....	....	....	....	....	....	....
2012-13	Albany Devils	AHL	11	2	3	5	4	....	....	....	....	....	....	....	....	....	....	....	....	....	....	....	....	....	....
	New Jersey	**NHL**	**48**	**4**	**10**	**14**	**14**	**0**	**0**	**0**	**58**	**6.9**	**2**	**390**	**35.1**	**13:02**	....	....	....	....	....	....	....	....	....
2013-14	**New Jersey**	**NHL**	**66**	**4**	**7**	**11**	**18**	**0**	**1**	**1**	**89**	**4.5**	**–8**	**581**	**41.0**	**12:28**	....	....	....	....	....	....	....	....	....
2014-15	**New Jersey**	**NHL**	**61**	**5**	**8**	**13**	**12**	**0**	**0**	**1**	**84**	**6.0**	**4**	**394**	**40.4**	**13:11**	....	....	....	....	....	....	....	....	....
2015-16	**New Jersey**	**NHL**	**82**	**1**	**10**	**11**	**43**	**0**	**0**	**0**	**62**	**1.6**	**–13**	**691**	**42.1**	**12:13**	....	....	....	....	....	....	....	....	....
2016-17	**NY Islanders**	**NHL**	**26**	**1**	**5**	**6**	**2**	**0**	**0**	**0**	**17**	**5.9**	**9**	**120**	**46.7**	**11:12**	....	....	....	....	....	....	....	....	....
	Bridgeport	AHL	7	1	2	3	6	....	....	....	....	....	....	....	....	....	....	....	....	....	....	....	....	....	....
	NHL Totals		**296**	**16**	**40**	**56**	**95**	**0**	**1**	**3**	**325**	**4.9**		**2184**	**40.6**	**12:23**	**24**	**3**	**4**	**7**	**4**	**0**	**0**	**0**	**9:14**

Signed to an ATO (amateur tryout) contract by **Albany** (AHL), April 12, 2006. Signed as a free agent by **New Jersey**, August 26, 2010. Signed as a free agent by **NY Islanders**, December 21, 2016.

GIORDANO, Mark
(jee-ohr-DAN-oh, MAHRK) **CGY**

Defense. Shoots left. 6', 198 lbs. Born, Toronto, ON, October 3, 1983.

Season	Club	League	GP	G	A	Pts	PIM	PP	SH	GW	S	S%	+/-	TF	F%	Min	GP	G	A	Pts	PIM	PP	SH	GW	Min
2001-02	Brampton	ON-Jr.A	48	11	26	37	59	....	....	....	....	....	....	....	....	....	....	....	....	....	....	....	....	....	....
2002-03	Owen Sound	OHL	68	18	30	48	109	....	....	....	....	....	....	....	....	....	4	1	3	4	2	....	....	....	....
2003-04	Owen Sound	OHL	65	14	35	49	72	....	....	....	....	....	....	....	....	....	7	1	3	4	5	....	....	....	....
2004-05	Lowell	AHL	66	6	10	16	85	....	....	....	....	....	....	....	....	....	11	0	1	1	41	....	....	....	....
2005-06	**Calgary**	**NHL**	**7**	**0**	**1**	**1**	**8**	**0**	**0**	**0**	**5**	**0.0**	**2**	**0**	**0.0**	**12:05**	....	....	....	....	....	....	....	....	....
	Omaha	AHL	73	16	42	58	141	....	....	....	....	....	....	....	....	....	....	....	....	....	....	....	....	....	....
2006-07	**Calgary**	**NHL**	**48**	**7**	**8**	**15**	**36**	**3**	**0**	**2**	**49**	**14.3**	**7**	**0**	**0.0**	**13:27**	**4**	**1**	**0**	**1**	**0**	**1**	**0**	**0**	**12:16**
	Omaha	AHL	5	0	2	2	8	....	....	....	....	....	....	....	....	....	3	0	1	1	2	....	....	....	....
2007-08	Dynamo Moscow	Russia	50	4	8	12	89	....	....	....	....	....	....	....	....	....	9	1	5	6	35	....	....	....	....
2008-09	**Calgary**	**NHL**	**58**	**2**	**17**	**19**	**59**	**2**	**0**	**0**	**82**	**2.4**	**2**	**0**	**0.0**	**16:13**	....	....	....	....	....	....	....	....	....
2009-10	**Calgary**	**NHL**	**82**	**11**	**19**	**30**	**81**	**5**	**0**	**1**	**111**	**9.9**	**17**	**0**	**0.0**	**20:50**	....	....	....	....	....	....	....	....	....

			Regular Season														Playoffs								
Season	Club	League	GP	G	A	Pts	PIM	PP	SH	GW	S	S%	+/-	TF	F%	Min	GP	G	A	Pts	PIM	PP	SH	GW	Min
2010-11	**Calgary**	**NHL**	**82**	**8**	**35**	**43**	**67**	**5**	**0**	**1**	**165**	**4.8**	**–8**	**0**	**0.0**	**23:08**	....	....	....	....	....	....	....	....	....
2011-12	**Calgary**	**NHL**	**61**	**9**	**18**	**27**	**75**	**5**	**0**	**0**	**125**	**7.2**	**0**	**0**	**0.0**	**23:01**	....	....	....	....	....	....	....	....	....
2012-13	**Calgary**	**NHL**	**47**	**4**	**11**	**15**	**40**	**1**	**1**	**1**	**58**	**6.9**	**–7**	**0**	**0.0**	**23:10**	....	....	....	....	....	....	....	....	....
2013-14	**Calgary**	**NHL**	**64**	**14**	**33**	**47**	**63**	**7**	**0**	**2**	**180**	**7.8**	**12**	**0**	**0.0**	**25:14**	....	....	....	....	....	....	....	....	....
2014-15	**Calgary**	**NHL**	**61**	**11**	**37**	**48**	**37**	**2**	**1**	**2**	**157**	**7.0**	**13**	**0**	**0.0**	**25:10**	....	....	....	....	....	....	....	....	....
2015-16	**Calgary**	**NHL**	**82**	**21**	**35**	**56**	**54**	**9**	**1**	**2**	**212**	**9.9**	**–5**	**0**	**0.0**	**24:48**	....	....	....	....	....	....	....	....	....
2016-17	**Calgary**	**NHL**	**81**	**12**	**27**	**39**	**59**	**3**	**2**	**4**	**151**	**7.9**	**22**	**0**	**0.0**	**23:35**	**4**	**0**	**1**	**1**	**2**	**0**	**0**	**0**	**25:31**
	NHL Totals		**673**	**99**	**241**	**340**	**579**	**42**	**5**	**15**	**1295**	**7.6**		**0**	**0.0**	**22:05**	**8**	**1**	**1**	**2**	**2**	**1**	**0**	**0**	**18:53**

NHL Foundation Player Award (2016)
Played in NHL All-Star Game (2015, 2016)
Signed as a free agent by **Calgary**, July 6, 2004. Signed as a free agent by **Dynamo Moscow** (Russia) August 28, 2007. Signed as a free agent by **Calgary**, July 1, 2008.

GIRARDI, Dan

(jih-RAHR-dee, DAN) **T.B.**

Defense. Shoots right. 6'1", 208 lbs. Born, Welland, ON, April 29, 1984.

Season	Club	League	GP	G	A	Pts	PIM	PP	SH	GW	S	S%	+/-	TF	F%	Min	GP	G	A	Pts	PIM	PP	SH	GW	Min
99-2000	Welland Cougars	Minor-ON	47	2	16	18	14	....	....	....	....	....	....	....	....	....	....	....	....	....	....	....	....	....	....
2000-01	Welland Cougars	Minor-ON	11	1	4	5	4	....	....	....	....	....	....	....	....	....	....	....	....	....	....	....	....	....	....
	Couchiching	ON-Jr.A	27	1	11	12	27	....	....	....	....	....	....	....	....	....	....	....	....	....	....	....	....	....	....
	Barrie Colts	OHL	6	0	0	0	0	....	....	....	....	....	....	....	....	....	....	....	....	....	....	....	....	....	....
2001-02	Barrie Colts	OHL	21	0	1	1	0	....	....	....	....	....	....	....	....	....	20	0	0	0	0	....	....	....	....
2002-03	Barrie Colts	OHL	31	3	13	16	24	....	....	....	....	....	....	....	....	....	....	....	....	....	....	....	....	....	....
	Guelph Storm	OHL	36	1	13	14	20	....	....	....	....	....	....	....	....	....	11	0	9	9	14	....	....	....	....
2003-04	Guelph Storm	OHL	68	8	39	47	55	....	....	....	....	....	....	....	....	....	22	2	17	19	10	....	....	....	....
2004-05	Guelph Storm	OHL	38	5	20	25	24	....	....	....	....	....	....	....	....	....	....	....	....	....	....	....	....	....	....
	London Knights	OHL	31	4	10	14	14	....	....	....	....	....	....	....	....	....	18	0	6	6	10	....	....	....	....
2005-06	Hartford	AHL	66	8	31	39	44	....	....	....	....	....	....	....	....	....	13	4	5	9	8	....	....	....	....
	Charlotte	ECHL	7	1	4	5	6	....	....	....	....	....	....	....	....	....	....	....	....	....	....	....	....	....	....
2006-07	**NY Rangers**	**NHL**	**34**	**0**	**6**	**6**	**8**	**0**	**0**	**0**	**33**	**0.0**	**7**	**0**	**0.0**	**15:50**	**10**	**0**	**0**	**0**	**4**	**0**	**0**	**0**	**19:52**
	Hartford	AHL	45	2	22	24	16	....	....	....	....	....	....	....	....	....	....	....	....	....	....	....	....	....	....
2007-08	**NY Rangers**	**NHL**	**82**	**10**	**18**	**28**	**14**	**5**	**0**	**1**	**147**	**6.8**	**0**	**1**	**0.0**	**21:12**	**10**	**0**	**3**	**3**	**6**	**0**	**0**	**0**	**20:42**
2008-09	**NY Rangers**	**NHL**	**82**	**4**	**18**	**22**	**53**	**2**	**0**	**1**	**122**	**3.3**	**–14**	**0**	**0.0**	**21:32**	**7**	**0**	**0**	**0**	**6**	**0**	**0**	**0**	**21:04**
2009-10	**NY Rangers**	**NHL**	**82**	**6**	**18**	**24**	**53**	**1**	**1**	**1**	**108**	**5.6**	**–2**	**0**	**0.0**	**21:29**	....	....	....	....	....	....	....	....	....
2010-11	**NY Rangers**	**NHL**	**80**	**4**	**27**	**31**	**37**	**2**	**0**	**1**	**110**	**3.6**	**7**	**0**	**0.0**	**24:35**	**5**	**0**	**0**	**0**	**0**	**0**	**0**	**0**	**27:01**
2011-12	**NY Rangers**	**NHL**	**82**	**5**	**24**	**29**	**20**	**1**	**0**	**2**	**122**	**4.1**	**13**	**0**	**0.0**	**26:15**	**20**	**3**	**9**	**12**	**2**	**1**	**0**	***3**	**26:52**
2012-13	**NY Rangers**	**NHL**	**46**	**2**	**12**	**14**	**16**	**0**	**0**	**1**	**81**	**2.5**	**–1**	**0**	**0.0**	**25:25**	**12**	**2**	**2**	**4**	**2**	**2**	**0**	**0**	**25:59**
2013-14	**NY Rangers**	**NHL**	**81**	**5**	**19**	**24**	**16**	**1**	**0**	**0**	**100**	**5.0**	**6**	**0**	**0.0**	**23:07**	**25**	**1**	**6**	**7**	**10**	**0**	**0**	**0**	**24:19**
2014-15	**NY Rangers**	**NHL**	**82**	**4**	**16**	**20**	**22**	**1**	**0**	**1**	**111**	**3.6**	**12**	**0**	**0.0**	**22:42**	**19**	**0**	**4**	**4**	**4**	**0**	**0**	**0**	**21:38**
2015-16	**NY Rangers**	**NHL**	**74**	**2**	**15**	**17**	**20**	**0**	**0**	**1**	**77**	**2.6**	**18**	**0**	**0.0**	**20:19**	**2**	**0**	**1**	**1**	**0**	**0**	**0**	**0**	**17:38**
2016-17	**NY Rangers**	**NHL**	**63**	**4**	**11**	**15**	**16**	**0**	**1**	**3**	**56**	**7.1**	**8**	**0**	**0.0**	**19:06**	**12**	**0**	**2**	**2**	**2**	**0**	**0**	**0**	**22:06**
	NHL Totals		**788**	**46**	**184**	**230**	**275**	**13**	**2**	**12**	**1067**	**4.3**		**1**	**0.0**	**22:15**	**122**	**6**	**27**	**33**	**36**	**3**	**0**	**3**	**23:25**

AHL All-Rookie Team (2006)
Played in NHL All-Star Game (2012)
Signed as a free agent by **NY Rangers**, July 1, 2006. Signed as a free agent by **Tampa Bay**, July 1, 2017.

GIRGENSONS, Zemgus

(GEER-gehn-suhnz, ZEHM-guhz) **BUF**

Center. Shoots left. 6'1", 203 lbs. Born, Riga, Latvia, January 5, 1994. Buffalo's 2nd pick, 14th overall, in 2012 NHL Draft.

Season	Club	League	GP	G	A	Pts	PIM	PP	SH	GW	S	S%	+/-	TF	F%	Min	GP	G	A	Pts	PIM	PP	SH	GW	Min
2009-10	Green Mountain	EmJHL	19	17	12	29	6	....	....	....	....	....	....	....	....	....	....	....	....	....	....	....	....	....	....
	Green Mountain	EJHL	23	11	17	28	13	....	....	....	....	....	....	....	....	....	2	0	2	2	0	....	....	....	....
2010-11	Dubuque	USHL	51	21	28	49	46	....	....	....	....	....	....	....	....	....	11	3	5	8	8	....	....	....	....
2011-12	Dubuque	USHL	49	24	31	55	69	....	....	....	....	....	....	....	....	....	2	2	2	4	0	....	....	....	....
2012-13	Rochester	AHL	61	6	11	17	28	....	....	....	....	....	....	....	....	....	3	3	0	3	0	....	....	....	....
2013-14	**Buffalo**	**NHL**	**70**	**8**	**14**	**22**	**14**	**0**	**1**	**1**	**115**	**7.0**	**–6**	**240**	**41.7**	**15:19**	....	....	....	....	....	....	....	....	....
	Latvia	Olympics	5	1	1	2	2	....	....	....	....	....	....	....	....	....	....	....	....	....	....	....	....	....	....
2014-15	**Buffalo**	**NHL**	**61**	**15**	**15**	**30**	**25**	**1**	**3**	**1**	**115**	**13.0**	**–16**	**1000**	**44.0**	**19:05**	....	....	....	....	....	....	....	....	....
2015-16	**Buffalo**	**NHL**	**71**	**7**	**11**	**18**	**20**	**1**	**0**	**1**	**110**	**6.4**	**0**	**335**	**45.7**	**15:02**	....	....	....	....	....	....	....	....	....
2016-17	**Buffalo**	**NHL**	**75**	**7**	**9**	**16**	**18**	**0**	**0**	**0**	**112**	**6.3**	**–7**	**579**	**47.2**	**13:10**	....	....	....	....	....	....	....	....	....
	NHL Totals		**277**	**37**	**49**	**86**	**77**	**2**	**4**	**3**	**452**	**8.2**		**2154**	**44.8**	**15:29**	....	....	....	....	....	....	....	....	....

USHL First All-Star Team (2012)
Played in NHL All-Star Game (2015)

GIROUX, Claude

(zhih-ROO, KLOHD) **PHI**

Center. Shoots right. 5'11", 185 lbs. Born, Hearst, ON, January 12, 1988. Philadelphia's 1st pick, 22nd overall, in 2006 NHL Draft.

Season	Club	League	GP	G	A	Pts	PIM	PP	SH	GW	S	S%	+/-	TF	F%	Min	GP	G	A	Pts	PIM	PP	SH	GW	Min
2004-05	Cumberland	ON-Jr.A	48	13	27	40	30	....	....	....	....	....	....	....	....	....	....	....	....	....	....	....	....	....	....
2005-06	Gatineau	QMJHL	69	39	64	103	64	....	....	....	....	....	....	....	....	....	17	5	15	20	24	....	....	....	....
2006-07	Gatineau	QMJHL	63	48	64	112	49	....	....	....	....	....	....	....	....	....	5	2	5	7	2	....	....	....	....
	Philadelphia	AHL	5	1	1	2	6	....	....	....	....	....	....	....	....	....	....	....	....	....	....	....	....	....	....
2007-08	**Philadelphia**	**NHL**	**2**	**0**	**0**	**0**	**0**	**0**	**0**	**0**	**2**	**0.0**	**–2**	**0**	**0.0**	**9:35**	....	....	....	....	....	....	....	....	....
	Gatineau	QMJHL	55	38	68	106	37	....	....	....	....	....	....	....	....	....	19	17	*34	*51	6	....	....	....	....
2008-09	**Philadelphia**	**NHL**	**42**	**9**	**18**	**27**	**14**	**2**	**0**	**0**	**67**	**13.4**	**10**	**309**	**47.3**	**15:10**	**6**	**2**	**3**	**5**	**6**	**0**	**0**	**0**	**15:57**
	Philadelphia	AHL	33	17	17	34	22	....	....	....	....	....	....	....	....	....	....	....	....	....	....	....	....	....	....
2009-10	**Philadelphia**	**NHL**	**82**	**16**	**31**	**47**	**23**	**8**	**0**	**2**	**145**	**11.0**	**–9**	**600**	**49.5**	**16:37**	**23**	**10**	**11**	**21**	**4**	**3**	**0**	**2**	**18:45**
2010-11	**Philadelphia**	**NHL**	**82**	**25**	**51**	**76**	**47**	**8**	**3**	**5**	**169**	**14.8**	**20**	**1095**	**50.1**	**19:24**	**11**	**1**	**11**	**12**	**8**	**0**	**0**	**0**	**21:57**
2011-12	**Philadelphia**	**NHL**	**77**	**28**	**65**	**93**	**29**	**6**	**0**	**5**	**242**	**11.6**	**6**	**1543**	**53.7**	**21:33**	**10**	***8**	**9**	**17**	**13**	**3**	***2**	**0**	**22:43**
2012-13	Eisbaren Berlin	Germany	9	4	15	19	6	....	....	....	....	....	....	....	....	....	....	....	....	....	....	....	....	....	....
	Philadelphia	**NHL**	**48**	**13**	**35**	**48**	**22**	**6**	**1**	**2**	**137**	**9.5**	**–7**	**1182**	**54.5**	**21:10**	....	....	....	....	....	....	....	....	....
2013-14	**Philadelphia**	**NHL**	**82**	**28**	**58**	**86**	**46**	**7**	**0**	**7**	**223**	**12.6**	**7**	**1760**	**52.9**	**20:26**	**7**	**2**	**4**	**6**	**2**	**0**	**0**	**0**	**19:24**
2014-15	**Philadelphia**	**NHL**	**81**	**25**	**48**	**73**	**36**	**14**	**0**	**4**	**279**	**9.0**	**–3**	**1878**	**56.6**	**20:34**	....	....	....	....	....	....	....	....	....
2015-16	**Philadelphia**	**NHL**	**78**	**22**	**45**	**67**	**53**	**6**	**1**	**5**	**241**	**9.1**	**–8**	**1881**	**57.5**	**20:33**	**6**	**0**	**1**	**1**	**2**	**0**	**0**	**0**	**20:48**
2016-17	**Philadelphia**	**NHL**	**82**	**14**	**44**	**58**	**38**	**5**	**0**	**3**	**199**	**7.0**	**–15**	**1748**	**55.9**	**19:07**	....	....	....	....	....	....	....	....	....
	NHL Totals		**656**	**180**	**395**	**575**	**308**	**62**	**5**	**33**	**1704**	**10.6**		**11996**	**54.3**	**19:30**	**63**	**23**	**39**	**62**	**35**	**6**	**2**	**2**	**19:56**

QMJHL All-Rookie Team (2006) • QMJHL First All-Star Team (2008) • Canadian Major Junior First All-Star Team (2008)
Played in NHL All-Star Game (2011, 2012, 2015, 2016)
Signed as a free agent by **Berlin** (Germany), October 4, 2012.

GLASS, Tanner

(GLAS, TA-nuhr)

Left wing. Shoots left. 6'1", 213 lbs. Born, Regina, SK, November 29, 1983. Florida's 13th pick, 265th overall, in 2003 NHL Draft.

Season	Club	League	GP	G	A	Pts	PIM	PP	SH	GW	S	S%	+/-	TF	F%	Min	GP	G	A	Pts	PIM	PP	SH	GW	Min
2000-01	Yorkton Mallers	SMHL	39	31	29	60	120	....	....	....	....	....	....	....	....	....	4	3	1	4	10	....	....	....	....
	Yorkton Terriers	SJHL	2	0	1	1	2	....	....	....	....	....	....	....	....	....	....	....	....	....	....	....	....	....	....
2001-02	Penticton	BCHL	57	11	28	39	171	....	....	....	....	....	....	....	....	....	....	....	....	....	....	....	....	....	....
2002-03	Penticton	BCHL	32	15	25	40	108	....	....	....	....	....	....	....	....	....	....	....	....	....	....	....	....	....	....
	Nanaimo Clippers	BCHL	18	8	14	22	46	....	....	....	....	....	....	....	....	....	....	....	....	....	....	....	....	....	....
2003-04	Dartmouth	ECAC	26	4	7	11	18	....	....	....	....	....	....	....	....	....	....	....	....	....	....	....	....	....	....
2004-05	Dartmouth	ECAC	33	7	8	15	32	....	....	....	....	....	....	....	....	....	....	....	....	....	....	....	....	....	....
2005-06	Dartmouth	ECAC	33	12	16	28	56	....	....	....	....	....	....	....	....	....	....	....	....	....	....	....	....	....	....
2006-07	Dartmouth	ECAC	32	8	20	28	92	....	....	....	....	....	....	....	....	....	....	....	....	....	....	....	....	....	....
	Rochester	AHL	4	0	1	1	5	....	....	....	....	....	....	....	....	....	....	....	....	....	....	....	....	....	....
2007-08	**Florida**	**NHL**	**41**	**1**	**1**	**2**	**39**	**0**	**0**	**0**	**11**	**9.1**	**–5**	**2**	**0.0**	**4:25**	....	....	....	....	....	....	....	....	....
	Rochester	AHL	43	6	5	11	84	....	....	....	....	....	....	....	....	....	....	....	....	....	....	....	....	....	....
2008-09	**Florida**	**NHL**	**3**	**0**	**0**	**0**	**7**	**0**	**0**	**0**	**1**	**0.0**	**0**	**1**	**100.0**	**6:45**	....	....	....	....	....	....	....	....	....
	Rochester	AHL	44	4	9	13	100	....	....	....	....	....	....	....	....	....	....	....	....	....	....	....	....	....	....
2009-10	**Vancouver**	**NHL**	**67**	**4**	**7**	**11**	**115**	**0**	**0**	**0**	**52**	**7.7**	**5**	**18**	**16.7**	**10:28**	**4**	**0**	**0**	**0**	**0**	**0**	**0**	**0**	**3:08**
2010-11	**Vancouver**	**NHL**	**73**	**3**	**7**	**10**	**72**	**0**	**0**	**1**	**45**	**6.7**	**–5**	**62**	**40.3**	**8:56**	**20**	**0**	**0**	**0**	**18**	**0**	**0**	**0**	**7:28**
2011-12	**Winnipeg**	**NHL**	**78**	**5**	**11**	**16**	**73**	**0**	**0**	**1**	**86**	**5.8**	**–12**	**73**	**39.7**	**13:25**	....	....	....	....	....	....	....	....	....

			Regular Season														Playoffs								
Season	Club	League	GP	G	A	Pts	PIM	PP	SH	GW	S	S%	+/-	TF	F%	Min	GP	G	A	Pts	PIM	PP	SH	GW	Min
2012-13	B. Bystrica	Slovakia	6	0	1	1	75	....	....	....	....	....	....	....	....	....	....	....	....	....	....	....	....	....	....
	Pittsburgh	**NHL**	**48**	**1**	**1**	**2**	**62**	**1**	**0**	**0**	**38**	**2.6**	**–11**	**51**	**43.1**	**10:04**	**5**	**1**	**0**	**1**	**4**	**0**	**0**	**0**	**8:13**
2013-14	**Pittsburgh**	**NHL**	**67**	**4**	**9**	**13**	**90**	**0**	**0**	**0**	**56**	**7.1**	**–8**	**19**	**47.4**	**11:47**	**8**	**0**	**0**	**0**	**4**	**0**	**0**	**0**	**9:50**
2014-15	**NY Rangers**	**NHL**	**66**	**1**	**5**	**6**	**98**	**0**	**0**	**0**	**53**	**1.9**	**–12**	**21**	**33.3**	**10:15**	**19**	**0**	**1**	**1**	**31**	**0**	**0**	**0**	**9:21**
2015-16	**NY Rangers**	**NHL**	**57**	**4**	**3**	**7**	**66**	**0**	**0**	**0**	**49**	**8.2**	**–3**	**20**	**30.0**	**10:17**	**4**	**0**	**0**	**0**	**4**	**0**	**0**	**0**	**9:28**
	Hartford	AHL	17	2	3	5	23	....	....	....	....	....	....	....	....	....	....	....	....	....	....	....	....	....	....
2016-17	**NY Rangers**	**NHL**	**11**	**1**	**1**	**2**	**17**	**0**	**0**	**0**	**8**	**12.5**	**0**	**2**	**100.0**	**10:55**	**7**	**1**	**3**	**4**	**7**	**0**	**0**	**1**	**9:52**
	Hartford	AHL	57	6	9	15	86	....	....	....	....	....	....	....	....	....	....	....	....	....	....	....	....	....	....
	NHL Totals		**511**	**24**	**45**	**69**	**639**	**1**	**0**	**2**	**399**	**6.0**		**269**	**38.7**	**10:17**	**67**	**2**	**4**	**6**	**68**	**0**	**0**	**1**	**8:27**

Signed as a free aget by **Vancouver**, July 22, 2009. Signed as a free agent by **Winnipeg**, July 2, 2011. Signed as a free agent by **Pittsburgh**, July 1, 2012. Signed as a free agent by **Banska Bystrica** (Slovakia), December 4, 2012. Signed as a free agent by **NY Rangers**, July 1, 2014.

GLENDENING, Luke

(glehn-DEHN-ihng , LEWK) **DET**

Right wing. Shoots right. 5'11", 199 lbs. Born, Grand Rapids, MI, April 28, 1989.

2008-09	U. of Michigan	CCHA	35	6	4	10	33	....	....	....	....	....	....	....	....	....	....	....	....	....	....	....	....	....	....
2009-10	U. of Michigan	CCHA	45	7	14	21	39	....	....	....	....	....	....	....	....	....	....	....	....	....	....	....	....	....	....
2010-11	U. of Michigan	CCHA	44	8	10	18	26	....	....	....	....	....	....	....	....	....	....	....	....	....	....	....	....	....	....
2011-12	U. of Michigan	CCHA	41	10	11	21	24	....	....	....	....	....	....	....	....	....	....	....	....	....	....	....	....	....	....
	Providence Bruins	AHL	3	0	0	0	0	....	....	....	....	....	....	....	....	....	....	....	....	....	....	....	....	....	....
2012-13	Toledo Walleye	ECHL	27	14	7	21	27	....	....	....	....	....	....	....	....	....	....	....	....	....	....	....	....	....	....
	Grand Rapids	AHL	51	8	18	26	50	....	....	....	....	....	....	....	....	....	24	6	10	16	30	....	....	....	....
2013-14	**Detroit**	**NHL**	**56**	**1**	**6**	**7**	**22**	**0**	**0**	**0**	**54**	**1.9**	**–8**	**678**	**48.5**	**13:55**	**5**	**1**	**0**	**1**	**0**	**0**	**0**	**0**	**14:11**
	Grand Rapids	AHL	18	5	7	12	18	....	....	....	....	....	....	....	....	....	....	....	....	....	....	....	....	....	....
2014-15	**Detroit**	**NHL**	**82**	**12**	**6**	**18**	**34**	**1**	**0**	**2**	**104**	**11.5**	**5**	**962**	**51.9**	**14:43**	**7**	**2**	**1**	**3**	**8**	**0**	**1**	**1**	**15:31**
2015-16	**Detroit**	**NHL**	**81**	**8**	**13**	**21**	**46**	**0**	**0**	**3**	**88**	**9.1**	**4**	**1125**	**54.6**	**14:35**	**5**	**0**	**1**	**1**	**0**	**0**	**0**	**0**	**16:36**
2016-17	**Detroit**	**NHL**	**74**	**3**	**11**	**14**	**26**	**0**	**0**	**0**	**76**	**3.9**	**–10**	**568**	**54.1**	**12:55**	....	....	....	....	....	....	....	....	....
	NHL Totals		**293**	**24**	**36**	**60**	**128**	**1**	**0**	**5**	**322**	**7.5**		**3333**	**52.5**	**14:04**	**17**	**3**	**2**	**5**	**8**	**0**	**1**	**1**	**15:26**

Signed as a free agent by **Detroit**, July 5, 2013.

GOLDOBIN, Nikolay

(gohl-DOH-bihn, NIH-koh-ligh) **VAN**

Right wing. Shoots left. 5'11", 185 lbs. Born, Moscow, Russia, October 7, 1995. San Jose's 1st pick, 27th overall, in 2014 NHL Draft.

2011-12	Chekhov Jr.	Russia-Jr.	50	13	9	22	8	....	....	....	....	....	....	....	....	....	9	2	1	3	0	....	....	....	....
2012-13	Sarnia Sting	OHL	68	30	38	68	12	....	....	....	....	....	....	....	....	....	4	0	1	1	0	....	....	....	....
	Sarnia Sting	OHL	68	30	38	68	12	....	....	....	....	....	....	....	....	....	4	0	1	1	0	....	....	....	....
2013-14	Sarnia Sting	OHL	67	38	56	94	21	....	....	....	....	....	....	....	....	....	....	....	....	....	....	....	....	....	....
2014-15	HIFK Helsinki	Finland	38	11	10	21	12	....	....	....	....	....	....	....	....	....	8	1	5	6	2	....	....	....	....
	Worcester Sharks	AHL	9	3	2	5	4	....	....	....	....	....	....	....	....	....	4	0	0	0	0	....	....	....	....
2015-16	**San Jose**	**NHL**	**9**	**1**	**1**	**2**	**0**	**0**	**0**	**0**	**7**	**14.3**	**1**	**0**	**0.0**	**11:11**	....	....	....	....	....	....	....	....	....
	San Jose	AHL	60	21	23	44	18	....	....	....	....	....	....	....	....	....	4	2	0	2	4	....	....	....	....
2016-17	**San Jose**	**NHL**	**2**	**0**	**0**	**0**	**0**	**0**	**0**	**0**	**4**	**0.0**	**–1**	**0**	**0.0**	**9:50**	....	....	....	....	....	....	....	....	....
	San Jose	AHL	46	15	26	41	16	....	....	....	....	....	....	....	....	....	....	....	....	....	....	....	....	....	....
	Vancouver	**NHL**	**12**	**3**	**0**	**3**	**0**	**0**	**0**	**1**	**10**	**30.0**	**1**	**0**	**0.0**	**11:38**	....	....	....	....	....	....	....	....	....
	Utica Comets	AHL	3	4	0	4	0	....	....	....	....	....	....	....	....	....	....	....	....	....	....	....	....	....	....
	NHL Totals		**23**	**4**	**1**	**5**	**0**	**0**	**0**	**1**	**21**	**19.0**		**0**	**0.0**	**11:18**	....	....	....	....	....	....	....	....	....

Traded to **Vancouver** by **San Jose** with San Jose's 4th round pick (later traded to Chicago – Chicago selected Tim Soderlund) in 2017 NHL Draft for Jannik Hansen, March 1, 2017.

GOLIGOSKI, Alex

(goh-lih-GAW-skee, AL-ehx) **ARI**

Defense. Shoots left. 5'11", 185 lbs. Born, Grand Rapids, MN, July 30, 1985. Pittsburgh's 3rd pick, 61st overall, in 2004 NHL Draft.

2002-03	Grand Rapids	High-MN	28	14	20	34	22	....	....	....	....	....	....	....	....	....	....	....	....	....	....	....	....	....	....
2003-04	Grand Rapids	High-MN	26	25	31	56	16	....	....	....	....	....	....	....	....	....	....	....	....	....	....	....	....	....	....
	Sioux Falls	USHL	10	0	2	2	6	....	....	....	....	....	....	....	....	....	....	....	....	....	....	....	....	....	....
2004-05	U. of Minnesota	WCHA	33	5	15	20	44	....	....	....	....	....	....	....	....	....	....	....	....	....	....	....	....	....	....
2005-06	U. of Minnesota	WCHA	41	11	28	39	63	....	....	....	....	....	....	....	....	....	....	....	....	....	....	....	....	....	....
2006-07	U. of Minnesota	WCHA	44	9	30	39	51	....	....	....	....	....	....	....	....	....	....	....	....	....	....	....	....	....	....
2007-08	**Pittsburgh**	**NHL**	**3**	**0**	**2**	**2**	**2**	**0**	**0**	**0**	**2**	**0.0**	**2**	**0**	**0.0**	**13:56**	....	....	....	....	....	....	....	....	....
	Wilkes-Barre	AHL	70	10	28	38	53	....	....	....	....	....	....	....	....	....	23	4	24	28	18	....	....	....	....
2008-09♦	**Pittsburgh**	**NHL**	**45**	**6**	**14**	**20**	**16**	**4**	**0**	**0**	**61**	**9.8**	**5**	**0**	**0.0**	**18:18**	**2**	**0**	**1**	**1**	**0**	**0**	**0**	**0**	**10:22**
	Wilkes-Barre	AHL	26	2	16	18	16	....	....	....	....	....	....	....	....	....	9	1	5	6	10	....	....	....	....
2009-10	**Pittsburgh**	**NHL**	**69**	**8**	**29**	**37**	**22**	**2**	**0**	**0**	**98**	**8.2**	**7**	**0**	**0.0**	**21:25**	**13**	**2**	**7**	**9**	**2**	**1**	**0**	**0**	**20:34**
2010-11	**Pittsburgh**	**NHL**	**60**	**9**	**22**	**31**	**28**	**4**	**0**	**4**	**101**	**8.9**	**20**	**0**	**0.0**	**20:46**	....	....	....	....	....	....	....	....	....
	Dallas	**NHL**	**23**	**5**	**10**	**15**	**12**	**3**	**0**	**0**	**61**	**8.2**	**0**	**0**	**0.0**	**26:04**	....	....	....	....	....	....	....	....	....
2011-12	**Dallas**	**NHL**	**71**	**9**	**21**	**30**	**16**	**2**	**0**	**1**	**140**	**6.4**	**0**	**0**	**0.0**	**22:46**	....	....	....	....	....	....	....	....	....
2012-13	**Dallas**	**NHL**	**47**	**3**	**24**	**27**	**18**	**0**	**0**	**0**	**80**	**3.8**	**4**	**0**	**0.0**	**22:23**	....	....	....	....	....	....	....	....	....
2013-14	**Dallas**	**NHL**	**81**	**6**	**36**	**42**	**28**	**3**	**0**	**0**	**141**	**4.3**	**9**	**1**	**0.0**	**24:19**	**6**	**1**	**3**	**4**	**8**	**0**	**0**	**0**	**28:30**
2014-15	**Dallas**	**NHL**	**81**	**4**	**32**	**36**	**24**	**0**	**0**	**0**	**122**	**3.3**	**0**	**0**	**0.0**	**23:49**	....	....	....	....	....	....	....	....	....
2015-16	**Dallas**	**NHL**	**82**	**5**	**32**	**37**	**34**	**1**	**0**	**1**	**127**	**3.9**	**21**	**0**	**0.0**	**23:50**	**13**	**4**	**3**	**7**	**6**	**0**	**0**	**1**	**23:14**
2016-17	**Arizona**	**NHL**	**82**	**6**	**30**	**36**	**28**	**1**	**1**	**0**	**112**	**5.4**	**–9**	**0**	**0.0**	**23:20**	....	....	....	....	....	....	....	....	....
	NHL Totals		**644**	**61**	**252**	**313**	**228**	**20**	**1**	**6**	**1045**	**5.8**		**1**	**0.0**	**22:42**	**34**	**7**	**14**	**21**	**16**	**1**	**0**	**1**	**22:24**

WCHA All-Rookie Team (2005) • WCHA Second All-Star Team (2006) • WCHA First All-Star Team (2007) • NCAA West First All-American Team (2007) • AHL All-Rookie Team (2008)
Traded to **Dallas** by **Pittsburgh** for James Neal and Matt Niskanen, February 21, 2011. Traded to **Arizona** by **Dallas** for Arizona's 5th round pick (Colton Point) in 2016 NHL Draft, June 16, 2016.

GOLOUBEF, Cody

(GOH-luh-behf, KOH-dee)

Defense. Shoots right. 6'1", 201 lbs. Born, Mississauga, ON, November 30, 1989. Columbus' 2nd pick, 37th overall, in 2008 NHL Draft.

2003-04	Tor. Marlboros	GTHL	89	10	27	37	44	....	....	....	....	....	....	....	....	....	....	....	....	....	....	....	....	....	....
2004-05	Tor. Marlboros	GTHL	69	14	47	61	56	....	....	....	....	....	....	....	....	....	....	....	....	....	....	....	....	....	....
2005-06	Milton Icehawks	ON-Jr.A	42	9	29	38	38	....	....	....	....	....	....	....	....	....	7	1	3	4	10	....	....	....	....
2006-07	Oakville Blades	ON-Jr.A	9	5	5	10	46	....	....	....	....	....	....	....	....	....	10	2	10	12	18	....	....	....	....
2007-08	U. of Wisconsin	WCHA	40	4	6	10	36	....	....	....	....	....	....	....	....	....	....	....	....	....	....	....	....	....	....
2008-09	U. of Wisconsin	WCHA	36	5	8	13	38	....	....	....	....	....	....	....	....	....	....	....	....	....	....	....	....	....	....
2009-10	U. of Wisconsin	WCHA	42	3	11	14	64	....	....	....	....	....	....	....	....	....	....	....	....	....	....	....	....	....	....
2010-11	Springfield	AHL	50	5	12	17	42	....	....	....	....	....	....	....	....	....	....	....	....	....	....	....	....	....	....
2011-12	**Columbus**	**NHL**	**1**	**0**	**0**	**0**	**0**	**0**	**0**	**0**	**0**	**0.0**	**1**	**0**	**0.0**	**6:00**	....	....	....	....	....	....	....	....	....
	Springfield	AHL	48	1	11	12	43	....	....	....	....	....	....	....	....	....	....	....	....	....	....	....	....	....	....
2012-13	Springfield	AHL	38	5	8	13	49	....	....	....	....	....	....	....	....	....	7	0	2	2	10	....	....	....	....
	Columbus	**NHL**	**11**	**1**	**0**	**1**	**0**	**0**	**0**	**1**	**14**	**7.1**	**–3**	**0**	**0.0**	**14:49**	....	....	....	....	....	....	....	....	....
2013-14	**Columbus**	**NHL**	**5**	**0**	**0**	**0**	**2**	**0**	**0**	**0**	**4**	**0.0**	**0**	**0**	**0.0**	**9:49**	....	....	....	....	....	....	....	....	....
	Springfield	AHL	62	7	21	28	98	....	....	....	....	....	....	....	....	....	5	0	0	0	6	....	....	....	....
2014-15	**Columbus**	**NHL**	**36**	**0**	**9**	**9**	**19**	**0**	**0**	**0**	**23**	**0.0**	**12**	**0**	**0.0**	**15:34**	....	....	....	....	....	....	....	....	....
	Springfield	AHL	3	0	0	0	0	....	....	....	....	....	....	....	....	....	....	....	....	....	....	....	....	....	....
2015-16	**Columbus**	**NHL**	**43**	**1**	**7**	**8**	**20**	**0**	**0**	**0**	**40**	**2.5**	**–3**	**0**	**0.0**	**15:08**	....	....	....	....	....	....	....	....	....
2016-17	Cleveland	AHL	16	2	5	7	22	....	....	....	....	....	....	....	....	....	....	....	....	....	....	....	....	....	....
	Colorado	**NHL**	**33**	**0**	**5**	**5**	**25**	**0**	**0**	**0**	**35**	**0.0**	**–11**	**0**	**0.0**	**16:59**	....	....	....	....	....	....	....	....	....
	San Antonio	AHL	2	0	1	1	2	....	....	....	....	....	....	....	....	....	....	....	....	....	....	....	....	....	....
	NHL Totals		**129**	**2**	**21**	**23**	**66**	**0**	**0**	**1**	**116**	**1.7**		**0**	**0.0**	**15:25**	....	....	....	....	....	....	....	....	....

• Missed majority of 2006-07 due to various injuries. • Missed majority of 2014-15 due to knee injury vs. Carolina, November 4, 2014 and as a healthy reserve. Traded to **Colorado** by **Columbus** for Ryan Stanton, November 28, 2016.

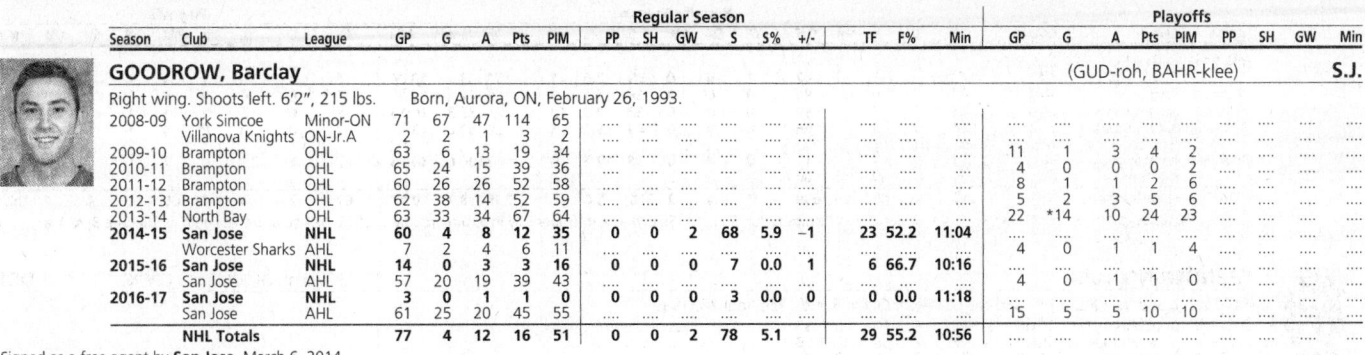

			Regular Season														Playoffs								
Season	Club	League	GP	G	A	Pts	PIM	PP	SH	GW	S	S%	+/-	TF	F%	Min	GP	G	A	Pts	PIM	PP	SH	GW	Min

GOODROW, Barclay

(GUD-roh, BAHR-klee) **S.J.**

Right wing. Shoots left. 6'2", 215 lbs. Born, Aurora, ON, February 26, 1993.

Season	Club	League	GP	G	A	Pts	PIM	PP	SH	GW	S	S%	+/-	TF	F%	Min	GP	G	A	Pts	PIM	PP	SH	GW	Min
2008-09	York Simcoe	Minor-ON	71	67	47	114	65	....	....	....	....	....	....	....	....	....	....	....	....	....	....	....	....	....	....
	Villanova Knights	ON-Jr.A	2	2	1	3	2	....	....	....	....	....	....	....	....	....	....	....	....	....	....	....	....	....	....
2009-10	Brampton	OHL	63	6	13	19	34	....	....	....	....	....	....	....	....	....	11	1	3	4	2	....	....	....	....
2010-11	Brampton	OHL	65	24	15	39	36	....	....	....	....	....	....	....	....	....	4	0	0	0	2	....	....	....	....
2011-12	Brampton	OHL	60	26	26	52	58	....	....	....	....	....	....	....	....	....	8	1	1	2	6	....	....	....	....
2012-13	Brampton	OHL	62	38	14	52	59	....	....	....	....	....	....	....	....	....	5	2	3	5	6	....	....	....	....
2013-14	North Bay	OHL	63	33	34	67	64	....	....	....	....	....	....	....	....	....	22	*14	10	24	23	....	....	....	....
2014-15	San Jose	NHL	60	4	8	12	35	0	0	2	68	5.9	–1	23	52.2	11:04	....	....	....	....	....	....	....	....	....
	Worcester Sharks	AHL	7	2	4	6	11	....	....	....	....	....	....	....	....	....	4	0	1	1	4	....	....	....	....
2015-16	San Jose	NHL	14	0	3	3	16	0	0	0	7	0.0	1	6	66.7	10:16	....	....	....	....	....	....	....	....	....
	San Jose	AHL	57	20	19	39	43	....	....	....	....	....	....	....	....	....	4	0	1	1	0	....	....	....	....
2016-17	San Jose	NHL	3	0	1	1	0	0	0	0	3	0.0	0	0	0.0	11:18	....	....	....	....	....	....	....	....	....
	San Jose	AHL	61	25	20	45	55	....	....	....	....	....	....	....	....	....	15	5	5	10	10	....	....	....	....
	NHL Totals		**77**	**4**	**12**	**16**	**51**	**0**	**0**	**2**	**78**	**5.1**		**29**	**55.2**	**10:56**	....	....	....	....	....	....	....	....	....

Signed as a free agent by **San Jose**, March 6, 2014.

GORDON, Boyd

(GOHR-duhn, BOID)

Center. Shoots right. 6', 200 lbs. Born, Unity, SK, October 19, 1983. Washington's 3rd pick, 17th overall, in 2002 NHL Draft.

Season	Club	League	GP	G	A	Pts	PIM	PP	SH	GW	S	S%	+/-	TF	F%	Min	GP	G	A	Pts	PIM	PP	SH	GW	Min
1998-99	Regina Rangers	SMBHL	60	70	102	172	53	....	....	....	....	....	....	....	....	....	....	....	....	....	....	....	....	....	....
99-2000	Red Deer Rebels	WHL	66	10	26	36	24	....	....	....	....	....	....	....	....	....	4	0	1	1	16	....	....	....	....
2000-01	Red Deer Rebels	WHL	72	12	27	39	39	....	....	....	....	....	....	....	....	....	22	3	6	9	2	....	....	....	....
2001-02	Red Deer Rebels	WHL	66	22	29	51	19	....	....	....	....	....	....	....	....	....	23	10	12	22	8	....	....	....	....
2002-03	Red Deer Rebels	WHL	56	33	48	81	28	....	....	....	....	....	....	....	....	....	23	8	12	20	14	....	....	....	....
2003-04	Washington	NHL	41	1	5	6	8	0	0	0	42	2.4	–9	328	43.0	13:11	....	....	....	....	....	....	....	....	....
	Portland Pirates	AHL	43	5	17	22	16	....	....	....	....	....	....	....	....	....	7	2	1	3	0	....	....	....	....
2004-05	Portland Pirates	AHL	80	17	22	39	35	....	....	....	....	....	....	....	....	....	....	....	....	....	....	....	....	....	....
2005-06	Washington	NHL	25	0	1	1	4	0	0	0	12	0.0	–4	216	46.3	11:40	....	....	....	....	....	....	....	....	....
	Hershey Bears	AHL	58	16	22	38	23	....	....	....	....	....	....	....	....	....	21	3	5	8	10	....	....	....	....
2006-07	Washington	NHL	71	7	22	29	14	0	2	0	104	6.7	10	1214	52.1	15:53	....	....	....	....	....	....	....	....	....
2007-08	Washington	NHL	67	7	9	16	12	0	1	0	100	7.0	5	904	55.8	15:44	7	0	0	0	0	0	0	0	13:23
2008-09	Washington	NHL	63	5	9	14	16	0	1	2	69	7.2	–4	667	56.1	13:28	14	0	3	3	4	0	0	0	11:17
2009-10	Washington	NHL	36	4	6	10	12	0	0	0	40	10.0	4	205	61.0	10:17	6	1	1	2	0	0	1	0	11:02
	Hershey Bears	AHL	2	0	2	2	0	....	....	....	....	....	....	....	....	....	....	....	....	....	....	....	....	....	....
2010-11	Washington	NHL	60	3	6	9	16	0	1	1	77	3.9	–5	719	58.0	13:03	9	0	0	0	6	0	0	0	12:54
2011-12	Phoenix	NHL	75	8	15	23	10	0	1	2	114	7.0	9	1177	56.8	15:56	16	0	2	2	6	0	0	0	17:49
2012-13	Phoenix	NHL	48	4	10	14	8	0	0	0	59	6.8	0	789	57.3	15:01	....	....	....	....	....	....	....	....	....
2013-14	Edmonton	NHL	74	8	13	21	20	1	1	1	80	10.0	–15	1492	56.5	14:45	....	....	....	....	....	....	....	....	....
2014-15	Edmonton	NHL	68	6	7	13	17	1	1	1	65	9.2	–5	1218	55.9	13:20	....	....	....	....	....	....	....	....	....
2015-16	Arizona	NHL	65	2	2	4	10	0	1	0	53	3.8	–7	909	57.9	12:12	....	....	....	....	....	....	....	....	....
2016-17	Philadelphia	NHL	13	1	0	1	2	0	0	0	8	12.5	–5	86	55.8	8:11	....	....	....	....	....	....	....	....	....
	Lehigh Valley	AHL	6	0	0	0	21	....	....	....	....	....	....	....	....	....	....	....	....	....	....	....	....	....	....
	NHL Totals		**706**	**56**	**105**	**161**	**149**	**2**	**9**	**7**	**823**	**6.8**		**9924**	**55.5**	**13:55**	**52**	**1**	**6**	**7**	**16**	**0**	**1**	**0**	**13:50**

WHL East First All-Star Team (2003)

• Missed majority of 2009-10 due to recurring back injury. Signed as a free agent by **Phoeniix**, July 1, 2011. Signed as a free agent by **Edmonton**, July 5, 2013. Traded to **Arizona** by **Edmonton** for Lauri Korpikoski, June 30, 2015. Signed as a free agent by **Philadelphia**, July 1, 2016. • Missed majority of 2016-17 due to recurring upper-body injury and as a healthy reserve.

GORGES, Josh

(JOHR-juhz, JAWSH) **BUF**

Defense. Shoots left. 6'1", 203 lbs. Born, Kelowna, BC, August 14, 1984.

Season	Club	League	GP	G	A	Pts	PIM	PP	SH	GW	S	S%	+/-	TF	F%	Min	GP	G	A	Pts	PIM	PP	SH	GW	Min
2000-01	Kelowna Rockets	WHL	57	4	6	10	24	....	....	....	....	....	....	....	....	....	6	1	1	2	4	....	....	....	....
2001-02	Kelowna Rockets	WHL	72	7	34	41	74	....	....	....	....	....	....	....	....	....	15	1	7	8	8	....	....	....	....
2002-03	Kelowna Rockets	WHL	54	11	48	59	76	....	....	....	....	....	....	....	....	....	19	3	17	20	16	....	....	....	....
2003-04	Kelowna Rockets	WHL	62	11	31	42	38	....	....	....	....	....	....	....	....	....	17	2	13	15	6	....	....	....	....
2004-05	Cleveland Barons	AHL	74	4	8	12	37	....	....	....	....	....	....	....	....	....	....	....	....	....	....	....	....	....	....
2005-06	San Jose	NHL	49	0	6	6	31	0	0	0	25	0.0	5	0	0.0	17:38	11	0	1	1	4	0	0	0	18:56
	Cleveland Barons	AHL	18	2	3	5	12	....	....	....	....	....	....	....	....	....	....	....	....	....	....	....	....	....	....
2006-07	San Jose	NHL	47	1	3	4	26	0	0	0	37	2.7	–3	0	0.0	17:48	....	....	....	....	....	....	....	....	....
	Worcester Sharks	AHL	7	0	1	1	2	....	....	....	....	....	....	....	....	....	....	....	....	....	....	....	....	....	....
	Montreal	NHL	7	0	0	0	0	0	0	0	3	0.0	–1	0	0.0	12:28	....	....	....	....	....	....	....	....	....
2007-08	Montreal	NHL	62	0	9	9	32	0	0	0	41	0.0	0	0	0.0	16:20	12	0	3	3	0	0	0	0	18:20
2008-09	Montreal	NHL	81	4	19	23	37	2	0	0	63	6.3	12	1	0.0	20:08	4	0	1	1	7	0	0	0	23:46
2009-10	Montreal	NHL	82	3	7	10	39	0	0	1	52	5.8	2	0	0.0	21:01	19	0	2	2	14	0	0	0	22:42
2010-11	Montreal	NHL	36	1	6	7	18	1	0	1	20	5.0	–3	0	0.0	21:10	....	....	....	....	....	....	....	....	....
2011-12	Montreal	NHL	82	2	14	16	39	0	0	1	59	3.4	14	0	0.0	22:38	....	....	....	....	....	....	....	....	....
2012-13	Montreal	NHL	48	2	7	9	15	0	0	0	40	5.0	4	0	0.0	21:23	5	0	0	0	4	0	0	0	21:18
2013-14	Montreal	NHL	66	1	13	14	12	0	0	0	35	2.9	6	1	0.0	21:15	17	0	2	2	6	0	0	0	23:27
2014-15	Buffalo	NHL	46	0	6	6	16	0	0	0	28	0.0	–28	0	0.0	22:22	....	....	....	....	....	....	....	....	....
2015-16	Buffalo	NHL	77	2	10	12	72	0	0	0	57	3.5	–7	0	0.0	20:28	....	....	....	....	....	....	....	....	....
2016-17	Buffalo	NHL	66	1	5	6	50	0	0	0	40	2.5	–3	1	0.0	18:27	....	....	....	....	....	....	....	....	....
	NHL Totals		**749**	**17**	**105**	**122**	**387**	**3**	**0**	**3**	**500**	**3.4**		**3**	**0.0**	**20:03**	**68**	**0**	**9**	**9**	**35**	**0**	**0**	**0**	**21:28**

WHL West Second All-Star Team (2003) • WHL West First All-Star Team (2004)

Signed as a free agent by **San Jose**, September 20, 2002. Traded to **Montreal** by **San Jose** with San Jose's 1st round pick (Max Pacioretty) in 2007 NHL Draft for Craig Rivet and Montreal's 5th round pick (Julien Demers) in 2008 NHL Draft, February 25, 2007. • Missed majority of 2010-11 due to knee injury at NY Islanders, December 26, 2010. Traded to **Buffalo** by **Montreal** for Minnesota' 2nd round pick (previously acquired, later traded to Chicago – Chicago selected Chad Krys) in 2016 NHL Draft, July 1, 2014.

GORMLEY, Brandon

(GOHRM-lee, BRAN-duhn)

Defense. Shoots left. 6'2", 195 lbs. Born, Murray River, PE, February 18, 1992. Phoenix's 1st pick, 13th overall, in 2010 NHL Draft.

Season	Club	League	GP	G	A	Pts	PIM	PP	SH	GW	S	S%	+/-	TF	F%	Min	GP	G	A	Pts	PIM	PP	SH	GW	Min
2007-08	Notre Dame	SMHL	42	23	33	56	63	....	....	....	....	....	....	....	....	....	9	1	6	7	18	....	....	....	....
2008-09	Moncton Wildcats	QMJHL	62	7	20	27	34	....	....	....	....	....	....	....	....	....	10	1	3	4	6	....	....	....	....
2009-10	Moncton Wildcats	QMJHL	58	9	34	43	54	....	....	....	....	....	....	....	....	....	21	2	15	17	10	....	....	....	....
2010-11	Moncton Wildcats	QMJHL	47	13	35	48	42	....	....	....	....	....	....	....	....	....	5	0	1	1	6	....	....	....	....
	San Antonio	AHL	4	1	0	1	0	....	....	....	....	....	....	....	....	....	....	....	....	....	....	....	....	....	....
2011-12	Moncton Wildcats	QMJHL	26	10	17	27	18	....	....	....	....	....	....	....	....	....	....	....	....	....	....	....	....	....	....
	Shawinigan	QMJHL	9	0	5	5	4	....	....	....	....	....	....	....	....	....	7	5	2	7	8	....	....	....	....
2012-13	Portland Pirates	AHL	68	5	24	29	44	....	....	....	....	....	....	....	....	....	3	1	2	3	0	....	....	....	....
2013-14	Phoenix	NHL	5	0	0	0	2	0	0	0	4	0.0	4	0	0.0	14:33	....	....	....	....	....	....	....	....	....
	Portland Pirates	AHL	54	7	29	36	34	....	....	....	....	....	....	....	....	....	....	....	....	....	....	....	....	....	....
2014-15	Arizona	NHL	27	2	2	4	10	1	0	0	39	5.1	–7	0	0.0	15:19	....	....	....	....	....	....	....	....	....
	Portland Pirates	AHL	23	3	7	10	18	....	....	....	....	....	....	....	....	....	5	1	4	5	2	....	....	....	....
2015-16	Colorado	NHL	26	0	1	1	8	0	0	0	11	0.0	–3	0	0.0	12:11	....	....	....	....	....	....	....	....	....
	San Antonio	AHL	39	4	2	6	26	....	....	....	....	....	....	....	....	....	....	....	....	....	....	....	....	....	....
2016-17	Albany Devils	AHL	35	2	8	10	30	....	....	....	....	....	....	....	....	....	....	....	....	....	....	....	....	....	....
	Binghamton	AHL	17	2	3	5	12	....	....	....	....	....	....	....	....	....	....	....	....	....	....	....	....	....	....
	NHL Totals		**58**	**2**	**3**	**5**	**20**	**1**	**0**	**0**	**54**	**3.7**		**0**	**0.0**	**13:51**	....	....	....	....	....	....	....	....	....

QMJHL All-Rookie Team (2009) • QMJHL Second All-Star Team (2010, 2011

Traded to **Colorado** by **Arizona** for Stefan Elliott, September 9, 2015. Signed as a free agent by **New Jersey**, July 28, 2016. Traded to **Ottawa** by **New Jersey** for future considerations, March 6, 2017.

GOSTISBEHERE, Shayne
(gaws-TIHS-bair, SHAYN) **PHI**

Defense. Shoots left. 5'11", 180 lbs. Born, Pembroke Pines, FL, April 20, 1993. Philadelphia's 3rd pick, 78th overall, in 2012 NHL Draft.

			Regular Season															Playoffs							
Season	Club	League	GP	G	A	Pts	PIM	PP	SH	GW	S	S%	+/-	TF	F%	Min	GP	G	A	Pts	PIM	PP	SH	GW	Min
2010-11	South Kent	High-CT	24	7	29	36	32	....	....	....	....	....	....	....	....	....	....	....	....	....	....	....	....	....	....
2011-12	Union College	ECAC	41	5	17	22	20	....	....	....	....	....	....	....	....	....	....	....	....	....	....	....	....	....	....
2012-13	Union College	ECAC	36	8	18	26	39	....	....	....	....	....	....	....	....	....	....	....	....	....	....	....	....	....	....
2013-14	Union College	ECAC	42	9	25	34	26	....	....	....	....	....	....	....	....	....	....	....	....	....	....	....	....	....	....
	Adirondack	AHL	2	0	0	0	0	....	....	....	....	....	....	....	....	....	....	....	....	....	....	....	....	....	....
2014-15	**Philadelphia**	**NHL**	**2**	**0**	**0**	**0**	**0**	**0**	**0**	**0**	**2**	**0.0**	**–2**	**0**	**0.0**	**12:34**	....	....	....	....	....	....	....	....	....
	Lehigh Valley	AHL	5	0	5	5	0	....	....	....	....	....	....	....	....	....	....	....	....	....	....	....	....	....	....
2015-16	**Philadelphia**	**NHL**	**64**	**17**	**29**	**46**	**24**	**8**	**0**	**5**	**152**	**11.2**	**8**	**1**	**100.0**	**20:05**	**6**	**1**	**1**	**2**	**4**	**1**	**0**	**0**	**20:33**
	Lehigh Valley	AHL	14	2	8	10	6	....	....	....	....	....	....	....	....	....	....	....	....	....	....	....	....	....	....
2016-17	**Philadelphia**	**NHL**	**76**	**7**	**32**	**39**	**32**	**2**	**0**	**1**	**198**	**3.5**	**–21**	**0**	**0.0**	**19:36**	....	....	....	....	....	....	....	....	....
	NHL Totals		**142**	**24**	**61**	**85**	**56**	**10**	**0**	**6**	**352**	**6.8**		**1**	**100.0**	**19:43**	**6**	**1**	**1**	**2**	**4**	**1**	**0**	**0**	**20:33**

ECAC All-Rookie Team (2012) • ECAC Second All-Star Team (2013) • NCAA East Second All-American Team (2013) • ECAC First All-Star Team (2014) • NCAA East First All-American Team (2014) • NCAA Championship All-Tournament Team (2014) • NCAA Championship Tournament MVP (2014) • NHL All-Rookie Team (2016)

• Missed majority of 2014-15 due to knee injury at Manchester (AHL), November 7, 2014.

GOURDE, Yanni
(GOHRD, YAH-nee) **T.B.**

Left wing. Shoots left. 5'9", 167 lbs. Born, St-Narcisse, QC, December 15, 1991.

			Regular Season															Playoffs							
Season	Club	League	GP	G	A	Pts	PIM	PP	SH	GW	S	S%	+/-	TF	F%	Min	GP	G	A	Pts	PIM	PP	SH	GW	Min
2007-08	Rive-Sud Express	Minor-QC	STATISTICS NOT AVAILABLE																						
	Levis	QAAA	2	0	0	0	0	....	....	....	....	....	....	....	....	....	....	....	....	....	....	....	....	....	....
2008-09	Jonquiere Elites	QAAA	41	23	30	53	50	....	....	....	....	....	....	....	....	....	4	1	5	6	6	....	....	....	....
	Victoriaville Tigres	QMJHL	4	0	1	1	0	....	....	....	....	....	....	....	....	....	....	....	....	....	....	....	....	....	....
2009-10	Victoriaville Tigres	QMJHL	59	11	17	28	36	....	....	....	....	....	....	....	....	....	16	2	3	5	20	....	....	....	....
2010-11	Victoriaville Tigres	QMJHL	68	26	42	68	48	....	....	....	....	....	....	....	....	....	9	4	6	10	12	....	....	....	....
2011-12	Victoriaville Tigres	QMJHL	68	37	87	124	70	....	....	....	....	....	....	....	....	....	4	1	2	3	6	....	....	....	....
	Worcester Sharks	AHL	4	1	2	3	0	....	....	....	....	....	....	....	....	....	....	....	....	....	....	....	....	....	....
2012-13	Worcester Sharks	AHL	54	8	6	14	41	....	....	....	....	....	....	....	....	....	....	....	....	....	....	....	....	....	....
	San Francisco	ECHL	8	4	6	10	9	....	....	....	....	....	....	....	....	....	....	....	....	....	....	....	....	....	....
2013-14	Worcester Sharks	AHL	25	4	20	24	26	....	....	....	....	....	....	....	....	....	....	....	....	....	....	....	....	....	....
	Kalamazoo Wings	ECHL	30	15	19	34	19	....	....	....	....	....	....	....	....	....	....	....	....	....	....	....	....	....	....
	Syracuse Crunch	AHL	18	2	6	8	16	....	....	....	....	....	....	....	....	....	....	....	....	....	....	....	....	....	....
2014-15	Syracuse Crunch	AHL	76	29	28	57	61	....	....	....	....	....	....	....	....	....	3	1	1	2	10	....	....	....	....
2015-16	**Tampa Bay**	**NHL**	**2**	**0**	**1**	**1**	**2**	**0**	**0**	**0**	**0**	**0.0**	**1**	**0**	**0.0**	**7:19**	....	....	....	....	....	....	....	....	....
	Syracuse Crunch	AHL	65	14	30	44	42	....	....	....	....	....	....	....	....	....	....	....	....	....	....	....	....	....	....
2016-17	**Tampa Bay**	**NHL**	**20**	**6**	**2**	**8**	**8**	**0**	**1**	**1**	**30**	**20.0**	**–1**	**163**	**36.8**	**15:22**	....	....	....	....	....	....	....	....	....
	Syracuse Crunch	AHL	56	22	26	48	54	....	....	....	....	....	....	....	....	....	22	9	*18	27	29	....	....	....	....
	NHL Totals		**22**	**6**	**3**	**9**	**10**	**0**	**1**	**1**	**30**	**20.0**		**163**	**36.8**	**14:38**	....	....	....	....	....	....	....	....	....

Signed as a free agent by **Tampa Bay**, March 10, 2014.

GRABNER, Michael
(GRAB-nuhr, MIGH-kuhl) **NYR**

Right wing. Shoots left. 6'1", 185 lbs. Born, Villach, Austria, October 5, 1987. Vancouver's 1st pick, 14th overall, in 2006 NHL Draft.

			Regular Season															Playoffs							
Season	Club	League	GP	G	A	Pts	PIM	PP	SH	GW	S	S%	+/-	TF	F%	Min	GP	G	A	Pts	PIM	PP	SH	GW	Min
2002-03	EC VSV Villach Jr.	Austria-Jr.	13	6	4	10	4	....	....	....	....	....	....	....	....	....	....	....	....	....	....	....	....	....	....
2003-04	EC VSV Villach Jr.	Austria-Jr.	23	32	5	37	58	....	....	....	....	....	....	....	....	....	....	....	....	....	....	....	....	....	....
	EC VSV Villach	Austria	18	2	1	3	0	....	....	....	....	....	....	....	....	....	....	....	....	....	....	....	....	....	....
	Austria	WJ18-B	5	3	1	4	4	....	....	....	....	....	....	....	....	....	....	....	....	....	....	....	....	....	....
2004-05	Spokane Chiefs	WHL	58	13	11	24	18	....	....	....	....	....	....	....	....	....	....	....	....	....	....	....	....	....	....
2005-06	Spokane Chiefs	WHL	67	36	14	50	28	....	....	....	....	....	....	....	....	....	....	....	....	....	....	....	....	....	....
2006-07	Spokane Chiefs	WHL	55	39	16	55	34	....	....	....	....	....	....	....	....	....	6	0	1	1	2	....	....	....	....
	Manitoba Moose	AHL	2	1	1	2	0	....	....	....	....	....	....	....	....	....	6	0	0	0	0	....	....	....	....
2007-08	Manitoba Moose	AHL	74	22	22	44	8	....	....	....	....	....	....	....	....	....	6	3	0	3	2	....	....	....	....
2008-09	Manitoba Moose	AHL	66	30	18	48	20	....	....	....	....	....	....	....	....	....	20	10	7	17	2	....	....	....	....
	Austria	Oly-Q	3	5	0	5	0	....	....	....	....	....	....	....	....	....	....	....	....	....	....	....	....	....	....
2009-10	**Vancouver**	**NHL**	**20**	**5**	**6**	**11**	**8**	**2**	**0**	**1**	**63**	**7.9**	**2**	**2**	**50.0**	**13:54**	**9**	**1**	**0**	**1**	**0**	**0**	**0**	**0**	**9:06**
	Manitoba Moose	AHL	38	15	11	26	6	....	....	....	....	....	....	....	....	....	....	....	....	....	....	....	....	....	....
2010-11	**NY Islanders**	**NHL**	**76**	**34**	**18**	**52**	**10**	**2**	**6**	**3**	**228**	**14.9**	**13**	**6**	**33.3**	**15:05**	....	....	....	....	....	....	....	....	....
2011-12	**NY Islanders**	**NHL**	**78**	**20**	**12**	**32**	**12**	**1**	**1**	**3**	**174**	**11.5**	**–18**	**5**	**60.0**	**15:33**	....	....	....	....	....	....	....	....	....
2012-13	EC VSV Villach	Austria	17	10	9	19	2	....	....	....	....	....	....	....	....	....	....	....	....	....	....	....	....	....	....
	NY Islanders	**NHL**	**45**	**16**	**5**	**21**	**12**	**2**	**1**	**3**	**108**	**14.8**	**4**	**22**	**45.5**	**14:48**	**6**	**1**	**3**	**4**	**0**	**0**	**0**	**0**	**12:30**
2013-14	**NY Islanders**	**NHL**	**64**	**12**	**14**	**26**	**12**	**0**	**3**	**2**	**137**	**8.8**	**–10**	**15**	**46.7**	**14:12**	....	....	....	....	....	....	....	....	....
	Austria	Olympics	4	5	1	6	0	....	....	....	....	....	....	....	....	....	....	....	....	....	....	....	....	....	....
2014-15	**NY Islanders**	**NHL**	**34**	**8**	**5**	**13**	**4**	**0**	**0**	**0**	**63**	**12.7**	**4**	**2**	**0.0**	**12:56**	**2**	**0**	**1**	**1**	**2**	**0**	**0**	**0**	**11:45**
2015-16	**Toronto**	**NHL**	**80**	**9**	**9**	**18**	**12**	**0**	**1**	**2**	**116**	**7.8**	**–4**	**13**	**23.1**	**14:28**	....	....	....	....	....	....	....	....	....
2016-17	**NY Rangers**	**NHL**	**76**	**27**	**13**	**40**	**10**	**0**	**1**	**3**	**162**	**16.7**	**22**	**13**	**53.9**	**14:06**	**12**	**4**	**2**	**6**	**0**	**0**	**1**	**1**	**14:02**
	NHL Totals		**473**	**131**	**82**	**213**	**80**	**7**	**13**	**17**	**1051**	**12.5**		**78**	**42.3**	**14:33**	**29**	**6**	**6**	**12**	**2**	**0**	**1**	**1**	**12:01**

NHL All-Rookie Team (2011)

Traded to **Florida** by **Vancouver** with Steve Bernier and Vancouver's 1st round pick (Quinton Howden) in 2010 NHL Draft for Keith Ballard and Victor Oreskovich, June 25, 2010. Claimed on waivers by **NY Islanders** from **Florida**, October 5, 2010. Signed as a free agent by **Villach** (Austria), October 4, 2012. • Missed majority of 2014-15 due to sports hernia surgery, October 9, 2014 and as a healthy reserve. Traded to **Toronto** by **NY Islanders** for Carter Verhaeghe, Christopher Gibson, Tom Nilsson, Taylor Beck and Matt Finn, September 17, 2015. Signed as a free agent by **NY Rangers**, July 1, 2016.

GRABOVSKI, Mikhail
(gra-BAWV-skee, mih-kigh-EHL) **VGK**

Center. Shoots left. 5'11", 186 lbs. Born, Potsdam, East Germany, January 31, 1984. Montreal's 4th pick, 150th overall, in 2004 NHL Draft.

			Regular Season															Playoffs							
Season	Club	League	GP	G	A	Pts	PIM	PP	SH	GW	S	S%	+/-	TF	F%	Min	GP	G	A	Pts	PIM	PP	SH	GW	Min
2001-02	HC Minsk	Belarus	26	10	7	17	16	....	....	....	....	....	....	....	....	....	....	....	....	....	....	....	....	....	....
	Belarus	WJC-A	6	0	1	1	2	....	....	....	....	....	....	....	....	....	....	....	....	....	....	....	....	....	....
2002-03	HC Minsk	Belarus	STATISTICS NOT AVAILABLE																						
2003-04	Nizhnekamsk	Russia	45	6	11	17	26	....	....	....	....	....	....	....	....	....	5	0	0	0	4	....	....	....	....
2004-05	Nizhnekamsk	Russia	60	16	20	36	32	....	....	....	....	....	....	....	....	....	3	2	0	2	2	....	....	....	....
	Belarus	Oly-Q	3	4	3	7	10	....	....	....	....	....	....	....	....	....	....	....	....	....	....	....	....	....	....
	Yunost-Minsk	BelOpen	....	....	....	....	....	....	....	....	....	....	....	....	....	....	5	2	4	6	6	....	....	....	....
2005-06	Dynamo Moscow	Russia	48	10	17	27	28	....	....	....	....	....	....	....	....	....	4	0	0	0	4	....	....	....	....
	Yunost-Minsk	BelOpen	8	6	8	14	10	....	....	....	....	....	....	....	....	....	....	....	....	....	....	....	....	....	....
2006-07	**Montreal**	**NHL**	**3**	**0**	**0**	**0**	**0**	**0**	**0**	**0**	**5**	**0.0**	**–2**	**31**	**41.9**	**13:18**	....	....	....	....	....	....	....	....	....
	Hamilton	AHL	66	17	37	54	34	....	....	....	....	....	....	....	....	....	20	4	7	11	21	....	....	....	....
2007-08	**Montreal**	**NHL**	**24**	**3**	**6**	**9**	**8**	**0**	**0**	**1**	**23**	**13.0**	**–4**	**154**	**33.1**	**11:14**	....	....	....	....	....	....	....	....	....
	Hamilton	AHL	12	8	12	20	6	....	....	....	....	....	....	....	....	....	....	....	....	....	....	....	....	....	....
2008-09	**Toronto**	**NHL**	**78**	**20**	**28**	**48**	**92**	**6**	**0**	**2**	**120**	**16.7**	**–8**	**957**	**44.5**	**16:13**	....	....	....	....	....	....	....	....	....
2009-10	**Toronto**	**NHL**	**59**	**10**	**25**	**35**	**10**	**2**	**1**	**3**	**126**	**7.9**	**3**	**735**	**49.8**	**16:48**	....	....	....	....	....	....	....	....	....
2010-11	**Toronto**	**NHL**	**81**	**29**	**29**	**58**	**60**	**10**	**0**	**4**	**239**	**12.1**	**14**	**1326**	**48.4**	**19:22**	....	....	....	....	....	....	....	....	....
2011-12	**Toronto**	**NHL**	**74**	**23**	**28**	**51**	**51**	**5**	**0**	**2**	**163**	**14.1**	**0**	**905**	**51.5**	**17:36**	....	....	....	....	....	....	....	....	....
2012-13	CSKA Moscow	KHL	29	12	12	24	10	....	....	....	....	....	....	....	....	....	....	....	....	....	....	....	....	....	....
	Toronto	**NHL**	**48**	**9**	**7**	**16**	**24**	**0**	**0**	**1**	**80**	**11.3**	**–10**	**638**	**50.6**	**15:34**	**7**	**0**	**2**	**2**	**2**	**0**	**0**	**0**	**19:06**
2013-14	**Washington**	**NHL**	**58**	**13**	**22**	**35**	**26**	**3**	**0**	**1**	**81**	**16.0**	**6**	**641**	**54.0**	**15:45**	....	....	....	....	....	....	....	....	....
2014-15	**NY Islanders**	**NHL**	**51**	**9**	**10**	**19**	**8**	**0**	**0**	**2**	**81**	**11.1**	**3**	**83**	**45.8**	**14:16**	**3**	**0**	**0**	**0**	**0**	**0**	**0**	**0**	**14:27**
2015-16	**NY Islanders**	**NHL**	**58**	**9**	**16**	**25**	**33**	**1**	**0**	**2**	**83**	**10.8**	**3**	**463**	**47.7**	**14:06**	....	....	....	....	....	....	....	....	....
2016-17			DID NOT PLAY – INJURED																						
	NHL Totals		**534**	**125**	**171**	**296**	**312**	**27**	**1**	**18**	**1001**	**12.5**		**5933**	**48.7**	**16:11**	**10**	**0**	**2**	**2**	**2**	**0**	**0**	**0**	**17:42**

Traded to **Toronto** by **Montreal** for Greg Pateryn and Toronto's 2nd round pick (later traded to Chicago, later traded back to Toronto, later traded to Boston - Boston selected Jared Knight) in 2010 NHL Draft, July 3, 2008. Signed as a free agent by **CSKA Moscow** (KHL), September 25, 2012. Signed as a free agent by **Washington**, August 22, 2013. Signed as a free agent by **NY Islanders**, July 2, 2014. • Missed remainder of 2015-1'6 and all of 2016-17 due to upper-body injury vs. Arizona, November 16, 2016. Traded to **Vegas** by **NY Islanders** with Jake Bischoff, NY Islanders' 1st round pick (Erik Brannstrom) in 2017 NHL Draft and NY Islanders' 2nd round pick in 2019 NHL Draft for Expansion Draft considerations, June 21, 2017.

			Regular Season														Playoffs								
Season	Club	League	GP	G	A	Pts	PIM	PP	SH	GW	S	S%	+/-	TF	F%	Min	GP	G	A	Pts	PIM	PP	SH	GW	Min

GRAGNANI, Marc-Andre

(GRUH-na-nee, MAHRK-AWN-dray)

Defense. Shoots left. 6'2", 200 lbs. Born, Montreal, QC, March 11, 1987. Buffalo's 3rd pick, 87th overall, in 2005 NHL Draft.

Season	Club	League	GP	G	A	Pts	PIM	PP	SH	GW	S	S%	+/-	TF	F%	Min	GP	G	A	Pts	PIM	PP	SH	GW	Min
2002-03	West Island Lions	QAAA	34	3	15	18	22	....	....	....	....	....	....	....	....	....	....	....	....	....	....	....	....	....	....
2003-04	P.E.I. Rocket	QMJHL	61	2	13	15	42	....	....	....	....	....	....	....	....	....	11	0	0	0	4	....	....	....	....
2004-05	P.E.I. Rocket	QMJHL	68	10	29	39	48	....	....	....	....	....	....	....	....	....	....	....	....	....	....	....	....	....	....
2005-06	P.E.I. Rocket	QMJHL	62	16	55	71	75	....	....	....	....	....	....	....	....	....	6	1	4	5	14	....	....	....	....
2006-07	P.E.I. Rocket	QMJHL	65	22	46	68	58	....	....	....	....	....	....	....	....	....	7	5	8	13	4	....	....	....	....
2007-08	**Buffalo**	**NHL**	**2**	**0**	**0**	**0**	**4**	**0**	**0**	**0**	**1**	**0.0**	**-2**	**0**	**0.0**	**6:18**	....	....	....	....	....	....	....	....	....
	Rochester	AHL	78	14	38	52	38	....	....	....	....	....	....	....	....	....	....	....	....	....	....	....	....	....	....
2008-09	**Buffalo**	**NHL**	**4**	**0**	**0**	**0**	**2**	**0**	**0**	**0**	**3**	**0.0**	**2**	**0**	**0.0**	**15:23**	....	....	....	....	....	....	....	....	....
	Portland Pirates	AHL	76	9	42	51	59	....	....	....	....	....	....	....	....	....	5	0	2	2	4	....	....	....	....
2009-10	Portland Pirates	AHL	66	12	31	43	37	....	....	....	....	....	....	....	....	....	4	0	2	2	0	....	....	....	....
2010-11	**Buffalo**	**NHL**	**9**	**1**	**2**	**3**	**2**	**0**	**0**	**1**	**11**	**9.1**	**0**	**0**	**0.0**	**15:17**	**7**	**1**	**6**	**7**	**4**	**1**	**0**	**0**	**21:53**
	Portland Pirates	AHL	63	12	48	60	51	....	....	....	....	....	....	....	....	....	....	....	....	....	....	....	....	....	....
2011-12	**Buffalo**	**NHL**	**44**	**1**	**11**	**12**	**20**	**1**	**0**	**0**	**35**	**2.9**	**10**	**1**	**100.0**	**16:23**	....	....	....	....	....	....	....	....	....
	Vancouver	**NHL**	**14**	**1**	**2**	**3**	**6**	**0**	**0**	**0**	**12**	**8.3**	**-4**	**0**	**0.0**	**15:25**	....	....	....	....	....	....	....	....	....
2012-13	Charlotte	AHL	42	3	25	28	29	....	....	....	....	....	....	....	....	....	....	....	....	....	....	....	....	....	....
	Carolina	**NHL**	**1**	**0**	**0**	**0**	**0**	**0**	**0**	**0**	**0**	**0.0**	**0**	**0**	**0.0**	**7:53**	....	....	....	....	....	....	....	....	....
2013-14	HC Lev Praha	KHL	42	2	7	9	43	....	....	....	....	....	....	....	....	....	22	0	4	4	0	....	....	....	....
2014-15	SC Bern	Swiss	49	8	29	37	18	....	....	....	....	....	....	....	....	....	11	1	4	5	0	....	....	....	....
2015-16	**New Jersey**	**NHL**	**4**	**0**	**0**	**0**	**2**	**0**	**0**	**0**	**0**	**0.0**	**-2**	**0**	**0.0**	**14:22**	....	....	....	....	....	....	....	....	....
	Albany Devils	AHL	57	1	30	31	16	....	....	....	....	....	....	....	....	....	11	0	3	3	16	....	....	....	....
2016-17	Dynamo Minsk	KHL	56	4	33	37	38	....	....	....	....	....	....	....	....	....	5	0	1	1	2	....	....	....	....
	NHL Totals		**78**	**3**	**15**	**18**	**36**	**1**	**0**	**1**	**62**	**4.8**		**1**	**100.0**	**15:33**	**7**	**1**	**6**	**7**	**4**	**1**	**0**	**0**	**21:54**

AHL First All-Star Team (2011) • Eddie Shore Award (AHL – Outstanding Defenseman) (2011)

Traded to **Vancouver** by **Buffalo** for Alexander Sulzer, February 27, 2012. Signed as a free agent by **Carolina**, July 11, 2012. Signed as a free agent by **Lev Praha** (KHL), May 22, 2013. Signed as a free agent by **Bern** (Swiss), July 10, 2014. Signed as a free agent by **New Jersey**, July 3, 2015. Signed as a free agent by **Minsk** (KHL), August 1, 2016.

GRANBERG, Petter

(GRAN-buhrg, PEH-tuhr) **NSH**

Defense. Shoots right. 6'3", 200 lbs. Born, Gallivare, Sweden, August 27, 1992. Toronto's 4th pick, 116th overall, in 2010 NHL Draft.

Season	Club	League	GP	G	A	Pts	PIM	PP	SH	GW	S	S%	+/-	TF	F%	Min	GP	G	A	Pts	PIM	PP	SH	GW	Min
2007-08	Skelleftea U18	Swe-U18	28	1	3	4	4	....	....	....	....	....	....	....	....	....	....	....	....	....	....	....	....	....	....
2008-09	Skelleftea AIK U18	Swe-U18	32	0	8	8	20	....	....	....	....	....	....	....	....	....	8	0	0	0	4	....	....	....	....
	Skelleftea AIK Jr.	Swe-Jr.	4	0	0	0	0	....	....	....	....	....	....	....	....	....	2	0	0	0	6	....	....	....	....
2009-10	Skelleftea AIK U18	Swe-U18	6	0	1	1	2	....	....	....	....	....	....	....	....	....	3	0	3	3	4	....	....	....	....
	Skelleftea AIK Jr.	Swe-Jr.	40	2	7	9	39	....	....	....	....	....	....	....	....	....	4	1	0	1	4	....	....	....	....
	Skelleftea AIK	Sweden	1	0	0	0	0	....	....	....	....	....	....	....	....	....	....	....	....	....	....	....	....	....	....
2010-11	Skelleftea AIK Jr.	Swe-Jr.	34	2	6	8	16	....	....	....	....	....	....	....	....	....	5	0	1	1	0	....	....	....	....
	Pitea HC	Sweden-3	1	0	0	0	0	....	....	....	....	....	....	....	....	....	....	....	....	....	....	....	....	....	....
	Skelleftea AIK	Sweden	23	0	1	1	6	....	....	....	....	....	....	....	....	....	11	0	1	1	2	....	....	....	....
2011-12	Skelleftea AIK Jr.	Swe-Jr.	5	2	4	6	6	....	....	....	....	....	....	....	....	....	....	....	....	....	....	....	....	....	....
	Sundsvall	Sweden-2	3	0	0	0	6	....	....	....	....	....	....	....	....	....	....	....	....	....	....	....	....	....	....
	Skelleftea AIK	Sweden	38	1	3	4	10	....	....	....	....	....	....	....	....	....	19	1	1	2	12	....	....	....	....
2012-13	Skelleftea AIK	Sweden	13	0	0	0	4	....	....	....	....	....	....	....	....	....	13	0	2	2	10	....	....	....	....
	Skelleftea AIK Jr.	Swe-Jr.	3	0	1	1	2	....	....	....	....	....	....	....	....	....	....	....	....	....	....	....	....	....	....
2013-14	**Toronto**	**NHL**	**1**	**0**	**0**	**0**	**0**	**0**	**0**	**0**	**0**	**0.0**	**0**	**0**	**0.0**	**11:46**	....	....	....	....	....	....	....	....	....
	Toronto Marlies	AHL	73	2	5	7	28	....	....	....	....	....	....	....	....	....	14	0	2	2	8	....	....	....	....
2014-15	**Toronto**	**NHL**	**7**	**0**	**0**	**0**	**6**	**0**	**0**	**0**	**1**	**0.0**	**1**	**0**	**0.0**	**11:27**	....	....	....	....	....	....	....	....	....
	Toronto Marlies	AHL	53	1	14	15	30	....	....	....	....	....	....	....	....	....	5	0	1	1	4	....	....	....	....
2015-16	**Nashville**	**NHL**	**27**	**0**	**2**	**2**	**13**	**0**	**0**	**0**	**12**	**0.0**	**1**	**0**	**0.0**	**13:43**	....	....	....	....	....	....	....	....	....
	Milwaukee	AHL	6	0	1	1	4	....	....	....	....	....	....	....	....	....	....	....	....	....	....	....	....	....	....
2016-17	**Nashville**	**NHL**	**10**	**0**	**0**	**0**	**10**	**0**	**0**	**0**	**4**	**0.0**	**0**	**0**	**0.0**	**9:38**	....	....	....	....	....	....	....	....	....
	Milwaukee	AHL	....	....	....	....	....	....	....	....	....	....	....	....	....	....	3	1	0	1	0	....	....	....	....
	NHL Totals		**45**	**0**	**2**	**2**	**29**	**0**	**0**	**0**	**17**	**0.0**		**0**	**0.0**	**12:25**	....	....	....	....	....	....	....	....	....

Claimed on waivers by **Nashville** from **Toronto**, November 22, 2015. • Missed majority of 2015-16 due to recurring ankle injury and as a healthy reserve.

GRANLUND, Markus

(GRAN-luhnd, mahr-KUHS) **VAN**

Center. Shoots left. 6', 178 lbs. Born, Oulu, Finland, April 16, 1993. Calgary's 2nd pick, 45th overall, in 2011 NHL Draft.

Season	Club	League	GP	G	A	Pts	PIM	PP	SH	GW	S	S%	+/-	TF	F%	Min	GP	G	A	Pts	PIM	PP	SH	GW	Min
2008-09	Karpat Oulu U18	Fin-U18	4	1	3	4	0	....	....	....	....	....	....	....	....	....	....	....	....	....	....	....	....	....	....
2009-10	HIFK Helsinki U18	Fin-U18	11	9	20	29	6	....	....	....	....	....	....	....	....	....	....	....	....	....	....	....	....	....	....
	HIFK Helsinki Jr.	Fin-Jr.	37	17	25	42	38	....	....	....	....	....	....	....	....	....	14	2	11	13	18	....	....	....	....
2010-11	Suomi U20	Finland-2	6	3	3	6	6	....	....	....	....	....	....	....	....	....	....	....	....	....	....	....	....	....	....
	HIFK Helsinki	Finland	2	0	0	0	0	....	....	....	....	....	....	....	....	....	....	....	....	....	....	....	....	....	....
	HIFK Helsinki Jr.	Fin-Jr.	40	20	32	52	49	....	....	....	....	....	....	....	....	....	5	4	5	9	6	....	....	....	....
2011-12	Kiekko-Vantaa	Finland-2	7	2	5	7	6	....	....	....	....	....	....	....	....	....	....	....	....	....	....	....	....	....	....
	HIFK Helsinki	Finland	47	15	19	34	18	....	....	....	....	....	....	....	....	....	3	0	0	0	0	....	....	....	....
	HIFK Helsinki Jr.	Fin-Jr.	....	....	....	....	....	....	....	....	....	....	....	....	....	....	1	1	0	1	0	....	....	....	....
2012-13	HIFK Helsinki	Finland	50	10	20	30	18	....	....	....	....	....	....	....	....	....	5	1	2	3	4	....	....	....	....
2013-14	**Calgary**	**NHL**	**7**	**2**	**1**	**3**	**0**	**0**	**1**	**0**	**9**	**22.2**	**2**	**54**	**51.9**	**12:05**	....	....	....	....	....	....	....	....	....
	Abbotsford Heat	AHL	52	25	21	46	22	....	....	....	....	....	....	....	....	....	4	2	3	5	2	....	....	....	....
2014-15	**Calgary**	**NHL**	**48**	**8**	**10**	**18**	**16**	**1**	**0**	**1**	**65**	**12.3**	**-4**	**524**	**36.8**	**13:22**	**3**	**0**	**1**	**1**	**0**	**0**	**0**	**0**	**7:44**
	Adirondack	AHL	21	9	8	17	14	....	....	....	....	....	....	....	....	....	....	....	....	....	....	....	....	....	....
2015-16	**Calgary**	**NHL**	**31**	**4**	**3**	**7**	**8**	**0**	**1**	**0**	**37**	**10.8**	**-1**	**282**	**44.7**	**12:58**	....	....	....	....	....	....	....	....	....
	Stockton Heat	AHL	12	5	4	9	10	....	....	....	....	....	....	....	....	....	....	....	....	....	....	....	....	....	....
	Vancouver	**NHL**	**16**	**2**	**1**	**3**	**6**	**0**	**0**	**1**	**19**	**10.5**	**-3**	**190**	**40.0**	**15:23**	....	....	....	....	....	....	....	....	....
2016-17	**Vancouver**	**NHL**	**69**	**19**	**13**	**32**	**14**	**3**	**0**	**3**	**122**	**15.6**	**-19**	**101**	**39.6**	**17:19**	....	....	....	....	....	....	....	....	....
	NHL Totals		**171**	**35**	**28**	**63**	**44**	**4**	**2**	**5**	**252**	**13.9**		**1151**	**40.2**	**15:01**	**3**	**0**	**1**	**1**	**0**	**0**	**0**	**0**	**7:44**

Traded to **Vancouver** by **Calgary** for Hunter Shinkaruk, February 22, 2016.

GRANLUND, Mikael

(GRAN-lund, mih-KIGH-ehl) **MIN**

Center. Shoots left. 5'10", 184 lbs. Born, Oulu, Finland, February 26, 1992. Minnesota's 1st pick, 9th overall, in 2010 NHL Draft.

Season	Club	League	GP	G	A	Pts	PIM	PP	SH	GW	S	S%	+/-	TF	F%	Min	GP	G	A	Pts	PIM	PP	SH	GW	Min
2007-08	Karpat Oulu U18	Fin-U18	31	22	27	49	20	....	....	....	....	....	....	....	....	....	5	3	5	8	0	....	....	....	....
2008-09	Suomi U20	Finland-2	6	4	3	7	0	....	....	....	....	....	....	....	....	....	....	....	....	....	....	....	....	....	....
	Karpat Oulu Jr.	Fin-Jr.	38	22	44	66	45	....	....	....	....	....	....	....	....	....	....	....	....	....	....	....	....	....	....
	Karpat Oulu	Finland	2	0	0	0	0	....	....	....	....	....	....	....	....	....	....	....	....	....	....	....	....	....	....
	Karpat Oulu U18	Fin-U18	....	....	....	....	....	....	....	....	....	....	....	....	....	....	3	2	4	6	2	....	....	....	....
2009-10	Suomi U20	Finland-2	1	0	0	0	0	....	....	....	....	....	....	....	....	....	....	....	....	....	....	....	....	....	....
	HIFK Helsinki	Finland	43	13	27	40	2	....	....	....	....	....	....	....	....	....	6	1	5	6	0	....	....	....	....
2010-11	HIFK Helsinki	Finland	39	8	28	36	14	....	....	....	....	....	....	....	....	....	15	5	*11	*16	4	....	....	....	....
2011-12	HIFK Helsinki	Finland	45	20	31	51	18	....	....	....	....	....	....	....	....	....	4	0	2	2	0	....	....	....	....
2012-13	Houston Aeros	AHL	29	10	18	28	8	....	....	....	....	....	....	....	....	....	5	1	1	2	4	....	....	....	....
	Minnesota	**NHL**	**27**	**2**	**6**	**8**	**6**	**0**	**0**	**0**	**36**	**5.6**	**-4**	**206**	**47.1**	**13:11**	....	....	....	....	....	....	....	....	....
2013-14	**Minnesota**	**NHL**	**63**	**8**	**33**	**41**	**22**	**2**	**0**	**2**	**104**	**7.7**	**-3**	**789**	**52.6**	**17:19**	**13**	**4**	**3**	**7**	**2**	**0**	**0**	**1**	**18:01**
	Finland	Olympics	6	3	4	7	4	....	....	....	....	....	....	....	....	....	....	....	....	....	....	....	....	....	....
2014-15	**Minnesota**	**NHL**	**68**	**8**	**31**	**39**	**20**	**0**	**0**	**2**	**99**	**8.1**	**17**	**984**	**48.4**	**17:54**	**10**	**2**	**4**	**6**	**0**	**0**	**0**	**1**	**17:50**
2015-16	**Minnesota**	**NHL**	**82**	**13**	**31**	**44**	**20**	**2**	**1**	**3**	**160**	**8.1**	**-12**	**1085**	**48.7**	**18:07**	**6**	**1**	**2**	**3**	**0**	**0**	**0**	**0**	**22:22**
2016-17	**Minnesota**	**NHL**	**81**	**26**	**43**	**69**	**12**	**7**	**3**	**4**	**177**	**14.7**	**23**	**33**	**48.5**	**18:49**	**5**	**0**	**2**	**2**	**2**	**0**	**0**	**0**	**20:32**
	NHL Totals		**321**	**57**	**144**	**201**	**80**	**11**	**4**	**11**	**576**	**9.9**		**3097**	**49.5**	**17:41**	**34**	**7**	**11**	**18**	**4**	**0**	**0**	**2**	**19:06**

Olympic All-Star Team (2014)

GRANT, Alex
(GRANT, AL-ehx) **MIN**

Defense. Shoots right. 6'4", 205 lbs. Born, Antigonish, NS, January 20, 1989. Pittsburgh's 6th pick, 118th overall, in 2007 NHL Draft.

			Regular Season														Playoffs								
Season	Club	League	GP	G	A	Pts	PIM	PP	SH	GW	S	S%	+/-	TF	F%	Min	GP	G	A	Pts	PIM	PP	SH	GW	Min
2004-05	Antigonish	MJrHL	50	7	9	16	36	....	....	....	....	....	....	....	....	....	3	1	1	2	2	....	....	....	....
2005-06	Saint John	QMJHL	47	4	9	13	58	....	....	....	....	....	....	....	....	....	....	....	....	....	....	....	....	....	....
2006-07	Saint John	QMJHL	68	12	20	32	108	....	....	....	....	....	....	....	....	....	....	....	....	....	....	....	....	....	....
2007-08	Saint John	QMJHL	70	15	33	48	96	....	....	....	....	....	....	....	....	....	14	3	11	14	12	....	....	....	....
2008-09	Saint John	QMJHL	37	9	22	31	51	....	....	....	....	....	....	....	....	....	....	....	....	....	....	....	....	....	....
	Shawinigan	QMJHL	23	4	15	19	11	....	....	....	....	....	....	....	....	....	21	4	5	9	18	....	....	....	....
2009-10	Wilkes-Barre	AHL	14	3	2	5	28	....	....	....	....	....	....	....	....	....	2	0	0	0	0	....	....	....	....
	Wheeling Nailers	ECHL	40	7	20	27	36	....	....	....	....	....	....	....	....	....	....	....	....	....	....	....	....	....	....
2010-11	Wilkes-Barre	AHL	4	0	0	0	0	....	....	....	....	....	....	....	....	....	....	....	....	....	....	....	....	....	....
	Wheeling Nailers	ECHL	14	3	2	5	6	....	....	....	....	....	....	....	....	....	17	2	0	2	13	....	....	....	....
2011-12	Wilkes-Barre	AHL	61	10	27	37	73	....	....	....	....	....	....	....	....	....	12	2	5	7	13	....	....	....	....
2012-13	Wilkes-Barre	AHL	46	4	16	20	73	....	....	....	....	....	....	....	....	....	13	2	2	4	27	....	....	....	....
2013-14	**Anaheim**	**NHL**	**2**	**2**	**0**	**2**	**2**	**0**	**0**	**0**	**2**	**100.0**	**3**	**0**	**0.0**	**12:11**	....	....	....	....	....	....	....	....	....
	Norfolk Admirals	AHL	52	7	20	27	46	....	....	....	....	....	....	....	....	....	....	....	....	....	....	....	....	....	....
	Binghamton	AHL	19	2	8	10	6	....	....	....	....	....	....	....	....	....	4	0	0	0	10	....	....	....	....
2014-15	Binghamton	AHL	58	6	27	33	57	....	....	....	....	....	....	....	....	....	....	....	....	....	....	....	....	....	....
2015-16	**Arizona**	**NHL**	**5**	**0**	**0**	**0**	**7**	**0**	**0**	**0**	**4**	**0.0**	**–2**	**0**	**0.0**	**13:14**	....	....	....	....	....	....	....	....	....
	Springfield	AHL	69	11	31	42	57	....	....	....	....	....	....	....	....	....	....	....	....	....	....	....	....	....	....
2016-17	Providence Bruins	AHL	70	17	32	49	36	....	....	....	....	....	....	....	....	....	17	2	6	8	12	....	....	....	....
	NHL Totals		**7**	**2**	**0**	**2**	**9**	**0**	**0**	**0**	**6**	**33.3**		**0**	**0.0**	**12:56**	....	....	....	....	....	....	....	....	....

• Missed majority of 2010-11 due to recurring wrist injury. Traded to **Anaheim** by **Pittsburgh** for Harry Zolnierczyk, June 24, 2013. Traded to **Ottawa** by **Anaheim** for Andre Petersson, March 5, 2014. Signed as a free agent by **Arizona**, July 2, 2015. Signed as a free agent by **Boston**, July 5, 2016. Signed as a free agent by **Minnesota**, July 1, 2017.

GRANT, Derek
(GRANT, DAIR-ihk) **ANA**

Center. Shoots left. 6'3", 202 lbs. Born, Abbotsford, BC, April 20, 1990. Ottawa's 5th pick, 119th overall, in 2008 NHL Draft.

			Regular Season														Playoffs								
Season	Club	League	GP	G	A	Pts	PIM	PP	SH	GW	S	S%	+/-	TF	F%	Min	GP	G	A	Pts	PIM	PP	SH	GW	Min
2006-07	Abbotsford Pilots	PIJHL	47	31	20	51	42	....	....	....	....	....	....	....	....	....	11	6	5	11	20	....	....	....	....
2007-08	Langley Chiefs	BCHL	57	24	39	63	44	....	....	....	....	....	....	....	....	....	12	5	5	10	15	....	....	....	....
2008-09	Langley Chiefs	BCHL	35	25	35	60	22	....	....	....	....	....	....	....	....	....	4	2	1	3	2	....	....	....	....
2009-10	Michigan State	CCHA	38	12	18	30	10	....	....	....	....	....	....	....	....	....	....	....	....	....	....	....	....	....	....
2010-11	Michigan State	CCHA	38	8	25	33	44	....	....	....	....	....	....	....	....	....	....	....	....	....	....	....	....	....	....
	Binghamton	AHL	14	1	5	6	0	....	....	....	....	....	....	....	....	....	7	1	1	2	2	....	....	....	....
2011-12	Binghamton	AHL	60	8	15	23	26	....	....	....	....	....	....	....	....	....	....	....	....	....	....	....	....	....	....
2012-13	Binghamton	AHL	63	19	9	28	37	....	....	....	....	....	....	....	....	....	3	0	0	0	6	....	....	....	....
	Ottawa	**NHL**	**5**	**0**	**0**	**0**	**0**	**0**	**0**	**0**	**5**	**0.0**	**–1**	**31**	**54.8**	**8:40**	....	....	....	....	....	....	....	....	....
2013-14	**Ottawa**	**NHL**	**20**	**0**	**2**	**2**	**4**	**0**	**0**	**0**	**31**	**0.0**	**–3**	**150**	**52.7**	**9:34**	....	....	....	....	....	....	....	....	....
	Binghamton	AHL	46	12	10	22	30	....	....	....	....	....	....	....	....	....	4	0	1	1	2	....	....	....	....
2014-15	Binghamton	AHL	73	21	17	38	45	....	....	....	....	....	....	....	....	....	....	....	....	....	....	....	....	....	....
2015-16	**Calgary**	**NHL**	**15**	**0**	**1**	**1**	**2**	**0**	**0**	**0**	**22**	**0.0**	**–7**	**111**	**55.0**	**10:53**	....	....	....	....	....	....	....	....	....
	Stockton Heat	AHL	36	27	18	45	36	....	....	....	....	....	....	....	....	....	....	....	....	....	....	....	....	....	....
2016-17	**Buffalo**	**NHL**	**35**	**0**	**3**	**3**	**19**	**0**	**0**	**0**	**31**	**0.0**	**–3**	**304**	**52.6**	**10:12**	....	....	....	....	....	....	....	....	....
	Rochester	AHL	23	11	8	19	22	....	....	....	....	....	....	....	....	....	....	....	....	....	....	....	....	....	....
	Nashville	**NHL**	**6**	**0**	**1**	**1**	**5**	**0**	**0**	**0**	**6**	**0.0**	**–2**	**52**	**53.9**	**8:41**	....	....	....	....	....	....	....	....	....
	Buffalo	**NHL**	**5**	**0**	**0**	**0**	**0**	**0**	**0**	**0**	**3**	**0.0**	**0**	**28**	**46.4**	**7:56**	....	....	....	....	....	....	....	....	....
	NHL Totals		**86**	**0**	**7**	**7**	**30**	**0**	**0**	**0**	**98**	**0.0**		**676**	**53.0**	**9:51**	....	....	....	....	....	....	....	....	....

Signed as a free agent by **Calgary**, July 1, 2015. Signed as a free agent by **Buffalo**, July 2, 2016. Claimed on waivers by **Nashville** from **Buffalo**, January 11, 2017. Claimed on waivers by **Buffalo** from **Nashville**, February 6, 2017. Signed as a free agent by **Anaheim**, July 2, 2017.

GRAOVAC, Tyler
(GRAW-vak, TIGH-luhr) **WSH**

Center. Shoots left. 6'5", 212 lbs. Born, Brampton, ON, April 27, 1993. Minnesota's 6th pick, 191st overall, in 2011 NHL Draft.

			Regular Season														Playoffs								
Season	Club	League	GP	G	A	Pts	PIM	PP	SH	GW	S	S%	+/-	TF	F%	Min	GP	G	A	Pts	PIM	PP	SH	GW	Min
2008-09	Mississauga Reps	GTHL	26	13	18	31	12	....	....	....	....	....	....	....	....	....	....	....	....	....	....	....	....	....	....
2009-10	Ottawa 67's	OHL	52	2	7	9	17	....	....	....	....	....	....	....	....	....	12	0	0	0	2	....	....	....	....
2010-11	Ottawa 67's	OHL	66	10	11	21	10	....	....	....	....	....	....	....	....	....	....	....	....	....	....	....	....	....	....
2011-12	Ottawa 67's	OHL	50	8	19	27	31	....	....	....	....	....	....	....	....	....	18	4	6	10	12	....	....	....	....
2012-13	Ottawa 67's	OHL	30	21	14	35	8	....	....	....	....	....	....	....	....	....	....	....	....	....	....	....	....	....	....
	Belleville Bulls	OHL	30	17	21	38	10	....	....	....	....	....	....	....	....	....	15	6	16	22	17	....	....	....	....
2013-14	Iowa Wild	AHL	64	13	12	25	29	....	....	....	....	....	....	....	....	....	....	....	....	....	....	....	....	....	....
2014-15	**Minnesota**	**NHL**	**3**	**0**	**0**	**0**	**0**	**0**	**0**	**0**	**4**	**0.0**	**0**	**22**	**27.3**	**9:13**	....	....	....	....	....	....	....	....	....
	Iowa Wild	AHL	73	21	25	46	26	....	....	....	....	....	....	....	....	....	....	....	....	....	....	....	....	....	....
2015-16	**Minnesota**	**NHL**	**2**	**0**	**0**	**0**	**0**	**0**	**0**	**0**	**2**	**0.0**	**–1**	**19**	**68.4**	**11:37**	....	....	....	....	....	....	....	....	....
	Iowa Wild	AHL	39	5	11	16	20	....	....	....	....	....	....	....	....	....	....	....	....	....	....	....	....	....	....
2016-17	**Minnesota**	**NHL**	**52**	**7**	**2**	**9**	**10**	**0**	**0**	**2**	**48**	**14.6**	**7**	**343**	**47.5**	**9:50**	....	....	....	....	....	....	....	....	....
	Iowa Wild	AHL	26	10	5	15	15	....	....	....	....	....	....	....	....	....	....	....	....	....	....	....	....	....	....
	NHL Totals		**57**	**7**	**2**	**9**	**10**	**0**	**0**	**2**	**54**	**13.0**		**384**	**47.4**	**9:52**	....	....	....	....	....	....	....	....	....

Canadian Major Junior Sportsman of the Year (2013)

• Missed majority of 2015-16 due to sports hernia surgery, October 9, 2016. Traded to **Washington** by **Minnesota** for Washington's 5th round pick in 2018 NHL Draft, June 14, 2017.

GRAVEL, Kevin
(gra-VEHL, KEH-vihn) **L.A.**

Defense. Shoots left. 6'4", 199 lbs. Born, Kingsford, MI, March 6, 1992. Los Angeles' 4th pick, 148th overall, in 2010 NHL Draft.

			Regular Season														Playoffs								
Season	Club	League	GP	G	A	Pts	PIM	PP	SH	GW	S	S%	+/-	TF	F%	Min	GP	G	A	Pts	PIM	PP	SH	GW	Min
2008-09	Marquette	NAHL	58	3	11	14	29	....	....	....	....	....	....	....	....	....	....	....	....	....	....	....	....	....	....
	USAHNTDP	U-17	3	0	1	1	4	....	....	....	....	....	....	....	....	....	....	....	....	....	....	....	....	....	....
2009-10	Sioux City	USHL	53	3	3	6	36	....	....	....	....	....	....	....	....	....	....	....	....	....	....	....	....	....	....
2010-11	St. Cloud State	WCHA	36	1	5	6	4	....	....	....	....	....	....	....	....	....	....	....	....	....	....	....	....	....	....
2011-12	St. Cloud State	WCHA	37	1	7	8	12	....	....	....	....	....	....	....	....	....	....	....	....	....	....	....	....	....	....
2012-13	St. Cloud State	WCHA	42	1	11	12	25	....	....	....	....	....	....	....	....	....	....	....	....	....	....	....	....	....	....
2013-14	St. Cloud State	NCHC	38	10	13	23	2	....	....	....	....	....	....	....	....	....	....	....	....	....	....	....	....	....	....
	Manchester	AHL	5	0	0	0	2	....	....	....	....	....	....	....	....	....	....	....	....	....	....	....	....	....	....
2014-15	Manchester	AHL	58	6	9	15	23	....	....	....	....	....	....	....	....	....	19	0	5	5	0	....	....	....	....
2015-16	**Los Angeles**	**NHL**	**5**	**0**	**0**	**0**	**0**	**0**	**0**	**0**	**2**	**0.0**	**0**	**0**	**0.0**	**11:41**	....	....	....	....	....	....	....	....	....
	Ontario Reign	AHL	55	7	13	20	30	....	....	....	....	....	....	....	....	....	12	1	6	7	4	....	....	....	....
2016-17	**Los Angeles**	**NHL**	**49**	**1**	**6**	**7**	**6**	**1**	**0**	**0**	**52**	**1.9**	**3**	**0**	**0.0**	**14:09**	....	....	....	....	....	....	....	....	....
	Ontario Reign	AHL	6	0	2	2	0	....	....	....	....	....	....	....	....	....	....	....	....	....	....	....	....	....	....
	NHL Totals		**54**	**1**	**6**	**7**	**6**	**1**	**0**	**0**	**54**	**1.9**		**0**	**0.0**	**13:55**	....	....	....	....	....	....	....	....	....

GREEN, Mike
(GREEN, MIGHK) **DET**

Defense. Shoots right. 6'1", 207 lbs. Born, Calgary, AB, October 12, 1985. Washington's 3rd pick, 29th overall, in 2004 NHL Draft.

			Regular Season														Playoffs								
Season	Club	League	GP	G	A	Pts	PIM	PP	SH	GW	S	S%	+/-	TF	F%	Min	GP	G	A	Pts	PIM	PP	SH	GW	Min
2000-01	Cgy. North Stars	AMHL	36	4	23	27	34	....	....	....	....	....	....	....	....	....	....	....	....	....	....	....	....	....	....
	Saskatoon Blades	WHL	5	0	2	2	0	....	....	....	....	....	....	....	....	....	....	....	....	....	....	....	....	....	....
2001-02	Saskatoon Blades	WHL	62	3	20	23	57	....	....	....	....	....	....	....	....	....	7	0	1	1	2	....	....	....	....
2002-03	Saskatoon Blades	WHL	72	6	36	42	70	....	....	....	....	....	....	....	....	....	6	0	2	2	6	....	....	....	....
2003-04	Saskatoon Blades	WHL	59	14	25	39	92	....	....	....	....	....	....	....	....	....	....	....	....	....	....	....	....	....	....
2004-05	Saskatoon Blades	WHL	67	14	52	66	105	....	....	....	....	....	....	....	....	....	4	0	0	0	6	....	....	....	....
2005-06	**Washington**	**NHL**	**22**	**1**	**2**	**3**	**18**	**0**	**0**	**0**	**13**	**7.7**	**–8**	**0**	**0.0**	**14:54**	....	....	....	....	....	....	....	....	....
	Hershey Bears	AHL	56	9	34	43	79	....	....	....	....	....	....	....	....	....	21	3	15	18	30	....	....	....	....
2006-07	**Washington**	**NHL**	**70**	**2**	**10**	**12**	**36**	**0**	**0**	**0**	**68**	**2.9**	**–10**	**0**	**0.0**	**15:29**	....	....	....	....	....	....	....	....	....
2007-08	**Washington**	**NHL**	**82**	**18**	**38**	**56**	**62**	**8**	**0**	**4**	**234**	**7.7**	**6**	**1**	**0.0**	**23:38**	**7**	**3**	**4**	**7**	**15**	**2**	**0**	**0**	**26:59**
2008-09	**Washington**	**NHL**	**68**	**31**	**42**	**73**	**68**	**18**	**1**	**4**	**243**	**12.8**	**24**	**0**	**0.0**	**25:46**	**14**	**1**	**8**	**9**	**12**	**1**	**0**	**0**	**24:59**
2009-10	**Washington**	**NHL**	**75**	**19**	**57**	**76**	**54**	**10**	**0**	**4**	**205**	**9.3**	**39**	**0**	**0.0**	**25:29**	**7**	**0**	**3**	**3**	**12**	**0**	**0**	**0**	**26:01**
2010-11	**Washington**	**NHL**	**49**	**8**	**16**	**24**	**48**	**5**	**0**	**1**	**115**	**7.0**	**6**	**0**	**0.0**	**25:12**	**8**	**1**	**5**	**6**	**8**	**1**	**0**	**0**	**21:27**
2011-12	**Washington**	**NHL**	**32**	**3**	**4**	**7**	**12**	**3**	**0**	**1**	**64**	**4.7**	**5**	**0**	**0.0**	**21:03**	**14**	**2**	**2**	**4**	**10**	**1**	**0**	**1**	**23:45**
2012-13	**Washington**	**NHL**	**35**	**12**	**14**	**26**	**20**	**4**	**0**	**2**	**96**	**12.5**	**–3**	**0**	**0.0**	**24:51**	**7**	**2**	**2**	**4**	**4**	**1**	**0**	**1**	**25:32**
2013-14	**Washington**	**NHL**	**70**	**9**	**29**	**38**	**64**	**3**	**0**	**2**	**172**	**5.2**	**–16**	**0**	**0.0**	**22:44**	....	....	....	....	....	....	....	....	....
2014-15	**Washington**	**NHL**	**72**	**10**	**35**	**45**	**34**	**1**	**0**	**2**	**159**	**6.3**	**15**	**0**	**0.0**	**19:06**	**14**	**0**	**2**	**2**	**14**	**0**	**0**	**0**	**18:24**

			Regular Season														Playoffs								
Season	Club	League	GP	G	A	Pts	PIM	PP	SH	GW	S	S%	+/-	TF	F%	Min	GP	G	A	Pts	PIM	PP	SH	GW	Min
2015-16	**Detroit**	**NHL**	**74**	**7**	**28**	**35**	**38**	**5**	**0**	**0**	**124**	**5.6**	**–6**	**2**	**0.0**	**19:46**	**5**	**1**	**1**	**2**	**10**	**0**	**0**	**0**	**16:46**
2016-17	**Detroit**	**NHL**	**72**	**14**	**22**	**36**	**40**	**3**	**0**	**2**	**125**	**11.2**	**–20**	**0**	**0.0**	**23:33**	....	....	....	....	....	....	....	....	....
	NHL Totals		**721**	**134**	**297**	**431**	**494**	**60**	**1**	**22**	**1618**	**8.3**		**3**	**0.0**	**22:05**	**76**	**10**	**27**	**37**	**85**	**6**	**0**	**2**	**22:58**

WHL East First All-Star Team (2005) • AHL All-Rookie Team (2006) • NHL First All-Star Team (2009, 2010)

Played in NHL All-Star Game (2011)

Signed as a free agent by **Detroit**, July 1, 2015.

GREENE, Andy

(GREEN, AN-dee) **N.J.**

Defense. Shoots left. 5'11", 190 lbs. Born, Trenton, MI, October 30, 1982.

Season	Club	League	GP	G	A	Pts	PIM	PP	SH	GW	S	S%	+/-	TF	F%	Min	GP	G	A	Pts	PIM	PP	SH	GW	Min
99-2000	Trenton Trojans	High-MI	STATISTICS NOT AVAILABLE																						
	Det. Compuware	NAHL	6	2	4	6	2	....	....	....	....	....	....	....	....	....	5	0	0	0	16	....	....	....	....
2000-01	Det. Compuware	NAHL	54	7	24	31	60	....	....	....	....	....	....	....	....	....	3	2	1	3	2	....	....	....	....
2001-02	Det. Compuware	NAHL	53	16	29	45	88	....	....	....	....	....	....	....	....	....	....	....	....	....	....	....	....	....	....
2002-03	Miami U.	CCHA	41	4	19	23	64	....	....	....	....	....	....	....	....	....	....	....	....	....	....	....	....	....	....
2003-04	Miami U.	CCHA	41	7	19	26	78	....	....	....	....	....	....	....	....	....	....	....	....	....	....	....	....	....	....
2004-05	Miami U.	CCHA	38	7	27	34	66	....	....	....	....	....	....	....	....	....	....	....	....	....	....	....	....	....	....
2005-06	Miami U.	CCHA	39	9	22	31	48	....	....	....	....	....	....	....	....	....	....	....	....	....	....	....	....	....	....
2006-07	**New Jersey**	**NHL**	**23**	**1**	**5**	**6**	**6**	**1**	**0**	**0**	**23**	**4.3**	**–1**	**0**	**0.0**	**14:15**	**11**	**2**	**1**	**3**	**2**	**0**	**0**	**1**	**17:04**
	Lowell Devils	AHL	52	5	16	21	28	....	....	....	....	....	....	....	....	....	....	....	....	....	....	....	....	....	....
2007-08	**New Jersey**	**NHL**	**59**	**2**	**8**	**10**	**22**	**2**	**0**	**0**	**50**	**4.0**	**0**	**0**	**0.0**	**19:30**	**2**	**0**	**0**	**0**	**0**	**0**	**0**	**0**	**15:11**
2008-09	**New Jersey**	**NHL**	**49**	**2**	**7**	**9**	**22**	**0**	**0**	**0**	**38**	**5.3**	**3**	**0**	**0.0**	**16:17**	**3**	**0**	**1**	**1**	**0**	**0**	**0**	**0**	**15:18**
2009-10	**New Jersey**	**NHL**	**78**	**6**	**31**	**37**	**14**	**4**	**0**	**4**	**86**	**7.0**	**9**	**0**	**0.0**	**23:32**	**5**	**1**	**1**	**2**	**6**	**1**	**0**	**0**	**19:42**
2010-11	**New Jersey**	**NHL**	**82**	**4**	**19**	**23**	**22**	**1**	**0**	**1**	**91**	**4.4**	**–23**	**0**	**0.0**	**22:22**	....	....	....	....	....	....	....	....	....
2011-12	**New Jersey**	**NHL**	**56**	**1**	**15**	**16**	**16**	**0**	**0**	**0**	**53**	**1.9**	**3**	**0**	**0.0**	**19:30**	**24**	**0**	**1**	**1**	**8**	**0**	**0**	**0**	**22:02**
2012-13	**New Jersey**	**NHL**	**48**	**4**	**12**	**16**	**20**	**2**	**1**	**1**	**63**	**6.3**	**12**	**0**	**0.0**	**23:02**	....	....	....	....	....	....	....	....	....
2013-14	**New Jersey**	**NHL**	**82**	**8**	**24**	**32**	**32**	**3**	**0**	**3**	**134**	**6.0**	**3**	**0**	**0.0**	**24:35**	....	....	....	....	....	....	....	....	....
2014-15	**New Jersey**	**NHL**	**82**	**3**	**19**	**22**	**20**	**0**	**0**	**1**	**83**	**3.6**	**1**	**0**	**0.0**	**23:33**	....	....	....	....	....	....	....	....	....
2015-16	**New Jersey**	**NHL**	**82**	**4**	**9**	**13**	**26**	**1**	**0**	**0**	**63**	**6.3**	**7**	**0**	**0.0**	**22:57**	....	....	....	....	....	....	....	....	....
2016-17	**New Jersey**	**NHL**	**66**	**4**	**9**	**13**	**8**	**1**	**1**	**1**	**83**	**4.8**	**–16**	**0**	**0.0**	**21:57**	....	....	....	....	....	....	....	....	....
	NHL Totals		**707**	**39**	**158**	**197**	**208**	**15**	**2**	**11**	**767**	**5.1**		**0**	**0.0**	**21:49**	**45**	**3**	**4**	**7**	**16**	**1**	**0**	**1**	**19:48**

CCHA All-Rookie Team (2003) • CCHA First All-Star Team (2004, 2005, 2006) • NCAA West Second All-American Team (2005) • NCAA West First All-American Team (2006)

Signed as a free agent by **New Jersey**, April 4, 2006.

GREENE, Matt

(GREEN, MAT)

Defense. Shoots right. 6'3", 229 lbs. Born, Grand Ledge, MI, May 13, 1983. Edmonton's 4th pick, 44th overall, in 2002 NHL Draft.

Season	Club	League	GP	G	A	Pts	PIM	PP	SH	GW	S	S%	+/-	TF	F%	Min	GP	G	A	Pts	PIM	PP	SH	GW	Min
2000-01	USAHNTDP	U-18	34	0	9	9	8	....	....	....	....	....	....	....	....	....	....	....	....	....	....	....	....	....	....
	USAHNTDP	USHL	20	0	1	1	51	....	....	....	....	....	....	....	....	....	....	....	....	....	....	....	....	....	....
2001-02	Green Bay	USHL	55	4	20	24	150	....	....	....	....	....	....	....	....	....	7	0	1	1	31	....	....	....	....
2002-03	North Dakota	WCHA	39	0	4	4	*135	....	....	....	....	....	....	....	....	....	....	....	....	....	....	....	....	....	....
2003-04	North Dakota	WCHA	40	1	16	17	86	....	....	....	....	....	....	....	....	....	....	....	....	....	....	....	....	....	....
2004-05	North Dakota	WCHA	43	2	8	10	*126	....	....	....	....	....	....	....	....	....	....	....	....	....	....	....	....	....	....
2005-06	**Edmonton**	**NHL**	**27**	**0**	**2**	**2**	**43**	**0**	**0**	**0**	**10**	**0.0**	**–6**	**0**	**0.0**	**11:13**	**18**	**0**	**1**	**1**	**34**	**0**	**0**	**0**	**10:03**
	Iowa Stars	AHL	26	2	5	7	47	....	....	....	....	....	....	....	....	....	....	....	....	....	....	....	....	....	....
2006-07	**Edmonton**	**NHL**	**78**	**1**	**9**	**10**	**109**	**0**	**0**	**0**	**52**	**1.9**	**–22**	**0**	**0.0**	**17:36**	....	....	....	....	....	....	....	....	....
2007-08	**Edmonton**	**NHL**	**46**	**0**	**1**	**1**	**53**	**0**	**0**	**0**	**28**	**0.0**	**–3**	**0**	**0.0**	**16:42**	....	....	....	....	....	....	....	....	....
	Springfield	AHL	1	0	0	0	0	....	....	....	....	....	....	....	....	....	....	....	....	....	....	....	....	....	....
2008-09	**Los Angeles**	**NHL**	**82**	**2**	**12**	**14**	**111**	**0**	**0**	**0**	**76**	**2.6**	**1**	**1**	**100.0**	**19:44**	....	....	....	....	....	....	....	....	....
2009-10	**Los Angeles**	**NHL**	**75**	**2**	**7**	**9**	**83**	**0**	**0**	**1**	**57**	**3.5**	**4**	**0**	**0.0**	**17:29**	**6**	**0**	**1**	**1**	**0**	**0**	**0**	**0**	**18:45**
2010-11	**Los Angeles**	**NHL**	**71**	**2**	**9**	**11**	**70**	**0**	**0**	**1**	**50**	**4.0**	**3**	**0**	**0.0**	**16:59**	**6**	**0**	**0**	**0**	**14**	**0**	**0**	**0**	**16:44**
2011-12 ♦	**Los Angeles**	**NHL**	**82**	**4**	**11**	**15**	**58**	**0**	**0**	**2**	**76**	**5.3**	**4**	**0**	**0.0**	**16:40**	**20**	**2**	**4**	**6**	**12**	**0**	**1**	**1**	**16:06**
2012-13	**Los Angeles**	**NHL**	**5**	**0**	**1**	**1**	**8**	**0**	**0**	**0**	**3**	**0.0**	**–1**	**0**	**0.0**	**15:17**	**9**	**0**	**2**	**2**	**6**	**0**	**0**	**0**	**15:29**
2013-14 ♦	**Los Angeles**	**NHL**	**38**	**2**	**4**	**6**	**47**	**0**	**0**	**0**	**38**	**5.3**	**6**	**1**	**0.0**	**15:53**	**20**	**0**	**4**	**4**	**16**	**0**	**0**	**0**	**14:28**
2014-15	**Los Angeles**	**NHL**	**82**	**3**	**6**	**9**	**54**	**0**	**0**	**0**	**69**	**4.3**	**1**	**0**	**0.0**	**15:48**	....	....	....	....	....	....	....	....	....
2015-16	**Los Angeles**	**NHL**	**3**	**0**	**0**	**0**	**8**	**0**	**0**	**0**	**3**	**0.0**	**0**	**0**	**0.0**	**11:45**	....	....	....	....	....	....	....	....	....
2016-17	**Los Angeles**	**NHL**	**26**	**1**	**1**	**2**	**19**	**0**	**0**	**0**	**14**	**7.1**	**3**	**0**	**0.0**	**13:11**	....	....	....	....	....	....	....	....	....
	NHL Totals		**615**	**17**	**63**	**80**	**663**	**0**	**0**	**4**	**476**	**3.6**		**2**	**50.0**	**16:45**	**79**	**2**	**12**	**14**	**82**	**0**	**1**	**1**	**14:29**

USHL Second All-Star Team (2002)

Traded to **Los Angeles** by **Edmonton** with Jarret Stoll for Lubomir Visnovsky, June 29, 2008. • Missed majority of 2012-13 due to back injury vs. Chicago, January 19, 2013. • Missed majority of 2013-14 due to upper-body injury vs. Nashville, November 2, 2013 and as a healthy reserve. • Missed majority of 2015-16 due to upper-body injury vs. Vancouver, October 3, 2016. • Missed majority of 2016-17 due to recurring back injury and resulting surgery, December, 2016.

GREENING, Colin

(GREEN-ihng, KAW-lihn) **TOR**

Center/Left wing. Shoots left. 6'2", 210 lbs. Born, St. John's, NL, March 9, 1986. Ottawa's 8th pick, 204th overall, in 2005 NHL Draft.

Season	Club	League	GP	G	A	Pts	PIM	PP	SH	GW	S	S%	+/-	TF	F%	Min	GP	G	A	Pts	PIM	PP	SH	GW	Min
2002-03	St. John's	NFAHA	60	24	34	58	48	....	....	....	....	....	....	....	....	....	....	....	....	....	....	....	....	....	....
2003-04	Upper Canada	High-ON	53	30	43	73	40	....	....	....	....	....	....	....	....	....	....	....	....	....	....	....	....	....	....
2004-05	Upper Canada	High-ON	35	24	22	46	24	....	....	....	....	....	....	....	....	....	....	....	....	....	....	....	....	....	....
2005-06	Nanaimo Clippers	BCHL	56	27	35	62	46	....	....	....	....	....	....	....	....	....	5	3	0	3	2	....	....	....	....
2006-07	Cornell Big Red	ECAC	31	11	8	19	26	....	....	....	....	....	....	....	....	....	....	....	....	....	....	....	....	....	....
2007-08	Cornell Big Red	ECAC	36	14	19	33	41	....	....	....	....	....	....	....	....	....	....	....	....	....	....	....	....	....	....
2008-09	Cornell Big Red	ECAC	36	15	16	31	28	....	....	....	....	....	....	....	....	....	....	....	....	....	....	....	....	....	....
2009-10	Cornell Big Red	ECAC	34	15	20	35	31	....	....	....	....	....	....	....	....	....	....	....	....	....	....	....	....	....	....
2010-11	**Ottawa**	**NHL**	**24**	**6**	**7**	**13**	**10**	**0**	**0**	**2**	**57**	**10.5**	**2**	**24**	**45.8**	**15:05**	....	....	....	....	....	....	....	....	....
	Binghamton	AHL	59	15	25	40	41	....	....	....	....	....	....	....	....	....	23	1	4	5	13	....	....	....	....
2011-12	**Ottawa**	**NHL**	**82**	**17**	**20**	**37**	**46**	**4**	**0**	**0**	**184**	**9.2**	**–4**	**62**	**41.9**	**15:35**	**7**	**0**	**1**	**1**	**0**	**0**	**0**	**0**	**13:59**
2012-13	Aalborg	Denmark	17	13	12	25	12	....	....	....	....	....	....	....	....	....	....	....	....	....	....	....	....	....	....
	Ottawa	**NHL**	**47**	**8**	**11**	**19**	**11**	**2**	**0**	**2**	**80**	**10.0**	**5**	**47**	**46.8**	**14:44**	**10**	**3**	**1**	**4**	**2**	**0**	**0**	**1**	**15:57**
2013-14	**Ottawa**	**NHL**	**76**	**6**	**11**	**17**	**41**	**2**	**0**	**1**	**108**	**5.6**	**–15**	**59**	**37.3**	**13:45**	....	....	....	....	....	....	....	....	....
2014-15	**Ottawa**	**NHL**	**26**	**1**	**0**	**1**	**29**	**0**	**0**	**0**	**39**	**2.6**	**–5**	**9**	**66.7**	**9:49**	....	....	....	....	....	....	....	....	....
	Binghamton	AHL	12	5	2	7	13	....	....	....	....	....	....	....	....	....	....	....	....	....	....	....	....	....	....
2015-16	**Ottawa**	**NHL**	**1**	**0**	**0**	**0**	**0**	**0**	**0**	**0**	**2**	**0.0**	**0**	**0**	**0.0**	**4:00**	....	....	....	....	....	....	....	....	....
	Binghamton	AHL	41	7	6	13	52	....	....	....	....	....	....	....	....	....	....	....	....	....	....	....	....	....	....
	Toronto	**NHL**	**30**	**7**	**8**	**15**	**13**	**1**	**0**	**0**	**56**	**12.5**	**–2**	**21**	**61.9**	**14:26**	....	....	....	....	....	....	....	....	....
2016-17	Toronto Marlies	AHL	69	10	14	24	49	....	....	....	....	....	....	....	....	....	11	2	2	4	0	....	....	....	....
	NHL Totals		**286**	**45**	**57**	**102**	**150**	**9**	**0**	**5**	**526**	**8.6**		**222**	**45.0**	**14:14**	**17**	**3**	**2**	**5**	**2**	**0**	**0**	**1**	**15:08**

ECAC Second All-Star Team (2008, 2009, 2010)

Signed as a free agent by **Aalborg** (Denmark), October 21, 2012. • Missed majority of 2014-15 as a healthy reserve. Traded to **Toronto** by **Ottawa** with Jared Cowen, Milan Michalek, Tobias Lindberg and Ottawa's 2nd round pick (Eemeli Rasanen) in 2017 NHL Draft for Dion Phaneuf, Matt Frattin, Casey Bailey, Ryan Rupert and Cody Donaghey, February 9, 2016.

GREER, A.J.

(GREER, AY-JAY) **COL**

Left wing. Shoots left. 6'3", 204 lbs. Born, Joliette, QC, December 14, 1996. Colorado's 2nd pick, 39th overall, in 2015 NHL Draft.

Season	Club	League	GP	G	A	Pts	PIM	PP	SH	GW	S	S%	+/-	TF	F%	Min	GP	G	A	Pts	PIM	PP	SH	GW	Min
2011-12	Esther-Blondin	QAAA	42	15	13	28	75	....	....	....	....	....	....	....	....	....	13	7	3	10	4	....	....	....	....
2012-13	Kimball Union	High-NH	30	16	19	35	....	....	....	....	....	....	....	....	....	....	....	....	....	....	....	....	....	....	....
2013-14	Boston Jr. Bruins	Minor-MA	8	2	4	6	0	....	....	....	....	....	....	....	....	....	....	....	....	....	....	....	....	....	....
	Kimball Union	High-NH	34	24	39	63	....	....	....	....	....	....	....	....	....	....	....	....	....	....	....	....	....	....	....
	Des Moines	USHL	2	2	1	3	2	....	....	....	....	....	....	....	....	....	....	....	....	....	....	....	....	....	....
2014-15	Boston University	H-East	37	3	4	7	18	....	....	....	....	....	....	....	....	....	....	....	....	....	....	....	....	....	....
2015-16	Boston University	H-East	18	1	4	5	10	....	....	....	....	....	....	....	....	....	....	....	....	....	....	....	....	....	....
	Rouyn-Noranda	QMJHL	33	16	11	27	57	....	....	....	....	....	....	....	....	....	20	12	10	22	28	....	....	....	....
2016-17	**Colorado**	**NHL**	**5**	**0**	**1**	**1**	**4**	**0**	**0**	**0**	**8**	**0.0**	**–2**	**0**	**0.0**	**13:39**	....	....	....	....	....	....	....	....	....
	San Antonio	AHL	63	15	23	38	78	....	....	....	....	....	....	....	....	....	....	....	....	....	....	....	....	....	....
	NHL Totals		**5**	**0**	**1**	**1**	**4**	**0**	**0**	**0**	**8**	**0.0**		**0**	**0.0**	**13:39**	....	....	....	....	....	....	....	....	....

GRENIER, Alexandre (GREHN-yay, al-ehx-AHN-druh) FLA

Right wing. Shoots right. 6'5", 200 lbs. Born, Laval, QC, September 5, 1991. Vancouver's 3rd pick, 90th overall, in 2011 NHL Draft.

Season	Club	League	GP	G	A	Pts	PIM	PP	SH	GW	S	S%	+/-	TF	F%	Min	GP	G	A	Pts	PIM	PP	SH	GW	Min
								Regular Season									Playoffs								
2009-10	St-Jerome	QJHL	51	26	28	54	63	....	....	....	....	....	....	....	....	....	7	1	3	4	2	....	....	....	....
2010-11	St-Jerome	QJHL	33	25	35	60	34	....	....	....	....	....	....	....	....	....	....	....	....	....	....	....	....	....	....
	Quebec Remparts	QMJHL	31	9	15	24	6	....	....	....	....	....	....	....	....	....	15	8	8	16	4	....	....	....	....
2011-12	Halifax	QMJHL	64	25	39	64	42	....	....	....	....	....	....	....	....	....	17	4	12	16	19	....	....	....	....
2012-13	Salzburg	Austria	25	5	8	13	21	....	....	....	....	....	....	....	....	....	....	....	....	....	....	....	....	....	....
	Chicago Wolves	AHL	4	0	0	0	2	....	....	....	....	....	....	....	....	....	....	....	....	....	....	....	....	....	....
	Kalamazoo Wings	ECHL	37	10	21	31	51	....	....	....	....	....	....	....	....	....	....	....	....	....	....	....	....	....	....
2013-14	Utica Comets	AHL	68	17	22	39	56	....	....	....	....	....	....	....	....	....	....	....	....	....	....	....	....	....	....
2014-15	Utica Comets	AHL	67	17	26	43	71	....	....	....	....	....	....	....	....	....	23	6	9	15	25	....	....	....	....
2015-16	**Vancouver**	**NHL**	**6**	**0**	**0**	**0**	**2**	**0**	**0**	**0**	**9**	**0.0**	**-4**	**2**	**50.0**	**11:29**	....	....	....	....	....	....	....	....	....
	Utica Comets	AHL	69	16	32	48	43	....	....	....	....	....	....	....	....	....	4	2	1	3	2	....	....	....	....
2016-17	**Vancouver**	**NHL**	**3**	**0**	**0**	**0**	**0**	**0**	**0**	**0**	**1**	**0.0**	**-1**	**2**	**100.0**	**6:29**	....	....	....	....	....	....	....	....	....
	Utica Comets	AHL	69	17	28	45	52	....	....	....	....	....	....	....	....	....	....	....	....	....	....	....	....	....	....
	NHL Totals		**9**	**0**	**0**	**0**	**2**	**0**	**0**	**0**	**10**	**0.0**		**4**	**75.0**	**9:49**	....	....	....	....	....	....	....	....	....

Signed as a free agent by **Salzburg** (Austria), June 1, 2012. Signed as a free agent by **Florida**, July 1, 2017.

GRIFFITH, Seth (GRIH-fihth, SEHTH) BUF

Center. Shoots right. 5'9", 191 lbs. Born, Wallaceburg, ON, January 4, 1993. Boston's 3rd pick, 131st overall, in 2012 NHL Draft.

Season	Club	League	GP	G	A	Pts	PIM	PP	SH	GW	S	S%	+/-	TF	F%	Min	GP	G	A	Pts	PIM	PP	SH	GW	Min
2008-09	Chatham-Kent	Minor-ON	52	42	45	87	112	....	....	....	....	....	....	....	....	....	....	....	....	....	....	....	....	....	....
	Chatham	ON-Jr.B	1	0	0	0	0	....	....	....	....	....	....	....	....	....	....	....	....	....	....	....	....	....	....
2009-10	St. Mary's Lincolns	ON-Jr.B	49	43	35	78	56	....	....	....	....	....	....	....	....	....	5	6	3	9	4	....	....	....	....
	London Knights	OHL	17	2	1	3	2	....	....	....	....	....	....	....	....	....	10	4	3	7	2	....	....	....	....
2010-11	London Knights	OHL	68	22	40	62	28	....	....	....	....	....	....	....	....	....	6	3	4	7	6	....	....	....	....
2011-12	London Knights	OHL	68	45	40	85	49	....	....	....	....	....	....	....	....	....	19	10	13	23	12	....	....	....	....
2012-13	London Knights	OHL	54	33	48	81	52	....	....	....	....	....	....	....	....	....	21	9	16	25	14	....	....	....	....
2013-14	Providence Bruins	AHL	69	20	30	50	28	....	....	....	....	....	....	....	....	....	12	4	7	11	8	....	....	....	....
2014-15	**Boston**	**NHL**	**30**	**6**	**4**	**10**	**6**	**1**	**0**	**1**	**33**	**18.2**	**-2**	**9**	**33.3**	**13:27**	....	....	....	....	....	....	....	....	....
	Providence Bruins	AHL	39	12	19	31	12	....	....	....	....	....	....	....	....	....	5	2	3	5	0	....	....	....	....
2015-16	**Boston**	**NHL**	**4**	**0**	**1**	**1**	**4**	**0**	**0**	**0**	**2**	**0.0**	**-4**	**0**	**0.0**	**9:58**	....	....	....	....	....	....	....	....	....
	Providence Bruins	AHL	57	24	*53	77	32	....	....	....	....	....	....	....	....	....	3	1	2	3	6	....	....	....	....
2016-17	**Toronto**	**NHL**	**3**	**0**	**0**	**0**	**0**	**0**	**0**	**0**	**3**	**0.0**	**0**	**0**	**0.0**	**9:28**	....	....	....	....	....	....	....	....	....
	Toronto Marlies	AHL	38	10	34	44	36	....	....	....	....	....	....	....	....	....	11	2	7	9	4	....	....	....	....
	Florida	**NHL**	**21**	**0**	**5**	**5**	**8**	**0**	**0**	**0**	**18**	**0.0**	**6**	**8**	**25.0**	**13:12**	....	....	....	....	....	....	....	....	....
	NHL Totals		**58**	**6**	**10**	**16**	**18**	**1**	**0**	**1**	**56**	**10.7**		**17**	**29.4**	**12:55**	....	....	....	....	....	....	....	....	....

OHL Second All-Star Team (2012) • OHL First All-Star Team (2013) • AHL First All-Star Team (2016)

Claimed on waivers by **Toronto** from **Boston**, October 11. 2016. Claimed on waivers by **Florida** from **Toronto**, November 12, 2016. Claimed on waivers by **Toronto** from **Florida**, January 20, 2017. Signed as a free agent by **Buffalo**, July 1, 2017.

GRIGORENKO, Mikhail (grih-gohr-EHN-koh, mih-khigh-IHL)

Center. Shoots left. 6'3", 209 lbs. Born, Khabarovsk, Russia, May 16, 1994. Buffalo's 1st pick, 12th overall, in 2012 NHL Draft.

Season	Club	League	GP	G	A	Pts	PIM	PP	SH	GW	S	S%	+/-	TF	F%	Min	GP	G	A	Pts	PIM	PP	SH	GW	Min
2010-11	CSKA Jr.	Russia-Jr.	43	17	18	35	22	....	....	....	....	....	....	....	....	....	10	1	4	5	4	....	....	....	....
2011-12	Quebec Remparts	QMJHL	59	40	45	85	12	....	....	....	....	....	....	....	....	....	11	3	7	10	4	....	....	....	....
2012-13	Quebec Remparts	QMJHL	33	30	24	54	8	....	....	....	....	....	....	....	....	....	11	5	9	14	0	....	....	....	....
	Buffalo	**NHL**	**25**	**1**	**4**	**5**	**0**	**0**	**0**	**0**	**31**	**3.2**	**-1**	**149**	**38.3**	**10:14**	....	....	....	....	....	....	....	....	....
	Rochester	AHL	....	....	....	....	....	....	....	....	....	....	....	....	....	....	2	0	0	0	0	....	....	....	....
2013-14	**Buffalo**	**NHL**	**18**	**2**	**1**	**3**	**2**	**0**	**0**	**0**	**20**	**10.0**	**-3**	**103**	**51.5**	**11:26**	....	....	....	....	....	....	....	....	....
	Quebec Remparts	QMJHL	23	15	24	39	6	....	....	....	....	....	....	....	....	....	5	1	8	9	6	....	....	....	....
	Rochester	AHL	9	0	4	4	0	....	....	....	....	....	....	....	....	....	5	0	0	0	2	....	....	....	....
2014-15	**Buffalo**	**NHL**	**25**	**3**	**3**	**6**	**2**	**1**	**0**	**0**	**35**	**8.6**	**-10**	**331**	**46.2**	**15:10**	....	....	....	....	....	....	....	....	....
	Rochester	AHL	43	14	22	36	27	....	....	....	....	....	....	....	....	....	....	....	....	....	....	....	....	....	....
2015-16	**Colorado**	**NHL**	**74**	**6**	**21**	**27**	**8**	**1**	**0**	**0**	**84**	**7.1**	**2**	**349**	**43.3**	**13:16**	....	....	....	....	....	....	....	....	....
2016-17	**Colorado**	**NHL**	**75**	**10**	**13**	**23**	**18**	**0**	**0**	**0**	**85**	**11.8**	**-14**	**192**	**57.8**	**14:05**	....	....	....	....	....	....	....	....	....
	NHL Totals		**217**	**22**	**42**	**64**	**30**	**2**	**0**	**0**	**255**	**8.6**		**1124**	**46.7**	**13:16**	....	....	....	....	....	....	....	....	....

QMJHL All-Rookie Team (2012) • QMJHL First All-Star Team (2012) • Canadian Major Junior Rookie of the Year (2012)

Traded to **Colorado** by **Buffalo** with Nikita Zadorov, J.T. Compher and Buffalo's 2nd round pick (later traded to San Jose – San Jose selected Jeremy Roy) in 2015 NHL Draft for Ryan O'Reilly and Jamie McGinn, June 26, 2015.

GRIMALDI, Rocco (grih-MAL-dee, RAW-koh) COL

Center. Shoots right. 5'6", 180 lbs. Born, Anaheim, CA, February 8, 1993. Florida's 2nd pick, 33rd overall, in 2011 NHL Draft.

Season	Club	League	GP	G	A	Pts	PIM	PP	SH	GW	S	S%	+/-	TF	F%	Min	GP	G	A	Pts	PIM	PP	SH	GW	Min
2008-09	Det. Lit. Caesars	T1EHL	32	11	9	20	22	....	....	....	....	....	....	....	....	....	7	1	5	6	0	....	....	....	....
	Det. Lit. Caesars	Other	19	19	15	34		....	....	....	....	....	....	....	....	....	....	....	....	....	....	....	....	....	....
2009-10	USAHNTDP	USHL	32	11	9	20	22	....	....	....	....	....	....	....	....	....	....	....	....	....	....	....	....	....	....
	USAHNTDP	U-17	16	7	18	25	20	....	....	....	....	....	....	....	....	....	....	....	....	....	....	....	....	....	....
	USAHNTDP	U-18	14	3	15	18	12	....	....	....	....	....	....	....	....	....	....	....	....	....	....	....	....	....	....
2010-11	USAHNTDP	USHL	23	12	13	25	18	....	....	....	....	....	....	....	....	....	....	....	....	....	....	....	....	....	....
	USAHNTDP	U-18	35	27	21	48	47	....	....	....	....	....	....	....	....	....	....	....	....	....	....	....	....	....	....
2011-12	North Dakota	WCHA	4	1	1	2	2	....	....	....	....	....	....	....	....	....	....	....	....	....	....	....	....	....	....
2012-13	North Dakota	WCHA	40	13	23	36	18	....	....	....	....	....	....	....	....	....	....	....	....	....	....	....	....	....	....
2013-14	North Dakota	NCHC	42	17	22	39	48	....	....	....	....	....	....	....	....	....	....	....	....	....	....	....	....	....	....
2014-15	**Florida**	**NHL**	**7**	**1**	**0**	**1**	**4**	**0**	**0**	**0**	**18**	**5.6**	**1**	**14**	**42.9**	**12:37**	....	....	....	....	....	....	....	....	....
	San Antonio	AHL	64	14	28	42	22	....	....	....	....	....	....	....	....	....	3	1	0	1	4	....	....	....	....
2015-16	**Florida**	**NHL**	**20**	**3**	**2**	**5**	**2**	**0**	**0**	**0**	**29**	**10.3**	**-4**	**108**	**43.5**	**11:52**	**2**	**0**	**0**	**0**	**2**	**0**	**0**	**0**	**10:30**
	Portland Pirates	AHL	52	16	17	33	20	....	....	....	....	....	....	....	....	....	5	0	4	4	0	....	....	....	....
2016-17	**Colorado**	**NHL**	**4**	**0**	**1**	**1**	**2**	**0**	**0**	**0**	**11**	**0.0**	**-3**	**0**	**0.0**	**11:00**	....	....	....	....	....	....	....	....	....
	San Antonio	AHL	72	31	24	55	39	....	....	....	....	....	....	....	....	....	....	....	....	....	....	....	....	....	....
	NHL Totals		**31**	**4**	**3**	**7**	**8**	**0**	**0**	**0**	**58**	**6.9**		**122**	**43.4**	**11:55**	**2**	**0**	**0**	**0**	**2**	**0**	**0**	**0**	**10:30**

WCHA All-Rookie Team (2013)

• Missed majority of 2011-12 due to knee injury in training camp. Traded to **Colorado** by **Florida** for Reto Berra, June 23, 2016.

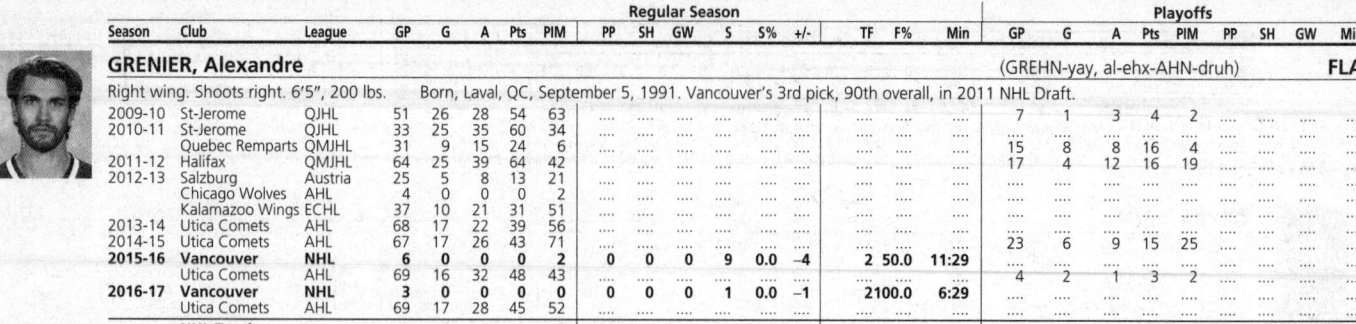

GROSSMANN, Nicklas (GROHS-man, NIHK-luhs)

Defense. Shoots left. 6'4", 230 lbs. Born, Stockholm, Sweden, January 22, 1985. Dallas' 4th pick, 56th overall, in 2004 NHL Draft.

Season	Club	League	GP	G	A	Pts	PIM	PP	SH	GW	S	S%	+/-	TF	F%	Min	GP	G	A	Pts	PIM	PP	SH	GW	Min
2002-03	Sodertalje SK Jr.	Swe-Jr.	34	1	1	2	32	....	....	....	....	....	....	....	....	....	....	....	....	....	....	....	....	....	....
2003-04	Sodertalje SK Jr.	Swe-Jr.	33	1	2	3	32	....	....	....	....	....	....	....	....	....	2	0	0	0	0	....	....	....	....
	Sodertalje SK	Sweden	1	0	0	0	0	....	....	....	....	....	....	....	....	....	....	....	....	....	....	....	....	....	....
2004-05	Sodertalje SK Jr.	Swe-Jr.	12	3	6	9	8	....	....	....	....	....	....	....	....	....	1	0	0	0	0	....	....	....	....
	Sodertalje SK	Sweden	31	0	2	2	14	....	....	....	....	....	....	....	....	....	9	0	0	0	0	....	....	....	....
2005-06	Iowa Stars	AHL	61	2	3	5	49	....	....	....	....	....	....	....	....	....	7	0	1	1	4	....	....	....	....
2006-07	**Dallas**	**NHL**	**8**	**0**	**0**	**0**	**4**	**0**	**0**	**0**	**8**	**0.0**	**-1**	**0**	**0.0**	**12:49**	....	....	....	....	....	....	....	....	....
	Iowa Stars	AHL	67	2	8	10	40	....	....	....	....	....	....	....	....	....	8	0	0	0	10	....	....	....	....
2007-08	**Dallas**	**NHL**	**62**	**0**	**7**	**7**	**22**	**0**	**0**	**0**	**34**	**0.0**	**10**	**0**	**0.0**	**15:33**	**18**	**1**	**1**	**2**	**6**	**0**	**0**	**0**	**18:37**
	Iowa Stars	AHL	10	0	0	0	10	....	....	....	....	....	....	....	....	....	....	....	....	....	....	....	....	....	....
2008-09	**Dallas**	**NHL**	**81**	**2**	**10**	**12**	**51**	**0**	**0**	**1**	**60**	**3.3**	**-8**	**0**	**0.0**	**17:39**	....	....	....	....	....	....	....	....	....
2009-10	**Dallas**	**NHL**	**71**	**0**	**7**	**7**	**32**	**0**	**0**	**0**	**58**	**0.0**	**-3**	**1**	**0.0**	**19:11**	....	....	....	....	....	....	....	....	....
2010-11	**Dallas**	**NHL**	**59**	**1**	**9**	**10**	**35**	**0**	**0**	**0**	**38**	**2.6**	**7**	**0**	**0.0**	**18:12**	....	....	....	....	....	....	....	....	....
2011-12	**Dallas**	**NHL**	**52**	**0**	**5**	**5**	**26**	**0**	**0**	**0**	**38**	**0.0**	**0**	**0**	**0.0**	**18:59**	....	....	....	....	....	....	....	....	....
	Philadelphia	**NHL**	**22**	**0**	**6**	**6**	**10**	**0**	**0**	**0**	**18**	**0.0**	**5**	**0**	**0.0**	**18:25**	**9**	**0**	**1**	**1**	**8**	**0**	**0**	**0**	**18:55**
2012-13	Sodertalje SK	Sweden-2	4	0	1	1	4	....	....	....	....	....	....	....	....	....	....	....	....	....	....	....	....	....	....
	Philadelphia	**NHL**	**30**	**1**	**3**	**4**	**21**	**0**	**0**	**0**	**21**	**4.8**	**-1**	**0**	**0.0**	**18:20**	....	....	....	....	....	....	....	....	....
2013-14	**Philadelphia**	**NHL**	**78**	**1**	**13**	**14**	**55**	**0**	**0**	**0**	**71**	**1.4**	**-6**	**0**	**0.0**	**19:07**	**4**	**0**	**0**	**0**	**2**	**0**	**0**	**0**	**16:24**
2014-15	**Philadelphia**	**NHL**	**68**	**5**	**9**	**14**	**32**	**0**	**0**	**0**	**43**	**11.6**	**8**	**0**	**0.0**	**17:39**	....	....	....	....	....	....	....	....	....
2015-16	**Arizona**	**NHL**	**58**	**3**	**4**	**7**	**24**	**0**	**0**	**1**	**42**	**7.1**	**-3**	**0**	**0.0**	**17:47**	....	....	....	....	....	....	....	....	....

Season	Club	League	GP	G	A	Pts	PIM	PP	SH	GW	S	S%	+/-	TF	F%	Min	GP	G	A	Pts	PIM	PP	SH	GW	Min
			Regular Season														Playoffs								
2016-17	Calgary	NHL	3	0	0	0	2	0	0	0	3	0.0	–4	0	0.0	13:01	....	....	....	....	....	....	....	....	....
	Orebro HK	Sweden	28	0	2	2	10	....	....	....	....	....	....	....	....	....	....	....	....	....	....	....	....	....	....
	NHL Totals		592	13	73	86	314	0	0	2	434	3.0		1	0.0	17:58	31	1	2	3	16	0	0	0	18:25

Traded to **Philadelphia** by **Dallas** for Los Angeles' 2nd round pick (previously acquired, Dallas selected Devin Shore) in 2012 NHL Draft and Minnesota's 3rd round pick (previously acquired, later traded to Pittsburgh – Pittsburgh selected Jake Guentzel) in 2013 NHL Draft, February 16, 2012. Signed as a free agent by **Sodertalje** (Sweden-2), November 14, 2012. Traded to **Arizona** by **Philadelphia** with Chris Pronger for Sam Gagner and Arizona's 3rd round pick (Otto Koivula) in 2016 NHL Draft, June 27, 2015. Signed as a free agent by **Calgary**, October 11, 2016. Signed as a free agent by **Orebro** (Sweden), December 1, 2016.

GRYBA, Eric (GREE-buh, AIR-ihk) EDM

Defense. Shoots right. 6'4", 225 lbs. Born, Saskatoon, SK, April 14, 1988. Ottawa's 2nd pick, 68th overall, in 2006 NHL Draft.

Season	Club	League	GP	G	A	Pts	PIM	PP	SH	GW	S	S%	+/-	TF	F%	Min	GP	G	A	Pts	PIM	PP	SH	GW	Min
2003-04	Sask. Contacts	SMHL	39	1	10	11	89	....	....	....	....	....	....	....	....	....	10	4	8	12	20	....	....	....	....
2004-05	Sask. Contacts	SMHL	32	11	29	40	83	....	....	....	....	....	....	....	....	....	11	5	7	12	22	....	....	....	....
2005-06	Green Bay	USHL	56	3	12	15	*205	....	....	....	....	....	....	....	....	....	3	1	1	2	27	....	....	....	....
2006-07	Boston University	H-East	38	1	3	4	76	....	....	....	....	....	....	....	....	....	....	....	....	....	....	....	....	....	....
2007-08	Boston University	H-East	32	1	1	2	54	....	....	....	....	....	....	....	....	....	....	....	....	....	....	....	....	....	....
2008-09	Boston University	H-East	45	0	6	6	106	....	....	....	....	....	....	....	....	....	....	....	....	....	....	....	....	....	....
2009-10	Boston University	H-East	38	4	6	10	*118	....	....	....	....	....	....	....	....	....	....	....	....	....	....	....	....	....	....
	Binghamton	AHL	6	1	0	1	2	....	....	....	....	....	....	....	....	....	....	....	....	....	....	....	....	....	....
2010-11	Binghamton	AHL	66	3	4	7	133	....	....	....	....	....	....	....	....	....	10	0	1	1	26	....	....	....	....
2011-12	Binghamton	AHL	73	5	15	20	95	....	....	....	....	....	....	....	....	....	....	....	....	....	....	....	....	....	....
2012-13	Binghamton	AHL	38	5	6	11	75	....	....	....	....	....	....	....	....	....	....	....	....	....	....	....	....	....	....
	Ottawa	NHL	33	2	4	6	26	0	0	0	51	3.9	–3	0	0.0	20:17	4	0	0	0	17	0	0	0	12:12
2013-14	Ottawa	NHL	57	2	9	11	64	0	0	0	57	3.5	9	0	0.0	17:31	....	....	....	....	....	....	....	....	....
2014-15	Ottawa	NHL	75	0	12	12	97	0	0	0	64	0.0	11	0	0.0	15:39	6	0	0	0	14	0	0	0	16:07
2015-16	Edmonton	NHL	53	1	5	6	75	0	0	0	58	1.7	0	0	0.0	17:53	....	....	....	....	....	....	....	....	....
2016-17	Edmonton	NHL	40	2	4	6	65	0	0	2	45	4.4	–5	0	0.0	16:08	3	0	0	0	4	0	0	0	14:08
	NHL Totals		258	7	34	41	327	0	0	2	275	2.5		0	0.0	17:11	13	0	0	0	35	0	0	0	14:27

Traded to **Edmonton** by **Ottawa** for Travis Ewanyk and Pittsburgh's 4th round pick (previously acquired, Ottawa selected Christian Wolanin) in 2015 NHL Draft, June 27, 2015. • Missed majority of 2016-17 as a healthy reserve.

GRZELCYK, Matt (GRIHZ-lihk, MAT) BOS

Defense. Shoots left. 5'9", 174 lbs. Born, Charlestown, MA, January 5, 1994. Boston's 2nd pick, 85th overall, in 2012 NHL Draft.

Season	Club	League	GP	G	A	Pts	PIM	PP	SH	GW	S	S%	+/-	TF	F%	Min	GP	G	A	Pts	PIM	PP	SH	GW	Min
2009-10	Belmont Hill	High-MA	31	2	18	20	30	....	....	....	....	....	....	....	....	....	....	....	....	....	....	....	....	....	....
2010-11	USAHNTDP	USHL	36	1	9	10	28	....	....	....	....	....	....	....	....	....	2	0	0	0	2	....	....	....	....
	USAHNTDP	U-17	17	1	7	8	10	....	....	....	....	....	....	....	....	....	....	....	....	....	....	....	....	....	....
2011-12	USAHNTDP	USHL	24	1	10	11	6	....	....	....	....	....	....	....	....	....	....	....	....	....	....	....	....	....	....
	USAHNTDP	U-18	36	2	19	21	16	....	....	....	....	....	....	....	....	....	....	....	....	....	....	....	....	....	....
2012-13	Boston University	H-East	38	3	20	23	26	....	....	....	....	....	....	....	....	....	....	....	....	....	....	....	....	....	....
2013-14	Boston University	H-East	19	3	8	11	16	....	....	....	....	....	....	....	....	....	....	....	....	....	....	....	....	....	....
2014-15	Boston University	H-East	41	10	28	38	36	....	....	....	....	....	....	....	....	....	....	....	....	....	....	....	....	....	....
2015-16	Boston University	H-East	27	10	13	23	36	....	....	....	....	....	....	....	....	....	....	....	....	....	....	....	....	....	....
2016-17	Boston	NHL	2	0	0	0	2	0	0	0	4	0.0	0	0	0.0	12:29	....	....	....	....	....	....	....	....	....
	Providence Bruins	AHL	70	6	26	32	18	....	....	....	....	....	....	....	....	....	17	0	3	3	8	....	....	....	....
	NHL Totals		2	0	0	0	2	0	0	0	4	0.0		0	0.0	12:29	....	....	....	....	....	....	....	....	....

Hockey East All-Rookie Team (2013) • Hockey East First All-Star Team (2015, 2016) • NCAA East First All-American Team (2015, 2016) • NCAA Championship All-Tournament Team (2015)

GUDAS, Radko (GOO-duhs, RAHD-koh) PHI

Defense. Shoots right. 6', 204 lbs. Born, Prague, Czech., June 5, 1990. Tampa Bay's 3rd pick, 66th overall, in 2010 NHL Draft.

Season	Club	League	GP	G	A	Pts	PIM	PP	SH	GW	S	S%	+/-	TF	F%	Min	GP	G	A	Pts	PIM	PP	SH	GW	Min
2004-05	HC Kladno U17	CzR-U17	46	1	5	6	70	....	....	....	....	....	....	....	....	....	7	0	0	0	10	....	....	....	....
2005-06	HC Kladno U17	CzR-U17	46	12	14	26	178	....	....	....	....	....	....	....	....	....	5	1	2	3	8	....	....	....	....
2006-07	HC Kladno U17	CzR-U17	16	6	7	13	34	....	....	....	....	....	....	....	....	....	7	4	1	5	14	....	....	....	....
	Kladno Jr.	CzRep-Jr.	15	0	1	1	18	....	....	....	....	....	....	....	....	....	1	0	0	0	0	....	....	....	....
	Beroun	CzRep-2	9	0	1	1	6	....	....	....	....	....	....	....	....	....	....	....	....	....	....	....	....	....	....
2007-08	Beroun	CzRep-2	43	1	5	6	90	....	....	....	....	....	....	....	....	....	....	....	....	....	....	....	....	....	....
	Kladno	CzRep	....	....	....	....	....	....	....	....	....	....	....	....	....	....	1	0	0	0	0	....	....	....	....
2008-09	Kladno Jr.	CzRep-Jr.	2	0	1	1	0	....	....	....	....	....	....	....	....	....	....	....	....	....	....	....	....	....	....
	Beroun	CzRep-2	32	1	6	7	110	....	....	....	....	....	....	....	....	....	....	....	....	....	....	....	....	....	....
	Kladno	CzRep	14	0	1	1	10	....	....	....	....	....	....	....	....	....	....	....	....	....	....	....	....	....	....
2009-10	Everett Silvertips	WHL	65	7	30	37	151	....	....	....	....	....	....	....	....	....	3	0	2	2	4	....	....	....	....
2010-11	Norfolk Admirals	AHL	76	4	13	17	165	....	....	....	....	....	....	....	....	....	6	0	0	0	7	....	....	....	....
2011-12	Norfolk Admirals	AHL	73	7	13	20	195	....	....	....	....	....	....	....	....	....	16	0	3	3	14	....	....	....	....
2012-13	Syracuse Crunch	AHL	57	4	16	20	207	....	....	....	....	....	....	....	....	....	12	2	1	3	34	....	....	....	....
	Tampa Bay	NHL	22	2	3	5	38	0	0	1	31	6.5	3	0	0.0	17:00	....	....	....	....	....	....	....	....	....
2013-14	Tampa Bay	NHL	73	3	19	22	152	1	0	1	114	2.6	2	0	0.0	19:08	3	0	1	1	9	0	0	0	19:07
	Czech Republic	Olympics	3	0	0	0	0	....	....	....	....	....	....	....	....	....	....	....	....	....	....	....	....	....	....
2014-15	Tampa Bay	NHL	31	2	3	5	34	0	0	1	63	3.2	–5	0	0.0	17:00	....	....	....	....	....	....	....	....	....
2015-16	Philadelphia	NHL	76	5	9	14	116	0	0	1	150	3.3	–3	0	0.0	19:51	6	0	0	0	18	0	0	0	19:37
2016-17	Philadelphia	NHL	67	6	17	23	93	0	0	0	113	5.3	8	0	0.0	19:18	....	....	....	....	....	....	....	....	....
	NHL Totals		269	18	51	69	433	1	0	4	471	3.8		0	0.0	18:57	9	0	1	1	27	0	0	0	19:27

WHL West Second All-Star Team (2010)

Traded to **Philadelphia** by **Tampa Bay** with Tampa Bay's 1st (later traded to Columbus – Columbus selected Gabriel Carlsson) and 3rd (Matej Tomek) round picks in 2015 NHL Draft for Braydon Coburn, March 2, 2015. • Missed majority of 2014-15 due to knee injury vs. Toronto, December 29, 2014.

GUDBRANSON, Erik (guhd-BRAN-suhn, AIR-ihk) VAN

Defense. Shoots right. 6'5", 216 lbs. Born, Ottawa, ON, January 7, 1992. Florida's 1st pick, 3rd overall, in 2010 NHL Draft.

Season	Club	League	GP	G	A	Pts	PIM	PP	SH	GW	S	S%	+/-	TF	F%	Min	GP	G	A	Pts	PIM	PP	SH	GW	Min
2007-08	Ottawa Jr. 67's	Minor-ON	70	15	40	55	118	....	....	....	....	....	....	....	....	....	....	....	....	....	....	....	....	....	....
2008-09	Kingston	OHL	63	3	19	22	69	....	....	....	....	....	....	....	....	....	....	....	....	....	....	....	....	....	....
2009-10	Kingston	OHL	41	2	21	23	68	....	....	....	....	....	....	....	....	....	7	1	2	3	6	....	....	....	....
2010-11	Kingston	OHL	44	12	22	34	105	....	....	....	....	....	....	....	....	....	5	1	3	4	10	....	....	....	....
2011-12	Florida	NHL	72	2	6	8	78	0	0	0	76	2.6	–19	0	0.0	14:12	7	0	0	0	8	0	0	0	17:07
2012-13	San Antonio	AHL	2	0	0	0	2	....	....	....	....	....	....	....	....	....	....	....	....	....	....	....	....	....	....
	Florida	NHL	32	0	4	4	47	0	0	0	49	0.0	–22	0	0.0	18:45	....	....	....	....	....	....	....	....	....
2013-14	Florida	NHL	65	3	6	9	114	0	0	0	92	3.3	–7	0	0.0	17:59	....	....	....	....	....	....	....	....	....
2014-15	Florida	NHL	76	4	9	13	58	0	0	0	110	3.6	–4	0	0.0	18:37	....	....	....	....	....	....	....	....	....
2015-16	Florida	NHL	64	2	7	9	49	0	0	0	73	2.7	3	0	0.0	20:07	6	0	0	0	2	0	0	0	26:54
2016-17	Vancouver	NHL	30	1	5	6	18	0	0	1	40	2.5	–14	0	0.0	20:20	....	....	....	....	....	....	....	....	....
	NHL Totals		339	12	37	49	364	0	0	1	440	2.7		0	0.0	18:00	13	0	0	0	10	0	0	0	21:38

Traded to **Vancouver** by **Florida** with NY Islanders' 5th round pick (previously acquired, Vancouver selected Cole Candella) in 2016 NHL Draft for Jared McCann, Vancouver's 2nd (later traded to Buffalo – Buffalo selected Rasmus Asplund) and 4th (Jonathan Ang) round picks in 2016 NHL Draft, May 25, 2016. • Missed majority of 2016-17 due to recurring wrist injury and resulting surgery.

GUENIN, Nate (GEH-nihn, NAYT)

Defense. Shoots right. 6'3", 207 lbs. Born, Alquippa, PA, December 10, 1982. NY Rangers' 3rd pick, 127th overall, in 2002 NHL Draft.

Season	Club	League	GP	G	A	Pts	PIM	PP	SH	GW	S	S%	+/-	TF	F%	Min	GP	G	A	Pts	PIM	PP	SH	GW	Min
99-2000	Pittsburgh	AAHA	40	3	10	13	122	....	....	....	....	....	....	....	....	....	....	....	....	....	....	....	....	....	....
2000-01	Green Bay	USHL	54	2	11	13	70	....	....	....	....	....	....	....	....	....	4	1	1	2	6	....	....	....	....
2001-02	Green Bay	USHL	56	4	11	15	150	....	....	....	....	....	....	....	....	....	7	3	3	6	10	....	....	....	....
2002-03	Ohio State	CCHA	42	2	9	11	75	....	....	....	....	....	....	....	....	....	....	....	....	....	....	....	....	....	....
2003-04	Ohio State	CCHA	29	2	15	17	92	....	....	....	....	....	....	....	....	....	....	....	....	....	....	....	....	....	....
2004-05	Ohio State	CCHA	41	2	12	14	136	....	....	....	....	....	....	....	....	....	....	....	....	....	....	....	....	....	....
2005-06	Ohio State	CCHA	39	0	11	11	87	....	....	....	....	....	....	....	....	....	....	....	....	....	....	....	....	....	....
2006-07	Philadelphia	NHL	9	0	2	2	4	0	0	0	0	0.0	0	0	0.0	8:40	....	....	....	....	....	....	....	....	....
	Philadelphia	AHL	68	3	9	12	92	....	....	....	....	....	....	....	....	....	....	....	....	....	....	....	....	....	....
2007-08	Philadelphia	NHL	2	0	0	0	2	0	0	0	0	0.0	2	0	0.0	9:57	....	....	....	....	....	....	....	....	....
	Philadelphia	AHL	77	4	13	17	146	....	....	....	....	....	....	....	....	....	12	0	1	1	18	....	....	....	....

			Regular Season														Playoffs								
Season	Club	League	GP	G	A	Pts	PIM	PP	SH	GW	S	S%	+/-	TF	F%	Min	GP	G	A	Pts	PIM	PP	SH	GW	Min
2008-09	Philadelphia	NHL	1	0	0	0	0	0	0	0	0	0.0	0	0	0.0	13:25	....	....	....	....	....	....	....	....	....
	Philadelphia	AHL	62	0	14	14	95	....	....	....	....	....	....	....	....	....	4	0	0	0	10	....	....	....	....
2009-10	Pittsburgh	NHL	2	0	0	0	0	0	0	0	1	0.0	-2	0	0.0	13:32	....	....	....	....	....	....	....	....	....
	Wilkes-Barre	AHL	41	3	2	5	63	....	....	....	....	....	....	....	....	....	....	....	....	....	....	....	....	....	....
	Peoria Rivermen	AHL	27	2	11	13	35	....	....	....	....	....	....	....	....	....	....	....	....	....	....	....	....	....	....
2010-11	Columbus	NHL	3	0	0	0	2	0	0	0	2	0.0	-3	0	0.0	14:48	....	....	....	....	....	....	....	....	....
	Springfield	AHL	30	0	5	5	21	....	....	....	....	....	....	....	....	....	....	....	....	....	....	....	....	....	....
	Syracuse Crunch	AHL	43	2	10	12	44	....	....	....	....	....	....	....	....	....	....	....	....	....	....	....	....	....	....
2011-12	Anaheim	NHL	15	2	0	2	6	0	0	1	5	40.0	6	0	0.0	11:09	....	....	....	....	....	....	....	....	....
	Syracuse Crunch	AHL	27	0	5	5	16	....	....	....	....	....	....	....	....	....	4	0	0	0	14	....	....	....	....
2012-13	Norfolk Admirals	AHL	66	4	20	24	38	....	....	....	....	....	....	....	....	....	....	....	....	....	....	....	....	....	....
2013-14	Colorado	NHL	68	1	8	9	46	0	0	0	52	1.9	3	0	0.0	17:17	7	0	1	1	4	0	0	0	16:00
2014-15	Colorado	NHL	76	2	13	15	32	0	0	0	38	5.3	-1	0	0.0	16:51	....	....	....	....	....	....	....	....	....
2015-16	Colorado	NHL	29	0	0	0	2	0	0	0	10	0.0	2	0	0.0	13:04	....	....	....	....	....	....	....	....	....
	San Antonio	AHL	24	2	9	11	14	....	....	....	....	....	....	....	....	....	....	....	....	....	....	....	....	....	....
2016-17	San Diego Gulls	AHL	56	2	10	12	28	....	....	....	....	....	....	....	....	....	10	1	1	2	0	....	....	....	....
	NHL Totals		205	5	23	28	94	0	0	1	108	4.6		0	0.0	15:32	7	0	1	1	4	0	0	0	16:00

USHL All-Rookie Team (2001) • CCHA Second All-Star Team (2005)

Signed as a free agent by **Philadelphia**, August 16, 2006. Signed as a free agent by **Pittsburgh**, July 3, 2009. Traded to **St. Louis** by **Pittsburgh** for Steve Wagner, February 11, 2010. Signed as a free agent by **Columbus**, July 2, 2010. Traded to **Anaheim** by **Columbus** for Trevor Smith, January 4, 2011. Signed as a free agent by **Colorado**, July 5, 2013. Signed as a free agent by **Anaheim**, July 2, 2016.

GUENTZEL, Jake

(GUHNT-zuhl, JAYK) **PIT**

Center. Shoots left. 5'10", 167 lbs. Born, Omaha, NE, October 6, 1994. Pittsburgh's 2nd pick, 77th overall, in 2013 NHL Draft.

Season	Club	League	GP	G	A	Pts	PIM	PP	SH	GW	S	S%	+/-	TF	F%	Min	GP	G	A	Pts	PIM	PP	SH	GW	Min
2010-11	Team Northwest	UMHSEL	15	6	5	11	4	....	....	....	....	....	....	....	....	....	3	0	0	0	0	....	....	....	....
	Hill-Murray	High-MN	25	15	28	43	10	....	....	....	....	....	....	....	....	....	3	4	2	6	4	....	....	....	....
2011-12	Team Southeast	UMHSEL	21	14	27	41	8	....	....	....	....	....	....	....	....	....	3	0	3	3	0	....	....	....	....
	Hill-Murray	High-MN	25	21	46	67	16	....	....	....	....	....	....	....	....	....	6	2	6	8	0	....	....	....	....
2012-13	Sioux City	USHL	60	29	44	73	24	....	....	....	....	....	....	....	....	....	....	....	....	....	....	....	....	....	....
2013-14	Nebraska-Omaha	NCHC	37	7	27	34	16	....	....	....	....	....	....	....	....	....	....	....	....	....	....	....	....	....	....
2014-15	Nebraska-Omaha	NCHC	36	14	25	39	34	....	....	....	....	....	....	....	....	....	....	....	....	....	....	....	....	....	....
2015-16	Nebraska-Omaha	NCHC	35	19	27	46	20	....	....	....	....	....	....	....	....	....	....	....	....	....	....	....	....	....	....
	Wilkes-Barre	AHL	11	2	4	6	0	....	....	....	....	....	....	....	....	....	10	5	9	14	0	....	....	....	....
2016-17 ♦	Pittsburgh	NHL	40	16	17	33	10	1	0	0	81	19.8	7	17	47.1	15:53	25	*13	8	21	10	1	1	*5	17:30
	Wilkes-Barre	AHL	33	21	21	42	12	....	....	....	....	....	....	....	....	....	....	....	....	....	....	....	....	....	....
	NHL Totals		40	16	17	33	10	1	0	0	81	19.8		17	47.1	15:53	25	13	8	21	10	1	1	5	17:30

USHL All-Rookie Team (2013) • USHL Second All-Star Team (2013) • USHL Rookie of the Year (2013) • NCHC All-Rookie Team (2014) • NCHC Second All-Star Team (2016) • AHL All-Rookie Team (2017)

GUHLE, Brendan

(GOO-lee, BREHN-duhn) **BUF**

Defense. Shoots left. 6'2", 192 lbs. Born, Edmonton, AB, July 29, 1997. Buffalo's 2nd pick, 51st overall, in 2015 NHL Draft.

Season	Club	League	GP	G	A	Pts	PIM	PP	SH	GW	S	S%	+/-	TF	F%	Min	GP	G	A	Pts	PIM	PP	SH	GW	Min
2012-13	Sherwood Park	AMHL	32	3	8	11	34	....	....	....	....	....	....	....	....	....	9	1	4	5	10	....	....	....	....
2013-14	Prince Albert	WHL	51	0	10	10	29	....	....	....	....	....	....	....	....	....	4	1	1	2	0	....	....	....	....
2014-15	Prince Albert	WHL	72	5	27	32	36	....	....	....	....	....	....	....	....	....	....	....	....	....	....	....	....	....	....
2015-16	Prince Albert	WHL	63	10	18	28	53	....	....	....	....	....	....	....	....	....	5	0	3	3	6	....	....	....	....
	Rochester	AHL	6	1	3	4	0	....	....	....	....	....	....	....	....	....	....	....	....	....	....	....	....	....	....
2016-17	Prince Albert	WHL	15	2	2	4	10	....	....	....	....	....	....	....	....	....	....	....	....	....	....	....	....	....	....
	Prince George	WHL	32	13	16	29	22	....	....	....	....	....	....	....	....	....	6	0	6	6	4	....	....	....	....
	Buffalo	NHL	3	0	0	0	0	0	0	0	4	0.0	1	0	0.0	16:21	....	....	....	....	....	....	....	....	....
	Rochester	AHL	6	1	1	2	2	....	....	....	....	....	....	....	....	....	....	....	....	....	....	....	....	....	....
	NHL Totals		3	0	0	0	0	0	0	0	4	0.0		0	0.0	16:21	....	....	....	....	....	....	....	....	....

• Called up by Buffalor on an emergency basis due to foot injury to D Josh Gorges, December 2, 2016.

GUNNARSSON, Carl

(GUHN-nuhr-suhn, KARL) **ST.L.**

Defense. Shoots left. 6'2", 196 lbs. Born, Orebro, Sweden, November 9, 1986. Toronto's 6th pick, 194th overall, in 2007 NHL Draft.

Season	Club	League	GP	G	A	Pts	PIM	PP	SH	GW	S	S%	+/-	TF	F%	Min	GP	G	A	Pts	PIM	PP	SH	GW	Min
2003-04	HC Orebro 90	Sweden-2	43	0	4	4	16	....	....	....	....	....	....	....	....	....	....	....	....	....	....	....	....	....	....
2004-05	Linkoping U18	Swe-U18	1	0	1	1	2	....	....	....	....	....	....	....	....	....	....	....	....	....	....	....	....	....	....
	Linkopings HC Jr.	Swe-Jr.	22	2	5	7	24	....	....	....	....	....	....	....	....	....	....	....	....	....	....	....	....	....	....
2005-06	Linkopings HC Jr.	Swe-Jr.	30	7	6	13	26	....	....	....	....	....	....	....	....	....	4	1	0	1	4	....	....	....	....
	IFK Arboga IK	Sweden-2	12	1	5	6	8	....	....	....	....	....	....	....	....	....	....	....	....	....	....	....	....	....	....
	Linkopings HC	Sweden	14	0	0	0	0	....	....	....	....	....	....	....	....	....	....	....	....	....	....	....	....	....	....
2006-07	Linkopings HC Jr.	Swe-Jr.	6	0	5	5	6	....	....	....	....	....	....	....	....	....	....	....	....	....	....	....	....	....	....
	VIK Vasteras HK	Sweden-2	15	2	3	5	14	....	....	....	....	....	....	....	....	....	....	....	....	....	....	....	....	....	....
	Linkopings HC	Sweden	30	2	2	4	8	....	....	....	....	....	....	....	....	....	15	0	4	4	4	....	....	....	....
2007-08	Linkopings HC	Sweden	53	2	7	9	26	....	....	....	....	....	....	....	....	....	16	0	4	4	10	....	....	....	....
2008-09	Linkopings HC	Sweden	53	6	10	16	26	....	....	....	....	....	....	....	....	....	7	0	1	1	2	....	....	....	....
2009-10	Toronto	NHL	43	3	12	15	10	0	0	0	45	6.7	8	1	0.0	21:26	....	....	....	....	....	....	....	....	....
	Toronto Marlies	AHL	12	0	2	2	2	....	....	....	....	....	....	....	....	....	....	....	....	....	....	....	....	....	....
2010-11	Toronto	NHL	68	4	16	20	14	1	0	1	69	5.8	-2	0	0.0	18:15	....	....	....	....	....	....	....	....	....
2011-12	Toronto	NHL	76	4	15	19	20	0	0	0	89	4.5	-9	1	0.0	21:42	....	....	....	....	....	....	....	....	....
2012-13	Orebro HK	Sweden-2	10	0	4	4	2	....	....	....	....	....	....	....	....	....	....	....	....	....	....	....	....	....	....
	Toronto	NHL	37	1	14	15	14	0	0	0	28	3.6	5	0	0.0	21:17	7	0	1	1	0	0	0	0	22:05
2013-14	Toronto	NHL	80	3	14	17	34	0	0	1	48	6.3	12	0	0.0	19:25	....	....	....	....	....	....	....	....	....
2014-15	St. Louis	NHL	61	2	10	12	2	0	0	0	54	3.7	10	0	0.0	18:04	6	0	0	0	0	0	0	0	17:51
2015-16	St. Louis	NHL	72	3	6	9	31	1	0	0	51	5.9	7	0	0.0	17:23	19	0	2	2	7	0	0	0	16:37
2016-17	St. Louis	NHL	56	0	6	6	4	0	0	0	32	0.0	-5	0	0.0	13:36	11	0	0	0	2	0	0	0	11:52
	NHL Totals		493	20	93	113	129	2	0	2	416	4.8		2	0.0	18:48	43	0	3	3	9	0	0	0	16:28

Signed as a free agent by **Orebro** (Sweden-2), November 12, 2012. Traded to **St. Louis** by **Toronto** with Calgary's 4th round pick (previously acquired, St. Louis selected Ville Husso) in 2014 NHL Draft for Roman Polak, June 28, 2014.

GURIANOV, Denis

(goo-REE-an-awv, deh-NEEZ) **DAL**

Right wing. Shoots left. 6'3", 200 lbs. Born, Togliatti, Russia, June 7, 1997. Dallas' 1st pick, 12th overall, in 2015 NHL Draft.

Season	Club	League	GP	G	A	Pts	PIM	PP	SH	GW	S	S%	+/-	TF	F%	Min	GP	G	A	Pts	PIM	PP	SH	GW	Min
2013-14	Ladja Togliatti Jr.	Russia-Jr.	37	7	9	16	6	....	....	....	....	....	....	....	....	....	....	....	....	....	....	....	....	....	....
2014-15	Lada Togliatti	KHL	8	0	1	1	2	....	....	....	....	....	....	....	....	....	....	....	....	....	....	....	....	....	....
	Ladja Togliatti Jr.	Russia-Jr.	23	15	10	25	39	....	....	....	....	....	....	....	....	....	4	3	1	4	12	....	....	....	....
2015-16	Ladja Togliatti Jr.	Russia-Jr.	7	4	2	6	4	....	....	....	....	....	....	....	....	....	....	....	....	....	....	....	....	....	....
	Lada Togliatti	KHL	47	4	1	5	6	....	....	....	....	....	....	....	....	....	....	....	....	....	....	....	....	....	....
2016-17	Dallas	NHL	1	0	0	0	0	0	0	0	0	0.0	-1	0	0.0	13:06	....	....	....	....	....	....	....	....	....
	Texas Stars	AHL	57	12	15	27	17	....	....	....	....	....	....	....	....	....	....	....	....	....	....	....	....	....	....
	NHL Totals		1	0	0	0	0	0	0	0	0	0.0		0	0.0	13:06	....	....	....	....	....	....	....	....	....

GUSTAFSSON, Erik

(GOOS-tahf-suhn, AIR-ihk) **CHI**

Defense. Shoots left. 6', 176 lbs. Born, Nynashamn, Sweden, March 14, 1992. Edmonton's 5th pick, 93rd overall, in 2012 NHL Draft.

Season	Club	League	GP	G	A	Pts	PIM	PP	SH	GW	S	S%	+/-	TF	F%	Min	GP	G	A	Pts	PIM	PP	SH	GW	Min
2008-09	Djurgarden U18	Swe-U18	33	2	8	10	22	....	....	....	....	....	....	....	....	....	2	0	0	0	0	....	....	....	....
2009-10	Djurgarden Jr.	Swe-Jr.	24	0	8	8	26	....	....	....	....	....	....	....	....	....	....	....	....	....	....	....	....	....	....
	Djurgarden U18	Swe-U18	27	7	13	20	54	....	....	....	....	....	....	....	....	....	3	0	0	0	0	....	....	....	....
2010-11	Djurgarden Jr.	Swe-Jr.	38	2	21	23	104	....	....	....	....	....	....	....	....	....	4	0	1	1	6	....	....	....	....
2011-12	Djurgarden Jr.	Swe-Jr.	21	3	11	14	14	....	....	....	....	....	....	....	....	....	....	....	....	....	....	....	....	....	....
	Djurgarden	Sweden	41	3	4	7	16	....	....	....	....	....	....	....	....	....	....	....	....	....	....	....	....	....	....
	Djurgarden	Sweden-Q	10	0	1	1	6	....	....	....	....	....	....	....	....	....	....	....	....	....	....	....	....	....	....
2012-13	Djurgarden	Sweden-2	55	8	16	24	82	....	....	....	....	....	....	....	....	....	....	....	....	....	....	....	....	....	....
2013-14	Frolunda	Sweden	50	2	18	20	16	....	....	....	....	....	....	....	....	....	....	....	....	....	....	....	....	....	....
2014-15	Frolunda	Sweden	55	4	25	29	22	....	....	....	....	....	....	....	....	....	12	1	2	3	31	....	....	....	....

			Regular Season														Playoffs								
Season	Club	League	GP	G	A	Pts	PIM	PP	SH	GW	S	S%	+/-	TF	F%	Min	GP	G	A	Pts	PIM	PP	SH	GW	Min
2015-16	**Chicago**	**NHL**	**41**	**0**	**14**	**14**	**4**	**0**	**0**	**0**	**58**	**0.0**	**11**	**0**	**0.0**	**15:27**	**5**	**0**	**1**	**1**	**0**	**0**	**0**	**0**	**11:21**
	Rockford IceHogs	AHL	27	3	8	11	38	....	....	....	....	....	....	....	....	....	....	....	....	....	....	....	....	....	....
2016-17	Rockford IceHogs	AHL	68	5	25	39	40	....	....	....	....	....	....	....	....	....	....	....	....	....	....	....	....	....	....
	NHL Totals		**41**	**0**	**14**	**14**	**4**	**0**	**0**	**0**	**58**	**0.0**		**0**	**0.0**	**15:27**	**5**	**0**	**1**	**1**	**0**	**0**	**0**	**0**	**11:21**

Signed as a free agent by **Chicago**, April 30, 2015.

HAGELIN, Carl (HAG-eh-lihn, KARL) PIT

Left wing. Shoots left. 5'11", 186 lbs. Born, Sodertalje, Sweden, August 23, 1988. NY Rangers' 4th pick, 168th overall, in 2007 NHL Draft.

Season	Club	League	GP	G	A	Pts	PIM	PP	SH	GW	S	S%	+/-	TF	F%	Min	GP	G	A	Pts	PIM	PP	SH	GW	Min
2004-05	Sodertalje SK U18	Swe-U18	14	10	7	17	16	....	....	....	....	....	....	....	....	....	2	0	2	2	0	....	....	....	....
2005-06	Sodertalje SK U18	Swe-U18	7	4	8	12	2	....	....	....	....	....	....	....	....	....	....	....	....	....	....	....	....	....	....
	Sodertalje SK Jr.	Swe-Jr.	41	20	20	40	42	....	....	....	....	....	....	....	....	....	4	1	2	3	22	....	....	....	....
2006-07	Sodertalje SK Jr.	Swe-Jr.	40	24	31	55	42	....	....	....	....	....	....	....	....	....	3	1	5	6	20	....	....	....	....
2007-08	U. of Michigan	CCHA	41	11	11	22	28	....	....	....	....	....	....	....	....	....	....	....	....	....	....	....	....	....	....
2008-09	U. of Michigan	CCHA	41	13	18	31	32	....	....	....	....	....	....	....	....	....	....	....	....	....	....	....	....	....	....
2009-10	U. of Michigan	CCHA	45	19	*31	*50	34	....	....	....	....	....	....	....	....	....	....	....	....	....	....	....	....	....	....
2010-11	U. of Michigan	CCHA	44	18	31	49	39	....	....	....	....	....	....	....	....	....	....	....	....	....	....	....	....	....	....
	Connecticut	AHL	....	....	....	....	....	....	....	....	....	....	....	....	....	....	5	1	1	2	4	....	....	....	....
2011-12	**NY Rangers**	**NHL**	**64**	**14**	**24**	**38**	**24**	**0**	**2**	**2**	**131**	**10.7**	**21**	**6**	**16.7**	**15:03**	**17**	**0**	**3**	**3**	**17**	**0**	**0**	**0**	**16:45**
	Connecticut	AHL	17	7	6	13	6	....	....	....	....	....	....	....	....	....	....	....	....	....	....	....	....	....	....
2012-13	Sodertalje SK	Sweden-2	8	5	6	11	0	....	....	....	....	....	....	....	....	....	....	....	....	....	....	....	....	....	....
	NY Rangers	**NHL**	**48**	**10**	**14**	**24**	**18**	**1**	**0**	**1**	**132**	**7.6**	**10**	**17**	**41.2**	**17:18**	**12**	**3**	**3**	**6**	**0**	**0**	**0**	**0**	**18:06**
2013-14	**NY Rangers**	**NHL**	**72**	**17**	**16**	**33**	**44**	**0**	**1**	**5**	**144**	**11.8**	**8**	**5**	**0.0**	**15:32**	**25**	**7**	**5**	**12**	**16**	**0**	***2**	**1**	**15:59**
	Sweden	Olympics	6	2	0	2	0	....	....	....	....	....	....	....	....	....	....	....	....	....	....	....	....	....	....
2014-15	**NY Rangers**	**NHL**	**82**	**17**	**18**	**35**	**46**	**1**	**0**	**4**	**185**	**9.2**	**18**	**17**	**35.3**	**15:14**	**19**	**2**	**3**	**5**	**6**	**0**	**0**	**1**	**16:38**
2015-16	**Anaheim**	**NHL**	**43**	**4**	**8**	**12**	**14**	**0**	**0**	**0**	**82**	**4.9**	**–10**	**7**	**42.9**	**15:00**	....	....	....	....	....	....	....	....	....
	♦ Pittsburgh	**NHL**	**37**	**10**	**17**	**27**	**18**	**0**	**0**	**6**	**96**	**10.4**	**18**	**7**	**42.9**	**16:32**	**24**	**6**	**10**	**16**	**14**	**1**	**0**	**1**	**16:23**
2016-17	**♦ Pittsburgh**	**NHL**	**61**	**6**	**16**	**22**	**16**	**0**	**0**	**2**	**128**	**4.7**	**10**	**6**	**50.0**	**15:29**	**15**	**2**	**0**	**2**	**19**	**0**	**0**	**0**	**12:09**
	NHL Totals		**407**	**78**	**113**	**191**	**180**	**2**	**3**	**20**	**898**	**8.7**		**65**	**35.4**	**15:38**	**112**	**20**	**24**	**44**	**72**	**1**	**2**	**3**	**16:00**

CCHA First All-Star Team (2011) • NCAA West Second All-American Team (2011)

Signed as a free agent by **Sodertalje** (Sweden-2), September 28, 2012. Traded to **Anaheim** by **NY Rangers** with NY Rangers' 2nd (Julius Naatinen) and 6th (Garrett Metcalf) round picks in 2015 NHL Draft for Emerson Etem and Florida's 2nd round pick (previously acquired, NY Rangers selected Ryan Gropp) in 2015 NHL Draft, June 27, 2015. Traded to **Pittsburgh** by **Anaheim** for David Perron and Adam Clendening, January 16, 2016.

HAGG, Robert (HAG, RAW-buhrt) PHI

Defense. Shoots left. 6'2", 201 lbs. Born, Uppsala, Sweden, February 8, 1995. Philadelphia's 2nd pick, 41st overall, in 2013 NHL Draft.

Season	Club	League	GP	G	A	Pts	PIM	PP	SH	GW	S	S%	+/-	TF	F%	Min	GP	G	A	Pts	PIM	PP	SH	GW	Min
2008-09	Gimo IF Hockey	Sweden-4	23	0	0	0	6	....	....	....	....	....	....	....	....	....	....	....	....	....	....	....	....	....	....
2009-10	Gimo IF	Sweden-4	32	7	9	16	28	....	....	....	....	....	....	....	....	....	....	....	....	....	....	....	....	....	....
2010-11	Tierps HK	Sweden-3	30	2	9	11	30	....	....	....	....	....	....	....	....	....	....	....	....	....	....	....	....	....	....
	MODO U18	Swe-U18	2	0	0	0	2	....	....	....	....	....	....	....	....	....	....	....	....	....	....	....	....	....	....
2011-12	MODO U18	Swe-U18	5	1	4	5	10	....	....	....	....	....	....	....	....	....	1	0	0	0	0	....	....	....	....
	MODO Jr.	Swe-Jr.	44	4	13	17	46	....	....	....	....	....	....	....	....	....	8	1	1	2	2	....	....	....	....
2012-13	MODO Jr.	Swe-Jr.	28	11	13	24	24	....	....	....	....	....	....	....	....	....	7	1	1	2	4	....	....	....	....
	MODO	Sweden	27	0	1	1	2	....	....	....	....	....	....	....	....	....	1	0	0	0	0	....	....	....	....
	MODO U18	Swe-U18	....	....	....	....	....	....	....	....	....	....	....	....	....	....	2	1	1	2	0	....	....	....	....
2013-14	MODO Jr.	Swe-Jr.	8	1	6	7	6	....	....	....	....	....	....	....	....	....	2	1	0	1	2	....	....	....	....
	MODO	Sweden	50	1	5	6	47	....	....	....	....	....	....	....	....	....	2	0	0	0	4	....	....	....	....
	Sweden	Olympics	7	1	0	1	12	....	....	....	....	....	....	....	....	....	....	....	....	....	....	....	....	....	....
	Adirondack	AHL	10	1	3	4	10	....	....	....	....	....	....	....	....	....	....	....	....	....	....	....	....	....	....
2014-15	Lehigh Valley	AHL	69	3	17	20	42	....	....	....	....	....	....	....	....	....	....	....	....	....	....	....	....	....	....
2015-16	Lehigh Valley	AHL	65	5	6	11	42	....	....	....	....	....	....	....	....	....	....	....	....	....	....	....	....	....	....
2016-17	**Philadelphia**	**NHL**	**1**	**0**	**0**	**0**	**0**	**0**	**0**	**0**	**5**	**0.0**	**0**	**0**	**0.0**	**21:19**	....	....	....	....	....	....	....	....	....
	Lehigh Valley	AHL	58	7	8	15	48	....	....	....	....	....	....	....	....	....	5	0	1	1	0	....	....	....	....
	NHL Totals		**1**	**0**	**0**	**0**	**0**	**0**	**0**	**0**	**5**	**0.0**		**0**	**0.0**	**21:19**	....	....	....	....	....	....	....	....	....

HAINSEY, Ron (HAYN-zee, RAWN) TOR

Defense. Shoots left. 6'3", 210 lbs. Born, Bolton, CT, March 24, 1981. Montreal's 1st pick, 13th overall, in 2000 NHL Draft.

Season	Club	League	GP	G	A	Pts	PIM	PP	SH	GW	S	S%	+/-	TF	F%	Min	GP	G	A	Pts	PIM	PP	SH	GW	Min
1997-98	USAHNTDP	U-17	18	2	7	9	28	....	....	....	....	....	....	....	....	....	....	....	....	....	....	....	....	....	....
	USAHNTDP	USHL	3	0	0	0	0	....	....	....	....	....	....	....	....	....	....	....	....	....	....	....	....	....	....
	USAHNTDP	NAHL	40	4	7	11	16	....	....	....	....	....	....	....	....	....	5	0	1	1	0	....	....	....	....
1998-99	USAHNTDP	USHL	48	5	12	17	45	....	....	....	....	....	....	....	....	....	....	....	....	....	....	....	....	....	....
99-2000	U. Mass Lowell	H-East	30	3	8	11	20	....	....	....	....	....	....	....	....	....	....	....	....	....	....	....	....	....	....
2000-01	U. Mass Lowell	H-East	33	10	26	36	51	....	....	....	....	....	....	....	....	....	....	....	....	....	....	....	....	....	....
	Quebec Citadelles	AHL	4	1	0	1	0	....	....	....	....	....	....	....	....	....	1	0	0	0	0	....	....	....	....
2001-02	Quebec Citadelles	AHL	63	7	24	31	26	....	....	....	....	....	....	....	....	....	3	0	0	0	0	....	....	....	....
2002-03	**Montreal**	**NHL**	**21**	**0**	**0**	**0**	**2**	**0**	**0**	**0**	**12**	**0.0**	**–1**	**0**	**0.0**	**12:25**	....	....	....	....	....	....	....	....	....
	Hamilton	AHL	33	2	11	13	26	....	....	....	....	....	....	....	....	....	23	1	10	11	20	....	....	....	....
2003-04	**Montreal**	**NHL**	**11**	**1**	**1**	**2**	**4**	**0**	**0**	**0**	**11**	**9.1**	**3**	**0**	**0.0**	**13:15**	....	....	....	....	....	....	....	....	....
	Hamilton	AHL	54	7	24	31	35	....	....	....	....	....	....	....	....	....	10	0	5	5	6	....	....	....	....
2004-05	Hamilton	AHL	68	9	14	23	45	....	....	....	....	....	....	....	....	....	4	1	1	2	0	....	....	....	....
2005-06	Hamilton	AHL	22	3	14	17	19	....	....	....	....	....	....	....	....	....	....	....	....	....	....	....	....	....	....
	Columbus	**NHL**	**55**	**2**	**15**	**17**	**43**	**1**	**0**	**0**	**81**	**2.5**	**13**	**1**	**0.0**	**17:47**	....	....	....	....	....	....	....	....	....
2006-07	**Columbus**	**NHL**	**80**	**9**	**25**	**34**	**69**	**7**	**0**	**0**	**136**	**6.6**	**–19**	**2**	**50.0**	**22:53**	....	....	....	....	....	....	....	....	....
2007-08	**Columbus**	**NHL**	**78**	**8**	**24**	**32**	**25**	**8**	**0**	**0**	**161**	**5.0**	**–7**	**0**	**0.0**	**22:34**	....	....	....	....	....	....	....	....	....
2008-09	**Atlanta**	**NHL**	**81**	**6**	**33**	**39**	**32**	**4**	**0**	**0**	**148**	**4.1**	**–16**	**0**	**0.0**	**22:22**	....	....	....	....	....	....	....	....	....
2009-10	**Atlanta**	**NHL**	**80**	**5**	**21**	**26**	**39**	**0**	**0**	**0**	**121**	**4.1**	**–6**	**0**	**0.0**	**22:08**	....	....	....	....	....	....	....	....	....
2010-11	**Atlanta**	**NHL**	**82**	**3**	**16**	**19**	**24**	**0**	**0**	**2**	**83**	**3.6**	**3**	**0**	**0.0**	**18:05**	....	....	....	....	....	....	....	....	....
2011-12	**Winnipeg**	**NHL**	**56**	**0**	**10**	**10**	**23**	**0**	**0**	**0**	**57**	**0.0**	**9**	**0**	**0.0**	**21:06**	....	....	....	....	....	....	....	....	....
2012-13	**Winnipeg**	**NHL**	**47**	**0**	**13**	**13**	**10**	**0**	**0**	**0**	**52**	**0.0**	**–8**	**0**	**0.0**	**22:52**	....	....	....	....	....	....	....	....	....
2013-14	**Carolina**	**NHL**	**82**	**4**	**11**	**15**	**45**	**0**	**0**	**1**	**72**	**5.6**	**–9**	**0**	**0.0**	**21:26**	....	....	....	....	....	....	....	....	....
2014-15	**Carolina**	**NHL**	**81**	**2**	**8**	**10**	**16**	**0**	**0**	**0**	**83**	**2.4**	**–14**	**1**	**100.0**	**21:06**	....	....	....	....	....	....	....	....	....
2015-16	**Carolina**	**NHL**	**81**	**5**	**14**	**19**	**37**	**0**	**0**	**2**	**131**	**3.8**	**–13**	**0**	**0.0**	**22:19**	....	....	....	....	....	....	....	....	....
2016-17	**Carolina**	**NHL**	**56**	**4**	**10**	**14**	**17**	**0**	**1**	**1**	**62**	**6.5**	**–16**	**0**	**0.0**	**22:20**	....	....	....	....	....	....	....	....	....
	♦ Pittsburgh	**NHL**	**16**	**0**	**3**	**3**	**4**	**0**	**0**	**0**	**9**	**0.0**	**8**	**0**	**0.0**	**21:00**	**25**	**2**	**6**	**8**	**6**	**0**	**0**	**0**	**21:07**
	NHL Totals		**907**	**49**	**204**	**253**	**390**	**20**	**1**	**6**	**1219**	**4.0**		**4**	**50.0**	**21:07**	**25**	**2**	**6**	**8**	**6**	**0**	**0**	**0**	**21:07**

Hockey East First All-Star Team (2001) • NCAA East Second All-American Team (2001) • AHL All-Rookie Team (2002)

Claimed on waivers by **Columbus** from **Montreal**, November 29, 2005. Signed as a free agent by **Atlanta**, July 2, 2008. • Transferred to **Winnipeg** after **Atlanta** franchise relocated, June 21, 2011. Signed as a free agent by **Carolina**, September 12, 2013. Traded to **Pittsburgh** by **Carolina** for Danny Kristo and Pittsburgh's 2nd round pick (later traded to Vegas – Vegas selected Jake Leschyshyn) in 2017 NHL Draft, February 23, 2017. Signed as a free agent by **Toronto**, July 1, 2017.

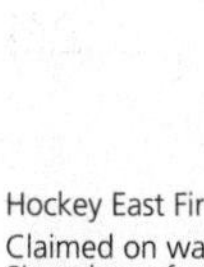

HALEY, Micheal (HAY-lee, MIGH-kuhl) FLA

Center. Shoots left. 5'10", 205 lbs. Born, Guelph, ON, March 30, 1986.

Season	Club	League	GP	G	A	Pts	PIM	PP	SH	GW	S	S%	+/-	TF	F%	Min	GP	G	A	Pts	PIM	PP	SH	GW	Min
2002-03	Sarnia Sting	OHL	43	3	3	6	32	....	....	....	....	....	....	....	....	....	6	0	0	0	2	....	....	....	....
2003-04	Sarnia Sting	OHL	51	8	8	16	69	....	....	....	....	....	....	....	....	....	....	....	....	....	....	....	....	....	....
2004-05	Sarnia Sting	OHL	61	14	16	30	122	....	....	....	....	....	....	....	....	....	....	....	....	....	....	....	....	....	....
2005-06	Sarnia Sting	OHL	23	2	6	8	83	....	....	....	....	....	....	....	....	....	....	....	....	....	....	....	....	....	....
	St. Michael's	OHL	30	12	0	12	78	....	....	....	....	....	....	....	....	....	4	0	1	1	11	....	....	....	....
2006-07	St. Michael's	OHL	68	30	24	54	174	....	....	....	....	....	....	....	....	....	....	....	....	....	....	....	....	....	....
	South Carolina	ECHL	7	5	1	6	13	....	....	....	....	....	....	....	....	....	....	....	....	....	....	....	....	....	....
2007-08	Bridgeport	AHL	36	2	2	4	75	....	....	....	....	....	....	....	....	....	....	....	....	....	....	....	....	....	....
	Utah Grizzlies	ECHL	28	11	8	19	115	....	....	....	....	....	....	....	....	....	14	7	6	13	49	....	....	....	....
2008-09	Bridgeport	AHL	45	5	3	8	99	....	....	....	....	....	....	....	....	....	5	1	0	1	10	....	....	....	....
2009-10	**NY Islanders**	**NHL**	**2**	**0**	**0**	**0**	**9**	**0**	**0**	**0**	**0**	**0.0**	**–3**	**5**	**20.0**	**7:37**	....	....	....	....	....	....	....	....	....
	Bridgeport	AHL	65	6	8	14	196	....	....	....	....	....	....	....	....	....	3	0	0	0	4	....	....	....	....
2010-11	**NY Islanders**	**NHL**	**27**	**2**	**1**	**3**	**85**	**0**	**0**	**0**	**13**	**15.4**	**–4**	**20**	**35.0**	**8:02**	....	....	....	....	....	....	....	....	....
	Bridgeport	AHL	50	12	10	22	144	....	....	....	....	....	....	....	....	....	....	....	....	....	....	....	....	....	....

			Regular Season														Playoffs								
Season	Club	League	GP	G	A	Pts	PIM	PP	SH	GW	S	S%	+/-	TF	F%	Min	GP	G	A	Pts	PIM	PP	SH	GW	Min
2011-12	**NY Islanders**	**NHL**	**14**	**0**	**0**	**0**	**57**	**0**	**0**	**0**	**13**	**0.0**	**−1**	**2**	**50.0**	**7:57**	....	....	....	....	....	....	....	....	....
	Bridgeport	AHL	51	15	10	25	125	....	....	....	....	....	....	....	....	....	3	0	0	0	2	....	....	....	....
2012-13	Connecticut	AHL	69	10	13	23	170	....	....	....	....	....	....	....	....	....	....	....	....	....	....	....	....	....	....
	NY Rangers	**NHL**	**9**	**0**	**0**	**0**	**12**	**0**	**0**	**0**	**4**	**0.0**	**−1**	**3**	**66.7**	**6:38**	**2**	**0**	**0**	**0**	**0**	**0**	**0**	**0**	**6:02**
2013-14	Hartford	AHL	53	7	11	18	131	....	....	....	....	....	....	....	....	....	....	....	....	....	....	....	....	....	....
2014-15	**San Jose**	**NHL**	**4**	**0**	**0**	**0**	**11**	**0**	**0**	**0**	**1**	**0.0**	**−1**	**2**	**100.0**	**7:31**	....	....	....	....	....	....	....	....	....
	Worcester Sharks	AHL	68	18	13	31	106	....	....	....	....	....	....	....	....	....	4	2	1	3	2	....	....	....	....
2015-16	**San Jose**	**NHL**	**16**	**1**	**0**	**1**	**48**	**0**	**0**	**0**	**10**	**10.0**	**−2**	**19**	**57.9**	**7:06**	....	....	....	....	....	....	....	....	....
	San Jose	AHL	41	12	11	23	52	....	....	....	....	....	....	....	....	....	....	....	....	....	....	....	....	....	....
2016-17	**San Jose**	**NHL**	**58**	**2**	**10**	**12**	**128**	**0**	**0**	**1**	**37**	**5.4**	**6**	**149**	**44.3**	**9:11**	....	....	....	....	....	....	....	....	....
	NHL Totals		**130**	**5**	**11**	**16**	**350**	**0**	**0**	**1**	**78**	**6.4**		**200**	**45.0**	**8:18**	**2**	**0**	**0**	**0**	**0**	**0**	**0**	**0**	**6:02**

Signed as a free agent by **NY Islanders**, May 19, 2008. Signed as a free agent by **NY Rangers**, July 1, 2012. Signed as a free agent by **San Jose**, July 10, 2014. Signed as a free agent by **Florida**, July 1, 2017.

HALL, Taylor (HAWL, TAY-luhr) N.J.

Left wing. Shoots left. 6'1", 205 lbs. Born, Calgary, AB, November 14, 1991. Edmonton's 1st pick, 1st overall, in 2010 NHL Draft.

Season	Club	League	GP	G	A	Pts	PIM	PP	SH	GW	S	S%	+/-	TF	F%	Min	GP	G	A	Pts	PIM	PP	SH	GW	Min
2006-07	Kingston Front.	Minor-ON	29	44	41	85	10	....	....	....	....	....	....	....	....	....	....	....	....	....	....	....	....	....	....
2007-08	Windsor Spitfires	OHL	63	45	39	84	22	....	....	....	....	....	....	....	....	....	5	2	3	5	2	....	....	....	....
2008-09	Windsor Spitfires	OHL	63	38	52	90	60	....	....	....	....	....	....	....	....	....	20	*16	20	*36	12	....	....	....	....
2009-10	Windsor Spitfires	OHL	57	40	*66	*106	56	....	....	....	....	....	....	....	....	....	19	17	18	*35	32	....	....	....	....
2010-11	**Edmonton**	**NHL**	**65**	**22**	**20**	**42**	**27**	**8**	**0**	**4**	**186**	**11.8**	**−9**	**105**	**40.0**	**18:13**	....	....	....	....	....	....	....	....	....
2011-12	**Edmonton**	**NHL**	**61**	**27**	**26**	**53**	**36**	**13**	**0**	**7**	**207**	**13.0**	**−3**	**57**	**40.4**	**18:13**	....	....	....	....	....	....	....	....	....
2012-13	Oklahoma City	AHL	26	14	20	34	33	....	....	....	....	....	....	....	....	....	....	....	....	....	....	....	....	....	....
	Edmonton	**NHL**	**45**	**16**	**34**	**50**	**33**	**4**	**0**	**4**	**154**	**10.4**	**5**	**53**	**54.7**	**18:37**	....	....	....	....	....	....	....	....	....
2013-14	**Edmonton**	**NHL**	**75**	**27**	**53**	**80**	**44**	**7**	**0**	**1**	**250**	**10.8**	**−15**	**81**	**45.7**	**20:01**	....	....	....	....	....	....	....	....	....
2014-15	**Edmonton**	**NHL**	**53**	**14**	**24**	**38**	**40**	**3**	**0**	**0**	**158**	**8.9**	**−1**	**98**	**45.9**	**19:13**	....	....	....	....	....	....	....	....	....
2015-16	**Edmonton**	**NHL**	**82**	**26**	**39**	**65**	**54**	**4**	**0**	**6**	**286**	**9.1**	**−4**	**39**	**35.9**	**19:12**	....	....	....	....	....	....	....	....	....
2016-17	**New Jersey**	**NHL**	**72**	**20**	**33**	**53**	**32**	**7**	**0**	**4**	**238**	**8.4**	**−9**	**18**	**44.4**	**19:20**	....	....	....	....	....	....	....	....	....
	NHL Totals		**453**	**152**	**229**	**381**	**266**	**46**	**0**	**26**	**1479**	**10.3**		**451**	**43.9**	**19:02**	....	....	....	....	....	....	....	....	....

Canadian Major Junior All-Rookie Team (2008) • Canadian Major Junior Rookie of the Year (2008) • OHL First All-Star Team (2009, 2010) • OHL Playoff MVP (2009)

Played in NHL All-Star Game (2016, 2017)

Traded to **New Jersey** by **Edmonton** for Adam Larsson, June 29, 2016.

HALMO, Mike (HAL-moh, MIGHK)

Left wing. Shoots left. 5'10", 205 lbs. Born, Waterloo, ON, May 11, 1991.

Season	Club	League	GP	G	A	Pts	PIM	PP	SH	GW	S	S%	+/-	TF	F%	Min	GP	G	A	Pts	PIM	PP	SH	GW	Min
2008-09	Owen Sound	OHL	62	5	3	8	90	....	....	....	....	....	....	....	....	....	4	0	1	1	2	....	....	....	....
2009-10	Owen Sound	OHL	60	11	18	29	121	....	....	....	....	....	....	....	....	....	....	....	....	....	....	....	....	....	....
2010-11	Owen Sound	OHL	59	20	23	43	121	....	....	....	....	....	....	....	....	....	22	5	10	15	36	....	....	....	....
2011-12	Owen Sound	OHL	66	40	45	85	162	....	....	....	....	....	....	....	....	....	....	....	....	....	....	....	....	....	....
	Bridgeport	AHL	5	1	0	1	5	....	....	....	....	....	....	....	....	....	....	....	....	....	....	....	....	....	....
2012-13	Bridgeport	AHL	46	5	9	14	46	....	....	....	....	....	....	....	....	....	....	....	....	....	....	....	....	....	....
2013-14	**NY Islanders**	**NHL**	**20**	**1**	**0**	**1**	**32**	**0**	**0**	**0**	**25**	**4.0**	**−1**	**20**	**20.0**	**9:30**	....	....	....	....	....	....	....	....	....
	Bridgeport	AHL	56	18	20	38	137	....	....	....	....	....	....	....	....	....	....	....	....	....	....	....	....	....	....
2014-15	Bridgeport	AHL	33	10	8	18	83	....	....	....	....	....	....	....	....	....	....	....	....	....	....	....	....	....	....
2015-16	Bridgeport	AHL	74	22	19	41	117	....	....	....	....	....	....	....	....	....	3	1	0	1	0	....	....	....	....
2016-17	Syracuse Crunch	AHL	69	16	12	28	100	....	....	....	....	....	....	....	....	....	....	....	....	....	....	....	....	....	....
	NHL Totals		**20**	**1**	**0**	**1**	**32**	**0**	**0**	**0**	**25**	**4.0**		**20**	**20.0**	**9:30**	....	....	....	....	....	....	....	....	....

Signed as a free agent by **NY Islanders**, March 10, 2012. • Missed majority of 2014-15 due to injury at Wilkes-Barre (AHL), December 12, 2014. Signed as a free agent by **Tampa Bay**, July 9, 2016.

HAMHUIS, Dan (HAM-HOOS, DAN) DAL

Defense. Shoots left. 6'1", 209 lbs. Born, Smithers, BC, December 13, 1982. Nashville's 1st pick, 12th overall, in 2001 NHL Draft.

Season	Club	League	GP	G	A	Pts	PIM	PP	SH	GW	S	S%	+/-	TF	F%	Min	GP	G	A	Pts	PIM	PP	SH	GW	Min
1997-98	Smithers A's	Minor-BC	59	59	72	131	59	....	....	....	....	....	....	....	....	....	....	....	....	....	....	....	....	....	....
1998-99	Prince George	WHL	56	1	3	4	45	....	....	....	....	....	....	....	....	....	7	1	2	3	8	....	....	....	....
99-2000	Prince George	WHL	70	10	23	33	140	....	....	....	....	....	....	....	....	....	13	2	3	5	35	....	....	....	....
2000-01	Prince George	WHL	62	13	47	60	125	....	....	....	....	....	....	....	....	....	6	2	3	5	15	....	....	....	....
2001-02	Prince George	WHL	59	10	50	60	135	....	....	....	....	....	....	....	....	....	7	0	5	5	16	....	....	....	....
2002-03	Milwaukee	AHL	68	6	21	27	81	....	....	....	....	....	....	....	....	....	6	0	3	3	2	....	....	....	....
2003-04	**Nashville**	**NHL**	**80**	**7**	**19**	**26**	**57**	**2**	**0**	**4**	**115**	**6.1**	**−12**	**0**	**0.0**	**22:08**	**6**	**0**	**2**	**2**	**6**	**0**	**0**	**0**	**20:29**
2004-05	Milwaukee	AHL	76	13	38	51	85	....	....	....	....	....	....	....	....	....	7	0	2	2	10	....	....	....	....
2005-06	**Nashville**	**NHL**	**82**	**7**	**31**	**38**	**70**	**4**	**1**	**1**	**135**	**5.2**	**11**	**0**	**0.0**	**22:34**	**5**	**0**	**2**	**2**	**2**	**0**	**0**	**0**	**19:41**
2006-07	**Nashville**	**NHL**	**81**	**6**	**14**	**20**	**66**	**0**	**0**	**1**	**84**	**7.1**	**8**	**1**	**0.0**	**21:20**	**5**	**0**	**1**	**1**	**2**	**0**	**0**	**0**	**21:36**
2007-08	**Nashville**	**NHL**	**80**	**4**	**23**	**27**	**66**	**1**	**0**	**1**	**127**	**3.1**	**−4**	**0**	**0.0**	**22:44**	**6**	**1**	**1**	**2**	**6**	**1**	**0**	**0**	**22:47**
2008-09	**Nashville**	**NHL**	**82**	**3**	**23**	**26**	**67**	**1**	**1**	**1**	**135**	**2.2**	**−4**	**0**	**0.0**	**22:50**	....	....	....	....	....	....	....	....	....
2009-10	**Nashville**	**NHL**	**78**	**5**	**19**	**24**	**49**	**0**	**0**	**0**	**115**	**4.3**	**4**	**0**	**0.0**	**21:15**	**6**	**0**	**2**	**2**	**2**	**0**	**0**	**0**	**22:25**
2010-11	**Vancouver**	**NHL**	**64**	**6**	**17**	**23**	**34**	**2**	**0**	**1**	**109**	**5.5**	**29**	**0**	**0.0**	**22:41**	**19**	**1**	**5**	**6**	**6**	**1**	**0**	**0**	**24:50**
2011-12	**Vancouver**	**NHL**	**82**	**4**	**33**	**37**	**46**	**1**	**0**	**0**	**140**	**2.9**	**29**	**0**	**0.0**	**23:26**	**5**	**0**	**3**	**3**	**6**	**0**	**0**	**0**	**24:23**
2012-13	**Vancouver**	**NHL**	**47**	**4**	**20**	**24**	**12**	**0**	**1**	**0**	**61**	**6.6**	**9**	**0**	**0.0**	**23:23**	**4**	**1**	**1**	**2**	**8**	**0**	**0**	**0**	**25:14**
2013-14	**Vancouver**	**NHL**	**79**	**5**	**17**	**22**	**26**	**0**	**0**	**0**	**150**	**3.3**	**13**	**0**	**0.0**	**23:57**	....	....	....	....	....	....	....	....	....
	Canada	Olympics	5	0	0	0	0	....	....	....	....	....	....	....	....	....	....	....	....	....	....	....	....	....	....
2014-15	**Vancouver**	**NHL**	**59**	**1**	**22**	**23**	**44**	**1**	**0**	**0**	**82**	**1.2**	**0**	**0**	**0.0**	**21:32**	**6**	**0**	**1**	**1**	**16**	**0**	**0**	**0**	**19:40**
2015-16	**Vancouver**	**NHL**	**58**	**3**	**10**	**13**	**28**	**1**	**0**	**1**	**72**	**4.2**	**−2**	**0**	**0.0**	**21:25**	....	....	....	....	....	....	....	....	....
2016-17	**Dallas**	**NHL**	**79**	**1**	**15**	**16**	**23**	**1**	**0**	**0**	**83**	**1.2**	**−7**	**0**	**0.0**	**19:22**	....	....	....	....	....	....	....	....	....
	NHL Totals		**951**	**56**	**263**	**319**	**588**	**14**	**3**	**10**	**1408**	**4.0**		**1**	**0.0**	**22:11**	**62**	**3**	**18**	**21**	**54**	**2**	**0**	**0**	**22:48**

WHL West First All-Star Team (2001, 2002) • WHL Player of the Year (2002) • Canadian Major Junior First All-Star Team (2002) • Canadian Major Junior Defenseman of the Year (2002) • AHL Second All-Star Team (2005)

Traded to **Philadelphia** by **Nashville** for Ryan Parent and future considerations, June 19, 2010. Traded to **Pittsburgh** by **Philadelphia** for Pittsburgh's 3rd round pick (later traded to Phoenix – Phoenix selected Harrison Ruopp) in 2011 NHL Draft, June 25, 2010. Signed as a free agent by **Vancouver**, July 1, 2010. Signed as a free agent by **Dallas**, July 1, 2016.

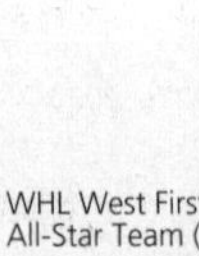

HAMILTON, Dougie (HAM-ihl-tuhn, DUH-gee) CGY

Defense. Shoots right. 6'6", 210 lbs. Born, Toronto, ON, June 17, 1993. Boston's 1st pick, 9th overall, in 2011 NHL Draft.

Season	Club	League	GP	G	A	Pts	PIM	PP	SH	GW	S	S%	+/-	TF	F%	Min	GP	G	A	Pts	PIM	PP	SH	GW	Min
2008-09	St. Cath. Falcons	Minor-ON	67	20	33	53	26	....	....	....	....	....	....	....	....	....	....	....	....	....	....	....	....	....	....
2009-10	Niagara Ice Dogs	OHL	64	3	13	16	36	....	....	....	....	....	....	....	....	....	5	0	1	1	4	....	....	....	....
2010-11	Niagara Ice Dogs	OHL	67	12	46	58	77	....	....	....	....	....	....	....	....	....	14	4	12	16	16	....	....	....	....
2011-12	Niagara Ice Dogs	OHL	50	17	55	72	47	....	....	....	....	....	....	....	....	....	20	5	18	23	16	....	....	....	....
2012-13	**Boston**	**NHL**	**42**	**5**	**11**	**16**	**14**	**2**	**0**	**0**	**83**	**6.0**	**4**	**0**	**0.0**	**17:08**	**7**	**0**	**3**	**3**	**0**	**0**	**0**	**0**	**15:47**
2013-14	**Boston**	**NHL**	**64**	**7**	**18**	**25**	**40**	**2**	**0**	**1**	**114**	**6.1**	**22**	**0**	**0.0**	**19:06**	**12**	**2**	**5**	**7**	**14**	**1**	**0**	**1**	**19:07**
2014-15	**Boston**	**NHL**	**72**	**10**	**32**	**42**	**41**	**5**	**0**	**2**	**188**	**5.3**	**−3**	**0**	**0.0**	**21:20**	....	....	....	....	....	....	....	....	....
2015-16	**Calgary**	**NHL**	**82**	**12**	**31**	**43**	**46**	**5**	**0**	**3**	**190**	**6.3**	**−14**	**0**	**0.0**	**19:46**	....	....	....	....	....	....	....	....	....
2016-17	**Calgary**	**NHL**	**81**	**13**	**37**	**50**	**64**	**2**	**0**	**5**	**222**	**5.9**	**12**	**0**	**0.0**	**19:41**	**4**	**0**	**1**	**1**	**8**	**0**	**0**	**0**	**22:16**
	NHL Totals		**341**	**47**	**129**	**176**	**205**	**16**	**0**	**11**	**797**	**5.9**		**0**	**0.0**	**19:38**	**23**	**2**	**9**	**11**	**22**	**1**	**0**	**1**	**18:39**

OHL Second All-Star Team (2011) • Canadian Major Junior Scholastic Player of the Year (2011) • OHL First All-Star Team (2012) • Canadian Major Junior Defenseman of the Year (2012)

Traded to **Calgary** by **Boston** for Calgary's 1st (Zachary Senyshyn) and 2nd (Jakob Forsbacks-Karlsson) round picks in 2015 NHL Draft and Washington's 2nd round pick (previously acquired, Boston selected Jeremy Lauzon) in 2015 NHL Draft, June 26, 2015.

HAMILTON, Freddie

Center. Shoots right. 6'1", 195 lbs. Born, Toronto, ON, January 1, 1992. San Jose's 4th pick, 129th overall, in 2010 NHL Draft.

(HAM-ihl-tuhn, FREH-dee) CGY

					Regular Season													Playoffs								
Season	Club	League	GP	G	A	Pts	PIM	PP	SH	GW	S	S%	+/-	TF	F%	Min	GP	G	A	Pts	PIM	PP	SH	GW	Min
2007-08	Tor. Marlboros	GTHL	51	39	42	81	4	…	…	…	…	…	…	…	…										
2008-09	Niagara Ice Dogs	OHL	65	10	18	28	8	…	…	…	…	…	…	…	…		12	2	2	4	4	…	…	…	
2009-10	Niagara Ice Dogs	OHL	64	25	30	55	12	…	…	…	…	…	…	…	…		5	1	1	2	6	…	…	…	
2010-11	Niagara Ice Dogs	OHL	68	38	45	83	20	…	…	…	…	…	…	…	…		14	4	10	14	4	…	…	…	
2011-12	Niagara Ice Dogs	OHL	61	35	51	86	31	…	…	…	…	…	…	…	…		20	7	17	24	9	…	…	…	
2012-13	Worcester Sharks	AHL	76	13	13	26	16	…	…	…	…	…	…	…	…										
2013-14	**San Jose**	**NHL**	**11**	**0**	**0**	**0**	**2**	0	0	0	13	0.0	-5	36	38.9	10:19									
	Worcester Sharks	AHL	64	22	21	43	6	…	…	…	…	…	…	…	…										
2014-15	**San Jose**	**NHL**	**1**	**0**	**0**	**0**	**0**	0	0	0	0	0.0	-1	2	50.0	8:27									
	Worcester Sharks	AHL	52	9	21	30	12	…	…	…	…	…	…	…	…										
	Colorado	**NHL**	**17**	**1**	**0**	**1**	**0**	0	0	1	11	9.1	-1	59	39.0	7:32									
	Lake Erie	AHL	5	2	2	4	0	…	…	…	…	…	…	…	…										
2015-16	**Calgary**	**NHL**	**4**	**1**	**1**	**2**	**0**	0	1	0	7	14.3	1	21	57.1	12:42									
	Stockton Heat	AHL	62	18	25	43	24	…	…	…	…	…	…	…	…										
2016-17	**Calgary**	**NHL**	**26**	**2**	**0**	**2**	**8**	0	0	1	30	6.7	-3	126	59.5	9:47	1	0	0	0	0	0	0	0	6:40
	NHL Totals		**59**	**4**	**1**	**5**	**10**	0	1	2	61	6.6		244	51.2	9:24	1	0	0	0	0	0	0	0	6:40

Traded to **Colorado** by **San Jose** for Karl Stollery, March 2, 2015. Traded to **Calgary** by **Colorado** for future considerations (conditions not met), October 4, 2015. • Missed majority of 2016-17 as a healthy reserve.

HAMILTON, Ryan

Left wing. Shoots left. 6'2", 219 lbs. Born, Oshawa, ON, April 15, 1985.

(HAM-ihl-tuhn, RIGH-uhn)

					Regular Season													Playoffs								
Season	Club	League	GP	G	A	Pts	PIM	PP	SH	GW	S	S%	+/-	TF	F%	Min	GP	G	A	Pts	PIM	PP	SH	GW	Min
2002-03	Couchiching	ON-Jr.A	11	5	8	13	2	…	…	…	…	…	…	…	…										
	Peterborough	ON-Jr.A	27	3	10	13	43	…	…	…	…	…	…	…	…										
	Trenton Sting	ON-Jr.A	17	3	8	11	24	…	…	…	…	…	…	…	…										
	Barrie Colts	OHL	24	3	2	5	10	…	…	…	…	…	…	…	…		6	1	0	1	0	…	…	…	
2003-04	Kingston	ON-Jr.A	14	1	5	6	23	…	…	…	…	…	…	…	…										
	Barrie Colts	OHL	46	17	10	27	21	…	…	…	…	…	…	…	…		7	0	1	1	8	…	…	…	
2004-05	Barrie Colts	OHL	37	13	11	24	6	…	…	…	…	…	…	…	…		6	2	0	2	2	…	…	…	
2005-06	Barrie Colts	OHL	63	46	26	72	58	…	…	…	…	…	…	…	…		14	8	9	17	11	…	…	…	
	Houston Aeros	AHL	…	…	…	…	…	…	…	…	…	…	…	…	…		1	0	0	0	0	…	…	…	
2006-07	Houston Aeros	AHL	62	7	9	16	36	…	…	…	…	…	…	…	…										
2007-08	Houston Aeros	AHL	72	20	19	39	38	…	…	…	…	…	…	…	…		2	1	0	1	0	…	…	…	
2008-09	Houston Aeros	AHL	29	8	4	12	24	…	…	…	…	…	…	…	…										
	Toronto Marlies	AHL	36	7	6	13	33	…	…	…	…	…	…	…	…		6	1	2	3	4	…	…	…	
2009-10	Toronto Marlies	AHL	47	16	9	25	37	…	…	…	…	…	…	…	…										
2010-11	Toronto Marlies	AHL	45	16	13	29	21	…	…	…	…	…	…	…	…										
2011-12	**Toronto**	**NHL**	**2**	**0**	**1**	**1**	**2**	0	0	0	1	0.0	-1	0	0.0	13:08									
	Toronto Marlies	AHL	74	25	26	51	36	…	…	…	…	…	…	…	…		17	2	3	5	6	…	…	…	
2012-13	Toronto Marlies	AHL	56	30	18	48	31	…	…	…	…	…	…	…	…		4	1	1	2	0	…	…	…	
	Toronto	**NHL**	**10**	**0**	**2**	**2**	**0**	0	0	0	6	0.0	1	18	22.2	10:51	2	0	1	1	0	0	0	0	8:08
2013-14	**Edmonton**	**NHL**	**2**	**0**	**0**	**0**	**0**	0	0	0	0	0.0	-2	0	0.0	10:02									
	Oklahoma City	AHL	30	7	9	16	26	…	…	…	…	…	…	…	…										
2014-15	**Edmonton**	**NHL**	**16**	**1**	**1**	**2**	**6**	1	0	0	12	8.3	-8	4	25.0	13:13									
	Oklahoma City	AHL	43	18	19	37	15	…	…	…	…	…	…	…	…		10	5	0	5	2	…	…	…	
2015-16	Bakersfield	AHL	60	20	13	33	41	…	…	…	…	…	…	…	…										
2016-17	Bakersfield	AHL	49	17	19	36	23	…	…	…	…	…	…	…	…										
	NHL Totals		**30**	**1**	**4**	**5**	**8**	1	0	0	19	5.3		22	22.7	12:12	2	0	1	1	0	0	0	0	8:08

Signed as a free agent by **Minnesota**, July 5, 2006. Traded to **Toronto** by **Minnesota** for Robbie Earl, January 21, 2009. Signed as a free agent by **Edmonton**, July 5, 2013. • Missed majority of 2013-14 due to knee and shoulder injuries and as a healthy reserve.

HAMONIC, Travis

Defense. Shoots right. 6'2", 205 lbs. Born, St. Malo, MB, August 16, 1990. NY Islanders' 4th pick, 53rd overall, in 2008 NHL Draft.

(HA-mohn-ihk, TRA-vihs) CGY

					Regular Season													Playoffs								
Season	Club	League	GP	G	A	Pts	PIM	PP	SH	GW	S	S%	+/-	TF	F%	Min	GP	G	A	Pts	PIM	PP	SH	GW	Min
2006-07	Winnipeg Saints	MJHL	32	2	13	15	62	…	…	…	…	…	…	…	…										
	Moose Jaw	WHL	22	0	3	3	30	…	…	…	…	…	…	…	…										
2007-08	Moose Jaw	WHL	61	5	17	22	101	…	…	…	…	…	…	…	…		6	0	1	1	6	…	…	…	
2008-09	Moose Jaw	WHL	57	13	27	40	126	…	…	…	…	…	…	…	…										
2009-10	Moose Jaw	WHL	31	10	29	39	48	…	…	…	…	…	…	…	…										
	Brandon	WHL	10	1	4	5	17	…	…	…	…	…	…	…	…		15	4	7	11	23	…	…	…	
2010-11	**NY Islanders**	**NHL**	**62**	**5**	**21**	**26**	**103**	1	0	0	118	4.2	4	0	0.0	21:34									
	Bridgeport	AHL	19	2	5	7	45	…	…	…	…	…	…	…	…										
2011-12	**NY Islanders**	**NHL**	**73**	**2**	**22**	**24**	**73**	1	0	0	124	1.6	6	0	0.0	22:26									
2012-13	Bridgeport	AHL	21	4	6	10	37	…	…	…	…	…	…	…	…										
	NY Islanders	**NHL**	**48**	**3**	**7**	**10**	**28**	1	0	1	83	3.6	-8	0	0.0	22:48	6	0	1	1	23	0	0	0	24:59
2013-14	**NY Islanders**	**NHL**	**69**	**5**	**15**	**18**	**68**	2	0	0	134	2.2	2	0	0.0	25:01									
2014-15	**NY Islanders**	**NHL**	**71**	**5**	**28**	**33**	**85**	1	0	0	132	3.8	15	0	0.0	21:47									
2015-16	**NY Islanders**	**NHL**	**72**	**5**	**16**	**21**	**35**	0	1	1	147	3.4	-5	0	0.0	23:49	11	1	2	3	8	0	0	0	26:08
2016-17	**NY Islanders**	**NHL**	**49**	**3**	**11**	**14**	**60**	0	0	0	74	4.1	-21	0	0.0	20:27									
	NHL Totals		**444**	**26**	**120**	**146**	**452**	6	1	2	812	3.2		0	0.0	22:39	17	1	3	4	31	0	0	0	25:44

WHL East Second All-Star Team (2010)• NHL Foundation Player Award (2017)

Traded to **Calgary** by **NY Islanders** with NY Islanders' 4th round pick in 2019 or 2020 NHL Draft for Calgary's 1st and 2nd round picks in 2018 NHL Draft and Calgary's 2nd round pick in 2019 or 2020 NHL Draft, June 24, 2017.

HANIFIN, Noah

Defense. Shoots left. 6'3", 206 lbs. Born, Boston, MA, January 25, 1997. Carolina's 1st pick, 5th overall, in 2015 NHL Draft.

(HAN-ih-fihn, NOH-uh) CAR

					Regular Season													Playoffs								
Season	Club	League	GP	G	A	Pts	PIM	PP	SH	GW	S	S%	+/-	TF	F%	Min	GP	G	A	Pts	PIM	PP	SH	GW	Min
2010-11	St. Sebastian's	High-MA	27	2	9	11	…	…	…	…	…	…	…	…	…										
2011-12	Bos. Adv. U18	T1EHL	9	1	1	2	5	…	…	…	…	…	…	…	…										
	St. Sebastian's	High-MA	28	5	24	29	…	…	…	…	…	…	…	…	…										
2012-13	Cape Cod	Minor-MA	10	1	2	3	19	…	…	…	…	…	…	…	…										
	St. Sebastian's	High-MA	28	10	24	34	…	…	…	…	…	…	…	…	…										
2013-14	USAHNTDP	USHL	31	6	14	20	18	…	…	…	…	…	…	…	…										
	USAHNTDP	U-17	20	3	17	20	16	…	…	…	…	…	…	…	…										
	USAHNTDP	U-18	8	1	4	5	4	…	…	…	…	…	…	…	…										
2014-15	Boston College	H-East	37	5	18	23	16	…	…	…	…	…	…	…	…										
2015-16	**Carolina**	**NHL**	**79**	**4**	**18**	**22**	**22**	1	0	0	122	3.3	-14	0	0.0	17:54									
2016-17	**Carolina**	**NHL**	**81**	**4**	**25**	**29**	**26**	2	0	1	108	3.7	-19	0	0.0	17:55									
	NHL Totals		**160**	**8**	**43**	**51**	**48**	3	0	1	230	3.5		0	0.0	17:55									

Hockey East All-Rookie Team (2015) • Hockey East Second All-Star Team (2015)

HANLEY, Joel

Defense. Shoots left. 6', 193 lbs. Born, Keswick, ON, June 8, 1991.

(HAN-lee, JOHL) ARI

					Regular Season													Playoffs								
Season	Club	League	GP	G	A	Pts	PIM	PP	SH	GW	S	S%	+/-	TF	F%	Min	GP	G	A	Pts	PIM	PP	SH	GW	Min
2007-08	Georgina Ice	ON-Jr.C	38	8	22	30	45	…	…	…	…	…	…	…	…		9	3	5	8	6	…	…	…	
	Newmarket	ON-Jr.A	2	0	0	0	0	…	…	…	…	…	…	…	…										
2008-09	Newmarket	ON-Jr.A	50	14	24	38	61	…	…	…	…	…	…	…	…										
2009-10	Newmarket	ON-Jr.A	23	5	15	20	11	…	…	…	…	…	…	…	…										
2010-11	Massachusetts	H-East	28	3	15	18	24	…	…	…	…	…	…	…	…										
2011-12	Massachusetts	H-East	36	7	18	25	18	…	…	…	…	…	…	…	…										
2012-13	Massachusetts	H-East	33	5	11	16	46	…	…	…	…	…	…	…	…										
2013-14	Massachusetts	H-East	34	2	14	16	39	…	…	…	…	…	…	…	…										
	Portland Pirates	AHL	15	0	5	5	6	…	…	…	…	…	…	…	…										
2014-15	Portland Pirates	AHL	63	2	15	17	34	…	…	…	…	…	…	…	…		5	0	1	1	0	…	…	…	
	Gwinnett	ECHL	3	1	0	1	0	…	…	…	…	…	…	…	…										

			Regular Season														Playoffs								
Season	Club	League	GP	G	A	Pts	PIM	PP	SH	GW	S	S%	+/-	TF	F%	Min	GP	G	A	Pts	PIM	PP	SH	GW	Min
2015-16	**Montreal**	**NHL**	**10**	**0**	**6**	**6**	**0**	**0**	**0**	**0**	**10**	**0.0**	**0**	**0**	**0.0**	**16:00**	....	....	....	....	....	....	....	....	....
	St. John's IceCaps	AHL	64	5	8	13	25	....	....	....	....	....	....	....	....	....	....	....	....	....	....	....	....	....	....
2016-17	**Montreal**	**NHL**	**7**	**0**	**0**	**0**	**4**	**0**	**0**	**0**	**5**	**0.0**	**–3**	**0**	**0.0**	**10:09**	....	....	....	....	....	....	....	....	....
	St. John's IceCaps	AHL	65	2	20	22	34	....	....	....	....	....	....	....	....	....	4	0	0	0	2	....	....	....	....
	NHL Totals		**17**	**0**	**6**	**6**	**4**	**0**	**0**	**0**	**15**	**0.0**		**0**	**0.0**	**13:36**	....	....	....	....	....	....	....	....	....

Signed to PTO (professional tryout) contract by **Portland** (AHL), March 11, 2014. Signed as a free agent by **Montreal**, July 1, 2015. Signed as a free agent by **Arizona**, July 1, 2017.

HANNIKAINEN, Markus

(hah-nih-KIGH-nehn, MAHR-kuhs) **CBJ**

Left wing. Shoots left. 6'2", 189 lbs. Born, Helsinki, Finland, March 26, 1993.

Season	Club	League	GP	G	A	Pts	PIM	PP	SH	GW	S	S%	+/-	TF	F%	Min	GP	G	A	Pts	PIM	PP	SH	GW	Min
2010-11	Jokerit U18	Fin-U18	7	1	4	5	2	....	....	....	....	....	....	....	....	....	2	0	4	4	0	....	....	....	....
	Jokerit Helsinki Jr.	Fin-Jr.	36	7	12	19	12	....	....	....	....	....	....	....	....	....	9	1	1	2	2	....	....	....	....
2011-12	Jokerit Helsinki Jr.	Fin-Jr.	16	6	7	13	12	....	....	....	....	....	....	....	....	....	12	5	5	10	2	....	....	....	....
	Kiekko-Vantaa	Finland-2	10	2	0	2	4	....	....	....	....	....	....	....	....	....	....	....	....	....	....	....	....	....	....
	Jokerit Helsinki	Finland	15	0	0	0	4	....	....	....	....	....	....	....	....	....	....	....	....	....	....	....	....	....	....
2012-13	Jokerit Helsinki Jr.	Fin-Jr.	11	7	7	14	4	....	....	....	....	....	....	....	....	....	....	....	....	....	....	....	....	....	....
	Kiekko-Vantaa	Finland-2	21	3	6	9	4	....	....	....	....	....	....	....	....	....	....	....	....	....	....	....	....	....	....
	Jokerit Helsinki	Finland	20	0	1	1	4	....	....	....	....	....	....	....	....	....	1	0	0	0	0	....	....	....	....
2013-14	Jokerit Helsinki Jr.	Fin-Jr.	4	3	0	3	0	....	....	....	....	....	....	....	....	....	4	1	3	4	0	....	....	....	....
	HPK Hameenlinna	Finland	4	0	0	0	4	....	....	....	....	....	....	....	....	....	....	....	....	....	....	....	....	....	....
	Kiekko-Vantaa	Finland-2	15	2	5	7	2	....	....	....	....	....	....	....	....	....	....	....	....	....	....	....	....	....	....
	Jokerit Helsinki	Finland	18	3	3	6	4	....	....	....	....	....	....	....	....	....	2	1	0	1	0	....	....	....	....
2014-15	JYP Jyvaskyla	Finland	60	19	27	51	22	....	....	....	....	....	....	....	....	....	....	....	....	....	....	....	....	....	....
2015-16	**Columbus**	**NHL**	**4**	**0**	**0**	**0**	**0**	**0**	**0**	**0**	**3**	**0.0**	**–2**	**0**	**0.0**	**7:09**	....	....	....	....	....	....	....	....	....
	Lake Erie	AHL	50	7	13	20	20	....	....	....	....	....	....	....	....	....	16	3	7	10	2	....	....	....	....
2016-17	**Columbus**	**NHL**	**10**	**1**	**1**	**2**	**6**	**0**	**0**	**0**	**8**	**12.5**	**0**	**0**	**0.0**	**9:08**	....	....	....	....	....	....	....	....	....
	Cleveland	AHL	57	19	18	37	22	....	....	....	....	....	....	....	....	....	....	....	....	....	....	....	....	....	....
	NHL Totals		**14**	**1**	**1**	**2**	**6**	**0**	**0**	**0**	**11**	**9.1**		**0**	**0.0**	**8:34**	....	....	....	....	....	....	....	....	....

Signed as a free agent by **Columbus**, April 20, 2015.

HANSEN, Jannik

(HAHN-suhn, YAH-nihk) **S.J.**

Right wing. Shoots right. 6'1", 195 lbs. Born, Rodovre, Denmark, March 15, 1986. Vancouver's 7th pick, 287th overall, in 2004 NHL Draft.

Season	Club	League	GP	G	A	Pts	PIM	PP	SH	GW	S	S%	+/-	TF	F%	Min	GP	G	A	Pts	PIM	PP	SH	GW	Min
2002-03	Rodovre	Denmark	15	0	0	0	0	....	....	....	....	....	....	....	....	....	....	....	....	....	....	....	....	....	....
	Malmo U18	Swe-U18	12	8	7	15	2	....	....	....	....	....	....	....	....	....	3	2	0	2	0	....	....	....	....
	Denmark	WJ18-B	5	2	5	7	14	....	....	....	....	....	....	....	....	....	....	....	....	....	....	....	....	....	....
2003-04	Rodovre	Denmark	35	12	7	19	48	....	....	....	....	....	....	....	....	....	....	....	....	....	....	....	....	....	....
	Denmark	WJC-B	3	0	1	1	12	....	....	....	....	....	....	....	....	....	....	....	....	....	....	....	....	....	....
	Denmark	WJ18-B	6	3	4	7	32	....	....	....	....	....	....	....	....	....	....	....	....	....	....	....	....	....	....
2004-05	Rodovre	Denmark	32	17	17	34	40	....	....	....	....	....	....	....	....	....	5	3	1	4	24	....	....	....	....
	Denmark	Oly-Q	3	0	1	1	4	....	....	....	....	....	....	....	....	....	....	....	....	....	....	....	....	....	....
2005-06	Portland	WHL	64	24	40	64	67	....	....	....	....	....	....	....	....	....	12	7	6	13	16	....	....	....	....
2006-07	Manitoba Moose	AHL	72	12	22	34	38	....	....	....	....	....	....	....	....	....	6	0	0	0	2	....	....	....	....
	Vancouver	**NHL**	....	....	....	....	....	....	....	....	....	....	....	....	....	....	**10**	**0**	**1**	**1**	**4**	**0**	**0**	**0**	**12:41**
2007-08	**Vancouver**	**NHL**	**5**	**0**	**0**	**0**	**2**	**0**	**0**	**0**	**3**	**0.0**	**0**	**1**	**100.0**	**11:34**	....	....	....	....	....	....	....	....	....
	Manitoba Moose	AHL	50	21	22	43	22	....	....	....	....	....	....	....	....	....	6	2	2	4	0	....	....	....	....
2008-09	**Vancouver**	**NHL**	**55**	**6**	**15**	**21**	**37**	**0**	**0**	**1**	**64**	**9.4**	**5**	**12**	**16.7**	**12:31**	**2**	**0**	**0**	**0**	**0**	**0**	**0**	**0**	**10:16**
	Manitoba Moose	AHL	2	1	0	1	2	....	....	....	....	....	....	....	....	....	....	....	....	....	....	....	....	....	....
2009-10	**Vancouver**	**NHL**	**47**	**9**	**6**	**15**	**18**	**0**	**1**	**3**	**67**	**13.4**	**–5**	**14**	**42.9**	**12:20**	**12**	**1**	**2**	**3**	**4**	**0**	**0**	**0**	**10:05**
	Manitoba Moose	AHL	5	0	2	2	5	....	....	....	....	....	....	....	....	....	....	....	....	....	....	....	....	....	....
2010-11	**Vancouver**	**NHL**	**82**	**9**	**20**	**29**	**32**	**0**	**0**	**2**	**113**	**8.0**	**13**	**19**	**42.1**	**14:43**	**25**	**3**	**6**	**9**	**18**	**0**	**0**	**0**	**15:50**
2011-12	**Vancouver**	**NHL**	**82**	**16**	**23**	**39**	**34**	**0**	**1**	**1**	**137**	**11.7**	**18**	**29**	**41.4**	**14:54**	**5**	**1**	**0**	**1**	**14**	**0**	**0**	**0**	**16:26**
2012-13	Tappara Tampere	Finland	20	7	10	17	43	....	....	....	....	....	....	....	....	....	....	....	....	....	....	....	....	....	....
	Vancouver	**NHL**	**47**	**10**	**17**	**27**	**8**	**1**	**0**	**2**	**99**	**10.1**	**12**	**31**	**9.7**	**17:33**	**4**	**0**	**0**	**0**	**2**	**0**	**0**	**0**	**18:12**
2013-14	**Vancouver**	**NHL**	**71**	**11**	**9**	**20**	**43**	**0**	**1**	**3**	**112**	**9.8**	**–9**	**29**	**41.4**	**15:40**	....	....	....	....	....	....	....	....	....
2014-15	**Vancouver**	**NHL**	**81**	**16**	**17**	**33**	**27**	**0**	**1**	**2**	**145**	**11.0**	**–6**	**6**	**16.7**	**13:58**	**6**	**2**	**2**	**4**	**0**	**0**	**0**	**0**	**16:27**
2015-16	**Vancouver**	**NHL**	**67**	**22**	**16**	**38**	**32**	**1**	**1**	**5**	**117**	**18.8**	**16**	**21**	**28.6**	**16:26**	....	....	....	....	....	....	....	....	....
2016-17	**Vancouver**	**NHL**	**28**	**6**	**7**	**13**	**27**	**0**	**0**	**1**	**56**	**10.7**	**2**	**0**	**0.0**	**16:21**	....	....	....	....	....	....	....	....	....
	San Jose	**NHL**	**15**	**2**	**5**	**7**	**7**	**0**	**0**	**0**	**17**	**11.8**	**0**	**1**	**0.0**	**15:30**	**6**	**0**	**1**	**1**	**0**	**0**	**0**	**0**	**15:41**
	NHL Totals		**580**	**107**	**135**	**242**	**267**	**2**	**5**	**20**	**930**	**11.5**		**163**	**31.3**	**14:51**	**70**	**7**	**12**	**19**	**42**	**0**	**0**	**0**	**14:27**

Signed as a free agent by **Tappara Tampere** (Finland), October 30, 2012. Traded to **San Jose** by **Vancouver** for Nikolay Goldobin and San Jose's 4th round pick (later traded to Chicago – Chicago selected Tim Soderlund) in 2017 NHL Draft, March 1, 2017.

HANZAL, Martin

(HAHN-zuhl, MAHR-tihn) **DAL**

Center. Shoots left. 6'6", 226 lbs. Born, Pisek, Czech., February 20, 1987. Phoenix's 1st pick, 17th overall, in 2005 NHL Draft.

Season	Club	League	GP	G	A	Pts	PIM	PP	SH	GW	S	S%	+/-	TF	F%	Min	GP	G	A	Pts	PIM	PP	SH	GW	Min
2002-03	C. Budejovice U17	CzR-U17	47	24	30	54	28	....	....	....	....	....	....	....	....	....	7	1	3	4	25	....	....	....	....
2003-04	C. Budejovice U17	CzR-U17	2	0	2	2	2	....	....	....	....	....	....	....	....	....	2	1	0	1	4	....	....	....	....
	C. Budejovice Jr.	CzRep-Jr.	53	15	7	22	32	....	....	....	....	....	....	....	....	....	....	....	....	....	....	....	....	....	....
2004-05	C. Budejovice Jr.	CzRep-Jr.	37	22	22	44	80	....	....	....	....	....	....	....	....	....	2	1	2	3	2	....	....	....	....
	C. Budejovice	CzRep-2	15	1	2	3	2	....	....	....	....	....	....	....	....	....	6	0	0	0	6	....	....	....	....
2005-06	C. Budejovice Jr.	CzRep-Jr.	7	3	5	8	20	....	....	....	....	....	....	....	....	....	....	....	....	....	....	....	....	....	....
	C. Budejovice	CzRep	19	0	1	1	10	....	....	....	....	....	....	....	....	....	....	....	....	....	....	....	....	....	....
	BK Mlada Boleslav	CzRep-2	5	2	0	2	0	....	....	....	....	....	....	....	....	....	....	....	....	....	....	....	....	....	....
	Omaha Lancers	USHL	19	4	15	19	30	....	....	....	....	....	....	....	....	....	5	1	0	1	4	....	....	....	....
2006-07	Red Deer Rebels	WHL	60	26	59	85	94	....	....	....	....	....	....	....	....	....	6	2	7	9	19	....	....	....	....
2007-08	**Phoenix**	**NHL**	**72**	**8**	**27**	**35**	**28**	**1**	**1**	**3**	**111**	**7.2**	**–7**	**1019**	**46.1**	**16:45**	....	....	....	....	....	....	....	....	....
2008-09	**Phoenix**	**NHL**	**74**	**11**	**20**	**31**	**40**	**0**	**2**	**2**	**97**	**11.3**	**–4**	**1078**	**48.3**	**16:21**	....	....	....	....	....	....	....	....	....
2009-10	**Phoenix**	**NHL**	**81**	**11**	**22**	**33**	**104**	**2**	**0**	**0**	**147**	**7.5**	**0**	**1104**	**50.6**	**18:29**	**7**	**0**	**3**	**3**	**10**	**0**	**0**	**0**	**18:58**
2010-11	**Phoenix**	**NHL**	**61**	**16**	**10**	**26**	**54**	**7**	**0**	**5**	**149**	**10.7**	**4**	**1029**	**50.3**	**19:30**	**4**	**1**	**2**	**3**	**8**	**1**	**0**	**0**	**19:50**
2011-12	**Phoenix**	**NHL**	**64**	**8**	**26**	**34**	**63**	**3**	**0**	**2**	**145**	**5.5**	**12**	**1097**	**52.1**	**18:27**	**12**	**3**	**3**	**6**	**29**	**0**	**0**	**2**	**16:35**
2012-13	C. Budejovice	CzRep	18	8	11	19	73	....	....	....	....	....	....	....	....	....	....	....	....	....	....	....	....	....	....
	Phoenix	**NHL**	**39**	**11**	**12**	**23**	**24**	**4**	**0**	**2**	**93**	**11.8**	**2**	**637**	**46.8**	**18:32**	....	....	....	....	....	....	....	....	....
2013-14	**Phoenix**	**NHL**	**65**	**15**	**25**	**40**	**73**	**5**	**0**	**2**	**169**	**8.9**	**–9**	**1099**	**54.5**	**18:41**	....	....	....	....	....	....	....	....	....
	Czech Republic	Olympics	4	0	1	1	4	....	....	....	....	....	....	....	....	....	....	....	....	....	....	....	....	....	....
2014-15	**Arizona**	**NHL**	**37**	**8**	**16**	**24**	**31**	**1**	**0**	**3**	**85**	**9.4**	**–1**	**612**	**56.5**	**17:44**	....	....	....	....	....	....	....	....	....
2015-16	**Arizona**	**NHL**	**64**	**13**	**28**	**41**	**77**	**3**	**1**	**2**	**141**	**9.2**	**–5**	**1047**	**56.0**	**17:48**	....	....	....	....	....	....	....	....	....
2016-17	**Arizona**	**NHL**	**51**	**16**	**10**	**26**	**43**	**4**	**0**	**2**	**126**	**12.7**	**–15**	**1064**	**56.0**	**18:35**	....	....	....	....	....	....	....	....	....
	Minnesota	**NHL**	**20**	**4**	**9**	**13**	**10**	**1**	**0**	**0**	**43**	**9.3**	**–2**	**296**	**57.8**	**15:31**	**5**	**1**	**0**	**1**	**0**	**0**	**0**	**0**	**18:45**
	NHL Totals		**628**	**121**	**205**	**326**	**547**	**31**	**4**	**23**	**1306**	**9.3**		**10082**	**51.9**	**17:57**	**28**	**5**	**8**	**13**	**47**	**1**	**0**	**2**	**18:02**

WHL East Second All-Star Team (2007)

Signed as a free agent by **Ceske Budejovice** (CzRep), October 28, 2012. Traded to **Minnesota** by **Arizona** with Ryan White and Arizona's 4th round pick (Mason Shaw) in 2017 NHL Draft for Grayson Downing, Minnesota's 1st round pick (Pierre-Olivier Joseph) in 2017 NHL Draft, Minnesoa's 2nd round pick in 2018 NHL Draft and Minnesota's 4th round pick in 2019 NHL Draft, February 26, 2017. Signed as a free agent by **Dallas**, July 1, 2017.

HARPER, Shane

(HAHR-puhr, SHAYN)

Right wing. Shoots right. 5'11", 193 lbs. Born, Valencia, CA, February 1, 1989.

Season	Club	League	GP	G	A	Pts	PIM	PP	SH	GW	S	S%	+/-	TF	F%	Min	GP	G	A	Pts	PIM	PP	SH	GW	Min
2005-06	Everett Silvertips	WHL	62	6	4	10	8	....	....	....	....	....	....	....	....	....	5	1	0	1	0	....	....	....	....
2006-07	Everett Silvertips	WHL	58	3	12	15	23	....	....	....	....	....	....	....	....	....	8	1	2	3	0	....	....	....	....
2007-08	Everett Silvertips	WHL	71	17	26	43	18	....	....	....	....	....	....	....	....	....	4	0	2	2	0	....	....	....	....
2008-09	Everett Silvertips	WHL	72	32	34	66	10	....	....	....	....	....	....	....	....	....	5	0	4	4	0	....	....	....	....
2009-10	Everett Silvertips	WHL	72	42	38	80	38	....	....	....	....	....	....	....	....	....	7	6	4	10	6	....	....	....	....
	Adirondack	AHL	5	1	0	1	2	....	....	....	....	....	....	....	....	....	....	....	....	....	....	....	....	....	....
2010-11	Adirondack	AHL	20	1	2	3	4	....	....	....	....	....	....	....	....	....	....	....	....	....	....	....	....	....	....
	Greenville	ECHL	48	22	23	45	20	....	....	....	....	....	....	....	....	....	11	4	6	10	2	....	....	....	....
2011-12	Adirondack	AHL	70	13	14	27	43	....	....	....	....	....	....	....	....	....	....	....	....	....	....	....	....	....	....
2012-13	Adirondack	AHL	48	5	5	10	35	....	....	....	....	....	....	....	....	....	....	....	....	....	....	....	....	....	....
	Trenton Titans	ECHL	15	14	13	27	2	....	....	....	....	....	....	....	....	....	....	....	....	....	....	....	....	....	....

			Regular Season														Playoffs								
Season	Club	League	GP	G	A	Pts	PIM	PP	SH	GW	S	S%	+/-	TF	F%	Min	GP	G	A	Pts	PIM	PP	SH	GW	Min
2013-14	Chicago Wolves	AHL	63	13	20	33	8	....	....	....	....	....	....	....	....	....	9	2	3	5	0	....	....	....	....
2014-15	Chicago Wolves	AHL	75	32	18	50	14	....	....	....	....	....	....	....	....	....	5	0	4	4	4	....	....	....	....
2015-16	Portland Pirates	AHL	59	12	25	37	18	....	....	....	....	....	....	....	....	....	5	2	0	2	0	....	....	....	....
2016-17	**Florida**	**NHL**	14	2	1	3	18	0	0	0	13	15.4	–1	0	0.0	10:18	....	....	....	....	....	....	....	....	....
	Springfield	AHL	39	7	12	19	6	....	....	....	....	....	....	....	....	....	....	....	....	....	....	....	....	....	....
	Albany Devils	AHL	19	1	2	3	2	....	....	....	....	....	....	....	....	....	....	....	....	....	....	....	....	....	....
	NHL Totals		14	2	1	3	18	0	0	0	13	15.4		0	0.0	10:18	....	....	....	....	....	....	....	....	....

WHL West Second All-Star Team (2010)

Signed as a free agent by **Philadelphia**, March 4, 2010. Traded to **NY Islanders** by **Philadelphia** with Philadelphia's 4th round pick (Devon Toews) in 2014 NHL Draft for Mark Streit, June 12, 2013. Signed as a free agent by **Florida**, July 1, 2015. Traded to **New Jersey** by **Florida** for Reece Scarlett, March 1, 2017.

HARPUR, Ben
(HAHR-puhr, BEHN) **OTT**

Defense. Shoots left. 6'6", 225 lbs. Born, Hamilton, ON, January 12, 1995. Ottawa's 4th pick, 108th overall, in 2013 NHL Draft.

Season	Club	League	GP	G	A	Pts	PIM	PP	SH	GW	S	S%	+/-	TF	F%	Min	GP	G	A	Pts	PIM	PP	SH	GW	Min
2010-11	N.F. Canucks	Minor-ON	43	6	12	18	111	....	....	....	....	....	....	....	....	....	....	....	....	....	....	....	....	....	....
2011-12	Guelph Storm	OHL	34	1	3	4	22	....	....	....	....	....	....	....	....	....	....	....	....	....	....	....	....	....	....
2012-13	Guelph Storm	OHL	67	3	12	15	59	....	....	....	....	....	....	....	....	....	5	0	0	0	2	....	....	....	....
2013-14	Guelph Storm	OHL	67	3	13	16	69	....	....	....	....	....	....	....	....	....	20	1	4	5	12	....	....	....	....
2014-15	Guelph Storm	OHL	28	4	16	20	40	....	....	....	....	....	....	....	....	....	....	....	....	....	....	....	....	....	....
	Barrie Colts	OHL	29	1	10	11	22	....	....	....	....	....	....	....	....	....	9	2	4	6	6	....	....	....	....
2015-16	**Ottawa**	**NHL**	5	0	1	1	2	0	0	0	3	0.0	1	0	0.0	13:40	....	....	....	....	....	....	....	....	....
	Binghamton	AHL	47	2	4	6	34	....	....	....	....	....	....	....	....	....	....	....	....	....	....	....	....	....	....
	Evansville IceMen	ECHL	4	0	2	2	2	....	....	....	....	....	....	....	....	....	....	....	....	....	....	....	....	....	....
2016-17	**Ottawa**	**NHL**	6	0	0	0	0	0	0	0	3	0.0	–1	0	0.0	17:48	9	0	2	2	4	0	0	0	18:28
	Binghamton	AHL	63	2	25	27	81	....	....	....	....	....	....	....	....	....	....	....	....	....	....	....	....	....	....
	NHL Totals		11	0	1	1	2	0	0	0	6	0.0		0	0.0	15:55	9	0	2	2	4	0	0	0	18:28

HARRINGTON, Scott
(HAIR-ihng-tuhn, SKAWT) **CBJ**

Defense. Shoots left. 6'2", 216 lbs. Born, Kingston, ON, March 10, 1993. Pittsburgh's 2nd pick, 54th overall, in 2011 NHL Draft.

Season	Club	League	GP	G	A	Pts	PIM	PP	SH	GW	S	S%	+/-	TF	F%	Min	GP	G	A	Pts	PIM	PP	SH	GW	Min
2008-09	Kingston Front.	Minor-ON	66	19	48	67	46	....	....	....	....	....	....	....	....	....	....	....	....	....	....	....	....	....	....
	Kingston	ON-Jr.A	2	1	0	1	2	....	....	....	....	....	....	....	....	....	18	1	6	7	6	....	....	....	....
2009-10	London Knights	OHL	55	1	13	14	20	....	....	....	....	....	....	....	....	....	12	0	2	2	4	....	....	....	....
2010-11	London Knights	OHL	67	6	16	22	51	....	....	....	....	....	....	....	....	....	6	0	1	1	0	....	....	....	....
2011-12	London Knights	OHL	44	3	23	26	32	....	....	....	....	....	....	....	....	....	19	1	6	7	6	....	....	....	....
2012-13	London Knights	OHL	50	3	16	19	26	....	....	....	....	....	....	....	....	....	17	0	4	4	14	....	....	....	....
	Wilkes-Barre	AHL	....	....	....	....	....	....	....	....	....	....	....	....	....	....	2	1	0	1	0	....	....	....	....
2013-14	Wilkes-Barre	AHL	76	5	19	24	55	....	....	....	....	....	....	....	....	....	16	0	1	1	12	....	....	....	....
2014-15	**Pittsburgh**	**NHL**	10	0	0	0	4	0	0	0	9	0.0	–10	0	0.0	15:48	....	....	....	....	....	....	....	....	....
	Wilkes-Barre	AHL	48	2	10	12	20	....	....	....	....	....	....	....	....	....	8	0	1	1	0	....	....	....	....
2015-16	**Toronto**	**NHL**	15	0	1	1	4	0	0	0	9	0.0	0	0	0.0	13:06	....	....	....	....	....	....	....	....	....
	Toronto Marlies	AHL	17	1	2	3	14	....	....	....	....	....	....	....	....	....	....	....	....	....	....	....	....	....	....
2016-17	**Columbus**	**NHL**	22	1	2	3	10	0	0	0	16	6.3	3	0	0.0	13:00	3	0	0	0	10	0	0	0	12:27
	Cleveland	AHL	2	0	0	0	0	....	....	....	....	....	....	....	....	....	....	....	....	....	....	....	....	....	....
	NHL Totals		47	1	3	4	18	0	0	0	34	2.9		0	0.0	13:38	3	0	0	0	10	0	0	0	12:27

OHL All-Rookie Team (2010) • OHL First All-Star Team (2012, 2013)

Traded to **Toronto** by **Pittsburgh** with Nick Spaling, Kasperi Kapanen, Pittsburgh's 1st round pick (later traded to Anaheim – Anaheim selected Sam Steel) in 2016 NHL Draft and New Jersey's 3rd round pick (previously acquired, Toronto selected James Greenway) in 2016 NHL Draft for Phil Kessel, Tyler Biggs, Tim Erixon and Pittsburgh's 2nd round pick (previously acquired, Pittsburgh selected Kasper Bjorkqvist) in 2016 NHL Draft, July 1, 2015. • Missed majority of 2015-16 due to recurring upper-body injury and as a healthy reserve. Traded to **Columbus** by **Toronto** with a conditional pick (conditions not met) in 2017 NHL Draft for Kerby Rychel, June 25, 2016.

HARTMAN, Ryan
(HAHRT-man, RIGH-uhn) **CHI**

Right wing. Shoots right. 6', 181 lbs. Born, Hilton Head Island, SC, September 20, 1994. Chicago's 1st pick, 30th overall, in 2013 NHL Draft.

Season	Club	League	GP	G	A	Pts	PIM	PP	SH	GW	S	S%	+/-	TF	F%	Min	GP	G	A	Pts	PIM	PP	SH	GW	Min
2009-10	Chicago Mission	T1EHL	38	25	19	44	64	....	....	....	....	....	....	....	....	....	....	....	....	....	....	....	....	....	....
	Chicago Mission	Other	25	21	30	51	....	....	....	....	....	....	....	....	....	....	....	....	....	....	....	....	....	....	....
2010-11	USAHNTDP	USHL	35	12	8	20	59	....	....	....	....	....	....	....	....	....	2	1	0	1	17	....	....	....	....
	USAHNTDP	U-17	17	9	5	14	12	....	....	....	....	....	....	....	....	....	....	....	....	....	....	....	....	....	....
	USAHNTDP	U-18	2	0	0	0	4	....	....	....	....	....	....	....	....	....	....	....	....	....	....	....	....	....	....
2011-12	USAHNTDP	USHL	24	7	9	16	46	....	....	....	....	....	....	....	....	....	....	....	....	....	....	....	....	....	....
	USAHNTDP	U-18	35	9	16	25	90	....	....	....	....	....	....	....	....	....	....	....	....	....	....	....	....	....	....
2012-13	Plymouth Whalers	OHL	56	23	37	60	120	....	....	....	....	....	....	....	....	....	9	4	2	6	16	....	....	....	....
2013-14	Plymouth Whalers	OHL	52	26	28	54	91	....	....	....	....	....	....	....	....	....	5	0	4	4	8	....	....	....	....
	Rockford IceHogs	AHL	9	3	4	7	8	....	....	....	....	....	....	....	....	....	....	....	....	....	....	....	....	....	....
2014-15	**Chicago**	**NHL**	5	0	0	0	2	0	0	0	8	0.0	–1	0	0.0	8:17	....	....	....	....	....	....	....	....	....
	Rockford IceHogs	AHL	69	13	24	37	120	....	....	....	....	....	....	....	....	....	8	2	1	3	8	....	....	....	....
2015-16	**Chicago**	**NHL**	3	0	1	1	0	0	0	0	3	0.0	–1	4	25.0	9:14	....	....	....	....	....	....	....	....	....
	Rockford IceHogs	AHL	61	15	20	35	129	....	....	....	....	....	....	....	....	....	3	1	0	1	4	....	....	....	....
2016-17	**Chicago**	**NHL**	76	19	12	31	70	1	0	4	170	11.2	13	62	40.3	12:46	4	0	0	0	14	0	0	0	11:34
	NHL Totals		84	19	13	32	72	1	0	4	181	10.5		66	39.4	12:22	4	0	0	0	14	0	0	0	11:34

HARTNELL, Scott
(HAHRT-nuhl, SKAWT) **NSH**

Left wing. Shoots left. 6'2", 214 lbs. Born, Regina, SK, April 18, 1982. Nashville's 1st pick, 6th overall, in 2000 NHL Draft.

Season	Club	League	GP	G	A	Pts	PIM	PP	SH	GW	S	S%	+/-	TF	F%	Min	GP	G	A	Pts	PIM	PP	SH	GW	Min
1997-98	Lloydminster	AJHL	56	9	25	34	82	....	....	....	....	....	....	....	....	....	4	2	1	3	8	....	....	....	....
	Prince Albert	WHL	1	0	1	1	2	....	....	....	....	....	....	....	....	....	....	....	....	....	....	....	....	....	....
1998-99	Prince Albert	WHL	65	10	34	44	104	....	....	....	....	....	....	....	....	....	14	0	5	5	22	....	....	....	....
99-2000	Prince Albert	WHL	62	27	55	82	124	....	....	....	....	....	....	....	....	....	6	3	2	5	6	....	....	....	....
2000-01	**Nashville**	**NHL**	75	2	14	16	48	0	0	0	92	2.2	–8	3	33.3	10:54	....	....	....	....	....	....	....	....	....
2001-02	**Nashville**	**NHL**	75	14	27	41	111	3	0	4	162	8.6	5	12	25.0	16:58	....	....	....	....	....	....	....	....	....
2002-03	**Nashville**	**NHL**	82	12	22	34	101	2	0	2	221	5.4	–3	23	30.4	15:17	....	....	....	....	....	....	....	....	....
2003-04	**Nashville**	**NHL**	59	18	15	33	87	5	0	3	154	11.7	–5	48	37.5	16:16	6	1	2	3	2	0	0	0	15:37
2004-05	Valerengen	Norway	28	17	12	29	103	....	....	....	....	....	....	....	....	....	11	12	7	19	24	....	....	....	....
2005-06	**Nashville**	**NHL**	81	25	23	48	101	10	2	8	211	11.8	8	58	37.9	16:05	5	1	0	1	4	0	0	0	12:12
2006-07	**Nashville**	**NHL**	64	22	17	39	96	10	0	2	150	14.7	19	134	47.0	15:43	5	1	1	2	28	1	0	0	14:23
2007-08	**Philadelphia**	**NHL**	80	24	19	43	159	10	1	6	176	13.6	2	32	40.6	16:11	17	3	4	7	20	0	0	0	15:28
2008-09	**Philadelphia**	**NHL**	82	30	30	60	143	6	1	5	210	14.3	14	36	50.0	17:48	6	1	1	2	23	1	0	0	18:36
2009-10	**Philadelphia**	**NHL**	81	14	30	44	155	8	0	4	171	8.2	–6	5	20.0	15:43	23	8	9	17	25	3	0	0	16:14
2010-11	**Philadelphia**	**NHL**	82	24	25	49	142	4	0	4	177	13.6	14	10	50.0	16:36	11	1	3	4	23	0	0	0	16:18
2011-12	**Philadelphia**	**NHL**	82	37	30	67	136	16	0	6	232	15.9	19	63	31.8	17:47	11	3	5	8	15	3	0	1	17:29
2012-13	**Philadelphia**	**NHL**	32	8	3	11	70	4	0	1	74	10.8	–5	4	75.0	15:52	....	....	....	....	....	....	....	....	....
2013-14	**Philadelphia**	**NHL**	78	20	32	52	103	9	0	3	207	9.7	11	18	22.2	16:53	7	0	3	3	6	0	0	0	16:52
2014-15	**Columbus**	**NHL**	77	28	32	60	100	8	0	2	204	13.7	1	14	50.0	17:18	....	....	....	....	....	....	....	....	....
2015-16	**Columbus**	**NHL**	79	23	26	49	112	10	0	1	150	15.3	–11	3	0.0	15:35	....	....	....	....	....	....	....	....	....
2016-17	**Columbus**	**NHL**	78	13	24	37	63	2	0	1	104	12.5	14	6	50.0	12:04	4	0	0	0	0	0	0	0	10:39
	NHL Totals		1187	314	369	683	1727	107	4	52	2695	11.7		469	40.1	15:50	95	19	28	47	146	8	0	1	15:52

Played in NHL All-Star Game (2012)

Signed as a free agent by **Oslo** (Norway), October 21, 2004. Traded to **Philadelphia** by **Nashville** with Kimmo Timonen for Nashville's 1st round pick (previously acquired, Nashville selected Jonathon Blum) in 2007 NHL Draft, June 18, 2007. Traded to **Columbus** by **Philadelphia** for RJ Umberger and Columbus' 4th round pick (later traded to Los Angeles – Los Angeles selected Austin Wagner) in 2015 NHL Draft, June 23, 2014. Signed as a free agent by **Nashville**, July 1, 2017.

HATHAWAY, Garnet (HATH-UH-way, GAHR-neht) CGY

Right wing. Shoots right. 6'2", 207 lbs. Born, Kennebunkport, ME, November 23, 1991.

Season	Club	League	GP	G	A	Pts	PIM	PP	SH	GW	S	S%	+/-	TF	F%	Min	GP	G	A	Pts	PIM	PP	SH	GW	Min
2008-09	Andover	High-MA	26	16	13	29	....																		
2009-10	Andover	High-MA	28	17	20	37	....																		
2010-11	Brown U.	ECAC	31	5	9	14	42																		
2011-12	Brown U.	ECAC	26	3	5	8	48																		
2012-13	Brown U.	ECAC	33	6	15	21	47																		
2013-14	Brown U.	ECAC	31	6	9	15	41																		
	Abbotsford Heat	AHL	8	0	0	0	10										1	0	0	0	10				
2014-15	Adirondack	AHL	72	19	17	36	77																		
2015-16	**Calgary**	**NHL**	14	0	3	3	31	0	0	0	11	0.0	-1	4	25.0	12:01									
	Stockton Heat	AHL	44	8	13	21	39																		
2016-17	**Calgary**	**NHL**	26	1	4	5	44	0	0	0	22	4.5	0	19	52.6	9:08	5	2	2	4	2				
	Stockton Heat	AHL	31	8	12	20	67																		
	NHL Totals		40	1	7	8	75	0	0	0	33	3.0		23	47.8	10:09									

Signed as a free agent by **Abbotsford** (AHL), March 14, 2014. Signed as a free agent by **Calgary**, April 13, 2015.

HAULA, Erik (HAWL-la, AIR-ihk) VGK

Left wing. Shoots left. 6', 193 lbs. Born, Pori, Finland, March 23, 1991. Minnesota's 7th pick, 182nd overall, in 2009 NHL Draft.

Season	Club	League	GP	G	A	Pts	PIM	PP	SH	GW	S	S%	+/-	TF	F%	Min	GP	G	A	Pts	PIM	PP	SH	GW	Min
2006-07	Assat Pori U18	Fin-U18	29	19	24	43	24										6	1	3	4	4				
2007-08	Assat Pori U18	Fin-U18	3	1	1	2	0										2	4	2	6	14				
	Assat Pori Jr.	Fin-Jr.	40	7	15	22	26										12	2	0	2	4				
2008-09	Shattuck	High-MN	53	26	58	84	46																		
2009-10	Omaha Lancers	USHL	56	28	44	72	59										8	2	9	11	2				
2010-11	U. of Minnesota	WCHA	34	6	18	24	22																		
2011-12	U. of Minnesota	WCHA	43	20	29	49	30																		
2012-13	U. of Minnesota	WCHA	37	16	35	51	14										5	1	1	2	4				
	Houston Aeros	AHL	6	0	2	2	2																		
2013-14	**Minnesota**	**NHL**	46	6	9	15	29	0	1	1	56	10.7	14	348	46.3	10:09	13	4	3	7	0	0	0	1	14:12
	Iowa Wild	AHL	31	14	13	27	14																		
2014-15	**Minnesota**	**NHL**	72	7	7	14	32	1	0	1	92	7.6	-7	573	45.4	12:09	2	1	0	1	0	0	0	0	11:00
2015-16	**Minnesota**	**NHL**	76	14	20	34	24	0	2	2	99	14.1	21	781	53.3	12:44	5	1	3	4	2	0	0	0	18:15
2016-17	**Minnesota**	**NHL**	72	15	11	26	28	1	0	4	134	11.2	5	750	53.9	13:49	4	0	1	1	0	0	0	0	15:24
	NHL Totals		266	42	47	89	113	2	3	8	381	11.0		2452	50.6	12:25	24	6	7	13	2	0	0	1	14:59

USHL All-Rookie Team (2010) • USHL Second All-Star Team (2010) • WCHA Second All-Star Team (2013)
Claimed by **Vegas** from **Minnesota** in Expansion Draft, June 21, 2017.

HAYDEN, John (HAY-duhn, JAWN) CHI

Center. Shoots right. 6'3", 223 lbs. Born, Chicago, IL, February 14, 1995. Chicago's 3rd pick, 74th overall, in 2013 NHL Draft.

Season	Club	League	GP	G	A	Pts	PIM	PP	SH	GW	S	S%	+/-	TF	F%	Min	GP	G	A	Pts	PIM	PP	SH	GW	Min
2010-11	Brunswick Bruins	High-CT	26	21	9	30	....																		
2011-12	USAHNTDP	USHL	36	8	7	15	51										2	0	2	2	2				
	USAHNTDP	U-17	17	3	6	9	12																		
2012-13	USAHNTDP	USHL	24	11	9	20	51																		
	USAHNTDP	U-18	29	6	8	14	29																		
2013-14	Yale	ECAC	33	6	10	16	18																		
2014-15	Yale	ECAC	29	7	11	18	10																		
2015-16	Yale	ECAC	32	16	7	23	26																		
2016-17	Yale	ECAC	33	21	13	34	62																		
	Chicago	**NHL**	12	1	3	4	4	0	0	0	22	4.5	3	0	0.0	11:41	1	0	0	0	0	0	0	0	5:39
	NHL Totals		12	1	3	4	4	0	0	0	22	4.5		0	0.0	11:41	1	0	0	0	0	0	0	0	5:39

ECAC Second All-Team (2017)

HAYES, Jimmy (HAYZ, JIH-mee)

Right wing. Shoots right. 6'5", 215 lbs. Born, Boston, MA, November 21, 1989. Toronto's 2nd pick, 60th overall, in 2008 NHL Draft.

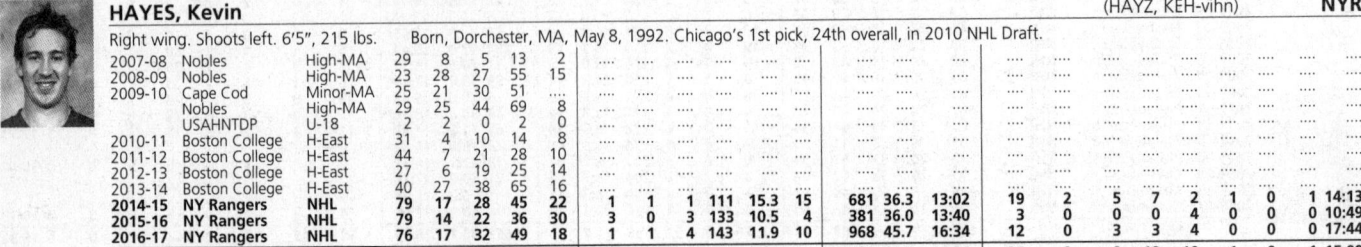

Season	Club	League	GP	G	A	Pts	PIM	PP	SH	GW	S	S%	+/-	TF	F%	Min	GP	G	A	Pts	PIM	PP	SH	GW	Min
2006-07	USAHNTDP	U-17	42	17	14	31	37																		
	USAHNTDP	NAHL	14	6	8	14	4																		
2007-08	USAHNTDP	U-18	18	2	5	7	6																		
	USAHNTDP	NAHL	19	2	8	10	6																		
	Lincoln Stars	USHL	21	4	11	15	18										8	4	5	9	8				
2008-09	Boston College	H-East	36	8	5	13	22																		
2009-10	Boston College	H-East	42	13	22	35	14																		
2010-11	Boston College	H-East	39	21	12	33	24																		
	Rockford IceHogs	AHL	7	0	0	0	2																		
2011-12	**Chicago**	**NHL**	31	5	4	9	16	1	0	0	41	12.2	-3	10	50.0	10:15	2	0	0	0	15	0	0	0	10:08
	Rockford IceHogs	AHL	33	7	16	23	11																		
2012-13	Rockford IceHogs	AHL	67	25	20	45	23																		
	Chicago	**NHL**	10	1	3	4	0	0	0	0	13	7.7	0	7	57.1	14:20									
2013-14	**Chicago**	**NHL**	2	0	0	0	0	0	0	0	1	0.0	1	0	0.0	11:51									
	Rockford IceHogs	AHL	13	4	4	8	2																		
	Florida	**NHL**	53	11	7	18	18	3	0	0	71	15.5	-6	30	36.7	10:56									
2014-15	**Florida**	**NHL**	72	19	16	35	20	4	0	3	166	11.4	-4	9	44.4	15:09									
2015-16	**Boston**	**NHL**	75	13	16	29	60	3	0	0	127	10.2	-12	112	37.5	13:50									
2016-17	**Boston**	**NHL**	58	2	3	5	29	0	0	1	74	2.7	-3	55	25.5	9:14									
	NHL Totals		301	51	49	100	143	11	0	4	493	10.3		223	35.9	12:23	2	0	0	0	15	0	0	0	10:08

Traded to **Chicago** by **Toronto** for Calgary's 2nd round pick (previously acquired, Toronto selected Brad Ross) in 2010 NHL Draft, June 25, 2010. Traded to **Florida** by **Chicago** with Dylan Olsen for Kris Versteeg and Phillipe Lefebvre, November 14, 2013. Traded to **Boston** by **Florida** for Reilly Smith and Marc Savard, July 1, 2015.

HAYES, Kevin (HAYZ, KEH-vihn) NYR

Right wing. Shoots left. 6'5", 215 lbs. Born, Dorchester, MA, May 8, 1992. Chicago's 1st pick, 24th overall, in 2010 NHL Draft.

Season	Club	League	GP	G	A	Pts	PIM	PP	SH	GW	S	S%	+/-	TF	F%	Min	GP	G	A	Pts	PIM	PP	SH	GW	Min
2007-08	Nobles	High-MA	29	8	5	13	2																		
2008-09	Nobles	High-MA	23	28	27	55	15																		
2009-10	Cape Cod	Minor-MA	25	21	30	51	....																		
	Nobles	High-MA	29	25	44	69	8																		
	USAHNTDP	U-18	2	0	0	2	0																		
2010-11	Boston College	H-East	31	4	10	14	8																		
2011-12	Boston College	H-East	44	7	21	28	10																		
2012-13	Boston College	H-East	27	6	19	25	14																		
2013-14	Boston College	H-East	40	27	38	65	16																		
2014-15	**NY Rangers**	**NHL**	79	17	28	45	22	1	1	1	111	15.3	15	681	36.3	13:02	19	2	5	7	2	1	0	1	14:13
2015-16	**NY Rangers**	**NHL**	79	14	22	36	30	3	0	3	133	10.5	4	381	36.0	13:40	3	0	0	0	4	0	0	0	10:49
2016-17	**NY Rangers**	**NHL**	76	17	32	49	18	1	1	4	143	11.9	10	968	45.7	16:34	12	0	3	3	4	0	0	0	17:44
	NHL Totals		234	48	82	130	70	5	2	8	387	12.4		2030	40.7	14:24	34	2	8	10	10	1	0	1	15:09

Hockey East First All-Star Team (2014) • NCAA East First All-American Team (2014)
Signed as a a free agent by **NY Rangers**, August 20, 2014.

HEDMAN, Victor

(HEHD-muhn, VIHK-tohr) **T.B.**

Defense. Shoots left. 6'6", 223 lbs. Born, Ornskoldsvik, Sweden, December 18, 1990. Tampa Bay's 1st pick, 2nd overall, in 2009 NHL Draft.

			Regular Season														Playoffs								
Season	Club	League	GP	G	A	Pts	PIM	PP	SH	GW	S	S%	+/-	TF	F%	Min	GP	G	A	Pts	PIM	PP	SH	GW	Min
2005-06	MODO U18	Swe-U18	8	3	3	6	14	....	....	....	....	....	....	....	....	....	2	0	0	0	0	....	....	....	....
	MODO Jr.	Swe-Jr.	10	0	1	1	8	....	....	....	....	....	....	....	....	....	....	....	....	....	....	....	....	....	....
2006-07	MODO U18	Swe-U18	3	3	0	3	29	....	....	....	....	....	....	....	....	....	....	....	....	....	....	....	....	....	....
	MODO Jr.	Swe-Jr.	34	13	12	25	30	....	....	....	....	....	....	....	....	....	5	1	1	2	44	....	....	....	....
2007-08	MODO Jr.	Swe-Jr.	6	2	1	3	26	....	....	....	....	....	....	....	....	....	3	2	0	2	4	....	....	....	....
	MODO	Sweden	39	2	2	4	44	....	....	....	....	....	....	....	....	....	5	1	0	1	4	....	....	....	....
2008-09	MODO Jr.	Swe-Jr.	2	0	2	2	10	....	....	....	....	....	....	....	....	....	5	0	1	1	2	....	....	....	....
	MODO	Sweden	43	7	14	21	52	....	....	....	....	....	....	....	....	....	....	....	....	....	....	....	....	....	....
2009-10	**Tampa Bay**	**NHL**	**74**	**4**	**16**	**20**	**79**	0	0	0	90	4.4	-3	0	0.0	20:51	....	....	....	....	....	....	....	....	....
2010-11	**Tampa Bay**	**NHL**	**79**	**3**	**23**	**26**	**70**	0	0	0	101	3.0	3	0	0.0	21:01	18	0	6	6	8	0	0	0	22:16
2011-12	**Tampa Bay**	**NHL**	**61**	**5**	**18**	**23**	**65**	0	0	0	82	6.1	-9	0	0.0	23:06	....	....	....	....	....	....	....	....	....
2012-13	Barys Astana	KHL	26	1	21	22	70	....	....	....	....	....	....	....	....	....	....	....	....	....	....	....	....	....	....
	Tampa Bay	**NHL**	**44**	**4**	**16**	**20**	**31**	0	0	0	76	5.3	1	0	0.0	22:40	....	....	....	....	....	....	....	....	....
2013-14	**Tampa Bay**	**NHL**	**75**	**13**	**42**	**55**	**53**	3	0	2	170	7.6	5	0	0.0	22:26	4	1	2	3	2	0	0	0	24:29
2014-15	**Tampa Bay**	**NHL**	**59**	**10**	**28**	**38**	**40**	3	0	2	115	8.7	12	0	0.0	22:41	26	1	13	14	6	1	0	0	23:58
2015-16	**Tampa Bay**	**NHL**	**78**	**10**	**37**	**47**	**46**	1	0	0	180	5.6	21	0	0.0	23:04	17	4	10	14	14	2	0	1	27:26
2016-17	**Tampa Bay**	**NHL**	**79**	**16**	**56**	**72**	**47**	4	0	5	166	9.6	3	0	0.0	24:31	....	....	....	....	....	....	....	....	....
	NHL Totals		**549**	**65**	**236**	**301**	**431**	11	0	9	980	6.6		0	0.0	22:31	65	6	31	37	30	3	0	1	24:26

Signed as a free agent by **Astana** (KHL), September 25, 2012.
NHL Second All-Star Team (2017)
Played in NHL All-Star Game (2017)

HEED, Tim

(HEH-ehd, TIHM) **S.J.**

Defense. Shoots right. 5'11", 175 lbs. Born, Gothenburg, Sweden, January 27, 1991. Anaheim's 5th pick, 132nd overall, in 2010 NHL Draft.

Season	Club	League	GP	G	A	Pts	PIM	PP	SH	GW	S	S%	+/-	TF	F%	Min	GP	G	A	Pts	PIM	PP	SH	GW	Min
2007-08	Sodertalje SK U18	Swe-U18	36	4	23	27	34	....	....	....	....	....	....	....	....	....	2	0	0	0	4	....	....	....	....
	Sodertalje SK Jr.	Swe-Jr.	2	0	0	0	0	....	....	....	....	....	....	....	....	....	....	....	....	....	....	....	....	....	....
2008-09	Sodertalje SK U18	Swe-U18	14	7	10	17	10	....	....	....	....	....	....	....	....	....	3	3	2	5	2	....	....	....	....
	Sodertalje SK Jr.	Swe-Jr.	32	1	7	8	10	....	....	....	....	....	....	....	....	....	2	0	1	1	0	....	....	....	....
2009-10	Sodertalje SK Jr.	Swe-Jr.	32	8	29	37	20	....	....	....	....	....	....	....	....	....	....	....	....	....	....	....	....	....	....
	Sodertalje SK	Sweden	27	1	9	10	2	....	....	....	....	....	....	....	....	....	....	....	....	....	....	....	....	....	....
	Sodertalje SK	Sweden-Q	10	0	4	4	0	....	....	....	....	....	....	....	....	....	....	....	....	....	....	....	....	....	....
2010-11	Sodertalje SK Jr.	Swe-Jr.	2	0	2	2	2	....	....	....	....	....	....	....	....	....	....	....	....	....	....	....	....	....	....
	Vaxjo Lakers HC	Sweden-2	29	3	20	23	8	....	....	....	....	....	....	....	....	....	....	....	....	....	....	....	....	....	....
	Sodertalje SK	Sweden	12	1	0	1	0	....	....	....	....	....	....	....	....	....	....	....	....	....	....	....	....	....	....
	Sodertalje SK	Sweden-Q	10	0	4	4	4	....	....	....	....	....	....	....	....	....	....	....	....	....	....	....	....	....	....
2011-12	Malmo	Sweden-2	53	5	28	33	10	....	....	....	....	....	....	....	....	....	....	....	....	....	....	....	....	....	....
2012-13	Vaxjo Jr.	Swe-Jr.	4	2	4	6	0	....	....	....	....	....	....	....	....	....	....	....	....	....	....	....	....	....	....
	Vaxjo Lakers HC	Sweden	10	0	0	0	2	....	....	....	....	....	....	....	....	....	....	....	....	....	....	....	....	....	....
	VIK Vasteras HK	Sweden-2	41	5	10	15	12	....	....	....	....	....	....	....	....	....	....	....	....	....	....	....	....	....	....
2013-14	Skelleftea AIK	Sweden	40	1	4	5	2	....	....	....	....	....	....	....	....	....	2	0	0	0	0	....	....	....	....
2014-15	Skelleftea AIK	Sweden	50	10	27	37	10	....	....	....	....	....	....	....	....	....	15	2	9	11	0	....	....	....	....
2015-16	Skelleftea AIK	Sweden	52	8	15	23	2	....	....	....	....	....	....	....	....	....	16	3	6	9	4	....	....	....	....
2016-17	**San Jose**	**NHL**	**1**	**0**	**0**	**0**	**0**	0	0	0	1	0.0	0	0	0.0	16:29	....	....	....	....	....	....	....	....	....
	San Jose	AHL	55	14	42	56	12	....	....	....	....	....	....	....	....	....	15	3	7	10	6	....	....	....	....
	NHL Totals		**1**	**0**	**0**	**0**	**0**	0	0	0	1	0.0		0	0.0	16:29	....	....	....	....	....	....	....	....	....

AHL Second All-Star Team (2017)
Signed as a free agent by **Skelleftea** (Sweden), May 17, 2013. Signed as a free agent by **San Jose**, May 20, 2016.

HEINEN, Danton

(HIGH-nehn, DAN-tuhn) **BOS**

Center/Left wing. Shoots left. 6'1", 193 lbs. Born, Langley, BC, July 5, 1995. Boston's 3rd pick, 116th overall, in 2014 NHL Draft.

Season	Club	League	GP	G	A	Pts	PIM	PP	SH	GW	S	S%	+/-	TF	F%	Min	GP	G	A	Pts	PIM	PP	SH	GW	Min
2011-12	Valley West	BCMML	39	19	24	43	6	....	....	....	....	....	....	....	....	....	2	2	0	2	0	....	....	....	....
2012-13	Richmond	PJHL	43	21	28	49	4	....	....	....	....	....	....	....	....	....	15	6	8	14	2	....	....	....	....
	Merritt	BCHL	2	0	2	2	0	....	....	....	....	....	....	....	....	....	....	....	....	....	....	....	....	....	....
2013-14	Surrey Eagles	BCHL	57	29	33	62	8	....	....	....	....	....	....	....	....	....	6	2	5	7	2	....	....	....	....
2014-15	U. of Denver	NCHC	40	16	29	*45	10	....	....	....	....	....	....	....	....	....	....	....	....	....	....	....	....	....	....
2015-16	U. of Denver	NCHC	41	20	28	48	10	....	....	....	....	....	....	....	....	....	....	....	....	....	....	....	....	....	....
	Providence Bruins	AHL	2	0	2	2	2	....	....	....	....	....	....	....	....	....	2	0	0	0	0	....	....	....	....
2016-17	**Boston**	**NHL**	**8**	**0**	**0**	**0**	**2**	0	0	0	7	0.0	-3	0	0.0	13:14	....	....	....	....	....	....	....	....	....
	Providence Bruins	AHL	64	14	30	44	14	....	....	....	....	....	....	....	....	....	17	9	9	18	0	....	....	....	....
	NHL Totals		**8**	**0**	**0**	**0**	**2**	0	0	0	7	0.0		0	0.0	13:14	....	....	....	....	....	....	....	....	....

NCHC All-Rookie Team (2015) • NCHC Second All-Star Team (2015) • NCHC Rookie of the Year (2015) • NCHC First All-Star Team (2016)

HELGESON, Seth

(HEHL-guh-suhn, SEHTH) **NYI**

Defense. Shoots left. 6'4", 210 lbs. Born, Faribault, MN, October 8, 1990. New Jersey's 4th pick, 114th overall, in 2009 NHL Draft.

Season	Club	League	GP	G	A	Pts	PIM	PP	SH	GW	S	S%	+/-	TF	F%	Min	GP	G	A	Pts	PIM	PP	SH	GW	Min
2006-07	Faribault Falcons	High-MN	27	19	17	36	....	....	....	....	....	....	....	....	....	....	....	....	....	....	....	....	....	....	....
2007-08	Sioux City	USHL	58	3	8	11	41	....	....	....	....	....	....	....	....	....	4	0	1	1	2	....	....	....	....
2008-09	Sioux City	USHL	58	4	12	16	64	....	....	....	....	....	....	....	....	....	....	....	....	....	....	....	....	....	....
2009-10	U. of Minnesota	WCHA	31	1	0	1	24	....	....	....	....	....	....	....	....	....	....	....	....	....	....	....	....	....	....
2010-11	U. of Minnesota	WCHA	36	1	6	7	66	....	....	....	....	....	....	....	....	....	....	....	....	....	....	....	....	....	....
2011-12	U. of Minnesota	WCHA	43	5	9	14	70	....	....	....	....	....	....	....	....	....	....	....	....	....	....	....	....	....	....
2012-13	U. of Minnesota	WCHA	40	0	5	5	62	....	....	....	....	....	....	....	....	....	....	....	....	....	....	....	....	....	....
2013-14	Albany Devils	AHL	75	1	9	10	100	....	....	....	....	....	....	....	....	....	4	0	0	0	2	....	....	....	....
2014-15	**New Jersey**	**NHL**	**22**	**0**	**2**	**2**	**18**	0	0	0	11	0.0	4	0	0.0	13:28	....	....	....	....	....	....	....	....	....
	Albany Devils	AHL	49	2	10	12	58	....	....	....	....	....	....	....	....	....	....	....	....	....	....	....	....	....	....
2015-16	**New Jersey**	**NHL**	**19**	**0**	**1**	**1**	**17**	0	0	0	9	0.0	-5	0	0.0	13:57	....	....	....	....	....	....	....	....	....
	Albany Devils	AHL	42	2	5	7	52	....	....	....	....	....	....	....	....	....	11	0	4	4	16	....	....	....	....
2016-17	**New Jersey**	**NHL**	**9**	**1**	**0**	**1**	**15**	0	0	0	3	33.3	2	0	0.0	13:28	....	....	....	....	....	....	....	....	....
	Albany Devils	AHL	48	2	7	9	50	....	....	....	....	....	....	....	....	....	4	0	1	1	2	....	....	....	....
	NHL Totals		**50**	**1**	**3**	**4**	**50**	0	0	0	23	4.3		0	0.0	13:39	....	....	....	....	....	....	....	....	....

Signed as a free agent by **NY Islanders**, July 1, 2017.

HELM, Darren

(HEHLM, DAIR-ehn) **DET**

Center/Left wing. Shoots left. 6', 196 lbs. Born, Winnipeg, MB, January 21, 1987. Detroit's 5th pick, 132nd overall, in 2005 NHL Draft.

Season	Club	League	GP	G	A	Pts	PIM	PP	SH	GW	S	S%	+/-	TF	F%	Min	GP	G	A	Pts	PIM	PP	SH	GW	Min
2003-04	Selkirk Fishermen	MJBHL	34	39	32	71	34	....	....	....	....	....	....	....	....	....	....	....	....	....	....	....	....	....	....
2004-05	Medicine Hat	WHL	72	10	14	24	27	....	....	....	....	....	....	....	....	....	13	2	6	8	10	....	....	....	....
2005-06	Medicine Hat	WHL	70	41	38	79	37	....	....	....	....	....	....	....	....	....	13	5	4	9	2	....	....	....	....
2006-07	Medicine Hat	WHL	59	25	39	64	53	....	....	....	....	....	....	....	....	....	23	10	12	22	14	....	....	....	....
2007-08 ♦	**Detroit**	**NHL**	**7**	**0**	**0**	**0**	**2**	0	0	0	7	0.0	-2	23	21.7	7:00	18	2	2	4	2	0	0	0	7:30
	Grand Rapids	AHL	67	16	15	31	30	....	....	....	....	....	....	....	....	....	....	....	....	....	....	....	....	....	....
2008-09	**Detroit**	**NHL**	**16**	**0**	**1**	**1**	**4**	0	0	0	29	0.0	-7	132	56.1	12:26	23	4	1	5	4	0	0	1	12:06
	Grand Rapids	AHL	55	13	24	37	24	....	....	....	....	....	....	....	....	....	....	....	....	....	....	....	....	....	....
2009-10	**Detroit**	**NHL**	**75**	**11**	**13**	**24**	**18**	0	3	3	165	6.7	-2	875	51.1	14:30	12	1	0	1	4	0	0	0	13:56
2010-11	**Detroit**	**NHL**	**82**	**12**	**20**	**32**	**16**	0	2	2	177	6.8	9	938	52.6	13:18	11	3	3	6	8	0	0	1	13:28
2011-12	**Detroit**	**NHL**	**68**	**9**	**17**	**26**	**12**	0	0	2	124	7.3	5	777	51.9	14:31	1	0	0	0	0	0	0	0	3:08
2012-13	**Detroit**	**NHL**	**1**	**0**	**0**	**0**	**2**	0	0	0	1	0.0	0	14	42.9	12:27	....	....	....	....	....	....	....	....	....
2013-14	**Detroit**	**NHL**	**42**	**12**	**8**	**20**	**14**	1	2	3	83	14.5	2	548	49.1	15:10	5	0	1	1	0	0	0	0	15:12
	Grand Rapids	AHL	2	0	0	0	0	....	....	....	....	....	....	....	....	....	....	....	....	....	....	....	....	....	....
2014-15	**Detroit**	**NHL**	**75**	**15**	**18**	**33**	**12**	3	2	1	160	9.4	7	421	53.0	15:50	7	0	3	3	4	0	0	0	19:17

			Regular Season														Playoffs								
Season	Club	League	GP	G	A	Pts	PIM	PP	SH	GW	S	S%	+/-	TF	F%	Min	GP	G	A	Pts	PIM	PP	SH	GW	Min
2015-16	**Detroit**	**NHL**	77	13	13	26	32	0	0	3	165	7.9	−2	77	50.7	15:04	5	1	0	1	6	0	0	0	13:02
2016-17	**Detroit**	**NHL**	50	8	9	17	20	2	0	1	98	8.2	−6	420	51.4	15:22	....	....	....	....	....	....	....	....	....
	NHL Totals		493	80	99	179	132	6	9	15	1009	7.9		4225	51.5	14:34	82	11	10	21	28	0	0	2	12:18

WHL East First All-Star Team (2006) • WHL East Second All-Star Team (2007)
• Missed majority of 2012-13 due to recurring back injury.

HEMSKY, Ales

(HEHM-skee, ahl-EHSH) **MTL**

Right wing. Shoots right. 6', 185 lbs. Born, Pardubice, Czech., August 13, 1983. Edmonton's 1st pick, 13th overall, in 2001 NHL Draft.

			Regular Season														Playoffs								
Season	Club	League	GP	G	A	Pts	PIM	PP	SH	GW	S	S%	+/-	TF	F%	Min	GP	G	A	Pts	PIM	PP	SH	GW	Min
99-2000	HC Pardubice Jr.	CzRep-Jr.	45	20	36	56	54	....	....	....	....	....	....	....	....	....	7	4	14	18	36	....	....	....	....
	Pardubice	CzRep	4	0	1	1	0	....	....	....	....	....	....	....	....	....	....	....	....	....	....	....	....	....	....
2000-01	Hull Olympiques	QMJHL	68	36	64	100	67	....	....	....	....	....	....	....	....	....	5	2	3	5	2	....	....	....	....
2001-02	Hull Olympiques	QMJHL	53	27	70	97	86	....	....	....	....	....	....	....	....	....	10	6	10	16	6	....	....	....	....
2002-03	**Edmonton**	**NHL**	59	6	24	30	14	0	0	1	50	12.0	5	3	33.3	12:04	6	0	0	0	0	0	0	0	12:46
2003-04	**Edmonton**	**NHL**	71	12	22	34	14	4	0	3	87	13.8	−7	3	33.3	14:26	....	....	....	....	....	....	....	....	....
2004-05	Pardubice	CzRep	47	13	18	31	28	....	....	....	....	....	....	....	....	....	16	4	*10	*14	26	....	....	....	....
2005-06	**Edmonton**	**NHL**	81	19	58	77	64	7	1	4	178	10.7	−5	7	42.9	16:59	24	6	11	17	14	4	0	2	16:06
	Czech Republic	Olympics	8	1	2	3	2	....	....	....	....	....	....	....	....	....	....	....	....	....	....	....	....	....	....
2006-07	**Edmonton**	**NHL**	64	13	40	53	40	5	0	1	122	10.7	−7	10	30.0	16:59	....	....	....	....	....	....	....	....	....
2007-08	**Edmonton**	**NHL**	74	20	51	71	34	8	0	2	184	10.9	−9	5	20.0	18:35	....	....	....	....	....	....	....	....	....
2008-09	**Edmonton**	**NHL**	72	23	43	66	32	4	0	2	185	12.4	1	4	0.0	18:39	....	....	....	....	....	....	....	....	....
2009-10	**Edmonton**	**NHL**	22	7	15	22	8	3	0	0	57	12.3	7	1	100.0	17:56	....	....	....	....	....	....	....	....	....
2010-11	**Edmonton**	**NHL**	47	14	28	42	18	1	1	1	100	14.0	3	7	14.3	18:17	....	....	....	....	....	....	....	....	....
2011-12	**Edmonton**	**NHL**	69	10	26	36	43	1	0	1	137	7.3	−13	6	33.3	17:36	....	....	....	....	....	....	....	....	....
2012-13	Pardubice	CzRep	27	14	18	32	52	....	....	....	....	....	....	....	....	....	....	....	....	....	....	....	....	....	....
	Edmonton	**NHL**	38	9	11	20	16	5	0	1	82	11.0	−6	24	50.0	15:42	....	....	....	....	....	....	....	....	....
2013-14	**Edmonton**	**NHL**	55	9	17	26	20	2	0	1	94	9.6	−13	4	25.0	16:05	....	....	....	....	....	....	....	....	....
	Czech Republic	Olympics	5	3	1	4	0	....	....	....	....	....	....	....	....	....	....	....	....	....	....	....	....	....	....
	Ottawa	**NHL**	20	4	13	17	4	0	0	0	44	9.1	−2	0	0.0	15:38	....	....	....	....	....	....	....	....	....
2014-15	**Dallas**	**NHL**	76	11	21	32	16	1	0	1	140	7.9	−8	0	0.0	13:38	....	....	....	....	....	....	....	....	....
2015-16	**Dallas**	**NHL**	75	13	26	39	20	1	0	0	155	8.4	3	6	33.3	13:06	13	1	3	4	2	1	0	0	15:24
2016-17	**Dallas**	**NHL**	15	4	3	7	0	1	0	0	30	13.3	−1	0	0.0	14:25	....	....	....	....	....	....	....	....	....
	NHL Totals		838	174	398	572	343	43	2	18	1645	10.6		80	35.0	16:00	43	7	14	21	16	5	0	2	15:25

QMJHL Second All-Star Team (2002)

Signed as a free agent by **Pardubice** (CzRep), September 18, 2004. • Missed majority of 2009-10 due to shoulder injury vs. Los Angeles, November 25, 2009. Signed as a free agent by **Pardubice** (CzRep), September 17, 2012. Traded to **Ottawa** by **Edmonton** for Ottawa's 5th round pick (Liam Coughlin) in 2014 NHL Draft and Ottawa's 3rd round pick (later traded to NY Rangers – NY Rangers selected Sergey Zobrovskiy) in 2015 NHL Draft, July 1, 2014. • Missed majority of 2016-17 due to hip injury in World Cup of Hockey 2016 and resulting surgery, October 31, 2016. Signed as a free agent by **Montreal**, July 3, 2017.

HENDRICKS, Matt

(HEHN-drihks, MAT)

Center. Shoots left. 6', 207 lbs. Born, Blaine, MN, June 17, 1981. Nashville's 5th pick, 131st overall, in 2000 NHL Draft.

			Regular Season														Playoffs								
Season	Club	League	GP	G	A	Pts	PIM	PP	SH	GW	S	S%	+/-	TF	F%	Min	GP	G	A	Pts	PIM	PP	SH	GW	Min
1998-99	Blaine Bengals	High-MN	22	23	34	57	42	....	....	....	....	....	....	....	....	....	....	....	....	....	....	....	....	....	....
99-2000	Blaine Bengals	High-MN	21	23	30	53	28	....	....	....	....	....	....	....	....	....	....	....	....	....	....	....	....	....	....
2000-01	St. Cloud State	WCHA	37	3	9	12	23	....	....	....	....	....	....	....	....	....	....	....	....	....	....	....	....	....	....
2001-02	St. Cloud State	WCHA	42	19	20	39	74	....	....	....	....	....	....	....	....	....	....	....	....	....	....	....	....	....	....
2002-03	St. Cloud State	WCHA	37	18	18	36	64	....	....	....	....	....	....	....	....	....	....	....	....	....	....	....	....	....	....
2003-04	St. Cloud State	WCHA	37	14	11	25	32	....	....	....	....	....	....	....	....	....	....	....	....	....	....	....	....	....	....
	Milwaukee	AHL	1	0	0	0	2	....	....	....	....	....	....	....	....	....	....	....	....	....	....	....	....	....	....
2004-05	Lowell	AHL	15	1	2	3	10	....	....	....	....	....	....	....	....	....	....	....	....	....	....	....	....	....	....
	Florida Everblades	ECHL	54	24	26	50	94	....	....	....	....	....	....	....	....	....	4	0	0	0	4	....	....	....	....
2005-06	Rochester	AHL	56	13	14	27	84	....	....	....	....	....	....	....	....	....	....	....	....	....	....	....	....	....	....
2006-07	Hershey Bears	AHL	65	18	26	44	105	....	....	....	....	....	....	....	....	....	19	8	4	12	18	....	....	....	....
2007-08	Providence Bruins	AHL	67	22	30	52	121	....	....	....	....	....	....	....	....	....	10	0	3	3	6	....	....	....	....
2008-09	**Colorado**	**NHL**	4	0	0	0	13	0	0	0	5	0.0	1	1	0.0	8:30	....	....	....	....	....	....	....	....	....
	Lake Erie	AHL	43	14	15	29	71	....	....	....	....	....	....	....	....	....	....	....	....	....	....	....	....	....	....
2009-10	**Colorado**	**NHL**	56	9	7	16	74	0	1	1	63	14.3	1	83	39.8	9:16	6	0	0	0	0	0	0	0	9:52
2010-11	**Washington**	**NHL**	77	9	16	25	110	1	0	3	113	8.0	−2	98	53.1	11:28	7	0	0	0	4	0	0	0	9:08
2011-12	**Washington**	**NHL**	78	4	5	9	95	0	0	0	97	4.1	−6	265	53.6	12:07	14	1	1	2	6	0	0	0	16:05
2012-13	**Washington**	**NHL**	48	5	3	8	73	0	0	1	54	9.3	−6	259	56.8	11:43	7	0	0	0	0	0	0	0	10:32
2013-14	**Nashville**	**NHL**	44	2	2	4	54	0	0	0	53	3.8	−5	26	53.9	11:33	....	....	....	....	....	....	....	....	....
	Edmonton	**NHL**	33	3	0	3	58	0	1	1	49	6.1	−6	37	54.1	14:19	....	....	....	....	....	....	....	....	....
2014-15	**Edmonton**	**NHL**	71	8	8	16	76	0	1	0	103	7.8	−14	198	49.5	13:09	....	....	....	....	....	....	....	....	....
2015-16	**Edmonton**	**NHL**	68	5	7	12	82	0	1	0	62	8.1	2	453	55.4	13:14	....	....	....	....	....	....	....	....	....
2016-17	**Edmonton**	**NHL**	42	4	3	7	29	0	0	1	42	9.5	−3	232	56.9	10:45	....	....	....	....	....	....	....	....	....
	NHL Totals		521	49	51	100	664	1	4	7	641	7.6		1652	53.8	11:55	34	1	1	2	10	0	0	0	12:25

Signed as a free agent by **Boston**, July 9, 2007. Traded to **Colorado** by **Boston** for Johnny Boychuk, June 24, 2008. Signed as a free agent by **Washington**, September 27, 2010. Signed as a free agent by **Nashville**, July 5, 2013. Traded to **Edmonton** by **Nashville** for Devan Dubnyk, January 15, 2014.

HENLEY, Samuel

(HEHN-lee, SAM-yewl)

Center. Shoots left. 6'4", 210 lbs. Born, Val-d'Or, QC, July 25, 1993.

			Regular Season														Playoffs								
Season	Club	League	GP	G	A	Pts	PIM	PP	SH	GW	S	S%	+/-	TF	F%	Min	GP	G	A	Pts	PIM	PP	SH	GW	Min
2008-09	Amos Forestiers	QAAA	13	1	4	5	2	....	....	....	....	....	....	....	....	....	6	1	2	3	0	....	....	....	....
2009-10	Lewiston	QMJHL	63	4	9	13	22	....	....	....	....	....	....	....	....	....	4	0	1	1	2	....	....	....	....
2010-11	Lewiston	QMJHL	64	13	18	31	37	....	....	....	....	....	....	....	....	....	15	0	2	2	4	....	....	....	....
2011-12	Val-d'Or Foreurs	QMJHL	63	13	14	27	71	....	....	....	....	....	....	....	....	....	4	1	2	3	9	....	....	....	....
2012-13	Val-d'Or Foreurs	QMJHL	58	22	23	45	59	....	....	....	....	....	....	....	....	....	10	1	2	3	6	....	....	....	....
2013-14	Val-d'Or Foreurs	QMJHL	51	30	39	69	42	....	....	....	....	....	....	....	....	....	24	8	20	28	25	....	....	....	....
2014-15	Lake Erie	AHL	54	6	4	10	47	....	....	....	....	....	....	....	....	....	....	....	....	....	....	....	....	....	....
2015-16	San Antonio	AHL	74	8	7	15	51	....	....	....	....	....	....	....	....	....	....	....	....	....	....	....	....	....	....
2016-17	**Colorado**	**NHL**	1	1	0	1	2	0	0	0	1	100.0	1	1	0.0	5:18	....	....	....	....	....	....	....	....	....
	San Antonio	AHL	55	3	6	9	39	....	....	....	....	....	....	....	....	....	....	....	....	....	....	....	....	....	....
	NHL Totals		1	1	0	1	2	0	0	0	1	100.0		1	0.0	5:18	....	....	....	....	....	....	....	....	....

Signed as a free agent by **Colorado**, May 5, 2014.

HENRIQUE, Adam

(HEHN-reek, A-duhm) **N.J.**

Center. Shoots left. 6', 195 lbs. Born, Brantford, ON, February 6, 1990. New Jersey's 4th pick, 82nd overall, in 2008 NHL Draft.

			Regular Season														Playoffs								
Season	Club	League	GP	G	A	Pts	PIM	PP	SH	GW	S	S%	+/-	TF	F%	Min	GP	G	A	Pts	PIM	PP	SH	GW	Min
2006-07	Windsor Spitfires	OHL	62	23	21	44	20	....	....	....	....	....	....	....	....	....	....	....	....	....	....	....	....	....	....
2007-08	Windsor Spitfires	OHL	66	20	24	44	28	....	....	....	....	....	....	....	....	....	5	2	3	5	4	....	....	....	....
2008-09	Windsor Spitfires	OHL	56	30	33	63	47	....	....	....	....	....	....	....	....	....	20	8	9	17	19	....	....	....	....
2009-10	Windsor Spitfires	OHL	54	38	39	77	57	....	....	....	....	....	....	....	....	....	19	*20	5	25	12	....	....	....	....
2010-11	**New Jersey**	**NHL**	1	0	0	0	0	0	0	0	3	0.0	1	1	0.0	13:21	....	....	....	....	....	....	....	....	....
	Albany Devils	AHL	73	25	25	50	26	....	....	....	....	....	....	....	....	....	....	....	....	....	....	....	....	....	....
2011-12	**New Jersey**	**NHL**	74	16	35	51	7	0	*4	3	130	12.3	8	1026	48.8	18:10	24	5	8	13	11	0	0	*3	17:15
	Albany Devils	AHL	3	0	1	1	2	....	....	....	....	....	....	....	....	....	....	....	....	....	....	....	....	....	....
2012-13	Albany Devils	AHL	16	5	3	8	12	....	....	....	....	....	....	....	....	....	....	....	....	....	....	....	....	....	....
	New Jersey	**NHL**	42	11	5	16	16	3	2	2	78	14.1	−3	680	49.0	18:19	....	....	....	....	....	....	....	....	....
2013-14	**New Jersey**	**NHL**	77	25	18	43	20	7	3	4	137	18.2	3	918	44.3	18:03	....	....	....	....	....	....	....	....	....
2014-15	**New Jersey**	**NHL**	75	16	27	43	34	5	0	3	127	12.6	−6	519	52.0	17:45	....	....	....	....	....	....	....	....	....
2015-16	**New Jersey**	**NHL**	80	30	20	50	23	7	2	8	149	20.1	10	1381	44.7	19:50	....	....	....	....	....	....	....	....	....
2016-17	**New Jersey**	**NHL**	82	20	20	40	38	6	2	2	142	14.1	−20	1214	48.2	18:10	....	....	....	....	....	....	....	....	....
	NHL Totals		431	118	125	243	138	28	13	22	766	15.4		5739	47.3	18:23	24	5	8	13	11	0	0	3	17:15

OHL Playoff MVP (2010) • NHL All-Rookie Team (2012)

HENSICK, T.J.

(HEHN-sihk, TEE-JAY)

Center. Shoots right. 5'10", 190 lbs. Born, Howell, MI, December 10, 1985. Colorado's 5th pick, 88th overall, in 2005 NHL Draft.

			Regular Season														Playoffs								
Season	Club	League	GP	G	A	Pts	PIM	PP	SH	GW	S	S%	+/-	TF	F%	Min	GP	G	A	Pts	PIM	PP	SH	GW	Min
2001-02	USAHNTDP	U-17	17	10	5	15	....	....	....	....	....	....	....	....	....	....	....	....	....	....	....	....	....	....	....
	USAHNTDP	NAHL	46	15	25	40	10	....	....	....	....	....	....	....	....	....	....	....	....	....	....	....	....	....	....
2002-03	USAHNTDP	U-18	48	24	24	48	11	....	....	....	....	....	....	....	....	....	....	....	....	....	....	....	....	....	....
	USAHNTDP	NAHL	10	6	7	13	0	....	....	....	....	....	....	....	....	....	....	....	....	....	....	....	....	....	....
2003-04	U. of Michigan	CCHA	43	12	*34	46	38	....	....	....	....	....	....	....	....	....	....	....	....	....	....	....	....	....	....
2004-05	U. of Michigan	CCHA	39	23	32	55	24	....	....	....	....	....	....	....	....	....	....	....	....	....	....	....	....	....	....
2005-06	U. of Michigan	CCHA	41	17	35	52	44	....	....	....	....	....	....	....	....	....	....	....	....	....	....	....	....	....	....
2006-07	U. of Michigan	CCHA	41	23	*46	*69	38	....	....	....	....	....	....	....	....	....	....	....	....	....	....	....	....	....	....
2007-08	**Colorado**	**NHL**	**31**	**6**	**5**	**11**	**2**	**4**	**0**	**1**	**52**	**11.5**	**–4**	**256**	**42.2**	**11:59**	**2**	**0**	**1**	**1**	**0**	**0**	**0**	**0**	**15:29**
	Lake Erie	AHL	50	12	33	45	18	....	....	....	....	....	....	....	....	....	....	....	....	....	....	....	....	....	....
2008-09	**Colorado**	**NHL**	**61**	**4**	**17**	**21**	**14**	**1**	**0**	**0**	**116**	**3.4**	**–7**	**510**	**47.3**	**12:54**	....	....	....	....	....	....	....	....	....
	Lake Erie	AHL	12	7	9	16	2	....	....	....	....	....	....	....	....	....	....	....	....	....	....	....	....	....	....
2009-10	**Colorado**	**NHL**	**7**	**1**	**2**	**3**	**0**	**0**	**0**	**0**	**13**	**7.7**	**0**	**14**	**42.9**	**9:27**	....	....	....	....	....	....	....	....	....
	Lake Erie	AHL	58	20	50	70	25	....	....	....	....	....	....	....	....	....	....	....	....	....	....	....	....	....	....
2010-11	**St. Louis**	**NHL**	**13**	**1**	**2**	**3**	**2**	**0**	**0**	**0**	**12**	**8.3**	**–5**	**29**	**37.9**	**9:05**	....	....	....	....	....	....	....	....	....
	Peoria Rivermen	AHL	59	21	48	69	27	....	....	....	....	....	....	....	....	....	4	2	1	3	2	....	....	....	....
2011-12	Peoria Rivermen	AHL	66	21	49	70	20	....	....	....	....	....	....	....	....	....	....	....	....	....	....	....	....	....	....
2012-13	Peoria Rivermen	AHL	76	19	48	67	50	....	....	....	....	....	....	....	....	....	....	....	....	....	....	....	....	....	....
2013-14	MODO	Sweden	31	4	11	15	2	....	....	....	....	....	....	....	....	....	....	....	....	....	....	....	....	....	....
	Hartford	AHL	42	11	23	34	0	....	....	....	....	....	....	....	....	....	....	....	....	....	....	....	....	....	....
2014-15	Hamilton	AHL	75	19	41	60	10	....	....	....	....	....	....	....	....	....	....	....	....	....	....	....	....	....	....
2015-16	Charlotte	AHL	46	7	18	25	8	....	....	....	....	....	....	....	....	....	....	....	....	....	....	....	....	....	....
	Utica Comets	AHL	19	2	13	15	4	....	....	....	....	....	....	....	....	....	4	1	1	2	0	....	....	....	....
2016-17	Ontario Reign	AHL	67	16	36	52	18	....	....	....	....	....	....	....	....	....	5	2	3	5	0	....	....	....	....
	NHL Totals		**112**	**12**	**26**	**38**	**18**	**5**	**0**	**1**	**193**	**6.2**		**809**	**45.2**	**11:59**	**2**	**0**	**1**	**1**	**0**	**0**	**0**	**0**	**15:29**

CCHA All-Rookie Team (2004) • CCHA First All-Star Team (2004, 2005, 2007) • CCHA Rookie of the Year (2004) • NCAA West First All-American Team (2005, 2007) • CCHA Second All-Star Team (2006) • AHL Second All-Star Team (2012)

Traded to **St. Louis** by **Colorado** for Julian Talbot, June 17, 2010. Signed as a free agent by **MODO** (Sweden), June 13, 2013. Signed as a free agent by **Hartford** (AHL), January 11, 2014. Signed as a free agent by **Hamilton** (AHL), July 3, 2014. Signed as a free agent by **Carolina**, July 1, 2015. • Re-assigned to **Utica** (AHL) by **Carolina**, March 7, 2016. Signed as a free agent by **Ontario** (AHL), July 6, 2016.

HERTL, Tomas

(HUHR-tuhl, TAW-muhsh) **S.J.**

Center. Shoots left. 6'2", 215 lbs. Born, Prague, Czech Rep., November 12, 1993. San Jose's 1st pick, 17th overall, in 2012 NHL Draft.

Season	Club	League	GP	G	A	Pts	PIM	PP	SH	GW	S	S%	+/-	TF	F%	Min	GP	G	A	Pts	PIM	PP	SH	GW	Min
2007-08	Slavia U17	CzR-U17	22	7	6	13	4	....	....	....	....	....	....	....	....	....	5	1	0	1	2	....	....	....	....
2008-09	Slavia U17	CzR-U17	35	16	15	31	12	....	....	....	....	....	....	....	....	....	8	5	2	7	4	....	....	....	....
2009-10	Slavia U18	CzR-U18	7	13	10	23	8	....	....	....	....	....	....	....	....	....	5	5	6	11	31	....	....	....	....
	Slavia Jr.	CzRep-Jr.	42	12	26	38	12	....	....	....	....	....	....	....	....	....	4	1	0	1	2	....	....	....	....
2010-11	Slavia U18	CzR-U18	4	2	6	8	0	....	....	....	....	....	....	....	....	....	....	....	....	....	....	....	....	....	....
	Slavia Jr.	CzRep-Jr.	33	14	27	41	49	....	....	....	....	....	....	....	....	....	4	4	2	6	0	....	....	....	....
	HC Slavia Praha	CzRep	1	0	0	0	0	....	....	....	....	....	....	....	....	....	....	....	....	....	....	....	....	....	....
2011-12	HC Slavia Praha	CzRep	50	15	13	28	28	....	....	....	....	....	....	....	....	....	....	....	....	....	....	....	....	....	....
	Usti nad Labem	CzRep-2	....	....	....	....	....	....	....	....	....	....	....	....	....	....	3	2	0	2	2	....	....	....	....
2012-13	HC Slavia Praha	CzRep	43	18	12	30	16	....	....	....	....	....	....	....	....	....	11	3	5	8	0	....	....	....	....
2013-14	**San Jose**	**NHL**	**37**	**15**	**10**	**25**	**4**	**3**	**0**	**3**	**98**	**15.3**	**11**	**51**	**56.9**	**15:20**	**7**	**2**	**3**	**5**	**2**	**0**	**0**	**0**	**13:35**
2014-15	**San Jose**	**NHL**	**82**	**13**	**18**	**31**	**16**	**3**	**0**	**4**	**145**	**9.0**	**–5**	**83**	**45.8**	**14:33**	....	....	....	....	....	....	....	....	....
	Worcester Sharks	AHL	2	0	2	2	0	....	....	....	....	....	....	....	....	....	....	....	....	....	....	....	....	....	....
2015-16	**San Jose**	**NHL**	**81**	**21**	**25**	**46**	**26**	**3**	**0**	**3**	**202**	**10.4**	**16**	**457**	**56.0**	**15:58**	**20**	**6**	**5**	**11**	**4**	**2**	**0**	**1**	**17:47**
2016-17	**San Jose**	**NHL**	**49**	**10**	**12**	**22**	**14**	**1**	**0**	**4**	**100**	**10.0**	**–8**	**474**	**51.7**	**17:13**	**6**	**0**	**2**	**2**	**2**	**0**	**0**	**0**	**19:18**
	NHL Totals		**249**	**59**	**65**	**124**	**60**	**10**	**0**	**14**	**545**	**10.8**		**1065**	**53.3**	**15:39**	**33**	**8**	**10**	**18**	**8**	**2**	**0**	**1**	**17:10**

• Missed majority of 2013-14 due to knee injury at Los Angeles, December 19, 2013 .

HICKEY, Thomas

(HIH-kee, TAW-muhs) **NYI**

Defense. Shoots left. 6', 189 lbs. Born, Calgary, AB, February 8, 1989. Los Angeles' 1st pick, 4th overall, in 2007 NHL Draft.

Season	Club	League	GP	G	A	Pts	PIM	PP	SH	GW	S	S%	+/-	TF	F%	Min	GP	G	A	Pts	PIM	PP	SH	GW	Min
2003-04	Calgary Royals	CBHL	32	13	25	38	51	....	....	....	....	....	....	....	....	....	....	....	....	....	....	....	....	....	....
2004-05	Calgary Royals	AMHL	33	9	13	22	36	....	....	....	....	....	....	....	....	....	....	....	....	....	....	....	....	....	....
	Seattle	WHL	5	2	1	3	6	....	....	....	....	....	....	....	....	....	....	....	....	....	....	....	....	....	....
2005-06	Seattle	WHL	69	1	27	28	53	....	....	....	....	....	....	....	....	....	7	1	3	4	10	....	....	....	....
2006-07	Seattle	WHL	68	9	41	50	70	....	....	....	....	....	....	....	....	....	11	3	4	7	4	....	....	....	....
2007-08	Seattle	WHL	63	11	34	45	49	....	....	....	....	....	....	....	....	....	9	1	9	10	4	....	....	....	....
2008-09	Seattle	WHL	57	16	35	51	30	....	....	....	....	....	....	....	....	....	5	2	1	3	4	....	....	....	....
	Manchester	AHL	7	1	6	7	2	....	....	....	....	....	....	....	....	....	....	....	....	....	....	....	....	....	....
2009-10	Manchester	AHL	19	1	5	6	12	....	....	....	....	....	....	....	....	....	4	0	3	3	0	....	....	....	....
2010-11	Manchester	AHL	77	6	18	24	38	....	....	....	....	....	....	....	....	....	7	0	2	2	0	....	....	....	....
2011-12	Manchester	AHL	76	3	23	26	36	....	....	....	....	....	....	....	....	....	4	0	4	4	2	....	....	....	....
2012-13	Manchester	AHL	33	3	9	12	12	....	....	....	....	....	....	....	....	....	....	....	....	....	....	....	....	....	....
	NY Islanders	**NHL**	**39**	**1**	**3**	**4**	**8**	**0**	**0**	**1**	**40**	**2.5**	**9**	**0**	**0.0**	**16:52**	**2**	**0**	**0**	**0**	**2**	**0**	**0**	**0**	**18:17**
2013-14	**NY Islanders**	**NHL**	**82**	**4**	**18**	**22**	**34**	**0**	**0**	**0**	**96**	**4.2**	**5**	**0**	**0.0**	**18:52**	....	....	....	....	....	....	....	....	....
2014-15	**NY Islanders**	**NHL**	**81**	**2**	**20**	**22**	**26**	**0**	**0**	**1**	**82**	**2.4**	**–12**	**2**	**50.0**	**18:56**	**7**	**0**	**1**	**1**	**2**	**0**	**0**	**0**	**21:25**
2015-16	**NY Islanders**	**NHL**	**62**	**6**	**12**	**18**	**30**	**0**	**0**	**2**	**55**	**10.9**	**9**	**0**	**0.0**	**17:24**	**11**	**1**	**4**	**5**	**8**	**0**	**0**	**1**	**19:54**
2016-17	**NY Islanders**	**NHL**	**76**	**4**	**16**	**20**	**35**	**0**	**0**	**2**	**87**	**4.6**	**–1**	**0**	**0.0**	**17:31**	....	....	....	....	....	....	....	....	....
	NHL Totals		**340**	**17**	**69**	**86**	**133**	**0**	**0**	**6**	**360**	**4.7**		**2**	**50.0**	**18:05**	**20**	**1**	**5**	**6**	**12**	**0**	**0**	**1**	**20:16**

WHL West Second All-Star Team (2007) • WHL West First All-Star Team (2008, 2009)

• Missed majority of 2009-10 due to shoulder injury vs. Providence (AHL), November 22, 2009. Claimed on waivers by **NY Islanders** from **Los Angeles**, January 15, 2013.

HINOSTROZA, Vinnie

(hihn-oh-STROH-za, VIH-nee) **CHI**

Center. Shoots right. 5'9", 173 lbs. Born, Chicago, IL, April 3, 1994. Chicago's 6th pick, 169th overall, in 2012 NHL Draft.

Season	Club	League	GP	G	A	Pts	PIM	PP	SH	GW	S	S%	+/-	TF	F%	Min	GP	G	A	Pts	PIM	PP	SH	GW	Min
2009-10	Chicago Mission	T1EHL	34	13	21	34	38	....	....	....	....	....	....	....	....	....	....	....	....	....	....	....	....	....	....
2010-11	Waterloo	USHL	50	8	14	22	36	....	....	....	....	....	....	....	....	....	....	....	....	....	....	....	....	....	....
2011-12	Waterloo	USHL	55	20	24	44	56	....	....	....	....	....	....	....	....	....	1	0	0	0	0	....	....	....	....
2012-13	Waterloo	USHL	46	25	35	60	14	....	....	....	....	....	....	....	....	....	5	4	3	7	8	....	....	....	....
2013-14	U. of Notre Dame	H-East	34	8	24	32	4	....	....	....	....	....	....	....	....	....	....	....	....	....	....	....	....	....	....
2014-15	U. of Notre Dame	H-East	42	11	33	44	48	....	....	....	....	....	....	....	....	....	....	....	....	....	....	....	....	....	....
	Rockford IceHogs	AHL	5	0	2	2	0	....	....	....	....	....	....	....	....	....	....	....	....	....	....	....	....	....	....
2015-16	**Chicago**	**NHL**	**7**	**0**	**0**	**0**	**6**	**0**	**0**	**0**	**6**	**0.0**	**–1**	**32**	**40.6**	**8:41**	....	....	....	....	....	....	....	....	....
	Rockford IceHogs	AHL	66	18	33	51	24	....	....	....	....	....	....	....	....	....	3	0	0	0	2	....	....	....	....
2016-17	**Chicago**	**NHL**	**49**	**6**	**8**	**14**	**17**	**0**	**0**	**2**	**76**	**7.9**	**–1**	**171**	**39.8**	**11:59**	**1**	**0**	**0**	**0**	**0**	**0**	**0**	**0**	**6:48**
	Rockford IceHogs	AHL	15	3	4	7	4	....	....	....	....	....	....	....	....	....	....	....	....	....	....	....	....	....	....
	NHL Totals		**56**	**6**	**8**	**14**	**23**	**0**	**0**	**2**	**82**	**7.3**		**203**	**39.9**	**11:34**	**1**	**0**	**0**	**0**	**0**	**0**	**0**	**0**	**6:48**

Hockey East First All-Star Team (2015)

HJALMARSSON, Niklas

(JAHL-muhr-suhn, NIHK-luhs) **ARI**

Defense. Shoots left. 6'3", 197 lbs. Born, Eksjo, Sweden, June 6, 1987. Chicago's 5th pick, 108th overall, in 2005 NHL Draft.

Season	Club	League	GP	G	A	Pts	PIM	PP	SH	GW	S	S%	+/-	TF	F%	Min	GP	G	A	Pts	PIM	PP	SH	GW	Min
2003-04	HV 71 Jr.	Swe-Jr.	15	1	3	4	14	....	....	....	....	....	....	....	....	....	2	0	0	0	8	....	....	....	....
2004-05	HV 71 U18	Swe-U18	3	0	2	2	4	....	....	....	....	....	....	....	....	....	....	....	....	....	....	....	....	....	....
	HV 71 Jr.	Swe-Jr.	31	4	11	15	87	....	....	....	....	....	....	....	....	....	....	....	....	....	....	....	....	....	....
	HV 71 Jonkoping	Sweden	14	0	0	0	0	....	....	....	....	....	....	....	....	....	....	....	....	....	....	....	....	....	....
2005-06	HV 71 Jr.	Swe-Jr.	7	3	2	5	12	....	....	....	....	....	....	....	....	....	....	....	....	....	....	....	....	....	....
	HV 71 Jonkoping	Sweden	4	1	2	3	0	....	....	....	....	....	....	....	....	....	12	0	1	1	4	....	....	....	....
2006-07	HV 71 Jonkoping	Sweden	37	2	0	2	24	....	....	....	....	....	....	....	....	....	14	1	1	2	0	....	....	....	....
	HV 71 Jr.	Swe-Jr.	7	0	2	2	14	....	....	....	....	....	....	....	....	....	....	....	....	....	....	....	....	....	....
	IK Oskarshamn	Sweden-2	8	1	2	3	6	....	....	....	....	....	....	....	....	....	....	....	....	....	....	....	....	....	....

			Regular Season														Playoffs								
Season	Club	League	GP	G	A	Pts	PIM	PP	SH	GW	S	S%	+/-	TF	F%	Min	GP	G	A	Pts	PIM	PP	SH	GW	Min
2007-08	Chicago	NHL	13	0	1	1	13	0	0	0	5	0.0	-2	0	0.0	13:37	....	....	....	....	....	....	....	....	....
	Rockford IceHogs	AHL	47	4	9	13	31	....	....	....	....	....	....	....	....	....	12	0	4	4	8	....	....	....	....
2008-09	Chicago	NHL	21	1	2	3	0	0	0	0	15	6.7	4	0	0.0	14:59	17	0	1	1	6	0	0	0	16:37
	Rockford IceHogs	AHL	52	2	16	18	53	....	....	....	....	....	....	....	....	....	....	....	....	....	....	....	....	....	....
2009-10♦	Chicago	NHL	77	2	15	17	20	0	0	1	62	3.2	9	0	0.0	19:40	22	1	7	8	6	0	0	0	21:01
2010-11	Chicago	NHL	80	3	7	10	39	0	0	0	64	4.7	13	0	0.0	18:29	7	0	2	2	2	0	0	0	18:55
2011-12	Chicago	NHL	69	1	14	15	14	0	0	0	65	1.5	9	0	0.0	20:11	6	0	1	1	4	0	0	0	18:10
2012-13	HC Bolzano	Italy	18	6	16	22	8	....	....	....	....	....	....	....	....	....	....	....	....	....	....	....	....	....	....
	♦ Chicago	NHL	46	2	8	10	22	0	0	0	43	4.7	15	0	0.0	20:54	23	0	5	5	4	0	0	0	23:15
2013-14	Chicago	NHL	81	4	22	26	34	0	1	1	98	4.1	11	0	0.0	21:17	19	0	4	4	14	0	0	0	22:58
	Sweden	Olympics	6	0	0	0	0	....	....	....	....	....	....	....	....	....	....	....	....	....	....	....	....	....	....
2014-15♦	Chicago	NHL	82	3	16	19	44	0	0	1	97	3.1	25	0	0.0	21:53	23	1	5	6	8	0	0	0	26:02
2015-16	Chicago	NHL	81	2	22	24	32	0	0	0	77	2.6	13	0	0.0	22:23	7	0	1	1	0	0	0	0	24:11
2016-17	Chicago	NHL	73	5	13	18	20	0	0	0	61	8.2	12	0	0.0	21:30	4	0	0	0	2	0	0	0	22:30
	NHL Totals		623	23	120	143	238	0	1	3	587	3.9		0	0.0	20:27	128	2	26	28	46	0	0	0	22:00

Signed as a free agent by **Bolzano** (Italy), November 8, 2012. Traded to **Arizona** by **Chicago** for Connor Murphy and Laurent Dauphin, June 23, 2017.

HOFFMAN, Mike (HAWF-muhn, MIGHK) OTT

Center/Left wing. Shoots left. 6'1", 180 lbs. Born, Kitchener, ON, November 24, 1989. Ottawa's 5th pick, 130th overall, in 2009 NHL Draft.

Season	Club	League	GP	G	A	Pts	PIM	PP	SH	GW	S	S%	+/-	TF	F%	Min	GP	G	A	Pts	PIM	PP	SH	GW	Min
2006-07	Kitchener	ON-Jr.B	47	28	29	57	70	....	....	....	....	....	....	....	....	....	6	3	5	8	6	....	....	....	....
	Kitchener Rangers	OHL	2	0	0	0	2	....	....	....	....	....	....	....	....	....	4	0	0	0	0	....	....	....	....
2007-08	Gatineau	QMJHL	19	5	7	12	16	....	....	....	....	....	....	....	....	....	....	....	....	....	....	....	....	....	....
	Drummondville	QMJHL	43	19	17	36	77	....	....	....	....	....	....	....	....	....	....	....	....	....	....	....	....	....	....
2008-09	Drummondville	QMJHL	62	52	42	94	86	....	....	....	....	....	....	....	....	....	19	21	13	34	26	....	....	....	....
2009-10	Saint John	QMJHL	56	46	39	85	38	....	....	....	....	....	....	....	....	....	21	11	13	24	23	....	....	....	....
2010-11	Binghamton	AHL	74	7	18	25	16	....	....	....	....	....	....	....	....	....	19	1	8	9	16	....	....	....	....
	Elmira Jackals	ECHL	4	0	3	3	0	....	....	....	....	....	....	....	....	....	....	....	....	....	....	....	....	....	....
2011-12	Ottawa	NHL	1	0	0	0	0	0	0	0	0	0.0	-1	0	0.0	9:01	....	....	....	....	....	....	....	....	....
	Binghamton	AHL	76	21	28	49	44	....	....	....	....	....	....	....	....	....	....	....	....	....	....	....	....	....	....
2012-13	Binghamton	AHL	41	13	15	28	38	....	....	....	....	....	....	....	....	....	....	....	....	....	....	....	....	....	....
	Ottawa	NHL	3	0	0	0	2	0	0	0	6	0.0	-1	2	100.0	12:19	....	....	....	....	....	....	....	....	....
2013-14	Ottawa	NHL	25	3	3	6	2	1	0	0	61	4.9	-2	9	66.7	13:11	....	....	....	....	....	....	....	....	....
	Binghamton	AHL	51	30	37	67	32	....	....	....	....	....	....	....	....	....	....	....	....	....	....	....	....	....	....
2014-15	Ottawa	NHL	79	27	21	48	14	1	0	4	199	13.6	16	14	50.0	14:33	6	1	2	3	2	0	0	1	13:01
2015-16	Ottawa	NHL	78	29	30	59	18	9	0	3	242	12.0	1	18	44.4	17:33	....	....	....	....	....	....	....	....	....
2016-17	Ottawa	NHL	74	26	35	61	51	13	0	8	224	11.6	17	21	57.1	17:36	19	6	5	11	10	1	0	1	18:23
	NHL Totals		260	85	89	174	87	24	0	15	732	11.6		64	54.7	16:08	25	7	7	14	12	1	0	2	17:06

QMJHL First All-Star Team (2009, 2010) • QMJHL Player of the Year (2010) • Canadian Major Junior Second All-Star Team (2010) • AHL First All-Star Team (2014)

HOLDEN, Nick (HOHL-dehn, NIHK) NYR

Defense. Shoots left. 6'4", 214 lbs. Born, St. Albert, AB, May 15, 1987.

Season	Club	League	GP	G	A	Pts	PIM	PP	SH	GW	S	S%	+/-	TF	F%	Min	GP	G	A	Pts	PIM	PP	SH	GW	Min
2004-05	St. Albert Raiders	AMHL	35	7	15	22	24	....	....	....	....	....	....	....	....	....	....	....	....	....	....	....	....	....	....
	Camrose Kodiaks	AJHL	4	0	0	0	0	....	....	....	....	....	....	....	....	....	....	....	....	....	....	....	....	....	....
2005-06	Camrose Kodiaks	AJHL	29	5	8	13	27	....	....	....	....	....	....	....	....	....	....	....	....	....	....	....	....	....	....
	Sherwood Park	AJHL	28	2	15	17	19	....	....	....	....	....	....	....	....	....	....	....	....	....	....	....	....	....	....
2006-07	Chilliwack Bruins	WHL	67	8	23	31	62	....	....	....	....	....	....	....	....	....	5	1	1	2	6	....	....	....	....
2007-08	Chilliwack Bruins	WHL	70	22	38	60	54	....	....	....	....	....	....	....	....	....	4	1	3	4	0	....	....	....	....
	Syracuse Crunch	AHL	1	0	0	0	2	....	....	....	....	....	....	....	....	....	....	....	....	....	....	....	....	....	....
2008-09	Syracuse Crunch	AHL	61	4	18	22	46	....	....	....	....	....	....	....	....	....	....	....	....	....	....	....	....	....	....
2009-10	Syracuse Crunch	AHL	68	6	17	23	52	....	....	....	....	....	....	....	....	....	....	....	....	....	....	....	....	....	....
2010-11	Columbus	NHL	5	0	0	0	0	0	0	0	6	0.0	0	0	0.0	17:11	....	....	....	....	....	....	....	....	....
	Springfield	AHL	67	4	21	25	63	....	....	....	....	....	....	....	....	....	....	....	....	....	....	....	....	....	....
2011-12	Springfield	AHL	25	3	6	9	14	....	....	....	....	....	....	....	....	....	....	....	....	....	....	....	....	....	....
2012-13	Springfield	AHL	73	9	30	39	58	....	....	....	....	....	....	....	....	....	8	0	3	3	6	....	....	....	....
	Columbus	NHL	2	0	0	0	0	0	0	0	2	0.0	1	0	0.0	8:35	....	....	....	....	....	....	....	....	....
2013-14	Colorado	NHL	54	10	15	25	22	2	0	2	66	15.2	12	0	0.0	18:41	7	3	1	4	8	2	0	0	22:09
2014-15	Colorado	NHL	78	5	9	14	28	2	0	2	94	5.3	-11	0	0.0	19:48	....	....	....	....	....	....	....	....	....
2015-16	Colorado	NHL	82	6	16	22	24	0	0	0	98	6.1	-1	0	0.0	21:53	....	....	....	....	....	....	....	....	....
2016-17	NY Rangers	NHL	80	11	23	34	35	3	0	2	84	13.1	13	1	0.0	20:37	11	2	2	4	4	0	0	0	19:20
	NHL Totals		301	32	63	95	109	7	0	6	350	9.1		1	0.0	20:16	18	5	3	8	12	2	0	0	20:26

Signed as a free agent by **Columbus**, March 28, 2008. • Missed majority of 2011-12 due to shoulder injury vs. Portland (AHL), January 13, 2012. Signed as a free agent by **Colorado**, July 6, 2013. Traded to **NY Rangers** by **Colorado** for NY Rangers' 4th round pick (Petr Kvaca) in 2017 NHL Draft, June 25, 2016.

HOLLAND, Peter (HAW-luhnd, PEE-tuhr) MTL

Center. Shoots left. 6'2", 201 lbs. Born, Toronto, ON, January 14, 1991. Anaheim's 1st pick, 15th overall, in 2009 NHL Draft.

Season	Club	League	GP	G	A	Pts	PIM	PP	SH	GW	S	S%	+/-	TF	F%	Min	GP	G	A	Pts	PIM	PP	SH	GW	Min
2006-07	Brampton	Minor-ON	60	59	60	119	107	....	....	....	....	....	....	....	....	....	....	....	....	....	....	....	....	....	....
2007-08	Guelph Storm	OHL	62	8	15	23	31	....	....	....	....	....	....	....	....	....	10	0	1	1	4	....	....	....	....
2008-09	Guelph Storm	OHL	68	28	39	67	42	....	....	....	....	....	....	....	....	....	4	4	0	4	2	....	....	....	....
2009-10	Guelph Storm	OHL	59	30	50	80	40	....	....	....	....	....	....	....	....	....	5	3	5	8	12	....	....	....	....
2010-11	Guelph Storm	OHL	67	37	51	88	57	....	....	....	....	....	....	....	....	....	6	3	6	9	4	....	....	....	....
	Syracuse Crunch	AHL	3	3	3	6	0	....	....	....	....	....	....	....	....	....	....	....	....	....	....	....	....	....	....
2011-12	Anaheim	NHL	4	1	0	1	2	0	0	1	1	100.0	0	18	38.9	7:42	....	....	....	....	....	....	....	....	....
	Syracuse Crunch	AHL	71	23	37	60	59	....	....	....	....	....	....	....	....	....	....	....	....	....	....	....	....	....	....
2012-13	Norfolk Admirals	AHL	45	19	20	39	68	....	....	....	....	....	....	....	....	....	....	....	....	....	....	....	....	....	....
	Anaheim	NHL	21	3	2	5	4	1	0	0	26	11.5	4	203	43.8	11:35	....	....	....	....	....	....	....	....	....
2013-14	Anaheim	NHL	4	1	0	1	2	0	0	0	3	33.3	-1	31	38.7	9:06	....	....	....	....	....	....	....	....	....
	Norfolk Admirals	AHL	10	5	4	9	22	....	....	....	....	....	....	....	....	....	....	....	....	....	....	....	....	....	....
	Toronto	NHL	39	5	5	10	16	1	0	0	40	12.5	1	364	46.7	11:35	....	....	....	....	....	....	....	....	....
	Toronto Marlies	AHL	14	5	5	10	10	....	....	....	....	....	....	....	....	....	11	7	8	15	6	....	....	....	....
2014-15	Toronto	NHL	62	11	14	25	31	1	1	3	93	11.8	0	685	45.6	14:31	....	....	....	....	....	....	....	....	....
2015-16	Toronto	NHL	65	9	18	27	28	5	0	1	138	6.5	-16	465	46.5	14:40	....	....	....	....	....	....	....	....	....
2016-17	Toronto	NHL	8	0	1	1	4	0	0	0	13	0.0	-2	56	46.4	10:43	....	....	....	....	....	....	....	....	....
	Arizona	NHL	40	5	6	11	18	1	0	0	66	7.6	-14	446	45.3	13:09	....	....	....	....	....	....	....	....	....
	NHL Totals		243	35	46	81	105	9	1	5	380	9.2		2268	45.6	13:17	....	....	....	....	....	....	....	....	....

Traded to **Toronto** by **Anaheim** with Brad Staubitz for Jesse Blacker, Toronto's 2nd round pick (Marcus Pettersson) in 2014 NHL Draft and Anaheim's 7th round pick (previously acquired, Anaheim selected Ondrej Kase) in 2014 NHL Draft, November 16, 2013. Traded to **Arizona** by **Toronto** for a conditional pick (conditions not met) in 2018 NHL Draft, December 9, 2016. Signed as a free agent by **Montreal**, July 1, 2017.

HOLMSTROM, Ben (HOHLM-struhm, BEHN)

Right wing. Shoots right. 6'1", 201 lbs. Born, Colorado Springs, CO, April 9, 1987.

Season	Club	League	GP	G	A	Pts	PIM	PP	SH	GW	S	S%	+/-	TF	F%	Min	GP	G	A	Pts	PIM	PP	SH	GW	Min
2003-04	Sioux Falls	USHL	54	3	5	8	53	....	....	....	....	....	....	....	....	....	....	....	....	....	....	....	....	....	....
2004-05	Sioux Falls	USHL	15	1	0	1	10	....	....	....	....	....	....	....	....	....	....	....	....	....	....	....	....	....	....
2005-06	Sioux Falls	USHL	56	10	9	19	115	....	....	....	....	....	....	....	....	....	14	3	3	6	22	....	....	....	....
2006-07	U. Mass Lowell	H-East	30	4	9	13	18	....	....	....	....	....	....	....	....	....	....	....	....	....	....	....	....	....	....
2007-08	U. Mass Lowell	H-East	37	7	20	27	62	....	....	....	....	....	....	....	....	....	....	....	....	....	....	....	....	....	....
2008-09	U. Mass Lowell	H-East	38	6	15	21	52	....	....	....	....	....	....	....	....	....	....	....	....	....	....	....	....	....	....
2009-10	U. Mass Lowell	H-East	39	9	14	23	69	....	....	....	....	....	....	....	....	....	....	....	....	....	....	....	....	....	....
	Adirondack	AHL	13	3	0	3	9	....	....	....	....	....	....	....	....	....	....	....	....	....	....	....	....	....	....
2010-11	Philadelphia	NHL	2	0	0	0	5	0	0	0	0	0.0	-1	16	31.3	9:04	....	....	....	....	....	....	....	....	....
	Adirondack	AHL	79	16	22	38	75	....	....	....	....	....	....	....	....	....	....	....	....	....	....	....	....	....	....
2011-12	Philadelphia	NHL	5	0	0	0	2	0	0	0	3	0.0	0	30	50.0	6:43	....	....	....	....	....	....	....	....	....
	Adirondack	AHL	67	15	26	41	134	....	....	....	....	....	....	....	....	....	....	....	....	....	....	....	....	....	....
2012-13	Adirondack	AHL	22	2	6	8	29	....	....	....	....	....	....	....	....	....	....	....	....	....	....	....	....	....	....
2013-14	Adirondack	AHL	75	13	19	32	146	....	....	....	....	....	....	....	....	....	....	....	....	....	....	....	....	....	....
2014-15	Charlotte	AHL	62	5	15	20	92	....	....	....	....	....	....	....	....	....	....	....	....	....	....	....	....	....	....

			Regular Season														Playoffs								
Season	Club	League	GP	G	A	Pts	PIM	PP	SH	GW	S	S%	+/-	TF	F%	Min	GP	G	A	Pts	PIM	PP	SH	GW	Min
2015-16	Bridgeport	AHL	76	4	20	24	138										3	0	0	0	0				
2016-17	Bridgeport	AHL	76	7	9	16	91																		
	NHL Totals		**7**	**0**	**0**	**0**	**7**	**0**	**0**	**0**	**3**	**0.0**		**46**	**43.5**	**7:24**									

Signed as a free agent by **Philadelphia**, March 17, 2010. • Missed majority of 2012-13 due to knee injury vs. Syracuse (AHL), December 8, 2012. Signed as a free agent by **Carolina**, July 4, 2014. Signed as a free agent by **NY Islanders**, July 2, 2015.

HOLZER, Korbinian

(HOHL-zuhr, kohr-BIHN-EE-uhn) **ANA**

Defense. Shoots right. 6'3", 215 lbs. Born, Munich, West Germany, February 16, 1988. Toronto's 4th pick, 111th overall, in 2006 NHL Draft.

2004-05	EC Bad Tolz Jr.	Ger-Jr.	34	7	11	18	66										5	0	2	2	2				
2005-06	EC Bad Tolz Jr.	Ger-Jr.	2	1	1	2	6																		
	Tolzer Lowen	German-2	46	3	3	6	94																		
2006-07	Regensburg	German-2	42	2	6	8	68										4	0	0	0	2				
2007-08	Dusseldorf	Germany	35	2	5	7	66										13	0	2	2	20				
2008-09	Dusseldorf	Germany	38	4	5	9	89										16	0	1	1	18				
2009-10	Dusseldorf	Germany	52	6	16	22	96										3	0	0	0	4				
	Germany	Olympics	4	0	0	0	2																		
2010-11	**Toronto**	**NHL**	**2**	**0**	**0**	**0**	**2**	**0**	**0**	**0**	**1**	**0.0**	**–1**	**0**	**0.0**	**13:01**									
	Toronto Marlies	AHL	73	3	10	13	88																		
2011-12	Toronto Marlies	AHL	67	1	19	20	68										17	1	4	5	39				
2012-13	Toronto Marlies	AHL	46	1	10	11	46										8	0	1	1	24				
	Toronto	**NHL**	**22**	**2**	**1**	**3**	**28**	**0**	**0**	**1**	**16**	**12.5**	**–12**	**0**	**0.0**	**18:30**									
2013-14	Toronto Marlies	AHL	72	5	18	23	104										10	2	5	7	4				
2014-15	**Toronto**	**NHL**	**34**	**0**	**6**	**6**	**25**	**0**	**0**	**0**	**32**	**0.0**	**3**	**0**	**0.0**	**17:06**									
	Toronto Marlies	AHL	9	0	2	2	10																		
2015-16	**Anaheim**	**NHL**	**29**	**0**	**3**	**3**	**10**	**0**	**0**	**0**	**17**	**0.0**	**–3**	**0**	**0.0**	**14:45**									
	San Diego Gulls	AHL	9	0	3	3	0																		
2016-17	**Anaheim**	**NHL**	**32**	**2**	**5**	**7**	**23**	**0**	**0**	**0**	**14**	**14.3**	**0**	**0**	**0.0**	**13:31**	**5**	**0**	**0**	**0**	**18**	**0**	**0**	**0**	**11:51**
	NHL Totals		**119**	**4**	**15**	**19**	**88**	**0**	**0**	**1**	**80**	**5.0**		**0**	**0.0**	**15:45**	**5**	**0**	**0**	**0**	**18**	**0**	**0**	**0**	**11:51**

Traded to **Anaheim** by **Toronto** for Eric Brewer and Anaheim's 5th round pick (later traded to Washington – Washington selected Beck Malenstyn) in 2016 NHL Draft, March 2, 2015. • Missed majority of 2015-16 and 2016-17 as a healthy reserve.

HONKA, Julius

(HOHN-kuh, YOO-lee-uhs) **DAL**

Defense. Shoots right. 5'11", 185 lbs. Born, Jyvaskyla, Finland, December 3, 1995. Dallas' 1st pick, 14th overall, in 2014 NHL Draft.

2011-12	JyP Jyvaskyla U18	Fin-U18	35	8	7	15	32																		
	JyP Jyvaskyla Jr.	Fin-Jr.	2	0	0	0	0																		
2012-13	JyP Jyvaskyla Jr.	Fin-Jr.	42	4	11	15	47										4	0	0	0	25				
2013-14	Swift Current	WHL	62	16	40	56	52										6	2	0	2	6				
2014-15	Texas Stars	AHL	68	8	23	31	55										3	1	1	2	4				
2015-16	Texas Stars	AHL	73	11	33	44	38										4	0	1	1	4				
2016-17	**Dallas**	**NHL**	**16**	**1**	**4**	**5**	**4**	**0**	**0**	**1**	**34**	**2.9**	**–4**	**0**	**0.0**	**16:52**									
	Texas Stars	AHL	50	7	24	31	59																		
	NHL Totals		**16**	**1**	**4**	**5**	**4**	**0**	**0**	**1**	**34**	**2.9**		**0**	**0.0**	**16:52**									

WHL East Second All-Star Team (2014)

HORNQVIST, Patric

(HOHRN-kwihst, PAT-rihk) **PIT**

Right wing. Shoots right. 5'11", 189 lbs. Born, Sollentuna, Sweden, January 1, 1987. Nashville's 7th pick, 230th overall, in 2005 NHL Draft.

2003-04	Vasby Jr.	Swe-Jr.	10	7	10	17	30																		
	Vasby	Sweden-3	32	8	5	13	26																		
2004-05	Vasby	Sweden-3	28	12	12	24	36																		
	Djurgarden Jr.	Swe-Jr.	5	3	0	3	2																		
2005-06	Djurgarden Jr.	Swe-Jr.	4	2	1	3	2										4	1	2	3	2				
	Djurgarden	Sweden	47	5	2	7	36																		
2006-07	Djurgarden	Sweden	49	23	11	34	38																		
	Djurgarden Jr.	Swe-Jr.															7	2	5	7	14				
2007-08	Djurgarden	Sweden	53	18	12	30	58										5	0	1	1	6				
2008-09	**Nashville**	**NHL**	**28**	**2**	**5**	**7**	**16**	**0**	**0**	**0**	**54**	**3.7**	**–3**	**5**	**20.0**	**11:24**									
	Milwaukee	AHL	49	17	18	35	44										11	4	4	8	6				
2009-10	**Nashville**	**NHL**	**80**	**30**	**21**	**51**	**40**	**10**	**0**	**8**	**275**	**10.9**	**18**	**18**	**27.8**	**15:41**	**2**	**0**	**1**	**1**	**4**	**0**	**0**	**0**	**13:10**
	Sweden	Olympics	4	1	0	1	4																		
2010-11	**Nashville**	**NHL**	**79**	**21**	**27**	**48**	**47**	**6**	**0**	**5**	**265**	**7.9**	**11**	**45**	**48.9**	**15:44**	**12**	**2**	**1**	**3**	**6**	**1**	**0**	**0**	**15:16**
2011-12	**Nashville**	**NHL**	**76**	**27**	**16**	**43**	**28**	**8**	**0**	**3**	**230**	**11.7**	**9**	**9**	**66.7**	**15:20**	**10**	**1**	**3**	**4**	**2**	**1**	**0**	**0**	**15:25**
2012-13	Martigny	Swiss-2	9	7	7	14	8																		
	Djurgarden	Sweden-2	10	2	3	5	6																		
	Nashville	**NHL**	**24**	**4**	**10**	**14**	**14**	**4**	**0**	**1**	**87**	**4.6**	**–1**	**2**	**50.0**	**16:14**									
2013-14	**Nashville**	**NHL**	**76**	**22**	**31**	**53**	**28**	**7**	**0**	**6**	**248**	**8.9**	**1**	**6**	**0.0**	**16:52**									
2014-15	**Pittsburgh**	**NHL**	**64**	**25**	**26**	**51**	**38**	**6**	**0**	**4**	**220**	**11.4**	**12**	**7**	**28.6**	**17:39**	**5**	**2**	**1**	**3**	**2**	**0**	**0**	**0**	**18:44**
2015-16♦	**Pittsburgh**	**NHL**	**82**	**22**	**29**	**51**	**36**	**9**	**0**	**3**	**257**	**8.6**	**15**	**8**	**62.5**	**16:51**	**24**	**9**	**4**	**13**	**10**	**2**	**0**	**1**	**17:23**
2016-17♦	**Pittsburgh**	**NHL**	**70**	**21**	**23**	**44**	**28**	**10**	**0**	**6**	**223**	**9.4**	**16**	**11**	**27.3**	**15:57**	**19**	**5**	**4**	**9**	**18**	**1**	**0**	**1**	**14:17**
	NHL Totals		**579**	**174**	**188**	**362**	**275**	**60**	**0**	**36**	**1859**	**9.4**		**111**	**40.5**	**16:02**	**72**	**19**	**14**	**33**	**42**	**5**	**0**	**2**	**15:55**

Signed as a free agent by **Martigny** (Swiss-2), October 2, 2012. Signed as a free agent by **Djurgarden** (Sweden-2), November 12, 2012. Traded to **Pittsburgh** by **Nashville** with Nick Spaling for James Neal, June 27, 2014.

HORTON, Nathan

(HOHR-tuhn, NAY-thuhn) **TOR**

Right wing. Shoots right. 6'2", 229 lbs. Born, Welland, ON, May 29, 1985. Florida's 1st pick, 3rd overall, in 2003 NHL Draft.

2000-01	Thorold	ON-Jr.B	41	16	31	47	75																		
2001-02	Oshawa Generals	OHL	64	31	36	67	84										5	1	2	3	10				
2002-03	Oshawa Generals	OHL	54	33	35	68	111										13	9	6	15	10				
2003-04	**Florida**	**NHL**	**55**	**14**	**8**	**22**	**57**	**6**	**1**	**0**	**81**	**17.3**	**–5**	**270**	**41.9**	**13:20**									
2004-05	San Antonio	AHL	21	5	4	9	21																		
2005-06	**Florida**	**NHL**	**71**	**28**	**19**	**47**	**89**	**3**	**0**	**1**	**162**	**17.3**	**8**	**24**	**45.8**	**16:53**									
2006-07	**Florida**	**NHL**	**82**	**31**	**31**	**62**	**61**	**7**	**1**	**3**	**217**	**14.3**	**15**	**31**	**48.4**	**18:04**									
2007-08	**Florida**	**NHL**	**82**	**27**	**35**	**62**	**85**	**9**	**0**	**3**	**212**	**12.7**	**15**	**73**	**39.7**	**18:44**									
2008-09	**Florida**	**NHL**	**67**	**22**	**23**	**45**	**48**	**5**	**1**	**5**	**131**	**16.8**	**–5**	**863**	**43.7**	**17:51**									
2009-10	**Florida**	**NHL**	**65**	**20**	**37**	**57**	**42**	**7**	**2**	**4**	**159**	**12.6**	**–1**	**85**	**56.5**	**20:53**									
2010-11♦	**Boston**	**NHL**	**80**	**26**	**27**	**53**	**85**	**6**	**0**	**2**	**188**	**13.8**	**29**	**19**	**42.1**	**16:17**	**21**	**8**	**9**	**17**	**35**	**1**	**0**	**3**	**16:54**
2011-12	**Boston**	**NHL**	**46**	**17**	**15**	**32**	**54**	**6**	**0**	**3**	**90**	**18.9**	**0**	**3**	**66.7**	**15:56**									
2012-13	**Boston**	**NHL**	**43**	**13**	**9**	**22**	**22**	**0**	**0**	**1**	**114**	**11.4**	**1**	**10**	**50.0**	**16:51**	**22**	**7**	**12**	**19**	**14**	**2**	**0**	**3**	**18:29**
2013-14	**Columbus**	**NHL**	**36**	**5**	**14**	**19**	**24**	**2**	**0**	**2**	**48**	**10.4**	**–3**	**1**	**100.0**	**15:27**									
2014-15	**Toronto**	**NHL**	DID NOT PLAY – INJURED																						
2015-16	**Toronto**	**NHL**	DID NOT PLAY – INJURED																						
2016-17	**Toronto**	**NHL**	DID NOT PLAY – INJURED																						
	NHL Totals		**627**	**203**	**218**	**421**	**567**	**51**	**5**	**24**	**1402**	**14.5**		**1379**	**44.2**	**17:16**	**43**	**15**	**21**	**36**	**49**	**3**	**0**	**6**	**17:43**

OHL All-Rookie Team (2002)

Signed as a free agent by **San Antonio** (AHL), October 28, 2004. Traded to **Boston** by **Florida** with Gregory Campbell for Dennis Wideman, Boston's 1st round pick (later traded to Los Angeles – Los Angeles selected Derek Forbort) in 2010 NHL Draft and Boston's 3rd round pick (Kyle Rau) in 2011 NHL Draft, June 22, 2010. Signed as a free agent by **Columbus**, July 5, 2013. • Missed majority of 2013-14 due to shoulder surgery, July 17, 2013. Traded to **Toronto** by **Columbus** for David Clarkson, February 26, 2015. • Missed all of 2014-15, 2015-16 and 2016-17 due to recurring back injury.

HORVAT, Bo
(HOHR-vat, BOH) **VAN**

Center. Shoots left. 6', 206 lbs. Born, Rodney, ON, April 5, 1995. Vancouver's 1st pick, 9th overall, in 2013 NHL Draft.

Season	Club	League	GP	G	A	Pts	PIM	PP	SH	GW	S	S%	+/-	TF	F%	Min	Playoffs GP	G	A	Pts	PIM	PP	SH	GW	Min
2010-11	Elgin-Mid. Chiefs	Minor-ON	30	30	31	61	12	....	....	....	....	....	....	....	....	....	12	5	7	12	4	....	....	....	....
	Elgin-Middlesex	Other	32	14	38	52	8	....	....	....	....	....	....	....	....	....	....	....	....	....	....	....	....	....	....
	St. Thomas Stars	ON-Jr.B	5	1	3	4	0	....	....	....	....	....	....	....	....	....	7	3	3	6	0	....	....	....	....
2011-12	London Knights	OHL	64	11	19	30	8	....	....	....	....	....	....	....	....	....	18	1	3	4	0	....	....	....	....
2012-13	London Knights	OHL	67	33	28	61	29	....	....	....	....	....	....	....	....	....	21	*16	7	23	10	....	....	....	....
2013-14	London Knights	OHL	54	30	44	74	36	....	....	....	....	....	....	....	....	....	9	5	6	11	4	....	....	....	....
2014-15	**Vancouver**	**NHL**	**68**	**13**	**12**	**25**	**16**	**0**	**1**	**1**	**93**	**14.0**	**–8**	**848**	**51.4**	**12:16**	**6**	**1**	**3**	**4**	**2**	**0**	**0**	**0**	**12:40**
	Utica Comets	AHL	5	0	0	0	4	....	....	....	....	....	....	....	....	....	....	....	....	....	....	....	....	....	....
2015-16	**Vancouver**	**NHL**	**82**	**16**	**24**	**40**	**18**	**4**	**0**	**4**	**155**	**10.3**	**–30**	**1493**	**50.9**	**17:08**	....	....	....	....	....	....	....	....	....
2016-17	**Vancouver**	**NHL**	**81**	**20**	**32**	**52**	**27**	**3**	**2**	**1**	**158**	**12.7**	**–7**	**1498**	**50.5**	**18:02**	....	....	....	....	....	....	....	....	....
	NHL Totals		**231**	**49**	**68**	**117**	**61**	**7**	**3**	**6**	**406**	**12.1**		**3839**	**50.8**	**16:01**	**6**	**1**	**3**	**4**	**2**	**0**	**0**	**0**	**12:40**

OHL Playoff MVP (2013
Played in NHL All-Star Game (2017)

HO-SANG, Joshua
(HOH-SANG, JAW-shoo-wah) **NYI**

Center/Right wing. Shoots right. 6', 175 lbs. Born, Toronto, ON, January 22, 1996. NY Islanders' 2nd pick, 28th overall, in 2014 NHL Draft.

Season	Club	League	GP	G	A	Pts	PIM	PP	SH	GW	S	S%	+/-	TF	F%	Min	Playoffs GP	G	A	Pts	PIM	PP	SH	GW	Min
2011-12	Tor. Marlboros	GTHL	30	31	48	79	24	....	....	....	....	....	....	....	....	....	....	....	....	....	....	....	....	....	....
2012-13	Windsor Spitfires	OHL	63	14	30	44	22	....	....	....	....	....	....	....	....	....	....	....	....	....	....	....	....	....	....
2013-14	Windsor Spitfires	OHL	67	32	53	85	44	....	....	....	....	....	....	....	....	....	4	1	2	3	10	....	....	....	....
2014-15	Windsor Spitfires	OHL	11	3	16	19	8	....	....	....	....	....	....	....	....	....	....	....	....	....	....	....	....	....	....
	Niagara Ice Dogs	OHL	49	14	48	62	38	....	....	....	....	....	....	....	....	....	11	1	15	16	18	....	....	....	....
2015-16	Niagara Ice Dogs	OHL	66	19	63	82	44	....	....	....	....	....	....	....	....	....	17	6	20	26	8	....	....	....	....
2016-17	**NY Islanders**	**NHL**	**21**	**4**	**6**	**10**	**12**	**1**	**0**	**0**	**22**	**18.2**	**1**	**2**	**0.0**	**16:27**	....	....	....	....	....	....	....	....	....
	Bridgeport	AHL	50	10	26	36	24	....	....	....	....	....	....	....	....	....	....	....	....	....	....	....	....	....	....
	NHL Totals		**21**	**4**	**6**	**10**	**12**	**1**	**0**	**0**	**22**	**18.2**		**2**	**0.0**	**16:27**	....	....	....	....	....	....	....	....	....

HOSSA, Marian
(HOH-sa, MAIR-ee-uhn) **CHI**

Right wing. Shoots left. 6'1", 207 lbs. Born, Stara Lubovna, Slovakia, January 12, 1979. Ottawa's 1st pick, 12th overall, in 1997 NHL Draft.

Season	Club	League	GP	G	A	Pts	PIM	PP	SH	GW	S	S%	+/-	TF	F%	Min	Playoffs GP	G	A	Pts	PIM	PP	SH	GW	Min
1995-96	Dukla Trencin Jr.	Slovak-Jr.	53	42	49	91	26	....	....	....	....	....	....	....	....	....	....	....	....	....	....	....	....	....	....
1996-97	Dukla Trencin	Slovakia	46	25	19	44	33	....	....	....	....	....	....	....	....	....	7	5	5	10	....	....	....	....	....
1997-98	Portland	WHL	53	45	40	85	50	....	....	....	....	....	....	....	....	....	16	13	6	19	6	....	....	....	....
	Ottawa	**NHL**	**7**	**0**	**1**	**1**	**0**	**0**	**0**	**0**	**10**	**0.0**	**–1**	....	....	....	....	....	....	....	....	....	....	....	....
1998-99	**Ottawa**	**NHL**	**60**	**15**	**15**	**30**	**37**	**1**	**0**	**2**	**124**	**12.1**	**18**	**4**	**25.0**	**13:59**	**4**	**0**	**2**	**2**	**4**	**0**	**0**	**0**	**16:46**
99-2000	**Ottawa**	**NHL**	**78**	**29**	**27**	**56**	**32**	**5**	**0**	**4**	**240**	**12.1**	**5**	**7**	**57.1**	**17:12**	**6**	**0**	**0**	**0**	**2**	**0**	**0**	**0**	**15:22**
2000-01	**Ottawa**	**NHL**	**81**	**32**	**43**	**75**	**44**	**11**	**2**	**7**	**249**	**12.9**	**19**	**14**	**42.9**	**18:01**	**4**	**1**	**1**	**2**	**4**	**0**	**0**	**0**	**19:02**
2001-02	Dukla Trencin	Slovakia	8	3	4	7	16	....	....	....	....	....	....	....	....	....	....	....	....	....	....	....	....	....	....
	Ottawa	**NHL**	**80**	**31**	**35**	**66**	**50**	**9**	**1**	**4**	**278**	**11.2**	**11**	**12**	**33.3**	**18:29**	**12**	**4**	**6**	**10**	**2**	**1**	**0**	**0**	**19:04**
	Slovakia	Olympics	2	4	2	6	0	....	....	....	....	....	....	....	....	....	....	....	....	....	....	....	....	....	....
2002-03	**Ottawa**	**NHL**	**80**	**45**	**35**	**80**	**34**	**14**	**0**	**10**	**229**	**19.7**	**8**	**19**	**36.8**	**18:31**	**18**	**5**	**11**	**16**	**6**	**3**	**0**	**1**	**18:41**
2003-04	**Ottawa**	**NHL**	**81**	**36**	**46**	**82**	**46**	**14**	**1**	**5**	**233**	**15.5**	**4**	**25**	**40.0**	**18:37**	**7**	**3**	**1**	**4**	**0**	**1**	**0**	**2**	**21:24**
2004-05	Dukla Trencin	Slovakia	25	22	20	42	38	....	....	....	....	....	....	....	....	....	5	4	5	9	14	....	....	....	....
	Mora IK	Sweden	24	18	14	32	22	....	....	....	....	....	....	....	....	....	....	....	....	....	....	....	....	....	....
2005-06	**Atlanta**	**NHL**	**80**	**39**	**53**	**92**	**67**	**14**	***7**	**7**	**341**	**11.4**	**17**	**15**	**26.7**	**21:41**	....	....	....	....	....	....	....	....	....
	Slovakia	Olympics	6	5	5	10	4	....	....	....	....	....	....	....	....	....	....	....	....	....	....	....	....	....	....
2006-07	**Atlanta**	**NHL**	**82**	**43**	**57**	**100**	**49**	**17**	**3**	**5**	**340**	**12.6**	**18**	**18**	**22.2**	**21:41**	**4**	**0**	**1**	**1**	**6**	**0**	**0**	**0**	**18:55**
2007-08	**Atlanta**	**NHL**	**60**	**26**	**30**	**56**	**30**	**8**	**2**	**4**	**229**	**11.4**	**–14**	**14**	**28.6**	**21:55**	....	....	....	....	....	....	....	....	....
	Pittsburgh	**NHL**	**12**	**3**	**7**	**10**	**6**	**0**	**0**	**0**	**35**	**8.6**	**0**	**1**	**0.0**	**18:34**	**20**	**12**	**14**	**26**	**12**	**5**	**0**	**2**	**21:00**
2008-09	**Detroit**	**NHL**	**74**	**40**	**31**	**71**	**63**	**10**	**0**	**8**	**307**	**13.0**	**27**	**19**	**21.1**	**17:48**	**23**	**6**	**9**	**15**	**10**	**2**	**1**	**1**	**18:38**
2009-10 ♦	**Chicago**	**NHL**	**57**	**24**	**27**	**51**	**18**	**2**	**5**	**2**	**199**	**12.1**	**24**	**1**	**0.0**	**18:44**	**22**	**3**	**12**	**15**	**25**	**0**	**0**	**1**	**18:25**
	Slovakia	Olympics	7	3	6	9	6	....	....	....	....	....	....	....	....	....	....	....	....	....	....	....	....	....	....
2010-11	**Chicago**	**NHL**	**65**	**25**	**32**	**57**	**32**	**8**	**2**	**2**	**205**	**12.2**	**9**	**4**	**75.0**	**19:42**	**7**	**2**	**4**	**6**	**2**	**1**	**0**	**1**	**18:35**
2011-12	**Chicago**	**NHL**	**81**	**29**	**48**	**77**	**20**	**9**	**2**	**4**	**248**	**11.7**	**18**	**9**	**33.3**	**19:58**	**3**	**0**	**0**	**0**	**0**	**0**	**0**	**0**	**17:21**
2012-13 ♦	**Chicago**	**NHL**	**40**	**17**	**14**	**31**	**16**	**4**	**1**	**6**	**116**	**14.7**	**20**	**3**	**33.3**	**18:02**	**22**	**7**	**9**	**16**	**2**	**3**	**0**	**2**	**19:57**
2013-14	**Chicago**	**NHL**	**72**	**30**	**30**	**60**	**20**	**4**	**3**	**4**	**241**	**12.4**	**28**	**3**	**33.3**	**18:16**	**19**	**2**	**12**	**14**	**8**	**1**	**0**	**0**	**20:25**
	Slovakia	Olympics	4	2	1	3	4	....	....	....	....	....	....	....	....	....	....	....	....	....	....	....	....	....	....
2014-15 ♦	**Chicago**	**NHL**	**82**	**22**	**39**	**61**	**32**	**6**	**1**	**2**	**247**	**8.9**	**17**	**7**	**57.1**	**18:33**	**23**	**4**	**13**	**17**	**10**	**1**	**1**	**2**	**19:52**
2015-16	**Chicago**	**NHL**	**64**	**13**	**20**	**33**	**24**	**2**	**3**	**2**	**191**	**6.8**	**10**	**2**	**0.0**	**17:16**	**7**	**3**	**2**	**5**	**0**	**0**	**1**	**0**	**17:59**
2016-17	**Chicago**	**NHL**	**73**	**26**	**19**	**45**	**8**	**5**	**1**	**7**	**167**	**15.6**	**7**	**14**	**35.7**	**16:51**	**4**	**0**	**0**	**0**	**2**	**0**	**0**	**0**	**19:01**
	NHL Totals		**1309**	**525**	**609**	**1134**	**628**	**143**	**34**	**85**	**4229**	**12.4**		**191**	**34.0**	**18:41**	**205**	**52**	**97**	**149**	**95**	**18**	**3**	**12**	**19:15**

WHL West First All-Star Team (1998) • WHL Rookie of the Year (1998) • Canadian Major Junior First All-Star Team (1998) •NHL All-Rookie Team (1999) • NHL Second All-Star Team (2009)
Played in NHL All-Star Game (2001, 2003, 2007, 2008, 2012)

Signed as a free agent by **Trencin** (Slovakia), September 16, 2004. Signed as a free agent by **Mora** (Sweden), November 11, 2004. Traded to **Atlanta** by **Ottawa** with Greg de Vries for Dany Heatley, August 23, 2005. Traded to **Pittsburgh** by **Atlanta** with Pascal Dupuis for Colby Armstrong, Erik Christensen, Angelo Esposito and Pittsburgh's 1st round pick (Daulton Leveille) in 2008 NHL Draft, February 26, 2008. Signed as a free agent by **Detroit**, July 2, 2008. Signed as a free agent by **Chicago**, July 1, 2009. • Announced by Marian Hossa and Chicago management that he will miss 2017-18 due to progressive skin disorder, June 21, 2017.

HOWDEN, Quinton
(HOW-duhn, KWIHN-tuhn)

Center. Shoots left. 6'2", 189 lbs. Born, Winnipeg, MB, January 21, 1992. Florida's 3rd pick, 25th overall, in 2010 NHL Draft.

Season	Club	League	GP	G	A	Pts	PIM	PP	SH	GW	S	S%	+/-	TF	F%	Min	Playoffs GP	G	A	Pts	PIM	PP	SH	GW	Min
2007-08	Eastman Selects	MMHL	37	23	27	50	36	....	....	....	....	....	....	....	....	....	....	....	....	....	....	....	....	....	....
	Moose Jaw	WHL	5	0	0	0	0	....	....	....	....	....	....	....	....	....	....	....	....	....	....	....	....	....	....
2008-09	Moose Jaw	WHL	62	13	17	30	22	....	....	....	....	....	....	....	....	....	2	0	2	2	2	....	....	....	....
2009-10	Moose Jaw	WHL	65	28	37	65	44	....	....	....	....	....	....	....	....	....	6	5	2	7	2	....	....	....	....
2010-11	Moose Jaw	WHL	60	40	39	79	43	....	....	....	....	....	....	....	....	....	14	5	10	15	6	....	....	....	....
2011-12	Moose Jaw	WHL	52	30	35	65	16	....	....	....	....	....	....	....	....	....	4	0	0	0	2	....	....	....	....
	San Antonio	AHL	....	....	....	....	....	....	....	....	....	....	....	....	....	....	....	....	....	....	....	....	....	....	....
2012-13	San Antonio	AHL	57	13	17	30	24	....	....	....	....	....	....	....	....	....	....	....	....	....	....	....	....	....	....
	Florida	**NHL**	**18**	**0**	**0**	**0**	**2**	**0**	**0**	**0**	**22**	**0.0**	**–11**	**4**	**25.0**	**10:27**	....	....	....	....	....	....	....	....	....
2013-14	**Florida**	**NHL**	**16**	**4**	**2**	**6**	**10**	**0**	**1**	**0**	**23**	**17.4**	**0**	**8**	**25.0**	**13:43**	....	....	....	....	....	....	....	....	....
	San Antonio	AHL	59	10	17	27	26	....	....	....	....	....	....	....	....	....	3	0	1	1	2	....	....	....	....
2014-15	San Antonio	AHL	33	3	15	18	16	....	....	....	....	....	....	....	....	....	....	....	....	....	....	....	....	....	....
2015-16	**Florida**	**NHL**	**58**	**6**	**5**	**11**	**18**	**0**	**0**	**0**	**54**	**11.1**	**–1**	**6**	**50.0**	**10:22**	....	....	....	....	....	....	....	....	....
2016-17	**Winnipeg**	**NHL**	**5**	**0**	**0**	**0**	**0**	**0**	**0**	**0**	**5**	**0.0**	**1**	**2**	**0.0**	**8:39**	....	....	....	....	....	....	....	....	....
	Manitoba Moose	AHL	58	13	11	24	10	....	....	....	....	....	....	....	....	....	....	....	....	....	....	....	....	....	....
	NHL Totals		**97**	**10**	**7**	**17**	**30**	**0**	**1**	**0**	**104**	**9.6**		**20**	**30.0**	**10:51**	....	....	....	....	....	....	....	....	....

WHL East Second All-Star Team (2011)
• Missed majority of 2014-15 due to recurring upper-body injury. Signed as a free agent by **Winnipeg**, July 1, 2016.

HRIVIK, Marek
(huh-RIHV-ihk, MAIR-ehk) **CGY**

Left wing. Shoots left. 6'2", 200 lbs. Born, Zilina, Slovakia, August 28, 1991.

Season	Club	League	GP	G	A	Pts	PIM	PP	SH	GW	S	S%	+/-	TF	F%	Min	Playoffs GP	G	A	Pts	PIM	PP	SH	GW	Min
2007-08	MsHK Zilina Jr.	Slovak-Jr.	47	17	17	34	24	....	....	....	....	....	....	....	....	....	....	....	....	....	....	....	....	....	....
2009-10	Moncton Wildcats	QMJHL	66	26	29	55	14	....	....	....	....	....	....	....	....	....	21	5	12	17	8	....	....	....	....
2010-11	Moncton Wildcats	QMJHL	59	38	41	79	18	....	....	....	....	....	....	....	....	....	4	0	6	6	11	....	....	....	....
2011-12	Moncton Wildcats	QMJHL	54	29	41	70	8	....	....	....	....	....	....	....	....	....	4	1	2	3	0	....	....	....	....
	Connecticut	AHL	8	1	0	1	0	....	....	....	....	....	....	....	....	....	9	5	4	9	10	....	....	....	....
2012-13	Connecticut	AHL	40	7	19	26	10	....	....	....	....	....	....	....	....	....	....	....	....	....	....	....	....	....	....
2013-14	Hartford	AHL	74	13	14	27	22	....	....	....	....	....	....	....	....	....	....	....	....	....	....	....	....	....	....
2014-15	Hartford	AHL	72	12	21	33	12	....	....	....	....	....	....	....	....	....	15	3	6	9	6	....	....	....	....
2015-16	**NY Rangers**	**NHL**	**5**	**0**	**1**	**1**	**0**	**0**	**0**	**0**	**3**	**0.0**	**3**	**5**	**60.0**	**10:43**	....	....	....	....	....	....	....	....	....
	Hartford	AHL	68	12	29	41	18	....	....	....	....	....	....	....	....	....	....	....	....	....	....	....	....	....	....

			Regular Season														Playoffs								
Season	Club	League	GP	G	A	Pts	PIM	PP	SH	GW	S	S%	+/-	TF	F%	Min	GP	G	A	Pts	PIM	PP	SH	GW	Min
2016-17	NY Rangers	NHL	16	0	2	2	2	0	0	0	15	0.0	–3	80	40.0	10:25	....	....	....	....	....	....	....	....	....
	Hartford	AHL	56	16	24	40	12	....	....	....	....	....	....	....	....	....	....	....	....	....	....	....	....	....	....
	NHL Totals		21	0	3	3	2	0	0	0	18	0.0		85	41.2	10:29	....	....	....	....	....	....	....	....	....

Signed as a free agent by **NY Rangers**, May 30, 2012. Signed as a free agent by **Calgary**, July 1, 2017.

HUBERDEAU, Jonathan

(hoo-BAIR-doh, JAWN-ah-thuhn) **FLA**

Center. Shoots left. 6'1", 188 lbs. Born, Saint-Jerome, QC, June 4, 1993. Florida's 1st pick, 3rd overall, in 2011 NHL Draft.

Season	Club	League	GP	G	A	Pts	PIM	PP	SH	GW	S	S%	+/-	TF	F%	Min	GP	G	A	Pts	PIM	PP	SH	GW	Min
2008-09	Saint-Eustache	QAAA	43	20	30	50	60	....	....	....	....	....	....	....	....	....	8	2	7	9	18	....	....	....	....
2009-10	Saint John	QMJHL	61	15	20	35	43	....	....	....	....	....	....	....	....	....	21	11	7	18	22	....	....	....	....
2010-11	Saint John	QMJHL	67	43	62	105	88	....	....	....	....	....	....	....	....	....	19	*16	14	30	16	....	....	....	....
2011-12	Saint John	QMJHL	37	30	42	72	50	....	....	....	....	....	....	....	....	....	15	10	11	21	18	....	....	....	....
2012-13	Saint John	QMJHL	30	16	29	45	48	....	....	....	....	....	....	....	....	....	....	....	....	....	....	....	....	....	....
	Florida	**NHL**	**48**	**14**	**17**	**31**	**18**	2	0	1	112	12.5	–15	33	33.3	16:56	....	....	....	....	....	....	....	....	....
2013-14	**Florida**	**NHL**	**69**	**9**	**19**	**28**	**37**	2	0	1	108	8.3	–5	11	45.5	15:40	....	....	....	....	....	....	....	....	....
2014-15	**Florida**	**NHL**	**79**	**15**	**39**	**54**	**38**	0	0	0	169	8.9	10	8	25.0	16:45	....	....	....	....	....	....	....	....	....
2015-16	**Florida**	**NHL**	**76**	**20**	**39**	**59**	**43**	4	1	2	174	11.5	17	18	38.9	18:09	6	1	2	3	10	0	0	0	23:31
2016-17	**Florida**	**NHL**	**31**	**10**	**16**	**26**	**13**	3	0	2	86	11.6	–2	9	44.4	17:55	....	....	....	....	....	....	....	....	....
	NHL Totals		**303**	**68**	**130**	**198**	**149**	11	1	6	649	10.5		79	36.7	17:00	6	1	2	3	10	0	0	0	23:31

QMJHL First All-Star Team (2011) • QMJHL Second All-Star Team (2012) • NHL All-Rookie Team (2013) • Calder Memorial Trophy (2013)
• Missed majority of 2016-17 due to lower-body injury in pre-season vs. New Jersey, October 8, 2016.

HUDLER, Jiri

(HOOD-luhr, YIH-ree) **DAL**

Center. Shoots left. 5'10", 183 lbs. Born, Olomouc, Czech., January 4, 1984. Detroit's 1st pick, 58th overall, in 2002 NHL Draft.

Season	Club	League	GP	G	A	Pts	PIM	PP	SH	GW	S	S%	+/-	TF	F%	Min	GP	G	A	Pts	PIM	PP	SH	GW	Min
1998-99	HC Vsetin U17	CzR-U17	46	57	57	114	....	....	....	....	....	....	....	....	....	....	....	....	....	....	....	....	....	....	....
99-2000	HC Vsetin Jr.	CzRep-Jr.	53	29	31	60	75	....	....	....	....	....	....	....	....	....	....	....	....	....	....	....	....	....	....
	Vsetin	CzRep	2	0	1	1	0	....	....	....	....	....	....	....	....	....	....	....	....	....	....	....	....	....	....
2000-01	HC Vsetin Jr.	CzRep-Jr.	16	8	14	22	16	....	....	....	....	....	....	....	....	....	....	....	....	....	....	....	....	....	....
	HC Slovnaft Vsetin	CzRep	22	1	4	5	10	....	....	....	....	....	....	....	....	....	....	....	....	....	....	....	....	....	....
	HC Femax Havirov	CzRep	15	5	1	6	12	....	....	....	....	....	....	....	....	....	....	....	....	....	....	....	....	....	....
2001-02	HC Vsetin	CzRep	46	15	31	46	54	....	....	....	....	....	....	....	....	....	....	....	....	....	....	....	....	....	....
	Liberec	CzRep-2	13	9	7	16	10	....	....	....	....	....	....	....	....	....	....	....	....	....	....	....	....	....	....
	HC Olomouc	CzRep-3	1	0	2	2	4	....	....	....	....	....	....	....	....	....	....	....	....	....	....	....	....	....	....
2002-03	HC Vsetin	CzRep	30	19	27	46	22	....	....	....	....	....	....	....	....	....	....	....	....	....	....	....	....	....	....
	Ak Bars Kazan	Russia	11	1	5	6	12	....	....	....	....	....	....	....	....	....	1	0	0	0	0	....	....	....	....
2003-04	**Detroit**	**NHL**	**12**	**1**	**2**	**3**	**10**	1	0	0	8	12.5	–1	50	30.0	8:10	....	....	....	....	....	....	....	....	....
	Grand Rapids	AHL	57	17	32	49	46	....	....	....	....	....	....	....	....	....	4	1	5	6	2	....	....	....	....
2004-05	Grand Rapids	AHL	52	12	22	34	10	....	....	....	....	....	....	....	....	....	....	....	....	....	....	....	....	....	....
	HC Vsetin	CzRep	7	5	2	7	10	....	....	....	....	....	....	....	....	....	....	....	....	....	....	....	....	....	....
2005-06	**Detroit**	**NHL**	**4**	**0**	**0**	**0**	**2**	0	0	0	3	0.0	0	0	0.0	7:13	....	....	....	....	....	....	....	....	....
	Grand Rapids	AHL	76	36	61	97	56	....	....	....	....	....	....	....	....	....	16	6	16	22	20	....	....	....	....
2006-07	**Detroit**	**NHL**	**76**	**15**	**10**	**25**	**36**	3	0	4	107	14.0	16	20	30.0	10:02	6	0	2	2	4	0	0	0	9:09
2007-08♦	**Detroit**	**NHL**	**81**	**13**	**29**	**42**	**26**	3	0	2	131	9.9	11	26	38.5	13:10	22	5	9	14	14	2	0	2	11:36
2008-09	**Detroit**	**NHL**	**82**	**23**	**34**	**57**	**16**	6	0	2	155	14.8	7	29	44.8	13:39	23	4	8	12	6	2	0	1	13:28
2009-10	Dynamo Moscow	KHL	54	19	35	54	18	....	....	....	....	....	....	....	....	....	4	0	1	1	4	....	....	....	....
2010-11	**Detroit**	**NHL**	**73**	**10**	**27**	**37**	**28**	3	0	2	105	9.5	–7	70	44.3	13:40	10	1	2	3	6	0	0	0	11:57
2011-12	**Detroit**	**NHL**	**81**	**25**	**25**	**50**	**42**	2	0	2	127	19.7	10	7	28.6	15:40	5	2	0	2	4	1	0	0	16:53
2012-13	HC Lev Praha	KHL	4	0	1	1	2	....	....	....	....	....	....	....	....	....	....	....	....	....	....	....	....	....	....
	HC Ocelari Trinec	CzRep	4	3	2	5	4	....	....	....	....	....	....	....	....	....	....	....	....	....	....	....	....	....	....
	Calgary	**NHL**	**42**	**10**	**17**	**27**	**22**	5	0	0	56	17.9	–13	31	32.3	17:10	....	....	....	....	....	....	....	....	....
2013-14	**Calgary**	**NHL**	**75**	**17**	**37**	**54**	**16**	2	0	1	109	15.6	4	22	18.2	18:51	....	....	....	....	....	....	....	....	....
2014-15	**Calgary**	**NHL**	**78**	**31**	**45**	**76**	**14**	6	0	5	158	19.6	17	46	45.7	18:01	11	4	4	8	2	3	0	1	16:22
2015-16	**Calgary**	**NHL**	**53**	**10**	**25**	**35**	**17**	1	0	0	80	12.5	–1	20	45.0	16:39	....	....	....	....	....	....	....	....	....
	Florida	**NHL**	**19**	**6**	**5**	**11**	**10**	2	0	1	29	20.7	0	6	33.3	13:18	6	0	1	1	4	0	0	0	14:56
2016-17	**Dallas**	**NHL**	**32**	**3**	**8**	**11**	**4**	1	0	1	27	11.1	–3	5	60.0	11:51	....	....	....	....	....	....	....	....	....
	NHL Totals		**708**	**164**	**264**	**428**	**243**	35	0	20	1095	15.0		332	38.0	14:41	83	16	26	42	40	8	0	4	13:10

AHL Second All-Star Team (2006) • Lady Byng Memorial Trophy (2015)

Signed as a free agent by **Vsetin** (CzRep), December 2, 2004. Signed as a free agent by **Dynamo Moscow** (KHL), July 10, 2009. Signed as a free agent by **Detroit**, May 24, 2010. Signed as a free agent by **Calgary**, July 2, 2012. Signed as a free agent by **Lev Praha** (KHL), September 20, 2012. Signed as a free agent by **Trinec** (CzRep), December 19, 2012. Traded to **Florida** by **Calgary** for Florida's 2nd round pick (Tyler Parsons) in 2016 NHL Draft and Florida's 4th round pick in 2018 NHL Draft, February 27, 2016. Signed as a free agent by **Dallas**, August 24, 2016. • Missed majority of 2016-17 due to recurring lower-body injury and as a healthy reserve.

HUDON, Charles

(OO-dawn, CHAR-uhlz) **MTL**

Left wing. Shoots left. 5'10", 195 lbs. Born, Alma, QC, June 23, 1994. Montreal's 6th pick, 122nd overall, in 2012 NHL Draft.

Season	Club	League	GP	G	A	Pts	PIM	PP	SH	GW	S	S%	+/-	TF	F%	Min	GP	G	A	Pts	PIM	PP	SH	GW	Min
2009-10	Saint-Eustache	QAAA	40	23	24	47	32	....	....	....	....	....	....	....	....	....	6	4	5	9	4	....	....	....	....
2010-11	Chicoutimi	QMJHL	63	23	37	60	42	....	....	....	....	....	....	....	....	....	4	0	3	3	4	....	....	....	....
2011-12	Chicoutimi	QMJHL	59	25	41	66	50	....	....	....	....	....	....	....	....	....	18	6	5	11	16	....	....	....	....
2012-13	Chicoutimi	QMJHL	56	30	41	71	66	....	....	....	....	....	....	....	....	....	6	5	5	10	8	....	....	....	....
	Hamilton	AHL	9	1	2	3	4	....	....	....	....	....	....	....	....	....	....	....	....	....	....	....	....	....	....
2013-14	Chicoutimi	QMJHL	33	14	27	41	57	....	....	....	....	....	....	....	....	....	....	....	....	....	....	....	....	....	....
	Baie-Comeau	QMJHL	24	12	23	35	26	....	....	....	....	....	....	....	....	....	22	10	11	21	30	....	....	....	....
2014-15	Hamilton	AHL	75	19	38	57	68	....	....	....	....	....	....	....	....	....	....	....	....	....	....	....	....	....	....
2015-16	**Montreal**	**NHL**	**3**	**0**	**2**	**2**	**0**	0	0	0	3	0.0	2	1	0.0	10:42	....	....	....	....	....	....	....	....	....
	St. John's IceCaps	AHL	67	28	25	53	79	....	....	....	....	....	....	....	....	....	....	....	....	....	....	....	....	....	....
2016-17	**Montreal**	**NHL**	**3**	**0**	**2**	**2**	**2**	0	0	0	3	0.0	1	0	0.0	11:56	....	....	....	....	....	....	....	....	....
	St. John's IceCaps	AHL	56	27	22	49	52	....	....	....	....	....	....	....	....	....	4	1	3	4	2	....	....	....	....
	NHL Totals		**6**	**0**	**4**	**4**	**2**	0	0	0	6	0.0		1	0.0	11:19	....	....	....	....	....	....	....	....	....

QMJHL All-Rookie Team (2011) • QMJHL Rookie of the Year (2011) • AHL All-Rookie Team (2015)

HUNT, Brad

(HUHNT, BRAD) **VGK**

Defense. Shoots left. 5'9", 187 lbs. Born, Ridge Meadows, BC, August 24, 1988.

Season	Club	League	GP	G	A	Pts	PIM	PP	SH	GW	S	S%	+/-	TF	F%	Min	GP	G	A	Pts	PIM	PP	SH	GW	Min
2005-06	Ridge Meadow	PIJHL	40	5	17	22	33	....	....	....	....	....	....	....	....	....	....	....	....	....	....	....	....	....	....
	Burnaby Express	BCHL	3	0	0	0	0	....	....	....	....	....	....	....	....	....	2	0	0	0	0	....	....	....	....
2006-07	Burnaby Express	BCHL	60	4	34	38	65	....	....	....	....	....	....	....	....	....	14	2	6	8	16	....	....	....	....
2007-08	Burnaby Express	BCHL	60	16	39	55	53	....	....	....	....	....	....	....	....	....	5	1	6	7	4	....	....	....	....
2008-09	Bemidji State	CHA	37	9	23	32	24	....	....	....	....	....	....	....	....	....	....	....	....	....	....	....	....	....	....
2009-10	Bemidji State	CHA	37	7	26	33	35	....	....	....	....	....	....	....	....	....	....	....	....	....	....	....	....	....	....
2010-11	Bemidji State	WCHA	38	3	18	21	33	....	....	....	....	....	....	....	....	....	....	....	....	....	....	....	....	....	....
2011-12	Bemidji State	WCHA	38	5	21	26	8	....	....	....	....	....	....	....	....	....	....	....	....	....	....	....	....	....	....
	Chicago Wolves	AHL	14	1	4	5	8	....	....	....	....	....	....	....	....	....	5	1	3	4	0	....	....	....	....
2012-13	Chicago Wolves	AHL	65	4	29	33	22	....	....	....	....	....	....	....	....	....	....	....	....	....	....	....	....	....	....
2013-14	**Edmonton**	**NHL**	**3**	**0**	**0**	**0**	**0**	0	0	0	1	0.0	–3	0	0.0	12:36	....	....	....	....	....	....	....	....	....
	Oklahoma City	AHL	66	11	39	50	34	....	....	....	....	....	....	....	....	....	3	1	0	1	4	....	....	....	....
2014-15	**Edmonton**	**NHL**	**11**	**1**	**2**	**3**	**0**	1	0	0	20	5.0	–6	0	0.0	19:29	....	....	....	....	....	....	....	....	....
	Oklahoma City	AHL	62	19	32	51	18	....	....	....	....	....	....	....	....	....	10	3	7	10	6	....	....	....	....
2015-16	**Edmonton**	**NHL**	**7**	**0**	**0**	**0**	**2**	0	0	0	12	0.0	–1	0	0.0	14:11	....	....	....	....	....	....	....	....	....
	Bakersfield	AHL	57	13	28	41	18	....	....	....	....	....	....	....	....	....	....	....	....	....	....	....	....	....	....
2016-17	**St. Louis**	**NHL**	**9**	**1**	**4**	**5**	**2**	1	0	0	12	8.3	–2	0	0.0	13:36	....	....	....	....	....	....	....	....	....
	Chicago Wolves	AHL	23	9	20	29	6	....	....	....	....	....	....	....	....	....	....	....	....	....	....	....	....	....	....
	Nashville	**NHL**	**3**	**0**	**1**	**1**	**0**	0	0	0	2	0.0	1	0	0.0	17:13	....	....	....	....	....	....	....	....	....
	NHL Totals		**33**	**2**	**7**	**9**	**4**	2	0	0	47	4.3		0	0.0	15:55	....	....	....	....	....	....	....	....	....

AHL Second All-Star Team (2014) • AHL First All-Star Team (2015)

Signed as a free agent by **Edmonton**, July 6, 2013. Signed as a free agent by **St. Louis**, July 2, 2016. Claimed on waivers by **Nashville** from **St. Louis**, January 17, 2017. Signed as a free agent by **Vegas**, July 1, 2017.

HUNWICK, Matt
(HUHN-wihk, MAT) **PIT**

Defense. Shoots left. 5'11", 191 lbs. Born, Warren, MI, May 21, 1985. Boston's 6th pick, 224th overall, in 2004 NHL Draft.

			Regular Season														Playoffs								
Season	Club	League	GP	G	A	Pts	PIM	PP	SH	GW	S	S%	+/-	TF	F%	Min	GP	G	A	Pts	PIM	PP	SH	GW	Min
2001-02	USAHNTDP	U-17	14	3	4	7	6	....	....	....	....	....	....	....	....	....	....	....	....	....	....	....	....	....	....
	USAHNTDP	NAHL	29	2	1	3	30	....	....	....	....	....	....	....	....	....	....	....	....	....	....	....	....	....	....
2002-03	USAHNTDP	U-18	40	6	16	22	40	....	....	....	....	....	....	....	....	....	....	....	....	....	....	....	....	....	....
	USAHNTDP	NAHL	8	2	2	4	23	....	....	....	....	....	....	....	....	....	....	....	....	....	....	....	....	....	....
2003-04	U. of Michigan	CCHA	41	1	14	15	62	....	....	....	....	....	....	....	....	....	....	....	....	....	....	....	....	....	....
2004-05	U. of Michigan	CCHA	40	6	19	25	60	....	....	....	....	....	....	....	....	....	....	....	....	....	....	....	....	....	....
2005-06	U. of Michigan	CCHA	41	11	19	30	70	....	....	....	....	....	....	....	....	....	....	....	....	....	....	....	....	....	....
2006-07	U. of Michigan	CCHA	41	6	21	27	64	....	....	....	....	....	....	....	....	....	....	....	....	....	....	....	....	....	....
2007-08	**Boston**	**NHL**	**13**	**0**	**1**	**1**	**4**	**0**	**0**	**0**	**6**	**0.0**	**–1**	**0**	**0.0**	**10:36**	....	....	....	....	....	....	....	....	....
	Providence Bruins	AHL	55	2	21	23	49	....	....	....	....	....	....	....	....	....	10	0	5	5	8	....	....	....	....
2008-09	**Boston**	**NHL**	**53**	**6**	**21**	**27**	**31**	**0**	**0**	**1**	**58**	**10.3**	**15**	**0**	**0.0**	**16:59**	**1**	**0**	**0**	**0**	**0**	**0**	**0**	**0**	**15:59**
	Providence Bruins	AHL	3	0	3	3	0	....	....	....	....	....	....	....	....	....	....	....	....	....	....	....	....	....	....
2009-10	**Boston**	**NHL**	**76**	**6**	**8**	**14**	**32**	**1**	**1**	**1**	**60**	**10.0**	**–16**	**1**	**0.0**	**17:58**	**13**	**0**	**6**	**6**	**2**	**0**	**0**	**0**	**21:57**
2010-11	**Boston**	**NHL**	**22**	**1**	**2**	**3**	**9**	**0**	**0**	**0**	**26**	**3.8**	**4**	**0**	**0.0**	**16:13**	....	....	....	....	....	....	....	....	....
	Colorado	**NHL**	**51**	**0**	**10**	**10**	**16**	**0**	**0**	**0**	**74**	**0.0**	**–19**	**0**	**0.0**	**19:30**	....	....	....	....	....	....	....	....	....
2011-12	**Colorado**	**NHL**	**33**	**3**	**3**	**6**	**8**	**0**	**0**	**0**	**40**	**7.5**	**–3**	**1**	**0.0**	**18:04**	....	....	....	....	....	....	....	....	....
2012-13	**Colorado**	**NHL**	**43**	**0**	**6**	**6**	**16**	**0**	**0**	**0**	**57**	**0.0**	**4**	**0**	**0.0**	**21:31**	....	....	....	....	....	....	....	....	....
2013-14	**Colorado**	**NHL**	**1**	**0**	**0**	**0**	**0**	**0**	**0**	**0**	**1**	**0.0**	**0**	**0**	**0.0**	**17:27**	....	....	....	....	....	....	....	....	....
	Lake Erie	AHL	52	10	21	31	33	....	....	....	....	....	....	....	....	....	....	....	....	....	....	....	....	....	....
2014-15	**NY Rangers**	**NHL**	**55**	**2**	**9**	**11**	**16**	**0**	**0**	**1**	**72**	**2.8**	**17**	**0**	**0.0**	**15:49**	**6**	**0**	**0**	**0**	**0**	**0**	**0**	**0**	**11:47**
2015-16	**Toronto**	**NHL**	**60**	**2**	**8**	**10**	**32**	**0**	**0**	**1**	**74**	**2.7**	**–17**	**0**	**0.0**	**22:34**	....	....	....	....	....	....	....	....	....
2016-17	**Toronto**	**NHL**	**72**	**1**	**18**	**19**	**18**	**0**	**0**	**0**	**73**	**1.4**	**8**	**0**	**0.0**	**17:59**	**6**	**0**	**1**	**1**	**2**	**0**	**0**	**0**	**25:39**
	NHL Totals		**479**	**21**	**86**	**107**	**182**	**1**	**1**	**4**	**541**	**3.9**		**2**	**0.0**	**18:24**	**26**	**0**	**7**	**7**	**4**	**0**	**0**	**0**	**20:14**

CCHA All-Rookie Team (2004) • CCHA Second All-Star Team (2005, 2006) • CCHA First All-Star Team (2007) • NCAA West Second All-American Team (2007)

Traded to **Colorado** by **Boston** for Colby Cohen, November 29, 2010. • Missed majority of 2011-12 as a healthy reserve. Signed as a free agent by **NY Rangers**, July 1, 2014. Signed as a free agent by **Toronto**, July 1, 2015. Signed as a free agent by **Pittsburgh**, July 1, 2017.

HUTTON, Ben
(HUH-tuhn, BEHN) **VAN**

Defense. Shoots left. 6'2", 183 lbs. Born, Prescott, ON, April 20, 1993. Vancouver's 3rd pick, 147th overall, in 2012 NHL Draft.

Season	Club	League	GP	G	A	Pts	PIM	PP	SH	GW	S	S%	+/-	TF	F%	Min	GP	G	A	Pts	PIM	PP	SH	GW	Min
2008-09	U.C. Cyclones	Minor-ON	54	6	21	27	20	....	....	....	....	....	....	....	....	....	....	....	....	....	....	....	....	....	....
	Kemptville 73's	ON-Jr.A	4	0	0	0	2	....	....	....	....	....	....	....	....	....	....	....	....	....	....	....	....	....	....
2009-10	Kemptville 73's	ON-Jr.A	60	16	18	34	6	....	....	....	....	....	....	....	....	....	4	0	0	0	2	....	....	....	....
2010-11	Kemptville 73's	ON-Jr.A	61	8	27	35	28	....	....	....	....	....	....	....	....	....	....	....	....	....	....	....	....	....	....
2011-12	Kemptville 73's	ON-Jr.A	35	7	20	27	25	....	....	....	....	....	....	....	....	....	....	....	....	....	....	....	....	....	....
	Nepean Raiders	ON-Jr.A	22	4	12	16	6	....	....	....	....	....	....	....	....	....	18	5	8	13	6	....	....	....	....
2012-13	U. of Maine	H-East	34	4	11	15	18	....	....	....	....	....	....	....	....	....	....	....	....	....	....	....	....	....	....
2013-14	U. of Maine	H-East	35	15	14	29	8	....	....	....	....	....	....	....	....	....	....	....	....	....	....	....	....	....	....
2014-15	U. of Maine	H-East	39	9	12	21	14	....	....	....	....	....	....	....	....	....	....	....	....	....	....	....	....	....	....
	Utica Comets	AHL	4	1	0	1	2	....	....	....	....	....	....	....	....	....	....	....	....	....	....	....	....	....	....
2015-16	**Vancouver**	**NHL**	**75**	**1**	**24**	**25**	**14**	**0**	**0**	**0**	**104**	**1.0**	**–21**	**0**	**0.0**	**19:52**	....	....	....	....	....	....	....	....	....
2016-17	**Vancouver**	**NHL**	**71**	**5**	**14**	**19**	**31**	**2**	**0**	**1**	**130**	**3.8**	**–22**	**0**	**0.0**	**20:30**	....	....	....	....	....	....	....	....	....
	NHL Totals		**146**	**6**	**38**	**44**	**45**	**2**	**0**	**1**	**234**	**2.6**		**0**	**0.0**	**20:11**	....	....	....	....	....	....	....	....	....

Hockey East First All-Star Team (2014) • NCAA East Second All-American Team (2014)

HYMAN, Zach
(HIGH-muhn, ZAK) **TOR**

Center. Shoots right. 6', 202 lbs. Born, Toronto, ON, June 9, 1992. Florida's 11th pick, 123rd overall, in 2010 NHL Draft.

Season	Club	League	GP	G	A	Pts	PIM	PP	SH	GW	S	S%	+/-	TF	F%	Min	GP	G	A	Pts	PIM	PP	SH	GW	Min
2008-09	Hamilton	ON-Jr.A	49	13	24	37	24	....	....	....	....	....	....	....	....	....	5	2	2	4	4	....	....	....	....
2009-10	Hamilton	ON-Jr.A	49	35	40	75	30	....	....	....	....	....	....	....	....	....	11	7	9	16	4	....	....	....	....
2010-11	Hamilton	ON-Jr.A	43	42	60	102	24	....	....	....	....	....	....	....	....	....	7	3	5	8	6	....	....	....	....
2011-12	U. of Michigan	CCHA	41	2	7	9	12	....	....	....	....	....	....	....	....	....	....	....	....	....	....	....	....	....	....
2012-13	U. of Michigan	CCHA	38	4	5	9	8	....	....	....	....	....	....	....	....	....	....	....	....	....	....	....	....	....	....
2013-14	U. of Michigan	Big Ten	35	7	10	17	12	....	....	....	....	....	....	....	....	....	....	....	....	....	....	....	....	....	....
2014-15	U. of Michigan	Big Ten	37	*22	32	*54	10	....	....	....	....	....	....	....	....	....	....	....	....	....	....	....	....	....	....
2015-16	**Toronto**	**NHL**	**16**	**4**	**2**	**6**	**18**	**0**	**0**	**0**	**37**	**10.8**	**0**	**3**	**33.3**	**15:41**	....	....	....	....	....	....	....	....	....
	Toronto Marlies	AHL	59	15	22	37	24	....	....	....	....	....	....	....	....	....	15	3	3	6	23	....	....	....	....
2016-17	**Toronto**	**NHL**	**82**	**10**	**18**	**28**	**30**	**0**	**4**	**3**	**156**	**6.4**	**2**	**29**	**37.9**	**16:42**	**6**	**1**	**3**	**4**	**4**	**0**	**0**	**0**	**18:29**
	NHL Totals		**98**	**14**	**20**	**34**	**48**	**0**	**4**	**3**	**193**	**7.3**		**32**	**37.5**	**16:32**	**6**	**1**	**3**	**4**	**4**	**0**	**0**	**0**	**18:29**

CJHL Player of the Year (2011) • NCAA West First All-American Team (2015)

Traded to **Toronto** by **Florida** with future considerations (conditions not met) for Greg McKegg, June 19, 2015.

IGINLA, Jarome
(ih-GIHN-lah, jah-ROHM)

Right wing. Shoots right. 6'1", 210 lbs. Born, Edmonton, AB, July 1, 1977. Dallas' 1st pick, 11th overall, in 1995 NHL Draft.

Season	Club	League	GP	G	A	Pts	PIM	PP	SH	GW	S	S%	+/-	TF	F%	Min	GP	G	A	Pts	PIM	PP	SH	GW	Min
1991-92	St. Albert Raiders	AMHL	36	26	30	56	22	....	....	....	....	....	....	....	....	....	....	....	....	....	....	....	....	....	....
1992-93	St. Albert Raiders	AMHL	36	34	53	*87	20	....	....	....	....	....	....	....	....	....	....	....	....	....	....	....	....	....	....
1993-94	Kamloops Blazers	WHL	48	6	23	29	33	....	....	....	....	....	....	....	....	....	19	3	6	9	10	....	....	....	....
1994-95	Kamloops Blazers	WHL	72	33	38	71	111	....	....	....	....	....	....	....	....	....	21	7	11	18	34	....	....	....	....
1995-96	Kamloops Blazers	WHL	63	63	73	136	120	....	....	....	....	....	....	....	....	....	16	16	13	29	44	....	....	....	....
	Calgary	**NHL**	....	....	....	....	....	....	....	....	....	....	....	....	....	....	**2**	**1**	**1**	**2**	**0**	**0**	**0**	**0**	....
1996-97	**Calgary**	**NHL**	**82**	**21**	**29**	**50**	**37**	**8**	**1**	**3**	**169**	**12.4**	**–4**	....	....	....	....	....	....	....	....	....	....	....	....
1997-98	**Calgary**	**NHL**	**70**	**13**	**19**	**32**	**29**	**0**	**2**	**1**	**154**	**8.4**	**–10**	....	....	....	....	....	....	....	....	....	....	....	....
1998-99	**Calgary**	**NHL**	**82**	**28**	**23**	**51**	**58**	**7**	**0**	**4**	**211**	**13.3**	**1**	**111**	**51.4**	**16:30**	....	....	....	....	....	....	....	....	....
99-2000	**Calgary**	**NHL**	**77**	**29**	**34**	**63**	**26**	**12**	**0**	**4**	**256**	**11.3**	**0**	**278**	**52.9**	**18:24**	....	....	....	....	....	....	....	....	....
2000-01	**Calgary**	**NHL**	**77**	**31**	**40**	**71**	**62**	**10**	**0**	**4**	**229**	**13.5**	**–2**	**638**	**51.7**	**19:58**	....	....	....	....	....	....	....	....	....
2001-02	**Calgary**	**NHL**	**82**	***52**	**44**	***96**	**77**	**16**	**1**	**7**	**311**	**16.7**	**27**	**308**	**55.2**	**22:22**	....	....	....	....	....	....	....	....	....
	Canada	Olympics	6	3	1	4	0	....	....	....	....	....	....	....	....	....	....	....	....	....	....	....	....	....	....
2002-03	**Calgary**	**NHL**	**75**	**35**	**32**	**67**	**49**	**11**	**3**	**6**	**316**	**11.1**	**–10**	**90**	**43.3**	**21:26**	....	....	....	....	....	....	....	....	....
2003-04	**Calgary**	**NHL**	**81**	***41**	**32**	**73**	**84**	**8**	**4**	***10**	**265**	**15.5**	**21**	**305**	**54.4**	**21:18**	**26**	***13**	**9**	**22**	**45**	**4**	***2**	**3**	**23:18**
2004-05			DID NOT PLAY																						
2005-06	**Calgary**	**NHL**	**82**	**35**	**32**	**67**	**86**	**17**	**1**	**6**	**293**	**11.9**	**5**	**541**	**54.2**	**21:42**	**7**	**5**	**3**	**8**	**11**	**1**	**1**	**1**	**24:14**
	Canada	Olympics	6	2	1	3	4	....	....	....	....	....	....	....	....	....	....	....	....	....	....	....	....	....	....
2006-07	**Calgary**	**NHL**	**70**	**39**	**55**	**94**	**40**	**13**	**1**	**7**	**264**	**14.8**	**12**	**406**	**53.0**	**22:04**	**6**	**2**	**2**	**4**	**12**	**0**	**0**	**1**	**23:45**
2007-08	**Calgary**	**NHL**	**82**	**50**	**48**	**98**	**83**	**15**	**0**	**9**	**338**	**14.8**	**27**	**445**	**55.1**	**21:26**	**7**	**4**	**5**	**9**	**2**	**3**	**0**	**0**	**22:43**
2008-09	**Calgary**	**NHL**	**82**	**35**	**54**	**89**	**37**	**10**	**0**	**4**	**289**	**12.1**	**–2**	**501**	**52.5**	**21:37**	**6**	**3**	**1**	**4**	**0**	**2**	**0**	**0**	**20:56**
2009-10	**Calgary**	**NHL**	**82**	**32**	**37**	**69**	**58**	**10**	**0**	**5**	**257**	**12.5**	**–2**	**323**	**47.1**	**20:36**	....	....	....	....	....	....	....	....	....
	Canada	Olympics	7	*5	2	7	0	....	....	....	....	....	....	....	....	....	....	....	....	....	....	....	....	....	....
2010-11	**Calgary**	**NHL**	**82**	**43**	**43**	**86**	**40**	**14**	**0**	**6**	**289**	**14.9**	**0**	**420**	**54.1**	**20:56**	....	....	....	....	....	....	....	....	....
2011-12	**Calgary**	**NHL**	**82**	**32**	**35**	**67**	**43**	**8**	**0**	**5**	**251**	**12.7**	**–10**	**426**	**50.2**	**20:36**	....	....	....	....	....	....	....	....	....
2012-13	**Calgary**	**NHL**	**31**	**9**	**13**	**22**	**22**	**2**	**0**	**2**	**100**	**9.0**	**–7**	**237**	**50.2**	**19:18**	....	....	....	....	....	....	....	....	....
	Pittsburgh	**NHL**	**13**	**5**	**6**	**11**	**9**	**4**	**0**	**1**	**34**	**14.7**	**2**	**10**	**40.0**	**17:40**	**15**	**4**	**8**	**12**	**16**	**2**	**0**	**0**	**15:45**
2013-14	**Boston**	**NHL**	**78**	**30**	**31**	**61**	**47**	**4**	**0**	**8**	**209**	**14.4**	**34**	**37**	**21.6**	**18:13**	**12**	**5**	**2**	**7**	**12**	**2**	**0**	**2**	**18:28**
2014-15	**Colorado**	**NHL**	**82**	**29**	**30**	**59**	**42**	**8**	**0**	**2**	**189**	**15.3**	**0**	**128**	**44.5**	**18:08**	....	....	....	....	....	....	....	....	....
2015-16	**Colorado**	**NHL**	**82**	**22**	**25**	**47**	**41**	**13**	**0**	**3**	**182**	**12.1**	**–22**	**115**	**53.0**	**15:52**	....	....	....	....	....	....	....	....	....

			Regular Season														Playoffs								
Season	Club	League	GP	G	A	Pts	PIM	PP	SH	GW	S	S%	+/-	TF	F%	Min	GP	G	A	Pts	PIM	PP	SH	GW	Min
2016-17	Colorado	NHL	61	8	10	18	54	4	0	0	120	6.7	−21	19	63.2	14:45	....	....	....	....	....	....	....	....	....
	Los Angeles	NHL	19	6	3	9	16	3	0	4	33	18.2	−9	11	36.4	16:20	....	....	....	....	....	....	....	....	....
	NHL Totals		1554	625	675	1300	1040	197	13	101	4759	13.1		5349	52.0	19:44	81	37	31	68	98	14	3	7	21:01

George Parsons Trophy (Memorial Cup - Most Sportsmanlike Player) (1995) • WHL West First All-Star Team (1996) • WHL Player of the Year (1996) • Canadian Major Junior First All-Star Team (1996) • NHL All-Rookie Team (1997) • NHL First All-Star Team (2002, 2008, 2009) • Maurice "Rocket" Richard Trophy (2002) • Art Ross Trophy (2002) • Lester B. Pearson Award (2002) • NHL Second All-Star Team (2004) • NHL Foundation Player Award (2004) • King Clancy Memorial Trophy (2004) • Maurice "Rocket" Richard Trophy (2004) (tied with Ilya Kovalchuk and Rick Nash) • Mark Messier NHL Leadership Award (2009)

Played in NHL All-Star Game (2002, 2003, 2004, 2008, 2009, 2012)

Traded to **Calgary** by **Dallas** with Corey Millen for Joe Nieuwendyk, December 19, 1995. Traded to **Pittsburgh** by **Calgary** for Kenny Agostino, Ben Hanowski and Pittsburgh's 1st round pick (Morgan Klimchuk) in 2013 NHL Draft, March 28, 2013. Signed as a free agent by **Boston**, July 5, 2013. Signed as a free agent by **Colorado**, July 1, 2014. Traded to **Los Angeles** by **Colorado** for a conditional 4th round pick in 2018 NHL Draft, March 1, 2017.

IRWIN, Matt

(UHR-wihn, MAT) **NSH**

Defense. Shoots left. 6'1", 207 lbs. Born, Brentwood Bay, BC, November 29, 1987.

Season	Club	League	GP	G	A	Pts	PIM	PP	SH	GW	S	S%	+/-	TF	F%	Min	GP	G	A	Pts	PIM	PP	SH	GW	Min
2004-05	Saanich Braves	VIJHL	46	7	10	17	74	....	....	....	....	....	....	....	....	....	....	....	....	....	....	....	....	....	....
	Nanaimo Clippers	BCHL	3	0	0	0	2	....	....	....	....	....	....	....	....	....	....	....	....	....	....	....	....	....	....
2005-06	Nanaimo Clippers	BCHL	56	3	6	9	41	....	....	....	....	....	....	....	....	....	5	0	1	1	4	....	....	....	....
2006-07	Nanaimo Clippers	BCHL	60	22	27	49	67	....	....	....	....	....	....	....	....	....	24	10	4	14	18	....	....	....	....
2007-08	Nanaimo Clippers	BCHL	59	16	37	53	40	....	....	....	....	....	....	....	....	....	14	6	7	13	22	....	....	....	....
2008-09	Massachusetts	H-East	31	7	11	18	8	....	....	....	....	....	....	....	....	....	....	....	....	....	....	....	....	....	....
2009-10	Massachusetts	H-East	36	7	17	24	16	....	....	....	....	....	....	....	....	....	....	....	....	....	....	....	....	....	....
	Worcester Sharks	AHL	3	0	0	0	2	....	....	....	....	....	....	....	....	....	1	0	0	0	0	....	....	....	....
2010-11	Worcester Sharks	AHL	72	10	21	31	43	....	....	....	....	....	....	....	....	....	....	....	....	....	....	....	....	....	....
2011-12	Worcester Sharks	AHL	71	11	31	42	48	....	....	....	....	....	....	....	....	....	....	....	....	....	....	....	....	....	....
2012-13	Worcester Sharks	AHL	35	1	14	15	26	....	....	....	....	....	....	....	....	....	....	....	....	....	....	....	....	....	....
	San Jose	**NHL**	**38**	**6**	**6**	**12**	**10**	**4**	**0**	**0**	**79**	**7.6**	**−1**	**0**	**0.0**	**19:06**	**11**	**0**	**1**	**1**	**4**	**0**	**0**	**0**	**17:47**
2013-14	**San Jose**	**NHL**	**62**	**2**	**17**	**19**	**35**	**1**	**0**	**0**	**147**	**1.4**	**5**	**1**	**0.0**	**18:49**	**2**	**1**	**0**	**1**	**0**	**0**	**0**	**0**	**19:48**
2014-15	**San Jose**	**NHL**	**53**	**8**	**11**	**19**	**18**	**1**	**0**	**1**	**93**	**8.6**	**3**	**0**	**0.0**	**17:01**	....	....	....	....	....	....	....	....	....
2015-16	**Boston**	**NHL**	**2**	**0**	**0**	**0**	**0**	**0**	**0**	**0**	**3**	**0.0**	**−5**	**0**	**0.0**	**14:56**	....	....	....	....	....	....	....	....	....
	Providence Bruins	AHL	64	5	25	30	27	....	....	....	....	....	....	....	....	....	2	0	0	0	0	....	....	....	....
2016-17	**Nashville**	**NHL**	**74**	**3**	**11**	**14**	**26**	**0**	**0**	**1**	**98**	**3.1**	**15**	**0**	**0.0**	**16:16**	**22**	**0**	**2**	**2**	**4**	**0**	**0**	**0**	**11:54**
	Milwaukee	AHL	4	0	1	1	4	....	....	....	....	....	....	....	....	....	....	....	....	....	....	....	....	....	....
	NHL Totals		**229**	**19**	**45**	**64**	**89**	**6**	**0**	**2**	**420**	**4.5**		**1**	**0.0**	**17:35**	**35**	**1**	**3**	**4**	**8**	**0**	**0**	**0**	**14:12**

Signed as a free agent by **San Jose**, March 23, 2010. Signed as a free agent by **Boston**, July 10, 2015. Signed as a free agent by **Nashville**, July 1, 2016.

JAGR, Jaromir

(YAH-guhr, YAIR-oh-MEER)

Right wing. Shoots left. 6'3", 230 lbs. Born, Kladno, Czech., February 15, 1972. Pittsburgh's 1st pick, 5th overall, in 1990 NHL Draft.

Season	Club	League	GP	G	A	Pts	PIM	PP	SH	GW	S	S%	+/-	TF	F%	Min	GP	G	A	Pts	PIM	PP	SH	GW	Min
1984-85	Kladno Jr.	Czech-Jr.	34	24	17	41	....	....	....	....	....	....	....	....	....	....	....	....	....	....	....	....	....	....	....
1985-86	Kladno Jr.	Czech-Jr.	36	41	29	70	....	....	....	....	....	....	....	....	....	....	....	....	....	....	....	....	....	....	....
1986-87	Kladno Jr.	Czech-Jr.	30	35	35	70	....	....	....	....	....	....	....	....	....	....	....	....	....	....	....	....	....	....	....
1987-88	Kladno Jr.	Czech-Jr.	35	57	27	84	....	....	....	....	....	....	....	....	....	....	....	....	....	....	....	....	....	....	....
1988-89	Kladno	Czech	29	3	3	6	4	....	....	....	....	....	....	....	....	....	10	5	7	12	0	....	....	....	....
1989-90	Poldi Kladno	Czech	42	22	28	50	....	....	....	....	....	....	....	....	....	....	9	*8	2	10	....	....	....	....	....
1990-91 ♦	**Pittsburgh**	**NHL**	**80**	**27**	**30**	**57**	**42**	**7**	**0**	**4**	**136**	**19.9**	**−4**	....	....	....	**24**	**3**	**10**	**13**	**6**	**1**	**0**	**1**	....
1991-92 ♦	**Pittsburgh**	**NHL**	**70**	**32**	**37**	**69**	**34**	**4**	**0**	**4**	**194**	**16.5**	**12**	....	....	....	**21**	**11**	**13**	**24**	**6**	**2**	**0**	**4**	....
1992-93	**Pittsburgh**	**NHL**	**81**	**34**	**60**	**94**	**61**	**10**	**1**	**9**	**242**	**14.0**	**30**	....	....	....	**12**	**5**	**4**	**9**	**23**	**1**	**0**	**1**	....
1993-94	**Pittsburgh**	**NHL**	**80**	**32**	**67**	**99**	**61**	**9**	**0**	**6**	**298**	**10.7**	**15**	....	....	....	**6**	**2**	**4**	**6**	**16**	**0**	**0**	**1**	....
1994-95	HC Kladno	CzRep	11	8	14	22	10	....	....	....	....	....	....	....	....	....	....	....	....	....	....	....	....	....	....
	HC Bolzano	Euroliga	5	8	8	16	4	....	....	....	....	....	....	....	....	....	....	....	....	....	....	....	....	....	....
	HC Bolzano	Italy	1	0	0	0	0	....	....	....	....	....	....	....	....	....	....	....	....	....	....	....	....	....	....
	Schalke	German-2	1	1	10	11	0	....	....	....	....	....	....	....	....	....	....	....	....	....	....	....	....	....	....
	Pittsburgh	**NHL**	**48**	**32**	**38**	***70**	**37**	**8**	**3**	**7**	**192**	**16.7**	**23**	....	....	....	**12**	**10**	**5**	**15**	**6**	**2**	**1**	**1**	....
1995-96	**Pittsburgh**	**NHL**	**82**	**62**	**87**	**149**	**96**	**20**	**1**	***12**	**403**	**15.4**	**31**	....	....	....	**18**	**11**	**12**	**23**	**18**	**5**	**1**	**1**	....
1996-97	**Pittsburgh**	**NHL**	**63**	**47**	**48**	**95**	**40**	**11**	**2**	**6**	**234**	**20.1**	**22**	....	....	....	**5**	**4**	**4**	**8**	**4**	**2**	**0**	**0**	....
1997-98	**Pittsburgh**	**NHL**	**77**	**35**	***67**	***102**	**64**	**7**	**0**	**8**	**262**	**13.4**	**17**	....	....	....	**6**	**4**	**5**	**9**	**2**	**1**	**0**	**0**	....
	Czech Republic	Olympics	6	1	4	5	2	....	....	....	....	....	....	....	....	....	....	....	....	....	....	....	....	....	....
1998-99	**Pittsburgh**	**NHL**	**81**	**44**	***83**	***127**	**66**	**10**	**1**	**7**	**343**	**12.8**	**17**	**4**	**50.0**	**25:51**	**9**	**5**	**7**	**12**	**16**	**1**	**0**	**1**	**25:32**
99-2000	**Pittsburgh**	**NHL**	**63**	**42**	**54**	***96**	**50**	**10**	**0**	**5**	**290**	**14.5**	**25**	**9**	**22.2**	**23:12**	**11**	**8**	**8**	**16**	**6**	**2**	**0**	***4**	**24:32**
2000-01	**Pittsburgh**	**NHL**	**81**	**52**	***69**	***121**	**42**	**14**	**1**	**10**	**317**	**16.4**	**19**	**2**	**0.0**	**23:19**	**16**	**2**	**10**	**12**	**18**	**2**	**0**	**0**	**22:15**
2001-02	**Washington**	**NHL**	**69**	**31**	**48**	**79**	**30**	**10**	**0**	**3**	**197**	**15.7**	**0**	**2**	**50.0**	**21:43**	....	....	....	....	....	....	....	....	....
	Czech Republic	Olympics	4	2	3	5	4	....	....	....	....	....	....	....	....	....	....	....	....	....	....	....	....	....	....
2002-03	**Washington**	**NHL**	**75**	**36**	**41**	**77**	**38**	**13**	**2**	**9**	**290**	**12.4**	**5**	**5**	**20.0**	**21:18**	**6**	**2**	**5**	**7**	**2**	**1**	**0**	**0**	**25:13**
2003-04	**Washington**	**NHL**	**46**	**16**	**29**	**45**	**26**	**6**	**0**	**1**	**159**	**10.1**	**−4**	**1**	**0.0**	**21:05**	....	....	....	....	....	....	....	....	....
	NY Rangers	**NHL**	**31**	**15**	**14**	**29**	**12**	**4**	**0**	**2**	**98**	**15.3**	**−1**	**0**	**0.0**	**20:45**	....	....	....	....	....	....	....	....	....
2004-05	HC Rabat Kladno	CzRep	17	11	17	28	16	....	....	....	....	....	....	....	....	....	....	....	....	....	....	....	....	....	....
	Avangard Omsk	Russia	32	16	22	38	63	....	....	....	....	....	....	....	....	....	11	4	*10	*14	22	....	....	....	....
2005-06	**NY Rangers**	**NHL**	**82**	**54**	**69**	**123**	**72**	**24**	**0**	**9**	**368**	**14.7**	**34**	**6**	**16.7**	**22:05**	**3**	**0**	**1**	**1**	**2**	**0**	**0**	**0**	**13:47**
	Czech Republic	Olympics	8	2	5	7	6	....	....	....	....	....	....	....	....	....	....	....	....	....	....	....	....	....	....
2006-07	**NY Rangers**	**NHL**	**82**	**30**	**66**	**96**	**78**	**7**	**0**	**5**	**324**	**9.3**	**26**	**6**	**16.7**	**21:46**	**10**	**5**	**6**	**11**	**12**	**2**	**0**	**0**	**22:07**
2007-08	**NY Rangers**	**NHL**	**82**	**25**	**46**	**71**	**58**	**7**	**0**	**5**	**249**	**10.0**	**8**	**3**	**33.3**	**20:28**	**10**	**5**	**10**	**15**	**12**	**2**	**0**	**1**	**19:54**
2008-09	Omsk	KHL	55	25	28	53	62	....	....	....	....	....	....	....	....	....	9	4	5	9	4	....	....	....	....
2009-10	Omsk	KHL	51	22	20	42	50	....	....	....	....	....	....	....	....	....	3	1	1	2	0	....	....	....	....
	Czech Republic	Olympics	5	2	1	3	6	....	....	....	....	....	....	....	....	....	....	....	....	....	....	....	....	....	....
2010-11	Omsk	KHL	49	19	31	50	48	....	....	....	....	....	....	....	....	....	14	2	7	9	8	....	....	....	....
2011-12	**Philadelphia**	**NHL**	**73**	**19**	**35**	**54**	**30**	**8**	**0**	**2**	**170**	**11.2**	**5**	**1**	**0.0**	**16:20**	**11**	**1**	**7**	**8**	**2**	**0**	**0**	**1**	**15:00**
2012-13	Rytiri Kladno	CzRep	34	24	33	57	28	....	....	....	....	....	....	....	....	....	....	....	....	....	....	....	....	....	....
	Dallas	**NHL**	**34**	**14**	**12**	**26**	**20**	**6**	**0**	**2**	**87**	**16.1**	**−5**	**1**	**0.0**	**18:18**	....	....	....	....	....	....	....	....	....
	Boston	**NHL**	**11**	**2**	**7**	**9**	**2**	**0**	**0**	**2**	**28**	**7.1**	**3**	**0**	**0.0**	**18:27**	**22**	**0**	**10**	**10**	**8**	**0**	**0**	**0**	**17:55**
2013-14	**New Jersey**	**NHL**	**82**	**24**	**43**	**67**	**46**	**5**	**0**	**6**	**231**	**10.4**	**16**	**2**	**0.0**	**19:10**	....	....	....	....	....	....	....	....	....
	Czech Republic	Olympics	5	2	1	3	2	....	....	....	....	....	....	....	....	....	....	....	....	....	....	....	....	....	....
2014-15	**New Jersey**	**NHL**	**57**	**11**	**18**	**29**	**42**	**2**	**0**	**3**	**119**	**9.2**	**−10**	**0**	**0.0**	**17:41**	....	....	....	....	....	....	....	....	....
	Florida	**NHL**	**20**	**6**	**12**	**18**	**6**	**2**	**0**	**2**	**50**	**12.0**	**7**	**1**	**100.0**	**17:15**	....	....	....	....	....	....	....	....	....
2015-16	**Florida**	**NHL**	**79**	**27**	**39**	**66**	**48**	**5**	**0**	**4**	**143**	**18.9**	**23**	**1**	**0.0**	**17:05**	**6**	**0**	**2**	**2**	**4**	**0**	**0**	**0**	**21:51**
2016-17	**Florida**	**NHL**	**82**	**16**	**30**	**46**	**56**	**8**	**0**	**2**	**181**	**8.8**	**2**	**2**	**50.0**	**17:00**	....	....	....	....	....	....	....	....	....
	NHL Totals		**1711**	**765**	**1149**	**1914**	**1157**	**217**	**11**	**135**	**5605**	**13.6**		**46**	**23.9**	**20:27**	**208**	**78**	**123**	**201**	**163**	**24**	**2**	**16**	**20:45**

NHL All-Rookie Team (1991) • NHL First All-Star Team (1995, 1996, 1998, 1999, 2000, 2001, 2006) • Art Ross Trophy (1995, 1998, 1999, 2000, 2001) • NHL Second All-Star Team (1997) • Lester B. Pearson Award (1999, 2000, 2006) • Hart Memorial Trophy (1999) • Bill Masterton Memorial Trophy (2016)

Played in NHL All-Star Game (1992, 1993, 1996, 1998, 1999, 2000, 2002, 2003, 2004, 2016)

Traded to **Washington** by **Pittsburgh** with Frantisek Kucera for Kris Beech, Michal Sivek, Ross Lupaschuk and future considerations, July 11, 2001. Traded to **NY Rangers** by **Washington** for Anson Carter, January 23, 2004. Signed as a free agent by **Kladno** (CzRep), September 17, 2004. Signed as a free agent by **Omsk** (Russia), November 7, 2004. Signed as a free agent by **Omsk** (KHL), July 4, 2008. Signed as a free agent by **Philadelphia**, July 1, 2011. Signed as a free agent by **Dallas**, July 3, 2012. Signed as a free agent by **Kladno** (CzRep), September 16, 2012. Traded to **Boston** by **Dallas** for Lane MacDermid, Cody Payne and Boston's 1st round pick (Jason Dickinson) in 2013 NHL Draft, April 2, 2013. Signed as a free agent by **New Jersey**, July 23, 2013. Traded to **Florida** by **New Jersey** for Florida's 2nd round pick (later traded to Anaheim, later traded to NY Rangers – NY Rangers selected Ryan Gropp) in 2015 NHL Draft and Minnesota's 3rd round pick (previously acquired, later traded to Anaheim, later traded to Buffalo, later traded to Nashville – Nashville selected Rem Pitlick) in 2016 NHL Draft, February 26, 2015.

JANKOWSKI, Mark

(jan-KOW-skee, MAHRK) **CGY**

Center. Shoots left. 6'4", 202 lbs. Born, Hamilton, ON, September 13, 1994. Calgary's 1st pick, 21st overall, in 2012 NHL Draft.

Season	Club	League	GP	G	A	Pts	PIM	PP	SH	GW	S	S%	+/-	TF	F%	Min	GP	G	A	Pts	PIM	PP	SH	GW	Min
2009-10	St. Cath. Falcons	Minor-ON	33	11	14	25	14	....	....	....	....	....	....	....	....	....	....	....	....	....	....	....	....	....	....
2010-11	Stanstead Coll.	MPHL	13	5	4	9	10	....	....	....	....	....	....	....	....	....	....	....	....	....	....	....	....	....	....
	Stanstead Coll.	High-QC	50	24	37	61	10	....	....	....	....	....	....	....	....	....	2	2	1	3	2	....	....	....	....
2011-12	Stanstead Coll.	MPHL	13	*19	11	*30	12	....	....	....	....	....	....	....	....	....	....	....	....	....	....	....	....	....	....
	Stanstead Coll.	High-QC	41	31	26	57	22	....	....	....	....	....	....	....	....	....	3	3	*4	*7	0	....	....	....	....
2012-13	Providence	H-East	34	7	11	18	10	....	....	....	....	....	....	....	....	....	....	....	....	....	....	....	....	....	....
2013-14	Providence	H-East	39	13	12	25	14	....	....	....	....	....	....	....	....	....	....	....	....	....	....	....	....	....	....
2014-15	Providence	H-East	37	8	19	27	14	....	....	....	....	....	....	....	....	....	....	....	....	....	....	....	....	....	....
2015-16	Providence	H-East	38	15	25	40	28	....	....	....	....	....	....	....	....	....	....	....	....	....	....	....	....	....	....
	Stockton Heat	AHL	8	2	4	6	0	....	....	....	....	....	....	....	....	....	....	....	....	....	....	....	....	....	....

			Regular Season														Playoffs								
Season	Club	League	GP	G	A	Pts	PIM	PP	SH	GW	S	S%	+/-	TF	F%	Min	GP	G	A	Pts	PIM	PP	SH	GW	Min
2016-17	Calgary	NHL	1	0	0	0	0	0	0	0	0	0.0	0	8	62.5	10:18	....	....	....	....	....	....	....	....	....
	Stockton Heat	AHL	64	27	29	56	29	....	....	....	....	....	....	....	....	....	5	1	4	5	0	....	....	....	....
	NHL Totals		**1**	**0**	**0**	**0**	**0**	**0**	**0**	**0**	**0**	**0.0**		**8**	**62.5**	**10:18**	....	....	....	....	....	....	....	....	....

NCAA Championship All-Tournament Team (2015) • Hockey East First All-Star Team (2016) • NCAA East Second All-American Team (2016) • AHL All-Rookie Team (2017)

JANMARK, Mattias (YAN-mahrk, mah-TEE-uhs) DAL

Center. Shoots left. 6'1", 195 lbs. Born, Stockholm, Sweden, December 8, 1992. Detroit's 4th pick, 79th overall, in 2013 NHL Draft.

Season	Club	League	GP	G	A	Pts	PIM	PP	SH	GW	S	S%	+/-	TF	F%	Min	GP	G	A	Pts	PIM	PP	SH	GW	Min
2007-08	SDE U18	Swe-U18	15	3	4	7	10	....	....	....	....	....	....	....	....	....	....	....	....	....	....	....	....	....	....
2008-09	SDE U18	Swe-U18	22	16	21	37	36	....	....	....	....	....	....	....	....	....	....	....	....	....	....	....	....	....	....
	AIK IF Solna U18	Swe-U18	12	2	6	8	4	....	....	....	....	....	....	....	....	....	7	5	5	10	2	....	....	....	....
2009-10	AIK IF Solna U18	Swe-U18	33	13	22	35	12	....	....	....	....	....	....	....	....	....	1	0	0	0	0	....	....	....	....
	AIK IF Solna Jr.	Swe-Jr.	13	4	7	11	6	....	....	....	....	....	....	....	....	....	4	0	1	1	0	....	....	....	....
2010-11	AIK IF Solna Jr.	Swe-Jr.	40	11	17	28	34	....	....	....	....	....	....	....	....	....	....	....	....	....	....	....	....	....	....
2011-12	AIK Solna Jr.	Swe-Jr.	40	23	38	61	30	....	....	....	....	....	....	....	....	....	3	0	0	0	4	....	....	....	....
	AIK Solna	Sweden	18	0	0	0	2	....	....	....	....	....	....	....	....	....	3	0	0	0	0	....	....	....	....
2012-13	AIK Solna	Sweden	55	14	17	31	32	....	....	....	....	....	....	....	....	....	....	....	....	....	....	....	....	....	....
2013-14	AIK Solna	Sweden	45	18	12	30	56	....	....	....	....	....	....	....	....	....	....	....	....	....	....	....	....	....	....
	AIK Solna	Sweden-Q	10	1	3	4	24	....	....	....	....	....	....	....	....	....	....	....	....	....	....	....	....	....	....
2014-15	Frolunda	Sweden	55	13	23	36	30	....	....	....	....	....	....	....	....	....	13	4	3	7	4	....	....	....	....
	Texas Stars	AHL	....	....	....	....	....	....	....	....	....	....	....	....	....	....	1	0	0	0	0	....	....	....	....
2015-16	**Dallas**	**NHL**	**73**	**15**	**14**	**29**	**16**	**0**	**1**	**3**	**108**	**13.9**	**12**	**260**	**36.2**	**14:10**	**12**	**2**	**3**	**5**	**2**	**0**	**0**	**0**	**14:41**
2016-17	**Dallas**	**NHL**	DID NOT PLAY – INJURED																						
	NHL Totals		**73**	**15**	**14**	**29**	**16**	**0**	**1**	**3**	**108**	**13.9**		**260**	**36.2**	**14:10**	**12**	**2**	**3**	**5**	**2**	**0**	**0**	**0**	**14:41**

Traded to **Dallas** by **Detroit** with Mattias Backman and Detroit's 2nd round pick (Roope Hintz) in 2015 NHL Draft for Erik Cole and Dallas' 3rd round pick (Vili Saarijarvi) in 2015 NHL Draft, March 1, 2015. • Missed 2016-17 due to recurring knee injury and resulting surgery, September 30. 2016.

JARNKROK, Calle (YARN-crock, KAHL-leh) NSH

Center. Shoots right. 5'11", 186 lbs. Born, Gavle, Sweden, September 25, 1991. Detroit's 2nd pick, 51st overall, in 2010 NHL Draft.

Season	Club	League	GP	G	A	Pts	PIM	PP	SH	GW	S	S%	+/-	TF	F%	Min	GP	G	A	Pts	PIM	PP	SH	GW	Min
2007-08	Brynas U18	Swe-U18	13	4	4	8	4	....	....	....	....	....	....	....	....	....	5	0	1	1	0	....	....	....	....
	Brynas IF Gavle Jr.	Swe-Jr.	2	0	0	0	2	....	....	....	....	....	....	....	....	....	....	....	....	....	....	....	....	....	....
2008-09	Brynas U18	Swe-U18	7	5	7	12	12	....	....	....	....	....	....	....	....	....	2	0	1	1	2	....	....	....	....
	Brynas IF Gavle Jr.	Swe-Jr.	41	8	18	26	37	....	....	....	....	....	....	....	....	....	7	4	3	7	2	....	....	....	....
2009-10	Brynas IF Gavle Jr.	Swe-Jr.	19	11	20	31	30	....	....	....	....	....	....	....	....	....	2	0	1	1	0	....	....	....	....
	Brynas IF Gavle	Sweden	33	4	6	10	2	....	....	....	....	....	....	....	....	....	5	1	1	2	0	....	....	....	....
2010-11	Brynas IF Gavle	Sweden	49	11	16	27	4	....	....	....	....	....	....	....	....	....	3	3	0	3	2	....	....	....	....
2011-12	Brynas IF Gavle	Sweden	50	16	23	39	22	....	....	....	....	....	....	....	....	....	16	4	12	16	12	....	....	....	....
2012-13	Brynas IF Gavle	Sweden	53	13	29	42	12	....	....	....	....	....	....	....	....	....	4	0	0	0	6	....	....	....	....
	Grand Rapids	AHL	9	0	3	3	0	....	....	....	....	....	....	....	....	....	....	....	....	....	....	....	....	....	....
2013-14	Grand Rapids	AHL	57	13	23	36	14	....	....	....	....	....	....	....	....	....	....	....	....	....	....	....	....	....	....
	Nashville	**NHL**	**12**	**2**	**7**	**9**	**4**	**0**	**0**	**0**	**13**	**15.4**	**7**	**147**	**39.5**	**14:04**	....	....	....	....	....	....	....	....	....
	Milwaukee	AHL	6	5	4	9	0	....	....	....	....	....	....	....	....	....	3	1	1	2	2	....	....	....	....
2014-15	**Nashville**	**NHL**	**74**	**7**	**11**	**18**	**18**	**0**	**0**	**1**	**95**	**7.4**	**2**	**641**	**46.2**	**12:51**	**6**	**0**	**2**	**2**	**0**	**0**	**0**	**0**	**16:29**
2015-16	**Nashville**	**NHL**	**81**	**16**	**14**	**30**	**14**	**3**	**1**	**4**	**125**	**12.8**	**1**	**799**	**45.8**	**16:08**	**14**	**0**	**1**	**1**	**4**	**0**	**0**	**0**	**14:55**
2016-17	**Nashville**	**NHL**	**81**	**15**	**16**	**31**	**25**	**2**	**1**	**1**	**134**	**11.2**	**−1**	**915**	**49.4**	**15:44**	**21**	**2**	**5**	**7**	**2**	**0**	**0**	**0**	**16:59**
	NHL Totals		**248**	**40**	**48**	**88**	**61**	**5**	**2**	**6**	**367**	**10.9**		**2502**	**46.8**	**14:55**	**41**	**2**	**8**	**10**	**6**	**0**	**0**	**0**	**16:12**

Traded to **Nashville** by **Detroit** with Patrick Eaves and Detroit's 2nd round pick (later traded to San Jose – San Jose selected Julius Bergman) in 2014 NHL Draft for David Legwand, March 5, 2014.

JASKIN, Dmitrij (YASH-kihn, dih-MEE-tree) ST.L.

Right wing. Shoots left. 6'2", 217 lbs. Born, Omsk, Russia, March 23, 1993. St. Louis' 2nd pick, 41st overall, in 2011 NHL Draft.

Season	Club	League	GP	G	A	Pts	PIM	PP	SH	GW	S	S%	+/-	TF	F%	Min	GP	G	A	Pts	PIM	PP	SH	GW	Min
2006-07	HC Vsetin U17	CzR-U17	4	1	0	1	0	....	....	....	....	....	....	....	....	....	....	....	....	....	....	....	....	....	....
2007-08	HC Vsetin U17	CzR-U17	40	15	25	40	72	....	....	....	....	....	....	....	....	....	2	2	0	2	6	....	....	....	....
2008-09	Slavia U17	CzR-U17	46	28	19	47	34	....	....	....	....	....	....	....	....	....	9	6	2	8	8	....	....	....	....
2009-10	Slavia U18	CzR-U18	12	15	12	27	36	....	....	....	....	....	....	....	....	....	2	1	3	4	4	....	....	....	....
	Slavia Jr.	CzRep-Jr.	40	13	10	23	67	....	....	....	....	....	....	....	....	....	7	2	5	7	26	....	....	....	....
2010-11	Slavia Jr.	CzRep-Jr.	1	0	0	0	0	....	....	....	....	....	....	....	....	....	2	2	3	5	2	....	....	....	....
	HC Slavia Praha	CzRep	33	3	7	10	16	....	....	....	....	....	....	....	....	....	17	2	1	3	31	....	....	....	....
2011-12	HC Slavia Praha	CzRep	37	4	2	6	18	....	....	....	....	....	....	....	....	....	....	....	....	....	....	....	....	....	....
	Beroun	CzRep-2	10	2	6	8	16	....	....	....	....	....	....	....	....	....	....	....	....	....	....	....	....	....	....
	Slavia Jr.	CzRep-Jr.	10	6	11	17	12	....	....	....	....	....	....	....	....	....	2	1	3	4	14	....	....	....	....
2012-13	Moncton Wildcats	QMJHL	51	46	53	99	73	....	....	....	....	....	....	....	....	....	5	1	2	3	16	....	....	....	....
	St. Louis	**NHL**	**2**	**0**	**0**	**0**	**0**	**0**	**0**	**0**	**2**	**0.0**	**−1**	**0**	**0.0**	**7:30**	....	....	....	....	....	....	....	....	....
2013-14	**St. Louis**	**NHL**	**18**	**1**	**1**	**2**	**8**	**0**	**0**	**0**	**18**	**5.6**	**−3**	**2**	**50.0**	**10:37**	....	....	....	....	....	....	....	....	....
	Chicago Wolves	AHL	42	15	14	29	28	....	....	....	....	....	....	....	....	....	9	4	5	9	10	....	....	....	....
2014-15	**St. Louis**	**NHL**	**54**	**13**	**5**	**18**	**16**	**3**	**0**	**4**	**108**	**12.0**	**7**	**7**	**42.9**	**13:28**	**6**	**0**	**1**	**1**	**2**	**0**	**0**	**0**	**12:56**
	Chicago Wolves	AHL	18	4	11	15	31	....	....	....	....	....	....	....	....	....	....	....	....	....	....	....	....	....	....
2015-16	**St. Louis**	**NHL**	**65**	**4**	**9**	**13**	**26**	**0**	**0**	**1**	**92**	**4.3**	**3**	**28**	**28.6**	**11:52**	**6**	**1**	**1**	**2**	**5**	**0**	**0**	**1**	**8:08**
	Chicago Wolves	AHL	3	1	1	2	4	....	....	....	....	....	....	....	....	....	....	....	....	....	....	....	....	....	....
2016-17	**St. Louis**	**NHL**	**51**	**1**	**10**	**11**	**18**	**0**	**0**	**0**	**55**	**1.8**	**5**	**10**	**50.0**	**11:33**	**2**	**1**	**0**	**1**	**4**	**0**	**0**	**0**	**14:02**
	NHL Totals		**190**	**19**	**25**	**44**	**68**	**3**	**0**	**5**	**275**	**6.9**		**47**	**36.2**	**12:04**	**14**	**2**	**2**	**4**	**11**	**0**	**0**	**1**	**11:02**

QMJHL First All-Star Team (2013)

JENNER, Boone (JEH-nuhr, BOON) CBJ

Center. Shoots left. 6'2", 215 lbs. Born, Dorchester, ON, June 15, 1993. Columbus' 1st pick, 37th overall, in 2011 NHL Draft.

Season	Club	League	GP	G	A	Pts	PIM	PP	SH	GW	S	S%	+/-	TF	F%	Min	GP	G	A	Pts	PIM	PP	SH	GW	Min
2008-09	Elgin-Mid. Chiefs	Minor-ON	54	49	54	103	72	....	....	....	....	....	....	....	....	....	15	10	19	29	22	....	....	....	....
	St. Thomas Stars	ON-Jr.B	4	0	0	0	16	....	....	....	....	....	....	....	....	....	....	....	....	....	....	....	....	....	....
2009-10	Oshawa Generals	OHL	65	19	30	49	91	....	....	....	....	....	....	....	....	....	....	....	....	....	....	....	....	....	....
2010-11	Oshawa Generals	OHL	63	25	41	66	57	....	....	....	....	....	....	....	....	....	10	7	5	12	14	....	....	....	....
2011-12	Oshawa Generals	OHL	43	22	27	49	59	....	....	....	....	....	....	....	....	....	6	4	7	11	10	....	....	....	....
	Springfield	AHL	5	1	0	1	2	....	....	....	....	....	....	....	....	....	....	....	....	....	....	....	....	....	....
2012-13	Oshawa Generals	OHL	56	45	37	82	58	....	....	....	....	....	....	....	....	....	9	2	6	8	8	....	....	....	....
	Springfield	AHL	5	3	1	4	0	....	....	....	....	....	....	....	....	....	8	2	3	5	8	....	....	....	....
2013-14	**Columbus**	**NHL**	**72**	**16**	**13**	**29**	**45**	**4**	**0**	**5**	**127**	**12.6**	**6**	**30**	**46.7**	**14:05**	**6**	**3**	**2**	**5**	**4**	**2**	**0**	**0**	**17:15**
2014-15	**Columbus**	**NHL**	**31**	**9**	**8**	**17**	**12**	**2**	**0**	**2**	**83**	**10.8**	**−5**	**306**	**49.4**	**18:16**	....	....	....	....	....	....	....	....	....
2015-16	**Columbus**	**NHL**	**82**	**30**	**19**	**49**	**77**	**9**	**1**	**3**	**225**	**13.3**	**−15**	**294**	**53.1**	**16:25**	....	....	....	....	....	....	....	....	....
2016-17	**Columbus**	**NHL**	**82**	**18**	**16**	**34**	**52**	**0**	**2**	**4**	**211**	**8.5**	**14**	**184**	**50.0**	**16:04**	**5**	**2**	**1**	**3**	**14**	**1**	**0**	**1**	**17:49**
	NHL Totals		**267**	**73**	**56**	**129**	**186**	**15**	**3**	**14**	**646**	**11.3**		**814**	**50.7**	**15:53**	**11**	**5**	**3**	**8**	**18**	**3**	**0**	**1**	**17:30**

OHL All-Rookie Team (2010)
• Missed majority of 2014-15 due to hand injury in practice, September 28, 2014 and recurring back injury.

JENSEN, Nick (JEHN-suhn, NIHK) DET

Defense. Shoots right. 6', 200 lbs. Born, St. Paul, MN, September 21, 1990. Detroit's 5th pick, 150th overall, in 2009 NHL Draft.

Season	Club	League	GP	G	A	Pts	PIM	PP	SH	GW	S	S%	+/-	TF	F%	Min	GP	G	A	Pts	PIM	PP	SH	GW	Min
2006-07	Rogers Royals	High-MN	21	20	17	37	....	....	....	....	....	....	....	....	....	....	....	....	....	....	....	....	....	....	....
2007-08	Rogers Royals	High-MN	14	14	13	27	....	....	....	....	....	....	....	....	....	....	....	....	....	....	....	....	....	....	....
2008-09	Green Bay	USHL	52	5	17	22	27	....	....	....	....	....	....	....	....	....	7	0	1	1	2	....	....	....	....
2009-10	Green Bay	USHL	53	6	21	27	35	....	....	....	....	....	....	....	....	....	12	2	6	8	6	....	....	....	....
2010-11	St. Cloud State	WCHA	38	5	18	23	18	....	....	....	....	....	....	....	....	....	....	....	....	....	....	....	....	....	....
2011-12	St. Cloud State	WCHA	39	6	26	32	4	....	....	....	....	....	....	....	....	....	....	....	....	....	....	....	....	....	....
2012-13	St. Cloud State	WCHA	42	4	27	31	14	....	....	....	....	....	....	....	....	....	....	....	....	....	....	....	....	....	....
2013-14	Grand Rapids	AHL	45	0	9	9	8	....	....	....	....	....	....	....	....	....	10	0	1	1	2	....	....	....	....
	Toledo Walleye	ECHL	3	0	0	0	0	....	....	....	....	....	....	....	....	....	....	....	....	....	....	....	....	....	....
2014-15	Grand Rapids	AHL	75	6	21	27	15	....	....	....	....	....	....	....	....	....	16	0	3	3	4	....	....	....	....
2015-16	Grand Rapids	AHL	75	3	16	19	17	....	....	....	....	....	....	....	....	....	9	0	2	2	0	....	....	....	....

Season	Club	League	GP	G	A	Pts	PIM	PP	SH	GW	S	S%	+/-	TF	F%	Min	GP	G	A	Pts	PIM	PP	SH	GW	Min
			Regular Season														Playoffs								
2016-17	**Detroit**	**NHL**	**49**	**4**	**9**	**13**	**12**	**0**	**0**	**0**	**59**	**6.8**	**-7**	**0**	**0.0**	**17:45**									
	Grand Rapids	AHL	27	1	5	6	6																		
	NHL Totals		**49**	**4**	**9**	**13**	**12**	**0**	**0**	**0**	**59**	**6.8**		**0**	**0.0**	**17:45**									

WCHA First All-Star Team (2013) • NCAA West First All-American Team (2013)

JENSEN, Nicklas

(YEHN-suhn, NIHK-luhs)

Left wing. Shoots left. 6'3", 217 lbs. Born, Herning, Denmark, March 6, 1993. Vancouver's 1st pick, 29th overall, in 2011 NHL Draft.

Season	Club	League	GP	G	A	Pts	PIM	PP	SH	GW	S	S%	+/-	TF	F%	Min	GP	G	A	Pts	PIM	PP	SH	GW	Min
2008-09	Herning IK Jr.	Den-Jr.	28	28	15	43	30																		
	Herning IK II	Den-2	4	3	0	3	0																		
2009-10	Herning Blue Fox	Denmark	34	12	14	26	28										10	6	4	10	8				
2010-11	Oshawa Generals	OHL	61	29	29	58	42										10	7	4	11	2				
2011-12	Oshawa Generals	OHL	57	25	33	58	29										6	1	4	5	0				
	Chicago Wolves	AHL	6	4	0	4	6										2	2	0	2	0				
2012-13	AIK Solna	Sweden	50	17	6	23	16																		
	Chicago Wolves	AHL	20	2	2	4	8																		
	Vancouver	**NHL**	**2**	**0**	**0**	**0**	**0**	**0**	**0**	**0**	**0**	**0.0**	**-1**	**0**	**0.0**	**13:51**									
2013-14	**Vancouver**	**NHL**	**17**	**3**	**3**	**6**	**10**	**0**	**0**	**1**	**30**	**10.0**	**-1**	**1**	**0.0**	**15:38**									
	Utica Comets	AHL	54	15	6	21	26																		
2014-15	**Vancouver**	**NHL**	**5**	**0**	**0**	**0**	**0**	**0**	**0**	**0**	**7**	**0.0**	**-1**	**0**	**0.0**	**9:33**									
	Utica Comets	AHL	59	14	14	28	39										18	4	1	5	10				
2015-16	Utica Comets	AHL	27	4	8	12	20																		
	Hartford	AHL	41	15	10	25	12																		
2016-17	**NY Rangers**	**NHL**	**7**	**0**	**0**	**0**	**0**	**0**	**0**	**0**	**8**	**0.0**	**-2**	**0**	**0.0**	**9:13**									
	Hartford	AHL	70	32	23	55	58																		
	NHL Totals		**31**	**3**	**3**	**6**	**10**	**0**	**0**	**1**	**45**	**6.7**		**1**	**0.0**	**13:06**									

Traded to **NY Rangers** by **Vancouver** with Vancouver's 6th round pick (Dominik Lakatos)in 2017 NHL Draft for Emerson Etem, January 8, 2016.

JOHANSEN, Ryan

(joh-HAN-suhn, RIGH-uhn) **NSH**

Center. Shoots right. 6'3", 218 lbs. Born, Port Moody, BC, July 31, 1992. Columbus' 1st pick, 4th overall, in 2010 NHL Draft.

Season	Club	League	GP	G	A	Pts	PIM	PP	SH	GW	S	S%	+/-	TF	F%	Min	GP	G	A	Pts	PIM	PP	SH	GW	Min
2007-08	Van. NE Chiefs	BCMML	41	18	30	48	26																		
2008-09	Penticton Vees	BCHL	47	5	12	17	21										10	4	3	7	2				
2009-10	Portland	WHL	71	25	44	69	53										13	6	12	18	18				
2010-11	Portland	WHL	63	40	52	92	64										21	13	15	*28	6				
2011-12	**Columbus**	**NHL**	**67**	**9**	**12**	**21**	**24**	**3**	**0**	**3**	**99**	**9.1**	**-2**	**215**	**45.1**	**12:44**									
2012-13	Springfield	AHL	40	17	16	33	20										5	0	1	1	2				
	Columbus	**NHL**	**40**	**5**	**7**	**12**	**12**	**0**	**0**	**2**	**84**	**6.0**	**-7**	**529**	**51.4**	**16:05**									
2013-14	**Columbus**	**NHL**	**82**	**33**	**30**	**63**	**43**	**7**	**0**	**5**	**237**	**13.9**	**3**	**1311**	**52.8**	**17:39**	**6**	**2**	**4**	**6**	**4**	**2**	**0**	**0**	**19:03**
2014-15	**Columbus**	**NHL**	**82**	**26**	**45**	**71**	**40**	**7**	**2**	**0**	**202**	**12.9**	**-6**	**1638**	**52.0**	**19:30**									
2015-16	**Columbus**	**NHL**	**38**	**6**	**20**	**26**	**25**	**1**	**0**	**0**	**88**	**6.8**	**-4**	**616**	**52.3**	**17:21**									
	Nashville	**NHL**	**42**	**8**	**26**	**34**	**36**	**3**	**0**	**2**	**97**	**8.2**	**10**	**630**	**52.4**	**17:46**	**14**	**4**	**4**	**8**	**16**	**0**	**0**	**0**	**18:42**
2016-17	**Nashville**	**NHL**	**82**	**14**	**47**	**61**	**60**	**4**	**1**	**3**	**154**	**9.1**	**1**	**1472**	**54.6**	**18:50**	**14**	**3**	**10**	**13**	**12**	**0**	**0**	**1**	**20:46**
	NHL Totals		**433**	**101**	**187**	**288**	**240**	**25**	**3**	**15**	**961**	**10.5**		**6411**	**52.5**	**17:18**	**34**	**9**	**18**	**27**	**32**	**2**	**0**	**1**	**19:37**

WHL West First All-Star Team (2011)
Played in NHL All-Star Game (2015)
Traded to **Nashville** by **Columbus** for Seth Jones, January 6, 2016.

JOHANSSON, Marcus

(yoh-HAHN-suhn, MAHR-kuhs) **N.J.**

Center/Wing. Shoots left. 6'1", 205 lbs. Born, Landskrona, Sweden, October 6, 1990. Washington's 1st pick, 24th overall, in 2009 NHL Draft.

Season	Club	League	GP	G	A	Pts	PIM	PP	SH	GW	S	S%	+/-	TF	F%	Min	GP	G	A	Pts	PIM	PP	SH	GW	Min
2005-06	Malmo U18	Swe-U18	12	0	7	7	0										6	0	4	4	0				
2006-07	Farjestad U18	Swe-U18	12	5	9	14	8										8	7	3	10	2				
2007-08	Farjestad U18	Swe-U18	24	12	26	38	16										8	4	8	12	0				
	Skare BK	Sweden-3	19	2	10	12	10																		
	Farjestad	Sweden															3	0	0	0	0				
2008-09	Farjestad U18	Swe-U18	2	2	0	2	0																		
	Skare BK Karlstad	Sweden-3	5	5	5	10	0																		
	Farjestad	Sweden	45	5	5	10	10										6	0	0	0	0				
2009-10	Farjestad	Sweden	42	10	10	20	10										7	0	5	5	2				
2010-11	**Washington**	**NHL**	**69**	**13**	**14**	**27**	**10**	**2**	**1**	**2**	**102**	**12.7**	**2**	**669**	**40.5**	**14:43**	**9**	**2**	**4**	**6**	**0**	**0**	**0**	**0**	**18:22**
	Hershey Bears	AHL	2	0	0	0	0																		
2011-12	**Washington**	**NHL**	**80**	**14**	**32**	**46**	**8**	**1**	**0**	**3**	**90**	**15.6**	**-5**	**710**	**43.2**	**16:48**	**14**	**1**	**2**	**3**	**0**	**0**	**0**	**0**	**19:35**
2012-13	Bofors	Sweden-2	16	8	10	18	8																		
	Washington	**NHL**	**34**	**6**	**16**	**22**	**4**	**3**	**0**	**1**	**40**	**15.0**	**3**	**87**	**46.0**	**16:35**	**7**	**1**	**1**	**2**	**0**	**0**	**0**	**1**	**16:59**
2013-14	**Washington**	**NHL**	**80**	**8**	**36**	**44**	**4**	**6**	**0**	**1**	**107**	**7.5**	**-21**	**274**	**34.7**	**17:32**									
	Sweden	Olympics	5	0	1	1	4																		
2014-15	**Washington**	**NHL**	**82**	**20**	**27**	**47**	**10**	**3**	**0**	**1**	**138**	**14.5**	**6**	**16**	**43.8**	**16:29**	**14**	**1**	**3**	**4**	**2**	**0**	**0**	**0**	**17:38**
2015-16	**Washington**	**NHL**	**74**	**17**	**29**	**46**	**16**	**6**	**0**	**7**	**132**	**12.9**	**12**	**278**	**46.0**	**16:38**	**12**	**2**	**5**	**7**	**2**	**2**	**0**	**0**	**16:41**
2016-17	**Washington**	**NHL**	**82**	**24**	**34**	**58**	**10**	**5**	**0**	**5**	**129**	**18.6**	**25**	**28**	**46.4**	**17:00**	**13**	**2**	**6**	**8**	**2**	**0**	**0**	**1**	**19:30**
	NHL Totals		**501**	**102**	**188**	**290**	**62**	**26**	**1**	**20**	**738**	**13.8**		**2062**	**41.8**	**16:34**	**69**	**9**	**21**	**30**	**6**	**2**	**0**	**2**	**18:15**

Signed as a free agent by **Karlskoga Bofors** (Sweden-2), October 30, 2012. Traded to **New Jersey** by **Washington** for Florida's 2nd round pick (previously acquired) in 2018 NHL Draft and Toronto's 3rd round pick (previously acquired) in 2018 NHL Draft. July 2, 2017.

JOHNS, Stephen

(JAWNZ, STEE-vehn) **DAL**

Defense. Shoots right. 6'4", 225 lbs. Born, Ellwood City, PA, April 18, 1992. Chicago's 5th pick, 60th overall, in 2010 NHL Draft.

Season	Club	League	GP	G	A	Pts	PIM	PP	SH	GW	S	S%	+/-	TF	F%	Min	GP	G	A	Pts	PIM	PP	SH	GW	Min
2007-08	Pittsburgh	MWEHL	26	4	7	11	24																		
	Pit. Hornets	Minor-PA	50	12	22	34	46																		
2008-09	USAHNTDP	NAHL	31	3	5	8	30																		
	USAHNTDP	U-17	16	2	6	8	20																		
2009-10	USAHNTDP	USHL	23	1	7	8	29																		
	USAHNTDP	U-18	39	2	9	11	38																		
2010-11	U. of Notre Dame	CCHA	44	2	11	13	*98																		
2011-12	U. of Notre Dame	CCHA	39	4	6	10	71																		
2012-13	U. of Notre Dame	CCHA	41	1	13	14	62																		
2013-14	U. of Notre Dame	H-East	40	8	12	20	69																		
	Rockford IceHogs	AHL	8	1	4	5	4																		
2014-15	Rockford IceHogs	AHL	51	4	17	21	44										8	3	4	7	4				
2015-16	**Dallas**	**NHL**	**14**	**1**	**2**	**3**	**6**	**0**	**0**	**0**	**13**	**7.7**	**-6**	**0**	**0.0**	**17:50**	**13**	**0**	**0**	**0**	**6**	**0**	**0**	**0**	**14:48**
	Texas Stars	AHL	55	4	20	24	43																		
2016-17	**Dallas**	**NHL**	**61**	**4**	**6**	**10**	**36**	**0**	**0**	**1**	**91**	**4.4**	**-10**	**0**	**0.0**	**18:15**									
	Texas Stars	AHL	2	3	0	3	0																		
	NHL Totals		**75**	**5**	**8**	**13**	**42**	**0**	**0**	**1**	**104**	**4.8**		**0**	**0.0**	**18:11**	**13**	**0**	**0**	**0**	**6**	**0**	**0**	**0**	**14:48**

Hockey East Second All-Star Team (2014)
Traded to **Dallas** by **Chicago** with Patrick Sharp for Trevor Daley and Ryan Garbutt, July 12, 2015.

JOHNSON, Erik

(JAWN-suhn, AIR-ihk) **COL**

Defense. Shoots right. 6'4", 225 lbs. Born, Bloomington, MN, March 21, 1988. St. Louis' 1st pick, 1st overall, in 2006 NHL Draft.

Season	Club	League	GP	G	A	Pts	PIM	PP	SH	GW	S	S%	+/-	TF	F%	Min	GP	G	A	Pts	PIM	PP	SH	GW	Min
2003-04	Holy Angels	High-MN	31	13	21	34																			
2004-05	USAHNTDP	U-17	26	5	9	14	14																		
	USAHNTDP	NAHL	31	6	6	12	12																		
2005-06	USAHNTDP	U-18	36	12	22	34	78																		
	USAHNTDP	NAHL	11	4	11	15	10																		
2006-07	U. of Minnesota	WCHA	41	4	20	24	50																		

			Regular Season														Playoffs								
Season	Club	League	GP	G	A	Pts	PIM	PP	SH	GW	S	S%	+/-	TF	F%	Min	GP	G	A	Pts	PIM	PP	SH	GW	Min
2007-08	St. Louis	NHL	69	5	28	33	28	4	0	3	105	4.8	–9	1	0.0	18:11	....	....	....	....	....	....	....	....	....
	Peoria Rivermen	AHL	1	0	0	0	2	....	....	....	....	....	....	....	....	....	....	....	....	....	....	....	....	....	....
2008-09	St. Louis	NHL	DID NOT PLAY – INJURED																						
2009-10	St. Louis	NHL	79	10	29	39	79	6	0	2	186	5.4	1	0	0.0	21:27	....	....	....	....	....	....	....	....	....
	United States	Olympics	6	1	0	1	4	....	....	....	....	....	....	....	....	....	....	....	....	....	....	....	....	....	....
2010-11	St. Louis	NHL	55	5	14	19	37	1	1	2	108	4.6	–8	0	0.0	22:08	....	....	....	....	....	....	....	....	....
	Colorado	NHL	22	3	7	10	19	2	0	0	53	5.7	–5	0	0.0	24:33	....	....	....	....	....	....	....	....	....
2011-12	Colorado	NHL	73	4	22	26	26	1	0	1	155	2.6	–7	0	0.0	20:50	....	....	....	....	....	....	....	....	....
2012-13	Colorado	NHL	31	0	4	4	18	0	0	0	64	0.0	–3	0	0.0	20:45	....	....	....	....	....	....	....	....	....
2013-14	Colorado	NHL	80	9	30	39	61	2	0	2	157	5.7	5	0	0.0	23:00	7	1	1	2	2	0	0	0	26:13
2014-15	Colorado	NHL	47	12	11	23	33	3	0	2	115	10.4	2	0	0.0	24:25	....	....	....	....	....	....	....	....	....
2015-16	Colorado	NHL	73	11	16	27	50	3	2	0	175	6.3	–19	1	0.0	23:27	....	....	....	....	....	....	....	....	....
2016-17	Colorado	NHL	46	2	15	17	9	0	0	1	96	2.1	–6	0	0.0	22:05	....	....	....	....	....	....	....	....	....
	NHL Totals		**575**	**61**	**176**	**237**	**360**	**22**	**3**	**13**	**1214**	**5.0**		**2**	**0.0**	**21:53**	**7**	**1**	**1**	**2**	**2**	**0**	**0**	**0**	**26:13**

WCHA All-Rookie Team (2007)

• Missed 2008-09 due to off-ice knee injury, September 16, 2008. Traded to **Colorado** by **St. Louis** with Jay McClement and St. Louis' 1st round pick (Duncan Siemens) in 2011 NHL Draft for Kevin Shattenkirk, Chris Stewart and Colorado's 2nd round pick (Ty Rattie) in 2011 NHL Draft, February 18, 2011.

JOHNSON, Jack

(JAWN-suhn, JAK) **CBJ**

Defense. Shoots left. 6'1", 230 lbs. Born, Indianapolis, IN, January 13, 1987. Carolina's 1st pick, 3rd overall, in 2005 NHL Draft.

Season	Club	League	GP	G	A	Pts	PIM	PP	SH	GW	S	S%	+/-	TF	F%	Min	GP	G	A	Pts	PIM	PP	SH	GW	Min
2002-03	Shattuck	High-MN	48	15	27	42	....	....	....	....	....	....	....	....	....	....	....	....	....	....	....	....	....	....	....
2003-04	USAHNTDP	U-17	31	12	9	21	78	....	....	....	....	....	....	....	....	....	....	....	....	....	....	....	....	....	....
	USAHNTDP	NAHL	29	3	12	15	93	....	....	....	....	....	....	....	....	....	....	....	....	....	....	....	....	....	....
2004-05	USAHNTDP	U-18	26	5	9	14	86	....	....	....	....	....	....	....	....	....	....	....	....	....	....	....	....	....	....
	USAHNTDP	NAHL	12	7	10	17	57	....	....	....	....	....	....	....	....	....	....	....	....	....	....	....	....	....	....
2005-06	U. of Michigan	CCHA	38	10	22	32	*149	....	....	....	....	....	....	....	....	....	....	....	....	....	....	....	....	....	....
2006-07	U. of Michigan	CCHA	36	16	23	39	87	....	....	....	....	....	....	....	....	....	....	....	....	....	....	....	....	....	....
	Los Angeles	**NHL**	**5**	**0**	**0**	**0**	**18**	0	0	0	5	0.0	–5	0	0.0	21:23	....	....	....	....	....	....	....	....	....
2007-08	**Los Angeles**	**NHL**	**74**	**3**	**8**	**11**	**76**	0	0	0	81	3.7	–19	5	60.0	21:42	....	....	....	....	....	....	....	....	....
2008-09	**Los Angeles**	**NHL**	**41**	**6**	**5**	**11**	**46**	3	0	0	50	12.0	–18	0	0.0	20:17	....	....	....	....	....	....	....	....	....
2009-10	**Los Angeles**	**NHL**	**80**	**8**	**28**	**36**	**48**	3	0	0	130	6.2	–15	0	0.0	22:37	6	0	7	7	6	0	0	0	23:42
	United States	Olympics	6	0	1	1	2	....	....	....	....	....	....	....	....	....	....	....	....	....	....	....	....	....	....
2010-11	**Los Angeles**	**NHL**	**82**	**5**	**37**	**42**	**44**	3	0	0	153	3.3	–21	0	0.0	23:12	6	1	4	5	0	1	0	1	22:48
2011-12	**Los Angeles**	**NHL**	**61**	**8**	**16**	**24**	**24**	5	0	4	120	6.7	–12	0	0.0	22:31	....	....	....	....	....	....	....	....	....
	Columbus	**NHL**	**21**	**4**	**10**	**14**	**15**	0	0	1	56	7.1	5	0	0.0	27:25	....	....	....	....	....	....	....	....	....
2012-13	**Columbus**	**NHL**	**44**	**5**	**14**	**19**	**12**	3	0	1	96	5.2	–5	0	0.0	25:58	....	....	....	....	....	....	....	....	....
2013-14	**Columbus**	**NHL**	**82**	**5**	**28**	**33**	**48**	4	0	0	147	3.4	–7	1	0.0	24:41	6	3	4	7	4	1	0	0	29:21
2014-15	**Columbus**	**NHL**	**79**	**8**	**32**	**40**	**44**	3	0	1	141	5.7	–13	0	0.0	24:10	....	....	....	....	....	....	....	....	....
2015-16	**Columbus**	**NHL**	**60**	**6**	**8**	**14**	**25**	3	0	2	86	7.0	–16	1	0.0	24:11	....	....	....	....	....	....	....	....	....
2016-17	**Columbus**	**NHL**	**82**	**5**	**18**	**23**	**32**	1	0	1	116	4.3	23	1	100.0	21:49	5	1	1	2	0	0	0	0	25:52
	NHL Totals		**711**	**63**	**204**	**267**	**432**	**28**	**0**	**10**	**1181**	**5.3**		**8**	**50.0**	**23:14**	**23**	**5**	**16**	**21**	**10**	**2**	**0**	**1**	**25:25**

CCHA All-Rookie Team (2006) • CCHA First All-Star Team (2007) • NCAA West First All-American Team (2007)

Traded to **Los Angeles** by **Carolina** with Oleg Tverdovsky for Eric Belanger and Tim Gleason, September 29, 2006. Traded to **Columbus** by **Los Angeles** with Los Angeles' 1st round pick (Marko Dano) in 2013 NHL Draft for Jeff Carter, February 23, 2012.

JOHNSON, Tyler

(JAWN-suhn, TIGH-luhr) **T.B.**

Center. Shoots right. 5'8", 185 lbs. Born, Spokane, WA, July 29, 1990.

Season	Club	League	GP	G	A	Pts	PIM	PP	SH	GW	S	S%	+/-	TF	F%	Min	GP	G	A	Pts	PIM	PP	SH	GW	Min
2005-06			STATISTICS NOT AVAILABLE																						
	Coeur d'Alene	NORPAC	11	4	3	7	2	....	....	....	....	....	....	....	....	....	2	1	1	2	4	....	....	....	....
2006-07	Coeur d'Alene	NORPAC	39	56	64	120	57	....	....	....	....	....	....	....	....	....	7	4	12	16	14	....	....	....	....
2007-08	Spokane Chiefs	WHL	69	13	22	35	34	....	....	....	....	....	....	....	....	....	21	5	3	8	24	....	....	....	....
2008-09	Spokane Chiefs	WHL	62	26	35	61	52	....	....	....	....	....	....	....	....	....	12	5	3	8	8	....	....	....	....
2009-10	Spokane Chiefs	WHL	64	36	35	71	32	....	....	....	....	....	....	....	....	....	7	3	5	8	0	....	....	....	....
2010-11	Spokane Chiefs	WHL	71	*53	62	115	48	....	....	....	....	....	....	....	....	....	14	7	7	14	9	....	....	....	....
2011-12	Norfolk Admirals	AHL	75	31	37	68	28	....	....	....	....	....	....	....	....	....	14	6	8	14	6	....	....	....	....
2012-13	Syracuse Crunch	AHL	62	*37	28	65	34	....	....	....	....	....	....	....	....	....	18	10	11	21	18	....	....	....	....
	Tampa Bay	**NHL**	**14**	**3**	**3**	**6**	**4**	0	0	0	11	27.3	3	121	59.5	13:04	....	....	....	....	....	....	....	....	....
2013-14	**Tampa Bay**	**NHL**	**82**	**24**	**26**	**50**	**26**	5	*5	4	181	13.3	23	1275	48.2	18:47	4	1	1	2	0	0	0	0	20:59
2014-15	**Tampa Bay**	**NHL**	**77**	**29**	**43**	**72**	**24**	8	0	6	203	14.3	33	1103	48.7	17:14	26	13	10	23	24	2	1	4	18:31
2015-16	**Tampa Bay**	**NHL**	**69**	**14**	**24**	**38**	**20**	3	0	7	167	8.4	4	986	48.6	17:08	17	7	10	17	12	0	0	3	17:46
2016-17	**Tampa Bay**	**NHL**	**66**	**19**	**26**	**45**	**28**	6	0	3	130	14.6	–5	1122	52.0	18:49	....	....	....	....	....	....	....	....	....
	NHL Totals		**308**	**89**	**122**	**211**	**102**	**22**	**5**	**20**	**692**	**12.9**		**4607**	**49.6**	**17:47**	**47**	**21**	**21**	**42**	**36**	**2**	**1**	**7**	**18:27**

WHL West First All-Star Team (2011) • AHL All-Rookie Team (2012) • Willie Marshall Award (AHL – Top Goal-scorer) (2013) • Les Cunningham Award (AHL – MVP) (2013) • NHL All-Rookie Team (2014)

Signed as a free agent by **Tampa Bay**, March 7, 2011.

JOHNSTON, Ross

(JAWN-stuhn, RAWS) **NYI**

Left wing. Shoots left. 6'5", 232 lbs. Born, Charlottetown, PEI, February 18, 1994.

Season	Club	League	GP	G	A	Pts	PIM	PP	SH	GW	S	S%	+/-	TF	F%	Min	GP	G	A	Pts	PIM	PP	SH	GW	Min
2010-11	Charlottetown	NBPEI	34	20	*37	57	109	....	....	....	....	....	....	....	....	....	5	5	3	8	20	....	....	....	....
	Summerside	MJrHL	2	2	1	3	4	....	....	....	....	....	....	....	....	....	....	....	....	....	....	....	....	....	....
2011-12	Summerside	MJrHL	23	12	17	29	55	....	....	....	....	....	....	....	....	....	....	....	....	....	....	....	....	....	....
	Moncton Wildcats	QMJHL	38	2	5	7	55	....	....	....	....	....	....	....	....	....	2	0	0	0	8	....	....	....	....
2012-13	Moncton Wildcats	QMJHL	53	12	15	27	96	....	....	....	....	....	....	....	....	....	3	0	0	0	4	....	....	....	....
2013-14	Victoriaville Tigres	QMJHL	60	10	15	25	139	....	....	....	....	....	....	....	....	....	5	0	3	3	6	....	....	....	....
2014-15	Charlottetown	QMJHL	44	18	14	32	124	....	....	....	....	....	....	....	....	....	10	4	7	11	28	....	....	....	....
	Bridgeport	AHL	2	0	0	0	0	....	....	....	....	....	....	....	....	....	....	....	....	....	....	....	....	....	....
2015-16	**NY Islanders**	**NHL**	**1**	**0**	**0**	**0**	**4**	0	0	0	0	0.0	0	0	0.0	16:17	....	....	....	....	....	....	....	....	....
	Bridgeport	AHL	39	1	3	4	79	....	....	....	....	....	....	....	....	....	....	....	....	....	....	....	....	....	....
	Missouri	ECHL	13	4	7	11	23	....	....	....	....	....	....	....	....	....	5	3	1	4	10	....	....	....	....
2016-17	Bridgeport	AHL	62	8	7	15	135	....	....	....	....	....	....	....	....	....	....	....	....	....	....	....	....	....	....
	NHL Totals		**1**	**0**	**0**	**0**	**4**	**0**	**0**	**0**	**0**	**0.0**		**0**	**0.0**	**16:17**	....	....	....	....	....	....	....	....	....

Signed as a free agent by **NY Islanders**, March 31, 2015.

JOHNSTON, Ryan

(JAWN-stuhn, RIGH-uhn)

Defense. Shoots right. 5'10", 182 lbs. Born, Sudbury, ON, February 14, 1992.

Season	Club	League	GP	G	A	Pts	PIM	PP	SH	GW	S	S%	+/-	TF	F%	Min	GP	G	A	Pts	PIM	PP	SH	GW	Min
2007-08	Sud. Wolves Mid.	Minor-ON	32	4	26	30	12	....	....	....	....	....	....	....	....	....	10	2	13	15	6	....	....	....	....
2008-09	Sud. Wolves Mid.	Minor-ON	33	10	18	28	22	....	....	....	....	....	....	....	....	....	11	4	5	9	12	....	....	....	....
2009-10	Elmira	ON-Jr.B	37	3	20	23	20	....	....	....	....	....	....	....	....	....	12	0	3	3	4	....	....	....	....
2010-11	Nepean Raiders	ON-Jr.A	58	11	31	42	32	....	....	....	....	....	....	....	....	....	7	1	3	4	6	....	....	....	....
2011-12	Nepean Raiders	ON-Jr.A	56	17	54	71	32	....	....	....	....	....	....	....	....	....	18	9	9	18	8	....	....	....	....
2012-13	Colgate	ECAC	34	0	8	8	30	....	....	....	....	....	....	....	....	....	....	....	....	....	....	....	....	....	....
2013-14	Colgate	ECAC	37	4	15	19	37	....	....	....	....	....	....	....	....	....	....	....	....	....	....	....	....	....	....
2014-15	Colgate	ECAC	38	1	14	15	26	....	....	....	....	....	....	....	....	....	....	....	....	....	....	....	....	....	....
2015-16	**Montreal**	**NHL**	**3**	**0**	**0**	**0**	**0**	0	0	0	1	0.0	1	0	0.0	16:17	....	....	....	....	....	....	....	....	....
	St. John's IceCaps	AHL	37	0	12	12	14	....	....	....	....	....	....	....	....	....	....	....	....	....	....	....	....	....	....
2016-17	**Montreal**	**NHL**	**7**	**0**	**0**	**0**	**4**	0	0	0	3	0.0	–3	0	0.0	9:52	....	....	....	....	....	....	....	....	....
	St. John's IceCaps	AHL	50	5	13	18	22	....	....	....	....	....	....	....	....	....	....	....	....	....	....	....	....	....	....
	NHL Totals		**10**	**0**	**0**	**0**	**4**	**0**	**0**	**0**	**4**	**0.0**		**0**	**0.0**	**11:48**	....	....	....	....	....	....	....	....	....

Signed as a free agent by **Montreal**, July 13, 2015.

JOKINEN, Jussi

(YOH-kih-nihn, YEW-see) **EDM**

Center. Shoots left. 5'11", 198 lbs. Born, Kalajoki, Finland, April 1, 1983. Dallas' 7th pick, 192nd overall, in 2001 NHL Draft.

			Regular Season														Playoffs								
Season	Club	League	GP	G	A	Pts	PIM	PP	SH	GW	S	S%	+/-	TF	F%	Min	GP	G	A	Pts	PIM	PP	SH	GW	Min
99-2000	Karpat Oulu U18	Fin-U18	15	6	25	31	14	....	....	....	....	....	....	....	....	....	6	2	3	5	0	....	....	....	....
	Karpat Oulu Jr.	Fin-Jr.	28	4	7	11	14	....	....	....	....	....	....	....	....	....	....	....	....	....	....	....	....	....	....
2000-01	Karpat Oulu U18	Fin-U18	1	2	1	3	0	....	....	....	....	....	....	....	....	....	....	....	....	....	....	....	....	....	....
	Karpat Oulu Jr.	Fin-Jr.	41	18	31	49	69	....	....	....	....	....	....	....	....	....	6	2	1	3	0	....	....	....	....
2001-02	Karpat Oulu Jr.	Fin-Jr.	2	4	1	5	2	....	....	....	....	....	....	....	....	....	1	1	1	2	0	....	....	....	....
	Karpat Oulu	Finland	54	10	6	16	38	....	....	....	....	....	....	....	....	....	4	1	0	1	0	....	....	....	....
2002-03	Karpat Oulu	Finland	51	14	23	37	10	....	....	....	....	....	....	....	....	....	15	2	1	3	33	....	....	....	....
2003-04	Karpat Oulu	Finland	55	15	23	38	20	....	....	....	....	....	....	....	....	....	15	3	4	7	6	....	....	....	....
2004-05	Karpat Oulu	Finland	56	23	24	47	24	....	....	....	....	....	....	....	....	....	12	3	4	7	2	....	....	....	....
2005-06	**Dallas**	**NHL**	**81**	**17**	**38**	**55**	**30**	**8**	**0**	**2**	**107**	**15.9**	**2**	**23**	**30.4**	**13:34**	**5**	**2**	**1**	**3**	**0**	**1**	**0**	**0**	**13:40**
	Finland	Olympics	8	1	3	4	2	....	....	....	....	....	....	....	....	....	....	....	....	....	....	....	....	....	....
2006-07	**Dallas**	**NHL**	**82**	**14**	**34**	**48**	**18**	**6**	**0**	**1**	**121**	**11.6**	**8**	**278**	**52.2**	**13:54**	**4**	**0**	**1**	**1**	**0**	**0**	**0**	**0**	**13:22**
2007-08	**Dallas**	**NHL**	**52**	**14**	**14**	**28**	**14**	**5**	**0**	**2**	**93**	**15.1**	**2**	**295**	**53.2**	**12:44**	....	....	....	....	....	....	....	....	....
	Tampa Bay	**NHL**	**20**	**2**	**12**	**14**	**4**	**1**	**0**	**0**	**38**	**5.3**	**–16**	**46**	**45.7**	**18:57**	....	....	....	....	....	....	....	....	....
2008-09	**Tampa Bay**	**NHL**	**46**	**6**	**10**	**16**	**16**	**2**	**0**	**0**	**64**	**9.4**	**–8**	**510**	**52.2**	**15:38**	....	....	....	....	....	....	....	....	....
	Carolina	**NHL**	**25**	**1**	**10**	**11**	**12**	**0**	**0**	**1**	**37**	**2.7**	**–2**	**163**	**58.3**	**14:43**	**18**	**7**	**4**	**11**	**2**	**2**	**0**	***3**	**15:35**
2009-10	**Carolina**	**NHL**	**81**	**30**	**35**	**65**	**36**	**10**	**0**	**6**	**160**	**18.8**	**3**	**265**	**51.3**	**16:49**	....	....	....	....	....	....	....	....	....
2010-11	**Carolina**	**NHL**	**70**	**19**	**33**	**52**	**24**	**8**	**0**	**1**	**136**	**14.0**	**3**	**320**	**52.8**	**17:13**	....	....	....	....	....	....	....	....	....
2011-12	**Carolina**	**NHL**	**79**	**12**	**34**	**46**	**54**	**3**	**2**	**3**	**118**	**10.2**	**–2**	**833**	**55.1**	**17:40**	....	....	....	....	....	....	....	....	....
2012-13	Karpat Oulu	Finland	21	7	14	21	10	....	....	....	....	....	....	....	....	....	....	....	....	....	....	....	....	....	....
	Carolina	**NHL**	**33**	**6**	**5**	**11**	**18**	**2**	**0**	**3**	**61**	**9.8**	**–8**	**283**	**59.4**	**15:35**	....	....	....	....	....	....	....	....	....
	Pittsburgh	**NHL**	**10**	**7**	**4**	**11**	**6**	**1**	**0**	**0**	**13**	**53.8**	**3**	**149**	**55.0**	**14:55**	**8**	**0**	**3**	**3**	**4**	**0**	**0**	**0**	**11:01**
2013-14	**Pittsburgh**	**NHL**	**81**	**21**	**36**	**57**	**18**	**6**	**0**	**4**	**172**	**12.2**	**12**	**299**	**53.5**	**15:42**	**13**	**7**	**3**	**10**	**10**	**1**	**0**	**3**	**15:43**
	Finland	Olympics	6	2	3	5	0	....	....	....	....	....	....	....	....	....	....	....	....	....	....	....	....	....	....
2014-15	**Florida**	**NHL**	**81**	**8**	**36**	**44**	**34**	**2**	**0**	**0**	**134**	**6.0**	**–2**	**250**	**50.4**	**16:44**	....	....	....	....	....	....	....	....	....
2015-16	**Florida**	**NHL**	**81**	**18**	**42**	**60**	**42**	**5**	**1**	**1**	**153**	**11.8**	**25**	**262**	**51.5**	**18:17**	**6**	**1**	**3**	**4**	**4**	**1**	**0**	**0**	**24:30**
2016-17	**Florida**	**NHL**	**69**	**11**	**17**	**28**	**39**	**4**	**1**	**2**	**118**	**9.3**	**–15**	**144**	**52.1**	**17:25**	....	....	....	....	....	....	....	....	....
	NHL Totals		**891**	**186**	**360**	**546**	**365**	**63**	**4**	**26**	**1525**	**12.2**		**4120**	**53.4**	**16:03**	**54**	**17**	**15**	**32**	**20**	**5**	**0**	**6**	**15:35**

Traded to **Tampa Bay** by **Dallas** with Jeff Halpern, Mike Smith and Dallas' 4th round pick (later traded to Minnesota, later traded to Edmonton – Edmonton selected Kyle Bigos) in 2009 NHL Draft for Brad Richards and Johan Holmqvist, February 26, 2008. Traded to **Carolina** by **Tampa Bay** for Wade Brookbank, Josef Melichar and future considerations, February 7, 2009. Signed as a free agent by **Oulu** (Finland), September 17, 2012. Traded to **Pittsburgh** by **Carolina** for future considerations, April 3, 2013. Signed as a free agent by **Florida**, July 1, 2014. Signed as a free agent by **Edmonton**, July 7, 2017.

JOKIPAKKA, Jyrki

(yoh-kih-PA-ka, YUHR-kee)

Defense. Shoots left. 6'3", 215 lbs. Born, Tampere, Finland, August 20, 1991. Dallas' 6th pick, 195th overall, in 2011 NHL Draft.

Season	Club	League	GP	G	A	Pts	PIM	PP	SH	GW	S	S%	+/-	TF	F%	Min	GP	G	A	Pts	PIM	PP	SH	GW	Min
2007-08	Ilves Tampere U17	Fin-U17	24	6	15	21	26	....	....	....	....	....	....	....	....	....	2	1	1	2	0	....	....	....	....
2008-09	Ilves Tampere U18	Fin-U18	33	4	7	11	12	....	....	....	....	....	....	....	....	....	....	....	....	....	....	....	....	....	....
	Ilves Tampere Jr.	Fin-Jr.	4	0	0	0	2	....	....	....	....	....	....	....	....	....	....	....	....	....	....	....	....	....	....
2009-10	Ilves Tampere Jr.	Fin-Jr.	38	3	12	15	77	....	....	....	....	....	....	....	....	....	5	1	0	1	2	....	....	....	....
2010-11	Suomi U20	Finland-2	6	0	3	3	2	....	....	....	....	....	....	....	....	....	....	....	....	....	....	....	....	....	....
	Ilves Tampere Jr.	Fin-Jr.	3	0	0	0	6	....	....	....	....	....	....	....	....	....	2	0	0	0	2	....	....	....	....
	LeKi Lempaala	Finland-2	1	0	0	0	0	....	....	....	....	....	....	....	....	....	....	....	....	....	....	....	....	....	....
	Ilves Tampere	Finland	48	1	8	9	18	....	....	....	....	....	....	....	....	....	5	0	0	0	2	....	....	....	....
2011-12	Ilves Tampere Jr.	Fin-Jr.	1	0	1	1	2	....	....	....	....	....	....	....	....	....	....	....	....	....	....	....	....	....	....
	LeKi Lempaala	Finland-2	3	1	0	1	0	....	....	....	....	....	....	....	....	....	....	....	....	....	....	....	....	....	....
	Ilves Tampere	Finland	52	9	8	17	18	....	....	....	....	....	....	....	....	....	....	....	....	....	....	....	....	....	....
	Ilves Tampere	Finland-Q	....	....	....	....	....	....	....	....	....	....	....	....	....	....	5	0	2	2	2	....	....	....	....
2012-13	Ilves Tampere	Finland	59	5	13	18	20	....	....	....	....	....	....	....	....	....	....	....	....	....	....	....	....	....	....
	Ilves Tampere	Finland-Q	....	....	....	....	....	....	....	....	....	....	....	....	....	....	5	0	0	0	0	....	....	....	....
2013-14	Texas Stars	AHL	68	5	16	21	32	....	....	....	....	....	....	....	....	....	21	0	5	5	8	....	....	....	....
2014-15	**Dallas**	**NHL**	**51**	**0**	**10**	**10**	**8**	**0**	**0**	**0**	**40**	**0.0**	**–2**	**0**	**0.0**	**16:31**	....	....	....	....	....	....	....	....	....
	Texas Stars	AHL	19	3	2	5	4	....	....	....	....	....	....	....	....	....	....	....	....	....	....	....	....	....	....
2015-16	**Dallas**	**NHL**	**40**	**2**	**4**	**6**	**6**	**0**	**0**	**1**	**26**	**7.7**	**1**	**0**	**0.0**	**14:30**	....	....	....	....	....	....	....	....	....
	Calgary	**NHL**	**18**	**0**	**6**	**6**	**8**	**0**	**0**	**0**	**19**	**0.0**	**3**	**0**	**0.0**	**17:54**	....	....	....	....	....	....	....	....	....
2016-17	**Calgary**	**NHL**	**38**	**1**	**5**	**6**	**12**	**0**	**0**	**0**	**29**	**3.4**	**–3**	**0**	**0.0**	**14:26**	....	....	....	....	....	....	....	....	....
	Ottawa	**NHL**	**3**	**0**	**0**	**0**	**0**	**0**	**0**	**0**	**0**	**0.0**	**–1**	**0**	**0.0**	**14:28**	....	....	....	....	....	....	....	....	....
	NHL Totals		**150**	**3**	**25**	**28**	**34**	**0**	**0**	**1**	**114**	**2.6**		**0**	**0.0**	**15:35**	....	....	....	....	....	....	....	....	....

Traded to **Calgary** by **Dallas** with Brent Pollock and Dallas' 2nd round pick (Dillon Dube) in 2016 NHL Draft for Kris Russell, February 29, 2016. Traded to **Ottawa** by **Calgary** with Calgary's 2nd round pick (Alex Formenton) in 2017 NHL Draft for Curtis Lazar and Michael Kostka, March 1, 2017.

JONES, Connor

(JOHNZ, KAW-nuhr) **NYI**

Left wing. Shoots left. 5'9", 176 lbs. Born, Montrose, BC, August 16, 1990.

Season	Club	League	GP	G	A	Pts	PIM	PP	SH	GW	S	S%	+/-	TF	F%	Min	GP	G	A	Pts	PIM	PP	SH	GW	Min
2005-06			STATISTICS NOT AVAILABLE																						
	Beaver Valley	KIJHL	5	2	1	3	4	....	....	....	....	....	....	....	....	....	10	1	2	3	6	....	....	....	....
2006-07	Beaver Valley	KIJHL	52	26	46	72	156	....	....	....	....	....	....	....	....	....	13	3	4	7	47	....	....	....	....
	Vernon Vipers	BCHL	2	1	2	3	2	....	....	....	....	....	....	....	....	....	16	3	6	9	6	....	....	....	....
2007-08	Vernon Vipers	BCHL	50	24	30	54	50	....	....	....	....	....	....	....	....	....	10	3	9	12	2	....	....	....	....
2008-09	Vernon Vipers	BCHL	60	19	41	60	49	....	....	....	....	....	....	....	....	....	17	9	9	18	18	....	....	....	....
2009-10	Vernon Vipers	BCHL	51	36	45	81	40	....	....	....	....	....	....	....	....	....	19	9	11	20	22	....	....	....	....
2010-11	Quinnipiac	ECAC	39	9	15	24	38	....	....	....	....	....	....	....	....	....	....	....	....	....	....	....	....	....	....
2011-12	Quinnipiac	ECAC	37	13	28	41	30	....	....	....	....	....	....	....	....	....	....	....	....	....	....	....	....	....	....
2012-13	Quinnipiac	ECAC	37	12	14	26	41	....	....	....	....	....	....	....	....	....	....	....	....	....	....	....	....	....	....
2013-14	Quinnipiac	ECAC	40	15	23	38	42	....	....	....	....	....	....	....	....	....	....	....	....	....	....	....	....	....	....
	Oklahoma City	AHL	5	0	0	0	2	....	....	....	....	....	....	....	....	....	....	....	....	....	....	....	....	....	....
2014-15	Oklahoma City	AHL	41	4	6	10	31	....	....	....	....	....	....	....	....	....	10	3	0	3	2	....	....	....	....
	Bakersfield	ECHL	27	10	16	26	29	....	....	....	....	....	....	....	....	....	....	....	....	....	....	....	....	....	....
2015-16	Bridgeport	AHL	51	6	7	13	21	....	....	....	....	....	....	....	....	....	3	0	0	0	0	....	....	....	....
2016-17	**NY Islanders**	**NHL**	**4**	**0**	**0**	**0**	**2**	**0**	**0**	**0**	**2**	**0.0**	**1**	**13**	**61.5**	**11:51**	....	....	....	....	....	....	....	....	....
	Bridgeport	AHL	58	5	14	19	89	....	....	....	....	....	....	....	....	....	....	....	....	....	....	....	....	....	....
	NHL Totals		**4**	**0**	**0**	**0**	**2**	**0**	**0**	**0**	**2**	**0.0**		**13**	**61.5**	**11:51**	....	....	....	....	....	....	....	....	....

Signed as a free agent by **NY Islanders**, February 22, 2017.

JONES, Seth

(JOHNZ, SEHTH) **CBJ**

Defense. Shoots right. 6'4", 208 lbs. Born, Arlington, TX, October 3, 1994. Nashville's 1st pick, 4th overall, in 2013 NHL Draft.

Season	Club	League	GP	G	A	Pts	PIM	PP	SH	GW	S	S%	+/-	TF	F%	Min	GP	G	A	Pts	PIM	PP	SH	GW	Min
2009-10	Dallas Stars	T1EHL	42	5	13	18	20	....	....	....	....	....	....	....	....	....	....	....	....	....	....	....	....	....	....
2010-11	USAHNTDP	USHL	28	1	13	14	20	....	....	....	....	....	....	....	....	....	....	....	....	....	....	....	....	....	....
	USAHNTDP	U-17	17	3	7	10	8	....	....	....	....	....	....	....	....	....	....	....	....	....	....	....	....	....	....
	USAHNTDP	U-18	12	0	7	7	4	....	....	....	....	....	....	....	....	....	....	....	....	....	....	....	....	....	....
2011-12	USAHNTDP	USHL	20	4	8	12	6	....	....	....	....	....	....	....	....	....	....	....	....	....	....	....	....	....	....
	USAHNTDP	U-18	32	4	15	19	12	....	....	....	....	....	....	....	....	....	....	....	....	....	....	....	....	....	....
2012-13	Portland	WHL	61	14	42	56	33	....	....	....	....	....	....	....	....	....	21	5	10	15	4	....	....	....	....
2013-14	**Nashville**	**NHL**	**77**	**6**	**19**	**25**	**24**	**2**	**0**	**2**	**100**	**6.0**	**–23**	**0**	**0.0**	**19:37**	....	....	....	....	....	....	....	....	....
2014-15	**Nashville**	**NHL**	**82**	**8**	**19**	**27**	**20**	**2**	**1**	**0**	**123**	**6.5**	**3**	**0**	**0.0**	**19:53**	**6**	**0**	**4**	**4**	**6**	**0**	**0**	**0**	**28:02**
2015-16	**Nashville**	**NHL**	**40**	**1**	**10**	**11**	**10**	**0**	**0**	**0**	**74**	**1.4**	**–5**	**0**	**0.0**	**19:39**	....	....	....	....	....	....	....	....	....
	Columbus	**NHL**	**41**	**2**	**18**	**20**	**12**	**1**	**0**	**0**	**83**	**2.4**	**–9**	**0**	**0.0**	**24:27**	....	....	....	....	....	....	....	....	....
2016-17	**Columbus**	**NHL**	**75**	**12**	**30**	**42**	**24**	**1**	**0**	**3**	**152**	**7.9**	**6**	**0**	**0.0**	**23:24**	**5**	**0**	**2**	**2**	**0**	**0**	**0**	**0**	**26:04**
	NHL Totals		**315**	**29**	**96**	**125**	**90**	**6**	**1**	**5**	**532**	**5.5**		**0**	**0.0**	**21:13**	**11**	**0**	**6**	**6**	**6**	**0**	**0**	**0**	**27:08**

WHL West First All-Star Team (2013) • WHL Rookie of the Year (2013) • Canadian Major Junior Top Prospect of the Year (2013)
Played in NHL All-Star Game (2017)
Traded to **Columbus** by **Nashvile** for Ryan Johansen, January 6, 2016.

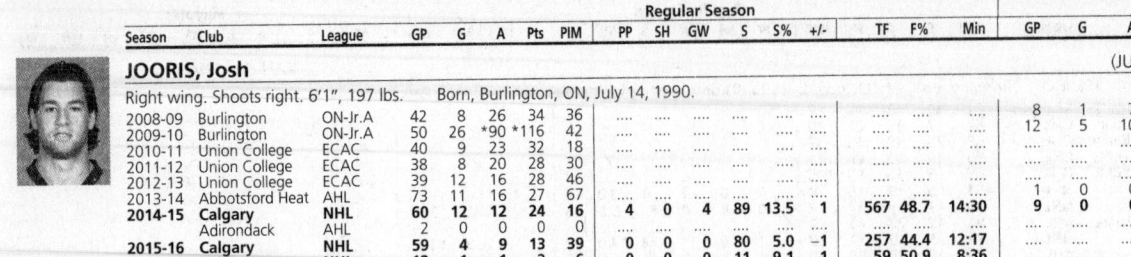

JOORIS, Josh
(JUHR-his, JAWSH) **CAR**

Right wing. Shoots right. 6'1", 197 lbs. Born, Burlington, ON, July 14, 1990.

			Regular Season														Playoffs								
Season	Club	League	GP	G	A	Pts	PIM	PP	SH	GW	S	S%	+/-	TF	F%	Min	GP	G	A	Pts	PIM	PP	SH	GW	Min
2008-09	Burlington	ON-Jr.A	42	8	26	34	36	....	....	....	....	....	....	....	....	....	8	1	7	8	12	....	....	....	....
2009-10	Burlington	ON-Jr.A	50	26	*90	*116	42	....	....	....	....	....	....	....	....	....	12	5	10	15	10	....	....	....	....
2010-11	Union College	ECAC	40	9	23	32	18	....	....	....	....	....	....	....	....	....	....	....	....	....	....	....	....	....	....
2011-12	Union College	ECAC	38	8	20	28	30	....	....	....	....	....	....	....	....	....	....	....	....	....	....	....	....	....	....
2012-13	Union College	ECAC	39	12	16	28	46	....	....	....	....	....	....	....	....	....	....	....	....	....	....	....	....	....	....
2013-14	Abbotsford Heat	AHL	73	11	16	27	67	....	....	....	....	....	....	....	....	....	1	0	0	0	2	....	....	....	....
2014-15	**Calgary**	**NHL**	**60**	**12**	**12**	**24**	**16**	**4**	**0**	**4**	**89**	**13.5**	**1**	**567**	**48.7**	**14:30**	**9**	**0**	**0**	**0**	**4**	**0**	**0**	**0**	**11:20**
	Adirondack	AHL	2	0	0	0	0	....	....	....	....	....	....	....	....	....	....	....	....	....	....	....	....	....	....
2015-16	**Calgary**	**NHL**	**59**	**4**	**9**	**13**	**39**	**0**	**0**	**0**	**80**	**5.0**	**-1**	**257**	**44.4**	**12:17**	....	....	....	....	....	....	....	....	....
2016-17	**NY Rangers**	**NHL**	**12**	**1**	**1**	**2**	**6**	**0**	**0**	**0**	**11**	**9.1**	**1**	**59**	**50.9**	**8:36**	....	....	....	....	....	....	....	....	....
	Arizona	**NHL**	**42**	**3**	**7**	**10**	**10**	**0**	**0**	**0**	**64**	**4.7**	**-3**	**391**	**49.1**	**13:13**	....	....	....	....	....	....	....	....	....
	NHL Totals		**173**	**20**	**29**	**49**	**71**	**4**	**0**	**4**	**244**	**8.2**		**1274**	**48.0**	**13:01**	**9**	**0**	**0**	**0**	**4**	**0**	**0**	**0**	**11:20**

Signed as a free agent by **Calgary**, July 30, 2013. Signed as a free agent by **NY Rangers**, July 15, 2016. Claimed on waivers by **Arizona** from **NY Rangers**, December 11, 2016. Signed as a free agent by **Carolina**, July 1, 2017.

JOSEFSON, Jacob
(JOH-sehf-suhn, YA-kuhb) **BUF**

Center. Shoots left. 6', 190 lbs. Born, Stockholm, Sweden, March 2, 1991. New Jersey's 1st pick, 20th overall, in 2009 NHL Draft.

			Regular Season														Playoffs								
Season	Club	League	GP	G	A	Pts	PIM	PP	SH	GW	S	S%	+/-	TF	F%	Min	GP	G	A	Pts	PIM	PP	SH	GW	Min
2005-06	Djurgarden U18	Swe-U18	5	1	1	2	0	....	....	....	....	....	....	....	....	....	....	....	....	....	....	....	....	....	....
2006-07	Djurgarden U18	Swe-U18	25	14	17	31	22	....	....	....	....	....	....	....	....	....	3	0	0	0	0	....	....	....	....
2007-08	Djurgarden U18	Swe-U18	4	1	2	3	12	....	....	....	....	....	....	....	....	....	6	0	6	6	4	....	....	....	....
	Djurgarden Jr.	Swe-Jr.	34	14	17	31	22	....	....	....	....	....	....	....	....	....	7	2	3	5	8	....	....	....	....
	Djurgarden	Sweden	1	0	0	0	0	....	....	....	....	....	....	....	....	....	....	....	....	....	....	....	....	....	....
2008-09	Djurgarden Jr.	Swe-Jr.	5	1	2	3	8	....	....	....	....	....	....	....	....	....	6	1	3	4	4	....	....	....	....
	Djurgarden	Sweden	50	5	11	16	14	....	....	....	....	....	....	....	....	....	....	....	....	....	....	....	....	....	....
	Djurgarden U18	Swe-U18	....	....	....	....	....	....	....	....	....	....	....	....	....	....	1	0	0	0	0	....	....	....	....
2009-10	Djurgarden	Sweden	43	8	12	20	20	....	....	....	....	....	....	....	....	....	14	3	2	5	4	....	....	....	....
2010-11	**New Jersey**	**NHL**	**28**	**3**	**7**	**10**	**6**	**0**	**0**	**1**	**31**	**9.7**	**5**	**202**	**47.0**	**13:14**	....	....	....	....	....	....	....	....	....
	Albany Devils	AHL	18	3	9	12	4	....	....	....	....	....	....	....	....	....	....	....	....	....	....	....	....	....	....
2011-12	**New Jersey**	**NHL**	**41**	**2**	**7**	**9**	**6**	**0**	**0**	**0**	**37**	**5.4**	**10**	**354**	**51.1**	**12:06**	**6**	**0**	**1**	**1**	**0**	**0**	**0**	**0**	**13:41**
	Albany Devils	AHL	4	2	1	3	2	....	....	....	....	....	....	....	....	....	....	....	....	....	....	....	....	....	....
2012-13	Albany Devils	AHL	38	10	15	25	29	....	....	....	....	....	....	....	....	....	....	....	....	....	....	....	....	....	....
	New Jersey	**NHL**	**22**	**1**	**2**	**3**	**2**	**0**	**0**	**0**	**20**	**5.0**	**-10**	**236**	**48.3**	**12:59**	....	....	....	....	....	....	....	....	....
2013-14	**New Jersey**	**NHL**	**27**	**1**	**2**	**3**	**4**	**0**	**1**	**0**	**21**	**4.8**	**0**	**168**	**49.4**	**10:08**	....	....	....	....	....	....	....	....	....
2014-15	**New Jersey**	**NHL**	**62**	**6**	**5**	**11**	**24**	**0**	**3**	**1**	**61**	**9.8**	**0**	**586**	**49.3**	**12:26**	....	....	....	....	....	....	....	....	....
2015-16	**New Jersey**	**NHL**	**58**	**4**	**10**	**14**	**20**	**3**	**0**	**1**	**86**	**4.7**	**-21**	**667**	**48.4**	**15:31**	....	....	....	....	....	....	....	....	....
2016-17	**New Jersey**	**NHL**	**38**	**1**	**9**	**10**	**16**	**0**	**0**	**1**	**44**	**2.3**	**-1**	**313**	**51.8**	**12:15**	....	....	....	....	....	....	....	....	....
	NHL Totals		**276**	**18**	**42**	**60**	**78**	**3**	**4**	**4**	**300**	**6.0**		**2526**	**49.4**	**12:54**	**6**	**0**	**1**	**1**	**0**	**0**	**0**	**0**	**13:41**

• Missed majority of 2013-14 as a healthy reserve. Signed as a free agent by **Buffalo**, July 1, 2017.

JOSI, Roman
(YOH-see, ROH-man) **NSH**

Defense. Shoots left. 6'1", 201 lbs. Born, Bern, Switzerland, June 1, 1990. Nashville's 3rd pick, 38th overall, in 2008 NHL Draft.

			Regular Season														Playoffs								
Season	Club	League	GP	G	A	Pts	PIM	PP	SH	GW	S	S%	+/-	TF	F%	Min	GP	G	A	Pts	PIM	PP	SH	GW	Min
2005-06	SC Bern Future Jr.	Swiss-Jr.	5	0	0	0	0	....	....	....	....	....	....	....	....	....	....	....	....	....	....	....	....	....	....
2006-07	SC Bern Future Jr.	Swiss-Jr.	33	14	16	30	28	....	....	....	....	....	....	....	....	....	14	1	3	4	2	....	....	....	....
	Switzerland U20	Swiss-2	5	1	1	2	2	....	....	....	....	....	....	....	....	....	....	....	....	....	....	....	....	....	....
	SC Bern	Swiss	3	0	1	1	0	....	....	....	....	....	....	....	....	....	....	....	....	....	....	....	....	....	....
2007-08	Switzerland U20	Swiss-2	2	0	1	1	0	....	....	....	....	....	....	....	....	....	....	....	....	....	....	....	....	....	....
	HC Neuchatel	Swiss-2	3	2	0	2	4	....	....	....	....	....	....	....	....	....	....	....	....	....	....	....	....	....	....
	SC Bern	Swiss	35	2	6	8	10	....	....	....	....	....	....	....	....	....	6	0	0	0	0	....	....	....	....
2008-09	SC Bern	Swiss	42	7	17	24	16	....	....	....	....	....	....	....	....	....	6	0	0	0	2	....	....	....	....
2009-10	SC Bern	Swiss	26	9	12	21	12	....	....	....	....	....	....	....	....	....	15	6	7	13	8	....	....	....	....
2010-11	Milwaukee	AHL	69	6	34	40	22	....	....	....	....	....	....	....	....	....	13	1	6	7	8	....	....	....	....
2011-12	**Nashville**	**NHL**	**52**	**5**	**11**	**16**	**14**	**1**	**0**	**0**	**64**	**7.8**	**1**	**0**	**0.0**	**18:23**	**10**	**0**	**0**	**0**	**10**	**0**	**0**	**0**	**18:48**
	Milwaukee	AHL	5	1	3	4	0	....	....	....	....	....	....	....	....	....	....	....	....	....	....	....	....	....	....
2012-13	SC Bern	Swiss	26	6	11	17	14	....	....	....	....	....	....	....	....	....	....	....	....	....	....	....	....	....	....
	Nashville	**NHL**	**48**	**5**	**13**	**18**	**8**	**1**	**0**	**1**	**96**	**5.2**	**-7**	**0**	**0.0**	**23:32**	....	....	....	....	....	....	....	....	....
2013-14	**Nashville**	**NHL**	**72**	**13**	**27**	**40**	**18**	**3**	**0**	**2**	**168**	**7.7**	**-2**	**0**	**0.0**	**26:25**	....	....	....	....	....	....	....	....	....
	Switzerland	Olympics	4	0	0	0	0	....	....	....	....	....	....	....	....	....	....	....	....	....	....	....	....	....	....
2014-15	**Nashville**	**NHL**	**81**	**15**	**40**	**55**	**26**	**3**	**0**	**4**	**201**	**7.5**	**15**	**1**	**0.0**	**26:28**	**6**	**1**	**0**	**1**	**0**	**0**	**0**	**0**	**31:37**
2015-16	**Nashville**	**NHL**	**81**	**14**	**47**	**61**	**43**	**6**	**1**	**3**	**198**	**7.1**	**-3**	**0**	**0.0**	**25:29**	**14**	**1**	**8**	**9**	**12**	**0**	**0**	**0**	**27:57**
2016-17	**Nashville**	**NHL**	**72**	**12**	**37**	**49**	**18**	**7**	**0**	**1**	**217**	**5.5**	**7**	**0**	**0.0**	**25:04**	**22**	**6**	**8**	**14**	**12**	**2**	**0**	**1**	**25:46**
	NHL Totals		**406**	**64**	**175**	**239**	**127**	**21**	**1**	**11**	**944**	**6.8**		**1**	**0.0**	**24:38**	**52**	**8**	**16**	**24**	**34**	**2**	**0**	**1**	**25:41**

Signed as a free agent by **Bern** (Swiss), September 20, 2012.
Played in NHL All-Star Game (2016)

JOST, Tyson
(JOHST, TIGH-suhn) **COL**

Center. Shoots left. 5'11", 191 lbs. Born, St. Albert, AB, March 14, 1998. Colorado's 1st pick, 10th overall, in 2016 NHL Draft.

			Regular Season														Playoffs								
Season	Club	League	GP	G	A	Pts	PIM	PP	SH	GW	S	S%	+/-	TF	F%	Min	GP	G	A	Pts	PIM	PP	SH	GW	Min
2013-14	Okan. Rockets	BCMML	36	*44	44	*88	65	....	....	....	....	....	....	....	....	....	7	9	*9	*18	14	....	....	....	....
	Penticton Vees	BCHL	3	0	0	0	0	....	....	....	....	....	....	....	....	....	....	....	....	....	....	....	....	....	....
	Okanagan	Tel-Cup	....	....	....	....	....	....	....	....	....	....	....	....	....	....	7	3	3	6	14	....	....	....	....
2014-15	Penticton Vees	BCHL	46	23	22	45	16	....	....	....	....	....	....	....	....	....	21	10	4	14	6	....	....	....	....
2015-16	Penticton Vees	BCHL	48	42	*62	104	43	....	....	....	....	....	....	....	....	....	11	6	8	14	4	....	....	....	....
2016-17	North Dakota	NCHC	33	16	19	35	44	....	....	....	....	....	....	....	....	....	....	....	....	....	....	....	....	....	....
	Colorado	**NHL**	**6**	**1**	**0**	**1**	**0**	**0**	**0**	**0**	**9**	**11.1**	**-5**	**70**	**40.0**	**15:41**	....	....	....	....	....	....	....	....	....
	NHL Totals		**6**	**1**	**0**	**1**	**0**	**0**	**0**	**0**	**9**	**11.1**		**70**	**40.0**	**15:41**	....	....	....	....	....	....	....	....	....

NCHC All-Rookie Team (2017)

JURCO, Tomas
(YUHR-koh, TAW-mahsh) **CHI**

Right wing. Shoots left. 6'2", 188 lbs. Born, Kosice, Slovakia, December 28, 1992. Detroit's 1st pick, 35th overall, in 2011 NHL Draft.

			Regular Season														Playoffs								
Season	Club	League	GP	G	A	Pts	PIM	PP	SH	GW	S	S%	+/-	TF	F%	Min	GP	G	A	Pts	PIM	PP	SH	GW	Min
2007-08	HC Kosice U18	Svk-U18	57	28	24	52	30	....	....	....	....	....	....	....	....	....	....	....	....	....	....	....	....	....	....
2008-09	HC Kosice U18	Svk-U18	5	8	5	13	2	....	....	....	....	....	....	....	....	....	....	....	....	....	....	....	....	....	....
	HC Kosice Jr.	Slovak-Jr.	48	19	30	49	20	....	....	....	....	....	....	....	....	....	3	5	0	5	0	....	....	....	....
2009-10	Saint John	QMJHL	64	26	25	51	24	....	....	....	....	....	....	....	....	....	21	7	10	17	8	....	....	....	....
2010-11	Saint John	QMJHL	60	31	25	56	17	....	....	....	....	....	....	....	....	....	19	6	12	18	8	....	....	....	....
2011-12	Saint John	QMJHL	48	30	38	68	37	....	....	....	....	....	....	....	....	....	16	13	16	29	12	....	....	....	....
2012-13	Grand Rapids	AHL	74	14	14	28	22	....	....	....	....	....	....	....	....	....	24	8	6	14	21	....	....	....	....
2013-14	**Detroit**	**NHL**	**36**	**8**	**7**	**15**	**14**	**2**	**0**	**0**	**77**	**10.4**	**0**	**0**	**0.0**	**13:28**	**3**	**0**	**0**	**0**	**0**	**0**	**0**	**0**	**12:52**
	Grand Rapids	AHL	32	13	19	32	14	....	....	....	....	....	....	....	....	....	8	5	2	7	11	....	....	....	....
	Slovakia	Olympics	4	1	0	1	2	....	....	....	....	....	....	....	....	....	....	....	....	....	....	....	....	....	....
2014-15	**Detroit**	**NHL**	**63**	**3**	**15**	**18**	**14**	**1**	**0**	**0**	**92**	**3.3**	**6**	**2**	**0.0**	**11:31**	**7**	**1**	**1**	**2**	**2**	**1**	**0**	**0**	**8:32**
2015-16	**Detroit**	**NHL**	**44**	**4**	**2**	**6**	**16**	**0**	**0**	**0**	**43**	**9.3**	**-6**	**1**	**100.0**	**9:11**	....	....	....	....	....	....	....	....	....
	Grand Rapids	AHL	5	5	4	9	4	....	....	....	....	....	....	....	....	....	....	....	....	....	....	....	....	....	....
2016-17	**Detroit**	**NHL**	**16**	**0**	**0**	**0**	**2**	**0**	**0**	**0**	**12**	**0.0**	**-8**	**1**	**0.0**	**10:02**	....	....	....	....	....	....	....	....	....
	Grand Rapids	AHL	2	1	1	2	6	....	....	....	....	....	....	....	....	....	....	....	....	....	....	....	....	....	....
	Chicago	**NHL**	**13**	**1**	**0**	**1**	**2**	**0**	**0**	**0**	**23**	**4.3**	**-4**	**0**	**0.0**	**11:22**	....	....	....	....	....	....	....	....	....
	NHL Totals		**172**	**16**	**24**	**40**	**48**	**3**	**0**	**0**	**247**	**6.5**		**4**	**25.0**	**11:11**	**10**	**1**	**1**	**2**	**2**	**1**	**0**	**0**	**9:50**

Traded to **Chicago** by **Detroit** for Chicago's 3rd round pick (Keith Petruzzelli) in 2017 NHL Draft, February 24, 2017.

Regular Season / Playoffs

KADRI, Nazem
(KAH-dree, NA-zihm) **TOR**

Center. Shoots left. 6', 192 lbs. Born, London, ON, October 6, 1990. Toronto's 1st pick, 7th overall, in 2009 NHL Draft.

Season	Club	League	GP	G	A	Pts	PIM	PP	SH	GW	S	S%	+/-	TF	F%	Min	GP	G	A	Pts	PIM	PP	SH	GW	Min
2005-06	Lon. Jr. Knights	Minor-ON	62	49	43	92	82	....	....	....	....	....	....	....	....	....	....	....	....	....	....	....	....	....	....
2006-07	Kitchener Rangers	OHL	62	7	15	22	30	....	....	....	....	....	....	....	....	....	9	0	2	2	4	....	....	....	....
2007-08	Kitchener Rangers	OHL	68	25	40	65	57	....	....	....	....	....	....	....	....	....	20	9	17	26	26	....	....	....	....
2008-09	London Knights	OHL	56	25	53	78	31	....	....	....	....	....	....	....	....	....	14	9	12	21	22	....	....	....	....
2009-10	London Knights	OHL	56	35	58	93	105	....	....	....	....	....	....	....	....	....	12	9	18	27	26	....	....	....	....
	Toronto	**NHL**	**1**	**0**	**0**	**0**	**0**	**0**	**0**	**0**	**0**	**0.0**	**–1**	**13**	**15.4**	**17:26**	....	....	....	....	....	....	....	....	....
2010-11	**Toronto**	**NHL**	**29**	**3**	**9**	**12**	**8**	**0**	**0**	**0**	**51**	**5.9**	**–3**	**121**	**40.5**	**15:47**	....	....	....	....	....	....	....	....	....
	Toronto Marlies	AHL	44	17	24	41	62	....	....	....	....	....	....	....	....	....	....	....	....	....	....	....	....	....	....
2011-12	**Toronto**	**NHL**	**21**	**5**	**2**	**7**	**8**	**1**	**0**	**1**	**28**	**17.9**	**2**	**15**	**26.7**	**14:10**	....	....	....	....	....	....	....	....	....
	Toronto Marlies	AHL	48	18	22	40	39	....	....	....	....	....	....	....	....	....	11	3	7	10	6	....	....	....	....
2012-13	Toronto Marlies	AHL	27	8	18	26	26	....	....	....	....	....	....	....	....	....	....	....	....	....	....	....	....	....	....
	Toronto	**NHL**	**48**	**18**	**26**	**44**	**23**	**5**	**0**	**1**	**107**	**16.8**	**15**	**565**	**44.3**	**16:03**	**7**	**1**	**3**	**4**	**10**	**0**	**0**	**0**	**13:35**
2013-14	**Toronto**	**NHL**	**78**	**20**	**30**	**50**	**67**	**7**	**0**	**2**	**148**	**13.5**	**–11**	**1127**	**45.3**	**17:23**	....	....	....	....	....	....	....	....	....
2014-15	**Toronto**	**NHL**	**73**	**18**	**21**	**39**	**28**	**3**	**1**	**1**	**176**	**10.2**	**–7**	**1144**	**46.2**	**17:36**	....	....	....	....	....	....	....	....	....
2015-16	**Toronto**	**NHL**	**76**	**17**	**28**	**45**	**73**	**4**	**0**	**2**	**260**	**6.5**	**–15**	**1304**	**49.2**	**18:16**	....	....	....	....	....	....	....	....	....
2016-17	**Toronto**	**NHL**	**82**	**32**	**29**	**61**	**95**	**12**	**0**	**6**	**236**	**13.6**	**–7**	**1134**	**48.0**	**16:35**	**6**	**1**	**1**	**2**	**8**	**0**	**0**	**0**	**19:22**
	NHL Totals		**408**	**113**	**145**	**258**	**302**	**32**	**1**	**13**	**1006**	**11.2**		**5423**	**46.6**	**16:59**	**13**	**2**	**4**	**6**	**18**	**0**	**0**	**0**	**16:15**

OHL Second All-Star Team (2010)

KALININ, Sergey
(kah-LIH-nihn, sair-GAY)

Right wing. Shoots left. 6'3", 200 lbs. Born, Omsk, Russia, March 17, 1991.

Season	Club	League	GP	G	A	Pts	PIM	PP	SH	GW	S	S%	+/-	TF	F%	Min	GP	G	A	Pts	PIM	PP	SH	GW	Min
2008-09	Avangard Omsk 2	Russia-3	41	5	13	18	16	....	....	....	....	....	....	....	....	....	....	....	....	....	....	....	....	....	....
2009-10	Omsk Jr.	Russia-Jr.	54	14	22	36	52	....	....	....	....	....	....	....	....	....	8	1	1	2	2	....	....	....	....
	Omsk	KHL	1	0	0	0	0	....	....	....	....	....	....	....	....	....	....	....	....	....	....	....	....	....	....
2010-11	Omsk Jr.	Russia-Jr.	5	1	4	5	4	....	....	....	....	....	....	....	....	....	....	....	....	....	....	....	....	....	....
	Omsk	KHL	24	0	1	1	0	....	....	....	....	....	....	....	....	....	8	0	1	1	0	....	....	....	....
2011-12	Omsk	KHL	53	9	9	18	20	....	....	....	....	....	....	....	....	....	19	2	1	3	10	....	....	....	....
2012-13	Omsk	KHL	26	2	6	8	10	....	....	....	....	....	....	....	....	....	6	1	0	1	4	....	....	....	....
2013-14	Omsk	KHL	51	8	9	17	32	....	....	....	....	....	....	....	....	....	11	2	5	7	4	....	....	....	....
2014-15	Omsk	KHL	58	12	13	25	49	....	....	....	....	....	....	....	....	....	6	0	0	0	2	....	....	....	....
2015-16	**New Jersey**	**NHL**	**78**	**8**	**7**	**15**	**33**	**3**	**0**	**2**	**70**	**11.4**	**–9**	**322**	**41.6**	**13:20**	....	....	....	....	....	....	....	....	....
2016-17	**New Jersey**	**NHL**	**43**	**2**	**2**	**4**	**15**	**0**	**0**	**0**	**38**	**5.3**	**–14**	**174**	**41.4**	**12:48**	....	....	....	....	....	....	....	....	....
	Toronto Marlies	AHL	19	2	2	4	9	....	....	....	....	....	....	....	....	....	11	1	0	1	4	....	....	....	....
	NHL Totals		**121**	**10**	**9**	**19**	**48**	**3**	**0**	**2**	**108**	**9.3**		**496**	**41.5**	**13:08**	....	....	....	....	....	....	....	....	....

Signed as a free agent by **New Jersey**, May 29, 2015. Traded to **Toronto** by **New Jersey** for Viktor Loov, February 18, 2017.

KAMENEV, Vladislav
KA-men-ehv, vla-dih-SLAHV) **NSH**

Left wing. Shoots left. 6'2", 194 lbs. Born, Orsk, Russia, August 12, 1996. Nashville's 2nd pick, 42nd overall, in 2014 NHL Draft.

Season	Club	League	GP	G	A	Pts	PIM	PP	SH	GW	S	S%	+/-	TF	F%	Min	GP	G	A	Pts	PIM	PP	SH	GW	Min
2012-13	Magnitogorsk Jr.	Russia-Jr.	36	9	6	15	22	....	....	....	....	....	....	....	....	....	3	0	0	0	0	....	....	....	....
2013-14	Yuzhny Ural Orsk	Russia-2	3	0	1	1	2	....	....	....	....	....	....	....	....	....	1	0	0	0	0	....	....	....	....
	Magnitogorsk	KHL	16	1	0	1	2	....	....	....	....	....	....	....	....	....	....	....	....	....	....	....	....	....	....
	Magnitogorsk Jr.	Russia-Jr.	15	4	6	10	12	....	....	....	....	....	....	....	....	....	5	1	2	3	4	....	....	....	....
2014-15	Magnitogorsk	KHL	41	6	4	10	10	....	....	....	....	....	....	....	....	....	10	1	0	1	0	....	....	....	....
2015-16	Milwaukee	AHL	57	15	22	37	35	....	....	....	....	....	....	....	....	....	3	1	0	1	0	....	....	....	....
2016-17	**Nashville**	**NHL**	**2**	**0**	**0**	**0**	**2**	**0**	**0**	**0**	**1**	**0.0**	**–1**	**13**	**46.2**	**10:04**	....	....	....	....	....	....	....	....	....
	Milwaukee	AHL	70	21	30	51	59	....	....	....	....	....	....	....	....	....	3	1	0	1	6	....	....	....	....
	NHL Totals		**2**	**0**	**0**	**0**	**2**	**0**	**0**	**0**	**1**	**0.0**		**13**	**46.2**	**10:04**	....	....	....	....	....	....	....	....	....

KAMPFER, Steven
(KAMP-fuhr, STEE-vehn) **NYR**

Defense. Shoots right. 5'11", 192 lbs. Born, Ann Arbor, MI, September 24, 1988. Anaheim's 5th pick, 93rd overall, in 2007 NHL Draft.

Season	Club	League	GP	G	A	Pts	PIM	PP	SH	GW	S	S%	+/-	TF	F%	Min	GP	G	A	Pts	PIM	PP	SH	GW	Min
2004-05	Sioux City	USHL	47	6	13	19	91	....	....	....	....	....	....	....	....	....	13	2	5	7	12	....	....	....	....
2005-06	Sioux City	USHL	56	6	10	16	99	....	....	....	....	....	....	....	....	....	....	....	....	....	....	....	....	....	....
2006-07	U. of Michigan	CCHA	35	1	3	4	24	....	....	....	....	....	....	....	....	....	....	....	....	....	....	....	....	....	....
2007-08	U. of Michigan	CCHA	42	2	15	17	36	....	....	....	....	....	....	....	....	....	....	....	....	....	....	....	....	....	....
2008-09	U. of Michigan	CCHA	25	1	12	13	24	....	....	....	....	....	....	....	....	....	....	....	....	....	....	....	....	....	....
2009-10	U. of Michigan	CCHA	45	3	23	26	50	....	....	....	....	....	....	....	....	....	....	....	....	....	....	....	....	....	....
	Providence Bruins	AHL	6	1	2	3	4	....	....	....	....	....	....	....	....	....	....	....	....	....	....	....	....	....	....
2010-11	**Boston**	**NHL**	**38**	**5**	**5**	**10**	**12**	**0**	**0**	**1**	**57**	**8.8**	**9**	**0**	**0.0**	**17:44**	....	....	....	....	....	....	....	....	....
	Providence Bruins	AHL	22	3	13	16	12	....	....	....	....	....	....	....	....	....	....	....	....	....	....	....	....	....	....
2011-12	**Boston**	**NHL**	**10**	**0**	**2**	**2**	**4**	**0**	**0**	**0**	**8**	**0.0**	**6**	**0**	**0.0**	**10:30**	....	....	....	....	....	....	....	....	....
	Providence Bruins	AHL	12	1	3	4	8	....	....	....	....	....	....	....	....	....	....	....	....	....	....	....	....	....	....
	Minnesota	**NHL**	**13**	**2**	**1**	**3**	**2**	**0**	**0**	**0**	**12**	**16.7**	**–7**	**0**	**0.0**	**18:17**	....	....	....	....	....	....	....	....	....
	Houston Aeros	AHL	12	1	3	4	8	....	....	....	....	....	....	....	....	....	4	0	0	0	2	....	....	....	....
2012-13	Houston Aeros	AHL	55	4	17	21	28	....	....	....	....	....	....	....	....	....	5	1	1	2	9	....	....	....	....
2013-14	Iowa Wild	AHL	69	6	20	26	48	....	....	....	....	....	....	....	....	....	....	....	....	....	....	....	....	....	....
2014-15	**Florida**	**NHL**	**25**	**2**	**2**	**4**	**12**	**0**	**0**	**1**	**28**	**7.1**	**–4**	**0**	**0.0**	**17:12**	....	....	....	....	....	....	....	....	....
	San Antonio	AHL	42	8	11	19	49	....	....	....	....	....	....	....	....	....	....	....	....	....	....	....	....	....	....
2015-16	**Florida**	**NHL**	**47**	**0**	**4**	**4**	**26**	**0**	**0**	**0**	**54**	**0.0**	**5**	**2**	**50.0**	**15:06**	....	....	....	....	....	....	....	....	....
2016-17	**NY Rangers**	**NHL**	**10**	**1**	**1**	**2**	**2**	**0**	**0**	**0**	**10**	**10.0**	**–1**	**0**	**0.0**	**12:54**	....	....	....	....	....	....	....	....	....
	Hartford	AHL	43	4	15	19	44	....	....	....	....	....	....	....	....	....	....	....	....	....	....	....	....	....	....
	Florida	**NHL**	**1**	**0**	**0**	**0**	**4**	**0**	**0**	**0**	**0**	**0.0**	**–1**	**0**	**0.0**	**16:48**	....	....	....	....	....	....	....	....	....
	NHL Totals		**144**	**10**	**15**	**25**	**62**	**0**	**0**	**2**	**169**	**5.9**		**2**	**50.0**	**15:59**	....	....	....	....	....	....	....	....	....

Traded to **Boston** by **Anaheim** for Boston's 4th round pick (later traded to Carolina - Carolina selected Justin Shugg) in 2010 NHL Draft, March 2, 2010. Traded to **Minnesota** by **Boston** for Greg Zanon, February 27, 2012. Signed as a free agent by **NY Rangers**, July 1, 2014. Traded to **Florida** by **NY Rangers** with Andrew Yogan for Joey Crabb, October 6, 2014. Traded to **NY Rangers** by **Florida** with a conditional 7th round pick (conditions not met) in 2018 NHL Draft for Dylan McIlrath, November 8, 2016.

KANE, Evander
(KAYN, ee-VAN-duhr) **BUF**

Left wing. Shoots left. 6'2", 204 lbs. Born, Vancouver, BC, August 2, 1991. Atlanta's 1st pick, 4th overall, in 2009 NHL Draft.

Season	Club	League	GP	G	A	Pts	PIM	PP	SH	GW	S	S%	+/-	TF	F%	Min	GP	G	A	Pts	PIM	PP	SH	GW	Min
2006-07	Greater Van.	BCMML	30	22	32	54	150	....	....	....	....	....	....	....	....	....	....	....	....	....	....	....	....	....	....
	Vancouver Giants	WHL	8	1	0	1	11	....	....	....	....	....	....	....	....	....	5	0	0	0	0	....	....	....	....
2007-08	Vancouver Giants	WHL	65	24	17	41	66	....	....	....	....	....	....	....	....	....	10	1	2	3	8	....	....	....	....
2008-09	Vancouver Giants	WHL	61	48	48	96	89	....	....	....	....	....	....	....	....	....	17	7	8	15	45	....	....	....	....
2009-10	**Atlanta**	**NHL**	**66**	**14**	**12**	**26**	**62**	**0**	**1**	**3**	**127**	**11.0**	**2**	**26**	**53.9**	**14:00**	....	....	....	....	....	....	....	....	....
2010-11	**Atlanta**	**NHL**	**73**	**19**	**24**	**43**	**68**	**4**	**0**	**2**	**234**	**8.1**	**–12**	**64**	**40.6**	**17:52**	....	....	....	....	....	....	....	....	....
2011-12	**Winnipeg**	**NHL**	**74**	**30**	**27**	**57**	**53**	**6**	**0**	**4**	**287**	**10.5**	**11**	**44**	**34.1**	**17:31**	....	....	....	....	....	....	....	....	....
2012-13	Dynamo Minsk	KHL	12	1	1	2	47	....	....	....	....	....	....	....	....	....	....	....	....	....	....	....	....	....	....
	Winnipeg	**NHL**	**48**	**17**	**16**	**33**	**80**	**2**	**0**	**4**	**190**	**8.9**	**–3**	**33**	**39.4**	**20:27**	....	....	....	....	....	....	....	....	....
2013-14	**Winnipeg**	**NHL**	**63**	**19**	**22**	**41**	**66**	**1**	**2**	**4**	**250**	**7.6**	**–7**	**105**	**42.9**	**20:17**	....	....	....	....	....	....	....	....	....
2014-15	**Winnipeg**	**NHL**	**37**	**10**	**12**	**22**	**56**	**4**	**1**	**1**	**126**	**7.9**	**–1**	**67**	**44.8**	**19:19**	....	....	....	....	....	....	....	....	....
2015-16	**Buffalo**	**NHL**	**65**	**20**	**15**	**35**	**91**	**2**	**1**	**3**	**271**	**7.4**	**–14**	**124**	**50.0**	**21:02**	....	....	....	....	....	....	....	....	....
2016-17	**Buffalo**	**NHL**	**70**	**28**	**15**	**43**	**113**	**3**	**0**	**5**	**260**	**10.8**	**–17**	**122**	**45.1**	**19:12**	....	....	....	....	....	....	....	....	....
	NHL Totals		**496**	**157**	**143**	**300**	**589**	**22**	**5**	**26**	**1745**	**9.0**		**585**	**44.4**	**18:34**	....	....	....	....	....	....	....	....	....

WHL West First All-Star Team (2009)

• Transferred to **Winnipeg** after **Atlanta** franchise relocated, June 21, 2011. Signed as a free agent by **Minsk** (KHL), September 28, 2012. Traded to **Buffalo** by **Winnipeg** with Zach Bogosian and Jason Kasdorf for Tyler Myers, Drew Stafford, Joel Armia, Brendan Lemieux and St. Louis' 1st round pick (previously acquired, Winnipeg selected Jack Roslovic) in 2015 NHL Draft, February 11, 2015. • Missed majority of 2014-15 due to recurring shoulder injury.

KANE, Patrick
(KAYN, PAT-rihk) **CHI**

Right wing. Shoots left. 5'11", 177 lbs. Born, Buffalo, NY, November 19, 1988. Chicago's 1st pick, 1st overall, in 2007 NHL Draft.

Season	Club	League	GP	G	A	Pts	PIM	PP	SH	GW	S	S%	+/-	TF	F%	Min	GP	G	A	Pts	PIM	PP	SH	GW	Min
			Regular Season														Playoffs								
2003-04	Det. Honeybaked	MWEHL	70	83	77	160	....	....	....	....	....	....	....	....	....	....	....	....	....	....	....	....	....	....	....
2004-05	USAHNTDP	U-17	23	16	17	33	8	....	....	....	....	....	....	....	....	....	....	....	....	....	....	....	....	....	....
	USAHNTDP	NAHL	40	16	21	37	8	....	....	....	....	....	....	....	....	....	9	7	8	15	2	....	....	....	....
2005-06	USAHNTDP	U-18	43	35	33	68	10	....	....	....	....	....	....	....	....	....	....	....	....	....	....	....	....	....	....
	USAHNTDP	NAHL	15	17	17	34	12	....	....	....	....	....	....	....	....	....	....	....	....	....	....	....	....	....	....
2006-07	London Knights	OHL	58	62	83	*145	52	....	....	....	....	....	....	....	....	....	16	10	21	*31	16	....	....	....	....
2007-08	**Chicago**	**NHL**	**82**	**21**	**51**	**72**	**52**	**7**	**0**	**4**	**191**	**11.0**	**-5**	**26**	**61.5**	**18:22**	....	....	....	....	....	....	....	....	....
2008-09	**Chicago**	**NHL**	**80**	**25**	**45**	**70**	**42**	**13**	**0**	**4**	**254**	**9.8**	**-2**	**31**	**41.9**	**18:40**	**16**	**9**	**5**	**14**	**12**	**2**	**0**	**0**	**16:36**
2009-10♦	**Chicago**	**NHL**	**82**	**30**	**58**	**88**	**20**	**9**	**0**	**6**	**261**	**11.5**	**16**	**22**	**40.9**	**19:12**	**22**	**10**	**18**	**28**	**6**	**1**	**1**	**1**	**18:55**
	United States	Olympics	6	3	2	5	2	....	....	....	....	....	....	....	....	....	....	....	....	....	....	....	....	....	....
2010-11	**Chicago**	**NHL**	**73**	**27**	**46**	**73**	**28**	**5**	**0**	**2**	**216**	**12.5**	**7**	**14**	**14.3**	**19:17**	**7**	**1**	**5**	**6**	**2**	**1**	**0**	**0**	**21:50**
2011-12	**Chicago**	**NHL**	**82**	**23**	**43**	**66**	**40**	**4**	**0**	**5**	**253**	**9.1**	**7**	**569**	**42.2**	**20:12**	**6**	**0**	**4**	**4**	**10**	**0**	**0**	**0**	**21:58**
2012-13	EHC Biel-Bienne	Swiss	20	13	10	23	6	....	....	....	....	....	....	....	....	....	....	....	....	....	....	....	....	....	....
	♦ Chicago	**NHL**	**47**	**23**	**32**	**55**	**8**	**8**	**0**	**3**	**138**	**16.7**	**11**	**10**	**20.0**	**20:03**	**23**	**9**	**10**	**19**	**8**	**0**	**0**	**2**	**20:56**
2013-14	**Chicago**	**NHL**	**69**	**29**	**40**	**69**	**22**	**10**	**0**	**6**	**227**	**12.8**	**7**	**8**	**50.0**	**19:37**	**19**	**8**	**12**	**20**	**8**	**1**	**0**	***4**	**21:23**
	United States	Olympics	6	0	4	4	6	....	....	....	....	....	....	....	....	....	....	....	....	....	....	....	....	....	....
2014-15♦	**Chicago**	**NHL**	**61**	**27**	**37**	**64**	**10**	**6**	**0**	**5**	**186**	**14.5**	**10**	**7**	**42.9**	**19:51**	**23**	**11**	**12**	**23**	**0**	**2**	**0**	**3**	**20:24**
2015-16	**Chicago**	**NHL**	**82**	**46**	**60**	***106**	**30**	**17**	**0**	**9**	**287**	**16.0**	**17**	**51**	**21.6**	**20:25**	**7**	**1**	**6**	**7**	**14**	**0**	**0**	**1**	**24:05**
2016-17	**Chicago**	**NHL**	**82**	**34**	**55**	**89**	**32**	**7**	**0**	**5**	**292**	**11.6**	**11**	**51**	**13.7**	**21:24**	**4**	**1**	**1**	**2**	**2**	**1**	**0**	**0**	**23:55**
	NHL Totals		**740**	**285**	**467**	**752**	**284**	**86**	**0**	**49**	**2305**	**12.4**		**789**	**38.9**	**19:41**	**127**	**50**	**73**	**123**	**62**	**8**	**1**	**11**	**20:22**

OHL All-Rookie Team (2007) • OHL First All-Star Team (2007) • OHL Rookie of the Year (2007) • Canadian Major Junior First All-Star Team (2007) • Canadian Major Junior Rookie of the Year (2007) • NHL All-Rookie Team (2008) • Calder Memorial Trophy (2008) • NHL First All-Star Team (2010, 2016, 2017) • Conn Smythe Trophy (2013) • Art Ross Trophy (2016) • Ted Lindsay Award (2016) • Hart Memorial Trophy (2016)

Played in NHL All-Star Game (2009, 2011, 2012, 2015, 2016, 2017)

Signed as a free agent by **Biel-Bienne** (Swiss), October 23, 2012.

KAPANEN, Kasperi
(KA-puh-nihn, kas-PAIR-ee) **TOR**

Right wing. Shoots right. 6', 185 lbs. Born, Kuopio, Finland, July 23, 1996. Pittsburgh's 1st pick, 22nd overall, in 2014 NHL Draft.

Season	Club	League	GP	G	A	Pts	PIM	PP	SH	GW	S	S%	+/-	TF	F%	Min	GP	G	A	Pts	PIM	PP	SH	GW	Min
2011-12	KalPa Kuopio U18	Fin-U18	27	13	11	24	8	....	....	....	....	....	....	....	....	....	2	0	0	0	0	....	....	....	....
2012-13	KalPa Kuopio U18	Fin-U18	3	3	3	6	0	....	....	....	....	....	....	....	....	....	....	....	....	....	....	....	....	....	....
	KalPa Kuopio Jr.	Fin-Jr.	36	14	15	29	16	....	....	....	....	....	....	....	....	....	....	....	....	....	....	....	....	....	....
	KalPa Kuopio	Finland	13	4	0	4	2	....	....	....	....	....	....	....	....	....	4	0	1	1	2	....	....	....	....
2013-14	KalPa Kuopio U18	Fin-U18	2	5	1	6	0	....	....	....	....	....	....	....	....	....	4	6	1	7	0	....	....	....	....
	KalPa Kuopio	Finland	47	7	7	14	10	....	....	....	....	....	....	....	....	....	....	....	....	....	....	....	....	....	....
2014-15	KalPa Kuopio	Finland	41	11	10	21	14	....	....	....	....	....	....	....	....	....	6	0	5	5	2	....	....	....	....
	Wilkes-Barre	AHL	4	1	1	2	0	....	....	....	....	....	....	....	....	....	7	3	2	5	0	....	....	....	....
2015-16	**Toronto**	**NHL**	**9**	**0**	**0**	**0**	**2**	**0**	**0**	**0**	**14**	**0.0**	**-3**	**0**	**0.0**	**14:47**	....	....	....	....	....	....	....	....	....
	Toronto Marlies	AHL	44	9	16	25	8	....	....	....	....	....	....	....	....	....	14	3	5	8	2	....	....	....	....
2016-17	**Toronto**	**NHL**	**8**	**1**	**0**	**1**	**0**	**0**	**0**	**0**	**11**	**9.1**	**-2**	**0**	**0.0**	**10:42**	**6**	**2**	**0**	**2**	**0**	**0**	**0**	**1**	**10:48**
	Toronto Marlies	AHL	43	18	25	43	16	....	....	....	....	....	....	....	....	....	9	2	6	8	8	....	....	....	....
	NHL Totals		**17**	**1**	**0**	**1**	**2**	**0**	**0**	**0**	**25**	**4.0**		**0**	**0.0**	**12:51**	**6**	**2**	**0**	**2**	**0**	**0**	**0**	**1**	**10:48**

Traded to **Toronto** by **Pittsburgh** with Nick Spaling, Scott Harrington, Pittsburgh's 1st round pick (later traded to Anahem – Anaheim selected Sam Steel) in 2016 NHL Draft and New Jersey's 3rd round pick (previously acquired, Toronto selected James Greenway) in 2016 NHL Draft for Phil Kessel, Tyler Biggs, Tim Erixon and Pittsburgh's 2nd round pick (previously acquired, Pittsburgh selected Kasper Bjorkqvist) in 2016 NHL Draft, July 1, 2015.

KAPLA, Michael
(KAP-lah, MIGH-kuhl) **N.J.**

Defense. Shoots left. 6', 200 lbs. Born, Eau Claire, WI, September 19, 1994.

Season	Club	League	GP	G	A	Pts	PIM	PP	SH	GW	S	S%	+/-	TF	F%	Min	GP	G	A	Pts	PIM	PP	SH	GW	Min
2010-11	Eau Claire Mem.	High-WI	24	3	32	35	16	....	....	....	....	....	....	....	....	....	5	1	10	11	2	....	....	....	....
2011-12	Team Wisconsin	UMHSEL	21	4	3	7	8	....	....	....	....	....	....	....	....	....	1	0	0	0	2	....	....	....	....
	Eau Claire Mem.	High-WI	24	6	35	41	6	....	....	....	....	....	....	....	....	....	4	1	4	5	2	....	....	....	....
	Sioux City	USHL	3	0	0	0	0	....	....	....	....	....	....	....	....	....	....	....	....	....	....	....	....	....	....
2012-13	Sioux City	USHL	51	9	17	26	25	....	....	....	....	....	....	....	....	....	....	....	....	....	....	....	....	....	....
2013-14	U. Mass Lowell	H-East	41	3	14	17	22	....	....	....	....	....	....	....	....	....	....	....	....	....	....	....	....	....	....
2014-15	U. Mass Lowell	H-East	39	7	18	25	28	....	....	....	....	....	....	....	....	....	....	....	....	....	....	....	....	....	....
2015-16	U. Mass Lowell	H-East	40	4	16	20	18	....	....	....	....	....	....	....	....	....	....	....	....	....	....	....	....	....	....
2016-17	U. Mass Lowell	H-East	41	3	27	30	34	....	....	....	....	....	....	....	....	....	....	....	....	....	....	....	....	....	....
	New Jersey	**NHL**	**5**	**0**	**0**	**0**	**0**	**0**	**0**	**0**	**4**	**0.0**	**-1**	**0**	**0.0**	**17:26**	....	....	....	....	....	....	....	....	....
	NHL Totals		**5**	**0**	**0**	**0**	**0**	**0**	**0**	**0**	**4**	**0.0**		**0**	**0.0**	**17:26**	....	....	....	....	....	....	....	....	....

Hockey East Second All-Star Team (2017)

Signed as a free agent by **New Jersey**, March 28, 2017.

KARLSSON, Erik
(KAHRL-suhn, AIR-ihk) **OTT**

Defense. Shoots right. 6', 192 lbs. Born, Landsbro, Sweden, May 31, 1990. Ottawa's 1st pick, 15th overall, in 2008 NHL Draft.

Season	Club	League	GP	G	A	Pts	PIM	PP	SH	GW	S	S%	+/-	TF	F%	Min	GP	G	A	Pts	PIM	PP	SH	GW	Min
2006-07	Sodertalje SK U18	Swe-U18	2	0	1	1	33	....	....	....	....	....	....	....	....	....	....	....	....	....	....	....	....	....	....
	Sodertalje SK Jr.	Swe-Jr.	10	2	8	10	8	....	....	....	....	....	....	....	....	....	....	....	....	....	....	....	....	....	....
2007-08	Frolunda U18	Swe-U18	3	1	2	3	2	....	....	....	....	....	....	....	....	....	2	0	1	1	10	....	....	....	....
	Frolunda Jr.	Swe-Jr.	38	13	24	37	68	....	....	....	....	....	....	....	....	....	5	1	0	1	4	....	....	....	....
	Frolunda	Sweden	7	1	0	1	0	....	....	....	....	....	....	....	....	....	6	0	0	0	0	....	....	....	....
2008-09	Frolunda Jr.	Swe-Jr.	1	0	2	2	2	....	....	....	....	....	....	....	....	....	....	....	....	....	....	....	....	....	....
	Boras HC	Sweden-2	7	0	1	1	14	....	....	....	....	....	....	....	....	....	....	....	....	....	....	....	....	....	....
	Frolunda	Sweden	45	5	5	10	10	....	....	....	....	....	....	....	....	....	11	1	2	3	24	....	....	....	....
2009-10	**Ottawa**	**NHL**	**60**	**5**	**21**	**26**	**24**	**1**	**0**	**0**	**112**	**4.5**	**-5**	**0**	**0.0**	**20:07**	**6**	**1**	**5**	**6**	**4**	**1**	**0**	**0**	**25:52**
	Binghamton	AHL	12	0	11	11	22	....	....	....	....	....	....	....	....	....	....	....	....	....	....	....	....	....	....
2010-11	**Ottawa**	**NHL**	**75**	**13**	**32**	**45**	**50**	**4**	**0**	**4**	**182**	**7.1**	**-30**	**0**	**0.0**	**23:31**	....	....	....	....	....	....	....	....	....
2011-12	**Ottawa**	**NHL**	**81**	**19**	**59**	**78**	**42**	**3**	**0**	**5**	**261**	**7.3**	**16**	**1**	**0.0**	**25:19**	**7**	**1**	**0**	**1**	**4**	**1**	**0**	**0**	**25:22**
2012-13	Jokerit Helsinki	Finland	30	9	25	34	24	....	....	....	....	....	....	....	....	....	....	....	....	....	....	....	....	....	....
	Ottawa	**NHL**	**17**	**6**	**8**	**14**	**8**	**2**	**1**	**2**	**79**	**7.6**	**8**	**0**	**0.0**	**27:09**	**10**	**1**	**7**	**8**	**6**	**0**	**0**	**0**	**26:44**
2013-14	**Ottawa**	**NHL**	**82**	**20**	**54**	**74**	**36**	**5**	**0**	**1**	**257**	**7.8**	**-15**	**0**	**0.0**	**27:04**	....	....	....	....	....	....	....	....	....
	Sweden	Olympics	6	4	4	8	0	....	....	....	....	....	....	....	....	....	....	....	....	....	....	....	....	....	....
2014-15	**Ottawa**	**NHL**	**82**	**21**	**45**	**66**	**42**	**6**	**0**	**3**	**292**	**7.2**	**7**	**0**	**0.0**	**27:15**	**6**	**1**	**3**	**4**	**2**	**1**	**0**	**0**	**28:58**
2015-16	**Ottawa**	**NHL**	**82**	**16**	***66**	**82**	**50**	**1**	**0**	**3**	**248**	**6.5**	**-2**	**1**	**0.0**	**28:58**	....	....	....	....	....	....	....	....	....
2016-17	**Ottawa**	**NHL**	**77**	**17**	**54**	**71**	**28**	**4**	**0**	**5**	**218**	**7.8**	**10**	**0**	**0.0**	**26:50**	**19**	**2**	**16**	**18**	**10**	**0**	**0**	**2**	**28:07**
	NHL Totals		**556**	**117**	**339**	**456**	**280**	**26**	**1**	**23**	**1649**	**7.1**		**2**	**0.0**	**25:52**	**48**	**6**	**31**	**37**	**26**	**3**	**0**	**2**	**27:15**

NHL First All-Star Team (2012, 2015, 2016, 2017) • James Norris Memorial Trophy (2012, 2015) • Olympic All-Star Team (2014) • Best Defenceman – Olympics (2014)

Played in NHL All-Star Game (2011, 2012, 2016, 2017)

Signed as a free agent by **Jokerit Helsinki** (Finland), September 26, 2012.

KARLSSON, Melker
(KAHRL-suhn, MEHL-kuhr) **S.J.**

Center. Shoots right. 6', 180 lbs. Born, Lycksele, Sweden, July 18, 1990.

Season	Club	League	GP	G	A	Pts	PIM	PP	SH	GW	S	S%	+/-	TF	F%	Min	GP	G	A	Pts	PIM	PP	SH	GW	Min
2006-07	Skelleftea U18	Swe-U18	14	5	4	9	20	....	....	....	....	....	....	....	....	....	....	....	....	....	....	....	....	....	....
	Skelleftea Jr.	Swe-Jr.	1	0	0	0	0	....	....	....	....	....	....	....	....	....	....	....	....	....	....	....	....	....	....
2007-08	Skelleftea U18	Swe-U18	30	21	13	34	14	....	....	....	....	....	....	....	....	....	....	....	....	....	....	....	....	....	....
	Skelleftea Jr.	Swe-Jr.	9	4	2	6	0	....	....	....	....	....	....	....	....	....	2	1	0	1	0	....	....	....	....
2008-09	Skelleftea AIK Jr.	Swe-Jr.	34	10	14	24	58	....	....	....	....	....	....	....	....	....	6	1	3	4	2	....	....	....	....
	Skelleftea AIK	Sweden	4	0	0	0	0	....	....	....	....	....	....	....	....	....	1	0	0	0	0	....	....	....	....
2009-10	Skelleftea AIK Jr.	Swe-Jr.	27	14	21	35	10	....	....	....	....	....	....	....	....	....	2	1	1	2	0	....	....	....	....
	Skelleftea AIK	Sweden	36	2	0	2	8	....	....	....	....	....	....	....	....	....	8	0	2	2	0	....	....	....	....
2010-11	Skelleftea AIK Jr.	Swe-Jr.	5	3	1	4	0	....	....	....	....	....	....	....	....	....	....	....	....	....	....	....	....	....	....
	Orebro HK	Sweden-2	10	2	4	6	12	....	....	....	....	....	....	....	....	....	....	....	....	....	....	....	....	....	....
	Skelleftea AIK	Sweden	40	4	2	6	2	....	....	....	....	....	....	....	....	....	16	1	3	4	2	....	....	....	....

			Regular Season														Playoffs								
Season	Club	League	GP	G	A	Pts	PIM	PP	SH	GW	S	S%	+/-	TF	F%	Min	GP	G	A	Pts	PIM	PP	SH	GW	Min
2011-12	Skelleftea AIK	Sweden	44	3	2	5	8	....	....	....	....	....	....	....	....	....	19	2	2	4	4	....	....	....	....
2012-13	Skelleftea AIK	Sweden	44	13	15	28	14	....	....	....	....	....	....	....	....	....	13	2	8	10	10	....	....	....	....
2013-14	Skelleftea AIK	Sweden	48	9	16	25	14	....	....	....	....	....	....	....	....	....	14	4	8	12	12	....	....	....	....
2014-15	**San Jose**	**NHL**	**53**	**13**	**11**	**24**	**20**	**1**	**0**	**2**	**100**	**13.0**	**-3**	**33**	**39.4**	**15:26**	....	....	....	....	....	....	....	....	....
	Worcester Sharks	AHL	20	5	5	10	6	....	....	....	....	....	....	....	....	....	....	....	....	....	....	....	....	....	....
2015-16	**San Jose**	**NHL**	**65**	**10**	**9**	**19**	**16**	**0**	**0**	**1**	**96**	**10.4**	**5**	**23**	**47.8**	**13:31**	**24**	**5**	**3**	**8**	**10**	**0**	**0**	**1**	**13:56**
	San Jose	AHL	4	0	2	2	0	....	....	....	....	....	....	....	....	....	....	....	....	....	....	....	....	....	....
2016-17	**San Jose**	**NHL**	**67**	**11**	**11**	**22**	**22**	**0**	**2**	**1**	**73**	**15.1**	**7**	**6**	**16.7**	**12:48**	**6**	**1**	**0**	**1**	**6**	**0**	**0**	**1**	**14:16**
	NHL Totals		**185**	**34**	**31**	**65**	**58**	**1**	**2**	**4**	**269**	**12.6**		**62**	**40.3**	**13:49**	**30**	**6**	**3**	**9**	**16**	**0**	**0**	**2**	**14:00**

Signed as a free agent by **San Jose**, May 30, 2014.

KARLSSON, William

(KAHRL-suhn, WIHL-yuhm) **VGK**

Center. Shoots left. 6'1", 188 lbs. Born, Marsta, Sweden, January 8, 1993. Anaheim's 3rd pick, 53rd overall, in 2011 NHL Draft.

Season	Club	League	GP	G	A	Pts	PIM	PP	SH	GW	S	S%	+/-	TF	F%	Min	GP	G	A	Pts	PIM	PP	SH	GW	Min
2007-08	Arlanda U18	Swe-U18	5	2	7	9	4	....	....	....	....	....	....	....	....	....	....	....	....	....	....	....	....	....	....
2008-09	Arlanda U18	Swe-U18	33	10	18	28	16	....	....	....	....	....	....	....	....	....	....	....	....	....	....	....	....	....	....
2009-10	Vasteras U18	Swe-U18	39	23	21	44	62	....	....	....	....	....	....	....	....	....	....	....	....	....	....	....	....	....	....
	Vasteras Jr.	Swe-Jr.	6	0	1	1	2	....	....	....	....	....	....	....	....	....	2	0	1	1	0	....	....	....	....
2010-11	Vasteras U18	Swe-U18	11	5	9	14	10	....	....	....	....	....	....	....	....	....	6	7	8	15	2	....	....	....	....
	Vasteras Jr.	Swe-Jr.	38	20	34	54	45	....	....	....	....	....	....	....	....	....	....	....	....	....	....	....	....	....	....
	VIK Vasteras HK	Sweden-2	14	1	3	4	2	....	....	....	....	....	....	....	....	....	....	....	....	....	....	....	....	....	....
2011-12	VIK Vasteras HK	Sweden-2	52	13	34	47	6	....	....	....	....	....	....	....	....	....	....	....	....	....	....	....	....	....	....
	Vasteras Jr.	Swe-Jr.	....	....	....	....	....	....	....	....	....	....	....	....	....	....	5	2	2	4	2	....	....	....	....
2012-13	HV 71 Jonkoping	Sweden	50	4	24	28	12	....	....	....	....	....	....	....	....	....	5	0	2	2	0	....	....	....	....
	HV 71 Jr.	Swe-Jr.	....	....	....	....	....	....	....	....	....	....	....	....	....	....	2	2	2	4	2	....	....	....	....
2013-14	HV 71 Jonkoping	Sweden	55	15	22	37	14	....	....	....	....	....	....	....	....	....	8	3	4	7	8	....	....	....	....
	Norfolk Admirals	AHL	9	2	7	9	6	....	....	....	....	....	....	....	....	....	8	1	2	3	2	....	....	....	....
2014-15	**Anaheim**	**NHL**	**18**	**2**	**1**	**3**	**2**	**0**	**0**	**1**	**24**	**8.3**	**1**	**164**	**48.8**	**12:09**	....	....	....	....	....	....	....	....	....
	Norfolk Admirals	AHL	37	8	16	24	2	....	....	....	....	....	....	....	....	....	....	....	....	....	....	....	....	....	....
	Columbus	**NHL**	**3**	**1**	**1**	**2**	**0**	**0**	**0**	**0**	**5**	**20.0**	**2**	**33**	**39.4**	**12:46**	....	....	....	....	....	....	....	....	....
	Springfield	AHL	15	0	0	0	0	....	....	....	....	....	....	....	....	....	....	....	....	....	....	....	....	....	....
2015-16	**Columbus**	**NHL**	**81**	**9**	**11**	**20**	**6**	**0**	**0**	**1**	**108**	**8.3**	**-9**	**911**	**45.7**	**14:28**	....	....	....	....	....	....	....	....	....
2016-17	**Columbus**	**NHL**	**81**	**6**	**19**	**25**	**10**	**1**	**0**	**3**	**96**	**6.3**	**10**	**960**	**45.3**	**13:23**	**5**	**2**	**1**	**3**	**0**	**0**	**0**	**0**	**16:06**
	NHL Totals		**183**	**18**	**32**	**50**	**18**	**1**	**0**	**5**	**233**	**7.7**		**2068**	**45.6**	**13:44**	**5**	**2**	**1**	**3**	**0**	**0**	**0**	**0**	**16:06**

Traded to **Columbus** by **Anaheim** with Rene Bourque and Anaheim's 2nd round pick (Kevin Stenlund) in 2015 NHL Draft for James Wisniewski and Detroit's 3rd round pick (previously acquired, Anaheim selected Brent Gates) in 2015 NHL Draft, March 2, 2015. Claimed by **Vegas** from **Columbus** in Expansion Draft, June 21, 2017.

KASE, Ondrej

(kah-SHEH, AWN-dray) **ANA**

Left wing. Shoots left. 6', 180 lbs. Born, Kadan, Czech Rep., November 8, 1995. Anaheim's 5th pick, 205th overall, in 2014 NHL Draft.

Season	Club	League	GP	G	A	Pts	PIM	PP	SH	GW	S	S%	+/-	TF	F%	Min	GP	G	A	Pts	PIM	PP	SH	GW	Min
2010-11	Chomutov U18	CzR-U18	8	3	3	6	2	....	....	....	....	....	....	....	....	....	....	....	....	....	....	....	....	....	....
2011-12	Chomutov U18	CzR-U18	38	18	26	44	14	....	....	....	....	....	....	....	....	....	2	0	2	2	0	....	....	....	....
2012-13	Chomutov U18	CzR-U18	14	10	16	26	6	....	....	....	....	....	....	....	....	....	....	....	....	....	....	....	....	....	....
	Chomutov Jr.	CzRep-Jr.	22	9	7	16	18	....	....	....	....	....	....	....	....	....	3	0	0	0	2	....	....	....	....
	SK Kadan	CzRep-2	9	2	1	3	2	....	....	....	....	....	....	....	....	....	4	1	0	1	0	....	....	....	....
2013-14	Chomutov Jr.	CzRep-Jr.	7	5	10	15	12	....	....	....	....	....	....	....	....	....	1	0	2	2	0	....	....	....	....
	SK Kadan	CzRep-2	5	3	1	4	0	....	....	....	....	....	....	....	....	....	....	....	....	....	....	....	....	....	....
	Pirati Chomutov	CzRep	43	5	5	10	10	....	....	....	....	....	....	....	....	....	....	....	....	....	....	....	....	....	....
	Pirati Chomutov	CzRep-Q	10	2	3	5	0	....	....	....	....	....	....	....	....	....	....	....	....	....	....	....	....	....	....
2014-15	Chomutov Jr.	CzRep-Jr.	3	1	7	8	0	....	....	....	....	....	....	....	....	....	....	....	....	....	....	....	....	....	....
	Pirati Chomutov	CzRep-2	49	10	17	27	8	....	....	....	....	....	....	....	....	....	11	6	5	11	4	....	....	....	....
2015-16	San Diego Gulls	AHL	25	8	6	14	6	....	....	....	....	....	....	....	....	....	9	1	3	4	0	....	....	....	....
2016-17	**Anaheim**	**NHL**	**53**	**5**	**10**	**15**	**18**	**0**	**0**	**2**	**77**	**6.5**	**-1**	**7**	**14.3**	**11:47**	**9**	**2**	**0**	**2**	**4**	**0**	**0**	**0**	**10:33**
	San Diego Gulls	AHL	14	6	6	12	4	....	....	....	....	....	....	....	....	....	3	0	1	1	0	....	....	....	....
	NHL Totals		**53**	**5**	**10**	**15**	**18**	**0**	**0**	**2**	**77**	**6.5**		**7**	**14.3**	**11:47**	**9**	**2**	**0**	**2**	**4**	**0**	**0**	**0**	**10:33**

KASSIAN, Zack

(KA-see-uhn, ZAK) **EDM**

Right wing. Shoots right. 6'3", 207 lbs. Born, Windsor, ON, January 24, 1991. Buffalo's 1st pick, 13th overall, in 2009 NHL Draft.

Season	Club	League	GP	G	A	Pts	PIM	PP	SH	GW	S	S%	+/-	TF	F%	Min	GP	G	A	Pts	PIM	PP	SH	GW	Min
2006-07	Wind. Jr. Spitfires	Minor-ON	57	32	48	80	136	....	....	....	....	....	....	....	....	....	....	....	....	....	....	....	....	....	....
	Leamington Flyers	ON-Jr.B	2	0	0	0	6	....	....	....	....	....	....	....	....	....	....	....	....	....	....	....	....	....	....
2007-08	Peterborough	OHL	58	9	12	21	74	....	....	....	....	....	....	....	....	....	5	1	0	1	2	....	....	....	....
2008-09	Peterborough	OHL	61	24	39	63	136	....	....	....	....	....	....	....	....	....	4	0	2	2	8	....	....	....	....
2009-10	Peterborough	OHL	33	8	19	27	58	....	....	....	....	....	....	....	....	....	....	....	....	....	....	....	....	....	....
	Windsor Spitfires	OHL	5	4	0	4	23	....	....	....	....	....	....	....	....	....	19	7	9	16	38	....	....	....	....
2010-11	Windsor Spitfires	OHL	56	26	51	77	67	....	....	....	....	....	....	....	....	....	16	6	10	16	37	....	....	....	....
	Portland Pirates	AHL	....	....	....	....	....	....	....	....	....	....	....	....	....	....	3	0	0	0	2	....	....	....	....
2011-12	**Buffalo**	**NHL**	**27**	**3**	**4**	**7**	**20**	**0**	**0**	**0**	**36**	**8.3**	**-1**	**14**	**50.0**	**11:56**	....	....	....	....	....	....	....	....	....
	Rochester	AHL	30	15	11	26	31	....	....	....	....	....	....	....	....	....	....	....	....	....	....	....	....	....	....
	Vancouver	**NHL**	**17**	**1**	**2**	**3**	**31**	**0**	**0**	**0**	**18**	**5.6**	**-1**	**9**	**44.4**	**10:17**	**4**	**0**	**0**	**0**	**2**	**0**	**0**	**0**	**4:51**
2012-13	Chicago Wolves	AHL	29	8	13	21	61	....	....	....	....	....	....	....	....	....	....	....	....	....	....	....	....	....	....
	Vancouver	**NHL**	**39**	**7**	**4**	**11**	**51**	**2**	**0**	**1**	**49**	**14.3**	**-7**	**14**	**42.9**	**13:29**	**4**	**0**	**0**	**0**	**4**	**0**	**0**	**0**	**12:05**
2013-14	**Vancouver**	**NHL**	**73**	**14**	**15**	**29**	**124**	**1**	**0**	**2**	**91**	**15.4**	**-4**	**21**	**28.6**	**12:56**	....	....	....	....	....	....	....	....	....
2014-15	**Vancouver**	**NHL**	**42**	**10**	**6**	**16**	**81**	**1**	**0**	**3**	**55**	**18.2**	**-5**	**6**	**0.0**	**12:37**	....	....	....	....	....	....	....	....	....
2015-16	**Edmonton**	**NHL**	**36**	**3**	**5**	**8**	**114**	**0**	**0**	**0**	**42**	**7.1**	**-7**	**4**	**25.0**	**12:27**	....	....	....	....	....	....	....	....	....
	Bakersfield	AHL	7	2	1	3	16	....	....	....	....	....	....	....	....	....	....	....	....	....	....	....	....	....	....
2016-17	**Edmonton**	**NHL**	**79**	**7**	**17**	**24**	**101**	**0**	**0**	**0**	**110**	**6.4**	**4**	**11**	**36.4**	**12:18**	**13**	**3**	**0**	**3**	**27**	**0**	**1**	**2**	**13:30**
	NHL Totals		**313**	**45**	**53**	**98**	**522**	**4**	**0**	**6**	**401**	**11.2**		**79**	**35.4**	**12:31**	**21**	**3**	**0**	**3**	**33**	**0**	**1**	**2**	**11:35**

Traded to **Vancouver** by **Buffalo** for Cody Hodgson, February 27, 2012. Traded to **Montreal** by **Vancouver** with Vancouver's 5th round pick (Casy Staum) in 2016 NHL Draft for Brandon Prust, July 1, 2015. Traded to **Edmonton** by **Montreal** for Ben Scrivens, December 28, 2015.

KEARNS, Bracken

(KUHNRZ, BRAK-en) **N.J.**

Center. Shoots right. 6', 195 lbs. Born, West Vancouver, BC, May 12, 1981.

Season	Club	League	GP	G	A	Pts	PIM	PP	SH	GW	S	S%	+/-	TF	F%	Min	GP	G	A	Pts	PIM	PP	SH	GW	Min
2000-01			STATISTICS NOT AVAILABLE																						
	Grandview	PIJHL	10	8	5	13	4	....	....	....	....	....	....	....	....	....	4	1	3	4	12	....	....	....	....
2001-02	U. of Calgary	CWUAA	26	0	8	8	2	....	....	....	....	....	....	....	....	....	....	....	....	....	....	....	....	....	....
2002-03	U. of Calgary	CWUAA	29	8	9	17	14	....	....	....	....	....	....	....	....	....	....	....	....	....	....	....	....	....	....
2003-04	U. of Calgary	CWUAA	38	11	12	23	22	....	....	....	....	....	....	....	....	....	....	....	....	....	....	....	....	....	....
2004-05	U. of Calgary	CWUAA	43	12	23	35	18	....	....	....	....	....	....	....	....	....	....	....	....	....	....	....	....	....	....
2005-06	Cleveland Barons	AHL	1	0	1	1	0	....	....	....	....	....	....	....	....	....	....	....	....	....	....	....	....	....	....
	Toledo Storm	ECHL	71	33	36	69	66	....	....	....	....	....	....	....	....	....	13	7	6	13	6	....	....	....	....
2006-07	Milwaukee	AHL	79	11	15	26	59	....	....	....	....	....	....	....	....	....	4	0	0	0	8	....	....	....	....
2007-08	Norfolk Admirals	AHL	53	9	16	25	40	....	....	....	....	....	....	....	....	....	....	....	....	....	....	....	....	....	....
	Reading Royals	ECHL	17	5	13	18	17	....	....	....	....	....	....	....	....	....	....	....	....	....	....	....	....	....	....
2008-09	Norfolk Admirals	AHL	53	12	10	22	63	....	....	....	....	....	....	....	....	....	....	....	....	....	....	....	....	....	....
2009-10	Rockford IceHogs	AHL	80	15	36	51	99	....	....	....	....	....	....	....	....	....	4	0	2	2	2	....	....	....	....
2010-11	San Antonio	AHL	72	20	23	43	104	....	....	....	....	....	....	....	....	....	....	....	....	....	....	....	....	....	....
2011-12	**Florida**	**NHL**	**5**	**0**	**0**	**0**	**10**	**0**	**0**	**0**	**0**	**0.0**	**0**	**2**	**50.0**	**7:14**	....	....	....	....	....	....	....	....	....
	San Antonio	AHL	69	22	30	52	58	....	....	....	....	....	....	....	....	....	10	2	5	7	4	....	....	....	....
2012-13	Worcester Sharks	AHL	66	21	25	46	73	....	....	....	....	....	....	....	....	....	....	....	....	....	....	....	....	....	....
	San Jose	**NHL**	**1**	**0**	**0**	**0**	**0**	**0**	**0**	**0**	**0**	**0.0**	**0**	**0**	**0.0**	**12:04**	**7**	**0**	**0**	**0**	**2**	**0**	**0**	**0**	**7:37**
2013-14	**San Jose**	**NHL**	**25**	**3**	**2**	**5**	**6**	**1**	**0**	**0**	**37**	**8.1**	**-2**	**71**	**42.3**	**13:12**	....	....	....	....	....	....	....	....	....
	Worcester Sharks	AHL	45	6	19	25	72	....	....	....	....	....	....	....	....	....	....	....	....	....	....	....	....	....	....
2014-15	Blues Espoo	Finland	45	10	10	20	38	....	....	....	....	....	....	....	....	....	4	0	0	0	0	....	....	....	....
2015-16	**NY Islanders**	**NHL**	**2**	**0**	**1**	**1**	**4**	**0**	**0**	**0**	**0**	**0.0**	**1**	**12**	**66.7**	**15:54**	....	....	....	....	....	....	....	....	....
	Bridgeport	AHL	73	23	30	53	76	....	....	....	....	....	....	....	....	....	3	0	2	2	2	....	....	....	....

			Regular Season														Playoffs								
Season	Club	League	GP	G	A	Pts	PIM	PP	SH	GW	S	S%	+/-	TF	F%	Min	GP	G	A	Pts	PIM	PP	SH	GW	Min
2016-17	**NY Islanders**	**NHL**	**2**	**0**	**0**	**0**	**2**	**0**	**0**	**0**	**3**	**0.0**	**–1**	**17**	**58.8**	**11:12**	....	....	....	....	....	....	....	....	....
	Bridgeport	AHL	74	23	28	51	43	....	....	....	....	....	....	....	....	....	....	....	....	....	....	....	....	....	....
	NHL Totals		**35**	**3**	**3**	**6**	**22**	**1**	**0**	**0**	**40**	**7.5**		**102**	**48.0**	**12:21**	**7**	**0**	**0**	**0**	**2**	**0**	**0**	**0**	**7:37**

Signed as a free agent by **Phoenix**, July 27, 2010. Signed as a free agent by **Florida**, July 14, 2011. Signed as a free agent by **San Jose**, July 2, 2012. Signed as a free agent by **Espoo** (Finland), October 23, 2014. Signed as a free agent by **NY Islanders**, July 2, 2015. Signed as a free agent by **New Jersey**, July 1, 2017.

KEITH, Duncan

(KEETH, DUHN-kuhn) **CHI**

Defense. Shoots left. 6'1", 192 lbs. Born, Winnipeg, MB, July 16, 1983. Chicago's 2nd pick, 54th overall, in 2002 NHL Draft.

1998-99	Penticton	Minor-BC	44	51	57	108	45	....	....	....	....	....	....	....	....	....	....	....	....	....	....	....	....	....	....
99-2000	Penticton	BCHL	59	9	27	36	37	....	....	....	....	....	....	....	....	....	6	0	0	0	6	....	....	....	....
2000-01	Penticton	BCHL	60	18	64	82	61	....	....	....	....	....	....	....	....	....	9	4	6	10	18	....	....	....	....
2001-02	Michigan State	CCHA	41	3	12	15	18	....	....	....	....	....	....	....	....	....	....	....	....	....	....	....	....	....	....
2002-03	Michigan State	CCHA	15	3	6	9	8	....	....	....	....	....	....	....	....	....	....	....	....	....	....	....	....	....	....
	Kelowna Rockets	WHL	37	11	35	46	60	....	....	....	....	....	....	....	....	....	19	3	11	14	12	....	....	....	....
2003-04	Norfolk Admirals	AHL	75	7	18	25	44	....	....	....	....	....	....	....	....	....	8	1	1	2	6	....	....	....	....
2004-05	Norfolk Admirals	AHL	79	9	17	26	78	....	....	....	....	....	....	....	....	....	6	0	0	0	14	....	....	....	....
2005-06	**Chicago**	**NHL**	**81**	**9**	**12**	**21**	**79**	**1**	**1**	**0**	**134**	**6.7**	**–11**	**0**	**0.0**	**23:26**	....	....	....	....	....	....	....	....	....
2006-07	**Chicago**	**NHL**	**82**	**2**	**29**	**31**	**76**	**0**	**0**	**0**	**122**	**1.6**	**0**	**0**	**0.0**	**23:36**	....	....	....	....	....	....	....	....	....
2007-08	**Chicago**	**NHL**	**82**	**12**	**20**	**32**	**56**	**1**	**1**	**0**	**148**	**8.1**	**30**	**0**	**0.0**	**25:34**	....	....	....	....	....	....	....	....	....
2008-09	**Chicago**	**NHL**	**77**	**8**	**36**	**44**	**60**	**2**	**1**	**1**	**173**	**4.6**	**33**	**0**	**0.0**	**25:34**	**17**	**0**	**6**	**6**	**10**	**0**	**0**	**0**	**24:39**
2009-10 ♦	**Chicago**	**NHL**	**82**	**14**	**55**	**69**	**51**	**3**	**1**	**1**	**213**	**6.6**	**21**	**0**	**0.0**	**26:36**	**22**	**2**	**15**	**17**	**10**	**0**	**0**	**0**	**28:11**
	Canada	Olympics	7	0	6	6	2	....	....	....	....	....	....	....	....	....	....	....	....	....	....	....	....	....	....
2010-11	**Chicago**	**NHL**	**82**	**7**	**38**	**45**	**22**	**3**	**1**	**1**	**173**	**4.0**	**–1**	**0**	**0.0**	**26:53**	**7**	**4**	**2**	**6**	**6**	**1**	**0**	**1**	**26:55**
2011-12	**Chicago**	**NHL**	**74**	**4**	**36**	**40**	**42**	**1**	**0**	**1**	**162**	**2.5**	**15**	**0**	**0.0**	**26:54**	**6**	**0**	**1**	**1**	**2**	**0**	**0**	**0**	**30:16**
2012-13 ♦	**Chicago**	**NHL**	**47**	**3**	**24**	**27**	**31**	**2**	**0**	**0**	**91**	**3.3**	**16**	**0**	**0.0**	**24:07**	**22**	**2**	**11**	**13**	**18**	**0**	**0**	**0**	**27:37**
2013-14	**Chicago**	**NHL**	**79**	**6**	**55**	**61**	**28**	**3**	**0**	**3**	**198**	**3.0**	**22**	**0**	**0.0**	**24:39**	**19**	**4**	**7**	**11**	**8**	**0**	**0**	**1**	**27:49**
	Canada	Olympics	6	0	1	1	4	....	....	....	....	....	....	....	....	....	....	....	....	....	....	....	....	....	....
2014-15 ♦	**Chicago**	**NHL**	**80**	**10**	**35**	**45**	**20**	**3**	**0**	**2**	**171**	**5.8**	**12**	**0**	**0.0**	**25:34**	**23**	**3**	**18**	**21**	**4**	**0**	**0**	**3**	**31:07**
2015-16	**Chicago**	**NHL**	**67**	**9**	**34**	**43**	**26**	**4**	**0**	**4**	**130**	**6.9**	**13**	**1**	**0.0**	**25:14**	**6**	**3**	**2**	**5**	**2**	**1**	**0**	**0**	**31:28**
2016-17	**Chicago**	**NHL**	**80**	**6**	**47**	**53**	**16**	**2**	**0**	**2**	**183**	**3.3**	**22**	**0**	**0.0**	**25:37**	**4**	**0**	**1**	**1**	**2**	**0**	**0**	**0**	**25:33**
	NHL Totals		**913**	**90**	**421**	**511**	**507**	**25**	**5**	**15**	**1898**	**4.7**		**1**	**0.0**	**25:21**	**126**	**18**	**63**	**81**	**62**	**2**	**0**	**5**	**28:11**

NHL First All-Star Team (2010, 2014) • James Norris Memorial Trophy (2010, 2014) • Conn Smythe Trophy (2015) • NHL Second All-Star Team (2017)

Played in NHL All-Star Game (2008, 2011, 2015, 2017)

• Left **Michigan State University** (CCHA) and signed as a free agent by **Kelowna** (WHL), December 27, 2002.

KELLER, Clayton

(KEH-luhr, KLAY-tuhn) **ARI**

Center/Left wing. Shoots left. 5'10", 169 lbs. Born, Chesterfield, MO, July 29, 1998. Arizona's 1st pick, 7th overall, in 2016 NHL Draft.

2013-14	Shattuck	High-MN	51	36	41	77	20	....	....	....	....	....	....	....	....	....	....	....	....	....	....	....	....	....	....
2014-15	USAHNTDP	USHL	32	14	23	37	10	....	....	....	....	....	....	....	....	....	....	....	....	....	....	....	....	....	....
	USAHNTDP	U-17	20	16	18	34	14	....	....	....	....	....	....	....	....	....	....	....	....	....	....	....	....	....	....
	USAHNTDP	U-18	8	4	7	11	4	....	....	....	....	....	....	....	....	....	....	....	....	....	....	....	....	....	....
2015-16	USAHNTDP	USHL	23	13	24	37	14	....	....	....	....	....	....	....	....	....	....	....	....	....	....	....	....	....	....
	USAHNTDP	U-18	39	24	46	70	40	....	....	....	....	....	....	....	....	....	....	....	....	....	....	....	....	....	....
2016-17	Boston University	H-East	31	21	24	45	26	....	....	....	....	....	....	....	....	....	....	....	....	....	....	....	....	....	....
	Arizona	**NHL**	**3**	**0**	**2**	**2**	**0**	**0**	**0**	**0**	**0**	**0.0**	**–3**	**0**	**0.0**	**12:40**	....	....	....	....	....	....	....	....	....
	NHL Totals		**3**	**0**	**2**	**2**	**0**	**0**	**0**	**0**	**0**	**0.0**		**0**	**0.0**	**12:40**	....	....	....	....	....	....	....	....	....

Hockey East All-Rookie Team (2017) • Hockey East Second All-Star Team (2017)

KELLY, Chris

(KEHL-lee, KRIHS)

Center/Left wing. Shoots left. 6', 193 lbs. Born, Toronto, ON, November 11, 1980. Ottawa's 4th pick, 94th overall, in 1999 NHL Draft.

1995-96	Toronto Marlies	MTHL	42	25	45	70	25	....	....	....	....	....	....	....	....	....	....	....	....	....	....	....	....	....	....
1996-97	Vaughan Vipers	ON-Jr.A	5	0	0	0	5	....	....	....	....	....	....	....	....	....	....	....	....	....	....	....	....	....	....
	Aurora Tigers	ON-Jr.A	49	14	20	34	11	....	....	....	....	....	....	....	....	....	....	....	....	....	....	....	....	....	....
1997-98	London Knights	OHL	54	15	14	29	4	....	....	....	....	....	....	....	....	....	16	4	5	9	12	....	....	....	....
1998-99	London Knights	OHL	68	36	41	77	60	....	....	....	....	....	....	....	....	....	25	9	17	26	22	....	....	....	....
99-2000	London Knights	OHL	63	29	43	72	57	....	....	....	....	....	....	....	....	....	....	....	....	....	....	....	....	....	....
2000-01	London Knights	OHL	31	21	34	55	46	....	....	....	....	....	....	....	....	....	....	....	....	....	....	....	....	....	....
	Sudbury Wolves	OHL	19	5	16	21	17	....	....	....	....	....	....	....	....	....	12	11	5	16	14	....	....	....	....
2001-02	Grand Rapids	AHL	31	3	3	6	20	....	....	....	....	....	....	....	....	....	5	1	1	2	5	....	....	....	....
	Muskegon Fury	UHL	4	1	2	3	0	....	....	....	....	....	....	....	....	....	....	....	....	....	....	....	....	....	....
2002-03	Binghamton	AHL	77	17	14	31	73	....	....	....	....	....	....	....	....	....	14	2	3	5	8	....	....	....	....
2003-04	**Ottawa**	**NHL**	**4**	**0**	**0**	**0**	**0**	**0**	**0**	**0**	**4**	**0.0**	**–2**	**5**	**40.0**	**9:29**	....	....	....	....	....	....	....	....	....
	Binghamton	AHL	54	15	19	34	40	....	....	....	....	....	....	....	....	....	2	0	0	0	4	....	....	....	....
2004-05	Binghamton	AHL	77	24	36	60	57	....	....	....	....	....	....	....	....	....	6	1	2	3	11	....	....	....	....
2005-06	**Ottawa**	**NHL**	**82**	**10**	**20**	**30**	**76**	**1**	**0**	**2**	**112**	**8.9**	**21**	**808**	**45.8**	**12:20**	**10**	**0**	**0**	**0**	**2**	**0**	**0**	**0**	**11:49**
2006-07	**Ottawa**	**NHL**	**82**	**15**	**23**	**38**	**40**	**1**	**2**	**0**	**131**	**11.5**	**28**	**564**	**49.8**	**15:18**	**20**	**3**	**4**	**7**	**4**	**0**	**0**	**0**	**15:28**
2007-08	**Ottawa**	**NHL**	**75**	**11**	**19**	**30**	**30**	**0**	**1**	**1**	**124**	**8.9**	**3**	**162**	**53.1**	**16:36**	....	....	....	....	....	....	....	....	....
2008-09	**Ottawa**	**NHL**	**82**	**12**	**11**	**23**	**38**	**0**	**1**	**1**	**118**	**10.2**	**–10**	**494**	**47.4**	**15:36**	....	....	....	....	....	....	....	....	....
2009-10	**Ottawa**	**NHL**	**81**	**15**	**17**	**32**	**38**	**0**	**0**	**3**	**112**	**13.4**	**–7**	**894**	**45.6**	**14:58**	**6**	**1**	**5**	**6**	**2**	**1**	**0**	**0**	**18:46**
2010-11	**Ottawa**	**NHL**	**57**	**12**	**11**	**23**	**27**	**0**	**1**	**2**	**89**	**13.5**	**–12**	**726**	**50.1**	**15:39**	....	....	....	....	....	....	....	....	....
	♦ Boston	**NHL**	**24**	**2**	**3**	**5**	**6**	**0**	**0**	**0**	**24**	**8.3**	**–1**	**190**	**53.7**	**14:52**	**25**	**5**	**8**	**13**	**6**	**0**	**0**	**0**	**15:28**
2011-12	**Boston**	**NHL**	**82**	**20**	**19**	**39**	**41**	**1**	**2**	**6**	**122**	**16.4**	**33**	**809**	**51.8**	**14:44**	**7**	**1**	**2**	**3**	**4**	**0**	**0**	**1**	**16:05**
2012-13	Martigny	Swiss-2	8	4	5	9	8	....	....	....	....	....	....	....	....	....	....	....	....	....	....	....	....	....	....
	Boston	**NHL**	**34**	**3**	**6**	**9**	**16**	**1**	**0**	**0**	**40**	**7.5**	**–8**	**373**	**57.9**	**14:58**	**22**	**2**	**1**	**3**	**19**	**0**	**0**	**0**	**15:40**
2013-14	**Boston**	**NHL**	**57**	**9**	**9**	**18**	**32**	**0**	**1**	**0**	**69**	**13.0**	**2**	**579**	**48.9**	**14:42**	....	....	....	....	....	....	....	....	....
2014-15	**Boston**	**NHL**	**80**	**7**	**21**	**28**	**48**	**0**	**1**	**2**	**112**	**6.3**	**6**	**539**	**48.6**	**15:08**	....	....	....	....	....	....	....	....	....
2015-16	**Boston**	**NHL**	**11**	**2**	**0**	**2**	**0**	**0**	**1**	**0**	**8**	**25.0**	**3**	**52**	**42.3**	**13:05**	....	....	....	....	....	....	....	....	....
2016-17	**Ottawa**	**NHL**	**82**	**5**	**7**	**12**	**23**	**0**	**1**	**2**	**85**	**5.9**	**–17**	**501**	**44.5**	**11:56**	**2**	**0**	**0**	**0**	**0**	**0**	**0**	**0**	**5:26**
	NHL Totals		**833**	**123**	**166**	**289**	**415**	**4**	**11**	**19**	**1150**	**10.7**		**6696**	**48.9**	**14:37**	**92**	**12**	**20**	**32**	**37**	**1**	**0**	**1**	**15:10**

Traded to **Boston** by **Ottawa** for Boston's 2nd round pick (Shane Prince) in 2011 NHL Draft, February 15, 2011. Signed as a free agent by **Martigny** (Swiss-2), October 31, 2012. • Missed majority of 2015-16 due to leg injury vs. Dallas, November 3, 2015. Signed as a free agent by **Ottawa**, July 7, 2016.

KEMPE, Adrian

(KEHM-peh, AY-dree-uhn) **L.A.**

Left wing. Shoots left. 6'1", 187 lbs. Born, Kramfors, Sweden, September 13, 1996. Los Angeles' 1st pick, 29th overall, in 2014 NHL Draft.

2010-11	Kramfors U18	Swe-U18	25	1	7	8	10	....	....	....	....	....	....	....	....	....	3	1	0	1	0	....	....	....	....
2011-12	Djurgarden U18	Swe-U18	34	10	10	20	24	....	....	....	....	....	....	....	....	....	4	0	2	2	0	....	....	....	....
2012-13	MODO U18	Swe-U18	3	1	1	2	2	....	....	....	....	....	....	....	....	....	2	0	2	2	0	....	....	....	....
	MODO Jr.	Swe-Jr.	39	6	7	13	36	....	....	....	....	....	....	....	....	....	7	1	0	1	4	....	....	....	....
2013-14	MODO Jr.	Swe-Jr.	20	3	16	19	32	....	....	....	....	....	....	....	....	....	5	1	1	2	6	....	....	....	....
	MODO	Sweden	45	5	6	11	12	....	....	....	....	....	....	....	....	....	2	0	1	1	0	....	....	....	....
	MODO U18	Swe-U18	....	....	....	....	....	....	....	....	....	....	....	....	....	....	4	5	3	8	6	....	....	....	....
2014-15	MODO	Sweden	50	5	12	17	42	....	....	....	....	....	....	....	....	....	....	....	....	....	....	....	....	....	....
	MODO	Sweden-Q	....	....	....	....	....	....	....	....	....	....	....	....	....	....	4	1	2	3	2	....	....	....	....
	Manchester	AHL	3	0	0	0	2	....	....	....	....	....	....	....	....	....	17	8	1	9	2	....	....	....	....
2015-16	Ontario Reign	AHL	55	11	17	28	27	....	....	....	....	....	....	....	....	....	13	4	1	5	2	....	....	....	....
2016-17	**Los Angeles**	**NHL**	**25**	**2**	**4**	**6**	**6**	**0**	**0**	**1**	**32**	**6.3**	**–3**	**153**	**43.8**	**12:14**	....	....	....	....	....	....	....	....	....
	Ontario Reign	AHL	46	12	8	20	44	....	....	....	....	....	....	....	....	....	5	0	2	2	2	....	....	....	....
	NHL Totals		**25**	**2**	**4**	**6**	**6**	**0**	**0**	**1**	**32**	**6.3**		**153**	**43.8**	**12:14**	....	....	....	....	....	....	....	....	....

KEMPNY, Michal
(KEHMP-nee, MEE-kuhl) **CHI**

Defense. Shoots left. 6', 194 lbs. Born, Hodonin, Czech., September 8, 1990.

Season	Club	League	GP	G	A	Pts	PIM	PP	SH	GW	S	S%	+/-	TF	F%	Min	GP	G	A	Pts	PIM	PP	SH	GW	Min
			Regular Season														Playoffs								
2005-06	HK 36 Skalica U18	Svk-U18	41	1	5	6	24	....	....	....	....	....	....	....	....	....	2	0	0	0	0	....	....	....	....
2006-07	HK 36 Skalica U18	Svk-U18	50	6	14	20	40	....	....	....	....	....	....	....	....	....	....	....	....	....	....	....	....	....	....
2007-08	HK 36 Skalica U18	Svk-U18	14	5	12	17	36	....	....	....	....	....	....	....	....	....	....	....	....	....	....	....	....	....	....
	HK 36 Skalica	Slovakia	1	0	0	0	0	....	....	....	....	....	....	....	....	....	....	....	....	....	....	....	....	....	....
2008-09	HC Kometa Brno	CzRep-2	18	1	0	1	6	....	....	....	....	....	....	....	....	....	14	1	0	1	6	....	....	....	....
2009-10	HC Kometa Brno	CzRep	24	0	0	0	18	....	....	....	....	....	....	....	....	....	....	....	....	....	....	....	....	....	....
2010-11	HC Kometa Brno	CzRep	21	0	0	0	14	....	....	....	....	....	....	....	....	....	....	....	....	....	....	....	....	....	....
2011-12	HC Kometa Brno	CzRep	23	1	1	2	14	....	....	....	....	....	....	....	....	....	....	....	....	....	....	....	....	....	....
2012-13	HC Slavia Praha	CzRep	51	5	9	14	32	....	....	....	....	....	....	....	....	....	11	1	3	4	12	....	....	....	....
2013-14	HC Kometa Brno	CzRep	51	7	8	15	74	....	....	....	....	....	....	....	....	....	18	2	4	6	20	....	....	....	....
2014-15	HC Kometa Brno	CzRep	43	8	21	29	94	....	....	....	....	....	....	....	....	....	2	1	0	1	2	....	....	....	....
2015-16	Omsk	KHL	59	5	16	21	46	....	....	....	....	....	....	....	....	....	11	2	2	4	12	....	....	....	....
2016-17	**Chicago**	**NHL**	**50**	**2**	**6**	**8**	**22**	**0**	**0**	**0**	**67**	**3.0**	**1**	**0**	**0.0**	**14:58**	**1**	**0**	**0**	**0**	**0**	**0**	**0**	**0**	**8:51**
	NHL Totals		**50**	**2**	**6**	**8**	**22**	**0**	**0**	**0**	**67**	**3.0**		**0**	**0.0**	**14:58**	**1**	**0**	**0**	**0**	**0**	**0**	**0**	**0**	**8:51**

Signed as a free agent by **Chicago**, May 24, 2016.

KERANEN, Michael
(kair-A-nehn, mih-KIGH-ehl)

Right wing. Shoots left. 6'1", 191 lbs. Born, Stockholm, Sweden, January 4, 1990.

Season	Club	League	GP	G	A	Pts	PIM	PP	SH	GW	S	S%	+/-	TF	F%	Min	GP	G	A	Pts	PIM	PP	SH	GW	Min
2006-07	Tappara U18	Fin-U18	18	0	1	1	16	....	....	....	....	....	....	....	....	....	....	....	....	....	....	....	....	....	....
	Ilves Tampere U18	Fin-U18	12	1	4	5	10	....	....	....	....	....	....	....	....	....	2	0	0	0	0	....	....	....	....
2007-08	Ilves Tampere U18	Fin-U18	35	13	28	41	30	....	....	....	....	....	....	....	....	....	....	....	....	....	....	....	....	....	....
	Ilves Tampere Jr.	Fin-Jr.	1	0	0	0	0	....	....	....	....	....	....	....	....	....	....	....	....	....	....	....	....	....	....
2008-09	Ilves Tampere Jr.	Fin-Jr.	35	6	6	12	22	....	....	....	....	....	....	....	....	....	....	....	....	....	....	....	....	....	....
2009-10	Ilves Tampere Jr.	Fin-Jr.	41	22	28	50	50	....	....	....	....	....	....	....	....	....	9	4	7	11	6	....	....	....	....
	Ilves Tampere	Finland	1	0	0	0	0	....	....	....	....	....	....	....	....	....	....	....	....	....	....	....	....	....	....
2010-11	Ilves Tampere Jr.	Fin-Jr.	4	3	4	7	0	....	....	....	....	....	....	....	....	....	6	4	2	6	2	....	....	....	....
	LeKi Lempaala	Finland-2	9	7	4	11	4	....	....	....	....	....	....	....	....	....	....	....	....	....	....	....	....	....	....
	Ilves Tampere	Finland	42	5	6	11	45	....	....	....	....	....	....	....	....	....	....	....	....	....	....	....	....	....	....
2011-12	Ilves Tampere	Finland	44	6	5	11	20	....	....	....	....	....	....	....	....	....	....	....	....	....	....	....	....	....	....
	Ilves Tampere	Finland-Q	....	....	....	....	....	....	....	....	....	....	....	....	....	....	5	0	0	0	2	....	....	....	....
2012-13	Ilves Tampere	Finland	56	13	14	27	10	....	....	....	....	....	....	....	....	....	....	....	....	....	....	....	....	....	....
	Ilves Tampere	Finland-Q	....	....	....	....	....	....	....	....	....	....	....	....	....	....	5	1	4	5	0	....	....	....	....
2013-14	Ilves Tampere	Finland	52	17	35	*52	47	....	....	....	....	....	....	....	....	....	....	....	....	....	....	....	....	....	....
2014-15	Iowa Wild	AHL	70	10	27	37	22	....	....	....	....	....	....	....	....	....	....	....	....	....	....	....	....	....	....
2015-16	**Minnesota**	**NHL**	**1**	**0**	**0**	**0**	**0**	**0**	**0**	**0**	**0**	**0.0**	**–1**	**0**	**0.0**	**6:09**	....	....	....	....	....	....	....	....	....
	Iowa Wild	AHL	45	8	15	23	22	....	....	....	....	....	....	....	....	....	....	....	....	....	....	....	....	....	....
	Binghamton	AHL	21	4	3	7	13	....	....	....	....	....	....	....	....	....	....	....	....	....	....	....	....	....	....
2016-17	Jokerit	KHL	25	2	5	7	6	....	....	....	....	....	....	....	....	....	....	....	....	....	....	....	....	....	....
	Ilves Tampere	Finland	31	7	6	13	14	....	....	....	....	....	....	....	....	....	10	1	2	3	4	....	....	....	....
	NHL Totals		**1**	**0**	**0**	**0**	**0**	**0**	**0**	**0**	**0**	**0.0**		**0**	**0.0**	**6:09**	....	....	....	....	....	....	....	....	....

Signed as a free agent by **Minnesota**, June 5, 2014. Traded to **Ottawa** by **Minnesota** for Conor Allen, February 29, 2016. Signed as a free agent by **Jokerit Helsinki** (KHL), April 28, 2016. Signed as a free agent by **Ilves Tampere** (Finland), December 6, 2016.

KERDILES, Nicolas
(kair-DEE-lihs, NIH-koh-las) **ANA**

Left wing. Shoots left. 6'2", 191 lbs. Born, Lewisville, TX, January 11, 1994. Anaheim's 2nd pick, 36th overall, in 2012 NHL Draft.

Season	Club	League	GP	G	A	Pts	PIM	PP	SH	GW	S	S%	+/-	TF	F%	Min	GP	G	A	Pts	PIM	PP	SH	GW	Min
2009-10	L.A. Selects	T1EHL	37	25	29	54	48	....	....	....	....	....	....	....	....	....	....	....	....	....	....	....	....	....	....
	L.A. Selects	Other	31	40	27	67	30	....	....	....	....	....	....	....	....	....	....	....	....	....	....	....	....	....	....
2010-11	USAHNTDP	USHL	32	12	8	20	52	....	....	....	....	....	....	....	....	....	....	....	....	....	....	....	....	....	....
	USAHNTDP	U-17	14	7	5	12	12	....	....	....	....	....	....	....	....	....	....	....	....	....	....	....	....	....	....
	USAHNTDP	U-18	14	1	4	5	2	....	....	....	....	....	....	....	....	....	....	....	....	....	....	....	....	....	....
2011-12	USAHNTDP	USHL	18	4	9	13	18	....	....	....	....	....	....	....	....	....	....	....	....	....	....	....	....	....	....
	USAHNTDP	U-18	36	18	17	35	20	....	....	....	....	....	....	....	....	....	....	....	....	....	....	....	....	....	....
2012-13	U. of Wisconsin	WCHA	32	11	22	33	37	....	....	....	....	....	....	....	....	....	....	....	....	....	....	....	....	....	....
2013-14	U. of Wisconsin	Big Ten	28	15	23	38	33	....	....	....	....	....	....	....	....	....	....	....	....	....	....	....	....	....	....
	Norfolk Admirals	AHL	6	1	3	4	2	....	....	....	....	....	....	....	....	....	10	3	1	4	2	....	....	....	....
2014-15	Norfolk Admirals	AHL	51	9	17	26	43	....	....	....	....	....	....	....	....	....	....	....	....	....	....	....	....	....	....
2015-16	San Diego Gulls	AHL	45	15	12	27	70	....	....	....	....	....	....	....	....	....	....	....	....	....	....	....	....	....	....
2016-17	**Anaheim**	**NHL**	**1**	**0**	**0**	**0**	**0**	**0**	**0**	**0**	**0**	**0.0**	**1**	**1**	**100.0**	**11:08**	**4**	**0**	**1**	**1**	**2**	**0**	**0**	**0**	**9:22**
	San Diego Gulls	AHL	27	7	8	15	25	....	....	....	....	....	....	....	....	....	8	4	4	8	6	....	....	....	....
	NHL Totals		**1**	**0**	**0**	**0**	**0**	**0**	**0**	**0**	**0**	**0.0**		**1**	**100.0**	**11:08**	**4**	**0**	**1**	**1**	**2**	**0**	**0**	**0**	**9:22**

Big Ten Second All-Star Team (2014)

KERO, Tanner
(KAIR-oh, TA-nuhr) **CHI**

Left wing. Shoots left. 6', 185 lbs. Born, Hancock, MI, July 24, 1992.

Season	Club	League	GP	G	A	Pts	PIM	PP	SH	GW	S	S%	+/-	TF	F%	Min	GP	G	A	Pts	PIM	PP	SH	GW	Min
2009-10	Marquette	NAHL	57	32	19	51	39	....	....	....	....	....	....	....	....	....	3	1	0	1	0	....	....	....	....
2010-11	Fargo Force	USHL	55	14	23	37	22	....	....	....	....	....	....	....	....	....	5	1	0	1	2	....	....	....	....
2011-12	Michigan Tech	WCHA	39	9	7	16	14	....	....	....	....	....	....	....	....	....	....	....	....	....	....	....	....	....	....
2012-13	Michigan Tech	WCHA	33	11	13	24	27	....	....	....	....	....	....	....	....	....	....	....	....	....	....	....	....	....	....
2013-14	Michigan Tech	WCHA	40	15	10	25	16	....	....	....	....	....	....	....	....	....	....	....	....	....	....	....	....	....	....
2014-15	Michigan Tech	WCHA	41	20	26	*46	10	....	....	....	....	....	....	....	....	....	....	....	....	....	....	....	....	....	....
	Rockford IceHogs	AHL	6	5	0	5	0	....	....	....	....	....	....	....	....	....	6	2	1	3	0	....	....	....	....
2015-16	**Chicago**	**NHL**	**17**	**1**	**2**	**3**	**2**	**0**	**0**	**0**	**26**	**3.8**	**–2**	**123**	**44.7**	**12:18**	....	....	....	....	....	....	....	....	....
	Rockford IceHogs	AHL	60	20	19	39	23	....	....	....	....	....	....	....	....	....	3	0	2	2	0	....	....	....	....
2016-17	**Chicago**	**NHL**	**47**	**6**	**10**	**16**	**8**	**0**	**0**	**0**	**60**	**10.0**	**15**	**471**	**44.4**	**13:29**	**4**	**0**	**0**	**0**	**0**	**0**	**0**	**0**	**13:38**
	Rockford IceHogs	AHL	28	7	13	20	14	....	....	....	....	....	....	....	....	....	....	....	....	....	....	....	....	....	....
	NHL Totals		**64**	**7**	**12**	**19**	**10**	**0**	**0**	**0**	**86**	**8.1**		**594**	**44.4**	**13:10**	**4**	**0**	**0**	**0**	**0**	**0**	**0**	**0**	**13:38**

WCHA First All-Star Team (2015) • WCHA Player of the Year (2015) • NCAA West First All-American Team (2015)

Signed as a free agent by **Chicago**, April 2, 2015.

KESLER, Ryan
(KEHZ-luhr, RIGH-uhn) **ANA**

Center. Shoots right. 6'2", 202 lbs. Born, Livonia, MI, August 31, 1984. Vancouver's 1st pick, 23rd overall, in 2003 NHL Draft.

Season	Club	League	GP	G	A	Pts	PIM	PP	SH	GW	S	S%	+/-	TF	F%	Min	GP	G	A	Pts	PIM	PP	SH	GW	Min
99-2000	Det. Honeybaked	MWEHL	72	44	73	117		....	....	....	....	....	....	....	....	....	....	....	....	....	....	....	....	....	....
2000-01	USAHNTDP	U-18	26	8	20	28	24	....	....	....	....	....	....	....	....	....	....	....	....	....	....	....	....	....	....
	USAHNTDP	NAHL	56	7	21	28	40	....	....	....	....	....	....	....	....	....	....	....	....	....	....	....	....	....	....
2001-02	USAHNTDP	U-18	46	11	33	44	23	....	....	....	....	....	....	....	....	....	....	....	....	....	....	....	....	....	....
	USAHNTDP	USHL	13	5	5	10	10	....	....	....	....	....	....	....	....	....	....	....	....	....	....	....	....	....	....
	USAHNTDP	NAHL	10	5	6	11	4	....	....	....	....	....	....	....	....	....	....	....	....	....	....	....	....	....	....
2002-03	Ohio State	CCHA	40	11	20	31	44	....	....	....	....	....	....	....	....	....	....	....	....	....	....	....	....	....	....
2003-04	**Vancouver**	**NHL**	**28**	**2**	**3**	**5**	**16**	**0**	**0**	**0**	**23**	**8.7**	**–2**	**194**	**40.2**	**10:42**	....	....	....	....	....	....	....	....	....
	Manitoba Moose	AHL	33	3	8	11	29	....	....	....	....	....	....	....	....	....	....	....	....	....	....	....	....	....	....
2004-05	Manitoba Moose	AHL	78	30	27	57	105	....	....	....	....	....	....	....	....	....	14	4	5	9	8	....	....	....	....
2005-06	**Vancouver**	**NHL**	**82**	**10**	**13**	**23**	**79**	**1**	**0**	**2**	**119**	**8.4**	**1**	**984**	**46.8**	**14:03**	....	....	....	....	....	....	....	....	....
2006-07	**Vancouver**	**NHL**	**48**	**6**	**10**	**16**	**40**	**0**	**0**	**0**	**88**	**6.8**	**1**	**690**	**46.1**	**16:26**	**1**	**0**	**0**	**0**	**0**	**0**	**0**	**0**	**27:51**
2007-08	**Vancouver**	**NHL**	**80**	**21**	**16**	**37**	**79**	**4**	**2**	**2**	**177**	**11.9**	**1**	**1358**	**53.0**	**19:03**	....	....	....	....	....	....	....	....	....
2008-09	**Vancouver**	**NHL**	**82**	**26**	**33**	**59**	**61**	**10**	**2**	**2**	**179**	**14.5**	**8**	**976**	**54.0**	**19:28**	**10**	**2**	**2**	**4**	**14**	**1**	**0**	**0**	**20:29**
2009-10	**Vancouver**	**NHL**	**82**	**25**	**50**	**75**	**104**	**12**	**1**	**5**	**214**	**11.7**	**1**	**1401**	**55.1**	**19:38**	**12**	**1**	**9**	**10**	**4**	**0**	**0**	**0**	**21:19**
	United States	Olympics	6	2	0	2	2	....	....	....	....	....	....	....	....	....	....	....	....	....	....	....	....	....	....
2010-11	**Vancouver**	**NHL**	**82**	**41**	**32**	**73**	**66**	**15**	**3**	**7**	**260**	**15.8**	**24**	**1496**	**57.4**	**20:30**	**25**	**7**	**12**	**19**	**47**	**4**	**0**	**2**	**22:34**
2011-12	**Vancouver**	**NHL**	**77**	**22**	**27**	**49**	**56**	**8**	**1**	**1**	**222**	**9.9**	**11**	**1351**	**53.6**	**20:06**	**5**	**0**	**3**	**3**	**6**	**0**	**0**	**0**	**22:04**
2012-13	**Vancouver**	**NHL**	**17**	**4**	**9**	**13**	**12**	**2**	**0**	**1**	**36**	**11.1**	**–5**	**303**	**57.4**	**18:57**	**4**	**2**	**0**	**2**	**0**	**1**	**0**	**0**	**23:06**
2013-14	**Vancouver**	**NHL**	**77**	**25**	**18**	**43**	**81**	**9**	**1**	**5**	**239**	**10.5**	**–15**	**1406**	**52.6**	**21:49**	....	....	....	....	....	....	....	....	....
	United States	Olympics	6	1	3	4	0	....	....	....	....	....	....	....	....	....	....	....	....	....	....	....	....	....	....

			Regular Season														Playoffs								
Season	Club	League	GP	G	A	Pts	PIM	PP	SH	GW	S	S%	+/-	TF	F%	Min	GP	G	A	Pts	PIM	PP	SH	GW	Min
2014-15	**Anaheim**	**NHL**	**81**	**20**	**27**	**47**	**75**	5	1	4	205	9.8	–5	1664	56.3	19:31	16	7	6	13	24	1	0	1	20:29
2015-16	**Anaheim**	**NHL**	**79**	**21**	**32**	**53**	**78**	5	1	4	164	12.8	5	1675	58.5	19:32	7	4	0	4	0	2	0	0	20:08
2016-17	**Anaheim**	**NHL**	**82**	**22**	**36**	**58**	**83**	8	0	2	186	11.8	8	1793	57.4	21:18	17	1	7	8	32	0	0	0	21:21
	NHL Totals		**897**	**245**	**306**	**551**	**830**	**79**	**12**	**35**	**2112**	**11.6**		**15291**	**54.4**	**19:02**	**97**	**24**	**39**	**63**	**127**	**9**	**0**	**3**	**21:31**

Frank J. Selke Trophy (2011)

Played in NHL All-Star Game (2011, 2017)

• Missed majority of 2012-13 due to recurring shoulder injury and foot injuriy vs. Dallas, February 15, 2013. Traded to **Anaheim** by **Vancouver** with Vancouver's 3rd round pick (Deven Sideroff) in 2015 NHL Draft for Nick Bonino, Luca Sbisa and Anaheim's 1st (Jared McCann) and 3rd (later traded to NY Rangers – NY Rangers selected Keegan Iverson) round picks in 2014 NHL Draft, June 27, 2014.

KESSEL, Phil

(KEH-suhl, FIHL) **PIT**

Right wing. Shoots right. 6', 202 lbs. Born, Madison, WI, October 2, 1987. Boston's 1st pick, 5th overall, in 2006 NHL Draft.

2003-04	USAHNTDP	U-17	32	31	18	49	8																		
	USAHNTDP	NAHL	30	21	12	33	18																		
2004-05	USAHNTDP	U-18	31	41	32	73	16																		
	USAHNTDP	NAHL	14	11	14	25	21																		
2005-06	U. of Minnesota	WCHA	39	18	33	51	28																		
2006-07	**Boston**	**NHL**	**70**	**11**	**18**	**29**	**12**	1	0	0	170	6.5	–12	373	40.8	14:04									
	Providence Bruins	AHL	2	1	0	1	2																		
2007-08	**Boston**	**NHL**	**82**	**19**	**18**	**37**	**28**	5	0	3	213	8.9	–6	326	42.3	15:14	4	3	1	4	2	1	0	0	14:31
2008-09	**Boston**	**NHL**	**70**	**36**	**24**	**60**	**16**	8	0	6	232	15.5	23	87	48.3	16:34	11	6	5	11	4	0	0	0	15:55
2009-10	**Toronto**	**NHL**	**70**	**30**	**25**	**55**	**21**	8	0	5	297	10.1	–8	122	48.4	19:33									
	United States	Olympics	6	1	1	2	0																		
2010-11	**Toronto**	**NHL**	**82**	**32**	**32**	**64**	**24**	12	1	6	325	9.8	–20	59	40.7	19:39									
2011-12	**Toronto**	**NHL**	**82**	**37**	**45**	**82**	**20**	10	0	6	295	12.5	–10	28	32.1	20:03									
2012-13	**Toronto**	**NHL**	**48**	**20**	**32**	**52**	**18**	6	0	4	161	12.4	–3	8	62.5	19:49	7	4	2	6	2	1	0	2	18:29
2013-14	**Toronto**	**NHL**	**82**	**37**	**43**	**80**	**27**	8	0	6	305	12.1	–5	14	14.3	20:40									
	United States	Olympics	6	5	3	8	4																		
2014-15	**Toronto**	**NHL**	**82**	**25**	**36**	**61**	**30**	8	0	4	280	8.9	–34	5	40.0	18:48									
2015-16♦	**Pittsburgh**	**NHL**	**82**	**26**	**33**	**59**	**18**	4	0	5	274	9.5	9	5	40.0	18:23	24	10	12	22	4	5	0	0	17:47
2016-17♦	**Pittsburgh**	**NHL**	**82**	**23**	**47**	**70**	**20**	8	0	4	229	10.0	3	15	33.3	17:56	25	8	15	23	2	*5	0	2	17:33
	NHL Totals		**832**	**296**	**353**	**649**	**234**	**78**	**1**	**49**	**2781**	**10.6**		**1042**	**42.2**	**18:15**	**71**	**31**	**35**	**66**	**14**	**12**	**0**	**4**	**17:18**

WCHA All-Rookie Team (2006) • WCHA Rookie of the Year (2006) • Bill Masterton Memorial Trophy (2007) • Olympic All-Star Team (2014) • Best Forward – Olympics (2014)

Played in NHL All-Star Game (2011, 2012, 2015)

Traded to **Toronto** by **Boston** for Toronto's 1st (Tyler Seguin) and 2nd (Jared Knight) round picks in 2010 NHL Draft and Toronto's 1st round pick (Dougie Hamilton) in 2011 NHL Draft, September 18, 2009. Traded to **Pittsburgh** by **Toronto** with Tim Erixon, Tyler Biggs and Pittsburgh's 2nd round pick (previously acquired, Pittsburgh selected Kasper Bjorkqvist) in 2016 NHL Draft for Nick Spaling, Kasperi Kapanen, Scott Harrington, Pittsburgh's 1st round pick (later traded to Anaheim – Anaheim selected Sam Steel) in 2016 NHL Draft and New Jersey's 3rd round pick (previously acquired, Toronto selected James Greenway) in 2016 NHL Draft, July 1, 2015.

KHAIRA, Jujhar

(KAIR-a, JOO-jahr) **EDM**

Left wing. Shoots left. 6'4", 219 lbs. Born, Surrey, BC, August 13, 1994. Edmonton's 3rd pick, 63rd overall, in 2012 NHL Draft.

2009-10	Cloverdale Colts	Minor-BC	STATISTICS NOT AVAILABLE																						
2010-11	Prince George	BCHL	58	10	32	42	21																		
2011-12	Prince George	BCHL	54	29	50	79	69										4	0	2	2	2				
2012-13	Michigan Tech	WCHA	37	6	19	25	49																		
2013-14	Everett Silvertips	WHL	59	16	27	43	59										5	3	1	4	8				
	Oklahoma City	AHL	6	0	0	0	2										3	1	0	1	0				
2014-15	Oklahoma City	AHL	51	4	6	10	62										8	3	1	4	4				
2015-16	**Edmonton**	**NHL**	**15**	**0**	**2**	**2**	**13**	0	0	0	14	0.0	–2	1	0.0	10:21									
	Bakersfield	AHL	49	10	17	27	69																		
2016-17	**Edmonton**	**NHL**	**10**	**1**	**0**	**1**	**2**	0	0	1	10	10.0	1	19	36.8	9:15									
	Bakersfield	AHL	27	8	12	20	31																		
	NHL Totals		**25**	**1**	**2**	**3**	**15**	**0**	**0**	**1**	**24**	**4.2**		**20**	**35.0**	**9:55**									

KHOKHLACHEV, Alex

(khohkh-luh-CHAWV, AL-ehx) **BOS**

Center. Shoots left. 5'10", 181 lbs. Born, Moscow, Russia, September 9, 1993. Boston's 2nd pick, 40th overall, in 2011 NHL Draft.

2009-10	Spartak Jr.	Russia-Jr.	51	15	25	40	22																		
2010-11	Windsor Spitfires	OHL	67	34	42	76	28										18	9	11	20	8				
2011-12	Windsor Spitfires	OHL	56	25	44	69	32																		
2012-13	Spartak Moscow	KHL	26	2	5	7	20																		
	Windsor Spitfires	OHL	29	22	26	48	20																		
	Providence Bruins	AHL	11	2	1	3	8																		
2013-14	**Boston**	**NHL**	**1**	**0**	**0**	**0**	**2**	0	0	0	2	0.0	0	17	47.1	15:14									
	Providence Bruins	AHL	65	21	36	57	28										12	*9	5	14	12				
2014-15	**Boston**	**NHL**	**3**	**0**	**0**	**0**	**0**	0	0	0	1	0.0	–2	17	52.9	8:12									
	Providence Bruins	AHL	61	15	28	43	28										5	2	1	3	4				
2015-16	**Boston**	**NHL**	**5**	**0**	**0**	**0**	**0**	0	0	0	4	0.0	–2	2	0.0	10:15									
	Providence Bruins	AHL	60	23	45	68	*12										3	0	2	2	2				
2016-17	St. Petersburg	KHL	25	5	5	10	2										9	0	1	1	11				
	NHL Totals		**9**	**0**	**0**	**0**	**2**	**0**	**0**	**0**	**7**	**0.0**		**36**	**47.2**	**10:07**									

Signed as a free agent by **Spartak Moscow** (KHL), July 1, 2012. Signed as a free agent by **St. Petersburg** (KHL), May 31, 2016.

KILLORN, Alex

(KIHL-ohrn, al-EHX) **T.B.**

Center. Shoots left. 6'2", 198 lbs. Born, Halifax, NS, September 14, 1989. Tampa Bay's 3rd pick, 77th overall, in 2007 NHL Draft.

2005-06	Lac St-Louis Lions	QAAA	43	18	34	52	94										10	9	6	15	8				
2006-07	Deerfield	High-MA	25	18	14	32	....																		
2007-08	Deerfield	High-MA	24	28	27	55	....																		
2008-09	Harvard Crimson	ECAC	30	6	8	14	46																		
2009-10	Harvard Crimson	ECAC	32	9	11	20	26																		
2010-11	Harvard Crimson	ECAC	34	15	14	29	36																		
2011-12	Harvard Crimson	ECAC	34	23	23	46	47																		
	Norfolk Admirals	AHL	10	2	4	6	2										17	3	9	12	8				
2012-13	Syracuse Crunch	AHL	44	16	22	38	32																		
	Tampa Bay	**NHL**	**38**	**7**	**12**	**19**	**14**	1	0	2	82	8.5	–6	28	39.3	16:49									
2013-14	**Tampa Bay**	**NHL**	**82**	**17**	**24**	**41**	**63**	3	0	2	173	9.8	8	172	43.0	16:47	4	1	1	2	4	0	0	0	18:41
2014-15	**Tampa Bay**	**NHL**	**71**	**15**	**23**	**38**	**36**	1	1	5	130	11.5	8	80	43.8	16:56	26	9	9	18	12	1	0	2	20:10
2015-16	**Tampa Bay**	**NHL**	**81**	**14**	**26**	**40**	**44**	3	0	3	154	9.1	14	80	38.8	16:48	17	5	8	13	*42	1	0	2	18:19
2016-17	**Tampa Bay**	**NHL**	**81**	**19**	**17**	**36**	**66**	4	1	4	176	10.8	–9	12	33.3	18:00									
	NHL Totals		**353**	**72**	**102**	**174**	**223**	**12**	**2**	**16**	**715**	**10.1**		**372**	**41.7**	**17:06**	**47**	**15**	**18**	**33**	**58**	**1**	**0**	**4**	**19:22**

NCAA East First All-American Team (2012)

KINDL, Jakub

(KIHN-duhl, YA-kuhb)

Defense. Shoots left. 6'3", 199 lbs. Born, Sumperk, Czech., February 10, 1987. Detroit's 1st pick, 19th overall, in 2005 NHL Draft.

2002-03	HC Pardubice U17	CzR-U17	3	0	3	3	10																		
	HC Pardubice Jr.	CzRep-Jr.	27	0	3	3	46																		
	Pardubice	CzRep	1	0	0	0	0																		
2003-04	HC Pardubice U17	CzR-U17	2	0	1	1	6																		
	HC Pardubice Jr.	CzRep-Jr.	48	4	14	18	108																		
	Hr. Kralove	CzRep-2	1	0	0	0	0										1	0	0	0	0				
2004-05	Kitchener Rangers	OHL	62	3	11	14	92										12	0	0	0	22				
2005-06	Kitchener Rangers	OHL	60	12	46	58	112										5	1	0	1	10				
	Grand Rapids	AHL	3	0	1	1	2																		

			Regular Season														Playoffs								
Season	Club	League	GP	G	A	Pts	PIM	PP	SH	GW	S	S%	+/-	TF	F%	Min	GP	G	A	Pts	PIM	PP	SH	GW	Min
2006-07	Kitchener Rangers	OHL	54	11	44	55	142	....	....	....	....	....	....	....	....	....	9	2	9	11	8	....	....	....	....
	Grand Rapids	AHL	....	....	....	....	....	....	....	....	....	....	....	....	....	....	7	0	2	2	0	....	....	....	....
2007-08	Grand Rapids	AHL	75	3	14	17	82	....	....	....	....	....	....	....	....	....	....	....	....	....	....	....	....	....	....
2008-09	Grand Rapids	AHL	78	6	27	33	76	....	....	....	....	....	....	....	....	....	10	2	1	3	2	....	....	....	....
2009-10	**Detroit**	**NHL**	**3**	**0**	**0**	**0**	**0**	**0**	**0**	**0**	**1**	**0.0**	**–2**	**0**	**0.0**	**10:50**	....	....	....	....	....	....	....	....	....
	Grand Rapids	AHL	73	3	30	33	59	....	....	....	....	....	....	....	....	....	....	....	....	....	....	....	....	....	....
2010-11	**Detroit**	**NHL**	**48**	**2**	**2**	**4**	**36**	**0**	**0**	**0**	**62**	**3.2**	**–6**	**0**	**0.0**	**13:37**	....	....	....	....	....	....	....	....	....
	Grand Rapids	AHL	8	1	4	5	6	....	....	....	....	....	....	....	....	....	....	....	....	....	....	....	....	....	....
2011-12	**Detroit**	**NHL**	**55**	**1**	**12**	**13**	**25**	**0**	**0**	**0**	**69**	**1.4**	**7**	**0**	**0.0**	**14:03**	....	....	....	....	....	....	....	....	....
2012-13	Pardubice	CzRep	27	1	10	11	26	....	....	....	....	....	....	....	....	....	....	....	....	....	....	....	....	....	....
	Detroit	**NHL**	**41**	**4**	**9**	**13**	**28**	**1**	**0**	**2**	**76**	**5.3**	**15**	**0**	**0.0**	**18:33**	**14**	**1**	**4**	**5**	**10**	**1**	**0**	**1**	**17:44**
2013-14	**Detroit**	**NHL**	**66**	**2**	**17**	**19**	**24**	**0**	**0**	**0**	**93**	**2.2**	**–4**	**0**	**0.0**	**17:14**	**4**	**0**	**0**	**0**	**2**	**0**	**0**	**0**	**17:16**
2014-15	**Detroit**	**NHL**	**35**	**5**	**8**	**13**	**22**	**2**	**0**	**0**	**54**	**9.3**	**2**	**0**	**0.0**	**15:55**	**1**	**0**	**0**	**0**	**0**	**0**	**0**	**0**	**16:37**
	Grand Rapids	AHL	2	1	0	1	2	....	....	....	....	....	....	....	....	....	....	....	....	....	....	....	....	....	....
2015-16	**Detroit**	**NHL**	**25**	**2**	**4**	**6**	**14**	**0**	**0**	**1**	**37**	**5.4**	**3**	**0**	**0.0**	**16:28**	....	....	....	....	....	....	....	....	....
	Grand Rapids	AHL	10	3	1	4	12	....	....	....	....	....	....	....	....	....	....	....	....	....	....	....	....	....	....
	Florida	**NHL**	**19**	**0**	**2**	**2**	**4**	**0**	**0**	**0**	**26**	**0.0**	**10**	**1**	**0.0**	**13:59**	**1**	**0**	**0**	**0**	**0**	**0**	**0**	**0**	**12:30**
2016-17	**Florida**	**NHL**	**39**	**0**	**4**	**4**	**28**	**0**	**0**	**0**	**41**	**0.0**	**–11**	**0**	**0.0**	**14:41**	....	....	....	....	....	....	....	....	....
	Springfield	AHL	13	1	6	7	16	....	....	....	....	....	....	....	....	....	....	....	....	....	....	....	....	....	....
	NHL Totals		**331**	**16**	**58**	**74**	**181**	**3**	**0**	**3**	**459**	**3.5**		**1**	**0.0**	**15:36**	**20**	**1**	**4**	**5**	**12**	**1**	**0**	**1**	**17:19**

OHL Second All-Star Team (2007)

Signed as a free agent by **Pardubice** (CzRep), September 23, 2012. • Missed majority of 2014-15 due to elbow injury at Ottawa, December 27, 2014 and as a healthy reserve. Traded to **Florida** by **Detroit** for Florida's 6th round pick (Reilly Webb) in 2017 NHL Draft, February 27, 2016.

KING, Dwight

(KIHNG, DWIGHT)

Left wing. Shoots left. 6'4", 232 lbs. Born, Meadow Lake, SK, July 5, 1989. Los Angeles' 6th pick, 109th overall, in 2007 NHL Draft.

Season	Club	League	GP	G	A	Pts	PIM	PP	SH	GW	S	S%	+/-	TF	F%	Min	GP	G	A	Pts	PIM	PP	SH	GW	Min
2004-05	Beardy's	SMHL	44	26	30	56	16	....	....	....	....	....	....	....	....	....	3	0	1	1	4	....	....	....	....
	Lethbridge	WHL	7	0	0	0	2	....	....	....	....	....	....	....	....	....	4	0	0	0	2	....	....	....	....
2005-06	Lethbridge	WHL	68	8	8	16	22	....	....	....	....	....	....	....	....	....	6	0	0	0	6	....	....	....	....
2006-07	Lethbridge	WHL	62	12	32	44	39	....	....	....	....	....	....	....	....	....	....	....	....	....	....	....	....	....	....
2007-08	Lethbridge	WHL	72	34	35	69	56	....	....	....	....	....	....	....	....	....	19	8	6	14	12	....	....	....	....
2008-09	Lethbridge	WHL	64	25	35	60	51	....	....	....	....	....	....	....	....	....	11	1	7	8	2	....	....	....	....
2009-10	Manchester	AHL	52	10	16	26	42	....	....	....	....	....	....	....	....	....	16	2	7	9	4	....	....	....	....
	Ontario Reign	ECHL	20	4	5	9	9	....	....	....	....	....	....	....	....	....	....	....	....	....	....	....	....	....	....
2010-11	**Los Angeles**	**NHL**	**6**	**0**	**0**	**0**	**2**	**0**	**0**	**0**	**3**	**0.0**	**–2**	**0**	**0.0**	**11:43**	....	....	....	....	....	....	....	....	....
	Manchester	AHL	72	24	28	52	58	....	....	....	....	....	....	....	....	....	7	2	3	5	2	....	....	....	....
2011-12♦	**Los Angeles**	**NHL**	**27**	**5**	**9**	**14**	**10**	**0**	**0**	**1**	**42**	**11.9**	**3**	**3**	**66.7**	**14:38**	**20**	**5**	**3**	**8**	**13**	**0**	**0**	**2**	**12:54**
	Manchester	AHL	50	11	18	29	20	....	....	....	....	....	....	....	....	....	....	....	....	....	....	....	....	....	....
2012-13	Manchester	AHL	28	5	12	17	13	....	....	....	....	....	....	....	....	....	....	....	....	....	....	....	....	....	....
	Los Angeles	**NHL**	**47**	**4**	**6**	**10**	**11**	**0**	**0**	**0**	**60**	**6.7**	**–3**	**6**	**33.3**	**12:45**	**18**	**2**	**3**	**5**	**2**	**0**	**1**	**0**	**14:47**
2013-14♦	**Los Angeles**	**NHL**	**77**	**15**	**15**	**30**	**18**	**0**	**2**	**3**	**111**	**13.5**	**16**	**5**	**40.0**	**15:03**	**26**	**3**	**8**	**11**	**20**	**0**	**0**	**0**	**14:56**
2014-15	**Los Angeles**	**NHL**	**81**	**13**	**13**	**26**	**21**	**0**	**0**	**1**	**127**	**10.2**	**–3**	**5**	**60.0**	**14:24**	....	....	....	....	....	....	....	....	....
2015-16	**Los Angeles**	**NHL**	**47**	**7**	**6**	**13**	**24**	**0**	**0**	**2**	**48**	**14.6**	**–6**	**7**	**28.6**	**14:26**	**5**	**0**	**1**	**1**	**2**	**0**	**0**	**0**	**14:27**
2016-17	**Los Angeles**	**NHL**	**63**	**8**	**7**	**15**	**10**	**0**	**0**	**1**	**89**	**9.0**	**0**	**13**	**30.8**	**15:00**	....	....	....	....	....	....	....	....	....
	Montreal	**NHL**	**17**	**1**	**0**	**1**	**2**	**0**	**0**	**0**	**21**	**4.8**	**–2**	**3**	**0.0**	**12:14**	**6**	**0**	**0**	**0**	**0**	**0**	**0**	**0**	**12:33**
	NHL Totals		**365**	**53**	**56**	**109**	**98**	**0**	**2**	**8**	**501**	**10.6**		**42**	**35.7**	**14:18**	**75**	**10**	**15**	**25**	**37**	**0**	**1**	**2**	**14:08**

Traded to **Montreal** by **Los Angeles** for Montreal's 4th round pick in 2018 NHL Draft, March 1, 2017.

KLEFBOM, Oscar

(KLEHF-bawm, AWS-kuhr) **EDM**

Defense. Shoots left. 6'3", 220 lbs. Born, Karlstad, Sweden, July 20, 1993. Edmonton's 2nd pick, 19th overall, in 2011 NHL Draft.

Season	Club	League	GP	G	A	Pts	PIM	PP	SH	GW	S	S%	+/-	TF	F%	Min	GP	G	A	Pts	PIM	PP	SH	GW	Min
2008-09	Farjestad U18	Swe-U18	15	2	2	4	4	....	....	....	....	....	....	....	....	....	4	0	1	1	2	....	....	....	....
2009-10	Farjestad U18	Swe-U18	31	10	18	28	37	....	....	....	....	....	....	....	....	....	6	0	0	0	0	....	....	....	....
	IFK Munkfors	Sweden-3	3	0	1	1	0	....	....	....	....	....	....	....	....	....	....	....	....	....	....	....	....	....	....
	Skare BK	Sweden-3	2	0	0	0	2	....	....	....	....	....	....	....	....	....	....	....	....	....	....	....	....	....	....
2010-11	Farjestad U18	Swe-U18	8	3	3	6	2	....	....	....	....	....	....	....	....	....	....	....	....	....	....	....	....	....	....
	Skare BK	Sweden-3	12	0	1	1	0	....	....	....	....	....	....	....	....	....	....	....	....	....	....	....	....	....	....
	Farjestad	Sweden	23	1	1	2	2	....	....	....	....	....	....	....	....	....	....	....	....	....	....	....	....	....	....
2011-12	Farjestad Jr.	Swe-Jr.	15	1	3	4	0	....	....	....	....	....	....	....	....	....	....	....	....	....	....	....	....	....	....
	Farjestad	Sweden	33	2	0	2	4	....	....	....	....	....	....	....	....	....	11	0	1	1	2	....	....	....	....
2012-13	Farjestad	Sweden	11	0	3	3	2	....	....	....	....	....	....	....	....	....	....	....	....	....	....	....	....	....	....
2013-14	**Edmonton**	**NHL**	**17**	**1**	**2**	**3**	**0**	**0**	**0**	**0**	**14**	**7.1**	**–6**	**0**	**0.0**	**15:48**	....	....	....	....	....	....	....	....	....
	Oklahoma City	AHL	48	1	9	10	10	....	....	....	....	....	....	....	....	....	2	0	1	1	4	....	....	....	....
2014-15	**Edmonton**	**NHL**	**60**	**2**	**18**	**20**	**4**	**0**	**0**	**0**	**98**	**2.0**	**–21**	**0**	**0.0**	**22:00**	....	....	....	....	....	....	....	....	....
	Oklahoma City	AHL	9	1	7	8	4	....	....	....	....	....	....	....	....	....	....	....	....	....	....	....	....	....	....
2015-16	**Edmonton**	**NHL**	**30**	**4**	**8**	**12**	**6**	**0**	**0**	**1**	**48**	**8.3**	**–4**	**0**	**0.0**	**21:53**	....	....	....	....	....	....	....	....	....
2016-17	**Edmonton**	**NHL**	**82**	**12**	**26**	**38**	**6**	**3**	**0**	**3**	**201**	**6.0**	**7**	**0**	**0.0**	**22:22**	**12**	**2**	**3**	**5**	**0**	**0**	**0**	**0**	**23:10**
	NHL Totals		**189**	**19**	**54**	**73**	**16**	**3**	**0**	**4**	**361**	**5.3**		**0**	**0.0**	**21:35**	**12**	**2**	**3**	**5**	**0**	**0**	**0**	**0**	**23:10**

• Missed majority of 2015-16 due to finger injury vs. NY Rangers, December 11, 2015 and recurring ankle injury.

KLEIN, Kevin

(KLIGHN, KEH-vihn)

Defense. Shoots right. 6'1", 202 lbs. Born, Kitchener, ON, December 13, 1984. Nashville's 3rd pick, 37th overall, in 2003 NHL Draft.

Season	Club	League	GP	G	A	Pts	PIM	PP	SH	GW	S	S%	+/-	TF	F%	Min	GP	G	A	Pts	PIM	PP	SH	GW	Min
99-2000	Kitchener Midget	Minor-ON	54	12	29	41	40	....	....	....	....	....	....	....	....	....	....	....	....	....	....	....	....	....	....
2000-01	St. Michael's	OHL	58	3	16	19	21	....	....	....	....	....	....	....	....	....	18	0	5	5	17	....	....	....	....
2001-02	St. Michael's	OHL	68	5	22	27	35	....	....	....	....	....	....	....	....	....	15	2	7	9	12	....	....	....	....
2002-03	St. Michael's	OHL	67	11	33	44	88	....	....	....	....	....	....	....	....	....	17	1	9	10	8	....	....	....	....
2003-04	St. Michael's	OHL	5	0	1	1	2	....	....	....	....	....	....	....	....	....	....	....	....	....	....	....	....	....	....
	Guelph Storm	OHL	46	6	23	29	40	....	....	....	....	....	....	....	....	....	22	10	11	21	12	....	....	....	....
2004-05	Milwaukee	AHL	65	4	12	16	22	....	....	....	....	....	....	....	....	....	7	0	0	0	11	....	....	....	....
	Rockford IceHogs	UHL	3	2	1	3	0	....	....	....	....	....	....	....	....	....	....	....	....	....	....	....	....	....	....
2005-06	**Nashville**	**NHL**	**2**	**0**	**0**	**0**	**0**	**0**	**0**	**0**	**0**	**0.0**	**–1**	**0**	**0.0**	**13:40**	....	....	....	....	....	....	....	....	....
	Milwaukee	AHL	76	10	33	43	31	....	....	....	....	....	....	....	....	....	21	3	7	10	31	....	....	....	....
2006-07	**Nashville**	**NHL**	**3**	**1**	**0**	**1**	**0**	**0**	**0**	**0**	**2**	**50.0**	**3**	**0**	**0.0**	**16:37**	....	....	....	....	....	....	....	....	....
	Milwaukee	AHL	70	5	15	20	67	....	....	....	....	....	....	....	....	....	4	1	0	1	0	....	....	....	....
2007-08	**Nashville**	**NHL**	**13**	**0**	**2**	**2**	**6**	**0**	**0**	**0**	**14**	**0.0**	**–3**	**0**	**0.0**	**14:24**	....	....	....	....	....	....	....	....	....
	Milwaukee	AHL	9	0	3	3	2	....	....	....	....	....	....	....	....	....	....	....	....	....	....	....	....	....	....
2008-09	**Nashville**	**NHL**	**63**	**4**	**8**	**12**	**19**	**1**	**0**	**0**	**41**	**9.8**	**–2**	**0**	**0.0**	**12:40**	....	....	....	....	....	....	....	....	....
2009-10	**Nashville**	**NHL**	**81**	**1**	**10**	**11**	**27**	**0**	**0**	**0**	**67**	**1.5**	**–13**	**0**	**0.0**	**19:55**	**6**	**0**	**2**	**2**	**4**	**0**	**0**	**0**	**17:43**
2010-11	**Nashville**	**NHL**	**81**	**2**	**16**	**18**	**24**	**0**	**0**	**0**	**99**	**2.0**	**9**	**0**	**0.0**	**20:48**	**12**	**1**	**2**	**3**	**6**	**0**	**0**	**0**	**20:14**
2011-12	**Nashville**	**NHL**	**66**	**4**	**17**	**21**	**4**	**0**	**0**	**2**	**91**	**4.4**	**–8**	**0**	**0.0**	**19:56**	**10**	**2**	**2**	**4**	**2**	**0**	**0**	**1**	**19:31**
2012-13	Herlev Eagles	Denmark	8	1	2	3	29	....	....	....	....	....	....	....	....	....	....	....	....	....	....	....	....	....	....
	Nashville	**NHL**	**47**	**3**	**11**	**14**	**9**	**0**	**0**	**0**	**54**	**5.6**	**–1**	**0**	**0.0**	**20:25**	....	....	....	....	....	....	....	....	....
2013-14	**Nashville**	**NHL**	**47**	**1**	**2**	**3**	**21**	**0**	**0**	**0**	**49**	**2.0**	**–11**	**0**	**0.0**	**18:48**	....	....	....	....	....	....	....	....	....
	NY Rangers	**NHL**	**30**	**1**	**5**	**6**	**0**	**0**	**0**	**0**	**24**	**4.2**	**4**	**0**	**0.0**	**15:01**	**25**	**1**	**3**	**4**	**6**	**0**	**0**	**0**	**13:17**
2014-15	**NY Rangers**	**NHL**	**65**	**9**	**17**	**26**	**25**	**0**	**0**	**4**	**76**	**11.8**	**24**	**1**	**0.0**	**18:29**	**14**	**0**	**4**	**4**	**2**	**0**	**0**	**0**	**19:05**
2015-16	**NY Rangers**	**NHL**	**69**	**9**	**17**	**26**	**19**	**0**	**0**	**4**	**69**	**13.0**	**16**	**0**	**0.0**	**20:23**	**5**	**0**	**1**	**1**	**7**	**0**	**0**	**0**	**19:02**
2016-17	**NY Rangers**	**NHL**	**60**	**3**	**11**	**14**	**31**	**0**	**0**	**0**	**54**	**5.6**	**5**	**0**	**0.0**	**17:38**	**1**	**0**	**1**	**1**	**0**	**0**	**0**	**0**	**18:15**
	NHL Totals		**627**	**38**	**116**	**154**	**185**	**1**	**0**	**10**	**640**	**5.9**		**1**	**0.0**	**18:34**	**73**	**4**	**15**	**19**	**27**	**0**	**0**	**1**	**17:13**

Signed as a free agent by **Herlev** (Denmark), November 14, 2012. Traded to **NY Rangers** by **Nashville** for Michael Del Zotto, January 22, 2014.

KLINGBERG, John
(KLIHNG-buhrg, JAWN) **DAL**

Defense. Shoots right. 6'2", 180 lbs. Born, Lerum, Sweden, August 14, 1992. Dallas' 5th pick, 131st overall, in 2010 NHL Draft.

			Regular Season														Playoffs								
Season	Club	League	GP	G	A	Pts	PIM	PP	SH	GW	S	S%	+/-	TF	F%	Min	GP	G	A	Pts	PIM	PP	SH	GW	Min
2008-09	Frolunda U18	Swe-U18	30	3	12	15	12	....	....	....	....	....	....	....	....	....	3	0	0	0	0	....	....	....	....
2009-10	Frolunda U18	Swe-U18	20	3	13	16	22	....	....	....	....	....	....	....	....	....	7	2	9	11	10	....	....	....	....
	Frolunda Jr.	Swe-Jr.	27	0	5	5	32	....	....	....	....	....	....	....	....	....	5	1	0	1	6	....	....	....	....
2010-11	Frolunda	Sweden	26	0	5	5	10	....	....	....	....	....	....	....	....	....	....	....	....	....	....	....	....	....	....
	Boras HC	Sweden-2	7	1	0	1	2	....	....	....	....	....	....	....	....	....	....	....	....	....	....	....	....	....	....
	Frolunda Jr.	Swe-Jr.	13	3	14	17	29	....	....	....	....	....	....	....	....	....	7	1	10	11	6	....	....	....	....
2011-12	Jokerit Helsinki	Finland	20	1	2	3	8	....	....	....	....	....	....	....	....	....	....	....	....	....	....	....	....	....	....
	Skelleftea AIK	Sweden	16	1	3	4	6	....	....	....	....	....	....	....	....	....	16	0	4	4	14	....	....	....	....
2012-13	Skelleftea AIK Jr.	Swe-Jr.	1	0	0	0	0	....	....	....	....	....	....	....	....	....	....	....	....	....	....	....	....	....	....
	Skelleftea AIK	Sweden	25	1	12	13	6	....	....	....	....	....	....	....	....	....	13	1	3	4	8	....	....	....	....
	Texas Stars	AHL	....	....	....	....	....	....	....	....	....	....	....	....	....	....	1	0	0	0	0	....	....	....	....
2013-14	Frolunda	Sweden	50	11	17	28	12	....	....	....	....	....	....	....	....	....	7	0	4	4	2	....	....	....	....
	Texas Stars	AHL	3	0	1	1	4	....	....	....	....	....	....	....	....	....	....	....	....	....	....	....	....	....	....
2014-15	**Dallas**	**NHL**	**65**	**11**	**29**	**40**	**32**	**2**	**0**	**3**	**98**	**11.2**	**5**	**0**	**0.0**	**21:50**	....	....	....	....	....	....	....	....	....
	Texas Stars	AHL	10	4	8	12	6	....	....	....	....	....	....	....	....	....	....	....	....	....	....	....	....	....	....
2015-16	**Dallas**	**NHL**	**76**	**10**	**48**	**58**	**30**	**2**	**0**	**4**	**171**	**5.8**	**22**	**0**	**0.0**	**22:41**	**13**	**1**	**3**	**4**	**2**	**1**	**0**	**0**	**24:48**
2016-17	**Dallas**	**NHL**	**80**	**13**	**36**	**49**	**34**	**4**	**0**	**3**	**124**	**10.5**	**2**	**1**	**100.0**	**23:21**	....	....	....	....	....	....	....	....	....
	NHL Totals		**221**	**34**	**113**	**147**	**96**	**8**	**0**	**10**	**393**	**8.7**		**1**	**100.0**	**22:41**	**13**	**1**	**3**	**4**	**2**	**1**	**0**	**0**	**24:48**

NHL All-Rookie Team (2015)

Signed as a free agent by **Frolunda** (Sweden), May 20, 2013.

KNIGHT, Corban
(NIGHT, KOHR-buhn) **PHI**

Center. Shoots right. 6'2", 195 lbs. Born, Oliver, BC, September 10, 1990. Florida's 5th pick, 135th overall, in 2009 NHL Draft.

			Regular Season														Playoffs								
Season	Club	League	GP	G	A	Pts	PIM	PP	SH	GW	S	S%	+/-	TF	F%	Min	GP	G	A	Pts	PIM	PP	SH	GW	Min
2006-07	UFA Bisons	AMHL	36	6	18	24	44	....	....	....	....	....	....	....	....	....	8	2	4	6	16	....	....	....	....
2007-08	UFA Bisons	AMHL	36	29	36	65	64	....	....	....	....	....	....	....	....	....	6	5	4	9	10	....	....	....	....
	Okotoks Oilers	AJHL	4	1	0	1	0	....	....	....	....	....	....	....	....	....	7	0	0	0	0	....	....	....	....
2008-09	Okotoks Oilers	AJHL	61	34	38	72	55	....	....	....	....	....	....	....	....	....	9	10	2	12	12	....	....	....	....
2009-10	North Dakota	WCHA	37	6	7	13	35	....	....	....	....	....	....	....	....	....	....	....	....	....	....	....	....	....	....
2010-11	North Dakota	WCHA	44	14	30	44	34	....	....	....	....	....	....	....	....	....	....	....	....	....	....	....	....	....	....
2011-12	North Dakota	WCHA	39	16	24	40	36	....	....	....	....	....	....	....	....	....	....	....	....	....	....	....	....	....	....
2012-13	North Dakota	WCHA	41	16	33	49	40	....	....	....	....	....	....	....	....	....	....	....	....	....	....	....	....	....	....
2013-14	**Calgary**	**NHL**	**7**	**1**	**0**	**1**	**0**	**0**	**0**	**0**	**4**	**25.0**	**–1**	**51**	**47.1**	**7:56**	....	....	....	....	....	....	....	....	....
	Abbotsford Heat	AHL	70	18	27	45	50	....	....	....	....	....	....	....	....	....	2	0	1	1	2	....	....	....	....
2014-15	**Calgary**	**NHL**	**2**	**0**	**0**	**0**	**0**	**0**	**0**	**0**	**2**	**0.0**	**0**	**11**	**81.8**	**6:24**	....	....	....	....	....	....	....	....	....
	Adirondack	AHL	22	8	4	12	12	....	....	....	....	....	....	....	....	....	....	....	....	....	....	....	....	....	....
	San Antonio	AHL	36	8	16	24	8	....	....	....	....	....	....	....	....	....	3	1	0	1	0	....	....	....	....
2015-16	**Florida**	**NHL**	**20**	**2**	**5**	**7**	**4**	**0**	**0**	**0**	**11**	**18.2**	**3**	**106**	**50.9**	**9:38**	....	....	....	....	....	....	....	....	....
	Portland Pirates	AHL	33	4	7	11	8	....	....	....	....	....	....	....	....	....	5	0	3	3	6	....	....	....	....
2016-17	Lehigh Valley	AHL	72	11	29	40	44	....	....	....	....	....	....	....	....	....	5	0	1	1	2	....	....	....	....
	NHL Totals		**29**	**3**	**5**	**8**	**4**	**0**	**0**	**0**	**17**	**17.6**		**168**	**51.8**	**9:00**	....	....	....	....	....	....	....	....	....

WCHA Second All-Star Team (2013) • NCAA West Second All-American Team (2013)

Traded to **Calgary** by **Florida** for Calgary's 4th round pick (Michael Downing) in 2013 NHL Draft, June 18, 2013. Traded to **Florida** by **Calgary** for Drew Shore, January 9, 2015. Signed as a free agent by **Lehigh Valley** (AHL), September 1, 2016. Signed as a free agent by **Philadelphia**, July 1, 2017.

KOEKKOEK, Slater
(KOO-KOO, SLAY-tuhr) **T.B.**

Defense. Shoots left. 6'2", 198 lbs. Born, Winchester, ON, February 18, 1994. Tampa Bay's 1st pick, 10th overall, in 2012 NHL Draft.

			Regular Season														Playoffs								
Season	Club	League	GP	G	A	Pts	PIM	PP	SH	GW	S	S%	+/-	TF	F%	Min	GP	G	A	Pts	PIM	PP	SH	GW	Min
2008-09	Notre Dame	Minor-SK	47	20	39	59	40	....	....	....	....	....	....	....	....	....	....	....	....	....	....	....	....	....	....
2009-10	Notre Dame	SMHL	44	16	27	43	91	....	....	....	....	....	....	....	....	....	13	3	4	7	6	....	....	....	....
2010-11	Peterborough	OHL	65	7	16	23	67	....	....	....	....	....	....	....	....	....	....	....	....	....	....	....	....	....	....
2011-12	Peterborough	OHL	26	5	13	18	17	....	....	....	....	....	....	....	....	....	....	....	....	....	....	....	....	....	....
2012-13	Peterborough	OHL	40	6	22	28	28	....	....	....	....	....	....	....	....	....	....	....	....	....	....	....	....	....	....
	Windsor Spitfires	OHL	2	0	1	1	0	....	....	....	....	....	....	....	....	....	....	....	....	....	....	....	....	....	....
2013-14	Windsor Spitfires	OHL	62	15	38	53	51	....	....	....	....	....	....	....	....	....	....	....	....	....	....	....	....	....	....
2014-15	**Tampa Bay**	**NHL**	**3**	**0**	**0**	**0**	**2**	**0**	**0**	**0**	**6**	**0.0**	**0**	**0**	**0.0**	**16:35**	....	....	....	....	....	....	....	....	....
	Syracuse Crunch	AHL	72	5	21	26	44	....	....	....	....	....	....	....	....	....	3	0	1	1	6	....	....	....	....
2015-16	**Tampa Bay**	**NHL**	**9**	**0**	**1**	**1**	**2**	**0**	**0**	**0**	**11**	**0.0**	**–1**	**0**	**0.0**	**10:19**	**10**	**0**	**1**	**1**	**2**	**0**	**0**	**0**	**10:04**
	Syracuse Crunch	AHL	60	5	10	15	26	....	....	....	....	....	....	....	....	....	....	....	....	....	....	....	....	....	....
2016-17	**Tampa Bay**	**NHL**	**29**	**0**	**4**	**4**	**8**	**0**	**0**	**0**	**27**	**0.0**	**–4**	**0**	**0.0**	**12:59**	....	....	....	....	....	....	....	....	....
	Syracuse Crunch	AHL	48	2	11	13	14	....	....	....	....	....	....	....	....	....	22	1	6	7	4	....	....	....	....
	NHL Totals		**41**	**0**	**5**	**5**	**12**	**0**	**0**	**0**	**44**	**0.0**		**0**	**0.0**	**12:40**	**10**	**0**	**1**	**1**	**2**	**0**	**0**	**0**	**10:04**

OHL First All-Star Team (2014)

• Missed majority of 2011-12 due to shoulder injury vs. Windsor (OHL), November 27, 2011.

KOIVU, Mikko
(KOI-voo, MEE-koh) **MIN**

Center. Shoots left. 6'3", 215 lbs. Born, Turku, Finland, March 12, 1983. Minnesota's 1st pick, 6th overall, in 2001 NHL Draft.

			Regular Season														Playoffs								
Season	Club	League	GP	G	A	Pts	PIM	PP	SH	GW	S	S%	+/-	TF	F%	Min	GP	G	A	Pts	PIM	PP	SH	GW	Min
99-2000	TPS Turku U18	Fin-U18	11	4	9	13	18	....	....	....	....	....	....	....	....	....	....	....	....	....	....	....	....	....	....
	TPS Turku Jr.	Fin-Jr.	30	4	8	12	22	....	....	....	....	....	....	....	....	....	13	1	4	5	8	....	....	....	....
2000-01	TPS Turku U18	Fin-U18	....	....	....	....	....	....	....	....	....	....	....	....	....	....	7	2	10	12	2	....	....	....	....
	TPS Turku Jr.	Fin-Jr.	26	9	36	45	26	....	....	....	....	....	....	....	....	....	3	1	1	2	6	....	....	....	....
	TPS Turku	Finland	21	0	1	1	2	....	....	....	....	....	....	....	....	....	....	....	....	....	....	....	....	....	....
2001-02	TPS Turku Jr.	Fin-Jr.	2	0	1	1	12	....	....	....	....	....	....	....	....	....	....	....	....	....	....	....	....	....	....
	TPS Turku	Finland	48	4	3	7	34	....	....	....	....	....	....	....	....	....	8	0	3	3	4	....	....	....	....
2002-03	TPS Turku	Finland	37	7	13	20	20	....	....	....	....	....	....	....	....	....	7	2	2	4	6	....	....	....	....
2003-04	TPS Turku	Finland	45	6	24	30	36	....	....	....	....	....	....	....	....	....	13	1	7	8	8	....	....	....	....
2004-05	Houston Aeros	AHL	67	20	28	48	47	....	....	....	....	....	....	....	....	....	5	1	0	1	2	....	....	....	....
2005-06	**Minnesota**	**NHL**	**64**	**6**	**15**	**21**	**40**	**3**	**0**	**0**	**96**	**6.3**	**–9**	**724**	**47.4**	**13:17**	....	....	....	....	....	....	....	....	....
	Finland	Olympics	8	0	0	0	6	....	....	....	....	....	....	....	....	....	....	....	....	....	....	....	....	....	....
2006-07	**Minnesota**	**NHL**	**82**	**20**	**34**	**54**	**58**	**9**	**2**	**2**	**162**	**12.3**	**6**	**1165**	**50.9**	**17:29**	**5**	**1**	**0**	**1**	**4**	**0**	**0**	**0**	**17:43**
2007-08	**Minnesota**	**NHL**	**57**	**11**	**31**	**42**	**42**	**2**	**0**	**2**	**144**	**7.6**	**13**	**1032**	**52.5**	**20:53**	**6**	**4**	**1**	**5**	**4**	**0**	**1**	**0**	**21:56**
2008-09	**Minnesota**	**NHL**	**79**	**20**	**47**	**67**	**66**	**5**	**4**	**3**	**236**	**8.5**	**2**	**1625**	**52.7**	**21:29**	....	....	....	....	....	....	....	....	....
2009-10	**Minnesota**	**NHL**	**80**	**22**	**49**	**71**	**50**	**8**	**1**	**2**	**246**	**8.9**	**–2**	**1518**	**56.9**	**20:45**	....	....	....	....	....	....	....	....	....
	Finland	Olympics	6	0	4	4	2	....	....	....	....	....	....	....	....	....	....	....	....	....	....	....	....	....	....
2010-11	**Minnesota**	**NHL**	**71**	**17**	**45**	**62**	**50**	**7**	**1**	**3**	**191**	**8.9**	**4**	**1293**	**52.8**	**19:29**	....	....	....	....	....	....	....	....	....
2011-12	**Minnesota**	**NHL**	**55**	**12**	**32**	**44**	**28**	**2**	**1**	**2**	**129**	**9.3**	**10**	**1123**	**52.3**	**21:21**	....	....	....	....	....	....	....	....	....
2012-13	TPS Turku	Finland	10	5	5	10	16	....	....	....	....	....	....	....	....	....	....	....	....	....	....	....	....	....	....
	Minnesota	**NHL**	**48**	**11**	**26**	**37**	**26**	**0**	**0**	**3**	**127**	**8.7**	**2**	**971**	**54.0**	**21:06**	**5**	**0**	**0**	**0**	**8**	**0**	**0**	**0**	**20:30**
2013-14	**Minnesota**	**NHL**	**65**	**11**	**43**	**54**	**24**	**2**	**0**	**4**	**147**	**7.5**	**0**	**1311**	**54.8**	**20:56**	**13**	**1**	**6**	**7**	**10**	**0**	**0**	**0**	**20:32**
2014-15	**Minnesota**	**NHL**	**80**	**14**	**34**	**48**	**38**	**4**	**0**	**4**	**179**	**7.8**	**2**	**1791**	**55.2**	**19:16**	**10**	**1**	**3**	**4**	**2**	**1**	**0**	**0**	**18:13**
2015-16	**Minnesota**	**NHL**	**82**	**17**	**39**	**56**	**40**	**10**	**1**	**2**	**141**	**12.1**	**6**	**1758**	**56.1**	**19:56**	**6**	**3**	**2**	**5**	**2**	**1**	**0**	**2**	**21:29**
2016-17	**Minnesota**	**NHL**	**80**	**18**	**40**	**58**	**34**	**2**	**0**	**4**	**139**	**12.9**	**27**	**1699**	**55.2**	**19:07**	**5**	**1**	**1**	**2**	**0**	**1**	**0**	**0**	**20:09**
	NHL Totals		**843**	**179**	**435**	**614**	**496**	**54**	**10**	**31**	**1937**	**9.2**		**16010**	**53.9**	**19:32**	**50**	**11**	**13**	**24**	**30**	**3**	**1**	**2**	**20:02**

Signed as a free agent by **TPS Turku** (Finland), October 22, 2012.

KOMAROV, Leo
(koh-mah-RAWV, L'YAY-oh) **TOR**

Center. Shoots left. 5'11", 211 lbs. Born, Narva, USSR, January 23, 1987. Toronto's 7th pick, 180th overall, in 2006 NHL Draft.

			Regular Season														Playoffs								
Season	Club	League	GP	G	A	Pts	PIM	PP	SH	GW	S	S%	+/-	TF	F%	Min	GP	G	A	Pts	PIM	PP	SH	GW	Min
2003-04	Sport Vaasa U18	Fin-U18	30	9	15	24	8	....	....	....	....	....	....	....	....	....	....	....	....	....	....	....	....	....	....
2004-05	Assat Pori U18	Fin-U18	9	4	5	9	62	....	....	....	....	....	....	....	....	....	....	....	....	....	....	....	....	....	....
	Assat Pori Jr.	Fin-Jr.	38	8	6	13	59	....	....	....	....	....	....	....	....	....	2	0	0	0	2	....	....	....	....
2005-06	Suomi U20	Finland-2	5	0	3	3	4	....	....	....	....	....	....	....	....	....	....	....	....	....	....	....	....	....	....
	Assat Pori Jr.	Fin-Jr.	10	5	6	11	59	....	....	....	....	....	....	....	....	....	2	2	1	3	10	....	....	....	....
	Assat Pori	Finland	44	3	3	6	106	....	....	....	....	....	....	....	....	....	14	1	3	4	22	....	....	....	....

			Regular Season														Playoffs								
Season	Club	League	GP	G	A	Pts	PIM	PP	SH	GW	S	S%	+/-	TF	F%	Min	GP	G	A	Pts	PIM	PP	SH	GW	Min
2006-07	Suomi U20	Finland-2	1	1	0	1	0	....	....	....	....	....	....	....	....	....	....	....	....	....	....	....	....	....	....
	Pelicans Lahti	Finland	49	3	9	12	108	....	....	....	....	....	....	....	....	....	6	1	0	1	6	....	....	....	....
2007-08	Pelicans Lahti Jr.	Fin-Jr.	2	0	3	3	0	....	....	....	....	....	....	....	....	....	....	....	....	....	....	....	....	....	....
	Pelicans Lahti	Finland	53	4	10	14	76	....	....	....	....	....	....	....	....	....	6	1	1	2	8	....	....	....	....
2008-09	Pelicans Lahti	Finland	56	8	16	24	144	....	....	....	....	....	....	....	....	....	10	0	1	1	16	....	....	....	....
2009-10	Dynamo Moscow	KHL	47	5	11	16	44	....	....	....	....	....	....	....	....	....	4	0	1	1	16	....	....	....	....
2010-11	Dynamo Moscow	KHL	52	14	12	26	70	....	....	....	....	....	....	....	....	....	6	4	2	6	2	....	....	....	....
2011-12	Dynamo Moscow	KHL	46	11	13	24	58	....	....	....	....	....	....	....	....	....	20	5	2	7	49	....	....	....	....
2012-13	Toronto Marlies	AHL	14	6	3	9	22	....	....	....	....	....	....	....	....	....	....	....	....	....	....	....	....	....	....
	Dynamo Moscow	KHL	13	2	8	10	42	....	....	....	....	....	....	....	....	....	....	....	....	....	....	....	....	....	....
	Toronto	**NHL**	**42**	**4**	**5**	**9**	**18**	**0**	**0**	**3**	**51**	**7.8**	**–1**	**57**	**50.9**	**13:56**	**7**	**0**	**0**	**0**	**17**	**0**	**0**	**0**	**9:13**
2013-14	Dynamo Moscow	KHL	52	12	22	34	42	....	....	....	....	....	....	....	....	....	7	3	1	4	22	....	....	....	....
	Finland	Olympics	6	0	0	0	0	....	....	....	....	....	....	....	....	....	....	....	....	....	....	....	....	....	....
2014-15	**Toronto**	**NHL**	**62**	**8**	**18**	**26**	**18**	**0**	**1**	**1**	**84**	**9.5**	**0**	**192**	**49.5**	**14:42**	....	....	....	....	....	....	....	....	....
2015-16	**Toronto**	**NHL**	**67**	**19**	**17**	**36**	**40**	**4**	**1**	**2**	**130**	**14.6**	**–12**	**127**	**48.8**	**17:50**	....	....	....	....	....	....	....	....	....
2016-17	**Toronto**	**NHL**	**82**	**14**	**18**	**32**	**31**	**4**	**1**	**1**	**114**	**12.3**	**6**	**202**	**45.1**	**17:04**	**6**	**0**	**1**	**1**	**2**	**0**	**0**	**0**	**19:37**
	NHL Totals		**253**	**45**	**58**	**103**	**107**	**8**	**3**	**7**	**379**	**11.9**		**578**	**47.9**	**16:10**	**13**	**0**	**1**	**1**	**19**	**0**	**0**	**0**	**14:01**

Played in NHL All-Star Game (2016)

Signed as a free agent by **Dynamo Moscow** (KHL), June 10, 2013. Signed as a free agent by **Toronto**, July 1, 2014.

KONECNY, Travis
(koh-NEH-kee, TRA-vihs) **PHI**

Center. Shoots right. 5'10", 177 lbs. Born, London, ON, March 11, 1997. Philadelphia's 2nd pick, 24th overall, in 2015 NHL Draft.

Season	Club	League	GP	G	A	Pts	PIM	PP	SH	GW	S	S%	+/-	TF	F%	Min	GP	G	A	Pts	PIM	PP	SH	GW	Min
2011-12	Elgin-Middl. Bant.	Minor-ON	63	78	74	152	137	....	....	....	....	....	....	....	....	....	....	....	....	....	....	....	....	....	....
	Elgin-Mid. Chiefs	Minor-ON	3	3	4	7	0	....	....	....	....	....	....	....	....	....	....	....	....	....	....	....	....	....	....
2012-13	Elgin-Mid. Chiefs	Minor-ON	27	31	35	66	72	....	....	....	....	....	....	....	....	....	11	7	11	18	42	....	....	....	....
	Elgin-Mid. Chiefs	Other	16	15	15	30	....	....	....	....	....	....	....	....	....	....	....	....	....	....	....	....	....	....	....
2013-14	Ottawa 67's	OHL	63	26	44	70	18	....	....	....	....	....	....	....	....	....	....	....	....	....	....	....	....	....	....
2014-15	Ottawa 67's	OHL	60	29	39	68	34	....	....	....	....	....	....	....	....	....	5	3	7	10	6	....	....	....	....
2015-16	Ottawa 67's	OHL	29	7	38	45	6	....	....	....	....	....	....	....	....	....	....	....	....	....	....	....	....	....	....
	Sarnia Sting	OHL	31	23	33	56	21	....	....	....	....	....	....	....	....	....	2	1	2	3	0	....	....	....	....
2016-17	**Philadelphia**	**NHL**	**70**	**11**	**17**	**28**	**49**	**3**	**0**	**0**	**133**	**8.3**	**–2**	**5**	**0.0**	**14:05**	....	....	....	....	....	....	....	....	....
	NHL Totals		**70**	**11**	**17**	**28**	**49**	**3**	**0**	**0**	**133**	**8.3**		**5**	**0.0**	**14:05**	....	....	....	....	....	....	....	....	....

OHL All-Rookie Team (2014) • OHL Rookie of the Year (2014) • E.J. McGuire Award of Excellence (2015)

KOPITAR, Anze
(KOH-pih-tahr, AHN-zheh) **L.A.**

Center. Shoots left. 6'3", 224 lbs. Born, Jesenice, Yugoslavia, August 24, 1987. Los Angeles' 1st pick, 11th overall, in 2005 NHL Draft.

Season	Club	League	GP	G	A	Pts	PIM	PP	SH	GW	S	S%	+/-	TF	F%	Min	GP	G	A	Pts	PIM	PP	SH	GW	Min
2002-03	Jesenice U18	Sloven-U18	14	38	38	76	10	....	....	....	....	....	....	....	....	....	....	....	....	....	....	....	....	....	....
	Jesenice Jr.	Sloven-Jr.	20	15	12	27	8	....	....	....	....	....	....	....	....	....	....	....	....	....	....	....	....	....	....
	Kranjska Gora	Slovenia	11	4	4	8	4	....	....	....	....	....	....	....	....	....	....	....	....	....	....	....	....	....	....
2003-04	Jesenice Jr.	Sloven-Jr.	25	32	28	60	16	....	....	....	....	....	....	....	....	....	....	....	....	....	....	....	....	....	....
	Kranjska Gora	Slovenia	21	14	11	25	10	....	....	....	....	....	....	....	....	....	4	1	1	2	0	....	....	....	....
2004-05	Sodertalje SK U18	Swe-U18	1	1	2	3	0	....	....	....	....	....	....	....	....	....	1	0	0	0	2	....	....	....	....
	Sodertalje SK Jr.	Swe-Jr.	30	28	21	49	26	....	....	....	....	....	....	....	....	....	2	1	1	2	0	....	....	....	....
	Sodertalje SK	Sweden	5	0	0	0	0	....	....	....	....	....	....	....	....	....	10	0	0	0	0	....	....	....	....
	Slovenia	Oly-Q	3	1	1	2	2	....	....	....	....	....	....	....	....	....	....	....	....	....	....	....	....	....	....
2005-06	Sodertalje SK	Sweden	47	8	12	20	28	....	....	....	....	....	....	....	....	....	....	....	....	....	....	....	....	....	....
	Sodertalje SK	Sweden-Q	10	7	4	11	6	....	....	....	....	....	....	....	....	....	....	....	....	....	....	....	....	....	....
2006-07	**Los Angeles**	**NHL**	**72**	**20**	**41**	**61**	**24**	**7**	**2**	**1**	**193**	**10.4**	**–12**	**1204**	**46.1**	**20:32**	....	....	....	....	....	....	....	....	....
2007-08	**Los Angeles**	**NHL**	**82**	**32**	**45**	**77**	**22**	**12**	**2**	**3**	**201**	**15.9**	**–15**	**1150**	**49.2**	**20:41**	....	....	....	....	....	....	....	....	....
2008-09	**Los Angeles**	**NHL**	**82**	**27**	**39**	**66**	**32**	**7**	**1**	**3**	**234**	**11.5**	**–17**	**1355**	**49.5**	**20:27**	....	....	....	....	....	....	....	....	....
2009-10	**Los Angeles**	**NHL**	**82**	**34**	**47**	**81**	**16**	**14**	**1**	**2**	**259**	**13.1**	**6**	**1211**	**49.7**	**21:47**	**6**	**2**	**3**	**5**	**2**	**1**	**0**	**1**	**21:13**
2010-11	**Los Angeles**	**NHL**	**75**	**25**	**48**	**73**	**20**	**6**	**1**	**6**	**233**	**10.7**	**25**	**1160**	**49.9**	**21:35**	....	....	....	....	....	....	....	....	....
2011-12♦	**Los Angeles**	**NHL**	**82**	**25**	**51**	**76**	**20**	**8**	**2**	**2**	**230**	**10.9**	**12**	**1418**	**53.8**	**21:20**	**20**	***8**	***12**	***20**	**9**	**0**	***2**	**1**	**22:03**
2012-13	Mora IK	Sweden-2	31	10	24	34	14	....	....	....	....	....	....	....	....	....	....	....	....	....	....	....	....	....	....
	Los Angeles	**NHL**	**47**	**10**	**32**	**42**	**16**	**0**	**0**	**1**	**98**	**10.2**	**14**	**888**	**53.3**	**20:29**	**18**	**3**	**6**	**9**	**12**	**1**	**0**	**1**	**21:15**
2013-14♦	**Los Angeles**	**NHL**	**82**	**29**	**41**	**70**	**24**	**10**	**0**	**9**	**200**	**14.5**	**34**	**1451**	**53.3**	**20:53**	**26**	**5**	***21**	***26**	**14**	**1**	**0**	**1**	**21:13**
	Slovenia	Olympics	5	2	1	3	4	....	....	....	....	....	....	....	....	....	....	....	....	....	....	....	....	....	....
2014-15	**Los Angeles**	**NHL**	**79**	**16**	**48**	**64**	**10**	**6**	**0**	**4**	**134**	**11.9**	**–2**	**1430**	**52.6**	**19:23**	....	....	....	....	....	....	....	....	....
2015-16	**Los Angeles**	**NHL**	**81**	**25**	**49**	**74**	**16**	**5**	**1**	**8**	**177**	**14.1**	**34**	**1776**	**53.5**	**20:52**	**5**	**2**	**2**	**4**	**2**	**1**	**0**	**0**	**22:26**
2016-17	**Los Angeles**	**NHL**	**76**	**12**	**40**	**52**	**28**	**5**	**0**	**0**	**150**	**8.0**	**–10**	**1693**	**52.7**	**20:46**	....	....	....	....	....	....	....	....	....
	NHL Totals		**840**	**255**	**481**	**736**	**228**	**80**	**10**	**39**	**2109**	**12.1**		**14736**	**51.4**	**20:49**	**75**	**20**	**44**	**64**	**39**	**4**	**2**	**4**	**21:32**

Frank J. Selke Trophy (2016) • Lady Byng Memorial Trophy (2016)

Played in NHL All-Star Game (2008, 2011, 2015)

Signed as a free agent by **Mora** (Sweden-2), September 19, 2012.

KORPIKOSKI, Lauri
(kohr-pih-KAWS-kee, LOW-ree)

Left wing. Shoots left. 6'1", 193 lbs. Born, Turku, Finland, July 28, 1986. NY Rangers' 2nd pick, 19th overall, in 2004 NHL Draft.

Season	Club	League	GP	G	A	Pts	PIM	PP	SH	GW	S	S%	+/-	TF	F%	Min	GP	G	A	Pts	PIM	PP	SH	GW	Min
2002-03	TPS Turku U18	Fin-U18	21	7	4	11	10	....	....	....	....	....	....	....	....	....	....	....	....	....	....	....	....	....	....
2003-04	TPS Turku U18	Fin-U18	....	....	....	....	....	....	....	....	....	....	....	....	....	....	4	5	3	8	16	....	....	....	....
	TPS Turku Jr.	Fin-Jr.	36	12	8	20	20	....	....	....	....	....	....	....	....	....	4	0	2	2	4	....	....	....	....
2004-05	TPS Turku Jr.	Fin-Jr.	3	3	0	3	0	....	....	....	....	....	....	....	....	....	....	....	....	....	....	....	....	....	....
	TPS Turku	Finland	41	0	6	6	12	....	....	....	....	....	....	....	....	....	6	1	0	1	0	....	....	....	....
2005-06	TPS Turku Jr.	Fin-Jr.	1	1	0	1	2	....	....	....	....	....	....	....	....	....	....	....	....	....	....	....	....	....	....
	Suomi U20	Finland-2	3	1	3	4	0	....	....	....	....	....	....	....	....	....	....	....	....	....	....	....	....	....	....
	TPS Turku	Finland	51	3	4	7	16	....	....	....	....	....	....	....	....	....	2	0	1	1	0	....	....	....	....
	Hartford	AHL	5	2	1	3	0	....	....	....	....	....	....	....	....	....	11	1	0	1	2	....	....	....	....
2006-07	Hartford	AHL	78	11	27	38	23	....	....	....	....	....	....	....	....	....	7	0	0	0	0	....	....	....	....
2007-08	Hartford	AHL	79	23	27	50	71	....	....	....	....	....	....	....	....	....	5	1	1	2	0	....	....	....	....
	NY Rangers	**NHL**	....	....	....	....	....	....	....	....	....	....	....	....	....	....	**1**	**1**	**0**	**1**	**0**	**0**	**0**	**0**	**7:14**
2008-09	**NY Rangers**	**NHL**	**68**	**6**	**8**	**14**	**14**	**0**	**0**	**1**	**63**	**9.5**	**–10**	**220**	**40.0**	**10:55**	**7**	**0**	**2**	**2**	**0**	**0**	**0**	**0**	**13:10**
	Hartford	AHL	4	4	2	6	0	....	....	....	....	....	....	....	....	....	....	....	....	....	....	....	....	....	....
2009-10	**Phoenix**	**NHL**	**71**	**5**	**6**	**11**	**16**	**0**	**0**	**1**	**68**	**7.4**	**–10**	**49**	**28.6**	**12:18**	**7**	**1**	**0**	**1**	**2**	**0**	**1**	**0**	**16:16**
2010-11	**Phoenix**	**NHL**	**79**	**19**	**21**	**40**	**20**	**0**	**2**	**4**	**103**	**18.4**	**17**	**244**	**43.9**	**15:32**	**4**	**0**	**1**	**1**	**2**	**0**	**0**	**0**	**16:33**
2011-12	**Phoenix**	**NHL**	**82**	**17**	**20**	**37**	**14**	**0**	**3**	**3**	**146**	**11.6**	**3**	**87**	**26.4**	**17:08**	**11**	**0**	**0**	**0**	**2**	**0**	**0**	**0**	**18:16**
2012-13	TPS Turku	Finland	11	6	11	17	10	....	....	....	....	....	....	....	....	....	....	....	....	....	....	....	....	....	....
	Phoenix	**NHL**	**36**	**6**	**5**	**11**	**12**	**1**	**0**	**0**	**83**	**7.2**	**–3**	**16**	**37.5**	**17:07**	....	....	....	....	....	....	....	....	....
2013-14	**Phoenix**	**NHL**	**64**	**9**	**16**	**25**	**24**	**1**	**0**	**0**	**109**	**8.3**	**–7**	**17**	**29.4**	**16:05**	....	....	....	....	....	....	....	....	....
	Finland	Olympics	6	2	2	4	2	....	....	....	....	....	....	....	....	....	....	....	....	....	....	....	....	....	....
2014-15	**Arizona**	**NHL**	**69**	**6**	**15**	**21**	**12**	**5**	**0**	**1**	**82**	**7.3**	**–27**	**33**	**33.3**	**15:15**	....	....	....	....	....	....	....	....	....
2015-16	**Edmonton**	**NHL**	**71**	**10**	**12**	**22**	**10**	**2**	**1**	**2**	**88**	**11.4**	**–17**	**34**	**52.9**	**13:56**	....	....	....	....	....	....	....	....	....
2016-17	**Dallas**	**NHL**	**60**	**8**	**12**	**20**	**10**	**0**	**0**	**0**	**104**	**7.7**	**5**	**7**	**0.0**	**13:02**	....	....	....	....	....	....	....	....	....
	Columbus	**NHL**	**9**	**0**	**0**	**0**	**0**	**0**	**0**	**0**	**4**	**0.0**	**0**	**0**	**0.0**	**8:15**	....	....	....	....	....	....	....	....	....
	NHL Totals		**609**	**86**	**115**	**201**	**132**	**9**	**6**	**12**	**850**	**10.1**		**707**	**38.5**	**14:26**	**30**	**2**	**3**	**5**	**6**	**0**	**1**	**0**	**16:01**

Traded to **Phoenix** by **NY Rangers** for Enver Lisin, July 13, 2009. Signed as a free agent by **TPS Turku** (Finland), October 2, 2012. Traded to **Edmonton** by **Arizona** for Boyd Gordon, June 30, 2015. Signed as a free agent by **Dallas**, September 23, 2016. Traded to **Columbus** by **Dallas** for Dillon Heatherington, March 1, 2017.

KOSMACHUK, Scott
(KAWZ-muh-chuk, SKAWT)

Right wing. Shoots right. 5'11", 185 lbs. Born, Richmond Hill, ON, January 24, 1994. Winnipeg's 3rd pick, 70th overall, in 2012 NHL Draft.

Season	Club	League	GP	G	A	Pts	PIM	PP	SH	GW	S	S%	+/-	TF	F%	Min	GP	G	A	Pts	PIM	PP	SH	GW	Min
2009-10	Tor. Marlboros	GTHL	79	39	33	72	108	....	....	....	....	....	....	....	....	....	....	....	....	....	....	....	....	....	....
2010-11	Guelph Storm	OHL	68	6	15	21	25	....	....	....	....	....	....	....	....	....	6	1	0	1	5	....	....	....	....
2011-12	Guelph Storm	OHL	67	30	29	59	110	....	....	....	....	....	....	....	....	....	6	2	3	5	12	....	....	....	....
2012-13	Guelph Storm	OHL	68	35	30	65	105	....	....	....	....	....	....	....	....	....	5	1	0	1	13	....	....	....	....
2013-14	Guelph Storm	OHL	68	49	52	101	83	....	....	....	....	....	....	....	....	....	20	10	18	28	27	....	....	....	....
2014-15	St. John's IceCaps	AHL	70	14	14	28	62	....	....	....	....	....	....	....	....	....	....	....	....	....	....	....	....	....	....

Season	Club	League	GP	G	A	Pts	PIM	PP	SH	GW	S	S%	+/-	TF	F%	Min	GP	G	A	Pts	PIM	PP	SH	GW	Min
			Regular Season														Playoffs								
2015-16	**Winnipeg**	**NHL**	**8**	**0**	**3**	**3**	**2**	0	0	0	9	0.0	1	0	0.0	11:32	....	....	....	....	....	....	....	....	....
	Manitoba Moose	AHL	67	19	17	36	41	....	....	....	....	....	....	....	....	....	....	....	....	....	....	....	....	....	....
2016-17	Manitoba Moose	AHL	58	11	17	28	47	....	....	....	....	....	....	....	....	....	....	....	....	....	....	....	....	....	....
	NHL Totals		**8**	**0**	**3**	**3**	**2**	**0**	**0**	**0**	**9**	**0.0**		**0**	**0.0**	**11:32**	....	....	....	....	....	....	....	....	....

OHL Second All-Star Team (2014)

KOSSILA, Kalle

(KOH-sih-la, KAL-ee) **ANA**

Left wing. Shoots left. 5'11", 175 lbs. Born, Kauniainen, Finland, April 14, 1993.

Season	Club	League	GP	G	A	Pts	PIM	PP	SH	GW	S	S%	+/-	TF	F%	Min	GP	G	A	Pts	PIM	PP	SH	GW	Min
2009-10	Blues Espoo U18	Fin-U18	33	10	16	26	10	....	....	....	....	....	....	....	....	....	11	5	6	11	4	....	....	....	....
2010-11	Blues Espoo U18	Fin-U18	5	4	10	14	2	....	....	....	....	....	....	....	....	....	4	3	4	7	0	....	....	....	....
	Blues Espoo Jr.	Fin-Jr.	30	8	11	19	6	....	....	....	....	....	....	....	....	....	12	3	5	8	0	....	....	....	....
2011-12	Blues Espoo Jr.	Fin-Jr.	42	20	37	57	22	....	....	....	....	....	....	....	....	....	4	1	1	2	0	....	....	....	....
2012-13	St. Cloud State	WCHA	40	15	18	33	12	....	....	....	....	....	....	....	....	....	....	....	....	....	....	....	....	....	....
2013-14	St. Cloud State	NCHC	38	13	27	40	16	....	....	....	....	....	....	....	....	....	....	....	....	....	....	....	....	....	....
2014-15	St. Cloud State	NCHC	38	6	20	26	29	....	....	....	....	....	....	....	....	....	....	....	....	....	....	....	....	....	....
2015-16	St. Cloud State	NCHC	41	14	*40	54	14	....	....	....	....	....	....	....	....	....	....	....	....	....	....	....	....	....	....
	San Diego Gulls	AHL	6	2	2	4	0	....	....	....	....	....	....	....	....	....	7	2	0	2	2	....	....	....	....
2016-17	**Anaheim**	**NHL**	**1**	**0**	**0**	**0**	**0**	0	0	0	1	0.0	0	7	42.9	6:54	....	....	....	....	....	....	....	....	....
	San Diego Gulls	AHL	65	14	34	48	8	....	....	....	....	....	....	....	....	....	10	2	4	6	2	....	....	....	....
	NHL Totals		**1**	**0**	**0**	**0**	**0**	**0**	**0**	**0**	**1**	**0.0**		**7**	**42.9**	**6:54**	....	....	....	....	....	....	....	....	....

NCHC Second All-Star Team (2016)

Signed as a free agent by **Anaheim**, March 30, 2016.

KOSTKA, Michael

(KOHST-kuh, MIGH-kuhl)

Defense. Shoots right. 6'1", 210 lbs. Born, Etobicoke, ON, November 28, 1985.

Season	Club	League	GP	G	A	Pts	PIM	PP	SH	GW	S	S%	+/-	TF	F%	Min	GP	G	A	Pts	PIM	PP	SH	GW	Min
2001-02	Ajax Axemen	ON-Jr.A	19	1	4	5	8	....	....	....	....	....	....	....	....	....	....	....	....	....	....	....	....	....	....
2002-03	Ajax Axemen	ON-Jr.A	39	4	11	15	32	....	....	....	....	....	....	....	....	....	....	....	....	....	....	....	....	....	....
2003-04	Aurora Tigers	ON-Jr.A	42	9	27	36	4	....	....	....	....	....	....	....	....	....	....	....	....	....	....	....	....	....	....
2004-05	Massachusetts	H-East	32	1	5	6	14	....	....	....	....	....	....	....	....	....	....	....	....	....	....	....	....	....	....
2005-06	Massachusetts	H-East	36	2	6	8	20	....	....	....	....	....	....	....	....	....	....	....	....	....	....	....	....	....	....
2006-07	Massachusetts	H-East	39	3	15	18	20	....	....	....	....	....	....	....	....	....	....	....	....	....	....	....	....	....	....
2007-08	Massachusetts	H-East	36	9	12	21	20	....	....	....	....	....	....	....	....	....	....	....	....	....	....	....	....	....	....
	Rochester	AHL	1	0	0	0	2	....	....	....	....	....	....	....	....	....	....	....	....	....	....	....	....	....	....
2008-09	Portland Pirates	AHL	80	4	26	30	33	....	....	....	....	....	....	....	....	....	4	1	0	1	6	....	....	....	....
2009-10	Portland Pirates	AHL	76	2	25	27	37	....	....	....	....	....	....	....	....	....	4	0	0	0	0	....	....	....	....
2010-11	Rochester	AHL	80	16	38	54	46	....	....	....	....	....	....	....	....	....	....	....	....	....	....	....	....	....	....
2011-12	San Antonio	AHL	18	2	4	6	14	....	....	....	....	....	....	....	....	....	....	....	....	....	....	....	....	....	....
	Norfolk Admirals	AHL	52	7	25	32	43	....	....	....	....	....	....	....	....	....	18	6	6	12	8	....	....	....	....
2012-13	Toronto Marlies	AHL	34	6	28	34	38	....	....	....	....	....	....	....	....	....	....	....	....	....	....	....	....	....	....
	Toronto	**NHL**	**35**	**0**	**8**	**8**	**27**	0	0	0	49	0.0	-7	0	0.0	22:05	1	0	0	0	0	0	0	0	22:22
2013-14	**Chicago**	**NHL**	**9**	**2**	**1**	**3**	**8**	0	0	1	18	11.1	3	0	0.0	14:26	....	....	....	....	....	....	....	....	....
	Tampa Bay	**NHL**	**19**	**2**	**6**	**8**	**0**	0	0	0	31	6.5	7	0	0.0	15:54	3	0	2	2	0	0	0	0	16:56
2014-15	**NY Rangers**	**NHL**	**7**	**0**	**1**	**1**	**0**	0	0	0	7	0.0	1	0	0.0	15:23	....	....	....	....	....	....	....	....	....
	Hartford	AHL	63	5	25	30	35	....	....	....	....	....	....	....	....	....	15	1	4	5	6	....	....	....	....
2015-16	**Ottawa**	**NHL**	**15**	**0**	**1**	**1**	**4**	0	0	0	9	0.0	6	0	0.0	14:51	....	....	....	....	....	....	....	....	....
	Binghamton	AHL	50	5	24	29	20	....	....	....	....	....	....	....	....	....	....	....	....	....	....	....	....	....	....
2016-17	Binghamton	AHL	46	1	11	12	32	....	....	....	....	....	....	....	....	....	....	....	....	....	....	....	....	....	....
	Stockton Heat	AHL	15	2	10	12	4	....	....	....	....	....	....	....	....	....	5	1	2	3	6	....	....	....	....
	NHL Totals		**85**	**4**	**17**	**21**	**39**	**0**	**0**	**1**	**114**	**3.5**		**0**	**0.0**	**18:04**	**4**	**0**	**2**	**2**	**0**	**0**	**0**	**0**	**18:17**

Hockey East Second All-Star Team (2008)

Signed as a free agent by **Buffalo**, March 25, 2008. Signed as a free agent by **Rochester** (AHL), August 25, 2010. Signed as a free agent by **Florida**, June 30, 2011. Traded to **Tampa Bay** by **Florida** with Evan Oberg for James Wright and Mike Vernace, December 2, 2011. Signed as a free agent by **Toronto**, July 1, 2012. Signed as a free agent by **Chicago**, July 19, 2013. Claimed on waivers by **Tampa Bay** from **Chicago**, February 23, 2014. • Missed majority of 2013-14 due to lower-body injury vs. Toronto, October 19, 2013 and as a healthy reserve. Signed as a free agent by **NY Rangers**, July 1, 2014. Signed as a free agent by **Ottawa**, July 1, 2015. Traded to **Calgary** by **Ottawa** with Curtis Lazar for Jyrki Jokipakka and Calgary's 2nd round pick (Alex Formenton) in 2017 NHL Draft, March 1, 2017.

KOSTOPOULOS, Tom

(kaw-STAWP-oh-lihs, TAWM)

Right wing. Shoots right. 6', 197 lbs. Born, Mississauga, ON, January 24, 1979. Pittsburgh's 9th pick, 204th overall, in 1999 NHL Draft.

Season	Club	League	GP	G	A	Pts	PIM	PP	SH	GW	S	S%	+/-	TF	F%	Min	GP	G	A	Pts	PIM	PP	SH	GW	Min
1995-96	Brampton	ON-Jr.A	24	9	9	18	28	....	....	....	....	....	....	....	....	....	....	....	....	....	....	....	....	....	....
1996-97	London Knights	OHL	64	13	12	25	67	....	....	....	....	....	....	....	....	....	....	....	....	....	....	....	....	....	....
1997-98	London Knights	OHL	66	24	26	50	108	....	....	....	....	....	....	....	....	....	16	6	4	10	26	....	....	....	....
1998-99	London Knights	OHL	66	27	60	87	114	....	....	....	....	....	....	....	....	....	25	19	16	35	32	....	....	....	....
99-2000	Wilkes-Barre	AHL	76	26	32	58	121	....	....	....	....	....	....	....	....	....	....	....	....	....	....	....	....	....	....
2000-01	Wilkes-Barre	AHL	80	16	36	52	120	....	....	....	....	....	....	....	....	....	21	3	9	12	6	....	....	....	....
2001-02	**Pittsburgh**	**NHL**	**11**	**1**	**2**	**3**	**9**	0	0	0	8	12.5	-1	0	0.0	12:03	....	....	....	....	....	....	....	....	....
	Wilkes-Barre	AHL	70	27	26	53	112	....	....	....	....	....	....	....	....	....	....	....	....	....	....	....	....	....	....
2002-03	**Pittsburgh**	**NHL**	**8**	**0**	**1**	**1**	**0**	0	0	0	6	0.0	-4	2	0.0	4:33	....	....	....	....	....	....	....	....	....
	Wilkes-Barre	AHL	71	21	42	63	131	....	....	....	....	....	....	....	....	....	6	1	2	3	7	....	....	....	....
2003-04	**Pittsburgh**	**NHL**	**60**	**9**	**13**	**22**	**67**	2	1	1	101	8.9	-14	10	30.0	14:26	....	....	....	....	....	....	....	....	....
	Wilkes-Barre	AHL	21	7	13	20	43	....	....	....	....	....	....	....	....	....	24	7	16	23	32	....	....	....	....
2004-05	Manchester	AHL	64	25	46	71	99	....	....	....	....	....	....	....	....	....	6	0	7	7	10	....	....	....	....
2005-06	**Los Angeles**	**NHL**	**76**	**8**	**14**	**22**	**100**	0	0	1	74	10.8	-8	30	36.7	12:56	....	....	....	....	....	....	....	....	....
2006-07	**Los Angeles**	**NHL**	**76**	**7**	**15**	**22**	**73**	0	0	0	90	7.8	-2	62	29.0	11:34	....	....	....	....	....	....	....	....	....
2007-08	**Montreal**	**NHL**	**67**	**7**	**6**	**13**	**113**	0	3	1	98	7.1	-3	28	28.6	11:16	12	3	1	4	6	0	0	1	13:35
2008-09	**Montreal**	**NHL**	**78**	**8**	**14**	**22**	**106**	0	1	0	121	6.6	-1	16	31.3	14:09	4	0	1	1	4	0	0	0	14:01
2009-10	**Carolina**	**NHL**	**82**	**8**	**13**	**21**	**106**	0	2	0	103	7.8	4	21	47.6	12:31	....	....	....	....	....	....	....	....	....
2010-11	**Carolina**	**NHL**	**17**	**1**	**3**	**4**	**30**	0	0	0	13	7.7	-1	14	28.6	11:17	....	....	....	....	....	....	....	....	....
	Calgary	**NHL**	**59**	**7**	**7**	**14**	**44**	2	0	0	66	10.6	-3	53	26.4	12:38	....	....	....	....	....	....	....	....	....
2011-12	**Calgary**	**NHL**	**81**	**4**	**8**	**12**	**57**	1	1	1	91	4.4	-15	84	29.8	12:19	....	....	....	....	....	....	....	....	....
2012-13	Wilkes-Barre	AHL	17	3	4	7	43	....	....	....	....	....	....	....	....	....	....	....	....	....	....	....	....	....	....
	New Jersey	**NHL**	**15**	**1**	**0**	**1**	**18**	0	0	0	13	7.7	0	5	60.0	9:06	....	....	....	....	....	....	....	....	....
2013-14	Wilkes-Barre	AHL	71	22	25	47	72	....	....	....	....	....	....	....	....	....	17	4	6	10	20	....	....	....	....
2014-15	Wilkes-Barre	AHL	72	16	28	44	62	....	....	....	....	....	....	....	....	....	8	3	2	5	12	....	....	....	....
2015-16	Wilkes-Barre	AHL	75	19	33	52	97	....	....	....	....	....	....	....	....	....	10	5	7	12	4	....	....	....	....
2016-17	Wilkes-Barre	AHL	74	24	30	54	49	....	....	....	....	....	....	....	....	....	5	0	2	2	4	....	....	....	....
	NHL Totals		**630**	**61**	**96**	**157**	**723**	**5**	**8**	**4**	**784**	**7.8**		**325**	**31.1**	**12:28**	**16**	**3**	**2**	**5**	**10**	**0**	**0**	**1**	**13:41**

Fred T. Hunt Memorial Award (AHL – Sportsmanship) (2016)

Signed as a free agent by **Manchester** (AHL), July 12, 2004. Signed as a free agent by **Los Angeles**, August 1, 2005. Signed as a free agent by **Montreal**, July 4, 2007.Signed as a free agent by **Carolina**, July 14, 2009. Traded to **Calgary** by **Carolina** with Anton Babchuk for Ian White and Brett Sutter, November 17, 2010. Signed as a free agent by **Wilkes-Barre** (AHL), January 23, 2013. Signed as a free agent by **Pittsburgh**, March 5, 2013. Claimed on waivers by **New Jersey** from **Pittsburgh**, March 6, 2013. Signed as a free agent by **Wilkes-Barre** (AHL), September 3, 2013.

KREIDER, Chris

(KRIGH-duhr, KRIHS) **NYR**

Center. Shoots left. 6'3", 228 lbs. Born, Boxford, MA, April 30, 1991. NY Rangers' 1st pick, 19th overall, in 2009 NHL Draft.

Season	Club	League	GP	G	A	Pts	PIM	PP	SH	GW	S	S%	+/-	TF	F%	Min	GP	G	A	Pts	PIM	PP	SH	GW	Min
2005-06	Masconomet	High-MA	19	5	10	15	....	....	....	....	....	....	....	....	....	....	....	....	....	....	....	....	....	....	....
2006-07	Masconomet	High-MA	20	28	13	41	....	....	....	....	....	....	....	....	....	....	....	....	....	....	....	....	....	....	....
2007-08	Andover	High-MA	24	26	15	41	....	....	....	....	....	....	....	....	....	....	....	....	....	....	....	....	....	....	....
2008-09	Andover	High-MA	26	33	23	56	10	....	....	....	....	....	....	....	....	....	....	....	....	....	....	....	....	....	....
	Valley Jr. Warriors	Minor-MA	5	4	2	6	....	....	....	....	....	....	....	....	....	....	....	....	....	....	....	....	....	....	....
2009-10	Boston College	H-East	38	15	8	23	26	....	....	....	....	....	....	....	....	....	....	....	....	....	....	....	....	....	....
2010-11	Boston College	H-East	32	11	13	24	37	....	....	....	....	....	....	....	....	....	....	....	....	....	....	....	....	....	....
2011-12	Boston College	H-East	44	23	22	45	66	....	....	....	....	....	....	....	....	....	....	....	....	....	....	....	....	....	....
	NY Rangers	**NHL**	....	....	....	....	....	....	....	....	....	....	....	....	....	....	**18**	**5**	**2**	**7**	**6**	**2**	**0**	**2**	**13:09**
2012-13	Connecticut	AHL	48	12	11	23	73	....	....	....	....	....	....	....	....	....	....	....	....	....	....	....	....	....	....
	NY Rangers	**NHL**	**23**	**2**	**1**	**3**	**6**	0	0	0	19	10.5	-1	1	0.0	10:07	8	1	1	2	0	0	0	1	9:42

			Regular Season														Playoffs								
Season	Club	League	GP	G	A	Pts	PIM	PP	SH	GW	S	S%	+/-	TF	F%	Min	GP	G	A	Pts	PIM	PP	SH	GW	Min
2013-14	NY Rangers	NHL	66	17	20	37	72	6	0	0	136	12.5	14	19	42.1	15:44	15	5	8	13	14	3	0	1	16:49
	Hartford	AHL	6	2	2	4	16	....	....	....	....	....	....	....	....	....	....	....	....	....	....	....	....	....	....
2014-15	NY Rangers	NHL	80	21	25	46	88	7	0	5	180	11.7	24	21	42.9	15:43	19	7	2	9	14	2	0	2	17:15
2015-16	NY Rangers	NHL	79	21	22	43	58	5	0	3	158	13.3	10	6	83.3	15:57	5	2	0	2	6	1	0	0	15:57
2016-17	NY Rangers	NHL	75	28	25	53	58	6	0	4	186	15.1	6	9	55.6	17:00	12	3	1	4	18	1	0	0	16:52
	NHL Totals		323	89	93	182	282	24	0	12	679	13.1		56	48.2	15:41	77	23	14	37	58	9	0	6	15:17

Hockey East All-Rookie Team (2010) • Hockey East Second All-Star Team (2012)

KREJCI, David
(KRAY-chee, DAY-vihd) **BOS**

Center. Shoots right. 6', 186 lbs. Born, Sternberk, Czech., April 28, 1986. Boston's 1st pick, 63rd overall, in 2004 NHL Draft.

Season	Club	League	GP	G	A	Pts	PIM	PP	SH	GW	S	S%	+/-	TF	F%	Min	GP	G	A	Pts	PIM	PP	SH	GW	Min
2000-01	HC Olomouc U17	CzR-U17	26	2	6	8	4	....	....	....	....	....	....	....	....	....	3	1	1	2	0	....	....	....	....
2001-02	HC Trinec U17	CzR-U17	48	32	27	59	30	....	....	....	....	....	....	....	....	....	6	2	4	6	2	....	....	....	....
2002-03	HC Trinec U17	CzR-U17	22	12	24	36	42	....	....	....	....	....	....	....	....	....	....	....	....	....	....	....	....	....	....
	HC Trinec Jr.	CzRep-Jr.	12	4	5	9	2	....	....	....	....	....	....	....	....	....	12	5	5	10	8	....	....	....	....
2003-04	HC Kladno Jr.	CzRep-Jr.	50	23	37	60	37	....	....	....	....	....	....	....	....	....	7	3	6	9	4	....	....	....	....
2004-05	Gatineau	QMJHL	62	22	41	63	31	....	....	....	....	....	....	....	....	....	10	2	7	9	10	....	....	....	....
2005-06	Gatineau	QMJHL	55	27	54	81	54	....	....	....	....	....	....	....	....	....	17	10	22	32	24	....	....	....	....
2006-07	Boston	NHL	6	0	0	0	2	0	0	0	2	0.0	-3	14	28.6	4:24	....	....	....	....	....	....	....	....	....
	Providence Bruins	AHL	69	31	43	74	47	....	....	....	....	....	....	....	....	....	13	3	13	16	22	....	....	....	....
2007-08	Boston	NHL	56	6	21	27	20	1	1	0	73	8.2	-3	635	48.2	14:55	7	1	4	5	2	1	0	0	19:09
	Providence Bruins	AHL	25	7	21	28	19	....	....	....	....	....	....	....	....	....	....	....	....	....	....	....	....	....	....
2008-09	Boston	NHL	82	22	51	73	26	5	2	6	146	15.1	*37	1048	50.3	16:52	11	2	6	8	2	0	0	1	17:18
2009-10	Boston	NHL	79	17	35	52	26	6	0	3	156	10.9	8	1104	50.7	18:15	9	4	4	8	2	2	0	0	19:06
	Czech Republic	Olympics	5	2	1	3	6	....	....	....	....	....	....	....	....	....	....	....	....	....	....	....	....	....	....
2010-11♦	Boston	NHL	75	13	49	62	28	1	0	2	157	8.3	23	1149	48.7	18:51	25	*12	11	*23	10	2	0	4	20:07
2011-12	Boston	NHL	79	23	39	62	36	2	0	2	145	15.9	-5	1045	52.1	18:25	7	1	2	3	4	1	0	0	21:29
2012-13	Pardubice	CzRep	24	16	11	27	22	....	....	....	....	....	....	....	....	....	....	....	....	....	....	....	....	....	....
	Boston	NHL	47	10	23	33	20	0	0	5	93	10.8	1	654	55.2	18:30	22	9	*17	*26	14	1	0	2	22:15
2013-14	Boston	NHL	80	19	50	69	28	3	0	6	169	11.2	39	1208	51.2	19:07	12	0	4	4	4	0	0	0	20:52
	Czech Republic	Olympics	5	1	2	3	0	....	....	....	....	....	....	....	....	....	....	....	....	....	....	....	....	....	....
2014-15	Boston	NHL	47	7	24	31	22	1	1	1	70	10.0	7	594	53.2	18:10	....	....	....	....	....	....	....	....	....
2015-16	Boston	NHL	72	17	46	63	32	4	0	3	143	11.9	4	1117	50.1	20:18	....	....	....	....	....	....	....	....	....
2016-17	Boston	NHL	82	23	31	54	26	8	0	3	158	14.6	-12	1279	51.5	18:16	3	0	0	0	0	0	0	0	13:25
	NHL Totals		705	157	369	526	266	31	4	31	1312	12.0		9847	50.9	18:07	96	29	48	77	38	7	0	7	20:06

Signed as a free agent by **Pardubice** (CzRep), October 3, 2012.

KRONWALL, Niklas
(KRAWN-wahl, NIHK-luhs) **DET**

Defense. Shoots left. 6', 194 lbs. Born, Stockholm, Sweden, January 12, 1981. Detroit's 1st pick, 29th overall, in 2000 NHL Draft.

Season	Club	League	GP	G	A	Pts	PIM	PP	SH	GW	S	S%	+/-	TF	F%	Min	GP	G	A	Pts	PIM	PP	SH	GW	Min
1996-97	Djurgarden Jr.	Swe-Jr.	1	0	0	0	0	....	....	....	....	....	....	....	....	....	....	....	....	....	....	....	....	....	....
1997-98	Djurgarden Jr.	Swe-Jr.	27	4	3	7	71	....	....	....	....	....	....	....	....	....	2	0	0	0	2	....	....	....	....
1998-99	Huddinge IK	Sweden-2	14	0	1	1	10	....	....	....	....	....	....	....	....	....	....	....	....	....	....	....	....	....	....
	Huddinge IK Jr.	Swe-Jr.	2	0	0	0	6	....	....	....	....	....	....	....	....	....	....	....	....	....	....	....	....	....	....
99-2000	Djurgarden	Sweden	37	1	4	5	16	....	....	....	....	....	....	....	....	....	8	0	0	0	8	....	....	....	....
2000-01	Djurgarden	Sweden	31	1	9	10	32	....	....	....	....	....	....	....	....	....	15	0	1	1	8	....	....	....	....
2001-02	Djurgarden	Sweden	48	5	7	12	34	....	....	....	....	....	....	....	....	....	5	0	0	0	0	....	....	....	....
2002-03	Djurgarden	Sweden	50	5	13	18	46	....	....	....	....	....	....	....	....	....	12	3	2	5	18	....	....	....	....
2003-04	Detroit	NHL	20	1	4	5	16	0	0	1	18	5.6	5	0	0.0	13:51	....	....	....	....	....	....	....	....	....
	Grand Rapids	AHL	25	2	11	13	20	....	....	....	....	....	....	....	....	....	....	....	....	....	....	....	....	....	....
2004-05	Grand Rapids	AHL	76	13	40	53	53	....	....	....	....	....	....	....	....	....	....	....	....	....	....	....	....	....	....
2005-06	Detroit	NHL	27	1	8	9	28	1	0	0	28	3.6	11	0	0.0	20:31	6	0	3	3	2	0	0	0	22:43
	Grand Rapids	AHL	1	0	0	0	0	....	....	....	....	....	....	....	....	....	....	....	....	....	....	....	....	....	....
	Sweden	Olympics	2	1	1	2	8	....	....	....	....	....	....	....	....	....	....	....	....	....	....	....	....	....	....
2006-07	Detroit	NHL	68	1	21	22	54	1	0	0	104	1.0	0	0	0.0	20:39	....	....	....	....	....	....	....	....	....
2007-08♦	Detroit	NHL	65	7	28	35	44	0	0	0	108	6.5	25	0	0.0	21:06	22	0	15	15	18	0	0	0	23:20
2008-09	Detroit	NHL	80	6	45	51	50	4	0	1	121	5.0	2	1	100.0	22:54	23	2	7	9	33	2	0	0	23:24
2009-10	Detroit	NHL	48	7	15	22	32	3	0	0	68	10.3	5	0	0.0	21:55	12	0	5	5	12	0	0	0	23:15
	Sweden	Olympics	4	0	0	0	2	....	....	....	....	....	....	....	....	....	....	....	....	....	....	....	....	....	....
2010-11	Detroit	NHL	77	11	26	37	36	5	0	3	131	8.4	5	0	0.0	22:52	11	2	4	6	4	1	0	0	23:04
2011-12	Detroit	NHL	82	15	21	36	38	7	0	4	141	10.6	-2	0	0.0	22:52	5	0	2	2	4	0	0	0	22:32
2012-13	Detroit	NHL	48	5	24	29	44	2	0	2	67	7.5	-5	0	0.0	24:22	14	0	2	2	4	0	0	0	25:21
2013-14	Detroit	NHL	79	8	41	49	44	5	0	0	110	7.3	0	0	0.0	24:19	5	1	1	2	0	1	0	0	25:58
	Sweden	Olympics	6	0	2	2	4	....	....	....	....	....	....	....	....	....	....	....	....	....	....	....	....	....	....
2014-15	Detroit	NHL	80	9	35	44	40	3	0	1	101	8.9	-4	1	100.0	23:50	6	0	2	2	4	0	0	0	23:35
2015-16	Detroit	NHL	64	3	23	26	30	0	0	2	61	4.9	-21	0	0.0	22:01	5	0	1	1	8	0	0	0	21:42
2016-17	Detroit	NHL	57	2	11	13	32	0	0	0	67	3.0	-7	0	0.0	19:27	....	....	....	....	....	....	....	....	....
	NHL Totals		795	76	302	378	488	31	0	14	1125	6.8		2	100.0	22:11	109	5	42	47	89	4	0	0	23:33

AHL First All-Star Team (2005) • Eddie Shore Award (AHL – Outstanding Defenseman) (2005)
• Missed majority of 2005-06 due to pre-season knee injury vs. Colorado, September 27, 2005.

KRUG, Torey
(KROOG, TOHR-ee) **BOS**

Defense. Shoots left. 5'9", 186 lbs. Born, Livonia, MI, April 12, 1991.

Season	Club	League	GP	G	A	Pts	PIM	PP	SH	GW	S	S%	+/-	TF	F%	Min	GP	G	A	Pts	PIM	PP	SH	GW	Min
2008-09	Indiana Ice	USHL	59	10	37	47	50	....	....	....	....	....	....	....	....	....	13	1	6	7	13	....	....	....	....
2009-10	Michigan State	CCHA	38	3	18	21	67	....	....	....	....	....	....	....	....	....	....	....	....	....	....	....	....	....	....
2010-11	Michigan State	CCHA	38	11	17	28	59	....	....	....	....	....	....	....	....	....	....	....	....	....	....	....	....	....	....
2011-12	Michigan State	CCHA	38	12	22	34	51	....	....	....	....	....	....	....	....	....	....	....	....	....	....	....	....	....	....
	Boston	NHL	2	0	1	1	0	0	0	0	3	0.0	0	0	0.0	17:08	....	....	....	....	....	....	....	....	....
2012-13	Providence Bruins	AHL	63	13	32	45	37	....	....	....	....	....	....	....	....	....	7	0	3	3	2	....	....	....	....
	Boston	NHL	1	0	1	1	0	0	0	0	0	0.0	-1	0	0.0	15:47	15	4	2	6	0	3	0	0	15:49
2013-14	Boston	NHL	79	14	26	40	28	6	0	2	183	7.7	18	2	50.0	17:31	12	2	8	10	6	1	0	0	19:37
2014-15	Boston	NHL	78	12	27	39	20	2	0	0	205	5.9	13	0	0.0	19:36	....	....	....	....	....	....	....	....	....
2015-16	Boston	NHL	81	4	40	44	33	1	0	1	244	1.6	9	2	100.0	21:37	....	....	....	....	....	....	....	....	....
2016-17	Boston	NHL	81	8	43	51	37	6	0	1	208	3.8	-10	1	0.0	21:36	....	....	....	....	....	....	....	....	....
	NHL Totals		322	38	138	176	118	15	0	4	843	4.5		5	60.0	20:04	27	6	10	16	6	4	0	0	17:31

CCHA All-Rookie Team (2010) • CCHA First All-Star Team (2011, 2012) • CCHA Player of the Year (2012) • NCAA West First All-American Team (2012) • NHL All-Rookie Team (2014)
Signed as a free agent by **Boston**, March 25, 2012.

KRUGER, Marcus
(KROO-guhr, MAHR-kuhs) **CAR**

Center. Shoots left. 6', 186 lbs. Born, Stockholm, Sweden, May 27, 1990. Chicago's 5th pick, 149th overall, in 2009 NHL Draft.

Season	Club	League	GP	G	A	Pts	PIM	PP	SH	GW	S	S%	+/-	TF	F%	Min	GP	G	A	Pts	PIM	PP	SH	GW	Min
2006-07	Djurgarden U18	Swe-U18	23	5	14	19	10	....	....	....	....	....	....	....	....	....	3	2	1	3	2	....	....	....	....
2007-08	Djurgarden U18	Swe-U18	22	11	20	31	22	....	....	....	....	....	....	....	....	....	7	3	8	11	6	....	....	....	....
	Djurgarden Jr.	Swe-Jr.	22	3	13	16	16	....	....	....	....	....	....	....	....	....	7	5	3	8	0	....	....	....	....
2008-09	Djurgarden Jr.	Swe-Jr.	34	9	30	39	24	....	....	....	....	....	....	....	....	....	6	1	5	6	2	....	....	....	....
	Djurgarden	Sweden	15	2	2	4	2	....	....	....	....	....	....	....	....	....	....	....	....	....	....	....	....	....	....
2009-10	Djurgarden	Sweden	38	11	20	31	14	....	....	....	....	....	....	....	....	....	16	3	7	10	6	....	....	....	....
2010-11	Djurgarden	Sweden	52	6	29	35	52	....	....	....	....	....	....	....	....	....	3	0	1	1	0	....	....	....	....
	Chicago	NHL	7	0	0	0	4	0	0	0	7	0.0	-4	39	35.9	11:58	5	0	1	1	0	0	0	0	11:51
2011-12	Chicago	NHL	71	9	17	26	22	0	0	1	89	10.1	11	619	45.9	15:24	6	0	0	0	0	0	0	0	17:48
2012-13	Rockford IceHogs	AHL	34	8	14	22	24	....	....	....	....	....	....	....	....	....	....	....	....	....	....	....	....	....	....
	♦ Chicago	NHL	47	4	9	13	24	0	0	2	50	8.0	3	493	46.3	14:10	23	3	2	5	2	0	0	1	13:48
2013-14	Chicago	NHL	81	8	20	28	36	0	0	2	96	8.3	6	773	56.7	13:52	19	1	3	4	6	0	0	0	15:39
	Sweden	Olympics	6	0	0	0	4	....	....	....	....	....	....	....	....	....	....	....	....	....	....	....	....	....	....
2014-15♦	Chicago	NHL	81	7	10	17	32	0	0	1	126	5.6	-5	670	53.3	13:05	23	2	2	4	4	0	0	1	15:06

			Regular Season														Playoffs								
Season	Club	League	GP	G	A	Pts	PIM	PP	SH	GW	S	S%	+/-	TF	F%	Min	GP	G	A	Pts	PIM	PP	SH	GW	Min
2015-16	**Chicago**	**NHL**	**41**	**0**	**4**	**4**	**24**	**0**	**0**	**0**	**50**	**0.0**	**–5**	**474**	**49.2**	**13:31**	**7**	**0**	**1**	**1**	**0**	**0**	**0**	**0**	**15:05**
2016-17	**Chicago**	**NHL**	**70**	**5**	**12**	**17**	**34**	**0**	**0**	**0**	**83**	**6.0**	**7**	**727**	**49.1**	**14:01**	**4**	**0**	**1**	**1**	**2**	**0**	**0**	**0**	**15:20**
	NHL Totals		**398**	**33**	**72**	**105**	**176**	**0**	**0**	**6**	**501**	**6.6**		**3795**	**50.4**	**13:59**	**87**	**6**	**10**	**16**	**14**	**0**	**0**	**2**	**14:53**

• Missed majority of 2015-16 due to wrist injury vs. Edmonton, December 17, 2015. Traded to **Vegas** by **Chicago** for future considerations, July 2, 2017. Traded to **Carolina** by **Vegas** for Carolina's 5th round pick in 2018 NHL Draft, July 4, 2017.

KUCHEROV, Nikita

(KOO-chuhr-awv, nih-KEE-tuh) **T.B.**

Left wing. Shoots left. 5'11", 178 lbs. Born, Maikop, Russia, June 17, 1993. Tampa Bay's 2nd pick, 58th overall, in 2011 NHL Draft.

Season	Club	League	GP	G	A	Pts	PIM	PP	SH	GW	S	S%	+/-	TF	F%	Min	GP	G	A	Pts	PIM	PP	SH	GW	Min
2009-10	CSKA Jr.	Russia-Jr.	53	29	25	54	40	....	....	....	....	....	....	....	....	....	5	0	2	2	2	....	....	....	....
2010-11	CSKA Jr.	Russia-Jr.	41	27	31	58	81	....	....	....	....	....	....	....	....	....	10	5	8	13	16	....	....	....	....
	CSKA Moscow	KHL	8	0	2	2	0	....	....	....	....	....	....	....	....	....	....	....	....	....	....	....	....	....	....
2011-12	CSKA Jr.	Russia-Jr.	23	24	19	43	40	....	....	....	....	....	....	....	....	....	7	3	1	4	0	....	....	....	....
	CSKA Moscow	KHL	18	1	4	5	4	....	....	....	....	....	....	....	....	....	....	....	....	....	....	....	....	....	....
2012-13	Quebec Remparts	QMJHL	6	3	7	10	2	....	....	....	....	....	....	....	....	....	....	....	....	....	....	....	....	....	....
	Rouyn-Noranda	QMJHL	27	26	27	53	12	....	....	....	....	....	....	....	....	....	14	9	15	24	10	....	....	....	....
2013-14	**Tampa Bay**	**NHL**	**52**	**9**	**9**	**18**	**14**	**3**	**0**	**3**	**102**	**8.8**	**3**	**1**	**100.0**	**13:07**	**2**	**1**	**0**	**1**	**0**	**0**	**0**	**0**	**11:37**
	Syracuse Crunch	AHL	17	13	11	24	10	....	....	....	....	....	....	....	....	....	....	....	....	....	....	....	....	....	....
2014-15	**Tampa Bay**	**NHL**	**82**	**29**	**36**	**65**	**37**	**2**	**0**	**2**	**191**	**15.2**	**38**	**2**	**0.0**	**14:57**	**26**	**10**	**12**	**22**	**14**	**3**	**0**	**3**	**16:59**
2015-16	**Tampa Bay**	**NHL**	**77**	**30**	**36**	**66**	**30**	**9**	**0**	**4**	**209**	**14.4**	**9**	**1**	**0.0**	**18:13**	**17**	**11**	**8**	**19**	**8**	**3**	**0**	**0**	**20:09**
2016-17	**Tampa Bay**	**NHL**	**74**	**40**	**45**	**85**	**38**	***17**	**0**	**7**	**246**	**16.3**	**13**	**0**	**0.0**	**19:26**	....	....	....	....	....	....	....	....	....
	NHL Totals		**285**	**108**	**126**	**234**	**119**	**31**	**0**	**16**	**748**	**14.4**		**4**	**25.0**	**16:40**	**45**	**22**	**20**	**42**	**22**	**6**	**0**	**3**	**17:57**

NHL Second All-Star Team (2017)
Played in NHL All-Star Game (2017)

KUHNHACKL, Tom

(koon-HAH-kuhl, TAWM) **PIT**

Center. Shoots left. 6'2", 196 lbs. Born, Landshut, Germany, January 21, 1992. Pittsburgh's 3rd pick, 110th overall, in 2010 NHL Draft.

Season	Club	League	GP	G	A	Pts	PIM	PP	SH	GW	S	S%	+/-	TF	F%	Min	GP	G	A	Pts	PIM	PP	SH	GW	Min
2007-08	EV Landshut Jr.	Ger-Jr.	30	21	20	41	102	....	....	....	....	....	....	....	....	....	3	1	0	1	2	....	....	....	....
2008-09	EV Landshut Jr.	Ger-Jr.	6	4	3	7	31	....	....	....	....	....	....	....	....	....	7	5	5	10	27	....	....	....	....
	Landshut Cann.	German-2	42	11	10	21	34	....	....	....	....	....	....	....	....	....	6	1	0	1	6	....	....	....	....
2009-10	EV Landshut Jr.	Ger-Jr.	2	1	3	4	0	....	....	....	....	....	....	....	....	....	3	4	4	8	12	....	....	....	....
	Landshut Cann.	German-2	38	12	9	21	38	....	....	....	....	....	....	....	....	....	6	0	0	0	2	....	....	....	....
	Augsburg	Germany	4	0	0	0	0	....	....	....	....	....	....	....	....	....	....	....	....	....	....	....	....	....	....
2010-11	Windsor Spitfires	OHL	63	39	29	68	47	....	....	....	....	....	....	....	....	....	18	11	12	23	10	....	....	....	....
2011-12	Windsor Spitfires	OHL	4	1	3	4	6	....	....	....	....	....	....	....	....	....	....	....	....	....	....	....	....	....	....
	Niagara Ice Dogs	OHL	30	7	18	25	29	....	....	....	....	....	....	....	....	....	20	6	5	11	14	....	....	....	....
2012-13	Wilkes-Barre	AHL	11	2	2	4	6	....	....	....	....	....	....	....	....	....	....	....	....	....	....	....	....	....	....
	Wheeling Nailers	ECHL	2	1	0	1	2	....	....	....	....	....	....	....	....	....	....	....	....	....	....	....	....	....	....
2013-14	Wilkes-Barre	AHL	48	8	2	10	22	....	....	....	....	....	....	....	....	....	2	0	0	0	2	....	....	....	....
	Wheeling Nailers	ECHL	16	7	7	14	12	....	....	....	....	....	....	....	....	....	10	6	0	6	6	....	....	....	....
2014-15	Wilkes-Barre	AHL	72	12	18	30	19	....	....	....	....	....	....	....	....	....	8	0	2	2	0	....	....	....	....
2015-16♦	**Pittsburgh**	**NHL**	**42**	**5**	**10**	**15**	**24**	**0**	**2**	**1**	**52**	**9.6**	**3**	**3**	**0.0**	**12:12**	**24**	**2**	**3**	**5**	**0**	**0**	**1**	**1**	**10:59**
	Wilkes-Barre	AHL	23	7	8	15	18	....	....	....	....	....	....	....	....	....	....	....	....	....	....	....	....	....	....
2016-17♦	**Pittsburgh**	**NHL**	**57**	**4**	**12**	**16**	**18**	**0**	**1**	**0**	**49**	**8.2**	**8**	**4**	**50.0**	**10:39**	**11**	**1**	**1**	**2**	**4**	**0**	**0**	**0**	**11:36**
	NHL Totals		**99**	**9**	**22**	**31**	**42**	**0**	**3**	**1**	**101**	**8.9**		**7**	**28.6**	**11:18**	**35**	**3**	**4**	**7**	**4**	**0**	**1**	**1**	**11:11**

KUKAN, Dean

(KOO-kahn, DEEN) **CBJ**

Defense. Shoots left. 6'2", 198 lbs. Born, Volketswil, Switzerland, July 8, 1993.

Season	Club	League	GP	G	A	Pts	PIM	PP	SH	GW	S	S%	+/-	TF	F%	Min	GP	G	A	Pts	PIM	PP	SH	GW	Min
2009-10	GCK Zurich Jr.	Swiss-Jr.	13	1	5	6	2	....	....	....	....	....	....	....	....	....	9	0	4	4	2	....	....	....	....
	GCK Lions Zurich	Swiss-2	29	0	6	6	14	....	....	....	....	....	....	....	....	....	....	....	....	....	....	....	....	....	....
2010-11	GCK Zurich Jr.	Swiss-Jr.	2	0	1	1	0	....	....	....	....	....	....	....	....	....	10	0	0	0	6	....	....	....	....
	ZSC Lions Zurich	Swiss	37	1	2	3	4	....	....	....	....	....	....	....	....	....	....	....	....	....	....	....	....	....	....
	GCK Lions Zurich	Swiss-2	2	0	0	0	0	....	....	....	....	....	....	....	....	....	....	....	....	....	....	....	....	....	....
2011-12	Lulea HF Jr.	Swe-Jr.	42	5	16	21	8	....	....	....	....	....	....	....	....	....	3	0	2	2	2	....	....	....	....
	Lulea HF	Sweden	3	0	0	0	0	....	....	....	....	....	....	....	....	....	....	....	....	....	....	....	....	....	....
2012-13	Lulea HF Jr.	Swe-Jr.	11	2	1	3	2	....	....	....	....	....	....	....	....	....	....	....	....	....	....	....	....	....	....
	Asploven	Sweden-2	2	0	0	0	4	....	....	....	....	....	....	....	....	....	....	....	....	....	....	....	....	....	....
	Tingsryds AIF	Sweden-2	16	0	2	2	2	....	....	....	....	....	....	....	....	....	....	....	....	....	....	....	....	....	....
	Lulea HF	Sweden	16	1	3	4	0	....	....	....	....	....	....	....	....	....	15	0	1	1	0	....	....	....	....
2013-14	Lulea HF	Sweden	54	4	8	12	12	....	....	....	....	....	....	....	....	....	6	1	1	2	....	....	....	....	....
2014-15	Lulea HF	Sweden	52	3	10	13	14	....	....	....	....	....	....	....	....	....	9	0	2	2	0	....	....	....	....
2015-16	**Columbus**	**NHL**	**8**	**0**	**0**	**0**	**0**	**0**	**0**	**0**	**3**	**0.0**	**9**	**0**	**0.0**	**17:21**	....	....	....	....	....	....	....	....	....
	Lake Erie	AHL	33	3	10	13	8	....	....	....	....	....	....	....	....	....	17	1	4	5	2	....	....	....	....
2016-17	Cleveland	AHL	72	4	25	29	43	....	....	....	....	....	....	....	....	....	....	....	....	....	....	....	....	....	....
	NHL Totals		**8**	**0**	**0**	**0**	**0**	**0**	**0**	**0**	**3**	**0.0**		**0**	**0.0**	**17:21**	....	....	....	....	....	....	....	....	....

Signed as a free agent by **Columbus**, June 1, 2015. • Missed majority of 2015-16 due to lower-body injury at Charlottte (AHL), December 20, 2016.

KULAK, Brett

(koo-LAK, BREHT) **CGY**

Defense. Shoots left. 6'2", 187 lbs. Born, Edmonton, AB, January 6, 1994. Calgary's 4th pick, 105th overall, in 2012 NHL Draft.

Season	Club	League	GP	G	A	Pts	PIM	PP	SH	GW	S	S%	+/-	TF	F%	Min	GP	G	A	Pts	PIM	PP	SH	GW	Min
2008-09	PAC T'Wolves	AMBHL	33	2	19	21	28	....	....	....	....	....	....	....	....	....	....	....	....	....	....	....	....	....	....
2009-10	PAC Saints	Minor-AB	32	4	34	38	42	....	....	....	....	....	....	....	....	....	10	2	8	10	14	....	....	....	....
2010-11	St. Albert Raiders	AMHL	31	9	18	27	71	....	....	....	....	....	....	....	....	....	5	1	1	2	0	....	....	....	....
	Vancouver Giants	WHL	3	0	0	0	0	....	....	....	....	....	....	....	....	....	....	....	....	....	....	....	....	....	....
2011-12	Vancouver Giants	WHL	72	9	15	24	22	....	....	....	....	....	....	....	....	....	6	0	4	4	2	....	....	....	....
2012-13	Vancouver Giants	WHL	72	12	32	44	34	....	....	....	....	....	....	....	....	....	....	....	....	....	....	....	....	....	....
	Abbotsford Heat	AHL	4	0	0	0	0	....	....	....	....	....	....	....	....	....	....	....	....	....	....	....	....	....	....
2013-14	Vancouver Giants	WHL	69	14	46	60	51	....	....	....	....	....	....	....	....	....	4	1	2	3	7	....	....	....	....
	Abbotsford Heat	AHL	6	1	2	3	2	....	....	....	....	....	....	....	....	....	4	0	0	0	2	....	....	....	....
2014-15	**Calgary**	**NHL**	**1**	**0**	**0**	**0**	**2**	**0**	**0**	**0**	**0**	**0.0**	**0**	**0**	**0.0**	**19:31**	....	....	....	....	....	....	....	....	....
	Adirondack	AHL	26	4	9	13	27	....	....	....	....	....	....	....	....	....	....	....	....	....	....	....	....	....	....
	Colorado Eagles	ECHL	39	9	21	30	15	....	....	....	....	....	....	....	....	....	....	....	....	....	....	....	....	....	....
2015-16	**Calgary**	**NHL**	**8**	**0**	**0**	**0**	**0**	**0**	**0**	**0**	**9**	**0.0**	**–2**	**0**	**0.0**	**12:21**	....	....	....	....	....	....	....	....	....
	Stockton Heat	AHL	59	3	14	17	36	....	....	....	....	....	....	....	....	....	....	....	....	....	....	....	....	....	....
2016-17	**Calgary**	**NHL**	**21**	**0**	**3**	**3**	**12**	**0**	**0**	**0**	**19**	**0.0**	**–3**	**0**	**0.0**	**14:15**	....	....	....	....	....	....	....	....	....
	Stockton Heat	AHL	22	2	8	10	14	....	....	....	....	....	....	....	....	....	5	0	4	4	4	....	....	....	....
	NHL Totals		**30**	**0**	**3**	**3**	**14**	**0**	**0**	**0**	**28**	**0.0**		**0**	**0.0**	**13:55**	....	....	....	....	....	....	....	....	....

KULEMIN, Nikolay

(KOOL-ay-mihn, NIH-koh-ligh) **NYI**

Left wing. Shoots left. 6'1", 225 lbs. Born, Magnitogorsk, USSR, July 14, 1986. Toronto's 2nd pick, 44th overall, in 2006 NHL Draft.

Season	Club	League	GP	G	A	Pts	PIM	PP	SH	GW	S	S%	+/-	TF	F%	Min	GP	G	A	Pts	PIM	PP	SH	GW	Min
2003-04	Magnitogorsk 2	Russia-3	43	8	18	26	91	....	....	....	....	....	....	....	....	....	....	....	....	....	....	....	....	....	....
2004-05	Magnitogorsk 2	Russia-3	43	9	13	22	44	....	....	....	....	....	....	....	....	....	....	....	....	....	....	....	....	....	....
2005-06	Magnitogorsk 2	Russia-3	4	3	1	4	6	....	....	....	....	....	....	....	....	....	....	....	....	....	....	....	....	....	....
	Magnitogorsk	Russia	31	5	7	12	8	....	....	....	....	....	....	....	....	....	11	2	4	6	6	....	....	....	....
2006-07	Magnitogorsk	Russia	54	27	12	39	42	....	....	....	....	....	....	....	....	....	15	10	1	11	10	....	....	....	....
2007-08	Magnitogorsk	Russia	57	21	12	33	63	....	....	....	....	....	....	....	....	....	11	2	2	4	29	....	....	....	....
2008-09	**Toronto**	**NHL**	**73**	**15**	**16**	**31**	**18**	**2**	**0**	**1**	**129**	**11.6**	**–8**	**66**	**53.0**	**13:48**	....	....	....	....	....	....	....	....	....
	Toronto Marlies	AHL	5	0	0	0	0	....	....	....	....	....	....	....	....	....	....	....	....	....	....	....	....	....	....
2009-10	**Toronto**	**NHL**	**78**	**16**	**20**	**36**	**16**	**0**	**1**	**3**	**145**	**11.0**	**0**	**66**	**40.9**	**16:22**	....	....	....	....	....	....	....	....	....
2010-11	**Toronto**	**NHL**	**82**	**30**	**27**	**57**	**26**	**5**	**1**	**5**	**173**	**17.3**	**7**	**111**	**54.1**	**17:19**	....	....	....	....	....	....	....	....	....
2011-12	**Toronto**	**NHL**	**70**	**7**	**21**	**28**	**6**	**1**	**0**	**1**	**107**	**6.5**	**2**	**78**	**41.0**	**15:13**	....	....	....	....	....	....	....	....	....
2012-13	Magnitogorsk	KHL	36	14	24	38	26	....	....	....	....	....	....	....	....	....	....	....	....	....	....	....	....	....	....
	Toronto	**NHL**	**48**	**7**	**16**	**23**	**22**	**0**	**0**	**0**	**72**	**9.7**	**–5**	**20**	**50.0**	**16:44**	**7**	**0**	**1**	**1**	**0**	**0**	**0**	**0**	**18:11**
2013-14	**Toronto**	**NHL**	**70**	**9**	**11**	**20**	**24**	**0**	**0**	**4**	**81**	**11.1**	**–4**	**108**	**35.2**	**16:13**	....	....	....	....	....	....	....	....	....
2014-15	**NY Islanders**	**NHL**	**82**	**15**	**16**	**31**	**21**	**0**	**3**	**0**	**115**	**13.0**	**7**	**24**	**29.2**	**14:52**	**7**	**1**	**1**	**2**	**2**	**0**	**0**	**1**	**15:42**

			Regular Season														Playoffs								
Season	Club	League	GP	G	A	Pts	PIM	PP	SH	GW	S	S%	+/-	TF	F%	Min	GP	G	A	Pts	PIM	PP	SH	GW	Min
2015-16	NY Islanders	NHL	81	9	13	22	22	0	0	3	92	9.8	13	59	39.0	14:04	11	1	3	4	2	1	0	0	17:56
2016-17	NY Islanders	NHL	72	12	11	23	18	1	1	4	74	16.2	3	27	51.9	13:49	....	....	....	....	....	....	....	....	....
	NHL Totals		656	120	151	271	173	9	6	21	988	12.1		559	44.0	15:20	25	2	5	7	4	1	0	1	17:23

Signed as a free agent by **Magnitogorsk** (KHL), September 15, 2012. Signed as a free agent by **NY Islanders**, July 2, 2014.

KULIKOV, Dmitry

(KOOL-ih-kawv, dih-MEE-tree) **WPG**

Defense. Shoots left. 6'1", 204 lbs. Born, Lipetsk, USSR, October 29, 1990. Florida's 1st pick, 14th overall, in 2009 NHL Draft.

Season	Club	League	GP	G	A	Pts	PIM	PP	SH	GW	S	S%	+/-	TF	F%	Min	GP	G	A	Pts	PIM	PP	SH	GW	Min
2007-08	Yaroslavl 2	Russia-3	36	6	13	19	54	....	....	....	....	....	....	....	....	....	....	....	....	....	....	....	....	....	....
2008-09	Drummondville	QMJHL	57	12	50	62	46	....	....	....	....	....	....	....	....	....	19	2	18	20	16	....	....	....	....
2009-10	Florida	NHL	68	3	13	16	32	1	0	0	87	3.4	–5	0	0.0	17:56	....	....	....	....	....	....	....	....	....
2010-11	Florida	NHL	72	6	20	26	45	1	0	1	83	7.2	–5	0	0.0	19:57	....	....	....	....	....	....	....	....	....
2011-12	Florida	NHL	58	4	24	28	36	2	0	1	104	3.8	–5	0	0.0	21:51	7	0	1	1	4	0	0	0	21:16
2012-13	Yaroslavl	KHL	22	3	4	7	28	....	....	....	....	....	....	....	....	....	....	....	....	....	....	....	....	....	....
	Florida	NHL	34	3	7	10	22	2	0	2	52	5.8	–5	0	0.0	20:59	....	....	....	....	....	....	....	....	....
2013-14	Florida	NHL	81	8	11	19	66	2	1	0	127	6.3	–26	0	0.0	21:42	....	....	....	....	....	....	....	....	....
2014-15	Florida	NHL	73	3	19	22	48	1	0	0	83	3.6	0	0	0.0	21:19	....	....	....	....	....	....	....	....	....
2015-16	Florida	NHL	74	1	16	17	51	0	0	1	99	1.0	8	0	0.0	21:02	6	1	3	4	4	0	0	0	25:09
2016-17	Buffalo	NHL	47	2	3	5	26	1	0	0	42	4.8	–26	0	0.0	21:54	....	....	....	....	....	....	....	....	....
	NHL Totals		507	30	113	143	326	10	1	5	677	4.4		0	0.0	20:47	13	1	4	5	8	0	0	0	23:04

QMJHL All-Rookie Team (2009) • QMJHL First All-Star Team (2009) • QMJHL Rookie of the Year (2009) • Canadian Major Junior Second All-Star Team (2009) • Canadian Major Junior All-Rookie Team (2009)

Signed as a free agent by **Yaroslavl** (KHL), September 25, 2012. Traded to **Buffalo** by **Florida** with Vancouver's 2nd round pick (previously acquired, Buffalo selected Rasmus Asplund) in 2016 NHL Draft for Mark Pysyk, Buffalo's 2nd round pick (Adam Mascherin) in 2016 NHL Draft and St. Louis' 3rd round pick (previously acquired, Florida selected Linus Nassen) in 2016 NHL Draft, June 25, 2016. Signed as a free agent by **Winnipeg**, July 1, 2017.

KUNITZ, Chris

(KOO-nihtz, KRIHS) **T.B.**

Left wing. Shoots left. 6', 195 lbs. Born, Regina, SK, September 26, 1979.

Season	Club	League	GP	G	A	Pts	PIM	PP	SH	GW	S	S%	+/-	TF	F%	Min	GP	G	A	Pts	PIM	PP	SH	GW	Min
1996-97	Yorkton Mallers	SMHL	64	38	38	76	233	....	....	....	....	....	....	....	....	....	....	....	....	....	....	....	....	....	....
1997-98	Melville	SJHL	60	30	27	57	151	....	....	....	....	....	....	....	....	....	....	....	....	....	....	....	....	....	....
1998-99	Melville	SJHL	63	57	32	89	222	....	....	....	....	....	....	....	....	....	4	4	1	5	19	....	....	....	....
99-2000	Ferris State	CCHA	38	20	9	29	70	....	....	....	....	....	....	....	....	....	....	....	....	....	....	....	....	....	....
2000-01	Ferris State	CCHA	37	16	13	29	81	....	....	....	....	....	....	....	....	....	....	....	....	....	....	....	....	....	....
2001-02	Ferris State	CCHA	35	*28	10	38	68	....	....	....	....	....	....	....	....	....	....	....	....	....	....	....	....	....	....
2002-03	Ferris State	CCHA	42	*35	*44	*79	56	....	....	....	....	....	....	....	....	....	....	....	....	....	....	....	....	....	....
2003-04	Anaheim	NHL	21	0	6	6	12	0	0	0	31	0.0	1	7	14.3	9:07	....	....	....	....	....	....	....	....	....
	Cincinnati	AHL	59	19	25	44	101	....	....	....	....	....	....	....	....	....	9	3	2	5	24	....	....	....	....
2004-05	Cincinnati	AHL	54	22	17	39	71	....	....	....	....	....	....	....	....	....	12	1	7	8	20	....	....	....	....
2005-06	Atlanta	NHL	2	0	0	0	2	0	0	0	0	0.0	–3	0	0.0	5:43	....	....	....	....	....	....	....	....	....
	Anaheim	NHL	67	19	22	41	69	5	1	2	149	12.8	19	15	46.7	14:08	16	3	5	8	8	0	0	0	12:30
	Portland Pirates	AHL	5	0	4	4	12	....	....	....	....	....	....	....	....	....	....	....	....	....	....	....	....	....	....
2006-07♦	Anaheim	NHL	81	25	35	60	81	11	0	5	180	13.9	23	13	30.8	17:03	13	1	5	6	19	0	0	0	17:47
2007-08	Anaheim	NHL	82	21	29	50	80	7	1	6	196	10.7	8	49	32.7	16:54	6	0	2	2	8	0	0	0	18:30
2008-09	Anaheim	NHL	62	16	19	35	55	3	0	2	139	11.5	9	22	45.5	16:29	....	....	....	....	....	....	....	....	....
♦	Pittsburgh	NHL	20	7	11	18	16	3	0	1	39	17.9	3	5	60.0	16:17	24	1	13	14	19	0	0	0	16:55
2009-10	Pittsburgh	NHL	50	13	19	32	39	2	1	0	131	9.9	3	15	40.0	16:26	13	4	7	11	8	1	0	0	17:26
2010-11	Pittsburgh	NHL	66	23	25	48	47	7	1	2	133	17.3	18	8	50.0	18:17	6	1	0	1	6	0	0	0	17:22
2011-12	Pittsburgh	NHL	82	26	35	61	49	6	0	3	230	11.3	16	38	52.6	18:19	6	2	4	6	8	2	0	0	19:03
2012-13	Pittsburgh	NHL	48	22	30	52	39	9	0	5	113	19.5	30	9	44.4	18:01	15	5	5	10	6	3	0	1	18:19
2013-14	Pittsburgh	NHL	78	35	33	68	66	13	0	8	218	16.1	25	4	75.0	19:09	13	3	5	8	16	2	0	0	19:01
	Canada	Olympics	6	1	0	1	6	....	....	....	....	....	....	....	....	....	....	....	....	....	....	....	....	....	....
2014-15	Pittsburgh	NHL	74	17	23	40	56	9	1	5	170	10.0	2	13	53.9	17:53	5	1	2	3	8	1	0	1	18:11
2015-16♦	Pittsburgh	NHL	80	17	23	40	41	2	0	1	150	11.3	29	11	45.5	16:49	24	4	8	12	15	2	0	0	14:20
2016-17♦	Pittsburgh	NHL	71	9	20	29	36	0	0	3	134	6.7	0	13	23.1	15:31	20	2	9	11	27	0	0	1	14:52
	NHL Totals		884	250	330	580	688	77	5	43	2013	12.4		222	41.9	16:53	161	27	65	92	148	11	0	3	16:27

CCHA First All-Star Team (2002, 2003) • CCHA Player of the Year (2003) • NCAA West First All-American Team (2003) • NHL First All-Star Team (2013)

Signed as a free agent by **Anaheim**, April 1, 2003. Claimed on waivers by **Atlanta** from **Anaheim**, October 4, 2005. Claimed on waivers by **Anaheim** from **Atlanta**, October 18, 2005. Traded to **Pittsburgh** by **Anaheim** with Eric Tangradi for Ryan Whitney, February 26, 2009. Signed as a free agent by **Tampa Bay**, July 1, 2017.

KUNYK, Cody

(KOO-nihk, KOH-dee)

Center. Shoots left. 5'11", 195 lbs. Born, Sherwood Park, AB, May 20, 1990.

Season	Club	League	GP	G	A	Pts	PIM	PP	SH	GW	S	S%	+/-	TF	F%	Min	GP	G	A	Pts	PIM	PP	SH	GW	Min
2003-04	Sherwood Park	AMBHL	31	16	20	36	19	....	....	....	....	....	....	....	....	....	....	....	....	....	....	....	....	....	....
2004-05	Sherwood Park	AMBHL	39	16	15	31	46	....	....	....	....	....	....	....	....	....	....	....	....	....	....	....	....	....	....
2005-06	Sherwood Park	Minor-AB	32	21	37	58	26	....	....	....	....	....	....	....	....	....	....	....	....	....	....	....	....	....	....
2006-07	Sherwood Park	AMHL	35	16	16	32	58	....	....	....	....	....	....	....	....	....	8	0	6	6	22	....	....	....	....
2007-08	Sherwood Park	AJHL	51	13	11	24	34	....	....	....	....	....	....	....	....	....	....	....	....	....	....	....	....	....	....
2008-09	Sherwood Park	AJHL	61	25	33	58	61	....	....	....	....	....	....	....	....	....	10	3	5	8	2	....	....	....	....
2009-10	Sherwood Park	AJHL	51	44	43	87	33	....	....	....	....	....	....	....	....	....	3	0	1	1	2	....	....	....	....
2010-11	Alaska	CCHA	38	12	18	30	28	....	....	....	....	....	....	....	....	....	....	....	....	....	....	....	....	....	....
2011-12	Alaska	CCHA	36	15	17	32	18	....	....	....	....	....	....	....	....	....	....	....	....	....	....	....	....	....	....
2012-13	Alaska	CCHA	37	11	17	28	22	....	....	....	....	....	....	....	....	....	....	....	....	....	....	....	....	....	....
2013-14	Alaska	WCHA	37	*22	21	43	22	....	....	....	....	....	....	....	....	....	....	....	....	....	....	....	....	....	....
	Tampa Bay	NHL	1	0	0	0	0	0	0	0	2	0.0	0	5	20.0	10:12	....	....	....	....	....	....	....	....	....
2014-15	Syracuse Crunch	AHL	69	10	16	26	38	....	....	....	....	....	....	....	....	....	2	0	0	0	0	....	....	....	....
2015-16	Gentofte Stars	Denmark	27	13	16	29	10	....	....	....	....	....	....	....	....	....	....	....	....	....	....	....	....	....	....
2016-17	Utica Comets	AHL	61	15	22	37	16	....	....	....	....	....	....	....	....	....	....	....	....	....	....	....	....	....	....
	Alaska Aces	ECHL	2	0	2	2	0	....	....	....	....	....	....	....	....	....	....	....	....	....	....	....	....	....	....
	NHL Totals		1	0	0	0	0	0	0	0	2	0.0		5	20.0	10:12	....	....	....	....	....	....	....	....	....

CCHA Second All-Star Team (2012) • WCHA First All-Star Team (2014) • WCHA Player of the Year (2014) • NCAA West Second All-American Team (2014)

Signed as a free agent by **Tampa Bay**, March 20, 2014. Signed as a free agent by **Gentofte** (Denmark), September 15, 2015, Signed as a free agent by **Utica** (AHL), July 25, 2016.

KURALY, Sean

(KUH-ra-lee, SHAWN) **BOS**

Center. Shoots left. 6'2", 212 lbs. Born, Lewiston, NY, January 20, 1993. San Jose's 3rd pick, 133rd overall, in 2011 NHL Draft.

Season	Club	League	GP	G	A	Pts	PIM	PP	SH	GW	S	S%	+/-	TF	F%	Min	GP	G	A	Pts	PIM	PP	SH	GW	Min
2009-10	Ohio Blue Jackets	T1EHL	37	19	30	49	24	....	....	....	....	....	....	....	....	....	....	....	....	....	....	....	....	....	....
	Indiana Ice	USHL	5	1	2	3	0	....	....	....	....	....	....	....	....	....	....	....	....	....	....	....	....	....	....
2010-11	Indiana Ice	USHL	51	8	21	29	45	....	....	....	....	....	....	....	....	....	5	1	1	2	4	....	....	....	....
2011-12	Indiana Ice	USHL	54	32	38	70	48	....	....	....	....	....	....	....	....	....	6	3	3	6	4	....	....	....	....
2012-13	Miami U.	CCHA	40	6	6	12	41	....	....	....	....	....	....	....	....	....	....	....	....	....	....	....	....	....	....
2013-14	Miami U.	NCHC	38	12	17	29	59	....	....	....	....	....	....	....	....	....	....	....	....	....	....	....	....	....	....
2014-15	Miami U.	NCHC	40	19	10	29	38	....	....	....	....	....	....	....	....	....	....	....	....	....	....	....	....	....	....
2015-16	Miami U.	NCHC	36	6	17	23	39	....	....	....	....	....	....	....	....	....	....	....	....	....	....	....	....	....	....
2016-17	Boston	NHL	8	0	1	1	2	0	0	0	11	0.0	–1	3	33.3	9:12	4	2	0	2	4	0	0	1	12:25
	Providence Bruins	AHL	54	14	12	26	37	....	....	....	....	....	....	....	....	....	6	0	1	1	23	....	....	....	....
	NHL Totals		8	0	1	1	2	0	0	0	11	0.0		3	33.3	9:12	4	2	0	2	4	0	0	1	12:25

USHL Second All-Star Team (2012)

Traded to **Boston** by **San Jose** with San Jose's 1st round pick (Trent Frederic) in 2016 NHL Draft for Martin Jones, June 30, 2015.

KUZNETSOV, Evgeny
(kooz-neht-SAWF, ehv-GEH-nee) **WSH**

Center. Shoots left. 6', 192 lbs. Born, Chelyabinsk, Russia, May 19, 1992. Washington's 1st pick, 26th overall, in 2010 NHL Draft.

Season	Club	League	GP	G	A	Pts	PIM	PP	SH	GW	S	S%	+/-	TF	F%	Min	Playoffs GP	G	A	Pts	PIM	PP	SH	GW	Min
2007-08	Chelyabinsk 2	Russia-3	2	0	0	0	0	....	....	....	....	....	....	....	....	....	....	....	....	....	....	....	....	....	....
2008-09	Chelyabinsk 2	Russia-3	22	5	11	16	40	....	....	....	....	....	....	....	....	....	....	....	....	....	....	....	....	....	....
2009-10	Chelyabinsk Jr.	Russia-Jr.	9	4	12	16	8	....	....	....	....	....	....	....	....	....	2	1	2	3	4	....	....	....	....
	Chelyabinsk	KHL	35	2	6	8	10	....	....	....	....	....	....	....	....	....	4	1	0	1	0	....	....	....	....
2010-11	Chelyabinsk	KHL	44	17	15	32	30	....	....	....	....	....	....	....	....	....	....	....	....	....	....	....	....	....	....
	Chelyabinsk Jr.	Russia-Jr.	8	10	5	15	4	....	....	....	....	....	....	....	....	....	5	0	2	2	10	....	....	....	....
2011-12	Chelyabinsk	KHL	49	19	22	41	30	....	....	....	....	....	....	....	....	....	12	7	2	9	10	....	....	....	....
2012-13	Chelyabinsk	KHL	51	19	25	44	42	....	....	....	....	....	....	....	....	....	25	5	6	11	28	....	....	....	....
2013-14	Chelyabinsk	KHL	31	8	13	21	12	....	....	....	....	....	....	....	....	....	....	....	....	....	....	....	....	....	....
	Washington	**NHL**	**17**	**3**	**6**	**9**	**6**	**0**	**1**	**0**	**22**	**13.6**	**–2**	**27**	**18.5**	**13:28**	....	....	....	....	....	....	....	....	....
2014-15	**Washington**	**NHL**	**80**	**11**	**26**	**37**	**24**	**4**	**0**	**1**	**127**	**8.7**	**10**	**681**	**44.6**	**13:20**	**14**	**5**	**2**	**7**	**8**	**0**	**0**	**1**	**16:37**
2015-16	**Washington**	**NHL**	**82**	**20**	**57**	**77**	**32**	**5**	**0**	**4**	**193**	**10.4**	**27**	**1137**	**47.8**	**17:25**	**12**	**1**	**1**	**2**	**8**	**1**	**0**	**0**	**17:27**
2016-17	**Washington**	**NHL**	**82**	**19**	**40**	**59**	**46**	**3**	**0**	**4**	**170**	**11.2**	**18**	**1037**	**44.0**	**16:57**	**13**	**5**	**5**	**10**	**8**	**0**	**0**	**1**	**19:49**
	NHL Totals		**261**	**53**	**129**	**182**	**108**	**12**	**1**	**9**	**512**	**10.4**		**2882**	**45.4**	**15:46**	**39**	**11**	**8**	**19**	**24**	**1**	**0**	**2**	**17:56**

Played in NHL All-Star Game (2016)

KYLINGTON, Oliver
(CHIH-lihng-tuhn, AW-lih-vuhr) **CGY**

Defense. Shoots left. 6', 183 lbs. Born, Stockholm, Sweden, May 19, 1997. Calgary's 2nd pick, 60th overall, in 2015 NHL Draft.

Season	Club	League	GP	G	A	Pts	PIM	PP	SH	GW	S	S%	+/-	TF	F%	Min	Playoffs GP	G	A	Pts	PIM	PP	SH	GW	Min
2011-12	Djurgarden U18	Swe-U18	13	0	3	3	4	....	....	....	....	....	....	....	....	....	....	....	....	....	....	....	....	....	....
2012-13	Sodertalje SK U18	Swe-U18	3	0	0	0	0	....	....	....	....	....	....	....	....	....	....	....	....	....	....	....	....	....	....
	Sodertalje SK Jr.	Swe-Jr.	39	3	10	13	12	....	....	....	....	....	....	....	....	....	3	0	1	1	0	....	....	....	....
2013-14	Farjestad U18	Swe-U18	2	1	2	3	2	....	....	....	....	....	....	....	....	....	....	....	....	....	....	....	....	....	....
	Farjestad Jr.	Swe-Jr.	21	5	16	21	22	....	....	....	....	....	....	....	....	....	2	3	0	3	0	....	....	....	....
	Farjestad	Sweden	32	2	4	6	6	....	....	....	....	....	....	....	....	....	12	0	2	2	2	....	....	....	....
2014-15	Farjestad Jr.	Swe-Jr.	10	4	3	7	2	....	....	....	....	....	....	....	....	....	6	0	5	5	6	....	....	....	....
	AIK Solna	Sweden-2	17	4	3	7	6	....	....	....	....	....	....	....	....	....	....	....	....	....	....	....	....	....	....
	Farjestad	Sweden	18	2	3	5	4	....	....	....	....	....	....	....	....	....	....	....	....	....	....	....	....	....	....
2015-16	**Calgary**	**NHL**	**1**	**0**	**0**	**0**	**0**	**0**	**0**	**0**	**1**	**0.0**	**0**	**0**	**0.0**	**17:22**	....	....	....	....	....	....	....	....	....
	Stockton Heat	AHL	47	5	7	12	14	....	....	....	....	....	....	....	....	....	....	....	....	....	....	....	....	....	....
2016-17	Stockton Heat	AHL	60	6	21	27	22	....	....	....	....	....	....	....	....	....	5	0	1	1	0	....	....	....	....
	NHL Totals		**1**	**0**	**0**	**0**	**0**	**0**	**0**	**0**	**1**	**0.0**		**0**	**0.0**	**17:22**	....	....	....	....	....	....	....	....	....

LABANC, Kevin
(luh-BAHNK, KEH-vuhn) **S.J.**

Right wing. Shoots right. 5'11", 185 lbs. Born, Brooklyn, NY, December 12, 1995. San Jose's 8th pick, 171st overall, in 2014 NHL Draft.

Season	Club	League	GP	G	A	Pts	PIM	PP	SH	GW	S	S%	+/-	TF	F%	Min	Playoffs GP	G	A	Pts	PIM	PP	SH	GW	Min
2009-10	N.J. Colonials	AYHL	37	18	41	59	24	....	....	....	....	....	....	....	....	....	....	....	....	....	....	....	....	....	....
2010-11	N.J. Rockets	AtJHL	5	0	1	1	2	....	....	....	....	....	....	....	....	....	....	....	....	....	....	....	....	....	....
	N.J. Rockets	MtJHL	36	13	33	46	16	....	....	....	....	....	....	....	....	....	2	1	0	1	0	....	....	....	....
2011-12	USAHNTDP	USHL	33	3	8	11	10	....	....	....	....	....	....	....	....	....	2	0	0	0	2	....	....	....	....
	USAHNTDP	U-17	17	2	9	11	12	....	....	....	....	....	....	....	....	....	....	....	....	....	....	....	....	....	....
2012-13	USAHNTDP	USHL	26	3	6	9	8	....	....	....	....	....	....	....	....	....	....	....	....	....	....	....	....	....	....
	USAHNTDP	U-18	41	7	8	15	12	....	....	....	....	....	....	....	....	....	....	....	....	....	....	....	....	....	....
2013-14	Barrie Colts	OHL	65	11	24	35	30	....	....	....	....	....	....	....	....	....	11	3	4	7	4	....	....	....	....
2014-15	Barrie Colts	OHL	68	31	76	107	55	....	....	....	....	....	....	....	....	....	9	2	4	6	8	....	....	....	....
2015-16	Barrie Colts	OHL	65	39	*88	*127	70	....	....	....	....	....	....	....	....	....	15	6	20	26	28	....	....	....	....
	San Jose	AHL	....	....	....	....	....	....	....	....	....	....	....	....	....	....	1	0	0	0	0	....	....	....	....
2016-17	**San Jose**	**NHL**	**55**	**8**	**12**	**20**	**22**	**0**	**0**	**2**	**70**	**11.4**	**9**	**4**	**50.0**	**13:41**	....	....	....	....	....	....	....	....	....
	San Jose	AHL	19	6	13	19	24	....	....	....	....	....	....	....	....	....	15	3	4	7	6	....	....	....	....
	NHL Totals		**55**	**8**	**12**	**20**	**22**	**0**	**0**	**2**	**70**	**11.4**		**4**	**50.0**	**13:41**	....	....	....	....	....	....	....	....	....

OHL Second All-Star Team (2016)

LABATE, Joseph
(luh-BA-tay, JOH-sehf) **VAN**

Center. Shoots left. 6'4", 190 lbs. Born, Eagan, MN, April 16, 1993. Vancouver's 4th pick, 101st overall, in 2011 NHL Draft.

Season	Club	League	GP	G	A	Pts	PIM	PP	SH	GW	S	S%	+/-	TF	F%	Min	Playoffs GP	G	A	Pts	PIM	PP	SH	GW	Min
2009-10	Holy Angels	High-MN	25	29	29	58	26	....	....	....	....	....	....	....	....	....	2	0	1	1	2	....	....	....	....
2010-11	Team Southeast	UMHSEL	5	2	6	8	2	....	....	....	....	....	....	....	....	....	3	4	2	6	0	....	....	....	....
	Holy Angels	High-MN	25	27	22	49	42	....	....	....	....	....	....	....	....	....	1	2	1	3	0	....	....	....	....
2011-12	U. of Wisconsin	WCHA	37	5	15	20	24	....	....	....	....	....	....	....	....	....	....	....	....	....	....	....	....	....	....
2012-13	U. of Wisconsin	WCHA	41	9	14	23	51	....	....	....	....	....	....	....	....	....	....	....	....	....	....	....	....	....	....
2013-14	U. of Wisconsin	Big Ten	37	11	11	22	22	....	....	....	....	....	....	....	....	....	....	....	....	....	....	....	....	....	....
2014-15	U. of Wisconsin	Big Ten	35	6	12	18	46	....	....	....	....	....	....	....	....	....	....	....	....	....	....	....	....	....	....
	Utica Comets	AHL	2	0	0	0	2	....	....	....	....	....	....	....	....	....	....	....	....	....	....	....	....	....	....
2015-16	Utica Comets	AHL	66	10	10	20	79	....	....	....	....	....	....	....	....	....	4	0	1	1	6	....	....	....	....
2016-17	**Vancouver**	**NHL**	**13**	**0**	**0**	**0**	**21**	**0**	**0**	**0**	**5**	**0.0**	**–2**	**1**	**100.0**	**6:46**	....	....	....	....	....	....	....	....	....
	Utica Comets	AHL	38	6	10	16	80	....	....	....	....	....	....	....	....	....	....	....	....	....	....	....	....	....	....
	NHL Totals		**13**	**0**	**0**	**0**	**21**	**0**	**0**	**0**	**5**	**0.0**		**1**	**100.0**	**6:46**	....	....	....	....	....	....	....	....	....

LABRIE, Pierre-Cedric
(la-BREE, pee-AIR-SEH-DRIHK) **NSH**

Left wing. Shoots left. 6'3", 226 lbs. Born, Baie Comeau, QC, June 12, 1986.

Season	Club	League	GP	G	A	Pts	PIM	PP	SH	GW	S	S%	+/-	TF	F%	Min	Playoffs GP	G	A	Pts	PIM	PP	SH	GW	Min
2002-03	Jonquiere Elites	QAAA	42	7	12	19	70	....	....	....	....	....	....	....	....	....	3	2	1	2	2	....	....	....	....
2003-04	Coaticook	QJHL	46	13	12	25	96	....	....	....	....	....	....	....	....	....	....	....	....	....	....	....	....	....	....
	Quebec Remparts	QMJHL	1	0	0	0	0	....	....	....	....	....	....	....	....	....	....	....	....	....	....	....	....	....	....
2004-05	Coaticook	QJHL	15	3	4	7	59	....	....	....	....	....	....	....	....	....	....	....	....	....	....	....	....	....	....
2005-06	Restigouche	MJrHL	54	43	43	86	153	....	....	....	....	....	....	....	....	....	4	3	2	5	16	....	....	....	....
	Baie-Comeau	QMJHL	....	....	....	....	....	....	....	....	....	....	....	....	....	....	4	2	2	4	6	....	....	....	....
2006-07	Baie-Comeau	QMJHL	68	35	28	63	113	....	....	....	....	....	....	....	....	....	11	8	6	14	35	....	....	....	....
2007-08	Manitoba Moose	AHL	67	7	11	18	108	....	....	....	....	....	....	....	....	....	3	0	0	0	2	....	....	....	....
2008-09	Manitoba Moose	AHL	63	6	9	15	79	....	....	....	....	....	....	....	....	....	14	0	1	1	37	....	....	....	....
2009-10	Manitoba Moose	AHL	45	5	1	6	69	....	....	....	....	....	....	....	....	....	....	....	....	....	....	....	....	....	....
	Peoria Rivermen	AHL	16	0	1	1	16	....	....	....	....	....	....	....	....	....	....	....	....	....	....	....	....	....	....
2010-11	Norfolk Admirals	AHL	64	7	19	26	148	....	....	....	....	....	....	....	....	....	6	0	1	1	4	....	....	....	....
2011-12	Norfolk Admirals	AHL	56	14	21	35	107	....	....	....	....	....	....	....	....	....	18	5	4	9	34	....	....	....	....
	Tampa Bay	**NHL**	**14**	**0**	**2**	**2**	**15**	**0**	**0**	**0**	**5**	**0.0**	**–2**	**5**	**60.0**	**5:54**	....	....	....	....	....	....	....	....	....
2012-13	Syracuse Crunch	AHL	39	11	7	18	83	....	....	....	....	....	....	....	....	....	....	....	....	....	....	....	....	....	....
	Tampa Bay	**NHL**	**19**	**2**	**1**	**3**	**30**	**0**	**0**	**0**	**16**	**12.5**	**2**	**4**	**50.0**	**8:33**	....	....	....	....	....	....	....	....	....
2013-14	**Tampa Bay**	**NHL**	**13**	**0**	**0**	**0**	**20**	**0**	**0**	**0**	**2**	**0.0**	**–4**	**2**	**100.0**	**6:53**	....	....	....	....	....	....	....	....	....
	Syracuse Crunch	AHL	38	2	4	6	112	....	....	....	....	....	....	....	....	....	....	....	....	....	....	....	....	....	....
2014-15	Rockford IceHogs	AHL	60	9	7	16	113	....	....	....	....	....	....	....	....	....	8	0	1	1	28	....	....	....	....
2015-16	Rockford IceHogs	AHL	66	20	14	34	102	....	....	....	....	....	....	....	....	....	....	....	....	....	....	....	....	....	....
2016-17	Rockford IceHogs	AHL	52	1	7	8	96	....	....	....	....	....	....	....	....	....	....	....	....	....	....	....	....	....	....
	NHL Totals		**46**	**2**	**3**	**5**	**65**	**0**	**0**	**0**	**23**	**8.7**		**11**	**63.6**	**7:16**	....	....	....	....	....	....	....	....	....

Signed as a free agent by **Vancouver**, July 3, 2007. Traded to **St. Louis** by **Vancouver** for Yan Stastny, March 3, 2010. Signed as a free agent by **Norfolk** (AHL), December 8, 2010. Signed as a free agent by **Tampa Bay**, December 29, 2011. Signed as a free agent by **Chicago**, July 1, 2014. Signed as a free agent by **Nashville**, July 1, 2017.

LADD, Andrew
(LAD, AN-droo) **NYI**

Left wing. Shoots left. 6'3", 200 lbs. Born, Maple Ridge, BC, December 12, 1985. Carolina's 1st pick, 4th overall, in 2004 NHL Draft.

Season	Club	League	GP	G	A	Pts	PIM	PP	SH	GW	S	S%	+/-	TF	F%	Min	Playoffs GP	G	A	Pts	PIM	PP	SH	GW	Min
2000-01	Port Coquitlam	Minor-BC	50	50	41	91	80	....	....	....	....	....	....	....	....	....	....	....	....	....	....	....	....	....	....
	Okanagan Chiefs	Minor-BC	6	4	8	12	10	....	....	....	....	....	....	....	....	....	....	....	....	....	....	....	....	....	....
2001-02	Port Coquitlam	Minor-BC	50	50	41	91	49	....	....	....	....	....	....	....	....	....	....	....	....	....	....	....	....	....	....
	Vancouver Giants	WHL	1	0	0	0	0	....	....	....	....	....	....	....	....	....	....	....	....	....	....	....	....	....	....
2002-03	Coquitlam	BCHL	58	15	40	55	61	....	....	....	....	....	....	....	....	....	....	....	....	....	....	....	....	....	....
2003-04	Calgary Hitmen	WHL	71	30	45	75	119	....	....	....	....	....	....	....	....	....	7	1	6	7	10	....	....	....	....
2004-05	Calgary Hitmen	WHL	65	19	26	45	167	....	....	....	....	....	....	....	....	....	12	7	4	11	18	....	....	....	....

Season	Club	League	GP	G	A	Pts	PIM	PP	SH	GW	S	S%	+/-	TF	F%	Min	GP	G	A	Pts	PIM	PP	SH	GW	Min
			Regular Season														Playoffs								
2005-06♦	Carolina	NHL	29	6	5	11	4	3	0	0	43	14.0	0	0	0.0	11:10	17	2	3	5	4	0	0	1	9:27
	Lowell	AHL	25	11	8	19	28	....	....	....	....	....	....	....	....	....	....	....	....	....	....	....	....	....	....
2006-07	Carolina	NHL	65	11	10	21	46	2	0	3	109	10.1	1	1	0.0	11:12	....	....	....	....	....	....	....	....	....
2007-08	Carolina	NHL	43	9	9	18	31	0	0	1	76	11.8	9	5	60.0	11:45	....	....	....	....	....	....	....	....	....
	Albany River Rats	AHL	2	1	0	1	4	....	....	....	....	....	....	....	....	....	....	....	....	....	....	....	....	....	....
	Chicago	NHL	20	5	7	12	4	1	0	0	55	9.1	4	3	33.3	14:58	....	....	....	....	....	....	....	....	....
2008-09	Chicago	NHL	82	15	34	49	28	0	0	2	195	7.7	26	42	23.8	14:24	17	3	1	4	12	0	0	1	12:55
2009-10♦	Chicago	NHL	82	17	21	38	67	0	0	1	148	11.5	2	12	41.7	13:42	19	3	3	6	12	0	0	0	12:48
2010-11	Atlanta	NHL	81	29	30	59	39	9	2	2	195	14.9	−10	44	34.1	20:04	....	....	....	....	....	....	....	....	....
2011-12	Winnipeg	NHL	82	28	22	50	64	4	0	6	265	10.6	−8	59	54.2	19:34	....	....	....	....	....	....	....	....	....
2012-13	Winnipeg	NHL	48	18	28	46	22	3	0	4	121	14.9	10	54	53.7	19:41	....	....	....	....	....	....	....	....	....
2013-14	Winnipeg	NHL	78	23	31	54	57	4	0	2	189	12.2	8	62	38.7	19:44	....	....	....	....	....	....	....	....	....
2014-15	Winnipeg	NHL	81	24	38	62	72	9	0	6	224	10.7	9	20	35.0	20:04	4	0	1	1	4	0	0	0	20:29
2015-16	Winnipeg	NHL	59	17	17	34	39	7	2	2	143	11.9	−10	10	70.0	19:27	....	....	....	....	....	....	....	....	....
	Chicago	NHL	19	8	4	12	6	3	0	1	38	21.1	−3	3	33.3	17:14	7	1	1	2	16	0	0	0	17:48
2016-17	NY Islanders	NHL	78	23	8	31	45	3	1	4	142	16.2	−14	10	40.0	16:11	....	....	....	....	....	....	....	....	....
	NHL Totals		847	233	264	497	524	48	5	34	1943	12.0		325	42.5	16:48	64	9	9	18	48	0	0	2	12:58

Traded to **Chicago** by **Carolina** for Tuomo Ruutu, February 26, 2008. Traded to **Atlanta** by **Chicago** for Ivan Vishnevskiy and Atlanta/Winnipeg's 2nd round pick (Adam Clendening) in 2011 NHL Draft, July 1, 2010. • Transferred to **Winnipeg** after **Atlanta** franchise relocated, June 21, 2011. Traded to **Chicago** by **Winnipeg** with Jay Harrison and Matt Fraser for Marko Dano and Chicago's 1st round pick (later traded to Philadelphia – Philadelphia selected German Rubtsov) in 2016 NHL Draft, February 25, 2016. Signed as a free agent by **NY Islanders**, July 1, 2016.

LADUE, Paul

(la-DOO, PAWL) **L.A.**

Defense. Shoots right. 6'1", 186 lbs. Born, Grand Forks, ND, September 6, 1992. Los Angeles' 5th pick, 181st overall, in 2012 NHL Draft.

Season	Club	League	GP	G	A	Pts	PIM	PP	SH	GW	S	S%	+/-	TF	F%	Min	GP	G	A	Pts	PIM	PP	SH	GW	Min
2009-10	Grand Forks C.K.	High-ND	25	....	....	30	....	....	....	....	....	....	....	....	....	....	....	....	....	....	....	....	....	....	....
2010-11	Alexandria	NAHL	56	3	19	22	58	....	....	....	....	....	....	....	....	....	3	0	2	2	2	....	....	....	....
2011-12	Lincoln Stars	USHL	56	9	25	34	27	....	....	....	....	....	....	....	....	....	8	1	2	3	2	....	....	....	....
2012-13	Lincoln Stars	USHL	62	12	37	49	20	....	....	....	....	....	....	....	....	....	5	1	1	2	0	....	....	....	....
2013-14	North Dakota	NCHC	41	6	15	21	23	....	....	....	....	....	....	....	....	....	....	....	....	....	....	....	....	....	....
2014-15	North Dakota	NCHC	41	5	17	22	31	....	....	....	....	....	....	....	....	....	....	....	....	....	....	....	....	....	....
2015-16	North Dakota	NCHC	41	5	14	19	14	....	....	....	....	....	....	....	....	....	....	....	....	....	....	....	....	....	....
	Ontario Reign	AHL	....	....	....	....	....	....	....	....	....	....	....	....	....	....	3	0	0	0	2	....	....	....	....
2016-17	Los Angeles	NHL	22	0	8	8	4	0	0	0	27	0.0	−5	0	0.0	15:24	....	....	....	....	....	....	....	....	....
	Ontario Reign	AHL	38	6	12	18	28	....	....	....	....	....	....	....	....	....	3	1	0	1	2	....	....	....	....
	NHL Totals		22	0	8	8	4	0	0	0	27	0.0		0	0.0	15:24	....	....	....	....	....	....	....	....	....

USHL First All-Star Team (2013) • NCHC All-Rookie Team (2014)

LAICH, Brooks

(LIGHK, BRUKS)

Center. Shoots left. 6'2", 200 lbs. Born, Wawota, SK, June 23, 1983. Ottawa's 7th pick, 193rd overall, in 2001 NHL Draft.

Season	Club	League	GP	G	A	Pts	PIM	PP	SH	GW	S	S%	+/-	TF	F%	Min	GP	G	A	Pts	PIM	PP	SH	GW	Min
99-2000	Tisdale Trojans	SMHL	57	51	52	103	....	....	....	....	....	....	....	....	....	....	....	....	....	....	....	....	....	....	....
2000-01	Moose Jaw	WHL	71	9	21	30	28	....	....	....	....	....	....	....	....	....	4	0	0	0	5	....	....	....	....
2001-02	Moose Jaw	WHL	28	6	14	20	12	....	....	....	....	....	....	....	....	....	....	....	....	....	....	....	....	....	....
	Seattle	WHL	47	22	36	58	42	....	....	....	....	....	....	....	....	....	11	5	3	8	11	....	....	....	....
2002-03	Seattle	WHL	60	41	53	94	65	....	....	....	....	....	....	....	....	....	15	5	14	19	24	....	....	....	....
2003-04	Ottawa	NHL	1	0	0	0	2	0	0	0	1	0.0	0	7	42.9	9:34	....	....	....	....	....	....	....	....	....
	Binghamton	AHL	44	15	18	33	16	....	....	....	....	....	....	....	....	....	....	....	....	....	....	....	....	....	....
	Washington	NHL	4	0	1	1	0	0	0	0	2	0.0	−1	49	51.0	10:50	....	....	....	....	....	....	....	....	....
	Portland Pirates	AHL	22	1	3	4	12	....	....	....	....	....	....	....	....	....	6	0	0	0	0	....	....	....	....
2004-05	Portland Pirates	AHL	68	16	10	26	33	....	....	....	....	....	....	....	....	....	....	....	....	....	....	....	....	....	....
2005-06	Washington	NHL	73	7	14	21	26	1	0	1	118	5.9	−9	666	49.7	11:13	....	....	....	....	....	....	....	....	....
	Hershey Bears	AHL	10	7	6	13	8	....	....	....	....	....	....	....	....	....	21	8	7	15	29	....	....	....	....
2006-07	Washington	NHL	73	8	10	18	29	2	3	0	119	6.7	−2	563	51.9	13:36	....	....	....	....	....	....	....	....	....
2007-08	Washington	NHL	82	21	16	37	35	8	2	4	122	17.2	−3	596	47.2	14:03	7	1	5	6	4	0	0	0	18:37
2008-09	Washington	NHL	82	23	30	53	31	9	1	3	185	12.4	−1	511	51.1	17:17	14	3	4	7	10	2	0	0	17:27
2009-10	Washington	NHL	78	25	34	59	34	12	1	4	222	11.3	16	337	45.1	18:17	7	2	1	3	4	0	0	1	19:57
2010-11	Washington	NHL	82	16	32	48	46	4	1	3	207	7.7	14	524	51.3	18:25	9	1	6	7	2	0	0	0	21:54
2011-12	Washington	NHL	82	16	25	41	34	5	1	5	191	8.4	−8	1394	47.6	18:30	14	2	5	7	6	0	0	0	20:13
2012-13	Kloten Flyers	Swiss	19	6	12	18	28	....	....	....	....	....	....	....	....	....	....	....	....	....	....	....	....	....	....
	Washington	NHL	9	1	3	4	6	0	0	0	10	10.0	2	81	50.6	16:32	....	....	....	....	....	....	....	....	....
2013-14	Washington	NHL	51	8	7	15	16	1	1	1	75	10.7	−7	460	44.1	17:15	....	....	....	....	....	....	....	....	....
2014-15	Washington	NHL	66	7	13	20	24	0	0	2	106	6.6	−2	198	43.9	14:43	14	1	1	2	0	0	0	0	11:56
2015-16	Washington	NHL	60	1	6	7	16	0	0	1	66	1.5	−7	109	34.9	10:33	....	....	....	....	....	....	....	....	....
	Toronto	NHL	21	1	6	7	2	0	0	0	35	2.9	−6	134	44.8	13:59	....	....	....	....	....	....	....	....	....
2016-17	Toronto Marlies	AHL	27	1	8	9	12	....	....	....	....	....	....	....	....	....	....	....	....	....	....	....	....	....	....
	NHL Totals		764	134	197	331	301	42	10	24	1459	9.2		5629	48.1	15:28	65	10	22	32	26	2	0	1	17:52

WHL West First All-Star Team (2003)

Traded to **Washington** by **Ottawa** with Ottawa's 2nd round pick (later traded to Colorado - Colorado selected Chris Durand) in 2005 NHL Draft for Peter Bondra, February 18, 2004. Signed as a free agent by **Kloten** (Swiss), September 28, 2012. • Missed majority of 2012-13 due to recurring groin injury and lower-body injury vs. NY Islanders, April 4, 2013. Traded to **Toronto** by **Washington** with Connor Carrick and Washington's 2nd round pick (Carl Grundstrom) in 2016 NHL Draft for Daniel Winnik and Anaheim's 5th round pick (previously acquired, Washington selected Beck Malenstyn) in 2016 NHL Draft, February 28, 2016. • Missed majority of 2016-17 due to recurring elbow injury and resulting surgery, April 12, 2017.

LAINE, Patrik

(LIGH-NAY, pa-TRIHK) **WPG**

Left wing. Shoots right. 6'5", 204 lbs. Born, Tampere, Finland, April 19, 1998. Winnipeg's 1st pick, 2nd overall, in 2016 NHL Draft.

Season	Club	League	GP	G	A	Pts	PIM	PP	SH	GW	S	S%	+/-	TF	F%	Min	GP	G	A	Pts	PIM	PP	SH	GW	Min
2012-13	Tappara U18	Fin-U18	27	17	9	26	6	....	....	....	....	....	....	....	....	....	3	2	1	3	0	....	....	....	....
2013-14	Tappara U18	Fin-U18	5	5	6	11	2	....	....	....	....	....	....	....	....	....	1	0	1	1	0	....	....	....	....
	Tappara Jr.	Fin-Jr.	42	26	11	37	43	....	....	....	....	....	....	....	....	....	1	0	0	0	0	....	....	....	....
2014-15	Tappara Jr.	Fin-Jr.	6	4	1	5	4	....	....	....	....	....	....	....	....	....	....	....	....	....	....	....	....	....	....
	Tappara Tampere	Finland	6	0	1	1	2	....	....	....	....	....	....	....	....	....	....	....	....	....	....	....	....	....	....
	LeKi Lempaala	Finland-2	36	5	7	12	14	....	....	....	....	....	....	....	....	....	2	0	0	0	2	....	....	....	....
2015-16	Tappara Tampere	Finland	46	17	16	33	6	....	....	....	....	....	....	....	....	....	18	*10	5	15	6	....	....	....	....
2016-17	Winnipeg	NHL	73	36	28	64	26	9	0	5	204	17.6	7	3	0.0	17:55	....	....	....	....	....	....	....	....	....
	NHL Totals		73	36	28	64	26	9	0	5	204	17.6		3	0.0	17:55	....	....	....	....	....	....	....	....	....

NHL All-Rookie Team (2017)

Played in NHL All-Star Game (2017)

LANDER, Anton

(LAN-duhr, AN-tawn)

Center. Shoots left. 6', 184 lbs. Born, Sundsvall, Sweden, April 24, 1991. Edmonton's 2nd pick, 40th overall, in 2009 NHL Draft.

Season	Club	League	GP	G	A	Pts	PIM	PP	SH	GW	S	S%	+/-	TF	F%	Min	GP	G	A	Pts	PIM	PP	SH	GW	Min
2005-06	Timra IK U18	Swe-U18	14	1	6	7	14	....	....	....	....	....	....	....	....	....	....	....	....	....	....	....	....	....	....
2006-07	Timra IK U18	Swe-U18	12	6	10	16	14	....	....	....	....	....	....	....	....	....	2	1	2	3	0	....	....	....	....
	Timra IK Jr.	Swe-Jr.	10	2	1	3	10	....	....	....	....	....	....	....	....	....	....	....	....	....	....	....	....	....	....
2007-08	Timra IK U18	Swe-U18	4	6	4	10	8	....	....	....	....	....	....	....	....	....	....	....	....	....	....	....	....	....	....
	Timra IK Jr.	Swe-Jr.	18	5	14	19	39	....	....	....	....	....	....	....	....	....	....	....	....	....	....	....	....	....	....
	Timra IK	Sweden	32	1	2	3	4	....	....	....	....	....	....	....	....	....	10	0	0	0	0	....	....	....	....
2008-09	Timra IK Jr.	Swe-Jr.	8	5	1	6	8	....	....	....	....	....	....	....	....	....	....	....	....	....	....	....	....	....	....
	Timra IK	Sweden	47	4	6	10	12	....	....	....	....	....	....	....	....	....	7	0	0	0	4	....	....	....	....
2009-10	Timra IK	Sweden	49	7	9	16	14	....	....	....	....	....	....	....	....	....	5	0	2	2	2	....	....	....	....
2010-11	Timra IK	Sweden	49	11	15	26	38	....	....	....	....	....	....	....	....	....	....	....	....	....	....	....	....	....	....
	Timra IK Jr.	Swe-Jr.	....	....	....	....	....	....	....	....	....	....	....	....	....	....	2	1	2	3	0	....	....	....	....
2011-12	Edmonton	NHL	56	2	4	6	12	0	1	0	54	3.7	−8	344	43.3	10:37	....	....	....	....	....	....	....	....	....
	Oklahoma City	AHL	14	1	4	5	10	....	....	....	....	....	....	....	....	....	14	2	2	4	4	....	....	....	....
2012-13	Oklahoma City	AHL	47	9	11	20	22	....	....	....	....	....	....	....	....	....	8	5	3	8	4	....	....	....	....
	Edmonton	NHL	11	0	1	1	2	0	0	0	11	0.0	−4	55	49.1	11:02	....	....	....	....	....	....	....	....	....
2013-14	Edmonton	NHL	27	0	1	1	4	0	0	0	18	0.0	−10	160	44.4	13:38	....	....	....	....	....	....	....	....	....
	Oklahoma City	AHL	46	18	34	52	30	....	....	....	....	....	....	....	....	....	3	1	1	2	0	....	....	....	....

			Regular Season														Playoffs								
Season	Club	League	GP	G	A	Pts	PIM	PP	SH	GW	S	S%	+/-	TF	F%	Min	GP	G	A	Pts	PIM	PP	SH	GW	Min
2014-15	Edmonton	NHL	38	6	14	20	14	4	0	2	61	9.8	–12	451	50.1	15:01	....	....	....	....	....	....	....	....	....
	Oklahoma City	AHL	29	9	22	31	20	....	....	....	....	....	....	....	....	....	....	....	....	....	....	....	....	....	....
2015-16	Edmonton	NHL	61	1	2	3	18	0	0	0	54	1.9	–9	693	54.6	12:05	....	....	....	....	....	....	....	....	....
2016-17	Edmonton	NHL	22	1	3	4	6	0	0	0	12	8.3	2	141	56.0	9:46	....	....	....	....	....	....	....	....	....
	Bakersfield	AHL	42	25	30	55	14	....	....	....	....	....	....	....	....	....	....	....	....	....	....	....	....	....	....
	NHL Totals		215	10	25	35	56	4	1	2	210	4.8		1844	50.4	12:07	....	....	....	....	....	....	....	....	....

LANDESKOG, Gabriel

(LAND-ehs-kawg, GAY-bree-ehl) **COL**

Left wing. Shoots left. 6'1", 215 lbs. Born, Stockholm, Sweden, November 23, 1992. Colorado's 1st pick, 2nd overall, in 2011 NHL Draft.

2007-08	Djurgarden U18	Swe-U18	23	12	10	22	4	....	....	....	....	....	....	....	....	....	2	0	0	0	0	....	....	....	....
	Djurgarden Jr.	Swe-Jr.	1	0	0	0	0	....	....	....	....	....	....	....	....	....	....	....	....	....	....	....	....	....	....
2008-09	Djurgarden U18	Swe-U18	8	5	7	12	41	....	....	....	....	....	....	....	....	....	2	0	0	0	0	....	....	....	....
	Djurgarden Jr.	Swe-Jr.	31	7	14	21	63	....	....	....	....	....	....	....	....	....	6	1	0	1	8	....	....	....	....
	Djurgarden	Sweden	3	0	1	1	2	....	....	....	....	....	....	....	....	....	....	....	....	....	....	....	....	....	....
2009-10	Kitchener Rangers	OHL	61	24	22	46	51	....	....	....	....	....	....	....	....	....	20	8	15	23	18	....	....	....	....
2010-11	Kitchener Rangers	OHL	53	36	30	66	61	....	....	....	....	....	....	....	....	....	7	6	4	10	4	....	....	....	....
2011-12	Colorado	NHL	82	22	30	52	51	6	0	5	270	8.1	20	36	22.2	18:37	....	....	....	....	....	....	....	....	....
2012-13	Djurgarden	Sweden-2	17	6	8	14	32	....	....	....	....	....	....	....	....	....	....	....	....	....	....	....	....	....	....
	Colorado	NHL	36	9	8	17	22	0	3	1	109	8.3	–4	18	33.3	19:20	....	....	....	....	....	....	....	....	....
2013-14	Colorado	NHL	81	26	39	65	71	5	0	4	222	11.7	21	18	72.2	18:41	7	3	1	4	8	0	0	1	21:12
	Sweden	Olympics	6	0	1	1	4	....	....	....	....	....	....	....	....	....	....	....	....	....	....	....	....	....	....
2014-15	Colorado	NHL	82	23	36	59	79	8	0	2	214	10.7	–2	45	35.6	18:30	....	....	....	....	....	....	....	....	....
2015-16	Colorado	NHL	75	20	33	53	69	4	1	2	169	11.8	–5	56	55.4	18:56	....	....	....	....	....	....	....	....	....
2016-17	Colorado	NHL	72	18	15	33	62	5	1	2	169	10.7	–25	125	49.6	18:47	....	....	....	....	....	....	....	....	....
	NHL Totals		428	118	161	279	354	28	5	16	1153	10.2		298	45.6	18:45	7	3	1	4	8	0	0	1	21:12

OHL All-Rookie Team (2010) • NHL All-Rookie Team (2012) • Calder Memorial Trophy (2012)

Signed as a free agent by **Djurgarden** (Sweden-2), October 3, 2012.

LAPPIN, Nick

(LA-pihn, NIK) **N.J.**

Right wing. Shoots right. 6'1", 175 lbs. Born, Geneva, IL, November 1, 1992.

2006-07	Chicago Mission	MWEHL	28	5	11	16	22	....	....	....	....	....	....	....	....	....	....	....	....	....	....	....	....	....	....
2007-08	Team Illinois	MWEHL	31	9	12	21	22	....	....	....	....	....	....	....	....	....	....	....	....	....	....	....	....	....	....
2008-09	Team Illinois	T1EHL	46	12	16	28	34	....	....	....	....	....	....	....	....	....	....	....	....	....	....	....	....	....	....
2009-10	Cedar Rapids	USHL	35	4	4	8	46	....	....	....	....	....	....	....	....	....	3	0	0	0	2	....	....	....	....
2010-11	Cedar Rapids	USHL	1	0	0	0	0	....	....	....	....	....	....	....	....	....	....	....	....	....	....	....	....	....	....
	Tri-City Storm	USHL	48	9	17	26	26	....	....	....	....	....	....	....	....	....	....	....	....	....	....	....	....	....	....
2011-12	Tri-City Storm	USHL	53	27	19	46	14	....	....	....	....	....	....	....	....	....	2	1	1	2	2	....	....	....	....
2012-13	Brown U.	ECAC	33	7	13	20	31	....	....	....	....	....	....	....	....	....	....	....	....	....	....	....	....	....	....
2013-14	Brown U.	ECAC	30	13	19	32	2	....	....	....	....	....	....	....	....	....	....	....	....	....	....	....	....	....	....
2014-15	Brown U.	ECAC	29	14	7	21	34	....	....	....	....	....	....	....	....	....	....	....	....	....	....	....	....	....	....
2015-16	Brown U.	ECAC	31	17	16	33	12	....	....	....	....	....	....	....	....	....	....	....	....	....	....	....	....	....	....
	Albany Devils	AHL	12	3	4	7	19	....	....	....	....	....	....	....	....	....	11	5	2	7	2	....	....	....	....
2016-17	New Jersey	NHL	43	4	3	7	17	0	0	0	57	7.0	–17	7	28.6	11:43	....	....	....	....	....	....	....	....	....
	Albany Devils	AHL	35	14	15	29	14	....	....	....	....	....	....	....	....	....	4	0	1	1	2	....	....	....	....
	NHL Totals		43	4	3	7	17	0	0	0	57	7.0		7	28.6	11:43	....	....	....	....	....	....	....	....	....

ECAC First All-Star Team (2016)

Signed as a free agent by **New Jersey**, March 8, 2016.

LARKIN, Dylan

(LAHR-kihn, DIH-luhn) **DET**

Center. Shoots left. 6'1", 190 lbs. Born, Waterford, MI, July 30, 1996. Detroit's 1st pick, 15th overall, in 2014 NHL Draft.

2011-12	Detroit Belle Tire	T1EHL	25	18	18	36	24	....	....	....	....	....	....	....	....	....	....	....	....	....	....	....	....	....	....
2012-13	USAHNTDP	USHL	37	7	7	14	40	....	....	....	....	....	....	....	....	....	....	....	....	....	....	....	....	....	....
	USAHNTDP	U-17	18	6	7	13	14	....	....	....	....	....	....	....	....	....	....	....	....	....	....	....	....	....	....
2013-14	USAHNTDP	USHL	26	17	9	26	24	....	....	....	....	....	....	....	....	....	....	....	....	....	....	....	....	....	....
	USAHNTDP	U-18	34	14	17	31	32	....	....	....	....	....	....	....	....	....	....	....	....	....	....	....	....	....	....
2014-15	U. of Michigan	Big Ten	35	15	32	47	38	....	....	....	....	....	....	....	....	....	....	....	....	....	....	....	....	....	....
	Grand Rapids	AHL	....	....	....	....	....	....	....	....	....	....	....	....	....	....	6	3	2	5	6	....	....	....	....
2015-16	Detroit	NHL	80	23	22	45	34	4	0	5	221	10.4	11	100	41.0	16:33	5	1	0	1	18	0	0	0	14:28
2016-17	Detroit	NHL	80	17	15	32	37	5	1	1	178	9.6	–28	432	45.4	16:09	....	....	....	....	....	....	....	....	....
	NHL Totals		160	40	37	77	71	9	1	6	399	10.0		532	44.5	16:21	5	1	0	1	18	0	0	0	14:28

NCAA West Second All-American Team (2015)

Played in NHL All-Star Game (2016)

LARSEN, Philip

(LAHR-suhn, FIHL-ihp)

Defense. Shoots right. 6', 182 lbs. Born, Esbjerg, Denmark, December 7, 1989. Dallas' 3rd pick, 149th overall, in 2008 NHL Draft.

2004-05	Esbjerg IK Jr.	Den-Jr.	10	1	0	1	2	....	....	....	....	....	....	....	....	....	....	....	....	....	....	....	....	....	....
2005-06	Rogle Jr.	Swe-Jr.	32	1	4	5	24	....	....	....	....	....	....	....	....	....	....	....	....	....	....	....	....	....	....
	Rogle	Sweden-2	13	0	0	0	0	....	....	....	....	....	....	....	....	....	....	....	....	....	....	....	....	....	....
2006-07	Frolunda U18	Swe-U18	3	1	2	3	2	....	....	....	....	....	....	....	....	....	4	2	1	3	8	....	....	....	....
	Frolunda Jr.	Swe-Jr.	37	3	15	18	50	....	....	....	....	....	....	....	....	....	8	0	1	1	6	....	....	....	....
	Frolunda	Sweden	5	0	0	0	0	....	....	....	....	....	....	....	....	....	....	....	....	....	....	....	....	....	....
2007-08	Frolunda Jr.	Swe-Jr.	8	1	4	5	12	....	....	....	....	....	....	....	....	....	7	0	4	4	6	....	....	....	....
	Boras HC	Sweden-2	24	5	5	10	32	....	....	....	....	....	....	....	....	....	....	....	....	....	....	....	....	....	....
	Frolunda	Sweden	16	0	0	0	2	....	....	....	....	....	....	....	....	....	....	....	....	....	....	....	....	....	....
2008-09	Frolunda Jr.	Swe-Jr.	1	1	0	1	0	....	....	....	....	....	....	....	....	....	....	....	....	....	....	....	....	....	....
	Frolunda	Sweden	53	2	15	17	18	....	....	....	....	....	....	....	....	....	11	2	1	3	4	....	....	....	....
2009-10	Frolunda	Sweden	42	1	9	10	20	....	....	....	....	....	....	....	....	....	7	0	0	0	4	....	....	....	....
	Dallas	NHL	2	0	1	1	0	0	0	0	1	0.0	1	0	0.0	12:27	....	....	....	....	....	....	....	....	....
2010-11	Dallas	NHL	6	0	2	2	0	0	0	0	11	0.0	1	0	0.0	13:26	....	....	....	....	....	....	....	....	....
	Texas Stars	AHL	54	4	18	22	12	....	....	....	....	....	....	....	....	....	6	2	3	5	4	....	....	....	....
2011-12	Dallas	NHL	55	3	8	11	16	1	0	0	69	4.3	11	0	0.0	17:57	....	....	....	....	....	....	....	....	....
	Texas Stars	AHL	12	1	9	10	6	....	....	....	....	....	....	....	....	....	....	....	....	....	....	....	....	....	....
2012-13	Lukko Rauma	Finland	27	5	10	15	24	....	....	....	....	....	....	....	....	....	....	....	....	....	....	....	....	....	....
	Dallas	NHL	32	2	3	5	18	1	0	0	30	6.7	–10	0	0.0	14:53	....	....	....	....	....	....	....	....	....
2013-14	Edmonton	NHL	30	3	9	12	8	1	0	0	47	6.4	–4	0	0.0	17:10	....	....	....	....	....	....	....	....	....
	Oklahoma City	AHL	7	1	6	7	4	....	....	....	....	....	....	....	....	....	....	....	....	....	....	....	....	....	....
2014-15	Khanty-Mansiisk	KHL	56	6	19	25	34	....	....	....	....	....	....	....	....	....	....	....	....	....	....	....	....	....	....
2015-16	Jokerit	KHL	52	11	25	36	39	....	....	....	....	....	....	....	....	....	4	3	1	4	0	....	....	....	....
2016-17	Vancouver	NHL	26	1	5	6	4	0	0	0	32	3.1	–8	0	0.0	16:28	....	....	....	....	....	....	....	....	....
	NHL Totals		151	9	28	37	46	3	0	0	190	4.7		0	0.0	16:38	....	....	....	....	....	....	....	....	....

Signed as a free agent by **Rauma** (Finland), September 27, 2012. Traded to **Edmonton** by **Dallas** with Dallas' 7th round pick (later traded to Tampa Bay – Tampa Bay selected Otto Somppi) in 2016 NHL Draft for Shawn Horcoff, July 5, 2013. • Missed majority of 2013-14 due to back injuries. Signed as a free agent by **Khanty-Mansiisk** (KHL), May 28, 2014. Signed as a free agent by **Jokerit Helsinki** (Finland), May 25, 2015. Traded to **Vancouver** by **Edmonton** for Vancouver's 5th round pick (later traded to Arizona – Arizona selected Michael Karow) in 2017 NHL Draft, February 24, 2016. • Missed majority of 2016-17 due to upper-body injury at New Jersey December 6, 2016.

			Regular Season														Playoffs								
Season	Club	League	GP	G	A	Pts	PIM	PP	SH	GW	S	S%	+/-	TF	F%	Min	GP	G	A	Pts	PIM	PP	SH	GW	Min

LARSSON, Adam

(LAHR-suhn, A-duhm) **EDM**

Defense. Shoots right. 6'3", 215 lbs. Born, Skelleftea, Sweden, November 12, 1992. New Jersey's 1st pick, 4th overall, in 2011 NHL Draft.

Season	Club	League	GP	G	A	Pts	PIM	PP	SH	GW	S	S%	+/-	TF	F%	Min	GP	G	A	Pts	PIM	PP	SH	GW	Min
2007-08	Skelleftea U18	Swe-U18	24	5	15	20	30	....	....	....	....	....	....	....	....	....	....	....	....	....	....	....	....	....	....
	Skelleftea Jr.	Swe-Jr.	3	0	5	5	6	....	....	....	....	....	....	....	....	....	....	....	....	....	....	....	....	....	....
2008-09	Skelleftea AIK U18	Swe-U18	7	3	8	11	6	....	....	....	....	....	....	....	....	....	8	0	6	6	6	....	....	....	....
	Skelleftea AIK Jr.	Swe-Jr.	26	2	7	9	28	....	....	....	....	....	....	....	....	....	5	0	4	4	2	....	....	....	....
	Skelleftea AIK	Sweden	1	0	0	0	0	....	....	....	....	....	....	....	....	....	....	....	....	....	....	....	....	....	....
2009-10	Skelleftea AIK Jr.	Swe-Jr.	1	1	0	1	2	....	....	....	....	....	....	....	....	....	....	....	....	....	....	....	....	....	....
	Skelleftea AIK	Sweden	49	4	13	17	18	....	....	....	....	....	....	....	....	....	11	0	1	1	31	....	....	....	....
2010-11	Skelleftea AIK	Sweden	37	1	8	9	41	....	....	....	....	....	....	....	....	....	17	0	4	4	12	....	....	....	....
2011-12	**New Jersey**	**NHL**	**65**	**2**	**16**	**18**	**20**	**0**	**0**	**0**	**68**	**2.9**	**−7**	**0**	**0.0**	**20:37**	**5**	**1**	**0**	**1**	**4**	**0**	**0**	**0**	**16:25**
2012-13	Albany Devils	AHL	33	4	15	19	24	....	....	....	....	....	....	....	....	....	....	....	....	....	....	....	....	....	....
	New Jersey	**NHL**	**37**	**0**	**6**	**6**	**12**	**0**	**0**	**0**	**30**	**0.0**	**4**	**0**	**0.0**	**18:06**	....	....	....	....	....	....	....	....	....
2013-14	**New Jersey**	**NHL**	**26**	**1**	**2**	**3**	**12**	**0**	**0**	**1**	**20**	**5.0**	**−1**	**0**	**0.0**	**17:47**	....	....	....	....	....	....	....	....	....
	Albany Devils	AHL	33	3	16	19	16	....	....	....	....	....	....	....	....	....	4	0	0	0	2	....	....	....	....
2014-15	**New Jersey**	**NHL**	**64**	**3**	**21**	**24**	**34**	**0**	**0**	**1**	**91**	**3.3**	**2**	**0**	**0.0**	**20:58**	....	....	....	....	....	....	....	....	....
	Albany Devils	AHL	1	0	2	2	0	....	....	....	....	....	....	....	....	....	....	....	....	....	....	....	....	....	....
2015-16	**New Jersey**	**NHL**	**82**	**3**	**15**	**18**	**77**	**0**	**0**	**1**	**65**	**4.6**	**15**	**0**	**0.0**	**22:31**	....	....	....	....	....	....	....	....	....
2016-17	**Edmonton**	**NHL**	**79**	**4**	**15**	**19**	**55**	**0**	**0**	**0**	**85**	**4.7**	**21**	**0**	**0.0**	**20:09**	**13**	**2**	**4**	**6**	**4**	**0**	**0**	**1**	**23:43**
	NHL Totals		**353**	**13**	**75**	**88**	**210**	**0**	**0**	**3**	**359**	**3.6**		**0**	**0.0**	**20:33**	**18**	**3**	**4**	**7**	**8**	**0**	**0**	**1**	**21:42**

Traded to **Edmonton** by **New Jersey** for Taylor Hall, June 29, 2016.

LARSSON, Jacob

(LAHR-suhn, YA-kuhb) **ANA**

Defense. Shoots left. 6'2", 191 lbs. Born, Ljungby, Sweden, April 29, 1997. Anaheim's 1st pick, 27th overall, in 2015 NHL Draft.

Season	Club	League	GP	G	A	Pts	PIM	PP	SH	GW	S	S%	+/-	TF	F%	Min	GP	G	A	Pts	PIM	PP	SH	GW	Min
2012-13	Troja U18	Swe-U18	10	0	0	0	0	....	....	....	....	....	....	....	....	....	2	0	1	1	2	....	....	....	....
	Troja Jr.	Swe-Jr.	19	5	5	10	2	....	....	....	....	....	....	....	....	....	....	....	....	....	....	....	....	....	....
2013-14	Frolunda U18	Swe-U18	38	9	16	25	55	....	....	....	....	....	....	....	....	....	5	2	4	6	8	....	....	....	....
	Frolunda Jr.	Swe-Jr.	13	0	0	0	0	....	....	....	....	....	....	....	....	....	3	0	0	0	0	....	....	....	....
2014-15	Frolunda U18	20 Elit	3	1	1	2	0	....	....	....	....	....	....	....	....	....	2	0	1	1	0	....	....	....	....
	Frolunda Jr.	Swe-Jr.	30	8	11	19	49	....	....	....	....	....	....	....	....	....	8	0	4	4	6	....	....	....	....
	Frolunda	Sweden	20	1	2	3	6	....	....	....	....	....	....	....	....	....	....	....	....	....	....	....	....	....	....
2015-16	Frolunda Jr.	Swe-Jr.	1	0	0	0	0	....	....	....	....	....	....	....	....	....	....	....	....	....	....	....	....	....	....
	Frolunda	Sweden	47	5	9	14	10	....	....	....	....	....	....	....	....	....	16	0	3	3	0	....	....	....	....
	San Diego Gulls	AHL	....	....	....	....	....	....	....	....	....	....	....	....	....	....	1	0	0	0	0	....	....	....	....
2016-17	**Anaheim**	**NHL**	**4**	**0**	**0**	**0**	**2**	**0**	**0**	**0**	**2**	**0.0**	**−1**	**0**	**0.0**	**16:26**	....	....	....	....	....	....	....	....	....
	San Diego Gulls	AHL	4	0	2	2	2	....	....	....	....	....	....	....	....	....	....	....	....	....	....	....	....	....	....
	Frolunda	Sweden	29	1	4	5	16	....	....	....	....	....	....	....	....	....	7	1	2	3	0	....	....	....	....
	NHL Totals		**4**	**0**	**0**	**0**	**2**	**0**	**0**	**0**	**2**	**0.0**		**0**	**0.0**	**16:26**	....	....	....	....	....	....	....	....	....

• Loaned to **Frolunda** (Sweden) by **Anaheim**, November 3, 2016.

LARSSON, Johan

(LAHR-suhn, YOH-han) **BUF**

Left wing. Shoots left. 5'11", 200 lbs. Born, Lau, Sweden, July 25, 1992. Minnesota's 3rd pick, 56th overall, in 2010 NHL Draft.

Season	Club	League	GP	G	A	Pts	PIM	PP	SH	GW	S	S%	+/-	TF	F%	Min	GP	G	A	Pts	PIM	PP	SH	GW	Min
2005-06	Sudrets	Sweden-4	2	0	2	2	2	....	....	....	....	....	....	....	....	....	....	....	....	....	....	....	....	....	....
2006-07	Sudrets	Sweden-4	29	13	7	20	40	....	....	....	....	....	....	....	....	....	....	....	....	....	....	....	....	....	....
2007-08	Sudrets	Sweden-4	25	11	11	22	71	....	....	....	....	....	....	....	....	....	....	....	....	....	....	....	....	....	....
2008-09	Brynas U18	Swe-U18	11	6	4	10	76	....	....	....	....	....	....	....	....	....	3	0	3	3	2	....	....	....	....
	Brynas IF Gavle Jr.	Swe-Jr.	33	4	5	9	55	....	....	....	....	....	....	....	....	....	5	0	0	0	2	....	....	....	....
2009-10	Brynas U18	Swe-U18	4	1	1	2	2	....	....	....	....	....	....	....	....	....	4	4	4	8	6	....	....	....	....
	Brynas IF Gavle Jr.	Swe-Jr.	40	15	19	34	80	....	....	....	....	....	....	....	....	....	5	1	1	2	2	....	....	....	....
2010-11	Brynas IF Gavle	Sweden	43	4	4	8	18	....	....	....	....	....	....	....	....	....	5	0	2	2	4	....	....	....	....
	Brynas IF Gavle Jr.	Swe-Jr.	10	6	9	15	8	....	....	....	....	....	....	....	....	....	1	0	0	0	0	....	....	....	....
2011-12	Brynas IF Gavle	Sweden	49	12	24	36	34	....	....	....	....	....	....	....	....	....	16	2	7	9	16	....	....	....	....
2012-13	Houston Aeros	AHL	62	15	22	37	38	....	....	....	....	....	....	....	....	....	....	....	....	....	....	....	....	....	....
	Minnesota	**NHL**	**1**	**0**	**0**	**0**	**0**	**0**	**0**	**0**	**2**	**0.0**	**0**	**0**	**0.0**	**14:02**	....	....	....	....	....	....	....	....	....
	Rochester	AHL	7	1	3	4	2	....	....	....	....	....	....	....	....	....	3	0	3	3	6	....	....	....	....
2013-14	**Buffalo**	**NHL**	**28**	**0**	**4**	**4**	**19**	**0**	**0**	**0**	**21**	**0.0**	**0**	**285**	**47.4**	**13:27**	....	....	....	....	....	....	....	....	....
	Rochester	AHL	51	15	26	41	75	....	....	....	....	....	....	....	....	....	5	1	2	3	4	....	....	....	....
2014-15	**Buffalo**	**NHL**	**39**	**6**	**10**	**16**	**12**	**1**	**0**	**0**	**50**	**12.0**	**0**	**341**	**44.0**	**14:31**	....	....	....	....	....	....	....	....	....
	Rochester	AHL	44	15	25	40	38	....	....	....	....	....	....	....	....	....	....	....	....	....	....	....	....	....	....
2015-16	**Buffalo**	**NHL**	**74**	**10**	**7**	**17**	**27**	**1**	**0**	**5**	**95**	**10.5**	**−4**	**759**	**51.1**	**14:49**	....	....	....	....	....	....	....	....	....
2016-17	**Buffalo**	**NHL**	**36**	**6**	**5**	**11**	**20**	**1**	**0**	**2**	**49**	**12.2**	**−7**	**533**	**49.0**	**16:51**	....	....	....	....	....	....	....	....	....
	NHL Totals		**178**	**22**	**26**	**48**	**78**	**3**	**0**	**7**	**217**	**10.1**		**1918**	**48.7**	**14:57**	....	....	....	....	....	....	....	....	....

Traded to **Buffalo** by **Minnesota** with Matt Hackett, Minnesota's 1st round pick (Nikita Zadorov) in 2013 NHL Draft and Minnesota's 2nd round pick (Vaclav Karabacek) in 2014 NHL Draft for Jason Pominville and Buffalo's 4th round pick (later traded to Edmonton – Edmonton selected William Lagesson) in 2014 NHL Draft, April 3, 2013. • Missed majority of 2016-17 due to wrist injury at Boston, December 31, 2016 and resulting surgery.

LASHOFF, Brian

(LASH-awf, BRIGH-uhn) **DET**

Defense. Shoots left. 6'3", 221 lbs. Born, Albany, NY, July 16, 1990.

Season	Club	League	GP	G	A	Pts	PIM	PP	SH	GW	S	S%	+/-	TF	F%	Min	GP	G	A	Pts	PIM	PP	SH	GW	Min
2006-07	Barrie Colts	OHL	47	2	10	12	20	....	....	....	....	....	....	....	....	....	5	0	1	1	2	....	....	....	....
2007-08	Barrie Colts	OHL	50	5	15	20	44	....	....	....	....	....	....	....	....	....	8	0	1	1	4	....	....	....	....
2008-09	Barrie Colts	OHL	25	1	12	13	19	....	....	....	....	....	....	....	....	....	....	....	....	....	....	....	....	....	....
	Kingston	OHL	35	6	13	19	32	....	....	....	....	....	....	....	....	....	....	....	....	....	....	....	....	....	....
	Grand Rapids	AHL	6	1	4	5	0	....	....	....	....	....	....	....	....	....	8	1	4	5	2	....	....	....	....
2009-10	Kingston	OHL	58	6	21	27	71	....	....	....	....	....	....	....	....	....	7	0	0	0	12	....	....	....	....
	Grand Rapids	AHL	6	0	2	2	2	....	....	....	....	....	....	....	....	....	....	....	....	....	....	....	....	....	....
2010-11	Grand Rapids	AHL	37	0	3	3	25	....	....	....	....	....	....	....	....	....	....	....	....	....	....	....	....	....	....
	Toledo Walleye	ECHL	3	0	1	1	0	....	....	....	....	....	....	....	....	....	....	....	....	....	....	....	....	....	....
2011-12	Grand Rapids	AHL	76	8	11	19	41	....	....	....	....	....	....	....	....	....	....	....	....	....	....	....	....	....	....
2012-13	Grand Rapids	AHL	37	2	4	6	23	....	....	....	....	....	....	....	....	....	18	0	1	1	10	....	....	....	....
	Detroit	**NHL**	**31**	**1**	**4**	**5**	**15**	**0**	**0**	**0**	**26**	**3.8**	**−10**	**0**	**0.0**	**17:47**	**3**	**0**	**0**	**0**	**0**	**0**	**0**	**0**	**18:00**
2013-14	**Detroit**	**NHL**	**75**	**1**	**5**	**6**	**36**	**0**	**0**	**0**	**38**	**2.6**	**−2**	**0**	**0.0**	**14:26**	**5**	**0**	**0**	**0**	**0**	**0**	**0**	**0**	**13:59**
2014-15	**Detroit**	**NHL**	**11**	**0**	**2**	**2**	**6**	**0**	**0**	**0**	**7**	**0.0**	**4**	**0**	**0.0**	**13:17**	....	....	....	....	....	....	....	....	....
	Grand Rapids	AHL	32	1	6	7	12	....	....	....	....	....	....	....	....	....	16	0	3	3	8	....	....	....	....
2015-16	Grand Rapids	AHL	74	1	15	16	30	....	....	....	....	....	....	....	....	....	9	2	1	3	0	....	....	....	....
2016-17	**Detroit**	**NHL**	**5**	**0**	**0**	**0**	**0**	**0**	**0**	**0**	**1**	**0.0**	**−3**	**0**	**0.0**	**12:31**	....	....	....	....	....	....	....	....	....
	Grand Rapids	AHL	62	3	8	11	32	....	....	....	....	....	....	....	....	....	17	1	3	4	12	....	....	....	....
	NHL Totals		**122**	**2**	**11**	**13**	**57**	**0**	**0**	**0**	**72**	**2.8**		**0**	**0.0**	**15:06**	**8**	**0**	**0**	**0**	**0**	**0**	**0**	**0**	**15:29**

Signed as a free agent by **Detroit**, October 1, 2008.

LATTA, Michael

(LA-tuh, MIGH-kuhl) **ARI**

Center. Shoots right. 6', 207 lbs. Born, Kitchener, ON, May 25, 1991. Nashville's 5th pick, 72nd overall, in 2009 NHL Draft.

Season	Club	League	GP	G	A	Pts	PIM	PP	SH	GW	S	S%	+/-	TF	F%	Min	GP	G	A	Pts	PIM	PP	SH	GW	Min
2006-07	Waterloo Wolves	Minor-ON	73	52	66	118	213	....	....	....	....	....	....	....	....	....	....	....	....	....	....	....	....	....	....
2007-08	Ottawa 67's	OHL	50	14	14	28	78	....	....	....	....	....	....	....	....	....	4	0	1	1	2	....	....	....	....
2008-09	Ottawa 67's	OHL	23	8	13	21	32	....	....	....	....	....	....	....	....	....	....	....	....	....	....	....	....	....	....
	Guelph Storm	OHL	42	14	22	36	60	....	....	....	....	....	....	....	....	....	4	0	2	2	12	....	....	....	....
2009-10	Guelph Storm	OHL	58	33	40	73	157	....	....	....	....	....	....	....	....	....	5	2	7	9	14	....	....	....	....
	Milwaukee	AHL	....	....	....	....	....	....	....	....	....	....	....	....	....	....	1	0	0	0	0	....	....	....	....
2010-11	Guelph Storm	OHL	68	34	55	89	158	....	....	....	....	....	....	....	....	....	6	5	5	10	11	....	....	....	....
	Milwaukee	AHL	4	0	1	1	2	....	....	....	....	....	....	....	....	....	7	0	0	0	12	....	....	....	....
2011-12	Milwaukee	AHL	51	14	13	27	100	....	....	....	....	....	....	....	....	....	3	0	1	1	2	....	....	....	....
2012-13	Milwaukee	AHL	67	9	26	35	184	....	....	....	....	....	....	....	....	....	....	....	....	....	....	....	....	....	....
	Hershey Bears	AHL	9	1	2	3	14	....	....	....	....	....	....	....	....	....	5	2	1	3	6	....	....	....	....
2013-14	**Washington**	**NHL**	**17**	**1**	**3**	**4**	**12**	**0**	**0**	**0**	**6**	**16.7**	**0**	**115**	**52.2**	**7:43**	....	....	....	....	....	....	....	....	....
	Hershey Bears	AHL	52	14	20	34	134	....	....	....	....	....	....	....	....	....	....	....	....	....	....	....	....	....	....

			Regular Season														Playoffs								
Season	Club	League	GP	G	A	Pts	PIM	PP	SH	GW	S	S%	+/-	TF	F%	Min	GP	G	A	Pts	PIM	PP	SH	GW	Min
2014-15	**Washington**	**NHL**	**53**	**0**	**6**	**6**	**68**	0	0	0	24	0.0	4	335	47.8	8:23	4	0	0	0	2	0	0	0	6:56
2015-16	**Washington**	**NHL**	**43**	**3**	**4**	**7**	**50**	0	0	0	29	10.3	0	198	51.5	8:05	....	....	....	....	....	....	....	....	....
2016-17	Ontario Reign	AHL	29	2	4	6	67	....	....	....	....	....	....	....	....	....	....	....	....	....	....	....	....	....	....
	Rockford IceHogs	AHL	32	3	13	16	61	....	....	....	....	....	....	....	....	....	....	....	....	....	....	....	....	....	....
	NHL Totals		**113**	**4**	**13**	**17**	**130**	**0**	**0**	**0**	**59**	**6.8**		**648**	**49.7**	**8:10**	**4**	**0**	**0**	**0**	**2**	**0**	**0**	**0**	**6:56**

Traded to **Washington** by **Nashville** with Martin Erat for Filip Forsberg, April 3, 2013. Signed as a free agent by **Los Angeles**, July 1, 2016. Traded to **Chicago** by **Los Angeles** for Cameron Schilling, January 21, 2017. Signed as a free agent by **Arizona**, July 4, 2017.

LAUGHTON, Scott

(LAW-tuhn, SKAWT) **PHI**

Center. Shoots left. 6'1", 190 lbs. Born, Oakville, ON, May 30, 1994. Philadelphia's 1st pick, 20th overall, in 2012 NHL Draft.

2009-10	Tor. Marlboros	GTHL	76	55	40	95	109	....	....	....	....	....	....	....	....	....	....	....	....	....	....	....	....	....	....
	St. Michael's	ON-Jr.A	2	0	0	0	4	....	....	....	....	....	....	....	....	....	....	....	....	....	....	....	....	....	....
2010-11	Oshawa Generals	OHL	63	12	11	23	58	....	....	....	....	....	....	....	....	....	10	1	1	2	11	....	....	....	....
2011-12	Oshawa Generals	OHL	64	21	32	53	101	....	....	....	....	....	....	....	....	....	6	2	3	5	17	....	....	....	....
2012-13	Oshawa Generals	OHL	49	23	33	56	72	....	....	....	....	....	....	....	....	....	7	7	6	13	11	....	....	....	....
	Philadelphia	**NHL**	**5**	**0**	**0**	**0**	**0**	0	0	0	10	0.0	0	43	44.2	11:31	....	....	....	....	....	....	....	....	....
	Adirondack	AHL	6	1	2	3	0	....	....	....	....	....	....	....	....	....	....	....	....	....	....	....	....	....	....
2013-14	Oshawa Generals	OHL	54	40	47	87	72	....	....	....	....	....	....	....	....	....	9	4	7	11	17	....	....	....	....
2014-15	**Philadelphia**	**NHL**	**31**	**2**	**4**	**6**	**17**	0	0	0	51	3.9	–1	283	47.4	12:43	....	....	....	....	....	....	....	....	....
	Lehigh Valley	AHL	39	14	13	27	31	....	....	....	....	....	....	....	....	....	....	....	....	....	....	....	....	....	....
2015-16	**Philadelphia**	**NHL**	**71**	**7**	**14**	**21**	**34**	0	0	0	85	8.2	–2	388	43.8	10:26	3	0	0	0	0	0	0	0	9:10
2016-17	**Philadelphia**	**NHL**	**2**	**0**	**0**	**0**	**0**	0	0	0	4	0.0	0	20	55.0	10:15	....	....	....	....	....	....	....	....	....
	Lehigh Valley	AHL	60	19	20	39	40	....	....	....	....	....	....	....	....	....	5	2	1	3	2	....	....	....	....
	NHL Totals		**109**	**9**	**18**	**27**	**51**	**0**	**0**	**0**	**150**	**6.0**		**734**	**45.5**	**11:08**	**3**	**0**	**0**	**0**	**0**	**0**	**0**	**0**	**9:10**

OHL First All-Star Team (2014)

LAZAR, Curtis

(lah-ZAHR, KUHR-tihs) **CGY**

Center/Right wing. Shoots right. 6', 209 lbs. Born, Salmon Arm, BC, February 2, 1995. Ottawa's 1st pick, 17th overall, in 2013 NHL Draft.

2009-10	PoE Academy	High-BC	51	57	58	115	....	....	....	....	....	....	....	....	....	....	....	....	....	....	....	....	....	....	....
2010-11	Okanagan H.A.	CSSHL	6	4	5	9	4	....	....	....	....	....	....	....	....	....	1	0	0	0	0	....	....	....	....
	Okanagan H.A.	High-BC	39	22	27	49	67	....	....	....	....	....	....	....	....	....	....	....	....	....	....	....	....	....	....
	Edmonton	WHL	6	0	1	1	0	....	....	....	....	....	....	....	....	....	4	1	0	1	0	....	....	....	....
2011-12	Edmonton	WHL	63	20	11	31	56	....	....	....	....	....	....	....	....	....	20	8	11	19	4	....	....	....	....
2012-13	Edmonton	WHL	72	38	23	61	47	....	....	....	....	....	....	....	....	....	22	9	2	11	20	....	....	....	....
2013-14	Edmonton	WHL	58	41	35	76	30	....	....	....	....	....	....	....	....	....	21	10	12	22	12	....	....	....	....
2014-15	**Ottawa**	**NHL**	**67**	**6**	**9**	**15**	**14**	0	0	0	92	6.5	1	273	47.3	12:54	6	0	0	0	2	0	0	0	13:52
2015-16	**Ottawa**	**NHL**	**76**	**6**	**14**	**20**	**18**	1	1	0	78	7.7	–1	384	43.8	13:52	....	....	....	....	....	....	....	....	....
2016-17	**Ottawa**	**NHL**	**33**	**0**	**1**	**1**	**4**	0	0	0	24	0.0	–10	75	37.3	8:49	....	....	....	....	....	....	....	....	....
	Binghamton	AHL	13	3	1	4	8	....	....	....	....	....	....	....	....	....	....	....	....	....	....	....	....	....	....
	Calgary	**NHL**	**4**	**1**	**2**	**3**	**0**	0	0	0	2	50.0	2	24	45.8	11:47	1	0	0	0	0	0	0	0	7:16
	NHL Totals		**180**	**13**	**26**	**39**	**36**	**1**	**1**	**0**	**196**	**6.6**		**756**	**44.4**	**12:32**	**7**	**0**	**0**	**0**	**2**	**0**	**0**	**0**	**12:55**

WHL East First All-Star Team (2014

Traded to **Calgary** by **Ottawa** with Michael Kostka for Jyrki Jokipakka and Calgary's 2nd round pick (Alex Formenton) in 2017 NHL Draft, March 1, 2017.

LEDDY, Nick

(LEH-dee, NIHK) **NYI**

Defense. Shoots left. 6', 199 lbs. Born, Eden Prairie, MN, March 20, 1991. Minnesota's 1st pick, 16th overall, in 2009 NHL Draft.

2006-07	Eden Prairie	High-MN	28	2	16	18	10	....	....	....	....	....	....	....	....	....	....	....	....	....	....	....	....	....	....
2007-08	Eden Prairie	High-MN	27	6	22	28	14	....	....	....	....	....	....	....	....	....	....	....	....	....	....	....	....	....	....
	USAHNTDP	U-18	4	0	2	2	....	....	....	....	....	....	....	....	....	....	....	....	....	....	....	....	....	....	....
2008-09	Eden Prairie	High-MN	31	12	33	45	26	....	....	....	....	....	....	....	....	....	....	....	....	....	....	....	....	....	....
	Team Southwest	UMHSEL	24	9	11	20	....	....	....	....	....	....	....	....	....	....	....	....	....	....	....	....	....	....	....
2009-10	U. of Minnesota	WCHA	30	3	8	11	4	....	....	....	....	....	....	....	....	....	....	....	....	....	....	....	....	....	....
2010-11	**Chicago**	**NHL**	**46**	**4**	**3**	**7**	**4**	0	0	0	37	10.8	–3	0	0.0	14:19	7	0	0	0	0	0	0	0	14:36
	Rockford IceHogs	AHL	22	2	8	10	2	....	....	....	....	....	....	....	....	....	....	....	....	....	....	....	....	....	....
2011-12	**Chicago**	**NHL**	**82**	**3**	**34**	**37**	**10**	0	0	0	94	3.2	–12	0	0.0	22:05	6	1	2	3	0	0	0	0	20:02
2012-13	Rockford IceHogs	AHL	31	3	13	16	12	....	....	....	....	....	....	....	....	....	....	....	....	....	....	....	....	....	....
	♦ **Chicago**	**NHL**	**48**	**6**	**12**	**18**	**10**	2	0	2	65	9.2	15	0	0.0	17:25	23	0	2	2	4	0	0	0	14:21
2013-14	**Chicago**	**NHL**	**82**	**7**	**24**	**31**	**10**	4	0	1	123	5.7	10	0	0.0	16:22	18	1	4	5	6	1	0	0	15:50
2014-15	**NY Islanders**	**NHL**	**78**	**10**	**27**	**37**	**14**	1	0	1	120	8.3	18	0	0.0	20:22	7	0	5	5	0	0	0	0	24:40
2015-16	**NY Islanders**	**NHL**	**81**	**5**	**35**	**40**	**25**	3	0	1	121	4.1	–9	0	0.0	22:37	11	1	3	4	0	0	0	0	27:04
2016-17	**NY Islanders**	**NHL**	**81**	**11**	**35**	**46**	**12**	3	0	1	137	8.0	–3	0	0.0	22:43	....	....	....	....	....	....	....	....	....
	NHL Totals		**498**	**46**	**170**	**216**	**85**	**13**	**0**	**6**	**697**	**6.6**		**0**	**0.0**	**19:54**	**72**	**3**	**16**	**19**	**10**	**1**	**0**	**0**	**18:10**

Traded to **Chicago** by **Minnesota** with Kim Johnsson for Cam Barker, February 12, 2010. Traded to **NY Islanders** by **Chicago** with Kent Simpson for T.J. Brennan, Ville Pokka and Anders Nilsson, October 4, 2014.

LEE, Anders

(LEE, AN-duhrz) **NYI**

Center. Shoots left. 6'3", 228 lbs. Born, Edina, MN, July 3, 1990. NY Islanders' 7th pick, 152nd overall, in 2009 NHL Draft.

2006-07	Saint Thomas	High-MN	31	24	17	41	....	....	....	....	....	....	....	....	....	....	....	....	....	....	....	....	....	....	....
2007-08	Edina Hornets	High-MN	31	32	22	54	....	....	....	....	....	....	....	....	....	....	....	....	....	....	....	....	....	....	....
2008-09	Edina Hornets	High-MN	31	25	59	84	30	....	....	....	....	....	....	....	....	....	....	....	....	....	....	....	....	....	....
	Team Southwest	UMHSEL	18	12	17	29	....	....	....	....	....	....	....	....	....	....	....	....	....	....	....	....	....	....	....
2009-10	Green Bay	USHL	59	35	31	66	54	....	....	....	....	....	....	....	....	....	12	*10	*12	*22	13	....	....	....	....
2010-11	U. of Notre Dame	CCHA	44	24	20	44	16	....	....	....	....	....	....	....	....	....	....	....	....	....	....	....	....	....	....
2011-12	U. of Notre Dame	CCHA	40	17	17	34	24	....	....	....	....	....	....	....	....	....	....	....	....	....	....	....	....	....	....
2012-13	U. of Notre Dame	CCHA	41	*20	18	38	37	....	....	....	....	....	....	....	....	....	....	....	....	....	....	....	....	....	....
	NY Islanders	**NHL**	**2**	**1**	**1**	**2**	**0**	0	0	0	2	50.0	–3	2	0.0	8:12	....	....	....	....	....	....	....	....	....
2013-14	**NY Islanders**	**NHL**	**22**	**9**	**5**	**14**	**14**	2	0	0	68	13.2	3	6	16.7	15:43	....	....	....	....	....	....	....	....	....
	Bridgeport	AHL	54	22	19	41	83	....	....	....	....	....	....	....	....	....	....	....	....	....	....	....	....	....	....
2014-15	**NY Islanders**	**NHL**	**76**	**25**	**16**	**41**	**33**	5	0	6	197	12.7	9	1	100.0	14:24	5	0	1	1	7	0	0	0	14:45
	Bridgeport	AHL	5	3	2	5	2	....	....	....	....	....	....	....	....	....	....	....	....	....	....	....	....	....	....
2015-16	**NY Islanders**	**NHL**	**80**	**15**	**21**	**36**	**51**	8	0	3	183	8.2	–2	6	16.7	14:35	....	....	....	....	....	....	....	....	....
2016-17	**NY Islanders**	**NHL**	**81**	**34**	**18**	**52**	**56**	9	0	6	191	17.8	9	18	38.9	15:35	....	....	....	....	....	....	....	....	....
	NHL Totals		**261**	**84**	**61**	**145**	**154**	**24**	**0**	**15**	**641**	**13.1**		**33**	**30.3**	**14:53**	**5**	**0**	**1**	**1**	**7**	**0**	**0**	**0**	**14:45**

USHL All-Rookie Team (2010) • USHL First All-Star Team (2010) • USHL Rookie of the Year (2010) • CCHA All-Rookie Team (2011) • CCHA Second All-Star Team (2011) • CCHA First All-Star Team (2013) • NCAA West Second All-American Team (2013)

LEHKONEN, Artturi

(lehch-KOH-nehn, AHR-tu-ree) **MTL**

Left wing. Shoots left. 6', 182 lbs. Born, Piikkio, Finland, April 7, 1995. Montreal's 4th pick, 55th overall, in 2013 NHL Draft.

2010-11	TPS Turku U18	Fin-U18	28	23	15	38	43	....	....	....	....	....	....	....	....	....	13	8	6	14	4	....	....	....	....
	TPS Turku Jr.	Fin-Jr.	2	0	1	1	0	....	....	....	....	....	....	....	....	....	....	....	....	....	....	....	....	....	....
2011-12	TPS Turku U18	Fin-U18	3	4	6	10	0	....	....	....	....	....	....	....	....	....	4	3	4	7	2	....	....	....	....
	TPS Turku Jr.	Fin-Jr.	40	28	26	54	54	....	....	....	....	....	....	....	....	....	....	....	....	....	....	....	....	....	....
	TPS Turku	Finland	18	2	2	4	8	....	....	....	....	....	....	....	....	....	2	0	0	0	0	....	....	....	....
2012-13	KalPa Kuopio	Finland	45	14	16	30	12	....	....	....	....	....	....	....	....	....	4	2	1	3	2	....	....	....	....
2013-14	KalPa Kuopio	Finland	33	7	13	20	4	....	....	....	....	....	....	....	....	....	....	....	....	....	....	....	....	....	....
2014-15	Frolunda	Sweden	47	8	8	16	12	....	....	....	....	....	....	....	....	....	13	3	3	6	0	....	....	....	....
2015-16	Frolunda	Sweden	49	16	17	33	12	....	....	....	....	....	....	....	....	....	16	*11	8	*19	4	....	....	....	....
2016-17	**Montreal**	**NHL**	**73**	**18**	**10**	**28**	**8**	2	1	3	158	11.4	–1	4	50.0	13:52	6	2	2	4	2	1	0	0	15:33
	NHL Totals		**73**	**18**	**10**	**28**	**8**	**2**	**1**	**3**	**158**	**11.4**		**4**	**50.0**	**13:52**	**6**	**2**	**2**	**4**	**2**	**1**	**0**	**0**	**15:33**

LEHTERA, Jori

(LEH-tuhr-a, YOHR-ee) **PHI**

Center. Shoots left. 6'2", 210 lbs. Born, Helsinki, Finland, December 23, 1987. St. Louis' 4th pick, 65th overall, in 2008 NHL Draft.

			Regular Season														Playoffs								
Season	Club	League	GP	G	A	Pts	PIM	PP	SH	GW	S	S%	+/-	TF	F%	Min	GP	G	A	Pts	PIM	PP	SH	GW	Min
2003-04	Jokerit U18	Fin-U18	19	0	6	6	2	....	....	....	....	....	....	....	....	....	5	3	1	4	0	....	....	....	....
2004-05	Jokerit U18	Fin-U18	30	13	37	50	24	....	....	....	....	....	....	....	....	....	7	6	5	11	2	....	....	....	....
2005-06	Suomi U20	Finland-2	2	0	0	0	0	....	....	....	....	....	....	....	....	....	....	....	....	....	....	....	....	....	....
	Jokerit Helsinki Jr.	Fin-Jr.	39	14	33	47	16	....	....	....	....	....	....	....	....	....	4	1	4	5	0	....	....	....	....
2006-07	Suomi U20	Finland-2	10	4	7	11	10	....	....	....	....	....	....	....	....	....	....	....	....	....	....	....	....	....	....
	Jokerit Helsinki Jr.	Fin-Jr.	24	18	48	66	20	....	....	....	....	....	....	....	....	....	5	1	7	8	2	....	....	....	....
	Jokerit Helsinki	Finland	28	6	6	12	14	....	....	....	....	....	....	....	....	....	....	....	....	....	....	....	....	....	....
2007-08	Tappara Tampere	Finland	54	13	29	42	32	....	....	....	....	....	....	....	....	....	11	4	2	6	8	....	....	....	....
2008-09	Tappara Tampere	Finland	58	9	38	47	34	....	....	....	....	....	....	....	....	....	3	4	5	9	4	....	....	....	....
	Peoria Rivermen	AHL	7	0	1	1	2	....	....	....	....	....	....	....	....	....	7	1	1	2	10	....	....	....	....
2009-10	Tappara Tampere	Finland	57	19	*50	*69	58	....	....	....	....	....	....	....	....	....	9	1	9	10	8	....	....	....	....
2010-11	Yaroslavl	KHL	53	16	21	37	38	....	....	....	....	....	....	....	....	....	18	0	3	3	14	....	....	....	....
2011-12	Sibir Novosibirsk	KHL	25	10	16	26	10	....	....	....	....	....	....	....	....	....	....	....	....	....	....	....	....	....	....
2012-13	Sibir Novosibirsk	KHL	52	17	29	46	46	....	....	....	....	....	....	....	....	....	3	0	2	2	0	....	....	....	....
2013-14	Novosibirsk	KHL	48	12	32	44	22	....	....	....	....	....	....	....	....	....	10	0	6	6	2	....	....	....	....
	Finland	Olympics	6	1	3	4	0	....	....	....	....	....	....	....	....	....	....	....	....	....	....	....	....	....	....
2014-15	**St. Louis**	**NHL**	**75**	**14**	**30**	**44**	**48**	**2**	**1**	**2**	**103**	**13.6**	**21**	**1061**	**51.2**	**16:13**	**5**	**0**	**2**	**2**	**0**	**0**	**0**	**0**	**14:53**
2015-16	**St. Louis**	**NHL**	**79**	**9**	**25**	**34**	**38**	**1**	**0**	**3**	**83**	**10.8**	**12**	**969**	**50.1**	**16:05**	**20**	**3**	**6**	**9**	**10**	**0**	**0**	**1**	**15:40**
2016-17	**St. Louis**	**NHL**	**64**	**7**	**15**	**22**	**34**	**0**	**0**	**1**	**67**	**10.4**	**-6**	**832**	**49.2**	**15:11**	**8**	**1**	**3**	**4**	**4**	**0**	**0**	**0**	**12:05**
	NHL Totals		**218**	**30**	**70**	**100**	**120**	**3**	**1**	**6**	**253**	**11.9**		**2862**	**50.2**	**15:52**	**33**	**4**	**11**	**15**	**14**	**0**	**0**	**1**	**14:41**

Traded to **Philadelphia** by **St. Louis** with Washington's 1st round pick (previously acquired, Philadelphia selected Morgan Frost) in 2017 NHL Draft for Brayden Schenn, June 23, 2017.

LEIER, Taylor

(LEER, TAY-luhr) **PHI**

Left wing. Shoots left. 5'11", 177 lbs. Born, Saskatoon, SK, February 15, 1994. Philadelphia's 5th pick, 117th overall, in 2012 NHL Draft.

2008-09	Sask. Bobcats	Minor-SK	STATISTICS NOT AVAILABLE																						
	Sask. Contacts	SMHL	2	2	0	2	0	....	....	....	....	....	....	....	....	....	....	....	....	....	....	....	....	....	....
2009-10	Sask. Contacts	SMHL	41	17	24	41	30	....	....	....	....	....	....	....	....	....	11	5	2	7	0	....	....	....	....
2010-11	Sask. Contacts	SMHL	44	31	43	74	32	....	....	....	....	....	....	....	....	....	9	7	6	13	8	....	....	....	....
2011-12	Portland	WHL	72	13	24	37	36	....	....	....	....	....	....	....	....	....	22	5	2	7	12	....	....	....	....
2012-13	Portland	WHL	64	27	35	62	63	....	....	....	....	....	....	....	....	....	21	9	7	16	12	....	....	....	....
2013-14	Portland	WHL	62	37	42	79	42	....	....	....	....	....	....	....	....	....	21	6	20	26	10	....	....	....	....
2014-15	Lehigh Valley	AHL	73	13	18	31	18	....	....	....	....	....	....	....	....	....	....	....	....	....	....	....	....	....	....
2015-16	**Philadelphia**	**NHL**	**6**	**0**	**0**	**0**	**0**	**0**	**0**	**0**	**3**	**0.0**	**0**	**0**	**0.0**	**7:43**	....	....	....	....	....	....	....	....	....
	Lehigh Valley	AHL	71	20	29	49	37	....	....	....	....	....	....	....	....	....	....	....	....	....	....	....	....	....	....
2016-17	**Philadelphia**	**NHL**	**10**	**1**	**1**	**2**	**4**	**0**	**0**	**0**	**7**	**14.3**	**-1**	**1**	**0.0**	**9:04**	....	....	....	....	....	....	....	....	....
	Lehigh Valley	AHL	48	13	24	37	16	....	....	....	....	....	....	....	....	....	5	1	0	1	2	....	....	....	....
	NHL Totals		**16**	**1**	**1**	**2**	**4**	**0**	**0**	**0**	**10**	**10.0**		**1**	**0.0**	**8:34**	....	....	....	....	....	....	....	....	....

LEIPSIC, Brendan

(LIGHP-sihk, BREHN-duhn) **VGK**

Left wing. Shoots left. 5'9", 165 lbs. Born, Winnipeg, MB, May 19, 1994. Nashville's 4th pick, 89th overall, in 2012 NHL Draft.

2009-10	Winnipeg Wild	MMHL	40	23	40	63	36	....	....	....	....	....	....	....	....	....	7	2	2	4	17	....	....	....	....
2010-11	Portland	WHL	68	16	17	33	50	....	....	....	....	....	....	....	....	....	21	3	4	7	14	....	....	....	....
2011-12	Portland	WHL	65	28	30	58	82	....	....	....	....	....	....	....	....	....	20	7	8	15	28	....	....	....	....
2012-13	Portland	WHL	68	*49	71	*120	103	....	....	....	....	....	....	....	....	....	21	10	14	24	41	....	....	....	....
2013-14	Portland	WHL	60	39	52	91	111	....	....	....	....	....	....	....	....	....	20	14	19	33	49	....	....	....	....
2014-15	Milwaukee	AHL	47	7	28	35	16	....	....	....	....	....	....	....	....	....	....	....	....	....	....	....	....	....	....
	Toronto Marlies	AHL	27	7	12	19	6	....	....	....	....	....	....	....	....	....	5	1	2	3	14	....	....	....	....
2015-16	**Toronto**	**NHL**	**6**	**1**	**2**	**3**	**2**	**0**	**0**	**1**	**11**	**9.1**	**-1**	**3**	**66.7**	**14:14**	....	....	....	....	....	....	....	....	....
	Toronto Marlies	AHL	65	20	34	54	55	....	....	....	....	....	....	....	....	....	13	2	2	4	12	....	....	....	....
2016-17	Toronto Marlies	AHL	49	18	33	51	30	....	....	....	....	....	....	....	....	....	11	4	1	5	21	....	....	....	....
	NHL Totals		**6**	**1**	**2**	**3**	**2**	**0**	**0**	**1**	**11**	**9.1**		**3**	**66.7**	**14:14**	....	....	....	....	....	....	....	....	....

WHL West Second All-Star Team (2013)

Traded to **Toronto** by **Nashville** with Olli Jokinen and Nashville's 1st round pick (later traded to Philadelphia – Philadelphia selected Travis Konecny) in 2015 NHL Draft for Cody Franson and Mike Santorelli, February 15, 2015. Claimed by **Vegas** from **Toronto** in Expansion Draft, June 21, 2017.

LEIVO, Josh

(LEE-voh, JAWSH) **TOR**

Left wing. Shoots right. 6'2", 205 lbs. Born, Innisfil, ON, May 26, 1993. Toronto's 3rd pick, 86th overall, in 2011 NHL Draft.

2008-09	Barrie Colts MM	Minor-ON	71	31	35	66	65	....	....	....	....	....	....	....	....	....	....	....	....	....	....	....	....	....	....
2009-10	Barrie Colts Mid.	Minor-ON	52	27	41	68	59	....	....	....	....	....	....	....	....	....	....	....	....	....	....	....	....	....	....
2010-11	Sudbury Wolves	OHL	64	13	17	30	37	....	....	....	....	....	....	....	....	....	8	6	7	13	4	....	....	....	....
2011-12	Sudbury Wolves	OHL	66	32	41	73	61	....	....	....	....	....	....	....	....	....	4	2	1	3	6	....	....	....	....
	Toronto Marlies	AHL	1	0	0	0	0	....	....	....	....	....	....	....	....	....	....	....	....	....	....	....	....	....	....
2012-13	Sudbury Wolves	OHL	34	19	25	44	34	....	....	....	....	....	....	....	....	....	....	....	....	....	....	....	....	....	....
	Kitchener Rangers	OHL	29	10	19	29	18	....	....	....	....	....	....	....	....	....	10	3	9	12	8	....	....	....	....
	Toronto Marlies	AHL	4	0	2	2	2	....	....	....	....	....	....	....	....	....	3	0	1	1	0	....	....	....	....
2013-14	**Toronto**	**NHL**	**7**	**1**	**1**	**2**	**0**	**0**	**0**	**0**	**4**	**25.0**	**0**	**1**	**0.0**	**9:52**	....	....	....	....	....	....	....	....	....
	Toronto Marlies	AHL	59	23	19	42	27	....	....	....	....	....	....	....	....	....	12	3	5	8	2	....	....	....	....
2014-15	**Toronto**	**NHL**	**9**	**1**	**0**	**1**	**4**	**0**	**0**	**0**	**10**	**10.0**	**-1**	**2**	**0.0**	**7:39**	....	....	....	....	....	....	....	....	....
	Toronto Marlies	AHL	51	11	21	32	44	....	....	....	....	....	....	....	....	....	5	1	5	6	0	....	....	....	....
2015-16	**Toronto**	**NHL**	**12**	**5**	**0**	**5**	**6**	**1**	**0**	**1**	**20**	**25.0**	**2**	**2**	**50.0**	**12:19**	....	....	....	....	....	....	....	....	....
	Toronto Marlies	AHL	51	17	31	48	14	....	....	....	....	....	....	....	....	....	15	4	8	12	12	....	....	....	....
2016-17	**Toronto**	**NHL**	**13**	**2**	**8**	**10**	**4**	**1**	**0**	**0**	**27**	**7.4**	**2**	**2**	**50.0**	**12:34**	....	....	....	....	....	....	....	....	....
	Toronto Marlies	AHL	5	0	0	0	6	....	....	....	....	....	....	....	....	....	....	....	....	....	....	....	....	....	....
	NHL Totals		**41**	**9**	**9**	**18**	**14**	**2**	**0**	**1**	**61**	**14.8**		**7**	**28.6**	**10:57**	....	....	....	....	....	....	....	....	....

LERG, Bryan

(LEHRG, BRIGH-uhn)

Center. Shoots left. 5'10", 175 lbs. Born, Livonia, MI, January 20, 1986.

2002-03	USAHNTDP	U-17	19	11	6	17	5	....	....	....	....	....	....	....	....	....	....	....	....	....	....	....	....	....	....
	USAHNTDP	NAHL	46	10	12	22	32	....	....	....	....	....	....	....	....	....	....	....	....	....	....	....	....	....	....
2003-04	USAHNTDP	U-18	46	22	25	47	....	....	....	....	....	....	....	....	....	....	....	....	....	....	....	....	....	....	....
	USAHNTDP	NAHL	11	5	7	12	10	....	....	....	....	....	....	....	....	....	....	....	....	....	....	....	....	....	....
2004-05	Michigan State	CCHA	41	10	5	15	14	....	....	....	....	....	....	....	....	....	....	....	....	....	....	....	....	....	....
2005-06	Michigan State	CCHA	45	15	23	38	26	....	....	....	....	....	....	....	....	....	....	....	....	....	....	....	....	....	....
2006-07	Michigan State	CCHA	41	23	13	36	21	....	....	....	....	....	....	....	....	....	....	....	....	....	....	....	....	....	....
2007-08	Michigan State	CCHA	42	20	19	39	18	....	....	....	....	....	....	....	....	....	....	....	....	....	....	....	....	....	....
	Springfield	AHL	4	0	2	2	2	....	....	....	....	....	....	....	....	....	....	....	....	....	....	....	....	....	....
2008-09	Springfield	AHL	42	9	8	17	24	....	....	....	....	....	....	....	....	....	....	....	....	....	....	....	....	....	....
	Stockton Thunder	ECHL	7	2	8	10	4	....	....	....	....	....	....	....	....	....	....	....	....	....	....	....	....	....	....
2009-10	Springfield	AHL	36	4	3	7	11	....	....	....	....	....	....	....	....	....	....	....	....	....	....	....	....	....	....
2010-11	Geneve	Swiss	1	0	0	0	0	....	....	....	....	....	....	....	....	....	....	....	....	....	....	....	....	....	....
	Wilkes-Barre	AHL	65	15	17	32	21	....	....	....	....	....	....	....	....	....	9	1	2	3	4	....	....	....	....
2011-12	Wilkes-Barre	AHL	70	27	26	53	32	....	....	....	....	....	....	....	....	....	12	0	2	2	4	....	....	....	....
2012-13	Lake Erie	AHL	28	9	7	16	6	....	....	....	....	....	....	....	....	....	....	....	....	....	....	....	....	....	....
2013-14	Lake Erie	AHL	35	12	15	27	4	....	....	....	....	....	....	....	....	....	....	....	....	....	....	....	....	....	....
2014-15	**San Jose**	**NHL**	**2**	**1**	**0**	**1**	**0**	**0**	**0**	**1**	**8**	**12.5**	**-1**	**4**	**100.0**	**12:36**	....	....	....	....	....	....	....	....	....
	Worcester Sharks	AHL	68	13	28	41	10	....	....	....	....	....	....	....	....	....	4	0	1	1	0	....	....	....	....
2015-16	**San Jose**	**NHL**	**6**	**0**	**0**	**0**	**0**	**0**	**0**	**0**	**4**	**0.0**	**1**	**33**	**51.5**	**8:53**	....	....	....	....	....	....	....	....	....
	San Jose	AHL	64	21	30	51	37	....	....	....	....	....	....	....	....	....	4	1	0	1	0	....	....	....	....

			Regular Season														Playoffs								
Season	Club	League	GP	G	A	Pts	PIM	PP	SH	GW	S	S%	+/-	TF	F%	Min	GP	G	A	Pts	PIM	PP	SH	GW	Min
2016-17	Rogle	Sweden	52	20	13	33	44	....	....	....	....	....	....	....	....	....	....	....	....	....	....	....	....	....	....
	Rogle	Sweden-Q	....	....	....	....	....	....	....	....	....	....	....	....	....	....	4	0	2	2	0	....	....	....	....
	NHL Totals		**8**	**1**	**0**	**1**	**0**	**0**	**0**	**1**	**12**	**8.3**		**37**	**56.8**	**9:48**	....	....	....	....	....	....	....	....	....

Signed as a free agent by **Edmonton**, April 2, 2008. Signed as a free agent by **Geneve** (Swiss), September 3, 2010. Signed as a free agent by **Wilkes-Barre** (AHL), December 8, 2010. Signed as a free agent by **Colorado**, July 13, 2012. Signed as a free agent by **San Jose**, July 10, 2014. Signed as a free agent by **Rogle** (Sweden), May 14, 2016.

LERNOUT, Brett

(luhr-NOWT, BREHT) **MTL**

Defense. Shoots right. 6'4", 213 lbs. Born, Winnipeg, MB, September 24, 1995. Montreal's 2nd pick, 73rd overall, in 2014 NHL Draft.

Season	Club	League	GP	G	A	Pts	PIM	PP	SH	GW	S	S%	+/-	TF	F%	Min	GP	G	A	Pts	PIM	PP	SH	GW	Min
2009-10	Winnipeg Sharks	Minor-MB	25	1	6	7	27	....	....	....	....	....	....	....	....	....	....	....	....	....	....	....	....	....	....
2010-11	Wpg. Warriors	Minor-MB	31	3	12	15	67	....	....	....	....	....	....	....	....	....	....	....	....	....	....	....	....	....	....
2011-12	Winnipeg Wild	MMHL	44	8	27	35	62	....	....	....	....	....	....	....	....	....	9	1	4	5	16	....	....	....	....
	Steinbach Pistons	MJHL	6	0	1	1	0	....	....	....	....	....	....	....	....	....	....	....	....	....	....	....	....	....	....
	Saskatoon Blades	WHL	2	0	0	0	0	....	....	....	....	....	....	....	....	....	....	....	....	....	....	....	....	....	....
2012-13	Saskatoon Blades	WHL	18	0	0	0	15	....	....	....	....	....	....	....	....	....	....	....	....	....	....	....	....	....	....
	Swift Current	WHL	41	1	1	2	43	....	....	....	....	....	....	....	....	....	....	0	0	0	0	....	....	....	....
2013-14	Swift Current	WHL	72	8	14	22	103	....	....	....	....	....	....	....	....	....	6	0	1	1	0	....	....	....	....
2014-15	Swift Current	WHL	72	14	28	42	68	....	....	....	....	....	....	....	....	....	4	1	0	1	4	....	....	....	....
	Hamilton	AHL	6	0	0	0	2	....	....	....	....	....	....	....	....	....	....	....	....	....	....	....	....	....	....
2015-16	**Montreal**	**NHL**	**1**	**0**	**0**	**0**	**0**	**0**	**0**	**0**	**0**	**0.0**	**0**	**0**	**0.0**	**6:30**	....	....	....	....	....	....	....	....	....
	St. John's IceCaps	AHL	69	2	10	12	73	....	....	....	....	....	....	....	....	....	....	....	....	....	....	....	....	....	....
2016-17	**Montreal**	**NHL**	**2**	**0**	**0**	**0**	**0**	**0**	**0**	**0**	**3**	**0.0**	**–1**	**0**	**0.0**	**19:00**	....	....	....	....	....	....	....	....	....
	St. John's IceCaps	AHL	74	3	13	16	63	....	....	....	....	....	....	....	....	....	4	0	1	1	2	....	....	....	....
	NHL Totals		**3**	**0**	**0**	**0**	**0**	**0**	**0**	**0**	**3**	**0.0**		**0**	**0.0**	**14:50**	....	....	....	....	....	....	....	....	....

LESSIO, Lucas

(LEH-see-oh, LOO-kuhs)

Left wing. Shoots left. 6'1", 212 lbs. Born, Maple, ON, January 23, 1993. Phoenix's 3rd pick, 56th overall, in 2011 NHL Draft.

Season	Club	League	GP	G	A	Pts	PIM	PP	SH	GW	S	S%	+/-	TF	F%	Min	GP	G	A	Pts	PIM	PP	SH	GW	Min
2008-09	Tor. Marlboros	GTHL	72	53	60	113	126	....	....	....	....	....	....	....	....	....	....	....	....	....	....	....	....	....	....
2009-10	St. Michael's	ON-Jr.A	41	30	42	72	87	....	....	....	....	....	....	....	....	....	5	0	3	3	10	....	....	....	....
2010-11	Oshawa Generals	OHL	66	27	27	54	66	....	....	....	....	....	....	....	....	....	10	5	4	9	6	....	....	....	....
2011-12	Oshawa Generals	OHL	66	34	28	62	71	....	....	....	....	....	....	....	....	....	6	3	2	5	6	....	....	....	....
2012-13	Oshawa Generals	OHL	35	19	15	34	38	....	....	....	....	....	....	....	....	....	9	1	2	3	20	....	....	....	....
	Portland Pirates	AHL	5	1	1	2	4	....	....	....	....	....	....	....	....	....	3	0	2	2	0	....	....	....	....
2013-14	**Phoenix**	**NHL**	**3**	**0**	**0**	**0**	**2**	**0**	**0**	**0**	**4**	**0.0**	**–2**	**0**	**0.0**	**11:32**	....	....	....	....	....	....	....	....	....
	Portland Pirates	AHL	69	29	25	54	63	....	....	....	....	....	....	....	....	....	....	....	....	....	....	....	....	....	....
2014-15	**Arizona**	**NHL**	**26**	**2**	**3**	**5**	**8**	**0**	**0**	**0**	**44**	**4.5**	**–10**	**2**	**0.0**	**12:45**	....	....	....	....	....	....	....	....	....
	Portland Pirates	AHL	49	15	16	31	26	....	....	....	....	....	....	....	....	....	5	0	3	3	0	....	....	....	....
2015-16	Springfield	AHL	24	7	5	12	25	....	....	....	....	....	....	....	....	....	....	....	....	....	....	....	....	....	....
	Montreal	**NHL**	**12**	**1**	**1**	**2**	**2**	**0**	**0**	**1**	**14**	**7.1**	**1**	**2**	**0.0**	**10:29**	....	....	....	....	....	....	....	....	....
	St. John's IceCaps	AHL	18	3	6	9	16	....	....	....	....	....	....	....	....	....	....	....	....	....	....	....	....	....	....
2016-17	Zagreb	KHL	40	12	10	22	93	....	....	....	....	....	....	....	....	....	....	....	....	....	....	....	....	....	....
	Orebro HK	Sweden	8	2	0	2	14	....	....	....	....	....	....	....	....	....	....	....	....	....	....	....	....	....	....
	NHL Totals		**41**	**3**	**4**	**7**	**12**	**0**	**0**	**1**	**62**	**4.8**		**4**	**0.0**	**12:00**	....	....	....	....	....	....	....	....	....

OHL All-Rookie Team (2011)

Traded to **Montreal** by **Arizona** for Christian Thomas, December 15, 2015. Signed as a free agent by **Zagreb** (KHL), October 14, 2016. Signed as a free agent by **Orebro** (Sweden), February 7, 2017. Signed as a free agent by **Riga** (KHL), June 20, 2017.

LETANG, Kris

(leh-TANG, KRIHS) **PIT**

Defense. Shoots right. 6', 201 lbs. Born, Montreal, QC, April 24, 1987. Pittsburgh's 3rd pick, 62nd overall, in 2005 NHL Draft.

Season	Club	League	GP	G	A	Pts	PIM	PP	SH	GW	S	S%	+/-	TF	F%	Min	GP	G	A	Pts	PIM	PP	SH	GW	Min
2002-03	Antoine-Girouard	QAAA	42	2	10	12	34	....	....	....	....	....	....	....	....	....	14	1	8	9	10	....	....	....	....
2003-04	Antoine-Girouard	QAAA	39	12	43	55	94	....	....	....	....	....	....	....	....	....	13	7	9	16	38	....	....	....	....
2004-05	Val-d'Or Foreurs	QMJHL	70	13	19	32	79	....	....	....	....	....	....	....	....	....	....	....	....	....	....	....	....	....	....
2005-06	Val-d'Or Foreurs	QMJHL	60	25	43	68	156	....	....	....	....	....	....	....	....	....	5	1	5	6	20	....	....	....	....
2006-07	**Pittsburgh**	**NHL**	**7**	**2**	**0**	**2**	**4**	**2**	**0**	**0**	**8**	**25.0**	**–3**	**0**	**0.0**	**11:33**	....	....	....	....	....	....	....	....	....
	Val-d'Or Foreurs	QMJHL	40	14	38	52	74	....	....	....	....	....	....	....	....	....	19	12	19	31	48	....	....	....	....
	Wilkes-Barre	AHL	....	....	....	....	....	....	....	....	....	....	....	....	....	....	1	0	1	1	2	....	....	....	....
2007-08	**Pittsburgh**	**NHL**	**63**	**6**	**11**	**17**	**23**	**1**	**0**	**3**	**68**	**8.8**	**–1**	**0**	**0.0**	**18:10**	**16**	**0**	**2**	**2**	**12**	**0**	**0**	**0**	**17:07**
	Wilkes-Barre	AHL	10	1	6	7	4	....	....	....	....	....	....	....	....	....	....	....	....	....	....	....	....	....	....
2008-09 ♦	**Pittsburgh**	**NHL**	**74**	**10**	**23**	**33**	**24**	**4**	**1**	**3**	**138**	**7.2**	**–7**	**1**	**0.0**	**21:09**	**23**	**4**	**9**	**13**	**26**	**2**	**0**	**1**	**19:18**
2009-10	**Pittsburgh**	**NHL**	**73**	**3**	**24**	**27**	**51**	**0**	**0**	**0**	**174**	**1.7**	**1**	**0**	**0.0**	**21:34**	**13**	**5**	**2**	**7**	**6**	**4**	**0**	**1**	**23:15**
2010-11	**Pittsburgh**	**NHL**	**82**	**8**	**42**	**50**	**101**	**4**	**0**	**2**	**236**	**3.4**	**15**	**1**	**100.0**	**24:02**	**7**	**0**	**4**	**4**	**10**	**0**	**0**	**0**	**26:32**
2011-12	**Pittsburgh**	**NHL**	**51**	**10**	**32**	**42**	**34**	**4**	**1**	**3**	**142**	**7.0**	**21**	**0**	**0.0**	**24:50**	**6**	**1**	**4**	**5**	**21**	**1**	**0**	**0**	**23:01**
2012-13	**Pittsburgh**	**NHL**	**35**	**5**	**33**	**38**	**8**	**1**	**0**	**1**	**95**	**5.3**	**16**	**0**	**0.0**	**25:38**	**15**	**3**	**13**	**16**	**8**	**2**	**0**	**1**	**27:38**
2013-14	**Pittsburgh**	**NHL**	**37**	**11**	**11**	**22**	**16**	**6**	**0**	**1**	**108**	**10.2**	**–8**	**0**	**0.0**	**24:14**	**13**	**2**	**4**	**6**	**14**	**0**	**0**	**1**	**24:10**
2014-15	**Pittsburgh**	**NHL**	**69**	**11**	**43**	**54**	**79**	**2**	**1**	**1**	**197**	**5.6**	**12**	**1**	**0.0**	**25:29**	....	....	....	....	....	....	....	....	....
2015-16 ♦	**Pittsburgh**	**NHL**	**71**	**16**	**51**	**67**	**66**	**5**	**0**	**2**	**218**	**7.3**	**9**	**0**	**0.0**	**26:57**	**23**	**3**	**12**	**15**	**22**	**0**	**0**	**1**	**28:53**
2016-17 ♦	**Pittsburgh**	**NHL**	**41**	**5**	**29**	**34**	**32**	**2**	**0**	**2**	**122**	**4.1**	**2**	**0**	**0.0**	**25:31**	....	....	....	....	....	....	....	....	....
	NHL Totals		**603**	**87**	**299**	**386**	**438**	**31**	**3**	**18**	**1506**	**5.8**		**3**	**33.3**	**23:24**	**116**	**18**	**50**	**68**	**119**	**9**	**0**	**5**	**23:36**

QMJHL All-Rookie Team (2005) • Canadian Major Junior All-Rookie Team (2005) • QMJHL First All-Star Team (2006, 2007) • Canadian Major Junior Second All-Star Team (2006. 2007) • NHL Second All-Star Team (2013, 2016)

Played in NHL All-Star Game (2011, 2012, 2016)

• Missed majority of 2013-14 due to pre-season knee injury and heart ailment, February 7, 2014.

LETESTU, Mark

(luh-TEHS- too, MAHRK) **EDM**

Center. Shoots right. 5'10", 197 lbs. Born, Elk Point, AB, February 4, 1985.

Season	Club	League	GP	G	A	Pts	PIM	PP	SH	GW	S	S%	+/-	TF	F%	Min	GP	G	A	Pts	PIM	PP	SH	GW	Min
2003-04	Bonnyville	AJHL	58	22	27	49	24	....	....	....	....	....	....	....	....	....	....	....	....	....	....	....	....	....	....
2004-05	Bonnyville	AJHL	63	39	47	86	32	....	....	....	....	....	....	....	....	....	....	....	....	....	....	....	....	....	....
2005-06	Bonnyville	AJHL	58	50	55	105	59	....	....	....	....	....	....	....	....	....	....	....	....	....	....	....	....	....	....
2006-07	Western Mich.	CCHA	37	24	22	46	14	....	....	....	....	....	....	....	....	....	....	....	....	....	....	....	....	....	....
2007-08	Wilkes-Barre	AHL	52	6	12	18	28	....	....	....	....	....	....	....	....	....	13	0	3	3	0	....	....	....	....
	Wheeling Nailers	ECHL	6	1	2	3	4	....	....	....	....	....	....	....	....	....	....	....	....	....	....	....	....	....	....
2008-09	Wilkes-Barre	AHL	73	24	37	61	6	....	....	....	....	....	....	....	....	....	12	2	8	10	4	....	....	....	....
2009-10	**Pittsburgh**	**NHL**	**10**	**1**	**0**	**1**	**2**	**0**	**0**	**0**	**9**	**11.1**	**–2**	**74**	**55.4**	**9:38**	**4**	**0**	**1**	**1**	**0**	**0**	**0**	**0**	**9:39**
	Wilkes-Barre	AHL	63	21	34	55	21	....	....	....	....	....	....	....	....	....	4	0	3	3	0	....	....	....	....
2010-11	**Pittsburgh**	**NHL**	**64**	**14**	**13**	**27**	**13**	**4**	**0**	**3**	**128**	**10.9**	**4**	**734**	**55.5**	**14:15**	**7**	**0**	**1**	**1**	**0**	**0**	**0**	**0**	**15:29**
2011-12	**Pittsburgh**	**NHL**	**11**	**0**	**1**	**1**	**2**	**0**	**0**	**0**	**9**	**0.0**	**–6**	**132**	**55.3**	**12:50**	....	....	....	....	....	....	....	....	....
	Columbus	**NHL**	**51**	**11**	**13**	**24**	**6**	**4**	**0**	**0**	**105**	**10.5**	**–3**	**590**	**51.2**	**16:15**	....	....	....	....	....	....	....	....	....
2012-13	Almtuna	Sweden-2	7	4	0	4	2	....	....	....	....	....	....	....	....	....	....	....	....	....	....	....	....	....	....
	Columbus	**NHL**	**46**	**13**	**14**	**27**	**10**	**3**	**2**	**2**	**92**	**14.1**	**7**	**487**	**50.1**	**16:31**	....	....	....	....	....	....	....	....	....
2013-14	**Columbus**	**NHL**	**82**	**12**	**22**	**34**	**20**	**5**	**1**	**1**	**122**	**9.8**	**1**	**730**	**51.2**	**14:41**	**6**	**1**	**1**	**2**	**0**	**1**	**0**	**0**	**16:51**
2014-15	**Columbus**	**NHL**	**54**	**7**	**6**	**13**	**0**	**0**	**1**	**1**	**63**	**11.1**	**–9**	**603**	**52.9**	**13:20**	....	....	....	....	....	....	....	....	....
2015-16	**Edmonton**	**NHL**	**82**	**10**	**15**	**25**	**10**	**3**	**2**	**0**	**107**	**9.3**	**–21**	**1162**	**51.3**	**15:47**	....	....	....	....	....	....	....	....	....
2016-17	**Edmonton**	**NHL**	**78**	**16**	**19**	**35**	**17**	**11**	**2**	**6**	**120**	**13.3**	**–2**	**896**	**50.5**	**14:14**	**13**	**5**	**6**	**11**	**2**	**4**	**0**	**0**	**17:36**
	NHL Totals		**478**	**84**	**103**	**187**	**80**	**30**	**8**	**13**	**755**	**11.1**		**5408**	**51.9**	**14:47**	**30**	**6**	**9**	**15**	**2**	**5**	**0**	**0**	**15:54**

Signed as a free agent by **Pittsburgh**, March 22, 2007. Traded to **Columbus** by **Pittsburgh** for Columbus' 4th round pick (Matia Marcantuoni) in 2012 NHL Draft, November 8, 2011. Signed as a free agent by **Almtuna** (Sweden-2), December 3, 2012. Signed as a free agent by **Edmonton**, July 1, 2015.

LETOURNEAU-LEBLOND, Pierre-Luc

(leh-TOOR-noh-leh-BLAWN)

Left wing. Shoots left. 6'1", 214 lbs. Born, Levis, QC, June 4, 1985. New Jersey's 4th pick, 216th overall, in 2004 NHL Draft.

			Regular Season														Playoffs								
Season	Club	League	GP	G	A	Pts	PIM	PP	SH	GW	S	S%	+/-	TF	F%	Min	GP	G	A	Pts	PIM	PP	SH	GW	Min
2003-04	Baie-Comeau	QMJHL	62	2	3	5	198	....	....	....	....	....	....	....	....	....	4	0	0	0	6	....	....	....	....
2004-05	Baie-Comeau	QMJHL	67	1	6	7	229	....	....	....	....	....	....	....	....	....	6	0	1	1	10	....	....	....	....
2005-06	Albany River Rats	AHL	27	1	1	2	130	....	....	....	....	....	....	....	....	....	....	....	....	....	....	....	....	....	....
	Adirondack	UHL	31	3	6	9	165	....	....	....	....	....	....	....	....	....	6	0	1	1	29	....	....	....	....
2006-07	Trenton Titans	ECHL	52	4	9	13	183	....	....	....	....	....	....	....	....	....	4	0	0	0	15	....	....	....	....
2007-08	Lowell Devils	AHL	36	3	3	6	98	....	....	....	....	....	....	....	....	....	....	....	....	....	....	....	....	....	....
	Trenton Devils	ECHL	6	0	1	1	46	....	....	....	....	....	....	....	....	....	....	....	....	....	....	....	....	....	....
2008-09	**New Jersey**	**NHL**	**8**	**0**	**1**	**1**	**22**	**0**	**0**	**0**	**3**	**0.0**	**3**	**0**	**0.0**	**4:51**	....	....	....	....	....	....	....	....	....
	Lowell Devils	AHL	60	5	5	10	216	....	....	....	....	....	....	....	....	....	....	....	....	....	....	....	....	....	....
2009-10	**New Jersey**	**NHL**	**27**	**0**	**2**	**2**	**48**	**0**	**0**	**0**	**9**	**0.0**	**–4**	**2**	**50.0**	**5:31**	**5**	**0**	**0**	**0**	**10**	**0**	**0**	**0**	**4:34**
	Lowell Devils	AHL	5	0	2	2	18	....	....	....	....	....	....	....	....	....	....	....	....	....	....	....	....	....	....
2010-11	**New Jersey**	**NHL**	**2**	**0**	**0**	**0**	**21**	**0**	**0**	**0**	**0**	**0.0**	**–2**	**0**	**0.0**	**3:28**	....	....	....	....	....	....	....	....	....
	Albany Devils	AHL	64	8	5	13	*334	....	....	....	....	....	....	....	....	....	....	....	....	....	....	....	....	....	....
2011-12	**Calgary**	**NHL**	**3**	**0**	**0**	**0**	**10**	**0**	**0**	**0**	**3**	**0.0**	**1**	**0**	**0.0**	**4:51**	....	....	....	....	....	....	....	....	....
	Abbotsford Heat	AHL	50	1	5	6	167	....	....	....	....	....	....	....	....	....	5	0	0	0	18	....	....	....	....
2012-13	Norfolk Admirals	AHL	33	3	5	8	98	....	....	....	....	....	....	....	....	....	....	....	....	....	....	....	....	....	....
2013-14	Wilkes-Barre	AHL	66	2	4	6	259	....	....	....	....	....	....	....	....	....	2	0	0	0	12	....	....	....	....
	Pittsburgh	**NHL**	**1**	**0**	**0**	**0**	**0**	**0**	**0**	**0**	**1**	**0.0**	**0**	**0**	**0.0**	**4:34**	....	....	....	....	....	....	....	....	....
2014-15	Wilkes-Barre	AHL	55	2	4	6	241	....	....	....	....	....	....	....	....	....	4	0	0	0	7	....	....	....	....
2015-16	Albany Devils	AHL	52	1	5	6	131	....	....	....	....	....	....	....	....	....	3	0	0	0	8	....	....	....	....
2016-17	Syracuse Crunch	AHL	37	1	4	5	121	....	....	....	....	....	....	....	....	....	....	....	....	....	....	....	....	....	....
	Toronto Marlies	AHL	1	0	0	0	7	....	....	....	....	....	....	....	....	....	....	....	....	....	....	....	....	....	....
	NHL Totals		**41**	**0**	**3**	**3**	**101**	**0**	**0**	**0**	**16**	**0.0**		**2**	**50.0**	**5:13**	**5**	**0**	**0**	**0**	**10**	**0**	**0**	**0**	**4:34**

• Missed majority of 2009-10 due to recurring upper-body injury and as a healthy reserve. Traded to **Calgary** by **New Jersey** for Calgary's 5th round pick (Graham Black) in 2012 NHL Draft, July 12, 2011. Signed as a free agent by **Anaheim**, January 15, 2013. Signed as a free agent by **Wilkes-Barre** (AHL), August 20, 2013. Signed as a free agent by **Pittsburgh**, November 7, 2013. Signed as a free agent by **New Jersey**, September 11, 2015. Signed as a free agent by **Tampa Bay**, July 1, 2016. • Loaned to **Toronto** (AHL) by **Tampa Bay**, February 27, 2017.

LEWIS, Trevor

(LOO-ihs, TREH-vuhr) **L.A.**

Center. Shoots right. 6'1", 199 lbs. Born, Salt Lake City, UT, January 8, 1987. Los Angeles' 2nd pick, 17th overall, in 2006 NHL Draft.

			Regular Season														Playoffs								
Season	Club	League	GP	G	A	Pts	PIM	PP	SH	GW	S	S%	+/-	TF	F%	Min	GP	G	A	Pts	PIM	PP	SH	GW	Min
2004-05	Des Moines	USHL	52	10	12	22	70	....	....	....	....	....	....	....	....	....	....	....	....	....	....	....	....	....	....
2005-06	Des Moines	USHL	56	35	40	75	69	....	....	....	....	....	....	....	....	....	11	3	*13	*16	16	....	....	....	....
2006-07	Owen Sound	OHL	62	29	44	73	51	....	....	....	....	....	....	....	....	....	4	1	2	3	0	....	....	....	....
	Manchester	AHL	8	4	2	6	2	....	....	....	....	....	....	....	....	....	2	0	0	0	0	....	....	....	....
2007-08	Manchester	AHL	76	12	16	28	43	....	....	....	....	....	....	....	....	....	4	0	0	0	2	....	....	....	....
2008-09	**Los Angeles**	**NHL**	**6**	**1**	**2**	**3**	**0**	**0**	**0**	**0**	**10**	**10.0**	**0**	**4**	**25.0**	**11:36**	....	....	....	....	....	....	....	....	....
	Manchester	AHL	75	20	31	51	30	....	....	....	....	....	....	....	....	....	....	....	....	....	....	....	....	....	....
2009-10	**Los Angeles**	**NHL**	**5**	**0**	**0**	**0**	**0**	**0**	**0**	**0**	**4**	**0.0**	**–3**	**5**	**0.0**	**9:08**	....	....	....	....	....	....	....	....	....
	Manchester	AHL	23	5	2	7	6	....	....	....	....	....	....	....	....	....	16	5	4	9	10	....	....	....	....
2010-11	**Los Angeles**	**NHL**	**72**	**3**	**10**	**13**	**6**	**0**	**0**	**2**	**105**	**2.9**	**–11**	**385**	**39.2**	**11:29**	**6**	**1**	**3**	**4**	**2**	**1**	**0**	**0**	**16:39**
2011-12♦	**Los Angeles**	**NHL**	**72**	**3**	**4**	**7**	**26**	**0**	**0**	**1**	**103**	**2.9**	**–3**	**199**	**43.7**	**13:14**	**20**	**3**	**6**	**9**	**2**	**1**	**0**	**0**	**14:54**
2012-13	Utah Grizzlies	ECHL	6	3	6	9	4	....	....	....	....	....	....	....	....	....	....	....	....	....	....	....	....	....	....
	Los Angeles	**NHL**	**48**	**5**	**9**	**14**	**19**	**0**	**1**	**2**	**92**	**5.4**	**5**	**64**	**48.4**	**15:12**	**18**	**1**	**2**	**3**	**2**	**1**	**0**	**1**	**16:25**
2013-14♦	**Los Angeles**	**NHL**	**73**	**6**	**5**	**11**	**6**	**0**	**1**	**2**	**111**	**5.4**	**–1**	**262**	**48.5**	**13:15**	**26**	**4**	**1**	**5**	**6**	**0**	**0**	**1**	**12:39**
2014-15	**Los Angeles**	**NHL**	**73**	**9**	**16**	**25**	**14**	**0**	**1**	**2**	**143**	**6.3**	**8**	**177**	**42.9**	**14:06**	....	....	....	....	....	....	....	....	....
2015-16	**Los Angeles**	**NHL**	**75**	**8**	**8**	**16**	**20**	**0**	**1**	**1**	**167**	**4.8**	**–10**	**257**	**40.1**	**14:34**	**5**	**2**	**0**	**2**	**4**	**0**	**1**	**0**	**10:37**
2016-17	**Los Angeles**	**NHL**	**82**	**12**	**12**	**24**	**30**	**1**	**0**	**3**	**145**	**8.3**	**–6**	**110**	**40.0**	**14:16**	....	....	....	....	....	....	....	....	....
	NHL Totals		**506**	**47**	**66**	**113**	**121**	**1**	**4**	**13**	**880**	**5.3**		**1463**	**42.4**	**13:36**	**75**	**11**	**12**	**23**	**16**	**3**	**1**	**2**	**14:20**

USHL Player of the Year (2006)

• Missed majority of 2009-10 due to lower-body injury and as a healthy reserve.

LIAMBAS, Michael

(lee-AM-buhs, MIGH-kuhl) **ANA**

Left wing. Shoots left. 5'10", 203 lbs. Born, Woodbridge, ON, February 16, 1989.

			Regular Season														Playoffs								
Season	Club	League	GP	G	A	Pts	PIM	PP	SH	GW	S	S%	+/-	TF	F%	Min	GP	G	A	Pts	PIM	PP	SH	GW	Min
2004-05	Tor. Nationals	GTHL	25	1	12	13	50	....	....	....	....	....	....	....	....	....	....	....	....	....	....	....	....	....	....
	St. Mike's B's	ON-Jr.A	5	1	0	1	16	....	....	....	....	....	....	....	....	....	....	....	....	....	....	....	....	....	....
2005-06	Tor. Nats Midget	GTHL	STATISTICS NOT AVAILABLE																						
2006-07	Erie Otters	OHL	55	4	1	5	169	....	....	....	....	....	....	....	....	....	....	....	....	....	....	....	....	....	....
2007-08	Erie Otters	OHL	60	0	5	5	169	....	....	....	....	....	....	....	....	....	....	....	....	....	....	....	....	....	....
2008-09	Erie Otters	OHL	5	1	0	1	2	....	....	....	....	....	....	....	....	....	5	0	0	0	6	....	....	....	....
	Bloomington	IHL	8	1	0	1	31	....	....	....	....	....	....	....	....	....	....	....	....	....	....	....	....	....	....
2009-10	Erie Otters	OHL	4	0	2	2	17	....	....	....	....	....	....	....	....	....	....	....	....	....	....	....	....	....	....
	Bloomington	IHL	17	0	3	3	115	....	....	....	....	....	....	....	....	....	....	....	....	....	....	....	....	....	....
2010-11	Cincinnati	ECHL	15	1	1	2	72	....	....	....	....	....	....	....	....	....	4	0	2	2	8	....	....	....	....
2011-12	Cincinnati	ECHL	39	0	9	9	160	....	....	....	....	....	....	....	....	....	....	....	....	....	....	....	....	....	....
2012-13	Cincinnati	ECHL	1	0	1	1	20	....	....	....	....	....	....	....	....	....	....	....	....	....	....	....	....	....	....
	Orlando	ECHL	32	2	7	9	151	....	....	....	....	....	....	....	....	....	....	....	....	....	....	....	....	....	....
	Milwaukee	AHL	27	1	0	1	74	....	....	....	....	....	....	....	....	....	2	0	1	1	32	....	....	....	....
2013-14	Milwaukee	AHL	60	3	5	8	267	....	....	....	....	....	....	....	....	....	2	0	0	0	2	....	....	....	....
2014-15	Milwaukee	AHL	54	5	3	8	158	....	....	....	....	....	....	....	....	....	....	....	....	....	....	....	....	....	....
2015-16	Rockford IceHogs	AHL	44	1	1	2	188	....	....	....	....	....	....	....	....	....	3	0	0	0	16	....	....	....	....
2016-17	**Nashville**	**NHL**	**1**	**0**	**0**	**0**	**0**	**0**	**0**	**0**	**0**	**0.0**	**–1**	**0**	**0.0**	**4:42**	....	....	....	....	....	....	....	....	....
	Milwaukee	AHL	72	3	8	11	*149	....	....	....	....	....	....	....	....	....	3	0	0	0	2	....	....	....	....
	NHL Totals		**1**	**0**	**0**	**0**	**0**	**0**	**0**	**0**	**0**	**0.0**		**0**	**0.0**	**4:42**	....	....	....	....	....	....	....	....	....

Signed as a free agent by **Chicago**, July 2, 2015. Signed as a free agent by **Nashville**, July 4, 2016. Signed as a free agent by **Anaheim**, July 2, 2017.

LILES, John-Michael

(LIGH-uhls, JAWN-MIGHK-uhl) **BOS**

Defense. Shoots left. 5'10", 185 lbs. Born, Indianapolis, IN, November 25, 1980. Colorado's 8th pick, 159th overall, in 2000 NHL Draft.

			Regular Season														Playoffs								
Season	Club	League	GP	G	A	Pts	PIM	PP	SH	GW	S	S%	+/-	TF	F%	Min	GP	G	A	Pts	PIM	PP	SH	GW	Min
1997-98	USAHNTDP	U-17	15	0	6	6	4	....	....	....	....	....	....	....	....	....	....	....	....	....	....	....	....	....	....
	USAHNTDP	USHL	5	0	1	1	0	....	....	....	....	....	....	....	....	....	....	....	....	....	....	....	....	....	....
	USAHNTDP	NAHL	42	4	7	11	40	....	....	....	....	....	....	....	....	....	5	2	0	2	0	....	....	....	....
1998-99	USAHNTDP	USHL	46	4	14	18	47	....	....	....	....	....	....	....	....	....	....	....	....	....	....	....	....	....	....
	USAHNTDP	NAHL	13	2	5	7	6	....	....	....	....	....	....	....	....	....	....	....	....	....	....	....	....	....	....
99-2000	Michigan State	CCHA	40	8	20	28	26	....	....	....	....	....	....	....	....	....	....	....	....	....	....	....	....	....	....
2000-01	Michigan State	CCHA	42	7	18	25	28	....	....	....	....	....	....	....	....	....	....	....	....	....	....	....	....	....	....
2001-02	Michigan State	CCHA	41	13	22	35	18	....	....	....	....	....	....	....	....	....	....	....	....	....	....	....	....	....	....
2002-03	Michigan State	CCHA	39	16	34	50	46	....	....	....	....	....	....	....	....	....	....	....	....	....	....	....	....	....	....
	Hershey Bears	AHL	5	0	1	1	4	....	....	....	....	....	....	....	....	....	5	0	0	0	2	....	....	....	....
2003-04	**Colorado**	**NHL**	**79**	**10**	**24**	**34**	**28**	**2**	**0**	**1**	**115**	**8.7**	**7**	**0**	**0.0**	**16:14**	**11**	**0**	**1**	**1**	**4**	**0**	**0**	**0**	**16:41**
2004-05	Iserlohn Roosters	Germany	17	5	6	11	24	....	....	....	....	....	....	....	....	....	....	....	....	....	....	....	....	....	....
2005-06	**Colorado**	**NHL**	**82**	**14**	**35**	**49**	**44**	**6**	**0**	**1**	**154**	**9.1**	**5**	**1**	**100.0**	**18:31**	**9**	**1**	**2**	**3**	**6**	**1**	**0**	**0**	**17:35**
	United States	Olympics	6	0	2	2	2	....	....	....	....	....	....	....	....	....	....	....	....	....	....	....	....	....	....
2006-07	**Colorado**	**NHL**	**71**	**14**	**30**	**44**	**24**	**8**	**0**	**3**	**128**	**10.9**	**0**	**0**	**0.0**	**17:46**	....	....	....	....	....	....	....	....	....
2007-08	**Colorado**	**NHL**	**81**	**6**	**26**	**32**	**26**	**5**	**0**	**1**	**163**	**3.7**	**2**	**0**	**0.0**	**19:40**	**10**	**2**	**3**	**5**	**2**	**1**	**0**	**0**	**19:08**
2008-09	**Colorado**	**NHL**	**75**	**12**	**27**	**39**	**31**	**6**	**0**	**1**	**146**	**8.2**	**–19**	**0**	**0.0**	**21:33**	....	....	....	....	....	....	....	....	....
2009-10	**Colorado**	**NHL**	**59**	**6**	**25**	**31**	**30**	**3**	**0**	**2**	**96**	**6.3**	**–2**	**0**	**0.0**	**18:28**	**6**	**1**	**1**	**2**	**4**	**1**	**0**	**0**	**19:01**
2010-11	**Colorado**	**NHL**	**76**	**6**	**40**	**46**	**35**	**3**	**0**	**0**	**163**	**3.7**	**–9**	**0**	**0.0**	**22:01**	....	....	....	....	....	....	....	....	....
2011-12	**Toronto**	**NHL**	**66**	**7**	**20**	**27**	**20**	**4**	**0**	**0**	**106**	**6.6**	**–14**	**0**	**0.0**	**21:21**	....	....	....	....	....	....	....	....	....
2012-13	**Toronto**	**NHL**	**32**	**2**	**9**	**11**	**4**	**0**	**0**	**0**	**47**	**4.3**	**–1**	**1**	**0.0**	**18:46**	**4**	**0**	**0**	**0**	**2**	**0**	**0**	**0**	**15:25**
2013-14	**Toronto**	**NHL**	**6**	**0**	**0**	**0**	**0**	**0**	**0**	**0**	**5**	**0.0**	**–2**	**1**	**100.0**	**17:04**	....	....	....	....	....	....	....	....	....
	Toronto Marlies	AHL	16	3	10	13	14	....	....	....	....	....	....	....	....	....	....	....	....	....	....	....	....	....	....
	Carolina	**NHL**	**35**	**2**	**7**	**9**	**8**	**1**	**0**	**0**	**51**	**3.9**	**7**	**0**	**0.0**	**20:06**	....	....	....	....	....	....	....	....	....
2014-15	**Carolina**	**NHL**	**57**	**2**	**20**	**22**	**14**	**0**	**0**	**0**	**90**	**2.2**	**–9**	**0**	**0.0**	**19:09**	....	....	....	....	....	....	....	....	....

			Regular Season														Playoffs								
Season	Club	League	GP	G	A	Pts	PIM	PP	SH	GW	S	S%	+/-	TF	F%	Min	GP	G	A	Pts	PIM	PP	SH	GW	Min
2015-16	Carolina	NHL	64	6	9	15	16	1	1	1	92	6.5	–3	0	0.0	20:34	....	....	....	....	....	....	....	....	....
	Boston	NHL	17	0	6	6	2	0	0	0	19	0.0	–7	0	0.0	19:19	....	....	....	....	....	....	....	....	....
2016-17	Boston	NHL	36	0	5	5	4	0	0	0	36	0.0	1	2	100.0	16:12	6	0	2	2	0	0	0	0	16:29
	NHL Totals		**836**	**87**	**283**	**370**	**286**	**39**	**1**	**10**	**1411**	**6.2**		**5**	**80.0**	**19:20**	**46**	**4**	**9**	**13**	**18**	**3**	**0**	**0**	**17:34**

CCHA Second All-Star Team (2001) • CCHA First All-Star Team (2002, 2003) • NCAA West Second All-American Team (2002) • NCAA West First All-American Team (2003) • NHL All-Rookie Team (2004)

Signed as a free agent by **Iserlohn** (Germany), December 29, 2004. Traded to **Toronto** by **Colorado** for Boston's 2nd round pick (previously acquired, later traded to Washington, later traded to Dallas – Dallas selected Mike Winther) in 2012 NHL Draft, June 24, 2011. Traded to **Carolina** by **Toronto** with Dennis Robertson for Tim Gleason, January 1, 2014. Traded to **Boston** by **Carolina** for Anthony Camara, Boston's 3rd round pick (Jack LaFontaine) in 2016 NHL Draft and Boston's 5th round pick (Jack Dugan) in 2017 NHL Draft, February 29, 2016.

LINDBERG, Oscar
(LIHND-buhrg, AWS-kuhr) **VGK**

Center. Shoots left. 6'1", 195 lbs. Born, Skelleftea, Sweden, October 29, 1991. Phoenix's 4th pick, 57th overall, in 2010 NHL Draft.

			Regular Season														Playoffs								
Season	Club	League	GP	G	A	Pts	PIM	PP	SH	GW	S	S%	+/-	TF	F%	Min	GP	G	A	Pts	PIM	PP	SH	GW	Min
2007-08	Skelleftea U18	Swe-U18	31	19	29	48	36	....	....	....	....	....	....	....	....	....	....	....	....	....	....	....	....	....	....
	Skelleftea Jr.	Swe-Jr.	1	0	0	0	2	....	....	....	....	....	....	....	....	....	2	0	1	1	0	....	....	....	....
2008-09	Skelleftea AIK U18	Swe-U18	6	8	10	18	14	....	....	....	....	....	....	....	....	....	7	4	5	9	8	....	....	....	....
	Skelleftea AIK Jr.	Swe-Jr.	38	14	19	33	54	....	....	....	....	....	....	....	....	....	5	0	1	1	4	....	....	....	....
2009-10	Skelleftea AIK Jr.	Swe-Jr.	30	14	23	37	44	....	....	....	....	....	....	....	....	....	1	1	1	2	12	....	....	....	....
	Skelleftea AIK	Sweden	36	1	1	2	35	....	....	....	....	....	....	....	....	....	10	2	0	2	2	....	....	....	....
2010-11	Skelleftea AIK Jr.	Swe-Jr.	9	8	4	12	8	....	....	....	....	....	....	....	....	....	....	....	....	....	....	....	....	....	....
	Skelleftea AIK	Sweden	41	5	9	14	31	....	....	....	....	....	....	....	....	....	18	3	4	7	4	....	....	....	....
2011-12	Skelleftea AIK Jr.	Swe-Jr.	2	1	3	4	2	....	....	....	....	....	....	....	....	....	....	....	....	....	....	....	....	....	....
	Sundsvall	Sweden-2	5	1	1	2	2	....	....	....	....	....	....	....	....	....	....	....	....	....	....	....	....	....	....
	Skelleftea AIK	Sweden	46	5	5	10	18	....	....	....	....	....	....	....	....	....	18	1	3	4	10	....	....	....	....
2012-13	Skelleftea AIK	Sweden	55	17	25	42	54	....	....	....	....	....	....	....	....	....	13	4	8	*12	16	....	....	....	....
2013-14	Hartford	AHL	75	18	26	44	58	....	....	....	....	....	....	....	....	....	....	....	....	....	....	....	....	....	....
2014-15	**NY Rangers**	**NHL**	**1**	**0**	**0**	**0**	**0**	**0**	**0**	**0**	**2**	**0.0**	**0**	**5**	**40.0**	**8:18**	....	....	....	....	....	....	....	....	....
	Hartford	AHL	75	28	28	56	68	....	....	....	....	....	....	....	....	....	15	3	13	16	6	....	....	....	....
2015-16	**NY Rangers**	**NHL**	**68**	**13**	**15**	**28**	**43**	**1**	**0**	**2**	**114**	**11.4**	**12**	**277**	**48.4**	**12:11**	**2**	**0**	**0**	**0**	**2**	**0**	**0**	**0**	**13:43**
2016-17	**NY Rangers**	**NHL**	**65**	**8**	**12**	**20**	**32**	**0**	**0**	**1**	**86**	**9.3**	**2**	**575**	**52.0**	**10:50**	**12**	**3**	**1**	**4**	**2**	**0**	**0**	**1**	**9:54**
	NHL Totals		**134**	**21**	**27**	**48**	**75**	**1**	**0**	**3**	**202**	**10.4**		**857**	**50.8**	**11:30**	**14**	**3**	**1**	**4**	**4**	**0**	**0**	**1**	**10:27**

Traded to **NY Rangers** by **Phoenix** for Ethan Werek, May 8, 2011. Claimed by **Vegas** from **NY Rangers** in Expansion Draft, June 21, 2017.

LINDBERG, Tobias
(LIHND-buhrg, toh-BEE-uhs) **TOR**

Right wing. Shoots left. 6'3", 227 lbs. Born, Stockholm, Sweden, July 22, 1995. Ottawa's 3rd pick, 102nd overall, in 2013 NHL Draft.

			Regular Season														Playoffs								
Season	Club	League	GP	G	A	Pts	PIM	PP	SH	GW	S	S%	+/-	TF	F%	Min	GP	G	A	Pts	PIM	PP	SH	GW	Min
2010-11	SDE U18	Swe-U18	9	0	2	2	18	....	....	....	....	....	....	....	....	....	....	....	....	....	....	....	....	....	....
2011-12	Djurgarden U18	Swe-U18	39	19	20	39	42	....	....	....	....	....	....	....	....	....	4	2	0	2	20	....	....	....	....
	Djurgarden Jr.	Swe-Jr.	1	0	0	0	0	....	....	....	....	....	....	....	....	....	3	0	1	1	0	....	....	....	....
2012-13	Djurgarden U18	Swe-U18	14	9	12	21	6	....	....	....	....	....	....	....	....	....	9	4	10	14	24	....	....	....	....
	Djurgarden Jr.	Swe-Jr.	43	9	13	22	30	....	....	....	....	....	....	....	....	....	2	0	2	2	2	....	....	....	....
	Djurgarden	Sweden-2	6	0	1	1	4	....	....	....	....	....	....	....	....	....	....	....	....	....	....	....	....	....	....
2013-14	Djurgarden Jr.	Swe-Jr.	38	7	15	22	93	....	....	....	....	....	....	....	....	....	4	2	1	3	12	....	....	....	....
	Djurgarden	Sweden-2	3	0	0	0	0	....	....	....	....	....	....	....	....	....	....	....	....	....	....	....	....	....	....
2014-15	Oshawa Generals	OHL	67	32	46	78	14	....	....	....	....	....	....	....	....	....	21	7	12	19	8	....	....	....	....
2015-16	Binghamton	AHL	34	5	17	22	8	....	....	....	....	....	....	....	....	....	....	....	....	....	....	....	....	....	....
	Toronto	**NHL**	**6**	**0**	**2**	**2**	**4**	**0**	**0**	**0**	**12**	**0.0**	**0**	**3**	**0.0**	**15:50**	....	....	....	....	....	....	....	....	....
	Toronto Marlies	AHL	22	6	6	12	12	....	....	....	....	....	....	....	....	....	3	0	0	0	2	....	....	....	....
2016-17	Toronto Marlies	AHL	44	6	10	16	34	....	....	....	....	....	....	....	....	....	....	....	....	....	....	....	....	....	....
	NHL Totals		**6**	**0**	**2**	**2**	**4**	**0**	**0**	**0**	**12**	**0.0**		**3**	**0.0**	**15:50**	....	....	....	....	....	....	....	....	....

Traded to **Toronto** by **Ottawa** with Jared Cowen, Colin Greening, Milan Michalek and Ottawa's 2nd round pick (Eemeli Rasanen) in 2017 NHL Draft for Dion Phaneuf, Matt Frattin, Casey Bailey, Ryan Rupert and Cody Donaghey, February 9, 2016.

LINDBOHM, Petteri
(LIHND-bawm, PEH-tuh-ree) **ST.L.**

Defense. Shoots left. 6'3", 198 lbs. Born, Helsinki, Finland, September 23, 1993. St. Louis' 7th pick, 176th overall, in 2012 NHL Draft.

			Regular Season														Playoffs								
Season	Club	League	GP	G	A	Pts	PIM	PP	SH	GW	S	S%	+/-	TF	F%	Min	GP	G	A	Pts	PIM	PP	SH	GW	Min
2009-10	K-Vantaa U18	Fin-U18	31	1	3	4	34	....	....	....	....	....	....	....	....	....	6	0	0	0	24	....	....	....	....
2010-11	Blues Espoo U18	Fin-U18	7	2	6	8	10	....	....	....	....	....	....	....	....	....	2	0	2	2	2	....	....	....	....
	Blues Espoo Jr.	Fin-Jr.	41	1	8	9	56	....	....	....	....	....	....	....	....	....	13	0	3	3	12	....	....	....	....
2011-12	Jokerit Helsinki Jr.	Fin-Jr.	41	3	7	10	98	....	....	....	....	....	....	....	....	....	12	0	3	3	12	....	....	....	....
	Kiekko-Vantaa	Finland-2	5	0	3	3	8	....	....	....	....	....	....	....	....	....	....	....	....	....	....	....	....	....	....
2012-13	Jokerit Helsinki Jr.	Fin-Jr.	2	0	1	1	2	....	....	....	....	....	....	....	....	....	....	....	....	....	....	....	....	....	....
	Kiekko-Vantaa	Finland-2	6	3	0	3	4	....	....	....	....	....	....	....	....	....	....	....	....	....	....	....	....	....	....
	Jokerit Helsinki	Finland	35	0	4	4	61	....	....	....	....	....	....	....	....	....	....	....	....	....	....	....	....	....	....
2013-14	Assat Pori	Finland	19	1	4	5	8	....	....	....	....	....	....	....	....	....	....	....	....	....	....	....	....	....	....
	Jokerit Helsinki Jr.	Fin-Jr.	3	0	0	0	4	....	....	....	....	....	....	....	....	....	....	....	....	....	....	....	....	....	....
	Kiekko-Vantaa	Finland-2	13	1	1	2	12	....	....	....	....	....	....	....	....	....	....	....	....	....	....	....	....	....	....
	Jokerit Helsinki	Finland	18	0	1	1	18	....	....	....	....	....	....	....	....	....	....	....	....	....	....	....	....	....	....
2014-15	**St. Louis**	**NHL**	**23**	**2**	**1**	**3**	**26**	**0**	**0**	**0**	**32**	**6.3**	**–1**	**0**	**0.0**	**15:34**	....	....	....	....	....	....	....	....	....
	Chicago Wolves	AHL	53	6	12	18	62	....	....	....	....	....	....	....	....	....	5	0	1	1	10	....	....	....	....
2015-16	**St. Louis**	**NHL**	**10**	**0**	**0**	**0**	**7**	**0**	**0**	**0**	**9**	**0.0**	**–4**	**0**	**0.0**	**13:47**	....	....	....	....	....	....	....	....	....
	Chicago Wolves	AHL	43	3	8	11	50	....	....	....	....	....	....	....	....	....	....	....	....	....	....	....	....	....	....
2016-17	**St. Louis**	**NHL**	**7**	**0**	**0**	**0**	**4**	**0**	**0**	**0**	**10**	**0.0**	**–4**	**0**	**0.0**	**12:59**	....	....	....	....	....	....	....	....	....
	Chicago Wolves	AHL	52	8	8	16	54	....	....	....	....	....	....	....	....	....	9	1	3	4	2	....	....	....	....
	NHL Totals		**40**	**2**	**1**	**3**	**37**	**0**	**0**	**0**	**51**	**3.9**		**0**	**0.0**	**14:40**	....	....	....	....	....	....	....	....	....

LINDELL, Esa
(lihn-DEHL, EH-suh) **DAL**

Defense. Shoots left. 6'3", 210 lbs. Born, Vantaa, Finland, May 23, 1994. Dallas' 5th pick, 74th overall, in 2012 NHL Draft.

			Regular Season														Playoffs								
Season	Club	League	GP	G	A	Pts	PIM	PP	SH	GW	S	S%	+/-	TF	F%	Min	GP	G	A	Pts	PIM	PP	SH	GW	Min
2009-10	Jokerit U18	Fin-U18	3	0	1	1	2	....	....	....	....	....	....	....	....	....	....	....	....	....	....	....	....	....	....
2010-11	Jokerit U18	Fin-U18	14	5	7	12	10	....	....	....	....	....	....	....	....	....	4	0	1	1	4	....	....	....	....
	Jokerit Helsinki Jr.	Fin-Jr.	....	....	....	....	....	....	....	....	....	....	....	....	....	....	3	1	1	2	2	....	....	....	....
2011-12	Jokerit Helsinki Jr.	Fin-Jr.	48	21	30	51	16	....	....	....	....	....	....	....	....	....	11	2	5	7	6	....	....	....	....
	Kiekko-Vantaa	Finland-2	2	0	0	0	0	....	....	....	....	....	....	....	....	....	....	....	....	....	....	....	....	....	....
2012-13	Jokerit Helsinki Jr.	Fin-Jr.	11	5	4	9	6	....	....	....	....	....	....	....	....	....	....	....	....	....	....	....	....	....	....
	Kiekko-Vantaa	Finland-2	22	4	6	10	16	....	....	....	....	....	....	....	....	....	....	....	....	....	....	....	....	....	....
	Jokerit Helsinki	Finland	19	0	0	0	4	....	....	....	....	....	....	....	....	....	....	....	....	....	....	....	....	....	....
2013-14	Kiekko-Vantaa	Finland-2	11	2	3	5	8	....	....	....	....	....	....	....	....	....	....	....	....	....	....	....	....	....	....
	Jokerit Helsinki	Finland	44	2	3	5	10	....	....	....	....	....	....	....	....	....	2	0	0	0	0	....	....	....	....
2014-15	Assat Pori	Finland	57	14	21	35	28	....	....	....	....	....	....	....	....	....	2	0	0	0	0	....	....	....	....
	Texas Stars	AHL	5	0	1	1	2	....	....	....	....	....	....	....	....	....	....	....	....	....	....	....	....	....	....
2015-16	**Dallas**	**NHL**	**4**	**0**	**0**	**0**	**0**	**0**	**0**	**0**	**2**	**0.0**	**–3**	**0**	**0.0**	**14:03**	....	....	....	....	....	....	....	....	....
	Texas Stars	AHL	73	14	28	42	56	....	....	....	....	....	....	....	....	....	4	2	2	4	0	....	....	....	....
2016-17	**Dallas**	**NHL**	**73**	**6**	**12**	**18**	**22**	**0**	**0**	**2**	**99**	**6.1**	**8**	**1**	**0.0**	**21:52**	....	....	....	....	....	....	....	....	....
	Texas Stars	AHL	2	0	1	1	0	....	....	....	....	....	....	....	....	....	....	....	....	....	....	....	....	....	....
	NHL Totals		**77**	**6**	**12**	**18**	**22**	**0**	**0**	**2**	**101**	**5.9**		**1**	**0.0**	**21:28**	....	....	....	....	....	....	....	....	....

LINDHOLM, Anton
(LIHND-hohlm, AN-tawn) **COL**

Defense. Shoots left. 5'11", 191 lbs. Born, Skelleftea, Sweden, November 29, 1994. Colorado's 5th pick, 144th overall, in 2014 NHL Draft.

			Regular Season														Playoffs								
Season	Club	League	GP	G	A	Pts	PIM	PP	SH	GW	S	S%	+/-	TF	F%	Min	GP	G	A	Pts	PIM	PP	SH	GW	Min
2009-10	Skelleftea AIK U18	Swe-U18	14	1	2	3	29	....	....	....	....	....	....	....	....	....	....	....	....	....	....	....	....	....	....
2010-11	Skelleftea AIK U18	Swe-U18	37	9	15	24	36	....	....	....	....	....	....	....	....	....	7	0	2	2	4	....	....	....	....
	Skelleftea AIK Jr.	Swe-Jr.	3	0	0	0	4	....	....	....	....	....	....	....	....	....	....	....	....	....	....	....	....	....	....
2011-12	Skelleftea AIK U18	Swe-U18	4	0	0	0	2	....	....	....	....	....	....	....	....	....	2	0	0	0	2	....	....	....	....
	Skelleftea AIK	Sweden	1	0	0	0	0	....	....	....	....	....	....	....	....	....	....	....	....	....	....	....	....	....	....
	Skelleftea AIK Jr.	Swe-Jr.	43	1	3	4	20	....	....	....	....	....	....	....	....	....	3	0	1	1	0	....	....	....	....
2012-13	Skelleftea AIK Jr.	Swe-Jr.	37	1	9	10	24	....	....	....	....	....	....	....	....	....	5	1	0	1	2	....	....	....	....
	Skelleftea AIK	Sweden	2	0	0	0	2	....	....	....	....	....	....	....	....	....	....	....	....	....	....	....	....	....	....

			Regular Season														Playoffs								
Season	Club	League	GP	G	A	Pts	PIM	PP	SH	GW	S	S%	+/-	TF	F%	Min	GP	G	A	Pts	PIM	PP	SH	GW	Min
2013-14	Skelleftea AIK Jr.	Swe-Jr.	39	1	5	6	34	....	....	....	....	....	....	....	....	....	....	....	....	....	....	....	....	....	....
	Pitea HC	Sweden-3	1	0	1	1	0	....	....	....	....	....	....	....	....	....	....	....	....	....	....	....	....	....	....
	Skelleftea AIK	Sweden	7	0	0	0	4	....	....	....	....	....	....	....	....	....	14	1	2	3	4	....	....	....	....
2014-15	Malmo	Sweden-2	5	1	2	3	2	....	....	....	....	....	....	....	....	....	....	....	....	....	....	....	....	....	....
	Skelleftea AIK	Sweden	35	0	7	7	35	....	....	....	....	....	....	....	....	....	15	1	4	5	8	....	....	....	....
2015-16	Skelleftea AIK	Sweden	30	0	4	4	18	....	....	....	....	....	....	....	....	....	16	0	1	1	6	....	....	....	....
2016-17	**Colorado**	**NHL**	**12**	**0**	**0**	**0**	**2**	**0**	**0**	**0**	**7**	**0.0**	**–8**	**0**	**0.0**	**14:45**	....	....	....	....	....	....	....	....	....
	San Antonio	AHL	62	2	11	13	39	....	....	....	....	....	....	....	....	....	....	....	....	....	....	....	....	....	....
	NHL Totals		**12**	**0**	**0**	**0**	**2**	**0**	**0**	**0**	**7**	**0.0**		**0**	**0.0**	**14:45**	....	....	....	....	....	....	....	....	....

LINDHOLM, Elias

(LIHND-hohlm, uh-LIGH-uhs) **CAR**

Center. Shoots right. 6'1", 192 lbs. Born, Boden , Sweden, December 2, 1994. Carolina's 1st pick, 5th overall, in 2013 NHL Draft.

2009-10	Brynas U18	Swe-U18	9	4	6	10	0	....	....	....	....	....	....	....	....	....	....	....	....	....	....	....	....	....	....
2010-11	Brynas U18	Swe-U18	40	17	44	61	32	....	....	....	....	....	....	....	....	....	4	3	3	6	29	....	....	....	....
	Brynas IF Gavle Jr.	Swe-Jr.	2	0	0	0	0	....	....	....	....	....	....	....	....	....	2	0	1	1	0	....	....	....	....
2011-12	Brynas U18	Swe-U18	4	1	6	7	0	....	....	....	....	....	....	....	....	....	3	1	2	3	0	....	....	....	....
	Brynas IF Gavle Jr.	Swe-Jr.	36	14	35	49	45	....	....	....	....	....	....	....	....	....	2	1	1	2	16	....	....	....	....
	Brynas IF Gavle	Sweden	12	0	0	0	0	....	....	....	....	....	....	....	....	....	2	0	0	0	0	....	....	....	....
2012-13	Brynas IF Gavle	Sweden	48	11	19	30	2	....	....	....	....	....	....	....	....	....	4	0	0	0	4	....	....	....	....
2013-14	**Carolina**	**NHL**	**58**	**9**	**12**	**21**	**4**	**4**	**0**	**2**	**70**	**12.9**	**–14**	**229**	**46.3**	**14:32**	....	....	....	....	....	....	....	....	....
2014-15	**Carolina**	**NHL**	**81**	**17**	**22**	**39**	**14**	**4**	**0**	**4**	**170**	**10.0**	**–23**	**220**	**52.3**	**16:25**	....	....	....	....	....	....	....	....	....
2015-16	**Carolina**	**NHL**	**82**	**11**	**28**	**39**	**24**	**2**	**0**	**3**	**176**	**6.3**	**–23**	**434**	**49.1**	**18:07**	....	....	....	....	....	....	....	....	....
2016-17	**Carolina**	**NHL**	**72**	**11**	**34**	**45**	**16**	**2**	**1**	**0**	**151**	**7.3**	**–2**	**635**	**55.6**	**18:11**	....	....	....	....	....	....	....	....	....
	NHL Totals		**293**	**48**	**96**	**144**	**58**	**12**	**1**	**9**	**567**	**8.5**		**1518**	**51.8**	**16:57**	....	....	....	....	....	....	....	....	....

LINDHOLM, Hampus

(LIHND-hohlm, HAM-puhs) **ANA**

Defense. Shoots left. 6'3", 205 lbs. Born, Helsingborg, Sweden, January 20, 1994. Anaheim's 1st pick, 6th overall, in 2012 NHL Draft.

2008-09	Jonstorps IF U18	Swe-U18	1	0	0	0	0	....	....	....	....	....	....	....	....	....	....	....	....	....	....	....	....	....	....
2009-10	Jonstorps IF U18	Swe-U18	15	3	4	7	8	....	....	....	....	....	....	....	....	....	....	....	....	....	....	....	....	....	....
	Jonstorps IF Jr.	Swe-Jr.	3	1	2	3	0	....	....	....	....	....	....	....	....	....	....	....	....	....	....	....	....	....	....
2010-11	Rogle U18	Swe-U18	11	2	3	5	10	....	....	....	....	....	....	....	....	....	3	0	2	2	0	....	....	....	....
	Rogle Jr.	Swe-Jr.	39	0	4	4	34	....	....	....	....	....	....	....	....	....	3	0	0	0	0	....	....	....	....
2011-12	Rogle U18	Swe-U18	1	1	3	4	2	....	....	....	....	....	....	....	....	....	....	....	....	....	....	....	....	....	....
	Rogle Jr.	Swe-Jr.	28	5	12	17	16	....	....	....	....	....	....	....	....	....	....	....	....	....	....	....	....	....	....
	Rogle	Sweden-2	36	2	7	9	18	....	....	....	....	....	....	....	....	....	....	....	....	....	....	....	....	....	....
2012-13	Norfolk Admirals	AHL	44	1	10	11	16	....	....	....	....	....	....	....	....	....	....	....	....	....	....	....	....	....	....
2013-14	**Anaheim**	**NHL**	**78**	**6**	**24**	**30**	**36**	**1**	**0**	**1**	**116**	**5.2**	**29**	**1**	**0.0**	**19:26**	**11**	**0**	**2**	**2**	**0**	**0**	**0**	**0**	**18:10**
2014-15	**Anaheim**	**NHL**	**78**	**7**	**27**	**34**	**32**	**0**	**0**	**1**	**107**	**6.5**	**25**	**5**	**0.0**	**21:46**	**16**	**2**	**8**	**10**	**10**	**0**	**0**	**0**	**23:15**
2015-16	**Anaheim**	**NHL**	**80**	**10**	**18**	**28**	**40**	**4**	**1**	**1**	**149**	**6.7**	**7**	**0**	**0.0**	**22:00**	**7**	**0**	**3**	**3**	**0**	**0**	**0**	**0**	**23:34**
2016-17	**Anaheim**	**NHL**	**66**	**6**	**14**	**20**	**36**	**1**	**0**	**2**	**94**	**6.4**	**13**	**2**	**100.0**	**22:27**	**17**	**1**	**3**	**4**	**10**	**0**	**0**	**0**	**22:00**
	NHL Totals		**302**	**29**	**83**	**112**	**144**	**6**	**1**	**5**	**466**	**6.2**		**8**	**25.0**	**21:22**	**51**	**3**	**16**	**19**	**20**	**0**	**0**	**0**	**21:47**

NHL All-Rookie Team (2014)

LIPON, JC

(lih-PAWN, JAY-SEE) **WPG**

Right wing. Shoots right. 6', 190 lbs. Born, Regina, SK, July 10, 1993. Winnipeg's 5th pick, 91st overall, in 2013 NHL Draft.

2008-09	Reg. Pat Cdns.	SMHL	43	4	9	13	26	....	....	....	....	....	....	....	....	....	5	2	1	3	4	....	....	....	....
2009-10	Kamloops Blazers	WHL	53	3	10	13	38	....	....	....	....	....	....	....	....	....	3	0	0	0	0	....	....	....	....
2010-11	Kamloops Blazers	WHL	65	3	18	21	111	....	....	....	....	....	....	....	....	....	....	....	....	....	....	....	....	....	....
2011-12	Kamloops Blazers	WHL	69	19	46	65	111	....	....	....	....	....	....	....	....	....	10	2	7	9	20	....	....	....	....
2012-13	Kamloops Blazers	WHL	61	36	53	89	115	....	....	....	....	....	....	....	....	....	15	6	17	23	20	....	....	....	....
2013-14	St. John's IceCaps	AHL	72	9	32	41	136	....	....	....	....	....	....	....	....	....	14	0	1	1	4	....	....	....	....
2014-15	St. John's IceCaps	AHL	75	5	21	26	163	....	....	....	....	....	....	....	....	....	....	....	....	....	....	....	....	....	....
2015-16	**Winnipeg**	**NHL**	**9**	**0**	**1**	**1**	**5**	**0**	**0**	**0**	**4**	**0.0**	**0**	**0**	**0.0**	**6:58**	....	....	....	....	....	....	....	....	....
	Manitoba Moose	AHL	45	13	17	30	87	....	....	....	....	....	....	....	....	....	....	....	....	....	....	....	....	....	....
2016-17	Manitoba Moose	AHL	71	12	18	30	129	....	....	....	....	....	....	....	....	....	....	....	....	....	....	....	....	....	....
	NHL Totals		**9**	**0**	**1**	**1**	**5**	**0**	**0**	**0**	**4**	**0.0**		**0**	**0.0**	**6:58**	....	....	....	....	....	....	....	....	....

LITTLE, Bryan

(LIH-tuhl, BRIGH-uhn) **WPG**

Center. Shoots right. 6', 191 lbs. Born, Edmonton, AB, November 12, 1987. Atlanta's 1st pick, 12th overall, in 2006 NHL Draft.

2003-04	Barrie Colts	OHL	64	34	24	58	18	....	....	....	....	....	....	....	....	....	12	5	5	10	7	....	....	....	....
2004-05	Barrie Colts	OHL	62	36	32	68	34	....	....	....	....	....	....	....	....	....	4	5	1	6	2	....	....	....	....
2005-06	Barrie Colts	OHL	64	42	67	109	99	....	....	....	....	....	....	....	....	....	14	8	15	23	19	....	....	....	....
2006-07	Barrie Colts	OHL	57	41	66	107	77	....	....	....	....	....	....	....	....	....	8	4	5	9	8	....	....	....	....
	Chicago Wolves	AHL	....	....	....	....	....	....	....	....	....	....	....	....	....	....	2	0	0	0	0	....	....	....	....
2007-08	**Atlanta**	**NHL**	**48**	**6**	**10**	**16**	**18**	**2**	**0**	**1**	**76**	**7.9**	**–2**	**505**	**45.2**	**15:37**	....	....	....	....	....	....	....	....	....
	Chicago Wolves	AHL	34	9	16	25	10	....	....	....	....	....	....	....	....	....	24	8	5	13	10	....	....	....	....
2008-09	**Atlanta**	**NHL**	**79**	**31**	**20**	**51**	**24**	**12**	**0**	**4**	**172**	**18.0**	**–5**	**214**	**43.5**	**16:55**	....	....	....	....	....	....	....	....	....
2009-10	**Atlanta**	**NHL**	**79**	**13**	**21**	**34**	**20**	**3**	**0**	**1**	**165**	**7.9**	**–6**	**154**	**44.2**	**15:45**	....	....	....	....	....	....	....	....	....
2010-11	**Atlanta**	**NHL**	**76**	**18**	**30**	**48**	**33**	**2**	**2**	**1**	**158**	**11.4**	**11**	**1331**	**46.3**	**18:27**	....	....	....	....	....	....	....	....	....
2011-12	**Winnipeg**	**NHL**	**74**	**24**	**22**	**46**	**26**	**6**	**0**	**6**	**162**	**14.8**	**–11**	**1479**	**49.6**	**20:13**	....	....	....	....	....	....	....	....	....
2012-13	**Winnipeg**	**NHL**	**48**	**7**	**25**	**32**	**4**	**2**	**0**	**2**	**84**	**8.3**	**8**	**842**	**51.2**	**19:48**	....	....	....	....	....	....	....	....	....
2013-14	**Winnipeg**	**NHL**	**82**	**23**	**41**	**64**	**58**	**8**	**2**	**1**	**170**	**13.5**	**8**	**1653**	**47.5**	**20:00**	....	....	....	....	....	....	....	....	....
2014-15	**Winnipeg**	**NHL**	**70**	**24**	**28**	**52**	**24**	**9**	**1**	**3**	**148**	**16.2**	**8**	**1551**	**49.1**	**19:55**	**4**	**2**	**1**	**3**	**0**	**1**	**0**	**0**	**19:16**
2015-16	**Winnipeg**	**NHL**	**57**	**17**	**25**	**42**	**12**	**2**	**2**	**2**	**127**	**13.4**	**–13**	**1314**	**51.3**	**19:36**	....	....	....	....	....	....	....	....	....
2016-17	**Winnipeg**	**NHL**	**59**	**21**	**26**	**47**	**18**	**6**	**0**	**3**	**119**	**17.6**	**–7**	**1097**	**55.6**	**17:33**	....	....	....	....	....	....	....	....	....
	NHL Totals		**672**	**184**	**248**	**432**	**237**	**52**	**7**	**24**	**1381**	**13.3**		**10140**	**49.3**	**18:24**	**4**	**2**	**1**	**3**	**0**	**1**	**0**	**0**	**19:16**

OHL Second All-Star Team (2007)

• Transferred to **Winnipeg** after **Atlanta** franchise relocated, June 21, 2011.

LOOV, Viktor

(LUHV, VIHK-tohr) **N.J.**

Defense. Shoots left. 6'3", 210 lbs. Born, Sodertalje, Sweden, November 16, 1992. Toronto's 6th pick, 209th overall, in 2012 NHL Draft.

2008-09	Sodertalje SK U18	Swe-U18	17	0	3	3	8	....	....	....	....	....	....	....	....	....	4	0	1	1	6	....	....	....	....
2009-10	Sodertalje SK U18	Swe-U18	21	4	14	18	32	....	....	....	....	....	....	....	....	....	2	0	0	0	4	....	....	....	....
	Sodertalje SK Jr.	Swe-Jr.	12	0	4	4	8	....	....	....	....	....	....	....	....	....	....	....	....	....	....	....	....	....	....
2010-11	Sodertalje SK Jr.	Swe-Jr.	42	4	19	23	36	....	....	....	....	....	....	....	....	....	2	0	0	0	2	....	....	....	....
	Sodertalje SK	Sweden-Q	1	0	0	0	0	....	....	....	....	....	....	....	....	....	....	....	....	....	....	....	....	....	....
2011-12	Sodertalje SK Jr.	Swe-Jr.	5	0	3	3	2	....	....	....	....	....	....	....	....	....	4	2	0	2	2	....	....	....	....
	Sodertalje SK	Sweden-2	50	3	3	6	42	....	....	....	....	....	....	....	....	....	....	....	....	....	....	....	....	....	....
2012-13	Sodertalje SK	Sweden-2	50	2	9	11	57	....	....	....	....	....	....	....	....	....	....	....	....	....	....	....	....	....	....
2013-14	MODO	Sweden	42	5	7	12	20	....	....	....	....	....	....	....	....	....	2	0	0	0	0	....	....	....	....
2014-15	Toronto Marlies	AHL	74	6	15	21	44	....	....	....	....	....	....	....	....	....	3	0	1	1	12	....	....	....	....
2015-16	**Toronto**	**NHL**	**4**	**0**	**2**	**2**	**0**	**0**	**0**	**0**	**1**	**0.0**	**4**	**0**	**0.0**	**10:28**	....	....	....	....	....	....	....	....	....
	Toronto Marlies	AHL	55	3	12	15	40	....	....	....	....	....	....	....	....	....	11	1	2	3	14	....	....	....	....
2016-17	Toronto Marlies	AHL	41	2	4	6	43	....	....	....	....	....	....	....	....	....	....	....	....	....	....	....	....	....	....
	Albany Devils	AHL	10	0	0	0	6	....	....	....	....	....	....	....	....	....	3	0	0	0	2	....	....	....	....
	NHL Totals		**4**	**0**	**2**	**2**	**0**	**0**	**0**	**0**	**1**	**0.0**		**0**	**0.0**	**10:28**	....	....	....	....	....	....	....	....	....

Traded to **New Jersey** by **Toronto** for Sergey Kalinin, February 18, 2017.

LORITO, Matt
(lohr-EE-toh, MAT) **DET**

Left wing. Shoots left. 5'9", 170 lbs. Born, Oakville, ON, July 3, 1990.

Season	Club	League	GP	G	A	Pts	PIM	PP	SH	GW	S	S%	+/-	TF	F%	Min	Playoffs GP	G	A	Pts	PIM	PP	SH	GW	Min
2009-10	Villanova Knights	ON-Jr.A	56	32	46	78	20	....	....	....	....	....	....	....	....	....	....	....	....	....	....	....	....	....	....
2010-11	Villanova Knights	ON-Jr.A	41	28	54	82	16	....	....	....	....	....	....	....	....	....	10	6	6	12	2	....	....	....	....
2011-12	Brown U.	ECAC	24	4	13	17	18	....	....	....	....	....	....	....	....	....	....	....	....	....	....	....	....	....	....
2012-13	Brown U.	ECAC	36	22	15	37	6	....	....	....	....	....	....	....	....	....	....	....	....	....	....	....	....	....	....
2013-14	Brown U.	ECAC	29	10	19	29	8	....	....	....	....	....	....	....	....	....	....	....	....	....	....	....	....	....	....
2014-15	Brown U.	ECAC	29	11	12	23	8	....	....	....	....	....	....	....	....	....	....	....	....	....	....	....	....	....	....
	Albany Devils	AHL	11	3	9	12	2	....	....	....	....	....	....	....	....	....	....	....	....	....	....	....	....	....	....
2015-16	Albany Devils	AHL	71	18	36	54	26	....	....	....	....	....	....	....	....	....	11	3	4	7	4	....	....	....	....
2016-17	**Detroit**	**NHL**	**2**	**0**	**1**	**1**	**0**	**0**	**0**	**0**	**6**	**0.0**	**0**	**0**	**0.0**	**14:26**	....	....	....	....	....	....	....	....	....
	Grand Rapids	AHL	61	22	34	56	25	....	....	....	....	....	....	....	....	....	19	7	6	13	4	....	....	....	....
	NHL Totals		**2**	**0**	**1**	**1**	**0**	**0**	**0**	**0**	**6**	**0.0**		**0**	**0.0**	**14:26**	....	....	....	....	....	....	....	....	....

Signed as a free agent by **Detroit**, July 1, 2016.

LOVEJOY, Ben
(LUHV-joi, BEHN) **N.J.**

Defense. Shoots right. 6'1", 205 lbs. Born, Concord, NH, February 20, 1984.

Season	Club	League	GP	G	A	Pts	PIM	PP	SH	GW	S	S%	+/-	TF	F%	Min	Playoffs GP	G	A	Pts	PIM	PP	SH	GW	Min
2002-03	Boston College	H-East	22	0	6	6	6	....	....	....	....	....	....	....	....	....	....	....	....	....	....	....	....	....	....
2003-04	Dartmouth	ECAC	DID NOT PLAY – TRANSFERRED COLLEGES																						
2004-05	Dartmouth	ECAC	32	2	11	13	28	....	....	....	....	....	....	....	....	....	....	....	....	....	....	....	....	....	....
2005-06	Dartmouth	ECAC	32	2	16	18	24	....	....	....	....	....	....	....	....	....	....	....	....	....	....	....	....	....	....
2006-07	Dartmouth	ECAC	32	7	16	23	28	....	....	....	....	....	....	....	....	....	....	....	....	....	....	....	....	....	....
	Norfolk Admirals	AHL	5	0	0	0	6	....	....	....	....	....	....	....	....	....	....	....	....	....	....	....	....	....	....
2007-08	Wilkes-Barre	AHL	72	2	18	20	63	....	....	....	....	....	....	....	....	....	23	2	8	10	18	....	....	....	....
2008-09	**Pittsburgh**	**NHL**	**2**	**0**	**0**	**0**	**0**	**0**	**0**	**0**	**1**	**0.0**	**0**	**0**	**0.0**	**11:53**	....	....	....	....	....	....	....	....	....
	Wilkes-Barre	AHL	76	7	24	31	84	....	....	....	....	....	....	....	....	....	12	1	1	2	14	....	....	....	....
2009-10	**Pittsburgh**	**NHL**	**12**	**0**	**3**	**3**	**2**	**0**	**0**	**0**	**14**	**0.0**	**8**	**0**	**0.0**	**16:37**	....	....	....	....	....	....	....	....	....
	Wilkes-Barre	AHL	65	9	20	29	92	....	....	....	....	....	....	....	....	....	2	0	2	2	2	....	....	....	....
2010-11	**Pittsburgh**	**NHL**	**47**	**3**	**14**	**17**	**48**	**0**	**0**	**0**	**60**	**5.0**	**11**	**0**	**0.0**	**15:00**	**7**	**0**	**2**	**2**	**4**	**0**	**0**	**0**	**10:54**
2011-12	**Pittsburgh**	**NHL**	**34**	**1**	**4**	**5**	**13**	**0**	**0**	**0**	**48**	**2.1**	**3**	**0**	**0.0**	**13:15**	**2**	**0**	**0**	**0**	**0**	**0**	**0**	**0**	**10:33**
2012-13	**Pittsburgh**	**NHL**	**3**	**0**	**0**	**0**	**0**	**0**	**0**	**0**	**7**	**0.0**	**–2**	**0**	**0.0**	**13:36**	....	....	....	....	....	....	....	....	....
	Anaheim	**NHL**	**32**	**0**	**10**	**10**	**29**	**0**	**0**	**0**	**51**	**0.0**	**6**	**0**	**0.0**	**18:13**	**7**	**0**	**2**	**2**	**0**	**0**	**0**	**0**	**21:05**
2013-14	**Anaheim**	**NHL**	**78**	**5**	**13**	**18**	**39**	**0**	**0**	**2**	**107**	**4.7**	**21**	**0**	**0.0**	**19:24**	**13**	**2**	**0**	**2**	**8**	**0**	**0**	**1**	**19:38**
2014-15	**Anaheim**	**NHL**	**40**	**1**	**10**	**11**	**17**	**0**	**0**	**0**	**50**	**2.0**	**3**	**0**	**0.0**	**18:33**	....	....	....	....	....	....	....	....	....
	Pittsburgh	**NHL**	**20**	**1**	**2**	**3**	**8**	**0**	**0**	**0**	**36**	**2.8**	**–7**	**0**	**0.0**	**21:13**	**5**	**0**	**2**	**2**	**0**	**0**	**0**	**0**	**22:55**
2015-16♦	**Pittsburgh**	**NHL**	**66**	**4**	**6**	**10**	**30**	**0**	**0**	**0**	**90**	**4.4**	**9**	**0**	**0.0**	**18:52**	**24**	**2**	**4**	**6**	**12**	**0**	**0**	**0**	**17:46**
2016-17	**New Jersey**	**NHL**	**82**	**1**	**6**	**7**	**39**	**0**	**0**	**1**	**84**	**1.2**	**–7**	**0**	**0.0**	**20:46**	....	....	....	....	....	....	....	....	....
	NHL Totals		**416**	**16**	**68**	**84**	**225**	**0**	**0**	**3**	**548**	**2.9**		**0**	**0.0**	**18:21**	**58**	**4**	**10**	**14**	**24**	**0**	**0**	**1**	**17:57**

AHL Second All-Star Team (2009)

Signed as a free agent by **Wilkes-Barre** (AHL), June 14, 2007. Signed as a free agent by **Pittsburgh**, July 7, 2008. • Missed majority of 2011-12 due to a broken wrist, knee surgery and as a healthy reserve. Traded to **Anaheim** by **Pittsburgh** for Anaheim's 5th round pick (Anthony Angello) in 2014 NHL Draft, February 6, 2013. Traded to **Pittsburgh** by **Anaheim** for Simon Despres, March 2, 2015. Signed as a free agent by **New Jersey**, July 1, 2016.

LOWE, Keegan
(LOH, KEE-guhn) **EDM**

Defense. Shoots left. 6'2", 195 lbs. Born, Greenwich, CT, March 29, 1993. Carolina's 3rd pick, 73rd overall, in 2011 NHL Draft.

Season	Club	League	GP	G	A	Pts	PIM	PP	SH	GW	S	S%	+/-	TF	F%	Min	Playoffs GP	G	A	Pts	PIM	PP	SH	GW	Min
2008-09	Shattuck U16	High-MN	55	7	26	33	77	....	....	....	....	....	....	....	....	....	....	....	....	....	....	....	....	....	....
2009-10	Edmonton	WHL	69	2	12	14	60	....	....	....	....	....	....	....	....	....	....	....	....	....	....	....	....	....	....
2010-11	Edmonton	WHL	71	2	22	24	123	....	....	....	....	....	....	....	....	....	4	1	0	1	4	....	....	....	....
2011-12	Edmonton	WHL	72	3	20	23	139	....	....	....	....	....	....	....	....	....	20	3	4	7	44	....	....	....	....
2012-13	Edmonton	WHL	64	15	16	31	148	....	....	....	....	....	....	....	....	....	22	1	7	8	28	....	....	....	....
2013-14	Charlotte	AHL	63	2	10	12	86	....	....	....	....	....	....	....	....	....	....	....	....	....	....	....	....	....	....
2014-15	**Carolina**	**NHL**	**2**	**0**	**0**	**0**	**10**	**0**	**0**	**0**	**0**	**0.0**	**–2**	**0**	**0.0**	**13:51**	....	....	....	....	....	....	....	....	....
	Charlotte	AHL	58	2	9	11	106	....	....	....	....	....	....	....	....	....	....	....	....	....	....	....	....	....	....
2015-16	Charlotte	AHL	67	3	11	14	75	....	....	....	....	....	....	....	....	....	....	....	....	....	....	....	....	....	....
2016-17	Charlotte	AHL	49	3	9	12	53	....	....	....	....	....	....	....	....	....	....	....	....	....	....	....	....	....	....
	St. John's IceCaps	AHL	22	3	3	6	21	....	....	....	....	....	....	....	....	....	3	0	0	0	0	....	....	....	....
	NHL Totals		**2**	**0**	**0**	**0**	**10**	**0**	**0**	**0**	**0**	**0.0**		**0**	**0.0**	**13:51**	....	....	....	....	....	....	....	....	....

WHL East Second All-Star Team (2013)

Traded to **Montreal** by **Carolina** for Philip Samuelsson, February 21, 2017. Signed as a free agent by **Edmonton**, July 1, 2017.

LOWRY, Adam
(LOW-ree, A-duhm) **WPG**

Center. Shoots left. 6'5", 210 lbs. Born, St. Louis, MO, March 29, 1993. Winnipeg's 2nd pick, 67th overall, in 2011 NHL Draft.

Season	Club	League	GP	G	A	Pts	PIM	PP	SH	GW	S	S%	+/-	TF	F%	Min	Playoffs GP	G	A	Pts	PIM	PP	SH	GW	Min
2007-08	Calgary Bisons	AMBHL	33	27	21	48	56	....	....	....	....	....	....	....	....	....	12	4	6	10	10	....	....	....	....
	Cgy. Blackhawks	Minor-AB	1	0	1	1	0	....	....	....	....	....	....	....	....	....	....	....	....	....	....	....	....	....	....
2008-09	Calgary Rangers	Minor-AB	29	29	25	54	51	....	....	....	....	....	....	....	....	....	....	....	....	....	....	....	....	....	....
2009-10	Swift Current	WHL	61	15	19	34	57	....	....	....	....	....	....	....	....	....	3	0	1	1	6	....	....	....	....
2010-11	Swift Current	WHL	66	18	27	45	84	....	....	....	....	....	....	....	....	....	....	....	....	....	....	....	....	....	....
2011-12	Swift Current	WHL	36	12	25	37	90	....	....	....	....	....	....	....	....	....	....	....	....	....	....	....	....	....	....
2012-13	Swift Current	WHL	72	45	43	88	102	....	....	....	....	....	....	....	....	....	5	3	2	5	4	....	....	....	....
	St. John's IceCaps	AHL	9	0	1	1	4	....	....	....	....	....	....	....	....	....	....	....	....	....	....	....	....	....	....
2013-14	St. John's IceCaps	AHL	64	17	16	33	49	....	....	....	....	....	....	....	....	....	17	2	3	5	16	....	....	....	....
2014-15	**Winnipeg**	**NHL**	**80**	**11**	**12**	**23**	**46**	**0**	**1**	**2**	**104**	**10.6**	**1**	**851**	**47.2**	**13:45**	**4**	**1**	**2**	**3**	**2**	**0**	**0**	**0**	**14:46**
2015-16	**Winnipeg**	**NHL**	**74**	**7**	**10**	**17**	**53**	**0**	**0**	**2**	**73**	**9.6**	**–9**	**845**	**46.3**	**14:01**	....	....	....	....	....	....	....	....	....
	Manitoba Moose	AHL	4	0	4	4	2	....	....	....	....	....	....	....	....	....	....	....	....	....	....	....	....	....	....
2016-17	**Winnipeg**	**NHL**	**82**	**15**	**14**	**29**	**52**	**5**	**0**	**1**	**122**	**12.3**	**1**	**1295**	**50.8**	**16:03**	....	....	....	....	....	....	....	....	....
	NHL Totals		**236**	**33**	**36**	**69**	**151**	**5**	**1**	**5**	**299**	**11.0**		**2991**	**48.5**	**14:38**	**4**	**1**	**2**	**3**	**2**	**0**	**0**	**0**	**14:46**

WHL East First All-Star Team (2013) • WHL Player of the Year (2013)

LUCIC, Milan
(LOO-cheech, MEE-lahn) **EDM**

Left wing. Shoots left. 6'3", 236 lbs. Born, Vancouver, BC, June 7, 1988. Boston's 3rd pick, 50th overall, in 2006 NHL Draft.

Season	Club	League	GP	G	A	Pts	PIM	PP	SH	GW	S	S%	+/-	TF	F%	Min	Playoffs GP	G	A	Pts	PIM	PP	SH	GW	Min
2004-05	Coquitlam	BCHL	50	9	14	23	100	....	....	....	....	....	....	....	....	....	....	....	....	....	....	....	....	....	....
	Vancouver Giants	WHL	1	0	0	0	2	....	....	....	....	....	....	....	....	....	2	0	0	0	0	....	....	....	....
2005-06	Vancouver Giants	WHL	62	9	10	19	149	....	....	....	....	....	....	....	....	....	18	3	4	7	23	....	....	....	....
2006-07	Vancouver Giants	WHL	70	30	38	68	147	....	....	....	....	....	....	....	....	....	22	7	12	19	26	....	....	....	....
2007-08	**Boston**	**NHL**	**77**	**8**	**19**	**27**	**89**	**1**	**0**	**4**	**88**	**9.1**	**–2**	**8**	**50.0**	**12:07**	**7**	**2**	**0**	**2**	**4**	**0**	**0**	**0**	**16:24**
2008-09	**Boston**	**NHL**	**72**	**17**	**25**	**42**	**136**	**2**	**0**	**3**	**97**	**17.5**	**17**	**10**	**60.0**	**14:57**	**10**	**3**	**6**	**9**	**43**	**0**	**0**	**0**	**15:14**
2009-10	**Boston**	**NHL**	**50**	**9**	**11**	**20**	**44**	**0**	**0**	**2**	**72**	**12.5**	**–7**	**14**	**21.4**	**14:21**	**13**	**5**	**4**	**9**	**19**	**2**	**0**	**1**	**16:27**
2010-11♦	**Boston**	**NHL**	**79**	**30**	**32**	**62**	**121**	**5**	**0**	**7**	**173**	**17.3**	**28**	**54**	**38.9**	**16:35**	**25**	**5**	**7**	**12**	**63**	**1**	**0**	**0**	**17:54**
2011-12	**Boston**	**NHL**	**81**	**26**	**35**	**61**	**135**	**7**	**0**	**1**	**149**	**17.4**	**7**	**30**	**46.7**	**17:02**	**7**	**0**	**3**	**3**	**8**	**0**	**0**	**0**	**20:17**
2012-13	**Boston**	**NHL**	**46**	**7**	**20**	**27**	**75**	**0**	**0**	**0**	**79**	**8.9**	**8**	**35**	**48.6**	**16:55**	**22**	**7**	**12**	**19**	**14**	**0**	**0**	**0**	**20:57**
2013-14	**Boston**	**NHL**	**80**	**24**	**35**	**59**	**91**	**3**	**0**	**5**	**153**	**15.7**	**30**	**131**	**46.6**	**17:23**	**12**	**4**	**3**	**7**	**4**	**0**	**0**	**1**	**18:27**
2014-15	**Boston**	**NHL**	**81**	**18**	**26**	**44**	**81**	**2**	**0**	**4**	**141**	**12.8**	**13**	**76**	**44.7**	**16:21**	....	....	....	....	....	....	....	....	....
2015-16	**Los Angeles**	**NHL**	**81**	**20**	**35**	**55**	**79**	**2**	**0**	**5**	**124**	**16.1**	**26**	**20**	**35.0**	**17:14**	**5**	**0**	**3**	**3**	**4**	**0**	**0**	**0**	**17:01**
2016-17	**Edmonton**	**NHL**	**82**	**23**	**27**	**50**	**50**	**12**	**0**	**3**	**175**	**13.1**	**–3**	**7**	**57.1**	**17:10**	**13**	**2**	**4**	**6**	**20**	**2**	**0**	**0**	**17:02**
	NHL Totals		**729**	**182**	**265**	**447**	**901**	**34**	**0**	**34**	**1251**	**14.5**		**385**	**44.4**	**16:04**	**114**	**28**	**42**	**70**	**179**	**5**	**0**	**2**	**18:04**

Traded to **Los Angeles** by **Boston** for Martin Jones, Colin Miller and Los Angeles' 1st round pick (Jakub Zboril) in 2015 NHL Draft, June 26, 2015. Signed as a free agent by **Edmonton**, July 1, 2016.

LUPUL, Joffrey

(LOO-puhl, JAWF-ree) **TOR**

Left wing. Shoots right. 6′1″, 211 lbs. Born, Fort Saskatchewan, AB, September 23, 1983. Anaheim's 1st pick, 7th overall, in 2002 NHL Draft.

			Regular Season														Playoffs								
Season	Club	League	GP	G	A	Pts	PIM	PP	SH	GW	S	S%	+/-	TF	F%	Min	GP	G	A	Pts	PIM	PP	SH	GW	Min
1998-99	Ft. Saskatchewan	Minor-AB	36	40	50	90	40	....	....	....	....	....	....	....	....	....	....	....	....	....	....	....	....	....	....
99-2000	Ft. Saskatchewan	AMHL	34	43	30	*73	47	....	....	....	....	....	....	....	....	....	4	0	1	1	2	....	....	....	....
2000-01	Medicine Hat	WHL	69	30	26	56	39	....	....	....	....	....	....	....	....	....	22	3	6	9	2	....	....	....	....
2001-02	Medicine Hat	WHL	72	*56	50	106	95	....	....	....	....	....	....	....	....	....	....	....	....	....	....	....	....	....	....
2002-03	Medicine Hat	WHL	50	41	37	78	82	....	....	....	....	....	....	....	....	....	11	4	11	15	20	....	....	....	....
2003-04	**Anaheim**	**NHL**	**75**	**13**	**21**	**34**	**28**	**4**	**0**	**2**	**137**	**9.5**	**–6**	**11**	**9.1**	**13:37**	....	....	....	....	....	....	....	....	....
	Cincinnati	AHL	3	3	2	5	2	....	....	....	....	....	....	....	....	....	....	....	....	....	....	....	....	....	....
2004-05	Cincinnati	AHL	65	30	26	56	58	....	....	....	....	....	....	....	....	....	12	3	9	12	27	....	....	....	....
2005-06	**Anaheim**	**NHL**	**81**	**28**	**25**	**53**	**48**	**12**	**2**	**2**	**296**	**9.5**	**–13**	**101**	**37.6**	**16:38**	**16**	**9**	**2**	**11**	**31**	**1**	**0**	**1**	**16:43**
2006-07	**Edmonton**	**NHL**	**81**	**16**	**12**	**28**	**45**	**5**	**0**	**1**	**172**	**9.3**	**–29**	**14**	**35.7**	**15:36**	....	....	....	....	....	....	....	....	....
2007-08	**Philadelphia**	**NHL**	**56**	**20**	**26**	**46**	**35**	**7**	**0**	**3**	**176**	**11.4**	**2**	**4**	**75.0**	**18:13**	**17**	**4**	**6**	**10**	**2**	**2**	**0**	**1**	**16:13**
2008-09	**Philadelphia**	**NHL**	**79**	**25**	**25**	**50**	**58**	**6**	**0**	**4**	**194**	**12.9**	**1**	**21**	**47.6**	**15:41**	**6**	**1**	**1**	**2**	**2**	**0**	**0**	**0**	**17:07**
2009-10	**Anaheim**	**NHL**	**23**	**10**	**4**	**14**	**18**	**0**	**0**	**0**	**66**	**15.2**	**3**	**5**	**20.0**	**15:58**	....	....	....	....	....	....	....	....	....
2010-11	**Anaheim**	**NHL**	**26**	**5**	**8**	**13**	**14**	**2**	**0**	**1**	**54**	**9.3**	**–4**	**14**	**50.0**	**13:13**	....	....	....	....	....	....	....	....	....
	Syracuse Crunch	AHL	3	1	3	4	0	....	....	....	....	....	....	....	....	....	....	....	....	....	....	....	....	....	....
	Toronto	**NHL**	**28**	**9**	**9**	**18**	**19**	**2**	**0**	**1**	**75**	**12.0**	**–7**	**18**	**27.8**	**17:51**	....	....	....	....	....	....	....	....	....
2011-12	**Toronto**	**NHL**	**66**	**25**	**42**	**67**	**48**	**8**	**0**	**3**	**191**	**13.1**	**1**	**58**	**36.2**	**18:37**	....	....	....	....	....	....	....	....	....
2012-13	Avtomobilist	KHL	9	1	3	4	4	....	....	....	....	....	....	....	....	....	....	....	....	....	....	....	....	....	....
	Toronto	**NHL**	**16**	**11**	**7**	**18**	**12**	**3**	**0**	**3**	**42**	**26.2**	**8**	**8**	**37.5**	**16:07**	**7**	**3**	**1**	**4**	**4**	**1**	**0**	**0**	**18:59**
2013-14	**Toronto**	**NHL**	**69**	**22**	**22**	**44**	**44**	**6**	**0**	**1**	**191**	**11.5**	**–15**	**55**	**43.6**	**18:27**	....	....	....	....	....	....	....	....	....
2014-15	**Toronto**	**NHL**	**55**	**10**	**11**	**21**	**26**	**2**	**0**	**1**	**97**	**10.3**	**–10**	**6**	**66.7**	**15:29**	....	....	....	....	....	....	....	....	....
2015-16	**Toronto**	**NHL**	**46**	**11**	**3**	**14**	**12**	**2**	**0**	**2**	**102**	**10.8**	**–10**	**4**	**0.0**	**14:37**	....	....	....	....	....	....	....	....	....
2016-17	**Toronto**	**NHL**	DID NOT PLAY – INJURED														....	....	....	....	....	....	....	....	....
	NHL Totals		**701**	**205**	**215**	**420**	**407**	**59**	**2**	**24**	**1793**	**11.4**		**319**	**38.2**	**16:14**	**46**	**17**	**10**	**27**	**39**	**4**	**0**	**2**	**16:56**

WHL East First All-Star Team (2002) • Canadian Major Junior First All-Star Team (2002)

Played in NHL All-Star Game (2012)

Traded to **Edmonton** by **Anaheim** with Ladislav Smid, Anaheim's 1st round pick (later traded to Phoenix - Phoenix selected Nick Ross) in 2007 NHL Draft and Anaheim's 1st (Jordan Eberle) and 2nd (later traded to NY Islanders - NY Islanders selected Travis Hamonic) round picks in 2008 NHL Draft for Chris Pronger, July 3, 2006. Traded to **Philadelphia** by **Edmonton** with Jason Smith for Joni Pitkanen, Geoff Sanderson and Philadelphia's 3rd round pick (Cameron Abney) in 2009 NHL Draft, July 1, 2007. Traded to **Anaheim** by **Philadelphia** with Luca Sbisa, Philadelphia's 1st round pick in 2009 (later traded to Columbus - Columbus selected John Moore) and 2010 (Emerson Etem) NHL Drafts and future considerations for Chris Pronger and Ryan Dingle, June 26, 2009. • Missed majority of 2009-10 due to back injury, December 16, 2009. Traded to **Toronto** by **Anaheim** with Jake Gardiner and Anaheim's 4th round pick (later traded to San Jose – San Jose selected Fredrik Bergvik) in 2013 NHL Draft for Francois Beauchemin, February 9, 2011. Signed as a free agent by **Avtomobilist Yekaterinburg** (KHL), October 30, 2012. • Missed majority of 2012-13 due to arm (January 23, 2013 at Pittsburgh) and head (April 4, 2013 vs. Philadelphia) injuries. • Missed 2016-17 due to recurring sports hernia injury and resulting surgery.

LYUBIMOV, Roman

(l'yoo-BEE-mawv, ROH-muhn)

Center. Shoots right. 6′2″, 207 lbs. Born, Tver, Russia, June 1, 1992.

Season	Club	League	GP	G	A	Pts	PIM	PP	SH	GW	S	S%	+/-	TF	F%	Min	GP	G	A	Pts	PIM	PP	SH	GW	Min
2010-11	CSKA Moscow	KHL	7	0	0	0	0	....	....	....	....	....	....	....	....	....	....	....	....	....	....	....	....	....	....
2011-12	CSKA Moscow	KHL	7	0	1	1	0	....	....	....	....	....	....	....	....	....	....	....	....	....	....	....	....	....	....
2012-13	CSKA Moscow	KHL	31	0	0	0	0	....	....	....	....	....	....	....	....	....	8	0	0	0	14	....	....	....	....
2013-14	CSKA Moscow	KHL	42	2	4	6	....	....	....	....	....	....	....	....	....	....	4	0	0	0	0	....	....	....	....
2014-15	CSKA Moscow	KHL	46	6	7	13	20	....	....	....	....	....	....	....	....	....	12	4	2	6	29	....	....	....	....
2015-16	CSKA Moscow	KHL	52	7	7	14	25	....	....	....	....	....	....	....	....	....	15	4	4	8	8	....	....	....	....
2016-17	**Philadelphia**	**NHL**	**47**	**4**	**2**	**6**	**8**	**0**	**0**	**1**	**41**	**9.8**	**–2**	**7**	**14.3**	**9:35**	....	....	....	....	....	....	....	....	....
	NHL Totals		**47**	**4**	**2**	**6**	**8**	**0**	**0**	**1**	**41**	**9.8**		**7**	**14.3**	**9:35**	....	....	....	....	....	....	....	....	....

Signed as a free agent by **Philadelphia**, July 11, 2016.

MAATTA, Olli

(MA-TA, OH-lee) **PIT**

Defense. Shoots left. 6′2″, 206 lbs. Born, Jyvaskyla, Finland, August 22, 1994. Pittsburgh's 2nd pick, 22nd overall, in 2012 NHL Draft.

Season	Club	League	GP	G	A	Pts	PIM	PP	SH	GW	S	S%	+/-	TF	F%	Min	GP	G	A	Pts	PIM	PP	SH	GW	Min
2009-10	JyP Jyvaskyla U18	Fin-U18	2	0	0	0	2	....	....	....	....	....	....	....	....	....	....	....	....	....	....	....	....	....	....
	JyP Jyvaskyla Jr.	Fin-Jr.	1	0	1	1	0	....	....	....	....	....	....	....	....	....	....	....	....	....	....	....	....	....	....
2010-11	Suomi U20	Finland-2	2	0	2	2	2	....	....	....	....	....	....	....	....	....	....	....	....	....	....	....	....	....	....
	JyP Jyvaskyla U18	Fin-U18	1	0	0	0	0	....	....	....	....	....	....	....	....	....	....	....	....	....	....	....	....	....	....
	D Team Jyvaskyla	Finland-2	23	1	5	6	6	....	....	....	....	....	....	....	....	....	....	....	....	....	....	....	....	....	....
	JyP Jyvaskyla Jr.	Fin-Jr.	19	2	6	8	8	....	....	....	....	....	....	....	....	....	12	1	4	5	6	....	....	....	....
2011-12	London Knights	OHL	58	5	27	32	25	....	....	....	....	....	....	....	....	....	19	6	17	23	2	....	....	....	....
2012-13	London Knights	OHL	57	8	30	38	30	....	....	....	....	....	....	....	....	....	21	4	10	14	8	....	....	....	....
	Wilkes-Barre	AHL	....	....	....	....	....	....	....	....	....	....	....	....	....	....	3	0	0	0	0	....	....	....	....
2013-14	**Pittsburgh**	**NHL**	**78**	**9**	**20**	**29**	**14**	**3**	**1**	**1**	**119**	**7.6**	**8**	**0**	**0.0**	**18:30**	**13**	**0**	**4**	**4**	**0**	**0**	**0**	**0**	**18:05**
	Finland	Olympics	6	3	2	5	0	....	....	....	....	....	....	....	....	....	....	....	....	....	....	....	....	....	....
2014-15	**Pittsburgh**	**NHL**	**20**	**1**	**8**	**9**	**10**	**0**	**0**	**0**	**27**	**3.7**	**1**	**0**	**0.0**	**20:43**	....	....	....	....	....	....	....	....	....
2015-16 ♦	**Pittsburgh**	**NHL**	**67**	**6**	**13**	**19**	**22**	**0**	**0**	**2**	**95**	**6.3**	**27**	**0**	**0.0**	**19:58**	**18**	**0**	**7**	**7**	**4**	**0**	**0**	**0**	**17:44**
2016-17 ♦	**Pittsburgh**	**NHL**	**55**	**1**	**6**	**7**	**12**	**0**	**0**	**0**	**66**	**1.5**	**17**	**0**	**0.0**	**18:04**	**25**	**2**	**6**	**8**	**12**	**0**	**0**	**1**	**20:37**
	NHL Totals		**220**	**17**	**47**	**64**	**58**	**3**	**1**	**3**	**307**	**5.5**		**0**	**0.0**	**19:02**	**56**	**2**	**17**	**19**	**16**	**0**	**0**	**1**	**19:06**

OHL All-Rookie Team (2012)

• Missed majority of 2014-15 due to shoulder injury vs. Ottawa, December 6, 2014.

MacARTHUR, Clarke

(muh-KAR-thuhr, KLAHRK) **OTT**

Left wing. Shoots left. 6′, 185 lbs. Born, Lloydminster, AB, April 6, 1985. Buffalo's 3rd pick, 74th overall, in 2003 NHL Draft.

Season	Club	League	GP	G	A	Pts	PIM	PP	SH	GW	S	S%	+/-	TF	F%	Min	GP	G	A	Pts	PIM	PP	SH	GW	Min
99-2000	Lloydminster	CABHL	24	19	45	64	51	....	....	....	....	....	....	....	....	....	5	9	6	15	4	....	....	....	....
2000-01	Strathcona	AMBHL	38	36	63	99	44	....	....	....	....	....	....	....	....	....	8	6	2	8	10	....	....	....	....
2001-02	Drayton Valley	AJHL	61	22	40	62	33	....	....	....	....	....	....	....	....	....	16	5	8	13	34	....	....	....	....
2002-03	Medicine Hat	WHL	70	23	52	75	104	....	....	....	....	....	....	....	....	....	11	3	6	9	8	....	....	....	....
2003-04	Medicine Hat	WHL	62	35	40	75	93	....	....	....	....	....	....	....	....	....	20	8	10	18	16	....	....	....	....
2004-05	Medicine Hat	WHL	58	30	44	74	100	....	....	....	....	....	....	....	....	....	13	3	8	11	18	....	....	....	....
	Rochester	AHL	....	....	....	....	....	....	....	....	....	....	....	....	....	....	3	0	1	1	0	....	....	....	....
2005-06	Rochester	AHL	69	21	32	53	71	....	....	....	....	....	....	....	....	....	....	....	....	....	....	....	....	....	....
2006-07	**Buffalo**	**NHL**	**19**	**3**	**4**	**7**	**4**	**0**	**0**	**0**	**16**	**18.8**	**4**	**50**	**46.0**	**8:54**	....	....	....	....	....	....	....	....	....
	Rochester	AHL	51	21	42	63	57	....	....	....	....	....	....	....	....	....	6	2	4	6	4	....	....	....	....
2007-08	**Buffalo**	**NHL**	**37**	**8**	**7**	**15**	**20**	**0**	**0**	**1**	**51**	**15.7**	**3**	**14**	**28.6**	**14:34**	....	....	....	....	....	....	....	....	....
	Rochester	AHL	43	14	28	42	26	....	....	....	....	....	....	....	....	....	....	....	....	....	....	....	....	....	....
2008-09	**Buffalo**	**NHL**	**71**	**17**	**14**	**31**	**56**	**5**	**0**	**0**	**108**	**15.7**	**–4**	**218**	**34.9**	**13:50**	....	....	....	....	....	....	....	....	....
2009-10	**Buffalo**	**NHL**	**60**	**13**	**13**	**26**	**47**	**3**	**0**	**3**	**99**	**13.1**	**–14**	**143**	**43.4**	**14:22**	....	....	....	....	....	....	....	....	....
	Atlanta	**NHL**	**21**	**3**	**6**	**9**	**2**	**1**	**1**	**0**	**30**	**10.0**	**–2**	**10**	**50.0**	**15:37**	....	....	....	....	....	....	....	....	....
2010-11	**Toronto**	**NHL**	**82**	**21**	**41**	**62**	**37**	**6**	**0**	**3**	**154**	**13.6**	**–3**	**16**	**56.3**	**17:07**	....	....	....	....	....	....	....	....	....
2011-12	**Toronto**	**NHL**	**73**	**20**	**23**	**43**	**37**	**3**	**0**	**4**	**148**	**13.5**	**3**	**11**	**45.5**	**15:51**	....	....	....	....	....	....	....	....	....
2012-13	Crimmitschau	German-2	9	4	7	11	16	....	....	....	....	....	....	....	....	....	....	....	....	....	....	....	....	....	....
	Toronto	**NHL**	**40**	**8**	**12**	**20**	**26**	**2**	**0**	**1**	**62**	**12.9**	**3**	**6**	**83.3**	**14:55**	**5**	**2**	**1**	**3**	**2**	**0**	**0**	**1**	**12:21**
2013-14	**Ottawa**	**NHL**	**79**	**24**	**31**	**55**	**78**	**8**	**1**	**5**	**159**	**15.1**	**12**	**32**	**46.9**	**17:38**	....	....	....	....	....	....	....	....	....
2014-15	**Ottawa**	**NHL**	**62**	**16**	**20**	**36**	**36**	**6**	**0**	**5**	**140**	**11.4**	**–6**	**22**	**36.4**	**17:00**	**6**	**2**	**0**	**2**	**18**	**0**	**0**	**0**	**15:59**
2015-16	**Ottawa**	**NHL**	**4**	**0**	**0**	**0**	**0**	**0**	**0**	**0**	**4**	**0.0**	**–1**	**1**	**0.0**	**10:52**	....	....	....	....	....	....	....	....	....
2016-17	**Ottawa**	**NHL**	**4**	**0**	**0**	**0**	**0**	**0**	**0**	**0**	**5**	**0.0**	**–1**	**1**	**0.0**	**13:29**	**19**	**3**	**6**	**9**	**12**	**2**	**0**	**1**	**15:10**
	NHL Totals		**552**	**133**	**171**	**304**	**343**	**34**	**2**	**22**	**976**	**13.6**		**524**	**40.5**	**15:33**	**30**	**7**	**7**	**14**	**32**	**2**	**0**	**2**	**14:52**

WHL East First All-Star Team (2005)

Traded to **Atlanta** by **Buffalo** for Atlanta's 3rd (Jerome Gauthier-Leduc) and 4th (Steven Shipley) round picks in 2010 NHL Draft, March 3, 2010. Signed as a free agent by **Toronto**, August 28, 2010. Signed as a free agent by **Crimmitschau** (German-2), October 23, 2012. Signed as a free agent by **Ottawa**, July 5, 2013. • Missed Majority of 2015-16 and 2016-17 due to upper-body injury at Columbus, October 14, 2015.

MacDONALD, Andrew
(MAK-DAWN-uhld, AN-droo) **PHI**

Defense. Shoots left. 6'1", 204 lbs. Born, Judique, NS, September 7, 1986. NY Islanders' 10th pick, 160th overall, in 2006 NHL Draft.

Season	Club	League	GP	G	A	Pts	PIM	PP	SH	GW	S	S%	+/-	TF	F%	Min	Playoffs GP	G	A	Pts	PIM	PP	SH	GW	Min
2003-04	Truro Bearcats	MJrHL	50	8	20	28	43	....	....	....	....	....	....	....	....	....	10	0	0	0	....	....	....	....	....
2004-05	Truro Bearcats	MJrHL	56	11	22	33	60	....	....	....	....	....	....	....	....	....	17	6	7	13	....	....	....	....	....
2005-06	Moncton Wildcats	QMJHL	68	6	40	46	62	....	....	....	....	....	....	....	....	....	21	2	11	13	10	....	....	....	....
2006-07	Moncton Wildcats	QMJHL	65	14	44	58	81	....	....	....	....	....	....	....	....	....	7	1	5	6	4	....	....	....	....
	Bridgeport	AHL	3	0	0	0	0	....	....	....	....	....	....	....	....	....	....	....	....	....	....	....	....	....	....
2007-08	Bridgeport	AHL	21	2	3	5	10	....	....	....	....	....	....	....	....	....	....	....	....	....	....	....	....	....	....
	Utah Grizzlies	ECHL	37	1	11	12	39	....	....	....	....	....	....	....	....	....	15	3	9	12	12	....	....	....	....
2008-09	**NY Islanders**	**NHL**	**3**	**0**	**0**	**0**	**2**	**0**	**0**	**0**	**1**	**0.0**	**2**	**0**	**0.0**	**10:10**	....	....	....	....	....	....	....	....	....
	Bridgeport	AHL	69	9	24	33	46	....	....	....	....	....	....	....	....	....	5	1	1	2	4	....	....	....	....
2009-10	**NY Islanders**	**NHL**	**46**	**1**	**6**	**7**	**20**	**0**	**0**	**0**	**43**	**2.3**	**4**	**1**	**0.0**	**20:05**	....	....	....	....	....	....	....	....	....
	Bridgeport	AHL	21	2	6	8	29	....	....	....	....	....	....	....	....	....	5	3	1	4	10	....	....	....	....
2010-11	**NY Islanders**	**NHL**	**60**	**4**	**23**	**27**	**37**	**1**	**0**	**1**	**72**	**5.6**	**9**	**0**	**0.0**	**23:25**	....	....	....	....	....	....	....	....	....
2011-12	**NY Islanders**	**NHL**	**75**	**5**	**14**	**19**	**26**	**1**	**0**	**0**	**71**	**7.0**	**−5**	**0**	**0.0**	**23:22**	....	....	....	....	....	....	....	....	....
2012-13	Karlovy Vary	CzRep	21	1	4	5	10	....	....	....	....	....	....	....	....	....	....	....	....	....	....	....	....	....	....
	HC Banik Sokolov	CzRep-3	1	0	0	0	0	....	....	....	....	....	....	....	....	....	....	....	....	....	....	....	....	....	....
	NY Islanders	**NHL**	**48**	**3**	**9**	**12**	**20**	**1**	**0**	**1**	**45**	**6.7**	**−2**	**0**	**0.0**	**23:31**	**4**	**0**	**0**	**0**	**4**	**0**	**0**	**0**	**23:26**
2013-14	**NY Islanders**	**NHL**	**63**	**4**	**20**	**24**	**34**	**2**	**0**	**2**	**72**	**5.6**	**−19**	**0**	**0.0**	**25:25**	....	....	....	....	....	....	....	....	....
	Philadelphia	**NHL**	**19**	**0**	**4**	**4**	**16**	**0**	**0**	**0**	**20**	**0.0**	**−3**	**0**	**0.0**	**22:00**	**7**	**1**	**1**	**2**	**8**	**0**	**0**	**0**	**22:37**
2014-15	**Philadelphia**	**NHL**	**58**	**2**	**10**	**12**	**41**	**1**	**0**	**0**	**62**	**3.2**	**−5**	**0**	**0.0**	**20:01**	....	....	....	....	....	....	....	....	....
2015-16	**Philadelphia**	**NHL**	**28**	**1**	**7**	**8**	**6**	**0**	**0**	**0**	**20**	**5.0**	**10**	**0**	**0.0**	**20:07**	**6**	**1**	**0**	**1**	**2**	**0**	**0**	**1**	**18:18**
	Lehigh Valley	AHL	43	5	31	36	30	....	....	....	....	....	....	....	....	....	....	....	....	....	....	....	....	....	....
2016-17	**Philadelphia**	**NHL**	**73**	**2**	**16**	**18**	**26**	**0**	**0**	**0**	**65**	**3.1**	**−5**	**0**	**0.0**	**20:06**	....	....	....	....	....	....	....	....	....
	NHL Totals		**473**	**22**	**109**	**131**	**228**	**6**	**0**	**4**	**471**	**4.7**		**1**	**0.0**	**22:06**	**17**	**2**	**1**	**3**	**14**	**0**	**0**	**1**	**21:17**

QMJHL First All-Star Team (2007)

Signed as a free agent by **Karlovy Vary** (CzRep), October 9, 2012. Traded to **Philadelphia** by **NY Islanders** for Matt Mangene, Philadelphia's 3rd round pick (Ilya Sorokin) in 2014 NHL Draft and Philadelphia's 2nd round pick in (later traded to Boston – Boston selected Brandon Carlo) 2015 NHL Draft, March 4, 2014.

MacKENZIE, Derek
(muh-KEHN-zee, DAIR-ihk) **FLA**

Center. Shoots left. 5'11", 181 lbs. Born, Sudbury, ON, June 11, 1981. Atlanta's 6th pick, 128th overall, in 1999 NHL Draft.

Season	Club	League	GP	G	A	Pts	PIM	PP	SH	GW	S	S%	+/-	TF	F%	Min	Playoffs GP	G	A	Pts	PIM	PP	SH	GW	Min
1996-97	Rayside-Balfour	NOJHA	40	23	32	55	40	....	....	....	....	....	....	....	....	....	....	....	....	....	....	....	....	....	....
1997-98	Sudbury Wolves	OHL	59	9	11	20	26	....	....	....	....	....	....	....	....	....	10	0	1	1	0	....	....	....	....
1998-99	Sudbury Wolves	OHL	68	22	65	87	74	....	....	....	....	....	....	....	....	....	4	2	4	6	2	....	....	....	....
99-2000	Sudbury Wolves	OHL	68	24	33	57	110	....	....	....	....	....	....	....	....	....	12	5	9	14	16	....	....	....	....
2000-01	Sudbury Wolves	OHL	62	40	49	89	89	....	....	....	....	....	....	....	....	....	12	6	8	14	16	....	....	....	....
2001-02	**Atlanta**	**NHL**	**1**	**0**	**0**	**0**	**2**	**0**	**0**	**0**	**1**	**0.0**	**−1**	**16**	**56.3**	**13:51**	....	....	....	....	....	....	....	....	....
	Chicago Wolves	AHL	68	13	12	25	80	....	....	....	....	....	....	....	....	....	25	4	2	6	20	....	....	....	....
2002-03	Chicago Wolves	AHL	80	14	18	32	97	....	....	....	....	....	....	....	....	....	9	0	0	0	4	....	....	....	....
2003-04	**Atlanta**	**NHL**	**12**	**0**	**1**	**1**	**10**	**0**	**0**	**0**	**7**	**0.0**	**0**	**63**	**46.0**	**6:38**	....	....	....	....	....	....	....	....	....
	Chicago Wolves	AHL	63	19	16	35	67	....	....	....	....	....	....	....	....	....	10	7	1	8	13	....	....	....	....
2004-05	Chicago Wolves	AHL	78	13	20	33	87	....	....	....	....	....	....	....	....	....	18	5	6	11	33	....	....	....	....
2005-06	**Atlanta**	**NHL**	**11**	**0**	**1**	**1**	**8**	**0**	**0**	**0**	**11**	**0.0**	**0**	**59**	**55.9**	**6:33**	....	....	....	....	....	....	....	....	....
	Chicago Wolves	AHL	36	10	12	22	48	....	....	....	....	....	....	....	....	....	....	....	....	....	....	....	....	....	....
2006-07	**Atlanta**	**NHL**	**4**	**0**	**0**	**0**	**0**	**0**	**0**	**0**	**3**	**0.0**	**1**	**16**	**56.3**	**5:00**	....	....	....	....	....	....	....	....	....
	Chicago Wolves	AHL	52	14	23	37	62	....	....	....	....	....	....	....	....	....	....	....	....	....	....	....	....	....	....
2007-08	**Columbus**	**NHL**	**17**	**2**	**0**	**2**	**8**	**0**	**0**	**0**	**19**	**10.5**	**−2**	**73**	**34.3**	**7:47**	....	....	....	....	....	....	....	....	....
	Syracuse Crunch	AHL	62	25	24	49	46	....	....	....	....	....	....	....	....	....	13	6	8	14	22	....	....	....	....
2008-09	**Columbus**	**NHL**	**1**	**0**	**0**	**0**	**2**	**0**	**0**	**0**	**1**	**0.0**	**−1**	**4**	**50.0**	**7:15**	....	....	....	....	....	....	....	....	....
	Syracuse Crunch	AHL	64	22	30	52	50	....	....	....	....	....	....	....	....	....	....	....	....	....	....	....	....	....	....
2009-10	**Columbus**	**NHL**	**18**	**1**	**3**	**4**	**0**	**0**	**0**	**0**	**14**	**7.1**	**3**	**104**	**54.8**	**8:42**	....	....	....	....	....	....	....	....	....
	Syracuse Crunch	AHL	47	17	30	47	30	....	....	....	....	....	....	....	....	....	....	....	....	....	....	....	....	....	....
2010-11	**Columbus**	**NHL**	**63**	**9**	**14**	**23**	**22**	**0**	**1**	**1**	**76**	**11.8**	**14**	**473**	**52.0**	**10:51**	....	....	....	....	....	....	....	....	....
2011-12	**Columbus**	**NHL**	**66**	**7**	**7**	**14**	**40**	**1**	**2**	**2**	**61**	**11.5**	**4**	**429**	**54.6**	**10:30**	....	....	....	....	....	....	....	....	....
2012-13	**Columbus**	**NHL**	**43**	**3**	**5**	**8**	**36**	**0**	**0**	**0**	**33**	**9.1**	**1**	**323**	**59.4**	**10:20**	....	....	....	....	....	....	....	....	....
2013-14	**Columbus**	**NHL**	**71**	**9**	**9**	**18**	**47**	**0**	**2**	**0**	**70**	**12.9**	**0**	**497**	**51.5**	**11:16**	**6**	**1**	**0**	**1**	**2**	**0**	**1**	**0**	**13:49**
2014-15	**Florida**	**NHL**	**82**	**5**	**6**	**11**	**45**	**1**	**0**	**0**	**72**	**6.9**	**−17**	**1022**	**53.1**	**12:27**	....	....	....	....	....	....	....	....	....
2015-16	**Florida**	**NHL**	**64**	**6**	**7**	**13**	**36**	**0**	**0**	**3**	**79**	**7.6**	**7**	**801**	**54.8**	**13:09**	**6**	**0**	**1**	**1**	**4**	**0**	**0**	**0**	**14:40**
2016-17	**Florida**	**NHL**	**82**	**6**	**10**	**16**	**50**	**0**	**2**	**1**	**91**	**6.6**	**−7**	**772**	**50.0**	**12:34**	....	....	....	....	....	....	....	....	....
	NHL Totals		**535**	**48**	**63**	**111**	**306**	**2**	**7**	**7**	**538**	**8.9**		**4652**	**52.9**	**11:12**	**12**	**1**	**1**	**2**	**6**	**0**	**1**	**0**	**14:14**

Signed as a free agent by **Columbus**, July 11, 2007. Signed as a free agent by **Florida**, July 1, 2014.

MacKINNON, Nathan
(muh-KIH-nuhn, NAY-thuhn) **COL**

Center. Shoots right. 6', 205 lbs. Born, Halifax, NS, September 1, 1995. Colorado's 1st pick, 1st overall, in 2013 NHL Draft.

Season	Club	League	GP	G	A	Pts	PIM	PP	SH	GW	S	S%	+/-	TF	F%	Min	Playoffs GP	G	A	Pts	PIM	PP	SH	GW	Min
2009-10	Shattuck Bantam	High-MN	58	54	47	101	56	....	....	....	....	....	....	....	....	....	....	....	....	....	....	....	....	....	....
2010-11	Shattuck Midget	High-MN	40	45	48	93	72	....	....	....	....	....	....	....	....	....	....	....	....	....	....	....	....	....	....
2011-12	Halifax	QMJHL	58	31	47	78	45	....	....	....	....	....	....	....	....	....	17	13	15	28	12	....	....	....	....
2012-13	Halifax	QMJHL	44	32	43	75	45	....	....	....	....	....	....	....	....	....	17	11	22	33	12	....	....	....	....
2013-14	**Colorado**	**NHL**	**82**	**24**	**39**	**63**	**26**	**8**	**0**	**5**	**241**	**10.0**	**20**	**452**	**42.9**	**17:21**	**7**	**2**	**8**	**10**	**4**	**0**	**0**	**1**	**20:34**
2014-15	**Colorado**	**NHL**	**64**	**14**	**24**	**38**	**34**	**3**	**0**	**2**	**192**	**7.3**	**−7**	**428**	**47.0**	**17:03**	....	....	....	....	....	....	....	....	....
2015-16	**Colorado**	**NHL**	**72**	**21**	**31**	**52**	**20**	**7**	**0**	**6**	**245**	**8.6**	**−4**	**1047**	**48.4**	**18:52**	....	....	....	....	....	....	....	....	....
2016-17	**Colorado**	**NHL**	**82**	**16**	**37**	**53**	**16**	**2**	**2**	**4**	**251**	**6.4**	**−14**	**1521**	**50.6**	**19:57**	....	....	....	....	....	....	....	....	....
	NHL Totals		**300**	**75**	**131**	**206**	**96**	**20**	**2**	**17**	**929**	**8.1**		**3448**	**48.5**	**18:21**	**7**	**2**	**8**	**10**	**4**	**0**	**0**	**1**	**20:34**

QMJHL Second All-Star Team (2013) • NHL All-Rookie Team (2014) • Calder Memorial Trophy (2014)

Played in NHL All-Star Game (2017)

MacWILLIAM, Andrew
(MAK-WIHL-yuhm, AN-droo)

Defense. Shoots left. 6'2", 225 lbs. Born, Calgary, AB, March 25, 1990. Toronto's 8th pick, 188th overall, in 2008 NHL Draft.

Season	Club	League	GP	G	A	Pts	PIM	PP	SH	GW	S	S%	+/-	TF	F%	Min	Playoffs GP	G	A	Pts	PIM	PP	SH	GW	Min
2006-07	Calgary Royals	AMHL	35	5	13	18	125	....	....	....	....	....	....	....	....	....	....	....	....	....	....	....	....	....	....
	Camrose Kodiaks	AJHL	2	0	0	0	0	....	....	....	....	....	....	....	....	....	1	0	0	0	0	....	....	....	....
2007-08	Camrose Kodiaks	AJHL	54	0	13	13	130	....	....	....	....	....	....	....	....	....	18	0	5	5	49	....	....	....	....
2008-09	Camrose Kodiaks	AJHL	57	8	21	29	220	....	....	....	....	....	....	....	....	....	11	0	4	4	39	....	....	....	....
2009-10	North Dakota	WCHA	43	0	3	3	87	....	....	....	....	....	....	....	....	....	....	....	....	....	....	....	....	....	....
2010-11	North Dakota	WCHA	37	0	8	8	49	....	....	....	....	....	....	....	....	....	....	....	....	....	....	....	....	....	....
2011-12	North Dakota	WCHA	42	2	5	7	75	....	....	....	....	....	....	....	....	....	....	....	....	....	....	....	....	....	....
2012-13	North Dakota	WCHA	41	2	11	13	*116	....	....	....	....	....	....	....	....	....	....	....	....	....	....	....	....	....	....
	Toronto Marlies	AHL	2	0	0	0	0	....	....	....	....	....	....	....	....	....	....	....	....	....	....	....	....	....	....
2013-14	Toronto Marlies	AHL	57	0	9	9	96	....	....	....	....	....	....	....	....	....	9	0	1	1	8	....	....	....	....
2014-15	**Toronto**	**NHL**	**12**	**0**	**2**	**2**	**12**	**0**	**0**	**0**	**5**	**0.0**	**−6**	**1**	**0.0**	**15:24**	....	....	....	....	....	....	....	....	....
	Toronto Marlies	AHL	58	3	4	7	47	....	....	....	....	....	....	....	....	....	4	0	1	1	6	....	....	....	....
2015-16	Manitoba Moose	AHL	72	1	14	15	86	....	....	....	....	....	....	....	....	....	....	....	....	....	....	....	....	....	....
2016-17	Albany Devils	AHL	63	0	5	5	100	....	....	....	....	....	....	....	....	....	....	....	....	....	....	....	....	....	....
	NHL Totals		**12**	**0**	**2**	**2**	**12**	**0**	**0**	**0**	**5**	**0.0**		**1**	**0.0**	**15:24**	....								

Signed as a free agent by **Winnipeg**, July 3, 2015. Signed as a free agent by **New Jersey**, July 1, 2016.

MALGIN, Denis
(mahl-GEEN, deh-NEEZ) **FLA**

Center. Shoots right. 5'9", 177 lbs. Born, Olten, Switzerland, January 18, 1997. Florida's 4th pick, 102nd overall, in 2015 NHL Draft.

Season	Club	League	GP	G	A	Pts	PIM	PP	SH	GW	S	S%	+/-	TF	F%	Min	Playoffs GP	G	A	Pts	PIM	PP	SH	GW	Min
2010-11	Zurich U17 II	Swiss-U17	16	13	9	22	6	....	....	....	....	....	....	....	....	....	....	....	....	....	....	....	....	....	....
2011-12	ZSC Zurich U17	Swiss-U17	25	17	19	36	34	....	....	....	....	....	....	....	....	....	8	2	7	9	2	....	....	....	....
2012-13	Zurich U17	Swiss-U17	7	6	10	16	16	....	....	....	....	....	....	....	....	....	5	4	5	9	4	....	....	....	....
	GCK Zurich Jr.	Swiss-Jr.	25	15	11	26	14	....	....	....	....	....	....	....	....	....	3	1	1	2	2	....	....	....	....
2013-14	GCK Zurich Jr.	Swiss-Jr.	....	....	....	....	....	....	....	....	....	....	....	....	....	....	7	5	1	6	8	....	....	....	....
	GCK Lions Zurich	Swiss-2	38	6	13	19	14	....	....	....	....	....	....	....	....	....	....	....	....	....	....	....	....	....	....

			Regular Season														Playoffs								
Season	Club	League	GP	G	A	Pts	PIM	PP	SH	GW	S	S%	+/-	TF	F%	Min	GP	G	A	Pts	PIM	PP	SH	GW	Min
2014-15	GCK Lions Zurich	Swiss-2	24	6	6	12	4	....	....	....	....	....	....	....	....	....	....	....	....	....	....	....	....	....	....
	ZSC Lions Zurich	Swiss	23	2	6	8	8	....	....	....	....	....	....	....	....	....	18	4	2	6	4	....	....	....	....
	GCK Zurich Jr.	Swiss-Jr.	....	....	....	....	....	....	....	....	....	....	....	....	....	....	5	1	8	9	4	....	....	....	....
2015-16	GCK Zurich Jr.	Swiss-Jr.	1	0	1	1	0	....	....	....	....	....	....	....	....	....	2	1	1	2	0	....	....	....	....
	GCK Lions Zurich	Swiss-2	7	2	3	5	0	....	....	....	....	....	....	....	....	....	....	....	....	....	....	....	....	....	....
	ZSC Lions Zurich	Swiss	38	5	12	17	12	....	....	....	....	....	....	....	....	....	3	0	0	0	0	....	....	....	....
2016-17	**Florida**	**NHL**	**47**	**6**	**4**	**10**	**8**	**2**	**0**	**1**	**67**	**9.0**	**–5**	**184**	**36.4**	**11:14**	....	....	....	....	....	....	....	....	....
	Springfield	AHL	15	3	9	12	14	....	....	....	....	....	....	....	....	....	....	....	....	....	....	....	....	....	....
	NHL Totals		**47**	**6**	**4**	**10**	**8**	**2**	**0**	**1**	**67**	**9.0**		**184**	**36.4**	**11:14**	....	....	....	....	....	....	....	....	....

MALKIN, Evgeni (MAHL-kihn, ehv-GEH-nee) PIT

Center. Shoots left. 6'3", 195 lbs. Born, Magnitogorsk, USSR, July 31, 1986. Pittsburgh's 1st pick, 2nd overall, in 2004 NHL Draft.

Season	Club	League	GP	G	A	Pts	PIM	PP	SH	GW	S	S%	+/-	TF	F%	Min	GP	G	A	Pts	PIM	PP	SH	GW	Min
2002-03	Magnitogorsk 2	Russia-3	STATISTICS NOT AVAILABLE																						
2003-04	Magnitogorsk 2	Russia-3	2	1	0	1	8	....	....	....	....	....	....	....	....	....									
	Magnitogorsk	Russia	34	3	9	12	12	....	....	....	....	....	....	....	....	....	....	....	....	....	....	....	....	....	....
2004-05	Magnitogorsk 2	Russia-3	2	1	1	2	2	....	....	....	....	....	....	....	....	....	....	....	....	....	....	....	....	....	....
	Magnitogorsk	Russia	52	12	20	32	24	....	....	....	....	....	....	....	....	....	5	0	4	4	0	....	....	....	....
2005-06	Magnitogorsk	Russia	46	21	26	47	46	....	....	....	....	....	....	....	....	....	11	5	10	15	41	....	....	....	....
	Russia	Olympics	7	2	4	6	31	....	....	....	....	....	....	....	....	....	....	....	....	....	....	....	....	....	....
2006-07	**Pittsburgh**	**NHL**	**78**	**33**	**52**	**85**	**80**	**16**	**0**	**6**	**242**	**13.6**	**2**	**728**	**43.3**	**19:10**	**5**	**0**	**4**	**4**	**8**	**0**	**0**	**0**	**19:34**
2007-08	**Pittsburgh**	**NHL**	**82**	**47**	**59**	**106**	**78**	**17**	**0**	**5**	**272**	**17.3**	**16**	**890**	**39.3**	**21:19**	**20**	**10**	**12**	**22**	**24**	**5**	**1**	**3**	**20:48**
2008-09♦	**Pittsburgh**	**NHL**	**82**	**35**	***78**	***113**	**80**	**14**	**2**	**4**	**290**	**12.1**	**17**	**668**	**42.4**	**22:31**	**24**	**14**	***22**	***36**	**51**	***7**	**0**	***3**	**20:57**
2009-10	**Pittsburgh**	**NHL**	**67**	**28**	**49**	**77**	**100**	**13**	**2**	**7**	**268**	**10.4**	**–6**	**498**	**40.0**	**20:51**	**13**	**5**	**6**	**11**	**6**	**4**	**0**	**1**	**21:54**
	Russia	Olympics	4	3	3	6	0	....	....	....	....	....	....	....	....	....	....	....	....	....	....	....	....	....	....
2010-11	**Pittsburgh**	**NHL**	**43**	**15**	**22**	**37**	**18**	**5**	**0**	**3**	**182**	**8.2**	**–4**	**200**	**38.5**	**19:49**	....	....	....	....	....	....	....	....	....
2011-12	**Pittsburgh**	**NHL**	**75**	**50**	**59**	***109**	**70**	**12**	**0**	**9**	**339**	**14.7**	**18**	**1210**	**47.5**	**21:01**	**6**	**3**	**5**	**8**	**6**	**1**	**0**	**0**	**22:15**
2012-13	Magnitogorsk	KHL	37	23	42	65	58	....	....	....	....	....	....	....	....	....	....	....	....	....	....	....	....	....	....
	Pittsburgh	**NHL**	**31**	**9**	**24**	**33**	**36**	**4**	**0**	**3**	**99**	**9.1**	**5**	**413**	**47.2**	**19:42**	**15**	**4**	**12**	**16**	**26**	**0**	**0**	**1**	**20:29**
2013-14	**Pittsburgh**	**NHL**	**60**	**23**	**49**	**72**	**62**	**7**	**0**	**3**	**191**	**12.0**	**10**	**621**	**48.8**	**20:04**	**13**	**6**	**8**	**14**	**8**	**1**	**0**	**1**	**21:00**
	Russia	Olympics	5	1	2	3	2	....	....	....	....	....	....	....	....	....	....	....	....	....	....	....	....	....	....
2014-15	**Pittsburgh**	**NHL**	**69**	**28**	**42**	**70**	**60**	**9**	**0**	**4**	**212**	**13.2**	**–2**	**755**	**42.7**	**18:58**	**5**	**0**	**0**	**0**	**0**	**0**	**0**	**0**	**19:19**
2015-16♦	**Pittsburgh**	**NHL**	**57**	**27**	**31**	**58**	**65**	**11**	**0**	**6**	**162**	**16.7**	**1**	**755**	**42.0**	**19:22**	**23**	**6**	**12**	**18**	**18**	**4**	**0**	**1**	**17:31**
2016-17♦	**Pittsburgh**	**NHL**	**62**	**33**	**39**	**72**	**77**	**11**	**0**	**6**	**191**	**17.3**	**18**	**846**	**43.1**	**18:37**	**25**	**10**	**18**	***28**	***53**	**1**	**0**	**0**	**18:04**
	NHL Totals		**706**	**328**	**504**	**832**	**726**	**119**	**4**	**56**	**2448**	**13.4**		**7584**	**43.5**	**20:15**	**149**	**58**	**99**	**157**	**200**	**23**	**1**	**10**	**19:54**

NHL All-Rookie Team (2007) • Calder Memorial Trophy (2007) • NHL First All-Star Team (2008, 2009, 2012) • Art Ross Trophy (2009, 2012) • Conn Smythe Trophy (2009) • Ted Lindsay Award (2012) • Hart Memorial Trophy (2012)

Played in NHL All-Star Game (2008, 2009, 2012, 2016)

Signed as a free agent by **Magnitogorsk** (KHL), September 16, 2012.

MALONE, Brad (ma-LOHN, BRAD) EDM

Center/Left wing. Shoots left. 6'2", 207 lbs. Born, Miramichi, NB, May 20, 1989. Colorado's 5th pick, 105th overall, in 2007 NHL Draft.

Season	Club	League	GP	G	A	Pts	PIM	PP	SH	GW	S	S%	+/-	TF	F%	Min	GP	G	A	Pts	PIM	PP	SH	GW	Min
2005-06	Cushing	High-MA	36	9	33	42	....	....	....	....	....	....	....	....	....	....	....	....	....	....	....	....	....	....	....
2006-07	Sioux Falls	USHL	57	14	19	33	134	....	....	....	....	....	....	....	....	....	8	3	1	4	24	....	....	....	....
2007-08	North Dakota	WCHA	34	1	2	3	44	....	....	....	....	....	....	....	....	....	....	....	....	....	....	....	....	....	....
2008-09	North Dakota	WCHA	41	5	12	17	75	....	....	....	....	....	....	....	....	....	....	....	....	....	....	....	....	....	....
2009-10	North Dakota	WCHA	43	11	14	25	*102	....	....	....	....	....	....	....	....	....	....	....	....	....	....	....	....	....	....
2010-11	North Dakota	WCHA	43	16	24	40	*108	....	....	....	....	....	....	....	....	....	....	....	....	....	....	....	....	....	....
	Lake Erie	AHL	....	....	....	....	....	....	....	....	....	....	....	....	....	....	3	0	1	1	2	....	....	....	....
2011-12	**Colorado**	**NHL**	**9**	**0**	**2**	**2**	**0**	**0**	**0**	**0**	**6**	**0.0**	**1**	**8**	**12.5**	**10:03**	....	....	....	....	....	....	....	....	....
	Lake Erie	AHL	67	11	25	36	89	....	....	....	....	....	....	....	....	....	....	....	....	....	....	....	....	....	....
2012-13	Lake Erie	AHL	63	10	14	24	99	....	....	....	....	....	....	....	....	....	....	....	....	....	....	....	....	....	....
	Colorado	**NHL**	**13**	**1**	**1**	**2**	**16**	**0**	**0**	**0**	**10**	**10.0**	**–7**	**46**	**47.8**	**8:47**	....	....	....	....	....	....	....	....	....
2013-14	**Colorado**	**NHL**	**32**	**3**	**2**	**5**	**23**	**0**	**0**	**0**	**16**	**18.8**	**–4**	**96**	**46.9**	**6:46**	**6**	**0**	**0**	**0**	**2**	**0**	**0**	**0**	**5:53**
	Lake Erie	AHL	35	8	7	15	75	....	....	....	....	....	....	....	....	....	....	....	....	....	....	....	....	....	....
2014-15	**Carolina**	**NHL**	**65**	**7**	**8**	**15**	**74**	**0**	**0**	**2**	**65**	**10.8**	**–8**	**49**	**61.2**	**10:09**	....	....	....	....	....	....	....	....	....
2015-16	**Carolina**	**NHL**	**57**	**2**	**4**	**6**	**75**	**0**	**0**	**0**	**31**	**6.5**	**–11**	**62**	**64.5**	**9:33**	....	....	....	....	....	....	....	....	....
2016-17	Hershey Bears	AHL	52	7	13	20	66	....	....	....	....	....	....	....	....	....	....	....	....	....	....	....	....	....	....
	Chicago Wolves	AHL	19	4	4	8	6	....	....	....	....	....	....	....	....	....	....	....	....	....	....	....	....	....	....
	NHL Totals		**176**	**13**	**17**	**30**	**188**	**0**	**0**	**2**	**128**	**10.2**		**261**	**52.9**	**9:14**	**6**	**0**	**0**	**0**	**2**	**0**	**0**	**0**	**5:53**

Signed as a free agent by **Carolina**, July 1, 2014. Signed as a free agent by **Washington**, July 2, 2016. Traded to **St. Louis** by **Washington** with Zach Sanford and Washington's 1st round pick (later traded to Philadelphia – Philadelphia selected Morgan Frost) in 2017 NHL Draft for Kevin Shattenkirk and Pheonix Copley, February 27, 2017. Signed as a free agent by **Edmonton**, July 3, 2017.

MALONE, Sean (mah-LOHN, SHAWN) BUF

Center. Shoots left. 6', 190 lbs. Born, Buffalo, NY, April 30, 1995. Buffalo's 10th pick, 159th overall, in 2013 NHL Draft.

Season	Club	League	GP	G	A	Pts	PIM	PP	SH	GW	S	S%	+/-	TF	F%	Min	GP	G	A	Pts	PIM	PP	SH	GW	Min
2010-11	Nichols	High-NY	14	3	9	12	4	....	....	....	....	....	....	....	....	....	3	3	3	6	0	....	....	....	....
	Buffalo Saints	Minor-NY	STATISTICS NOT AVAILABLE																						
2011-12	Nichols	High-NY	15	17	18	35	6	....	....	....	....	....	....	....	....	....	1	0	1	1	0	....	....	....	....
	Nichols	Other	16	17	17	34	....	....	....	....	....	....	....	....	....	....	....	....	....	....	....	....	....	....	....
	Buffalo Saints	Minor-NY	....	27	27	54	....	....	....	....	....	....	....	....	....	....	....	....	....	....	....	....	....	....	....
2012-13	USAHNTDP	USHL	15	5	8	13	17	....	....	....	....	....	....	....	....	....	....	....	....	....	....	....	....	....	....
	USAHNTDP	U-18	35	9	11	20	2	....	....	....	....	....	....	....	....	....	....	....	....	....	....	....	....	....	....
2013-14	Harvard Crimson	ECAC	31	6	14	20	16	....	....	....	....	....	....	....	....	....	....	....	....	....	....	....	....	....	....
2014-15	Harvard Crimson	ECAC	21	8	10	18	12	....	....	....	....	....	....	....	....	....	....	....	....	....	....	....	....	....	....
2015-16	Harvard Crimson	ECAC	27	10	9	19	8	....	....	....	....	....	....	....	....	....	....	....	....	....	....	....	....	....	....
2016-17	Harvard Crimson	ECAC	36	18	24	42	16	....	....	....	....	....	....	....	....	....	....	....	....	....	....	....	....	....	....
	Buffalo	**NHL**	**1**	**0**	**0**	**0**	**0**	**0**	**0**	**0**	**1**	**0.0**	**0**	**8**	**62.5**	**12:12**	....	....	....	....	....	....	....	....	....
	NHL Totals		**1**	**0**	**0**	**0**	**0**	**0**	**0**	**0**	**1**	**0.0**		**8**	**62.5**	**12:12**	....	....	....	....	....	....	....	....	....

MANNING, Brandon (MAN-nihng, BRAN-duhn) PHI

Defense. Shoots left. 6'1", 205 lbs. Born, Prince George, BC, June 4, 1990.

Season	Club	League	GP	G	A	Pts	PIM	PP	SH	GW	S	S%	+/-	TF	F%	Min	GP	G	A	Pts	PIM	PP	SH	GW	Min
2007-08	Prince George	BCHL	58	7	19	26	107	....	....	....	....	....	....	....	....	....	4	0	3	3	6	....	....	....	....
	Chilliwack Bruins	WHL	6	0	0	0	8	....	....	....	....	....	....	....	....	....	4	0	0	0	4	....	....	....	....
2008-09	Chilliwack Bruins	WHL	72	11	18	29	140	....	....	....	....	....	....	....	....	....	....	....	....	....	....	....	....	....	....
2009-10	Chilliwack Bruins	WHL	69	13	41	54	138	....	....	....	....	....	....	....	....	....	6	0	6	6	10	....	....	....	....
2010-11	Chilliwack Bruins	WHL	53	21	32	53	129	....	....	....	....	....	....	....	....	....	5	1	0	1	8	....	....	....	....
2011-12	**Philadelphia**	**NHL**	**4**	**0**	**0**	**0**	**0**	**0**	**0**	**0**	**6**	**0.0**	**1**	**0**	**0.0**	**13:44**	....	....	....	....	....	....	....	....	....
	Adirondack	AHL	46	6	13	19	81	....	....	....	....	....	....	....	....	....	....	....	....	....	....	....	....	....	....
2012-13	Adirondack	AHL	65	6	15	21	135	....	....	....	....	....	....	....	....	....	....	....	....	....	....	....	....	....	....
	Philadelphia	**NHL**	**6**	**0**	**2**	**2**	**0**	**0**	**0**	**0**	**5**	**0.0**	**4**	**0**	**0.0**	**14:48**	....	....	....	....	....	....	....	....	....
2013-14	Adirondack	AHL	73	8	23	31	231	....	....	....	....	....	....	....	....	....	....	....	....	....	....	....	....	....	....
2014-15	**Philadelphia**	**NHL**	**11**	**0**	**3**	**3**	**7**	**0**	**0**	**0**	**10**	**0.0**	**3**	**0**	**0.0**	**17:10**	....	....	....	....	....	....	....	....	....
	Lehigh Valley	AHL	60	11	32	43	150	....	....	....	....	....	....	....	....	....	....	....	....	....	....	....	....	....	....
2015-16	**Philadelphia**	**NHL**	**56**	**1**	**6**	**7**	**66**	**0**	**0**	**1**	**67**	**1.5**	**2**	**1**	**0.0**	**16:32**	**6**	**0**	**1**	**1**	**4**	**0**	**0**	**0**	**18:24**
2016-17	**Philadelphia**	**NHL**	**65**	**3**	**9**	**12**	**83**	**0**	**1**	**1**	**84**	**3.6**	**–12**	**1**	**0.0**	**18:03**	....	....	....	....	....	....	....	....	....
	NHL Totals		**142**	**4**	**20**	**24**	**156**	**0**	**1**	**2**	**172**	**2.3**		**2**	**0.0**	**17:07**	**6**	**0**	**1**	**1**	**4**	**0**	**0**	**0**	**18:24**

Signed as a free agent by **Philadelphia**, November 23, 2010.

			Regular Season															Playoffs							
Season	Club	League	GP	G	A	Pts	PIM	PP	SH	GW	S	S%	+/-	TF	F%	Min	GP	G	A	Pts	PIM	PP	SH	GW	Min

MANSON, Josh — (MAN-suhn, JAWSH) — ANA

Defense. Shoots right. 6'3", 215 lbs.　Born, Prince Albert, SK, October 7, 1991. Anaheim's 7th pick, 160th overall, in 2011 NHL Draft.

Season	Club	League	GP	G	A	Pts	PIM	PP	SH	GW	S	S%	+/-	TF	F%	Min	GP	G	A	Pts	PIM	PP	SH	GW	Min
2008-09	Prince Albert	SMHL	40	19	16	35	64	....	....	....	....	....	....				3	1	0	1	4	....	....	....	....
	Flin Flon Bombers	SJHL	2	0	0	0	0	....	....	....	....	....	....				....	....	....	....	....	....	....	....	....
2009-10	Salmon Arm	BCHL	54	10	14	24	75	....	....	....	....	....	....				6	1	0	1	15	....	....	....	....
2010-11	Salmon Arm	BCHL	57	12	35	47	80	....	....	....	....	....	....				14	2	7	9	15	....	....	....	....
2011-12	Northeastern	H-East	33	0	4	4	48	....	....	....	....	....	....				....	....	....	....	....	....	....	....	....
2012-13	Northeastern	H-East	33	3	4	7	45	....	....	....	....	....	....				....	....	....	....	....	....	....	....	....
2013-14	Northeastern	H-East	33	3	7	10	65	....	....	....	....	....	....				....	....	....	....	....	....	....	....	....
	Norfolk Admirals	AHL	9	1	0	1	26	....	....	....	....	....	....				10	1	0	1	6	....	....	....	....
2014-15	**Anaheim**	**NHL**	28	0	3	3	31	0	0	0	26	0.0	1	0	0.0	18:26	....	....	....	....	....	....	....	....	....
	Norfolk Admirals	AHL	36	3	9	12	47	....	....	....	....	....	....				....	....	....	....	....	....	....	....	....
2015-16	**Anaheim**	**NHL**	71	5	10	15	74	0	0	1	88	5.7	11	0	0.0	18:47	1	0	0	0	0	0	0	0	4:44
2016-17	**Anaheim**	**NHL**	82	5	12	17	82	0	1	1	88	5.7	14	0	0.0	18:38	17	0	3	3	20	0	0	0	20:33
	NHL Totals		181	10	25	35	187	0	1	2	202	5.0		0	0.0	18:39	18	0	3	3	20	0	0	0	19:40

Hockey East Second All-Star Team (2014)

MANTHA, Anthony — (MAN-tha, AN-thuh-nee) — DET

Right wing. Shoots left. 6'5", 221 lbs.　Born, Longueuil, QC, September 16, 1994. Detroit's 1st pick, 20th overall, in 2013 NHL Draft.

Season	Club	League	GP	G	A	Pts	PIM	PP	SH	GW	S	S%	+/-	TF	F%	Min	GP	G	A	Pts	PIM	PP	SH	GW	Min
2010-11	C.C. Lemoyne	QAAA	37	20	24	44	42	....	....	....	....	....	....				3	0	1	1	12	....	....	....	....
	Val-d'Or Foreurs	QMJHL	2	0	0	0	0	....	....	....	....	....	....				....	....	....	....	....	....	....	....	....
2011-12	Val-d'Or Foreurs	QMJHL	63	22	29	51	39	....	....	....	....	....	....				4	2	2	4	6	....	....	....	....
2012-13	Val-d'Or Foreurs	QMJHL	67	*50	39	89	71	....	....	....	....	....	....				9	5	7	12	13	....	....	....	....
2013-14	Val-d'Or Foreurs	QMJHL	57	*57	63	*120	75	....	....	....	....	....	....				24	*24	14	38	*52	....	....	....	....
2014-15	Grand Rapids	AHL	62	15	18	33	64	....	....	....	....	....	....				16	4	12	16	4	....	....	....	....
2015-16	**Detroit**	**NHL**	10	2	1	3	2	2	0	1	18	11.1	-6	0	0.0	11:42	....	....	....	....	....	....	....	....	....
	Grand Rapids	AHL	60	21	24	45	32	....	....	....	....	....	....				9	4	7	11	8	....	....	....	....
2016-17	**Detroit**	**NHL**	60	17	19	36	53	1	0	3	133	12.8	10	11	45.5	15:54	....	....	....	....	....	....	....	....	....
	Grand Rapids	AHL	10	8	2	10	6	....	....	....	....	....	....				....	....	....	....	....	....	....	....	....
	NHL Totals		70	19	20	39	55	3	0	4	151	12.6		11	45.5	15:18									

QMJHL Second All-Star Team (2013) • QMJHL First All-Star Team (2014) • QMJHL Player of the Year (2014) • Canadian Major Junior Player of the Year (2014)

MARCHAND, Brad — (mahr-SHAND, BRAD) — BOS

Left wing. Shoots left. 5'9", 181 lbs.　Born, Halifax, NS, May 11, 1988. Boston's 4th pick, 71st overall, in 2006 NHL Draft.

Season	Club	League	GP	G	A	Pts	PIM	PP	SH	GW	S	S%	+/-	TF	F%	Min	GP	G	A	Pts	PIM	PP	SH	GW	Min
2003-04	Dartmouth	NSMHL	60	47	47	94	104	....	....	....	....	....	....				11	1	0	1	7	....	....	....	....
2004-05	Moncton Wildcats	QMJHL	61	9	20	29	52	....	....	....	....	....	....				20	5	14	19	34	....	....	....	....
2005-06	Moncton Wildcats	QMJHL	68	29	37	66	83	....	....	....	....	....	....				20	*16	*24	*40	36	....	....	....	....
2006-07	Val-d'Or Foreurs	QMJHL	57	33	47	80	108	....	....	....	....	....	....				14	3	16	19	18	....	....	....	....
2007-08	Val-d'Or Foreurs	QMJHL	33	21	23	44	36	....	....	....	....	....	....				16	7	8	15	26	....	....	....	....
	Halifax	QMJHL	26	10	19	29	40	....	....	....	....	....	....				....	....	....	....	....	....	....	....	....
2008-09	Providence Bruins	AHL	79	18	41	59	67	....	....	....	....	....	....				....	....	....	....	....	....	....	....	....
2009-10	**Boston**	**NHL**	20	0	1	1	20	0	0	0	32	0.0	-3	11	27.3	11:58	....	....	....	....	....	....	....	....	....
	Providence Bruins	AHL	34	13	19	32	51	....	....	....	....	....	....				....	....	....	....	....	....	....	....	....
2010-11♦	Boston	NHL	77	21	20	41	51	2	5	2	149	14.1	25	25	32.0	13:59	25	11	8	19	40	0	1	1	16:46
2011-12	Boston	NHL	76	28	27	55	87	5	1	3	167	16.8	31	9	55.6	17:37	7	1	1	2	2	0	0	0	18:04
2012-13	Boston	NHL	45	18	18	36	27	4	2	5	91	19.8	23	12	50.0	16:58	22	4	9	13	21	0	0	1	19:35
2013-14	Boston	NHL	82	25	28	53	64	1	*5	2	149	16.8	36	23	26.1	15:57	12	0	5	5	18	0	0	0	17:38
2014-15	Boston	NHL	77	24	18	42	95	2	2	5	180	13.3	5	33	39.4	16:54	....	....	....	....	....	....	....	....	....
2015-16	Boston	NHL	77	37	24	61	90	6	4	6	250	14.8	21	56	37.5	18:36	....	....	....	....	....	....	....	....	....
2016-17	Boston	NHL	80	39	46	85	81	9	3	8	226	17.3	18	36	36.1	19:26	6	1	3	4	6	0	0	1	23:31
	NHL Totals		534	192	182	374	515	29	22	34	1244	15.4		205	36.6	16:53	72	17	26	43	87	0	1	3	18:28

NHL First All-Star Team (2017)
Played in NHL All-Star Game (2017)

MARCHENKO, Alexey — (MAHR-chehn-koh, al-EHX-ay) — TOR

Defense. Shoots right. 6'3", 210 lbs.　Born, Moscow, Russia, January 2, 1992. Detroit's 9th pick, 205th overall, in 2011 NHL Draft.

Season	Club	League	GP	G	A	Pts	PIM	PP	SH	GW	S	S%	+/-	TF	F%	Min	GP	G	A	Pts	PIM	PP	SH	GW	Min
2009-10	CSKA Jr.	Russia-Jr.	43	11	23	34	59	....	....	....	....	....	....				2	0	0	0	4	....	....	....	....
	CSKA Moscow	KHL	10	0	0	0	0	....	....	....	....	....	....				....	....	....	....	....	....	....	....	....
2010-11	CSKA Jr.	Russia-Jr.	36	5	33	38	28	....	....	....	....	....	....				15	3	8	11	31	....	....	....	....
	CSKA Moscow	KHL	22	0	2	2	4	....	....	....	....	....	....				....	....	....	....	....	....	....	....	....
2011-12	CSKA Jr.	Russia-Jr.	5	2	4	6	10	....	....	....	....	....	....				19	4	14	18	18	....	....	....	....
	CSKA Moscow	KHL	6	0	0	0	2	....	....	....	....	....	....				5	0	1	1	4	....	....	....	....
2012-13	CSKA Moscow	KHL	44	4	5	9	6	....	....	....	....	....	....				7	0	0	0	0	....	....	....	....
2013-14	**Detroit**	**NHL**	1	0	0	0	2	0	0	0	0	0.0	2	0	0.0	13:21	....	....	....	....	....	....	....	....	....
	Grand Rapids	AHL	49	3	15	18	14	....	....	....	....	....	....				....	....	....	....	....	....	....	....	....
2014-15	**Detroit**	**NHL**	13	1	1	2	2	0	0	0	7	14.3	1	0	0.0	15:26	3	0	0	0	0	0	0	0	16:52
	Grand Rapids	AHL	51	3	17	20	26	....	....	....	....	....	....				11	0	4	4	2	....	....	....	....
2015-16	**Detroit**	**NHL**	66	2	9	11	10	0	0	0	40	5.0	-5	0	0.0	16:50	3	0	0	0	10	0	0	0	16:01
	Grand Rapids	AHL	4	0	0	0	0	....	....	....	....	....	....				....	....	....	....	....	....	....	....	....
2016-17	**Detroit**	**NHL**	30	0	6	6	12	0	0	0	27	0.0	6	0	0.0	17:59	....	....	....	....	....	....	....	....	....
	Toronto	**NHL**	11	1	1	2	0	0	0	0	9	11.1	1	0	0.0	14:09	....	....	....	....	....	....	....	....	....
	NHL Totals		121	4	17	21	26	0	0	0	83	4.8		0	0.0	16:42	6	0	0	0	10	0	0	0	16:27

Claimed on waivers by **Toronto** from **Detroit**, February 4, 2017.

MARCHESSAULT, Jonathan — (mahr-SHUH-sohn, JAWN-ah-thuhn) — VGK

Center. Shoots right. 5'9", 174 lbs.　Born, Cap-Rouge, QC, December 27, 1990.

Season	Club	League	GP	G	A	Pts	PIM	PP	SH	GW	S	S%	+/-	TF	F%	Min	GP	G	A	Pts	PIM	PP	SH	GW	Min
2007-08	Quebec Remparts	QMJHL	56	10	10	20	18	....	....	....	....	....	....				11	1	0	1	6	....	....	....	....
2008-09	Quebec Remparts	QMJHL	62	18	35	53	75	....	....	....	....	....	....				14	2	4	6	10	....	....	....	....
2009-10	Quebec Remparts	QMJHL	68	30	41	71	54	....	....	....	....	....	....				9	3	11	14	14	....	....	....	....
2010-11	Quebec Remparts	QMJHL	68	40	55	95	41	....	....	....	....	....	....				18	11	22	33	12	....	....	....	....
2011-12	Connecticut	AHL	76	24	40	64	50	....	....	....	....	....	....				9	4	0	4	26	....	....	....	....
2012-13	Springfield	AHL	74	21	46	67	65	....	....	....	....	....	....				8	0	3	3	8	....	....	....	....
	Columbus	**NHL**	2	0	0	0	0	0	0	0	0	0.0	-1	0	0.0	10:57	....	....	....	....	....	....	....	....	....
2013-14	Springfield	AHL	56	14	27	41	51	....	....	....	....	....	....				....	....	....	....	....	....	....	....	....
	Syracuse Crunch	AHL	21	9	6	15	8	....	....	....	....	....	....				....	....	....	....	....	....	....	....	....
2014-15	**Tampa Bay**	**NHL**	2	1	0	1	0	0	0	0	3	33.3	1	3	33.3	11:57	2	0	0	0	0	0	0	0	11:28
	Syracuse Crunch	AHL	68	24	43	67	38	....	....	....	....	....	....				3	0	0	0	0	....	....	....	....
2015-16	**Tampa Bay**	**NHL**	45	7	11	18	17	4	0	1	81	8.6	-10	79	48.1	12:05	5	0	1	1	6	0	0	0	7:06
	Syracuse Crunch	AHL	11	6	3	9	6	....	....	....	....	....	....				....	....	....	....	....	....	....	....	....
2016-17	**Florida**	**NHL**	75	30	21	51	38	8	0	6	193	15.5	-21	270	45.2	16:55	....	....	....	....	....	....	....	....	....
	NHL Totals		124	38	32	70	55	12	0	7	277	13.7		352	45.7	14:59	7	0	1	1	6	0	0	0	8:21

QMJHL First All-Star Team (2011) • AHL First All-Star Team (2013)

Signed as a free agent by **Columbus**, July 1, 2012. Traded to **Tampa Bay** by **Columbus** with Dalton Smith for Matt Taormina and Dana Tyrell, March 5, 2014. Signed as a free agent by **Florida**, July 1, 2016. Claimed by **Vegas** from **Florida** in Expansion Draft, June 21, 2017.

MARINCIN, Martin

(mah-RIHN-chihn, MAHR-tihn) **TOR**

Defense. Shoots left. 6'4", 201 lbs. Born, Kosice, Czech., February 18, 1992. Edmonton's 3rd pick, 46th overall, in 2010 NHL Draft.

			Regular Season														Playoffs								
Season	Club	League	GP	G	A	Pts	PIM	PP	SH	GW	S	S%	+/-	TF	F%	Min	GP	G	A	Pts	PIM	PP	SH	GW	Min
2006-07	HC Kosice U18	Svk-U18	16	0	3	3	6	....	....	....	....	....	....	....	....	....	....	....	....	....	....	....	....	....	....
2007-08	HC Kosice U18	Svk-U18	59	3	29	32	36	....	....	....	....	....	....	....	....	....	....	....	....	....	....	....	....	....	....
2008-09	HC Kosice U18	Svk-U18	5	4	4	8	35	....	....	....	....	....	....	....	....	....	....	....	....	....	....	....	....	....	....
	HC Kosice Jr.	Slovak-Jr.	46	11	15	26	50	....	....	....	....	....	....	....	....	....	3	0	0	0	0	....	....	....	....
2009-10	Slovakia U20	Slovakia	35	2	4	6	71	....	....	....	....	....	....	....	....	....	....	....	....	....	....	....	....	....	....
	HC Kosice Jr.	Slovak-Jr.	....	....	....	....	....	....	....	....	....	....	....	....	....	....	2	0	0	0	0	....	....	....	....
2010-11	Prince George	WHL	67	14	42	56	65	....	....	....	....	....	....	....	....	....	4	1	4	5	6	....	....	....	....
	Oklahoma City	AHL	1	0	0	0	2	....	....	....	....	....	....	....	....	....	....	....	....	....	....	....	....	....	....
2011-12	Prince George	WHL	30	4	13	17	25	....	....	....	....	....	....	....	....	....	....	....	....	....	....	....	....	....	....
	Regina Pats	WHL	28	7	16	23	10	....	....	....	....	....	....	....	....	....	5	2	0	2	6	....	....	....	....
	Oklahoma City	AHL	6	0	1	1	2	....	....	....	....	....	....	....	....	....	....	....	....	....	....	....	....	....	....
2012-13	Oklahoma City	AHL	69	7	23	30	40	....	....	....	....	....	....	....	....	....	17	1	6	7	2	....	....	....	....
2013-14	**Edmonton**	**NHL**	**44**	**0**	**6**	**6**	**16**	**0**	**0**	**0**	**28**	**0.0**	**–2**	**0**	**0.0**	**19:10**	....	....	....	....	....	....	....	....	....
	Oklahoma City	AHL	24	3	4	7	4	....	....	....	....	....	....	....	....	....	....	....	....	....	....	....	....	....	....
	Slovakia	Olympics	4	0	0	0	4	....	....	....	....	....	....	....	....	....	....	....	....	....	....	....	....	....	....
2014-15	**Edmonton**	**NHL**	**41**	**1**	**4**	**5**	**16**	**0**	**0**	**0**	**38**	**2.6**	**–4**	**1**	**100.0**	**18:39**	....	....	....	....	....	....	....	....	....
	Oklahoma City	AHL	28	0	7	7	20	....	....	....	....	....	....	....	....	....	8	0	2	2	6	....	....	....	....
2015-16	**Toronto**	**NHL**	**65**	**1**	**6**	**7**	**34**	**0**	**0**	**0**	**55**	**1.8**	**–3**	**0**	**0.0**	**16:46**	....	....	....	....	....	....	....	....	....
2016-17	**Toronto**	**NHL**	**25**	**1**	**6**	**7**	**16**	**0**	**0**	**0**	**22**	**4.5**	**3**	**0**	**0.0**	**18:03**	**6**	**0**	**0**	**0**	**2**	**0**	**0**	**0**	**16:53**
	NHL Totals		**175**	**3**	**22**	**25**	**82**	**0**	**0**	**0**	**143**	**2.1**		**1**	**100.0**	**18:00**	**6**	**0**	**0**	**0**	**2**	**0**	**0**	**0**	**16:53**

Traded to **Toronto** by **Edmonton** for Brad Ross and Pittsburgh's 4th round pick (previously acquired, later traded to Ottawa – Ottawa selected Christian Wolanin) in 2015 NHL Draft, June 27, 2015. • Missed majority of 2016-17 due to lower-body injury at. Boston, December 10. 2016.

MARKOV, Andrei

(MAHR-kahf, AHN-dray)

Defense. Shoots left. 6', 194 lbs. Born, Voskresensk, USSR, December 20, 1978. Montreal's 6th pick, 162nd overall, in 1998 NHL Draft.

			Regular Season														Playoffs								
Season	Club	League	GP	G	A	Pts	PIM	PP	SH	GW	S	S%	+/-	TF	F%	Min	GP	G	A	Pts	PIM	PP	SH	GW	Min
1995-96	Voskresensk	CIS	38	0	0	0	14	....	....	....	....	....	....	....	....	....	....	....	....	....	....	....	....	....	....
1996-97	Voskresensk	Russia	43	8	4	12	32	....	....	....	....	....	....	....	....	....	2	1	1	2	0	....	....	....	....
1997-98	Voskresensk	Russia	43	10	5	15	83	....	....	....	....	....	....	....	....	....	....	....	....	....	....	....	....	....	....
1998-99	Dynamo Moscow	Russia	38	10	11	21	32	....	....	....	....	....	....	....	....	....	16	3	6	9	6	....	....	....	....
	Dynamo Moscow	EuroHL	12	7	5	12	12	....	....	....	....	....	....	....	....	....	6	2	2	4	4	....	....	....	....
99-2000	Dynamo Moscow	Russia	29	11	12	23	28	....	....	....	....	....	....	....	....	....	17	4	3	7	8	....	....	....	....
2000-01	**Montreal**	**NHL**	**63**	**6**	**17**	**23**	**18**	**2**	**0**	**0**	**82**	**7.3**	**–6**	**2**	**50.0**	**16:53**	....	....	....	....	....	....	....	....	....
	Quebec Citadelles	AHL	14	0	5	5	4	....	....	....	....	....	....	....	....	....	7	1	1	2	2	....	....	....	....
2001-02	**Montreal**	**NHL**	**56**	**5**	**19**	**24**	**24**	**2**	**0**	**1**	**73**	**6.8**	**–1**	**0**	**0.0**	**17:15**	**12**	**1**	**3**	**4**	**8**	**0**	**0**	**1**	**15:53**
	Quebec Citadelles	AHL	12	4	6	10	7	....	....	....	....	....	....	....	....	....	....	....	....	....	....	....	....	....	....
2002-03	**Montreal**	**NHL**	**79**	**13**	**24**	**37**	**34**	**3**	**0**	**2**	**159**	**8.2**	**13**	**1**	**0.0**	**23:17**	....	....	....	....	....	....	....	....	....
2003-04	**Montreal**	**NHL**	**69**	**6**	**22**	**28**	**20**	**2**	**0**	**0**	**105**	**5.7**	**–2**	**2**	**50.0**	**21:29**	**11**	**1**	**4**	**5**	**8**	**0**	**0**	**1**	**22:52**
2004-05	Dynamo Moscow	Russia	42	7	16	23	76	....	....	....	....	....	....	....	....	....	10	2	0	2	22	....	....	....	....
2005-06	**Montreal**	**NHL**	**67**	**10**	**36**	**46**	**74**	**6**	**1**	**1**	**88**	**11.4**	**13**	**1**	**0.0**	**23:33**	**6**	**0**	**1**	**1**	**4**	**0**	**0**	**0**	**25:29**
	Russia	Olympics	8	1	2	3	6	....	....	....	....	....	....	....	....	....	....	....	....	....	....	....	....	....	....
2006-07	**Montreal**	**NHL**	**77**	**6**	**43**	**49**	**56**	**5**	**0**	**2**	**128**	**4.7**	**2**	**1**	**0.0**	**24:29**	....	....	....	....	....	....	....	....	....
2007-08	**Montreal**	**NHL**	**82**	**16**	**42**	**58**	**63**	**10**	**1**	**2**	**145**	**11.0**	**1**	**0**	**0.0**	**24:58**	**12**	**1**	**3**	**4**	**8**	**0**	**0**	**0**	**24:54**
2008-09	**Montreal**	**NHL**	**78**	**12**	**52**	**64**	**36**	**7**	**0**	**3**	**165**	**7.3**	**–2**	**0**	**0.0**	**24:38**	....	....	....	....	....	....	....	....	....
2009-10	**Montreal**	**NHL**	**45**	**6**	**28**	**34**	**32**	**4**	**0**	**1**	**85**	**7.1**	**11**	**0**	**0.0**	**23:48**	**8**	**0**	**4**	**4**	**0**	**0**	**0**	**0**	**23:47**
	Russia	Olympics	4	0	2	2	0	....	....	....	....	....	....	....	....	....	....	....	....	....	....	....	....	....	....
2010-11	**Montreal**	**NHL**	**7**	**1**	**2**	**3**	**4**	**0**	**0**	**1**	**20**	**5.0**	**2**	**0**	**0.0**	**22:55**	....	....	....	....	....	....	....	....	....
2011-12	**Montreal**	**NHL**	**13**	**0**	**3**	**3**	**4**	**0**	**0**	**0**	**17**	**0.0**	**–4**	**0**	**0.0**	**18:00**	....	....	....	....	....	....	....	....	....
2012-13	Vityaz Chekhov	KHL	21	1	7	8	16	....	....	....	....	....	....	....	....	....	....	....	....	....	....	....	....	....	....
	Montreal	**NHL**	**48**	**10**	**20**	**30**	**14**	**8**	**0**	**4**	**79**	**12.7**	**–9**	**0**	**0.0**	**24:08**	**5**	**0**	**1**	**1**	**0**	**0**	**0**	**0**	**23:54**
2013-14	**Montreal**	**NHL**	**81**	**7**	**36**	**43**	**34**	**2**	**1**	**1**	**131**	**5.3**	**12**	**0**	**0.0**	**25:14**	**17**	**1**	**9**	**10**	**10**	**0**	**0**	**0**	**26:00**
	Russia	Olympics	5	0	2	2	0	....	....	....	....	....	....	....	....	....	....	....	....	....	....	....	....	....	....
2014-15	**Montreal**	**NHL**	**81**	**10**	**40**	**50**	**38**	**4**	**0**	**1**	**135**	**7.4**	**22**	**0**	**0.0**	**24:55**	**12**	**1**	**1**	**2**	**8**	**0**	**0**	**0**	**24:04**
2015-16	**Montreal**	**NHL**	**82**	**5**	**39**	**44**	**38**	**4**	**0**	**0**	**117**	**4.3**	**–6**	**0**	**0.0**	**23:50**	....	....	....	....	....	....	....	....	....
2016-17	**Montreal**	**NHL**	**62**	**6**	**30**	**36**	**16**	**1**	**0**	**1**	**98**	**6.1**	**18**	**0**	**0.0**	**21:50**	**6**	**0**	**1**	**1**	**10**	**0**	**0**	**0**	**26:09**
	NHL Totals		**990**	**119**	**453**	**572**	**505**	**60**	**3**	**20**	**1627**	**7.3**		**7**	**28.6**	**23:00**	**89**	**5**	**27**	**32**	**56**	**0**	**0**	**2**	**23:30**

Played in NHL All-Star Game (2008, 2009)

Signed as a free agent by **Dynamo Moscow** (Russia), June 19, 2004. • Missed majority of 2010-11 and 2011-12 due to knee injury vs. Carolina, November 13, 2010. Signed as a free agent by **Chekhov** (KHL), October 3, 2012.

MARLEAU, Patrick

(mahr-LOH, PAT-rihk) **TOR**

Center. Shoots left. 6'2", 215 lbs. Born, Swift Current, SK, September 15, 1979. San Jose's 1st pick, 2nd overall, in 1997 NHL Draft.

			Regular Season														Playoffs								
Season	Club	League	GP	G	A	Pts	PIM	PP	SH	GW	S	S%	+/-	TF	F%	Min	GP	G	A	Pts	PIM	PP	SH	GW	Min
1993-94	Swift Current	SMHL	53	72	95	167	....	....	....	....	....	....	....	....	....	....	....	....	....	....	....	....	....	....	....
1994-95	Swift Current	SMHL	31	30	22	52	18	....	....	....	....	....	....	....	....	....	....	....	....	....	....	....	....	....	....
1995-96	Seattle	WHL	72	32	42	74	22	....	....	....	....	....	....	....	....	....	5	3	4	7	4	....	....	....	....
1996-97	Seattle	WHL	71	51	74	125	37	....	....	....	....	....	....	....	....	....	15	7	16	23	12	....	....	....	....
1997-98	**San Jose**	**NHL**	**74**	**13**	**19**	**32**	**14**	**1**	**0**	**2**	**90**	**14.4**	**5**	....	....	....	**5**	**0**	**1**	**1**	**0**	**0**	**0**	**0**	....
1998-99	**San Jose**	**NHL**	**81**	**21**	**24**	**45**	**24**	**4**	**0**	**4**	**134**	**15.7**	**10**	**1121**	**43.4**	**15:11**	**6**	**2**	**1**	**3**	**4**	**2**	**0**	**0**	**11:08**
99-2000	**San Jose**	**NHL**	**81**	**17**	**23**	**40**	**36**	**3**	**0**	**3**	**161**	**10.6**	**–9**	**851**	**42.0**	**14:11**	**5**	**1**	**1**	**2**	**2**	**1**	**0**	**0**	**11:51**
2000-01	**San Jose**	**NHL**	**81**	**25**	**27**	**52**	**22**	**5**	**0**	**6**	**146**	**17.1**	**7**	**1088**	**44.8**	**16:17**	**6**	**2**	**0**	**2**	**4**	**0**	**0**	**0**	**14:50**
2001-02	**San Jose**	**NHL**	**79**	**21**	**23**	**44**	**40**	**3**	**0**	**5**	**121**	**17.4**	**9**	**897**	**47.3**	**14:04**	**12**	**6**	**5**	**11**	**6**	**1**	**0**	**3**	**15:50**
2002-03	**San Jose**	**NHL**	**82**	**28**	**29**	**57**	**33**	**8**	**1**	**3**	**172**	**16.3**	**–10**	**1403**	**47.3**	**18:31**	....	....	....	....	....	....	....	....	....
2003-04	**San Jose**	**NHL**	**80**	**28**	**29**	**57**	**24**	**9**	**0**	**5**	**220**	**12.7**	**–5**	**1014**	**41.6**	**18:12**	**17**	**8**	**4**	**12**	**6**	**4**	**1**	**2**	**19:16**
2004-05			DID NOT PLAY																						
2005-06	**San Jose**	**NHL**	**82**	**34**	**52**	**86**	**26**	**20**	**1**	**4**	**260**	**13.1**	**–12**	**1216**	**46.8**	**19:56**	**11**	**9**	**5**	**14**	**8**	**4**	**0**	**2**	**21:07**
2006-07	**San Jose**	**NHL**	**77**	**32**	**46**	**78**	**33**	**14**	**0**	**9**	**180**	**17.8**	**9**	**693**	**50.5**	**18:34**	**11**	**3**	**3**	**6**	**2**	**1**	**0**	**1**	**18:59**
2007-08	**San Jose**	**NHL**	**78**	**19**	**29**	**48**	**33**	**7**	**0**	**2**	**185**	**10.3**	**–19**	**605**	**52.4**	**18:14**	**13**	**4**	**4**	**8**	**2**	**0**	***2**	**0**	**23:04**
2008-09	**San Jose**	**NHL**	**76**	**38**	**33**	**71**	**18**	**11**	**5**	**10**	**251**	**15.1**	**16**	**591**	**52.5**	**21:21**	**6**	**2**	**1**	**3**	**8**	**1**	**0**	**2**	**20:29**
2009-10	**San Jose**	**NHL**	**82**	**44**	**39**	**83**	**22**	**12**	**4**	**6**	**274**	**16.1**	**21**	**615**	**51.4**	**21:13**	**14**	**8**	**5**	**13**	**8**	**3**	**1**	**2**	**22:07**
	Canada	Olympics	7	2	3	5	0	....	....	....	....	....	....	....	....	....	....	....	....	....	....	....	....	....	....
2010-11	**San Jose**	**NHL**	**82**	**37**	**36**	**73**	**16**	**11**	**2**	**9**	**279**	**13.3**	**–3**	**549**	**52.5**	**20:47**	**18**	**7**	**6**	**13**	**9**	**3**	**0**	**1**	**22:21**
2011-12	**San Jose**	**NHL**	**82**	**30**	**34**	**64**	**26**	**10**	**0**	**8**	**251**	**12.0**	**10**	**467**	**52.0**	**20:29**	**5**	**0**	**0**	**0**	**4**	**0**	**0**	**0**	**20:21**
2012-13	**San Jose**	**NHL**	**48**	**17**	**14**	**31**	**24**	**6**	**1**	**3**	**150**	**11.3**	**–2**	**150**	**47.3**	**19:07**	**11**	**5**	**3**	**8**	**2**	**1**	**0**	**1**	**21:18**
2013-14	**San Jose**	**NHL**	**82**	**33**	**37**	**70**	**18**	**11**	**2**	**4**	**285**	**11.6**	**0**	**308**	**52.9**	**20:31**	**7**	**3**	**4**	**7**	**2**	**0**	**0**	**1**	**20:07**
	Canada	Olympics	6	0	4	4	2	....	....	....	....	....	....	....	....	....	....	....	....	....	....	....	....	....	....
2014-15	**San Jose**	**NHL**	**82**	**19**	**38**	**57**	**12**	**7**	**0**	**4**	**233**	**8.2**	**–17**	**356**	**48.0**	**19:35**	....	....	....	....	....	....	....	....	....
2015-16	**San Jose**	**NHL**	**82**	**25**	**23**	**48**	**10**	**11**	**1**	**5**	**216**	**11.6**	**–22**	**525**	**50.9**	**19:02**	**24**	**5**	**8**	**13**	**8**	**1**	**0**	**1**	**16:47**
2016-17	**San Jose**	**NHL**	**82**	**27**	**19**	**46**	**28**	**7**	**0**	**6**	**190**	**14.2**	**4**	**215**	**53.5**	**17:09**	**6**	**3**	**1**	**4**	**0**	**1**	**0**	**0**	**19:08**
	NHL Totals		**1493**	**508**	**574**	**1082**	**459**	**160**	**17**	**98**	**3798**	**13.4**		**12664**	**47.5**	**18:27**	**177**	**68**	**52**	**120**	**75**	**23**	**4**	**16**	**19:12**

WHL West First All-Star Team (1997)

Played in NHL All-Star Game (2004, 2007, 2009)

Signed as a free agent by **Toronto**, July 2, 2017.

MARNER, Mitch

(MAHR-nuhr, MIHTCH) **TOR**

Center. Shoots right. 5'11", 160 lbs. Born, Markham, ON, May 5, 1997. Toronto's 1st pick, 4th overall, in 2015 NHL Draft.

			Regular Season														Playoffs								
Season	Club	League	GP	G	A	Pts	PIM	PP	SH	GW	S	S%	+/-	TF	F%	Min	GP	G	A	Pts	PIM	PP	SH	GW	Min
2012-13	Don Mills Flyers	GTHL	55	41	45	86	34	....	....	....	....	....	....	....	....	....	....	....	....	....	....	....	....	....	....
	St. Michael's	ON-Jr.A	6	1	3	4	0	....	....	....	....	....	....	....	....	....	14	3	1	4	0	....	....	....	....
2013-14	London Knights	OHL	64	13	46	59	24	....	....	....	....	....	....	....	....	....	9	3	6	9	4	....	....	....	....
2014-15	London Knights	OHL	63	44	82	126	53	....	....	....	....	....	....	....	....	....	7	9	7	16	8	....	....	....	....
2015-16	London Knights	OHL	57	39	77	116	68	....	....	....	....	....	....	....	....	....	18	16	*28	*44	8	....	....	....	....
2016-17	**Toronto**	**NHL**	**77**	**19**	**42**	**61**	**38**	**4**	**0**	**5**	**176**	**10.8**	**0**	**37**	**37.8**	**16:49**	**6**	**1**	**3**	**4**	**0**	**0**	**0**	**0**	**17:48**
	NHL Totals		**77**	**19**	**42**	**61**	**38**	**4**	**0**	**5**	**176**	**10.8**		**37**	**37.8**	**16:49**	**6**	**1**	**3**	**4**	**0**	**0**	**0**	**0**	**17:48**

OHL First All-Star Team (2015, 2016) • OHL Playoff MVP (2016) • NHL All-Rookie Team (2017)

MAROON, Patrick (ma-ROON, PAT-rihk) EDM

Left wing. Shoots left. 6'3", 227 lbs. Born, St Louis, MO, April 23, 1988. Philadelphia's 6th pick, 161st overall, in 2007 NHL Draft.

Season	Club	League	GP	G	A	Pts	PIM	PP	SH	GW	S	S%	+/-	TF	F%	Min	Playoffs GP	G	A	Pts	PIM	PP	SH	GW	Min
2005-06	Texarkana Bandits	NAHL	57	23	37	60	61	....	....	....	....	....	....	....	....	....	8	3	1	4	22	....	....	....	....
2006-07	St. Louis Bandits	NAHL	57	40	55	*95	152	....	....	....	....	....	....	....	....	....	12	*10	*13	*23	12	....	....	....	....
2007-08	London Knights	OHL	64	35	55	90	57	....	....	....	....	....	....	....	....	....	5	0	1	1	10	....	....	....	....
	Philadelphia	AHL	1	0	0	0	0	....	....	....	....	....	....	....	....	....	....	....	....	....	....	....	....	....	....
2008-09	Philadelphia	AHL	80	23	31	54	62	....	....	....	....	....	....	....	....	....	4	1	2	3	13	....	....	....	....
2009-10	Adirondack	AHL	67	11	33	44	125	....	....	....	....	....	....	....	....	....	....	....	....	....	....	....	....	....	....
2010-11	Adirondack	AHL	9	5	3	8	30	....	....	....	....	....	....	....	....	....	....	....	....	....	....	....	....	....	....
	Syracuse Crunch	AHL	57	21	27	48	68	....	....	....	....	....	....	....	....	....	....	....	....	....	....	....	....	....	....
2011-12	**Anaheim**	**NHL**	**2**	**0**	**0**	**0**	**2**	**0**	**0**	**0**	**1**	**0.0**	**0**	**0**	**0.0**	**12:33**	....	....	....	....	....	....	....	....	....
	Syracuse Crunch	AHL	75	32	42	74	120	....	....	....	....	....	....	....	....	....	4	0	0	0	4	....	....	....	....
2012-13	Norfolk Admirals	AHL	64	26	24	50	139	....	....	....	....	....	....	....	....	....	....	....	....	....	....	....	....	....	....
	Anaheim	**NHL**	**13**	**2**	**1**	**3**	**10**	**0**	**0**	**0**	**21**	**9.5**	**–1**	**14**	**28.6**	**9:47**	....	....	....	....	....	....	....	....	....
2013-14	**Anaheim**	**NHL**	**62**	**11**	**18**	**29**	**101**	**1**	**0**	**3**	**93**	**11.8**	**11**	**15**	**46.7**	**12:19**	**13**	**2**	**5**	**7**	**38**	**1**	**0**	**0**	**13:04**
2014-15	**Anaheim**	**NHL**	**71**	**9**	**25**	**34**	**82**	**1**	**0**	**1**	**120**	**7.5**	**–5**	**21**	**33.3**	**14:17**	**16**	**7**	**4**	**11**	**6**	**3**	**0**	**1**	**17:56**
2015-16	**Anaheim**	**NHL**	**56**	**4**	**9**	**13**	**54**	**3**	**0**	**0**	**65**	**6.2**	**–13**	**49**	**32.7**	**11:23**	....	....	....	....	....	....	....	....	....
	Edmonton	**NHL**	**16**	**8**	**6**	**14**	**34**	**2**	**0**	**1**	**39**	**20.5**	**6**	**4**	**25.0**	**15:41**	....	....	....	....	....	....	....	....	....
2016-17	**Edmonton**	**NHL**	**81**	**27**	**15**	**42**	**95**	**3**	**0**	**5**	**178**	**15.2**	**13**	**15**	**40.0**	**16:44**	**13**	**3**	**5**	**8**	**28**	**1**	**0**	**1**	**17:21**
	NHL Totals		**301**	**61**	**74**	**135**	**378**	**10**	**0**	**10**	**517**	**11.8**		**118**	**34.7**	**13:52**	**42**	**12**	**14**	**26**	**72**	**5**	**0**	**2**	**16:15**

Traded to **Anaheim** by **Philadelphia** with David Laliberte for Danny Syvret and Rob Bordson, November 21, 2010. Traded to **Edmonton** by **Anaheim** for Martin Gernat and Edmonton's 4th round pick (Jack Kopacka) in 2016 NHL Draft, February 29, 2016.

MARTIN, Matt (MAHR-tihn, MAT) TOR

Left wing. Shoots left. 6'3", 220 lbs. Born, Windsor, ON, May 8, 1989. NY Islanders' 11th pick, 148th overall, in 2008 NHL Draft.

Season	Club	League	GP	G	A	Pts	PIM	PP	SH	GW	S	S%	+/-	TF	F%	Min	Playoffs GP	G	A	Pts	PIM	PP	SH	GW	Min
2005-06	Blenheim Blast	ON-Jr.C	40	11	12	23	102	....	....	....	....	....	....	....	....	....	....	....	....	....	....	....	....	....	....
2006-07	Sarnia Blast	ON-Jr.B	9	2	5	7	16	....	....	....	....	....	....	....	....	....	....	....	....	....	....	....	....	....	....
	Sarnia Sting	OHL	39	3	3	6	52	....	....	....	....	....	....	....	....	....	4	0	0	0	0	....	....	....	....
2007-08	Sarnia Sting	OHL	66	25	13	38	155	....	....	....	....	....	....	....	....	....	9	3	3	6	16	....	....	....	....
2008-09	Sarnia Sting	OHL	61	35	30	65	142	....	....	....	....	....	....	....	....	....	5	3	0	3	10	....	....	....	....
2009-10	**NY Islanders**	**NHL**	**5**	**0**	**2**	**2**	**26**	**0**	**0**	**0**	**10**	**0.0**	**–1**	**0**	**0.0**	**13:14**	....	....	....	....	....	....	....	....	....
	Bridgeport	AHL	76	12	19	31	113	....	....	....	....	....	....	....	....	....	5	1	2	3	4	....	....	....	....
2010-11	**NY Islanders**	**NHL**	**68**	**5**	**9**	**14**	**147**	**0**	**0**	**1**	**60**	**8.3**	**–13**	**27**	**37.0**	**10:57**	....	....	....	....	....	....	....	....	....
	Bridgeport	AHL	7	1	2	3	11	....	....	....	....	....	....	....	....	....	....	....	....	....	....	....	....	....	....
2011-12	**NY Islanders**	**NHL**	**80**	**7**	**7**	**14**	**121**	**0**	**0**	**1**	**130**	**5.4**	**–17**	**23**	**43.5**	**12:09**	....	....	....	....	....	....	....	....	....
2012-13	**NY Islanders**	**NHL**	**48**	**4**	**7**	**11**	**63**	**1**	**0**	**1**	**67**	**6.0**	**–2**	**18**	**33.3**	**11:54**	**6**	**1**	**0**	**1**	**14**	**0**	**0**	**0**	**12:10**
2013-14	**NY Islanders**	**NHL**	**79**	**8**	**6**	**14**	**90**	**0**	**0**	**3**	**120**	**6.7**	**–11**	**9**	**33.3**	**11:54**	....	....	....	....	....	....	....	....	....
2014-15	**NY Islanders**	**NHL**	**78**	**8**	**6**	**14**	**114**	**0**	**0**	**2**	**90**	**8.9**	**–4**	**10**	**50.0**	**11:16**	**7**	**0**	**1**	**1**	**12**	**0**	**0**	**0**	**11:55**
2015-16	**NY Islanders**	**NHL**	**80**	**10**	**9**	**19**	**119**	**0**	**0**	**1**	**86**	**11.6**	**2**	**4**	**25.0**	**10:33**	**11**	**0**	**0**	**0**	**12**	**0**	**0**	**0**	**12:29**
2016-17	**Toronto**	**NHL**	**82**	**5**	**4**	**9**	**123**	**0**	**0**	**0**	**66**	**7.6**	**0**	**11**	**0.0**	**8:54**	**6**	**0**	**2**	**2**	**6**	**0**	**0**	**0**	**9:57**
	NHL Totals		**520**	**47**	**50**	**97**	**803**	**1**	**0**	**9**	**629**	**7.5**		**102**	**34.3**	**11:03**	**30**	**1**	**3**	**4**	**44**	**0**	**0**	**0**	**11:47**

Signed as a free agent by **Toronto**, July 1, 2016.

MARTIN, Paul (MAHR-tihn, PAWL) S.J.

Defense. Shoots left. 6'1", 200 lbs. Born, Minneapolis, MN, March 5, 1981. New Jersey's 5th pick, 62nd overall, in 2000 NHL Draft.

Season	Club	League	GP	G	A	Pts	PIM	PP	SH	GW	S	S%	+/-	TF	F%	Min	Playoffs GP	G	A	Pts	PIM	PP	SH	GW	Min
1998-99	Elk River Elks	High-MN	24	9	11	20	....	....	....	....	....	....	....	....	....	....	....	....	....	....	....	....	....	....	....
99-2000	Elk River Elks	High-MN	24	15	35	50	26	....	....	....	....	....	....	....	....	....	....	....	....	....	....	....	....	....	....
2000-01	U. of Minnesota	WCHA	38	3	17	20	8	....	....	....	....	....	....	....	....	....	....	....	....	....	....	....	....	....	....
2001-02	U. of Minnesota	WCHA	44	8	30	38	22	....	....	....	....	....	....	....	....	....	....	....	....	....	....	....	....	....	....
2002-03	U. of Minnesota	WCHA	45	9	30	39	32	....	....	....	....	....	....	....	....	....	....	....	....	....	....	....	....	....	....
2003-04	**New Jersey**	**NHL**	**70**	**6**	**18**	**24**	**4**	**2**	**0**	**2**	**82**	**7.3**	**12**	**0**	**0.0**	**20:08**	**5**	**1**	**1**	**2**	**4**	**1**	**0**	**0**	**23:40**
2004-05	Fribourg	Swiss	11	3	4	7	2	....	....	....	....	....	....	....	....	....	....	....	....	....	....	....	....	....	....
2005-06	**New Jersey**	**NHL**	**80**	**5**	**32**	**37**	**32**	**3**	**0**	**0**	**97**	**5.2**	**1**	**0**	**0.0**	**23:37**	**9**	**0**	**3**	**3**	**4**	**0**	**0**	**0**	**24:17**
2006-07	**New Jersey**	**NHL**	**82**	**3**	**23**	**26**	**18**	**1**	**0**	**0**	**84**	**3.6**	**–9**	**0**	**0.0**	**25:13**	**11**	**0**	**4**	**4**	**6**	**0**	**0**	**0**	**25:09**
2007-08	**New Jersey**	**NHL**	**73**	**5**	**27**	**32**	**22**	**2**	**0**	**2**	**93**	**5.4**	**20**	**0**	**0.0**	**23:53**	**5**	**1**	**2**	**3**	**2**	**1**	**0**	**0**	**25:35**
2008-09	**New Jersey**	**NHL**	**73**	**5**	**28**	**33**	**36**	**2**	**0**	**1**	**107**	**4.7**	**21**	**0**	**0.0**	**24:22**	**7**	**0**	**4**	**4**	**2**	**0**	**0**	**0**	**26:20**
2009-10	**New Jersey**	**NHL**	**22**	**2**	**9**	**11**	**2**	**1**	**0**	**0**	**21**	**9.5**	**10**	**0**	**0.0**	**22:30**	**5**	**0**	**0**	**0**	**0**	**0**	**0**	**0**	**22:24**
2010-11	**Pittsburgh**	**NHL**	**77**	**3**	**21**	**24**	**16**	**2**	**0**	**1**	**104**	**2.9**	**9**	**0**	**0.0**	**23:22**	**7**	**0**	**2**	**2**	**2**	**0**	**0**	**0**	**24:42**
2011-12	**Pittsburgh**	**NHL**	**73**	**2**	**25**	**27**	**18**	**0**	**0**	**0**	**93**	**2.2**	**9**	**0**	**0.0**	**23:00**	**3**	**1**	**0**	**1**	**0**	**0**	**0**	**0**	**22:08**
2012-13	**Pittsburgh**	**NHL**	**34**	**6**	**17**	**23**	**16**	**2**	**0**	**1**	**38**	**15.8**	**14**	**0**	**0.0**	**25:20**	**15**	**2**	**9**	**11**	**4**	**1**	**0**	**0**	**26:38**
2013-14	**Pittsburgh**	**NHL**	**39**	**3**	**12**	**15**	**10**	**1**	**0**	**2**	**54**	**5.6**	**–4**	**0**	**0.0**	**24:34**	**13**	**0**	**8**	**8**	**6**	**0**	**0**	**0**	**27:20**
	United States	Olympics	4	0	0	0	0	....	....	....	....	....	....	....	....	....	....	....	....	....	....	....	....	....	....
2014-15	**Pittsburgh**	**NHL**	**74**	**3**	**17**	**20**	**20**	**0**	**0**	**0**	**61**	**4.9**	**17**	**0**	**0.0**	**22:47**	**5**	**0**	**2**	**2**	**2**	**0**	**0**	**0**	**24:36**
2015-16	**San Jose**	**NHL**	**78**	**3**	**17**	**20**	**22**	**1**	**0**	**0**	**49**	**6.1**	**13**	**0**	**0.0**	**20:44**	**24**	**0**	**5**	**5**	**6**	**0**	**0**	**0**	**22:04**
2016-17	**San Jose**	**NHL**	**81**	**4**	**22**	**26**	**20**	**0**	**0**	**1**	**57**	**7.0**	**10**	**0**	**0.0**	**19:14**	**6**	**1**	**0**	**1**	**4**	**0**	**0**	**0**	**19:24**
	NHL Totals		**856**	**50**	**268**	**318**	**236**	**17**	**0**	**10**	**940**	**5.3**		**0**	**0.0**	**22:50**	**115**	**6**	**40**	**46**	**42**	**3**	**0**	**0**	**24:21**

Minnesota High School Player of the Year (1999) • WCHA All-Rookie Team (2001) • WCHA Second All-Star Team (2002, 2003) • NCAA West Second All-American Team (2003) • NCAA Championship All-Tournament Team (2003)

Signed as a free agent by **Fribourg** (Swiss), November 4, 2004. • Missed majority of 2009-10 due to arm injury at Pittsburgh, October 24, 2009. Signed as a free agent by **Pittsburgh**, July 1, 2010. • Missed majority of 2013-14 due to leg (November 25, 2013 vs. Ottawa) and hand (February 19, 2014 vs. Czech Republic) injuries. Signed as a free agent by **San Jose**, July 1, 2015.

MARTINEZ, Alec (mar-TEE-nehz, AL-ehk) L.A.

Defense. Shoots left. 6'1", 210 lbs. Born, Rochester Hills, MI, July 26, 1987. Los Angeles' 5th pick, 95th overall, in 2007 NHL Draft.

Season	Club	League	GP	G	A	Pts	PIM	PP	SH	GW	S	S%	+/-	TF	F%	Min	Playoffs GP	G	A	Pts	PIM	PP	SH	GW	Min
2004-05	Cedar Rapids	USHL	58	10	11	21	30	....	....	....	....	....	....	....	....	....	11	1	2	3	8	....	....	....	....
2005-06	Miami U.	CCHA	39	3	8	11	31	....	....	....	....	....	....	....	....	....	....	....	....	....	....	....	....	....	....
2006-07	Miami U.	CCHA	42	9	15	24	40	....	....	....	....	....	....	....	....	....	....	....	....	....	....	....	....	....	....
2007-08	Miami U.	CCHA	42	9	23	32	42	....	....	....	....	....	....	....	....	....	....	....	....	....	....	....	....	....	....
2008-09	Manchester	AHL	72	8	15	23	42	....	....	....	....	....	....	....	....	....	....	....	....	....	....	....	....	....	....
2009-10	**Los Angeles**	**NHL**	**4**	**0**	**0**	**0**	**2**	**0**	**0**	**0**	**6**	**0.0**	**–2**	**0**	**0.0**	**15:25**	....	....	....	....	....	....	....	....	....
	Manchester	AHL	55	7	23	30	26	....	....	....	....	....	....	....	....	....	16	0	3	3	10	....	....	....	....
2010-11	**Los Angeles**	**NHL**	**60**	**5**	**11**	**16**	**18**	**1**	**0**	**0**	**74**	**6.8**	**11**	**0**	**0.0**	**15:17**	**6**	**0**	**1**	**1**	**2**	**0**	**0**	**0**	**13:29**
	Manchester	AHL	20	5	11	16	14	....	....	....	....	....	....	....	....	....	....	....	....	....	....	....	....	....	....
2011-12♦	**Los Angeles**	**NHL**	**51**	**6**	**6**	**12**	**8**	**3**	**0**	**0**	**78**	**7.7**	**–1**	**1**	**0.0**	**14:43**	**20**	**1**	**2**	**3**	**8**	**0**	**0**	**1**	**14:28**
2012-13	TPS Turku	Finland	11	1	1	2	8	....	....	....	....	....	....	....	....	....	....	....	....	....	....	....	....	....	....
	Allen Americans	CHL	3	1	1	2	0	....	....	....	....	....	....	....	....	....	....	....	....	....	....	....	....	....	....
	Los Angeles	**NHL**	**27**	**1**	**4**	**5**	**10**	**0**	**0**	**0**	**30**	**3.3**	**–2**	**0**	**0.0**	**16:01**	**7**	**0**	**2**	**2**	**8**	**0**	**0**	**0**	**13:14**
2013-14♦	**Los Angeles**	**NHL**	**61**	**11**	**11**	**22**	**14**	**3**	**0**	**2**	**79**	**13.9**	**17**	**0**	**0.0**	**15:41**	**26**	**5**	**5**	**10**	**12**	**2**	**0**	**3**	**16:37**
2014-15	**Los Angeles**	**NHL**	**56**	**6**	**16**	**22**	**10**	**1**	**0**	**1**	**103**	**5.8**	**9**	**0**	**0.0**	**19:56**	....	....	....	....	....	....	....	....	....
2015-16	**Los Angeles**	**NHL**	**78**	**10**	**21**	**31**	**40**	**4**	**0**	**4**	**124**	**8.1**	**16**	**0**	**0.0**	**21:09**	**1**	**0**	**0**	**0**	**0**	**0**	**0**	**0**	**11:43**
2016-17	**Los Angeles**	**NHL**	**82**	**9**	**30**	**39**	**24**	**2**	**1**	**3**	**144**	**6.3**	**–17**	**1**	**0.0**	**21:38**	....	....	....	....	....	....	....	....	....
	NHL Totals		**419**	**48**	**99**	**147**	**126**	**14**	**1**	**10**	**638**	**7.5**		**2**	**0.0**	**18:17**	**60**	**6**	**10**	**16**	**30**	**2**	**0**	**4**	**15:07**

CCHA First All-Star Team (2008) • NCAA West Second All-American Team (2008)

Signed as a free agent by **TPS Turku** (Finland), October 5, 2012. Signed as a free agent by **Allen** (CHL), December 31, 2012.

MARTINOOK, Jordan (mahr-TIHN-ook, JOHR-dahn) ARI

Left wing. Shoots left. 6', 202 lbs. Born, Brandon, MB, July 25, 1992. Phoenix's 2nd pick, 58th overall, in 2012 NHL Draft.

Season	Club	League	GP	G	A	Pts	PIM	PP	SH	GW	S	S%	+/-	TF	F%	Min	Playoffs GP	G	A	Pts	PIM	PP	SH	GW	Min
2006-07	Leduc Oil Kings	AMBHL	30	19	14	33	32	....	....	....	....	....	....	....	....	....	....	....	....	....	....	....	....	....	....
2007-08	Leduc Oil Kings	Minor-AB	STATISTICS NOT AVAILABLE					....	....	....	....	....	....	....	....	....	....	....	....	....	....	....	....	....	....
	Leduc Oil Kings	AMHL	3	1	0	1	0	....	....	....	....	....	....	....	....	....	....	....	....	....	....	....	....	....	....
2008-09	Leduc Oil Kings	AMHL	33	7	13	20	38	....	....	....	....	....	....	....	....	....	....	....	....	....	....	....	....	....	....
2009-10	Drayton Valley	AJHL	59	21	19	40	48	....	....	....	....	....	....	....	....	....	....	....	....	....	....	....	....	....	....
2010-11	Vancouver Giants	WHL	72	11	17	28	67	....	....	....	....	....	....	....	....	....	4	1	0	1	8	....	....	....	....
2011-12	Vancouver Giants	WHL	72	40	24	64	80	....	....	....	....	....	....	....	....	....	6	3	6	9	2	....	....	....	....

			Regular Season														Playoffs								
Season	Club	League	GP	G	A	Pts	PIM	PP	SH	GW	S	S%	+/-	TF	F%	Min	GP	G	A	Pts	PIM	PP	SH	GW	Min
2012-13	Portland Pirates	AHL	53	9	10	19	30	....	....	....	....	....	....	....	....	....	3	0	1	1	0	....	....	....	....
2013-14	Portland Pirates	AHL	67	14	16	30	48	....	....	....	....	....	....	....	....	....	....	....	....	....	....	....	....	....	....
2014-15	**Arizona**	**NHL**	**8**	**0**	**1**	**1**	**0**	0	0	0	8	0.0	-3	1	100.0	11:42	....	....	....	....	....	....	....	....	....
	Portland Pirates	AHL	62	15	28	43	41	....	....	....	....	....	....	....	....	....	....	....	....	....	....	....	....	....	....
2015-16	**Arizona**	**NHL**	**81**	**9**	**15**	**24**	**18**	0	1	2	109	8.3	-9	33	54.6	15:11	....	....	....	....	....	....	....	....	....
2016-17	**Arizona**	**NHL**	**77**	**11**	**14**	**25**	**40**	1	1	2	109	10.1	-8	1037	44.4	15:41	....	....	....	....	....	....	....	....	....
	NHL Totals		**166**	**20**	**30**	**50**	**58**	**1**	**2**	**4**	**226**	**8.8**		**1071**	**44.7**	**15:15**	....	....	....	....	....	....	....	....	....

MARTINSEN, Andreas

(MAHR-tihn-sehn, an-DRAY-uhs) **MTL**

Left wing. Shoots left. 6'3", 220 lbs. Born, Baerum, Norway, June 13, 1990.

2009-10	Leksands IF	Sweden-2	22	3	2	5	8	....	....	....	....	....	....	....	....	....	....	....	....	....	....	....	....	....	....
	Leksands IF Jr.	Swe-Jr.	8	2	3	5	37	....	....	....	....	....	....	....	....	....	....	....	....	....	....	....	....	....	....
2012-13	Dusseldorf	Germany	52	6	16	22	72	....	....	....	....	....	....	....	....	....	....	....	....	....	....	....	....	....	....
2013-14	Dusseldorfer EG	Germany	42	9	8	17	124	....	....	....	....	....	....	....	....	....	....	....	....	....	....	....	....	....	....
2014-15	Dusseldorfer EG	Germany	50	18	23	41	99	....	....	....	....	....	....	....	....	....	12	1	4	5	8	....	....	....	....
2015-16	**Colorado**	**NHL**	**55**	**4**	**7**	**11**	**47**	0	0	1	52	7.7	-4	4	25.0	11:06	....	....	....	....	....	....	....	....	....
	San Antonio	AHL	10	1	1	2	8	....	....	....	....	....	....	....	....	....	....	....	....	....	....	....	....	....	....
2016-17	**Colorado**	**NHL**	**55**	**3**	**4**	**7**	**32**	0	0	0	59	5.1	-10	3	100.0	9:38	....	....	....	....	....	....	....	....	....
	Montreal	**NHL**	**9**	**0**	**0**	**0**	**0**	0	0	0	14	0.0	-4	1	0.0	11:54	2	0	0	0	0	0	0	0	10:13
	NHL Totals		**119**	**7**	**11**	**18**	**79**	**0**	**0**	**1**	**125**	**5.6**		**8**	**50.0**	**10:29**	**2**	**0**	**0**	**0**	**0**	**0**	**0**	**0**	**10:13**

Signed as a free agent by **Colorado**, May 15, 2015. Traded to **Montreal** by **Colorado** for Sven Andrighetto, March 1, 2017.

MASHINTER, Brandon

(ma-SHIHN-tuhr, BRAN-duhn)

Left wing. Shoots left. 6'4", 212 lbs. Born, Bradford, ON, September 20, 1988.

2004-05	Tor. T-Birds	ON-Jr.A	49	3	6	9	19	....	....	....	....	....	....	....	....	....	....	....	....	....	....	....	....	....	....
	Sarnia Sting	OHL	8	0	0	0	9	....	....	....	....	....	....	....	....	....	....	....	....	....	....	....	....	....	....
2005-06	Sarnia Sting	OHL	65	6	1	7	65	....	....	....	....	....	....	....	....	....	....	....	....	....	....	....	....	....	....
2006-07	Sarnia Sting	OHL	55	7	8	15	49	....	....	....	....	....	....	....	....	....	4	0	2	2	0	....	....	....	....
2007-08	Kitchener Rangers	OHL	62	10	10	20	84	....	....	....	....	....	....	....	....	....	20	2	2	4	16	....	....	....	....
2008-09	Kitchener Rangers	OHL	21	14	12	26	24	....	....	....	....	....	....	....	....	....	....	....	....	....	....	....	....	....	....
	Belleville Bulls	OHL	31	20	12	32	32	....	....	....	....	....	....	....	....	....	17	8	3	11	13	....	....	....	....
2009-10	Worcester Sharks	AHL	79	22	15	37	117	....	....	....	....	....	....	....	....	....	11	1	5	6	6	....	....	....	....
2010-11	**San Jose**	**NHL**	**13**	**0**	**0**	**0**	**17**	0	0	0	5	0.0	-2	0	0.0	6:23	....	....	....	....	....	....	....	....	....
	Worcester Sharks	AHL	62	14	19	33	96	....	....	....	....	....	....	....	....	....	....	....	....	....	....	....	....	....	....
2011-12	Worcester Sharks	AHL	65	16	17	33	67	....	....	....	....	....	....	....	....	....	....	....	....	....	....	....	....	....	....
2012-13	Worcester Sharks	AHL	30	2	3	5	44	....	....	....	....	....	....	....	....	....	....	....	....	....	....	....	....	....	....
	NY Rangers	**NHL**	**4**	**0**	**0**	**0**	**0**	0	0	0	2	0.0	-2	1	100.0	5:55	....	....	....	....	....	....	....	....	....
	Connecticut	AHL	35	10	9	19	52	....	....	....	....	....	....	....	....	....	....	....	....	....	....	....	....	....	....
2013-14	**NY Rangers**	**NHL**	**6**	**0**	**0**	**0**	**10**	0	0	0	3	0.0	-1	0	0.0	4:34	....	....	....	....	....	....	....	....	....
	Hartford	AHL	11	1	6	7	15	....	....	....	....	....	....	....	....	....	....	....	....	....	....	....	....	....	....
	Rockford IceHogs	AHL	47	14	14	28	79	....	....	....	....	....	....	....	....	....	....	....	....	....	....	....	....	....	....
2014-15	Rockford IceHogs	AHL	69	17	15	32	57	....	....	....	....	....	....	....	....	....	8	3	3	6	4	....	....	....	....
2015-16	**Chicago**	**NHL**	**41**	**4**	**1**	**5**	**23**	0	0	0	25	16.0	-7	0	0.0	7:30	2	0	0	0	2	0	0	0	8:33
	Rockford IceHogs	AHL	12	4	3	7	11	....	....	....	....	....	....	....	....	....	....	....	....	....	....	....	....	....	....
2016-17	Rockford IceHogs	AHL	61	15	15	30	70	....	....	....	....	....	....	....	....	....	....	....	....	....	....	....	....	....	....
	NHL Totals		**64**	**4**	**1**	**5**	**50**	**0**	**0**	**0**	**35**	**11.4**		**1**	**100.0**	**6:54**	**2**	**0**	**0**	**0**	**2**	**0**	**0**	**0**	**8:33**

Signed as a free agent by **San Jose**, March 3, 2009. Traded to **NY Rangers** by **San Jose** for Tommy Grant and NY Rangers' 6th round pick (later traded to Chicago – Chicago selected Ivan Nalimov) in 2014 NHL Draft, January 16, 2013. Traded to **Chicago** by **NY Rangers** for Kyle Beach, December 6, 2013.

MATHESON, Mike

(MA-thuh-suhn, MIGHK) **FLA**

Defense. Shoots left. 6'2", 192 lbs. Born, Pointe-Claire, QC, February 27, 1994. Florida's 1st pick, 23rd overall, in 2012 NHL Draft.

2009-10	Lac St-Louis Lions	QAAA	30	5	6	11	33	....	....	....	....	....	....	....	....	....	17	6	7	13	10	....	....	....	....
2010-11	Lac St-Louis Lions	QAAA	35	14	24	38	72	....	....	....	....	....	....	....	....	....	15	7	18	25	16	....	....	....	....
2011-12	Dubuque	USHL	53	11	16	27	84	....	....	....	....	....	....	....	....	....	5	4	1	5	4	....	....	....	....
2012-13	Boston College	H-East	36	8	17	25	78	....	....	....	....	....	....	....	....	....	....	....	....	....	....	....	....	....	....
2013-14	Boston College	H-East	38	3	18	21	49	....	....	....	....	....	....	....	....	....	....	....	....	....	....	....	....	....	....
2014-15	Boston College	H-East	38	3	22	25	26	....	....	....	....	....	....	....	....	....	....	....	....	....	....	....	....	....	....
	San Antonio	AHL	5	0	2	2	8	....	....	....	....	....	....	....	....	....	....	....	....	....	....	....	....	....	....
2015-16	**Florida**	**NHL**	**3**	**0**	**0**	**0**	**2**	0	0	0	4	0.0	1	0	0.0	17:32	5	0	1	1	0	0	0	0	21:41
	Portland Pirates	AHL	54	8	12	20	30	....	....	....	....	....	....	....	....	....	3	0	1	1	2	....	....	....	....
2016-17	**Florida**	**NHL**	**81**	**7**	**10**	**17**	**36**	0	0	0	179	3.9	-5	1	100.0	21:03	....	....	....	....	....	....	....	....	....
	NHL Totals		**84**	**7**	**10**	**17**	**38**	**0**	**0**	**0**	**183**	**3.8**		**1**	**100.0**	**20:56**	**5**	**0**	**1**	**1**	**0**	**0**	**0**	**0**	**21:41**

Hockey East All-Rookie Team (2013) • Hockey East First All-Star Team (2014) • NCAA East Second All-American Team (2014)

MATTEAU, Stefan

(mah-TOH, steh-FAN) **VGK**

Left wing. Shoots left. 6'2", 220 lbs. Born, Chicago, IL, February 23, 1994. New Jersey's 1st pick, 29th overall, in 2012 NHL Draft.

2009-10	Notre Dame	SMHL	40	15	22	37	67	....	....	....	....	....	....	....	....	....	13	4	8	12	6	....	....	....	....
2010-11	USAHNTDP	USHL	28	4	5	9	47	....	....	....	....	....	....	....	....	....	2	0	0	0	2	....	....	....	....
	USAHNTDP	U-17	17	3	6	9	18	....	....	....	....	....	....	....	....	....	....	....	....	....	....	....	....	....	....
2011-12	USAHNTDP	USHL	18	6	4	10	93	....	....	....	....	....	....	....	....	....	....	....	....	....	....	....	....	....	....
	USAHNTDP	U-18	28	9	13	22	73	....	....	....	....	....	....	....	....	....	....	....	....	....	....	....	....	....	....
2012-13	Blainville-Bois.	QMJHL	35	18	10	28	70	....	....	....	....	....	....	....	....	....	11	3	6	9	16	....	....	....	....
	New Jersey	**NHL**	**17**	**1**	**2**	**3**	**6**	0	0	0	22	4.5	-1	4	0.0	9:11	....	....	....	....	....	....	....	....	....
2013-14	Albany Devils	AHL	67	13	13	26	66	....	....	....	....	....	....	....	....	....	4	1	0	1	4	....	....	....	....
2014-15	Albany Devils	AHL	61	12	15	27	40	....	....	....	....	....	....	....	....	....	....	....	....	....	....	....	....	....	....
	New Jersey	**NHL**	**7**	**1**	**0**	**1**	**4**	0	0	0	8	12.5	0	0	0.0	11:52	....	....	....	....	....	....	....	....	....
2015-16	**New Jersey**	**NHL**	**20**	**1**	**0**	**1**	**13**	0	0	0	22	4.5	-9	0	0.0	10:05	....	....	....	....	....	....	....	....	....
	Albany Devils	AHL	1	0	0	0	4	....	....	....	....	....	....	....	....	....	....	....	....	....	....	....	....	....	....
	Montreal	**NHL**	**12**	**0**	**1**	**1**	**4**	0	0	0	5	0.0	-4	0	0.0	10:38	....	....	....	....	....	....	....	....	....
2016-17	St. John's IceCaps	AHL	67	12	13	25	122	....	....	....	....	....	....	....	....	....	4	3	1	4	2	....	....	....	....
	NHL Totals		**56**	**3**	**3**	**6**	**27**	**0**	**0**	**0**	**57**	**5.3**		**4**	**0.0**	**10:09**	....	....	....	....	....	....	....	....	....

Traded to **Montreal** by **New Jersey** for Devante Smith-Pelly, February 29, 2016. • Missed majority of 2015-16 as a healthy reserve. Signed as a free agent by **Vegas**, July 1, 2017.

MATTHEWS, Auston

(MA-thewz, AW-stuhn) **TOR**

Center. Shoots left. 6'2", 216 lbs. Born, San Ramon, CA, September 17, 1997. Toronto's 1st pick, 1st overall, in 2016 NHL Draft.

2012-13	Arizona Bobcats	Minor-AZ	48	55	45	100	16	....	....	....	....	....	....	....	....	....	4	4	2	6	....	....	....	....	....
2013-14	USAHNTDP	USHL	20	10	10	20	4	....	....	....	....	....	....	....	....	....	....	....	....	....	....	....	....	....	....
	USAHNTDP	U-17	14	8	12	20	10	....	....	....	....	....	....	....	....	....	....	....	....	....	....	....	....	....	....
	USAHNTDP	U-18	10	6	3	9	4	....	....	....	....	....	....	....	....	....	....	....	....	....	....	....	....	....	....
2014-15	USAHNTDP	USHL	24	20	28	48	10	....	....	....	....	....	....	....	....	....	....	....	....	....	....	....	....	....	....
	USAHNTDP	U-18	36	35	34	69	30	....	....	....	....	....	....	....	....	....	....	....	....	....	....	....	....	....	....
2015-16	ZSC Lions Zurich	Swiss	36	24	22	46	6	....	....	....	....	....	....	....	....	....	4	0	3	3	2	....	....	....	....
2016-17	**Toronto**	**NHL**	**82**	**40**	**29**	**69**	**14**	8	0	8	279	14.3	2	1132	46.8	17:38	6	4	1	5	0	0	0	0	20:18
	NHL Totals		**82**	**40**	**29**	**69**	**14**	**8**	**0**	**8**	**279**	**14.3**		**1132**	**46.8**	**17:38**	**6**	**4**	**1**	**5**	**0**	**0**	**0**	**0**	**20:18**

NHL All-Rookie Team (2017) • Calder Memorial Trophy (2017)

Played in NHL All-Star Game (2017)

Signed as a free agent by **Zurich** (Swiss), August 7, 2015.

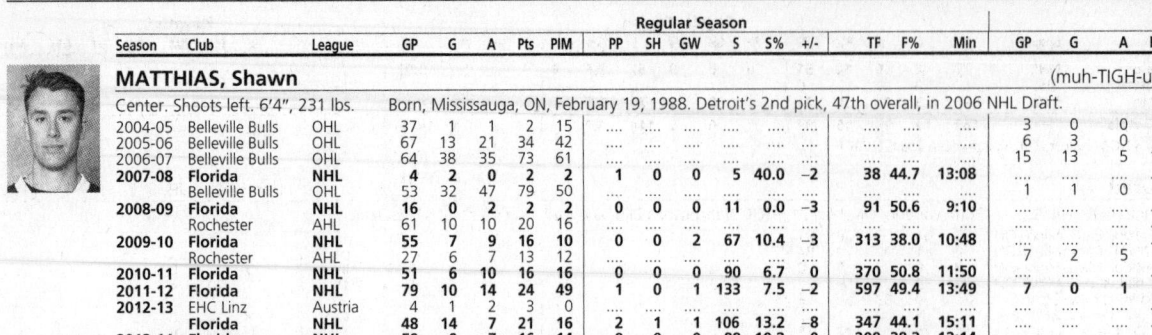

MATTHIAS, Shawn

(muh-TIGH-uhs, SHAWN) **WPG**

Center. Shoots left. 6'4", 231 lbs. Born, Mississauga, ON, February 19, 1988. Detroit's 2nd pick, 47th overall, in 2006 NHL Draft.

			Regular Season														Playoffs								
Season	Club	League	GP	G	A	Pts	PIM	PP	SH	GW	S	S%	+/-	TF	F%	Min	GP	G	A	Pts	PIM	PP	SH	GW	Min
2004-05	Belleville Bulls	OHL	37	1	1	2	15										3	0	0	0	0				
2005-06	Belleville Bulls	OHL	67	13	21	34	42										6	3	0	3	2				
2006-07	Belleville Bulls	OHL	64	38	35	73	61										15	13	5	18	10				
2007-08	**Florida**	**NHL**	**4**	**2**	**0**	**2**	**2**	**1**	**0**	**0**	**5**	**40.0**	**–2**	**38**	**44.7**	**13:08**									
	Belleville Bulls	OHL	53	32	47	79	50										1	1	0	1	0				
2008-09	**Florida**	**NHL**	**16**	**0**	**2**	**2**	**2**	**0**	**0**	**0**	**11**	**0.0**	**–3**	**91**	**50.6**	**9:10**									
	Rochester	AHL	61	10	10	20	16																		
2009-10	**Florida**	**NHL**	**55**	**7**	**9**	**16**	**10**	**0**	**0**	**2**	**67**	**10.4**	**–3**	**313**	**38.0**	**10:48**									
	Rochester	AHL	27	6	7	13	12										7	2	5	7	7				
2010-11	**Florida**	**NHL**	**51**	**6**	**10**	**16**	**16**	**0**	**0**	**0**	**90**	**6.7**	**0**	**370**	**50.8**	**11:50**									
2011-12	**Florida**	**NHL**	**79**	**10**	**14**	**24**	**49**	**1**	**0**	**1**	**133**	**7.5**	**–2**	**597**	**49.4**	**13:49**	**7**	**0**	**1**	**1**	**6**	**0**	**0**	**0**	**11:08**
2012-13	EHC Linz	Austria	4	1	2	3	0																		
	Florida	**NHL**	**48**	**14**	**7**	**21**	**16**	**2**	**1**	**1**	**106**	**13.2**	**–8**	**347**	**44.1**	**15:11**									
2013-14	**Florida**	**NHL**	**59**	**9**	**7**	**16**	**14**	**0**	**0**	**0**	**88**	**10.2**	**0**	**209**	**38.3**	**12:14**									
	Vancouver	**NHL**	**18**	**3**	**4**	**7**	**12**	**0**	**0**	**0**	**39**	**7.7**	**–3**	**224**	**46.0**	**15:35**									
2014-15	**Vancouver**	**NHL**	**78**	**18**	**9**	**27**	**16**	**1**	**0**	**0**	**132**	**13.6**	**–3**	**187**	**44.9**	**13:06**	**6**	**1**	**1**	**2**	**10**	**0**	**0**	**0**	**12:12**
2015-16	**Toronto**	**NHL**	**51**	**6**	**11**	**17**	**12**	**0**	**0**	**1**	**66**	**9.1**	**–10**	**16**	**31.3**	**13:01**									
	Colorado	**NHL**	**20**	**6**	**5**	**11**	**8**	**0**	**0**	**1**	**35**	**17.1**	**–7**	**8**	**50.0**	**14:48**									
2016-17	**Winnipeg**	**NHL**	**45**	**8**	**4**	**12**	**13**	**0**	**1**	**1**	**51**	**15.7**	**0**	**16**	**31.3**	**13:34**									
	NHL Totals		**524**	**89**	**82**	**171**	**170**	**5**	**2**	**7**	**823**	**10.8**		**2416**	**45.5**	**13:00**	**13**	**1**	**2**	**3**	**16**	**0**	**0**	**0**	**11:38**

Traded to **Florida** by **Detroit** with Detroit's 2nd round pick (later traded to Nashville - Nashville selected Nick Spaling) in 2007 NHL Draft for Todd Bertuzzi, February 27, 2007. Signed as a free agent by **Linz** (Austria), December 3, 2012. Traded to **Vancouver** by **Florida** with Jacob Markstrom for Roberto Luongo and Steven Anthony, March 4, 2014. Signed as a free agent by **Toronto**, July 6, 2015. Traded to **Colorado** by **Toronto** for Colin Smith and Colorado's 4th round pick (Keaton Middleton) in 2016 NHL Draft, February 22, 2016. Signed as a free agent by **Winnipeg**, July 1, 2016.

MAYFIELD, Scott

(MAY-feeld, SKAWT) **NYI**

Defense. Shoots right. 6'4", 224 lbs. Born, St. Louis, MO, October 14, 1992. NY Islanders' 2nd pick, 34th overall, in 2011 NHL Draft.

			Regular Season														Playoffs								
Season	Club	League	GP	G	A	Pts	PIM	PP	SH	GW	S	S%	+/-	TF	F%	Min	GP	G	A	Pts	PIM	PP	SH	GW	Min
2008-09	St.L. AAA Blues	Minor-MO	62	10	20	30	84																		
2009-10	Youngstown	USHL	59	10	12	22	145																		
2010-11	Youngstown	USHL	52	7	9	16	159																		
2011-12	U. of Denver	WCHA	42	3	9	12	76																		
2012-13	U. of Denver	WCHA	39	4	13	17	112																		
	Bridgeport	AHL	6	0	0	0	2																		
2013-14	**NY Islanders**	**NHL**	**5**	**0**	**0**	**0**	**7**	**0**	**0**	**0**	**7**	**0.0**	**–3**	**0**	**0.0**	**17:22**									
	Bridgeport	AHL	71	3	15	18	129																		
2014-15	**NY Islanders**	**NHL**															**2**	**0**	**0**	**0**	**0**	**0**	**0**	**0**	**12:25**
	Bridgeport	AHL	69	1	13	14	173																		
2015-16	**NY Islanders**	**NHL**	**6**	**1**	**0**	**1**	**11**	**0**	**0**	**0**	**4**	**25.0**	**–4**	**0**	**0.0**	**17:07**									
	Bridgeport	AHL	54	5	7	12	80										3	0	0	0	6				
2016-17	**NY Islanders**	**NHL**	**25**	**2**	**7**	**9**	**35**	**0**	**0**	**0**	**39**	**5.1**	**–1**	**0**	**0.0**	**14:08**									
	Bridgeport	AHL	23	3	3	6	27																		
	NHL Totals		**36**	**3**	**7**	**10**	**53**	**0**	**0**	**0**	**50**	**6.0**		**0**	**0.0**	**15:05**	**2**	**0**	**0**	**0**	**0**	**0**	**0**	**0**	**12:25**

McAVOY, Charlie

(mak-A-voy, CHAHR-lee) **BOS**

Defense. Shoots right. 6'1", 208 lbs. Born, Long Beach, NY, December 21, 1997. Boston's 1st pick, 14th overall, in 2016 NHL Draft.

			Regular Season														Playoffs								
Season	Club	League	GP	G	A	Pts	PIM	PP	SH	GW	S	S%	+/-	TF	F%	Min	GP	G	A	Pts	PIM	PP	SH	GW	Min
2012-13	N.J. Rockets	MtJHL	42	15	39	54	47																		
	N.J. Rockets	AtJHL	4	0	0	0	0																		
	N.J. Rockets	Other	40	6	11	17	68																		
2013-14	USAHNTDP	USHL	34	4	6	10	56																		
	USAHNTDP	U-17	20	3	6	9	4																		
2014-15	USAHNTDP	USHL	23	3	16	19	33																		
	USAHNTDP	U-18	40	4	17	21	18																		
2015-16	Boston University	H-East	37	3	22	25	56																		
2016-17	Boston University	H-East	38	5	21	26	51																		
	Boston	**NHL**															**6**	**0**	**3**	**3**	**2**	**0**	**0**	**0**	**26:12**
	NHL Totals																**6**	**0**	**3**	**3**	**2**	**0**	**0**	**0**	**26:12**

Hockey East All-Rookie Team (2016) • Hockey East First All-Star Team (2017) • NCAA East First All-American Team (2017)

McBAIN, Jamie

(muhk-BAYN, JAY-mee) **T.B.**

Defense. Shoots right. 6'1", 193 lbs. Born, Edina, MN, February 25, 1988. Carolina's 1st pick, 63rd overall, in 2006 NHL Draft.

			Regular Season														Playoffs								
Season	Club	League	GP	G	A	Pts	PIM	PP	SH	GW	S	S%	+/-	TF	F%	Min	GP	G	A	Pts	PIM	PP	SH	GW	Min
2003-04	Shattuck	High-MN	73	6	27	33																			
2004-05	USAHNTDP	U-17	14	1	6	7	16																		
	USAHNTDP	NAHL	38	2	7	9	22										10	0	3	3	4				
2005-06	USAHNTDP	U-18	41	9	16	25	35																		
	USAHNTDP	NAHL	14	0	5	5	6																		
2006-07	U. of Wisconsin	WCHA	36	3	15	18	36																		
2007-08	U. of Wisconsin	WCHA	35	5	19	24	18																		
2008-09	U. of Wisconsin	WCHA	40	7	30	37	30																		
	Albany River Rats	AHL	10	1	1	2	2																		
2009-10	**Carolina**	**NHL**	**14**	**3**	**7**	**10**	**0**	**1**	**0**	**1**	**29**	**10.3**	**6**	**0**	**0.0**	**25:47**									
	Albany River Rats	AHL	68	7	33	40	10										8	4	2	6	8				
2010-11	**Carolina**	**NHL**	**76**	**7**	**23**	**30**	**32**	**1**	**0**	**2**	**95**	**7.4**	**–8**	**0**	**0.0**	**19:06**									
2011-12	**Carolina**	**NHL**	**76**	**8**	**19**	**27**	**4**	**5**	**0**	**1**	**127**	**6.3**	**–7**	**0**	**0.0**	**19:48**									
2012-13	Pelicans Lahti	Finland	7	0	1	1	6																		
	Carolina	**NHL**	**40**	**1**	**7**	**8**	**12**	**0**	**0**	**0**	**46**	**2.2**	**0**	**0**	**0.0**	**18:25**									
2013-14	**Buffalo**	**NHL**	**69**	**6**	**11**	**17**	**14**	**2**	**0**	**0**	**98**	**6.1**	**–13**	**0**	**0.0**	**20:10**									
2014-15	**Los Angeles**	**NHL**	**26**	**3**	**6**	**9**	**4**	**1**	**0**	**0**	**18**	**16.7**	**4**	**0**	**0.0**	**12:41**									
	Manchester	AHL	5	1	2	3	2																		
2015-16	**Los Angeles**	**NHL**	**44**	**2**	**7**	**9**	**6**	**1**	**0**	**0**	**32**	**6.3**	**2**	**0**	**0.0**	**12:14**	**4**	**0**	**0**	**0**	**2**	**0**	**0**	**0**	**10:52**
	Ontario Reign	AHL	3	1	1	2	0																		
2016-17	**Arizona**	**NHL**	**3**	**0**	**0**	**0**	**0**	**0**	**0**	**0**	**3**	**0.0**	**–1**	**0**	**0.0**	**16:40**									
	Tucson	AHL	64	8	35	43	48																		
	NHL Totals		**348**	**30**	**80**	**110**	**72**	**11**	**0**	**4**	**448**	**6.7**		**0**	**0.0**	**18:17**	**4**	**0**	**0**	**0**	**2**	**0**	**0**	**0**	**10:52**

WCHA All-Rookie Team (2007) • WCHA First All-Star Team (2009) • WCHA Player of the Year (2009) • NCAA West First All-American Team (2009)

Signed as a free agent by **Lahti** (Finland), November 2, 2012. Traded to **Buffalo** by **Carolina** with Carolina's 2nd round pick (J.T. Compher) in 2013 NHL Draft for Andrej Sekera, June 30, 2013. Signed as a free agent by **Los Angeles**, November 11, 2014. Signed as a free agent by **Arizona**, July 1, 2016. Signed as a free agent by **Tampa Bay**, July 1, 2017.

McCABE, Jake

(muh-KAYB, JAYK) **BUF**

Defense. Shoots left. 6', 214 lbs. Born, Eau Claire, WI, October 12, 1993. Buffalo's 3rd pick, 44th overall, in 2012 NHL Draft.

			Regular Season														Playoffs								
Season	Club	League	GP	G	A	Pts	PIM	PP	SH	GW	S	S%	+/-	TF	F%	Min	GP	G	A	Pts	PIM	PP	SH	GW	Min
2008-09	Eau Claire Mem.	High-WI	23	2	20	22	16																		
	Team Wisconsin	UMHSEL	22	3	7	10																			
2009-10	USAHNTDP	USHL	35	0	5	5	34																		
	USAHNTDP	U-17	16	0	3	3	16																		
	USAHNTDP	U-18	1	0	0	0	2																		
2010-11	USAHNTDP	USHL	19	2	4	6	4																		
	USAHNTDP	U-18	27	2	8	10	10																		
2011-12	U. of Wisconsin	WCHA	26	3	9	12	12																		
2012-13	U. of Wisconsin	WCHA	38	3	18	21	50																		
2013-14	U. of Wisconsin	Big Ten	36	8	17	25	53																		
	Buffalo	**NHL**	**7**	**0**	**1**	**1**	**15**	**0**	**0**	**0**	**1**	**0.0**	**–3**	**0**	**0.0**	**15:13**									
2014-15	**Buffalo**	**NHL**	**2**	**0**	**0**	**0**	**0**	**0**	**0**	**0**	**2**	**0.0**	**0**	**0**	**0.0**	**11:08**									
	Rochester	AHL	57	5	24	29	50																		

			Regular Season														Playoffs								
Season	Club	League	GP	G	A	Pts	PIM	PP	SH	GW	S	S%	+/-	TF	F%	Min	GP	G	A	Pts	PIM	PP	SH	GW	Min
2015-16	**Buffalo**	**NHL**	**77**	**4**	**10**	**14**	**51**	**0**	**0**	**0**	**62**	**6.5**	**6**	**2**	**0.0**	**19:07**	....	....	....	....	....	....	....	....	....
	Rochester	AHL	1	0	0	0	0	....	....	....	....	....	....	....	....	....	....	....	....	....	....	....	....	....	....
2016-17	**Buffalo**	**NHL**	**76**	**3**	**17**	**20**	**26**	**1**	**0**	**1**	**79**	**3.8**	**–7**	**0**	**0.0**	**20:42**	....	....	....	....	....	....	....	....	....
	NHL Totals		**162**	**7**	**28**	**35**	**92**	**1**	**0**	**1**	**144**	**4.9**		**2**	**0.0**	**19:36**	....	....	....	....	....	....	....	....	....

Big Ten First All-Star Team (2014) • NCAA West First All-American Team (2014)

McCANN, Jared (muh-KAN, JAIR-uhd) FLA

Center. Shoots left. 6'1", 198 lbs. Born, London, ON, May 31, 1996. Vancouver's 2nd pick, 24th overall, in 2014 NHL Draft.

Season	Club	League	GP	G	A	Pts	PIM	PP	SH	GW	S	S%	+/-	TF	F%	Min	GP	G	A	Pts	PIM	PP	SH	GW	Min
2009-10	Elgin-Middl. Bant.	Minor-ON	62	61	69	130	91	....	....	....	....	....	....	....	....	....	....	....	....	....	....	....	....	....	....
2010-11	Elgin-Middl. Bant.	Minor-ON	78	81	98	179	84	....	....	....	....	....	....	....	....	....	....	....	....	....	....	....	....	....	....
	Elgin-Middl. MM	Minor-ON	3	0	0	0	0	....	....	....	....	....	....	....	....	....	3	3	0	3	0	....	....	....	....
2011-12	Lon. Knights MM	Minor-ON	29	33	26	59	22	....	....	....	....	....	....	....	....	....	11	9	11	20	4	....	....	....	....
	Lon. Knights MM	Other	27	19	33	52	6	....	....	....	....	....	....	....	....	....	....	....	....	....	....	....	....	....	....
	London Nationals	ON-Jr.B	4	1	0	1	2	....	....	....	....	....	....	....	....	....	4	2	1	3	0	....	....	....	....
2012-13	Sault Ste. Marie	OHL	64	21	23	44	35	....	....	....	....	....	....	....	....	....	1	0	0	0	0	....	....	....	....
2013-14	Sault Ste. Marie	OHL	64	27	35	62	51	....	....	....	....	....	....	....	....	....	9	2	5	7	4	....	....	....	....
2014-15	Sault Ste. Marie	OHL	56	34	47	81	27	....	....	....	....	....	....	....	....	....	14	6	10	16	12	....	....	....	....
2015-16	**Vancouver**	**NHL**	**69**	**9**	**9**	**18**	**32**	**1**	**0**	**1**	**106**	**8.5**	**–6**	**522**	**34.7**	**12:31**	....	....	....	....	....	....	....	....	....
2016-17	**Florida**	**NHL**	**29**	**1**	**6**	**7**	**4**	**0**	**0**	**0**	**44**	**2.3**	**–1**	**105**	**39.1**	**11:38**	....	....	....	....	....	....	....	....	....
	Springfield	AHL	42	11	14	25	55	....	....	....	....	....	....	....	....	....	....	....	....	....	....	....	....	....	....
	NHL Totals		**98**	**10**	**15**	**25**	**36**	**1**	**0**	**1**	**150**	**6.7**		**627**	**35.4**	**12:16**	....	....	....	....	....	....	....	....	....

Traded to **Florida** by **Vancouver** with Vancouver's 2nd (later traded to Buffalo – Buffalo selected Rasmus Asplund) and 4th (Jonathan Ang) round picks in 2016 NHL Draft for Erik Gudbranson and NY Islanders' 5th round pick (previously acquired, Vancouver selected Cole Candella) in 2016 NHL Draft, May 25, 2016.

McCARRON, Michael (muh-KAIR-uhn, MIGH-kuhl) MTL

Right wing. Shoots right. 6'6", 231 lbs. Born, Grosse Pointe, MI, March 7, 1995. Montreal's 1st pick, 25th overall, in 2013 NHL Draft.

Season	Club	League	GP	G	A	Pts	PIM	PP	SH	GW	S	S%	+/-	TF	F%	Min	GP	G	A	Pts	PIM	PP	SH	GW	Min
2009-10	Det. Honeybaked	T1EHL	29	12	20	32	44	....	....	....	....	....	....	....	....	....	....	....	....	....	....	....	....	....	....
2010-11	Det. Honeybaked	T1EHL	38	6	12	18	88	....	....	....	....	....	....	....	....	....	....	....	....	....	....	....	....	....	....
2011-12	USAHNTDP	USHL	35	3	14	17	112	....	....	....	....	....	....	....	....	....	1	0	1	1	2	....	....	....	....
	USAHNTDP	U-17	17	3	6	9	14	....	....	....	....	....	....	....	....	....	....	....	....	....	....	....	....	....	....
2012-13	USAHNTDP	USHL	19	5	5	10	84	....	....	....	....	....	....	....	....	....	....	....	....	....	....	....	....	....	....
	USAHNTDP	U-18	40	11	16	27	98	....	....	....	....	....	....	....	....	....	....	....	....	....	....	....	....	....	....
2013-14	London Knights	OHL	66	14	20	34	120	....	....	....	....	....	....	....	....	....	9	3	2	5	22	....	....	....	....
2014-15	London Knights	OHL	25	22	19	41	58	....	....	....	....	....	....	....	....	....	....	....	....	....	....	....	....	....	....
	Oshawa Generals	OHL	31	6	21	27	70	....	....	....	....	....	....	....	....	....	21	9	9	18	33	....	....	....	....
2015-16	**Montreal**	**NHL**	**20**	**1**	**1**	**2**	**37**	**0**	**0**	**0**	**41**	**2.4**	**–10**	**169**	**50.3**	**11:41**	....	....	....	....	....	....	....	....	....
	St. John's IceCaps	AHL	58	17	21	38	91	....	....	....	....	....	....	....	....	....	....	....	....	....	....	....	....	....	....
2016-17	**Montreal**	**NHL**	**31**	**1**	**4**	**5**	**41**	**0**	**0**	**0**	**31**	**3.2**	**–4**	**175**	**43.4**	**9:53**	**1**	**0**	**0**	**0**	**0**	**0**	**0**	**0**	**6:54**
	St. John's IceCaps	AHL	32	7	12	19	66	....	....	....	....	....	....	....	....	....	2	0	0	0	6	....	....	....	....
	NHL Totals		**51**	**2**	**5**	**7**	**78**	**0**	**0**	**0**	**72**	**2.8**		**344**	**46.8**	**10:36**	**1**	**0**	**0**	**0**	**0**	**0**	**0**	**0**	**6:54**

Memorial Cup All-Star Team (2015)

McCARTHY, John (muh-KAHR-thee, JAWN)

Left wing. Shoots left. 6'1", 195 lbs. Born, Boston, MA, August 9, 1986. San Jose's 5th pick, 202nd overall, in 2006 NHL Draft.

Season	Club	League	GP	G	A	Pts	PIM	PP	SH	GW	S	S%	+/-	TF	F%	Min	GP	G	A	Pts	PIM	PP	SH	GW	Min
2004-05	Des Moines	USHL	60	8	10	18	32	....	....	....	....	....	....	....	....	....	....	....	....	....	....	....	....	....	....
2005-06	Boston University	H-East	32	2	2	4	12	....	....	....	....	....	....	....	....	....	....	....	....	....	....	....	....	....	....
2006-07	Boston University	H-East	39	2	3	5	18	....	....	....	....	....	....	....	....	....	....	....	....	....	....	....	....	....	....
2007-08	Boston University	H-East	38	4	3	7	24	....	....	....	....	....	....	....	....	....	....	....	....	....	....	....	....	....	....
2008-09	Boston University	H-East	45	6	23	29	24	....	....	....	....	....	....	....	....	....	....	....	....	....	....	....	....	....	....
2009-10	**San Jose**	**NHL**	**4**	**0**	**0**	**0**	**0**	**0**	**0**	**0**	**3**	**0.0**	**–3**	**0**	**0.0**	**9:08**	....	....	....	....	....	....	....	....	....
	Worcester Sharks	AHL	74	15	27	42	39	....	....	....	....	....	....	....	....	....	11	2	3	5	10	....	....	....	....
2010-11	**San Jose**	**NHL**	**37**	**2**	**2**	**4**	**8**	**0**	**0**	**0**	**41**	**4.9**	**–8**	**36**	**36.1**	**8:45**	....	....	....	....	....	....	....	....	....
	Worcester Sharks	AHL	25	7	5	12	13	....	....	....	....	....	....	....	....	....	....	....	....	....	....	....	....	....	....
2011-12	**San Jose**	**NHL**	**10**	**0**	**0**	**0**	**10**	**0**	**0**	**0**	**14**	**0.0**	**–2**	**43**	**41.9**	**9:26**	....	....	....	....	....	....	....	....	....
	Worcester Sharks	AHL	65	20	27	47	41	....	....	....	....	....	....	....	....	....	....	....	....	....	....	....	....	....	....
2012-13	Worcester Sharks	AHL	65	9	16	25	12	....	....	....	....	....	....	....	....	....	....	....	....	....	....	....	....	....	....
2013-14	**San Jose**	**NHL**	**36**	**1**	**1**	**2**	**4**	**0**	**0**	**0**	**49**	**2.0**	**–11**	**133**	**53.4**	**11:03**	....	....	....	....	....	....	....	....	....
	Worcester Sharks	AHL	13	3	4	7	9	....	....	....	....	....	....	....	....	....	....	....	....	....	....	....	....	....	....
2014-15	Chicago Wolves	AHL	25	5	3	8	11	....	....	....	....	....	....	....	....	....	....	....	....	....	....	....	....	....	....
	Worcester Sharks	AHL	35	9	9	18	8	....	....	....	....	....	....	....	....	....	....	....	....	....	....	....	....	....	....
2015-16	**San Jose**	**NHL**	**1**	**0**	**0**	**0**	**0**	**0**	**0**	**0**	**0**	**0.0**	**0**	**1**	**0.0**	**7:05**	....	....	....	....	....	....	....	....	....
	San Jose	AHL	67	16	29	45	22	....	....	....	....	....	....	....	....	....	4	0	0	0	0	....	....	....	....
2016-17	San Jose	AHL	67	19	14	33	26	....	....	....	....	....	....	....	....	....	15	2	5	7	18	....	....	....	....
	NHL Totals		**88**	**3**	**3**	**6**	**22**	**0**	**0**	**0**	**107**	**2.8**		**213**	**47.9**	**9:46**	....	....	....	....	....	....	....	....	....

Signed as a free agent by **St. Louis**, July 4, 2014. Signed as a free agent by **San Jose**, July 2, 2015.

McCLEMENT, Jay (muh-KLEHM-ehnt, JAY)

Center. Shoots left. 6'1", 205 lbs. Born, Kingston, ON, March 2, 1983. St. Louis' 1st pick, 57th overall, in 2001 NHL Draft.

Season	Club	League	GP	G	A	Pts	PIM	PP	SH	GW	S	S%	+/-	TF	F%	Min	GP	G	A	Pts	PIM	PP	SH	GW	Min
1997-98	Kingston	ON-Jr.A	48	3	8	11	15	....	....	....	....	....	....	....	....	....	....	....	....	....	....	....	....	....	....
1998-99	Kingston	ON-Jr.A	51	25	28	53	34	....	....	....	....	....	....	....	....	....	....	....	....	....	....	....	....	....	....
99-2000	Brampton	OHL	63	13	16	29	34	....	....	....	....	....	....	....	....	....	6	0	4	4	8	....	....	....	....
2000-01	Brampton	OHL	66	30	19	49	61	....	....	....	....	....	....	....	....	....	9	4	2	6	10	....	....	....	....
2001-02	Brampton	OHL	61	26	29	55	43	....	....	....	....	....	....	....	....	....	....	....	....	....	....	....	....	....	....
2002-03	Brampton	OHL	45	22	27	49	37	....	....	....	....	....	....	....	....	....	11	3	4	7	11	....	....	....	....
	Worcester IceCats	AHL	....	....	....	....	....	....	....	....	....	....	....	....	....	....	1	0	0	0	0	....	....	....	....
2003-04	Worcester IceCats	AHL	69	12	13	25	20	....	....	....	....	....	....	....	....	....	10	0	3	3	0	....	....	....	....
2004-05	Worcester IceCats	AHL	79	17	34	51	45	....	....	....	....	....	....	....	....	....	....	....	....	....	....	....	....	....	....
2005-06	**St. Louis**	**NHL**	**67**	**6**	**21**	**27**	**30**	**1**	**0**	**2**	**76**	**7.9**	**–23**	**691**	**46.9**	**13:56**	....	....	....	....	....	....	....	....	....
	Peoria Rivermen	AHL	11	4	5	9	4	....	....	....	....	....	....	....	....	....	4	0	2	2	2	....	....	....	....
2006-07	**St. Louis**	**NHL**	**81**	**8**	**28**	**36**	**55**	**0**	**0**	**0**	**104**	**7.7**	**3**	**839**	**52.7**	**13:53**	....	....	....	....	....	....	....	....	....
2007-08	**St. Louis**	**NHL**	**81**	**9**	**13**	**22**	**26**	**0**	**0**	**2**	**110**	**8.2**	**–17**	**700**	**52.3**	**13:55**	....	....	....	....	....	....	....	....	....
2008-09	**St. Louis**	**NHL**	**82**	**12**	**14**	**26**	**29**	**0**	**3**	**3**	**137**	**8.8**	**–10**	**1451**	**52.1**	**16:36**	**4**	**0**	**0**	**0**	**4**	**0**	**0**	**0**	**16:28**
2009-10	**St. Louis**	**NHL**	**82**	**11**	**18**	**29**	**22**	**0**	**0**	**3**	**109**	**10.1**	**0**	**1412**	**49.7**	**16:44**	....	....	....	....	....	....	....	....	....
2010-11	**St. Louis**	**NHL**	**56**	**6**	**10**	**16**	**18**	**1**	**0**	**1**	**89**	**6.7**	**–13**	**831**	**51.4**	**17:08**	....	....	....	....	....	....	....	....	....
	Colorado	**NHL**	**24**	**1**	**3**	**4**	**12**	**0**	**0**	**0**	**38**	**2.6**	**–8**	**321**	**52.3**	**15:39**	....	....	....	....	....	....	....	....	....
2011-12	**Colorado**	**NHL**	**80**	**10**	**7**	**17**	**31**	**0**	**1**	**1**	**95**	**10.5**	**–8**	**873**	**51.3**	**13:45**	....	....	....	....	....	....	....	....	....
2012-13	**Toronto**	**NHL**	**48**	**8**	**9**	**17**	**11**	**0**	**0**	**0**	**48**	**16.7**	**0**	**393**	**51.7**	**15:15**	**7**	**0**	**0**	**0**	**0**	**0**	**0**	**0**	**14:44**
2013-14	**Toronto**	**NHL**	**81**	**4**	**6**	**10**	**32**	**0**	**0**	**1**	**67**	**6.0**	**–8**	**1260**	**53.7**	**14:46**	....	....	....	....	....	....	....	....	....
2014-15	**Carolina**	**NHL**	**82**	**7**	**14**	**21**	**17**	**0**	**0**	**2**	**68**	**10.3**	**–7**	**990**	**55.5**	**13:35**	....	....	....	....	....	....	....	....	....
2015-16	**Carolina**	**NHL**	**77**	**3**	**8**	**11**	**24**	**0**	**1**	**0**	**64**	**4.7**	**–17**	**678**	**55.3**	**11:36**	....	....	....	....	....	....	....	....	....
2016-17	**Carolina**	**NHL**	**65**	**5**	**3**	**8**	**18**	**0**	**1**	**1**	**37**	**13.5**	**–8**	**525**	**48.2**	**11:23**	....	....	....	....	....	....	....	....	....
	NHL Totals		**906**	**90**	**154**	**244**	**325**	**2**	**6**	**16**	**1042**	**8.6**		**10964**	**51.9**	**14:23**	**11**	**0**	**0**	**0**	**4**	**0**	**0**	**0**	**15:22**

Traded to **Colorado** by **St. Louis** with Erik Johnson and St. Louis' 1st round pick (Duncan Siemens) in 2011 NHL Draft for Kevin Shattenkirk, Chris Stewart and Colorado's 2nd round pick (Ty Rattie) in 2011 NHL Draft, February 18, 2011. Signed as a free agent by **Toronto**, July 1, 2012. Signed as a free agent by **Carolina**, July 2, 2014.

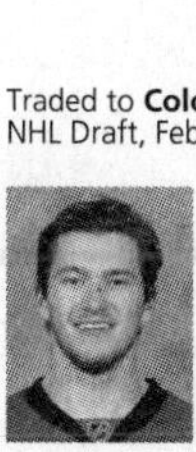

McCORMICK, Max (muh-KOHR-mihk, MAX) OTT

Left wing. Shoots left. 5'11", 188 lbs. Born, De Pere, WI, May 1, 1992. Ottawa's 8th pick, 171st overall, in 2011 NHL Draft.

Season	Club	League	GP	G	A	Pts	PIM	PP	SH	GW	S	S%	+/-	TF	F%	Min	GP	G	A	Pts	PIM	PP	SH	GW	Min
2007-08	Notre Dame Acad.	High-WI	16	19	20	39	....	....	....	....	....	....	....	....	....	....	....	....	....	....	....	....	....	....	....
2008-09	Team Wisconsin	UMHSEL	STATISTICS NOT AVAILABLE																						
	Notre Dame Acad.	High-WI	18	19	38	57	....	....	....	....	....	....	....	....	....	....	....	....	....	....	....	....	....	....	....
2009-10	Team Wisconsin	UMHSEL	24	....	....	24	....	....	....	....	....	....	....	....	....	....	....	....	....	....	....	....	....	....	....
	Notre Dame Acad.	High-WI	29	38	37	75	74	....	....	....	....	....	....	....	....	....	....	....	....	....	....	....	....	....	....
2010-11	Sioux City	USHL	55	21	21	42	102	....	....	....	....	....	....	....	....	....	3	1	2	3	4	....	....	....	....

					Regular Season												Playoffs								
Season	Club	League	GP	G	A	Pts	PIM	PP	SH	GW	S	S%	+/-	TF	F%	Min	GP	G	A	Pts	PIM	PP	SH	GW	Min
2011-12	Ohio State	CCHA	27	10	12	22	31	....	....	....	....	....	....	....	....	....	....	....	....	....	....	....	....	....	....
2012-13	Ohio State	CCHA	40	15	16	31	26	....	....	....	....	....	....	....	....	....	....	....	....	....	....	....	....	....	....
2013-14	Ohio State	Big Ten	37	11	24	35	40	....	....	....	....	....	....	....	....	....	....	....	....	....	....	....	....	....	....
2014-15	Binghamton	AHL	62	10	10	20	133	....	....	....	....	....	....	....	....	....	....	....	....	....	....	....	....	....	....
2015-16	**Ottawa**	**NHL**	**20**	**2**	**2**	**4**	**37**	**0**	**0**	**0**	**37**	**5.4**	**–4**	**76**	**51.3**	**10:28**	....	....	....	....	....	....	....	....	....
	Binghamton	AHL	57	15	15	30	143	....	....	....	....	....	....	....	....	....	....	....	....	....	....	....	....	....	....
2016-17	**Ottawa**	**NHL**	**7**	**0**	**0**	**0**	**0**	**0**	**0**	**0**	**7**	**0.0**	**–3**	**24**	**62.5**	**6:46**	....	....	....	....	....	....	....	....	....
	Binghamton	AHL	66	21	15	36	105	....	....	....	....	....	....	....	....	....	....	....	....	....	....	....	....	....	....
	NHL Totals		**27**	**2**	**2**	**4**	**37**	**0**	**0**	**0**	**44**	**4.5**		**100**	**54.0**	**9:30**	....	....	....	....	....	....	....	....	....

CCHA All-Rookie Team (2012)

McCOSHEN, Ian

(muh-KOH-shuhn, EE-uhn) **FLA**

Defense. Shoots left. 6'3", 217 lbs. Born, Anaheim, CA, August 5, 1995. Florida's 2nd pick, 31st overall, in 2013 NHL Draft.

2009-10	Shattuck Bantam	High-MN	58	21	35	56	46	....	....	....	....	....	....	....	....	....	....	....	....	....	....	....	....	....	....
2010-11	Waterloo	USHL	42	0	6	6	38	....	....	....	....	....	....	....	....	....	2	0	0	0	0	....	....	....	....
2011-12	Waterloo	USHL	55	8	12	20	43	....	....	....	....	....	....	....	....	....	15	4	3	7	6	....	....	....	....
2012-13	Waterloo	USHL	53	11	33	44	48	....	....	....	....	....	....	....	....	....	5	2	2	4	4	....	....	....	....
2013-14	Boston College	H-East	35	5	8	13	48	....	....	....	....	....	....	....	....	....	....	....	....	....	....	....	....	....	....
2014-15	Boston College	H-East	35	6	10	16	63	....	....	....	....	....	....	....	....	....	....	....	....	....	....	....	....	....	....
2015-16	Boston College	H-East	40	6	15	21	*86	....	....	....	....	....	....	....	....	....	....	....	....	....	....	....	....	....	....
2016-17	**Florida**	**NHL**	**3**	**0**	**1**	**1**	**0**	**0**	**0**	**0**	**0**	**0.0**	**0**	**0**	**0.0**	**13:15**	....	....	....	....	....	....	....	....	....
	Springfield	AHL	68	4	12	16	37	....	....	....	....	....	....	....	....	....	....	....	....	....	....	....	....	....	....
	NHL Totals		**3**	**0**	**1**	**1**	**0**	**0**	**0**	**0**	**0**	**0.0**		**0**	**0.0**	**13:15**	....	....	....	....	....	....	....	....	....

USHL First All-Star Team (2013) • Hockey East Second All-Star Team (2016)

McDAVID, Connor

(muhk-DAY-vihd, KAW-nuhr) **EDM**

Center. Shoots left. 6'1", 200 lbs. Born, Richmond Hill, ON, January 13, 1997. Edmonton's 1st pick, 1st overall, in 2015 NHL Draft.

2011-12	Tor. Marlboros	GTHL	33	27	50	77	....	....	....	....	....	....	....	....	....	....	14	11	15	26	....	....	....	....	....
	Tor. Marlboros	Other	41	41	65	106	....	....	....	....	....	....	....	....	....	....	....	....	....	....	....	....	....	....	....
	PEAC Piranhas	Other	17	31	32	63	....	....	....	....	....	....	....	....	....	....	....	....	....	....	....	....	....	....	....
2012-13	Erie Otters	OHL	63	25	41	66	36	....	....	....	....	....	....	....	....	....	....	....	....	....	....	....	....	....	....
2013-14	Erie Otters	OHL	56	28	71	99	20	....	....	....	....	....	....	....	....	....	14	4	15	19	2	....	....	....	....
2014-15	Erie Otters	OHL	47	44	76	120	48	....	....	....	....	....	....	....	....	....	20	21	28	49	12	....	....	....	....
2015-16	**Edmonton**	**NHL**	**45**	**16**	**32**	**48**	**18**	**3**	**0**	**5**	**105**	**15.2**	**–1**	**604**	**41.2**	**18:53**	....	....	....	....	....	....	....	....	....
2016-17	**Edmonton**	**NHL**	**82**	**30**	***70**	***100**	**26**	**3**	**1**	**6**	**251**	**12.0**	**27**	**806**	**43.2**	**21:08**	**13**	**5**	**4**	**9**	**2**	**1**	**1**	**0**	**22:25**
	NHL Totals		**127**	**46**	**102**	**148**	**44**	**6**	**1**	**11**	**356**	**12.9**		**1410**	**42.3**	**20:20**	**13**	**5**	**4**	**9**	**2**	**1**	**1**	**0**	**22:25**

OHL All-Rookie Team (2013) • OHL Rookie of the Year (2013) • OHL Second All-Star Team (2014) • OHL First All-Star Team (2015) • OHL Player of the Year (2015) • OHL Playoff MVP (2015) • NHL All-Rookie Team (2016) • NHL First All-Star Team (2017) • Art Ross Trophy (2017) • Ted Lindsay Award (2017) • Hart Memorial Trophy (2017)

Played in NHL All-Star Game (2017)

McDONAGH, Ryan

(muhk-DUHN-uh, RIGH-uhn) **NYR**

Defense. Shoots left. 6'1", 216 lbs. Born, St.Paul, MN, June 13, 1989. Montreal's 1st pick, 12th overall, in 2007 NHL Draft.

2004-05	Cretin-Derham	High-MN	28	12	18	30	....	....	....	....	....	....	....	....	....	....	....	....	....	....	....	....	....	....	....
2005-06	Cretin-Derham	High-MN	25	12	33	45	....	....	....	....	....	....	....	....	....	....	....	....	....	....	....	....	....	....	....
2006-07	Cretin-Derham	High-MN	26	14	26	40	....	....	....	....	....	....	....	....	....	....	....	....	....	....	....	....	....	....	....
2007-08	U. of Wisconsin	WCHA	40	5	7	12	42	....	....	....	....	....	....	....	....	....	....	....	....	....	....	....	....	....	....
2008-09	U. of Wisconsin	WCHA	36	5	11	16	59	....	....	....	....	....	....	....	....	....	....	....	....	....	....	....	....	....	....
2009-10	U. of Wisconsin	WCHA	43	4	14	18	73	....	....	....	....	....	....	....	....	....	....	....	....	....	....	....	....	....	....
2010-11	**NY Rangers**	**NHL**	**40**	**1**	**8**	**9**	**14**	**0**	**0**	**1**	**27**	**3.7**	**16**	**0**	**0.0**	**18:44**	**5**	**0**	**0**	**0**	**4**	**0**	**0**	**0**	**22:49**
	Connecticut	AHL	38	1	7	8	12	....	....	....	....	....	....	....	....	....	....	....	....	....	....	....	....	....	....
2011-12	**NY Rangers**	**NHL**	**82**	**7**	**25**	**32**	**44**	**0**	**0**	**1**	**123**	**5.7**	**25**	**2**	**50.0**	**24:44**	**20**	**0**	**4**	**4**	**11**	**0**	**0**	**0**	**26:49**
2012-13	Barys Astana	KHL	10	0	3	3	6	....	....	....	....	....	....	....	....	....	....	....	....	....	....	....	....	....	....
	NY Rangers	**NHL**	**47**	**4**	**15**	**19**	**22**	**0**	**0**	**1**	**83**	**4.8**	**13**	**1**	**0.0**	**24:21**	**12**	**1**	**3**	**4**	**6**	**0**	**0**	**0**	**25:53**
2013-14	**NY Rangers**	**NHL**	**77**	**14**	**29**	**43**	**36**	**2**	**3**	**4**	**177**	**7.9**	**11**	**0**	**0.0**	**24:49**	**25**	**4**	**13**	**17**	**8**	**2**	**0**	**0**	**26:49**
	United States	Olympics	6	1	1	2	0	....	....	....	....	....	....	....	....	....	....	....	....	....	....	....	....	....	....
2014-15	**NY Rangers**	**NHL**	**71**	**8**	**25**	**33**	**26**	**3**	**0**	**2**	**148**	**5.4**	**23**	**0**	**0.0**	**23:08**	**19**	**3**	**6**	**9**	**8**	**2**	**0**	**2**	**23:31**
2015-16	**NY Rangers**	**NHL**	**73**	**9**	**25**	**34**	**22**	**2**	**0**	**0**	**113**	**8.0**	**26**	**1**	**100.0**	**22:21**	**3**	**0**	**0**	**0**	**0**	**0**	**0**	**0**	**20:41**
2016-17	**NY Rangers**	**NHL**	**77**	**6**	**36**	**42**	**37**	**1**	**1**	**1**	**153**	**3.9**	**20**	**0**	**0.0**	**24:21**	**12**	**2**	**5**	**7**	**12**	**1**	**0**	**0**	**27:21**
	NHL Totals		**467**	**49**	**163**	**212**	**201**	**8**	**4**	**10**	**824**	**5.9**		**4**	**50.0**	**23:31**	**96**	**10**	**31**	**41**	**49**	**5**	**0**	**2**	**25:43**

WCHA All-Rookie Team (2008) • WCHA Second All-Star Team (2010)

Played in NHL All-Star Game (2016, 2017)

Traded to **NY Rangers** by **Montreal** with Chris Higgins and Pavel Valentenko for Scott Gomez, Tom Pyatt and Michael Busto, June 30, 2009. Signed as a free agent by **Astana** (KHL), October 9, 2012.

McDONALD, Colin

(muhk-DAWN-uhld, KAW-lihn) **PHI**

Right wing. Shoots right. 6'2", 220 lbs. Born, Wethersfield, CT, September 30, 1984. Edmonton's 2nd pick, 51st overall, in 2003 NHL Draft.

2001-02	N.E. Jr. Coyotes	EJHL	39	16	20	36	50	....	....	....	....	....	....	....	....	....	....	....	....	....	....	....	....	....	....
2002-03	N.E. Jr. Coyotes	EJHL	44	28	40	*68	59	....	....	....	....	....	....	....	....	....	....	....	....	....	....	....	....	....	....
2003-04	Providence	H-East	37	10	6	16	47	....	....	....	....	....	....	....	....	....	....	....	....	....	....	....	....	....	....
2004-05	Providence	H-East	26	11	5	16	14	....	....	....	....	....	....	....	....	....	....	....	....	....	....	....	....	....	....
2005-06	Providence	H-East	36	9	19	28	29	....	....	....	....	....	....	....	....	....	....	....	....	....	....	....	....	....	....
2006-07	Providence	H-East	36	13	4	17	30	....	....	....	....	....	....	....	....	....	....	....	....	....	....	....	....	....	....
2007-08	Springfield	AHL	73	12	11	23	46	....	....	....	....	....	....	....	....	....	....	....	....	....	....	....	....	....	....
2008-09	Springfield	AHL	77	10	12	22	65	....	....	....	....	....	....	....	....	....	....	....	....	....	....	....	....	....	....
	Stockton Thunder	ECHL	3	0	2	2	0	....	....	....	....	....	....	....	....	....	....	....	....	....	....	....	....	....	....
2009-10	**Edmonton**	**NHL**	**2**	**1**	**0**	**1**	**0**	**0**	**0**	**0**	**3**	**33.3**	**1**	**0**	**0.0**	**6:42**	....	....	....	....	....	....	....	....	....
	Springfield	AHL	76	12	11	23	38	....	....	....	....	....	....	....	....	....	....	....	....	....	....	....	....	....	....
2010-11	Oklahoma City	AHL	80	*42	16	58	63	....	....	....	....	....	....	....	....	....	6	1	1	2	6	....	....	....	....
2011-12	**Pittsburgh**	**NHL**	**5**	**0**	**0**	**0**	**0**	**0**	**0**	**0**	**6**	**0.0**	**0**	**0**	**0.0**	**8:28**	....	....	....	....	....	....	....	....	....
	Wilkes-Barre	AHL	68	14	35	49	41	....	....	....	....	....	....	....	....	....	12	6	7	13	2	....	....	....	....
2012-13	Bridgeport	AHL	35	6	21	27	32	....	....	....	....	....	....	....	....	....	....	....	....	....	....	....	....	....	....
	NY Islanders	**NHL**	**45**	**7**	**10**	**17**	**32**	**1**	**0**	**0**	**82**	**8.5**	**–1**	**8**	**50.0**	**11:22**	**6**	**2**	**1**	**3**	**2**	**0**	**0**	**0**	**11:57**
2013-14	**NY Islanders**	**NHL**	**70**	**8**	**10**	**18**	**34**	**0**	**0**	**0**	**96**	**8.3**	**–22**	**15**	**46.7**	**12:23**	....	....	....	....	....	....	....	....	....
2014-15	**NY Islanders**	**NHL**	**18**	**2**	**6**	**8**	**0**	**0**	**0**	**0**	**29**	**6.9**	**–3**	**4**	**50.0**	**10:30**	**2**	**0**	**0**	**0**	**2**	**0**	**0**	**0**	**11:45**
	Bridgeport	AHL	40	14	21	35	28	....	....	....	....	....	....	....	....	....	....	....	....	....	....	....	....	....	....
2015-16	**Philadelphia**	**NHL**	**5**	**1**	**0**	**1**	**7**	**0**	**0**	**0**	**4**	**25.0**	**0**	**0**	**0.0**	**8:09**	**3**	**0**	**0**	**0**	**0**	**0**	**0**	**0**	**8:52**
	Lehigh Valley	AHL	51	14	18	32	30	....	....	....	....	....	....	....	....	....	....	....	....	....	....	....	....	....	....
2016-17	**Philadelphia**	**NHL**	**3**	**1**	**0**	**1**	**0**	**0**	**0**	**0**	**5**	**20.0**	**1**	**1**	**0.0**	**9:01**	....	....	....	....	....	....	....	....	....
	Lehigh Valley	AHL	72	25	19	44	27	....	....	....	....	....	....	....	....	....	5	2	1	3	0	....	....	....	....
	NHL Totals		**148**	**20**	**26**	**46**	**73**	**1**	**0**	**0**	**225**	**8.9**		**28**	**46.4**	**11:26**	**11**	**2**	**1**	**3**	**4**	**0**	**0**	**0**	**11:04**

Hockey East All-Rookie Team (2004) • Willie Marshall Award (AHL – Top Goal-scorer) (2011)

Signed as a free agent by **Oklahoma City** (AHL). July 9, 2010. Signed as a free agent by **Pittsburgh**, July 1, 2011. Signed as a free agent by **NY Islanders**, July 2, 2012. Signed as a free agent by **Philadelphia**, July 3, 2015.

McENENY, Evan

(muhk-EHN-ehn-ee, EH-vuhn) **VAN**

Defense. Shoots left. 6'2", 203 lbs. Born, Hamilton, ON, May 22, 1994.

2009-10	Ham. Bulldogs	Minor-ON	59	13	37	50	50	....	....	....	....	....	....	....	....	....	....	....	....	....	....	....	....	....	....
	Burlington	ON-Jr.A	4	0	1	1	0	....	....	....	....	....	....	....	....	....	....	....	....	....	....	....	....	....	....
2010-11	Kitchener Rangers	OHL	44	0	4	4	14	....	....	....	....	....	....	....	....	....	4	0	0	0	0	....	....	....	....
2011-12	Kitchener Rangers	OHL	2	0	2	2	4	....	....	....	....	....	....	....	....	....	....	....	....	....	....	....	....	....	....
2012-13	Kitchener Rangers	OHL	65	6	28	34	42	....	....	....	....	....	....	....	....	....	10	1	3	4	14	....	....	....	....

Season	Club	League	GP	G	A	Pts	PIM	PP	SH	GW	S	S%	+/-	TF	F%	Min	GP	G	A	Pts	PIM	PP	SH	GW	Min
			Regular Season														Playoffs								
2013-14	Kitchener Rangers	OHL	15	2	5	7	23	....	....	....	....	....	....	....	....	....	....	....	....	....	....	....	....	....	....
	Kingston	OHL	46	5	30	35	55	....	....	....	....	....	....	....	....	....	7	1	1	2	6	....	....	....	....
	Utica Comets	AHL	1	0	0	0	2	....	....	....	....	....	....	....	....	....	....	....	....	....	....	....	....	....	....
2014-15	Kingston	OHL	68	9	36	45	71	....	....	....	....	....	....	....	....	....	4	1	1	2	0	....	....	....	....
2015-16	Utica Comets	AHL	2	0	0	0	0	....	....	....	....	....	....	....	....	....	....	....	....	....	....	....	....	....	....
	Kalamazoo Wings	ECHL	36	1	24	25	19	....	....	....	....	....	....	....	....	....	5	0	1	1	6	....	....	....	....
2016-17	**Vancouver**	**NHL**	**1**	**0**	**0**	**0**	**0**	**0**	**0**	**0**	**1**	**0.0**	**-1**	**0**	**0.0**	**15:08**	....	....	....	....	....	....	....	....	....
	Utica Comets	AHL	64	8	15	23	20	....	....	....	....	....	....	....	....	....	....	....	....	....	....	....	....	....	....
	NHL Totals		**1**	**0**	**0**	**0**	**0**	**0**	**0**	**0**	**1**	**0.0**		**0**	**0.0**	**15:08**	....	....	....	....	....	....	....	....	....

• Missed majority of 2011-12 due to knee injury at Sarnia (OHL), September 23, 2011. Signed as a free agent by **Vancouver**, September 13, 2012.

McFARLAND, John

(muhk-FAHR-luhnd, JAWN)

Left wing. Shoots right. 6', 211 lbs. Born, Richmond Hill, ON, April 2, 1992. Florida's 4th pick, 33rd overall, in 2010 NHL Draft.

Season	Club	League	GP	G	A	Pts	PIM	PP	SH	GW	S	S%	+/-	TF	F%	Min	GP	G	A	Pts	PIM	PP	SH	GW	Min
2007-08	Tor. Jr. Canadiens	GTHL	76	96	69	165	176	....	....	....	....	....	....	....	....	....	....	....	....	....	....	....	....	....	....
2008-09	Sudbury Wolves	OHL	58	21	31	52	36	....	....	....	....	....	....	....	....	....	6	1	3	4	2	....	....	....	....
2009-10	Sudbury Wolves	OHL	64	20	30	50	70	....	....	....	....	....	....	....	....	....	4	3	0	3	2	....	....	....	....
2010-11	Sudbury Wolves	OHL	12	6	4	10	13	....	....	....	....	....	....	....	....	....	....	....	....	....	....	....	....	....	....
	Saginaw Spirit	OHL	37	19	9	28	33	....	....	....	....	....	....	....	....	....	12	5	4	9	6	....	....	....	....
2011-12	Saginaw Spirit	OHL	36	20	21	41	18	....	....	....	....	....	....	....	....	....	....	....	....	....	....	....	....	....	....
	Ottawa 67's	OHL	12	4	5	9	10	....	....	....	....	....	....	....	....	....	....	....	....	....	....	....	....	....	....
2012-13	San Antonio	AHL	43	5	9	14	10	....	....	....	....	....	....	....	....	....	....	....	....	....	....	....	....	....	....
	Cincinnati	ECHL	23	12	13	25	12	....	....	....	....	....	....	....	....	....	12	4	5	9	6	....	....	....	....
2013-14	San Antonio	AHL	45	10	14	24	17	....	....	....	....	....	....	....	....	....	....	....	....	....	....	....	....	....	....
	Cincinnati	ECHL	20	8	5	13	4	....	....	....	....	....	....	....	....	....	....	....	....	....	....	....	....	....	....
2014-15	San Antonio	AHL	46	10	9	19	8	....	....	....	....	....	....	....	....	....	3	1	0	1	6	....	....	....	....
2015-16	**Florida**	**NHL**	**3**	**0**	**0**	**0**	**0**	**0**	**0**	**0**	**2**	**0.0**	**-1**	**0**	**0.0**	**9:55**	....	....	....	....	....	....	....	....	....
	Portland Pirates	AHL	56	14	10	24	47	....	....	....	....	....	....	....	....	....	4	0	0	0	0	....	....	....	....
2016-17	SaiPa	Finland	21	3	6	9	4	....	....	....	....	....	....	....	....	....	....	....	....	....	....	....	....	....	....
	NHL Totals		**3**	**0**	**0**	**0**	**0**	**0**	**0**	**0**	**2**	**0.0**		**0**	**0.0**	**9:55**	....	....	....	....	....	....	....	....	....

Signed as a free agent by **SaiPa Lappeenranta** (Finland), July 25, 2016.

McGINN, Brock

(muh-GIHN, BRAWK) **CAR**

Left wing. Shoots left. 6', 185 lbs. Born, Fergus, ON, February 2, 1994. Carolina's 2nd pick, 47th overall, in 2012 NHL Draft.

Season	Club	League	GP	G	A	Pts	PIM	PP	SH	GW	S	S%	+/-	TF	F%	Min	GP	G	A	Pts	PIM	PP	SH	GW	Min
2009-10	Guelph Jr. Storm	Minor-ON	STATISTICS NOT AVAILABLE																						
	Orangeville	ON-Jr.A	3	0	0	0	0	....	....	....	....	....	....	....	....	....	1	0	0	0	0	....	....	....	....
2010-11	Guelph Storm	OHL	68	10	4	14	38	....	....	....	....	....	....	....	....	....	6	0	0	0	2	....	....	....	....
2011-12	Guelph Storm	OHL	33	12	7	19	25	....	....	....	....	....	....	....	....	....	6	1	1	2	8	....	....	....	....
2012-13	Guelph Storm	OHL	68	28	26	54	71	....	....	....	....	....	....	....	....	....	3	2	2	4	11	....	....	....	....
	Charlotte	AHL	4	0	0	0	0	....	....	....	....	....	....	....	....	....	2	0	0	0	2	....	....	....	....
2013-14	Guelph Storm	OHL	58	43	42	85	45	....	....	....	....	....	....	....	....	....	12	6	6	12	21	....	....	....	....
2014-15	Charlotte	AHL	73	15	12	27	38	....	....	....	....	....	....	....	....	....	....	....	....	....	....	....	....	....	....
2015-16	**Carolina**	**NHL**	**21**	**3**	**1**	**4**	**10**	**0**	**0**	**0**	**25**	**12.0**	**-14**	**1**	**0.0**	**11:11**	....	....	....	....	....	....	....	....	....
	Charlotte	AHL	48	19	16	35	29	....	....	....	....	....	....	....	....	....	....	....	....	....	....	....	....	....	....
2016-17	**Carolina**	**NHL**	**57**	**7**	**9**	**16**	**6**	**0**	**0**	**1**	**74**	**9.5**	**-11**	**4**	**25.0**	**12:00**	....	....	....	....	....	....	....	....	....
	Charlotte	AHL	9	5	3	8	6	....	....	....	....	....	....	....	....	....	....	....	....	....	....	....	....	....	....
	NHL Totals		**78**	**10**	**10**	**20**	**16**	**0**	**0**	**1**	**99**	**10.1**		**5**	**20.0**	**11:47**	....	....	....	....	....	....	....	....	....

McGINN, Jamie

(muh-GIHN, JAY-mee) **ARI**

Left wing. Shoots left. 6'1", 205 lbs. Born, Fergus, ON, August 5, 1988. San Jose's 2nd pick, 36th overall, in 2006 NHL Draft.

Season	Club	League	GP	G	A	Pts	PIM	PP	SH	GW	S	S%	+/-	TF	F%	Min	GP	G	A	Pts	PIM	PP	SH	GW	Min
2003-04	Tor. Jr. Canadiens	GTHL	31	....	....	48	....	....	....	....	....	....	....	....	....	....	18	14	18	32	....	....	....	....	....
2004-05	Ottawa 67's	OHL	59	10	12	22	35	....	....	....	....	....	....	....	....	....	18	4	7	11	0	....	....	....	....
2005-06	Ottawa 67's	OHL	65	26	31	57	113	....	....	....	....	....	....	....	....	....	6	2	2	4	4	....	....	....	....
2006-07	Ottawa 67's	OHL	68	46	43	89	49	....	....	....	....	....	....	....	....	....	5	5	1	6	2	....	....	....	....
	Worcester Sharks	AHL	4	1	1	2	4	....	....	....	....	....	....	....	....	....	6	0	0	0	8	....	....	....	....
2007-08	Ottawa 67's	OHL	51	29	29	58	54	....	....	....	....	....	....	....	....	....	4	2	2	4	4	....	....	....	....
	Worcester Sharks	AHL	8	0	2	2	0	....	....	....	....	....	....	....	....	....	....	....	....	....	....	....	....	....	....
2008-09	**San Jose**	**NHL**	**35**	**4**	**2**	**6**	**2**	**1**	**0**	**1**	**27**	**14.8**	**-6**	**7**	**85.7**	**8:55**	....	....	....	....	....	....	....	....	....
	Worcester Sharks	AHL	47	19	11	30	52	....	....	....	....	....	....	....	....	....	6	4	0	4	19	....	....	....	....
2009-10	**San Jose**	**NHL**	**59**	**10**	**3**	**13**	**38**	**0**	**0**	**2**	**76**	**13.2**	**-3**	**16**	**43.8**	**10:00**	**15**	**0**	**0**	**0**	**8**	**0**	**0**	**0**	**7:45**
	Worcester Sharks	AHL	27	7	14	21	15	....	....	....	....	....	....	....	....	....	....	....	....	....	....	....	....	....	....
2010-11	**San Jose**	**NHL**	**49**	**1**	**5**	**6**	**33**	**0**	**0**	**0**	**63**	**1.6**	**-6**	**11**	**72.7**	**11:35**	**7**	**0**	**1**	**1**	**30**	**0**	**0**	**0**	**6:33**
	Worcester Sharks	AHL	30	9	11	20	27	....	....	....	....	....	....	....	....	....	....	....	....	....	....	....	....	....	....
2011-12	**San Jose**	**NHL**	**61**	**12**	**12**	**24**	**26**	**3**	**0**	**0**	**104**	**11.5**	**1**	**3**	**66.7**	**12:33**	....	....	....	....	....	....	....	....	....
	Colorado	**NHL**	**17**	**8**	**5**	**13**	**11**	**3**	**0**	**2**	**55**	**14.5**	**-4**	**4**	**100.0**	**16:40**	....	....	....	....	....	....	....	....	....
2012-13	**Colorado**	**NHL**	**47**	**11**	**11**	**22**	**26**	**3**	**0**	**2**	**128**	**8.6**	**-13**	**6**	**50.0**	**17:17**	....	....	....	....	....	....	....	....	....
2013-14	**Colorado**	**NHL**	**79**	**19**	**19**	**38**	**30**	**5**	**0**	**3**	**167**	**11.4**	**-3**	**2**	**50.0**	**15:47**	**7**	**2**	**3**	**5**	**2**	**0**	**0**	**0**	**17:18**
2014-15	**Colorado**	**NHL**	**19**	**4**	**2**	**6**	**6**	**1**	**0**	**0**	**36**	**11.1**	**-9**	**1**	**100.0**	**14:46**	....	....	....	....	....	....	....	....	....
2015-16	**Buffalo**	**NHL**	**63**	**14**	**13**	**27**	**10**	**6**	**0**	**3**	**109**	**12.8**	**-10**	**3**	**66.7**	**14:10**	....	....	....	....	....	....	....	....	....
	Anaheim	**NHL**	**21**	**8**	**4**	**12**	**23**	**3**	**0**	**2**	**47**	**17.0**	**3**	**4**	**50.0**	**14:41**	**7**	**2**	**0**	**2**	**2**	**0**	**0**	**1**	**10:06**
2016-17	**Arizona**	**NHL**	**72**	**9**	**8**	**17**	**23**	**0**	**0**	**2**	**116**	**7.8**	**-23**	**3**	**33.3**	**13:10**	....	....	....	....	....	....	....	....	....
	NHL Totals		**522**	**100**	**84**	**184**	**228**	**25**	**0**	**17**	**928**	**10.8**		**60**	**61.7**	**13:25**	**36**	**4**	**4**	**8**	**42**	**0**	**0**	**1**	**9:50**

Traded to **Colorado** by **San Jose** with Michael Sgarbossa and Mike Connolly for T.J. Galiardi, Daniel Winnik and Anaheim's 7th round pick (previously acquired, San Jose selected Emil Galimov) in 2013 NHL Draft, February 27, 2012. • Missed majority of 2014-15 due to back injury at New Jersey, November 15, 2014. Traded to **Buffalo** by **Colorado** with Ryan O'Reilly for Nikita Zadorov, Mikhail Grigorenko, J.T. Compher and Buffalo's 2nd round pick (later traded to San Jose – San Jose selected Jeremy Roy) in 2015 NHL Draft, June 26, 2015. Traded to **Anaheim** by **Buffalo** for Minnesota's 3rd round pick (previously acquired, later traded to Nashville – Nashville selected Rem Pitlick) in 2016 NHL Draft, February 29, 2016. Signed as a free agent by **Arizona**, July 1, 2016.

McGINN, Tye

(muhk-GIHN, TIGH) **T.B.**

Left wing. Shoots left. 6'3", 205 lbs. Born, Fergus, ON, July 29, 1990. Philadelphia's 2nd pick, 119th overall, in 2010 NHL Draft.

Season	Club	League	GP	G	A	Pts	PIM	PP	SH	GW	S	S%	+/-	TF	F%	Min	GP	G	A	Pts	PIM	PP	SH	GW	Min
2006-07	Waterloo Wolves	Minor-ON	62	41	55	96	42	....	....	....	....	....	....	....	....	....	....	....	....	....	....	....	....	....	....
2007-08	Ottawa 67's	OHL	59	3	8	11	25	....	....	....	....	....	....	....	....	....	4	0	0	0	2	....	....	....	....
2008-09	Listowel Cyclones	ON-Jr.B	14	10	18	28	10	....	....	....	....	....	....	....	....	....	....	....	....	....	....	....	....	....	....
	Gatineau	QMJHL	48	8	22	30	25	....	....	....	....	....	....	....	....	....	10	7	6	13	19	....	....	....	....
2009-10	Gatineau	QMJHL	50	27	35	62	50	....	....	....	....	....	....	....	....	....	10	2	5	7	12	....	....	....	....
2010-11	Gatineau	QMJHL	42	31	33	64	39	....	....	....	....	....	....	....	....	....	14	5	8	13	17	....	....	....	....
2011-12	Adirondack	AHL	63	12	6	18	45	....	....	....	....	....	....	....	....	....	....	....	....	....	....	....	....	....	....
2012-13	Adirondack	AHL	46	14	12	26	54	....	....	....	....	....	....	....	....	....	....	....	....	....	....	....	....	....	....
	Philadelphia	**NHL**	**18**	**3**	**2**	**5**	**19**	**0**	**0**	**1**	**33**	**9.1**	**0**	**0**	**0.0**	**12:43**	....	....	....	....	....	....	....	....	....
2013-14	**Philadelphia**	**NHL**	**18**	**4**	**1**	**5**	**4**	**0**	**0**	**0**	**16**	**25.0**	**-1**	**0**	**0.0**	**11:11**	....	....	....	....	....	....	....	....	....
	Adirondack	AHL	54	20	15	35	62	....	....	....	....	....	....	....	....	....	....	....	....	....	....	....	....	....	....
2014-15	**San Jose**	**NHL**	**33**	**1**	**4**	**5**	**11**	**0**	**0**	**0**	**35**	**2.9**	**1**	**1**	**100.0**	**10:20**	....	....	....	....	....	....	....	....	....
	Arizona	**NHL**	**18**	**1**	**1**	**2**	**10**	**0**	**0**	**0**	**25**	**4.0**	**-1**	**1**	**0.0**	**9:40**	....	....	....	....	....	....	....	....	....
2015-16	**Tampa Bay**	**NHL**	**2**	**0**	**0**	**0**	**0**	**0**	**0**	**0**	**1**	**0.0**	**0**	**0**	**0.0**	**8:33**	....	....	....	....	....	....	....	....	....
	Syracuse Crunch	AHL	72	20	24	44	53	....	....	....	....	....	....	....	....	....	....	....	....	....	....	....	....	....	....
2016-17	Syracuse Crunch	AHL	21	10	9	19	16	....	....	....	....	....	....	....	....	....	22	5	11	16	12	....	....	....	....
	NHL Totals		**89**	**9**	**8**	**17**	**44**	**0**	**0**	**1**	**110**	**8.2**		**2**	**50.0**	**10:49**	....	....	....	....	....	....	....	....	....

Traded to **San Jose** by **Philadelphia** for San Jose's 3rd round pick (Felix Sandstrom) in 2015 NHL Draft, July 2, 2014. Claimed on waivers by **Arizona** from **San Jose**, March 2, 2015. Signed as a free agent by **Tampa Bay**, July 21, 2015. • Missed majority of 2016-17 due to shoulder injury at Rochester (AHL), October 21, 2016 and resulting surgery.

			Regular Season														Playoffs								
Season	Club	League	GP	G	A	Pts	PIM	PP	SH	GW	S	S%	+/-	TF	F%	Min	GP	G	A	Pts	PIM	PP	SH	GW	Min

McILRATH, Dylan
(MAK-ihl-rayth, DIH-luhn) **DET**

Defense. Shoots right. 6'5", 236 lbs. Born, Winnipeg, MB, April 20, 1992. NY Rangers' 1st pick, 10th overall, in 2010 NHL Draft.

2007-08	Wpg. Warriors	Minor-MB	34	5	17	22	68	....	....	....	....	....	....	....	....	....	....	....	....	....	....	....	....	....	....
2008-09	Moose Jaw	WHL	53	1	3	4	102	....	....	....	....	....	....	....	....	....	....	....	....	....	....	....	....	....	....
2009-10	Moose Jaw	WHL	65	7	17	24	169	....	....	....	....	....	....	....	....	....	7	0	1	1	21	....	....	....	....
2010-11	Moose Jaw	WHL	62	5	18	23	153	....	....	....	....	....	....	....	....	....	6	0	0	0	15	....	....	....	....
	Connecticut	AHL	2	0	0	0	7	....	....	....	....	....	....	....	....	....	....	....	....	....	....	....	....	....	....
2011-12	Moose Jaw	WHL	52	3	20	23	127	....	....	....	....	....	....	....	....	....	14	0	6	6	12	....	....	....	....
	Connecticut	AHL	....	....	....	....	....	....	....	....	....	....	....	....	....	....	5	0	0	0	9	....	....	....	....
2012-13	Connecticut	AHL	45	0	5	5	125	....	....	....	....	....	....	....	....	....	....	....	....	....	....	....	....	....	....
2013-14	**NY Rangers**	**NHL**	**2**	**0**	**0**	**0**	**7**	**0**	**0**	**0**	**0**	**0.0**	**–1**	**0**	**0.0**	**7:02**	....	....	....	....	....	....	....	....	....
	Hartford	AHL	62	6	11	17	165	....	....	....	....	....	....	....	....	....	....	....	....	....	....	....	....	....	....
2014-15	**NY Rangers**	**NHL**	**1**	**0**	**0**	**0**	**9**	**0**	**0**	**0**	**0**	**0.0**	**0**	**0**	**0.0**	**8:02**	....	....	....	....	....	....	....	....	....
	Hartford	AHL	73	6	11	17	165	....	....	....	....	....	....	....	....	....	15	0	2	2	23	....	....	....	....
2015-16	**NY Rangers**	**NHL**	**34**	**2**	**2**	**4**	**64**	**0**	**0**	**0**	**28**	**7.1**	**7**	**0**	**0.0**	**14:07**	**1**	**0**	**0**	**0**	**0**	**0**	**0**	**0**	**9:07**
2016-17	**NY Rangers**	**NHL**	**1**	**0**	**0**	**0**	**4**	**0**	**0**	**0**	**0**	**0.0**	**0**	**0**	**0.0**	**9:14**	....	....	....	....	....	....	....	....	....
	Hartford	AHL	4	0	0	0	11	....	....	....	....	....	....	....	....	....	....	....	....	....	....	....	....	....	....
	Florida	**NHL**	**5**	**1**	**0**	**1**	**10**	**0**	**0**	**0**	**3**	**33.3**	**–2**	**0**	**0.0**	**9:34**	....	....	....	....	....	....	....	....	....
	Springfield	AHL	18	1	3	4	28	....	....	....	....	....	....	....	....	....	....	....	....	....	....	....	....	....	....
	Grand Rapids	AHL	21	0	4	4	42	....	....	....	....	....	....	....	....	....	19	0	5	5	25	....	....	....	....
	NHL Totals		**43**	**3**	**2**	**5**	**94**	**0**	**0**	**0**	**31**	**9.7**		**0**	**0.0**	**13:01**	**1**	**0**	**0**	**0**	**0**	**0**	**0**	**0**	**9:07**

Traded to **Florida** by **NY Rangers** for Steven Kampfer and a conditional 7th round pick (conditions not met) in 2018 NHL Draft, November 8, 2016. Traded to **Detroit** by **Florida** with Florida's 3rd round pick (Kasper Kotkansalo) in 2017 NHL Draft for Thomas Vanek. March 1, 2017.

McKEGG, Greg
(muh-KEHG, GREHG) **PIT**

Center. Shoots left. 6', 191 lbs. Born, St.Thomas, ON, June 17, 1992. Toronto's 2nd pick, 62nd overall, in 2010 NHL Draft.

2007-08	Elgin-Mid. Chiefs	Minor-ON	64	73	53	126		....	....	....	....	....	....	....	....	....	....	....	....	....	....	....	....	....	....
	St. Thomas Stars	ON-Jr.B	3	4	1	5	2	....	....	....	....	....	....	....	....	....	....	....	....	....	....	....	....	....	....
2008-09	Erie Otters	OHL	64	8	10	18	22	....	....	....	....	....	....	....	....	....	5	2	1	3	4	....	....	....	....
2009-10	Erie Otters	OHL	67	37	48	85	32	....	....	....	....	....	....	....	....	....	4	2	1	3	0	....	....	....	....
2010-11	Erie Otters	OHL	66	49	43	92	35	....	....	....	....	....	....	....	....	....	7	4	1	5	12	....	....	....	....
	Toronto Marlies	AHL	2	1	0	1	0	....	....	....	....	....	....	....	....	....	....	....	....	....	....	....	....	....	....
2011-12	Erie Otters	OHL	35	12	22	34	32	....	....	....	....	....	....	....	....	....	....	....	....	....	....	....	....	....	....
	London Knights	OHL	30	19	22	41	22	....	....	....	....	....	....	....	....	....	15	4	7	11	2	....	....	....	....
2012-13	Toronto Marlies	AHL	61	8	15	23	22	....	....	....	....	....	....	....	....	....	9	3	3	6	10	....	....	....	....
2013-14	**Toronto**	**NHL**	**1**	**0**	**0**	**0**	**0**	**0**	**0**	**0**	**1**	**0.0**	**0**	**6**	**16.7**	**3:43**	....	....	....	....	....	....	....	....	....
	Toronto Marlies	AHL	65	19	28	47	31	....	....	....	....	....	....	....	....	....	14	3	3	6	10	....	....	....	....
2014-15	**Toronto**	**NHL**	**3**	**0**	**0**	**0**	**0**	**0**	**0**	**0**	**1**	**0.0**	**0**	**33**	**51.5**	**9:11**	....	....	....	....	....	....	....	....	....
	Toronto Marlies	AHL	62	22	15	37	39	....	....	....	....	....	....	....	....	....	5	2	0	2	12	....	....	....	....
2015-16	**Florida**	**NHL**	**15**	**2**	**0**	**2**	**2**	**0**	**0**	**0**	**14**	**14.3**	**1**	**111**	**45.1**	**8:15**	**1**	**0**	**0**	**0**	**2**	**0**	**0**	**0**	**6:02**
	Portland Pirates	AHL	47	10	13	23	22	....	....	....	....	....	....	....	....	....	3	1	0	1	2	....	....	....	....
2016-17	**Florida**	**NHL**	**31**	**3**	**3**	**6**	**11**	**0**	**0**	**0**	**28**	**10.7**	**–5**	**83**	**51.8**	**10:13**	....	....	....	....	....	....	....	....	....
	Springfield	AHL	7	2	2	4	2	....	....	....	....	....	....	....	....	....	....	....	....	....	....	....	....	....	....
	Tampa Bay	**NHL**	**15**	**0**	**1**	**1**	**11**	**0**	**0**	**0**	**8**	**0.0**	**2**	**97**	**48.5**	**9:16**	....	....	....	....	....	....	....	....	....
	NHL Totals		**65**	**5**	**4**	**9**	**24**	**0**	**0**	**0**	**52**	**9.6**		**330**	**47.9**	**9:24**	**1**	**0**	**0**	**0**	**2**	**0**	**0**	**0**	**6:02**

Traded to **Florida** by **Toronto** for Zach Hyman and future considerations (conditions not met), June 19, 2015. Claimed on waivers by **Tampa Bay** from **Florida**, February 27, 2017. Signed as a free agent by **Pittsburgh**, July 1, 2017.

McKENZIE, Curtis
(muh-KEHN-zee, KUHR-tihs) **DAL**

Left wing. Shoots left. 6'2", 205 lbs. Born, Golden, BC, February 22, 1991. Dallas' 5th pick, 159th overall, in 2009 NHL Draft.

2007-08	Penticton Vees	BCHL	49	3	7	10	81	....	....	....	....	....	....	....	....	....	7	0	1	1	9	....	....	....	....
2008-09	Penticton Vees	BCHL	53	30	34	64	90	....	....	....	....	....	....	....	....	....	10	3	7	10	81	....	....	....	....
2009-10	Miami U.	CCHA	42	6	21	27	88	....	....	....	....	....	....	....	....	....	....	....	....	....	....	....	....	....	....
2010-11	Miami U.	CCHA	37	7	5	12	57	....	....	....	....	....	....	....	....	....	....	....	....	....	....	....	....	....	....
2011-12	Miami U.	CCHA	40	5	12	17	60	....	....	....	....	....	....	....	....	....	....	....	....	....	....	....	....	....	....
2012-13	Miami U.	CCHA	39	11	13	24	80	....	....	....	....	....	....	....	....	....	....	....	....	....	....	....	....	....	....
	Texas Stars	AHL	5	0	1	1	14	....	....	....	....	....	....	....	....	....	2	0	0	0	0	....	....	....	....
2013-14	Texas Stars	AHL	75	27	38	65	92	....	....	....	....	....	....	....	....	....	21	3	11	14	21	....	....	....	....
2014-15	**Dallas**	**NHL**	**36**	**4**	**1**	**5**	**48**	**0**	**0**	**0**	**41**	**9.8**	**–8**	**8**	**37.5**	**11:32**	....	....	....	....	....	....	....	....	....
	Texas Stars	AHL	31	6	15	21	46	....	....	....	....	....	....	....	....	....	3	1	1	2	18	....	....	....	....
2015-16	**Dallas**	**NHL**	**3**	**0**	**0**	**0**	**0**	**0**	**0**	**0**	**3**	**0.0**	**–1**	**0**	**0.0**	**8:48**	**1**	**0**	**0**	**0**	**5**	**0**	**0**	**0**	**7:18**
	Texas Stars	AHL	61	24	31	55	120	....	....	....	....	....	....	....	....	....	4	1	1	2	8	....	....	....	....
2016-17	**Dallas**	**NHL**	**53**	**6**	**10**	**16**	**72**	**0**	**0**	**3**	**66**	**9.1**	**5**	**6**	**50.0**	**10:51**	....	....	....	....	....	....	....	....	....
	NHL Totals		**92**	**10**	**11**	**21**	**120**	**0**	**0**	**3**	**110**	**9.1**		**14**	**42.9**	**11:03**	**1**	**0**	**0**	**0**	**5**	**0**	**0**	**0**	**7:18**

AHL All-Rookie Team (2014) • Dudley "Red" Garrett Memorial Award (AHL – Rookie of the Year) (2014)

McLEOD, Cody
(muh-KLOWD, KOH-dee) **NSH**

Left wing. Shoots left. 6'2", 210 lbs. Born, Binscarth, MB, June 26, 1984.

99-2000	Waywayseecappo	MJHL	5	0	2	2	0	....	....	....	....	....	....	....	....	....	....	....	....	....	....	....	....	....	....
2000-01	Waywayseecappo	MJHL	59	27	29	56	42	....	....	....	....	....	....	....	....	....	....	....	....	....	....	....	....	....	....
2001-02	Portland	WHL	47	10	3	13	86	....	....	....	....	....	....	....	....	....	5	0	0	0	0	....	....	....	....
2002-03	Portland	WHL	71	15	18	33	153	....	....	....	....	....	....	....	....	....	7	1	1	2	13	....	....	....	....
2003-04	Portland	WHL	69	13	18	31	227	....	....	....	....	....	....	....	....	....	5	2	2	4	6	....	....	....	....
2004-05	Portland	WHL	70	31	29	60	195	....	....	....	....	....	....	....	....	....	7	0	3	3	8	....	....	....	....
	Adirondack	UHL	1	0	0	0	0	....	....	....	....	....	....	....	....	....	5	0	0	0	11	....	....	....	....
2005-06	Lowell	AHL	33	4	5	9	87	....	....	....	....	....	....	....	....	....	....	....	....	....	....	....	....	....	....
	San Diego Gulls	ECHL	16	4	5	9	48	....	....	....	....	....	....	....	....	....	2	2	1	3	14	....	....	....	....
2006-07	Albany River Rats	AHL	73	11	8	19	180	....	....	....	....	....	....	....	....	....	5	0	0	0	4	....	....	....	....
2007-08	**Colorado**	**NHL**	**49**	**4**	**5**	**9**	**120**	**0**	**0**	**0**	**60**	**6.7**	**–6**	**3**	**0.0**	**10:07**	**10**	**1**	**1**	**2**	**26**	**0**	**0**	**0**	**12:23**
	Lake Erie	AHL	27	6	7	13	101	....	....	....	....	....	....	....	....	....	....	....	....	....	....	....	....	....	....
2008-09	**Colorado**	**NHL**	**79**	**15**	**5**	**20**	**162**	**0**	**0**	**3**	**118**	**12.7**	**–11**	**5**	**40.0**	**11:35**	....	....	....	....	....	....	....	....	....
2009-10	**Colorado**	**NHL**	**74**	**7**	**11**	**18**	**138**	**0**	**0**	**1**	**117**	**6.0**	**–13**	**13**	**30.8**	**12:56**	**6**	**0**	**0**	**0**	**5**	**0**	**0**	**0**	**11:03**
2010-11	**Colorado**	**NHL**	**71**	**5**	**3**	**8**	**189**	**2**	**0**	**0**	**73**	**6.8**	**–7**	**8**	**37.5**	**9:47**	....	....	....	....	....	....	....	....	....
2011-12	**Colorado**	**NHL**	**75**	**6**	**5**	**11**	**164**	**0**	**0**	**0**	**62**	**9.7**	**0**	**3**	**66.7**	**7:12**	....	....	....	....	....	....	....	....	....
2012-13	**Colorado**	**NHL**	**48**	**8**	**4**	**12**	**83**	**0**	**0**	**0**	**79**	**10.1**	**4**	**17**	**41.2**	**13:05**	....	....	....	....	....	....	....	....	....
2013-14	**Colorado**	**NHL**	**71**	**5**	**8**	**13**	**122**	**0**	**1**	**0**	**76**	**6.6**	**2**	**10**	**20.0**	**10:20**	**7**	**1**	**0**	**1**	**22**	**0**	**1**	**0**	**10:50**
2014-15	**Colorado**	**NHL**	**82**	**7**	**5**	**12**	**191**	**0**	**1**	**2**	**94**	**7.4**	**–2**	**9**	**11.1**	**11:11**	....	....	....	....	....	....	....	....	....
2015-16	**Colorado**	**NHL**	**82**	**8**	**5**	**13**	**138**	**1**	**0**	**1**	**73**	**11.0**	**1**	**1**	**100.0**	**10:32**	....	....	....	....	....	....	....	....	....
2016-17	**Colorado**	**NHL**	**28**	**1**	**0**	**1**	**52**	**0**	**0**	**0**	**12**	**8.3**	**–2**	**0**	**0.0**	**5:53**	....	....	....	....	....	....	....	....	....
	Nashville	**NHL**	**31**	**4**	**1**	**5**	**93**	**0**	**0**	**0**	**18**	**22.2**	**–1**	**1**	**0.0**	**8:20**	**15**	**1**	**0**	**1**	**27**	**0**	**0**	**1**	**6:50**
	NHL Totals		**690**	**70**	**52**	**122**	**1452**	**3**	**2**	**7**	**782**	**9.0**		**70**	**31.4**	**10:23**	**38**	**3**	**1**	**4**	**80**	**0**	**1**	**1**	**9:42**

Signed as a free agent by **Colorado**, July 6, 2006. Traded to **Nashville** by **Colorado** for Felix Girard, January 13, 2017.

McNABB, Brayden
(muhk-NAB, BRAY-duhn) **VGK**

Defense. Shoots left. 6'4", 216 lbs. Born, Davidson, SK, January 21, 1991. Buffalo's 2nd pick, 66th overall, in 2009 NHL Draft.

2006-07	Notre Dame	SMHL	41	5	13	18	72	....	....	....	....	....	....	....	....	....	....	....	....	....	....	....	....	....	....
	Kootenay Ice	WHL	3	0	0	0	0	....	....	....	....	....	....	....	....	....	....	....	....	....	....	....	....	....	....
2007-08	Kootenay Ice	WHL	65	2	9	11	63	....	....	....	....	....	....	....	....	....	10	0	1	1	10	....	....	....	....
2008-09	Kootenay Ice	WHL	67	10	26	36	140	....	....	....	....	....	....	....	....	....	4	0	5	5	2	....	....	....	....
2009-10	Kootenay Ice	WHL	64	17	40	57	121	....	....	....	....	....	....	....	....	....	6	0	4	4	18	....	....	....	....
2010-11	Kootenay Ice	WHL	59	21	51	72	95	....	....	....	....	....	....	....	....	....	19	3	*24	27	37	....	....	....	....
2011-12	**Buffalo**	**NHL**	**25**	**1**	**7**	**8**	**15**	**1**	**0**	**0**	**23**	**4.3**	**–1**	**0**	**0.0**	**17:50**	....	....	....	....	....	....	....	....	....
	Rochester	AHL	45	5	25	30	31	....	....	....	....	....	....	....	....	....	3	0	1	1	0	....	....	....	....
2012-13	Rochester	AHL	62	5	31	36	50	....	....	....	....	....	....	....	....	....	....	....	....	....	....	....	....	....	....

			Regular Season														Playoffs								
Season	Club	League	GP	G	A	Pts	PIM	PP	SH	GW	S	S%	+/-	TF	F%	Min	GP	G	A	Pts	PIM	PP	SH	GW	Min
2013-14	Buffalo	NHL	12	0	0	0	6	0	0	0	10	0.0	1	0	0.0	17:14									
	Rochester	AHL	38	7	22	29	45																		
	Manchester	AHL	14	3	4	7	18										4	0	1	1	2				
2014-15	Los Angeles	NHL	71	2	22	24	52	0	0	1	74	2.7	11	1	100.0	15:54									
2015-16	Los Angeles	NHL	81	2	12	14	92	0	0	1	91	2.2	11	0	0.0	18:49	5	0	0	0	2	0	0	0	16:54
2016-17	Los Angeles	NHL	49	2	2	4	54	0	0	0	47	4.3	1	0	0.0	15:04									
	NHL Totals		238	7	43	50	219	1	0	2	245	2.9		1	100.0	16:59	5	0	0	0	2	0	0	0	16:54

WHL East First All-Star Team (2010, 2011)
Traded to **Los Angeles** by **Buffalo** with Jonathan Parker and Los Angeles' 2nd round pick (previously acquired, Los Angeles selected Alex Lintuniemi) in 2014 NHL Draft and Los Angeles' 2nd round pick (previously acquired, Los Angeles selected Erik Cernak) in 2015 NHL Draft for Nicolas Deslauriers and Hudson Fasching, March 5, 2014. Claimed by **Vegas** from **Los Angeles** in Expansion Draft, June 21, 2017.

McNEILL, Mark

Right wing. Shoots right. 6'2", 214 lbs. Born, Langley, BC, February 22, 1993. Chicago's 1st pick, 18th overall, in 2011 NHL Draft. (muhk-NEEL, MAHRK) **DAL**

			Regular Season														Playoffs								
Season	Club	League	GP	G	A	Pts	PIM	PP	SH	GW	S	S%	+/-	TF	F%	Min	GP	G	A	Pts	PIM	PP	SH	GW	Min
2008-09	SSAC Athletics	AMHL	33	21	18	39	38										4	2	0	2	2				
	Prince Albert	WHL	4	0	0	0	0																		
2009-10	Prince Albert	WHL	68	9	15	24	27																		
2010-11	Prince Albert	WHL	70	32	49	81	53										6	2	3	5	2				
2011-12	Prince Albert	WHL	69	31	40	71	48																		
	Rockford IceHogs	AHL	7	0	0	0	12																		
2012-13	Prince Albert	WHL	65	25	42	67	43										4	1	3	4	4				
	Rockford IceHogs	AHL	5	0	0	0	0																		
2013-14	Rockford IceHogs	AHL	76	18	19	37	46																		
2014-15	Rockford IceHogs	AHL	63	23	21	44	23										8	2	2	4	2				
2015-16	Chicago	NHL	1	0	0	0	0	0	0	0	0	0.0	0	1	0.0	12:44									
	Rockford IceHogs	AHL	64	25	23	48	33										3	1	1	2	0				
2016-17	Rockford IceHogs	AHL	58	6	22	28	23																		
	Dallas	NHL	1	0	0	0	0	0	0	0	1	0.0	-1	2	0.0	13:49									
	Texas Stars	AHL	21	3	8	11	6																		
	NHL Totals		2	0	0	0	0	0	0	0	1	0.0		3	0.0	13:17									

Traded to **Dallas** by **Chicago** with Dallas' 4th round pick in 2018 NHL Draft for Johnny Oduya, February 28, 2017.

McQUAID, Adam

Defense. Shoots right. 6'4", 212 lbs. Born, Charlottetown, PE, October 12, 1986. Columbus' 2nd pick, 55th overall, in 2005 NHL Draft. (muh-KWAYD, A-duhm) **BOS**

			Regular Season														Playoffs								
Season	Club	League	GP	G	A	Pts	PIM	PP	SH	GW	S	S%	+/-	TF	F%	Min	GP	G	A	Pts	PIM	PP	SH	GW	Min
2003-04	Sudbury Wolves	OHL	47	3	6	9	25										7	0	1	1	2				
2004-05	Sudbury Wolves	OHL	66	3	16	19	98										8	0	2	2	10				
2005-06	Sudbury Wolves	OHL	68	3	14	17	107										10	0	1	1	16				
2006-07	Sudbury Wolves	OHL	65	9	22	31	110										21	1	5	6	24				
2007-08	Providence Bruins	AHL	68	1	8	9	73										10	0	0	0	9				
2008-09	Providence Bruins	AHL	78	4	11	15	141										16	0	3	3	26				
2009-10	Boston	NHL	19	1	0	1	21	0	0	1	10	10.0	-5	0	0.0	10:44	9	0	0	0	6	0	0	0	10:12
	Providence Bruins	AHL	32	3	7	10	66																		
2010-11♦	Boston	NHL	67	3	12	15	96	0	0	0	46	6.5	30	0	0.0	14:52	23	0	4	4	14	0	0	0	13:01
2011-12	Boston	NHL	72	2	8	10	99	0	0	0	63	3.2	16	0	0.0	14:57									
2012-13	Boston	NHL	32	1	3	4	60	0	0	0	26	3.8	0	0	0.0	14:18	22	2	2	4	10	0	0	1	14:47
2013-14	Boston	NHL	30	1	5	6	69	0	0	0	25	4.0	12	0	0.0	16:03									
2014-15	Boston	NHL	63	1	6	7	85	0	0	0	60	1.7	-2	1	0.0	18:26									
2015-16	Boston	NHL	64	1	8	9	89	0	0	0	42	2.4	6	0	0.0	18:02									
2016-17	Boston	NHL	77	2	8	10	71	0	0	1	64	3.1	4	0	0.0	18:15	2	0	1	1	0	0	0	0	11:49
	NHL Totals		424	12	50	62	590	0	0	2	336	3.6		1	0.0	16:22	56	2	7	9	30	0	0	1	13:13

Traded to **Boston** by **Columbus** for Boston's 5th round pick (later traded to Dallas – Dallas selected Jamie Benn) in 2007 NHL Draft, May 16, 2007. • Missed majority of 2013-14 with a blood clot near his right shoulder and resulting surgery.

McRAE, Philip

Center. Shoots left. 6'2", 200 lbs. Born, Minneapolis, MN, March 15, 1990. St. Louis' 2nd pick, 33rd overall, in 2008 NHL Draft. (muh-KRAY, FIHL-ihp)

			Regular Season														Playoffs								
Season	Club	League	GP	G	A	Pts	PIM	PP	SH	GW	S	S%	+/-	TF	F%	Min	GP	G	A	Pts	PIM	PP	SH	GW	Min
2005-06	USAHNTDP	U-17	15	1	1	2	0																		
	USAHNTDP	NAHL	33	8	8	16	9										10	1	2	3	2				
2006-07	London Knights	OHL	63	2	8	10	27										16	0	0	0	6				
2007-08	London Knights	OHL	66	18	28	46	61										4	0	0	0	7				
2008-09	London Knights	OHL	59	29	31	60	54										14	5	5	10	12				
2009-10	London Knights	OHL	33	11	26	37	43																		
	Plymouth Whalers	OHL	19	5	9	14	21										9	6	9	15	11				
2010-11	St. Louis	NHL	15	1	2	3	2	0	0	0	13	7.7	-10	64	53.1	9:02									
	Peoria Rivermen	AHL	46	12	14	26	23																		
2011-12	Peoria Rivermen	AHL	71	23	16	39	26																		
2012-13	Peoria Rivermen	AHL	45	7	11	18	19																		
2013-14	Tappara Tampere	Finland	8	0	1	1	2																		
	Blues Espoo	Finland	45	8	12	20	12										7	3	1	4	2				
2014-15	Chicago Wolves	AHL	67	15	18	33	21																		
2015-16	Bakersfield	AHL	35	9	6	15	33																		
2016-17	Hartford	AHL	76	8	11	19	20																		
	NHL Totals		15	1	2	3	2	0	0	0	13	7.7		64	53.1	9:02									

Signed as a free agent by **Tappara Tampere** (Finland), July 12, 2013. Signed as a free agent by **Espoo** (Finland), October 17, 2013. Signed as a free agent by **Bakersfield** (AHL), August 7, 2015. Signed as a free agent by **Hartford** (AHL), August 24, 2016. Signed as a free agent by **Assat Pori** (Finland), June 1, 2017.

MEDVEDEV, Evgeni

Defense. Shoots left. 6'3", 187 lbs. Born, Chelyabinsk, Russia, August 27, 1987. (mehd-VEH-dehv, ehv-GEH-nee)

			Regular Season														Playoffs								
Season	Club	League	GP	G	A	Pts	PIM	PP	SH	GW	S	S%	+/-	TF	F%	Min	GP	G	A	Pts	PIM	PP	SH	GW	Min
2002-03	Mechel	Russia	11	0	0	0	6																		
2003-04	Chelyabinsk	Russia-2	34	7	11	18	24																		
2004-05	Chelyabinsk	Russia-2	44	5	6	11	42										5	1	0	1	8				
2005-06	Cherepovets	Russia	49	4	5	9	54										2	0	0	0	6				
2006-07	Cherepovets	Russia	50	10	10	20	115										3	0	0	0	6				
2007-08	Ak Bars Kazan	Russia	41	6	20	26	89										8	2	1	3	4				
2008-09	Ak Bars Kazan	KHL	48	8	11	19	64										21	2	5	7	32				
2009-10	Ak Bars Kazan	KHL	48	2	10	12	40										17	2	3	5	6				
2010-11	Ak Bars Kazan	KHL	49	4	16	20	26										9	0	3	3	6				
2011-12	Ak Bars Kazan	KHL	45	5	19	24	36										6	0	1	1	6				
2012-13	Ak Bars Kazan	KHL	49	6	20	26	44										18	0	7	7	12				
2013-14	Ak Bars Kazan	KHL	50	3	21	24	55										5	1	0	1	31				
	Russia	Olympics	5	0	1	1	2																		
2014-15	Ak Bars Kazan	KHL	43	3	13	16	26										14	1	3	4	12				
2015-16	Philadelphia	NHL	45	4	8	12	34	1	0	1	71	5.6	5	0	0.0	18:50	12	2	6	8	6				
2016-17	Omsk	KHL	56	2	20	22	36																		
	NHL Totals		45	4	8	12	34	1	0	1	71	5.6		0	0.0	18:50									

Signed as a free agent by **Philadelphia**, May 20, 2015. Signed as a free agent by **Omsk** (KHL), July 9, 2016.

Season	Club	League	GP	G	A	Pts	PIM	PP	SH	GW	S	S%	+/-	TF	F%	Min	GP	G	A	Pts	PIM	PP	SH	GW	Min
			Regular Season														Playoffs								

MEGAN, Wade (MEE-guhn, WAYD) ST.L.

Center. Shoots left. 6'1", 195 lbs. Born, Canton, NY, July 22, 1990. Florida's 6th pick, 138th overall, in 2009 NHL Draft.

Season	Club	League	GP	G	A	Pts	PIM	PP	SH	GW	S	S%	+/-	TF	F%	Min	GP	G	A	Pts	PIM	PP	SH	GW	Min
2007-08	Kent Prep School	High-CT	34	24	29	53	....	....	....	....	....	....	....	....	....	....	....	....	....	....	....	....	....	....	....
2008-09	Kent Prep School	High-CT	32	27	36	63	18	....	....	....	....	....	....	....	....	....	....	....	....	....	....	....	....	....	....
	Neponset Valley	Minor-MA	16	8	8	16	....	....	....	....	....	....	....	....	....	....	....	....	....	....	....	....	....	....	....
2009-10	Boston University	H-East	35	5	7	12	22	....	....	....	....	....	....	....	....	....	....	....	....	....	....	....	....	....	....
2010-11	Boston University	H-East	39	8	5	13	32	....	....	....	....	....	....	....	....	....	....	....	....	....	....	....	....	....	....
2011-12	Boston University	H-East	39	20	9	29	57	....	....	....	....	....	....	....	....	....	....	....	....	....	....	....	....	....	....
2012-13	Boston University	H-East	38	16	13	29	50	....	....	....	....	....	....	....	....	....	....	....	....	....	....	....	....	....	....
	San Antonio	AHL	13	1	0	1	0	....	....	....	....	....	....	....	....	....	....	....	....	....	....	....	....	....	....
2013-14	San Antonio	AHL	43	11	6	17	18	....	....	....	....	....	....	....	....	....	....	....	....	....	....	....	....	....	....
	Cincinnati	ECHL	16	13	7	20	11	....	....	....	....	....	....	....	....	....	22	10	3	13	12	....	....	....	....
2014-15	San Antonio	AHL	59	8	5	13	44	....	....	....	....	....	....	....	....	....	3	0	0	0	0	....	....	....	....
	Cincinnati	ECHL	5	4	3	7	12	....	....	....	....	....	....	....	....	....	....	....	....	....	....	....	....	....	....
2015-16	Portland Pirates	AHL	75	14	9	23	53	....	....	....	....	....	....	....	....	....	5	0	0	0	10	....	....	....	....
2016-17	**St. Louis**	**NHL**	**3**	**1**	**0**	**1**	**0**	**0**	**0**	**0**	**6**	**16.7**	**1**	**27**	**48.2**	**8:48**	....	....	....	....	....	....	....	....	....
	Chicago Wolves	AHL	73	*33	33	66	57	....	....	....	....	....	....	....	....	....	5	0	1	1	4	....	....	....	....
	NHL Totals		**3**	**1**	**0**	**1**	**0**	**0**	**0**	**0**	**6**	**16.7**		**27**	**48.1**	**8:48**	....	....	....	....	....	....	....	....	....

AHL First All-Star Team (2017)

Signed as a free agent by **Portland** (AHL), June 9, 2015. Signed as a free agent by **St. Louis**, July 2, 2016.

MEGNA, Jaycob (MEHG-na, JAY-kuhb) ANA

Defense. Shoots left. 6'6", 225 lbs. Born, Plantation, FL, December 10, 1992. Anaheim's 8th pick, 210th overall, in 2012 NHL Draft.

Season	Club	League	GP	G	A	Pts	PIM	PP	SH	GW	S	S%	+/-	TF	F%	Min	GP	G	A	Pts	PIM	PP	SH	GW	Min
2009-10	Team Illinois	T1EHL	48	1	12	13	8	....	....	....	....	....	....	....	....	....	....	....	....	....	....	....	....	....	....
	Team Illinois	Other	25	1	19	20	4	....	....	....	....	....	....	....	....	....	....	....	....	....	....	....	....	....	....
2010-11	Muskegon	USHL	55	1	17	18	24	....	....	....	....	....	....	....	....	....	6	0	3	3	0	....	....	....	....
2011-12	Nebraska-Omaha	WCHA	35	2	3	5	8	....	....	....	....	....	....	....	....	....	....	....	....	....	....	....	....	....	....
2012-13	Nebraska-Omaha	WCHA	38	2	5	7	14	....	....	....	....	....	....	....	....	....	....	....	....	....	....	....	....	....	....
2013-14	Nebraska-Omaha	NCHC	32	0	10	10	18	....	....	....	....	....	....	....	....	....	....	....	....	....	....	....	....	....	....
	Norfolk Admirals	AHL	2	0	0	0	2	....	....	....	....	....	....	....	....	....	....	....	....	....	....	....	....	....	....
2014-15	Norfolk Admirals	AHL	32	1	4	5	4	....	....	....	....	....	....	....	....	....	....	....	....	....	....	....	....	....	....
2015-16	San Diego Gulls	AHL	67	0	12	12	14	....	....	....	....	....	....	....	....	....	9	1	0	1	0	....	....	....	....
2016-17	**Anaheim**	**NHL**	**1**	**0**	**0**	**0**	**0**	**0**	**0**	**0**	**0**	**0.0**	**1**	**0**	**0.0**	**15:20**	....	....	....	....	....	....	....	....	....
	San Diego Gulls	AHL	62	5	22	27	37	....	....	....	....	....	....	....	....	....	10	0	4	4	8	....	....	....	....
	NHL Totals		**1**	**0**	**0**	**0**	**0**	**0**	**0**	**0**	**0**	**0.0**		**0**	**0.0**	**15:20**	....	....	....	....	....	....	....	....	....

WCHA All-Rookie Team (2012)

MEGNA, Jayson (MEHG-na, JAY-suhn) VAN

Right wing. Shoots right. 6'1", 195 lbs. Born, Fort Lauderdale, FL, February 1, 1990.

Season	Club	League	GP	G	A	Pts	PIM	PP	SH	GW	S	S%	+/-	TF	F%	Min	GP	G	A	Pts	PIM	PP	SH	GW	Min
2009-10	Cedar Rapids	USHL	56	11	15	26	62	....	....	....	....	....	....	....	....	....	5	0	0	0	6	....	....	....	....
2010-11	Cedar Rapids	USHL	60	30	28	58	45	....	....	....	....	....	....	....	....	....	8	4	3	7	4	....	....	....	....
2011-12	Nebraska-Omaha	WCHA	38	13	18	31	27	....	....	....	....	....	....	....	....	....	....	....	....	....	....	....	....	....	....
2012-13	Wilkes-Barre	AHL	56	5	7	12	28	....	....	....	....	....	....	....	....	....	12	2	3	5	0	....	....	....	....
2013-14	**Pittsburgh**	**NHL**	**36**	**5**	**4**	**9**	**6**	**0**	**0**	**2**	**36**	**13.9**	**1**	**10**	**20.0**	**10:29**	**2**	**0**	**0**	**0**	**0**	**0**	**0**	**0**	**9:10**
	Wilkes-Barre	AHL	25	9	6	15	4	....	....	....	....	....	....	....	....	....	13	1	2	3	4	....	....	....	....
2014-15	**Pittsburgh**	**NHL**	**12**	**0**	**1**	**1**	**14**	**0**	**0**	**0**	**13**	**0.0**	**–2**	**0**	**0.0**	**11:02**	....	....	....	....	....	....	....	....	....
	Wilkes-Barre	AHL	63	26	13	39	40	....	....	....	....	....	....	....	....	....	8	1	4	5	2	....	....	....	....
2015-16	**NY Rangers**	**NHL**	**6**	**1**	**1**	**2**	**2**	**0**	**0**	**0**	**9**	**11.1**	**–1**	**1**	**100.0**	**12:15**	....	....	....	....	....	....	....	....	....
	Hartford	AHL	68	15	29	44	22	....	....	....	....	....	....	....	....	....	....	....	....	....	....	....	....	....	....
2016-17	**Vancouver**	**NHL**	**58**	**4**	**4**	**8**	**6**	**0**	**0**	**0**	**72**	**5.6**	**–4**	**16**	**12.5**	**12:26**	....	....	....	....	....	....	....	....	....
	Utica Comets	AHL	4	1	2	3	0	....	....	....	....	....	....	....	....	....	....	....	....	....	....	....	....	....	....
	NHL Totals		**112**	**10**	**10**	**20**	**28**	**0**	**0**	**2**	**130**	**7.7**		**27**	**18.5**	**11:39**	**2**	**0**	**0**	**0**	**0**	**0**	**0**	**0**	**9:10**

USHL First All-Star Team (2011)

Signed as a free agent by **Pittsburgh**, August 1, 2012. Signed as a free agent by **NY Rangers**, July 1, 2015. Signed as a free agent by **Vancouver**, July 1, 2016.

MEIER, Timo (MIGH-uhr, TEE-moh) S.J.

Right wing. Shoots left. 6', 210 lbs. Born, St. Gallen, Switzerland, October 8, 1996. San Jose's 1st pick, 9th overall, in 2015 NHL Draft.

Season	Club	League	GP	G	A	Pts	PIM	PP	SH	GW	S	S%	+/-	TF	F%	Min	GP	G	A	Pts	PIM	PP	SH	GW	Min
2009-10	SC Herisau U17	Swiss-U17	20	15	9	24	18	....	....	....	....	....	....	....	....	....	....	....	....	....	....	....	....	....	....
2010-11	Pikes U17	Swiss-U17	23	7	2	9	8	....	....	....	....	....	....	....	....	....	2	0	0	0	2	....	....	....	....
2011-12	Pikes U17	Swiss-U17	29	23	23	46	22	....	....	....	....	....	....	....	....	....	10	10	6	16	8	....	....	....	....
	Pikes II	Swiss-6	1	2	2	4	0	....	....	....	....	....	....	....	....	....	....	....	....	....	....	....	....	....	....
2012-13	Rapperswil U17	Swiss-U17	10	11	17	28	2	....	....	....	....	....	....	....	....	....	2	1	2	3	0	....	....	....	....
	Rapperswil Jr.	Swiss-Jr.	39	16	22	38	60	....	....	....	....	....	....	....	....	....	....	....	....	....	....	....	....	....	....
2013-14	Halifax	QMJHL	66	17	17	34	48	....	....	....	....	....	....	....	....	....	12	1	3	4	8	....	....	....	....
2014-15	Halifax	QMJHL	61	44	46	90	59	....	....	....	....	....	....	....	....	....	14	10	11	21	18	....	....	....	....
2015-16	Halifax	QMJHL	23	11	25	36	22	....	....	....	....	....	....	....	....	....	....	....	....	....	....	....	....	....	....
	Rouyn-Noranda	QMJHL	29	23	28	51	24	....	....	....	....	....	....	....	....	....	18	11	12	23	30	....	....	....	....
2016-17	**San Jose**	**NHL**	**34**	**3**	**3**	**6**	**10**	**0**	**0**	**1**	**85**	**3.5**	**1**	**5**	**20.0**	**12:28**	**5**	**0**	**0**	**0**	**2**	**0**	**0**	**0**	**12:04**
	San Jose	AHL	33	14	9	23	40	....	....	....	....	....	....	....	....	....	14	4	3	7	41	....	....	....	....
	NHL Totals		**34**	**3**	**3**	**6**	**10**	**0**	**0**	**1**	**85**	**3.5**		**5**	**20.0**	**12:28**	**5**	**0**	**0**	**0**	**2**	**0**	**0**	**0**	**12:04**

QMJHL Second All-Star Team (2015)

MELCHIORI, Julian (mehl-KEE-awr-ee, JOO-lee-ehn) WPG

Defense. Shoots left. 6'5", 214 lbs. Born, Richmond Hill, ON, December 6, 1991. Atlanta's 2nd pick, 87th overall, in 2010 NHL Draft.

Season	Club	League	GP	G	A	Pts	PIM	PP	SH	GW	S	S%	+/-	TF	F%	Min	GP	G	A	Pts	PIM	PP	SH	GW	Min
2007-08	Tor. Marlboros	GTHL	43	2	13	15	36	....	....	....	....	....	....	....	....	....	....	....	....	....	....	....	....	....	....
2008-09	Newmarket	ON-Jr.A	48	2	20	22	34	....	....	....	....	....	....	....	....	....	9	1	2	3	14	....	....	....	....
2009-10	Newmarket	ON-Jr.A	39	7	16	23	16	....	....	....	....	....	....	....	....	....	20	2	9	11	10	....	....	....	....
2010-11	Kitchener Rangers	OHL	63	1	18	19	55	....	....	....	....	....	....	....	....	....	3	0	0	0	0	....	....	....	....
2011-12	Kitchener Rangers	OHL	35	2	17	19	42	....	....	....	....	....	....	....	....	....	....	....	....	....	....	....	....	....	....
	Oshawa Generals	OHL	26	0	17	17	22	....	....	....	....	....	....	....	....	....	6	2	1	3	2	....	....	....	....
	St. John's IceCaps	AHL	1	0	0	0	0	....	....	....	....	....	....	....	....	....	....	....	....	....	....	....	....	....	....
2012-13	St. John's IceCaps	AHL	52	1	7	8	39	....	....	....	....	....	....	....	....	....	....	....	....	....	....	....	....	....	....
2013-14	**Winnipeg**	**NHL**	**1**	**0**	**0**	**0**	**0**	**0**	**0**	**0**	**0**	**0.0**	**–1**	**0**	**0.0**	**8:41**	....	....	....	....	....	....	....	....	....
	St. John's IceCaps	AHL	50	1	10	11	32	....	....	....	....	....	....	....	....	....	....	....	....	....	....	....	....	....	....
2014-15	St. John's IceCaps	AHL	70	1	5	6	54	....	....	....	....	....	....	....	....	....	....	....	....	....	....	....	....	....	....
2015-16	**Winnipeg**	**NHL**	**11**	**0**	**0**	**0**	**0**	**0**	**0**	**0**	**12**	**0.0**	**1**	**0**	**0.0**	**13:36**	....	....	....	....	....	....	....	....	....
	Manitoba Moose	AHL	62	3	4	7	46	....	....	....	....	....	....	....	....	....	....	....	....	....	....	....	....	....	....
2016-17	**Winnipeg**	**NHL**	**18**	**0**	**2**	**2**	**8**	**0**	**0**	**0**	**15**	**0.0**	**0**	**0**	**0.0**	**18:22**	....	....	....	....	....	....	....	....	....
	Manitoba Moose	AHL	40	2	6	8	18	....	....	....	....	....	....	....	....	....	....	....	....	....	....	....	....	....	....
	NHL Totals		**30**	**0**	**2**	**2**	**8**	**0**	**0**	**0**	**27**	**0.0**		**0**	**0.0**	**16:18**	....	....	....	....	....	....	....	....	....

• Transferred to **Winnipeg** after **Atlanta** franchise relocated, June 21, 2011.

MERRILL, Jon (MAIR-ihl, JAWN) VGK

Defense. Shoots left. 6'3", 205 lbs. Born, Oklahoma City, OK, February 3, 1992. New Jersey's 1st pick, 38th overall, in 2010 NHL Draft.

Season	Club	League	GP	G	A	Pts	PIM	PP	SH	GW	S	S%	+/-	TF	F%	Min	GP	G	A	Pts	PIM	PP	SH	GW	Min
2007-08	Det. Caesars	MWEHL	25	2	9	11	26	....	....	....	....	....	....	....	....	....	....	....	....	....	....	....	....	....	....
	Little Caesars	Minor-MI	....	7	21	28	....	....	....	....	....	....	....	....	....	....	....	....	....	....	....	....	....	....	....
2008-09	USAHNTDP	NAHL	26	2	2	4	14	....	....	....	....	....	....	....	....	....	....	....	....	....	....	....	....	....	....
	USAHNTDP	U-17	8	0	1	1	6	....	....	....	....	....	....	....	....	....	....	....	....	....	....	....	....	....	....
	USAHNTDP	U-18	9	1	2	3	4	....	....	....	....	....	....	....	....	....	....	....	....	....	....	....	....	....	....
2009-10	USAHNTDP	USHL	22	1	8	9	12	....	....	....	....	....	....	....	....	....	....	....	....	....	....	....	....	....	....
	USAHNTDP	U-18	34	4	19	23	6	....	....	....	....	....	....	....	....	....	....	....	....	....	....	....	....	....	....
2010-11	U. of Michigan	CCHA	42	7	18	25	16	....	....	....	....	....	....	....	....	....	....	....	....	....	....	....	....	....	....

			Regular Season														Playoffs								
Season	Club	League	GP	G	A	Pts	PIM	PP	SH	GW	S	S%	+/-	TF	F%	Min	GP	G	A	Pts	PIM	PP	SH	GW	Min
2011-12	U. of Michigan	CCHA	19	2	9	11	15	....	....	....	....	....	....	....	....	....	....	....	....	....	....	....	....	....	....
2012-13	U. of Michigan	CCHA	21	2	9	11	14	....	....	....	....	....	....	....	....	....	....	....	....	....	....	....	....	....	....
	Albany Devils	AHL	12	1	7	8	4	....	....	....	....	....	....	....	....	....	....	....	....	....	....	....	....	....	....
2013-14	**New Jersey**	**NHL**	**52**	**2**	**9**	**11**	**12**	**0**	**0**	**2**	**45**	**4.4**	**–3**	**0**	**0.0**	**19:14**	....	....	....	....	....	....	....	....	....
	Albany Devils	AHL	15	2	8	10	0	....	....	....	....	....	....	....	....	....	4	1	1	2	10	....	....	....	....
2014-15	**New Jersey**	**NHL**	**66**	**2**	**12**	**14**	**24**	**2**	**0**	**0**	**47**	**4.3**	**–14**	**0**	**0.0**	**20:33**	....	....	....	....	....	....	....	....	....
2015-16	**New Jersey**	**NHL**	**47**	**1**	**4**	**5**	**28**	**0**	**0**	**1**	**30**	**3.3**	**–15**	**0**	**0.0**	**16:54**	....	....	....	....	....	....	....	....	....
2016-17	**New Jersey**	**NHL**	**51**	**1**	**5**	**6**	**24**	**0**	**0**	**0**	**48**	**2.1**	**–9**	**0**	**0.0**	**18:34**	....	....	....	....	....	....	....	....	....
	NHL Totals		**216**	**6**	**30**	**36**	**88**	**2**	**0**	**3**	**170**	**3.5**		**0**	**0.0**	**18:58**	....	....	....	....	....	....	....	....	....

CCHA All-Rookie Team (2011) • CCHA Second All-Star Team (2011) • NCAA Championship All-Tournament Team (2011)

Signed as a free agent by **New Jersey**, July 1, 2016. Claimed by **Vegas** from **New Jersey** in Expansion Draft, June 21, 2017.

MERSCH, Michael

(MUHRSH, MIGH-kuhl) **L.A.**

Left wing. Shoots left. 6'2", 218 lbs. Born, Park Ridge, IL, October 2, 1992. Los Angeles' 4th pick, 110th overall, in 2011 NHL Draft.

Season	Club	League	GP	G	A	Pts	PIM	PP	SH	GW	S	S%	+/-	TF	F%	Min	GP	G	A	Pts	PIM	PP	SH	GW	Min
2007-08	Team Illinois	MWEHL	31	13	16	29	46	....	....	....	....	....	....	....	....	....	....	....	....	....	....	....	....	....	....
	Team Illinois	Other	....	22	24	46	29	....	....	....	....	....	....	....	....	....	....	....	....	....	....	....	....	....	....
2008-09	USAHNTDP	NAHL	42	15	13	28	50	....	....	....	....	....	....	....	....	....	9	5	2	7	4	....	....	....	....
	USAHNTDP	U-17	14	7	4	11	4	....	....	....	....	....	....	....	....	....	....	....	....	....	....	....	....	....	....
2009-10	USAHNTDP	USHL	26	4	4	8	22	....	....	....	....	....	....	....	....	....	....	....	....	....	....	....	....	....	....
	USAHNTDP	U-18	23	0	6	6	8	....	....	....	....	....	....	....	....	....	....	....	....	....	....	....	....	....	....
2010-11	U. of Wisconsin	WCHA	41	8	11	19	32	....	....	....	....	....	....	....	....	....	....	....	....	....	....	....	....	....	....
2011-12	U. of Wisconsin	WCHA	37	14	16	30	37	....	....	....	....	....	....	....	....	....	....	....	....	....	....	....	....	....	....
2012-13	U. of Wisconsin	WCHA	42	23	13	36	22	....	....	....	....	....	....	....	....	....	....	....	....	....	....	....	....	....	....
2013-14	U. of Wisconsin	Big Ten	37	*22	13	35	18	....	....	....	....	....	....	....	....	....	....	....	....	....	....	....	....	....	....
	Manchester	AHL	7	2	1	3	2	....	....	....	....	....	....	....	....	....	4	0	1	1	2	....	....	....	....
2014-15	Manchester	AHL	76	22	23	45	25	....	....	....	....	....	....	....	....	....	18	13	9	22	8	....	....	....	....
2015-16	**Los Angeles**	**NHL**	**17**	**1**	**2**	**3**	**0**	**0**	**0**	**0**	**23**	**4.3**	**1**	**4**	**25.0**	**10:23**	....	....	....	....	....	....	....	....	....
	Ontario Reign	AHL	52	24	19	43	26	....	....	....	....	....	....	....	....	....	13	2	4	6	4	....	....	....	....
2016-17	Ontario Reign	AHL	48	16	17	33	46	....	....	....	....	....	....	....	....	....	5	0	3	3	0	....	....	....	....
	NHL Totals		**17**	**1**	**2**	**3**	**0**	**0**	**0**	**0**	**23**	**4.3**		**4**	**25.0**	**10:23**	....	....	....	....	....	....	....	....	....

Big Ten First All-Star Team (2014) • NCAA West Second All-American Team (2014)

METHOT, Marc

(meh-THAWT, MAHRK) **DAL**

Defense. Shoots left. 6'3", 228 lbs. Born, Ottawa, ON, June 21, 1985. Columbus' 7th pick, 168th overall, in 2003 NHL Draft.

Season	Club	League	GP	G	A	Pts	PIM	PP	SH	GW	S	S%	+/-	TF	F%	Min	GP	G	A	Pts	PIM	PP	SH	GW	Min
2001-02	Kanata Valley	ON-Jr.A	50	3	10	13	22	....	....	....	....	....	....	....	....	....	11	0	1	1	24	....	....	....	....
2002-03	London Knights	OHL	68	2	13	15	46	....	....	....	....	....	....	....	....	....	14	2	4	6	6	....	....	....	....
2003-04	London Knights	OHL	63	2	9	11	66	....	....	....	....	....	....	....	....	....	15	0	3	3	18	....	....	....	....
2004-05	London Knights	OHL	67	4	12	16	88	....	....	....	....	....	....	....	....	....	18	2	1	3	32	....	....	....	....
2005-06	Syracuse Crunch	AHL	70	2	11	13	75	....	....	....	....	....	....	....	....	....	5	0	0	0	8	....	....	....	....
2006-07	**Columbus**	**NHL**	**20**	**0**	**4**	**4**	**12**	**0**	**0**	**0**	**11**	**0.0**	**5**	**0**	**0.0**	**14:38**	....	....	....	....	....	....	....	....	....
	Syracuse Crunch	AHL	59	1	15	16	58	....	....	....	....	....	....	....	....	....	....	....	....	....	....	....	....	....	....
2007-08	**Columbus**	**NHL**	**9**	**0**	**0**	**0**	**8**	**0**	**0**	**0**	**9**	**0.0**	**–1**	**0**	**0.0**	**14:14**	....	....	....	....	....	....	....	....	....
	Syracuse Crunch	AHL	66	7	6	13	130	....	....	....	....	....	....	....	....	....	13	0	6	6	14	....	....	....	....
2008-09	**Columbus**	**NHL**	**66**	**4**	**13**	**17**	**55**	**0**	**0**	**0**	**58**	**6.9**	**7**	**0**	**0.0**	**17:57**	**4**	**0**	**0**	**0**	**2**	**0**	**0**	**0**	**16:15**
2009-10	**Columbus**	**NHL**	**60**	**2**	**6**	**8**	**51**	**0**	**0**	**0**	**42**	**4.8**	**–8**	**0**	**0.0**	**19:31**	....	....	....	....	....	....	....	....	....
2010-11	**Columbus**	**NHL**	**74**	**0**	**15**	**15**	**58**	**0**	**0**	**0**	**58**	**0.0**	**2**	**0**	**0.0**	**19:53**	....	....	....	....	....	....	....	....	....
2011-12	**Columbus**	**NHL**	**46**	**1**	**6**	**7**	**24**	**0**	**0**	**0**	**42**	**2.4**	**–11**	**0**	**0.0**	**20:03**	....	....	....	....	....	....	....	....	....
2012-13	**Ottawa**	**NHL**	**47**	**2**	**9**	**11**	**31**	**0**	**0**	**0**	**53**	**3.8**	**2**	**0**	**0.0**	**22:14**	**10**	**1**	**4**	**5**	**6**	**0**	**0**	**1**	**22:44**
2013-14	**Ottawa**	**NHL**	**75**	**6**	**17**	**23**	**28**	**0**	**0**	**1**	**117**	**5.1**	**0**	**0**	**0.0**	**21:45**	....	....	....	....	....	....	....	....	....
2014-15	**Ottawa**	**NHL**	**45**	**1**	**10**	**11**	**18**	**0**	**0**	**0**	**49**	**2.0**	**22**	**1**	**0.0**	**22:40**	**6**	**0**	**0**	**0**	**6**	**0**	**0**	**0**	**23:48**
	Binghamton	AHL	1	0	0	0	0	....	....	....	....	....	....	....	....	....	....	....	....	....	....	....	....	....	....
2015-16	**Ottawa**	**NHL**	**69**	**5**	**7**	**12**	**34**	**0**	**0**	**0**	**74**	**6.8**	**12**	**0**	**0.0**	**20:39**	....	....	....	....	....	....	....	....	....
2016-17	**Ottawa**	**NHL**	**68**	**0**	**12**	**12**	**24**	**0**	**0**	**0**	**69**	**0.0**	**13**	**0**	**0.0**	**19:49**	**18**	**2**	**2**	**4**	**10**	**0**	**0**	**1**	**22:13**
	NHL Totals		**579**	**21**	**99**	**120**	**343**	**0**	**0**	**1**	**582**	**3.6**		**1**	**0.0**	**20:06**	**38**	**3**	**6**	**9**	**24**	**0**	**0**	**2**	**21:59**

Traded to **Ottawa** by **Columbus** for Nick Foligno, July 1, 2012. Claimed by **Vegas** from **Ottawa** in Expansion Draft, June 21, 2017. Traded to **Dallas** by **Vegas** for Dylan Ferguson and Dallas's 2nd round pick in 2020 NHL Draft, June 26, 2017.

MICHALEK, Milan

(mih-KHAL-ihk, MEE-lan)

Right wing. Shoots left. 6'2", 227 lbs. Born, Jindrichuv Hradec, Czech., December 7, 1984. San Jose's 1st pick, 6th overall, in 2003 NHL Draft.

Season	Club	League	GP	G	A	Pts	PIM	PP	SH	GW	S	S%	+/-	TF	F%	Min	GP	G	A	Pts	PIM	PP	SH	GW	Min
99-2000	C. Budejovice Jr.	CzRep-Jr.	48	16	26	42	42	....	....	....	....	....	....	....	....	....	6	3	1	4	4	....	....	....	....
2000-01	C. Budejovice Jr.	CzRep-Jr.	30	10	13	23	30	....	....	....	....	....	....	....	....	....	4	1	3	4	2	....	....	....	....
	C. Budejovice	CzRep	5	0	0	0	0	....	....	....	....	....	....	....	....	....	....	....	....	....	....	....	....	....	....
2001-02	C. Budejovice	CzRep	47	6	11	17	12	....	....	....	....	....	....	....	....	....	....	....	....	....	....	....	....	....	....
	C. Budejovice Jr.	CzRep-Jr.	5	3	2	5	4	....	....	....	....	....	....	....	....	....	7	5	4	9	14	....	....	....	....
2002-03	C. Budejovice	CzRep	46	3	5	8	14	....	....	....	....	....	....	....	....	....	4	1	0	1	2	....	....	....	....
	Kladno	CzRep-2	....	....	....	....	....	....	....	....	....	....	....	....	....	....	6	2	2	4	16	....	....	....	....
2003-04	**San Jose**	**NHL**	**2**	**1**	**0**	**1**	**4**	**0**	**0**	**0**	**1**	**100.0**	**1**	**0**	**0.0**	**9:05**	....	....	....	....	....	....	....	....	....
	Cleveland Barons	AHL	7	2	2	4	4	....	....	....	....	....	....	....	....	....	....	....	....	....	....	....	....	....	....
2004-05			DID NOT PLAY																						
2005-06	**San Jose**	**NHL**	**81**	**17**	**18**	**35**	**45**	**4**	**0**	**2**	**159**	**10.7**	**1**	**4**	**0.0**	**15:46**	**9**	**1**	**4**	**5**	**8**	**1**	**0**	**0**	**15:11**
2006-07	**San Jose**	**NHL**	**78**	**26**	**40**	**66**	**36**	**11**	**0**	**9**	**191**	**13.6**	**17**	**11**	**18.2**	**16:46**	**11**	**4**	**2**	**6**	**4**	**0**	**0**	**1**	**18:50**
2007-08	**San Jose**	**NHL**	**79**	**24**	**31**	**55**	**47**	**5**	**1**	**8**	**233**	**10.3**	**19**	**10**	**60.0**	**18:05**	**13**	**4**	**0**	**4**	**4**	**1**	**0**	**1**	**17:34**
2008-09	**San Jose**	**NHL**	**77**	**23**	**34**	**57**	**52**	**6**	**0**	**6**	**179**	**12.8**	**11**	**30**	**46.7**	**18:27**	**6**	**1**	**0**	**1**	**2**	**1**	**0**	**0**	**19:22**
2009-10	**Ottawa**	**NHL**	**66**	**22**	**12**	**34**	**18**	**8**	**2**	**3**	**163**	**13.5**	**–12**	**8**	**50.0**	**18:15**	**1**	**0**	**0**	**0**	**0**	**0**	**0**	**0**	**12:08**
	Czech Republic	Olympics	5	2	0	2	0	....	....	....	....	....	....	....	....	....	....	....	....	....	....	....	....	....	....
2010-11	**Ottawa**	**NHL**	**66**	**18**	**15**	**33**	**49**	**1**	**4**	**0**	**167**	**10.8**	**–12**	**13**	**30.8**	**18:04**	....	....	....	....	....	....	....	....	....
2011-12	**Ottawa**	**NHL**	**77**	**35**	**25**	**60**	**32**	**10**	**1**	**3**	**212**	**16.5**	**4**	**6**	**16.7**	**19:33**	**7**	**1**	**1**	**2**	**4**	**0**	**0**	**0**	**21:54**
2012-13	C. Budejovice	CzRep	21	13	11	24	26	....	....	....	....	....	....	....	....	....	....	....	....	....	....	....	....	....	....
	Ottawa	**NHL**	**23**	**4**	**10**	**14**	**17**	**0**	**0**	**0**	**58**	**6.9**	**8**	**4**	**50.0**	**18:11**	**10**	**3**	**2**	**5**	**2**	**0**	**1**	**0**	**17:51**
2013-14	**Ottawa**	**NHL**	**82**	**17**	**22**	**39**	**41**	**4**	**0**	**1**	**169**	**10.1**	**–25**	**14**	**42.9**	**17:35**	....	....	....	....	....	....	....	....	....
	Czech Republic	Olympics	5	0	0	0	0	....	....	....	....	....	....	....	....	....	....	....	....	....	....	....	....	....	....
2014-15	**Ottawa**	**NHL**	**66**	**13**	**21**	**34**	**33**	**5**	**1**	**1**	**130**	**10.0**	**3**	**23**	**47.8**	**16:22**	**6**	**1**	**0**	**1**	**4**	**0**	**0**	**0**	**16:44**
2015-16	**Ottawa**	**NHL**	**32**	**6**	**4**	**10**	**12**	**3**	**0**	**0**	**56**	**10.7**	**1**	**5**	**40.0**	**16:48**	....	....	....	....	....	....	....	....	....
	Toronto	**NHL**	**13**	**1**	**5**	**6**	**6**	**0**	**0**	**0**	**8**	**12.5**	**–1**	**3**	**33.3**	**14:25**	....	....	....	....	....	....	....	....	....
2016-17	**Toronto**	**NHL**	**5**	**1**	**1**	**2**	**2**	**0**	**0**	**0**	**6**	**16.7**	**–2**	**1**	**0.0**	**14:16**	....	....	....	....	....	....	....	....	....
	Toronto Marlies	AHL	16	2	3	5	20	....	....	....	....	....	....	....	....	....	....	....	....	....	....	....	....	....	....
	NHL Totals		**747**	**208**	**238**	**446**	**394**	**57**	**9**	**33**	**1732**	**12.0**		**132**	**40.2**	**17:32**	**63**	**15**	**9**	**24**	**28**	**3**	**1**	**2**	**17:59**

Played in NHL All-Star Game (2012)

• Missed majority of 2003-04 due to knee injury vs. Calgary, October 11, 2003. Traded to **Ottawa** by **San Jose** with Jonathan Cheechoo and San Jose's 2nd round pick (later traded to NY Islanders, later traded to Chicago - Chicago selected Kent Simpson) in 2010 NHL Draft for Dany Heatley and Ottawa's 5th round pick (Isaac MacLeod) in 2010 NHL Draft, September 12, 2009. Signed as a free agent by **Ceske Budejovice** (CzRep), October 28, 2012. Traded to **Toronto** by **Ottawa** with Jared Cowen, Colin Greening, Tobias Lindberg and Ottawa's 2nd round pick (Eemeli Rasanen) in 2017 NHL Draft for Dion Phaneuf, Matt Frattin, Casey Bailey, Ryan Rupert and Cody Donaghey, February 9, 2016. • Missed majority of 2016-17 due to recurring knee injury.

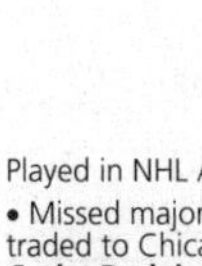

MICHALEK, Zbynek

(mih-KHAL-ihk, z'BIGH-nehk)

Defense. Shoots right. 6'2", 210 lbs. Born, Jindrichuv Hradec, Czech., December 23, 1982.

Season	Club	League	GP	G	A	Pts	PIM	PP	SH	GW	S	S%	+/-	TF	F%	Min	GP	G	A	Pts	PIM	PP	SH	GW	Min
99-2000	Karlovy Vary Jr.	CzRep-Jr.	40	2	10	12	20	....	....	....	....	....	....	....	....	....	....	....	....	....	....	....	....	....	....
2000-01	Shawinigan	QMJHL	69	10	29	39	52	....	....	....	....	....	....	....	....	....	3	0	0	0	0	....	....	....	....
2001-02	Shawinigan	QMJHL	68	16	35	51	54	....	....	....	....	....	....	....	....	....	12	8	9	17	17	....	....	....	....
2002-03	Houston Aeros	AHL	62	4	10	14	26	....	....	....	....	....	....	....	....	....	23	1	1	2	6	....	....	....	....
2003-04	**Minnesota**	**NHL**	**22**	**1**	**1**	**2**	**4**	**0**	**0**	**0**	**17**	**5.9**	**–7**	**0**	**0.0**	**14:13**	....	....	....	....	....	....	....	....	....
	Houston Aeros	AHL	55	5	16	21	32	....	....	....	....	....	....	....	....	....	2	1	0	1	0	....	....	....	....
2004-05	Houston Aeros	AHL	76	7	17	24	48	....	....	....	....	....	....	....	....	....	5	1	2	3	4	....	....	....	....
2005-06	**Phoenix**	**NHL**	**82**	**9**	**15**	**24**	**62**	**5**	**0**	**2**	**105**	**8.6**	**4**	**0**	**0.0**	**22:50**	....	....	....	....	....	....	....	....	....
2006-07	**Phoenix**	**NHL**	**82**	**4**	**24**	**28**	**34**	**3**	**0**	**0**	**144**	**2.8**	**–20**	**1**	**100.0**	**23:40**	....	....	....	....	....	....	....	....	....
2007-08	**Phoenix**	**NHL**	**75**	**4**	**13**	**17**	**34**	**0**	**0**	**2**	**92**	**4.3**	**9**	**0**	**0.0**	**21:36**	....	....	....	....	....	....	....	....	....

			Regular Season														Playoffs								
Season	Club	League	GP	G	A	Pts	PIM	PP	SH	GW	S	S%	+/-	TF	F%	Min	GP	G	A	Pts	PIM	PP	SH	GW	Min
2008-09	Phoenix	NHL	82	6	21	27	28	0	0	0	106	5.7	–13	0	0.0	22:43									
2009-10	Phoenix	NHL	72	3	14	17	30	2	0	1	104	2.9	5	0	0.0	22:39	7	0	2	2	2	0	0	0	20:28
	Czech Republic	Olympics	5	0	0	0	2																		
2010-11	Pittsburgh	NHL	73	5	14	19	30	1	0	2	104	4.8	0	0	0.0	21:50	7	0	1	1	0	0	0	0	27:20
2011-12	Pittsburgh	NHL	62	2	11	13	24	0	0	0	77	2.6	0	0	0.0	21:39	6	0	1	1	0	0	0	0	21:08
2012-13	Phoenix	NHL	34	0	2	2	14	0	0	0	42	0.0	4	0	0.0	21:18									
2013-14	Phoenix	NHL	59	2	8	10	24	0	0	1	78	2.6	6	0	0.0	20:59									
	Czech Republic	Olympics	5	0	1	1	2																		
2014-15	Arizona	NHL	53	2	6	8	12	0	0	0	67	3.0	–6	0	0.0	21:05									
	St. Louis	NHL	15	2	2	4	6	0	0	0	19	10.5	3	0	0.0	19:37	6	0	0	0	4	0	0	0	16:21
2015-16	Arizona	NHL	70	2	5	7	20	0	0	0	69	2.9	3	0	0.0	17:01									
2016-17	Arizona	NHL	3	0	0	0	0	0	0	0	3	0.0	1	0	0.0	17:40									
	Tucson	AHL	43	6	8	14	32																		
	NHL Totals		784	42	136	178	322	11	0	8	1027	4.1		1	100.0	21:25	26	0	4	4	6	0	0	0	21:31

Signed as a free agent by **Minnesota**, September 29, 2001. Traded to **Phoenix** by **Minnesota** for Erik Westrum and Dustin Wood, August 26, 2005. Signed as a free agent by **Pittsburgh**, July 1, 2010. Traded to **Phoenix** by **Pittsburgh** for Harrison Ruopp, Marc Cheverie and Philadelphia's 3rd round pick (previously acquired, Pittsburgh selected Oskar Sundqvist) in 2012 NHL Draft, June 22, 2012. Traded to **St. Louis** by **Arizona** with future considerations for Maxim Letunov. March 2. 2015. Signed as a free agent by **Arizona**, July 1, 2015.

MIELE, Andy

(MEE-lee, AN-dee)

Left wing. Shoots left. 5'7", 169 lbs. Born, Grosse Pointe Woods, MI, April 15, 1988.

Season	Club	League	GP	G	A	Pts	PIM	PP	SH	GW	S	S%	+/-	TF	F%	Min	GP	G	A	Pts	PIM	PP	SH	GW	Min
2005-06	Cedar Rapids	USHL	52	10	17	27	41										8	0	4	4	4				
2006-07	Cedar Rapids	USHL	13	7	8	15	15																		
	Chicago Steel	USHL	45	13	29	42	70										4	2	4	6	14				
2007-08	Chicago Steel	USHL	29	30	11	41	78																		
	Miami U.	CCHA	18	6	8	14	4																		
2008-09	Miami U.	CCHA	41	15	16	31	34																		
2009-10	Miami U.	CCHA	43	15	29	44	61																		
2010-11	Miami U.	CCHA	39	24	*47	*71	35																		
2011-12	Phoenix	NHL	7	0	0	0	6	0	0	0	4	0.0	–3	28	25.0	8:56									
	Portland Pirates	AHL	69	16	38	54	43																		
2012-13	Portland Pirates	AHL	70	19	34	53	72										3	1	2	3	15				
	Phoenix	NHL	1	0	0	0	0	0	0	0	0	0.0	1	3	66.7	9:02									
2013-14	Phoenix	NHL	7	0	2	2	5	0	0	0	6	0.0	4	42	35.7	9:21									
	Portland Pirates	AHL	70	27	45	72	66																		
2014-15	Grand Rapids	AHL	71	26	44	70	42										16	3	11	14	20				
2015-16	Grand Rapids	AHL	75	18	44	62	77										9	2	5	7	12				
2016-17	Lehigh Valley	AHL	65	13	44	57	54										5	1	2	3	4				
	NHL Totals		15	0	2	2	11	0	0	0	10	0.0		73	32.9	9:08									

CCHA Second All-Star Team (2010) • CCHA First All-Star Team (2011) • CCHA Player of the Year (2011) • NCAA West First All-American Team (2011) • Hobey Baker Memorial Award (Top U.S. Collegiate Player) (2011) • AHL Second All-Star Team (2014) • AHL First All-Star Team (2015)

Signed as a free agent by **Phoenix**, April 2, 2011. Signed as a free agent by **Detroit**, July 3, 2014. Signed as a free agent by **Philadelphia**, July 1, 2016.

MILANO, Sonny

(mih-LA-noh, SUH-nee) **CBJ**

Left wing. Shoots left. 6'1", 196 lbs. Born, Massapequa, NY, May 12, 1996. Columbus' 1st pick, 16th overall, in 2014 NHL Draft.

Season	Club	League	GP	G	A	Pts	PIM	PP	SH	GW	S	S%	+/-	TF	F%	Min	GP	G	A	Pts	PIM	PP	SH	GW	Min
2011-12	Cleveland Barons	T1EHL	40	44	43	87	10																		
2012-13	USAHNTDP	USHL	38	10	12	22	12																		
	USAHNTDP	U-17	18	10	15	25	8																		
2013-14	USAHNTDP	USHL	25	14	25	39	21																		
	USAHNTDP	U-18	33	15	33	48	8																		
2014-15	Plymouth Whalers	OHL	50	22	46	68	24																		
	Springfield	AHL	10	0	5	5	0																		
2015-16	Columbus	NHL	3	0	1	1	0	0	0	0	2	0.0	1	0	0.0	13:23									
	Lake Erie	AHL	54	14	17	31	22										17	4	4	8	4				
2016-17	Columbus	NHL	4	0	0	0	0	0	0	0	2	0.0	–3	0	0.0	11:41	1	0	0	0	0	0	0	0	6:47
	Cleveland	AHL	63	18	29	47	24																		
	NHL Totals		7	0	1	1	0	0	0	0	4	0.0		0	0.0	12:25	1	0	0	0	0	0	0	0	6:47

MILLER, Andrew

(MIH-luhr, AN-droo) **CAR**

Center. Shoots right. 5'10", 181 lbs. Born, Bloomfield Hills, MI, September 18, 1988.

Season	Club	League	GP	G	A	Pts	PIM	PP	SH	GW	S	S%	+/-	TF	F%	Min	GP	G	A	Pts	PIM	PP	SH	GW	Min
2007-08	Chicago Steel	USHL	59	14	27	41	28										7	2	4	6	4				
2008-09	Chicago Steel	USHL	58	32	50	82	76																		
2009-10	Yale	ECAC	34	5	29	34	12																		
2010-11	Yale	ECAC	36	12	33	45	18																		
2011-12	Yale	ECAC	34	7	29	36	8																		
2012-13	Yale	ECAC	37	18	23	41	15																		
2013-14	Oklahoma City	AHL	52	8	26	34	14										3	0	0	0	4				
2014-15	Edmonton	NHL	9	1	5	6	0	0	0	0	14	7.1	–2	2	50.0	13:45									
	Oklahoma City	AHL	63	27	33	60	16										10	3	3	6	8				
2015-16	Edmonton	NHL	6	0	0	0	0	0	0	0	3	0.0	–1	29	44.8	9:07									
	Bakersfield	AHL	44	15	24	39	18																		
	Charlotte	AHL	11	3	3	6	0																		
2016-17	Charlotte	AHL	55	11	30	41	10										5	3	2	5	2				
	NHL Totals		15	1	5	6	0	0	0	0	17	5.9		31	45.2	11:54									

USHL Player of the Year (2009) • ECAC First All-Star Team (2011, 2013) • NCAA East Second All-American Team (2013) • NCAA Championship All-Tournament Team (2013) • NCAA Championship Tournament MVP (2013)

Signed as a free agent by **Edmonton**, April 17, 2013. • Re-assigned to **Charlotte** (AHL) by **Edmonton**, March 7, 2016. Signed as a free agent by **Carolina**, July 1, 2016.

MILLER, Colin

(MIH-luhr, KAW-lihn) **VGK**

Defense. Shoots right. 6'1", 196 lbs. Born, Sault Ste. Marie, ON, October 29, 1992. Los Angeles' 3rd pick, 151st overall, in 2012 NHL Draft.

Season	Club	League	GP	G	A	Pts	PIM	PP	SH	GW	S	S%	+/-	TF	F%	Min	GP	G	A	Pts	PIM	PP	SH	GW	Min
2008-09	Soo North Stars	Minor-ON	32	6	15	21	42										10	2	7	9	14				
2009-10	Soo Thunderbirds	NOJHL	46	7	23	30	38										14	5	9	14	6				
2010-11	Sault Ste. Marie	OHL	66	3	19	22	44																		
2011-12	Sault Ste. Marie	OHL	54	8	20	28	79																		
2012-13	Sault Ste. Marie	OHL	54	20	35	55	78										6	1	6	7	0				
2013-14	Manchester	AHL	65	5	12	17	35										3	0	0	0	6				
2014-15	Manchester	AHL	70	19	33	52	82										19	2	8	10	12				
2015-16	Boston	NHL	42	3	13	16	39	0	0	0	59	5.1	0	0	0.0	15:48									
	Providence Bruins	AHL	20	4	8	12	16										2	0	0	0	0				
2016-17	Boston	NHL	61	6	7	13	55	1	0	0	85	7.1	0	0	0.0	15:49	4	0	1	1	2	0	0	0	15:33
	NHL Totals		103	9	20	29	94	1	0	0	144	6.3		0	0.0	15:48	4	0	1	1	2	0	0	0	15:33

AHL Second All-Star Team (2015)

Traded to **Boston** by **Los Angeles** with Martin Jones and Los Angeles' 1st round pick (Jakub Zboril) in 2015 NHL Draft for Milan Lucic, June 26, 2015. Claimed by **Vegas** from **Boston** in Expansion Draft, June 21, 2017.

MILLER, Drew

(MIH-luhr, DROO)

Left wing. Shoots left. 6'2", 180 lbs. Born, Dover, NJ, February 17, 1984. Anaheim's 6th pick, 186th overall, in 2003 NHL Draft.

Season	Club	League	GP	G	A	Pts	PIM	PP	SH	GW	S	S%	+/-	TF	F%	Min	GP	G	A	Pts	PIM	PP	SH	GW	Min
2000-01	Capital Centre	NAHL	37	4	3	7	22																		
2001-02	Capital Centre	NAHL	54	18	16	34	56																		
2002-03	Capital Centre	NAHL	14	9	9	18	12																		
	River City Lancers	USHL	49	14	11	25	22										11	5	4	9	6				
2003-04	Michigan State	CCHA	41	4	6	10	39																		
2004-05	Michigan State	CCHA	40	17	16	33	20																		

Season	Club	League	GP	G	A	Pts	PIM	PP	SH	GW	S	S%	+/-	TF	F%	Min	GP	G	A	Pts	PIM	PP	SH	GW	Min
			Regular Season														Playoffs								
2005-06	Michigan State	CCHA	44	18	25	43	30																		
	Portland Pirates	AHL															1	0	0	0	0				
2006-07	Portland Pirates	AHL	79	16	20	36	51																		
	♦ Anaheim	**NHL**															**3**	**0**	**0**	**0**	**2**	**0**	**0**	**0**	**7:00**
2007-08	**Anaheim**	**NHL**	**26**	**2**	**3**	**5**	**6**	**0**	**0**	**0**	**30**	**6.7**	**−1**	**9**	**33.3**	**11:11**									
	Portland Pirates	AHL	31	16	20	36	12										16	1	7	8	12				
2008-09	**Anaheim**	**NHL**	**27**	**4**	**6**	**10**	**17**	**0**	**0**	**0**	**45**	**8.9**	**0**	**14**	**21.4**	**12:59**	**13**	**2**	**1**	**3**	**2**	**0**	**0**	**1**	**16:09**
	Iowa Chops	AHL	53	23	15	38	10																		
2009-10	**Tampa Bay**	**NHL**	**14**	**0**	**0**	**0**	**2**	**0**	**0**	**0**	**10**	**0.0**	**−3**	**2**	**0.0**	**12:14**									
	Detroit	**NHL**	**66**	**10**	**9**	**19**	**10**	**1**	**1**	**3**	**93**	**10.8**	**5**	**41**	**34.2**	**12:42**	**12**	**1**	**1**	**2**	**4**	**0**	**0**	**0**	**12:35**
2010-11	**Detroit**	**NHL**	**67**	**10**	**8**	**18**	**13**	**0**	**1**	**2**	**85**	**11.8**	**−2**	**17**	**23.5**	**11:45**	**9**	**1**	**1**	**2**	**4**	**0**	**0**	**0**	**10:17**
2011-12	**Detroit**	**NHL**	**80**	**14**	**11**	**25**	**20**	**0**	**0**	**4**	**131**	**10.7**	**6**	**25**	**20.0**	**12:52**	**5**	**0**	**1**	**1**	**2**	**0**	**0**	**0**	**11:32**
2012-13	Braehead Clan	Britain	23	15	15	30	7																		
	Detroit	**NHL**	**44**	**4**	**4**	**8**	**2**	**1**	**0**	**2**	**54**	**7.4**	**−8**	**4**	**25.0**	**13:49**	**6**	**1**	**1**	**2**	**2**	**0**	**0**	**1**	**13:13**
2013-14	**Detroit**	**NHL**	**82**	**7**	**8**	**15**	**21**	**0**	**0**	**1**	**117**	**6.0**	**−11**	**23**	**39.1**	**14:08**	**5**	**0**	**1**	**1**	**0**	**0**	**0**	**0**	**14:33**
2014-15	**Detroit**	**NHL**	**82**	**5**	**8**	**13**	**25**	**0**	**1**	**0**	**98**	**5.1**	**−3**	**19**	**31.6**	**13:26**	**7**	**1**	**1**	**2**	**2**	**0**	**0**	**0**	**16:44**
2015-16	**Detroit**	**NHL**	**28**	**1**	**1**	**2**	**2**	**0**	**0**	**0**	**27**	**3.7**	**−5**	**2**	**50.0**	**12:58**									
2016-17	**Detroit**	**NHL**	**55**	**5**	**2**	**7**	**18**	**0**	**0**	**1**	**43**	**11.6**	**−12**	**3**	**66.7**	**10:17**									
	Grand Rapids	AHL	7	2	1	3	0																		
	NHL Totals		**571**	**62**	**60**	**122**	**136**	**2**	**3**	**13**	**733**	**8.5**		**159**	**30.2**	**12:44**	**60**	**6**	**7**	**13**	**18**	**0**	**0**	**2**	**13:21**

Traded to **Tampa Bay** by **Anaheim** with Anaheim's 3rd round pick (Adam Janosik) in 2010 NHL Draft for Evgeny Artyukhin, August 13, 2009. Claimed on waivers by **Detroit** from **Tampa Bay**, November 11, 2009. Signed as a free agent by **Braehead** (Britain), October 8, 2012. • Missed majority of 2015-16 due to jaw (December 3, 2015 vs. Arizona) and knee (January 10, 2016 at Anaheim) injuries.

MILLER, J.T.

(MIH-luhr, JAY-TEE) **NYR**

Center. Shoots left. 6'1", 206 lbs. Born, East Palestine, OH, March 14, 1993. NY Rangers' 1st pick, 15th overall, in 2011 NHL Draft.

Season	Club	League	GP	G	A	Pts	PIM	PP	SH	GW	S	S%	+/-	TF	F%	Min	GP	G	A	Pts	PIM	PP	SH	GW	Min
2008-09	Pit. Hornets	T1EHL	45	21	21	42	76																		
2009-10	USAHNTDP	USHL	29	5	7	12	32																		
	USAHNTDP	U-17	17	10	9	19	47																		
	USAHNTDP	U-18	1	0	0	0	0																		
2010-11	USAHNTDP	USHL	21	3	12	15	48																		
	USAHNTDP	U-18	35	12	23	35	38																		
2011-12	Plymouth Whalers	OHL	61	25	37	62	61										13	2	8	10	18				
	Connecticut	AHL															8	0	1	1	2				
2012-13	Connecticut	AHL	42	8	15	23	29																		
	NY Rangers	**NHL**	**26**	**2**	**2**	**4**	**8**	**1**	**0**	**0**	**43**	**4.7**	**−7**	**118**	**53.4**	**13:31**									
2013-14	**NY Rangers**	**NHL**	**30**	**3**	**3**	**6**	**18**	**0**	**0**	**0**	**46**	**6.5**	**−6**	**51**	**51.0**	**11:27**	**4**	**0**	**2**	**2**	**2**	**0**	**0**	**0**	**9:16**
	Hartford	AHL	41	15	27	42	47																		
2014-15	**NY Rangers**	**NHL**	**58**	**10**	**13**	**23**	**23**	**2**	**0**	**3**	**92**	**10.9**	**5**	**205**	**45.4**	**12:42**	**19**	**1**	**7**	**8**	**2**	**0**	**0**	**0**	**14:39**
	Hartford	AHL	18	6	9	15	12																		
2015-16	**NY Rangers**	**NHL**	**82**	**22**	**21**	**43**	**46**	**2**	**0**	**5**	**135**	**16.3**	**10**	**157**	**43.3**	**15:02**	**5**	**0**	**3**	**3**	**4**	**0**	**0**	**0**	**16:10**
2016-17	**NY Rangers**	**NHL**	**82**	**22**	**34**	**56**	**21**	**2**	**3**	**6**	**132**	**16.7**	**17**	**357**	**44.0**	**16:22**	**12**	**0**	**3**	**3**	**21**	**0**	**0**	**0**	**16:33**
	NHL Totals		**278**	**59**	**73**	**132**	**116**	**7**	**3**	**14**	**448**	**13.2**		**888**	**45.8**	**14:25**	**40**	**1**	**15**	**16**	**29**	**0**	**0**	**0**	**14:52**

MILLER, Kevan

(MIH-luhr, KEH-vuhn) **BOS**

Defense. Shoots right. 6'2", 210 lbs. Born, Los Angeles, CA, November 15, 1987.

Season	Club	League	GP	G	A	Pts	PIM	PP	SH	GW	S	S%	+/-	TF	F%	Min	GP	G	A	Pts	PIM	PP	SH	GW	Min
2007-08	U. of Vermont	H-East	39	2	5	7	12																		
2008-09	U. of Vermont	H-East	39	1	7	8	30																		
2009-10	U. of Vermont	H-East	39	1	10	11	26																		
2010-11	U. of Vermont	H-East	27	1	3	4	29																		
	Providence Bruins	AHL	6	0	0	0	9																		
2011-12	Providence Bruins	AHL	65	3	21	24	98																		
2012-13	Providence Bruins	AHL	64	2	14	16	71										9	0	5	5	10				
2013-14	**Boston**	**NHL**	**47**	**1**	**5**	**6**	**38**	**0**	**0**	**1**	**41**	**2.4**	**20**	**0**	**0.0**	**17:28**	**11**	**0**	**2**	**2**	**8**	**0**	**0**	**0**	**19:26**
	Providence Bruins	AHL	19	2	3	5	39																		
2014-15	**Boston**	**NHL**	**41**	**2**	**5**	**7**	**15**	**0**	**0**	**1**	**37**	**5.4**	**20**	**0**	**0.0**	**18:02**									
2015-16	**Boston**	**NHL**	**71**	**5**	**13**	**18**	**53**	**0**	**0**	**0**	**64**	**7.8**	**15**	**0**	**0.0**	**19:04**									
2016-17	**Boston**	**NHL**	**58**	**3**	**10**	**13**	**50**	**0**	**0**	**1**	**49**	**6.1**	**1**	**0**	**0.0**	**17:48**	**6**	**0**	**0**	**0**	**4**	**0**	**0**	**0**	**25:15**
	NHL Totals		**217**	**11**	**33**	**44**	**156**	**0**	**0**	**3**	**191**	**5.8**		**0**	**0.0**	**18:11**	**17**	**0**	**2**	**2**	**12**	**0**	**0**	**0**	**21:29**

Signed as a free agent by **Providence** (AHL), March 18, 2011. Signed as a free agent by **Boston**, October 21, 2011.

MITCHELL, Garrett

(MIH-chuhl, GAIR-reht)

Right wing. Shoots right. 5'11", 183 lbs. Born, Regina, SK, September 2, 1991. Washington's 6th pick, 175th overall, in 2009 NHL Draft.

Season	Club	League	GP	G	A	Pts	PIM	PP	SH	GW	S	S%	+/-	TF	F%	Min	GP	G	A	Pts	PIM	PP	SH	GW	Min
2006-07	Reg. Pat Cdns.	SMHL	42	14	11	25	140																		
	Regina Pats	WHL	4	0	1	1	2																		
2007-08	Regina Pats	WHL	62	8	5	13	73										6	1	0	1	6				
2008-09	Regina Pats	WHL	71	10	5	15	140																		
2009-10	Regina Pats	WHL	57	15	16	31	110																		
	Hershey Bears	AHL	1	0	0	0	0																		
2010-11	Regina Pats	WHL	70	18	34	52	140																		
	Hershey Bears	AHL	2	0	0	0	5																		
2011-12	Hershey Bears	AHL	65	6	9	15	85										5	1	0	1	0				
	South Carolina	ECHL	2	0	0	0	7																		
2012-13	Hershey Bears	AHL	75	15	15	30	94										5	1	0	1	4				
2013-14	Hershey Bears	AHL	17	0	2	2	44																		
2014-15	Hershey Bears	AHL	64	4	4	8	121										10	1	2	3	10				
2015-16	Hershey Bears	AHL	58	11	16	27	90										20	1	4	5	23				
2016-17	**Washington**	**NHL**	**1**	**0**	**0**	**0**	**0**	**0**	**0**	**0**	**0**	**0.0**	**0**	**1**	**0.0**	**8:48**									
	Hershey Bears	AHL	71	10	10	20	121										12	0	0	0	6				
	NHL Totals		**1**	**0**	**0**	**0**	**0**	**0**	**0**	**0**	**0**	**0.0**		**1**	**0.0**	**8:48**									

MITCHELL, John

(MIH-chuhl, JAWN)

Center. Shoots left. 6'1", 204 lbs. Born, Oakville, ON, January 22, 1985. Toronto's 4th pick, 158th overall, in 2003 NHL Draft.

Season	Club	League	GP	G	A	Pts	PIM	PP	SH	GW	S	S%	+/-	TF	F%	Min	GP	G	A	Pts	PIM	PP	SH	GW	Min
2000-01	Waterloo Siskens	ON-Jr.A	47	15	29	44	33																		
2001-02	Plymouth Whalers	OHL	62	9	9	18	23										6	1	0	1	4				
2002-03	Plymouth Whalers	OHL	68	18	37	55	31										18	2	10	12	8				
2003-04	Plymouth Whalers	OHL	65	28	54	82	45										9	6	6	12	6				
2004-05	Plymouth Whalers	OHL	63	25	50	75	59										4	1	1	2	0				
	St. John's	AHL	2	0	0	0	0																		
2005-06	Toronto Marlies	AHL	51	5	12	17	22										2	0	0	0	0				
2006-07	Toronto Marlies	AHL	73	16	20	36	46																		
2007-08	Toronto Marlies	AHL	79	20	31	51	56										19	8	4	12	12				
2008-09	**Toronto**	**NHL**	**76**	**12**	**17**	**29**	**33**	**2**	**0**	**0**	**98**	**12.2**	**−16**	**669**	**48.7**	**13:48**									
2009-10	**Toronto**	**NHL**	**60**	**6**	**17**	**23**	**31**	**1**	**0**	**1**	**90**	**6.7**	**−7**	**477**	**51.2**	**15:49**									
2010-11	**Toronto**	**NHL**	**23**	**2**	**1**	**3**	**12**	**1**	**0**	**1**	**28**	**7.1**	**−7**	**149**	**55.7**	**12:31**									
	Toronto Marlies	AHL	10	1	4	5	2																		
	Connecticut	AHL	14	7	5	12	10										6	3	3	6	0				
2011-12	**NY Rangers**	**NHL**	**63**	**5**	**11**	**16**	**8**	**0**	**0**	**0**	**64**	**7.8**	**10**	**199**	**51.8**	**10:10**	**18**	**0**	**1**	**1**	**2**	**0**	**0**	**0**	**7:05**
	Connecticut	AHL	17	7	7	14	20																		
2012-13	**Colorado**	**NHL**	**47**	**10**	**10**	**20**	**18**	**1**	**0**	**1**	**72**	**13.9**	**5**	**344**	**49.7**	**16:45**									
2013-14	**Colorado**	**NHL**	**75**	**11**	**21**	**32**	**36**	**3**	**0**	**2**	**107**	**10.3**	**13**	**748**	**50.0**	**16:16**									
2014-15	**Colorado**	**NHL**	**68**	**11**	**15**	**26**	**32**	**3**	**1**	**1**	**105**	**10.5**	**−9**	**735**	**50.9**	**15:51**									

			Regular Season														Playoffs								
Season	Club	League	GP	G	A	Pts	PIM	PP	SH	GW	S	S%	+/-	TF	F%	Min	GP	G	A	Pts	PIM	PP	SH	GW	Min
2015-16	Colorado	NHL	71	10	11	21	52	0	0	3	101	9.9	–7	849	48.9	15:15	....	....	....	....	....	....	....	....	....
2016-17	Colorado	NHL	65	3	4	7	45	0	0	1	57	5.3	–12	538	55.4	12:33	....	....	....	....	....	....	....	....	....
	NHL Totals		548	70	107	177	267	11	1	10	722	9.7		4708	50.7	14:26	18	0	1	1	2	0	0	0	7:05

Traded to **NY Rangers** by **Toronto** for NY Rangers' 7th round pick (Viktor Loov) in 2012 NHL Draft, February 28, 2011. Signed as a free agent by **Colorado**, July 1, 2012.

MITCHELL, Torrey

(MIH-chuhl, TOH-ree) **MTL**

Center. Shoots right. 5'11", 190 lbs. Born, Greenfield Park, QC, January 30, 1985. San Jose's 3rd pick, 126th overall, in 2004 NHL Draft.

2001-02	C.C. Lemoyne	QAAA	41	15	41	56	54	....	....	....	....	....	....	....	....	....	19	13	14	27	18	....	....	....	....
2002-03	Hotchkiss School	High-CT	26	19	30	49	33	....	....	....	....	....	....	....	....	....	....	....	....	....	....	....	....	....	....
2003-04	Hotchkiss School	High-CT	25	25	37	62	42	....	....	....	....	....	....	....	....	....	....	....	....	....	....	....	....	....	....
2004-05	U. of Vermont	ECAC	38	11	19	30	74	....	....	....	....	....	....	....	....	....	....	....	....	....	....	....	....	....	....
2005-06	U. of Vermont	H-East	38	12	28	40	34	....	....	....	....	....	....	....	....	....	....	....	....	....	....	....	....	....	....
2006-07	U. of Vermont	H-East	39	12	23	35	46	....	....	....	....	....	....	....	....	....	....	....	....	....	....	....	....	....	....
	Worcester Sharks	AHL	11	2	5	7	27	....	....	....	....	....	....	....	....	....	6	1	1	2	15	....	....	....	....
2007-08	San Jose	NHL	82	10	10	20	50	1	2	0	110	9.1	–3	692	49.4	14:19	13	1	2	3	10	1	0	0	14:00
2008-09	Worcester Sharks	AHL	2	1	0	1	0	....	....	....	....	....	....	....	....	....	....	....	....	....	....	....	....	....	....
	San Jose	NHL	....	....	....	....	....	....	....	....	....	....	....	....	....	....	4	0	0	0	2	0	0	0	9:38
2009-10	San Jose	NHL	56	2	9	11	27	0	0	0	59	3.4	6	205	43.4	11:26	15	0	2	2	2	0	0	0	13:05
	Worcester Sharks	AHL	5	1	2	3	10	....	....	....	....	....	....	....	....	....	....	....	....	....	....	....	....	....	....
2010-11	San Jose	NHL	66	9	14	23	46	0	0	1	116	7.8	10	203	48.8	13:21	18	1	4	5	10	0	0	0	15:02
2011-12	San Jose	NHL	76	9	10	19	29	0	0	0	100	9.0	–6	83	43.4	12:26	5	0	1	1	6	0	0	0	13:02
2012-13	San Francisco	ECHL	2	1	0	1	0	....	....	....	....	....	....	....	....	....	....	....	....	....	....	....	....	....	....
	Minnesota	NHL	45	4	4	8	21	0	0	1	39	10.3	–8	42	50.0	10:30	5	1	0	1	0	0	0	0	11:24
2013-14	Minnesota	NHL	58	1	8	9	21	0	0	0	47	2.1	–3	24	37.5	10:08	....	....	....	....	....	....	....	....	....
	Buffalo	NHL	9	1	0	1	4	0	0	0	9	11.1	0	7	42.9	15:39	....	....	....	....	....	....	....	....	....
2014-15	Buffalo	NHL	51	6	7	13	26	0	0	2	45	13.3	–6	661	47.2	15:20	....	....	....	....	....	....	....	....	....
	Montreal	NHL	14	0	1	1	8	0	0	0	10	0.0	–2	153	56.9	10:03	12	1	4	5	6	0	0	0	12:31
2015-16	Montreal	NHL	71	11	8	19	51	0	1	3	69	15.9	2	717	51.6	12:41	....	....	....	....	....	....	....	....	....
2016-17	Montreal	NHL	78	8	9	17	38	0	0	1	68	11.8	5	752	54.5	12:36	3	1	0	1	0	0	0	0	11:33
	NHL Totals		606	61	80	141	321	1	3	8	672	9.1		3539	50.2	12:37	75	5	13	18	36	1	0	0	13:16

ECAC All-Rookie Team (2005)

• Missed majority of 2008-09 due to leg injury in training camp, September 18, 2008. Signed as a free agent by **Minnesota**, July 1, 2012. Traded to **Buffalo** by **Minnesota** with Winnipeg's 2nd round pick (previously acquired, later traded to Washington – Washington selected Vitek Vanecek) in 2014 NHL Draft and Minnesota's 2nd round pick (later traded to Montreal, later traded to Chicago – Chicago selected Chad Krys) in 2016 NHL Draft for Matt Moulson and Cody McCormick, March 5, 2014. Traded to **Montreal** by **Buffalo** for Jack Nevins and Montreal's 7th round pick (Vasili Glotov) in 2016 NHL Draft, March 2, 2015.

MITCHELL, Zack

(MIH-chuhl, ZAK) **MIN**

Right wing. Shoots right. 6'1", 194 lbs. Born, Caledon, ON, January 7, 1993.

2008-09	Tor. Marlboros	GTHL	77	42	48	90	74	....	....	....	....	....	....	....	....	....	....	....	....	....	....	....	....	....	....
2009-10	Guelph Storm	OHL	59	3	7	10	25	....	....	....	....	....	....	....	....	....	5	2	0	2	0	....	....	....	....
2010-11	Guelph Storm	OHL	61	9	10	19	24	....	....	....	....	....	....	....	....	....	6	1	6	7	2	....	....	....	....
2011-12	Guelph Storm	OHL	67	37	38	75	32	....	....	....	....	....	....	....	....	....	6	2	2	4	2	....	....	....	....
2012-13	Guelph Storm	OHL	68	22	34	56	34	....	....	....	....	....	....	....	....	....	5	1	1	2	4	....	....	....	....
2013-14	Guelph Storm	OHL	67	31	52	83	40	....	....	....	....	....	....	....	....	....	20	12	18	30	12	....	....	....	....
2014-15	Iowa Wild	AHL	76	17	18	35	12	....	....	....	....	....	....	....	....	....	....	....	....	....	....	....	....	....	....
2015-16	Iowa Wild	AHL	70	22	20	42	26	....	....	....	....	....	....	....	....	....	....	....	....	....	....	....	....	....	....
2016-17	Minnesota	NHL	11	0	0	0	0	0	0	0	10	0.0	–1	19	57.9	8:26	....	....	....	....	....	....	....	....	....
	Iowa Wild	AHL	62	11	11	22	10	....	....	....	....	....	....	....	....	....	....	....	....	....	....	....	....	....	....
	NHL Totals		11	0	0	0	0	0	0	0	10	0.0		19	57.9	8:26	....	....	....	....	....	....	....	....	....

Signed as a free agent by **Minnesota**, March 4, 2014.

MOLINO, Griffen

(muh-LEE-noh, GRIHF-uhn) **VAN**

Center. Shoots left. 6', 185 lbs. Born, Trenton, MI, January 21, 1994.

2009-10	Det. L.C. U16	T1EHL	38	3	14	17	16	....	....	....	....	....	....	....	....	....	....	....	....	....	....	....	....	....	....
2010-11	Det. L.C. U16	T1EHL	22	7	15	22	4	....	....	....	....	....	....	....	....	....	....	....	....	....	....	....	....	....	....
2011-12	Det. L.C. U18	HPHL	26	4	10	14	22	....	....	....	....	....	....	....	....	....	....	....	....	....	....	....	....	....	....
2012-13	Brockville Braves	ON-Jr.A	61	14	20	34	38	....	....	....	....	....	....	....	....	....	6	2	1	3	2	....	....	....	....
2013-14	Sioux Falls	USHL	59	8	31	39	31	....	....	....	....	....	....	....	....	....	2	0	0	0	2	....	....	....	....
2014-15	Muskegon	USHL	57	18	46	64	39	....	....	....	....	....	....	....	....	....	12	3	6	9	10	....	....	....	....
2015-16	Western Mich.	NCHC	36	11	14	25	12	....	....	....	....	....	....	....	....	....	....	....	....	....	....	....	....	....	....
2016-17	Western Mich.	NCHC	40	15	18	33	29	....	....	....	....	....	....	....	....	....	....	....	....	....	....	....	....	....	....
	Vancouver	NHL	5	0	0	0	0	0	0	0	3	0.0	–2	0	0.0	10:35	....	....	....	....	....	....	....	....	....
	NHL Totals		5	0	0	0	0	0	0	0	3	0.0		0	0.0	10:35	....	....	....	....	....	....	....	....	....

Signed as a free agent by **Vancouver**, March 28, 2017.

MONAHAN, Sean

(MAWN-ah-han, SHAWN) **CGY**

Center. Shoots left. 6'3", 195 lbs. Born, Brampton, ON, October 12, 1994. Calgary's 1st pick, 6th overall, in 2013 NHL Draft.

2009-10	Miss. Rebels	GTHL	47	46	44	90	48	....	....	....	....	....	....	....	....	....	....	....	....	....	....	....	....	....	....
2010-11	Ottawa 67's	OHL	65	20	27	47	32	....	....	....	....	....	....	....	....	....	4	2	2	4	0	....	....	....	....
2011-12	Ottawa 67's	OHL	62	33	45	78	38	....	....	....	....	....	....	....	....	....	18	8	7	15	12	....	....	....	....
2012-13	Ottawa 67's	OHL	58	31	47	78	24	....	....	....	....	....	....	....	....	....	....	....	....	....	....	....	....	....	....
2013-14	Calgary	NHL	75	22	12	34	8	3	0	2	140	15.7	–20	1036	46.0	15:59	....	....	....	....	....	....	....	....	....
2014-15	Calgary	NHL	81	31	31	62	12	10	1	8	191	16.2	8	1830	49.3	19:37	11	3	3	6	2	1	0	0	19:47
2015-16	Calgary	NHL	81	27	36	63	18	7	0	5	197	13.7	–6	1739	51.0	19:10	....	....	....	....	....	....	....	....	....
2016-17	Calgary	NHL	82	27	31	58	20	8	1	4	199	13.6	–1	1444	51.5	17:35	4	4	1	5	0	4	0	0	18:30
	NHL Totals		319	107	110	217	58	28	2	19	727	14.7		6049	49.7	18:07	15	7	4	11	2	5	0	0	19:27

OHL Second All-Star Team (2012)

MONTOUR, Brandon

(MAWN-toor, BRAN-duhn) **ANA**

Defense. Shoots right. 6', 192 lbs. Born, Brantford, ON, April 11, 1994. Anaheim's 3rd pick, 55th overall, in 2014 NHL Draft.

2009-10	Cambridge	Minor-ON	30	4	14	18	12	....	....	....	....	....	....	....	....	....	11	0	2	2	6	....	....	....	....
2010-11	Camb. Hawks Mid.	Minor-ON	19	3	8	11		38	....	....	....	....	....	....	....	....	....	....	....	....	....	....	....	....	....
....																									
	Brantford	ON-Jr.B	37	1	13	14	22	....	....	....	....	....	....	....	....	....	10	0	3	3	6	....	....	....	....
2011-12	Brantford	ON-Jr.B	51	14	22	36	65	....	....	....	....	....	....	....	....	....	19	6	12	18	30	....	....	....	....
2012-13	Caledonia	ON-Jr.B	49	18	49	67	94	....	....	....	....	....	....	....	....	....	12	4	11	15	22	....	....	....	....
2013-14	Waterloo	USHL	60	14	48	62	36	....	....	....	....	....	....	....	....	....	12	6	*10	*16	10	....	....	....	....
2014-15	Massachusetts	H-East	21	3	17	20	30	....	....	....	....	....	....	....	....	....	....	....	....	....	....	....	....	....	....
	Norfolk Admirals	AHL	14	1	9	10	8	....	....	....	....	....	....	....	....	....	....	....	....	....	....	....	....	....	....
2015-16	San Diego Gulls	AHL	68	12	45	57	42	....	....	....	....	....	....	....	....	....	9	0	5	5	8	....	....	....	....
2016-17	Anaheim	NHL	27	2	4	6	14	0	0	0	50	4.0	11	0	0.0	17:23	17	0	7	7	4	0	0	0	19:11
	San Diego Gulls	AHL	36	13	19	32	34	....	....	....	....	....	....	....	....	....	....	....	....	....	....	....	....	....	....
	NHL Totals		27	2	4	6	14	0	0	0	50	4.0		0	0.0	17:23	17	0	7	7	4	0	0	0	19:11

USHL First All-Star Team (2014) • USHL Player of the Year (2014) • Hockey East All-Rookie Team (2015) • AHL All-Rookie Team (2016) • AHL First All-Star Team (2016)

MOORE, Dominic
(MOOR, DOHM-ihn-ihk) **TOR**

Center. Shoots left. 6', 192 lbs. Born, Sarnia, ON, August 3, 1980. NY Rangers' 2nd pick, 95th overall, in 2000 NHL Draft.

			Regular Season														Playoffs								
Season	Club	League	GP	G	A	Pts	PIM	PP	SH	GW	S	S%	+/-	TF	F%	Min	GP	G	A	Pts	PIM	PP	SH	GW	Min
1996-97	Thornhill Rattlers	ON-Jr.A	29	4	6	10	48	....	....	....	....	....	....	....	....	....	1	0	1	1	0	....	....	....	....
1997-98	Aurora Tigers	ON-Jr.A	51	10	15	25	16	....	....	....	....	....	....	....	....	....	....	....	....	....	....	....	....	....	....
1998-99	Aurora Tigers	ON-Jr.A	51	34	53	87	70	....	....	....	....	....	....	....	....	....	....	....	....	....	....	....	....	....	....
99-2000	Harvard Crimson	ECAC	30	12	12	24	28	....	....	....	....	....	....	....	....	....	....	....	....	....	....	....	....	....	....
2000-01	Harvard Crimson	ECAC	32	15	28	43	40	....	....	....	....	....	....	....	....	....	....	....	....	....	....	....	....	....	....
2001-02	Harvard Crimson	ECAC	32	13	16	29	37	....	....	....	....	....	....	....	....	....	....	....	....	....	....	....	....	....	....
2002-03	Harvard Crimson	ECAC	34	*24	27	*51	30	....	....	....	....	....	....	....	....	....	....	....	....	....	....	....	....	....	....
2003-04	**NY Rangers**	**NHL**	**5**	**0**	**3**	**3**	**0**	**0**	**0**	**0**	**3**	**0.0**	**0**	**36**	**30.6**	**9:18**	....	....	....	....	....	....	....	....	....
	Hartford	AHL	70	14	25	39	60	....	....	....	....	....	....	....	....	....	16	3	3	6	8	....	....	....	....
2004-05	Hartford	AHL	78	19	31	50	78	....	....	....	....	....	....	....	....	....	6	1	1	2	4	....	....	....	....
2005-06	**NY Rangers**	**NHL**	**82**	**9**	**9**	**18**	**28**	**2**	**0**	**1**	**139**	**6.5**	**4**	**814**	**46.3**	**12:28**	**4**	**0**	**0**	**0**	**2**	**0**	**0**	**0**	**11:21**
2006-07	**Pittsburgh**	**NHL**	**59**	**6**	**9**	**15**	**46**	**0**	**0**	**0**	**100**	**6.0**	**1**	**678**	**51.6**	**13:04**	....	....	....	....	....	....	....	....	....
	Minnesota	**NHL**	**10**	**2**	**0**	**2**	**10**	**0**	**0**	**1**	**11**	**18.2**	**3**	**66**	**62.1**	**10:12**	....	....	....	....	....	....	....	....	....
2007-08	**Minnesota**	**NHL**	**30**	**1**	**2**	**3**	**10**	**0**	**0**	**0**	**28**	**3.6**	**−11**	**311**	**52.4**	**11:57**	....	....	....	....	....	....	....	....	....
	Toronto	**NHL**	**38**	**4**	**10**	**14**	**14**	**1**	**0**	**0**	**72**	**5.6**	**7**	**393**	**50.6**	**14:21**	....	....	....	....	....	....	....	....	....
2008-09	**Toronto**	**NHL**	**63**	**12**	**29**	**41**	**69**	**4**	**1**	**1**	**132**	**9.1**	**−1**	**1007**	**54.8**	**17:18**	....	....	....	....	....	....	....	....	....
	Buffalo	**NHL**	**18**	**1**	**3**	**4**	**23**	**0**	**0**	**0**	**33**	**3.0**	**−1**	**237**	**51.1**	**15:12**	....	....	....	....	....	....	....	....	....
2009-10	**Florida**	**NHL**	**48**	**8**	**9**	**17**	**35**	**2**	**1**	**0**	**81**	**9.9**	**−7**	**462**	**55.8**	**14:55**	....	....	....	....	....	....	....	....	....
	Montreal	**NHL**	**21**	**2**	**9**	**11**	**8**	**0**	**1**	**0**	**38**	**5.3**	**4**	**201**	**53.2**	**14:40**	**19**	**4**	**1**	**5**	**6**	**0**	**0**	**1**	**14:34**
2010-11	**Tampa Bay**	**NHL**	**77**	**18**	**14**	**32**	**52**	**6**	**0**	**3**	**175**	**10.3**	**−12**	**892**	**53.3**	**15:36**	**18**	**3**	**8**	**11**	**18**	**1**	**0**	**0**	**17:46**
2011-12	**Tampa Bay**	**NHL**	**56**	**4**	**15**	**19**	**48**	**0**	**1**	**1**	**74**	**5.4**	**−10**	**573**	**55.7**	**16:17**	....	....	....	....	....	....	....	....	....
	San Jose	**NHL**	**23**	**0**	**6**	**6**	**6**	**0**	**0**	**0**	**29**	**0.0**	**−8**	**189**	**52.9**	**13:43**	**3**	**0**	**0**	**0**	**5**	**0**	**0**	**0**	**15:08**
2012-13			DID NOT PLAY																						
2013-14	**NY Rangers**	**NHL**	**73**	**6**	**12**	**18**	**18**	**0**	**1**	**1**	**96**	**6.3**	**0**	**648**	**54.6**	**11:43**	**25**	**3**	**5**	**8**	**24**	**0**	**0**	**2**	**13:28**
2014-15	**NY Rangers**	**NHL**	**82**	**10**	**17**	**27**	**28**	**0**	**2**	**3**	**116**	**8.6**	**5**	**1074**	**54.5**	**13:49**	**19**	**1**	**2**	**3**	**12**	**0**	**0**	**1**	**14:49**
2015-16	**NY Rangers**	**NHL**	**80**	**6**	**9**	**15**	**32**	**0**	**0**	**2**	**94**	**6.4**	**−2**	**861**	**55.3**	**13:18**	**5**	**1**	**0**	**1**	**6**	**0**	**0**	**0**	**12:41**
2016-17	**Boston**	**NHL**	**82**	**11**	**14**	**25**	**44**	**0**	**3**	**1**	**96**	**11.5**	**2**	**654**	**54.6**	**12:57**	**6**	**0**	**1**	**1**	**4**	**0**	**0**	**0**	**16:09**
	NHL Totals		**847**	**100**	**170**	**270**	**471**	**15**	**10**	**14**	**1317**	**7.6**		**9096**	**53.3**	**13:54**	**99**	**12**	**17**	**29**	**77**	**1**	**0**	**4**	**14:48**

ECAC All-Rookie Team (2000) • ECAC Second All-Star Team (2001) • ECAC First All-Star Team (2003) • NCAA East First All-American Team (2003) • Bill Masterton Memorial Trophy (2014)

Traded to **Nashville** by **NY Rangers** for Adam Hall, July 19, 2006. Traded to **Pittsburgh** by **Nashville** with Libor Pivko for Pittsburgh's 3rd round pick (Ryan Thang) in 2007 NHL Draft, July 19, 2006. Traded to **Minnesota** by **Pittsburgh** for Minnesota's 3rd round pick (Casey Pierro-Zabotel) in 2007 NHL Draft, February 27, 2007. Claimed on waivers by **Toronto** from **Minnesota**, January 11, 2008. Traded to **Buffalo** by **Toronto** for Carolina's 2nd round pick (previously acquired, Toronto selected Jesse Blacker) in 2009 NHL Draft, March 4, 2009. Signed as a free agent by **Florida**, October 5, 2009. Traded to **Montreal** by **Florida** for Montreal's 2nd round pick (later traded to San Jose – San Jose selected Matthew Nieto) in 2011 NHL Draft, February 11, 2010. Signed as a free agent by **Tampa Bay**, July 30, 2010. Traded to **San Jose** by **Tampa Bay** with Tampa Bay's 7th round pick (later traded to Chicago – Chicago selected Brandon Whitney) in 2012 NHL Draft for Minnesota's 2nd round pick (previously acquired, later traded to Nashville – Nashville selected Pontus Aberg) in 2012 NHL Draft, February 16, 2012. • Missed 2012-13 due to personal reasons. Signed as a free agent by **NY Rangers**, July 5, 2013. Signed as a free agent by **Boston**, August 30, 2016. Signed as a free agent by **Toronto**, July 1, 2017.

MOORE, John
(MOOR, JAWN) **N.J.**

Defense. Shoots left. 6'3", 210 lbs. Born, Winnetka, IL, November 19, 1990. Columbus' 1st pick, 21st overall, in 2009 NHL Draft.

Season	Club	League	GP	G	A	Pts	PIM	PP	SH	GW	S	S%	+/-	TF	F%	Min	GP	G	A	Pts	PIM	PP	SH	GW	Min
2006-07	Chicago Mission	MWEHL	31	1	12	13	26	....	....	....	....	....	....	....	....	....	....	....	....	....	....	....	....	....	....
2007-08	Chicago Steel	USHL	56	4	11	15	26	....	....	....	....	....	....	....	....	....	7	0	2	2	2	....	....	....	....
2008-09	Chicago Steel	USHL	57	14	25	39	50	....	....	....	....	....	....	....	....	....	....	....	....	....	....	....	....	....	....
2009-10	Kitchener Rangers	OHL	61	10	37	47	53	....	....	....	....	....	....	....	....	....	20	4	12	16	2	....	....	....	....
2010-11	**Columbus**	**NHL**	**2**	**0**	**0**	**0**	**0**	**0**	**0**	**0**	**0**	**0.0**	**0**	**0**	**0.0**	**11:28**	....	....	....	....	....	....	....	....	....
	Springfield	AHL	73	5	19	24	23	....	....	....	....	....	....	....	....	....	....	....	....	....	....	....	....	....	....
2011-12	**Columbus**	**NHL**	**67**	**2**	**5**	**7**	**8**	**0**	**0**	**0**	**64**	**3.1**	**−23**	**0**	**0.0**	**15:49**	....	....	....	....	....	....	....	....	....
	Springfield	AHL	5	1	1	2	2	....	....	....	....	....	....	....	....	....	....	....	....	....	....	....	....	....	....
2012-13	Springfield	AHL	24	3	6	9	10	....	....	....	....	....	....	....	....	....	....	....	....	....	....	....	....	....	....
	Columbus	**NHL**	**17**	**0**	**1**	**1**	**2**	**0**	**0**	**0**	**14**	**0.0**	**−5**	**0**	**0.0**	**14:31**	....	....	....	....	....	....	....	....	....
	NY Rangers	**NHL**	**13**	**1**	**5**	**6**	**5**	**0**	**0**	**0**	**15**	**6.7**	**9**	**0**	**0.0**	**11:46**	**12**	**0**	**1**	**1**	**2**	**0**	**0**	**0**	**17:08**
2013-14	**NY Rangers**	**NHL**	**74**	**4**	**11**	**15**	**25**	**0**	**0**	**2**	**115**	**3.5**	**7**	**0**	**0.0**	**15:20**	**21**	**0**	**2**	**2**	**16**	**0**	**0**	**0**	**14:32**
2014-15	**NY Rangers**	**NHL**	**38**	**1**	**5**	**6**	**19**	**0**	**0**	**0**	**56**	**1.8**	**7**	**0**	**0.0**	**15:06**	....	....	....	....	....	....	....	....	....
	Arizona	**NHL**	**19**	**1**	**4**	**5**	**11**	**0**	**0**	**0**	**21**	**4.8**	**−11**	**0**	**0.0**	**18:43**	....	....	....	....	....	....	....	....	....
2015-16	**New Jersey**	**NHL**	**73**	**4**	**15**	**19**	**28**	**1**	**0**	**3**	**106**	**3.8**	**−12**	**0**	**0.0**	**19:50**	....	....	....	....	....	....	....	....	....
2016-17	**New Jersey**	**NHL**	**63**	**12**	**10**	**22**	**39**	**1**	**0**	**1**	**102**	**11.8**	**−7**	**0**	**0.0**	**18:59**	....	....	....	....	....	....	....	....	....
	NHL Totals		**366**	**25**	**56**	**81**	**137**	**2**	**0**	**6**	**493**	**5.1**		**0**	**0.0**	**16:55**	**33**	**0**	**3**	**3**	**18**	**0**	**0**	**0**	**15:29**

USHL First All-Star Team (2009) • USHL Defenseman of the Year (2009)

Traded to **NY Rangers** by **Columbus** with Derek Dorsett, Derick Brassard and Columbus' 6th round pick (later traded to Minnesota – Minnesota selected Chase Lang) in 2014 NHL Draft for Marian Gaborik, Blake Parlett and Steven Delisle, April 3, 2013. Traded to **Arizona** by **NY Rangers** with Anthony Duclair, Tampa Bay's 2nd round pick (previously acquired, later traded to Calgary – Calgary selected Oliver Kylington) in 2015 NHL Draft and NY Rangers' 1st round pick (later traded to Detroit – Detroit selected Dennis Cholowski) in 2016 NHL Draft for Keith Yandle, Chris Summers and Arizona's 4th round pick (Tarmo Reunanen) in 2016 NHL Draft, March 1, 2015. Signed as a free agent by **New Jersey**, July 1, 2015.

MOORE, Mike
(MOOR, MIGHK)

Defense. Shoots left. 6'1", 210 lbs. Born, Calgary, AB, December 12, 1984.

Season	Club	League	GP	G	A	Pts	PIM	PP	SH	GW	S	S%	+/-	TF	F%	Min	GP	G	A	Pts	PIM	PP	SH	GW	Min
2002-03	South Surrey	BCHL	55	3	10	13	187	....	....	....	....	....	....	....	....	....	....	....	....	....	....	....	....	....	....
2003-04	Surrey Eagles	BCHL	52	6	21	27	148	....	....	....	....	....	....	....	....	....	10	0	2	2	6	....	....	....	....
2004-05	Princeton	ECAC	25	3	7	10	22	....	....	....	....	....	....	....	....	....	....	....	....	....	....	....	....	....	....
2005-06	Princeton	ECAC	30	0	4	4	42	....	....	....	....	....	....	....	....	....	....	....	....	....	....	....	....	....	....
2006-07	Princeton	ECAC	32	4	10	14	50	....	....	....	....	....	....	....	....	....	....	....	....	....	....	....	....	....	....
2007-08	Princeton	ECAC	34	7	17	24	40	....	....	....	....	....	....	....	....	....	....	....	....	....	....	....	....	....	....
	Worcester Sharks	AHL	3	0	0	0	16	....	....	....	....	....	....	....	....	....	....	....	....	....	....	....	....	....	....
2008-09	Worcester Sharks	AHL	76	5	13	18	132	....	....	....	....	....	....	....	....	....	12	0	1	1	17	....	....	....	....
2009-10	Worcester Sharks	AHL	64	3	19	22	82	....	....	....	....	....	....	....	....	....	11	0	0	0	14	....	....	....	....
2010-11	**San Jose**	**NHL**	**6**	**1**	**0**	**1**	**7**	**0**	**0**	**0**	**5**	**20.0**	**−1**	**0**	**0.0**	**10:07**	....	....	....	....	....	....	....	....	....
	Worcester Sharks	AHL	49	2	10	12	50	....	....	....	....	....	....	....	....	....	....	....	....	....	....	....	....	....	....
2011-12	Worcester Sharks	AHL	61	4	16	20	85	....	....	....	....	....	....	....	....	....	....	....	....	....	....	....	....	....	....
2012-13	Milwaukee	AHL	50	5	11	16	42	....	....	....	....	....	....	....	....	....	4	1	0	1	2	....	....	....	....
2013-14	Providence Bruins	AHL	75	7	14	21	106	....	....	....	....	....	....	....	....	....	12	0	2	2	22	....	....	....	....
2014-15	Hershey Bears	AHL	41	3	11	14	47	....	....	....	....	....	....	....	....	....	9	0	1	1	10	....	....	....	....
2015-16	Hershey Bears	AHL	48	5	5	10	59	....	....	....	....	....	....	....	....	....	....	....	....	....	....	....	....	....	....
2016-17	Bremerhaven	Germany	45	2	13	15	95	....	....	....	....	....	....	....	....	....	6	1	0	1	8	....	....	....	....
	NHL Totals		**6**	**1**	**0**	**1**	**7**	**0**	**0**	**0**	**5**	**20.0**		**0**	**0.0**	**10:07**	....	....	....	....	....	....	....	....	....

ECAC First All-Star Team (2008) • NCAA East First All-American Team (2008)

Signed as a free agent by **San Jose**, April 8, 2008. Signed as a free agent by **Nashville**, July 3, 2012. Signed as a free agent by **Boston**, July 5, 2013. Signed as a free agent by **Washington**, July 1, 2014. Signed as a free agent by **Bremerhaven** (Germany), July 17, 2016.

MORIN, Jeremy
(moh-REHN, JAIR-eh-mee)

Right wing. Shoots right. 6'1", 189 lbs. Born, Auburn, NY, April 16, 1991. Atlanta's 3rd pick, 45th overall, in 2009 NHL Draft.

Season	Club	League	GP	G	A	Pts	PIM	PP	SH	GW	S	S%	+/-	TF	F%	Min	GP	G	A	Pts	PIM	PP	SH	GW	Min
2006-07	Rochester	EJHL	45	26	28	54	80	....	....	....	....	....	....	....	....	....	....	....	....	....	....	....	....	....	....
2007-08	USAHNTDP	NAHL	30	17	17	34	26	....	....	....	....	....	....	....	....	....	....	....	....	....	....	....	....	....	....
	USAHNTDP	U-17	7	11	1	12	4	....	....	....	....	....	....	....	....	....	....	....	....	....	....	....	....	....	....
	USAHNTDP	U-18	28	20	14	34	36	....	....	....	....	....	....	....	....	....	....	....	....	....	....	....	....	....	....
2008-09	USAHNTDP	NAHL	14	12	15	27	28	....	....	....	....	....	....	....	....	....	....	....	....	....	....	....	....	....	....
	USAHNTDP	U-18	41	21	11	32	79	....	....	....	....	....	....	....	....	....	....	....	....	....	....	....	....	....	....
2009-10	Kitchener Rangers	OHL	58	47	36	83	76	....	....	....	....	....	....	....	....	....	20	12	9	21	32	....	....	....	....
2010-11	**Chicago**	**NHL**	**9**	**2**	**1**	**3**	**9**	**0**	**0**	**0**	**13**	**15.4**	**2**	**0**	**0.0**	**12:06**	....	....	....	....	....	....	....	....	....
	Rockford IceHogs	AHL	22	8	4	12	34	....	....	....	....	....	....	....	....	....	....	....	....	....	....	....	....	....	....
2011-12	**Chicago**	**NHL**	**3**	**0**	**0**	**0**	**0**	**0**	**0**	**0**	**2**	**0.0**	**−1**	**0**	**0.0**	**8:52**	....	....	....	....	....	....	....	....	....
	Rockford IceHogs	AHL	69	18	22	40	121	....	....	....	....	....	....	....	....	....	....	....	....	....	....	....	....	....	....
2012-13	Rockford IceHogs	AHL	67	30	28	58	86	....	....	....	....	....	....	....	....	....	....	....	....	....	....	....	....	....	....
	Chicago	**NHL**	**3**	**1**	**1**	**2**	**0**	**0**	**0**	**0**	**7**	**14.3**	**1**	**4**	**0.0**	**13:01**	....	....	....	....	....	....	....	....	....
2013-14	**Chicago**	**NHL**	**24**	**5**	**6**	**11**	**32**	**0**	**0**	**0**	**46**	**10.9**	**5**	**6**	**66.7**	**9:10**	**2**	**0**	**0**	**0**	**2**	**0**	**0**	**0**	**6:26**
	Rockford IceHogs	AHL	47	24	23	47	58	....	....	....	....	....	....	....	....	....	....	....	....	....	....	....	....	....	....

			Regular Season														Playoffs								
Season	Club	League	GP	G	A	Pts	PIM	PP	SH	GW	S	S%	+/-	TF	F%	Min	GP	G	A	Pts	PIM	PP	SH	GW	Min
2014-15	Chicago	NHL	15	0	0	0	15	0	0	0	28	0.0	0	1	100.0	7:44									
	Rockford IceHogs	AHL	3	1	0	1	2																		
	Columbus	NHL	28	2	4	6	13	0	0	0	45	4.4	1	4	25.0	11:31									
2015-16	Rockford IceHogs	AHL	28	9	13	22	24																		
	Toronto Marlies	AHL	13	2	4	6	8																		
	San Jose	AHL	18	5	9	14	12										4	0	0	0	2				
2016-17	Syracuse Crunch	AHL	43	9	12	21	22																		
	Tucson	AHL	20	7	2	9	23																		
	NHL Totals		82	10	12	22	69	0	0	0	141	7.1		15	40.0	10:10	2	0	0	0	2	0	0	0	6:26

OHL Second All-Star Team (2010)

Traded to **Chicago** by **Atlanta** with Marty Reasoner, Joey Crabb and New Jersey's 1st (previously acquired, Chicago selected Kevin Hayes) and 2nd (previously acquired, Chicago selected Justin Holl) round picks in 2010 NHL Draft for Dustin Byfuglien, Brent Sopel, Ben Eager and Akim Aliu, June 24, 2010. • Missed majority of 2010-11 due to recurring upper-body injury. Traded to **Columbus** by **Chicago** for Tim Erixon, December 14, 2014. Traded to **Chicago** by **Columbus** with Artem Anisimov, Corey Tropp, Marko Dano and Columbus' 4th round pick (later traded to NY Islanders – NY Islanders selected Anatoli Golyshev) in 2016 NHL Draft for Brandon Saad, Michael Paliotta and Alex Broadhurst, June 30, 2015. Traded to **Toronto** by **Chicago** for Richard Panik, January 3, 2016. Traded to **San Jose** by **Toronto** with James Reimer for Alex Stalock, Ben Smith and San Jose's 3rd round pick in 2018 NHL Draft, February 28, 2016. Signed as a free agent by **Tampa Bay**, July 1, 2016. Traded to **Arizona** by **Tampa Bay** for Stefan Fournier, February 25, 2017.

MORIN, Samuel

(moh-REHN, SAM-yewl) **PHI**

Defense. Shoots left. 6'7", 227 lbs. Born, Lac-Beauport, QC, July 12, 1995. Philadelphia's 1st pick, 11th overall, in 2013 NHL Draft.

2010-11	Levis	QAAA	36	0	12	12	40										4	0	0	0	4				
2011-12	Rimouski Oceanic	QMJHL	62	0	8	8	57										10	0	1	1	8				
2012-13	Rimouski Oceanic	QMJHL	46	4	12	16	117										6	1	6	7	16				
2013-14	Rimouski Oceanic	QMJHL	54	7	24	31	121										11	4	4	8	30				
2014-15	Rimouski Oceanic	QMJHL	38	5	27	32	68										19	1	10	11	28				
2015-16	Lehigh Valley	AHL	76	4	15	19	118																		
2016-17	Philadelphia	NHL	1	0	0	0	0	0	0	0	2	0.0	0	0	0.0	17:47									
	Lehigh Valley	AHL	74	3	13	16	129										5	0	2	2	2				
	NHL Totals		1	0	0	0	0	0	0	0	2	0.0		0	0.0	17:47									

MORIN, Travis

(moh-REHN, TRA-vihs) **DAL**

Center. Shoots left. 6'1", 190 lbs. Born, Minneapolis, MN, January 9, 1984. Washington's 13th pick, 263rd overall, in 2004 NHL Draft.

2001-02	Chicago Steel	USHL	20	5	8	13											4	0	0	0	2				
2002-03	Chicago Steel	USHL	60	21	26	47	46																		
2003-04	Minnesota State	WCHA	38	9	12	21	14																		
2004-05	Minnesota State	WCHA	36	12	19	31	20																		
2005-06	Minnesota State	WCHA	39	20	22	42	16																		
2006-07	Minnesota State	WCHA	38	17	22	39	34																		
	South Carolina	ECHL	8	2	1	3	0																		
2007-08	Hershey Bears	AHL	4	0	0	0	0																		
	South Carolina	ECHL	68	34	50	84	30										20	*10	7	17	18				
2008-09	Hershey Bears	AHL	1	0	1	1	0																		
	South Carolina	ECHL	71	26	*62	88	46										19	4	*18	22	12				
2009-10	Texas Stars	AHL	80	21	31	52	30										24	4	12	16	6				
2010-11	Dallas	NHL	3	0	0	0	0	0	0	0	2	0.0	0	14	57.1	8:52									
	Texas Stars	AHL	64	21	24	45	30										6	3	4	7	0				
2011-12	Texas Stars	AHL	76	13	53	66	46																		
2012-13	Texas Stars	AHL	59	12	32	44	14										7	0	3	3	4				
2013-14	Dallas	NHL	4	0	1	1	0	0	0	0	4	0.0	2	38	50.0	10:20									
	Texas Stars	AHL	66	32	*56	*88	52										21	*9	*13	*22	12				
2014-15	Dallas	NHL	6	0	0	0	0	0	0	0	10	0.0	1	60	46.7	12:06									
	Texas Stars	AHL	63	22	41	63	40										3	0	0	0	0				
2015-16	Texas Stars	AHL	63	15	39	54	36										4	0	1	1	8				
2016-17	Texas Stars	AHL	72	21	34	55	42																		
	NHL Totals		13	0	1	1	0	0	0	0	16	0.0		112	49.1	10:48									

WCHA Second All-Star Team (2007) • ECHL First All-Star Team (2009) • AHL First All-Star Team (2014) • John P. Sollenberger Trophy (AHL - Top Scorer) (2014) • Les Cunningham Award (AHL – MVP) (2014) • Jack A. Butterfield Trophy (AHL - Playoff MVP) (2014)

Signed as a free agent by **Texas** (AHL), October 21, 2009. Signed as a free agent by **Dallas**, July 12, 2010.

MORRISSEY, Josh

(MOHR-ih-see, JAWSH) **WPG**

Defense. Shoots left. 6', 195 lbs. Born, Calgary, AB, March 28, 1995. Winnipeg's 1st pick, 13th overall, in 2013 NHL Draft.

2008-09	Calgary Royals	AMBHL	33	6	18	24	56																		
2009-10	Calgary Royals	AMBHL	32	21	28	49	108																		
2010-11	Calgary Royals	AMHL	30	17	22	39	11										6	1	3	4	10				
	Prince Albert	WHL	5	0	0	0	4																		
2011-12	Prince Albert	WHL	68	10	28	38	60																		
2012-13	Prince Albert	WHL	70	15	32	47	91										4	0	1	1	9				
2013-14	Prince Albert	WHL	59	28	45	73	59										4	1	2	3	6				
	St. John's IceCaps	AHL	8	0	1	1	2										20	2	7	9	20				
2014-15	Prince Albert	WHL	27	7	14	21	28																		
	Kelowna Rockets	WHL	20	6	11	17	34										13	2	12	14	24				
2015-16	Winnipeg	NHL	1	0	0	0	0	0	0	0	1	0.0	0	0	0.0	15:54									
	Manitoba Moose	AHL	57	3	19	22	47																		
2016-17	Winnipeg	NHL	82	6	14	20	38	1	0	3	99	6.1	6	0	0.0	19:29									
	NHL Totals		83	6	14	20	38	1	0	3	100	6.0		0	0.0	19:27									

Canadian Major Junior Scholastic Player of the Year (2013) • WHL East First All-Star Team (2014) • WHL West Second All-Star Team (2015)

MORROW, Joe

(MOH-row, JOH) **MTL**

Defense. Shoots left. 6', 199 lbs. Born, Edmonton, AB, December 9, 1992. Pittsburgh's 1st pick, 23rd overall, in 2011 NHL Draft.

2006-07	Strathcona	AMBHL	32	16	16	32	75										4	2	3	5	8				
2007-08	Sherwood Park	Minor-AB	24	7	11	18	57																		
	Portland	WHL	1	0	0	0	0																		
2008-09	Portland	WHL	41	0	7	7	26																		
2009-10	Portland	WHL	63	7	24	31	59										13	0	2	2	6				
2010-11	Portland	WHL	60	9	40	49	67										21	6	14	20	27				
2011-12	Portland	WHL	62	17	47	64	99										22	4	13	17	35				
2012-13	Wilkes-Barre	AHL	57	4	11	15	35																		
	Texas Stars	AHL	9	1	3	4	4										8	2	1	3	8				
2013-14	Providence Bruins	AHL	56	6	23	29	28										10	2	5	7	8				
2014-15	Boston	NHL	15	1	0	1	4	0	0	0	20	5.0	3	0	0.0	16:41									
	Providence Bruins	AHL	33	3	9	12	14										5	0	0	0	6				
2015-16	Boston	NHL	33	1	6	7	4	0	0	0	44	2.3	–7	0	0.0	15:54									
2016-17	Boston	NHL	17	0	1	1	8	0	0	0	19	0.0	–4	0	0.0	15:32	5	0	1	1	2	0	0	0	22:13
	Providence Bruins	AHL	3	1	0	1	2																		
	NHL Totals		65	2	7	9	16	0	0	0	83	2.4		0	0.0	15:59	5	0	1	1	2	0	0	0	22:13

WHL West First All-Star Team (2012)

Traded to **Dallas** by **Pittsburgh** with Pittsburgh's 5th round pick (Matej Paulovic) in 2013 NHL Draft for Brenden Morrow and Minnesota's 3rd round pick (previously acquired, Philadelphia selected Jake Guentzel) in 2013 NHL Draft, March 24, 2013. Traded to **Boston** by **Dallas** with Loui Eriksson, Reilly Smith and Matt Fraser for Tyler Seguin, Rich Peverley and Ryan Button, July 4, 2013. • Missed majority of 2015-16 as a healthy reserve. Signed as a free agent by **Montreal**, July 1, 2017.

			Regular Season														Playoffs								
Season	Club	League	GP	G	A	Pts	PIM	PP	SH	GW	S	S%	+/-	TF	F%	Min	GP	G	A	Pts	PIM	PP	SH	GW	Min

MOTTE, Tyler

(MAWT, TIGH-luhr) **CBJ**

Center. Shoots left. 5'9", 188 lbs. Born, Port Huron, MI, March 10, 1995. Chicago's 5th pick, 121st overall, in 2013 NHL Draft.

Season	Club	League	GP	G	A	Pts	PIM	PP	SH	GW	S	S%	+/-	TF	F%	Min	GP	G	A	Pts	PIM	PP	SH	GW	Min
2010-11	Det. Honeybaked	T1EHL	34	23	14	37	20	....	....	....	....	....	....	....	....	....	....	....	....	....	....	....	....	....	....
2011-12	USAHNTDP	USHL	36	15	13	28	32	....	....	....	....	....	....	....	....	....	2	2	0	2	0	....	....	....	....
	USAHNTDP	U-17	17	8	3	11	30	....	....	....	....	....	....	....	....	....	....	....	....	....	....	....	....	....	....
	USAHNTDP	U-18	2	1	0	1	0	....	....	....	....	....	....	....	....	....	....	....	....	....	....	....	....	....	....
2012-13	USAHNTDP	USHL	26	11	6	17	6	....	....	....	....	....	....	....	....	....	....	....	....	....	....	....	....	....	....
	USAHNTDP	U-18	41	15	13	28	44	....	....	....	....	....	....	....	....	....	....	....	....	....	....	....	....	....	....
2013-14	U. of Michigan	Big Ten	34	9	9	18	22	....	....	....	....	....	....	....	....	....	....	....	....	....	....	....	....	....	....
2014-15	U. of Michigan	Big Ten	35	9	22	31	14	....	....	....	....	....	....	....	....	....	....	....	....	....	....	....	....	....	....
2015-16	U. of Michigan	Big Ten	38	32	24	56	36	....	....	....	....	....	....	....	....	....	....	....	....	....	....	....	....	....	....
	Rockford IceHogs	AHL	5	2	3	5	2	....	....	....	....	....	....	....	....	....	3	2	0	2	0	....	....	....	....
2016-17	**Chicago**	**NHL**	**33**	**4**	**3**	**7**	**14**	**0**	**0**	**0**	**46**	**8.7**	**2**	**10**	**40.0**	**11:23**	....	....	....	....	....	....	....	....	....
	Rockford IceHogs	AHL	43	10	6	16	20	....	....	....	....	....	....	....	....	....	....	....	....	....	....	....	....	....	....
	NHL Totals		**33**	**4**	**3**	**7**	**14**	**0**	**0**	**0**	**46**	**8.7**		**10**	**40.0**	**11:23**	....	....	....	....	....	....	....	....	....

Big Ten First All-Star Team (2016) • NCAA West First All-American Team (2016

Traded to **Columbus** by **Chicago** with Artemi Panarin and NY Islanders' 6th round pick (previously acquired, Columbus selected Jonathan Davidsson) in 2017 NHL Draft for Brandon Saad, Anton Forsberg and Columbus' 5th round pick in 2018 NHL Draft, June 23, 2017.

MOULSON, Matt

(MOHL-suhn, MAT) **BUF**

Left wing. Shoots left. 6'1", 212 lbs. Born, North York, ON, November 1, 1983. Pittsburgh's 11th pick, 263rd overall, in 2003 NHL Draft.

Season	Club	League	GP	G	A	Pts	PIM	PP	SH	GW	S	S%	+/-	TF	F%	Min	GP	G	A	Pts	PIM	PP	SH	GW	Min
2001-02	Guelph	ON-Jr.B	42	56	46	102	80	....	....	....	....	....	....	....	....	....	....	....	....	....	....	....	....	....	....
2002-03	Cornell Big Red	ECAC	33	13	10	23	22	....	....	....	....	....	....	....	....	....	....	....	....	....	....	....	....	....	....
2003-04	Cornell Big Red	ECAC	32	18	17	35	37	....	....	....	....	....	....	....	....	....	....	....	....	....	....	....	....	....	....
2004-05	Cornell Big Red	ECAC	34	22	20	42	33	....	....	....	....	....	....	....	....	....	....	....	....	....	....	....	....	....	....
2005-06	Cornell Big Red	ECAC	35	18	20	38	14	....	....	....	....	....	....	....	....	....	....	....	....	....	....	....	....	....	....
2006-07	Manchester	AHL	77	25	32	57	23	....	....	....	....	....	....	....	....	....	16	2	3	5	8	....	....	....	....
2007-08	**Los Angeles**	**NHL**	**22**	**5**	**4**	**9**	**4**	**0**	**0**	**0**	**35**	**14.3**	**2**	**4**	**25.0**	**12:05**	....	....	....	....	....	....	....	....	....
	Manchester	AHL	57	28	28	56	29	....	....	....	....	....	....	....	....	....	4	2	0	2	4	....	....	....	....
2008-09	**Los Angeles**	**NHL**	**7**	**1**	**0**	**1**	**2**	**0**	**0**	**1**	**6**	**16.7**	**-4**	**0**	**0.0**	**14:30**	....	....	....	....	....	....	....	....	....
	Manchester	AHL	54	21	26	47	35	....	....	....	....	....	....	....	....	....	....	....	....	....	....	....	....	....	....
2009-10	**NY Islanders**	**NHL**	**82**	**30**	**18**	**48**	**16**	**8**	**0**	**5**	**208**	**14.4**	**-1**	**4**	**75.0**	**16:38**	....	....	....	....	....	....	....	....	....
2010-11	**NY Islanders**	**NHL**	**82**	**31**	**22**	**53**	**24**	**9**	**0**	**3**	**237**	**13.1**	**-10**	**9**	**55.6**	**18:52**	....	....	....	....	....	....	....	....	....
2011-12	**NY Islanders**	**NHL**	**82**	**36**	**33**	**69**	**6**	**14**	**0**	**5**	**219**	**16.4**	**1**	**4**	**50.0**	**19:18**	....	....	....	....	....	....	....	....	....
2012-13	**NY Islanders**	**NHL**	**47**	**15**	**29**	**44**	**4**	**8**	**0**	**0**	**154**	**9.7**	**-3**	**1**	**100.0**	**19:09**	**6**	**2**	**1**	**3**	**10**	**1**	**0**	**0**	**17:23**
2013-14	**NY Islanders**	**NHL**	**11**	**6**	**3**	**9**	**6**	**5**	**0**	**0**	**28**	**21.4**	**3**	**3**	**0.0**	**17:39**	....	....	....	....	....	....	....	....	....
	Buffalo	**NHL**	**44**	**11**	**18**	**29**	**20**	**3**	**0**	**2**	**105**	**10.5**	**-8**	**4**	**25.0**	**18:44**	....	....	....	....	....	....	....	....	....
	Minnesota	**NHL**	**20**	**6**	**7**	**13**	**8**	**1**	**0**	**3**	**43**	**14.0**	**7**	**2**	**50.0**	**16:27**	**10**	**1**	**2**	**3**	**4**	**0**	**0**	**0**	**15:00**
2014-15	**Buffalo**	**NHL**	**77**	**13**	**28**	**41**	**4**	**3**	**0**	**2**	**156**	**8.3**	**-11**	**22**	**59.1**	**17:41**	....	....	....	....	....	....	....	....	....
2015-16	**Buffalo**	**NHL**	**81**	**8**	**13**	**21**	**16**	**2**	**0**	**1**	**111**	**7.2**	**-5**	**5**	**0.0**	**11:54**	....	....	....	....	....	....	....	....	....
2016-17	**Buffalo**	**NHL**	**81**	**14**	**18**	**32**	**10**	**11**	**0**	**2**	**134**	**10.4**	**-4**	**4**	**25.0**	**11:36**	....	....	....	....	....	....	....	....	....
	NHL Totals		**636**	**176**	**193**	**369**	**120**	**64**	**0**	**24**	**1436**	**12.3**		**62**	**45.2**	**16:19**	**16**	**3**	**3**	**6**	**14**	**1**	**0**	**0**	**15:54**

ECAC First All-Star Team (2005) • NCAA East Second All-American Team (2005) • ECAC Second All-Star Team (2006)

Signed as a free agent by **Los Angeles**, September 1, 2006. Signed as a free agent by **NY Islanders**, July 6, 2009. Traded to **Buffalo** by **NY Islanders** with NY Islanders' 1st (later traded to Ottawa – Ottawa selected Colin White) in 2015 NHL Draft and 2nd (Brendan Guhle) round picks in 2015 NHL Draft for Thomas Vanek, October 27, 2013. Traded to **Minnesota** by **Buffalo** with Cody McCormick for Torrey Mitchell, Winnipeg's 2nd round pick (previously acquired, later traded to Washington – Washington selected Vitek Vanecek) in 2014 NHL Draft and Minnesota's 2nd round pick (later traded to Montreal, later traded to Chicago – Chicago selected Chad Krys) in 2016 NHL Draft, March 5, 2014. Signed as a free agent by **Buffalo**, July 1, 2014.

MOZIK, Vojtech

(MOH-zihk, VOI-tehk) **N.J.**

Defense. Shoots right. 6'3", 200 lbs. Born, Praha, Czech Rep., December 26, 1992.

Season	Club	League	GP	G	A	Pts	PIM	PP	SH	GW	S	S%	+/-	TF	F%	Min	GP	G	A	Pts	PIM	PP	SH	GW	Min
2009-10	Ml. Boleslav U18	CzR-U18	50	9	23	32	83	....	....	....	....	....	....	....	....	....	2	0	0	0	14	....	....	....	....
	Ml. Boleslav Jr.	CzRep-Jr.	3	0	1	1	2	....	....	....	....	....	....	....	....	....	....	....	....	....	....	....	....	....	....
2010-11	Ml. Boleslav Jr.	CzRep-Jr.	52	3	12	15	48	....	....	....	....	....	....	....	....	....	....	....	....	....	....	....	....	....	....
2011-12	Ml. Boleslav Jr.	CzRep-Jr.	11	0	3	3	14	....	....	....	....	....	....	....	....	....	....	....	....	....	....	....	....	....	....
	BK Mlada Boleslav	CzRep	39	3	5	8	16	....	....	....	....	....	....	....	....	....	....	....	....	....	....	....	....	....	....
	BK Mlada Boleslav	CzRep-Q	....	....	....	....	....	....	....	....	....	....	....	....	....	....	7	0	2	2	8	....	....	....	....
2012-13	BK Mlada Boleslav	CzRep-2	5	0	0	0	2	....	....	....	....	....	....	....	....	....	....	....	....	....	....	....	....	....	....
	HC Skoda Plzen	CzRep	28	0	1	1	20	....	....	....	....	....	....	....	....	....	....	....	....	....	....	....	....	....	....
2013-14	HC Skoda Plzen	CzRep	51	8	6	14	60	....	....	....	....	....	....	....	....	....	6	0	1	1	2	....	....	....	....
2014-15	HC Skoda Plzen	CzRep	51	10	19	29	94	....	....	....	....	....	....	....	....	....	4	1	1	2	6	....	....	....	....
2015-16	**New Jersey**	**NHL**	**7**	**0**	**0**	**0**	**4**	**0**	**0**	**0**	**6**	**0.0**	**0**	**0**	**0.0**	**13:14**	....	....	....	....	....	....	....	....	....
	Albany Devils	AHL	53	2	15	17	40	....	....	....	....	....	....	....	....	....	11	0	2	2	7	....	....	....	....
2016-17	Albany Devils	AHL	65	11	11	22	56	....	....	....	....	....	....	....	....	....	4	0	0	0	0	....	....	....	....
	NHL Totals		**7**	**0**	**0**	**0**	**4**	**0**	**0**	**0**	**6**	**0.0**		**0**	**0.0**	**13:14**	....	....	....	....	....	....	....	....	....

Signed as a free agent by **New Jersey**, June 15, 2015.

MUELLER, Chris

(MEW-luhr, KRIHS) **TOR**

Center. Shoots right. 5'11", 210 lbs. Born, West Seneca, NY, March 6, 1986.

Season	Club	League	GP	G	A	Pts	PIM	PP	SH	GW	S	S%	+/-	TF	F%	Min	GP	G	A	Pts	PIM	PP	SH	GW	Min
2004-05	Michigan State	CCHA	41	2	16	18	32	....	....	....	....	....	....	....	....	....	....	....	....	....	....	....	....	....	....
2005-06	Michigan State	CCHA	41	11	16	27	47	....	....	....	....	....	....	....	....	....	....	....	....	....	....	....	....	....	....
2006-07	Michigan State	CCHA	42	16	16	32	30	....	....	....	....	....	....	....	....	....	....	....	....	....	....	....	....	....	....
2007-08	Michigan State	CCHA	42	13	14	27	32	....	....	....	....	....	....	....	....	....	....	....	....	....	....	....	....	....	....
	Grand Rapids	AHL	2	0	0	0	0	....	....	....	....	....	....	....	....	....	....	....	....	....	....	....	....	....	....
2008-09	Lake Erie	AHL	59	5	11	16	23	....	....	....	....	....	....	....	....	....	....	....	....	....	....	....	....	....	....
	Johnstown Chiefs	ECHL	3	3	3	6	2	....	....	....	....	....	....	....	....	....	....	....	....	....	....	....	....	....	....
2009-10	Milwaukee	AHL	67	13	14	27	37	....	....	....	....	....	....	....	....	....	7	3	2	5	4	....	....	....	....
	Cincinnati	ECHL	5	4	1	5	0	....	....	....	....	....	....	....	....	....	....	....	....	....	....	....	....	....	....
2010-11	Milwaukee	AHL	67	24	26	50	34	....	....	....	....	....	....	....	....	....	13	4	7	11	13	....	....	....	....
	Nashville	**NHL**	**15**	**0**	**3**	**3**	**2**	**0**	**0**	**0**	**7**	**0.0**	**0**	**89**	**48.3**	**8:38**	....	....	....	....	....	....	....	....	....
2011-12	**Nashville**	**NHL**	**4**	**0**	**0**	**0**	**0**	**0**	**0**	**0**	**4**	**0.0**	**-1**	**27**	**55.6**	**9:09**	....	....	....	....	....	....	....	....	....
	Milwaukee	AHL	73	32	28	60	30	....	....	....	....	....	....	....	....	....	3	1	0	1	0	....	....	....	....
2012-13	Milwaukee	AHL	55	18	18	36	35	....	....	....	....	....	....	....	....	....	2	0	0	0	2	....	....	....	....
	Nashville	**NHL**	**18**	**2**	**3**	**5**	**6**	**0**	**0**	**1**	**22**	**9.1**	**-4**	**185**	**49.7**	**10:42**	....	....	....	....	....	....	....	....	....
2013-14	**Dallas**	**NHL**	**9**	**0**	**0**	**0**	**0**	**0**	**0**	**0**	**8**	**0.0**	**-2**	**54**	**53.7**	**9:15**	**4**	**0**	**0**	**0**	**2**	**0**	**0**	**0**	**6:28**
	Texas Stars	AHL	60	25	32	57	29	....	....	....	....	....	....	....	....	....	19	6	5	11	12	....	....	....	....
2014-15	**NY Rangers**	**NHL**	**7**	**1**	**1**	**2**	**0**	**1**	**0**	**0**	**10**	**10.0**	**-1**	**64**	**59.4**	**10:27**	....	....	....	....	....	....	....	....	....
	Hartford	AHL	64	14	26	40	26	....	....	....	....	....	....	....	....	....	15	5	4	9	6	....	....	....	....
2015-16	San Diego Gulls	AHL	63	20	37	57	50	....	....	....	....	....	....	....	....	....	9	4	7	11	6	....	....	....	....
2016-17	Tucson	AHL	68	19	48	67	48	....	....	....	....	....	....	....	....	....	....	....	....	....	....	....	....	....	....
	NHL Totals		**53**	**3**	**7**	**10**	**8**	**1**	**0**	**1**	**51**	**5.9**		**419**	**51.8**	**9:43**	**4**	**0**	**0**	**0**	**2**	**0**	**0**	**0**	**6:28**

Signed as a free agent by **Nashville**, December 27, 2010. Signed as a free agent by **Dallas**, July 8, 2013. Signed as a free agent by **NY Rangers**, July 1, 2014. Signed as a free agent by **Anaheim**, July 1, 2015. Signed as a free agent by **Arizona**, July 1, 2016. Signed as a free agent by **Toronto**, July 1, 2017.

MUELLER, Mirco

(MEW-luhr, MIHR-koh) **N.J.**

Defense. Shoots left. 6'3", 210 lbs. Born, Winterthur, Switz., March 21, 1995. San Jose's 1st pick, 18th overall, in 2013 NHL Draft.

Season	Club	League	GP	G	A	Pts	PIM	PP	SH	GW	S	S%	+/-	TF	F%	Min	GP	G	A	Pts	PIM	PP	SH	GW	Min
2009-10	Winterthur U17	Swiss-U17	12	0	4	4	0	....	....	....	....	....	....	....	....	....	....	....	....	....	....	....	....	....	....
2010-11	Kloten Flyers U17	Swiss-U17	32	12	19	31	14	....	....	....	....	....	....	....	....	....	10	0	6	6	12	....	....	....	....
	Kloten Flyers Jr.	Swiss-Jr.	1	0	0	0	0	....	....	....	....	....	....	....	....	....	....	....	....	....	....	....	....	....	....
2011-12	Kloten Flyers U17	Swiss-U17	4	1	3	4	0	....	....	....	....	....	....	....	....	....	....	....	....	....	....	....	....	....	....
	Kloten Flyers Jr.	Swiss-Jr.	26	3	3	6	8	....	....	....	....	....	....	....	....	....	4	1	2	3	2	....	....	....	....
	Kloten Flyers	Swiss	7	1	0	1	0	....	....	....	....	....	....	....	....	....	....	....	....	....	....	....	....	....	....
2012-13	Everett Silvertips	WHL	63	6	25	31	57	....	....	....	....	....	....	....	....	....	6	0	1	1	6	....	....	....	....

Season	Club	League	GP	G	A	Pts	PIM	PP	SH	GW	S	S%	+/-	TF	F%	Min	GP	G	A	Pts	PIM	PP	SH	GW	Min
																	Regular Season								

Season	Club	League	GP	G	A	Pts	PIM	PP	SH	GW	S	S%	+/-	TF	F%	Min	GP	G	A	Pts	PIM	PP	SH	GW	Min
2013-14	Everett Silvertips	WHL	60	5	22	27	31										5	1	1	2	4				
	Worcester Sharks	AHL	9	0	2	2	2																		
2014-15	**San Jose**	**NHL**	39	1	3	4	10	0	0	0	31	3.2	-8	0	0.0	16:58									
	Worcester Sharks	AHL	3	1	0	1	4																		
2015-16	**San Jose**	**NHL**	11	0	0	0	7	0	0	0	8	0.0	-4	0	0.0	10:36									
	San Jose	AHL	50	1	10	11	35										4	0	0	0	0				
2016-17	**San Jose**	**NHL**	4	1	1	2	0	0	0	0	3	33.3	2	0	0.0	9:36									
	San Jose	AHL	62	2	18	20	22										15	0	5	5	6				
	NHL Totals		54	2	4	6	17	0	0	0	42	4.8		0	0.0	15:07									

Traded to **New Jersey** by **San Jose** with San Jose's 5th round pick (Marian Studenic) in 2017 NHL Draft for Boston's 2nd round pick (previously acquired, San Jose selected Mario Ferraro) in 2017 NHL Draft and Nashville's 4th round pick (previously acquired, later traded to NY Rangers – NY Rangers selected Brandon Crawley) in 2017 NHL Draft, June 17, 2017.

MURPHY, Connor
(MUHR-fee, KAW-nuhr)   **CHI**

Defense. Shoots right. 6'4", 212 lbs.   Born, Dublin, OH, March 26, 1993. Phoenix's 1st pick, 20th overall, in 2011 NHL Draft.

Season	Club	League	GP	G	A	Pts	PIM	PP	SH	GW	S	S%	+/-	TF	F%	Min	GP	G	A	Pts	PIM	PP	SH	GW	Min
2008-09	Ohio Blue Jackets	Ind.	35	7	11	18																			
2009-10	USAHNTDP	USHL	2	0	0	0	2																		
	USAHNTDP	U-17	6	1	0	1	2																		
2010-11	USAHNTDP	USHL	9	3	1	4	6																		
	USAHNTDP	U-18	13	3	3	6	0																		
2011-12	Sarnia Sting	OHL	35	8	18	26	26										6	1	2	3	6				
2012-13	Sarnia Sting	OHL	33	6	12	18	32																		
2013-14	**Phoenix**	**NHL**	30	1	7	8	10	0	0	1	30	3.3	5	0	0.0	17:59									
	Portland Pirates	AHL	36	0	13	13	48																		
2014-15	**Arizona**	**NHL**	73	4	3	7	42	0	0	0	72	5.6	-27	1	0.0	16:48									
2015-16	**Arizona**	**NHL**	78	6	11	17	48	1	0	1	101	5.9	5	0	0.0	20:31									
2016-17	**Arizona**	**NHL**	77	2	15	17	45	0	1	1	81	2.5	-13	0	0.0	19:11									
	NHL Totals		258	13	36	49	145	1	1	3	284	4.6		1	0.0	18:46									

• Missed majority of 2009-10 and 2010-11 due to recurring back injury. Traded to **Chicago** by **Arizona** with Laurent Dauphin for Niklas Hjalmarsson, June 23, 2017.

MURPHY, Ryan
(MUHR-fee, RIGH-uhn)   **MIN**

Defense. Shoots right. 5'11", 185 lbs.   Born, Aurora, ON, March 31, 1993. Carolina's 1st pick, 12th overall, in 2011 NHL Draft.

Season	Club	League	GP	G	A	Pts	PIM	PP	SH	GW	S	S%	+/-	TF	F%	Min	GP	G	A	Pts	PIM	PP	SH	GW	Min
2008-09	York Simcoe	Minor-ON	73	30	65	95	52																		
	Villanova Knights	ON-Jr.A	4	4	2	6	0																		
2009-10	Kitchener Rangers	OHL	62	6	33	39	22										20	5	12	17	16				
2010-11	Kitchener Rangers	OHL	63	26	53	79	36										7	2	9	11	8				
2011-12	Kitchener Rangers	OHL	49	11	43	54	30										16	2	20	22	12				
2012-13	Kitchener Rangers	OHL	54	10	38	48	34										10	3	4	7	8				
	Carolina	**NHL**	4	0	0	0	2	0	0	0	7	0.0	-4	0	0.0	21:04									
	Charlotte	AHL	3	0	2	2	0										5	0	2	2	2				
2013-14	**Carolina**	**NHL**	48	2	10	12	10	1	0	0	81	2.5	-9	0	0.0	18:17									
	Charlotte	AHL	22	3	19	22	8																		
2014-15	**Carolina**	**NHL**	37	4	9	13	8	3	0	1	61	6.6	-11	0	0.0	18:17									
	Charlotte	AHL	25	0	17	17	10																		
2015-16	**Carolina**	**NHL**	35	0	10	10	10	0	0	0	47	0.0	-1	0	0.0	17:15									
	Charlotte	AHL	32	7	17	24	18																		
2016-17	**Carolina**	**NHL**	27	0	2	2	8	0	0	0	17	0.0	-11	0	0.0	13:10									
	Charlotte	AHL	7	0	1	1	4																		
	NHL Totals		151	6	31	37	38	4	0	1	213	2.8		0	0.0	17:12									

OHL All-Rookie Team (2010) • OHL First All-Star Team (2011) • OHL Second All-Star Team (2012, 2013)

Traded to **Calgary** by **Carolina** with Eddie Lack and Carolina's 7th round pick in 2019 NHL Draft for Keegan Kanzig and Calgary's 6th round pick in 2019 NHL Draft, June 29, 2017. Signed as a free agent by **Minnesota**, July 1, 2017.

MURRAY, Ryan
(MUHR-ee, RIGH-uhn)   **CBJ**

Defense. Shoots left. 6'1", 208 lbs.   Born, Regina, SK, September 27, 1993. Columbus' 1st pick, 2nd overall, in 2012 NHL Draft.

Season	Club	League	GP	G	A	Pts	PIM	PP	SH	GW	S	S%	+/-	TF	F%	Min	GP	G	A	Pts	PIM	PP	SH	GW	Min
2007-08	Balgonie	SMBHL	25	11	31	42	26																		
	Balgonie	Minor-SK	10	2	5	7																			
2008-09	Moose Jaw	SMHL	41	12	26	38	12										5	1	6	7	6				
	Everett Silvertips	WHL															5	0	1	1	2				
2009-10	Everett Silvertips	WHL	52	5	22	27	31										7	2	5	7	2				
2010-11	Everett Silvertips	WHL	70	6	40	46	45										4	1	2	3	4				
2011-12	Everett Silvertips	WHL	46	9	22	31	31										4	3	2	5	0				
2012-13	Everett Silvertips	WHL	23	2	15	17	14																		
2013-14	**Columbus**	**NHL**	66	4	17	21	10	3	0	0	62	6.5	-0	0	0.0	19:52	5	0	1	1	0	0	0	0	22:44
2014-15	**Columbus**	**NHL**	12	1	2	3	8	1	0	0	8	12.5	1	0	0.0	18:55									
2015-16	**Columbus**	**NHL**	82	4	21	25	40	1	0	0	90	4.4	-10	0	0.0	22:51									
2016-17	**Columbus**	**NHL**	60	2	9	11	24	0	0	0	52	3.8	-3	0	0.0	18:20									
	NHL Totals		220	11	49	60	82	5	0	0	212	5.2		0	0.0	20:30	5	0	1	1	0	0	0	0	22:44

WHL West Second All-Star Team (2011, 2012)

• Missed majority of 2012-13 due to shoulder surgery, January 20, 2013. • Missed majority of 2014-15 due to recurring knee injury and ankle injury vs. St. Louis, February 6, 2015.

MUSIL, David
(moo-SIHL, DAY-vihd)   **EDM**

Defense. Shoots left. 6'4", 207 lbs.   Born, Calgary, AB, AB, April 9, 1993. Edmonton's 3rd pick, 31st overall, in 2011 NHL Draft.

Season	Club	League	GP	G	A	Pts	PIM	PP	SH	GW	S	S%	+/-	TF	F%	Min	GP	G	A	Pts	PIM	PP	SH	GW	Min
2005-06	Jihlava U17	CzR-U17	5	0	0	0	0																		
2006-07	Jihlava U17	CzR-U17	36	7	23	30	42																		
	Trebic U17	CzR-U17	14	1	3	4	26																		
2007-08	Jihlava U17	CzR-U17	42	8	27	35	98										3	0	1	1	6				
	Jihlava Jr.	CzRep-Jr.	9	0	5	5	6																		
2008-09	Jihlava U17	CzR-U17	9	3	3	6	46																		
	Jihlava Jr.	CzRep-Jr.	27	9	12	21	46										8	3	3	6	10				
	HC Dukla Jihlava	CzRep-2	14	0	1	1	4										4	0	0	0	4				
2009-10	Vancouver Giants	WHL	71	7	25	32	67										16	2	2	4	8				
2010-11	Vancouver Giants	WHL	62	6	19	25	83										4	0	1	1	2				
2011-12	Vancouver Giants	WHL	59	6	21	27	104																		
2012-13	Vancouver Giants	WHL	14	2	6	8	18																		
	Edmonton	AHL	48	7	16	23	56										22	0	6	6	26				
2013-14	Oklahoma City	AHL	61	2	10	12	54										2	0	1	1	0				
	Bakersfield	ECHL	3	1	0	1	2																		
2014-15	**Edmonton**	**NHL**	4	0	2	2	2	0	0	0	3	0.0	-2	0	0.0	19:48									
	Oklahoma City	AHL	65	2	9	11	35										6	0	0	0	6				
2015-16	Bakersfield	AHL	67	3	11	14	39																		
2016-17	Bakersfield	AHL	47	4	10	14	34																		
	Tucson	AHL	13	0	4	4	6																		
	NHL Totals		4	0	2	2	2	0	0	0	3	0.0		0	0.0	19:48									

• Loaned to **Tucson** (AHL) by **Bakersfield** (AHL), March 6, 2017.

MUZZIN, Jake

(MUH-zihn, JAYK) **L.A.**

Defense. Shoots left. 6'3", 216 lbs. Born, Woodstock, ON, February 21, 1989. Pittsburgh's 7th pick, 141st overall, in 2007 NHL Draft.

			Regular Season														Playoffs								
Season	Club	League	GP	G	A	Pts	PIM	PP	SH	GW	S	S%	+/-	TF	F%	Min	GP	G	A	Pts	PIM	PP	SH	GW	Min
2004-05	Brantford 99ers	Minor-ON	57	20	23	43	78																		
2005-06	Sault Ste. Marie	OHL	DID NOT PLAY – INJURED																						
2006-07	Soo Thunderbirds	NOJHL	4	0	3	3	2																		
	Sault Ste. Marie	OHL	37	1	3	4	10										13	0	4	4	6				
2007-08	Sault Ste. Marie	OHL	67	6	12	18	53										10	1	3	4	4				
2008-09	Sault Ste. Marie	OHL	62	6	23	29	57																		
2009-10	Sault Ste. Marie	OHL	64	15	52	67	76										5	0	1	1	2				
	Manchester	AHL	1	0	1	1	0										13	1	3	4	6				
2010-11	Los Angeles	NHL	11	0	1	1	0	0	0	0	8	0.0	–2	0	0.0	13:43									
	Manchester	AHL	45	3	15	18	39										7	3	1	4	2				
2011-12	Manchester	AHL	71	7	24	31	40										3	0	1	1	2				
2012-13	Manchester	AHL	29	2	9	11	24																		
	Los Angeles	NHL	45	7	9	16	35	3	0	1	77	9.1	16	0	0.0	17:54	17	0	3	3	6	0	0	0	15:50
2013-14♦	Los Angeles	NHL	76	5	19	24	58	1	0	0	175	2.9	8	0	0.0	19:02	26	6	6	12	8	3	0	1	23:24
2014-15	Los Angeles	NHL	76	10	31	41	22	4	0	3	173	5.8	–4	0	0.0	22:42									
2015-16	Los Angeles	NHL	82	8	32	40	64	1	0	1	203	3.9	7	0	0.0	23:04	5	1	4	5	2	0	0	0	25:33
2016-17	Los Angeles	NHL	82	9	19	28	46	4	0	1	184	4.9	–21	0	0.0	22:18									
	NHL Totals		372	39	111	150	225	13	0	6	820	4.8		0	0.0	21:06	48	7	13	20	16	3	0	1	20:57

OHL First All-Star Team (2010) • Canadian Major Junior First All-Star Team (2010)

• Missed 2005-06 due to off-season back surgery. Signed as a free agent by **Los Angeles**, January 4, 2010.

MYERS, Tyler

(MIGH-uhrz, TIGH-luhr) **WPG**

Defense. Shoots right. 6'8", 229 lbs. Born, Houston, TX, February 1, 1990. Buffalo's 1st pick, 12th overall, in 2008 NHL Draft.

Season	Club	League	GP	G	A	Pts	PIM	PP	SH	GW	S	S%	+/-	TF	F%	Min	GP	G	A	Pts	PIM	PP	SH	GW	Min
2005-06	Notre Dame	SMHL	34	4	6	10	78																		
	Kelowna Rockets	WHL	9	0	1	1	2										8	1	0	1	2				
2006-07	Kelowna Rockets	WHL	59	2	13	15	78																		
2007-08	Kelowna Rockets	WHL	65	6	13	19	97										7	1	2	3	12				
2008-09	Kelowna Rockets	WHL	58	9	33	42	105										22	5	15	20	29				
2009-10	Buffalo	NHL	82	11	37	48	32	3	0	1	104	10.6	13	0	0.0	23:44	6	1	0	1	4	0	0	0	25:54
2010-11	Buffalo	NHL	80	10	27	37	40	3	0	5	122	8.2	0	0	0.0	22:27	7	1	5	6	16	0	0	0	23:52
2011-12	Buffalo	NHL	55	8	15	23	33	3	0	1	84	9.5	5	0	0.0	22:29									
2012-13	Klagenfurter AC	Austria	17	3	7	10	37																		
	Buffalo	NHL	39	3	5	8	32	1	0	2	48	6.3	–8	0	0.0	21:19									
2013-14	Buffalo	NHL	62	9	13	22	58	3	0	0	99	9.1	–26	0	0.0	21:54									
2014-15	Buffalo	NHL	47	4	9	13	61	1	0	0	72	5.6	–15	0	0.0	25:04									
	Winnipeg	NHL	24	3	12	15	16	1	0	0	52	5.8	9	0	0.0	23:49	4	1	0	1	2	1	0	0	24:23
2015-16	Winnipeg	NHL	73	9	18	27	72	0	0	0	140	6.4	6	1	0.0	22:37									
2016-17	Winnipeg	NHL	11	2	3	5	13	0	0	0	16	12.5	5	0	0.0	22:12									
	NHL Totals		473	59	139	198	357	15	0	9	737	8.0		1	0.0	22:52	17	3	5	8	22	1	0	0	24:42

WHL West Second All-Star Team (2009) • NHL All-Rookie Team (2010) • Calder Memorial Trophy (2010)

Signed as a free agent by **Klagenfurt** (Austria), October 15, 2012. Traded to **Winnipeg** by **Buffalo** with Drew Stafford, Joel Armia, Brendan Lemieux and St. Louis' 1st round pick (previously acquired, Winnipeg selected Jack Roslovic) in 2015 NHL Draft for Evander Kane, Zach Bogosian and Jason Kasdorf, February 11, 2015. • Missed majority of 2016-17 due to lower-body injury at Arizona, November 19, 2016.

NAKLADAL, Jakub

(nahk-LA-dahl, YA-kuhb)

Defense. Shoots right. 6'2", 212 lbs. Born, Hradec Kralove, Czech Rep., December 30, 1987.

Season	Club	League	GP	G	A	Pts	PIM	PP	SH	GW	S	S%	+/-	TF	F%	Min	GP	G	A	Pts	PIM	PP	SH	GW	Min
2007-08	Pardubice	CzRep	14	1	2	3	20																		
	HC Vrchlabi	CzRep-2	11	0	1	1	6																		
2008-09	Pardubice	CzRep	42	2	7	9	38																		
	HC Chrudim	CzRep-2	3	0	0	0	4										1	0	0	0	2				
2009-10	Pardubice	CzRep	45	5	9	15	58										13	1	3	4	26				
2010-11	Pardubice	CzRep	45	5	6	11	32										9	1	2	3	18				
2011-12	Pardubice	CzRep	12	2	3	5	4																		
	Ufa	KHL	32	1	7	8	30										6	1	0	1	20				
2012-13	Spartak Moscow	KHL	37	0	4	4	26																		
	HC Lev Praha	KHL	14	1	4	5	8										4	0	0	0	2				
2013-14	HC Lev Praha	KHL	34	0	3	3	26																		
2014-15	TPS Turku	Finland	50	3	12	15	63																		
2015-16	Calgary	NHL	27	2	3	5	6	0	0	0	42	4.8	–5	0	0.0	14:11									
	Stockton Heat	AHL	35	2	12	14	30																		
2016-17	Carolina	NHL	3	0	0	0	0	0	0	0	3	0.0	–4	0	0.0	14:30									
	Yaroslavl	KHL	24	3	6	9	21										15	6	5	11	21				
	NHL Totals		30	2	3	5	6	0	0	0	45	4.4		0	0.0	14:13									

Signed as a free agent by **Calgary**, May 19, 2015. Signed as a free agent by **Carolina**, October 9, 2016. Signed as a free agent by **Yaroslavl** (KHL), December 2, 2016.

NAMESTNIKOV, Vladislav

(nah-MEHST-nih-kawv, vla-dih-SLAHV) **T.B.**

Center. Shoots left. 5'11", 180 lbs. Born, Zhukovsky, Russia, November 22, 1992. Tampa Bay's 1st pick, 27th overall, in 2011 NHL Draft.

Season	Club	League	GP	G	A	Pts	PIM	PP	SH	GW	S	S%	+/-	TF	F%	Min	GP	G	A	Pts	PIM	PP	SH	GW	Min
2009-10	Khimik	Russia-2	33	12	9	21	18										2	1	0	1	2				
2010-11	London Knights	OHL	68	30	39	69	49										6	1	4	5	6				
2011-12	London Knights	OHL	63	22	49	71	50										19	4	14	18	20				
2012-13	Syracuse Crunch	AHL	44	7	14	21	32										18	2	5	7	10				
2013-14	Tampa Bay	NHL	4	0	0	0	4	0	0	0	4	0.0	–1	26	46.2	9:28									
	Syracuse Crunch	AHL	56	19	29	48	40																		
2014-15	Tampa Bay	NHL	43	9	7	16	13	1	0	3	46	19.6	1	155	45.2	12:00	12	0	1	1	4	0	0	0	7:52
	Syracuse Crunch	AHL	34	14	21	35	12																		
2015-16	Tampa Bay	NHL	80	14	21	35	45	1	0	2	106	13.2	17	391	44.8	14:07	17	1	2	3	0	0	0	0	10:15
2016-17	Tampa Bay	NHL	74	10	18	28	31	3	0	0	114	8.8	–4	480	43.5	14:47									
	NHL Totals		201	33	46	79	93	5	0	5	270	12.2		1052	44.3	13:49	29	1	3	4	4	0	0	0	9:16

NASH, Rick

(NASH, RIHK) **NYR**

Left wing. Shoots left. 6'4", 212 lbs. Born, Brampton, ON, June 16, 1984. Columbus' 1st pick, 1st overall, in 2002 NHL Draft.

Season	Club	League	GP	G	A	Pts	PIM	PP	SH	GW	S	S%	+/-	TF	F%	Min	GP	G	A	Pts	PIM	PP	SH	GW	Min
99-2000	Tor. Marlboros	GTHL	34	61	54	115	34																		
2000-01	London Knights	OHL	58	31	35	66	56										4	3	3	6	8				
2001-02	London Knights	OHL	54	32	40	72	88										12	10	9	19	21				
2002-03	Columbus	NHL	74	17	22	39	78	6	0	2	154	11.0	–27	14	35.7	13:57									
2003-04	Columbus	NHL	80	*41	16	57	87	*19	0	7	269	15.2	–35	21	28.6	17:38									
2004-05	HC Davos	Swiss	44	26	20	46	83										15	9	2	11	26				
2005-06	Columbus	NHL	54	31	23	54	51	11	0	4	170	18.2	5	38	50.0	18:16									
	Canada	Olympics	6	0	1	1	10																		
2006-07	Columbus	NHL	75	27	30	57	73	9	1	5	228	11.8	–8	143	42.7	19:12									
2007-08	Columbus	NHL	80	38	31	69	95	10	4	6	329	11.6	2	44	31.8	20:29									
2008-09	Columbus	NHL	78	40	39	79	52	6	5	5	263	15.2	11	18	27.8	21:10	4	1	2	3	2	0	0	0	20:52
2009-10	Columbus	NHL	76	33	34	67	58	10	2	6	254	13.0	–2	22	50.0	20:56									
	Canada	Olympics	7	2	3	5	0																		
2010-11	Columbus	NHL	75	32	34	66	34	6	0	7	305	10.5	2	24	29.2	18:56									
2011-12	Columbus	NHL	82	30	29	59	40	6	2	2	306	9.8	–19	19	31.6	19:05									
2012-13	HC Davos	Swiss	17	12	6	18	8																		
	NY Rangers	NHL	44	21	21	42	26	3	1	3	176	11.9	16	12	41.7	19:58	12	1	4	5	0	0	0	0	20:28
2013-14	NY Rangers	NHL	65	26	13	39	36	4	2	9	258	10.1	10	2	100.0	17:01	25	3	7	10	8	1	0	1	17:25
	Canada	Olympics	6	0	1	1	2																		
2014-15	NY Rangers	NHL	79	42	27	69	36	6	4	8	304	13.8	29	4	50.0	17:27	19	5	9	14	4	2	0	0	18:30

			Regular Season														Playoffs								
Season	Club	League	GP	G	A	Pts	PIM	PP	SH	GW	S	S%	+/-	TF	F%	Min	GP	G	A	Pts	PIM	PP	SH	GW	Min
2015-16	NY Rangers	NHL	60	15	21	36	30	4	0	4	183	8.2	8	1	0.0	16:56	5	2	2	4	4	0	1	0	18:09
2016-17	NY Rangers	NHL	67	23	15	38	26	6	1	3	195	11.8	9	1	0.0	16:28	12	3	2	5	4	0	0	1	18:25
	NHL Totals		989	416	355	771	722	106	22	71	3394	12.3		363	39.4	18:25	77	15	26	41	22	3	1	2	18:32

OHL All-Rookie Team (2001) • OHL Rookie of the Year (2001) • CHL All-Rookie Team (2001) • NHL All-Rookie Team (2003) • Maurice "Rocket" Richard Trophy (2004) (tied with Jarome Iginla and Ilya Kovalchuk) • NHL Foundation Player Award (2009)

Played in NHL All-Star Game (2004, 2007, 2008, 2009, 2011, 2015)

Signed as a free agent by **Davos** (Swiss), August 3, 2004. Traded to **NY Rangers** by **Columbus** with Steven Delisle and Columbus' 3rd round pick (Pavel Buchnevich) in 2013 NHL Draft for Brandon Dubinsky, Artem Anisimov, Tim Erixon and NY Rangers' 1st round pick (Kerby Rychel) in 2013 NHL Draft, July 23, 2012. Signed as a free agent by **Davos** (Swiss), September 18, 2012.

NASH, Riley (NASH, RIGH-lee) BOS

Center. Shoots right. 6'1", 200 lbs. Born, Consort, AB, May 9, 1989. Edmonton's 3rd pick, 21st overall, in 2007 NHL Draft.

Season	Club	League	GP	G	A	Pts	PIM	PP	SH	GW	S	S%	+/-	TF	F%	Min	GP	G	A	Pts	PIM	PP	SH	GW	Min
2005-06	Thompson Blazers	BCMML	31	29	31	60	100	....	....	....	....	....	....	....	....	....	....	....	....	....	....	....	....	....	....
	Salmon Arm	BCHL	1	0	0	0	0	....	....	....	....	....	....	....	....	....	5	1	2	3	0	....	....	....	....
2006-07	Salmon Arm	BCHL	55	38	46	84	87	....	....	....	....	....	....	....	....	....	11	4	7	11	31	....	....	....	....
2007-08	Cornell Big Red	ECAC	36	12	20	32	28	....	....	....	....	....	....	....	....	....	....	....	....	....	....	....	....	....	....
2008-09	Cornell Big Red	ECAC	36	13	22	35	34	....	....	....	....	....	....	....	....	....	....	....	....	....	....	....	....	....	....
2009-10	Cornell Big Red	ECAC	30	12	23	35	39	....	....	....	....	....	....	....	....	....	....	....	....	....	....	....	....	....	....
2010-11	Charlotte	AHL	79	14	18	32	26	....	....	....	....	....	....	....	....	....	16	1	3	4	16	....	....	....	....
2011-12	Carolina	NHL	5	0	1	1	2	0	0	0	2	0.0	1	35	31.4	10:34	....	....	....	....	....	....	....	....	....
	Charlotte	AHL	58	8	12	20	26	....	....	....	....	....	....	....	....	....	....	....	....	....	....	....	....	....	....
2012-13	Charlotte	AHL	51	13	24	37	20	....	....	....	....	....	....	....	....	....	5	1	2	3	0	....	....	....	....
	Carolina	NHL	32	4	5	9	8	0	0	0	36	11.1	-4	289	44.3	12:48	....	....	....	....	....	....	....	....	....
2013-14	Carolina	NHL	73	10	14	24	29	1	0	3	86	11.6	0	666	46.0	12:40	....	....	....	....	....	....	....	....	....
2014-15	Carolina	NHL	68	8	17	25	12	1	0	0	94	8.5	-10	958	50.9	16:19	....	....	....	....	....	....	....	....	....
2015-16	Carolina	NHL	64	9	13	22	18	2	0	1	76	11.8	-5	390	49.5	12:57	....	....	....	....	....	....	....	....	....
2016-17	Boston	NHL	81	7	10	17	14	0	1	2	125	5.6	-1	562	49.1	13:48	6	0	2	2	2	0	0	0	17:28
	NHL Totals		323	38	60	98	83	4	1	6	419	9.1		2900	48.3	13:46	6	0	2	2	2	0	0	0	17:28

ECAC All-Rookie Team (2008) • ECAC Rookie of the Year (2008) • ECAC First All-Star Team (2009)

Traded to **Carolina** by **Edmonton** for Ottawa's 2nd round pick (previously acquired, Edmonton selected Martin Marincin) in 2010 NHL Draft, June 25, 2010. Signed as a free agent by **Boston**, July 1, 2016.

NATTINEN, Joonas (na-TIH-nehn, YOH-nuhs) MTL

Center. Shoots right. 6'3", 192 lbs. Born, Jamsa, Finland, January 3, 1991. Montreal's 2nd pick, 65th overall, in 2009 NHL Draft.

Season	Club	League	GP	G	A	Pts	PIM	PP	SH	GW	S	S%	+/-	TF	F%	Min	GP	G	A	Pts	PIM	PP	SH	GW	Min
2006-07	JyP Jyvaskyla U18	Fin-U18	30	10	25	35	22	....	....	....	....	....	....	....	....	....	8	5	7	12	0	....	....	....	....
2007-08	JyP Jyvaskyla U18	Fin-U18	34	14	34	48	22	....	....	....	....	....	....	....	....	....	2	0	0	0	0	....	....	....	....
	JyP Jyvaskyla Jr.	Fin-Jr.	8	0	2	2	2	....	....	....	....	....	....	....	....	....	3	0	2	2	2	....	....	....	....
2008-09	Suomi U20	Finland-2	5	2	2	4	0	....	....	....	....	....	....	....	....	....	....	....	....	....	....	....	....	....	....
	Blues Espoo Jr.	Fin-Jr.	30	9	29	38	6	....	....	....	....	....	....	....	....	....	10	3	10	13	4	....	....	....	....
	Blues Espoo	Finland	14	0	0	0	4	....	....	....	....	....	....	....	....	....	....	....	....	....	....	....	....	....	....
2009-10	Blues Espoo	Finland	23	0	3	3	4	....	....	....	....	....	....	....	....	....	1	0	0	0	0	....	....	....	....
	Suomi U20	Finland-2	7	0	8	8	6	....	....	....	....	....	....	....	....	....	....	....	....	....	....	....	....	....	....
	Hokki Kajaani	Finland-2	10	2	2	4	4	....	....	....	....	....	....	....	....	....	....	....	....	....	....	....	....	....	....
	Blues Espoo Jr.	Fin-Jr.	11	7	6	13	2	....	....	....	....	....	....	....	....	....	....	....	....	....	....	....	....	....	....
2010-11	Suomi U20	Finland-2	2	0	0	0	0	....	....	....	....	....	....	....	....	....	....	....	....	....	....	....	....	....	....
	Blues Espoo Jr.	Fin-Jr.	2	0	2	2	0	....	....	....	....	....	....	....	....	....	....	....	....	....	....	....	....	....	....
	Blues Espoo	Finland	11	0	0	0	6	....	....	....	....	....	....	....	....	....	....	....	....	....	....	....	....	....	....
	HPK Hameenlinna	Finland	10	0	2	2	6	....	....	....	....	....	....	....	....	....	1	0	1	1	0	....	....	....	....
2011-12	Hamilton	AHL	63	11	10	21	30	....	....	....	....	....	....	....	....	....	....	....	....	....	....	....	....	....	....
2012-13	Hamilton	AHL	24	5	4	9	8	....	....	....	....	....	....	....	....	....	....	....	....	....	....	....	....	....	....
2013-14	Montreal	NHL	1	0	0	0	0	0	0	0	0	0.0	0	2	0.0	1:45	....	....	....	....	....	....	....	....	....
	Hamilton	AHL	69	8	7	15	22	....	....	....	....	....	....	....	....	....	....	....	....	....	....	....	....	....	....
2014-15	MODO	Sweden	55	7	11	18	38	....	....	....	....	....	....	....	....	....	....	....	....	....	....	....	....	....	....
	MODO	Sweden-Q	....	....	....	....	....	....	....	....	....	....	....	....	....	....	4	0	0	0	2	....	....	....	....
2015-16	JYP Jyvaskyla	Finland	46	9	12	21	16	....	....	....	....	....	....	....	....	....	13	2	2	4	8	....	....	....	....
2016-17	JYP Jyvaskyla	Finland	46	8	23	31	51	....	....	....	....	....	....	....	....	....	15	3	4	7	6	....	....	....	....
	NHL Totals		1	0	0	0	0	0	0	0	0	0.0		2	0.0	1:45	....	....	....	....	....	....	....	....	....

• Missed majority of 2012-13 due to upper-body injury vs. St. Johns (AHL), December 28, 2012. Signed as a free agent by **MODO** (Sweden), June 3, 2014. Signed as a free agent by **Jyvaskyla** (Finland), April 21, 2015.

NEAL, James (NEEL, JAYMS) VGK

Left wing. Shoots left. 6'2", 221 lbs. Born, Whitby, ON, September 3, 1987. Dallas' 2nd pick, 33rd overall, in 2005 NHL Draft.

Season	Club	League	GP	G	A	Pts	PIM	PP	SH	GW	S	S%	+/-	TF	F%	Min	GP	G	A	Pts	PIM	PP	SH	GW	Min
2003-04	Bowmanville	ON-Jr.A	43	28	27	55	....	....	....	....	....	....	....	....	....	....	....	....	....	....	....	....	....	....	....
	Plymouth Whalers	OHL	9	2	4	6	0	....	....	....	....	....	....	....	....	....	....	....	....	....	....	....	....	....	....
2004-05	Plymouth Whalers	OHL	67	18	26	44	32	....	....	....	....	....	....	....	....	....	4	1	1	2	6	....	....	....	....
2005-06	Plymouth Whalers	OHL	66	21	37	58	109	....	....	....	....	....	....	....	....	....	13	9	7	16	33	....	....	....	....
2006-07	Plymouth Whalers	OHL	45	27	38	65	94	....	....	....	....	....	....	....	....	....	20	13	12	25	54	....	....	....	....
2007-08	Iowa Stars	AHL	62	18	19	37	63	....	....	....	....	....	....	....	....	....	....	....	....	....	....	....	....	....	....
2008-09	Dallas	NHL	77	24	13	37	51	9	0	2	171	14.0	-11	31	35.5	15:52	....	....	....	....	....	....	....	....	....
	Manitoba Moose	AHL	5	4	1	5	2	....	....	....	....	....	....	....	....	....	....	....	....	....	....	....	....	....	....
2009-10	Dallas	NHL	78	27	28	55	64	2	1	4	200	13.5	-5	60	31.7	18:12	....	....	....	....	....	....	....	....	....
2010-11	Dallas	NHL	59	21	18	39	60	5	0	3	160	13.1	8	17	41.2	17:42	....	....	....	....	....	....	....	....	....
	Pittsburgh	NHL	20	1	5	6	6	0	0	0	52	1.9	-1	6	16.7	16:54	7	1	1	2	6	0	0	1	17:25
2011-12	Pittsburgh	NHL	80	40	41	81	87	*18	0	4	329	12.2	6	15	26.7	19:08	5	2	4	6	12	1	0	0	19:50
2012-13	Pittsburgh	NHL	40	21	15	36	26	9	0	6	136	15.4	5	6	16.7	17:28	13	6	4	10	8	2	0	1	17:43
2013-14	Pittsburgh	NHL	59	27	34	61	55	11	0	4	238	11.3	15	18	27.8	18:27	13	2	2	4	24	0	0	0	18:26
2014-15	Nashville	NHL	67	23	14	37	57	3	0	6	221	10.4	12	17	41.2	18:05	6	4	1	5	8	1	0	0	20:37
2015-16	Nashville	NHL	82	31	27	58	65	4	0	3	268	11.6	27	27	29.6	19:04	14	4	4	8	8	1	0	1	21:29
2016-17	Nashville	NHL	70	23	18	41	35	5	0	5	202	11.4	-10	6	50.0	17:42	22	6	3	9	14	1	0	2	17:55
	NHL Totals		632	238	213	451	506	66	1	37	1977	12.0		203	32.5	17:58	80	25	19	44	80	6	0	5	18:52

OHL First All-Star Team (2007) • Canadian Major Junior Second All-Star Team (2007) • NHL First All-Star Team (2012)

Played in NHL All-Star Game (2012, 2016)

Traded to **Pittsburgh** by **Dallas** with Matt Niskanen for Alex Goligoski, February 21, 2011. Traded to **Nashville** by **Pittsburgh** for Patric Hornqvist and Nick Spaling, June 27, 2014. Claimed by **Vegas** from **Nashville** in Expansion Draft, June 21, 2017.

NEIL, Chris (NEEL, KRIHS)

Right wing. Shoots right. 6'1", 206 lbs. Born, Markdale, ON, June 18, 1979. Ottawa's 7th pick, 161st overall, in 1998 NHL Draft.

Season	Club	League	GP	G	A	Pts	PIM	PP	SH	GW	S	S%	+/-	TF	F%	Min	GP	G	A	Pts	PIM	PP	SH	GW	Min
1995-96	Orangeville	ON-Jr.B	43	15	15	30	50	....	....	....	....	....	....	....	....	....	....	....	....	....	....	....	....	....	....
1996-97	North Bay	OHL	65	13	16	29	150	....	....	....	....	....	....	....	....	....	....	....	....	....	....	....	....	....	....
1997-98	North Bay	OHL	59	26	29	55	231	....	....	....	....	....	....	....	....	....	....	....	....	....	....	....	....	....	....
1998-99	North Bay	OHL	66	26	46	72	215	....	....	....	....	....	....	....	....	....	4	1	0	1	15	....	....	....	....
99-2000	Mobile Mysticks	ECHL	4	0	2	2	39	....	....	....	....	....	....	....	....	....	....	....	....	....	....	....	....	....	....
	Grand Rapids	IHL	51	9	10	19	301	....	....	....	....	....	....	....	....	....	8	0	2	2	24	....	....	....	....
2000-01	Grand Rapids	IHL	78	15	21	36	354	....	....	....	....	....	....	....	....	....	10	2	2	4	22	....	....	....	....
2001-02	Ottawa	NHL	72	10	7	17	231	1	0	0	56	17.9	5	0	0.0	8:22	12	0	0	0	12	0	0	0	7:12
2002-03	Ottawa	NHL	68	6	4	10	147	0	0	0	62	9.7	8	5	60.0	7:40	15	1	0	1	24	0	0	0	7:57
2003-04	Ottawa	NHL	82	8	8	16	194	0	0	1	76	10.5	13	14	42.9	8:51	7	0	1	1	19	0	0	0	6:45
2004-05	Binghamton	AHL	22	4	6	10	132	....	....	....	....	....	....	....	....	....	6	1	1	2	26	....	....	....	....
2005-06	Ottawa	NHL	79	16	17	33	204	8	0	0	126	12.7	9	9	22.2	12:18	10	1	0	1	14	0	0	0	6:58
2006-07	Ottawa	NHL	82	12	16	28	177	3	0	3	139	8.6	6	13	38.5	13:08	20	2	2	4	20	0	0	0	10:40
2007-08	Ottawa	NHL	68	6	14	20	199	0	0	1	78	7.7	-3	0	0.0	12:46	4	0	1	1	22	0	0	0	11:17
2008-09	Ottawa	NHL	60	3	7	10	146	0	0	0	59	5.1	-13	6	16.7	10:58	....	....	....	....	....	....	....	....	....
2009-10	Ottawa	NHL	68	10	12	22	175	1	0	2	100	10.0	-1	4	50.0	11:59	6	3	1	4	20	0	0	0	14:11
2010-11	Ottawa	NHL	80	6	10	16	210	0	0	2	105	5.7	-14	6	50.0	12:46	....	....	....	....	....	....	....	....	....
2011-12	Ottawa	NHL	72	13	15	28	178	2	0	0	127	10.2	-10	2	0.0	12:48	7	2	1	3	22	1	0	1	13:35

			Regular Season														Playoffs								
Season	Club	League	GP	G	A	Pts	PIM	PP	SH	GW	S	S%	+/-	TF	F%	Min	GP	G	A	Pts	PIM	PP	SH	GW	Min
2012-13	**Ottawa**	**NHL**	**48**	**4**	**8**	**12**	**144**	**0**	**0**	**3**	**87**	**4.6**	**0**	**6**	**50.0**	**13:52**	**10**	**0**	**4**	**4**	***39**	**0**	**0**	**0**	**12:42**
2013-14	**Ottawa**	**NHL**	**76**	**8**	**6**	**14**	**211**	**0**	**0**	**0**	**99**	**8.1**	**−10**	**3**	**33.3**	**11:48**	....	....	....	....	....	....	....	....	....
2014-15	**Ottawa**	**NHL**	**38**	**4**	**3**	**7**	**78**	**1**	**0**	**0**	**23**	**17.4**	**5**	**5**	**60.0**	**9:44**	**2**	**0**	**0**	**0**	**0**	**0**	**0**	**0**	**7:15**
2015-16	**Ottawa**	**NHL**	**80**	**5**	**8**	**13**	**165**	**0**	**0**	**0**	**70**	**7.1**	**−3**	**2**	**50.0**	**9:18**	....	....	....	....	....	....	....	....	....
2016-17	**Ottawa**	**NHL**	**53**	**1**	**3**	**4**	**63**	**0**	**0**	**0**	**42**	**2.4**	**−11**	**0**	**0.0**	**7:34**	**2**	**0**	**0**	**0**	**12**	**0**	**0**	**0**	**2:08**
	NHL Totals		**1026**	**112**	**138**	**250**	**2522**	**16**	**0**	**12**	**1249**	**9.0**		**75**	**40.0**	**10:58**	**95**	**9**	**10**	**19**	**204**	**1**	**0**	**1**	**9:33**

Signed as a free agent by **Binghamton** (AHL), March 2, 2005. • Missed majority of 2014-15 due to lower-body (December 11, 2014 vs. Los Angeles) and thumb (February 14, 2015 vs. Edmonton) injuries.

NELSON, Brock

(NEHL-suhn, BRAWK) **NYI**

Center. Shoots left. 6'3", 206 lbs. Born, Warroad, MN, October 15, 1991. NY Islanders' 2nd pick, 30th overall, in 2010 NHL Draft.

Season	Club	League	GP	G	A	Pts	PIM	PP	SH	GW	S	S%	+/-	TF	F%	Min	GP	G	A	Pts	PIM	PP	SH	GW	Min
2007-08	Warroad Warriors	High-MN	31	14	9	23	....	....	....	....	....	....	....	....	....	....	....	....	....	....	....	....	....	....	....
2008-09	Warroad Warriors	High-MN	31	45	36	81	....	....	....	....	....	....	....	....	....	....	....	....	....	....	....	....	....	....	....
2009-10	Team Great Plains	UMHSEL	24	5	10	15	....	....	....	....	....	....	....	....	....	....	....	....	....	....	....	....	....	....	....
	Warroad Warriors	High-MN	25	39	34	73	38	....	....	....	....	....	....	....	....	....	6	14	8	22	8	....	....	....	....
2010-11	North Dakota	WCHA	42	8	13	21	27	....	....	....	....	....	....	....	....	....	....	....	....	....	....	....	....	....	....
2011-12	North Dakota	WCHA	42	28	19	47	4	....	....	....	....	....	....	....	....	....	....	....	....	....	....	....	....	....	....
	Bridgeport	AHL	4	0	0	0	0	....	....	....	....	....	....	....	....	....	2	0	0	0	0	....	....	....	....
2012-13	Bridgeport	AHL	66	25	27	52	34	....	....	....	....	....	....	....	....	....	....	....	....	....	....	....	....	....	....
	NY Islanders	**NHL**	....	....	....	....	....	....	....	....	....	....	....	....	....	....	**1**	**0**	**0**	**0**	**0**	**0**	**0**	**0**	**7:44**
2013-14	**NY Islanders**	**NHL**	**72**	**14**	**12**	**26**	**12**	**3**	**0**	**1**	**132**	**10.6**	**−10**	**451**	**42.4**	**14:16**	....	....	....	....	....	....	....	....	....
	Bridgeport	AHL	1	0	1	1	2	....	....	....	....	....	....	....	....	....	....	....	....	....	....	....	....	....	....
2014-15	**NY Islanders**	**NHL**	**82**	**20**	**22**	**42**	**24**	**10**	**0**	**3**	**190**	**10.5**	**6**	**799**	**44.3**	**15:53**	**6**	**2**	**0**	**2**	**2**	**0**	**0**	**0**	**14:20**
2015-16	**NY Islanders**	**NHL**	**81**	**26**	**14**	**40**	**30**	**3**	**0**	**3**	**165**	**15.8**	**−3**	**388**	**47.9**	**15:48**	**11**	**1**	**4**	**5**	**6**	**0**	**0**	**0**	**16:49**
2016-17	**NY Islanders**	**NHL**	**81**	**20**	**25**	**45**	**36**	**1**	**0**	**4**	**173**	**11.6**	**−6**	**791**	**43.7**	**15:39**	....	....	....	....	....	....	....	....	....
	NHL Totals		**316**	**80**	**73**	**153**	**102**	**17**	**0**	**11**	**660**	**12.1**		**2429**	**44.3**	**15:26**	**18**	**3**	**4**	**7**	**8**	**0**	**0**	**0**	**15:29**

NELSON, Casey

(NEHL-sun, KAY-see) **BUF**

Defense. Shoots right. 6'2", 183 lbs. Born, Wisconsin Rapids, WI, July 18, 1992.

Season	Club	League	GP	G	A	Pts	PIM	PP	SH	GW	S	S%	+/-	TF	F%	Min	GP	G	A	Pts	PIM	PP	SH	GW	Min
2009-10	Wisc. Rapids	High-WI	STATISTICS NOT AVAILABLE																						
2010-11	Alaska Avalanche	NAHL	29	1	5	6	8	....	....	....	....	....	....	....	....	....	....	....	....	....	....	....	....	....	....
2011-12	Alaska Avalanche	NAHL	56	1	19	20	14	....	....	....	....	....	....	....	....	....	5	0	0	0	0	....	....	....	....
2012-13	Johnstown	NAHL	56	10	22	32	42	....	....	....	....	....	....	....	....	....	2	0	0	0	0	....	....	....	....
2013-14	Minnesota State	WCHA	19	1	4	5	6	....	....	....	....	....	....	....	....	....	....	....	....	....	....	....	....	....	....
2014-15	Minnesota State	WCHA	40	7	26	33	16	....	....	....	....	....	....	....	....	....	....	....	....	....	....	....	....	....	....
2015-16	Minnesota State	WCHA	40	6	16	22	22	....	....	....	....	....	....	....	....	....	....	....	....	....	....	....	....	....	....
	Buffalo	**NHL**	**7**	**0**	**4**	**4**	**8**	**0**	**0**	**0**	**5**	**0.0**	**1**	**0**	**0.0**	**14:49**	....	....	....	....	....	....	....	....	....
2016-17	**Buffalo**	**NHL**	**11**	**0**	**0**	**0**	**4**	**0**	**0**	**0**	**10**	**0.0**	**−3**	**0**	**0.0**	**12:36**	....	....	....	....	....	....	....	....	....
	Rochester	AHL	58	7	14	21	24	....	....	....	....	....	....	....	....	....	....	....	....	....	....	....	....	....	....
	NHL Totals		**18**	**0**	**4**	**4**	**12**	**0**	**0**	**0**	**15**	**0.0**		**0**	**0.0**	**13:28**	....	....	....	....	....	....	....	....	....

WCHA First All-Star Team (2016)

Signed as a free agent by **Buffalo**, March 22, 2016.

NEMETH, Patrik

(NEH-meht, PAHT-rihk) **DAL**

Defense. Shoots left. 6'3", 230 lbs. Born, Stockholm, Sweden, February 8, 1992. Dallas' 2nd pick, 41st overall, in 2010 NHL Draft.

Season	Club	League	GP	G	A	Pts	PIM	PP	SH	GW	S	S%	+/-	TF	F%	Min	GP	G	A	Pts	PIM	PP	SH	GW	Min
2007-08	Hammarby U18	Swe-U18	13	1	3	4	12	....	....	....	....	....	....	....	....	....	....	....	....	....	....	....	....	....	....
2008-09	AIK IF Solna U18	Swe-U18	27	3	10	13	123	....	....	....	....	....	....	....	....	....	4	1	0	1	29	....	....	....	....
	AIK IF Solna Jr.	Swe-Jr.	19	0	0	0	43	....	....	....	....	....	....	....	....	....	....	....	....	....	....	....	....	....	....
	AIK IF Solna	Sweden-2	1	0	1	1	0	....	....	....	....	....	....	....	....	....	....	....	....	....	....	....	....	....	....
2009-10	AIK IF Solna U18	Swe-U18	3	0	1	1	4	....	....	....	....	....	....	....	....	....	1	0	1	1	0	....	....	....	....
	AIK IF Solna Jr.	Swe-Jr.	38	1	19	20	120	....	....	....	....	....	....	....	....	....	5	1	2	3	10	....	....	....	....
	AIK IF Solna	Sweden-2	19	0	3	3	8	....	....	....	....	....	....	....	....	....	....	....	....	....	....	....	....	....	....
2010-11	AIK IF Solna	Sweden	38	1	6	7	18	....	....	....	....	....	....	....	....	....	7	0	0	0	2	....	....	....	....
2011-12	AIK Solna	Sweden	46	0	3	3	55	....	....	....	....	....	....	....	....	....	11	0	1	1	8	....	....	....	....
2012-13	Texas Stars	AHL	47	1	11	12	40	....	....	....	....	....	....	....	....	....	....	....	....	....	....	....	....	....	....
2013-14	**Dallas**	**NHL**	**8**	**0**	**0**	**0**	**6**	**0**	**0**	**0**	**3**	**0.0**	**−3**	**0**	**0.0**	**13:46**	**5**	**0**	**0**	**0**	**12**	**0**	**0**	**0**	**15:16**
	Texas Stars	AHL	37	3	7	10	32	....	....	....	....	....	....	....	....	....	18	1	4	5	8	....	....	....	....
2014-15	**Dallas**	**NHL**	**22**	**0**	**3**	**3**	**6**	**0**	**0**	**0**	**16**	**0.0**	**0**	**0**	**0.0**	**16:13**	....	....	....	....	....	....	....	....	....
	Texas Stars	AHL	8	0	2	2	6	....	....	....	....	....	....	....	....	....	3	0	1	1	4	....	....	....	....
2015-16	**Dallas**	**NHL**	**38**	**0**	**8**	**8**	**14**	**0**	**0**	**0**	**36**	**0.0**	**−1**	**0**	**0.0**	**15:38**	....	....	....	....	....	....	....	....	....
	Texas Stars	AHL	8	0	1	1	2	....	....	....	....	....	....	....	....	....	....	....	....	....	....	....	....	....	....
2016-17	**Dallas**	**NHL**	**40**	**0**	**3**	**3**	**14**	**0**	**0**	**0**	**46**	**0.0**	**−4**	**0**	**0.0**	**15:47**	....	....	....	....	....	....	....	....	....
	Texas Stars	AHL	4	1	2	3	2	....	....	....	....	....	....	....	....	....	....	....	....	....	....	....	....	....	....
	NHL Totals		**108**	**0**	**14**	**14**	**40**	**0**	**0**	**0**	**101**	**0.0**		**0**	**0.0**	**15:40**	**5**	**0**	**0**	**0**	**12**	**0**	**0**	**0**	**15:16**

• Missed majority of 2014-15 due to arm injury vs. Philadelphia, October 18, 2014.

NESS, Aaron

(NEHS, AIR-uhn) **WSH**

Defense. Shoots left. 5'10", 187 lbs. Born, Roseau, MN, May 18, 1990. NY Islanders' 3rd pick, 40th overall, in 2008 NHL Draft.

Season	Club	League	GP	G	A	Pts	PIM	PP	SH	GW	S	S%	+/-	TF	F%	Min	GP	G	A	Pts	PIM	PP	SH	GW	Min
2005-06	Roseau Rams	High-MN	30	3	18	21	8	....	....	....	....	....	....	....	....	....	....	....	....	....	....	....	....	....	....
2006-07	Roseau Rams	High-MN	31	13	38	51	12	....	....	....	....	....	....	....	....	....	....	....	....	....	....	....	....	....	....
	Team Great Plains	UMWEHL	11	0	8	8	....	....	....	....	....	....	....	....	....	....	....	....	....	....	....	....	....	....	....
2007-08	Roseau Rams	High-MN	31	28	44	72	16	....	....	....	....	....	....	....	....	....	....	....	....	....	....	....	....	....	....
	Team Great Plains	UMWEHL	11	2	11	13	....	....	....	....	....	....	....	....	....	....	....	....	....	....	....	....	....	....	....
2008-09	U. of Minnesota	WCHA	37	2	15	17	16	....	....	....	....	....	....	....	....	....	....	....	....	....	....	....	....	....	....
2009-10	U. of Minnesota	WCHA	39	2	10	12	24	....	....	....	....	....	....	....	....	....	....	....	....	....	....	....	....	....	....
2010-11	U. of Minnesota	WCHA	35	2	12	14	41	....	....	....	....	....	....	....	....	....	....	....	....	....	....	....	....	....	....
	Bridgeport	AHL	13	1	3	4	4	....	....	....	....	....	....	....	....	....	....	....	....	....	....	....	....	....	....
2011-12	**NY Islanders**	**NHL**	**9**	**0**	**0**	**0**	**2**	**0**	**0**	**0**	**6**	**0.0**	**0**	**0**	**0.0**	**16:56**	....	....	....	....	....	....	....	....	....
	Bridgeport	AHL	69	5	22	27	36	....	....	....	....	....	....	....	....	....	3	0	0	0	4	....	....	....	....
2012-13	Bridgeport	AHL	76	3	24	27	30	....	....	....	....	....	....	....	....	....	....	....	....	....	....	....	....	....	....
2013-14	**NY Islanders**	**NHL**	**20**	**1**	**2**	**3**	**10**	**0**	**0**	**0**	**23**	**4.3**	**−13**	**0**	**0.0**	**14:48**	....	....	....	....	....	....	....	....	....
	Bridgeport	AHL	48	6	14	20	47	....	....	....	....	....	....	....	....	....	....	....	....	....	....	....	....	....	....
2014-15	Bridgeport	AHL	74	8	37	45	62	....	....	....	....	....	....	....	....	....	....	....	....	....	....	....	....	....	....
2015-16	**Washington**	**NHL**	**8**	**0**	**2**	**2**	**2**	**0**	**0**	**0**	**8**	**0.0**	**4**	**0**	**0.0**	**12:23**	....	....	....	....	....	....	....	....	....
	Hershey Bears	AHL	62	6	21	27	22	....	....	....	....	....	....	....	....	....	21	0	*12	12	12	....	....	....	....
2016-17	**Washington**	**NHL**	**2**	**0**	**0**	**0**	**0**	**0**	**0**	**0**	**0**	**0.0**	**−1**	**0**	**0.0**	**12:50**	....	....	....	....	....	....	....	....	....
	Hershey Bears	AHL	51	5	12	17	24	....	....	....	....	....	....	....	....	....	9	0	1	1	0	....	....	....	....
	NHL Totals		**39**	**1**	**4**	**5**	**14**	**0**	**0**	**0**	**37**	**2.7**		**0**	**0.0**	**14:42**	....	....	....	....	....	....	....	....	....

Signed as a free agent by **Washington**, July 1, 2015.

NESTEROV, Nikita

(NEHS-tehr-awf, nih-KEE-tuh)

Defense. Shoots left. 5'11", 191 lbs. Born, Chelyabinsk, Russia, March 28, 1993. Tampa Bay's 3rd pick, 148th overall, in 2011 NHL Draft.

Season	Club	League	GP	G	A	Pts	PIM	PP	SH	GW	S	S%	+/-	TF	F%	Min	GP	G	A	Pts	PIM	PP	SH	GW	Min
2009-10	Chelyabinsk Jr.	Russia-Jr.	9	5	2	7	8	....	....	....	....	....	....	....	....	....	4	0	0	0	6	....	....	....	....
2010-11	Chelyabinsk Jr.	Russia-Jr.	46	5	14	19	72	....	....	....	....	....	....	....	....	....	5	0	0	0	6	....	....	....	....
2011-12	Chelyabinsk Jr.	Russia-Jr.	41	11	20	31	66	....	....	....	....	....	....	....	....	....	4	0	5	5	6	....	....	....	....
	Chelyabinsk	KHL	10	0	1	1	4	....	....	....	....	....	....	....	....	....	3	0	0	0	0	....	....	....	....
2012-13	Chelyabinsk Jr.	Russia-Jr.	2	0	1	1	2	....	....	....	....	....	....	....	....	....	4	2	1	3	0	....	....	....	....
	Chelyabinsk	KHL	35	0	0	0	14	....	....	....	....	....	....	....	....	....	19	0	4	4	6	....	....	....	....
2013-14	Syracuse Crunch	AHL	54	4	12	16	39	....	....	....	....	....	....	....	....	....	....	....	....	....	....	....	....	....	....
2014-15	**Tampa Bay**	**NHL**	**27**	**2**	**5**	**7**	**16**	**1**	**0**	**0**	**44**	**4.5**	**6**	**0**	**0.0**	**16:03**	**17**	**1**	**5**	**6**	**8**	**0**	**0**	**0**	**10:46**
	Syracuse Crunch	AHL	32	3	11	14	26	....	....	....	....	....	....	....	....	....	....	....	....	....	....	....	....	....	....
2015-16	**Tampa Bay**	**NHL**	**57**	**3**	**6**	**9**	**41**	**2**	**0**	**0**	**57**	**5.3**	**−6**	**0**	**0.0**	**14:53**	**9**	**0**	**1**	**1**	**9**	**0**	**0**	**0**	**11:59**
	Syracuse Crunch	AHL	10	1	3	4	4	....	....	....	....	....	....	....	....	....	....	....	....	....	....	....	....	....	....

			Regular Season														Playoffs								
Season	Club	League	GP	G	A	Pts	PIM	PP	SH	GW	S	S%	+/-	TF	F%	Min	GP	G	A	Pts	PIM	PP	SH	GW	Min
2016-17	Tampa Bay	NHL	35	3	9	12	20	1	0	0	46	6.5	–3	0	0.0	16:35	....	....	....	....	....	....	....	....	....
	Montreal	NHL	13	1	4	5	4	0	0	0	17	5.9	3	0	0.0	15:29	2	0	0	0	0	0	0	0	14:28
	NHL Totals		132	9	24	33	81	4	0	0	164	5.5		0	0.0	15:38	28	1	6	7	17	0	0	0	11:25

Traded to **Montreal** by **Tampa Bay** for Jonathan Racine and Montreal's 6th round pick (Cole Guttman) in 2017 NHL Draft, January 26, 2017.

NESTRASIL, Andrej

(NEHS-tra-shihl, ahn-DRAY)

Right wing. Shoots left. 6'3", 200 lbs. Born, Prague, Czech., February 22, 1991. Detroit's 3rd pick, 75th overall, in 2009 NHL Draft.

Season	Club	League	GP	G	A	Pts	PIM	PP	SH	GW	S	S%	+/-	TF	F%	Min	GP	G	A	Pts	PIM	PP	SH	GW	Min
2004-05	Slavia U17	CzR-U17	3	0	1	1	2	....	....	....	....	....	....	....	....	....	....	....	....	....	....	....	....	....	....
2005-06	Slavia U17	CzR-U17	41	6	12	18	18	....	....	....	....	....	....	....	....	....	....	....	....	....	....	....	....	....	....
2006-07	Slavia U17	CzR-U17	43	24	37	61	75	....	....	....	....	....	....	....	....	....	5	2	2	4	6	....	....	....	....
2007-08	Slavia U17	CzR-U17	....	....	....	....	....	....	....	....	....	....	....	....	....	....	2	1	0	1	2	....	....	....	....
	Slavia Jr.	CzRep-Jr.	40	12	16	28	58	....	....	....	....	....	....	....	....	....	5	1	2	3	4	....	....	....	....
2008-09	Victoriaville Tigres	QMJHL	66	22	35	57	67	....	....	....	....	....	....	....	....	....	4	2	1	3	10	....	....	....	....
2009-10	Victoriaville Tigres	QMJHL	50	16	35	51	40	....	....	....	....	....	....	....	....	....	16	2	4	6	10	....	....	....	....
2010-11	P.E.I. Rocket	QMJHL	58	19	51	70	40	....	....	....	....	....	....	....	....	....	5	1	5	6	2	....	....	....	....
2011-12	Grand Rapids	AHL	25	3	1	4	6	....	....	....	....	....	....	....	....	....	....	....	....	....	....	....	....	....	....
	Toledo Walleye	ECHL	51	7	22	29	20	....	....	....	....	....	....	....	....	....	....	....	....	....	....	....	....	....	....
2012-13	Toledo Walleye	ECHL	40	11	30	41	26	....	....	....	....	....	....	....	....	....	4	1	2	3	0	....	....	....	....
	Grand Rapids	AHL	25	3	3	6	2	....	....	....	....	....	....	....	....	....	1	0	0	0	0	....	....	....	....
2013-14	Grand Rapids	AHL	70	16	20	36	24	....	....	....	....	....	....	....	....	....	10	4	2	6	4	....	....	....	....
2014-15	Detroit	NHL	13	0	2	2	4	0	0	0	16	0.0	–3	2	100.0	11:04	....	....	....	....	....	....	....	....	....
	Carolina	NHL	41	7	11	18	4	2	0	0	66	10.6	2	92	57.6	14:05	....	....	....	....	....	....	....	....	....
	Charlotte	AHL	3	0	0	0	17	....	....	....	....	....	....	....	....	....	....	....	....	....	....	....	....	....	....
2015-16	Carolina	NHL	55	9	14	23	8	2	0	1	105	8.6	4	25	32.0	14:21	....	....	....	....	....	....	....	....	....
2016-17	Carolina	NHL	19	1	4	5	2	0	0	0	27	3.7	–3	10	30.0	10:54	....	....	....	....	....	....	....	....	....
	Charlotte	AHL	39	5	9	14	6	....	....	....	....	....	....	....	....	....	5	0	1	1	0	....	....	....	....
	NHL Totals		128	17	31	48	18	4	0	1	214	7.9		129	51.2	13:25	....	....	....	....	....	....	....	....	....

Claimed on waivers by **Carolina** from **Detroit**, November 20, 2014.

NEWBURY, Kris

(new-BUHR-ee, KRIHS)

Center. Shoots left. 5'11", 205 lbs. Born, Brampton, ON, February 19, 1982. San Jose's 4th pick, 139th overall, in 2002 NHL Draft.

Season	Club	League	GP	G	A	Pts	PIM	PP	SH	GW	S	S%	+/-	TF	F%	Min	GP	G	A	Pts	PIM	PP	SH	GW	Min
1996-97	Brampton	ON-Jr.A	28	9	4	13	36	....	....	....	....	....	....	....	....	....	....	....	....	....	....	....	....	....	....
1997-98	Brampton	ON-Jr.A	46	11	21	32	161	....	....	....	....	....	....	....	....	....	....	....	....	....	....	....	....	....	....
1998-99	Belleville Bulls	OHL	51	6	8	14	89	....	....	....	....	....	....	....	....	....	21	4	6	10	0	....	....	....	....
99-2000	Belleville Bulls	OHL	34	6	18	24	72	....	....	....	....	....	....	....	....	....	....	....	....	....	....	....	....	....	....
	Sarnia Sting	OHL	27	6	8	14	44	....	....	....	....	....	....	....	....	....	7	0	3	3	16	....	....	....	....
2000-01	Sarnia Sting	OHL	64	28	30	58	126	....	....	....	....	....	....	....	....	....	4	1	3	4	20	....	....	....	....
2001-02	Sarnia Sting	OHL	66	42	62	104	141	....	....	....	....	....	....	....	....	....	5	1	3	4	15	....	....	....	....
2002-03	Sarnia Sting	OHL	64	34	58	92	149	....	....	....	....	....	....	....	....	....	6	4	4	8	16	....	....	....	....
2003-04	St. John's	AHL	72	5	15	20	153	....	....	....	....	....	....	....	....	....	....	....	....	....	....	....	....	....	....
2004-05	St. John's	AHL	55	4	9	13	103	....	....	....	....	....	....	....	....	....	5	0	0	0	36	....	....	....	....
	Pensacola	ECHL	6	2	4	6	20	....	....	....	....	....	....	....	....	....	....	....	....	....	....	....	....	....	....
2005-06	Toronto Marlies	AHL	74	22	37	59	215	....	....	....	....	....	....	....	....	....	5	0	1	1	12	....	....	....	....
2006-07	Toronto	NHL	15	2	2	4	26	0	0	0	30	6.7	4	20	45.0	7:42	....	....	....	....	....	....	....	....	....
	Toronto Marlies	AHL	37	12	24	36	87	....	....	....	....	....	....	....	....	....	....	....	....	....	....	....	....	....	....
2007-08	Toronto	NHL	28	1	1	2	32	0	0	0	14	7.1	–7	55	40.0	4:22	....	....	....	....	....	....	....	....	....
	Toronto Marlies	AHL	54	16	27	43	101	....	....	....	....	....	....	....	....	....	19	4	9	13	*73	....	....	....	....
2008-09	Toronto	NHL	1	0	0	0	2	0	0	0	0	0.0	0	3	33.3	4:55	....	....	....	....	....	....	....	....	....
	Toronto Marlies	AHL	33	6	23	29	72	....	....	....	....	....	....	....	....	....	....	....	....	....	....	....	....	....	....
2009-10	Detroit	NHL	4	1	0	1	4	0	0	0	3	33.3	1	18	38.9	8:41	....	....	....	....	....	....	....	....	....
	Grand Rapids	AHL	52	11	22	33	144	....	....	....	....	....	....	....	....	....	....	....	....	....	....	....	....	....	....
	Hartford	AHL	18	4	14	18	61	....	....	....	....	....	....	....	....	....	....	....	....	....	....	....	....	....	....
2010-11	NY Rangers	NHL	11	0	1	1	35	0	0	0	6	0.0	–1	56	60.7	7:38	....	....	....	....	....	....	....	....	....
	Connecticut	AHL	69	17	44	61	139	....	....	....	....	....	....	....	....	....	6	2	2	4	2	....	....	....	....
2011-12	NY Rangers	NHL	7	0	0	0	24	0	0	0	2	0.0	–1	17	35.3	5:53	....	....	....	....	....	....	....	....	....
	Connecticut	AHL	65	25	39	64	130	....	....	....	....	....	....	....	....	....	9	1	3	4	20	....	....	....	....
2012-13	Connecticut	AHL	70	20	42	62	127	....	....	....	....	....	....	....	....	....	....	....	....	....	....	....	....	....	....
	NY Rangers	NHL	6	0	1	1	9	0	0	0	4	0.0	1	32	50.0	7:53	3	0	0	0	2	0	0	0	6:10
2013-14	Philadelphia	NHL	4	0	1	1	7	0	0	0	1	0.0	0	14	42.9	5:02	....	....	....	....	....	....	....	....	....
	Adirondack	AHL	46	14	22	36	182	....	....	....	....	....	....	....	....	....	....	....	....	....	....	....	....	....	....
	Hershey Bears	AHL	17	4	9	13	25	....	....	....	....	....	....	....	....	....	....	....	....	....	....	....	....	....	....
2014-15	Hershey Bears	AHL	68	18	30	48	171	....	....	....	....	....	....	....	....	....	10	0	4	4	16	....	....	....	....
2015-16	Ontario Reign	AHL	44	10	16	26	79	....	....	....	....	....	....	....	....	....	12	1	2	3	17	....	....	....	....
2016-17	Reading Royals	ECHL	1	1	2	3	2	....	....	....	....	....	....	....	....	....	....	....	....	....	....	....	....	....	....
	Bakersfield	AHL	14	3	2	5	17	....	....	....	....	....	....	....	....	....	....	....	....	....	....	....	....	....	....
	Charlotte	AHL	38	8	7	15	33	....	....	....	....	....	....	....	....	....	....	....	....	....	....	....	....	....	....
	NHL Totals		76	4	6	10	139	0	0	0	60	6.7		215	47.0	6:11	3	0	0	0	2	0	0	0	6:10

OHL Second All-Star Team (2002)

Signed as a free agent by **St. John's** (AHL), October 2, 2003. Signed as a free agent by **Toronto**, July 17, 2006. Signed as a free agent by **Detroit**, July 7, 2009. Traded to **NY Rangers** by **Detroit** for Jordan Owens, March 3, 2010. Traded to **Philadelphia** by **NY Rangers** for Danny Syvret, July 1, 2013. Signed as a free agent by **Washington**, July 4, 2014. Signed as a free agent by **Ontario** (AHL), July 26, 2015. Signed as a free agent by **Reading** (ECHL), October 15, 2016. • Loaned to **Bakersfield** (AHL) by **Reading** (ECHL), October 18, 2016. • Loaned to **Charlotte** (AHL) by **Reading** (ECHL), November 29, 2016.

NICHUSHKIN, Valeri

(nih-CHOOSH-kihn, val-AIR-ee) **DAL**

Right wing. Shoots left. 6'4", 205 lbs. Born, Chelyabinsk, Russia, March 4, 1995. Dallas' 1st pick, 10th overall, in 2013 NHL Draft.

Season	Club	League	GP	G	A	Pts	PIM	PP	SH	GW	S	S%	+/-	TF	F%	Min	GP	G	A	Pts	PIM	PP	SH	GW	Min
2011-12	Chelyabinsk Jr.	Russia-Jr.	38	4	6	10	6	....	....	....	....	....	....	....	....	....	....	....	....	....	....	....	....	....	....
2012-13	Chelyabinsk Jr.	Russia-Jr.	9	4	4	8	0	....	....	....	....	....	....	....	....	....	....	....	....	....	....	....	....	....	....
	Chelmet	Russia-2	15	8	2	10	4	....	....	....	....	....	....	....	....	....	....	....	....	....	....	....	....	....	....
	Chelyabinsk	KHL	18	4	2	6	0	....	....	....	....	....	....	....	....	....	25	6	3	9	0	....	....	....	....
2013-14	Dallas	NHL	79	14	20	34	8	2	0	2	128	10.9	20	1	0.0	14:58	6	1	1	2	2	0	0	0	13:28
	Russia	Olympics	5	1	0	1	0	....	....	....	....	....	....	....	....	....	....	....	....	....	....	....	....	....	....
2014-15	Dallas	NHL	8	0	1	1	2	0	0	0	6	0.0	–5	0	0.0	13:46	....	....	....	....	....	....	....	....	....
	Texas Stars	AHL	5	0	4	4	12	....	....	....	....	....	....	....	....	....	....	....	....	....	....	....	....	....	....
2015-16	Dallas	NHL	79	9	20	29	12	1	0	1	139	6.5	2	1	0.0	13:56	10	0	1	1	2	0	0	0	13:31
2016-17	CSKA Moscow	KHL	36	11	13	24	9	....	....	....	....	....	....	....	....	....	9	1	4	5	4	....	....	....	....
	NHL Totals		166	23	41	64	22	3	0	3	273	8.4		2	0.0	14:25	16	1	2	3	4	0	0	0	13:29

• Missed majority of 2014-15 due to recurring hip and groin injuries. Signed as a free agent by **CSKA Moscow** (KHL), September 20, 2016.

NIEDERREITER, Nino

(nee-duhr-RIGH-tuhr, NEE-noh) **MIN**

Right wing. Shoots left. 6'2", 211 lbs. Born, Chur, Switzerland, September 8, 1992. NY Islanders' 1st pick, 5th overall, in 2010 NHL Draft.

Season	Club	League	GP	G	A	Pts	PIM	PP	SH	GW	S	S%	+/-	TF	F%	Min	GP	G	A	Pts	PIM	PP	SH	GW	Min
2006-07	HC Davos U18	Swiss-U18	32	43	19	62	38	....	....	....	....	....	....	....	....	....	....	....	....	....	....	....	....	....	....
	HC Davos Jr.	Swiss-Jr.	....	....	....	....	....	....	....	....	....	....	....	....	....	....	1	0	0	0	4	....	....	....	....
2007-08	HC Davos U18	Swiss-U18	32	39	26	65	62	....	....	....	....	....	....	....	....	....	5	6	3	9	4	....	....	....	....
	HC Davos Jr.	Swiss-Jr.	8	7	3	10	4	....	....	....	....	....	....	....	....	....	3	0	1	1	8	....	....	....	....
2008-09	HC Davos U18	Swiss-U18	6	6	6	12	6	....	....	....	....	....	....	....	....	....	....	....	....	....	....	....	....	....	....
	HC Davos Jr.	Swiss-Jr.	30	20	14	34	44	....	....	....	....	....	....	....	....	....	8	5	6	11	12	....	....	....	....
	HC Davos	Swiss	....	....	....	....	....	....	....	....	....	....	....	....	....	....	3	0	1	1	0	....	....	....	....
2009-10	Portland	WHL	65	36	24	60	68	....	....	....	....	....	....	....	....	....	13	8	8	16	16	....	....	....	....
2010-11	NY Islanders	NHL	9	1	1	2	8	0	0	0	12	8.3	–1	0	0.0	13:36	....	....	....	....	....	....	....	....	....
	Portland	WHL	55	41	29	70	67	....	....	....	....	....	....	....	....	....	21	9	18	27	30	....	....	....	....
2011-12	NY Islanders	NHL	55	1	0	1	12	0	0	0	74	1.4	–29	2	0.0	10:07	....	....	....	....	....	....	....	....	....
	Bridgeport	AHL	6	3	1	4	4	....	....	....	....	....	....	....	....	....	....	....	....	....	....	....	....	....	....
2012-13	Bridgeport	AHL	74	28	22	50	38	....	....	....	....	....	....	....	....	....	....	....	....	....	....	....	....	....	....
2013-14	Minnesota	NHL	81	14	22	36	44	2	0	1	143	9.8	12	26	26.9	14:06	13	3	3	6	8	0	0	2	14:40
	Switzerland	Olympics	4	0	0	0	2	....	....	....	....	....	....	....	....	....	....	....	....	....	....	....	....	....	....

Season	Club	League	GP	G	A	Pts	PIM	PP	SH	GW	S	S%	+/-	TF	F%	Min	GP	G	A	Pts	PIM	PP	SH	GW	Min
											Regular Season									Playoffs					
2014-15	Minnesota	NHL	80	24	13	37	28	6	1	5	149	16.1	2	7	28.6	14:33	10	4	1	5	10	0	0	1	15:06
2015-16	Minnesota	NHL	82	20	23	43	36	2	0	1	159	12.6	9	27	40.7	15:33	6	1	5	6	4	0	0	0	15:26
2016-17	Minnesota	NHL	82	25	32	57	53	8	0	3	186	13.4	17	1	0.0	15:04	5	0	1	1	2	0	0	0	15:58
	NHL Totals		389	85	91	176	181	18	1	10	723	11.8		63	31.7	14:07	34	8	10	18	24	0	0	3	15:07

WHL West Second All-Star Team (2010)
Traded to **Minnesota** by **NY Islanders** for Cal Clutterbuck and New Jersey's 3rd round pick (previously acquired, Minnesota selected Eamon McAdam) in 2013 NHL Draft, June 30, 2013.

NIELSEN, Frans
(NEEL-sehn, FRAHNZ) **DET**

Center. Shoots left. 6'1", 188 lbs. Born, Herning, Denmark, April 24, 1984. NY Islanders' 2nd pick, 87th overall, in 2002 NHL Draft.

Season	Club	League	GP	G	A	Pts	PIM	PP	SH	GW	S	S%	+/-	TF	F%	Min	GP	G	A	Pts	PIM	PP	SH	GW	Min
99-2000	Herning IK Jr.	Den-Jr.	36	18	16	34	6																		
	Denmark	WJ18-B	5	3	4	7	0																		
2000-01	Herning IK	Denmark	38	18	19	37	6																		
	Denmark	WJ18-B	3	2	1	3	0																		
2001-02	Malmo	Sweden	20	0	1	1	0																		
	Malmo Jr.	Swe-Jr.	29	15	27	42	8																		
2002-03	Malmo	Sweden	47	3	6	9	10											7	3	7	10	2				
	Malmo Jr.	Swe-Jr.	2	1	3	4	0																		
	Denmark	WJC-B	5	3	7	10	0																		
	Denmark	WC-A	6	0	0	0	4																		
2003-04	Malmo	Sweden	50	9	7	16	28																		
	Malmo	Sweden-Q	10	3	5	8	2																		
2004-05	Malmo	Sweden	49	8	7	15	6																		
	Malmo	Sweden-Q	10	7	2	9	0																		
	Denmark	Oly-Q	3	2	3	5	0																		
2005-06	Timra IK	Sweden	50	5	13	18	22																		
2006-07	NY Islanders	NHL	15	1	1	2	0	0	0	1	16	6.3	-2	53	45.3	5:13									
	Bridgeport	AHL	54	20	24	44	10																		
2007-08	NY Islanders	NHL	16	2	1	3	0	0	0	0	17	11.8	1	111	48.7	8:42									
	Bridgeport	AHL	48	10	28	38	18																		
2008-09	NY Islanders	NHL	59	9	24	33	18	3	1	2	101	8.9	-4	758	47.2	16:32									
2009-10	NY Islanders	NHL	76	12	26	38	6	0	1	1	136	8.8	4	1165	50.0	17:13									
2010-11	NY Islanders	NHL	71	13	31	44	38	0	*7	1	156	8.3	13	965	46.2	17:46									
2011-12	NY Islanders	NHL	82	17	30	47	6	5	0	1	133	12.8	-3	1156	45.2	17:27									
2012-13	Lukko Rauma	Finland	27	4	20	24	10																		
	NY Islanders	NHL	48	6	23	29	12	2	1	1	93	6.5	-3	558	48.0	18:01	6	0	2	2	0	0	0	0	18:00
2013-14	NY Islanders	NHL	80	25	33	58	8	5	2	0	167	15.0	-11	1084	49.3	18:20									
2014-15	NY Islanders	NHL	78	14	29	43	12	4	1	4	157	8.9	8	1050	48.2	16:35	7	1	1	2	0	0	0	0	16:11
2015-16	NY Islanders	NHL	81	20	32	52	12	7	2	2	181	11.0	1	1169	50.1	17:43	11	3	3	6	2	2	0	0	21:42
2016-17	Detroit	NHL	79	17	24	41	18	4	2	0	162	10.5	-19	1214	53.8	17:09									
	NHL Totals		685	136	254	390	130	30	17	13	1319	10.3		9283	48.9	16:57	24	4	6	10	2	2	0	0	19:10

Signed as a free agent by **Rauma** (Finland), September 26, 2012. Signed as a free agent by **Detroit**, July 1, 2016.
Played in NHL All-Star Game (2017)

NIETO, Matt
(NEE-eh-toh, MAT) **COL**

Left wing. Shoots left. 5'11", 190 lbs. Born, Long Beach, CA, November 5, 1992. San Jose's 1st pick, 47th overall, in 2011 NHL Draft.

Season	Club	League	GP	G	A	Pts	PIM	PP	SH	GW	S	S%	+/-	TF	F%	Min	GP	G	A	Pts	PIM	PP	SH	GW	Min
2007-08	Salisbury School	High-CT	23	8	10	18																			
2008-09	USAHNTDP	NAHL	38	11	24	35	14																		
	USAHNTDP	U-17	14	9	9	18	8																		
	USAHNTDP	U-18	13	6	8	14	14																		
2009-10	USAHNTDP	USHL	24	15	14	29	19																		
	USAHNTDP	U-18	30	13	12	25	12																		
2010-11	Boston University	H-East	39	10	13	23	16																		
2011-12	Boston University	H-East	37	16	26	42	26																		
2012-13	Boston University	H-East	39	18	19	37	24																		
2013-14	San Jose	NHL	66	10	14	24	16	1	0	2	124	8.1	-4	11	27.3	14:05	7	2	3	5	0	0	0	0	14:20
2014-15	San Jose	NHL	72	10	17	27	20	1	0	1	135	7.4	-12	1	0.0	15:15									
2015-16	San Jose	NHL	67	8	9	17	10	0	2	1	90	8.9	-8	8	25.0	13:10	16	1	2	3	8	0	0	0	12:21
2016-17	San Jose	NHL	16	0	2	2	4	0	0	0	24	0.0	-3	2	0.0	12:13									
	Colorado	NHL	43	7	4	11	4	0	0	1	61	11.5	-9	4	50.0	15:56									
	NHL Totals		264	35	46	81	54	2	2	5	434	8.1		26	26.9	14:21	23	3	5	8	8	0	0	0	12:57

Claimed on waivers by **Colorado** from **San Jose**, January 5, 2017.

NIEVES, Cristoval
(noo-EH-vehz, KRIHS-TOH-vahl) **NYR**

Center. Shoots left. 6'3", 219 lbs. Born, Syracuse, NY, January 23, 1994. NY Rangers' 2nd pick, 59th overall, in 2012 NHL Draft.

Season	Club	League	GP	G	A	Pts	PIM	PP	SH	GW	S	S%	+/-	TF	F%	Min	GP	G	A	Pts	PIM	PP	SH	GW	Min
2009-10	Syr. Nationals	Minor-NY	60	30	42	72																			
2010-11	Kent Prep School	High-CT	22	11	28	39	6																		
2011-12	Kent Prep School	High-CT	26	7	32	39	24																		
	Indiana Ice	USHL	13	2	8	10	2																		
2012-13	U. of Michigan	CCHA	40	8	21	29	18																		
2013-14	U. of Michigan	Big Ten	34	3	19	22	18																		
2014-15	U. of Michigan	Big Ten	35	7	21	28	18																		
2015-16	Hartford	AHL	8	2	3	5	0																		
	U. of Michigan	Big Ten	35	10	21	31	18																		
2016-17	NY Rangers	NHL	1	0	0	0	0	0	0	0	0	0.0	-1	10	30.0	11:44									
	Hartford	AHL	40	6	12	18	10																		
	NHL Totals		1	0	0	0	0	0	0	0	0	0.0		10	30.0	11:44									

NISKANEN, Matt
(NIHS-kah-nehn, MAT) **WSH**

Defense. Shoots right. 6', 200 lbs. Born, Virginia, MN, December 6, 1986. Dallas' 1st pick, 28th overall, in 2005 NHL Draft.

Season	Club	League	GP	G	A	Pts	PIM	PP	SH	GW	S	S%	+/-	TF	F%	Min	GP	G	A	Pts	PIM	PP	SH	GW	Min
2003-04	Virginia	High-MN		24	37	61																			
2004-05	Virginia	High-MN	29	27	38	65	34																		
2005-06	U. Minn-Duluth	WCHA	38	1	13	14	40																		
2006-07	U. Minn-Duluth	WCHA	39	9	22	31	42																		
	Iowa Stars	AHL	13	0	3	3	6											12	2	5	7	10				
2007-08	Dallas	NHL	78	7	19	26	36	2	0	0	99	7.1	22	0	0.0	20:30	16	0	3	3	10	0	0	0	16:23
2008-09	Dallas	NHL	80	6	29	35	52	2	0	0	111	5.4	-11	0	0.0	19:58									
2009-10	Dallas	NHL	74	3	12	15	18	0	0	2	110	2.7	-15	0	0.0	18:16									
2010-11	Dallas	NHL	45	0	6	6	30	0	0	0	51	0.0	-1	0	0.0	15:44									
	Pittsburgh	NHL	18	1	3	4	20	0	0	0	26	3.8	-2	0	0.0	18:31	7	0	1	1	0	0	0	0	12:58
2011-12	Pittsburgh	NHL	75	4	17	21	47	3	0	0	118	3.4	9	0	0.0	17:56	4	1	2	3	6	1	0	0	18:31
2012-13	Pittsburgh	NHL	40	4	10	14	12	0	0	2	67	6.0	4	0	0.0	20:21	15	0	2	2	11	0	0	0	18:55
2013-14	Pittsburgh	NHL	81	10	36	46	51	3	0	0	162	6.2	33	0	0.0	21:18	13	2	7	9	8	2	0	0	19:54
2014-15	Washington	NHL	82	4	27	31	47	2	0	0	117	3.4	7	0	0.0	22:21	14	0	4	4	0	0	0	0	23:47
2015-16	Washington	NHL	82	5	27	32	38	2	0	3	150	3.3	10	0	0.0	24:40	12	0	3	3	6	0	0	0	26:32
2016-17	Washington	NHL	78	5	34	39	32	1	0	2	154	3.2	20	0	0.0	22:11	13	1	3	4	19	1	0	0	22:38
	NHL Totals		733	49	220	269	383	15	0	15	1165	4.2		0	0.0	20:33	94	4	25	29	60	4	0	0	20:22

WCHA First All-Star Team (2007)
Traded to **Pittsburgh** by **Dallas** with James Neal for Alex Goligoski, February 21, 2011. Signed as a free agent by **Washington**, July 1, 2014.

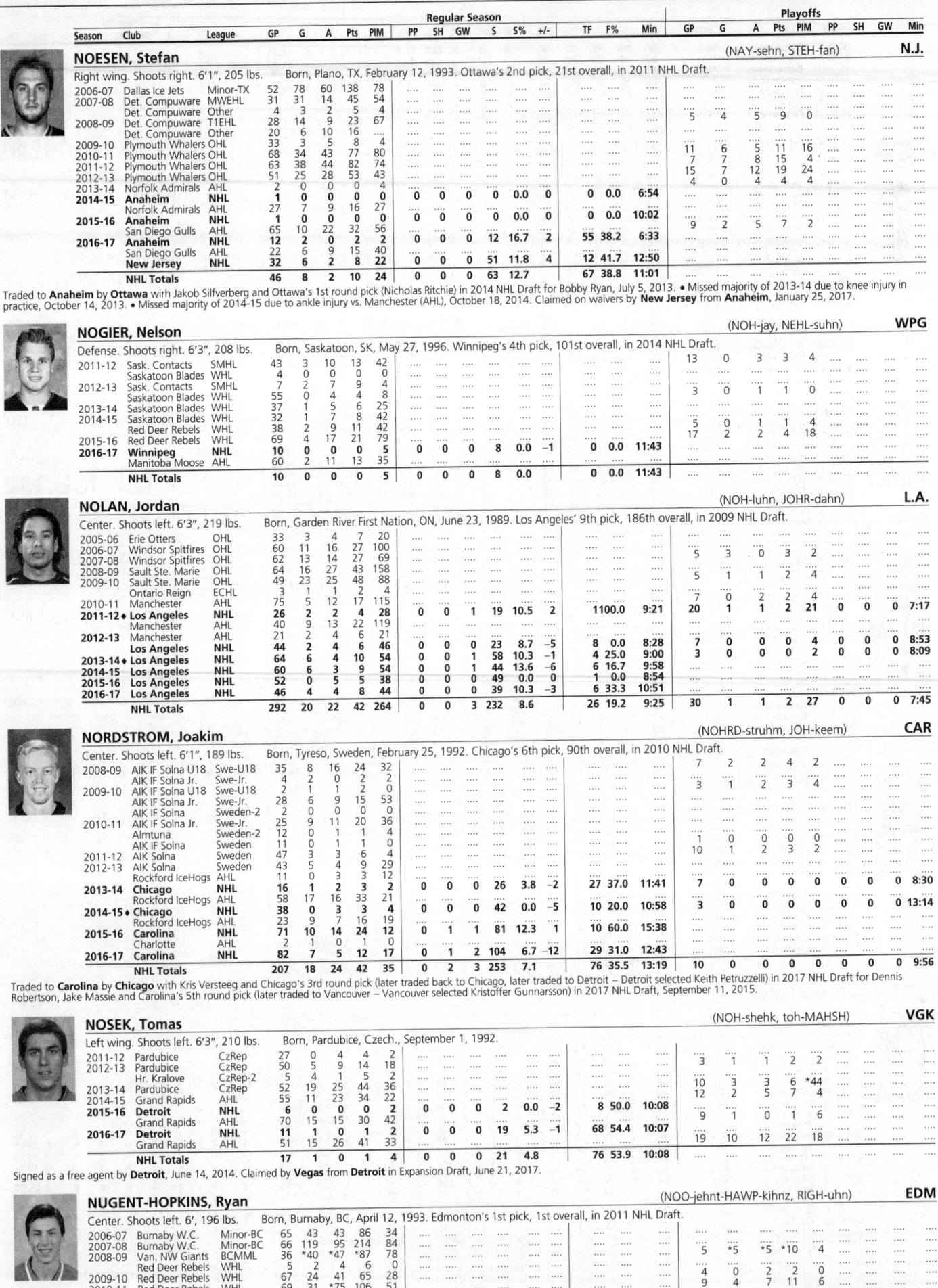

NOESEN, Stefan

(NAY-sehn, STEH-fan) **N.J.**

Right wing. Shoots right. 6'1", 205 lbs. Born, Plano, TX, February 12, 1993. Ottawa's 2nd pick, 21st overall, in 2011 NHL Draft.

			Regular Season														Playoffs								
Season	Club	League	GP	G	A	Pts	PIM	PP	SH	GW	S	S%	+/-	TF	F%	Min	GP	G	A	Pts	PIM	PP	SH	GW	Min
2006-07	Dallas Ice Jets	Minor-TX	52	78	60	138	78	....	....	....	....	....	....	....	....	....	....	....	....	....	....	....	....	....	....
2007-08	Det. Compuware	MWEHL	31	31	14	45	54	....	....	....	....	....	....	....	....	....	....	....	....	....	....	....	....	....	....
	Det. Compuware	Other	4	3	2	5	4	....	....	....	....	....	....	....	....	....	....	....	....	....	....	....	....	....	....
2008-09	Det. Compuware	T1EHL	28	14	9	23	67	....	....	....	....	....	....	....	....	....	5	4	5	9	0	....	....	....	....
	Det. Compuware	Other	20	6	10	16	....	....	....	....	....	....	....	....	....	....	....	....	....	....	....	....	....	....	....
2009-10	Plymouth Whalers	OHL	33	3	5	8	4	....	....	....	....	....	....	....	....	....	....	....	....	....	....	....	....	....	....
2010-11	Plymouth Whalers	OHL	68	34	43	77	80	....	....	....	....	....	....	....	....	....	11	6	5	11	16	....	....	....	....
2011-12	Plymouth Whalers	OHL	63	38	44	82	74	....	....	....	....	....	....	....	....	....	7	7	8	15	4	....	....	....	....
2012-13	Plymouth Whalers	OHL	51	25	28	53	43	....	....	....	....	....	....	....	....	....	15	7	12	19	24	....	....	....	....
2013-14	Norfolk Admirals	AHL	2	0	0	0	4	....	....	....	....	....	....	....	....	....	4	0	4	4	4	....	....	....	....
2014-15	**Anaheim**	**NHL**	**1**	**0**	**0**	**0**	**0**	**0**	**0**	**0**	**0**	**0.0**	**0**	**0**	**0.0**	**6:54**	....	....	....	....	....	....	....	....	....
	Norfolk Admirals	AHL	27	7	9	16	27	....	....	....	....	....	....	....	....	....	....	....	....	....	....	....	....	....	....
2015-16	**Anaheim**	**NHL**	**1**	**0**	**0**	**0**	**0**	**0**	**0**	**0**	**0**	**0.0**	**0**	**0**	**0.0**	**10:02**	....	....	....	....	....	....	....	....	....
	San Diego Gulls	AHL	65	10	22	32	56	....	....	....	....	....	....	....	....	....	9	2	5	7	2	....	....	....	....
2016-17	**Anaheim**	**NHL**	**12**	**2**	**0**	**2**	**2**	**0**	**0**	**0**	**12**	**16.7**	**2**	**55**	**38.2**	**6:33**	....	....	....	....	....	....	....	....	....
	San Diego Gulls	AHL	22	6	9	15	40	....	....	....	....	....	....	....	....	....	....	....	....	....	....	....	....	....	....
	New Jersey	**NHL**	**32**	**6**	**2**	**8**	**22**	**0**	**0**	**0**	**51**	**11.8**	**4**	**12**	**41.7**	**12:50**	....	....	....	....	....	....	....	....	....
	NHL Totals		**46**	**8**	**2**	**10**	**24**	**0**	**0**	**0**	**63**	**12.7**		**67**	**38.8**	**11:01**	....	....	....	....	....	....	....	....	....

Traded to **Anaheim** by **Ottawa** wirh Jakob Silfverberg and Ottawa's 1st round pick (Nicholas Ritchie) in 2014 NHL Draft for Bobby Ryan, July 5, 2013. • Missed majority of 2013-14 due to knee injury in practice, October 14, 2013. • Missed majority of 2014-15 due to ankle injury vs. Manchester (AHL), October 18, 2014. Claimed on waivers by **New Jersey** from **Anaheim**, January 25, 2017.

NOGIER, Nelson

(NOH-jay, NEHL-suhn) **WPG**

Defense. Shoots right. 6'3", 208 lbs. Born, Saskatoon, SK, May 27, 1996. Winnipeg's 4th pick, 101st overall, in 2014 NHL Draft.

			Regular Season														Playoffs								
Season	Club	League	GP	G	A	Pts	PIM	PP	SH	GW	S	S%	+/-	TF	F%	Min	GP	G	A	Pts	PIM	PP	SH	GW	Min
2011-12	Sask. Contacts	SMHL	43	3	10	13	42	....	....	....	....	....	....	....	....	....	13	0	3	3	4	....	....	....	....
	Saskatoon Blades	WHL	4	0	0	0	0	....	....	....	....	....	....	....	....	....	....	....	....	....	....	....	....	....	....
2012-13	Sask. Contacts	SMHL	7	2	7	9	4	....	....	....	....	....	....	....	....	....	....	....	....	....	....	....	....	....	....
	Saskatoon Blades	WHL	55	0	4	4	8	....	....	....	....	....	....	....	....	....	3	0	1	1	0	....	....	....	....
2013-14	Saskatoon Blades	WHL	37	1	5	6	25	....	....	....	....	....	....	....	....	....	....	....	....	....	....	....	....	....	....
2014-15	Saskatoon Blades	WHL	32	1	7	8	42	....	....	....	....	....	....	....	....	....	....	....	....	....	....	....	....	....	....
	Red Deer Rebels	WHL	38	2	9	11	42	....	....	....	....	....	....	....	....	....	5	0	1	1	4	....	....	....	....
2015-16	Red Deer Rebels	WHL	69	4	17	21	79	....	....	....	....	....	....	....	....	....	17	2	2	4	18	....	....	....	....
2016-17	**Winnipeg**	**NHL**	**10**	**0**	**0**	**0**	**5**	**0**	**0**	**0**	**8**	**0.0**	**–1**	**0**	**0.0**	**11:43**	....	....	....	....	....	....	....	....	....
	Manitoba Moose	AHL	60	2	11	13	35	....	....	....	....	....	....	....	....	....	....	....	....	....	....	....	....	....	....
	NHL Totals		**10**	**0**	**0**	**0**	**5**	**0**	**0**	**0**	**8**	**0.0**		**0**	**0.0**	**11:43**	....	....	....	....	....	....	....	....	....

NOLAN, Jordan

(NOH-luhn, JOHR-dahn) **L.A.**

Center. Shoots left. 6'3", 219 lbs. Born, Garden River First Nation, ON, June 23, 1989. Los Angeles' 9th pick, 186th overall, in 2009 NHL Draft.

			Regular Season														Playoffs								
Season	Club	League	GP	G	A	Pts	PIM	PP	SH	GW	S	S%	+/-	TF	F%	Min	GP	G	A	Pts	PIM	PP	SH	GW	Min
2005-06	Erie Otters	OHL	33	3	4	7	20	....	....	....	....	....	....	....	....	....	....	....	....	....	....	....	....	....	....
2006-07	Windsor Spitfires	OHL	60	11	16	27	100	....	....	....	....	....	....	....	....	....	....	....	....	....	....	....	....	....	....
2007-08	Windsor Spitfires	OHL	62	13	14	27	69	....	....	....	....	....	....	....	....	....	5	3	0	3	2	....	....	....	....
2008-09	Sault Ste. Marie	OHL	64	16	27	43	158	....	....	....	....	....	....	....	....	....	....	....	....	....	....	....	....	....	....
2009-10	Sault Ste. Marie	OHL	49	23	25	48	88	....	....	....	....	....	....	....	....	....	5	1	1	2	4	....	....	....	....
	Ontario Reign	ECHL	3	1	1	2	4	....	....	....	....	....	....	....	....	....	....	....	....	....	....	....	....	....	....
2010-11	Manchester	AHL	75	5	12	17	115	....	....	....	....	....	....	....	....	....	7	0	2	2	4	....	....	....	....
2011-12 ♦	**Los Angeles**	**NHL**	**26**	**2**	**2**	**4**	**28**	**0**	**0**	**1**	**19**	**10.5**	**2**	**1**	**100.0**	**9:21**	**20**	**1**	**1**	**2**	**21**	**0**	**0**	**0**	**7:17**
	Manchester	AHL	40	9	13	22	119	....	....	....	....	....	....	....	....	....	....	....	....	....	....	....	....	....	....
2012-13	Manchester	AHL	21	2	4	6	21	....	....	....	....	....	....	....	....	....	....	....	....	....	....	....	....	....	....
	Los Angeles	**NHL**	**44**	**2**	**4**	**6**	**46**	**0**	**0**	**0**	**23**	**8.7**	**–5**	**8**	**0.0**	**8:28**	**7**	**0**	**0**	**0**	**4**	**0**	**0**	**0**	**8:53**
2013-14 ♦	**Los Angeles**	**NHL**	**64**	**6**	**4**	**10**	**54**	**0**	**0**	**1**	**58**	**10.3**	**–1**	**4**	**25.0**	**9:00**	**3**	**0**	**0**	**0**	**2**	**0**	**0**	**0**	**8:09**
2014-15	**Los Angeles**	**NHL**	**60**	**6**	**3**	**9**	**54**	**0**	**0**	**1**	**44**	**13.6**	**–6**	**6**	**16.7**	**9:58**	....	....	....	....	....	....	....	....	....
2015-16	**Los Angeles**	**NHL**	**52**	**0**	**5**	**5**	**38**	**0**	**0**	**0**	**49**	**0.0**	**0**	**1**	**0.0**	**8:54**	....	....	....	....	....	....	....	....	....
2016-17	**Los Angeles**	**NHL**	**46**	**4**	**4**	**8**	**44**	**0**	**0**	**0**	**39**	**10.3**	**–3**	**6**	**33.3**	**10:51**	....	....	....	....	....	....	....	....	....
	NHL Totals		**292**	**20**	**22**	**42**	**264**	**0**	**0**	**3**	**232**	**8.6**		**26**	**19.2**	**9:25**	**30**	**1**	**1**	**2**	**27**	**0**	**0**	**0**	**7:45**

NORDSTROM, Joakim

(NOHRD-struhm, JOH-keem) **CAR**

Center. Shoots left. 6'1", 189 lbs. Born, Tyreso, Sweden, February 25, 1992. Chicago's 6th pick, 90th overall, in 2010 NHL Draft.

			Regular Season														Playoffs								
Season	Club	League	GP	G	A	Pts	PIM	PP	SH	GW	S	S%	+/-	TF	F%	Min	GP	G	A	Pts	PIM	PP	SH	GW	Min
2008-09	AIK IF Solna U18	Swe-U18	35	8	16	24	32	....	....	....	....	....	....	....	....	....	7	2	2	4	2	....	....	....	....
	AIK IF Solna Jr.	Swe-Jr.	4	2	0	2	2	....	....	....	....	....	....	....	....	....	....	....	....	....	....	....	....	....	....
2009-10	AIK IF Solna U18	Swe-U18	2	1	1	2	0	....	....	....	....	....	....	....	....	....	3	1	2	3	4	....	....	....	....
	AIK IF Solna Jr.	Swe-Jr.	28	6	9	15	53	....	....	....	....	....	....	....	....	....	....	....	....	....	....	....	....	....	....
	AIK IF Solna	Sweden-2	2	0	0	0	0	....	....	....	....	....	....	....	....	....	....	....	....	....	....	....	....	....	....
2010-11	AIK IF Solna Jr.	Swe-Jr.	25	9	11	20	36	....	....	....	....	....	....	....	....	....	....	....	....	....	....	....	....	....	....
	Almtuna	Sweden-2	12	0	1	1	4	....	....	....	....	....	....	....	....	....	....	....	....	....	....	....	....	....	....
	AIK IF Solna	Sweden	11	0	1	1	0	....	....	....	....	....	....	....	....	....	1	0	0	0	0	....	....	....	....
2011-12	AIK Solna	Sweden	47	3	3	6	4	....	....	....	....	....	....	....	....	....	10	1	2	3	2	....	....	....	....
2012-13	AIK Solna	Sweden	43	5	4	9	29	....	....	....	....	....	....	....	....	....	....	....	....	....	....	....	....	....	....
	Rockford IceHogs	AHL	11	0	3	3	12	....	....	....	....	....	....	....	....	....	....	....	....	....	....	....	....	....	....
2013-14	**Chicago**	**NHL**	**16**	**1**	**2**	**3**	**2**	**0**	**0**	**0**	**26**	**3.8**	**–2**	**27**	**37.0**	**11:41**	**7**	**0**	**0**	**0**	**0**	**0**	**0**	**0**	**8:30**
	Rockford IceHogs	AHL	58	17	16	33	21	....	....	....	....	....	....	....	....	....	....	....	....	....	....	....	....	....	....
2014-15 ♦	**Chicago**	**NHL**	**38**	**0**	**3**	**3**	**4**	**0**	**0**	**0**	**42**	**0.0**	**–5**	**10**	**20.0**	**10:58**	**3**	**0**	**0**	**0**	**0**	**0**	**0**	**0**	**13:14**
	Rockford IceHogs	AHL	23	9	7	16	19	....	....	....	....	....	....	....	....	....	....	....	....	....	....	....	....	....	....
2015-16	**Carolina**	**NHL**	**71**	**10**	**14**	**24**	**12**	**0**	**1**	**1**	**81**	**12.3**	**1**	**10**	**60.0**	**15:38**	....	....	....	....	....	....	....	....	....
	Charlotte	AHL	2	1	0	1	0	....	....	....	....	....	....	....	....	....	....	....	....	....	....	....	....	....	....
2016-17	**Carolina**	**NHL**	**82**	**7**	**5**	**12**	**17**	**0**	**1**	**2**	**104**	**6.7**	**–12**	**29**	**31.0**	**12:43**	....	....	....	....	....	....	....	....	....
	NHL Totals		**207**	**18**	**24**	**42**	**35**	**0**	**2**	**3**	**253**	**7.1**		**76**	**35.5**	**13:19**	**10**	**0**	**0**	**0**	**0**	**0**	**0**	**0**	**9:56**

Traded to **Carolina** by **Chicago** with Kris Versteeg and Chicago's 3rd round pick (later traded back to Chicago, later traded to Detroit – Detroit selected Keith Petruzzelli) in 2017 NHL Draft for Dennis Robertson, Jake Massie and Carolina's 5th round pick (later traded to Vancouver – Vancouver selected Kristoffer Gunnarsson) in 2017 NHL Draft, September 11, 2015.

NOSEK, Tomas

(NOH-shehk, toh-MAHSH) **VGK**

Left wing. Shoots left. 6'3", 210 lbs. Born, Pardubice, Czech., September 1, 1992.

			Regular Season														Playoffs								
Season	Club	League	GP	G	A	Pts	PIM	PP	SH	GW	S	S%	+/-	TF	F%	Min	GP	G	A	Pts	PIM	PP	SH	GW	Min
2011-12	Pardubice	CzRep	27	0	4	4	2	....	....	....	....	....	....	....	....	....	....	....	....	....	....	....	....	....	....
2012-13	Pardubice	CzRep	50	5	9	14	18	....	....	....	....	....	....	....	....	....	3	1	1	2	2	....	....	....	....
	Hr. Kralove	CzRep-2	5	4	1	5	2	....	....	....	....	....	....	....	....	....	....	....	....	....	....	....	....	....	....
2013-14	Pardubice	CzRep	52	19	25	44	36	....	....	....	....	....	....	....	....	....	10	3	3	6	*44	....	....	....	....
2014-15	Grand Rapids	AHL	55	11	23	34	22	....	....	....	....	....	....	....	....	....	12	2	5	7	4	....	....	....	....
2015-16	**Detroit**	**NHL**	**6**	**0**	**0**	**0**	**2**	**0**	**0**	**0**	**2**	**0.0**	**–2**	**8**	**50.0**	**10:08**	....	....	....	....	....	....	....	....	....
	Grand Rapids	AHL	70	15	15	30	42	....	....	....	....	....	....	....	....	....	9	1	0	1	6	....	....	....	....
2016-17	**Detroit**	**NHL**	**11**	**1**	**0**	**1**	**2**	**0**	**0**	**0**	**19**	**5.3**	**–1**	**68**	**54.4**	**10:07**	....	....	....	....	....	....	....	....	....
	Grand Rapids	AHL	51	15	26	41	33	....	....	....	....	....	....	....	....	....	19	10	12	22	18	....	....	....	....
	NHL Totals		**17**	**1**	**0**	**1**	**4**	**0**	**0**	**0**	**21**	**4.8**		**76**	**53.9**	**10:08**	....	....	....	....	....	....	....	....	....

Signed as a free agent by **Detroit**, June 14, 2014. Claimed by **Vegas** from **Detroit** in Expansion Draft, June 21, 2017.

NUGENT-HOPKINS, Ryan

(NOO-jehnt-HAWP-kihnz, RIGH-uhn) **EDM**

Center. Shoots left. 6', 196 lbs. Born, Burnaby, BC, April 12, 1993. Edmonton's 1st pick, 1st overall, in 2011 NHL Draft.

			Regular Season														Playoffs								
Season	Club	League	GP	G	A	Pts	PIM	PP	SH	GW	S	S%	+/-	TF	F%	Min	GP	G	A	Pts	PIM	PP	SH	GW	Min
2006-07	Burnaby W.C.	Minor-BC	65	43	43	86	34	....	....	....	....	....	....	....	....	....	....	....	....	....	....	....	....	....	....
2007-08	Burnaby W.C.	Minor-BC	66	119	95	214	84	....	....	....	....	....	....	....	....	....	....	....	....	....	....	....	....	....	....
2008-09	Van. NW Giants	BCMML	36	*40	*47	*87	78	....	....	....	....	....	....	....	....	....	5	*5	*5	*10	4	....	....	....	....
	Red Deer Rebels	WHL	5	2	4	6	0	....	....	....	....	....	....	....	....	....	....	....	....	....	....	....	....	....	....
2009-10	Red Deer Rebels	WHL	67	24	41	65	28	....	....	....	....	....	....	....	....	....	4	0	2	2	0	....	....	....	....
2010-11	Red Deer Rebels	WHL	69	31	*75	106	51	....	....	....	....	....	....	....	....	....	9	4	7	11	6	....	....	....	....

			Regular Season														Playoffs								
Season	Club	League	GP	G	A	Pts	PIM	PP	SH	GW	S	S%	+/-	TF	F%	Min	GP	G	A	Pts	PIM	PP	SH	GW	Min
2011-12	**Edmonton**	**NHL**	**62**	**18**	**34**	**52**	**16**	**3**	**0**	**2**	**134**	**13.4**	**–2**	**605**	**37.5**	**17:36**									
2012-13	Oklahoma City	AHL	19	8	12	20	6																		
	Edmonton	**NHL**	**40**	**4**	**20**	**24**	**8**	**2**	**0**	**0**	**78**	**5.1**	**3**	**551**	**41.0**	**18:52**									
2013-14	**Edmonton**	**NHL**	**80**	**19**	**37**	**56**	**26**	**6**	**0**	**4**	**178**	**10.7**	**–12**	**1280**	**42.4**	**20:24**									
2014-15	**Edmonton**	**NHL**	**76**	**24**	**32**	**56**	**25**	**2**	**0**	**2**	**189**	**12.7**	**–12**	**1356**	**45.7**	**20:38**									
2015-16	**Edmonton**	**NHL**	**55**	**12**	**22**	**34**	**18**	**4**	**0**	**1**	**108**	**11.1**	**–9**	**823**	**44.8**	**19:04**									
2016-17	**Edmonton**	**NHL**	**82**	**18**	**25**	**43**	**29**	**5**	**0**	**4**	**200**	**9.0**	**–10**	**1268**	**43.9**	**17:42**	**13**	**0**	**4**	**4**	**2**	**0**	**0**	**0**	**18:25**
	NHL Totals		**395**	**95**	**170**	**265**	**122**	**22**	**0**	**13**	**887**	**10.7**		**5883**	**43.2**	**19:06**	**13**	**0**	**4**	**4**	**2**	**0**	**0**	**0**	**18:25**

WHL Rookie of the Year (2010) • Canadian Major Junior All-Rookie Team (2010) • WHL East First All-Star Team (2011) • NHL All-Rookie Team (2012)
Played in NHL All-Star Game (2015)

NURSE, Darnell

(NUHRS, dahr-NEHL) **EDM**

Defense. Shoots left. 6'4", 213 lbs. Born, Hamilton, ON, February 4, 1995. Edmonton's 1st pick, 7th overall, in 2013 NHL Draft.

Season	Club	League	GP	G	A	Pts	PIM	PP	SH	GW	S	S%	+/-	TF	F%	Min	GP	G	A	Pts	PIM	PP	SH	GW	Min
2010-11	Don Mills Flyers	GTHL	38	11	18	29	72																		
	St. Michael's	ON-Jr.A	2	0	0	0	4																		
2011-12	Sault Ste. Marie	OHL	53	1	9	10	61																		
2012-13	Sault Ste. Marie	OHL	68	12	29	41	116										6	1	3	4	6				
2013-14	Sault Ste. Marie	OHL	64	13	37	50	91										9	3	5	8	12				
	Oklahoma City	AHL	4	0	1	1	0										3	0	1	1	7				
2014-15	**Edmonton**	**NHL**	**2**	**0**	**0**	**0**	**0**	**0**	**0**	**0**	**2**	**0.0**	**–2**	**0**	**0.0**	**17:00**									
	Sault Ste. Marie	OHL	36	10	23	33	58										14	3	5	8	26				
	Oklahoma City	AHL															4	0	4	4	4				
2015-16	**Edmonton**	**NHL**	**69**	**3**	**7**	**10**	**60**	**0**	**0**	**0**	**120**	**2.5**	**–13**	**0**	**0.0**	**20:14**									
	Bakersfield	AHL	9	0	2	2	7																		
2016-17	**Edmonton**	**NHL**	**44**	**5**	**6**	**11**	**33**	**0**	**0**	**0**	**85**	**5.9**	**0**	**0**	**0.0**	**17:01**	**13**	**0**	**2**	**2**	**6**	**0**	**0**	**0**	**17:25**
	NHL Totals		**115**	**8**	**13**	**21**	**93**	**0**	**0**	**0**	**207**	**3.9**		**0**	**0.0**	**18:57**	**13**	**0**	**2**	**2**	**6**	**0**	**0**	**0**	**17:25**

OHL Second All-Star Team (2015)

• Missed majority of 2014-15 due to leg injury vs. Saginaw (OHL), February 13, 2015.

NUTIVAARA, Markus

(noo-tih-VAH-ruh, MAHR-kuhs) **CBJ**

Defense. Shoots left. 6'1", 185 lbs. Born, Oulu, Finland, June 6, 1994. Columbus' 9th pick, 189th overall, in 2015 NHL Draft.

Season	Club	League	GP	G	A	Pts	PIM	PP	SH	GW	S	S%	+/-	TF	F%	Min	GP	G	A	Pts	PIM	PP	SH	GW	Min
2010-11	Ahmat U18	Fin-U18	22	10	13	23	43																		
	Ahmat Haukipudas	Finland-4	3	0	0	0	2																		
....																									
2011-12	Karpat Oulu U18	Fin-U18	41	10	20	30	14										9	2	4	6	4				
2012-13	Pelicans Lahti Jr.	Fin-Jr.	42	4	11	15	14																		
2013-14	Karpat Oulu Jr.	Fin-Jr.	19	2	9	11	10										12	1	4	5	2				
	Jokipojat Joensuu	Finland-2	11	0	3	3	4																		
2014-15	Karpat Oulu Jr.	Fin-Jr.	7	2	6	8	0										5	3	2	5	0				
	Hokki Kajaani	Finland-2	2	0	2	2	2																		
	Karpat Oulu	Finland	35	0	2	2	4										16	1	5	6	0				
2015-16	Karpat Oulu	Finland	50	6	16	22	14										7	1	4	5	0				
2016-17	**Columbus**	**NHL**	**66**	**2**	**5**	**7**	**6**	**0**	**0**	**0**	**66**	**3.0**	**7**	**0**	**0.0**	**13:13**	**2**	**1**	**1**	**2**	**0**	**0**	**0**	**0**	**11:56**
	NHL Totals		**66**	**2**	**5**	**7**	**6**	**0**	**0**	**0**	**66**	**3.0**		**0**	**0.0**	**13:13**	**2**	**1**	**1**	**2**	**0**	**0**	**0**	**0**	**11:56**

NYLANDER, Alexander

(NEE-lan-duhr, al-ehx-AN-duhr) **BUF**

Left wing. Shoots right. 6'1", 178 lbs. Born, Calgary, AB, Canada, March 2, 1998. Buffalo's 1st pick, 8th overall, in 2016 NHL Draft.

Season	Club	League	GP	G	A	Pts	PIM	PP	SH	GW	S	S%	+/-	TF	F%	Min	GP	G	A	Pts	PIM	PP	SH	GW	Min
2013-14	SDE U18	Swe-U18	21	9	27	36	2																		
	Sodertalje SK U18	Swe-U18	17	12	10	22	6																		
2014-15	AIK Solna U18	Swe-U18	7	2	13	15	2										2	0	0	0	4				
	AIK Solna Jr.	Swe-Jr.	42	15	25	40	12										2	0	1	1	0				
	AIK Solna	Sweden-2	7	1	1	2	0																		
2015-16	Mississauga	OHL	57	28	47	75	18										6	6	6	12	2				
2016-17	**Buffalo**	**NHL**	**4**	**0**	**1**	**1**	**0**	**0**	**0**	**0**	**4**	**0.0**	**–2**	**2**	**0.0**	**12:20**									
	Rochester	AHL	65	10	18	28	6																		
	NHL Totals		**4**	**0**	**1**	**1**	**0**	**0**	**0**	**0**	**4**	**0.0**		**2**	**0.0**	**12:20**									

OHL All-Rookie Team (2016)

NYLANDER, William

(NEE-lan-duhr, WIHL-yuhm) **TOR**

Center. Shoots right. 5'11", 190 lbs. Born, Calgary, AB, May 1, 1996. Toronto's 1st pick, 8th overall, in 2014 NHL Draft.

Season	Club	League	GP	G	A	Pts	PIM	PP	SH	GW	S	S%	+/-	TF	F%	Min	GP	G	A	Pts	PIM	PP	SH	GW	Min
2011-12	SDE U18	Swe-U18	18	12	14	26	14																		
	Sodertalje SK U18	Swe-U18	9	7	5	12	2																		
	Sodertalje SK Jr.	Swe-Jr.	8	1	3	4	2										4	0	5	5	2				
2012-13	Sodertalje SK U18	Swe-U18	1	2	1	3	2																		
	Sodertalje SK Jr.	Swe-Jr.	27	15	28	43	14																		
	Sodertalje SK	Sweden-2	18	6	3	9	6																		
2013-14	Sodertalje SK	Sweden-2	17	11	8	19	6																		
	Rogle	Sweden-2	18	4	4	8	10																		
	MODO Jr.	Swe-Jr.	3	0	3	3	4										5	3	5	8	2				
	MODO	Sweden	22	1	6	7	6										2	0	0	0	0				
	MODO U18	Swe-U18															4	3	4	7	4				
2014-15	MODO	Sweden	21	8	12	20	6																		
	Toronto Marlies	AHL	37	14	18	32	4										5	0	3	3	0				
2015-16	**Toronto**	**NHL**	**22**	**6**	**7**	**13**	**4**	**1**	**0**	**1**	**43**	**14.0**	**1**	**291**	**49.1**	**16:20**									
	Toronto Marlies	AHL	38	18	27	45	10										14	7	4	11	2				
2016-17	**Toronto**	**NHL**	**81**	**22**	**39**	**61**	**32**	**9**	**0**	**2**	**205**	**10.7**	**–3**	**122**	**40.2**	**16:01**	**6**	**1**	**3**	**4**	**2**	**0**	**0**	**0**	**18:41**
	NHL Totals		**103**	**28**	**46**	**74**	**36**	**10**	**0**	**3**	**248**	**11.3**		**413**	**46.5**	**16:05**	**6**	**1**	**3**	**4**	**2**	**0**	**0**	**0**	**18:41**

• Loaned to **MODO** (Sweden) by **Toronto**, October 6, 2014.

NYQUIST, Gustav

(NEW-kwihst, GUS-TAHV) **DET**

Right wing. Shoots left. 5'11", 183 lbs. Born, Halmstad, Sweden, September 1, 1989. Detroit's 3rd pick, 121st overall, in 2008 NHL Draft.

Season	Club	League	GP	G	A	Pts	PIM	PP	SH	GW	S	S%	+/-	TF	F%	Min	GP	G	A	Pts	PIM	PP	SH	GW	Min
2005-06	Malmo U18	Swe-U18	14	9	3	12	10										6	1	3	4	0				
2006-07	Malmo Jr.	Swe-Jr.	42	21	23	44	57										4	2	2	4	6				
2007-08	Malmo Jr.	Swe-Jr.	24	11	20	31	20										7	5	5	10	6				
2008-09	U. of Maine	H-East	38	13	19	32	28																		
2009-10	U. of Maine	H-East	39	19	*42	*61	20																		
2010-11	U. of Maine	H-East	36	18	*33	51	20																		
	Grand Rapids	AHL	8	1	3	4	2																		
2011-12	**Detroit**	**NHL**	**18**	**1**	**6**	**7**	**2**	**0**	**0**	**0**	**19**	**5.3**	**2**	**0**	**0.0**	**10:36**	**4**	**0**	**0**	**0**	**0**	**0**	**0**	**0**	**8:52**
	Grand Rapids	AHL	56	22	36	58	18																		
2012-13	Grand Rapids	AHL	58	23	37	60	34										10	2	5	7	19				
	Detroit	**NHL**	**22**	**3**	**3**	**6**	**6**	**0**	**0**	**0**	**46**	**6.5**	**0**	**4**	**25.0**	**13:02**	**14**	**2**	**3**	**5**	**2**	**1**	**0**	**1**	**12:36**
2013-14	**Detroit**	**NHL**	**57**	**28**	**20**	**48**	**10**	**6**	**0**	**6**	**153**	**18.3**	**16**	**9**	**55.6**	**16:51**	**5**	**0**	**0**	**0**	**0**	**0**	**0**	**0**	**15:23**
	Grand Rapids	AHL	15	7	14	21	6																		
	Sweden	Olympics	6	0	0	0	0																		
2014-15	**Detroit**	**NHL**	**82**	**27**	**27**	**54**	**26**	**14**	**0**	**4**	**195**	**13.8**	**–11**	**9**	**11.1**	**16:39**	**7**	**1**	**1**	**2**	**2**	**0**	**0**	**0**	**15:39**
2015-16	**Detroit**	**NHL**	**82**	**17**	**26**	**43**	**34**	**7**	**0**	**3**	**161**	**10.6**	**–2**	**2**	**0.0**	**15:10**	**5**	**1**	**0**	**1**	**6**	**0**	**0**	**0**	**16:51**
2016-17	**Detroit**	**NHL**	**76**	**12**	**36**	**48**	**18**	**2**	**0**	**2**	**165**	**7.3**	**0**	**5**	**80.0**	**17:26**									
	NHL Totals		**337**	**88**	**118**	**206**	**96**	**29**	**0**	**15**	**739**	**11.9**		**29**	**37.9**	**15:57**	**35**	**4**	**4**	**8**	**10**	**1**	**0**	**1**	**13:47**

Hockey East All-Rookie Team (2009) • Hockey East First All-Star Team (2010, 2011) • NCAA East First All-American Team (2010) • NCAA East Second All-American Team (2011) • AHL All-Rookie Team (2012) • AHL First All-Star Team (2013)

O'BRIEN, Jim

(oh-BRIGH-uhn, JIHM)

Center. Shoots right. 6'3", 195 lbs. Born, Maplewood, MN, January 29, 1989. Ottawa's 1st pick, 29th overall, in 2007 NHL Draft.

			Regular Season													Playoffs								
Season	Club	League	GP	G	A	Pts	PIM	PP	SH	GW	S	S%	+/-	TF	F%	Min	GP	G	A	Pts	PIM	PP	SH	GW	Min
2003-04	Det. Caesars	MWEHL	68	19	24	43	72	....	....	....	....	....	....	....	....	....	....	....	....	....	....	....	....	....	....
2004-05	USAHNTDP	U-17	13	6	6	12	10	....	....	....	....	....	....	....	....	....	....	....	....	....	....	....	....	....	....
	USAHNTDP	NAHL	40	10	12	22	41	....	....	....	....	....	....	....	....	....	1	0	0	0	0	....	....	....	....
2005-06	USAHNTDP	U-18	38	11	14	25	62	....	....	....	....	....	....	....	....	....	....	....	....	....	....	....	....	....	....
	USAHNTDP	NAHL	13	6	10	16	14	....	....	....	....	....	....	....	....	....	....	....	....	....	....	....	....	....	....
2006-07	U. of Minnesota	WCHA	43	7	8	15	51	....	....	....	....	....	....	....	....	....	....	....	....	....	....	....	....	....	....
2007-08	Seattle	WHL	70	21	34	55	66	....	....	....	....	....	....	....	....	....	12	2	6	8	14	....	....	....	....
2008-09	Seattle	WHL	63	27	35	62	55	....	....	....	....	....	....	....	....	....	5	1	0	1	10	....	....	....	....
	Binghamton	AHL	6	0	1	1	0	....	....	....	....	....	....	....	....	....	....	....	....	....	....	....	....	....	....
2009-10	Binghamton	AHL	76	8	9	17	49	....	....	....	....	....	....	....	....	....	....	....	....	....	....	....	....	....	....
2010-11	**Ottawa**	**NHL**	**6**	**0**	**0**	**0**	**2**	**0**	**0**	**0**	**11**	**0.0**	**–3**	**16**	**50.0**	**9:40**	....	....	....	....	....	....	....	....	....
	Binghamton	AHL	74	24	32	56	67	....	....	....	....	....	....	....	....	....	23	3	4	7	12	....	....	....	....
2011-12	**Ottawa**	**NHL**	**28**	**3**	**3**	**6**	**4**	**0**	**0**	**1**	**37**	**8.1**	**6**	**256**	**47.3**	**11:45**	**7**	**0**	**1**	**1**	**0**	**0**	**0**	**0**	**8:38**
	Binghamton	AHL	27	7	7	14	10	....	....	....	....	....	....	....	....	....	....	....	....	....	....	....	....	....	....
2012-13	**Ottawa**	**NHL**	**29**	**5**	**1**	**6**	**8**	**1**	**0**	**0**	**38**	**13.2**	**–2**	**219**	**45.7**	**11:25**	....	....	....	....	....	....	....	....	....
2013-14	Binghamton	AHL	51	11	18	29	46	....	....	....	....	....	....	....	....	....	2	1	1	2	2	....	....	....	....
2014-15	Novokuznetsk	KHL	22	2	10	12	30	....	....	....	....	....	....	....	....	....	....	....	....	....	....	....	....	....	....
	Hershey Bears	AHL	32	10	19	29	26	....	....	....	....	....	....	....	....	....	10	3	1	4	8	....	....	....	....
2015-16	**New Jersey**	**NHL**	**4**	**0**	**0**	**0**	**2**	**0**	**0**	**0**	**3**	**0.0**	**–4**	**49**	**59.2**	**13:31**	....	....	....	....	....	....	....	....	....
	Albany Devils	AHL	56	19	19	38	48	....	....	....	....	....	....	....	....	....	6	2	3	5	4	....	....	....	....
2016-17	San Antonio	AHL	53	9	15	24	42	....	....	....	....	....	....	....	....	....	....	....	....	....	....	....	....	....	....
	NHL Totals		**67**	**8**	**4**	**12**	**16**	**1**	**0**	**1**	**89**	**9.0**		**540**	**47.8**	**11:32**	**7**	**0**	**1**	**1**	**0**	**0**	**0**	**0**	**8:38**

Signed as a free agent by **Novokuznetsk** (KHL), September 19, 2014. Signed as a free agent by **Hershey**, (AHL), December 26, 2014. Signed as a free agent by **New Jersey**, July 1, 2015. Signed as a free agent by **Colorado**, July 1, 2016.

O'BRIEN, Liam

(oh-BRIGH-uhn, LEE-uhm) **WSH**

Left wing. Shoots left. 6'1", 205 lbs. Born, Halifax, NS, July 29, 1994.

Season	Club	League	GP	G	A	Pts	PIM	PP	SH	GW	S	S%	+/-	TF	F%	Min	GP	G	A	Pts	PIM	PP	SH	GW	Min
2010-11	Rimouski Oceanic	QMJHL	61	2	8	10	45	....	....	....	....	....	....	....	....	....	5	0	0	0	6	....	....	....	....
2011-12	Rimouski Oceanic	QMJHL	40	7	9	16	67	....	....	....	....	....	....	....	....	....	....	....	....	....	....	....	....	....	....
	Rouyn-Noranda	QMJHL	27	3	7	10	69	....	....	....	....	....	....	....	....	....	4	1	0	1	11	....	....	....	....
2012-13	Rouyn-Noranda	QMJHL	65	10	14	24	164	....	....	....	....	....	....	....	....	....	12	2	1	3	17	....	....	....	....
2013-14	Rouyn-Noranda	QMJHL	68	20	15	35	148	....	....	....	....	....	....	....	....	....	9	1	3	4	12	....	....	....	....
2014-15	**Washington**	**NHL**	**13**	**1**	**1**	**2**	**23**	**0**	**0**	**0**	**16**	**6.3**	**4**	**2**	**50.0**	**7:33**	....	....	....	....	....	....	....	....	....
	Hershey Bears	AHL	45	4	4	8	121	....	....	....	....	....	....	....	....	....	10	3	3	6	14	....	....	....	....
2015-16	Hershey Bears	AHL	59	7	9	16	120	....	....	....	....	....	....	....	....	....	20	4	2	6	*65	....	....	....	....
2016-17	**Washington**	**NHL**	**1**	**0**	**0**	**0**	**0**	**0**	**0**	**0**	**0**	**0.0**	**0**	**0**	**0.0**	**6:08**	....	....	....	....	....	....	....	....	....
	Hershey Bears	AHL	64	10	20	30	117	....	....	....	....	....	....	....	....	....	6	0	0	0	13	....	....	....	....
	NHL Totals		**14**	**1**	**1**	**2**	**23**	**0**	**0**	**0**	**16**	**6.3**		**2**	**50.0**	**7:27**	....	....	....	....	....	....	....	....	....

Signed as a free agent by **Washington**, October 6, 2014.

ODUYA, Johnny

(oh-DOO-yuh, JAW-nee) **OTT**

Defense. Shoots left. 6', 195 lbs. Born, Stockholm, Sweden, October 1, 1981. Washington's 6th pick, 221st overall, in 2001 NHL Draft.

Season	Club	League	GP	G	A	Pts	PIM	PP	SH	GW	S	S%	+/-	TF	F%	Min	GP	G	A	Pts	PIM	PP	SH	GW	Min
1996-97	Hammarby Jr.	Swe-Jr.	13	0	0	0	....	....	....	....	....	....	....	....	....	....	....	....	....	....	....	....	....	....	....
1997-98	Hammarby Jr.	Swe-Jr.	26	3	11	14	70	....	....	....	....	....	....	....	....	....	....	....	....	....	....	....	....	....	....
1998-99	Hammarby Jr.	Swe-Jr.	38	14	31	45	45	....	....	....	....	....	....	....	....	....	....	....	....	....	....	....	....	....	....
99-2000	Hammarby Jr.	Swe-Jr.	32	3	18	21	48	....	....	....	....	....	....	....	....	....	6	1	2	3	4	....	....	....	....
	Hammarby	Sweden-2	1	0	0	0	0	....	....	....	....	....	....	....	....	....	1	0	0	0	0	....	....	....	....
2000-01	Moncton Wildcats	QMJHL	44	11	38	49	147	....	....	....	....	....	....	....	....	....	....	....	....	....	....	....	....	....	....
	Victoriaville Tigres	QMJHL	24	3	16	19	112	....	....	....	....	....	....	....	....	....	13	4	9	13	10	....	....	....	....
2001-02	Hammarby	Sweden-2	46	11	14	25	66	....	....	....	....	....	....	....	....	....	2	1	0	1	4	....	....	....	....
2002-03	Hammarby	Sweden-2	48	15	25	40	200	....	....	....	....	....	....	....	....	....	....	....	....	....	....	....	....	....	....
2003-04	Djurgarden	Sweden	42	4	4	8	*173	....	....	....	....	....	....	....	....	....	4	0	0	0	6	....	....	....	....
2004-05	Djurgarden	Sweden	49	2	4	6	139	....	....	....	....	....	....	....	....	....	12	0	2	2	39	....	....	....	....
2005-06	Frolunda	Sweden	47	8	11	19	95	....	....	....	....	....	....	....	....	....	17	1	2	3	16	....	....	....	....
2006-07	**New Jersey**	**NHL**	**76**	**2**	**9**	**11**	**61**	**0**	**0**	**0**	**55**	**3.6**	**–5**	**0**	**0.0**	**18:31**	**6**	**0**	**1**	**1**	**6**	**0**	**0**	**0**	**12:59**
2007-08	**New Jersey**	**NHL**	**75**	**6**	**20**	**26**	**46**	**2**	**0**	**0**	**63**	**9.5**	**27**	**0**	**0.0**	**19:02**	**5**	**0**	**1**	**1**	**6**	**0**	**0**	**0**	**20:40**
2008-09	**New Jersey**	**NHL**	**82**	**7**	**22**	**29**	**30**	**1**	**1**	**4**	**108**	**6.5**	**21**	**0**	**0.0**	**20:52**	**7**	**0**	**0**	**0**	**2**	**0**	**0**	**0**	**20:19**
2009-10	**New Jersey**	**NHL**	**40**	**2**	**2**	**4**	**18**	**0**	**0**	**0**	**44**	**4.5**	**2**	**0**	**0.0**	**21:11**	....	....	....	....	....	....	....	....	....
	Atlanta	**NHL**	**27**	**1**	**8**	**9**	**12**	**0**	**0**	**0**	**24**	**4.2**	**6**	**0**	**0.0**	**21:22**	....	....	....	....	....	....	....	....	....
	Sweden	Olympics	4	0	0	0	12	....	....	....	....	....	....	....	....	....	....	....	....	....	....	....	....	....	....
2010-11	**Atlanta**	**NHL**	**82**	**2**	**15**	**17**	**22**	**0**	**0**	**0**	**90**	**2.2**	**–15**	**0**	**0.0**	**20:43**	....	....	....	....	....	....	....	....	....
2011-12	**Winnipeg**	**NHL**	**63**	**2**	**11**	**13**	**33**	**0**	**0**	**1**	**52**	**3.8**	**–9**	**0**	**0.0**	**19:20**	....	....	....	....	....	....	....	....	....
	Chicago	**NHL**	**18**	**1**	**4**	**5**	**0**	**0**	**0**	**0**	**30**	**3.3**	**3**	**0**	**0.0**	**24:25**	**6**	**0**	**3**	**3**	**0**	**0**	**0**	**0**	**23:14**
2012-13	Flying Farangs	Thailand	6	4	4	8	0	....	....	....	....	....	....	....	....	....	....	....	....	....	....	....	....	....	....
	♦ Chicago	**NHL**	**48**	**3**	**9**	**12**	**10**	**0**	**0**	**0**	**52**	**5.8**	**12**	**0**	**0.0**	**20:31**	**23**	**3**	**5**	**8**	**16**	**0**	**0**	**1**	**22:45**
2013-14	**Chicago**	**NHL**	**77**	**3**	**13**	**16**	**38**	**0**	**0**	**1**	**83**	**3.6**	**11**	**1**	**100.0**	**20:06**	**19**	**2**	**5**	**7**	**8**	**0**	**0**	**0**	**21:54**
	Sweden	Olympics	6	0	1	1	0	....	....	....	....	....	....	....	....	....	....	....	....	....	....	....	....	....	....
2014-15	**♦ Chicago**	**NHL**	**76**	**2**	**8**	**10**	**26**	**0**	**0**	**0**	**76**	**2.6**	**5**	**0**	**0.0**	**20:17**	**23**	**0**	**5**	**5**	**6**	**0**	**0**	**0**	**24:45**
2015-16	**Dallas**	**NHL**	**82**	**4**	**17**	**21**	**26**	**0**	**1**	**0**	**63**	**6.3**	**8**	**0**	**0.0**	**20:23**	**13**	**1**	**2**	**3**	**2**	**0**	**0**	**0**	**18:39**
2016-17	**Dallas**	**NHL**	**37**	**1**	**6**	**7**	**10**	**0**	**0**	**0**	**24**	**4.2**	**–2**	**0**	**0.0**	**18:10**	....	....	....	....	....	....	....	....	....
	Chicago	**NHL**	**15**	**1**	**1**	**2**	**8**	**0**	**0**	**0**	**13**	**7.7**	**–2**	**0**	**0.0**	**18:31**	**4**	**0**	**0**	**0**	**0**	**0**	**0**	**0**	**19:21**
	NHL Totals		**798**	**37**	**145**	**182**	**340**	**3**	**2**	**6**	**777**	**4.8**		**1**	**100.0**	**20:05**	**106**	**6**	**22**	**28**	**46**	**0**	**0**	**1**	**21:37**

Signed as a free agent by **New Jersey**, July 24, 2006. Traded to **Atlanta** by **New Jersey** with Niclas Bergfors, Patrice Cormier and New Jersey's 1st (later traded to Chicago - Chicago selected Kevin Hayes) and 2nd (later traded to Chicago - Chicago selected Justin Holl) round picks in 2010 NHL Draft for Ilya Kovalchuk, Anssi Salmela and Atlanta's 2nd round pick (Jonathon Merrill) in 2010 NHL Draft, February 4, 2010. • Transferred to **Winnipeg** after **Atlanta** franchise relocated, June 21, 2011. Signed as a free agent by **Flying Farangs Bangkok** (Thailand), October 31, 2012. Traded to **Chicago** by **Winnipeg** for Chicago's 2nd (later traded to Washington – Washington selected Zachary Sanford) and 3rd (J.C. Lipon) round picks in 2013 NHL Draft, February 27, 2012. Signed as a free agent by **Dallas**, July 15, 2015. Traded to **Chicago** by **Dallas** for Mark McNeill and Dallas' 4th round pck in 2018 NHL Draft, February 28, 2017. Signed as a free agent by **Ottawa**, July 24, 2017.

OESTERLE, Jordan

(OH-stuhr-lee, JOHR-duhn) **CHI**

Defense. Shoots left. 6', 182 lbs. Born, Dearborn Heights, MI, June 25, 1992.

Season	Club	League	GP	G	A	Pts	PIM	PP	SH	GW	S	S%	+/-	TF	F%	Min	GP	G	A	Pts	PIM	PP	SH	GW	Min
2008-09	Detroit Belle Tire	T1EHL	31	5	15	20	10	....	....	....	....	....	....	....	....	....	....	....	....	....	....	....	....	....	....
	Detroit Belle Tire	Other	3	0	2	2	15	....	....	....	....	....	....	....	....	....	....	....	....	....	....	....	....	....	....
2009-10	Detroit Belle Tire	T1EHL	47	5	25	30	42	....	....	....	....	....	....	....	....	....	4	0	1	1	0	....	....	....	....
	Detroit Belle Tire	Other	6	1	3	4	4	....	....	....	....	....	....	....	....	....	....	....	....	....	....	....	....	....	....
2010-11	Sioux Falls	USHL	54	2	13	15	16	....	....	....	....	....	....	....	....	....	10	2	3	5	0	....	....	....	....
2011-12	Western Mich.	CCHA	41	2	6	8	8	....	....	....	....	....	....	....	....	....	....	....	....	....	....	....	....	....	....
2012-13	Western Mich.	CCHA	38	3	6	9	14	....	....	....	....	....	....	....	....	....	....	....	....	....	....	....	....	....	....
2013-14	Western Mich.	NCHC	34	2	15	17	27	....	....	....	....	....	....	....	....	....	....	....	....	....	....	....	....	....	....
	Oklahoma City	AHL	4	1	0	1	2	....	....	....	....	....	....	....	....	....	1	0	0	0	0	....	....	....	....
2014-15	**Edmonton**	**NHL**	**6**	**0**	**1**	**1**	**0**	**0**	**0**	**0**	**7**	**0.0**	**–4**	**0**	**0.0**	**14:42**	....	....	....	....	....	....	....	....	....
	Oklahoma City	AHL	65	8	17	25	8	....	....	....	....	....	....	....	....	....	10	1	3	4	8	....	....	....	....
2015-16	**Edmonton**	**NHL**	**17**	**0**	**5**	**5**	**0**	**0**	**0**	**0**	**24**	**0.0**	**1**	**0**	**0.0**	**21:41**	....	....	....	....	....	....	....	....	....
	Bakersfield	AHL	44	4	21	25	10	....	....	....	....	....	....	....	....	....	....	....	....	....	....	....	....	....	....
2016-17	**Edmonton**	**NHL**	**2**	**0**	**0**	**0**	**0**	**0**	**0**	**0**	**2**	**0.0**	**–1**	**0**	**0.0**	**17:17**	....	....	....	....	....	....	....	....	....
	Bakersfield	AHL	44	7	25	32	10	....	....	....	....	....	....	....	....	....	....	....	....	....	....	....	....	....	....
	NHL Totals		**25**	**0**	**6**	**6**	**0**	**0**	**0**	**0**	**33**	**0.0**		**0**	**0.0**	**19:39**	....	....	....	....	....	....	....	....	....

Signed as a free agent by **Edmonton**, April 3, 2014. Signed as a free agent by **Chicago**, July 1, 2017.

			Regular Season														Playoffs								
Season	Club	League	GP	G	A	Pts	PIM	PP	SH	GW	S	S%	+/-	TF	F%	Min	GP	G	A	Pts	PIM	PP	SH	GW	Min

O'GARA, Rob

(OH-GAR-uh, RAWB)   BOS

Defense. Shoots left. 6'4", 207 lbs.   Born, Massapequa, NY, July 6, 1993. Boston's 5th pick, 151st overall, in 2011 NHL Draft.

Season	Club	League	GP	G	A	Pts	PIM	PP	SH	GW	S	S%	+/-	TF	F%	Min	GP	G	A	Pts	PIM	PP	SH	GW	Min
2007-08	Long Island Bant.	AYHL	27	1	6	7	22	....	....	....	....	....	....	....	....	....	....	....	....	....	....	....	....	....	....
2008-09	Long Island Mid.	AYHL	17	1	4	5	16	....	....	....	....	....	....	....	....	....	....	....	....	....	....	....	....	....	....
2009-10	Long Island Mid.	AYHL	33	8	17	25	48	....	....	....	....	....	....	....	....	....	....	....	....	....	....	....	....	....	....
2010-11	Milton Academy	High-MA	30	2	7	9	22	....	....	....	....	....	....	....	....	....	....	....	....	....	....	....	....	....	....
2011-12	Milton Academy	High-MA	STATISTICS NOT AVAILABLE																						
2012-13	Yale	ECAC	37	0	7	7	32	....	....	....	....	....	....	....	....	....	....	....	....	....	....	....	....	....	....
2013-14	Yale	ECAC	33	4	7	11	30	....	....	....	....	....	....	....	....	....	....	....	....	....	....	....	....	....	....
2014-15	Yale	ECAC	33	6	15	21	31	....	....	....	....	....	....	....	....	....	....	....	....	....	....	....	....	....	....
2015-16	Yale	ECAC	30	4	8	12	41	....	....	....	....	....	....	....	....	....	....	....	....	....	....	....	....	....	....
	Providence Bruins	AHL	5	1	0	1	4	....	....	....	....	....	....	....	....	....	....	....	....	....	....	....	....	....	....
2016-17	**Boston**	**NHL**	**3**	**0**	**0**	**0**	**0**	0	0	0	2	0.0	1	0	0.0	16:01	....	....	....	....	....	....	....	....	....
	Providence Bruins	AHL	59	4	9	13	30	....	....	....	....	....	....	....	....	....	3	0	0	0	4	....	....	....	....
	NHL Totals		**3**	**0**	**0**	**0**	**0**	0	0	0	2	0.0		0	0.0	16:01	....	....	....	....	....	....	....	....	....

ECAC First All-Star Team (2015, 2016) • NCAA East First All-American Team (2015) • NCAA East Second All-American Team (2016)

OKPOSO, Kyle

(oh-POH-soh, KIGHL)   BUF

Right wing. Shoots right. 6', 217 lbs.   Born, St. Paul, MN, April 16, 1988. NY Islanders' 1st pick, 7th overall, in 2006 NHL Draft.

Season	Club	League	GP	G	A	Pts	PIM	PP	SH	GW	S	S%	+/-	TF	F%	Min	GP	G	A	Pts	PIM	PP	SH	GW	Min
2004-05	Shattuck	High-MN	65	47	45	92	72	....	....	....	....	....	....	....	....	....	....	....	....	....	....	....	....	....	....
2005-06	Des Moines	USHL	50	27	31	58	56	....	....	....	....	....	....	....	....	....	11	5	11	*16	8	....	....	....	....
2006-07	U. of Minnesota	WCHA	40	19	21	40	34	....	....	....	....	....	....	....	....	....	....	....	....	....	....	....	....	....	....
2007-08	U. of Minnesota	WCHA	18	7	4	11	6	....	....	....	....	....	....	....	....	....	....	....	....	....	....	....	....	....	....
	NY Islanders	**NHL**	**9**	**2**	**3**	**5**	**2**	1	0	1	15	13.3	3	0	0.0	16:28	....	....	....	....	....	....	....	....	....
	Bridgeport	AHL	35	9	19	28	12	....	....	....	....	....	....	....	....	....	....	....	....	....	....	....	....	....	....
2008-09	**NY Islanders**	**NHL**	**65**	**18**	**21**	**39**	**36**	9	0	3	165	10.9	−6	15	33.3	18:01	....	....	....	....	....	....	....	....	....
	Bridgeport	AHL	....	....	....	....	....	....	....	....	....	....	....	....	....	....	2	1	0	1	2	....	....	....	....
2009-10	**NY Islanders**	**NHL**	**80**	**19**	**33**	**52**	**34**	4	0	4	249	7.6	−22	69	47.8	20:32	....	....	....	....	....	....	....	....	....
2010-11	**NY Islanders**	**NHL**	**38**	**5**	**15**	**20**	**40**	0	0	2	72	6.9	3	87	41.4	16:35	....	....	....	....	....	....	....	....	....
2011-12	**NY Islanders**	**NHL**	**79**	**24**	**21**	**45**	**46**	3	0	5	152	15.8	−15	142	47.9	17:04	....	....	....	....	....	....	....	....	....
2012-13	**NY Islanders**	**NHL**	**48**	**4**	**20**	**24**	**38**	0	0	0	101	4.0	−2	186	55.9	16:57	6	3	1	4	5	0	1	1	19:13
2013-14	**NY Islanders**	**NHL**	**71**	**27**	**42**	**69**	**51**	5	0	4	195	13.8	−9	204	47.6	20:26	....	....	....	....	....	....	....	....	....
2014-15	**NY Islanders**	**NHL**	**60**	**18**	**33**	**51**	**12**	6	0	2	195	9.2	−8	161	49.7	19:33	7	2	1	3	2	0	0	0	18:31
2015-16	**NY Islanders**	**NHL**	**79**	**22**	**42**	**64**	**51**	7	0	4	202	10.9	−4	63	36.5	18:12	11	2	6	8	4	1	0	0	22:03
2016-17	**Buffalo**	**NHL**	**65**	**19**	**26**	**45**	**24**	7	0	2	156	12.2	−7	99	54.6	18:58	....	....	....	....	....	....	....	....	....
	NHL Totals		**594**	**158**	**256**	**414**	**334**	42	0	24	1502	10.5		1026	48.7	18:36	24	7	8	15	11	1	1	1	20:19

USHL All-Rookie Team (2006) • USHL First All-Star Team (2006) • USHL Rookie of the Year (2006) • WCHA All-Rookie Team (2007) • WCHA Second All-Star Team (2007)
Played in NHL All-Star Game (2017)
• Missed majority of 2010-11 due to training camp shoulder injury. Signed as a free agent by **Buffalo**, July 1, 2016.

OLEKSIAK, Jamie

(oh-LEHK-see-ak, JAY-mih)   DAL

Defense. Shoots left. 6'7", 260 lbs.   Born, Toronto, ON, December 21, 1992. Dallas' 1st pick, 14th overall, in 2011 NHL Draft.

Season	Club	League	GP	G	A	Pts	PIM	PP	SH	GW	S	S%	+/-	TF	F%	Min	GP	G	A	Pts	PIM	PP	SH	GW	Min
2007-08	Tor. Young Nats	GTHL	51	1	10	11	46	....	....	....	....	....	....	....	....	....	....	....	....	....	....	....	....	....	....
2008-09	Det. Lit. Caesars	T1EHL	30	3	7	10	31	....	....	....	....	....	....	....	....	....	....	....	....	....	....	....	....	....	....
	Chicago Steel	USHL	29	0	4	4	47	....	....	....	....	....	....	....	....	....	....	....	....	....	....	....	....	....	....
2009-10	Chicago Steel	USHL	29	0	10	10	43	....	....	....	....	....	....	....	....	....	....	....	....	....	....	....	....	....	....
	Sioux Falls	USHL	24	2	2	4	32	....	....	....	....	....	....	....	....	....	3	0	1	1	2	....	....	....	....
2010-11	Northeastern	H-East	38	4	9	13	57	....	....	....	....	....	....	....	....	....	....	....	....	....	....	....	....	....	....
2011-12	Saginaw Spirit	OHL	31	6	5	11	24	....	....	....	....	....	....	....	....	....	....	....	....	....	....	....	....	....	....
	Niagara Ice Dogs	OHL	28	6	15	21	23	....	....	....	....	....	....	....	....	....	20	0	4	4	6	....	....	....	....
2012-13	Texas Stars	AHL	59	6	27	33	29	....	....	....	....	....	....	....	....	....	9	0	1	1	6	....	....	....	....
	Dallas	**NHL**	**16**	**0**	**2**	**2**	**14**	0	0	0	11	0.0	−5	0	0.0	14:50	....	....	....	....	....	....	....	....	....
2013-14	**Dallas**	**NHL**	**7**	**0**	**0**	**0**	**2**	0	0	0	5	0.0	−3	0	0.0	17:47	....	....	....	....	....	....	....	....	....
	Texas Stars	AHL	69	5	18	23	31	....	....	....	....	....	....	....	....	....	21	0	5	5	8	....	....	....	....
2014-15	**Dallas**	**NHL**	**36**	**1**	**7**	**8**	**8**	0	0	0	36	2.8	0	0	0.0	13:24	....	....	....	....	....	....	....	....	....
	Texas Stars	AHL	35	4	12	16	12	....	....	....	....	....	....	....	....	....	3	0	0	0	0	....	....	....	....
2015-16	**Dallas**	**NHL**	**19**	**0**	**2**	**2**	**21**	0	0	0	13	0.0	−5	0	0.0	12:43	....	....	....	....	....	....	....	....	....
	Texas Stars	AHL	8	0	2	2	2	....	....	....	....	....	....	....	....	....	....	....	....	....	....	....	....	....	....
2016-17	**Dallas**	**NHL**	**41**	**5**	**2**	**7**	**37**	0	0	1	33	15.2	−4	0	0.0	16:13	....	....	....	....	....	....	....	....	....
	NHL Totals		**119**	**6**	**13**	**19**	**82**	0	0	1	98	6.1		0	0.0	14:43	....	....	....	....	....	....	....	....	....

• Missed majority of 2015-16 and 2016-17 as a healthy reserve.

OLEKSY, Steve

(oh-LEHK-see, STEEV)   ANA

Defense. Shoots right. 6', 190 lbs.   Born, Chesterfield, MI, February 4, 1986.

Season	Club	League	GP	G	A	Pts	PIM	PP	SH	GW	S	S%	+/-	TF	F%	Min	GP	G	A	Pts	PIM	PP	SH	GW	Min
2005-06	Traverse City	NAHL	57	11	19	30	140	....	....	....	....	....	....	....	....	....	....	....	....	....	....	....	....	....	....
2006-07	Lake Superior	CCHA	39	2	2	4	24	....	....	....	....	....	....	....	....	....	....	....	....	....	....	....	....	....	....
2007-08	Lake Superior	CCHA	36	1	6	7	36	....	....	....	....	....	....	....	....	....	....	....	....	....	....	....	....	....	....
2008-09	Lake Superior	CCHA	38	0	9	9	50	....	....	....	....	....	....	....	....	....	....	....	....	....	....	....	....	....	....
	Las Vegas	ECHL	2	0	0	0	0	....	....	....	....	....	....	....	....	....	....	....	....	....	....	....	....	....	....
2009-10	Toledo Walleye	ECHL	3	0	0	0	2	....	....	....	....	....	....	....	....	....	....	....	....	....	....	....	....	....	....
	Port Huron	IHL	28	1	1	2	35	....	....	....	....	....	....	....	....	....	....	....	....	....	....	....	....	....	....
	Idaho Steelheads	ECHL	33	1	8	9	72	....	....	....	....	....	....	....	....	....	8	0	0	0	25	....	....	....	....
2010-11	Idaho Steelheads	ECHL	55	7	14	21	134	....	....	....	....	....	....	....	....	....	....	....	....	....	....	....	....	....	....
	Lake Erie	AHL	17	0	4	4	39	....	....	....	....	....	....	....	....	....	3	0	1	1	2	....	....	....	....
2011-12	Idaho Steelheads	ECHL	14	1	7	8	47	....	....	....	....	....	....	....	....	....	....	....	....	....	....	....	....	....	....
	Bridgeport	AHL	50	1	14	15	98	....	....	....	....	....	....	....	....	....	3	0	0	0	2	....	....	....	....
2012-13	Hershey Bears	AHL	55	2	12	14	151	....	....	....	....	....	....	....	....	....	....	....	....	....	....	....	....	....	....
	Washington	**NHL**	**28**	**1**	**8**	**9**	**33**	0	0	0	25	4.0	9	0	0.0	17:16	7	0	1	1	4	0	0	0	15:09
2013-14	**Washington**	**NHL**	**33**	**2**	**8**	**10**	**53**	0	0	1	27	7.4	7	0	0.0	15:16	....	....	....	....	....	....	....	....	....
	Hershey Bears	AHL	30	0	6	6	39	....	....	....	....	....	....	....	....	....	....	....	....	....	....	....	....	....	....
2014-15	**Washington**	**NHL**	**1**	**0**	**0**	**0**	**0**	0	0	0	1	0.0	−1	0	0.0	12:11	....	....	....	....	....	....	....	....	....
	Hershey Bears	AHL	68	4	11	15	147	....	....	....	....	....	....	....	....	....	8	0	3	3	8	....	....	....	....
2015-16	Wilkes-Barre	AHL	63	2	17	19	123	....	....	....	....	....	....	....	....	....	9	0	1	1	38	....	....	....	....
2016-17	**Pittsburgh**	**NHL**	**11**	**0**	**1**	**1**	**24**	0	0	0	11	0.0	2	0	0.0	13:42	....	....	....	....	....	....	....	....	....
	Wilkes-Barre	AHL	16	1	4	5	16	....	....	....	....	....	....	....	....	....	....	....	....	....	....	....	....	....	....
	Toronto Marlies	AHL	20	3	6	9	39	....	....	....	....	....	....	....	....	....	11	1	2	3	14	....	....	....	....
	NHL Totals		**73**	**3**	**17**	**20**	**110**	0	0	1	64	4.7		0	0.0	15:45	7	0	1	1	4	0	0	0	15:09

Signed as a free agent by **Hershey** (AHL), July 2, 2012. Signed as a free agent by **Washington**, March 4, 2013. Signed as a free agent by **Pittsburgh**, July 1, 2015. Traded to **Toronto** by **Pittsburgh** with Eric Fehr and Pittsburgh's 4th round pick (Vladislav Kara) in 2017 NHL Draft for Frank Corrado, March 1, 2017. Signed as a free agent by **Anaheim**, July 2, 2017.

OLOFSSON, Gustav

(OH-lawf-suhn, GOO-stahv)   MIN

Defense. Shoots left. 6'3", 197 lbs.   Born, Boras, Sweden, December 1, 1994. Minnesota's 1st pick, 46th overall, in 2013 NHL Draft.

Season	Club	League	GP	G	A	Pts	PIM	PP	SH	GW	S	S%	+/-	TF	F%	Min	GP	G	A	Pts	PIM	PP	SH	GW	Min
2010-11	Col. T-birds U16	T1EHL	35	5	10	15	18	....	....	....	....	....	....	....	....	....	....	....	....	....	....	....	....	....	....
2011-12	Col. T-birds U18	T1EHL	38	5	25	30	10	....	....	....	....	....	....	....	....	....	....	....	....	....	....	....	....	....	....
	Green Bay	USHL	3	0	1	1	0	....	....	....	....	....	....	....	....	....	....	....	....	....	....	....	....	....	....
2012-13	Green Bay	USHL	63	2	21	23	59	....	....	....	....	....	....	....	....	....	4	0	0	0	0	....	....	....	....
2013-14	Colorado College	NCHC	30	4	4	8	20	....	....	....	....	....	....	....	....	....	....	....	....	....	....	....	....	....	....
	Iowa Wild	AHL	8	1	0	1	2	....	....	....	....	....	....	....	....	....	....	....	....	....	....	....	....	....	....
	Sweden	Olympics	7	1	4	5	2	....	....	....	....	....	....	....	....	....	....	....	....	....	....	....	....	....	....
2014-15	Iowa Wild	AHL	1	0	0	0	0	....	....	....	....	....	....	....	....	....	....	....	....	....	....	....	....	....	....
2015-16	**Minnesota**	**NHL**	**2**	**0**	**0**	**0**	**0**	0	0	0	1	0.0	0	0	0.0	9:12	....	....	....	....	....	....	....	....	....
	Iowa Wild	AHL	52	2	15	17	12	....	....	....	....	....	....	....	....	....	....	....	....	....	....	....	....	....	....

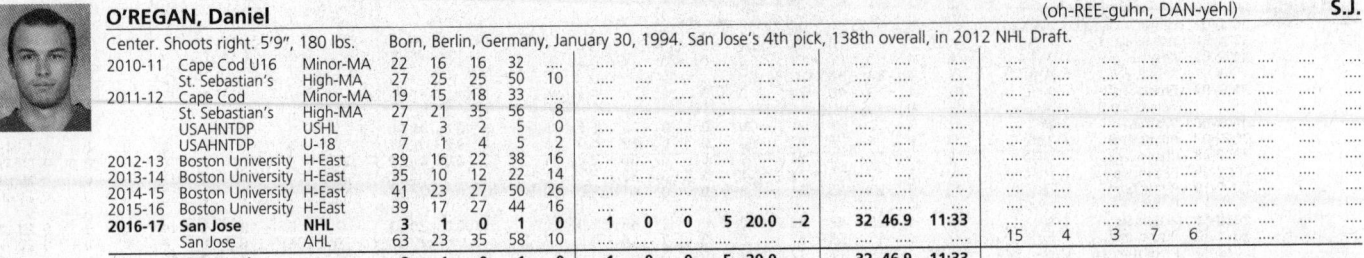

			Regular Season														Playoffs								
Season	Club	League	GP	G	A	Pts	PIM	PP	SH	GW	S	S%	+/-	TF	F%	Min	GP	G	A	Pts	PIM	PP	SH	GW	Min
2016-17	**Minnesota**	**NHL**	**13**	**0**	**3**	**3**	**2**	**0**	**0**	**0**	**7**	**0.0**	**–1**	**0**	**0.0**	**13:29**									
	Iowa Wild	AHL	59	6	18	24	32																		
	NHL Totals		**15**	**0**	**3**	**3**	**2**	**0**	**0**	**0**	**8**	**0.0**		**0**	**0.0**	**12:55**									

USHL All-Rookie Team (2013)

O'REGAN, Daniel

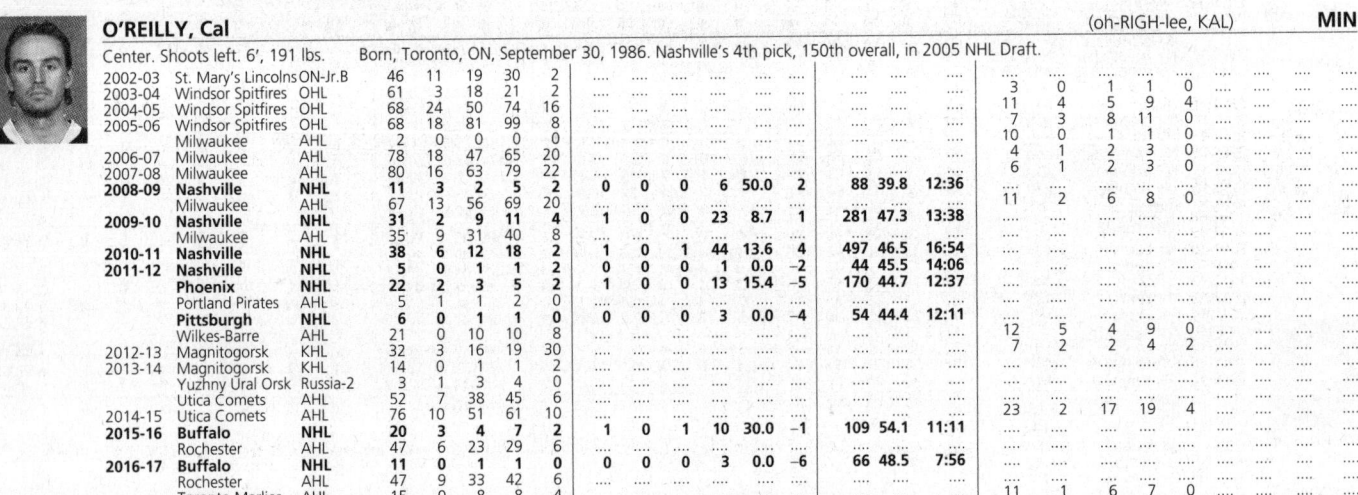

(oh-REE-guhn, DAN-yehl) **S.J.**

Center. Shoots right. 5'9", 180 lbs. Born, Berlin, Germany, January 30, 1994. San Jose's 4th pick, 138th overall, in 2012 NHL Draft.

Season	Club	League	GP	G	A	Pts	PIM	PP	SH	GW	S	S%	+/-	TF	F%	Min	GP	G	A	Pts	PIM	PP	SH	GW	Min
2010-11	Cape Cod U16	Minor-MA	22	16	16	32																			
	St. Sebastian's	High-MA	27	25	25	50	10																		
2011-12	Cape Cod	Minor-MA	19	15	18	33																			
	St. Sebastian's	High-MA	27	21	35	56	8																		
	USAHNTDP	USHL	7	3	2	5	0																		
	USAHNTDP	U-18	7	1	4	5	2																		
2012-13	Boston University	H-East	39	16	22	38	16																		
2013-14	Boston University	H-East	35	10	12	22	14																		
2014-15	Boston University	H-East	41	23	27	50	26																		
2015-16	Boston University	H-East	39	17	27	44	16																		
2016-17	**San Jose**	**NHL**	**3**	**1**	**0**	**1**	**0**	**1**	**0**	**0**	**5**	**20.0**	**–2**	**32**	**46.9**	**11:33**									
	San Jose	AHL	63	23	35	58	10										15	4	3	7	6				
	NHL Totals		**3**	**1**	**0**	**1**	**0**	**1**	**0**	**0**	**5**	**20.0**		**32**	**46.9**	**11:33**									

Hockey East All-Rookie Team (2013) • Hockey East Second All-Star Team (2015) • Hockey East First All-Star Team (2016) • NCAA East Second All-American Team (2016) • AHL All-Rookie Team (2017) • Dudley "Red" Garrett Memorial Award (AHL – Rookie of the Year) (2017)

O'REILLY, Cal

(oh-RIGH-lee, KAL) **MIN**

Center. Shoots left. 6', 191 lbs. Born, Toronto, ON, September 30, 1986. Nashville's 4th pick, 150th overall, in 2005 NHL Draft.

Season	Club	League	GP	G	A	Pts	PIM	PP	SH	GW	S	S%	+/-	TF	F%	Min	GP	G	A	Pts	PIM	PP	SH	GW	Min
2002-03	St. Mary's Lincolns	ON-Jr.B	46	11	19	30	2																		
2003-04	Windsor Spitfires	OHL	61	3	18	21	2										3	0	1	1	0				
2004-05	Windsor Spitfires	OHL	68	24	50	74	16										11	4	5	9	4				
2005-06	Windsor Spitfires	OHL	68	18	81	99	8										7	3	8	11	0				
	Milwaukee	AHL	2	0	0	0	0										10	0	1	1	0				
2006-07	Milwaukee	AHL	78	18	47	65	20										4	1	2	3	0				
2007-08	Milwaukee	AHL	80	16	63	79	22										6	1	2	3	0				
2008-09	**Nashville**	**NHL**	**11**	**3**	**2**	**5**	**2**	**0**	**0**	**0**	**6**	**50.0**	**2**	**88**	**39.8**	**12:36**									
	Milwaukee	AHL	67	13	56	69	20										11	2	6	8	0				
2009-10	**Nashville**	**NHL**	**31**	**2**	**9**	**11**	**4**	**1**	**0**	**0**	**23**	**8.7**	**1**	**281**	**47.3**	**13:38**									
	Milwaukee	AHL	35	9	31	40	8																		
2010-11	**Nashville**	**NHL**	**38**	**6**	**12**	**18**	**2**	**1**	**0**	**1**	**44**	**13.6**	**4**	**497**	**46.5**	**16:54**									
2011-12	**Nashville**	**NHL**	**5**	**0**	**1**	**1**	**2**	**0**	**0**	**0**	**1**	**0.0**	**–2**	**44**	**45.5**	**14:06**									
	Phoenix	**NHL**	**22**	**2**	**3**	**5**	**2**	**1**	**0**	**0**	**13**	**15.4**	**–5**	**170**	**44.7**	**12:37**									
	Portland Pirates	AHL	5	1	1	2	0																		
	Pittsburgh	**NHL**	**6**	**0**	**1**	**1**	**0**	**0**	**0**	**0**	**3**	**0.0**	**–4**	**54**	**44.4**	**12:11**									
	Wilkes-Barre	AHL	21	0	10	10	8										12	5	4	9	0				
2012-13	Magnitogorsk	KHL	32	3	16	19	30										7	2	2	4	2				
2013-14	Magnitogorsk	KHL	14	0	1	1	2																		
	Yuzhny Ural Orsk	Russia-2	3	1	3	4	0																		
	Utica Comets	AHL	52	7	38	45	6																		
2014-15	Utica Comets	AHL	76	10	51	61	10										23	2	17	19	4				
2015-16	**Buffalo**	**NHL**	**20**	**3**	**4**	**7**	**2**	**1**	**0**	**1**	**10**	**30.0**	**–1**	**109**	**54.1**	**11:11**									
	Rochester	AHL	47	6	23	29	6																		
2016-17	**Buffalo**	**NHL**	**11**	**0**	**1**	**1**	**0**	**0**	**0**	**0**	**3**	**0.0**	**–6**	**66**	**48.5**	**7:56**									
	Rochester	AHL	47	9	33	42	6																		
	Toronto Marlies	AHL	15	0	8	8	4										11	1	6	7	0				
	NHL Totals		**144**	**16**	**33**	**49**	**14**	**4**	**0**	**2**	**103**	**15.5**		**1309**	**46.6**	**13:26**									

• Missed majority of 2010-11 due to recurring leg injury. Traded to **Phoenix** by **Nashville** for Phoenix's 4th round pick (Mikko Vainonen) in 2012 NHL Draft, October 28, 2011. Claimed on waivers by **Pittsburgh** from **Phoenix**, February 1, 2012. Signed as a free agent by **Magnitogorsk** (KHL), July 18, 2012. Signed as a free agent by **Utica** (AHL), November 19, 2013. Signed as a free agent by **Vancouver**, July 3, 2014. Signed as a free agent by **Buffalo**, July 3, 2015. • Loaned to **Toronto** (AHL) by **Buffalo** for cash, March 8, 2017. Signed as a free agent by **Minnesota**, July 1, 2017.

O'REILLY, Ryan

(oh-RIGH-lee, RIGH-uhn) **BUF**

Center. Shoots left. 6'1", 210 lbs. Born, Clinton, ON, February 7, 1991. Colorado's 2nd pick, 33rd overall, in 2009 NHL Draft.

Season	Club	League	GP	G	A	Pts	PIM	PP	SH	GW	S	S%	+/-	TF	F%	Min	GP	G	A	Pts	PIM	PP	SH	GW	Min
2006-07	Tor. Jr. Canadiens	GTHL	50	31	43	74																			
	Tor. Canadiens	ON-Jr.A	1	1	0	1	0																		
2007-08	Erie Otters	OHL	61	19	33	52	14																		
2008-09	Erie Otters	OHL	68	16	50	66	26										5	0	5	5	2				
2009-10	**Colorado**	**NHL**	**81**	**8**	**18**	**26**	**18**	**0**	**2**	**2**	**135**	**5.9**	**4**	**1014**	**47.8**	**16:46**	**6**	**1**	**0**	**1**	**2**	**0**	**0**	**1**	**17:05**
2010-11	**Colorado**	**NHL**	**74**	**13**	**13**	**26**	**16**	**2**	**1**	**0**	**119**	**10.9**	**–7**	**1025**	**51.8**	**16:03**									
2011-12	**Colorado**	**NHL**	**81**	**18**	**37**	**55**	**12**	**4**	**0**	**3**	**189**	**9.5**	**–1**	**1443**	**52.8**	**19:32**									
2012-13	Magnitogorsk	KHL	12	5	5	10	2																		
	Colorado	**NHL**	**29**	**6**	**14**	**20**	**4**	**3**	**0**	**0**	**66**	**9.1**	**–3**	**456**	**52.9**	**18:30**									
2013-14	**Colorado**	**NHL**	**80**	**28**	**36**	**64**	**2**	**9**	**0**	**6**	**201**	**13.9**	**–1**	**371**	**51.8**	**19:49**	**7**	**2**	**4**	**6**	**0**	**0**	**0**	**0**	**22:21**
2014-15	**Colorado**	**NHL**	**82**	**17**	**38**	**55**	**12**	**2**	**1**	**1**	**171**	**9.9**	**–5**	**1334**	**53.5**	**19:43**									
2015-16	**Buffalo**	**NHL**	**71**	**21**	**39**	**60**	**8**	**8**	**1**	**2**	**157**	**13.4**	**–16**	**1812**	**56.5**	**21:44**									
2016-17	**Buffalo**	**NHL**	**72**	**20**	**35**	**55**	**10**	**8**	**1**	**3**	**189**	**10.6**	**–1**	**1791**	**58.0**	**21:28**									
	NHL Totals		**570**	**131**	**230**	**361**	**82**	**36**	**6**	**17**	**1227**	**10.7**		**9246**	**53.9**	**19:13**	**13**	**3**	**4**	**7**	**2**	**0**	**0**	**1**	**19:55**

Lady Byng Memorial Trophy (2014)

Played in NHL All-Star Game (2016)

Signed as a free agent by **Magnitogorsk** (KHL), December 7, 2012. Traded to **Buffalo** by **Colorado** with Jamie McGinn for Nikita Zadorov, Mikhail Grigorenko, J.T. Compher and Buffalo's 2nd round pick (later traded to San Jose – San Jose selected Jeremy Roy) in 2015 NHL Draft, June 26, 2015.

ORLOV, Dmitry

(ohr-LAWF, dih-MEE-tree) **WSH**

Defense. Shoots left. 6', 212 lbs. Born, Novokuznetsk, USSR, July 23, 1991. Washington's 2nd pick, 55th overall, in 2009 NHL Draft.

Season	Club	League	GP	G	A	Pts	PIM	PP	SH	GW	S	S%	+/-	TF	F%	Min	GP	G	A	Pts	PIM	PP	SH	GW	Min
2007-08	Novokuznetsk	Russia	6	0	0	0	0																		
2008-09	Novokuznetsk 2	Russia-3	STATISTICS NOT AVAILABLE																						
	Novokuznetsk	KHL	16	1	0	1	4																		
2009-10	Novokuznetsk	KHL	41	4	3	7	49																		
	Novokuznetsk Jr.	Russia-Jr.	7	7	6	13	6										17	9	10	19	26				
2010-11	Novokuznetsk	KHL	45	2	11	13	43																		
	Novokuznetsk Jr.	Russia-Jr.	1	0	0	0	0																		
	Hershey Bears	AHL	19	2	7	9	12										6	0	1	1	4				
2011-12	**Washington**	**NHL**	**60**	**3**	**16**	**19**	**18**	**0**	**0**	**1**	**51**	**5.9**	**1**	**1**	**0.0**	**16:52**									
	Hershey Bears	AHL	15	4	5	9	12																		
2012-13	Hershey Bears	AHL	31	3	14	17	20										4	1	2	3	4				
	Washington	**NHL**	**5**	**0**	**1**	**1**	**0**	**0**	**0**	**0**	**1**	**0.0**	**5**	**0**	**0.0**	**14:57**									
2013-14	**Washington**	**NHL**	**54**	**3**	**8**	**11**	**19**	**0**	**0**	**0**	**59**	**5.1**	**–1**	**0**	**0.0**	**19:36**									
	Hershey Bears	AHL	11	3	6	9	4																		
2014-15	Hershey Bears	AHL	3	0	3	3	4																		
2015-16	**Washington**	**NHL**	**82**	**8**	**21**	**29**	**26**	**0**	**0**	**3**	**90**	**8.9**	**8**	**0**	**0.0**	**16:02**	**11**	**0**	**1**	**1**	**2**	**0**	**0**	**0**	**13:18**
2016-17	**Washington**	**NHL**	**82**	**6**	**27**	**33**	**51**	**1**	**0**	**0**	**125**	**4.8**	**30**	**0**	**0.0**	**19:32**	**13**	**0**	**3**	**3**	**2**	**0**	**0**	**0**	**21:25**
	NHL Totals		**283**	**20**	**73**	**93**	**114**	**1**	**0**	**4**	**326**	**6.1**		**1**	**0.0**	**17:53**	**24**	**0**	**4**	**4**	**4**	**0**	**0**	**0**	**17:41**

• Missed majority of 2014-15 due to wrist injury while playing for Russia in 2014 World Championship (WC-A) vs. USA, May 12, 2014.

ORPIK, Brooks

(OHR-pihk, BRUKS) **WSH**

Defense. Shoots left. 6'2", 221 lbs. Born, San Francisco, CA, September 26, 1980. Pittsburgh's 1st pick, 18th overall, in 2000 NHL Draft.

Season	Club	League	GP	G	A	Pts	PIM	PP	SH	GW	S	S%	+/-	TF	F%	Min	Playoffs GP	G	A	Pts	PIM	PP	SH	GW	Min
			Regular Season														Playoffs								
1996-97	Thayer Academy	High-MA	20	4	1	5	....	....	....	....	....	....	....	....	....	....	....	....	....	....	....	....	....	....	....
1997-98	Thayer Academy	High-MA	22	0	7	7	....	....	....	....	....	....	....	....	....	....	....	....	....	....	....	....	....	....	....
1998-99	Boston College	H-East	41	1	10	11	*96	....	....	....	....	....	....	....	....	....	....	....	....	....	....	....	....	....	....
99-2000	Boston College	H-East	38	1	9	10	102	....	....	....	....	....	....	....	....	....	....	....	....	....	....	....	....	....	....
2000-01	Boston College	H-East	40	0	20	20	*124	....	....	....	....	....	....	....	....	....	....	....	....	....	....	....	....	....	....
2001-02	Wilkes-Barre	AHL	78	2	18	20	99	....	....	....	....	....	....	....	....	....	....	....	....	....	....	....	....	....	....
2002-03	**Pittsburgh**	**NHL**	**6**	**0**	**0**	**0**	**2**	**0**	**0**	**0**	**2**	**0.0**	**–5**	**0**	**0.0**	**18:19**	....	....	....	....	....	....	....	....	....
	Wilkes-Barre	AHL	71	4	14	18	105	....	....	....	....	....	....	....	....	....	6	0	0	0	14	....	....	....	....
2003-04	**Pittsburgh**	**NHL**	**79**	**1**	**9**	**10**	**127**	**0**	**0**	**0**	**56**	**1.8**	**–36**	**0**	**0.0**	**18:25**	....	....	....	....	....	....	....	....	....
	Wilkes-Barre	AHL	3	0	0	0	2	....	....	....	....	....	....	....	....	....	24	0	4	4	53	....	....	....	....
2005-06	**Pittsburgh**	**NHL**	**64**	**2**	**7**	**9**	**124**	**0**	**0**	**0**	**32**	**6.3**	**–3**	**0**	**0.0**	**18:50**	....	....	....	....	....	....	....	....	....
2006-07	**Pittsburgh**	**NHL**	**70**	**0**	**6**	**6**	**82**	**0**	**0**	**0**	**59**	**0.0**	**4**	**0**	**0.0**	**16:37**	**5**	**0**	**0**	**0**	**8**	**0**	**0**	**0**	**15:43**
2007-08	**Pittsburgh**	**NHL**	**78**	**1**	**10**	**11**	**57**	**0**	**0**	**0**	**50**	**2.0**	**11**	**0**	**0.0**	**16:58**	**20**	**0**	**2**	**2**	**18**	**0**	**0**	**0**	**20:47**
2008-09 ♦	**Pittsburgh**	**NHL**	**79**	**2**	**17**	**19**	**73**	**1**	**0**	**0**	**39**	**5.1**	**10**	**0**	**0.0**	**20:20**	**24**	**0**	**4**	**4**	**22**	**0**	**0**	**0**	**20:04**
2009-10	**Pittsburgh**	**NHL**	**73**	**2**	**23**	**25**	**64**	**0**	**0**	**0**	**61**	**3.3**	**6**	**0**	**0.0**	**20:06**	**13**	**0**	**2**	**2**	**12**	**0**	**0**	**0**	**21:40**
	United States	Olympics	6	0	0	0	0	....	....	....	....	....	....	....	....	....	....	....	....	....	....	....	....	....	....
2010-11	**Pittsburgh**	**NHL**	**63**	**1**	**12**	**13**	**66**	**0**	**0**	**0**	**56**	**1.8**	**12**	**1**	**100.0**	**20:53**	**7**	**0**	**3**	**3**	**14**	**0**	**0**	**0**	**24:11**
2011-12	**Pittsburgh**	**NHL**	**73**	**2**	**16**	**18**	**61**	**0**	**0**	**0**	**44**	**4.5**	**19**	**0**	**0.0**	**22:33**	**6**	**0**	**0**	**0**	**4**	**0**	**0**	**0**	**22:17**
2012-13	**Pittsburgh**	**NHL**	**46**	**0**	**8**	**8**	**32**	**0**	**0**	**0**	**32**	**0.0**	**17**	**0**	**0.0**	**22:17**	**12**	**1**	**1**	**2**	**10**	**0**	**0**	**1**	**25:08**
2013-14	**Pittsburgh**	**NHL**	**72**	**2**	**11**	**13**	**46**	**0**	**0**	**0**	**50**	**4.0**	**–3**	**0**	**0.0**	**21:12**	**5**	**1**	**1**	**2**	**0**	**0**	**0**	**0**	**19:55**
	United States	Olympics	6	0	0	0	2	....	....	....	....	....	....	....	....	....	....	....	....	....	....	....	....	....	....
2014-15	**Washington**	**NHL**	**78**	**0**	**19**	**19**	**66**	**0**	**0**	**0**	**66**	**0.0**	**5**	**0**	**0.0**	**21:48**	**14**	**0**	**2**	**2**	**8**	**0**	**0**	**0**	**22:17**
2015-16	**Washington**	**NHL**	**41**	**3**	**7**	**10**	**24**	**0**	**0**	**1**	**31**	**9.7**	**11**	**0**	**0.0**	**19:49**	**6**	**0**	**0**	**0**	**10**	**0**	**0**	**0**	**21:05**
2016-17	**Washington**	**NHL**	**79**	**0**	**14**	**14**	**48**	**0**	**0**	**0**	**93**	**0.0**	**32**	**0**	**0.0**	**17:47**	**13**	**0**	**2**	**2**	**11**	**0**	**0**	**0**	**15:56**
	NHL Totals		**901**	**16**	**159**	**175**	**872**	**1**	**0**	**1**	**671**	**2.4**		**1**	**100.0**	**19:43**	**125**	**2**	**17**	**19**	**117**	**0**	**0**	**1**	**20:52**

Signed as a free agent by **Washington**, July 1, 2014.

OSHIE, T.J.

(OH-shee, TEE-JAY) **WSH**

Center. Shoots right. 5'11", 189 lbs. Born, Mt. Vernon, WA, December 23, 1986. St. Louis' 1st pick, 24th overall, in 2005 NHL Draft.

Season	Club	League	GP	G	A	Pts	PIM	PP	SH	GW	S	S%	+/-	TF	F%	Min	Playoffs GP	G	A	Pts	PIM	PP	SH	GW	Min
2004-05	Warroad Warriors	High-MN	31	37	62	99	22	....	....	....	....	....	....	....	....	....	....	....	....	....	....	....	....	....	....
	Sioux Falls	USHL	11	3	2	5	6	....	....	....	....	....	....	....	....	....	....	....	....	....	....	....	....	....	....
2005-06	North Dakota	WCHA	44	24	21	45	33	....	....	....	....	....	....	....	....	....	....	....	....	....	....	....	....	....	....
2006-07	North Dakota	WCHA	43	17	*35	52	30	....	....	....	....	....	....	....	....	....	....	....	....	....	....	....	....	....	....
2007-08	North Dakota	WCHA	42	18	27	45	57	....	....	....	....	....	....	....	....	....	....	....	....	....	....	....	....	....	....
2008-09	**St. Louis**	**NHL**	**57**	**14**	**25**	**39**	**30**	**6**	**1**	**1**	**101**	**13.9**	**16**	**109**	**43.1**	**16:35**	**4**	**0**	**0**	**0**	**2**	**0**	**0**	**0**	**19:01**
2009-10	**St. Louis**	**NHL**	**76**	**18**	**30**	**48**	**36**	**1**	**1**	**3**	**158**	**11.4**	**–1**	**153**	**41.8**	**18:19**	....	....	....	....	....	....	....	....	....
2010-11	**St. Louis**	**NHL**	**49**	**12**	**22**	**34**	**15**	**3**	**1**	**3**	**103**	**11.7**	**10**	**227**	**44.1**	**19:11**	....	....	....	....	....	....	....	....	....
2011-12	**St. Louis**	**NHL**	**80**	**19**	**35**	**54**	**50**	**3**	**1**	**3**	**188**	**10.1**	**15**	**53**	**45.3**	**19:32**	**9**	**0**	**3**	**3**	**6**	**0**	**0**	**0**	**18:49**
2012-13	**St. Louis**	**NHL**	**30**	**7**	**13**	**20**	**15**	**2**	**1**	**1**	**65**	**10.8**	**–5**	**13**	**38.5**	**19:06**	**6**	**2**	**0**	**2**	**2**	**1**	**0**	**0**	**18:31**
2013-14	**St. Louis**	**NHL**	**79**	**21**	**39**	**60**	**42**	**5**	**2**	**5**	**152**	**13.8**	**19**	**66**	**42.4**	**18:59**	**5**	**2**	**0**	**2**	**2**	**0**	**0**	**0**	**24:22**
	United States	Olympics	6	1	3	4	4	....	....	....	....	....	....	....	....	....	....	....	....	....	....	....	....	....	....
2014-15	**St. Louis**	**NHL**	**72**	**19**	**36**	**55**	**51**	**3**	**0**	**4**	**162**	**11.7**	**17**	**13**	**23.1**	**18:50**	**6**	**1**	**1**	**2**	**0**	**0**	**0**	**0**	**19:08**
2015-16	**Washington**	**NHL**	**80**	**26**	**25**	**51**	**34**	**11**	**0**	**5**	**185**	**14.1**	**16**	**262**	**52.7**	**18:58**	**12**	**6**	**4**	**10**	**11**	**2**	**0**	**2**	**19:00**
2016-17	**Washington**	**NHL**	**68**	**33**	**23**	**56**	**36**	**7**	**1**	**4**	**143**	**23.1**	**28**	**180**	**48.3**	**17:51**	**13**	**4**	**8**	**12**	**4**	**2**	**0**	**1**	**20:53**
	NHL Totals		**591**	**169**	**248**	**417**	**309**	**41**	**8**	**29**	**1257**	**13.4**		**1076**	**46.1**	**18:37**	**55**	**15**	**16**	**31**	**27**	**5**	**0**	**3**	**19:52**

WCHA All-Rookie Team (2006) • WCHA First All-Star Team (2008) • NCAA West First All-American Team (2008)

Traded to **Washington** by **St. Louis** for Troy Brouwer, Pheonix Copley and Washington's 3rd round pick (later traded back to Washington – Washington selcted Garrett Pilon) in 2016 NHL Draft, July 2, 2015.

OTT, Steve

(AWT, STEEV)

Center. Shoots left. 6', 189 lbs. Born, Summerside, PE, August 19, 1982. Dallas' 1st pick, 25th overall, in 2000 NHL Draft.

Season	Club	League	GP	G	A	Pts	PIM	PP	SH	GW	S	S%	+/-	TF	F%	Min	Playoffs GP	G	A	Pts	PIM	PP	SH	GW	Min
1998-99	Leamington Flyers	ON-Jr.B	48	14	30	44	110	....	....	....	....	....	....	....	....	....	....	....	....	....	....	....	....	....	....
99-2000	Windsor Spitfires	OHL	66	23	39	62	131	....	....	....	....	....	....	....	....	....	12	3	5	8	21	....	....	....	....
2000-01	Windsor Spitfires	OHL	55	50	37	87	164	....	....	....	....	....	....	....	....	....	9	3	8	11	27	....	....	....	....
2001-02	Windsor Spitfires	OHL	53	43	45	88	178	....	....	....	....	....	....	....	....	....	14	6	10	16	49	....	....	....	....
2002-03	**Dallas**	**NHL**	**26**	**3**	**4**	**7**	**31**	**0**	**0**	**0**	**25**	**12.0**	**6**	**4**	**50.0**	**8:46**	**1**	**0**	**0**	**0**	**0**	**0**	**0**	**0**	**6:57**
	Utah Grizzlies	AHL	40	9	11	20	98	....	....	....	....	....	....	....	....	....	....	....	....	....	....	....	....	....	....
2003-04	**Dallas**	**NHL**	**73**	**2**	**10**	**12**	**152**	**0**	**0**	**1**	**74**	**2.7**	**–2**	**59**	**49.2**	**10:14**	**4**	**1**	**0**	**1**	**0**	**0**	**0**	**1**	**6:55**
2004-05	Hamilton	AHL	67	18	21	39	279	....	....	....	....	....	....	....	....	....	4	0	0	0	20	....	....	....	....
2005-06	**Dallas**	**NHL**	**82**	**5**	**17**	**22**	**178**	**0**	**0**	**1**	**89**	**5.6**	**1**	**535**	**49.2**	**11:54**	**5**	**0**	**1**	**1**	**2**	**0**	**0**	**0**	**7:41**
2006-07	**Dallas**	**NHL**	**19**	**0**	**4**	**4**	**35**	**0**	**0**	**0**	**17**	**0.0**	**–4**	**39**	**59.0**	**9:11**	**6**	**0**	**0**	**0**	**8**	**0**	**0**	**0**	**6:43**
	Iowa Stars	AHL	3	0	0	0	8	....	....	....	....	....	....	....	....	....	....	....	....	....	....	....	....	....	....
2007-08	**Dallas**	**NHL**	**73**	**11**	**11**	**22**	**147**	**0**	**1**	**2**	**89**	**12.4**	**2**	**311**	**58.8**	**14:28**	**18**	**2**	**1**	**3**	**22**	**1**	**0**	**1**	**13:46**
2008-09	**Dallas**	**NHL**	**64**	**19**	**27**	**46**	**135**	**5**	**0**	**0**	**132**	**14.4**	**3**	**172**	**46.5**	**17:35**	....	....	....	....	....	....	....	....	....
2009-10	**Dallas**	**NHL**	**73**	**22**	**14**	**36**	**153**	**8**	**1**	**2**	**146**	**15.1**	**–14**	**352**	**56.8**	**16:28**	....	....	....	....	....	....	....	....	....
2010-11	**Dallas**	**NHL**	**82**	**12**	**20**	**32**	**183**	**3**	**2**	**4**	**120**	**10.0**	**–9**	**1138**	**56.6**	**17:09**	....	....	....	....	....	....	....	....	....
2011-12	**Dallas**	**NHL**	**74**	**11**	**28**	**39**	**156**	**4**	**0**	**2**	**108**	**10.2**	**5**	**1011**	**55.5**	**18:21**	....	....	....	....	....	....	....	....	....
2012-13	**Buffalo**	**NHL**	**48**	**9**	**15**	**24**	**93**	**2**	**0**	**3**	**73**	**12.3**	**3**	**535**	**55.7**	**18:33**	....	....	....	....	....	....	....	....	....
2013-14	**Buffalo**	**NHL**	**59**	**9**	**11**	**20**	**55**	**6**	**0**	**1**	**99**	**9.1**	**–26**	**701**	**52.1**	**19:42**	....	....	....	....	....	....	....	....	....
	St. Louis	**NHL**	**23**	**0**	**3**	**3**	**37**	**0**	**0**	**0**	**28**	**0.0**	**–12**	**216**	**59.7**	**14:27**	**6**	**0**	**2**	**2**	**14**	**0**	**0**	**0**	**19:05**
2014-15	**St. Louis**	**NHL**	**78**	**3**	**9**	**12**	**86**	**0**	**0**	**0**	**49**	**6.1**	**–8**	**284**	**56.3**	**11:38**	**6**	**0**	**0**	**0**	**26**	**0**	**0**	**0**	**11:15**
2015-16	**St. Louis**	**NHL**	**21**	**0**	**2**	**2**	**34**	**0**	**0**	**0**	**21**	**0.0**	**–3**	**70**	**55.7**	**10:55**	**9**	**0**	**1**	**1**	**8**	**0**	**0**	**0**	**6:53**
2016-17	**Detroit**	**NHL**	**42**	**3**	**3**	**6**	**63**	**0**	**0**	**0**	**33**	**9.1**	**–6**	**176**	**58.0**	**10:28**	....	....	....	....	....	....	....	....	....
	Montreal	**NHL**	**11**	**0**	**1**	**1**	**17**	**0**	**0**	**0**	**12**	**0.0**	**–2**	**102**	**50.0**	**11:56**	**6**	**0**	**0**	**0**	**0**	**0**	**0**	**0**	**12:22**
	NHL Totals		**848**	**109**	**179**	**288**	**1555**	**28**	**4**	**16**	**1115**	**9.8**		**5705**	**54.8**	**14:35**	**61**	**3**	**5**	**8**	**80**	**1**	**0**	**2**	**11:08**

Canadian Major Junior Second All-Star Team (2001) • OHL Second All-Star Team (2002)

• Missed majority of 2006-07 due to ankle injury vs. Los Angeles, October 28, 2006. Traded to **Buffalo** by **Dallas** with Adam Pardy for Derek Roy, July 2, 2012. Traded to **St. Louis** by **Buffalo** with Ryan Miller for Jaroslav Halak, Chris Stewart, William Carrier, St. Louis' 1st round pick (later traded to Winnipeg – Winnipeg selected Jack Roslovic) in 2015 NHL Draft and St. Louis' 3rd round pick (later traded to Florida – Florida selected Linus Nassen) in 2016 NHL Draft, February 28, 2014. • Missed majority of 2015-16 due to leg injury vs. Toronto, December 5, 2015 and as a healthy reserve. Signed as a free agent by **Detroit**, July 1, 2016. Traded to **Montreal** by **Detroit** for Montreal's 6th round pick in 2018 NHL Draft, March 1, 2017. • Officially announced his retirement, May 25, 2017.

OUELLET, Xavier

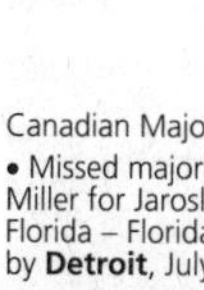

(OO-leht, ehx-AV-ee-ay) **DET**

Defense. Shoots left. 6'1", 200 lbs. Born, Bayonne, France, July 29, 1993. Detroit's 2nd pick, 48th overall, in 2011 NHL Draft.

Season	Club	League	GP	G	A	Pts	PIM	PP	SH	GW	S	S%	+/-	TF	F%	Min	Playoffs GP	G	A	Pts	PIM	PP	SH	GW	Min
2008-09	Esther-Blondin	QAAA	41	2	9	11	49	....	....	....	....	....	....	....	....	....	14	1	3	4	24	....	....	....	....
2009-10	Montreal	QMJHL	43	2	14	16	22	....	....	....	....	....	....	....	....	....	7	0	3	3	12	....	....	....	....
2010-11	Montreal	QMJHL	67	8	35	43	44	....	....	....	....	....	....	....	....	....	10	0	8	8	6	....	....	....	....
2011-12	Blainville-Bois.	QMJHL	63	21	39	60	67	....	....	....	....	....	....	....	....	....	11	3	7	10	14	....	....	....	....
2012-13	Blainville-Bois.	QMJHL	50	10	31	41	44	....	....	....	....	....	....	....	....	....	15	7	9	16	22	....	....	....	....
2013-14	**Detroit**	**NHL**	**4**	**0**	**0**	**0**	**2**	**0**	**0**	**0**	**4**	**0.0**	**0**	**0**	**0.0**	**14:34**	**1**	**0**	**0**	**0**	**0**	**0**	**0**	**0**	**9:20**
	Grand Rapids	AHL	70	4	13	17	22	....	....	....	....	....	....	....	....	....	8	0	0	0	4	....	....	....	....
2014-15	**Detroit**	**NHL**	**21**	**2**	**1**	**3**	**2**	**0**	**0**	**0**	**27**	**7.4**	**4**	**0**	**0.0**	**16:23**	....	....	....	....	....	....	....	....	....
	Grand Rapids	AHL	52	1	15	16	24	....	....	....	....	....	....	....	....	....	16	1	5	6	8	....	....	....	....
2015-16	**Detroit**	**NHL**	**5**	**0**	**1**	**1**	**2**	**0**	**0**	**0**	**4**	**0.0**	**–2**	**0**	**0.0**	**16:15**	....	....	....	....	....	....	....	....	....
	Grand Rapids	AHL	61	4	25	29	66	....	....	....	....	....	....	....	....	....	9	2	2	4	6	....	....	....	....
2016-17	**Detroit**	**NHL**	**66**	**3**	**9**	**12**	**51**	**0**	**0**	**0**	**89**	**3.4**	**2**	**2**	**0.0**	**17:58**	....	....	....	....	....	....	....	....	....
	NHL Totals		**96**	**5**	**11**	**16**	**57**	**0**	**0**	**0**	**124**	**4.0**		**2**	**0.0**	**17:24**	**1**	**0**	**0**	**0**	**0**	**0**	**0**	**0**	**9:20**

QMJHL All-Rookie Team (2010) • QMJHL First All-Star Team (2012, 2013)

			Regular Season														Playoffs								
Season	Club	League	GP	G	A	Pts	PIM	PP	SH	GW	S	S%	+/-	TF	F%	Min	GP	G	A	Pts	PIM	PP	SH	GW	Min

OVECHKIN, Alex

(oh-VEHCH-kihn, AL-ehx) **WSH**

Left wing. Shoots right. 6'3", 239 lbs. Born, Moscow, USSR, September 17, 1985. Washington's 1st pick, 1st overall, in 2004 NHL Draft.

Season	Club	League	GP	G	A	Pts	PIM	PP	SH	GW	S	S%	+/-	TF	F%	Min	GP	G	A	Pts	PIM	PP	SH	GW	Min
2001-02	Dyn'o Moscow 2	Russia-3	19	18	8	26	20	....	....	....	....	....	....	....	....	....	....	....	....	....	....	....	....	....	....
	Dynamo Moscow	Russia	22	2	2	4	4	....	....	....	....	....	....	....	....	....	3	0	0	0	0	....	....	....	....
2002-03	Dynamo Moscow	Russia	40	8	7	15	28	....	....	....	....	....	....	....	....	....	5	0	0	0	2	....	....	....	....
2003-04	Dynamo Moscow	Russia	53	13	11	24	40	....	....	....	....	....	....	....	....	....	3	0	0	0	2	....	....	....	....
2004-05	Dynamo Moscow	Russia	37	13	13	26	32	....	....	....	....	....	....	....	....	....	10	2	4	6	31	....	....	....	....
2005-06	**Washington**	**NHL**	**81**	**52**	**54**	**106**	**52**	**21**	**3**	**5**	**425**	**12.2**	**2**	**16**	**12.5**	**21:37**	....	....	....	....	....	....	....	....	....
	Russia	Olympics	8	5	0	5	8	....	....	....	....	....	....	....	....	....	....	....	....	....	....	....	....	....	....
2006-07	**Washington**	**NHL**	**82**	**46**	**46**	**92**	**52**	**16**	**0**	**8**	**392**	**11.7**	**–19**	**17**	**47.1**	**21:23**	....	....	....	....	....	....	....	....	....
2007-08	**Washington**	**NHL**	**82**	***65**	**47**	***112**	**40**	***22**	**0**	***11**	**446**	**14.6**	**28**	**18**	**38.9**	**23:06**	**7**	**4**	**5**	**9**	**0**	**1**	**0**	**2**	**24:03**
2008-09	**Washington**	**NHL**	**79**	***56**	**54**	**110**	**72**	**19**	**1**	**10**	**528**	**10.6**	**8**	**32**	**25.0**	**23:00**	**14**	**11**	**10**	**21**	**8**	**3**	**0**	**1**	**23:21**
2009-10	**Washington**	**NHL**	**72**	**50**	**59**	**109**	**89**	**13**	**0**	**7**	**368**	**13.6**	**45**	**22**	**45.5**	**21:48**	**7**	**5**	**5**	**10**	**0**	**1**	**0**	**0**	**23:06**
	Russia	Olympics	4	2	2	4	2	....	....	....	....	....	....	....	....	....	....	....	....	....	....	....	....	....	....
2010-11	**Washington**	**NHL**	**79**	**32**	**53**	**85**	**41**	**7**	**0**	***11**	**367**	**8.7**	**24**	**18**	**33.3**	**21:22**	**9**	**5**	**5**	**10**	**10**	**1**	**0**	**1**	**23:30**
2011-12	**Washington**	**NHL**	**78**	**38**	**27**	**65**	**26**	**13**	**0**	**3**	**303**	**12.5**	**–8**	**15**	**40.0**	**19:48**	**14**	**5**	**4**	**9**	**8**	**2**	**0**	**1**	**19:51**
2012-13	Dynamo Moscow	KHL	31	19	21	40	14	....	....	....	....	....	....	....	....	....	....	....	....	....	....	....	....	....	....
	Washington	**NHL**	**48**	***32**	**24**	**56**	**36**	***16**	**0**	**4**	**220**	**14.5**	**2**	**1**	**0.0**	**20:53**	**7**	**1**	**1**	**2**	**4**	**1**	**0**	**0**	**20:44**
2013-14	**Washington**	**NHL**	**78**	***51**	**28**	**79**	**48**	***24**	**0**	**10**	**386**	**13.2**	**–35**	**3**	**66.7**	**20:33**	....	....	....	....	....	....	....	....	....
	Russia	Olympics	5	1	1	2	0	....	....	....	....	....	....	....	....	....	....	....	....	....	....	....	....	....	....
2014-15	**Washington**	**NHL**	**81**	***53**	**28**	**81**	**58**	**25**	**0**	**11**	**395**	**13.4**	**10**	**5**	**40.0**	**20:20**	**14**	**5**	**4**	**9**	**6**	**1**	**0**	**0**	**19:57**
2015-16	**Washington**	**NHL**	**79**	***50**	**21**	**71**	**53**	**19**	**0**	**8**	**398**	**12.6**	**21**	**0**	**0.0**	**20:19**	**12**	**5**	**7**	**12**	**2**	**3**	**0**	**1**	**21:19**
2016-17	**Washington**	**NHL**	**82**	**33**	**36**	**69**	**50**	***17**	**0**	**7**	**313**	**10.5**	**6**	**1**	**0.0**	**18:22**	**13**	**5**	**3**	**8**	**8**	**2**	**0**	**0**	**19:30**
	NHL Totals		**921**	**558**	**477**	**1035**	**617**	**212**	**4**	**95**	**4541**	**12.3**		**148**	**34.5**	**21:03**	**97**	**46**	**44**	**90**	**46**	**15**	**0**	**6**	**21:27**

Olympic All-Star Team (2006) • NHL All-Rookie Team (2006) • NHL First All-Star Team (2006, 2007, 2008, 2009, 2010, 2013, 2015) • Calder Memorial Trophy (2006) • Maurice "Rocket" Richard Trophy (2008, 2009, 2013, 2014, 2015, 2016) • Art Ross Trophy (2008) • Lester B. Pearson Award (2008, 2009) • Hart Memorial Trophy (2008, 2009, 2013) • Ted Lindsay Award (2010) • NHL Second All-Star Team (2011, 2013, 2014, 2016)

Played in NHL All-Star Game (2007, 2008, 2009, 2011, 2015, 2017)

Signed as a free agent by **Dynamo Moscow** (KHL), September 19, 2012. • In 2012-13 Ovechkin was voted to the NHL First All-Star Team as a Right wing and voted to the NHL Second All-Star Team as a Left wing.

PAAJARVI, Magnus

(pe-ya-YAR-vee, MAG-nuhs) **ST.L.**

Left wing. Shoots left. 6'3", 208 lbs. Born, Norrkoping, Sweden, April 12, 1991. Edmonton's 1st pick, 10th overall, in 2009 NHL Draft.

Season	Club	League	GP	G	A	Pts	PIM	PP	SH	GW	S	S%	+/-	TF	F%	Min	GP	G	A	Pts	PIM	PP	SH	GW	Min
2005-06	Malmo U18	Swe-U18	13	2	3	5	4	....	....	....	....	....	....	....	....	....	1	0	0	0	0	....	....	....	....
	Malmo Jr.	Swe-Jr.	2	0	0	0	0	....	....	....	....	....	....	....	....	....	....	....	....	....	....	....	....	....	....
2006-07	Malmo U18	Swe-U18	3	3	3	6	0	....	....	....	....	....	....	....	....	....	....	....	....	....	....	....	....	....	....
	Malmo Jr.	Swe-Jr.	20	4	2	6	6	....	....	....	....	....	....	....	....	....	4	0	1	1	0	....	....	....	....
2007-08	Timra IK U18	Swe-U18	5	1	6	7	4	....	....	....	....	....	....	....	....	....	....	....	....	....	....	....	....	....	....
	Timra IK Jr.	Swe-Jr.	18	7	15	22	6	....	....	....	....	....	....	....	....	....	....	....	....	....	....	....	....	....	....
	Timra IK	Sweden	35	1	2	3	2	....	....	....	....	....	....	....	....	....	11	0	0	0	2	....	....	....	....
2008-09	Timra IK Jr.	Swe-Jr.	1	0	0	0	0	....	....	....	....	....	....	....	....	....	....	....	....	....	....	....	....	....	....
	Timra IK	Sweden	50	7	10	17	4	....	....	....	....	....	....	....	....	....	7	1	0	1	0	....	....	....	....
2009-10	Timra IK	Sweden	49	12	17	29	6	....	....	....	....	....	....	....	....	....	5	0	1	1	2	....	....	....	....
2010-11	**Edmonton**	**NHL**	**80**	**15**	**19**	**34**	**16**	**3**	**0**	**0**	**180**	**8.3**	**–13**	**5**	**20.0**	**15:23**	....	....	....	....	....	....	....	....	....
2011-12	**Edmonton**	**NHL**	**41**	**2**	**6**	**8**	**4**	**0**	**0**	**0**	**79**	**2.5**	**–7**	**7**	**28.6**	**13:11**	....	....	....	....	....	....	....	....	....
	Oklahoma City	AHL	34	7	18	25	4	....	....	....	....	....	....	....	....	....	14	2	9	11	2	....	....	....	....
2012-13	Oklahoma City	AHL	38	4	16	20	10	....	....	....	....	....	....	....	....	....	....	....	....	....	....	....	....	....	....
	Edmonton	**NHL**	**42**	**9**	**7**	**16**	**14**	**2**	**1**	**2**	**75**	**12.0**	**–1**	**12**	**33.3**	**14:08**	....	....	....	....	....	....	....	....	....
2013-14	**St. Louis**	**NHL**	**55**	**6**	**6**	**12**	**6**	**0**	**0**	**1**	**60**	**10.0**	**–6**	**6**	**33.3**	**10:15**	....	....	....	....	....	....	....	....	....
2014-15	**St. Louis**	**NHL**	**10**	**0**	**1**	**1**	**6**	**0**	**0**	**0**	**9**	**0.0**	**–2**	**1**	**100.0**	**9:48**	....	....	....	....	....	....	....	....	....
	Chicago Wolves	AHL	36	11	18	29	6	....	....	....	....	....	....	....	....	....	5	3	1	4	0	....	....	....	....
2015-16	**St. Louis**	**NHL**	**48**	**3**	**6**	**9**	**8**	**0**	**0**	**1**	**88**	**3.4**	**–9**	**2**	**0.0**	**12:51**	**3**	**0**	**1**	**1**	**0**	**0**	**0**	**0**	**8:12**
	Chicago Wolves	AHL	7	4	3	7	2	....	....	....	....	....	....	....	....	....	....	....	....	....	....	....	....	....	....
2016-17	**St. Louis**	**NHL**	**32**	**8**	**5**	**13**	**6**	**1**	**0**	**3**	**51**	**15.7**	**9**	**3**	**33.3**	**12:09**	**8**	**1**	**2**	**3**	**2**	**0**	**0**	**1**	**12:36**
	Chicago Wolves	AHL	26	7	11	18	2	....	....	....	....	....	....	....	....	....	....	....	....	....	....	....	....	....	....
	NHL Totals		**308**	**43**	**50**	**93**	**60**	**6**	**1**	**7**	**542**	**7.9**		**36**	**30.6**	**13:05**	**11**	**1**	**3**	**4**	**2**	**0**	**0**	**1**	**11:24**

Traded to **St. Louis** by **Edmonton** with Edmonton's 2nd round pick (Ivan Barbashev) in 2014 NHL Draft and Edmonton's 4th round pick (Adam Musil) in 2015 NHL Draft for David Perron and St. Louis' 3rd round pick (later forfieited to San Jose as a result of Edmonton's hiring of Todd McLellan as head coach – San Jose selected Mike Robinson) in 2015 NHL Draft, July 10, 2014.

PACIORETTY, Max

(pahk-OHR-eht-tee, MAX) **MTL**

Left wing. Shoots left. 6'2", 215 lbs. Born, New Canaan, CT, November 20, 1988. Montreal's 2nd pick, 22nd overall, in 2007 NHL Draft.

Season	Club	League	GP	G	A	Pts	PIM	PP	SH	GW	S	S%	+/-	TF	F%	Min	GP	G	A	Pts	PIM	PP	SH	GW	Min
2004-05	Taft Rhinos	High-CT	23	5	14	19	....	....	....	....	....	....	....	....	....	....	....	....	....	....	....	....	....	....	....
2005-06	Taft Rhinos	High-CT	26	7	26	33	....	....	....	....	....	....	....	....	....	....	....	....	....	....	....	....	....	....	....
2006-07	Sioux City	USHL	60	21	42	63	119	....	....	....	....	....	....	....	....	....	7	4	6	10	10	....	....	....	....
2007-08	U. of Michigan	CCHA	37	15	24	39	59	....	....	....	....	....	....	....	....	....	....	....	....	....	....	....	....	....	....
2008-09	**Montreal**	**NHL**	**34**	**3**	**8**	**11**	**27**	**1**	**0**	**0**	**57**	**5.3**	**–3**	**2**	**50.0**	**12:37**	....	....	....	....	....	....	....	....	....
	Hamilton	AHL	37	6	23	29	43	....	....	....	....	....	....	....	....	....	....	....	....	....	....	....	....	....	....
2009-10	**Montreal**	**NHL**	**52**	**3**	**11**	**14**	**20**	**0**	**0**	**0**	**74**	**4.1**	**–5**	**7**	**14.3**	**12:43**	....	....	....	....	....	....	....	....	....
	Hamilton	AHL	18	2	9	11	10	....	....	....	....	....	....	....	....	....	5	1	0	1	2	....	....	....	....
2010-11	**Montreal**	**NHL**	**37**	**14**	**10**	**24**	**39**	**7**	**0**	**2**	**112**	**12.5**	**–1**	**1**	**0.0**	**15:54**	....	....	....	....	....	....	....	....	....
	Hamilton	AHL	27	17	15	32	20	....	....	....	....	....	....	....	....	....	....	....	....	....	....	....	....	....	....
2011-12	**Montreal**	**NHL**	**79**	**33**	**32**	**65**	**56**	**4**	**0**	**5**	**286**	**11.5**	**2**	**5**	**20.0**	**18:16**	....	....	....	....	....	....	....	....	....
2012-13	HC Ambri-Piotta	Swiss	5	1	0	1	4	....	....	....	....	....	....	....	....	....	....	....	....	....	....	....	....	....	....
	Montreal	**NHL**	**44**	**15**	**24**	**39**	**28**	**4**	**0**	**0**	**163**	**9.2**	**8**	**7**	**28.6**	**16:31**	**4**	**0**	**0**	**0**	**4**	**0**	**0**	**0**	**17:16**
2013-14	**Montreal**	**NHL**	**73**	**39**	**21**	**60**	**35**	**10**	**1**	***11**	**270**	**14.4**	**8**	**10**	**60.0**	**18:29**	**17**	**5**	**6**	**11**	**8**	**1**	**0**	**2**	**19:19**
	United States	Olympics	5	0	1	1	4	....	....	....	....	....	....	....	....	....	....	....	....	....	....	....	....	....	....
2014-15	**Montreal**	**NHL**	**80**	**37**	**30**	**67**	**32**	**7**	**3**	**10**	**302**	**12.3**	**38**	**9**	**22.2**	**19:24**	**11**	**5**	**2**	**7**	**16**	**1**	**1**	**0**	**19:51**
2015-16	**Montreal**	**NHL**	**82**	**30**	**34**	**64**	**34**	**8**	**1**	**6**	**303**	**9.9**	**–10**	**13**	**46.2**	**18:32**	....	....	....	....	....	....	....	....	....
2016-17	**Montreal**	**NHL**	**81**	**35**	**32**	**67**	**38**	**8**	**1**	**7**	**268**	**13.1**	**15**	**50**	**54.0**	**19:11**	**6**	**0**	**1**	**1**	**7**	**0**	**0**	**0**	**20:44**
	NHL Totals		**562**	**209**	**202**	**411**	**309**	**49**	**6**	**41**	**1835**	**11.4**		**104**	**44.2**	**17:29**	**38**	**10**	**9**	**19**	**35**	**2**	**1**	**2**	**19:29**

USHL All-Rookie Team (2007) • USHL Rookie of the Year (2007) • CCHA All-Rookie Team (2008) • CCHA Rookie of the Year (2008) • Bill Masterton Memorial Trophy (2012)

Signed as a free agent by **Ambri-Piotta** (Swiss), September 24, 2012.

PAETSCH, Nathan

(PASH, NAY-thuhn)

Defense. Shoots left. 6', 195 lbs. Born, Humboldt, SK, March 30, 1983. Buffalo's 8th pick, 202nd overall, in 2003 NHL Draft.

Season	Club	League	GP	G	A	Pts	PIM	PP	SH	GW	S	S%	+/-	TF	F%	Min	GP	G	A	Pts	PIM	PP	SH	GW	Min
1998-99	Tisdale Trojans	SMHL	74	20	55	75	120	....	....	....	....	....	....	....	....	....	....	....	....	....	....	....	....	....	....
	Moose Jaw	WHL	2	0	0	0	0	....	....	....	....	....	....	....	....	....	1	0	0	0	0	....	....	....	....
99-2000	Moose Jaw	WHL	68	9	35	44	49	....	....	....	....	....	....	....	....	....	4	0	1	1	0	....	....	....	....
2000-01	Moose Jaw	WHL	70	8	54	62	118	....	....	....	....	....	....	....	....	....	4	1	2	3	6	....	....	....	....
2001-02	Moose Jaw	WHL	59	16	36	52	86	....	....	....	....	....	....	....	....	....	12	0	4	4	16	....	....	....	....
2002-03	Moose Jaw	WHL	59	15	39	54	81	....	....	....	....	....	....	....	....	....	13	3	10	13	6	....	....	....	....
2003-04	Rochester	AHL	54	5	5	10	49	....	....	....	....	....	....	....	....	....	16	1	1	2	28	....	....	....	....
2004-05	Rochester	AHL	80	4	19	23	150	....	....	....	....	....	....	....	....	....	9	1	1	2	16	....	....	....	....
2005-06	**Buffalo**	**NHL**	**1**	**0**	**1**	**1**	**0**	**0**	**0**	**0**	**0**	**0.0**	**–1**	**0**	**0.0**	**15:38**	**1**	**0**	**0**	**0**	**0**	**0**	**0**	**0**	**12:06**
	Rochester	AHL	72	11	39	50	90	....	....	....	....	....	....	....	....	....	....	....	....	....	....	....	....	....	....
2006-07	**Buffalo**	**NHL**	**63**	**2**	**22**	**24**	**50**	**0**	**0**	**0**	**62**	**3.2**	**10**	**0**	**0.0**	**15:15**	....	....	....	....	....	....	....	....	....
2007-08	**Buffalo**	**NHL**	**59**	**2**	**7**	**9**	**27**	**0**	**0**	**0**	**49**	**4.1**	**3**	**0**	**0.0**	**13:38**	....	....	....	....	....	....	....	....	....
2008-09	**Buffalo**	**NHL**	**23**	**2**	**4**	**6**	**25**	**0**	**0**	**0**	**21**	**9.5**	**3**	**0**	**0.0**	**12:11**	....	....	....	....	....	....	....	....	....
2009-10	**Buffalo**	**NHL**	**11**	**1**	**1**	**2**	**6**	**0**	**0**	**0**	**9**	**11.1**	**2**	**0**	**0.0**	**9:39**	....	....	....	....	....	....	....	....	....
	Columbus	**NHL**	**10**	**0**	**0**	**0**	**6**	**0**	**0**	**0**	**8**	**0.0**	**–5**	**0**	**0.0**	**11:14**	....	....	....	....	....	....	....	....	....
2010-11	Rochester	AHL	9	1	2	3	2	....	....	....	....	....	....	....	....	....	....	....	....	....	....	....	....	....	....
	Syracuse Crunch	AHL	34	8	9	17	12	....	....	....	....	....	....	....	....	....	....	....	....	....	....	....	....	....	....
2011-12	Wolfsburg	Germany	52	7	18	25	46	....	....	....	....	....	....	....	....	....	2	0	0	0	0	....	....	....	....
2012-13	Grand Rapids	AHL	70	4	27	31	32	....	....	....	....	....	....	....	....	....	24	0	11	11	21	....	....	....	....
2013-14	Grand Rapids	AHL	68	4	27	31	40	....	....	....	....	....	....	....	....	....	10	0	5	5	4	....	....	....	....

			Regular Season														Playoffs								
Season	Club	League	GP	G	A	Pts	PIM	PP	SH	GW	S	S%	+/-	TF	F%	Min	GP	G	A	Pts	PIM	PP	SH	GW	Min
2014-15	Grand Rapids	AHL	75	8	30	38	42	....	....	....	....	....	....	....	....	....	16	0	4	4	2	....	....	....	....
2015-16	Grand Rapids	AHL	73	4	20	24	26	....	....	....	....	....	....	....	....	....	9	1	2	3	4	....	....	....	....
2016-17	Grand Rapids	AHL	73	1	17	18	30	....	....	....	....	....	....	....	....	....	19	2	5	7	8	....	....	....	....
	NHL Totals		**167**	**7**	**35**	**42**	**114**	**0**	**0**	**0**	**149**	**4.7**		**0**	**0.0**	**13:39**	**1**	**0**	**0**	**0**	**0**	**0**	**0**	**0**	**12:06**

• Re-entered NHL Entry Draft. Originally Washington's 1st pick, 58th overall, in 2001 NHL Draft.

WHL East Second All-Star Team (2003)

• Missed majority of 2008-09 and 2009-10 as a healthy reserve. Traded to **Columbus** by **Buffalo** with Vancouver's 2nd round pick (previously acquired, Columbus selected Petr Straka) in 2010 NHL Draft for Raffi Torres, March 3, 2010. Signed as a free agent by **Florida**, July 7, 2010. Traded to **Vancouver** by **Florida** for Sean Zimmerman, October 7, 2010. Signed as a free agent by **Wolfsburg** (Germany), June 22, 2011. Signed as a free agent by **Grand Rapids** (AHL), July 9, 2012.

PAGEAU, Jean-Gabriel

(pah-ZHOH, ZHAWN-ga-BREE-ehl) **OTT**

Center. Shoots right. 5'10", 180 lbs. Born, Ottawa, ON, November 11, 1992. Ottawa's 5th pick, 96th overall, in 2011 NHL Draft.

Season	Club	League	GP	G	A	Pts	PIM	PP	SH	GW	S	S%	+/-	TF	F%	Min	GP	G	A	Pts	PIM	PP	SH	GW	Min
2008-09	Gatineau	QAAA	37	15	16	31	6	....	....	....	....	....	....	....	....	....	....	....	....	....	....	....	....	....	....
2009-10	Gatineau	QMJHL	62	16	15	31	20	....	....	....	....	....	....	....	....	....	4	1	0	1	0	....	....	....	....
2010-11	Gatineau	QMJHL	67	32	47	79	22	....	....	....	....	....	....	....	....	....	24	13	16	29	20	....	....	....	....
2011-12	Gatineau	QMJHL	23	23	16	39	12	....	....	....	....	....	....	....	....	....	....	....	....	....	....	....	....	....	....
	Chicoutimi	QMJHL	23	9	17	26	13	....	....	....	....	....	....	....	....	....	16	4	10	14	6	....	....	....	....
2012-13	Binghamton	AHL	69	7	22	29	33	....	....	....	....	....	....	....	....	....	....	....	....	....	....	....	....	....	....
	Ottawa	**NHL**	**9**	**2**	**2**	**4**	**0**	**0**	**0**	**2**	**14**	**14.3**	**3**	**82**	**48.8**	**11:30**	**10**	**4**	**2**	**6**	**8**	**1**	**0**	**1**	**12:52**
2013-14	**Ottawa**	**NHL**	**28**	**2**	**0**	**2**	**12**	**0**	**0**	**0**	**31**	**6.5**	**-5**	**246**	**48.0**	**10:15**	....	....	....	....	....	....	....	....	....
	Binghamton	AHL	46	20	24	44	23	....	....	....	....	....	....	....	....	....	4	1	0	1	2	....	....	....	....
2014-15	**Ottawa**	**NHL**	**50**	**10**	**9**	**19**	**9**	**0**	**2**	**2**	**97**	**10.3**	**4**	**681**	**49.2**	**14:11**	**6**	**0**	**0**	**0**	**0**	**0**	**0**	**0**	**15:34**
	Binghamton	AHL	27	11	10	21	27	....	....	....	....	....	....	....	....	....	....	....	....	....	....	....	....	....	....
2015-16	**Ottawa**	**NHL**	**82**	**19**	**24**	**43**	**26**	**1**	**7**	**2**	**133**	**14.3**	**17**	**1177**	**52.2**	**16:42**	....	....	....	....	....	....	....	....	....
2016-17	**Ottawa**	**NHL**	**82**	**12**	**21**	**33**	**24**	**0**	**0**	**2**	**169**	**7.1**	**13**	**1018**	**54.8**	**16:08**	**19**	**8**	**2**	**10**	**16**	**0**	**0**	**1**	**18:18**
	NHL Totals		**251**	**45**	**56**	**101**	**71**	**1**	**9**	**8**	**444**	**10.1**		**3204**	**52.0**	**15:06**	**35**	**12**	**4**	**16**	**24**	**1**	**0**	**2**	**16:17**

PAILLE, Daniel

(PIGH-yay, DAN-yehl)

Left wing. Shoots left. 6'1", 200 lbs. Born, Welland, ON, April 15, 1984. Buffalo's 2nd pick, 20th overall, in 2002 NHL Draft.

Season	Club	League	GP	G	A	Pts	PIM	PP	SH	GW	S	S%	+/-	TF	F%	Min	GP	G	A	Pts	PIM	PP	SH	GW	Min
99-2000	Welland Cougars	ON-Jr.B	42	14	17	31	19	....	....	....	....	....	....	....	....	....	16	16	16	32	....	....	....	....	....
2000-01	Guelph Storm	OHL	64	22	31	53	57	....	....	....	....	....	....	....	....	....	4	2	0	2	2	....	....	....	....
2001-02	Guelph Storm	OHL	62	27	30	57	54	....	....	....	....	....	....	....	....	....	9	5	2	7	9	....	....	....	....
2002-03	Guelph Storm	OHL	54	30	27	57	28	....	....	....	....	....	....	....	....	....	11	8	6	14	6	....	....	....	....
2003-04	Guelph Storm	OHL	59	37	43	80	63	....	....	....	....	....	....	....	....	....	22	9	9	18	14	....	....	....	....
2004-05	Rochester	AHL	79	14	15	29	54	....	....	....	....	....	....	....	....	....	9	2	2	4	6	....	....	....	....
2005-06	**Buffalo**	**NHL**	**14**	**1**	**2**	**3**	**2**	**0**	**0**	**0**	**15**	**6.7**	**5**	**4**	**25.0**	**10:24**	....	....	....	....	....	....	....	....	....
	Rochester	AHL	45	14	13	27	29	....	....	....	....	....	....	....	....	....	....	....	....	....	....	....	....	....	....
2006-07	**Buffalo**	**NHL**	**29**	**3**	**8**	**11**	**18**	**0**	**0**	**0**	**45**	**6.7**	**5**	**6**	**33.3**	**12:47**	**1**	**0**	**0**	**0**	**0**	**0**	**0**	**0**	**4:52**
	Rochester	AHL	29	7	14	21	12	....	....	....	....	....	....	....	....	....	....	....	....	....	....	....	....	....	....
2007-08	**Buffalo**	**NHL**	**77**	**19**	**16**	**35**	**14**	**0**	**3**	**2**	**110**	**17.3**	**9**	**41**	**36.6**	**13:16**	....	....	....	....	....	....	....	....	....
2008-09	**Buffalo**	**NHL**	**73**	**12**	**15**	**27**	**20**	**0**	**0**	**2**	**80**	**15.0**	**0**	**17**	**17.7**	**11:54**	....	....	....	....	....	....	....	....	....
2009-10	**Buffalo**	**NHL**	**2**	**0**	**1**	**1**	**0**	**0**	**0**	**0**	**2**	**0.0**	**1**	**0**	**0.0**	**10:22**	....	....	....	....	....	....	....	....	....
	Boston	**NHL**	**74**	**10**	**9**	**19**	**12**	**0**	**1**	**0**	**118**	**8.5**	**-4**	**13**	**30.8**	**13:49**	**13**	**0**	**2**	**2**	**2**	**0**	**0**	**0**	**16:01**
2010-11 ♦	**Boston**	**NHL**	**43**	**6**	**7**	**13**	**28**	**0**	**1**	**0**	**48**	**12.5**	**3**	**0**	**0.0**	**11:18**	**25**	**3**	**3**	**6**	**4**	**0**	**1**	**0**	**8:43**
2011-12	**Boston**	**NHL**	**69**	**9**	**6**	**15**	**15**	**0**	**2**	**1**	**86**	**10.5**	**-5**	**7**	**28.6**	**11:30**	**7**	**1**	**0**	**1**	**2**	**0**	**0**	**0**	**9:39**
2012-13	Ilves Tampere	Finland	9	2	4	6	6	....	....	....	....	....	....	....	....	....	....	....	....	....	....	....	....	....	....
	Boston	**NHL**	**46**	**10**	**7**	**17**	**8**	**0**	**2**	**1**	**70**	**14.3**	**3**	**10**	**20.0**	**12:41**	**22**	**4**	**5**	**9**	**0**	**0**	**1**	**3**	**12:32**
2013-14	**Boston**	**NHL**	**72**	**9**	**9**	**18**	**6**	**0**	**1**	**1**	**71**	**12.7**	**9**	**17**	**64.7**	**10:58**	**7**	**1**	**0**	**1**	**2**	**0**	**0**	**0**	**11:31**
2014-15	**Boston**	**NHL**	**71**	**6**	**7**	**13**	**12**	**0**	**1**	**1**	**66**	**9.1**	**-9**	**7**	**28.6**	**11:31**	....	....	....	....	....	....	....	....	....
2015-16	Rockford IceHogs	AHL	31	1	3	4	2	....	....	....	....	....	....	....	....	....	....	....	....	....	....	....	....	....	....
	NY Rangers	**NHL**	**12**	**0**	**0**	**0**	**0**	**0**	**0**	**0**	**11**	**0.0**	**-2**	**1**	**0.0**	**11:25**	....	....	....	....	....	....	....	....	....
	Hartford	AHL	23	5	6	11	6	....	....	....	....	....	....	....	....	....	....	....	....	....	....	....	....	....	....
2016-17	Brynas IF Gavle	Sweden	45	12	13	25	22	....	....	....	....	....	....	....	....	....	20	5	5	10	0	....	....	....	....
	NHL Totals		**582**	**85**	**87**	**172**	**135**	**0**	**11**	**8**	**722**	**11.8**		**123**	**34.1**	**12:07**	**75**	**9**	**10**	**19**	**10**	**0**	**2**	**3**	**11:24**

Traded to **Boston** by **Buffalo** for Boston's 3rd round pick (Kevin Sundher) in 2010 NHL Draft, October 20, 2009. Signed as a free agent by **Ilves Tampere** (Finland), December 2, 2012. Signed to a PTO (professional tryout) contract by **Rockford** (AHL), September 29, 2015. Signed as a free agent by **NY Rangers**, January 21, 2016. Signed as a free agent by **Gavle** (Sweden), May 19, 2016.

PAKARINEN, Iiro

(pa-ka-REE-nehn, YEE-roh) **EDM**

Right wing. Shoots right. 6'1", 215 lbs. Born, Suonenjoki, Finland, August 25, 1991. Florida's 10th pick, 184th overall, in 2011 NHL Draft.

Season	Club	League	GP	G	A	Pts	PIM	PP	SH	GW	S	S%	+/-	TF	F%	Min	GP	G	A	Pts	PIM	PP	SH	GW	Min
2006-07	KalPa Kuopio U18	Fin-U18	2	1	1	2	0	....	....	....	....	....	....	....	....	....	....	....	....	....	....	....	....	....	....
2007-08	KalPa Kuopio U18	Fin-U18	20	14	14	28	59	....	....	....	....	....	....	....	....	....	2	0	0	0	4	....	....	....	....
	KalPa Kuopio Jr.	Fin-Jr.	1	0	0	0	0	....	....	....	....	....	....	....	....	....	....	....	....	....	....	....	....	....	....
2008-09	KalPa Kuopio Jr.	Fin-Jr.	37	11	10	21	44	....	....	....	....	....	....	....	....	....	5	1	0	1	2	....	....	....	....
2009-10	Suomi U20	Finland-2	6	1	2	3	6	....	....	....	....	....	....	....	....	....	....	....	....	....	....	....	....	....	....
	KalPa Kuopio Jr.	Fin-Jr.	11	8	4	12	10	....	....	....	....	....	....	....	....	....	....	....	....	....	....	....	....	....	....
	KalPa Kuopio	Finland	38	3	5	8	37	....	....	....	....	....	....	....	....	....	12	3	0	3	8	....	....	....	....
2010-11	Suomi U20	Finland-2	3	0	0	0	0	....	....	....	....	....	....	....	....	....	....	....	....	....	....	....	....	....	....
	KalPa Kuopio Jr.	Fin-Jr.	4	3	2	5	6	....	....	....	....	....	....	....	....	....	....	....	....	....	....	....	....	....	....
	KalPa Kuopio	Finland	47	7	3	10	34	....	....	....	....	....	....	....	....	....	7	1	0	1	37	....	....	....	....
2011-12	KalPa Kuopio	Finland	54	10	3	13	47	....	....	....	....	....	....	....	....	....	7	2	2	4	0	....	....	....	....
2012-13	HIFK Helsinki	Finland	33	5	7	12	6	....	....	....	....	....	....	....	....	....	6	3	0	3	4	....	....	....	....
2013-14	HIFK Helsinki	Finland	60	20	10	30	32	....	....	....	....	....	....	....	....	....	2	0	0	0	2	....	....	....	....
2014-15	**Edmonton**	**NHL**	**17**	**1**	**2**	**3**	**2**	**0**	**0**	**0**	**34**	**2.9**	**-4**	**1**	**100.0**	**10:08**	....	....	....	....	....	....	....	....	....
	Oklahoma City	AHL	39	17	11	28	20	....	....	....	....	....	....	....	....	....	....	....	....	....	....	....	....	....	....
2015-16	**Edmonton**	**NHL**	**63**	**5**	**8**	**13**	**8**	**0**	**0**	**0**	**76**	**6.6**	**-10**	**13**	**38.5**	**10:45**	....	....	....	....	....	....	....	....	....
	Bakersfield	AHL	4	1	2	3	4	....	....	....	....	....	....	....	....	....	....	....	....	....	....	....	....	....	....
2016-17	**Edmonton**	**NHL**	**14**	**2**	**2**	**4**	**2**	**0**	**0**	**1**	**15**	**13.3**	**2**	**1**	**0.0**	**8:55**	**1**	**0**	**0**	**0**	**0**	**0**	**0**	**0**	**8:26**
	Bakersfield	AHL	5	0	1	1	4	....	....	....	....	....	....	....	....	....	....	....	....	....	....	....	....	....	....
	NHL Totals		**94**	**8**	**12**	**20**	**12**	**0**	**0**	**1**	**125**	**6.4**		**15**	**40.0**	**10:22**	**1**	**0**	**0**	**0**	**0**	**0**	**0**	**0**	**8:26**

Signed as a free agent by **Edmonton**, June 16, 2014.

PALAT, Ondrej

(PAL-at, AWN-dray) **T.B.**

Left wing. Shoots left. 6', 188 lbs. Born, Frydek-Mistek, Czech., March 28, 1991. Tampa Bay's 6th pick, 208th overall, in 2011 NHL Draft.

Season	Club	League	GP	G	A	Pts	PIM	PP	SH	GW	S	S%	+/-	TF	F%	Min	GP	G	A	Pts	PIM	PP	SH	GW	Min
2005-06	HC Vitkovice U17	CzR-U17	22	2	7	9	4	....	....	....	....	....	....	....	....	....	1	0	0	0	0	....	....	....	....
2006-07	HC Vitkovice U17	CzR-U17	33	32	24	56	18	....	....	....	....	....	....	....	....	....	9	3	6	9	4	....	....	....	....
	HC Vitkovice Jr.	CzRep-Jr.	13	5	2	7	12	....	....	....	....	....	....	....	....	....	3	0	0	0	0	....	....	....	....
2007-08	HC Vitkovice U17	CzR-U17	4	2	3	5	0	....	....	....	....	....	....	....	....	....	2	1	1	2	2	....	....	....	....
	HC Vitkovice Jr.	CzRep-Jr.	42	19	18	37	28	....	....	....	....	....	....	....	....	....	2	1	0	1	2	....	....	....	....
2008-09	HC Vitkovice Jr.	CzRep-Jr.	42	23	33	56	14	....	....	....	....	....	....	....	....	....	10	8	6	14	12	....	....	....	....
2009-10	Drummondville	QMJHL	59	17	23	40	24	....	....	....	....	....	....	....	....	....	7	1	1	2	0	....	....	....	....
2010-11	Drummondville	QMJHL	61	39	57	96	24	....	....	....	....	....	....	....	....	....	10	4	7	11	6	....	....	....	....
2011-12	Norfolk Admirals	AHL	61	9	21	30	10	....	....	....	....	....	....	....	....	....	18	4	5	9	6	....	....	....	....
2012-13	Syracuse Crunch	AHL	56	13	39	52	35	....	....	....	....	....	....	....	....	....	18	7	*19	*26	12	....	....	....	....
	Tampa Bay	**NHL**	**14**	**2**	**2**	**4**	**0**	**0**	**0**	**1**	**16**	**12.5**	**5**	**6**	**0.0**	**11:44**	....	....	....	....	....	....	....	....	....
2013-14	**Tampa Bay**	**NHL**	**81**	**23**	**36**	**59**	**20**	**3**	**2**	**3**	**165**	**13.9**	**32**	**37**	**13.5**	**18:02**	**3**	**2**	**1**	**3**	**0**	**1**	**1**	**0**	**18:02**
	Czech Republic	Olympics	4	0	0	0	0	....	....	....	....	....	....	....	....	....	....	....	....	....	....	....	....	....	....
2014-15	**Tampa Bay**	**NHL**	**75**	**16**	**47**	**63**	**24**	**3**	**1**	**5**	**139**	**11.5**	**31**	**35**	**28.6**	**17:26**	**26**	**8**	**8**	**16**	**12**	**4**	**0**	**0**	**19:10**
2015-16	**Tampa Bay**	**NHL**	**62**	**16**	**24**	**40**	**20**	**1**	**2**	**4**	**117**	**13.7**	**10**	**8**	**25.0**	**17:55**	**17**	**4**	**6**	**10**	**14**	**2**	**0**	**2**	**19:28**
2016-17	**Tampa Bay**	**NHL**	**75**	**17**	**35**	**52**	**39**	**5**	**0**	**3**	**162**	**10.5**	**8**	**34**	**26.5**	**19:07**	....	....	....	....	....	....	....	....	....
	NHL Totals		**307**	**74**	**144**	**218**	**103**	**12**	**5**	**16**	**599**	**12.4**		**120**	**21.7**	**17:50**	**46**	**14**	**15**	**29**	**26**	**7**	**1**	**2**	**19:12**

NHL All-Rookie Team (2014)

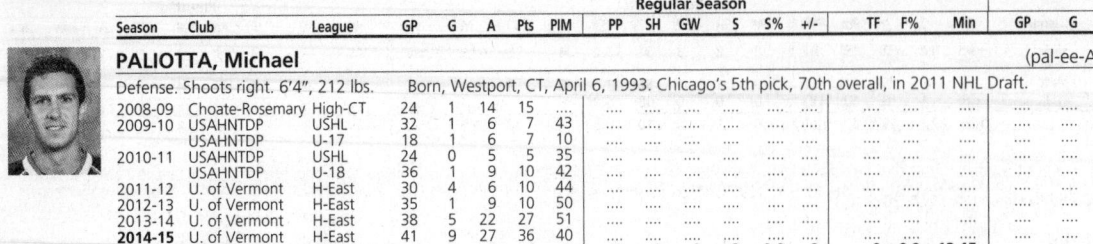

PALIOTTA, Michael
(pal-ee-AW-tuh, MIGH-kuhl)

Defense. Shoots right. 6'4", 212 lbs. Born, Westport, CT, April 6, 1993. Chicago's 5th pick, 70th overall, in 2011 NHL Draft.

			Regular Season														Playoffs								
Season	Club	League	GP	G	A	Pts	PIM	PP	SH	GW	S	S%	+/-	TF	F%	Min	GP	G	A	Pts	PIM	PP	SH	GW	Min
2008-09	Choate-Rosemary	High-CT	24	1	14	15	....	....	....	....	....	....	....	....	....	....	....	....	....	....	....	....	....	....	....
2009-10	USAHNTDP	USHL	32	1	6	7	43	....	....	....	....	....	....	....	....	....	....	....	....	....	....	....	....	....	....
	USAHNTDP	U-17	18	1	6	7	10	....	....	....	....	....	....	....	....	....	....	....	....	....	....	....	....	....	....
2010-11	USAHNTDP	USHL	24	0	5	5	35	....	....	....	....	....	....	....	....	....	....	....	....	....	....	....	....	....	....
	USAHNTDP	U-18	36	1	9	10	42	....	....	....	....	....	....	....	....	....	....	....	....	....	....	....	....	....	....
2011-12	U. of Vermont	H-East	30	4	6	10	44	....	....	....	....	....	....	....	....	....	....	....	....	....	....	....	....	....	....
2012-13	U. of Vermont	H-East	35	1	9	10	50	....	....	....	....	....	....	....	....	....	....	....	....	....	....	....	....	....	....
2013-14	U. of Vermont	H-East	38	5	22	27	51	....	....	....	....	....	....	....	....	....	....	....	....	....	....	....	....	....	....
2014-15	U. of Vermont	H-East	41	9	27	36	40	....	....	....	....	....	....	....	....	....	....	....	....	....	....	....	....	....	....
	Chicago	NHL	1	0	1	1	0	0	0	0	2	0.0	0	0	0.0	12:45	....	....	....	....	....	....	....	....	....
2015-16	Columbus	NHL	1	0	0	0	4	0	0	0	2	0.0	0	0	0.0	7:32	....	....	....	....	....	....	....	....	....
	Lake Erie	AHL	68	8	15	23	29	....	....	....	....	....	....	....	....	....	8	0	0	0	0	....	....	....	....
2016-17	Hartford	AHL	52	1	13	14	20	....	....	....	....	....	....	....	....	....	....	....	....	....	....	....	....	....	....
	NHL Totals		2	0	1	1	4	0	0	0	4	0.0		0	0.0	10:09	....	....	....	....	....	....	....	....	....

Hockey East Second All-Star Team (2015) • NCAA East Second All-American Team (2015)

Traded to **Columbus** by **Chicago** with Brandon Saad and Alex Broadhurst for Artem Anisimov, Jeremy Morin, Corey Tropp, Marko Dano and Columbus' 4th round pick (later traded to NY Islanders – NY Islanders selected Anatoli Golyshev) in 2016 NHL Draft, June 30, 2015. Signed as a free agent by **NY Rangers**, July 1, 2016.

PALMIERI, Kyle
(pawl-mee-AIR-ee, KIGHL) **N.J.**

Right wing. Shoots right. 5'11", 185 lbs. Born, Smithtown, NY, February 1, 1991. Anaheim's 2nd pick, 26th overall, in 2009 NHL Draft.

			Regular Season														Playoffs								
Season	Club	League	GP	G	A	Pts	PIM	PP	SH	GW	S	S%	+/-	TF	F%	Min	GP	G	A	Pts	PIM	PP	SH	GW	Min
2007-08	USAHNTDP	NAHL	32	15	10	25	43	....	....	....	....	....	....	....	....	....	....	....	....	....	....	....	....	....	....
	USAHNTDP	U-17	7	5	0	5	8	....	....	....	....	....	....	....	....	....	....	....	....	....	....	....	....	....	....
	USAHNTDP	U-18	27	9	9	18	20	....	....	....	....	....	....	....	....	....	....	....	....	....	....	....	....	....	....
2008-09	USAHNTDP	NAHL	5	1	1	2	2	....	....	....	....	....	....	....	....	....	....	....	....	....	....	....	....	....	....
	USAHNTDP	U-18	28	14	14	28	49	....	....	....	....	....	....	....	....	....	....	....	....	....	....	....	....	....	....
2009-10	U. of Notre Dame	CCHA	33	9	8	17	36	....	....	....	....	....	....	....	....	....	....	....	....	....	....	....	....	....	....
2010-11	Anaheim	NHL	10	1	0	1	0	0	0	0	10	10.0	–1	0	0.0	8:41	1	0	0	0	0	0	0	0	10:07
	Syracuse Crunch	AHL	62	29	22	51	56	....	....	....	....	....	....	....	....	....	....	....	....	....	....	....	....	....	....
2011-12	Anaheim	NHL	18	4	3	7	6	0	0	0	34	11.8	3	2	100.0	11:31	....	....	....	....	....	....	....	....	....
	Syracuse Crunch	AHL	51	33	25	58	53	....	....	....	....	....	....	....	....	....	4	1	1	2	0	....	....	....	....
2012-13	Norfolk Admirals	AHL	33	13	12	25	54	....	....	....	....	....	....	....	....	....	....	....	....	....	....	....	....	....	....
	Anaheim	NHL	42	10	11	21	9	2	0	5	92	10.9	2	12	8.3	12:20	7	3	2	5	4	0	0	0	10:34
2013-14	Anaheim	NHL	71	14	17	31	38	0	0	4	147	9.5	9	23	39.1	11:57	9	3	0	3	14	0	0	0	10:12
2014-15	Anaheim	NHL	57	14	15	29	37	5	0	4	112	12.5	–2	12	50.0	14:06	16	1	3	4	4	0	0	1	13:12
	Norfolk Admirals	AHL	2	0	0	0	4	....	....	....	....	....	....	....	....	....	....	....	....	....	....	....	....	....	....
2015-16	New Jersey	NHL	82	30	27	57	39	11	0	4	222	13.5	3	27	37.0	17:48	....	....	....	....	....	....	....	....	....
2016-17	New Jersey	NHL	80	26	27	53	46	8	1	3	192	13.5	2	29	41.4	17:21	....	....	....	....	....	....	....	....	....
	NHL Totals		360	99	100	199	175	26	1	20	809	12.2		105	38.1	14:45	33	7	5	12	22	0	0	1	11:44

AHL First All-Star Team (2012)

Traded to **New Jersey** by **Anaheim** for Florida's 2nd round pick (previously acquired, later traded to NY Rangers – NY Rangers selected Ryan Gropp) in 2015 NHL Draft and Minnesota's 3rd round pick (previously acquired, later traded to Buffalo, later traded to Nashville – Nashville selected Rem Pitlick) in 2016 NHL Draft, June 27, 2015.

PANARIN, Artemi
(pah-NAHR-ihn, ahr-TEHM-ee) **CBJ**

Left wing. Shoots right. 5'11", 170 lbs. Born, Korkino, USSR, October 30, 1991.

			Regular Season														Playoffs								
Season	Club	League	GP	G	A	Pts	PIM	PP	SH	GW	S	S%	+/-	TF	F%	Min	GP	G	A	Pts	PIM	PP	SH	GW	Min
2008-09	Vityaz Chekhov 2	Russia-3	62	29	39	68	70	....	....	....	....	....	....	....	....	....	13	4	5	9	28	....	....	....	....
	Vityaz Chekhov	KHL	5	0	1	1	2	....	....	....	....	....	....	....	....	....	....	....	....	....	....	....	....	....	....
2009-10	Chekhov Jr.	Russia-Jr.	38	20	24	44	55	....	....	....	....	....	....	....	....	....	4	1	2	3	12	....	....	....	....
	Vityaz Chekhov	KHL	20	1	8	9	16	....	....	....	....	....	....	....	....	....	....	....	....	....	....	....	....	....	....
2010-11	Chekhov Jr.	Russia-Jr.	13	5	12	17	22	....	....	....	....	....	....	....	....	....	....	....	....	....	....	....	....	....	....
	Vityaz Chekhov	KHL	40	5	16	21	8	....	....	....	....	....	....	....	....	....	....	....	....	....	....	....	....	....	....
2011-12	Vityaz Chekhov	KHL	38	12	14	26	49	....	....	....	....	....	....	....	....	....	....	....	....	....	....	....	....	....	....
	Ak Bars Kazan	KHL	12	1	4	5	4	....	....	....	....	....	....	....	....	....	3	0	0	0	0	....	....	....	....
2012-13	Vityaz Chekhov	KHL	40	11	7	18	22	....	....	....	....	....	....	....	....	....	....	....	....	....	....	....	....	....	....
	St. Petersburg	KHL	3	0	1	1	2	....	....	....	....	....	....	....	....	....	14	2	7	9	0	....	....	....	....
2013-14	St. Petersburg	KHL	51	20	20	40	30	....	....	....	....	....	....	....	....	....	4	0	0	0	2	....	....	....	....
2014-15	St. Petersburg	KHL	54	26	36	62	37	....	....	....	....	....	....	....	....	....	20	5	*15	20	4	....	....	....	....
2015-16	Chicago	NHL	80	30	47	77	32	8	0	7	187	16.0	8	0	0.0	18:31	7	2	5	7	14	0	0	1	20:10
2016-17	Chicago	NHL	82	31	43	74	21	9	0	5	211	14.7	18	10	20.0	19:28	4	0	1	1	0	0	0	0	20:52
	NHL Totals		162	61	90	151	53	17	0	12	398	15.3		10	20.0	19:00	11	2	6	8	14	0	0	1	20:25

NHL All-Rookie Team (2016) • Calder Memorial Trophy (2016) • NHL Second All-Star Team (2017)

Signed as a free agent by **Chicago**, May 1, 2015. Traded to **Columbus** by **Chicago** with Tyler Motte and NY Islanders' 6th round pick (previously acquired, Columbus selected Jonathan Davidsson) in 2017 NHL Draft for Brandon Saad, Anton Forsberg and Columbus' 5th round pick in 2018 NHL Draft, June 23, 2017.

PANIK, Richard
(PAH-nihk, RIH-chuhrd) **CHI**

Right wing. Shoots left. 6'1", 208 lbs. Born, Martin, Slovakia, February 7, 1991. Tampa Bay's 3rd pick, 52nd overall, in 2009 NHL Draft.

			Regular Season														Playoffs								
Season	Club	League	GP	G	A	Pts	PIM	PP	SH	GW	S	S%	+/-	TF	F%	Min	GP	G	A	Pts	PIM	PP	SH	GW	Min
2005-06	MHC Martin U18	Svk-U18	40	11	13	24	20	....	....	....	....	....	....	....	....	....	4	4	2	6	4	....	....	....	....
2006-07	HC Trinec U17	CzR-U17	12	10	6	16	48	....	....	....	....	....	....	....	....	....	3	1	4	5	8	....	....	....	....
	HC Trinec Jr.	CzRep-Jr.	27	16	9	25	30	....	....	....	....	....	....	....	....	....	4	1	4	5	6	....	....	....	....
2007-08	HC Trinec Jr.	CzRep-Jr.	39	35	27	62	70	....	....	....	....	....	....	....	....	....	8	8	4	12	52	....	....	....	....
	HC Ocelari Trinec	CzRep	6	0	0	0	0	....	....	....	....	....	....	....	....	....	....	....	....	....	....	....	....	....	....
2008-09	HC Trinec Jr.	CzRep-Jr.	16	10	9	19	36	....	....	....	....	....	....	....	....	....	8	6	1	7	41	....	....	....	....
	HC Havirov	CzRep-2	3	2	1	3	0	....	....	....	....	....	....	....	....	....	....	....	....	....	....	....	....	....	....
	HC Ocelari Trinec	CzRep	15	1	1	2	4	....	....	....	....	....	....	....	....	....	4	0	0	0	0	....	....	....	....
2009-10	Windsor Spitfires	OHL	33	9	9	18	19	....	....	....	....	....	....	....	....	....	....	....	....	....	....	....	....	....	....
	Belleville Bulls	OHL	27	12	11	23	36	....	....	....	....	....	....	....	....	....	....	....	....	....	....	....	....	....	....
	Norfolk Admirals	AHL	5	0	1	1	0	....	....	....	....	....	....	....	....	....	....	....	....	....	....	....	....	....	....
2010-11	Belleville Bulls	OHL	27	14	17	31	33	....	....	....	....	....	....	....	....	....	....	....	....	....	....	....	....	....	....
	Guelph Storm	OHL	24	13	12	25	42	....	....	....	....	....	....	....	....	....	6	1	2	3	10	....	....	....	....
2011-12	Norfolk Admirals	AHL	64	19	22	41	62	....	....	....	....	....	....	....	....	....	18	5	1	6	23	....	....	....	....
2012-13	Syracuse Crunch	AHL	51	22	19	41	81	....	....	....	....	....	....	....	....	....	16	9	5	14	59	....	....	....	....
	Tampa Bay	NHL	25	5	4	9	4	1	0	1	34	14.7	–2	3	33.3	11:20	....	....	....	....	....	....	....	....	....
2013-14	Tampa Bay	NHL	50	3	10	13	21	0	0	0	56	5.4	–9	8	37.5	12:42	2	0	0	0	4	0	0	0	15:03
	Syracuse Crunch	AHL	13	3	8	11	8	....	....	....	....	....	....	....	....	....	....	....	....	....	....	....	....	....	....
	Slovakia	Olympics	4	0	0	0	0	....	....	....	....	....	....	....	....	....	....	....	....	....	....	....	....	....	....
2014-15	Toronto	NHL	76	11	6	17	49	2	0	1	87	12.6	–8	7	28.6	11:39	....	....	....	....	....	....	....	....	....
2015-16	Toronto Marlies	AHL	33	9	16	25	34	....	....	....	....	....	....	....	....	....	....	....	....	....	....	....	....	....	....
	Chicago	NHL	30	6	2	8	6	0	0	1	39	15.4	4	2	50.0	10:50	6	0	3	3	6	0	0	0	12:49
2016-17	Chicago	NHL	82	22	22	44	58	4	0	5	155	14.2	14	7	28.6	14:44	4	0	1	1	2	0	0	0	15:46
	NHL Totals		263	47	44	91	138	7	0	8	371	12.7		27	33.3	12:41	12	0	4	4	12	0	0	0	14:10

Claimed on waivers by **Toronto** from **Tampa Bay**, October 8, 2014. Traded to **Chicago** by **Toronto** for Jeremy Morin, January 3, 2016.

PAQUETTE, Cedric
(pah-KEHT, SEH-drihk) **T.B.**

Center. Shoots left. 6'1", 199 lbs. Born, Gaspe, QC, August 13, 1993. Tampa Bay's 6th pick, 101st overall, in 2012 NHL Draft.

			Regular Season														Playoffs								
Season	Club	League	GP	G	A	Pts	PIM	PP	SH	GW	S	S%	+/-	TF	F%	Min	GP	G	A	Pts	PIM	PP	SH	GW	Min
2008-09	Ecole Notre Dame	QAAA	45	12	6	18	34	....	....	....	....	....	....	....	....	....	4	0	0	0	4	....	....	....	....
2009-10	Ecole Notre Dame	QAAA	32	10	18	28	83	....	....	....	....	....	....	....	....	....	8	5	2	7	24	....	....	....	....
2010-11	Ecole Notre Dame	QAAA	34	28	27	55	102	....	....	....	....	....	....	....	....	....	17	5	11	16	36	....	....	....	....
2011-12	Blainville-Bois.	QMJHL	63	31	17	48	88	....	....	....	....	....	....	....	....	....	11	7	10	17	22	....	....	....	....
2012-13	Blainville-Bois.	QMJHL	63	27	56	83	103	....	....	....	....	....	....	....	....	....	15	7	5	12	33	....	....	....	....
	Syracuse Crunch	AHL	....	....	....	....	....	....	....	....	....	....	....	....	....	....	3	0	0	0	0	....	....	....	....
2013-14	Tampa Bay	NHL	2	0	1	1	0	0	0	0	1	0.0	1	29	55.2	14:33	4	0	2	2	16	0	0	0	10:34
	Syracuse Crunch	AHL	70	20	24	44	153	....	....	....	....	....	....	....	....	....	....	....	....	....	....	....	....	....	....

			Regular Season														Playoffs								
Season	Club	League	GP	G	A	Pts	PIM	PP	SH	GW	S	S%	+/-	TF	F%	Min	GP	G	A	Pts	PIM	PP	SH	GW	Min
2014-15	Tampa Bay	NHL	64	12	7	19	51	0	2	3	91	13.2	4	235	47.7	13:37	24	3	0	3	28	0	1	1	12:48
	Syracuse Crunch	AHL	5	4	3	7	7																		
2015-16	Tampa Bay	NHL	56	6	5	11	51	0	1	1	50	12.0	–2	283	49.8	12:44	17	0	1	1	24	0	0	0	10:29
2016-17	Tampa Bay	NHL	58	4	6	10	80	0	0	0	68	5.9	–6	434	46.1	11:31									
	NHL Totals		180	22	19	41	182	0	3	4	210	10.5		981	47.8	12:41	45	3	3	6	68	0	1	1	11:43

PARAYKO, Colton

(pa-RAY-koh, KOHL-tuhn) **ST.L.**

Defense. Shoots right. 6'6", 226 lbs. Born, St. Albert, AB, May 12, 1993. St. Louis' 4th pick, 86th overall, in 2012 NHL Draft.

Season	Club	League	GP	G	A	Pts	PIM	PP	SH	GW	S	S%	+/-	TF	F%	Min	GP	G	A	Pts	PIM	PP	SH	GW	Min
2008-09	St. Albert Flyers	Minor-AB	33	1	16	17	10										2	0	2	2	0				
2009-10	St. Albert	Minor-AB	33	5	8	13	10																		
2010-11	Fort McMurray	AJHL	42	3	9	12	12										12	2	1	3	2				
2011-12	Fort McMurray	AJHL	53	9	33	42	65										21	3	9	12	14				
2012-13	Alaska	CCHA	33	4	13	17	23																		
2013-14	Alaska	WCHA	37	7	19	26	16																		
2014-15	Alaska	WCHA	34	6	17	23	16																		
	Chicago Wolves	AHL	17	4	3	7	6										5	0	0	0	6				
2015-16	St. Louis	NHL	79	9	24	33	29	3	0	3	165	5.5	28	0	0.0	19:23	20	2	5	7	4	1	0	0	20:07
2016-17	St. Louis	NHL	81	4	31	35	32	4	0	2	188	2.1	7	0	0.0	21:12	11	2	3	5	2	0	0	0	23:44
	NHL Totals		160	13	55	68	61	7	0	5	353	3.7		0	0.0	20:18	31	4	8	12	6	1	0	0	21:24

WCHA First All-Star Team (2014, 2015) • NCAA West Second All-American Team (2014, 2015) • NHL All-Rookie Team (2016)

PARDY, Adam

(PAHR-dee, A-duhm)

Defense. Shoots left. 6'4", 227 lbs. Born, Bonavista, NL, March 29, 1984. Calgary's 6th pick, 173rd overall, in 2004 NHL Draft.

Season	Club	League	GP	G	A	Pts	PIM	PP	SH	GW	S	S%	+/-	TF	F%	Min	GP	G	A	Pts	PIM	PP	SH	GW	Min
2002-03	Yarmouth	MJrHL	1	0	0	0	2																		
	Antigonish	MJrHL	31	5	16	21	42																		
	Cape Breton	QMJHL	7	0	1	1	2										2	0	0	0	0				
2003-04	Cape Breton	QMJHL	68	4	12	16	137										5	0	1	1	8				
2004-05	Cape Breton	QMJHL	69	12	27	39	163										5	2	2	4	8				
2005-06	Omaha	AHL	24	0	0	0	18																		
	Las Vegas	ECHL	41	1	11	12	55										10	2	1	3	12				
2006-07	Omaha	AHL	70	2	6	8	60										6	1	1	2	0				
2007-08	Quad City Flames	AHL	65	5	13	18	67																		
2008-09	Calgary	NHL	60	1	9	10	69	0	0	0	38	2.6	3	0	0.0	15:00	6	0	2	2	5	0	0	0	14:51
2009-10	Calgary	NHL	57	2	7	9	48	0	0	0	40	5.0	–3	0	0.0	15:51									
2010-11	Calgary	NHL	30	1	6	7	24	0	0	0	36	2.8	3	0	0.0	14:41									
2011-12	Dallas	NHL	36	0	3	3	16	0	0	0	29	0.0	–5	0	0.0	16:28									
	Texas Stars	AHL	2	0	4	4	2																		
2012-13	Rochester	AHL	21	2	7	9	22																		
	Buffalo	NHL	17	0	4	4	14	0	0	0	6	0.0	4	0	0.0	16:30									
2013-14	Winnipeg	NHL	60	0	6	6	38	0	0	0	47	0.0	4	0	0.0	14:25									
	St. John's IceCaps	AHL	3	0	0	0	9																		
2014-15	Winnipeg	NHL	55	0	9	9	40	0	0	0	29	0.0	9	0	0.0	15:01	2	1	0	1	2	0	0	0	18:16
2015-16	Winnipeg	NHL	14	0	1	1	8	0	0	0	10	0.0	–3	0	0.0	13:06									
	Edmonton	NHL	9	0	3	3	6	0	0	0	12	0.0	–4	0	0.0	20:13									
2016-17	Nashville	NHL	4	0	0	0	6	0	0	0	4	0.0	–1	0	0.0	11:00									
	Milwaukee	AHL	31	3	4	7	20										3	0	0	0	6				
	NHL Totals		342	4	48	52	269	0	0	0	251	1.6		0	0.0	15:15	8	1	2	3	7	0	0	0	15:43

• Missed majority of 2010-11 due to shoulder (October 10, 2010 vs. Los Angeles) and upper-body (February 7, 2011 vs. Chicago) injuries. Signed as a free agent by **Dallas**, July 1, 2011. Traded to **Buffalo** by **Dallas** with Steve Ott for Derek Roy, July 2, 2012. Signed as a free agent by **Winnipeg**, July 6, 2013. Claimed on waivers by **Edmonton** from **Winnipeg**, February 29, 2016. • Missed majority of 2015-16 as a healthy reserve. Signed as a free agent by **Nashville**, November 30, 2016.

PARENTEAU, PA

(pair-ehn-TOH, PEE—EH

Left wing. Shoots right. 6', 200 lbs. Born, Hull, QC, March 24, 1983. Anaheim's 11th pick, 264th overall, in 2001 NHL Draft.

Season	Club	League	GP	G	A	Pts	PIM	PP	SH	GW	S	S%	+/-	TF	F%	Min	GP	G	A	Pts	PIM	PP	SH	GW	Min
99-2000	C.C. Lemoyne	QAAA	40	25	40	65	18										16	4	9	13	8				
2000-01	Moncton Wildcats	QMJHL	45	10	19	29	38																		
	Chicoutimi	QMJHL	28	10	13	23	14										7	4	7	11	2				
2001-02	Chicoutimi	QMJHL	68	51	67	118	120										4	3	1	4	10				
2002-03	Chicoutimi	QMJHL	31	20	35	55	56																		
	Sherbrooke	QMJHL	28	13	35	48	84										12	8	11	19	6				
2003-04	Cincinnati	AHL	66	14	16	30	20										7	1	2	3	6				
2004-05	Cincinnati	AHL	76	17	24	41	58										9	2	0	2	8				
2005-06	Portland Pirates	AHL	56	22	27	49	42										19	5	17	22	24				
	Augusta Lynx	ECHL	2	0	1	1	0																		
2006-07	Portland Pirates	AHL	28	15	13	28	35																		
	Chicago	NHL	5	0	1	1	2	0	0	0	7	0.0	–1	2	50.0	11:05									
	Norfolk Admirals	AHL	40	15	36	51	12										6	2	1	3	2				
2007-08	Hartford	AHL	75	34	47	81	81										5	3	2	5	13				
2008-09	Hartford	AHL	74	29	49	78	142																		
2009-10	NY Rangers	NHL	22	3	5	8	4	1	0	0	38	7.9	–2	12	33.3	13:42									
	Hartford	AHL	35	20	25	45	63																		
2010-11	NY Islanders	NHL	81	20	33	53	46	9	0	2	161	12.4	–8	30	36.7	18:13									
2011-12	NY Islanders	NHL	80	18	49	67	89	6	0	2	167	10.8	–8	26	38.5	18:39									
2012-13	Colorado	NHL	48	18	25	43	38	6	0	1	105	17.1	–11	13	7.7	19:09									
2013-14	Colorado	NHL	55	14	19	33	30	1	0	1	110	12.7	3	14	14.3	16:57	7	1	2	3	2	0	0	0	17:53
2014-15	Montreal	NHL	56	8	14	22	30	3	0	1	97	8.2	0	26	38.5	14:59	8	1	1	2	2	0	0	1	14:22
2015-16	Toronto	NHL	77	20	21	41	68	7	0	3	168	11.9	0	18	22.2	16:16									
2016-17	New Jersey	NHL	59	13	14	27	35	4	0	2	109	11.9	–16	19	31.6	14:59									
	Nashville	NHL	8	0	1	1	0	0	0	0	14	0.0	–2	1	0.0	12:34	5	0	0	0	0	0	0	0	9:23
	NHL Totals		491	114	182	296	342	37	0	12	976	11.7		161	30.4	16:48	20	2	3	5	4	0	0	1	14:21

AHL Second All-Star Team (2008) • AHL First All-Star Team (2009)

Traded to **Chicago** by **Anaheim** with Bruno St. Jacques for Sebastien Caron, Matt Keith and Chris Durno, December 28, 2006. Traded to **NY Rangers** by **Chicago** for future considerations, October 11, 2007. Signed as a free agent by **NY Islanders**, July 2, 2010. Signed as a free agent by **Colorado**, July 1, 2012. Traded to **Montreal** by **Colorado** with Colorado's 5th round pick (Matthew Bradley) in 2015 NHL Draft for Daniel Briere, June 30, 2014. Signed as a free agent by **Toronto**, July 1, 2015. Signed as a free agent by **NY Islanders**, July 2, 2016. Claimed on waivers by **New Jersey** from **NY Islanders**, October 11, 2016. Traded to **Nashville** by **New Jersey** for Nashville's 6th round pick (later traded to San Jose – San Jose selected Alexander Chmelevski) in 2017 NHL Draft, March 1, 2017.

PARISE, Zach

(pah-REE-say, ZAK) **MIN**

Left wing. Shoots left. 5'11", 196 lbs. Born, Minneapolis, MN, July 28, 1984. New Jersey's 1st pick, 17th overall, in 2003 NHL Draft.

Season	Club	League	GP	G	A	Pts	PIM	PP	SH	GW	S	S%	+/-	TF	F%	Min	GP	G	A	Pts	PIM	PP	SH	GW	Min
2000-01	Shattuck	High-MN	58	69	93	162																			
2001-02	Shattuck	High-MN	67	77	101	178	58																		
	USAHNTDP	U-18	12	7	7	14	6																		
2002-03	North Dakota	WCHA	39	26	35	61	34																		
2003-04	North Dakota	WCHA	37	23	32	55	24																		
2004-05	Albany River Rats	AHL	73	18	40	58	56																		
2005-06	New Jersey	NHL	81	14	18	32	28	2	0	5	133	10.5	–1	162	42.6	13:08	9	1	2	3	2	0	0	0	15:03
2006-07	New Jersey	NHL	82	31	31	62	30	9	0	7	247	12.6	–3	52	44.2	17:32	11	7	3	10	8	2	0	1	19:08
2007-08	New Jersey	NHL	81	32	33	65	25	10	1	8	266	12.0	13	104	48.1	18:04	5	1	4	5	2	1	0	0	18:29
2008-09	New Jersey	NHL	82	45	49	94	24	14	0	8	364	12.4	30	121	44.6	18:45	7	3	3	6	2	1	0	1	19:02
2009-10	New Jersey	NHL	81	38	44	82	32	9	1	5	347	11.0	24	48	37.5	19:46	5	1	3	4	0	0	1	0	20:44
	United States	Olympics	6	4	4	8	0																		
2010-11	New Jersey	NHL	13	3	3	6	6	0	0	1	49	6.1	–1	11	36.4	19:51									
2011-12	New Jersey	NHL	82	31	38	69	32	7	3	3	293	10.6	–5	63	47.6	21:29	24	*8	7	15	4	3	0	1	20:53
2012-13	Minnesota	NHL	48	18	20	38	16	7	0	4	182	9.9	2	9	33.3	20:40	5	1	0	1	2	0	0	0	21:24
2013-14	Minnesota	NHL	67	29	27	56	30	14	1	5	245	11.8	10	24	41.7	20:26	13	4	10	14	6	2	0	1	20:29
	United States	Olympics	6	1	0	1	0																		
2014-15	Minnesota	NHL	74	33	29	62	41	11	0	3	259	12.7	21	12	16.7	19:11	10	4	6	10	4	1	1	0	18:53

			Regular Season														Playoffs								
Season	Club	League	GP	G	A	Pts	PIM	PP	SH	GW	S	S%	+/-	TF	F%	Min	GP	G	A	Pts	PIM	PP	SH	GW	Min
2015-16	Minnesota	NHL	70	25	28	53	36	7	0	7	234	10.7	–3	4	0.0	19:18	....	....	....	....	....	....	....	....	....
2016-17	Minnesota	NHL	69	19	23	42	30	6	0	4	194	9.8	–3	13	61.5	17:26	5	2	1	3	8	1	0	0	19:28
	NHL Totals		830	318	343	661	330	96	6	60	2813	11.3		623	43.5	18:37	94	32	39	71	38	11	2	4	19:32

WCHA All-Rookie Team (2003) • WCHA First All-Star Team (2004) • NCAA West First All-American Team (2004) • NHL Second All-Star Team (2009) • Olympic All-Star Team (2010)

Played in NHL All-Star Game (2009)

• Missed majority of 2010-11 due to knee injury at Los Angeles, October 30, 2010. Signed as a free agent by **Minnesota**, July 4, 2012.

PASTRNAK, David

(PAS-tuhr-nak, DAY-vihd) **BOS**

Left wing. Shoots right. 6', 181 lbs. Born, Havirov, Czech Rep., May 25, 1996. Boston's 1st pick, 25th overall, in 2014 NHL Draft.

Season	Club	League	GP	G	A	Pts	PIM	PP	SH	GW	S	S%	+/-	TF	F%	Min	GP	G	A	Pts	PIM	PP	SH	GW	Min
2010-11	HC Havirov U18	CzR-U18	16	7	12	19	4	....	....	....	....	....	....	....	....	....	1	0	0	0	0	....	....	....	....
2011-12	HC Havirov U18	CzR-U18	17	18	22	40	28	....	....	....	....	....	....	....	....	....	....	....	....	....	....	....	....	....	....
	HC Trinec U18	CzR-U18	31	33	14	47	6	....	....	....	....	....	....	....	....	....	....	....	....	....	....	....	....	....	....
	AZ Havirov Jr.	CzRep-Jr.	3	0	1	1	2	....	....	....	....	....	....	....	....	....	....	....	....	....	....	....	....	....	....
	AZ Havirov	CzRep-3	2	0	0	0	0	....	....	....	....	....	....	....	....	....	4	0	0	0	0	....	....	....	....
2012-13	Sodertalje SK U18	Swe-U18	7	6	8	14	4	....	....	....	....	....	....	....	....	....	....	....	....	....	....	....	....	....	....
	Sodertalje SK Jr.	Swe-Jr.	36	12	17	29	67	....	....	....	....	....	....	....	....	....	4	2	2	4	10	....	....	....	....
	Sodertalje SK	Sweden-2	16	2	1	3	0	....	....	....	....	....	....	....	....	....	....	....	....	....	....	....	....	....	....
2013-14	Sodertalje SK Jr.	Swe-Jr.	1	1	1	2	0	....	....	....	....	....	....	....	....	....	2	0	0	0	0	....	....	....	....
	Sodertalje SK	Sweden-2	36	8	16	24	24	....	....	....	....	....	....	....	....	....	....	....	....	....	....	....	....	....	....
2014-15	**Boston**	**NHL**	**46**	**10**	**17**	**27**	**8**	**2**	**0**	**3**	**93**	**10.8**	**12**	**17**	**29.4**	**13:58**	....	....	....	....	....	....	....	....	....
	Providence Bruins	AHL	25	11	17	28	12	....	....	....	....	....	....	....	....	....	3	0	0	0	0	....	....	....	....
2015-16	**Boston**	**NHL**	**51**	**15**	**11**	**26**	**20**	**0**	**0**	**2**	**108**	**13.9**	**3**	**3**	**0.0**	**13:57**	....	....	....	....	....	....	....	....	....
	Providence Bruins	AHL	3	1	3	4	2	....	....	....	....	....	....	....	....	....	....	....	....	....	....	....	....	....	....
2016-17	**Boston**	**NHL**	**75**	**34**	**36**	**70**	**34**	**10**	**0**	**6**	**262**	**13.0**	**11**	**3**	**66.7**	**17:59**	**6**	**2**	**2**	**4**	**6**	**1**	**0**	**0**	**21:04**
	NHL Totals		**172**	**59**	**64**	**123**	**62**	**12**	**0**	**11**	**463**	**12.7**		**23**	**30.4**	**15:43**	**6**	**2**	**2**	**4**	**6**	**1**	**0**	**0**	**21:04**

PATERYN, Greg

(PA-tuhr-ihn, GREHG) **DAL**

Defense. Shoots right. 6'2", 223 lbs. Born, Sterling Heights, MI, June 20, 1990. Toronto's 4th pick, 128th overall, in 2008 NHL Draft.

Season	Club	League	GP	G	A	Pts	PIM	PP	SH	GW	S	S%	+/-	TF	F%	Min	GP	G	A	Pts	PIM	PP	SH	GW	Min
2004-05	Brother Rice	High-MI	29	2	8	10	42	....	....	....	....	....	....	....	....	....	....	....	....	....	....	....	....	....	....
2005-06	Brother Rice	High-MI	24	0	8	8	34	....	....	....	....	....	....	....	....	....	....	....	....	....	....	....	....	....	....
2006-07	Brother Rice	High-MI	27	9	19	28	44	....	....	....	....	....	....	....	....	....	....	....	....	....	....	....	....	....	....
2007-08	Ohio	USHL	60	3	24	27	145	....	....	....	....	....	....	....	....	....	....	....	....	....	....	....	....	....	....
2008-09	U. of Michigan	CCHA	28	0	5	5	32	....	....	....	....	....	....	....	....	....	....	....	....	....	....	....	....	....	....
2009-10	U. of Michigan	CCHA	33	1	5	6	18	....	....	....	....	....	....	....	....	....	....	....	....	....	....	....	....	....	....
2010-11	U. of Michigan	CCHA	40	3	14	17	28	....	....	....	....	....	....	....	....	....	....	....	....	....	....	....	....	....	....
2011-12	U. of Michigan	CCHA	41	2	13	15	65	....	....	....	....	....	....	....	....	....	....	....	....	....	....	....	....	....	....
2012-13	Hamilton	AHL	39	7	5	12	27	....	....	....	....	....	....	....	....	....	....	....	....	....	....	....	....	....	....
	Montreal	**NHL**	**3**	**0**	**0**	**0**	**0**	**0**	**0**	**0**	**0**	**0.0**	**0**	**0**	**0.0**	**9:36**	....	....	....	....	....	....	....	....	....
2013-14	Hamilton	AHL	68	15	19	34	67	....	....	....	....	....	....	....	....	....	....	....	....	....	....	....	....	....	....
2014-15	**Montreal**	**NHL**	**17**	**0**	**0**	**0**	**6**	**0**	**0**	**0**	**10**	**0.0**	**0**	**0**	**0.0**	**12:39**	**7**	**0**	**3**	**3**	**0**	**0**	**0**	**0**	**10:58**
	Hamilton	AHL	53	3	12	15	56	....	....	....	....	....	....	....	....	....	....	....	....	....	....	....	....	....	....
2015-16	**Montreal**	**NHL**	**38**	**1**	**6**	**7**	**49**	**0**	**0**	**0**	**32**	**3.1**	**–8**	**0**	**0.0**	**16:45**	....	....	....	....	....	....	....	....	....
	St. John's IceCaps	AHL	3	0	0	0	0	....	....	....	....	....	....	....	....	....	....	....	....	....	....	....	....	....	....
2016-17	**Montreal**	**NHL**	**24**	**1**	**5**	**6**	**4**	**0**	**0**	**0**	**28**	**3.6**	**1**	**0**	**0.0**	**14:23**	....	....	....	....	....	....	....	....	....
	Dallas	**NHL**	**12**	**0**	**3**	**3**	**6**	**0**	**0**	**0**	**14**	**0.0**	**–2**	**0**	**0.0**	**17:31**	....	....	....	....	....	....	....	....	....
	NHL Totals		**94**	**2**	**14**	**16**	**65**	**0**	**0**	**0**	**84**	**2.4**		**0**	**0.0**	**15:16**	**7**	**0**	**3**	**3**	**0**	**0**	**0**	**0**	**10:58**

Traded to **Montreal** by **Toronto** with Toronto's 2nd round pick (later traded to Chicago, later traded back to Toronto, later traded to Boston - Boston selected Jared Knight) in 2010 NHL Draft for Mikhail Grabovski, July 3, 2008. • Missed majority of 2015-16 as a healthy reserve. Traded to **Dallas** by **Montreal** with Montreal's 4th round pick (later traded to Los Angeles – Los Angeles selected Markus Phillips) in 2017 NHL Draft for Jordie Benn, February 27, 2017.

PAUL, Nick

(PAWL, NIHK) **OTT**

Left wing. Shoots left. 6'4", 221 lbs. Born, Mississauga, ON, March 20, 1995. Dallas' 6th pick, 101st overall, in 2013 NHL Draft.

Season	Club	League	GP	G	A	Pts	PIM	PP	SH	GW	S	S%	+/-	TF	F%	Min	GP	G	A	Pts	PIM	PP	SH	GW	Min
2010-11	Miss. Senators	GTHL	37	14	11	25	12	....	....	....	....	....	....	....	....	....	....	....	....	....	....	....	....	....	....
2011-12	Mississauga Reps	GTHL	33	25	32	57	....	....	....	....	....	....	....	....	....	....	....	....	....	....	....	....	....	....	....
	Mississauga Reps	Other	30	23	28	51	....	....	....	....	....	....	....	....	....	....	....	....	....	....	....	....	....	....	....
	Mississauga	ON-Jr.A	9	3	2	5	4	....	....	....	....	....	....	....	....	....	....	....	....	....	....	....	....	....	....
2012-13	Brampton	OHL	66	12	16	28	21	....	....	....	....	....	....	....	....	....	5	0	1	1	0	....	....	....	....
2013-14	North Bay	OHL	67	26	20	46	39	....	....	....	....	....	....	....	....	....	22	12	6	18	10	....	....	....	....
2014-15	North Bay	OHL	58	37	29	66	49	....	....	....	....	....	....	....	....	....	15	7	8	15	6	....	....	....	....
2015-16	**Ottawa**	**NHL**	**24**	**2**	**3**	**5**	**6**	**0**	**0**	**0**	**28**	**7.1**	**–3**	**60**	**51.7**	**12:12**	....	....	....	....	....	....	....	....	....
	Binghamton	AHL	45	6	11	17	10	....	....	....	....	....	....	....	....	....	....	....	....	....	....	....	....	....	....
2016-17	**Ottawa**	**NHL**	**1**	**0**	**0**	**0**	**0**	**0**	**0**	**0**	**4**	**0.0**	**–2**	**13**	**38.5**	**16:29**	....	....	....	....	....	....	....	....	....
	Binghamton	AHL	72	15	22	37	30	....	....	....	....	....	....	....	....	....	....	....	....	....	....	....	....	....	....
	NHL Totals		**25**	**2**	**3**	**5**	**6**	**0**	**0**	**0**	**32**	**6.3**		**73**	**49.3**	**12:22**	....	....	....	....	....	....	....	....	....

Traded to **Ottawa** by **Dallas** with Alex Chiasson, Alexander Guptill and Dallas' 2nd round pick (later traded to New Jersey – New Jersey selected Mackenzie Blackwood) in 2015 NHL Draft for Jason Spezza and Ludwig Karlsson, July 1, 2014.

PAVELSKI, Joe

(pah-VEHL-skee, JOH) **S.J.**

Center. Shoots right. 5'11", 190 lbs. Born, Plover, WI, July 11, 1984. San Jose's 7th pick, 205th overall, in 2003 NHL Draft.

Season	Club	League	GP	G	A	Pts	PIM	PP	SH	GW	S	S%	+/-	TF	F%	Min	GP	G	A	Pts	PIM	PP	SH	GW	Min
2001-02	Stevens Point High	High-WI	STATISTICS NOT AVAILABLE																						
2002-03	Waterloo	USHL	60	36	33	69	32	....	....	....	....	....	....	....	....	....	7	5	7	12	8	....	....	....	....
2003-04	Waterloo	USHL	54	21	31	52	58	....	....	....	....	....	....	....	....	....	12	6	6	12	10	....	....	....	....
2004-05	U. of Wisconsin	WCHA	41	16	29	45	26	....	....	....	....	....	....	....	....	....	....	....	....	....	....	....	....	....	....
2005-06	U. of Wisconsin	WCHA	43	23	33	56	34	....	....	....	....	....	....	....	....	....	....	....	....	....	....	....	....	....	....
2006-07	**San Jose**	**NHL**	**46**	**14**	**14**	**28**	**18**	**5**	**0**	**3**	**111**	**12.6**	**4**	**389**	**48.6**	**15:02**	**6**	**1**	**0**	**1**	**0**	**0**	**0**	**0**	**10:27**
	Worcester Sharks	AHL	16	8	18	26	8	....	....	....	....	....	....	....	....	....	....	....	....	....	....	....	....	....	....
2007-08	**San Jose**	**NHL**	**82**	**19**	**21**	**40**	**28**	**8**	**1**	**4**	**207**	**9.2**	**1**	**501**	**53.5**	**14:07**	**13**	**5**	**4**	**9**	**0**	**2**	**0**	**3**	**22:03**
2008-09	**San Jose**	**NHL**	**80**	**25**	**34**	**59**	**46**	**8**	**3**	**3**	**266**	**9.4**	**5**	**1274**	**56.3**	**18:58**	**6**	**0**	**1**	**1**	**9**	**0**	**0**	**0**	**19:21**
2009-10	**San Jose**	**NHL**	**67**	**25**	**26**	**51**	**26**	**3**	**1**	**5**	**228**	**11.0**	**1**	**821**	**58.1**	**19:29**	**15**	**9**	**8**	**17**	**6**	**5**	**0**	**3**	**21:32**
	United States	Olympics	6	0	3	3	4	....	....	....	....	....	....	....	....	....	....	....	....	....	....	....	....	....	....
2010-11	**San Jose**	**NHL**	**74**	**20**	**46**	**66**	**24**	**11**	**1**	**5**	**282**	**7.1**	**10**	**1020**	**54.3**	**19:39**	**18**	**5**	**5**	**10**	**10**	**1**	**0**	**1**	**21:08**
2011-12	**San Jose**	**NHL**	**82**	**31**	**30**	**61**	**31**	**8**	**1**	**2**	**269**	**11.5**	**18**	**864**	**58.7**	**20:37**	**5**	**0**	**0**	**0**	**5**	**0**	**0**	**0**	**21:00**
2012-13	Dynamo Minsk	KHL	17	7	8	15	10	....	....	....	....	....	....	....	....	....	....	....	....	....	....	....	....	....	....
	San Jose	**NHL**	**48**	**16**	**15**	**31**	**10**	**5**	**0**	**5**	**130**	**12.3**	**2**	**660**	**51.8**	**18:55**	**11**	**4**	**8**	**12**	**0**	**3**	**0**	**0**	**21:13**
2013-14	**San Jose**	**NHL**	**82**	**41**	**38**	**79**	**32**	**16**	**1**	**3**	**225**	**18.2**	**23**	**1206**	**56.0**	**19:51**	**7**	**2**	**4**	**6**	**2**	**1**	**0**	**0**	**20:33**
	United States	Olympics	6	1	4	5	0	....	....	....	....	....	....	....	....	....	....	....	....	....	....	....	....	....	....
2014-15	**San Jose**	**NHL**	**82**	**37**	**33**	**70**	**29**	**19**	**0**	**5**	**261**	**14.2**	**12**	**1147**	**56.0**	**20:08**	....	....	....	....	....	....	....	....	....
2015-16	**San Jose**	**NHL**	**82**	**38**	**40**	**78**	**30**	**12**	**0**	**11**	**224**	**17.0**	**25**	**938**	**55.0**	**19:49**	**24**	***14**	**9**	**23**	**4**	**5**	**0**	**4**	**20:47**
2016-17	**San Jose**	**NHL**	**81**	**29**	**39**	**68**	**34**	**7**	**1**	**7**	**233**	**12.4**	**11**	**856**	**52.5**	**19:07**	**6**	**2**	**2**	**4**	**0**	**1**	**0**	**1**	**21:12**
	NHL Totals		**806**	**295**	**336**	**631**	**308**	**102**	**9**	**53**	**2436**	**12.1**		**9676**	**55.1**	**18:50**	**111**	**42**	**41**	**83**	**36**	**18**	**0**	**12**	**20:31**

USHL All-Rookie Team (2003) • USHL First All-Star Team (2003) • USHL Rookie of the Year (2003) • WCHA All-Rookie Team (2005) • WCHA Second All-Star Team (2006) • NCAA West Second All-American Team (2006) • NHL Second All-Star Team (2014)

Played in NHL All-Star Game (2016, 2017)

Signed as a free agent by **Minsk** (KHL), October 5, 2012.

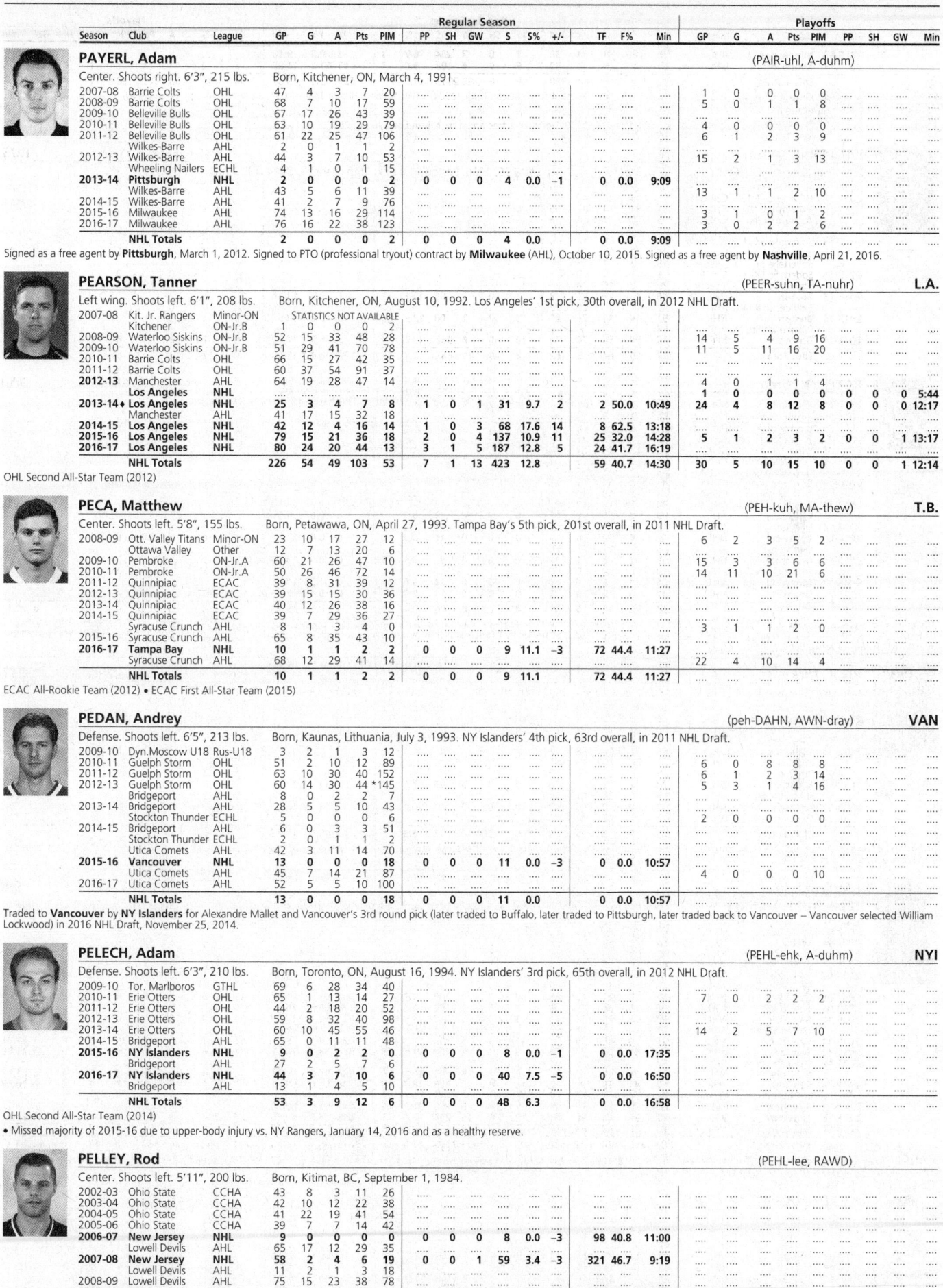

PAYERL, Adam
(PAIR-uhl, A-duhm)

Center. Shoots right. 6'3", 215 lbs. Born, Kitchener, ON, March 4, 1991.

Season	Club	League	GP	G	A	Pts	PIM	PP	SH	GW	S	S%	+/-	TF	F%	Min	GP	G	A	Pts	PIM	PP	SH	GW	Min
			Regular Season														Playoffs								
2007-08	Barrie Colts	OHL	47	4	3	7	20	....	....	....	....	....	....	....	....	....	1	0	0	0	0	....	....	....	....
2008-09	Barrie Colts	OHL	68	7	10	17	59	....	....	....	....	....	....	....	....	....	5	0	1	1	8	....	....	....	....
2009-10	Belleville Bulls	OHL	67	17	26	43	39	....	....	....	....	....	....	....	....	....	....	....	....	....	....	....	....	....	....
2010-11	Belleville Bulls	OHL	63	10	19	29	79	....	....	....	....	....	....	....	....	....	4	0	0	0	0	....	....	....	....
2011-12	Belleville Bulls	OHL	61	22	25	47	106	....	....	....	....	....	....	....	....	....	6	1	2	3	9	....	....	....	....
	Wilkes-Barre	AHL	2	0	1	1	2	....	....	....	....	....	....	....	....	....	....	....	....	....	....	....	....	....	....
2012-13	Wilkes-Barre	AHL	44	3	7	10	53	....	....	....	....	....	....	....	....	....	15	2	1	3	13	....	....	....	....
	Wheeling Nailers	ECHL	4	1	0	1	15	....	....	....	....	....	....	....	....	....	....	....	....	....	....	....	....	....	....
2013-14	**Pittsburgh**	**NHL**	**2**	**0**	**0**	**0**	**2**	**0**	**0**	**0**	**4**	**0.0**	**-1**	**0**	**0.0**	**9:09**	....	....	....	....	....	....	....	....	....
	Wilkes-Barre	AHL	43	5	6	11	39	....	....	....	....	....	....	....	....	....	13	1	1	2	10	....	....	....	....
2014-15	Wilkes-Barre	AHL	41	2	7	9	76	....	....	....	....	....	....	....	....	....	....	....	....	....	....	....	....	....	....
2015-16	Milwaukee	AHL	74	13	16	29	114	....	....	....	....	....	....	....	....	....	3	1	0	1	2	....	....	....	....
2016-17	Milwaukee	AHL	76	16	22	38	123	....	....	....	....	....	....	....	....	....	3	0	2	2	6	....	....	....	....
	NHL Totals		**2**	**0**	**0**	**0**	**2**	**0**	**0**	**0**	**4**	**0.0**		**0**	**0.0**	**9:09**	....	....	....	....	....	....	....	....	....

Signed as a free agent by **Pittsburgh**, March 1, 2012. Signed to PTO (professional tryout) contract by **Milwaukee** (AHL), October 10, 2015. Signed as a free agent by **Nashville**, April 21, 2016.

PEARSON, Tanner
(PEER-suhn, TA-nuhr) **L.A.**

Left wing. Shoots left. 6'1", 208 lbs. Born, Kitchener, ON, August 10, 1992. Los Angeles' 1st pick, 30th overall, in 2012 NHL Draft.

Season	Club	League	GP	G	A	Pts	PIM	PP	SH	GW	S	S%	+/-	TF	F%	Min	GP	G	A	Pts	PIM	PP	SH	GW	Min
2007-08	Kit. Jr. Rangers	Minor-ON	STATISTICS NOT AVAILABLE																						
	Kitchener	ON-Jr.B	1	0	0	0	2	....	....	....	....	....	....	....	....	....	....	....	....	....	....	....	....	....	....
2008-09	Waterloo Siskins	ON-Jr.B	52	15	33	48	28	....	....	....	....	....	....	....	....	....	14	5	4	9	16	....	....	....	....
2009-10	Waterloo Siskins	ON-Jr.B	51	29	41	70	78	....	....	....	....	....	....	....	....	....	11	5	11	16	20	....	....	....	....
2010-11	Barrie Colts	OHL	66	15	27	42	35	....	....	....	....	....	....	....	....	....	....	....	....	....	....	....	....	....	....
2011-12	Barrie Colts	OHL	60	37	54	91	37	....	....	....	....	....	....	....	....	....	....	....	....	....	....	....	....	....	....
2012-13	Manchester	AHL	64	19	28	47	14	....	....	....	....	....	....	....	....	....	4	0	1	1	4	....	....	....	....
	Los Angeles	**NHL**	....	....	....	....	....	....	....	....	....	....	....	....	....	....	**1**	**0**	**0**	**0**	**0**	**0**	**0**	**0**	**5:44**
2013-14♦	**Los Angeles**	**NHL**	**25**	**3**	**4**	**7**	**8**	**1**	**0**	**1**	**31**	**9.7**	**2**	**2**	**50.0**	**10:49**	**24**	**4**	**8**	**12**	**8**	**0**	**0**	**0**	**12:17**
	Manchester	AHL	41	17	15	32	18	....	....	....	....	....	....	....	....	....	....	....	....	....	....	....	....	....	....
2014-15	**Los Angeles**	**NHL**	**42**	**12**	**4**	**16**	**14**	**1**	**0**	**3**	**68**	**17.6**	**14**	**8**	**62.5**	**13:18**	....	....	....	....	....	....	....	....	....
2015-16	**Los Angeles**	**NHL**	**79**	**15**	**21**	**36**	**18**	**2**	**0**	**4**	**137**	**10.9**	**11**	**25**	**32.0**	**14:28**	**5**	**1**	**2**	**3**	**2**	**0**	**0**	**1**	**13:17**
2016-17	**Los Angeles**	**NHL**	**80**	**24**	**20**	**44**	**13**	**3**	**1**	**5**	**187**	**12.8**	**5**	**24**	**41.7**	**16:19**	....	....	....	....	....	....	....	....	....
	NHL Totals		**226**	**54**	**49**	**103**	**53**	**7**	**1**	**13**	**423**	**12.8**		**59**	**40.7**	**14:30**	**30**	**5**	**10**	**15**	**10**	**0**	**0**	**1**	**12:14**

OHL Second All-Star Team (2012)

PECA, Matthew
(PEH-kuh, MA-thew) **T.B.**

Center. Shoots left. 5'8", 155 lbs. Born, Petawawa, ON, April 27, 1993. Tampa Bay's 5th pick, 201st overall, in 2011 NHL Draft.

Season	Club	League	GP	G	A	Pts	PIM	PP	SH	GW	S	S%	+/-	TF	F%	Min	GP	G	A	Pts	PIM	PP	SH	GW	Min
2008-09	Ott. Valley Titans	Minor-ON	23	10	17	27	12	....	....	....	....	....	....	....	....	....	6	2	3	5	2	....	....	....	....
	Ottawa Valley	Other	12	7	13	20	6	....	....	....	....	....	....	....	....	....	....	....	....	....	....	....	....	....	....
2009-10	Pembroke	ON-Jr.A	60	21	26	47	10	....	....	....	....	....	....	....	....	....	15	3	3	6	6	....	....	....	....
2010-11	Pembroke	ON-Jr.A	50	26	46	72	14	....	....	....	....	....	....	....	....	....	14	11	10	21	6	....	....	....	....
2011-12	Quinnipiac	ECAC	39	8	31	39	12	....	....	....	....	....	....	....	....	....	....	....	....	....	....	....	....	....	....
2012-13	Quinnipiac	ECAC	39	15	15	30	36	....	....	....	....	....	....	....	....	....	....	....	....	....	....	....	....	....	....
2013-14	Quinnipiac	ECAC	40	12	26	38	16	....	....	....	....	....	....	....	....	....	....	....	....	....	....	....	....	....	....
2014-15	Quinnipiac	ECAC	39	7	29	36	27	....	....	....	....	....	....	....	....	....	....	....	....	....	....	....	....	....	....
	Syracuse Crunch	AHL	8	1	3	4	0	....	....	....	....	....	....	....	....	....	3	1	1	2	0	....	....	....	....
2015-16	Syracuse Crunch	AHL	65	8	35	43	10	....	....	....	....	....	....	....	....	....	....	....	....	....	....	....	....	....	....
2016-17	**Tampa Bay**	**NHL**	**10**	**1**	**1**	**2**	**2**	**0**	**0**	**0**	**9**	**11.1**	**-3**	**72**	**44.4**	**11:27**	....	....	....	....	....	....	....	....	....
	Syracuse Crunch	AHL	68	12	29	41	14	....	....	....	....	....	....	....	....	....	22	4	10	14	4	....	....	....	....
	NHL Totals		**10**	**1**	**1**	**2**	**2**	**0**	**0**	**0**	**9**	**11.1**		**72**	**44.4**	**11:27**	....	....	....	....	....	....	....	....	....

ECAC All-Rookie Team (2012) • ECAC First All-Star Team (2015)

PEDAN, Andrey
(peh-DAHN, AWN-dray) **VAN**

Defense. Shoots left. 6'5", 213 lbs. Born, Kaunas, Lithuania, July 3, 1993. NY Islanders' 4th pick, 63rd overall, in 2011 NHL Draft.

Season	Club	League	GP	G	A	Pts	PIM	PP	SH	GW	S	S%	+/-	TF	F%	Min	GP	G	A	Pts	PIM	PP	SH	GW	Min
2009-10	Dyn.Moscow U18	Rus-U18	3	2	1	3	12	....	....	....	....	....	....	....	....	....	....	....	....	....	....	....	....	....	....
2010-11	Guelph Storm	OHL	51	2	10	12	89	....	....	....	....	....	....	....	....	....	6	0	8	8	8	....	....	....	....
2011-12	Guelph Storm	OHL	63	10	30	40	152	....	....	....	....	....	....	....	....	....	6	1	2	3	14	....	....	....	....
2012-13	Guelph Storm	OHL	60	14	30	44	*145	....	....	....	....	....	....	....	....	....	5	3	1	4	16	....	....	....	....
	Bridgeport	AHL	8	0	2	2	7	....	....	....	....	....	....	....	....	....	....	....	....	....	....	....	....	....	....
2013-14	Bridgeport	AHL	28	5	5	10	43	....	....	....	....	....	....	....	....	....	....	....	....	....	....	....	....	....	....
	Stockton Thunder	ECHL	5	0	0	0	6	....	....	....	....	....	....	....	....	....	2	0	0	0	0	....	....	....	....
2014-15	Bridgeport	AHL	6	0	3	3	51	....	....	....	....	....	....	....	....	....	....	....	....	....	....	....	....	....	....
	Stockton Thunder	ECHL	2	0	1	1	2	....	....	....	....	....	....	....	....	....	....	....	....	....	....	....	....	....	....
	Utica Comets	AHL	42	3	11	14	70	....	....	....	....	....	....	....	....	....	....	....	....	....	....	....	....	....	....
2015-16	**Vancouver**	**NHL**	**13**	**0**	**0**	**0**	**18**	**0**	**0**	**0**	**11**	**0.0**	**-3**	**0**	**0.0**	**10:57**	....	....	....	....	....	....	....	....	....
	Utica Comets	AHL	45	7	14	21	87	....	....	....	....	....	....	....	....	....	4	0	0	0	10	....	....	....	....
2016-17	Utica Comets	AHL	52	5	5	10	100	....	....	....	....	....	....	....	....	....	....	....	....	....	....	....	....	....	....
	NHL Totals		**13**	**0**	**0**	**0**	**18**	**0**	**0**	**0**	**11**	**0.0**		**0**	**0.0**	**10:57**	....	....	....	....	....	....	....	....	....

Traded to **Vancouver** by **NY Islanders** for Alexandre Mallet and Vancouver's 3rd round pick (later traded to Buffalo, later traded to Pittsburgh, later traded back to Vancouver – Vancouver selected William Lockwood) in 2016 NHL Draft, November 25, 2014.

PELECH, Adam
(PEHL-ehk, A-duhm) **NYI**

Defense. Shoots left. 6'3", 210 lbs. Born, Toronto, ON, August 16, 1994. NY Islanders' 3rd pick, 65th overall, in 2012 NHL Draft.

Season	Club	League	GP	G	A	Pts	PIM	PP	SH	GW	S	S%	+/-	TF	F%	Min	GP	G	A	Pts	PIM	PP	SH	GW	Min
2009-10	Tor. Marlboros	GTHL	69	6	28	34	40	....	....	....	....	....	....	....	....	....	....	....	....	....	....	....	....	....	....
2010-11	Erie Otters	OHL	65	1	13	14	27	....	....	....	....	....	....	....	....	....	7	0	2	2	2	....	....	....	....
2011-12	Erie Otters	OHL	44	2	18	20	52	....	....	....	....	....	....	....	....	....	....	....	....	....	....	....	....	....	....
2012-13	Erie Otters	OHL	59	8	32	40	98	....	....	....	....	....	....	....	....	....	....	....	....	....	....	....	....	....	....
2013-14	Erie Otters	OHL	60	10	45	55	46	....	....	....	....	....	....	....	....	....	14	2	5	7	10	....	....	....	....
2014-15	Bridgeport	AHL	65	0	11	11	48	....	....	....	....	....	....	....	....	....	....	....	....	....	....	....	....	....	....
2015-16	**NY Islanders**	**NHL**	**9**	**0**	**2**	**2**	**0**	**0**	**0**	**0**	**8**	**0.0**	**-1**	**0**	**0.0**	**17:35**	....	....	....	....	....	....	....	....	....
	Bridgeport	AHL	27	2	5	7	6	....	....	....	....	....	....	....	....	....	....	....	....	....	....	....	....	....	....
2016-17	**NY Islanders**	**NHL**	**44**	**3**	**7**	**10**	**6**	**0**	**0**	**0**	**40**	**7.5**	**-5**	**0**	**0.0**	**16:50**	....	....	....	....	....	....	....	....	....
	Bridgeport	AHL	13	1	4	5	10	....	....	....	....	....	....	....	....	....	....	....	....	....	....	....	....	....	....
	NHL Totals		**53**	**3**	**9**	**12**	**6**	**0**	**0**	**0**	**48**	**6.3**		**0**	**0.0**	**16:58**	....	....	....	....	....	....	....	....	....

OHL Second All-Star Team (2014)

• Missed majority of 2015-16 due to upper-body injury vs. NY Rangers, January 14, 2016 and as a healthy reserve.

PELLEY, Rod
(PEHL-lee, RAWD)

Center. Shoots left. 5'11", 200 lbs. Born, Kitimat, BC, September 1, 1984.

Season	Club	League	GP	G	A	Pts	PIM	PP	SH	GW	S	S%	+/-	TF	F%	Min	GP	G	A	Pts	PIM	PP	SH	GW	Min
2002-03	Ohio State	CCHA	43	8	3	11	26	....	....	....	....	....	....	....	....	....	....	....	....	....	....	....	....	....	....
2003-04	Ohio State	CCHA	42	10	12	22	38	....	....	....	....	....	....	....	....	....	....	....	....	....	....	....	....	....	....
2004-05	Ohio State	CCHA	41	22	19	41	54	....	....	....	....	....	....	....	....	....	....	....	....	....	....	....	....	....	....
2005-06	Ohio State	CCHA	39	7	7	14	42	....	....	....	....	....	....	....	....	....	....	....	....	....	....	....	....	....	....
2006-07	**New Jersey**	**NHL**	**9**	**0**	**0**	**0**	**0**	**0**	**0**	**0**	**8**	**0.0**	**-3**	**98**	**40.8**	**11:00**	....	....	....	....	....	....	....	....	....
	Lowell Devils	AHL	65	17	12	29	35	....	....	....	....	....	....	....	....	....	....	....	....	....	....	....	....	....	....
2007-08	**New Jersey**	**NHL**	**58**	**2**	**4**	**6**	**19**	**0**	**0**	**1**	**59**	**3.4**	**-3**	**321**	**46.7**	**9:19**	....	....	....	....	....	....	....	....	....
	Lowell Devils	AHL	11	2	1	3	18	....	....	....	....	....	....	....	....	....	....	....	....	....	....	....	....	....	....
2008-09	Lowell Devils	AHL	75	15	23	38	78	....	....	....	....	....	....	....	....	....	....	....	....	....	....	....	....	....	....
2009-10	**New Jersey**	**NHL**	**63**	**2**	**8**	**10**	**40**	**0**	**0**	**0**	**74**	**2.7**	**-4**	**198**	**49.5**	**7:52**	**3**	**0**	**0**	**0**	**2**	**0**	**0**	**0**	**9:12**
2010-11	**New Jersey**	**NHL**	**74**	**3**	**7**	**10**	**27**	**1**	**0**	**0**	**88**	**3.4**	**-9**	**320**	**52.8**	**11:48**	....	....	....	....	....	....	....	....	....

			Regular Season														Playoffs								
Season	Club	League	GP	G	A	Pts	PIM	PP	SH	GW	S	S%	+/-	TF	F%	Min	GP	G	A	Pts	PIM	PP	SH	GW	Min
2011-12	**New Jersey**	**NHL**	**7**	**0**	**0**	**0**	**7**	**0**	**0**	**0**	**3**	**0.0**	**0**	**10**	**30.0**	**6:12**	....	....	....	....	....	....	....	....	....
	Anaheim	**NHL**	**45**	**2**	**1**	**3**	**9**	**0**	**0**	**0**	**41**	**4.9**	**–3**	**244**	**50.0**	**8:00**	....	....	....	....	....	....	....	....	....
2012-13	Norfolk Admirals	AHL	60	3	7	10	34	....	....	....	....	....	....	....	....	....	....	....	....	....	....	....	....	....	....
2013-14	Albany Devils	AHL	74	13	7	20	55	....	....	....	....	....	....	....	....	....	4	0	0	0	2	....	....	....	....
2014-15	Albany Devils	AHL	70	7	6	13	65	....	....	....	....	....	....	....	....	....	....	....	....	....	....	....	....	....	....
2015-16	Albany Devils	AHL	65	8	5	13	40	....	....	....	....	....	....	....	....	....	11	2	0	2	0	....	....	....	....
2016-17	Albany Devils	AHL	71	6	7	13	34	....	....	....	....	....	....	....	....	....	4	0	0	0	2	....	....	....	....
	NHL Totals		**256**	**9**	**20**	**29**	**102**	**1**	**0**	**1**	**273**	**3.3**		**1191**	**48.9**	**9:25**	**3**	**0**	**0**	**0**	**2**	**0**	**0**	**0**	**9:12**

CCHA Second All-Star Team (2005)

Signed as a free agent by **New Jersey**, July 17, 2006. Traded to **Anaheim** by **New Jersey** with Mark Fraser and New Jersey's 7th round pick (Jaycob Megna) in 2012 NHL Draft for Kurtis Foster and Timo Pielmeier, December 12, 2011. Signed as a free agent by **New Jersey**, July 8, 2013. Signed as a free agent by **Albany** (AHL), July 6, 2016. Signed as a free agent by **Stockton** (AHL), July 19, 2017.

PELUSO, Anthony

(puh-LOO-soh, AN-toh-nee) **WSH**

Right wing. Shoots right. 6'3", 235 lbs. Born, North York, ON, April 18, 1989. St. Louis' 9th pick, 160th overall, in 2007 NHL Draft.

Season	Club	League	GP	G	A	Pts	PIM	PP	SH	GW	S	S%	+/-	TF	F%	Min	GP	G	A	Pts	PIM	PP	SH	GW	Min
2004-05	Rich. Hill Stars	Minor-ON	30	22	20	42	80	....	....	....	....	....	....	....	....	....	....	....	....	....	....	....	....	....	....
2005-06	Erie Otters	OHL	68	5	3	8	66	....	....	....	....	....	....	....	....	....	....	....	....	....	....	....	....	....	....
2006-07	Erie Otters	OHL	52	7	3	10	176	....	....	....	....	....	....	....	....	....	....	....	....	....	....	....	....	....	....
2007-08	Erie Otters	OHL	21	3	3	6	41	....	....	....	....	....	....	....	....	....	....	....	....	....	....	....	....	....	....
	Sault Ste. Marie	OHL	42	4	11	15	83	....	....	....	....	....	....	....	....	....	14	2	1	3	12	....	....	....	....
2008-09	Sault Ste. Marie	OHL	36	9	6	15	68	....	....	....	....	....	....	....	....	....	....	....	....	....	....	....	....	....	....
	Brampton	OHL	27	11	11	22	57	....	....	....	....	....	....	....	....	....	21	8	7	15	29	....	....	....	....
2009-10	Peoria Rivermen	AHL	22	1	1	2	57	....	....	....	....	....	....	....	....	....	....	....	....	....	....	....	....	....	....
	Alaska Aces	ECHL	27	4	7	11	48	....	....	....	....	....	....	....	....	....	4	1	0	1	6	....	....	....	....
2010-11	Peoria Rivermen	AHL	62	5	2	7	102	....	....	....	....	....	....	....	....	....	4	1	0	1	0	....	....	....	....
2011-12	Peoria Rivermen	AHL	61	4	5	9	159	....	....	....	....	....	....	....	....	....	....	....	....	....	....	....	....	....	....
2012-13	Peoria Rivermen	AHL	36	5	6	11	58	....	....	....	....	....	....	....	....	....	....	....	....	....	....	....	....	....	....
	Winnipeg	**NHL**	**5**	**0**	**2**	**2**	**14**	**0**	**0**	**0**	**4**	**0.0**	**1**	**0**	**0.0**	**5:00**	....	....	....	....	....	....	....	....	....
2013-14	**Winnipeg**	**NHL**	**53**	**2**	**3**	**5**	**65**	**0**	**0**	**0**	**24**	**8.3**	**–5**	**3**	**33.3**	**5:46**	....	....	....	....	....	....	....	....	....
2014-15	**Winnipeg**	**NHL**	**49**	**1**	**1**	**2**	**86**	**0**	**0**	**0**	**23**	**4.3**	**–3**	**1**	**0.0**	**5:53**	....	....	....	....	....	....	....	....	....
2015-16	**Winnipeg**	**NHL**	**35**	**1**	**4**	**5**	**44**	**0**	**0**	**0**	**16**	**6.3**	**4**	**0**	**0.0**	**6:23**	....	....	....	....	....	....	....	....	....
2016-17	Manitoba Moose	AHL	22	0	2	2	6	....	....	....	....	....	....	....	....	....	....	....	....	....	....	....	....	....	....
	NHL Totals		**142**	**4**	**10**	**14**	**209**	**0**	**0**	**0**	**67**	**6.0**		**4**	**25.0**	**5:56**	....	....	....	....	....	....	....	....	....

Signed as a free agent by **Winnipeg**, July 24, 2013. • Missed majority of 2015-16 due to upper-body injury vs. NY Islanders, March 3, 2016 and as a healthy reserve. • Missed majority of 2016-17 as a healthy reserve. Signed as a free agent by **Washington**, July 1, 2017.

PERCY, Stuart

(PUHR-see, STEW-uhrt)

Defense. Shoots left. 6'1", 187 lbs. Born, Oakville, ON, May 18, 1993. Toronto's 2nd pick, 25th overall, in 2011 NHL Draft.

Season	Club	League	GP	G	A	Pts	PIM	PP	SH	GW	S	S%	+/-	TF	F%	Min	GP	G	A	Pts	PIM	PP	SH	GW	Min
2008-09	Tor. Marlboros	GTHL	79	13	44	57	42	....	....	....	....	....	....	....	....	....	....	....	....	....	....	....	....	....	....
2009-10	St. Michael's	OHL	52	3	15	18	40	....	....	....	....	....	....	....	....	....	16	0	1	1	12	....	....	....	....
2010-11	St. Michael's	OHL	64	4	30	34	50	....	....	....	....	....	....	....	....	....	20	2	10	12	14	....	....	....	....
2011-12	St. Michael's	OHL	34	5	20	25	41	....	....	....	....	....	....	....	....	....	6	1	1	2	4	....	....	....	....
	Toronto Marlies	AHL	1	0	1	1	0	....	....	....	....	....	....	....	....	....	3	0	0	0	0	....	....	....	....
2012-13	Mississauga	OHL	68	13	32	45	44	....	....	....	....	....	....	....	....	....	6	0	2	2	4	....	....	....	....
	Toronto Marlies	AHL	4	1	2	3	2	....	....	....	....	....	....	....	....	....	....	....	....	....	....	....	....	....	....
2013-14	Toronto Marlies	AHL	71	4	21	25	30	....	....	....	....	....	....	....	....	....	14	0	2	2	4	....	....	....	....
2014-15	**Toronto**	**NHL**	**9**	**0**	**3**	**3**	**2**	**0**	**0**	**0**	**13**	**0.0**	**–4**	**0**	**0.0**	**18:05**	....	....	....	....	....	....	....	....	....
	Toronto Marlies	AHL	43	1	10	11	14	....	....	....	....	....	....	....	....	....	4	0	2	2	2	....	....	....	....
2015-16	**Toronto**	**NHL**	**3**	**0**	**0**	**0**	**0**	**0**	**0**	**0**	**1**	**0.0**	**–2**	**0**	**0.0**	**13:10**	....	....	....	....	....	....	....	....	....
	Toronto Marlies	AHL	58	4	20	24	47	....	....	....	....	....	....	....	....	....	14	0	4	4	12	....	....	....	....
2016-17	Wilkes-Barre	AHL	37	1	7	8	18	....	....	....	....	....	....	....	....	....	....	....	....	....	....	....	....	....	....
	NHL Totals		**12**	**0**	**3**	**3**	**2**	**0**	**0**	**0**	**14**	**0.0**		**0**	**0.0**	**16:51**	....	....	....	....	....	....	....	....	....

Signed as a free agent by **Pittsburgh**, July 1, 2016. • Missed majority of 2016-17 as a healthy reserve.

PERLINI, Brendan

(puhr-LEE-nee, BREHN-duhn) **ARI**

Left wing. Shoots left. 6'4", 207 lbs. Born, Guildford, UK, April 27, 1996. Arizona's 1st pick, 12th overall, in 2014 NHL Draft.

Season	Club	League	GP	G	A	Pts	PIM	PP	SH	GW	S	S%	+/-	TF	F%	Min	GP	G	A	Pts	PIM	PP	SH	GW	Min
2009-10	Soo Greyhounds	Minor-ON	18	19	15	34	12	....	....	....	....	....	....	....	....	....	....	....	....	....	....	....	....	....	....
2010-11	Detroit Belle Tire	T1EHL	31	18	17	35	17	....	....	....	....	....	....	....	....	....	....	....	....	....	....	....	....	....	....
2011-12	Detroit Belle Tire	T1EHL	40	21	23	44	20	....	....	....	....	....	....	....	....	....	7	4	3	7	4	....	....	....	....
2012-13	Barrie Colts	OHL	32	1	1	2	4	....	....	....	....	....	....	....	....	....	....	....	....	....	....	....	....	....	....
	Niagara Ice Dogs	OHL	27	7	3	10	4	....	....	....	....	....	....	....	....	....	5	1	2	3	4	....	....	....	....
2013-14	Niagara Ice Dogs	OHL	58	34	37	71	36	....	....	....	....	....	....	....	....	....	7	0	1	1	6	....	....	....	....
2014-15	Niagara Ice Dogs	OHL	43	26	34	60	22	....	....	....	....	....	....	....	....	....	11	7	5	12	7	....	....	....	....
	Portland Pirates	AHL	....	....	....	....	....	....	....	....	....	....	....	....	....	....	4	1	0	1	0	....	....	....	....
2015-16	Niagara Ice Dogs	OHL	57	25	20	45	28	....	....	....	....	....	....	....	....	....	14	6	3	9	9	....	....	....	....
2016-17	**Arizona**	**NHL**	**57**	**14**	**7**	**21**	**20**	**3**	**0**	**2**	**92**	**15.2**	**–4**	**2**	**50.0**	**14:50**	....	....	....	....	....	....	....	....	....
	Tucson	AHL	17	14	5	19	14	....	....	....	....	....	....	....	....	....	....	....	....	....	....	....	....	....	....
	NHL Totals		**57**	**14**	**7**	**21**	**20**	**3**	**0**	**2**	**92**	**15.2**		**2**	**50.0**	**14:50**	....	....	....	....	....	....	....	....	....

PERREAULT, Mathieu

(pair-OH, MA-tyew) **WPG**

Center. Shoots left. 5'10", 188 lbs. Born, Drummondville, QC, January 5, 1988. Washington's 10th pick, 177th overall, in 2006 NHL Draft.

Season	Club	League	GP	G	A	Pts	PIM	PP	SH	GW	S	S%	+/-	TF	F%	Min	GP	G	A	Pts	PIM	PP	SH	GW	Min
2004-05	Magog	QAAA	41	25	47	72	68	....	....	....	....	....	....	....	....	....	9	5	10	15	12	....	....	....	....
2005-06	Acadie-Bathurst	QMJHL	62	18	34	52	42	....	....	....	....	....	....	....	....	....	17	10	11	21	8	....	....	....	....
2006-07	Acadie-Bathurst	QMJHL	67	41	78	119	66	....	....	....	....	....	....	....	....	....	12	6	8	14	8	....	....	....	....
2007-08	Acadie-Bathurst	QMJHL	65	34	*80	*114	61	....	....	....	....	....	....	....	....	....	12	3	19	22	6	....	....	....	....
	Hershey Bears	AHL	....	....	....	....	....	....	....	....	....	....	....	....	....	....	3	0	0	0	0	....	....	....	....
2008-09	Hershey Bears	AHL	77	11	39	50	36	....	....	....	....	....	....	....	....	....	21	2	6	8	8	....	....	....	....
2009-10	**Washington**	**NHL**	**21**	**4**	**5**	**9**	**6**	**1**	**0**	**0**	**27**	**14.8**	**4**	**210**	**45.2**	**11:21**	....	....	....	....	....	....	....	....	....
	Hershey Bears	AHL	56	16	34	50	34	....	....	....	....	....	....	....	....	....	21	7	12	19	18	....	....	....	....
2010-11	**Washington**	**NHL**	**35**	**7**	**7**	**14**	**20**	**1**	**0**	**1**	**41**	**17.1**	**–3**	**305**	**45.6**	**11:53**	....	....	....	....	....	....	....	....	....
	Hershey Bears	AHL	34	11	24	35	38	....	....	....	....	....	....	....	....	....	6	3	3	6	6	....	....	....	....
2011-12	**Washington**	**NHL**	**64**	**16**	**14**	**30**	**24**	**2**	**0**	**4**	**60**	**26.7**	**9**	**451**	**50.8**	**12:02**	**4**	**0**	**0**	**0**	**0**	**0**	**0**	**0**	**10:43**
2012-13	HIFK Helsinki	Finland	7	1	6	7	6	....	....	....	....	....	....	....	....	....	....	....	....	....	....	....	....	....	....
	Washington	**NHL**	**39**	**6**	**11**	**17**	**20**	**2**	**0**	**1**	**47**	**12.8**	**7**	**325**	**51.7**	**11:40**	**7**	**1**	**3**	**4**	**0**	**0**	**0**	**0**	**13:38**
2013-14	**Anaheim**	**NHL**	**69**	**18**	**25**	**43**	**36**	**4**	**0**	**1**	**120**	**15.0**	**13**	**830**	**52.7**	**13:52**	**11**	**2**	**3**	**5**	**18**	**2**	**0**	**1**	**12:36**
2014-15	**Winnipeg**	**NHL**	**62**	**18**	**23**	**41**	**38**	**5**	**0**	**2**	**129**	**14.0**	**7**	**438**	**51.6**	**16:15**	**3**	**0**	**2**	**2**	**0**	**0**	**0**	**0**	**17:03**
2015-16	**Winnipeg**	**NHL**	**71**	**9**	**32**	**41**	**36**	**6**	**0**	**1**	**133**	**6.8**	**–11**	**203**	**46.3**	**16:33**	....	....	....	....	....	....	....	....	....
2016-17	**Winnipeg**	**NHL**	**65**	**13**	**32**	**45**	**30**	**3**	**0**	**3**	**134**	**9.7**	**–11**	**189**	**51.3**	**16:17**	....	....	....	....	....	....	....	....	....
	NHL Totals		**426**	**91**	**149**	**240**	**210**	**24**	**0**	**13**	**691**	**13.2**		**2951**	**50.3**	**14:16**	**25**	**3**	**8**	**11**	**18**	**2**	**0**	**1**	**13:07**

QMJHL First All-Star Team (2007) • QMJHL Player of the Year (2007) • QMJHL Second All-Star Team (2008) • Canadian Major Junior Second All-Star Team (2007, 2008)

Signed as a free agent by **HIFK Helsinki** (Finland), November 24, 2012. Traded to **Anaheim** by **Washington** for John Mitchell and Anaheim's 4th round pick (later traded back to Anaheim, later traded to Dallas – Dallas selected Brent Moran) in 2014 NHL Draft, September 29, 2013. Signed as a free agent by **Winnipeg**, July 1, 2014.

PERRON, David

(peh-RAWN, DAY-vihd) **VGK**

Left wing. Shoots right. 6', 200 lbs. Born, Sherbrooke, QC, May 28, 1988. St. Louis' 3rd pick, 26th overall, in 2007 NHL Draft.

Season	Club	League	GP	G	A	Pts	PIM	PP	SH	GW	S	S%	+/-	TF	F%	Min	GP	G	A	Pts	PIM	PP	SH	GW	Min
2005-06	St-Jerome	QJHL	51	24	45	69	92	....	....	....	....	....	....	....	....	....	8	4	5	9	8	....	....	....	....
2006-07	Lewiston	QMJHL	70	39	44	83	75	....	....	....	....	....	....	....	....	....	17	12	16	28	22	....	....	....	....
2007-08	**St. Louis**	**NHL**	**62**	**13**	**14**	**27**	**38**	**3**	**0**	**1**	**68**	**19.1**	**16**	**14**	**35.7**	**12:33**	....	....	....	....	....	....	....	....	....
2008-09	**St. Louis**	**NHL**	**81**	**15**	**35**	**50**	**50**	**4**	**0**	**3**	**161**	**9.3**	**13**	**6**	**16.7**	**14:32**	**4**	**1**	**1**	**2**	**4**	**0**	**0**	**0**	**17:12**
2009-10	**St. Louis**	**NHL**	**82**	**20**	**27**	**47**	**60**	**5**	**1**	**2**	**166**	**12.0**	**–10**	**21**	**38.1**	**16:09**	....	....	....	....	....	....	....	....	....
2010-11	**St. Louis**	**NHL**	**10**	**5**	**2**	**7**	**12**	**0**	**0**	**0**	**29**	**17.2**	**7**	**0**	**0.0**	**18:25**	....	....	....	....	....	....	....	....	....
2011-12	**St. Louis**	**NHL**	**57**	**21**	**21**	**42**	**28**	**5**	**1**	**4**	**114**	**18.4**	**19**	**10**	**20.0**	**18:17**	**9**	**1**	**4**	**5**	**10**	**0**	**0**	**1**	**17:06**
2012-13	**St. Louis**	**NHL**	**48**	**10**	**15**	**25**	**44**	**2**	**0**	**2**	**84**	**11.9**	**0**	**22**	**36.4**	**18:00**	**6**	**0**	**2**	**2**	**6**	**0**	**0**	**0**	**17:11**

							Regular Season										Playoffs								
Season	Club	League	GP	G	A	Pts	PIM	PP	SH	GW	S	S%	+/-	TF	F%	Min	GP	G	A	Pts	PIM	PP	SH	GW	Min
2013-14	Edmonton	NHL	78	28	29	57	90	8	1	2	220	12.7	–16	39	33.3	19:08	....	....	....	....	....	....	....	....	....
2014-15	Edmonton	NHL	38	5	14	19	20	0	0	1	74	6.8	–17	9	33.3	17:00	....	....	....	....	....	....	....	....	....
	Pittsburgh	NHL	43	12	10	22	42	3	0	1	122	9.8	–8	3	0.0	17:37	5	0	1	1	4	0	0	0	17:17
2015-16	Pittsburgh	NHL	43	4	12	16	28	1	0	0	96	4.2	–13	5	20.0	15:28	....	....	....	....	....	....	....	....	....
	Anaheim	NHL	28	8	12	20	34	3	0	1	51	15.7	12	5	20.0	14:49	7	1	2	3	8	0	0	0	15:47
2016-17	St. Louis	NHL	82	18	28	46	54	3	1	3	151	11.9	–2	66	48.5	17:18	11	0	1	1	8	0	0	0	14:27
	NHL Totals		652	159	219	378	500	37	4	20	1336	11.9		200	37.0	16:31	42	3	11	14	40	0	0	1	16:14

• Missed majority of 2010-11 due to head injury vs. San Jose, November 4, 2010. Traded to **Edmonton** by **St. Louis** with St. Louis' 3rd round pick (later forfieited to San Jose as a result of Edmonton's hiring of Todd McLellan as head coach – San Jose selected Mike Robinson) in 2015 NHL Draft for Magnus Paajarvi, Edmonton's 2nd round pick (Ivan Barbashev) in 2014 NHL Draft and Edmonton's 4th round pick (Adam Musil) in 2015 NHL Draft, July 10, 2013. Traded to **Pittsburgh** by **Edmonton** for Rob Klinkhammer and Pittsburgh's 1st round pick (later traded to NY Islanders – NY Islanders selected Matthew Barzal) in 2015 NHL Draft, January 2, 2015. Traded to **Anaheim** by **Pittsburgh** with Adam Clendening for Carl Hagelin, January 16, 2016. Signed as a free agent by **St. Louis**, July 1, 2016. Claimed by **Vegas** from **St. Louis** in Expansion Draft, June 21, 2017.

PERRY, Corey

(PAIR-ee, KOH-ree) **ANA**

Right wing. Shoots right. 6'3", 210 lbs. Born, Peterborough, ON, May 16, 1985. Anaheim's 2nd pick, 28th overall, in 2003 NHL Draft.

Season	Club	League	GP	G	A	Pts	PIM	PP	SH	GW	S	S%	+/-	TF	F%	Min	GP	G	A	Pts	PIM	PP	SH	GW	Min
2000-01	Peterborough	Minor-ON	64	69	46	115	20	....	....	....	....	....	....	....	....	....	3	3	0	3	0	....	....	....	....
2001-02	London Knights	OHL	67	28	31	59	56	....	....	....	....	....	....	....	....	....	12	2	3	5	30	....	....	....	....
2002-03	London Knights	OHL	67	25	53	78	145	....	....	....	....	....	....	....	....	....	14	7	16	23	27	....	....	....	....
2003-04	London Knights	OHL	66	40	*73	113	98	....	....	....	....	....	....	....	....	....	15	7	15	22	20	....	....	....	....
	Cincinnati	AHL	....	....	....	....	....	....	....	....	....	....	....	....	....	....	3	1	1	2	4	....	....	....	....
2004-05	London Knights	OHL	60	*47	*83	*130	117	....	....	....	....	....	....	....	....	....	18	11	*27	*38	46	....	....	....	....
2005-06	Anaheim	NHL	56	13	12	25	50	4	0	2	98	13.3	1	11	27.3	11:34	11	0	3	3	16	0	0	0	9:33
	Portland Pirates	AHL	19	16	18	34	32	....	....	....	....	....	....	....	....	....	1	1	0	1	0	....	....	....	....
2006-07♦	Anaheim	NHL	82	17	27	44	55	4	0	3	194	8.8	12	21	42.9	12:28	21	6	9	15	37	1	0	1	16:30
2007-08	Anaheim	NHL	70	29	25	54	108	11	0	4	200	14.5	12	16	18.8	17:57	3	2	1	3	8	0	0	0	14:55
2008-09	Anaheim	NHL	78	32	40	72	109	10	0	8	283	11.3	10	31	29.0	18:36	13	8	6	14	36	2	0	1	22:00
2009-10	Anaheim	NHL	82	27	49	76	111	6	1	2	270	10.0	0	28	21.4	21:04	....	....	....	....	....	....	....	....	....
	Canada	Olympics	7	4	1	5	2	....	....	....	....	....	....	....	....	....	....	....	....	....	....	....	....	....	....
2010-11	Anaheim	NHL	82	*50	48	98	104	14	4	*11	290	17.2	9	22	40.9	22:19	6	2	6	8	4	1	1	1	25:15
2011-12	Anaheim	NHL	80	37	23	60	127	14	1	6	277	13.4	–7	48	39.6	21:23	....	....	....	....	....	....	....	....	....
2012-13	Anaheim	NHL	44	15	21	36	72	5	0	5	128	11.7	10	29	20.7	19:04	7	0	2	2	4	0	0	0	20:20
2013-14	Anaheim	NHL	81	43	39	82	65	8	0	9	280	15.4	32	25	36.0	19:29	13	4	7	11	19	2	0	0	19:41
	Canada	Olympics	6	0	1	1	2	....	....	....	....	....	....	....	....	....	....	....	....	....	....	....	....	....	....
2014-15	Anaheim	NHL	67	33	22	55	67	4	0	3	193	17.1	13	12	25.0	18:06	16	10	8	18	14	2	0	2	19:54
2015-16	Anaheim	NHL	82	34	28	62	68	12	0	6	215	15.8	2	10	20.0	17:42	7	0	4	4	6	0	0	0	17:49
2016-17	Anaheim	NHL	82	19	34	53	76	5	0	3	215	8.8	2	20	35.0	17:43	17	4	7	11	34	1	0	3	17:52
	NHL Totals		886	349	368	717	1012	97	6	62	2643	13.2		273	31.1	18:16	114	36	53	89	178	9	1	8	18:14

OHL First All-Star Team (2004, 2005) • Canadian Major Junior Second All-Star Team (2004) • Canadian Major Junior First All-Star Team (2005) • OHL Playoff MVP (2005) • NHL First All-Star Team (2011, 2014) • Maurice "Rocket" Richard Trophy (2011) • Hart Memorial Trophy (2011)

Played in NHL All-Star Game (2008, 2011, 2012, 2016)

PESCE, Brett

(PEH-SHEE, BREHT) **CAR**

Defense. Shoots right. 6'3", 200 lbs. Born, Tarrytown, NY, November 15, 1994. Carolina's 2nd pick, 66th overall, in 2013 NHL Draft.

Season	Club	League	GP	G	A	Pts	PIM	PP	SH	GW	S	S%	+/-	TF	F%	Min	GP	G	A	Pts	PIM	PP	SH	GW	Min
2011-12	Jersey Hitmen	EJHL	17	1	5	6	18	....	....	....	....	....	....	....	....	....	....	....	....	....	....	....	....	....	....
	USAHNTDP	U-18	6	0	0	0	2	....	....	....	....	....	....	....	....	....	....	....	....	....	....	....	....	....	....
2012-13	New Hampshire	H-East	38	1	5	6	10	....	....	....	....	....	....	....	....	....	....	....	....	....	....	....	....	....	....
2013-14	New Hampshire	H-East	41	7	14	21	6	....	....	....	....	....	....	....	....	....	....	....	....	....	....	....	....	....	....
2014-15	New Hampshire	H-East	31	3	13	16	32	....	....	....	....	....	....	....	....	....	....	....	....	....	....	....	....	....	....
	Charlotte	AHL	4	0	1	1	6	....	....	....	....	....	....	....	....	....	....	....	....	....	....	....	....	....	....
2015-16	Carolina	NHL	69	4	12	16	16	1	0	1	85	4.7	–7	1	0.0	18:46	....	....	....	....	....	....	....	....	....
	Charlotte	AHL	3	1	2	3	0	....	....	....	....	....	....	....	....	....	....	....	....	....	....	....	....	....	....
2016-17	Carolina	NHL	82	2	18	20	20	0	0	0	109	1.8	23	0	0.0	21:12	....	....	....	....	....	....	....	....	....
	NHL Totals		151	6	30	36	36	1	0	1	194	3.1		1	0.0	20:05	....	....	....	....	....	....	....	....	....

PETAN, Nic

(peh-TAN, NIHK) **WPG**

Center. Shoots left. 5'9", 179 lbs. Born, Delta, BC, March 22, 1995. Winnipeg's 2nd pick, 43rd overall, in 2013 NHL Draft.

Season	Club	League	GP	G	A	Pts	PIM	PP	SH	GW	S	S%	+/-	TF	F%	Min	GP	G	A	Pts	PIM	PP	SH	GW	Min
2010-11	Greater Van.	BCMML	35	19	30	49	36	....	....	....	....	....	....	....	....	....	6	3	3	6	18	....	....	....	....
	Portland	WHL	3	0	1	1	0	....	....	....	....	....	....	....	....	....	7	0	0	0	0	....	....	....	....
2011-12	Portland	WHL	61	14	21	35	22	....	....	....	....	....	....	....	....	....	22	0	0	0	4	....	....	....	....
2012-13	Portland	WHL	71	46	*74	*120	43	....	....	....	....	....	....	....	....	....	21	9	*19	28	16	....	....	....	....
2013-14	Portland	WHL	63	35	*78	113	69	....	....	....	....	....	....	....	....	....	21	7	21	28	38	....	....	....	....
2014-15	Portland	WHL	54	15	74	89	41	....	....	....	....	....	....	....	....	....	17	10	18	28	20	....	....	....	....
2015-16	Winnipeg	NHL	26	2	4	6	10	0	0	0	25	8.0	2	21	57.1	11:45	....	....	....	....	....	....	....	....	....
	Manitoba Moose	AHL	47	9	23	32	26	....	....	....	....	....	....	....	....	....	....	....	....	....	....	....	....	....	....
2016-17	Winnipeg	NHL	54	1	12	13	12	0	0	0	57	1.8	–13	315	46.0	10:54	....	....	....	....	....	....	....	....	....
	Manitoba Moose	AHL	9	4	1	5	4	....	....	....	....	....	....	....	....	....	....	....	....	....	....	....	....	....	....
	NHL Totals		80	3	16	19	22	0	0	0	82	3.7		336	46.7	11:11	....	....	....	....	....	....	....	....	....

WHL West First All-Star Team (2013, 2014) • WHL West Second All-Star Team (2015)

PETROVIC, Alex

(peh-TROH-vihk, AL-ehx) **FLA**

Defense. Shoots right. 6'4", 206 lbs. Born, Edmonton, AB, March 3, 1992. Florida's 5th pick, 36th overall, in 2010 NHL Draft.

Season	Club	League	GP	G	A	Pts	PIM	PP	SH	GW	S	S%	+/-	TF	F%	Min	GP	G	A	Pts	PIM	PP	SH	GW	Min
2007-08	Edmonton MLAC	AMHL	31	3	8	11	80	....	....	....	....	....	....	....	....	....	....	....	....	....	....	....	....	....	....
	Red Deer Rebels	WHL	10	1	0	1	2	....	....	....	....	....	....	....	....	....	....	....	....	....	....	....	....	....	....
2008-09	Red Deer Rebels	WHL	66	1	12	13	70	....	....	....	....	....	....	....	....	....	....	....	....	....	....	....	....	....	....
2009-10	Red Deer Rebels	WHL	57	8	19	27	87	....	....	....	....	....	....	....	....	....	4	0	0	0	4	....	....	....	....
2010-11	Red Deer Rebels	WHL	69	7	50	57	140	....	....	....	....	....	....	....	....	....	9	0	6	6	23	....	....	....	....
2011-12	Red Deer Rebels	WHL	68	12	36	48	141	....	....	....	....	....	....	....	....	....	....	....	....	....	....	....	....	....	....
	San Antonio	AHL	5	0	1	1	0	....	....	....	....	....	....	....	....	....	9	2	4	6	14	....	....	....	....
2012-13	San Antonio	AHL	55	4	13	17	102	....	....	....	....	....	....	....	....	....	....	....	....	....	....	....	....	....	....
	Florida	NHL	6	0	0	0	25	0	0	0	5	0.0	–8	0	0.0	18:47	....	....	....	....	....	....	....	....	....
2013-14	Florida	NHL	7	0	1	1	8	0	0	0	4	0.0	3	0	0.0	12:14	....	....	....	....	....	....	....	....	....
	San Antonio	AHL	43	2	11	13	79	....	....	....	....	....	....	....	....	....	....	....	....	....	....	....	....	....	....
2014-15	Florida	NHL	33	0	3	3	34	0	0	0	29	0.0	–4	0	0.0	16:16	....	....	....	....	....	....	....	....	....
	San Antonio	AHL	41	3	17	20	59	....	....	....	....	....	....	....	....	....	3	0	1	1	0	....	....	....	....
2015-16	Florida	NHL	66	2	15	17	90	0	0	0	53	3.8	17	0	0.0	16:57	6	1	3	4	4	0	0	1	19:55
2016-17	Florida	NHL	49	1	13	14	79	0	0	0	55	1.8	–1	0	0.0	18:09	....	....	....	....	....	....	....	....	....
	NHL Totals		161	3	32	35	236	0	0	0	146	2.1		0	0.0	17:02	6	1	3	4	4	0	0	1	19:55

WHL East Second All-Star Team (2011) • WHL East First All-Star Team (2012) • WHL Defenseman of the Year (2012)

PETRY, Jeff

(PEH-tree, JEHF) **MTL**

Defense. Shoots right. 6'3", 204 lbs. Born, Ann Arbor, MI, December 9, 1987. Edmonton's 1st pick, 45th overall, in 2006 NHL Draft.

Season	Club	League	GP	G	A	Pts	PIM	PP	SH	GW	S	S%	+/-	TF	F%	Min	GP	G	A	Pts	PIM	PP	SH	GW	Min
2004-05	St. Mary's Prep	High-MI	23	2	8	10	....	....	....	....	....	....	....	....	....	....	6	2	5	7	....	....	....	....	....
2005-06	Det. Caesers	MWEHL	33	7	21	28	24	....	....	....	....	....	....	....	....	....	....	....	....	....	....	....	....	....	....
	Des Moines	USHL	48	1	14	15	68	....	....	....	....	....	....	....	....	....	11	2	5	7	8	....	....	....	....
2006-07	Des Moines	USHL	55	18	27	45	71	....	....	....	....	....	....	....	....	....	8	0	6	6	10	....	....	....	....
2007-08	Michigan State	CCHA	42	3	21	24	28	....	....	....	....	....	....	....	....	....	....	....	....	....	....	....	....	....	....
2008-09	Michigan State	CCHA	38	2	12	14	32	....	....	....	....	....	....	....	....	....	....	....	....	....	....	....	....	....	....
2009-10	Michigan State	CCHA	38	4	25	29	26	....	....	....	....	....	....	....	....	....	....	....	....	....	....	....	....	....	....
	Springfield	AHL	8	0	3	3	2	....	....	....	....	....	....	....	....	....	....	....	....	....	....	....	....	....	....
2010-11	Edmonton	NHL	35	1	4	5	10	0	0	0	41	2.4	–12	0	0.0	20:22	....	....	....	....	....	....	....	....	....
	Oklahoma City	AHL	41	7	17	24	18	....	....	....	....	....	....	....	....	....	6	0	1	1	4	....	....	....	....
2011-12	Edmonton	NHL	73	2	23	25	26	1	0	0	111	1.8	–7	0	0.0	21:46	....	....	....	....	....	....	....	....	....
	Oklahoma City	AHL	2	0	1	1	2	....	....	....	....	....	....	....	....	....	....	....	....	....	....	....	....	....	....

			Regular Season														Playoffs								
Season	Club	League	GP	G	A	Pts	PIM	PP	SH	GW	S	S%	+/-	TF	F%	Min	GP	G	A	Pts	PIM	PP	SH	GW	Min
2012-13	**Edmonton**	**NHL**	**48**	**3**	**9**	**12**	**29**	**0**	**1**	**0**	**66**	**4.5**	**1**	**1**	**0.0**	**21:55**	....	....	....	....	....	....	....	....	....
2013-14	**Edmonton**	**NHL**	**80**	**7**	**10**	**17**	**42**	**1**	**0**	**0**	**96**	**7.3**	**–22**	**0**	**0.0**	**21:35**	....	....	....	....	....	....	....	....	....
2014-15	**Edmonton**	**NHL**	**59**	**4**	**11**	**15**	**32**	**1**	**0**	**1**	**103**	**3.9**	**–25**	**0**	**0.0**	**20:57**	....	....	....	....	....	....	....	....	....
	Montreal	**NHL**	**19**	**3**	**4**	**7**	**10**	**0**	**0**	**0**	**23**	**13.0**	**–3**	**0**	**0.0**	**22:11**	**12**	**2**	**1**	**3**	**4**	**1**	**0**	**0**	**22:17**
2015-16	**Montreal**	**NHL**	**51**	**5**	**11**	**16**	**16**	**1**	**0**	**2**	**98**	**5.1**	**–6**	**1**	**100.0**	**21:21**	....	....	....	....	....	....	....	....	....
2016-17	**Montreal**	**NHL**	**80**	**8**	**20**	**28**	**22**	**2**	**0**	**1**	**172**	**4.7**	**3**	**0**	**0.0**	**22:07**	**6**	**1**	**0**	**1**	**2**	**0**	**0**	**0**	**24:44**
	NHL Totals		**445**	**33**	**92**	**125**	**187**	**6**	**1**	**4**	**710**	**4.6**		**2**	**50.0**	**21:34**	**18**	**3**	**1**	**4**	**6**	**1**	**0**	**0**	**23:06**

USHL First All-Star Team (2007) • USHL Defenseman of the Year (2007) • CCHA All-Rookie Team (2008) • CCHA Second All-Star Team (2010) • NCAA West Second All-American Team (2010)

Traded to **Montreal** by **Edmonton** for Montreal's 2nd (later traded to NY Rangers, later traded to Washington – Washington selected Jonas Siegenthaler) and 4th (Caleb Jones) round picks in 2015 NHL Draft, March 2, 2015.

PHANEUF, Dion (fah-NUF, DEE-awn) OTT

Defense. Shoots left. 6'3", 227 lbs. Born, Edmonton, AB, April 10, 1985. Calgary's 1st pick, 9th overall, in 2003 NHL Draft.

Season	Club	League	GP	G	A	Pts	PIM	PP	SH	GW	S	S%	+/-	TF	F%	Min	GP	G	A	Pts	PIM	PP	SH	GW	Min
2000-01	Southgate	AMBHL	35	15	50	65	208	....	....	....	....	....	....	....	....	....	4	3	4	7	15	....	....	....	....
2001-02	Red Deer Rebels	WHL	67	5	12	17	170	....	....	....	....	....	....	....	....	....	21	0	2	2	14	....	....	....	....
2002-03	Red Deer Rebels	WHL	71	16	14	30	185	....	....	....	....	....	....	....	....	....	23	7	7	14	34	....	....	....	....
2003-04	Red Deer Rebels	WHL	62	19	24	43	126	....	....	....	....	....	....	....	....	....	19	2	9	11	30	....	....	....	....
2004-05	Red Deer Rebels	WHL	55	24	32	56	73	....	....	....	....	....	....	....	....	....	7	1	4	5	12	....	....	....	....
2005-06	**Calgary**	**NHL**	**82**	**20**	**29**	**49**	**93**	**16**	**0**	**7**	**242**	**8.3**	**5**	**0**	**0.0**	**21:44**	**7**	**1**	**0**	**1**	**7**	**1**	**0**	**0**	**18:37**
2006-07	**Calgary**	**NHL**	**79**	**17**	**33**	**50**	**98**	**13**	**0**	**4**	**230**	**7.4**	**10**	**0**	**0.0**	**25:40**	**6**	**1**	**0**	**1**	**7**	**1**	**0**	**0**	**26:24**
2007-08	**Calgary**	**NHL**	**82**	**17**	**43**	**60**	**182**	**10**	**1**	**4**	**263**	**6.5**	**12**	**0**	**0.0**	**26:25**	**7**	**3**	**4**	**7**	**4**	**1**	**0**	**0**	**27:07**
2008-09	**Calgary**	**NHL**	**80**	**11**	**36**	**47**	**100**	**4**	**0**	**4**	**277**	**4.0**	**–11**	**0**	**0.0**	**26:32**	**5**	**0**	**3**	**3**	**4**	**0**	**0**	**0**	**24:48**
2009-10	**Calgary**	**NHL**	**55**	**10**	**12**	**22**	**49**	**5**	**0**	**2**	**138**	**7.2**	**3**	**0**	**0.0**	**23:14**	....	....	....	....	....	....	....	....	....
	Toronto	**NHL**	**26**	**2**	**8**	**10**	**34**	**0**	**0**	**1**	**87**	**2.3**	**–2**	**0**	**0.0**	**26:22**	....	....	....	....	....	....	....	....	....
2010-11	**Toronto**	**NHL**	**66**	**8**	**22**	**30**	**88**	**3**	**0**	**1**	**190**	**4.2**	**–2**	**0**	**0.0**	**25:18**	....	....	....	....	....	....	....	....	....
2011-12	**Toronto**	**NHL**	**82**	**12**	**32**	**44**	**92**	**7**	**0**	**1**	**202**	**5.9**	**–10**	**0**	**0.0**	**25:17**	....	....	....	....	....	....	....	....	....
2012-13	**Toronto**	**NHL**	**48**	**9**	**19**	**28**	**65**	**3**	**0**	**1**	**88**	**10.2**	**–4**	**0**	**0.0**	**25:11**	**7**	**1**	**2**	**3**	**6**	**0**	**0**	**0**	**25:22**
2013-14	**Toronto**	**NHL**	**80**	**8**	**23**	**31**	**144**	**2**	**0**	**0**	**145**	**5.5**	**2**	**1**	**0.0**	**23:34**	....	....	....	....	....	....	....	....	....
2014-15	**Toronto**	**NHL**	**70**	**3**	**26**	**29**	**108**	**2**	**0**	**1**	**138**	**2.2**	**–11**	**0**	**0.0**	**23:43**	....	....	....	....	....	....	....	....	....
2015-16	**Toronto**	**NHL**	**51**	**3**	**21**	**24**	**67**	**0**	**0**	**0**	**116**	**2.6**	**–4**	**0**	**0.0**	**22:02**	....	....	....	....	....	....	....	....	....
	Ottawa	**NHL**	**20**	**1**	**7**	**8**	**23**	**0**	**0**	**0**	**28**	**3.6**	**–3**	**0**	**0.0**	**23:10**	....	....	....	....	....	....	....	....	....
2016-17	**Ottawa**	**NHL**	**81**	**9**	**21**	**30**	**100**	**4**	**1**	**2**	**156**	**5.8**	**–6**	**0**	**0.0**	**23:02**	**19**	**1**	**4**	**5**	**17**	**0**	**0**	**1**	**23:18**
	NHL Totals		**902**	**130**	**332**	**462**	**1243**	**69**	**2**	**28**	**2300**	**5.7**		**1**	**0.0**	**24:24**	**51**	**7**	**13**	**20**	**45**	**3**	**0**	**1**	**23:59**

WHL East First All-Star Team (2004, 2005) • WHL Defenseman of the Year (2004, 2005) • Canadian Major Junior First All-Star Team (2004, 2005) • NHL All-Rookie Team (2006) • NHL First All-Star Team (2008)

Played in NHL All-Star Game (2007, 2008, 2012)

Traded to **Toronto** by **Calgary** with Fredrik Sjostrom and Keith Aulie for Matt Stajan, Niklas Hagman, Jamal Mayers and Ian White, January 31, 2010. Traded to **Ottawa** by **Toronto** with Matt Frattin, Casey Bailey, Ryan Rupert and Cody Donaghey for Jared Cowen, Colin Greening, Milan Michalek, Tobias Lindberg and Ottawa's 2nd round pick (Eemeli Rasanen) in 2017 NHL Draft, February 9, 2016.

PIETILA, Blake (pee-EH-tihl-a, BLAYK) N.J.

Left wing. Shoots left. 5'11", 200 lbs. Born, Milford, MI, February 20, 1993. New Jersey's 5th pick, 129th overall, in 2011 NHL Draft.

Season	Club	League	GP	G	A	Pts	PIM	PP	SH	GW	S	S%	+/-	TF	F%	Min	GP	G	A	Pts	PIM	PP	SH	GW	Min
2008-09	Det. Compuware	T1EHL	31	8	11	19	8	....	....	....	....	....	....	....	....	....	5	1	5	6	0	....	....	....	....
2009-10	USAHNTDP	USHL	28	5	3	8	27	....	....	....	....	....	....	....	....	....	....	....	....	....	....	....	....	....	....
	USAHNTDP	U-17	18	1	6	7	10	....	....	....	....	....	....	....	....	....	....	....	....	....	....	....	....	....	....
	USAHNTDP	U-18	1	0	0	0	0	....	....	....	....	....	....	....	....	....	....	....	....	....	....	....	....	....	....
2010-11	USAHNTDP	USHL	24	4	5	9	20	....	....	....	....	....	....	....	....	....	....	....	....	....	....	....	....	....	....
	USAHNTDP	U-18	13	10	4	14	33	....	....	....	....	....	....	....	....	....	....	....	....	....	....	....	....	....	....
2011-12	Michigan Tech	WCHA	39	10	14	24	46	....	....	....	....	....	....	....	....	....	....	....	....	....	....	....	....	....	....
2012-13	Michigan Tech	WCHA	35	14	10	24	44	....	....	....	....	....	....	....	....	....	....	....	....	....	....	....	....	....	....
2013-14	Michigan Tech	WCHA	39	8	20	28	84	....	....	....	....	....	....	....	....	....	....	....	....	....	....	....	....	....	....
2014-15	Michigan Tech	WCHA	40	14	16	30	56	....	....	....	....	....	....	....	....	....	....	....	....	....	....	....	....	....	....
2015-16	**New Jersey**	**NHL**	**7**	**1**	**1**	**2**	**2**	**0**	**0**	**0**	**10**	**10.0**	**0**	**0**	**0.0**	**12:02**	....	....	....	....	....	....	....	....	....
	Albany Devils	AHL	58	10	7	17	41	....	....	....	....	....	....	....	....	....	8	3	3	6	8	....	....	....	....
2016-17	**New Jersey**	**NHL**	**10**	**0**	**1**	**1**	**4**	**0**	**0**	**0**	**9**	**0.0**	**–5**	**45**	**51.1**	**13:02**	....	....	....	....	....	....	....	....	....
	Albany Devils	AHL	49	17	16	33	38	....	....	....	....	....	....	....	....	....	4	0	2	2	0	....	....	....	....
	NHL Totals		**17**	**1**	**2**	**3**	**6**	**0**	**0**	**0**	**19**	**5.3**		**45**	**51.1**	**12:37**	....	....	....	....	....	....	....	....	....

PIETRANGELO, Alex (puh-TRAN-geh-loh, AL-ehx) ST.L.

Defense. Shoots right. 6'3", 210 lbs. Born, King City, ON, January 18, 1990. St. Louis' 1st pick, 4th overall, in 2008 NHL Draft.

Season	Club	League	GP	G	A	Pts	PIM	PP	SH	GW	S	S%	+/-	TF	F%	Min	GP	G	A	Pts	PIM	PP	SH	GW	Min
2005-06	Tor. Jr. Canadiens	GTHL	44	13	31	44	33	....	....	....	....	....	....	....	....	....	....	....	....	....	....	....	....	....	....
2006-07	Mississauga	OHL	59	7	45	52	45	....	....	....	....	....	....	....	....	....	4	0	0	0	8	....	....	....	....
2007-08	Niagara Ice Dogs	OHL	60	13	40	53	94	....	....	....	....	....	....	....	....	....	6	5	4	9	4	....	....	....	....
2008-09	Niagara Ice Dogs	OHL	36	8	21	29	32	....	....	....	....	....	....	....	....	....	12	1	5	6	20	....	....	....	....
	St. Louis	**NHL**	**8**	**0**	**1**	**1**	**2**	**0**	**0**	**0**	**7**	**0.0**	**0**	**0**	**0.0**	**16:31**	....	....	....	....	....	....	....	....	....
	Peoria Rivermen	AHL	1	0	0	0	4	....	....	....	....	....	....	....	....	....	7	0	3	3	2	....	....	....	....
2009-10	**St. Louis**	**NHL**	**9**	**1**	**1**	**2**	**6**	**0**	**0**	**0**	**7**	**14.3**	**–9**	**0**	**0.0**	**16:34**	....	....	....	....	....	....	....	....	....
	Barrie Colts	OHL	25	9	20	29	27	....	....	....	....	....	....	....	....	....	17	2	12	14	8	....	....	....	....
2010-11	**St. Louis**	**NHL**	**79**	**11**	**32**	**43**	**19**	**4**	**0**	**1**	**161**	**6.8**	**18**	**0**	**0.0**	**22:00**	....	....	....	....	....	....	....	....	....
2011-12	**St. Louis**	**NHL**	**81**	**12**	**39**	**51**	**36**	**6**	**0**	**6**	**202**	**5.9**	**16**	**0**	**0.0**	**24:44**	**8**	**0**	**5**	**5**	**0**	**0**	**0**	**0**	**25:26**
2012-13	**St. Louis**	**NHL**	**47**	**5**	**19**	**24**	**10**	**2**	**0**	**0**	**93**	**5.4**	**0**	**0**	**0.0**	**25:07**	**6**	**1**	**1**	**2**	**2**	**0**	**0**	**0**	**26:34**
2013-14	**St. Louis**	**NHL**	**81**	**8**	**43**	**51**	**32**	**2**	**0**	**1**	**164**	**4.9**	**20**	**0**	**0.0**	**25:22**	**6**	**1**	**2**	**3**	**0**	**0**	**0**	**0**	**30:15**
	Canada	Olympics	6	0	1	1	0	....	....	....	....	....	....	....	....	....	....	....	....	....	....	....	....	....	....
2014-15	**St. Louis**	**NHL**	**81**	**7**	**39**	**46**	**28**	**1**	**0**	**2**	**195**	**3.6**	**–2**	**0**	**0.0**	**25:25**	**6**	**0**	**2**	**2**	**0**	**0**	**0**	**0**	**26:48**
2015-16	**St. Louis**	**NHL**	**73**	**7**	**30**	**37**	**20**	**1**	**0**	**1**	**182**	**3.8**	**10**	**0**	**0.0**	**26:18**	**20**	**2**	**8**	**10**	**16**	**0**	**0**	**0**	**28:48**
2016-17	**St. Louis**	**NHL**	**80**	**14**	**34**	**48**	**24**	**6**	**0**	**4**	**181**	**7.7**	**3**	**1**	**0.0**	**25:17**	**11**	**0**	**4**	**4**	**8**	**0**	**0**	**0**	**28:16**
	NHL Totals		**539**	**65**	**238**	**303**	**177**	**22**	**0**	**15**	**1192**	**5.5**		**1**	**0.0**	**24:36**	**57**	**4**	**22**	**26**	**26**	**0**	**0**	**0**	**27:56**

NHL Second All-Star Team (2012, 2014)

• Missed majority of 2009-10 as a healthy reserve.

PIRRI, Brandon (PIHR-ee, BRAN-duhn) NYR

Center. Shoots left. 6', 183 lbs. Born, Toronto, ON, April 10, 1991. Chicago's 2nd pick, 59th overall, in 2009 NHL Draft.

Season	Club	League	GP	G	A	Pts	PIM	PP	SH	GW	S	S%	+/-	TF	F%	Min	GP	G	A	Pts	PIM	PP	SH	GW	Min
2006-07	Tor. Young Nats	GTHL	44	54	72	128	18	....	....	....	....	....	....	....	....	....	....	....	....	....	....	....	....	....	....
2007-08	Streetsville Derbys	ON-Jr.A	40	18	32	50	42	....	....	....	....	....	....	....	....	....	....	....	....	....	....	....	....	....	....
2008-09	Streetsville Derbys	ON-Jr.A	18	21	28	49	24	....	....	....	....	....	....	....	....	....	....	....	....	....	....	....	....	....	....
	Georgetown	ON-Jr.A	26	25	20	45	22	....	....	....	....	....	....	....	....	....	14	8	13	21	10	....	....	....	....
2009-10	RPI Engineers	ECAC	39	11	*32	43	67	....	....	....	....	....	....	....	....	....	....	....	....	....	....	....	....	....	....
2010-11	**Chicago**	**NHL**	**1**	**0**	**0**	**0**	**0**	**0**	**0**	**0**	**1**	**0.0**	**–1**	**6**	**33.3**	**8:56**	....	....	....	....	....	....	....	....	....
	Rockford IceHogs	AHL	70	12	31	43	50	....	....	....	....	....	....	....	....	....	....	....	....	....	....	....	....	....	....
2011-12	**Chicago**	**NHL**	**5**	**0**	**2**	**2**	**0**	**0**	**0**	**0**	**5**	**0.0**	**2**	**54**	**48.2**	**13:31**	....	....	....	....	....	....	....	....	....
	Rockford IceHogs	AHL	66	23	33	56	36	....	....	....	....	....	....	....	....	....	....	....	....	....	....	....	....	....	....
2012-13	Rockford IceHogs	AHL	76	22	*53	*75	72	....	....	....	....	....	....	....	....	....	....	....	....	....	....	....	....	....	....
	Chicago	**NHL**	**1**	**0**	**0**	**0**	**0**	**0**	**0**	**0**	**2**	**0.0**	**0**	**14**	**42.9**	**17:55**	....	....	....	....	....	....	....	....	....
2013-14	**Chicago**	**NHL**	**28**	**6**	**5**	**11**	**6**	**1**	**0**	**0**	**34**	**17.6**	**6**	**247**	**42.9**	**12:15**	....	....	....	....	....	....	....	....	....
	Rockford IceHogs	AHL	26	11	15	26	10	....	....	....	....	....	....	....	....	....	....	....	....	....	....	....	....	....	....
	Florida	**NHL**	**21**	**7**	**7**	**14**	**2**	**2**	**0**	**0**	**46**	**15.2**	**0**	**207**	**47.3**	**13:56**	....	....	....	....	....	....	....	....	....
2014-15	**Florida**	**NHL**	**49**	**22**	**2**	**24**	**14**	**7**	**0**	**4**	**143**	**15.4**	**6**	**175**	**49.1**	**14:46**	....	....	....	....	....	....	....	....	....

			Regular Season														Playoffs								
Season	Club	League	GP	G	A	Pts	PIM	PP	SH	GW	S	S%	+/-	TF	F%	Min	GP	G	A	Pts	PIM	PP	SH	GW	Min
2015-16	**Florida**	**NHL**	**52**	**11**	**13**	**24**	**30**	**3**	**0**	**2**	**111**	**9.9**	**–4**	**141**	**46.8**	**14:50**	....	....	....	....	....	....	....	....	....
	Anaheim	**NHL**	**9**	**3**	**2**	**5**	**0**	**0**	**0**	**1**	**17**	**17.6**	**0**	**2**	**0.0**	**12:44**	....	....	....	....	....	....	....	....	....
2016-17	**NY Rangers**	**NHL**	**60**	**8**	**10**	**18**	**25**	**5**	**0**	**3**	**96**	**8.3**	**–8**	**243**	**57.6**	**12:17**	....	....	....	....	....	....	....	....	....
	NHL Totals		**226**	**57**	**41**	**98**	**77**	**18**	**0**	**10**	**455**	**12.5**		**1089**	**48.7**	**13:37**	....	....	....	....	....	....	....	....	....

ECAC All-Rookie Team (2010) • John P. Sollenberger Trophy (AHL - Top Scorer) (2013)

Traded to **Florida** by **Chicago** for Florida's 3rd round pick (later traded to Nashville – Nashville selected Justin Kirkland) in 2014 NHL Draft and Florida's 5th round pick (later traded to St. Louis – St. Louis selected Conner Bleackley) in 2016 NHL Draft, March 2, 2014. Traded to **Anaheim** by **Florida** for Anaheim's 6th round pick (Maxim Mamin) in 2016 NHL Draft, February 29, 2016. Signed as a free agent by **NY Rangers**, August 25, 2016.

PITLICK, Tyler (PIHT-lihk, TIGH-luhr) DAL

Center. Shoots right. 6', 202 lbs. Born, Minneapolis, MN, November 1, 1991. Edmonton's 2nd pick, 31st overall, in 2010 NHL Draft.

Season	Club	League	GP	G	A	Pts	PIM	PP	SH	GW	S	S%	+/-	TF	F%	Min	GP	G	A	Pts	PIM	PP	SH	GW	Min
2007-08	Centennial	High-MN	....	25	34	59	....	....	....	....	....	....	....	....	....	....	....	....	....	....	....	....	....	....	....
2008-09	Centennial	High-MN	25	31	33	64	....	....	....	....	....	....	....	....	....	....	....	....	....	....	....	....	....	....	....
2009-10	Minnesota State	WCHA	38	11	8	19	27	....	....	....	....	....	....	....	....	....	....	....	....	....	....	....	....	....	....
2010-11	Medicine Hat	WHL	56	27	35	62	31	....	....	....	....	....	....	....	....	....	....	....	....	....	....	....	....	....	....
2011-12	Oklahoma City	AHL	62	7	16	23	28	....	....	....	....	....	....	....	....	....	13	2	5	7	2	....	....	....	....
2012-13	Oklahoma City	AHL	44	3	7	10	10	....	....	....	....	....	....	....	....	....	16	2	4	6	8	....	....	....	....
2013-14	**Edmonton**	**NHL**	**10**	**1**	**0**	**1**	**0**	**0**	**0**	**0**	**9**	**11.1**	**–2**	**3**	**33.3**	**8:58**	....	....	....	....	....	....	....	....	....
	Oklahoma City	AHL	39	8	14	22	10	....	....	....	....	....	....	....	....	....	2	0	0	0	0	....	....	....	....
2014-15	**Edmonton**	**NHL**	**17**	**2**	**0**	**2**	**4**	**0**	**0**	**1**	**18**	**11.1**	**–3**	**9**	**55.6**	**12:27**	....	....	....	....	....	....	....	....	....
	Oklahoma City	AHL	14	3	6	9	8	....	....	....	....	....	....	....	....	....	....	....	....	....	....	....	....	....	....
2015-16	Bakersfield	AHL	37	7	14	21	4	....	....	....	....	....	....	....	....	....	....	....	....	....	....	....	....	....	....
2016-17	**Edmonton**	**NHL**	**31**	**8**	**3**	**11**	**6**	**0**	**0**	**1**	**54**	**14.8**	**0**	**15**	**53.3**	**9:55**	....	....	....	....	....	....	....	....	....
	NHL Totals		**58**	**11**	**3**	**14**	**10**	**0**	**0**	**2**	**81**	**13.6**		**27**	**51.9**	**10:30**	....	....	....	....	....	....	....	....	....

• Missed majority of 2014-15 due to spleen injury at Calgary, December 31, 2014. • Missed majority of 2015-16 and 2016-17 due to various injuries and as a healthy reserve. Signed as a free agent by **Dallas**, July 1, 2017.

PLEKANEC, Tomas (pleh-KA-nehts, TAW-muhs) MTL

Left wing. Shoots left. 5'11", 196 lbs. Born, Kladno, Czech., October 31, 1982. Montreal's 4th pick, 71st overall, in 2001 NHL Draft.

Season	Club	League	GP	G	A	Pts	PIM	PP	SH	GW	S	S%	+/-	TF	F%	Min	GP	G	A	Pts	PIM	PP	SH	GW	Min
1996-97	Kladno U17	CzR-U17	13	1	3	4	....	....	....	....	....	....	....	....	....	....	....	....	....	....	....	....	....	....	....
1997-98	HC Kladno U17	CzR-U17	45	38	26	64	....	....	....	....	....	....	....	....	....	....	....	....	....	....	....	....	....	....	....
1998-99	HC Kladno Jr.	CzRep-Jr.	53	22	20	42	....	....	....	....	....	....	....	....	....	....	....	....	....	....	....	....	....	....	....
99-2000	HC Kladno Jr.	CzRep-Jr.	43	14	16	30	....	....	....	....	....	....	....	....	....	....	....	....	....	....	....	....	....	....	....
	Kralupy	CzRep-3	6	2	2	4	2	....	....	....	....	....	....	....	....	....	....	....	....	....	....	....	....	....	....
	HC CKD Slany	CzRep-3	3	0	1	1	6	....	....	....	....	....	....	....	....	....	....	....	....	....	....	....	....	....	....
2000-01	Kladno	CzRep	47	9	9	18	24	....	....	....	....	....	....	....	....	....	....	....	....	....	....	....	....	....	....
	HC Kladno Jr.	CzRep-Jr.	9	6	4	10	4	....	....	....	....	....	....	....	....	....	....	....	....	....	....	....	....	....	....
2001-02	Kladno	CzRep	48	7	16	23	28	....	....	....	....	....	....	....	....	....	....	....	....	....	....	....	....	....	....
	BK Mlada Boleslav	CzRep-3	6	6	3	9	14	....	....	....	....	....	....	....	....	....	....	....	....	....	....	....	....	....	....
	Kladno	CzRep-Q	5	0	1	1	0	....	....	....	....	....	....	....	....	....	....	....	....	....	....	....	....	....	....
2002-03	Hamilton	AHL	77	19	27	46	74	....	....	....	....	....	....	....	....	....	13	3	2	5	8	....	....	....	....
2003-04	**Montreal**	**NHL**	**2**	**0**	**0**	**0**	**0**	**0**	**0**	**0**	**0**	**0.0**	**0**	**11**	**45.5**	**9:02**	....	....	....	....	....	....	....	....	....
	Hamilton	AHL	74	23	43	66	90	....	....	....	....	....	....	....	....	....	10	2	5	7	6	....	....	....	....
2004-05	Hamilton	AHL	80	29	35	64	68	....	....	....	....	....	....	....	....	....	4	2	4	6	6	....	....	....	....
2005-06	**Montreal**	**NHL**	**67**	**9**	**20**	**29**	**32**	**1**	**0**	**0**	**99**	**9.1**	**4**	**708**	**50.3**	**13:15**	**6**	**0**	**4**	**4**	**6**	**0**	**0**	**0**	**18:00**
	Hamilton	AHL	2	0	0	0	2	....	....	....	....	....	....	....	....	....	....	....	....	....	....	....	....	....	....
2006-07	**Montreal**	**NHL**	**81**	**20**	**27**	**47**	**36**	**5**	**2**	**1**	**150**	**13.3**	**10**	**1159**	**48.3**	**15:59**	....	....	....	....	....	....	....	....	....
2007-08	**Montreal**	**NHL**	**81**	**29**	**40**	**69**	**42**	**12**	**2**	**6**	**186**	**15.6**	**15**	**1381**	**49.5**	**18:05**	**12**	**4**	**5**	**9**	**2**	**2**	**0**	**0**	**18:02**
2008-09	**Montreal**	**NHL**	**80**	**20**	**19**	**39**	**54**	**6**	**3**	**2**	**202**	**9.9**	**–9**	**1351**	**50.6**	**17:15**	**3**	**0**	**0**	**0**	**4**	**0**	**0**	**0**	**13:36**
2009-10	**Montreal**	**NHL**	**82**	**25**	**45**	**70**	**50**	**3**	**1**	**4**	**216**	**11.6**	**5**	**1615**	**49.0**	**19:58**	**19**	**4**	**7**	**11**	**20**	**1**	**0**	**1**	**19:57**
	Czech Republic	Olympics	5	2	1	3	2	....	....	....	....	....	....	....	....	....	....	....	....	....	....	....	....	....	....
2010-11	**Montreal**	**NHL**	**77**	**22**	**35**	**57**	**60**	**3**	**1**	**4**	**227**	**9.7**	**8**	**1577**	**50.0**	**20:15**	**7**	**2**	**3**	**5**	**2**	**0**	**1**	**0**	**23:20**
2011-12	**Montreal**	**NHL**	**81**	**17**	**35**	**52**	**56**	**5**	**3**	**2**	**220**	**7.7**	**–15**	**1678**	**49.1**	**20:45**	....	....	....	....	....	....	....	....	....
2012-13	Rytiri Kladno	CzRep	32	21	25	46	38	....	....	....	....	....	....	....	....	....	....	....	....	....	....	....	....	....	....
	Montreal	**NHL**	**47**	**14**	**19**	**33**	**24**	**4**	**0**	**2**	**133**	**10.5**	**3**	**961**	**50.6**	**19:13**	**5**	**0**	**4**	**4**	**2**	**0**	**0**	**0**	**20:53**
2013-14	**Montreal**	**NHL**	**81**	**20**	**23**	**43**	**38**	**3**	**3**	**5**	**199**	**10.1**	**11**	**1713**	**48.0**	**19:47**	**17**	**4**	**5**	**9**	**8**	**0**	**0**	**1**	**20:19**
	Czech Republic	Olympics	5	1	3	4	0	....	....	....	....	....	....	....	....	....	....	....	....	....	....	....	....	....	....
2014-15	**Montreal**	**NHL**	**82**	**26**	**34**	**60**	**46**	**7**	**3**	**5**	**248**	**10.5**	**8**	**1557**	**49.9**	**19:09**	**12**	**1**	**3**	**4**	**6**	**0**	**0**	**0**	**20:23**
2015-16	**Montreal**	**NHL**	**82**	**14**	**40**	**54**	**36**	**1**	**0**	**1**	**189**	**7.4**	**4**	**1615**	**49.8**	**18:32**	....	....	....	....	....	....	....	....	....
2016-17	**Montreal**	**NHL**	**78**	**10**	**18**	**28**	**24**	**3**	**2**	**3**	**139**	**7.2**	**10**	**1352**	**51.2**	**16:49**	**6**	**1**	**2**	**3**	**0**	**0**	**0**	**0**	**18:32**
	NHL Totals		**921**	**226**	**355**	**581**	**498**	**53**	**20**	**35**	**2208**	**10.2**		**16678**	**49.6**	**18:16**	**87**	**16**	**33**	**49**	**50**	**3**	**1**	**2**	**19:42**

Signed as a free agent by **Kladno** (CzRep), September 16, 2012.

POINT, Brayden (POYNT, BRAY-duhn) T.B.

Center. Shoots right. 5'10", 160 lbs. Born, Calgary, AB, March 13, 1996. Tampa Bay's 4th pick, 79th overall, in 2014 NHL Draft.

Season	Club	League	GP	G	A	Pts	PIM	PP	SH	GW	S	S%	+/-	TF	F%	Min	GP	G	A	Pts	PIM	PP	SH	GW	Min
2009-10	Calgary Bisons	AMBHL	33	21	12	33	26	....	....	....	....	....	....	....	....	....	12	7	5	12	31	....	....	....	....
2010-11	Calgary Bisons	AMBHL	33	42	*60	*102	12	....	....	....	....	....	....	....	....	....	....	....	....	....	....	....	....	....	....
2011-12	Calgary Buffaloes	AMHL	32	19	22	41	22	....	....	....	....	....	....	....	....	....	5	1	0	1	2	....	....	....	....
	Canmore Eagles	AJHL	4	2	1	3	0	....	....	....	....	....	....	....	....	....	....	....	....	....	....	....	....	....	....
	Moose Jaw	WHL	5	1	0	1	0	....	....	....	....	....	....	....	....	....	14	7	3	10	2	....	....	....	....
2012-13	Moose Jaw	WHL	67	24	33	57	26	....	....	....	....	....	....	....	....	....	....	....	....	....	....	....	....	....	....
2013-14	Moose Jaw	WHL	72	36	55	91	53	....	....	....	....	....	....	....	....	....	....	....	....	....	....	....	....	....	....
2014-15	Moose Jaw	WHL	60	38	49	87	46	....	....	....	....	....	....	....	....	....	....	....	....	....	....	....	....	....	....
	Syracuse Crunch	AHL	9	2	2	4	2	....	....	....	....	....	....	....	....	....	2	0	0	0	0	....	....	....	....
2015-16	Moose Jaw	WHL	48	35	53	88	36	....	....	....	....	....	....	....	....	....	10	6	10	16	10	....	....	....	....
2016-17	**Tampa Bay**	**NHL**	**68**	**18**	**22**	**40**	**14**	**5**	**0**	**2**	**122**	**14.8**	**4**	**532**	**44.7**	**17:08**	....	....	....	....	....	....	....	....	....
	NHL Totals		**68**	**18**	**22**	**40**	**14**	**5**	**0**	**2**	**122**	**14.8**		**532**	**44.7**	**17:08**	....	....	....	....	....	....	....	....	....

WHL East First All-Star Team (2015, 2016)

POIRIER, Emile (p'wah-REE-ay, eh-MEEL) CGY

Left wing. Shoots left. 6'2", 196 lbs. Born, Montreal, QC, December 14, 1994. Calgary's 2nd pick, 22nd overall, in 2013 NHL Draft.

Season	Club	League	GP	G	A	Pts	PIM	PP	SH	GW	S	S%	+/-	TF	F%	Min	GP	G	A	Pts	PIM	PP	SH	GW	Min
2010-11	Laval-Montreal	QAAA	42	27	24	51	30	....	....	....	....	....	....	....	....	....	5	1	2	3	4	....	....	....	....
2011-12	Gatineau	QMJHL	67	15	25	40	53	....	....	....	....	....	....	....	....	....	4	1	0	1	8	....	....	....	....
2012-13	Gatineau	QMJHL	65	32	38	70	101	....	....	....	....	....	....	....	....	....	10	6	4	10	14	....	....	....	....
2013-14	Gatineau	QMJHL	63	43	44	87	129	....	....	....	....	....	....	....	....	....	9	7	3	10	26	....	....	....	....
	Abbotsford Heat	AHL	2	2	2	4	0	....	....	....	....	....	....	....	....	....	3	1	0	1	2	....	....	....	....
2014-15	**Calgary**	**NHL**	**6**	**0**	**1**	**1**	**0**	**0**	**0**	**0**	**2**	**0.0**	**1**	**1**	**0.0**	**7:59**	....	....	....	....	....	....	....	....	....
	Adirondack	AHL	55	19	23	42	50	....	....	....	....	....	....	....	....	....	....	....	....	....	....	....	....	....	....
2015-16	**Calgary**	**NHL**	**2**	**0**	**0**	**0**	**2**	**0**	**0**	**0**	**3**	**0.0**	**–1**	**0**	**0.0**	**13:54**	....	....	....	....	....	....	....	....	....
	Stockton Heat	AHL	60	12	17	29	51	....	....	....	....	....	....	....	....	....	....	....	....	....	....	....	....	....	....
2016-17	Stockton Heat	AHL	43	6	11	17	64	....	....	....	....	....	....	....	....	....	....	....	....	....	....	....	....	....	....
	NHL Totals		**8**	**0**	**1**	**1**	**2**	**0**	**0**	**0**	**5**	**0.0**		**1**	**0.0**	**9:28**	....	....	....	....	....	....	....	....	....

POLAK, Roman (POH-lahk, ROH-muhn)

Defense. Shoots right. 6', 237 lbs. Born, Ostrava, Czech., April 28, 1986. St. Louis' 6th pick, 180th overall, in 2004 NHL Draft.

Season	Club	League	GP	G	A	Pts	PIM	PP	SH	GW	S	S%	+/-	TF	F%	Min	GP	G	A	Pts	PIM	PP	SH	GW	Min
2001-02	HC Ostrava Jr.	CzRep-Jr.	46	4	9	13	84	....	....	....	....	....	....	....	....	....	....	....	....	....	....	....	....	....	....
2002-03	HC Ostrava Jr.	CzRep-Jr.	32	3	12	15	34	....	....	....	....	....	....	....	....	....	....	....	....	....	....	....	....	....	....
2003-04	HC Vitkovice Jr.	CzRep-Jr.	52	4	8	12	48	....	....	....	....	....	....	....	....	....	....	....	....	....	....	....	....	....	....
2004-05	Kootenay Ice	WHL	65	5	18	23	85	....	....	....	....	....	....	....	....	....	9	0	0	0	6	....	....	....	....
2005-06	HC Vitkovice Jr.	CzRep-Jr.	1	0	0	0	4	....	....	....	....	....	....	....	....	....	....	....	....	....	....	....	....	....	....
	Vitkovice	CzRep	37	0	1	1	16	....	....	....	....	....	....	....	....	....	6	0	0	0	6	....	....	....	....
2006-07	**St. Louis**	**NHL**	**19**	**0**	**0**	**0**	**6**	**0**	**0**	**0**	**13**	**0.0**	**–3**	**0**	**0.0**	**13:38**	....	....	....	....	....	....	....	....	....
	Peoria Rivermen	AHL	53	4	8	12	66	....	....	....	....	....	....	....	....	....	....	....	....	....	....	....	....	....	....

			Regular Season														Playoffs								
Season	Club	League	GP	G	A	Pts	PIM	PP	SH	GW	S	S%	+/-	TF	F%	Min	GP	G	A	Pts	PIM	PP	SH	GW	Min
2007-08	**St. Louis**	**NHL**	**6**	**0**	**1**	**1**	**0**	**0**	**0**	**0**	**2**	**0.0**	**1**	**0**	**0.0**	**11:32**	....	....	....	....	....	....	....	....	....
	Peoria Rivermen	AHL	34	0	7	7	33	....	....	....	....	....	....	....	....	....	....	....	....	....	....	....	....	....	....
2008-09	**St. Louis**	**NHL**	**69**	**1**	**14**	**15**	**45**	**0**	**0**	**1**	**73**	**1.4**	**-15**	**1**	**0.0**	**21:32**	**4**	**0**	**0**	**0**	**0**	**0**	**0**	**0**	**21:49**
2009-10	**St. Louis**	**NHL**	**78**	**4**	**17**	**21**	**59**	**0**	**0**	**1**	**73**	**5.5**	**7**	**0**	**0.0**	**19:59**	....	....	....	....	....	....	....	....	....
	Czech Republic	Olympics	5	0	0	0	4	....	....	....	....	....	....	....	....	....	....	....	....	....	....	....	....	....	....
2010-11	**St. Louis**	**NHL**	**55**	**3**	**9**	**12**	**33**	**0**	**0**	**1**	**54**	**5.6**	**-4**	**1**	**0.0**	**19:57**	....	....	....	....	....	....	....	....	....
2011-12	**St. Louis**	**NHL**	**77**	**0**	**11**	**11**	**57**	**0**	**0**	**0**	**88**	**0.0**	**6**	**0**	**0.0**	**18:52**	**9**	**0**	**0**	**0**	**19**	**0**	**0**	**0**	**20:41**
2012-13	Vitkovice	CzRep	22	2	6	8	79	....	....	....	....	....	....	....	....	....	....	....	....	....	....	....	....	....	....
	St. Louis	**NHL**	**48**	**1**	**5**	**6**	**48**	**0**	**0**	**1**	**39**	**2.6**	**-2**	**0**	**0.0**	**18:25**	**6**	**0**	**1**	**1**	**2**	**0**	**0**	**0**	**20:09**
2013-14	**St. Louis**	**NHL**	**72**	**4**	**9**	**13**	**71**	**0**	**0**	**0**	**83**	**4.8**	**3**	**0**	**0.0**	**17:20**	**6**	**0**	**1**	**1**	**4**	**0**	**0**	**0**	**18:38**
2014-15	**Toronto**	**NHL**	**56**	**5**	**4**	**9**	**48**	**0**	**0**	**1**	**61**	**8.2**	**-22**	**1**	**100.0**	**21:05**	....	....	....	....	....	....	....	....	....
2015-16	**Toronto**	**NHL**	**55**	**1**	**12**	**13**	**56**	**0**	**0**	**0**	**56**	**1.8**	**8**	**1**	**100.0**	**19:44**	....	....	....	....	....	....	....	....	....
	San Jose	**NHL**	**24**	**0**	**3**	**3**	**16**	**0**	**0**	**0**	**35**	**0.0**	**-2**	**0**	**0.0**	**17:49**	**24**	**0**	**0**	**0**	**15**	**0**	**0**	**0**	**15:46**
2016-17	**Toronto**	**NHL**	**75**	**4**	**7**	**11**	**65**	**0**	**0**	**1**	**64**	**6.3**	**10**	**1**	**0.0**	**17:55**	**2**	**0**	**0**	**0**	**0**	**0**	**0**	**0**	**17:37**
	NHL Totals		**634**	**23**	**92**	**115**	**504**	**0**	**0**	**6**	**641**	**3.6**		**5**	**40.0**	**19:05**	**51**	**0**	**2**	**2**	**40**	**0**	**0**	**0**	**18:02**

Signed as a free agent by **Vitkovice** (CzRep), September 20, 2012. Traded to **Toronto** by **St. Louis** for Carl Gunnarsson and Calgary's 4th round pick (previously acquired, St. Louis selected Ville Husso) in 2014 NHL Draft, June 28, 2014. Traded to **San Jose** by **Toronto** with Nick Spaling for Raffi Torres, San Jose's 2nd round pick (later traded to Anaheim – Anaheim selected Maxime Comtois) in 2017 NHL Draft and San Jose's 2nd round pick in 2018 NHL Draft, February 22, 2016. Signed as a free agent by **Toronto**, July 2, 2016.

POMINVILLE, Jason

(paw-MIHN-vihl, JAY-suhn) **BUF**

Right wing. Shoots right. 6', 184 lbs. Born, Repentigny, QC, November 30, 1982. Buffalo's 4th pick, 55th overall, in 2001 NHL Draft.

Season	Club	League	GP	G	A	Pts	PIM	PP	SH	GW	S	S%	+/-	TF	F%	Min	GP	G	A	Pts	PIM	PP	SH	GW	Min
1997-98	Cap-d-Madeleine	QAAA	13	3	7	10	....	....	....	....	....	....	....	....	....	....	....	....	....	....	....	....	....	....	....
1998-99	Cap-d-Madeleine	QAAA	41	18	38	56	16	....	....	....	....	....	....	....	....	....	7	2	7	9	0	....	....	....	....
	Shawinigan	QMJHL	2	0	0	0	0	....	....	....	....	....	....	....	....	....	....	....	....	....	....	....	....	....	....
99-2000	Shawinigan	QMJHL	60	4	17	21	12	....	....	....	....	....	....	....	....	....	13	2	3	5	0	....	....	....	....
2000-01	Shawinigan	QMJHL	71	46	67	113	24	....	....	....	....	....	....	....	....	....	10	6	6	12	0	....	....	....	....
2001-02	Shawinigan	QMJHL	66	57	64	121	32	....	....	....	....	....	....	....	....	....	2	0	0	0	0	....	....	....	....
2002-03	Rochester	AHL	73	13	21	34	16	....	....	....	....	....	....	....	....	....	3	1	1	2	0	....	....	....	....
2003-04	**Buffalo**	**NHL**	**1**	**0**	**0**	**0**	**0**	**0**	**0**	**0**	**3**	**0.0**	**0**	**0**	**0.0**	**14:22**	....	....	....	....	....	....	....	....	....
	Rochester	AHL	66	34	30	64	30	....	....	....	....	....	....	....	....	....	16	9	10	19	6	....	....	....	....
2004-05	Rochester	AHL	78	30	38	68	43	....	....	....	....	....	....	....	....	....	....	....	....	....	....	....	....	....	....
2005-06	**Buffalo**	**NHL**	**57**	**18**	**12**	**30**	**22**	**10**	**2**	**2**	**124**	**14.5**	**-4**	**5**	**20.0**	**14:07**	**18**	**5**	**5**	**10**	**8**	**0**	**1**	**1**	**12:11**
	Rochester	AHL	18	19	7	26	11	....	....	....	....	....	....	....	....	....	....	....	....	....	....	....	....	....	....
2006-07	**Buffalo**	**NHL**	**82**	**34**	**34**	**68**	**30**	**2**	**2**	**5**	**212**	**16.0**	**25**	**14**	**42.9**	**17:25**	**16**	**4**	**6**	**10**	**0**	**0**	**0**	**0**	**17:54**
2007-08	**Buffalo**	**NHL**	**82**	**27**	**53**	**80**	**20**	**2**	**1**	**1**	**232**	**11.6**	**16**	**67**	**37.3**	**19:58**	....	....	....	....	....	....	....	....	....
2008-09	**Buffalo**	**NHL**	**82**	**20**	**46**	**66**	**18**	**6**	**1**	**2**	**239**	**8.4**	**-4**	**67**	**37.3**	**19:46**	....	....	....	....	....	....	....	....	....
2009-10	**Buffalo**	**NHL**	**82**	**24**	**38**	**62**	**22**	**8**	**0**	**2**	**252**	**9.5**	**13**	**120**	**35.0**	**18:45**	**6**	**2**	**2**	**4**	**2**	**0**	**0**	**1**	**20:17**
2010-11	**Buffalo**	**NHL**	**73**	**22**	**30**	**52**	**15**	**5**	**1**	**2**	**215**	**10.2**	**1**	**155**	**43.2**	**18:09**	**5**	**1**	**3**	**4**	**2**	**0**	**0**	**1**	**15:51**
2011-12	**Buffalo**	**NHL**	**82**	**30**	**43**	**73**	**12**	**8**	**2**	**5**	**235**	**12.8**	**-7**	**375**	**47.7**	**19:41**	....	....	....	....	....	....	....	....	....
2012-13	Adler Mannheim	Germany	7	5	7	12	0	....	....	....	....	....	....	....	....	....	....	....	....	....	....	....	....	....	....
	Buffalo	**NHL**	**37**	**10**	**15**	**25**	**8**	**1**	**1**	**1**	**94**	**10.6**	**1**	**86**	**46.5**	**20:54**	....	....	....	....	....	....	....	....	....
	Minnesota	**NHL**	**10**	**4**	**5**	**9**	**0**	**1**	**0**	**1**	**24**	**16.7**	**0**	**19**	**57.9**	**17:31**	**2**	**0**	**0**	**0**	**0**	**0**	**0**	**0**	**13:32**
2013-14	**Minnesota**	**NHL**	**82**	**30**	**30**	**60**	**16**	**7**	**0**	**5**	**226**	**13.3**	**3**	**159**	**54.7**	**18:35**	**13**	**2**	**7**	**9**	**0**	**0**	**0**	**0**	**18:16**
2014-15	**Minnesota**	**NHL**	**82**	**18**	**36**	**54**	**8**	**3**	**0**	**4**	**252**	**7.1**	**9**	**87**	**44.8**	**18:17**	**10**	**3**	**3**	**6**	**0**	**2**	**0**	**1**	**17:29**
2015-16	**Minnesota**	**NHL**	**75**	**11**	**25**	**36**	**12**	**3**	**0**	**2**	**187**	**5.9**	**10**	**82**	**45.1**	**16:22**	**6**	**4**	**3**	**7**	**6**	**0**	**0**	**0**	**15:56**
2016-17	**Minnesota**	**NHL**	**78**	**13**	**34**	**47**	**4**	**0**	**0**	**2**	**176**	**7.4**	**2**	**78**	**50.0**	**14:14**	**5**	**0**	**1**	**1**	**0**	**0**	**0**	**0**	**14:05**
	NHL Totals		**905**	**261**	**401**	**662**	**187**	**56**	**10**	**34**	**2471**	**10.6**		**1314**	**45.5**	**18:00**	**81**	**21**	**30**	**51**	**18**	**2**	**1**	**4**	**16:12**

QMJHL First All-Star Team (2002)

Played in NHL All-Star Game (2012)

Signed as a free agent by **Mannheim** (Germany), December 4, 2012. Traded to **Minnesota** by **Buffalo** with Buffalo's 4th round pick (later traded to Edmonton – Edmonton selected William Lagesson) in 2014 NHL Draft for Matt Hackett, Johan Larsson, Minnesota's 1st round pick (Nikita Zadorov) in 2013 NHL Draft and Minnesota's 2nd round pick (Vaclav Karabacek) in 2014 NHL Draft, April 3, 2013. Traded to **Buffalo** by **Minnesota** with Marco Scandella and Minnesota's 4th round pick in 2018 NHL Draft for Tyler Ennis, Marcus Foligno and Buffalo's 3rd round pick in 2018 NHL Draft, June 30. 2017.

PORTER, Chris

(POHR-tuhr, KRIHS)

Center. Shoots left. 6'1", 206 lbs. Born, Toronto, ON, May 29, 1984. Chicago's 10th pick, 282nd overall, in 2003 NHL Draft.

Season	Club	League	GP	G	A	Pts	PIM	PP	SH	GW	S	S%	+/-	TF	F%	Min	GP	G	A	Pts	PIM	PP	SH	GW	Min
2001-02	Shattuck	High-MN	75	10	25	35	32	....	....	....	....	....	....	....	....	....	....	....	....	....	....	....	....	....	....
2002-03	Lincoln Stars	USHL	59	13	22	35	74	....	....	....	....	....	....	....	....	....	10	4	3	7	10	....	....	....	....
2003-04	North Dakota	WCHA	41	10	15	25	46	....	....	....	....	....	....	....	....	....	....	....	....	....	....	....	....	....	....
2004-05	North Dakota	WCHA	45	12	3	15	36	....	....	....	....	....	....	....	....	....	....	....	....	....	....	....	....	....	....
2005-06	North Dakota	WCHA	46	7	16	23	40	....	....	....	....	....	....	....	....	....	....	....	....	....	....	....	....	....	....
2006-07	North Dakota	WCHA	43	13	17	30	38	....	....	....	....	....	....	....	....	....	....	....	....	....	....	....	....	....	....
2007-08	Peoria Rivermen	AHL	80	12	25	37	72	....	....	....	....	....	....	....	....	....	....	....	....	....	....	....	....	....	....
2008-09	**St. Louis**	**NHL**	**6**	**1**	**1**	**2**	**0**	**0**	**0**	**0**	**7**	**14.3**	**-1**	**3**	**33.3**	**10:32**	....	....	....	....	....	....	....	....	....
	Peoria Rivermen	AHL	74	7	16	23	72	....	....	....	....	....	....	....	....	....	7	1	1	2	0	....	....	....	....
2009-10	Peoria Rivermen	AHL	80	13	18	31	53	....	....	....	....	....	....	....	....	....	....	....	....	....	....	....	....	....	....
2010-11	**St. Louis**	**NHL**	**45**	**3**	**4**	**7**	**16**	**0**	**0**	**1**	**55**	**5.5**	**-4**	**22**	**54.6**	**10:23**	....	....	....	....	....	....	....	....	....
	Peoria Rivermen	AHL	36	9	11	20	63	....	....	....	....	....	....	....	....	....	....	....	....	....	....	....	....	....	....
2011-12	**St. Louis**	**NHL**	**47**	**4**	**3**	**7**	**11**	**0**	**0**	**1**	**61**	**6.6**	**-1**	**19**	**42.1**	**10:24**	....	....	....	....	....	....	....	....	....
	Peoria Rivermen	AHL	2	0	1	1	2	....	....	....	....	....	....	....	....	....	....	....	....	....	....	....	....	....	....
2012-13	Peoria Rivermen	AHL	12	7	3	10	11	....	....	....	....	....	....	....	....	....	....	....	....	....	....	....	....	....	....
	St. Louis	**NHL**	**29**	**2**	**6**	**8**	**0**	**0**	**0**	**2**	**46**	**4.3**	**5**	**58**	**43.1**	**11:38**	**6**	**1**	**0**	**1**	**0**	**0**	**0**	**0**	**9:14**
2013-14	**St. Louis**	**NHL**	**22**	**0**	**1**	**1**	**0**	**0**	**0**	**0**	**24**	**0.0**	**-3**	**10**	**30.0**	**10:23**	**6**	**1**	**2**	**3**	**0**	**0**	**0**	**0**	**12:14**
	Chicago Wolves	AHL	38	7	11	18	37	....	....	....	....	....	....	....	....	....	....	....	....	....	....	....	....	....	....
2014-15	**St. Louis**	**NHL**	**24**	**1**	**1**	**2**	**6**	**0**	**0**	**1**	**24**	**4.2**	**-3**	**9**	**44.4**	**9:33**	**3**	**0**	**1**	**1**	**0**	**0**	**0**	**0**	**8:11**
2015-16	**Minnesota**	**NHL**	**61**	**4**	**3**	**7**	**6**	**0**	**0**	**0**	**45**	**8.9**	**-6**	**1**	**0.0**	**9:38**	**6**	**1**	**0**	**1**	**0**	**0**	**0**	**0**	**10:14**
2016-17	Providence Bruins	AHL	67	8	17	25	28	....	....	....	....	....	....	....	....	....	17	5	4	9	8	....	....	....	....
	NHL Totals		**234**	**15**	**19**	**34**	**39**	**0**	**0**	**5**	**262**	**5.7**		**122**	**43.4**	**10:16**	**21**	**3**	**3**	**6**	**0**	**0**	**0**	**0**	**10:13**

Signed as a free agent by **St. Louis**, August 21, 2007. • Missed majority of 2014-15 due to lower-body injury vs. Coloradro, December 29, 2014 and as a healthy reserve. Signed as a free agent by **Philadelphia**, August 8, 2015. Claimed on waivers by **Minnesota** from **Philadelphia**, October 1, 2015. Signed as a free agent by **Providence** (AHL) November 5, 2016.

PORTER, Kevin

(POHR-tuhr, KEH-vihn) **BUF**

Center. Shoots left. 6', 190 lbs. Born, Detroit, MI, March 12, 1986. Phoenix's 5th pick, 119th overall, in 2004 NHL Draft.

Season	Club	League	GP	G	A	Pts	PIM	PP	SH	GW	S	S%	+/-	TF	F%	Min	GP	G	A	Pts	PIM	PP	SH	GW	Min
2002-03	USAHNTDP	U-17	19	9	11	20	8	....	....	....	....	....	....	....	....	....	....	....	....	....	....	....	....	....	....
	USAHNTDP	U-18	13	1	2	3	2	....	....	....	....	....	....	....	....	....	....	....	....	....	....	....	....	....	....
	USAHNTDP	NAHL	40	19	9	28	17	....	....	....	....	....	....	....	....	....	....	....	....	....	....	....	....	....	....
2003-04	USAHNTDP	U-18	44	5	21	26	26	....	....	....	....	....	....	....	....	....	....	....	....	....	....	....	....	....	....
	USAHNTDP	NAHL	11	3	8	11	4	....	....	....	....	....	....	....	....	....	....	....	....	....	....	....	....	....	....
2004-05	U. of Michigan	CCHA	39	11	13	24	51	....	....	....	....	....	....	....	....	....	....	....	....	....	....	....	....	....	....
2005-06	U. of Michigan	CCHA	39	17	21	38	30	....	....	....	....	....	....	....	....	....	....	....	....	....	....	....	....	....	....
2006-07	U. of Michigan	CCHA	41	24	34	58	16	....	....	....	....	....	....	....	....	....	....	....	....	....	....	....	....	....	....
2007-08	U. of Michigan	CCHA	43	*33	30	*63	18	....	....	....	....	....	....	....	....	....	....	....	....	....	....	....	....	....	....
	San Antonio	AHL	....	....	....	....	....	....	....	....	....	....	....	....	....	....	7	0	4	4	0	....	....	....	....
2008-09	**Phoenix**	**NHL**	**34**	**5**	**5**	**10**	**4**	**1**	**0**	**2**	**39**	**12.8**	**-2**	**95**	**29.5**	**13:38**	....	....	....	....	....	....	....	....	....
	San Antonio	AHL	42	13	22	35	14	....	....	....	....	....	....	....	....	....	....	....	....	....	....	....	....	....	....
2009-10	**Phoenix**	**NHL**	**4**	**0**	**0**	**0**	**0**	**0**	**0**	**0**	**3**	**0.0**	**1**	**15**	**33.3**	**7:22**	....	....	....	....	....	....	....	....	....
	San Antonio	AHL	52	15	25	40	31	....	....	....	....	....	....	....	....	....	....	....	....	....	....	....	....	....	....
	Colorado	**NHL**	**16**	**2**	**1**	**3**	**0**	**0**	**1**	**0**	**18**	**11.1**	**-4**	**27**	**48.2**	**13:13**	**4**	**0**	**0**	**0**	**0**	**0**	**0**	**0**	**10:38**
	Lake Erie	AHL	4	1	0	1	2	....	....	....	....	....	....	....	....	....	....	....	....	....	....	....	....	....	....
2010-11	**Colorado**	**NHL**	**74**	**14**	**11**	**25**	**27**	**1**	**0**	**3**	**102**	**13.7**	**-11**	**58**	**32.8**	**13:49**	....	....	....	....	....	....	....	....	....
2011-12	**Colorado**	**NHL**	**35**	**4**	**3**	**7**	**17**	**0**	**0**	**0**	**32**	**12.5**	**-2**	**46**	**30.4**	**9:11**	....	....	....	....	....	....	....	....	....
2012-13	Rochester	AHL	48	15	29	44	38	....	....	....	....	....	....	....	....	....	....	....	....	....	....	....	....	....	....
	Buffalo	**NHL**	**31**	**4**	**5**	**9**	**10**	**0**	**1**	**0**	**37**	**10.8**	**-1**	**271**	**40.2**	**15:14**	....	....	....	....	....	....	....	....	....
2013-14	**Buffalo**	**NHL**	**12**	**0**	**1**	**1**	**2**	**0**	**0**	**0**	**3**	**0.0**	**-5**	**53**	**34.0**	**11:38**	....	....	....	....	....	....	....	....	....
	Rochester	AHL	50	19	17	36	24	....	....	....	....	....	....	....	....	....	5	0	3	3	0	....	....	....	....
2014-15	Grand Rapids	AHL	76	16	23	39	25	....	....	....	....	....	....	....	....	....	16	1	3	4	14	....	....	....	....
2015-16 ♦	**Pittsburgh**	**NHL**	**41**	**0**	**3**	**3**	**0**	**0**	**0**	**0**	**34**	**0.0**	**-2**	**87**	**50.6**	**11:19**	....	....	....	....	....	....	....	....	....
	Wilkes-Barre	AHL	16	5	4	9	4	....	....	....	....	....	....	....	....	....	....	....	....	....	....	....	....	....	....

			Regular Season														Playoffs								
Season	Club	League	GP	G	A	Pts	PIM	PP	SH	GW	S	S%	+/-	TF	F%	Min	GP	G	A	Pts	PIM	PP	SH	GW	Min
2016-17	**Pittsburgh**	**NHL**	**2**	**0**	**0**	**0**	**0**	**0**	**0**	**0**	**0**	**0.0**	**–1**	**19**	**36.8**	**11:15**	....	....	....	....	....	....	....	....	....
	Wilkes-Barre	AHL	69	11	35	46	50	....	....	....	....	....	....	....	....	....	5	0	6	6	2	....	....	....	....
	NHL Totals		**249**	**29**	**29**	**58**	**60**	**2**	**2**	**5**	**268**	**10.8**		**671**	**38.3**	**12:38**	**4**	**0**	**0**	**0**	**0**	**0**	**0**	**0**	**10:38**

CCHA Second All-Star Team (2007) • CCHA First All-Star Team (2008) • CCHA Player of the Year (2008) • NCAA West First All-American Team (2008)

Traded to **Colorado** by **Phoenix** with Peter Mueller for Wojtek Wolski, March 3, 2010. Signed as a free agent by **Buffalo**, July 6, 2012. • Missed majority of 2011-12 as a healthy reserve. Signed as a free agent by **Detroit**, July 3, 2014. Signed as a free agent by **Pittsburgh**, July 1, 2015. Signed as a free agent by **Buffalo**, July 1, 2017.

POSTMA, Paul

(POHST-muh, PAWL) **BOS**

Defense. Shoots right. 6'3", 195 lbs. Born, Red Deer, AB, February 22, 1989. Atlanta's 4th pick, 205th overall, in 2007 NHL Draft.

Season	Club	League	GP	G	A	Pts	PIM	PP	SH	GW	S	S%	+/-	TF	F%	Min	GP	G	A	Pts	PIM	PP	SH	GW	Min
2004-05	Red Deer	AMHL	36	6	5	11	24	....	....	....	....	....	....	....	....	....	....	....	....	....	....	....	....	....	....
	Swift Current	WHL	4	0	0	0	0	....	....	....	....	....	....	....	....	....	....	....	....	....	....	....	....	....	....
2005-06	Swift Current	WHL	58	2	9	11	6	....	....	....	....	....	....	....	....	....	4	0	0	0	0	....	....	....	....
2006-07	Swift Current	WHL	70	5	19	24	42	....	....	....	....	....	....	....	....	....	6	0	1	1	0	....	....	....	....
2007-08	Swift Current	WHL	2	0	0	0	2	....	....	....	....	....	....	....	....	....	....	....	....	....	....	....	....	....	....
	Calgary Hitmen	WHL	66	14	28	42	30	....	....	....	....	....	....	....	....	....	16	6	4	10	4	....	....	....	....
2008-09	Calgary Hitmen	WHL	70	23	61	84	28	....	....	....	....	....	....	....	....	....	18	5	8	13	10	....	....	....	....
2009-10	Chicago Wolves	AHL	63	15	14	29	24	....	....	....	....	....	....	....	....	....	7	0	2	2	0	....	....	....	....
2010-11	**Atlanta**	**NHL**	**1**	**0**	**0**	**0**	**0**	**0**	**0**	**0**	**1**	**0.0**	**0**	**0**	**0.0**	**9:55**	....	....	....	....	....	....	....	....	....
	Chicago Wolves	AHL	69	12	33	45	20	....	....	....	....	....	....	....	....	....	....	....	....	....	....	....	....	....	....
2011-12	**Winnipeg**	**NHL**	**3**	**0**	**0**	**0**	**0**	**0**	**0**	**0**	**3**	**0.0**	**0**	**0**	**0.0**	**8:31**	....	....	....	....	....	....	....	....	....
	St. John's IceCaps	AHL	56	13	31	44	32	....	....	....	....	....	....	....	....	....	15	1	9	10	14	....	....	....	....
2012-13	St. John's IceCaps	AHL	27	7	11	18	16	....	....	....	....	....	....	....	....	....	....	....	....	....	....	....	....	....	....
	Winnipeg	**NHL**	**34**	**4**	**5**	**9**	**6**	**2**	**0**	**0**	**32**	**12.5**	**–5**	**0**	**0.0**	**15:02**	....	....	....	....	....	....	....	....	....
2013-14	**Winnipeg**	**NHL**	**20**	**1**	**2**	**3**	**8**	**0**	**0**	**1**	**19**	**5.3**	**1**	**0**	**0.0**	**16:08**	....	....	....	....	....	....	....	....	....
	St. John's IceCaps	AHL	4	1	5	6	4	....	....	....	....	....	....	....	....	....	....	....	....	....	....	....	....	....	....
2014-15	**Winnipeg**	**NHL**	**42**	**2**	**4**	**6**	**16**	**2**	**0**	**0**	**40**	**5.0**	**1**	**0**	**0.0**	**14:08**	....	....	....	....	....	....	....	....	....
2015-16	**Winnipeg**	**NHL**	**26**	**2**	**0**	**2**	**4**	**0**	**0**	**0**	**24**	**8.3**	**–3**	**0**	**0.0**	**11:27**	....	....	....	....	....	....	....	....	....
	Manitoba Moose	AHL	7	1	2	3	2	....	....	....	....	....	....	....	....	....	....	....	....	....	....	....	....	....	....
2016-17	**Winnipeg**	**NHL**	**65**	**1**	**13**	**14**	**15**	**0**	**0**	**0**	**50**	**2.0**	**3**	**0**	**0.0**	**10:51**	....	....	....	....	....	....	....	....	....
	NHL Totals		**191**	**10**	**24**	**34**	**49**	**4**	**0**	**1**	**169**	**5.9**		**0**	**0.0**	**12:55**	....	....	....	....	....	....	....	....	....

WHL East First All-Star Team (2009) • Canadian Major Junior Second All-Star Team (2009) • AHL First All-Star Team (2012)

• Transferred to **Winnipeg** after **Atlanta** franchise relocated, June 21, 2011. • Missed majority of 2013-14 due to blood clot in his leg. • Missed majority of 2014-15 due to lower-body injury at Tampa Bay, March 14, 2015 and as a healthy reserve. • Missed majority of 2015-16 as a healthy reserve. Signed as a free agent by **Boston**, July 1, 2017.

POTURALSKI, Andrew

(POHT-uhr-AL-skee, AN-droo) **CAR**

Right wing. Shoots right. 5'10", 180 lbs. Born, Williamsville, NY, January 14, 1994.

Season	Club	League	GP	G	A	Pts	PIM	PP	SH	GW	S	S%	+/-	TF	F%	Min	GP	G	A	Pts	PIM	PP	SH	GW	Min
2008-09	Nichols	High-NY	21	13	16	19	....	....	....	....	....	....	....	....	....	....	....	....	....	....	....	....	....	....	....
2009-10	Nichols	High-NY	29	28	25	53	8	....	....	....	....	....	....	....	....	....	....	....	....	....	....	....	....	....	....
2010-11	Nichols	High-NY	22	19	10	29	....	....	....	....	....	....	....	....	....	....	....	....	....	....	....	....	....	....	....
	Nichols	CISAA	14	13	10	23	26	....	....	....	....	....	....	....	....	....	4	8	0	8	4	....	....	....	....
2011-12	Buffalo Jr. Sabres	ON-Jr.A	33	16	22	38	32	....	....	....	....	....	....	....	....	....	8	5	2	7	4	....	....	....	....
	Cedar Rapids	USHL	2	2	1	3	0	....	....	....	....	....	....	....	....	....	....	....	....	....	....	....	....	....	....
2012-13	Cedar Rapids	USHL	53	12	21	33	43	....	....	....	....	....	....	....	....	....	....	....	....	....	....	....	....	....	....
2013-14	Cedar Rapids	USHL	60	27	37	64	28	....	....	....	....	....	....	....	....	....	4	2	1	3	2	....	....	....	....
2014-15	New Hampshire	H-East	40	14	15	29	16	....	....	....	....	....	....	....	....	....	....	....	....	....	....	....	....	....	....
2015-16	New Hampshire	H-East	37	22	30	*52	24	....	....	....	....	....	....	....	....	....	....	....	....	....	....	....	....	....	....
	Charlotte	AHL	16	2	3	5	0	....	....	....	....	....	....	....	....	....	....	....	....	....	....	....	....	....	....
2016-17	**Carolina**	**NHL**	**2**	**0**	**0**	**0**	**0**	**0**	**0**	**0**	**1**	**0.0**	**–3**	**24**	**50.0**	**12:16**	....	....	....	....	....	....	....	....	....
	Charlotte	AHL	74	19	33	52	34	....	....	....	....	....	....	....	....	....	5	0	0	0	5	....	....	....	....
	NHL Totals		**2**	**0**	**0**	**0**	**0**	**0**	**0**	**0**	**1**	**0.0**		**24**	**50.0**	**12:16**	....	....	....	....	....	....	....	....	....

Hockey East First All-Star Team (2016) • NCAA East First All-American Team (2016)

Signed as a free agent by **Carolina**, March 8, 2016.

POULIOT, Benoit

(POO-lee-oh, BEHN-wah) **BUF**

Left wing. Shoots Left. 6'3", 200 lbs. Born, Alfred, ON, September 29, 1986. Minnesota's 1st pick, 4th overall, in 2005 NHL Draft.

Season	Club	League	GP	G	A	Pts	PIM	PP	SH	GW	S	S%	+/-	TF	F%	Min	GP	G	A	Pts	PIM	PP	SH	GW	Min
2002-03	Clarence Beavers	ON-Jr.B	38	13	17	30	86	....	....	....	....	....	....	....	....	....	5	0	2	2	8	....	....	....	....
	Hawkesbury	ON-Jr.A	1	1	0	1	0	....	....	....	....	....	....	....	....	....	....	....	....	....	....	....	....	....	....
2003-04	Hawkesbury	ON-Jr.A	45	21	21	42	85	....	....	....	....	....	....	....	....	....	6	3	7	10	10	....	....	....	....
	Sudbury Wolves	OHL	4	2	2	4	0	....	....	....	....	....	....	....	....	....	4	2	1	3	0	....	....	....	....
2004-05	Sudbury Wolves	OHL	67	29	38	67	102	....	....	....	....	....	....	....	....	....	12	6	8	14	20	....	....	....	....
2005-06	Sudbury Wolves	OHL	51	35	30	65	141	....	....	....	....	....	....	....	....	....	8	8	3	11	16	....	....	....	....
	Houston Aeros	AHL	....	....	....	....	....	....	....	....	....	....	....	....	....	....	2	0	0	0	2	....	....	....	....
2006-07	**Minnesota**	**NHL**	**3**	**0**	**0**	**0**	**0**	**0**	**0**	**0**	**1**	**0.0**	**–1**	**2**	**0.0**	**6:58**	....	....	....	....	....	....	....	....	....
	Houston Aeros	AHL	67	19	17	36	109	....	....	....	....	....	....	....	....	....	....	....	....	....	....	....	....	....	....
2007-08	**Minnesota**	**NHL**	**11**	**2**	**1**	**3**	**0**	**0**	**0**	**0**	**10**	**20.0**	**–1**	**65**	**40.0**	**8:49**	**1**	**0**	**0**	**0**	**0**	**0**	**0**	**0**	**10:16**
	Houston Aeros	AHL	46	10	14	24	67	....	....	....	....	....	....	....	....	....	3	0	0	0	2	....	....	....	....
2008-09	**Minnesota**	**NHL**	**37**	**5**	**6**	**11**	**18**	**2**	**0**	**1**	**34**	**14.7**	**1**	**217**	**42.9**	**11:51**	....	....	....	....	....	....	....	....	....
	Houston Aeros	AHL	30	9	15	24	20	....	....	....	....	....	....	....	....	....	20	1	7	8	28	....	....	....	....
2009-10	**Minnesota**	**NHL**	**14**	**2**	**2**	**4**	**12**	**0**	**0**	**0**	**19**	**10.5**	**0**	**8**	**50.0**	**11:56**	....	....	....	....	....	....	....	....	....
	Montreal	**NHL**	**39**	**15**	**9**	**24**	**31**	**4**	**0**	**3**	**92**	**16.3**	**8**	**3**	**33.3**	**16:44**	**18**	**0**	**2**	**2**	**6**	**0**	**0**	**0**	**11:45**
	Hamilton	AHL	3	1	2	3	4	....	....	....	....	....	....	....	....	....	....	....	....	....	....	....	....	....	....
2010-11	**Montreal**	**NHL**	**79**	**13**	**17**	**30**	**87**	**1**	**0**	**4**	**129**	**10.1**	**2**	**22**	**45.5**	**11:32**	**3**	**0**	**0**	**0**	**7**	**0**	**0**	**0**	**6:12**
2011-12	**Boston**	**NHL**	**74**	**16**	**16**	**32**	**38**	**1**	**0**	**5**	**107**	**15.0**	**18**	**18**	**44.4**	**12:13**	**7**	**1**	**1**	**2**	**6**	**0**	**0**	**0**	**12:40**
2012-13	**Tampa Bay**	**NHL**	**34**	**8**	**12**	**20**	**15**	**0**	**0**	**1**	**60**	**13.3**	**8**	**31**	**32.3**	**13:14**	....	....	....	....	....	....	....	....	....
2013-14	**NY Rangers**	**NHL**	**80**	**15**	**21**	**36**	**56**	**7**	**0**	**4**	**141**	**10.6**	**10**	**39**	**51.3**	**13:26**	**25**	**5**	**5**	**10**	**26**	**1**	**0**	**1**	**15:42**
2014-15	**Edmonton**	**NHL**	**58**	**19**	**15**	**34**	**28**	**4**	**1**	**3**	**105**	**18.1**	**–1**	**34**	**38.2**	**16:37**	....	....	....	....	....	....	....	....	....
2015-16	**Edmonton**	**NHL**	**55**	**14**	**22**	**36**	**30**	**5**	**1**	**0**	**109**	**12.8**	**–6**	**49**	**40.8**	**16:03**	....	....	....	....	....	....	....	....	....
2016-17	**Edmonton**	**NHL**	**67**	**8**	**6**	**14**	**34**	**0**	**0**	**1**	**77**	**10.4**	**–5**	**28**	**25.0**	**14:03**	**13**	**0**	**0**	**0**	**4**	**0**	**0**	**0**	**12:40**
	NHL Totals		**551**	**117**	**127**	**244**	**349**	**24**	**2**	**22**	**884**	**13.2**		**516**	**41.1**	**13:37**	**67**	**6**	**8**	**14**	**49**	**1**	**0**	**1**	**13:14**

OHL All-Rookie Team (2005) • OHL First All-Star Team (2005) • OHL Rookie of the Year (2005) • Canadian Major Junior All-Rookie Team (2005) • Canadian Major Junior Rookie of the Year (2005)

Traded to **Montreal** by **Minnesota** for Guillaume Latendresse, November 23, 2009. Signed as a free agent by **Boston**, July 1, 2011. Traded to **Tampa Bay** by **Boston** for Michel Ouellet and Tampa Bay's 5th round pick (Seth Griffith) in 2012 NHL Draft, June 23, 2012. Signed as a free agent by **NY Rangers**, July 5, 2013. Signed as a free agent by **Edmonton**, July 1, 2014. Signed as a free agent by **Buffalo**, July 1, 2017.

POULIOT, Derrick

(POO-lee-oh, DAIR-ihk) **PIT**

Defense. Shoots left. 6', 208 lbs. Born, Estevan, SK, January 16, 1994. Pittsburgh's 1st pick, 8th overall, in 2012 NHL Draft.

Season	Club	League	GP	G	A	Pts	PIM	PP	SH	GW	S	S%	+/-	TF	F%	Min	GP	G	A	Pts	PIM	PP	SH	GW	Min
2008-09	Weyburn Wings	Minor-SK	26	25	38	63	24	....	....	....	....	....	....	....	....	....	5	5	1	6	....	....	....	....	....
	Moose Jaw	SMHL	5	1	1	2	0	....	....	....	....	....	....	....	....	....	....	....	....	....	....	....	....	....	....
2009-10	Moose Jaw	SMHL	43	14	29	43	38	....	....	....	....	....	....	....	....	....	4	0	2	2	4	....	....	....	....
	Portland	WHL	7	0	1	1	0	....	....	....	....	....	....	....	....	....	....	....	....	....	....	....	....	....	....
2010-11	Portland	WHL	66	5	25	30	38	....	....	....	....	....	....	....	....	....	21	1	3	4	16	....	....	....	....
2011-12	Portland	WHL	72	11	48	59	79	....	....	....	....	....	....	....	....	....	22	3	14	17	18	....	....	....	....
2012-13	Portland	WHL	44	9	36	45	60	....	....	....	....	....	....	....	....	....	21	4	16	20	12	....	....	....	....
	Wilkes-Barre	AHL	....	....	....	....	....	....	....	....	....	....	....	....	....	....	1	0	0	0	0	....	....	....	....
2013-14	Portland	WHL	58	17	53	70	74	....	....	....	....	....	....	....	....	....	21	5	*27	32	13	....	....	....	....
2014-15	**Pittsburgh**	**NHL**	**34**	**2**	**5**	**7**	**4**	**1**	**0**	**2**	**56**	**3.6**	**–11**	**0**	**0.0**	**17:33**	....	....	....	....	....	....	....	....	....
	Wilkes-Barre	AHL	31	7	17	24	20	....	....	....	....	....	....	....	....	....	6	1	2	3	2	....	....	....	....
2015-16	**Pittsburgh**	**NHL**	**22**	**0**	**7**	**7**	**2**	**0**	**0**	**0**	**25**	**0.0**	**4**	**0**	**0.0**	**15:27**	**2**	**0**	**0**	**0**	**2**	**0**	**0**	**0**	**14:41**
	Wilkes-Barre	AHL	37	6	17	23	26	....	....	....	....	....	....	....	....	....	....	....	....	....	....	....	....	....	....
2016-17	**Pittsburgh**	**NHL**	**11**	**0**	**0**	**0**	**4**	**0**	**0**	**0**	**11**	**0.0**	**–4**	**0**	**0.0**	**14:53**	....	....	....	....	....	....	....	....	....
	Wilkes-Barre	AHL	46	7	16	23	26	....	....	....	....	....	....	....	....	....	5	1	1	2	2	....	....	....	....
	NHL Totals		**67**	**2**	**12**	**14**	**10**	**1**	**0**	**2**	**92**	**2.2**		**0**	**0.0**	**16:25**	**2**	**0**	**0**	**0**	**2**	**0**	**0**	**0**	**14:41**

WHL West First All-Star Team (2014) • WHL Defenseman of the Year (2014) • Canadian Major Junior Defenseman of the Year (2014)

PRINCE, Shane
(PRIHNS, SHAYN) **NYI**

Center. Shoots left. 5'11", 185 lbs. Born, Rochester, NY, November 16, 1992. Ottawa's 4th pick, 61st overall, in 2011 NHL Draft.

			Regular Season													Playoffs								
Season	Club	League	GP	G	A	Pts	PIM	PP	SH	GW	S	S%	+/-	TF	F%	Min	GP	G	A	Pts	PIM	PP	SH	GW	Min
2007-08	Maksymum	EmJHL	34	15	31	46	10	....	....	....	....	....	....	....	....	....	....	....	....	....	....	....	....	....	....
	Maksymum	Other	10	3	4	7	4	....	....	....	....	....	....	....	....	....	....	....	....	....	....	....	....	....	....
	Rochester	EJHL	11	3	3	6	4	....	....	....	....	....	....	....	....	....	....	....	....	....	....	....	....	....	....
2008-09	Kitchener Rangers	OHL	63	3	9	12	34	....	....	....	....	....	....	....	....	....	....	....	....	....	....	....	....	....	....
2009-10	Kitchener Rangers	OHL	39	8	9	17	32	....	....	....	....	....	....	....	....	....	....	....	....	....	....	....	....	....	....
	Ottawa 67's	OHL	26	7	6	13	13	....	....	....	....	....	....	....	....	....	12	2	2	4	4	....	....	....	....
2010-11	Ottawa 67's	OHL	59	25	63	88	18	....	....	....	....	....	....	....	....	....	3	1	0	1	0	....	....	....	....
2011-12	Ottawa 67's	OHL	57	43	47	90	12	....	....	....	....	....	....	....	....	....	18	7	9	16	6	....	....	....	....
2012-13	Binghamton	AHL	65	18	17	35	24	....	....	....	....	....	....	....	....	....	3	1	0	1	0	....	....	....	....
2013-14	Binghamton	AHL	69	21	27	48	53	....	....	....	....	....	....	....	....	....	4	1	1	2	0	....	....	....	....
2014-15	**Ottawa**	**NHL**	**2**	**0**	**1**	**1**	**0**	**0**	**0**	**0**	**2**	**0.0**	**1**	**0**	**0.0**	**10:29**	....	....	....	....	....	....	....	....	....
	Binghamton	AHL	72	28	37	65	31	....	....	....	....	....	....	....	....	....	....	....	....	....	....	....	....	....	....
2015-16	**Ottawa**	**NHL**	**42**	**3**	**9**	**12**	**6**	**0**	**0**	**1**	**62**	**4.8**	**2**	**3**	**66.7**	**10:38**	....	....	....	....	....	....	....	....	....
	NY Islanders	**NHL**	**20**	**3**	**2**	**5**	**4**	**0**	**0**	**0**	**26**	**11.5**	**3**	**2**	**100.0**	**12:30**	**11**	**3**	**1**	**4**	**0**	**0**	**0**	**0**	**13:44**
2016-17	**NY Islanders**	**NHL**	**50**	**5**	**13**	**18**	**18**	**1**	**0**	**2**	**71**	**7.0**	**-9**	**7**	**57.1**	**12:58**	....	....	....	....	....	....	....	....	....
	NHL Totals		**114**	**11**	**25**	**36**	**28**	**1**	**0**	**3**	**161**	**6.8**		**12**	**66.7**	**11:59**	**11**	**3**	**1**	**4**	**0**	**0**	**0**	**0**	**13:44**

AHL Second All-Star Team (2015)

Traded to **NY Islanders** by **Ottawa** with Ottawa's 7th round pick (Nick Pastujov) in 2016 NHL Draft for NY Islanders' 3rd round pick (later traded to New Jersey – New Jersey selected Brandon Gignac) in 2016 NHL Draft, February 29, 2016.

PROSSER, Nate
(PRAW-suhr, NAYT) **ST.L.**

Defense. Shoots right. 6'2", 202 lbs. Born, Elk River, MN, May 7, 1986.

			Regular Season													Playoffs								
Season	Club	League	GP	G	A	Pts	PIM	PP	SH	GW	S	S%	+/-	TF	F%	Min	GP	G	A	Pts	PIM	PP	SH	GW	Min
2006-07	Colorado College	WCHA	21	0	3	3	8	....	....	....	....	....	....	....	....	....	....	....	....	....	....	....	....	....	....
2007-08	Colorado College	WCHA	39	3	17	20	51	....	....	....	....	....	....	....	....	....	....	....	....	....	....	....	....	....	....
2008-09	Colorado College	WCHA	38	5	8	13	61	....	....	....	....	....	....	....	....	....	....	....	....	....	....	....	....	....	....
2009-10	**Minnesota**	**NHL**	**3**	**0**	**1**	**1**	**8**	**0**	**0**	**0**	**4**	**0.0**	**2**	**0**	**0.0**	**19:37**	....	....	....	....	....	....	....	....	....
	Colorado College	WCHA	39	4	24	28	58	....	....	....	....	....	....	....	....	....	....	....	....	....	....	....	....	....	....
2010-11	**Minnesota**	**NHL**	**2**	**0**	**0**	**0**	**0**	**0**	**0**	**0**	**1**	**0.0**	**0**	**0**	**0.0**	**14:48**	....	....	....	....	....	....	....	....	....
	Houston Aeros	AHL	73	8	19	27	31	....	....	....	....	....	....	....	....	....	24	2	2	4	16	....	....	....	....
2011-12	**Minnesota**	**NHL**	**51**	**1**	**11**	**12**	**57**	**0**	**0**	**0**	**32**	**3.1**	**-17**	**0**	**0.0**	**19:15**	....	....	....	....	....	....	....	....	....
	Houston Aeros	AHL	23	0	4	4	10	....	....	....	....	....	....	....	....	....	2	1	0	1	2	....	....	....	....
2012-13	**Minnesota**	**NHL**	**17**	**0**	**0**	**0**	**4**	**0**	**0**	**0**	**5**	**0.0**	**4**	**0**	**0.0**	**11:15**	....	....	....	....	....	....	....	....	....
2013-14	**Minnesota**	**NHL**	**53**	**2**	**6**	**8**	**58**	**0**	**0**	**2**	**30**	**6.7**	**2**	**0**	**0.0**	**14:32**	**10**	**0**	**0**	**0**	**12**	**0**	**0**	**0**	**12:31**
2014-15	**Minnesota**	**NHL**	**63**	**2**	**5**	**7**	**32**	**0**	**0**	**1**	**38**	**5.3**	**-1**	**0**	**0.0**	**12:48**	**1**	**0**	**0**	**0**	**2**	**0**	**0**	**0**	**4:02**
2015-16	**Minnesota**	**NHL**	**54**	**0**	**3**	**3**	**39**	**0**	**0**	**0**	**20**	**0.0**	**1**	**0**	**0.0**	**11:23**	**6**	**0**	**1**	**1**	**0**	**0**	**0**	**0**	**11:54**
2016-17	**Minnesota**	**NHL**	**39**	**2**	**5**	**7**	**12**	**0**	**0**	**0**	**20**	**10.0**	**0**	**0**	**0.0**	**12:44**	**3**	**0**	**1**	**1**	**2**	**0**	**0**	**0**	**9:47**
	NHL Totals		**282**	**7**	**31**	**38**	**210**	**0**	**0**	**3**	**150**	**4.7**		**0**	**0.0**	**14:00**	**20**	**0**	**2**	**2**	**16**	**0**	**0**	**0**	**11:30**

WCHA Second All-Star Team (2010)

Signed as a free agent by **Minnesota**, March 18, 2010. • Missed majority of 2012-13 as a healthy reserve. Signed as a free agent by **St. Louis**, July 21, 2014. Claimed on waivers by **Minnesota** from **St. Louis**, October 2, 2014. • Missed majority of 2016-17 as a healthy reserve. Signed as a free agent by **St. Louis**, August 3, 2017.

PROUT, Dalton
(PROWT, DAHL-tuhn) **N.J.**

Defense. Shoots right. 6'3", 230 lbs. Born, Kingsville, ON, March 13, 1990. Columbus' 7th pick, 154th overall, in 2010 NHL Draft.

			Regular Season													Playoffs								
Season	Club	League	GP	G	A	Pts	PIM	PP	SH	GW	S	S%	+/-	TF	F%	Min	GP	G	A	Pts	PIM	PP	SH	GW	Min
2005-06	Wind. Jr. Spitfires	Minor-ON	58	11	19	30	78	....	....	....	....	....	....	....	....	....	....	....	....	....	....	....	....	....	....
2006-07	Sarnia Sting	OHL	49	1	2	3	36	....	....	....	....	....	....	....	....	....	4	0	0	0	0	....	....	....	....
2007-08	Sarnia Sting	OHL	32	0	2	2	43	....	....	....	....	....	....	....	....	....	....	....	....	....	....	....	....	....	....
	Barrie Colts	OHL	25	0	3	3	39	....	....	....	....	....	....	....	....	....	8	0	2	2	16	....	....	....	....
2008-09	Barrie Colts	OHL	65	0	6	6	98	....	....	....	....	....	....	....	....	....	5	0	1	1	10	....	....	....	....
2009-10	Barrie Colts	OHL	63	7	14	21	121	....	....	....	....	....	....	....	....	....	17	1	6	7	20	....	....	....	....
2010-11	Barrie Colts	OHL	23	7	14	21	55	....	....	....	....	....	....	....	....	....	....	....	....	....	....	....	....	....	....
	Saginaw Spirit	OHL	29	2	8	10	44	....	....	....	....	....	....	....	....	....	12	2	0	2	27	....	....	....	....
2011-12	**Columbus**	**NHL**	**5**	**0**	**0**	**0**	**0**	**0**	**0**	**0**	**2**	**0.0**	**1**	**0**	**0.0**	**11:48**	....	....	....	....	....	....	....	....	....
	Springfield	AHL	62	4	9	13	54	....	....	....	....	....	....	....	....	....	....	....	....	....	....	....	....	....	....
2012-13	Springfield	AHL	40	1	8	9	73	....	....	....	....	....	....	....	....	....	6	0	1	1	14	....	....	....	....
	Columbus	**NHL**	**28**	**1**	**6**	**7**	**25**	**0**	**0**	**0**	**16**	**6.3**	**15**	**0**	**0.0**	**18:32**	....	....	....	....	....	....	....	....	....
2013-14	**Columbus**	**NHL**	**49**	**2**	**4**	**6**	**37**	**0**	**0**	**0**	**56**	**3.6**	**-7**	**1**	**0.0**	**17:12**	**2**	**0**	**0**	**0**	**2**	**0**	**0**	**0**	**13:12**
	Springfield	AHL	15	0	3	3	11	....	....	....	....	....	....	....	....	....	....	....	....	....	....	....	....	....	....
2014-15	**Columbus**	**NHL**	**63**	**0**	**8**	**8**	**85**	**0**	**0**	**0**	**64**	**0.0**	**-14**	**0**	**0.0**	**18:25**	....	....	....	....	....	....	....	....	....
2015-16	**Columbus**	**NHL**	**64**	**3**	**6**	**9**	**102**	**0**	**0**	**0**	**69**	**4.3**	**-6**	**1**	**0.0**	**16:10**	....	....	....	....	....	....	....	....	....
2016-17	**Columbus**	**NHL**	**15**	**0**	**3**	**3**	**14**	**0**	**0**	**0**	**6**	**0.0**	**4**	**0**	**0.0**	**13:04**	....	....	....	....	....	....	....	....	....
	Cleveland	AHL	7	0	2	2	6	....	....	....	....	....	....	....	....	....	....	....	....	....	....	....	....	....	....
	New Jersey	**NHL**	**14**	**0**	**3**	**3**	**30**	**0**	**0**	**0**	**7**	**0.0**	**-5**	**0**	**0.0**	**14:56**	....	....	....	....	....	....	....	....	....
	NHL Totals		**238**	**6**	**30**	**36**	**293**	**0**	**0**	**0**	**220**	**2.7**		**2**	**0.0**	**16:54**	**2**	**0**	**0**	**0**	**2**	**0**	**0**	**0**	**13:12**

Traded to **New Jersey** by **Columbus** for Kyle Quincey, March 1, 2017.

PROVOROV, Ivan
(PROH-voh-rawv, ih-VAHN) **PHI**

Defense. Shoots left. 6', 200 lbs. Born, Yaroslavl, Russia, January 13, 1997. Philadelphia's 1st pick, 7th overall, in 2015 NHL Draft.

			Regular Season													Playoffs								
Season	Club	League	GP	G	A	Pts	PIM	PP	SH	GW	S	S%	+/-	TF	F%	Min	GP	G	A	Pts	PIM	PP	SH	GW	Min
2011-12	Wilkes Barre Bant.	AYHL	27	28	33	61	39	....	....	....	....	....	....	....	....	....	....	....	....	....	....	....	....	....	....
2012-13	Wilkes Barre U16	AYHL	24	14	22	36	47	....	....	....	....	....	....	....	....	....	....	....	....	....	....	....	....	....	....
	Wilkes Barre U16	Other	27	28	33	61	....	....	....	....	....	....	....	....	....	....	....	....	....	....	....	....	....	....	....
2013-14	Cedar Rapids	USHL	56	6	13	19	32	....	....	....	....	....	....	....	....	....	....	....	....	....	....	....	....	....	....
2014-15	Brandon	WHL	60	15	46	61	42	....	....	....	....	....	....	....	....	....	19	2	11	13	10	....	....	....	....
2015-16	Brandon	WHL	62	21	52	73	16	....	....	....	....	....	....	....	....	....	21	3	10	13	14	....	....	....	....
2016-17	**Philadelphia**	**NHL**	**82**	**6**	**24**	**30**	**34**	**0**	**0**	**1**	**161**	**3.7**	**-7**	**0**	**0.0**	**21:59**	....	....	....	....	....	....	....	....	....
	NHL Totals		**82**	**6**	**24**	**30**	**34**	**0**	**0**	**1**	**161**	**3.7**		**0**	**0.0**	**21:59**	....	....	....	....	....	....	....	....	....

WHL East First All-Star Team (2015, 2016)

PRUST, Brandon
(PROOST, BRAN-duhn)

Left wing. Shoots left. 6', 194 lbs. Born, London, ON, March 16, 1984. Calgary's 2nd pick, 70th overall, in 2004 NHL Draft.

			Regular Season													Playoffs								
Season	Club	League	GP	G	A	Pts	PIM	PP	SH	GW	S	S%	+/-	TF	F%	Min	GP	G	A	Pts	PIM	PP	SH	GW	Min
2001-02	London Nationals	ON-Jr.B	52	17	35	52	38	....	....	....	....	....	....	....	....	....	....	....	....	....	....	....	....	....	....
2002-03	London Knights	OHL	65	12	17	29	94	....	....	....	....	....	....	....	....	....	14	2	1	3	21	....	....	....	....
2003-04	London Knights	OHL	64	19	33	52	269	....	....	....	....	....	....	....	....	....	15	7	13	20	33	....	....	....	....
2004-05	London Knights	OHL	48	10	20	30	174	....	....	....	....	....	....	....	....	....	15	3	5	8	*71	....	....	....	....
2005-06	Omaha	AHL	79	12	14	26	294	....	....	....	....	....	....	....	....	....	....	....	....	....	....	....	....	....	....
2006-07	**Calgary**	**NHL**	**10**	**0**	**0**	**0**	**25**	**0**	**0**	**0**	**1**	**0.0**	**1**	**0**	**0.0**	**6:03**	....	....	....	....	....	....	....	....	....
	Omaha	AHL	63	17	10	27	211	....	....	....	....	....	....	....	....	....	6	0	3	3	20	....	....	....	....
2007-08	Quad City Flames	AHL	79	10	27	37	248	....	....	....	....	....	....	....	....	....	....	....	....	....	....	....	....	....	....
2008-09	**Calgary**	**NHL**	**25**	**1**	**1**	**2**	**79**	**0**	**0**	**1**	**15**	**6.7**	**-4**	**15**	**53.3**	**6:21**	....	....	....	....	....	....	....	....	....
	Phoenix	**NHL**	**11**	**0**	**1**	**1**	**29**	**0**	**0**	**0**	**8**	**0.0**	**-4**	**16**	**56.3**	**9:59**	....	....	....	....	....	....	....	....	....
2009-10	**Calgary**	**NHL**	**43**	**1**	**4**	**5**	**98**	**0**	**0**	**1**	**23**	**4.3**	**6**	**29**	**37.9**	**6:33**	....	....	....	....	....	....	....	....	....
	NY Rangers	**NHL**	**26**	**4**	**5**	**9**	**65**	**0**	**0**	**2**	**21**	**19.0**	**3**	**2**	**100.0**	**9:20**	....	....	....	....	....	....	....	....	....
2010-11	**NY Rangers**	**NHL**	**82**	**13**	**16**	**29**	**160**	**0**	**5**	**1**	**87**	**14.9**	**2**	**9**	**44.4**	**13:49**	**5**	**0**	**1**	**1**	**4**	**0**	**0**	**0**	**16:24**
2011-12	**NY Rangers**	**NHL**	**82**	**5**	**12**	**17**	**156**	**0**	**2**	**2**	**68**	**7.4**	**-1**	**5**	**60.0**	**11:57**	**19**	**1**	**1**	**2**	**31**	**0**	**0**	**0**	**12:47**
2012-13	**Montreal**	**NHL**	**38**	**5**	**9**	**14**	**110**	**0**	**0**	**1**	**39**	**12.8**	**11**	**55**	**45.5**	**13:38**	**4**	**0**	**1**	**1**	**14**	**0**	**0**	**0**	**15:27**
2013-14	**Montreal**	**NHL**	**52**	**6**	**7**	**13**	**121**	**0**	**0**	**3**	**49**	**12.2**	**-1**	**125**	**52.0**	**12:49**	**13**	**0**	**2**	**2**	**32**	**0**	**0**	**0**	**12:13**
2014-15	**Montreal**	**NHL**	**82**	**4**	**14**	**18**	**134**	**0**	**0**	**0**	**78**	**5.1**	**6**	**31**	**51.6**	**12:58**	**12**	**1**	**3**	**4**	**35**	**0**	**0**	**0**	**13:47**

Season	Club	League	GP	G	A	Pts	PIM	PP	SH	GW	S	S%	+/-	TF	F%	Min	GP	G	A	Pts	PIM	PP	SH	GW	Min
			Regular Season														Playoffs								
2015-16	**Vancouver**	**NHL**	**35**	**1**	**6**	**7**	**59**	**0**	**0**	**1**	**19**	**5.3**	**–3**	**11**	**54.6**	**12:47**									
	Utica Comets	AHL	9	1	6	7	5																		
2016-17	Nurnberg	Germany	29	3	5	8	67										11	2	4	6	*51				
	NHL Totals		**486**	**40**	**75**	**115**	**1036**	**0**	**7**	**12**	**408**	**9.8**		**298**	**50.0**	**11:39**	**53**	**2**	**8**	**10**	**116**	**0**	**0**	**0**	**13:25**

Traded to **Phoenix** by **Calgary** with Matthew Lombardi and Calgary's 1st round pick (Brandon Gormley) in 2010 NHL Draft for Olli Jokinen and Phoenix's 3rd round pick (later traded to Florida – Florida selected Josh Birkholz) in 2009 NHL Draft, March 4, 2009. Traded to **Calgary** by **Phoenix** for Jim Vandermeer, June 27, 2009. Traded to **NY Rangers** by **Calgary** with Olli Jokinen for Chris Higgins and Ales Kotalik, February 2, 2010. Signed as a free agent by **Montreal**, July 1, 2012. Traded to **Vancouver** by **Montreal** for Zack Kassian and Vancouver's 5th round pick (Casey Staum) in 2016 NHL Draft, July 1, 2015. Signed as a free agent by **Nurnberg** (Germany), November 26, 2016.

PUEMPEL, Matt

(PUHM-puhl, MAT) **NYR**

Left wing. Shoots left. 6'1", 205 lbs. Born, Windsor, ON, January 24, 1993. Ottawa's 3rd pick, 24th overall, in 2011 NHL Draft.

Season	Club	League	GP	G	A	Pts	PIM	PP	SH	GW	S	S%	+/-	TF	F%	Min	GP	G	A	Pts	PIM	PP	SH	GW	Min
2008-09	Sun County	Minor-ON	76	88	56	144																			
	Leamington Flyers	ON-Jr.B	1	2	0	2	0																		
2009-10	Peterborough	OHL	59	33	31	64	43										4	1	1	2	6				
2010-11	Peterborough	OHL	55	34	35	69	49																		
2011-12	Peterborough	OHL	30	17	16	33	31																		
	Binghamton	AHL	9	1	0	1	2																		
2012-13	Kitchener Rangers	OHL	51	35	12	47	43										10	3	4	7	10				
	Binghamton	AHL	2	0	0	0	0										3	2	0	2	0				
2013-14	Binghamton	AHL	74	30	18	48	94										1	0	0	0	0				
2014-15	**Ottawa**	**NHL**	**13**	**2**	**1**	**3**	**8**	**0**	**0**	**0**	**14**	**14.3**	**6**	**1**	**0.0**	**8:02**									
	Binghamton	AHL	51	12	20	32	31																		
2015-16	**Ottawa**	**NHL**	**26**	**2**	**1**	**3**	**9**	**0**	**0**	**1**	**26**	**7.7**	**–3**	**2**	**50.0**	**11:20**									
	Binghamton	AHL	34	17	13	30	15																		
2016-17	**Ottawa**	**NHL**	**13**	**0**	**0**	**0**	**7**	**0**	**0**	**0**	**12**	**0.0**	**–5**	**1**	**0.0**	**8:34**									
	NY Rangers	**NHL**	**27**	**6**	**3**	**9**	**4**	**3**	**0**	**1**	**32**	**18.8**	**–6**	**0**	**0.0**	**10:10**									
	NHL Totals		**79**	**10**	**5**	**15**	**28**	**3**	**0**	**2**	**84**	**11.9**		**4**	**25.0**	**9:56**									

OHL All-Rookie Team (2010) • OHL Rookie of the Year (2010) • Canadian Major Junior All-Rookie Team (2010) • Canadian Major Junior Rookie of the Year (2010)

Claimed on waivers by **NY Rangers** from **Ottawa**, November 21, 2016.

PULJUJARVI, Jesse

(poo-LEE-ahr-vee, yeh-SEH) **EDM**

Right wing. Shoots right. 6'4", 203 lbs. Born, Alvkarleby, Sweden, May 7, 1998. Edmonton's 1st pick, 4th overall, in 2016 NHL Draft.

Season	Club	League	GP	G	A	Pts	PIM	PP	SH	GW	S	S%	+/-	TF	F%	Min	GP	G	A	Pts	PIM	PP	SH	GW	Min
2012-13	Karpat Oulu U18	Fin-U18	42	31	20	51	14										3	0	1	1	0				
2013-14	Karpat Oulu U18	Fin-U18	8	7	7	14	8																		
	Karpat Oulu Jr.	Fin-Jr.	18	12	11	23	4										12	7	0	7	2				
2014-15	Karpat Oulu Jr.	Fin-Jr.	11	12	6	18	10										5	2	1	3	4				
	Karpat Oulu	Finland	21	4	7	11	10																		
	Hokki Kajaani	Finland-2	15	8	5	13	8										3	0	1	1	0				
2015-16	Karpat Oulu	Finland	50	13	15	28	22										10	4	5	9	2				
2016-17	**Edmonton**	**NHL**	**28**	**1**	**7**	**8**	**10**	**1**	**0**	**0**	**41**	**2.4**	**5**	**1**	**0.0**	**11:15**									
	Bakersfield	AHL	39	12	16	28	10																		
	NHL Totals		**28**	**1**	**7**	**8**	**10**	**1**	**0**	**0**	**41**	**2.4**		**1**	**0.0**	**11:15**									

PULKKINEN, Teemu

(PUHL-kih-nuhn, TEE-moo) **VGK**

Left wing. Shoots right. 5'11", 183 lbs. Born, Vantaa, Finland, January 2, 1992. Detroit's 4th pick, 111th overall, in 2010 NHL Draft.

Season	Club	League	GP	G	A	Pts	PIM	PP	SH	GW	S	S%	+/-	TF	F%	Min	GP	G	A	Pts	PIM	PP	SH	GW	Min
2007-08	Jokerit U18	Fin-U18	32	36	24	60	8										6	11	6	17	6				
2008-09	Suomi U20	Finland-2	1	0	0	0	0																		
	Jokerit U18	Fin-U18	9	16	19	35	4																		
	Jokerit Helsinki Jr.	Fin-Jr.	24	15	13	28	12																		
	Jokerit Helsinki	Finland	3	0	0	0	6																		
2009-10	Jokerit Helsinki Jr.	Fin-Jr.	17	20	21	41	41										4	3	3	6	0				
	Jokerit Helsinki	Finland	12	1	2	3	6																		
2010-11	Suomi U20	Finland-2	1	1	0	1	0																		
	Jokerit Helsinki	Finland	55	18	36	54	32										3	0	1	1	0				
2011-12	Jokerit Helsinki	Finland	56	16	21	37	41										4	0	1	1	2				
2012-13	Jokerit Helsinki	Finland	59	14	20	34	49										6	2	3	5	22				
	Grand Rapids	AHL	2	0	1	1	2										14	3	2	5	10				
2013-14	**Detroit**	**NHL**	**3**	**0**	**0**	**0**	**2**	**0**	**0**	**0**	**4**	**0.0**	**0**	**0**	**0.0**	**7:28**									
	Grand Rapids	AHL	71	31	28	59	34										10	5	6	11	10				
2014-15	**Detroit**	**NHL**	**31**	**5**	**3**	**8**	**10**	**1**	**0**	**2**	**67**	**7.5**	**5**	**0**	**0.0**	**11:29**									
	Grand Rapids	AHL	46	*34	27	61	30										16	14	4	18	22				
2015-16	**Detroit**	**NHL**	**36**	**6**	**6**	**12**	**14**	**1**	**0**	**1**	**65**	**9.2**	**2**	**1**	**0.0**	**11:34**									
2016-17	**Minnesota**	**NHL**	**9**	**1**	**0**	**1**	**2**	**0**	**0**	**0**	**4**	**25.0**	**–1**	**0**	**0.0**	**9:23**									
	Iowa Wild	AHL	47	18	18	36	36																		
	Arizona	**NHL**	**4**	**1**	**0**	**1**	**4**	**0**	**0**	**0**	**6**	**16.7**	**–1**	**1**	**0.0**	**9:46**									
	NHL Totals		**83**	**13**	**9**	**22**	**32**	**2**	**0**	**3**	**146**	**8.9**		**2**	**0.0**	**11:04**									

AHL All-Rookie Team (2014) • AHL First All-Star Team (2015) • Willie Marshall Award (AHL – Top Goal-scorer) (2015)

• Missed majority of 2015-16 due to shoulder injury vs. Arizona, December 3, 2015 and as a healthy reserve. Claimed on waivers by **Minnesota** from **Detroit**, October 11, 2016. Traded to **Arizona** by **Minnesota** for future considerations, February 27, 2017. Claimed by **Vegas** from **Arizona** in Expansion Draft, June 21, 2017.

PULOCK, Ryan

(POO-lawk, RIGH-uhn) **NYI**

Defense. Shoots right. 6'2", 215 lbs. Born, Dauphin, MB, October 6, 1994. NY Islanders' 1st pick, 15th overall, in 2013 NHL Draft.

Season	Club	League	GP	G	A	Pts	PIM	PP	SH	GW	S	S%	+/-	TF	F%	Min	GP	G	A	Pts	PIM	PP	SH	GW	Min
2009-10	Parkland Rangers	MMHL	39	9	10	19	8										3	0	1	1	0				
2010-11	Brandon	WHL	63	8	34	42	4										6	2	4	6	2				
2011-12	Brandon	WHL	71	19	41	60	20										9	3	2	5	0				
2012-13	Brandon	WHL	61	14	31	45	22																		
2013-14	Brandon	WHL	66	23	40	63	18										9	2	2	4	6				
	Bridgeport	AHL	3	0	1	1	2																		
2014-15	Bridgeport	AHL	54	17	12	29	6																		
2015-16	**NY Islanders**	**NHL**	**15**	**2**	**2**	**4**	**5**	**0**	**0**	**0**	**15**	**13.3**	**1**	**0**	**0.0**	**15:44**	**6**	**1**	**2**	**3**	**0**	**1**	**0**	**0**	**14:34**
	Bridgeport	AHL	51	7	17	24	12																		
2016-17	**NY Islanders**	**NHL**	**1**	**0**	**0**	**0**	**0**	**0**	**0**	**0**	**0**	**0.0**	**1**	**0**	**0.0**	**3:57**									
	Bridgeport	AHL	55	15	31	46	18																		
	NHL Totals		**16**	**2**	**2**	**4**	**5**	**0**	**0**	**0**	**15**	**13.3**		**0**	**0.0**	**15:00**	**6**	**1**	**2**	**3**	**0**	**1**	**0**	**0**	**14:34**

WHL East First All-Star Team (2012, 2014) • AHL All-Rookie Team (2015)

PURCELL, Teddy

(PUHR-sihl, TEH-dee)

Right wing. Shoots right. 6'2", 195 lbs. Born, St. Johns, NL, September 8, 1985.

Season	Club	League	GP	G	A	Pts	PIM	PP	SH	GW	S	S%	+/-	TF	F%	Min	GP	G	A	Pts	PIM	PP	SH	GW	Min
2003-04	Notre Dame	SJHL	51	21	25	46	8																		
2004-05	Cedar Rapids	USHL	58	20	47	67	22										11	5	9	14	4				
2005-06	Cedar Rapids	USHL	55	19	*52	71	14										8	3	8	11	4				
2006-07	U. of Maine	H-East	40	16	27	43	34																		
2007-08	**Los Angeles**	**NHL**	**10**	**1**	**2**	**3**	**0**	**0**	**0**	**0**	**10**	**10.0**	**2**	**0**	**0.0**	**11:59**									
	Manchester	AHL	67	25	58	83	34										4	0	3	3	0				
2008-09	**Los Angeles**	**NHL**	**40**	**4**	**12**	**16**	**4**	**2**	**0**	**1**	**68**	**5.9**	**–4**	**29**	**17.2**	**13:31**									
	Manchester	AHL	38	16	22	38	12																		
2009-10	**Los Angeles**	**NHL**	**41**	**3**	**3**	**6**	**4**	**1**	**0**	**1**	**55**	**5.5**	**–1**	**3**	**33.3**	**11:22**									
	Tampa Bay	**NHL**	**19**	**3**	**6**	**9**	**6**	**1**	**0**	**0**	**46**	**6.5**	**–8**	**1**	**100.0**	**16:05**									
2010-11	**Tampa Bay**	**NHL**	**81**	**17**	**34**	**51**	**10**	**3**	**0**	**1**	**196**	**8.7**	**5**	**37**	**32.4**	**14:06**	**18**	**6**	**11**	**17**	**2**	**1**	**0**	**1**	**13:42**
2011-12	**Tampa Bay**	**NHL**	**81**	**24**	**41**	**65**	**16**	**8**	**0**	**3**	**152**	**15.8**	**9**	**17**	**17.7**	**16:08**									
2012-13	**Tampa Bay**	**NHL**	**48**	**11**	**25**	**36**	**12**	**3**	**0**	**2**	**94**	**11.7**	**–1**	**6**	**33.3**	**16:45**									
2013-14	**Tampa Bay**	**NHL**	**81**	**12**	**30**	**42**	**14**	**3**	**0**	**4**	**157**	**7.6**	**–3**	**16**	**25.0**	**16:28**	**4**	**1**	**0**	**1**	**0**	**1**	**0**	**0**	**15:32**
2014-15	**Edmonton**	**NHL**	**82**	**12**	**22**	**34**	**24**	**5**	**0**	**0**	**146**	**8.2**	**–33**	**7**	**57.1**	**17:10**									

Season	Club	League	GP	G	A	Pts	PIM	PP	SH	GW	S	S%	+/-	TF	F%	Min	Playoffs GP	G	A	Pts	PIM	PP	SH	GW	Min
2015-16	**Edmonton**	**NHL**	**61**	**11**	**21**	**32**	**10**	**2**	**0**	**2**	**130**	**8.5**	**-9**	**5**	**20.0**	**17:27**	....	....	....	....	....	....	....	....	....
	Florida	**NHL**	**15**	**3**	**8**	**11**	**2**	**0**	**0**	**0**	**19**	**15.8**	**-2**	**1**	**100.0**	**14:19**	**6**	**2**	**0**	**2**	**0**	**1**	**0**	**0**	**15:33**
2016-17	**Los Angeles**	**NHL**	**12**	**0**	**2**	**2**	**0**	**0**	**0**	**0**	**10**	**0.0**	**0**	**3**	**100.0**	**12:54**	....	....	....	....	....	....	....	....	....
	Ontario Reign	AHL	38	10	28	38	2	....	....	....	....	....	....	....	....	....	5	0	2	2	2	....	....	....	....
	NHL Totals		**571**	**101**	**206**	**307**	**102**	**28**	**0**	**14**	**1083**	**9.3**		**125**	**29.6**	**15:31**	**28**	**9**	**11**	**20**	**2**	**3**	**0**	**1**	**14:22**

AHL All-Rookie Team (2008) • AHL First All-Star Team (2008) • Dudley "Red" Garrett Memorial Award (AHL) (AHL – Rookie of the Year) (2008)

Signed as a free agent by **Los Angeles**, April 27, 2007. Traded to **Tampa Bay** by **Los Angeles** with Florida's 3rd round pick (previously acquired, Tampa Bay selected Brock Beukeboom) in 2010 NHL Draft for Jeff Halpern, March 3, 2010. Traded to **Edmonton** by **Tampa Bay** for Sam Gagner, June 29, 2014. Traded to **Florida** by **Edmonton** for Florida's 3rd round pick (Matthew Cairns) in 2016 NHL Draft, February 27, 2016. Signed as a free agent by **Los Angeles**, July 1, 2016.

PYATT, Tom (PIGH-at, TAWM) OTT

Center. Shoots left. 5'11", 188 lbs. Born, Thunder Bay, ON, February 14, 1987. NY Rangers' 6th pick, 107th overall, in 2005 NHL Draft.

Season	Club	League	GP	G	A	Pts	PIM	PP	SH	GW	S	S%	+/-	TF	F%	Min	Playoffs GP	G	A	Pts	PIM	PP	SH	GW	Min
2003-04	Saginaw Spirit	OHL	67	9	9	18	21	....	....	....	....	....	....	....	....	....	....	....	....	....	....	....	....	....	....
2004-05	Saginaw Spirit	OHL	57	18	30	48	14	....	....	....	....	....	....	....	....	....	....	....	....	....	....	....	....	....	....
2005-06	Saginaw Spirit	OHL	58	24	29	53	29	....	....	....	....	....	....	....	....	....	4	1	2	3	4	....	....	....	....
2006-07	Saginaw Spirit	OHL	58	43	38	81	18	....	....	....	....	....	....	....	....	....	6	3	5	8	0	....	....	....	....
	Hartford	AHL	1	0	0	0	0	....	....	....	....	....	....	....	....	....	....	....	....	....	....	....	....	....	....
2007-08	Hartford	AHL	41	4	7	11	6	....	....	....	....	....	....	....	....	....	3	0	0	0	0	....	....	....	....
	Charlotte	ECHL	16	6	9	15	8	....	....	....	....	....	....	....	....	....	3	0	0	0	0	....	....	....	....
2008-09	Hartford	AHL	73	15	22	37	22	....	....	....	....	....	....	....	....	....	4	0	0	0	2	....	....	....	....
2009-10	**Montreal**	**NHL**	**40**	**2**	**3**	**5**	**10**	**0**	**0**	**0**	**48**	**4.2**	**-5**	**50**	**42.0**	**11:04**	**18**	**2**	**2**	**4**	**2**	**0**	**0**	**1**	**13:03**
	Hamilton	AHL	41	13	22	35	8	....	....	....	....	....	....	....	....	....	....	....	....	....	....	....	....	....	....
2010-11	**Montreal**	**NHL**	**61**	**2**	**5**	**7**	**9**	**0**	**0**	**0**	**65**	**3.1**	**-1**	**110**	**50.0**	**10:38**	**7**	**0**	**0**	**0**	**0**	**0**	**0**	**0**	**9:54**
2011-12	**Tampa Bay**	**NHL**	**74**	**12**	**7**	**19**	**8**	**1**	**0**	**1**	**95**	**12.6**	**-19**	**281**	**45.6**	**14:48**	....	....	....	....	....	....	....	....	....
2012-13	**Tampa Bay**	**NHL**	**43**	**8**	**8**	**16**	**12**	**0**	**0**	**1**	**60**	**13.3**	**5**	**290**	**50.0**	**13:35**	....	....	....	....	....	....	....	....	....
2013-14	**Tampa Bay**	**NHL**	**27**	**3**	**4**	**7**	**4**	**0**	**0**	**1**	**27**	**11.1**	**-2**	**193**	**52.3**	**11:28**	**1**	**0**	**0**	**0**	**0**	**0**	**0**	**0**	**7:54**
2014-15	Geneve	Swiss	50	11	22	33	10	....	....	....	....	....	....	....	....	....	11	2	8	10	0	....	....	....	....
2015-16	Geneve	Swiss	42	11	18	29	8	....	....	....	....	....	....	....	....	....	5	1	3	4	0	....	....	....	....
2016-17	**Ottawa**	**NHL**	**82**	**9**	**14**	**23**	**16**	**0**	**0**	**1**	**95**	**9.5**	**9**	**49**	**42.9**	**15:38**	**14**	**2**	**0**	**2**	**0**	**0**	**0**	**0**	**13:15**
	NHL Totals		**327**	**36**	**41**	**77**	**59**	**1**	**0**	**4**	**390**	**9.2**		**973**	**48.4**	**13:20**	**40**	**4**	**2**	**6**	**2**	**0**	**0**	**1**	**12:27**

Traded to **Montreal** by **NY Rangers** with Scott Gomez and Michael Busto for Chris Higgins, Ryan McDonagh and Pavel Valentenko, June 30, 2009. Signed as a free agent by **Tampa Bay**, July 6, 2011. • Missed majority of 2013-14 due to collarbone injury at Buffalo, October 8, 2013 and as a healthy reserve. Signed as a free agent by **Geneve** (Swiss), August 4, 2014. Signed as a free agent by **Ottawa**, May 24, 2016.

PYSYK, Mark (PEHS-ihk, MAHRK) FLA

Defense. Shoots right. 6'1", 192 lbs. Born, Edmonton, AB, January 11, 1992. Buffalo's 1st pick, 23rd overall, in 2010 NHL Draft.

Season	Club	League	GP	G	A	Pts	PIM	PP	SH	GW	S	S%	+/-	TF	F%	Min	Playoffs GP	G	A	Pts	PIM	PP	SH	GW	Min
2007-08	Sherwood Park	AMHL	34	10	10	20	60	....	....	....	....	....	....	....	....	....	2	1	0	1	16	....	....	....	....
	Edmonton	WHL	14	1	2	3	8	....	....	....	....	....	....	....	....	....	....	....	....	....	....	....	....	....	....
2008-09	Edmonton	WHL	61	5	15	20	27	....	....	....	....	....	....	....	....	....	4	0	0	0	2	....	....	....	....
2009-10	Edmonton	WHL	48	7	17	24	47	....	....	....	....	....	....	....	....	....	....	....	....	....	....	....	....	....	....
2010-11	Edmonton	WHL	63	6	34	40	88	....	....	....	....	....	....	....	....	....	4	0	0	0	6	....	....	....	....
2011-12	Edmonton	WHL	57	6	32	38	83	....	....	....	....	....	....	....	....	....	20	3	8	11	16	....	....	....	....
2012-13	Rochester	AHL	57	4	14	18	20	....	....	....	....	....	....	....	....	....	3	0	0	0	2	....	....	....	....
	Buffalo	**NHL**	**19**	**1**	**4**	**5**	**0**	**1**	**0**	**0**	**21**	**4.8**	**-7**	**0**	**0.0**	**16:17**	....	....	....	....	....	....	....	....	....
2013-14	**Buffalo**	**NHL**	**44**	**1**	**6**	**7**	**16**	**0**	**0**	**1**	**51**	**2.0**	**-11**	**0**	**0.0**	**19:37**	....	....	....	....	....	....	....	....	....
	Rochester	AHL	31	1	11	12	28	....	....	....	....	....	....	....	....	....	5	0	0	0	14	....	....	....	....
2014-15	**Buffalo**	**NHL**	**7**	**2**	**1**	**3**	**2**	**0**	**0**	**1**	**4**	**50.0**	**4**	**0**	**0.0**	**18:11**	....	....	....	....	....	....	....	....	....
	Rochester	AHL	54	3	14	17	32	....	....	....	....	....	....	....	....	....	....	....	....	....	....	....	....	....	....
2015-16	**Buffalo**	**NHL**	**55**	**1**	**10**	**11**	**32**	**0**	**0**	**0**	**44**	**2.3**	**-1**	**0**	**0.0**	**15:54**	....	....	....	....	....	....	....	....	....
	Rochester	AHL	3	0	1	1	2	....	....	....	....	....	....	....	....	....	....	....	....	....	....	....	....	....	....
2016-17	**Florida**	**NHL**	**82**	**4**	**13**	**17**	**10**	**0**	**0**	**0**	**86**	**4.7**	**0**	**1**	**0.0**	**18:34**	....	....	....	....	....	....	....	....	....
	NHL Totals		**207**	**9**	**34**	**43**	**60**	**1**	**0**	**2**	**206**	**4.4**		**1**	**0.0**	**17:51**	....	....	....	....	....	....	....	....	....

WHL East Second All-Star Team (2012)

Traded to **Florida** by **Buffalo** with Buffalo's 2nd round pick (Adam Mascherin) in 2016 NHL Draft and St. Louis' 3rd round pick (previously acquired, Florida selected Linus Nassen) in 2016 NHL Draft for Dmitry Kulikov and Vancouver's 2nd round pick (previously acquired, Buffalo selected Rasmus Asplund) in 2016 NHL Draft, June 25, 2016.

QUENNEVILLE, John (KWEHN-vihl, JAWN) N.J.

Center. Shoots left. 6'1", 195 lbs. Born, Edmonton, AB, April 16, 1996. New Jersey's 1st pick, 30th overall, in 2014 NHL Draft.

Season	Club	League	GP	G	A	Pts	PIM	PP	SH	GW	S	S%	+/-	TF	F%	Min	Playoffs GP	G	A	Pts	PIM	PP	SH	GW	Min
2009-10	Sherwood Park	AMBHL	29	15	15	30	51	....	....	....	....	....	....	....	....	....	....	....	....	....	....	....	....	....	....
2010-11	SSAC Lions	AMBHL	33	35	40	75	52	....	....	....	....	....	....	....	....	....	2	2	2	4	0	....	....	....	....
	SSAC Bulldogs	Minor-AB	2	1	3	4	0	....	....	....	....	....	....	....	....	....	....	....	....	....	....	....	....	....	....
2011-12	SSAC Athletics	AMHL	30	15	18	33	40	....	....	....	....	....	....	....	....	....	6	2	1	3	20	....	....	....	....
	Sherwood Park	AJHL	9	0	3	3	0	....	....	....	....	....	....	....	....	....	2	2	0	2	0	....	....	....	....
2012-13	Brandon	WHL	47	8	11	19	14	....	....	....	....	....	....	....	....	....	....	....	....	....	....	....	....	....	....
2013-14	Brandon	WHL	61	25	33	58	71	....	....	....	....	....	....	....	....	....	9	5	8	13	10	....	....	....	....
2014-15	Brandon	WHL	57	17	30	47	63	....	....	....	....	....	....	....	....	....	19	10	9	19	18	....	....	....	....
2015-16	Brandon	WHL	57	31	42	73	71	....	....	....	....	....	....	....	....	....	21	*16	11	27	8	....	....	....	....
2016-17	**New Jersey**	**NHL**	**12**	**1**	**3**	**4**	**2**	**1**	**0**	**0**	**21**	**4.8**	**1**	**0**	**0.0**	**13:42**	....	....	....	....	....	....	....	....	....
	Albany Devils	AHL	58	14	32	46	53	....	....	....	....	....	....	....	....	....	4	3	1	4	4	....	....	....	....
	NHL Totals		**12**	**1**	**3**	**4**	**2**	**1**	**0**	**0**	**21**	**4.8**		**0**	**0.0**	**13:42**	....	....	....	....	....	....	....	....	....

QUINCEY, Kyle (KWIHN-see, KIGHL) MIN

Defense. Shoots left. 6'2", 216 lbs. Born, Kitchener, ON, August 12, 1985. Detroit's 2nd pick, 132nd overall, in 2003 NHL Draft.

Season	Club	League	GP	G	A	Pts	PIM	PP	SH	GW	S	S%	+/-	TF	F%	Min	Playoffs GP	G	A	Pts	PIM	PP	SH	GW	Min
2001-02	Mississauga	ON-Jr.A	27	5	14	19	31	....	....	....	....	....	....	....	....	....	....	....	....	....	....	....	....	....	....
2002-03	London Knights	OHL	66	6	12	18	77	....	....	....	....	....	....	....	....	....	14	3	4	7	11	....	....	....	....
2003-04	London Knights	OHL	3	0	2	2	4	....	....	....	....	....	....	....	....	....	....	....	....	....	....	....	....	....	....
	Mississauga	OHL	61	14	23	37	135	....	....	....	....	....	....	....	....	....	24	3	13	16	32	....	....	....	....
2004-05	Mississauga	OHL	59	15	31	46	111	....	....	....	....	....	....	....	....	....	5	0	3	3	4	....	....	....	....
2005-06	**Detroit**	**NHL**	**1**	**0**	**0**	**0**	**0**	**0**	**0**	**0**	**1**	**0.0**	**0**	**0**	**0.0**	**11:37**	....	....	....	....	....	....	....	....	....
	Grand Rapids	AHL	70	7	26	33	107	....	....	....	....	....	....	....	....	....	16	0	1	1	27	....	....	....	....
2006-07	**Detroit**	**NHL**	**6**	**1**	**0**	**1**	**0**	**0**	**0**	**0**	**7**	**14.3**	**0**	**0**	**0.0**	**11:26**	**13**	**0**	**0**	**0**	**2**	**0**	**0**	**0**	**8:11**
	Grand Rapids	AHL	65	4	18	22	126	....	....	....	....	....	....	....	....	....	2	0	0	0	0	....	....	....	....
2007-08	**Detroit**	**NHL**	**6**	**0**	**0**	**0**	**4**	**0**	**0**	**0**	**5**	**0.0**	**-3**	**0**	**0.0**	**13:58**	....	....	....	....	....	....	....	....	....
	Grand Rapids	AHL	66	5	15	20	149	....	....	....	....	....	....	....	....	....	....	....	....	....	....	....	....	....	....
2008-09	**Los Angeles**	**NHL**	**72**	**4**	**34**	**38**	**63**	**2**	**0**	**2**	**150**	**2.7**	**-5**	**0**	**0.0**	**20:59**	....	....	....	....	....	....	....	....	....
2009-10	**Colorado**	**NHL**	**79**	**6**	**23**	**29**	**76**	**1**	**0**	**0**	**139**	**4.3**	**9**	**1**	**0.0**	**23:37**	**6**	**0**	**0**	**0**	**8**	**0**	**0**	**0**	**22:06**
2010-11	**Colorado**	**NHL**	**21**	**0**	**1**	**1**	**18**	**0**	**0**	**0**	**39**	**0.0**	**-5**	**0**	**0.0**	**19:35**	....	....	....	....	....	....	....	....	....
2011-12	**Colorado**	**NHL**	**54**	**5**	**18**	**23**	**60**	**3**	**0**	**1**	**131**	**3.8**	**-1**	**1**	**0.0**	**22:21**	....	....	....	....	....	....	....	....	....
	Detroit	**NHL**	**18**	**2**	**1**	**3**	**29**	**1**	**0**	**0**	**37**	**5.4**	**0**	**0**	**0.0**	**20:22**	**5**	**0**	**2**	**2**	**6**	**0**	**0**	**0**	**16:29**
2012-13	Denver	CHL	12	2	9	11	6	....	....	....	....	....	....	....	....	....	....	....	....	....	....	....	....	....	....
	Detroit	**NHL**	**36**	**1**	**2**	**3**	**18**	**0**	**0**	**0**	**36**	**2.8**	**7**	**0**	**0.0**	**19:13**	**14**	**0**	**2**	**2**	**12**	**0**	**0**	**0**	**19:02**
2013-14	**Detroit**	**NHL**	**82**	**4**	**9**	**13**	**88**	**0**	**0**	**1**	**106**	**3.8**	**-5**	**0**	**0.0**	**20:48**	**5**	**0**	**0**	**0**	**2**	**0**	**0**	**0**	**21:25**
2014-15	**Detroit**	**NHL**	**73**	**3**	**15**	**18**	**77**	**0**	**0**	**0**	**90**	**3.3**	**10**	**0**	**0.0**	**19:29**	**7**	**0**	**3**	**3**	**4**	**0**	**0**	**0**	**19:39**
2015-16	**Detroit**	**NHL**	**47**	**4**	**7**	**11**	**36**	**0**	**0**	**2**	**62**	**6.5**	**1**	**0**	**0.0**	**19:46**	**4**	**0**	**1**	**1**	**4**	**0**	**0**	**0**	**18:53**
2016-17	**New Jersey**	**NHL**	**53**	**4**	**8**	**12**	**39**	**0**	**0**	**0**	**61**	**6.6**	**4**	**0**	**0.0**	**18:38**	....	....	....	....	....	....	....	....	....
	Columbus	**NHL**	**20**	**2**	**1**	**3**	**12**	**0**	**0**	**0**	**18**	**11.1**	**0**	**0**	**0.0**	**15:55**	**2**	**0**	**1**	**1**	**2**	**0**	**0**	**0**	**19:02**
	NHL Totals		**568**	**36**	**119**	**155**	**520**	**7**	**0**	**6**	**882**	**4.1**		**2**	**0.0**	**20:23**	**56**	**0**	**9**	**9**	**40**	**0**	**0**	**0**	**16:54**

OHL Second All-Star Team (2005)

Claimed on waivers by **Los Angeles** from **Detroit**, October 13, 2008. Traded to **Colorado** by **Los Angeles** with Tom Preissing and Los Angeles' 5th round pick (Luke Walker) in 2010 NHL Draft for Ryan Smyth, July 3, 2009. • Missed majority of 2010-11 due to shoulder injury at Atlanta, December 10, 2010. Traded to **Tampa Bay** by **Colorado** for Steve Downie, February 21, 2012. Traded to **Detroit** by **Tampa Bay** for Sebastien Piche and Detroit's 1st round pick (Andrei Vasilevskiy) in 2012 NHL Draft, February 21, 2012. Signed as a free agent by **Denver** (CHL), October 12, 2012. Signed as a free agent by **New Jesey**, September 28, 2016. Traded to **Columbus** by **New Jersey** for Dalton Prout, March 1, 2017. Signed as a free agent by **Minnesota**, July 1, 2017.

QUINE, Alan
(KWIH-nee, AL-uhn) **NYI**

Center. Shoots left. 6', 200 lbs. Born, Orleans, ON, February 25, 1993. NY Islanders' 6th pick, 166th overall, in 2013 NHL Draft.

			Regular Season														Playoffs								
Season	Club	League	GP	G	A	Pts	PIM	PP	SH	GW	S	S%	+/-	TF	F%	Min	GP	G	A	Pts	PIM	PP	SH	GW	Min
2008-09	Tor. Jr. Canadiens	GTHL	35	26	26	52	8																		
	Tor. Canadiens	ON-Jr.A	2	1	1	2	0																		
2009-10	Kingston	OHL	64	11	17	28	8										7	1	2	3	0				
2010-11	Kingston	OHL	17	4	7	11	2																		
	Peterborough	OHL	52	22	20	42	6																		
2011-12	Peterborough	OHL	65	30	40	70	21																		
	Grand Rapids	AHL	3	0	1	1	0																		
2012-13	Peterborough	OHL	26	9	17	26	14																		
	Belleville Bulls	OHL	28	14	27	41	6										17	8	7	15	6				
2013-14	Bridgeport	AHL	61	8	19	27	23																		
	Stockton Thunder	ECHL	7	2	6	8	2										8	3	1	4	0				
2014-15	Bridgeport	AHL	75	23	38	61	34																		
2015-16	**NY Islanders**	**NHL**	**2**	**1**	**0**	**1**	**0**	**0**	**1**	**0**	**5**	**20.0**	**0**	**26**	**61.5**	**17:46**	**10**	**1**	**4**	**5**	**2**	**1**	**0**	**1**	**15:23**
	Bridgeport	AHL	56	19	29	48	24																		
2016-17	**NY Islanders**	**NHL**	**61**	**5**	**13**	**18**	**8**	**2**	**0**	**1**	**82**	**6.1**	**-2**	**550**	**48.0**	**12:31**									
	NHL Totals		**63**	**6**	**13**	**19**	**8**	**2**	**1**	**1**	**87**	**6.9**		**576**	**48.6**	**12:41**	**10**	**1**	**4**	**5**	**2**	**1**	**0**	**1**	**15:23**

• Re-entered NHL Entry Draft. Originally Detroit's 4th pick, 85th overall, in 2011 NHL Draft.

RACINE, Jonathan
(RAY-seen, JAWN-ah-thuhn)

Defense. Shoots left. 6'2", 194 lbs. Born, Montreal, QC, May 28, 1993. Florida's 6th pick, 87th overall, in 2011 NHL Draft.

Season	Club	League	GP	G	A	Pts	PIM	PP	SH	GW	S	S%	+/-	TF	F%	Min	GP	G	A	Pts	PIM	PP	SH	GW	Min
2008-09	Saint-Eustache	QAAA	45	5	7	12	74										8	0	2	2	12				
2009-10	Shawinigan	QMJHL	55	0	4	4	43										6	0	0	0	0				
2010-11	Shawinigan	QMJHL	68	2	5	7	86										12	0	1	1	22				
2011-12	Shawinigan	QMJHL	61	3	10	13	107										11	1	5	6	22				
2012-13	Moncton Wildcats	QMJHL	61	8	13	21	138										5	0	0	0	7				
	San Antonio	AHL	8	0	0	0	4																		
2013-14	**Florida**	**NHL**	**1**	**0**	**0**	**0**	**2**	**0**	**0**	**0**	**0**	**0.0**	**-1**	**0**	**0.0**	**15:35**									
	San Antonio	AHL	51	0	6	6	91																		
2014-15	San Antonio	AHL	70	0	7	7	149										3	0	1	1	4				
2015-16	Portland Pirates	AHL	69	1	8	9	89										5	0	0	0	4				
2016-17	St. John's IceCaps	AHL	26	0	3	3	58																		
	Syracuse Crunch	AHL	29	1	2	3	78										5	1	1	2	2				
	NHL Totals		**1**	**0**	**0**	**0**	**2**	**0**	**0**	**0**	**0**	**0.0**		**0**	**0.0**	**15:35**									

Traded to **Montreal** by **Florida** for Tim Bozon, October 8, 2016. Traded to **Tampa Bay** by **Montreal** with Montreal's 6th round pick (Cole Guttman) in 2017 NHL Draft for Nikita Nesterov, January 26, 2017.

RADULOV, Alexander
(ra-DEW-lahf, al-EHX-AN-duhr) **DAL**

Right wing. Shoots left. 6'1", 200 lbs. Born, Nizhny Tagil, USSR, July 5, 1986. Nashville's 1st pick, 15th overall, in 2004 NHL Draft.

Season	Club	League	GP	G	A	Pts	PIM	PP	SH	GW	S	S%	+/-	TF	F%	Min	GP	G	A	Pts	PIM	PP	SH	GW	Min
2002-03	Dyn'o Moscow 2	Russia-3	STATISTICS NOT AVAILABLE																						
2003-04	Dyn'o Moscow 2	Russia-3	STATISTICS NOT AVAILABLE																						
	THK Tver	Russia-2	42	15	16	31	102																		
	Dynamo Moscow	Russia	1	0	0	0	2																		
2004-05	Quebec Remparts	QMJHL	65	32	43	75	64										13	6	5	11	15				
2005-06	Quebec Remparts	QMJHL	62	61	*91	*152	101										23	21	*34	*55	30				
2006-07	**Nashville**	**NHL**	**64**	**18**	**19**	**37**	**26**	**5**	**0**	**4**	**96**	**18.8**	**19**	**0**	**0.0**	**11:38**	**4**	**3**	**1**	**4**	**19**	**0**	**0**	**0**	**13:10**
	Milwaukee	AHL	11	6	12	18	26																		
2007-08	**Nashville**	**NHL**	**81**	**26**	**32**	**58**	**44**	**4**	**0**	**2**	**183**	**14.2**	**7**	**1**	**0.0**	**16:24**	**6**	**2**	**2**	**4**	**6**	**1**	**0**	**0**	**15:59**
2008-09	Ufa	KHL	52	22	26	48	92										4	0	2	2	4				
2009-10	Ufa	KHL	54	24	39	63	62										16	8	*11	*19	10				
	Russia	Olympics	4	1	1	2	4																		
2010-11	Ufa	KHL	54	20	*60	*80	83										21	3	*15	18	42				
2011-12	Ufa	KHL	50	25	38	63	64										6	0	6	6	2				
	Nashville	**NHL**	**9**	**3**	**4**	**7**	**4**	**0**	**0**	**0**	**21**	**14.3**	**3**	**0**	**0.0**	**19:21**	**8**	**1**	**5**	**6**	**4**	**0**	**0**	**0**	**18:08**
2012-13	CSKA Moscow	KHL	48	22	*46	68	86										9	1	6	7	0				
2013-14	CSKA Moscow	KHL	34	9	25	34	75																		
	Russia	Olympics	5	3	3	6	4																		
2014-15	CSKA Moscow	KHL	46	24	*47	*71	143										16	8	13	*21	20				
2015-16	CSKA Moscow	KHL	53	23	42	65	73										20	4	12	16	26				
2016-17	**Montreal**	**NHL**	**76**	**18**	**36**	**54**	**62**	**6**	**0**	**2**	**147**	**12.2**	**10**	**12**	**50.0**	**18:17**	**6**	**2**	**5**	**7**	**6**	**0**	**0**	**1**	**19:55**
	NHL Totals		**230**	**65**	**91**	**156**	**136**	**15**	**0**	**8**	**447**	**14.5**		**13**	**46.2**	**15:49**	**24**	**8**	**13**	**21**	**35**	**1**	**0**	**1**	**17:13**

QMJHL All-Rookie Team (2005) • QMJHL First All-Star Team (2006) • QMJHL Player of the Year (2006) • Canadian Major Junior First All-Star Team (2006) • Canadian Major Junior Player of the Year (2006)

Signed as a free agent by **Ufa** (KHL), July 11, 2008. Signed as a free agent by **CSKA Moscow** (KHL), July 2, 2012. Signed as a free agent by **Montreal**, July 1, 2016. Signed as a free agent by **Dallas**, July 3, 2017.

RAFFL, Michael
(RA-fuhl, mi-KHIGH-ehl) **PHI**

Left wing. Shoots left. 6', 200 lbs. Born, Villach, Austria, December 1, 1988.

Season	Club	League	GP	G	A	Pts	PIM	PP	SH	GW	S	S%	+/-	TF	F%	Min	GP	G	A	Pts	PIM	PP	SH	GW	Min
2005-06	EC VSV Villach Jr.	Austria-Jr.	26	11	27	38	91										4	6	6	12	10				
	EC VSV Villach	Austria	5	0	0	0	0										3	0	0	0	0				
2006-07	EC VSV Villach Jr.	Austria-Jr.	21	23	24	47	82																		
	EC VSV Villach	Austria	43	4	2	6	22										4	0	0	0	0				
2007-08	EC VSV Villach Jr.	Austria-Jr.	6	5	7	12	28																		
	EC VSV Villach	Austria	40	3	6	9	24										5	2	0	2	2				
2008-09	EC VSV Villach	Austria	49	9	10	19	77										6	0	2	2	12				
2009-10	EC VSV Villach	Austria	42	25	18	43	54										5	1	0	1	14				
2010-11	EC VSV Villach	Austria	50	26	29	55	62										8	5	4	9	20				
2011-12	Leksands IF	Sweden-2	45	10	14	24	26																		
2012-13	Leksands IF	Sweden-2	59	27	25	52	44																		
2013-14	**Philadelphia**	**NHL**	**68**	**9**	**13**	**22**	**28**	**0**	**0**	**3**	**101**	**8.9**	**2**	**93**	**55.9**	**12:59**	**7**	**0**	**1**	**1**	**0**	**0**	**0**	**0**	**12:35**
	Adirondack	AHL	2	1	2	3	0																		
	Austria	Olympics	4	1	2	3	4																		
2014-15	**Philadelphia**	**NHL**	**67**	**21**	**7**	**28**	**34**	**2**	**1**	**2**	**134**	**15.7**	**6**	**97**	**45.4**	**14:12**									
2015-16	**Philadelphia**	**NHL**	**82**	**13**	**18**	**31**	**30**	**1**	**0**	**4**	**132**	**9.8**	**9**	**82**	**40.2**	**14:18**	**6**	**1**	**0**	**1**	**2**	**0**	**0**	**0**	**12:35**
2016-17	**Philadelphia**	**NHL**	**52**	**8**	**3**	**11**	**20**	**0**	**0**	**3**	**63**	**12.7**	**-7**	**10**	**30.0**	**13:16**									
	NHL Totals		**269**	**51**	**41**	**92**	**112**	**3**	**1**	**12**	**430**	**11.9**		**282**	**46.8**	**13:45**	**13**	**1**	**1**	**2**	**2**	**0**	**0**	**0**	**12:35**

Signed as a free agent by **Philadelphia**, May 31, 2013.

RAKELL, Rickard
(ra-KEHL, REE-kahrd) **ANA**

Right wing. Shoots right. 6'2", 201 lbs. Born, Sundbyberg, Sweden, May 5, 1993. Anaheim's 1st pick, 30th overall, in 2011 NHL Draft.

Season	Club	League	GP	G	A	Pts	PIM	PP	SH	GW	S	S%	+/-	TF	F%	Min	GP	G	A	Pts	PIM	PP	SH	GW	Min
2007-08	Spanga Hockey	Sweden-4	24	4	3	7	12																		
2008-09	AIK IF Solna U18	Swe-U18	16	2	3	5	22																		
2009-10	AIK IF Solna U18	Swe-U18	30	25	16	41	18										3	2	2	4	0				
	AIK IF Solna Jr.	Swe-Jr.	8	3	1	4	2										2	1	0	1	0				
2010-11	Plymouth Whalers	OHL	49	20	25	45	12										1	0	0	0	0				
2011-12	Plymouth Whalers	OHL	60	28	34	62	12										13	2	10	12	0				
2012-13	Plymouth Whalers	OHL	40	21	23	44	12										15	6	9	15	10				
	Anaheim	**NHL**	**4**	**0**	**0**	**0**	**0**	**0**	**0**	**0**	**3**	**0.0**	**-2**	**21**	**47.6**	**8:57**									
2013-14	**Anaheim**	**NHL**	**18**	**0**	**4**	**4**	**2**	**0**	**0**	**0**	**22**	**0.0**	**-3**	**194**	**49.0**	**11:43**	**4**	**1**	**1**	**2**	**0**	**1**	**0**	**0**	**10:58**
	Norfolk Admirals	AHL	46	14	23	37	12										1	0	1	1	0				
2014-15	**Anaheim**	**NHL**	**71**	**9**	**22**	**31**	**10**	**2**	**0**	**1**	**105**	**8.6**	**6**	**665**	**46.6**	**12:34**	**16**	**1**	**0**	**1**	**2**	**0**	**0**	**1**	**11:32**
	Norfolk Admirals	AHL	2	1	3	4	0																		

			Regular Season														Playoffs								
Season	Club	League	GP	G	A	Pts	PIM	PP	SH	GW	S	S%	+/-	TF	F%	Min	GP	G	A	Pts	PIM	PP	SH	GW	Min
2015-16	**Anaheim**	**NHL**	**72**	**20**	**23**	**43**	**19**	**4**	**0**	**7**	**169**	**11.8**	**–1**	**451**	**43.7**	**16:04**	**7**	**1**	**1**	**2**	**0**	**0**	**0**	**0**	**15:03**
2016-17	**Anaheim**	**NHL**	**71**	**33**	**18**	**51**	**12**	**5**	**0**	***10**	**177**	**18.6**	**10**	**147**	**42.2**	**17:23**	**15**	**7**	**6**	**13**	**0**	**0**	**0**	**0**	**19:03**
	NHL Totals		**236**	**62**	**67**	**129**	**43**	**11**	**0**	**18**	**476**	**13.0**		**1478**	**45.6**	**14:58**	**42**	**10**	**8**	**18**	**2**	**1**	**0**	**1**	**14:45**

RAMAGE, John

(RAM-ihj, JAWN) **CBJ**

Defense. Shoots right. 6', 200 lbs. Born, Mississauga, ON, February 7, 1991. Calgary's 3rd pick, 103rd overall, in 2010 NHL Draft.

2007-08	St. Louis Bandits	NAHL	45	4	5	9	75	....	....	....	....	....	....	....	....	....	11	0	2	2	2	....	....	....	....
	USAHNTDP	U-17	3	0	0	0	0	....	....	....	....	....	....	....	....	....	....	....	....	....	....	....	....	....	....
2008-09	USAHNTDP	NAHL	14	1	4	5	12	....	....	....	....	....	....	....	....	....	....	....	....	....	....	....	....	....	....
	USAHNTDP	U-18	40	1	4	5	32	....	....	....	....	....	....	....	....	....	....	....	....	....	....	....	....	....	....
2009-10	U. of Wisconsin	WCHA	41	2	10	12	51	....	....	....	....	....	....	....	....	....	....	....	....	....	....	....	....	....	....
2010-11	U. of Wisconsin	WCHA	37	1	10	11	59	....	....	....	....	....	....	....	....	....	....	....	....	....	....	....	....	....	....
2011-12	U. of Wisconsin	WCHA	37	3	7	10	62	....	....	....	....	....	....	....	....	....	....	....	....	....	....	....	....	....	....
2012-13	U. of Wisconsin	WCHA	42	8	12	20	65	....	....	....	....	....	....	....	....	....	....	....	....	....	....	....	....	....	....
2013-14	Abbotsford Heat	AHL	50	0	1	1	46	....	....	....	....	....	....	....	....	....	....	....	....	....	....	....	....	....	....
	Alaska Aces	ECHL	6	1	0	1	6	....	....	....	....	....	....	....	....	....	20	4	9	13	20	....	....	....	....
2014-15	**Calgary**	**NHL**	**1**	**0**	**0**	**0**	**0**	**0**	**0**	**0**	**4**	**0.0**	**–1**	**0**	**0.0**	**18:10**	....	....	....	....	....	....	....	....	....
	Adirondack	AHL	57	3	12	15	81	....	....	....	....	....	....	....	....	....	....	....	....	....	....	....	....	....	....
2015-16	**Columbus**	**NHL**	**1**	**0**	**0**	**0**	**0**	**0**	**0**	**0**	**0**	**0.0**	**–2**	**0**	**0.0**	**14:09**	....	....	....	....	....	....	....	....	....
	Lake Erie	AHL	68	8	19	27	67	....	....	....	....	....	....	....	....	....	1	0	0	0	0	....	....	....	....
2016-17	Cleveland	AHL	69	4	21	25	67	....	....	....	....	....	....	....	....	....	....	....	....	....	....	....	....	....	....
	NHL Totals		**2**	**0**	**0**	**0**	**0**	**0**	**0**	**0**	**4**	**0.0**		**0**	**0.0**	**16:10**	....	....	....	....	....	....	....	....	....

Signed as a free agent by **Columbus**, July 3, 2015.

RANDELL, Tyler

(RAN-duhl, TIGH-luhr) **OTT**

Right wing. Shoots right. 6'1", 198 lbs. Born, Scarborough, ON, June 15, 1991. Boston's 4th pick, 176th overall, in 2009 NHL Draft.

2006-07	Brampton	Minor-ON	63	53	38	91	81	....	....	....	....	....	....	....	....	....	....	....	....	....	....	....	....	....	....
2007-08	Belleville Bulls	OHL	62	5	6	11	24	....	....	....	....	....	....	....	....	....	19	0	0	0	0	....	....	....	....
2008-09	Belleville Bulls	OHL	36	10	5	15	60	....	....	....	....	....	....	....	....	....	....	....	....	....	....	....	....	....	....
	Kitchener Rangers	OHL	37	14	8	22	39	....	....	....	....	....	....	....	....	....	....	....	....	....	....	....	....	....	....
2009-10	Kitchener Rangers	OHL	47	9	12	21	88	....	....	....	....	....	....	....	....	....	20	1	4	5	19	....	....	....	....
2010-11	Kitchener Rangers	OHL	68	20	12	32	160	....	....	....	....	....	....	....	....	....	7	0	0	0	7	....	....	....	....
2011-12	Kitchener Rangers	OHL	17	9	1	10	21	....	....	....	....	....	....	....	....	....	6	7	1	8	14	....	....	....	....
	Providence Bruins	AHL	30	2	0	2	45	....	....	....	....	....	....	....	....	....	....	....	....	....	....	....	....	....	....
2012-13	Providence Bruins	AHL	23	0	0	0	56	....	....	....	....	....	....	....	....	....	....	....	....	....	....	....	....	....	....
	South Carolina	ECHL	22	2	2	4	46	....	....	....	....	....	....	....	....	....	....	....	....	....	....	....	....	....	....
2013-14	Providence Bruins	AHL	43	4	7	11	93	....	....	....	....	....	....	....	....	....	8	1	0	1	6	....	....	....	....
2014-15	Providence Bruins	AHL	74	11	9	20	120	....	....	....	....	....	....	....	....	....	5	0	0	0	4	....	....	....	....
2015-16	**Boston**	**NHL**	**27**	**6**	**0**	**6**	**47**	**0**	**0**	**1**	**18**	**33.3**	**–2**	**0**	**0.0**	**6:59**	....	....	....	....	....	....	....	....	....
	Providence Bruins	AHL	2	0	0	0	0	....	....	....	....	....	....	....	....	....	....	....	....	....	....	....	....	....	....
2016-17	Providence Bruins	AHL	59	1	9	10	81	....	....	....	....	....	....	....	....	....	12	0	0	0	20	....	....	....	....
	NHL Totals		**27**	**6**	**0**	**6**	**47**	**0**	**0**	**1**	**18**	**33.3**		**0**	**0.0**	**6:59**	....	....	....	....	....	....	....	....	....

• Missed majority of 2015-16 as a healthy reserve. Signed as a free agent by **Ottawa**, July 1, 2017.

RANFORD, Brendan

(RAN-fohrd, BREHN-duhn)

Left wing. Shoots left. 5'10", 190 lbs. Born, Edmonton, AB, May 3, 1992. Philadelphia's 6th pick, 209th overall, in 2010 NHL Draft.

2007-08	CAC Canadians	AMHL	35	*33	46	*79	58	....	....	....	....	....	....	....	....	....	12	10	5	15	6	....	....	....	....
	Kamloops Blazers	WHL	3	0	0	0	0	....	....	....	....	....	....	....	....	....	....	....	....	....	....	....	....	....	....
2008-09	Kamloops Blazers	WHL	66	13	14	27	46	....	....	....	....	....	....	....	....	....	4	0	3	3	2	....	....	....	....
2009-10	Kamloops Blazers	WHL	72	29	36	65	83	....	....	....	....	....	....	....	....	....	4	2	3	5	4	....	....	....	....
2010-11	Kamloops Blazers	WHL	68	33	53	86	68	....	....	....	....	....	....	....	....	....	....	....	....	....	....	....	....	....	....
2011-12	Kamloops Blazers	WHL	69	40	52	92	73	....	....	....	....	....	....	....	....	....	11	5	9	14	8	....	....	....	....
2012-13	Kamloops Blazers	WHL	70	22	65	87	28	....	....	....	....	....	....	....	....	....	15	5	15	20	0	....	....	....	....
2013-14	Texas Stars	AHL	65	12	21	33	14	....	....	....	....	....	....	....	....	....	21	8	8	16	12	....	....	....	....
2014-15	**Dallas**	**NHL**	**1**	**0**	**0**	**0**	**0**	**0**	**0**	**0**	**0**	**0.0**	**0**	**0**	**0.0**	**9:19**	....	....	....	....	....	....	....	....	....
	Texas Stars	AHL	73	18	33	51	22	....	....	....	....	....	....	....	....	....	3	0	1	1	0	....	....	....	....
2015-16	Texas Stars	AHL	76	19	40	59	49	....	....	....	....	....	....	....	....	....	4	1	3	4	4	....	....	....	....
2016-17	Texas Stars	AHL	36	6	11	17	4	....	....	....	....	....	....	....	....	....	....	....	....	....	....	....	....	....	....
	Tucson	AHL	10	0	0	0	4	....	....	....	....	....	....	....	....	....	....	....	....	....	....	....	....	....	....
	San Antonio	AHL	21	4	13	17	8	....	....	....	....	....	....	....	....	....	....	....	....	....	....	....	....	....	....
	NHL Totals		**1**	**0**	**0**	**0**	**0**	**0**	**0**	**0**	**0**	**0.0**		**0**	**0.0**	**9:19**	....	....	....	....	....	....	....	....	....

WHL West Second All-Star Team (2011)

Signed as a free agent by **Texas** (AHL), May 24, 2013. Signed as a free agent by **Dallas**, July 3, 2014. Traded to **Arizona** by **Dallas** with Brandon Troock for Justin Peters and Justin Hache, February 1, 2017. Traded to **Colorado** by **Arizona** for Joe Whitney, March 1, 2017.

RANTANEN, Mikko

(ran-TA-nehn, MEE-koh) **COL**

Right wing. Shoots left. 6'4", 211 lbs. Born, Nousiainen, Finland, October 29, 1996. Colorado's 1st pick, 10th overall, in 2015 NHL Draft.

2011-12	TPS Turku U18	Fin-U18	22	5	8	13	6	....	....	....	....	....	....	....	....	....	7	1	1	2	2	....	....	....	....
2012-13	TPS Turku U18	Fin-U18	5	2	6	8	0	....	....	....	....	....	....	....	....	....	1	1	0	1	0	....	....	....	....
	TPS Turku Jr.	Fin-Jr.	35	10	14	24	14	....	....	....	....	....	....	....	....	....	9	2	4	6	4	....	....	....	....
	TPS Turku	Finland	15	2	1	3	4	....	....	....	....	....	....	....	....	....	....	....	....	....	....	....	....	....	....
2013-14	TPS Turku U18	Fin-U18	2	0	2	2	0	....	....	....	....	....	....	....	....	....	....	....	....	....	....	....	....	....	....
	TPS Turku Jr.	Fin-Jr.	17	5	13	18	8	....	....	....	....	....	....	....	....	....	3	2	1	3	0	....	....	....	....
	TPS Turku	Finland	37	5	4	9	10	....	....	....	....	....	....	....	....	....	....	....	....	....	....	....	....	....	....
2014-15	TPS Turku	Finland	56	9	19	28	22	....	....	....	....	....	....	....	....	....	....	....	....	....	....	....	....	....	....
	TPS Turku Jr.	Fin-Jr.	....	....	....	....	....	....	....	....	....	....	....	....	....	....	7	6	8	14	2	....	....	....	....
2015-16	**Colorado**	**NHL**	**9**	**0**	**0**	**0**	**2**	**0**	**0**	**0**	**9**	**0.0**	**–7**	**24**	**54.2**	**8:57**	....	....	....	....	....	....	....	....	....
	San Antonio	AHL	52	24	36	60	42	....	....	....	....	....	....	....	....	....	....	....	....	....	....	....	....	....	....
2016-17	**Colorado**	**NHL**	**75**	**20**	**18**	**38**	**22**	**4**	**0**	**2**	**133**	**15.0**	**–25**	**50**	**58.0**	**18:03**	....	....	....	....	....	....	....	....	....
	San Antonio	AHL	4	0	2	2	4	....	....	....	....	....	....	....	....	....	....	....	....	....	....	....	....	....	....
	NHL Totals		**84**	**20**	**18**	**38**	**24**	**4**	**0**	**2**	**142**	**14.1**		**74**	**56.8**	**17:05**	....	....	....	....	....	....	....	....	....

AHL All-Rookie Team (2016) • AHL Second All-Star Team (2016) • Dudley "Red" Garrett Memorial Award (AHL – Rookie of the Year) (2016) (co-winner - Frank Vatrano)

RASK, Victor

(RASK, VIHK-tohr) **CAR**

Center. Shoots left. 6'2", 200 lbs. Born, Leksand, Sweden, March 1, 1993. Carolina's 2nd pick, 42nd overall, in 2011 NHL Draft.

2007-08	Leksands IF U18	Swe-U18	8	0	2	2	2	....	....	....	....	....	....	....	....	....	2	0	0	0	0	....	....	....	....
2008-09	Leksands IF U18	Swe-U18	26	9	6	15	8	....	....	....	....	....	....	....	....	....	....	....	....	....	....	....	....	....	....
2009-10	Leksands IF U18	Swe-U18	10	6	3	9	4	....	....	....	....	....	....	....	....	....	4	4	3	7	2	....	....	....	....
	Leksands IF Jr.	Swe-Jr.	39	22	19	41	35	....	....	....	....	....	....	....	....	....	5	3	2	5	2	....	....	....	....
	Leksands IF	Sweden-2	8	0	0	0	0	....	....	....	....	....	....	....	....	....	....	....	....	....	....	....	....	....	....
2010-11	Leksands IF U18	Swe-U18	4	4	4	8	0	....	....	....	....	....	....	....	....	....	6	3	2	5	6	....	....	....	....
	Leksands IF Jr.	Swe-Jr.	13	3	9	12	2	....	....	....	....	....	....	....	....	....	....	....	....	....	....	....	....	....	....
	Leksands IF	Sweden-2	37	5	6	11	8	....	....	....	....	....	....	....	....	....	....	....	....	....	....	....	....	....	....
2011-12	Calgary Hitmen	WHL	64	33	30	63	21	....	....	....	....	....	....	....	....	....	....	....	....	....	....	....	....	....	....
2012-13	Calgary Hitmen	WHL	37	14	27	41	16	....	....	....	....	....	....	....	....	....	17	6	10	16	10	....	....	....	....
	Charlotte	AHL	10	1	4	5	0	....	....	....	....	....	....	....	....	....	....	....	....	....	....	....	....	....	....
2013-14	Charlotte	AHL	76	16	23	39	20	....	....	....	....	....	....	....	....	....	....	....	....	....	....	....	....	....	....
2014-15	**Carolina**	**NHL**	**80**	**11**	**22**	**33**	**16**	**2**	**0**	**2**	**172**	**6.4**	**–14**	**918**	**51.0**	**16:20**	....	....	....	....	....	....	....	....	....
2015-16	**Carolina**	**NHL**	**80**	**21**	**27**	**48**	**24**	**5**	**0**	**5**	**160**	**13.1**	**–6**	**935**	**51.2**	**16:59**	....	....	....	....	....	....	....	....	....
2016-17	**Carolina**	**NHL**	**82**	**16**	**29**	**45**	**16**	**4**	**0**	**3**	**186**	**8.6**	**–10**	**918**	**49.8**	**17:18**	....	....	....	....	....	....	....	....	....
	NHL Totals		**242**	**48**	**78**	**126**	**56**	**11**	**0**	**10**	**518**	**9.3**		**2771**	**50.7**	**16:52**	....	....	....	....	....	....	....	....	....

RASMUSSEN, Dennis

(rahz-MOO-suhn, DEH-nihs) **ANA**

Center. Shoots left. 6'3", 205 lbs. Born, Vasteras, Sweden, July 3, 1990.

			Regular Season														Playoffs								
Season	Club	League	GP	G	A	Pts	PIM	PP	SH	GW	S	S%	+/-	TF	F%	Min	GP	G	A	Pts	PIM	PP	SH	GW	Min
2007-08	Vasteras Jr.	Swe-Jr.	39	8	11	19	38	....	....	....	....	....	....	....	....	....	3	1	2	3	8	....	....	....	....
2008-09	Vasteras Jr.	Swe-Jr.	40	19	25	44	18	....	....	....	....	....	....	....	....	....	3	1	3	4	0	....	....	....	....
	VIK Vasteras HK	Sweden-2	20	5	2	7	4	....	....	....	....	....	....	....	....	....	....	....	....	....	....	....	....	....	....
2009-10	Vasteras Jr.	Swe-Jr.	3	1	3	4	29	....	....	....	....	....	....	....	....	....	5	1	4	5	2	....	....	....	....
	VIK Vasteras HK	Sweden-2	44	4	13	17	20	....	....	....	....	....	....	....	....	....	....	....	....	....	....	....	....	....	....
2010-11	VIK Vasteras HK	Sweden-2	54	13	25	38	16	....	....	....	....	....	....	....	....	....	....	....	....	....	....	....	....	....	....
2011-12	Vaxjo Lakers HC	Sweden	55	8	9	17	10	....	....	....	....	....	....	....	....	....	....	....	....	....	....	....	....	....	....
2012-13	Vaxjo Lakers HC	Sweden	42	16	12	28	28	....	....	....	....	....	....	....	....	....	....	....	....	....	....	....	....	....	....
2013-14	Vaxjo Lakers HC	Sweden	52	16	24	40	20	....	....	....	....	....	....	....	....	....	12	2	4	6	6	....	....	....	....
2014-15	Rockford IceHogs	AHL	73	13	14	27	30	....	....	....	....	....	....	....	....	....	7	0	0	0	2	....	....	....	....
2015-16	**Chicago**	**NHL**	**44**	**4**	**5**	**9**	**4**	**0**	**0**	**1**	**42**	**9.5**	**9**	**307**	**46.9**	**9:10**	....	....	....	....	....	....	....	....	....
	Rockford IceHogs	AHL	25	7	9	16	18	....	....	....	....	....	....	....	....	....	3	1	1	2	0	....	....	....	....
2016-17	**Chicago**	**NHL**	**68**	**4**	**4**	**8**	**12**	**0**	**0**	**0**	**77**	**5.2**	**–4**	**370**	**44.6**	**11:50**	**3**	**1**	**0**	**1**	**0**	**0**	**0**	**0**	**13:36**
	NHL Totals		**112**	**8**	**9**	**17**	**16**	**0**	**0**	**1**	**119**	**6.7**		**677**	**45.6**	**10:47**	**3**	**1**	**0**	**1**	**0**	**0**	**0**	**0**	**13:36**

Signed as a free agent by **Chicago**, June 10, 2014. Signed as a free agent by **Anaheim**, July 7, 2017.

RATTIE, Ty

(RA-tee, TIGH) **EDM**

Right wing. Shoots right. 6', 178 lbs. Born, Calgary, AB, February 5, 1993. St. Louis' 1st pick, 32nd overall, in 2011 NHL Draft.

			Regular Season														Playoffs								
Season	Club	League	GP	G	A	Pts	PIM	PP	SH	GW	S	S%	+/-	TF	F%	Min	GP	G	A	Pts	PIM	PP	SH	GW	Min
2007-08	Airdrie Xtreme	AMBHL	33	*75	56	*131	24	....	....	....	....	....	....	....	....	....	10	12	*11	*23	16	....	....	....	....
2008-09	UFA Bisons	AMHL	34	29	25	54	12	....	....	....	....	....	....	....	....	....	3	1	4	5	2	....	....	....	....
	Portland	WHL	10	1	0	1	0	....	....	....	....	....	....	....	....	....	....	....	....	....	....	....	....	....	....
	Brooks Bandits	AJHL	2	0	0	0	0	....	....	....	....	....	....	....	....	....	2	0	1	1	0	....	....	....	....
2009-10	Portland	WHL	61	17	20	37	38	....	....	....	....	....	....	....	....	....	13	2	2	4	12	....	....	....	....
2010-11	Portland	WHL	67	28	51	79	55	....	....	....	....	....	....	....	....	....	21	9	13	22	22	....	....	....	....
2011-12	Portland	WHL	69	57	64	121	54	....	....	....	....	....	....	....	....	....	21	19	14	33	12	....	....	....	....
2012-13	Portland	WHL	62	48	62	110	27	....	....	....	....	....	....	....	....	....	21	*20	16	*36	17	....	....	....	....
2013-14	**St. Louis**	**NHL**	**2**	**0**	**0**	**0**	**0**	**0**	**0**	**0**	**4**	**0.0**	**–2**	**0**	**0.0**	**11:03**	....	....	....	....	....	....	....	....	....
	Chicago Wolves	AHL	72	31	17	48	37	....	....	....	....	....	....	....	....	....	9	1	2	3	4	....	....	....	....
2014-15	**St. Louis**	**NHL**	**11**	**0**	**2**	**2**	**2**	**0**	**0**	**0**	**8**	**0.0**	**0**	**0**	**0.0**	**9:06**	....	....	....	....	....	....	....	....	....
	Chicago Wolves	AHL	59	21	21	42	12	....	....	....	....	....	....	....	....	....	3	0	0	0	2	....	....	....	....
2015-16	**St. Louis**	**NHL**	**13**	**4**	**2**	**6**	**4**	**0**	**0**	**0**	**16**	**25.0**	**1**	**0**	**0.0**	**9:17**	....	....	....	....	....	....	....	....	....
	Chicago Wolves	AHL	62	17	29	46	28	....	....	....	....	....	....	....	....	....	....	....	....	....	....	....	....	....	....
2016-17	**St. Louis**	**NHL**	**4**	**0**	**0**	**0**	**0**	**0**	**0**	**0**	**1**	**0.0**	**0**	**0**	**0.0**	**7:20**	....	....	....	....	....	....	....	....	....
	Chicago Wolves	AHL	22	2	3	5	2	....	....	....	....	....	....	....	....	....	9	2	2	4	14	....	....	....	....
	Carolina	**NHL**	**5**	**0**	**2**	**2**	**0**	**0**	**0**	**0**	**9**	**0.0**	**–2**	**0**	**0.0**	**13:28**	....	....	....	....	....	....	....	....	....
	NHL Totals		**35**	**4**	**6**	**10**	**6**	**0**	**0**	**0**	**38**	**10.5**		**0**	**0.0**	**9:42**	....	....	....	....	....	....	....	....	....

WHL West First All-Star Team (2012) • WHL West Second All-Star Team (2013)

Claimed on waivers by **Carolina** from **St. Louis**, January 4, 2017. Claimed on waivers by **St. Louis** from **Carolina**, February 19, 2017. Signed as a free agent by **Edmonton**, July 1, 2017.

RAU, Kyle

(ROW, KIGHL) **MIN**

Center. Shoots left. 5'8", 178 lbs. Born, Eden Prairie, MN, October 24, 1992. Florida's 7th pick, 91st overall, in 2011 NHL Draft.

			Regular Season														Playoffs								
Season	Club	League	GP	G	A	Pts	PIM	PP	SH	GW	S	S%	+/-	TF	F%	Min	GP	G	A	Pts	PIM	PP	SH	GW	Min
2009-10	Eden Prairie	High-MN	25	38	39	77	12	....	....	....	....	....	....	....	....	....	3	2	2	4	0	....	....	....	....
2010-11	Team Southwest	UMHSEL	19	16	7	23	14	....	....	....	....	....	....	....	....	....	3	0	0	0	0	....	....	....	....
	Eden Prairie	High-MN	25	33	36	69	16	....	....	....	....	....	....	....	....	....	6	8	4	12	2	....	....	....	....
	Sioux Falls	USHL	11	4	6	10	15	....	....	....	....	....	....	....	....	....	10	*7	5	*12	4	....	....	....	....
2011-12	U. of Minnesota	WCHA	40	18	25	43	29	....	....	....	....	....	....	....	....	....	....	....	....	....	....	....	....	....	....
2012-13	U. of Minnesota	WCHA	40	15	25	40	22	....	....	....	....	....	....	....	....	....	....	....	....	....	....	....	....	....	....
2013-14	U. of Minnesota	Big Ten	41	14	26	40	16	....	....	....	....	....	....	....	....	....	....	....	....	....	....	....	....	....	....
2014-15	U. of Minnesota	Big Ten	39	20	21	41	18	....	....	....	....	....	....	....	....	....	....	....	....	....	....	....	....	....	....
	San Antonio	AHL	7	2	1	3	0	....	....	....	....	....	....	....	....	....	1	0	0	0	2	....	....	....	....
2015-16	**Florida**	**NHL**	**9**	**0**	**0**	**0**	**2**	**0**	**0**	**0**	**15**	**0.0**	**–1**	**0**	**0.0**	**12:35**	....	....	....	....	....	....	....	....	....
	Portland Pirates	AHL	63	17	14	31	24	....	....	....	....	....	....	....	....	....	5	1	1	2	2	....	....	....	....
2016-17	**Florida**	**NHL**	**24**	**2**	**1**	**3**	**4**	**0**	**0**	**0**	**21**	**9.5**	**–3**	**3**	**66.7**	**9:36**	....	....	....	....	....	....	....	....	....
	Springfield	AHL	48	10	14	24	32	....	....	....	....	....	....	....	....	....	....	....	....	....	....	....	....	....	....
	NHL Totals		**33**	**2**	**1**	**3**	**6**	**0**	**0**	**0**	**36**	**5.6**		**3**	**66.7**	**10:25**	....	....	....	....	....	....	....	....	....

WCHA All-Rookie Team (2012) • Big Ten Second All-Star Team (2014) • NCAA West Second All-American Team (2014) • NCAA Championship All-Tournament Team (2014)

Signed as a free agent by **Minnesota**, July 1, 2017.

RAYMOND, Mason

(RAY-muhnd, MAY-sohn)

Left wing. Shoots left. 6'1", 179 lbs. Born, Cochrane, AB, September 17, 1985. Vancouver's 2nd pick, 51st overall, in 2005 NHL Draft.

			Regular Season														Playoffs								
Season	Club	League	GP	G	A	Pts	PIM	PP	SH	GW	S	S%	+/-	TF	F%	Min	GP	G	A	Pts	PIM	PP	SH	GW	Min
2003-04	Camrose Kodiaks	AJHL	57	27	35	62	32	....	....	....	....	....	....	....	....	....	11	2	5	7	24	....	....	....	....
2004-05	Camrose Kodiaks	AJHL	55	*41	41	82	80	....	....	....	....	....	....	....	....	....	15	8	*12	20	....	....	....	....	....
2005-06	U. Minn-Duluth	WCHA	40	11	17	28	30	....	....	....	....	....	....	....	....	....	....	....	....	....	....	....	....	....	....
2006-07	U. Minn-Duluth	WCHA	39	14	32	46	45	....	....	....	....	....	....	....	....	....	....	....	....	....	....	....	....	....	....
	Manitoba Moose	AHL	11	2	2	4	6	....	....	....	....	....	....	....	....	....	13	0	1	1	0	....	....	....	....
2007-08	**Vancouver**	**NHL**	**49**	**9**	**12**	**21**	**2**	**1**	**0**	**0**	**80**	**11.3**	**1**	**63**	**38.1**	**12:31**	....	....	....	....	....	....	....	....	....
	Manitoba Moose	AHL	20	7	10	17	6	....	....	....	....	....	....	....	....	....	....	....	....	....	....	....	....	....	....
2008-09	**Vancouver**	**NHL**	**72**	**11**	**12**	**23**	**24**	**4**	**0**	**0**	**145**	**7.6**	**2**	**50**	**34.0**	**13:43**	**10**	**2**	**1**	**3**	**2**	**0**	**0**	**0**	**15:12**
2009-10	**Vancouver**	**NHL**	**82**	**25**	**28**	**53**	**48**	**8**	**0**	**4**	**217**	**11.5**	**0**	**23**	**34.8**	**17:20**	**12**	**3**	**1**	**4**	**6**	**0**	**0**	**1**	**17:36**
2010-11	**Vancouver**	**NHL**	**70**	**15**	**24**	**39**	**10**	**2**	**1**	**5**	**197**	**7.6**	**8**	**65**	**40.0**	**15:48**	**24**	**2**	**6**	**8**	**6**	**0**	**0**	**0**	**17:29**
2011-12	**Vancouver**	**NHL**	**55**	**10**	**10**	**20**	**18**	**1**	**1**	**2**	**125**	**8.0**	**4**	**25**	**28.0**	**15:35**	**5**	**0**	**1**	**1**	**0**	**0**	**0**	**0**	**12:34**
2012-13	Orebro HK	Sweden-2	2	0	1	1	2	....	....	....	....	....	....	....	....	....	....	....	....	....	....	....	....	....	....
	Vancouver	**NHL**	**46**	**10**	**12**	**22**	**16**	**4**	**0**	**1**	**79**	**12.7**	**2**	**50**	**34.0**	**15:49**	**4**	**1**	**1**	**2**	**0**	**0**	**0**	**0**	**16:49**
2013-14	**Toronto**	**NHL**	**82**	**19**	**26**	**45**	**22**	**6**	**1**	**4**	**178**	**10.7**	**–6**	**16**	**43.8**	**17:21**	....	....	....	....	....	....	....	....	....
2014-15	**Calgary**	**NHL**	**57**	**12**	**11**	**23**	**8**	**0**	**0**	**1**	**123**	**9.8**	**–8**	**3**	**0.0**	**14:49**	**8**	**0**	**2**	**2**	**0**	**0**	**0**	**0**	**9:41**
2015-16	**Calgary**	**NHL**	**29**	**4**	**1**	**5**	**8**	**0**	**0**	**0**	**53**	**7.5**	**–3**	**7**	**42.9**	**12:20**	....	....	....	....	....	....	....	....	....
	Stockton Heat	AHL	15	6	9	15	2	....	....	....	....	....	....	....	....	....	....	....	....	....	....	....	....	....	....
2016-17	**Anaheim**	**NHL**	**4**	**0**	**0**	**0**	**0**	**0**	**0**	**0**	**3**	**0.0**	**–2**	**1**	**0.0**	**8:55**	....	....	....	....	....	....	....	....	....
	NHL Totals		**546**	**115**	**136**	**251**	**156**	**26**	**3**	**17**	**1200**	**9.6**		**303**	**36.0**	**15:20**	**63**	**8**	**12**	**20**	**14**	**0**	**0**	**1**	**15:43**

AJHL MVP (2005) • WCHA All-Rookie Team (2006) • WCHA First All-Star Team (2007)

Signed as a free agent by **Orebro** (Sweden-2), December 26, 2012. Signed as a free agent by **Toronto**, September 23, 2013. Signed as a free agent by **Calgary**, July 1, 2014. Signed as a free agent by **Anaheim**, July 4, 2016.

READ, Matt

(REED, MAT) **PHI**

Right wing. Shoots right. 5'10", 185 lbs. Born, Ilderton, ON, June 14, 1986.

			Regular Season														Playoffs								
Season	Club	League	GP	G	A	Pts	PIM	PP	SH	GW	S	S%	+/-	TF	F%	Min	GP	G	A	Pts	PIM	PP	SH	GW	Min
2005-06	Milton Icehawks	ON-Jr.A	48	34	34	68	52	....	....	....	....	....	....	....	....	....	11	6	13	19	6	....	....	....	....
2006-07	Des Moines	USHL	58	28	34	62	110	....	....	....	....	....	....	....	....	....	8	2	0	2	6	....	....	....	....
2007-08	Bemidji State	CHA	36	9	18	27	37	....	....	....	....	....	....	....	....	....	....	....	....	....	....	....	....	....	....
2008-09	Bemidji State	CHA	37	15	25	40	50	....	....	....	....	....	....	....	....	....	....	....	....	....	....	....	....	....	....
2009-10	Bemidji State	CHA	37	19	22	41	32	....	....	....	....	....	....	....	....	....	....	....	....	....	....	....	....	....	....
2010-11	Bemidji State	WCHA	37	22	13	35	34	....	....	....	....	....	....	....	....	....	....	....	....	....	....	....	....	....	....
	Adirondack	AHL	11	7	6	13	6	....	....	....	....	....	....	....	....	....	....	....	....	....	....	....	....	....	....
2011-12	**Philadelphia**	**NHL**	**79**	**24**	**23**	**47**	**12**	**4**	**2**	**6**	**155**	**15.5**	**13**	**346**	**41.0**	**17:04**	**11**	**3**	**2**	**5**	**4**	**1**	**0**	**1**	**15:14**
2012-13	Sodertalje SK	Sweden-2	20	6	18	24	12	....	....	....	....	....	....	....	....	....	....	....	....	....	....	....	....	....	....
	Philadelphia	**NHL**	**42**	**11**	**13**	**24**	**2**	**1**	**0**	**2**	**72**	**15.3**	**1**	**48**	**29.2**	**18:01**	....	....	....	....	....	....	....	....	....
2013-14	**Philadelphia**	**NHL**	**75**	**22**	**18**	**40**	**16**	**0**	**4**	**3**	**151**	**14.6**	**–4**	**28**	**42.9**	**18:48**	**7**	**1**	**2**	**3**	**4**	**0**	**0**	**0**	**19:04**
2014-15	**Philadelphia**	**NHL**	**80**	**8**	**22**	**30**	**14**	**2**	**0**	**2**	**142**	**5.6**	**–4**	**21**	**52.4**	**17:34**	....	....	....	....	....	....	....	....	....

					Regular Season													Playoffs								
Season	Club	League	GP	G	A	Pts	PIM	PP	SH	GW	S	S%	+/-	TF	F%	Min	GP	G	A	Pts	PIM	PP	SH	GW	Min
2015-16	Philadelphia	NHL	79	11	15	26	27	2	0	2	127	8.7	-5	50	48.0	15:15	6	0	0	0	2	0	0	0	12:19
2016-17	Philadelphia	NHL	63	10	9	19	8	2	1	2	92	10.9	3	15	33.3	13:48									
	NHL Totals		418	86	100	186	79	11	7	17	739	11.6		508	40.9	16:44	24	4	4	8	10	1	0	1	15:37

CHA All-Rookie Team (2008) • CHA Rookie of the Year (2008) • CHA First All-Star Team (2009) • NCAA West Second All-American Team (2010)
Signed as a free agent by **Philadelphia**, March 24, 2011. Signed as a free agent by **Sodertalje** (Sweden-2), September 30. 2012.

REAVES, Ryan
(REEVZ, RIGH-uhn) **PIT**

Right wing. Shoots right. 6'1", 224 lbs.   Born, Winnipeg, MB, January 20, 1987. St. Louis' 4th pick, 156th overall, in 2005 NHL Draft.

Season	Club	League	GP	G	A	Pts	PIM	PP	SH	GW	S	S%	+/-	TF	F%	Min	GP	G	A	Pts	PIM	PP	SH	GW	Min
2004-05	Brandon	WHL	64	7	9	16	79										23	2	4	6	43				
2005-06	Brandon	WHL	68	14	14	28	91										6	0	1	1	8				
2006-07	Brandon	WHL	69	15	20	35	76										11	1	4	5	19				
2007-08	Peoria Rivermen	AHL	31	4	3	7	46										2	0	0	0	22				
	Alaska Aces	ECHL	9	2	0	2	42										4	0	0	0	22				
2008-09	Peoria Rivermen	AHL	57	8	9	17	130																		
2009-10	Peoria Rivermen	AHL	76	4	7	11	167																		
2010-11	**St. Louis**	**NHL**	28	2	2	4	78	0	0	1	16	12.5	-1	2	0.0	6:48									
	Peoria Rivermen	AHL	50	4	6	10	146																		
2011-12	**St. Louis**	**NHL**	60	3	1	4	124	0	0	1	32	9.4	0	2	50.0	6:32	2	0	0	0	0	0	0	0	7:47
2012-13	Orlando	ECHL	13	6	3	9	34																		
	St. Louis	**NHL**	43	4	2	6	79	0	0	1	24	16.7	3	3	100.0	7:27	6	0	0	0	2	0	0	0	7:30
2013-14	**St. Louis**	**NHL**	63	2	6	8	126	0	0	0	25	8.0	-1	8	75.0	8:31	6	0	0	0	6	0	0	0	6:08
2014-15	**St. Louis**	**NHL**	81	6	6	12	116	0	0	1	55	10.9	-3	0	0.0	8:31	6	1	0	1	0	0	0	0	8:43
2015-16	**St. Louis**	**NHL**	64	3	1	4	68	0	0	0	31	9.7	-6	2	50.0	8:02	5	0	0	0	7	0	0	0	6:10
2016-17	**St. Louis**	**NHL**	80	7	6	13	104	0	0	1	58	12.1	4	5	0.0	8:53	11	0	0	0	8	0	0	0	9:34
	NHL Totals		419	27	24	51	695	0	0	5	241	11.2		22	50.0	8:00	36	1	0	1	23	0	0	0	7:56

Signed as a free agent by **Orlando** (ECHL), December 8, 2012. Traded to **Pittsburgh** by **St. Louis** with St. Louis' 2nd round pick (Zachary Lauzon) in 2017 NHL Draft for Oscar Sundqvist and Pittsburgh's 1st round pick (Klim Kostin) in 2017 NHL Draft, June 23, 2017.

REDMOND, Zach
(REHD-muhnd, ZAK) **MTL**

Defense. Shoots right. 6'2", 205 lbs.   Born, Traverse City, MI, July 26, 1988. Atlanta's 7th pick, 184th overall, in 2008 NHL Draft.

Season	Club	League	GP	G	A	Pts	PIM	PP	SH	GW	S	S%	+/-	TF	F%	Min	GP	G	A	Pts	PIM	PP	SH	GW	Min
2005-06	Sioux Falls	USHL	48	4	7	11	57										11	1	2	3	4				
2006-07	Sioux Falls	USHL	60	8	31	39	37										8	3	7	10	8				
2007-08	Ferris State	CCHA	37	6	13	19	33																		
2008-09	Ferris State	CCHA	38	3	21	24	48																		
2009-10	Ferris State	CCHA	40	6	21	27	46																		
2010-11	Ferris State	CCHA	26	7	13	20	20																		
	Chicago Wolves	AHL	3	0	0	0	4																		
2011-12	St. John's IceCaps	AHL	72	8	23	31	33											10	1	2	3	10				
2012-13	St. John's IceCaps	AHL	38	8	11	19	34																		
	Winnipeg	**NHL**	8	1	3	4	12	0	1	0	13	7.7	0	0	0.0	19:35									
2013-14	**Winnipeg**	**NHL**	10	1	2	3	0	0	0	0	10	10.0	1	0	0.0	15:20									
	St. John's IceCaps	AHL	40	6	19	25	26											21	2	12	14	16				
2014-15	**Colorado**	**NHL**	59	5	15	20	24	1	0	1	93	5.4	-1	0	0.0	17:09									
2015-16	**Colorado**	**NHL**	37	2	6	8	10	1	0	0	22	9.1	5	0	0.0	11:47									
	San Antonio	AHL	11	3	4	7	6																		
2016-17	**Montreal**	**NHL**	16	0	5	5	2	0	0	0	12	0.0	6	0	0.0	12:19									
	St. John's IceCaps	AHL	26	4	14	18	8											4	1	1	2	2				
	NHL Totals		130	9	29	38	48	2	1	1	150	6.0		0	0.0	15:02									

CCHA Second All-Star Team (2010) • CCHA First All-Star Team (2011) • NCAA West Second All-American Team (2011)
• Transferred to **Winnipeg** after **Atlanta** franchise relocated, June 21, 2011. Signed as a free agent by **Colorado**, July 1, 2014. Signed as a free agent by **Montreal**, July 1, 2016.

REGNER, Brent
(REHG-nuhr, BREHNT) **DAL**

Defense. Shoots right. 5'11", 189 lbs.   Born, Westlock, AB, May 17, 1989. Columbus' 7th pick, 137th overall, in 2008 NHL Draft.

Season	Club	League	GP	G	A	Pts	PIM	PP	SH	GW	S	S%	+/-	TF	F%	Min	GP	G	A	Pts	PIM	PP	SH	GW	Min
2004-05	Ft. Saskatchewan	AMHL	36	2	13	15	24										14	1	7	8	2				
2005-06	Ft. Saskatchewan	AMHL	36	9	25	34	30																		
	Vancouver Giants	WHL	1	0	0	0	0																		
2006-07	Vancouver Giants	WHL	64	1	5	6	19										22	0	6	6	10				
2007-08	Vancouver Giants	WHL	72	8	39	47	45										10	0	10	10	10				
2008-09	Vancouver Giants	WHL	70	15	52	67	42										17	2	11	13	6				
2009-10	Syracuse Crunch	AHL	50	4	16	20	22																		
2010-11	Springfield	AHL	56	6	13	19	17																		
2011-12	Springfield	AHL	75	2	29	31	26																		
2012-13	Peoria Rivermen	AHL	66	3	15	18	22																		
	Evansville IceMen	ECHL	2	1	0	1	0																		
	Chicago Wolves	AHL	7	0	1	1	7																		
2013-14	Chicago Wolves	AHL	63	3	21	24	36											9	2	4	6	6				
2014-15	Chicago Wolves	AHL	71	6	23	29	29											3	1	1	2	0				
2015-16	**Florida**	**NHL**	7	0	0	0	4	0	0	0	7	0.0	-2	0	0.0	11:35									
	Portland Pirates	AHL	65	5	18	23	34											5	0	3	3	0				
2016-17	Springfield	AHL	28	2	11	13	8																		
	NHL Totals		7	0	0	0	4	0	0	0	7	0.0		0	0.0	11:35									

WHL West Second All-Star Team (2009)
Signed as a free agent by **St. Louis**, July 3, 2014. Signed as a free agent by **Florida**, July 1, 2015. • Missed majority of 2016-17 as a healthy reserve. Signed as a free agent by **Dallas**, July 1, 2017.

REILLY, Mike
(RIGH-lee, MIGHK) **MIN**

Defense. Shoots left. 6'2", 191 lbs.   Born, Chicago, IL, July 13, 1993. Columbus' 3rd pick, 98th overall, in 2011 NHL Draft.

Season	Club	League	GP	G	A	Pts	PIM	PP	SH	GW	S	S%	+/-	TF	F%	Min	GP	G	A	Pts	PIM	PP	SH	GW	Min
2009-10	Holy Angels	High-MN	24	4	29	33	19										2	3	2	5	0				
2010-11	Shattuck	High-MN	54	14	34	48	30																		
2011-12	Penticton Vees	BCHL	51	24	59	83	42										15	1	8	9	10				
2012-13	U. of Minnesota	WCHA	37	3	11	14	14																		
2013-14	U. of Minnesota	Big Ten	41	9	24	33	18																		
2014-15	U. of Minnesota	Big Ten	39	6	*36	42	44																		
2015-16	**Minnesota**	**NHL**	29	1	6	7	8	0	0	0	27	3.7	-4	0	0.0	12:05									
	Iowa Wild	AHL	45	5	18	23	10																		
2016-17	**Minnesota**	**NHL**	17	1	0	1	2	0	0	0	19	5.3	1	0	0.0	12:23									
	Iowa Wild	AHL	57	5	25	30	48																		
	NHL Totals		46	2	6	8	10	0	0	0	46	4.3		0	0.0	12:12									

Big Ten First All-Star Team (2014) • NCAA West First All-American Team (2014, 2015)
Signed as a free agent by **Minnesota**, July 3, 2015.

REINHART, Griffin
(RIGHN-hart, GRIHF-uhn) **VGK**

Defense. Shoots left. 6'4", 212 lbs.   Born, North Vancouver, BC, January 24, 1994. NY Islanders' 1st pick, 4th overall, in 2012 NHL Draft.

Season	Club	League	GP	G	A	Pts	PIM	PP	SH	GW	S	S%	+/-	TF	F%	Min	GP	G	A	Pts	PIM	PP	SH	GW	Min
2008-09	Hollyburn Huskies	Minor-BC		STATISTICS NOT AVAILABLE																				
	Van. NW Giants	BCMML	3	1	3	4	0										2	0	0	0	0				
2009-10	Van. NW Giants	BCMML	32	9	25	34	24										5	3	5	8	14				
	Edmonton	WHL	2	0	0	0	0																		
2010-11	Edmonton	WHL	45	6	19	25	36										4	0	0	0	0				
2011-12	Edmonton	WHL	58	12	24	36	38										20	2	6	8	20				
2012-13	Edmonton	WHL	59	8	21	29	35										12	3	4	7	12				
2013-14	Edmonton	WHL	45	4	17	21	55										21	4	9	13	18				
2014-15	**NY Islanders**	**NHL**	8	0	1	1	6	0	0	0	4	0.0	1	0	0.0	14:10	1	0	0	0	0	0	0	0	12:42
	Bridgeport	AHL	59	7	15	22	64																		

			Regular Season														Playoffs								
Season	Club	League	GP	G	A	Pts	PIM	PP	SH	GW	S	S%	+/-	TF	F%	Min	GP	G	A	Pts	PIM	PP	SH	GW	Min
2015-16	**Edmonton**	**NHL**	29	0	1	1	20	0	0	0	24	0.0	–6	0	0.0	18:04	....	....	....	....	....	....	....	....	....
	Bakersfield	AHL	30	2	8	10	16	....	....	....	....	....	....	....	....	....	....	....	....	....	....	....	....	....	....
2016-17	Bakersfield	AHL	54	7	14	21	42	....	....	....	....	....	....	....	....	....	....	....	....	....	....	....	....	....	....
	Edmonton	**NHL**	....	....	....	....	....	....	....	....	....	....	....	....	....	....	1	0	1	1	0	0	0	0	13:23
	NHL Totals		37	0	2	2	26	0	0	0	28	0.0		0	0.0	17:14	2	0	1	1	0	0	0	0	13:02

WHL East Second All-Star Team (2014)

Traded to **Edmonton** by **NY Islanders** for Pittsburgh's 1st round pick (previously acquired, NY Islanders selected Matthew Barzal) in 2015 NHL Draft and Edmonton's 2nd round pick (later traded to Tampa Bay – Tampa Bay selected Mitchell Stephens) in 2015 NHL Draft, June 26, 2015. Claimed by **Vegas** from **Edmonton** in Expansion Draft, June 21, 2017.

REINHART, Max

(RIGHN-hart, MAX) **OTT**

Center. Shoots left. 6'1", 195 lbs. Born, West Vancouver, BC, February 4, 1992. Calgary's 1st pick, 64th overall, in 2010 NHL Draft.

Season	Club	League	GP	G	A	Pts	PIM	PP	SH	GW	S	S%	+/-	TF	F%	Min	GP	G	A	Pts	PIM	PP	SH	GW	Min
2007-08	Van. NW Giants	BCMML	40	17	8	25	28	....	....	....	....	....	....	....	....	....	2	0	1	1	0	....	....	....	....
	Langley Chiefs	BCHL	1	0	0	0	2	....	....	....	....	....	....	....	....	....	....	....	....	....	....	....	....	....	....
2008-09	Kootenay Ice	WHL	62	11	16	27	21	....	....	....	....	....	....	....	....	....	4	1	0	1	2	....	....	....	....
2009-10	Kootenay Ice	WHL	72	21	30	51	38	....	....	....	....	....	....	....	....	....	6	1	1	2	6	....	....	....	....
2010-11	Kootenay Ice	WHL	71	34	45	79	41	....	....	....	....	....	....	....	....	....	19	15	12	27	12	....	....	....	....
2011-12	Kootenay Ice	WHL	61	28	50	78	40	....	....	....	....	....	....	....	....	....	3	0	2	2	6	....	....	....	....
	Abbotsford Heat	AHL	1	2	0	2	0	....	....	....	....	....	....	....	....	....	4	1	1	2	0	....	....	....	....
2012-13	Abbotsford Heat	AHL	67	7	14	21	32	....	....	....	....	....	....	....	....	....	....	....	....	....	....	....	....	....	....
	Calgary	**NHL**	11	1	2	3	4	0	0	0	26	3.8	–3	91	37.4	14:25	....	....	....	....	....	....	....	....	....
2013-14	**Calgary**	**NHL**	8	0	2	2	2	0	0	0	7	0.0	1	9	22.2	10:42	....	....	....	....	....	....	....	....	....
	Abbotsford Heat	AHL	66	21	42	63	47	....	....	....	....	....	....	....	....	....	4	1	3	4	4	....	....	....	....
2014-15	**Calgary**	**NHL**	4	0	0	0	0	0	0	0	3	0.0	–3	29	20.7	8:05	....	....	....	....	....	....	....	....	....
	Adirondack	AHL	69	15	24	39	38	....	....	....	....	....	....	....	....	....	....	....	....	....	....	....	....	....	....
2015-16	Milwaukee	AHL	73	23	15	38	32	....	....	....	....	....	....	....	....	....	3	0	0	0	4	....	....	....	....
2016-17	Kolner Haie	Germany	52	6	17	23	26	....	....	....	....	....	....	....	....	....	3	0	0	0	4	....	....	....	....
	NHL Totals		23	1	4	5	6	0	0	0	36	2.8		129	32.6	12:01	....	....	....	....	....	....	....	....	....

WHL East Second All-Star Team (2012)

Traded to **Nashville** by **Calgary** for future considerations, July 1, 2015. Signed as a free agent by **Koln** (Germany), June 6, 2016. Signed as a free agent by **Ottawa**, July 1, 2017.

REINHART, Sam

(RIGHN-hahrt, SAM) **BUF**

Center. Shoots right. 6'1", 189 lbs. Born, North Vancouver, BC, November 6, 1995. Buffalo's 1st pick, 2nd overall, in 2014 NHL Draft.

Season	Club	League	GP	G	A	Pts	PIM	PP	SH	GW	S	S%	+/-	TF	F%	Min	GP	G	A	Pts	PIM	PP	SH	GW	Min
2009-10	Hollyburn Huskies	Minor-BC	STATISTICS NOT AVAILABLE																						
	Van. NW Giants	BCMML	5	2	0	2	0	....	....	....	....	....	....	....	....	....	5	0	1	1	2	....	....	....	....
2010-11	Van. NW Giants	BCMML	34	38	40	78	6	....	....	....	....	....	....	....	....	....	5	5	4	9	....	....	....	....	....
	Kootenay Ice	WHL	4	2	0	2	0	....	....	....	....	....	....	....	....	....	7	0	0	0	0	....	....	....	....
2011-12	Kootenay Ice	WHL	67	28	34	62	2	....	....	....	....	....	....	....	....	....	4	1	1	2	0	....	....	....	....
2012-13	Kootenay Ice	WHL	72	35	50	85	22	....	....	....	....	....	....	....	....	....	5	0	1	1	4	....	....	....	....
2013-14	Kootenay Ice	WHL	60	36	69	105	11	....	....	....	....	....	....	....	....	....	13	6	17	23	2	....	....	....	....
2014-15	**Buffalo**	**NHL**	9	0	1	1	2	0	0	0	3	0.0	–1	86	24.4	10:22	....	....	....	....	....	....	....	....	....
	Kootenay Ice	WHL	47	19	46	65	20	....	....	....	....	....	....	....	....	....	7	6	3	9	8	....	....	....	....
	Rochester	AHL	3	0	3	3	0	....	....	....	....	....	....	....	....	....	....	....	....	....	....	....	....	....	....
2015-16	**Buffalo**	**NHL**	79	23	19	42	8	8	0	3	165	13.9	–8	108	33.3	16:50	....	....	....	....	....	....	....	....	....
2016-17	**Buffalo**	**NHL**	79	17	30	47	8	9	0	3	178	9.6	–11	210	41.0	17:13	....	....	....	....	....	....	....	....	....
	NHL Totals		167	40	50	90	18	17	0	6	346	11.6		404	35.4	16:40	....	....	....	....	....	....	....	....	....

WHL Rookie of the Year (2012) • WHL East Second All-Star Team (2013, 2015) • WHL East First All-Star Team (2014)

RENDULIC, Borna

(REHN-dew-LIHCH, BOHR-na)

Right wing. Shoots right. 6'2", 200 lbs. Born, Zagreb, Croatia, March 25, 1992.

Season	Club	League	GP	G	A	Pts	PIM	PP	SH	GW	S	S%	+/-	TF	F%	Min	GP	G	A	Pts	PIM	PP	SH	GW	Min
2010-11	Assat Pori Jr.	Fin-Jr.	31	4	14	18	36	....	....	....	....	....	....	....	....	....	....	....	....	....	....	....	....	....	....
	Medvescak Zagreb	Austria	12	1	1	2	2	....	....	....	....	....	....	....	....	....	....	....	....	....	....	....	....	....	....
	Zagreb 2	Croatia	....	....	....	....	....	....	....	....	....	....	....	....	....	....	4	1	5	6	2	....	....	....	....
2011-12	Assat Pori Jr.	Fin-Jr.	34	21	28	49	41	....	....	....	....	....	....	....	....	....	5	4	8	12	27	....	....	....	....
	Assat Pori	Finland	3	0	0	0	0	....	....	....	....	....	....	....	....	....	....	....	....	....	....	....	....	....	....
	SaPKo Savonlinna	Finland-2	7	2	3	5	14	....	....	....	....	....	....	....	....	....	....	....	....	....	....	....	....	....	....
2012-13	HPK Jr.	Fin-Jr.	1	0	0	0	0	....	....	....	....	....	....	....	....	....	....	....	....	....	....	....	....	....	....
	Peliitat Heinola	Finland-2	5	2	2	4	0	....	....	....	....	....	....	....	....	....	....	....	....	....	....	....	....	....	....
	HPK Hameenlinna	Finland	37	8	4	12	6	....	....	....	....	....	....	....	....	....	5	0	1	1	0	....	....	....	....
2013-14	HPK Hameenlinna	Finland	57	11	21	32	34	....	....	....	....	....	....	....	....	....	6	3	0	3	2	....	....	....	....
2014-15	**Colorado**	**NHL**	11	1	1	2	6	0	0	0	6	16.7	1	0	0.0	9:24	....	....	....	....	....	....	....	....	....
	Lake Erie	AHL	26	4	4	8	12	....	....	....	....	....	....	....	....	....	....	....	....	....	....	....	....	....	....
2015-16	**Colorado**	**NHL**	3	0	0	0	0	0	0	0	1	0.0	–2	3	0.0	7:32	....	....	....	....	....	....	....	....	....
	San Antonio	AHL	68	16	22	38	41	....	....	....	....	....	....	....	....	....	....	....	....	....	....	....	....	....	....
2016-17	**Vancouver**	**NHL**	1	0	0	0	0	0	0	0	1	0.0	0	0	0.0	4:51	....	....	....	....	....	....	....	....	....
	Utica Comets	AHL	69	12	11	23	30	....	....	....	....	....	....	....	....	....	....	....	....	....	....	....	....	....	....
	NHL Totals		15	1	1	2	6	0	0	0	8	12.5		3	0.0	8:43	....	....	....	....	....	....	....	....	....

Signed as a free agent by **Colorado**, May 19, 2014. • Missed majority of 2014-15 due to leg injury vs. Florida, January 15, 2015. Signed as a free agent by **Vancouver**, July 1, 2016.

RENOUF, Dan

(reh-NUF, DAN-yehl) **DET**

Defense. Shoots left. 6'3", 209 lbs. Born, Pickering, ON, June 1, 1994.

Season	Club	League	GP	G	A	Pts	PIM	PP	SH	GW	S	S%	+/-	TF	F%	Min	GP	G	A	Pts	PIM	PP	SH	GW	Min
2009-10	Ajax-Pickering	Minor-ON	73	17	39	56	60	....	....	....	....	....	....	....	....	....	....	....	....	....	....	....	....	....	....
	Whitby Fury	ON-Jr.A	2	0	0	0	0	....	....	....	....	....	....	....	....	....	....	....	....	....	....	....	....	....	....
2010-11	The Hill Academy	High-ON	62	10	43	53	34	....	....	....	....	....	....	....	....	....	....	....	....	....	....	....	....	....	....
2011-12	Youngstown	USHL	58	1	14	15	53	....	....	....	....	....	....	....	....	....	6	0	2	2	4	....	....	....	....
2012-13	Youngstown	USHL	57	10	18	28	83	....	....	....	....	....	....	....	....	....	9	0	1	1	7	....	....	....	....
2013-14	U. of Maine	H-East	34	1	10	11	12	....	....	....	....	....	....	....	....	....	....	....	....	....	....	....	....	....	....
2014-15	U. of Maine	H-East	39	3	9	12	24	....	....	....	....	....	....	....	....	....	....	....	....	....	....	....	....	....	....
2015-16	U. of Maine	H-East	38	6	9	15	36	....	....	....	....	....	....	....	....	....	....	....	....	....	....	....	....	....	....
	Grand Rapids	AHL	6	0	1	1	5	....	....	....	....	....	....	....	....	....	....	....	....	....	....	....	....	....	....
2016-17	**Detroit**	**NHL**	1	0	0	0	0	0	0	0	1	0.0	0	0	0.0	13:35	....	....	....	....	....	....	....	....	....
	Grand Rapids	AHL	67	3	13	16	95	....	....	....	....	....	....	....	....	....	19	2	2	4	6	....	....	....	....
	NHL Totals		1	0	0	0	0	0	0	0	1	0.0		0	0.0	13:35	....	....	....	....	....	....	....	....	....

Signed as a free agent by **Detroit**, March 10, 2016.

RIBEIRO, Mike

(rih-BAIR-roh, MIGHK)

Center. Shoots left. 6', 179 lbs. Born, Montreal, QC, February 10, 1980. Montreal's 2nd pick, 45th overall, in 1998 NHL Draft.

Season	Club	League	GP	G	A	Pts	PIM	PP	SH	GW	S	S%	+/-	TF	F%	Min	GP	G	A	Pts	PIM	PP	SH	GW	Min
1995-96	Mtl-Bourassa	QAAA	43	13	26	39	18	....	....	....	....	....	....	....	....	....	....	....	....	....	....	....	....	....	....
1996-97	Mtl-Bourassa	QAAA	43	32	57	89	48	....	....	....	....	....	....	....	....	....	16	15	23	38	14	....	....	....	....
1997-98	Rouyn-Noranda	QMJHL	67	40	*85	125	55	....	....	....	....	....	....	....	....	....	6	3	1	4	0	....	....	....	....
1998-99	Rouyn-Noranda	QMJHL	69	*67	*100	*167	137	....	....	....	....	....	....	....	....	....	11	5	11	16	12	....	....	....	....
	Fredericton	AHL	....	....	....	....	....	....	....	....	....	....	....	....	....	....	5	0	1	1	2	....	....	....	....
99-2000	**Montreal**	**NHL**	19	1	1	2	2	1	0	0	18	5.6	–6	95	34.7	10:40	....	....	....	....	....	....	....	....	....
	Quebec Citadelles	AHL	3	0	0	0	2	....	....	....	....	....	....	....	....	....	....	....	....	....	....	....	....	....	....
	Rouyn-Noranda	QMJHL	2	1	3	4	0	....	....	....	....	....	....	....	....	....	....	....	....	....	....	....	....	....	....
	Quebec Remparts	QMJHL	21	17	28	45	30	....	....	....	....	....	....	....	....	....	11	3	20	23	38	....	....	....	....
2000-01	**Montreal**	**NHL**	2	0	0	0	2	0	0	0	3	0.0	0	11	18.2	10:38	....	....	....	....	....	....	....	....	....
	Quebec Citadelles	AHL	74	26	40	66	44	....	....	....	....	....	....	....	....	....	9	1	5	6	23	....	....	....	....
2001-02	**Montreal**	**NHL**	43	8	10	18	12	3	0	0	48	16.7	–11	141	44.0	13:55	....	....	....	....	....	....	....	....	....
	Quebec Citadelles	AHL	23	9	14	23	36	....	....	....	....	....	....	....	....	....	3	0	3	3	0	....	....	....	....
2002-03	**Montreal**	**NHL**	52	5	12	17	6	2	0	0	57	8.8	–3	358	50.3	11:07	....	....	....	....	....	....	....	....	....
	Hamilton	AHL	3	0	1	1	0	....	....	....	....	....	....	....	....	....	....	....	....	....	....	....	....	....	....
2003-04	**Montreal**	**NHL**	81	20	45	65	34	7	0	5	103	19.4	15	913	44.8	17:05	11	2	1	3	18	0	0	0	16:31

			Regular Season														Playoffs								
Season	Club	League	GP	G	A	Pts	PIM	PP	SH	GW	S	S%	+/-	TF	F%	Min	GP	G	A	Pts	PIM	PP	SH	GW	Min
2004-05	Blues Espoo	Finland	17	8	9	17	4	....	....	....	....	....	....	....	....	....	....	....	....	....	....	....	....	....	....
2005-06	**Montreal**	**NHL**	**79**	**16**	**35**	**51**	**36**	**8**	**0**	**2**	**130**	**12.3**	**-6**	**843**	**44.7**	**16:35**	**6**	**0**	**2**	**2**	**0**	**0**	**0**	**0**	**18:22**
2006-07	**Dallas**	**NHL**	**81**	**18**	**41**	**59**	**22**	**6**	**0**	**3**	**111**	**16.2**	**3**	**678**	**46.6**	**14:56**	**7**	**0**	**3**	**3**	**4**	**0**	**0**	**0**	**18:28**
2007-08	**Dallas**	**NHL**	**76**	**27**	**56**	**83**	**46**	**7**	**0**	**5**	**107**	**25.2**	**21**	**883**	**45.0**	**18:26**	**18**	**3**	**14**	**17**	**16**	**0**	**0**	**0**	**21:45**
2008-09	**Dallas**	**NHL**	**82**	**22**	**56**	**78**	**52**	**7**	**0**	**1**	**163**	**13.5**	**-4**	**1240**	**45.5**	**20:57**	....	....	....	....	....	....	....	....	....
2009-10	**Dallas**	**NHL**	**66**	**19**	**34**	**53**	**38**	**8**	**2**	**0**	**155**	**12.3**	**-5**	**1102**	**44.8**	**19:32**	....	....	....	....	....	....	....	....	....
2010-11	**Dallas**	**NHL**	**82**	**19**	**52**	**71**	**28**	**7**	**0**	**4**	**161**	**11.8**	**-4**	**1213**	**46.6**	**19:58**	....	....	....	....	....	....	....	....	....
2011-12	**Dallas**	**NHL**	**74**	**18**	**45**	**63**	**66**	**2**	**0**	**5**	**142**	**12.7**	**5**	**808**	**42.2**	**20:03**	....	....	....	....	....	....	....	....	....
2012-13	**Washington**	**NHL**	**48**	**13**	**36**	**49**	**53**	**6**	**0**	**1**	**63**	**20.6**	**-4**	**505**	**44.8**	**17:50**	**7**	**1**	**1**	**2**	**10**	**0**	**0**	**1**	**18:33**
2013-14	**Phoenix**	**NHL**	**80**	**16**	**31**	**47**	**52**	**4**	**0**	**3**	**110**	**14.5**	**-13**	**903**	**43.3**	**18:00**	....	....	....	....	....	....	....	....	....
2014-15	**Nashville**	**NHL**	**82**	**15**	**47**	**62**	**52**	**1**	**0**	**3**	**96**	**15.6**	**11**	**1348**	**43.2**	**18:45**	**6**	**1**	**4**	**5**	**4**	**0**	**0**	**0**	**23:22**
2015-16	**Nashville**	**NHL**	**81**	**7**	**43**	**50**	**62**	**2**	**0**	**0**	**76**	**9.2**	**11**	**760**	**37.9**	**17:27**	**12**	**0**	**2**	**2**	**16**	**0**	**0**	**0**	**15:22**
2016-17	**Nashville**	**NHL**	**46**	**4**	**21**	**25**	**14**	**2**	**0**	**0**	**38**	**10.5**	**-5**	**444**	**41.2**	**15:58**	....	....	....	....	....	....	....	....	....
	Milwaukee	AHL	28	5	21	26	18	....	....	....	....	....	....	....	....	....	3	0	3	3	0	....	....	....	....
	NHL Totals		**1074**	**228**	**565**	**793**	**577**	**73**	**2**	**32**	**1581**	**14.4**		**12245**	**44.2**	**17:31**	**67**	**7**	**27**	**34**	**68**	**0**	**0**	**1**	**18:54**

QMJHL Second All-Star Team (1998) • QMJHL First All-Star Team (1999) • Canadian Major Junior First All-Star Team (1999)

Played in NHL All-Star Game (2008)

Signed as a free agent by **Espoo** (Finland), January 17, 2005. Traded to **Dallas** by **Montreal** with Montreal's 6th round pick (Matthew Tassone) in 2008 NHL Draft for Janne Niinimaa and Dallas' 5th round pick (Andrew Conboy) in 2007 NHL Draft, September 30, 2006. Traded to **Washington** by **Dallas** for Cody Eakin and Boston's 2nd round pick (previously acquired, Dallas selected Mike Winther) in 2012 NHL Draft, June 22, 2012. Signed as a free agent by **Phoenix**, July 5, 2013. Signed as a free agent by **Nashville**, July 15, 2014.

RICHARD, Tanner

(rih-SHARD, TA-nuhr)

Center. Shoots left. 6', 176 lbs. Born, Markham, ON, April 6, 1993. Tampa Bay's 5th pick, 71st overall, in 2012 NHL Draft.

Season	Club	League	GP	G	A	Pts	PIM	PP	SH	GW	S	S%	+/-	TF	F%	Min	GP	G	A	Pts	PIM	PP	SH	GW	Min
2010-11	Rapperswil	Swiss	4	0	0	0	0	....	....	....	....	....	....	....	....	....	4	0	1	1	0	....	....	....	....
2011-12	Guelph Storm	OHL	43	13	35	48	46	....	....	....	....	....	....	....	....	....	6	1	4	5	6	....	....	....	....
2012-13	Guelph Storm	OHL	52	11	51	62	94	....	....	....	....	....	....	....	....	....	5	0	3	3	6	....	....	....	....
	Syracuse Crunch	AHL	8	0	3	3	6	....	....	....	....	....	....	....	....	....	....	....	....	....	....	....	....	....	....
2013-14	Syracuse Crunch	AHL	65	2	15	17	95	....	....	....	....	....	....	....	....	....	....	....	....	....	....	....	....	....	....
2014-15	Syracuse Crunch	AHL	70	13	25	38	135	....	....	....	....	....	....	....	....	....	2	1	0	1	2	....	....	....	....
2015-16	Syracuse Crunch	AHL	71	11	43	54	57	....	....	....	....	....	....	....	....	....	....	....	....	....	....	....	....	....	....
2016-17	**Tampa Bay**	**NHL**	**3**	**0**	**0**	**0**	**2**	**0**	**0**	**0**	**1**	**0.0**	**-2**	**30**	**43.3**	**12:42**	....	....	....	....	....	....	....	....	....
	Syracuse Crunch	AHL	47	14	20	34	50	....	....	....	....	....	....	....	....	....	....	....	....	....	....	....	....	....	....
	NHL Totals		**3**	**0**	**0**	**0**	**2**	**0**	**0**	**0**	**1**	**0.0**		**30**	**43.3**	**12:42**	....	....	....	....	....	....	....	....	....

RICHARDSON, Brad

(RIH-chuhrd-suhn, BRAD) **ARI**

Center. Shoots left. 6', 197 lbs. Born, Belleville, ON, February 4, 1985. Colorado's 4th pick, 163rd overall, in 2003 NHL Draft.

Season	Club	League	GP	G	A	Pts	PIM	PP	SH	GW	S	S%	+/-	TF	F%	Min	GP	G	A	Pts	PIM	PP	SH	GW	Min
2001-02	Owen Sound	OHL	58	12	21	33	20	....	....	....	....	....	....	....	....	....	....	....	....	....	....	....	....	....	....
2002-03	Owen Sound	OHL	67	27	40	67	54	....	....	....	....	....	....	....	....	....	4	1	1	2	10	....	....	....	....
2003-04	Owen Sound	OHL	15	7	9	16	4	....	....	....	....	....	....	....	....	....	....	....	....	....	....	....	....	....	....
2004-05	Owen Sound	OHL	68	41	56	97	60	....	....	....	....	....	....	....	....	....	8	6	4	10	8	....	....	....	....
2005-06	**Colorado**	**NHL**	**41**	**3**	**10**	**13**	**12**	**1**	**0**	**0**	**51**	**5.9**	**0**	**305**	**41.0**	**10:44**	**9**	**1**	**0**	**1**	**6**	**0**	**0**	**0**	**11:41**
	Lowell	AHL	29	4	13	17	20	....	....	....	....	....	....	....	....	....	....	....	....	....	....	....	....	....	....
2006-07	**Colorado**	**NHL**	**73**	**14**	**8**	**22**	**28**	**0**	**3**	**3**	**129**	**10.9**	**4**	**358**	**40.8**	**13:10**	....	....	....	....	....	....	....	....	....
	Albany River Rats	AHL	3	0	1	1	2	....	....	....	....	....	....	....	....	....	....	....	....	....	....	....	....	....	....
2007-08	**Colorado**	**NHL**	**22**	**2**	**3**	**5**	**8**	**0**	**0**	**0**	**32**	**6.3**	**-3**	**60**	**43.3**	**13:29**	....	....	....	....	....	....	....	....	....
	Lake Erie	AHL	38	14	26	40	18	....	....	....	....	....	....	....	....	....	....	....	....	....	....	....	....	....	....
2008-09	**Los Angeles**	**NHL**	**31**	**0**	**5**	**5**	**11**	**0**	**0**	**0**	**37**	**0.0**	**-6**	**95**	**54.7**	**10:48**	....	....	....	....	....	....	....	....	....
	Manchester	AHL	3	1	2	3	0	....	....	....	....	....	....	....	....	....	....	....	....	....	....	....	....	....	....
2009-10	**Los Angeles**	**NHL**	**81**	**11**	**16**	**27**	**37**	**0**	**1**	**4**	**148**	**7.4**	**1**	**391**	**48.1**	**12:51**	**6**	**1**	**1**	**2**	**2**	**0**	**0**	**1**	**14:41**
2010-11	**Los Angeles**	**NHL**	**68**	**7**	**12**	**19**	**47**	**0**	**1**	**1**	**103**	**6.8**	**-13**	**181**	**50.8**	**11:46**	**6**	**2**	**3**	**5**	**2**	**0**	**0**	**0**	**15:37**
2011-12 ♦	**Los Angeles**	**NHL**	**59**	**5**	**3**	**8**	**30**	**0**	**1**	**0**	**98**	**5.1**	**-6**	**56**	**58.9**	**12:52**	**13**	**1**	**0**	**1**	**4**	**0**	**0**	**0**	**8:35**
2012-13	**Los Angeles**	**NHL**	**16**	**1**	**5**	**6**	**10**	**0**	**0**	**0**	**27**	**3.7**	**2**	**56**	**48.2**	**10:54**	**11**	**0**	**1**	**1**	**0**	**0**	**0**	**0**	**10:46**
2013-14	**Vancouver**	**NHL**	**73**	**11**	**12**	**23**	**39**	**1**	**2**	**2**	**85**	**12.9**	**1**	**966**	**55.2**	**14:54**	....	....	....	....	....	....	....	....	....
2014-15	**Vancouver**	**NHL**	**45**	**8**	**13**	**21**	**34**	**0**	**1**	**1**	**66**	**12.1**	**0**	**578**	**47.8**	**14:28**	**5**	**0**	**0**	**0**	**15**	**0**	**0**	**0**	**12:37**
2015-16	**Arizona**	**NHL**	**82**	**11**	**20**	**31**	**46**	**0**	**0**	**3**	**117**	**9.4**	**8**	**961**	**54.4**	**15:37**	....	....	....	....	....	....	....	....	....
2016-17	**Arizona**	**NHL**	**16**	**5**	**4**	**9**	**15**	**0**	**2**	**0**	**25**	**20.0**	**-1**	**230**	**52.6**	**15:21**	....	....	....	....	....	....	....	....	....
	NHL Totals		**607**	**78**	**111**	**189**	**317**	**2**	**11**	**14**	**918**	**8.5**		**4237**	**50.6**	**13:18**	**50**	**5**	**5**	**10**	**29**	**0**	**0**	**1**	**11:36**

Traded to **Los Angeles** by **Colorado** for Detroit's 2nd round pick (previously acquired, Colorado selected Peter Delmas) in 2008 NHL Draft, June 21, 2008. • Missed majority of 2012-13 as a healthy reserve. Signed as a free agent by **Vancouver**, July 5, 2013. Signed as a free agent by **Arizona**, July 1, 2015.

RIEDER, Tobias

(REE-duhr, TOH-bee-uhs) **ARI**

Right wing. Shoots left. 5'11", 185 lbs. Born, Landshut, Germany, January 10, 1993. Edmonton's 7th pick, 114th overall, in 2011 NHL Draft.

Season	Club	League	GP	G	A	Pts	PIM	PP	SH	GW	S	S%	+/-	TF	F%	Min	GP	G	A	Pts	PIM	PP	SH	GW	Min
2008-09	EV Landshut Jr.	Ger-Jr.	36	27	24	51	18	....	....	....	....	....	....	....	....	....	9	6	8	14	10	....	....	....	....
2009-10	EV Landshut Jr.	Ger-Jr.	5	6	3	9	25	....	....	....	....	....	....	....	....	....	4	5	1	6	2	....	....	....	....
	Landshut Cann.	German-2	45	10	13	23	28	....	....	....	....	....	....	....	....	....	6	0	0	0	0	....	....	....	....
2010-11	Kitchener Rangers	OHL	65	23	26	49	35	....	....	....	....	....	....	....	....	....	7	0	2	2	4	....	....	....	....
2011-12	Kitchener Rangers	OHL	60	42	43	85	25	....	....	....	....	....	....	....	....	....	16	13	14	27	4	....	....	....	....
2012-13	Kitchener Rangers	OHL	52	27	29	56	12	....	....	....	....	....	....	....	....	....	9	2	10	12	4	....	....	....	....
2013-14	Portland Pirates	AHL	64	28	20	48	10	....	....	....	....	....	....	....	....	....	....	....	....	....	....	....	....	....	....
2014-15	**Arizona**	**NHL**	**72**	**13**	**8**	**21**	**14**	**0**	**3**	**1**	**189**	**6.9**	**-19**	**5**	**20.0**	**16:54**	....	....	....	....	....	....	....	....	....
	Portland Pirates	AHL	9	4	1	5	0	....	....	....	....	....	....	....	....	....	....	....	....	....	....	....	....	....	....
2015-16	**Arizona**	**NHL**	**82**	**14**	**23**	**37**	**10**	**2**	**0**	**1**	**189**	**7.4**	**-21**	**29**	**34.5**	**17:18**	....	....	....	....	....	....	....	....	....
2016-17	**Arizona**	**NHL**	**80**	**16**	**18**	**34**	**6**	**2**	**1**	**1**	**155**	**10.3**	**-8**	**13**	**30.8**	**17:19**	....	....	....	....	....	....	....	....	....
	NHL Totals		**234**	**43**	**49**	**92**	**30**	**4**	**4**	**3**	**533**	**8.1**		**47**	**31.9**	**17:11**	....	....	....	....	....	....	....	....	....

Traded to **Phoenix** by **Edmonton** for Kale Kessy, March 30, 2013.

RIELLY, Morgan

(RIGH-lee, MOHR-guhn) **TOR**

Defense. Shoots left. 6'1", 214 lbs. Born, Vancouver, BC, March 9, 1994. Toronto's 1st pick, 5th overall, in 2012 NHL Draft.

Season	Club	League	GP	G	A	Pts	PIM	PP	SH	GW	S	S%	+/-	TF	F%	Min	GP	G	A	Pts	PIM	PP	SH	GW	Min
2008-09	Notre Dame	Minor-SK	43	41	43	84	10	....	....	....	....	....	....	....	....	....	....	....	....	....	....	....	....	....	....
2009-10	Notre Dame	SMHL	43	18	37	55	20	....	....	....	....	....	....	....	....	....	13	7	2	9	0	....	....	....	....
2010-11	Moose Jaw	WHL	65	6	22	28	21	....	....	....	....	....	....	....	....	....	6	0	6	6	0	....	....	....	....
2011-12	Moose Jaw	WHL	18	3	15	18	2	....	....	....	....	....	....	....	....	....	5	0	3	3	0	....	....	....	....
2012-13	Moose Jaw	WHL	60	12	42	54	19	....	....	....	....	....	....	....	....	....	....	....	....	....	....	....	....	....	....
	Toronto Marlies	AHL	14	1	2	3	0	....	....	....	....	....	....	....	....	....	8	1	0	1	0	....	....	....	....
2013-14	**Toronto**	**NHL**	**73**	**2**	**25**	**27**	**12**	**1**	**0**	**0**	**96**	**2.1**	**-13**	**0**	**0.0**	**17:38**	....	....	....	....	....	....	....	....	....
2014-15	**Toronto**	**NHL**	**81**	**8**	**21**	**29**	**14**	**1**	**0**	**0**	**148**	**5.4**	**-16**	**0**	**0.0**	**20:20**	....	....	....	....	....	....	....	....	....
2015-16	**Toronto**	**NHL**	**82**	**9**	**27**	**36**	**28**	**2**	**1**	**0**	**167**	**5.4**	**-17**	**0**	**0.0**	**23:14**	....	....	....	....	....	....	....	....	....
2016-17	**Toronto**	**NHL**	**76**	**6**	**21**	**27**	**21**	**1**	**0**	**1**	**171**	**3.5**	**-20**	**0**	**0.0**	**22:10**	**6**	**1**	**4**	**5**	**2**	**1**	**0**	**0**	**26:53**
	NHL Totals		**312**	**25**	**94**	**119**	**75**	**5**	**1**	**1**	**582**	**4.3**		**0**	**0.0**	**20:55**	**6**	**1**	**4**	**5**	**2**	**1**	**0**	**0**	**26:53**

WHL East First All-Star Team (2013)

• Missed majority of 2011-12 due to knee injury vs. Calgary (WHL), November 6, 2011.

RINALDO, Zac

(rih-NAL-doh, ZAK) **ARI**

Center. Shoots left. 5'10", 188 lbs. Born, Mississauga, ON, June 15, 1990. Philadelphia's 4th pick, 178th overall, in 2008 NHL Draft.

Season	Club	League	GP	G	A	Pts	PIM	PP	SH	GW	S	S%	+/-	TF	F%	Min	GP	G	A	Pts	PIM	PP	SH	GW	Min
2006-07	Hamilton	ON-Jr.A	44	16	16	32	193	....	....	....	....	....	....	....	....	....	16	4	4	8	48	....	....	....	....
	St. Michael's	OHL	6	0	0	0	2	....	....	....	....	....	....	....	....	....	....	....	....	....	....	....	....	....	....
2007-08	St. Michael's	OHL	63	7	7	14	191	....	....	....	....	....	....	....	....	....	4	0	0	0	9	....	....	....	....
2008-09	St. Michael's	OHL	34	6	7	13	*112	....	....	....	....	....	....	....	....	....	....	....	....	....	....	....	....	....	....
	London Knights	OHL	22	4	13	17	*89	....	....	....	....	....	....	....	....	....	8	1	1	2	26	....	....	....	....
2009-10	London Knights	OHL	34	8	7	15	*148	....	....	....	....	....	....	....	....	....	....	....	....	....	....	....	....	....	....
	Barrie Colts	OHL	26	2	8	10	*107	....	....	....	....	....	....	....	....	....	4	2	0	2	11	....	....	....	....

			Regular Season														Playoffs								
Season	Club	League	GP	G	A	Pts	PIM	PP	SH	GW	S	S%	+/-	TF	F%	Min	GP	G	A	Pts	PIM	PP	SH	GW	Min
2010-11	Adirondack	AHL	60	3	6	9	331																		
	Philadelphia	**NHL**															2	0	0	0	12	0	0	0	2:53
2011-12	**Philadelphia**	**NHL**	66	2	7	9	232	0	0	0	54	3.7	−1	9	66.7	7:29	5	0	0	0	48	0	0	0	5:41
	Adirondack	AHL	4	1	1	2	11																		
2012-13	Adirondack	AHL	31	2	3	5	92																		
	Philadelphia	**NHL**	32	3	2	5	85	0	0	0	15	20.0	−7	2	50.0	8:23									
2013-14	**Philadelphia**	**NHL**	67	2	2	4	153	0	0	1	54	3.7	−13	3	66.7	7:42	7	0	0	0	4	0	0	0	6:51
2014-15	**Philadelphia**	**NHL**	58	1	5	6	102	0	0	0	45	2.2	−9	3	33.3	8:55									
2015-16	**Boston**	**NHL**	52	1	2	3	83	0	0	0	38	2.6	−5	1	0.0	8:18									
	Providence Bruins	AHL	2	0	0	0	12																		
2016-17	Providence Bruins	AHL	29	5	2	7	20																		
	NHL Totals		275	9	18	27	655	0	0	1	206	4.4		18	55.6	8:06	14	0	0	0	64	0	0	0	5:52

Traded to **Boston** by **Philadelphia** for Boston's 3rd round pick (Kirill Ustimenko) in 2017 NHL Draft, June 29, 2015. • Missed majority of 2016-17 as a healthy reserve. Signed as a free agent by **Arizona**, July 1, 2017.

RISTOLAINEN, Rasmus

(rihs-toh-LIGH-nehn, RAZ-muhs) **BUF**

Defense. Shoots right. 6'4", 207 lbs. Born, Turku, Finland, October 27, 1994. Buffalo's 1st pick, 8th overall, in 2013 NHL Draft.

2009-10	TPS Turku U18	Fin-U18	32	3	7	10	28										3	1	0	1	4				
	TPS Turku Jr.	Fin-Jr.	5	1	1	2	0																		
2010-11	TPS Turku U18	Fin-U18	2	1	2	3	0										13	5	3	8	8				
	TPS Turku Jr.	Fin-Jr.	27	0	12	12	30																		
	TPS Turku	Finland	1	0	0	0	0																		
2011-12	TPS Turku Jr.	Fin-Jr.	8	0	4	4	6																		
	TPS Turku	Finland	40	3	5	8	78										2	0	0	0	0				
2012-13	TPS Turku	Finland	52	3	12	15	32																		
	TPS Turku Jr.	Fin-Jr.															5	2	1	3	2				
2013-14	**Buffalo**	**NHL**	34	2	2	4	6	0	0	0	52	3.8	−15	1	0.0	19:07									
	Rochester	AHL	34	6	14	20	22										5	0	2	2	2				
2014-15	**Buffalo**	**NHL**	78	8	12	20	26	4	0	0	121	6.6	−32	1	100.0	20:37									
2015-16	**Buffalo**	**NHL**	82	9	32	41	33	4	0	1	202	4.5	−21	0	0.0	25:17									
2016-17	**Buffalo**	**NHL**	79	6	39	45	58	1	0	2	186	3.2	−9	0	0.0	26:28									
	NHL Totals		273	25	85	110	123	9	0	3	561	4.5		2	50.0	23:31									

RITCHIE, Brett

(RIH-chee, BREHT) **DAL**

Right wing. Shoots right. 6'3", 220 lbs. Born, Orangeville, ON, July 1, 1993. Dallas' 2nd pick, 44th overall, in 2011 NHL Draft.

2008-09	Tor. Marlboros	GTHL	71	36	33	69	67																		
2009-10	Sarnia Sting	OHL	65	13	16	29	35																		
2010-11	Sarnia Sting	OHL	49	21	20	41	47																		
2011-12	Sarnia Sting	OHL	23	8	7	15	30																		
	Niagara Ice Dogs	OHL	30	16	14	30	24										20	3	8	11	14				
2012-13	Niagara Ice Dogs	OHL	53	41	35	76	40										4	1	3	4	9				
	Texas Stars	AHL	5	3	1	4	0										9	2	0	2	2				
2013-14	Texas Stars	AHL	68	22	26	48	53										13	7	4	11	10				
2014-15	**Dallas**	**NHL**	31	6	3	9	12	0	0	1	78	7.7	−1	4	25.0	13:59									
	Texas Stars	AHL	33	14	7	21	40										3	1	1	2	2				
2015-16	**Dallas**	**NHL**	8	0	1	1	7	0	0	0	15	0.0	−3	0	0.0	11:36	2	0	0	0	0	0	0	0	6:46
	Texas Stars	AHL	35	14	14	28	26										3	1	1	2	0				
2016-17	**Dallas**	**NHL**	78	16	8	24	38	1	0	2	167	9.6	11	2	50.0	12:54									
	NHL Totals		117	22	12	34	57	1	0	3	260	8.5		6	33.3	13:06	2	0	0	0	0	0	0	0	6:46

OHL Second All-Star Team (2013)

RITCHIE, Nick

(RIH-chee, NIHK) **ANA**

Left wing. Shoots left. 6'2", 232 lbs. Born, Orangeville, ON, December 5, 1995. Anaheim's 1st pick, 10th overall, in 2014 NHL Draft.

2010-11	Tor. Marlboros	GTHL	68	50	45	95	119																		
	Georgetown	ON-Jr.A	1	0	0	0	0																		
2011-12	Peterborough	OHL	63	16	23	39	60																		
2012-13	Peterborough	OHL	41	18	17	35	50																		
2013-14	Peterborough	OHL	61	39	35	74	136										11	5	5	10	24				
2014-15	Peterborough	OHL	25	14	18	32	69																		
	Sault Ste. Marie	OHL	23	15	15	30	44										14	13	13	26	28				
2015-16	**Anaheim**	**NHL**	33	2	2	4	37	0	0	0	55	3.6	−2	3	33.3	11:46									
	San Diego Gulls	AHL	38	16	14	30	59										9	5	3	8	20				
2016-17	**Anaheim**	**NHL**	77	14	14	28	62	1	0	3	149	9.4	4	8	50.0	12:59	15	4	0	4	46	0	0	2	13:26
	NHL Totals		110	16	16	32	99	1	0	3	204	7.8		11	45.5	12:37	15	4	0	4	46	0	0	2	13:26

ROBAK, Colby

(ROH-bak, KOHL-bee)

Defense. Shoots left. 6'3", 194 lbs. Born, Dauphin, MB, April 24, 1990. Florida's 2nd pick, 46th overall, in 2008 NHL Draft.

2005-06	Parkland Rangers	MMHL	40	14	20	34	14																		
2006-07	Brandon	WHL	39	2	3	5	12										1	0	0	0	0				
2007-08	Brandon	WHL	71	6	24	30	25										6	0	2	2	8				
2008-09	Brandon	WHL	65	13	29	42	41										12	6	8	14	4				
2009-10	Brandon	WHL	71	16	50	66	9										15	3	9	12	2				
2010-11	Rochester	AHL	76	7	17	24	22																		
2011-12	**Florida**	**NHL**	3	0	0	0	0	0	0	0	1	0.0	1	0	0.0	12:34									
	San Antonio	AHL	73	9	30	39	30										8	1	4	5	4				
2012-13	San Antonio	AHL	63	5	18	23	50																		
	Florida	**NHL**	16	0	1	1	17	0	0	0	15	0.0	−1	0	0.0	15:11									
2013-14	**Florida**	**NHL**	16	0	2	2	6	0	0	0	15	0.0	−4	0	0.0	18:34									
	San Antonio	AHL	56	8	13	21	24																		
2014-15	**Florida**	**NHL**	7	0	0	0	2	0	0	0	6	0.0	−1	0	0.0	12:58									
	Anaheim	**NHL**	5	0	1	1	0	0	0	0	2	0.0	3	0	0.0	15:15									
	Norfolk Admirals	AHL	29	1	5	6	18																		
2015-16	Rochester	AHL	73	5	15	20	50																		
2016-17	Stockton Heat	AHL	6	0	5	5	6																		
	Utica Comets	AHL	64	3	25	28	54																		
	NHL Totals		47	0	4	4	25	0	0	0	39	0.0		0	0.0	15:51									

WHL East Second All-Star Team (2010)

Traded to **Anaheim** by **Florida** for Jesse Blacker and Anaheim's 6th round pick (Sebastian Repo) in 2017 NHL Draft, December 4, 2014. Signed as a free agent by **Rochester** (AHL), September 28, 2015. Signed as a free agent by **Stockton** (AHL), October 14, 2016. Signed as a free agent by **Utica** (AHL), November 2, 2016.

ROBINSON, Buddy

(RAW-bihn-suhn, BUH-dee) **WPG**

Right wing. Shoots right. 6'6", 232 lbs. Born, Bellmawr, NJ, September 30, 1991.

2009-10	Hamilton	ON-Jr.A	49	11	12	23	62																		
2010-11	Hamilton	ON-Jr.A	32	15	23	38	39																		
	Nepean Raiders	ON-Jr.A	19	5	19	24	20																		
2011-12	Lake Superior	CCHA	39	5	5	10	37																		
2012-13	Lake Superior	CCHA	38	8	8	16	48																		
	Binghamton	AHL	6	2	2	4	8										2	0	0	0	0				
2013-14	Binghamton	AHL	69	15	16	31	49										4	0	0	0	4				
	Elmira Jackals	ECHL	1	0	0	0	0																		
2014-15	Binghamton	AHL	75	12	22	34	69																		
2015-16	**Ottawa**	**NHL**	3	1	1	2	4	0	0	1	5	20.0	2	1	0.0	8:36									
	Binghamton	AHL	62	13	10	23	66																		

			Regular Season														Playoffs								
Season	Club	League	GP	G	A	Pts	PIM	PP	SH	GW	S	S%	+/-	TF	F%	Min	GP	G	A	Pts	PIM	PP	SH	GW	Min
2016-17	**Ottawa**	**NHL**	**4**	**0**	**0**	**0**	**2**	**0**	**0**	**0**	**4**	**0.0**	**0**	**0**	**0.0**	**6:57**									
	Binghamton	AHL	33	7	5	12	18																		
	San Jose	AHL	33	10	9	19	53										15	4	5	9	12				
	NHL Totals		**7**	**1**	**1**	**2**	**6**	**0**	**0**	**1**	**9**	**11.1**		**1**	**0.0**	**7:39**									

Signed as a free agent by **Ottawa**, March 25, 2013. Traded to **San Jose** by **Ottawa** with Zack Stortini and Ottawa's 7th round pick (later traded to New Jersey – New Jersey selected Matthew Hellickson) in 2017 NHL Draft for Tommy Wingels, January 24, 2017. Signed as a free agent by **Winnipeg**, July 1, 2017.

RODIN, Anton (ROH-dihn, AN-tawn) VAN

Right wing. Shoots left. 5'11", 181 lbs. Born, Stockholm, Sweden, November 21, 1990. Vancouver's 2nd pick, 53rd overall, in 2009 NHL Draft.

2006-07	Brynas U18	Swe-U18	14	7	4	11	4										3	0	0	0	2				
	Brynas IF Gavle Jr.	Swe-Jr.	1	0	0	0	0																		
2007-08	Brynas U18	Swe-U18	6	2	7	9	8										5	2	5	7	0				
	Brynas IF Gavle Jr.	Swe-Jr.	35	8	11	19	36										7	1	0	1	0				
2008-09	Brynas IF Gavle Jr.	Swe-Jr.	37	29	26	55	34										7	2	10	12	4				
	IK Oskarshamn	Sweden-2	6	0	0	0	2																		
2009-10	Brynas IF Gavle Jr.	Swe-Jr.	4	0	3	3	4										3	0	3	3	0				
	Brynas IF Gavle	Sweden	36	1	4	5	8										5	1	0	1	4				
	Mora IK	Sweden-2	8	2	2	4	0																		
2010-11	Brynas IF Gavle	Sweden	53	7	19	26	16										5	1	1	2	0				
2011-12	Chicago Wolves	AHL	62	10	17	27	18																		
2012-13	Chicago Wolves	AHL	49	4	10	14	22																		
2013-14	Brynas IF Gavle	Sweden	47	12	23	35	38										5	2	1	3	6				
2014-15	Brynas IF Gavle	Sweden	54	19	21	40	32										7	5	2	7	6				
2015-16	Brynas IF Gavle	Sweden	33	16	21	37	18																		
2016-17	**Vancouver**	**NHL**	**3**	**0**	**1**	**1**	**0**	**0**	**0**	**0**	**2**	**0.0**	**1**	**0**	**0.0**	**8:55**									
	Utica Comets	AHL	3	0	1	1	0																		
	NHL Totals		**3**	**0**	**1**	**1**	**0**	**0**	**0**	**0**	**2**	**0.0**		**0**	**0.0**	**8:55**									

Signed as a free agent by **Gavle** (Sweden), May 28, 2013. • Missed majority of 2016-17 due to recurring knee injury.

RODRIGUES, Evan (rawd-REE-gehz, EH-vuhn) BUF

Left wing. Shoots right. 5'11", 174 lbs. Born, Etobicoke, ON, July 28, 1993.

2008-09	Tor. Marlboros	GTHL	73	39	54	93	80																		
2009-10	Georgetown	ON-Jr.A	56	20	31	51	22										11	4	2	6	2				
2010-11	Georgetown	ON-Jr.A	37	21	33	54	42										5	1	3	4	0				
2011-12	Boston University	H-East	36	2	10	12	24																		
2012-13	Boston University	H-East	38	14	20	34	28																		
2013-14	Boston University	H-East	31	5	9	14	20																		
2014-15	Boston University	H-East	41	21	40	61	31																		
2015-16	**Buffalo**	**NHL**	**2**	**1**	**1**	**2**	**0**	**0**	**0**	**0**	**8**	**12.5**	**2**	**0**	**0.0**	**11:45**									
	Rochester	AHL	72	9	21	30	39																		
2016-17	**Buffalo**	**NHL**	**30**	**4**	**2**	**6**	**4**	**1**	**0**	**0**	**51**	**7.8**	**–7**	**250**	**41.6**	**12:56**									
	Rochester	AHL	48	9	21	30	27																		
	NHL Totals		**32**	**5**	**3**	**8**	**4**	**1**	**0**	**0**	**59**	**8.5**		**250**	**41.6**	**12:51**									

Hockey East Second All-Star Team (2013, 2015)

Signed as a free agent by **Buffalo**, April 22, 2015.

ROONEY, Kevin (ROO-nee, KEH-vihn) N.J.

Center. Shoots left. 6'2", 190 lbs. Born, Canton, MA, May 21, 1993.

2010-11	Berkshire Bears	High-MA	25	12	14	26																			
2011-12	Berkshire Bears	High-MA	30	14	12	26																			
2012-13	Providence	H-East	29	1	3	4	18																		
2013-14	Providence	H-East	36	3	4	7	20																		
2014-15	Providence	H-East	41	7	8	15	12																		
2015-16	Providence	H-East	38	6	4	10	20																		
	Albany Devils	AHL	7	0	3	3	0																		
2016-17	**New Jersey**	**NHL**	**4**	**0**	**0**	**0**	**4**	**0**	**0**	**0**	**2**	**0.0**	**–3**	**27**	**37.0**	**10:11**									
	Albany Devils	AHL	71	13	8	21	39										4	1	0	1	2				
	NHL Totals		**4**	**0**	**0**	**0**	**4**	**0**	**0**	**0**	**2**	**0.0**		**27**	**37.0**	**10:11**									

Signed as a free agent by **Albany** (AHL), July 5, 2016. Signed as a free agent by **New Jersey**, February 27, 2017.

ROSLOVIC, Jack (raws-LOH-vihk, JAK) WPG

Center. Shoots right. 6'1", 188 lbs. Born, Columbus, OH, January 29, 1997. Winnipeg's 2nd pick, 25th overall, in 2015 NHL Draft.

2012-13	Ohio B-Jack. U16	T1EHL	40	23	30	53	22										4	3	2	5	0				
	Ohio B-Jack. Midg.		T1EHL	4	0	0	0	2																	
....																									
2013-14	USAHNTDP	USHL	34	4	10	14	14																		
	USAHNTDP	U-17	20	9	8	17	16																		
2014-15	USAHNTDP	USHL	25	11	27	38	8																		
	USAHNTDP	U-18	40	16	26	42	20																		
2015-16	Miami U.	NCHC	36	10	16	26	18																		
2016-17	**Winnipeg**	**NHL**	**1**	**0**	**0**	**0**	**0**	**0**	**0**	**0**	**1**	**0.0**	**–1**	**6**	**16.7**	**8:24**									
	Manitoba Moose	AHL	65	13	35	48	22																		
	NHL Totals		**1**	**0**	**0**	**0**	**0**	**0**	**0**	**0**	**1**	**0.0**		**6**	**16.7**	**8:24**									

NCHC All-Rookie Team (2016)

ROUSSEL, Antoine (roo-SEHL, an-TWAHN) DAL

Left wing. Shoots left. 6', 200 lbs. Born, Roubaix, France, November 21, 1989.

2006-07	C.C. Lemoyne	QAAA	12	4	10	14	18																		
	Chicoutimi	QMJHL	56	7	13	20	55										4	0	0	0	14				
2007-08	Chicoutimi	QMJHL	70	13	24	37	121										5	0	4	4	29				
2008-09	Chicoutimi	QMJHL	58	15	20	35	110										4	0	2	2	15				
2009-10	Chicoutimi	QMJHL	68	24	23	47	131										7	4	5	9	10				
2010-11	Providence Bruins	AHL	42	1	7	8	88																		
	Reading Royals	ECHL	5	0	1	1	7										8	0	3	3	14				
2011-12	Chicago Wolves	AHL	61	4	5	9	177										2	0	0	0	6				
2012-13	Texas Stars	AHL	43	8	11	19	107																		
	Dallas	**NHL**	**39**	**7**	**7**	**14**	**85**	**0**	**0**	**0**	**46**	**15.2**	**3**	**55**	**54.6**	**9:24**									
2013-14	**Dallas**	**NHL**	**81**	**14**	**15**	**29**	**209**	**0**	**0**	**2**	**113**	**12.4**	**–1**	**44**	**43.2**	**13:20**	**6**	**0**	**3**	**3**	**27**	**0**	**0**	**0**	**13:26**
2014-15	**Dallas**	**NHL**	**80**	**13**	**12**	**25**	**148**	**0**	**0**	**1**	**113**	**11.5**	**–20**	**17**	**17.7**	**14:31**									
2015-16	**Dallas**	**NHL**	**80**	**13**	**16**	**29**	**123**	**0**	**0**	**6**	**111**	**11.7**	**11**	**35**	**42.9**	**13:51**	**13**	**2**	**0**	**2**	**16**	**0**	**0**	**0**	**14:16**
2016-17	**Dallas**	**NHL**	**60**	**12**	**15**	**27**	**115**	**0**	**0**	**3**	**82**	**14.6**	**1**	**16**	**43.8**	**15:31**									
	NHL Totals		**340**	**59**	**65**	**124**	**680**	**0**	**0**	**12**	**465**	**12.7**		**167**	**44.3**	**13:40**	**19**	**2**	**3**	**5**	**43**	**0**	**0**	**0**	**14:00**

Signed as a free agent by **Chicago** (AHL), October 2, 2011. Signed as a free agent by **Dallas**, July 2, 2012.

			Regular Season														Playoffs								
Season	Club	League	GP	G	A	Pts	PIM	PP	SH	GW	S	S%	+/-	TF	F%	Min	GP	G	A	Pts	PIM	PP	SH	GW	Min

ROWNEY, Carter

(ROW-nee, KAR-tuhr) **PIT**

Right wing. Shoots righr. 6'2", 200 lbs. Born, Grand Prairie, AB, May 10, 1989.

2003-04	Grand Prairie	AMBHL	37	18	18	36	40	....	....	....	....	....	....	....	....	....	....	....	....	....	....	....	....	....	....
2004-05	Grand Prairie	Minor-AB	23	6	3	9	2	....	....	....	....	....	....	....	....	....	....	....	....	....	....	....	....	....	....
2005-06	Grand Prairie	Minor-AB	39	*48	25	73	39	....	....	....	....	....	....	....	....	....	4	5	0	5	6	....	....	....	....
	Grande Prairie	AJHL	1	0	1	1	0	....	....	....	....	....	....	....	....	....	....	....	....	....	....	....	....	....	....
2006-07	Grande Prairie	AJHL	42	7	12	19	28	....	....	....	....	....	....	....	....	....	6	0	0	0	2	....	....	....	....
2007-08	Grande Prairie	AJHL	52	16	15	31	47	....	....	....	....	....	....	....	....	....	....	....	....	....	....	....	....	....	....
2008-09	Grande Prairie	AJHL	62	35	43	78	71	....	....	....	....	....	....	....	....	....	19	12	6	18	10	....	....	....	....
2009-10	North Dakota	WCHA	39	1	7	8	23	....	....	....	....	....	....	....	....	....	....	....	....	....	....	....	....	....	....
2010-11	North Dakota	WCHA	28	3	2	5	14	....	....	....	....	....	....	....	....	....	....	....	....	....	....	....	....	....	....
2011-12	North Dakota	WCHA	42	18	15	33	18	....	....	....	....	....	....	....	....	....	....	....	....	....	....	....	....	....	....
2012-13	North Dakota	WCHA	41	10	17	27	10	....	....	....	....	....	....	....	....	....	....	....	....	....	....	....	....	....	....
	Abbotsford Heat	AHL	4	1	0	1	0	....	....	....	....	....	....	....	....	....	....	....	....	....	....	....	....	....	....
2013-14	Wheeling Nailers	ECHL	39	13	31	44	19	....	....	....	....	....	....	....	....	....	....	....	....	....	....	....	....	....	....
	Wilkes-Barre	AHL	24	2	2	4	6	....	....	....	....	....	....	....	....	....	7	0	2	2	2	....	....	....	....
2014-15	Wheeling Nailers	ECHL	5	1	6	7	2	....	....	....	....	....	....	....	....	....	....	....	....	....	....	....	....	....	....
	Wilkes-Barre	AHL	63	10	21	31	31	....	....	....	....	....	....	....	....	....	8	2	2	4	4	....	....	....	....
2015-16	Wilkes-Barre	AHL	74	24	32	56	37	....	....	....	....	....	....	....	....	....	10	4	8	12	6	....	....	....	....
2016-17	**Pittsburgh**	**NHL**	**27**	**3**	**4**	**7**	**4**	**0**	**0**	**1**	**24**	**12.5**	**2**	**198**	**48.0**	**10:58**	**20**	**0**	**3**	**3**	**4**	**0**	**0**	**0**	**12:17**
	Wilkes-Barre	AHL	26	10	11	21	15	....	....	....	....	....	....	....	....	....	....	....	....	....	....	....	....	....	....
	NHL Totals		**27**	**3**	**4**	**7**	**4**	**0**	**0**	**1**	**24**	**12.5**		**198**	**48.0**	**10:58**	**20**	**0**	**3**	**3**	**4**	**0**	**0**	**0**	**12:17**

Signed as a free agent by **Pittsburgh**, March 9, 2016.

ROZSIVAL, Michal

(roh-ZIH-vahl, MEE-khahl) **CHI**

Defense. Shoots right. 6'1", 210 lbs. Born, Vlasim, Czech., September 3, 1978. Pittsburgh's 5th pick, 105th overall, in 1996 NHL Draft.

1994-95	Jihlava Jr.	CzRep-Jr.	31	8	13	21	....	....	....	....	....	....	....	....	....	....	....	....	....	....	....	....	....	....	....
1995-96	HC Dukla Jihlava	CzRep	36	3	4	7	....	....	....	....	....	....	....	....	....	....	....	....	....	....	....	....	....	....	....
1996-97	Swift Current	WHL	63	8	31	39	69	....	....	....	....	....	....	....	....	....	10	0	6	6	15	....	....	....	....
1997-98	Swift Current	WHL	71	14	55	69	122	....	....	....	....	....	....	....	....	....	12	0	5	5	33	....	....	....	....
1998-99	Syracuse Crunch	AHL	49	3	22	25	72	....	....	....	....	....	....	....	....	....	....	....	....	....	....	....	....	....	....
99-2000	**Pittsburgh**	**NHL**	**75**	**4**	**17**	**21**	**48**	**1**	**0**	**1**	**73**	**5.5**	**11**	**1**	**0.0**	**19:01**	**2**	**0**	**0**	**0**	**4**	**0**	**0**	**0**	**30:56**
2000-01	**Pittsburgh**	**NHL**	**30**	**1**	**4**	**5**	**26**	**0**	**0**	**0**	**17**	**5.9**	**3**	**1**	**100.0**	**17:06**	....	....	....	....	....	....	....	....	....
	Wilkes-Barre	AHL	29	8	8	16	32	....	....	....	....	....	....	....	....	....	21	3	*19	22	23	....	....	....	....
2001-02	**Pittsburgh**	**NHL**	**79**	**9**	**20**	**29**	**47**	**4**	**0**	**4**	**89**	**10.1**	**–6**	**0**	**0.0**	**20:01**	....	....	....	....	....	....	....	....	....
2002-03	**Pittsburgh**	**NHL**	**53**	**4**	**6**	**10**	**40**	**1**	**0**	**0**	**61**	**6.6**	**–5**	**0**	**0.0**	**20:25**	....	....	....	....	....	....	....	....	....
2003-04	Wilkes-Barre	AHL	1	0	0	0	2	....	....	....	....	....	....	....	....	....	....	....	....	....	....	....	....	....	....
2004-05	HC Ocelari Trinec	CzRep	35	1	10	11	40	....	....	....	....	....	....	....	....	....	....	....	....	....	....	....	....	....	....
	Pardubice	CzRep	16	1	3	4	30	....	....	....	....	....	....	....	....	....	16	1	2	3	34	....	....	....	....
2005-06	**NY Rangers**	**NHL**	**82**	**5**	**25**	**30**	**90**	**3**	**0**	**3**	**115**	**4.3**	***35**	**1**	**0.0**	**22:27**	**4**	**0**	**1**	**1**	**8**	**0**	**0**	**0**	**24:31**
2006-07	**NY Rangers**	**NHL**	**80**	**10**	**30**	**40**	**52**	**7**	**0**	**3**	**104**	**9.6**	**10**	**3**	**0.0**	**23:46**	**10**	**3**	**4**	**7**	**10**	**2**	**0**	**1**	**24:45**
2007-08	**NY Rangers**	**NHL**	**80**	**13**	**25**	**38**	**80**	**6**	**2**	**0**	**127**	**10.2**	**0**	**0**	**0.0**	**24:33**	**10**	**1**	**5**	**6**	**10**	**0**	**0**	**0**	**25:05**
2008-09	**NY Rangers**	**NHL**	**76**	**8**	**22**	**30**	**52**	**3**	**0**	**2**	**120**	**6.7**	**–7**	**0**	**0.0**	**22:31**	**7**	**0**	**0**	**0**	**4**	**0**	**0**	**0**	**22:41**
2009-10	**NY Rangers**	**NHL**	**82**	**3**	**20**	**23**	**78**	**1**	**0**	**1**	**80**	**3.8**	**3**	**1**	**100.0**	**21:26**	....	....	....	....	....	....	....	....	....
2010-11	**NY Rangers**	**NHL**	**32**	**3**	**12**	**15**	**22**	**0**	**0**	**1**	**24**	**12.5**	**3**	**0**	**0.0**	**22:03**	....	....	....	....	....	....	....	....	....
	Phoenix	**NHL**	**33**	**3**	**3**	**6**	**20**	**2**	**0**	**2**	**31**	**9.7**	**3**	**0**	**0.0**	**19:59**	**4**	**0**	**0**	**0**	**2**	**0**	**0**	**0**	**19:54**
2011-12	**Phoenix**	**NHL**	**54**	**1**	**12**	**13**	**34**	**0**	**0**	**0**	**49**	**2.0**	**8**	**0**	**0.0**	**19:20**	**15**	**0**	**0**	**0**	**2**	**0**	**0**	**0**	**21:48**
2012-13♦	**Chicago**	**NHL**	**27**	**0**	**12**	**12**	**14**	**0**	**0**	**0**	**13**	**0.0**	**18**	**2**	**0.0**	**18:07**	**23**	**0**	**4**	**4**	**16**	**0**	**0**	**0**	**19:16**
2013-14	**Chicago**	**NHL**	**42**	**1**	**7**	**8**	**32**	**0**	**0**	**0**	**39**	**2.6**	**7**	**0**	**0.0**	**16:39**	**17**	**1**	**5**	**6**	**8**	**0**	**0**	**0**	**17:37**
	Czech Republic	Olympics	5	0	0	0	0	....	....	....	....	....	....	....	....	....	....	....	....	....	....	....	....	....	....
2014-15♦	**Chicago**	**NHL**	**65**	**1**	**12**	**13**	**22**	**0**	**0**	**0**	**56**	**1.8**	**0**	**0**	**0.0**	**17:01**	**10**	**0**	**1**	**1**	**6**	**0**	**0**	**0**	**17:26**
2015-16	**Chicago**	**NHL**	**51**	**1**	**12**	**13**	**33**	**0**	**0**	**0**	**41**	**2.4**	**3**	**0**	**0.0**	**16:10**	**4**	**0**	**0**	**0**	**2**	**0**	**0**	**0**	**16:13**
2016-17	**Chicago**	**NHL**	**22**	**1**	**2**	**3**	**14**	**0**	**0**	**1**	**16**	**6.3**	**–3**	**0**	**0.0**	**15:30**	....	....	....	....	....	....	....	....	....
	NHL Totals		**963**	**68**	**241**	**309**	**704**	**28**	**2**	**18**	**1055**	**6.4**		**9**	**22.2**	**20:24**	**106**	**5**	**20**	**25**	**72**	**2**	**0**	**1**	**20:48**

WHL East First All-Star Team (1998)

• Missed majority of 2003-04 due to training camp knee injury, September 18, 2003. Signed as a free agent by **Trinec** (CzRep), September 17, 2004. Signed as a free agent by **Pardubice** (CzRep), January, 2005. Signed as a free agent by **NY Rangers**, August 29, 2005. Traded to **Phoenix** by **NY Rangers** for Wojtek Wolski, January 10, 2011. Signed as a free agent by **Chicago**, September 11, 2012. • Missed majority of 2016-17 due to lower-body injury vs. Winnipeg, January 26, 2017.

RUHWEDEL, Chad

(ROO-WEE-dehl, CHAD) **PIT**

Defense. Shoots right. 5'11", 191 lbs. Born, San Diego, CA, May 7, 1990.

2008-09	Sioux Falls	USHL	55	0	11	11	30	....	....	....	....	....	....	....	....	....	4	0	1	1	4	....	....	....	....
2009-10	Sioux Falls	USHL	59	5	17	22	55	....	....	....	....	....	....	....	....	....	3	0	1	1	2	....	....	....	....
2010-11	U. Mass Lowell	H-East	32	2	13	15	10	....	....	....	....	....	....	....	....	....	....	....	....	....	....	....	....	....	....
2011-12	U. Mass Lowell	H-East	37	6	19	25	26	....	....	....	....	....	....	....	....	....	....	....	....	....	....	....	....	....	....
2012-13	U. Mass Lowell	H-East	41	7	16	23	20	....	....	....	....	....	....	....	....	....	....	....	....	....	....	....	....	....	....
	Buffalo	**NHL**	**7**	**0**	**0**	**0**	**0**	**0**	**0**	**0**	**8**	**0.0**	**0**	**0**	**0.0**	**14:12**	....	....	....	....	....	....	....	....	....
2013-14	**Buffalo**	**NHL**	**21**	**0**	**1**	**1**	**2**	**0**	**0**	**0**	**35**	**0.0**	**–3**	**0**	**0.0**	**17:53**	....	....	....	....	....	....	....	....	....
	Rochester	AHL	47	4	24	28	22	....	....	....	....	....	....	....	....	....	5	2	3	5	4	....	....	....	....
2014-15	**Buffalo**	**NHL**	**4**	**0**	**1**	**1**	**0**	**0**	**0**	**0**	**4**	**0.0**	**3**	**0**	**0.0**	**12:28**	....	....	....	....	....	....	....	....	....
	Rochester	AHL	72	10	26	36	22	....	....	....	....	....	....	....	....	....	....	....	....	....	....	....	....	....	....
2015-16	**Buffalo**	**NHL**	**1**	**0**	**0**	**0**	**2**	**0**	**0**	**0**	**1**	**0.0**	**0**	**0**	**0.0**	**15:30**	....	....	....	....	....	....	....	....	....
	Rochester	AHL	59	10	16	26	26	....	....	....	....	....	....	....	....	....	....	....	....	....	....	....	....	....	....
2016-17	**Pittsburgh**	**NHL**	**34**	**2**	**8**	**10**	**8**	**0**	**0**	**0**	**45**	**4.4**	**9**	**0**	**0.0**	**17:20**	**6**	**0**	**0**	**0**	**4**	**0**	**0**	**0**	**14:07**
	Wilkes-Barre	AHL	28	4	12	16	12	....	....	....	....	....	....	....	....	....	....	....	....	....	....	....	....	....	....
	NHL Totals		**67**	**2**	**10**	**12**	**12**	**0**	**0**	**0**	**93**	**2.2**		**0**	**0.0**	**16:52**	**6**	**0**	**0**	**0**	**4**	**0**	**0**	**0**	**14:07**

Hockey East First All-Star Team (2013) • NCAA East First All-American Team (2013)

Signed as a free agent by **Buffalo**, April 13, 2013. Signed as a free agent by **Pittsburgh**, July 1, 2016.

RUSSELL, Kris

(RUH-sehl, KRIHS) **EDM**

Defense. Shoots left. 5'10", 170 lbs. Born, Caroline, AB, May 2, 1987. Columbus' 3rd pick, 67th overall, in 2005 NHL Draft.

2003-04	Medicine Hat	WHL	55	4	15	19	30	....	....	....	....	....	....	....	....	....	20	3	2	5	4	....	....	....	....
2004-05	Medicine Hat	WHL	72	26	35	61	37	....	....	....	....	....	....	....	....	....	10	2	1	3	4	....	....	....	....
2005-06	Medicine Hat	WHL	55	14	33	47	18	....	....	....	....	....	....	....	....	....	13	4	8	12	11	....	....	....	....
2006-07	Medicine Hat	WHL	59	32	37	69	56	....	....	....	....	....	....	....	....	....	23	4	15	19	24	....	....	....	....
2007-08	**Columbus**	**NHL**	**67**	**2**	**8**	**10**	**14**	**1**	**0**	**1**	**90**	**2.2**	**–12**	**0**	**0.0**	**14:47**	....	....	....	....	....	....	....	....	....
2008-09	**Columbus**	**NHL**	**66**	**2**	**19**	**21**	**28**	**1**	**0**	**1**	**86**	**2.3**	**–10**	**0**	**0.0**	**16:07**	**4**	**1**	**1**	**2**	**2**	**0**	**0**	**0**	**16:40**
	Syracuse Crunch	AHL	14	3	5	8	0	....	....	....	....	....	....	....	....	....	....	....	....	....	....	....	....	....	....
2009-10	**Columbus**	**NHL**	**70**	**7**	**15**	**22**	**32**	**0**	**0**	**1**	**108**	**6.5**	**3**	**0**	**0.0**	**18:35**	....	....	....	....	....	....	....	....	....
2010-11	**Columbus**	**NHL**	**73**	**5**	**18**	**23**	**37**	**1**	**0**	**0**	**88**	**5.7**	**–9**	**0**	**0.0**	**17:31**	....	....	....	....	....	....	....	....	....
2011-12	**Columbus**	**NHL**	**12**	**2**	**1**	**3**	**13**	**0**	**0**	**0**	**20**	**10.0**	**–1**	**0**	**0.0**	**17:34**	....	....	....	....	....	....	....	....	....
	St. Louis	**NHL**	**43**	**4**	**5**	**9**	**12**	**0**	**0**	**1**	**36**	**11.1**	**13**	**0**	**0.0**	**16:51**	**9**	**0**	**3**	**3**	**5**	**0**	**0**	**0**	**19:27**
2012-13	TPS Turku	Finland	15	2	12	14	8	....	....	....	....	....	....	....	....	....	....	....	....	....	....	....	....	....	....
	St. Louis	**NHL**	**33**	**1**	**6**	**7**	**9**	**1**	**0**	**0**	**41**	**2.4**	**6**	**0**	**0.0**	**16:03**	....	....	....	....	....	....	....	....	....
2013-14	**Calgary**	**NHL**	**68**	**7**	**22**	**29**	**15**	**4**	**0**	**1**	**109**	**6.4**	**–11**	**0**	**0.0**	**23:08**	....	....	....	....	....	....	....	....	....
2014-15	**Calgary**	**NHL**	**79**	**4**	**30**	**34**	**17**	**1**	**0**	**0**	**111**	**3.6**	**18**	**0**	**0.0**	**23:57**	**11**	**2**	**5**	**7**	**7**	**1**	**0**	**1**	**26:45**
2015-16	**Calgary**	**NHL**	**51**	**4**	**11**	**15**	**8**	**2**	**0**	**1**	**56**	**7.1**	**–4**	**1**	**0.0**	**22:52**	....	....	....	....	....	....	....	....	....
	Dallas	**NHL**	**11**	**0**	**4**	**4**	**2**	**0**	**0**	**0**	**14**	**0.0**	**–1**	**0**	**0.0**	**24:02**	**12**	**0**	**4**	**4**	**4**	**0**	**0**	**0**	**19:57**
2016-17	**Edmonton**	**NHL**	**68**	**1**	**12**	**13**	**23**	**0**	**0**	**1**	**68**	**1.5**	**5**	**0**	**0.0**	**21:13**	**13**	**0**	**4**	**4**	**4**	**0**	**0**	**0**	**22:02**
	NHL Totals		**641**	**39**	**151**	**190**	**210**	**11**	**0**	**7**	**827**	**4.7**		**1**	**0.0**	**19:24**	**49**	**3**	**17**	**20**	**22**	**1**	**0**	**1**	**21:40**

WHL East Second All-Star Team (2005) • WHL East First All-Star Team (2006, 2007) • WHL Defenseman of the Year (2006, 2007) • Canadian Major Junior Second All-Star Team (2006) • Canadian Major Junior Sportsman of the Year (2006) • WHL Player of the Year (2007) • Canadian Major Junior First All-Star Team (2007) • Canadian Major Junior Defenseman of the Year (2007)

Traded to **St. Louis** by **Columbus** for Nikita Nikitin, November 11, 2011. Signed as a free agent by **TPS Turku** (Finland), September 26, 2012. Traded to **Calgary** by **St. Louis** for Calgary's 5th round pick (Jaedon Descheneau) in 2014 NHL Draft, July 5, 2013. Traded to **Dallas** by **Calgary** for Jyrki Jokipakka, Brett Pollock and Dallas' 2nd round pick (Dillon Dube) in 2016 NHL Draft, February 29, 2016. Signed as a free agent by **Edmonton**, October 7, 2016.

			Regular Season														Playoffs								
Season	Club	League	GP	G	A	Pts	PIM	PP	SH	GW	S	S%	+/-	TF	F%	Min	GP	G	A	Pts	PIM	PP	SH	GW	Min

RUSSO, Robbie

(ROO-soh, RAW-bee)

Defense. Shoots right. 6', 189 lbs. Born, Westmount, IL, February 15, 1993. NY Islanders' 5th pick, 95th overall, in 2011 NHL Draft.

2008-09	Chicago Mission	T1EHL	46	5	17	22	10	....	....	....	....	....	....	....	....	....	....	....	....	....	....	....	....	....	....
	Chicago Mission	Other	....	5	3	8	10	....	....	....	....	....	....	....	....	....	....	....	....	....	....	....	....	....	....
2009-10	USAHNTDP	USHL	34	3	17	20	36	....	....	....	....	....	....	....	....	....	....	....	....	....	....	....	....	....	....
	USAHNTDP	U-17	18	4	7	11	22	....	....	....	....	....	....	....	....	....	....	....	....	....	....	....	....	....	....
2010-11	USAHNTDP	USHL	24	0	6	6	11	....	....	....	....	....	....	....	....	....	....	....	....	....	....	....	....	....	....
	USAHNTDP	U-18	36	4	20	24	16	....	....	....	....	....	....	....	....	....	....	....	....	....	....	....	....	....	....
2011-12	U. of Notre Dame	CCHA	40	4	11	15	14	....	....	....	....	....	....	....	....	....	....	....	....	....	....	....	....	....	....
2012-13	U. of Notre Dame	CCHA	41	5	18	23	40	....	....	....	....	....	....	....	....	....	....	....	....	....	....	....	....	....	....
2013-14	U. of Notre Dame	H-East	21	4	11	15	8	....	....	....	....	....	....	....	....	....	....	....	....	....	....	....	....	....	....
2014-15	U. of Notre Dame	H-East	40	15	26	41	20	....	....	....	....	....	....	....	....	....	....	....	....	....	....	....	....	....	....
2015-16	Grand Rapids	AHL	71	5	34	39	42	....	....	....	....	....	....	....	....	....	9	1	4	5	9	....	....	....	....
2016-17	**Detroit**	**NHL**	**19**	**0**	**0**	**0**	**2**	**0**	**0**	**0**	**18**	**0.0**	**2**	**0**	**0.0**	**16:04**	....	....	....	....	....	....	....	....	....
	Grand Rapids	AHL	58	7	25	32	37	....	....	....	....	....	....	....	....	....	19	0	7	7	22	....	....	....	....
	NHL Totals		**19**	**0**	**0**	**0**	**2**	**0**	**0**	**0**	**18**	**0.0**		**0**	**0.0**	**16:04**	....	....	....	....	....	....	....	....	....

CCHA All-Rookie Team (2012) • Hockey East First All-Star Team (2015) • NCAA East Second All-American Team (2015) • AHL All-Rookie Team (2016) • AHL Second All-Star Team (2016)

Signed as a free agent by **Detroit**, August 16, 2015.

RUST, Bryan

(RUHST, BRIGH-uhn) **PIT**

Right wing. Shoots right. 5'11", 192 lbs. Born, Pontiac, MI, May 11, 1992. Pittsburgh's 2nd pick, 80th overall, in 2010 NHL Draft.

2007-08	Det. Honeybaked	MWEHL	31	17	28	45	6	....	....	....	....	....	....	....	....	....	....	....	....	....	....	....	....	....	....
	Det. Honeybaked	Minor-MI	37	27	20	47	....	....	....	....	....	....	....	....	....	....	....	....	....	....	....	....	....	....	....
2008-09	USAHNTDP	NAHL	42	6	9	15	18	....	....	....	....	....	....	....	....	....	9	0	2	2	4	....	....	....	....
	USAHNTDP	U-17	16	3	2	5	4	....	....	....	....	....	....	....	....	....	....	....	....	....	....	....	....	....	....
2009-10	USAHNTDP	USHL	27	10	13	23	6	....	....	....	....	....	....	....	....	....	....	....	....	....	....	....	....	....	....
	USAHNTDP	U-17	1	0	0	0	0	....	....	....	....	....	....	....	....	....	....	....	....	....	....	....	....	....	....
	USAHNTDP	U-18	38	16	13	29	18	....	....	....	....	....	....	....	....	....	....	....	....	....	....	....	....	....	....
2010-11	U. of Notre Dame	CCHA	40	6	13	19	4	....	....	....	....	....	....	....	....	....	....	....	....	....	....	....	....	....	....
2011-12	U. of Notre Dame	CCHA	40	5	6	11	14	....	....	....	....	....	....	....	....	....	....	....	....	....	....	....	....	....	....
2012-13	U. of Notre Dame	CCHA	41	15	19	34	4	....	....	....	....	....	....	....	....	....	....	....	....	....	....	....	....	....	....
2013-14	U. of Notre Dame	H-East	40	17	16	33	12	....	....	....	....	....	....	....	....	....	....	....	....	....	....	....	....	....	....
	Wilkes-Barre	AHL	2	0	0	0	0	....	....	....	....	....	....	....	....	....	1	0	0	0	0	....	....	....	....
2014-15	**Pittsburgh**	**NHL**	**14**	**1**	**1**	**2**	**4**	**0**	**0**	**0**	**34**	**2.9**	**–3**	**0**	**0.0**	**12:02**	....	....	....	....	....	....	....	....	....
	Wilkes-Barre	AHL	45	13	14	27	14	....	....	....	....	....	....	....	....	....	3	2	0	2	0	....	....	....	....
2015-16 ♦	**Pittsburgh**	**NHL**	**41**	**4**	**7**	**11**	**12**	**0**	**0**	**1**	**68**	**5.9**	**1**	**4**	**25.0**	**12:30**	**23**	**6**	**3**	**9**	**6**	**0**	**0**	**1**	**11:31**
	Wilkes-Barre	AHL	16	3	3	6	2	....	....	....	....	....	....	....	....	....	....	....	....	....	....	....	....	....	....
2016-17 ♦	**Pittsburgh**	**NHL**	**57**	**15**	**13**	**28**	**8**	**0**	**0**	**1**	**110**	**13.6**	**4**	**5**	**40.0**	**13:38**	**23**	**7**	**2**	**9**	**10**	**0**	**0**	**2**	**15:57**
	NHL Totals		**112**	**20**	**21**	**41**	**24**	**0**	**0**	**2**	**212**	**9.4**		**9**	**33.3**	**13:01**	**46**	**13**	**5**	**18**	**16**	**0**	**0**	**3**	**13:44**

RYAN, Bobby

(RIGH-uhn, BAW-bee) **OTT**

Left wing. Shoots right. 6'2", 209 lbs. Born, Cherry Hill, NJ, March 17, 1987. Anaheim's 1st pick, 2nd overall, in 2005 NHL Draft.

2003-04	Owen Sound	OHL	65	22	17	39	52	....	....	....	....	....	....	....	....	....	7	1	2	3	2	....	....	....	....
2004-05	Owen Sound	OHL	62	37	52	89	51	....	....	....	....	....	....	....	....	....	8	2	7	9	8	....	....	....	....
2005-06	Owen Sound	OHL	59	31	64	95	44	....	....	....	....	....	....	....	....	....	11	5	7	12	14	....	....	....	....
	Portland Pirates	AHL	....	....	....	....	....	....	....	....	....	....	....	....	....	....	19	1	7	8	22	....	....	....	....
2006-07	Owen Sound	OHL	63	43	59	102	63	....	....	....	....	....	....	....	....	....	4	1	1	2	2	....	....	....	....
	Portland Pirates	AHL	8	3	6	9	6	....	....	....	....	....	....	....	....	....	....	....	....	....	....	....	....	....	....
2007-08	**Anaheim**	**NHL**	**23**	**5**	**5**	**10**	**6**	**3**	**0**	**0**	**37**	**13.5**	**–1**	**1**	**100.0**	**11:16**	**2**	**0**	**0**	**0**	**2**	**0**	**0**	**0**	**11:09**
	Portland Pirates	AHL	48	21	28	49	38	....	....	....	....	....	....	....	....	....	16	8	12	20	18	....	....	....	....
2008-09	**Anaheim**	**NHL**	**64**	**31**	**26**	**57**	**33**	**12**	**0**	**3**	**174**	**17.8**	**13**	**13**	**46.2**	**15:26**	**13**	**5**	**2**	**7**	**0**	**2**	**0**	**1**	**19:41**
	Iowa Chops	AHL	14	9	10	19	19	....	....	....	....	....	....	....	....	....	....	....	....	....	....	....	....	....	....
2009-10	**Anaheim**	**NHL**	**81**	**35**	**29**	**64**	**81**	**11**	**0**	**3**	**258**	**13.6**	**9**	**93**	**44.1**	**18:29**	....	....	....	....	....	....	....	....	....
	United States	Olympics	6	1	1	2	2	....	....	....	....	....	....	....	....	....	....	....	....	....	....	....	....	....	....
2010-11	**Anaheim**	**NHL**	**82**	**34**	**37**	**71**	**61**	**5**	**1**	**5**	**270**	**12.6**	**15**	**219**	**39.7**	**20:11**	**4**	**3**	**1**	**4**	**2**	**0**	**0**	**0**	**20:29**
2011-12	**Anaheim**	**NHL**	**82**	**31**	**26**	**57**	**53**	**3**	**2**	**3**	**204**	**15.2**	**1**	**69**	**29.0**	**18:21**	....	....	....	....	....	....	....	....	....
2012-13	Mora IK	Sweden-2	11	10	3	13	8	....	....	....	....	....	....	....	....	....	....	....	....	....	....	....	....	....	....
	Anaheim	**NHL**	**46**	**11**	**19**	**30**	**17**	**2**	**0**	**1**	**101**	**10.9**	**3**	**81**	**30.9**	**16:35**	**7**	**2**	**2**	**4**	**0**	**0**	**0**	**0**	**16:17**
2013-14	**Ottawa**	**NHL**	**70**	**23**	**25**	**48**	**45**	**6**	**0**	**2**	**190**	**12.1**	**7**	**13**	**61.5**	**16:52**	....	....	....	....	....	....	....	....	....
2014-15	**Ottawa**	**NHL**	**78**	**18**	**36**	**54**	**24**	**4**	**0**	**5**	**221**	**8.1**	**5**	**11**	**36.4**	**17:28**	**6**	**2**	**0**	**2**	**0**	**1**	**0**	**0**	**15:18**
2015-16	**Ottawa**	**NHL**	**81**	**22**	**34**	**56**	**28**	**6**	**0**	**2**	**183**	**12.0**	**–9**	**11**	**27.3**	**17:10**	....	....	....	....	....	....	....	....	....
2016-17	**Ottawa**	**NHL**	**62**	**13**	**12**	**25**	**24**	**2**	**0**	**0**	**111**	**11.7**	**–3**	**9**	**66.7**	**15:32**	**19**	**6**	**9**	**15**	**14**	**3**	**0**	**3**	**17:13**
	NHL Totals		**669**	**223**	**249**	**472**	**372**	**54**	**3**	**24**	**1749**	**12.8**		**520**	**38.7**	**17:17**	**51**	**18**	**14**	**32**	**18**	**6**	**0**	**4**	**17:31**

OHL First All-Star Team (2005) • AHL All-Rookie Team (2008) • NHL All-Rookie Team (2009)

Played in NHL All-Star Game (2015)

Signed as a free agent by **Mora** (Sweden-2), November 21, 2012. Traded to **Ottawa** by **Anaheim** for Jakob Silfverberg, Stefan Noesen and Ottawa's 1st round pick (Nicholas Ritchie) in 2014 NHL Draft, July 5, 2013.

RYAN, Derek

(RIGH-uhn, DAIR-ihk) **CAR**

Center. Shoots right. 5'10", 170 lbs. Born, Spokane, WA, December 29, 1986.

2003-04	Spokane Chiefs	WHL	1	1	0	1	0	....	....	....	....	....	....	....	....	....	4	1	0	1	0	....	....	....	....
2004-05	Spokane Chiefs	WHL	71	14	32	46	39	....	....	....	....	....	....	....	....	....	....	....	....	....	....	....	....	....	....
2005-06	Spokane Chiefs	WHL	72	24	37	61	50	....	....	....	....	....	....	....	....	....	....	....	....	....	....	....	....	....	....
2006-07	Spokane Chiefs	WHL	72	28	31	59	50	....	....	....	....	....	....	....	....	....	6	3	2	5	2	....	....	....	....
	Kalamazoo Wings	UHL	3	0	2	2	0	....	....	....	....	....	....	....	....	....	13	4	1	5	8	....	....	....	....
2007-08	U. of Alberta	CIS	44	15	23	38	48	....	....	....	....	....	....	....	....	....	....	....	....	....	....	....	....	....	....
2008-09	U. of Alberta	CIS	39	23	28	51	22	....	....	....	....	....	....	....	....	....	....	....	....	....	....	....	....	....	....
2009-10	U. of Alberta	CIS	42	19	33	52	40	....	....	....	....	....	....	....	....	....	....	....	....	....	....	....	....	....	....
2010-11	U. of Alberta	CIS	40	29	37	66	20	....	....	....	....	....	....	....	....	....	....	....	....	....	....	....	....	....	....
2011-12	Szekesfehervar	Austria	50	25	24	49	20	....	....	....	....	....	....	....	....	....	6	1	3	4	6	....	....	....	....
2012-13	EC VSV Villach	Austria	54	27	39	66	22	....	....	....	....	....	....	....	....	....	7	3	8	11	6	....	....	....	....
2013-14	EC VSV Villach	Austria	54	38	46	84	50	....	....	....	....	....	....	....	....	....	....	....	....	....	....	....	....	....	....
2014-15	Orebro HK	Sweden	55	15	*45	*60	18	....	....	....	....	....	....	....	....	....	6	0	1	1	2	....	....	....	....
2015-16	**Carolina**	**NHL**	**6**	**2**	**0**	**2**	**2**	**1**	**0**	**0**	**5**	**40.0**	**1**	**59**	**59.3**	**12:12**	....	....	....	....	....	....	....	....	....
	Charlotte	AHL	70	23	32	55	24	....	....	....	....	....	....	....	....	....	....	....	....	....	....	....	....	....	....
2016-17	**Carolina**	**NHL**	**67**	**11**	**18**	**29**	**22**	**4**	**1**	**3**	**73**	**15.1**	**–8**	**707**	**55.3**	**14:53**	....	....	....	....	....	....	....	....	....
	Charlotte	AHL	9	5	8	13	0	....	....	....	....	....	....	....	....	....	....	....	....	....	....	....	....	....	....
	NHL Totals		**73**	**13**	**18**	**31**	**24**	**5**	**1**	**3**	**78**	**16.7**		**766**	**55.6**	**14:40**	....	....	....	....	....	....	....	....	....

Signed as a free agent by **Carolina**, June 15, 2015.

RYCHEL, Kerby

(RIGH-kuhl, KUHR-bee) **TOR**

Left wing. Shoots left. 6'1", 213 lbs. Born, Torrance, CA, October 7, 1994. Columbus' 2nd pick, 19th overall, in 2013 NHL Draft.

2008-09	Sun County	Minor-ON	26	11	17	28	24	....	....	....	....	....	....	....	....	....	12	8	5	13	2	....	....	....	....
2009-10	Detroit Belle Tire	T1EHL	29	13	10	23	29	....	....	....	....	....	....	....	....	....	....	....	....	....	....	....	....	....	....
	Detroit Belle Tire	Other	26	17	9	26	29	....	....	....	....	....	....	....	....	....	....	....	....	....	....	....	....	....	....
2010-11	St. Michael's	OHL	30	2	6	8	47	....	....	....	....	....	....	....	....	....	....	....	....	....	....	....	....	....	....
	Windsor Spitfires	OHL	32	5	8	13	26	....	....	....	....	....	....	....	....	....	18	2	4	6	14	....	....	....	....
2011-12	Windsor Spitfires	OHL	68	41	33	74	54	....	....	....	....	....	....	....	....	....	4	2	0	2	5	....	....	....	....
2012-13	Windsor Spitfires	OHL	68	40	47	87	94	....	....	....	....	....	....	....	....	....	....	....	....	....	....	....	....	....	....
2013-14	Windsor Spitfires	OHL	27	16	23	39	15	....	....	....	....	....	....	....	....	....	....	....	....	....	....	....	....	....	....
	Guelph Storm	OHL	31	18	33	51	28	....	....	....	....	....	....	....	....	....	20	11	*21	*32	23	....	....	....	....
2014-15	**Columbus**	**NHL**	**5**	**0**	**3**	**3**	**2**	**0**	**0**	**0**	**4**	**0.0**	**3**	**0**	**0.0**	**10:42**	....	....	....	....	....	....	....	....	....
	Springfield	AHL	51	12	21	33	43	....	....	....	....	....	....	....	....	....	....	....	....	....	....	....	....	....	....

			Regular Season														Playoffs								
Season	Club	League	GP	G	A	Pts	PIM	PP	SH	GW	S	S%	+/-	TF	F%	Min	GP	G	A	Pts	PIM	PP	SH	GW	Min
2015-16	**Columbus**	**NHL**	**32**	**2**	**7**	**9**	**15**	**0**	**0**	**0**	**32**	**6.3**	**5**	**3**	**33.3**	**9:31**									
	Lake Erie	AHL	37	6	21	27	53										17	1	5	6	26				
2016-17	Toronto Marlies	AHL	73	19	33	52	118										11	2	3	5	2				
	NHL Totals		**37**	**2**	**10**	**12**	**17**	**0**	**0**	**0**	**36**	**5.6**		**3**	**33.3**	**9:40**									

Traded to **Toronto** by **Columbus** for Scott Harrington and a conditional pick (conditions not met) in 2017 NHL Draft, June 25, 2016.

SAAD, Brandon

(SAHD, BRAN-duhn) **CHI**

Left wing. Shoots left. 6'1", 206 lbs. Born, Pittsburgh, PA, October 27, 1992. Chicago's 4th pick, 43rd overall, in 2011 NHL Draft.

Season	Club	League	GP	G	A	Pts	PIM	PP	SH	GW	S	S%	+/-	TF	F%	Min	GP	G	A	Pts	PIM	PP	SH	GW	Min
2007-08	Pittsburgh	MWEHL	26	11	19	30	16																		
2008-09	Mahoning Valley	NAHL	47	29	18	47	48										7	5	1	6	10				
	USAHNTDP	U-17	7	6	5	11	2																		
2009-10	USAHNTDP	USHL	24	12	14	26	18																		
	USAHNTDP	U-18	39	17	15	32	16																		
2010-11	Saginaw Spirit	OHL	59	27	28	55	47										12	3	9	12	10				
2011-12	Saginaw Spirit	OHL	44	34	42	76	38										12	8	9	17	4				
	Chicago	**NHL**	**2**	**0**	**0**	**0**	**0**	**0**	**0**	**0**	**3**	**0.0**	**0**	**0**	**0.0**	**14:01**	**2**	**0**	**1**	**1**	**0**	**0**	**0**	**0**	**12:21**
2012-13	Rockford IceHogs	AHL	31	8	12	20	10																		
	♦ Chicago	**NHL**	**46**	**10**	**17**	**27**	**12**	**0**	**1**	**2**	**98**	**10.2**	**17**	**46**	**37.0**	**16:28**	**23**	**1**	**5**	**6**	**4**	**0**	**0**	**0**	**16:24**
2013-14	**Chicago**	**NHL**	**78**	**19**	**28**	**47**	**20**	**3**	**0**	**2**	**159**	**11.9**	**20**	**122**	**41.0**	**16:17**	**19**	**6**	**10**	**16**	**6**	**1**	**0**	**1**	**17:31**
2014-15♦	**Chicago**	**NHL**	**82**	**23**	**29**	**52**	**12**	**2**	**0**	**6**	**203**	**11.3**	**7**	**88**	**43.2**	**17:15**	**23**	**8**	**3**	**11**	**6**	**0**	**1**	**2**	**20:16**
2015-16	**Columbus**	**NHL**	**78**	**31**	**22**	**53**	**14**	**6**	**0**	**7**	**233**	**13.3**	**1**	**34**	**55.9**	**17:13**									
2016-17	**Columbus**	**NHL**	**82**	**24**	**29**	**53**	**8**	**1**	**0**	**4**	**210**	**11.4**	**23**	**9**	**44.4**	**17:02**	**5**	**1**	**2**	**3**	**0**	**0**	**0**	**0**	**15:58**
	NHL Totals		**368**	**107**	**125**	**232**	**66**	**12**	**1**	**21**	**906**	**11.8**		**299**	**42.8**	**16:53**	**72**	**16**	**21**	**37**	**16**	**1**	**1**	**3**	**17:47**

OHL First All-Star Team (2012) • NHL All-Rookie Team (2013)

Played in NHL All-Star Game (2016)

Traded to **Columbus** by **Chicago** with Michael Paliotta and Alex Broadhurst for Artem Anisimov, Jeremy Morin, Corey Tropp, Marko Dano and Columbus' 4th round pick (later traded to NY Islanders – NY Islanders selected Anatoli Golyshev) in 2016 NHL Draft, June 30, 2015. Traded to **Chicago** by **Columbus** with Anton Forsberg and Columbus' 5th round pick in 2018 NHL Draft for Artemi Panarin, Tyler Motte and NY Islanders' 6th round pick (previously acquired, Columbus selected Jonathan Davidsson) in 2017 NHL Draft, June 23, 2017.

SALOMAKI, Miikka

(sa-loh-MYA-kee, MEEKA) **NSH**

Right wing. Shoots left. 5'11", 203 lbs. Born, Raahe, Finland, March 9, 1993. Nashville's 2nd pick, 52nd overall, in 2011 NHL Draft.

Season	Club	League	GP	G	A	Pts	PIM	PP	SH	GW	S	S%	+/-	TF	F%	Min	GP	G	A	Pts	PIM	PP	SH	GW	Min
2008-09	Laser HT U18	Fin-U18	23	13	30	43	71																		
2009-10	Karpat Oulu U18	Fin-U18	3	4	2	6	4																		
	Karpat Oulu Jr.	Fin-Jr.	37	18	25	43	93																		
2010-11	Suomi U20	Finland-2	3	1	1	2	27																		
	Karpat Oulu	Finland	40	4	6	10	53										3	0	1	1	27				
	Karpat Oulu U18	Fin-U18															2	0	1	1	2				
2011-12	Karpat Oulu	Finland	40	12	9	21	56										7	1	0	1	56				
2012-13	Karpat Oulu	Finland	42	9	10	19	44										3	2	0	2	14				
2013-14	Milwaukee	AHL	75	20	30	50	83										3	0	0	0	6				
2014-15	**Nashville**	**NHL**	**1**	**1**	**0**	**1**	**0**	**0**	**0**	**0**	**4**	**25.0**	**1**	**0**	**0.0**	**10:49**									
	Milwaukee	AHL	38	7	11	18	30																		
2015-16	**Nashville**	**NHL**	**61**	**5**	**5**	**10**	**28**	**0**	**0**	**1**	**61**	**8.2**	**–1**	**3**	**66.7**	**12:00**	**14**	**1**	**1**	**2**	**6**	**0**	**0**	**0**	**13:01**
	Milwaukee	AHL	4	1	1	2	4																		
2016-17	**Nashville**	**NHL**	**5**	**0**	**0**	**0**	**2**	**0**	**0**	**0**	**3**	**0.0**	**–1**	**0**	**0.0**	**12:13**	**6**	**0**	**0**	**0**	**2**	**0**	**0**	**0**	**8:12**
	Milwaukee	AHL	4	1	0	1	4																		
	NHL Totals		**67**	**6**	**5**	**11**	**30**	**0**	**0**	**1**	**68**	**8.8**		**3**	**66.7**	**12:00**	**20**	**1**	**1**	**2**	**8**	**0**	**0**	**0**	**11:34**

• Missed majority of 2014-15 as a healthy reserve.

SAMUELSSON, Henrik

(SAM-yuhl-suhn, HEHN-rihk) **EDM**

Center/Right wing. Shoots right. 6'3", 210 lbs. Born, Pittsburgh, PA, February 7, 1994. Phoenix's 1st pick, 27th overall, in 2012 NHL Draft.

Season	Club	League	GP	G	A	Pts	PIM	PP	SH	GW	S	S%	+/-	TF	F%	Min	GP	G	A	Pts	PIM	PP	SH	GW	Min
2009-10	P.F. Chang's	T1EHL	37	12	23	35	73																		
	P.F. Chang's	Other	11	15	13	28	....																		
	P.F. Chang's U18	T1EHL	8	2	6	8	25																		
2010-11	USAHNTDP	USHL	27	4	7	11	78																		
	USAHNTDP	U-17	17	8	10	18	24																		
	USAHNTDP	U-18	10	3	3	6	10																		
2011-12	MODO U18	Swe-U18	3	4	1	5	8																		
	MODO Jr.	Swe-Jr.	16	4	5	9	22																		
	MODO	Sweden	15	0	2	2	12																		
	Edmonton	WHL	28	7	16	23	42										17	4	10	14	20				
2012-13	Edmonton	WHL	69	33	47	80	97										22	11	8	19	*43				
2013-14	Edmonton	WHL	65	35	60	95	97										21	8	15	23	*51				
2014-15	**Arizona**	**NHL**	**3**	**0**	**0**	**0**	**2**	**0**	**0**	**0**	**4**	**0.0**	**–2**	**2**	**100.0**	**13:16**									
	Portland Pirates	AHL	68	18	22	40	56										5	2	3	5	13				
2015-16	Springfield	AHL	43	3	9	12	30																		
2016-17	Tucson	AHL	20	2	1	3	16																		
	Bakersfield	AHL	5	0	0	0	4																		
	NHL Totals		**3**	**0**	**0**	**0**	**2**	**0**	**0**	**0**	**4**	**0.0**		**2**	**100.0**	**13:16**									

Traded to **Edmonton** by **Arizona** for Mitchell Moroz, February 1, 2017. • Missed majority of 2016-17 due to recurring lower-body injury and as a healthy reserve.

SAMUELSSON, Philip

(SAM-yuhl-suhn, FIHL-ihp) **CAR**

Defense. Shoots left. 6'2", 194 lbs. Born, Leksand, Sweden, July 26, 1991. Pittsburgh's 2nd pick, 61st overall, in 2009 NHL Draft.

Season	Club	League	GP	G	A	Pts	PIM	PP	SH	GW	S	S%	+/-	TF	F%	Min	GP	G	A	Pts	PIM	PP	SH	GW	Min
2006-07	P.F. Chang's	Minor-AZ	54	9	31	40	70																		
2007-08	P.F. Chang's	Minor-AZ	41	8	25	33	48																		
2008-09	Chicago Steel	USHL	54	0	22	22	60																		
	USAHNTDP	U-18	4	0	0	0	6																		
2010-11	Boston College	H-East	39	4	12	16	72																		
2011-12	Wilkes-Barre	AHL	46	1	8	9	26										10	0	1	1	18				
	Wheeling Nailers	ECHL	5	0	1	1	11										3	1	0	1	0				
2012-13	Wilkes-Barre	AHL	65	2	8	10	70										15	0	2	2	8				
2013-14	**Pittsburgh**	**NHL**	**5**	**0**	**0**	**0**	**0**	**0**	**0**	**0**	**5**	**0.0**	**–1**	**0**	**0.0**	**15:34**									
	Wilkes-Barre	AHL	64	3	19	22	66										8	0	1	1	8				
2014-15	Wilkes-Barre	AHL	22	0	4	4	20																		
	Arizona	**NHL**	**4**	**0**	**0**	**0**	**0**	**0**	**0**	**0**	**4**	**0.0**	**–3**	**0**	**0.0**	**16:53**									
	Portland Pirates	AHL	51	5	15	20	31										5	1	2	3	4				
2015-16	**Arizona**	**NHL**	**4**	**0**	**0**	**0**	**2**	**0**	**0**	**0**	**5**	**0.0**	**0**	**0**	**0.0**	**15:53**									
	Springfield	AHL	56	4	27	31	32																		
2016-17	St. John's IceCaps	AHL	40	1	4	5	21																		
	Charlotte	AHL	25	3	11	14	14										5	1	1	2	2				
	NHL Totals		**13**	**0**	**0**	**0**	**2**	**0**	**0**	**0**	**14**	**0.0**		**0**	**0.0**	**16:04**									

Traded to **Arizona** by **Pittsburgh** for Rob Klinkhammer and future considerations, December 5, 2014. Signed as a free agent by **Montreal**, July 2, 2016. Traded to **Carolina** by **Montreal** for Keegan Lowe, February 21, 2017.

SANFORD, Zach

(SAN-fohrd, ZAK) **ST.L.**

Left wing. Shoots left. 6'3", 185 lbs. Born, Salem, MA, November 9, 1994. Washington's 3rd pick, 61st overall, in 2013 NHL Draft.

Season	Club	League	GP	G	A	Pts	PIM	PP	SH	GW	S	S%	+/-	TF	F%	Min	GP	G	A	Pts	PIM	PP	SH	GW	Min
2009-10	Pinkerton	High-NH	23	14	11	25	48																		
2010-11	Pinkerton	High-NH	21	15	16	31	39																		
2011-12	Pinkerton	High-NH	21	36	33	69	40																		
2012-13	Islanders H.C.	EJHL	37	12	24	36	22																		
2013-14	Waterloo	USHL	52	17	18	35	60										7	4	4	8	8				
2014-15	Boston College	H-East	38	7	17	24	30										12	5	7	12	8				

			Regular Season														Playoffs								
Season	Club	League	GP	G	A	Pts	PIM	PP	SH	GW	S	S%	+/-	TF	F%	Min	GP	G	A	Pts	PIM	PP	SH	GW	Min
2015-16	Boston College	H-East	41	13	26	39	44	....	....	....	....	....	....	....	....	....	....	....	....	....	....	....	....	....	....
2016-17	Washington	NHL	26	2	1	3	6	0	0	1	23	8.7	0	18	55.6	10:09	....	....	....	....	....	....	....	....	....
	Hershey Bears	AHL	25	11	5	16	14	....	....	....	....	....	....	....	....	....	....	....	....	....	....	....	....	....	....
	St. Louis	NHL	13	2	3	5	4	0	0	1	13	15.4	2	21	33.3	12:14	4	0	0	0	0	0	0	0	10:55
	Chicago Wolves	AHL	....	....	....	....	....	....	....	....	....	....	....	....	....	....	2	0	0	0	0	....	....	....	....
	NHL Totals		39	4	4	8	10	0	0	2	36	11.1		39	43.6	10:51	4	0	0	0	0	0	0	0	10:55

Traded to **St. Louis** by **Washington** with Brad Malone and Washington's 1st round pick (later traded to Philadelphia – Philadelphia selected Morgan Frost) in 2017 NHL Draft for Kevin Shattenkirk and Pheonix Copley, February 27, 2017.

SANTINI, Steven

(san-TEE-nee, STEE-vehn) **N.J.**

Defense. Shoots right. 6'2", 205 lbs. Born, Bronxville, NY, March 7, 1995. New Jersey's 1st pick, 42nd overall, in 2013 NHL Draft.

Season	Club	League	GP	G	A	Pts	PIM	PP	SH	GW	S	S%	+/-	TF	F%	Min	GP	G	A	Pts	PIM	PP	SH	GW	Min
2010-11	NY Apple Core	EJHL	44	3	14	17	26	....	....	....	....	....	....	....	....	....	5	0	1	1	0	....	....	....	....
2011-12	USAHNTDP	USHL	36	1	4	5	41	....	....	....	....	....	....	....	....	....	2	0	1	1	0	....	....	....	....
	USAHNTDP	U-17	17	1	3	4	28	....	....	....	....	....	....	....	....	....	....	....	....	....	....	....	....	....	....
2012-13	USAHNTDP	USHL	25	0	5	5	6	....	....	....	....	....	....	....	....	....	....	....	....	....	....	....	....	....	....
	USAHNTDP	U-18	41	0	10	10	38	....	....	....	....	....	....	....	....	....	....	....	....	....	....	....	....	....	....
2013-14	Boston College	H-East	35	3	8	11	52	....	....	....	....	....	....	....	....	....	....	....	....	....	....	....	....	....	....
2014-15	Boston College	H-East	22	1	4	5	20	....	....	....	....	....	....	....	....	....	....	....	....	....	....	....	....	....	....
2015-16	Boston College	H-East	41	1	18	19	50	....	....	....	....	....	....	....	....	....	....	....	....	....	....	....	....	....	....
	New Jersey	NHL	1	0	0	0	2	0	0	0	1	0.0	2	0	0.0	14:35	....	....	....	....	....	....	....	....	....
2016-17	New Jersey	NHL	38	2	5	7	14	0	0	0	46	4.3	-6	0	0.0	16:05	....	....	....	....	....	....	....	....	....
	Albany Devils	AHL	20	0	2	2	35	....	....	....	....	....	....	....	....	....	4	0	2	2	0	....	....	....	....
	NHL Totals		39	2	5	7	16	0	0	0	47	4.3		0	0.0	16:03	....	....	....	....	....	....	....	....	....

SAVARD, David

(suh-VAHRD, DAY-vihd) **CBJ**

Defense. Shoots right. 6'2", 227 lbs. Born, St. Hyacinthe, QC, October 22, 1990. Columbus' 3rd pick, 94th overall, in 2009 NHL Draft.

Season	Club	League	GP	G	A	Pts	PIM	PP	SH	GW	S	S%	+/-	TF	F%	Min	GP	G	A	Pts	PIM	PP	SH	GW	Min
2006-07	Sem. St-Francois	QAAA	44	10	16	26	52	....	....	....	....	....	....	....	....	....	18	1	12	13	10	....	....	....	....
2007-08	Baie-Comeau	QMJHL	35	1	6	7	22	....	....	....	....	....	....	....	....	....	....	....	....	....	....	....	....	....	....
	Moncton Wildcats	QMJHL	32	0	5	5	18	....	....	....	....	....	....	....	....	....	....	....	....	....	....	....	....	....	....
2008-09	Moncton Wildcats	QMJHL	68	9	35	44	33	....	....	....	....	....	....	....	....	....	10	5	5	10	10	....	....	....	....
2009-10	Moncton Wildcats	QMJHL	64	13	*64	77	36	....	....	....	....	....	....	....	....	....	21	1	14	15	8	....	....	....	....
2010-11	Springfield	AHL	72	11	32	43	18	....	....	....	....	....	....	....	....	....	....	....	....	....	....	....	....	....	....
2011-12	Columbus	NHL	31	2	8	10	16	1	0	0	34	5.9	0	0	0.0	16:34	....	....	....	....	....	....	....	....	....
	Springfield	AHL	44	4	18	22	72	....	....	....	....	....	....	....	....	....	....	....	....	....	....	....	....	....	....
2012-13	Springfield	AHL	60	5	26	31	40	....	....	....	....	....	....	....	....	....	8	2	3	5	8	....	....	....	....
	Columbus	NHL	4	0	0	0	0	0	0	0	1	0.0	-3	0	0.0	13:12	....	....	....	....	....	....	....	....	....
2013-14	Columbus	NHL	70	5	10	15	28	1	0	1	63	7.9	2	1	100.0	17:50	6	0	4	4	4	0	0	0	23:20
2014-15	Columbus	NHL	82	11	25	36	71	3	0	3	112	9.8	0	1	100.0	22:57	....	....	....	....	....	....	....	....	....
2015-16	Columbus	NHL	65	4	21	25	45	1	0	0	122	3.3	-7	0	0.0	23:10	....	....	....	....	....	....	....	....	....
2016-17	Columbus	NHL	74	6	17	23	44	0	0	0	135	4.4	33	0	0.0	21:50	5	0	1	1	4	0	0	0	24:53
	NHL Totals		326	28	81	109	204	6	0	4	467	6.0		2	100.0	20:55	11	0	5	5	8	0	0	0	24:02

QMJHL First All-Star Team (2010) • Canadian Major Junior First All-Star Team (2010) • Canadian Major Junior Defenseman of the Year (2010)

SBISA, Luca

(S'BEE-za, LOO-ka) **VGK**

Defense. Shoots left. 6'2", 198 lbs. Born, Ozieri, Italy, January 30, 1990. Philadelphia's 1st pick, 19th overall, in 2008 NHL Draft.

Season	Club	League	GP	G	A	Pts	PIM	PP	SH	GW	S	S%	+/-	TF	F%	Min	GP	G	A	Pts	PIM	PP	SH	GW	Min
2005-06	EV Zug Jr.	Swiss-Jr.	18	0	3	3	18	....	....	....	....	....	....	....	....	....	....	....	....	....	....	....	....	....	....
2006-07	EV Zug Jr.	Swiss-Jr.	STATISTICS NOT AVAILABLE																						
	EHC Seewen	Swiss-3	6	1	2	3	4	....	....	....	....	....	....	....	....	....	....	....	....	....	....	....	....	....	....
	EV Zug	Swiss	7	0	0	0	0	....	....	....	....	....	....	....	....	....	1	0	0	0	0	....	....	....	....
2007-08	Lethbridge	WHL	62	6	27	33	63	....	....	....	....	....	....	....	....	....	19	3	12	15	17	....	....	....	....
2008-09	Philadelphia	NHL	39	0	7	7	36	0	0	0	38	0.0	-6	0	0.0	17:29	1	0	0	0	2	0	0	0	5:37
	Lethbridge	WHL	18	4	11	15	19	....	....	....	....	....	....	....	....	....	11	2	1	3	12	....	....	....	....
	Philadelphia	AHL	2	1	1	2	2	....	....	....	....	....	....	....	....	....	....	....	....	....	....	....	....	....	....
2009-10	Anaheim	NHL	8	0	0	0	6	0	0	0	3	0.0	-1	0	0.0	12:38	....	....	....	....	....	....	....	....	....
	Lethbridge	WHL	17	1	12	13	18	....	....	....	....	....	....	....	....	....	....	....	....	....	....	....	....	....	....
	Portland	WHL	12	3	2	5	11	....	....	....	....	....	....	....	....	....	13	2	2	4	26	....	....	....	....
	Switzerland	Olympics	5	0	0	0	0	....	....	....	....	....	....	....	....	....	....	....	....	....	....	....	....	....	....
2010-11	Anaheim	NHL	68	2	9	11	43	1	0	0	76	2.6	-11	0	0.0	16:48	6	0	1	1	8	0	0	0	16:29
	Syracuse Crunch	AHL	8	2	7	9	4	....	....	....	....	....	....	....	....	....	....	....	....	....	....	....	....	....	....
2011-12	Anaheim	NHL	80	5	19	24	66	0	0	0	88	5.7	-5	0	0.0	17:56	....	....	....	....	....	....	....	....	....
2012-13	HC Lugano	Swiss	30	5	7	12	14	....	....	....	....	....	....	....	....	....	....	....	....	....	....	....	....	....	....
	Anaheim	NHL	41	1	7	8	23	0	0	1	39	2.6	0	0	0.0	19:50	5	0	0	0	4	0	0	0	21:26
2013-14	Anaheim	NHL	30	1	5	6	43	0	0	0	30	3.3	0	0	0.0	17:03	2	0	1	1	5	0	0	0	14:20
	Norfolk Admirals	AHL	4	0	2	2	0	....	....	....	....	....	....	....	....	....	....	....	....	....	....	....	....	....	....
2014-15	Vancouver	NHL	76	3	8	11	46	0	0	2	79	3.8	-8	0	0.0	18:47	6	1	1	2	7	0	0	0	17:27
2015-16	Vancouver	NHL	41	2	6	8	26	0	0	1	29	6.9	5	0	0.0	17:23	....	....	....	....	....	....	....	....	....
2016-17	Vancouver	NHL	82	2	11	13	40	0	0	1	75	2.7	-1	0	0.0	18:59	....	....	....	....	....	....	....	....	....
	NHL Totals		465	16	72	88	329	1	0	5	457	3.5		0	0.0	18:01	20	1	3	4	26	0	0	0	17:15

Traded to **Anaheim** by **Philadelphia** with Joffrey Lupul, Philadelphia's 1st round picks in 2009 (later traded to Columbus - Columbus selected John Moore) and 2010 (Emerson Etem) NHL Drafts and future considerations for Chris Pronger and Ryan Dingle, June 26, 2009. Signed as a free agent by **Lugano** (Swiss), September 19, 2012. • Missed majority of 2013-14 due to hand injury vs. Tampa Bay, November 22, 2013 and as a healthy reserve. Traded to **Vancouver** by **Anaheim** with Nick Bonino and Anaheim's 1st (Jared McCann) and 3rd (later traded to NY Rangers – NY Rangers selected Keegan Iverson) round picks in 2014 NHL Draft for Ryan Kesler and Vancouver's 3rd round pick (Deven Sideroff) in 2015 NHL Draft, June 27, 2014. Claimed by **Vegas** from **Vancouver** in Expansion Draft, June 21, 2017.

SCANDELLA, Marco

(skan-DEHL-a, MAHR-koh) **BUF**

Defense. Shoots left. 6'3", 211 lbs. Born, Montreal, QC, February 23, 1990. Minnesota's 2nd pick, 55th overall, in 2008 NHL Draft.

Season	Club	League	GP	G	A	Pts	PIM	PP	SH	GW	S	S%	+/-	TF	F%	Min	GP	G	A	Pts	PIM	PP	SH	GW	Min
2005-06	Ecole Montpetit	QAAA	42	3	4	7	40	....	....	....	....	....	....	....	....	....	3	0	0	0	2	....	....	....	....
2006-07	Mtl. Predateurs	QAAA	42	7	13	20	66	....	....	....	....	....	....	....	....	....	3	0	1	1	10	....	....	....	....
2007-08	Val-d'Or Foreurs	QMJHL	65	4	10	14	35	....	....	....	....	....	....	....	....	....	4	0	1	1	4	....	....	....	....
2008-09	Val-d'Or Foreurs	QMJHL	58	10	27	37	64	....	....	....	....	....	....	....	....	....	....	....	....	....	....	....	....	....	....
	Houston Aeros	AHL	2	0	0	0	0	....	....	....	....	....	....	....	....	....	6	0	0	0	2	....	....	....	....
2009-10	Val-d'Or Foreurs	QMJHL	31	9	22	31	41	....	....	....	....	....	....	....	....	....	6	2	4	6	4	....	....	....	....
	Houston Aeros	AHL	7	0	1	1	7	....	....	....	....	....	....	....	....	....	....	....	....	....	....	....	....	....	....
2010-11	Minnesota	NHL	20	0	2	2	2	0	0	0	13	0.0	-9	0	0.0	14:58	....	....	....	....	....	....	....	....	....
	Houston Aeros	AHL	33	3	16	19	17	....	....	....	....	....	....	....	....	....	20	2	6	8	8	....	....	....	....
2011-12	Minnesota	NHL	63	3	9	12	19	1	0	1	77	3.9	-22	0	0.0	21:47	....	....	....	....	....	....	....	....	....
	Houston Aeros	AHL	9	2	3	5	4	....	....	....	....	....	....	....	....	....	....	....	....	....	....	....	....	....	....
2012-13	Houston Aeros	AHL	45	2	15	17	23	....	....	....	....	....	....	....	....	....	2	1	0	1	2	....	....	....	....
	Minnesota	NHL	6	1	0	1	4	0	0	0	7	14.3	-1	0	0.0	14:26	5	1	1	2	0	0	0	0	18:01
2013-14	Minnesota	NHL	76	3	14	17	20	0	0	1	80	3.8	10	0	0.0	18:49	13	2	1	3	0	0	1	0	21:28
2014-15	Minnesota	NHL	64	11	12	23	56	1	0	4	112	9.8	8	0	0.0	21:43	10	2	1	3	0	0	0	0	20:44
2015-16	Minnesota	NHL	73	5	16	21	22	2	0	0	126	4.0	6	0	0.0	20:42	6	1	0	1	4	1	0	0	19:34
2016-17	Minnesota	NHL	71	4	9	13	25	0	0	0	88	4.5	-2	0	0.0	18:20	5	0	0	0	2	0	0	0	22:55
	NHL Totals		373	27	62	89	148	4	0	6	503	5.4		0	0.0	19:49	39	6	3	9	6	1	1	0	20:44

Traded to **Buffalo** by **Minnesota** with Jason Pominville and Minnesota's 4th round pick in 2018 NHL Draft for Tyler Ennis, Marcus Foligno and Buffalo's 3rd round pick in 2018 NHL Draft, June 30. 2017.

SCEVIOUR, Colton

(SEE-vee-yuhr, KOHL-tuhn) **FLA**

Center/Right wing. Shoots right. 6', 195 lbs. Born, Red Deer, AB, April 20, 1989. Dallas' 3rd pick, 112th overall, in 2007 NHL Draft.

Season	Club	League	GP	G	A	Pts	PIM	PP	SH	GW	S	S%	+/-	TF	F%	Min	GP	G	A	Pts	PIM	PP	SH	GW	Min
2004-05	Red Deer	AMHL	36	15	22	37	32	....	....	....	....	....	....	....	....	....	....	....	....	....	....	....	....	....	....
	Portland	WHL	6	1	0	1	6	....	....	....	....	....	....	....	....	....	4	0	0	0	0	....	....	....	....
2005-06	Portland	WHL	58	3	6	9	25	....	....	....	....	....	....	....	....	....	12	0	1	1	4	....	....	....	....
2006-07	Portland	WHL	49	12	26	38	38	....	....	....	....	....	....	....	....	....	....	....	....	....	....	....	....	....	....
2007-08	Portland	WHL	17	2	8	10	9	....	....	....	....	....	....	....	....	....	....	....	....	....	....	....	....	....	....
	Lethbridge	WHL	52	31	23	54	36	....	....	....	....	....	....	....	....	....	19	3	10	13	15	....	....	....	....

								Regular Season									Playoffs								
Season	Club	League	GP	G	A	Pts	PIM	PP	SH	GW	S	S%	+/-	TF	F%	Min	GP	G	A	Pts	PIM	PP	SH	GW	Min
2008-09	Lethbridge	WHL	69	29	51	80	48	....	....	....	....	....	....	....	....	....	11	4	3	7	12	....	....	....	....
2009-10	Texas Stars	AHL	80	9	22	31	19	....	....	....	....	....	....	....	....	....	24	1	7	8	12	....	....	....	....
2010-11	**Dallas**	**NHL**	**1**	**0**	**0**	**0**	**0**	**0**	**0**	**0**	**0**	**0.0**	**–1**	**0**	**0.0**	**5:09**	....	....	....	....	....	....	....	....	....
	Texas Stars	AHL	77	16	25	41	17	....	....	....	....	....	....	....	....	....	6	1	0	1	0	....	....	....	....
2011-12	Texas Stars	AHL	75	21	32	53	25	....	....	....	....	....	....	....	....	....	....	....	....	....	....	....	....	....	....
2012-13	Texas Stars	AHL	62	21	31	52	20	....	....	....	....	....	....	....	....	....	9	1	3	4	4	....	....	....	....
	Dallas	**NHL**	**1**	**0**	**1**	**1**	**0**	**0**	**0**	**0**	**0**	**0.0**	**–1**	**3**	**33.3**	**4:51**	....	....	....	....	....	....	....	....	....
2013-14	**Dallas**	**NHL**	**26**	**8**	**4**	**12**	**4**	**2**	**0**	**2**	**69**	**11.6**	**–3**	**43**	**39.5**	**14:53**	**6**	**1**	**2**	**3**	**0**	**0**	**0**	**0**	**15:02**
	Texas Stars	AHL	54	32	31	63	31	....	....	....	....	....	....	....	....	....	....	....	....	....	....	....	....	....	....
2014-15	**Dallas**	**NHL**	**71**	**9**	**17**	**26**	**13**	**0**	**0**	**2**	**113**	**8.0**	**1**	**71**	**42.3**	**12:43**	....	....	....	....	....	....	....	....	....
2015-16	**Dallas**	**NHL**	**71**	**11**	**12**	**23**	**21**	**1**	**0**	**1**	**125**	**8.8**	**6**	**24**	**37.5**	**12:41**	**11**	**2**	**3**	**5**	**0**	**0**	**0**	**0**	**12:43**
2016-17	**Florida**	**NHL**	**80**	**9**	**15**	**24**	**25**	**1**	**3**	**1**	**172**	**5.2**	**–16**	**58**	**53.5**	**14:38**	....	....	....	....	....	....	....	....	....
	NHL Totals		**250**	**37**	**49**	**86**	**63**	**4**	**3**	**6**	**479**	**7.7**		**199**	**44.2**	**13:29**	**17**	**3**	**5**	**8**	**0**	**0**	**0**	**0**	**13:32**

AHL First All-Star Team (2014)

Signed as a free agent by **Florida**, July 1, 2016.

SCHALLER, Tim

(SHAL-uhr, TIHM) **BOS**

Left wing. Shoots left. 6'2", 219 lbs. Born, Merrimack, NH, November 16, 1990.

2007-08	N.E. Jr. Huskies	EJHL	44	8	25	33	29	....	....	....	....	....	....	....	....	....	....	....	....	....	....	....	....	....	....
2008-09	Islanders H.C.	EJHL	45	16	23	39	54	....	....	....	....	....	....	....	....	....	2	0	1	1	0	....	....	....	....
2009-10	Providence	H-East	33	2	3	5	40	....	....	....	....	....	....	....	....	....	....	....	....	....	....	....	....	....	....
2010-11	Providence	H-East	34	5	14	19	36	....	....	....	....	....	....	....	....	....	....	....	....	....	....	....	....	....	....
2011-12	Providence	H-East	26	14	7	21	24	....	....	....	....	....	....	....	....	....	....	....	....	....	....	....	....	....	....
2012-13	Providence	H-East	38	8	15	23	61	....	....	....	....	....	....	....	....	....	....	....	....	....	....	....	....	....	....
2013-14	Rochester	AHL	72	11	7	18	36	....	....	....	....	....	....	....	....	....	5	0	1	1	2	....	....	....	....
2014-15	**Buffalo**	**NHL**	**18**	**1**	**1**	**2**	**2**	**0**	**0**	**0**	**19**	**5.3**	**–5**	**186**	**39.8**	**11:21**	....	....	....	....	....	....	....	....	....
	Rochester	AHL	65	15	28	43	116	....	....	....	....	....	....	....	....	....	....	....	....	....	....	....	....	....	....
2015-16	**Buffalo**	**NHL**	**17**	**1**	**2**	**3**	**2**	**0**	**1**	**1**	**18**	**5.6**	**3**	**113**	**35.4**	**8:19**	....	....	....	....	....	....	....	....	....
	Rochester	AHL	37	12	14	26	48	....	....	....	....	....	....	....	....	....	....	....	....	....	....	....	....	....	....
2016-17	**Boston**	**NHL**	**59**	**7**	**7**	**14**	**23**	**0**	**0**	**2**	**89**	**7.9**	**–6**	**57**	**49.1**	**12:16**	**6**	**1**	**0**	**1**	**2**	**0**	**1**	**0**	**13:29**
	NHL Totals		**94**	**9**	**10**	**19**	**27**	**0**	**1**	**3**	**126**	**7.1**		**356**	**39.9**	**11:23**	**6**	**1**	**0**	**1**	**2**	**0**	**1**	**0**	**13:29**

Signed as a free agent by **Buffalo**, April 2, 2013. Signed as a free agent by **Boston**, July 1, 2016.

SCHEIFELE, Mark

(SHIHF-lee, MAHRK) **WPG**

Center. Shoots right. 6'3", 207 lbs. Born, Kitchener, ON, March 15, 1993. Winnipeg's 1st pick, 7th overall, in 2011 NHL Draft.

2008-09	Kit. Jr. Rangers	Minor-ON	31	20	19	39	16	....	....	....	....	....	....	....	....	....	....	....	....	....	....	....	....	....	....
	Kit. Jr. Rangers	Other	18	20	20	40	14	....	....	....	....	....	....	....	....	....	....	....	....	....	....	....	....	....	....
2009-10	Kitchener	ON-Jr.B	51	18	37	55	20	....	....	....	....	....	....	....	....	....	5	0	3	3	6	....	....	....	....
2010-11	Barrie Colts	OHL	66	22	53	75	35	....	....	....	....	....	....	....	....	....	....	....	....	....	....	....	....	....	....
2011-12	**Winnipeg**	**NHL**	**7**	**1**	**0**	**1**	**0**	**1**	**0**	**0**	**5**	**20.0**	**0**	**51**	**35.3**	**10:57**	....	....	....	....	....	....	....	....	....
	Barrie Colts	OHL	47	23	40	63	36	....	....	....	....	....	....	....	....	....	13	5	7	12	12	....	....	....	....
	St. John's IceCaps	AHL	....	....	....	....	....	....	....	....	....	....	....	....	....	....	10	0	1	1	2	....	....	....	....
2012-13	Barrie Colts	OHL	45	39	40	79	30	....	....	....	....	....	....	....	....	....	21	15	*26	*41	14	....	....	....	....
	Winnipeg	**NHL**	**4**	**0**	**0**	**0**	**0**	**0**	**0**	**0**	**6**	**0.0**	**0**	**14**	**71.4**	**11:32**	....	....	....	....	....	....	....	....	....
2013-14	**Winnipeg**	**NHL**	**63**	**13**	**21**	**34**	**14**	**1**	**0**	**2**	**100**	**13.0**	**9**	**785**	**42.2**	**16:21**	....	....	....	....	....	....	....	....	....
2014-15	**Winnipeg**	**NHL**	**82**	**15**	**34**	**49**	**24**	**3**	**0**	**2**	**170**	**8.8**	**11**	**1148**	**42.9**	**18:35**	**4**	**0**	**1**	**1**	**4**	**0**	**0**	**0**	**17:40**
2015-16	**Winnipeg**	**NHL**	**71**	**29**	**32**	**61**	**48**	**7**	**0**	**3**	**194**	**14.9**	**16**	**1166**	**44.2**	**18:33**	....	....	....	....	....	....	....	....	....
2016-17	**Winnipeg**	**NHL**	**79**	**32**	**50**	**82**	**38**	**7**	**0**	**5**	**160**	**20.0**	**18**	**1461**	**43.5**	**20:34**	....	....	....	....	....	....	....	....	....
	NHL Totals		**306**	**90**	**137**	**227**	**124**	**19**	**0**	**12**	**635**	**14.2**		**4625**	**43.3**	**18:22**	**4**	**0**	**1**	**1**	**4**	**0**	**0**	**0**	**17:40**

SCHENN, Brayden

(SHEHN, BRAY-duhn) **ST.L.**

Center. Shoots left. 6'1", 195 lbs. Born, Saskatoon, SK, August 22, 1991. Los Angeles' 1st pick, 5th overall, in 2009 NHL Draft.

2006-07	Sask. Contacts	SMHL	41	27	43	70	63	....	....	....	....	....	....	....	....	....	....	....	....	....	....	....	....	....	....
2007-08	Brandon	WHL	66	28	43	71	48	....	....	....	....	....	....	....	....	....	6	2	1	3	14	....	....	....	....
2008-09	Brandon	WHL	70	32	56	88	82	....	....	....	....	....	....	....	....	....	12	8	10	18	12	....	....	....	....
2009-10	Brandon	WHL	59	34	65	99	55	....	....	....	....	....	....	....	....	....	15	8	11	19	2	....	....	....	....
	Los Angeles	**NHL**	**1**	**0**	**0**	**0**	**0**	**0**	**0**	**0**	**0**	**0.0**	**–1**	**14**	**28.6**	**12:31**	....	....	....	....	....	....	....	....	....
2010-11	**Los Angeles**	**NHL**	**8**	**0**	**2**	**2**	**0**	**0**	**0**	**0**	**11**	**0.0**	**–1**	**51**	**33.3**	**11:15**	....	....	....	....	....	....	....	....	....
	Brandon	WHL	2	1	3	4	2	....	....	....	....	....	....	....	....	....	....	....	....	....	....	....	....	....	....
	Saskatoon Blades	WHL	27	21	32	53	23	....	....	....	....	....	....	....	....	....	10	6	5	11	14	....	....	....	....
	Manchester	AHL	7	3	4	7	4	....	....	....	....	....	....	....	....	....	5	1	3	4	0	....	....	....	....
2011-12	**Philadelphia**	**NHL**	**54**	**12**	**6**	**18**	**34**	**4**	**0**	**3**	**97**	**12.4**	**–7**	**436**	**46.1**	**14:07**	**11**	**3**	**6**	**9**	**8**	**2**	**0**	**0**	**14:16**
	Adirondack	AHL	7	6	6	12	4	....	....	....	....	....	....	....	....	....	....	....	....	....	....	....	....	....	....
2012-13	Adirondack	AHL	33	13	20	33	15	....	....	....	....	....	....	....	....	....	....	....	....	....	....	....	....	....	....
	Philadelphia	**NHL**	**47**	**8**	**18**	**26**	**24**	**2**	**0**	**0**	**79**	**10.1**	**–8**	**453**	**45.5**	**15:32**	....	....	....	....	....	....	....	....	....
2013-14	**Philadelphia**	**NHL**	**82**	**20**	**21**	**41**	**54**	**4**	**0**	**6**	**178**	**11.2**	**0**	**685**	**43.2**	**15:45**	**7**	**0**	**3**	**3**	**8**	**0**	**0**	**0**	**14:12**
2014-15	**Philadelphia**	**NHL**	**82**	**18**	**29**	**47**	**34**	**7**	**0**	**6**	**156**	**11.5**	**–5**	**184**	**46.7**	**17:05**	....	....	....	....	....	....	....	....	....
2015-16	**Philadelphia**	**NHL**	**80**	**26**	**33**	**59**	**33**	**11**	**0**	**5**	**178**	**14.6**	**3**	**116**	**44.8**	**16:54**	**6**	**0**	**2**	**2**	**7**	**0**	**0**	**0**	**18:58**
2016-17	**Philadelphia**	**NHL**	**79**	**25**	**30**	**55**	**38**	***17**	**0**	**7**	**178**	**14.0**	**–13**	**494**	**47.0**	**17:48**	....	....	....	....	....	....	....	....	....
	NHL Totals		**433**	**109**	**139**	**248**	**217**	**45**	**0**	**27**	**877**	**12.4**		**2433**	**45.0**	**16:16**	**24**	**3**	**11**	**14**	**23**	**2**	**0**	**0**	**15:26**

WHL Rookie of the Year (2008) • Canadian Major Junior All-Rookie Team (2008) • WHL East Second All-Star Team (2009, 2011) • WHL East First All-Star Team (2010)

Traded to **Philadelphia** by **Los Angeles** with Wayne Simmonds and Los Angeles' 2nd round pick (Devin Shore) in 2012 NHL Draft for Mike Richards and Rob Bordson, June 23, 2011. Traded to **St. Louis** by **Philadelphia** for Jori Lehtera and Washington's 1st round pick (previously acqured, Philadelphia selected Morgan Frost) in 2017 NHL Draft, June 23, 2017.

SCHENN, Luke

(SHEHN, LEWK) **ARI**

Defense. Shoots right. 6'2", 229 lbs. Born, Saskatoon, SK, November 2, 1989. Toronto's 1st pick, 5th overall, in 2008 NHL Draft.

2004-05	Sask. Contacts	SMHL	41	5	22	27	69	....	....	....	....	....	....	....	....	....	....	....	....	....	....	....	....	....	....
2005-06	Kelowna Rockets	WHL	60	3	8	11	86	....	....	....	....	....	....	....	....	....	12	0	0	0	14	....	....	....	....
2006-07	Kelowna Rockets	WHL	72	2	27	29	139	....	....	....	....	....	....	....	....	....	....	....	....	....	....	....	....	....	....
2007-08	Kelowna Rockets	WHL	57	7	21	28	100	....	....	....	....	....	....	....	....	....	7	2	2	4	6	....	....	....	....
2008-09	**Toronto**	**NHL**	**70**	**2**	**12**	**14**	**71**	**1**	**0**	**0**	**102**	**2.0**	**–12**	**0**	**0.0**	**21:32**	....	....	....	....	....	....	....	....	....
2009-10	**Toronto**	**NHL**	**79**	**5**	**12**	**17**	**50**	**0**	**0**	**1**	**101**	**5.0**	**2**	**0**	**0.0**	**16:53**	....	....	....	....	....	....	....	....	....
2010-11	**Toronto**	**NHL**	**82**	**5**	**17**	**22**	**34**	**0**	**0**	**0**	**128**	**3.9**	**–7**	**0**	**0.0**	**22:22**	....	....	....	....	....	....	....	....	....
2011-12	**Toronto**	**NHL**	**79**	**2**	**20**	**22**	**62**	**0**	**0**	**0**	**81**	**2.5**	**–6**	**0**	**0.0**	**16:02**	....	....	....	....	....	....	....	....	....
2012-13	**Philadelphia**	**NHL**	**47**	**3**	**8**	**11**	**34**	**0**	**0**	**0**	**81**	**3.7**	**3**	**0**	**0.0**	**21:52**	....	....	....	....	....	....	....	....	....
2013-14	**Philadelphia**	**NHL**	**79**	**4**	**8**	**12**	**58**	**0**	**0**	**0**	**78**	**5.1**	**0**	**0**	**0.0**	**16:32**	**7**	**1**	**0**	**1**	**0**	**0**	**0**	**1**	**17:22**
2014-15	**Philadelphia**	**NHL**	**58**	**3**	**11**	**14**	**18**	**0**	**0**	**0**	**67**	**4.5**	**–2**	**0**	**0.0**	**18:04**	....	....	....	....	....	....	....	....	....
2015-16	**Philadelphia**	**NHL**	**29**	**2**	**3**	**5**	**30**	**0**	**0**	**0**	**19**	**10.5**	**–7**	**2**	**50.0**	**17:35**	....	....	....	....	....	....	....	....	....
	Los Angeles	**NHL**	**43**	**2**	**9**	**11**	**52**	**1**	**0**	**0**	**57**	**3.5**	**5**	**0**	**0.0**	**17:34**	**5**	**1**	**1**	**2**	**6**	**0**	**0**	**0**	**18:07**
2016-17	**Arizona**	**NHL**	**78**	**1**	**7**	**8**	**85**	**0**	**0**	**0**	**94**	**1.1**	**–9**	**0**	**0.0**	**18:03**	....	....	....	....	....	....	....	....	....
	NHL Totals		**644**	**29**	**107**	**136**	**494**	**2**	**0**	**1**	**808**	**3.6**		**2**	**50.0**	**18:38**	**12**	**2**	**1**	**3**	**6**	**0**	**0**	**1**	**17:40**

WHL West Second All-Star Team (2008) • NHL All-Rookie Team (2009)

Traded to **Philadelphia** by **Toronto** for James van Riemsdyk, June 23, 2012. Traded to **Los Angeles** by **Philadelphia** with Vincent Lecavalier for Jordan Weal and Los Angeles' 3rd round pick (Carsen Twarynski) in 2016 NHL Draft, January 6, 2016. Signed as a free agent by **Arizona**, July 23, 2016.

						Regular Season													Playoffs						
Season	Club	League	GP	G	A	Pts	PIM	PP	SH	GW	S	S%	+/-	TF	F%	Min	GP	G	A	Pts	PIM	PP	SH	GW	Min

SCHERBAK, Nikita
(shair-BAK, nih-KEE-tuh) **MTL**

Right wing. Shoots left. 6'2", 200 lbs.   Born, Moscow, Russia, December 30, 1995. Montreal's 1st pick, 26th overall, in 2014 NHL Draft.

Season	Club	League	GP	G	A	Pts	PIM	PP	SH	GW	S	S%	+/-	TF	F%	Min	GP	G	A	Pts	PIM	PP	SH	GW	Min
2012-13	Stupino Jr.	Russia-Jr.	50	7	7	14	14																			
2013-14	Saskatoon Blades	WHL	65	28	50	78	46																			
2014-15	Everett Silvertips	WHL	65	27	55	82	60											11	3	5	8	10				
2015-16	St. John's IceCaps	AHL	48	7	16	23	20																			
2016-17	**Montreal**	**NHL**	3	1	0	1	0	1	0	0	3	33.3	1	0	0.0	11:23									
	St. John's IceCaps	AHL	66	13	28	41	32											4	1	1	2	4				
	NHL Totals		3	1	0	1	0	1	0	0	3	33.3		0	0.0	11:23									

SCHILLING, Cameron
(SHIHL-ihng, KAM-ruhn) **WPG**

Defense. Shoots left. 6'2", 196 lbs.   Born, Carmel, IN, October 7, 1988.

Season	Club	League	GP	G	A	Pts	PIM	PP	SH	GW	S	S%	+/-	TF	F%	Min	GP	G	A	Pts	PIM	PP	SH	GW	Min
2007-08	Indiana Ice	USHL	55	2	8	10	91											4	0	0	0	2				
2008-09	Miami U.	CCHA	25	0	7	7	43																			
2009-10	Miami U.	CCHA	42	4	15	19	58																			
2010-11	Miami U.	CCHA	38	3	14	17	34																			
2011-12	Miami U.	CCHA	39	1	13	14	20																			
	Hershey Bears	AHL	7	0	0	0	14											4	2	0	2	4				
2012-13	Hershey Bears	AHL	70	7	9	16	61											5	0	1	1	4				
	Washington	**NHL**	1	0	0	0	0	0	0	0	0	0.0	-1	0	0.0	11:58									
2013-14	**Washington**	**NHL**	1	0	0	0	0	0	0	0	2	0.0	-2	0	0.0	17:45									
	Hershey Bears	AHL	70	3	13	16	89																			
2014-15	**Washington**	**NHL**	4	0	0	0	4	0	0	0	2	0.0	1	0	0.0	11:23									
	Hershey Bears	AHL	63	3	15	18	63											10	3	5	8	2				
2015-16	Rockford IceHogs	AHL	73	5	17	22	38											3	0	1	1	0				
2016-17	Rockford IceHogs	AHL	40	7	10	17	18																			
	Ontario Reign	AHL	32	1	8	9	31											5	0	2	2	0				
	NHL Totals		6	0	0	0	4	0	0	0	4	0.0		0	0.0	12:32									

Signed as a free agent by **Washington**, March 27, 2012. Signed as a free agent by **Chicago**, July 2, 2015. Traded to **Los Angeles** by **Chicago** for Michael Latta, January 21, 2017. Signed as a free agent by **Winnipeg**, July 1, 2017.

SCHLEMKO, David
(SHLEHM-koh, DAY-vihd) **MTL**

Defense. Shoots left. 6', 190 lbs.   Born, Edmonton, AB, May 7, 1987.

Season	Club	League	GP	G	A	Pts	PIM	PP	SH	GW	S	S%	+/-	TF	F%	Min	GP	G	A	Pts	PIM	PP	SH	GW	Min
2004-05	Medicine Hat	WHL	65	5	24	29	23											13	0	3	3	10				
2005-06	Medicine Hat	WHL	69	9	35	44	44											13	2	5	7	15				
2006-07	Medicine Hat	WHL	64	8	50	58	78											23	3	13	16	12				
2007-08	San Antonio	AHL	1	0	0	0	4																			
	Arizona Sundogs	CHL	58	10	29	39	24											14	3	5	8	6				
2008-09	**Phoenix**	**NHL**	3	0	1	1	0	0	0	0	3	0.0	-2	0	0.0	19:16									
	San Antonio	AHL	68	7	22	29	20																			
2009-10	**Phoenix**	**NHL**	17	1	4	5	8	0	0	0	19	5.3	1	0	0.0	17:49									
	San Antonio	AHL	55	5	26	31	30																			
2010-11	**Phoenix**	**NHL**	43	4	10	14	24	0	0	0	47	8.5	8	0	0.0	16:02	4	1	0	1	4	1	0	0	15:54
	San Antonio	AHL	3	0	0	0	2																			
2011-12	**Phoenix**	**NHL**	46	1	10	11	10	0	0	0	58	1.7	7	0	0.0	18:21	5	0	0	0	0	0	0	0	16:13
2012-13	Arizona Sundogs	CHL	14	3	7	10	4																			
	Phoenix	**NHL**	30	1	5	6	12	0	0	0	35	2.9	8	0	0.0	17:13									
2013-14	**Phoenix**	**NHL**	48	1	8	9	18	0	0	0	61	1.6	2	0	0.0	16:24									
2014-15	**Arizona**	**NHL**	20	1	3	4	4	0	0	0	24	4.2	-5	0	0.0	18:07									
	Portland Pirates	AHL	2	1	3	4	0																			
	Dallas	**NHL**	5	0	0	0	0	0	0	0	6	0.0	0	0	0.0	14:25									
	Calgary	**NHL**	19	0	0	0	8	0	0	0	15	0.0	6	0	0.0	12:39	11	0	1	1	2	0	0	0	14:06
2015-16	**New Jersey**	**NHL**	67	6	13	19	16	1	0	3	104	5.8	-22	0	0.0	18:39									
2016-17	**San Jose**	**NHL**	62	2	16	18	14	1	0	1	118	1.7	4	0	0.0	16:45	6	2	1	3	2	1	0	0	16:50
	NHL Totals		360	17	70	87	114	2	0	4	490	3.5		0	0.0	17:07	26	3	2	5	8	2	0	0	15:25

WHL East Second All-Star Team (2007)

Signed as a free agent by **Phoenix**, July 19, 2007. Signed as a free agent by **Arizona** (CHL), October 2, 2012. Claimed on waivers by **Dallas** from **Arizona**, January 3, 2015. Claimed on waivers by **Calgary** from **Dallas**, March 1, 2015. Signed as a free agent by **New Jersey**, September 11, 2015. Signed as a free agent by **San Jose**, July 1, 2016. Claimed by **Vegas** from **San Jose** in Expansion Draft, June 21, 2017. Traded to **Montreal** by **Vegas** for Montreal's 5th round pick in 2019 NHL Draft, June 22, 2017.

SCHMALTZ, Jordan
(SHMAHLTZ, JOHR-dahn) **ST.L.**

Defense. Shoots right. 6'2", 190 lbs.   Born, Madison, WI, October 8, 1993. St. Louis' 1st pick, 25th overall, in 2012 NHL Draft.

Season	Club	League	GP	G	A	Pts	PIM	PP	SH	GW	S	S%	+/-	TF	F%	Min	GP	G	A	Pts	PIM	PP	SH	GW	Min
2008-09	Chi. Mission U16	T1EHL	25	3	10	13	33																			
2009-10	Chicago Mission	T1EHL	39	10	21	31	30																			
2010-11	Sioux City	USHL	53	13	31	44	22											3	0	1	1	4				
2011-12	Sioux City	USHL	9	3	3	6	9																			
	Green Bay	USHL	46	7	28	35	20											12	2	5	7	8				
2012-13	North Dakota	WCHA	42	3	9	12	31																			
2013-14	North Dakota	NCHC	41	6	18	24	10																			
2014-15	North Dakota	NCHC	42	4	24	28	8																			
2015-16	Chicago Wolves	AHL	71	6	30	36	24																			
2016-17	**St. Louis**	**NHL**	9	0	2	2	4	0	0	0	5	0.0	0	0	0.0	14:20	1	0	0	0	0	0	0	0	9:18
	Chicago Wolves	AHL	42	3	22	25	22											8	1	4	5	4				
	NHL Totals		9	0	2	2	4	0	0	0	5	0.0		0	0.0	14:20	1	0	0	0	0	0	0	0	9:18

USHL All-Rookie Team (2011) • USHL First All-Star Team (2011, 2012) • NCHC Second All-Star Team (2014, 2015)

SCHMALTZ, Nick
(SHMAHLTZ, NIHK) **CHI**

Center. Shoots right. 6', 177 lbs.   Born, Madison, WI, February 23, 1996. Chicago's 1st pick, 20th overall, in 2014 NHL Draft.

Season	Club	League	GP	G	A	Pts	PIM	PP	SH	GW	S	S%	+/-	TF	F%	Min	GP	G	A	Pts	PIM	PP	SH	GW	Min
2011-12	Chicago Mission	HPHL	13	9	11	20	4																			
	Green Bay	USHL	11	1	3	4	2											4	1	1	2	0				
2012-13	Green Bay	USHL	64	18	34	52	15																			
2013-14	Green Bay	USHL	55	18	45	63	16											4	1	2	3	17				
	USAHNTDP	U-18	2	0	0	0	0																			
2014-15	North Dakota	NCHC	38	5	21	26	12																			
2015-16	North Dakota	NCHC	37	11	35	46	6																			
2016-17	**Chicago**	**NHL**	61	6	22	28	6	0	0	0	66	9.1	10	272	30.9	13:16	4	0	0	0	2	0	0	0	15:22
	Rockford IceHogs	AHL	12	6	3	9	2																			
	NHL Totals		61	6	22	28	6	0	0	0	66	9.1		272	30.9	13:16	4	0	0	0	2	0	0	0	15:22

USHL All-Rookie Team (2013) • NCHC All-Rookie Team (2015)

SCHMIDT, Nate
(SHMIHT, NAYT) **VGK**

Defense. Shoots left. 6', 191 lbs.   Born, St. Cloud, MN, July 16, 1991.

Season	Club	League	GP	G	A	Pts	PIM	PP	SH	GW	S	S%	+/-	TF	F%	Min	GP	G	A	Pts	PIM	PP	SH	GW	Min
2009-10	Fargo Force	USHL	57	14	23	37	81											13	0	6	6	6				
2010-11	U. of Minnesota	WCHA	13	0	1	1	6																			
2011-12	U. of Minnesota	WCHA	43	3	38	41	14																			
2012-13	U. of Minnesota	WCHA	40	9	23	32	16											5	0	2	2	0				
	Hershey Bears	AHL	8	1	3	4	2																			
2013-14	**Washington**	**NHL**	29	2	4	6	8	0	0	0	41	4.9	4	0	0.0	18:42									
	Hershey Bears	AHL	38	2	11	13	12																			
2014-15	**Washington**	**NHL**	39	1	3	4	10	0	0	0	40	2.5	-2	0	0.0	13:53									
	Hershey Bears	AHL	19	3	6	9	6											8	4	5	9	0				

			Regular Season														Playoffs								
Season	Club	League	GP	G	A	Pts	PIM	PP	SH	GW	S	S%	+/-	TF	F%	Min	GP	G	A	Pts	PIM	PP	SH	GW	Min
2015-16	Washington	NHL	72	2	14	16	16	0	0	1	80	2.5	12	0	0.0	18:04	10	0	1	1	2	0	0	0	12:30
2016-17	Washington	NHL	60	3	14	17	16	0	0	0	60	5.0	22	0	0.0	15:29	11	1	3	4	4	0	0	0	16:39
	NHL Totals		200	8	35	43	48	0	0	1	221	3.6		0	0.0	16:34	21	1	4	5	6	0	0	0	14:40

WCHA Second All-Star Team (2012) • WCHA First All-Star Team (2013) • NCAA West Second All-American Team (2013)

Signed as a free agent by **Washington**, April 3, 2013. Claimed by **Vegas** from **Washington** in Expansion Draft, June 21, 2017.

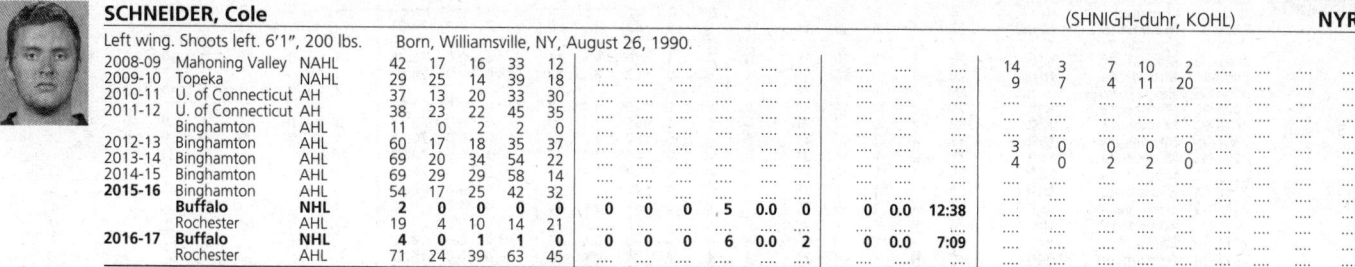

SCHNEIDER, Cole

(SHNIGH-duhr, KOHL) **NYR**

Left wing. Shoots left. 6'1", 200 lbs. Born, Williamsville, NY, August 26, 1990.

Season	Club	League	GP	G	A	Pts	PIM	PP	SH	GW	S	S%	+/-	TF	F%	Min	GP	G	A	Pts	PIM	PP	SH	GW	Min
2008-09	Mahoning Valley	NAHL	42	17	16	33	12	....	....	....	....	....	....	....	....	....	14	3	7	10	2	....	....	....	....
2009-10	Topeka	NAHL	29	25	14	39	18	....	....	....	....	....	....	....	....	....	9	7	4	11	20	....	....	....	....
2010-11	U. of Connecticut	AH	37	13	20	33	30	....	....	....	....	....	....	....	....	....	....	....	....	....	....	....	....	....	....
2011-12	U. of Connecticut	AH	38	23	22	45	35	....	....	....	....	....	....	....	....	....	....	....	....	....	....	....	....	....	....
	Binghamton	AHL	11	0	2	2	0	....	....	....	....	....	....	....	....	....	....	....	....	....	....	....	....	....	....
2012-13	Binghamton	AHL	60	17	18	35	37	....	....	....	....	....	....	....	....	....	3	0	0	0	0	....	....	....	....
2013-14	Binghamton	AHL	69	20	34	54	22	....	....	....	....	....	....	....	....	....	4	0	2	2	0	....	....	....	....
2014-15	Binghamton	AHL	69	29	29	58	14	....	....	....	....	....	....	....	....	....	....	....	....	....	....	....	....	....	....
2015-16	Binghamton	AHL	54	17	25	42	32	....	....	....	....	....	....	....	....	....	....	....	....	....	....	....	....	....	....
	Buffalo	NHL	2	0	0	0	0	0	0	0	5	0.0	0	0	0.0	12:38	....	....	....	....	....	....	....	....	....
	Rochester	AHL	19	4	10	14	21	....	....	....	....	....	....	....	....	....	....	....	....	....	....	....	....	....	....
2016-17	Buffalo	NHL	4	0	1	1	0	0	0	0	6	0.0	2	0	0.0	7:09	....	....	....	....	....	....	....	....	....
	Rochester	AHL	71	24	39	63	45	....	....	....	....	....	....	....	....	....	....	....	....	....	....	....	....	....	....
	NHL Totals		6	0	1	1	0	0	0	0	11	0.0		0	0.0	8:58	....	....	....	....	....	....	....	....	....

Signed as a free agent by **Ottawa**, March 14, 2012. Traded to **Buffalo** by **Ottawa** with Michael Sdao, Eric O'Dell, and Alexander Guptill for Jason Akeson, Phil Varone, Jerome Leduc and future considerations (conditions not met), February 27, 2016. Signed as a free agent by **NY Rangers**, July 1, 2017.

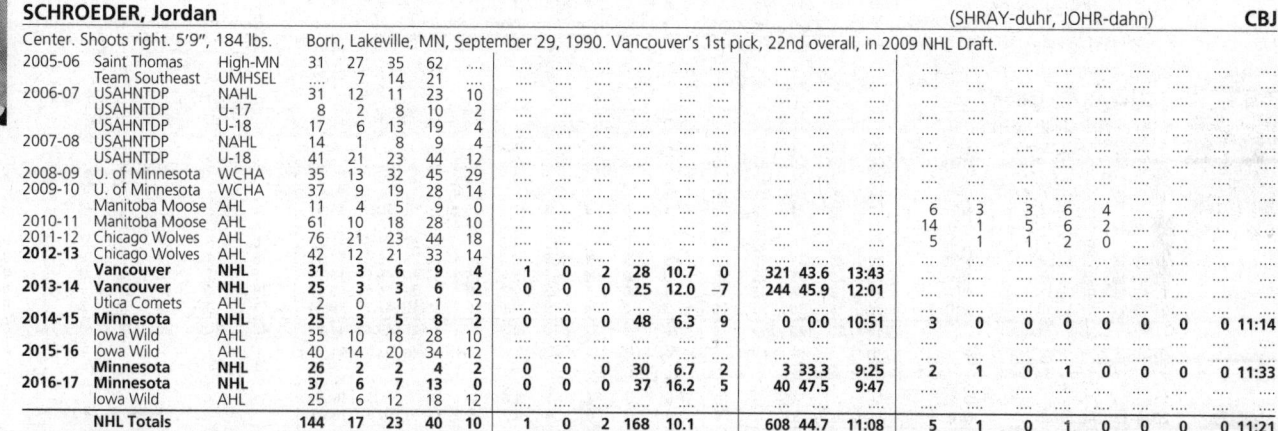

SCHROEDER, Jordan

(SHRAY-duhr, JOHR-dahn) **CBJ**

Center. Shoots right. 5'9", 184 lbs. Born, Lakeville, MN, September 29, 1990. Vancouver's 1st pick, 22nd overall, in 2009 NHL Draft.

Season	Club	League	GP	G	A	Pts	PIM	PP	SH	GW	S	S%	+/-	TF	F%	Min	GP	G	A	Pts	PIM	PP	SH	GW	Min
2005-06	Saint Thomas	High-MN	31	27	35	62	....	....	....	....	....	....	....	....	....	....	....	....	....	....	....	....	....	....	....
	Team Southeast	UMHSEL	....	7	14	21	....	....	....	....	....	....	....	....	....	....	....	....	....	....	....	....	....	....	....
2006-07	USAHNTDP	NAHL	31	12	11	23	10	....	....	....	....	....	....	....	....	....	....	....	....	....	....	....	....	....	....
	USAHNTDP	U-17	8	2	8	10	2	....	....	....	....	....	....	....	....	....	....	....	....	....	....	....	....	....	....
	USAHNTDP	U-18	17	6	13	19	4	....	....	....	....	....	....	....	....	....	....	....	....	....	....	....	....	....	....
2007-08	USAHNTDP	NAHL	14	1	8	9	4	....	....	....	....	....	....	....	....	....	....	....	....	....	....	....	....	....	....
	USAHNTDP	U-18	41	21	23	44	12	....	....	....	....	....	....	....	....	....	....	....	....	....	....	....	....	....	....
2008-09	U. of Minnesota	WCHA	35	13	32	45	29	....	....	....	....	....	....	....	....	....	....	....	....	....	....	....	....	....	....
2009-10	U. of Minnesota	WCHA	37	9	19	28	14	....	....	....	....	....	....	....	....	....	....	....	....	....	....	....	....	....	....
	Manitoba Moose	AHL	11	4	5	9	0	....	....	....	....	....	....	....	....	....	6	3	3	6	4	....	....	....	....
2010-11	Manitoba Moose	AHL	61	10	18	28	10	....	....	....	....	....	....	....	....	....	14	1	5	6	2	....	....	....	....
2011-12	Chicago Wolves	AHL	76	21	23	44	18	....	....	....	....	....	....	....	....	....	5	1	1	2	0	....	....	....	....
2012-13	Chicago Wolves	AHL	42	12	21	33	14	....	....	....	....	....	....	....	....	....	....	....	....	....	....	....	....	....	....
	Vancouver	NHL	31	3	6	9	4	1	0	2	28	10.7	0	321	43.6	13:43	....	....	....	....	....	....	....	....	....
2013-14	Vancouver	NHL	25	3	3	6	2	0	0	0	25	12.0	–7	244	45.9	12:01	....	....	....	....	....	....	....	....	....
	Utica Comets	AHL	2	0	1	1	2	....	....	....	....	....	....	....	....	....	....	....	....	....	....	....	....	....	....
2014-15	Minnesota	NHL	25	3	5	8	2	0	0	0	48	6.3	9	0	0.0	10:51	3	0	0	0	0	0	0	0	11:14
	Iowa Wild	AHL	35	10	18	28	10	....	....	....	....	....	....	....	....	....	....	....	....	....	....	....	....	....	....
2015-16	Iowa Wild	AHL	40	14	20	34	12	....	....	....	....	....	....	....	....	....	....	....	....	....	....	....	....	....	....
	Minnesota	NHL	26	2	2	4	2	0	0	0	30	6.7	2	3	33.3	9:25	2	1	0	1	0	0	0	0	11:33
2016-17	Minnesota	NHL	37	6	7	13	0	0	0	0	37	16.2	5	40	47.5	9:47	....	....	....	....	....	....	....	....	....
	Iowa Wild	AHL	25	6	12	18	12	....	....	....	....	....	....	....	....	....	....	....	....	....	....	....	....	....	....
	NHL Totals		144	17	23	40	10	1	0	2	168	10.1		608	44.7	11:08	5	1	0	1	0	0	0	0	11:21

WCHA All-Rookie Team (2009) • WCHA Second All-Star Team (2009) • WCHA Rookie of the Year (2009)

• Missed majority of 2013-14 due to ankle inury at Pittsburgh, October 19. 2013. Signed as a free agent by **Minnesota**, July 14, 2014. Traded to **Columbus** by **Minnesota** for Dante Salituro, June 23, 2017.

SCHULTZ, Jeff

(SHUHLTZ, JEHF)

Defense. Shoots left. 6'6", 222 lbs. Born, Calgary, AB, February 25, 1986. Washington's 2nd pick, 27th overall, in 2004 NHL Draft.

Season	Club	League	GP	G	A	Pts	PIM	PP	SH	GW	S	S%	+/-	TF	F%	Min	GP	G	A	Pts	PIM	PP	SH	GW	Min
2000-01	Calgary Hawks	CBHL	27	7	8	15	20	....	....	....	....	....	....	....	....	....	....	....	....	....	....	....	....	....	....
2001-02	Calgary Rangers	CBHL	27	5	18	23	42	....	....	....	....	....	....	....	....	....	....	....	....	....	....	....	....	....	....
2002-03	Calgary Hitmen	WHL	50	2	1	3	4	....	....	....	....	....	....	....	....	....	4	0	0	0	0	....	....	....	....
2003-04	Calgary Hitmen	WHL	72	11	24	35	33	....	....	....	....	....	....	....	....	....	7	1	1	2	0	....	....	....	....
2004-05	Calgary Hitmen	WHL	72	2	27	29	31	....	....	....	....	....	....	....	....	....	12	2	1	3	6	....	....	....	....
2005-06	Calgary Hitmen	WHL	68	7	33	40	36	....	....	....	....	....	....	....	....	....	13	4	6	10	6	....	....	....	....
	Hershey Bears	AHL	....	....	....	....	....	....	....	....	....	....	....	....	....	....	7	1	3	4	4	....	....	....	....
2006-07	Washington	NHL	38	0	3	3	16	0	0	0	22	0.0	5	0	0.0	18:13	....	....	....	....	....	....	....	....	....
	Hershey Bears	AHL	44	2	10	12	39	....	....	....	....	....	....	....	....	....	19	0	1	1	18	....	....	....	....
2007-08	Washington	NHL	72	5	13	18	28	0	0	0	36	13.9	12	1	100.0	18:05	2	0	0	0	2	0	0	0	10:25
	Hershey Bears	AHL	1	0	0	0	0	....	....	....	....	....	....	....	....	....	....	....	....	....	....	....	....	....	....
2008-09	Washington	NHL	64	1	11	12	21	0	1	0	40	2.5	13	0	0.0	19:46	1	0	0	0	0	0	0	0	12:26
2009-10	Washington	NHL	73	3	20	23	32	0	0	0	43	7.0	50	0	0.0	19:52	7	0	1	1	4	0	0	0	19:43
2010-11	Washington	NHL	72	1	9	10	12	0	0	1	34	2.9	6	0	0.0	19:47	9	0	0	0	6	0	0	0	20:45
2011-12	Washington	NHL	54	1	5	6	12	0	0	0	22	4.5	–2	0	0.0	15:18	10	0	0	0	2	0	0	0	15:35
2012-13	Washington	NHL	26	0	3	3	12	0	0	0	12	0.0	–6	0	0.0	14:15	....	....	....	....	....	....	....	....	....
2013-14	Manchester	AHL	67	2	11	13	32	....	....	....	....	....	....	....	....	....	2	0	0	0	2	....	....	....	....
	♦ Los Angeles	NHL	....	....	....	....	....	....	....	....	....	....	....	....	....	....	7	0	0	0	0	0	0	0	18:51
2014-15	Los Angeles	NHL	9	0	1	1	4	0	0	0	7	0.0	1	0	0.0	16:45	....	....	....	....	....	....	....	....	....
	Manchester	AHL	52	3	13	16	30	....	....	....	....	....	....	....	....	....	14	0	3	3	10	....	....	....	....
2015-16	Los Angeles	NHL	1	0	0	0	0	0	0	0	1	0.0	–1	0	0.0	18:15	....	....	....	....	....	....	....	....	....
	Ontario Reign	AHL	66	3	15	18	24	....	....	....	....	....	....	....	....	....	13	1	3	4	2	....	....	....	....
2016-17	San Diego Gulls	AHL	65	0	15	15	18	....	....	....	....	....	....	....	....	....	10	0	1	1	2	....	....	....	....
	NHL Totals		409	11	65	76	137	0	1	1	217	5.1		1	100.0	18:20	36	0	1	1	14	0	0	0	17:57

WHL East Second All-Star Team (2006)

• Missed majority of 2012-13 as a healthy reserve. Signed as a free agent by **Los Angeles**, July 5, 2013. Signed as a free agent by **Anaheim**, July 5, 2016.

SCHULTZ, Justin

(SHUHLTZ, JUHS-tihn) **PIT**

Defense. Shoots right. 6'2", 193 lbs. Born, Kelowna, BC, July 6, 1990. Anaheim's 4th pick, 43rd overall, in 2008 NHL Draft.

Season	Club	League	GP	G	A	Pts	PIM	PP	SH	GW	S	S%	+/-	TF	F%	Min	GP	G	A	Pts	PIM	PP	SH	GW	Min
2006-07	Westside Warriors	Minor-BC	....	29	29	58	29	....	....	....	....	....	....	....	....	....	....	....	....	....	....	....	....	....	....
2007-08	Westside Warriors	BCHL	57	9	31	40	28	....	....	....	....	....	....	....	....	....	11	3	5	8	4	....	....	....	....
2008-09	Westside Warriors	BCHL	49	15	35	50	29	....	....	....	....	....	....	....	....	....	6	1	2	3	2	....	....	....	....
2009-10	U. of Wisconsin	WCHA	43	6	16	22	12	....	....	....	....	....	....	....	....	....	....	....	....	....	....	....	....	....	....
2010-11	U. of Wisconsin	WCHA	41	18	29	47	28	....	....	....	....	....	....	....	....	....	....	....	....	....	....	....	....	....	....
2011-12	U. of Wisconsin	WCHA	37	16	28	44	12	....	....	....	....	....	....	....	....	....	....	....	....	....	....	....	....	....	....
2012-13	Oklahoma City	AHL	34	18	30	48	6	....	....	....	....	....	....	....	....	....	....	....	....	....	....	....	....	....	....
	Edmonton	NHL	48	8	19	27	8	4	0	3	85	9.4	–17	1	0.0	21:27	....	....	....	....	....	....	....	....	....
2013-14	Edmonton	NHL	74	11	22	33	16	1	0	3	109	10.1	–22	1	0.0	23:21	....	....	....	....	....	....	....	....	....
2014-15	Edmonton	NHL	81	6	25	31	12	0	0	1	122	4.9	–17	1	100.0	22:37	....	....	....	....	....	....	....	....	....
2015-16	Edmonton	NHL	45	3	7	10	14	1	0	0	59	5.1	–22	2	0.0	20:08	....	....	....	....	....	....	....	....	....
	♦ Pittsburgh	NHL	18	1	7	8	2	1	0	0	23	4.3	7	0	0.0	14:14	15	0	4	4	0	0	0	0	13:01
2016-17	♦ Pittsburgh	NHL	78	12	39	51	34	3	0	1	154	7.8	27	0	0.0	20:27	21	4	9	13	4	3	0	2	19:44
	NHL Totals		344	41	119	160	86	10	0	8	552	7.4		5	20.0	21:21	36	4	13	17	4	3	0	2	16:56

WCHA All-Rookie Team (2010) • WCHA First All-Star Team (2011, 2012) • NCAA West First All-American Team (2011, 2012) • AHL All-Rookie Team (2013) • AHL First All-Star Team (2013) • Eddie Shore Award (AHL - Outstanding Defenseman) (2013) • NHL All-Rookie Team (2013)

Signed as a free agent by **Edmonton**, July 1, 2012. Traded to **Pittsburgh** by **Edmonton** for Pittsburgh's 3rd round pick (Filip Berglund) in 2016 NHL Draft, February 27, 2016.

SCHULTZ, Nick

(SHUHLTZ, NIHK)

Defense. Shoots left. 6'1", 203 lbs. Born, Strasbourg, SK, August 25, 1982. Minnesota's 2nd pick, 33rd overall, in 2000 NHL Draft.

			Regular Season														Playoffs								
Season	Club	League	GP	G	A	Pts	PIM	PP	SH	GW	S	S%	+/-	TF	F%	Min	GP	G	A	Pts	PIM	PP	SH	GW	Min
1997-98	Yorkton Mallers	SMHL	59	10	30	40	74	....	....	....	....	....	....	....	....	....	....	....	....	....	....	....	....	....	....
1998-99	Prince Albert	WHL	58	5	18	23	37	....	....	....	....	....	....	....	....	....	14	0	7	7	0	....	....	....	....
99-2000	Prince Albert	WHL	72	11	33	44	38	....	....	....	....	....	....	....	....	....	6	0	3	3	2	....	....	....	....
2000-01	Prince Albert	WHL	59	17	30	47	120	....	....	....	....	....	....	....	....	....	....	....	....	....	....	....	....	....	....
	Cleveland	IHL	4	1	1	2	2	....	....	....	....	....	....	....	....	....	3	0	1	1	0	....	....	....	....
2001-02	**Minnesota**	**NHL**	**52**	**4**	**6**	**10**	**14**	**1**	**0**	**1**	**47**	**8.5**	**0**	**0**	**0.0**	**16:08**	....	....	....	....	....	....	....	....	....
	Houston Aeros	AHL	....	....	....	....	....	....	....	....	....	....	....	....	....	....	14	1	5	6	2	....	....	....	....
2002-03	**Minnesota**	**NHL**	**75**	**3**	**7**	**10**	**23**	**0**	**0**	**1**	**70**	**4.3**	**11**	**0**	**0.0**	**18:28**	**18**	**0**	**1**	**1**	**10**	**0**	**0**	**0**	**19:39**
2003-04	**Minnesota**	**NHL**	**79**	**6**	**10**	**16**	**16**	**1**	**0**	**0**	**72**	**8.3**	**12**	**0**	**0.0**	**20:19**	....	....	....	....	....	....	....	....	....
2004-05	Kassel Huskies	Germany	46	7	15	22	26	....	....	....	....	....	....	....	....	....	7	0	4	4	6	....	....	....	....
2005-06	**Minnesota**	**NHL**	**79**	**2**	**12**	**14**	**43**	**0**	**0**	**0**	**45**	**4.4**	**2**	**0**	**0.0**	**17:58**	....	....	....	....	....	....	....	....	....
2006-07	**Minnesota**	**NHL**	**82**	**2**	**10**	**12**	**42**	**0**	**0**	**1**	**69**	**2.9**	**0**	**0**	**0.0**	**20:13**	**5**	**0**	**1**	**1**	**0**	**0**	**0**	**0**	**18:06**
2007-08	**Minnesota**	**NHL**	**81**	**2**	**13**	**15**	**42**	**0**	**0**	**0**	**52**	**3.8**	**9**	**0**	**0.0**	**20:10**	**1**	**0**	**0**	**0**	**0**	**0**	**0**	**0**	**16:11**
2008-09	**Minnesota**	**NHL**	**79**	**2**	**9**	**11**	**31**	**0**	**0**	**0**	**48**	**4.2**	**–4**	**1**	**0.0**	**20:33**	....	....	....	....	....	....	....	....	....
2009-10	**Minnesota**	**NHL**	**80**	**1**	**19**	**20**	**43**	**1**	**0**	**0**	**83**	**1.2**	**–8**	**0**	**0.0**	**20:58**	....	....	....	....	....	....	....	....	....
2010-11	**Minnesota**	**NHL**	**74**	**3**	**14**	**17**	**38**	**0**	**0**	**0**	**46**	**6.5**	**–4**	**1**	**100.0**	**20:13**	....	....	....	....	....	....	....	....	....
2011-12	**Minnesota**	**NHL**	**62**	**1**	**2**	**3**	**30**	**1**	**0**	**0**	**38**	**2.6**	**–10**	**0**	**0.0**	**19:36**	....	....	....	....	....	....	....	....	....
	Edmonton	**NHL**	**20**	**0**	**4**	**4**	**10**	**0**	**0**	**0**	**13**	**0.0**	**–2**	**0**	**0.0**	**20:04**	....	....	....	....	....	....	....	....	....
2012-13	**Edmonton**	**NHL**	**48**	**1**	**8**	**9**	**24**	**0**	**0**	**0**	**33**	**3.0**	**–13**	**2**	**0.0**	**18:38**	....	....	....	....	....	....	....	....	....
2013-14	**Edmonton**	**NHL**	**60**	**0**	**4**	**4**	**24**	**0**	**0**	**0**	**27**	**0.0**	**–11**	**0**	**0.0**	**16:58**	....	....	....	....	....	....	....	....	....
	Columbus	**NHL**	**9**	**0**	**1**	**1**	**4**	**0**	**0**	**0**	**8**	**0.0**	**–2**	**0**	**0.0**	**11:54**	**2**	**0**	**0**	**0**	**0**	**0**	**0**	**0**	**9:44**
2014-15	**Philadelphia**	**NHL**	**80**	**2**	**13**	**15**	**47**	**0**	**0**	**1**	**69**	**2.9**	**2**	**0**	**0.0**	**19:03**	....	....	....	....	....	....	....	....	....
2015-16	**Philadelphia**	**NHL**	**81**	**1**	**9**	**10**	**42**	**0**	**0**	**0**	**70**	**1.4**	**–1**	**1**	**100.0**	**17:57**	**6**	**0**	**0**	**0**	**2**	**0**	**0**	**0**	**16:48**
2016-17	**Philadelphia**	**NHL**	**28**	**0**	**4**	**4**	**10**	**0**	**0**	**0**	**25**	**0.0**	**1**	**0**	**0.0**	**15:15**	....	....	....	....	....	....	....	....	....
	NHL Totals		**1069**	**30**	**145**	**175**	**483**	**4**	**0**	**4**	**815**	**3.7**		**5**	**40.0**	**19:04**	**32**	**0**	**2**	**2**	**12**	**0**	**0**	**0**	**18:08**

Signed as a free agent by **Kassel** (Germany), September 24, 2004. Traded to **Edmonton** by **Minnesota** for Tom Gilbert, February 27, 2012. Traded to **Columbus** by **Edmonton** for Columbus's 5th round pick (later traded back to Columbus – Columbus selected Tyler Bird) in 2014 NHL Draft. March 5, 2014. Signed as a free agent by **Philadelphia**, July 2, 2014. • Missed majority of 2016-17 due to various injuries.

SCHWARTZ, Jaden

(SHWOHRTZ, JAY-duhn) **ST.L.**

Center. Shoots left. 5'10", 190 lbs. Born, Melfort, SK, June 25, 1992. St. Louis' 1st pick, 14th overall, in 2010 NHL Draft.

Season	Club	League	GP	G	A	Pts	PIM	PP	SH	GW	S	S%	+/-	TF	F%	Min	GP	G	A	Pts	PIM	PP	SH	GW	Min
2008-09	Notre Dame	SJHL	46	34	42	76	15	....	....	....	....	....	....	....	....	....	....	....	....	....	....	....	....	....	....
2009-10	Tri-City Storm	USHL	60	33	50	*83	18	....	....	....	....	....	....	....	....	....	3	3	0	3	0	....	....	....	....
2010-11	Colorado College	WCHA	30	17	30	47	22	....	....	....	....	....	....	....	....	....	....	....	....	....	....	....	....	....	....
2011-12	Colorado College	WCHA	30	15	26	41	18	....	....	....	....	....	....	....	....	....	....	....	....	....	....	....	....	....	....
	St. Louis	**NHL**	**7**	**2**	**1**	**3**	**0**	**1**	**0**	**1**	**6**	**33.3**	**1**	**2**	**50.0**	**11:41**	....	....	....	....	....	....	....	....	....
2012-13	Peoria Rivermen	AHL	33	9	10	19	14	....	....	....	....	....	....	....	....	....	....	....	....	....	....	....	....	....	....
	St. Louis	**NHL**	**45**	**7**	**6**	**13**	**4**	**0**	**0**	**1**	**50**	**14.0**	**–4**	**27**	**55.6**	**12:28**	**6**	**0**	**1**	**1**	**2**	**0**	**0**	**0**	**16:06**
2013-14	**St. Louis**	**NHL**	**80**	**25**	**31**	**56**	**27**	**5**	**3**	**1**	**188**	**13.3**	**28**	**78**	**56.4**	**17:32**	**6**	**1**	**2**	**3**	**0**	**0**	**0**	**0**	**22:10**
2014-15	**St. Louis**	**NHL**	**75**	**28**	**35**	**63**	**16**	**8**	**0**	**4**	**184**	**15.2**	**13**	**146**	**46.6**	**18:15**	**6**	**1**	**2**	**3**	**0**	**0**	**0**	**0**	**18:01**
2015-16	**St. Louis**	**NHL**	**33**	**8**	**14**	**22**	**8**	**1**	**0**	**1**	**63**	**12.7**	**8**	**32**	**46.9**	**17:12**	**20**	**4**	**10**	**14**	**6**	**3**	**0**	**1**	**18:08**
2016-17	**St. Louis**	**NHL**	**78**	**19**	**36**	**55**	**18**	**3**	**0**	**4**	**179**	**10.6**	**14**	**140**	**47.9**	**18:54**	**11**	**4**	**5**	**9**	**2**	**1**	**0**	**3**	**21:33**
	NHL Totals		**318**	**89**	**123**	**212**	**73**	**18**	**3**	**12**	**670**	**13.3**		**425**	**49.4**	**17:09**	**49**	**10**	**20**	**30**	**10**	**4**	**0**	**4**	**19:08**

USHL First All-Star Team (2010) • WCHA All-Rookie Team (2011) • WCHA Second All-Star Team (2012) • NCAA West First All-American Team (2012)
• Missed majority of 2015-16 due to ankle injury at Montreal, October 20, 2015 and as a healthy reserve.

SCUDERI, Rob

(SKUD-uh-ree, RAWB)

Defense. Shoots left. 6'1", 212 lbs. Born, Syosset, NY, December 30, 1978. Pittsburgh's 5th pick, 134th overall, in 1998 NHL Draft.

Season	Club	League	GP	G	A	Pts	PIM	PP	SH	GW	S	S%	+/-	TF	F%	Min	GP	G	A	Pts	PIM	PP	SH	GW	Min
1995-96	NY Apple Core	MtJHL	76	18	60	78	....	....	....	....	....	....	....	....	....	....	....	....	....	....	....	....	....	....	....
1996-97	NY Apple Core	MtJHL	82	42	70	112	64	....	....	....	....	....	....	....	....	....	....	....	....	....	....	....	....	....	....
1997-98	Boston College	H-East	42	0	24	24	12	....	....	....	....	....	....	....	....	....	....	....	....	....	....	....	....	....	....
1998-99	Boston College	H-East	41	2	8	10	20	....	....	....	....	....	....	....	....	....	....	....	....	....	....	....	....	....	....
99-2000	Boston College	H-East	42	1	12	13	22	....	....	....	....	....	....	....	....	....	....	....	....	....	....	....	....	....	....
2000-01	Boston College	H-East	43	4	19	23	42	....	....	....	....	....	....	....	....	....	....	....	....	....	....	....	....	....	....
2001-02	Wilkes-Barre	AHL	75	1	22	23	66	....	....	....	....	....	....	....	....	....	....	....	....	....	....	....	....	....	....
2002-03	Wilkes-Barre	AHL	74	4	17	21	44	....	....	....	....	....	....	....	....	....	6	0	1	1	4	....	....	....	....
2003-04	**Pittsburgh**	**NHL**	**13**	**1**	**2**	**3**	**4**	**0**	**0**	**0**	**4**	**25.0**	**2**	**0**	**0.0**	**20:06**	....	....	....	....	....	....	....	....	....
	Wilkes-Barre	AHL	64	1	15	16	54	....	....	....	....	....	....	....	....	....	24	0	3	3	14	....	....	....	....
2004-05	Wilkes-Barre	AHL	79	2	18	20	34	....	....	....	....	....	....	....	....	....	11	2	1	3	2	....	....	....	....
2005-06	**Pittsburgh**	**NHL**	**57**	**0**	**4**	**4**	**36**	**0**	**0**	**0**	**28**	**0.0**	**–18**	**0**	**0.0**	**20:15**	....	....	....	....	....	....	....	....	....
	Wilkes-Barre	AHL	13	0	8	8	8	....	....	....	....	....	....	....	....	....	....	....	....	....	....	....	....	....	....
2006-07	**Pittsburgh**	**NHL**	**78**	**1**	**10**	**11**	**28**	**0**	**0**	**0**	**31**	**3.2**	**3**	**0**	**0.0**	**18:49**	**5**	**0**	**0**	**0**	**2**	**0**	**0**	**0**	**17:14**
2007-08	**Pittsburgh**	**NHL**	**71**	**0**	**5**	**5**	**26**	**0**	**0**	**0**	**28**	**0.0**	**3**	**0**	**0.0**	**18:45**	**20**	**0**	**3**	**3**	**2**	**0**	**0**	**0**	**19:02**
2008-09 ♦	**Pittsburgh**	**NHL**	**81**	**1**	**15**	**16**	**18**	**0**	**0**	**0**	**51**	**2.0**	**23**	**0**	**0.0**	**19:10**	**24**	**1**	**4**	**5**	**6**	**0**	**0**	**0**	**20:30**
2009-10	**Los Angeles**	**NHL**	**73**	**0**	**11**	**11**	**21**	**0**	**0**	**0**	**38**	**0.0**	**16**	**0**	**0.0**	**19:16**	**6**	**0**	**0**	**0**	**6**	**0**	**0**	**0**	**20:40**
2010-11	**Los Angeles**	**NHL**	**82**	**2**	**13**	**15**	**16**	**0**	**0**	**1**	**46**	**4.3**	**1**	**0**	**0.0**	**20:17**	**6**	**0**	**2**	**2**	**0**	**0**	**0**	**0**	**20:49**
2011-12 ♦	**Los Angeles**	**NHL**	**82**	**1**	**8**	**9**	**16**	**0**	**0**	**0**	**63**	**1.6**	**–7**	**0**	**0.0**	**20:37**	**20**	**0**	**1**	**1**	**4**	**0**	**0**	**0**	**21:44**
2012-13	**Los Angeles**	**NHL**	**48**	**1**	**11**	**12**	**4**	**0**	**0**	**0**	**33**	**3.0**	**–6**	**1**	**0.0**	**21:47**	**18**	**0**	**3**	**3**	**0**	**0**	**0**	**0**	**23:18**
2013-14	**Pittsburgh**	**NHL**	**53**	**0**	**4**	**4**	**2**	**0**	**0**	**0**	**28**	**0.0**	**–8**	**0**	**0.0**	**18:55**	**13**	**0**	**0**	**0**	**6**	**0**	**0**	**0**	**17:45**
2014-15	**Pittsburgh**	**NHL**	**82**	**1**	**9**	**10**	**17**	**0**	**0**	**0**	**52**	**1.9**	**9**	**0**	**0.0**	**19:09**	**5**	**0**	**0**	**0**	**0**	**0**	**0**	**0**	**22:00**
2015-16	**Pittsburgh**	**NHL**	**25**	**0**	**4**	**4**	**8**	**0**	**0**	**0**	**9**	**0.0**	**4**	**1**	**0.0**	**17:05**	....	....	....	....	....	....	....	....	....
	Chicago	**NHL**	**17**	**0**	**0**	**0**	**0**	**0**	**0**	**0**	**14**	**0.0**	**–6**	**0**	**0.0**	**11:06**	....	....	....	....	....	....	....	....	....
	Rockford IceHogs	AHL	3	0	0	0	2	....	....	....	....	....	....	....	....	....	....	....	....	....	....	....	....	....	....
	Los Angeles	**NHL**	**21**	**0**	**6**	**6**	**2**	**0**	**0**	**0**	**12**	**0.0**	**9**	**0**	**0.0**	**18:07**	**5**	**0**	**0**	**0**	**2**	**0**	**0**	**0**	**19:20**
2016-17	Ontario Reign	AHL	15	0	3	3	4	....	....	....	....	....	....	....	....	....	....	....	....	....	....	....	....	....	....
	NHL Totals		**783**	**8**	**102**	**110**	**198**	**0**	**0**	**1**	**437**	**1.8**		**2**	**0.0**	**19:20**	**122**	**1**	**13**	**14**	**28**	**0**	**0**	**0**	**20:29**

NCAA Championship All-Tournament Team (2001)

Signed as a free agent by **Los Angeles** July 2, 2009. Signed as a free agent by **Pittsburgh**, July 5, 2013. Traded to **Chicago** by **Pittsburgh** for Trevor Daley, December 14, 2015. Traded to **Los Angeles** by **Chicago** for Christian Ehrhoff, February 26, 2016. • Missed majority of 2016-17 due to various injuries and as a healthy reserve.

SEABROOK, Brent

(SEE-bruk, BREHNT) **CHI**

Defense. Shoots right. 6'3", 220 lbs. Born, Richmond, BC, April 20, 1985. Chicago's 1st pick, 14th overall, in 2003 NHL Draft.

Season	Club	League	GP	G	A	Pts	PIM	PP	SH	GW	S	S%	+/-	TF	F%	Min	GP	G	A	Pts	PIM	PP	SH	GW	Min
2000-01	Delta Ice Hawks	PIJHL	54	16	26	42	55	....	....	....	....	....	....	....	....	....	....	....	....	....	....	....	....	....	....
	Lethbridge	WHL	4	0	0	0	0	....	....	....	....	....	....	....	....	....	....	....	....	....	....	....	....	....	....
2001-02	Lethbridge	WHL	67	6	33	39	70	....	....	....	....	....	....	....	....	....	4	1	1	2	2	....	....	....	....
2002-03	Lethbridge	WHL	69	9	33	42	113	....	....	....	....	....	....	....	....	....	....	....	....	....	....	....	....	....	....
2003-04	Lethbridge	WHL	61	12	29	41	107	....	....	....	....	....	....	....	....	....	....	....	....	....	....	....	....	....	....
2004-05	Lethbridge	WHL	63	12	42	54	107	....	....	....	....	....	....	....	....	....	5	1	2	3	10	....	....	....	....
	Norfolk Admirals	AHL	3	0	0	0	2	....	....	....	....	....	....	....	....	....	6	0	1	1	6	....	....	....	....
2005-06	**Chicago**	**NHL**	**69**	**5**	**27**	**32**	**60**	**1**	**0**	**2**	**114**	**4.4**	**5**	**0**	**0.0**	**20:02**	....	....	....	....	....	....	....	....	....
2006-07	**Chicago**	**NHL**	**81**	**4**	**20**	**24**	**104**	**0**	**0**	**0**	**144**	**2.8**	**–6**	**2**	**50.0**	**20:46**	....	....	....	....	....	....	....	....	....
2007-08	**Chicago**	**NHL**	**82**	**9**	**23**	**32**	**90**	**4**	**0**	**2**	**152**	**5.9**	**13**	**1**	**0.0**	**21:30**	....	....	....	....	....	....	....	....	....
2008-09	**Chicago**	**NHL**	**82**	**8**	**18**	**26**	**62**	**3**	**1**	**1**	**132**	**6.1**	**23**	**0**	**0.0**	**23:19**	**17**	**1**	**11**	**12**	**14**	**1**	**0**	**0**	**26:00**
2009-10 ♦	**Chicago**	**NHL**	**78**	**4**	**26**	**30**	**59**	**0**	**0**	**2**	**129**	**3.1**	**20**	**0**	**0.0**	**23:13**	**22**	**4**	**7**	**11**	**14**	**1**	**0**	**0**	**24:11**
	Canada	Olympics	7	0	1	1	2	....	....	....	....	....	....	....	....	....	....	....	....	....	....	....	....	....	....
2010-11	**Chicago**	**NHL**	**82**	**9**	**39**	**48**	**47**	**5**	**0**	**1**	**135**	**6.7**	**0**	**0**	**0.0**	**24:23**	**5**	**0**	**1**	**1**	**6**	**0**	**0**	**0**	**22:57**
2011-12	**Chicago**	**NHL**	**78**	**9**	**25**	**34**	**22**	**2**	**0**	**3**	**156**	**5.8**	**21**	**0**	**0.0**	**24:43**	**6**	**1**	**2**	**3**	**0**	**0**	**0**	**0**	**30:01**
2012-13 ♦	**Chicago**	**NHL**	**47**	**8**	**12**	**20**	**23**	**3**	**0**	**1**	**65**	**12.3**	**12**	**0**	**0.0**	**22:00**	**23**	**3**	**1**	**4**	**4**	**0**	**0**	**2**	**23:05**
2013-14	**Chicago**	**NHL**	**82**	**7**	**34**	**41**	**22**	**3**	**1**	**0**	**149**	**4.7**	**23**	**0**	**0.0**	**22:16**	**16**	**3**	**12**	**15**	**21**	**2**	**0**	**0**	**23:22**
2014-15 ♦	**Chicago**	**NHL**	**82**	**8**	**23**	**31**	**27**	**4**	**0**	**2**	**181**	**4.4**	**–3**	**0**	**0.0**	**22:11**	**23**	**7**	**4**	**11**	**10**	**1**	**0**	**1**	**26:17**

			Regular Season														Playoffs								
Season	Club	League	GP	G	A	Pts	PIM	PP	SH	GW	S	S%	+/-	TF	F%	Min	GP	G	A	Pts	PIM	PP	SH	GW	Min
2015-16	**Chicago**	**NHL**	81	14	35	49	32	6	0	3	167	8.4	6	0	0.0	22:49	7	1	1	2	12	1	0	0	27:09
2016-17	**Chicago**	**NHL**	79	3	36	39	26	2	0	0	131	2.3	5	1	0.0	21:54	4	0	0	0	2	0	0	0	22:25
	NHL Totals		923	88	318	406	574	33	2	17	1655	5.3		4	25.0	22:28	123	20	39	59	83	6	0	3	24:52

WHL East Second All-Star Team (2005)
Played in NHL All-Star Game (2015)

SEDIN, Daniel
(suh-DEEN, DAN-yehl) **VAN**

Left wing. Shoots left. 6'1", 187 lbs. Born, Ornskoldsvik, Sweden, September 26, 1980. Vancouver's 1st pick, 2nd overall, in 1999 NHL Draft.

Season	Club	League	GP	G	A	Pts	PIM	PP	SH	GW	S	S%	+/-	TF	F%	Min	GP	G	A	Pts	PIM	PP	SH	GW	Min
1997-98	Malmo Jr.	Swe-Jr.	4	3	3	6	4	....	....	....	....	....	....	....	....	....	....	....	....	....	....	....	....	....	....
	MoDo Jr.	Swe-Jr.	26	26	14	40	....	....	....	....	....	....	....	....	....	....	....	....	....	....	....	....	....	....	....
	MoDo	Sweden	45	4	8	12	26	....	....	....	....	....	....	....	....	....	9	0	0	0	2	....	....	....	....
1998-99	MoDo	Sweden	50	21	21	42	20	....	....	....	....	....	....	....	....	....	13	4	8	12	14	....	....	....	....
99-2000	MoDo	Sweden	50	19	26	45	28	....	....	....	....	....	....	....	....	....	13	*8	6	14	18	....	....	....	....
	MoDo	EuroHL	4	3	3	6	0	....	....	....	....	....	....	....	....	....	2	0	0	0	0	....	....	....	....
2000-01	**Vancouver**	**NHL**	75	20	14	34	24	10	0	3	127	15.7	–3	10	60.0	13:00	4	1	2	3	0	0	0	0	16:15
2001-02	**Vancouver**	**NHL**	79	9	23	32	32	4	0	2	117	7.7	1	18	33.3	12:22	6	0	1	1	0	0	0	0	10:44
2002-03	**Vancouver**	**NHL**	79	14	17	31	34	4	0	2	134	10.4	8	24	45.8	12:26	14	1	5	6	8	1	0	1	12:23
2003-04	**Vancouver**	**NHL**	82	18	36	54	18	1	0	3	153	11.8	18	71	47.9	13:33	7	1	2	3	0	1	0	0	16:03
2004-05	MODO	Sweden	49	13	20	33	40	....	....	....	....	....	....	....	....	....	6	0	3	3	6	....	....	....	....
2005-06	**Vancouver**	**NHL**	82	22	49	71	34	11	0	4	204	10.8	7	49	42.9	16:40	....	....	....	....	....	....	....	....	....
	Sweden	Olympics	8	1	3	4	2	....	....	....	....	....	....	....	....	....	....	....	....	....	....	....	....	....	....
2006-07	**Vancouver**	**NHL**	81	36	48	84	36	16	0	8	236	15.3	19	44	22.7	18:04	12	2	3	5	4	0	0	0	21:31
2007-08	**Vancouver**	**NHL**	82	29	45	74	50	12	0	7	247	11.7	6	38	44.7	19:03	....	....	....	....	....	....	....	....	....
2008-09	**Vancouver**	**NHL**	82	31	51	82	36	9	0	7	285	10.9	24	35	40.0	18:48	10	4	6	10	8	2	0	0	18:37
2009-10	**Vancouver**	**NHL**	63	29	56	85	28	8	0	8	225	12.9	36	33	33.3	19:08	12	5	9	14	12	1	0	2	19:46
	Sweden	Olympics	4	1	2	3	0	....	....	....	....	....	....	....	....	....	....	....	....	....	....	....	....	....	....
2010-11	**Vancouver**	**NHL**	82	41	63	*104	32	*18	0	10	266	15.4	30	17	23.5	18:33	25	9	11	20	32	*5	0	2	20:12
2011-12	**Vancouver**	**NHL**	72	30	37	67	40	10	0	6	229	13.1	14	19	31.6	18:49	2	0	2	2	0	0	0	0	20:07
2012-13	**Vancouver**	**NHL**	47	12	28	40	18	3	0	3	138	8.7	12	7	42.9	19:01	4	0	3	3	14	0	0	0	20:43
2013-14	**Vancouver**	**NHL**	73	16	31	47	38	5	0	4	224	7.1	0	27	29.6	20:36	....	....	....	....	....	....	....	....	....
	Sweden	Olympics	6	1	4	5	4	....	....	....	....	....	....	....	....	....	....	....	....	....	....	....	....	....	....
2014-15	**Vancouver**	**NHL**	82	20	56	76	18	4	0	5	226	8.8	5	5	40.0	18:21	6	2	2	4	0	0	0	1	18:22
2015-16	**Vancouver**	**NHL**	82	28	33	61	36	8	0	6	258	10.9	7	19	26.3	18:20	....	....	....	....	....	....	....	....	....
2016-17	**Vancouver**	**NHL**	82	15	29	44	32	6	0	3	216	6.9	–16	6	50.0	18:23	....	....	....	....	....	....	....	....	....
	NHL Totals		1225	370	616	986	506	129	0	81	3285	11.3		422	38.2	17:07	102	25	46	71	78	10	0	6	18:00

NHL Second All-Star Team (2010) • NHL First All-Star Team (2011) • Art Ross Trophy (2011) • Ted Lindsay Award (2011)
Played in NHL All-Star Game (2011, 2012, 2016)
Signed as a free agent by **MODO** (Sweden), September 18, 2004.

SEDIN, Henrik
(suh-DEEN, HEHN-rihk) **VAN**

Center. Shoots left. 6'2", 188 lbs. Born, Ornskoldsvik, Sweden, September 26, 1980. Vancouver's 2nd pick, 3rd overall, in 1999 NHL Draft.

Season	Club	League	GP	G	A	Pts	PIM	PP	SH	GW	S	S%	+/-	TF	F%	Min	GP	G	A	Pts	PIM	PP	SH	GW	Min
1997-98	Malmo Jr.	Swe-Jr.	8	4	7	11	6	....	....	....	....	....	....	....	....	....	....	....	....	....	....	....	....	....	....
	MoDo Jr.	Swe-Jr.	26	14	22	36	....	....	....	....	....	....	....	....	....	....	....	....	....	....	....	....	....	....	....
	MoDo	Sweden	39	1	4	5	8	....	....	....	....	....	....	....	....	....	7	0	0	0	0	....	....	....	....
1998-99	MoDo	Sweden	49	12	22	34	32	....	....	....	....	....	....	....	....	....	13	2	8	10	6	....	....	....	....
99-2000	MoDo	Sweden	50	9	38	47	22	....	....	....	....	....	....	....	....	....	13	5	9	14	2	....	....	....	....
2000-01	**Vancouver**	**NHL**	82	9	20	29	38	2	0	1	98	9.2	–2	1020	44.1	13:31	4	0	4	4	0	0	0	0	16:31
2001-02	**Vancouver**	**NHL**	82	16	20	36	36	3	0	1	78	20.5	9	785	47.4	12:48	6	3	0	3	0	0	0	1	11:55
2002-03	**Vancouver**	**NHL**	78	8	31	39	38	4	1	1	81	9.9	9	995	48.2	13:58	14	3	2	5	8	1	0	0	13:01
2003-04	**Vancouver**	**NHL**	76	11	31	42	32	2	0	2	99	11.1	23	961	50.0	14:02	7	2	2	4	2	2	0	0	16:02
2004-05	MODO	Sweden	44	14	22	36	50	....	....	....	....	....	....	....	....	....	6	1	3	4	6	....	....	....	....
2005-06	**Vancouver**	**NHL**	82	18	57	75	56	5	1	0	113	15.9	11	1238	50.7	16:54	....	....	....	....	....	....	....	....	....
	Sweden	Olympics	8	3	1	4	2	....	....	....	....	....	....	....	....	....	....	....	....	....	....	....	....	....	....
2006-07	**Vancouver**	**NHL**	82	10	71	81	66	1	0	2	134	7.5	19	1220	52.5	18:26	12	2	2	4	14	1	0	1	22:12
2007-08	**Vancouver**	**NHL**	82	15	61	76	56	4	1	2	141	10.6	6	1369	47.0	19:31	....	....	....	....	....	....	....	....	....
2008-09	**Vancouver**	**NHL**	82	22	60	82	48	4	0	8	143	15.4	22	1364	49.6	19:31	10	4	6	10	2	1	0	0	20:07
2009-10	**Vancouver**	**NHL**	82	29	*83	*112	48	4	2	5	166	17.5	35	1527	49.5	19:41	12	3	11	14	6	0	0	1	20:38
	Sweden	Olympics	4	0	2	2	2	....	....	....	....	....	....	....	....	....	....	....	....	....	....	....	....	....	....
2010-11	**Vancouver**	**NHL**	82	19	*75	94	40	8	0	4	157	12.1	26	1387	52.0	19:16	25	3	*19	22	16	2	0	1	20:56
2011-12	**Vancouver**	**NHL**	82	14	*67	81	52	8	0	6	113	12.4	23	1302	50.1	19:05	5	2	3	5	4	2	0	0	21:21
2012-13	**Vancouver**	**NHL**	48	11	34	45	24	1	1	1	70	15.7	19	891	49.4	19:21	4	0	3	3	4	0	0	0	20:45
2013-14	**Vancouver**	**NHL**	70	11	39	50	42	4	0	1	97	11.3	3	1097	52.3	20:40	....	....	....	....	....	....	....	....	....
2014-15	**Vancouver**	**NHL**	82	18	55	73	22	5	0	0	101	17.8	11	1565	45.0	18:37	6	1	3	4	2	1	0	0	18:50
2015-16	**Vancouver**	**NHL**	74	11	44	55	24	5	1	0	99	11.1	0	1347	46.0	18:23	....	....	....	....	....	....	....	....	....
2016-17	**Vancouver**	**NHL**	82	15	35	50	28	1	0	4	99	15.2	–27	1246	49.0	19:02	....	....	....	....	....	....	....	....	....
	NHL Totals		1248	237	783	1020	650	61	7	38	1789	13.2		19314	48.9	17:38	105	23	55	78	58	10	0	4	18:48

NHL First All-Star Team (2010, 2011) • Art Ross Trophy (2010) • Hart Memorial Trophy (2010) • King Clancy Memorial Trophy (2016)
Played in NHL All-Star Game (2008, 2011, 2012)
Signed as a free agent by **MODO** (Sweden), September 18, 2004.

SEDLAK, Lukas
(SEHD-lak, LOO-kuhsh) **CBJ**

Center. Shoots left. 6', 213 lbs. Born, Ceske Budejovice, Czech Rep., February 25, 1993. Columbus' 5th pick, 158th overall, in 2011 NHL Draft.

Season	Club	League	GP	G	A	Pts	PIM	PP	SH	GW	S	S%	+/-	TF	F%	Min	GP	G	A	Pts	PIM	PP	SH	GW	Min
2007-08	C. Budejovice U17	CzR-U17	6	0	2	2	4	....	....	....	....	....	....	....	....	....	2	0	0	0	2	....	....	....	....
2008-09	C. Budejovice U17	CzR-U17	44	12	17	29	14	....	....	....	....	....	....	....	....	....	4	0	0	0	4	....	....	....	....
2009-10	C. Budejovice U18	CzR-U18	37	29	27	56	76	....	....	....	....	....	....	....	....	....	4	5	1	6	39	....	....	....	....
	C. Budejovice Jr.	CzRep-Jr.	11	4	8	12	4	....	....	....	....	....	....	....	....	....	....	....	....	....	....	....	....	....	....
2010-11	C. Budejovice Jr.	CzRep-Jr.	47	14	13	27	65	....	....	....	....	....	....	....	....	....	....	....	....	....	....	....	....	....	....
	C. Budejovice U18	CzR-U18	....	....	....	....	....	....	....	....	....	....	....	....	....	....	1	0	1	1	0	....	....	....	....
2011-12	Chicoutimi	QMJHL	50	17	28	45	57	....	....	....	....	....	....	....	....	....	18	5	3	8	18	....	....	....	....
2012-13	Chicoutimi	QMJHL	48	15	19	34	64	....	....	....	....	....	....	....	....	....	6	1	4	5	8	....	....	....	....
2013-14	Springfield	AHL	54	8	6	14	26	....	....	....	....	....	....	....	....	....	4	0	1	1	0	....	....	....	....
2014-15	Springfield	AHL	51	6	10	16	30	....	....	....	....	....	....	....	....	....	....	....	....	....	....	....	....	....	....
2015-16	Lake Erie	AHL	54	14	4	18	27	....	....	....	....	....	....	....	....	....	17	9	7	16	18	....	....	....	....
2016-17	**Columbus**	**NHL**	62	7	6	13	25	0	1	0	57	12.3	10	443	52.4	9:43	2	0	0	0	0	0	0	0	8:16
	NHL Totals		62	7	6	13	25	0	1	0	57	12.3		443	52.4	9:43	2	0	0	0	0	0	0	0	8:16

SEGUIN, Tyler
(SAY-gihn, TIGH-luhr) **DAL**

Center. Shoots right. 6'1", 200 lbs. Born, Brampton, ON, January 31, 1992. Boston's 1st pick, 2nd overall, in 2010 NHL Draft.

Season	Club	League	GP	G	A	Pts	PIM	PP	SH	GW	S	S%	+/-	TF	F%	Min	GP	G	A	Pts	PIM	PP	SH	GW	Min
2007-08	Tor. Young Nats	GTHL	51	39	47	86	56	....	....	....	....	....	....	....	....	....	....	....	....	....	....	....	....	....	....
2008-09	Plymouth Whalers	OHL	61	21	46	67	28	....	....	....	....	....	....	....	....	....	11	5	11	16	8	....	....	....	....
2009-10	Plymouth Whalers	OHL	63	48	58	*106	54	....	....	....	....	....	....	....	....	....	9	5	5	10	8	....	....	....	....
2010-11 ♦	**Boston**	**NHL**	74	11	11	22	18	1	0	0	131	8.4	–4	303	49.5	12:13	13	3	4	7	2	0	0	0	10:35
2011-12	**Boston**	**NHL**	81	29	38	67	30	5	0	7	242	12.0	34	106	43.4	16:56	7	2	1	3	0	0	0	1	18:14
2012-13	EHC Biel-Bienne	Swiss	29	25	15	40	24	....	....	....	....	....	....	....	....	....	....	....	....	....	....	....	....	....	....
	Boston	**NHL**	48	16	16	32	16	4	0	2	161	9.9	23	45	48.9	17:01	22	1	7	8	4	0	0	0	16:03
2013-14	**Dallas**	**NHL**	80	37	47	84	18	11	0	8	294	12.6	16	677	41.5	19:21	6	1	2	3	0	0	0	0	19:57
2014-15	**Dallas**	**NHL**	71	37	40	77	20	13	0	5	280	13.2	–1	511	53.8	19:33	....	....	....	....	....	....	....	....	....
2015-16	**Dallas**	**NHL**	72	33	40	73	16	7	0	6	278	11.9	2	846	55.6	19:27	1	0	0	0	0	0	0	0	15:40
2016-17	**Dallas**	**NHL**	82	26	46	72	22	11	0	4	301	8.6	–15	786	51.0	18:28	....	....	....	....	....	....	....	....	....
	NHL Totals		508	189	238	427	140	52	0	32	1687	11.2		3274	50.2	17:36	49	7	14	21	6	0	0	1	15:23

OHL First All-Star Team (2010) • OHL Player of the Year (2010) • Canadian Major Junior First All-Star Team (2010)
Played in NHL All-Star Game (2012, 2015, 2016, 2017)
Signed as a free agent by **Biel-Bienne** (Swiss), September 20, 2012. Traded to **Dallas** by **Boston** with Rich Peverley and Ryan Button for Loui Eriksson, Joe Morrow, Reilly Smith and Matt Fraser, July 4, 2013.

SEIDENBERG, Dennis
(SIGH-dehn-buhrg, DEH-nihs) **NYI**

Defense. Shoots left. 6', 198 lbs. Born, Schwenningen, West Germany, July 18, 1981. Philadelphia's 6th pick, 172nd overall, in 2001 NHL Draft.

Season	Club	League	GP	G	A	Pts	PIM	PP	SH	GW	S	S%	+/-	TF	F%	Min	GP	G	A	Pts	PIM	PP	SH	GW	Min
			Regular Season														Playoffs								
99-2000	Mannheim Jr.	Ger-Jr.	52	12	28	40	28	....	....	....	....	....	....	....	....	....	....	....	....	....	....	....	....	....	....
	Adler Mannheim	Germany	3	0	0	0	0	....	....	....	....	....	....	....	....	....	....	....	....	....	....	....	....	....	....
2000-01	Mannheim Jr.	Ger-Jr.	9	3	8	11	20	....	....	....	....	....	....	....	....	....	....	....	....	....	....	....	....	....	....
	Adler Mannheim	Germany	55	2	5	7	6	....	....	....	....	....	....	....	....	....	12	0	1	1	10	....	....	....	....
2001-02	Adler Mannheim	Germany	55	7	13	20	56	....	....	....	....	....	....	....	....	....	8	0	0	0	2	....	....	....	....
2002-03	**Philadelphia**	**NHL**	**58**	**4**	**9**	**13**	**20**	**1**	**0**	**0**	**123**	**3.3**	**8**	**1**	**0.0**	**16:50**	....	....	....	....	....	....	....	....	....
	Philadelphia	AHL	19	5	6	11	17	....	....	....	....	....	....	....	....	....	....	....	....	....	....	....	....	....	....
2003-04	**Philadelphia**	**NHL**	**5**	**0**	**0**	**0**	**2**	**0**	**0**	**0**	**14**	**0.0**	**-4**	**0**	**0.0**	**17:20**	**3**	**0**	**0**	**0**	**0**	**0**	**0**	**0**	**7:36**
	Philadelphia	AHL	33	7	12	19	31	....	....	....	....	....	....	....	....	....	9	2	2	4	4	....	....	....	....
2004-05	Philadelphia	AHL	79	13	28	41	47	....	....	....	....	....	....	....	....	....	18	2	8	10	19	....	....	....	....
2005-06	**Philadelphia**	**NHL**	**29**	**2**	**5**	**7**	**4**	**1**	**0**	**0**	**34**	**5.9**	**-4**	**1**	**0.0**	**14:22**	....	....	....	....	....	....	....	....	....
	Phoenix	**NHL**	**34**	**1**	**10**	**11**	**14**	**1**	**0**	**0**	**49**	**2.0**	**-9**	**0**	**0.0**	**19:13**	....	....	....	....	....	....	....	....	....
	Germany	Olympics	5	0	0	0	6	....	....	....	....	....	....	....	....	....	....	....	....	....	....	....	....	....	....
2006-07	**Phoenix**	**NHL**	**32**	**1**	**1**	**2**	**16**	**0**	**0**	**0**	**36**	**2.8**	**-4**	**0**	**0.0**	**14:43**	....	....	....	....	....	....	....	....	....
	Carolina	**NHL**	**20**	**1**	**5**	**6**	**2**	**0**	**0**	**0**	**47**	**2.1**	**-12**	**0**	**0.0**	**18:29**	....	....	....	....	....	....	....	....	....
2007-08	**Carolina**	**NHL**	**47**	**0**	**15**	**15**	**18**	**0**	**0**	**0**	**80**	**0.0**	**6**	**1**	**100.0**	**18:50**	....	....	....	....	....	....	....	....	....
2008-09	**Carolina**	**NHL**	**70**	**5**	**25**	**30**	**37**	**2**	**0**	**1**	**129**	**3.9**	**-9**	**0**	**0.0**	**22:20**	**16**	**1**	**5**	**6**	**16**	**0**	**0**	**0**	**22:25**
2009-10	**Florida**	**NHL**	**62**	**2**	**21**	**23**	**33**	**1**	**0**	**0**	**116**	**1.7**	**-3**	**1**	**0.0**	**22:55**	....	....	....	....	....	....	....	....	....
	Boston	**NHL**	**17**	**2**	**7**	**9**	**6**	**1**	**0**	**1**	**37**	**5.4**	**9**	**0**	**0.0**	**22:57**	....	....	....	....	....	....	....	....	....
	Germany	Olympics	4	1	0	1	2	....	....	....	....	....	....	....	....	....	....	....	....	....	....	....	....	....	....
2010-11♦	**Boston**	**NHL**	**81**	**7**	**25**	**32**	**41**	**1**	**0**	**2**	**166**	**4.2**	**3**	**0**	**0.0**	**23:33**	**25**	**1**	**10**	**11**	**31**	**0**	**0**	**0**	**27:37**
2011-12	**Boston**	**NHL**	**80**	**5**	**18**	**23**	**39**	**0**	**0**	**2**	**174**	**2.9**	**15**	**0**	**0.0**	**24:02**	**7**	**1**	**2**	**3**	**2**	**0**	**0**	**0**	**26:43**
2012-13	Adler Mannheim	Germany	26	2	18	20	20	....	....	....	....	....	....	....	....	....	....	....	....	....	....	....	....	....	....
	Boston	**NHL**	**46**	**4**	**13**	**17**	**10**	**0**	**0**	**2**	**83**	**4.8**	**18**	**0**	**0.0**	**23:48**	**18**	**0**	**1**	**1**	**4**	**0**	**0**	**0**	**25:59**
2013-14	**Boston**	**NHL**	**34**	**1**	**9**	**10**	**10**	**0**	**0**	**0**	**53**	**1.9**	**11**	**0**	**0.0**	**21:50**	....	....	....	....	....	....	....	....	....
2014-15	**Boston**	**NHL**	**82**	**3**	**11**	**14**	**34**	**0**	**0**	**0**	**103**	**2.9**	**-1**	**0**	**0.0**	**22:06**	....	....	....	....	....	....	....	....	....
2015-16	**Boston**	**NHL**	**61**	**1**	**11**	**12**	**24**	**0**	**0**	**0**	**66**	**1.5**	**-1**	**0**	**0.0**	**19:24**	....	....	....	....	....	....	....	....	....
2016-17	**NY Islanders**	**NHL**	**73**	**5**	**17**	**22**	**32**	**0**	**0**	**0**	**89**	**5.6**	**25**	**0**	**0.0**	**19:26**	....	....	....	....	....	....	....	....	....
	NHL Totals		**831**	**44**	**202**	**246**	**342**	**8**	**0**	**8**	**1399**	**3.1**		**4**	**25.0**	**20:50**	**69**	**3**	**18**	**21**	**53**	**0**	**0**	**0**	**25:02**

• Missed majority of 2003-04 due to leg injury vs. Edmonton, January 10, 2004. Traded to **Phoenix** by **Philadelphia** with Philadelphia's 4th round pick (later traded to NY Islanders - NY Islanders selected Tomas Marcinko) in 2006 NHL Draft for Petr Nedved and Phoenix's 4th round pick (Joonas Lehtivuori) in 2006 NHL Draft, January 20, 2006. Traded to **Carolina** by **Phoenix** for Kevyn Adams, January 8, 2007. Signed as a free agent by **Florida**, September 14, 2009. Traded to **Boston** by **Florida** with Matt Bartkowski for Byron Bitz, Craig Weller and Tampa Bay's 2nd round pick (previously acquired, Florida selected Alexander Petrovic) in 2010 NHL Draft, March 3, 2010. Signed as a free agent by **Mannheim** (Germany), September 21, 2012. • Missed majority of 2013-14 due to knee (December 27, 2013 vs. Ottawa) and lower-body (January 17, 2014 at Chicago) injuries. Signed as a free agent by **NY Islanders**, September 28, 2016.

SEKERA, Andrej
(seh-KAIR-ah, AWN-dray) **EDM**

Defense. Shoots left. 6', 198 lbs. Born, Bojnice, Czech., June 8, 1986. Buffalo's 3rd pick, 71st overall, in 2004 NHL Draft.

Season	Club	League	GP	G	A	Pts	PIM	PP	SH	GW	S	S%	+/-	TF	F%	Min	GP	G	A	Pts	PIM	PP	SH	GW	Min
			Regular Season														Playoffs								
2001-02	Dukla Trencin Jr.	Slovak-Jr.	52	5	10	15	10	....	....	....	....	....	....	....	....	....	....	....	....	....	....	....	....	....	....
2002-03	Dukla Trencin Jr.	Slovak-Jr.	48	9	15	24	20	....	....	....	....	....	....	....	....	....	....	....	....	....	....	....	....	....	....
2003-04	Dukla Trencin Jr.	Slovak-Jr.	42	5	12	17	40	....	....	....	....	....	....	....	....	....	2	0	1	1	4	....	....	....	....
	Dukla Trencin	Slovakia	3	0	0	0	2	....	....	....	....	....	....	....	....	....	....	....	....	....	....	....	....	....	....
	Dukla Trencin U18	Svk-U18	5	0	0	0	0	....	....	....	....	....	....	....	....	....	....	....	....	....	....	....	....	....	....
2004-05	Owen Sound	OHL	51	7	21	28	18	....	....	....	....	....	....	....	....	....	6	0	4	4	4	....	....	....	....
2005-06	Owen Sound	OHL	51	21	34	55	54	....	....	....	....	....	....	....	....	....	11	5	8	13	9	....	....	....	....
2006-07	**Buffalo**	**NHL**	**2**	**0**	**0**	**0**	**2**	**0**	**0**	**0**	**0**	**0.0**	**1**	**0**	**0.0**	**7:31**	....	....	....	....	....	....	....	....	....
	Rochester	AHL	54	3	16	19	28	....	....	....	....	....	....	....	....	....	....	....	....	....	....	....	....	....	....
2007-08	**Buffalo**	**NHL**	**37**	**2**	**6**	**8**	**16**	**0**	**0**	**1**	**28**	**7.1**	**5**	**0**	**0.0**	**19:37**	....	....	....	....	....	....	....	....	....
	Rochester	AHL	40	2	15	17	22	....	....	....	....	....	....	....	....	....	....	....	....	....	....	....	....	....	....
2008-09	**Buffalo**	**NHL**	**69**	**3**	**16**	**19**	**22**	**1**	**0**	**1**	**84**	**3.6**	**-11**	**1**	**0.0**	**20:42**	....	....	....	....	....	....	....	....	....
2009-10	**Buffalo**	**NHL**	**49**	**4**	**7**	**11**	**6**	**0**	**0**	**0**	**59**	**6.8**	**-1**	**1**	**0.0**	**17:27**	**6**	**0**	**0**	**0**	**7**	**0**	**0**	**0**	**13:55**
	Slovakia	Olympics	7	1	0	1	0	....	....	....	....	....	....	....	....	....	....	....	....	....	....	....	....	....	....
2010-11	**Buffalo**	**NHL**	**76**	**3**	**26**	**29**	**34**	**0**	**0**	**0**	**88**	**3.4**	**11**	**0**	**0.0**	**21:06**	**2**	**1**	**0**	**1**	**4**	**0**	**0**	**0**	**16:18**
2011-12	**Buffalo**	**NHL**	**69**	**3**	**10**	**13**	**18**	**1**	**0**	**0**	**88**	**3.4**	**3**	**1**	**0.0**	**19:36**	....	....	....	....	....	....	....	....	....
2012-13	Bratislava	KHL	25	3	9	12	8	....	....	....	....	....	....	....	....	....	....	....	....	....	....	....	....	....	....
	Buffalo	**NHL**	**37**	**2**	**10**	**12**	**4**	**0**	**0**	**0**	**33**	**6.1**	**-2**	**0**	**0.0**	**21:12**	....	....	....	....	....	....	....	....	....
2013-14	**Carolina**	**NHL**	**74**	**11**	**33**	**44**	**20**	**4**	**1**	**1**	**142**	**7.7**	**4**	**0**	**0.0**	**23:41**	....	....	....	....	....	....	....	....	....
	Slovakia	Olympics	4	0	2	2	0	....	....	....	....	....	....	....	....	....	....	....	....	....	....	....	....	....	....
2014-15	**Carolina**	**NHL**	**57**	**2**	**17**	**19**	**8**	**1**	**0**	**0**	**77**	**2.6**	**-7**	**0**	**0.0**	**22:46**	....	....	....	....	....	....	....	....	....
	Los Angeles	**NHL**	**16**	**1**	**3**	**4**	**6**	**0**	**0**	**0**	**23**	**4.3**	**4**	**0**	**0.0**	**19:13**	....	....	....	....	....	....	....	....	....
2015-16	**Edmonton**	**NHL**	**81**	**6**	**24**	**30**	**12**	**2**	**0**	**2**	**155**	**3.9**	**-15**	**0**	**0.0**	**21:50**	....	....	....	....	....	....	....	....	....
2016-17	**Edmonton**	**NHL**	**80**	**8**	**27**	**35**	**18**	**1**	**1**	**1**	**128**	**6.3**	**14**	**0**	**0.0**	**21:29**	**11**	**1**	**2**	**3**	**2**	**0**	**0**	**0**	**21:10**
	NHL Totals		**647**	**45**	**179**	**224**	**166**	**10**	**2**	**6**	**905**	**5.0**		**3**	**0.0**	**21:02**	**19**	**2**	**2**	**4**	**13**	**0**	**0**	**0**	**18:22**

OHL All-Rookie Team (2005) • OHL First All-Star Team (2006)

Signed as a free agent by **Bratislava** (KHL), September 27, 2012. Traded to **Carolina** by **Buffalo** for Jamie McBain and Carolina's 2nd round pick (J.T. Compher) in 2013 NHL Draft, June 30, 2013. Traded to **Los Angeles** by **Carolina** for Roland McKeown and Los Angeles' 1st round pick (Julien Gauthier) in 2016 NHL Draft, February 25, 2015. Signed as a free agent by **Edmonton**, July 1, 2015.

SELLECK, Eric
(SEHL-ehk, AIR-ihk)

Left wing. Shoots left. 6'2", 208 lbs. Born, Spencerville, ON, October 20, 1987.

Season	Club	League	GP	G	A	Pts	PIM	PP	SH	GW	S	S%	+/-	TF	F%	Min	GP	G	A	Pts	PIM	PP	SH	GW	Min
			Regular Season														Playoffs								
2006-07	Pembroke	ON-Jr.A	53	23	24	47	137	....	....	....	....	....	....	....	....	....	15	4	8	12	29	....	....	....	....
2007-08	Pembroke	ON-Jr.A	49	43	38	81	120	....	....	....	....	....	....	....	....	....	14	8	21	29	28	....	....	....	....
2008-09	Oswego State	NCAA-3	26	13	13	26	45	....	....	....	....	....	....	....	....	....	....	....	....	....	....	....	....	....	....
2009-10	Oswego State	NCAA-3	28	21	33	54	48	....	....	....	....	....	....	....	....	....	....	....	....	....	....	....	....	....	....
2010-11	Rochester	AHL	67	5	11	16	214	....	....	....	....	....	....	....	....	....	....	....	....	....	....	....	....	....	....
2011-12	San Antonio	AHL	71	5	4	9	204	....	....	....	....	....	....	....	....	....	9	0	0	0	4	....	....	....	....
2012-13	San Antonio	AHL	60	5	11	16	181	....	....	....	....	....	....	....	....	....	....	....	....	....	....	....	....	....	....
	Florida	**NHL**	**2**	**0**	**1**	**1**	**17**	**0**	**0**	**0**	**2**	**0.0**	**2**	**0**	**0.0**	**7:55**	....	....	....	....	....	....	....	....	....
2013-14	San Antonio	AHL	42	3	4	7	93	....	....	....	....	....	....	....	....	....	....	....	....	....	....	....	....	....	....
	Chicago Wolves	AHL	18	3	2	5	70	....	....	....	....	....	....	....	....	....	9	0	1	1	17	....	....	....	....
2014-15	Portland Pirates	AHL	74	8	15	23	185	....	....	....	....	....	....	....	....	....	5	1	1	2	8	....	....	....	....
2015-16	**Arizona**	**NHL**	**1**	**0**	**0**	**0**	**5**	**0**	**0**	**0**	**1**	**0.0**	**0**	**0**	**0.0**	**9:33**	....	....	....	....	....	....	....	....	....
	Springfield	AHL	60	10	12	22	137	....	....	....	....	....	....	....	....	....	....	....	....	....	....	....	....	....	....
2016-17	Tucson	AHL	46	5	4	9	103	....	....	....	....	....	....	....	....	....	....	....	....	....	....	....	....	....	....
	NHL Totals		**3**	**0**	**1**	**1**	**22**	**0**	**0**	**0**	**3**	**0.0**		**0**	**0.0**	**8:28**	....	....	....	....	....	....	....	....	....

SUNYAC (NCAA-3) Rookie of the Year (2009) • SUNYAC (NCAA-3) Player of the Year (2010) • NCAA-3 East All-American Team (2010)

Signed as a free agent by **Florida**, April 21, 2010. Traded to **St. Louis** by **Florida** for Mark Mancari, March 2, 2014. Signed as a free agent by **Arizona**, July 3, 2015.

SERGACHEV, Mikhail
(sair-ga-CHEHV, mih-KIGH-ehl) **T.B.**

Defense. Shoots left. 6'3", 223 lbs. Born, Nizhnekamsk, Russia, June 25, 1998. Montreal's 1st pick, 9th overall, in 2016 NHL Draft.

Season	Club	League	GP	G	A	Pts	PIM	PP	SH	GW	S	S%	+/-	TF	F%	Min	GP	G	A	Pts	PIM	PP	SH	GW	Min
			Regular Season														Playoffs								
2014-15	Irbis Kazan Jr.	Russia-Jr.	25	2	6	8	18	....	....	....	....	....	....	....	....	....	2	0	0	0	0	....	....	....	....
2015-16	Windsor Spitfires	OHL	67	17	40	57	56	....	....	....	....	....	....	....	....	....	5	2	3	5	8	....	....	....	....
2016-17	**Montreal**	**NHL**	**4**	**0**	**0**	**0**	**0**	**0**	**0**	**0**	**2**	**0.0**	**1**	**0**	**0.0**	**12:08**	....	....	....	....	....	....	....	....	....
	Windsor Spitfires	OHL	50	10	34	44	71	....	....	....	....	....	....	....	....	....	7	1	2	3	10	....	....	....	....
	NHL Totals		**4**	**0**	**0**	**0**	**0**	**0**	**0**	**0**	**2**	**0.0**		**0**	**0.0**	**12:08**	....	....	....	....	....	....	....	....	....

OHL First All-Star Team (2016) • OHL Second All-Star Team (2017)

Traded to **Tampa Bay** by **Montreal** with a conditional 2nd round pick in 2018 NHL Draft for Jonathan Drouin and a conditional 6th round pick in 2018 NHL Draft, June 15, 2017.

			Regular Season															Playoffs							
Season	Club	League	GP	G	A	Pts	PIM	PP	SH	GW	S	S%	+/-	TF	F%	Min	GP	G	A	Pts	PIM	PP	SH	GW	Min

SESTITO, Tom

(sehs-TEE-toh, TAWM)   **PIT**

Left wing. Shoots left. 6'5", 228 lbs.   Born, Rome, NY, September 28, 1987. Columbus' 3rd pick, 85th overall, in 2006 NHL Draft.

Season	Club	League	GP	G	A	Pts	PIM	PP	SH	GW	S	S%	+/-	TF	F%	Min	GP	G	A	Pts	PIM	PP	SH	GW	Min
2003-04	Syracuse Jr. Stars	EmJHL	31	13	16	29	137										6	5	6	11	32				
2004-05	Plymouth Whalers	OHL	35	1	3	4	88																		
2005-06	Plymouth Whalers	OHL	57	10	10	20	176										13	5	2	7	29				
2006-07	Plymouth Whalers	OHL	60	42	22	64	135										19	11	6	17	57				
2007-08	**Columbus**	**NHL**	1	0	0	0	17	0	0	0	0	0.0	0	0	0.0	4:36									
	Syracuse Crunch	AHL	66	7	16	23	202										9	3	0	3	57				
2008-09	Syracuse Crunch	AHL	52	8	12	20	168																		
2009-10	**Columbus**	**NHL**	3	0	0	0	7	0	0	0	0	0.0	0	0	0.0	5:34									
	Syracuse Crunch	AHL	36	10	7	17	138																		
2010-11	**Columbus**	**NHL**	9	2	2	4	40	1	0	0	7	28.6	-4		1100.0	9:32									
	Springfield	AHL	46	11	21	32	192																		
	Adirondack	AHL	11	2	1	3	45																		
2011-12	**Philadelphia**	**NHL**	14	0	1	1	83	0	0	0	4	0.0	-3	4	50.0	6:54									
	Adirondack	AHL	34	9	8	17	120																		
2012-13	Sheffield Steelers	Britain	17	8	11	19	69																		
	Philadelphia	**NHL**	7	2	0	2	12	0	0	1	3	66.7	1		1100.0	5:46									
	Adirondack	AHL	1	0	0	0	2																		
	Vancouver	**NHL**	23	1	0	1	53	0	0	0	11	9.1	-3	1	0.0	6:38	1	0	0	0	2	0	0	0	5:51
2013-14	**Vancouver**	**NHL**	77	5	4	9	*213	1	0	0	31	16.1	-14	11	27.3	6:27									
2014-15	**Vancouver**	**NHL**	3	0	1	1	7	0	0	0	1	0.0	1	0	0.0	6:14									
	Utica Comets	AHL	10	1	0	1	20																		
2015-16	**Pittsburgh**	**NHL**	4	0	1	1	19	0	0	0	1	0.0	1	0	0.0	5:48									
	Wilkes-Barre	AHL	41	5	9	14	104										7	1	3	4	52				
2016-17	**Pittsburgh**	**NHL**	13	0	2	2	48	0	0	0	3	0.0	0	0	0.0	5:32									
	Wilkes-Barre	AHL	33	6	10	16	121										5	1	0	1	13				
	NHL Totals		**154**	**10**	**11**	**21**	**499**	**2**	**0**	**1**	**61**	**16.4**		**18**	**38.9**	**6:33**	**1**	**0**	**0**	**0**	**2**	**0**	**0**	**0**	**5:51**

Traded to **Philadelphia** by **Columbus** for Michael Chaput and Greg Moore, February 28, 2011. Signed as a free agent by **Sheffield** (Britain), October 8, 2012. Claimed on waivers by **Vancouver** from **Philadelphia**, March 1, 2013. • Missed majority of 2014-15 due to leg injury vs. Nashville, November 2, 2014 and as a healthy reserve. Signed to a PTO (professional tryout) contact by **Pittsburgh**, August 22, 2015. Signed as a free agent by **Pittsburgh**, February 16, 2016.

SETOGUCHI, Devin

(SEHT-oh-GOO-chee, DEH-vihn)

Right wing. Shoots right. 6'", 205 lbs.   Born, Taber, AB, January 1, 1987. San Jose's 1st pick, 8th overall, in 2005 NHL Draft.

Season	Club	League	GP	G	A	Pts	PIM	PP	SH	GW	S	S%	+/-	TF	F%	Min	GP	G	A	Pts	PIM	PP	SH	GW	Min
2003-04	Saskatoon Blades	WHL	66	13	18	31	53																		
2004-05	Saskatoon Blades	WHL	69	33	31	64	34										4	0	1	1	0				
2005-06	Saskatoon Blades	WHL	65	36	47	83	69										10	8	4	12	8				
2006-07	Prince George	WHL	55	36	29	65	55										15	*11	10	21	24				
2007-08	**San Jose**	**NHL**	44	11	6	17	8	3	0	2	105	10.5	6	17	64.7	14:15	9	1	1	2	2	0	0	0	10:25
	Worcester Sharks	AHL	23	8	11	19	25																		
2008-09	**San Jose**	**NHL**	81	31	34	65	25	11	0	3	246	12.6	16	21	28.6	16:13	6	1	2	3	2	0	0	0	16:21
2009-10	**San Jose**	**NHL**	70	20	16	36	19	8	0	4	165	12.1	0	10	30.0	15:18	15	5	4	9	6	1	0	1	18:25
2010-11	**San Jose**	**NHL**	72	22	19	41	37	4	0	5	199	11.1	22	11	45.5	15:12	18	7	3	10	12	3	0	2	17:26
2011-12	**Minnesota**	**NHL**	69	19	17	36	28	7	0	2	174	10.9	-17	11	27.3	17:36									
2012-13	Ontario Reign	ECHL	10	4	9	13	2																		
	Minnesota	**NHL**	48	13	14	27	20	5	0	3	97	13.4	5	17	41.2	14:26	5	1	0	1	0	0	0	0	16:04
2013-14	**Winnipeg**	**NHL**	75	11	16	27	22	2	0	3	129	8.5	-7	20	25.0	15:03									
2014-15	**Calgary**	**NHL**	12	0	0	0	4	0	0	0	12	0.0	-7	2	50.0	12:09									
	Adirondack	AHL	19	3	7	10	4																		
2015-16	HC Davos	Swiss	30	11	13	24	2										7	5	3	8	10				
2016-17	**Los Angeles**	**NHL**	45	4	8	12	14	0	0	0	60	6.7	-5	4	50.0	12:27									
	Ontario Reign	AHL	9	0	3	3	10																		
	NHL Totals		**516**	**131**	**130**	**261**	**177**	**40**	**0**	**22**	**1187**	**11.0**		**113**	**38.1**	**15:13**	**53**	**15**	**10**	**25**	**22**	**4**	**0**	**3**	**16:16**

WHL East Second All-Star Team (2006)

Traded to **Minnesota** by **San Jose** with Charlie Coyle and San Jose's 1st round pick (Zack Phillips) in 2011 NHL Draft for Brent Burns and Minnesota's 2nd round pick (later traded to Tampa Bay – later traded to Nashville – Nashville selected Pontius Aberg) in 2012 NHL Draft, June 24, 2011. Signed as a free agent by **Ontario** (ECHL), October 30, 2012. Traded to **Winnipeg** by **Minnesota** for Winnipeg's 2nd round pick (later traded to Buffalo, later traded to Washington – Washington selected Vitak Vanecek) in 2014 NHL Draft, July 5, 2013. Signed as a free agent by **Calgary**, August 23, 2014. • Missed majority of 2014-15 due to upper-body injury at Florida, November 8, 2014. Signed as a free agent by **Davos** (Swiss), October 6, 2015. Signed as a free agent by **Ambri-Piotta** (Swiss), May 9, 2016. Signed as a free agent by **Los Angeles**, October 11, 2016.

SEVERSON, Damon

(SEE-vuhr-suhn, DAY-muhn)   **N.J.**

Defense. Shoots right. 6'2", 205 lbs.   Born, Melville, SK, August 7, 1994. New Jersey's 2nd pick, 60th overall, in 2012 NHL Draft.

Season	Club	League	GP	G	A	Pts	PIM	PP	SH	GW	S	S%	+/-	TF	F%	Min	GP	G	A	Pts	PIM	PP	SH	GW	Min
2009-10	Yorkton Harvest	SMHL	44	9	25	34	53										4	1	1	2	18				
	Melville	SJHL	1	0	1	1	2																		
	Kelowna Rockets	WHL	5	0	0	0	0																		
2010-11	Kelowna Rockets	WHL	64	4	13	17	53										10	2	0	2	13				
2011-12	Kelowna Rockets	WHL	56	7	30	37	80										4	2	0	2	2				
2012-13	Kelowna Rockets	WHL	71	10	42	52	74										11	1	9	10	18				
	Albany Devils	AHL	2	0	2	2	0																		
2013-14	Kelowna Rockets	WHL	64	15	46	61	63										14	4	14	18	18				
2014-15	**New Jersey**	**NHL**	51	5	12	17	22	0	0	0	93	5.4	-13	1	0.0	21:58									
2015-16	**New Jersey**	**NHL**	72	1	20	21	32	0	0	0	94	1.1	-8	0	0.0	18:10									
	Albany Devils	AHL	3	0	1	1	9										11	0	8	8	14				
2016-17	**New Jersey**	**NHL**	80	3	28	31	58	0	0	1	125	2.4	-31	0	0.0	20:21									
	NHL Totals		**203**	**9**	**60**	**69**	**112**	**0**	**0**	**1**	**312**	**2.9**		**1**	**0.0**	**19:59**									

WHL West Second All-Star Team (2014)

SGARBOSSA, Michael

(s'gahr-BOH-suh, MIGH-kuhl)   **WPG**

Center. Shoots left. 6', 186 lbs.   Born, Campbellville, ON, July 25, 1992.

Season	Club	League	GP	G	A	Pts	PIM	PP	SH	GW	S	S%	+/-	TF	F%	Min	GP	G	A	Pts	PIM	PP	SH	GW	Min
2008-09	Barrie Colts	OHL	67	10	33	43	43										5	3	3	6	10				
2009-10	Barrie Colts	OHL	19	7	13	20	14										6	0	2	2	4				
	Saginaw Spirit	OHL	48	13	19	32	49																		
2010-11	Saginaw Spirit	OHL	26	7	13	20	24																		
	Sudbury Wolves	OHL	37	29	33	62	53										8	5	9	14	16				
2011-12	Sudbury Wolves	OHL	66	47	55	*102	68										4	2	1	3	6				
2012-13	Lake Erie	AHL	57	19	25	44	71																		
	Colorado	**NHL**	6	0	0	0	4	0	0	0	6	0.0	-3	25	36.0	10:22									
2013-14	Lake Erie	AHL	49	5	15	20	56																		
2014-15	**Colorado**	**NHL**	3	0	1	1	10	0	0	0	2	0.0	0	20	45.0	7:06									
	Lake Erie	AHL	40	4	19	23	35																		
	Norfolk Admirals	AHL	20	6	9	15	29																		
2015-16	**Anaheim**	**NHL**	1	0	0	0	0	0	0	0	0	0.0	0	4	50.0	8:21									
	San Diego Gulls	AHL	62	17	27	44	48										5	1	4	5	2				
2016-17	**Anaheim**	**NHL**	9	0	2	2	0	0	0	0	7	0.0	-2	81	42.0	9:28									
	San Diego Gulls	AHL	2	1	0	1	0																		
	Florida	**NHL**	29	2	5	7	9	1	0	0	26	7.7	-3	233	44.6	11:41									
	Springfield	AHL	14	4	8	12	16																		
	NHL Totals		**48**	**2**	**8**	**10**	**23**	**1**	**0**	**0**	**41**	**4.9**		**363**	**43.5**	**10:45**									

OHL First All-Star Team (2012)

Signed as a free agent by **San Jose**, September 20, 2010. Traded to **Colorado** by **San Jose** with Jamie McGinn and Mike Connolly for T.J. Galiardi, Daniel Winnik and Anaheim's 7th round pick (previously acquired, San Jose selected Emil Galimov) in 2013 NHL Draft, February 27, 2012. Traded to **Anaheim** by **Colorado** for Mat Clark, March 2, 2015. Traded to **Florida** by **Anaheim** for Logan Shaw, November 16, 2016. Signed as a free agent by **Winnipeg**, July 1, 2017.

SHARP, Patrick

(SHAHRP, PAT-rihk) **CHI**

Left wing. Shoots right. 6'1", 200 lbs. Born, Winnipeg, MB, December 27, 1981. Philadelphia's 2nd pick, 95th overall, in 2001 NHL Draft.

			Regular Season														Playoffs								
Season	Club	League	GP	G	A	Pts	PIM	PP	SH	GW	S	S%	+/-	TF	F%	Min	GP	G	A	Pts	PIM	PP	SH	GW	Min
1997-98	Kanata Valley	ON-Jr.A	54	11	23	34	22	....	....	....	....	....	....	....	....	....	7	0	5	5	0	....	....	....	....
1998-99	Thunder Bay	USHL	55	19	24	43	48	....	....	....	....	....	....	....	....	....	3	1	1	2	0	....	....	....	....
99-2000	Thunder Bay	USHL	56	20	35	55	41	....	....	....	....	....	....	....	....	....	....	....	....	....	....	....	....	....	....
2000-01	U. of Vermont	ECAC	34	12	15	27	36	....	....	....	....	....	....	....	....	....	....	....	....	....	....	....	....	....	....
2001-02	U. of Vermont	ECAC	31	13	13	26	50	....	....	....	....	....	....	....	....	....	....	....	....	....	....	....	....	....	....
2002-03	**Philadelphia**	**NHL**	**3**	**0**	**0**	**0**	**2**	**0**	**0**	**0**	**3**	**0.0**	**0**	**7**	**42.9**	**5:59**	....	....	....	....	....	....	....	....	....
	Philadelphia	AHL	53	14	19	33	39	....	....	....	....	....	....	....	....	....	....	....	....	....	....	....	....	....	....
2003-04	**Philadelphia**	**NHL**	**41**	**5**	**2**	**7**	**55**	**0**	**0**	**1**	**44**	**11.4**	**–3**	**272**	**46.7**	**9:56**	**12**	**1**	**0**	**1**	**2**	**0**	**0**	**0**	**6:12**
	Philadelphia	AHL	35	15	14	29	45	....	....	....	....	....	....	....	....	....	1	2	0	2	0	....	....	....	....
2004-05	Philadelphia	AHL	75	23	29	52	80	....	....	....	....	....	....	....	....	....	21	8	13	*21	20	....	....	....	....
2005-06	**Philadelphia**	**NHL**	**22**	**5**	**3**	**8**	**10**	**1**	**0**	**3**	**33**	**15.2**	**4**	**38**	**52.6**	**7:43**	....	....	....	....	....	....	....	....	....
	Chicago	**NHL**	**50**	**9**	**14**	**23**	**36**	**0**	**1**	**2**	**111**	**8.1**	**1**	**664**	**48.0**	**16:19**	....	....	....	....	....	....	....	....	....
2006-07	**Chicago**	**NHL**	**80**	**20**	**15**	**35**	**74**	**5**	**3**	**1**	**160**	**12.5**	**–15**	**1008**	**46.5**	**17:04**	....	....	....	....	....	....	....	....	....
2007-08	**Chicago**	**NHL**	**80**	**36**	**26**	**62**	**55**	**9**	***7**	**7**	**209**	**17.2**	**23**	**594**	**51.4**	**18:47**	....	....	....	....	....	....	....	....	....
2008-09	**Chicago**	**NHL**	**61**	**26**	**18**	**44**	**41**	**9**	**0**	**4**	**184**	**14.1**	**6**	**566**	**45.8**	**17:57**	**17**	**7**	**4**	**11**	**6**	**3**	**0**	**2**	**16:17**
2009-10♦	**Chicago**	**NHL**	**82**	**25**	**41**	**66**	**28**	**4**	**2**	**4**	**266**	**9.4**	**24**	**466**	**51.7**	**18:07**	**22**	**11**	**11**	**22**	**16**	**3**	**1**	**1**	**17:52**
2010-11	**Chicago**	**NHL**	**74**	**34**	**37**	**71**	**38**	**12**	**2**	**6**	**268**	**12.7**	**–1**	**508**	**48.0**	**19:25**	**7**	**3**	**2**	**5**	**2**	**3**	**0**	**0**	**18:55**
2011-12	**Chicago**	**NHL**	**74**	**33**	**36**	**69**	**38**	**7**	**1**	**8**	**282**	**11.7**	**28**	**291**	**47.8**	**19:54**	**6**	**1**	**0**	**1**	**4**	**0**	**0**	**0**	**20:18**
2012-13♦	**Chicago**	**NHL**	**28**	**6**	**14**	**20**	**14**	**1**	**0**	**1**	**88**	**6.8**	**8**	**62**	**64.5**	**18:50**	**23**	***10**	**6**	**16**	**8**	**2**	**0**	**2**	**18:15**
2013-14	**Chicago**	**NHL**	**82**	**34**	**44**	**78**	**40**	**10**	**0**	**3**	**313**	**10.9**	**13**	**152**	**54.6**	**18:53**	**19**	**5**	**5**	**10**	**6**	**1**	**0**	**0**	**18:35**
	Canada	Olympics	5	1	0	1	4	....	....	....	....	....	....	....	....	....	....	....	....	....	....	....	....	....	....
2014-15♦	**Chicago**	**NHL**	**68**	**16**	**27**	**43**	**33**	**8**	**0**	**2**	**230**	**7.0**	**–8**	**108**	**49.1**	**16:49**	**23**	**5**	**10**	**15**	**8**	**1**	**0**	**0**	**15:35**
2015-16	**Dallas**	**NHL**	**76**	**20**	**35**	**55**	**27**	**7**	**0**	**6**	**226**	**8.8**	**–3**	**33**	**48.5**	**17:37**	**13**	**4**	**2**	**6**	**0**	**1**	**0**	**0**	**18:32**
2016-17	**Dallas**	**NHL**	**48**	**8**	**10**	**18**	**31**	**1**	**1**	**0**	**146**	**5.5**	**–22**	**61**	**47.5**	**15:57**	....	....	....	....	....	....	....	....	....
	NHL Totals		**869**	**277**	**322**	**599**	**522**	**74**	**17**	**48**	**2563**	**10.8**		**4830**	**48.6**	**17:22**	**142**	**47**	**40**	**87**	**52**	**14**	**1**	**5**	**16:42**

Played in NHL All-Star Game (2011)

Traded to **Chicago** by **Philadelphia** with Eric Meloche for Matt Ellison and Chicago's 3rd round pick (later traded to Montreal - Montreal selected Ryan White) in 2006 NHL Draft, December 5, 2005. Traded to **Dallas** by **Chicago** with Stephen Johns for Trevor Daley and Ryan Garbutt, July 12, 2015. Signed as a free agent by **Chicago**, July 1, 2017.

SHATTENKIRK, Kevin

(SHAH-tehn-kuhrk, KEH-vihn) **NYR**

Defense. Shoots right. 6', 200 lbs. Born, New Rochelle, NY, January 29, 1989. Colorado's 1st pick, 14th overall, in 2007 NHL Draft.

			Regular Season														Playoffs								
Season	Club	League	GP	G	A	Pts	PIM	PP	SH	GW	S	S%	+/-	TF	F%	Min	GP	G	A	Pts	PIM	PP	SH	GW	Min
2004-05	Brunswick Bruins	High-CT	22	10	18	28	....	....	....	....	....	....	....	....	....	....	....	....	....	....	....	....	....	....	....
2005-06	USAHNTDP	U-17	13	4	4	8	4	....	....	....	....	....	....	....	....	....	....	....	....	....	....	....	....	....	....
	USAHNTDP	NAHL	28	6	9	15	17	....	....	....	....	....	....	....	....	....	12	3	7	10	10	....	....	....	....
2006-07	USAHNTDP	U-18	43	8	19	27	36	....	....	....	....	....	....	....	....	....	....	....	....	....	....	....	....	....	....
	USAHNTDP	NAHL	14	5	8	13	26	....	....	....	....	....	....	....	....	....	....	....	....	....	....	....	....	....	....
2007-08	Boston University	H-East	40	4	17	21	38	....	....	....	....	....	....	....	....	....	....	....	....	....	....	....	....	....	....
2008-09	Boston University	H-East	43	7	21	28	40	....	....	....	....	....	....	....	....	....	....	....	....	....	....	....	....	....	....
2009-10	Boston University	H-East	38	7	22	29	38	....	....	....	....	....	....	....	....	....	....	....	....	....	....	....	....	....	....
	Lake Erie	AHL	3	0	2	2	0	....	....	....	....	....	....	....	....	....	....	....	....	....	....	....	....	....	....
2010-11	**Colorado**	**NHL**	**46**	**7**	**19**	**26**	**20**	**2**	**0**	**1**	**67**	**10.4**	**–11**	**0**	**0.0**	**19:50**	....	....	....	....	....	....	....	....	....
	Lake Erie	AHL	10	0	0	0	10	....	....	....	....	....	....	....	....	....	....	....	....	....	....	....	....	....	....
	St. Louis	**NHL**	**26**	**2**	**15**	**17**	**16**	**1**	**0**	**1**	**41**	**4.9**	**7**	**0**	**0.0**	**19:51**	....	....	....	....	....	....	....	....	....
2011-12	**St. Louis**	**NHL**	**81**	**9**	**34**	**43**	**60**	**5**	**0**	**2**	**178**	**5.1**	**20**	**4**	**25.0**	**21:36**	**9**	**1**	**1**	**2**	**6**	**0**	**0**	**0**	**21:26**
2012-13	TPS Turku	Finland	12	2	4	6	22	....	....	....	....	....	....	....	....	....	....	....	....	....	....	....	....	....	....
	St. Louis	**NHL**	**48**	**5**	**18**	**23**	**20**	**2**	**0**	**0**	**84**	**6.0**	**2**	**0**	**0.0**	**21:18**	**6**	**0**	**2**	**2**	**6**	**0**	**0**	**0**	**18:38**
2013-14	**St. Louis**	**NHL**	**81**	**10**	**35**	**45**	**38**	**7**	**0**	**5**	**188**	**5.3**	**1**	**0**	**0.0**	**20:34**	**6**	**1**	**4**	**5**	**2**	**0**	**0**	**0**	**25:39**
	United States	Olympics	6	0	3	3	0	....	....	....	....	....	....	....	....	....	....	....	....	....	....	....	....	....	....
2014-15	**St. Louis**	**NHL**	**56**	**8**	**36**	**44**	**52**	**4**	**0**	**1**	**135**	**5.9**	**19**	**0**	**0.0**	**22:34**	**6**	**0**	**8**	**8**	**2**	**0**	**0**	**0**	**22:55**
2015-16	**St. Louis**	**NHL**	**72**	**14**	**30**	**44**	**51**	**6**	**0**	**1**	**180**	**7.8**	**–14**	**0**	**0.0**	**22:25**	**20**	**2**	**9**	**11**	**19**	**0**	**0**	**0**	**21:04**
2016-17	**St. Louis**	**NHL**	**61**	**11**	**31**	**42**	**37**	**7**	**0**	**0**	**115**	**9.6**	**–11**	**0**	**0.0**	**19:51**	....	....	....	....	....	....	....	....	....
	Washington	**NHL**	**19**	**2**	**12**	**14**	**10**	**1**	**0**	**2**	**46**	**4.3**	**4**	**0**	**0.0**	**20:12**	**13**	**1**	**5**	**6**	**6**	**1**	**0**	**1**	**18:27**
	NHL Totals		**490**	**68**	**230**	**298**	**304**	**35**	**0**	**13**	**1034**	**6.6**		**4**	**25.0**	**21:06**	**60**	**5**	**29**	**34**	**41**	**1**	**0**	**1**	**20:57**

Hockey East All-Rookie Team (2008) • Hockey East Second All-Star Team (2009) • NCAA East Second All-American Team (2009)

Played in NHL All-Star Game (2015)

Traded to **St. Louis** by **Colorado** with Chris Stewart and Colorado's 2nd round pick (Ty Rattie) in 2011 NHL Draft for Erik Johnson, Jay McClement and St. Louis' 1st round pick (Duncan Siemens) in 2011 NHL Draft, February 18, 2011. Signed as a free agent by **TPS Turku** (Finland), November 24, 2012. Traded to **Washington** by **St. Louis** with Pheonix Copley for Zach Sanford, Brad Malone and Washington's 1st round pick (later traded to Philadelphia – Philadelphia selected Morgan Frost) in 2017 NHL Draft, February 27, 2017. Signed as a free agent by **NY Rangers**, July 1, 2017.

SHAW, Andrew

(SHAW, AN-droo) **MTL**

Center. Shoots right. 5'11", 179 lbs. Born, Belleville, ON, July 20, 1991. Chicago's 8th pick, 139th overall, in 2011 NHL Draft.

			Regular Season														Playoffs								
Season	Club	League	GP	G	A	Pts	PIM	PP	SH	GW	S	S%	+/-	TF	F%	Min	GP	G	A	Pts	PIM	PP	SH	GW	Min
2006-07	Quinte Red Devils	Minor-ON	32	24	27	51	88	....	....	....	....	....	....	....	....	....	3	1	2	3	....	....	....	....	....
	Quinte Red Devils	Other	18	14	18	32	....	....	....	....	....	....	....	....	....	....	....	....	....	....	....	....	....	....	....
2007-08	Quinte Red Devils	Minor-ON	STATISTICS NOT AVAILABLE																						
2008-09	Niagara Ice Dogs	OHL	56	8	9	17	97	....	....	....	....	....	....	....	....	....	12	2	1	3	22	....	....	....	....
2009-10	Niagara Ice Dogs	OHL	68	11	25	36	129	....	....	....	....	....	....	....	....	....	5	0	0	0	4	....	....	....	....
2010-11	Owen Sound	OHL	66	22	32	54	135	....	....	....	....	....	....	....	....	....	20	10	7	17	*53	....	....	....	....
2011-12	**Chicago**	**NHL**	**37**	**12**	**11**	**23**	**50**	**0**	**0**	**2**	**74**	**16.2**	**–1**	**88**	**46.6**	**15:12**	**3**	**0**	**0**	**0**	**15**	**0**	**0**	**0**	**13:55**
	Rockford IceHogs	AHL	38	12	11	23	99	....	....	....	....	....	....	....	....	....	....	....	....	....	....	....	....	....	....
2012-13	Rockford IceHogs	AHL	28	8	6	14	84	....	....	....	....	....	....	....	....	....	....	....	....	....	....	....	....	....	....
♦	**Chicago**	**NHL**	**48**	**9**	**6**	**15**	**38**	**2**	**0**	**2**	**64**	**14.1**	**6**	**457**	**44.0**	**15:03**	**23**	**5**	**4**	**9**	**35**	**1**	**0**	**2**	**14:49**
2013-14	**Chicago**	**NHL**	**80**	**20**	**19**	**39**	**76**	**5**	**0**	**2**	**149**	**13.4**	**12**	**684**	**43.3**	**15:41**	**12**	**2**	**6**	**8**	**12**	**1**	**0**	**0**	**17:06**
2014-15♦	**Chicago**	**NHL**	**79**	**15**	**11**	**26**	**67**	**5**	**0**	**2**	**146**	**10.3**	**–8**	**712**	**50.1**	**14:57**	**23**	**5**	**7**	**12**	**36**	**2**	**0**	**0**	**15:33**
2015-16	**Chicago**	**NHL**	**78**	**14**	**20**	**34**	**69**	**4**	**0**	**2**	**153**	**9.2**	**11**	**314**	**46.5**	**14:39**	**6**	**4**	**2**	**6**	**18**	**3**	**0**	**0**	**13:55**
2016-17	**Montreal**	**NHL**	**68**	**12**	**17**	**29**	**110**	**1**	**0**	**1**	**127**	**9.4**	**4**	**438**	**54.6**	**15:12**	**5**	**0**	**0**	**0**	**7**	**0**	**0**	**0**	**15:02**
	NHL Totals		**390**	**82**	**84**	**166**	**410**	**17**	**0**	**11**	**713**	**11.5**		**2693**	**47.5**	**15:07**	**72**	**16**	**19**	**35**	**123**	**7**	**0**	**2**	**15:20**

Traded to **Montreal** by **Chicago** for Montreal's 2nd round pick (Alexander DeBrincat) in 2016 NHL Draft and Minnesota's 2nd round pick (previously acquired, later traded to Chicago – Chicago selected Chad Krys) in 2016 NHL Draft, June 24, 2016.

SHAW, Logan

(SHAW, LOH-guhn) **ANA**

Right wing. Shoots right. 6'3", 202 lbs. Born, Glace Bay, NS, October 5, 1992. Florida's 5th pick, 76th overall, in 2011 NHL Draft.

			Regular Season														Playoffs								
Season	Club	League	GP	G	A	Pts	PIM	PP	SH	GW	S	S%	+/-	TF	F%	Min	GP	G	A	Pts	PIM	PP	SH	GW	Min
2007-08	Cape Breton	NSMHL	34	17	22	39	55	....	....	....	....	....	....	....	....	....	10	3	9	12	8	....	....	....	....
	Cape Breton	Other	2	1	0	1	0	....	....	....	....	....	....	....	....	....	....	....	....	....	....	....	....	....	....
2008-09	Cape Breton	QMJHL	49	5	3	8	22	....	....	....	....	....	....	....	....	....	8	0	0	0	0	....	....	....	....
2009-10	Cape Breton	QMJHL	67	9	15	24	31	....	....	....	....	....	....	....	....	....	5	0	0	0	4	....	....	....	....
2010-11	Cape Breton	QMJHL	68	26	20	46	37	....	....	....	....	....	....	....	....	....	4	0	1	1	4	....	....	....	....
2011-12	Cape Breton	QMJHL	37	14	12	26	27	....	....	....	....	....	....	....	....	....	....	....	....	....	....	....	....	....	....
	Quebec Remparts	QMJHL	23	6	9	15	19	....	....	....	....	....	....	....	....	....	11	6	5	11	12	....	....	....	....
2012-13	Quebec Remparts	QMJHL	67	26	42	68	37	....	....	....	....	....	....	....	....	....	11	3	5	8	8	....	....	....	....
2013-14	San Antonio	AHL	46	1	7	8	24	....	....	....	....	....	....	....	....	....	....	....	....	....	....	....	....	....	....
	Cincinnati	ECHL	20	8	10	18	8	....	....	....	....	....	....	....	....	....	24	5	1	6	4	....	....	....	....
2014-15	San Antonio	AHL	69	13	12	25	25	....	....	....	....	....	....	....	....	....	2	0	0	0	0	....	....	....	....
2015-16	**Florida**	**NHL**	**53**	**5**	**2**	**7**	**13**	**1**	**0**	**1**	**72**	**6.9**	**–7**	**37**	**43.2**	**12:14**	**3**	**0**	**0**	**0**	**0**	**0**	**0**	**0**	**11:37**
	Portland Pirates	AHL	19	11	3	14	4	....	....	....	....	....	....	....	....	....	3	0	0	0	0	....	....	....	....
2016-17	Springfield	AHL	13	4	2	6	2	....	....	....	....	....	....	....	....	....	....	....	....	....	....	....	....	....	....
	Anaheim	**NHL**	**55**	**3**	**7**	**10**	**10**	**0**	**1**	**1**	**59**	**5.1**	**3**	**145**	**37.9**	**9:43**	**9**	**0**	**0**	**0**	**4**	**0**	**0**	**0**	**9:31**
	San Diego Gulls	AHL	2	0	0	0	0	....	....	....	....	....	....	....	....	....	....	....	....	....	....	....	....	....	....
	NHL Totals		**108**	**8**	**9**	**17**	**23**	**1**	**1**	**2**	**131**	**6.1**		**182**	**39.0**	**10:57**	**12**	**0**	**0**	**0**	**4**	**0**	**0**	**0**	**10:03**

Traded to **Anaheim** by **Florida** for Michael Sgarbossa, November 16, 2016.

SHEAHAN, Riley

(SHAY-an, RIGH-lee) **DET**

Center. Shoots left. 6'3", 226 lbs. Born, St. Catharines, ON, December 7, 1991. Detroit's 1st pick, 21st overall, in 2010 NHL Draft.

			Regular Season														Playoffs								
Season	Club	League	GP	G	A	Pts	PIM	PP	SH	GW	S	S%	+/-	TF	F%	Min	GP	G	A	Pts	PIM	PP	SH	GW	Min
2007-08	St. Catharines	ON-Jr.B	45	22	39	61	39	....	....	....	....	....	....	....	....	....	16	5	10	15	14	....	....	....	....
2008-09	St. Catharines	ON-Jr.B	40	27	46	73	55	....	....	....	....	....	....	....	....	....	11	8	5	13	30	....	....	....	....
2009-10	U. of Notre Dame	CCHA	37	6	11	17	22	....	....	....	....	....	....	....	....	....	....	....	....	....	....	....	....	....	....
2010-11	U. of Notre Dame	CCHA	40	5	17	22	28	....	....	....	....	....	....	....	....	....	....	....	....	....	....	....	....	....	....
2011-12	U. of Notre Dame	CCHA	37	9	16	25	24	....	....	....	....	....	....	....	....	....	....	....	....	....	....	....	....	....	....
	Detroit	**NHL**	**1**	**0**	**0**	**0**	**4**	**0**	**0**	**0**	**3**	**0.0**	**0**	**0**	**0.0**	**6:03**	....	....	....	....	....	....	....	....	....
	Grand Rapids	AHL	7	1	1	2	0	....	....	....	....	....	....	....	....	....	....	....	....	....	....	....	....	....	....
2012-13	Grand Rapids	AHL	72	16	20	36	33	....	....	....	....	....	....	....	....	....	24	3	13	16	10	....	....	....	....
	Detroit	**NHL**	**1**	**0**	**0**	**0**	**0**	**0**	**0**	**0**	**1**	**0.0**	**0**	**1**	**0.0**	**6:47**	....	....	....	....	....	....	....	....	....
2013-14	**Detroit**	**NHL**	**42**	**9**	**15**	**24**	**6**	**2**	**0**	**1**	**59**	**15.3**	**8**	**512**	**49.0**	**14:27**	**5**	**0**	**0**	**0**	**0**	**0**	**0**	**0**	**14:24**
	Grand Rapids	AHL	31	8	10	18	12	....	....	....	....	....	....	....	....	....	8	1	4	5	0	....	....	....	....
2014-15	**Detroit**	**NHL**	**79**	**13**	**23**	**36**	**16**	**5**	**0**	**0**	**123**	**10.6**	**–3**	**970**	**49.9**	**15:39**	**7**	**2**	**1**	**3**	**2**	**2**	**0**	**1**	**14:08**
2015-16	**Detroit**	**NHL**	**81**	**14**	**11**	**25**	**12**	**3**	**1**	**2**	**128**	**10.9**	**–8**	**782**	**45.8**	**15:14**	**5**	**0**	**1**	**1**	**4**	**0**	**0**	**0**	**16:21**
2016-17	**Detroit**	**NHL**	**80**	**2**	**11**	**13**	**14**	**1**	**0**	**0**	**109**	**1.8**	**–29**	**466**	**50.6**	**13:58**	....	....	....	....	....	....	....	....	....
	NHL Totals		**284**	**38**	**60**	**98**	**52**	**11**	**1**	**3**	**423**	**9.0**		**2731**	**48.7**	**14:49**	**17**	**2**	**2**	**4**	**6**	**2**	**0**	**1**	**14:52**

SHEARY, Conor

(SHEER-ee, KAW-nuhr) **PIT**

Left wing. Shoots left. 5'8", 175 lbs. Born, Melrose, MA, June 8, 1992.

Season	Club	League	GP	G	A	Pts	PIM	PP	SH	GW	S	S%	+/-	TF	F%	Min	GP	G	A	Pts	PIM	PP	SH	GW	Min
2007-08	Cushing	High-MA	29	2	2	4	....	....	....	....	....	....	....	....	....	....	....	....	....	....	....	....	....	....	....
2008-09	Cushing	High-MA	31	16	27	43	....	....	....	....	....	....	....	....	....	....	....	....	....	....	....	....	....	....	....
2009-10	Cushing	High-MA	31	31	41	72	....	....	....	....	....	....	....	....	....	....	....	....	....	....	....	....	....	....	....
2010-11	Massachusetts	H-East	34	6	8	14	12	....	....	....	....	....	....	....	....	....	....	....	....	....	....	....	....	....	....
2011-12	Massachusetts	H-East	36	12	23	35	10	....	....	....	....	....	....	....	....	....	....	....	....	....	....	....	....	....	....
2012-13	Massachusetts	H-East	34	11	16	27	29	....	....	....	....	....	....	....	....	....	....	....	....	....	....	....	....	....	....
2013-14	Massachusetts	H-East	34	9	19	28	2	....	....	....	....	....	....	....	....	....	....	....	....	....	....	....	....	....	....
	Wilkes-Barre	AHL	2	0	0	0	0	....	....	....	....	....	....	....	....	....	15	6	5	11	0	....	....	....	....
2014-15	Wilkes-Barre	AHL	58	20	25	45	8	....	....	....	....	....	....	....	....	....	8	5	7	12	2	....	....	....	....
2015-16♦	**Pittsburgh**	**NHL**	**44**	**7**	**3**	**10**	**8**	**0**	**0**	**0**	**51**	**13.7**	**–1**	**8**	**12.5**	**9:45**	**23**	**4**	**6**	**10**	**8**	**0**	**0**	**1**	**13:58**
	Wilkes-Barre	AHL	30	7	29	36	4	....	....	....	....	....	....	....	....	....	....	....	....	....	....	....	....	....	....
2016-17♦	**Pittsburgh**	**NHL**	**61**	**23**	**30**	**53**	**22**	**2**	**0**	**6**	**154**	**14.9**	**24**	**0**	**0.0**	**15:56**	**22**	**2**	**5**	**7**	**4**	**0**	**0**	**0**	**14:08**
	NHL Totals		**105**	**30**	**33**	**63**	**30**	**2**	**0**	**6**	**205**	**14.6**		**8**	**12.5**	**13:21**	**45**	**6**	**11**	**17**	**12**	**0**	**0**	**1**	**14:03**

Signed to an ATO (amateur tryout) contract by **Wilkes-Barre** (AHL), March 17, 2014. Signed as a free agent by **Wilkes-Barre** (AHL), October 9, 2014. Signed as a free agent by **Pittsburgh**, July 1, 2015.

SHINKARUK, Hunter

(shinh-KA-ruhk, HUHN-tuhr) **CGY**

Center/Left wing. Shoots left. 5'10", 181 lbs. Born, Calgary, AB, October 13, 1994. Vancouver's 2nd pick, 24th overall, in 2013 NHL Draft.

Season	Club	League	GP	G	A	Pts	PIM	PP	SH	GW	S	S%	+/-	TF	F%	Min	GP	G	A	Pts	PIM	PP	SH	GW	Min
2007-08	Calgary Royals	AMBHL	33	10	30	40	24	....	....	....	....	....	....	....	....	....	3	2	2	4	0	....	....	....	....
2008-09	Calgary Royals	AMBHL	27	32	31	63	10	....	....	....	....	....	....	....	....	....	10	11	11	22	6	....	....	....	....
2009-10	Calgary Royals	AMHL	3	0	1	1	0	....	....	....	....	....	....	....	....	....	....	....	....	....	....	....	....	....	....
2010-11	Medicine Hat	WHL	63	14	28	42	24	....	....	....	....	....	....	....	....	....	14	4	5	9	0	....	....	....	....
2011-12	Medicine Hat	WHL	66	49	42	91	38	....	....	....	....	....	....	....	....	....	8	2	9	11	6	....	....	....	....
2012-13	Medicine Hat	WHL	64	37	49	86	44	....	....	....	....	....	....	....	....	....	8	3	3	6	8	....	....	....	....
2013-14	Medicine Hat	WHL	18	5	11	16	29	....	....	....	....	....	....	....	....	....	....	....	....	....	....	....	....	....	....
2014-15	Utica Comets	AHL	74	16	15	31	28	....	....	....	....	....	....	....	....	....	23	4	2	6	4	....	....	....	....
2015-16	**Vancouver**	**NHL**	**1**	**0**	**0**	**0**	**0**	**0**	**0**	**0**	**0**	**0.0**	**0**	**0**	**0.0**	**9:35**	....	....	....	....	....	....	....	....	....
	Utica Comets	AHL	45	21	18	39	18	....	....	....	....	....	....	....	....	....	....	....	....	....	....	....	....	....	....
	Calgary	**NHL**	**7**	**2**	**1**	**3**	**2**	**1**	**0**	**0**	**12**	**16.7**	**–4**	**1**	**0.0**	**15:44**	....	....	....	....	....	....	....	....	....
	Stockton Heat	AHL	17	6	6	12	2	....	....	....	....	....	....	....	....	....	....	....	....	....	....	....	....	....	....
2016-17	**Calgary**	**NHL**	**7**	**0**	**1**	**1**	**2**	**0**	**0**	**0**	**5**	**0.0**	**–3**	**0**	**0.0**	**10:35**	....	....	....	....	....	....	....	....	....
	Stockton Heat	AHL	52	15	20	35	20	....	....	....	....	....	....	....	....	....	5	2	1	3	4	....	....	....	....
	NHL Totals		**15**	**2**	**2**	**4**	**4**	**1**	**0**	**0**	**17**	**11.8**		**1**	**0.0**	**12:55**	....	....	....	....	....	....	....	....	....

WHL East Second All-Star Team (2013)

• Missed majority of 2009-10 season due to leg injury at Fort Saskatchewan (AMHL), October, 2009. • Missed majority of 2013-14 due to recurring hip injury and resulting surgery, January 7, 2014. Traded to **Calgary** by **Vancouver** for Markus Granlund, February 22, 2016.

SHORE, Devin

(SHOHR, DEH-vihn) **DAL**

Center. Shoots left. 6'1", 205 lbs. Born, Ajax, ON, July 19, 1994. Dallas' 4th pick, 61st overall, in 2012 NHL Draft.

Season	Club	League	GP	G	A	Pts	PIM	PP	SH	GW	S	S%	+/-	TF	F%	Min	GP	G	A	Pts	PIM	PP	SH	GW	Min
2009-10	Ajax-Pickering	Minor-ON	68	40	48	88	35	....	....	....	....	....	....	....	....	....	....	....	....	....	....	....	....	....	....
2010-11	The Hill Academy	High-ON	61	33	62	95	18	....	....	....	....	....	....	....	....	....	....	....	....	....	....	....	....	....	....
2011-12	Whitby Fury	ON-Jr.A	41	29	29	58	26	....	....	....	....	....	....	....	....	....	23	7	25	32	10	....	....	....	....
2012-13	U. of Maine	H-East	38	6	20	26	10	....	....	....	....	....	....	....	....	....	....	....	....	....	....	....	....	....	....
2013-14	U. of Maine	H-East	35	14	29	43	38	....	....	....	....	....	....	....	....	....	....	....	....	....	....	....	....	....	....
2014-15	U. of Maine	H-East	39	14	21	35	20	....	....	....	....	....	....	....	....	....	....	....	....	....	....	....	....	....	....
	Texas Stars	AHL	19	4	2	6	4	....	....	....	....	....	....	....	....	....	3	1	0	1	0	....	....	....	....
2015-16	**Dallas**	**NHL**	**3**	**0**	**0**	**0**	**0**	**0**	**0**	**0**	**1**	**0.0**	**2**	**1**	**0.0**	**12:07**	....	....	....	....	....	....	....	....	....
	Texas Stars	AHL	23	15	11	26	8	....	....	....	....	....	....	....	....	....	....	....	....	....	....	....	....	....	....
2016-17	**Dallas**	**NHL**	**82**	**13**	**20**	**33**	**14**	**1**	**0**	**0**	**115**	**11.3**	**–4**	**470**	**47.0**	**14:08**	....	....	....	....	....	....	....	....	....
	NHL Totals		**85**	**13**	**20**	**33**	**14**	**1**	**0**	**0**	**116**	**11.2**		**471**	**46.9**	**14:04**	....	....	....	....	....	....	....	....	....

Hockey East First All-Star Team (2014) • NCAA East Second All-American Team (2014) • Hockey East Second All-Star Team (2015)

• Missed majority of 2015-16 due to shoulder injury vs. Charlotte (AHL), December 11, 2015.

SHORE, Drew

(SHOHR, DROO)

Center. Shoots right. 6'3", 205 lbs. Born, Denver, CO, January 29, 1991. Florida's 2nd pick, 44th overall, in 2009 NHL Draft.

Season	Club	League	GP	G	A	Pts	PIM	PP	SH	GW	S	S%	+/-	TF	F%	Min	GP	G	A	Pts	PIM	PP	SH	GW	Min
2006-07	Det. Honeybaked	MWEHL	31	9	25	34	20	....	....	....	....	....	....	....	....	....	....	....	....	....	....	....	....	....	....
	Det. Honeybaked	Other	34	17	23	40	....	....	....	....	....	....	....	....	....	....	....	....	....	....	....	....	....	....	....
2007-08	USAHNTDP	NAHL	35	9	16	25	12	....	....	....	....	....	....	....	....	....	3	0	1	1	0	....	....	....	....
	USAHNTDP	U-17	16	4	8	12	6	....	....	....	....	....	....	....	....	....	....	....	....	....	....	....	....	....	....
2008-09	USAHNTDP	NAHL	15	7	7	14	16	....	....	....	....	....	....	....	....	....	....	....	....	....	....	....	....	....	....
	USAHNTDP	U-18	47	10	25	35	30	....	....	....	....	....	....	....	....	....	....	....	....	....	....	....	....	....	....
2009-10	U. of Denver	WCHA	41	5	14	19	18	....	....	....	....	....	....	....	....	....	....	....	....	....	....	....	....	....	....
2010-11	U. of Denver	WCHA	40	23	23	46	38	....	....	....	....	....	....	....	....	....	....	....	....	....	....	....	....	....	....
2011-12	U. of Denver	WCHA	42	22	31	53	45	....	....	....	....	....	....	....	....	....	....	....	....	....	....	....	....	....	....
	San Antonio	AHL	8	1	2	3	4	....	....	....	....	....	....	....	....	....	9	2	0	2	2	....	....	....	....
2012-13	San Antonio	AHL	41	10	20	30	18	....	....	....	....	....	....	....	....	....	....	....	....	....	....	....	....	....	....
	Florida	**NHL**	**43**	**3**	**10**	**13**	**14**	**1**	**1**	**1**	**96**	**3.1**	**–10**	**443**	**47.9**	**15:48**	....	....	....	....	....	....	....	....	....
2013-14	**Florida**	**NHL**	**24**	**5**	**2**	**7**	**8**	**1**	**1**	**1**	**23**	**21.7**	**–1**	**208**	**41.4**	**12:00**	....	....	....	....	....	....	....	....	....
	San Antonio	AHL	50	6	26	32	25	....	....	....	....	....	....	....	....	....	....	....	....	....	....	....	....	....	....
2014-15	San Antonio	AHL	35	9	21	30	16	....	....	....	....	....	....	....	....	....	....	....	....	....	....	....	....	....	....
	Calgary	**NHL**	**11**	**1**	**2**	**3**	**0**	**0**	**0**	**0**	**13**	**7.7**	**–5**	**59**	**49.2**	**10:40**	**1**	**0**	**0**	**0**	**2**	**0**	**0**	**0**	**14:17**
	Adirondack	AHL	12	3	4	7	8	....	....	....	....	....	....	....	....	....	....	....	....	....	....	....	....	....	....
2015-16	**Calgary**	**NHL**	**2**	**0**	**1**	**1**	**2**	**0**	**0**	**0**	**3**	**0.0**	**0**	**10**	**40.0**	**14:00**	....	....	....	....	....	....	....	....	....
	Stockton Heat	AHL	59	10	28	38	22	....	....	....	....	....	....	....	....	....	....	....	....	....	....	....	....	....	....
2016-17	EHC Kloten	Swiss	53	24	27	51	28	....	....	....	....	....	....	....	....	....	....	....	....	....	....	....	....	....	....
	Vancouver	**NHL**	**14**	**0**	**2**	**2**	**4**	**0**	**0**	**0**	**11**	**0.0**	**–3**	**71**	**53.5**	**11:58**	....	....	....	....	....	....	....	....	....
	NHL Totals		**94**	**9**	**17**	**26**	**28**	**2**	**2**	**2**	**146**	**6.2**		**791**	**46.6**	**13:37**	**1**	**0**	**0**	**0**	**2**	**0**	**0**	**0**	**14:17**

WCHA Second All-Star Team (2011, 2012)

Traded to **Calgary** by **Florida** for Corban Knight, January 9, 2015. Signed as a free agent by **Kloten** (Swiss), August 12, 2016. Signed as a free agent by **Vancouver**, March 12, 2017. Signed as a free agent by **Zurich** (Swiss), May 30, 2017.

					Regular Season														Playoffs							
Season	Club	League	GP	G	A	Pts	PIM	PP	SH	GW	S	S%	+/-	TF	F%	Min	GP	G	A	Pts	PIM	PP	SH	GW	Min

SHORE, Nick — (SHOHR, NIHK) — L.A.

Center. Shoots right. 6'1", 194 lbs. Born, Denver, CO, September 26, 1992. Los Angeles' 3rd pick, 82nd overall, in 2011 NHL Draft.

Season	Club	League	GP	G	A	Pts	PIM	PP	SH	GW	S	S%	+/-	TF	F%	Min	GP	G	A	Pts	PIM	PP	SH	GW	Min
2007-08	Colorado T-birds	Minor-CO	....	64	71	135	....										9	2	2	4	6				
2008-09	USAHNTDP	NAHL	42	10	11	21	30																		
	USAHNTDP	U-17	16	7	6	13	18																		
2009-10	USAHNTDP	USHL	26	6	14	20	10																		
	USAHNTDP	U-18	39	13	24	37	30																		
2010-11	U. of Denver	WCHA	33	7	11	18	37																		
2011-12	U. of Denver	WCHA	43	13	28	41	16																		
2012-13	U. of Denver	WCHA	39	14	20	34	47																		
2013-14	Manchester	AHL	68	14	24	38	36										4	0	1	1	0				
2014-15	**Los Angeles**	**NHL**	34	1	6	7	10	0	0	0	33	3.0	0	236	53.8	11:05									
	Manchester	AHL	38	20	22	42	16										19	4	14	18	2				
2015-16	**Los Angeles**	**NHL**	68	3	7	10	32	0	0	1	90	3.3	-10	741	51.8	12:24	1	0	0	0	0	0	0	0	9:16
2016-17	**Los Angeles**	**NHL**	70	6	11	17	20	0	1	1	79	7.6	-2	721	50.2	12:47									
	NHL Totals		172	10	24	34	62	0	1	2	202	5.0		1698	51.4	12:18	1	0	0	0	0	0	0	0	9:16

SIELOFF, Patrick — (SEE-lawf, PAT-rihk) — OTT

Defense. Shoots left. 6'1", 205 lbs. Born, Ann Arbor, MI, May 15, 1994. Calgary's 2nd pick, 42nd overall, in 2012 NHL Draft.

Season	Club	League	GP	G	A	Pts	PIM	PP	SH	GW	S	S%	+/-	TF	F%	Min	GP	G	A	Pts	PIM	PP	SH	GW	Min
2009-10	Det. Compuware	T1EHL	37	2	8	10	52										5	0	3	3	0				
	Det. Compuware	Other	6	0	3	3	2																		
2010-11	USAHNTDP	USHL	36	1	3	4	66										2	0	0	0	0				
	USAHNTDP	U-17	17	2	3	5	10																		
2011-12	USAHNTDP	USHL	24	0	2	2	55																		
	USAHNTDP	U-18	36	3	5	8	58																		
2012-13	Windsor Spitfires	OHL	45	3	8	11	85																		
2013-14	Abbotsford Heat	AHL	2	0	0	0	0																		
2014-15	Adirondack	AHL	48	2	3	5	78																		
2015-16	**Calgary**	**NHL**	1	1	0	1	2	0	0	1	1	100.0	1	0	0.0	17:59									
	Stockton Heat	AHL	52	2	9	11	44																		
2016-17	Binghamton	AHL	52	2	10	12	93																		
	NHL Totals		1	1	0	1	2	0	0	1	1	100.0		0	0.0	17:59									

• Missed majority of 2013-14 due to broken cheekbone in pre-seaon game vs. Ottawa, September 20, 2013. Traded to **Ottawa** by **Calgary** for Alex Chiasson, June 27, 2016.

SIEMENS, Duncan — (SEE-muhns, DUHN-kuhn) — COL

Defense. Shoots left. 6'3", 210 lbs. Born, Edmonton, AB, September 7, 1993. Colorado's 2nd pick, 11th overall, in 2011 NHL Draft.

Season	Club	League	GP	G	A	Pts	PIM	PP	SH	GW	S	S%	+/-	TF	F%	Min	GP	G	A	Pts	PIM	PP	SH	GW	Min
2007-08	Sherwood Park	AMBHL	32	14	22	36	54										12	5	7	12	32				
2008-09	Sherwood Park	AMHL	34	5	13	18	68										11	2	6	8	24				
	Saskatoon Blades	WHL	2	0	1	1	2																		
2009-10	Saskatoon Blades	WHL	57	3	17	20	89										7	0	0	0	11				
2010-11	Saskatoon Blades	WHL	72	5	38	43	121										10	1	3	4	15				
2011-12	Saskatoon Blades	WHL	57	6	22	28	91										4	1	1	2	10				
	Lake Erie	AHL	3	0	0	0	2																		
2012-13	Saskatoon Blades	WHL	70	3	29	32	109										4	0	1	1	2				
2013-14	Lake Erie	AHL	46	1	3	4	45																		
2014-15	**Colorado**	**NHL**	1	0	0	0	0	0	0	0	0	0.0	0	0	0.0	14:00									
	Lake Erie	AHL	54	0	6	6	57																		
2015-16	San Antonio	AHL	53	1	6	7	90																		
2016-17	**Colorado**	**NHL**	3	0	0	0	2	0	0	0	2	0.0	-2	0	0.0	12:19									
	San Antonio	AHL	73	2	5	7	100																		
	NHL Totals		4	0	0	0	2	0	0	0	2	0.0		0	0.0	12:44									

WHL East Second All-Star Team (2011)

SIFERS, Jaime — (SIH-fuhrs, JAY-mee)

Defense. Shoots right. 5'11", 200 lbs. Born, Stratford, CT, January 18, 1983.

Season	Club	League	GP	G	A	Pts	PIM	PP	SH	GW	S	S%	+/-	TF	F%	Min	GP	G	A	Pts	PIM	PP	SH	GW	Min
2002-03	U. of Vermont	ECAC	34	4	14	18	66																		
2003-04	U. of Vermont	ECAC	35	4	14	18	93																		
2004-05	U. of Vermont	ECAC	36	4	12	16	57																		
2005-06	U. of Vermont	H-East	38	3	15	18	60																		
	Toronto Marlies	AHL	2	0	0	0	2																		
2006-07	Toronto Marlies	AHL	80	7	18	25	75																		
2007-08	Toronto Marlies	AHL	80	3	10	13	57										19	2	3	5	6				
2008-09	**Toronto**	**NHL**	23	0	2	2	18	0	0	0	25	0.0	-4	0	0.0	12:50									
	Toronto Marlies	AHL	43	4	16	20	47										4	0	1	1	4				
2009-10	**Minnesota**	**NHL**	14	0	0	0	6	0	0	0	9	0.0	1	0	0.0	12:59									
	Houston Aeros	AHL	54	3	5	8	58																		
2010-11	Chicago Wolves	AHL	68	4	18	22	66																		
2011-12	Adler Mannheim	Germany	52	5	19	24	59										14	0	3	3	8				
2012-13	Adler Mannheim	Germany	52	1	14	15	64										6	0	1	1	2				
2013-14	Adler Mannheim	Germany	50	3	21	24	62																		
2014-15	Springfield	AHL	76	3	19	22	82																		
2015-16	Lake Erie	AHL	67	5	14	19	86										14	0	5	5	10				
2016-17	Cleveland	AHL	74	6	14	20	74																		
	NHL Totals		37	0	2	2	24	0	0	0	34	0.0		0	0.0	12:53									

ECAC Second All-Star Team (2005)

Signed as a free agent by **Toronto**, July 20, 2006. Signed as a free agent by **Minnesota**, July 8, 2009. Signed as a free agent by **Atlanta**, July 7, 2010. Signed as a free agent by **Mannheim** (Germany), May 26, 2011. • Transferred to **Winnipeg** after **Atlanta** franchise relocated, June 21, 2011. Signed as a free agent by **Columbus**, July 2, 2015.

SILFVERBERG, Jakob — (SIHL-vuhr-buhrg, JA-kuhb) — ANA

Left wing. Shoots right. 6'2", 196 lbs. Born, Gavle, Sweden, October 13, 1990. Ottawa's 2nd pick, 39th overall, in 2009 NHL Draft.

Season	Club	League	GP	G	A	Pts	PIM	PP	SH	GW	S	S%	+/-	TF	F%	Min	GP	G	A	Pts	PIM	PP	SH	GW	Min
2005-06	Brynas U18	Swe-U18	8	0	0	0	0																		
2006-07	Brynas U18	Swe-U18	14	3	8	11	6										3	0	0	0	0				
	Brynas IF Gavle Jr.	Swe-Jr.	6	1	3	4	0																		
2007-08	Brynas U18	Swe-U18	5	5	3	8	2										5	3	4	7	2				
	Brynas IF Gavle Jr.	Swe-Jr.	30	8	12	20	8										7	3	0	3	2				
2008-09	Brynas IF Gavle Jr.	Swe-Jr.	30	14	24	38	6										4	0	0	0	2				
2009-10	Brynas IF Gavle Jr.	Swe-Jr.	1	1	1	2	0										3	3	2	5	0				
	Brynas IF Gavle	Sweden	48	8	8	16	4										5	0	4	4	2				
2010-11	Brynas IF Gavle	Sweden	53	18	16	34	16										5	0	4	4	2				
2011-12	Brynas IF Gavle	Sweden	49	24	30	54	10										17	13	7	20	4				
	Ottawa	**NHL**	....	....	....	....	....										2	0	0	0	2	0	0	0	9:11
2012-13	Binghamton	AHL	34	13	16	29	2																		
	Ottawa	**NHL**	48	10	9	19	12	2	1	2	134	7.5	9	13	38.5	16:14	10	2	2	4	2	1	0	0	16:39
2013-14	**Anaheim**	**NHL**	52	10	13	23	12	1	2	1	119	8.4	5	12	8.3	14:16	13	2	0	2	4	0	1	1	14:56
	Sweden	Olympics	6	0	1	1	2																		
2014-15	**Anaheim**	**NHL**	81	13	26	39	24	2	1	2	189	6.9	15	50	46.0	15:40	16	4	14	18	16	1	0	0	15:40
2015-16	**Anaheim**	**NHL**	82	20	19	39	32	2	0	2	215	9.3	8	20	20.0	16:58	7	0	5	5	6	0	0	0	16:56
2016-17	**Anaheim**	**NHL**	79	23	26	49	20	5	1	5	227	10.1	10	7	14.3	18:29	17	9	5	14	6	2	0	2	19:54
	NHL Totals		342	76	93	169	100	12	5	12	884	8.6		102	33.3	16:30	65	17	26	43	36	4	0	4	17:32

Traded to **Anaheim** by **Ottawa** wirh Stefan Noesen and Ottawa's 1st round pick (Nicholas Ritchie) in 2014 NHL Draft for Bobby Ryan, July 5, 2013.

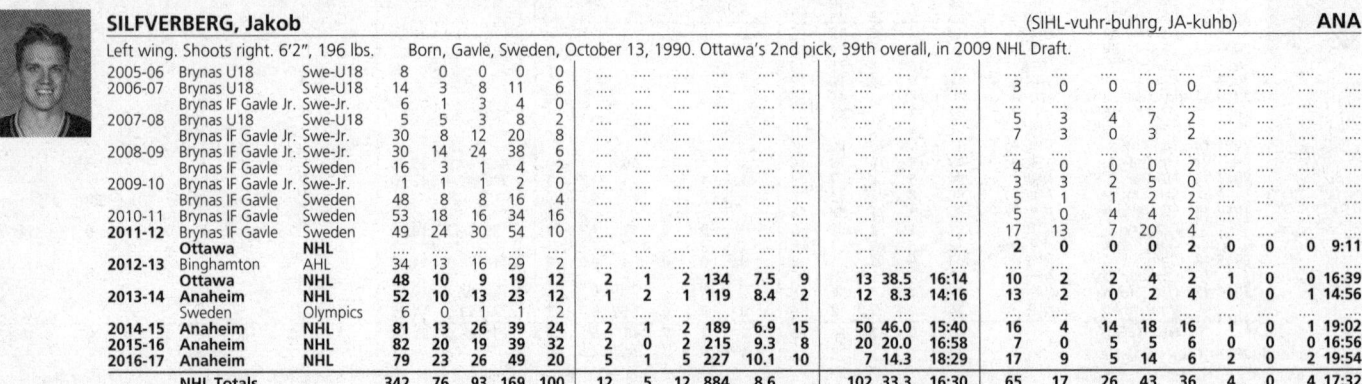

			Regular Season														Playoffs								
Season	Club	League	GP	G	A	Pts	PIM	PP	SH	GW	S	S%	+/-	TF	F%	Min	GP	G	A	Pts	PIM	PP	SH	GW	Min

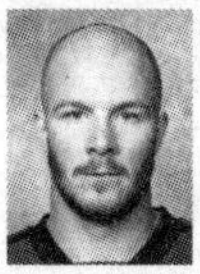

SILL, Zach
(SIHL, ZAK) **WSH**

Center. Shoots left. 6', 202 lbs. Born, Truro, NS, May 24, 1988.

Season	Club	League	GP	G	A	Pts	PIM	PP	SH	GW	S	S%	+/-	TF	F%	Min	GP	G	A	Pts	PIM	PP	SH	GW	Min
2005-06	Truro Bearcats	MJrHL	48	12	8	20	68	....	....	....	....	....	....	....	....	....	2	0	0	0	0	....	....	....	....
2006-07	U. of Maine	H-East	6	1	1	2	2	....	....	....	....	....	....	....	....	....	....	....	....	....	....	....	....	....	....
	Truro Bearcats	MJrHL	6	1	0	1	18	....	....	....	....	....	....	....	....	....	13	5	5	10	31	....	....	....	....
2007-08	Moncton Wildcats	QMJHL	66	18	8	26	95	....	....	....	....	....	....	....	....	....	....	....	....	....	....	....	....	....	....
2008-09	Moncton Wildcats	QMJHL	58	9	15	24	78	....	....	....	....	....	....	....	....	....	10	4	1	5	10	....	....	....	....
2009-10	Wheeling Nailers	ECHL	6	1	2	3	15	....	....	....	....	....	....	....	....	....	....	....	....	....	....	....	....	....	....
	Wilkes-Barre	AHL	54	5	6	11	48	....	....	....	....	....	....	....	....	....	4	0	0	0	2	....	....	....	....
2010-11	Wilkes-Barre	AHL	80	11	19	30	85	....	....	....	....	....	....	....	....	....	12	1	2	3	6	....	....	....	....
2011-12	Wilkes-Barre	AHL	68	10	7	17	40	....	....	....	....	....	....	....	....	....	12	3	1	4	0	....	....	....	....
2012-13	Wilkes-Barre	AHL	57	4	5	9	108	....	....	....	....	....	....	....	....	....	15	2	2	4	6	....	....	....	....
2013-14	**Pittsburgh**	**NHL**	**20**	**0**	**0**	**0**	**12**	**0**	**0**	**0**	**14**	**0.0**	**-4**	**90**	**37.8**	**10:48**	....	....	....	....	....	....	....	....	....
	Wilkes-Barre	AHL	18	3	3	6	34	....	....	....	....	....	....	....	....	....	17	1	2	3	18	....	....	....	....
2014-15	**Pittsburgh**	**NHL**	**42**	**1**	**2**	**3**	**60**	**0**	**0**	**0**	**26**	**3.8**	**-3**	**1**	**0.0**	**8:18**	....	....	....	....	....	....	....	....	....
	Toronto	**NHL**	**21**	**0**	**1**	**1**	**24**	**0**	**0**	**0**	**17**	**0.0**	**-2**	**92**	**50.0**	**8:34**	....	....	....	....	....	....	....	....	....
2015-16	**Washington**	**NHL**	**10**	**1**	**0**	**1**	**2**	**0**	**0**	**0**	**13**	**7.7**	**0**	**77**	**42.9**	**9:56**	....	....	....	....	....	....	....	....	....
	Hershey Bears	AHL	63	9	13	22	49	....	....	....	....	....	....	....	....	....	21	6	4	10	26	....	....	....	....
2016-17	Hershey Bears	AHL	67	7	9	16	30	....	....	....	....	....	....	....	....	....	12	0	0	0	12	....	....	....	....
	NHL Totals		**93**	**2**	**3**	**5**	**98**	**0**	**0**	**0**	**70**	**2.9**		**260**	**43.5**	**9:04**	....	....	....	....	....	....	....	....	....

Signed as a free agent by **Pittsburgh**, May 16, 2011. • Missed majority of 2013-14 due to wrist injury at Norfolk (AHL), January 25, 2014. Traded to **Toronto** by **Pittsburgh** with Pittsburgh's 4th round pick (later traded to Edmonton, later traded to Ottawa – Ottawa selected Christian Wolanin) in 2015 NHL Draft and Pittsburgh's 2nd round pick (later traded back to Pittsburgh – Pittsburgh selected Kasper Bjorkqvist) in 2016 NHL Draft for Daniel Winnik, February 25, 2015. Signed as a free agent by **Washington**, July 16, 2015.

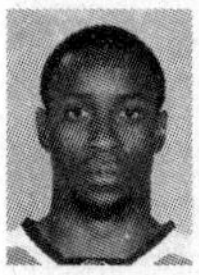

SIMMONDS, Wayne
(SIH-muhnds, WAYN) **PHI**

Right wing. Shoots right. 6'2", 185 lbs. Born, Scarborough, ON, August 26, 1988. Los Angeles' 3rd pick, 61st overall, in 2007 NHL Draft.

Season	Club	League	GP	G	A	Pts	PIM	PP	SH	GW	S	S%	+/-	TF	F%	Min	GP	G	A	Pts	PIM	PP	SH	GW	Min
2004-05	Tor. Jr. Canadiens	GTHL	67	32	40	72	97	....	....	....	....	....	....	....	....	....	....	....	....	....	....	....	....	....	....
2005-06	Brockville Braves	ON-Jr.A	49	24	19	43	127	....	....	....	....	....	....	....	....	....	7	4	2	6	12	....	....	....	....
2006-07	Owen Sound	OHL	66	23	26	49	112	....	....	....	....	....	....	....	....	....	4	1	1	2	4	....	....	....	....
2007-08	Owen Sound	OHL	29	17	22	39	43	....	....	....	....	....	....	....	....	....	....	....	....	....	....	....	....	....	....
	Sault Ste. Marie	OHL	31	16	20	36	68	....	....	....	....	....	....	....	....	....	14	5	9	14	22	....	....	....	....
2008-09	**Los Angeles**	**NHL**	**82**	**9**	**14**	**23**	**73**	**2**	**0**	**2**	**127**	**7.1**	**-8**	**25**	**36.0**	**13:50**	....	....	....	....	....	....	....	....	....
2009-10	**Los Angeles**	**NHL**	**78**	**16**	**24**	**40**	**116**	**0**	**0**	**2**	**127**	**12.6**	**22**	**10**	**30.0**	**14:29**	**6**	**2**	**1**	**3**	**9**	**0**	**0**	**0**	**14:21**
2010-11	**Los Angeles**	**NHL**	**80**	**14**	**16**	**30**	**75**	**1**	**0**	**3**	**117**	**12.0**	**-2**	**19**	**36.8**	**13:27**	**6**	**1**	**2**	**3**	**20**	**0**	**0**	**0**	**14:44**
2011-12	**Philadelphia**	**NHL**	**82**	**28**	**21**	**49**	**114**	**11**	**0**	**4**	**197**	**14.2**	**-1**	**17**	**41.2**	**15:55**	**11**	**1**	**5**	**6**	**38**	**1**	**0**	**0**	**14:52**
2012-13	Crimmitschau	German-2	9	4	10	14	35	....	....	....	....	....	....	....	....	....	....	....	....	....	....	....	....	....	....
	Liberec	CzRep	6	4	2	6	16	....	....	....	....	....	....	....	....	....	....	....	....	....	....	....	....	....	....
	Philadelphia	**NHL**	**45**	**15**	**17**	**32**	**82**	**6**	**0**	**4**	**110**	**13.6**	**-7**	**3**	**66.7**	**15:38**	....	....	....	....	....	....	....	....	....
2013-14	**Philadelphia**	**NHL**	**82**	**29**	**31**	**60**	**106**	**15**	**0**	**4**	**209**	**13.9**	**-4**	**2**	**50.0**	**16:46**	**7**	**4**	**1**	**5**	**20**	**3**	**0**	**0**	**15:23**
2014-15	**Philadelphia**	**NHL**	**75**	**28**	**22**	**50**	**66**	**14**	**0**	**6**	**188**	**14.9**	**-5**	**5**	**80.0**	**16:48**	....	....	....	....	....	....	....	....	....
2015-16	**Philadelphia**	**NHL**	**81**	**32**	**28**	**60**	**147**	**13**	**0**	**5**	**229**	**14.0**	**-7**	**7**	**71.4**	**17:14**	**6**	**0**	**2**	**2**	**13**	**0**	**0**	**0**	**17:48**
2016-17	**Philadelphia**	**NHL**	**82**	**31**	**23**	**54**	**122**	**16**	**2**	**4**	**224**	**13.8**	**-18**	**17**	**47.1**	**18:58**	....	....	....	....	....	....	....	....	....
	NHL Totals		**687**	**202**	**196**	**398**	**901**	**78**	**2**	**34**	**1528**	**13.2**		**105**	**43.8**	**15:55**	**36**	**8**	**11**	**19**	**100**	**4**	**0**	**0**	**15:21**

Traded to **Philadelphia** by **Los Angeles** with Brayden Schenn and Los Angeles' 2nd round pick (later traded to Dallas – Dallas selected Devin Shore) in 2012 NHL Draft for Mike Richards and Rob Bordson, June 23, 2011. Signed as a free agent by **Crimmitschau** (German-2), September 24, 2012. Signed as a free agent by **Liberec** (CzRep), October 23, 2012.

Played in NHL All-Star Game (2017)

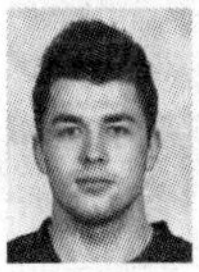

SIMON, Dominik
(see-MAWN, DOHM-ihn-ihk) **PIT**

Center. Shoots left. 5'11", 176 lbs. Born, Prague, Czech Rep., August 8, 1994. Pittsburgh's 2nd pick, 137th overall, in 2015 NHL Draft.

Season	Club	League	GP	G	A	Pts	PIM	PP	SH	GW	S	S%	+/-	TF	F%	Min	GP	G	A	Pts	PIM	PP	SH	GW	Min
2009-10	Sparta U18	CzR-U18	4	1	1	2	0	....	....	....	....	....	....	....	....	....	....	....	....	....	....	....	....	....	....
2010-11	Sparta U18	CzR-U18	38	24	16	40	10	....	....	....	....	....	....	....	....	....	5	2	1	3	4	....	....	....	....
2011-12	Sparta U18	CzR-U18	14	17	13	30	12	....	....	....	....	....	....	....	....	....	7	3	5	8	4	....	....	....	....
	Sparta Jr.	CzRep-Jr.	34	11	10	21	2	....	....	....	....	....	....	....	....	....	....	....	....	....	....	....	....	....	....
2012-13	Sparta Jr.	CzRep-Jr.	11	9	8	17	2	....	....	....	....	....	....	....	....	....	7	7	0	7	2	....	....	....	....
	HC Sparta Praha	CzRep	18	1	1	2	0	....	....	....	....	....	....	....	....	....	....	....	....	....	....	....	....	....	....
	Litomerice	CzRep-2	25	9	10	19	24	....	....	....	....	....	....	....	....	....	....	....	....	....	....	....	....	....	....
2013-14	HC Sparta Praha	CzRep	46	7	4	11	4	....	....	....	....	....	....	....	....	....	10	1	1	2	6	....	....	....	....
	Litomerice	CzRep-2	3	0	1	1	12	....	....	....	....	....	....	....	....	....	....	....	....	....	....	....	....	....	....
2014-15	HC Skoda Plzen	CzRep	52	18	12	30	20	....	....	....	....	....	....	....	....	....	4	1	2	3	4	....	....	....	....
2015-16	**Pittsburgh**	**NHL**	**3**	**0**	**1**	**1**	**0**	**0**	**0**	**0**	**2**	**0.0**	**0**	**0**	**0.0**	**6:04**	....	....	....	....	....	....	....	....	....
	Wilkes-Barre	AHL	68	25	23	48	36	....	....	....	....	....	....	....	....	....	7	1	1	2	2	....	....	....	....
2016-17	**Pittsburgh**	**NHL**	**2**	**0**	**1**	**1**	**0**	**0**	**0**	**0**	**2**	**0.0**	**-1**	**0**	**0.0**	**13:03**	....	....	....	....	....	....	....	....	....
	Wilkes-Barre	AHL	70	15	31	46	18	....	....	....	....	....	....	....	....	....	5	0	3	3	0	....	....	....	....
	NHL Totals		**5**	**0**	**2**	**2**	**0**	**0**	**0**	**0**	**4**	**0.0**		**0**	**0.0**	**8:52**	....	....	....	....	....	....	....	....	....

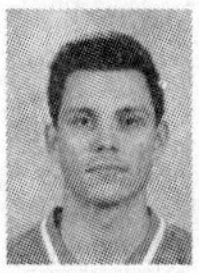

SIMPSON, Dillon
(SIHMP-suhn, DIH-luhn) **EDM**

Defense. Shoots left. 6'2", 194 lbs. Born, Edmonton, AB, February 10, 1993. Edmonton's 6th pick, 92nd overall, in 2011 NHL Draft.

Season	Club	League	GP	G	A	Pts	PIM	PP	SH	GW	S	S%	+/-	TF	F%	Min	GP	G	A	Pts	PIM	PP	SH	GW	Min
2007-08	Southgate	AMBHL	33	7	31	38	32	....	....	....	....	....	....	....	....	....	4	4	2	6	2	....	....	....	....
2008-09	SSAC Athletics	AMHL	34	3	12	15	8	....	....	....	....	....	....	....	....	....	4	0	0	0	0	....	....	....	....
	Spruce Grove	AJHL	1	0	0	0	0	....	....	....	....	....	....	....	....	....	1	0	0	0	2	....	....	....	....
2009-10	Spruce Grove	AJHL	58	12	29	41	19	....	....	....	....	....	....	....	....	....	16	0	6	6	6	....	....	....	....
2010-11	North Dakota	WCHA	30	2	8	10	8	....	....	....	....	....	....	....	....	....	....	....	....	....	....	....	....	....	....
2011-12	North Dakota	WCHA	42	2	16	18	8	....	....	....	....	....	....	....	....	....	....	....	....	....	....	....	....	....	....
2012-13	North Dakota	WCHA	42	5	19	24	12	....	....	....	....	....	....	....	....	....	....	....	....	....	....	....	....	....	....
2013-14	North Dakota	NCHC	42	7	16	23	20	....	....	....	....	....	....	....	....	....	....	....	....	....	....	....	....	....	....
2014-15	Oklahoma City	AHL	71	3	14	17	14	....	....	....	....	....	....	....	....	....	10	0	0	0	0	....	....	....	....
2015-16	Bakersfield	AHL	57	4	16	20	20	....	....	....	....	....	....	....	....	....	....	....	....	....	....	....	....	....	....
2016-17	**Edmonton**	**NHL**	**3**	**0**	**0**	**0**	**2**	**0**	**0**	**0**	**2**	**0.0**	**0**	**0**	**0.0**	**10:53**	....	....	....	....	....	....	....	....	....
	Bakersfield	AHL	53	3	8	11	26	....	....	....	....	....	....	....	....	....	....	....	....	....	....	....	....	....	....
	NHL Totals		**3**	**0**	**0**	**0**	**2**	**0**	**0**	**0**	**2**	**0.0**		**0**	**0.0**	**10:53**	....	....	....	....	....	....	....	....	....

NCHC First All-Star Team (2014)

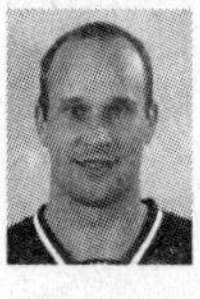

SISLO, Mike
(SIHS-loh, MIGHK) **ARI**

Right wing. Shoots right. 5'11", 190 lbs. Born, Superior, WI, January 20, 1988.

Season	Club	League	GP	G	A	Pts	PIM	PP	SH	GW	S	S%	+/-	TF	F%	Min	GP	G	A	Pts	PIM	PP	SH	GW	Min
2005-06	Green Bay	USHL	57	3	3	6	36	....	....	....	....	....	....	....	....	....	3	0	0	0	5	....	....	....	....
2006-07	Green Bay	USHL	60	23	26	49	28	....	....	....	....	....	....	....	....	....	4	3	1	4	2	....	....	....	....
2007-08	New Hampshire	H-East	38	3	5	8	12	....	....	....	....	....	....	....	....	....	....	....	....	....	....	....	....	....	....
2008-09	New Hampshire	H-East	38	19	12	31	12	....	....	....	....	....	....	....	....	....	....	....	....	....	....	....	....	....	....
2009-10	New Hampshire	H-East	39	14	15	29	20	....	....	....	....	....	....	....	....	....	....	....	....	....	....	....	....	....	....
2010-11	New Hampshire	H-East	39	15	*33	48	38	....	....	....	....	....	....	....	....	....	....	....	....	....	....	....	....	....	....
	Albany Devils	AHL	3	0	0	0	0	....	....	....	....	....	....	....	....	....	....	....	....	....	....	....	....	....	....
2011-12	Albany Devils	AHL	59	9	18	27	20	....	....	....	....	....	....	....	....	....	....	....	....	....	....	....	....	....	....
2012-13	Albany Devils	AHL	61	13	13	26	46	....	....	....	....	....	....	....	....	....	....	....	....	....	....	....	....	....	....
2013-14	**New Jersey**	**NHL**	**14**	**0**	**0**	**0**	**0**	**0**	**0**	**0**	**20**	**0.0**	**-1**	**6**	**83.3**	**8:51**	....	....	....	....	....	....	....	....	....
	Albany Devils	AHL	59	23	18	41	26	....	....	....	....	....	....	....	....	....	4	1	1	2	0	....	....	....	....
2014-15	**New Jersey**	**NHL**	**10**	**0**	**1**	**1**	**2**	**0**	**0**	**0**	**13**	**0.0**	**-2**	**0**	**0.0**	**12:13**	....	....	....	....	....	....	....	....	....
	Albany Devils	AHL	65	20	20	40	53	....	....	....	....	....	....	....	....	....	....	....	....	....	....	....	....	....	....
2015-16	**New Jersey**	**NHL**	**18**	**3**	**1**	**4**	**4**	**1**	**0**	**0**	**29**	**10.3**	**-2**	**2**	**0.0**	**12:26**	....	....	....	....	....	....	....	....	....
	Albany Devils	AHL	57	27	26	53	18	....	....	....	....	....	....	....	....	....	9	2	5	7	6	....	....	....	....

			Regular Season														Playoffs								
Season	Club	League	GP	G	A	Pts	PIM	PP	SH	GW	S	S%	+/-	TF	F%	Min	GP	G	A	Pts	PIM	PP	SH	GW	Min
2016-17	San Antonio	AHL	54	6	15	21	18	....	....	....	....	....	....	....	....	....	....	....	....	....	....	....	....	....	....
	Toronto Marlies	AHL	18	8	8	16	8	....	....	....	....	....	....	....	....	....	5	0	0	0	0	....	....	....	....
	NHL Totals		**42**	**3**	**2**	**5**	**6**	**1**	**0**	**0**	**62**	**4.8**		**8**	**62.5**	**11:11**	....	....	....	....	....	....	....	....	....

AHL Second All-Star Team (2016)

Signed as a free agent by **New Jersey**, April 6, 2011. Signed as a free agent by **Colorado**, July 1, 2016. • Loaned to **Toronto** (AHL) by **Colorado**, March 3, 2017. Signed as a free agent by **Arizona**, July 1, 2017.

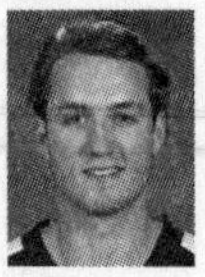

SISSONS, Colton (SIH-suhnz, KOHL-tuhn) NSH

Center. Shoots right. 6'1", 200 lbs. Born, North Vancouver, BC, November 5, 1993. Nashville's 2nd pick, 50th overall, in 2012 NHL Draft.

2008-09	Van. NW Giants	BCMML	39	30	24	54	44	....	....	....	....	....	....	....	....	....	....	....	....	....	....	....	....	....	....
2009-10	Westside Warriors	BCHL	58	6	16	22	29	....	....	....	....	....	....	....	....	....	11	1	1	2	4	....	....	....	....
2010-11	Kelowna Rockets	WHL	63	17	24	41	46	....	....	....	....	....	....	....	....	....	10	3	3	6	6	....	....	....	....
2011-12	Kelowna Rockets	WHL	58	26	15	41	62	....	....	....	....	....	....	....	....	....	4	1	1	2	2	....	....	....	....
2012-13	Kelowna Rockets	WHL	61	28	39	67	54	....	....	....	....	....	....	....	....	....	....	....	....	....	....	....	....	....	....
2013-14	**Nashville**	**NHL**	**17**	**1**	**3**	**4**	**4**	**0**	**0**	**0**	**13**	**7.7**	**0**	**144**	**48.6**	**10:37**	....	....	....	....	....	....	....	....	....
	Milwaukee	AHL	62	25	19	44	8	....	....	....	....	....	....	....	....	....	3	0	1	1	2	....	....	....	....
2014-15	Milwaukee	AHL	76	25	17	42	27	....	....	....	....	....	....	....	....	....	....	....	....	....	....	....	....	....	....
2015-16	**Nashville**	**NHL**	**34**	**4**	**2**	**6**	**12**	**0**	**0**	**0**	**25**	**16.0**	**5**	**252**	**56.0**	**9:58**	**10**	**0**	**0**	**0**	**8**	**0**	**0**	**0**	**10:34**
	Milwaukee	AHL	38	8	11	19	31	....	....	....	....	....	....	....	....	....	....	....	....	....	....	....	....	....	....
2016-17	**Nashville**	**NHL**	**58**	**8**	**2**	**10**	**12**	**0**	**1**	**1**	**42**	**19.0**	**11**	**384**	**50.0**	**11:07**	**22**	**6**	**6**	**12**	**16**	**1**	**0**	**2**	**15:04**
	NHL Totals		**109**	**13**	**7**	**20**	**28**	**0**	**1**	**1**	**80**	**16.3**		**780**	**51.7**	**10:41**	**32**	**6**	**6**	**12**	**24**	**1**	**0**	**2**	**13:39**

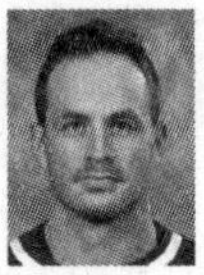

SKILLE, Jack (SKIH-lee, JAK)

Right wing. Shoots right. 6'1", 216 lbs. Born, Madison, WI, May 19, 1987. Chicago's 1st pick, 7th overall, in 2005 NHL Draft.

2003-04	USAHNTDP	NAHL	28	11	9	20	31	....	....	....	....	....	....	....	....	....	....	....	....	....	....	....	....	....	....
	USAHNTDP	U-17	33	14	10	24	30	....	....	....	....	....	....	....	....	....	....	....	....	....	....	....	....	....	....
2004-05	USAHNTDP	NAHL	16	6	11	17	20	....	....	....	....	....	....	....	....	....	....	....	....	....	....	....	....	....	....
	USAHNTDP	U-18	26	9	11	20	36	....	....	....	....	....	....	....	....	....	....	....	....	....	....	....	....	....	....
2005-06	U. of Wisconsin	WCHA	41	13	8	21	37	....	....	....	....	....	....	....	....	....	....	....	....	....	....	....	....	....	....
2006-07	U. of Wisconsin	WCHA	26	8	10	18	12	....	....	....	....	....	....	....	....	....	....	....	....	....	....	....	....	....	....
	Norfolk Admirals	AHL	9	4	4	8	0	....	....	....	....	....	....	....	....	....	3	0	0	0	2	....	....	....	....
2007-08	**Chicago**	**NHL**	**16**	**3**	**2**	**5**	**0**	**0**	**0**	**0**	**23**	**13.0**	**1**	**4**	**50.0**	**11:59**	....	....	....	....	....	....	....	....	....
	Rockford IceHogs	AHL	59	16	18	34	44	....	....	....	....	....	....	....	....	....	12	2	1	3	6	....	....	....	....
2008-09	**Chicago**	**NHL**	**8**	**1**	**0**	**1**	**5**	**0**	**0**	**0**	**14**	**7.1**	**–3**	**0**	**0.0**	**9:26**	....	....	....	....	....	....	....	....	....
	Rockford IceHogs	AHL	58	20	25	45	56	....	....	....	....	....	....	....	....	....	....	....	....	....	....	....	....	....	....
2009-10	**Chicago**	**NHL**	**6**	**1**	**1**	**2**	**0**	**0**	**0**	**0**	**9**	**11.1**	**–3**	**0**	**0.0**	**7:40**	....	....	....	....	....	....	....	....	....
	Rockford IceHogs	AHL	63	23	26	49	50	....	....	....	....	....	....	....	....	....	4	0	0	0	0	....	....	....	....
2010-11	**Chicago**	**NHL**	**49**	**7**	**10**	**17**	**25**	**1**	**0**	**1**	**121**	**5.8**	**3**	**4**	**50.0**	**10:44**	....	....	....	....	....	....	....	....	....
	Florida	**NHL**	**13**	**1**	**1**	**2**	**4**	**0**	**0**	**0**	**33**	**3.0**	**–12**	**6**	**16.7**	**16:25**	....	....	....	....	....	....	....	....	....
2011-12	**Florida**	**NHL**	**46**	**4**	**6**	**10**	**28**	**0**	**1**	**1**	**76**	**5.3**	**–9**	**16**	**50.0**	**11:58**	....	....	....	....	....	....	....	....	....
2012-13	Rosenborg Elite	Norway	9	6	6	12	20	....	....	....	....	....	....	....	....	....	....	....	....	....	....	....	....	....	....
	Florida	**NHL**	**40**	**3**	**9**	**12**	**11**	**0**	**0**	**0**	**69**	**4.3**	**–9**	**16**	**50.0**	**13:19**	....	....	....	....	....	....	....	....	....
2013-14	**Columbus**	**NHL**	**16**	**4**	**0**	**4**	**6**	**0**	**0**	**1**	**23**	**17.4**	**2**	**1**	**100.0**	**8:40**	**6**	**0**	**1**	**1**	**0**	**0**	**0**	**0**	**11:01**
	Springfield	AHL	22	13	11	24	9	....	....	....	....	....	....	....	....	....	....	....	....	....	....	....	....	....	....
2014-15	**Columbus**	**NHL**	**45**	**6**	**2**	**8**	**16**	**0**	**0**	**0**	**95**	**6.3**	**–18**	**8**	**37.5**	**12:31**	....	....	....	....	....	....	....	....	....
2015-16	**Colorado**	**NHL**	**74**	**8**	**6**	**14**	**11**	**0**	**0**	**0**	**106**	**7.5**	**–4**	**19**	**21.1**	**8:50**	....	....	....	....	....	....	....	....	....
2016-17	**Vancouver**	**NHL**	**55**	**5**	**4**	**9**	**12**	**0**	**0**	**0**	**73**	**6.8**	**0**	**2**	**100.0**	**8:48**	....	....	....	....	....	....	....	....	....
	NHL Totals		**368**	**43**	**41**	**84**	**118**	**1**	**1**	**3**	**642**	**6.7**		**76**	**40.8**	**10:48**	**6**	**0**	**1**	**1**	**0**	**0**	**0**	**0**	**11:01**

Traded to **Florida** by **Chicago** with Hugh Jessiman and David Pacan for Michael Frolik and Alexander Salak, February 9, 2011. Signed as a free agent by **Rosenborg** (Norway), October 11, 2012. Signed as a free agent by **Columbus**, July 7, 2013. • Missed majority of 2013-14 due to upper-body injury at Colorado, December 31, 2013. Signed as a free agent by **NY Islanders**, July 1, 2014. Claimed on waivers by **Columbus** from **NY Islanders**, October 5, 2014. Signed as a free agent by **Colorado**, October 6, 2015. Signed as a free agent by **Vancouver**, October 13, 2016.

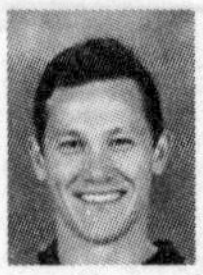

SKINNER, Jeff (SKIH-nuhr, JEHF) CAR

Center. Shoots left. 5'11", 200 lbs. Born, Markham, ON, May 16, 1992. Carolina's 1st pick, 7th overall, in 2010 NHL Draft.

2007-08	Tor. Young Nats	GTHL	56	65	44	109	163	....	....	....	....	....	....	....	....	....	....	....	....	....	....	....	....	....	....
2008-09	Kitchener Rangers	OHL	63	27	24	51	34	....	....	....	....	....	....	....	....	....	....	....	....	....	....	....	....	....	....
2009-10	Kitchener Rangers	OHL	64	50	40	90	72	....	....	....	....	....	....	....	....	....	20	*20	13	33	14	....	....	....	....
2010-11	**Carolina**	**NHL**	**82**	**31**	**32**	**63**	**46**	**6**	**0**	**2**	**215**	**14.4**	**3**	**157**	**36.9**	**16:44**	....	....	....	....	....	....	....	....	....
2011-12	**Carolina**	**NHL**	**64**	**20**	**24**	**44**	**56**	**4**	**0**	**5**	**210**	**9.5**	**–8**	**159**	**42.1**	**18:37**	....	....	....	....	....	....	....	....	....
2012-13	**Carolina**	**NHL**	**42**	**13**	**11**	**24**	**26**	**5**	**0**	**0**	**159**	**8.2**	**–21**	**44**	**47.7**	**18:28**	....	....	....	....	....	....	....	....	....
2013-14	**Carolina**	**NHL**	**71**	**33**	**21**	**54**	**22**	**11**	**0**	**6**	**274**	**12.0**	**–14**	**51**	**45.1**	**17:12**	....	....	....	....	....	....	....	....	....
2014-15	**Carolina**	**NHL**	**77**	**18**	**13**	**31**	**18**	**4**	**0**	**2**	**235**	**7.7**	**–24**	**46**	**45.7**	**16:03**	....	....	....	....	....	....	....	....	....
2015-16	**Carolina**	**NHL**	**82**	**28**	**23**	**51**	**38**	**4**	**0**	**7**	**258**	**10.9**	**–2**	**47**	**42.6**	**16:17**	....	....	....	....	....	....	....	....	....
2016-17	**Carolina**	**NHL**	**79**	**37**	**26**	**63**	**28**	**7**	**0**	**4**	**281**	**13.2**	**–3**	**27**	**37.0**	**17:44**	....	....	....	....	....	....	....	....	....
	NHL Totals		**497**	**180**	**150**	**330**	**234**	**41**	**0**	**26**	**1632**	**11.0**		**531**	**41.4**	**17:10**	....	....	....	....	....	....	....	....	....

NHL All-Rookie Team (2011) • Calder Memorial Trophy (2011)
Played in NHL All-Star Game (2011)

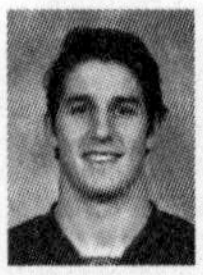

SKJEI, Brady (SHAY, BRAY-dee) NYR

Defense. Shoots left. 6'3", 211 lbs. Born, Lakeville, MN, March 26, 1994. NY Rangers' 1st pick, 28th overall, in 2012 NHL Draft.

2009-10	Lakeville North	High-MN	25	7	16	23	24	....	....	....	....	....	....	....	....	....	5	4	2	6	6	....	....	....	....
2010-11	USAHNTDP	USHL	36	1	5	6	14	....	....	....	....	....	....	....	....	....	2	0	0	0	0	....	....	....	....
	USAHNTDP	U-17	17	4	9	13	10	....	....	....	....	....	....	....	....	....	....	....	....	....	....	....	....	....	....
2011-12	USAHNTDP	USHL	24	3	9	12	12	....	....	....	....	....	....	....	....	....	....	....	....	....	....	....	....	....	....
	USAHNTDP	U-18	36	1	10	11	24	....	....	....	....	....	....	....	....	....	....	....	....	....	....	....	....	....	....
2012-13	U. of Minnesota	WCHA	36	1	2	3	14	....	....	....	....	....	....	....	....	....	....	....	....	....	....	....	....	....	....
2013-14	U. of Minnesota	Big Ten	40	6	8	14	30	....	....	....	....	....	....	....	....	....	....	....	....	....	....	....	....	....	....
2014-15	U. of Minnesota	Big Ten	33	1	9	10	32	....	....	....	....	....	....	....	....	....	....	....	....	....	....	....	....	....	....
	Hartford	AHL	8	0	0	0	0	....	....	....	....	....	....	....	....	....	15	1	2	3	16	....	....	....	....
2015-16	**NY Rangers**	**NHL**	**7**	**0**	**0**	**0**	**4**	**0**	**0**	**0**	**6**	**0.0**	**1**	**0**	**0.0**	**17:44**	**5**	**0**	**2**	**2**	**2**	**0**	**0**	**0**	**18:28**
	Hartford	AHL	68	4	24	28	36	....	....	....	....	....	....	....	....	....	....	....	....	....	....	....	....	....	....
2016-17	**NY Rangers**	**NHL**	**80**	**5**	**34**	**39**	**42**	**0**	**0**	**0**	**127**	**3.9**	**11**	**1**	**0.0**	**17:28**	**12**	**4**	**1**	**5**	**10**	**0**	**0**	**0**	**19:15**
	NHL Totals		**87**	**5**	**34**	**39**	**46**	**0**	**0**	**0**	**133**	**3.8**		**1**	**0.0**	**17:29**	**17**	**4**	**3**	**7**	**12**	**0**	**0**	**0**	**19:01**

NHL All-Rookie Team (2017)

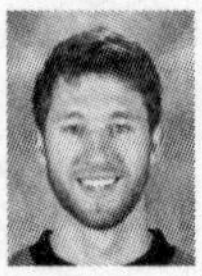

SLAVIN, Jaccob (SLA-vihn, JAY-kuhb) CAR

Defense. Shoots left. 6'3", 205 lbs. Born, Denver, CO, May 1, 1994. Carolina's 6th pick, 120th overall, in 2012 NHL Draft.

2010-11	Col. Thunderbirds	T1EHL	34	5	21	26	12	....	....	....	....	....	....	....	....	....	....	....	....	....	....	....	....	....	....
	Chicago Steel	USHL	17	1	0	1	10	....	....	....	....	....	....	....	....	....	....	....	....	....	....	....	....	....	....
2011-12	Chicago Steel	USHL	60	3	27	30	12	....	....	....	....	....	....	....	....	....	....	....	....	....	....	....	....	....	....
2012-13	Chicago Steel	USHL	62	5	28	33	6	....	....	....	....	....	....	....	....	....	....	....	....	....	....	....	....	....	....
2013-14	Colorado College	NCHC	32	5	20	25	11	....	....	....	....	....	....	....	....	....	....	....	....	....	....	....	....	....	....
2014-15	Colorado College	NCHC	34	5	12	17	2	....	....	....	....	....	....	....	....	....	....	....	....	....	....	....	....	....	....
2015-16	**Carolina**	**NHL**	**63**	**2**	**18**	**20**	**8**	**0**	**0**	**0**	**84**	**2.4**	**1**	**0**	**0.0**	**20:59**	....	....	....	....	....	....	....	....	....
	Charlotte	AHL	14	0	7	7	0	....	....	....	....	....	....	....	....	....	....	....	....	....	....	....	....	....	....
2016-17	**Carolina**	**NHL**	**82**	**5**	**29**	**34**	**12**	**0**	**1**	**0**	**99**	**5.1**	**23**	**0**	**0.0**	**23:26**	....	....	....	....	....	....	....	....	....
	NHL Totals		**145**	**7**	**47**	**54**	**20**	**0**	**1**	**0**	**183**	**3.8**		**0**	**0.0**	**22:22**	....	....	....	....	....	....	....	....	....

NCHC All-Rookie Team (2014) • NCHC Second All-Star Team (2014) • NCHC Rookie of the Year (2014) • NCHC First All-Star Team (2015)

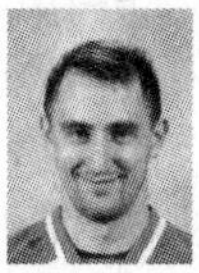

SLEPYSHEV, Anton (SLEHP-ih-shehv, an-TAWN) EDM

Left wing. Shoots left. 6'2", 218 lbs. Born, Penza, Russia, May 13, 1994. Edmonton's 4th pick, 88th overall, in 2013 NHL Draft.

			Regular Season														Playoffs								
Season	Club	League	GP	G	A	Pts	PIM	PP	SH	GW	S	S%	+/-	TF	F%	Min	GP	G	A	Pts	PIM	PP	SH	GW	Min
2009-10	Dizel Penza 2	Russia-3	39	12	9	21	10										4	1	1	2	4				
2010-11	Dizel Penza 2	Russia-3	20	8	4	12	10																		
2011-12	Novokuznetsk Jr.	Russia-Jr.	13	7	2	9	6										3	1	0	1	0				
	Novokuznetsk	KHL	39	4	3	7	2																		
2012-13	Novokuznetsk Jr.	Russia-Jr.	1	0	0	0	0																		
	Novokuznetsk	KHL	15	3	0	3	2																		
	Ufa	KHL	11	4	2	6	2										14	0	0	0	0				
	Tolpar Ufa Jr.	Russia-Jr.															3	0	1	1	12				
2013-14	Tolpar Ufa Jr.	Russia-Jr.	2	2	2	4	0																		
	Ufa	KHL	36	3	5	8	4										18	2	1	3	6				
2014-15	Ufa	KHL	58	15	10	25	12										5	0	2	2	0				
2015-16	**Edmonton**	**NHL**	**11**	**0**	**1**	**1**	**2**	**0**	**0**	**0**	**5**	**0.0**	**–5**	**1**	**100.0**	**8:41**									
	Bakersfield	AHL	49	13	8	21	28																		
2016-17	**Edmonton**	**NHL**	**41**	**4**	**6**	**10**	**4**	**0**	**0**	**0**	**55**	**7.3**	**5**	**5**	**40.0**	**11:07**	**12**	**3**	**0**	**3**	**4**	**0**	**0**	**1**	**11:21**
	Bakersfield	AHL	9	3	7	10	6																		
	NHL Totals		**52**	**4**	**7**	**11**	**6**	**0**	**0**	**0**	**60**	**6.7**		**6**	**50.0**	**10:36**	**12**	**3**	**0**	**3**	**4**	**0**	**0**	**1**	**11:21**

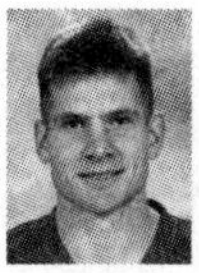

SMITH, Ben (SMIHTH, BEHN) TOR

Right wing. Shoots right. 5'11", 198 lbs. Born, Winston-Salem, NC, July 11, 1988. Chicago's 5th pick, 169th overall, in 2008 NHL Draft.

			Regular Season														Playoffs								
Season	Club	League	GP	G	A	Pts	PIM	PP	SH	GW	S	S%	+/-	TF	F%	Min	GP	G	A	Pts	PIM	PP	SH	GW	Min
2006-07	Boston College	H-East	42	10	8	18	10																		
2007-08	Boston College	H-East	44	25	25	50	12																		
2008-09	Boston College	H-East	37	6	11	17	6																		
2009-10	Boston College	H-East	42	16	21	37	8																		
	Rockford IceHogs	AHL															3	1	0	1	0				
2010-11	**Chicago**	**NHL**	**6**	**1**	**0**	**1**	**0**	**0**	**0**	**0**	**6**	**16.7**	**1**	**8**	**75.0**	**13:47**	**7**	**3**	**0**	**3**	**0**	**0**	**0**	**1**	**14:50**
	Rockford IceHogs	AHL	63	19	12	31	16																		
2011-12	**Chicago**	**NHL**	**13**	**2**	**0**	**2**	**0**	**0**	**0**	**0**	**18**	**11.1**	**–5**	**14**	**50.0**	**9:49**									
	Rockford IceHogs	AHL	38	15	16	31	10																		
2012-13	Rockford IceHogs	AHL	54	27	20	47	13																		
	♦ **Chicago**	**NHL**	**1**	**1**	**0**	**1**	**0**	**0**	**0**	**0**	**1**	**100.0**	**1**	**2**	**0.0**	**18:21**	**1**	**0**	**0**	**0**	**0**	**0**	**0**	**0**	**10:23**
2013-14	**Chicago**	**NHL**	**75**	**14**	**12**	**26**	**2**	**1**	**0**	**2**	**90**	**15.6**	**3**	**394**	**50.8**	**12:44**	**19**	**4**	**2**	**6**	**2**	**0**	**0**	**0**	**15:14**
2014-15	**Chicago**	**NHL**	**61**	**5**	**4**	**9**	**2**	**0**	**0**	**0**	**77**	**6.5**	**–1**	**452**	**51.1**	**13:35**									
	San Jose	**NHL**	**19**	**2**	**3**	**5**	**0**	**0**	**0**	**1**	**15**	**13.3**	**3**	**142**	**55.6**	**11:20**									
2015-16	**San Jose**	**NHL**	**6**	**0**	**0**	**0**	**0**	**0**	**0**	**0**	**1**	**0.0**	**–1**	**17**	**29.4**	**5:59**									
	St. John's IceCaps	AHL	14	8	2	10	4																		
	Toronto	**NHL**	**16**	**2**	**4**	**6**	**0**	**0**	**0**	**1**	**16**	**12.5**	**3**	**168**	**56.6**	**14:23**									
	Toronto Marlies	AHL	5	4	2	6	0										15	2	7	9	2				
2016-17	**Colorado**	**NHL**	**4**	**0**	**0**	**0**	**0**	**0**	**0**	**0**	**1**	**0.0**	**–2**	**40**	**52.5**	**10:46**									
	Toronto	**NHL**	**36**	**2**	**2**	**4**	**4**	**0**	**0**	**0**	**29**	**6.9**	**–5**	**428**	**51.4**	**11:33**									
	NHL Totals		**237**	**29**	**25**	**54**	**8**	**1**	**0**	**4**	**254**	**11.4**		**1665**	**51.9**	**12:28**	**27**	**7**	**2**	**9**	**2**	**0**	**0**	**1**	**14:57**

NCAA Championship All-Tournament Team (2008, 2010) • NCAA Championship Tournament MVP (2010)

Traded to **San Jose** by **Chicago** with Chicago's 7th round pick (Ivan Chekhovich) in 2017 NHL Draft for Andrew Desjardins, March 2, 2015. Traded to **Toronto** by **San Jose** with Alex Stalock and San Jose's 3rd round pick in 2018 NHL Draft for James Reimer and Jeremy Morin, February 28, 2016. Signed as a free agent by **Colorado**, August 16, 2016. Claimed on waivers by **Toronto** from **Colorado**, October 24, 2016.

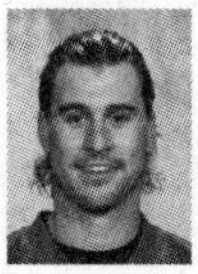

SMITH, Brendan (SMIHTH, BREHN-duhn) NYR

Defense. Shoots left. 6'2", 211 lbs. Born, Mimico, ON, February 8, 1989. Detroit's 1st pick, 27th overall, in 2007 NHL Draft.

			Regular Season														Playoffs								
Season	Club	League	GP	G	A	Pts	PIM	PP	SH	GW	S	S%	+/-	TF	F%	Min	GP	G	A	Pts	PIM	PP	SH	GW	Min
2004-05	Tor. Marlboros	GTHL	66	22	63	85	120																		
2005-06	St. Michael's	ON-Jr.A	39	5	21	26	55										17	1	5	6	44				
2006-07	St. Michael's	ON-Jr.A	39	12	24	36	90										16	6	14	20	30				
2007-08	U. of Wisconsin	WCHA	22	2	10	12	26																		
2008-09	U. of Wisconsin	WCHA	31	9	14	23	75																		
2009-10	U. of Wisconsin	WCHA	42	15	37	52	76																		
2010-11	Grand Rapids	AHL	63	12	20	32	124																		
2011-12	**Detroit**	**NHL**	**14**	**1**	**6**	**7**	**13**	**0**	**0**	**0**	**13**	**7.7**	**3**	**0**	**0.0**	**15:38**									
	Grand Rapids	AHL	57	10	24	34	90																		
2012-13	Grand Rapids	AHL	32	5	15	20	49																		
	Detroit	**NHL**	**34**	**0**	**8**	**8**	**36**	**0**	**0**	**0**	**33**	**0.0**	**1**	**0**	**0.0**	**18:24**	**14**	**2**	**3**	**5**	**10**	**0**	**0**	**1**	**19:08**
2013-14	**Detroit**	**NHL**	**71**	**5**	**14**	**19**	**68**	**1**	**0**	**0**	**90**	**5.6**	**–2**	**0**	**0.0**	**18:23**	**5**	**0**	**0**	**0**	**8**	**0**	**0**	**0**	**19:37**
2014-15	**Detroit**	**NHL**	**76**	**4**	**9**	**13**	**68**	**0**	**0**	**1**	**88**	**4.5**	**–2**	**0**	**0.0**	**17:53**	**5**	**0**	**0**	**0**	**6**	**0**	**0**	**0**	**16:05**
2015-16	**Detroit**	**NHL**	**63**	**3**	**12**	**15**	**62**	**1**	**0**	**0**	**82**	**3.7**	**1**	**0**	**0.0**	**17:36**	**3**	**0**	**1**	**1**	**0**	**0**	**0**	**0**	**16:14**
2016-17	**Detroit**	**NHL**	**33**	**2**	**3**	**5**	**34**	**1**	**0**	**1**	**39**	**5.1**	**–1**	**0**	**0.0**	**18:44**									
	NY Rangers	**NHL**	**18**	**1**	**3**	**4**	**29**	**0**	**0**	**0**	**23**	**4.3**	**2**	**0**	**0.0**	**20:10**	**12**	**0**	**4**	**4**	**20**	**0**	**0**	**0**	**19:41**
	NHL Totals		**309**	**16**	**55**	**71**	**310**	**3**	**0**	**2**	**368**	**4.3**		**0**	**0.0**	**18:07**	**39**	**2**	**8**	**10**	**44**	**0**	**0**	**1**	**18:45**

WCHA First All-Star Team (2010) • NCAA West First All-American Team (2010) • NCAA Championship All-Tournament Team (2010) • AHL All-Rookie Team (2011)

Traded to **NY Rangers** by **Detroit** for NY Rangers' 3rd round pick (Zach Gallant) in 2017 NHL Draft and NY Rangers' 2nd round pick in 2018 NHL Draft, February 28, 2017.

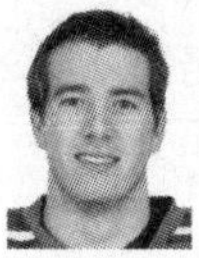

SMITH, C.J. (SMIHTH, SEE-JAY) BUF

Left wing. Shoots left. 5'11", 185 lbs. Born, Des Moines, IA, December 1, 1994.

			Regular Season														Playoffs								
Season	Club	League	GP	G	A	Pts	PIM	PP	SH	GW	S	S%	+/-	TF	F%	Min	GP	G	A	Pts	PIM	PP	SH	GW	Min
2010-11	Holy Angels	High-MN	25	17	20	37	18										1	0	0	0	10				
2011-12	Austin Bruins	NAHL	53	13	14	27	20																		
2012-13	Austin Bruins	NAHL	60	30	29	59	22										8	4	1	5	4				
2013-14	Muskegon	USHL	13	4	1	5	6																		
	Chicago Steel	USHL	46	23	17	40	10																		
2014-15	U. Mass Lowell	H-East	39	16	19	35	28																		
2015-16	U. Mass Lowell	H-East	40	17	22	39	50																		
2016-17	U. Mass Lowell	H-East	41	23	28	51	46																		
	Buffalo	**NHL**	**2**	**0**	**1**	**1**	**0**	**0**	**0**	**0**	**2**	**0.0**	**–1**	**0**	**0.0**	**11:32**									
	NHL Totals		**2**	**0**	**1**	**1**	**0**	**0**	**0**	**0**	**2**	**0.0**		**0**	**0.0**	**11:32**									

Signed as a free agent by **Buffalo**, March 30, 2017.

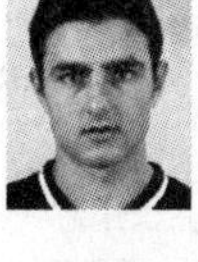

SMITH, Colin (SMIHTH, KAW-lihn)

Center. Shoots right. 5'10", 175 lbs. Born, Edmonton, AB, June 20, 1993. Colorado's 5th pick, 192nd overall, in 2012 NHL Draft.

			Regular Season														Playoffs								
Season	Club	League	GP	G	A	Pts	PIM	PP	SH	GW	S	S%	+/-	TF	F%	Min	GP	G	A	Pts	PIM	PP	SH	GW	Min
2006-07	CAC Lehigh	AMBHL	30	24	37	61	8																		
2007-08	CAC Lehigh	AMBHL	33	36	*70	106	28										2	2	1	3	0				
2008-09	CAC Canadians	AMHL	34	23	32	55	10										5	3	4	7	2				
	Kamloops Blazers	WHL	8	0	4	4	4										4	1	0	1	0				
2009-10	Kamloops Blazers	WHL	48	5	21	26	46										4	2	2	4	2				
2010-11	Kamloops Blazers	WHL	72	21	29	50	61																		
2011-12	Kamloops Blazers	WHL	72	35	50	85	51										11	3	7	10	12				
2012-13	Kamloops Blazers	WHL	72	41	65	106	72										12	2	12	14	2				
2013-14	Lake Erie	AHL	76	8	26	34	66																		
2014-15	**Colorado**	**NHL**	**1**	**0**	**0**	**0**	**0**	**0**	**0**	**0**	**1**	**0.0**	**0**	**10**	**40.0**	**6:06**									
	Lake Erie	AHL	53	12	19	31	22																		
2015-16	San Antonio	AHL	54	13	21	34	33																		
	Toronto Marlies	AHL	23	7	15	22	4										9	1	4	5	2				

			Regular Season														Playoffs								
Season	Club	League	GP	G	A	Pts	PIM	PP	SH	GW	S	S%	+/-	TF	F%	Min	GP	G	A	Pts	PIM	PP	SH	GW	Min
2016-17	Toronto Marlies	AHL	52	8	20	28	22	....	....	....	....	....	....	....	....	....	....	....	....	....	....	....	....	....	....
	San Antonio	AHL	21	6	13	19	10	....	....	....	....	....	....	....	....	....	....	....	....	....	....	....	....	....	....
	NHL Totals		**1**	**0**	**0**	**0**	**0**	**0**	**0**	**0**	**1**	**0.0**		**10**	**40.0**	**6:06**	....	....	....	....	....	....	....	....	....

WHL West First All-Star Team (2013)

Traded to **Toronto** by **Colorado** with Colorado's 4th round pick (Keaton Middleton) in 2016 NHL Draft for Shawn Matthias, February 22, 2016. Signed as a free agent by **Toronto** (AHL), July 4, 2016. Signed as a free agent by **San Antonio** (AHL), March 1, 2017.

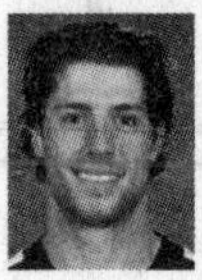

SMITH, Craig

(SMIHTH, KRAYG) **NSH**

Center. Shoots right. 6'1", 208 lbs. Born, Madison, WI, September 5, 1989. Nashville's 6th pick, 98th overall, in 2009 NHL Draft.

Season	Club	League	GP	G	A	Pts	PIM	PP	SH	GW	S	S%	+/-	TF	F%	Min	GP	G	A	Pts	PIM	PP	SH	GW	Min
2004-05	Madison Lancers	High-WI	20	16	24	40	....	....	....	....	....	....	....	....	....	....	....	....	....	....	....	....	....	....	....
2005-06	Madison Lancers	High-WI	20	35	26	61	....	....	....	....	....	....	....	....	....	....	....	....	....	....	....	....	....	....	....
2006-07	Waterloo	USHL	45	8	10	18	28	....	....	....	....	....	....	....	....	....	4	0	1	1	8	....	....	....	....
2007-08	Waterloo	USHL	58	13	10	23	90	....	....	....	....	....	....	....	....	....	11	2	3	5	8	....	....	....	....
2008-09	Waterloo	USHL	54	28	48	76	108	....	....	....	....	....	....	....	....	....	3	1	3	4	26	....	....	....	....
2009-10	U. of Wisconsin	WCHA	41	8	25	33	72	....	....	....	....	....	....	....	....	....	....	....	....	....	....	....	....	....	....
2010-11	U. of Wisconsin	WCHA	41	19	24	43	87	....	....	....	....	....	....	....	....	....	....	....	....	....	....	....	....	....	....
2011-12	**Nashville**	**NHL**	**72**	**14**	**22**	**36**	**30**	**6**	**0**	**1**	**172**	**8.1**	**-9**	**393**	**44.0**	**14:11**	**2**	**0**	**1**	**1**	**0**	**0**	**0**	**0**	**8:25**
2012-13	KalPa Kuopio	Finland	8	4	4	8	20	....	....	....	....	....	....	....	....	....	....	....	....	....	....	....	....	....	....
	Nashville	**NHL**	**44**	**4**	**8**	**12**	**20**	**2**	**0**	**0**	**83**	**4.8**	**-11**	**200**	**39.5**	**13:51**	....	....	....	....	....	....	....	....	....
	Milwaukee	AHL	4	1	4	5	0	....	....	....	....	....	....	....	....	....	....	....	....	....	....	....	....	....	....
2013-14	**Nashville**	**NHL**	**79**	**24**	**28**	**52**	**22**	**7**	**0**	**4**	**215**	**11.2**	**16**	**19**	**15.8**	**16:24**	....	....	....	....	....	....	....	....	....
2014-15	**Nashville**	**NHL**	**82**	**23**	**21**	**44**	**44**	**6**	**0**	**4**	**252**	**9.1**	**11**	**30**	**40.0**	**15:44**	**6**	**2**	**3**	**5**	**0**	**0**	**0**	**1**	**20:34**
2015-16	**Nashville**	**NHL**	**82**	**21**	**16**	**37**	**40**	**2**	**0**	**6**	**199**	**10.6**	**4**	**230**	**33.0**	**15:11**	**11**	**1**	**1**	**2**	**4**	**0**	**0**	**0**	**15:17**
2016-17	**Nashville**	**NHL**	**78**	**12**	**17**	**29**	**30**	**2**	**0**	**1**	**155**	**7.7**	**7**	**111**	**46.0**	**13:49**	**10**	**1**	**2**	**3**	**2**	**0**	**0**	**0**	**12:50**
	NHL Totals		**437**	**98**	**112**	**210**	**186**	**25**	**0**	**16**	**1076**	**9.1**		**983**	**40.1**	**14:58**	**29**	**4**	**7**	**11**	**6**	**0**	**0**	**1**	**15:04**

USHL First All-Star Team (2009) • WCHA All-Rookie Team (2010)

Signed as a free agent by **Kuopio** (Finland), October 2, 2012.

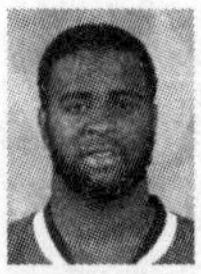

SMITH, Gemel

(SMIHTH, juh-MEHL) **DAL**

Center. Shoots left. 5'10", 195 lbs. Born, Toronto, ON, April 16, 1994. Dallas' 6th pick, 104th overall, in 2012 NHL Draft.

Season	Club	League	GP	G	A	Pts	PIM	PP	SH	GW	S	S%	+/-	TF	F%	Min	GP	G	A	Pts	PIM	PP	SH	GW	Min
2009-10	North York	GTHL	52	31	51	82	....	....	....	....	....	....	....	....	....	....	....	....	....	....	....	....	....	....	....
2010-11	Owen Sound	OHL	66	8	8	16	14	....	....	....	....	....	....	....	....	....	21	1	2	3	2	....	....	....	....
2011-12	Owen Sound	OHL	68	21	39	60	51	....	....	....	....	....	....	....	....	....	5	1	2	3	10	....	....	....	....
2012-13	Owen Sound	OHL	61	23	29	52	54	....	....	....	....	....	....	....	....	....	12	7	3	10	10	....	....	....	....
2013-14	Owen Sound	OHL	40	26	22	48	37	....	....	....	....	....	....	....	....	....	....	....	....	....	....	....	....	....	....
	London Knights	OHL	29	11	16	27	10	....	....	....	....	....	....	....	....	....	9	3	9	12	9	....	....	....	....
2014-15	Texas Stars	AHL	68	10	17	27	38	....	....	....	....	....	....	....	....	....	....	....	....	....	....	....	....	....	....
2015-16	Texas Stars	AHL	65	13	13	26	24	....	....	....	....	....	....	....	....	....	3	0	0	0	2	....	....	....	....
	Idaho Steelheads	ECHL	4	1	3	4	2	....	....	....	....	....	....	....	....	....	....	....	....	....	....	....	....	....	....
2016-17	**Dallas**	**NHL**	**17**	**3**	**3**	**6**	**21**	**0**	**1**	**0**	**19**	**15.8**	**-1**	**59**	**42.4**	**13:35**	....	....	....	....	....	....	....	....	....
	Texas Stars	AHL	53	12	21	33	44	....	....	....	....	....	....	....	....	....	....	....	....	....	....	....	....	....	....
	NHL Totals		**17**	**3**	**3**	**6**	**21**	**0**	**1**	**0**	**19**	**15.8**		**59**	**42.4**	**13:35**	....	....	....	....	....	....	....	....	....

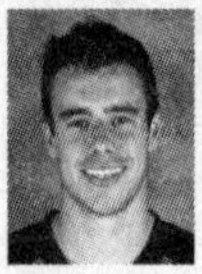

SMITH, Reilly

(SMIHTH, RIGH-lee) **VGK**

Right wing. Shoots left. 6', 185 lbs. Born, Toronto, ON, April 1, 1991. Dallas' 3rd pick, 69th overall, in 2009 NHL Draft.

Season	Club	League	GP	G	A	Pts	PIM	PP	SH	GW	S	S%	+/-	TF	F%	Min	GP	G	A	Pts	PIM	PP	SH	GW	Min
2007-08	Tor. Young Nats	GTHL	70	80	77	157	56	....	....	....	....	....	....	....	....	....	....	....	....	....	....	....	....	....	....
	St. Michael's	ON-Jr.A	13	2	7	9	22	....	....	....	....	....	....	....	....	....	1	0	0	0	2	....	....	....	....
2008-09	St. Michael's	ON-Jr.A	49	27	48	75	44	....	....	....	....	....	....	....	....	....	6	9	6	15	10	....	....	....	....
2009-10	Miami U.	CCHA	44	8	12	20	24	....	....	....	....	....	....	....	....	....	....	....	....	....	....	....	....	....	....
2010-11	Miami U.	CCHA	38	28	26	54	18	....	....	....	....	....	....	....	....	....	....	....	....	....	....	....	....	....	....
2011-12	Miami U.	CCHA	39	30	18	48	22	....	....	....	....	....	....	....	....	....	....	....	....	....	....	....	....	....	....
	Dallas	**NHL**	**3**	**0**	**0**	**0**	**2**	**0**	**0**	**0**	**2**	**0.0**	**-3**	**1**	**100.0**	**8:24**	....	....	....	....	....	....	....	....	....
2012-13	Texas Stars	AHL	45	14	21	35	20	....	....	....	....	....	....	....	....	....	7	0	4	4	0	....	....	....	....
	Dallas	**NHL**	**37**	**3**	**6**	**9**	**8**	**0**	**0**	**0**	**34**	**8.8**	**0**	**4**	**75.0**	**10:55**	....	....	....	....	....	....	....	....	....
2013-14	**Boston**	**NHL**	**82**	**20**	**31**	**51**	**14**	**6**	**0**	**3**	**146**	**13.7**	**28**	**2**	**0.0**	**14:42**	**12**	**4**	**1**	**5**	**0**	**2**	**0**	**2**	**15:46**
2014-15	**Boston**	**NHL**	**81**	**13**	**27**	**40**	**20**	**1**	**0**	**0**	**143**	**9.1**	**7**	**8**	**25.0**	**15:24**	....	....	....	....	....	....	....	....	....
2015-16	**Florida**	**NHL**	**82**	**25**	**25**	**50**	**31**	**5**	**0**	**3**	**173**	**14.5**	**19**	**2**	**0.0**	**18:37**	**6**	**4**	**4**	**8**	**0**	**0**	**0**	**0**	**24:50**
2016-17	**Florida**	**NHL**	**80**	**15**	**22**	**37**	**17**	**6**	**1**	**3**	**160**	**9.4**	**-13**	**6**	**50.0**	**18:21**	....	....	....	....	....	....	....	....	....
	NHL Totals		**365**	**76**	**111**	**187**	**92**	**18**	**1**	**9**	**658**	**11.6**		**23**	**39.1**	**16:06**	**18**	**8**	**5**	**13**	**0**	**2**	**0**	**2**	**18:47**

CCHA First All-Star Team (2011, 2012) • NCAA West First All-American Team (2012)

Traded to **Boston** by **Dallas** with Loui Eriksson, Joe Morrow and Matt Fraser for Tyler Seguin, Rich Peverley and Ryan Button, July 4, 2013. Traded to **Florida** by **Boston** with Marc Savard for Jimmy Hayes, July 1, 2015. Traded to **Vegas** by **Florida** for Vegas' 4th round pick in 2018 NHL Draft and Expansion Draft considerations, June 21, 2017.

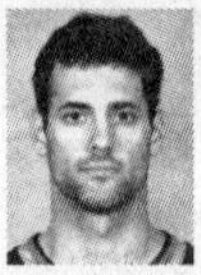

SMITH, Trevor

(SMIHTH, TREH-vuhr) **NSH**

Center. Shoots left. 6'1", 195 lbs. Born, Ottawa, ON, February 8, 1985.

Season	Club	League	GP	G	A	Pts	PIM	PP	SH	GW	S	S%	+/-	TF	F%	Min	GP	G	A	Pts	PIM	PP	SH	GW	Min
2003-04	Quesnel	BCHL	44	28	19	47	50	....	....	....	....	....	....	....	....	....	....	....	....	....	....	....	....	....	....
2004-05	Omaha Lancers	USHL	60	29	39	68	78	....	....	....	....	....	....	....	....	....	5	3	1	4	2	....	....	....	....
2005-06	New Hampshire	H-East	39	10	10	20	34	....	....	....	....	....	....	....	....	....	....	....	....	....	....	....	....	....	....
2006-07	New Hampshire	H-East	39	21	22	43	39	....	....	....	....	....	....	....	....	....	....	....	....	....	....	....	....	....	....
	Bridgeport	AHL	8	1	2	3	2	....	....	....	....	....	....	....	....	....	....	....	....	....	....	....	....	....	....
2007-08	Bridgeport	AHL	53	20	17	37	16	....	....	....	....	....	....	....	....	....	....	....	....	....	....	....	....	....	....
	Utah Grizzlies	ECHL	22	11	14	25	28	....	....	....	....	....	....	....	....	....	....	....	....	....	....	....	....	....	....
2008-09	**NY Islanders**	**NHL**	**7**	**1**	**0**	**1**	**0**	**0**	**0**	**0**	**7**	**14.3**	**-3**	**9**	**66.7**	**11:48**	....	....	....	....	....	....	....	....	....
	Bridgeport	AHL	76	30	32	62	40	....	....	....	....	....	....	....	....	....	5	1	3	4	0	....	....	....	....
2009-10	Bridgeport	AHL	77	21	26	47	73	....	....	....	....	....	....	....	....	....	5	1	2	3	2	....	....	....	....
2010-11	Syracuse Crunch	AHL	35	12	15	27	16	....	....	....	....	....	....	....	....	....	....	....	....	....	....	....	....	....	....
	Springfield	AHL	33	8	8	16	10	....	....	....	....	....	....	....	....	....	....	....	....	....	....	....	....	....	....
2011-12	**Tampa Bay**	**NHL**	**16**	**2**	**3**	**5**	**4**	**0**	**0**	**0**	**17**	**11.8**	**2**	**83**	**41.0**	**12:28**	....	....	....	....	....	....	....	....	....
	Norfolk Admirals	AHL	64	26	43	69	70	....	....	....	....	....	....	....	....	....	18	5	11	16	20	....	....	....	....
2012-13	Wilkes-Barre	AHL	75	23	31	54	64	....	....	....	....	....	....	....	....	....	15	5	8	13	9	....	....	....	....
	Pittsburgh	**NHL**	**1**	**0**	**0**	**0**	**0**	**0**	**0**	**0**	**0**	**0.0**	**0**	**0**	**0.0**	**10:24**	....	....	....	....	....	....	....	....	....
2013-14	**Toronto**	**NHL**	**28**	**4**	**5**	**9**	**4**	**0**	**0**	**2**	**24**	**16.7**	**-3**	**258**	**44.6**	**10:22**	....	....	....	....	....	....	....	....	....
	Toronto Marlies	AHL	24	10	16	26	10	....	....	....	....	....	....	....	....	....	14	3	8	11	2	....	....	....	....
2014-15	**Toronto**	**NHL**	**54**	**2**	**3**	**5**	**12**	**0**	**0**	**0**	**46**	**4.3**	**-9**	**561**	**52.2**	**11:04**	....	....	....	....	....	....	....	....	....
	Toronto Marlies	AHL	8	2	3	5	12	....	....	....	....	....	....	....	....	....	....	....	....	....	....	....	....	....	....
2015-16	SC Bern	Swiss	17	3	2	5	14	....	....	....	....	....	....	....	....	....	1	0	0	0	0	....	....	....	....
2016-17	**Nashville**	**NHL**	**1**	**0**	**0**	**0**	**0**	**0**	**0**	**0**	**0**	**0.0**	**0**	**8**	**0.0**	**7:20**	....	....	....	....	....	....	....	....	....
	Milwaukee	AHL	74	14	35	49	47	....	....	....	....	....	....	....	....	....	3	0	1	1	0	....	....	....	....
	NHL Totals		**107**	**9**	**11**	**20**	**20**	**0**	**0**	**2**	**94**	**9.6**		**919**	**48.7**	**11:06**	....	....	....	....	....	....	....	....	....

NCAA East Second All-American Team (2007)

Signed as a free agent by **NY Islanders**, April 2, 2007. Signed as a free agent by **Anaheim**, July 2, 2010. Traded to **Columbus** by **Anaheim** for Nate Guenin, January 4, 2011. Signed as a free agent by **Tampa Bay**, July 5, 2011. Signed as a free agent by **Pittsburgh**, July 1, 2012. Signed as a free agent by **Toronto**, July 5, 2013. Signed as a free agent by **Bern** (Swiss), July 2, 2015. Signed as a free agent by **Nashville**, July 2, 2016.

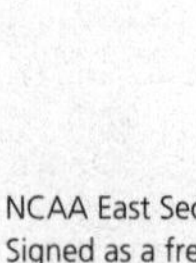

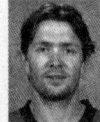

SMITH, Zack

(SMIHTH, ZAK) **OTT**

Center. Shoots left. 6'2", 209 lbs. Born, Medicine Hat, AB, April 5, 1988. Ottawa's 3rd pick, 79th overall, in 2008 NHL Draft.

Season	Club	League	GP	G	A	Pts	PIM	PP	SH	GW	S	S%	+/-	TF	F%	Min	GP	G	A	Pts	PIM	PP	SH	GW	Min
2004-05	Swift Current	SMHL	43	15	27	42	83	....	....	....	....	....	....	....	....	....	....	....	....	....	....	....	....	....	....
	Swift Current	WHL	14	1	1	2	0	....	....	....	....	....	....	....	....	....	....	....	....	....	....	....	....	....	....
2005-06	Swift Current	WHL	64	2	5	7	78	....	....	....	....	....	....	....	....	....	3	0	0	0	9	....	....	....	....
2006-07	Swift Current	WHL	71	16	15	31	130	....	....	....	....	....	....	....	....	....	6	0	2	2	11	....	....	....	....
2007-08	Swift Current	WHL	72	22	47	69	136	....	....	....	....	....	....	....	....	....	12	5	5	10	29	....	....	....	....
	Manitoba Moose	AHL	....	....	....	....	....	....	....	....	....	....	....	....	....	....	6	0	1	1	0	....	....	....	....

			Regular Season														Playoffs								
Season	Club	League	GP	G	A	Pts	PIM	PP	SH	GW	S	S%	+/-	TF	F%	Min	GP	G	A	Pts	PIM	PP	SH	GW	Min
2008-09	**Ottawa**	**NHL**	**1**	**0**	**0**	**0**	**0**	**0**	**0**	**0**	**0**	**0.0**	**0**	**1**	**0.0**	**7:01**	....	....	....	....	....	....	....	....	....
	Binghamton	AHL	79	24	24	48	132	....	....	....	....	....	....	....	....	....	....	....	....	....	....	....	....	....	....
2009-10	**Ottawa**	**NHL**	**15**	**2**	**1**	**3**	**14**	**0**	**1**	**0**	**11**	**18.2**	**1**	**61**	**47.5**	**9:03**	**6**	**0**	**0**	**0**	**5**	**0**	**0**	**0**	**7:25**
	Binghamton	AHL	68	14	27	41	100	....	....	....	....	....	....	....	....	....	....	....	....	....	....	....	....	....	....
2010-11	**Ottawa**	**NHL**	**55**	**4**	**5**	**9**	**120**	**0**	**0**	**0**	**78**	**5.1**	**-11**	**388**	**53.9**	**12:36**	....	....	....	....	....	....	....	....	....
	Binghamton	AHL	22	7	5	12	32	....	....	....	....	....	....	....	....	....	23	8	12	20	36	....	....	....	....
2011-12	**Ottawa**	**NHL**	**81**	**14**	**12**	**26**	**98**	**1**	**2**	**3**	**134**	**10.4**	**4**	**990**	**48.9**	**14:04**	**7**	**0**	**1**	**1**	**10**	**0**	**0**	**0**	**13:22**
2012-13	Frederikshavn	Denmark	7	4	6	10	18	....	....	....	....	....	....	....	....	....	....	....	....	....	....	....	....	....	....
	Ottawa	**NHL**	**48**	**4**	**11**	**15**	**56**	**0**	**0**	**0**	**94**	**4.3**	**-9**	**731**	**51.9**	**15:09**	**10**	**1**	**1**	**2**	**31**	**0**	**0**	**0**	**13:17**
2013-14	**Ottawa**	**NHL**	**82**	**13**	**9**	**22**	**111**	**0**	**1**	**4**	**154**	**8.4**	**-9**	**1291**	**52.7**	**15:32**	....	....	....	....	....	....	....	....	....
2014-15	**Ottawa**	**NHL**	**37**	**2**	**1**	**3**	**18**	**0**	**0**	**0**	**38**	**5.3**	**-8**	**231**	**44.6**	**12:02**	**3**	**0**	**0**	**0**	**0**	**0**	**0**	**0**	**9:53**
	Binghamton	AHL	2	1	1	2	2	....	....	....	....	....	....	....	....	....	....	....	....	....	....	....	....	....	....
2015-16	**Ottawa**	**NHL**	**81**	**25**	**11**	**36**	**80**	**4**	**5**	**4**	**121**	**20.7**	**16**	**729**	**52.1**	**15:24**	....	....	....	....	....	....	....	....	....
2016-17	**Ottawa**	**NHL**	**74**	**16**	**16**	**32**	**61**	**1**	**4**	**1**	**137**	**11.7**	**6**	**609**	**52.1**	**16:23**	**19**	**1**	**5**	**6**	**12**	**0**	**0**	**0**	**16:11**
	NHL Totals		**474**	**80**	**66**	**146**	**558**	**6**	**13**	**12**	**767**	**10.4**		**5031**	**51.3**	**14:31**	**45**	**2**	**7**	**9**	**58**	**0**	**0**	**0**	**13:31**

Signed as a free agent by **Frederikshavn** (Denmark), November 26, 2012. • Missed majority of 2014-15 due to wrist injury at Boston, December 13, 2014.

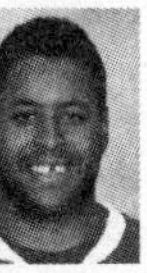

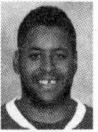

SMITH-PELLY, Devante

(SMIHTH-PEH-lee, deh-VAHN-tay) **WSH**

Right wing. Shoots right. 6', 215 lbs. Born, Scarborough, ON, June 14, 1992. Anaheim's 3rd pick, 42nd overall, in 2010 NHL Draft.

Season	Club	League	GP	G	A	Pts	PIM	PP	SH	GW	S	S%	+/-	TF	F%	Min	GP	G	A	Pts	PIM	PP	SH	GW	Min
2007-08	Tor. Jr. Canadiens	GTHL	85	38	39	77	159	....	....	....	....	....	....	....	....	....	....	....	....	....	....	....	....	....	....
2008-09	St. Michael's	OHL	57	13	12	25	24	....	....	....	....	....	....	....	....	....	11	2	3	5	4	....	....	....	....
2009-10	St. Michael's	OHL	60	29	33	62	35	....	....	....	....	....	....	....	....	....	16	8	6	14	20	....	....	....	....
2010-11	St. Michael's	OHL	67	36	30	66	50	....	....	....	....	....	....	....	....	....	20	*15	6	21	16	....	....	....	....
2011-12	**Anaheim**	**NHL**	**49**	**7**	**6**	**13**	**16**	**1**	**1**	**1**	**66**	**10.6**	**-7**	**21**	**28.6**	**12:03**	....	....	....	....	....	....	....	....	....
	Syracuse Crunch	AHL	4	0	1	1	2	....	....	....	....	....	....	....	....	....	....	....	....	....	....	....	....	....	....
2012-13	Norfolk Admirals	AHL	65	14	18	32	65	....	....	....	....	....	....	....	....	....	....	....	....	....	....	....	....	....	....
	Anaheim	**NHL**	**7**	**0**	**0**	**0**	**0**	**0**	**0**	**0**	**5**	**0.0**	**-4**	**0**	**0.0**	**9:00**	....	....	....	....	....	....	....	....	....
2013-14	**Anaheim**	**NHL**	**19**	**2**	**8**	**10**	**2**	**0**	**0**	**0**	**23**	**8.7**	**5**	**4**	**0.0**	**12:39**	**12**	**5**	**0**	**5**	**24**	**2**	**0**	**1**	**14:42**
	Norfolk Admirals	AHL	55	27	16	43	29	....	....	....	....	....	....	....	....	....	....	....	....	....	....	....	....	....	....
2014-15	**Anaheim**	**NHL**	**54**	**5**	**12**	**17**	**12**	**0**	**1**	**1**	**76**	**6.6**	**1**	**82**	**28.1**	**14:39**	....	....	....	....	....	....	....	....	....
	Montreal	**NHL**	**20**	**1**	**2**	**3**	**12**	**0**	**0**	**0**	**28**	**3.6**	**-2**	**1**	**0.0**	**13:18**	**12**	**1**	**2**	**3**	**2**	**0**	**0**	**0**	**12:19**
2015-16	**Montreal**	**NHL**	**46**	**6**	**6**	**12**	**22**	**0**	**0**	**3**	**60**	**10.0**	**-2**	**2**	**0.0**	**11:00**	....	....	....	....	....	....	....	....	....
	New Jersey	**NHL**	**18**	**8**	**5**	**13**	**8**	**0**	**0**	**2**	**34**	**23.5**	**-1**	**3**	**66.7**	**15:35**	....	....	....	....	....	....	....	....	....
2016-17	**New Jersey**	**NHL**	**53**	**4**	**5**	**9**	**12**	**0**	**0**	**0**	**76**	**5.3**	**-19**	**71**	**40.9**	**13:30**	....	....	....	....	....	....	....	....	....
	NHL Totals		**266**	**33**	**44**	**77**	**84**	**1**	**2**	**7**	**368**	**9.0**		**184**	**32.6**	**12:59**	**24**	**6**	**2**	**8**	**26**	**2**	**0**	**1**	**13:30**

Traded to **Montreal** by **Anaheim** for Jiri Sekac, February 24, 2014. Traded to **New Jersey** by **Montreal** for Stefan Matteau, February 29, 2016. Signed as a free agent by **Washington**, July 3, 2017.

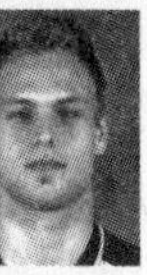

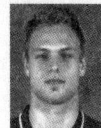

SOBOTKA, Vladimir

(suh-BOHT-kah, vla-DIH-meer) **ST.L.**

Center. Shoots left. 5'10", 197 lbs. Born, Trebic, Czech., July 2, 1987. Boston's 5th pick, 106th overall, in 2005 NHL Draft.

Season	Club	League	GP	G	A	Pts	PIM	PP	SH	GW	S	S%	+/-	TF	F%	Min	GP	G	A	Pts	PIM	PP	SH	GW	Min
2002-03	Slavia U17	CzR-U17	46	16	24	40	48	....	....	....	....	....	....	....	....	....	8	1	1	2	29	....	....	....	....
2003-04	Slavia U17	CzR-U17	35	24	41	65	109	....	....	....	....	....	....	....	....	....	7	7	12	19	8	....	....	....	....
	Slavia Jr.	CzRep-Jr.	18	6	6	12	16	....	....	....	....	....	....	....	....	....	....	....	....	....	....	....	....	....	....
	HC Slavia Praha	CzRep	1	0	0	0	0	....	....	....	....	....	....	....	....	....	....	....	....	....	....	....	....	....	....
2004-05	Slavia Jr.	CzRep-Jr.	27	12	21	33	93	....	....	....	....	....	....	....	....	....	....	....	....	....	....	....	....	....	....
	HC Slavia Praha	CzRep	18	0	1	1	8	....	....	....	....	....	....	....	....	....	....	....	....	....	....	....	....	....	....
	Havl. Brod	CzRep-3	7	3	0	3	31	....	....	....	....	....	....	....	....	....	7	1	5	6	0	....	....	....	....
2005-06	Slavia Jr.	CzRep-Jr.	8	10	4	14	42	....	....	....	....	....	....	....	....	....	....	....	....	....	....	....	....	....	....
	HC Slavia Praha	CzRep	33	1	9	10	28	....	....	....	....	....	....	....	....	....	11	2	3	5	10	....	....	....	....
2006-07	HC Slavia Praha	CzRep	33	7	6	13	38	....	....	....	....	....	....	....	....	....	....	....	....	....	....	....	....	....	....
2007-08	**Boston**	**NHL**	**48**	**1**	**6**	**7**	**24**	**0**	**0**	**1**	**40**	**2.5**	**1**	**247**	**48.6**	**8:50**	**6**	**2**	**0**	**2**	**0**	**0**	**0**	**0**	**8:37**
	Providence Bruins	AHL	18	10	10	20	37	....	....	....	....	....	....	....	....	....	6	0	4	4	0	....	....	....	....
2008-09	**Boston**	**NHL**	**25**	**1**	**4**	**5**	**10**	**0**	**0**	**0**	**19**	**5.3**	**-10**	**52**	**57.7**	**10:33**	....	....	....	....	....	....	....	....	....
	Providence Bruins	AHL	44	20	24	44	83	....	....	....	....	....	....	....	....	....	14	2	11	13	43	....	....	....	....
2009-10	**Boston**	**NHL**	**61**	**4**	**6**	**10**	**30**	**0**	**0**	**0**	**67**	**6.0**	**-7**	**361**	**54.3**	**11:06**	**13**	**0**	**2**	**2**	**15**	**0**	**0**	**0**	**13:20**
	Providence Bruins	AHL	6	4	6	10	4	....	....	....	....	....	....	....	....	....	....	....	....	....	....	....	....	....	....
2010-11	**St. Louis**	**NHL**	**65**	**7**	**22**	**29**	**69**	**1**	**1**	**0**	**75**	**9.3**	**-4**	**419**	**51.6**	**16:11**	....	....	....	....	....	....	....	....	....
2011-12	**St. Louis**	**NHL**	**73**	**5**	**15**	**20**	**42**	**0**	**1**	**1**	**117**	**4.3**	**12**	**501**	**56.1**	**15:51**	**9**	**1**	**1**	**2**	**15**	**0**	**0**	**1**	**13:09**
2012-13	HC Slavia Praha	CzRep	27	10	15	25	8	....	....	....	....	....	....	....	....	....	....	....	....	....	....	....	....	....	....
	St. Louis	**NHL**	**48**	**8**	**11**	**19**	**35**	**1**	**0**	**2**	**69**	**11.6**	**-4**	**506**	**56.5**	**15:27**	**6**	**0**	**3**	**3**	**0**	**0**	**0**	**0**	**16:37**
2013-14	**St. Louis**	**NHL**	**61**	**9**	**24**	**33**	**72**	**1**	**0**	**1**	**102**	**8.8**	**14**	**813**	**61.9**	**16:45**	**6**	**0**	**3**	**3**	**4**	**0**	**0**	**0**	**21:12**
2014-15	Omsk	KHL	53	10	28	38	51	....	....	....	....	....	....	....	....	....	4	1	1	2	0	....	....	....	....
2015-16	Omsk	KHL	44	18	16	34	22	....	....	....	....	....	....	....	....	....	2	0	2	2	0	....	....	....	....
2016-17	Omsk	KHL	41	9	21	30	30	....	....	....	....	....	....	....	....	....	12	3	7	10	16	....	....	....	....
	St. Louis	**NHL**	**1**	**1**	**0**	**1**	**0**	**0**	**0**	**0**	**2**	**50.0**	**0**	**12**	**50.0**	**16:41**	**11**	**2**	**4**	**6**	**2**	**0**	**0**	**0**	**17:27**
	NHL Totals		**382**	**36**	**88**	**124**	**282**	**3**	**2**	**5**	**491**	**7.3**		**2911**	**56.3**	**14:01**	**51**	**5**	**13**	**18**	**36**	**0**	**0**	**1**	**14:57**

Traded to **St. Louis** by **Boston** for David Warsofsky, June 26, 2010. Signed as a free agent by **Slavia Praha** (CzRep), September 15, 2012. Signed as a free agent by **Omsk** (KHL), July 10, 2014. Signed as a free agent by **St. Louis**, April 7, 2017.

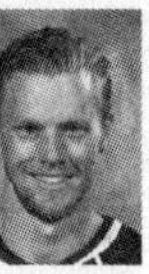

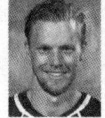

SODERBERG, Carl

(SOH-dehr-buhrg, KAHRL) **COL**

Center. Shoots left. 6'3", 210 lbs. Born, Malmo, Sweden, October 12, 1985. St. Louis' 2nd pick, 49th overall, in 2004 NHL Draft.

Season	Club	League	GP	G	A	Pts	PIM	PP	SH	GW	S	S%	+/-	TF	F%	Min	GP	G	A	Pts	PIM	PP	SH	GW	Min
2000-01	Skane	Other	8	1	2	3	2	....	....	....	....	....	....	....	....	....	....	....	....	....	....	....	....	....	....
	Malmo U18	Swe-U18	3	1	1	2	0	....	....	....	....	....	....	....	....	....	....	....	....	....	....	....	....	....	....
2001-02	Malmo U18	Swe-U18	13	9	20	29	18	....	....	....	....	....	....	....	....	....	....	....	....	....	....	....	....	....	....
	Malmo Jr.	Swe-Jr.	4	0	2	2	2	....	....	....	....	....	....	....	....	....	7	0	2	2	4	....	....	....	....
2002-03	Malmo U18	Swe-U18	4	6	3	9	25	....	....	....	....	....	....	....	....	....	....	....	....	....	....	....	....	....	....
	Malmo Jr.	Swe-Jr.	28	17	18	35	22	....	....	....	....	....	....	....	....	....	6	2	4	6	8	....	....	....	....
2003-04	Malmo U18	Swe-U18	27	23	25	48	30	....	....	....	....	....	....	....	....	....	6	1	2	3	10	....	....	....	....
	Malmo	Sweden	24	1	1	2	8	....	....	....	....	....	....	....	....	....	....	....	....	....	....	....	....	....	....
	Malmo	Sweden-Q	8	1	1	2	4	....	....	....	....	....	....	....	....	....	....	....	....	....	....	....	....	....	....
2004-05	Morrums GoIS IK	Sweden-2	14	5	6	11	8	....	....	....	....	....	....	....	....	....	....	....	....	....	....	....	....	....	....
	Malmo Jr.	Swe-Jr.	12	13	6	19	43	....	....	....	....	....	....	....	....	....	3	2	1	3	12	....	....	....	....
	Malmo	Sweden	38	0	5	5	8	....	....	....	....	....	....	....	....	....	....	....	....	....	....	....	....	....	....
	Malmo	Sweden-Q	7	0	0	0	0	....	....	....	....	....	....	....	....	....	....	....	....	....	....	....	....	....	....
2005-06	Malmo	Sweden-2	49	20	27	47	47	....	....	....	....	....	....	....	....	....	....	....	....	....	....	....	....	....	....
2006-07	Malmo	Sweden	31	12	18	30	14	....	....	....	....	....	....	....	....	....	....	....	....	....	....	....	....	....	....
2007-08	Malmo	Sweden-2	42	22	36	58	18	....	....	....	....	....	....	....	....	....	....	....	....	....	....	....	....	....	....
2008-09	Malmo	Sweden-2	45	18	41	59	26	....	....	....	....	....	....	....	....	....	....	....	....	....	....	....	....	....	....
2009-10	Malmo	Sweden-2	51	20	31	51	53	....	....	....	....	....	....	....	....	....	5	0	1	1	0	....	....	....	....
2010-11	Malmo	Sweden-2	52	12	34	46	18	....	....	....	....	....	....	....	....	....	....	....	....	....	....	....	....	....	....
2011-12	Linkopings HC	Sweden	42	14	21	35	20	....	....	....	....	....	....	....	....	....	....	....	....	....	....	....	....	....	....
2012-13	Linkopings HC	Sweden	54	*31	29	60	48	....	....	....	....	....	....	....	....	....	6	1	1	2	27	....	....	....	....
	Boston	**NHL**	**6**	**0**	**2**	**2**	**6**	**0**	**0**	**0**	**6**	**0.0**	**-2**	**13**	**53.9**	**14:44**	**2**	**0**	**0**	**0**	**0**	**0**	**0**	**0**	**12:15**
2013-14	**Boston**	**NHL**	**73**	**16**	**32**	**48**	**36**	**5**	**0**	**3**	**129**	**12.4**	**4**	**328**	**42.4**	**14:16**	**12**	**1**	**5**	**6**	**2**	**0**	**0**	**0**	**15:41**
2014-15	**Boston**	**NHL**	**82**	**13**	**31**	**44**	**26**	**5**	**0**	**3**	**163**	**8.0**	**10**	**766**	**48.2**	**16:49**	....	....	....	....	....	....	....	....	....
2015-16	**Colorado**	**NHL**	**82**	**12**	**39**	**51**	**32**	**3**	**1**	**0**	**163**	**7.4**	**-7**	**719**	**47.2**	**18:01**	....	....	....	....	....	....	....	....	....
2016-17	**Colorado**	**NHL**	**80**	**6**	**8**	**14**	**22**	**1**	**0**	**0**	**128**	**4.7**	**-26**	**702**	**52.0**	**13:27**	....	....	....	....	....	....	....	....	....
	NHL Totals		**323**	**47**	**112**	**159**	**122**	**14**	**1**	**6**	**589**	**8.0**		**2528**	**48.2**	**15:40**	**14**	**1**	**5**	**6**	**2**	**0**	**0**	**0**	**15:12**

Traded to **Boston** by **St. Louis** for Hannu Toivonen, July 23, 2007. Traded to **Colorado** by **Boston** for Boston's 6th round pick (previously acquired, Boston selected Oskar Steen) in 2016 NHL Draft, June 25, 2015.

						Regular Season												Playoffs							
Season	Club	League	GP	G	A	Pts	PIM	PP	SH	GW	S	S%	+/-	TF	F%	Min	GP	G	A	Pts	PIM	PP	SH	GW	Min

SORENSEN, Marcus (SOHR-ehn-suhn, MAHR-kuhs) **S.J.**

Right wing. Shoots left. 5'11", 175 lbs. Born, Sodertalje, Sweden, April 7, 1992. Ottawa's 2nd pick, 106th overall, in 2010 NHL Draft.

Season	Club	League	GP	G	A	Pts	PIM	PP	SH	GW	S	S%	+/-	TF	F%	Min	GP	G	A	Pts	PIM	PP	SH	GW	Min
2008-09	Sodertalje SK U18	Swe-U18	32	16	12	28	92	….	….	….	….	….	….	….	….	….	4	2	3	5	6	….	….	….	….
2009-10	Sodertalje SK U18	Swe-U18	15	15	27	42	61	….	….	….	….	….	….	….	….	….	2	1	1	2	2	….	….	….	….
	Sodertalje SK Jr.	Swe-Jr.	27	7	10	17	54	….	….	….	….	….	….	….	….	….	….	….	….	….	….	….	….	….	….
2010-11	Djurgarden	Sweden	8	1	1	2	0	….	….	….	….	….	….	….	….	….	….	….	….	….	….	….	….	….	….
	Djurgarden Jr.	Swe-Jr.	31	14	22	36	53	….	….	….	….	….	….	….	….	….	4	3	0	3	2	….	….	….	….
2011-12	Skelleftea AIK Jr.	Swe-Jr.	8	2	3	5	57	….	….	….	….	….	….	….	….	….	….	….	….	….	….	….	….	….	….
	Skelleftea AIK	Sweden	1	0	0	0	0	….	….	….	….	….	….	….	….	….	….	….	….	….	….	….	….	….	….
	Boras HC	Sweden-2	36	10	9	19	63	….	….	….	….	….	….	….	….	….	….	….	….	….	….	….	….	….	….
2012-13	Djurgarden	Sweden-2	46	10	13	23	38	….	….	….	….	….	….	….	….	….	….	….	….	….	….	….	….	….	….
	Djurgarden Jr.	Swe-Jr.	2	1	2	3	0	….	….	….	….	….	….	….	….	….	….	….	….	….	….	….	….	….	….
2013-14	Djurgarden	Sweden-2	43	13	17	30	34	….	….	….	….	….	….	….	….	….	….	….	….	….	….	….	….	….	….
2014-15	Djurgarden	Sweden	50	17	15	32	30	….	….	….	….	….	….	….	….	….	….	….	….	….	….	….	….	….	….
2015-16	Djurgarden	Sweden	47	15	19	34	34	….	….	….	….	….	….	….	….	….	8	1	5	6	14	….	….	….	….
2016-17	**San Jose**	**NHL**	**19**	**1**	**3**	**4**	**4**	0	0	1	27	3.7	-1	4	75.0	10:49	6	1	1	2	0	0	0	0	10:58
	San Jose	AHL	43	17	17	34	23	….	….	….	….	….	….	….	….	….	10	0	1	1	10	….	….	….	….
	NHL Totals		**19**	**1**	**3**	**4**	**4**	**0**	**0**	**1**	**27**	**3.7**		**4**	**75.0**	**10:49**	**6**	**1**	**1**	**2**	**0**	**0**	**0**	**0**	**10:58**

Signed as a free agent by **San Jose**, May 13, 2016.

SORENSEN, Nick (SOHR-ehn-sehn, NIHK) **ANA**

Right wing. Shoots right. 6'1", 182 lbs. Born, Holback, Denmark, October 23, 1994. Anaheim's 2nd pick, 45th overall, in 2013 NHL Draft.

Season	Club	League	GP	G	A	Pts	PIM	PP	SH	GW	S	S%	+/-	TF	F%	Min	GP	G	A	Pts	PIM	PP	SH	GW	Min
2009-10	Rogle U18	Swe-U18	30	22	17	39	22	….	….	….	….	….	….	….	….	….	2	0	0	0	0	….	….	….	….
2010-11	Rogle U18	Swe-U18	6	7	3	10	4	….	….	….	….	….	….	….	….	….	4	1	0	1	2	….	….	….	….
	Rogle Jr.	Swe-Jr.	30	18	11	29	34	….	….	….	….	….	….	….	….	….	….	….	….	….	….	….	….	….	….
	Rogle	Sweden-2	6	0	0	0	2	….	….	….	….	….	….	….	….	….	….	….	….	….	….	….	….	….	….
2011-12	Quebec Remparts	QMJHL	8	5	4	9	2	….	….	….	….	….	….	….	….	….	….	….	….	….	….	….	….	….	….
2012-13	Quebec Remparts	QMJHL	46	20	27	47	18	….	….	….	….	….	….	….	….	….	8	7	3	10	10	….	….	….	….
2013-14	Quebec Remparts	QMJHL	44	31	30	61	43	….	….	….	….	….	….	….	….	….	5	6	3	9	8	….	….	….	….
	Sweden	Olympics	7	2	4	6	4	….	….	….	….	….	….	….	….	….	….	….	….	….	….	….	….	….	….
2014-15	Skelleftea AIK	Sweden	14	1	3	4	4	….	….	….	….	….	….	….	….	….	8	0	0	0	2	….	….	….	….
2015-16	Linkopings HC	Sweden	37	10	13	23	37	….	….	….	….	….	….	….	….	….	6	0	3	3	2	….	….	….	….
2016-17	**Anaheim**	**NHL**	**5**	**0**	**1**	**1**	**2**	0	0	0	7	0.0	-1	1100.0		10:53	….	….	….	….	….	….	….	….	….
	San Diego Gulls	AHL	48	10	12	22	38	….	….	….	….	….	….	….	….	….	8	2	2	4	8	….	….	….	….
	NHL Totals		**5**	**0**	**1**	**1**	**2**	**0**	**0**	**0**	**7**	**0.0**		**1100.0**		**10:53**	….	….	….	….	….	….	….	….	….

SOSHNIKOV, Nikita (sohsh-NIH-kauf, nih-kee-tuh) **TOR**

Right wing. Shoots left. 5'11", 190 lbs. Born, Nizhny Tagil, Russia, October 14, 1993.

Season	Club	League	GP	G	A	Pts	PIM	PP	SH	GW	S	S%	+/-	TF	F%	Min	GP	G	A	Pts	PIM	PP	SH	GW	Min
2010-11	Mytischi	KHL	48	17	10	27	14	….	….	….	….	….	….	….	….	….	6	0	1	1	6	….	….	….	….
2011-12	Mytischi	KHL	47	14	20	34	12	….	….	….	….	….	….	….	….	….	11	1	4	5	25	….	….	….	….
2012-13	Mytischi	KHL	59	38	34	72	47	….	….	….	….	….	….	….	….	….	8	5	4	9	4	….	….	….	….
2013-14	Mytischi	KHL	33	2	3	5	27	….	….	….	….	….	….	….	….	….	3	1	0	1	2	….	….	….	….
	Buran Voronezh	Russia-2	4	2	2	4	0	….	….	….	….	….	….	….	….	….	….	….	….	….	….	….	….	….	….
	Mytischi Jr.	Russia-Jr.	10	5	8	13	4	….	….	….	….	….	….	….	….	….	2	2	0	2	0	….	….	….	….
2014-15	Mytischi	KHL	57	14	18	32	22	….	….	….	….	….	….	….	….	….	….	….	….	….	….	….	….	….	….
2015-16	**Toronto**	**NHL**	**11**	**2**	**3**	**5**	**6**	1	0	0	33	6.1	-4	1	0.0	15:37	….	….	….	….	….	….	….	….	….
	Toronto Marlies	AHL	52	18	10	28	18	….	….	….	….	….	….	….	….	….	11	5	2	7	4	….	….	….	….
2016-17	**Toronto**	**NHL**	**56**	**5**	**4**	**9**	**16**	0	0	0	70	7.1	1	17	11.8	10:51	….	….	….	….	….	….	….	….	….
	Toronto Marlies	AHL	6	1	2	3	6	….	….	….	….	….	….	….	….	….	….	….	….	….	….	….	….	….	….
	NHL Totals		**67**	**7**	**7**	**14**	**22**	**1**	**0**	**0**	**103**	**6.8**		**18**	**11.1**	**11:38**	….	….	….	….	….	….	….	….	….

Signed as a free agent by **Toronto**, March 20, 2015.

SPALING, Nick (SPAHL-ihng, NIHK)

Center. Shoots left. 6'1", 198 lbs. Born, Palmerston, ON, September 19, 1988. Nashville's 3rd pick, 58th overall, in 2007 NHL Draft.

Season	Club	League	GP	G	A	Pts	PIM	PP	SH	GW	S	S%	+/-	TF	F%	Min	GP	G	A	Pts	PIM	PP	SH	GW	Min
2004-05	Listowel Cyclones	ON-Jr.B	61	25	27	52	58	….	….	….	….	….	….	….	….	….	5	0	3	3	0	….	….	….	….
2005-06	Kitchener Rangers	OHL	62	10	15	25	22	….	….	….	….	….	….	….	….	….	9	2	3	5	4	….	….	….	….
2006-07	Kitchener Rangers	OHL	61	23	36	59	41	….	….	….	….	….	….	….	….	….	20	14	16	30	9	….	….	….	….
2007-08	Kitchener Rangers	OHL	56	38	34	72	18	….	….	….	….	….	….	….	….	….	11	0	3	3	8	….	….	….	….
2008-09	Milwaukee	AHL	79	12	23	35	28	….	….	….	….	….	….	….	….	….	11	0	3	3	8	….	….	….	….
2009-10	**Nashville**	**NHL**	**28**	**0**	**3**	**3**	**0**	0	0	0	26	0.0	3	95	41.1	11:03	6	0	0	0	0	0	0	0	8:24
	Milwaukee	AHL	48	7	10	17	21	….	….	….	….	….	….	….	….	….	….	….	….	….	….	….	….	….	….
2010-11	**Nashville**	**NHL**	**74**	**8**	**6**	**14**	**20**	1	0	2	75	10.7	-10	497	50.9	13:56	12	2	4	6	0	0	0	1	15:19
	Milwaukee	AHL	4	1	1	2	2	….	….	….	….	….	….	….	….	….	….	….	….	….	….	….	….	….	….
2011-12	**Nashville**	**NHL**	**77**	**10**	**12**	**22**	**18**	0	0	3	107	9.3	-7	894	50.1	15:43	10	0	3	3	0	0	0	0	15:49
2012-13	**Nashville**	**NHL**	**47**	**9**	**4**	**13**	**18**	1	0	2	57	15.8	-10	482	46.3	15:52	….	….	….	….	….	….	….	….	….
2013-14	**Nashville**	**NHL**	**71**	**13**	**19**	**32**	**14**	3	1	1	85	15.3	2	167	52.7	16:01	….	….	….	….	….	….	….	….	….
2014-15	**Pittsburgh**	**NHL**	**82**	**9**	**18**	**27**	**26**	1	0	0	90	10.0	-2	174	48.3	15:14	5	1	1	2	4	0	0	0	13:40
2015-16	**Toronto**	**NHL**	**35**	**1**	**6**	**7**	**18**	0	0	0	32	3.1	-7	508	51.0	15:16	….	….	….	….	….	….	….	….	….
	San Jose	**NHL**	**23**	**2**	**4**	**6**	**6**	0	0	0	21	9.5	5	93	53.8	12:47	24	0	1	1	6	0	0	0	12:44
2016-17	Geneve	Swiss	41	14	24	38	14	….	….	….	….	….	….	….	….	….	4	2	2	4	0	….	….	….	….
	NHL Totals		**437**	**52**	**72**	**124**	**120**	**6**	**1**	**8**	**493**	**10.5**		**2910**	**49.6**	**14:54**	**57**	**3**	**9**	**12**	**10**	**0**	**0**	**1**	**13:27**

Traded to **Pittsburgh** by **Nashville** with Patric Hornqvist for James Neal, June 27, 2014. Traded to **Toronto** by **Pittsburgh** with Kasperi Kapanen, Scott Harrington, Pittsburgh's 1st round pick (later traded to Anaheim — Anaheim selected Sam Steel) in 2016 NHL Draft and New Jersey's 3rd round pick (previously acquired, Toronto selected James Greenway) in 2016 NHL Draft for Phil Kessel, Tim Erixon, Tyler Biggs and Pittsburgh's 2nd round pick (previously acquired, Pittsburgh selected Kasper Bjorkqvist) in 2016 NHL Draft, July 1, 2015. Traded to **San Jose** by **Toronto** with Roman Polak for Raffi Torres, San Jose's 2nd round pick (later traded to Anaheim — Anaheim selected Maxime Comtois) in 2017 NHL Draft and San Jose's 2nd round pick in 2018 NHL Draft, February 22, 2016. Signed as a free agent by **Geneve** (Swiss), August 10, 2016.

SPEERS, Blake (SPEERZ, BLAYK) **N.J.**

Center. Shoots right. 5'11", 185 lbs. Born, Sault Ste. Marie, ON, January 2, 1997. New Jersey's 3rd pick, 67th overall, in 2015 NHL Draft.

Season	Club	League	GP	G	A	Pts	PIM	PP	SH	GW	S	S%	+/-	TF	F%	Min	GP	G	A	Pts	PIM	PP	SH	GW	Min
2012-13	Soo Thunder MM	Minor-ON	61	43	70	113	56	….	….	….	….	….	….	….	….	….	….	….	….	….	….	….	….	….	….
2013-14	Sault Ste. Marie	OHL	62	19	21	40	12	….	….	….	….	….	….	….	….	….	9	0	3	3	0	….	….	….	….
2014-15	Sault Ste. Marie	OHL	57	24	43	67	12	….	….	….	….	….	….	….	….	….	14	3	6	9	4	….	….	….	….
2015-16	Sault Ste. Marie	OHL	68	26	48	74	42	….	….	….	….	….	….	….	….	….	12	6	4	10	8	….	….	….	….
2016-17	**New Jersey**	**NHL**	**3**	**0**	**0**	**0**	**0**	0	0	0	3	0.0	0	2	0.0	9:29	….	….	….	….	….	….	….	….	….
	Sault Ste. Marie	OHL	30	15	19	34	16	….	….	….	….	….	….	….	….	….	11	1	7	8	12	….	….	….	….
	Albany Devils	AHL	….	….	….	….	….	….	….	….	….	….	….	….	….	….	2	0	0	0	0	….	….	….	….
	NHL Totals		**3**	**0**	**0**	**0**	**0**	**0**	**0**	**0**	**3**	**0.0**		**2**	**0.0**	**9:29**	….	….	….	….	….	….	….	….	….

OHL All-Rookie Team (2014)

SPEZZA, Jason (SPEHT-zuh, JAY-suhn) **DAL**

Center. Shoots right. 6'3", 220 lbs. Born, Mississauga, ON, June 13, 1983. Ottawa's 1st pick, 2nd overall, in 2001 NHL Draft.

Season	Club	League	GP	G	A	Pts	PIM	PP	SH	GW	S	S%	+/-	TF	F%	Min	GP	G	A	Pts	PIM	PP	SH	GW	Min
1997-98	Toronto Marlies	MTHL	54	53	61	114	42	….	….	….	….	….	….	….	….	….	….	….	….	….	….	….	….	….	….
1998-99	Brampton	OHL	67	22	49	71	18	….	….	….	….	….	….	….	….	….	….	….	….	….	….	….	….	….	….
99-2000	Mississauga	OHL	52	24	37	61	33	….	….	….	….	….	….	….	….	….	….	….	….	….	….	….	….	….	….
2000-01	Mississauga	OHL	15	7	23	30	11	….	….	….	….	….	….	….	….	….	….	….	….	….	….	….	….	….	….
	Windsor Spitfires	OHL	41	36	50	86	32	….	….	….	….	….	….	….	….	….	9	4	5	9	10	….	….	….	….
2001-02	Windsor Spitfires	OHL	27	19	26	45	16	….	….	….	….	….	….	….	….	….	….	….	….	….	….	….	….	….	….
	Belleville Bulls	OHL	26	23	37	60	26	….	….	….	….	….	….	….	….	….	11	5	6	11	18	….	….	….	….
	Grand Rapids	AHL	….	….	….	….	….	….	….	….	….	….	….	….	….	….	3	1	0	1	2	….	….	….	….
2002-03	**Ottawa**	**NHL**	**33**	**7**	**14**	**21**	**8**	3	0	0	65	10.8	-3	330	45.8	12:40	3	1	1	2	0	1	0	0	11:34
	Binghamton	AHL	43	22	32	54	71	….	….	….	….	….	….	….	….	….	2	1	2	3	4	….	….	….	….
2003-04	**Ottawa**	**NHL**	**78**	**22**	**33**	**55**	**71**	5	0	3	142	15.5	22	956	47.7	14:38	3	0	0	0	2	0	0	0	9:44

Season	Club	League	GP	G	A	Pts	PIM	PP	SH	GW	S	S%	+/-	TF	F%	Min	GP	G	A	Pts	PIM	PP	SH	GW	Min
			Regular Season														Playoffs								
2004-05	Binghamton	AHL	80	32	*85	*117	50	....	....	....	....	....	....	....	....	....	6	1	3	4	6	....	....	....	....
2005-06	**Ottawa**	**NHL**	**68**	**19**	**71**	**90**	**33**	**7**	**0**	**5**	**156**	**12.2**	**23**	**1220**	**52.6**	**19:00**	**10**	**5**	**9**	**14**	**2**	**3**	**0**	**1**	**17:59**
2006-07	**Ottawa**	**NHL**	**67**	**34**	**53**	**87**	**45**	**13**	**1**	**5**	**162**	**21.0**	**19**	**1261**	**53.0**	**19:17**	**20**	**7**	***15**	***22**	**10**	**3**	**0**	**0**	**20:58**
2007-08	**Ottawa**	**NHL**	**76**	**34**	**58**	**92**	**66**	**11**	**0**	**6**	**210**	**16.2**	**26**	**1445**	**50.5**	**20:40**	**4**	**0**	**1**	**1**	**0**	**0**	**0**	**0**	**19:45**
2008-09	**Ottawa**	**NHL**	**82**	**32**	**41**	**73**	**79**	**13**	**1**	**3**	**246**	**13.0**	**-14**	**1477**	**53.3**	**19:41**	....	....	....	....	....	....	....	....	....
2009-10	**Ottawa**	**NHL**	**60**	**23**	**34**	**57**	**20**	**11**	**0**	**5**	**165**	**13.9**	**0**	**1018**	**50.5**	**19:04**	**6**	**1**	**6**	**7**	**4**	**1**	**0**	**0**	**22:46**
2010-11	**Ottawa**	**NHL**	**62**	**21**	**36**	**57**	**28**	**7**	**0**	**2**	**188**	**11.2**	**-7**	**1210**	**56.3**	**20:12**	....	....	....	....	....	....	....	....	....
2011-12	**Ottawa**	**NHL**	**80**	**34**	**50**	**84**	**36**	**10**	**0**	**2**	**232**	**14.7**	**11**	**1700**	**53.5**	**19:55**	**7**	**3**	**2**	**5**	**8**	**0**	**0**	**1**	**20:59**
2012-13	Rapperswil	Swiss	28	9	21	30	12	....	....	....	....	....	....	....	....	....	....	....	....	....	....	....	....	....	....
	Ottawa	**NHL**	**5**	**2**	**3**	**5**	**2**	**1**	**0**	**0**	**12**	**16.7**	**3**	**119**	**57.1**	**19:11**	**3**	**0**	**1**	**1**	**0**	**0**	**0**	**0**	**18:27**
2013-14	**Ottawa**	**NHL**	**75**	**23**	**43**	**66**	**46**	**9**	**0**	**5**	**223**	**10.3**	**-26**	**1436**	**54.0**	**18:13**	....	....	....	....	....	....	....	....	....
2014-15	**Dallas**	**NHL**	**82**	**17**	**45**	**62**	**28**	**4**	**0**	**1**	**204**	**8.3**	**-7**	**1262**	**54.0**	**17:13**	....	....	....	....	....	....	....	....	....
2015-16	**Dallas**	**NHL**	**75**	**33**	**30**	**63**	**22**	**9**	**0**	**7**	**202**	**16.3**	**4**	**981**	**54.8**	**16:31**	**13**	**5**	**8**	**13**	**2**	**1**	**0**	**2**	**17:35**
2016-17	**Dallas**	**NHL**	**68**	**15**	**35**	**50**	**29**	**2**	**1**	**4**	**149**	**10.1**	**-18**	**678**	**52.2**	**16:10**	....	....	....	....	....	....	....	....	....
	NHL Totals		**911**	**316**	**546**	**862**	**513**	**105**	**3**	**48**	**2356**	**13.4**		**15093**	**52.7**	**18:09**	**69**	**22**	**43**	**65**	**28**	**9**	**0**	**4**	**18:59**

OHL All-Rookie Team (1999) • AHL All-Rookie Team (2003) • AHL First All-Star Team (2005) • John P. Sollenberger Trophy (AHL - Top Scorer) (2005) • Les Cunningham Award (AHL – MVP) (2005)
Played in NHL All-Star Game (2008, 2012)

Signed as a free agent by **Rapperswil** (Swiss), September 19, 2012. Traded to **Dallas** by **Ottawa** with Ludwig Karlsson for Alex Chiasson. Alexander Guptill, Nicholas Paul and Dallas' 2nd round pick (later traded to New Jersey – New Jersey selected Mackenzie Blackwood) in 2015 NHL Draft, July 1, 2014.

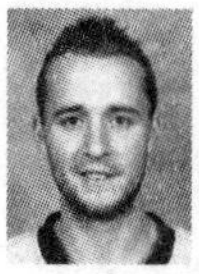

SPOONER, Ryan (SPOO-nuhr, RIGH-uhn) BOS

Center. Shoots left. 5'10", 184 lbs. Born, Ottawa, ON, January 30, 1992. Boston's 3rd pick, 45th overall, in 2010 NHL Draft.

Season	Club	League	GP	G	A	Pts	PIM	PP	SH	GW	S	S%	+/-	TF	F%	Min	GP	G	A	Pts	PIM	PP	SH	GW	Min
2007-08	Ott. Jr. Senators	Minor-ON	53	52	45	97	16	....	....	....	....	....	....	....	....	....	....	....	....	....	....	....	....	....	....
2008-09	Peterborough	OHL	62	30	28	58	8	....	....	....	....	....	....	....	....	....	4	0	1	1	0	....	....	....	....
2009-10	Peterborough	OHL	47	19	35	54	12	....	....	....	....	....	....	....	....	....	3	0	1	1	2	....	....	....	....
2010-11	Peterborough	OHL	14	10	9	19	2	....	....	....	....	....	....	....	....	....	....	....	....	....	....	....	....	....	....
	Kingston	OHL	50	25	37	62	6	....	....	....	....	....	....	....	....	....	5	4	2	6	2	....	....	....	....
	Providence Bruins	AHL	3	2	1	3	0	....	....	....	....	....	....	....	....	....	....	....	....	....	....	....	....	....	....
2011-12	Kingston	OHL	27	14	18	32	8	....	....	....	....	....	....	....	....	....	....	....	....	....	....	....	....	....	....
	Sarnia Sting	OHL	30	15	19	34	8	....	....	....	....	....	....	....	....	....	6	1	2	3	8	....	....	....	....
	Providence Bruins	AHL	5	1	3	4	0	....	....	....	....	....	....	....	....	....	....	....	....	....	....	....	....	....	....
2012-13	Providence Bruins	AHL	59	17	40	57	14	....	....	....	....	....	....	....	....	....	12	2	3	5	4	....	....	....	....
	Boston	**NHL**	**4**	**0**	**0**	**0**	**0**	**0**	**0**	**0**	**4**	**0.0**	**0**	**24**	**45.8**	**9:07**	....	....	....	....	....	....	....	....	....
2013-14	**Boston**	**NHL**	**23**	**0**	**11**	**11**	**6**	**0**	**0**	**0**	**42**	**0.0**	**0**	**145**	**40.7**	**12:49**	....	....	....	....	....	....	....	....	....
	Providence Bruins	AHL	49	11	35	46	8	....	....	....	....	....	....	....	....	....	12	6	9	15	2	....	....	....	....
2014-15	**Boston**	**NHL**	**29**	**8**	**10**	**18**	**2**	**3**	**0**	**1**	**73**	**11.0**	**2**	**220**	**45.5**	**14:32**	....	....	....	....	....	....	....	....	....
	Providence Bruins	AHL	34	8	18	26	10	....	....	....	....	....	....	....	....	....	5	0	4	4	0	....	....	....	....
2015-16	**Boston**	**NHL**	**80**	**13**	**36**	**49**	**35**	**6**	**0**	**4**	**162**	**8.0**	**-9**	**711**	**42.8**	**15:08**	....	....	....	....	....	....	....	....	....
2016-17	**Boston**	**NHL**	**78**	**11**	**28**	**39**	**14**	**3**	**0**	**3**	**145**	**7.6**	**-8**	**203**	**38.9**	**14:06**	**4**	**0**	**2**	**2**	**0**	**0**	**0**	**0**	**13:03**
	NHL Totals		**214**	**32**	**85**	**117**	**57**	**12**	**0**	**8**	**426**	**7.5**		**1303**	**42.4**	**14:19**	**4**	**0**	**2**	**2**	**0**	**0**	**0**	**0**	**13:02**

AHL All-Rookie Team (2013)

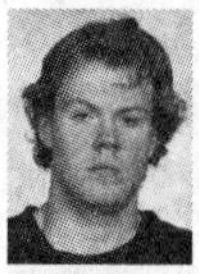

SPRONG, Daniel (SPRAWNG, DAN-yuhl) PIT

Right wing. Shoots right. 6', 180 lbs. Born, Amsterdam, Netherlands, March 17, 1997. Pittsburgh's 1st pick, 46th overall, in 2015 NHL Draft.

Season	Club	League	GP	G	A	Pts	PIM	PP	SH	GW	S	S%	+/-	TF	F%	Min	GP	G	A	Pts	PIM	PP	SH	GW	Min
2012-13	Lac St-L. Tigres	Minor-QC	30	48	56	104	36	....	....	....	....	....	....	....	....	....	3	5	3	8	0	....	....	....	....
2013-14	Charlottetown	QMJHL	67	30	38	68	20	....	....	....	....	....	....	....	....	....	4	4	1	5	0	....	....	....	....
2014-15	Charlottetown	QMJHL	68	39	49	88	18	....	....	....	....	....	....	....	....	....	10	7	4	11	6	....	....	....	....
2015-16	**Pittsburgh**	**NHL**	**18**	**2**	**0**	**2**	**0**	**0**	**0**	**0**	**23**	**8.7**	**-1**	**2**	**50.0**	**8:44**	....	....	....	....	....	....	....	....	....
	Charlottetown	QMJHL	33	16	30	46	22	....	....	....	....	....	....	....	....	....	12	4	11	15	12	....	....	....	....
	Wilkes-Barre	AHL	....	....	....	....	....	....	....	....	....	....	....	....	....	....	10	5	2	7	2	....	....	....	....
2016-17	Charlottetown	QMJHL	31	32	27	59	8	....	....	....	....	....	....	....	....	....	12	9	11	20	17	....	....	....	....
	NHL Totals		**18**	**2**	**0**	**2**	**0**	**0**	**0**	**0**	**23**	**8.7**		**2**	**50.0**	**8:44**	....	....	....	....	....	....	....	....	....

QMJHL All-Rookie Team (2014)
• Missed majority of 2016-17 due to recurring shoulder injury and resulting surgery, June, 2016.

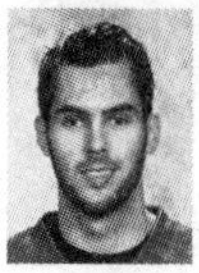

SPROUL, Ryan (SPROHL, RIGH-uhn) DET

Defense. Shoots right. 6'4", 211 lbs. Born, Mississauga, ON, January 13, 1993. Detroit's 3rd pick, 55th overall, in 2011 NHL Draft.

Season	Club	League	GP	G	A	Pts	PIM	PP	SH	GW	S	S%	+/-	TF	F%	Min	GP	G	A	Pts	PIM	PP	SH	GW	Min
2008-09	Vaughan Kings	GTHL	31	2	7	9	14	....	....	....	....	....	....	....	....	....	....	....	....	....	....	....	....	....	....
2009-10	Bramalea Blues	ON-Jr.A	6	0	1	1	6	....	....	....	....	....	....	....	....	....	....	....	....	....	....	....	....	....	....
	Vaughan Vipers	ON-Jr.A	8	1	1	2	0	....	....	....	....	....	....	....	....	....	2	0	0	0	0	....	....	....	....
2010-11	Vaughan Vipers	ON-Jr.A	3	1	2	3	4	....	....	....	....	....	....	....	....	....	....	....	....	....	....	....	....	....	....
	Sault Ste. Marie	OHL	61	14	19	33	36	....	....	....	....	....	....	....	....	....	....	....	....	....	....	....	....	....	....
2011-12	Sault Ste. Marie	OHL	61	23	31	54	53	....	....	....	....	....	....	....	....	....	....	....	....	....	....	....	....	....	....
2012-13	Sault Ste. Marie	OHL	50	20	46	66	45	....	....	....	....	....	....	....	....	....	6	2	3	5	0	....	....	....	....
	Grand Rapids	AHL	2	0	0	0	2	....	....	....	....	....	....	....	....	....	....	....	....	....	....	....	....	....	....
2013-14	**Detroit**	**NHL**	**1**	**0**	**0**	**0**	**0**	**0**	**0**	**0**	**3**	**0.0**	**0**	**0**	**0.0**	**18:25**	....	....	....	....	....	....	....	....	....
	Grand Rapids	AHL	72	11	21	32	49	....	....	....	....	....	....	....	....	....	10	2	3	5	4	....	....	....	....
2014-15	Grand Rapids	AHL	66	5	19	24	26	....	....	....	....	....	....	....	....	....	5	0	0	0	0	....	....	....	....
2015-16	Grand Rapids	AHL	75	12	23	35	22	....	....	....	....	....	....	....	....	....	9	2	7	9	8	....	....	....	....
2016-17	**Detroit**	**NHL**	**27**	**1**	**6**	**7**	**6**	**1**	**0**	**0**	**46**	**2.2**	**-8**	**0**	**0.0**	**15:09**	....	....	....	....	....	....	....	....	....
	NHL Totals		**28**	**1**	**6**	**7**	**6**	**1**	**0**	**0**	**49**	**2.0**		**0**	**0.0**	**15:16**	....	....	....	....	....	....	....	....	....

OHL First All-Star Team (2013) • Canadian Major Junior Defenseman of the Year (2013) • AHL All-Rookie Team (2014)

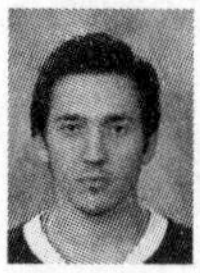

SPURGEON, Jared (SPUHR-juhn, JAIR-uhd) MIN

Defense. Shoots right. 5'9", 164 lbs. Born, Edmonton, AB, November 29, 1989. NY Islanders' 12th pick, 156th overall, in 2008 NHL Draft.

Season	Club	League	GP	G	A	Pts	PIM	PP	SH	GW	S	S%	+/-	TF	F%	Min	GP	G	A	Pts	PIM	PP	SH	GW	Min
2004-05	K of C Pats	AMHL	26	9	21	30	16	....	....	....	....	....	....	....	....	....	....	....	....	....	....	....	....	....	....
2005-06	Spokane Chiefs	WHL	46	3	9	12	28	....	....	....	....	....	....	....	....	....	....	....	....	....	....	....	....	....	....
2006-07	Spokane Chiefs	WHL	38	4	15	19	16	....	....	....	....	....	....	....	....	....	....	....	....	....	....	....	....	....	....
2007-08	Spokane Chiefs	WHL	69	12	31	43	19	....	....	....	....	....	....	....	....	....	21	0	5	5	16	....	....	....	....
2008-09	Spokane Chiefs	WHL	59	10	35	45	37	....	....	....	....	....	....	....	....	....	12	2	3	5	10	....	....	....	....
2009-10	Spokane Chiefs	WHL	54	8	43	51	18	....	....	....	....	....	....	....	....	....	7	0	4	4	2	....	....	....	....
2010-11	**Minnesota**	**NHL**	**53**	**4**	**8**	**12**	**2**	**2**	**0**	**1**	**38**	**10.5**	**-1**	**0**	**0.0**	**15:04**	....	....	....	....	....	....	....	....	....
	Houston Aeros	AHL	23	2	7	9	10	....	....	....	....	....	....	....	....	....	23	1	10	11	10	....	....	....	....
2011-12	**Minnesota**	**NHL**	**70**	**3**	**20**	**23**	**6**	**2**	**0**	**1**	**92**	**3.3**	**-4**	**0**	**0.0**	**21:36**	....	....	....	....	....	....	....	....	....
2012-13	Langnau	Swiss	12	3	4	7	6	....	....	....	....	....	....	....	....	....	....	....	....	....	....	....	....	....	....
	Minnesota	**NHL**	**39**	**5**	**10**	**15**	**4**	**4**	**0**	**2**	**67**	**7.5**	**1**	**0**	**0.0**	**21:33**	**5**	**0**	**0**	**0**	**2**	**0**	**0**	**0**	**21:15**
2013-14	**Minnesota**	**NHL**	**67**	**5**	**21**	**26**	**16**	**2**	**0**	**1**	**91**	**5.5**	**15**	**0**	**0.0**	**22:38**	**13**	**3**	**3**	**6**	**2**	**1**	**0**	**0**	**24:04**
2014-15	**Minnesota**	**NHL**	**66**	**9**	**16**	**25**	**6**	**3**	**0**	**2**	**128**	**7.0**	**3**	**0**	**0.0**	**22:37**	**10**	**1**	**3**	**4**	**4**	**1**	**0**	**0**	**21:20**
2015-16	**Minnesota**	**NHL**	**77**	**11**	**18**	**29**	**14**	**5**	**0**	**2**	**122**	**9.0**	**11**	**0**	**0.0**	**22:41**	**6**	**2**	**3**	**5**	**4**	**2**	**0**	**0**	**26:00**
2016-17	**Minnesota**	**NHL**	**76**	**10**	**28**	**38**	**20**	**1**	**0**	**2**	**144**	**6.9**	**33**	**0**	**0.0**	**24:02**	**5**	**0**	**1**	**1**	**0**	**0**	**0**	**0**	**25:20**
	NHL Totals		**448**	**47**	**121**	**168**	**68**	**19**	**0**	**11**	**682**	**6.9**		**0**	**0.0**	**21:44**	**39**	**6**	**10**	**16**	**12**	**4**	**0**	**0**	**23:28**

Signed as a free agent by **Minnesota**, September 23, 2010. Signed as a free agent by **Langnau** (Swiss), September 21, 2012.

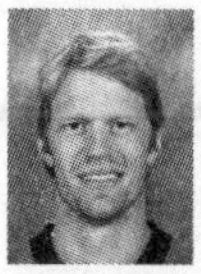

STAAL, Eric (STAWL, AIR-ihk) MIN

Center. Shoots left. 6'4", 205 lbs. Born, Thunder Bay, ON, October 29, 1984. Carolina's 1st pick, 2nd overall, in 2003 NHL Draft.

Season	Club	League	GP	G	A	Pts	PIM	PP	SH	GW	S	S%	+/-	TF	F%	Min	GP	G	A	Pts	PIM	PP	SH	GW	Min
99-2000	Thunder Bay	Other	7	4	8	12	0	....	....	....	....	....	....	....	....	....	....	....	....	....	....	....	....	....	....
2000-01	Peterborough	OHL	63	19	30	49	23	....	....	....	....	....	....	....	....	....	7	2	5	7	4	....	....	....	....
2001-02	Peterborough	OHL	56	23	39	62	40	....	....	....	....	....	....	....	....	....	6	3	6	9	10	....	....	....	....
2002-03	Peterborough	OHL	66	39	59	98	36	....	....	....	....	....	....	....	....	....	7	9	5	14	6	....	....	....	....
2003-04	**Carolina**	**NHL**	**81**	**11**	**20**	**31**	**40**	**2**	**1**	**3**	**164**	**6.7**	**-6**	**669**	**43.1**	**16:40**	....	....	....	....	....	....	....	....	....
2004-05	Lowell	AHL	77	26	51	77	88	....	....	....	....	....	....	....	....	....	11	2	8	10	12	....	....	....	....
2005-06 ♦	**Carolina**	**NHL**	**82**	**45**	**55**	**100**	**81**	**19**	**4**	**4**	**279**	**16.1**	**-8**	**1309**	**42.6**	**19:39**	**25**	**9**	***19**	***28**	**8**	***7**	**0**	**1**	**19:48**

Season	Club	League	GP	G	A	Pts	PIM	PP	SH	GW	S	S%	+/-	TF	F%	Min	GP	G	A	Pts	PIM	PP	SH	GW	Min
			Regular Season														Playoffs								
2006-07	Carolina	NHL	82	30	40	70	68	12	1	1	288	10.4	-6	1238	45.2	20:08	....	....	....	....	....	....	....	....	....
2007-08	Carolina	NHL	82	38	44	82	50	14	0	7	310	12.3	-2	1708	44.9	21:38	....	....	....	....	....	....	....	....	....
2008-09	Carolina	NHL	82	40	35	75	50	14	1	8	372	10.8	15	1586	45.3	21:03	18	10	5	15	4	3	0	1	21:31
2009-10	Carolina	NHL	70	29	41	70	68	13	0	5	277	10.5	4	1162	41.8	20:43	....	....	....	....	....	....	....	....	....
	Canada	Olympics	7	1	5	6	6	....	....	....	....	....	....	....	....	....	....	....	....	....	....	....	....	....	....
2010-11	Carolina	NHL	81	33	43	76	72	12	3	8	296	11.1	-10	1751	48.0	21:56	....	....	....	....	....	....	....	....	....
2011-12	Carolina	NHL	82	24	46	70	48	7	3	3	262	9.2	-20	1681	52.5	21:33	....	....	....	....	....	....	....	....	....
2012-13	Carolina	NHL	48	18	35	53	54	3	1	4	152	11.8	5	1014	52.0	21:00	....	....	....	....	....	....	....	....	....
2013-14	Carolina	NHL	79	21	40	61	74	1	2	0	230	9.1	-13	1430	52.7	20:17	....	....	....	....	....	....	....	....	....
2014-15	Carolina	NHL	77	23	31	54	41	7	0	4	244	9.4	-13	669	51.3	18:51	....	....	....	....	....	....	....	....	....
2015-16	Carolina	NHL	63	10	23	33	32	1	0	0	159	6.3	-3	601	53.7	19:17	....	....	....	....	....	....	....	....	....
	NY Rangers	NHL	20	3	3	6	2	0	0	0	40	7.5	1	241	51.0	16:15	5	0	0	0	4	0	0	0	16:05
2016-17	Minnesota	NHL	82	28	37	65	34	4	1	8	211	13.3	17	1174	49.2	18:36	5	0	1	1	0	0	0	0	18:54
	NHL Totals		1011	353	493	846	714	109	17	55	3284	10.7		16233	47.7	20:01	53	19	25	44	16	10	0	2	19:57

OHL Second All-Star Team (2003) • Canadian Major Junior First All-Star Team (2003) • NHL Second All-Star Team (2006)

Played in NHL All-Star Game (2007, 2008, 2009, 2011)

Traded to **NY Rangers** by **Carolina** for Aleksi Saarela, NY Rangers' 2nd round pick (later traded to Chicago – Chicago selected Artur Kayumov) in 2016 NHL Draft and NY Rangers' 2nd round pick (Luke Martin) in 2017 NHL Draft, February 28, 2016. Signed as a free agent by **Minnesota**, July 1, 2016.

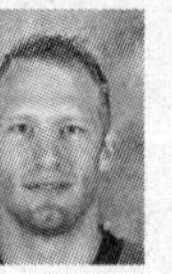

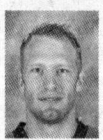

STAAL, Jordan

(STAWL, JOHR-dahn) **CAR**

Center. Shoots left. 6'4", 220 lbs. Born, Thunder Bay, ON, September 10, 1988. Pittsburgh's 1st pick, 2nd overall, in 2006 NHL Draft.

Season	Club	League	GP	G	A	Pts	PIM	PP	SH	GW	S	S%	+/-	TF	F%	Min	GP	G	A	Pts	PIM	PP	SH	GW	Min
2004-05	Peterborough	OHL	66	9	19	28	29	....	....	....	....	....	....	....	....	....	14	5	5	10	16	....	....	....	....
2005-06	Peterborough	OHL	68	28	40	68	69	....	....	....	....	....	....	....	....	....	19	10	6	16	16	....	....	....	....
2006-07	Pittsburgh	NHL	81	29	13	42	24	4	*7	4	131	22.1	16	383	37.1	14:56	5	3	0	3	2	0	0	0	16:00
2007-08	Pittsburgh	NHL	82	12	16	28	55	3	0	4	183	6.6	-5	1202	42.2	18:16	20	6	1	7	14	1	0	1	18:16
2008-09•	Pittsburgh	NHL	82	22	27	49	37	2	1	3	166	13.3	5	1206	47.0	19:51	24	4	5	9	8	0	1	0	19:13
2009-10	Pittsburgh	NHL	82	21	28	49	57	1	2	1	195	10.8	19	1324	48.3	19:24	11	3	2	5	6	2	0	0	18:14
2010-11	Pittsburgh	NHL	42	11	19	30	24	3	0	4	91	12.1	7	801	46.9	21:21	7	1	2	3	2	0	0	0	21:28
2011-12	Pittsburgh	NHL	62	25	25	50	34	5	3	0	149	16.8	11	1158	51.0	20:03	6	6	3	9	2	1	0	1	19:49
2012-13	Carolina	NHL	48	10	21	31	32	1	0	1	114	8.8	-18	914	50.1	20:06	....	....	....	....	....	....	....	....	....
2013-14	Carolina	NHL	82	15	25	40	34	2	1	2	165	9.1	2	1477	54.4	18:57	....	....	....	....	....	....	....	....	....
2014-15	Carolina	NHL	46	6	18	24	14	1	0	1	92	6.5	-6	885	56.4	18:33	....	....	....	....	....	....	....	....	....
2015-16	Carolina	NHL	82	20	28	48	34	6	0	4	151	13.2	6	1395	57.8	18:18	....	....	....	....	....	....	....	....	....
2016-17	Carolina	NHL	75	16	29	45	38	4	1	3	164	9.8	-1	1166	59.1	18:40	....	....	....	....	....	....	....	....	....
	NHL Totals		764	187	249	436	383	32	15	27	1601	11.7		11911	51.0	18:46	73	23	13	36	34	4	1	2	18:51

NHL All-Rookie Team (2007)

Traded to **Carolina** by **Pittsburgh** for Brandon Sutter, Brian Dumoulin and Carolina's 1st round pick (Derrick Pouliot) in 2012 NHL Draft, June 22, 2012.

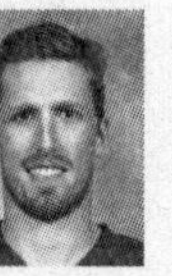

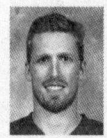

STAAL, Marc

(STAWL, MAHRK) **NYR**

Defense. Shoots left. 6'4", 209 lbs. Born, Thunder Bay, ON, January 13, 1987. NY Rangers' 1st pick, 12th overall, in 2005 NHL Draft.

Season	Club	League	GP	G	A	Pts	PIM	PP	SH	GW	S	S%	+/-	TF	F%	Min	GP	G	A	Pts	PIM	PP	SH	GW	Min
2003-04	Sudbury Wolves	OHL	61	1	13	14	34	....	....	....	....	....	....	....	....	....	7	1	2	3	2	....	....	....	....
2004-05	Sudbury Wolves	OHL	65	6	20	26	53	....	....	....	....	....	....	....	....	....	12	0	4	4	15	....	....	....	....
2005-06	Sudbury Wolves	OHL	57	11	38	49	60	....	....	....	....	....	....	....	....	....	10	0	8	8	8	....	....	....	....
	Hartford	AHL	....	....	....	....	....	....	....	....	....	....	....	....	....	....	12	0	2	2	8	....	....	....	....
2006-07	Sudbury Wolves	OHL	53	5	29	34	68	....	....	....	....	....	....	....	....	....	21	5	15	20	22	....	....	....	....
2007-08	NY Rangers	NHL	80	2	8	10	42	0	0	0	78	2.6	2	0	0.0	18:48	10	1	2	3	8	0	0	1	22:21
2008-09	NY Rangers	NHL	82	3	12	15	64	0	0	1	96	3.1	-7	0	0.0	21:08	7	1	0	1	0	0	0	0	21:33
2009-10	NY Rangers	NHL	82	8	19	27	44	0	0	2	78	10.3	11	0	0.0	23:08	....	....	....	....	....	....	....	....	....
2010-11	NY Rangers	NHL	77	7	22	29	50	4	2	2	116	6.0	8	0	0.0	25:44	5	0	1	1	0	0	0	0	28:01
2011-12	NY Rangers	NHL	46	2	3	5	16	1	0	0	61	3.3	-7	0	0.0	19:54	20	3	3	6	12	2	0	1	25:18
2012-13	NY Rangers	NHL	21	2	9	11	14	1	0	0	20	10.0	4	0	0.0	24:27	1	0	0	0	0	0	0	0	17:17
2013-14	NY Rangers	NHL	72	3	11	14	24	1	0	0	92	3.3	-1	1	100.0	20:32	25	1	4	5	6	0	0	0	21:49
2014-15	NY Rangers	NHL	80	5	15	20	42	0	0	0	97	5.2	18	2	50.0	21:08	19	0	1	1	10	0	0	0	20:41
2015-16	NY Rangers	NHL	77	2	13	15	36	0	0	1	65	3.1	2	4	25.0	19:41	5	0	2	2	4	0	0	0	19:09
2016-17	NY Rangers	NHL	72	3	7	10	34	0	0	0	70	4.3	9	1	0.0	19:11	12	0	0	0	2	0	0	0	19:15
	NHL Totals		689	37	119	156	366	7	2	6	773	4.8		8	37.5	21:12	104	6	13	19	42	2	0	2	22:09

OHL First All-Star Team (2006, 2007) • Canadian Major Junior First All-Star Team (2006, 2007) • OHL Playoff MVP (2007)

Played in NHL All-Star Game (2011)

• Missed majority of 2012-13 due to eye injury vs. Philadelphia, March 5, 2013.

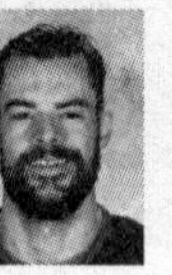

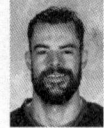

STAFFORD, Drew

(STA-fuhrd, DROO)

Right wing. Shoots right. 6'2", 214 lbs. Born, Milwaukee, WI, October 30, 1985. Buffalo's 1st pick, 13th overall, in 2004 NHL Draft.

Season	Club	League	GP	G	A	Pts	PIM	PP	SH	GW	S	S%	+/-	TF	F%	Min	GP	G	A	Pts	PIM	PP	SH	GW	Min
2001-02	Shattuck	High-MN	45	35	53	88	30	....	....	....	....	....	....	....	....	....	....	....	....	....	....	....	....	....	....
2002-03	Shattuck	High-MN	65	49	67	116	....	....	....	....	....	....	....	....	....	....	....	....	....	....	....	....	....	....	....
2003-04	North Dakota	WCHA	36	11	21	32	30	....	....	....	....	....	....	....	....	....	....	....	....	....	....	....	....	....	....
2004-05	North Dakota	WCHA	42	13	25	38	34	....	....	....	....	....	....	....	....	....	....	....	....	....	....	....	....	....	....
2005-06	North Dakota	WCHA	42	24	24	48	63	....	....	....	....	....	....	....	....	....	....	....	....	....	....	....	....	....	....
2006-07	Buffalo	NHL	41	13	14	27	33	3	0	3	67	19.4	5	13	46.2	13:08	10	2	2	4	4	0	0	0	11:52
	Rochester	AHL	34	22	22	44	30	....	....	....	....	....	....	....	....	....	....	....	....	....	....	....	....	....	....
2007-08	Buffalo	NHL	64	16	22	38	51	1	0	5	103	15.5	3	21	38.1	13:32	....	....	....	....	....	....	....	....	....
2008-09	Buffalo	NHL	79	20	25	45	29	9	0	0	183	10.9	3	20	20.0	15:38	....	....	....	....	....	....	....	....	....
2009-10	Buffalo	NHL	71	14	20	34	35	5	0	1	181	7.7	4	86	47.7	14:28	3	0	0	0	0	0	0	0	14:06
2010-11	Buffalo	NHL	62	31	21	52	34	11	0	4	179	17.3	13	56	30.4	16:32	7	1	2	3	2	1	0	0	20:01
2011-12	Buffalo	NHL	80	20	30	50	46	3	1	4	226	8.8	5	86	52.3	17:39	....	....	....	....	....	....	....	....	....
2012-13	Buffalo	NHL	46	6	12	18	21	0	0	0	121	5.0	-16	84	44.1	17:01	....	....	....	....	....	....	....	....	....
2013-14	Buffalo	NHL	70	16	18	34	39	2	1	1	185	8.6	-19	197	53.8	18:38	....	....	....	....	....	....	....	....	....
2014-15	Buffalo	NHL	50	9	15	24	39	2	0	1	91	9.9	-18	160	50.0	15:59	....	....	....	....	....	....	....	....	....
	Winnipeg	NHL	26	9	10	19	8	2	0	0	56	16.1	6	14	42.9	17:30	4	1	1	2	0	0	0	0	17:19
2015-16	Winnipeg	NHL	78	21	17	38	28	6	1	6	187	11.2	-23	101	50.5	17:52	....	....	....	....	....	....	....	....	....
2016-17	Winnipeg	NHL	40	4	9	13	12	2	0	1	68	5.9	-2	12	25.0	13:18	....	....	....	....	....	....	....	....	....
	Boston	NHL	18	4	4	8	12	1	0	2	41	9.8	8	10	40.0	14:16	6	2	0	2	2	1	0	0	13:44
	NHL Totals		725	183	217	400	387	47	3	28	1688	10.8		860	47.4	16:02	30	6	5	11	8	2	0	0	15:05

Traded to **Winnipeg** by **Buffalo** with Tyler Myers, Joel Armia, Brendan Lemieux and St. Louis' 1st round pick (previously acquired, Winnipeg selected Jack Roslovic) in 2015 NHL Draft for Evander Kane, Zach Bogosian and Jason Kasdorf, February 11, 2015. Traded to **Boston** by **Winnipeg** for Boston's 5th round pick in 2018 NHL Draft, March 1, 2017.

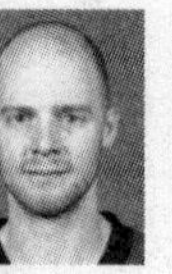

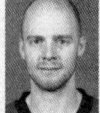

STAJAN, Matt

(STAY-juhn, MAT) **CGY**

Center. Shoots left. 6'1", 195 lbs. Born, Mississauga, ON, December 19, 1983. Toronto's 2nd pick, 57th overall, in 2002 NHL Draft.

Season	Club	League	GP	G	A	Pts	PIM	PP	SH	GW	S	S%	+/-	TF	F%	Min	GP	G	A	Pts	PIM	PP	SH	GW	Min
99-2000	Miss. Senators	GTHL	STATISTICS NOT AVAILABLE																						
2000-01	Belleville Bulls	OHL	57	9	18	27	27	....	....	....	....	....	....	....	....	....	7	1	6	7	5	....	....	....	....
2001-02	Belleville Bulls	OHL	68	33	52	85	50	....	....	....	....	....	....	....	....	....	11	3	8	11	14	....	....	....	....
2002-03	Belleville Bulls	OHL	57	34	60	94	75	....	....	....	....	....	....	....	....	....	7	5	8	13	16	....	....	....	....
	St. John's	AHL	1	0	1	1	0	....	....	....	....	....	....	....	....	....	....	....	....	....	....	....	....	....	....
	Toronto	NHL	1	1	0	1	0	0	0	0	1	100.0	1	12	33.3	11:00	....	....	....	....	....	....	....	....	....
2003-04	Toronto	NHL	69	14	13	27	22	0	0	0	63	22.2	7	450	38.9	11:00	3	0	0	0	2	0	0	0	11:13
2004-05	St. John's	AHL	80	23	43	66	43	....	....	....	....	....	....	....	....	....	5	2	2	4	6	....	....	....	....
2005-06	Toronto	NHL	80	15	12	27	50	3	4	5	83	18.1	5	373	44.5	11:38	....	....	....	....	....	....	....	....	....
2006-07	Toronto	NHL	82	10	29	39	44	1	1	1	132	7.6	3	985	46.1	16:09	....	....	....	....	....	....	....	....	....
2007-08	Toronto	NHL	82	16	17	33	47	2	1	3	127	12.6	-11	1293	47.6	18:54	....	....	....	....	....	....	....	....	....
2008-09	Toronto	NHL	76	15	40	55	54	5	1	1	114	13.2	-4	1177	51.4	16:56	....	....	....	....	....	....	....	....	....
2009-10	Toronto	NHL	55	16	25	41	30	7	0	2	99	16.2	-3	926	51.6	18:47	....	....	....	....	....	....	....	....	....
	Calgary	NHL	27	3	13	16	2	0	0	2	33	9.1	-3	408	52.0	19:11	....	....	....	....	....	....	....	....	....
2010-11	Calgary	NHL	76	6	25	31	32	0	1	0	81	7.4	1	845	51.6	14:14	....	....	....	....	....	....	....	....	....
2011-12	Calgary	NHL	61	8	10	18	29	0	0	1	77	10.4	-3	639	51.8	13:01	....	....	....	....	....	....	....	....	....

			Regular Season														Playoffs								
Season	Club	League	GP	G	A	Pts	PIM	PP	SH	GW	S	S%	+/-	TF	F%	Min	GP	G	A	Pts	PIM	PP	SH	GW	Min
2012-13	Calgary	NHL	43	5	18	23	26	0	0	1	44	11.4	7	770	46.2	17:10	....	....	....	....	....	....	....	....	....
2013-14	Calgary	NHL	63	14	19	33	42	0	1	2	70	20.0	-13	1096	48.1	18:22	....	....	....	....	....	....	....	....	....
2014-15	Calgary	NHL	59	7	10	17	28	0	0	0	46	15.2	7	602	50.3	12:00	11	1	3	4	21	0	0	1	16:07
2015-16	Calgary	NHL	80	6	11	17	52	0	2	0	58	10.3	-4	788	47.3	12:42	....	....	....	....	....	....	....	....	....
2016-17	Calgary	NHL	81	6	17	23	40	0	0	3	59	10.2	3	768	50.1	12:41	3	0	0	0	0	0	0	0	10:16
	NHL Totals		935	142	259	401	498	18	11	21	1087	13.1		11132	48.7	14:54	17	1	3	4	23	0	0	1	14:13

• Scored a goal in his first NHL game (April 5, 2003 vs. Ottawa).

Traded to **Calgary** by **Toronto** with Niklas Hagman, Jamal Mayers and Ian White for Dion Phaneuf, Fredrik Sjostrom and Keith Aulie, January 31, 2010.

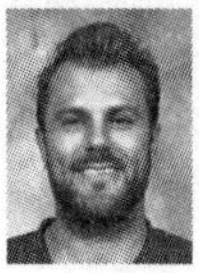

STALBERG, Viktor

(STAHL-buhrg, VIHK-tuhr)

Left wing. Shoots left. 6'3", 209 lbs. Born, Stockholm, Sweden, January 17, 1986. Toronto's 5th pick, 161st overall, in 2006 NHL Draft.

Season	Club	League	GP	G	A	Pts	PIM	PP	SH	GW	S	S%	+/-	TF	F%	Min	GP	G	A	Pts	PIM	PP	SH	GW	Min
2003-04	Molndal U18	Swe-U18	13	14	13	27	....	....	....	....	....	....	....	....	....	....	....	....	....	....	....	....	....	....	....
	Molndal Jr.	Swe-Jr.	18	25	10	35	....	....	....	....	....	....	....	....	....	....	....	....	....	....	....	....	....	....	....
	Molndal	Sweden-4	....	11	9	20	....	....	....	....	....	....	....	....	....	....	....	....	....	....	....	....	....	....	....
2004-05	Molndal Jr.	Swe-Jr.	11	16	7	23	....	....	....	....	....	....	....	....	....	....	....	....	....	....	....	....	....	....	....
	Molndal	Sweden-3	29	6	9	15	54	....	....	....	....	....	....	....	....	....	....	....	....	....	....	....	....	....	....
2005-06	Frolunda Jr.	Swe-Jr.	41	27	26	53	89	....	....	....	....	....	....	....	....	....	7	6	5	11	6	....	....	....	....
2006-07	U. of Vermont	H-East	39	7	8	15	53	....	....	....	....	....	....	....	....	....	....	....	....	....	....	....	....	....	....
2007-08	U. of Vermont	H-East	39	10	13	23	34	....	....	....	....	....	....	....	....	....	....	....	....	....	....	....	....	....	....
2008-09	U. of Vermont	H-East	39	24	22	46	32	....	....	....	....	....	....	....	....	....	....	....	....	....	....	....	....	....	....
	Toronto Marlies	AHL	....	....	....	....	....	....	....	....	....	....	....	....	....	....	2	0	1	1	0	....	....	....	....
2009-10	Toronto	NHL	40	9	5	14	30	0	0	0	117	7.7	-13	9	33.3	14:37	....	....	....	....	....	....	....	....	....
	Toronto Marlies	AHL	39	12	21	33	36	....	....	....	....	....	....	....	....	....	....	....	....	....	....	....	....	....	....
2010-11	Chicago	NHL	77	12	12	24	43	0	0	3	135	8.9	2	9	55.6	10:42	7	1	0	1	5	0	0	0	12:17
2011-12	Chicago	NHL	79	22	21	43	34	0	0	6	215	10.2	6	11	45.5	14:04	6	0	2	2	8	0	0	0	14:54
2012-13	Frolunda	Sweden	11	7	5	12	10	....	....	....	....	....	....	....	....	....	....	....	....	....	....	....	....	....	....
	Mytischi	KHL	14	3	7	10	4	....	....	....	....	....	....	....	....	....	....	....	....	....	....	....	....	....	....
	♦ Chicago	NHL	47	9	14	23	25	0	0	1	113	8.0	16	1	0.0	14:07	19	0	3	3	6	0	0	0	10:35
2013-14	Nashville	NHL	70	8	10	18	32	0	0	1	114	7.0	-14	3	33.3	12:35	....	....	....	....	....	....	....	....	....
2014-15	Nashville	NHL	25	2	8	10	18	0	0	1	27	7.4	0	1	100.0	11:53	6	1	2	3	0	0	0	0	14:08
	Milwaukee	AHL	20	11	6	17	14	....	....	....	....	....	....	....	....	....	....	....	....	....	....	....	....	....	....
2015-16	NY Rangers	NHL	75	9	11	20	22	0	0	0	125	7.2	6	6	33.3	12:12	5	0	0	0	6	0	0	0	10:55
2016-17	Carolina	NHL	57	9	3	12	33	0	2	2	71	12.7	-6	3	0.0	11:42	....	....	....	....	....	....	....	....	....
	Ottawa	NHL	18	2	2	4	8	1	0	0	30	6.7	-3	0	0.0	13:48	17	0	2	2	2	0	0	0	13:46
	NHL Totals		488	82	86	168	245	1	2	14	947	8.7		43	39.5	12:41	60	2	9	11	27	0	0	0	12:30

Hockey East First All-Star Team (2009) • NCAA East First All-American Team (2009)

Traded to **Chicago** by **Toronto** with Chris Didomenico and Phillipe Paradis for Kris Versteeg and Bill Sweatt, June 30, 2010. Signed as a free agent by **Frolunda** (Sweden), October 11, 2012. Signed as a free agent by **Mytischi** (KHL), November 20, 2012. Signed as a free agent by **Nashville**, July 5, 2013. Signed as a free agent by **NY Rangers**, July 1, 2015. Signed as a free agent by **Carolina**, July 1, 2016. Traded to **Ottawa** by **Carolina** for Ottawa's 3rd round pick (later traded to Chicago – Chicago selected Evan Barratt) in 2017 NHL Draft, February 28, 2017.

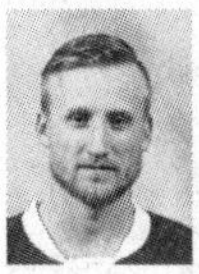

STAMKOS, Steven

(STAM-kohs, STEE-vehn) **T.B.**

Center. Shoots right. 6'1", 194 lbs. Born, Markham, ON, February 7, 1990. Tampa Bay's 1st pick, 1st overall, in 2008 NHL Draft.

Season	Club	League	GP	G	A	Pts	PIM	PP	SH	GW	S	S%	+/-	TF	F%	Min	GP	G	A	Pts	PIM	PP	SH	GW	Min
2005-06	Markham Waxers	Minor-ON	66	105	92	197	87	....	....	....	....	....	....	....	....	....	....	....	....	....	....	....	....	....	....
2006-07	Sarnia Sting	OHL	63	42	50	92	56	....	....	....	....	....	....	....	....	....	4	3	3	6	0	....	....	....	....
2007-08	Sarnia Sting	OHL	61	58	47	105	88	....	....	....	....	....	....	....	....	....	9	11	0	11	20	....	....	....	....
2008-09	Tampa Bay	NHL	79	23	23	46	39	9	1	1	181	12.7	-13	557	45.4	14:56	....	....	....	....	....	....	....	....	....
2009-10	Tampa Bay	NHL	82	*51	44	95	38	24	1	5	297	17.2	-2	1004	47.9	20:33	....	....	....	....	....	....	....	....	....
2010-11	Tampa Bay	NHL	82	45	46	91	74	17	0	8	272	16.5	3	927	46.5	20:12	18	6	7	13	6	3	0	1	19:43
2011-12	Tampa Bay	NHL	82	*60	37	97	66	12	0	*12	303	19.8	7	1227	45.5	22:01	....	....	....	....	....	....	....	....	....
2012-13	Tampa Bay	NHL	48	29	28	57	32	10	0	2	157	18.5	-4	819	49.6	22:01	....	....	....	....	....	....	....	....	....
2013-14	Tampa Bay	NHL	37	25	15	40	18	9	1	5	124	20.2	9	529	49.2	20:15	4	2	2	4	6	0	0	0	21:50
2014-15	Tampa Bay	NHL	82	43	29	72	49	13	0	6	268	16.0	2	943	49.7	19:22	26	7	11	18	20	2	0	1	18:33
2015-16	Tampa Bay	NHL	77	36	28	64	38	14	1	8	216	16.7	3	927	50.0	19:45	1	0	0	0	0	0	0	0	11:55
2016-17	Tampa Bay	NHL	17	9	11	20	14	3	0	1	58	15.5	3	198	53.5	17:53	....	....	....	....	....	....	....	....	....
	NHL Totals		586	321	261	582	368	111	3	48	1876	17.1		7131	48.1	19:42	49	15	20	35	32	5	0	2	19:07

OHL Second All-Star Team (2008) • Canadian Major Junior First All-Star Team (2008) • Maurice "Rocket" Richard Trophy (2010) (tied with Sidney Crosby) • NHL Second All-Star Team (2011, 2012) • Maurice "Rocket" Richard Trophy (2012)

Played in NHL All-Star Game (2011, 2012, 2015, 2016)

• Missed majority of 2013-14 due to leg injury at Boston, November 11, 2013. • Missed majority of 2016-17 due to knee injury at Detroit, November 15, 2016.

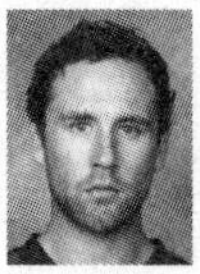

STANTON, Ryan

(STAN-tuhn, RIGH-uhn) **EDM**

Defense. Shoots left. 6'2", 196 lbs. Born, St. Albert, AB, July 20, 1989.

Season	Club	League	GP	G	A	Pts	PIM	PP	SH	GW	S	S%	+/-	TF	F%	Min	GP	G	A	Pts	PIM	PP	SH	GW	Min
2004-05	St. Albert	Minor-AB	32	4	10	14	77	....	....	....	....	....	....	....	....	....	....	....	....	....	....	....	....	....	....
	St. Albert Raiders	AMHL	8	0	0	0	2	....	....	....	....	....	....	....	....	....	....	....	....	....	....	....	....	....	....
2005-06	St. Albert Raiders	AMHL	35	3	15	18	64	....	....	....	....	....	....	....	....	....	....	....	....	....	....	....	....	....	....
	Moose Jaw	WHL	2	0	0	0	2	....	....	....	....	....	....	....	....	....	....	....	....	....	....	....	....	....	....
2006-07	Moose Jaw	WHL	54	0	8	8	75	....	....	....	....	....	....	....	....	....	....	....	....	....	....	....	....	....	....
2007-08	Moose Jaw	WHL	58	4	16	20	68	....	....	....	....	....	....	....	....	....	6	0	0	0	2	....	....	....	....
2008-09	Moose Jaw	WHL	69	5	29	34	111	....	....	....	....	....	....	....	....	....	....	....	....	....	....	....	....	....	....
2009-10	Moose Jaw	WHL	59	10	30	40	81	....	....	....	....	....	....	....	....	....	7	0	6	6	4	....	....	....	....
	Rockford IceHogs	AHL	2	0	1	1	0	....	....	....	....	....	....	....	....	....	2	0	0	0	0	....	....	....	....
2010-11	Rockford IceHogs	AHL	73	3	14	17	76	....	....	....	....	....	....	....	....	....	....	....	....	....	....	....	....	....	....
2011-12	Rockford IceHogs	AHL	76	3	14	17	130	....	....	....	....	....	....	....	....	....	....	....	....	....	....	....	....	....	....
2012-13	Rockford IceHogs	AHL	73	3	22	25	126	....	....	....	....	....	....	....	....	....	....	....	....	....	....	....	....	....	....
	Chicago	NHL	1	0	0	0	2	0	0	0	1	0.0	1	0	0.0	17:05	....	....	....	....	....	....	....	....	....
2013-14	Vancouver	NHL	64	1	15	16	32	0	0	0	65	1.5	5	1	100.0	14:43	....	....	....	....	....	....	....	....	....
2014-15	Vancouver	NHL	54	3	8	11	35	0	0	0	59	5.1	9	0	0.0	16:00	....	....	....	....	....	....	....	....	....
2015-16	Washington	NHL	1	0	0	0	2	0	0	0	0	0.0	-1	0	0.0	8:41	....	....	....	....	....	....	....	....	....
	Hershey Bears	AHL	60	4	12	16	69	....	....	....	....	....	....	....	....	....	21	3	2	5	32	....	....	....	....
2016-17	San Antonio	AHL	15	1	3	4	29	....	....	....	....	....	....	....	....	....	....	....	....	....	....	....	....	....	....
	Cleveland	AHL	33	1	7	8	40	....	....	....	....	....	....	....	....	....	....	....	....	....	....	....	....	....	....
	NHL Totals		120	4	23	27	71	0	0	0	125	3.2		1	100.0	15:16	....	....	....	....	....	....	....	....	....

Signed as a free agent by **Chicago**, March 12, 2010. Claimed on waivers by **Vancouver** from **Chicago**, September 30, 2013. Signed as a free agent by **Washington**, July 24, 2015. Signed as a free agent by **Colorado**, July 1, 2016. Traded to **Columbus** by **Colorado** for Cody Golubef, November 28, 2016. Signed as a free agent by **Edmonton**, July 1, 2017.

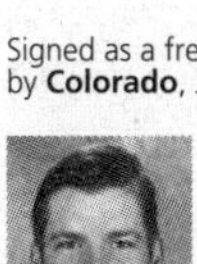

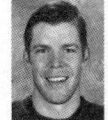

STASTNY, Paul

(STAS-nee, PAWL) **ST.L.**

Center. Shoots left. 6', 205 lbs. Born, Quebec City, QC, December 27, 1985. Colorado's 2nd pick, 44th overall, in 2005 NHL Draft.

Season	Club	League	GP	G	A	Pts	PIM	PP	SH	GW	S	S%	+/-	TF	F%	Min	GP	G	A	Pts	PIM	PP	SH	GW	Min
2002-03	River City Lancers	USHL	57	10	20	30	39	....	....	....	....	....	....	....	....	....	8	0	1	1	2	....	....	....	....
2003-04	River City Lancers	USHL	56	30	*47	77	46	....	....	....	....	....	....	....	....	....	3	1	2	3	0	....	....	....	....
2004-05	U. of Denver	WCHA	42	17	28	45	30	....	....	....	....	....	....	....	....	....	....	....	....	....	....	....	....	....	....
2005-06	U. of Denver	WCHA	39	19	34	53	79	....	....	....	....	....	....	....	....	....	....	....	....	....	....	....	....	....	....
2006-07	Colorado	NHL	82	28	50	78	42	11	0	6	185	15.1	4	1226	48.5	18:10	....	....	....	....	....	....	....	....	....
2007-08	Colorado	NHL	66	24	47	71	24	3	0	4	138	17.4	22	1101	51.0	21:05	9	2	1	3	6	0	0	1	19:56
2008-09	Colorado	NHL	45	11	25	36	22	7	0	2	118	9.3	-9	850	51.8	21:14	....	....	....	....	....	....	....	....	....
2009-10	Colorado	NHL	81	20	59	79	50	9	0	2	199	10.1	2	1703	50.0	21:24	6	1	4	5	4	1	0	0	20:23
	United States	Olympics	6	1	2	3	0	....	....	....	....	....	....	....	....	....	....	....	....	....	....	....	....	....	....
2010-11	Colorado	NHL	74	22	35	57	56	4	1	3	181	12.2	-7	1524	53.2	19:44	....	....	....	....	....	....	....	....	....
2011-12	Colorado	NHL	79	21	32	53	34	7	0	2	190	11.1	-8	1424	55.4	18:50	....	....	....	....	....	....	....	....	....
2012-13	EHC Munchen	Germany	13	7	11	18	20	....	....	....	....	....	....	....	....	....	....	....	....	....	....	....	....	....	....
	Colorado	NHL	40	9	15	24	14	2	0	1	87	10.3	-7	781	52.4	19:21	....	....	....	....	....	....	....	....	....
2013-14	Colorado	NHL	71	25	35	60	22	4	0	4	150	16.7	9	1210	54.1	18:24	7	5	5	10	4	1	1	1	22:13
	United States	Olympics	6	2	0	2	0	....	....	....	....	....	....	....	....	....	....	....	....	....	....	....	....	....	....
2014-15	St. Louis	NHL	74	16	30	46	40	7	0	7	143	11.2	5	1158	57.9	17:38	6	1	0	1	4	0	0	0	17:28

			Regular Season														Playoffs								
Season	Club	League	GP	G	A	Pts	PIM	PP	SH	GW	S	S%	+/-	TF	F%	Min	GP	G	A	Pts	PIM	PP	SH	GW	Min
2015-16	**St. Louis**	**NHL**	**64**	**10**	**39**	**49**	**26**	**2**	**0**	**2**	**103**	**9.7**	**3**	**1220**	**56.1**	**19:09**	**20**	**3**	**10**	**13**	**16**	**1**	**0**	**1**	**20:05**
2016-17	**St. Louis**	**NHL**	**66**	**18**	**22**	**40**	**36**	**5**	**0**	**5**	**112**	**16.1**	**4**	**1410**	**55.7**	**19:08**	**7**	**2**	**1**	**3**	**2**	**0**	**0**	**0**	**21:24**
	NHL Totals		**742**	**204**	**389**	**593**	**366**	**61**	**1**	**38**	**1606**	**12.7**		**13607**	**53.3**	**19:24**	**55**	**14**	**21**	**35**	**36**	**3**	**1**	**3**	**20:15**

WCHA All-Rookie Team (2005) • WCHA Rookie of the Year (2005) • NCAA Championship All-Tournament Team (2005) • WCHA First All-Star Team (2006) • NCAA West Second All-American Team (2006) • NHL All-Rookie Team (2007)

Played in NHL All-Star Game (2011)

Signed as a free agent by **Munchen** (Germany), November 16, 2012. Signed as a free agent by **St. Louis**, July 1, 2014.

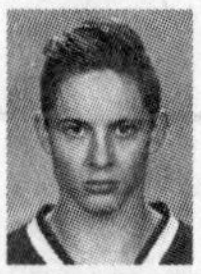

STECHER, Troy

(STEH-chur, TROI) **VAN**

Defense. Shoots right. 5'11", 191 lbs. Born, Richmond, BC, April 7, 1994.

Season	Club	League	GP	G	A	Pts	PIM	PP	SH	GW	S	S%	+/-	TF	F%	Min	GP	G	A	Pts	PIM	PP	SH	GW	Min
2008-09	Richmond Bant.	Minor-BC	71	17	51	68	30																		
2009-10	Greater Van.	BCMML	38	4	27	31	22										5	1	1	2	6				
2010-11	Penticton Vees	BCHL	54	5	15	20	47										9	2	3	5	6				
2011-12	Penticton Vees	BCHL	53	5	37	42	42										15	2	8	10	8				
2012-13	Penticton Vees	BCHL	52	8	39	47	40										15	0	6	6	10				
2013-14	North Dakota	NCHC	42	2	9	11	14																		
2014-15	North Dakota	NCHC	34	3	10	13	22																		
2015-16	North Dakota	NCHC	43	8	21	29	37																		
2016-17	**Vancouver**	**NHL**	**71**	**3**	**21**	**24**	**25**	**1**	**0**	**0**	**125**	**2.4**	**–16**	**0**	**0.0**	**19:59**									
	Utica Comets	AHL	4	0	1	1	4																		
	NHL Totals		**71**	**3**	**21**	**24**	**25**	**1**	**0**	**0**	**125**	**2.4**		**0**	**0.0**	**19:59**									

NCHC Second All-Star Team (2016) • NCAA West Second All-American Team (2016) • NCAA Championship All-Tournament Team (2016)

Signed as a free agent by **Vancouver**, April 13, 2016.

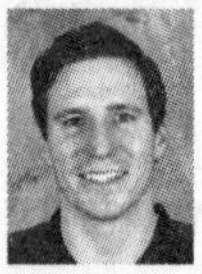

STEEN, Alexander

(STEEN, al-ehx-AN-duhr) **ST.L.**

Center. Shoots left. 5'11", 212 lbs. Born, Winnipeg, MB, March 1, 1984. Toronto's 1st pick, 24th overall, in 2002 NHL Draft.

Season	Club	League	GP	G	A	Pts	PIM	PP	SH	GW	S	S%	+/-	TF	F%	Min	GP	G	A	Pts	PIM	PP	SH	GW	Min
99-2000	V.Frolunda Jr.	Swe-Jr.	8	5	7	12	0																		
	V.Frolunda U18	Swe-U18	14	3	5	8	16																		
2000-01	V.Frolunda Jr.	Swe-Jr.	23	11	12	23	15										3	1	0	1	2				
	V.Frolunda U18	Swe-U18	6	3	3	6	9																		
2001-02	V.Frolunda Jr.	Swe-Jr.	23	21	17	38	47										2	1	1	2	2				
	V.Frolunda	Sweden	26	0	3	3	14										10	1	2	3	0				
2002-03	V.Frolunda	Sweden	45	5	10	15	18										16	2	3	5	4				
	V.Frolunda Jr.	Swe-Jr.	2	0	2	2	0																		
2003-04	V.Frolunda	Sweden	48	10	14	24	50										10	4	6	10	14				
2004-05	MODO	Sweden	50	9	8	17	26										6	1	0	1	4				
2005-06	**Toronto**	**NHL**	**75**	**18**	**27**	**45**	**42**	**9**	**1**	**3**	**176**	**10.2**	**–9**	**29**	**24.1**	**17:37**									
2006-07	**Toronto**	**NHL**	**82**	**15**	**20**	**35**	**26**	**4**	**0**	**5**	**192**	**7.8**	**5**	**44**	**34.1**	**15:42**									
2007-08	**Toronto**	**NHL**	**76**	**15**	**27**	**42**	**32**	**2**	**1**	**2**	**169**	**8.9**	**0**	**179**	**33.0**	**18:05**									
2008-09	**Toronto**	**NHL**	**20**	**2**	**2**	**4**	**6**	**1**	**0**	**0**	**31**	**6.5**	**–4**	**82**	**52.4**	**15:38**									
	St. Louis	**NHL**	**61**	**6**	**18**	**24**	**24**	**2**	**1**	**0**	**117**	**5.1**	**–6**	**154**	**41.6**	**16:34**	**4**	**0**	**1**	**1**	**0**	**0**	**0**	**0**	**17:47**
2009-10	**St. Louis**	**NHL**	**68**	**24**	**23**	**47**	**30**	**7**	**2**	**4**	**189**	**12.7**	**6**	**73**	**41.1**	**16:17**									
2010-11	**St. Louis**	**NHL**	**72**	**20**	**31**	**51**	**26**	**1**	**2**	**5**	**218**	**9.2**	**–3**	**106**	**38.7**	**19:33**									
2011-12	**St. Louis**	**NHL**	**43**	**15**	**13**	**28**	**28**	**3**	**0**	**3**	**134**	**11.2**	**24**	**95**	**55.8**	**19:08**	**9**	**1**	**2**	**3**	**6**	**1**	**0**	**1**	**20:54**
2012-13	MODO	Sweden	20	8	15	23	28																		
	St. Louis	**NHL**	**40**	**8**	**19**	**27**	**14**	**3**	**0**	**3**	**129**	**6.2**	**5**	**204**	**46.1**	**19:00**	**6**	**3**	**0**	**3**	**6**	**1**	**1**	**1**	**20:56**
2013-14	**St. Louis**	**NHL**	**68**	**33**	**29**	**62**	**46**	**7**	**1**	**9**	**211**	**15.6**	**17**	**541**	**49.0**	**20:17**	**6**	**1**	**2**	**3**	**6**	**0**	**0**	**1**	**25:24**
	Sweden	Olympics	6	1	3	4	4																		
2014-15	**St. Louis**	**NHL**	**74**	**24**	**40**	**64**	**33**	**8**	**0**	**5**	**223**	**10.8**	**8**	**433**	**50.0**	**19:59**	**6**	**1**	**3**	**4**	**2**	**0**	**1**	**0**	**19:35**
2015-16	**St. Louis**	**NHL**	**67**	**17**	**35**	**52**	**48**	**2**	**1**	**2**	**172**	**9.9**	**3**	**357**	**44.5**	**20:22**	**20**	**4**	**6**	**10**	**30**	**1**	**0**	**1**	**21:21**
2016-17	**St. Louis**	**NHL**	**76**	**16**	**35**	**51**	**53**	**3**	**0**	**2**	**117**	**13.7**	**–2**	**247**	**40.9**	**19:18**	**10**	**3**	**4**	**7**	**4**	**0**	**0**	**0**	**19:12**
	NHL Totals		**822**	**213**	**319**	**532**	**408**	**52**	**9**	**43**	**2078**	**10.3**		**2544**	**45.2**	**18:22**	**61**	**13**	**18**	**31**	**54**	**3**	**2**	**4**	**20:53**

Traded to **St. Louis** by **Toronto** with Carlo Colaiacovo for Lee Stempniak, November 24, 2008. Signed as a free agent by **MODO** (Sweden), September 25, 2012.

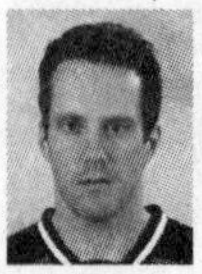

STEMPNIAK, Lee

(STEHMP-nee-ak, LEE) **CAR**

Right wing. Shoots right. 5'11", 195 lbs. Born, Buffalo, NY, February 4, 1983. St. Louis' 7th pick, 148th overall, in 2003 NHL Draft.

Season	Club	League	GP	G	A	Pts	PIM	PP	SH	GW	S	S%	+/-	TF	F%	Min	GP	G	A	Pts	PIM	PP	SH	GW	Min
2000-01	Buffalo Lightning	ON-Jr.A	48	34	51	86	36																		
2001-02	Dartmouth	ECAC	32	12	9	21	8																		
2002-03	Dartmouth	ECAC	34	21	28	49	32																		
2003-04	Dartmouth	ECAC	34	16	22	38	42																		
2004-05	Dartmouth	ECAC	35	14	*29	43	34																		
2005-06	**St. Louis**	**NHL**	**57**	**14**	**13**	**27**	**22**	**5**	**0**	**2**	**100**	**14.0**	**–10**	**7**	**42.9**	**14:22**									
	Peoria Rivermen	AHL	26	8	7	15	32										3	0	3	3	2				
2006-07	**St. Louis**	**NHL**	**82**	**27**	**25**	**52**	**33**	**8**	**0**	**4**	**166**	**16.3**	**–2**	**7**	**14.3**	**14:43**									
2007-08	**St. Louis**	**NHL**	**80**	**13**	**25**	**38**	**40**	**3**	**0**	**2**	**162**	**8.0**	**0**	**11**	**36.4**	**15:53**									
2008-09	**St. Louis**	**NHL**	**14**	**3**	**10**	**13**	**2**	**0**	**0**	**1**	**43**	**7.0**	**–3**	**1**	**0.0**	**19:28**									
	Toronto	**NHL**	**61**	**11**	**20**	**31**	**31**	**3**	**0**	**0**	**128**	**8.6**	**–9**	**12**	**33.3**	**15:52**									
2009-10	**Toronto**	**NHL**	**62**	**14**	**16**	**30**	**18**	**5**	**1**	**1**	**164**	**8.5**	**–10**	**25**	**36.0**	**17:53**									
	Phoenix	**NHL**	**18**	**14**	**4**	**18**	**8**	**4**	**0**	**1**	**48**	**29.2**	**10**	**14**	**57.1**	**15:22**	**7**	**0**	**2**	**2**	**0**	**0**	**0**	**0**	**14:28**
2010-11	**Phoenix**	**NHL**	**82**	**19**	**19**	**38**	**19**	**2**	**0**	**0**	**199**	**9.5**	**4**	**45**	**40.0**	**15:15**	**4**	**0**	**0**	**0**	**0**	**0**	**0**	**0**	**12:13**
2011-12	**Calgary**	**NHL**	**61**	**14**	**14**	**28**	**16**	**2**	**0**	**2**	**130**	**10.8**	**–2**	**26**	**26.9**	**16:14**									
2012-13	**Calgary**	**NHL**	**47**	**9**	**23**	**32**	**12**	**4**	**0**	**2**	**113**	**8.0**	**2**	**23**	**13.0**	**17:54**									
2013-14	**Calgary**	**NHL**	**52**	**8**	**15**	**23**	**28**	**0**	**2**	**0**	**144**	**5.6**	**–21**	**28**	**32.1**	**19:24**									
	Pittsburgh	**NHL**	**21**	**4**	**7**	**11**	**4**	**0**	**0**	**1**	**34**	**11.8**	**5**	**5**	**20.0**	**16:08**	**13**	**2**	**1**	**3**	**6**	**0**	**0**	**0**	**15:03**
2014-15	**NY Rangers**	**NHL**	**53**	**9**	**9**	**18**	**18**	**0**	**0**	**1**	**86**	**10.5**	**7**	**25**	**44.0**	**12:26**									
	Winnipeg	**NHL**	**18**	**6**	**4**	**10**	**2**	**0**	**0**	**2**	**29**	**20.7**	**1**	**7**	**14.3**	**13:33**	**4**	**1**	**0**	**1**	**0**	**0**	**0**	**0**	**12:45**
2015-16	**New Jersey**	**NHL**	**63**	**16**	**25**	**41**	**34**	**3**	**1**	**3**	**120**	**13.3**	**3**	**10**	**20.0**	**18:44**									
	Boston	**NHL**	**19**	**3**	**7**	**10**	**4**	**0**	**0**	**1**	**26**	**11.5**	**1**	**3**	**0.0**	**15:20**									
2016-17	**Carolina**	**NHL**	**82**	**16**	**24**	**40**	**32**	**2**	**0**	**2**	**131**	**12.2**	**2**	**8**	**37.5**	**15:51**									
	NHL Totals		**872**	**200**	**260**	**460**	**323**	**41**	**4**	**25**	**1823**	**11.0**		**257**	**32.7**	**16:05**	**28**	**3**	**3**	**6**	**6**	**0**	**0**	**0**	**14:10**

ECAC All-Rookie Team (2002) • ECAC First All-Star Team (2004, 2005) • NCAA East First All-American Team (2004) • NCAA East Second All-American Team (2005)

Traded to **Toronto** by **St. Louis** for Alexander Steen and Carlo Colaiacovo, November 24, 2008. Traded to **Phoenix** by **Toronto** for Matt Jones and Phoenix's 4th (later traded to Washington – Washington selected Philipp Grubauer) and 7th (later traded to Edmonton – Edmonton selected Kellen Jones) round picks in 2010 NHL Draft, March 3, 2010. Traded to **Calgary** by **Phoenix** for Daymond Langkow, August 29, 2011. Traded to **Pittsburgh** by **Calgary** for Pittsburgh's 3rd round pick (later traded to Chicago – Chicago selected Matt Iacopelli) in 2014 NHL Draft, March 5, 2014. Signed as a free agent by **NY Rangers**, July 19, 2014. Traded to **Winnipeg** by **NY Rangers** for Carl Klingberg, March 1, 2015. Signed as a free agent by **New Jersey**, October 3, 2015. Traded to **Boston** by **New Jersey** for Boston's 4th round pick (Evan Cormier) in 2016 NHL Draft and Boston's 2nd round pick (later traded to San Jose – San Jose selected Mario Ferraro) in 2017 NHL Draft, February 29, 2016. Signed as a free agent by **Carolina**, July 1, 2016.

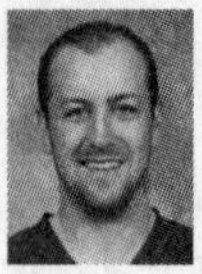

STEPAN, Derek

(STEH-pan, DAIR-ihk) **ARI**

Center. Shoots right. 6', 196 lbs. Born, Hastings, MN, June 18, 1990. NY Rangers' 2nd pick, 51st overall, in 2008 NHL Draft.

Season	Club	League	GP	G	A	Pts	PIM	PP	SH	GW	S	S%	+/-	TF	F%	Min	GP	G	A	Pts	PIM	PP	SH	GW	Min
2006-07	Shattuck	High-MN	63	38	32	70	22																		
2007-08	Shattuck	High-MN	60	44	67	111	22																		
2008-09	U. of Wisconsin	WCHA	40	9	24	33	6																		
2009-10	U. of Wisconsin	WCHA	41	12	*42	*54	8																		
2010-11	**NY Rangers**	**NHL**	**82**	**21**	**24**	**45**	**20**	**3**	**0**	**3**	**166**	**12.7**	**8**	**719**	**38.5**	**16:27**	**5**	**0**	**0**	**0**	**2**	**0**	**0**	**0**	**20:29**
2011-12	**NY Rangers**	**NHL**	**82**	**17**	**34**	**51**	**22**	**4**	**0**	**4**	**169**	**10.1**	**14**	**867**	**44.5**	**18:57**	**20**	**1**	**8**	**9**	**4**	**1**	**0**	**0**	**19:07**
2012-13	KalPa Kuopio	Finland	12	2	2	4	0																		
	NY Rangers	**NHL**	**48**	**18**	**26**	**44**	**12**	**4**	**1**	**6**	**108**	**16.7**	**25**	**977**	**45.9**	**20:55**	**12**	**4**	**1**	**5**	**2**	**0**	**0**	**2**	**22:30**
2013-14	**NY Rangers**	**NHL**	**82**	**17**	**40**	**57**	**18**	**5**	**0**	**2**	**199**	**8.5**	**12**	**1512**	**45.2**	**18:03**	**24**	**5**	**10**	**15**	**2**	**2**	**0**	**0**	**19:47**
	United States	Olympics	1	0	0	0	0																		
2014-15	**NY Rangers**	**NHL**	**68**	**16**	**39**	**55**	**22**	**3**	**2**	**3**	**155**	**10.3**	**26**	**1232**	**44.1**	**18:11**	**19**	**5**	**7**	**12**	**10**	**2**	**0**	**1**	**19:31**

			Regular Season														Playoffs								
Season	Club	League	GP	G	A	Pts	PIM	PP	SH	GW	S	S%	+/-	TF	F%	Min	GP	G	A	Pts	PIM	PP	SH	GW	Min
2015-16	NY Rangers	NHL	72	22	31	53	20	5	3	5	192	11.5	5	1103	46.7	17:45	5	2	0	2	0	1	0	0	17:11
2016-17	NY Rangers	NHL	81	17	38	55	16	4	1	2	209	8.1	19	1522	47.0	18:37	12	2	4	6	4	0	1	0	20:59
	NHL Totals		515	128	232	360	130	28	7	25	1198	10.7		7932	45.0	18:16	97	19	30	49	24	6	1	3	19:59

Signed as a free agent by **Kuopio** (Finland), November 11, 2012. Traded to **Arizona** by **NY Rangers** with Antti Raanta for Tony DeAngelo and Arizona's 1st round pick (Lias Andersson) in 2017 NHL Draft, June 23, 2017.

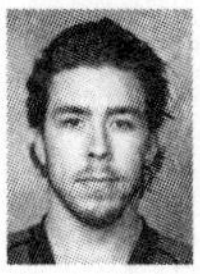

STEPHENSON, Chandler (STEE-vehn-suhn, CHAND-luhr) WSH

Center/Left wing. Shoots left. 5'11", 190 lbs. Born, Saskatoon, SK, April 22, 1994. Washington's 3rd pick, 77th overall, in 2012 NHL Draft.

Season	Club	League	GP	G	A	Pts	PIM	PP	SH	GW	S	S%	+/-	TF	F%	Min	GP	G	A	Pts	PIM	PP	SH	GW	Min
2008-09	Sask. Generals	Minor-SK	46	49	61	110	72	....	....	....	....	....	....	....	....	....	....	....	....	....	....	....	....	....	....
	Saskatoon Blazers	SMHL	9	2	1	3	2	....	....	....	....	....	....	....	....	....	....	....	....	....	....	....	....	....	....
2009-10	Sask. Contacts	SMHL	42	17	37	54	34	....	....	....	....	....	....	....	....	....	11	5	14	19	4	....	....	....	....
2010-11	Regina Pats	WHL	60	7	12	19	6	....	....	....	....	....	....	....	....	....	....	....	....	....	....	....	....	....	....
2011-12	Regina Pats	WHL	55	22	20	42	24	....	....	....	....	....	....	....	....	....	5	1	3	4	0	....	....	....	....
2012-13	Regina Pats	WHL	46	14	31	45	37	....	....	....	....	....	....	....	....	....	....	....	....	....	....	....	....	....	....
2013-14	Regina Pats	WHL	69	30	59	89	65	....	....	....	....	....	....	....	....	....	4	0	4	4	0	....	....	....	....
	Hershey Bears	AHL	2	1	0	1	0	....	....	....	....	....	....	....	....	....	....	....	....	....	....	....	....	....	....
2014-15	Hershey Bears	AHL	54	7	7	14	10	....	....	....	....	....	....	....	....	....	10	1	4	5	2	....	....	....	....
2015-16	Washington	NHL	9	0	0	0	2	0	0	0	2	0.0	-3	55	54.6	7:51	....	....	....	....	....	....	....	....	....
	Hershey Bears	AHL	46	7	21	28	26	....	....	....	....	....	....	....	....	....	17	1	5	6	2	....	....	....	....
2016-17	Washington	NHL	4	0	0	0	0	0	0	0	3	0.0	0	25	48.0	8:53	....	....	....	....	....	....	....	....	....
	Hershey Bears	AHL	72	10	28	38	42	....	....	....	....	....	....	....	....	....	9	3	2	5	6	....	....	....	....
	NHL Totals		13	0	0	0	2	0	0	0	5	0.0		80	52.5	8:10	....	....	....	....	....	....	....	....	....

WHL East Second All-Star Team (2014)

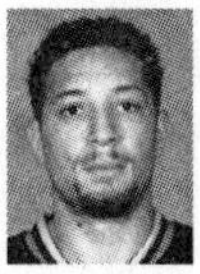

STEWART, Chris (STEW-ahrt, KRIHS) MIN

Right wing. Shoots right. 6'2", 231 lbs. Born, Toronto, ON, October 30, 1987. Colorado's 1st pick, 18th overall, in 2006 NHL Draft.

Season	Club	League	GP	G	A	Pts	PIM	PP	SH	GW	S	S%	+/-	TF	F%	Min	GP	G	A	Pts	PIM	PP	SH	GW	Min
2004-05	Kingston	OHL	64	18	12	30	45	....	....	....	....	....	....	....	....	....	....	....	....	....	....	....	....	....	....
2005-06	Kingston	OHL	62	37	50	87	118	....	....	....	....	....	....	....	....	....	6	2	0	2	13	....	....	....	....
2006-07	Kingston	OHL	61	36	46	82	108	....	....	....	....	....	....	....	....	....	5	4	2	6	6	....	....	....	....
	Albany River Rats	AHL	5	1	2	3	2	....	....	....	....	....	....	....	....	....	1	0	0	0	0	....	....	....	....
2007-08	Lake Erie	AHL	77	25	19	44	93	....	....	....	....	....	....	....	....	....	....	....	....	....	....	....	....	....	....
2008-09	Colorado	NHL	53	11	8	19	54	1	1	1	98	11.2	-18	21	33.3	12:20	....	....	....	....	....	....	....	....	....
	Lake Erie	AHL	19	5	6	11	23	....	....	....	....	....	....	....	....	....	....	....	....	....	....	....	....	....	....
2009-10	Colorado	NHL	77	28	36	64	73	3	0	5	221	12.7	4	8	37.5	16:42	6	3	0	3	4	0	0	1	18:00
	Lake Erie	AHL	2	0	0	0	2	....	....	....	....	....	....	....	....	....	....	....	....	....	....	....	....	....	....
2010-11	Colorado	NHL	36	13	17	30	38	5	0	3	95	13.7	-10	6	33.3	16:56	....	....	....	....	....	....	....	....	....
	St. Louis	NHL	26	15	8	23	15	7	0	2	67	22.4	4	26	42.3	18:16	....	....	....	....	....	....	....	....	....
2011-12	St. Louis	NHL	79	15	15	30	109	2	0	1	166	9.0	1	13	23.1	15:26	7	2	0	2	12	0	0	0	10:47
2012-13	Crimmitschau	German-2	15	6	14	20	24	....	....	....	....	....	....	....	....	....	....	....	....	....	....	....	....	....	....
	Liberec	CzRep	5	0	1	1	2	....	....	....	....	....	....	....	....	....	....	....	....	....	....	....	....	....	....
	St. Louis	NHL	48	18	18	36	40	6	0	3	97	18.6	0	27	29.6	15:49	6	0	1	1	0	0	0	0	16:32
2013-14	St. Louis	NHL	58	15	11	26	112	3	0	3	107	14.0	2	25	32.0	13:42	....	....	....	....	....	....	....	....	....
	Buffalo	NHL	5	0	0	0	6	0	0	0	3	0.0	-2	10	40.0	13:36	....	....	....	....	....	....	....	....	....
2014-15	Buffalo	NHL	61	11	14	25	63	5	0	0	116	9.5	-30	37	27.0	16:00	....	....	....	....	....	....	....	....	....
	Minnesota	NHL	20	3	8	11	25	0	0	0	39	7.7	4	4	0.0	15:31	8	0	2	2	2	0	0	0	15:59
2015-16	Anaheim	NHL	56	8	12	20	73	1	0	1	78	10.3	2	9	33.3	10:48	7	1	2	3	0	0	0	0	9:33
2016-17	Minnesota	NHL	79	13	8	21	94	0	0	0	82	15.9	3	11	18.2	10:23	5	0	0	0	0	0	0	0	7:50
	NHL Totals		598	150	155	305	702	33	1	19	1169	12.8		197	31.0	14:20	39	6	5	11	18	0	0	1	13:15

Traded to **St. Louis** by **Colorado** with Kevin Shattenkirk and Colorado's 2nd round pick (Ty Rattie) in 2011 NHL Draft for Erik Johnson, Jay McClement and St. Louis' 1st round pick (Duncan Siemens) in 2011 NHL Draft, February 18, 2011. Signed as a free agent by **Crimmitschau** (German-2), September 24, 2012. Signed as a free agent by **Liberec** (CzRep), October 23, 2012. Traded to **Buffalo** by **St. Louis** with Jaroslav Halak, William Carrier, St. Louis' 1st round pick (later traded to Winnipeg – Winnipeg selected Jack Roslovic) in 2015 NHL Draft and St. Louis' 3rd round pick (later traded to Florida – Florida selected Linus Nassen) in 2016 NHL Draft for Ryan Miller and Steve Ott, February 28, 2014. Traded to **Minnesota** by **Buffalo** for Minnesota's 2nd round pick (Ukko-Pekka Luukkonen) in 2017 NHL Draft, March 2, 2015. Signed as a free agent by **Anaheim**, July 12, 2015. Signed as a free agent by **Minnesota**, July 1, 2016.

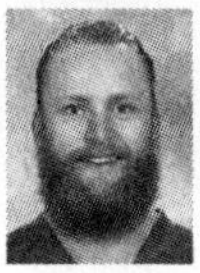

STOLLERY, Karl (STAW-luh-ree, KAHRL)

Defense. Shoots left. 5'11", 180 lbs. Born, Camrose, AB, November 21, 1987.

Season	Club	League	GP	G	A	Pts	PIM	PP	SH	GW	S	S%	+/-	TF	F%	Min	GP	G	A	Pts	PIM	PP	SH	GW	Min
2004-05	Camrose AA	Minor-AB	STATISTICS NOT AVAILABLE																						
	Camrose Kodiaks	AJHL	4	0	0	0	0	....	....	....	....	....	....	....	....	....	....	....	....	....	....	....	....	....	....
2005-06	Camrose Kodiaks	AJHL	42	1	5	6	40	....	....	....	....	....	....	....	....	....	11	1	2	3	6	....	....	....	....
2006-07	Camrose Kodiaks	AJHL	59	11	24	35	57	....	....	....	....	....	....	....	....	....	17	2	7	9	26	....	....	....	....
2007-08	Camrose Kodiaks	AJHL	52	3	24	27	40	....	....	....	....	....	....	....	....	....	18	5	10	15	18	....	....	....	....
2008-09	Merrimack	H-East	34	5	11	16	26	....	....	....	....	....	....	....	....	....	....	....	....	....	....	....	....	....	....
2009-10	Merrimack	H-East	35	4	15	19	42	....	....	....	....	....	....	....	....	....	....	....	....	....	....	....	....	....	....
2010-11	Merrimack	H-East	39	6	21	27	48	....	....	....	....	....	....	....	....	....	....	....	....	....	....	....	....	....	....
2011-12	Merrimack	H-East	37	7	14	21	58	....	....	....	....	....	....	....	....	....	....	....	....	....	....	....	....	....	....
	Lake Erie	AHL	9	2	5	7	4	....	....	....	....	....	....	....	....	....	....	....	....	....	....	....	....	....	....
2012-13	Lake Erie	AHL	72	5	29	34	62	....	....	....	....	....	....	....	....	....	....	....	....	....	....	....	....	....	....
2013-14	Colorado	NHL	2	0	0	0	2	0	0	0	1	0.0	1	0	0.0	6:31	....	....	....	....	....	....	....	....	....
	Lake Erie	AHL	68	7	23	30	42	....	....	....	....	....	....	....	....	....	....	....	....	....	....	....	....	....	....
2014-15	Colorado	NHL	5	0	0	0	2	0	0	0	3	0.0	3	0	0.0	11:25	....	....	....	....	....	....	....	....	....
	Lake Erie	AHL	46	5	9	14	55	....	....	....	....	....	....	....	....	....	....	....	....	....	....	....	....	....	....
	San Jose	NHL	5	0	0	0	4	0	0	0	6	0.0	-4	0	0.0	18:02	....	....	....	....	....	....	....	....	....
	Worcester Sharks	AHL	14	2	4	6	8	....	....	....	....	....	....	....	....	....	4	1	1	2	6	....	....	....	....
2015-16	San Jose	AHL	67	6	18	24	65	....	....	....	....	....	....	....	....	....	4	0	0	0	0	....	....	....	....
2016-17	New Jersey	NHL	11	0	3	3	13	0	0	0	11	0.0	-5	0	0.0	16:55	....	....	....	....	....	....	....	....	....
	Albany Devils	AHL	59	1	16	17	53	....	....	....	....	....	....	....	....	....	3	0	1	1	2	....	....	....	....
	NHL Totals		23	0	3	3	21	0	0	0	21	0.0		0	0.0	15:04	....	....	....	....	....	....	....	....	....

Hockey East All-Rookie Team (2009) • Hockey East Second All-Star Team (2012)

Signed to a ATO (amateur tryout) contract by **Lake Erie** (AHL), March 23, 2012. Signed as a free agent by **Colorado**, May 2, 2013. Traded to **San Jose** by **Colorado** for Freddie Hamilton, March 2, 2015. Signed as a free agent by **New Jersey**, July 1, 2016.

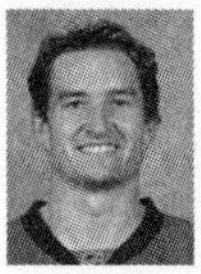

STONE, Mark (STOHN, MAHRK) OTT

Right wing. Shoots right. 6'3", 205 lbs. Born, Winnipeg, MB, May 13, 1992. Ottawa's 3rd pick, 178th overall, in 2010 NHL Draft.

Season	Club	League	GP	G	A	Pts	PIM	PP	SH	GW	S	S%	+/-	TF	F%	Min	GP	G	A	Pts	PIM	PP	SH	GW	Min
2007-08	Wpg. Thrashers	MMHL	40	22	31	53	28	....	....	....	....	....	....	....	....	....	9	7	7	14	2	....	....	....	....
2008-09	Brandon	WHL	56	17	22	39	27	....	....	....	....	....	....	....	....	....	12	1	3	4	4	....	....	....	....
2009-10	Brandon	WHL	39	11	17	28	25	....	....	....	....	....	....	....	....	....	15	1	3	4	4	....	....	....	....
2010-11	Brandon	WHL	71	37	69	106	28	....	....	....	....	....	....	....	....	....	6	1	9	10	4	....	....	....	....
2011-12	Brandon	WHL	66	41	*82	123	22	....	....	....	....	....	....	....	....	....	8	2	4	6	6	....	....	....	....
	Ottawa	NHL	....	....	....	....	....	....	....	....	....	....	....	....	....	....	1	0	1	1	0	0	0	0	8:43
2012-13	Binghamton	AHL	54	15	23	38	14	....	....	....	....	....	....	....	....	....	3	1	2	3	0	....	....	....	....
	Ottawa	NHL	4	0	0	0	2	0	0	0	3	0.0	-1	1	100.0	10:00	1	0	0	0	0	0	0	0	11:23
2013-14	Ottawa	NHL	19	4	4	8	4	1	0	0	36	11.1	5	1	100.0	14:29	....	....	....	....	....	....	....	....	....
	Binghamton	AHL	37	15	26	41	6	....	....	....	....	....	....	....	....	....	4	1	3	4	0	....	....	....	....
2014-15	Ottawa	NHL	80	26	38	64	14	5	1	6	157	16.6	21	18	38.9	17:01	6	0	4	4	2	0	0	0	19:10
2015-16	Ottawa	NHL	75	23	38	61	38	5	1	1	151	15.2	-4	19	42.1	20:07	....	....	....	....	....	....	....	....	....
2016-17	Ottawa	NHL	71	22	32	54	25	6	0	5	134	16.4	12	25	40.0	18:34	19	5	3	8	20	0	0	0	20:41
	NHL Totals		249	75	112	187	83	17	2	12	481	15.6		64	42.2	18:05	27	5	8	13	22	0	0	0	19:34

WHL East First All-Star Team (2011, 2012) • Canadian Major Junior Sportsman of the Year (2012) • NHL All-Rookie Team (2015)

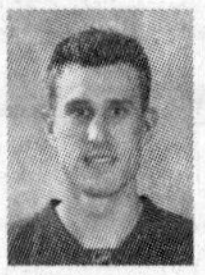

STONE, Michael (STOHN, MIGH-kuhl) CGY

Defense. Shoots right. 6'3", 215 lbs. Born, Winnipeg, MB, June 7, 1990. Phoenix's 4th pick, 69th overall, in 2008 NHL Draft.

			Regular Season														Playoffs								
Season	Club	League	GP	G	A	Pts	PIM	PP	SH	GW	S	S%	+/-	TF	F%	Min	GP	G	A	Pts	PIM	PP	SH	GW	Min
2005-06	Wpg. Thrashers	MMHL	40	14	18	32	14	....	....	....	....	....	....	....	....	....	....	....	....	....	....	....	....	....	....
2006-07	Calgary Hitmen	WHL	55	2	18	20	32	....	....	....	....	....	....	....	....	....	17	0	3	3	14	....	....	....	....
2007-08	Calgary Hitmen	WHL	71	10	25	35	28	....	....	....	....	....	....	....	....	....	14	3	4	7	10	....	....	....	....
2008-09	Calgary Hitmen	WHL	69	19	42	61	87	....	....	....	....	....	....	....	....	....	18	2	11	13	16	....	....	....	....
2009-10	Calgary Hitmen	WHL	69	21	44	65	91	....	....	....	....	....	....	....	....	....	23	5	15	20	26	....	....	....	....
2010-11	San Antonio	AHL	70	2	11	13	27	....	....	....	....	....	....	....	....	....	....	....	....	....	....	....	....	....	....
2011-12	**Phoenix**	**NHL**	**13**	**1**	**2**	**3**	**2**	**0**	**0**	**0**	**13**	**7.7**	**7**	**0**	**0.0**	**13:53**	**2**	**0**	**0**	**0**	**0**	**0**	**0**	**0**	**11:19**
	Portland Pirates	AHL	51	9	13	22	24	....	....	....	....	....	....	....	....	....	....	....	....	....	....	....	....	....	....
2012-13	Portland Pirates	AHL	36	6	22	28	20	....	....	....	....	....	....	....	....	....	1	0	1	1	4	....	....	....	....
	Phoenix	**NHL**	**40**	**5**	**4**	**9**	**16**	**1**	**0**	**0**	**50**	**10.0**	**2**	**0**	**0.0**	**16:41**	....	....	....	....	....	....	....	....	....
2013-14	**Phoenix**	**NHL**	**70**	**8**	**13**	**21**	**38**	**2**	**0**	**1**	**105**	**7.6**	**-10**	**0**	**0.0**	**18:12**	....	....	....	....	....	....	....	....	....
2014-15	**Arizona**	**NHL**	**81**	**3**	**15**	**18**	**60**	**0**	**0**	**0**	**144**	**2.1**	**-24**	**1**	**100.0**	**20:52**	....	....	....	....	....	....	....	....	....
2015-16	**Arizona**	**NHL**	**75**	**6**	**30**	**36**	**62**	**0**	**0**	**1**	**161**	**3.7**	**-10**	**2**	**0.0**	**22:28**	....	....	....	....	....	....	....	....	....
2016-17	**Arizona**	**NHL**	**45**	**1**	**8**	**9**	**12**	**1**	**0**	**0**	**57**	**1.8**	**-5**	**1**	**100.0**	**20:13**	....	....	....	....	....	....	....	....	....
	Calgary	**NHL**	**19**	**2**	**4**	**6**	**20**	**0**	**0**	**0**	**24**	**8.3**	**5**	**0**	**0.0**	**18:51**	**4**	**1**	**0**	**1**	**0**	**0**	**0**	**0**	**18:46**
	NHL Totals		**343**	**26**	**76**	**102**	**210**	**4**	**0**	**2**	**554**	**4.7**		**4**	**50.0**	**19:44**	**6**	**1**	**0**	**1**	**0**	**0**	**0**	**0**	**16:17**

WHL East Second All-Star Team (2009) • WHL East First All-Star Team (2010)

Traded to **Calgary** by **Arizona** for Calgary's 3rd round pick (later traded to Edmonton – Edmonton selected Stuart Skinner) in 2017 NHL Draft and Calgary's 5th round pick in 2018 NHL Draft, February 20, 2017.

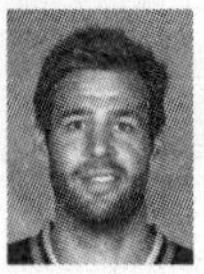

STONER, Clayton (STOH-nuhr, KLAY-tuhn) VGK

Defense. Shoots left. 6'4", 216 lbs. Born, Port McNeill, BC, February 19, 1985. Minnesota's 4th pick, 79th overall, in 2004 NHL Draft.

			Regular Season														Playoffs								
Season	Club	League	GP	G	A	Pts	PIM	PP	SH	GW	S	S%	+/-	TF	F%	Min	GP	G	A	Pts	PIM	PP	SH	GW	Min
2000-01	Campbell River	VIJHL	47	4	16	20	57	....	....	....	....	....	....	....	....	....	....	....	....	....	....	....	....	....	....
2001-02	Campbell River	VIJHL	42	12	35	47	199	....	....	....	....	....	....	....	....	....	....	....	....	....	....	....	....	....	....
2002-03	Tri-City	WHL	58	4	12	16	85	....	....	....	....	....	....	....	....	....	....	....	....	....	....	....	....	....	....
2003-04	Tri-City	WHL	71	7	24	31	109	....	....	....	....	....	....	....	....	....	11	1	1	2	8	....	....	....	....
2004-05	Tri-City	WHL	60	12	34	46	81	....	....	....	....	....	....	....	....	....	4	0	3	3	2	....	....	....	....
2005-06	Houston Aeros	AHL	73	6	18	24	92	....	....	....	....	....	....	....	....	....	3	1	1	2	7	....	....	....	....
2006-07	Houston Aeros	AHL	65	1	6	7	104	....	....	....	....	....	....	....	....	....	....	....	....	....	....	....	....	....	....
2007-08	Houston Aeros	AHL	56	3	12	15	78	....	....	....	....	....	....	....	....	....	....	....	....	....	....	....	....	....	....
2008-09	Houston Aeros	AHL	63	2	22	24	81	....	....	....	....	....	....	....	....	....	20	1	4	5	27	....	....	....	....
2009-10	**Minnesota**	**NHL**	**8**	**0**	**2**	**2**	**12**	**0**	**0**	**0**	**5**	**0.0**	**1**	**0**	**0.0**	**13:19**	....	....	....	....	....	....	....	....	....
	Houston Aeros	AHL	26	3	7	10	52	....	....	....	....	....	....	....	....	....	....	....	....	....	....	....	....	....	....
2010-11	**Minnesota**	**NHL**	**57**	**2**	**7**	**9**	**96**	**0**	**0**	**1**	**40**	**5.0**	**5**	**0**	**0.0**	**16:52**	....	....	....	....	....	....	....	....	....
2011-12	**Minnesota**	**NHL**	**51**	**1**	**4**	**5**	**62**	**0**	**0**	**0**	**47**	**2.1**	**3**	**0**	**0.0**	**17:36**	....	....	....	....	....	....	....	....	....
2012-13	B. Bystrica	Slovakia	8	1	4	5	16	....	....	....	....	....	....	....	....	....	....	....	....	....	....	....	....	....	....
	Minnesota	**NHL**	**48**	**0**	**10**	**10**	**42**	**0**	**0**	**0**	**40**	**0.0**	**0**	**0**	**0.0**	**18:13**	**1**	**0**	**1**	**1**	**0**	**0**	**0**	**0**	**8:18**
2013-14	**Minnesota**	**NHL**	**63**	**1**	**4**	**5**	**84**	**0**	**0**	**0**	**48**	**2.1**	**-6**	**0**	**0.0**	**13:20**	**13**	**1**	**2**	**3**	**26**	**0**	**0**	**0**	**12:17**
2014-15	**Anaheim**	**NHL**	**69**	**1**	**7**	**8**	**68**	**0**	**0**	**1**	**68**	**1.5**	**-2**	**0**	**0.0**	**17:39**	**16**	**1**	**0**	**1**	**10**	**0**	**0**	**0**	**18:14**
2015-16	**Anaheim**	**NHL**	**50**	**1**	**5**	**6**	**67**	**0**	**0**	**0**	**32**	**3.1**	**4**	**0**	**0.0**	**15:22**	**1**	**0**	**0**	**0**	**0**	**0**	**0**	**0**	**7:32**
2016-17	**Anaheim**	**NHL**	**14**	**1**	**2**	**3**	**28**	**0**	**0**	**0**	**16**	**6.3**	**0**	**0**	**0.0**	**17:33**	....	....	....	....	....	....	....	....	....
	San Diego Gulls	AHL	3	1	0	1	12	....	....	....	....	....	....	....	....	....	....	....	....	....	....	....	....	....	....
	NHL Totals		**360**	**7**	**41**	**48**	**459**	**0**	**0**	**2**	**296**	**2.4**		**0**	**0.0**	**16:25**	**31**	**2**	**3**	**5**	**36**	**0**	**0**	**0**	**15:04**

WHL West Second All-Star Team (2005)

• Missed majority of 2009-10 due to recurring groin injury. Signed as a free agent by **Banska Bystrica** (Slovakia), November 29, 2012. Signed as a free agent by **Anaheim**, July 1, 2014. Claimed by **Vegas** from **Anaheim** in Expansion Draft, June 21, 2017.

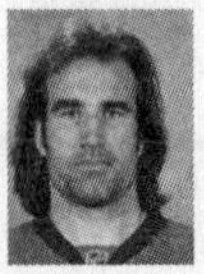

STORTINI, Zack (stohr-TEE-nee, ZAK)

Right wing. Shoots right. 6'4", 215 lbs. Born, Elliot Lake, ON, September 11, 1985. Edmonton's 5th pick, 94th overall, in 2003 NHL Draft.

			Regular Season														Playoffs								
Season	Club	League	GP	G	A	Pts	PIM	PP	SH	GW	S	S%	+/-	TF	F%	Min	GP	G	A	Pts	PIM	PP	SH	GW	Min
2000-01	Newmarket	ON-Jr.A	34	3	10	13	68	....	....	....	....	....	....	....	....	....	....	....	....	....	....	....	....	....	....
2001-02	Sudbury Wolves	OHL	65	8	6	14	187	....	....	....	....	....	....	....	....	....	5	1	0	1	24	....	....	....	....
2002-03	Sudbury Wolves	OHL	62	13	16	29	222	....	....	....	....	....	....	....	....	....	....	....	....	....	....	....	....	....	....
2003-04	Sudbury Wolves	OHL	62	21	16	37	151	....	....	....	....	....	....	....	....	....	7	1	1	2	14	....	....	....	....
	Toronto	AHL	2	0	0	0	7	....	....	....	....	....	....	....	....	....	3	0	0	0	4	....	....	....	....
2004-05	Sudbury Wolves	OHL	58	13	27	40	186	....	....	....	....	....	....	....	....	....	12	2	5	7	27	....	....	....	....
2005-06	Iowa Stars	AHL	27	2	1	3	108	....	....	....	....	....	....	....	....	....	....	....	....	....	....	....	....	....	....
	Milwaukee	AHL	37	0	7	7	153	....	....	....	....	....	....	....	....	....	17	2	0	2	19	....	....	....	....
2006-07	**Edmonton**	**NHL**	**29**	**1**	**0**	**1**	**105**	**0**	**0**	**0**	**17**	**5.9**	**-7**	**3**	**100.0**	**7:09**	....	....	....	....	....	....	....	....	....
	Hamilton	AHL	47	9	6	15	195	....	....	....	....	....	....	....	....	....	22	3	0	3	*56	....	....	....	....
2007-08	**Edmonton**	**NHL**	**66**	**3**	**9**	**12**	**201**	**0**	**0**	**0**	**38**	**7.9**	**3**	**7**	**42.9**	**8:10**	....	....	....	....	....	....	....	....	....
	Springfield	AHL	4	3	2	5	21	....	....	....	....	....	....	....	....	....	....	....	....	....	....	....	....	....	....
2008-09	**Edmonton**	**NHL**	**52**	**6**	**5**	**11**	**181**	**0**	**0**	**0**	**23**	**26.1**	**-3**	**11**	**63.6**	**7:17**	....	....	....	....	....	....	....	....	....
2009-10	**Edmonton**	**NHL**	**77**	**4**	**9**	**13**	**155**	**1**	**0**	**1**	**46**	**8.7**	**3**	**183**	**47.5**	**9:17**	....	....	....	....	....	....	....	....	....
2010-11	**Edmonton**	**NHL**	**32**	**0**	**4**	**4**	**76**	**0**	**0**	**0**	**16**	**0.0**	**-2**	**33**	**42.4**	**7:06**	....	....	....	....	....	....	....	....	....
	Oklahoma City	AHL	29	1	2	3	53	....	....	....	....	....	....	....	....	....	5	1	0	1	6	....	....	....	....
2011-12	**Nashville**	**NHL**	**1**	**0**	**0**	**0**	**7**	**0**	**0**	**0**	**1**	**0.0**	**0**	**0**	**0.0**	**4:53**	....	....	....	....	....	....	....	....	....
	Milwaukee	AHL	74	9	6	15	146	....	....	....	....	....	....	....	....	....	3	0	1	1	2	....	....	....	....
2012-13	Hamilton	AHL	73	2	4	6	241	....	....	....	....	....	....	....	....	....	....	....	....	....	....	....	....	....	....
2013-14	Norfolk Admirals	AHL	73	4	5	9	*299	....	....	....	....	....	....	....	....	....	9	0	2	2	4	....	....	....	....
2014-15	Lehigh Valley	AHL	76	13	12	25	184	....	....	....	....	....	....	....	....	....	....	....	....	....	....	....	....	....	....
2015-16	Binghamton	AHL	66	8	8	16	182	....	....	....	....	....	....	....	....	....	....	....	....	....	....	....	....	....	....
2016-17	Binghamton	AHL	22	2	1	3	20	....	....	....	....	....	....	....	....	....	....	....	....	....	....	....	....	....	....
	San Jose	AHL	26	1	0	1	96	....	....	....	....	....	....	....	....	....	6	0	1	1	14	....	....	....	....
	NHL Totals		**257**	**14**	**27**	**41**	**725**	**1**	**0**	**1**	**141**	**9.9**		**237**	**48.1**	**8:04**	....	....	....	....	....	....	....	....	....

Signed as a free agent by **Nashville**, July 5, 2011. Signed as a free agent by **Hamilton** (AHL), September 21, 2012. Signed as a free agent by **Anaheim**, July 8, 2013. Signed as a free agent by **Philadelphia**, July 2, 2014. Signed as a free agent by **Ottawa**, July 1, 2015. Traded to **San Jose** by **Ottawa** with Buddy Robinson and Ottawa's 7th round pick (later traded to New Jersey – New Jersey selected Matthew Hellickson) in 2017 NHL Draft for Tommy Wingels, January 24, 2017.

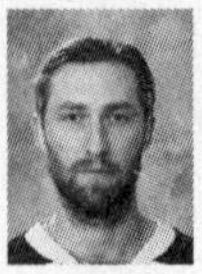

STRACHAN, Tyson (STRAWN, TIGH-suhn)

Defense. Shoots right. 6'3", 210 lbs. Born, Melfort, SK, October 30, 1984. Carolina's 6th pick, 137th overall, in 2003 NHL Draft.

			Regular Season														Playoffs								
Season	Club	League	GP	G	A	Pts	PIM	PP	SH	GW	S	S%	+/-	TF	F%	Min	GP	G	A	Pts	PIM	PP	SH	GW	Min
2001-02	Tisdale Trojans	SMHL	42	5	18	23	70	....	....	....	....	....	....	....	....	....	....	....	....	....	....	....	....	....	....
	Melville	SJHL	2	0	0	0	0	....	....	....	....	....	....	....	....	....	....	....	....	....	....	....	....	....	....
2002-03	Vernon Vipers	BCHL	56	6	22	28	99	....	....	....	....	....	....	....	....	....	....	....	....	....	....	....	....	....	....
2003-04	Ohio State	CCHA	30	2	5	7	8	....	....	....	....	....	....	....	....	....	....	....	....	....	....	....	....	....	....
2004-05	Ohio State	CCHA	31	1	4	5	32	....	....	....	....	....	....	....	....	....	....	....	....	....	....	....	....	....	....
2005-06	Ohio State	CCHA	23	3	2	5	37	....	....	....	....	....	....	....	....	....	....	....	....	....	....	....	....	....	....
2006-07	Ohio State	CCHA	35	7	11	18	55	....	....	....	....	....	....	....	....	....	....	....	....	....	....	....	....	....	....
	Albany River Rats	AHL	1	0	0	0	0	....	....	....	....	....	....	....	....	....	....	....	....	....	....	....	....	....	....
2007-08	Peoria Rivermen	AHL	34	1	2	3	61	....	....	....	....	....	....	....	....	....	....	....	....	....	....	....	....	....	....
	Las Vegas	ECHL	25	2	7	9	68	....	....	....	....	....	....	....	....	....	16	0	4	4	12	....	....	....	....
2008-09	**St. Louis**	**NHL**	**30**	**0**	**3**	**3**	**39**	**0**	**0**	**0**	**21**	**0.0**	**8**	**0**	**0.0**	**13:26**	....	....	....	....	....	....	....	....	....
	Peoria Rivermen	AHL	29	2	3	5	67	....	....	....	....	....	....	....	....	....	3	0	0	0	11	....	....	....	....
2009-10	**St. Louis**	**NHL**	**8**	**0**	**2**	**2**	**4**	**0**	**0**	**0**	**7**	**0.0**	**3**	**0**	**0.0**	**14:02**	....	....	....	....	....	....	....	....	....
	Peoria Rivermen	AHL	65	5	21	26	75	....	....	....	....	....	....	....	....	....	....	....	....	....	....	....	....	....	....
2010-11	**St. Louis**	**NHL**	**29**	**0**	**1**	**1**	**39**	**0**	**0**	**0**	**28**	**0.0**	**-10**	**0**	**0.0**	**12:08**	....	....	....	....	....	....	....	....	....
	Peoria Rivermen	AHL	13	0	8	8	4	....	....	....	....	....	....	....	....	....	1	0	0	0	2	....	....	....	....
2011-12	**Florida**	**NHL**	**15**	**1**	**2**	**3**	**5**	**0**	**0**	**0**	**14**	**7.1**	**1**	**0**	**0.0**	**14:21**	**2**	**0**	**1**	**1**	**0**	**0**	**0**	**0**	**13:30**
	San Antonio	AHL	50	3	14	17	41	....	....	....	....	....	....	....	....	....	7	1	3	4	0	....	....	....	....
2012-13	San Antonio	AHL	24	1	8	9	22	....	....	....	....	....	....	....	....	....	....	....	....	....	....	....	....	....	....
	Florida	**NHL**	**38**	**0**	**4**	**4**	**40**	**0**	**0**	**0**	**42**	**0.0**	**-13**	**0**	**0.0**	**18:58**	....	....	....	....	....	....	....	....	....
2013-14	**Washington**	**NHL**	**18**	**0**	**2**	**2**	**28**	**0**	**0**	**0**	**7**	**0.0**	**-2**	**0**	**0.0**	**17:20**	....	....	....	....	....	....	....	....	....
	Hershey Bears	AHL	60	4	15	19	56	....	....	....	....	....	....	....	....	....	....	....	....	....	....	....	....	....	....
2014-15	**Buffalo**	**NHL**	**46**	**0**	**5**	**5**	**44**	**0**	**0**	**0**	**38**	**0.0**	**-30**	**0**	**0.0**	**18:59**	....	....	....	....	....	....	....	....	....

			Regular Season														Playoffs								
Season	Club	League	GP	G	A	Pts	PIM	PP	SH	GW	S	S%	+/-	TF	F%	Min	GP	G	A	Pts	PIM	PP	SH	GW	Min
2015-16	**Minnesota**	**NHL**	**2**	**0**	**0**	**0**	**0**	**0**	**0**	**0**	**0**	**0.0**	**1**	**0**	**0.0**	**7:33**	....	....	....	....	....	....	....	....	....
	Iowa Wild	AHL	67	1	12	13	68	....	....	....	....	....	....	....	....	....	....	....	....	....	....	....	....	....	....
2016-17	Rochester	AHL	61	1	11	12	36	....	....	....	....	....	....	....	....	....	....	....	....	....	....	....	....	....	....
	NHL Totals		**186**	**1**	**19**	**20**	**199**	**0**	**0**	**0**	**157**	**0.6**		**0**	**0.0**	**16:09**	**2**	**0**	**1**	**1**	**0**	**0**	**0**	**0**	**13:30**

Signed as a free agent by **St. Louis**, October 9, 2008. Signed as a free agent by **Florida**, July 12, 2011. Signed as a free agent by **Washington**, July 8, 2013. Signed as a free agent by **Buffalo**, July 3, 2014. Signed as a free agent by **Minnesota**, July 2, 2015. Signed as a free agent by **Rochester** (AHL), September 14, 2016.

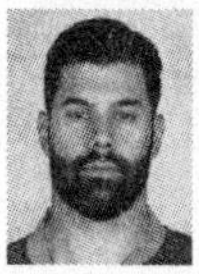

STRAIT, Brian

(STRAYT, BRIGH-uhn) **N.J.**

Defense. Shoots left. 6'1", 205 lbs. Born, Boston, MA, January 4, 1988. Pittsburgh's 3rd pick, 65th overall, in 2006 NHL Draft.

Season	Club	League	GP	G	A	Pts	PIM	PP	SH	GW	S	S%	+/-	TF	F%	Min	GP	G	A	Pts	PIM	PP	SH	GW	Min
2003-04	NMH School	High-MA	30	5	15	20	....	....	....	....	....	....	....	....	....	....	....	....	....	....	....	....	....	....	....
2004-05	USAHNTDP	U-17	18	1	5	6	8	....	....	....	....	....	....	....	....	....	....	....	....	....	....	....	....	....	....
	USAHNTDP	NAHL	42	4	8	12	42	....	....	....	....	....	....	....	....	....	10	0	2	2	2	....	....	....	....
2005-06	USAHNTDP	U-18	40	2	7	9	31	....	....	....	....	....	....	....	....	....	....	....	....	....	....	....	....	....	....
	USAHNTDP	NAHL	15	0	5	5	41	....	....	....	....	....	....	....	....	....	....	....	....	....	....	....	....	....	....
2006-07	Boston University	H-East	36	3	3	6	47	....	....	....	....	....	....	....	....	....	....	....	....	....	....	....	....	....	....
2007-08	Boston University	H-East	37	0	10	10	20	....	....	....	....	....	....	....	....	....	....	....	....	....	....	....	....	....	....
2008-09	Boston University	H-East	38	2	5	7	67	....	....	....	....	....	....	....	....	....	....	....	....	....	....	....	....	....	....
2009-10	Wilkes-Barre	AHL	78	2	12	14	73	....	....	....	....	....	....	....	....	....	4	0	1	1	0	....	....	....	....
2010-11	**Pittsburgh**	**NHL**	**3**	**0**	**0**	**0**	**0**	**0**	**0**	**0**	**0**	**0.0**	**–1**	**0**	**0.0**	**13:32**	....	....	....	....	....	....	....	....	....
	Wilkes-Barre	AHL	75	2	8	10	49	....	....	....	....	....	....	....	....	....	12	1	3	4	10	....	....	....	....
2011-12	**Pittsburgh**	**NHL**	**9**	**0**	**1**	**1**	**4**	**0**	**0**	**0**	**4**	**0.0**	**–2**	**0**	**0.0**	**12:53**	**3**	**0**	**0**	**0**	**0**	**0**	**0**	**0**	**9:35**
	Wilkes-Barre	AHL	41	4	12	16	26	....	....	....	....	....	....	....	....	....	2	0	1	1	0	....	....	....	....
2012-13	Wilkes-Barre	AHL	26	0	0	0	34	....	....	....	....	....	....	....	....	....	....	....	....	....	....	....	....	....	....
	NY Islanders	**NHL**	**19**	**0**	**4**	**4**	**10**	**0**	**0**	**0**	**13**	**0.0**	**4**	**0**	**0.0**	**17:09**	**6**	**1**	**0**	**1**	**12**	**0**	**0**	**0**	**20:35**
2013-14	**NY Islanders**	**NHL**	**47**	**3**	**6**	**9**	**14**	**0**	**0**	**0**	**40**	**7.5**	**–14**	**0**	**0.0**	**17:57**	....	....	....	....	....	....	....	....	....
2014-15	**NY Islanders**	**NHL**	**52**	**2**	**5**	**7**	**32**	**0**	**0**	**0**	**59**	**3.4**	**–1**	**1**	**0.0**	**18:22**	**7**	**0**	**0**	**0**	**4**	**0**	**0**	**0**	**18:50**
2015-16	**NY Islanders**	**NHL**	**52**	**1**	**5**	**6**	**31**	**0**	**0**	**0**	**43**	**2.3**	**1**	**0**	**0.0**	**15:26**	....	....	....	....	....	....	....	....	....
2016-17	**Winnipeg**	**NHL**	**5**	**0**	**2**	**2**	**0**	**0**	**0**	**0**	**3**	**0.0**	**–1**	**0**	**0.0**	**15:56**	....	....	....	....	....	....	....	....	....
	Manitoba Moose	AHL	58	2	12	14	36	....	....	....	....	....	....	....	....	....	....	....	....	....	....	....	....	....	....
	NHL Totals		**187**	**6**	**23**	**29**	**91**	**0**	**0**	**0**	**162**	**3.7**		**1**	**0.0**	**16:55**	**16**	**1**	**0**	**1**	**16**	**0**	**0**	**0**	**17:45**

Claimed on waivers by **NY Islanders** from **Pittsburgh**, January 18, 2013. • Missed majority of 2012-13 due to ankle injury vs. Philadelphia, February 18, 2013. Signed as a free agent by **Winnipeg**, July 1, 2016. Signed as a free agent by **New Jersey**, July 1, 2017.

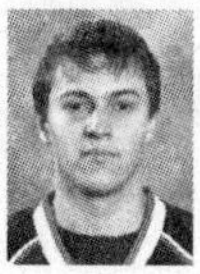

STRAKA, Petr

(STRAH-kuh, PEH-tuhr)

Right wing. Shoots left. 6'1", 185 lbs. Born, Plzen, Czech., June 15, 1992. Columbus' 3rd pick, 55th overall, in 2010 NHL Draft.

Season	Club	League	GP	G	A	Pts	PIM	PP	SH	GW	S	S%	+/-	TF	F%	Min	GP	G	A	Pts	PIM	PP	SH	GW	Min
2006-07	HC Plzen U17	CzR-U17	22	5	6	11	14	....	....	....	....	....	....	....	....	....	7	0	0	0	0	....	....	....	....
2007-08	HC Plzen U17	CzR-U17	46	40	34	74	42	....	....	....	....	....	....	....	....	....	8	5	9	14	4	....	....	....	....
2008-09	HC Plzen U17	CzR-U17	1	1	2	3	4	....	....	....	....	....	....	....	....	....	1	0	2	2	2	....	....	....	....
	HC Plzen Jr.	CzRep-Jr.	27	13	10	23	6	....	....	....	....	....	....	....	....	....	5	3	1	4	2	....	....	....	....
2009-10	Rimouski Oceanic	QMJHL	62	28	36	64	54	....	....	....	....	....	....	....	....	....	12	5	9	14	10	....	....	....	....
2010-11	Rimouski Oceanic	QMJHL	41	10	15	25	33	....	....	....	....	....	....	....	....	....	5	2	2	4	0	....	....	....	....
2011-12	Rimouski Oceanic	QMJHL	54	18	19	37	41	....	....	....	....	....	....	....	....	....	21	10	12	22	6	....	....	....	....
2012-13	Baie-Comeau	QMJHL	55	41	41	82	34	....	....	....	....	....	....	....	....	....	19	11	14	25	12	....	....	....	....
2013-14	Adirondack	AHL	60	9	18	27	22	....	....	....	....	....	....	....	....	....	....	....	....	....	....	....	....	....	....
2014-15	**Philadelphia**	**NHL**	**3**	**0**	**2**	**2**	**0**	**0**	**0**	**0**	**2**	**0.0**	**1**	**0**	**0.0**	**9:27**	....	....	....	....	....	....	....	....	....
	Lehigh Valley	AHL	68	14	10	24	26	....	....	....	....	....	....	....	....	....	....	....	....	....	....	....	....	....	....
2015-16	Lehigh Valley	AHL	64	19	18	37	25	....	....	....	....	....	....	....	....	....	....	....	....	....	....	....	....	....	....
2016-17	Albany Devils	AHL	38	4	9	13	14	....	....	....	....	....	....	....	....	....	....	....	....	....	....	....	....	....	....
	NHL Totals		**3**	**0**	**2**	**2**	**0**	**0**	**0**	**0**	**2**	**0.0**		**0**	**0.0**	**9:27**	....	....	....	....	....	....	....	....	....

QMJHL All-Rookie Team (2010) • Canadian Major Junior All-Rookie Team (2010)

Signed as a free agent by **Philadelphia**, April 24, 2013. Traded to **New Jersey** by **Philadelphia** for a conditional 7th round pick in 2017 NHL Draft (conditions not met), November 12, 2016. • Missed majority of 2016-17 due to various injuries and as a healthy reserve. Signed as a free agent by **Plzen** (Czech Rep.), June 20, 2017.

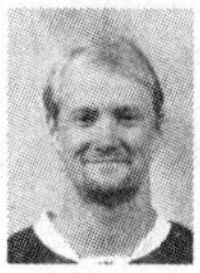

STRALMAN, Anton

(STROHL-muhn, AN-tawn) **T.B.**

Defense. Shoots right. 5'11", 190 lbs. Born, Tibro, Sweden, August 1, 1986. Toronto's 5th pick, 216th overall, in 2005 NHL Draft.

Season	Club	League	GP	G	A	Pts	PIM	PP	SH	GW	S	S%	+/-	TF	F%	Min	GP	G	A	Pts	PIM	PP	SH	GW	Min
2002-03	Skovde IK Jr.	Swe-Jr.	46	20	9	29	38	....	....	....	....	....	....	....	....	....	....	....	....	....	....	....	....	....	....
2003-04	Skovde IK	Sweden-3	27	4	8	12	18	....	....	....	....	....	....	....	....	....	....	....	....	....	....	....	....	....	....
2004-05	Skovde IK	Sweden-2	50	10	11	21	40	....	....	....	....	....	....	....	....	....	....	....	....	....	....	....	....	....	....
2005-06	Timra IK	Sweden	45	1	4	5	28	....	....	....	....	....	....	....	....	....	....	....	....	....	....	....	....	....	....
	Timra IK Jr.	Swe-Jr.	....	....	....	....	....	....	....	....	....	....	....	....	....	....	3	0	0	0	4	....	....	....	....
2006-07	Timra IK	Sweden	53	10	11	21	34	....	....	....	....	....	....	....	....	....	7	1	3	4	10	....	....	....	....
2007-08	**Toronto**	**NHL**	**50**	**3**	**6**	**9**	**18**	**0**	**0**	**0**	**40**	**7.5**	**–10**	**0**	**0.0**	**12:49**	....	....	....	....	....	....	....	....	....
	Toronto Marlies	AHL	21	0	11	11	22	....	....	....	....	....	....	....	....	....	....	....	....	....	....	....	....	....	....
2008-09	**Toronto**	**NHL**	**38**	**1**	**12**	**13**	**20**	**0**	**0**	**1**	**43**	**2.3**	**–2**	**1**	**100.0**	**15:34**	....	....	....	....	....	....	....	....	....
	Toronto Marlies	AHL	36	7	9	16	24	....	....	....	....	....	....	....	....	....	6	1	2	3	0	....	....	....	....
2009-10	**Columbus**	**NHL**	**73**	**6**	**28**	**34**	**37**	**4**	**0**	**0**	**121**	**5.0**	**–17**	**0**	**0.0**	**20:29**	....	....	....	....	....	....	....	....	....
2010-11	**Columbus**	**NHL**	**51**	**1**	**17**	**18**	**22**	**1**	**0**	**1**	**80**	**1.3**	**–11**	**0**	**0.0**	**19:44**	....	....	....	....	....	....	....	....	....
2011-12	**NY Rangers**	**NHL**	**53**	**2**	**16**	**18**	**20**	**0**	**0**	**0**	**55**	**3.6**	**9**	**0**	**0.0**	**17:06**	**20**	**3**	**3**	**6**	**4**	**2**	**0**	**0**	**16:56**
2012-13	**NY Rangers**	**NHL**	**48**	**4**	**3**	**7**	**16**	**0**	**0**	**0**	**66**	**6.1**	**14**	**1**	**0.0**	**18:03**	**10**	**0**	**0**	**0**	**0**	**0**	**0**	**0**	**21:06**
2013-14	**NY Rangers**	**NHL**	**81**	**1**	**12**	**13**	**26**	**0**	**0**	**0**	**104**	**1.0**	**9**	**0**	**0.0**	**19:25**	**25**	**0**	**5**	**5**	**4**	**0**	**0**	**0**	**21:03**
2014-15	**Tampa Bay**	**NHL**	**82**	**9**	**30**	**39**	**26**	**2**	**0**	**0**	**138**	**6.5**	**22**	**0**	**0.0**	**21:57**	**26**	**1**	**8**	**9**	**8**	**0**	**0**	**0**	**22:31**
2015-16	**Tampa Bay**	**NHL**	**73**	**9**	**25**	**34**	**20**	**1**	**0**	**0**	**127**	**7.1**	**16**	**0**	**0.0**	**22:05**	**6**	**1**	**0**	**1**	**2**	**0**	**0**	**0**	**20:14**
2016-17	**Tampa Bay**	**NHL**	**73**	**5**	**17**	**22**	**20**	**1**	**0**	**0**	**130**	**3.8**	**1**	**0**	**0.0**	**22:54**	....	....	....	....	....	....	....	....	....
	NHL Totals		**622**	**41**	**166**	**207**	**225**	**9**	**0**	**2**	**904**	**4.5**		**2**	**50.0**	**19:33**	**87**	**5**	**16**	**21**	**18**	**2**	**0**	**0**	**20:29**

Traded to **Calgary** by **Toronto** with Colin Stuart and Toronto's 7th round pick (Matt DeBlouw) in 2012 NHL Draft for Wayne Primeau and Calgary's 2nd round pick (later traded to Chicago – Chicago selected Brandon Saad) in 2011 NHL Draft, July 27, 2009. Traded to **Columbus** by **Calgary** for Columbus' 3rd round pick (Max Reinhart) in 2010 NHL Draft, September 29, 2009. Signed as a free agent by **NY Rangers**, November 5, 2011. Signed as a free agent by **Tampa Bay**, July 1, 2014.

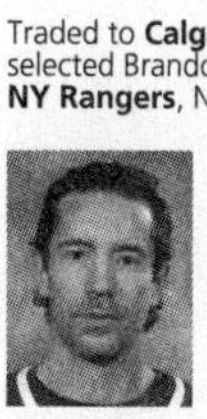

STREET, Ben

(STREET, BEHN) **DET**

Center. Shoots left. 5'11", 185 lbs. Born, Coquitlam, BC, February 13, 1987.

Season	Club	League	GP	G	A	Pts	PIM	PP	SH	GW	S	S%	+/-	TF	F%	Min	GP	G	A	Pts	PIM	PP	SH	GW	Min
2003-04	Salmon Arm	BCHL	54	13	21	34	14	....	....	....	....	....	....	....	....	....	13	1	9	10	0	....	....	....	....
2004-05	Salmon Arm	BCHL	56	29	39	68	21	....	....	....	....	....	....	....	....	....	11	7	8	15	0	....	....	....	....
2005-06	U. of Wisconsin	WCHA	43	10	5	15	0	....	....	....	....	....	....	....	....	....	....	....	....	....	....	....	....	....	....
2006-07	U. of Wisconsin	WCHA	41	10	7	17	16	....	....	....	....	....	....	....	....	....	....	....	....	....	....	....	....	....	....
2007-08	U. of Wisconsin	WCHA	40	13	17	30	36	....	....	....	....	....	....	....	....	....	....	....	....	....	....	....	....	....	....
2008-09	U. of Wisconsin	WCHA	4	1	0	1	8	....	....	....	....	....	....	....	....	....	....	....	....	....	....	....	....	....	....
2009-10	U. of Wisconsin	WCHA	43	14	16	30	30	....	....	....	....	....	....	....	....	....	....	....	....	....	....	....	....	....	....
2010-11	Wilkes-Barre	AHL	36	12	11	23	8	....	....	....	....	....	....	....	....	....	8	0	1	1	0	....	....	....	....
	Wheeling Nailers	ECHL	38	24	27	51	10	....	....	....	....	....	....	....	....	....	....	....	....	....	....	....	....	....	....
2011-12	Wilkes-Barre	AHL	71	27	30	57	24	....	....	....	....	....	....	....	....	....	12	1	2	3	2	....	....	....	....
2012-13	Abbotsford Heat	AHL	69	15	22	37	22	....	....	....	....	....	....	....	....	....	....	....	....	....	....	....	....	....	....
	Calgary	**NHL**	**6**	**0**	**1**	**1**	**0**	**0**	**0**	**0**	**13**	**0.0**	**–1**	**51**	**47.1**	**13:37**	....	....	....	....	....	....	....	....	....
2013-14	**Calgary**	**NHL**	**13**	**0**	**1**	**1**	**4**	**0**	**0**	**0**	**17**	**0.0**	**–2**	**137**	**46.0**	**10:36**	....	....	....	....	....	....	....	....	....
	Abbotsford Heat	AHL	58	28	32	60	24	....	....	....	....	....	....	....	....	....	4	0	1	1	2	....	....	....	....
2014-15	**Colorado**	**NHL**	**3**	**0**	**0**	**0**	**0**	**0**	**0**	**0**	**4**	**0.0**	**0**	**32**	**53.1**	**11:36**	....	....	....	....	....	....	....	....	....
	Lake Erie	AHL	44	9	30	39	10	....	....	....	....	....	....	....	....	....	....	....	....	....	....	....	....	....	....
2015-16	**Colorado**	**NHL**	**7**	**0**	**0**	**0**	**4**	**0**	**0**	**0**	**8**	**0.0**	**–1**	**47**	**55.3**	**7:21**	....	....	....	....	....	....	....	....	....
	San Antonio	AHL	15	7	14	21	4	....	....	....	....	....	....	....	....	....	....	....	....	....	....	....	....	....	....
2016-17	**Detroit**	**NHL**	**6**	**0**	**1**	**1**	**0**	**0**	**0**	**0**	**8**	**0.0**	**1**	**0**	**0.0**	**8:15**	....	....	....	....	....	....	....	....	....
	Grand Rapids	AHL	62	25	30	55	16	....	....	....	....	....	....	....	....	....	19	8	13	21	2	....	....	....	....
	NHL Totals		**35**	**0**	**3**	**3**	**8**	**0**	**0**	**0**	**50**	**0.0**		**267**	**48.7**	**10:09**	....	....	....	....	....	....	....	....	....

Signed as a free agent by **Calgary**, July 2, 2012. Signed as a free agent by **Colorado**, July 1, 2014. • Missed majority of 2015-16 due to chest injury at Toronto, November 17, 2015. Signed as a free agent by **Detroit**, July 1, 2016.

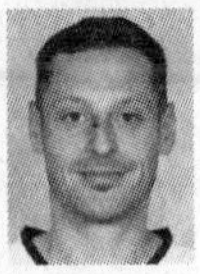

STREIT, Mark

(STRIGHT, MAHRK) **MTL**

Defense. Shoots left. 5'11", 191 lbs. Born, Bern, Switz., December 11, 1977. Montreal's 8th pick, 262nd overall, in 2004 NHL Draft.

			Regular Season														Playoffs								
Season	Club	League	GP	G	A	Pts	PIM	PP	SH	GW	S	S%	+/-	TF	F%	Min	GP	G	A	Pts	PIM	PP	SH	GW	Min
1995-96	Fribourg	Swiss	34	2	2	4	6										4	0	0	0	2				
1996-97	HC Davos	Swiss	46	2	9	11	18										6	0	0	0	0				
1997-98	HC Ambri-Piotta	Swiss	2	0	0	0	0																		
	HC Davos	Swiss	38	4	10	14	14										18	1	5	6	20				
1998-99	HC Davos	Swiss	44	7	18	25	42										6	3	3	6	8				
99-2000	Springfield	AHL	43	3	12	15	18										5	0	0	0	2				
	Utah Grizzlies	IHL	1	0	1	1	2																		
	Tallahassee	ECHL	14	0	5	5	16																		
2000-01	ZSC Lions Zurich	Swiss	44	5	11	16	48										16	2	5	7	37				
2001-02	ZSC Lions Zurich	Swiss	28	6	17	23	36										16	0	6	6	14				
	Switzerland	Olympics	4	1	1	2	0																		
2002-03	ZSC Lions Zurich	Swiss	37	4	19	23	62										12	1	7	8	2				
2003-04	ZSC Lions Zurich	Swiss	48	12	24	36	78										13	5	2	7	14				
2004-05	ZSC Lions Zurich	Swiss	44	14	29	43	46										15	4	11	15	20				
2005-06	**Montreal**	**NHL**	**48**	**2**	**9**	**11**	**28**	**2**	**0**	**0**	**52**	**3.8**	**–6**	**1**	**0.0**	**14:36**	**1**	**0**	**0**	**0**	**0**	**0**	**0**	**0**	**3:29**
	Switzerland	Olympics	6	2	1	3	6																		
2006-07	**Montreal**	**NHL**	**76**	**10**	**26**	**36**	**14**	**2**	**1**	**1**	**102**	**9.8**	**–5**	**12**	**33.3**	**14:01**									
2007-08	**Montreal**	**NHL**	**81**	**13**	**49**	**62**	**28**	**7**	**0**	**3**	**165**	**7.9**	**–6**	**1**	**0.0**	**17:31**	**11**	**1**	**3**	**4**	**8**	**0**	**0**	**0**	**14:48**
2008-09	**NY Islanders**	**NHL**	**74**	**16**	**40**	**56**	**62**	**10**	**1**	**1**	**150**	**10.7**	**5**	**0**	**0.0**	**25:13**									
2009-10	**NY Islanders**	**NHL**	**82**	**11**	**38**	**49**	**48**	**9**	**0**	**2**	**187**	**5.9**	**0**	**1**	**0.0**	**25:42**									
	Switzerland	Olympics	5	0	3	3	0																		
2010-11			DID NOT PLAY – INJURED																						
2011-12	**NY Islanders**	**NHL**	**82**	**7**	**40**	**47**	**46**	**3**	**0**	**1**	**149**	**4.7**	**–27**	**1**	**0.0**	**23:23**									
2012-13	SC Bern	Swiss	32	7	19	26	30																		
	NY Islanders	**NHL**	**48**	**6**	**21**	**27**	**22**	**3**	**0**	**1**	**83**	**7.2**	**–14**	**0**	**0.0**	**23:21**	**6**	**2**	**3**	**5**	**4**	**1**	**0**	**0**	**20:18**
2013-14	**Philadelphia**	**NHL**	**82**	**10**	**34**	**44**	**44**	**4**	**0**	**2**	**121**	**8.3**	**3**	**0**	**0.0**	**20:39**	**7**	**1**	**2**	**3**	**0**	**0**	**0**	**0**	**19:59**
	Switzerland	Olympics	4	0	1	1	2																		
2014-15	**Philadelphia**	**NHL**	**81**	**9**	**43**	**52**	**36**	**4**	**0**	**0**	**144**	**6.3**	**–8**	**0**	**0.0**	**22:22**									
2015-16	**Philadelphia**	**NHL**	**62**	**6**	**17**	**23**	**18**	**2**	**0**	**1**	**110**	**5.5**	**–1**	**0**	**0.0**	**21:52**	**6**	**0**	**1**	**1**	**6**	**0**	**0**	**0**	**20:38**
2016-17	**Philadelphia**	**NHL**	**49**	**5**	**16**	**21**	**22**	**1**	**0**	**1**	**88**	**5.7**	**–10**	**0**	**0.0**	**19:23**									
	♦ Pittsburgh	**NHL**	**19**	**1**	**5**	**6**	**6**	**0**	**0**	**1**	**26**	**3.8**	**–2**	**0**	**0.0**	**17:06**	**3**	**0**	**2**	**2**	**0**	**0**	**0**	**0**	**15:03**
	NHL Totals		**784**	**96**	**338**	**434**	**374**	**47**	**2**	**14**	**1377**	**7.0**		**16**	**25.0**	**20:50**	**34**	**4**	**11**	**15**	**18**	**1**	**0**	**0**	**17:33**

Played in NHL All-Star Game (2009)

Signed as a free agent by **NY Islanders**, July 1, 2008. • Missed 2010-11 due to shoulder injury in training camp, September 25, 2010. Signed as a free agent by **Bern** (Swiss), September 15, 2012. Traded to **Philadelphia** by **NY Islanders** for Shane Harper and Philadelphia's 4th round pick (Devon Toews) in 2014 NHL Draft, June 12, 2013. Traded to **Tampa Bay** by **Philadelphia** for Valtteri Filppula, Tampa Bay's 4th round pick (Maksim Sushko) in 2017 NHL Draft and Los Angeles' 7th round pick (previously acquired, Philadelphia selected Wyatt Kalynuk) in 2017 NHL Draft, March 1, 2017. Traded to **Pittsburgh** by **Tampa Bay** for Pittsburgh's 4th round pick (later traded to Vegas) in 2018 NHL Draft, March 1, 2017. Signed as a free agent by **Montreal**, July 25, 2017.

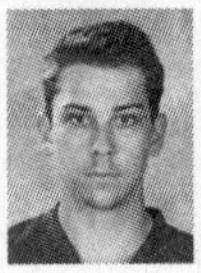

STROME, Dylan

(STROHM, DIH-luhn) **ARI**

Center. Shoots left. 6'3", 197 lbs. Born, Mississauga, ON, March 7, 1997. Arizona's 1st pick, 3rd overall, in 2015 NHL Draft.

			Regular Season														Playoffs								
Season	Club	League	GP	G	A	Pts	PIM	PP	SH	GW	S	S%	+/-	TF	F%	Min	GP	G	A	Pts	PIM	PP	SH	GW	Min
2012-13	Tor. Marlboros	GTHL	60	65	78	143	8																		
2013-14	Erie Otters	OHL	60	10	29	39	11										14	3	6	9	0				
2014-15	Erie Otters	OHL	68	45	*84	*129	32										20	10	12	22	12				
2015-16	Erie Otters	OHL	56	37	74	111	44										13	10	11	21	12				
2016-17	**Arizona**	**NHL**	**7**	**0**	**1**	**1**	**0**	**0**	**0**	**0**	**6**	**0.0**	**–5**	**77**	**40.3**	**13:41**									
	Erie Otters	OHL	35	22	53	75	18										22	14	20	34	14				
	NHL Totals		**7**	**0**	**1**	**1**	**0**	**0**	**0**	**0**	**6**	**0.0**		**77**	**40.3**	**13:41**									

OHL Second All-Star Team (2015) • OHL First All-Star Team (2017)

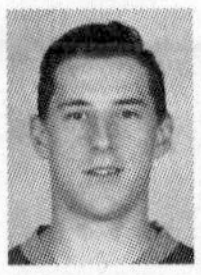

STROME, Ryan

(STROHM, RIGH-uhn) **EDM**

Center. Shoots right. 6'1", 199 lbs. Born, Mississauga, ON, July 11, 1993. NY Islanders' 1st pick, 5th overall, in 2011 NHL Draft.

			Regular Season														Playoffs								
Season	Club	League	GP	G	A	Pts	PIM	PP	SH	GW	S	S%	+/-	TF	F%	Min	GP	G	A	Pts	PIM	PP	SH	GW	Min
2008-09	Tor. Marlboros	GTHL	76	41	63	104	86																		
2009-10	Barrie Colts	OHL	34	5	9	14	35																		
	Niagara Ice Dogs	OHL	27	3	10	13	26										5	0	3	3	0				
2010-11	Niagara Ice Dogs	OHL	65	33	73	106	82										14	6	6	12	19				
2011-12	Niagara Ice Dogs	OHL	46	30	38	68	47										20	7	16	23	31				
2012-13	Niagara Ice Dogs	OHL	53	34	60	94	59										5	2	1	3	8				
	Bridgeport	AHL	10	2	5	7	4																		
2013-14	**NY Islanders**	**NHL**	**37**	**7**	**11**	**18**	**8**	**4**	**0**	**1**	**89**	**7.9**	**–1**	**374**	**44.1**	**15:11**									
	Bridgeport	AHL	37	13	36	49	41																		
2014-15	**NY Islanders**	**NHL**	**81**	**17**	**33**	**50**	**47**	**1**	**1**	**2**	**179**	**9.5**	**23**	**319**	**46.7**	**15:24**	**7**	**2**	**2**	**4**	**2**	**0**	**0**	**1**	**17:33**
2015-16	**NY Islanders**	**NHL**	**71**	**8**	**20**	**28**	**28**	**1**	**0**	**0**	**132**	**6.1**	**–9**	**95**	**41.1**	**15:39**	**8**	**1**	**3**	**4**	**2**	**0**	**0**	**1**	**13:49**
	Bridgeport	AHL	8	2	2	4	10																		
2016-17	**NY Islanders**	**NHL**	**69**	**13**	**17**	**30**	**40**	**2**	**0**	**2**	**114**	**11.4**	**–8**	**344**	**42.7**	**14:36**									
	NHL Totals		**258**	**45**	**81**	**126**	**123**	**8**	**1**	**5**	**514**	**8.8**		**1132**	**44.2**	**15:14**	**15**	**3**	**5**	**8**	**4**	**0**	**0**	**2**	**15:33**

OHL Second All-Star Team (2011) • AHL All-Rookie Team (2014)

Traded to **Edmonton** by **NY Islanders** for Jordan Eberle, June 22, 2017.

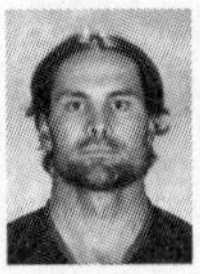

STUART, Mark

(STEW-uhrt, MAHRK)

Defense. Shoots left. 6'2", 215 lbs. Born, Rochester, MN, April 27, 1984. Boston's 1st pick, 21st overall, in 2003 NHL Draft.

			Regular Season														Playoffs								
Season	Club	League	GP	G	A	Pts	PIM	PP	SH	GW	S	S%	+/-	TF	F%	Min	GP	G	A	Pts	PIM	PP	SH	GW	Min
99-2000	Roch. Lourdes	High-MN	28	19	22	41																			
2000-01	USAHNTDP	U-17	12	1	5	6	6																		
	USAHNTDP	NAHL	52	2	11	13	114																		
2001-02	USAHNTDP	U-18	40	9	9	18																			
	USAHNTDP	USHL	12	0	1	1	25																		
	USAHNTDP	NAHL	9	0	1	1	18																		
2002-03	Colorado College	WCHA	38	3	17	20	81																		
2003-04	Colorado College	WCHA	37	4	11	15	100																		
2004-05	Colorado College	WCHA	43	5	14	19	94																		
2005-06	**Boston**	**NHL**	**17**	**1**	**1**	**2**	**10**	**0**	**0**	**0**	**9**	**11.1**	**–1**	**0**	**0.0**	**17:46**									
	Providence Bruins	AHL	60	4	3	7	76										6	0	0	0	25				
2006-07	**Boston**	**NHL**	**15**	**0**	**1**	**1**	**14**	**0**	**0**	**0**	**4**	**0.0**	**7**	**0**	**0.0**	**10:23**									
	Providence Bruins	AHL	49	4	16	20	62										3	0	1	1	9				
2007-08	**Boston**	**NHL**	**82**	**4**	**4**	**8**	**81**	**0**	**0**	**1**	**60**	**6.7**	**2**	**0**	**0.0**	**15:22**	**7**	**0**	**1**	**1**	**8**	**0**	**0**	**0**	**16:00**
2008-09	**Boston**	**NHL**	**82**	**5**	**12**	**17**	**76**	**0**	**0**	**1**	**61**	**8.2**	**20**	**0**	**0.0**	**15:25**	**11**	**0**	**1**	**1**	**7**	**0**	**0**	**0**	**17:57**
2009-10	**Boston**	**NHL**	**56**	**2**	**5**	**7**	**80**	**0**	**0**	**0**	**53**	**3.8**	**1**	**0**	**0.0**	**17:01**	**4**	**0**	**0**	**0**	**6**	**0**	**0**	**0**	**14:39**
2010-11	**Boston**	**NHL**	**31**	**1**	**4**	**5**	**23**	**0**	**0**	**1**	**20**	**5.0**	**8**	**1**	**100.0**	**16:15**									
	Atlanta	**NHL**	**23**	**1**	**0**	**1**	**24**	**0**	**0**	**0**	**21**	**4.8**	**–8**	**0**	**0.0**	**14:51**									
2011-12	**Winnipeg**	**NHL**	**80**	**3**	**11**	**14**	**98**	**0**	**1**	**1**	**60**	**5.0**	**–4**	**0**	**0.0**	**17:12**									
2012-13	Florida Everblades	ECHL	9	2	1	3	12																		
	Winnipeg	**NHL**	**42**	**2**	**2**	**4**	**53**	**0**	**0**	**0**	**40**	**5.0**	**5**	**0**	**0.0**	**16:42**									
2013-14	**Winnipeg**	**NHL**	**69**	**2**	**11**	**13**	**101**	**0**	**0**	**0**	**73**	**2.7**	**11**	**0**	**0.0**	**18:38**									
2014-15	**Winnipeg**	**NHL**	**70**	**2**	**12**	**14**	**69**	**0**	**0**	**1**	**51**	**3.9**	**5**	**1**	**0.0**	**19:13**	**4**	**1**	**1**	**2**	**2**	**0**	**0**	**0**	**17:46**
2015-16	**Winnipeg**	**NHL**	**64**	**1**	**2**	**3**	**66**	**0**	**0**	**0**	**39**	**2.6**	**–7**	**0**	**0.0**	**16:21**									
2016-17	**Winnipeg**	**NHL**	**42**	**2**	**2**	**4**	**27**	**0**	**0**	**1**	**24**	**8.3**	**4**	**0**	**0.0**	**12:27**									
	NHL Totals		**673**	**26**	**67**	**93**	**722**	**0**	**1**	**6**	**515**	**5.0**		**2**	**50.0**	**16:26**	**26**	**1**	**3**	**4**	**23**	**0**	**0**	**0**	**16:53**

WCHA All-Rookie Team (2003) • WCHA Second All-Star Team (2005) • NCAA West First All-American Team (2005)

Traded to **Atlanta** by **Boston** with Blake Wheeler for Rich Peverley and Boris Valabik, February 18, 2011. • Transferred to **Winnipeg** after **Atlanta** franchise relocated, June 21, 2011. Signed as a free agent by **Florida** (ECHL), December 11, 2012.

			Regular Season														Playoffs								
Season	Club	League	GP	G	A	Pts	PIM	PP	SH	GW	S	S%	+/-	TF	F%	Min	GP	G	A	Pts	PIM	PP	SH	GW	Min

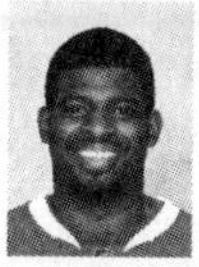

SUBBAN, P.K.

(soo-BAN, PEE-KAY) **NSH**

Defense. Shoots right. 6', 210 lbs. Born, Toronto, ON, May 13, 1989. Montreal's 3rd pick, 43rd overall, in 2007 NHL Draft.

Season	Club	League	GP	G	A	Pts	PIM	PP	SH	GW	S	S%	+/-	TF	F%	Min	GP	G	A	Pts	PIM	PP	SH	GW	Min
2004-05	Markham	GTHL	67	15	28	43	179	....	....	....	....	....	....	....	....	....	....	....	....	....	....	....	....	....	....
2005-06	Belleville Bulls	OHL	52	5	7	12	70	....	....	....	....	....	....	....	....	....	3	0	0	0	2	....	....	....	....
2006-07	Belleville Bulls	OHL	68	15	41	56	89	....	....	....	....	....	....	....	....	....	15	5	8	13	26	....	....	....	....
2007-08	Belleville Bulls	OHL	58	8	38	46	100	....	....	....	....	....	....	....	....	....	21	8	15	23	28	....	....	....	....
2008-09	Belleville Bulls	OHL	56	14	62	76	94	....	....	....	....	....	....	....	....	....	17	3	12	15	22	....	....	....	....
2009-10	**Montreal**	**NHL**	**2**	**0**	**2**	**2**	**2**	**0**	**0**	**0**	**4**	**0.0**	**1**	**0**	**0.0**	**20:06**	**14**	**1**	**7**	**8**	**6**	**0**	**0**	**0**	**20:44**
	Hamilton	AHL	77	18	35	53	82	....	....	....	....	....	....	....	....	....	7	3	7	10	6	....	....	....	....
2010-11	**Montreal**	**NHL**	**77**	**14**	**24**	**38**	**124**	**9**	**0**	**3**	**197**	**7.1**	**–8**	**0**	**0.0**	**22:16**	**7**	**2**	**2**	**4**	**2**	**2**	**0**	**0**	**28:33**
2011-12	**Montreal**	**NHL**	**81**	**7**	**29**	**36**	**119**	**5**	**0**	**0**	**205**	**3.4**	**9**	**0**	**0.0**	**24:18**	....	....	....	....	....	....	....	....	....
2012-13	**Montreal**	**NHL**	**42**	**11**	**27**	**38**	**57**	**7**	**0**	**0**	**126**	**8.7**	**12**	**0**	**0.0**	**23:15**	**5**	**2**	**2**	**4**	**31**	**1**	**0**	**0**	**23:56**
2013-14	**Montreal**	**NHL**	**82**	**10**	**43**	**53**	**81**	**4**	**0**	**1**	**204**	**4.9**	**–4**	**0**	**0.0**	**24:37**	**17**	**5**	**9**	**14**	**24**	***4**	**0**	**1**	**27:26**
	Canada	Olympics	1	0	0	0	0	....	....	....	....	....	....	....	....	....	....	....	....	....	....	....	....	....	....
2014-15	**Montreal**	**NHL**	**82**	**15**	**45**	**60**	**74**	**8**	**0**	**5**	**170**	**8.8**	**21**	**0**	**0.0**	**26:12**	**12**	**1**	**7**	**8**	**31**	**0**	**0**	**0**	**26:45**
2015-16	**Montreal**	**NHL**	**68**	**6**	**45**	**51**	**75**	**2**	**0**	**0**	**176**	**3.4**	**4**	**0**	**0.0**	**26:22**	....	....	....	....	....	....	....	....	....
2016-17	**Nashville**	**NHL**	**66**	**10**	**30**	**40**	**44**	**3**	**0**	**2**	**142**	**7.0**	**–8**	**0**	**0.0**	**24:24**	**22**	**2**	**10**	**12**	**29**	**0**	**0**	**0**	**25:32**
	NHL Totals		**500**	**73**	**245**	**318**	**576**	**38**	**0**	**11**	**1224**	**6.0**		**0**	**0.0**	**24:32**	**77**	**13**	**37**	**50**	**123**	**7**	**0**	**1**	**25:27**

OHL First All-Star Team (2009) • AHL All-Rookie Team (2010) • AHL First All-Star Team (2010) • NHL All-Rookie Team (2011) • NHL First All-Star Team (2013, 2015) • James Norris Memorial Trophy (2013)
Played in NHL All-Star Game (2016, 2017)
Traded to **Nashville** by **Montreal** for Shea Weber, June 29, 2016.

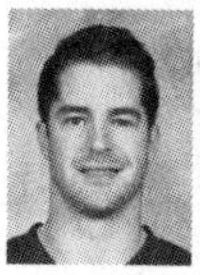

SUMMERS, Chris

(SUHM-mehrs, KRIHS) **PIT**

Defense. Shoots left. 6'2", 209 lbs. Born, Ann Arbor, MI, February 5, 1988. Phoenix's 2nd pick, 29th overall, in 2006 NHL Draft.

Season	Club	League	GP	G	A	Pts	PIM	PP	SH	GW	S	S%	+/-	TF	F%	Min	GP	G	A	Pts	PIM	PP	SH	GW	Min
2004-05	USAHNTDP	U-17	13	2	2	4	10	....	....	....	....	....	....	....	....	....	....	....	....	....	....	....	....	....	....
	USAHNTDP	NAHL	31	2	5	7	20	....	....	....	....	....	....	....	....	....	7	1	0	1	0	....	....	....	....
2005-06	USAHNTDP	U-18	42	4	9	13	67	....	....	....	....	....	....	....	....	....	....	....	....	....	....	....	....	....	....
	USAHNTDP	NAHL	17	2	2	4	20	....	....	....	....	....	....	....	....	....	....	....	....	....	....	....	....	....	....
2006-07	U. of Michigan	CCHA	41	6	8	14	58	....	....	....	....	....	....	....	....	....	....	....	....	....	....	....	....	....	....
2007-08	U. of Michigan	CCHA	41	2	11	13	65	....	....	....	....	....	....	....	....	....	....	....	....	....	....	....	....	....	....
2008-09	U. of Michigan	CCHA	41	4	13	17	40	....	....	....	....	....	....	....	....	....	....	....	....	....	....	....	....	....	....
2009-10	U. of Michigan	CCHA	40	4	12	16	28	....	....	....	....	....	....	....	....	....	....	....	....	....	....	....	....	....	....
	San Antonio	AHL	6	1	0	1	0	....	....	....	....	....	....	....	....	....	....	....	....	....	....	....	....	....	....
2010-11	**Phoenix**	**NHL**	**2**	**0**	**0**	**0**	**4**	**0**	**0**	**0**	**0**	**0.0**	**–3**	**0**	**0.0**	**13:52**	....	....	....	....	....	....	....	....	....
	San Antonio	AHL	75	1	9	10	54	....	....	....	....	....	....	....	....	....	....	....	....	....	....	....	....	....	....
2011-12	**Phoenix**	**NHL**	**21**	**0**	**3**	**3**	**11**	**0**	**0**	**0**	**10**	**0.0**	**–4**	**0**	**0.0**	**12:27**	....	....	....	....	....	....	....	....	....
	Portland Pirates	AHL	28	0	2	2	37	....	....	....	....	....	....	....	....	....	....	....	....	....	....	....	....	....	....
2012-13	Portland Pirates	AHL	60	2	10	12	53	....	....	....	....	....	....	....	....	....	3	0	0	0	0	....	....	....	....
	Phoenix	**NHL**	**6**	**0**	**0**	**0**	**9**	**0**	**0**	**0**	**5**	**0.0**	**–3**	**0**	**0.0**	**12:39**	....	....	....	....	....	....	....	....	....
2013-14	**Phoenix**	**NHL**	**18**	**2**	**1**	**3**	**15**	**0**	**0**	**0**	**17**	**11.8**	**0**	**0**	**0.0**	**14:55**	....	....	....	....	....	....	....	....	....
	Portland Pirates	AHL	48	2	7	9	47	....	....	....	....	....	....	....	....	....	....	....	....	....	....	....	....	....	....
2014-15	**Arizona**	**NHL**	**17**	**0**	**3**	**3**	**8**	**0**	**0**	**0**	**13**	**0.0**	**–12**	**0**	**0.0**	**13:43**	....	....	....	....	....	....	....	....	....
	Portland Pirates	AHL	8	0	1	1	6	....	....	....	....	....	....	....	....	....	....	....	....	....	....	....	....	....	....
	NY Rangers	**NHL**	**3**	**0**	**0**	**0**	**0**	**0**	**0**	**0**	**2**	**0.0**	**0**	**0**	**0.0**	**17:15**	....	....	....	....	....	....	....	....	....
	Hartford	AHL	13	0	1	1	17	....	....	....	....	....	....	....	....	....	....	....	....	....	....	....	....	....	....
2015-16	**NY Rangers**	**NHL**	**3**	**0**	**0**	**0**	**4**	**0**	**0**	**0**	**5**	**0.0**	**–2**	**0**	**0.0**	**15:23**	....	....	....	....	....	....	....	....	....
	Hartford	AHL	74	3	8	11	51	....	....	....	....	....	....	....	....	....	....	....	....	....	....	....	....	....	....
2016-17	Hartford	AHL	74	4	8	12	71	....	....	....	....	....	....	....	....	....	....	....	....	....	....	....	....	....	....
	NHL Totals		**70**	**2**	**7**	**9**	**51**	**0**	**0**	**0**	**52**	**3.8**		**0**	**0.0**	**13:47**	....	....	....	....	....	....	....	....	....

Traded to **NY Rangers** by **Arizona** with Keith Yandle and Arizona's 4th round pick (Tarmo Reunanen) in 2016 NHL Draft for John Moore, Anthony Duclair, Tampa Bay's 2nd round pick (previously acquired, later traded to Calgary – Calgary selected Oliver Kylington) in 2015 NHL Draft and NY Rangers' 1st round pick (later traded to Detroit – Detroit selected Dennis Cholowski) in 2016 NHL Draft, March 1, 2015. Signed as a free agent by **Pittsburgh**, July 1, 2017.

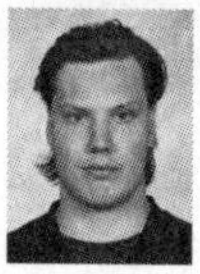

SUNDQVIST, Oskar

(SUHND-qvihst, AWS-kuhr) **ST.L.**

Center. Shoots right. 6'3", 209 lbs. Born, Boden, Sweden, March 23, 1994. Pittsburgh's 4th pick, 81st overall, in 2012 NHL Draft.

Season	Club	League	GP	G	A	Pts	PIM	PP	SH	GW	S	S%	+/-	TF	F%	Min	GP	G	A	Pts	PIM	PP	SH	GW	Min
2010-11	Skelleftea AIK Jr.	Swe-Jr.	1	0	0	0	0	....	....	....	....	....	....	....	....	....	....	....	....	....	....	....	....	....	....
	Skelleftea AIK U18	Swe-U18	38	19	16	35	100	....	....	....	....	....	....	....	....	....	8	1	0	1	29	....	....	....	....
2011-12	Skelleftea AIK Jr.	Swe-Jr.	2	1	0	1	0	....	....	....	....	....	....	....	....	....	....	....	....	....	....	....	....	....	....
	Skelleftea AIK U18	Swe-U18	39	21	32	53	129	....	....	....	....	....	....	....	....	....	7	5	5	10	14	....	....	....	....
2012-13	Skelleftea AIK	Sweden	14	1	0	1	8	....	....	....	....	....	....	....	....	....	....	....	....	....	....	....	....	....	....
	Skelleftea AIK Jr.	Swe-Jr.	38	17	16	33	48	....	....	....	....	....	....	....	....	....	5	3	2	5	4	....	....	....	....
2013-14	Skelleftea AIK	Sweden	51	6	10	16	16	....	....	....	....	....	....	....	....	....	13	4	2	6	16	....	....	....	....
	Sweden	Olympics	7	2	0	2	4	....	....	....	....	....	....	....	....	....	....	....	....	....	....	....	....	....	....
2014-15	Skelleftea AIK	Sweden	41	9	10	19	34	....	....	....	....	....	....	....	....	....	15	1	4	5	18	....	....	....	....
2015-16	**Pittsburgh**	**NHL**	**18**	**1**	**3**	**4**	**4**	**0**	**1**	**1**	**13**	**7.7**	**0**	**139**	**46.0**	**10:19**	**2**	**0**	**0**	**0**	**0**	**0**	**0**	**0**	**9:18**
	Wilkes-Barre	AHL	45	5	12	17	30	....	....	....	....	....	....	....	....	....	....	....	....	....	....	....	....	....	....
2016-17	**Pittsburgh**	**NHL**	**10**	**0**	**0**	**0**	**2**	**0**	**0**	**0**	**9**	**0.0**	**–4**	**44**	**36.4**	**9:10**	....	....	....	....	....	....	....	....	....
	Wilkes-Barre	AHL	63	20	26	46	52	....	....	....	....	....	....	....	....	....	5	0	1	1	19	....	....	....	....
	NHL Totals		**28**	**1**	**3**	**4**	**6**	**0**	**1**	**1**	**22**	**4.5**		**183**	**43.7**	**9:54**	**2**	**0**	**0**	**0**	**0**	**0**	**0**	**0**	**9:18**

Traded to **St. Louis** by **Pittsburgh** with Pittsburgh's 1st round pick (Klim Kostin) in 2017 NHL Draft for Ryan Reaves and St. Louis' 2nd round pick (Zachary Lauzon) in 2017 NHL Draft, June 23, 2017.

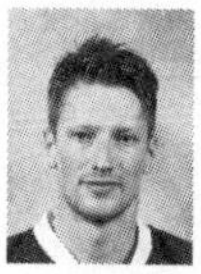

SUSTR, Andrej

(SHOO-stuhr, an-DRAY) **T.B.**

Defense. Shoots right. 6'7", 220 lbs. Born, Plzen, Czech., November 29, 1990.

Season	Club	League	GP	G	A	Pts	PIM	PP	SH	GW	S	S%	+/-	TF	F%	Min	GP	G	A	Pts	PIM	PP	SH	GW	Min
2006-07	Jihlava U17	CzR-U17	37	5	15	20	56	....	....	....	....	....	....	....	....	....	....	....	....	....	....	....	....	....	....
	Jihlava Jr.	CzRep-Jr.	5	0	0	0	4	....	....	....	....	....	....	....	....	....	....	....	....	....	....	....	....	....	....
2007-08	HC Plzen Jr.	CzRep-Jr.	41	2	8	10	44	....	....	....	....	....	....	....	....	....	5	1	0	1	4	....	....	....	....
2008-09	HC Plzen Jr.	CzRep-Jr.	13	1	4	5	14	....	....	....	....	....	....	....	....	....	....	....	....	....	....	....	....	....	....
	HC Rokycany	CzRep-3	2	0	0	0	2	....	....	....	....	....	....	....	....	....	....	....	....	....	....	....	....	....	....
	Kenai River	NAHL	36	1	7	8	58	....	....	....	....	....	....	....	....	....	2	0	0	0	2	....	....	....	....
2009-10	Youngstown	USHL	50	1	18	19	95	....	....	....	....	....	....	....	....	....	....	....	....	....	....	....	....	....	....
2010-11	Nebraska-Omaha	WCHA	39	2	7	9	38	....	....	....	....	....	....	....	....	....	....	....	....	....	....	....	....	....	....
2011-12	Nebraska-Omaha	WCHA	33	4	13	17	26	....	....	....	....	....	....	....	....	....	....	....	....	....	....	....	....	....	....
2012-13	Nebraska-Omaha	WCHA	39	9	16	25	53	....	....	....	....	....	....	....	....	....	....	....	....	....	....	....	....	....	....
	Tampa Bay	**NHL**	**2**	**0**	**0**	**0**	**0**	**0**	**0**	**0**	**2**	**0.0**	**1**	**0**	**0.0**	**10:43**	....	....	....	....	....	....	....	....	....
	Syracuse Crunch	AHL	8	2	1	3	8	....	....	....	....	....	....	....	....	....	18	2	5	7	25	....	....	....	....
2013-14	**Tampa Bay**	**NHL**	**43**	**1**	**7**	**8**	**16**	**0**	**0**	**0**	**39**	**2.6**	**3**	**0**	**0.0**	**15:48**	**3**	**0**	**0**	**0**	**2**	**0**	**0**	**0**	**18:26**
	Syracuse Crunch	AHL	12	1	3	4	2	....	....	....	....	....	....	....	....	....	....	....	....	....	....	....	....	....	....
2014-15	**Tampa Bay**	**NHL**	**72**	**0**	**13**	**13**	**34**	**0**	**0**	**0**	**55**	**0.0**	**10**	**0**	**0.0**	**17:42**	**26**	**1**	**1**	**2**	**18**	**0**	**0**	**0**	**15:14**
2015-16	**Tampa Bay**	**NHL**	**77**	**4**	**17**	**21**	**30**	**0**	**0**	**1**	**65**	**6.2**	**–2**	**0**	**0.0**	**16:50**	**17**	**1**	**2**	**3**	**16**	**0**	**0**	**0**	**17:18**
2016-17	**Tampa Bay**	**NHL**	**80**	**3**	**11**	**14**	**43**	**0**	**0**	**1**	**93**	**3.2**	**–10**	**1**	**0.0**	**17:35**	....	....	....	....	....	....	....	....	....
	NHL Totals		**274**	**8**	**48**	**56**	**123**	**0**	**0**	**2**	**254**	**3.1**		**1**	**0.0**	**17:05**	**46**	**2**	**3**	**5**	**36**	**0**	**0**	**0**	**16:12**

Signed as a free agent by **Tampa Bay** March 21, 2013.

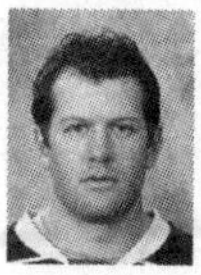

SUTER, Ryan

(SOO-tuhr, RIGH-uhn) **MIN**

Defense. Shoots left. 6'2", 206 lbs. Born, Madison, WI, January 21, 1985. Nashville's 1st pick, 7th overall, in 2003 NHL Draft.

Season	Club	League	GP	G	A	Pts	PIM	PP	SH	GW	S	S%	+/-	TF	F%	Min	GP	G	A	Pts	PIM	PP	SH	GW	Min
2000-01	Culver Academy	High-IN	26	13	32	45	....	....	....	....	....	....	....	....	....	....	....	....	....	....	....	....	....	....	....
2001-02	USAHNTDP	U-17	8	2	11	13	21	....	....	....	....	....	....	....	....	....	....	....	....	....	....	....	....	....	....
	USAHNTDP	U-18	27	4	10	14	6	....	....	....	....	....	....	....	....	....	....	....	....	....	....	....	....	....	....
	USAHNTDP	NAHL	35	2	10	12	75	....	....	....	....	....	....	....	....	....	....	....	....	....	....	....	....	....	....
2002-03	USAHNTDP	NAHL	9	2	5	7	12	....	....	....	....	....	....	....	....	....	....	....	....	....	....	....	....	....	....
	USAHNTDP	U-18	42	7	17	24	124	....	....	....	....	....	....	....	....	....	....	....	....	....	....	....	....	....	....
2003-04	U. of Wisconsin	WCHA	39	3	16	19	93	....	....	....	....	....	....	....	....	....	....	....	....	....	....	....	....	....	....
2004-05	Milwaukee	AHL	63	7	16	23	70	....	....	....	....	....	....	....	....	....	7	1	5	6	16	....	....	....	....

Season	Club	League	GP	G	A	Pts	PIM	PP	SH	GW	S	S%	+/-	TF	F%	Min	Playoffs GP	G	A	Pts	PIM	PP	SH	GW	Min
			Regular Season														Playoffs								
2005-06	**Nashville**	**NHL**	**71**	**1**	**15**	**16**	**66**	**0**	**0**	**0**	**84**	**1.2**	**7**	**0**	**0.0**	**17:21**	....	....	....	....	....	....	....	....	....
2006-07	**Nashville**	**NHL**	**82**	**8**	**16**	**24**	**54**	**1**	**0**	**0**	**87**	**9.2**	**10**	**0**	**0.0**	**20:09**	**5**	**1**	**0**	**1**	**8**	**0**	**0**	**0**	**23:19**
2007-08	**Nashville**	**NHL**	**76**	**7**	**24**	**31**	**71**	**1**	**0**	**1**	**138**	**5.1**	**3**	**0**	**0.0**	**20:35**	**6**	**1**	**1**	**2**	**4**	**0**	**0**	**0**	**21:12**
2008-09	**Nashville**	**NHL**	**82**	**7**	**38**	**45**	**73**	**3**	**0**	**3**	**143**	**4.9**	**–16**	**0**	**0.0**	**24:16**	....	....	....	....	....	....	....	....	....
2009-10	**Nashville**	**NHL**	**82**	**4**	**33**	**37**	**48**	**2**	**0**	**1**	**125**	**3.2**	**4**	**1**	**0.0**	**23:59**	**6**	**0**	**0**	**0**	**0**	**0**	**0**	**0**	**24:09**
	United States	Olympics	6	0	4	4	2	....	....	....	....	....	....	....	....	....	....	....	....	....	....	....	....	....	....
2010-11	**Nashville**	**NHL**	**70**	**4**	**35**	**39**	**54**	**1**	**0**	**1**	**115**	**3.5**	**20**	**1**	**0.0**	**25:12**	**12**	**1**	**5**	**6**	**6**	**0**	**0**	**0**	**28:51**
2011-12	**Nashville**	**NHL**	**79**	**7**	**39**	**46**	**30**	**3**	**1**	**1**	**134**	**5.2**	**15**	**1**	**0.0**	**26:30**	**10**	**1**	**3**	**4**	**4**	**1**	**0**	**0**	**28:50**
2012-13	**Minnesota**	**NHL**	**48**	**4**	**28**	**32**	**24**	**3**	**0**	**1**	**91**	**4.4**	**2**	**0**	**0.0**	**27:17**	**5**	**0**	**0**	**0**	**4**	**0**	**0**	**0**	**31:37**
2013-14	**Minnesota**	**NHL**	**82**	**8**	**35**	**43**	**34**	**3**	**0**	**0**	**150**	**5.3**	**15**	**1**	**100.0**	**29:25**	**13**	**1**	**6**	**7**	**4**	**1**	**0**	**0**	**29:13**
	United States	Olympics	6	0	3	3	4	....	....	....	....	....	....	....	....	....	....	....	....	....	....	....	....	....	....
2014-15	**Minnesota**	**NHL**	**77**	**2**	**36**	**38**	**48**	**1**	**0**	**1**	**150**	**1.3**	**7**	**0**	**0.0**	**29:04**	**10**	**0**	**3**	**3**	**0**	**0**	**0**	**0**	**26:59**
2015-16	**Minnesota**	**NHL**	**82**	**8**	**43**	**51**	**30**	**3**	**1**	**2**	**188**	**4.3**	**10**	**0**	**0.0**	**28:36**	**6**	**0**	**3**	**3**	**4**	**0**	**0**	**0**	**29:17**
2016-17	**Minnesota**	**NHL**	**82**	**9**	**31**	**40**	**36**	**4**	**1**	**1**	**164**	**5.5**	***34**	**0**	**0.0**	**26:55**	**5**	**1**	**2**	**3**	**10**	**1**	**0**	**0**	**29:06**
	NHL Totals		**913**	**69**	**373**	**442**	**568**	**25**	**3**	**12**	**1569**	**4.4**		**4**	**25.0**	**24:57**	**78**	**6**	**23**	**29**	**44**	**3**	**0**	**0**	**27:36**

WCHA All-Rookie Team (2004) • NHL First All-Star Team (2013)
Played in NHL All-Star Game (2012, 2015, 2017)
Signed as a free agent by **Minnesota**, July 4, 2012.

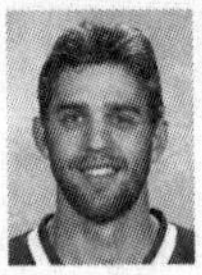

SUTTER, Brandon

(SUH-tuhr, BRAN-duhn) **VAN**

Center/Right wing. Shoots right. 6'3", 190 lbs. Born, Huntington, NY, February 14, 1989. Carolina's 1st pick, 11th overall, in 2007 NHL Draft.

Season	Club	League	GP	G	A	Pts	PIM	PP	SH	GW	S	S%	+/-	TF	F%	Min	Playoffs GP	G	A	Pts	PIM	PP	SH	GW	Min
2003-04	Red Deer Chiefs	AMBHL	35	25	34	59	28	....	....	....	....	....	....	....	....	....	11	5	4	9	....	....	....	....	....
2004-05	Red Deer	AMHL	34	4	16	20	28	....	....	....	....	....	....	....	....	....	....	....	....	....	....	....	....	....	....
	Red Deer Rebels	WHL	7	0	2	2	8	....	....	....	....	....	....	....	....	....	7	1	4	5	2	....	....	....	....
2005-06	Red Deer Rebels	WHL	68	22	24	46	36	....	....	....	....	....	....	....	....	....	....	....	....	....	....	....	....	....	....
2006-07	Red Deer Rebels	WHL	71	20	37	57	54	....	....	....	....	....	....	....	....	....	7	0	3	3	14	....	....	....	....
2007-08	Red Deer Rebels	WHL	59	26	23	49	38	....	....	....	....	....	....	....	....	....	....	....	....	....	....	....	....	....	....
	Albany River Rats	AHL	7	1	1	2	2	....	....	....	....	....	....	....	....	....	7	0	2	2	4	....	....	....	....
2008-09	**Carolina**	**NHL**	**50**	**1**	**5**	**6**	**16**	**0**	**0**	**0**	**57**	**1.8**	**–1**	**332**	**38.6**	**8:50**	....	....	....	....	....	....	....	....	....
	Albany River Rats	AHL	22	4	8	12	6	....	....	....	....	....	....	....	....	....	....	....	....	....	....	....	....	....	....
2009-10	**Carolina**	**NHL**	**72**	**21**	**19**	**40**	**2**	**5**	**0**	**3**	**168**	**12.5**	**–1**	**997**	**49.1**	**16:33**	....	....	....	....	....	....	....	....	....
	Albany River Rats	AHL	7	1	3	4	2	....	....	....	....	....	....	....	....	....	....	....	....	....	....	....	....	....	....
2010-11	**Carolina**	**NHL**	**82**	**14**	**15**	**29**	**25**	**1**	**0**	**3**	**145**	**9.7**	**13**	**1349**	**44.3**	**16:51**	....	....	....	....	....	....	....	....	....
2011-12	**Carolina**	**NHL**	**82**	**17**	**15**	**32**	**21**	**2**	**3**	**0**	**171**	**9.9**	**–3**	**1295**	**50.5**	**17:24**	....	....	....	....	....	....	....	....	....
2012-13	**Pittsburgh**	**NHL**	**48**	**11**	**8**	**19**	**4**	**3**	**0**	**5**	**82**	**13.4**	**3**	**761**	**50.2**	**16:24**	**15**	**2**	**1**	**3**	**0**	**0**	**0**	**0**	**16:18**
2013-14	**Pittsburgh**	**NHL**	**81**	**13**	**13**	**26**	**12**	**2**	**3**	**1**	**144**	**9.0**	**–9**	**1150**	**47.7**	**15:46**	**13**	**5**	**2**	**7**	**2**	**0**	**1**	**1**	**15:53**
2014-15	**Pittsburgh**	**NHL**	**80**	**21**	**12**	**33**	**14**	**3**	**4**	**4**	**180**	**11.7**	**6**	**1359**	**50.6**	**17:19**	**5**	**1**	**1**	**2**	**2**	**1**	**0**	**0**	**15:57**
2015-16	**Vancouver**	**NHL**	**20**	**5**	**4**	**9**	**2**	**1**	**1**	**2**	**45**	**11.1**	**3**	**278**	**52.5**	**17:59**	....	....	....	....	....	....	....	....	....
2016-17	**Vancouver**	**NHL**	**81**	**17**	**17**	**34**	**12**	**4**	**0**	**1**	**160**	**10.6**	**–20**	**1452**	**54.3**	**18:48**	....	....	....	....	....	....	....	....	....
	NHL Totals		**596**	**120**	**108**	**228**	**108**	**21**	**11**	**19**	**1152**	**10.4**		**8973**	**49.3**	**16:24**	**33**	**8**	**4**	**12**	**4**	**1**	**1**	**1**	**16:05**

Traded to **Pittsburgh** by **Carolina** with Brian Dumoulin and Carolina's 1st round pick (Derrick Pouliot) in 2012 NHL Draft for Jordan Staal, June 22, 2012. Traded to **Vancouver** by **Pittsburgh** with Vancouver's 3rd round pick (previously acquired, Vancouver selected William Lockwood) in 2016 NHL Draft for Nick Bonino, Adam Clendening and Anaheim's 2nd round pick (previously acquired, Pittsburgh selected Filip Gustavsson) in 2016 NHL Draft, July 28, 2015. • Missed majority of 2015-16 due to sports hernia surgery and broken jaw at Colorado, February 9, 2015.

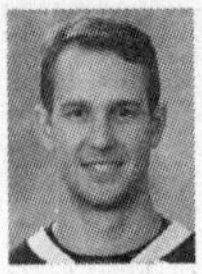

SUTTER, Brett

(SUH-tuhr, BREHT)

Left wing. Shoots left. 6', 200 lbs. Born, Viking, AB, June 2, 1987. Calgary's 7th pick, 179th overall, in 2005 NHL Draft.

Season	Club	League	GP	G	A	Pts	PIM	PP	SH	GW	S	S%	+/-	TF	F%	Min	Playoffs GP	G	A	Pts	PIM	PP	SH	GW	Min
2003-04	Kootenay Ice	WHL	44	5	7	12	26	....	....	....	....	....	....	....	....	....	4	0	0	0	4	....	....	....	....
2004-05	Kootenay Ice	WHL	70	8	11	19	70	....	....	....	....	....	....	....	....	....	16	1	2	3	16	....	....	....	....
2005-06	Kootenay Ice	WHL	16	8	7	15	21	....	....	....	....	....	....	....	....	....	....	....	....	....	....	....	....	....	....
	Red Deer Rebels	WHL	57	9	26	35	80	....	....	....	....	....	....	....	....	....	....	....	....	....	....	....	....	....	....
2006-07	Red Deer Rebels	WHL	67	28	29	57	77	....	....	....	....	....	....	....	....	....	7	3	4	7	11	....	....	....	....
2007-08	Quad City Flames	AHL	75	4	6	10	63	....	....	....	....	....	....	....	....	....	....	....	....	....	....	....	....	....	....
2008-09	**Calgary**	**NHL**	**4**	**1**	**0**	**1**	**2**	**0**	**0**	**0**	**6**	**16.7**	**–2**	**1**	**0.0**	**8:04**	....	....	....	....	....	....	....	....	....
	Quad City Flames	AHL	71	10	15	25	50	....	....	....	....	....	....	....	....	....	....	....	....	....	....	....	....	....	....
2009-10	**Calgary**	**NHL**	**10**	**0**	**0**	**0**	**5**	**0**	**0**	**0**	**9**	**0.0**	**–1**	**5**	**20.0**	**9:40**	....	....	....	....	....	....	....	....	....
	Abbotsford Heat	AHL	66	9	15	24	69	....	....	....	....	....	....	....	....	....	13	4	7	11	20	....	....	....	....
2010-11	**Calgary**	**NHL**	**4**	**0**	**1**	**1**	**5**	**0**	**0**	**0**	**3**	**0.0**	**–1**	**23**	**52.2**	**10:07**	....	....	....	....	....	....	....	....	....
	Charlotte	AHL	60	9	12	21	84	....	....	....	....	....	....	....	....	....	16	4	10	14	15	....	....	....	....
	Carolina	**NHL**	**1**	**0**	**0**	**0**	**0**	**0**	**0**	**0**	**0**	**0.0**	**0**	**3**	**33.3**	**4:09**	....	....	....	....	....	....	....	....	....
2011-12	**Carolina**	**NHL**	**15**	**0**	**3**	**3**	**11**	**0**	**0**	**0**	**11**	**0.0**	**–1**	**21**	**66.7**	**7:34**	....	....	....	....	....	....	....	....	....
	Charlotte	AHL	63	13	16	29	58	....	....	....	....	....	....	....	....	....	....	....	....	....	....	....	....	....	....
2012-13	Charlotte	AHL	70	19	29	48	62	....	....	....	....	....	....	....	....	....	5	0	0	0	0	....	....	....	....
	Carolina	**NHL**	**3**	**0**	**0**	**0**	**4**	**0**	**0**	**0**	**2**	**0.0**	**–1**	**14**	**57.1**	**8:21**	....	....	....	....	....	....	....	....	....
2013-14	**Carolina**	**NHL**	**17**	**1**	**1**	**2**	**9**	**0**	**0**	**1**	**16**	**6.3**	**–4**	**73**	**50.7**	**7:34**	....	....	....	....	....	....	....	....	....
	Charlotte	AHL	62	15	29	44	69	....	....	....	....	....	....	....	....	....	....	....	....	....	....	....	....	....	....
2014-15	**Minnesota**	**NHL**	**6**	**0**	**3**	**3**	**4**	**0**	**0**	**0**	**6**	**0.0**	**1**	**0**	**0.0**	**9:19**	....	....	....	....	....	....	....	....	....
	Iowa Wild	AHL	71	12	17	29	37	....	....	....	....	....	....	....	....	....	....	....	....	....	....	....	....	....	....
2015-16	Iowa Wild	AHL	57	4	10	14	37	....	....	....	....	....	....	....	....	....	....	....	....	....	....	....	....	....	....
	Ontario Reign	AHL	17	5	2	7	25	....	....	....	....	....	....	....	....	....	5	0	1	1	2	....	....	....	....
2016-17	Ontario Reign	AHL	66	18	18	36	52	....	....	....	....	....	....	....	....	....	5	1	1	2	2	....	....	....	....
	NHL Totals		**60**	**2**	**8**	**10**	**40**	**0**	**0**	**1**	**53**	**3.8**		**140**	**52.1**	**8:17**	....	....	....	....	....	....	....	....	....

Traded to **Carolina** by **Calgary** with Ian White for Anton Babchuk and Tom Kostopoulos, November 17, 2010. Signed as a free agent by **Minnesota**, July 1, 2014. Traded to **Los Angeles** by **Minnesota** for Scott Sabourin, February 29, 2016. Signed as a free agent by **Ontario** (AHL), July 2, 2016.

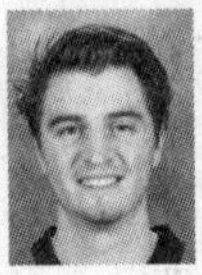

SUTTER, Brody

(SUH-tuhr, BROH-dee)

Center. Shoots right. 6'5", 203 lbs. Born, Viking, AB, September 26, 1991. Carolina's 6th pick, 193rd overall, in 2011 NHL Draft.

Season	Club	League	GP	G	A	Pts	PIM	PP	SH	GW	S	S%	+/-	TF	F%	Min	Playoffs GP	G	A	Pts	PIM	PP	SH	GW	Min
2007-08	Calgary Buffaloes	AMHL	32	8	11	19	24	....	....	....	....	....	....	....	....	....	12	4	6	10	4	....	....	....	....
2008-09	Saskatoon Blades	WHL	18	0	2	2	4	....	....	....	....	....	....	....	....	....	....	....	....	....	....	....	....	....	....
	Lethbridge	WHL	30	4	3	7	7	....	....	....	....	....	....	....	....	....	10	0	0	0	2	....	....	....	....
2009-10	Lethbridge	WHL	72	5	9	14	42	....	....	....	....	....	....	....	....	....	....	....	....	....	....	....	....	....	....
2010-11	Lethbridge	WHL	46	18	24	42	35	....	....	....	....	....	....	....	....	....	....	....	....	....	....	....	....	....	....
2011-12	Lethbridge	WHL	65	30	30	60	49	....	....	....	....	....	....	....	....	....	....	....	....	....	....	....	....	....	....
	Charlotte	AHL	4	1	0	1	0	....	....	....	....	....	....	....	....	....	....	....	....	....	....	....	....	....	....
2012-13	Florida Everblades	ECHL	37	8	8	16	13	....	....	....	....	....	....	....	....	....	....	....	....	....	....	....	....	....	....
	Charlotte	AHL	23	3	2	5	13	....	....	....	....	....	....	....	....	....	5	2	3	5	2	....	....	....	....
2013-14	Charlotte	AHL	69	8	20	28	29	....	....	....	....	....	....	....	....	....	....	....	....	....	....	....	....	....	....
2014-15	**Carolina**	**NHL**	**4**	**0**	**0**	**0**	**0**	**0**	**0**	**0**	**0**	**0.0**	**–2**	**14**	**50.0**	**7:26**	....	....	....	....	....	....	....	....	....
	Charlotte	AHL	45	12	13	25	17	....	....	....	....	....	....	....	....	....	....	....	....	....	....	....	....	....	....
2015-16	**Carolina**	**NHL**	**8**	**0**	**0**	**0**	**0**	**0**	**0**	**0**	**7**	**0.0**	**–4**	**13**	**69.2**	**8:58**	....	....	....	....	....	....	....	....	....
	Charlotte	AHL	70	13	11	24	37	....	....	....	....	....	....	....	....	....	....	....	....	....	....	....	....	....	....
2016-17	Springfield	AHL	19	4	5	9	6	....	....	....	....	....	....	....	....	....	....	....	....	....	....	....	....	....	....
	NHL Totals		**12**	**0**	**0**	**0**	**0**	**0**	**0**	**0**	**7**	**0.0**		**27**	**59.3**	**8:27**	....	....	....	....	....	....	....	....	....

Traded to **Florida** by **Carolina** for Connor Brickley, October 11, 2016. • Missed majority of 2016-17 due to various injuries.

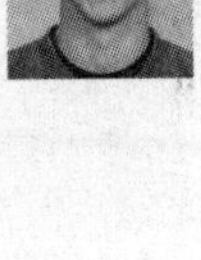

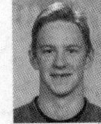

SVECHNIKOV, Evgeni

(svech-NIH-kawv, ehv-GEH-nee) **DET**

Left wing. Shoots left. 6'3", 205 lbs. Born, Neftegorsk, Russia, October 31, 1996. Detroit's 1st pick, 19th overall, in 2015 NHL Draft.

Season	Club	League	GP	G	A	Pts	PIM	PP	SH	GW	S	S%	+/-	TF	F%	Min	Playoffs GP	G	A	Pts	PIM	PP	SH	GW	Min
2012-13	Irbis Kazan Jr.	Rus.-Jr. B	6	2	2	4	6	....	....	....	....	....	....	....	....	....	....	....	....	....	....	....	....	....	....
	Bars Kazan Jr.	Russia-Jr.	34	9	9	18	34	....	....	....	....	....	....	....	....	....	4	1	1	2	2	....	....	....	....
2013-14	Ak Bars Kazan	KHL	3	0	0	0	0	....	....	....	....	....	....	....	....	....	....	....	....	....	....	....	....	....	....
	Bars Kazan Jr.	Russia-Jr.	29	14	13	27	68	....	....	....	....	....	....	....	....	....	6	4	1	5	14	....	....	....	....
2014-15	Cape Breton	QMJHL	55	32	46	78	70	....	....	....	....	....	....	....	....	....	7	1	6	7	14	....	....	....	....
2015-16	Cape Breton	QMJHL	50	32	47	79	97	....	....	....	....	....	....	....	....	....	13	4	11	15	8	....	....	....	....
	Grand Rapids	AHL	....	....	....	....	....	....	....	....	....	....	....	....	....	....	2	0	1	1	0	....	....	....	....

Season	Club	League	GP	G	A	Pts	PIM	PP	SH	GW	S	S%	+/-	TF	F%	Min	GP	G	A	Pts	PIM	PP	SH	GW	Min
2016-17	Detroit	NHL	2	0	0	0	0	0	0	0	4	0.0	0	0	0.0	13:09									
	Grand Rapids	AHL	74	20	31	51	62										19	5	7	12	20				
	NHL Totals		2	0	0	0	0	0	0	0	4	0.0		0	0.0	13:09									

SVEDBERG, Viktor

Defense. Shoots left. 6'8", 238 lbs. Born, Gothenburg, Sweden, May 24, 1991. (SVEHD-buhrg, VIHK-tuhr) **CHI**

Season	Club	League	GP	G	A	Pts	PIM	PP	SH	GW	S	S%	+/-	TF	F%	Min	GP	G	A	Pts	PIM	PP	SH	GW	Min
2009-10	Frolunda Jr.	Swe-Jr.	40	4	10	14	85																		
2010-11	Frolunda Jr.	Swe-Jr.	41	5	17	22	73										7	0	1	1	10				
	Frolunda	Sweden	9	0	0	0	0																		
2011-12	Frolunda Jr.	Swe-Jr.	6	1	2	3	4																		
	Frolunda	Sweden	55	3	2	5	20										6	0	0	0	0				
2012-13	Frolunda Jr.	Swe-Jr.	1	0	0	0	2																		
	Frolunda	Sweden	51	0	2	2	24										6	0	0	0	4				
2013-14	Rockford IceHogs	AHL	35	2	7	9	26																		
2014-15	Rockford IceHogs	AHL	49	3	11	14	41										8	0	4	4	8				
2015-16	**Chicago**	**NHL**	27	2	2	4	4	0	0	0	40	5.0	-5	0	0.0	15:45	3	0	0	0	6	0	0	0	8:02
	Rockford IceHogs	AHL	40	1	14	15	39																		
2016-17	Rockford IceHogs	AHL	51	2	9	11	70																		
	NHL Totals		27	2	2	4	4	0	0	0	40	5.0		0	0.0	15:45	3	0	0	0	6	0	0	0	8:02

Signed as a free agent by **Rockford** (AHL), May 16, 2013. Signed as a free agent by **Chicago**, October 19, 2013. • Missed majority of 2013-14 due to shoulder injury vs. Chicago (AHL), February 14, 2014.

SZWARZ, Jordan

Right wing. Shoots right. 5'11", 196 lbs. Born, Burlington, ON, May 14, 1991. Phoenix's 4th pick, 97th overall, in 2009 NHL Draft. (SWAWRZ, JOHR-dahn) **BOS**

Season	Club	League	GP	G	A	Pts	PIM	PP	SH	GW	S	S%	+/-	TF	F%	Min	GP	G	A	Pts	PIM	PP	SH	GW	Min
2006-07	Burlington Eagles	Minor-ON	66	56	54	110	88																		
2007-08	Saginaw Spirit	OHL	65	12	21	33	56										4	0	0	0	2				
2008-09	Saginaw Spirit	OHL	67	17	34	51	76										8	1	5	6	10				
2009-10	Saginaw Spirit	OHL	65	26	28	54	82										6	1	2	3	0				
	San Antonio	AHL	1	0	0	0	0																		
2010-11	Saginaw Spirit	OHL	65	27	39	66	90										12	4	9	13	8				
2011-12	Portland Pirates	AHL	58	7	13	20	28																		
2012-13	Portland Pirates	AHL	60	11	22	33	31																		
2013-14	**Phoenix**	**NHL**	26	3	0	3	19	0	0	1	25	12.0	-6	3	33.3	8:39									
	Portland Pirates	AHL	27	8	6	14	55																		
2014-15	**Arizona**	**NHL**	9	1	0	1	2	0	0	0	8	12.5	-2	0	0.0	13:28									
	Portland Pirates	AHL	45	9	13	22	65										5	1	2	3	8				
2015-16	Springfield	AHL	56	12	11	23	31																		
2016-17	Providence Bruins	AHL	65	22	32	54	76										17	6	5	11	18				
	NHL Totals		35	4	0	4	21	0	0	1	33	12.1		3	33.3	9:53									

Signed as a free agent by **Providence** (AHL), October 14, 2016. Signed as a free agent by **Boston**, July 1, 2017.

TANEV, Brandon

Left wing. Shoots left. 6', 180 lbs. Born, Toronto, ON, December 31, 1991. ((TA-nehv, BRAN-duhn) **WPG**

Season	Club	League	GP	G	A	Pts	PIM	PP	SH	GW	S	S%	+/-	TF	F%	Min	GP	G	A	Pts	PIM	PP	SH	GW	Min
2010-11	Markham Waxers	ON-Jr.A	46	16	26	42	16										6	2	2	4	0				
2011-12	Surrey Eagles	BCHL	58	11	22	33	27										10	3	1	4	2				
2012-13	Providence	H-East	33	4	7	11	6																		
2013-14	Providence	H-East	39	6	9	15	20																		
2014-15	Providence	H-East	39	10	13	23	20																		
2015-16	Providence	H-East	38	15	13	28	35																		
	Winnipeg	**NHL**	3	0	0	0	2	0	0	0	4	0.0	0	0	0.0	12:03									
2016-17	**Winnipeg**	**NHL**	51	2	2	4	26	0	0	1	54	3.7	-6	1	100.0	10:41									
	Manitoba Moose	AHL	23	2	7	9	13																		
	NHL Totals		54	2	2	4	28	0	0	1	58	3.4		1	100.0	10:45									

Signed as a free agent by **Winnipeg**, March 30, 2016.

TANEV, Chris

Defense. Shoots right. 6'2", 185 lbs. Born, Toronto, ON, December 20, 1989. (TA-nehv, KRIHS) **VAN**

Season	Club	League	GP	G	A	Pts	PIM	PP	SH	GW	S	S%	+/-	TF	F%	Min	GP	G	A	Pts	PIM	PP	SH	GW	Min
2006-07	Durham Fury	ON-Jr.A	40	0	9	9	8										4	0	3	3	6				
2007-08	Durham Fury	ON-Jr.A	19	1	6	7	12																		
	Stouffville Spirit	ON-Jr.A	4	0	0	0	0																		
	Markham Waxers	ON-Jr.A	26	1	9	10	12										23	1	2	3	4				
2008-09	Markham Waxers	ON-Jr.A	50	4	37	41	33										14	1	5	6	8				
2009-10	RIT Tigers	AH	41	10	18	28	4																		
2010-11	**Vancouver**	**NHL**	29	0	1	1	0	0	0	0	15	0.0	0	0	0.0	13:47	5	0	0	0	0	0	0	0	14:40
	Manitoba Moose	AHL	39	1	8	9	16										14	1	2	3	4				
2011-12	**Vancouver**	**NHL**	25	0	2	2	8	0	0	0	15	0.0	10	0	0.0	16:43	5	0	0	0	0	0	0	0	15:11
	Chicago Wolves	AHL	34	0	14	14	6																		
2012-13	Chicago Wolves	AHL	29	2	10	12	6																		
	Vancouver	**NHL**	38	2	5	7	10	0	0	1	20	10.0	4	0	0.0	17:17									
2013-14	**Vancouver**	**NHL**	64	6	11	17	8	0	1	2	65	9.2	12	0	0.0	20:44									
2014-15	**Vancouver**	**NHL**	70	2	18	20	12	0	0	1	53	3.8	8	0	0.0	21:05	6	0	3	3	0	0	0	0	22:00
2015-16	**Vancouver**	**NHL**	69	4	14	18	8	2	0	0	42	9.5	-8	0	0.0	21:45									
2016-17	**Vancouver**	**NHL**	53	2	8	10	14	0	0	1	39	5.1	3	0	0.0	20:21									
	NHL Totals		348	16	59	75	54	2	1	5	249	6.4		0	0.0	19:42	16	0	3	3	0	0	0	0	17:35

Signed as a free agent by **Vancouver**, May 31, 2010.

TANGRADI, Eric

Left wing. Shoots left. 6'4", 221 lbs. Born, Philadelphia, PA, February 10, 1989. Anaheim's 2nd pick, 42nd overall, in 2007 NHL Draft. (tan-GRAY-dee, AIR-ihk) **DET**

Season	Club	League	GP	G	A	Pts	PIM	PP	SH	GW	S	S%	+/-	TF	F%	Min	GP	G	A	Pts	PIM	PP	SH	GW	Min
2005-06	Wyoming Prep	High-PA	38	21	23	44	120																		
2006-07	Belleville Bulls	OHL	65	5	15	20	32										15	8	9	17	14				
2007-08	Belleville Bulls	OHL	56	24	36	60	41										21	7	11	18	20				
2008-09	Belleville Bulls	OHL	55	38	50	88	61										16	8	13	21	12				
2009-10	**Pittsburgh**	**NHL**	1	0	0	0	0	0	0	0	3	0.0	0	0	0.0	13:49									
	Wilkes-Barre	AHL	65	17	22	39	31										4	1	1	2	6				
2010-11	**Pittsburgh**	**NHL**	15	1	2	3	10	0	0	0	18	5.6	-4	3	33.3	11:12	1	0	0	0	0	0	0	0	15:12
	Wilkes-Barre	AHL	42	18	15	33	86																		
2011-12	**Pittsburgh**	**NHL**	24	0	2	2	16	0	0	0	20	0.0	-4	2	0.0	8:56	2	0	1	1	0	0	0	0	8:07
	Wilkes-Barre	AHL	37	15	16	31	40										10	4	5	9	14				
2012-13	Wilkes-Barre	AHL	34	10	8	18	57																		
	Pittsburgh	**NHL**	5	0	0	0	0	0	0	0	0	0.0	0	0	0.0	8:32									
	Winnipeg	**NHL**	36	1	3	4	22	0	0	0	44	2.3	-4	2	0.0	10:18									
2013-14	**Winnipeg**	**NHL**	55	3	3	6	21	0	0	0	52	5.8	-6	3	100.0	8:39									
2014-15	**Montreal**	**NHL**	7	0	0	0	17	0	0	0	5	0.0	-3	1	100.0	7:44									
	Hamilton	AHL	48	14	17	31	56																		
2015-16	**Detroit**	**NHL**	1	0	0	0	0	0	0	0	0	0.0	0	1	0.0	6:55									
	Grand Rapids	AHL	72	28	28	56	66										7	2	3	5	4				
2016-17	Grand Rapids	AHL	54	17	27	44	53										19	2	17	19	12				
	NHL Totals		144	5	10	15	86	0	0	0	146	3.4		12	41.7	9:21	3	0	1	1	0	0	0	0	10:29

Traded to **Pittsburgh** by **Anaheim** with Chris Kunitz for Ryan Whitney, February 26, 2009. Traded to **Winnipeg** by **Pittsburgh** for Winnipeg's 6th round pick (Dane Birks) in 2013 NHL Draft, February 13, 2013. Traded to **Montreal** by **Winnipeg** for Peter Budaj and Patrick Holland, October 5, 2014. Signed as a free agent by **Detroit**, July 8, 2015.

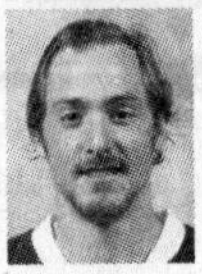

TAORMINA, Matt

(tah'ohr-MEE-nah, MAT) **MTL**

Defense. Shoots left. 5'10", 182 lbs. Born, Warren, MI, October 20, 1986.

			Regular Season														Playoffs								
Season	Club	League	GP	G	A	Pts	PIM	PP	SH	GW	S	S%	+/-	TF	F%	Min	GP	G	A	Pts	PIM	PP	SH	GW	Min
2004-05	Texarkana Bandits	NAHL	52	14	30	44	44	....	....	....	....	....	....	....	....	....	9	3	3	6	6	....	....	....	....
2005-06	Providence	H-East	36	1	10	11	16	....	....	....	....	....	....	....	....	....	....	....	....	....	....	....	....	....	....
2006-07	Providence	H-East	35	5	2	7	6	....	....	....	....	....	....	....	....	....	....	....	....	....	....	....	....	....	....
2007-08	Providence	H-East	36	9	18	27	12	....	....	....	....	....	....	....	....	....	....	....	....	....	....	....	....	....	....
2008-09	Providence	H-East	34	5	15	20	16	....	....	....	....	....	....	....	....	....	....	....	....	....	....	....	....	....	....
	Binghamton	AHL	11	2	3	5	4	....	....	....	....	....	....	....	....	....	....	....	....	....	....	....	....	....	....
2009-10	Lowell Devils	AHL	75	10	40	50	45	....	....	....	....	....	....	....	....	....	5	1	3	4	4	....	....	....	....
2010-11	**New Jersey**	**NHL**	**17**	**3**	**2**	**5**	**2**	**1**	**0**	**0**	**38**	**7.9**	**-2**	**0**	**0.0**	**20:40**	....	....	....	....	....	....	....	....	....
2011-12	**New Jersey**	**NHL**	**30**	**1**	**6**	**7**	**4**	**0**	**0**	**0**	**33**	**3.0**	**6**	**0**	**0.0**	**16:32**	....	....	....	....	....	....	....	....	....
	Albany Devils	AHL	33	6	10	16	12	....	....	....	....	....	....	....	....	....	....	....	....	....	....	....	....	....	....
2012-13	Syracuse Crunch	AHL	55	4	20	24	21	....	....	....	....	....	....	....	....	....	18	2	10	12	4	....	....	....	....
	Tampa Bay	**NHL**	**2**	**0**	**0**	**0**	**0**	**0**	**0**	**0**	**0**	**0.0**	**-1**	**0**	**0.0**	**16:39**	....	....	....	....	....	....	....	....	....
2013-14	**Tampa Bay**	**NHL**	**7**	**0**	**0**	**0**	**0**	**0**	**0**	**0**	**6**	**0.0**	**0**	**0**	**0.0**	**13:24**	....	....	....	....	....	....	....	....	....
	Syracuse Crunch	AHL	41	6	12	18	20	....	....	....	....	....	....	....	....	....	....	....	....	....	....	....	....	....	....
	Springfield	AHL	17	3	5	8	2	....	....	....	....	....	....	....	....	....	4	0	1	1	0	....	....	....	....
2014-15	Worcester Sharks	AHL	76	11	27	38	24	....	....	....	....	....	....	....	....	....	4	1	0	1	0	....	....	....	....
2015-16	**Tampa Bay**	**NHL**	**3**	**0**	**0**	**0**	**0**	**0**	**0**	**0**	**2**	**0.0**	**0**	**0**	**0.0**	**13:56**	**3**	**0**	**0**	**0**	**0**	**0**	**0**	**0**	**3:38**
	Syracuse Crunch	AHL	61	13	28	41	10	....	....	....	....	....	....	....	....	....	....	....	....	....	....	....	....	....	....
2016-17	Syracuse Crunch	AHL	70	15	45	60	22	....	....	....	....	....	....	....	....	....	22	5	15	20	11	....	....	....	....
	NHL Totals		**59**	**4**	**8**	**12**	**6**	**1**	**0**	**0**	**79**	**5.1**		**0**	**0.0**	**17:13**	**3**	**0**	**0**	**0**	**0**	**0**	**0**	**0**	**3:38**

AHL First All-Star Team (2017) • Eddie Shore Award (AHL – Outstanding Defenseman) (2017)

Signed as a free agent by **Binghamton** (AHL), March 10, 2009. Signed as a free agent by **Lowell** (AHL), August 14, 2009. Signed as a free agent by **New Jersey**, February 26, 2010. • Missed majority of 2010-11 due to ankle injury at Boston, November 15, 2010. Signed as a free agent by **Tampa Bay**, July 6, 2012. Traded to **Columbus** by **Tampa Bay** with Dana Tyrell for Jon Marchessault and Dalton Smith, March 5, 2014. Signed as a free agent by **Worcester** (AHL). September 26, 2014. Signed as a free agent by **Tampa Bay**, July 1, 2015. Signed as a free agent by **Montreal**, July 1, 2017.

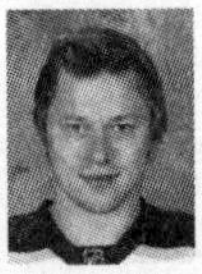

TARASENKO, Vladimir

(ta-rah-SEHN-koh, vla-DIH-meer) **ST.L.**

Right wing. Shoots left. 6', 219 lbs. Born, Yaroslavl, USSR, December 13, 1991. St. Louis' 2nd pick, 16th overall, in 2010 NHL Draft.

Season	Club	League	GP	G	A	Pts	PIM	PP	SH	GW	S	S%	+/-	TF	F%	Min	GP	G	A	Pts	PIM	PP	SH	GW	Min
2007-08	Sibir Novosibirsk 2	Russia-3	17	6	4	10	2	....	....	....	....	....	....	....	....	....	....	....	....	....	....	....	....	....	....
2008-09	Sibir Novosibirsk 2	Russia-3	STATISTICS NOT AVAILABLE																						
	Sibir Novosibirsk	KHL	38	7	3	10	2	....	....	....	....	....	....	....	....	....	....	....	....	....	....	....	....	....	....
2009-10	Novosibirsk Jr.	Russia-Jr.	1	1	0	1	0	....	....	....	....	....	....	....	....	....	....	....	....	....	....	....	....	....	....
	Sibir Novosibirsk	KHL	42	13	11	24	18	....	....	....	....	....	....	....	....	....	....	....	....	....	....	....	....	....	....
2010-11	Sibir Novosibirsk	KHL	42	9	10	19	8	....	....	....	....	....	....	....	....	....	3	0	0	0	0	....	....	....	....
	Novosibirsk Jr.	Russia-Jr.	3	2	2	4	2	....	....	....	....	....	....	....	....	....	....	....	....	....	....	....	....	....	....
2011-12	Sibir Novosibirsk	KHL	39	18	20	38	15	....	....	....	....	....	....	....	....	....	....	....	....	....	....	....	....	....	....
	St. Petersburg	KHL	15	5	4	9	0	....	....	....	....	....	....	....	....	....	15	10	6	16	6	....	....	....	....
2012-13	St. Petersburg	KHL	31	14	18	32	8	....	....	....	....	....	....	....	....	....	....	....	....	....	....	....	....	....	....
	St. Louis	**NHL**	**38**	**8**	**11**	**19**	**10**	**3**	**0**	**1**	**75**	**10.7**	**1**	**1**	**100.0**	**13:25**	**1**	**0**	**0**	**0**	**0**	**0**	**0**	**0**	**5:51**
2013-14	**St. Louis**	**NHL**	**64**	**21**	**22**	**43**	**16**	**5**	**0**	**3**	**136**	**15.4**	**20**	**6**	**33.3**	**15:10**	**6**	**4**	**0**	**4**	**0**	**2**	**0**	**0**	**18:58**
	Russia	Olympics	5	0	1	1	0	....	....	....	....	....	....	....	....	....	....	....	....	....	....	....	....	....	....
2014-15	**St. Louis**	**NHL**	**77**	**37**	**36**	**73**	**31**	**8**	**0**	**6**	**264**	**14.0**	**27**	**3**	**0.0**	**17:37**	**6**	**6**	**1**	**7**	**0**	**2**	**0**	**2**	**17:23**
2015-16	**St. Louis**	**NHL**	**80**	**40**	**34**	**74**	**37**	**12**	**0**	**7**	**292**	**13.7**	**7**	**1**	**0.0**	**18:38**	**20**	**9**	**6**	**15**	**2**	**1**	**0**	**0**	**18:01**
2016-17	**St. Louis**	**NHL**	**82**	**39**	**36**	**75**	**12**	**9**	**0**	**8**	**286**	**13.6**	**-1**	**10**	**50.0**	**18:28**	**11**	**3**	**3**	**6**	**0**	**1**	**0**	**1**	**20:50**
	NHL Totals		**341**	**145**	**139**	**284**	**106**	**37**	**0**	**25**	**1053**	**13.8**		**21**	**38.1**	**17:08**	**44**	**22**	**10**	**32**	**2**	**6**	**0**	**3**	**18:29**

NHL Second All-Star Team (2015, 2016)

Played in NHL All-Star Game (2015, 2016, 2017)

Signed as a free agent by **St. Petersburg** (KHL), September 24, 2012.

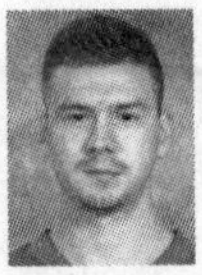

TARASOV, Daniil

(TAIR-ah-sawv, DAN-ihl) **S.J.**

Right wing. Shoots right. 6', 180 lbs. Born, Moscow, USSR, June 20, 1991.

Season	Club	League	GP	G	A	Pts	PIM	PP	SH	GW	S	S%	+/-	TF	F%	Min	GP	G	A	Pts	PIM	PP	SH	GW	Min
2010-11	Indiana Ice	USHL	57	37	38	75	46	....	....	....	....	....	....	....	....	....	5	2	4	6	6	....	....	....	....
2011-12	Indiana Ice	USHL	60	47	41	88	86	....	....	....	....	....	....	....	....	....	6	5	5	10	8	....	....	....	....
2012-13	Worcester Sharks	AHL	43	14	14	28	20	....	....	....	....	....	....	....	....	....	....	....	....	....	....	....	....	....	....
	San Francisco	ECHL	17	3	11	14	5	....	....	....	....	....	....	....	....	....	....	....	....	....	....	....	....	....	....
2013-14	Worcester Sharks	AHL	47	17	14	31	40	....	....	....	....	....	....	....	....	....	....	....	....	....	....	....	....	....	....
2014-15	**San Jose**	**NHL**	**5**	**0**	**1**	**1**	**0**	**0**	**0**	**0**	**5**	**0.0**	**2**	**1**	**100.0**	**7:34**	....	....	....	....	....	....	....	....	....
	Worcester Sharks	AHL	54	16	17	33	27	....	....	....	....	....	....	....	....	....	4	0	3	3	2	....	....	....	....
2015-16	Dynamo Moscow	KHL	37	4	4	8	14	....	....	....	....	....	....	....	....	....	10	3	0	3	29	....	....	....	....
2016-17	Dynamo Moscow	KHL	34	5	2	7	20	....	....	....	....	....	....	....	....	....	9	1	1	2	2	....	....	....	....
	NHL Totals		**5**	**0**	**1**	**1**	**0**	**0**	**0**	**0**	**5**	**0.0**		**1**	**100.0**	**7:34**	....	....	....	....	....	....	....	....	....

USHL All-Rookie Team (2011) • USHL Second All-Star Team (2011) • USHL First All-Star Team (2012)

Signed as a free agent by **Worcester** (AHL), June 1, 2012. Signed as a free agent by **San Jose**, April 2, 2013. Signed as a free agent by **Dynamo Moscow**, July 17, 2015.

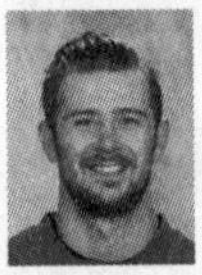

TATAR, Tomas

(TAH-tahr, TAW-mahsh) **DET**

Center. Shoots left. 5'10", 185 lbs. Born, Ilava, Czech., December 1, 1990. Detroit's 2nd pick, 60th overall, in 2009 NHL Draft.

Season	Club	League	GP	G	A	Pts	PIM	PP	SH	GW	S	S%	+/-	TF	F%	Min	GP	G	A	Pts	PIM	PP	SH	GW	Min
2004-05	Dubnica U18	Svk-U18	1	0	0	0	0	....	....	....	....	....	....	....	....	....	....	....	....	....	....	....	....	....	....
2005-06	Dubnica U18	Svk-U18	43	11	15	26	18	....	....	....	....	....	....	....	....	....	....	....	....	....	....	....	....	....	....
2006-07	Dubnica Jr.	Slovak-Jr.	6	3	0	3	2	....	....	....	....	....	....	....	....	....	....	....	....	....	....	....	....	....	....
	Dukla Trencin U18	Svk-U18	48	33	44	77	42	....	....	....	....	....	....	....	....	....	....	....	....	....	....	....	....	....	....
2007-08	Dukla Trencin U18	Svk-U18	4	9	4	13	0	....	....	....	....	....	....	....	....	....	....	....	....	....	....	....	....	....	....
	Dukla Trencin Jr.	Slovak-Jr.	42	41	35	76	32	....	....	....	....	....	....	....	....	....	....	....	....	....	....	....	....	....	....
2008-09	HC 07 Detva	Slovak-2	1	1	1	2	2	....	....	....	....	....	....	....	....	....	....	....	....	....	....	....	....	....	....
	HKm Zvolen	Slovakia	48	7	8	15	20	....	....	....	....	....	....	....	....	....	13	5	3	8	4	....	....	....	....
2009-10	Grand Rapids	AHL	58	16	16	32	12	....	....	....	....	....	....	....	....	....	....	....	....	....	....	....	....	....	....
2010-11	**Detroit**	**NHL**	**9**	**1**	**0**	**1**	**0**	**0**	**0**	**0**	**6**	**16.7**	**0**	**0**	**0.0**	**9:36**	....	....	....	....	....	....	....	....	....
	Grand Rapids	AHL	70	24	33	57	45	....	....	....	....	....	....	....	....	....	....	....	....	....	....	....	....	....	....
2011-12	Grand Rapids	AHL	76	24	34	58	45	....	....	....	....	....	....	....	....	....	....	....	....	....	....	....	....	....	....
2012-13	SHK 37 Piestany	Slovakia	8	5	5	10	6	....	....	....	....	....	....	....	....	....	....	....	....	....	....	....	....	....	....
	Grand Rapids	AHL	61	23	26	49	50	....	....	....	....	....	....	....	....	....	24	*16	5	21	23	....	....	....	....
	Detroit	**NHL**	**18**	**4**	**3**	**7**	**4**	**1**	**0**	**0**	**32**	**12.5**	**2**	**1**	**100.0**	**11:22**	....	....	....	....	....	....	....	....	....
2013-14	**Detroit**	**NHL**	**73**	**19**	**20**	**39**	**30**	**2**	**0**	**3**	**158**	**12.0**	**12**	**52**	**50.0**	**14:21**	**5**	**0**	**0**	**0**	**8**	**0**	**0**	**0**	**15:07**
	Slovakia	Olympics	4	1	1	2	2	....	....	....	....	....	....	....	....	....	....	....	....	....	....	....	....	....	....
2014-15	**Detroit**	**NHL**	**82**	**29**	**27**	**56**	**28**	**9**	**0**	**7**	**211**	**13.7**	**6**	**12**	**50.0**	**16:13**	**7**	**3**	**1**	**4**	**2**	**1**	**0**	**0**	**15:45**
2015-16	**Detroit**	**NHL**	**81**	**21**	**24**	**45**	**24**	**7**	**0**	**3**	**165**	**12.7**	**4**	**24**	**25.0**	**14:21**	**5**	**0**	**3**	**3**	**2**	**0**	**0**	**0**	**15:02**
2016-17	**Detroit**	**NHL**	**82**	**25**	**21**	**46**	**26**	**5**	**0**	**5**	**166**	**15.1**	**-8**	**13**	**61.5**	**17:17**	....	....	....	....	....	....	....	....	....
	NHL Totals		**345**	**99**	**95**	**194**	**112**	**24**	**0**	**18**	**738**	**13.4**		**102**	**46.1**	**15:13**	**17**	**3**	**4**	**7**	**12**	**1**	**0**	**0**	**15:21**

Jack A. Butterfield Trophy (AHL - Playoff MVP) (2013)

Signed as a free agent by **Piestany** (Slovakia), September 20, 2012.

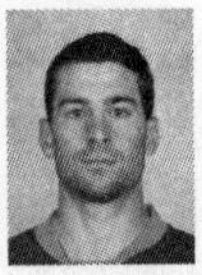

TAVARES, John

(tah-VAIR-ehs, JAWN) **NYI**

Center. Shoots left. 6'1", 211 lbs. Born, Mississauga, ON, September 20, 1990. NY Islanders' 1st pick, 1st overall, in 2009 NHL Draft.

Season	Club	League	GP	G	A	Pts	PIM	PP	SH	GW	S	S%	+/-	TF	F%	Min	GP	G	A	Pts	PIM	PP	SH	GW	Min
2004-05	Tor. Marlboros	GTHL	72	91	67	158	....	....	....	....	....	....	....	....	....	....	....	....	....	....	....	....	....	....	....
	Milton Icehawks	ON-Jr.A	20	13	15	28	10	....	....	....	....	....	....	....	....	....	....	....	....	....	....	....	....	....	....
2005-06	Oshawa Generals	OHL	65	45	32	77	72	....	....	....	....	....	....	....	....	....	....	....	....	....	....	....	....	....	....
2006-07	Oshawa Generals	OHL	67	*72	62	134	60	....	....	....	....	....	....	....	....	....	9	7	12	19	6	....	....	....	....
2007-08	Oshawa Generals	OHL	59	40	78	118	69	....	....	....	....	....	....	....	....	....	15	3	13	16	20	....	....	....	....
2008-09	Oshawa Generals	OHL	32	*26	28	*54	32	....	....	....	....	....	....	....	....	....	....	....	....	....	....	....	....	....	....
	London Knights	OHL	24	*32	18	*50	22	....	....	....	....	....	....	....	....	....	14	10	11	21	8	....	....	....	....
2009-10	**NY Islanders**	**NHL**	**82**	**24**	**30**	**54**	**22**	**11**	**0**	**2**	**186**	**12.9**	**-15**	**1129**	**47.5**	**18:00**	....	....	....	....	....	....	....	....	....
2010-11	**NY Islanders**	**NHL**	**79**	**29**	**38**	**67**	**53**	**9**	**0**	**4**	**243**	**11.9**	**-16**	**1319**	**52.5**	**19:15**	....	....	....	....	....	....	....	....	....
2011-12	**NY Islanders**	**NHL**	**82**	**31**	**50**	**81**	**26**	**7**	**0**	**8**	**286**	**10.8**	**-6**	**1586**	**51.3**	**20:34**	....	....	....	....	....	....	....	....	....

			Regular Season														Playoffs								
Season	Club	League	GP	G	A	Pts	PIM	PP	SH	GW	S	S%	+/-	TF	F%	Min	GP	G	A	Pts	PIM	PP	SH	GW	Min
2012-13	SC Bern	Swiss	28	17	25	42	28	....	....	....	....	....	....	....	....	....	....	....	....	....	....	....	....	....	....
	NY Islanders	NHL	48	28	19	47	18	9	0	5	162	17.3	–2	930	49.4	20:46	6	3	2	5	4	0	0	1	20:34
2013-14	NY Islanders	NHL	59	24	42	66	40	8	0	4	188	12.8	–6	1129	49.1	21:15	....	....	....	....	....	....	....	....	....
	Canada	Olympics	4	0	0	0	0	....	....	....	....	....	....	....	....	....	....	....	....	....	....	....	....	....	....
2014-15	NY Islanders	NHL	82	38	48	86	46	13	0	8	278	13.7	5	1442	52.2	20:40	7	2	4	6	2	0	0	1	19:19
2015-16	NY Islanders	NHL	78	33	37	70	38	7	0	5	250	13.2	6	1370	54.1	20:00	11	6	5	11	6	2	0	2	22:54
2016-17	NY Islanders	NHL	77	28	38	66	38	7	1	3	260	10.8	4	1628	50.6	20:25	....	....	....	....	....	....	....	....	....
	NHL Totals		587	235	302	537	281	71	1	39	1853	12.7		10533	51.0	20:02	24	11	11	22	12	2	0	4	21:16

OHL All-Rookie Team (2006) • Canadian Major Junior Rookie of the Year (2006) • OHL First All-Star Team (2007) • OHL Player of the Year (2007) • Canadian Major Junior First All-Star Team (2007, 2009) • Canadian Major Junior Player of the Year (2007) • OHL Second All-Star Team (2009) • NHL All-Rookie Team (2010) • NHL First All-Star Team (2015)

Played in NHL All-Star Game (2012, 2015, 2016, 2017)

Signed as a free agent by **Bern** (Swiss), September 28, 2012.

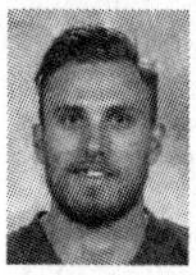

TENNYSON, Matt (TEHN-ihs-suhn, MAT) BUF

Defense. Shoots right. 6'2", 205 lbs. Born, Pleasanton, CA, April 23, 1990.

2007-08	Texas Tornado	NAHL	58	4	10	14	80	....	....	....	....	....	....	....	....	....	....	....	....	....	....	....	....	....	....
2008-09	Cedar Rapids	USHL	57	4	6	10	51	....	....	....	....	....	....	....	....	....	5	0	0	0	2	....	....	....	....
2009-10	Western Mich.	CCHA	34	2	7	9	30	....	....	....	....	....	....	....	....	....	....	....	....	....	....	....	....	....	....
2010-11	Western Mich.	CCHA	42	9	12	21	38	....	....	....	....	....	....	....	....	....	....	....	....	....	....	....	....	....	....
2011-12	Western Mich.	CCHA	41	11	13	24	28	....	....	....	....	....	....	....	....	....	....	....	....	....	....	....	....	....	....
	Worcester Sharks	AHL	7	1	1	2	0	....	....	....	....	....	....	....	....	....	....	....	....	....	....	....	....	....	....
2012-13	Worcester Sharks	AHL	60	5	22	27	44	....	....	....	....	....	....	....	....	....	....	....	....	....	....	....	....	....	....
	San Jose	NHL	4	0	2	2	2	0	0	0	8	0.0	2	0	0.0	15:43	....	....	....	....	....	....	....	....	....
2013-14	Worcester Sharks	AHL	54	7	14	21	33	....	....	....	....	....	....	....	....	....	....	....	....	....	....	....	....	....	....
2014-15	San Jose	NHL	27	2	6	8	16	1	0	0	37	5.4	0	0	0.0	17:34	....	....	....	....	....	....	....	....	....
	Worcester Sharks	AHL	43	4	11	15	30	....	....	....	....	....	....	....	....	....	4	0	0	0	0	....	....	....	....
2015-16	San Jose	NHL	29	1	3	4	0	1	0	0	23	4.3	1	0	0.0	10:31	....	....	....	....	....	....	....	....	....
	San Jose	AHL	5	0	0	0	0	....	....	....	....	....	....	....	....	....	1	0	0	0	2	....	....	....	....
2016-17	Carolina	NHL	45	0	6	6	6	0	0	0	36	0.0	–13	0	0.0	13:17	....	....	....	....	....	....	....	....	....
	Charlotte	AHL	9	3	4	7	5	....	....	....	....	....	....	....	....	....	....	....	....	....	....	....	....	....	....
	NHL Totals		105	3	17	20	24	2	0	0	104	2.9		0	0.0	13:43	....	....	....	....	....	....	....	....	....

CCHA Second All-Star Team (2012)

Signed as a free agent by **San Jose**, March 29, 2012. • Missed majority of of 2015-16 due to head injury at St. Louis, February 22, 2016 and as a healthy reserve. Signed as a free agent by **Carolina**, July 3, 2016. Signed as a free agent by **Buffalo**, July 1, 2017.

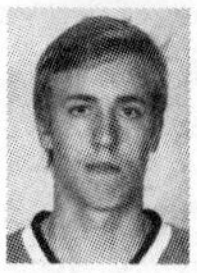

TERAVAINEN, Teuvo (tair-uh-VIGH-nehn, TAY-voh) CAR

Center. Shoots left. 5'11", 178 lbs. Born, Helsinki, Finland, September 11, 1994. Chicago's 1st pick, 18th overall, in 2012 NHL Draft.

2009-10	Jokerit U18	Fin-U18	29	16	14	30	6	....	....	....	....	....	....	....	....	....	4	0	4	4	0	....	....	....	....
2010-11	Jokerit U18	Fin-U18	4	1	3	4	2	....	....	....	....	....	....	....	....	....	1	0	1	1	25	....	....	....	....
	Jokerit Helsinki Jr.	Fin-Jr.	26	3	17	20	8	....	....	....	....	....	....	....	....	....	8	1	4	5	4	....	....	....	....
2011-12	Jokerit Helsinki Jr.	Fin-Jr.	11	12	8	20	4	....	....	....	....	....	....	....	....	....	2	1	1	2	0	....	....	....	....
	Kiekko-Vantaa	Finland-2	3	1	2	3	0	....	....	....	....	....	....	....	....	....	....	....	....	....	....	....	....	....	....
	Jokerit Helsinki	Finland	40	11	7	18	6	....	....	....	....	....	....	....	....	....	9	2	4	6	0	....	....	....	....
2012-13	Kiekko-Vantaa	Finland-2	1	0	1	1	0	....	....	....	....	....	....	....	....	....	....	....	....	....	....	....	....	....	....
	Jokerit Helsinki	Finland	44	13	18	31	6	....	....	....	....	....	....	....	....	....	6	1	1	2	0	....	....	....	....
2013-14	Jokerit Helsinki	Finland	49	9	35	44	12	....	....	....	....	....	....	....	....	....	2	0	0	0	0	....	....	....	....
	Chicago	NHL	3	0	0	0	0	0	0	0	4	0.0	0	25	52.0	14:06	....	....	....	....	....	....	....	....	....
	Rockford IceHogs	AHL	5	2	0	2	2	....	....	....	....	....	....	....	....	....	....	....	....	....	....	....	....	....	....
2014-15♦	Chicago	NHL	34	4	5	9	2	0	0	1	66	6.1	4	62	46.8	12:47	18	4	6	10	0	1	0	1	13:28
	Rockford IceHogs	AHL	39	6	19	25	6	....	....	....	....	....	....	....	....	....	....	....	....	....	....	....	....	....	....
2015-16	Chicago	NHL	78	13	22	35	20	2	0	3	136	9.6	–2	309	40.5	15:21	7	0	1	1	0	0	0	0	12:05
2016-17	Carolina	NHL	81	15	27	42	16	5	0	2	169	8.9	–6	413	46.7	16:14	....	....	....	....	....	....	....	....	....
	NHL Totals		196	32	54	86	38	7	0	6	375	8.5		809	44.5	15:15	25	4	7	11	0	1	0	1	13:05

Traded to **Carolina** by **Chicago** with Bryan Bickell for NY Rangers' 2nd round pick (previously acquired, Chicago selected Artur Kayumov) in 2016 NHL Draft and Chicago's 3rd round pick (previously acquired, later traded to Detroit – Detroit selected Keith Petruzzelli) in 2017 NHL Draft, June 15, 2016.

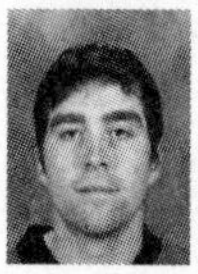

TERRY, Chris (TAIR-ee, KRIHS) MTL

Left wing. Shoots left. 5'10", 197 lbs. Born, Brampton, ON, April 7, 1989. Carolina's 4th pick, 132nd overall, in 2007 NHL Draft.

2003-04	Markham	GTHL	66	39	50	89	....	....	....	....	....	....	....	....	....	....	....	....	....	....	....	....	....	....	....
2004-05	Markham	GTHL	60	42	53	95	113	....	....	....	....	....	....	....	....	....	9	0	9	9	14	....	....	....	....
2005-06	Plymouth Whalers	OHL	64	9	19	28	72	....	....	....	....	....	....	....	....	....	11	3	2	5	4	....	....	....	....
2006-07	Plymouth Whalers	OHL	68	22	44	66	98	....	....	....	....	....	....	....	....	....	20	8	10	18	21	....	....	....	....
2007-08	Plymouth Whalers	OHL	68	44	57	101	107	....	....	....	....	....	....	....	....	....	4	4	3	7	6	....	....	....	....
	Albany River Rats	AHL	1	0	0	0	0	....	....	....	....	....	....	....	....	....	....	....	....	....	....	....	....	....	....
2008-09	Plymouth Whalers	OHL	53	39	55	94	75	....	....	....	....	....	....	....	....	....	11	7	9	16	18	....	....	....	....
2009-10	Albany River Rats	AHL	80	17	30	47	47	....	....	....	....	....	....	....	....	....	8	2	4	6	0	....	....	....	....
2010-11	Charlotte	AHL	80	34	30	64	52	....	....	....	....	....	....	....	....	....	16	6	3	9	14	....	....	....	....
2011-12	Charlotte	AHL	74	16	43	59	67	....	....	....	....	....	....	....	....	....	....	....	....	....	....	....	....	....	....
2012-13	Charlotte	AHL	70	25	35	60	40	....	....	....	....	....	....	....	....	....	5	2	2	4	8	....	....	....	....
	Carolina	NHL	3	1	0	1	0	0	0	1	1	100.0	0	1	100.0	9:36	....	....	....	....	....	....	....	....	....
2013-14	Carolina	NHL	10	0	2	2	0	0	0	0	13	0.0	–4	0	0.0	12:05	....	....	....	....	....	....	....	....	....
	Charlotte	AHL	70	28	41	69	62	....	....	....	....	....	....	....	....	....	....	....	....	....	....	....	....	....	....
2014-15	Carolina	NHL	57	11	9	20	14	3	0	0	71	15.5	–4	11	54.6	12:43	....	....	....	....	....	....	....	....	....
	Charlotte	AHL	5	1	1	2	4	....	....	....	....	....	....	....	....	....	....	....	....	....	....	....	....	....	....
2015-16	Carolina	NHL	68	8	3	11	16	0	0	0	78	10.3	–12	9	11.1	11:16	....	....	....	....	....	....	....	....	....
2016-17	Montreal	NHL	14	2	2	4	4	0	0	0	15	13.3	–1	2	50.0	9:53	....	....	....	....	....	....	....	....	....
	St. John's IceCaps	AHL	58	30	38	68	36	....	....	....	....	....	....	....	....	....	4	1	0	1	4	....	....	....	....
	NHL Totals		152	22	16	38	34	3	0	1	178	12.4		23	39.1	11:43	....	....	....	....	....	....	....	....	....

AHL Second All-Star Team (2017)

Signed as a free agent by **Montreal**, July 2, 2016.

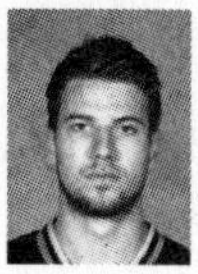

THEODORE, Shea (THEE-oh-dohr, SHAY) VGK

Defense. Shoots left. 6'2", 195 lbs. Born, Langley, BC, August 3, 1995. Anaheim's 1st pick, 26th overall, in 2013 NHL Draft.

2010-11	Fraser Valley	BCMML	35	5	24	29	28	....	....	....	....	....	....	....	....	....	....	....	....	....	....	....	....	....	....
	Seattle	WHL	4	0	0	0	2	....	....	....	....	....	....	....	....	....	....	....	....	....	....	....	....	....	....
2011-12	Seattle	WHL	69	4	31	35	30	....	....	....	....	....	....	....	....	....	....	....	....	....	....	....	....	....	....
2012-13	Seattle	WHL	71	19	31	50	32	....	....	....	....	....	....	....	....	....	7	0	2	2	4	....	....	....	....
2013-14	Seattle	WHL	70	22	57	79	39	....	....	....	....	....	....	....	....	....	9	0	5	5	4	....	....	....	....
	Norfolk Admirals	AHL	4	0	0	0	0	....	....	....	....	....	....	....	....	....	4	1	2	3	2	....	....	....	....
2014-15	Seattle	WHL	43	13	35	48	16	....	....	....	....	....	....	....	....	....	6	3	6	9	0	....	....	....	....
	Norfolk Admirals	AHL	9	4	7	11	2	....	....	....	....	....	....	....	....	....	....	....	....	....	....	....	....	....	....
2015-16	Anaheim	NHL	19	3	5	8	2	2	0	1	28	10.7	7	0	0.0	19:07	6	0	0	0	0	0	0	0	14:18
	San Diego Gulls	AHL	50	9	28	37	34	....	....	....	....	....	....	....	....	....	7	2	3	5	4	....	....	....	....
2016-17	Anaheim	NHL	34	2	7	9	28	1	0	1	60	3.3	–6	0	0.0	17:19	14	2	6	8	4	0	0	0	17:25
	San Diego Gulls	AHL	26	5	15	20	12	....	....	....	....	....	....	....	....	....	....	....	....	....	....	....	....	....	....
	NHL Totals		53	5	12	17	30	3	0	2	88	5.7		0	0.0	17:57	20	2	6	8	4	0	0	0	16:29

WHL West First All-Star Team (2014, 2015)

Traded to **Vegas** by **Anaheim** for Expansion Draft considerations, June 21, 2017.

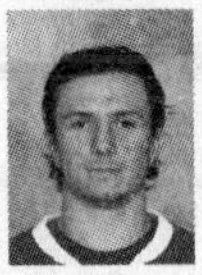

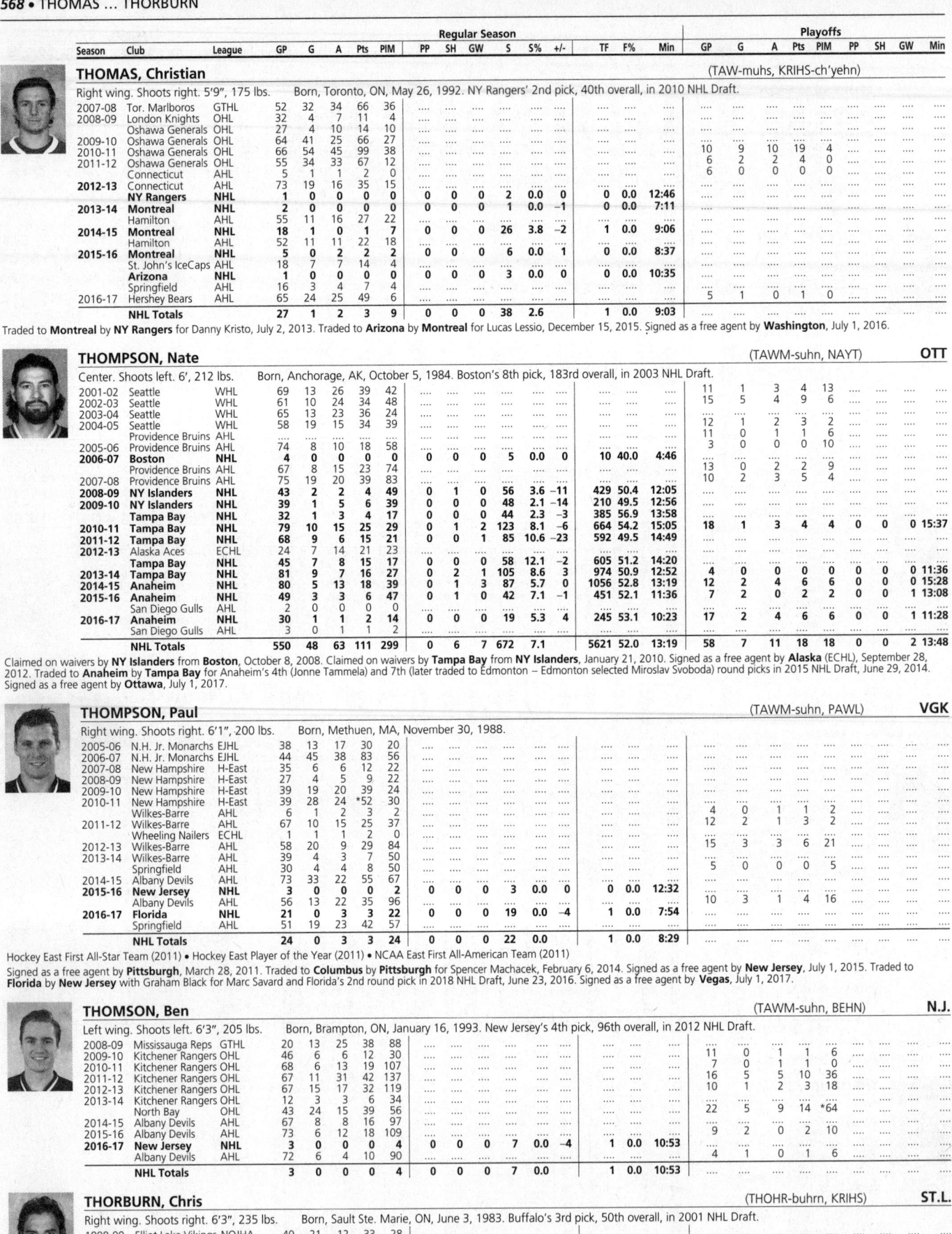

THOMAS, Christian

(TAW-muhs, KRIHS-ch'yehn)

Right wing. Shoots right. 5'9", 175 lbs. Born, Toronto, ON, May 26, 1992. NY Rangers' 2nd pick, 40th overall, in 2010 NHL Draft.

			Regular Season														Playoffs								
Season	Club	League	GP	G	A	Pts	PIM	PP	SH	GW	S	S%	+/-	TF	F%	Min	GP	G	A	Pts	PIM	PP	SH	GW	Min
2007-08	Tor. Marlboros	GTHL	52	32	34	66	36	....	....	....	....	....	....	....	....	....	....	....	....	....	....	....	....	....	....
2008-09	London Knights	OHL	32	4	7	11	4	....	....	....	....	....	....	....	....	....	....	....	....	....	....	....	....	....	....
	Oshawa Generals	OHL	27	4	10	14	10	....	....	....	....	....	....	....	....	....	....	....	....	....	....	....	....	....	....
2009-10	Oshawa Generals	OHL	64	41	25	66	27	....	....	....	....	....	....	....	....	....	....	....	....	....	....	....	....	....	....
2010-11	Oshawa Generals	OHL	66	54	45	99	38	....	....	....	....	....	....	....	....	....	10	9	10	19	4	....	....	....	....
2011-12	Oshawa Generals	OHL	55	34	33	67	12	....	....	....	....	....	....	....	....	....	6	2	2	4	0	....	....	....	....
	Connecticut	AHL	5	1	1	2	0	....	....	....	....	....	....	....	....	....	6	0	0	0	0	....	....	....	....
2012-13	Connecticut	AHL	73	19	16	35	15	....	....	....	....	....	....	....	....	....	....	....	....	....	....	....	....	....	....
	NY Rangers	**NHL**	**1**	**0**	**0**	**0**	**0**	**0**	**0**	**0**	**2**	**0.0**	**0**	**0**	**0.0**	**12:46**	....	....	....	....	....	....	....	....	....
2013-14	**Montreal**	**NHL**	**2**	**0**	**0**	**0**	**0**	**0**	**0**	**0**	**1**	**0.0**	**-1**	**0**	**0.0**	**7:11**	....	....	....	....	....	....	....	....	....
	Hamilton	AHL	55	11	16	27	22	....	....	....	....	....	....	....	....	....	....	....	....	....	....	....	....	....	....
2014-15	**Montreal**	**NHL**	**18**	**1**	**0**	**1**	**7**	**0**	**0**	**0**	**26**	**3.8**	**-2**	**1**	**0.0**	**9:06**	....	....	....	....	....	....	....	....	....
	Hamilton	AHL	52	11	11	22	18	....	....	....	....	....	....	....	....	....	....	....	....	....	....	....	....	....	....
2015-16	**Montreal**	**NHL**	**5**	**0**	**2**	**2**	**2**	**0**	**0**	**0**	**6**	**0.0**	**1**	**0**	**0.0**	**8:37**	....	....	....	....	....	....	....	....	....
	St. John's IceCaps	AHL	18	7	7	14	4	....	....	....	....	....	....	....	....	....	....	....	....	....	....	....	....	....	....
	Arizona	**NHL**	**1**	**0**	**0**	**0**	**0**	**0**	**0**	**0**	**3**	**0.0**	**0**	**0**	**0.0**	**10:35**	....	....	....	....	....	....	....	....	....
	Springfield	AHL	16	3	4	7	4	....	....	....	....	....	....	....	....	....	....	....	....	....	....	....	....	....	....
2016-17	Hershey Bears	AHL	65	24	25	49	6	....	....	....	....	....	....	....	....	....	5	1	0	1	0	....	....	....	....
	NHL Totals		**27**	**1**	**2**	**3**	**9**	**0**	**0**	**0**	**38**	**2.6**		**1**	**0.0**	**9:03**	....	....	....	....	....	....	....	....	....

Traded to **Montreal** by **NY Rangers** for Danny Kristo, July 2, 2013. Traded to **Arizona** by **Montreal** for Lucas Lessio, December 15, 2015. Signed as a free agent by **Washington**, July 1, 2016.

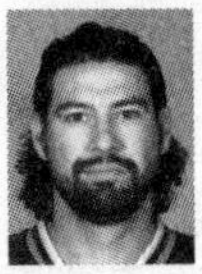

THOMPSON, Nate

(TAWM-suhn, NAYT) **OTT**

Center. Shoots left. 6', 212 lbs. Born, Anchorage, AK, October 5, 1984. Boston's 8th pick, 183rd overall, in 2003 NHL Draft.

Season	Club	League	GP	G	A	Pts	PIM	PP	SH	GW	S	S%	+/-	TF	F%	Min	GP	G	A	Pts	PIM	PP	SH	GW	Min
2001-02	Seattle	WHL	69	13	26	39	42	....	....	....	....	....	....	....	....	....	11	1	3	4	13	....	....	....	....
2002-03	Seattle	WHL	61	10	24	34	48	....	....	....	....	....	....	....	....	....	15	5	4	9	6	....	....	....	....
2003-04	Seattle	WHL	65	13	23	36	24	....	....	....	....	....	....	....	....	....	....	....	....	....	....	....	....	....	....
2004-05	Seattle	WHL	58	19	15	34	39	....	....	....	....	....	....	....	....	....	12	1	2	3	2	....	....	....	....
	Providence Bruins	AHL	....	....	....	....	....	....	....	....	....	....	....	....	....	....	11	0	1	1	6	....	....	....	....
2005-06	Providence Bruins	AHL	74	8	10	18	58	....	....	....	....	....	....	....	....	....	3	0	0	0	10	....	....	....	....
2006-07	**Boston**	**NHL**	**4**	**0**	**0**	**0**	**0**	**0**	**0**	**0**	**5**	**0.0**	**0**	**10**	**40.0**	**4:46**	....	....	....	....	....	....	....	....	....
	Providence Bruins	AHL	67	8	15	23	74	....	....	....	....	....	....	....	....	....	13	0	2	2	9	....	....	....	....
2007-08	Providence Bruins	AHL	75	19	20	39	83	....	....	....	....	....	....	....	....	....	10	2	3	5	4	....	....	....	....
2008-09	**NY Islanders**	**NHL**	**43**	**2**	**2**	**4**	**49**	**0**	**1**	**0**	**56**	**3.6**	**-11**	**429**	**50.4**	**12:05**	....	....	....	....	....	....	....	....	....
2009-10	**NY Islanders**	**NHL**	**39**	**1**	**5**	**6**	**39**	**0**	**0**	**0**	**48**	**2.1**	**-14**	**210**	**49.5**	**12:56**	....	....	....	....	....	....	....	....	....
	Tampa Bay	**NHL**	**32**	**1**	**3**	**4**	**17**	**0**	**0**	**0**	**44**	**2.3**	**-3**	**385**	**56.9**	**13:58**	....	....	....	....	....	....	....	....	....
2010-11	**Tampa Bay**	**NHL**	**79**	**10**	**15**	**25**	**29**	**0**	**1**	**2**	**123**	**8.1**	**-6**	**664**	**54.2**	**15:05**	**18**	**1**	**3**	**4**	**4**	**0**	**0**	**0**	**15:37**
2011-12	**Tampa Bay**	**NHL**	**68**	**9**	**6**	**15**	**21**	**0**	**0**	**1**	**85**	**10.6**	**-23**	**592**	**49.5**	**14:49**	....	....	....	....	....	....	....	....	....
2012-13	Alaska Aces	ECHL	24	7	14	21	23	....	....	....	....	....	....	....	....	....	....	....	....	....	....	....	....	....	....
	Tampa Bay	**NHL**	**45**	**7**	**8**	**15**	**17**	**0**	**0**	**0**	**58**	**12.1**	**-2**	**605**	**51.2**	**14:20**	....	....	....	....	....	....	....	....	....
2013-14	**Tampa Bay**	**NHL**	**81**	**9**	**7**	**16**	**27**	**0**	**2**	**1**	**105**	**8.6**	**3**	**974**	**50.9**	**12:52**	**4**	**0**	**0**	**0**	**0**	**0**	**0**	**0**	**11:36**
2014-15	**Anaheim**	**NHL**	**80**	**5**	**13**	**18**	**39**	**0**	**1**	**3**	**87**	**5.7**	**0**	**1056**	**52.8**	**13:19**	**12**	**2**	**4**	**6**	**6**	**0**	**0**	**0**	**15:28**
2015-16	**Anaheim**	**NHL**	**49**	**3**	**3**	**6**	**47**	**0**	**1**	**0**	**42**	**7.1**	**-1**	**451**	**52.1**	**11:36**	**7**	**2**	**0**	**2**	**2**	**0**	**0**	**1**	**13:08**
	San Diego Gulls	AHL	2	0	0	0	0	....	....	....	....	....	....	....	....	....	....	....	....	....	....	....	....	....	....
2016-17	**Anaheim**	**NHL**	**30**	**1**	**1**	**2**	**14**	**0**	**0**	**0**	**19**	**5.3**	**4**	**245**	**53.1**	**10:23**	**17**	**2**	**4**	**6**	**6**	**0**	**0**	**1**	**11:28**
	San Diego Gulls	AHL	3	0	1	1	2	....	....	....	....	....	....	....	....	....	....	....	....	....	....	....	....	....	....
	NHL Totals		**550**	**48**	**63**	**111**	**299**	**0**	**6**	**7**	**672**	**7.1**		**5621**	**52.0**	**13:19**	**58**	**7**	**11**	**18**	**18**	**0**	**0**	**2**	**13:48**

Claimed on waivers by **NY Islanders** from **Boston**, October 8, 2008. Claimed on waivers by **Tampa Bay** from **NY Islanders**, January 21, 2010. Signed as a free agent by **Alaska** (ECHL), September 28, 2012. Traded to **Anaheim** by **Tampa Bay** for Anaheim's 4th (Jonne Tammela) and 7th (later traded to Edmonton – Edmonton selected Miroslav Svoboda) round picks in 2015 NHL Draft, June 29, 2014. Signed as a free agent by **Ottawa**, July 1, 2017.

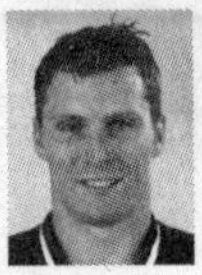

THOMPSON, Paul

(TAWM-suhn, PAWL) **VGK**

Right wing. Shoots right. 6'1", 200 lbs. Born, Methuen, MA, November 30, 1988.

Season	Club	League	GP	G	A	Pts	PIM	PP	SH	GW	S	S%	+/-	TF	F%	Min	GP	G	A	Pts	PIM	PP	SH	GW	Min
2005-06	N.H. Jr. Monarchs	EJHL	38	13	17	30	20	....	....	....	....	....	....	....	....	....	....	....	....	....	....	....	....	....	....
2006-07	N.H. Jr. Monarchs	EJHL	44	45	38	83	56	....	....	....	....	....	....	....	....	....	....	....	....	....	....	....	....	....	....
2007-08	New Hampshire	H-East	35	6	6	12	22	....	....	....	....	....	....	....	....	....	....	....	....	....	....	....	....	....	....
2008-09	New Hampshire	H-East	27	4	5	9	22	....	....	....	....	....	....	....	....	....	....	....	....	....	....	....	....	....	....
2009-10	New Hampshire	H-East	39	19	20	39	24	....	....	....	....	....	....	....	....	....	....	....	....	....	....	....	....	....	....
2010-11	New Hampshire	H-East	39	28	24	*52	30	....	....	....	....	....	....	....	....	....	....	....	....	....	....	....	....	....	....
	Wilkes-Barre	AHL	6	1	2	3	2	....	....	....	....	....	....	....	....	....	4	0	1	1	2	....	....	....	....
2011-12	Wilkes-Barre	AHL	67	10	15	25	37	....	....	....	....	....	....	....	....	....	12	2	1	3	2	....	....	....	....
	Wheeling Nailers	ECHL	1	1	1	2	0	....	....	....	....	....	....	....	....	....	....	....	....	....	....	....	....	....	....
2012-13	Wilkes-Barre	AHL	58	20	9	29	84	....	....	....	....	....	....	....	....	....	15	3	3	6	21	....	....	....	....
2013-14	Wilkes-Barre	AHL	39	4	3	7	50	....	....	....	....	....	....	....	....	....	....	....	....	....	....	....	....	....	....
	Springfield	AHL	30	4	4	8	50	....	....	....	....	....	....	....	....	....	5	0	0	0	5	....	....	....	....
2014-15	Albany Devils	AHL	73	33	22	55	67	....	....	....	....	....	....	....	....	....	....	....	....	....	....	....	....	....	....
2015-16	**New Jersey**	**NHL**	**3**	**0**	**0**	**0**	**2**	**0**	**0**	**0**	**3**	**0.0**	**0**	**0**	**0.0**	**12:32**	....	....	....	....	....	....	....	....	....
	Albany Devils	AHL	56	13	22	35	96	....	....	....	....	....	....	....	....	....	10	3	1	4	16	....	....	....	....
2016-17	**Florida**	**NHL**	**21**	**0**	**3**	**3**	**22**	**0**	**0**	**0**	**19**	**0.0**	**-4**	**1**	**0.0**	**7:54**	....	....	....	....	....	....	....	....	....
	Springfield	AHL	51	19	23	42	57	....	....	....	....	....	....	....	....	....	....	....	....	....	....	....	....	....	....
	NHL Totals		**24**	**0**	**3**	**3**	**24**	**0**	**0**	**0**	**22**	**0.0**		**1**	**0.0**	**8:29**	....	....	....	....	....	....	....	....	....

Hockey East First All-Star Team (2011) • Hockey East Player of the Year (2011) • NCAA East First All-American Team (2011)

Signed as a free agent by **Pittsburgh**, March 28, 2011. Traded to **Columbus** by **Pittsburgh** for Spencer Machacek, February 6, 2014. Signed as a free agent by **New Jersey**, July 1, 2015. Traded to **Florida** by **New Jersey** with Graham Black for Marc Savard and Florida's 2nd round pick in 2018 NHL Draft, June 23, 2016. Signed as a free agent by **Vegas**, July 1, 2017.

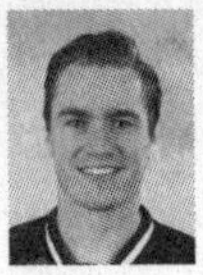

THOMSON, Ben

(TAWM-suhn, BEHN) **N.J.**

Left wing. Shoots left. 6'3", 205 lbs. Born, Brampton, ON, January 16, 1993. New Jersey's 4th pick, 96th overall, in 2012 NHL Draft.

Season	Club	League	GP	G	A	Pts	PIM	PP	SH	GW	S	S%	+/-	TF	F%	Min	GP	G	A	Pts	PIM	PP	SH	GW	Min
2008-09	Mississauga Reps	GTHL	20	13	25	38	88	....	....	....	....	....	....	....	....	....	....	....	....	....	....	....	....	....	....
2009-10	Kitchener Rangers	OHL	46	6	6	12	30	....	....	....	....	....	....	....	....	....	11	0	1	1	6	....	....	....	....
2010-11	Kitchener Rangers	OHL	68	6	13	19	107	....	....	....	....	....	....	....	....	....	7	0	1	1	0	....	....	....	....
2011-12	Kitchener Rangers	OHL	67	11	31	42	137	....	....	....	....	....	....	....	....	....	16	5	5	10	36	....	....	....	....
2012-13	Kitchener Rangers	OHL	67	15	17	32	119	....	....	....	....	....	....	....	....	....	10	1	2	3	18	....	....	....	....
2013-14	Kitchener Rangers	OHL	12	3	3	6	34	....	....	....	....	....	....	....	....	....	....	....	....	....	....	....	....	....	....
	North Bay	OHL	43	24	15	39	56	....	....	....	....	....	....	....	....	....	22	5	9	14	*64	....	....	....	....
2014-15	Albany Devils	AHL	67	8	8	16	97	....	....	....	....	....	....	....	....	....	....	....	....	....	....	....	....	....	....
2015-16	Albany Devils	AHL	73	6	12	18	109	....	....	....	....	....	....	....	....	....	9	2	0	2	10	....	....	....	....
2016-17	**New Jersey**	**NHL**	**3**	**0**	**0**	**0**	**4**	**0**	**0**	**0**	**7**	**0.0**	**-4**	**1**	**0.0**	**10:53**	....	....	....	....	....	....	....	....	....
	Albany Devils	AHL	72	6	4	10	90	....	....	....	....	....	....	....	....	....	4	1	0	1	6	....	....	....	....
	NHL Totals		**3**	**0**	**0**	**0**	**4**	**0**	**0**	**0**	**7**	**0.0**		**1**	**0.0**	**10:53**	....	....	....	....	....	....	....	....	....

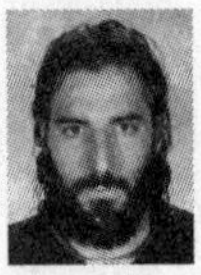

THORBURN, Chris

(THOHR-buhrn, KRIHS) **ST.L.**

Right wing. Shoots right. 6'3", 235 lbs. Born, Sault Ste. Marie, ON, June 3, 1983. Buffalo's 3rd pick, 50th overall, in 2001 NHL Draft.

Season	Club	League	GP	G	A	Pts	PIM	PP	SH	GW	S	S%	+/-	TF	F%	Min	GP	G	A	Pts	PIM	PP	SH	GW	Min
1998-99	Elliot Lake Vikings	NOJHA	40	21	12	33	28	....	....	....	....	....	....	....	....	....	....	....	....	....	....	....	....	....	....
99-2000	North Bay	OHL	56	12	8	20	33	....	....	....	....	....	....	....	....	....	6	0	2	2	0	....	....	....	....
2000-01	North Bay	OHL	66	22	32	54	64	....	....	....	....	....	....	....	....	....	4	0	1	1	9	....	....	....	....
2001-02	North Bay	OHL	67	15	43	58	112	....	....	....	....	....	....	....	....	....	5	1	2	3	8	....	....	....	....
2002-03	Saginaw Spirit	OHL	37	19	19	38	68	....	....	....	....	....	....	....	....	....	....	....	....	....	....	....	....	....	....
	Plymouth Whalers	OHL	27	11	22	33	56	....	....	....	....	....	....	....	....	....	18	11	9	20	10	....	....	....	....
2003-04	Rochester	AHL	58	6	16	22	77	....	....	....	....	....	....	....	....	....	16	3	2	5	18	....	....	....	....
2004-05	Rochester	AHL	73	12	17	29	185	....	....	....	....	....	....	....	....	....	4	0	1	1	2	....	....	....	....
2005-06	**Buffalo**	**NHL**	**2**	**0**	**1**	**1**	**7**	**0**	**0**	**0**	**1**	**0.0**	**-1**	**1**	**0.0**	**6:52**	....	....	....	....	....	....	....	....	....
	Rochester	AHL	77	23	27	50	134	....	....	....	....	....	....	....	....	....	....	....	....	....	....	....	....	....	....

			Regular Season														Playoffs								
Season	Club	League	GP	G	A	Pts	PIM	PP	SH	GW	S	S%	+/-	TF	F%	Min	GP	G	A	Pts	PIM	PP	SH	GW	Min
2006-07	Pittsburgh	NHL	39	3	2	5	69	0	0	1	40	7.5	1	8	25.0	7:54	....	....	....	....	....	....	....	....	....
	Wilkes-Barre	AHL	3	0	1	1	2	....	....	....	....	....	....	....	....	....	....	....	....	....	....	....	....	....	....
2007-08	Atlanta	NHL	73	5	13	18	92	0	0	1	72	6.9	–4	20	60.0	8:56	....	....	....	....	....	....	....	....	....
2008-09	Atlanta	NHL	82	7	8	15	104	0	0	1	85	8.2	–10	37	40.5	9:35	....	....	....	....	....	....	....	....	....
2009-10	Atlanta	NHL	76	4	9	13	89	0	3	0	63	6.3	6	29	55.2	9:59	....	....	....	....	....	....	....	....	....
2010-11	Atlanta	NHL	82	9	10	19	77	2	0	0	114	7.9	–4	251	49.8	13:48	....	....	....	....	....	....	....	....	....
2011-12	Winnipeg	NHL	72	4	7	11	83	0	0	0	69	5.8	–6	67	58.2	10:11	....	....	....	....	....	....	....	....	....
2012-13	Winnipeg	NHL	42	2	2	4	70	0	0	0	13	15.4	–5	46	43.5	6:19	....	....	....	....	....	....	....	....	....
2013-14	Winnipeg	NHL	55	2	9	11	65	0	0	1	26	7.7	0	33	60.6	8:57	....	....	....	....	....	....	....	....	....
2014-15	Winnipeg	NHL	81	7	7	14	76	0	0	2	67	10.4	–5	56	64.3	8:05	4	0	0	0	0	0	0	0	7:29
2015-16	Winnipeg	NHL	82	6	6	12	81	0	1	2	70	8.6	–1	122	55.7	10:07	....	....	....	....	....	....	....	....	....
2016-17	Winnipeg	NHL	64	3	1	4	95	0	1	0	36	8.3	–7	26	50.0	6:59	....	....	....	....	....	....	....	....	....
	NHL Totals		750	52	75	127	908	2	5	8	656	7.9		696	52.6	9:26	4	0	0	0	0	0	0	0	7:29

Claimed on waivers by **Pittsburgh** from **Buffalo**, October 3, 2006. Traded to **Atlanta** by **Pittsburgh** for NY Rangers' 3rd round pick (previously acquired, Pittsburgh selected Robert Bortuzzo) in 2007 NHL Draft, June 22, 2007. • Transferred to **Winnipeg** after **Atlanta** franchise relocated, June 21, 2011. Claimed by **Vegas** from **Winnipeg** in Expansion Draft, June 21, 2017. Signed as a free agent by **St. Louis**, July 1, 2017.

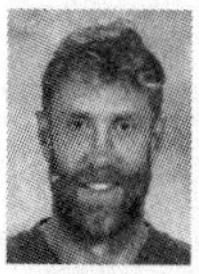

THORNTON, Joe

(THOHRN-tuhn, JOH) **S.J.**

Center. Shoots left. 6'4", 220 lbs. Born, London, ON, July 2, 1979. Boston's 1st pick, 1st overall, in 1997 NHL Draft.

Season	Club	League	GP	G	A	Pts	PIM	PP	SH	GW	S	S%	+/-	TF	F%	Min	GP	G	A	Pts	PIM	PP	SH	GW	Min
1993-94	Elgin-Mid. Chiefs	Minor-ON	67	*83	*85	*168	45	....	....	....	....	....	....	....	....	....	....	....	....	....	....	....	....	....	....
	St. Thomas Stars	ON-Jr.B	6	2	6	8	2	....	....	....	....	....	....	....	....	....	....	....	....	....	....	....	....	....	....
1994-95	St. Thomas Stars	ON-Jr.B	50	40	64	104	53	....	....	....	....	....	....	....	....	....	....	....	....	....	....	....	....	....	....
1995-96	Sault Ste. Marie	OHL	66	30	46	76	53	....	....	....	....	....	....	....	....	....	4	1	1	2	11	....	....	....	....
1996-97	Sault Ste. Marie	OHL	59	41	81	122	123	....	....	....	....	....	....	....	....	....	11	11	8	19	24	....	....	....	....
1997-98	Boston	NHL	55	3	4	7	19	0	0	1	33	9.1	–6	....	....	....	6	0	0	0	9	0	0	0	....
1998-99	Boston	NHL	81	16	25	41	69	7	0	1	128	12.5	3	1073	48.7	15:21	11	3	6	9	4	2	0	2	19:52
99-2000	Boston	NHL	81	23	37	60	82	5	0	3	171	13.5	–5	1861	49.5	21:18	....	....	....	....	....	....	....	....	....
2000-01	Boston	NHL	72	37	34	71	107	19	1	5	181	20.4	–4	1651	52.1	21:45	....	....	....	....	....	....	....	....	....
2001-02	Boston	NHL	66	22	46	68	127	6	0	5	152	14.5	7	1341	49.1	19:59	6	2	4	6	10	0	0	0	21:09
2002-03	Boston	NHL	77	36	65	101	109	12	2	4	196	18.4	12	1766	49.5	22:33	5	1	2	3	4	1	0	0	20:13
2003-04	Boston	NHL	77	23	50	73	98	4	0	6	187	12.3	18	1671	56.3	21:38	7	0	0	0	14	0	0	0	21:30
2004-05	HC Davos	Swiss	40	10	44	54	80	....	....	....	....	....	....	....	....	....	14	4	*20	*24	29	....	....	....	....
2005-06	Boston	NHL	23	9	*24	*33	6	3	0	2	60	15.0	0	511	52.3	21:33	....	....	....	....	....	....	....	....	....
	San Jose	NHL	58	20	*72	*92	55	8	0	4	135	14.8	31	1287	50.9	21:15	11	2	7	9	12	1	0	1	25:09
	Canada	Olympics	6	1	2	3	0	....	....	....	....	....	....	....	....	....	....	....	....	....	....	....	....	....	....
2006-07	San Jose	NHL	82	22	*92	114	44	10	0	5	213	10.3	24	1522	51.1	20:19	11	1	10	11	10	0	0	0	22:00
2007-08	San Jose	NHL	82	29	*67	96	59	11	0	5	178	16.3	18	1485	52.9	21:24	13	2	8	10	2	1	0	1	24:42
2008-09	San Jose	NHL	82	25	61	86	56	11	0	3	139	18.0	16	1295	55.4	19:28	6	1	4	5	5	1	0	0	19:14
2009-10	San Jose	NHL	79	20	69	89	54	4	1	2	141	14.2	17	1228	53.9	19:51	15	3	9	12	18	1	0	1	21:20
	Canada	Olympics	7	1	1	2	0	....	....	....	....	....	....	....	....	....	....	....	....	....	....	....	....	....	....
2010-11	San Jose	NHL	80	21	49	70	47	9	2	3	149	14.1	4	1240	54.4	19:52	18	3	14	17	16	0	0	2	22:15
2011-12	San Jose	NHL	82	18	59	77	31	4	0	2	156	11.5	17	993	56.1	20:28	5	2	3	5	2	0	0	0	21:54
2012-13	HC Davos	Swiss	33	12	24	36	43	....	....	....	....	....	....	....	....	....	....	....	....	....	....	....	....	....	....
	San Jose	NHL	48	7	33	40	26	2	0	1	85	8.2	6	701	58.5	18:23	11	2	8	10	2	1	0	0	20:17
2013-14	San Jose	NHL	82	11	65	76	32	2	0	3	122	9.0	20	1099	56.1	18:56	7	2	1	3	8	1	0	0	19:19
2014-15	San Jose	NHL	78	16	49	65	30	4	0	0	131	12.2	–4	955	58.0	18:25	....	....	....	....	....	....	....	....	....
2015-16	San Jose	NHL	82	19	63	82	54	8	0	6	121	15.7	25	753	53.0	18:22	24	3	18	21	10	1	0	1	19:40
2016-17	San Jose	NHL	79	7	43	50	51	1	0	0	81	8.6	7	737	50.9	18:04	4	0	2	2	0	0	0	0	18:50
	NHL Totals		1446	384	1007	1391	1156	130	6	61	2759	13.9		23169	52.8	19:52	160	27	96	123	126	10	0	8	21:21

OHL All-Rookie Team (1996) • OHL Rookie of the Year (1996) • Canadian Major Junior Rookie of the Year (1996) • OHL Second All-Star Team (1997) • NHL Second All-Star Team (2003, 2008, 2016) • NHL First All-Star Team (2006) • Art Ross Trophy (2006) • Hart Memorial Trophy (2006)

Played in NHL All-Star Game (2002, 2003, 2004, 2007, 2008, 2009)

Signed as a free agent by **Davos** (Swiss), July 8, 2004. Traded to **San Jose** by **Boston** for Brad Stuart, Marco Sturm and Wayne Primeau, November 30, 2005. Signed as a free agent by **Davos** (Swiss), September 16, 2012.

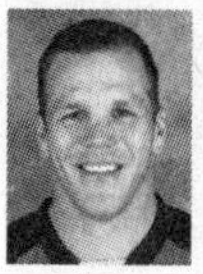

THORNTON, Shawn

(THOHRN-tuhn, SHAWN)

Right wing. Shoots right. 6'2", 217 lbs. Born, Oshawa, ON, July 23, 1977. Toronto's 6th pick, 190th overall, in 1997 NHL Draft.

Season	Club	League	GP	G	A	Pts	PIM	PP	SH	GW	S	S%	+/-	TF	F%	Min	GP	G	A	Pts	PIM	PP	SH	GW	Min
1995-96	Peterborough	OHL	63	4	10	14	192	....	....	....	....	....	....	....	....	....	24	3	0	3	25	....	....	....	....
1996-97	Peterborough	OHL	61	19	10	29	204	....	....	....	....	....	....	....	....	....	11	2	4	6	20	....	....	....	....
1997-98	St. John's	AHL	59	0	3	3	225	....	....	....	....	....	....	....	....	....	....	....	....	....	....	....	....	....	....
1998-99	St. John's	AHL	78	8	11	19	354	....	....	....	....	....	....	....	....	....	5	0	0	0	9	....	....	....	....
99-2000	St. John's	AHL	60	4	12	16	316	....	....	....	....	....	....	....	....	....	....	....	....	....	....	....	....	....	....
2000-01	St. John's	AHL	79	5	12	17	320	....	....	....	....	....	....	....	....	....	3	1	2	3	2	....	....	....	....
2001-02	Norfolk Admirals	AHL	70	8	14	22	281	....	....	....	....	....	....	....	....	....	4	0	0	0	4	....	....	....	....
2002-03	Chicago	NHL	13	1	1	2	31	0	0	0	15	6.7	–4	3	66.7	8:30	....	....	....	....	....	....	....	....	....
	Norfolk Admirals	AHL	50	11	2	13	213	....	....	....	....	....	....	....	....	....	9	0	2	2	28	....	....	....	....
2003-04	Chicago	NHL	8	1	0	1	23	0	0	0	14	7.1	2	19	42.1	11:14	....	....	....	....	....	....	....	....	....
	Norfolk Admirals	AHL	64	6	11	17	259	....	....	....	....	....	....	....	....	....	8	1	1	2	6	....	....	....	....
2004-05	Norfolk Admirals	AHL	71	5	9	14	253	....	....	....	....	....	....	....	....	....	6	0	0	0	8	....	....	....	....
2005-06	Chicago	NHL	10	0	0	0	16	0	0	0	16	0.0	–5	17	58.8	7:18	....	....	....	....	....	....	....	....	....
	Norfolk Admirals	AHL	59	10	22	32	192	....	....	....	....	....	....	....	....	....	4	0	0	0	35	....	....	....	....
2006-07 ♦	Anaheim	NHL	48	2	7	9	88	0	0	0	60	3.3	3	8	25.0	8:26	15	0	0	0	19	0	0	0	3:58
	Portland Pirates	AHL	15	4	4	8	55	....	....	....	....	....	....	....	....	....	....	....	....	....	....	....	....	....	....
2007-08	Boston	NHL	58	4	3	7	74	0	0	1	65	6.2	–1	7	28.6	7:24	7	0	0	0	6	0	0	0	8:04
2008-09	Boston	NHL	79	6	5	11	123	0	0	2	136	4.4	–2	5	20.0	10:02	10	1	0	1	6	0	0	0	9:07
2009-10	Boston	NHL	74	1	9	10	141	0	0	0	119	0.8	–9	23	47.8	9:03	12	0	0	0	4	0	0	0	7:08
2010-11 ♦	Boston	NHL	79	10	10	20	122	0	0	2	151	6.6	8	31	54.8	10:05	18	0	1	1	24	0	0	0	6:57
2011-12	Boston	NHL	81	5	8	13	154	0	0	0	114	4.4	–7	38	42.1	9:11	5	0	0	0	0	0	0	0	7:30
2012-13	Boston	NHL	45	3	4	7	60	0	1	0	55	5.5	1	17	41.2	8:06	22	0	4	4	18	0	0	0	7:21
2013-14	Boston	NHL	64	5	3	8	74	0	0	1	93	5.4	3	9	33.3	8:48	12	0	1	1	4	0	0	0	7:22
2014-15	Florida	NHL	46	1	4	5	50	0	0	0	53	1.9	–13	12	25.0	9:35	....	....	....	....	....	....	....	....	....
2015-16	Florida	NHL	50	1	4	5	80	0	0	0	58	1.7	–2	13	46.2	8:41	4	0	0	0	2	0	0	0	7:10
2016-17	Florida	NHL	50	2	2	4	67	0	0	0	42	4.8	–7	15	33.3	7:41	....	....	....	....	....	....	....	....	....
	NHL Totals		705	42	60	102	1103	0	1	6	991	4.2		217	42.9	8:56	105	1	6	7	83	0	0	0	7:00

Traded to **Chicago** by **Toronto** for Marty Wilford, September 30, 2001. Signed as a free agent by **Anaheim**, July 14, 2006. Signed as a free agent by **Boston**, July 1, 2007. Signed as a free agent by **Florida**, July 1, 2014. • Officially announced his retirement, April 10, 2017.

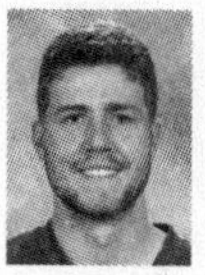

TIERNEY, Chris

(TEER-nee, KRIHS) **S.J.**

Center. Shoots left. 6'1", 195 lbs. Born, Keswick, ON, July 1, 1994. San Jose's 2nd pick, 55th overall, in 2012 NHL Draft.

Season	Club	League	GP	G	A	Pts	PIM	PP	SH	GW	S	S%	+/-	TF	F%	Min	GP	G	A	Pts	PIM	PP	SH	GW	Min
2009-10	York Simcoe	Minor-ON	57	35	55	90	28	....	....	....	....	....	....	....	....	....	....	....	....	....	....	....	....	....	....
	York Simcoe	Other	6	2	1	3	0	....	....	....	....	....	....	....	....	....	....	....	....	....	....	....	....	....	....
2010-11	London Knights	OHL	47	3	8	11	12	....	....	....	....	....	....	....	....	....	4	0	1	1	0	....	....	....	....
2011-12	London Knights	OHL	65	11	23	34	20	....	....	....	....	....	....	....	....	....	19	5	2	7	4	....	....	....	....
2012-13	London Knights	OHL	68	18	39	57	12	....	....	....	....	....	....	....	....	....	21	6	15	21	6	....	....	....	....
2013-14	London Knights	OHL	67	40	49	89	12	....	....	....	....	....	....	....	....	....	9	6	11	17	0	....	....	....	....
2014-15	San Jose	NHL	43	6	15	21	6	1	0	1	48	12.5	3	342	43.9	12:15	....	....	....	....	....	....	....	....	....
	Worcester Sharks	AHL	29	8	21	29	10	....	....	....	....	....	....	....	....	....	4	1	2	3	0	....	....	....	....
2015-16	San Jose	NHL	79	7	13	20	20	1	1	2	96	7.3	–16	805	45.7	13:12	24	5	4	9	6	0	0	0	14:46
	San Jose	AHL	2	1	2	3	0	....	....	....	....	....	....	....	....	....	....	....	....	....	....	....	....	....	....
2016-17	San Jose	NHL	80	11	12	23	6	1	1	2	90	12.2	0	826	48.6	14:36	6	0	1	1	0	0	0	0	13:51
	NHL Totals		202	24	40	64	32	3	2	5	234	10.3		1973	46.6	13:33	30	5	5	10	6	0	0	0	14:35

			Regular Season														Playoffs								
Season	Club	League	GP	G	A	Pts	PIM	PP	SH	GW	S	S%	+/-	TF	F%	Min	GP	G	A	Pts	PIM	PP	SH	GW	Min

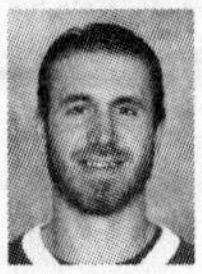

TINORDI, Jarred

(tih-NOHR-dee, JAIR-uhd) **PIT**

Defense. Shoots left. 6'6", 230 lbs. Born, Burnsville, MN, February 20, 1992. Montreal's 1st pick, 22nd overall, in 2010 NHL Draft.

2008-09	USAHNTDP	NAHL	42	2	13	15	53	....	....	....	....	....	....	....	....	....	9	1	0	1	6	....	....	....	....
	USAHNTDP	U-17	16	3	1	4	12	....	....	....	....	....	....	....	....	....	....	....	....	....	....	....	....	....	....
	USAHNTDP	U-18	1	0	1	1	0	....	....	....	....	....	....	....	....	....	....	....	....	....	....	....	....	....	....
2009-10	USAHNTDP	USHL	26	4	5	9	68	....	....	....	....	....	....	....	....	....	....	....	....	....	....	....	....	....	....
	USAHNTDP	U-18	39	2	6	8	37	....	....	....	....	....	....	....	....	....	....	....	....	....	....	....	....	....	....
2010-11	London Knights	OHL	63	1	13	14	140	....	....	....	....	....	....	....	....	....	6	0	0	0	17	....	....	....	....
2011-12	London Knights	OHL	48	2	14	16	63	....	....	....	....	....	....	....	....	....	19	3	5	8	27	....	....	....	....
2012-13	**Montreal**	**NHL**	**8**	**0**	**2**	**2**	**2**	**0**	**0**	**0**	**5**	**0.0**	**5**	**0**	**0.0**	**11:43**	**5**	**0**	**1**	**1**	**15**	**0**	**0**	**0**	**13:05**
	Hamilton	AHL	67	2	11	13	71	....	....	....	....	....	....	....	....	....	....	....	....	....	....	....	....	....	....
2013-14	**Montreal**	**NHL**	**22**	**0**	**2**	**2**	**40**	**0**	**0**	**0**	**10**	**0.0**	**-2**	**0**	**0.0**	**14:32**	....	....	....	....	....	....	....	....	....
	Hamilton	AHL	47	3	6	9	70	....	....	....	....	....	....	....	....	....	....	....	....	....	....	....	....	....	....
2014-15	**Montreal**	**NHL**	**13**	**0**	**2**	**2**	**19**	**0**	**0**	**0**	**5**	**0.0**	**-5**	**0**	**0.0**	**12:04**	....	....	....	....	....	....	....	....	....
	Hamilton	AHL	44	1	6	7	36	....	....	....	....	....	....	....	....	....	....	....	....	....	....	....	....	....	....
2015-16	**Montreal**	**NHL**	**3**	**0**	**0**	**0**	**5**	**0**	**0**	**0**	**0**	**0.0**	**-3**	**0**	**0.0**	**13:06**	....	....	....	....	....	....	....	....	....
	St. John's IceCaps	AHL	6	0	2	2	6	....	....	....	....	....	....	....	....	....	....	....	....	....	....	....	....	....	....
	Arizona	**NHL**	**7**	**0**	**0**	**0**	**12**	**0**	**0**	**0**	**3**	**0.0**	**-2**	**0**	**0.0**	**14:49**	....	....	....	....	....	....	....	....	....
2016-17	Tucson	AHL	64	1	10	11	102	....	....	....	....	....	....	....	....	....	....	....	....	....	....	....	....	....	....
	NHL Totals		**53**	**0**	**6**	**6**	**78**	**0**	**0**	**0**	**23**	**0.0**		**0**	**0.0**	**13:27**	**5**	**0**	**1**	**1**	**15**	**0**	**0**	**0**	**13:05**

Traded to **Arizona** by **Montreal** with Stefan Fournier for Victor Bartley and John Scott, January 15, 2016. • Suspended by the NHL for 20 games for violating the terms of the NHL/NHLPA Performance Enhancing Substances Program, March 9, 2016. • Missed majority of 2015-16 as a healthy reserve. Signed as a free agent by **Pittsburgh**, July 1, 2017.

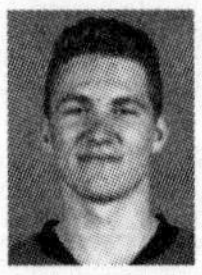

TKACHUK, Matthew

(KUH-chuhk, MA-thew) **CGY**

Left wing. Shoots left. 6'2", 202 lbs. Born, Scottsdale, AZ, December 11, 1997. Calgary's 1st pick, 6th overall, in 2016 NHL Draft.

2012-13	St.L. AAA Blues	T1EHL	41	25	57	82	26	....	....	....	....	....	....	....	....	....	5	4	9	13	2	....	....	....	....
2013-14	USAHNTDP	USHL	33	5	12	17	18	....	....	....	....	....	....	....	....	....	....	....	....	....	....	....	....	....	....
	USAHNTDP	U-17	20	8	9	17	23	....	....	....	....	....	....	....	....	....	....	....	....	....	....	....	....	....	....
2014-15	USAHNTDP	USHL	24	13	20	33	70	....	....	....	....	....	....	....	....	....	....	....	....	....	....	....	....	....	....
	USAHNTDP	U-18	41	25	37	62	44	....	....	....	....	....	....	....	....	....	....	....	....	....	....	....	....	....	....
2015-16	London Knights	OHL	57	30	77	107	80	....	....	....	....	....	....	....	....	....	18	*20	20	40	*42	....	....	....	....
2016-17	**Calgary**	**NHL**	**76**	**13**	**35**	**48**	**105**	**3**	**0**	**2**	**142**	**9.2**	**14**	**23**	**34.8**	**14:40**	**4**	**0**	**0**	**0**	**4**	**0**	**0**	**0**	**15:32**
	NHL Totals		**76**	**13**	**35**	**48**	**105**	**3**	**0**	**2**	**142**	**9.2**		**23**	**34.8**	**14:40**	**4**	**0**	**0**	**0**	**4**	**0**	**0**	**0**	**15:32**

OHL First All-Star Team (2016)

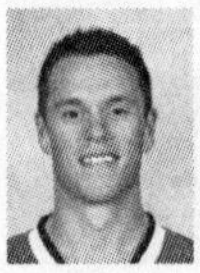

TOEWS, Jonathan

(TAYVZ, JAWN-ah-thuhn) **CHI**

Center. Shoots left. 6'2", 201 lbs. Born, Winnipeg, MB, April 29, 1988. Chicago's 1st pick, 3rd overall, in 2006 NHL Draft.

2004-05	Shattuck	High-MN	64	48	62	110	38	....	....	....	....	....	....	....	....	....	....	....	....	....	....	....	....	....	....
2005-06	North Dakota	WCHA	42	22	17	39	22	....	....	....	....	....	....	....	....	....	....	....	....	....	....	....	....	....	....
2006-07	North Dakota	WCHA	34	18	28	46	10	....	....	....	....	....	....	....	....	....	....	....	....	....	....	....	....	....	....
2007-08	**Chicago**	**NHL**	**64**	**24**	**30**	**54**	**44**	**7**	**0**	**4**	**144**	**16.7**	**11**	**956**	**53.2**	**18:40**	....	....	....	....	....	....	....	....	....
2008-09	**Chicago**	**NHL**	**82**	**34**	**35**	**69**	**51**	**12**	**0**	**7**	**195**	**17.4**	**12**	**1287**	**54.7**	**18:38**	**17**	**7**	**6**	**13**	**26**	**5**	**0**	**2**	**16:14**
2009-10♦	**Chicago**	**NHL**	**76**	**25**	**43**	**68**	**47**	**9**	**1**	**3**	**202**	**12.4**	**22**	**1397**	**57.3**	**20:00**	**22**	**7**	***22**	**29**	**4**	**5**	**0**	**3**	**20:58**
	Canada	Olympics	7	1	*7	8	2	....	....	....	....	....	....	....	....	....	....	....	....	....	....	....	....	....	....
2010-11	**Chicago**	**NHL**	**80**	**32**	**44**	**76**	**26**	**10**	**1**	**8**	**233**	**13.7**	**25**	**1653**	**56.7**	**20:46**	**7**	**1**	**3**	**4**	**2**	**0**	**1**	**0**	**22:31**
2011-12	**Chicago**	**NHL**	**59**	**29**	**28**	**57**	**28**	**5**	**1**	**4**	**185**	**15.7**	**17**	**1137**	**59.4**	**20:51**	**6**	**2**	**2**	**4**	**6**	**0**	**0**	**1**	**22:17**
2012-13♦	**Chicago**	**NHL**	**47**	**23**	**25**	**48**	**27**	**2**	**2**	**5**	**143**	**16.1**	**28**	**933**	**59.9**	**19:21**	**23**	**3**	**11**	**14**	**18**	**1**	**0**	**0**	**21:33**
2013-14	**Chicago**	**NHL**	**76**	**28**	**40**	**68**	**34**	**5**	**3**	**5**	**193**	**14.5**	**26**	**1544**	**57.3**	**20:28**	**19**	**9**	**8**	**17**	**8**	**2**	**1**	***4**	**21:43**
	Canada	Olympics	6	1	2	3	0	....	....	....	....	....	....	....	....	....	....	....	....	....	....	....	....	....	....
2014-15♦	**Chicago**	**NHL**	**81**	**28**	**38**	**66**	**36**	**6**	**2**	**7**	**192**	**14.6**	**30**	**1675**	**56.5**	**19:34**	**23**	**10**	**11**	**21**	**8**	**3**	**1**	**0**	**20:54**
2015-16	**Chicago**	**NHL**	**80**	**28**	**30**	**58**	**62**	**6**	**4**	**8**	**179**	**15.6**	**16**	**1573**	**58.6**	**19:15**	**7**	**0**	**6**	**6**	**10**	**0**	**1**	**0**	**22:41**
2016-17	**Chicago**	**NHL**	**72**	**21**	**37**	**58**	**35**	**6**	**0**	**5**	**199**	**10.6**	**7**	**1552**	**54.9**	**20:09**	**4**	**1**	**1**	**2**	**0**	**1**	**0**	**0**	**20:34**
	NHL Totals		**717**	**272**	**350**	**622**	**390**	**68**	**14**	**56**	**1865**	**14.6**		**13707**	**56.8**	**19:46**	**128**	**40**	**70**	**110**	**82**	**17**	**3**	**10**	**20:46**

WCHA Second All-Star Team (2007) • NCAA West First All-American Team (2007) • NHL All-Rookie Team (2008) • Olympic All-Star Team (2010) • Best Forward – Olympics (2010) • Conn Smythe Trophy (2010) • Frank J. Selke Trophy (2013) • NHL Second All-Star Team (2013) • Mark Messier NHL Leadership Award (2015)

Played in NHL All-Star Game (2009, 2011, 2015, 2017)

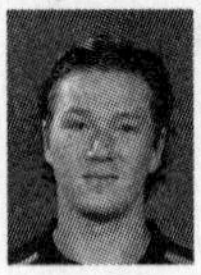

TOFFOLI, Tyler

(TAW-foh-lee, TIGH-luhr) **L.A.**

Right wing. Shoots right. 6'1", 200 lbs. Born, Scarborough, ON, April 24, 1992. Los Angeles' 2nd pick, 47th overall, in 2010 NHL Draft.

2007-08	Tor. Jr. Canadiens	GTHL	83	68	106	174	72	....	....	....	....	....	....	....	....	....	....	....	....	....	....	....	....	....	....
2008-09	Ottawa 67's	OHL	54	17	29	46	16	....	....	....	....	....	....	....	....	....	7	2	6	8	4	....	....	....	....
2009-10	Ottawa 67's	OHL	65	37	42	79	54	....	....	....	....	....	....	....	....	....	12	7	6	13	10	....	....	....	....
2010-11	Ottawa 67's	OHL	68	*57	51	*108	33	....	....	....	....	....	....	....	....	....	4	3	5	8	4	....	....	....	....
	Manchester	AHL	1	1	0	1	0	....	....	....	....	....	....	....	....	....	5	1	0	1	6	....	....	....	....
2011-12	Ottawa 67's	OHL	65	*52	48	100	22	....	....	....	....	....	....	....	....	....	18	11	7	18	21	....	....	....	....
2012-13	Manchester	AHL	58	28	23	51	18	....	....	....	....	....	....	....	....	....	....	....	....	....	....	....	....	....	....
	Los Angeles	**NHL**	**10**	**2**	**3**	**5**	**2**	**1**	**0**	**0**	**20**	**10.0**	**3**	**0**	**0.0**	**11:59**	**12**	**2**	**4**	**6**	**0**	**1**	**0**	**0**	**10:46**
2013-14♦	**Los Angeles**	**NHL**	**62**	**12**	**17**	**29**	**10**	**1**	**0**	**5**	**124**	**9.7**	**21**	**9**	**22.2**	**12:56**	**26**	**7**	**7**	**14**	**10**	**0**	**0**	**2**	**13:18**
	Manchester	AHL	18	15	8	23	4	....	....	....	....	....	....	....	....	....	....	....	....	....	....	....	....	....	....
2014-15	**Los Angeles**	**NHL**	**76**	**23**	**26**	**49**	**37**	**3**	**5**	**3**	**200**	**11.5**	**25**	**9**	**44.4**	**14:35**	....	....	....	....	....	....	....	....	....
2015-16	**Los Angeles**	**NHL**	**82**	**31**	**27**	**58**	**20**	**9**	**1**	**4**	**213**	**14.6**	***35**	**4**	**0.0**	**17:19**	**5**	**0**	**1**	**1**	**2**	**0**	**0**	**0**	**16:43**
2016-17	**Los Angeles**	**NHL**	**63**	**16**	**18**	**34**	**22**	**4**	**0**	**2**	**165**	**9.7**	**6**	**5**	**40.0**	**16:35**	....	....	....	....	....	....	....	....	....
	NHL Totals		**293**	**84**	**91**	**175**	**91**	**18**	**6**	**14**	**722**	**11.6**		**27**	**29.6**	**15:21**	**43**	**9**	**12**	**21**	**12**	**1**	**0**	**2**	**13:00**

OHL First All-Star Team (2011, 2012) • AHL All-Rookie Team (2013) • Dudley "Red" Garrett Memorial Trophy (AHL – Rookie of the Year) (2013)

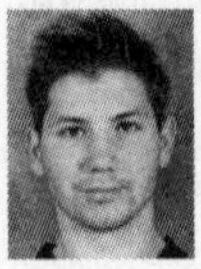

TOLCHINSKY, Sergey

(tohl-CHIHN-skee, SIHR-gay) **CAR**

Left wing. Shoots left. 5'8", 170 lbs. Born, Moscow, Russia, February 3, 1995.

2011-12	CSKA Jr.	Russia-Jr.	51	19	15	34	26	....	....	....	....	....	....	....	....	....	15	2	2	4	6	....	....	....	....
2012-13	Sault Ste. Marie	OHL	62	26	25	51	12	....	....	....	....	....	....	....	....	....	6	2	2	4	4	....	....	....	....
2013-14	Sault Ste. Marie	OHL	66	31	60	91	22	....	....	....	....	....	....	....	....	....	9	2	4	6	4	....	....	....	....
	Charlotte	AHL	1	0	0	0	0	....	....	....	....	....	....	....	....	....	....	....	....	....	....	....	....	....	....
2014-15	Sault Ste. Marie	OHL	61	30	65	95	10	....	....	....	....	....	....	....	....	....	14	4	10	14	2	....	....	....	....
2015-16	**Carolina**	**NHL**	**2**	**0**	**1**	**1**	**0**	**0**	**0**	**0**	**1**	**0.0**	**1**	**1**	**0.0**	**11:48**	....	....	....	....	....	....	....	....	....
	Charlotte	AHL	72	14	22	36	28	....	....	....	....	....	....	....	....	....	....	....	....	....	....	....	....	....	....
2016-17	**Carolina**	**NHL**	**2**	**0**	**1**	**1**	**0**	**0**	**0**	**0**	**2**	**0.0**	**0**	**0**	**0.0**	**11:29**	....	....	....	....	....	....	....	....	....
	Charlotte	AHL	59	7	16	23	41	....	....	....	....	....	....	....	....	....	1	0	1	1	0	....	....	....	....
	NHL Totals		**4**	**0**	**2**	**2**	**0**	**0**	**0**	**0**	**3**	**0.0**		**1**	**0.0**	**11:38**	....	....	....	....	....	....	....	....	....

Signed as a free agent by **Carolina**, August 22, 2013.

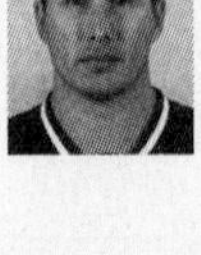

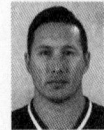

TOOTOO, Jordin

(TOO-TOO, JOHR-dahn) **CHI**

Right wing. Shoots right. 5'9", 195 lbs. Born, Churchill, MB, February 2, 1983. Nashville's 6th pick, 98th overall, in 2001 NHL Draft.

1997-98	Spruce Grove	AMBHL	34	20	10	30	149	....	....	....	....	....	....	....	....	....	....	....	....	....	....	....	....	....	....
1998-99	OCN Blizzard	MJHL	47	16	21	37	251	....	....	....	....	....	....	....	....	....	....	....	....	....	....	....	....	....	....
99-2000	Brandon	WHL	45	6	10	16	214	....	....	....	....	....	....	....	....	....	....	....	....	....	....	....	....	....	....
2000-01	Brandon	WHL	60	20	28	48	172	....	....	....	....	....	....	....	....	....	6	2	4	6	18	....	....	....	....
2001-02	Brandon	WHL	64	32	39	71	272	....	....	....	....	....	....	....	....	....	16	4	3	7	*58	....	....	....	....
2002-03	Brandon	WHL	51	35	39	74	216	....	....	....	....	....	....	....	....	....	17	6	3	9	49	....	....	....	....
2003-04	**Nashville**	**NHL**	**70**	**4**	**4**	**8**	**137**	**2**	**0**	**0**	**92**	**4.3**	**-6**	**18**	**55.6**	**8:29**	**5**	**0**	**0**	**0**	**4**	**0**	**0**	**0**	**5:09**
2004-05	Milwaukee	AHL	59	10	12	22	266	....	....	....	....	....	....	....	....	....	6	0	0	0	41	....	....	....	....
2005-06	**Nashville**	**NHL**	**34**	**4**	**6**	**10**	**55**	**0**	**0**	**0**	**61**	**6.6**	**9**	**17**	**70.6**	**9:15**	**3**	**0**	**0**	**0**	**0**	**0**	**0**	**0**	**4:04**
	Milwaukee	AHL	41	13	14	27	133	....	....	....	....	....	....	....	....	....	15	9	2	11	35	....	....	....	....

			Regular Season														Playoffs								
Season	Club	League	GP	G	A	Pts	PIM	PP	SH	GW	S	S%	+/-	TF	F%	Min	GP	G	A	Pts	PIM	PP	SH	GW	Min
2006-07	**Nashville**	**NHL**	**65**	**3**	**6**	**9**	**116**	**0**	**0**	**0**	**77**	**3.9**	**–11**	**12**	**33.3**	**8:24**	**4**	**0**	**1**	**1**	**21**	**0**	**0**	**0**	**9:32**
2007-08	**Nashville**	**NHL**	**63**	**11**	**7**	**18**	**100**	**0**	**0**	**1**	**98**	**11.2**	**–8**	**4**	**50.0**	**9:54**	**6**	**2**	**0**	**2**	**4**	**0**	**0**	**0**	**12:31**
2008-09	**Nashville**	**NHL**	**72**	**4**	**12**	**16**	**124**	**0**	**0**	**1**	**138**	**2.9**	**–15**	**16**	**56.3**	**12:05**	....	....	....	....	....	....	....	....	....
2009-10	**Nashville**	**NHL**	**51**	**6**	**10**	**16**	**40**	**0**	**0**	**1**	**101**	**5.9**	**2**	**8**	**25.0**	**10:50**	**6**	**0**	**1**	**1**	**2**	**0**	**0**	**0**	**7:58**
2010-11	**Nashville**	**NHL**	**54**	**8**	**10**	**18**	**61**	**0**	**0**	**1**	**85**	**9.4**	**8**	**3**	**66.7**	**11:53**	**12**	**1**	**5**	**6**	**28**	**0**	**0**	**0**	**13:26**
2011-12	**Nashville**	**NHL**	**77**	**6**	**24**	**30**	**92**	**1**	**0**	**1**	**136**	**4.4**	**–5**	**12**	**33.3**	**13:09**	**3**	**0**	**0**	**0**	**4**	**0**	**0**	**0**	**7:46**
2012-13	**Detroit**	**NHL**	**42**	**3**	**5**	**8**	**78**	**0**	**0**	**1**	**45**	**6.7**	**0**	**0**	**0.0**	**9:05**	**1**	**0**	**0**	**0**	**2**	**0**	**0**	**0**	**6:24**
2013-14	**Detroit**	**NHL**	**11**	**0**	**1**	**1**	**5**	**0**	**0**	**0**	**11**	**0.0**	**–3**	**0**	**0.0**	**6:59**	....	....	....	....	....	....	....	....	....
	Grand Rapids	AHL	51	6	12	18	104	....	....	....	....	....	....	....	....	....	4	0	1	1	4	....	....	....	....
2014-15	**New Jersey**	**NHL**	**68**	**10**	**5**	**15**	**72**	**1**	**0**	**1**	**75**	**13.3**	**1**	**1**	**100.0**	**10:27**	....	....	....	....	....	....	....	....	....
2015-16	**New Jersey**	**NHL**	**66**	**4**	**5**	**9**	**102**	**2**	**0**	**0**	**90**	**4.4**	**–26**	**2**	**0.0**	**11:32**	....	....	....	....	....	....	....	....	....
2016-17	**Chicago**	**NHL**	**50**	**2**	**1**	**3**	**28**	**0**	**0**	**0**	**43**	**4.7**	**–6**	**1**	**100.0**	**6:45**	**2**	**0**	**0**	**0**	**0**	**0**	**0**	**0**	**6:13**
	NHL Totals		**723**	**65**	**96**	**161**	**1010**	**6**	**0**	**7**	**1052**	**6.2**		**94**	**50.0**	**10:16**	**42**	**3**	**7**	**10**	**65**	**0**	**0**	**0**	**9:35**

WHL East First All-Star Team (2003)

Signed as a free agent by **Detroit**, July 1, 2012. Signed as a free agent by **New Jersey**, October 7, 2014. Signed as a free agent by **Chicago**, July 5, 2016.

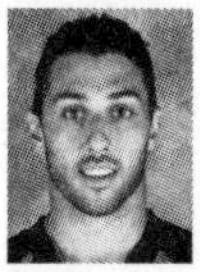

TROCHECK, Vincent
(TROH-chehk, VIHN-sihnt) **FLA**

Center. Shoots right. 5'10", 182 lbs. Born, Pittsburgh, PA, July 11, 1993. Florida's 4th pick, 64th overall, in 2011 NHL Draft.

Season	Club	League	GP	G	A	Pts	PIM	PP	SH	GW	S	S%	+/-	TF	F%	Min	GP	G	A	Pts	PIM	PP	SH	GW	Min
2008-09	Det. Lit. Caesars	T1EHL	44	27	19	46	32	....	....	....	....	....	....	....	....	....	7	1	4	5	0	....	....	....	....
2009-10	Saginaw Spirit	OHL	68	15	28	43	56	....	....	....	....	....	....	....	....	....	6	2	2	4	2	....	....	....	....
2010-11	Saginaw Spirit	OHL	68	26	36	62	60	....	....	....	....	....	....	....	....	....	12	6	5	11	4	....	....	....	....
2011-12	Saginaw Spirit	OHL	65	29	56	85	65	....	....	....	....	....	....	....	....	....	12	5	6	11	10	....	....	....	....
2012-13	Saginaw Spirit	OHL	35	24	26	*50	34	....	....	....	....	....	....	....	....	....	....	....	....	....	....	....	....	....	....
	Plymouth Whalers	OHL	28	26	33	*59	24	....	....	....	....	....	....	....	....	....	15	10	14	24	8	....	....	....	....
2013-14	**Florida**	**NHL**	**20**	**5**	**3**	**8**	**6**	**1**	**1**	**0**	**38**	**13.2**	**–11**	**348**	**47.7**	**18:53**	....	....	....	....	....	....	....	....	....
	San Antonio	AHL	55	16	26	42	32	....	....	....	....	....	....	....	....	....	....	....	....	....	....	....	....	....	....
2014-15	**Florida**	**NHL**	**50**	**7**	**15**	**22**	**24**	**1**	**0**	**0**	**89**	**7.9**	**9**	**481**	**48.7**	**14:00**	....	....	....	....	....	....	....	....	....
	San Antonio	AHL	23	8	11	19	19	....	....	....	....	....	....	....	....	....	3	1	1	2	2	....	....	....	....
2015-16	**Florida**	**NHL**	**76**	**25**	**28**	**53**	**44**	**4**	**1**	**4**	**174**	**14.4**	**15**	**1106**	**49.5**	**17:46**	**2**	**0**	**1**	**1**	**0**	**0**	**0**	**0**	**31:33**
2016-17	**Florida**	**NHL**	**82**	**23**	**31**	**54**	**43**	**2**	**0**	**2**	**230**	**10.0**	**–13**	**1664**	**50.2**	**20:50**	....	....	....	....	....	....	....	....	....
	NHL Totals		**228**	**60**	**77**	**137**	**117**	**8**	**2**	**6**	**531**	**11.3**		**3599**	**49.5**	**18:09**	**2**	**0**	**1**	**1**	**0**	**0**	**0**	**0**	**31:33**

OHL First All-Star Team (2013) • OHL Player of the Year (2013)

Played in NHL All-Star Game (2017)

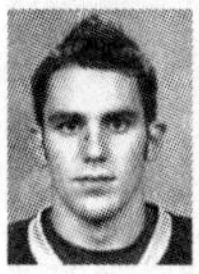

TROPP, Corey
(TROHP, KOHR-ee) **ANA**

Right wing. Shoots right. 6', 185 lbs. Born, Grosse Pointe, MI, July 25, 1989. Buffalo's 3rd pick, 89th overall, in 2007 NHL Draft.

Season	Club	League	GP	G	A	Pts	PIM	PP	SH	GW	S	S%	+/-	TF	F%	Min	GP	G	A	Pts	PIM	PP	SH	GW	Min
2005-06	Sioux Falls	USHL	46	7	8	15	21	....	....	....	....	....	....	....	....	....	14	2	3	5	8	....	....	....	....
2006-07	Sioux Falls	USHL	54	26	36	62	76	....	....	....	....	....	....	....	....	....	8	4	9	*13	0	....	....	....	....
2007-08	Michigan State	CCHA	42	6	11	17	16	....	....	....	....	....	....	....	....	....	....	....	....	....	....	....	....	....	....
2008-09	Michigan State	CCHA	21	3	8	11	45	....	....	....	....	....	....	....	....	....	....	....	....	....	....	....	....	....	....
2009-10	Michigan State	CCHA	37	20	22	42	50	....	....	....	....	....	....	....	....	....	....	....	....	....	....	....	....	....	....
2010-11	Portland Pirates	AHL	76	10	30	40	113	....	....	....	....	....	....	....	....	....	12	2	5	7	12	....	....	....	....
2011-12	**Buffalo**	**NHL**	**34**	**3**	**5**	**8**	**20**	**0**	**0**	**1**	**32**	**9.4**	**0**	**5**	**0.0**	**10:05**	....	....	....	....	....	....	....	....	....
	Rochester	AHL	27	9	13	22	46	....	....	....	....	....	....	....	....	....	3	0	0	0	8	....	....	....	....
2012-13	Rochester	AHL	6	2	2	4	7	....	....	....	....	....	....	....	....	....	....	....	....	....	....	....	....	....	....
2013-14	**Buffalo**	**NHL**	**9**	**0**	**1**	**1**	**0**	**0**	**0**	**0**	**7**	**0.0**	**–8**	**0**	**0.0**	**10:29**	....	....	....	....	....	....	....	....	....
	Columbus	**NHL**	**44**	**2**	**8**	**10**	**37**	**0**	**0**	**0**	**28**	**7.1**	**11**	**1**	**0.0**	**8:37**	**2**	**0**	**0**	**0**	**0**	**0**	**0**	**0**	**6:11**
2014-15	**Columbus**	**NHL**	**61**	**1**	**7**	**8**	**76**	**0**	**0**	**0**	**22**	**4.5**	**–14**	**2**	**50.0**	**8:45**	....	....	....	....	....	....	....	....	....
2015-16	Albany Devils	AHL	51	11	17	28	61	....	....	....	....	....	....	....	....	....	....	....	....	....	....	....	....	....	....
	San Diego Gulls	AHL	15	5	6	11	16	....	....	....	....	....	....	....	....	....	8	1	1	2	20	....	....	....	....
2016-17	**Anaheim**	**NHL**	**1**	**0**	**0**	**0**	**0**	**0**	**0**	**0**	**0**	**0.0**	**–1**	**0**	**0.0**	**9:28**	....	....	....	....	....	....	....	....	....
	San Diego Gulls	AHL	62	21	33	54	48	....	....	....	....	....	....	....	....	....	1	0	0	0	0	....	....	....	....
	NHL Totals		**149**	**6**	**21**	**27**	**133**	**0**	**0**	**1**	**89**	**6.7**		**8**	**12.5**	**9:08**	**2**	**0**	**0**	**0**	**0**	**0**	**0**	**0**	**6:11**

CCHA Second All-Star Team (2010)

Claimed on waivers by **Columbus** from **Buffalo**, November 28, 2013. Traded to **Chicago** by **Columbus** with Artem Anisimov, Jeremy Morin, Marko Dano and Columbus' 4th round pick (later traded to NY Islanders – NY Islanders selected Anatoli Golyshev) in 2016 NHL Draft for Brandon Saad, Michael Paliotta and Alex Broadhurst, June 30, 2015. • Loaned to **Albany** (AHL) by **Chicago**, October 8, 2015. Traded to **Anaheim** by **Chicago** for Tim Jackman and Anaheim's 7th round pick (Joshua Ess) in 2017 NHL Draft, February 29, 2016.

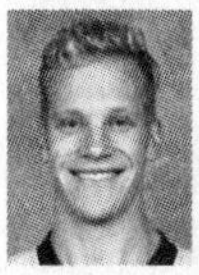

TROTMAN, Zach
(TRAWT-muhn, ZAK) **PIT**

Defense. Shoots right. 6'3", 217 lbs. Born, Novi, MI, August 26, 1990. Boston's 8th pick, 210th overall, in 2010 NHL Draft.

Season	Club	League	GP	G	A	Pts	PIM	PP	SH	GW	S	S%	+/-	TF	F%	Min	GP	G	A	Pts	PIM	PP	SH	GW	Min
2008-09	Wichita Falls	NAHL	47	2	4	6	79	....	....	....	....	....	....	....	....	....	5	0	1	1	8	....	....	....	....
2009-10	Lake Superior	CCHA	36	2	6	8	18	....	....	....	....	....	....	....	....	....	....	....	....	....	....	....	....	....	....
2010-11	Lake Superior	CCHA	38	6	14	20	12	....	....	....	....	....	....	....	....	....	....	....	....	....	....	....	....	....	....
2011-12	Lake Superior	CCHA	40	11	10	21	12	....	....	....	....	....	....	....	....	....	....	....	....	....	....	....	....	....	....
	Providence Bruins	AHL	9	1	2	3	2	....	....	....	....	....	....	....	....	....	....	....	....	....	....	....	....	....	....
2012-13	Providence Bruins	AHL	48	2	14	16	19	....	....	....	....	....	....	....	....	....	4	0	0	0	0	....	....	....	....
2013-14	**Boston**	**NHL**	**2**	**0**	**0**	**0**	**0**	**0**	**0**	**0**	**4**	**0.0**	**0**	**0**	**0.0**	**15:00**	....	....	....	....	....	....	....	....	....
	Providence Bruins	AHL	53	8	16	24	21	....	....	....	....	....	....	....	....	....	8	0	4	4	14	....	....	....	....
2014-15	**Boston**	**NHL**	**27**	**1**	**4**	**5**	**0**	**0**	**0**	**1**	**46**	**2.2**	**–2**	**0**	**0.0**	**16:24**	....	....	....	....	....	....	....	....	....
	Providence Bruins	AHL	40	2	11	13	27	....	....	....	....	....	....	....	....	....	5	1	0	1	2	....	....	....	....
2015-16	**Boston**	**NHL**	**38**	**2**	**5**	**7**	**22**	**0**	**0**	**0**	**60**	**3.3**	**3**	**0**	**0.0**	**18:33**	....	....	....	....	....	....	....	....	....
2016-17	Ontario Reign	AHL	9	0	2	2	26	....	....	....	....	....	....	....	....	....	....	....	....	....	....	....	....	....	....
	NHL Totals		**67**	**3**	**9**	**12**	**22**	**0**	**0**	**1**	**110**	**2.7**		**0**	**0.0**	**17:35**	....	....	....	....	....	....	....	....	....

• Missed majority of 2015-16 as a healthy reserve. Signed as a free agent by **Los Angeles**, July 1, 2016. • Missed majority of 2016-17 due to upper body injury. Signed as a free agent by **Pittsburgh**, July 1, 2017.

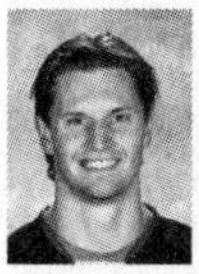

TROUBA, Jacob
(TROO-buh, JAY-kuhb) **WPG**

Defense. Shoots right. 6'3", 202 lbs. Born, Rochester, MI, February 26, 1994. Winnipeg's 1st pick, 9th overall, in 2012 NHL Draft.

Season	Club	League	GP	G	A	Pts	PIM	PP	SH	GW	S	S%	+/-	TF	F%	Min	GP	G	A	Pts	PIM	PP	SH	GW	Min
2009-10	Det. Compuware	T1EHL	38	14	14	28	40	....	....	....	....	....	....	....	....	....	....	....	....	....	....	....	....	....	....
	Det. Compuware	Other	6	3	5	8	12	....	....	....	....	....	....	....	....	....	....	....	....	....	....	....	....	....	....
	Det. Comp. U18	T1EHL	3	3	0	3	2	....	....	....	....	....	....	....	....	....	....	....	....	....	....	....	....	....	....
2010-11	USAHNTDP	USHL	31	3	4	7	31	....	....	....	....	....	....	....	....	....	....	....	....	....	....	....	....	....	....
	USAHNTDP	U-17	17	4	12	16	18	....	....	....	....	....	....	....	....	....	....	....	....	....	....	....	....	....	....
	USAHNTDP	U-18	10	1	2	3	10	....	....	....	....	....	....	....	....	....	....	....	....	....	....	....	....	....	....
2011-12	USAHNTDP	USHL	22	4	14	18	35	....	....	....	....	....	....	....	....	....	....	....	....	....	....	....	....	....	....
	USAHNTDP	U-18	32	5	9	14	36	....	....	....	....	....	....	....	....	....	....	....	....	....	....	....	....	....	....
2012-13	U. of Michigan	CCHA	37	12	17	29	88	....	....	....	....	....	....	....	....	....	....	....	....	....	....	....	....	....	....
2013-14	**Winnipeg**	**NHL**	**65**	**10**	**19**	**29**	**43**	**0**	**1**	**1**	**121**	**8.3**	**4**	**0**	**0.0**	**22:26**	....	....	....	....	....	....	....	....	....
2014-15	**Winnipeg**	**NHL**	**65**	**7**	**15**	**22**	**46**	**1**	**0**	**0**	**133**	**5.3**	**2**	**1**	**0.0**	**23:19**	**4**	**0**	**2**	**2**	**2**	**0**	**0**	**0**	**19:06**
2015-16	**Winnipeg**	**NHL**	**81**	**6**	**15**	**21**	**62**	**0**	**1**	**0**	**133**	**4.5**	**10**	**1**	**0.0**	**22:04**	....	....	....	....	....	....	....	....	....
2016-17	**Winnipeg**	**NHL**	**60**	**8**	**25**	**33**	**54**	**2**	**0**	**1**	**154**	**5.2**	**4**	**0**	**0.0**	**24:58**	....	....	....	....	....	....	....	....	....
	NHL Totals		**271**	**31**	**74**	**105**	**205**	**3**	**2**	**2**	**541**	**5.7**		**2**	**0.0**	**23:06**	**4**	**0**	**2**	**2**	**2**	**0**	**0**	**0**	**19:06**

CCHA All-Rookie Team (2013) • CCHA First All-Star Team (2013) • NCAA West First All-American Team (2013)

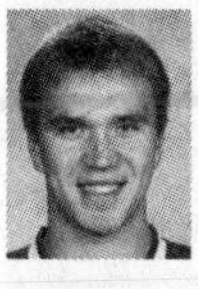

TRYAMKIN, Nikita
(tree-AM-kihn, nih-KEE-tuh)

Defense. Shoots left. 6'7", 228 lbs. Born, Sysert, Russia, August 30, 1994. Vancouver's 4th pick, 66th overall, in 2014 NHL Draft.

Season	Club	League	GP	G	A	Pts	PIM	PP	SH	GW	S	S%	+/-	TF	F%	Min	GP	G	A	Pts	PIM	PP	SH	GW	Min
2011-12	Avtomobilist Jr.	Russia-Jr.	60	3	9	12	82	....	....	....	....	....	....	....	....	....	9	0	0	0	8	....	....	....	....
2012-13	Avtomobilist Jr.	Russia-Jr.	28	8	10	18	58	....	....	....	....	....	....	....	....	....	8	1	2	3	40	....	....	....	....
	Avtomobilist	KHL	32	3	1	4	12	....	....	....	....	....	....	....	....	....	8	2	0	2	8	....	....	....	....
2013-14	Avtomobilist Jr.	Russia-Jr.	2	2	1	3	4	....	....	....	....	....	....	....	....	....	1	0	0	0	0	....	....	....	....
	Avtomobilist	KHL	45	1	6	7	38	....	....	....	....	....	....	....	....	....	4	0	0	0	2	....	....	....	....

Season	Club	League	GP	G	A	Pts	PIM	PP	SH	GW	S	S%	+/-	TF	F%	Min	GP	G	A	Pts	PIM	PP	SH	GW	Min
2014-15	Avtomobilist Jr.	Russia-Jr.	3	1	3	4	8										1	0	0	0	12				
	Avtomobilist	KHL	58	1	5	6	37										5	0	0	0	12				
2015-16	Avtomobilist	KHL	53	4	7	11	71										6	0	1	1	4				
	Vancouver	NHL	13	1	1	2	10	0	0	0	11	9.1	-3	0	0.0	17:31									
2016-17	Vancouver	NHL	66	2	7	9	64	0	0	0	65	3.1	-7	0	0.0	16:44									
	NHL Totals		79	3	8	11	74	0	0	0	76	3.9		0	0.0	16:52									

TUCH, Alex
(TUHK, AL-ehx) **VGK**

Right wing. Shoots right. 6'4", 222 lbs. Born, Syracuse, NY, May 10, 1996. Minnesota's 1st pick, 18th overall, in 2014 NHL Draft.

Season	Club	League	GP	G	A	Pts	PIM	PP	SH	GW	S	S%	+/-	TF	F%	Min	GP	G	A	Pts	PIM	PP	SH	GW	Min
2011-12	Syracuse Jr. Stars	EmJHL	40	44	57	*101	26										4	1	3	4	4				
2012-13	USAHNTDP	USHL	38	4	6	10	24																		
	USAHNTDP	U-17	18	7	9	16	8																		
2013-14	USAHNTDP	USHL	26	13	19	32	36																		
	USAHNTDP	U-18	35	16	15	31	36																		
2014-15	Boston College	H-East	37	14	14	28	28																		
2015-16	Boston College	H-East	40	18	16	34	33																		
2016-17	**Minnesota**	**NHL**	6	0	0	0	0	0	0	0	8	0.0	-3	0	0.0	10:42									
	Iowa Wild	AHL	57	18	19	37	28																		
	NHL Totals		6	0	0	0	0	0	0	0	8	0.0		0	0.0	10:42									

Traded to **Vegas** by **Minnesota** for Vegas' 3rd round pick in 2018 NHL Draft and Expansion Draft considerations, June 21, 2017.
Hockey East All-Rookie Team (2015)

TURRIS, Kyle
(TUH-rihs, KIGHL) **OTT**

Center. Shoots right. 6'1", 190 lbs. Born, New Westminster, BC, August 14, 1989. Phoenix's 1st pick, 3rd overall, in 2007 NHL Draft.

Season	Club	League	GP	G	A	Pts	PIM	PP	SH	GW	S	S%	+/-	TF	F%	Min	GP	G	A	Pts	PIM	PP	SH	GW	Min
2004-05	Grandview	Minor-BC	30	13	20	33											12	3	6	9					
2005-06	Burnaby Express	BCHL	57	36	36	72	32										20	10	13	23	6				
2006-07	Burnaby Express	BCHL	53	66	55	121	83										14	12	14	26	16				
2007-08	U. of Wisconsin	WCHA	36	11	24	35	38																		
	Phoenix	**NHL**	3	0	1	1	2	0	0	0	11	0.0	-5	42	40.5	19:45									
2008-09	**Phoenix**	**NHL**	63	8	12	20	21	3	0	3	91	8.8	-15	567	42.9	12:55									
	San Antonio	AHL	8	4	3	7	6																		
2009-10	San Antonio	AHL	76	24	39	63	60																		
2010-11	**Phoenix**	**NHL**	65	11	14	25	16	0	0	1	116	9.5	0	540	50.0	11:16	4	1	2	3	2	0	0	0	13:49
	San Antonio	AHL	2	0	1	1	2																		
2011-12	**Phoenix**	**NHL**	6	0	0	0	4	0	0	0	9	0.0	-2	51	41.2	12:45									
	Ottawa	**NHL**	49	12	17	29	16	1	0	2	133	9.0	12	672	47.2	17:21	7	1	2	3	2	0	0	1	16:37
2012-13	Karpat Oulu	Finland	21	7	12	19	24																		
	Ottawa	**NHL**	48	12	17	29	24	3	0	2	118	10.2	6	920	49.0	19:38	10	6	3	9	13	1	1	1	19:58
2013-14	**Ottawa**	**NHL**	82	26	32	58	39	6	2	5	215	12.1	22	1429	50.7	18:44									
2014-15	**Ottawa**	**NHL**	82	24	40	64	36	4	1	6	215	11.2	5	1472	50.1	19:13	6	1	1	2	18	1	0	0	19:50
2015-16	**Ottawa**	**NHL**	57	13	17	30	32	3	0	2	122	10.7	-15	1044	51.3	19:42									
2016-17	**Ottawa**	**NHL**	78	27	28	55	47	6	0	6	185	14.6	-3	1225	53.1	19:30	19	4	6	10	25	0	0	1	21:19
	NHL Totals		533	133	178	311	248	26	3	27	1215	10.9		7962	49.8	17:19	46	13	14	27	60	2	1	3	19:28

WCHA All-Rookie Team (2008)
Traded to **Ottawa** by **Phoenix** for David Rundblad and Ottawa's 2nd round pick (later traded to Columbus, later traded to Philadelphia – Philadelphia selected Anthony Stolarz) in 2012 NHL Draft, December 17, 2011. Signed as a free agent by **Oulu** (Finland), October 6, 2012.

TYNAN, TJ
(TIGH-nuhn, TEE-JAY) **VGK**

Center. Shoots right. 5'8", 165 lbs. Born, Orland Park, IL, February 25, 1992. Columbus' 2nd pick, 66th overall, in 2011 NHL Draft.

Season	Club	League	GP	G	A	Pts	PIM	PP	SH	GW	S	S%	+/-	TF	F%	Min	GP	G	A	Pts	PIM	PP	SH	GW	Min
2009-10	Des Moines	USHL	60	17	*55	72	55																		
2010-11	U. of Notre Dame	CCHA	44	23	31	54	36																		
2011-12	U. of Notre Dame	CCHA	39	13	28	41	38																		
2012-13	U. of Notre Dame	CCHA	41	10	18	28	28																		
2013-14	U. of Notre Dame	H-East	40	8	30	38	30																		
	Springfield	AHL	3	0	0	0	2																		
2014-15	Springfield	AHL	75	13	35	48	48																		
2015-16	Lake Erie	AHL	76	6	40	46	38										17	1	5	6	8				
2016-17	**Columbus**	**NHL**	3	0	0	0	0	0	0	0	3	0.0	-1	0	0.0	7:29									
	Cleveland	AHL	72	12	29	41	34																		
	NHL Totals		3	0	0	0	0	0	0	0	3	0.0		0	0.0	7:29									

USHL All-Rookie Team (2010) • CCHA All-Rookie Team (2011) • CCHA Second All-Star Team (2011) • CCHA Rookie of the Year (2011) • CCHA First All-Star Team (2012)
Signed as a free agent by **Vegas**, July 1, 2017.

TYUTIN, Fedor
(T'YOO-tihn, FEH-duhr) **COL**

Defense. Shoots left. 6'2", 221 lbs. Born, Izhevsk, USSR, July 19, 1983. NY Rangers' 2nd pick, 40th overall, in 2001 NHL Draft.

Season	Club	League	GP	G	A	Pts	PIM	PP	SH	GW	S	S%	+/-	TF	F%	Min	GP	G	A	Pts	PIM	PP	SH	GW	Min
1998-99	Magnitogorsk 2	Russia-4	7	0	1	1	2																		
99-2000	Izhstal Izhevsk 2	Russia-3	38	11	8	19	68																		
	Izhstal Izhevsk	Russia-2	10	0	1	1	12																		
2000-01	St. Petersburg	Russia	34	2	4	6	20																		
2001-02	Guelph Storm	OHL	53	19	40	59	54										9	2	8	10	8				
2002-03	St. Petersburg	Russia	10	1	1	2	16																		
	Ak Bars Kazan	Russia	10	0	0	0	8										5	0	0	0	4				
2003-04	**NY Rangers**	**NHL**	25	2	5	7	14	0	1	0	33	6.1	-4	1	0.0	20:08									
	Hartford	AHL	43	5	9	14	50										16	0	5	5	18				
2004-05	Hartford	AHL	13	2	1	3	10																		
	St. Petersburg	Russia	35	5	3	8	24																		
2005-06	**NY Rangers**	**NHL**	77	6	19	25	58	4	0	2	102	5.9	1	1	0.0	20:33	4	0	1	1	0	0	0	0	17:50
	Russia	Olympics	8	0	1	1	4																		
2006-07	**NY Rangers**	**NHL**	66	2	12	14	44	1	1	0	75	2.7	-8	1	0.0	20:02	10	0	5	5	8	0	0	0	19:30
2007-08	**NY Rangers**	**NHL**	82	5	15	20	43	1	0	0	131	3.8	5	0	0.0	20:27	10	0	3	3	4	0	0	0	19:52
2008-09	**Columbus**	**NHL**	82	9	25	34	81	5	1	0	167	5.4	1	1	100.0	23:31	4	0	0	0	0	0	0	0	23:16
2009-10	**Columbus**	**NHL**	80	6	26	32	49	3	0	2	149	4.0	-7	3	33.3	23:31									
	Russia	Olympics	4	0	2	2	2																		
2010-11	**Columbus**	**NHL**	80	7	20	27	32	1	0	0	128	5.5	-12	2	50.0	22:42									
2011-12	**Columbus**	**NHL**	66	5	21	26	49	1	0	0	124	4.0	-21	0	0.0	24:09									
2012-13	Mytischi	KHL	17	1	2	3	8																		
	Columbus	**NHL**	48	4	18	22	28	0	0	1	56	7.1	9	1	100.0	24:06									
2013-14	**Columbus**	**NHL**	69	4	22	26	44	1	0	0	87	4.6	6	0	0.0	21:25	4	1	1	2	4	1	0	0	14:56
	Russia	Olympics	5	0	0	0	4																		
2014-15	**Columbus**	**NHL**	67	3	12	15	40	0	0	0	56	5.4	8	0	0.0	19:55									
2015-16	**Columbus**	**NHL**	61	1	2	3	28	0	0	0	25	4.0	-6	0	0.0	17:35									
2016-17	**Colorado**	**NHL**	69	1	12	13	38	0	0	0	46	2.2	-25	0	0.0	18:56									
	NHL Totals		872	55	209	264	548	17	3	5	1179	4.7		10	40.0	21:23	32	1	10	11	30	1	0	0	19:18

Signed as a free agent by **St. Petersburg** (Russia), November 11, 2004. Traded to **Columbus** by **NY Rangers** with Christian Backman for Nikolai Zherdev and Dan Fritsche, July 2, 2008. Signed as a free agent by **Mytischi** (KHL), November 12, 2012. Signed as a free agent by **Colorado**, July 1, 2016.

UPSHALL, Scottie

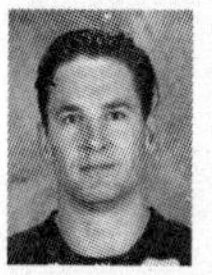

(UHP-shuhl, SKAW-tee)

Left wing. Shoots left. 6', 200 lbs. Born, Fort McMurray, AB, October 7, 1983. Nashville's 1st pick, 6th overall, in 2002 NHL Draft.

Season	Club	League	GP	G	A	Pts	PIM	PP	SH	GW	S	S%	+/-	TF	F%	Min	Playoffs GP	G	A	Pts	PIM	PP	SH	GW	Min
1998-99	Fort McMurray	AMHL	28	62	40	102	100																		
99-2000	Fort McMurray	AJHL	52	26	26	52	65																		
2000-01	Kamloops Blazers	WHL	70	42	45	87	111										4	0	2	2	10				
2001-02	Kamloops Blazers	WHL	61	32	51	83	139										4	1	2	3	21				
2002-03	**Nashville**	**NHL**	**8**	**1**	**0**	**1**	**0**	**0**	**0**	**0**	**6**	**16.7**	**2**	**2**	**0.0**	**8:42**									
	Kamloops Blazers	WHL	42	25	31	56	111										6	0	2	2	34				
	Milwaukee	AHL	2	1	0	1	2										6	0	0	0	2				
2003-04	**Nashville**	**NHL**	**7**	**0**	**1**	**1**	**0**	**0**	**0**	**0**	**6**	**0.0**	**-2**	**8**	**37.5**	**9:11**									
	Milwaukee	AHL	31	13	11	24	42										8	3	0	3	4				
2004-05	Milwaukee	AHL	62	19	27	46	108										5	2	2	4	8				
2005-06	**Nashville**	**NHL**	**48**	**8**	**16**	**24**	**34**	**1**	**0**	**2**	**72**	**11.1**	**14**	**11**	**45.5**	**10:26**	**2**	**0**	**0**	**0**	**0**	**0**	**0**	**0**	**11:57**
	Milwaukee	AHL	23	17	16	33	44										14	6	10	16	20				
2006-07	**Nashville**	**NHL**	**14**	**2**	**1**	**3**	**18**	**0**	**0**	**2**	**27**	**7.4**	**-1**	**0**	**0.0**	**10:28**									
	Milwaukee	AHL	5	0	1	1	6																		
	Philadelphia	**NHL**	**18**	**6**	**7**	**13**	**8**	**1**	**1**	**2**	**60**	**10.0**	**4**	**18**	**44.4**	**18:05**									
2007-08	**Philadelphia**	**NHL**	**61**	**14**	**16**	**30**	**74**	**3**	**0**	**1**	**128**	**10.9**	**2**	**7**	**28.6**	**13:20**	**17**	**3**	**4**	**7**	***44**	**1**	**0**	**1**	**13:57**
2008-09	**Philadelphia**	**NHL**	**55**	**7**	**14**	**21**	**63**	**2**	**0**	**0**	**126**	**5.6**	**5**	**10**	**10.0**	**13:13**									
	Phoenix	**NHL**	**19**	**8**	**5**	**13**	**26**	**3**	**0**	**1**	**66**	**12.1**	**2**	**9**	**44.4**	**18:35**									
2009-10	**Phoenix**	**NHL**	**49**	**18**	**14**	**32**	**50**	**2**	**0**	**4**	**119**	**15.1**	**5**	**17**	**41.2**	**15:03**									
2010-11	**Phoenix**	**NHL**	**61**	**16**	**11**	**27**	**42**	**2**	**0**	**2**	**144**	**11.1**	**5**	**19**	**21.1**	**13:27**									
	Columbus	**NHL**	**21**	**6**	**1**	**7**	**10**	**0**	**0**	**0**	**47**	**12.8**	**-12**	**6**	**66.7**	**15:46**									
2011-12	**Florida**	**NHL**	**26**	**2**	**3**	**5**	**29**	**1**	**0**	**1**	**53**	**3.8**	**-3**	**6**	**50.0**	**12:43**	**7**	**1**	**2**	**3**	**4**	**0**	**0**	**0**	**13:22**
2012-13	**Florida**	**NHL**	**27**	**4**	**1**	**5**	**25**	**1**	**0**	**1**	**54**	**7.4**	**-8**	**14**	**64.3**	**13:30**									
2013-14	**Florida**	**NHL**	**76**	**15**	**22**	**37**	**73**	**1**	**1**	**3**	**161**	**9.3**	**1**	**71**	**45.1**	**15:55**									
2014-15	**Florida**	**NHL**	**63**	**8**	**7**	**15**	**28**	**0**	**0**	**2**	**93**	**8.6**	**-8**	**65**	**52.3**	**12:41**									
2015-16	**St. Louis**	**NHL**	**70**	**6**	**8**	**14**	**44**	**0**	**0**	**1**	**113**	**5.3**	**5**	**34**	**35.3**	**10:57**	**17**	**1**	**2**	**3**	**10**	**0**	**0**	**0**	**8:47**
2016-17	**St. Louis**	**NHL**	**73**	**10**	**8**	**18**	**45**	**0**	**2**	**1**	**85**	**11.8**	**-1**	**12**	**25.0**	**10:59**	**11**	**0**	**0**	**0**	**8**	**0**	**0**	**0**	**11:35**
	NHL Totals		**696**	**131**	**135**	**266**	**569**	**17**	**4**	**23**	**1360**	**9.6**		**309**	**42.4**	**13:10**	**54**	**5**	**8**	**13**	**66**	**1**	**0**	**1**	**11:41**

WHL All-Rookie Team (2001) • WHL Rookie of the Year (2001) • CHL All-Rookie Team (2001) • Canadian Major Junior Rookie of the Year (2001) • WHL West Second All-Star Team (2002)

• Missed majority of 2003-04 due to knee injury vs. Phoenix, December 22, 2003. Traded to **Philadelphia** by **Nashville** with Ryan Parent and Nashville's 1st (later traded back to Nashville – Nashville selected Jonathon Blum) and 3rd (later traded to Washington – Washington selected Phil Desimone) round picks in 2007 NHL Draft for Peter Forsberg, February 15, 2007. Traded to **Phoenix** by **Philadelphia** with Philadelphia's 2nd round pick (Lucas Lessio) in 2011 NHL Draft for Daniel Carcillo, March 4, 2009. Traded to **Columbus** by **Phoenix** with Sami Lepisto for Rostislav Klesla and Dane Byers, February 28, 2011. Signed as a free agent by **Florida**, July 1, 2011. Signed as a free agent by **St. Louis**, October 5, 2015.

VALIEV, Rinat

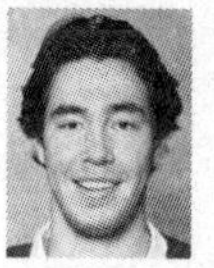

(va-LEE'yev, rin-NAT) **TOR**

Defense. Shoots left. 6'2", 214 lbs. Born, Nizhnekamsk, Russia, May 11, 1995. Toronto's 2nd pick, 68th overall, in 2014 NHL Draft.

Season	Club	League	GP	G	A	Pts	PIM	PP	SH	GW	S	S%	+/-	TF	F%	Min	Playoffs GP	G	A	Pts	PIM	PP	SH	GW	Min
2011-12	Bars Kazan Jr.	Russia-Jr.	15	1	1	2	10										1	1	0	1	0				
	Irbis Kazan Jr.	Rus.-Jr. B	26	2	7	9	38										4	0	2	2	6				
2012-13	Indiana Ice	USHL	36	6	7	13	43																		
	Bars Kazan Jr.	Russia-Jr.	6	0	0	0	0																		
2013-14	Kootenay Ice	WHL	55	5	23	28	68										13	1	8	9	16				
2014-15	Kootenay Ice	WHL	52	9	37	46	53										7	3	2	5	0				
	Toronto Marlies	AHL	2	0	0	0	0																		
2015-16	**Toronto**	**NHL**	**10**	**0**	**0**	**0**	**0**	**0**	**0**	**0**	**7**	**0.0**	**0**	**0**	**0.0**	**12:15**									
	Toronto Marlies	AHL	60	4	19	23	30										12	0	0	0	4				
2016-17	Toronto Marlies	AHL	47	3	10	13	79										9	0	1	1	10				
	NHL Totals		**10**	**0**	**0**	**0**	**0**	**0**	**0**	**0**	**7**	**0.0**		**0**	**0.0**	**12:15**									

WHL East Second All-Star Team (2015)

van RIEMSDYK, James

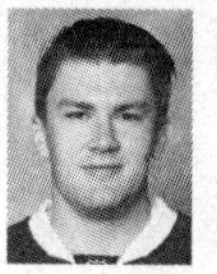

(VAN REEMZ-dighk, JAYMZ) **TOR**

Left wing. Shoots left. 6'3", 209 lbs. Born, Middletown, NJ, May 4, 1989. Philadelphia's 1st pick, 2nd overall, in 2007 NHL Draft.

Season	Club	League	GP	G	A	Pts	PIM	PP	SH	GW	S	S%	+/-	TF	F%	Min	Playoffs GP	G	A	Pts	PIM	PP	SH	GW	Min
2004-05	Christian Bros.	High-NJ	30	36	24	60	....																		
2005-06	USAHNTDP	U-17	11	7	5	12	18																		
	USAHNTDP	U-18	14	1	3	4	6																		
	USAHNTDP	NAHL	37	18	11	29	26										7	1	0	1	8				
2006-07	USAHNTDP	U-18	39	25	28	53	48																		
	USAHNTDP	NAHL	12	13	12	25	37																		
2007-08	New Hampshire	H-East	31	11	23	34	36																		
2008-09	New Hampshire	H-East	36	17	23	40	47																		
	Philadelphia	AHL	7	1	1	2	2										4	0	0	0	2				
2009-10	**Philadelphia**	**NHL**	**78**	**15**	**20**	**35**	**30**	**4**	**0**	**6**	**173**	**8.7**	**-1**	**2**	**0.0**	**12:58**	**21**	**3**	**3**	**6**	**4**	**0**	**0**	**0**	**11:54**
2010-11	**Philadelphia**	**NHL**	**75**	**21**	**19**	**40**	**35**	**3**	**0**	**4**	**173**	**12.1**	**15**	**3**	**0.0**	**14:32**	**11**	**7**	**0**	**7**	**4**	**2**	**0**	**1**	**19:23**
2011-12	**Philadelphia**	**NHL**	**43**	**11**	**13**	**24**	**24**	**2**	**0**	**1**	**121**	**9.1**	**-1**	**5**	**40.0**	**15:10**	**7**	**1**	**1**	**2**	**4**	**0**	**0**	**0**	**13:45**
2012-13	**Toronto**	**NHL**	**48**	**18**	**14**	**32**	**26**	**5**	**0**	**3**	**140**	**12.9**	**-7**	**43**	**55.8**	**19:12**	**7**	**2**	**5**	**7**	**4**	**1**	**0**	**0**	**19:41**
2013-14	**Toronto**	**NHL**	**80**	**30**	**31**	**61**	**50**	**9**	**2**	**3**	**279**	**10.8**	**-9**	**113**	**40.7**	**21:03**									
	United States	Olympics	6	1	6	7	2																		
2014-15	**Toronto**	**NHL**	**82**	**27**	**29**	**56**	**43**	**9**	**1**	**4**	**248**	**10.9**	**-33**	**54**	**38.9**	**19:05**									
2015-16	**Toronto**	**NHL**	**40**	**14**	**15**	**29**	**6**	**5**	**0**	**0**	**129**	**10.9**	**3**	**2**	**50.0**	**17:46**									
2016-17	**Toronto**	**NHL**	**82**	**29**	**33**	**62**	**37**	**6**	**0**	**5**	**238**	**12.2**	**-2**	**5**	**20.0**	**15:53**	**6**	**2**	**1**	**3**	**0**	**1**	**0**	**0**	**17:38**
	NHL Totals		**528**	**165**	**174**	**339**	**251**	**43**	**3**	**26**	**1501**	**11.0**		**227**	**41.9**	**16:56**	**52**	**15**	**10**	**25**	**16**	**4**	**0**	**1**	**15:27**

Hockey East All-Rookie Team (2008) • Hockey East Second All-Star Team (2009)

Traded to **Toronto** by **Philadelphia** for Luke Schenn, June 23, 2012. • Missed majority of 2015-16 due to foot injury at San Jose, January 9, 2016.

van RIEMSDYK, Trevor

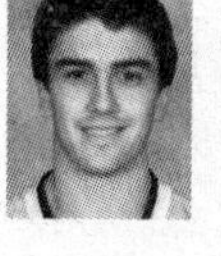

(VAN REEMZ-dighk,TREH-vuhr) **CAR**

Defense. Shoots right. 6'2", 188 lbs. Born, Middletown, NJ, July 24, 1991.

Season	Club	League	GP	G	A	Pts	PIM	PP	SH	GW	S	S%	+/-	TF	F%	Min	Playoffs GP	G	A	Pts	PIM	PP	SH	GW	Min
2007-08	Christian Bros.	High-NJ	27	9	39	48	12																		
2008-09	Christian Bros.	High-NJ	29	11	47	58	18																		
2009-10	N.H. Jr. Monarchs	EJHL	31	8	27	35	4										4	0	3	3	0				
2010-11	N.H. Jr. Monarchs	EJHL	39	16	22	38	20										6	2	3	5	4				
2011-12	New Hampshire	H-East	37	4	15	19	24																		
2012-13	New Hampshire	H-East	39	8	25	33	8																		
2013-14	New Hampshire	H-East	26	4	19	23	10																		
2014-15♦	**Chicago**	**NHL**	**18**	**0**	**1**	**1**	**2**	**0**	**0**	**0**	**21**	**0.0**	**0**	**0**	**0.0**	**13:32**	**4**	**0**	**0**	**0**	**0**	**0**	**0**	**0**	**7:02**
	Rockford IceHogs	AHL	8	0	3	3	0																		
2015-16	**Chicago**	**NHL**	**82**	**3**	**11**	**14**	**31**	**0**	**0**	**1**	**85**	**3.5**	**-5**	**0**	**0.0**	**19:59**	**7**	**1**	**0**	**1**	**2**	**0**	**0**	**0**	**23:53**
2016-17	**Chicago**	**NHL**	**58**	**5**	**11**	**16**	**29**	**0**	**0**	**2**	**73**	**6.8**	**17**	**0**	**0.0**	**18:25**	**4**	**0**	**0**	**0**	**0**	**0**	**0**	**0**	**19:02**
	NHL Totals		**158**	**8**	**23**	**31**	**62**	**0**	**0**	**3**	**179**	**4.5**		**0**	**0.0**	**18:40**	**15**	**1**	**0**	**1**	**2**	**0**	**0**	**0**	**18:06**

Hockey East All-Rookie Team (2012) • Hockey East First All-Star Team (2013) • NCAA East First All-American Team (2013)

Signed as a free agent by **Chicago**, March 24, 2014. • Missed majority of 2014-15 due to knee injury vs. Dallas, November 16, 2014. Claimed by **Vegas** from **Chicago** in Expansion Draft, June 21, 2017. Traded to **Carolina** by **Vegas** with Vegas' 7th round pick in 2018 NHL Draft for Pittsburgh's 2nd round pick (previously acquired, Vegas selected Jake Leschyshyn) in 2017 NHL Draft, June 22, 2017.

VAN BRABANT, Bryce

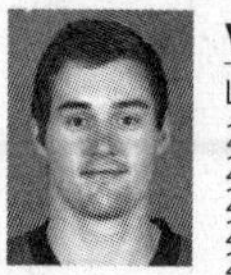

(VAN-BRAY-behnt, BRIGHS)

Left wing. Shoots left. 6'3", 207 lbs. Born, Morinville, AB, November 12, 1991.

Season	Club	League	GP	G	A	Pts	PIM	PP	SH	GW	S	S%	+/-	TF	F%	Min	Playoffs GP	G	A	Pts	PIM	PP	SH	GW	Min
2007-08	Ft. Saskatchewan	AMHL	33	11	4	15	65										12	3	4	7	22				
2008-09	Spruce Grove	AJHL	46	4	7	11	84										4	2	2	4	6				
2009-10	Spruce Grove	AJHL	51	8	6	14	137										16	1	4	5	16				
2010-11	Spruce Grove	AJHL	54	10	12	22	163										13	2	3	5	41				
2011-12	Quinnipiac	ECAC	33	4	3	7	51																		
2012-13	Quinnipiac	ECAC	42	5	8	13	48																		
2013-14	Quinnipiac	ECAC	40	15	7	22	*113																		
	Calgary	**NHL**	**6**	**0**	**0**	**0**	**2**	**0**	**0**	**0**	**4**	**0.0**	**-1**	**0**	**0.0**	**9:09**									

			Regular Season														Playoffs								
Season	Club	League	GP	G	A	Pts	PIM	PP	SH	GW	S	S%	+/-	TF	F%	Min	GP	G	A	Pts	PIM	PP	SH	GW	Min
2014-15	Adirondack	AHL	52	8	7	15	54	....	....	....	....	....	....	....	....	....	....	....	....	....	....	....	....	....	....
2015-16	Stockton Heat	AHL	62	7	9	16	51	....	....	....	....	....	....	....	....	....	....	....	....	....	....	....	....	....	....
2016-17	Idaho Steelheads	ECHL	15	4	5	9	10	....	....	....	....	....	....	....	....	....	5	0	0	0	4	....	....	....	....
	Texas Stars	AHL	21	1	1	2	41	....	....	....	....	....	....	....	....	....	....	....	....	....	....	....	....	....	....
	NHL Totals		**6**	**0**	**0**	**0**	**2**	**0**	**0**	**0**	**4**	**0.0**		**0**	**0.0**	**9:09**	....	....	....	....	....	....	....	....	....

Signed as a free agent by **Calgary**, March 29, 2014. Signed as a free agent by **Idaho** (ECHL), September 15, 2016. • Loaned to **Texas** (AHL) by **Idaho** (ECHL), October 12, 2016.

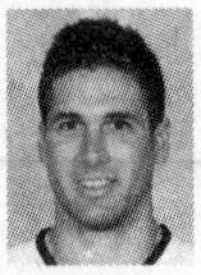

VANDEVELDE, Chris

(van-duh-VEHL-dee, KRIHS)

Center. Shoots left. 6'2", 190 lbs. Born, Moorhead, MN, March 15, 1987. Edmonton's 5th pick, 97th overall, in 2005 NHL Draft.

Season	Club	League	GP	G	A	Pts	PIM	PP	SH	GW	S	S%	+/-	TF	F%	Min	GP	G	A	Pts	PIM	PP	SH	GW	Min
2003-04	Moorhead Spuds	High-MN	29	19	24	43	....	....	....	....	....	....	....	....	....	....	....	....	....	....	....	....	....	....	....
2004-05	Moorhead Spuds	High-MN	30	35	32	67	28	....	....	....	....	....	....	....	....	....	....	....	....	....	....	....	....	....	....
	Lincoln Stars	USHL	7	1	4	5	0	....	....	....	....	....	....	....	....	....	4	0	2	2	0	....	....	....	....
2005-06	Lincoln Stars	USHL	56	16	20	36	70	....	....	....	....	....	....	....	....	....	9	1	3	4	10	....	....	....	....
2006-07	North Dakota	WCHA	38	3	6	9	37	....	....	....	....	....	....	....	....	....	....	....	....	....	....	....	....	....	....
2007-08	North Dakota	WCHA	43	15	17	32	38	....	....	....	....	....	....	....	....	....	....	....	....	....	....	....	....	....	....
2008-09	North Dakota	WCHA	43	18	17	35	69	....	....	....	....	....	....	....	....	....	....	....	....	....	....	....	....	....	....
2009-10	North Dakota	WCHA	42	16	25	41	22	....	....	....	....	....	....	....	....	....	....	....	....	....	....	....	....	....	....
2010-11	**Edmonton**	**NHL**	**12**	**0**	**2**	**2**	**12**	**0**	**0**	**0**	**16**	**0.0**	**-6**	**159**	**52.8**	**17:17**	....	....	....	....	....	....	....	....	....
	Oklahoma City	AHL	67	12	4	16	45	....	....	....	....	....	....	....	....	....	6	1	0	1	6	....	....	....	....
2011-12	**Edmonton**	**NHL**	**5**	**1**	**0**	**1**	**2**	**0**	**0**	**0**	**1**	**100.0**	**2**	**40**	**45.0**	**9:52**	....	....	....	....	....	....	....	....	....
	Oklahoma City	AHL	68	7	16	23	33	....	....	....	....	....	....	....	....	....	14	6	0	6	10	....	....	....	....
2012-13	Oklahoma City	AHL	57	7	13	20	27	....	....	....	....	....	....	....	....	....	17	2	2	4	10	....	....	....	....
	Edmonton	**NHL**	**11**	**0**	**0**	**0**	**4**	**0**	**0**	**0**	**7**	**0.0**	**-3**	**44**	**47.7**	**7:03**	....	....	....	....	....	....	....	....	....
2013-14	Adirondack	AHL	41	10	14	24	27	....	....	....	....	....	....	....	....	....	....	....	....	....	....	....	....	....	....
	Philadelphia	**NHL**	**18**	**0**	**1**	**1**	**6**	**0**	**0**	**0**	**8**	**0.0**	**-3**	**40**	**40.0**	**7:44**	....	....	....	....	....	....	....	....	....
2014-15	**Philadelphia**	**NHL**	**72**	**9**	**6**	**15**	**28**	**0**	**0**	**0**	**70**	**12.9**	**-6**	**56**	**37.5**	**11:44**	....	....	....	....	....	....	....	....	....
	Lehigh Valley	AHL	1	2	0	2	0	....	....	....	....	....	....	....	....	....	....	....	....	....	....	....	....	....	....
2015-16	**Philadelphia**	**NHL**	**79**	**2**	**12**	**14**	**27**	**0**	**1**	**0**	**77**	**2.6**	**-7**	**21**	**28.6**	**13:33**	**6**	**1**	**0**	**1**	**0**	**0**	**0**	**0**	**15:12**
2016-17	**Philadelphia**	**NHL**	**81**	**6**	**9**	**15**	**16**	**0**	**0**	**0**	**69**	**8.7**	**-5**	**42**	**52.4**	**11:34**	....	....	....	....	....	....	....	....	....
	NHL Totals		**278**	**18**	**30**	**48**	**95**	**0**	**1**	**0**	**248**	**7.3**		**402**	**46.8**	**11:58**	**6**	**1**	**0**	**1**	**0**	**0**	**0**	**0**	**15:12**

Signed as a free agent by **Adirondack** (AHL), October 3, 2013. Signed as a free agent by **Philadelphia**, December 12, 2013.

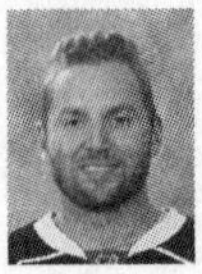

VANEK, Thomas

(VAN-ehk, TAW-muhs)

Left wing. Shoots right. 6'2", 214 lbs. Born, Vienna, Austria, January 19, 1984. Buffalo's 1st pick, 5th overall, in 2003 NHL Draft.

Season	Club	League	GP	G	A	Pts	PIM	PP	SH	GW	S	S%	+/-	TF	F%	Min	GP	G	A	Pts	PIM	PP	SH	GW	Min
99-2000	Sioux Falls	USHL	35	15	18	33	12	....	....	....	....	....	....	....	....	....	3	0	1	1	0	....	....	....	....
2000-01	Sioux Falls	USHL	20	19	10	29	15	....	....	....	....	....	....	....	....	....	8	5	4	9	2	....	....	....	....
2001-02	Sioux Falls	USHL	53	46	45	91	54	....	....	....	....	....	....	....	....	....	3	0	0	0	9	....	....	....	....
2002-03	U. of Minnesota	WCHA	45	31	31	62	60	....	....	....	....	....	....	....	....	....	....	....	....	....	....	....	....	....	....
	Austria	WJC-B	5	9	4	13	10	....	....	....	....	....	....	....	....	....	....	....	....	....	....	....	....	....	....
2003-04	U. of Minnesota	WCHA	38	26	25	51	72	....	....	....	....	....	....	....	....	....	....	....	....	....	....	....	....	....	....
2004-05	Rochester	AHL	74	42	26	68	62	....	....	....	....	....	....	....	....	....	5	2	3	5	10	....	....	....	....
	Austria	Oly-Q	3	1	0	1	0	....	....	....	....	....	....	....	....	....	....	....	....	....	....	....	....	....	....
2005-06	**Buffalo**	**NHL**	**81**	**25**	**23**	**48**	**72**	**11**	**0**	**4**	**204**	**12.3**	**-11**	**23**	**21.7**	**14:44**	**10**	**2**	**0**	**2**	**6**	**2**	**0**	**0**	**10:45**
2006-07	**Buffalo**	**NHL**	**82**	**43**	**41**	**84**	**40**	**15**	**0**	**5**	**237**	**18.1**	***47**	**39**	**28.2**	**16:47**	**16**	**6**	**4**	**10**	**10**	**1**	**0**	**2**	**16:27**
2007-08	**Buffalo**	**NHL**	**82**	**36**	**28**	**64**	**64**	**19**	**0**	**9**	**240**	**15.0**	**-5**	**13**	**46.2**	**16:51**	....	....	....	....	....	....	....	....	....
2008-09	**Buffalo**	**NHL**	**73**	**40**	**24**	**64**	**44**	***20**	**2**	**5**	**211**	**19.0**	**-1**	**6**	**16.7**	**17:12**	....	....	....	....	....	....	....	....	....
2009-10	**Buffalo**	**NHL**	**71**	**28**	**25**	**53**	**42**	**10**	**0**	**6**	**182**	**15.4**	**9**	**9**	**22.2**	**16:46**	**3**	**2**	**1**	**3**	**2**	**0**	**0**	**0**	**13:38**
2010-11	**Buffalo**	**NHL**	**80**	**32**	**41**	**73**	**24**	**11**	**0**	**5**	**238**	**13.4**	**2**	**26**	**30.8**	**17:21**	**7**	**5**	**0**	**5**	**0**	**4**	**0**	**0**	**17:10**
2011-12	**Buffalo**	**NHL**	**78**	**26**	**35**	**61**	**52**	**10**	**0**	**5**	**204**	**12.7**	**-6**	**6**	**50.0**	**16:56**	....	....	....	....	....	....	....	....	....
2012-13	Graz 99ers	Austria	11	5	10	15	4	....	....	....	....	....	....	....	....	....	....	....	....	....	....	....	....	....	....
	Buffalo	**NHL**	**38**	**20**	**21**	**41**	**20**	**9**	**1**	**2**	**119**	**16.8**	**-1**	**12**	**66.7**	**18:24**	....	....	....	....	....	....	....	....	....
2013-14	**Buffalo**	**NHL**	**13**	**4**	**5**	**9**	**4**	**1**	**0**	**0**	**50**	**8.0**	**-5**	**5**	**40.0**	**18:37**	....	....	....	....	....	....	....	....	....
	NY Islanders	**NHL**	**47**	**17**	**27**	**44**	**34**	**5**	**0**	**2**	**137**	**12.4**	**4**	**1**	**100.0**	**20:00**	....	....	....	....	....	....	....	....	....
	Austria	Olympics	4	0	1	1	4	....	....	....	....	....	....	....	....	....	....	....	....	....	....	....	....	....	....
	Montreal	**NHL**	**18**	**6**	**9**	**15**	**8**	**2**	**0**	**2**	**61**	**9.8**	**8**	**40**	**42.5**	**18:11**	**17**	**5**	**5**	**10**	**4**	**3**	**0**	**0**	**14:53**
2014-15	**Minnesota**	**NHL**	**80**	**21**	**31**	**52**	**37**	**5**	**0**	**2**	**171**	**12.3**	**-6**	**20**	**50.0**	**16:13**	**10**	**0**	**4**	**4**	**2**	**0**	**0**	**0**	**14:12**
2015-16	**Minnesota**	**NHL**	**74**	**18**	**23**	**41**	**22**	**6**	**0**	**5**	**146**	**12.3**	**-10**	**38**	**31.6**	**15:37**	....	....	....	....	....	....	....	....	....
2016-17	**Detroit**	**NHL**	**48**	**15**	**23**	**38**	**16**	**5**	**0**	**2**	**99**	**15.2**	**2**	**15**	**40.0**	**14:37**	....	....	....	....	....	....	....	....	....
	Florida	**NHL**	**20**	**2**	**8**	**10**	**6**	**0**	**0**	**0**	**34**	**5.9**	**-7**	**0**	**0.0**	**13:54**	....	....	....	....	....	....	....	....	....
	NHL Totals		**885**	**333**	**364**	**697**	**485**	**129**	**3**	**54**	**2333**	**14.3**		**253**	**36.4**	**16:40**	**63**	**20**	**14**	**34**	**24**	**10**	**0**	**2**	**14:43**

USHL First All-Star Team (2002) • USHL MVP (2002) • WCHA All-Rookie Team (2003) • WCHA Second All-Star Team (2003, 2004) • WCHA Rookie of the Year (2003) • NCAA Championship All-Tournament Team (2003) • NCAA Championship Tournament MVP (2003) • NCAA West Second All-American Team (2004) • AHL All-Rookie Team (2005) • NHL Second All-Star Team (2007)

Played in NHL All-Star Game (2009)

Signed as a free agent by **Graz** (Austria), October 1, 2012. Traded to **NY Islanders** by **Buffalo** for Matt Moulson and NY Islanders' 1st (later traded to Ottawa – Ottawa selected Colin White) and 2nd (Brendan Guhle) round picks in 2015 NHL Draft, October 27, 2013. Traded to **Montreal** by **NY Islanders** with NY Islanders' 5th round pick (Nikolas Koberstein) in 2014 NHL Draft for Sebastian Collberg and Montreal's 2nd round pick (later traded to Tampa Bay – Tampa Bay selected Johnathan MacLeod) in 2014 NHL Draft, March 5, 2014. Signed as a free agent by **Minnesota**, July 1, 2014. Signed as a free agent by **Detroit**, July 1, 2016. Traded to **Florida** by **Detroit** for Dylan McIlrath and Florida's 3rd round pick (Kasper Kotkansalo) in 2017 NHL Draft, March 1, 2017.

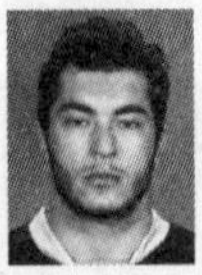

VARONE, Phil

(vah-ROH-nee, FIHL) **PHI**

Center. Shoots left. 5'10", 185 lbs. Born, Vaughan, ON, December 4, 1990. San Jose's 3rd pick, 147th overall, in 2009 NHL Draft.

Season	Club	League	GP	G	A	Pts	PIM	PP	SH	GW	S	S%	+/-	TF	F%	Min	GP	G	A	Pts	PIM	PP	SH	GW	Min
2005-06	Vaughan M.M.	GTHL	49	34	29	63	....	....	....	....	....	....	....	....	....	....	....	....	....	....	....	....	....	....	....
	Vaughan Midget	GTHL	4	6	1	7	2	....	....	....	....	....	....	....	....	....	....	....	....	....	....	....	....	....	....
2006-07	Kitchener	ON-Jr.B	20	10	11	21	21	....	....	....	....	....	....	....	....	....	....	....	....	....	....	....	....	....	....
	Kitchener Rangers	OHL	13	1	3	4	2	....	....	....	....	....	....	....	....	....	....	....	....	....	....	....	....	....	....
2007-08	Kitchener Rangers	OHL	35	5	20	25	12	....	....	....	....	....	....	....	....	....	....	....	....	....	....	....	....	....	....
	London Knights	OHL	31	10	26	36	14	....	....	....	....	....	....	....	....	....	5	1	1	2	7	....	....	....	....
2008-09	London Knights	OHL	58	19	33	52	32	....	....	....	....	....	....	....	....	....	14	10	9	19	19	....	....	....	....
2009-10	London Knights	OHL	31	9	22	31	17	....	....	....	....	....	....	....	....	....	....	....	....	....	....	....	....	....	....
2010-11	London Knights	OHL	4	1	0	1	2	....	....	....	....	....	....	....	....	....	....	....	....	....	....	....	....	....	....
	Erie Otters	OHL	55	33	48	81	30	....	....	....	....	....	....	....	....	....	7	3	10	13	4	....	....	....	....
2011-12	Rochester	AHL	76	11	41	52	42	....	....	....	....	....	....	....	....	....	3	2	1	3	0	....	....	....	....
2012-13	Rochester	AHL	62	11	24	35	42	....	....	....	....	....	....	....	....	....	3	0	0	0	2	....	....	....	....
2013-14	**Buffalo**	**NHL**	**9**	**1**	**1**	**2**	**4**	**0**	**0**	**0**	**15**	**6.7**	**-3**	**56**	**46.4**	**11:24**	....	....	....	....	....	....	....	....	....
	Rochester	AHL	69	18	43	61	58	....	....	....	....	....	....	....	....	....	5	0	3	3	0	....	....	....	....
2014-15	**Buffalo**	**NHL**	**28**	**3**	**2**	**5**	**10**	**0**	**0**	**0**	**28**	**10.7**	**-14**	**326**	**45.1**	**13:27**	....	....	....	....	....	....	....	....	....
	Rochester	AHL	55	15	29	44	22	....	....	....	....	....	....	....	....	....	....	....	....	....	....	....	....	....	....
2015-16	**Buffalo**	**NHL**	**5**	**1**	**1**	**2**	**2**	**0**	**0**	**0**	**2**	**50.0**	**1**	**9**	**66.7**	**8:19**	....	....	....	....	....	....	....	....	....
	Rochester	AHL	44	13	19	32	20	....	....	....	....	....	....	....	....	....	....	....	....	....	....	....	....	....	....
	Ottawa	**NHL**	**1**	**0**	**1**	**1**	**0**	**0**	**0**	**0**	**0**	**0.0**	**1**	**9**	**44.4**	**9:29**	....	....	....	....	....	....	....	....	....
	Binghamton	AHL	21	6	17	23	8	....	....	....	....	....	....	....	....	....	....	....	....	....	....	....	....	....	....
2016-17	**Ottawa**	**NHL**	**7**	**0**	**0**	**0**	**2**	**0**	**0**	**0**	**1**	**0.0**	**-3**	**27**	**55.6**	**7:59**	....	....	....	....	....	....	....	....	....
	Binghamton	AHL	65	15	36	51	22	....	....	....	....	....	....	....	....	....	....	....	....	....	....	....	....	....	....
	NHL Totals		**50**	**5**	**5**	**10**	**18**	**0**	**0**	**0**	**46**	**10.9**		**427**	**46.4**	**11:43**	....	....	....	....	....	....	....	....	....

Signed as a free agent by **Rochester** (AHL), September 27, 2011. Signed as a free agent by **Buffalo**, March 19, 2012. Traded to **Ottawa** by **Buffalo** with Jason Akeson, Jerome Leduc and future considerations (conditions not met) for Michael Sdao, Eric O'Dell, Cole Schneider and Alexander Guptill, February 27, 2016. Signed as a free agent by **Philadelphia**, July 1, 2017.

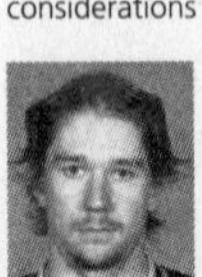

VATANEN, Sami

(VAH-ta-nehn, SA-mee) **ANA**

Defense. Shoots right. 5'10", 183 lbs. Born, Jyvaskyla, Finland, June 3, 1991. Anaheim's 5th pick, 106th overall, in 2009 NHL Draft.

Season	Club	League	GP	G	A	Pts	PIM	PP	SH	GW	S	S%	+/-	TF	F%	Min	GP	G	A	Pts	PIM	PP	SH	GW	Min
2006-07	JyP Jyvaskyla U18	Fin-U18	....	....	....	....	....	....	....	....	....	....	....	....	....	....	7	1	0	1	2	....	....	....	....
2007-08	JyP Jyvaskyla U18	Fin-U18	35	9	29	38	30	....	....	....	....	....	....	....	....	....	1	0	0	0	0	....	....	....	....
	JyP Jyvaskyla Jr.	Fin-Jr.	....	....	....	....	....	....	....	....	....	....	....	....	....	....	2	0	0	0	0	....	....	....	....

			Regular Season														Playoffs								
Season	Club	League	GP	G	A	Pts	PIM	PP	SH	GW	S	S%	+/-	TF	F%	Min	GP	G	A	Pts	PIM	PP	SH	GW	Min
2008-09	JyP Jyvaskyla U18	Fin-U18	2	0	0	0	0	....	....	....	....	....	....	....	....	....	1	1	1	2	14	....	....	....	....
	Suomi U20	Finland-2	2	0	0	0	2	....	....	....	....	....	....	....	....	....	....	....	....	....	....	....	....	....	....
	D Team Jyvaskyla	Finland-2	5	1	1	2	8	....	....	....	....	....	....	....	....	....	....	....	....	....	....	....	....	....	....
	JyP Jyvaskyla Jr.	Fin-Jr.	20	3	7	10	22	....	....	....	....	....	....	....	....	....	....	....	....	....	....	....	....	....	....
2009-10	Suomi U20	Finland-2	1	0	0	0	2	....	....	....	....	....	....	....	....	....	....	....	....	....	....	....	....	....	....
	JYP Jyvaskyla	Finland	55	7	23	30	44	....	....	....	....	....	....	....	....	....	14	3	4	7	6	....	....	....	....
2010-11	Suomi U20	Finland-2	1	0	0	0	0	....	....	....	....	....	....	....	....	....	....	....	....	....	....	....	....	....	....
	JYP Jyvaskyla	Finland	52	11	20	31	30	....	....	....	....	....	....	....	....	....	3	1	1	2	0	....	....	....	....
2011-12	JYP Jyvaskyla	Finland	49	14	28	42	40	....	....	....	....	....	....	....	....	....	4	2	0	2	4	....	....	....	....
2012-13	Norfolk Admirals	AHL	62	9	36	45	44	....	....	....	....	....	....	....	....	....	....	....	....	....	....	....	....	....	....
	Anaheim	**NHL**	**8**	**2**	**0**	**2**	**0**	**1**	**0**	**0**	**6**	**33.3**	**3**	**0**	**0.0**	**15:49**	....	....	....	....	....	....	....	....	....
2013-14	**Anaheim**	**NHL**	**48**	**6**	**15**	**21**	**22**	**2**	**0**	**0**	**73**	**8.2**	**9**	**0**	**0.0**	**17:27**	**5**	**0**	**1**	**1**	**0**	**0**	**0**	**0**	**20:14**
	Norfolk Admirals	AHL	8	2	5	7	4	....	....	....	....	....	....	....	....	....	5	0	3	3	4	....	....	....	....
	Finland	Olympics	6	0	5	5	0	....	....	....	....	....	....	....	....	....	....	....	....	....	....	....	....	....	....
2014-15	**Anaheim**	**NHL**	**67**	**12**	**25**	**37**	**36**	**7**	**1**	**1**	**122**	**9.8**	**5**	**2**	**50.0**	**21:28**	**16**	**3**	**8**	**11**	**8**	**0**	**0**	**0**	**21:14**
2015-16	**Anaheim**	**NHL**	**71**	**9**	**29**	**38**	**20**	**4**	**0**	**2**	**140**	**6.4**	**8**	**0**	**0.0**	**21:19**	**7**	**1**	**3**	**4**	**6**	**0**	**0**	**1**	**23:03**
2016-17	**Anaheim**	**NHL**	**71**	**3**	**21**	**24**	**30**	**2**	**0**	**0**	**117**	**2.6**	**3**	**0**	**0.0**	**21:40**	**12**	**1**	**5**	**6**	**4**	**1**	**0**	**0**	**22:08**
	NHL Totals		**265**	**32**	**90**	**122**	**108**	**16**	**1**	**3**	**458**	**7.0**		**2**	**50.0**	**20:35**	**40**	**5**	**17**	**22**	**18**	**1**	**0**	**1**	**21:42**

AHL All-Rookie Team (2013) • AHL First All-Star Team (2013)

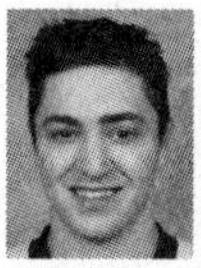

VATRANO, Frank

(vuh-TRAH-noh, FRANK) **BOS**

Left wing. Shoots left. 5'9", 201 lbs. Born, East Longmeadow, MA, March 14, 1994.

Season	Club	League	GP	G	A	Pts	PIM	PP	SH	GW	S	S%	+/-	TF	F%	Min	GP	G	A	Pts	PIM	PP	SH	GW	Min
2009-10	Bos. Jr. Bruins	EJHL	8	0	2	2	2	....	....	....	....	....	....	....	....	....	....	....	....	....	....	....	....	....	....
2010-11	USAHNTDP	USHL	34	11	4	15	22	....	....	....	....	....	....	....	....	....	2	1	0	1	0	....	....	....	....
	USAHNTDP	U-17	17	7	7	14	28	....	....	....	....	....	....	....	....	....	....	....	....	....	....	....	....	....	....
2011-12	USAHNTDP	USHL	24	7	11	18	8	....	....	....	....	....	....	....	....	....	....	....	....	....	....	....	....	....	....
	USAHNTDP	U-18	36	9	8	17	16	....	....	....	....	....	....	....	....	....	....	....	....	....	....	....	....	....	....
2012-13	USAHNTDP	USHL	1	0	1	1	2	....	....	....	....	....	....	....	....	....	....	....	....	....	....	....	....	....	....
	USAHNTDP	U-18	4	0	3	3	19	....	....	....	....	....	....	....	....	....	....	....	....	....	....	....	....	....	....
	Bos. Jr. Bruins	EJHL	19	13	9	22	20	....	....	....	....	....	....	....	....	....	....	....	....	....	....	....	....	....	....
2013-14	U. Mass Lowell	H-East	1	0	0	0	0	....	....	....	....	....	....	....	....	....	....	....	....	....	....	....	....	....	....
2014-15	U. Mass Lowell	H-East	36	18	10	28	28	....	....	....	....	....	....	....	....	....	....	....	....	....	....	....	....	....	....
	Providence Bruins	AHL	5	1	0	1	0	....	....	....	....	....	....	....	....	....	....	....	....	....	....	....	....	....	....
2015-16	**Boston**	**NHL**	**39**	**8**	**3**	**11**	**14**	**0**	**0**	**1**	**99**	**8.1**	**–3**	**3**	**0.0**	**11:53**	....	....	....	....	....	....	....	....	....
	Providence Bruins	AHL	36	*36	19	55	22	....	....	....	....	....	....	....	....	....	3	1	0	1	2	....	....	....	....
2016-17	**Boston**	**NHL**	**44**	**10**	**8**	**18**	**14**	**4**	**0**	**1**	**116**	**8.6**	**–3**	**7**	**28.6**	**13:29**	**6**	**1**	**0**	**1**	**4**	**0**	**0**	**0**	**11:21**
	Providence Bruins	AHL	2	2	0	2	4	....	....	....	....	....	....	....	....	....	....	....	....	....	....	....	....	....	....
	NHL Totals		**83**	**18**	**11**	**29**	**28**	**4**	**0**	**2**	**215**	**8.4**		**10**	**20.0**	**12:44**	**6**	**1**	**0**	**1**	**4**	**0**	**0**	**0**	**11:21**

AHL All-Rookie Team (2016) • AHL First All-Star Team (2016) • Willie Marshall Award (AHL – Top Goal-scorer) (2016) • Dudley "Red" Garrett Memorial Award (AHL – Rookie of the Year) (2016) (co -winner - Mikko Rantanen)

Signed as a free agent by **Boston**, March 13, 2015.

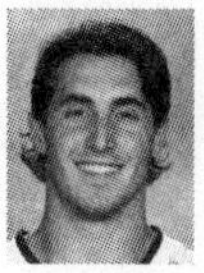

VECCHIONE, Mike

(veh-KEE-OH-nee, MIGHK) **PHI**

Center. Shoots right. 5'10", 195 lbs. Born, Saugas, MA, February 25, 1993.

Season	Club	League	GP	G	A	Pts	PIM	PP	SH	GW	S	S%	+/-	TF	F%	Min	GP	G	A	Pts	PIM	PP	SH	GW	Min
2008-09	Malden Cath.	High-MA	....	8	15	23	....	....	....	....	....	....	....	....	....	....	....	0	0	0	....	....	....	....	....
2009-10	Malden Catholic	High-MA	....	24	30	54	....	....	....	....	....	....	....	....	....	....	....	2	0	2	....	....	....	....	....
2010-11	Malden Catholic	High-MA	....	26	44	70	....	....	....	....	....	....	....	....	....	....	....	0	8	8	....	....	....	....	....
2011-12	Tri-City Storm	USHL	49	10	19	29	28	....	....	....	....	....	....	....	....	....	2	0	2	2	0	....	....	....	....
2012-13	Tri-City Storm	USHL	63	26	34	60	75	....	....	....	....	....	....	....	....	....	....	....	....	....	....	....	....	....	....
2013-14	Union College	ECAC	38	14	20	34	32	....	....	....	....	....	....	....	....	....	....	....	....	....	....	....	....	....	....
2014-15	Union College	ECAC	39	19	*31	50	18	....	....	....	....	....	....	....	....	....	....	....	....	....	....	....	....	....	....
2015-16	Union College	ECAC	34	9	20	29	30	....	....	....	....	....	....	....	....	....	....	....	....	....	....	....	....	....	....
2016-17	Union College	ECAC	38	*29	34	*63	45	....	....	....	....	....	....	....	....	....	....	....	....	....	....	....	....	....	....
	Philadelphia	**NHL**	**2**	**0**	**0**	**0**	**0**	**0**	**0**	**0**	**1**	**0.0**	**–1**	**12**	**66.7**	**8:30**	....	....	....	....	....	....	....	....	....
	NHL Totals		**2**	**0**	**0**	**0**	**0**	**0**	**0**	**0**	**1**	**0.0**		**12**	**66.7**	**8:30**	....	....	....	....	....	....	....	....	....

ECAC First All-Team (2017) • NCAA East First All-American Team (2017)

Signed as a free agent by **Philadelphia**, March 31, 2017.

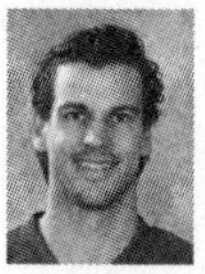

VERMETTE, Antoine

(vuhr-MEHT, AN-twuhn) **ANA**

Center. Shoots left. 6'1", 198 lbs. Born, St-Agapit, QC, July 20, 1982. Ottawa's 3rd pick, 55th overall, in 2000 NHL Draft.

Season	Club	League	GP	G	A	Pts	PIM	PP	SH	GW	S	S%	+/-	TF	F%	Min	GP	G	A	Pts	PIM	PP	SH	GW	Min
1997-98	Quebec Select	QAHA	19	11	20	31	36	....	....	....	....	....	....	....	....	....	....	....	....	....	....	....	....	....	....
	Levis	QAAA	8	1	1	2	4	....	....	....	....	....	....	....	....	....	1	0	0	0	0	....	....	....	....
1998-99	Quebec Remparts	QMJHL	57	9	17	26	32	....	....	....	....	....	....	....	....	....	13	0	0	0	2	....	....	....	....
99-2000	Victoriaville Tigres	QMJHL	71	30	41	71	87	....	....	....	....	....	....	....	....	....	6	0	1	1	6	....	....	....	....
2000-01	Victoriaville Tigres	QMJHL	71	57	62	119	102	....	....	....	....	....	....	....	....	....	9	4	6	10	14	....	....	....	....
2001-02	Victoriaville Tigres	QMJHL	4	0	2	2	6	....	....	....	....	....	....	....	....	....	22	10	16	26	10	....	....	....	....
2002-03	Binghamton	AHL	80	34	28	62	57	....	....	....	....	....	....	....	....	....	14	2	9	11	10	....	....	....	....
2003-04	**Ottawa**	**NHL**	**57**	**7**	**7**	**14**	**16**	**0**	**1**	**0**	**63**	**11.1**	**5**	**100**	**44.0**	**11:59**	**4**	**0**	**1**	**1**	**4**	**0**	**0**	**0**	**11:35**
	Binghamton	AHL	3	0	0	0	6	....	....	....	....	....	....	....	....	....	....	....	....	....	....	....	....	....	....
2004-05	Binghamton	AHL	78	28	45	73	36	....	....	....	....	....	....	....	....	....	6	1	4	5	10	....	....	....	....
2005-06	**Ottawa**	**NHL**	**82**	**21**	**12**	**33**	**44**	**1**	**6**	**4**	**123**	**17.1**	**17**	**537**	**57.9**	**12:35**	**10**	**2**	**0**	**2**	**4**	**0**	**0**	**1**	**15:00**
2006-07	**Ottawa**	**NHL**	**77**	**19**	**20**	**39**	**52**	**2**	**3**	**2**	**151**	**12.6**	**–2**	**834**	**53.0**	**15:42**	**20**	**2**	**3**	**5**	**6**	**0**	**0**	**0**	**16:20**
2007-08	**Ottawa**	**NHL**	**81**	**24**	**29**	**53**	**51**	**4**	**3**	**3**	**175**	**13.7**	**3**	**1217**	**56.7**	**17:35**	**4**	**0**	**0**	**0**	**4**	**0**	**0**	**0**	**20:33**
2008-09	**Ottawa**	**NHL**	**62**	**9**	**19**	**28**	**42**	**2**	**0**	**0**	**141**	**6.4**	**–12**	**771**	**58.4**	**18:03**	....	....	....	....	....	....	....	....	....
	Columbus	**NHL**	**17**	**7**	**6**	**13**	**8**	**1**	**1**	**1**	**33**	**21.2**	**5**	**341**	**56.3**	**19:29**	**4**	**0**	**0**	**0**	**10**	**0**	**0**	**0**	**16:47**
2009-10	**Columbus**	**NHL**	**82**	**27**	**38**	**65**	**32**	**6**	**2**	**1**	**156**	**17.3**	**2**	**1573**	**54.2**	**20:09**	....	....	....	....	....	....	....	....	....
2010-11	**Columbus**	**NHL**	**82**	**19**	**28**	**47**	**60**	**3**	**1**	**3**	**183**	**10.4**	**0**	**1540**	**55.6**	**18:49**	....	....	....	....	....	....	....	....	....
2011-12	**Columbus**	**NHL**	**60**	**8**	**19**	**27**	**12**	**2**	**1**	**3**	**106**	**7.5**	**–17**	**804**	**56.3**	**17:14**	....	....	....	....	....	....	....	....	....
	Phoenix	**NHL**	**22**	**3**	**7**	**10**	**16**	**2**	**0**	**1**	**43**	**7.0**	**4**	**336**	**57.1**	**17:07**	**16**	**5**	**5**	**10**	**24**	**3**	**0**	**0**	**18:04**
2012-13	**Phoenix**	**NHL**	**48**	**13**	**8**	**21**	**36**	**3**	**0**	**3**	**91**	**14.3**	**–3**	**839**	**57.5**	**18:15**	....	....	....	....	....	....	....	....	....
2013-14	**Phoenix**	**NHL**	**82**	**24**	**21**	**45**	**44**	**7**	**3**	**4**	**160**	**15.0**	**0**	**1783**	**56.4**	**19:13**	....	....	....	....	....	....	....	....	....
2014-15	**Arizona**	**NHL**	**63**	**13**	**22**	**35**	**34**	**6**	**0**	**1**	**85**	**15.3**	**–23**	**1381**	**56.1**	**18:59**	....	....	....	....	....	....	....	....	....
	♦ Chicago	**NHL**	**19**	**0**	**3**	**3**	**6**	**0**	**0**	**0**	**24**	**0.0**	**–2**	**196**	**50.0**	**14:04**	**20**	**4**	**3**	**7**	**4**	**0**	**0**	**3**	**13:08**
2015-16	**Arizona**	**NHL**	**76**	**17**	**21**	**38**	**93**	**6**	**1**	**2**	**123**	**13.8**	**–14**	**1351**	**55.8**	**16:38**	....	....	....	....	....	....	....	....	....
2016-17	**Anaheim**	**NHL**	**72**	**9**	**19**	**28**	**42**	**5**	**0**	**1**	**88**	**10.2**	**–7**	**1195**	**62.3**	**15:54**	**17**	**1**	**2**	**3**	**2**	**0**	**0**	**0**	**13:59**
	NHL Totals		**982**	**220**	**279**	**499**	**588**	**50**	**22**	**29**	**1745**	**12.6**		**14798**	**56.4**	**17:02**	**95**	**14**	**14**	**28**	**58**	**3**	**0**	**4**	**15:23**

AHL All-Rookie Team (2003)

• Missed majority of 2001-02 due to neck injury in Team Canada Jr. Selection Camp, June 3, 2001. Traded to **Columbus** by **Ottawa** for Pascal Leclaire and Columbus' 2nd round pick (Robin Lehner) in 2009 NHL Draft, March 4, 2009. Traded to **Phoenix** by **Columbus** for Curtis McElhinney, Ottawa's 2nd round pick (previously acquired, later traded to Philadelphia – Philadelphia selected Anthony Stolarz) in 2012 NHL Draft and Phoenix's 4th round pick (later traded to Philadelphia, later traded to Los Angeles – Los Angeles selected Justin Auger) in 2013 NHL Draft, February 22, 2012. Traded to **Chicago** by **Arizona** for Klas Dahlbeck and Chicago's 1st round pick (Nick Merkley) in 2015 NHL Draft, February 28, 2015. Signed as a free agent by **Arizona**, July 1, 2015. Signed as a free agent by **Anaheim**, August 15, 2016.

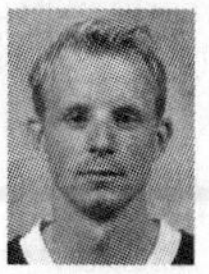

VERMIN, Joel

(VAIR-mihn, JOHL)

Right wing. Shoots left. 5'11", 192 lbs. Born, Bern, Switz., February 5, 1992. Tampa Bay's 6th pick, 186th overall, in 2013 NHL Draft.

Season	Club	League	GP	G	A	Pts	PIM	PP	SH	GW	S	S%	+/-	TF	F%	Min	GP	G	A	Pts	PIM	PP	SH	GW	Min
2007-08	SC Bern U17	Swiss-U17	32	24	21	45	22	....	....	....	....	....	....	....	....	....	13	2	8	10	2	....	....	....	....
	SC Bern Future Jr.	Swiss-Jr.	4	0	0	0	6	....	....	....	....	....	....	....	....	....	....	....	....	....	....	....	....	....	....
2008-09	SC Bern U17	Swiss-U17	28	29	25	54	50	....	....	....	....	....	....	....	....	....	8	7	9	16	12	....	....	....	....
	SC Bern Future Jr.	Swiss-Jr.	13	3	5	8	2	....	....	....	....	....	....	....	....	....	....	....	....	....	....	....	....	....	....
2009-10	SC Bern Future Jr.	Swiss-Jr.	34	28	27	55	59	....	....	....	....	....	....	....	....	....	7	3	8	11	2	....	....	....	....
	SC Bern	Swiss	12	0	0	0	0	....	....	....	....	....	....	....	....	....	....	....	....	....	....	....	....	....	....
2010-11	SC Bern Future Jr.	Swiss-Jr.	6	4	6	10	2	....	....	....	....	....	....	....	....	....	....	....	....	....	....	....	....	....	....
	SC Bern	Swiss	36	1	7	8	6	....	....	....	....	....	....	....	....	....	11	3	3	6	0	....	....	....	....
2011-12	SC Bern	Swiss	33	11	10	21	0	....	....	....	....	....	....	....	....	....	17	2	3	5	2	....	....	....	....

			Regular Season														Playoffs								
Season	Club	League	GP	G	A	Pts	PIM	PP	SH	GW	S	S%	+/-	TF	F%	Min	GP	G	A	Pts	PIM	PP	SH	GW	Min
2012-13	SC Bern	Swiss	47	13	22	35	14	....	....	....	....	....	....	....	....	....	19	3	6	9	8	....	....	....	....
2013-14	SC Bern	Swiss	55	8	14	22	18	....	....	....	....	....	....	....	....	....	....	....	....	....	....	....	....	....	....
	Syracuse Crunch	AHL	8	1	0	1	0	....	....	....	....	....	....	....	....	....	....	....	....	....	....	....	....	....	....
2014-15	Syracuse Crunch	AHL	73	12	21	33	16	....	....	....	....	....	....	....	....	....	3	0	1	1	0	....	....	....	....
2015-16	**Tampa Bay**	**NHL**	**6**	**0**	**1**	**1**	**0**	**0**	**0**	**0**	**1**	**0.0**	**1**	**1**	**100.0**	**9:08**	....	....	....	....	....	....	....	....	....
	Syracuse Crunch	AHL	37	9	12	21	6	....	....	....	....	....	....	....	....	....	....	....	....	....	....	....	....	....	....
2016-17	**Tampa Bay**	**NHL**	**18**	**0**	**3**	**3**	**4**	**0**	**0**	**0**	**12**	**0.0**	**2**	**3**	**66.7**	**10:56**	....	....	....	....	....	....	....	....	....
	Syracuse Crunch	AHL	46	13	19	32	17	....	....	....	....	....	....	....	....	....	22	9	2	11	8	....	....	....	....
	NHL Totals		**24**	**0**	**4**	**4**	**4**	**0**	**0**	**0**	**13**	**0.0**		**4**	**75.0**	**10:29**	....	....	....	....	....	....	....	....	....

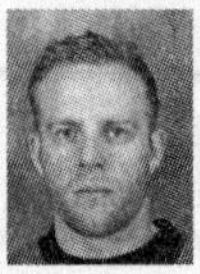

VERSTEEG, Kris

(vuhr-STEEG, KRIHS) **CGY**

Left wing. Shoots right. 5'11", 176 lbs. Born, Lethbridge, AB, May 13, 1986. Boston's 4th pick, 134th overall, in 2004 NHL Draft.

Season	Club	League	GP	G	A	Pts	PIM	PP	SH	GW	S	S%	+/-	TF	F%	Min	GP	G	A	Pts	PIM	PP	SH	GW	Min
2002-03	Lethbridge	WHL	57	8	10	18	32	....	....	....	....	....	....	....	....	....	....	....	....	....	....	....	....	....	....
2003-04	Lethbridge	WHL	68	16	33	49	85	....	....	....	....	....	....	....	....	....	....	....	....	....	....	....	....	....	....
2004-05	Lethbridge	WHL	68	22	30	52	68	....	....	....	....	....	....	....	....	....	5	0	1	1	4	....	....	....	....
2005-06	Kamloops Blazers	WHL	14	6	6	12	24	....	....	....	....	....	....	....	....	....	....	....	....	....	....	....	....	....	....
	Red Deer Rebels	WHL	57	10	26	36	103	....	....	....	....	....	....	....	....	....	....	....	....	....	....	....	....	....	....
	Providence Bruins	AHL	13	2	4	6	13	....	....	....	....	....	....	....	....	....	3	0	0	0	6	....	....	....	....
2006-07	Providence Bruins	AHL	43	22	27	49	19	....	....	....	....	....	....	....	....	....	....	....	....	....	....	....	....	....	....
	Norfolk Admirals	AHL	27	4	19	23	20	....	....	....	....	....	....	....	....	....	2	0	0	0	2	....	....	....	....
2007-08	**Chicago**	**NHL**	**13**	**2**	**2**	**4**	**6**	**0**	**0**	**0**	**21**	**9.5**	**–1**	**3**	**66.7**	**15:52**	....	....	....	....	....	....	....	....	....
	Rockford IceHogs	AHL	56	18	31	49	174	....	....	....	....	....	....	....	....	....	12	6	5	11	6	....	....	....	....
2008-09	**Chicago**	**NHL**	**78**	**22**	**31**	**53**	**55**	**6**	**4**	**3**	**139**	**15.8**	**15**	**266**	**46.6**	**17:02**	**17**	**4**	**8**	**12**	**22**	**3**	**0**	**0**	**16:14**
2009-10 ♦	**Chicago**	**NHL**	**79**	**20**	**24**	**44**	**35**	**4**	**3**	**4**	**184**	**10.9**	**8**	**183**	**42.1**	**15:44**	**22**	**6**	**8**	**14**	**14**	**0**	**0**	**2**	**17:13**
2010-11	**Toronto**	**NHL**	**53**	**14**	**21**	**35**	**29**	**5**	**0**	**0**	**128**	**10.9**	**–13**	**77**	**52.0**	**18:56**	....	....	....	....	....	....	....	....	....
	Philadelphia	**NHL**	**27**	**7**	**4**	**11**	**24**	**1**	**1**	**0**	**52**	**13.5**	**4**	**53**	**43.4**	**15:22**	**11**	**1**	**5**	**6**	**12**	**0**	**0**	**0**	**15:00**
2011-12	**Florida**	**NHL**	**71**	**23**	**31**	**54**	**49**	**8**	**1**	**5**	**181**	**12.7**	**4**	**65**	**32.3**	**19:55**	**7**	**3**	**2**	**5**	**8**	**2**	**0**	**1**	**20:34**
2012-13	**Florida**	**NHL**	**10**	**2**	**2**	**4**	**8**	**0**	**0**	**0**	**20**	**10.0**	**–8**	**5**	**0.0**	**16:53**	....	....	....	....	....	....	....	....	....
2013-14	**Florida**	**NHL**	**18**	**2**	**5**	**7**	**9**	**0**	**0**	**0**	**47**	**4.3**	**–9**	**19**	**47.4**	**15:42**	....	....	....	....	....	....	....	....	....
	Chicago	**NHL**	**63**	**10**	**19**	**29**	**27**	**1**	**0**	**1**	**110**	**9.1**	**9**	**100**	**47.0**	**14:06**	**15**	**1**	**2**	**3**	**4**	**0**	**0**	**0**	**11:56**
2014-15 ♦	**Chicago**	**NHL**	**61**	**14**	**20**	**34**	**35**	**2**	**0**	**1**	**134**	**10.4**	**11**	**48**	**31.3**	**15:51**	**12**	**1**	**1**	**2**	**6**	**0**	**0**	**0**	**13:21**
2015-16	**Carolina**	**NHL**	**63**	**11**	**22**	**33**	**36**	**2**	**0**	**2**	**136**	**8.1**	**–6**	**13**	**46.2**	**16:23**	....	....	....	....	....	....	....	....	....
	Los Angeles	**NHL**	**14**	**4**	**1**	**5**	**9**	**0**	**0**	**2**	**20**	**20.0**	**6**	**3**	**66.7**	**10:54**	**5**	**1**	**1**	**2**	**0**	**0**	**0**	**0**	**9:47**
2016-17	**Calgary**	**NHL**	**69**	**15**	**22**	**37**	**46**	**8**	**0**	**1**	**136**	**11.0**	**–3**	**102**	**52.0**	**14:44**	**4**	**1**	**3**	**4**	**4**	**1**	**0**	**0**	**15:20**
	NHL Totals		**619**	**146**	**204**	**350**	**368**	**37**	**9**	**19**	**1308**	**11.2**		**937**	**44.7**	**16:21**	**93**	**18**	**30**	**48**	**70**	**6**	**0**	**3**	**15:12**

NHL All-Rookie Team (2009)

Traded to **Chicago** by **Boston** with future considerations for Brandon Bochenski, February 3, 2007. Traded to **Toronto** by **Chicago** with Bill Sweatt for Viktor Stalberg, Chris Didomenico and Phillipe Paradis, June 30, 2010. Traded to **Philadelphia** by **Toronto** for Philadelphia's 1st (Stuart Percy) and 3rd (Josh Leivo) round picks in 2011 NHL Draft, February 14, 2011. Traded to **Florida** by **Philadelphia** for Florida's 2nd round pick (later traded to Tampa Bay – Tampa Bay selected Brian Hart) in 2012 NHL Draft and San Jose's 3rd round pick (previously acquired, Philadelphia selected Shayne Gostibehere) in 2012 NHL Draft, July 1, 2011. • Missed majority of 2012-13 due to recurring chest injury and knee injury vs. Tampa Bay, March 12, 2013. Traded to **Chicago** by **Florida** with Phillipe Lefebvre for Jimmy Hayes and Dylan Olsen, November 14, 2013. Traded to **Carolina** by **Chicago** with Joakim Nordstrom and Chicago's 3rd round pick (later traded back to Chicago, later traded to Detroit – Detroit selected Keith Petruzzelli) in 2017 NHL Draft for Dennis Robertson, Jake Massie and Carolina's 5th round pick (later traded to Vancouver –Vancouver selected Kristoffer Gunnarsson) in 2017 NHL Draft, September 11, 2015. Traded to **Los Angeles** by **Carolina** for Valentin Zykov and future considerations (conditions not met), February 28, 2016. Signed as a free agent by **Calgary**, October 11, 2016.

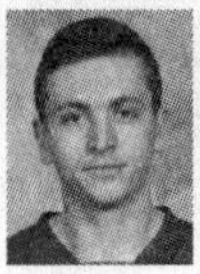

VESEY, Jimmy

(VEE-see, JIHM-mee) **NYR**

Left wing. Shoots left. 6'3", 207 lbs. Born, North Reading, MA, May 26, 1993. Nashville's 3rd pick, 66th overall, in 2012 NHL Draft.

Season	Club	League	GP	G	A	Pts	PIM	PP	SH	GW	S	S%	+/-	TF	F%	Min	GP	G	A	Pts	PIM	PP	SH	GW	Min
2009-10	Belmont Hill	High-MA	30	13	17	30	....	....	....	....	....	....	....	....	....	....	....	....	....	....	....	....	....	....	....
2010-11	Belmont Hill	High-MA	32	23	12	35	90	....	....	....	....	....	....	....	....	....	....	....	....	....	....	....	....	....	....
2011-12	South Shore	EJHL	45	*48	43	*91	52	....	....	....	....	....	....	....	....	....	6	5	3	8	2	....	....	....	....
2012-13	Harvard Crimson	ECAC	27	11	7	18	25	....	....	....	....	....	....	....	....	....	....	....	....	....	....	....	....	....	....
2013-14	Harvard Crimson	ECAC	31	13	9	22	14	....	....	....	....	....	....	....	....	....	....	....	....	....	....	....	....	....	....
2014-15	Harvard Crimson	ECAC	37	*32	26	*58	21	....	....	....	....	....	....	....	....	....	....	....	....	....	....	....	....	....	....
2015-16	Harvard Crimson	ECAC	33	*24	22	46	6	....	....	....	....	....	....	....	....	....	....	....	....	....	....	....	....	....	....
2016-17	**NY Rangers**	**NHL**	**80**	**16**	**11**	**27**	**26**	**5**	**0**	**6**	**116**	**13.8**	**–13**	**7**	**28.6**	**13:38**	**12**	**1**	**4**	**5**	**9**	**0**	**0**	**0**	**14:26**
	NHL Totals		**80**	**16**	**11**	**27**	**26**	**5**	**0**	**6**	**116**	**13.8**		**7**	**28.6**	**13:38**	**12**	**1**	**4**	**5**	**9**	**0**	**0**	**0**	**14:26**

ECAC All-Rookie Team (2013) • ECAC First All-Star Team (2015, 2016) • ECAC Player of the Year (2015, 2016) • NCAA East First All-American Team (2015, 2016) • Hobey Baker Memorial Award (Top U.S. Collegiate Player) (2016)

• Rights traded to **Buffalo** by **Nashville** for Minnesota's 3rd round pick (previously acquired, Nashville selected Rem Pitlick) in 2016 NHL Draft, June 20, 2016. Signed as a free agent by **NY Rangers**, August 19, 2016.

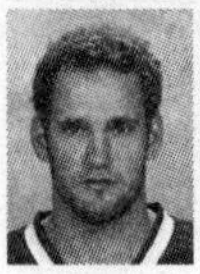

VEY, Linden

(VAY, LIHN-duhn)

Right wing. Shoots right. 6', 189 lbs. Born, Wakaw, SK, July 17, 1991. Los Angeles' 5th pick, 96th overall, in 2009 NHL Draft.

Season	Club	League	GP	G	A	Pts	PIM	PP	SH	GW	S	S%	+/-	TF	F%	Min	GP	G	A	Pts	PIM	PP	SH	GW	Min
2006-07	Beardy's	SMHL	44	28	44	72	26	....	....	....	....	....	....	....	....	....	....	....	....	....	....	....	....	....	....
	Medicine Hat	WHL	2	0	0	0	2	....	....	....	....	....	....	....	....	....	....	....	....	....	....	....	....	....	....
2007-08	Medicine Hat	WHL	48	8	9	17	21	....	....	....	....	....	....	....	....	....	5	0	1	1	2	....	....	....	....
2008-09	Medicine Hat	WHL	71	24	48	72	20	....	....	....	....	....	....	....	....	....	11	2	5	7	2	....	....	....	....
2009-10	Medicine Hat	WHL	72	24	51	75	34	....	....	....	....	....	....	....	....	....	12	2	6	8	8	....	....	....	....
2010-11	Medicine Hat	WHL	69	46	70	*116	36	....	....	....	....	....	....	....	....	....	15	12	13	25	8	....	....	....	....
2011-12	Manchester	AHL	74	19	24	43	16	....	....	....	....	....	....	....	....	....	4	2	4	6	0	....	....	....	....
2012-13	Manchester	AHL	74	22	45	67	32	....	....	....	....	....	....	....	....	....	4	2	0	2	4	....	....	....	....
2013-14	**Los Angeles**	**NHL**	**18**	**0**	**5**	**5**	**0**	**0**	**0**	**0**	**8**	**0.0**	**0**	**124**	**44.4**	**12:08**	....	....	....	....	....	....	....	....	....
	Manchester	AHL	43	14	34	48	20	....	....	....	....	....	....	....	....	....	4	0	2	2	4	....	....	....	....
2014-15	**Vancouver**	**NHL**	**75**	**10**	**14**	**24**	**18**	**4**	**0**	**2**	**61**	**16.4**	**–3**	**502**	**42.8**	**13:10**	**1**	**0**	**0**	**0**	**0**	**0**	**0**	**0**	**9:59**
2015-16	**Vancouver**	**NHL**	**41**	**4**	**11**	**15**	**6**	**3**	**0**	**0**	**40**	**10.0**	**–14**	**449**	**43.0**	**15:45**	....	....	....	....	....	....	....	....	....
	Utica Comets	AHL	26	3	12	15	8	....	....	....	....	....	....	....	....	....	....	....	....	....	....	....	....	....	....
2016-17	**Calgary**	**NHL**	**4**	**0**	**0**	**0**	**0**	**0**	**0**	**0**	**1**	**0.0**	**–2**	**24**	**37.5**	**11:01**	....	....	....	....	....	....	....	....	....
	Stockton Heat	AHL	61	15	40	55	40	....	....	....	....	....	....	....	....	....	5	4	1	5	2	....	....	....	....
	NHL Totals		**138**	**14**	**30**	**44**	**24**	**7**	**0**	**2**	**110**	**12.7**		**1099**	**42.9**	**13:44**	**1**	**0**	**0**	**0**	**0**	**0**	**0**	**0**	**9:59**

WHL East First All-Star Team (2011)

Traded to **Vancouver** by **Los Angeles** for Tampa Bay's 2nd round pick (previously acquired, Los Angeles selected Roland McKeown) in 2014 NHL Draft, June 28, 2014. Signed as a free agent by **Calgary**, July 5, 2016.

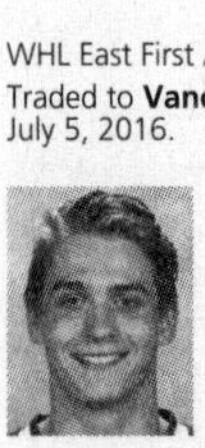

VIRTANEN, Jake

(vuhr-TA-nehn, JAYK) **VAN**

Right wing. Shoots right. 6'1", 208 lbs. Born, New Westminster, BC, August 17, 1996. Vancouver's 1st pick, 6th overall, in 2014 NHL Draft.

Season	Club	League	GP	G	A	Pts	PIM	PP	SH	GW	S	S%	+/-	TF	F%	Min	GP	G	A	Pts	PIM	PP	SH	GW	Min
2010-11	Abbots. Hawks	Minor-BC	62	70	49	119	153	....	....	....	....	....	....	....	....	....	....	....	....	....	....	....	....	....	....
	Yale Lions	High-BC	....	....	....	....	....	....	....	....	....	....	....	....	....	....	1	1	1	2	....	....	....	....	....
2011-12	Fraser Valley	BCMML	39	17	22	39	120	....	....	....	....	....	....	....	....	....	....	....	....	....	....	....	....	....	....
	Yale Lions	High-BC	6	10	3	13	....	....	....	....	....	....	....	....	....	....	....	....	....	....	....	....	....	....	....
	Calgary Hitmen	WHL	9	3	1	4	4	....	....	....	....	....	....	....	....	....	5	0	0	0	4	....	....	....	....
2012-13	Calgary Hitmen	WHL	62	16	18	34	67	....	....	....	....	....	....	....	....	....	15	2	4	6	27	....	....	....	....
2013-14	Calgary Hitmen	WHL	71	45	26	71	100	....	....	....	....	....	....	....	....	....	6	1	3	4	4	....	....	....	....
2014-15	Calgary Hitmen	WHL	50	21	31	52	82	....	....	....	....	....	....	....	....	....	14	5	8	13	28	....	....	....	....
	Utica Comets	AHL	....	....	....	....	....	....	....	....	....	....	....	....	....	....	10	0	1	1	6	....	....	....	....
2015-16	**Vancouver**	**NHL**	**55**	**7**	**6**	**13**	**45**	**1**	**0**	**1**	**94**	**7.4**	**–7**	**5**	**40.0**	**11:34**	....	....	....	....	....	....	....	....	....
	Utica Comets	AHL	2	0	0	0	0	....	....	....	....	....	....	....	....	....	....	....	....	....	....	....	....	....	....
2016-17	**Vancouver**	**NHL**	**10**	**0**	**1**	**1**	**2**	**0**	**0**	**0**	**13**	**0.0**	**1**	**3**	**100.0**	**10:09**	....	....	....	....	....	....	....	....	....
	Utica Comets	AHL	65	9	10	19	48	....	....	....	....	....	....	....	....	....	....	....	....	....	....	....	....	....	....
	NHL Totals		**65**	**7**	**7**	**14**	**47**	**1**	**0**	**1**	**107**	**6.5**		**8**	**62.5**	**11:21**	....	....	....	....	....	....	....	....	....

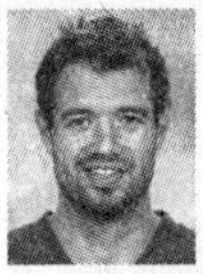

VLASIC, Marc-Edouard
(vih-LASH-ihc, MAHRK-EHD-wahrd) **S.J.**

Defense. Shoots left. 6'1", 205 lbs. Born, Montreal, QC, March 30, 1987. San Jose's 2nd pick, 35th overall, in 2005 NHL Draft.

Season	Club	League	GP	G	A	Pts	PIM	PP	SH	GW	S	S%	+/-	TF	F%	Min	GP	G	A	Pts	PIM	PP	SH	GW	Min
			Regular Season														Playoffs								
2002-03	West Island Lions	QAAA	41	4	6	10	14	....	....	....	....	....	....	....	....	....	9	0	3	3	0	....	....	....	....
2003-04	West Island Lions	QAAA	2	1	1	2	0	....	....	....	....	....	....	....	....	....	....	....	....	....	....	....	....	....	....
	Quebec Remparts	QMJHL	41	1	9	10	4	....	....	....	....	....	....	....	....	....	5	0	1	1	0	....	....	....	....
2004-05	Quebec Remparts	QMJHL	70	5	25	30	33	....	....	....	....	....	....	....	....	....	13	2	7	9	2	....	....	....	....
2005-06	Quebec Remparts	QMJHL	66	16	57	73	57	....	....	....	....	....	....	....	....	....	23	5	24	29	10	....	....	....	....
2006-07	San Jose	NHL	81	3	23	26	18	2	0	0	66	4.5	13	0	0.0	22:12	11	0	1	1	2	0	0	0	22:52
2007-08	San Jose	NHL	82	2	12	14	24	1	0	0	72	2.8	–12	0	0.0	21:37	13	0	1	1	0	0	0	0	24:39
	Worcester Sharks	AHL	1	0	2	2	0	....	....	....	....	....	....	....	....	....	....	....	....	....	....	....	....	....	....
2008-09	San Jose	NHL	82	6	30	36	42	3	0	1	104	5.8	15	0	0.0	23:54	6	0	1	1	0	0	0	0	20:39
2009-10	San Jose	NHL	64	3	13	16	33	1	0	0	74	4.1	21	0	0.0	22:05	15	0	3	3	4	0	0	0	21:53
2010-11	San Jose	NHL	80	4	14	18	18	0	0	2	116	3.4	14	0	0.0	20:52	18	0	3	3	4	0	0	0	21:45
2011-12	San Jose	NHL	82	4	19	23	40	0	0	1	119	3.4	11	0	0.0	23:09	5	0	0	0	2	0	0	0	20:53
2012-13	San Jose	NHL	48	3	4	7	29	0	0	0	59	5.1	5	0	0.0	20:49	11	1	1	2	6	0	0	0	20:40
2013-14	San Jose	NHL	81	5	19	24	38	0	1	0	138	3.6	31	0	0.0	20:43	5	1	2	3	0	1	0	0	17:00
	Canada	Olympics	6	0	0	0	0	....	....	....	....	....	....	....	....	....	....	....	....	....	....	....	....	....	....
2014-15	San Jose	NHL	70	9	14	23	23	0	0	3	98	9.2	12	0	0.0	22:07	....	....	....	....	....	....	....	....	....
2015-16	San Jose	NHL	67	8	31	39	48	2	0	0	116	6.9	15	0	0.0	23:08	24	1	11	12	12	0	0	0	23:34
2016-17	San Jose	NHL	75	6	22	28	35	1	0	2	144	4.2	4	0	0.0	21:14	6	0	3	3	2	0	0	0	23:16
	NHL Totals		812	53	201	254	348	10	1	9	1106	4.8		0	0.0	22:01	114	3	26	29	32	1	0	0	22:16

NHL All-Rookie Team (2007)

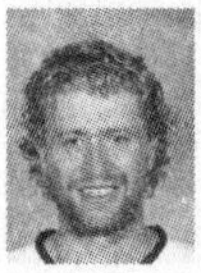

VORACEK, Jakub
(VOHR-rah-chehk, YA-kuhb) **PHI**

Right wing. Shoots left. 6'2", 214 lbs. Born, Kladno, Czech., August 15, 1989. Columbus' 1st pick, 7th overall, in 2007 NHL Draft.

Season	Club	League	GP	G	A	Pts	PIM	PP	SH	GW	S	S%	+/-	TF	F%	Min	GP	G	A	Pts	PIM	PP	SH	GW	Min
			Regular Season														Playoffs								
2002-03	HC Kladno U17	CzR-U17	2	1	1	2	2	....	....	....	....	....	....	....	....	....	2	1	1	2	0	....	....	....	....
2003-04	HC Kladno U17	CzR-U17	52	30	24	54	26	....	....	....	....	....	....	....	....	....	2	0	0	0	2	....	....	....	....
2004-05	HC Kladno U17	CzR-U17	30	23	39	62	44	....	....	....	....	....	....	....	....	....	7	5	4	9	14	....	....	....	....
	HC Kladno Jr.	CzRep-Jr.	16	5	7	12	6	....	....	....	....	....	....	....	....	....	1	1	0	1	2	....	....	....	....
2005-06	HC Kladno U17	CzR-U17	....	....	....	....	....	....	....	....	....	....	....	....	....	....	2	1	3	4	31	....	....	....	....
	HC Kladno Jr.	CzRep-Jr.	46	21	38	59	54	....	....	....	....	....	....	....	....	....	6	7	4	11	2	....	....	....	....
	HC Rabat Kladno	CzRep	1	0	0	0	0	....	....	....	....	....	....	....	....	....	....	....	....	....	....	....	....	....	....
2006-07	Halifax	QMJHL	59	23	63	86	26	....	....	....	....	....	....	....	....	....	12	7	17	24	6	....	....	....	....
2007-08	Halifax	QMJHL	53	33	68	101	42	....	....	....	....	....	....	....	....	....	15	5	13	18	14	....	....	....	....
2008-09	Columbus	NHL	80	9	29	38	44	0	0	1	101	8.9	11	3	0.0	12:40	4	0	1	1	8	0	0	0	12:06
2009-10	Columbus	NHL	81	16	34	50	26	4	0	1	154	10.4	–7	6	33.3	15:37	....	....	....	....	....	....	....	....	....
2010-11	Columbus	NHL	80	14	32	46	26	2	0	2	183	7.7	–3	65	36.9	16:58	....	....	....	....	....	....	....	....	....
2011-12	Philadelphia	NHL	78	18	31	49	32	0	0	2	190	9.5	11	23	30.4	16:17	11	2	8	10	8	1	0	1	15:58
2012-13	HC Lev Praha	KHL	23	7	13	20	22	....	....	....	....	....	....	....	....	....	....	....	....	....	....	....	....	....	....
	Philadelphia	NHL	48	22	24	46	35	8	0	3	129	17.1	–7	5	40.0	17:14	....	....	....	....	....	....	....	....	....
2013-14	Philadelphia	NHL	82	23	39	62	22	8	0	2	235	9.8	11	6	66.7	17:15	7	2	2	4	4	1	0	1	16:57
	Czech Republic	Olympics	5	1	1	2	2	....	....	....	....	....	....	....	....	....	....	....	....	....	....	....	....	....	....
2014-15	Philadelphia	NHL	82	22	59	81	78	11	0	3	221	10.0	1	9	66.7	18:36	....	....	....	....	....	....	....	....	....
2015-16	Philadelphia	NHL	73	11	44	55	38	1	0	2	213	5.2	–5	6	50.0	18:35	6	1	0	1	4	0	0	0	17:53
2016-17	Philadelphia	NHL	82	20	41	61	56	5	0	3	253	7.9	–24	14	21.4	19:05	....	....	....	....	....	....	....	....	....
	NHL Totals		686	155	333	488	357	39	0	19	1679	9.2		137	37.2	16:54	28	5	11	16	24	2	0	2	16:04

QMJHL All-Rookie Team (2007) • QMJHL Rookie of the Year (2007) • QMJHL Second All-Star Team (2008) • NHL First All-Star Team (2015)

Played in NHL All-Star Game (2015)

Traded to **Philadelphia** by **Columbus** with Columbus' 1st (Sean Couturier) and 3rd (Nick Cousins) round picks in 2011 NHL Draft for Jeff Carter, June 23, 2011. Signed as a free agent by **Lev Praha** (KHL), September 16, 2012.

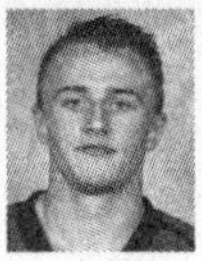

VRANA, Jakub
(vuh-RA-nuh, YA-kuhb) **WSH**

Right wing. Shoots left. 5'11", 185 lbs. Born, Prague, Czech Rep., February 28, 1996. Washington's 1st pick, 13th overall, in 2014 NHL Draft.

Season	Club	League	GP	G	A	Pts	PIM	PP	SH	GW	S	S%	+/-	TF	F%	Min	GP	G	A	Pts	PIM	PP	SH	GW	Min
			Regular Season														Playoffs								
2010-11	HC Letnany U18	CzR-U18	26	19	10	29	10	....	....	....	....	....	....	....	....	....	....	....	....	....	....	....	....	....	....
2011-12	Linkoping U18	Swe-U18	32	28	17	45	6	....	....	....	....	....	....	....	....	....	3	2	2	4	12	....	....	....	....
	Linkopings HC Jr.	Swe-Jr.	3	1	0	1	2	....	....	....	....	....	....	....	....	....	....	....	....	....	....	....	....	....	....
2012-13	Linkoping U18	Swe-U18	3	3	2	5	2	....	....	....	....	....	....	....	....	....	2	1	0	1	12	....	....	....	....
	Linkopings HC Jr.	Swe-Jr.	32	20	12	32	49	....	....	....	....	....	....	....	....	....	5	1	0	1	0	....	....	....	....
	Linkopings HC	Sweden	5	0	0	0	0	....	....	....	....	....	....	....	....	....	....	....	....	....	....	....	....	....	....
2013-14	Linkoping U18	Swe-U18	1	0	0	0	0	....	....	....	....	....	....	....	....	....	3	1	2	3	4	....	....	....	....
	Linkopings HC Jr.	Swe-Jr.	24	14	11	25	26	....	....	....	....	....	....	....	....	....	....	....	....	....	....	....	....	....	....
	Linkopings HC	Sweden	24	2	1	3	2	....	....	....	....	....	....	....	....	....	14	1	1	2	6	....	....	....	....
2014-15	Linkopings HC	Sweden	44	12	12	24	12	....	....	....	....	....	....	....	....	....	11	4	1	5	2	....	....	....	....
	Hershey Bears	AHL	3	0	5	5	0	....	....	....	....	....	....	....	....	....	10	2	4	6	2	....	....	....	....
2015-16	Hershey Bears	AHL	36	16	18	34	20	....	....	....	....	....	....	....	....	....	21	8	6	14	2	....	....	....	....
2016-17	Washington	NHL	21	3	3	6	2	3	0	2	32	9.4	2	3	0.0	11:07	....	....	....	....	....	....	....	....	....
	Hershey Bears	AHL	49	19	17	36	28	....	....	....	....	....	....	....	....	....	7	0	0	0	4	....	....	....	....
	NHL Totals		21	3	3	6	2	3	0	2	32	9.4		3	0.0	11:07	....	....	....	....	....	....	....	....	....

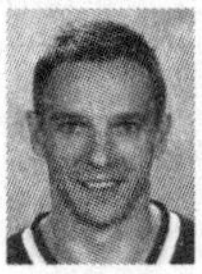

VRBATA, Radim
(vuhr-BA-tuh, RA-dihm) **FLA**

Right wing. Shoots right. 6'1", 194 lbs. Born, Mlada Boleslav, Czech., June 13, 1981. Colorado's 10th pick, 212th overall, in 1999 NHL Draft.

Season	Club	League	GP	G	A	Pts	PIM	PP	SH	GW	S	S%	+/-	TF	F%	Min	GP	G	A	Pts	PIM	PP	SH	GW	Min
			Regular Season														Playoffs								
1997-98	Ml. Boleslav Jr.	CzRep-Jr.	35	42	31	73	4	....	....	....	....	....	....	....	....	....	....	....	....	....	....	....	....	....	....
1998-99	Hull Olympiques	QMJHL	54	22	38	60	16	....	....	....	....	....	....	....	....	....	23	6	13	19	6	....	....	....	....
99-2000	Hull Olympiques	QMJHL	58	29	45	74	26	....	....	....	....	....	....	....	....	....	15	3	9	12	8	....	....	....	....
2000-01	Shawinigan	QMJHL	55	56	64	120	67	....	....	....	....	....	....	....	....	....	10	4	7	11	4	....	....	....	....
	Hershey Bears	AHL	....	....	....	....	....	....	....	....	....	....	....	....	....	....	1	0	1	1	2	....	....	....	....
2001-02	Colorado	NHL	52	18	12	30	14	6	0	3	112	16.1	7	8	37.5	14:32	9	0	0	0	0	0	0	0	13:05
	Hershey Bears	AHL	20	8	14	22	8	....	....	....	....	....	....	....	....	....	....	....	....	....	....	....	....	....	....
2002-03	Colorado	NHL	66	11	19	30	16	3	0	4	171	6.4	0	14	50.0	13:55	....	....	....	....	....	....	....	....	....
	Carolina	NHL	10	5	0	5	2	3	0	0	44	11.4	–7	15	46.7	19:00	....	....	....	....	....	....	....	....	....
2003-04	Carolina	NHL	80	12	13	25	24	4	0	2	195	6.2	–10	21	38.1	13:42	....	....	....	....	....	....	....	....	....
2004-05	Liberec	CzRep	45	18	21	39	91	....	....	....	....	....	....	....	....	....	12	3	2	5	0	....	....	....	....
2005-06	Carolina	NHL	16	2	3	5	6	1	0	0	38	5.3	0	3	33.3	12:37	....	....	....	....	....	....	....	....	....
	Chicago	NHL	45	13	21	34	16	5	0	0	147	8.8	4	6	50.0	15:43	....	....	....	....	....	....	....	....	....
2006-07	Chicago	NHL	77	14	27	41	26	5	0	2	215	6.5	–4	12	33.3	16:53	....	....	....	....	....	....	....	....	....
2007-08	Phoenix	NHL	76	27	29	56	14	7	3	5	246	11.0	6	19	36.8	18:12	....	....	....	....	....	....	....	....	....
2008-09	Tampa Bay	NHL	18	3	3	6	8	1	0	0	41	7.3	–1	3	33.3	14:13	....	....	....	....	....	....	....	....	....
	BK Mlada Boleslav	CzRep	11	5	3	8	18	....	....	....	....	....	....	....	....	....	....	....	....	....	....	....	....	....	....
	Liberec	CzRep	7	7	2	9	2	....	....	....	....	....	....	....	....	....	3	0	1	1	2	....	....	....	....
2009-10	Phoenix	NHL	82	24	19	43	24	7	0	4	266	9.0	6	8	25.0	16:13	7	2	2	4	4	1	0	1	15:42
2010-11	Phoenix	NHL	79	19	29	48	20	10	0	2	240	7.9	5	7	28.6	16:22	4	2	3	5	0	1	0	0	19:55
2011-12	Phoenix	NHL	77	35	27	62	24	9	1	*12	232	15.1	24	67	40.3	18:39	16	2	3	5	8	1	0	0	17:20
2012-13	BK Mlada Boleslav	CzRep-2	2	1	1	2	0	....	....	....	....	....	....	....	....	....	....	....	....	....	....	....	....	....	....
	Phoenix	NHL	34	12	16	28	14	2	1	1	106	11.3	6	32	31.3	18:19	....	....	....	....	....	....	....	....	....
2013-14	Phoenix	NHL	80	20	31	51	22	10	0	2	263	7.6	–6	43	39.5	17:57	....	....	....	....	....	....	....	....	....
2014-15	Vancouver	NHL	79	31	32	63	20	12	0	7	267	11.6	6	9	55.6	16:37	6	2	2	4	0	1	0	0	16:10

			Regular Season													Playoffs								
Season	Club	League	GP	G	A	Pts	PIM	PP	SH	GW	S	S%	+/-	TF	F%	Min	GP	G	A	Pts	PIM	PP	SH	GW	Min
2015-16	Vancouver	NHL	63	13	14	27	12	5	0	0	199	6.5	–30	14	28.6	16:03	....	....	....	....	....	....	....	....	....
2016-17	Arizona	NHL	81	20	35	55	16	4	0	4	233	8.6	–18	47	36.2	16:54	....	....	....	....	....	....	....	....	....
	NHL Totals		1015	279	330	609	278	94	5	48	3015	9.3		328	38.1	16:22	42	8	10	18	12	4	0	1	16:14

QMJHL First All-Star Team (2001)

Played in NHL All-Star Game (2015)

Traded to **Carolina** by **Colorado** for Bates Battaglia, March 11, 2003. Signed as a free agent by **Liberec** (CzRep), September 4, 2004. Traded to **Chicago** by **Carolina** for Chicago's 4th round pick (later traded to St. Louis - St. Louis selected Cade Fairchild) in 2007 NHL Draft, December 29, 2005. Traded to **Phoenix** by **Chicago** for Kevyn Adams, August 11, 2007. Signed as a free agent by **Tampa Bay**, July 1, 2008. • Re-assigned to **Mlada Boleslav** (CzRep) by **Tampa Bay**, December 9, 2008. • Loaned to **Liberec** (CzRep) by **Mlada Boleslav** (CzRep), January 29, 2009. Traded to **Phoenix** by **Tampa Bay** for Todd Fedoruk and David Hale, July 21, 2009. Signed as a free agent by **Mlada Boleslav** (CzRep-2), November 1, 2012. Signed as a free agent by **Vancouver**, July 3, 2014. Signed as a free agent by **Arizona**, August 16, 2016. Signed as a free agent by **Florida**, July 1, 2017.

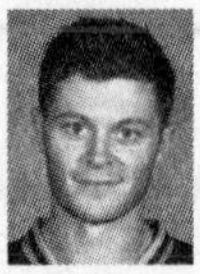

WAGNER, Chris (WAG-nuhr, KRIHS) ANA

Center. Shoots right. 6', 195 lbs. Born, Wellesley, MA, May 27, 1991. Anaheim's 4th pick, 122nd overall, in 2010 NHL Draft.

Season	Club	League	GP	G	A	Pts	PIM	PP	SH	GW	S	S%	+/-	TF	F%	Min	GP	G	A	Pts	PIM	PP	SH	GW	Min
2008-09	South Shore	EJHL	38	20	14	34	72	....	....	....	....	....	....	....	....	....	2	2	0	2	0	....	....	....	....
2009-10	South Shore	EJHL	44	34	49	*83	70	....	....	....	....	....	....	....	....	....	4	3	6	9	8	....	....	....	....
2010-11	Colgate	ECAC	41	9	10	19	26	....	....	....	....	....	....	....	....	....	....	....	....	....	....	....	....	....	....
2011-12	Colgate	ECAC	38	17	34	51	69	....	....	....	....	....	....	....	....	....	....	....	....	....	....	....	....	....	....
2012-13	Norfolk Admirals	AHL	70	8	13	21	65	....	....	....	....	....	....	....	....	....	....	....	....	....	....	....	....	....	....
2013-14	Norfolk Admirals	AHL	76	14	14	28	68	....	....	....	....	....	....	....	....	....	10	2	3	5	10	....	....	....	....
2014-15	Anaheim	NHL	9	0	0	0	2	0	0	0	7	0.0	–2	55	60.0	8:47	2	0	0	0	0	0	0	0	5:33
	Norfolk Admirals	AHL	48	15	13	28	65	....	....	....	....	....	....	....	....	....	....	....	....	....	....	....	....	....	....
2015-16	Anaheim	NHL	11	0	0	0	17	0	0	0	17	0.0	–2	73	53.4	9:46	....	....	....	....	....	....	....	....	....
	Anaheim	NHL	6	0	2	2	2	0	0	0	11	0.0	2	16	50.0	12:01	2	0	0	0	0	0	0	0	7:39
	Colorado	NHL	26	4	0	4	9	0	0	1	27	14.8	–2	185	54.6	8:14	....	....	....	....	....	....	....	....	....
	San Diego Gulls	AHL	15	6	4	10	22	....	....	....	....	....	....	....	....	....	7	2	2	4	4	....	....	....	....
2016-17	Anaheim	NHL	43	6	1	7	6	0	0	0	40	15.0	2	148	41.9	9:21	17	3	0	3	6	0	0	1	11:00
	San Diego Gulls	AHL	30	12	7	19	18	....	....	....	....	....	....	....	....	....	....	....	....	....	....	....	....	....	....
	NHL Totals		95	10	3	13	36	0	0	1	102	9.8		477	50.9	7:19	21	3	0	3	6	0	0	1	10:09

ECAC Second All-Star Team (2012)

Claimed on waivers by **Colorado** from **Anaheim**, November 15, 2015. Claimed on waivers by **Anaheim** from **Colorado**, February 25, 2016.

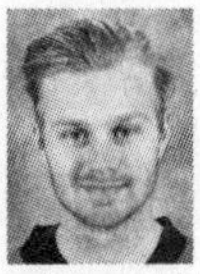

WALLMARK, Lucas (VAWL-mahrk, LOO-kuhs) CAR

Center. Shoots left. 6', 176 lbs. Born, Umea, Sweden, September 5, 1995. Carolina's 5th pick, 97th overall, in 2014 NHL Draft.

Season	Club	League	GP	G	A	Pts	PIM	PP	SH	GW	S	S%	+/-	TF	F%	Min	GP	G	A	Pts	PIM	PP	SH	GW	Min
2009-10	Tegs U18	Swe-U18	16	3	6	9	37	....	....	....	....	....	....	....	....	....	....	....	....	....	....	....	....	....	....
	Bjorkloven U18	Swe-U18	10	1	3	4	0	....	....	....	....	....	....	....	....	....	....	....	....	....	....	....	....	....	....
2010-11	Skelleftea AIK U18	Swe-U18	36	18	49	67	18	....	....	....	....	....	....	....	....	....	2	1	0	1	0	....	....	....	....
2011-12	Skelleftea AIK U18	Swe-U18	2	1	1	2	0	....	....	....	....	....	....	....	....	....	3	3	2	5	2	....	....	....	....
	Skelleftea AIK Jr.	Swe-Jr.	37	11	26	37	14	....	....	....	....	....	....	....	....	....	3	1	2	3	4	....	....	....	....
2012-13	Skelleftea AIK Jr.	Swe-Jr.	14	5	11	16	18	....	....	....	....	....	....	....	....	....	....	....	....	....	....	....	....	....	....
	Skelleftea AIK	Sweden	2	0	0	0	0	....	....	....	....	....	....	....	....	....	....	....	....	....	....	....	....	....	....
	Karlskrona HK	Sweden-2	23	5	10	15	6	....	....	....	....	....	....	....	....	....	....	....	....	....	....	....	....	....	....
2013-14	Asploven	Sweden-2	11	1	7	8	6	....	....	....	....	....	....	....	....	....	....	....	....	....	....	....	....	....	....
	Lulea HF	Sweden	41	3	7	10	2	....	....	....	....	....	....	....	....	....	1	0	0	0	0	....	....	....	....
2014-15	Lulea HF	Sweden	50	5	13	18	14	....	....	....	....	....	....	....	....	....	9	0	5	5	2	....	....	....	....
2015-16	Lulea HF	Sweden	48	8	24	32	20	....	....	....	....	....	....	....	....	....	11	7	2	9	4	....	....	....	....
2016-17	Carolina	NHL	8	0	2	2	2	0	0	0	11	0.0	1	58	53.5	10:52	....	....	....	....	....	....	....	....	....
	Charlotte	AHL	67	24	22	46	28	....	....	....	....	....	....	....	....	....	5	3	3	6	2	....	....	....	....
	NHL Totals		8	0	2	2	2	0	0	0	11	0.0		58	53.4	10:52	....	....	....	....	....	....	....	....	....

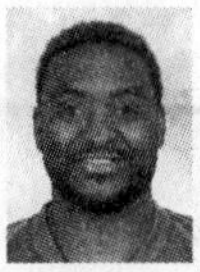

WARD, Joel (WOHRD, JOHL) S.J.

Right wing. Shoots right. 6'1", 225 lbs. Born, Toronto, ON, December 2, 1980.

Season	Club	League	GP	G	A	Pts	PIM	PP	SH	GW	S	S%	+/-	TF	F%	Min	GP	G	A	Pts	PIM	PP	SH	GW	Min
1997-98	Owen Sound	OHL	47	8	4	12	14	....	....	....	....	....	....	....	....	....	11	1	1	2	5	....	....	....	....
1998-99	Owen Sound	OHL	58	19	16	35	23	....	....	....	....	....	....	....	....	....	16	2	4	6	0	....	....	....	....
99-2000	Owen Sound	OHL	63	23	20	43	51	....	....	....	....	....	....	....	....	....	....	....	....	....	....	....	....	....	....
2000-01	Owen Sound	OHL	67	26	36	62	45	....	....	....	....	....	....	....	....	....	5	2	4	6	4	....	....	....	....
	Long Beach	WCHL	....	....	....	....	....	....	....	....	....	....	....	....	....	....	8	0	0	0	0	....	....	....	....
2001-02	U. of P.E.I.	CIS	22	13	14	27	16	....	....	....	....	....	....	....	....	....	....	....	....	....	....	....	....	....	....
2002-03	U. of P.E.I.	CIS	19	11	15	26	24	....	....	....	....	....	....	....	....	....	....	....	....	....	....	....	....	....	....
2003-04	U. of P.E.I.	CIS	27	14	24	38	42	....	....	....	....	....	....	....	....	....	....	....	....	....	....	....	....	....	....
2004-05	U. of P.E.I.	CIS	28	16	28	44	42	....	....	....	....	....	....	....	....	....	....	....	....	....	....	....	....	....	....
2005-06	Houston Aeros	AHL	66	8	14	22	34	....	....	....	....	....	....	....	....	....	8	4	2	6	4	....	....	....	....
2006-07	Minnesota	NHL	11	0	1	1	0	0	0	0	12	0.0	0	1	0.0	7:42	....	....	....	....	....	....	....	....	....
	Houston Aeros	AHL	64	9	14	23	45	....	....	....	....	....	....	....	....	....	....	....	....	....	....	....	....	....	....
2007-08	Houston Aeros	AHL	79	21	20	41	47	....	....	....	....	....	....	....	....	....	4	0	2	2	0	....	....	....	....
2008-09	Nashville	NHL	79	17	18	35	29	3	2	2	133	12.8	1	46	43.5	16:01	....	....	....	....	....	....	....	....	....
2009-10	Nashville	NHL	71	13	21	34	18	3	1	1	134	9.7	–5	81	38.3	17:33	6	2	2	4	2	0	1	0	19:54
2010-11	Nashville	NHL	80	10	19	29	42	5	0	4	157	6.4	–1	168	48.8	17:04	12	7	6	13	6	2	0	1	20:25
2011-12	Washington	NHL	73	6	12	18	20	0	0	0	79	7.6	12	52	55.8	12:26	14	1	4	5	6	0	0	1	10:57
2012-13	Washington	NHL	39	8	12	20	12	1	1	1	52	15.4	7	65	58.5	15:08	7	1	3	4	6	1	0	0	13:11
2013-14	Washington	NHL	82	24	25	49	32	6	2	4	133	18.0	7	199	45.2	16:04	....	....	....	....	....	....	....	....	....
2014-15	Washington	NHL	82	19	15	34	30	6	0	4	138	13.8	–4	127	47.2	16:52	14	3	6	9	2	0	0	1	19:03
2015-16	San Jose	NHL	79	21	22	43	28	5	1	3	138	15.2	–15	493	48.1	16:58	24	7	6	13	16	1	0	1	15:52
2016-17	San Jose	NHL	78	10	19	29	30	1	2	2	105	9.5	–2	456	48.9	15:57	6	1	3	4	4	1	0	0	14:43
	NHL Totals		674	128	164	292	241	30	9	21	1081	11.8		1688	48.0	15:56	83	22	30	52	42	5	1	4	16:13

Signed as a free agent by **Houston** (AHL), December 4, 2005. Signed as a free agent by **Minnesota**, September 27, 2006. Signed as a free agent by **Nashville**, July 14, 2008. Signed as a free agent by **Washington**, July 1, 2011. Signed as a free agent by **San Jose**, July 3, 2015.

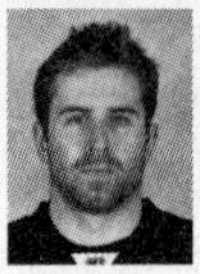

WARSOFSKY, David (wawr-SAWF-skee, DAY-vihd) COL

Defense. Shoots left. 5'9", 170 lbs. Born, Marshfield, MA, May 30, 1990. St. Louis' 7th pick, 95th overall, in 2008 NHL Draft.

Season	Club	League	GP	G	A	Pts	PIM	PP	SH	GW	S	S%	+/-	TF	F%	Min	GP	G	A	Pts	PIM	PP	SH	GW	Min
2005-06	Cushing	High-MA	....	8	26	34	....	....	....	....	....	....	....	....	....	....	....	....	....	....	....	....	....	....	....
2006-07	Cushing	High-MA	29	15	34	49	55	....	....	....	....	....	....	....	....	....	....	....	....	....	....	....	....	....	....
2007-08	USAHNTDP	U-18	41	5	29	34	26	....	....	....	....	....	....	....	....	....	....	....	....	....	....	....	....	....	....
	USAHNTDP	NAHL	15	4	2	6	8	....	....	....	....	....	....	....	....	....	....	....	....	....	....	....	....	....	....
2008-09	Boston University	H-East	45	3	20	23	28	....	....	....	....	....	....	....	....	....	....	....	....	....	....	....	....	....	....
2009-10	Boston University	H-East	34	12	11	23	48	....	....	....	....	....	....	....	....	....	....	....	....	....	....	....	....	....	....
2010-11	Boston University	H-East	34	7	15	22	46	....	....	....	....	....	....	....	....	....	....	....	....	....	....	....	....	....	....
	Providence Bruins	AHL	10	0	3	3	6	....	....	....	....	....	....	....	....	....	....	....	....	....	....	....	....	....	....
2011-12	Providence Bruins	AHL	66	5	24	29	18	....	....	....	....	....	....	....	....	....	....	....	....	....	....	....	....	....	....
2012-13	Providence Bruins	AHL	58	3	13	16	17	....	....	....	....	....	....	....	....	....	12	0	3	3	0	....	....	....	....
2013-14	Boston	NHL	6	1	1	2	0	0	0	0	10	10.0	1	0	0.0	16:10	....	....	....	....	....	....	....	....	....
	Providence Bruins	AHL	56	6	26	32	11	....	....	....	....	....	....	....	....	....	12	2	7	9	2	....	....	....	....
2014-15	Boston	NHL	4	0	1	1	0	0	0	0	7	0.0	1	0	0.0	17:46	....	....	....	....	....	....	....	....	....
	Providence Bruins	AHL	40	4	11	15	20	....	....	....	....	....	....	....	....	....	5	0	1	1	0	....	....	....	....
2015-16	Pittsburgh	NHL	12	1	0	1	0	1	0	0	21	4.8	–6	0	0.0	17:45	....	....	....	....	....	....	....	....	....
	Wilkes-Barre	AHL	17	2	4	6	6	....	....	....	....	....	....	....	....	....	....	....	....	....	....	....	....	....	....
	New Jersey	NHL	10	0	1	1	2	0	0	0	19	0.0	–3	0	0.0	16:22	....	....	....	....	....	....	....	....	....
2016-17	Pittsburgh	NHL	7	0	1	1	6	0	0	0	14	0.0	–3	0	0.0	15:44	....	....	....	....	....	....	....	....	....
	Wilkes-Barre	AHL	58	16	31	47	32	....	....	....	....	....	....	....	....	....	5	3	3	6	0	....	....	....	....
	NHL Totals		39	2	4	6	8	1	0	0	71	2.8		0	0.0	16:48	....	....	....	....	....	....	....	....	....

Hockey East Second All-Star Team (2011) • AHL Second All-Star Team (2017)

Traded to **Boston** by **St. Louis** for Vladimir Sobotka, June 26, 2010. Signed as a free agent by **Pittsburgh**, July 1, 2015. Claimed on waivers by **New Jersey** from **Pittsburgh**, February 29, 2016. • Missed majority of 2015-16 as a healthy reserve. Signed as a free agent by **Pittsburgh**, July 1, 2016. Signed as a free agent by **Colorado**, July 1, 2017.

			Regular Season														Playoffs								
Season	Club	League	GP	G	A	Pts	PIM	PP	SH	GW	S	S%	+/-	TF	F%	Min	GP	G	A	Pts	PIM	PP	SH	GW	Min

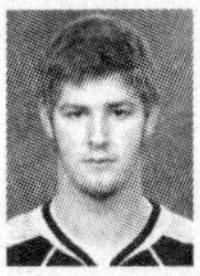

WATSON, Austin

(WAWT-suhn, AW-stuhn) **NSH**

Left wing. Shoots right. 6'4", 204 lbs. Born, Ann Arbor, MI, January 13, 1992. Nashville's 1st pick, 18th overall, in 2010 NHL Draft.

Season	Club	League	GP	G	A	Pts	PIM	PP	SH	GW	S	S%	+/-	TF	F%	Min	GP	G	A	Pts	PIM	PP	SH	GW	Min
2007-08	Det. Compuware	Minor-MI	....	45	104	149	....	....	....	....	....	....	....	....	....	....	....	....	....	....	....	....	....	....	....
2008-09	Windsor Spitfires	OHL	63	10	19	29	41	....	....	....	....	....	....	....	....	....	20	0	3	3	15	....	....	....	....
2009-10	Windsor Spitfires	OHL	42	11	23	34	14	....	....	....	....	....	....	....	....	....	....	....	....	....	....	....	....	....	....
	Peterborough	OHL	10	9	11	20	8	....	....	....	....	....	....	....	....	....	4	2	0	2	2	....	....	....	....
2010-11	Peterborough	OHL	68	34	34	68	54	....	....	....	....	....	....	....	....	....	....	....	....	....	....	....	....	....	....
	Milwaukee	AHL	5	0	0	0	0	....	....	....	....	....	....	....	....	....	3	0	0	0	0	....	....	....	....
2011-12	Peterborough	OHL	32	14	19	33	33	....	....	....	....	....	....	....	....	....	....	....	....	....	....	....	....	....	....
	London Knights	OHL	29	11	24	35	14	....	....	....	....	....	....	....	....	....	19	10	7	17	10	....	....	....	....
2012-13	Milwaukee	AHL	72	20	17	37	22	....	....	....	....	....	....	....	....	....	4	1	0	1	0	....	....	....	....
	Nashville	**NHL**	**6**	**1**	**0**	**1**	**0**	**0**	**0**	**0**	**4**	**25.0**	**-2**	**44**	**43.2**	**12:42**	....	....	....	....	....	....	....	....	....
2013-14	Milwaukee	AHL	76	22	24	46	24	....	....	....	....	....	....	....	....	....	3	0	0	0	6	....	....	....	....
2014-15	Milwaukee	AHL	76	26	18	44	34	....	....	....	....	....	....	....	....	....	....	....	....	....	....	....	....	....	....
2015-16	**Nashville**	**NHL**	**57**	**3**	**7**	**10**	**32**	**0**	**0**	**0**	**55**	**5.5**	**-4**	**13**	**46.2**	**10:00**	....	....	....	....	....	....	....	....	....
2016-17	**Nashville**	**NHL**	**77**	**5**	**12**	**17**	**99**	**0**	**0**	**0**	**90**	**5.6**	**14**	**42**	**40.5**	**12:26**	**22**	**4**	**5**	**9**	**28**	**0**	**0**	**0**	**13:40**
	Milwaukee	AHL	3	1	0	1	9	....	....	....	....	....	....	....	....	....	....	....	....	....	....	....	....	....	....
	NHL Totals		**140**	**9**	**19**	**28**	**131**	**0**	**0**	**0**	**149**	**6.0**		**99**	**42.4**	**11:27**	**22**	**4**	**5**	**9**	**28**	**0**	**0**	**0**	**13:40**

OHL Playoff MVP (2012)

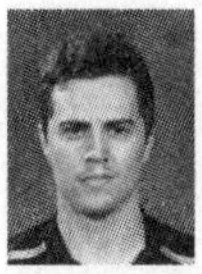

WEAL, Jordan

(WEEL, JOHR-dahn) **PHI**

Center. Shoots right. 5'10", 179 lbs. Born, North Vancouver, BC, April 15, 1992. Los Angeles' 3rd pick, 70th overall, in 2010 NHL Draft.

Season	Club	League	GP	G	A	Pts	PIM	PP	SH	GW	S	S%	+/-	TF	F%	Min	GP	G	A	Pts	PIM	PP	SH	GW	Min
2007-08	Van. NW Giants	BCMML	40	*39	*61	*100	44	....	....	....	....	....	....	....	....	....	2	0	2	2	2	....	....	....	....
	Regina Pats	WHL	3	0	1	1	0	....	....	....	....	....	....	....	....	....	4	0	0	0	0	....	....	....	....
2008-09	Regina Pats	WHL	65	16	54	70	26	....	....	....	....	....	....	....	....	....	....	....	....	....	....	....	....	....	....
2009-10	Regina Pats	WHL	72	35	67	102	54	....	....	....	....	....	....	....	....	....	....	....	....	....	....	....	....	....	....
2010-11	Regina Pats	WHL	72	43	53	96	70	....	....	....	....	....	....	....	....	....	....	....	....	....	....	....	....	....	....
	Manchester	AHL	7	0	1	1	0	....	....	....	....	....	....	....	....	....	....	....	....	....	....	....	....	....	....
2011-12	Regina Pats	WHL	70	41	75	116	36	....	....	....	....	....	....	....	....	....	5	1	4	5	0	....	....	....	....
	Manchester	AHL	2	0	0	0	0	....	....	....	....	....	....	....	....	....	....	....	....	....	....	....	....	....	....
2012-13	Manchester	AHL	63	15	18	33	38	....	....	....	....	....	....	....	....	....	4	0	2	2	4	....	....	....	....
2013-14	Manchester	AHL	76	23	47	70	42	....	....	....	....	....	....	....	....	....	4	0	3	3	2	....	....	....	....
2014-15	Manchester	AHL	73	20	49	69	56	....	....	....	....	....	....	....	....	....	19	10	12	22	16	....	....	....	....
2015-16	**Los Angeles**	**NHL**	**10**	**0**	**0**	**0**	**2**	**0**	**0**	**0**	**1**	**0.0**	**0**	**44**	**45.5**	**8:07**	....	....	....	....	....	....	....	....	....
	Philadelphia	**NHL**	**4**	**0**	**0**	**0**	**0**	**0**	**0**	**0**	**3**	**0.0**	**1**	**24**	**54.2**	**12:28**	....	....	....	....	....	....	....	....	....
2016-17	**Philadelphia**	**NHL**	**23**	**8**	**4**	**12**	**10**	**1**	**0**	**1**	**49**	**16.3**	**5**	**28**	**50.0**	**14:19**	....	....	....	....	....	....	....	....	....
	Lehigh Valley	AHL	43	15	32	47	30	....	....	....	....	....	....	....	....	....	....	....	....	....	....	....	....	....	....
	NHL Totals		**37**	**8**	**4**	**12**	**12**	**1**	**0**	**1**	**53**	**15.1**		**96**	**49.0**	**12:26**	....	....	....	....	....	....	....	....	....

WHL East First All-Star Team (2012) • AHL Second All-Star Team (2015) • Jack A. Butterfield Trophy (AHL - Playoff MVP) (2015)

Traded to **Philadelphia** by **Los Angeles** with Los Angeles' 3rd round pick (Carsen Twarynski) in 2016 NHL Draft for Vincent Lecavalier and Luke Schenn, January 6, 2016. • Missed majority of 2015-16 as a healthy reserve.

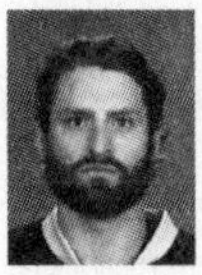

WEBER, Mike

(WEH-buhr, MIGHK) **MIN**

Defense. Shoots left. 6'2", 217 lbs. Born, Pittsburgh, PA, December 16, 1987. Buffalo's 3rd pick, 57th overall, in 2006 NHL Draft.

Season	Club	League	GP	G	A	Pts	PIM	PP	SH	GW	S	S%	+/-	TF	F%	Min	GP	G	A	Pts	PIM	PP	SH	GW	Min
2002-03	Jr. Penguins	EmJHL	28	4	11	15	109	....	....	....	....	....	....	....	....	....	3	0	0	0	20	....	....	....	....
2003-04	Windsor Spitfires	OHL	65	0	2	2	49	....	....	....	....	....	....	....	....	....	....	....	....	....	....	....	....	....	....
2004-05	Windsor Spitfires	OHL	68	2	6	8	132	....	....	....	....	....	....	....	....	....	11	0	1	1	18	....	....	....	....
2005-06	Windsor Spitfires	OHL	68	5	21	26	181	....	....	....	....	....	....	....	....	....	7	0	0	0	12	....	....	....	....
2006-07	Windsor Spitfires	OHL	30	3	16	19	86	....	....	....	....	....	....	....	....	....	....	....	....	....	....	....	....	....	....
	Barrie Colts	OHL	30	3	12	15	86	....	....	....	....	....	....	....	....	....	7	0	6	6	10	....	....	....	....
2007-08	**Buffalo**	**NHL**	**16**	**0**	**3**	**3**	**14**	**0**	**0**	**0**	**12**	**0.0**	**12**	**0**	**0.0**	**16:41**	....	....	....	....	....	....	....	....	....
	Rochester	AHL	59	1	13	14	178	....	....	....	....	....	....	....	....	....	....	....	....	....	....	....	....	....	....
2008-09	**Buffalo**	**NHL**	**7**	**0**	**0**	**0**	**19**	**0**	**0**	**0**	**2**	**0.0**	**-3**	**0**	**0.0**	**14:10**	....	....	....	....	....	....	....	....	....
	Portland Pirates	AHL	42	1	7	8	94	....	....	....	....	....	....	....	....	....	....	....	....	....	....	....	....	....	....
2009-10	Portland Pirates	AHL	80	5	16	21	153	....	....	....	....	....	....	....	....	....	4	1	0	1	14	....	....	....	....
2010-11	**Buffalo**	**NHL**	**58**	**4**	**13**	**17**	**69**	**0**	**0**	**0**	**53**	**7.5**	**13**	**0**	**0.0**	**16:54**	**7**	**0**	**1**	**1**	**6**	**0**	**0**	**0**	**15:51**
2011-12	**Buffalo**	**NHL**	**51**	**1**	**4**	**5**	**64**	**0**	**0**	**0**	**51**	**2.0**	**-19**	**0**	**0.0**	**18:35**	....	....	....	....	....	....	....	....	....
2012-13	Lorenskog IK	Norway	5	1	5	6	10	....	....	....	....	....	....	....	....	....	....	....	....	....	....	....	....	....	....
	Buffalo	**NHL**	**42**	**1**	**6**	**7**	**70**	**0**	**0**	**0**	**25**	**4.0**	**3**	**0**	**0.0**	**18:22**	....	....	....	....	....	....	....	....	....
2013-14	**Buffalo**	**NHL**	**68**	**1**	**8**	**9**	**73**	**0**	**0**	**0**	**47**	**2.1**	**-29**	**0**	**0.0**	**17:49**	....	....	....	....	....	....	....	....	....
2014-15	**Buffalo**	**NHL**	**64**	**1**	**6**	**7**	**68**	**0**	**0**	**0**	**41**	**2.4**	**-22**	**0**	**0.0**	**18:45**	....	....	....	....	....	....	....	....	....
2015-16	**Buffalo**	**NHL**	**35**	**1**	**4**	**5**	**32**	**0**	**0**	**0**	**28**	**3.6**	**3**	**0**	**0.0**	**15:55**	....	....	....	....	....	....	....	....	....
	Washington	**NHL**	**10**	**0**	**0**	**0**	**28**	**0**	**0**	**0**	**12**	**0.0**	**-1**	**0**	**0.0**	**13:59**	**2**	**0**	**0**	**0**	**0**	**0**	**0**	**0**	**9:51**
2016-17	Iowa Wild	AHL	56	1	7	8	92	....	....	....	....	....	....	....	....	....	....	....	....	....	....	....	....	....	....
	NHL Totals		**351**	**9**	**44**	**53**	**437**	**0**	**0**	**0**	**271**	**3.3**		**0**	**0.0**	**17:35**	**9**	**0**	**1**	**1**	**6**	**0**	**0**	**0**	**14:31**

Signed as a free agent by **Lorenskog** (Norway), November 15, 2012. Traded to **Washington** by **Buffalo** for Washington's 3rd round pick (Oskari Laaksonen) in 2017 NHL Draft, February 23, 2016. Signed as a free agent by **Iowa** (AHL), October 20, 2016. Signed as a free agent by **Minnesota**, February 28, 2017.

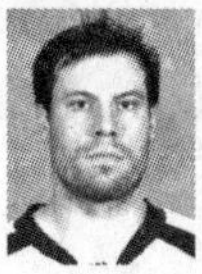

WEBER, Shea

(WEH-buhr, SHAY) **MTL**

Defense. Shoots right. 6'4", 232 lbs. Born, Sicamous, BC, August 14, 1985. Nashville's 4th pick, 49th overall, in 2003 NHL Draft.

Season	Club	League	GP	G	A	Pts	PIM	PP	SH	GW	S	S%	+/-	TF	F%	Min	GP	G	A	Pts	PIM	PP	SH	GW	Min
2000-01	Sicamous Bantam	Minor-BC	STATISTICS NOT AVAILABLE																						
	Sicamous Eagles	KIJHL	5	0	6	6	2	....	....	....	....	....	....	....	....	....	....	....	....	....	....	....	....	....	....
2001-02	Sicamous Eagles	KIJHL	47	9	33	42	87	....	....	....	....	....	....	....	....	....	....	....	....	....	....	....	....	....	....
	Kelowna Rockets	WHL	5	0	0	0	0	....	....	....	....	....	....	....	....	....	....	....	....	....	....	....	....	....	....
2002-03	Kelowna Rockets	WHL	70	2	16	18	167	....	....	....	....	....	....	....	....	....	19	1	4	5	26	....	....	....	....
2003-04	Kelowna Rockets	WHL	60	12	20	32	126	....	....	....	....	....	....	....	....	....	17	3	14	17	16	....	....	....	....
2004-05	Kelowna Rockets	WHL	55	12	29	41	95	....	....	....	....	....	....	....	....	....	18	9	8	17	25	....	....	....	....
2005-06	**Nashville**	**NHL**	**28**	**2**	**8**	**10**	**42**	**2**	**0**	**1**	**46**	**4.3**	**8**	**0**	**0.0**	**17:00**	**4**	**2**	**0**	**2**	**8**	**1**	**0**	**0**	**14:12**
	Milwaukee	AHL	46	12	15	27	49	....	....	....	....	....	....	....	....	....	14	6	5	11	16	....	....	....	....
2006-07	**Nashville**	**NHL**	**79**	**17**	**23**	**40**	**60**	**6**	**0**	**2**	**152**	**11.2**	**13**	**0**	**0.0**	**19:23**	**5**	**0**	**3**	**3**	**2**	**0**	**0**	**0**	**21:41**
2007-08	**Nashville**	**NHL**	**54**	**6**	**14**	**20**	**49**	**5**	**0**	**2**	**152**	**3.9**	**-6**	**0**	**0.0**	**19:30**	**6**	**1**	**3**	**4**	**6**	**0**	**0**	**0**	**19:30**
2008-09	**Nashville**	**NHL**	**81**	**23**	**30**	**53**	**80**	**10**	**1**	**4**	**251**	**9.2**	**1**	**0**	**0.0**	**23:58**	....	....	....	....	....	....	....	....	....
2009-10	**Nashville**	**NHL**	**78**	**16**	**27**	**43**	**36**	**7**	**0**	**3**	**222**	**7.2**	**0**	**0**	**0.0**	**23:10**	**6**	**2**	**1**	**3**	**4**	**0**	**0**	**0**	**24:27**
	Canada	Olympics	7	2	4	6	2	....	....	....	....	....	....	....	....	....	....	....	....	....	....	....	....	....	....
2010-11	**Nashville**	**NHL**	**82**	**16**	**32**	**48**	**56**	**6**	**1**	**3**	**254**	**6.3**	**7**	**0**	**0.0**	**25:19**	**12**	**3**	**2**	**5**	**8**	**2**	**0**	**0**	**27:58**
2011-12	**Nashville**	**NHL**	**78**	**19**	**30**	**49**	**46**	**10**	**2**	**1**	**230**	**8.3**	**21**	**0**	**0.0**	**26:10**	**10**	**2**	**1**	**3**	**9**	**1**	**0**	**0**	**28:27**
2012-13	**Nashville**	**NHL**	**48**	**9**	**19**	**28**	**48**	**3**	**0**	**1**	**124**	**7.3**	**-2**	**0**	**0.0**	**25:55**	....	....	....	....	....	....	....	....	....
2013-14	**Nashville**	**NHL**	**79**	**23**	**33**	**56**	**52**	**12**	**0**	**4**	**195**	**11.8**	**-2**	**0**	**0.0**	**26:54**	....	....	....	....	....	....	....	....	....
	Canada	Olympics	6	3	3	6	0	....	....	....	....	....	....	....	....	....	....	....	....	....	....	....	....	....	....
2014-15	**Nashville**	**NHL**	**78**	**15**	**30**	**45**	**72**	**5**	**1**	**2**	**237**	**6.3**	**15**	**0**	**0.0**	**26:22**	**2**	**0**	**1**	**1**	**2**	**0**	**0**	**0**	**25:49**
2015-16	**Nashville**	**NHL**	**78**	**20**	**31**	**51**	**27**	**14**	**0**	**1**	**189**	**10.6**	**-7**	**0**	**0.0**	**25:23**	**14**	**3**	**4**	**7**	**18**	**1**	**0**	**2**	**27:10**
2016-17	**Montreal**	**NHL**	**78**	**17**	**25**	**42**	**38**	**12**	**0**	**4**	**183**	**9.3**	**20**	**0**	**0.0**	**25:04**	**6**	**1**	**2**	**3**	**5**	**1**	**0**	**1**	**27:59**
	NHL Totals		**841**	**183**	**302**	**485**	**606**	**92**	**5**	**28**	**2235**	**8.2**		**0**	**0.0**	**24:07**	**65**	**14**	**17**	**31**	**62**	**6**	**0**	**3**	**25:22**

WHL West Second All-Star Team (2004) • WHL West First All-Star Team (2005) • Canadian Major Junior Second All-Star Team (2005) • Olympic All-Star Team (2010) • NHL First All-Star Team (2011, 2012) • NHL Second All-Star Team (2014, 2015) • Mark Messier NHL Leadership Award (2016)

Played in NHL All-Star Game (2009, 2011, 2012, 2015, 2016, 2017)

Traded to **Montreal** by **Nashville** for P.K. Subban, June 29, 2016.

			Regular Season														Playoffs								
Season	Club	League	GP	G	A	Pts	PIM	PP	SH	GW	S	S%	+/-	TF	F%	Min	GP	G	A	Pts	PIM	PP	SH	GW	Min

WEBER, Yannick (WEH-buhr, YAH-nihk) NSH

Defense. Shoots right. 5'11", 200 lbs. Born, Morges, Switz., September 23, 1988. Montreal's 5th pick, 73rd overall, in 2007 NHL Draft.

Season	Club	League	GP	G	A	Pts	PIM	PP	SH	GW	S	S%	+/-	TF	F%	Min	GP	G	A	Pts	PIM	PP	SH	GW	Min
2003-04	SC Bern Jr.	Swiss-Jr.	32	2	3	5	39	....	....	....	....	....	....	....	....	....	8	2	0	2	8	....	....	....	....
2004-05	SC Bern Jr.	Swiss-Jr.	37	5	4	9	62	....	....	....	....	....	....	....	....	....	5	0	0	0	22	....	....	....	....
2005-06	SC Bern Future Jr.	Swiss-Jr.	17	1	6	7	46	....	....	....	....	....	....	....	....	....	....	....	....	....	....	....	....	....	....
	SC Langenthal	Swiss-2	28	3	0	3	8	....	....	....	....	....	....	....	....	....	....	....	....	....	....	....	....	....	....
2006-07	SC Bern Future Jr.	Swiss-Jr.	1	0	0	0	2	....	....	....	....	....	....	....	....	....	....	....	....	....	....	....	....	....	....
	Kitchener Rangers	OHL	51	13	28	41	42	....	....	....	....	....	....	....	....	....	9	3	6	9	8	....	....	....	....
2007-08	Kitchener Rangers	OHL	59	20	35	55	79	....	....	....	....	....	....	....	....	....	17	4	13	17	24	....	....	....	....
2008-09	**Montreal**	**NHL**	3	0	1	1	2	0	0	0	6	0.0	-1	0	0.0	15:06	3	1	1	2	0	0	0	0	13:36
	Hamilton	AHL	68	16	28	44	42	....	....	....	....	....	....	....	....	....	2	0	1	1	10	....	....	....	....
2009-10	**Montreal**	**NHL**	5	0	0	0	4	0	0	0	2	0.0	-5	0	0.0	13:53	....	....	....	....	....	....	....	....	....
	Hamilton	AHL	65	7	25	32	58	....	....	....	....	....	....	....	....	....	3	0	0	0	2	....	....	....	....
	Switzerland	Olympics	5	0	0	0	6	....	....	....	....	....	....	....	....	....	....	....	....	....	....	....	....	....	....
2010-11	**Montreal**	**NHL**	41	1	10	11	14	0	0	0	63	1.6	0	0	0.0	16:34	3	2	0	2	0	1	0	0	8:46
	Hamilton	AHL	15	8	4	12	10	....	....	....	....	....	....	....	....	....	....	....	....	....	....	....	....	....	....
2011-12	**Montreal**	**NHL**	60	4	14	18	30	4	0	0	88	4.5	-7	0	0.0	15:37	....	....	....	....	....	....	....	....	....
2012-13	Geneve	Swiss	32	5	16	21	40	....	....	....	....	....	....	....	....	....	....	....	....	....	....	....	....	....	....
	Montreal	**NHL**	6	0	2	2	2	0	0	0	3	0.0	-1	0	0.0	13:45	....	....	....	....	....	....	....	....	....
2013-14	**Vancouver**	**NHL**	49	6	4	10	16	3	0	2	70	8.6	-7	0	0.0	11:55	....	....	....	....	....	....	....	....	....
	Utica Comets	AHL	7	2	5	7	0	....	....	....	....	....	....	....	....	....	....	....	....	....	....	....	....	....	....
	Switzerland	Olympics	4	0	0	0	2	....	....	....	....	....	....	....	....	....	....	....	....	....	....	....	....	....	....
2014-15	**Vancouver**	**NHL**	65	11	10	21	30	5	0	1	117	9.4	4	0	0.0	17:11	6	0	0	0	12	0	0	0	19:10
2015-16	**Vancouver**	**NHL**	45	0	7	7	24	0	0	0	65	0.0	-17	0	0.0	18:50	....	....	....	....	....	....	....	....	....
2016-17	**Nashville**	**NHL**	73	1	7	8	25	0	0	1	72	1.4	1	0	0.0	11:55	22	0	1	1	5	0	0	0	11:09
	NHL Totals		347	23	55	78	147	12	0	4	486	4.7		0	0.0	15:05	34	3	2	5	17	1	0	0	12:35

OHL Second All-Star Team (2008) • AHL All-Rookie Team (2009)
Signed as a free agent by **Geneve** (Swiss), September 18, 2012. Signed as a free agent by **Vancouver**, July 5, 2013. Signed as a free agent by **Nashville**, July 1, 2016.

WEEGAR, MacKenzie (WEE-guhr, muh-KEHN-zee) FLA

Defense. Shoots right. 6', 212 lbs. Born, Ottawa, ON, January 7, 1994. Florida's 8th pick, 206th overall, in 2013 NHL Draft.

Season	Club	League	GP	G	A	Pts	PIM	PP	SH	GW	S	S%	+/-	TF	F%	Min	GP	G	A	Pts	PIM	PP	SH	GW	Min
2010-11	Winchester	ON-Jr.B	40	10	23	33	94	....	....	....	....	....	....	....	....	....	13	3	6	9	83	....	....	....	....
	Nepean Raiders	ON-Jr.A	5	0	2	2	0	....	....	....	....	....	....	....	....	....	....	....	....	....	....	....	....	....	....
2011-12	Nepean Raiders	ON-Jr.A	53	13	37	50	61	....	....	....	....	....	....	....	....	....	18	2	4	6	24	....	....	....	....
2012-13	Halifax	QMJHL	62	8	36	44	58	....	....	....	....	....	....	....	....	....	17	0	5	5	10	....	....	....	....
2013-14	Halifax	QMJHL	61	12	47	59	97	....	....	....	....	....	....	....	....	....	16	5	17	22	14	....	....	....	....
2014-15	San Antonio	AHL	31	2	8	10	40	....	....	....	....	....	....	....	....	....	....	....	....	....	....	....	....	....	....
	Cincinnati	ECHL	21	1	12	13	13	....	....	....	....	....	....	....	....	....	....	....	....	....	....	....	....	....	....
2015-16	Portland Pirates	AHL	62	7	17	24	60	....	....	....	....	....	....	....	....	....	1	0	0	0	0	....	....	....	....
2016-17	**Florida**	**NHL**	3	0	0	0	4	0	0	0	3	0.0	0	0	0.0	17:27	....	....	....	....	....	....	....	....	....
	Springfield	AHL	60	14	22	36	70	....	....	....	....	....	....	....	....	....	....	....	....	....	....	....	....	....	....
	NHL Totals		3	0	0	0	4	0	0	0	3	0.0		0	0.0	17:27	....	....	....	....	....	....	....	....	....

QMJHL All-Rookie Team (2013) • QMJHL Second All-Star Team (2014)

WEISE, Dale (WEES, DAYL) PHI

Right wing. Shoots right. 6'2", 206 lbs. Born, Winnipeg, MB, August 5, 1988. NY Rangers' 5th pick, 111th overall, in 2008 NHL Draft.

Season	Club	League	GP	G	A	Pts	PIM	PP	SH	GW	S	S%	+/-	TF	F%	Min	GP	G	A	Pts	PIM	PP	SH	GW	Min
2005-06	Swift Current	WHL	53	4	14	18	57	....	....	....	....	....	....	....	....	....	4	0	0	0	2	....	....	....	....
2006-07	Swift Current	WHL	67	18	25	43	94	....	....	....	....	....	....	....	....	....	6	0	1	1	8	....	....	....	....
2007-08	Swift Current	WHL	53	29	22	51	84	....	....	....	....	....	....	....	....	....	12	7	6	13	20	....	....	....	....
2008-09	Hartford	AHL	74	11	12	23	64	....	....	....	....	....	....	....	....	....	6	3	1	4	2	....	....	....	....
2009-10	Hartford	AHL	73	28	22	50	114	....	....	....	....	....	....	....	....	....	....	....	....	....	....	....	....	....	....
2010-11	**NY Rangers**	**NHL**	10	0	0	0	19	0	0	0	9	0.0	-1	0	0.0	6:30	....	....	....	....	....	....	....	....	....
	Connecticut	AHL	47	18	20	38	73	....	....	....	....	....	....	....	....	....	5	2	1	3	8	....	....	....	....
2011-12	**Vancouver**	**NHL**	68	4	4	8	81	0	0	0	48	8.3	-1	4	0.0	8:10	2	0	0	0	0	0	0	0	4:16
2012-13	Trappers Tilburg	Nether.	19	22	26	48	79	....	....	....	....	....	....	....	....	....	....	....	....	....	....	....	....	....	....
	Vancouver	**NHL**	40	3	3	6	43	0	0	2	35	8.6	-7	8	12.5	9:33	4	0	0	0	4	0	0	0	5:38
2013-14	**Vancouver**	**NHL**	44	3	9	12	42	1	0	0	29	10.3	-1	4	0.0	7:46	....	....	....	....	....	....	....	....	....
	Montreal	**NHL**	17	3	1	4	17	0	0	1	12	25.0	4	0	0.0	10:07	16	3	4	7	4	0	0	2	10:14
2014-15	**Montreal**	**NHL**	79	10	19	29	34	0	0	1	91	11.0	21	12	41.7	12:11	12	2	1	3	16	0	0	1	12:31
2015-16	**Montreal**	**NHL**	56	14	12	26	22	3	0	1	117	12.0	0	30	50.0	14:21	....	....	....	....	....	....	....	....	....
	Chicago	**NHL**	15	0	1	1	2	0	0	0	19	0.0	4	5	20.0	9:57	4	1	0	1	0	0	0	1	8:24
2016-17	**Philadelphia**	**NHL**	64	8	7	15	39	1	0	2	94	8.5	1		3100.0	12:53	....	....	....	....	....	....	....	....	....
	NHL Totals		393	45	56	101	299	5	0	7	454	9.9		66	37.9	10:50	38	6	5	11	24	0	0	4	9:58

Claimed on waivers by **Vancouver** from **NY Rangers**, October 4, 2011. Signed as a free agent by **Tilburg** (Netherlands), October 10, 2012. Traded to **Montreal** by **Vancouver** for Raphael Diaz, February 3, 2014. Traded to **Chicago** by **Montreal** with Tomas Fleischmann for Phillip Danault and Chicago's 2nd round pick in 2018 NHL Draft, February 26, 2016. Signed as a free agent by **Philadelphia**, July 1, 2016.

WENNBERG, Alexander (WEHN-buhrg, al-ehx-AN-duhr) CBJ

Center. Shoots left. 6'2", 197 lbs. Born, Stockholm, Sweden, September 22, 1994. Columbus' 1st pick, 14th overall, in 2013 NHL Draft.

Season	Club	League	GP	G	A	Pts	PIM	PP	SH	GW	S	S%	+/-	TF	F%	Min	GP	G	A	Pts	PIM	PP	SH	GW	Min
2010-11	Djurgarden U18	Swe-U18	40	11	23	34	6	....	....	....	....	....	....	....	....	....	5	1	2	3	2	....	....	....	....
2011-12	Djurgarden U18	Swe-U18	10	4	2	6	4	....	....	....	....	....	....	....	....	....	2	0	1	1	0	....	....	....	....
	Djurgarden Jr.	Swe-Jr.	42	1	18	19	6	....	....	....	....	....	....	....	....	....	3	0	1	1	0	....	....	....	....
	Djurgarden	Sweden	1	0	0	0	0	....	....	....	....	....	....	....	....	....	....	....	....	....	....	....	....	....	....
2012-13	Djurgarden Jr.	Swe-Jr.	2	1	1	2	0	....	....	....	....	....	....	....	....	....	1	0	1	1	0	....	....	....	....
	Djurgarden	Sweden-2	46	14	18	32	14	....	....	....	....	....	....	....	....	....	3	0	3	3	0	....	....	....	....
2013-14	Frolunda	Sweden	50	16	5	21	8	....	....	....	....	....	....	....	....	....	7	1	0	1	0	....	....	....	....
	Sweden	Olympics	7	3	4	7	2	....	....	....	....	....	....	....	....	....	....	....	....	....	....	....	....	....	....
2014-15	**Columbus**	**NHL**	68	4	16	20	22	1	0	0	85	4.7	-19	674	42.7	15:37	....	....	....	....	....	....	....	....	....
	Springfield	AHL	6	0	3	3	12	....	....	....	....	....	....	....	....	....	....	....	....	....	....	....	....	....	....
2015-16	**Columbus**	**NHL**	69	8	32	40	2	1	0	1	97	8.2	-1	922	43.4	15:52	....	....	....	....	....	....	....	....	....
2016-17	**Columbus**	**NHL**	80	13	46	59	21	2	0	5	109	11.9	9	1285	47.4	18:23	5	0	1	1	2	0	0	0	19:27
	NHL Totals		217	25	94	119	45	4	0	6	291	8.6		2881	45.0	16:43	5	0	1	1	2	0	0	0	19:27

WERENSKI, Zach (wuh-REHN-skee, ZAK) CBJ

Defense. Shoots left. 6'2", 218 lbs. Born, Grosse Pointe, MI, July 19, 1997. Columbus' 1st pick, 8th overall, in 2015 NHL Draft.

Season	Club	League	GP	G	A	Pts	PIM	PP	SH	GW	S	S%	+/-	TF	F%	Min	GP	G	A	Pts	PIM	PP	SH	GW	Min
2011-12	Det. B. Tire U16	T1EHL	35	8	20	28	18	....	....	....	....	....	....	....	....	....	7	3	5	8	4	....	....	....	....
2012-13	Det. L.C. U18	HPHL	28	7	14	21	18	....	....	....	....	....	....	....	....	....	....	....	....	....	....	....	....	....	....
2013-14	USAHNTDP	USHL	35	6	13	19	17	....	....	....	....	....	....	....	....	....	....	....	....	....	....	....	....	....	....
	USAHNTDP	U-17	16	2	11	13	25	....	....	....	....	....	....	....	....	....	....	....	....	....	....	....	....	....	....
2014-15	U. of Michigan	Big Ten	35	9	16	25	8	....	....	....	....	....	....	....	....	....	....	....	....	....	....	....	....	....	....
2015-16	U. of Michigan	Big Ten	36	11	25	36	20	....	....	....	....	....	....	....	....	....	....	....	....	....	....	....	....	....	....
	Lake Erie	AHL	7	1	0	1	0	....	....	....	....	....	....	....	....	....	17	5	9	14	2	....	....	....	23:29
2016-17	**Columbus**	**NHL**	78	11	36	47	14	4	0	1	188	5.9	17	0	0.0	20:55	3	1	0	1	0	1	0	0	23:29
	NHL Totals		78	11	36	47	14	4	0	1	188	5.9		0	0.0	20:55	3	1	0	1	0	1	0	0	23:29

Big Ten First All-Star Team (2016) • NCAA West First All-American Team (2016) • NHL All-Rookie Team (2017)

Season	Club	League	GP	G	A	Pts	PIM	PP	SH	GW	S	S%	+/-	TF	F%	Min	GP	G	A	Pts	PIM	PP	SH	GW	Min
			Regular Season														Playoffs								

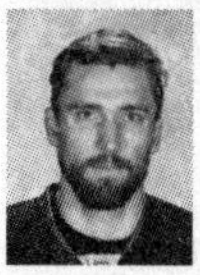

WHEELER, Blake

(WEE-luhr, BLAYK) **WPG**

Right wing. Shoots right. 6'5", 225 lbs. Born, Plymouth, MN, August 31, 1986. Phoenix's 1st pick, 5th overall, in 2004 NHL Draft.

Season	Club	League	GP	G	A	Pts	PIM	PP	SH	GW	S	S%	+/-	TF	F%	Min	GP	G	A	Pts	PIM	PP	SH	GW	Min
2002-03	Breck Mustangs	High-MN	26	15	27	42	....	....	....	....	....	....	....	....	....	....	....	....	....	....	....	....	....	....	....
2003-04	Team Northwest	UMEHL	24	5	6	11	....	....	....	....	....	....	....	....	....	....	....	....	....	....	....	....	....	....	....
	Breck Mustangs	High-MN	27	39	50	89	34	....	....	....	....	....	....	....	....	....	3	6	5	11	0	....	....	....	....
2004-05	Green Bay	USHL	58	19	28	47	43	....	....	....	....	....	....	....	....	....	....	....	....	....	....	....	....	....	....
2005-06	U. of Minnesota	WCHA	39	9	14	23	41	....	....	....	....	....	....	....	....	....	....	....	....	....	....	....	....	....	....
2006-07	U. of Minnesota	WCHA	44	18	20	38	42	....	....	....	....	....	....	....	....	....	....	....	....	....	....	....	....	....	....
2007-08	U. of Minnesota	WCHA	44	15	20	35	72	....	....	....	....	....	....	....	....	....	....	....	....	....	....	....	....	....	....
2008-09	**Boston**	**NHL**	**81**	**21**	**24**	**45**	**46**	**3**	**2**	**3**	**150**	**14.0**	**36**	**34**	**38.2**	**13:41**	**8**	**0**	**0**	**0**	**0**	**0**	**0**	**0**	**12:08**
2009-10	**Boston**	**NHL**	**82**	**18**	**20**	**38**	**53**	**3**	**1**	**2**	**159**	**11.3**	**-4**	**27**	**48.2**	**15:47**	**13**	**1**	**5**	**6**	**6**	**0**	**0**	**0**	**14:14**
2010-11	**Boston**	**NHL**	**58**	**11**	**16**	**27**	**32**	**0**	**0**	**2**	**101**	**10.9**	**8**	**136**	**38.2**	**15:12**	....	....	....	....	....	....	....	....	....
	Atlanta	**NHL**	**23**	**7**	**10**	**17**	**14**	**0**	**0**	**0**	**78**	**9.0**	**2**	**12**	**0.0**	**18:53**	....	....	....	....	....	....	....	....	....
2011-12	**Winnipeg**	**NHL**	**80**	**17**	**47**	**64**	**55**	**6**	**0**	**3**	**208**	**8.2**	**3**	**10**	**40.0**	**19:05**	....	....	....	....	....	....	....	....	....
2012-13	EHC Munchen	Germany	15	6	14	20	51	....	....	....	....	....	....	....	....	....	....	....	....	....	....	....	....	....	....
	Winnipeg	**NHL**	**48**	**19**	**22**	**41**	**28**	**2**	**0**	**2**	**129**	**14.7**	**-3**	**18**	**22.2**	**18:48**	....	....	....	....	....	....	....	....	....
2013-14	**Winnipeg**	**NHL**	**82**	**28**	**41**	**69**	**63**	**8**	**0**	**4**	**225**	**12.4**	**4**	**40**	**37.5**	**18:41**	....	....	....	....	....	....	....	....	....
	United States	Olympics	6	0	1	1	2	....	....	....	....	....	....	....	....	....	....	....	....	....	....	....	....	....	....
2014-15	**Winnipeg**	**NHL**	**79**	**26**	**35**	**61**	**73**	**2**	**4**	**6**	**244**	**10.7**	**26**	**48**	**45.8**	**19:40**	**4**	**1**	**0**	**1**	**2**	**0**	**0**	**0**	**19:15**
2015-16	**Winnipeg**	**NHL**	**82**	**26**	**52**	**78**	**49**	**3**	**2**	**5**	**256**	**10.2**	**8**	**28**	**35.7**	**19:47**	....	....	....	....	....	....	....	....	....
2016-17	**Winnipeg**	**NHL**	**82**	**26**	**48**	**74**	**47**	**5**	**2**	**4**	**259**	**10.0**	**6**	**94**	**45.7**	**20:09**	....	....	....	....	....	....	....	....	....
	NHL Totals		**697**	**199**	**315**	**514**	**460**	**32**	**11**	**31**	**1809**	**11.0**		**447**	**39.4**	**17:57**	**25**	**2**	**5**	**7**	**8**	**0**	**0**	**0**	**14:21**

USHL All-Rookie Team (2005)

Signed as a free agent by **Boston**, July 1, 2008. Traded to **Atlanta** by **Boston** with Mark Stuart for Rich Peverley and Boris Valabik, February 18, 2011. • Transferred to **Winnipeg** after **Atlanta** franchise relocated, June 21, 2011. Signed as a free agent by **Munchen** (Germany), October 28, 2012.

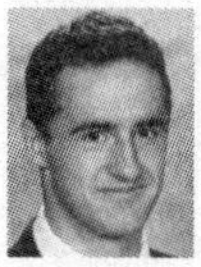

WHITE, Colin

(WIGHT, KAWL-ihn) **OTT**

Center. Shoots right. 6'1", 185 lbs. Born, Boston, MA, January 30, 1997. Ottawa's 2nd pick, 21st overall, in 2015 NHL Draft.

Season	Club	League	GP	G	A	Pts	PIM	PP	SH	GW	S	S%	+/-	TF	F%	Min	GP	G	A	Pts	PIM	PP	SH	GW	Min
2011-12	Nobles	High-MA	29	16	18	44	....	....	....	....	....	....	....	....	....	....	....	....	....	....	....	....	....	....	....
2012-13	Cape Cod	Minor-MA	9	3	6	9	0	....	....	....	....	....	....	....	....	....	....	....	....	....	....	....	....	....	....
	Nobles	High-MA	22	18	14	32	10	....	....	....	....	....	....	....	....	....	....	....	....	....	....	....	....	....	....
2013-14	USAHNTDP	USHL	35	14	14	28	50	....	....	....	....	....	....	....	....	....	....	....	....	....	....	....	....	....	....
	USAHNTDP	U-17	20	20	19	39	35	....	....	....	....	....	....	....	....	....	....	....	....	....	....	....	....	....	....
2014-15	USAHNTDP	USHL	20	4	13	17	10	....	....	....	....	....	....	....	....	....	....	....	....	....	....	....	....	....	....
	USAHNTDP	U-18	34	19	19	38	18	....	....	....	....	....	....	....	....	....	....	....	....	....	....	....	....	....	....
2015-16	Boston College	H-East	37	19	24	43	46	....	....	....	....	....	....	....	....	....	....	....	....	....	....	....	....	....	....
2016-17	Boston College	H-East	35	16	17	33	46	....	....	....	....	....	....	....	....	....	....	....	....	....	....	....	....	....	....
	Ottawa	**NHL**	**2**	**0**	**0**	**0**	**0**	**0**	**0**	**0**	**1**	**0.0**	**0**	**21**	**33.3**	**13:43**	**1**	**0**	**0**	**0**	**0**	**0**	**0**	**0**	**2:39**
	Binghamton	AHL	3	1	2	3	2	....	....	....	....	....	....	....	....	....	....	....	....	....	....	....	....	....	....
	NHL Totals		**2**	**0**	**0**	**0**	**0**	**0**	**0**	**0**	**1**	**0.0**		**21**	**33.3**	**13:43**	**1**	**0**	**0**	**0**	**0**	**0**	**0**	**0**	**2:39**

Hockey East All-Rookie Team (2016) • Hockey East Second All-Star Team (2016)

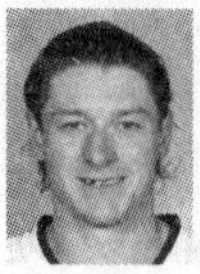

WHITE, Ryan

(WIGHT, RIGH-uhn)

Center. Shoots right. 6', 200 lbs. Born, Brandon, MB, March 17, 1988. Montreal's 4th pick, 66th overall, in 2006 NHL Draft.

Season	Club	League	GP	G	A	Pts	PIM	PP	SH	GW	S	S%	+/-	TF	F%	Min	GP	G	A	Pts	PIM	PP	SH	GW	Min
2003-04	Brandon	MMHL	39	21	41	62	90	....	....	....	....	....	....	....	....	....	11	7	7	14	22	....	....	....	....
2004-05	Calgary Hitmen	WHL	63	9	14	23	95	....	....	....	....	....	....	....	....	....	12	2	1	3	26	....	....	....	....
2005-06	Calgary Hitmen	WHL	72	20	33	53	121	....	....	....	....	....	....	....	....	....	13	3	4	7	18	....	....	....	....
2006-07	Calgary Hitmen	WHL	72	34	55	89	97	....	....	....	....	....	....	....	....	....	18	6	8	14	36	....	....	....	....
2007-08	Calgary Hitmen	WHL	68	28	44	72	98	....	....	....	....	....	....	....	....	....	16	6	11	17	8	....	....	....	....
2008-09	Hamilton	AHL	80	11	18	29	68	....	....	....	....	....	....	....	....	....	6	3	1	4	9	....	....	....	....
2009-10	**Montreal**	**NHL**	**16**	**0**	**2**	**2**	**16**	**0**	**0**	**0**	**5**	**0.0**	**-6**	**10**	**70.0**	**11:09**	....	....	....	....	....	....	....	....	....
	Hamilton	AHL	62	17	17	34	173	....	....	....	....	....	....	....	....	....	19	4	5	9	47	....	....	....	....
2010-11	**Montreal**	**NHL**	**27**	**2**	**3**	**5**	**38**	**0**	**0**	**0**	**30**	**6.7**	**5**	**32**	**40.6**	**8:55**	**7**	**0**	**0**	**0**	**2**	**0**	**0**	**0**	**6:35**
	Hamilton	AHL	33	3	9	12	77	....	....	....	....	....	....	....	....	....	13	2	6	8	37	....	....	....	....
2011-12	**Montreal**	**NHL**	**20**	**0**	**3**	**3**	**61**	**0**	**0**	**0**	**12**	**0.0**	**-7**	**59**	**49.2**	**14:31**	....	....	....	....	....	....	....	....	....
	Hamilton	AHL	4	4	1	5	26	....	....	....	....	....	....	....	....	....	....	....	....	....	....	....	....	....	....
2012-13	**Montreal**	**NHL**	**26**	**1**	**0**	**1**	**67**	**0**	**0**	**0**	**16**	**6.3**	**1**	**167**	**54.5**	**9:25**	**3**	**1**	**0**	**1**	**23**	**0**	**0**	**0**	**9:06**
2013-14	**Montreal**	**NHL**	**52**	**2**	**4**	**6**	**50**	**0**	**0**	**1**	**51**	**3.9**	**-8**	**388**	**50.8**	**9:41**	....	....	....	....	....	....	....	....	....
2014-15	**Philadelphia**	**NHL**	**34**	**6**	**6**	**12**	**30**	**0**	**0**	**1**	**45**	**13.3**	**4**	**123**	**52.9**	**11:43**	....	....	....	....	....	....	....	....	....
	Lehigh Valley	AHL	11	1	2	3	39	....	....	....	....	....	....	....	....	....	....	....	....	....	....	....	....	....	....
2015-16	**Philadelphia**	**NHL**	**73**	**11**	**5**	**16**	**101**	**3**	**0**	**0**	**88**	**12.5**	**-9**	**351**	**52.4**	**12:34**	**6**	**1**	**0**	**1**	**28**	**0**	**0**	**1**	**12:39**
2016-17	**Arizona**	**NHL**	**46**	**7**	**6**	**13**	**70**	**0**	**0**	**1**	**43**	**16.3**	**-8**	**81**	**43.2**	**10:57**	....	....	....	....	....	....	....	....	....
	Minnesota	**NHL**	**19**	**2**	**1**	**3**	**14**	**0**	**0**	**0**	**17**	**11.8**	**-8**	**10**	**40.0**	**9:57**	**3**	**0**	**0**	**0**	**4**	**0**	**0**	**0**	**7:04**
	NHL Totals		**313**	**31**	**30**	**61**	**447**	**3**	**0**	**3**	**307**	**10.1**		**1221**	**51.2**	**11:05**	**19**	**2**	**0**	**2**	**57**	**0**	**0**	**1**	**8:58**

WHL East First All-Star Team (2007) • WHL East Second All-Star Team (2008)

• Missed majority of 2011-12 due to sports hernia injury in training camp. Signed as a free agent by **Philadelphia**, August 7, 2014. Signed as a free agent by **Arizona**, July 1, 2016. Traded to **Minnesota** by **Arizona** with Martin Hanzal and Arizona's 4th round pick (Mason Shaw) in 2017 NHL Draft for Grayson Downing, Minnesota's 1st round pick (Pierre-Olivier Joseph) in 2017 NHL Draft, Minnesota's 2nd round pick in 2018 NHL Draft and Minnesota's 4th round pick in 2019 NHL Draft, February 26, 2017.

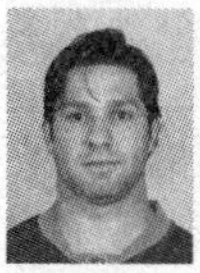

WHITNEY, Joe

(WHIHT-nee, JOH)

Right wing. Shoots left. 5'6", 167 lbs. Born, Reading, MA, February 6, 1988.

Season	Club	League	GP	G	A	Pts	PIM	PP	SH	GW	S	S%	+/-	TF	F%	Min	GP	G	A	Pts	PIM	PP	SH	GW	Min
2007-08	Boston College	H-East	44	11	*40	51	50	....	....	....	....	....	....	....	....	....	....	....	....	....	....	....	....	....	....
2008-09	Boston College	H-East	36	7	8	15	36	....	....	....	....	....	....	....	....	....	....	....	....	....	....	....	....	....	....
2009-10	Boston College	H-East	42	17	28	45	61	....	....	....	....	....	....	....	....	....	....	....	....	....	....	....	....	....	....
2010-11	Boston College	H-East	39	5	26	31	60	....	....	....	....	....	....	....	....	....	....	....	....	....	....	....	....	....	....
	Portland Pirates	AHL	1	0	1	1	0	....	....	....	....	....	....	....	....	....	....	....	....	....	....	....	....	....	....
2011-12	Albany Devils	AHL	72	15	29	44	36	....	....	....	....	....	....	....	....	....	....	....	....	....	....	....	....	....	....
2012-13	Albany Devils	AHL	66	26	25	51	32	....	....	....	....	....	....	....	....	....	....	....	....	....	....	....	....	....	....
2013-14	**New Jersey**	**NHL**	**1**	**0**	**0**	**0**	**0**	**0**	**0**	**0**	**0**	**0.0**	**0**	**1**	**0.0**	**8:00**	....	....	....	....	....	....	....	....	....
	Albany Devils	AHL	73	22	31	53	34	....	....	....	....	....	....	....	....	....	4	1	0	1	0	....	....	....	....
2014-15	**New Jersey**	**NHL**	**4**	**1**	**0**	**1**	**0**	**0**	**0**	**0**	**1**	**100.0**	**-1**	**0**	**0.0**	**6:53**	....	....	....	....	....	....	....	....	....
	Albany Devils	AHL	66	23	37	60	64	....	....	....	....	....	....	....	....	....	....	....	....	....	....	....	....	....	....
2015-16	Bridgeport	AHL	36	14	19	33	29	....	....	....	....	....	....	....	....	....	....	....	....	....	....	....	....	....	....
2016-17	San Antonio	AHL	55	11	17	28	41	....	....	....	....	....	....	....	....	....	....	....	....	....	....	....	....	....	....
	Tucson	AHL	19	3	5	8	8	....	....	....	....	....	....	....	....	....	....	....	....	....	....	....	....	....	....
	NHL Totals		**5**	**1**	**0**	**1**	**0**	**0**	**0**	**0**	**1**	**100.0**		**1**	**0.0**	**7:06**	....	....	....	....	....	....	....	....	....

Hockey East All-Rookie Team (2008) • NCAA Championship All-Tournament Team (2010)

Signed as a free agent by **Albany** (AHL), July 28, 2011. Signed as a free agent by **New Jersey**, May 1, 2013. Signed as a free agent by **NY Islanders**, July 2, 2015. • Missed majority of 2015-16 as a healthy reserve. Signed as a free agent by **Colorado**, July 1, 2016. Traded to **Arizona** by **Colorado** for Brendan Ranford, March 1, 2017.

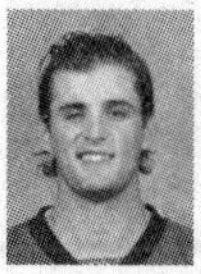

WIDEMAN, Chris

(WIGHD-muhn, KRIHS) **OTT**

Defense. Shoots right. 5'10", 180 lbs. Born, St. Louis, MO, January 7, 1990. Ottawa's 4th pick, 100th overall, in 2009 NHL Draft.

Season	Club	League	GP	G	A	Pts	PIM	PP	SH	GW	S	S%	+/-	TF	F%	Min	GP	G	A	Pts	PIM	PP	SH	GW	Min
2006-07	St.L. AAA Blues	Minor-MO	62	9	21	30	122	....	....	....	....	....	....	....	....	....	....	....	....	....	....	....	....	....	....
	St. Louis Bandits	NAHL	1	0	0	0	0	....	....	....	....	....	....	....	....	....	7	0	1	1	4	....	....	....	....
2007-08	Cedar Rapids	USHL	53	2	12	14	51	....	....	....	....	....	....	....	....	....	1	0	0	0	0	....	....	....	....
2008-09	Miami U.	CCHA	39	0	26	26	56	....	....	....	....	....	....	....	....	....	....	....	....	....	....	....	....	....	....
2009-10	Miami U.	CCHA	44	5	17	22	63	....	....	....	....	....	....	....	....	....	....	....	....	....	....	....	....	....	....
2010-11	Miami U.	CCHA	39	3	20	23	32	....	....	....	....	....	....	....	....	....	....	....	....	....	....	....	....	....	....
2011-12	Miami U.	CCHA	41	4	20	24	40	....	....	....	....	....	....	....	....	....	....	....	....	....	....	....	....	....	....
2012-13	Binghamton	AHL	60	2	16	18	46	....	....	....	....	....	....	....	....	....	3	1	2	3	2	....	....	....	....
	Elmira Jackals	ECHL	5	0	5	5	7	....	....	....	....	....	....	....	....	....	....	....	....	....	....	....	....	....	....
2013-14	Binghamton	AHL	73	9	42	51	101	....	....	....	....	....	....	....	....	....	4	1	0	1	6	....	....	....	....
2014-15	Binghamton	AHL	75	19	42	61	116	....	....	....	....	....	....	....	....	....	....	....	....	....	....	....	....	....	....

Season	Club	League	GP	G	A	Pts	PIM	PP	SH	GW	S	S%	+/-	TF	F%	Min	GP	G	A	Pts	PIM	PP	SH	GW	Min
			Regular Season														Playoffs								
2015-16	Ottawa	NHL	64	6	7	13	34	1	0	2	87	6.9	4	0	0.0	13:57	....	....	....	....	....	....	....	....	....
2016-17	Ottawa	NHL	76	5	12	17	46	1	0	1	123	4.1	7	0	0.0	13:58	15	1	3	4	4	0	0	0	13:01
	NHL Totals		140	11	19	30	80	2	0	3	210	5.2		0	0.0	13:57	15	1	3	4	4	0	0	0	13:01

CCHA All-Rookie Team (2009) • CCHA Second All-Star Team (2011) • AHL First All-Star Team (2015) • Eddie Shore Award (AHL – Outstanding Defenseman) (2015)

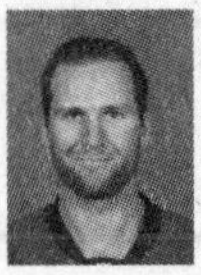

WIDEMAN, Dennis
(WIGHD-muhn, DEH-nihs)

Defense. Shoots right. 6', 202 lbs. Born, Kitchener, ON, March 20, 1983. Buffalo's 9th pick, 241st overall, in 2002 NHL Draft.

Season	Club	League	GP	G	A	Pts	PIM	PP	SH	GW	S	S%	+/-	TF	F%	Min	GP	G	A	Pts	PIM	PP	SH	GW	Min
1998-99	Elmira	ON-Jr.B	47	18	30	48	142	....	....	....	....	....	....	....	....	....	....	....	....	....	....	....	....	....	....
99-2000	Sudbury Wolves	OHL	63	10	26	36	64	....	....	....	....	....	....	....	....	....	12	1	2	3	22	....	....	....	....
2000-01	Sudbury Wolves	OHL	25	7	11	18	37	....	....	....	....	....	....	....	....	....	....	....	....	....	....	....	....	....	....
	London Knights	OHL	24	8	8	16	38	....	....	....	....	....	....	....	....	....	5	0	4	4	6	....	....	....	....
2001-02	London Knights	OHL	65	27	42	69	141	....	....	....	....	....	....	....	....	....	12	4	9	13	26	....	....	....	....
2002-03	London Knights	OHL	55	20	27	47	83	....	....	....	....	....	....	....	....	....	14	6	6	12	10	....	....	....	....
2003-04	London Knights	OHL	60	24	41	65	85	....	....	....	....	....	....	....	....	....	15	7	10	17	17	....	....	....	....
2004-05	Worcester IceCats	AHL	79	13	30	43	65	....	....	....	....	....	....	....	....	....	....	....	....	....	....	....	....	....	....
2005-06	St. Louis	NHL	67	8	16	24	83	5	1	1	150	5.3	–31	1	0.0	21:41	....	....	....	....	....	....	....	....	....
	Peoria Rivermen	AHL	12	2	4	6	31	....	....	....	....	....	....	....	....	....	....	....	....	....	....	....	....	....	....
2006-07	St. Louis	NHL	55	5	17	22	44	4	0	1	94	5.3	–7	0	0.0	20:12	....	....	....	....	....	....	....	....	....
	Boston	NHL	20	1	2	3	27	0	0	0	28	3.6	–3	1	0.0	17:20	....	....	....	....	....	....	....	....	....
2007-08	Boston	NHL	81	13	23	36	70	9	0	1	171	7.6	11	0	0.0	25:09	6	0	3	3	0	0	0	0	24:21
2008-09	Boston	NHL	79	13	37	50	34	6	1	2	169	7.7	32	0	0.0	24:39	11	0	7	7	4	0	0	0	24:42
2009-10	Boston	NHL	76	6	24	30	34	2	0	2	146	4.1	–14	0	0.0	23:33	13	1	11	12	4	0	0	0	26:02
2010-11	Florida	NHL	61	9	24	33	33	8	0	1	135	6.7	–26	1	100.0	23:58	....	....	....	....	....	....	....	....	....
	Washington	NHL	14	1	6	7	6	1	0	0	25	4.0	7	0	0.0	24:05	....	....	....	....	....	....	....	....	....
2011-12	Washington	NHL	82	11	35	46	46	4	0	3	175	6.3	–8	0	0.0	23:54	14	0	3	3	2	0	0	0	20:44
2012-13	Calgary	NHL	46	6	16	22	12	4	0	1	94	6.4	–9	1	0.0	25:01	....	....	....	....	....	....	....	....	....
2013-14	Calgary	NHL	46	4	17	21	18	2	0	0	102	3.9	–15	0	0.0	22:42	....	....	....	....	....	....	....	....	....
2014-15	Calgary	NHL	80	15	41	56	34	6	0	2	173	8.7	6	0	0.0	24:39	11	0	7	7	12	0	0	0	26:29
2015-16	Calgary	NHL	51	2	17	19	30	2	0	0	75	2.7	–9	0	0.0	20:37	....	....	....	....	....	....	....	....	....
2016-17	Calgary	NHL	57	5	13	18	32	2	0	1	87	5.7	–6	0	0.0	20:14	....	....	....	....	....	....	....	....	....
	NHL Totals		815	99	288	387	503	55	2	15	1624	6.1		4	25.0	23:05	55	1	31	32	22	0	0	0	24:20

OHL First All-Star Team (2004) • Canadian Major Junior Second All-Star Team (2004)

Played in NHL All-Star Game (2012)

Signed as a free agent by **St. Louis**, June 30, 2004. Traded to **Boston** by **St. Louis** for Brad Boyes, February 27, 2007. Traded to **Florida** by **Boston** with Boston's 1st round pick (later traded to Los Angeles – Los Angeles selected Derek Forbert) in 2010 NHL Draft and Boston's 3rd round pick (Kyle Rau) in 2011 NHL Draft for Nathan Horton and Gregory Campbell, June 22, 2010. Traded to **Washington** by **Florida** for Jake Hauswirth and Washington's 3rd round pick (Jonathan Racine) in 2011 NHL Draft, February 28, 2011. Traded to **Calgary** by **Washington** for Jordan Henry and Calgary's 5th round pick (later traded to Winnipeg – Winnipeg selected Tucker Poolman) in 2013 NHL Draft, June 27, 2012.

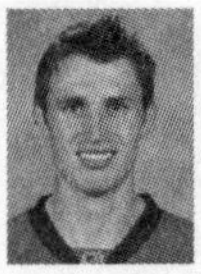

WIERCIOCH, Patrick
(WEER-kawsh, PAT-rihk) **VAN**

Defense. Shoots left. 6'5", 202 lbs. Born, Burnaby, BC, September 12, 1990. Ottawa's 2nd pick, 42nd overall, in 2008 NHL Draft.

Season	Club	League	GP	G	A	Pts	PIM	PP	SH	GW	S	S%	+/-	TF	F%	Min	GP	G	A	Pts	PIM	PP	SH	GW	Min
2006-07	Burnaby Express	BCHL	42	9	16	25	46	....	....	....	....	....	....	....	....	....	14	3	4	7	10	....	....	....	....
2007-08	Omaha Lancers	USHL	40	3	18	21	24	....	....	....	....	....	....	....	....	....	14	2	9	11	22	....	....	....	....
2008-09	U. of Denver	WCHA	36	12	23	35	26	....	....	....	....	....	....	....	....	....	....	....	....	....	....	....	....	....	....
2009-10	U. of Denver	WCHA	39	6	21	27	34	....	....	....	....	....	....	....	....	....	....	....	....	....	....	....	....	....	....
2010-11	Ottawa	NHL	8	0	2	2	4	0	0	0	3	0.0	0	0	0.0	13:54	....	....	....	....	....	....	....	....	....
	Binghamton	AHL	67	4	14	18	25	....	....	....	....	....	....	....	....	....	15	0	1	1	0	....	....	....	....
2011-12	Binghamton	AHL	57	4	16	20	34	....	....	....	....	....	....	....	....	....	....	....	....	....	....	....	....	....	....
2012-13	Binghamton	AHL	32	10	9	19	22	....	....	....	....	....	....	....	....	....	....	....	....	....	....	....	....	....	....
	Ottawa	NHL	42	5	14	19	39	3	0	0	81	6.2	9	0	0.0	15:42	1	0	0	0	0	0	0	0	1:47
2013-14	Ottawa	NHL	53	4	19	23	20	3	0	0	97	4.1	–1	2	0.0	16:22	....	....	....	....	....	....	....	....	....
2014-15	Ottawa	NHL	56	3	10	13	28	1	0	2	79	3.8	3	0	0.0	18:03	6	2	2	4	4	1	0	1	19:18
2015-16	Ottawa	NHL	52	0	5	5	24	0	0	0	56	0.0	2	0	0.0	17:20	....	....	....	....	....	....	....	....	....
2016-17	Colorado	NHL	57	4	8	12	23	0	0	0	63	6.3	–18	0	0.0	16:40	....	....	....	....	....	....	....	....	....
	NHL Totals		268	16	58	74	138	7	0	2	379	4.2		2	0.0	16:48	7	2	2	4	4	1	0	1	16:47

WCHA All-Rookie Team (2009) • WCHA Second All-Star Team (2009) • WCHA First All-Star Team (2010) • NCAA West First All-American Team (2010)

Signed as a free agent by **Colorado**, July 1, 2016. Signed as a free agent by **Vancouver**, July 1, 2017.

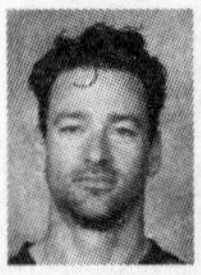

WILLIAMS, Justin
(WIHL-yuhms, JUHS-tihn) **CAR**

Right wing. Shoots right. 6'1", 186 lbs. Born, Cobourg, ON, October 4, 1981. Philadelphia's 1st pick, 28th overall, in 2000 NHL Draft.

Season	Club	League	GP	G	A	Pts	PIM	PP	SH	GW	S	S%	+/-	TF	F%	Min	GP	G	A	Pts	PIM	PP	SH	GW	Min
1997-98	Colborne Colts	ON-Jr.C	36	32	35	67	26	....	....	....	....	....	....	....	....	....	....	....	....	....	....	....	....	....	....
	Cobourg Cougars	ON-Jr.A	17	0	3	3	5	....	....	....	....	....	....	....	....	....	....	....	....	....	....	....	....	....	....
1998-99	Plymouth Whalers	OHL	47	4	8	12	28	....	....	....	....	....	....	....	....	....	7	1	2	3	0	....	....	....	....
99-2000	Plymouth Whalers	OHL	68	37	46	83	46	....	....	....	....	....	....	....	....	....	23	*14	16	*30	10	....	....	....	....
2000-01	Philadelphia	NHL	63	12	13	25	22	0	0	0	99	12.1	6	13	53.9	12:31	....	....	....	....	....	....	....	....	....
2001-02	Philadelphia	NHL	75	17	23	40	32	0	0	1	162	10.5	11	16	25.0	14:27	5	0	0	0	4	0	0	0	16:42
2002-03	Philadelphia	NHL	41	8	16	24	22	0	0	2	105	7.6	15	16	50.0	15:57	12	1	5	6	8	0	0	1	14:11
2003-04	Philadelphia	NHL	47	6	20	26	32	3	0	1	107	5.6	10	38	31.6	15:30	....	....	....	....	....	....	....	....	....
	Carolina	NHL	32	5	13	18	32	1	0	0	96	5.2	2	25	36.0	18:52	....	....	....	....	....	....	....	....	....
2004-05	Lulea HF	Sweden	49	14	18	32	61	....	....	....	....	....	....	....	....	....	4	0	1	1	29	....	....	....	....
2005-06 ♦	Carolina	NHL	82	31	45	76	60	8	4	4	255	12.2	1	17	29.4	21:08	25	7	11	18	34	0	1	1	21:36
2006-07	Carolina	NHL	82	33	34	67	73	12	2	8	258	12.8	–11	24	37.5	20:51	....	....	....	....	....	....	....	....	....
2007-08	Carolina	NHL	37	9	21	30	43	2	0	0	106	8.5	2	13	38.5	19:18	....	....	....	....	....	....	....	....	....
2008-09	Carolina	NHL	32	3	7	10	9	2	0	0	80	3.8	–9	20	30.0	15:08	....	....	....	....	....	....	....	....	....
	Los Angeles	NHL	12	1	3	4	8	1	0	0	28	3.6	1	2	50.0	17:51	....	....	....	....	....	....	....	....	....
2009-10	Los Angeles	NHL	49	10	19	29	39	1	0	1	140	7.1	3	11	36.4	16:23	3	0	1	1	2	0	0	0	11:24
2010-11	Los Angeles	NHL	73	22	35	57	59	5	0	3	213	10.3	14	14	50.0	17:15	6	3	1	4	2	1	0	0	16:44
2011-12 ♦	Los Angeles	NHL	82	22	37	59	44	9	0	2	241	9.1	10	25	44.0	17:09	20	4	11	15	12	1	0	0	18:24
2012-13	Los Angeles	NHL	48	11	22	33	22	1	0	3	142	7.7	15	6	33.3	16:59	18	6	3	9	8	1	0	2	18:36
2013-14 ♦	Los Angeles	NHL	82	19	24	43	48	4	0	1	239	7.9	14	10	20.0	16:57	26	9	16	25	35	2	0	2	16:49
2014-15	Los Angeles	NHL	81	18	23	41	29	4	0	2	174	10.3	8	6	50.0	15:49	....	....	....	....	....	....	....	....	....
2015-16	Washington	NHL	82	22	30	52	36	3	0	3	201	10.9	15	109	52.3	16:39	12	3	4	7	14	0	0	0	15:28
2016-17	Washington	NHL	80	24	24	48	50	5	0	4	167	14.4	14	117	54.7	15:29	13	3	6	9	6	1	0	1	18:38
	NHL Totals		1080	273	409	682	660	61	6	35	2813	9.7		482	44.8	16:55	140	36	58	94	125	6	1	7	17:50

Conn Smythe Trophy (2014)

Played in NHL All-Star Game (2007)

• Missed majority of 2002-03 due to shoulder (November 15, 2002 vs. Carolina) and knee (January 18, 2003 vs. Tampa Bay) injuries. Traded to **Carolina** by **Philadelphia** for Danny Markov, January 20, 2004. Signed as a free agent by **Lulea** (Sweden), September 21, 2004. • Missed majority of 2007-08 due to knee injury at Florida, December 20, 2007. Traded to **Los Angeles** by **Carolina** for Patrick O'Sullivan and Calgary's 2nd round pick (previously acquired, Carolina selected Brian Dumoulin) in 2009 NHL Draft, March 4. 2009. Signed as a free agent by **Washington**, July 1, 2015. Signed as a free agent by **Carolina**, July 1, 2017.

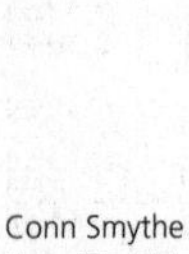

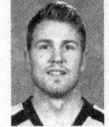

WILSON, Colin
(WIHL-suhn, KAW-lihn) **COL**

Center. Shoots left. 6'1", 221 lbs. Born, Greenwich, CT, October 20, 1989. Nashville's 1st pick, 7th overall, in 2008 NHL Draft.

Season	Club	League	GP	G	A	Pts	PIM	PP	SH	GW	S	S%	+/-	TF	F%	Min	GP	G	A	Pts	PIM	PP	SH	GW	Min
2005-06	USAHNTDP	U-17	15	9	7	16	2	....	....	....	....	....	....	....	....	....	....	....	....	....	....	....	....	....	....
	USAHNTDP	U-18	16	2	4	6	8	....	....	....	....	....	....	....	....	....	....	....	....	....	....	....	....	....	....
	USAHNTDP	NAHL	34	10	11	21	10	....	....	....	....	....	....	....	....	....	2	0	0	0	2	....	....	....	....
2006-07	USAHNTDP	U-18	41	19	31	50	32	....	....	....	....	....	....	....	....	....	....	....	....	....	....	....	....	....	....
	USAHNTDP	NAHL	15	11	13	24	21	....	....	....	....	....	....	....	....	....	....	....	....	....	....	....	....	....	....
2007-08	Boston University	H-East	37	12	23	35	22	....	....	....	....	....	....	....	....	....	....	....	....	....	....	....	....	....	....
2008-09	Boston University	H-East	43	17	*38	*55	52	....	....	....	....	....	....	....	....	....	....	....	....	....	....	....	....	....	....
2009-10	Nashville	NHL	35	8	7	15	7	1	0	3	58	13.8	–2	124	50.0	15:10	6	0	1	1	0	0	0	0	13:43
	Milwaukee	AHL	40	13	21	34	19	....	....	....	....	....	....	....	....	....	....	....	....	....	....	....	....	....	....
2010-11	Nashville	NHL	82	16	18	34	17	2	0	2	101	15.8	9	228	47.4	13:18	3	0	0	0	0	0	0	0	11:37
2011-12	Nashville	NHL	68	15	20	35	21	5	0	5	114	13.2	5	77	50.7	16:08	4	1	0	1	0	0	0	0	13:25

Season	Club	League	GP	G	A	Pts	PIM	PP	SH	GW	S	S%	+/-	TF	F%	Min	GP	G	A	Pts	PIM	PP	SH	GW	Min
2012-13	Nashville	NHL	25	7	12	19	4	2	0	1	26	26.9	1	21	38.1	16:34	....								
2013-14	Nashville	NHL	81	11	22	33	21	2	0	3	112	9.8	-1	343	48.4	15:13	....								
2014-15	Nashville	NHL	77	20	22	42	22	3	0	5	172	11.6	19	178	39.9	16:13	6	5	0	5	0	4	0	1	19:44
2015-16	Nashville	NHL	64	6	18	24	14	1	0	0	108	5.6	-1	35	40.0	14:27	14	5	8	13	0	0	0	0	17:00
2016-17	Nashville	NHL	70	12	23	35	18	6	0	0	113	10.6	7	39	41.0	14:57	14	2	2	4	2	2	0	0	15:16
	NHL Totals		**502**	**95**	**142**	**237**	**124**	**22**	**0**	**19**	**804**	**11.8**		**1045**	**46.3**	**15:07**	**47**	**13**	**11**	**24**	**2**	**6**	**0**	**1**	**15:46**

Hockey East All-Rookie Team (2008) • Hockey East Rookie of the Year (2008) • Hockey East First All-Star Team (2009) • NCAA East First All-American Team (2009) • NCAA Championship All-Tournament Team (2009

Traded to **Colorado** by **Nashville** for Coloradio's 4th round pick in 2019 NHL Draft, July 1. 2017.

WILSON, Garrett
(WIHL-suhn, GAIR-reht)   **PIT**

Left wing. Shoots left. 6'2", 199 lbs.   Born, Barrie, ON, March 16, 1991. Florida's 4th pick, 107th overall, in 2009 NHL Draft.

Season	Club	League	GP	G	A	Pts	PIM	PP	SH	GW	S	S%	+/-	TF	F%	Min	GP	G	A	Pts	PIM	PP	SH	GW	Min
2007-08	Tecumseh Chiefs	ON-Jr.B	46	11	26	37	40	....						....			14	13	8	21	22	....			
	Windsor Spitfires	OHL	7	1	0	1	2	....						....			3	0	0	0	0	....			
2008-09	Owen Sound	OHL	53	17	18	35	44	....						....			4	1	3	4	7	....			
2009-10	Owen Sound	OHL	65	36	26	62	80	....						....			....								
2010-11	Owen Sound	OHL	66	40	46	86	114	....						....			22	11	10	21	28	....			
2011-12	San Antonio	AHL	11	1	0	1	2	....						....			....								
	Cincinnati	ECHL	63	17	18	35	50	....						....			....								
2012-13	Cincinnati	ECHL	38	19	10	29	56	....						....			15	4	1	5	17	....			
	San Antonio	AHL	26	3	2	5	19	....						....			....								
2013-14	**Florida**	**NHL**	**3**	**0**	**0**	**0**	**0**	0	0	0	4	0.0	-1	0	0.0	10:20	....								
	San Antonio	AHL	71	14	16	30	58	....						....			....								
2014-15	**Florida**	**NHL**	**2**	**0**	**0**	**0**	**0**	0	0	0	5	0.0	-2	0	0.0	8:51	....								
	San Antonio	AHL	71	23	15	38	80	....						....			3	0	2	2	2	....			
2015-16	**Florida**	**NHL**	**29**	**0**	**0**	**0**	**24**	0	0	0	28	0.0	-3	1	0.0	9:22	6	0	1	1	4	0	0	0	8:55
	Portland Pirates	AHL	37	7	13	20	55	....						....			....								
2016-17	Wilkes-Barre	AHL	59	11	20	31	83	....						....			5	0	2	2	0	....			
	NHL Totals		**34**	**0**	**0**	**0**	**24**	**0**	**0**	**0**	**37**	**0.0**		**1**	**0.0**	**9:26**	**6**	**0**	**1**	**1**	**4**	**0**	**0**	**0**	**8:55**

OHL First All-Star Team (2011)

Signed as a free agent by **Pittsburgh**, July 7, 2016.

WILSON, Scott
(WIHL-suhn, SKAWT)   **PIT**

Center/Left wing. Shoots left. 5'11", 183 lbs.   Born, Oakville, ON, April 24, 1992. Pittsburgh's 5th pick, 209th overall, in 2011 NHL Draft.

Season	Club	League	GP	G	A	Pts	PIM	PP	SH	GW	S	S%	+/-	TF	F%	Min	GP	G	A	Pts	PIM	PP	SH	GW	Min
2008-09	Oakville Rangers	Minor-ON	STATISTICS NOT AVAILABLE															1	0	0	0	0	....			
	Georgetown	ON-Jr.A	6	0	1	1	2	....						....			1	0	0	0	0	....			
2009-10	Georgetown	ON-Jr.A	56	24	43	67	28	....						....			11	9	8	17	2	....			
2010-11	Georgetown	ON-Jr.A	42	20	41	61	59	....						....			4	1	2	3	8	....			
2011-12	U. Mass Lowell	H-East	37	16	22	38	26	....						....			....								
2012-13	U. Mass Lowell	H-East	41	16	22	38	32	....						....			....								
2013-14	U. Mass Lowell	H-East	31	7	12	19	24	....						....			....								
	Wilkes-Barre	AHL	1	0	0	0	0	....						....			....								
2014-15	**Pittsburgh**	**NHL**	**1**	**0**	**0**	**0**	**0**	0	0	0	0	0.0	0	0	0.0	4:21	3	0	0	0	0	0	0	0	6:44
	Wilkes-Barre	AHL	55	19	22	41	30	....						....			3	2	2	4	0	....			
2015-16	**Pittsburgh**	**NHL**	**24**	**5**	**1**	**6**	**12**	0	0	1	39	12.8	0	0	0.0	10:41	....								
	Wilkes-Barre	AHL	34	22	14	36	19	....						....			....								
2016-17 ♦	**Pittsburgh**	**NHL**	**78**	**8**	**18**	**26**	**32**	0	0	1	127	6.3	0	31	00.0	10:57	20	3	3	6	11	0	0	0	11:58
	NHL Totals		**103**	**13**	**19**	**32**	**44**	**0**	**0**	**2**	**166**	**7.8**		**31**	**00.0**	**10:49**	**23**	**3**	**3**	**6**	**11**	**0**	**0**	**0**	**11:17**

Hockey East All-Rookie Team (2012)

WILSON, Tom
(WIHL-suhn, TAWM)   **WSH**

Right wing. Shoots right. 6'4", 215 lbs.   Born, Toronto, ON, March 29, 1994. Washington's 2nd pick, 16th overall, in 2012 NHL Draft.

Season	Club	League	GP	G	A	Pts	PIM	PP	SH	GW	S	S%	+/-	TF	F%	Min	GP	G	A	Pts	PIM	PP	SH	GW	Min
2009-10	Tor. Jr. Canadiens	GTHL	73	44	61	105	140	....						....			....								
2010-11	Plymouth Whalers	OHL	28	3	3	6	71	....						....			....								
2011-12	Plymouth Whalers	OHL	49	9	18	27	141	....						....			13	7	6	13	39	....			
2012-13	Plymouth Whalers	OHL	48	23	35	58	104	....						....			12	9	8	17	41	....			
	Hershey Bears	AHL	....					....						....			3	1	0	1	6	....			
	Washington	**NHL**	....					....						....			3	0	0	0	0	0	0	0	6:53
2013-14	**Washington**	**NHL**	**82**	**3**	**7**	**10**	**151**	1	0	0	63	4.8	1	3	0.0	7:56	....								
2014-15	**Washington**	**NHL**	**67**	**4**	**13**	**17**	**172**	0	0	0	79	5.1	-1	11	18.2	10:56	13	0	1	1	25	0	0	0	7:44
	Hershey Bears	AHL	2	0	0	0	0	....						....			....								
2015-16	**Washington**	**NHL**	**82**	**7**	**16**	**23**	**163**	0	0	1	99	7.1	3	14	57.1	12:55	12	0	1	1	13	0	0	1	12:01
2016-17	**Washington**	**NHL**	**82**	**7**	**12**	**19**	**133**	0	0	0	95	7.4	6	10	30.0	12:56	13	3	0	3	34	0	0	1	13:52
	NHL Totals		**313**	**21**	**48**	**69**	**619**	**1**	**0**	**1**	**336**	**6.3**		**38**	**34.2**	**11:11**	**41**	**3**	**2**	**5**	**72**	**0**	**0**	**1**	**10:52**

WINGELS, Tommy
(WIHN-guhls, TAW-mee)   **CHI**

Center. Shoots right. 6', 200 lbs.   Born, Evanston, IL, April 12, 1988. San Jose's 5th pick, 177th overall, in 2008 NHL Draft.

Season	Club	League	GP	G	A	Pts	PIM	PP	SH	GW	S	S%	+/-	TF	F%	Min	GP	G	A	Pts	PIM	PP	SH	GW	Min
2006-07	Cedar Rapids	USHL	47	10	18	28	52	....						....			6	3	0	3	6	....			
2007-08	Miami U.	CCHA	42	15	14	29	22	....						....			....								
2008-09	Miami U.	CCHA	41	11	17	28	66	....						....			....								
2009-10	Miami U.	CCHA	44	17	25	42	49	....						....			....								
2010-11	**San Jose**	**NHL**	**5**	**0**	**0**	**0**	**0**	0	0	0	1	0.0	-1	3	33.3	5:07	....								
	Worcester Sharks	AHL	69	17	16	33	69	....						....			....								
2011-12	**San Jose**	**NHL**	**33**	**3**	**6**	**9**	**18**	0	0	0	71	4.2	-1	17	41.2	13:45	5	0	1	1	7	0	0	0	10:30
	Worcester Sharks	AHL	29	13	8	21	28	....						....			....								
2012-13	KooKoo Kouvola	Finland-2	18	8	14	22	33	....						....			....								
	San Jose	**NHL**	**42**	**5**	**8**	**13**	**26**	0	1	0	69	7.2	-9	16	25.0	14:14	11	0	2	2	6	0	0	0	13:53
2013-14	**San Jose**	**NHL**	**77**	**16**	**22**	**38**	**35**	0	2	7	163	9.8	11	56	35.7	16:07	7	0	3	3	4	0	0	0	16:47
2014-15	**San Jose**	**NHL**	**75**	**15**	**21**	**36**	**40**	4	1	1	158	9.5	-7	154	45.5	16:28	....								
2015-16	**San Jose**	**NHL**	**68**	**7**	**11**	**18**	**63**	1	0	0	111	6.3	-10	93	40.9	13:38	22	2	0	2	21	0	0	1	9:46
2016-17	**San Jose**	**NHL**	**37**	**5**	**3**	**8**	**15**	0	0	2	42	11.9	-2	147	40.1	10:03	....								
	Ottawa	**NHL**	**36**	**2**	**2**	**4**	**12**	0	0	0	39	5.1	-9	113	46.0	10:58	9	0	0	0	4	0	0	0	9:53
	NHL Totals		**373**	**53**	**73**	**126**	**209**	**5**	**4**	**10**	**654**	**8.1**		**599**	**41.9**	**14:04**	**54**	**2**	**6**	**8**	**42**	**0**	**0**	**1**	**11:36**

NCAA Championship All-Tournament Team (2009) • CCHA Second All-Star Team (2010)

Signed as a free agent by **Kouvola** (Finland-2), October 4, 2012. Traded to **Ottawa** by **San Jose** for Buddy Robinson, Zach Stortini and Ottawa's 7th round pick (later traded to New Jersey – New Jersey selected Matthew Hellickson) in 2017 NHL Draft, January 24, 2017. Signed as a free agent by **Chicago**, July 1, 2017.

WINNIK, Daniel
(WIHN-ihk, DAN-yehl)

Center/Left wing. Shoots left. 6'2", 203 lbs.   Born, Toronto, ON, March 6, 1985. Phoenix's 10th pick, 265th overall, in 2004 NHL Draft.

Season	Club	League	GP	G	A	Pts	PIM	PP	SH	GW	S	S%	+/-	TF	F%	Min	GP	G	A	Pts	PIM	PP	SH	GW	Min
2002-03	Wexford Raiders	ON-Jr.A	47	20	33	53	70	....						....			18	11	11	22	24	....			
2003-04	New Hampshire	H-East	38	4	10	14	12	....						....			....								
2004-05	New Hampshire	H-East	42	18	22	40	26	....						....			....								
2005-06	New Hampshire	H-East	39	15	26	41	44	....						....			....								
	San Antonio	AHL	7	1	1	2	8	....						....			....								
2006-07	San Antonio	AHL	66	9	12	21	34	....						....			....								
	Phoenix	ECHL	5	0	6	6	9	....						....			....								
2007-08	**Phoenix**	**NHL**	**79**	**11**	**15**	**26**	**25**	0	0	1	122	9.0	-3	154	42.2	14:06	....								
2008-09	**Phoenix**	**NHL**	**49**	**3**	**4**	**7**	**63**	0	0	0	66	4.5	1	138	37.0	13:04	....								
	San Antonio	AHL	5	0	0	0	4	....						....			....								
2009-10	**Phoenix**	**NHL**	**74**	**4**	**15**	**19**	**12**	0	0	0	83	4.8	1	110	45.5	13:09	7	0	0	0	0	0	0	0	12:45
2010-11	**Colorado**	**NHL**	**80**	**11**	**15**	**26**	**35**	2	2	1	167	6.6	-2	69	36.2	16:33	....								

			Regular Season														Playoffs								
Season	Club	League	GP	G	A	Pts	PIM	PP	SH	GW	S	S%	+/-	TF	F%	Min	GP	G	A	Pts	PIM	PP	SH	GW	Min
2011-12	Colorado	NHL	63	5	13	18	42	0	1	0	155	3.2	–11	47	46.8	17:42	....	....	....	....	....	....	....	....	....
	San Jose	NHL	21	3	2	5	10	0	0	1	29	10.3	0	19	57.9	13:40	5	0	1	1	6	0	0	0	12:25
2012-13	Anaheim	NHL	48	6	13	19	16	0	0	1	95	6.3	13	53	30.2	16:50	7	0	1	1	7	0	0	0	15:04
2013-14	Anaheim	NHL	76	6	24	30	23	0	2	2	115	5.2	6	196	43.4	15:23	9	0	1	1	2	0	0	0	13:37
2014-15	Toronto	NHL	58	7	18	25	19	0	0	0	70	10.0	15	186	48.4	16:50	....	....	....	....	....	....	....	....	....
	Pittsburgh	NHL	21	2	7	9	8	0	0	1	27	7.4	8	42	40.5	16:07	5	0	0	0	2	0	0	0	13:53
2015-16	Toronto	NHL	56	4	10	14	16	0	0	0	85	4.7	–3	16	37.5	14:16	....	....	....	....	....	....	....	....	....
	Washington	NHL	20	2	3	5	22	0	0	0	16	12.5	7	4	50.0	12:11	12	0	0	0	4	0	0	0	11:22
2016-17	Washington	NHL	72	12	13	25	49	0	2	3	82	14.6	15	21	42.9	12:55	13	0	0	0	0	0	0	0	10:59
	NHL Totals		717	76	152	228	340	2	7	11	1112	6.8		1055	42.6	14:57	58	0	3	3	21	0	0	0	12:33

Hockey East Second All-Star Team (2006)

Traded to **Colorado** by **Phoenix** for Colorado's 4th round pick (Rhett Holland) in 2012 NHL Draft, June 28, 2010. Traded to **San Jose** by **Colorado** with T.J. Galiardi and Anaheim's 7th round pick (previously acquired, San Jose selected Emil Galimov) in 2013 NHL Draft for Jamie McGinn, Michael Sgarbossa and Mike Connolly, February 27, 2012. Signed as a free agent by **Anaheim**, July 20, 2012. Signed as a free agent by **Toronto**, July 28, 2014. Traded to **Pittsburgh** by **Toronto** for Zach Sill, Pittsburgh's 4th round pick (later traded to Edmonton, later traded to Ottawa – Ottawa selected Christian Wolanin) in 2015 NHL Draft and Pittsburgh's 2nd round pick (later traded back to Pittsburgh – Pittsburgh selected Kasper Bjorkqvist) in 2016 NHL Draft, February 25, 2015. Signed as a free agent by **Toronto**, July 1, 2015. Traded to **Washington** by **Toronto** with Anaheim's 5th round pick (previously acquired, Washington selected Beck Malenstyn) in 2016 NHL Draft for Brooks Laich, Connor Carrick and Washington's 2nd round pick (Carl Grundstrom) in 2016 NHL Draft, February 28, 2015.

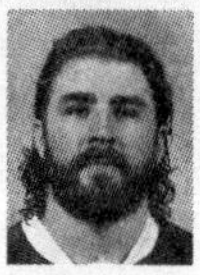

WITKOWSKI, Luke

(wiht-KOW-skee, LEWK) **DET**

Defense. Shoots right. 6'2", 200 lbs. Born, Holland, MI, April 14, 1990. Tampa Bay's 6th pick, 160th overall, in 2008 NHL Draft.

Season	Club	League	GP	G	A	Pts	PIM	PP	SH	GW	S	S%	+/-	TF	F%	Min	GP	G	A	Pts	PIM	PP	SH	GW	Min
2006-07	Team nXi Majors	Minor-MI	59	18	22	40	172	....	....	....	....	....	....	....	....	....	....	....	....	....	....	....	....	....	....
2007-08	Ohio	USHL	58	3	10	13	139	....	....	....	....	....	....	....	....	....	....	....	....	....	....	....	....	....	....
2008-09	Fargo Force	USHL	55	6	16	22	118	....	....	....	....	....	....	....	....	....	10	2	1	3	29	....	....	....	....
2009-10	Western Mich.	CCHA	32	2	4	6	67	....	....	....	....	....	....	....	....	....	....	....	....	....	....	....	....	....	....
2010-11	Western Mich.	CCHA	42	1	8	9	56	....	....	....	....	....	....	....	....	....	....	....	....	....	....	....	....	....	....
2011-12	Western Mich.	CCHA	40	2	11	13	66	....	....	....	....	....	....	....	....	....	....	....	....	....	....	....	....	....	....
2012-13	Western Mich.	CCHA	38	2	8	10	46	....	....	....	....	....	....	....	....	....	....	....	....	....	....	....	....	....	....
	Syracuse Crunch	AHL	3	0	0	0	4	....	....	....	....	....	....	....	....	....	....	....	....	....	....	....	....	....	....
2013-14	Syracuse Crunch	AHL	76	2	10	12	204	....	....	....	....	....	....	....	....	....	....	....	....	....	....	....	....	....	....
2014-15	Tampa Bay	NHL	16	0	0	0	15	0	0	0	10	0.0	0	0	0.0	15:11	....	....	....	....	....	....	....	....	....
	Syracuse Crunch	AHL	50	2	6	8	91	....	....	....	....	....	....	....	....	....	3	0	1	1	4	....	....	....	....
2015-16	Tampa Bay	NHL	4	0	0	0	4	0	0	0	1	0.0	0	0	0.0	7:08	2	0	0	0	0	0	0	0	3:16
	Syracuse Crunch	AHL	70	3	11	14	166	....	....	....	....	....	....	....	....	....	....	....	....	....	....	....	....	....	....
2016-17	Tampa Bay	NHL	34	0	4	4	39	0	0	0	24	0.0	–1	0	0.0	9:52	....	....	....	....	....	....	....	....	....
	Syracuse Crunch	AHL	19	0	5	5	59	....	....	....	....	....	....	....	....	....	....	....	....	....	....	....	....	....	....
	NHL Totals		54	0	4	4	58	0	0	0	35	0.0		0	0.0	11:15	2	0	0	0	0	0	0	0	3:16

CCHA Second All-Star Team (2013)

Signed as a free agent by **Detroit**, July 1, 2017.

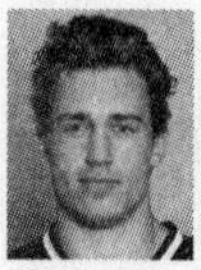

WOOD, Miles

(WUD, MIGH-uhlz) **N.J.**

Left wing. Shoots left. 6'2", 195 lbs. Born, Buffalo, NY, September 13, 1995. New Jersey's 3rd pick, 100th overall, in 2013 NHL Draft.

Season	Club	League	GP	G	A	Pts	PIM	PP	SH	GW	S	S%	+/-	TF	F%	Min	GP	G	A	Pts	PIM	PP	SH	GW	Min
2010-11	Salem Ice Dogs	EmJHL	13	4	5	9	8	....	....	....	....	....	....	....	....	....	2	0	0	0	0	....	....	....	....
2011-12	Salem Ice Dogs	EmJHL	14	8	1	9	28	....	....	....	....	....	....	....	....	....	....	....	....	....	....	....	....	....	....
2012-13	Cape Cod	Minor-MA	6	0	0	0	0	....	....	....	....	....	....	....	....	....	....	....	....	....	....	....	....	....	....
	Nobles	High-MA	15	8	10	18	18	....	....	....	....	....	....	....	....	....	....	....	....	....	....	....	....	....	....
2013-14	Nobles	High-MA	27	29	24	53	....	....	....	....	....	....	....	....	....	....	....	....	....	....	....	....	....	....	....
2014-15	Nobles	High-MA	17	17	18	35	....	....	....	....	....	....	....	....	....	....	....	....	....	....	....	....	....	....	....
2015-16	Boston College	H-East	37	10	25	35	76	....	....	....	....	....	....	....	....	....	....	....	....	....	....	....	....	....	....
	New Jersey	NHL	1	0	0	0	0	0	0	0	2	0.0	0	0	0.0	13:06	....	....	....	....	....	....	....	....	....
2016-17	New Jersey	NHL	60	8	9	17	86	2	0	0	105	7.6	–21	2	50.0	12:51	....	....	....	....	....	....	....	....	....
	Albany Devils	AHL	15	4	4	8	34	....	....	....	....	....	....	....	....	....	2	0	0	0	10	....	....	....	....
	NHL Totals		61	8	9	17	86	2	0	0	107	7.5		2	50.0	12:51	....	....	....	....	....	....	....	....	....

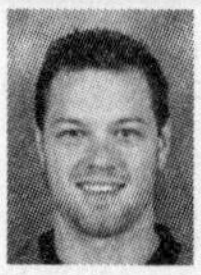

WOODS, Brendan

(WOODZ, BREHN-duhn)

Left wing. Shoots left. 6'4", 210 lbs. Born, Humboldt, SK, June 11, 1992. Carolina's 7th pick, 129th overall, in 2012 NHL Draft.

Season	Club	League	GP	G	A	Pts	PIM	PP	SH	GW	S	S%	+/-	TF	F%	Min	GP	G	A	Pts	PIM	PP	SH	GW	Min
2008-09	Williston North.	High-MA	29	8	11	19	28	....	....	....	....	....	....	....	....	....	....	....	....	....	....	....	....	....	....
2009-10	Chicago Steel	USHL	34	6	4	10	32	....	....	....	....	....	....	....	....	....	....	....	....	....	....	....	....	....	....
2010-11	Muskegon	USHL	57	14	12	26	86	....	....	....	....	....	....	....	....	....	6	1	1	2	14	....	....	....	....
2011-12	U. of Wisconsin	WCHA	34	5	5	10	67	....	....	....	....	....	....	....	....	....	....	....	....	....	....	....	....	....	....
2012-13	U. of Wisconsin	WCHA	41	5	7	12	47	....	....	....	....	....	....	....	....	....	....	....	....	....	....	....	....	....	....
	Charlotte	AHL	2	0	0	0	2	....	....	....	....	....	....	....	....	....	....	....	....	....	....	....	....	....	....
2013-14	Charlotte	AHL	42	5	3	8	40	....	....	....	....	....	....	....	....	....	....	....	....	....	....	....	....	....	....
2014-15	Carolina	NHL	2	0	0	0	0	0	0	0	3	0.0	–1	0	0.0	6:02	....	....	....	....	....	....	....	....	....
	Charlotte	AHL	68	13	17	30	101	....	....	....	....	....	....	....	....	....	....	....	....	....	....	....	....	....	....
2015-16	Carolina	NHL	5	0	0	0	7	0	0	0	5	0.0	0	1	0.0	8:42	....	....	....	....	....	....	....	....	....
	Charlotte	AHL	59	9	11	20	39	....	....	....	....	....	....	....	....	....	....	....	....	....	....	....	....	....	....
2016-17	Charlotte	AHL	24	3	3	6	41	....	....	....	....	....	....	....	....	....	3	1	0	1	8	....	....	....	....
	NHL Totals		7	0	0	0	7	0	0	0	8	0.0		1	0.0	7:57	....	....	....	....	....	....	....	....	....

• Missed majority of 2016-17 as a healthy reserve.

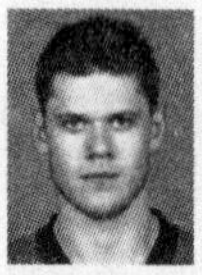

WOTHERSPOON, Tyler

(WUH-thuhr-spoon, TIGH-luhr) **CGY**

Defense. Shoots left. 6'2", 207 lbs. Born, Burnaby, BC, March 12, 1993. Calgary's 3rd pick, 57th overall, in 2011 NHL Draft.

Season	Club	League	GP	G	A	Pts	PIM	PP	SH	GW	S	S%	+/-	TF	F%	Min	GP	G	A	Pts	PIM	PP	SH	GW	Min
2008-09	Valley West	BCMML	37	11	13	24	85	....	....	....	....	....	....	....	....	....	....	....	....	....	....	....	....	....	....
	Portland	WHL	4	0	0	0	0	....	....	....	....	....	....	....	....	....	....	....	....	....	....	....	....	....	....
2009-10	Portland	WHL	43	1	4	5	21	....	....	....	....	....	....	....	....	....	2	0	0	0	0	....	....	....	....
2010-11	Portland	WHL	64	2	10	12	73	....	....	....	....	....	....	....	....	....	20	3	1	4	10	....	....	....	....
2011-12	Portland	WHL	67	7	21	28	42	....	....	....	....	....	....	....	....	....	22	1	6	7	6	....	....	....	....
2012-13	Portland	WHL	61	7	30	37	30	....	....	....	....	....	....	....	....	....	21	2	8	10	20	....	....	....	....
2013-14	Calgary	NHL	14	0	4	4	4	0	0	0	3	0.0	–3	0	0.0	13:27	....	....	....	....	....	....	....	....	....
	Abbotsford Heat	AHL	48	1	8	9	12	....	....	....	....	....	....	....	....	....	....	....	....	....	....	....	....	....	....
2014-15	Calgary	NHL	1	0	0	0	0	0	0	0	1	0.0	–3	0	0.0	20:19	6	0	0	0	0	0	0	0	6:39
	Adirondack	AHL	61	2	22	24	20	....	....	....	....	....	....	....	....	....	....	....	....	....	....	....	....	....	....
2015-16	Calgary	NHL	11	0	1	1	0	0	0	0	9	0.0	0	0	0.0	14:10	....	....	....	....	....	....	....	....	....
	Stockton Heat	AHL	53	2	8	10	16	....	....	....	....	....	....	....	....	....	....	....	....	....	....	....	....	....	....
2016-17	Calgary	NHL	4	0	0	0	0	0	0	0	4	0.0	–2	0	0.0	10:54	....	....	....	....	....	....	....	....	....
	Stockton Heat	AHL	56	6	12	18	24	....	....	....	....	....	....	....	....	....	5	0	0	0	2	....	....	....	....
	NHL Totals		30	0	5	5	4	0	0	0	17	0.0		0	0.0	13:36	6	0	0	0	0	0	0	0	6:39

WHL West Second All-Star Team (2013)

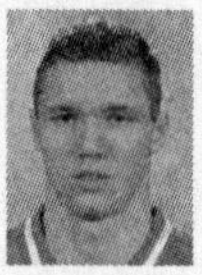

YAKIMOV, Bogdan

(ya-KIH-mawv, bawg-DAHN) **EDM**

Center. Shoots left. 6'5", 232 lbs. Born, Nizhnekamsk, Russia, October 4, 1994. Edmonton's 3rd pick, 83rd overall, in 2013 NHL Draft.

Season	Club	League	GP	G	A	Pts	PIM	PP	SH	GW	S	S%	+/-	TF	F%	Min	GP	G	A	Pts	PIM	PP	SH	GW	Min
2011-12	Nizhnekamsk Jr.	Russia-Jr.	46	15	10	25	10	....	....	....	....	....	....	....	....	....	2	2	1	3	0	....	....	....	....
2012-13	Dizel Penza	Russia-2	21	3	6	9	12	....	....	....	....	....	....	....	....	....	....	....	....	....	....	....	....	....	....
	Izhstal Izhevsk	Russia-2	16	5	8	13	4	....	....	....	....	....	....	....	....	....	....	....	....	....	....	....	....	....	....
	Nizhnekamsk Jr.	Russia-Jr.	11	6	7	13	2	....	....	....	....	....	....	....	....	....	....	....	....	....	....	....	....	....	....
2013-14	Nizhnekamsk Jr.	Russia-Jr.	5	4	2	6	0	....	....	....	....	....	....	....	....	....	3	0	2	2	0	....	....	....	....
	Nizhnekamsk	KHL	33	7	5	12	2	....	....	....	....	....	....	....	....	....	2	0	1	1	0	....	....	....	....
2014-15	Edmonton	NHL	1	0	0	0	0	0	0	0	1	0.0	–1	7	42.9	11:19	....	....	....	....	....	....	....	....	....
	Oklahoma City	AHL	57	12	16	28	18	....	....	....	....	....	....	....	....	....	....	....	....	....	....	....	....	....	....

Season	Club	League	GP	G	A	Pts	PIM	PP	SH	GW	S	S%	+/-	TF	F%	Min	GP	G	A	Pts	PIM	PP	SH	GW	Min
			Regular Season														Playoffs								
2015-16	Bakersfield	AHL	36	5	10	15	10	....	....	....	....	....	....	....	....	....	....	....	....	....	....	....	....	....	....
	Nizhnekamsk	KHL	11	3	1	4	2	....	....	....	....	....	....	....	....	....	4	1	1	2	0	....	....	....	....
2016-17	Nizhnekamsk	KHL	50	3	8	11	4	....	....	....	....	....	....	....	....	....	....	....	....	....	....	....	....	....	....
	NHL Totals		**1**	**0**	**0**	**0**	**0**	**0**	**0**	**0**	**1**	**0.0**		**7**	**42.9**	**11:19**	....	....	....	....	....	....	....	....	....

• Loaned to **Nizhnekamsk** (KHL) by **Edmonton**, December 21, 2015.

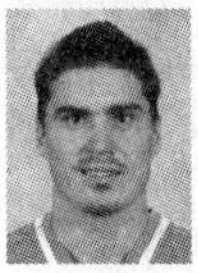

YAKUPOV, Nail

(YA-kuh-pawv, NAY-uhl) **COL**

Right wing. Shoots left. 5'11", 195 lbs. Born, Nizhnekamsk, Russia, October 6, 1993. Edmonton's 1st pick, 1st overall, in 2012 NHL Draft.

Season	Club	League	GP	G	A	Pts	PIM	PP	SH	GW	S	S%	+/-	TF	F%	Min	GP	G	A	Pts	PIM	PP	SH	GW	Min
2009-10	Nizhnekamsk Jr.	Russia-Jr.	14	4	2	6	26	....	....	....	....	....	....	....	....	....	....	....	....	....	....	....	....	....	....
2010-11	Sarnia Sting	OHL	65	49	52	101	71	....	....	....	....	....	....	....	....	....	....	....	....	....	....	....	....	....	....
2011-12	Sarnia Sting	OHL	42	31	38	69	30	....	....	....	....	....	....	....	....	....	6	2	3	5	4	....	....	....	....
2012-13	Nizhnekamsk	KHL	22	9	9	18	33	....	....	....	....	....	....	....	....	....	....	....	....	....	....	....	....	....	....
	Edmonton	**NHL**	**48**	**17**	**14**	**31**	**24**	**6**	**0**	**2**	**81**	**21.0**	**-4**	**6**	**0.0**	**14:34**	....	....	....	....	....	....	....	....	....
2013-14	**Edmonton**	**NHL**	**63**	**11**	**13**	**24**	**36**	**4**	**0**	**1**	**122**	**9.0**	**-33**	**0**	**0.0**	**14:19**	....	....	....	....	....	....	....	....	....
2014-15	**Edmonton**	**NHL**	**81**	**14**	**19**	**33**	**18**	**5**	**0**	**1**	**191**	**7.3**	**-35**	**1**	**0.0**	**15:27**	....	....	....	....	....	....	....	....	....
2015-16	**Edmonton**	**NHL**	**60**	**8**	**15**	**23**	**24**	**1**	**0**	**1**	**127**	**6.3**	**-16**	**1**	**0.0**	**14:13**	....	....	....	....	....	....	....	....	....
2016-17	**St. Louis**	**NHL**	**40**	**3**	**6**	**9**	**14**	**0**	**0**	**0**	**35**	**8.6**	**-3**	**0**	**0.0**	**10:39**	....	....	....	....	....	....	....	....	....
	NHL Totals		**292**	**53**	**67**	**120**	**116**	**16**	**0**	**5**	**556**	**9.5**		**8**	**0.0**	**14:09**	....	....	....	....	....	....	....	....	....

OHL All-Rookie Team (2011) • OHL Rookie of the Year (2011) • Canadian Major Junior Rookie of the Year (2011) • Canadian Major Junior Top Prospect of the Year (2012)

Signed as a free agent by **Nizhnekamsk** (KHL), September 20, 2012. Traded to **St. Louis** by **Edmonton** for Zach Pochiro and St. Louis' 3rd round pick (later traded to Arizona – Arizona selected Cameron Crotty) in 2017 NHL Draft, October 7, 2016. Signed as a free agent by **Colorado**, July 4, 2017.

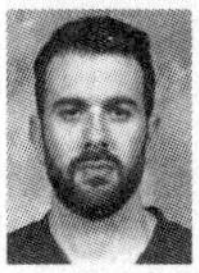

YANDLE, Keith

(YAN-DUHL, KEETH) **FLA**

Defense. Shoots left. 6'1", 196 lbs. Born, Boston, MA, September 9, 1986. Phoenix's 3rd pick, 105th overall, in 2005 NHL Draft.

Season	Club	League	GP	G	A	Pts	PIM	PP	SH	GW	S	S%	+/-	TF	F%	Min	GP	G	A	Pts	PIM	PP	SH	GW	Min
2004-05	Cushing	High-MA	34	14	40	54	52	....	....	....	....	....	....	....	....	....	....	....	....	....	....	....	....	....	....
2005-06	Moncton Wildcats	QMJHL	66	25	59	84	109	....	....	....	....	....	....	....	....	....	21	6	14	20	36	....	....	....	....
2006-07	**Phoenix**	**NHL**	**7**	**0**	**2**	**2**	**8**	**0**	**0**	**0**	**10**	**0.0**	**0**	**0**	**0.0**	**20:10**	....	....	....	....	....	....	....	....	....
	San Antonio	AHL	69	6	27	33	97	....	....	....	....	....	....	....	....	....	....	....	....	....	....	....	....	....	....
2007-08	**Phoenix**	**NHL**	**43**	**5**	**7**	**12**	**14**	**4**	**0**	**0**	**72**	**6.9**	**-12**	**0**	**0.0**	**14:04**	....	....	....	....	....	....	....	....	....
	San Antonio	AHL	30	1	14	15	80	....	....	....	....	....	....	....	....	....	5	0	0	0	8	....	....	....	....
2008-09	**Phoenix**	**NHL**	**69**	**4**	**26**	**30**	**37**	**1**	**0**	**0**	**118**	**3.4**	**-4**	**0**	**0.0**	**16:37**	....	....	....	....	....	....	....	....	....
2009-10	**Phoenix**	**NHL**	**82**	**12**	**29**	**41**	**45**	**5**	**0**	**2**	**145**	**8.3**	**16**	**0**	**0.0**	**20:14**	**7**	**2**	**3**	**5**	**4**	**1**	**0**	**0**	**17:12**
2010-11	**Phoenix**	**NHL**	**82**	**11**	**48**	**59**	**68**	**3**	**0**	**0**	**199**	**5.5**	**12**	**0**	**0.0**	**24:23**	**4**	**0**	**5**	**5**	**0**	**0**	**0**	**0**	**25:50**
2011-12	**Phoenix**	**NHL**	**82**	**11**	**32**	**43**	**51**	**0**	**0**	**2**	**196**	**5.6**	**5**	**0**	**0.0**	**22:20**	**16**	**1**	**8**	**9**	**10**	**0**	**0**	**0**	**21:27**
2012-13	**Phoenix**	**NHL**	**48**	**10**	**20**	**30**	**54**	**5**	**0**	**3**	**130**	**7.7**	**4**	**0**	**0.0**	**22:15**	....	....	....	....	....	....	....	....	....
2013-14	**Phoenix**	**NHL**	**82**	**8**	**45**	**53**	**63**	**3**	**0**	**2**	**241**	**3.3**	**-23**	**0**	**0.0**	**24:09**	....	....	....	....	....	....	....	....	....
2014-15	**Arizona**	**NHL**	**63**	**4**	**37**	**41**	**32**	**2**	**0**	**0**	**185**	**2.2**	**-32**	**0**	**0.0**	**23:55**	....	....	....	....	....	....	....	....	....
	NY Rangers	**NHL**	**21**	**2**	**9**	**11**	**8**	**0**	**0**	**2**	**47**	**4.3**	**6**	**0**	**0.0**	**19:56**	**19**	**2**	**9**	**11**	**10**	**0**	**0**	**0**	**18:01**
2015-16	**NY Rangers**	**NHL**	**82**	**5**	**42**	**47**	**40**	**2**	**0**	**1**	**160**	**3.1**	**-4**	**0**	**0.0**	**19:58**	**5**	**1**	**0**	**1**	**2**	**0**	**0**	**0**	**20:43**
2016-17	**Florida**	**NHL**	**82**	**5**	**36**	**41**	**39**	**2**	**0**	**0**	**178**	**2.8**	**-6**	**0**	**0.0**	**22:02**	....	....	....	....	....	....	....	....	....
	NHL Totals		**743**	**77**	**333**	**410**	**459**	**27**	**0**	**12**	**1681**	**4.6**		**0**	**0.0**	**21:16**	**51**	**6**	**25**	**31**	**26**	**1**	**0**	**0**	**19:51**

QMJHL First All-Star Team (2006) • Canadian Major Junior First All-Star Team (2006) • Canadian Major Junior Defenseman of the Year (2006)

Played in NHL All-Star Game (2011, 2012)

Traded to **NY Rangers** by **Arizona** with Chris Summers and Arizona's 4th round pick (Tarmo Reunanen) in 2016 NHL Draft for John Moore, Anthony Duclair, Tampa Bay's 2nd round pick (previously acquired, later traded to Calgary – Calgary selected Oliver Kylington) in 2015 NHL Draft and NY Rangers' 1st round pick (later traded to Detroit – Detroit selected Dennis Cholowski) in 2016 NHL Draft, March 1, 2015. Traded to **Florida** by **NY Rangers** for Florida's 6th round pick (Tyler Wall) in 2016 NHL Draft and Florida's 4th round pick (later traded to San Jose – San Jose selected Scott Reedy) in 2017 NHL Draft, June 20, 2016.

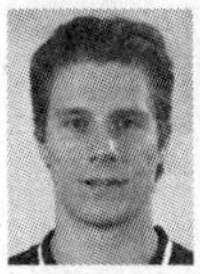

ZACHA, Pavel

(zah-KHUH, PAH-vehl) **N.J.**

Center. Shoots left. 6'3", 210 lbs. Born, Brno, Czech Rep., April 6, 1997. New Jersey's 1st pick, 6th overall, in 2015 NHL Draft.

Season	Club	League	GP	G	A	Pts	PIM	PP	SH	GW	S	S%	+/-	TF	F%	Min	GP	G	A	Pts	PIM	PP	SH	GW	Min
2010-11	HC Liberec U18	CzR-U18	3	1	0	1	0	....	....	....	....	....	....	....	....	....	....	....	....	....	....	....	....	....	....
2011-12	HC Liberec U18	CzR-U18	36	10	15	25	20	....	....	....	....	....	....	....	....	....	7	2	3	5	6	....	....	....	....
	HC Liberec Jr.	CzRep-Jr.	1	0	0	0	0	....	....	....	....	....	....	....	....	....	....	....	....	....	....	....	....	....	....
2012-13	HC Liberec U18	CzR-U18	6	6	7	13	4	....	....	....	....	....	....	....	....	....	1	1	0	1	10	....	....	....	....
	Benatky	CzRep-2	1	0	0	0	0	....	....	....	....	....	....	....	....	....	....	....	....	....	....	....	....	....	....
	HC Liberec Jr.	CzRep-Jr.	39	14	26	40	26	....	....	....	....	....	....	....	....	....	5	2	2	4	0	....	....	....	....
2013-14	HC Liberec Jr.	CzRep-Jr.	10	6	11	17	64	....	....	....	....	....	....	....	....	....	3	1	1	2	4	....	....	....	....
	Benatky	CzRep-2	12	4	5	9	6	....	....	....	....	....	....	....	....	....	....	....	....	....	....	....	....	....	....
	Liberec	CzRep	38	4	4	8	10	....	....	....	....	....	....	....	....	....	3	0	0	0	0	....	....	....	....
2014-15	Sarnia Sting	OHL	37	16	18	34	56	....	....	....	....	....	....	....	....	....	5	2	1	3	10	....	....	....	....
2015-16	Sarnia Sting	OHL	51	28	36	64	97	....	....	....	....	....	....	....	....	....	7	6	7	13	16	....	....	....	....
	New Jersey	**NHL**	**1**	**0**	**2**	**2**	**0**	**0**	**0**	**0**	**3**	**0.0**	**4**	**9**	**33.3**	**16:51**	....	....	....	....	....	....	....	....	....
	Albany Devils	AHL	3	1	2	3	2	....	....	....	....	....	....	....	....	....	5	1	2	3	2	....	....	....	....
2016-17	**New Jersey**	**NHL**	**70**	**8**	**16**	**24**	**19**	**5**	**0**	**2**	**83**	**9.6**	**-17**	**457**	**40.3**	**14:18**	....	....	....	....	....	....	....	....	....
	NHL Totals		**71**	**8**	**18**	**26**	**19**	**5**	**0**	**2**	**86**	**9.3**		**466**	**40.1**	**14:21**	....	....	....	....	....	....	....	....	....

OHL All-Rookie Team (2015)

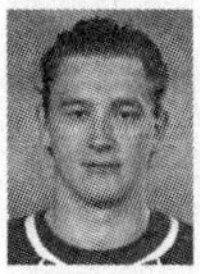

ZADOROV, Nikita

(za-DOHR-awv, nih-KEE-tuh) **COL**

Defense. Shoots left. 6'5", 230 lbs. Born, Moscow, Russia, April 16, 1995. Buffalo's 2nd pick, 16th overall, in 2013 NHL Draft.

Season	Club	League	GP	G	A	Pts	PIM	PP	SH	GW	S	S%	+/-	TF	F%	Min	GP	G	A	Pts	PIM	PP	SH	GW	Min
2011-12	CSKA Jr.	Russia-Jr.	41	2	4	6	63	....	....	....	....	....	....	....	....	....	8	0	0	0	8	....	....	....	....
2012-13	London Knights	OHL	63	6	19	25	54	....	....	....	....	....	....	....	....	....	20	2	4	6	36	....	....	....	....
2013-14	**Buffalo**	**NHL**	**7**	**1**	**0**	**1**	**4**	**0**	**0**	**0**	**4**	**25.0**	**-4**	**0**	**0.0**	**17:10**	....	....	....	....	....	....	....	....	....
	London Knights	OHL	36	11	19	30	43	....	....	....	....	....	....	....	....	....	9	4	5	9	16	....	....	....	....
2014-15	**Buffalo**	**NHL**	**60**	**3**	**12**	**15**	**51**	**2**	**0**	**1**	**52**	**5.8**	**-10**	**1**	**100.0**	**17:42**	....	....	....	....	....	....	....	....	....
2015-16	**Colorado**	**NHL**	**22**	**0**	**2**	**2**	**12**	**0**	**0**	**0**	**18**	**0.0**	**-5**	**0**	**0.0**	**16:56**	....	....	....	....	....	....	....	....	....
	San Antonio	AHL	52	10	19	29	90	....	....	....	....	....	....	....	....	....	....	....	....	....	....	....	....	....	....
2016-17	**Colorado**	**NHL**	**56**	**0**	**10**	**10**	**73**	**0**	**0**	**0**	**61**	**0.0**	**-20**	**0**	**0.0**	**19:02**	....	....	....	....	....	....	....	....	....
	NHL Totals		**145**	**4**	**24**	**28**	**140**	**2**	**0**	**1**	**135**	**3.0**		**1**	**100.0**	**18:05**	....	....	....	....	....	....	....	....	....

OHL All-Rookie Team (2013) • OHL Second All-Star Team (2014)

Traded to **Colorado** by **Buffalo** with Mikhail Grigorenko, J.T. Compher and Buffalo's 2nd round pick (later traded to San Jose – San Jose selected Jeremy Roy) in 2015 NHL Draft for Ryan O'Reilly and Jamie McGinn, June 26, 2015.

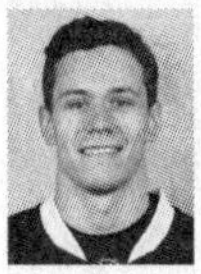

ZAITSEV, Nikita

(ZIGH-t'sehv, nih-KEE-tuh) **TOR**

Defense. Shoots right. 6'2", 196 lbs. Born, Moscow, USSR, October 29, 1991.

Season	Club	League	GP	G	A	Pts	PIM	PP	SH	GW	S	S%	+/-	TF	F%	Min	GP	G	A	Pts	PIM	PP	SH	GW	Min
2009-10	Novosibirsk Jr.	Russia-Jr.	4	0	1	1	2	....	....	....	....	....	....	....	....	....	....	....	....	....	....	....	....	....	....
	Sibir Novosibirsk	KHL	40	0	1	1	6	....	....	....	....	....	....	....	....	....	....	....	....	....	....	....	....	....	....
2010-11	Novosibirsk Jr.	Russia-Jr.	4	1	2	3	0	....	....	....	....	....	....	....	....	....	....	....	....	....	....	....	....	....	....
	Sibir Novosibirsk	KHL	39	0	2	2	12	....	....	....	....	....	....	....	....	....	4	0	0	0	2	....	....	....	....
	Zauralje Kurgan	Russia-2	....	....	....	....	....	....	....	....	....	....	....	....	....	....	4	0	2	2	4	....	....	....	....
2011-12	Novosibirsk Jr.	Russia-Jr.	4	4	0	4	0	....	....	....	....	....	....	....	....	....	1	0	0	0	10	....	....	....	....
	Sibir Novosibirsk	KHL	53	1	3	4	28	....	....	....	....	....	....	....	....	....	....	....	....	....	....	....	....	....	....
2012-13	Sibir Novosibirsk	KHL	49	7	11	18	41	....	....	....	....	....	....	....	....	....	7	1	0	1	8	....	....	....	....
2013-14	CSKA Moscow	KHL	33	4	8	12	18	....	....	....	....	....	....	....	....	....	4	1	1	2	27	....	....	....	....
2014-15	CSKA Moscow	KHL	57	12	20	32	31	....	....	....	....	....	....	....	....	....	16	1	7	8	2	....	....	....	....
2015-16	CSKA Moscow	KHL	46	8	18	26	20	....	....	....	....	....	....	....	....	....	20	4	9	13	10	....	....	....	....
2016-17	**Toronto**	**NHL**	**82**	**4**	**32**	**36**	**38**	**1**	**0**	**0**	**106**	**3.8**	**-22**	**0**	**0.0**	**22:01**	**4**	**0**	**0**	**0**	**0**	**0**	**0**	**0**	**21:45**
	NHL Totals		**82**	**4**	**32**	**36**	**38**	**1**	**0**	**0**	**106**	**3.8**		**0**	**0.0**	**22:01**	**4**	**0**	**0**	**0**	**0**	**0**	**0**	**0**	**21:45**

Signed as a free agent by **Toronto**, May 2, 2016.

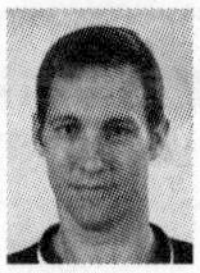

ZAJAC, Travis

(ZAY-jak, TRA-vihs) **N.J.**

Center. Shoots right. 6'2", 185 lbs. Born, Winnipeg, MB, May 13, 1985. New Jersey's 1st pick, 20th overall, in 2004 NHL Draft.

			Regular Season														Playoffs								
Season	Club	League	GP	G	A	Pts	PIM	PP	SH	GW	S	S%	+/-	TF	F%	Min	GP	G	A	Pts	PIM	PP	SH	GW	Min
2002-03	Salmon Arm	BCHL	59	16	36	52	27	....	....	....	....	....	....	....	....	....	11	2	4	6	6	....	....	....	....
2003-04	Salmon Arm	BCHL	59	43	69	112	110	....	....	....	....	....	....	....	....	....	14	10	13	23	10	....	....	....	....
2004-05	North Dakota	WCHA	45	20	19	39	16	....	....	....	....	....	....	....	....	....	....	....	....	....	....	....	....	....	....
2005-06	North Dakota	WCHA	46	18	29	47	20	....	....	....	....	....	....	....	....	....	....	....	....	....	....	....	....	....	....
	Albany River Rats	AHL	2	0	1	1	2	....	....	....	....	....	....	....	....	....	....	....	....	....	....	....	....	....	....
2006-07	**New Jersey**	**NHL**	**80**	**17**	**25**	**42**	**16**	**6**	**0**	**2**	**134**	**12.7**	**1**	**904**	**46.9**	**16:03**	**11**	**1**	**4**	**5**	**4**	**0**	**0**	**0**	**16:22**
2007-08	**New Jersey**	**NHL**	**82**	**14**	**20**	**34**	**31**	**5**	**0**	**1**	**155**	**9.0**	**–11**	**1032**	**51.2**	**16:44**	**5**	**0**	**1**	**1**	**4**	**0**	**0**	**0**	**13:35**
2008-09	**New Jersey**	**NHL**	**82**	**20**	**42**	**62**	**29**	**5**	**1**	**2**	**185**	**10.8**	**33**	**1287**	**53.1**	**18:39**	**7**	**1**	**3**	**4**	**6**	**0**	**0**	**1**	**17:51**
2009-10	**New Jersey**	**NHL**	**82**	**25**	**42**	**67**	**24**	**6**	**0**	**4**	**210**	**11.9**	**22**	**1373**	**52.9**	**20:13**	**5**	**1**	**1**	**2**	**2**	**0**	**0**	**0**	**21:46**
2010-11	**New Jersey**	**NHL**	**82**	**13**	**31**	**44**	**24**	**2**	**1**	**1**	**173**	**7.5**	**–6**	**1278**	**55.3**	**19:47**	....	....	....	....	....	....	....	....	....
2011-12	**New Jersey**	**NHL**	**15**	**2**	**4**	**6**	**4**	**1**	**0**	**1**	**25**	**8.0**	**–3**	**204**	**57.8**	**17:22**	**24**	**7**	**7**	**14**	**4**	**1**	**0**	**2**	**20:29**
2012-13	**New Jersey**	**NHL**	**48**	**7**	**13**	**20**	**22**	**1**	**1**	**1**	**82**	**8.5**	**–5**	**881**	**57.4**	**19:32**	....	....	....	....	....	....	....	....	....
2013-14	**New Jersey**	**NHL**	**80**	**18**	**30**	**48**	**28**	**3**	**0**	**3**	**165**	**10.9**	**3**	**1394**	**54.6**	**20:19**	....	....	....	....	....	....	....	....	....
2014-15	**New Jersey**	**NHL**	**74**	**11**	**14**	**25**	**29**	**4**	**2**	**0**	**112**	**9.8**	**–3**	**1200**	**53.4**	**19:04**	....	....	....	....	....	....	....	....	....
2015-16	**New Jersey**	**NHL**	**74**	**14**	**28**	**42**	**25**	**6**	**2**	**2**	**111**	**12.6**	**3**	**1387**	**51.6**	**19:51**	....	....	....	....	....	....	....	....	....
2016-17	**New Jersey**	**NHL**	**80**	**14**	**31**	**45**	**33**	**6**	**1**	**1**	**126**	**11.1**	**–8**	**1617**	**54.7**	**19:44**	....	....	....	....	....	....	....	....	....
	NHL Totals		**779**	**155**	**280**	**435**	**265**	**45**	**8**	**18**	**1478**	**10.5**		**12557**	**53.3**	**18:56**	**52**	**10**	**16**	**26**	**20**	**1**	**0**	**3**	**18:43**

WCHA All-Rookie Team (2005) • NCAA Championship All-Tournament Team (2005)

• Missed majority of 2011-12 due to leg injury during off-ice workout, August 17, 2011.

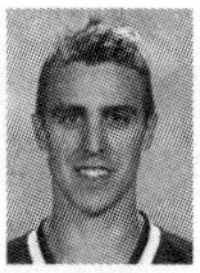

ZALEWSKI, Mike

(zuh-LEH-skee, MIGHK)

Left wing. Shoots left. 6'2", 205 lbs. Born, New Hartford, NY, August 18, 1992.

Season	Club	League	GP	G	A	Pts	PIM	PP	SH	GW	S	S%	+/-	TF	F%	Min	GP	G	A	Pts	PIM	PP	SH	GW	Min
2008-09	New Hartford	High-NY	....	44	43	87	....	....	....	....	....	....	....	....	....	....	....	....	....	....	....	....	....	....	....
2009-10	Syracuse Jr. Stars	EJHL	43	16	32	48	28	....	....	....	....	....	....	....	....	....	2	0	1	1	4	....	....	....	....
2010-11	Vernon Vipers	BCHL	46	12	17	29	34	....	....	....	....	....	....	....	....	....	16	5	3	8	4	....	....	....	....
2011-12	Vernon Vipers	BCHL	60	38	37	75	83	....	....	....	....	....	....	....	....	....	....	....	....	....	....	....	....	....	....
2012-13	RPI Engineers	ECAC	36	12	9	21	22	....	....	....	....	....	....	....	....	....	....	....	....	....	....	....	....	....	....
2013-14	RPI Engineers	ECAC	35	9	17	26	53	....	....	....	....	....	....	....	....	....	....	....	....	....	....	....	....	....	....
	Vancouver	**NHL**	**2**	**0**	**1**	**1**	**0**	**0**	**0**	**0**	**2**	**0.0**	**2**	**0**	**0.0**	**12:08**	....	....	....	....	....	....	....	....	....
2014-15	Utica Comets	AHL	55	3	9	12	18	....	....	....	....	....	....	....	....	....	23	1	2	3	14	....	....	....	....
2015-16	**Vancouver**	**NHL**	**3**	**0**	**1**	**1**	**2**	**0**	**0**	**0**	**2**	**0.0**	**1**	**10**	**60.0**	**11:51**	....	....	....	....	....	....	....	....	....
	Utica Comets	AHL	58	16	17	33	46	....	....	....	....	....	....	....	....	....	4	0	1	1	2	....	....	....	....
2016-17	**Vancouver**	**NHL**	**1**	**0**	**0**	**0**	**0**	**0**	**0**	**0**	**0**	**0.0**	**–1**	**0**	**0.0**	**8:03**	....	....	....	....	....	....	....	....	....
	Utica Comets	AHL	54	5	13	18	36	....	....	....	....	....	....	....	....	....	....	....	....	....	....	....	....	....	....
	NHL Totals		**6**	**0**	**2**	**2**	**2**	**0**	**0**	**0**	**4**	**0.0**		**10**	**60.0**	**11:19**	....	....	....	....	....	....	....	....	....

Signed as a free agent by **Vancouver**, March 14, 2014. Signed as a free agent by **Utica** (AHL), July 8, 2015.

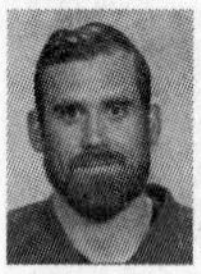

ZETTERBERG, Henrik

(ZEH-tuhr-buhrg, HEHN-rihk) **DET**

Left wing. Shoots left. 6', 195 lbs. Born, Njurunda, Sweden, October 9, 1980. Detroit's 4th pick, 210th overall, in 1999 NHL Draft.

Season	Club	League	GP	G	A	Pts	PIM	PP	SH	GW	S	S%	+/-	TF	F%	Min	GP	G	A	Pts	PIM	PP	SH	GW	Min
1997-98	Timra IK Jr.	Swe-Jr.	18	9	5	14	4	....	....	....	....	....	....	....	....	....	....	....	....	....	....	....	....	....	....
	Timra IK	Sweden-2	16	1	2	3	4	....	....	....	....	....	....	....	....	....	4	0	1	1	0	....	....	....	....
1998-99	Timra IK	Sweden-2	37	15	13	28	2	....	....	....	....	....	....	....	....	....	4	2	1	3	2	....	....	....	....
99-2000	Timra IK	Sweden-2	32	20	14	34	20	....	....	....	....	....	....	....	....	....	10	10	4	14	4	....	....	....	....
2000-01	Timra IK	Sweden	47	15	31	46	24	....	....	....	....	....	....	....	....	....	....	....	....	....	....	....	....	....	....
2001-02	Timra IK	Sweden	48	10	22	32	20	....	....	....	....	....	....	....	....	....	....	....	....	....	....	....	....	....	....
	Sweden	Olympics	4	0	1	1	0	....	....	....	....	....	....	....	....	....	....	....	....	....	....	....	....	....	....
2002-03	**Detroit**	**NHL**	**79**	**22**	**22**	**44**	**8**	**5**	**1**	**4**	**135**	**16.3**	**6**	**401**	**46.1**	**16:19**	**4**	**1**	**0**	**1**	**0**	**0**	**0**	**0**	**18:19**
2003-04	**Detroit**	**NHL**	**61**	**15**	**28**	**43**	**14**	**7**	**1**	**2**	**137**	**10.9**	**15**	**627**	**45.6**	**18:15**	**12**	**2**	**2**	**4**	**4**	**0**	**0**	**0**	**17:17**
2004-05	Timra IK	Sweden	50	19	31	*50	24	....	....	....	....	....	....	....	....	....	7	6	2	8	2	....	....	....	....
2005-06	**Detroit**	**NHL**	**77**	**39**	**46**	**85**	**30**	**17**	**1**	**9**	**270**	**14.4**	**29**	**583**	**50.3**	**18:57**	**6**	**6**	**0**	**6**	**2**	**4**	**0**	**0**	**21:43**
	Sweden	Olympics	8	3	3	6	0	....	....	....	....	....	....	....	....	....	....	....	....	....	....	....	....	....	....
2006-07	**Detroit**	**NHL**	**63**	**33**	**35**	**68**	**36**	**11**	**1**	***10**	**224**	**14.7**	**26**	**888**	**52.5**	**20:50**	**18**	**6**	**8**	**14**	**12**	**3**	**0**	**1**	**22:45**
2007-08 ♦	**Detroit**	**NHL**	**75**	**43**	**49**	**92**	**34**	**16**	**1**	**7**	**358**	**12.0**	**30**	**1210**	**55.0**	**22:04**	**22**	***13**	**14**	***27**	**16**	**4**	***2**	**4**	**22:36**
2008-09	**Detroit**	**NHL**	**77**	**31**	**42**	**73**	**36**	**12**	**2**	**5**	**309**	**10.0**	**13**	**1189**	**53.3**	**19:53**	**23**	**11**	**13**	**24**	**13**	**4**	**0**	**0**	**22:10**
2009-10	**Detroit**	**NHL**	**74**	**23**	**47**	**70**	**26**	**3**	**0**	**6**	**309**	**7.4**	**12**	**1098**	**49.5**	**20:04**	**12**	**7**	**8**	**15**	**6**	**2**	**0**	**2**	**20:25**
	Sweden	Olympics	4	1	0	1	2	....	....	....	....	....	....	....	....	....	....	....	....	....	....	....	....	....	....
2010-11	**Detroit**	**NHL**	**80**	**24**	**56**	**80**	**40**	**10**	**0**	**3**	**306**	**7.8**	**–1**	**984**	**52.4**	**19:35**	**7**	**3**	**5**	**8**	**2**	**1**	**0**	**0**	**21:59**
2011-12	**Detroit**	**NHL**	**82**	**22**	**47**	**69**	**47**	**3**	**0**	**4**	**267**	**8.2**	**14**	**1115**	**49.2**	**19:50**	**5**	**2**	**1**	**3**	**4**	**2**	**0**	**0**	**23:05**
2012-13	EV Zug	Swiss	23	16	16	32	20	....	....	....	....	....	....	....	....	....	....	....	....	....	....	....	....	....	....
	Detroit	**NHL**	**46**	**11**	**37**	**48**	**18**	**4**	**2**	**5**	**173**	**6.4**	**2**	**544**	**48.4**	**20:31**	**14**	**4**	**8**	**12**	**8**	**1**	**0**	**1**	**19:59**
2013-14	**Detroit**	**NHL**	**45**	**16**	**32**	**48**	**20**	**3**	**0**	**1**	**151**	**10.6**	**19**	**489**	**53.0**	**20:33**	**2**	**1**	**1**	**2**	**0**	**0**	**0**	**0**	**19:32**
	Sweden	Olympics	1	1	0	1	0	....	....	....	....	....	....	....	....	....	....	....	....	....	....	....	....	....	....
2014-15	**Detroit**	**NHL**	**77**	**17**	**49**	**66**	**32**	**4**	**0**	**3**	**227**	**7.5**	**–6**	**1064**	**50.9**	**19:07**	**7**	**0**	**3**	**3**	**8**	**0**	**0**	**0**	**18:02**
2015-16	**Detroit**	**NHL**	**82**	**13**	**37**	**50**	**24**	**2**	**0**	**3**	**214**	**6.1**	**–15**	**1075**	**50.1**	**19:25**	**5**	**1**	**0**	**1**	**4**	**0**	**0**	**0**	**19:36**
2016-17	**Detroit**	**NHL**	**82**	**17**	**51**	**68**	**22**	**2**	**0**	**0**	**195**	**8.7**	**15**	**1362**	**51.8**	**19:43**	....	....	....	....	....	....	....	....	....
	NHL Totals		**1000**	**326**	**578**	**904**	**387**	**99**	**9**	**62**	**3275**	**10.0**		**12629**	**51.0**	**19:35**	**137**	**57**	**63**	**120**	**79**	**21**	**2**	**8**	**21:03**

Swedish Elite League Rookie of the Year (2001) • NHL All-Rookie Team (2003) • NHL Second All-Star Team (2008) • Conn Smythe Trophy (2008) • NHL Foundation Player Award (2013) • King Clancy Memorial Trophy (2015)

Signed as a free agent by **Timra** (Sweden), September 20, 2004. Signed as a free agent by **Zug** (Swiss), October 8, 2012.

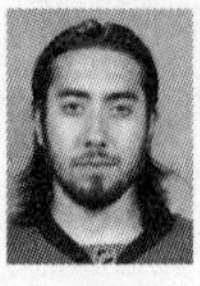

ZIBANEJAD, Mika

(zih-BAN-ih-jad, MEEKA) **NYR**

Center. Shoots right. 6'2", 215 lbs. Born, Huddinge, Sweden, April 18, 1993. Ottawa's 1st pick, 6th overall, in 2011 NHL Draft.

Season	Club	League	GP	G	A	Pts	PIM	PP	SH	GW	S	S%	+/-	TF	F%	Min	GP	G	A	Pts	PIM	PP	SH	GW	Min
2008-09	AIK IF Solna U18	Swe-U18	11	2	2	4	2	....	....	....	....	....	....	....	....	....	....	....	....	....	....	....	....	....	....
2009-10	Djurgarden U18	Swe-U18	28	14	22	36	18	....	....	....	....	....	....	....	....	....	5	5	4	9	4	....	....	....	....
	Djurgarden Jr.	Swe-Jr.	14	2	2	4	4	....	....	....	....	....	....	....	....	....	....	....	....	....	....	....	....	....	....
2010-11	Djurgarden U18	Swe-U18	2	3	2	5	2	....	....	....	....	....	....	....	....	....	....	....	....	....	....	....	....	....	....
	Djurgarden Jr.	Swe-Jr.	27	12	9	21	12	....	....	....	....	....	....	....	....	....	3	1	2	3	0	....	....	....	....
	Djurgarden	Sweden	26	5	4	9	2	....	....	....	....	....	....	....	....	....	7	1	1	2	2	....	....	....	....
2011-12	**Ottawa**	**NHL**	**9**	**0**	**1**	**1**	**2**	**0**	**0**	**0**	**12**	**0.0**	**–3**	**50**	**44.0**	**12:54**	....	....	....	....	....	....	....	....	....
	Djurgarden	Sweden	26	5	8	13	4	....	....	....	....	....	....	....	....	....	....	....	....	....	....	....	....	....	....
	Djurgarden Jr.	Swe-Jr.	1	0	0	0	2	....	....	....	....	....	....	....	....	....	....	....	....	....	....	....	....	....	....
	Djurgarden	Sweden-Q	10	4	2	6	2	....	....	....	....	....	....	....	....	....	....	....	....	....	....	....	....	....	....
2012-13	**Ottawa**	**NHL**	**42**	**7**	**13**	**20**	**6**	**3**	**0**	**0**	**90**	**7.8**	**9**	**343**	**46.4**	**13:34**	**10**	**1**	**3**	**4**	**0**	**0**	**0**	**0**	**13:36**
2013-14	**Ottawa**	**NHL**	**69**	**16**	**17**	**33**	**18**	**3**	**0**	**0**	**153**	**10.5**	**–15**	**397**	**46.1**	**14:20**	....	....	....	....	....	....	....	....	....
	Binghamton	AHL	6	2	5	7	2	....	....	....	....	....	....	....	....	....	....	....	....	....	....	....	....	....	....
2014-15	**Ottawa**	**NHL**	**80**	**20**	**26**	**46**	**20**	**4**	**0**	**0**	**150**	**13.3**	**0**	**1261**	**48.8**	**16:26**	**6**	**1**	**3**	**4**	**0**	**1**	**0**	**0**	**15:43**
2015-16	**Ottawa**	**NHL**	**81**	**21**	**30**	**51**	**18**	**2**	**2**	**7**	**184**	**11.4**	**–2**	**1306**	**50.5**	**17:46**	....	....	....	....	....	....	....	....	....
2016-17	**NY Rangers**	**NHL**	**56**	**14**	**23**	**37**	**16**	**4**	**0**	**2**	**119**	**11.8**	**9**	**950**	**52.0**	**17:04**	**12**	**2**	**7**	**9**	**0**	**0**	**0**	**1**	**17:53**
	NHL Totals		**337**	**78**	**110**	**188**	**80**	**16**	**2**	**9**	**708**	**11.0**		**4307**	**49.5**	**15:59**	**28**	**4**	**13**	**17**	**0**	**1**	**0**	**1**	**15:53**

• Re-assigned to **Djurgarden** (Sweden) by **Ottawa**, October 26, 2011. Traded to **NY Rangers** by **Ottawa** with Ottawa's 2nd round pick in 2018 NHL Draft for Derick Brassard and NY Rangers' 7th round pick in 2018 NHL Draft, July 18, 2016.

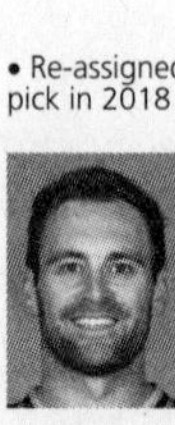

ZOLNIERCZYK, Harry

(ZOHL-nuhr-chuhk, HAIR-ee)

Left wing. Shoots left. 5'11", 180 lbs. Born, Toronto, ON, September 1, 1987.

Season	Club	League	GP	G	A	Pts	PIM	PP	SH	GW	S	S%	+/-	TF	F%	Min	GP	G	A	Pts	PIM	PP	SH	GW	Min
2005-06	Alberni Valley	BCHL	53	9	13	22	40	....	....	....	....	....	....	....	....	....	6	1	3	4	10	....	....	....	....
2006-07	Alberni Valley	BCHL	47	20	18	38	85	....	....	....	....	....	....	....	....	....	5	3	2	5	10	....	....	....	....
2007-08	Brown U.	ECAC	16	0	3	3	2	....	....	....	....	....	....	....	....	....	....	....	....	....	....	....	....	....	....
2008-09	Brown U.	ECAC	31	1	1	2	30	....	....	....	....	....	....	....	....	....	....	....	....	....	....	....	....	....	....
2009-10	Brown U.	ECAC	37	13	20	33	78	....	....	....	....	....	....	....	....	....	....	....	....	....	....	....	....	....	....
2010-11	Brown U.	ECAC	30	16	15	31	*128	....	....	....	....	....	....	....	....	....	....	....	....	....	....	....	....	....	....
	Adirondack	AHL	16	3	2	5	37	....	....	....	....	....	....	....	....	....	....	....	....	....	....	....	....	....	....

					Regular Season												Playoffs							
Season	Club	League	GP	G	A	Pts	PIM	PP	SH	GW	S	S%	+/-	TF	F%	Min	GP	G	A	Pts	PIM	PP	SH	GW	Min
2011-12	Philadelphia	NHL	37	3	3	6	35	0	0	0	49	6.1	-11	28	42.9	7:42	....								
	Adirondack	AHL	39	8	13	21	37										....								
2012-13	Adirondack	AHL	52	9	8	17	54										....								
	Philadelphia	NHL	7	0	1	1	36	0	0	0	4	0.0	0	0	0.0	7:22	....								
	Norfolk Admirals	AHL	9	2	0	2	14										....								
2013-14	**Pittsburgh**	NHL	13	2	0	2	12	0	0	0	12	16.7	0	2	100.0	10:08	....								
	Wilkes-Barre	AHL	57	18	18	36	75										17	3	7	10	10				
2014-15	**NY Islanders**	NHL	2	0	0	0	0	0	0	0	1	0.0	-1	2	0.0	11:08	....								
	Bridgeport	AHL	60	18	26	44	78										....								
2015-16	**Anaheim**	NHL	1	0	0	0	0	0	0	0	1	0.0	-1	0	0.0	8:48	....								
	San Diego Gulls	AHL	24	6	3	9	31										4	0	0	0	0				
2016-17	**Nashville**	NHL	24	2	2	4	10	0	0	0	19	10.5	-2	19	42.1	8:52	11	1	2	3	0	0	0	0	8:49
	Milwaukee	AHL	24	6	10	16	20										....								
	NHL Totals		84	7	6	13	93	0	0	0	86	8.1		51	43.1	8:29	11	1	2	3	0	0	0	0	8:49

Signed as a free agent by **Philadelphia**, March 8, 2011. Traded to **Anaheim** by **Philadelphia** for Jay Rosehill, April 1, 2013. Traded to **Pittsburgh** by **Anaheim** for Alex Grant, June 24, 2013. Signed as a free agent by **NY Islanders**, July 2, 2014. Signed as a free agent by **Anaheim**, July 3, 2015. • Missed majority of 2015-16 as a healthy reserve. Signed as a free agent by **Nashville**, July 1, 2016.

ZUCCARELLO, Mats

(zoo-ka-REHL-oh, MATS) **NYR**

Left wing. Shoots left. 5'8", 179 lbs.   Born, Oslo, Norway, September 1, 1987.

Season	Club	League	GP	G	A	Pts	PIM	PP	SH	GW	S	S%	+/-	TF	F%	Min	GP	G	A	Pts	PIM	PP	SH	GW	Min
2003-04	Frisk-Asker U18	Nor-U18	24	23	14	37	44										2	3	1	4	0				
	Frisk-Asker Jr.	Nor-Jr.	20	7	14	21	14										3	0	2	2	0				
2004-05	Frisk-Asker U18	Nor-U18	12	11	18	29	50										....								
	Frisk-Asker Jr.	Nor-Jr.	27	19	17	36	16										5	3	3	6	6				
	Frisk-Asker IF	Norway	1	0	0	0	0										....								
2005-06	Frisk Asker IF/NTG	Nor-Jr.	2	7	0	7	0										2	2	3	5	0				
	Frisk-Asker IF	Norway	21	5	3	8	12										4	0	0	0	2				
2006-07	Frisk-Asker IF/NTG	Nor-Jr.	....														1	3	4	7	2				
	Frisk-Asker IF	Norway	43	34	25	59	36										7	4	4	8	2				
2007-08	Frisk-Asker IF	Norway	33	24	40	64	48										15	12	15	27	24				
2008-09	MODO	Sweden	35	12	28	40	38										....								
2009-10	MODO	Sweden	55	23	41	*64	62										....								
	Norway	Olympics	4	1	2	3	2										....								
2010-11	**NY Rangers**	NHL	42	6	17	23	4	0	0	2	74	8.1	3	15	53.3	14:10	1	0	0	0	2	0	0	0	7:34
	Connecticut	AHL	36	13	16	29	16										2	1	1	2	4				
2011-12	**NY Rangers**	NHL	10	2	1	3	6	1	0	1	10	20.0	0	0	0.0	10:03	....								
	Connecticut	AHL	37	12	24	36	22										....								
2012-13	Magnitogorsk	KHL	44	11	17	28	30										7	2	2	4	10				
	NY Rangers	NHL	15	3	5	8	8	0	0	0	27	11.1	10	4	0.0	16:25	12	1	6	7	4	0	0	0	16:22
2013-14	**NY Rangers**	NHL	77	19	40	59	32	4	1	4	170	11.2	11	8	37.5	17:08	25	5	8	13	20	0	0	0	17:41
	Norway	Olympics	3	0	0	0	2										....								
2014-15	**NY Rangers**	NHL	78	15	34	49	45	0	0	3	154	9.7	17	37	43.2	17:16	5	0	2	2	0	0	0	0	14:35
2015-16	**NY Rangers**	NHL	81	26	35	61	34	7	0	4	166	15.7	2	11	45.5	18:29	5	1	1	2	4	0	0	1	18:21
2016-17	**NY Rangers**	NHL	80	15	44	59	26	5	0	3	189	7.9	15	13	46.2	18:50	12	4	3	7	16	1	0	1	20:33
	NHL Totals		383	86	176	262	155	17	1	17	790	10.9		88	43.2	17:16	60	11	20	31	46	1	0	2	17:37

Signed as a free agent by **NY Rangers**, May 26, 2010. Signed as a free agent by **Magnitogorsk** (KHL), May 26, 2012. Signed as a free agent by **NY Rangers**, March 28, 2013.

ZUCKER, Jason

(ZUH-KUHR, JAY-suhn) **MIN**

Left wing. Shoots left. 5'11", 185 lbs.   Born, Newport Beach, CA, January 16, 1992. Minnesota's 4th pick, 59th overall, in 2010 NHL Draft.

Season	Club	League	GP	G	A	Pts	PIM	PP	SH	GW	S	S%	+/-	TF	F%	Min	GP	G	A	Pts	PIM	PP	SH	GW	Min
2007-08	Det. Compuware	MWEHL	30	17	21	38	30										....								
	Det. Compuware	Minor-MI	42	29	35	64											....								
2008-09	USAHNTDP	NAHL	36	11	4	15	55										....								
	USAHNTDP	U-17	12	8	6	14											....								
	USAHNTDP	U-18	16	2	6	8	8										....								
2009-10	USAHNTDP	USHL	22	11	7	18	23										....								
	USAHNTDP	U-18	38	18	17	35	24										....								
2010-11	U. of Denver	WCHA	40	23	22	45	59										....								
2011-12	U. of Denver	WCHA	38	22	24	46	38										....								
	Minnesota	NHL	6	0	2	2	2	0	0	0	10	0.0	-2	0	0.0	11:02	....								
2012-13	Houston Aeros	AHL	55	24	26	50	43										1	0	0	0	4				
	Minnesota	NHL	20	4	1	5	8	0	0	0	34	11.8	4	1	0.0	11:16	5	1	1	2	0	0	0	1	13:29
2013-14	**Minnesota**	NHL	21	4	1	5	2	1	0	1	40	10.0	2	0	0.0	12:59	....								
	Iowa Wild	AHL	22	8	5	13	55										....								
2014-15	**Minnesota**	NHL	51	21	5	26	18	1	1	3	124	16.9	-9	7	28.6	15:04	10	2	1	3	2	0	0	0	14:11
2015-16	**Minnesota**	NHL	71	13	10	23	20	0	1	1	158	8.2	-4	1	100.0	15:35	6	0	2	2	2	0	0	0	13:56
2016-17	**Minnesota**	NHL	79	22	25	47	30	1	0	3	172	12.8	*34	5	20.0	15:17	5	1	0	1	2	0	0	0	17:15
	NHL Totals		248	64	44	108	80	3	2	8	538	11.9		14	28.6	14:42	26	4	4	8	6	0	0	1	14:35

WCHA All-Rookie Team (2011) • WCHA Second All-Star Team (2011, 2012) • WCHA Rookie of the Year (2011) • NCAA West Second All-American Team (2012) • AHL All-Rookie Team (2013)

ZYKOV, Valentin

(ZIH-kawv, val-ehn-TEEN) **CAR**

Left wing. Shoots right. 6'1", 224 lbs.   Born, St. Petersburg, Russia, May 15, 1995. Los Angeles' 1st pick, 37th overall, in 2013 NHL Draft.

Season	Club	League	GP	G	A	Pts	PIM	PP	SH	GW	S	S%	+/-	TF	F%	Min	GP	G	A	Pts	PIM	PP	SH	GW	Min
2011-12	CSKA Jr.	Russia-Jr.	52	5	6	11	105										18	0	2	2	4				
2012-13	Baie-Comeau	QMJHL	67	40	35	75	60										19	10	9	19	18				
2013-14	Baie-Comeau	QMJHL	53	23	40	63	70										22	7	15	22	14				
2014-15	Baie-Comeau	QMJHL	16	6	12	18	22										....								
	Gatineau	QMJHL	26	15	13	28	38										11	3	4	7	20				
2015-16	Ontario Reign	AHL	43	7	7	14	20										....								
	Charlotte	AHL	2	0	0	0	0										....								
2016-17	**Carolina**	NHL	2	1	0	1	0	0	0	0	3	33.3	1	0	0.0	6:15	....								
	Charlotte	AHL	66	16	18	34	57										5	0	2	2	2				
	NHL Totals		2	1	0	1	0	0	0	0	3	33.3		0	0.0	6:15	....								

QMJHL All-Rookie Team (2013) • QMJHL Rookie of the Year (2013) • Canadian Major Junior Rookie of the Year (2013)
Traded to **Carolina** by **Los Angeles** with future considerations (conditions not met) for Kris Versteeg, February 28, 2016.

NHL Goaltenders

 Jake Allen
 Frederik Andersen
 Craig Anderson
 Richard Bachman
 Jonathan Bernier
 Reto Berra
 Jean-Francois Berube
 Ben Bishop
 Sergei Bobrovsky

 Peter Budaj
 Mike Condon
 Jared Coreau
 Corey Crawford
 Scott Darling
 Aaron Dell
 Louis Domingue
 Devan Dubnyk
 Brian Elliott

 Jhonas Enroth
 Marc-Andre Fleury
 John Gibson
 Thomas Greiss
 Philipp Grubauer
 Jonas Gustavsson
 Jaroslav Halak
 Andrew Hammond
 Connor Hellebuyck

 Braden Holtby
 Jimmy Howard
 Michael Hutchinson
 Carter Hutton
 Chad Johnson
 Martin Jones
 Anton Khudobin
 Keith Kinkaid
 Joonas Korpisalo

 Darcy Kuemper
 Eddie Lack
 Robin Lehner
 Kari Lehtonen
 Henrik Lundqvist
 Roberto Luongo
 Jacob Markstrom
 Spencer Martin
 Steve Mason

 Curtis McElhinney
 Ryan Miller
 Al Montoya
 Petr Mrazek
 Matt Murray
 Michal Neuvirth
 Antti Niemi
 Anders Nilsson
 Ondrej Pavelec

 Justin Peters
 Calvin Pickard
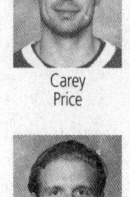 Carey Price
 Jonathan Quick
 Antti Raanta
 Tuukka Rask
 James Reimer
 Pekka Rinne
 Juuse Saros

Cory Schneider
Mike Smith
Garret Sparks
Alex Stalock
Cam Talbot
Semyon Varlamov
Andrei Vasilevskiy
Cam Ward
Jeff Zatkoff

2017-18 Goaltender Register

Note: The 2017-18 Goaltender Register lists all active NHL goaltenders, every goaltender drafted in the 2017 NHL Draft, goaltenders on NHL Reserve Lists and other goaltenders.

Trades and roster changes are current as of August 14, 2017.

To calculate a goaltender's goals-against per game average **(Avg)**, divide goals against **(GA)** by minutes played **(Mins)** and multiply this result by **60**.

Abbreviations: GP – games played; **W** – wins; **L** – losses; **O/T** – overtime losses/ties; **Mins** – minutes played; **GA** – goals against; **SO** – shutouts;
Avg – goals-against-per-game average; ***** – league-leading total
♦ – member of Stanley Cup-winning team.

NHL Player Register begins on page 351.
Prospect Register begins on page 279.
Retired Player Index begins on page 616.
Retired Goaltender Index begins on page 665.
League Abbreviations are listed on page 678.

ALLEN, Jake (AL-luhn, JAYK) ST.L.

Goaltender. Catches left. 6'2", 195 lbs. Born, Fredericton, NB, August 7, 1990.
(St. Louis' 3rd pick, 34th overall, in 2008 NHL Draft).

			Regular Season								Playoffs						
Season	Club	League	GP	W	L	O/T	Mins	GA	SO	Avg	GP	W	L	Mins	GA	SO	Avg
2006-07	Fredericton	NBPEI	STATISTICS NOT AVAILABLE														
2007-08	St. John's	QMJHL	30	9	12	0	1507	79	2	3.14	4	2	1	128	8	0	3.74
2008-09	Montreal	QMJHL	53	28	25	0	3023	144	3	2.86	10	4	6	585	35	1	3.59
2009-10	Montreal	QMJHL	23	11	11	0	1241	55	1	2.66	....	....	....	....	....	....	....
	Drummondville	QMJHL	22	18	3	0	1271	37	3	1.75	14	9	5	840	34	1	2.43
2010-11	Peoria Rivermen	AHL	47	25	19	3	2805	118	6	2.52	3	0	3	189	12	0	3.80
2011-12	Peoria Rivermen	AHL	38	13	20	2	2148	105	1	2.93	....	....	....	....	....	....	....
	St. Louis	**NHL**	....	....	....	....	....	....	....	....	**1**	**0**	**0**	**1**	**0**	**0**	**0.00**
2012-13	Peoria Rivermen	AHL	35	13	19	2	2054	99	2	2.89	....	....	....	....	....	....	....
	St. Louis	**NHL**	**15**	**9**	**4**	**0**	**804**	**33**	**1**	**2.46**	....	....	....	....	....	....	....
2013-14	Chicago Wolves	AHL	*52	*33	16	3	*3138	106	*7	*2.03	9	3	6	511	28	1	3.29
2014-15	**St. Louis**	**NHL**	**37**	**22**	**7**	**4**	**2077**	**79**	**4**	**2.28**	**6**	**2**	**4**	**328**	**12**	**0**	**2.20**
2015-16	**St. Louis**	**NHL**	**47**	**26**	**15**	**3**	**2583**	**101**	**6**	**2.35**	**5**	**1**	**1**	**169**	**7**	**0**	**2.49**
2016-17	**St. Louis**	**NHL**	**61**	**33**	**20**	**5**	**3418**	**138**	**4**	**2.42**	**11**	**6**	**5**	**675**	**22**	**0**	**1.96**
	NHL Totals		**160**	**90**	**46**	**12**	**8882**	**351**	**15**	**2.37**	**23**	**9**	**10**	**1173**	**41**	**0**	**2.10**

QMJHL First All-Star Team (2010) • Canadian Major Junior First All-Star Team (2010) • Canadian Major Junior Goaltender of the Year (2010) • NHL All-Rookie Team (2013) • AHL First All-Star Team (2014) • Aldege "Baz" Bastien Award (AHL – Outstanding Goaltender) (2014) • NHL All-Rookie Team (2015)

ALTSHULLER, Daniel (awl-SHOO-luhr, DAN-yehl)

Goaltender. Catches left. 6'3", 205 lbs. Born, Ottawa, ON, July 24, 1994.
(Carolina's 3rd pick, 69th overall, in 2012 NHL Draft).

			Regular Season								Playoffs						
Season	Club	League	GP	W	L	O/T	Mins	GA	SO	Avg	GP	W	L	Mins	GA	SO	Avg
2009-10	Ott. Jr. 67's MM	Minor-ON	24	....	....	....	1080	40	3	1.74	....	....	....	....	....	....	....
	Nepean Raiders	ON-Jr.A	1	0	1	0	60	2	0	2.00	....	....	....	....	....	....	....
2010-11	Nepean Raiders	ON-Jr.A	43	19	13	10	2515	135	1	3.22	....	....	....	....	....	....	....
2011-12	Oshawa Generals	OHL	30	11	16	3	1756	104	0	3.55	5	2	2	279	18	0	3.87
2012-13	Oshawa Generals	OHL	58	*36	18	2	3363	147	3	2.62	9	4	5	541	27	0	3.00
2013-14	Oshawa Generals	OHL	52	31	13	3	2907	124	2	2.56	11	8	3	699	22	*3	*1.89
2014-15	Florida Everblades	ECHL	14	8	3	1	767	41	0	3.21	6	2	3	288	16	1	3.34
2015-16	Charlotte Checkers	AHL	28	10	10	5	1473	69	1	2.81	....	....	....	....	....	....	....
	Florida Everblades	ECHL	15	10	4	0	818	24	3	1.76	....	....	....	....	....	....	....
2016-17	Charlotte Checkers	AHL	15	7	5	0	729	35	0	2.88	....	....	....	....	....	....	....
	Florida Everblades	ECHL	9	6	0	3	555	18	0	1.94	....	....	....	....	....	....	....

OHL All-Rookie Team (2012)

ALVES, Jorge (AL-vehz, HOHR-geh)

Goaltender. Catches left. 5'9", 185 lbs. Born, Boston, MA, January 30, 1979.

			Regular Season								Playoffs						
Season	Club	League	GP	W	L	O/T	Mins	GA	SO	Avg	GP	W	L	Mins	GA	SO	Avg
2016-17	**Carolina**	**NHL**	**1**	**0**	**0**	**0**	**1**	**0**	**0**	**0.00**	....	....	....	....	....	....	....
	NHL Totals		**1**	**0**	**0**	**0**	**1**	**0**	**0**	**0.00**	....	....	....	....	....	....	....

• **Carolina's** equipment manager/practice goaltender signed to a PTO (professional tryout) contract by **Carolina**, December 31, 2016 and played the last 7.6 seconds of the game that night vs. Tampa Bay.

ANDERSEN, Frederik (AHN-duhr-suhn, FREH-duhr-ihk) TOR

Goaltender. Catches left. 6'4", 220 lbs. Born, Herning, Denmark, October 2, 1989.
(Anaheim's 3rd pick, 87th overall, in 2012 NHL Draft).

			Regular Season								Playoffs						
Season	Club	League	GP	W	L	O/T	Mins	GA	SO	Avg	GP	W	L	Mins	GA	SO	Avg
2005-06	Herning IK Jr.	Den-Jr.	29	....	....	....	....	....	....	....	6	....	....	....	....	....	....
	Herning IK II	Den-2	3	....	....	....	....	....	....	....	....	....	....	....	....	....	....
2006-07	Herning IK Jr.	Den-Jr.	27	....	....	....	....	....	....	....	....	....	....	....	....	....	....
	Herning IK II	Den-2	18	....	....	....	....	....	....	....	....	....	....	....	....	....	....
2007-08	Herning IK Jr.	Den-Jr.	17	....	....	....	....	....	....	....	....	....	....	....	....	....	....
	Herning IK II	Den-2	9	....	....	....	....	....	....	....	....	....	....	....	....	....	....
2008-09	Herning IK II	Den-2	1	....	....	....	....	....	....	....	....	....	....	....	....	....	....
	Herning Blue Fox	Denmark	22	....	....	....	1249	51	1	2.45	....	....	....	....	....	....	....
2009-10	Frederikshavn	Denmark	30	....	....	....	1754	64	6	2.19	10	....	....	607	29	0	2.86
2010-11	Frederikshavn	Denmark	35	....	....	....	1953	81	....	2.49	11	....	....	666	26	....	2.34
2011-12	Frolunda	Sweden	39	....	....	....	2335	65	7	1.67	6	....	....	379	17	0	2.69
2012-13	Norfolk Admirals	AHL	47	24	18	1	2685	98	4	2.19	....	....	....	....	....	....	....
2013-14	**Anaheim**	**NHL**	**28**	**20**	**5**	**0**	**1569**	**60**	**0**	**2.29**	**7**	**3**	**2**	**368**	**19**	**0**	**3.10**
	Norfolk Admirals	AHL	4	3	1	0	245	8	1	1.96	....	....	....	....	....	....	....
2014-15	**Anaheim**	**NHL**	**54**	**35**	**12**	**5**	**3106**	**123**	**3**	**2.38**	**16**	**11**	**5**	**1050**	**41**	**1**	**2.34**
2015-16	**Anaheim**	**NHL**	**43**	**22**	**9**	**7**	**2298**	**88**	**3**	**2.30**	**5**	**3**	**2**	**297**	**7**	**1**	**1.41**
2016-17	**Toronto**	**NHL**	**66**	**33**	**16**	**14**	**3799**	**169**	**4**	**2.67**	**6**	**2**	**4**	**403**	**18**	**0**	**2.68**
	NHL Totals		**191**	**110**	**42**	**26**	**10772**	**440**	**10**	**2.45**	**34**	**19**	**13**	**2118**	**85**	**2**	**2.41**

• Re-entered NHL Entry Draft. Originally Carolina's 8th pick, 187th overall, in 2010 NHL Draft.

NHL All-Rookie Team (2014) • William M. Jennings Trophy (2016) (shared with John Gibson)

Traded to **Toronto** by **Anaheim** for Pittsburgh's 1st round pick (previously acquired, Anaheim selected Sam Steel) in 2016 NHL Draft and San Jose's 2nd round pick (previously acquired, Anaheim selected Maxime Comtois) in 2017 NHL Draft, June 20, 2016.

ANDERSON, Craig (AN-duhr-suhn, KRAYG) OTT

Goaltender. Catches left. 6'2", 184 lbs. Born, Park Ridge, IL, May 21, 1981.
(Chicago's 4th pick, 73rd overall, in 2001 NHL Draft).

			Regular Season								Playoffs						
Season	Club	League	GP	W	L	O/T	Mins	GA	SO	Avg	GP	W	L	Mins	GA	SO	Avg
1997-98	Chicago Jets	MEHL	50	....	....	....	2991	143	2	2.86	....	....	....	....	....	....	....
1998-99	Chicago Freeze	NAHL	14	11	3	0	840	40	0	2.56	....	....	....	....	....	....	....
	Guelph Storm	OHL	21	12	5	1	1006	52	1	3.10	3	0	2	114	9	0	4.74
99-2000	Guelph Storm	OHL	38	12	17	2	1955	117	0	3.59	3	0	1	110	5	0	2.73
2000-01	Guelph Storm	OHL	59	30	19	9	3555	156	3	2.63	4	0	4	240	17	0	4.25
2001-02	Norfolk Admirals	AHL	28	9	13	4	1568	77	2	2.95	1	0	1	21	1	0	2.83
2002-03	**Chicago**	**NHL**	**6**	**0**	**3**	**2**	**270**	**18**	**0**	**4.00**	....	....	....	....	....	....	....
	Norfolk Admirals	AHL	32	15	11	5	1795	58	4	1.94	5	2	3	345	15	0	2.61
2003-04	**Chicago**	**NHL**	**21**	**6**	**14**	**0**	**1205**	**57**	**1**	**2.84**	....	....	....	....	....	....	....
	Norfolk Admirals	AHL	37	17	20	0	2108	74	3	2.11	5	2	3	327	10	0	1.84
2004-05	Norfolk Admirals	AHL	15	9	4	1	886	27	2	1.83	6	2	4	356	14	0	2.36
2005-06	**Chicago**	**NHL**	**29**	**6**	**12**	**4**	**1554**	**86**	**1**	**3.32**	....	....	....	....	....	....	....
2006-07	**Florida**	**NHL**	**5**	**1**	**1**	**1**	**217**	**8**	**0**	**2.21**	....	....	....	....	....	....	....
	Rochester	AHL	34	23	10	1	2060	88	1	2.56	6	2	4	376	18	0	2.87
2007-08	**Florida**	**NHL**	**17**	**8**	**6**	**1**	**935**	**35**	**2**	**2.25**	....	....	....	....	....	....	....
2008-09	**Florida**	**NHL**	**31**	**15**	**7**	**5**	**1636**	**74**	**3**	**2.71**	....	....	....	....	....	....	....
2009-10	**Colorado**	**NHL**	**71**	**38**	**25**	**7**	**4235**	**186**	**7**	**2.64**	**6**	**2**	**4**	**366**	**16**	**1**	**2.62**
2010-11	**Colorado**	**NHL**	**33**	**13**	**15**	**3**	**1810**	**99**	**0**	**3.28**	....	....	....	....	....	....	....
	Ottawa	**NHL**	**18**	**11**	**5**	**1**	**1055**	**36**	**2**	**2.05**	....	....	....	....	....	....	....
2011-12	**Ottawa**	**NHL**	**63**	**33**	**22**	**6**	**3492**	**165**	**3**	**2.84**	**7**	**3**	**4**	**419**	**14**	**1**	**2.00**
2012-13	**Ottawa**	**NHL**	**24**	**12**	**9**	**2**	**1421**	**40**	**3**	***1.69**	**10**	**5**	**4**	**578**	**29**	**0**	**3.01**
2013-14	**Ottawa**	**NHL**	**53**	**25**	**16**	**8**	**3000**	**150**	**4**	**3.00**	....	....	....	....	....	....	....
2014-15	**Ottawa**	**NHL**	**35**	**14**	**13**	**8**	**2093**	**87**	**3**	**2.49**	**4**	**2**	**2**	**247**	**4**	**1**	**0.97**
2015-16	**Ottawa**	**NHL**	**60**	**31**	**23**	**5**	**3477**	**161**	**4**	**2.78**	....	....	....	....	....	....	....
2016-17	**Ottawa**	**NHL**	**40**	**25**	**11**	**4**	**2421**	**92**	**5**	**2.28**	**19**	**11**	**8**	**1178**	**46**	**1**	**2.34**
	NHL Totals		**506**	**238**	**182**	**57**	**28821**	**1294**	**38**	**2.69**	**46**	**23**	**22**	**2788**	**109**	**4**	**2.35**

• Re-entered NHL Entry Draft. Originally Calgary's 3rd pick, 77th overall, in 1999 NHL Draft.

OHL First All-Star Team (2001) • Bill Masterton Memorial Trophy (2017)

Claimed on waivers by **Boston** from **Chicago**, January 19, 2006. Claimed on waivers by **St. Louis** from **Boston**, January 31, 2006. Claimed on waivers by **Chicago** from **St. Louis**, February 3, 2006. Traded to **Florida** by **Chicago** for Florida's 6th round pick (later traded to Tampa Bay - Tampa Bay selected Luke Witkowski) in 2008 NHL Draft, June 24, 2006. Signed as a free agent by **Colorado**, July 1, 2009. Traded to **Ottawa** by **Colorado** for Brian Elliott, February 18, 2011.

APPLEBY, Ken (A-puhl-bee, KEHN) N.J.

Goaltender. Catches left. 6'4", 210 lbs. Born, North Bay, ON, April 10, 1995.

			Regular Season								Playoffs						
Season	Club	League	GP	W	L	O/T	Mins	GA	SO	Avg	GP	W	L	Mins	GA	SO	Avg
2010-11	North Bay Trappers	Minor-ON	21	....	....	....	....	....	....	2.92	1	0	1	59	4	0	4.07
2011-12	Kirkland Lake	ON-Jr.A	14	2	11	1	811	66	1	4.88	....	....	....	....	....	....	....
2012-13	Oshawa Generals	OHL	18	6	4	2	756	34	0	2.70	....	....	....	....	....	....	....
2013-14	Oshawa Generals	OHL	24	11	7	3	1234	51	3	2.48	....	....	....	....	....	....	....
2014-15	Oshawa Generals	OHL	50	38	7	4	2935	102	6	2.04	21	16	5	1259	47	2	2.24
2015-16	Adirondack	ECHL	29	17	9	2	1712	64	3	2.24	12	7	5	754	29	1	2.31
	Albany Devils	AHL	8	3	3	2	486	21	1	2.59	....	....	....	....	....	....	....
2016-17	Albany Devils	AHL	32	17	14	1	1917	84	0	2.63	1	0	0	33	2	0	3.61
	Adirondack	ECHL	6	4	1	1	363	12	1	1.98	....	....	....	....	....	....	....

Signed as a free agent by **New Jersey**, October 4, 2015. • Re-assigned to **Adirondack** (ECHL) by **New Jersey**, October 5, 2015.

BACHMAN, Richard (BAWK-mahn, RIH-chuhrd) VAN

Goaltender. Catches left. 5'10", 183 lbs. Born, Salt Lake City, UT, July 25, 1987.
(Dallas' 3rd pick, 120th overall, in 2006 NHL Draft).

			Regular Season								Playoffs						
Season	Club	League	GP	W	L	O/T	Mins	GA	SO	Avg	GP	W	L	Mins	GA	SO	Avg
2004-05	Cushing	High-MA	28	....	....	....	1498	53	3	1.89	....	....	....	....	....	....	....
	Junior Bruins	EmJHL	25	....	....	....	....	....	....	....	....	....	....	....	....	....	....
2005-06	Cushing	High-MA	30	....	....	....	1598	60	4	2.25	....	....	....	....	....	....	....
	Junior Bruins	EmJHL	....	31	1	2	....	....	....	1.69	....	....	....	....	....	....	....
2006-07	Chicago Steel	USHL	7	2	5	0	359	29	0	4.85	....	....	....	....	....	....	....
	Cedar Rapids	USHL	26	14	10	2	1565	78	4	2.99	6	4	1	329	7	*2	*1.28
2007-08	Colorado College	WCHA	35	25	9	1	2103	65	4	1.85	....	....	....	....	....	....	....
2008-09	Colorado College	WCHA	35	14	11	10	2073	91	3	2.63	....	....	....	....	....	....	....
2009-10	Texas Stars	AHL	8	4	4	0	446	16	1	2.15	....	....	....	....	....	....	....
	Idaho Steelheads	ECHL	35	22	7	4	2028	77	*4	*2.28	8	6	2	492	13	1	1.59
2010-11	**Dallas**	**NHL**	**1**	**0**	**0**	**0**	**10**	**0**	**0**	**0.00**	....	....	....	....	....	....	....
	Texas Stars	AHL	55	28	19	5	3191	117	6	2.20	6	2	4	394	15	0	2.29
2011-12	**Dallas**	**NHL**	**18**	**8**	**5**	**1**	**933**	**43**	**1**	**2.77**	....	....	....	....	....	....	....
	Texas Stars	AHL	15	7	6	1	844	44	2	3.13	....	....	....	....	....	....	....
2012-13	Texas Stars	AHL	6	5	1	0	363	14	0	2.31	....	....	....	....	....	....	....
	Dallas	**NHL**	**13**	**6**	**5**	**0**	**609**	**33**	**0**	**3.25**	....	....	....	....	....	....	....
2013-14	**Edmonton**	**NHL**	**3**	**0**	**2**	**1**	**139**	**7**	**0**	**3.02**	....	....	....	....	....	....	....
	Oklahoma City	AHL	*52	26	19	6	3074	153	2	2.99	3	0	3	200	9	0	2.70
2014-15	**Edmonton**	**NHL**	**7**	**3**	**2**	**0**	**317**	**15**	**1**	**2.84**	....	....	....	....	....	....	....
	Oklahoma City	AHL	23	14	5	3	1338	53	3	2.38	9	5	4	581	15	0	1.55
2015-16	**Vancouver**	**NHL**	**1**	**1**	**0**	**0**	**60**	**3**	**0**	**3.00**	....	....	....	....	....	....	....
	Utica Comets	AHL	35	17	12	5	2010	92	1	2.75	3	0	2	106	7	0	3.96
2016-17	**Vancouver**	**NHL**	**5**	**2**	**3**	**0**	**295**	**13**	**0**	**2.64**	....	....	....	....	....	....	....
	Utica Comets	AHL	27	13	11	3	1584	70	1	2.65	....	....	....	....	....	....	....
	NHL Totals		**48**	**20**	**17**	**2**	**2363**	**114**	**2**	**2.89**	....	....	....	....	....	....	....

WCHA All-Rookie Team (2008) • WCHA First All-Star Team (2008) • WCHA Rookie of the Year (2008) • WCHA Player of the Year (2008) • NCAA West First All-American Team (2008) • NCAA Rookie of the Year (2008)

Signed as a free agent by **Edmonton**, July 6, 2013. Signed as a free agent by **Vancouver**, July 1, 2015.

BEDNARD, Ryan (BEHD-nahrd, RIGH-uhn) FLA

Goaltender. Catches left. 6'5", 200 lbs. Born, Macomb, MI, March 31, 1997.
(Florida's 8th pick, 206th overall, in 2015 NHL Draft).

			Regular Season								Playoffs						
Season	Club	League	GP	W	L	O/T	Mins	GA	SO	Avg	GP	W	L	Mins	GA	SO	Avg
2013-14	Det. Vic. Honda	T1EHL	18	12	6	0	933	28	4	1.62	....	....	....	....	....	....	....
2014-15	Johnstown	NAHL	37	16	16	5	2184	97	1	2.66	....	....	....	....	....	....	....
	Youngstown	USHL	1	0	1	0	59	4	0	4.08	....	....	....	....	....	....	....
2015-16	Youngstown	USHL	39	22	8	5	2168	86	2	2.38	....	....	....	....	....	....	....
2016-17	Bowling Green	WCHA	7	4	3	0	378	17	1	2.70	....	....	....	....	....	....	....

BERDIN, Mikhail (BAIR-dihn, mih-KIGH-ehl) WPG

Goaltender. Catches left. 6'2", 163 lbs. Born, Ufa, Russia, March 1, 1998.
(Winnipeg's 6th pick, 157th overall, in 2016 NHL Draft).

			Regular Season								Playoffs						
Season	Club	League	GP	W	L	O/T	Mins	GA	SO	Avg	GP	W	L	Mins	GA	SO	Avg
2014-15	Cherepovets Jr.	Russia-Jr.	13	3	5	0	545	30	0	3.30	....	....	....	....	....	....	....
2015-16	Russia U18	Russia-Jr.	22	12	6	0	1188	41	4	2.07	....	....	....	....	....	....	....
2016-17	Sioux Falls	USHL	31	14	12	3	1781	81	2	2.73	....	....	....	....	....	....	....

BERNIER, Jonathan (BUHRN-yay, JAWN-ah-thuhn) COL

Goaltender. Catches left. 6', 184 lbs. Born, Laval, QC, August 7, 1988.
(Los Angeles' 1st pick, 11th overall, in 2006 NHL Draft).

			Regular Season								Playoffs						
Season	Club	League	GP	W	L	O/T	Mins	GA	SO	Avg	GP	W	L	Mins	GA	SO	Avg
2003-04	Laval Regents	QAAA	27	16	4	0	1329	62	2	2.80	3	1	2	180	5	0	1.67
2004-05	Lewiston	QMJHL	23	7	12	3	1353	67	0	2.97	1	0	0	20	0	0	0.00
2005-06	Lewiston	QMJHL	54	27	26	0	3241	146	2	2.70	6	2	4	359	17	1	2.84
2006-07	Lewiston	QMJHL	37	26	10	0	2186	94	2	2.58	17	*16	1	1025	40	1	2.34
2007-08	**Los Angeles**	**NHL**	**4**	**1**	**3**	**0**	**238**	**16**	**0**	**4.03**	....	....	....	....	....	....	....
	Lewiston	QMJHL	34	18	15	0	2024	92	0	2.73	6	2	4	348	17	0	2.93
	Manchester	AHL	3	1	1	1	184	5	0	1.63	3	0	3	195	9	0	2.76
2008-09	Manchester	AHL	54	23	24	4	3101	124	5	2.40	....	....	....	....	....	....	....
2009-10	**Los Angeles**	**NHL**	**3**	**3**	**0**	**0**	**185**	**4**	**1**	**1.30**	....	....	....	....	....	....	....
	Manchester	AHL	58	30	21	6	3424	116	*9	2.03	16	10	6	996	30	*3	*1.81
2010-11	**Los Angeles**	**NHL**	**25**	**11**	**8**	**3**	**1378**	**57**	**3**	**2.48**	....	....	....	....	....	....	....
2011-12 ♦	**Los Angeles**	**NHL**	**16**	**5**	**6**	**2**	**890**	**35**	**1**	**2.36**	....	....	....	....	....	....	....
2012-13	Heilbronner Falken	German-2	13	6	7	0	793	34	1	2.57	....	....	....	....	....	....	....
	Los Angeles	**NHL**	**14**	**9**	**3**	**1**	**768**	**24**	**1**	**1.88**	**1**	**0**	**0**	**30**	**0**	**0**	**0.00**
2013-14	**Toronto**	**NHL**	**55**	**26**	**19**	**7**	**3084**	**138**	**1**	**2.68**	....	....	....	....	....	....	....
2014-15	**Toronto**	**NHL**	**58**	**21**	**28**	**7**	**3177**	**152**	**2**	**2.87**	....	....	....	....	....	....	....
2015-16	**Toronto**	**NHL**	**38**	**12**	**21**	**3**	**2147**	**103**	**3**	**2.88**	....	....	....	....	....	....	....
	Toronto Marlies	AHL	4	3	0	1	240	5	3	1.25	....	....	....	....	....	....	....
2016-17	**Anaheim**	**NHL**	**39**	**21**	**7**	**4**	**1993**	**83**	**2**	**2.50**	**4**	**1**	**2**	**183**	**10**	**0**	**3.28**
	NHL Totals		**252**	**109**	**95**	**27**	**13860**	**612**	**14**	**2.65**	**5**	**1**	**2**	**213**	**10**	**0**	**2.82**

QMJHL Second All-Star Team (2007) • Canadian Major Junior Second All-Star Team (2007) • AHL First All-Star Team (2010) • Aldege "Baz" Bastien Award (AHL – Outstanding Goaltender) (2010)

Signed as a free agent by **Heilbronner** (German-2), October 10, 2012. Traded to **Toronto** by **Los Angeles** for Ben Scrivens, Matt Frattin and Toronto's 2nd round pick (later traded to Columbus, later traded back to Toronto – Toronto selected Travis Dermott) in 2015 NHL Draft, June 23, 2013. Traded to **Anaheim** by **Toronto** for future considerations (conditions not met), July 8, 2016. Signed as a free agent by **Colorado**, July 1, 2017.

BERRA, Reto (BAIR-uh, REH-toh) ANA

Goaltender. Catches left. 6'4", 210 lbs. Born, Bulach, Switz., January 3, 1987.
(St. Louis' 6th pick, 106th overall, in 2006 NHL Draft).

			Regular Season								Playoffs						
Season	Club	League	GP	W	L	O/T	Mins	GA	SO	Avg	GP	W	L	Mins	GA	SO	Avg
2004-05	GCK Zurich Jr.	Swiss-Jr.	22	....	....	....	....	....	....	....	....	....	....	....	....	....	....
	GCK Lions Zurich	Swiss-2	3	....	....	....	180	12	0	4.00	....	....	....	....	....	....	....
	EHC Dubendorf	Swiss-3					STATISTICS NOT AVAILABLE										
2005-06	GCK Zurich Jr.	Swiss-Jr.	23	....	....	....	....	....	....	....	....	....	....	....	....	....	....
	GCK Lions Zurich	Swiss-2	15	....	....	....	835	51	1	3.56	....	....	....	....	....	....	....
	ZSC Lions Zurich	Swiss	2	0	1	0	90	6	0	3.99	....	....	....	....	....	....	....
2006-07	Switzerland U20	Swiss-2	3	0	3	0	179	13	0	4.69	....	....	....	....	....	....	....
	GCK Lions Zurich	Swiss-2	6	4	2	0	359	18	0	3.01	....	....	....	....	....	....	....
	ZSC Lions Zurich	Swiss	2	1	0	0	78	4	0	3.08	4	0	3	188	9	0	2.87
2007-08	HC Davos	Swiss	16	9	7	0	966	44	0	2.73	....	....	....	....	....	....	....
2008-09	EV Zug	Swiss	6	1	5	0	368	17	0	2.77	....	....	....	....	....	....	....
	SCL Tigers Langnau	Swiss	2	1	1	0	120	9	0	4.50	....	....	....	....	....	....	....
	HC Davos	Swiss	8	3	4	0	445	20	0	2.70	4	3	1	216	5	0	1.39
2009-10	EHC Biel-Bienne	Swiss	40	16	20	0	2319	130	3	3.36	10	3	7	582	33	0	3.40
	EHC Biel-Bienne	Swiss-Q	....	....	....	....	....	....	....	....	7	4	3	419	20	0	2.86
2010-11	EHC Biel-Bienne	Swiss	41	17	24	0	2452	122	3	2.99	....	....	....	....	....	....	....
2011-12	EHC Biel-Bienne	Swiss	49	23	26	0	2865	117	7	2.45	5	1	4	302	18	0	3.57
2012-13	EHC Biel-Bienne	Swiss	49	24	25	0	*2973	149	3	3.01	7	3	4	455	24	0	3.17
2013-14	**Calgary**	**NHL**	**29**	**9**	**17**	**2**	**1648**	**81**	**0**	**2.95**	....	....	....	....	....	....	....
	Abbotsford Heat	AHL	9	4	3	1	473	21	0	2.66	....	....	....	....	....	....	....
	Switzerland	Olympics	1	0	1	0	59	1	0	1.02	....	....	....	....	....	....	....
	Colorado	**NHL**	**2**	**0**	**1**	**1**	**72**	**7**	**0**	**5.83**	....	....	....	....	....	....	....
2014-15	**Colorado**	**NHL**	**19**	**5**	**4**	**1**	**748**	**33**	**1**	**2.65**	....	....	....	....	....	....	....
	Lake Erie Monsters	AHL	5	3	1	1	303	13	0	2.57	....	....	....	....	....	....	....
2015-16	**Colorado**	**NHL**	**14**	**5**	**8**	**0**	**721**	**29**	**2**	**2.41**	....	....	....	....	....	....	....
	San Antonio	AHL	16	7	7	0	884	50	0	3.39	....	....	....	....	....	....	....
2016-17	**Florida**	**NHL**	**7**	**0**	**5**	**0**	**313**	**18**	**0**	**3.45**	....	....	....	....	....	....	....
	Springfield	AHL	31	12	14	3	1758	74	3	2.53	....	....	....	....	....	....	....
	NHL Totals		**71**	**19**	**35**	**4**	**3502**	**168**	**3**	**2.88**	....	....	....	....	....	....	....

Traded to **Calgary** by **St. Louis** with Mark Cundari and St. Louis' 1st round pick (Emile Poirier) in 2013 NHL Draft for Jay Bouwmeester, April 1, 2013. Traded to **Colorado** by **Calgary** for Colorado's 2nd round pick (Hunter Smith) in 2014 NHL Draft, March 5, 2014. Traded to **Florida** by **Colorado** for Rocco Grimaldi, June 23, 2016. Signed as a free agent by **Anaheim**, July 5, 2017.

BERUBE, Jean-Francois (beh-ROO-bay, ZHAWN-fran-SWUH) CHI

Goaltender. Catches left. 6'1", 177 lbs. Born, Repentigny, QC, July 13, 1991.
(Los Angeles' 4th pick, 95th overall, in 2009 NHL Draft).

			Regular Season								Playoffs						
Season	Club	League	GP	W	L	O/T	Mins	GA	SO	Avg	GP	W	L	Mins	GA	SO	Avg
2007-08	Laurentides	QAAA	10	0	6	1	511	35	0	4.11	....	....	....	....	....	....	....
	Lachute Stars	QueAA					STATISTICS NOT AVAILABLE										
2008-09	Montreal	QMJHL	20	6	9	0	1059	51	1	2.89	1	0	0	20	1	0	3.00
2009-10	Montreal	QMJHL	45	17	23	0	2394	121	1	3.03	7	3	4	449	18	0	2.40
	Manchester	AHL	3	2	1	0	180	11	0	3.67	....	....	....	....	....	....	....
2010-11	Montreal	QMJHL	50	32	7	8	2935	127	3	2.60	10	6	4	623	29	*2	2.79
2011-12	Ontario Reign	ECHL	37	17	13	4	2091	100	4	2.87	4	1	2	206	11	0	3.20
2012-13	Ontario Reign	ECHL	24	15	6	2	1418	53	1	2.24	10	6	4	608	21	1	2.07
	Manchester	AHL	2	0	2	0	97	7	0	4.32	....	....	....	....	....	....	....
2013-14	Manchester	AHL	48	28	17	2	2790	110	3	2.37	4	1	3	252	7	1	1.67
2014-15	Manchester	AHL	52	37	9	4	3025	110	2	2.18	17	13	3	1019	39	0	2.30
2015-16	**NY Islanders**	**NHL**	**7**	**3**	**2**	**1**	**399**	**18**	**0**	**2.71**	**1**	**0**	**0**	**5**	**0**	**0**	**0.00**
	Bridgeport	AHL	5	4	1	0	287	6	1	1.25	....	....	....	....	....	....	....
2016-17	**NY Islanders**	**NHL**	**14**	**3**	**2**	**2**	**527**	**30**	**0**	**3.42**	....	....	....	....	....	....	....
	NHL Totals		**21**	**6**	**4**	**3**	**926**	**48**	**0**	**3.11**	**1**	**0**	**0**	**5**	**0**	**0**	**0.00**

Claimed on waivers by **NY Islanders** from **Los Angeles**, October 6, 2015.. Claimed by **Vegas** from **NY Islanders** in Expansion Draft, June 21, 2017. Signed as a free agent by **Chicago**, July 1, 2017.

BIBEAU, Antoine (Bee-BOH, an-TWAHN) S.J.

Goaltender. Catches left. 6'3", 205 lbs. Born, Victoriaville, QC, May 1, 1994.
(Toronto's 4th pick, 172nd overall, in 2013 NHL Draft).

			Regular Season								Playoffs						
Season	Club	League	GP	W	L	O/T	Mins	GA	SO	Avg	GP	W	L	Mins	GA	SO	Avg
2009-10	Trois-Rivieres	QAAA	22	8	4	3	1023	59	0	3.46	2	0	1	79	4	0	3.05
2010-11	Trois-Rivieres	QAAA	29	16	8	2	1521	83	0	3.27	5	2	3	266	21	0	4.74
	Lewiston	QMJHL	3	2	0	0	144	5	0	2.10	....	....	....	....	....	....	....
2011-12	P.E.I. Rocket	QMJHL	29	7	9	1	1183	88	0	4.46	....	....	....	....	....	....	....
2012-13	P.E.I. Rocket	QMJHL	46	28	11	3	2521	118	*5	2.81	6	2	4	374	21	0	3.37
2013-14	Charlottetown	QMJHL	26	8	11	5	1424	78	1	3.29	....	....	....	....	....	....	....
	Val-d'Or Foreurs	QMJHL	22	13	7	1	1267	64	1	3.03	*24	*16	8	*1476	69	1	2.80
2014-15	Toronto Marlies	AHL	31	15	10	5	1809	81	4	2.69	1	0	1	57	3	0	3.13
2015-16	Toronto Marlies	AHL	40	28	9	1	2354	106	3	2.70	12	6	5	682	31	1	2.73
2016-17	**Toronto**	**NHL**	**2**	**1**	**1**	**0**	**121**	**4**	**0**	**1.98**	....	....	....	....	....	....	....
	Toronto Marlies	AHL	32	13	14	5	1892	97	3	3.08	1	0	1	37	2	0	3.23
	NHL Totals		**2**	**1**	**1**	**0**	**121**	**4**	**0**	**1.98**	....	....	....	....	....	....	....

Signed as a free agent by **San Jose**, July 1, 2017.

BINNINGTON, Jordan (BIHN-ihng-tuhn, JOHR-duhn) ST.L.

Goaltender. Catches left. 6'1", 167 lbs. Born, Richmond Hill, ON, July 11, 1993.
(St. Louis' 4th pick, 88th overall, in 2011 NHL Draft).

			Regular Season								Playoffs						
Season	Club	League	GP	W	L	O/T	Mins	GA	SO	Avg	GP	W	L	Mins	GA	SO	Avg
2008-09	Vaughan Kings	GTHL	....	34	15	....	....	....	....	2.18	....	....	....	....	....	....	....
	Dixie Beehives	ON-Jr.A	1	0	1	0	59	3	0	3.04	....	....	....	....	....	....	....

2009-10	Owen Sound	OHL	22	6	10	2	1068	78	0	4.38	....	....	....	....	....	....	....
2010-11	Owen Sound	OHL	46	27	12	5	2596	132	1	3.05	7	4	2	355	19	0	3.21
2011-12	Owen Sound	OHL	39	21	17	1	2304	115	1	2.99	2	0	2	120	10	0	5.00
	Peoria Rivermen	AHL	1	0	1	0	60	3	0	3.02	....	....	....	....	....	....	....
2012-13	Owen Sound	OHL	50	32	12	6	3011	109	*7	2.17	12	6	6	705	33	0	2.81
2013-14	Kalamazoo Wings	ECHL	40	23	13	3	2398	94	1	2.35	3	1	2	223	7	0	1.89
	Chicago Wolves	AHL	1	1	0	0	65	3	0	2.78	....	....	....	....	....	....	....
2014-15	Chicago Wolves	AHL	45	25	15	1	2555	100	3	2.35	5	2	3	333	12	0	2.16
2015-16	**St. Louis**	**NHL**	**1**	**0**	**0**	**0**	**13**	**1**	**0**	**4.62**	....	....	....	....	....	....	....
	Chicago Wolves	AHL	41	17	18	5	2340	111	1	2.85	....	....	....	....	....	....	....
2016-17	Chicago Wolves	AHL	32	16	7	8	1879	85	2	2.71	2	0	0	65	2	0	1.86
	NHL Totals		**1**	**0**	**0**	**0**	**13**	**1**	**0**	**4.62**	....	....	....	....	....	....	....

OHL First All-Star Team (2013)

BISHOP, Ben (BIH-shuhp, BEHN) DAL

Goaltender. Catches left. 6'7", 216 lbs. Born, Denver, CO, November 21, 1986.
(St. Louis' 3rd pick, 85th overall, in 2005 NHL Draft).

			Regular Season								Playoffs						
Season	**Club**	**League**	**GP**	**W**	**L**	**O/T**	**Mins**	**GA**	**SO**	**Avg**	**GP**	**W**	**L**	**Mins**	**GA**	**SO**	**Avg**
2003-04	St.L. AAA Blues	MAHL	11	8	1	2	660	19	1	1.73	....	....	....	....	....	....	....
	St.L. AAA Blues	Other	26	15	7	4	1480	62	3	2.51	....	....	....	....	....	....	....
2004-05	Texas Tornado	NAHL	45	*35	8	0	2577	83	5	1.93	*11	*9	2	*660	30	0	2.73
2005-06	University of Maine	H-East	31	21	8	2	1788	68	0	2.28	....	....	....	....	....	....	....
2006-07	University of Maine	H-East	34	21	9	2	1907	68	3	2.14	....	....	....	....	....	....	....
2007-08	University of Maine	H-East	34	13	18	3	1972	80	2	2.43	....	....	....	....	....	....	....
	Peoria Rivermen	AHL	5	2	2	1	302	12	0	2.38	....	....	....	....	....	....	....
2008-09	**St. Louis**	**NHL**	**6**	**1**	**1**	**1**	**245**	**12**	**0**	**2.94**	....	....	....	....	....	....	....
	Peoria Rivermen	AHL	33	15	16	1	1898	89	1	2.81	....	....	....	....	....	....	....
2009-10	Peoria Rivermen	AHL	48	23	18	4	2793	129	0	2.77	....	....	....	....	....	....	....
2010-11	**St. Louis**	**NHL**	**7**	**3**	**4**	**0**	**369**	**17**	**1**	**2.76**	....	....	....	....	....	....	....
	Peoria Rivermen	AHL	35	17	14	2	2043	87	2	2.55	1	0	1	59	2	0	2.04
2011-12	Peoria Rivermen	AHL	38	24	14	0	2258	85	*6	2.26	....	....	....	....	....	....	....
	Ottawa	**NHL**	**10**	**3**	**3**	**2**	**532**	**22**	**0**	**2.48**	....	....	....	....	....	....	....
	Binghamton	AHL	3	2	1	0	179	7	0	2.35	....	....	....	....	....	....	....
2012-13	Binghamton	AHL	13	8	3	2	787	34	0	2.59	....	....	....	....	....	....	....
	Ottawa	**NHL**	**13**	**8**	**5**	**0**	**758**	**31**	**1**	**2.45**	....	....	....	....	....	....	....
	Tampa Bay	**NHL**	**9**	**3**	**4**	**1**	**502**	**25**	**1**	**2.99**	....	....	....	....	....	....	....
2013-14	**Tampa Bay**	**NHL**	**63**	**37**	**14**	**7**	**3586**	**133**	**5**	**2.23**	....	....	....	....	....	....	....
2014-15	**Tampa Bay**	**NHL**	**62**	**40**	**13**	**5**	**3519**	**136**	**4**	**2.32**	**25**	**13**	**11**	**1459**	**53**	**3**	**2.18**
2015-16	**Tampa Bay**	**NHL**	**61**	**35**	**21**	**4**	**3585**	**123**	**6**	***2.06**	**11**	**8**	**2**	**582**	**18**	**2**	**1.86**
2016-17	**Tampa Bay**	**NHL**	**32**	**16**	**12**	**3**	**1813**	**77**	**1**	**2.55**	....	....	....	....	....	....	....
	Los Angeles	**NHL**	**7**	**2**	**3**	**2**	**410**	**17**	**0**	**2.49**	....	....	....	....	....	....	....
	NHL Totals		**270**	**148**	**80**	**25**	**15319**	**593**	**19**	**2.32**	**36**	**21**	**13**	**2041**	**71**	**5**	**2.09**

Hockey East All-Rookie Team (2006) • Hockey East Second All-Star Team (2008) • AHL Second All-Star Team (2012) • NHL Second All-Star Team (2016)

Played in NHL All-Star Game (2016)

Traded to **Ottawa** by **St. Louis** for Ottawa's 2nd round pick (Thomas Vannelli) in 2013 NHL Draft, February 26. 2012. Traded to **Tampa Bay** by **Ottawa** for Cory Conacher and Philadelphia's 4th round pick (previously acquired, Ottawa selected Tobias Lindberg) in 2013 NHL Draft, April 3, 2013. Traded to **Los Angeles** by **Tampa Bay** with Tampa Bay's 5th round pick (Drake Rymsha) in 2017 NHL Draft for Peter Budaj, Erik Cernak and Los Angeles' 7th round pick (later traded to Philadelphia – Philadelphia selected Wyatt Kalynuk) in 2017 NHL Draft, February 28, 2017. Traded to **Dallas** by **Los Angeles** for Montreal's 4th round pick (previously acquired, Los Angeles selected Markus Phillips) in 2017 NHL Draft, May 9, 2017.

BLACKWOOD, Mackenzie (BLAK-wud, muh-KEHN-zee) N.J.

Goaltender. Catches left. 6'4", 225 lbs. Born, Thunder Bay, ON, December 9, 1996.
(New Jersey's 2nd pick, 42nd overall, in 2015 NHL Draft).

			Regular Season								Playoffs						
Season	**Club**	**League**	**GP**	**W**	**L**	**O/T**	**Mins**	**GA**	**SO**	**Avg**	**GP**	**W**	**L**	**Mins**	**GA**	**SO**	**Avg**
2011-12	Thunder Bay Kings	Minor-ON	38	15	13	2	1766	121	1	3.08	....	....	....	....	....	....	....
2012-13	Elmira Sugar Kings	ON-Jr.B	24	10	8	2	1309	74	0	3.39	....	....	....	....	....	....	....
2013-14	Barrie Colts	OHL	45	23	15	2	2497	124	1	2.98	10	5	4	552	24	1	2.61
2014-15	Barrie Colts	OHL	51	33	14	2	2953	152	2	3.09	9	5	4	562	27	0	2.88
2015-16	Barrie Colts	OHL	43	28	13	0	2452	111	3	2.72	13	6	5	796	36	1	2.71
2016-17	Albany Devils	AHL	36	17	14	4	2048	87	3	2.55	4	1	3	254	9	1	2.13

OHL All-Rookie Team (2014) • OHL First All-Star Team (2016)

BOBROVSKY, Sergei (bawb-RAWF-skee, SAIR-gay) CBJ

Goaltender. Catches left. 6'2", 182 lbs. Born, Novokuznetsk, USSR, September 20, 1988.

			Regular Season								Playoffs						
Season	**Club**	**League**	**GP**	**W**	**L**	**O/T**	**Mins**	**GA**	**SO**	**Avg**	**GP**	**W**	**L**	**Mins**	**GA**	**SO**	**Avg**
2006-07	Novokuznetsk	Russia	8	....	....	....	280	13	0	2.78	....	....	....	....	....	....	....
2007-08	Novokuznetsk	Russia	24	....	....	....	1153	57	1	2.97	....	....	....	....	....	....	....
2008-09	Novokuznetsk	KHL	32	....	....	....	1636	69	1	2.53	....	....	....	....	....	....	....
2009-10	Novokuznetsk	KHL	35	....	....	....	1964	89	1	2.72	....	....	....	....	....	....	....
2010-11	**Philadelphia**	**NHL**	**54**	**28**	**13**	**8**	**3017**	**130**	**0**	**2.59**	**6**	**0**	**2**	**186**	**10**	**0**	**3.23**
2011-12	**Philadelphia**	**NHL**	**29**	**14**	**10**	**2**	**1550**	**78**	**0**	**3.02**	**1**	**0**	**0**	**37**	**5**	**0**	**8.11**
2012-13	SKA St. Petersburg	KHL	24	18	3	0	1420	46	4	1.94	....	....	....	....	....	....	....
	Columbus	**NHL**	**38**	**21**	**11**	**6**	**2219**	**74**	**4**	**2.00**	....	....	....	....	....	....	....
2013-14	**Columbus**	**NHL**	**58**	**32**	**20**	**5**	**3299**	**131**	**5**	**2.38**	**6**	**2**	**4**	**378**	**20**	**0**	**3.17**
	Russia	Olympics	3	....	....	....	157	3	....	1.15	....	....	....	....	....	....	....
2014-15	**Columbus**	**NHL**	**51**	**30**	**17**	**3**	**2994**	**134**	**2**	**2.69**	....	....	....	....	....	....	....
2015-16	**Columbus**	**NHL**	**37**	**15**	**19**	**1**	**2116**	**97**	**1**	**2.75**	....	....	....	....	....	....	....
2016-17	**Columbus**	**NHL**	**63**	**41**	**17**	**5**	**3707**	**127**	**7**	***2.06**	**5**	**1**	**4**	**309**	**20**	**0**	**3.88**
	NHL Totals		**330**	**181**	**107**	**30**	**18902**	**771**	**19**	**2.45**	**18**	**3**	**10**	**910**	**55**	**0**	**3.63**

NHL First All-Star Team (2013, 2017) • Vezina Trophy (2013, 2017)

Played in NHL All-Star Game (2017)

Signed as a free agent by **Philadelphia**, May 6, 2010. Traded to **Columbus** by **Philadelphia** for Ottawa's 2nd round pick (previously acquired, Philadelphia selected Anthony Stolarz) in 2012 NHL Draft, Vancouver's 4th round pick (previously acquired, Philadelphia selected Taylor Leier) in 2012 NHL Draft and Phoenix's 4th round pick (previously acquired, later traded to Los Angeles – Los Angeles selected Justin Auger) in 2013 NHL Draft, June 22, 2012. Signed as a free agent by **St. Petersburg** (KHL), September 21, 2012.

BOOTH, Callum (BOOTH, KAL-uhm) CAR

Goaltender. Catches left. 6'3", 191 lbs. Born, Montreal, QC, May 21, 1997.
(Carolina's 3rd pick, 93rd overall, in 2015 NHL Draft).

			Regular Season								Playoffs						
Season	**Club**	**League**	**GP**	**W**	**L**	**O/T**	**Mins**	**GA**	**SO**	**Avg**	**GP**	**W**	**L**	**Mins**	**GA**	**SO**	**Avg**
2012-13	Salisbury School	High-CT	....	....	....	....	1200	41	....	2.08	....	....	....	....	....	....	....
2013-14	Quebec Remparts	QMJHL	25	11	5	3	1120	50	1	2.68	1	0	1	59	5	0	5.08
2014-15	Quebec Remparts	QMJHL	41	23	13	2	2280	116	2	3.05	4	1	1	169	7	1	2.49
2015-16	Quebec Remparts	QMJHL	39	16	15	5	2192	115	3	3.15	....	....	....	....	....	....	....
2016-17	Quebec Remparts	QMJHL	21	*13	6	2	1212	58	1	2.87	....	....	....	....	....	....	....
	Saint John	QMJHL	26	*18	6	1	1456	57	3	2.35	*18	*16	2	*1115	31	*4	*1.67

QMJHL All-Rookie Team (2014)

BOW, Landon (BOH, LAN-duhn) DAL

Goaltender. Catches left. 6'5", 208 lbs. Born, St. Albert, AB, August 24, 1995.

			Regular Season								Playoffs						
Season	**Club**	**League**	**GP**	**W**	**L**	**O/T**	**Mins**	**GA**	**SO**	**Avg**	**GP**	**W**	**L**	**Mins**	**GA**	**SO**	**Avg**
2010-11	St. Albert Flyers	AMMHL	....	17	3	1	1241	46	1	2.22	....	....	....	....	....	....	....
2011-12	St. Albert Raiders	AMHL	....	9	3	2	801	33	1	2.47	....	0	0	13	2	0	9.23
2012-13	Swift Current	WHL	14	5	4	1	642	33	1	3.09	....	....	....	....	....	....	....
2013-14	Swift Current	WHL	27	13	5	3	1405	73	0	3.12	....	....	....	....	....	....	....
2014-15	Swift Current	WHL	66	31	27	5	3614	189	7	3.14	4	0	4	244	15	0	3.69
2015-16	Swift Current	WHL	30	9	14	4	1593	82	*2	3.09	....	....	....	....	....	....	....
	Seattle	WHL	23	16	6	0	1293	38	*5	1.76	18	13	5	1131	37	*2	*1.96
2016-17	Texas Stars	AHL	16	7	7	0	870	46	0	3.17	....	....	....	....	....	....	....
	Idaho Steelheads	ECHL	27	19	6	2	1556	54	3	*2.08	4	1	3	241	14	0	3.49

Signed as a free agent by **Texas** (AHL), June 1, 2016. Signed as a free agent by **Dallas**, March 10, 2017.

BOYLE, Kevin (BOIL, KEH-vuhn) ANA

Goaltender. Catches left. 6'2", 200 lbs. Born, Manalapan, NJ, May 30, 1992.

			Regular Season								Playoffs						
Season	**Club**	**League**	**GP**	**W**	**L**	**O/T**	**Mins**	**GA**	**SO**	**Avg**	**GP**	**W**	**L**	**Mins**	**GA**	**SO**	**Avg**
2007-08	N.J. Rockets	MtJHL	19	....	....	....	919	58	1	3.78	2	1	1	133	7	0	3.15
2008-09	N.J. Rockets	MtJHL	30	....	....	....	1618	86	1	3.30	3	1	2	190	8	0	2.53
	N.J. Rockets	AtJHL	1	1	0	0	60	2	0	2.00	....	....	....	....	....	....	....
	Tri-City Storm	USHL	1	0	1	0	60	4	0	4.00	....	....	....	....	....	....	....
2009-10	N.J. Rockets	AtJHL	19	....	....	....	1192	57	2	2.71	....	....	....	....	....	....	....
2010-11	Westside Warriors	BCHL	39	20	15	1	2205	110	1	2.99	12	6	6	700	35	1	3.00
2011-12	Massachusetts	H-East	21	8	7	4	1141	57	0	3.00	....	....	....	....	....	....	....
2012-13	Massachusetts	H-East	20	8	10	2	1185	54	1	2.73	....	....	....	....	....	....	....
2013-14							DID NOT PLAY – TRANSFERRED COLLEGES										
2014-15	U. Mass Lowell	H-East	34	18	9	6	1962	79	3	2.42	....	....	....	....	....	....	....
2015-16	U. Mass Lowell	H-East	*39	24	10	5	*2364	72	7	1.83	....	....	....	....	....	....	....
2016-17	San Diego Gulls	AHL	19	10	5	4	1111	42	1	2.27	....	....	....	....	....	....	....
	Utah Grizzlies	ECHL	16	9	6	1	967	44	0	2.73	5	1	4	289	16	0	3.32

Hockey East Second All-Star Team (2016)

Signed as a free agent by **Anaheim**, March 30, 2016.

BRITTAIN, Sam (brih-TAYN, SAM)

Goaltender. Catches left. 6'3", 226 lbs. Born, Calgary, AB, May 10, 1992.
(Florida's 8th pick, 92nd overall, in 2010 NHL Draft).

			Regular Season								Playoffs						
Season	**Club**	**League**	**GP**	**W**	**L**	**O/T**	**Mins**	**GA**	**SO**	**Avg**	**GP**	**W**	**L**	**Mins**	**GA**	**SO**	**Avg**
2008-09	Calgary Buffaloes	AMHL	26	14	9	3	1542	67	....	2.61	15	11	4	901	45	....	3.00
	Canmore Eagles	AJHL	3	1	2	0	179	9	0	3.02	....	....	....	....	....	....	....
2009-10	Canmore Eagles	AJHL	52	23	19	8	3065	167	2	3.27	9	5	4	559	28	0	3.01
2010-11	U. of Denver	WCHA	33	19	9	5	1998	76	1	2.28	....	....	....	....	....	....	....
2011-12	U. of Denver	WCHA	12	8	4	0	736	29	1	2.36	....	....	....	....	....	....	....
2012-13	U. of Denver	WCHA	13	5	7	0	752	37	0	2.95	....	....	....	....	....	....	....
2013-14	U. of Denver	NCHC	*39	19	14	6	*2348	87	*5	2.22	....	....	....	....	....	....	....
2014-15	San Antonio	AHL	7	4	2	1	374	11	1	1.76	....	....	....	....	....	....	....
	Cincinnati	ECHL	27	14	11	1	1547	70	4	2.71	....	....	....	....	....	....	....
2015-16	Portland Pirates	AHL	25	8	10	3	1313	61	0	2.79	....	....	....	....	....	....	....
2016-17	Springfield	AHL	10	4	5	0	546	22	0	2.42	....	....	....	....	....	....	....
	Manchester	ECHL	36	20	9	5	2011	110	0	3.28	19	11	8	1132	44	1	2.33

WCHA All-Rookie Team (2011) • NCHC First All-Star Team (2014) • NCAA West First All-American Team (2014)

BROSSOIT, Laurent (BRAH-sah, LAWR-ehnt) EDM

Goaltender. Catches left. 6'3", 204 lbs. Born, Port Alberni, BC, March 23, 1993.
(Calgary's 5th pick, 164th overall, in 2011 NHL Draft).

			Regular Season								Playoffs						
Season	**Club**	**League**	**GP**	**W**	**L**	**O/T**	**Mins**	**GA**	**SO**	**Avg**	**GP**	**W**	**L**	**Mins**	**GA**	**SO**	**Avg**
2008-09	Valley West Hawks	BCMML					STATISTICS NOT AVAILABLE										
	Edmonton	WHL	1	0	0	0	37	5	0	8.11	....	....	....	....	....	....	....
2009-10	Cowichan Valley	BCHL	21	10	8	0	999	61	2	3.66	5	1	3	259	17	0	3.93
	Edmonton	WHL	2	0	1	0	86	4	0	2.79	....	....	....	....	....	....	....
2010-11	Edmonton	WHL	34	13	12	2	1664	92	2	3.32	2	0	2	117	7	0	3.59
2011-12	Edmonton	WHL	61	*42	13	5	3574	147	3	2.47	20	*16	4	1204	41	*2	*2.04
2012-13	Edmonton	WHL	49	33	8	6	2854	107	5	2.25	*22	14	8	*1322	40	*5	1.82
2013-14	Abbotsford Heat	AHL	2	0	1	0	94	9	0	5.72	....	....	....	....	....	....	....
	Alaska Aces	ECHL	3	*2	0	0	126	0	*2	*0.00	....	....	....	....	....	....	....
	Oklahoma City	AHL	8	2	5	0	416	25	0	3.60	....	....	....	....	....	....	....
	Bakersfield	ECHL	35	*24	9	2	2079	74	*6	*2.14	16	10	6	976	37	*3	2.27
2014-15	**Edmonton**	**NHL**	**1**	**0**	**1**	**0**	**60**	**2**	**0**	**2.00**	....	....	....	....	....	....	....
	Oklahoma City	AHL	53	25	22	4	3049	130	4	2.56	2	1	0	87	5	0	3.46
2015-16	**Edmonton**	**NHL**	**5**	**0**	**4**	**1**	**300**	**18**	**0**	**3.60**	....	....	....	....	....	....	....
	Bakersfield	AHL	31	18	9	3	1807	80	3	2.66	....	....	....	....	....	....	....
2016-17	**Edmonton**	**NHL**	**8**	**4**	**1**	**0**	**332**	**11**	**0**	**1.99**	**1**	**0**	**0**	**27**	**2**	**0**	**4.44**
	Bakersfield	AHL	21	9	8	3	1189	53	2	2.67	....	....	....	....	....	....	....
	NHL Totals		**14**	**4**	**6**	**1**	**692**	**31**	**0**	**2.69**	**1**	**0**	**0**	**27**	**2**	**0**	**4.44**

WHL East Second All-Star Team (2013)

Traded to **Edmonton** by **Calgary** with Roman Horak for Olivier Roy and Ladislav Smid, November 8, 2013.

BUDAJ, Peter (BOO-digh, PEE-tuhr) T.B.

Goaltender. Catches left. 6'1", 192 lbs. Born, Banska Bystrica, Czech., September 18, 1982.
(Colorado's 1st pick, 63rd overall, in 2001 NHL Draft).

			Regular Season								Playoffs						
Season	Club	League	GP	W	L	O/T	Mins	GA	SO	Avg	GP	W	L	Mins	GA	SO	Avg
99-2000	St. Michael's	OHL	34	6	18	1	1676	112	1	4.01	....	....	....	....	....	....	....
2000-01	St. Michael's	OHL	37	17	12	3	1996	95	3	2.86	11	6	4	621	26	1	2.51
2001-02	St. Michael's	OHL	42	26	9	5	2329	89	2	*2.29	12	5	6	621	34	*1	3.29
2002-03	Hershey Bears	AHL	28	10	10	2	1467	65	2	2.66	1	0	0	6	2	0	20.81
2003-04	Hershey Bears	AHL	46	17	20	6	2574	120	3	2.80	....	....	....	....	....	....	....
2004-05	Hershey Bears	AHL	59	29	25	2	3356	148	5	2.65	....	....	....	....	....	....	....
2005-06	Colorado	NHL	34	14	10	6	1803	86	2	2.86	....	....	....	....	....	....	....
	Slovakia	Olympics	3	2	1	0	179	6	0	2.01	....	....	....	....	....	....	....
2006-07	Colorado	NHL	57	31	16	6	3199	143	3	2.68	....	....	....	....	....	....	....
2007-08	Colorado	NHL	35	16	10	4	1912	82	0	2.57	3	0	0	108	6	0	3.33
2008-09	Colorado	NHL	56	20	29	5	3232	154	2	2.86	....	....	....	....	....	....	....
2009-10	Colorado	NHL	15	5	5	2	728	32	1	2.64	1	0	0	9	1	0	6.67
	Slovakia	Olympics	DID NOT PLAY – SPARE GOALTENDER														
2010-11	Colorado	NHL	45	15	21	4	2439	130	1	3.20	....	....	....	....	....	....	....
2011-12	Montreal	NHL	17	5	7	5	1037	44	0	2.55	....	....	....	....	....	....	....
2012-13	Montreal	NHL	13	8	1	1	656	25	1	2.29	2	0	2	63	7	0	6.67
2013-14	Montreal	NHL	24	10	8	3	1338	56	1	2.51	1	0	0	20	3	0	9.00
	Slovakia	Olympics	1	0	0	0	27	2	....	4.53	....	....	....	....	....	....	....
2014-15	St. John's IceCaps	AHL	19	0	9	6	913	54	0	3.55	....	....	....	....	....	....	....
2015-16	Los Angeles	NHL	1	1	0	0	62	4	0	3.87	....	....	....	....	....	....	....
	Ontario Reign	AHL	*60	*42	14	4	*3575	104	*9	*1.75	13	7	6	800	29	0	2.18
2016-17	Los Angeles	NHL	53	27	20	3	3029	107	7	2.12	....	....	....	....	....	....	....
	Tampa Bay	NHL	7	3	1	0	279	13	0	2.80	....	....	....	....	....	....	....
	NHL Totals		**357**	**155**	**128**	**39**	**19714**	**876**	**18**	**2.67**	**7**	**0**	**2**	**200**	**17**	**0**	**5.10**

OHL Second All-Star Team (2002) • AHL First All-Star Team (2016) • Harry "Hap" Holmes Memorial Award (AHL – fewest goals against) (2016) • Aldege "Baz" Bastien Award (AHL) – Outstanding Goaltender) (2016)

Signed as a free agent by **Montreal**, July 1, 2011. Traded to **Winnipeg** by **Montreal** with Patrick Holland for Eric Tangradi, October 5, 2014. Signed as a free agent by **Los Angeles**, October 9, 2015. Traded to **Tampa Bay** by **Los Angeles** with Erik Cernak and Los Angeles' 7th round pick (later traded to Philadelphia – Philadelphia selected Wyatt Kalynuk) in 2017 NHL Draft for Ben Bishop and Tampa Bay's 5th round pick (Drake Rymsha) in 2017 NHL Draft, February 26, 2017.

CAMPBELL, Jack (KAM-buhl, JAK) L.A.

Goaltender. Catches left. 6'3", 200 lbs. Born, Port Huron, MI, January 9, 1992.
(Dallas' 1st pick, 11th overall, in 2010 NHL Draft).

			Regular Season								Playoffs						
Season	Club	League	GP	W	L	O/T	Mins	GA	SO	Avg	GP	W	L	Mins	GA	SO	Avg
2007-08	Det. Honeybaked	MWEHL	12	8	2	2	630	24	2	2.06	....	....	....	....	....	....	....
	Det. Honeybaked	Minor-MI	25	20	4	1	....	....	....	....	....	....	....	....	....	....	....
2008-09	USAHNTDP	NAHL	21	14	6	1	1262	53	1	2.52	....	....	....	....	....	....	....
	USAHNTDP	U-17	7	6	0	1	394	7	3	1.07	....	....	....	....	....	....	....
	USAHNTDP	U-18	7	7	0	0	421	12	2	1.71	....	....	....	....	....	....	....
2009-10	USAHNTDP	USHL	11	6	3	1	569	21	1	2.21	....	....	....	....	....	....	....
	USAHNTDP	U-18	25	16	9	0	1469	54	3	2.21	....	....	....	....	....	....	....
2010-11	Windsor Spitfires	OHL	45	24	14	4	2447	155	0	3.80	18	9	9	1124	70	2	3.74
2011-12	Windsor Spitfires	OHL	12	6	3	2	729	38	1	3.13	....	....	....	....	....	....	....
	Sault Ste. Marie	OHL	34	15	12	5	1945	116	1	3.58	....	....	....	....	....	....	....
	Texas Stars	AHL	12	4	7	0	676	34	1	3.02	....	....	....	....	....	....	....
2012-13	Texas Stars	AHL	40	19	13	3	2108	93	2	2.65	....	....	....	....	....	....	....
2013-14	Dallas	NHL	1	0	1	0	60	6	0	6.00	....	....	....	....	....	....	....
	Texas Stars	AHL	16	12	2	2	966	24	4	1.49	4	2	1	237	10	0	2.54
2014-15	Texas Stars	AHL	35	14	14	5	1958	99	2	3.03	1	0	1	59	3	0	3.03
	Idaho Steelheads	ECHL	7	5	2	0	417	12	1	1.73	....	....	....	....	....	....	....
2015-16	Texas Stars	AHL	19	7	7	5	1035	63	0	3.65	3	1	2	148	11	0	4.45
	Idaho Steelheads	ECHL	20	14	5	1	1211	34	4	1.68	....	....	....	....	....	....	....
2016-17	Los Angeles	NHL	1	0	0	0	20	0	0	0.00	....	....	....	....	....	....	....
	Ontario Reign	AHL	52	*31	15	6	3072	129	5	2.52	5	2	2	282	8	0	*1.70
	NHL Totals		**2**	**0**	**1**	**0**	**80**	**6**	**0**	**4.50**	....	....	....	....	....	....	....

Traded to **Los Angeles** by **Dallas** for Nick Ebert, June 25, 2016.

CANNATA, Joe (ka-NA-tuh, JOH) COL

Goaltender. Catches left. 6'1", 200 lbs. Born, Wakefield, MA, January 2, 1990.
(Vancouver's 6th pick, 173rd overall, in 2009 NHL Draft).

			Regular Season								Playoffs						
Season	Club	League	GP	W	L	O/T	Mins	GA	SO	Avg	GP	W	L	Mins	GA	SO	Avg
2007-08	USAHNTDP	NAHL	5	3	1	1	307	12	0	2.35	....	....	....	....	....	....	....
	USAHNTDP	U-18	28	13	13	2	1474	64	1	2.61	....	....	....	....	....	....	....
2008-09	Merrimack College	H-East	23	7	11	4	1353	53	2	2.35	....	....	....	....	....	....	....
2009-10	Merrimack College	H-East	24	10	13	1	1362	69	2	3.04	....	....	....	....	....	....	....
2010-11	Merrimack College	H-East	*39	25	10	4	2252	93	1	2.48	....	....	....	....	....	....	....
2011-12	Merrimack College	H-East	36	17	12	7	2179	79	2	2.18	....	....	....	....	....	....	....
	Chicago Wolves	AHL	1	1	0	0	60	2	0	2.00	....	....	....	....	....	....	....
2012-13	Kalamazoo Wings	ECHL	7	3	4	0	419	23	0	3.29	....	....	....	....	....	....	....
	Chicago Wolves	AHL	14	6	6	0	747	33	0	2.65	....	....	....	....	....	....	....
2013-14	Utica Comets	AHL	28	11	12	1	1484	70	0	2.83	....	....	....	....	....	....	....
2014-15	Utica Comets	AHL	5	3	2	0	302	10	0	1.99	....	....	....	....	....	....	....
	Ontario Reign	ECHL	21	12	6	2	1249	42	1	2.02	9	4	4	515	20	2	2.33
2015-16	Utica Comets	AHL	40	20	13	6	2381	100	2	2.52	3	1	1	141	7	0	2.98
2016-17	Hershey Bears	AHL	22	11	5	4	1265	68	0	3.22	....	....	....	....	....	....	....
	South Carolina	ECHL	3	3	0	0	180	7	0	2.33	....	....	....	....	....	....	....
	San Antonio	AHL	6	2	3	0	316	19	0	3.60	....	....	....	....	....	....	....

Hockey East First All-Star Team (2012) • NCAA East Second All-American Team (2012)

Signed as a free agent by **Washington**, July 1, 2016. Traded to **Colorado** by **Washington** for Cody Corbett, March 1, 2017.

CARLSON, Adam (KAHRL-suhn, A-duhm) WSH

Goaltender. Catches . 6'3", 175 lbs. Born, Edina, MN, February 13, 1994.

			Regular Season								Playoffs						
Season	Club	League	GP	W	L	O/T	Mins	GA	SO	Avg	GP	W	L	Mins	GA	SO	Avg
2011-12	Edina Junior Gold A	Minor-MN	STATISTICS NOT AVAILABLE														
2012-13	North Iowa Bulls	NA3HL	1	0	0	0	11	2	0	10.94	....	....	....	....	....	....	....
	Steele County	MNJHL	34	13	15	0	1720	90	3	3.14	5	2	3	296	20	0	4.05
2013-14	Coulee Region	NAHL	32	13	12	1	1616	72	1	2.67	....	....	....	....	....	....	....
2014-15	Coulee Region	NAHL	*49	25	15	9	*2947	120	6	2.44	5	2	2	234	19	0	4.87
2015-16	Mercyhurst College	AH	17	7	7	3	989	47	0	2.85	....	....	....	....	....	....	....
2016-17	South Carolina	ECHL	23	9	11	2	1315	65	1	2.97	1	0	0	3	0	0	0.00

Signed as a free agent by **Washington**, March 28, 2016.

COMRIE, Eric (KAWM-ree, AIR-ihk) WPG

Goaltender. Catches left. 6'1", 175 lbs. Born, Edmonton, AB, July 6, 1995.
(Winnipeg's 3rd pick, 59th overall, in 2013 NHL Draft).

			Regular Season								Playoffs						
Season	Club	League	GP	W	L	O/T	Mins	GA	SO	Avg	GP	W	L	Mins	GA	SO	Avg
2010-11	L.A. Selects	T1EHL	19	16	2	0	966	24	5	1.34	....	....	....	....	....	....	....
	Tri-City Americans	WHL	....	....	....	....	....	....	....	....	1	0	0	20	1	0	3.00
2011-12	Tri-City Americans	WHL	31	19	6	2	1663	74	3	2.67	....	....	....	....	....	....	....
2012-13	Tri-City Americans	WHL	37	20	14	3	2178	95	2	2.62	0	0	0	0	0	0	0.00
2013-14	Tri-City Americans	WHL	60	26	25	9	3523	151	4	2.57	5	1	4	295	17	0	3.46
	St. John's IceCaps	AHL	2	0	2	0	113	12	0	6.35	....	....	....	....	....	....	....
2014-15	Tri-City Americans	WHL	40	20	19	1	2402	115	1	2.87	4	0	4	256	18	0	4.22
	St. John's IceCaps	AHL	3	2	1	0	185	7	0	2.27	....	....	....	....	....	....	....
2015-16	Manitoba Moose	AHL	46	13	25	7	2600	135	1	3.12	....	....	....	....	....	....	....
2016-17	Winnipeg	NHL	1	1	0	0	59	4	0	4.07	....	....	....	....	....	....	....
	Manitoba Moose	AHL	51	19	26	6	2920	144	3	2.96	....	....	....	....	....	....	....
	NHL Totals		**1**	**1**	**0**	**0**	**59**	**4**	**0**	**4.07**	....	....	....	....	....	....	....

WHL West Second All-Star Team (2014, 2015)

CONDON, Mike (KAWN-duhn, MIGHK) OTT

Goaltender. Catches left. 6'2", 197 lbs. Born, Holliston, MA, April 27, 1990.

			Regular Season								Playoffs						
Season	Club	League	GP	W	L	O/T	Mins	GA	SO	Avg	GP	W	L	Mins	GA	SO	Avg
2008-09	Belmont Hill	High-MA	31	....	....	....	....	....	....	2.12	....	....	....	....	....	....	....
2009-10	Princeton	ECAC	4	0	1	0	123	5	0	2.44	....	....	....	....	....	....	....
2010-11	Princeton	ECAC	11	6	4	1	660	31	1	2.82	....	....	....	....	....	....	....
2011-12	Princeton	ECAC	14	4	6	3	832	40	0	2.88	....	....	....	....	....	....	....
2012-13	Princeton	ECAC	24	8	11	4	1354	56	2	2.48	....	....	....	....	....	....	....
	Ontario Reign	ECHL	4	3	1	0	243	6	1	1.48	....	....	....	....	....	....	....
	Houston Aeros	AHL	5	3	0	0	226	9	0	2.39	....	....	....	....	....	....	....
2013-14	Wheeling Nailers	ECHL	39	23	12	4	2315	84	6	2.18	10	6	4	625	26	2	2.50
2014-15	Hamilton Bulldogs	AHL	48	23	19	0	2857	116	4	2.44	....	....	....	....	....	....	....
2015-16	Montreal	NHL	55	21	25	6	3123	141	1	2.71	....	....	....	....	....	....	....
2016-17	Pittsburgh	NHL	1	0	0	0	20	0	0	0.00	....	....	....	....	....	....	....
	Ottawa	NHL	40	19	14	6	2304	96	5	2.50	2	0	0	61	4	0	3.93
	NHL Totals		**96**	**40**	**39**	**12**	**5447**	**237**	**6**	**2.61**	**2**	**0**	**0**	**61**	**4**	**0**	**3.93**

Signed to an ATO (amateur tryout) contract by **Ontario** (ECHL), March 20, 2013. Signed to a PTO (professional tryout) contract by **Houston** (AHL), April 7, 2013. Signed as a free agent by **Montreal**, May 8, 2013. Claimed on waivers by **Pittsburgh** from **Montreal**, October 11, 2016. Traded to **Ottawa** by **Pittsburgh** for Ottawa's 5th round pick (Jan Drozg) in 2017 NHL Draft, November 2, 2016.

COPLEY, Pheonix (KAWP-lee, FEE-nihks) WSH

Goaltender. Catches left. 6'4", 196 lbs. Born, North Pole, AK, January 18, 1992.

			Regular Season								Playoffs						
Season	Club	League	GP	W	L	O/T	Mins	GA	SO	Avg	GP	W	L	Mins	GA	SO	Avg
2009-10	So. Cal Titans	NAPHL	10	6	1	1	429	22	1	2.62	....	....	....	....	....	....	....
	So. Cal Titans	Minor-CA	8	4	2	1	442	24	....	2.71	....	....	....	....	....	....	....
2010-11	Corpus Christi	NAHL	42	14	23	4	2376	165	0	4.17	....	....	....	....	....	....	....
2011-12	Tri-City Storm	USHL	25	9	13	0	1451	76	2	3.14	....	....	....	....	....	....	....
	Des Moines	USHL	20	7	11	1	1163	60	0	3.09	....	....	....	....	....	....	....
2012-13	Michigan Tech	WCHA	24	8	15	1	1323	71	3	3.22	....	....	....	....	....	....	....
2013-14	Michigan Tech	WCHA	30	10	13	6	1724	72	1	2.51	....	....	....	....	....	....	....
	South Carolina	ECHL	3	2	1	0	147	8	0	3.26	1	0	1	70	3	0	2.58
2014-15	Hershey Bears	AHL	26	17	4	3	1520	55	3	2.17	5	3	1	229	7	0	1.83
2015-16	St. Louis	NHL	1	0	0	0	24	1	0	2.50	....	....	....	....	....	....	....
	Chicago Wolves	AHL	37	15	16	3	2088	97	3	2.79	....	....	....	....	....	....	....
2016-17	St. Louis	NHL	1	0	1	0	59	5	0	5.08	....	....	....	....	....	....	....
	Chicago Wolves	AHL	25	15	6	3	1452	56	1	2.31	....	....	....	....	....	....	....
	Hershey Bears	AHL	16	11	5	0	920	33	0	2.15	9	5	4	534	19	1	2.13
	NHL Totals		**2**	**0**	**1**	**0**	**83**	**6**	**0**	**4.34**	....	....	....	....	....	....	....

Signed as a free agent by **Washington**, March 20, 2014. Traded to **St. Louis** by **Washington** with Troy Brouwer and Washington's 3rd round pick (later traded back to Washington – Washington selected Garrett Pilon) in 2016 NHL Draft for T.J. Oshie, July 2, 2015. Traded to **Washington** by **St. Louis** with Kevin Shattenkirk for Zach Sanford, Brad Malone and Washington's 1st round pick (later traded to Philadelphia – Philadelphia selected Morgan Frost) in 2017 NHL Draft, February 27, 2017.

COREAU, Jared (KOHR-oh, JAIR-uhd) DET

Goaltender. Catches left. 6'6", 220 lbs. Born, Perth, ON, November 5, 1991.

			Regular Season								Playoffs						
Season	Club	League	GP	W	L	O/T	Mins	GA	SO	Avg	GP	W	L	Mins	GA	SO	Avg
2008-09	Peterborough Stars	ON-Jr.A	12	8	1	1	304	23	0	2.16	2	0	0	22	0	0	0.00
2009-10	Lincoln Stars	USHL	38	7	22	4	1988	120	1	3.62	....	....	....	....	....	....	....
2010-11	Northern Mich.	CCHA	15	5	5	2	662	41	0	3.71	....	....	....	....	....	....	....
2011-12	Northern Mich.	CCHA	23	12	7	2	1244	46	1	2.22	....	....	....	....	....	....	....
2012-13	Northern Mich.	CCHA	38	15	19	4	2182	98	1	2.70	....	....	....	....	....	....	....
2013-14	Grand Rapids	AHL	5	0	4	0	205	15	0	4.39	....	....	....	....	....	....	....
	Toledo Walleye	ECHL	21	1	12	6	1146	77	0	4.03	....	....	....	....	....	....	....
2014-15	Grand Rapids	AHL	25	16	8	1	1475	54	3	2.20	1	0	1	58	3	0	3.10
	Toledo Walleye	ECHL	8	5	2	0	439	22	0	3.01	....	....	....	....	....	....	....
2015-16	Grand Rapids	AHL	47	29	15	2	2742	111	6	2.43	3	2	1	159	5	0	1.89
2016-17	Detroit	NHL	14	5	4	3	712	41	2	3.46	....	....	....	....	....	....	....
	Grand Rapids	AHL	33	19	11	3	1979	77	2	2.33	19	*15	4	1141	54	0	2.84
	NHL Totals		**14**	**5**	**4**	**3**	**712**	**41**	**2**	**3.46**	....	....	....	....	....	....	....

Signed as a free agent by **Detroit**, April 3, 2013.

CORMIER, Evan (kohr-ME-ay, EH-vuhn) N.J.

Goaltender. Catches left. 6'3", 200 lbs. Born, Bowmanville, ON, November 6, 1997.
(New Jersey's 6th pick, 105th overall, in 2016 NHL Draft).

			Regular Season								Playoffs						
Season	Club	League	GP	W	L	O/T	Mins	GA	SO	Avg	GP	W	L	Mins	GA	SO	Avg
2012-13	Clarington Toros	Minor-ON	25	7	12	3	....	....	....	2.40	....	....	....	....	....	....	....
	Cobourg Cougars	ON-Jr.A	....	....	....	....	....	....	....	....	4	1	1	172	13	0	4.53
2013-14	North Bay Trappers	NOJHL	37	8	28	0	2007	127	0	3.80	4	0	4	220	18	0	4.91
	North Bay Battalion	OHL	3	1	0	0	83	1	0	0.72	....	....	....	....	....	....	....
2014-15	North Bay Battalion	OHL	8	3	2	1	408	17	2	2.50	....	....	....	....	....	....	....
	Saginaw Spirit	OHL	22	9	10	0	1224	71	1	3.48	4	0	4	238	21	0	5.30
2015-16	Saginaw Spirit	OHL	58	21	27	7	3246	201	1	3.72	4	0	3	166	20	0	7.22
2016-17	Saginaw Spirit	OHL	49	23	19	7	2858	154	2	3.23	....	....	....	....	....	....	....

CRAWFORD, Corey (KRAW-fohrd, KOH-ree) CHI

Goaltender. Catches left. 6'2", 216 lbs. Born, Montreal, QC, December 31, 1984.
(Chicago's 2nd pick, 52nd overall, in 2003 NHL Draft).

			Regular Season								Playoffs						
Season	Club	League	GP	W	L	O/T	Mins	GA	SO	Avg	GP	W	L	Mins	GA	SO	Avg
2000-01	Gatineau Intrepide	QAAA	21	17	3	1	1346	43	5	1.92	....	....	....	....	....	....	....
2001-02	Moncton Wildcats	QMJHL	38	9	20	3	1863	116	1	3.74	....	....	....	....	....	....	....
2002-03	Moncton Wildcats	QMJHL	50	24	17	6	2855	130	2	2.73	6	2	3	303	20	0	3.97
2003-04	Moncton Wildcats	QMJHL	54	*35	15	3	3019	132	2	2.62	*20	*13	6	*1170	42	0	2.15
2004-05	Moncton Wildcats	QMJHL	51	28	16	6	2942	121	*5	2.47	12	6	6	725	33	*1	2.73
2005-06	**Chicago**	**NHL**	**2**	**0**	**0**	**1**	**86**	**5**	**0**	**3.49**	....	....	....	....	....	....	....
	Norfolk Admirals	AHL	48	22	23	1	2734	134	1	2.94	1	0	0	17	1	0	3.49
2006-07	Norfolk Admirals	AHL	60	38	20	2	3467	164	1	2.84	6	2	4	363	20	0	3.31
2007-08	**Chicago**	**NHL**	**5**	**1**	**2**	**0**	**224**	**8**	**1**	**2.14**	....	....	....	....	....	....	....
	Rockford IceHogs	AHL	55	29	19	5	3028	143	3	2.83	12	7	5	741	27	0	2.19
2008-09	Rockford IceHogs	AHL	47	22	20	3	2686	116	2	2.59	2	0	2	117	5	0	2.57
	Chicago	**NHL**	....	....	....	....	....	....	....	....	**1**	**0**	**0**	**16**	**1**	**0**	**3.75**
2009-10	**Chicago**	**NHL**	**1**	**0**	**1**	**0**	**59**	**3**	**0**	**3.05**	....	....	....	....	....	....	....
	Rockford IceHogs	AHL	45	24	16	2	2521	112	1	2.67	4	0	4	216	13	0	3.61
2010-11	**Chicago**	**NHL**	**57**	**33**	**18**	**6**	**3337**	**128**	**4**	**2.30**	**7**	**3**	**4**	**435**	**16**	**1**	**2.21**
2011-12	**Chicago**	**NHL**	**57**	**30**	**17**	**7**	**3218**	**146**	**0**	**2.72**	**6**	**2**	**4**	**396**	**17**	**0**	**2.58**
2012-13♦	**Chicago**	**NHL**	**30**	**19**	**5**	**5**	**1761**	**57**	**3**	**1.94**	***23**	***16**	**7**	***1504**	**46**	**1**	***1.84**
2013-14	**Chicago**	**NHL**	**59**	**32**	**16**	**10**	**3395**	**128**	**2**	**2.26**	**19**	**11**	**8**	**1234**	**52**	**1**	**2.53**
2014-15♦	**Chicago**	**NHL**	**57**	**32**	**20**	**5**	**3333**	**126**	**2**	**2.27**	**20**	**13**	**6**	**1223**	**47**	**2**	**2.31**
2015-16	**Chicago**	**NHL**	**58**	**35**	**18**	**5**	**3323**	**131**	***7**	**2.37**	**7**	**3**	**4**	**448**	**19**	**0**	**2.54**
2016-17	**Chicago**	**NHL**	**55**	**32**	**18**	**4**	**3247**	**138**	**2**	**2.55**	**4**	**0**	**4**	**254**	**12**	**0**	**2.83**
	NHL Totals		**381**	**214**	**115**	**43**	**21983**	**870**	**21**	**2.37**	**87**	**48**	**37**	**5510**	**210**	**5**	**2.29**

QMJHL Second All-Star Team (2004, 2005) • NHL All-Rookie Team (2011) • William M. Jennings Trophy (2013) (shared with Ray Emery) • William M. Jennings Trophy (2015) (tied with Carey Price)
Played in NHL All-Star Game (2017)

DACCORD, Joel (DA-kohrd, JOHL) OTT

Goaltender. Catches left. 6'3", 205 lbs. Born, Boston, MA, August 19, 1996.
(Ottawa's 8th pick, 199th overall, in 2015 NHL Draft).

			Regular Season								Playoffs						
Season	Club	League	GP	W	L	O/T	Mins	GA	SO	Avg	GP	W	L	Mins	GA	SO	Avg
2011-12	North Andover	High-MA	25	....	....	....	1125	....	4	1.53	....	....	....	....	....	....	....
2012-13	Cushing	High-MA	10	....	....	....	526	19	4	1.95	....	....	....	....	....	....	....
2013-14	Cushing	High-MA	....	....	....	....	1442	62	....	2.58	....	....	....	....	....	....	....
2014-15	Boston Jr. Bruins	Minor-MA	11	5	3	0	317	8	2	1.14	....	....	....	....	....	....	....
	Cushing	High-MA	....	....	....	....	1413	47	....	1.80	....	....	....	....	....	....	....
2015-16	Muskegon	USHL	48	21	20	5	2764	143	2	3.10	....	....	....	....	....	....	....
2016-17	Arizona State	NCAA	15	3	8	1	730	49	0	4.03	....	....	....	....	....	....	....

DANIS, Yann (DA-nihs, YAN)

Goaltender. Catches left. 6', 185 lbs. Born, Lafontaine, QC, June 21, 1981.

			Regular Season								Playoffs						
Season	Club	League	GP	W	L	O/T	Mins	GA	SO	Avg	GP	W	L	Mins	GA	SO	Avg
1997-98	St-Jerome	Minor-QC	STATISTICS NOT AVAILABLE														
	Amos Foresters	QAAA	3	2	0	0	144	2	0	0.83	2	0	1	78	6	0	4.62
99-2000	Cornwall Colts	ON-Jr.A	26	15	5	0	1367	71	0	3.12	13	11	2	786	37	0	2.82
2000-01	Brown U.	ECAC	12	2	8	1	667	40	0	3.60	....	....	....	....	....	....	....
2001-02	Brown U.	ECAC	24	11	10	2	1451	45	3	1.86	....	....	....	....	....	....	....
2002-03	Brown U.	ECAC	*34	15	14	5	*2074	80	5	2.31	....	....	....	....	....	....	....
2003-04	Brown U.	ECAC	30	15	11	4	1821	55	*5	*1.81	....	....	....	....	....	....	....
	Hamilton Bulldogs	AHL	2	2	0	0	120	3	1	1.50	1	0	0	12	0	0	0.00
2004-05	Hamilton Bulldogs	AHL	53	28	17	6	3075	120	5	2.34	4	0	4	237	13	0	3.29
2005-06	**Montreal**	**NHL**	**6**	**3**	**2**	**0**	**312**	**14**	**1**	**2.69**	....	....	....	....	....	....	....
	Hamilton Bulldogs	AHL	39	17	17	3	2242	111	0	2.97	....	....	....	....	....	....	....
2006-07	Hamilton Bulldogs	AHL	44	23	14	5	2540	119	1	2.81	1	1	0	54	1	0	1.12
2007-08	Hamilton Bulldogs	AHL	38	11	19	4	2064	113	0	3.28	....	....	....	....	....	....	....
2008-09	**NY Islanders**	**NHL**	**31**	**10**	**17**	**3**	**1760**	**84**	**2**	**2.86**	....	....	....	....	....	....	....
	Bridgeport	AHL	10	7	3	0	611	23	0	2.26	....	....	....	....	....	....	....
2009-10	**New Jersey**	**NHL**	**12**	**3**	**2**	**1**	**467**	**16**	**0**	**2.06**	....	....	....	....	....	....	....
2010-11	Amur Khabarovsk	KHL	31	....	....	....	1652	84	2	3.05	....	....	....	....	....	....	....
2011-12	**Edmonton**	**NHL**	**1**	**0**	**0**	**0**	**32**	**2**	**0**	**3.75**	....	....	....	....	....	....	....
	Oklahoma City	AHL	43	26	14	2	2545	88	5	2.07	14	8	6	842	33	1	2.35
2012-13	Oklahoma City	AHL	47	26	15	6	2775	120	2	2.59	17	10	7	1019	41	1	2.41
	Edmonton	**NHL**	**3**	**1**	**0**	**0**	**110**	**7**	**0**	**3.82**	....	....	....	....	....	....	....
2013-14	Adirondack	AHL	31	9	11	4	1514	76	2	3.01	....	....	....	....	....	....	....
2014-15	Norfolk Admirals	AHL	11	5	6	0	640	29	2	2.72	....	....	....	....	....	....	....
	Hartford Wolf Pack	AHL	24	12	7	4	1428	56	2	2.35	14	7	7	887	35	0	2.37
2015-16	**New Jersey**	**NHL**	**2**	**0**	**1**	**0**	**51**	**4**	**0**	**4.71**	....	....	....	....	....	....	....
	Albany Devils	AHL	47	28	12	5	2681	99	8	2.22	1	0	0	20	2	0	6.00
2016-17	St. John's IceCaps	AHL	25	11	9	4	1487	74	1	2.99	....	....	....	....	....	....	....
	NHL Totals		**55**	**17**	**22**	**4**	**2732**	**127**	**3**	**2.79**	....	....	....	....	....	....	....

ECAC Second All-Star Team (2002, 2003) • ECAC First All-Star Team (2004) • ECAC Goaltender of the Year (2004) • ECAC Player of the Year (2004) • NCAA East First All-American Team (2004) • AHL First All-Star Team (2012) • Baz Bastien Memorial Trophy (AHL – Top Goaltender) (2012)

Signed as a free agent by **Montreal**, March 19, 2004. Signed as a free agent by **NY Islanders**, July 2, 2008. Signed as a free agent by **New Jersey**, July 10, 2009. Signed as a free agent by **Khabarovsk** (KHL), July 27, 2010. Signed as a free agent by **Edmonton**, July 4, 2011. Signed as a free agent by **Philadelphia**, July 5, 2013. Signed to a PTO (professional tryout) contract by **Norfolk** (AHL), November 10, 2014. Signed to a PTO (professional tryout) contract by **Hartford** (AHL), January 1, 2015. Signed as a free agent by **New Jersey**, July 3, 2015. Signed as a free agent by **St. John's** (AHL), October 17, 2016.

DANSK, Oscar (DANSK, AWS-kuhr) VGK

Goaltender. Catches left. 6'3", 195 lbs. Born, Stockholm, Sweden, February 28, 1994.
(Columbus' 2nd pick, 31st overall, in 2012 NHL Draft).

			Regular Season								Playoffs						
Season	Club	League	GP	W	L	O/T	Mins	GA	SO	Avg	GP	W	L	Mins	GA	SO	Avg
2007-08	Shattuck Bantam	High-MN	39	....	....	....	....	....	....	1.98	....	....	....	....	....	....	....
2008-09	Shattuck Bantam	High-MN	32	....	....	....	....	....	....	1.43	....	....	....	....	....	....	....
2009-10	Shattuck	High-MN	18	13	2	1	....	....	....	1.89	....	....	....	....	....	....	....
2010-11	Brynas U18	Swe-U18	17	....	....	....	1017	30	2	1.77	5	....	....	317	20	0	3.78
	Brynas IF Gavle Jr.	Swe-Jr.	21	....	....	....	1157	52	1	2.70	1	....	....	57	5	0	5.22
2011-12	Brynas U18	Swe-U18	2	....	....	....	121	4	0	1.98	3	....	....	180	3	1	1.00
	Brynas IF Gavle Jr.	Swe-Jr.	28	....	....	....	1511	71	2	2.82	2	....	....	120	7	0	3.49
2012-13	Erie Otters	OHL	43	11	23	6	2393	164	0	4.11	....	....	....	....	....	....	....
2013-14	Erie Otters	OHL	42	29	9	1	2405	96	*6	*2.39	3	0	1	124	14	0	6.79
2014-15	Springfield Falcons	AHL	21	7	7	5	1144	68	0	3.57	....	....	....	....	....	....	....
	Kalamazoo Wings	ECHL	11	1	8	0	530	33	0	3.73	....	....	....	....	....	....	....
2015-16	Rogle	Sweden	36	13	21	0	1947	87	2	2.68	....	....	....	....	....	....	....
2016-17	Rogle	Sweden	24	6	16	0	1341	67	2	3.00	....	....	....	....	....	....	....

• Loaned to **Rogle** (Sweden) by **Columbus**, May 23, 2015. Signed as a free agent by **Vegas**, July 3, 2017.

DARLING, Scott (DAHR-lihng, SKAWT) CAR

Goaltender. Catches left. 6'6", 232 lbs. Born, Lemont, IL, December 22, 1988.
(Phoenix's 7th pick, 153rd overall, in 2007 NHL Draft).

			Regular Season								Playoffs						
Season	Club	League	GP	W	L	O/T	Mins	GA	SO	Avg	GP	W	L	Mins	GA	SO	Avg
2005-06	Chicago Y.A.	MWEHL	2	0	2	0	120	10	0	5.00	....	....	....	....	....	....	....
	North Iowa	NAHL	8	2	4	0	405	28	0	4.15	....	....	....	....	....	....	....
2006-07	Capital District	EJHL	22	9	9	3	1243	70	1	3.38	....	....	....	....	....	....	....
	North Iowa	NAHL	1	0	0	0	15	3	0	12.00	....	....	....	....	....	....	....
2007-08	Indiana Ice	USHL	42	27	10	2	2391	121	1	3.04	3	1	2	179	11	0	3.69
2008-09	University of Maine	H-East	27	10	14	3	1566	72	*3	2.76	....	....	....	....	....	....	....
2009-10	University of Maine	H-East	27	15	6	3	1511	78	0	3.10	....	....	....	....	....	....	....
2010-11	Louisiana	SPHL	30	6	22	0	1598	102	0	3.83	....	....	....	....	....	....	....
2011-12	Florida Everblades	ECHL	1	0	1	0	58	5	0	5.14	....	....	....	....	....	....	....
2012-13	Hamilton Bulldogs	AHL	1	0	0	0	25	0	0	0.00	....	....	....	....	....	....	....
	Wheeling Nailers	ECHL	32	13	12	4	1819	85	2	2.80	....	....	....	....	....	....	....
2013-14	Milwaukee	AHL	26	13	6	2	1347	45	6	2.00	....	....	....	....	....	....	....
2014-15♦	**Chicago**	**NHL**	**14**	**9**	**4**	**0**	**833**	**27**	**1**	**1.94**	**5**	**3**	**1**	**298**	**11**	**0**	**2.21**
	Rockford IceHogs	AHL	26	14	8	2	1419	52	2	2.20	....	....	....	....	....	....	....
2015-16	**Chicago**	**NHL**	**29**	**12**	**8**	**4**	**1560**	**67**	**1**	**2.58**	....	....	....	....	....	....	....
2016-17	**Chicago**	**NHL**	**32**	**18**	**5**	**5**	**1689**	**67**	**2**	**2.38**	....	....	....	....	....	....	....
	NHL Totals		**75**	**39**	**17**	**9**	**4082**	**161**	**4**	**2.37**	**5**	**3**	**1**	**298**	**11**	**0**	**2.21**

Signed as a free agent by **Hamilton** (AHL), September 26, 2012. Signed as a free agent by **Chicago**, July 1, 2014. Traded to **Carolina** by **Chicago** for Ottawa's 3rd round pick (previously acquired, Chicago selected Evan Barratt) in 2017 NHL Draft, April 28, 2017.

DELIA, Collin (DEE-LEE-ah, KAW-lihn) CHI

Goaltender. Catches left. 6'2", 190 lbs. Born, Rancho Cucamonga, CA, June 20, 1994.

			Regular Season								Playoffs						
Season	Club	League	GP	W	L	O/T	Mins	GA	SO	Avg	GP	W	L	Mins	GA	SO	Avg
2012-13	Amarillo Bulls	NAHL	19	11	2	2	981	37	3	2.26	2	0	0	43	4	0	5.65
2013-14	Amarillo Bulls	NAHL	31	22	7	0	1723	46	7	1.60	6	4	2	328	13	0	2.38
2014-15	Merrimack College	H-East	9	4	4	1	517	16	1	1.86	....	....	....	....	....	....	....
2015-16	Merrimack College	H-East	26	8	12	6	1521	75	0	2.96	....	....	....	....	....	....	....
2016-17	Merrimack College	H-East	21	9	8	3	1202	43	3	2.15	....	....	....	....	....	....	....

Signed as a free agent by **Chicago**, July 28, 2017.

DELL, Aaron (DEHL, AIR-uhn) S.J.

Goaltender. Catches left. 6', 205 lbs. Born, Airdrie, AB, May 4, 1989.

			Regular Season								Playoffs						
Season	Club	League	GP	W	L	O/T	Mins	GA	SO	Avg	GP	W	L	Mins	GA	SO	Avg
2007-08	Calgary Canucks	AJHL	23	5	11	2	1245	65	0	3.13	....	....	....	....	....	....	....
2008-09	Calgary Canucks	AJHL	51	25	17	8	2986	126	3	2.53	4	1	3	253	13	0	3.08
2009-10	North Dakota	WCHA	5	1	3	1	199	6	1	1.81	....	....	....	....	....	....	....
2010-11	North Dakota	WCHA	40	30	7	2	2349	70	6	1.79	....	....	....	....	....	....	....
2011-12	North Dakota	WCHA	33	18	10	2	1800	80	2	2.67	....	....	....	....	....	....	....
2012-13	Allen Americans	CHL	44	22	11	6	2344	90	3	2.30	19	12	7	1097	45	1	2.46
2013-14	Utah Grizzlies	ECHL	29	19	7	3	1735	62	2	2.14	3	1	1	188	6	0	1.92
	Abbotsford Heat	AHL	6	1	2	0	262	10	0	2.29	....	....	....	....	....	....	....
2014-15	Allen Americans	ECHL	12	8	1	2	676	32	1	2.84	....	....	....	....	....	....	....
	Worcester Sharks	AHL	26	15	8	2	1544	53	4	2.06	3	0	3	149	12	0	4.83
2015-16	San Jose Barracuda	AHL	40	17	16	6	2281	92	4	2.42	4	1	3	231	10	0	2.59
2016-17	**San Jose**	**NHL**	**20**	**11**	**6**	**1**	**1111**	**37**	**1**	**2.00**	....	....	....	....	....	....	....
	NHL Totals		**20**	**11**	**6**	**1**	**1111**	**37**	**1**	**2.00**	....	....	....	....	....	....	....

WCHA First All-Star Team (2011) • NCAA East Second All-American Team (2011) • CHL All-Rookie Team (2013) • CHL First All-Star Team (2013)

Signed as a free agent by **Allen** (ECHL), October 20, 2012. Signed as a free agent by **Utah** (ECHL), September 9, 2013. • Loaned to **Abbotsford** (AHL) by **Utah** (ECHL), March 8, 2014. Signed as a free agent by **Allen** (ECHL), October 11, 2014. • Loaned to **Worcester** (AHL) by **Allen** (ECHL), November 11, 2014. Signed as a free agent by **San Jose**, March 4, 2015.

DEMKO, Thatcher (DEHM-koh, THA-chur) VAN

Goaltender. Catches left. 6'4", 192 lbs. Born, San Diego, CA, December 8, 1995.
(Vancouver's 3rd pick, 36th overall, in 2014 NHL Draft).

			Regular Season								Playoffs						
Season	Club	League	GP	W	L	O/T	Mins	GA	SO	Avg	GP	W	L	Mins	GA	SO	Avg
2010-11	San Diego Gulls	Minor-CA	25	12	12	1	....	....	....	2.47	....	....	....	....	....	....	....
2011-12	L.A. Jr. Kings	T1EHL	7	3	0	3	330	14	0	2.29	....	....	....	....	....	....	....
	L.A. Jr. Kings	Minor-CA	3	3	0	0	....	....	....	....	....	....	....	....	....	....	....
	Omaha Lancers	USHL	15	9	3	0	754	36	1	2.87	....	....	....	....	....	....	....
	USAHNTDP	U-17	3	2	0	0	140	3	0	1.29	....	....	....	....	....	....	....
2012-13	USAHNTDP	USHL	19	15	3	0	1059	39	1	2.21	....	....	....	....	....	....	....
	USAHNTDP	U-17	1	1	0	0	60	1	0	1.00	....	....	....	....	....	....	....
	USAHNTDP	U-18	28	17	6	3	1620	52	5	1.93	....	....	....	....	....	....	....

2013-14	Boston College	H-East	24	16	5	3	1446	54	2	2.24	....	....	....	....	....	....	....
2014-15	Boston College	H-East	35	19	13	3	2107	77	1	2.19	....	....	....	....	....	....	....
2015-16	Boston College	H-East	*39	*27	8	4	2362	74	*10	1.88	....	....	....	....	....	....	....
2016-17	Utica Comets	AHL	45	22	17	4	2555	114	2	2.68	....	....	....	....	....	....	....

Hockey East First All-Star Team (2016) • NCAA East Second All-American Team (2016)

DESMITH, Casey (duh-SMIHTH, KAY-see) PIT

Goaltender. Catches left. 6', 181 lbs. Born, Rochester, NH, August 13, 1991.

			Regular Season								Playoffs						
Season	Club	League	GP	W	L	O/T	Mins	GA	SO	Avg	GP	W	L	Mins	GA	SO	Avg
2006-07	Berwick Acad.	High-MA	6	....	....	....	120	7	....	....	....	....	....	....	....	....	....
2007-08	Berwick Acad.	High-MA	24	....	....	....	1097	56	....	....	....	....	....	....	....	....	....
2008-09	Deerfield Academy	High-MA	20	....	....	....	1053	53	....	....	....	....	....	....	....	....	....
2009-10	Indiana Ice	USHL	27	11	11	1	1434	76	0	3.18	8	4	3	412	17	0	2.48
2010-11	Indiana Ice	USHL	37	22	13	2	2174	92	3	2.54	4	2	2	229	10	1	2.63
2011-12	New Hampshire	H-East	22	9	10	1	1286	50	1	2.33	....	....	....	....	....	....	....
2012-13	New Hampshire	H-East	*38	19	10	7	2204	82	5	2.23	....	....	....	....	....	....	....
2013-14	New Hampshire	H-East	37	20	16	0	2148	86	3	2.40	....	....	....	....	....	....	....
2014-15							STATISTICS NOT AVAILABLE										
2015-16	Wilkes-Barre	AHL	6	2	2	0	309	10	0	1.94	....	....	....	....	....	....	....
	Wheeling Nailers	ECHL	13	5	2	2	611	26	0	2.55	....	....	....	....	....	....	....
2016-17	Wilkes-Barre	AHL	29	21	5	1	1731	58	1	*2.01	5	2	3	303	14	0	2.78

Harry "Hap" Holmes Memorial Award (AHL – fewest goals against) (2017) (shared with Tristan Jarry)

Signed as a free agent by **Pittsburgh**, July 1, 2017.

DESROSIERS, Philippe (duh-ROHZ-ee-yay, fihl-EEP) DAL

Goaltender. Catches left. 6'1", 185 lbs. Born, Saint-Hyacinthe, QC, August 16, 1995.
(Dallas' 4th pick, 54th overall, in 2013 NHL Draft).

			Regular Season								Playoffs						
Season	Club	League	GP	W	L	O/T	Mins	GA	SO	Avg	GP	W	L	Mins	GA	SO	Avg
2010-11	Antoine-Girouard	QAAA	20	10	9	0	1100	65	2	3.54	3	1	2	139	8	0	3.45
2011-12	Antoine-Girouard	QAAA	23	16	4	3	1320	61	1	2.77	11	6	3	673	29	0	2.58
	Rimouski Oceanic	QMJHL	3	1	2	0	155	9	0	3.48	....	....	....	....	....	....	....
2012-13	Rimouski Oceanic	QMJHL	43	22	8	5	2305	118	1	3.07	4	2	2	239	9	0	2.26
2013-14	Rimouski Oceanic	QMJHL	52	31	14	7	2921	129	5	2.65	11	7	3	640	25	2	2.34
2014-15	Rimouski Oceanic	QMJHL	44	29	9	3	2469	103	5	2.50	9	5	3	411	17	0	2.48
2015-16	Texas Stars	AHL	10	5	5	0	596	28	0	2.82	....	....	....	....	....	....	....
	Idaho Steelheads	ECHL	31	15	7	6	1744	68	2	2.34	7	3	4	390	16	0	2.47
2016-17	Texas Stars	AHL	8	3	2	0	373	17	1	2.73	....	....	....	....	....	....	....
	Idaho Steelheads	ECHL	13	5	3	2	678	43	0	3.81	....	....	....	....	....	....	....
	Norfolk Admirals	ECHL	20	8	11	0	1156	72	0	3.74	....	....	....	....	....	....	....

• Re-assigned to **Norfolk** (AHL) by **Dallas**, February 3, 2017.

DIPIETRO, Michael (dee-pee-EHT-roh, MIGH-kuhl) VAN

Goaltender. Catches left. 6', 202 lbs. Born, Windsor, ON, September 6, 1999.
(Vancouver's 4th pick, 64th overall, in 2017 NHL Draft).

			Regular Season								Playoffs						
Season	Club	League	GP	W	L	O/T	Mins	GA	SO	Avg	GP	W	L	Mins	GA	SO	Avg
2014-15	Sun County MM	Minor-ON	21	6	11	0	893	42	4	2.12	9	4	4	404	17	1	1.89
	Leamington Flyers	ON-Jr.B	1	1	0	0	60	2	0	2.00	....	....	....	....	....	....	....
2015-16	Windsor Spitfires	OHL	29	16	8	2	1644	67	2	2.45	3	1	2	190	11	0	3.48
2016-17	Windsor Spitfires	OHL	51	30	12	6	2935	115	*6	2.35	7	3	4	436	18	0	2.48

DOMINGUE, Louis (doh-MING, LOO-ee) ARI

Goaltender. Catches right. 6'3", 210 lbs. Born, St-Hyacinthe, QC, March 6, 1992.
(Phoenix's 5th pick, 138th overall, in 2010 NHL Draft).

			Regular Season								Playoffs						
Season	Club	League	GP	W	L	O/T	Mins	GA	SO	Avg	GP	W	L	Mins	GA	SO	Avg
2007-08	Lac St-Louis Lions	QAAA	35	22	9	0	1732	90	2	3.12	13	8	4	761	33	1	2.60
2008-09	Moncton Wildcats	QMJHL	12	5	5	0	621	26	0	2.51	....	....	....	....	....	....	....
2009-10	Moncton Wildcats	QMJHL	22	11	9	0	1196	56	1	2.81	....	....	....	....	....	....	....
	Quebec Remparts	QMJHL	19	9	8	0	1017	43	2	2.54	9	3	5	455	33	0	4.35
2010-11	Quebec Remparts	QMJHL	*57	*37	12	3	3033	134	2	2.65	18	11	6	996	41	1	2.47
2011-12	Quebec Remparts	QMJHL	39	23	8	4	2162	94	4	2.61	11	7	4	679	30	0	2.65
2012-13	Portland Pirates	AHL	2	1	0	0	100	4	0	2.40	....	....	....	....	....	....	....
	Gwinnett	ECHL	34	23	9	2	2051	92	3	2.69	10	6	4	619	23	2	2.23
2013-14	Portland Pirates	AHL	36	9	18	2	1783	108	1	3.63	....	....	....	....	....	....	....
	Gwinnett	ECHL	7	1	3	2	388	13	1	2.01	....	....	....	....	....	....	....
2014-15	**Arizona**	**NHL**	**7**	**1**	**2**	**1**	**308**	**14**	**0**	**2.73**	....	....	....	....	....	....	....
	Portland Pirates	AHL	20	11	6	2	1121	50	0	2.68	5	2	2	253	10	1	2.37
	Gwinnett	ECHL	2	1	1	0	119	2	1	1.01	....	....	....	....	....	....	....
2015-16	**Arizona**	**NHL**	**39**	**15**	**18**	**5**	**2206**	**101**	**2**	**2.75**	....	....	....	....	....	....	....
	Springfield Falcons	AHL	13	6	6	1	778	33	1	2.55	....	....	....	....	....	....	....
2016-17	**Arizona**	**NHL**	**31**	**11**	**15**	**1**	**1599**	**82**	**0**	**3.08**	....	....	....	....	....	....	....
	NHL Totals		**77**	**27**	**35**	**7**	**4113**	**197**	**2**	**2.87**	....	....	....	....	....	....	....

DRIEDGER, Chris (DREE-guhr, KRIHS) OTT

Goaltender. Catches left. 6'4", 205 lbs. Born, Winnipeg, MB, May 18, 1994.
(Ottawa's 2nd pick, 76th overall, in 2012 NHL Draft).

			Regular Season								Playoffs						
Season	Club	League	GP	W	L	O/T	Mins	GA	SO	Avg	GP	W	L	Mins	GA	SO	Avg
2009-10	Wpg. Monarchs	Minor-MB	12	....	....	....	....	....	....	1.75	....	....	....	....	....	....	....
2010-11	Tri-City Americans	WHL	22	6	6	1	977	57	0	3.50	....	....	....	....	....	....	....
2011-12	Calgary Hitmen	WHL	44	24	12	3	2294	107	3	2.80	2	0	2	82	9	0	6.59
2012-13	Calgary Hitmen	WHL	54	36	14	4	3199	134	2	2.51	17	11	6	1006	40	1	2.39
2013-14	Calgary Hitmen	WHL	50	28	14	7	2892	127	3	2.64	6	2	3	328	24	1	4.39
	Binghamton	AHL	1	0	0	0	26	2	0	4.58	....	....	....	....	....	....	....
	Elmira Jackals	ECHL	4	1	2	....	199	13	0	3.92	....	....	....	....	....	....	....
2014-15	**Ottawa**	**NHL**	**1**	**0**	**0**	**0**	**23**	**0**	**0**	**0.00**	....	....	....	....	....	....	....
	Binghamton	AHL	8	6	0	0	401	17	0	2.55	....	....	....	....	....	....	....
	Evansville IceMen	ECHL	40	8	27	4	2253	142	2	3.78	....	....	....	....	....	....	....
2015-16	**Ottawa**	**NHL**	**1**	**0**	**0**	**0**	**32**	**0**	**0**	**0.00**	....	....	....	....	....	....	....
	Binghamton	AHL	39	18	15	4	2228	105	1	2.83	....	....	....	....	....	....	....
2016-17	**Ottawa**	**NHL**	**1**	**0**	**1**	**0**	**40**	**4**	**0**	**6.00**	....	....	....	....	....	....	....
	Binghamton	AHL	34	12	19	2	1918	103	1	3.22	....	....	....	....	....	....	....
	Wichita Thunder	ECHL	2	0	2	0	120	9	0	4.51	....	....	....	....	....	....	....
	NHL Totals		**3**	**0**	**1**	**0**	**95**	**4**	**0**	**2.53**	....	....	....	....	....	....	....

DUBNYK, Devan (DOOB-nihk, DEH-vuhn) MIN

Goaltender. Catches left. 6'6", 212 lbs. Born, Regina, SK, May 4, 1986.
(Edmonton's 1st pick, 14th overall, in 2004 NHL Draft).

			Regular Season								Playoffs						
Season	Club	League	GP	W	L	O/T	Mins	GA	SO	Avg	GP	W	L	Mins	GA	SO	Avg
2000-01	Calgary Bruins	CBHL	14	....	....	....	815	39	2	3.10	....	....	....	....	....	....	....
2001-02	Calgary Bruins	CBHL	18	7	9	2	1105	68	1	3.69	....	....	....	....	....	....	....
	Kamloops Blazers	WHL	3	1	1	0	143	13	0	5.44	....	....	....	....	....	....	....
2002-03	Kamloops Blazers	WHL	26	12	8	1	1278	66	2	3.10	....	....	....	....	....	....	....
2003-04	Kamloops Blazers	WHL	44	20	18	5	2532	106	6	2.51	4	1	3	245	12	0	2.94
2004-05	Kamloops Blazers	WHL	*65	23	34	7	3699	166	6	2.69	6	2	4	362	22	0	3.65
2005-06	Kamloops Blazers	WHL	54	27	26	1	3207	136	1	2.54	....	....	....	....	....	....	....
2006-07	Wilkes-Barre	AHL	4	2	1	0	204	10	0	2.94	....	....	....	....	....	....	....
	Stockton Thunder	ECHL	43	24	11	7	2529	108	2	2.56	6	2	4	395	18	0	2.73
2007-08	Springfield Falcons	AHL	33	9	17	0	1772	92	0	3.12	....	....	....	....	....	....	....
2008-09	Springfield Falcons	AHL	*62	18	41	2	*3635	180	3	2.97	....	....	....	....	....	....	....
2009-10	**Edmonton**	**NHL**	**19**	**4**	**10**	**2**	**1075**	**64**	**0**	**3.57**	....	....	....	....	....	....	....
	Springfield Falcons	AHL	33	13	17	2	1985	100	0	3.02	....	....	....	....	....	....	....
2010-11	**Edmonton**	**NHL**	**35**	**12**	**13**	**8**	**2061**	**93**	**2**	**2.71**	....	....	....	....	....	....	....
2011-12	**Edmonton**	**NHL**	**47**	**20**	**20**	**3**	**2653**	**118**	**2**	**2.67**	....	....	....	....	....	....	....
2012-13	**Edmonton**	**NHL**	**38**	**14**	**16**	**6**	**2101**	**90**	**2**	**2.57**	....	....	....	....	....	....	....
2013-14	**Edmonton**	**NHL**	**32**	**11**	**17**	**2**	**1678**	**94**	**2**	**3.36**	....	....	....	....	....	....	....
	Nashville	**NHL**	**2**	**0**	**1**	**1**	**124**	**9**	**0**	**4.35**	....	....	....	....	....	....	....
	Hamilton Bulldogs	AHL	8	2	5	0	415	23	0	3.33	....	....	....	....	....	....	....
2014-15	**Arizona**	**NHL**	**19**	**9**	**5**	**2**	**1035**	**47**	**1**	**2.72**	....	....	....	....	....	....	....
	Minnesota	**NHL**	**39**	**27**	**9**	**2**	**2293**	**68**	**5**	**1.78**	**10**	**4**	**6**	**570**	**24**	**1**	**2.53**
2015-16	**Minnesota**	**NHL**	**67**	**32**	**26**	**6**	**3861**	**150**	**5**	**2.33**	**6**	**2**	**4**	**359**	**20**	**0**	**3.34**
2016-17	**Minnesota**	**NHL**	**65**	**40**	**19**	**5**	**3758**	**141**	**5**	**2.25**	**5**	**1**	**4**	**322**	**10**	**1**	**1.86**
	NHL Totals		**363**	**169**	**136**	**37**	**20639**	**874**	**24**	**2.54**	**21**	**7**	**14**	**1251**	**54**	**2**	**2.59**

Canadian Major Junior Scholastic Player of the Year (2004) • NHL Second All-Star Team (2015) • Bill Masterton Memorial Trophy (2015)

Played in NHL All-Star Game (2016, 2017)

Traded to **Nashville** by **Edmonton** for Matt Hendricks, January 15, 2014. Traded to **Montreal** by **Nashville** for future considerations, March 5, 2014. Signed as a free agent by **Arizona**, July 1, 2014. Traded to **Minnesota** by **Arizona** for Minnesota's 3rd round pick (Brendan Warren) in 2015 NHL Draft, January 15, 2015.

ELLIOTT, Brian (EHL-lee-awt, BRIGH-uhn) PHI

Goaltender. Catches left. 6'2", 209 lbs. Born, Newmarket, ON, April 9, 1985.
(Ottawa's 9th pick, 291st overall, in 2003 NHL Draft).

			Regular Season								Playoffs						
Season	Club	League	GP	W	L	O/T	Mins	GA	SO	Avg	GP	W	L	Mins	GA	SO	Avg
2002-03	Ajax Axemen	ON-Jr.A	39	....	....	....	2097	135	0	3.86	....	....	....	....	....	....	....
2003-04	U. of Wisconsin	WCHA	6	3	3	0	336	12	0	2.14	....	....	....	....	....	....	....
2004-05	U. of Wisconsin	WCHA	9	6	2	1	467	9	3	1.16	....	....	....	....	....	....	....
2005-06	U. of Wisconsin	WCHA	35	*27	5	3	2128	55	*8	*1.55	....	....	....	....	....	....	....
2006-07	U. of Wisconsin	WCHA	36	15	17	2	2053	72	*5	2.10	....	....	....	....	....	....	....
	Binghamton	AHL	8	3	4	0	425	30	0	4.24	....	....	....	....	....	....	....
2007-08	**Ottawa**	**NHL**	**1**	**1**	**0**	**0**	**60**	**1**	**0**	**1.00**	....	....	....	....	....	....	....
	Binghamton	AHL	44	18	19	1	2394	112	2	2.81	....	....	....	....	....	....	....
2008-09	**Ottawa**	**NHL**	**31**	**16**	**8**	**3**	**1667**	**77**	**1**	**2.77**	....	....	....	....	....	....	....
	Binghamton	AHL	30	18	8	1	1691	65	2	2.31	....	....	....	....	....	....	....
2009-10	**Ottawa**	**NHL**	**55**	**29**	**18**	**4**	**3038**	**130**	**5**	**2.57**	**4**	**1**	**2**	**203**	**14**	**0**	**4.14**
2010-11	**Ottawa**	**NHL**	**43**	**13**	**19**	**8**	**2293**	**122**	**3**	**3.19**	....	....	....	....	....	....	....
	Colorado	**NHL**	**12**	**2**	**8**	**1**	**690**	**44**	**0**	**3.83**	....	....	....	....	....	....	....
2011-12	**St. Louis**	**NHL**	**38**	**23**	**10**	**4**	**2235**	**58**	**9**	***1.56**	**8**	**3**	**4**	**455**	**18**	**0**	**2.37**
2012-13	**St. Louis**	**NHL**	**24**	**14**	**8**	**1**	**1292**	**49**	**3**	**2.28**	**6**	**2**	**4**	**378**	**12**	**0**	**1.90**
	Peoria Rivermen	AHL	2	1	1	0	119	3	1	1.51	....	....	....	....	....	....	....
2013-14	**St. Louis**	**NHL**	**31**	**18**	**6**	**2**	**1624**	**53**	**4**	**1.96**	....	....	....	....	....	....	....
2014-15	**St. Louis**	**NHL**	**46**	**26**	**14**	**3**	**2546**	**96**	**5**	**2.26**	**1**	**0**	**0**	**26**	**1**	**0**	**2.31**
2015-16	**St. Louis**	**NHL**	**42**	**23**	**8**	**6**	**2263**	**78**	**4**	**2.07**	**18**	**9**	**9**	**1058**	**43**	**1**	**2.44**
2016-17	**Calgary**	**NHL**	**49**	**26**	**18**	**3**	**2844**	**121**	**2**	**2.55**	**4**	**0**	**3**	**185**	**12**	**0**	**3.89**
	NHL Totals		**372**	**191**	**117**	**35**	**20552**	**829**	**36**	**2.42**	**41**	**15**	**22**	**2305**	**100**	**1**	**2.60**

WCHA Second All-Star Team (2006, 2007) • NCAA West First All-American Team (2006) • NCAA Championship All-Tournament Team (2006) • William M. Jennings Trophy (2012) (shared with Jaroslav Halak)

Played in NHL All-Star Game (2012, 2015}

Traded to **Colorado** by **Ottawa** for Craig Anderson, February 18, 2011. Signed as a free agent by **St. Louis**, July 1, 2011. Traded to **Calgary** by **St. Louis** for Calgary's 2nd round pick (Jordan Kyrou) in 2016 NHL Draft and a 3rd round pick in 2018 NHL Draft, June 24, 2016. Signed as a free agent by **Philadelphia**, July 1, 2017.

ELLIS, Nick (EHL-ihs, NIHK) EDM

Goaltender. Catches left. 6'1", 180 lbs. Born, Millersville, MD, January 18, 1994.

			Regular Season								Playoffs						
Season	Club	League	GP	W	L	O/T	Mins	GA	SO	Avg	GP	W	L	Mins	GA	SO	Avg
2009-10	Team Maryland	AYHL	26	....	....	....	1265	92	1	3.86	....	....	....	....	....	....	....
2010-11	Pomfret	High-CT	25	....	....	....	1330	81	1	3.65	....	....	....	....	....	....	....
2011-12	Pomfret	High-CT	25	....	....	....	1323	94	0	4.26	....	....	....	....	....	....	....
2012-13	Des Moines	USHL	37	12	12	4	1882	107	0	3.41	....	....	....	....	....	....	....
2013-14	Providence College	H-East	7	3	2	1	331	13	0	2.35	....	....	....	....	....	....	....
2014-15	Providence College	H-East	5	2	0	0	189	7	1	2.22	....	....	....	....	....	....	....
2015-16	Providence College	H-East	36	25	7	4	2196	66	4	*1.80	....	....	....	....	....	....	....
2016-17	Bakersfield	AHL	34	16	12	2	1781	80	1	2.69	....	....	....	....	....	....	....

Signed as a free agent by **Edmonton**, April 7, 2016.

ENROTH, Jhonas (EHN-rawth, YOH-nuhs)

Goaltender. Catches left. 5'10", 171 lbs. Born, Stockholm, Sweden, June 25, 1988.
(Buffalo's 2nd pick, 46th overall, in 2006 NHL Draft).

			Regular Season								Playoffs						
Season	Club	League	GP	W	L	O/T	Mins	GA	SO	Avg	GP	W	L	Mins	GA	SO	Avg
2003-04	Huddinge IK U18	Swe-U18	6	....	....	....	324	15	0	2.77	....	....	....	....	....	....	....
2004-05	Huddinge IK Jr.	Swe-Jr.	19	....	....	....	1144	49	3	2.57	3	....	....	186	6	1	1.93
	Huddinge IK U18	Swe-U18	2	....	....	....	125	5	0	2.40	....	....	....	....	....	....	....
	Huddinge IK	Sweden-2	2	....	....	....	51	6	0	6.95	....	....	....	....	....	....	....
2005-06	Sodertalje SK Jr.	Swe-Jr.	39	....	....	....	2378	86	1	2.17	4	....	....	243	9	0	2.22
	Sodertalje SK U18	Swe-U18	2	....	....	....	120	5	0	2.50	....	....	....	....	....	....	....
2006-07	Sodertalje SK Jr.	Swe-Jr.	3	....	....	....	180	4	0	1.33	....	....	....	....	....	....	....
	Sodertalje SK	Sweden-2	33	....	....	....	1938	57	3	1.76	....	....	....	....	....	....	....

2007-08	Sodertalje SK Jr.	Swe-Jr.	1	....	....	....	59	4	0	4.05	....	....	....	....	....	....	....
	Sodertalje SK	Sweden	27	....	....	....	1578	56	2	*2.13	....	....	....	....	....	....	....
2008-09	Portland Pirates	AHL	58	26	23	6	3424	157	3	2.75	5	1	4	264	10	1	2.27
2009-10	**Buffalo**	**NHL**	**1**	**0**	**1**	**0**	**58**	**4**	**0**	**4.14**	....	....	....	....	....	....	....
	Portland Pirates	AHL	48	28	18	1	2781	110	5	2.37	....	....	....	....	....	....	....
2010-11	**Buffalo**	**NHL**	**14**	**9**	**2**	**2**	**769**	**35**	**1**	**2.73**	**1**	**0**	**0**	**17**	**1**	**0**	**3.53**
	Portland Pirates	AHL	41	20	17	2	2393	111	0	2.78	4	1	2	217	10	0	2.77
2011-12	**Buffalo**	**NHL**	**26**	**8**	**11**	**4**	**1399**	**63**	**1**	**2.70**	....	....	....	....	....	....	....
2012-13	Huddinge IK	Sweden-3	2	2	0	0	120	5	0	2.50	....	....	....	....	....	....	....
	Almtuna	Sweden-2	14	....	....	....	....	....	....	2.31	....	....	....	....	....	....	....
	Buffalo	**NHL**	**12**	**4**	**4**	**1**	**623**	**27**	**1**	**2.60**	....	....	....	....	....	....	....
2013-14	**Buffalo**	**NHL**	**28**	**4**	**17**	**5**	**1574**	**74**	**0**	**2.82**	....	....	....	....	....	....	....
	Sweden	Olympics					DID NOT PLAY – SPARE GOALTENDER										
2014-15	**Buffalo**	**NHL**	**37**	**13**	**21**	**2**	**2204**	**120**	**1**	**3.27**	....	....	....	....	....	....	....
	Dallas	**NHL**	**13**	**5**	**5**	**0**	**630**	**25**	**1**	**2.38**	....	....	....	....	....	....	....
2015-16	**Los Angeles**	**NHL**	**16**	**7**	**5**	**1**	**856**	**31**	**2**	**2.17**	....	....	....	....	....	....	....
2016-17	**Toronto**	**NHL**	**6**	**0**	**3**	**1**	**274**	**18**	**0**	**3.94**	....	....	....	....	....	....	....
	Toronto Marlies	AHL	3	2	1	0	178	9	0	3.03	....	....	....	....	....	....	....
	San Diego Gulls	AHL	18	14	4	0	1077	31	2	1.73	10	4	6	580	26	0	2.69
	NHL Totals		**153**	**50**	**69**	**16**	**8387**	**397**	**7**	**2.84**	**1**	**0**	**0**	**17**	**1**	**0**	**3.53**

NHL All-Rookie Team (2012)

Signed as a free agent by **Huddinge** (Sweden-3), October 25, 2012. Signed as a free agent by **Almtuna** (Sweden-2), November 5, 2012. Traded to **Dallas** by **Buffalo** for Anders Lindback and Dallas' 3rd round pick (Casey Fitzgerald) in 2016 NHL Draft, February 11, 2015. Signed as a free agent by **Los Angeles**, July 1, 2015. Signed as a free agent by **Toronto**, August 22, 2016. Traded to **Anaheim** by **Toronto** for Anaheim's 7th round pick in 2018 NHL Draft, January 11, 2017.

ERIKSSON EK, Olle (AIR-ihk-suhn EHK, OH-leh) ANA

Goaltender. Catches left. 6'3", 178 lbs. Born, Karlstad, Sweden, June 22, 1999.
(Anaheim's 5th pick, 153rd overall, in 2017 NHL Draft).

			Regular Season								Playoffs						
Season	**Club**	**League**	**GP**	**W**	**L**	**O/T**	**Mins**	**GA**	**SO**	**Avg**	**GP**	**W**	**L**	**Mins**	**GA**	**SO**	**Avg**
2013-14	Farjestad U18	Swe-U18	1	1	0	0	60	0	1	0.00	....	....	....	....	....	....	....
2014-15	Farjestad U18	Swe-U18	15	9	6	0	893	46	1	3.09	....	....	....	....	....	....	....
2015-16	Farjestad U18	Swe-U18	26	12	12	0	1494	82	0	3.29	....	....	....	....	....	....	....
	Farjestad Jr.	Swe-Jr.	2	1	1	0	123	6	0	2.93	....	....	....	....	....	....	....
2016-17	Farjestad Jr.	Swe-Jr.	30	18	11	0	1718	62	5	2.16	1	0	1	60	5	0	5.00
	Farjestad U18	Swe-U18	....	....	....	....	....	....	....	....	1	0	1	24	4	0	10.02

FAGERBLOM, Hugo (FAG-uhr-blawm, HEW-goh) FLA

Goaltender. Catches left. 6'6", 202 lbs. Born, Boras, Sweden, January 9, 1996.
(Florida's 6th pick, 182nd overall, in 2014 NHL Draft).

			Regular Season								Playoffs						
Season	**Club**	**League**	**GP**	**W**	**L**	**O/T**	**Mins**	**GA**	**SO**	**Avg**	**GP**	**W**	**L**	**Mins**	**GA**	**SO**	**Avg**
2012-13	Frolunda U18	Swe-U18	21	15	5	0	1193	33	5	1.66	1	0	1	34	2	0	3.54
2013-14	Frolunda U18	Swe-U18	20	15	5	0	1200	45	4	2.25	2	1	1	120	4	0	2.01
2014-15	Boras HC	Sweden-4	3	3	0	0	180	7	0	2.33	....	....	....	....	....	....	....
	Frolunda Jr.	Swe-Jr.	21	12	6	0	1147	49	2	2.56	4	2	1	209	7	0	2.01
2015-16	Grastorps IK	Sweden-3	4	1	3	0	225	12	0	3.20	....	....	....	....	....	....	....
	Frolunda Jr.	Swe-Jr.	20	9	8	0	1108	69	0	3.74	2	0	2	106	11	0	6.23
2016-17	Wings HC Arlanda	Sweden-3	20	9	9	0	1105	62	0	3.36	....	....	....	....	....	....	....

FEDOTOV, Ivan (feh-DOH-tawv, ih-VAHN) PHI

Goaltender. Catches left. 6'6", 191 lbs. Born, St. Petersburg, Russia, November 28, 1996.
(Philadelphia's 9th pick, 188th overall, in 2015 NHL Draft).

			Regular Season								Playoffs						
Season	**Club**	**League**	**GP**	**W**	**L**	**O/T**	**Mins**	**GA**	**SO**	**Avg**	**GP**	**W**	**L**	**Mins**	**GA**	**SO**	**Avg**
2013-14	Nizhnekamsk Jr.	Russia-Jr.	24	7	11	0	1273	70	0	3.30	....	....	....	....	....	....	....
2014-15	Nizhnekamsk	KHL	1	0	0	0	20	2	0	6.00	....	....	....	....	....	....	....
	Nizhnekamsk Jr.	Russia-Jr.	41	21	10	0	2305	75	6	1.95	10	6	4	578	29	0	3.01
2015-16	Nizhnekamsk Jr.	Russia-Jr.	29	18	5	0	1646	61	5	2.22	5	2	2	326	10	0	1.84
2016-17	Toros Neftekamsk	Russia-2	7	5	2	0	419	12	0	1.72	1	0	0	22	2	0	5.47

FERGUSON, Dylan (FUHR-guh-suhn, DIH-luhn) VGK

Goaltender. Catches left. 6'1", 195 lbs. Born, Lantzville, BC, September 20, 1998.
(Dallas' 8th pick, 194th overall, in 2017 NHL Draft).

			Regular Season								Playoffs						
Season	**Club**	**League**	**GP**	**W**	**L**	**O/T**	**Mins**	**GA**	**SO**	**Avg**	**GP**	**W**	**L**	**Mins**	**GA**	**SO**	**Avg**
2013-14	Notre Dame Argos	SMHL	24	18	4	0	1351	59	0	2.62	6	6	0	362	10	0	1.66
2014-15	Notre Dame	SMHL	25	17	7	0	1420	64	3	2.70	4	2	2	237	8	0	2.02
2015-16	Kamloops Blazers	WHL	16	4	10	0	814	56	1	4.13	....	....	....	....	....	....	....
2016-17	Kamloops Blazers	WHL	31	16	10	2	1706	78	0	2.74	....	....	....	....	....	....	....

Traded to **Vegas** by **Dallas** with Dallas's 2nd round pick in 2020 NHL Draft for Marc Methot, June 26, 2017.

FITZPATRICK, Evan (fihtz-PA-trihk, EH-vuhn) ST.L.

Goaltender. Catches left. 6'2", 203 lbs. Born, St. Johns, NL, January 28, 1998.
(St. Louis' 3rd pick, 59th overall, in 2016 NHL Draft).

			Regular Season								Playoffs						
Season	**Club**	**League**	**GP**	**W**	**L**	**O/T**	**Mins**	**GA**	**SO**	**Avg**	**GP**	**W**	**L**	**Mins**	**GA**	**SO**	**Avg**
2013-14	Dartmouth	NSMHL	18	12	6	0	1093	42	4	2.31	11	6	5	647	31	1	2.87
2014-15	Sherbrooke	QMJHL	32	13	11	0	1689	96	1	3.41	3	1	1	145	11	0	4.56
2015-16	Sherbrooke	QMJHL	54	18	26	8	3067	175	2	3.42	5	1	4	317	18	0	3.41
2016-17	Sherbrooke	QMJHL	49	16	27	4	2741	158	1	3.46	....	....	....	....	....	....	....

FLEURY, Marc-Andre (fluh-REE, MAHRK-AWN-dray) VGK

Goaltender. Catches left. 6'2", 180 lbs. Born, Sorel, QC, November 28, 1984.
(Pittsburgh's 1st pick, 1st overall, in 2003 NHL Draft).

			Regular Season								Playoffs						
Season	**Club**	**League**	**GP**	**W**	**L**	**O/T**	**Mins**	**GA**	**SO**	**Avg**	**GP**	**W**	**L**	**Mins**	**GA**	**SO**	**Avg**
99-2000	C.C. Lemoyne	QAAA	15	4	9	0	780	36	1	2.77	....	....	....	....	....	....	....
2000-01	Cape Breton	QMJHL	35	12	13	2	1705	115	0	4.05	2	0	1	32	4	0	7.50
2001-02	Cape Breton	QMJHL	55	26	14	8	3043	141	2	2.78	16	9	7	1003	55	0	3.29
2002-03	Cape Breton	QMJHL	51	17	24	6	2889	162	2	3.36	4	0	4	228	17	0	4.47
2003-04	**Pittsburgh**	**NHL**	**21**	**4**	**14**	**2**	**1154**	**70**	**1**	**3.64**	....	....	....	....	....	....	....
	Cape Breton	QMJHL	10	8	1	1	606	20	0	1.98	4	1	3	251	13	0	3.10
	Wilkes-Barre	AHL	....	....	....	....	....	....	....	....	2	0	1	92	6	0	3.90
2004-05	Wilkes-Barre	AHL	54	26	19	4	3029	127	5	2.52	4	0	2	151	11	0	4.36
2005-06	**Pittsburgh**	**NHL**	**50**	**13**	**27**	**6**	**2809**	**152**	**1**	**3.25**	....	....	....	....	....	....	....
	Wilkes-Barre	AHL	12	10	2	0	727	19	0	1.57	5	2	3	311	18	0	3.48
2006-07	**Pittsburgh**	**NHL**	**67**	**40**	**16**	**9**	**3905**	**184**	**5**	**2.83**	**5**	**1**	**4**	**287**	**18**	**0**	**3.76**
2007-08	**Pittsburgh**	**NHL**	**35**	**19**	**10**	**2**	**1857**	**72**	**4**	**2.33**	***20**	***14**	**6**	***1251**	**41**	***3**	**1.97**
	Wilkes-Barre	AHL	5	3	2	0	297	7	0	1.42	....	....	....	....	....	....	....
2008-09 ♦	**Pittsburgh**	**NHL**	**62**	**35**	**18**	**7**	**3641**	**162**	**4**	**2.67**	***24**	***16**	**8**	***1447**	**63**	**0**	**2.61**
2009-10	**Pittsburgh**	**NHL**	**67**	**37**	**21**	**6**	**3798**	**168**	**1**	**2.65**	**13**	**7**	**6**	**798**	**37**	**1**	**2.78**
	Canada	Olympics					DID NOT PLAY – SPARE GOALTENDER										
2010-11	**Pittsburgh**	**NHL**	**65**	**36**	**20**	**5**	**3695**	**143**	**3**	**2.32**	**7**	**3**	**4**	**405**	**17**	**1**	**2.52**
2011-12	**Pittsburgh**	**NHL**	**67**	**42**	**17**	**4**	**3896**	**153**	**3**	**2.36**	**6**	**2**	**4**	**337**	**26**	**0**	**4.63**
2012-13	**Pittsburgh**	**NHL**	**33**	**23**	**8**	**0**	**1858**	**74**	**1**	**2.39**	**5**	**2**	**2**	**290**	**17**	**1**	**3.52**
2013-14	**Pittsburgh**	**NHL**	**64**	**39**	**18**	**5**	**3792**	**150**	**5**	**2.37**	**13**	**7**	**6**	**800**	**32**	***2**	**2.40**
2014-15	**Pittsburgh**	**NHL**	**64**	**34**	**20**	**9**	**3776**	**146**	**10**	**2.32**	**5**	**1**	**4**	**312**	**11**	**0**	**2.12**
2015-16 ♦	**Pittsburgh**	**NHL**	**58**	**35**	**17**	**6**	**3463**	**132**	**5**	**2.29**	**2**	**0**	**1**	**79**	**4**	**0**	**3.04**
2016-17 ♦	**Pittsburgh**	**NHL**	**38**	**18**	**10**	**7**	**2125**	**107**	**1**	**3.02**	**15**	**9**	**6**	**867**	**37**	**2**	**2.56**
	NHL Totals		**691**	**375**	**216**	**68**	**39769**	**1713**	**44**	**2.58**	**115**	**62**	**51**	**6873**	**303**	**10**	**2.65**

Claimed by **Vegas** from **Pittsburgh** in Expansion Draft, June 21, 2017.

QMJHL Second All-Star Team (2003)

Played in NHL All-Star Game (2011, 2015)

FORSBERG, Anton (FOHRZ-buhrg, AN-tawn) CHI

Goaltender. Catches left. 6'3", 192 lbs. Born, Harnosand, Sweden, November 27, 1992.
(Columbus' 6th pick, 188th overall, in 2011 NHL Draft).

			Regular Season								Playoffs						
Season	**Club**	**League**	**GP**	**W**	**L**	**O/T**	**Mins**	**GA**	**SO**	**Avg**	**GP**	**W**	**L**	**Mins**	**GA**	**SO**	**Avg**
2007-08	Harnosand Jr.	Swe-Jr.	9	....	....	....	....	....	....	....	....	....	....	....	....	....	....
	Harnosand	Sweden-3	1	....	....	....	20	2	0	6.00	....	....	....	....	....	....	....
2008-09	MODO U18	Swe-U18	12	....	....	....	619	34	0	3.29	5	....	....	225	11	1	2.93
2009-10	MODO U18	Swe-U18	9	....	....	....	538	26	0	2.90	2	....	....	120	5	0	2.50
	MODO Jr.	Swe-Jr.	21	....	....	....	1183	73	1	3.70	3	....	....	177	7	0	2.37
2010-11	MODO Jr.	Swe-Jr.	33	....	....	....	1942	94	3	2.90	6	....	....	358	17	0	2.85
	AIK Harnosand	Sweden-3	1	....	....	....	59	5	0	5.11	....	....	....	....	....	....	....
2011-12	MODO	Sweden	14	....	....	....	609	32	0	3.15	....	....	....	....	....	....	....
	MODO Jr.	Swe-Jr.	14	....	....	....	847	31	2	2.19	4	....	....	248	14	0	3.39
2012-13	Sodertalje SK	Sweden-2	41	26	14	0	2432	90	3	2.22	....	....	....	....	....	....	....
2013-14	MODO	Sweden	22	11	11	0	1304	53	1	2.44	....	....	....	....	....	....	....
	Springfield Falcons	AHL	4	3	0	0	212	4	0	1.13	2	0	1	59	3	0	3.03
2014-15	**Columbus**	**NHL**	**5**	**0**	**4**	**0**	**256**	**20**	**0**	**4.69**	....	....	....	....	....	....	....
	Springfield Falcons	AHL	30	20	8	1	1764	59	3	2.01	....	....	....	....	....	....	....
2015-16	**Columbus**	**NHL**	**4**	**1**	**3**	**0**	**178**	**9**	**0**	**3.03**	....	....	....	....	....	....	....
	Lake Erie Monsters	AHL	41	23	10	5	2302	92	2	2.40	10	9	0	584	13	*2	*1.34
2016-17	**Columbus**	**NHL**	**1**	**0**	**1**	**0**	**59**	**4**	**0**	**4.07**	....	....	....	....	....	....	....
	Cleveland	AHL	51	27	17	4	2977	113	4	2.28	....	....	....	....	....	....	....
	NHL Totals		**10**	**1**	**8**	**0**	**493**	**33**	**0**	**4.02**	....	....	....	....	....	....	....

Traded to **Chicago** by **Columbus** with Brandon Saad and Columbus' 5th round pick in 2018 NHL Draft for Artemi Panarin, Tyler Motte and NY Islanders 6th round pick (previously acquired, Columbus selected Jonathan Davidsson) in 2017 NHL Draft, June 23, 2017.

FUCALE, Zachary (fuh-KAL-ee, za-KAH-ree) MTL

Goaltender. Catches left. 6'2", 191 lbs. Born, Rosemere, QC, May 28, 1995.
(Montreal's 3rd pick, 36th overall, in 2013 NHL Draft).

			Regular Season								Playoffs						
Season	**Club**	**League**	**GP**	**W**	**L**	**O/T**	**Mins**	**GA**	**SO**	**Avg**	**GP**	**W**	**L**	**Mins**	**GA**	**SO**	**Avg**
2010-11	Saint-Eustache	QAAA	28	15	5	3	1513	78	3	3.09	10	7	3	664	40	0	3.61
2011-12	Halifax	QMJHL	58	32	18	6	3249	171	2	3.16	17	10	7	1022	49	0	2.88
2012-13	Halifax	QMJHL	55	*45	5	3	3162	124	2	2.35	17	*16	1	*1042	35	*3	*2.02
2013-14	Halifax	QMJHL	50	*36	9	3	2917	110	6	*2.26	15	9	4	797	37	0	2.79
2014-15	Halifax	QMJHL	24	13	9	2	1426	76	2	3.20	....	....	....	....	....	....	....
	Quebec Remparts	QMJHL	17	8	8	0	933	50	1	3.22	20	14	6	1194	51	1	2.56
2015-16	St. John's IceCaps	AHL	42	16	19	4	2376	124	1	3.13	....	....	....	....	....	....	....
2016-17	St. John's IceCaps	AHL	3	1	2	0	178	7	1	2.36	....	....	....	....	....	....	....
	Brampton Beast	ECHL	46	25	12	4	2539	134	4	3.17	11	6	5	704	25	0	2.13

QMJHL First All-Star Team (2013) • QMJHL Second All-Star Team (2014)

GEORGIEV, Alexandar (ZHOHR-zhee-ehv, al-EHX-AN-duhr) NYR

Goaltender. Catches left. 6'1", 180 lbs. Born, Moscow, Russia, February 10, 1996.

			Regular Season								Playoffs						
Season	**Club**	**League**	**GP**	**W**	**L**	**O/T**	**Mins**	**GA**	**SO**	**Avg**	**GP**	**W**	**L**	**Mins**	**GA**	**SO**	**Avg**
2014-15	TPS Turku Jr.	Fin-Jr.	25	....	....	....	1490	56	....	2.25	12	....	....	739	32	....	2.60
	TPS Turku	Finland	14	2	8	2	759	28	2	2.21	....	....	....	....	....	....	....
2015-16	TPS Turku Jr.	Fin-Jr.	9	....	....	....	547	26	....	2.85	....	....	....	....	....	....	....
	SaPKo Savonlinna	Finland-2	13	....	....	....	722	30	....	2.49	....	....	....	....	....	....	....
	TPS Turku	Finland	10	3	4	0	395	15	1	2.28	2	0	1	79	5	0	3.78
2016-17	TPS Turku	Finland	27	13	8	4	1554	44	2	*1.70	1	0	0	2	0	0	0.00

Signed as a free agent by **NY Rangers**, July 17, 2017.

GIBSON, Christopher (GIHB-suhn, KRIHS-tuh-fuhr) NYI

Goaltender. Catches left. 6'1", 188 lbs. Born, Karkkila, Finland, December 27, 1992.
(Los Angeles' 1st pick, 49th overall, in 2011 NHL Draft).

			Regular Season								Playoffs						
Season	**Club**	**League**	**GP**	**W**	**L**	**O/T**	**Mins**	**GA**	**SO**	**Avg**	**GP**	**W**	**L**	**Mins**	**GA**	**SO**	**Avg**
2008-09	Notre Dame	SMHL	18	16	1	0	1049	46	1	2.63	6	6	0	360	11	1	1.83
2009-10	Chicoutimi	QMJHL	29	8	19	0	1592	93	2	3.50	4	2	1	230	13	0	3.39
2010-11	Chicoutimi	QMJHL	37	14	15	8	2235	90	4	2.42	4	0	4	219	19	0	5.20
2011-12	Chicoutimi	QMJHL	48	27	17	4	2809	139	3	2.97	18	9	9	1116	58	*1	3.12
2012-13	Chicoutimi	QMJHL	41	17	18	4	2279	117	4	3.08	6	2	4	356	23	0	3.87
2013-14	Toronto Marlies	AHL	12	5	6	0	640	26	0	2.44	....	....	....	....	....	....	....
	Orlando	ECHL	20	8	9	2	1178	62	0	3.16	2	1	1	123	4	0	1.94
2014-15	Toronto Marlies	AHL	45	24	17	3	2605	105	2	2.42	4	2	2	231	15	0	3.90
2015-16	**NY Islanders**	**NHL**	**4**	**1**	**1**	**1**	**194**	**11**	**0**	**3.40**	....	....	....	....	....	....	....
	Bridgeport	AHL	42	19	11	6	2351	106	2	2.70	1	0	1	59	6	0	6.15
2016-17	Bridgeport	AHL	7	6	0	0	380	16	0	2.52	....	....	....	....	....	....	....
	NHL Totals		**4**	**1**	**1**	**1**	**194**	**11**	**0**	**3.40**	....	....	....	....	....	....	....

QMJHL First All-Star Team (2011)

Signed as a free agent by **Toronto**, July 21, 2013. Traded to **NY Islanders** by **Toronto** with Carter Verhaeghe, Tom Nilsson, Taylor Beck and Matt Finn for Michael Grabner, September 17, 2015. • Missed majority of 2016-17 due to recurring knee injury.

GIBSON, John (GIHB-suhn, JAWN) ANA

Goaltender. Catches left. 6'3", 226 lbs. Born, Pittsburgh, PA, July 14, 1993.
(Anaheim's 2nd pick, 39th overall, in 2011 NHL Draft).

			Regular Season								Playoffs						
Season	Club	League	GP	W	L	O/T	Mins	GA	SO	Avg	GP	W	L	Mins	GA	SO	Avg
2009-10	USAHNTDP	USHL	18	7	9	0	1023	63	0	3.69	....	....	....	....	....	....	....
	USAHNTDP	U-17	6	3	1	1	335	16	0	2.87	....	....	....	....	....	....	....
	USAHNTDP	U-18	2	2	0	0	120	4	0	2.00	....	....	....	....	....	....	....
2010-11	USAHNTDP	USHL	17	9	4	3	983	39	1	2.38	....	....	....	....	....	....	....
	USAHNTDP	U-18	23	15	7	0	1255	56	0	2.68	....	....	....	....	....	....	....
2011-12	Kitchener Rangers	OHL	32	21	10	0	1897	87	1	2.75	16	8	7	898	40	1	2.67
2012-13	Kitchener Rangers	OHL	27	17	9	1	1615	65	1	2.41	10	5	5	609	22	1	2.17
	Norfolk Admirals	AHL	1	0	0	0	40	3	0	4.50	....	....	....	....	....	....	....
2013-14	**Anaheim**	**NHL**	**3**	**3**	**0**	**0**	**181**	**4**	**1**	**1.33**	**4**	**2**	**2**	**200**	**9**	**1**	**2.70**
	Norfolk Admirals	AHL	45	21	17	4	2587	101	5	2.34	6	4	2	373	9	1	*1.45
2014-15	**Anaheim**	**NHL**	**23**	**13**	**8**	**0**	**1340**	**58**	**1**	**2.60**	....	....	....	....	....	....	....
	Norfolk Admirals	AHL	11	6	3	2	665	23	1	2.07	....	....	....	....	....	....	....
2015-16	**Anaheim**	**NHL**	**40**	**21**	**13**	**4**	**2295**	**79**	**4**	**2.07**	**2**	**0**	**2**	**117**	**6**	**0**	**3.08**
	San Diego Gulls	AHL	13	7	4	1	775	34	1	2.63	....	....	....	....	....	....	....
2016-17	**Anaheim**	**NHL**	**52**	**25**	**16**	**9**	**2950**	**109**	**6**	**2.22**	**16**	**9**	**5**	**879**	**38**	**0**	**2.59**
	NHL Totals		**118**	**62**	**37**	**13**	**6766**	**250**	**12**	**2.22**	**22**	**11**	**9**	**1196**	**53**	**1**	**2.66**

OHL Second All-Star Team (2013) • NHL All-Rookie Team (2016) • William M. Jennings Trophy (2016) (shared with Frederik Andersen)

Played in NHL All-Star Game (2016)

GILLIES, Jon (GIHL-eez, JAWN) CGY

Goaltender. Catches left. 6'6", 225 lbs. Born, Concord, NH, January 22, 1994.
(Calgary's 3rd pick, 75th overall, in 2012 NHL Draft).

			Regular Season								Playoffs						
Season	Club	League	GP	W	L	O/T	Mins	GA	SO	Avg	GP	W	L	Mins	GA	SO	Avg
2009-10	Salisbury School	High-CT	8	....	....	....	313	....	1	1.99	....	....	....	....	....	....	....
	Neponset Valley	Minor-MA					STATISTICS NOT AVAILABLE										
2010-11	Indiana Ice	USHL	25	15	6	2	1447	68	3	2.82	2	0	1	82	3	0	2.20
2011-12	Indiana Ice	USHL	53	31	11	9	2967	137	3	2.77	6	3	3	359	17	0	2.84
2012-13	Providence College	H-East	35	17	12	6	2105	73	5	2.08	....	....	....	....	....	....	....
2013-14	Providence College	H-East	34	19	9	5	2027	73	4	2.16	....	....	....	....	....	....	....
2014-15	Providence College	H-East	*39	24	13	2	*2301	77	*4	*2.01	....	....	....	....	....	....	....
2015-16	Stockton Heat	AHL	7	2	3	1	363	14	2	2.31	....	....	....	....	....	....	....
2016-17	**Calgary**	**NHL**	**1**	**1**	**0**	**0**	**60**	**1**	**0**	**1.00**	....	....	....	....	....	....	....
	Stockton Heat	AHL	39	18	14	4	2215	108	1	2.93	3	0	2	137	8	0	3.49
	NHL Totals		**1**	**1**	**0**	**0**	**60**	**1**	**0**	**1.00**	....	....	....	....	....	....	....

Hockey East All-Rookie Team (2013) • Hockey East First All-Star Team (2013, 2015) • Hockey East Rookie of the Year (2013) • NCAA East Second All-American Team (2013, 2015) • NCAA Championship All-Tournament Team (2015) • NCAA Championship Tournament MVP (2015)

• Missed majority of 2015-16 due to hip injury vs. Bakersfield (AHL), November 6, 2015.

GLASS, Jeff (GLAS, JEHF) CHI

Goaltender. Catches left. 6'3", 206 lbs. Born, Calgary, AB, November 19, 1985.
(Ottawa's 5th pick, 89th overall, in 2004 NHL Draft).

			Regular Season								Playoffs						
Season	Club	League	GP	W	L	O/T	Mins	GA	SO	Avg	GP	W	L	Mins	GA	SO	Avg
2001-02	Crowsnest Pass	AJHL	34	....	....	....	1802	126	0	4.20	....	....	....	....	....	....	....
2002-03	Kootenay Ice	WHL	35	15	16	3	1884	77	4	2.45	9	4	5	643	23	0	2.15
2003-04	Kootenay Ice	WHL	57	26	20	6	3263	128	5	2.35	4	0	4	239	14	0	3.51
2004-05	Kootenay Ice	WHL	51	34	11	5	3061	90	8	1.76	16	10	6	1027	39	0	2.28
2005-06	Binghamton	AHL	6	1	4	0	312	20	0	3.85	....	....	....	....	....	....	....
	Charlotte Checkers	ECHL	39	19	15	4	2221	119	2	3.22	3	1	2	178	11	0	3.71
2006-07	Binghamton	AHL	43	9	24	2	2174	149	1	4.11	....	....	....	....	....	....	....
2007-08	Binghamton	AHL	45	15	20	4	2313	111	2	2.88	....	....	....	....	....	....	....
2008-09	Binghamton	AHL	41	17	19	3	2219	119	0	3.22	....	....	....	....	....	....	....
2009-10	Barys Astana	KHL	41	....	....	....	2113	101	1	2.87	3	....	....	223	10	0	2.69
2010-11	Barys Astana	KHL	23	....	....	....	1240	61	1	2.95	2	....	....	119	6	0	3.02
2011-12	Barys Astana	KHL	28	12	12	0	1546	83	1	3.22	....	....	....	....	....	....	....
2012-13	Sibir Novosibirsk	KHL	38	16	11	0	2198	74	4	2.02	7	3	4	407	12	2	1.77
2013-14	Spartak Moscow	KHL	37	12	19	0	2098	81	4	2.32	....	....	....	....	....	....	....
	CSKA Moscow	KHL	6	2	2	0	366	8	1	1.31	4	0	4	212	11	0	3.11
2014-15	Lada Togliatti	KHL	14	1	9	0	677	39	0	3.46	....	....	....	....	....	....	....
2015-16	Dynamo Minsk	KHL	31	12	14	0	1756	81	4	2.77	....	....	....	....	....	....	....
2016-17	Toronto Marlies	AHL	2	1	1	0	117	4	0	2.05	....	....	....	....	....	....	....
	Rockford IceHogs	AHL	20	8	10	2	1165	51	2	2.63	....	....	....	....	....	....	....

WHL West First All-Star Team (2005) • WHL Goaltender of the Year (2005) • Canadian Major Junior First All-Star Team (2005) • Canadian Major Junior Goaltender of the Year (2005)

Signed as a free agent by **Astana** (KHL), August 31, 2009. Signed to a PTO (professional try-out) contract by **Toronto** (AHL), September 27, 2016. Signed as a free agent by **Rockford** (AHL), January 10, 2017. Signed as a free agent by **Chicago**, February 23, 2017.

GREISS, Thomas (GRIGHS, TAW-muhs) NYI

Goaltender. Catches left. 6'1", 228 lbs. Born, Fussen, West Germany, January 29, 1986.
(San Jose's 2nd pick, 94th overall, in 2004 NHL Draft).

			Regular Season								Playoffs						
Season	Club	League	GP	W	L	O/T	Mins	GA	SO	Avg	GP	W	L	Mins	GA	SO	Avg
2001-02	EV Fussen Jr.	Ger-Jr.					STATISTICS NOT AVAILABLE										
2002-03	Koln Jr.	Ger-Jr.	25	....	....	....	1613	58	0	2.16	3	1	2	180	8	1	2.67
2003-04	Koln Jr.	Ger-Jr.	24	....	....	....	1286	56	....	2.61	....	....	....	....	....	....	....
	Kolner Haie	Germany	1	....	....	....	20	4	0	12.00	....	....	....	....	....	....	....
2004-05	Kolner Haie	Germany	8	....	....	....	459	16	0	2.09	....	....	....	....	....	....	....
	Regensburg	German-2	1	....	....	....	60	2	0	2.00	2	....	....	56	2	0	2.14
2005-06	Kolner Haie	Germany	27	....	....	....	1560	64	1	2.46	9	....	....	533	27	*1	3.04
	Germany	Olympics	1	0	1	0	60	5	0	5.00	....	....	....	....	....	....	....
2006-07	Worcester Sharks	AHL	43	26	15	2	2555	111	0	2.61	3	0	3	172	12	0	4.18
	Fresno Falcons	ECHL	3	1	2	0	180	7	0	2.34	....	....	....	....	....	....	....
2007-08	**San Jose**	**NHL**	**3**	**0**	**1**	**1**	**129**	**7**	**0**	**3.26**	....	....	....	....	....	....	....
	Worcester Sharks	AHL	41	18	21	2	2424	125	0	3.09	....	....	....	....	....	....	....
2008-09	Worcester Sharks	AHL	57	30	24	2	3346	138	1	2.47	12	6	6	742	30	2	2.43
2009-10	**San Jose**	**NHL**	**16**	**7**	**4**	**1**	**782**	**35**	**0**	**2.69**	**1**	**0**	**0**	**40**	**2**	**0**	**3.00**
	Germany	Olympics	3	0	3	0	179	15	0	5.03	....	....	....	....	....	....	....
2010-11	Brynas IF Gavle	Sweden	32	....	....	....	1850	90	2	2.92	5	....	....	317	18	0	3.40
2011-12	**San Jose**	**NHL**	**19**	**9**	**7**	**1**	**1043**	**40**	**0**	**2.30**	....	....	....	....	....	....	....
2012-13	Hannover Scorp.	Germany	9	3	6	0	535	31	0	3.47	....	....	....	....	....	....	....
	San Jose	**NHL**	**6**	**1**	**4**	**0**	**308**	**13**	**1**	**2.53**	....	....	....	....	....	....	....
	Worcester Sharks	AHL	1	0	1	0	60	5	0	5.04	....	....	....	....	....	....	....
2013-14	**Phoenix**	**NHL**	**25**	**10**	**8**	**5**	**1312**	**50**	**2**	**2.29**	....	....	....	....	....	....	....
2014-15	**Pittsburgh**	**NHL**	**20**	**9**	**6**	**3**	**1159**	**50**	**0**	**2.59**	....	....	....	....	....	....	....
2015-16	**NY Islanders**	**NHL**	**41**	**23**	**11**	**4**	**2287**	**90**	**1**	**2.36**	**11**	**5**	**6**	**733**	**30**	**0**	**2.46**
2016-17	**NY Islanders**	**NHL**	**51**	**26**	**18**	**5**	**2813**	**126**	**3**	**2.69**	....	....	....	....	....	....	....
	NHL Totals		**181**	**85**	**59**	**20**	**9833**	**411**	**7**	**2.51**	**12**	**5**	**6**	**773**	**32**	**0**	**2.48**

• Re-assigned to **Gavle** (Sweden) by **San Jose**, October 21, 2010. Signed as a free agent by **Hannover** (Germany), November 20, 2012. Signed as a free agent by **Phoenix**, July 5, 2013. Signed as a free agent by **Pittsburgh**, July 1, 2014. Signed as a free agent by **NY Islanders**, July 1, 2015.

GROSENICK, Troy (GOHS-nihk, TROI) S.J.

Goaltender. Catches left. 6'1", 185 lbs. Born, Brookfield, WI, August 27, 1989.

			Regular Season								Playoffs						
Season	Club	League	GP	W	L	O/T	Mins	GA	SO	Avg	GP	W	L	Mins	GA	SO	Avg
2010-11	Union College	ECAC	3	0	0	1	85	3	0	2.12	....	....	....	....	....	....	....
2011-12	Union College	ECAC	34	22	6	3	1922	53	5	1.65	....	....	....	....	....	....	....
2012-13	Union College	ECAC	34	17	10	5	1929	68	2	2.12	....	....	....	....	....	....	....
2013-14	Worcester Sharks	AHL	35	18	14	0	1966	86	2	2.62	....	....	....	....	....	....	....
2014-15	**San Jose**	**NHL**	**2**	**1**	**1**	**0**	**118**	**3**	**1**	**1.53**	....	....	....	....	....	....	....
	Worcester Sharks	AHL	36	20	13	3	2167	95	1	2.63	2	1	0	88	5	0	3.41
2015-16	San Jose Barracuda	AHL	28	11	10	4	1574	83	0	3.16	1	0	0	4	0	0	0.00
2016-17	San Jose Barracuda	AHL	49	30	10	5	2729	93	*10	2.04	15	8	7	914	41	*2	2.69
	NHL Totals		**2**	**1**	**1**	**0**	**118**	**3**	**1**	**1.53**	....	....	....	....	....	....	....

ECAC First All-Star Team (2012) • NCAA East First All-American Team (2012) • AHL First All-Star Team (2017) • Aldege "Baz" Bastien Award (AHL – Outstanding Goaltender) (2017)

Signed as a free agent by **San Jose**, April 8, 2013.

GRUBAUER, Philipp (groo-BAHW-uhr, FIHL-ihp) WSH

Goaltender. Catches left. 6'1", 182 lbs. Born, Rosenheim, Germany, November 25, 1991.
(Washington's 3rd pick, 112th overall, in 2010 NHL Draft).

			Regular Season								Playoffs						
Season	Club	League	GP	W	L	O/T	Mins	GA	SO	Avg	GP	W	L	Mins	GA	SO	Avg
2006-07	Rosenheim Jr.	Ger-Jr.	6	....	....	....	354	49	....	8.32	3	....	....	180	12	....	4.00
2007-08	Rosenheim Jr.	Ger-Jr.	23	....	....	....	1288	71	....	3.31	3	....	....	181	8	....	2.65
	Rosenheim	German-3	5	....	....	....	307	14	1	2.74	7	....	....	420	12	....	1.71
2008-09	Belleville Bulls	OHL	17	7	8	0	947	62	1	3.93	1	0	0	56	4	0	4.26
2009-10	Belleville Bulls	OHL	31	10	14	5	1717	90	5	3.14	....	....	....	....	....	....	....
	Windsor Spitfires	OHL	19	13	1	2	1011	40	2	2.37	18	*16	2	1094	49	0	2.69
2010-11	Kingston	OHL	38	22	13	3	2239	135	2	3.62	....	....	....	....	....	....	....
2011-12	South Carolina	ECHL	43	23	13	5	2536	94	1	2.22	....	....	....	....	....	....	....
2012-13	Reading Royals	ECHL	26	19	5	1	1542	59	0	2.30	....	....	....	....	....	....	....
	Hershey Bears	AHL	28	15	9	2	1624	61	2	2.25	5	2	3	301	19	0	3.79
	Washington	**NHL**	**2**	**0**	**1**	**0**	**84**	**5**	**0**	**3.57**	....	....	....	....	....	....	....
2013-14	**Washington**	**NHL**	**17**	**6**	**5**	**5**	**883**	**35**	**0**	**2.38**	....	....	....	....	....	....	....
	Hershey Bears	AHL	28	13	13	2	1685	73	3	2.60	....	....	....	....	....	....	....
2014-15	**Washington**	**NHL**	**1**	**1**	**0**	**0**	**65**	**2**	**0**	**1.85**	**1**	**1**	**0**	**60**	**3**	**0**	**3.00**
	Hershey Bears	AHL	49	27	17	5	2918	112	6	2.30	7	2	4	394	22	0	3.35
2015-16	**Washington**	**NHL**	**22**	**8**	**9**	**1**	**1111**	**43**	**0**	**2.32**	....	....	....	....	....	....	....
2016-17	**Washington**	**NHL**	**24**	**13**	**6**	**2**	**1265**	**43**	**3**	**2.04**	**1**	**0**	**0**	**19**	**2**	**0**	**6.32**
	NHL Totals		**66**	**28**	**21**	**8**	**3408**	**128**	**3**	**2.25**	**2**	**1**	**0**	**79**	**5**	**0**	**3.80**

GUDLEVSKIS, Kristers (guhd-LEHV-skihz, KRIHS-tuhrs) NYI

Goaltender. Catches left. 6'3", 223 lbs. Born, Aizkraukle, Latvia, July 31, 1992.
(Tampa Bay's 3rd pick, 124th overall, in 2013 NHL Draft).

			Regular Season								Playoffs						
Season	Club	League	GP	W	L	O/T	Mins	GA	SO	Avg	GP	W	L	Mins	GA	SO	Avg
2009-10	HK Ogre	Latvia	9	....	....	....	....	....	....	6.12	....	....	....	....	....	....	....
	Ozolnieki-Juniors	Belarus-2	31	....	....	....	....	157	....	....	....	....	....	....	....	....	....
2010-11	HK Riga Jr.	Russia-Jr.	49	....	....	....	2760	101	7	2.20	3	....	....	188	13	0	4.16
2011-12	HK Riga Jr.	Russia-Jr.	40	....	....	....	2285	91	1	2.39	4	....	....	257	15	0	3.50
2012-13	Dynamo Riga	KHL	2	1	1	0	82	3	0	2.18	....	....	....	....	....	....	....
	HK Riga Jr.	Russia-Jr.	56	....	....	....	3190	111	3	2.09	3	....	....	154	19	0	7.42
	Juniors Riga Jr.	Rus.-Jr. B	2	....	....	....	120	6	0	3.00	....	....	....	....	....	....	....
	HK Juniors Riga Jr.	Latvia	....	....	....	....	....	....	....	....	1	....	....	59	1	0	1.02
2013-14	**Tampa Bay**	**NHL**	**1**	**1**	**0**	**0**	**60**	**2**	**0**	**2.00**	**2**	**0**	**1**	**40**	**2**	**0**	**3.00**
	Syracuse Crunch	AHL	34	18	11	4	1901	85	5	2.68	....	....	....	....	....	....	....
	Florida Everblades	ECHL	11	7	4	0	656	20	2	1.83	....	....	....	....	....	....	....
	Latvia	Olympics	2	0	2	0	119	7	0	3.54	....	....	....	....	....	....	....
2014-15	Syracuse Crunch	AHL	46	25	14	4	2673	125	2	2.81	3	0	3	145	12	0	4.96
2015-16	**Tampa Bay**	**NHL**	**1**	**0**	**0**	**1**	**60**	**1**	**0**	**1.00**	....	....	....	....	....	....	....
	Syracuse Crunch	AHL	41	16	12	8	2333	110	1	2.83	....	....	....	....	....	....	....
2016-17	**Tampa Bay**	**NHL**	**1**	**0**	**0**	**0**	**11**	**0**	**0**	**0.00**	....	....	....	....	....	....	....
	Syracuse Crunch	AHL	37	15	10	7	1947	86	0	2.65	1	0	0	38	0	0	0.00
	NHL Totals		**3**	**1**	**0**	**1**	**131**	**3**	**0**	**1.37**	**2**	**0**	**1**	**40**	**2**	**0**	**3.00**

Traded to **NY Islanders** by **Tampa Bay** for Carter Verhaeghe, July 1, 2017.

GUSTAFSSON, Johan (GUHS-tahf-suhn, YOH-han) MIN

Goaltender. Catches left. 6'2", 199 lbs. Born, Koping, Sweden, February 28, 1992.
(Minnesota's 5th pick, 159th overall, in 2010 NHL Draft).

			Regular Season								Playoffs						
Season	Club	League	GP	W	L	O/T	Mins	GA	SO	Avg	GP	W	L	Mins	GA	SO	Avg
2006-07	IFK Arboga IK	Sweden-2	4	....	....	....	201	22	0	6.55	....	....	....	....	....	....	....
2007-08	Kopings HC	Sweden-4					STATISTICS NOT AVAILABLE										
2008-09	Farjestad U18	Swe-U18	27	....	....	....	1581	47	5	1.78	4	....	....	228	14	0	3.68
2009-10	Farjestad U18	Swe-U18	10	....	....	....	600	34	1	3.40	7	....	....	417	22	0	3.16
	Farjestad	Sweden	3	....	....	....	136	9	0	3.96	....	....	....	....	....	....	....
	Skare BK	Sweden-3	26	....	....	....	1553	74	2	2.86	....	....	....	....	....	....	....
2010-11	VIK Vasteras HK Jr.	Swe-Jr.	7	....	....	....	424	20	1	2.83	....	....	....	....	....	....	....
	VIK Vasteras HK	Sweden-2	28	....	....	....	1632	64	2	2.35	....	....	....	....	....	....	....
2011-12	Lulea HF	Sweden	29	....	....	....	1754	51	6	1.74	3	....	....	179	10	0	3.36
2012-13	Lulea HF	Sweden	33	20	13	0	2016	57	4	1.70	*15	8	7	*946	32	0	2.03
2013-14	Iowa Wild	AHL	40	12	20	4	2253	112	1	2.98	....	....	....	....	....	....	....
2014-15	Iowa Wild	AHL	35	8	22	1	1842	107	0	3.48	....	....	....	....	....	....	....
	Alaska Aces	ECHL	5	4	1	0	304	15	0	2.96	....	....	....	....	....	....	....

2015-16	Frolunda	Sweden	22	10	9	0	1157	51	1	2.65	9	6	2	506	19	0	2.25
2016-17	Frolunda	Sweden	38	22	13	0	2074	73	2	2.11	14	7	7	804	34	2	2.54

Signed as a free agent by **Frolunda** (Sweden), May 4, 2015.

GUSTAVSSON, Filip (GUHS-tahf-suhn, FIHL-ihp) PIT

Goaltender. Catches left. 6'2", 190 lbs. Born, Skelleftea, Sweden, June 7, 1998.
(Pittsburgh's 1st pick, 55th overall, in 2016 NHL Draft).

			Regular Season								Playoffs						
Season	Club	League	GP	W	L	O/T	Mins	GA	SO	Avg	GP	W	L	Mins	GA	SO	Avg
2012-13	Skelleftea AIK U18	Swe-U18	1	1	0	0	60	3	0	3.00	....	....	....	....	....	....	....
2013-14	Skelleftea AIK U18	Swe-U18	18	15	3	0	1082	28	4	1.55	....	....	....	....	....	....	....
2014-15	Lulea HF U18	Swe-U18	18	9	9	0	1092	40	2	2.20	....	....	....	....	....	....	....
	Lulea HF Jr.	Swe-Jr.	7	1	6	0	424	28	0	3.96	....	....	....	....	....	....	....
2015-16	Lulea HF Jr.	Swe-Jr.	20	8	11	0	1154	62	0	3.22	1	0	1	60	3	0	3.00
	Lulea HF	Sweden	6	4	2	0	359	13	0	2.17	1	0	0	1	0	0	0.00
2016-17	Lulea HF Jr.	Swe-Jr.	6	3	3	0	373	13	0	2.09	3	1	2	189	3	1	0.95
	Lulea HF	Sweden	15	4	10	0	845	38	0	2.70	2	0	1	51	3	0	3.53

GUSTAVSSON, Jonas (GUHS-tahv-suhn, YOH-nuhs)

Goaltender. Catches left. 6'4", 201 lbs. Born, Danderyd, Sweden, October 24, 1984.

			Regular Season								Playoffs						
Season	Club	League	GP	W	L	O/T	Mins	GA	SO	Avg	GP	W	L	Mins	GA	SO	Avg
2000-01	AIK Solna U18	Swe-U18	12	....	....	....	667	42	1	3.78	....	....	....	....	....	....	....
2001-02	AIK Solna U18	Swe-U18	8	....	....	....	439	13	2	1.78	4	....	....	239	12	0	3.01
2002-03	AIK Solna Jr.	Swe-Jr.	21	....	....	....	1261	69	0	3.28	4	....	....	198	9	0	2.72
2003-04	AIK Solna Jr.	Swe-Jr.	9	....	....	....	505	24	0	2.85	....	....	....	....	....	....	....
	AIK Solna	Sweden-2	1	....	....	....	20	1	0	2.95	....	....	....	....	....	....	....
2004-05	AIK Solna Jr.	Swe-Jr.	10	....	....	....	557	32	0	3.45	....	....	....	....	....	....	....
	AIK Solna	Sweden-3	22	....	....	....	1270	32	4	1.51	....	....	....	....	....	....	....
2005-06	AIK Solna Jr.	Swe-Jr.	5	....	....	....	258	14	0	3.26	....	....	....	....	....	....	....
	AIK Solna	Sweden-2	6	....	....	....	351	14	0	2.39	....	....	....	....	....	....	....
2006-07	AIK IF Solna	Sweden-2	23	....	....	....	1269	59	2	2.79	....	....	....	....	....	....	....
2007-08	Skare BK	Sweden-3	6	....	....	....	368	16	0	2.61	....	....	....	....	....	....	....
	Farjestad	Sweden	20	....	....	....	1102	44	2	2.40	10	....	....	517	31	0	3.60
2008-09	Farjestad	Sweden	42	....	....	....	2475	81	3	*1.96	13	....	....	819	14	*5	*1.03
2009-10	**Toronto**	**NHL**	**42**	**16**	**15**	**9**	**2340**	**112**	**1**	**2.87**	....	....	....	....	....	....	....
	Sweden	Olympics	1	1	0	0	60	2	0	2.00	....	....	....	....	....	....	....
2010-11	**Toronto**	**NHL**	**23**	**6**	**13**	**2**	**1242**	**68**	**0**	**3.29**	....	....	....	....	....	....	....
	Toronto Marlies	AHL	5	3	1	1	263	5	0	1.14	....	....	....	....	....	....	....
2011-12	**Toronto**	**NHL**	**42**	**17**	**17**	**4**	**2301**	**112**	**4**	**2.92**	....	....	....	....	....	....	....
2012-13	**Detroit**	**NHL**	**7**	**2**	**2**	**1**	**349**	**17**	**0**	**2.92**	....	....	....	....	....	....	....
	Grand Rapids	AHL	1	1	0	0	60	1	0	1.00	....	....	....	....	....	....	....
2013-14	**Detroit**	**NHL**	**27**	**16**	**5**	**4**	**1551**	**68**	**0**	**2.63**	**2**	**0**	**2**	**133**	**6**	**0**	**2.71**
	Sweden	Olympics	DID NOT PLAY – SPARE GOALTENDER														
2014-15	**Detroit**	**NHL**	**7**	**3**	**3**	**1**	**351**	**15**	**1**	**2.56**	....	....	....	....	....	....	....
	Grand Rapids	AHL	2	1	1	0	119	4	0	2.02	....	....	....	....	....	....	....
2015-16	**Boston**	**NHL**	**24**	**11**	**9**	**1**	**1258**	**57**	**1**	**2.72**	....	....	....	....	....	....	....
2016-17	**Edmonton**	**NHL**	**7**	**1**	**3**	**1**	**329**	**17**	**0**	**3.10**	....	....	....	....	....	....	....
	Bakersfield	AHL	20	8	9	1	1114	45	1	2.42	....	....	....	....	....	....	....
	NHL Totals		**179**	**72**	**67**	**23**	**9721**	**466**	**7**	**2.88**	**2**	**0**	**2**	**133**	**6**	**0**	**2.71**

Signed as a free agent by **Toronto**, July 7, 2009. Traded to **Winnipeg** by **Toronto** for a conditional 7th round pick (conditions not met) in 2012 NHL Draft, June 23, 2012. Signed as a free agent by **Detroit**, July 1, 2012. • Missed majority of 2014-15 due to shoulder injury vs. NY Rangers, November 5, 2014. Signed as a free agent by **Boston**, October 5, 2015. Signed as a free agent by **Edmonton**, July 1, 2016. Signed as a free agent by **Linkoping** (Sweden), May 4, 2017.

HACKETT, Matt (HA-keht, MA-thew)

Goaltender. Catches left. 6'2", 179 lbs. Born, London, ON, March 7, 1990.
(Minnesota's 2nd pick, 77th overall, in 2009 NHL Draft).

			Regular Season								Playoffs						
Season	Club	League	GP	W	L	O/T	Mins	GA	SO	Avg	GP	W	L	Mins	GA	SO	Avg
2006-07	London Jr. Knights	Minor-ON	38	28	7	3	....	52	20	1.39	6	5	1	....	12	2	2.00
	St. Catharines	ON-Jr.B	16	7	7	0	902	63	0	4.19	....	....	....	....	....	....	....
	Windsor Spitfires	OHL	7	0	7	0	429	36	0	5.04	....	....	....	....	....	....	....
2007-08	Windsor Spitfires	OHL	4	1	1	0	130	10	0	4.61	....	....	....	....	....	....	....
	Plymouth Whalers	OHL	18	6	9	1	978	56	0	3.44	1	0	0	16	0	0	0.00
2008-09	Plymouth Whalers	OHL	55	34	15	3	3036	154	2	3.04	11	6	5	638	32	*1	3.01
2009-10	Plymouth Whalers	OHL	56	33	18	3	3165	138	4	2.62	8	3	4	429	24	0	3.36
2010-11	Houston Aeros	AHL	45	23	16	4	2552	101	2	2.37	*24	*14	10	*1465	61	1	2.50
2011-12	**Minnesota**	**NHL**	**12**	**3**	**6**	**0**	**556**	**22**	**0**	**2.37**	....	....	....	....	....	....	....
	Houston Aeros	AHL	44	20	17	6	2546	101	1	2.38	2	0	2	61	6	0	5.93
2012-13	Houston Aeros	AHL	43	19	20	3	2574	114	0	2.66	....	....	....	....	....	....	....
	Minnesota	**NHL**	**1**	**0**	**1**	**0**	**59**	**5**	**0**	**5.08**	....	....	....	....	....	....	....
	Rochester	AHL	3	3	0	0	185	5	0	1.62	1	0	1	58	2	0	2.08
2013-14	**Buffalo**	**NHL**	**8**	**1**	**6**	**1**	**426**	**22**	**0**	**3.10**	....	....	....	....	....	....	....
	Rochester	AHL	33	13	17	2	1952	100	0	3.07	....	....	....	....	....	....	....
2014-15	**Buffalo**	**NHL**	**5**	**0**	**4**	**1**	**250**	**18**	**0**	**4.32**	....	....	....	....	....	....	....
	Rochester	AHL	16	8	5	3	934	43	0	2.76	....	....	....	....	....	....	....
2015-16	San Diego Gulls	AHL	22	10	7	2	1129	57	1	3.03	6	2	4	370	14	1	2.27
	Utah Grizzlies	ECHL	2	2	0	0	127	4	0	1.89	....	....	....	....	....	....	....
2016-17	San Diego Gulls	AHL	7	2	3	0	340	19	1	3.35	....	....	....	....	....	....	....
	NHL Totals		**26**	**4**	**17**	**2**	**1291**	**67**	**0**	**3.11**	....	....	....	....	....	....	....

OHL Second All-Star Team (2010)

Traded to **Buffalo** by **Minnesota** with Johan Larsson, Minnesota's 1st round pick (Nikita Zadorov) in 2013 NHL Draft and Minnesota's 2nd round pick (Vaclav Karabacek) in 2014 NHL Draft for Jason Pominville and Buffalo's 4th round pick (later traded to Edmonton – Edmonton selected William Lagesson) in 2014 NHL Draft, April 3, 2013. Signed as a free agent by **Anaheim**, July 1, 2015. • Missed majority of 2016-17 due to recurring shoulder injury and resulting surgery, December 2, 2016.

HALAK, Jaroslav (HA-lak, YAHR-roh-slav) NYI

Goaltender. Catches left. 5'11", 181 lbs. Born, Bratislava, Czech., May 13, 1985.
(Montreal's 11th pick, 271st overall, in 2003 NHL Draft).

			Regular Season								Playoffs						
Season	Club	League	GP	W	L	O/T	Mins	GA	SO	Avg	GP	W	L	Mins	GA	SO	Avg
2001-02	Bratislava Jr.	Slovak-Jr.	22	....	....	....	1257	41	0	1.96	6	6	0	353	7	2	1.19
2002-03	Bratislava Jr.	Slovak-Jr.	20	13	3	3	1200	41	1	2.02	....	....	....	....	....	....	....
2003-04	Bratislava Jr.	Slovak-Jr.	29	....	....	....	1694	51	....	1.81	....	....	....	....	....	....	....
	HK 91 Senica	Slovak-2	21	....	....	....	1240	54	....	2.61	....	....	....	....	....	....	....
	Bratislava	Slovakia	12	....	....	....	650	18	0	1.66	1	....	....	45	6	0	8.00
2004-05	Lewiston	QMJHL	47	24	17	4	2697	125	4	2.78	8	4	4	460	27	0	3.52
2005-06	Hamilton Bulldogs	AHL	13	7	6	0	786	30	3	2.29	....	....	....	....	....	....	....
	Long Beach	ECHL	20	11	4	2	1026	35	2	2.05	4	2	2	252	13	0	3.10
2006-07	**Montreal**	**NHL**	**16**	**10**	**6**	**0**	**912**	**44**	**2**	**2.89**	....	....	....	....	....	....	....
	Hamilton Bulldogs	AHL	28	16	11	0	1618	54	6	*2.00	....	....	....	....	....	....	....
2007-08	**Montreal**	**NHL**	**6**	**2**	**1**	**1**	**285**	**10**	**1**	**2.11**	**2**	**0**	**1**	**77**	**3**	**0**	**2.34**
	Hamilton Bulldogs	AHL	28	15	10	2	1630	57	2	2.10	....	....	....	....	....	....	....
2008-09	**Montreal**	**NHL**	**34**	**18**	**14**	**1**	**1931**	**92**	**1**	**2.86**	**1**	**0**	**0**	**20**	**0**	**0**	**0.00**
2009-10	**Montreal**	**NHL**	**45**	**26**	**13**	**5**	**2630**	**105**	**5**	**2.40**	**18**	**9**	**9**	**1013**	**43**	**0**	**2.55**
	Slovakia	Olympics	7	3	4	0	423	17	1	2.41	....	....	....	....	....	....	....
2010-11	**St. Louis**	**NHL**	**57**	**27**	**21**	**7**	**3294**	**136**	**7**	**2.48**	....	....	....	....	....	....	....
2011-12	**St. Louis**	**NHL**	**46**	**26**	**12**	**7**	**2747**	**90**	**6**	**1.97**	**2**	**1**	**1**	**104**	**3**	**0**	**1.73**
2012-13	Weiswasser	German-2	1	1	0	0	65	1	0	0.92	....	....	....	....	....	....	....
	St. Louis	**NHL**	**16**	**6**	**5**	**1**	**813**	**29**	**3**	**2.14**	....	....	....	....	....	....	....
2013-14	**St. Louis**	**NHL**	**40**	**24**	**9**	**4**	**2238**	**83**	**4**	**2.23**	....	....	....	....	....	....	....
	Slovakia	Olympics	2	....	....	....	94	8	0	5.13	....	....	....	....	....	....	....
	Washington	**NHL**	**12**	**5**	**4**	**3**	**701**	**27**	**1**	**2.31**	....	....	....	....	....	....	....
2014-15	**NY Islanders**	**NHL**	**59**	**38**	**17**	**4**	**3550**	**144**	**6**	**2.43**	**7**	**3**	**4**	**418**	**16**	**0**	**2.30**
2015-16	**NY Islanders**	**NHL**	**36**	**18**	**13**	**4**	**2091**	**80**	**3**	**2.30**	....	....	....	....	....	....	....
2016-17	**NY Islanders**	**NHL**	**28**	**12**	**9**	**5**	**1605**	**75**	**2**	**2.80**	....	....	....	....	....	....	....
	Bridgeport	AHL	27	17	7	3	1536	55	2	2.15	....	....	....	....	....	....	....
	NHL Totals		**395**	**212**	**124**	**42**	**22797**	**915**	**41**	**2.41**	**30**	**13**	**15**	**1632**	**65**	**0**	**2.39**

AHL All-Rookie Team (2007) • William M. Jennings Trophy (2012) (shared with Brian Elliott)

Played in NHL All-Star Game (2015)

Traded to **St. Louis** by **Montreal** for Lars Eller and Ian Schultz, June 17, 2010. Signed as a free agent by **Weiswasser** (German-2), November 21, 2012. Traded to **Buffalo** by **St. Louis** with Chris Stewart, William Carrier, St. Louis' 1st round pick (later traded to Winnipeg – Winnipeg selected Jack Roslovic) in 2015 NHL Draft and St. Louis' 3rd round pick (later traded to Florida – Florida selected Linus Nassen) in 2016 NHL Draft for Ryan Miller and Steve Ott, February 28, 2014. Traded to **Washington** by **Buffalo** with Buffalo's 3rd round pick (later traded to NY Rangers – NY Rangers selected Robin Kovacs) in 2015 NHL Draft for Michal Neuvirth and Rostislav Klesla, March 5, 2014. Traded to **NY Islanders** by **Washington** for Chicago's 4th round pick (previously acquired, later traded to NY Rangers – NY Rangers selected Igor Shesterkin) in 2014 NHL Draft, May 1, 2014.

HALVERSON, Brandon (HAL-vuhr-suhn, BRAN-duhn) NYR

Goaltender. Catches left. 6'4", 212 lbs. Born, Traverse City, MI, March 29, 1996.
(NY Rangers' 1st pick, 59th overall, in 2014 NHL Draft).

			Regular Season								Playoffs						
Season	Club	League	GP	W	L	O/T	Mins	GA	SO	Avg	GP	W	L	Mins	GA	SO	Avg
2010-11	Det. Vic. Honda	T1EHL	22	4	10	6	882	61	1	3.11	....	....	....	....	....	....	....
	Det. Vic. Honda	Minor-MI	3	1	2	0	144	9	1	3.00	....	....	....	....	....	....	....
2011-12	Det. L.C. U16	HPHL	20	6	10	2	874	45	1	3.09	....	....	....	....	....	....	....
2012-13	Oak. Grizzlies U18	T1EHL	21	9	9	2	1069	57	0	2.88	4	2	1	209	6	0	1.46
2013-14	Sault Ste. Marie	OHL	19	12	6	1	1136	56	2	2.96	....	....	....	....	....	....	....
2014-15	Sault Ste. Marie	OHL	50	40	5	2	2784	122	6	2.63	14	10	4	796	39	1	2.94
2015-16	Sault Ste. Marie	OHL	43	20	17	4	2517	126	0	3.00	12	5	7	744	40	0	3.23
2016-17	Hartford Wolf Pack	AHL	26	9	16	0	1443	83	0	3.45	....	....	....	....	....	....	....
	Greenville	ECHL	9	4	5	0	471	27	1	3.43	....	....	....	....	....	....	....

HAMMOND, Andrew (HAM-uhnd, AN-droo) OTT

Goaltender. Catches left. 6'1", 220 lbs. Born, Surrey, BC, February 11, 1988.

			Regular Season								Playoffs						
Season	Club	League	GP	W	L	O/T	Mins	GA	SO	Avg	GP	W	L	Mins	GA	SO	Avg
2006-07	Grandview Steelers	PIJHL	28	17	5	3	1568	60	3	2.30	16	9	7	988	44	1	2.67
	Alberni Valley	BCHL	1	0	1	0	34	4	0	7.03	....	....	....	....	....	....	....
2007-08	Surrey Eagles	BCHL	32	15	14	1	1568	90	2	3.44	....	....	....	....	....	....	....
	Vernon Vipers	BCHL	9	6	3	0	538	22	1	2.45	7	3	3	412	20	0	2.91
2008-09	Vernon Vipers	BCHL	43	27	12	1	2479	95	5	2.30	17	12	5	1082	27	4	1.50
2009-10	Bowling Green	CCHA	19	0	12	2	837	60	0	4.30	....	....	....	....	....	....	....
2010-11	Bowling Green	CCHA	27	6	17	3	1528	68	2	2.67	....	....	....	....	....	....	....
2011-12	Bowling Green	CCHA	44	14	24	5	2615	119	2	2.73	....	....	....	....	....	....	....
2012-13	Bowling Green	CCHA	29	10	15	3	1625	67	3	2.47	....	....	....	....	....	....	....
2013-14	**Ottawa**	**NHL**	**1**	**0**	**0**	**0**	**35**	**0**	**0**	**0.00**	....	....	....	....	....	....	....
	Binghamton	AHL	48	25	19	3	2733	128	1	2.81	4	1	3	265	13	0	2.95
2014-15	**Ottawa**	**NHL**	**24**	**20**	**1**	**2**	**1411**	**42**	**3**	**1.79**	**2**	**0**	**2**	**122**	**7**	**0**	**3.44**
	Binghamton	AHL	25	7	13	2	1369	80	2	3.51	....	....	....	....	....	....	....
2015-16	**Ottawa**	**NHL**	**24**	**7**	**11**	**4**	**1382**	**61**	**1**	**2.65**	....	....	....	....	....	....	....
	Binghamton	AHL	2	0	2	0	119	8	0	4.05	....	....	....	....	....	....	....
2016-17	**Ottawa**	**NHL**	**6**	**0**	**2**	**0**	**206**	**14**	**0**	**4.08**	....	....	....	....	....	....	....
	Binghamton	AHL	5	2	3	0	297	16	0	3.24	....	....	....	....	....	....	....
	NHL Totals		**55**	**27**	**14**	**6**	**3034**	**117**	**4**	**2.31**	**2**	**0**	**2**	**122**	**7**	**0**	**3.44**

Signed as a free agent by **Ottawa**, March 20, 2013. • Missed majority of 2016-17 due to lower-body injury at NY Islanders, December 18, 2016.

HART, Carter (HAHRT, KAHR-tuhr) PHI

Goaltender. Catches left. 6'1", 176 lbs. Born, Sherwood Park, AB, August 13, 1998.
(Philadelphia's 3rd pick, 48th overall, in 2016 NHL Draft).

			Regular Season								Playoffs						
Season	Club	League	GP	W	L	O/T	Mins	GA	SO	Avg	GP	W	L	Mins	GA	SO	Avg
2011-12	Ft. Saskatchewan	AMBHL	....	3	14	2	985	69	0	4.20	....	....	....	....	....	....	....
2012-13	Sherwood Park	AMBHL	....	11	5	4	1285	72	1	3.36	....	2	2	297	19	0	3.84
2013-14	Sherwood Park	Minor-AB	....	14	3	4	1275	41	*4	*1.93	....	....	....	....	....	....	....
	Sherwood Park	AMHL	1	0	1	0	59	4	0	4.07	....	....	....	....	....	....	....
	Everett Silvertips	WHL	2	0	1	1	103	6	0	3.49	....	....	....	....	....	....	....
2014-15	Everett Silvertips	WHL	30	18	5	5	1648	63	4	2.29	....	....	....	....	....	....	....
2015-16	Everett Silvertips	WHL	63	*35	23	4	3693	132	6	2.14	6	2	4	352	14	1	2.39
2016-17	Everett Silvertips	WHL	54	32	11	8	3078	102	*9	*1.99	10	4	6	691	28	1	2.43

WHL West First All-Star Team (2016, 2017)

HAWKEY, Hayden (HAW-kee, HAY-duhn) MTL

Goaltender. Catches left. 6'2", 187 lbs. Born, Fremont, CA, March 1, 1995.
(Montreal's 5th pick, 177th overall, in 2014 NHL Draft).

			Regular Season								Playoffs						
Season	Club	League	GP	W	L	O/T	Mins	GA	SO	Avg	GP	W	L	Mins	GA	SO	Avg
2011-12	Col. T-birds U16	T1EHL	20	16	0	3	1060	20	6	1.02	....	....	....	....	....	....	....
	Col. T-birds U18	T1EHL	2	2	0	0	108	3	0	1.50	....	....	....	....	....	....	....

Season	Club	League	GP	W	L	O/T	Mins	GA	SO	Avg	GP	W	L	Mins	GA	SO	Avg
2012-13	Col. T-birds U18	T1EHL	26	18	7	0	1391	50	4	1.94	3	0	1	163	8	0	2.50
2013-14	Omaha Lancers	USHL	33	22	6	3	1901	63	3	*1.99	4	1	3	256	12	0	2.82
2014-15	Omaha Lancers	USHL	15	5	7	2	801	40	1	2.99	....	....	....	....	....	....	....
2015-16	Providence College	H-East	5	2	0	0	180	5	1	1.67	....	....	....	....	....	....	....
2016-17	Providence College	H-East	39	22	12	5	2352	86	3	2.19	....	....	....	....	....	....	....

USHL All-Rookie Team (2014) • USHL First All-Star Team (2014) • USHL Goaltender of the Year (2014)

HELLBERG, Magnus (HEHL-buhrg, MAG-nuhs)

Goaltender. Catches left. 6'6", 200 lbs. Born, Uppsala, Sweden, April 4, 1991.
(Nashville's 1st pick, 38th overall, in 2011 NHL Draft).

			Regular Season								Playoffs						
Season	Club	League	GP	W	L	O/T	Mins	GA	SO	Avg	GP	W	L	Mins	GA	SO	Avg
2007-08	Arlanda U18	Swe-U18	11	....	....	....	....	....	....	....	....	....	....	....	....	....	....
	Arlanda Jr.	Swe-Jr.	1	....	....	....	....	....	....	8.00	....	....	....	....	....	....	....
2008-09	Arlanda U18	Swe-U18	33	....	....	....	1979	103	2	3.12	....	....	....	....	....	....	....
	Wings HC Arlanda	Sweden-3	2	....	....	....	119	7	0	3.52	....	....	....	....	....	....	....
2009-10	Almtuna Jr.	Swe-Jr.	22	....	....	....	1339	44	2	1.97	....	....	....	....	....	....	....
	IF Vallentuna BK	Sweden-3	1	....	....	....	24	3	0	7.57	....	....	....	....	....	....	....
2010-11	IFK Kumla IK	Sweden-3	3	....	....	....	179	6	0	2.01	....	....	....	....	....	....	....
	Almtuna	Sweden-2	31	....	....	....	1790	61	5	2.04	5	....	....	277	15	0	3.24
2011-12	Frolunda	Sweden	17	....	....	....	1016	44	2	2.60	....	....	....	....	....	....	....
	Frolunda Jr.	Swe-Jr.	2	....	....	....	120	8	0	4.00	....	....	....	....	....	....	....
	Orebro HK	Sweden-2	3	....	....	....	180	10	0	3.33	....	....	....	....	....	....	....
2012-13	Milwaukee	AHL	39	22	13	0	2107	75	6	2.14	4	1	3	248	7	1	1.69
	Cincinnati	ECHL	2	1	1	0	119	5	0	2.52	....	....	....	....	....	....	....
2013-14	**Nashville**	**NHL**	**1**	**0**	**0**	**0**	**12**	**1**	**0**	**5.00**	....	....	....	....	....	....	....
	Milwaukee	AHL	21	5	13	1	1168	55	1	2.82	....	....	....	....	....	....	....
	Cincinnati	ECHL	7	5	1	1	394	19	0	2.89							....
2014-15	Milwaukee	AHL	38	15	10	6	2007	78	3	2.33	....	....	....	....	....	....	....
2015-16	**NY Rangers**	**NHL**	**1**	**0**	**0**	**0**	**20**	**2**	**0**	**6.00**	....	....	....	....	....	....	....
	Hartford Wolf Pack	AHL	53	30	20	3	3098	124	3	2.40	....	....	....	....	....	....	....
2016-17	**NY Rangers**	**NHL**	**2**	**1**	**0**	**0**	**79**	**2**	**0**	**1.52**	....	....	....	....	....	....	....
	Hartford Wolf Pack	AHL	36	12	15	5	1990	98	1	2.95	....	....	....	....	....	....	....
	NHL Totals		**4**	**1**	**0**	**0**	**111**	**5**	**0**	**2.70**	....	....	....	....	....	....	....

Traded to **NY Rangers** by **Nashville** for NY Rangers' 6th round pick (Pavel Koltygin) in 2017 NHL Draft, July 1, 2015.

HELLEBUYCK, Connor (hehl-ee-BUHK, KAW-nuhr) WPG

Goaltender. Catches left. 6'4", 207 lbs. Born, Commerce, MI, May 19, 1993.
(Winnipeg's 4th pick, 130th overall, in 2012 NHL Draft).

			Regular Season								Playoffs						
Season	Club	League	GP	W	L	O/T	Mins	GA	SO	Avg	GP	W	L	Mins	GA	SO	Avg
2010-11	Walled Lake	High-MI	STATISTICS NOT AVAILABLE														
	Team Michigan	Other	STATISTICS NOT AVAILABLE														
2011-12	Odessa Jackalopes	NAHL	*53	26	21	5	*3085	128	3	2.49	4	1	3	243	14	0	3.46
2012-13	U. Mass Lowell	H-East	24	20	3	0	1397	32	*6	*1.37	....	....	....	....	....	....	....
2013-14	U. Mass Lowell	H-East	29	18	9	2	1748	52	6	*1.79	....	....	....	....	....	....	....
2014-15	St. John's IceCaps	AHL	58	28	22	5	3332	143	6	2.58	....	....	....	....	....	....	....
2015-16	**Winnipeg**	**NHL**	**26**	**13**	**11**	**1**	**1433**	**56**	**2**	**2.34**	....	....	....	....	....	....	....
	Manitoba Moose	AHL	30	13	15	1	1735	72	4	2.49	....	....	....	....	....	....	....
2016-17	**Winnipeg**	**NHL**	**56**	**26**	**19**	**4**	**3034**	**146**	**4**	**2.89**	....	....	....	....	....	....	....
	NHL Totals		**82**	**39**	**30**	**5**	**4467**	**202**	**6**	**2.71**	....	....	....	....	....	....	....

NAHL Rookie of the Year (2012) • NAHL Goaltender of the Year (2012) • Hockey East All-Rookie Team (2013) • Hockey East Second All-Star Team (2013) • Hockey East First All-Star Team (2014) • NCAA East First All-American Team (2014)

HELVIG, Jeremy (HEHL-vihg, JAIR-eh-mee) CAR

Goaltender. Catches left. 6'4", 217 lbs. Born, Markham, ON, May 25, 1997.
(Carolina's 8th pick, 134th overall, in 2016 NHL Draft).

			Regular Season								Playoffs						
Season	Club	League	GP	W	L	O/T	Mins	GA	SO	Avg	GP	W	L	Mins	GA	SO	Avg
2012-13	Tor. Red Wings	GTHL	25	10	11	4	1125	46	3	1.84	14	8	6	590	29	2	2.07
	Tor. Red Wings	Other	13	4	7	2	562	21	2	1.68	....	....	....	....	....	....	....
2013-14	Tor. Patriots	ON-Jr.A	28	17	7	1	1516	68	1	2.69	....	....	....	....	....	....	....
2014-15	Kingston	OHL	14	2	8	2	699	53	0	4.55	1	0	0	23	2	0	5.15
2015-16	Kingston	OHL	27	19	3	1	1437	51	2	2.13	7	3	1	325	13	*2	2.40
2016-17	Kingston	OHL	*59	29	22	7	*3446	156	*6	2.72	11	4	7	663	32	0	2.90

HILL, Adin (HIHL, AY-dihn) ARI

Goaltender. Catches left. 6'4", 198 lbs. Born, Comox, BC, May 11, 1996.
(Arizona's 5th pick, 76th overall, in 2015 NHL Draft).

			Regular Season								Playoffs						
Season	Club	League	GP	W	L	O/T	Mins	GA	SO	Avg	GP	W	L	Mins	GA	SO	Avg
2012-13	Calgary Buffaloes	AMHL	....	9	6	2	927	47	0	3.04	....	0	1	39	5	0	6.15
2013-14	Calgary Canucks	AJHL	19	2	14	1	1041	45	0	3.92	....	....	....	....	....	....	....
	Portland	WHL	4	4	0	0	218	6	0	1.65	....	....	....	....	....	....	....
2014-15	Portland	WHL	46	31	11	1	2604	122	2	2.81	17	10	7	1074	53	1	2.96
2015-16	Portland	WHL	65	32	27	6	3897	192	3	2.96	4	0	4	234	14	0	3.58
	Springfield Falcons	AHL	4	1	3	0	236	12	0	3.05	....	....	....	....	....	....	....
2016-17	Tucson	AHL	40	16	14	6	2243	118	1	3.16	....	....	....	....	....	....	....
	Rapid City Rush	ECHL	5	1	3	1	301	18	1	3.59	....	....	....	....	....	....	....

HILLER, Jonas (HIHL-uhr, YOH-nuhs)

Goaltender. Catches right. 6'2", 191 lbs. Born, Felben Wellhausen, Switz., February 12, 1982.

			Regular Season								Playoffs						
Season	Club	League	GP	W	L	O/T	Mins	GA	SO	Avg	GP	W	L	Mins	GA	SO	Avg
2000-01	HC Davos	Swiss	1	0	0	0	9	0	0	0.00	....	....	....	....	....	....	....
2001-02	HC Davos	Swiss	DID NOT PLAY														
2002-03	HC Davos	Swiss	DID NOT PLAY														
2003-04	Lausanne HC	Swiss	21	....	....	....	1161	64	1	3.31	....	....	....	....	....	....	....
	Chaux-de-Fonds	Swiss-2	1	0	1	0	60	4	0	4.00	....	....	....	....	....	....	....
	Lausanne HC	Swiss-Q	....	....	....	....	....	....	....	....	4	4	0	251	7	0	1.67
2004-05	HC Davos	Swiss	43	26	12	4	2519	95	*8	2.26	*15	12	3	*932	34	0	*2.19
2005-06	HC Davos	Swiss	*44	23	16	5	*2676	110	3	2.47	15	9	6	900	45	1	3.00
2006-07	HC Davos	Swiss	*44	*28	16	0	*2656	115	3	2.60	*19	*12	7	*1138	39	3	2.05
2007-08	**Anaheim**	**NHL**	**23**	**10**	**7**	**1**	**1223**	**42**	**0**	**2.06**	....	....	....	....	....	....	....
	Portland Pirates	AHL	6	3	2	1	370	13	0	2.11	....	....	....	....	....	....	....
2008-09	**Anaheim**	**NHL**	**46**	**23**	**15**	**1**	**2486**	**99**	**4**	**2.39**	**13**	**7**	**6**	**807**	**30**	***2**	**2.23**
2009-10	**Anaheim**	**NHL**	**59**	**30**	**23**	**4**	**3338**	**152**	**2**	**2.73**	....	....	....	....	....	....	....
	Switzerland	Olympics	5	2	3	0	316	13	0	2.47	....	....	....	....	....	....	....
2010-11	**Anaheim**	**NHL**	**49**	**26**	**16**	**3**	**2672**	**114**	**5**	**2.56**	....	....	....	....	....	....	....
2011-12	**Anaheim**	**NHL**	***73**	**29**	**30**	**12**	***4253**	**182**	**4**	**2.57**	....	....	....	....	....	....	....
2012-13	**Anaheim**	**NHL**	**26**	**15**	**6**	**4**	**1498**	**59**	**1**	**2.36**	**7**	**3**	**4**	**439**	**18**	**1**	**2.46**
2013-14	**Anaheim**	**NHL**	**50**	**29**	**13**	**7**	**2909**	**120**	**5**	**2.48**	**6**	**2**	**2**	**219**	**8**	**0**	**2.19**
	Switzerland	Olympics	3	2	1	0	179	2	2	0.67	....	....	....	....	....	....	....
2014-15	**Calgary**	**NHL**	**52**	**26**	**19**	**4**	**2871**	**113**	**1**	**2.36**	**7**	**3**	**3**	**322**	**14**	**0**	**2.61**
2015-16	**Calgary**	**NHL**	**26**	**9**	**11**	**1**	**1351**	**79**	**1**	**3.51**	....	....	....	....	....	....	....
2016-17	EHC Biel-Bienne	Swiss	47	22	24	0	2803	127	2	2.72	5	1	4	307	14	0	2.73
	NHL Totals		**404**	**197**	**140**	**37**	**22601**	**960**	**23**	**2.55**	**33**	**15**	**15**	**1787**	**70**	**3**	**2.35**

Played in NHL All-Star Game (2011)

Signed as a free agent by **Anaheim**, May 25, 2007. Signed as a free agent by **Calgary**, July 1, 2014. Signed as a free agent by **Biel-Bienne** (Swiss), April 19, 2016.

HOGBERG, Marcus (HOHG-buhrg, MAHR-kuhs) OTT

Goaltender. Catches left. 6'5", 218 lbs. Born, Orebro, Sweden, November 25, 1994.
(Ottawa's 2nd pick, 78th overall, in 2013 NHL Draft).

			Regular Season								Playoffs						
Season	Club	League	GP	W	L	O/T	Mins	GA	SO	Avg	GP	W	L	Mins	GA	SO	Avg
2010-11	Linkopings HC U18	Swe-U18	27	....	....	....	1631	53	4	1.95	5	....	....	305	13	0	2.55
	Linkopings HC Jr.	Swe-Jr.	4	....	....	....	163	12	0	4.42	....	....	....	....	....	....	....
2011-12	Linkopings HC U18	Swe-U18	3	....	....	....	179	9	0	3.01	1	....	....	60	2	0	2.00
	Linkopings HC Jr.	Swe-Jr.	35	....	....	....	2055	85	4	2.48	6	....	....	366	10	2	1.64
2012-13	Linkopings HC Jr.	Swe-Jr.	23	13	9	0	1369	55	2	2.41	....	....	....	....	....	....	....
	Linkopings HC	Sweden	3	1	1	0	140	6	0	2.57	....	....	....	....	....	....	....
2013-14	Linkopings HC Jr.	Swe-Jr.	5	4	1	0	304	14	0	2.76	....	....	....	....	....	....	....
	Mora IK	Sweden-2	15	5	8	0	778	38	0	2.93	....	....	....	....	....	....	....
	Linkopings HC	Sweden	4	4	0	0	222	4	0	1.08	11	4	5	569	28	2	2.95
2014-15	Linkopings HC Jr.	Swe-Jr.	1	1	0	0	63	1	0	0.96	....	....	....	....	....	....	....
	Linkopings HC	Sweden	27	12	12	0	1463	56	3	2.30	6	1	4	283	15	0	3.18
	IK Oskarshamn	Sweden-2	2	2	0	0	123	6	0	2.92	....	....	....	....	....	....	....
2015-16	Linkopings HC	Sweden	28	15	12	0	1581	61	2	2.31	....	....	....	....	....	....	....
2016-17	Linkopings HC	Sweden	33	19	14	0	2000	63	4	1.89	6	2	4	340	14	0	2.47
	Binghamton	AHL	3	0	3	0	180	13	0	4.34	....	....	....	....	....	....	....

HOLLETT, Jordan (HAWL-eht, JOHR-duhn) OTT

Goaltender. Catches left. 6'4", 203 lbs. Born, Langley, BC, March 31, 1999.
(Ottawa's 4th pick, 183rd overall, in 2017 NHL Draft).

			Regular Season								Playoffs						
Season	Club	League	GP	W	L	O/T	Mins	GA	SO	Avg	GP	W	L	Mins	GA	SO	Avg
2014-15	Okan. H.A. White	CSSHL	12	9	3	0	716	25	2	2.10	....	....	....	....	....	....	....
	Regina Pats	WHL	1	0	1	0	60	5	0	5.00	....	....	....	....	....	....	....
2015-16	Ridge Meadows	PJHL	8	3	4	1	474	26	0	3.29	....	....	....	....	....	....	....
	Regina Pats	WHL	23	10	6	1	1144	70	0	3.67	1	0	0	7	0	0	0.00
2016-17	Regina Pats	WHL	19	15	2	2	1143	54	2	2.83	1	0	0	20	0	0	0.00

HOLM, Arvid (HOHLM, AHR-vihd) WPG

Goaltender. Catches left. 6'4", 213 lbs. Born, Ljungby, Sweden, November 3, 1998.
(Winnipeg's 6th pick, 167th overall, in 2017 NHL Draft).

			Regular Season								Playoffs						
Season	Club	League	GP	W	L	O/T	Mins	GA	SO	Avg	GP	W	L	Mins	GA	SO	Avg
2014-15	Troja U18	Swe-U18	8	5	3	0	480	17	2	2.12	....	....	....	....	....	....	....
2015-16	Troja U18	Swe-U18	18	8	10	0	1088	53	4	2.92	....	....	....	....	....	....	....
	IF Troja-Ljungby Jr.	Swe-Jr.	29	23	5	0	1706	74	4	2.60	3	1	2	180	9	0	2.99
2016-17	Karlskrona HK Jr.	Swe-Jr.	26	7	17	0	1483	72	1	2.91	2	2	0	130	2	1	0.92

HOLTBY, Braden (HOHLT-bee, BRAY-duhn) WSH

Goaltender. Catches left. 6'2", 217 lbs. Born, Lloydminster, SK, September 16, 1989.
(Washington's 5th pick, 93rd overall, in 2008 NHL Draft).

			Regular Season								Playoffs						
Season	Club	League	GP	W	L	O/T	Mins	GA	SO	Avg	GP	W	L	Mins	GA	SO	Avg
2005-06	Saskatoon Blazers	SMHL	STATISTICS NOT AVAILABLE														
	Saskatoon Blades	WHL	1	0	1	0	59	4	0	4.07	....	....	....	....	....	....	....
2006-07	Saskatoon Blades	WHL	51	17	29	3	2725	146	0	3.21	....	....	....	....	....	....	....
2007-08	Saskatoon Blades	WHL	*64	25	29	8	3632	172	1	2.84	....	....	....	....	....	....	....
2008-09	Saskatoon Blades	WHL	*61	40	16	4	*3571	156	6	2.62	7	3	4	414	16	0	2.32
2009-10	Hershey Bears	AHL	37	25	8	2	2146	83	2	2.32	3	2	1	200	12	0	3.60
	South Carolina	ECHL	12	7	2	3	712	35	0	2.95	....	....	....	....	....	....	....
2010-11	**Washington**	**NHL**	**14**	**10**	**2**	**2**	**736**	**22**	**2**	**1.79**	....	....	....	....	....	....	....
	Hershey Bears	AHL	30	17	10	2	1785	68	5	2.29	6	2	4	359	18	0	3.01
2011-12	**Washington**	**NHL**	**7**	**4**	**2**	**1**	**361**	**15**	**1**	**2.49**	**14**	**7**	**7**	**922**	**30**	**0**	**1.95**
	Hershey Bears	AHL	40	20	15	2	2322	101	3	2.61	....	....	....	....	....	....	....
2012-13	Hershey Bears	AHL	25	12	12	1	1458	52	4	2.14	....	....	....	....	....	....	....
	Washington	**NHL**	**36**	**23**	**12**	**1**	**2089**	**90**	**4**	**2.58**	**7**	**3**	**4**	**433**	**16**	**1**	**2.22**
2013-14	**Washington**	**NHL**	**48**	**23**	**15**	**4**	**2656**	**126**	**4**	**2.85**	....	....	....	....	....	....	....
2014-15	**Washington**	**NHL**	**73**	**41**	**20**	**10**	**4247**	**157**	**9**	**2.22**	**13**	**6**	**7**	**806**	**23**	**1**	**1.71**
2015-16	**Washington**	**NHL**	**66**	***48**	**9**	**7**	**3841**	**141**	**3**	**2.20**	**12**	**6**	**6**	**732**	**21**	**2**	***1.72**
2016-17	**Washington**	**NHL**	**63**	***42**	**13**	**6**	**3680**	**127**	***9**	**2.07**	**13**	**7**	**6**	**803**	**33**	**0**	**2.47**
	NHL Totals		**307**	**191**	**73**	**31**	**17610**	**678**	**32**	**2.31**	**59**	**29**	**30**	**3696**	**123**	**4**	**2.00**

WHL East First All-Star Team (2009) • NHL First All-Star Team (2016) • Vezina Trophy (2016) • NHL Second All-Star Team (2017) • William M. Jennings Trophy (2017)

Played in NHL All-Star Game (2016, 2017)

HOWARD, Jimmy (HOW-uhrd, JIHM-ee) DET

Goaltender. Catches left. 6'1", 218 lbs. Born, Syracuse, NY, March 26, 1984.
(Detroit's 1st pick, 64th overall, in 2003 NHL Draft).

			Regular Season								Playoffs						
Season	Club	League	GP	W	L	O/T	Mins	GA	SO	Avg	GP	W	L	Mins	GA	SO	Avg
2000-01	Kanata Valley	ON-Jr.A	25	10	10	2	1350	83	1	3.69	....	....	....	....	....	....	....
2001-02	USAHNTDP	U-18	19	15	4	1	1170	37	4	1.90	....	....	....	....	....	....	....
	USAHNTDP	USHL	8	4	3	0	425	14	0	1.98	....	....	....	....	....	....	....
	USAHNTDP	NAHL	8	3	4	0	381	25	0	3.93	....	....	....	....	....	....	....
2002-03	University of Maine	H-East	21	14	6	0	1151	47	3	2.45	....	....	....	....	....	....	....
2003-04	University of Maine	H-East	23	14	4	3	1364	27	*6	*1.19	....	....	....	....	....	....	....
2004-05	University of Maine	H-East	*39	*19	13	7	*2310	74	*6	1.92	....	....	....	....	....	....	....
2005-06	**Detroit**	**NHL**	**4**	**1**	**2**	**0**	**201**	**10**	**0**	**2.99**	....	....	....	....	....	....	....
	Grand Rapids	AHL	38	27	6	2	2140	92	2	2.58	13	5	7	763	44	0	3.46

2006-07	Grand Rapids	AHL	49	21	21	3	2776	125	6	2.70	7	3	4	434	14	0	*1.93
2007-08	**Detroit**	**NHL**	**4**	**0**	**2**	**0**	**197**	**7**	**0**	**2.13**	....	....	....	....	....	....	....
	Grand Rapids	AHL	54	21	28	2	3097	146	2	2.83	....	....	....	....	....	....	....
2008-09	**Detroit**	**NHL**	**1**	**0**	**1**	**0**	**59**	**4**	**0**	**4.07**	....	....	....	....	....	....	....
	Grand Rapids	AHL	45	21	18	4	2644	112	4	2.54	10	4	6	598	24	0	2.41
2009-10	**Detroit**	**NHL**	**63**	**37**	**15**	**10**	**3740**	**141**	**3**	**2.26**	**12**	**5**	**7**	**720**	**33**	**1**	**2.75**
2010-11	**Detroit**	**NHL**	**63**	**37**	**17**	**5**	**3615**	**168**	**2**	**2.79**	**11**	**7**	**4**	**673**	**28**	**0**	**2.50**
2011-12	**Detroit**	**NHL**	**57**	**35**	**17**	**4**	**3360**	**119**	**6**	**2.13**	**5**	**1**	**4**	**295**	**13**	**0**	**2.64**
2012-13	**Detroit**	**NHL**	**42**	**21**	**13**	**7**	**2446**	**87**	***5**	**2.13**	**14**	**7**	**7**	**859**	**35**	**1**	**2.44**
2013-14	**Detroit**	**NHL**	**51**	**21**	**19**	**11**	**3004**	**133**	**2**	**2.66**	**3**	**1**	**2**	**178**	**6**	**1**	**2.02**
	United States	Olympics	DID NOT PLAY – SPARE GOALTENDER														
2014-15	**Detroit**	**NHL**	**53**	**23**	**13**	**11**	**2971**	**121**	**2**	**2.44**	**1**	**0**	**0**	**20**	**1**	**0**	**3.00**
2015-16	**Detroit**	**NHL**	**37**	**14**	**14**	**5**	**1974**	**92**	**2**	**2.80**	**2**	**0**	**2**	**117**	**7**	**0**	**3.59**
2016-17	**Detroit**	**NHL**	**26**	**10**	**11**	**1**	**1397**	**49**	**1**	**2.10**	....	....	....	....	....	....	....
	Grand Rapids	AHL	4	3	1	0	227	8	1	2.11	....	....	....	....	....	....	....
	NHL Totals		**401**	**199**	**124**	**54**	**22964**	**931**	**23**	**2.43**	**48**	**21**	**26**	**2862**	**123**	**3**	**2.58**

Hockey East All-Rookie Team (2003) • Hockey East Rookie of the Year (2003) • Hockey East First All-Star Team (2004) • NCAA East Second All-American Team (2004) • AHL All-Rookie Team (2006) • NHL All-Rookie Team (2010)

Played in NHL All-Star Game (2012)

HUSKA, Adam (HUHS-kuh, A-duhm) NYR

Goaltender. Catches left. 6'4", 199 lbs. Born, Zvolen, Slovakia, May 12, 1997.
(NY Rangers' 7th pick, 184th overall, in 2015 NHL Draft).

			Regular Season								Playoffs						
Season	Club	League	GP	W	L	O/T	Mins	GA	SO	Avg	GP	W	L	Mins	GA	SO	Avg
2011-12	HKm Zvolen U18	Svk-U18	3	....	....	....	18	3	0	10.08	....	....	....	....	....	....	....
	HC 07 Detva	Svk-U18	2	....	....	....	60	8	0	7.95	....	....	....	....	....	....	....
2012-13	HKm Zvolen U18	Svk-U18	21	....	....	....	1267	53	1	2.51	2	....	....	90	2	0	1.33
2013-14	Slovakia U18	Slovak-2	14	....	....	....	748	48	0	3.85	....	....	....	....	....	....	....
	HKm Zvolen U18	Svk-U18	27	....	....	....	1461	80	0	3.28	5	....	....	147	11	0	4.49
2014-15	SR 18	Slovak-2	25	....	....	....	1296	79	0	3.66	....	....	....	....	....	....	....
	Green Bay	USHL	5	0	3	1	245	19	0	4.65	....	....	....	....	....	....	....
2015-16	Green Bay	USHL	37	26	9	2	2138	65	4	*1.82	....	....	....	....	....	....	....
2016-17	U. of Connecticut	H-East	21	7	9	4	1235	59	1	2.87	....	....	....	....	....	....	....

USHL First All-Star Team (2016)

HUSSO, Ville (HOO-soh, VIHL-ee) ST.L.

Goaltender. Catches left. 6'3", 205 lbs. Born, Helsinki, Finland, February 6, 1995.
(St. Louis' 5th pick, 94th overall, in 2014 NHL Draft).

			Regular Season								Playoffs						
Season	Club	League	GP	W	L	O/T	Mins	GA	SO	Avg	GP	W	L	Mins	GA	SO	Avg
2010-11	HIFK Helsinki U18	Fin-U18	16	12	3	0	962	37	3	2.31	3	1	2	174	14	0	4.83
2011-12	HIFK Helsinki U18	Fin-U18	15	9	4	0	892	40	2	2.69	1	0	1	60	5	0	5.00
	HIFK Helsinki Jr.	Fin-Jr.	27	14	9	0	1618	65	3	2.41	10	9	1	604	18	0	1.79
2012-13	HIFK Helsinki Jr.	Fin-Jr.	41	....	....	....	2459	108	7	2.63	5	....	....	322	12	0	2.23
2013-14	HIFK Helsinki	Finland	41	20	14	5	2355	78	2	1.99	2	0	2	144	3	0	1.25
	HCK	Finland-2	6	....	....	....	364	13	....	2.14	....	....	....	....	....	....	....
2014-15	HIFK Helsinki	Finland	41	16	11	10	2338	92	3	2.36	3	1	2	159	6	0	2.27
2015-16	HIFK Helsinki	Finland	39	*25	8	6	2328	74	5	*1.91	15	9	6	889	23	*4	*1.55
2016-17	Chicago Wolves	AHL	22	13	6	2	1267	50	1	2.37	10	4	6	535	30	0	3.36
	Missouri Mavericks	ECHL	13	4	4	3	688	37	1	3.23	....	....	....	....	....	....	....

HUTCHINSON, Michael (HUH-chihn-suhn, MIGH-kuhl) WPG

Goaltender. Catches right. 6'3", 202 lbs. Born, Barrie, ON, March 2, 1990.
(Boston's 3rd pick, 77th overall, in 2008 NHL Draft).

			Regular Season								Playoffs						
Season	Club	League	GP	W	L	O/T	Mins	GA	SO	Avg	GP	W	L	Mins	GA	SO	Avg
2005-06	Markham Majors	GTHL	34	....	....	....	1530	69	9	2.02	....	....	....	....	....	....	....
2006-07	Orangeville	ON-Jr.A	8	1	4	0	289	24	0	4.99	....	....	....	....	....	....	....
	Barrie Colts	OHL	14	8	3	0	768	27	0	2.11	1	1	0	45	1	0	1.33
2007-08	Barrie Colts	OHL	32	12	15	4	1826	92	1	3.02	8	4	4	500	22	1	2.64
2008-09	Barrie Colts	OHL	38	15	20	1	2146	108	5	3.02	3	0	2	112	10	0	5.37
2009-10	London Knights	OHL	46	32	12	2	2667	127	3	2.86	12	7	5	686	47	0	4.11
2010-11	Providence Bruins	AHL	28	13	10	1	1476	77	1	3.13	....	....	....	....	....	....	....
	Reading Royals	ECHL	18	9	5	4	1049	50	1	2.86	....	....	....	....	....	....	....
2011-12	Providence Bruins	AHL	29	13	14	1	1680	66	3	2.36	....	....	....	....	....	....	....
	Reading Royals	ECHL	2	1	1	0	120	7	0	3.50	....	....	....	....	....	....	....
2012-13	Providence Bruins	AHL	30	13	13	3	1749	67	3	2.30	2	0	0	49	1	0	1.22
2013-14	**Winnipeg**	**NHL**	**3**	**2**	**1**	**0**	**183**	**5**	**0**	**1.64**	....	....	....	....	....	....	....
	St. John's IceCaps	AHL	24	17	5	1	1383	53	3	2.30	*21	12	9	*1290	42	*3	1.95
	Ontario Reign	ECHL	28	22	4	2	1671	58	3	2.08	....	....	....	....	....	....	....
2014-15	**Winnipeg**	**NHL**	**38**	**21**	**10**	**5**	**2138**	**85**	**2**	**2.39**	....	....	....	....	....	....	....
2015-16	**Winnipeg**	**NHL**	**30**	**9**	**15**	**3**	**1586**	**75**	**0**	**2.84**	....	....	....	....	....	....	....
2016-17	**Winnipeg**	**NHL**	**28**	**9**	**12**	**3**	**1378**	**67**	**1**	**2.92**	....	....	....	....	....	....	....
	NHL Totals		**99**	**41**	**38**	**11**	**5285**	**232**	**3**	**2.63**	....	....	....	....	....	....	....

Jack A. Butterfield Trophy (AHL - Playoff MVP) (2014)

Signed as a free agent by **Winnipeg**, July 19, 2013.

HUTTON, Carter (HUH-tuhn, KAR-tuhr) ST.L.

Goaltender. Catches left. 6'1", 201 lbs. Born, Thunder Bay, ON, December 19, 1985.

			Regular Season								Playoffs						
Season	Club	League	GP	W	L	O/T	Mins	GA	SO	Avg	GP	W	L	Mins	GA	SO	Avg
2005-06	F-Wm. North Stars	ON-Jr.A	36	33	1	0	2053	63	10	1.84	15	12	3	928	36	2	2.33
2006-07	U. Mass Lowell	H-East	19	3	10	5	1097	52	1	2.84	....	....	....	....	....	....	....
2007-08	U. Mass Lowell	H-East	20	7	11	2	1187	49	2	2.48	....	....	....	....	....	....	....
2008-09	U. Mass Lowell	H-East	19	9	8	1	1106	38	*3	2.06	....	....	....	....	....	....	....
2009-10	U. Mass Lowell	H-East	27	13	12	2	1614	55	*4	*2.04	....	....	....	....	....	....	....
	Adirondack	AHL	4	1	2	1	244	11	0	2.71	....	....	....	....	....	....	....
2010-11	Worcester Sharks	AHL	22	11	7	2	1174	59	2	3.01	....	....	....	....	....	....	....
2011-12	Toledo Walleye	ECHL	14	7	7	0	819	43	0	3.15	....	....	....	....	....	....	....
	Rockford IceHogs	AHL	43	22	13	4	2372	93	3	2.35	....	....	....	....	....	....	....
2012-13	Rockford IceHogs	AHL	51	26	22	1	2908	132	2	2.72	....	....	....	....	....	....	....
	Chicago	**NHL**	**1**	**0**	**1**	**0**	**59**	**3**	**0**	**3.05**	....	....	....	....	....	....	....
2013-14	**Nashville**	**NHL**	**40**	**20**	**11**	**4**	**2085**	**91**	**1**	**2.62**	....	....	....	....	....	....	....
2014-15	**Nashville**	**NHL**	**18**	**6**	**7**	**4**	**1010**	**44**	**1**	**2.61**	....	....	....	....	....	....	....
2015-16	**Nashville**	**NHL**	**17**	**7**	**5**	**4**	**979**	**38**	**2**	**2.33**	**3**	**0**	**0**	**20**	**1**	**0**	**3.00**
2016-17	**St. Louis**	**NHL**	**30**	**13**	**8**	**2**	**1459**	**58**	**4**	**2.39**	....	....	....	....	....	....	....
	NHL Totals		**106**	**46**	**32**	**14**	**5592**	**234**	**8**	**2.51**	**3**	**0**	**0**	**20**	**1**	**0**	**3.00**

Hockey East Second All-Star Team (2010)

Signed to an ATO (amateur tryout) contract by **Adirondack** (AHL), March 20, 2010. Signed as a free agent by **San Jose**, June 1, 2010. Signed as a free agent by **Chicago**, February 24, 2012. Signed as a free agent by **Nashville**, July 5, 2013. Signed as a free agent by **St. Louis**, July 1, 2016.

INGRAM, Connor (IHN-gruhm, KAW-nuhr) T.B.

Goaltender. Catches left. 6', 212 lbs. Born, Imperial, SK, March 31, 1997.
(Tampa Bay's 5th pick, 88th overall, in 2016 NHL Draft).

			Regular Season								Playoffs						
Season	Club	League	GP	W	L	O/T	Mins	GA	SO	Avg	GP	W	L	Mins	GA	SO	Avg
2011-12	Sask Valley Vipers	SBHL	14	9	1	3	820	38	2	2.85	6	3	3	378	19	0	3.02
2012-13	Humboldt Broncos	Minor-SK	12	3	4	4	705	35	0	2.98	8	5	2	480	18	0	2.25
2013-14	Prince Albert	SMHL	23	16	4	3	1364	45	2	1.98	7	3	3	418	18	0	2.58
	Flin Flon Bombers	SJHL	2	0	1	0	68	3	0	2.63	....	....	....	....	....	....	....
2014-15	Kamloops Blazers	WHL	52	21	21	5	2915	144	3	2.96	....	....	....	....	....	....	....
2015-16	Kamloops Blazers	WHL	61	34	15	9	3539	154	4	2.61	7	3	4	424	15	1	2.12
2016-17	Kamloops Blazers	WHL	45	26	14	4	2577	105	5	2.44	6	2	4	357	13	0	2.18

WHL West Second All-Star Team (2016, 2017)

JARRY, Tristan (JAIR-ee, TRIH-STAN) PIT

Goaltender. Catches left. 6'2", 194 lbs. Born, Surrey, BC, April 29, 1995.
(Pittsburgh's 1st pick, 44th overall, in 2013 NHL Draft).

			Regular Season								Playoffs						
Season	Club	League	GP	W	L	O/T	Mins	GA	SO	Avg	GP	W	L	Mins	GA	SO	Avg
2009-10	North Delta	Minor-BC	26	....	....	....	....	....	....	1.65	....	....	....	....	....	....	....
2010-11	Greater Van.	BCMML	20	....	....	....	....	....	....	2.31	6	....	....	....	....	....	....
2011-12	Edmonton	WHL	14	8	2	1	718	35	0	2.93	....	....	....	....	....	....	....
2012-13	Edmonton	WHL	27	18	7	0	1495	40	6	*1.61	1	0	0	27	0	0	0.00
2013-14	Edmonton	WHL	63	*44	14	3	3703	138	*8	*2.24	*21	*16	5	*1261	46	*3	2.19
2014-15	Edmonton	WHL	55	23	26	6	3216	147	3	2.74	5	1	4	312	15	0	2.88
2015-16	Wilkes-Barre	AHL	33	17	13	3	1943	87	5	2.69	3	1	0	107	4	0	2.24
2016-17	**Pittsburgh**	**NHL**	**1**	**0**	**1**	**0**	**59**	**3**	**0**	**3.05**	....	....	....	....	....	....	....
	Wilkes-Barre	AHL	45	28	15	2	2707	97	3	2.15	....	....	....	....	....	....	....
	NHL Totals		**1**	**0**	**1**	**0**	**59**	**3**	**0**	**3.05**	....	....	....	....	....	....	....

WHL East First All-Star Team (2014, 2015) • Harry ''Hap'' Holmes Memorial Award (AHL – fewest goals against) (2017) (shared with Casey DeSmith)

JOHANSSON, Jonas (yoh-HAHN-suhn, YOH-nuhs) BUF

Goaltender. Catches left. 6'5", 212 lbs. Born, Gavle, Sweden, September 19, 1995.
(Buffalo's 5th pick, 61st overall, in 2014 NHL Draft).

			Regular Season								Playoffs						
Season	Club	League	GP	W	L	O/T	Mins	GA	SO	Avg	GP	W	L	Mins	GA	SO	Avg
2010-11	Brynas U18	Swe-U18	1	....	....	....	37	1	0	1.63	....	....	....	....	....	....	....
2011-12	Brynas U18	Swe-U18	21	....	....	....	1239	46	2	2.23	3	....	....	178	7	0	2.36
	Brynas IF Gavle Jr.	Swe-Jr.	5	....	....	....	237	13	0	3.29	....	....	....	....	....	....	....
2012-13	Brynas U18	Swe-U18	6	5	1	0	365	14	0	2.30	7	6	1	430	21	0	2.93
	Brynas IF Gavle Jr.	Swe-Jr.	29	14	15	0	1689	84	0	2.98	2	0	2	124	4	0	1.93
2013-14	Brynas IF Gavle Jr.	Swe-Jr.	23	13	9	0	1345	52	1	2.32	7	5	2	433	17	0	2.36
	Brynas IF Gavle	Sweden	4	2	2	0	243	12	0	2.96	....	....	....	....	....	....	....
2014-15	Brynas IF Gavle	Sweden	2	0	2	0	105	11	0	6.30	....	....	....	....	....	....	....
	Brynas IF Gavle Jr.	Swe-Jr.	13	6	6	0	763	46	0	3.62	2	1	1	119	7	0	3.52
2015-16	Almtuna	Sweden-2	46	25	20	0	2795	114	2	2.45	....	....	....	....	....	....	....
2016-17	Brynas IF Gavle	Sweden	2	1	1	0	120	4	1	2.00	....	....	....	....	....	....	....
	Almtuna	Sweden-2	41	18	21	0	2387	89	3	2.24	....	....	....	....	....	....	....
	Rochester	AHL	7	3	3	1	421	20	0	2.85	....	....	....	....	....	....	....

JOHNSON, Chad (JAWN-suhn, CHAD) BUF

Goaltender. Catches left. 6'3", 196 lbs. Born, Calgary, AB, June 10, 1986.
(Pittsburgh's 4th pick, 125th overall, in 2006 NHL Draft).

			Regular Season								Playoffs						
Season	Club	League	GP	W	L	O/T	Mins	GA	SO	Avg	GP	W	L	Mins	GA	SO	Avg
2002-03	Calgary Buffaloes	AMHL	....	8	8	2	1145	62	....	3.25	1	0	1	60	3	0	3.00
2003-04	Brooks Bandits	AJHL	31	6	20	3	1782	117	0	3.94	....	....	....	....	....	....	....
2004-05	Brooks Bandits	AJHL	43	25	16	2	2505	109	2	2.61	119	4	5	493	....	....	....
2005-06	Alaska	CCHA	18	6	7	4	985	42	0	2.56	....	....	....	....	....	....	....
2006-07	Alaska	CCHA	19	5	6	2	1002	52	1	3.11	....	....	....	....	....	....	....
2007-08	Alaska	CCHA	7	0	6	0	357	20	0	3.36	....	....	....	....	....	....	....
2008-09	Alaska	CCHA	35	14	16	5	2062	57	6	*1.66	....	....	....	....	....	....	....
2009-10	**NY Rangers**	**NHL**	**5**	**1**	**2**	**1**	**281**	**11**	**0**	**2.35**	....	....	....	....	....	....	....
	Hartford Wolf Pack	AHL	47	24	18	2	2649	112	3	2.54	....	....	....	....	....	....	....
2010-11	**NY Rangers**	**NHL**	**1**	**0**	**0**	**0**	**20**	**2**	**0**	**6.00**	....	....	....	....	....	....	....
	Connecticut Whale	AHL	40	16	19	3	2271	103	2	2.72	....	....	....	....	....	....	....
2011-12	Connecticut Whale	AHL	49	22	18	6	2775	115	1	2.49	....	....	....	....	....	....	....
2012-13	Portland Pirates	AHL	34	16	15	1	1938	97	2	3.00	3	0	3	204	12	0	3.53
	Phoenix	**NHL**	**4**	**2**	**0**	**2**	**247**	**5**	**1**	**1.21**	....	....	....	....	....	....	....
2013-14	**Boston**	**NHL**	**27**	**17**	**4**	**3**	**1511**	**53**	**2**	**2.10**	....	....	....	....	....	....	....
2014-15	**NY Islanders**	**NHL**	**19**	**8**	**8**	**1**	**1053**	**54**	**0**	**3.08**	....	....	....	....	....	....	....
2015-16	**Buffalo**	**NHL**	**45**	**22**	**16**	**4**	**2591**	**102**	**1**	**2.36**	....	....	....	....	....	....	....
2016-17	**Calgary**	**NHL**	**36**	**18**	**15**	**1**	**2013**	**87**	**3**	**2.59**	**1**	**0**	**1**	**52**	**1**	**0**	**1.15**
	NHL Totals		**137**	**68**	**45**	**12**	**7716**	**314**	**7**	**2.44**	**1**	**0**	**1**	**52**	**1**	**0**	**1.15**

AJHL South Division First All-Star Team (2005) • CCHA First All-Star Team (2009) • CCHA Rookie of the Year (2009) • NCAA West Second All-American Team (2009)

Traded to **NY Rangers** by **Pittsburgh** for Pittsburgh's 5th round pick (previously acquired, Pittsburgh selected Andy Bathgate) in 2009 NHL Draft, June 27, 2009. Signed as a free agent by **Phoenix**, July 1. 2012. Signed as a free agent by **Boston**, July 5, 2013. Signed as a free agent by **NY Islanders**, July 1, 2014. Traded to **Buffalo** by **NY Islanders** with Vancouver's 3rd round pick (previously acquired, later traded to Pittsburgh, later traded back to Vancouver – Vancouver selected William Lockwood) in 2016 NHL Draft for Michael Neuvirth, March 2, 2015. Signed as a free agent by **Calgary**, July 1, 2016. Traded to **Arizona** by **Calgary** wiith Brandon Hickey and a conditional 3rd round pick in 2018 NHL Draft for Mike Smith, June 17, 2017. Signed as a free agent by **Buffalo**, July 1, 2017.

JONES, Martin (JOHNZ, MAR-tihn) S.J.

Goaltender. Catches left. 6'4", 190 lbs. Born, North Vancouver, BC, January 10, 1990.

			Regular Season								Playoffs						
Season	**Club**	**League**	**GP**	**W**	**L**	**O/T**	**Mins**	**GA**	**SO**	**Avg**	**GP**	**W**	**L**	**Mins**	**GA**	**SO**	**Avg**
2006-07	Calgary Hitmen	WHL	18	9	4	3	1029	52	0	3.03	....	....	....	....	....	....	....
2007-08	Calgary Hitmen	WHL	27	18	8	1	1529	54	1	2.12	5	2	1	250	12	0	2.88
2008-09	Calgary Hitmen	WHL	55	*45	5	4	3295	114	*7	2.08	18	14	4	1095	34	2	1.86
2009-10	Calgary Hitmen	WHL	48	36	11	1	2851	105	*8	*2.21	*23	*16	7	*1401	55	*2	*2.36
2010-11	Manchester	AHL	39	23	12	1	2187	82	4	2.25	4	2	1	213	9	0	2.54
	Ontario Reign	ECHL	1	1	0	0	64	4	0	3.76	....	....	....	....	....	....	....
2011-12	Manchester	AHL	41	18	17	2	2166	94	1	2.60	3	1	1	155	6	0	2.33
2012-13	Manchester	AHL	56	27	25	4	3347	141	5	2.53	4	1	3	277	10	0	2.16
2013-14♦	**Los Angeles**	**NHL**	**19**	**12**	**6**	**0**	**1095**	**33**	**4**	**1.81**	**2**	**0**	**0**	**56**	**0**	**0**	**0.00**
	Manchester	AHL	22	16	3	3	1351	48	2	2.13	....	....	....	....	....	....	....
2014-15	**Los Angeles**	**NHL**	**15**	**4**	**5**	**2**	**775**	**29**	**3**	**2.25**	....	....	....	....	....	....	....
2015-16	**San Jose**	**NHL**	**65**	**37**	**23**	**4**	**3786**	**143**	**6**	**2.27**	***24**	**14**	**10**	***1473**	**53**	***3**	**2.16**
2016-17	**San Jose**	**NHL**	**65**	**35**	**23**	**6**	**3800**	**152**	**2**	**2.40**	**6**	**2**	**4**	**377**	**11**	**1**	**1.75**
	NHL Totals		**164**	**88**	**57**	**12**	**9456**	**357**	**15**	**2.27**	**32**	**16**	**14**	**1906**	**64**	**4**	**2.01**

WHL East Second All-Star Team (2009) • WHL East First All-Star Team (2010) • WHL Goaltender of the Year (2010) • Canadian Major Junior Second All-Star Team (2010)

Played in NHL All-Star Game (2017)

Signed as a free agent by **Los Angeles**, October 2, 2008. Traded to **Boston** by **Los Angeles** with Colin Miller and Los Angeles' 1st round pick (Jakub Zboril) in 2015 NHL Draft for Milan Lucic, June 26, 2015. Traded to **San Jose** by **Boston** for Sean Kuraly and San Jose's 1st round pick (Trent Frederic) in 2016 NHL Draft, June 30, 2015.

KAHKONEN, Kaapo (kakh-KOH-nihn, KA-poh) MIN

Goaltender. Catches left. 6'2", 222 lbs. Born, Helsinki, Finland, August 16, 1996.
(Minnesota's 3rd pick, 109th overall, in 2014 NHL Draft).

			Regular Season								Playoffs						
Season	**Club**	**League**	**GP**	**W**	**L**	**O/T**	**Mins**	**GA**	**SO**	**Avg**	**GP**	**W**	**L**	**Mins**	**GA**	**SO**	**Avg**
2011-12	Blues Espoo U18	Fin-U18	1	1	0	0	60	2	0	2.00	....	....	....	....	....	....	....
2012-13	Blues Espoo U18	Fin-U18	2	....	....	....	120	6	0	3.00	....	....	....	....	....	....	....
	Blues Espoo Jr.	Fin-Jr.	28	....	....	....	1676	68	4	2.43	12	....	....	628	28	2	2.68
2013-14	Blues Espoo Jr.	Fin-Jr.	38	....	....	....	2279	91	....	2.39	10	....	....	599	21	....	2.10
2014-15	TuTo Turku	Finland-2	47	....	....	....	2610	92	....	2.11	13	....	....	801	26	....	1.95
2015-16	Blues Espoo	Finland	27	6	15	5	1581	71	1	2.69	....	....	....	....	....	....	....
	TuTo Turku	Finland-2	1	....	....	....	60	0	1	0.00	6	....	....	356	18	....	3.03
2016-17	Lukko Rauma	Finland	34	12	12	10	2020	87	2	2.58	....	....	....	....	....	....	....

KALLGREN, Erik (KAHL-grehn, AIR-ihk) ARI

Goaltender. Catches left. 6'2", 188 lbs. Born, Stockholm, Sweden, October 14, 1996.
(Arizona's 9th pick, 183rd overall, in 2015 NHL Draft).

			Regular Season								Playoffs						
Season	**Club**	**League**	**GP**	**W**	**L**	**O/T**	**Mins**	**GA**	**SO**	**Avg**	**GP**	**W**	**L**	**Mins**	**GA**	**SO**	**Avg**
2012-13	Linkopings HC U18	Swe-U18	17	13	3	0	994	35	4	2.11	....	....	....	....	....	....	....
	Linkopings HC Jr.	Swe-Jr.	2	0	2	0	97	4	0	2.46	....	....	....	....	....	....	....
2013-14	Linkopings HC U18	Swe-U18	25	19	6	0	1507	55	4	2.19	5	3	2	330	11	0	2.00
	Linkopings HC Jr.	Swe-Jr.	2	1	1	0	119	7	0	3.53	1	0	1	47	5	0	6.36
2014-15	Linkopings HC Jr.	Swe-Jr.	34	27	7	0	2052	60	6	1.75	7	5	2	428	18	0	2.52
	IK Oskarshamn	Sweden-2	3	2	1	0	145	6	0	2.49	....	....	....	....	....	....	....
2015-16	IK Oskarshamn	Sweden-2	21	9	10	0	1169	54	1	2.77	....	....	....	....	....	....	....
	Linkopings HC Jr.	Swe-Jr.	....	....	....	....	....	....	....	....	3	1	2	159	10	0	3.77
2016-17	IK Oskarshamn	Sweden-2	22	11	10	0	1165	49	1	2.52	....	....	....	....	....	....	....

KASDORF, Jason (KAZ-dawrf, JAY-suhn) BUF

Goaltender. Catches left. 6'3", 172 lbs. Born, Winnipeg, MB, May 18, 1992.
(Winnipeg's 6th pick, 157th overall, in 2011 NHL Draft).

			Regular Season								Playoffs						
Season	**Club**	**League**	**GP**	**W**	**L**	**O/T**	**Mins**	**GA**	**SO**	**Avg**	**GP**	**W**	**L**	**Mins**	**GA**	**SO**	**Avg**
2008-09	Wpg. Thrashers	MMHL	44	....	....	....	1032	36	4	2.09	....	....	....	....	....	....	....
2009-10	Portage Terriers	MJHL	....	19	10	5	2094	89	2	2.55	....	....	....	....	....	....	....
2010-11	Portage Terriers	MJHL	34	24	10	0	2018	85	2	2.53	16	10	5	930	34	2	2.19
2011-12	Des Moines	USHL	33	10	16	5	1750	100	3	3.43	....	....	....	....	....	....	....
2012-13	RPI Engineers	ECAC	23	14	5	2	1330	36	3	1.62	....	....	....	....	....	....	....
2013-14	RPI Engineers	ECAC	2	1	1	0	103	6	1	3.49	....	....	....	....	....	....	....
2014-15	RPI Engineers	ECAC	33	11	19	2	1816	90	1	2.97	....	....	....	....	....	....	....
2015-16	RPI Engineers	ECAC	30	12	12	5	1777	68	2	2.30	....	....	....	....	....	....	....
	Buffalo	**NHL**	**1**	**0**	**1**	**0**	**60**	**4**	**0**	**4.00**	....	....	....	....	....	....	....
2016-17	Rochester	AHL	3	0	3	0	177	17	0	5.75	....	....	....	....	....	....	....
	Elmira Jackals	ECHL	31	5	20	1	1621	107	1	3.96	....	....	....	....	....	....	....
	NHL Totals		**1**	**0**	**1**	**0**	**60**	**4**	**0**	**4.00**	....	....	....	....	....	....	....

ECAC All-Rookie Team (2013) • ECAC Second All-Star Team (2013, 2016)

• Missed majority of 2013-14 due to shoulder injury in practice, October 1, 2013. Traded to **Buffalo** by **Winnipeg** with Evander Kane and Zach Bogosian for Tyler Myers, Drew Stafford, Joel Armia, Brendan Lemieux and St. Louis' 1st round pick (previously acquired, Winnipeg selected Jack Roslovic) in 2015 NHL Draft, February 11, 2015.

KASKISUO, Kasimir (kas-KIH-soo-oh), KAS-ih-mihr) TOR

Goaltender. Catches left. 6'3", 195 lbs. Born, Vantaa, Finland, October 2, 1993.

			Regular Season								Playoffs						
Season	**Club**	**League**	**GP**	**W**	**L**	**O/T**	**Mins**	**GA**	**SO**	**Avg**	**GP**	**W**	**L**	**Mins**	**GA**	**SO**	**Avg**
2011-12	Jokerit Helsinki Jr.	Fin-Jr.	9	5	1	0	425	20	0	2.82	....	....	....	....	....	....	....
	Bewe Helsinki	Finland-4	2	....	....	....	120	5	0	2.50	....	....	....	....	....	....	....
2012-13	Jokerit Helsinki Jr.	Fin-Jr.	13	....	....	....	751	34	1	2.72	....	....	....	....	....	....	....
2013-14	Min. Wilderness	NAHL	32	21	6	5	1951	48	9	*1.48	5	2	2	274	8	1	1.75
2014-15	U. Minn-Duluth	NCHC	36	18	14	3	2114	81	1	2.30	....	....	....	....	....	....	....
2015-16	U. Minn-Duluth	NCHC	39	19	15	5	*2350	75	*5	1.92	....	....	....	....	....	....	....
	Toronto Marlies	AHL	2	1	0	1	125	5	0	2.40	....	....	....	....	....	....	....
2016-17	Toronto Marlies	AHL	7	5	1	0	391	12	1	1.84	10	5	3	564	25	0	2.66
	Orlando	ECHL	32	14	11	5	1842	106	1	3.45	....	....	....	....	....	....	....

NCHC All-Rookie Team (2015)

Signed as a free agent by **Toronto**, March 28, 2016.

KHUDOBIN, Anton (hoo-DOH-bihn, AN-tawn) BOS

Goaltender. Catches left. 5'11", 195 lbs. Born, Ust-Kamenogorsk, USSR, May 7, 1986.
(Minnesota's 11th pick, 206th overall, in 2004 NHL Draft).

			Regular Season								Playoffs						
Season	**Club**	**League**	**GP**	**W**	**L**	**O/T**	**Mins**	**GA**	**SO**	**Avg**	**GP**	**W**	**L**	**Mins**	**GA**	**SO**	**Avg**
2003-04	Magnitogorsk 2	Russia-3	38	....	....	....	....	80	....	....	....	....	....	....	....	....	....
2004-05	Magnitogorsk	Russia	4	....	....	....	133	0	1	0.00	....	....	....	....	....	....	....
	Magnitogorsk 2	Russia-3	27	....	....	....	....	52	....	....	....	....	....	....	....	....	....
2005-06	Saskatoon Blades	WHL	44	23	13	3	2362	114	4	2.90	10	4	6	685	32	0	2.80
2006-07	Magnitogorsk	Russia	16	....	....	....	618	28	0	2.72	3	....	....	26	1	0	2.30
2007-08	Houston Aeros	AHL	12	2	2	1	482	16	1	1.99	....	....	....	....	....	....	....
	Texas Wildcatters	ECHL	27	20	1	4	1549	51	3	*1.98	9	5	4	547	20	1	2.19
2008-09	Houston Aeros	AHL	10	3	6	1	512	26	0	3.04	17	8	8	890	40	2	2.70
	Florida Everblades	ECHL	33	18	10	1	1706	77	4	2.71	....	....	....	....	....	....	....
2009-10	**Minnesota**	**NHL**	**2**	**2**	**0**	**0**	**69**	**1**	**0**	**0.87**	....	....	....	....	....	....	....
	Houston Aeros	AHL	40	14	19	4	2247	91	4	2.43	....	....	....	....	....	....	....
2010-11	**Minnesota**	**NHL**	**4**	**2**	**1**	**0**	**189**	**5**	**1**	**1.59**	....	....	....	....	....	....	....
	Houston Aeros	AHL	34	19	12	1	1883	81	1	2.58	....	....	....	....	....	....	....
	Providence Bruins	AHL	16	9	4	1	901	36	1	2.40	....	....	....	....	....	....	....
2011-12	**Boston**	**NHL**	**1**	**1**	**0**	**0**	**60**	**1**	**0**	**1.00**	....	....	....	....	....	....	....
	Providence Bruins	AHL	44	21	19	3	2597	113	2	2.61	....	....	....	....	....	....	....
2012-13	Mytischi	KHL	26	6	14	0	1500	74	1	2.96	....	....	....	....	....	....	....
	Boston	**NHL**	**14**	**9**	**4**	**1**	**803**	**31**	**1**	**2.32**	....	....	....	....	....	....	....
2013-14	**Carolina**	**NHL**	**36**	**19**	**14**	**1**	**2084**	**80**	**1**	**2.30**	....	....	....	....	....	....	....
	Charlotte Checkers	AHL	2	1	1	0	119	6	0	3.03	....	....	....	....	....	....	....
2014-15	**Carolina**	**NHL**	**34**	**8**	**17**	**6**	**1920**	**87**	**1**	**2.72**	....	....	....	....	....	....	....
2015-16	**Anaheim**	**NHL**	**9**	**3**	**3**	**0**	**356**	**16**	**1**	**2.70**	....	....	....	....	....	....	....
	San Diego Gulls	AHL	31	19	8	3	1807	74	0	2.46	4	2	1	185	7	0	2.26
2016-17	**Boston**	**NHL**	**16**	**7**	**6**	**1**	**885**	**39**	**0**	**2.64**	....	....	....	....	....	....	....
	Providence Bruins	AHL	11	7	3	1	626	28	2	2.69	....	....	....	....	....	....	....
	NHL Totals		**116**	**51**	**45**	**9**	**6366**	**260**	**5**	**2.45**	....	....	....	....	....	....	....

ECHL First All-Star Team (2008) • ECHL Goaltender of the Year (2008)

Traded to **Boston** by **Minnesota** for Jeff Penner and Mikko Lehtonen, February 28, 2011. Signed as a free agent by **Mytischi** (KHL), September 21, 2012. Signed as a free agent by **Carolina**, July 5, 2013. Traded to **Anaheim** by **Carolina** for James Wisniewski, June 27, 2015. Signed as a free agent by **Boston**, July 1, 2016.

KINKAID, Keith (kihn-KAID, KEETH) N.J.

Goaltender. Catches left. 6'3", 195 lbs. Born, Farmingville, NY, July 4, 1989.

			Regular Season								Playoffs						
Season	**Club**	**League**	**GP**	**W**	**L**	**O/T**	**Mins**	**GA**	**SO**	**Avg**	**GP**	**W**	**L**	**Mins**	**GA**	**SO**	**Avg**
2007-08	New York Bobcats	AtJHL	29	20	5	0	1458	58	....	2.39	....	....	....	....	....	....	....
	Des Moines	USHL	15	4	9	2	844	48	0	3.41	....	....	....	....	....	....	....
2008-09	St. Louis Bandits	NAHL	40	*30	5	4	2393	71	*7	*1.78	*12	*10	2	*728	14	*3	*1.15
2009-10	Union College	ECAC	25	12	8	3	1478	61	1	2.48	....	....	....	....	....	....	....
2010-11	Union College	ECAC	*38	25	10	3	*2266	75	3	1.99	....	....	....	....	....	....	....
2011-12	Albany Devils	AHL	42	17	20	3	2347	115	3	2.94	....	....	....	....	....	....	....
2012-13	Albany Devils	AHL	45	21	17	6	2644	120	2	2.72	....	....	....	....	....	....	....
	New Jersey	**NHL**	**1**	**0**	**0**	**0**	**26**	**1**	**0**	**2.31**	....	....	....	....	....	....	....
2013-14	Albany Devils	AHL	43	24	13	5	2519	96	4	2.29	4	1	3	238	9	0	2.26
2014-15	**New Jersey**	**NHL**	**19**	**6**	**5**	**4**	**925**	**40**	**0**	**2.59**	....	....	....	....	....	....	....
	Albany Devils	AHL	13	7	2	3	713	26	1	2.19	....	....	....	....	....	....	....
2015-16	**New Jersey**	**NHL**	**23**	**9**	**9**	**1**	**1240**	**58**	**2**	**2.81**	....	....	....	....	....	....	....
2016-17	**New Jersey**	**NHL**	**26**	**8**	**13**	**3**	**1476**	**65**	**1**	**2.64**	....	....	....	....	....	....	....
	NHL Totals		**69**	**23**	**27**	**8**	**3667**	**164**	**3**	**2.68**	....	....	....	....	....	....	....

ECAC All-Rookie Team (2010) • ECAC First All-Star Team (2011) • NCAA East First All-American Team (2011)

Signed as a free agent by **New Jersey**, April 18, 2011.

KIVLENIEKS, Matiss (kihv-LEH-nihx, MAH-tihs) CBJ

Goaltender. Catches left. 6'2", 190 lbs. Born, Riga, Latvia, August 26, 1996.

			Regular Season								Playoffs						
Season	**Club**	**League**	**GP**	**W**	**L**	**O/T**	**Mins**	**GA**	**SO**	**Avg**	**GP**	**W**	**L**	**Mins**	**GA**	**SO**	**Avg**
2012-13	Prizma Riga U18	LatviaU18	13	....	....	....	659	28	....	2.55	....	....	....	....	....	....	....
2013-14	Edina Lakers	MNJHL	39	11	27	1	2218	146	2	3.95	2	0	2	120	9	0	4.50
2014-15	Forest Lake Lakers	MNJHL	33	21	12	0	1940	72	4	2.23	4	2	2	240	7	1	1.75
	Coulee Region	NAHL	1	0	1	0	59	4	0	4.05	....	....	....	....	....	....	....
2015-16	Coulee Region	NAHL	29	16	10	1	1618	65	2	2.41	....	....	....	....	....	....	....
2016-17	Sioux City	USHL	49	*36	7	2	2991	92	*5	*1.85	*13	8	3	*807	28	2	2.08

Signed as a free agent by **Columbus**, May 25, 2017.

KORENAR, Josef (KOH-REH-nahr, JOH-sehf) S.J.

Goaltender. Catches left. 6'1", 175 lbs. Born, Vystrkov, Czech Rep., January 31, 1998.

			Regular Season								Playoffs						
Season	**Club**	**League**	**GP**	**W**	**L**	**O/T**	**Mins**	**GA**	**SO**	**Avg**	**GP**	**W**	**L**	**Mins**	**GA**	**SO**	**Avg**
2014-15	Jihlava U18	CzR-U18	23	....	....	....	1386	52	3	2.25	2	....	....	119	5	0	2.52
	Jihlava Jr.	CzRep-Jr.	6	....	....	....	260	20	0	4.61	....	....	....	....	....	....	....
2015-16	Jihlava U18	CzR-U18	3	....	....	....	180	6	0	2.00	....	....	....	....	....	....	....
	Jihlava Jr.	CzRep-Jr.	24	....	....	....	1409	77	0	3.28	3	....	....	179	9	0	3.02
2016-17	Lincoln Stars	USHL	32	14	11	0	1783	66	2	2.22	....	....	....	....	....	....	....

Signed as a free agent by **San Jose**, July 13, 2017.

KORPISALO, Joonas (kohr-pih-SAL-loh, YOH-nuhs) CBJ

Goaltender. Catches left. 6'3", 191 lbs. Born, Pori, Finland, April 28, 1994.
(Columbus' 3rd pick, 62nd overall, in 2012 NHL Draft).

			Regular Season								Playoffs						
Season	**Club**	**League**	**GP**	**W**	**L**	**O/T**	**Mins**	**GA**	**SO**	**Avg**	**GP**	**W**	**L**	**Mins**	**GA**	**SO**	**Avg**
2010-11	Jokerit U18	Fin-U18	20	16	4	0	1200	53	0	2.65	8	5	3	460	22	0	2.87
2011-12	Jokerit Helsinki Jr.	Fin-Jr.	38	28	11	0	2295	78	4	2.04	4	3	1	270	8	1	1.77
2012-13	Jokerit Helsinki Jr.	Fin-Jr.	13	....	....	....	787	35	1	2.67	....	....	....	....	....	....	....
	Kiekko-Vantaa	Finland-2	18	....	....	....	997	45	0	2.71	....	....	....	....	....	....	....
	Jokerit Helsinki	Finland	1	0	0	0	15	0	0	0.00	....	....	....	....	....	....	....
2013-14	Jokerit Helsinki Jr.	Fin-Jr.	1	....	....	....	60	1	0	1.00	....	....	....	....	....	....	....
	Jokerit Helsinki	Finland	1	0	1	0	34	3	0	5.32	....	....	....	....	....	....	....
	Kiekko-Vantaa	Finland-2	4	....	....	....	199	11	....	3.31	....	....	....	....	....	....	....
	Ilves Tampere Jr.	Fin-Jr.	2	....	....	....	120	5	0	2.50	....	....	....	....	....	....	....
	Ilves Tampere	Finland	8	3	1	0	337	8	1	1.42	....	....	....	....	....	....	....
	LeKi Lempaala	Finland-2	2	....	....	....	68	7	....	6.13	....	....	....	....	....	....	....

2014-15	Springfield Falcons	AHL	3	0	2	0	169	9	0	3.20	....	....	....	....	....	....	....
	Ilves Tampere	Finland	38	14	13	7	2132	83	2	2.34	2	0	2	193	4	0	1.24
2015-16	**Columbus**	**NHL**	**31**	**16**	**11**	**4**	**1803**	**78**	**0**	**2.60**	....	....	....	....	....	....	....
	Lake Erie Monsters	AHL	18	8	8	2	1066	42	2	2.36	9	6	2	507	25	0	2.96
2016-17	**Columbus**	**NHL**	**14**	**7**	**5**	**1**	**791**	**38**	**1**	**2.88**	....	....	....	....	....	....	....
	Cleveland	AHL	16	7	6	3	935	42	0	2.69	....	....	....	....	....	....	....
	NHL Totals		**45**	**23**	**16**	**5**	**2594**	**116**	**1**	**2.68**	....	....	....	....	....	....	....

KUEMPER, Darcy (KEHM-puhr, DAHR-see) L.A.

Goaltender. Catches left. 6'5", 212 lbs. Born, Saskatoon, SK, May 5, 1990.
(Minnesota's 5th pick, 161st overall, in 2009 NHL Draft).

			Regular Season								Playoffs						
Season	Club	League	GP	W	L	O/T	Mins	GA	SO	Avg	GP	W	L	Mins	GA	SO	Avg
2006-07	Sask. Contacts	SMHL	25	8	14	3	1489	87	1	3.51	4	1	3	200	19	0	5.70
	Spokane Chiefs	WHL	....	....	....	....	....	....	....	....	1	0	0	0	0	0	0.00
2007-08	Saskatoon Blazers	SMHL	26	15	7	4	1578	62	1	2.36	13	7	6	781	34	1	2.61
2008-09	Red Deer Rebels	WHL	55	21	25	8	3167	156	3	2.96	....	....	....	....	....	....	....
2009-10	Red Deer Rebels	WHL	61	28	23	4	3234	147	3	2.73	2	0	2	61	6	0	5.90
	Houston Aeros	AHL	4	2	1	0	199	8	0	2.41	....	....	....	....	....	....	....
2010-11	Red Deer Rebels	WHL	62	*45	12	5	3685	114	*13	*1.86	7	4	3	403	19	0	2.83
2011-12	Houston Aeros	AHL	19	6	6	4	1070	42	1	2.36	....	....	....	....	....	....	....
	Ontario Reign	ECHL	8	7	1	0	484	14	0	1.74	....	....	....	....	....	....	....
2012-13	Houston Aeros	AHL	21	13	8	0	1210	38	4	1.88	2	1	1	119	3	1	1.51
	Orlando	ECHL	3	0	2	1	184	8	0	2.61	....	....	....	....	....	....	....
	Minnesota	**NHL**	**6**	**1**	**2**	**0**	**288**	**10**	**0**	**2.08**	**2**	**0**	**0**	**73**	**4**	**0**	**3.29**
2013-14	**Minnesota**	**NHL**	**26**	**12**	**8**	**4**	**1480**	**60**	**2**	**2.43**	**6**	**3**	**1**	**325**	**11**	**1**	**2.03**
	Iowa Wild	AHL	17	7	10	0	997	41	1	2.47	....	....	....	....	....	....	....
2014-15	**Minnesota**	**NHL**	**31**	**14**	**12**	**2**	**1569**	**68**	**3**	**2.60**	**1**	**0**	**0**	**23**	**0**	**0**	**0.00**
	Iowa Wild	AHL	5	2	3	0	279	15	1	3.22	....	....	....	....	....	....	....
2015-16	**Minnesota**	**NHL**	**21**	**6**	**7**	**5**	**1063**	**43**	**2**	**2.43**	....	....	....	....	....	....	....
2016-17	**Minnesota**	**NHL**	**18**	**8**	**5**	**3**	**1053**	**55**	**0**	**3.13**	....	....	....	....	....	....	....
	NHL Totals		**102**	**41**	**34**	**14**	**5453**	**236**	**7**	**2.60**	**9**	**3**	**1**	**421**	**15**	**1**	**2.14**

WHL East Second All-Star Team (2010) • WHL East First All-Star Team (2011) • Canadian Major Junior Goaltender of the Year (2011)

Signed as a free agent by **Los Angeles**, July 1, 2017.

KUPSKY, Jake (KUHP-skee, JAYK) S.J.

Goaltender. Catches right. 6'3", 205 lbs. Born, Waukeshaw, WI, October 27, 1995.
(San Jose's 9th pick, 193rd overall, in 2015 NHL Draft).

			Regular Season								Playoffs						
Season	Club	League	GP	W	L	O/T	Mins	GA	SO	Avg	GP	W	L	Mins	GA	SO	Avg
2010-11	Waukesha Wings	High-WI	4	0	0	0	59	4	0	4.02	....	....	....	....	....	....	....
2011-12	Waukesha Wings	High-WI	10	8	2	0	493	15	2	1.55	1	0	1	50	2	0	2.04
2012-13	Waukesha Wings	High-WI	23	16	6	1	1164	52	3	2.28	3	2	1	158	6	1	1.94
2013-14	Waukesha Wings	High-WI	22	17	4	1	1113	35	8	1.60	3	2	1	153	3	2	1.00
2014-15	Lone Star Brahmas	NAHL	30	19	4	4	1670	60	2	2.16	9	6	3	581	18	0	1.86
2015-16	Union College	ECAC	10	2	3	1	450	24	1	3.20	....	....	....	....	....	....	....
2016-17	Union College	ECAC	9	3	4	1	468	31	0	3.98	....	....	....	....	....	....	....

KVACA, Petr (K'VAH-chuh, PEH-tuhr) COL

Goaltender. Catches left. 6'1", 174 lbs. Born, Brandys nad Labem, Czech Rep., September 12, 1997.
(Colorado's 4th pick, 114th overall, in 2017 NHL Draft).

			Regular Season								Playoffs						
Season	Club	League	GP	W	L	O/T	Mins	GA	SO	Avg	GP	W	L	Mins	GA	SO	Avg
2012-13	C. Budejovice U18	CzR-U18	3	....	....	....	156	11	0	4.23	....	....	....	....	....	....	....
2013-14	C. Budejovice U18	CzR-U18	41	....	....	....	2226	119	3	3.21	9	....	....	547	23	0	2.52
2014-15	C. Budejovice U18	CzR-U18	25	....	....	....	1455	57	2	2.34	....	....	....	....	....	....	....
	C. Budejovice Jr.	CzRep-Jr.	17	....	....	....	979	49	1	3.00	....	....	....	....	....	....	....
2015-16	C. Budejovice Jr.	CzRep-Jr.	37	....	....	....	2155	113	4	3.15	2	....	....	125	5	0	2.40
	CEZ C. Budejovice	CzRep-2	3	....	....	....	138	4	1	1.74	1	....	....	0	0	0	0.00
2016-17	C. Budejovice Jr.	CzRep-Jr.	2	....	....	....	120	7	1	3.50	....	....	....	....	....	....	....
	Benatky	CzRep-2	7	....	....	....	425	20	0	2.82	....	....	....	....	....	....	....
	CEZ C. Budejovice	CzRep-2	29	....	....	....	1719	49	3	1.71	9	....	....	502	11	3	1.31

LACK, Eddie (LAK, EH-dee) CGY

Goaltender. Catches left. 6'4", 200 lbs. Born, Norrtalje, Sweden, January 5, 1988.

			Regular Season								Playoffs						
Season	Club	League	GP	W	L	O/T	Mins	GA	SO	Avg	GP	W	L	Mins	GA	SO	Avg
2004-05	Djurgarden U18	Swe-U18	9	....	....	....	527	21	1	2.39	3	....	....	140	6	0	2.57
	Djurgarden Jr.	Swe-Jr.	1	....	....	....	60	6	0	6.00	....	....	....	....	....	....	....
2005-06	Djurgarden Jr.	Swe-Jr.	23	....	....	....	1400	49	3	2.10	....	....	....	....	....	....	....
2006-07	Leksands IF Jr.	Swe-Jr.	30	....	....	....	1782	85	0	2.86	....	....	....	....	....	....	....
	Leksands IF	Sweden-2	3	....	....	....	137	7	0	3.06	....	....	....	....	....	....	....
2007-08	Leksands IF Jr.	Swe-Jr.	18	....	....	....	1077	47	4	2.62	3	....	....	179	8	0	2.68
	Leksands IF	Sweden-2	26	....	....	....	1530	50	4	1.96	....	....	....	....	....	....	....
2008-09	Leksands IF Jr.	Swe-Jr.	2	....	....	....	120	4	1	2.00	....	....	....	....	....	....	....
	Leksands IF	Sweden-2	38	....	....	....	2260	78	4	2.07	....	....	....	....	....	....	....
2009-10	Brynas IF Gavle Jr.	Swe-Jr.	6	....	....	....	359	21	0	....	....	....	....	....	....	....	....
	Brynas IF Gavle	Sweden	14	....	....	....	809	36	0	2.67	2	....	....	79	2	0	1.53
2010-11	Manitoba Moose	AHL	53	28	21	4	3135	118	5	2.26	12	6	5	752	25	2	1.99
2011-12	Chicago Wolves	AHL	46	21	20	3	2703	104	4	2.31	5	2	2	304	11	0	2.17
2012-13	Chicago Wolves	AHL	13	7	4	1	760	38	1	3.00	....	....	....	....	....	....	....
2013-14	**Vancouver**	**NHL**	**41**	**16**	**17**	**5**	**2319**	**93**	**4**	**2.41**	....	....	....	....	....	....	....
2014-15	**Vancouver**	**NHL**	**41**	**18**	**13**	**4**	**2324**	**95**	**2**	**2.45**	**4**	**1**	**3**	**198**	**10**	**0**	**3.03**
2015-16	**Carolina**	**NHL**	**34**	**12**	**14**	**6**	**1920**	**90**	**2**	**2.81**	....	....	....	....	....	....	....
2016-17	**Carolina**	**NHL**	**20**	**8**	**7**	**3**	**1090**	**48**	**1**	**2.64**	....	....	....	....	....	....	....
	Charlotte Checkers	AHL	2	1	1	0	120	3	0	1.50	....	....	....	....	....	....	....
	NHL Totals		**136**	**54**	**51**	**18**	**7653**	**326**	**9**	**2.56**	**4**	**1**	**3**	**198**	**10**	**0**	**3.03**

AHL All-Rookie Team (2011)

Signed as a free agent by **Vancouver**, April 6, 2010. Traded to **Carolina** by **Vancouver** for Carolina's 3rd round pick (Guillaume Brisebois) in 2015 NHL Draft and Carolina's 7th round pick (Brett McKenzie) in 2016 NHL Draft, June 26, 2015. Traded to **Calgary** by **Carolina** with Ryan Murphy and Carolina's 7th round pick in 2019 NHL Draft for Keegan Kanzig and Calgary's 6th round pick in 2019 NHL Draft, June 29, 2017.

LaFONTAINE, Jack (lah-fawn-TAYN, JAK) CAR

Goaltender. Catches left. 6'2", 204 lbs. Born, Mississauga, ON, January 6, 1998.
(Carolina's 6th pick, 75th overall, in 2016 NHL Draft).

			Regular Season								Playoffs						
Season	Club	League	GP	W	L	O/T	Mins	GA	SO	Avg	GP	W	L	Mins	GA	SO	Avg
2012-13	Don Mills Flyers	GTHL	26	10	9	6	1056	60	1	2.56	5	2	1	172	12	0	3.14
	Don Mills Flyers	Other	9	4	3	2	383	24	1	2.82	....	....	....	....	....	....	....
2013-14	Don Mills Flyers	GTHL	22	9	10	3	987	53	4	2.42	7	2	3	288	18	0	2.81
	Don Mills Flyers	Other	15	9	3	1	586	32	2	2.46	....	....	....	....	....	....	....
2014-15	Georgetown	ON-Jr.A	30	20	6	0	1635	58	2	2.13	8	4	4	430	17	2	2.37
2015-16	Janesville Jets	NAHL	41	24	8	7	2356	85	4	2.16	4	1	3	286	9	0	1.89
2016-17	U. of Michigan	Big Ten	11	1	7	1	594	33	0	3.34	....	....	....	....	....	....	....

LAGACE, Maxime (luh-ga-SEE, max-EEM) VGK

Goaltender. Catches left. 6'2", 190 lbs. Born, St-Augustin, QC, January 12, 1993.

			Regular Season								Playoffs						
Season	Club	League	GP	W	L	O/T	Mins	GA	SO	Avg	GP	W	L	Mins	GA	SO	Avg
2008-09	Quebec Typhons	Minor-QC					STATISTICS NOT AVAILABLE										
	St-Francois Blizzard	QAAA	8	1	1	2	346	27	0	4.68	....	....	....	....	....	....	....
2009-10	St-Francois Blizzard	QAAA	22	18	3	1	1256	39	1	1.86	3	1	2	180	10	0	3.33
2010-11	P.E.I. Rocket	QMJHL	18	8	4	0	870	52	1	3.59	....	....	....	....	....	....	....
2011-12	P.E.I. Rocket	QMJHL	56	12	34	5	2912	219	1	4.51	....	....	....	....	....	....	....
2012-13	P.E.I. Rocket	QMJHL	33	13	12	1	1571	106	1	4.05	1	0	0	27	1	0	2.19
2013-14	Cape Breton	QMJHL	8	3	3	1	464	25	0	3.23	....	....	....	....	....	....	....
	Shawinigan	QMJHL	3	1	2	0	180	12	1	4.00	....	....	....	....	....	....	....
	Sherbrooke	QMJHL	15	2	9	3	827	56	0	4.06	....	....	....	....	....	....	....
2014-15	Texas Stars	AHL	1	0	0	0	17	1	0	3.55	....	....	....	....	....	....	....
	Missouri Mavericks	ECHL	15	5	6	3	779	39	1	3.01	....	....	....	....	....	....	....
	Bakersfield	ECHL	13	6	4	1	718	32	1	2.68	....	....	....	....	....	....	....
2015-16	Texas Stars	AHL	36	19	10	3	2051	99	1	2.90	2	0	1	88	4	0	2.74
	Idaho Steelheads	ECHL	11	3	5	2	582	30	0	3.09	....	....	....	....	....	....	....
2016-17	Texas Stars	AHL	32	11	12	3	1567	93	1	3.56	....	....	....	....	....	....	....

Signed as a free agent by **Dallas**, July 23, 2012. Signed as a free agent by **Vegas**, July 1, 2017.

LANGHAMER, Marek (lang-HAHM-uhr, MAHR-ehk) ARI

Goaltender. Catches left. 6'3", 187 lbs. Born, Moravska Trebova, Czech Rep., July 22, 1994.
(Phoenix's 7th pick, 184th overall, in 2012 NHL Draft).

			Regular Season								Playoffs						
Season	Club	League	GP	W	L	O/T	Mins	GA	SO	Avg	GP	W	L	Mins	GA	SO	Avg
2008-09	HC Pardubice U17	CzR-U17	29	....	....	....	1433	87	0	3.64	6	....	....	352	12	0	2.05
2009-10	HC Pardubice U18	CzR-U18	35	....	....	....	2031	83	4	2.45	6	....	....	327	14	1	2.57
	HC Pardubice Jr.	CzRep-Jr.	2	....	....	....	30	0	0	0.00	....	....	....	....	....	....	....
2010-11	HC Pardubice U18	CzR-U18	17	....	....	....	1028	43	1	2.51	5	....	....	320	12	0	2.25
	HC Pardubice Jr.	CzRep-Jr.	37	....	....	....	2162	113	3	3.14	....	....	....	....	....	....	....
	HC Chrudim	CzRep-2	4	....	....	....	172	5	0	1.74	....	....	....	....	....	....	....
2011-12	HC Pardubice Jr.	CzRep-Jr.	33	....	....	....	1916	105	0	3.29	....	....	....	....	....	....	....
2012-13	Medicine Hat	WHL	30	15	12	1	1450	83	2	3.44	1	0	0	38	5	0	7.83
2013-14	Medicine Hat	WHL	40	23	14	3	2392	103	2	2.58	18	9	9	1071	42	0	2.35
2014-15	Medicine Hat	WHL	50	30	16	3	2904	136	2	2.81	....	....	....	....	....	....	....
2015-16	Springfield Falcons	AHL	19	7	9	2	1027	65	0	3.80	....	....	....	....	....	....	....
	Rapid City Rush	ECHL	8	5	2	1	484	18	1	2.23	....	....	....	....	....	....	....
2016-17	**Arizona**	**NHL**	**1**	**0**	**0**	**0**	**16**	**1**	**0**	**3.75**	....	....	....	....	....	....	....
	Tucson	AHL	25	8	11	2	1267	71	0	3.36	....	....	....	....	....	....	....
	Rapid City Rush	ECHL	7	5	2	0	419	19	1	2.72	....	....	....	....	....	....	....
	NHL Totals		**1**	**0**	**0**	**0**	**16**	**1**	**0**	**3.75**	....	....	....	....	....	....	....

LARSSON, Filip (LAHR-suhn, FIHL-ihp) DET

Goaltender. Catches left. 6'2", 185 lbs. Born, Stockholm, Sweden, August 17, 1998.
(Detroit's 6th pick, 167th overall, in 2016 NHL Draft).

			Regular Season								Playoffs						
Season	Club	League	GP	W	L	O/T	Mins	GA	SO	Avg	GP	W	L	Mins	GA	SO	Avg
2014-15	Djurgarden U18	Swe-U18	34	21	13	0	1978	75	3	2.27	5	3	2	300	9	2	1.80
	Djurgarden Jr.	Swe-Jr.	1	0	1	0	65	4	0	3.69	....	....	....	....	....	....	....
2015-16	Djurgarden U18	Swe-U18	4	2	2	0	243	13	0	3.21	4	2	2	258	11	0	2.56
	Djurgarden Jr.	Swe-Jr.	19	9	10	0	1120	72	0	3.86	....	....	....	....	....	....	....
2016-17	Djurgarden Jr.	Swe-Jr.	31	17	14	0	1820	68	2	2.24	2	0	2	117	4	0	2.06

LEHNER, Robin (LEH-nuhr, RAW-bihn) BUF

Goaltender. Catches left. 6'5", 240 lbs. Born, Goteborg, Sweden, July 24, 1991.
(Ottawa's 3rd pick, 46th overall, in 2009 NHL Draft).

			Regular Season								Playoffs						
Season	Club	League	GP	W	L	O/T	Mins	GA	SO	Avg	GP	W	L	Mins	GA	SO	Avg
2007-08	Frolunda U18	Swe-U18	19	....	....	....	1147	34	6	1.78	4	....	....	243	15	0	3.70
2008-09	Frolunda U18	Swe-U18	2	....	....	....	117	5	0	2.56	7	....	....	438	19	0	2.60
	Frolunda Jr.	Swe-Jr.	22	....	....	....	1318	67	1	3.05	1	....	....	58	3	0	3.08
2009-10	Sault Ste. Marie	OHL	47	27	13	3	2574	120	*5	2.80	5	1	4	279	20	0	4.30
	Binghamton	AHL	2	2	0	0	120	6	0	3.00	....	....	....	....	....	....	....
2010-11	**Ottawa**	**NHL**	**8**	**1**	**4**	**0**	**341**	**20**	**0**	**3.52**	....	....	....	....	....	....	....
	Binghamton	AHL	22	10	8	2	1246	56	3	2.70	19	*14	4	1112	39	*3	2.10
2011-12	**Ottawa**	**NHL**	**5**	**3**	**2**	**0**	**299**	**10**	**1**	**2.01**	....	....	....	....	....	....	....
	Binghamton	AHL	40	13	22	1	2192	119	2	3.26	....	....	....	....	....	....	....
2012-13	Binghamton	AHL	31	18	10	2	1841	65	3	2.12	....	....	....	....	....	....	....
	Ottawa	**NHL**	**12**	**5**	**3**	**4**	**735**	**27**	**0**	**2.20**	**2**	**0**	**1**	**49**	**2**	**0**	**2.45**
2013-14	**Ottawa**	**NHL**	**36**	**12**	**15**	**6**	**1942**	**99**	**1**	**3.06**	....	....	....	....	....	....	....
2014-15	**Ottawa**	**NHL**	**25**	**9**	**12**	**3**	**1471**	**74**	**0**	**3.02**	....	....	....	....	....	....	....
2015-16	**Buffalo**	**NHL**	**21**	**5**	**9**	**5**	**1164**	**48**	**1**	**2.47**	....	....	....	....	....	....	....
	Rochester	AHL	3	1	2	0	179	10	0	3.36	....	....	....	....	....	....	....
2016-17	**Buffalo**	**NHL**	**59**	**23**	**26**	**8**	**3405**	**152**	**2**	**2.68**	....	....	....	....	....	....	....
	NHL Totals		**166**	**58**	**71**	**26**	**9357**	**430**	**5**	**2.76**	**2**	**0**	**1**	**49**	**2**	**0**	**2.45**

Jack A. Butterfield Trophy (AHL – Playoff MVP) (2011)

Traded to **Buffalo** by **Ottawa** with David Legwand for NY Islanders' 1st round pick (previously acquired, Ottawa selected Colin White) in 2015 NHL Draft, June 26, 2015.

LEHTONEN, Kari (LEH-tuh-nehn, KAH-ree) DAL

Goaltender. Catches left. 6'4", 205 lbs. Born, Helsinki, Finland, November 16, 1983.
(Atlanta's 1st pick, 2nd overall, in 2002 NHL Draft).

			Regular Season								Playoffs						
Season	Club	League	GP	W	L	O/T	Mins	GA	SO	Avg	GP	W	L	Mins	GA	SO	Avg
1998-99	Jokerit U18	Fin-U18	2	....	....	....	....	....	....	....	4	2	2	240	7	0	1.75
99-2000	Jokerit Helsinki Jr.	Fin-Jr.	33	21	9	3	1974	86	2	2.61	12	9	3	758	14	4	1.11
2000-01	Jokerit U18	Fin-U18	....	....	....	....	....	....	....	....	6	....	....	....	....	....	....
	Jokerit Helsinki Jr.	Fin-Jr.	31	20	9	1	1799	71	3	2.37	1	0	1	54	4	0	4.44
	Jokerit Helsinki	Finland	4	3	1	0	189	6	0	1.90	....	....	....	....	....	....	....
2001-02	Jokerit Helsinki Jr.	Fin-Jr.	6	5	1	0	360	11	1	1.83	....	....	....	....	....	....	....
	Jokerit Helsinki	Finland	23	13	5	2	1242	37	4	1.79	11	8	2	623	18	3	1.73
2002-03	Jokerit Helsinki	Finland	45	23	14	6	2634	87	5	1.98	10	6	4	626	17	2	1.63
2003-04	**Atlanta**	**NHL**	**4**	**4**	**0**	**0**	**240**	**5**	**1**	**1.25**	....	....	....	....	....	....	....
	Chicago Wolves	AHL	39	20	14	2	2192	88	3	2.41	10	6	4	663	23	1	2.08
2004-05	Chicago Wolves	AHL	57	38	17	2	3378	128	5	2.27	16	10	6	983	28	2	*1.71
2005-06	**Atlanta**	**NHL**	**38**	**20**	**15**	**0**	**2166**	**106**	**2**	**2.94**	....	....	....	....	....	....	....
	Finland	Olympics	DID NOT PLAY – INJURED														
2006-07	**Atlanta**	**NHL**	**68**	**34**	**24**	**9**	**3934**	**183**	**4**	**2.79**	**2**	**0**	**2**	**118**	**11**	**0**	**5.59**
2007-08	**Atlanta**	**NHL**	**48**	**17**	**22**	**5**	**2707**	**131**	**4**	**2.90**	....	....	....	....	....	....	....
	Chicago Wolves	AHL	2	2	0	0	124	4	0	1.93	....	....	....	....	....	....	....
2008-09	**Atlanta**	**NHL**	**46**	**19**	**22**	**3**	**2624**	**134**	**3**	**3.06**	....	....	....	....	....	....	....
2009-10	**Dallas**	**NHL**	**12**	**6**	**4**	**0**	**663**	**31**	**0**	**2.81**	....	....	....	....	....	....	....
	Chicago Wolves	AHL	4	1	1	2	247	11	0	2.67	....	....	....	....	....	....	....
2010-11	**Dallas**	**NHL**	**69**	**34**	**24**	**11**	**4119**	**175**	**3**	**2.55**	....	....	....	....	....	....	....
2011-12	**Dallas**	**NHL**	**59**	**32**	**22**	**4**	**3497**	**136**	**4**	**2.33**	....	....	....	....	....	....	....
2012-13	**Dallas**	**NHL**	**36**	**15**	**14**	**3**	**1986**	**88**	**1**	**2.66**	....	....	....	....	....	....	....
2013-14	**Dallas**	**NHL**	***65**	**33**	**20**	**10**	***3804**	**153**	**5**	**2.41**	**6**	**2**	**4**	**346**	**19**	**1**	**3.29**
	Finland	Olympics	2	....	....	....	119	3	0	1.51	....	....	....	....	....	....	....
2014-15	**Dallas**	**NHL**	**65**	**34**	**17**	**10**	**3698**	**181**	**5**	**2.94**	....	....	....	....	....	....	....
2015-16	**Dallas**	**NHL**	**43**	**25**	**10**	**2**	**2279**	**105**	**2**	**2.76**	**11**	**6**	**3**	**555**	**26**	**1**	**2.81**
2016-17	**Dallas**	**NHL**	**59**	**22**	**25**	**7**	**3177**	**151**	**3**	**2.85**	....	....	....	....	....	....	....
	NHL Totals		**612**	**295**	**219**	**64**	**34894**	**1579**	**37**	**2.72**	**19**	**8**	**9**	**1019**	**56**	**2**	**3.30**

AHL Second All-Star Team (2005)

Traded to **Dallas** by **Atlanta** for Ivan Vishnevskiy and Dallas' 4th round pick (Ivan Telegin) in 2010 NHL Draft, February 9, 2010.

LEIGHTON, Michael (LAY-tohn, MIGH-kuhl) T.B.

Goaltender. Catches left. 6'3", 186 lbs. Born, Petrolia, ON, May 19, 1981.
(Chicago's 5th pick, 165th overall, in 1999 NHL Draft).

			Regular Season								Playoffs						
Season	Club	League	GP	W	L	O/T	Mins	GA	SO	Avg	GP	W	L	Mins	GA	SO	Avg
1997-98	Petrolia Jets	ON-Jr.B	30	....	....	....	1583	87	2	3.30	....	....	....	....	....	....	....
1998-99	Windsor Spitfires	OHL	28	4	15	9	1390	112	0	4.83	3	0	1	81	10	0	7.43
99-2000	Windsor Spitfires	OHL	42	17	17	2	2272	118	1	3.12	12	5	6	617	32	0	3.11
2000-01	Windsor Spitfires	OHL	54	32	13	5	3035	138	2	2.73	9	4	5	519	27	1	3.12
2001-02	Norfolk Admirals	AHL	52	27	16	8	3114	111	6	2.14	4	1	2	238	8	0	2.02
2002-03	**Chicago**	**NHL**	**8**	**2**	**3**	**2**	**447**	**21**	**1**	**2.82**	....	....	....	....	....	....	....
	Norfolk Admirals	AHL	36	18	13	5	2184	91	4	2.50	4	3	1	240	7	1	1.75
2003-04	**Chicago**	**NHL**	**34**	**6**	**18**	**8**	**1988**	**99**	**2**	**2.99**	....	....	....	....	....	....	....
	Norfolk Admirals	AHL	18	10	7	1	1081	33	1	1.83	4	2	1	212	2	2	0.57
2004-05	Norfolk Admirals	AHL	41	20	16	3	2319	78	7	2.02	....	....	....	....	....	....	....
2005-06	Rochester	AHL	40	15	22	1	2318	124	2	3.21	....	....	....	....	....	....	....
2006-07	Portland Pirates	AHL	16	8	6	1	962	37	2	2.31	....	....	....	....	....	....	....
	Nashville	**NHL**	**1**	**0**	**0**	**0**	**20**	**2**	**0**	**6.00**	....	....	....	....	....	....	....
	Philadelphia	**NHL**	**4**	**2**	**2**	**0**	**195**	**12**	**0**	**3.69**	....	....	....	....	....	....	....
	Philadelphia	AHL	5	2	0	2	270	7	0	1.56	....	....	....	....	....	....	....
2007-08	**Carolina**	**NHL**	**3**	**1**	**1**	**0**	**158**	**7**	**0**	**2.66**	....	....	....	....	....	....	....
	Albany River Rats	AHL	58	28	25	4	3451	121	*7	2.10	7	3	4	510	10	*2	*1.18
2008-09	**Carolina**	**NHL**	**19**	**6**	**7**	**2**	**1029**	**50**	**0**	**2.92**	....	....	....	....	....	....	....
2009-10	**Carolina**	**NHL**	**7**	**1**	**4**	**0**	**350**	**25**	**0**	**4.29**	....	....	....	....	....	....	....
	Philadelphia	**NHL**	**27**	**16**	**5**	**2**	**1449**	**60**	**1**	**2.48**	**14**	**8**	**3**	**757**	**31**	***3**	***2.46**
2010-11	**Philadelphia**	**NHL**	**1**	**1**	**0**	**0**	**60**	**4**	**0**	**4.00**	**2**	**0**	**1**	**70**	**4**	**0**	**3.43**
	Adirondack	AHL	30	14	12	3	1783	66	5	2.22	....	....	....	....	....	....	....
2011-12	Adirondack	AHL	*56	28	26	1	3237	139	2	2.58	....	....	....	....	....	....	....
2012-13	**Philadelphia**	**NHL**	**1**	**0**	**1**	**0**	**59**	**5**	**0**	**5.08**	....	....	....	....	....	....	....
	Adirondack	AHL	2	1	1	0	119	4	0	2.02	....	....	....	....	....	....	....
2013-14	Donetsk	KHL	42	20	16	0	2448	71	6	1.74	8	3	4	467	20	0	2.57
2014-15	Rockford IceHogs	AHL	42	22	13	4	2391	90	5	2.26	8	4	3	440	19	0	2.59
2015-16	**Chicago**	**NHL**	**1**	**0**	**0**	**0**	**39**	**1**	**0**	**1.54**	....	....	....	....	....	....	....
	Rockford IceHogs	AHL	46	28	8	8	2585	105	5	2.44	....	....	....	....	....	....	....
2016-17	**Carolina**	**NHL**	**4**	**2**	**2**	**0**	**210**	**12**	**0**	**3.43**	....	....	....	....	....	....	....
	Charlotte Checkers	AHL	23	11	7	3	1326	48	3	2.17	1	0	1	52	1	0	1.15
	NHL Totals		**110**	**37**	**43**	**14**	**6004**	**298**	**4**	**2.98**	**16**	**8**	**4**	**827**	**35**	**3**	**2.54**

AHL All-Rookie Team (2002) • AHL First All-Star Team (2008) • Aldege "Baz" Bastien Memorial Award (AHL – Outstanding Goaltender) (2008)

Traded to **Buffalo** by **Chicago** for Milan Bartovic, October 4, 2005. Signed as a free agent by **Anaheim**, July 13, 2006. Claimed on waivers by **Nashville** from **Anaheim**, November 27, 2006. Claimed on waivers by **Philadelphia** from **Nashville**, January 11, 2007. Claimed on waivers by **Montreal** from **Philadelphia**, February 27, 2007. Traded to **Carolina** by **Montreal** for Carolina's 7th round pick (Scott Kishel) in 2007 NHL Draft, June 23, 2007. Claimed on waivers by **Philadelphia** from **Carolina**, December 15, 2009. Traded to **Columbus** by **Philadelphia** with Philadelphia's 3rd round pick (later traded to Toronto – Toronto selected Martins Dzierkals) in 2015 NHL Draft for Steve Mason, April 3, 2013. Signed as a free agent by **Donetsk** (KHL), August 19, 2013. Signed as a free agent by **Chicago**, August 18, 2014. Signed as a free agent by **Carolina**, September 7, 2016. Signed as a free agent by **Tampa Bay**, July 1, 2017.

LINDBACK, Anders (LIHND-bak, AN-duhrs) NSH

Goaltender. Catches left. 6'6", 215 lbs. Born, Gavle, Sweden, May 3, 1988.
(Nashville's 7th pick, 207th overall, in 2008 NHL Draft).

			Regular Season								Playoffs						
Season	Club	League	GP	W	L	O/T	Mins	GA	SO	Avg	GP	W	L	Mins	GA	SO	Avg
2003-04	Brynas U18	Swe-U18	3	....	....	....	178	13	0	4.38	....	....	....	....	....	....	....
2004-05	Brynas U18	Swe-U18	49	....	....	....	2940	108	7	2.20	....	....	....	....	....	....	....
2005-06	Brynas U18	Swe-U18	11	....	....	....	666	36	2	3.24	....	....	....	....	....	....	....
	Brynas IF Gavle Jr.	Swe-Jr.	5	....	....	....	257	7	2	1.64	....	....	....	....	....	....	....
2006-07	Brynas IF Gavle Jr.	Swe-Jr.	36	....	....	....	2143	81	5	2.27	3	....	....	180	6	0	2.00
2007-08	Almtuna	Sweden-2	18	....	....	....	1034	53	0	3.07	....	....	....	....	....	....	....
2008-09	Brynas IF Gavle Jr.	Swe-Jr.	3	....	....	....	179	7	0	2.35	....	....	....	....	....	....	....
	Brynas IF Gavle	Sweden	24	....	....	....	1332	57	1	2.57	3	....	....	177	7	0	2.37
2009-10	Timra IK	Sweden	42	....	....	....	2537	104	3	2.46	5	....	....	306	15	0	2.94
2010-11	**Nashville**	**NHL**	**22**	**11**	**5**	**2**	**1131**	**49**	**2**	**2.60**	**1**	**0**	**0**	**13**	**0**	**0**	**0.00**
	Milwaukee	AHL	4	2	2	0	241	11	0	2.73	....	....	....	....	....	....	....
2011-12	**Nashville**	**NHL**	**16**	**5**	**8**	**0**	**792**	**32**	**0**	**2.42**	....	....	....	....	....	....	....
	Milwaukee	AHL	2	1	1	0	119	7	0	3.53	....	....	....	....	....	....	....
2012-13	Ilves Tampere	Finland	13	3	6	4	797	31	3	2.33	....	....	....	....	....	....	....
	Tampa Bay	**NHL**	**24**	**10**	**10**	**1**	**1304**	**63**	**0**	**2.90**	....	....	....	....	....	....	....
2013-14	**Tampa Bay**	**NHL**	**23**	**8**	**12**	**2**	**1302**	**63**	**1**	**2.90**	**4**	**0**	**3**	**215**	**14**	**0**	**3.91**
	Syracuse Crunch	AHL	2	1	1	0	117	3	1	1.54	....	....	....	....	....	....	....
2014-15	**Dallas**	**NHL**	**10**	**2**	**8**	**0**	**517**	**32**	**0**	**3.71**	....	....	....	....	....	....	....
	Texas Stars	AHL	7	4	2	1	429	12	0	1.68	....	....	....	....	....	....	....
	Buffalo	**NHL**	**16**	**4**	**8**	**2**	**891**	**41**	**0**	**2.76**	....	....	....	....	....	....	....
2015-16	**Arizona**	**NHL**	**19**	**5**	**7**	**1**	**906**	**47**	**0**	**3.11**	....	....	....	....	....	....	....
2016-17	Ontario Reign	AHL	4	2	1	1	247	14	0	3.40	....	....	....	....	....	....	....
	Rogle	Sweden	23	7	15	0	1344	59	0	2.63	....	....	....	....	....	....	....
	Rogle	Sweden-Q	....	....	....	....	....	....	....	....	4	4	0	292	8	0	1.64
	NHL Totals		**130**	**45**	**58**	**8**	**6843**	**327**	**3**	**2.87**	**5**	**0**	**3**	**228**	**14**	**0**	**3.68**

Traded to **Tampa Bay** by **Nashville** with Kyle Wilson and Nashville's 7th round pick (Nikita Gusev) in 2012 NHL Draft for Sebastian Caron, Minnesota's 2nd round pick (previously acquired, Nashville selected Pontus Aberg) in 2012 NHL Draft, Philadelphia's 2nd round pick (previously acquired, Nashville selected Colton Sissons) in 2012 NHL Draft and Tampa Bay's 3rd round pick (Jonathan Diaby) in 2013 NHL Draft, June 15, 2012. Signed as a free agent by **Ilves Tampere** (Finland), October 27, 2012. Signed as a free agent by **Dallas**, July 1, 2014. Traded to **Buffalo** by **Dallas** for Jhonas Enroth and Dallas' 3rd round pick (Casey Fitzgerald) in 2016 NHL Draft, February 11, 2015. Signed as a free agent by **Arizona**, July 1, 2015. Signed to a PTO (professional try-out) contract by **Ontario** (AHL), October 26, 2016. Signed as a free agent by **Rogle** (Sweden), December 14, 2016. Signed as a free agent by **Nashville**, July 1, 2017.

LINDGREN, Charlie (LIHND-gruhn, CHAHR-lee) MTL

Goaltender. Catches right. 6'2", 182 lbs. Born, Lakeville, MN, December 18, 1993.

			Regular Season								Playoffs						
Season	Club	League	GP	W	L	O/T	Mins	GA	SO	Avg	GP	W	L	Mins	GA	SO	Avg
2009-10	Lakeville North	High-MN	15	4	7	2	669	41	1	3.13	4	2	1	164	8	1	2.93
2010-11	Team Southeast	UMHSEL	13	7	3	2	596	31	0	3.12	2	1	0	92	8	0	5.22
	Lakeville North	High-MN	18	8	9	1	912	59	2	3.30	6	5	1	356	11	1	1.85
2011-12	Sioux Falls	USHL	33	9	19	3	1821	101	0	3.33	....	....	....	....	....	....	....
2012-13	Sioux Falls	USHL	52	*35	14	2	2853	133	2	2.80	*10	5	5	595	25	*1	2.52
2013-14	St. Cloud State	NCHC	10	2	2	1	323	13	1	2.42	....	....	....	....	....	....	....
2014-15	St. Cloud State	NCHC	38	19	18	1	2226	84	2	2.26	....	....	....	....	....	....	....
2015-16	St. Cloud State	NCHC	*40	*30	9	1	2343	83	*5	2.13	....	....	....	....	....	....	....
	Montreal	**NHL**	**1**	**1**	**0**	**0**	**60**	**2**	**0**	**2.00**	....	....	....	....	....	....	....
2016-17	**Montreal**	**NHL**	**2**	**2**	**0**	**0**	**122**	**3**	**0**	**1.48**	....	....	....	....	....	....	....
	St. John's IceCaps	AHL	48	24	18	6	2860	122	5	2.56	4	1	3	272	10	0	2.21
	NHL Totals		**3**	**3**	**0**	**0**	**182**	**5**	**0**	**1.65**	....	....	....	....	....	....	....

NCHC All-Rookie Team (2014) • NCHC First All-Star Team (2016) • NCHC Goaltender of the Year (2016) • NCAA West First All-American Team (2016)

Signed as a free agent by **Montreal**, March 30, 2016.

LUNDQVIST, Henrik (LUHND-kvihst, HEHN-rihk) NYR

Goaltender. Catches left. 6'1", 188 lbs. Born, Are, Sweden, March 2, 1982.
(NY Rangers' 7th pick, 205th overall, in 2000 NHL Draft).

			Regular Season								Playoffs						
Season	Club	League	GP	W	L	O/T	Mins	GA	SO	Avg	GP	W	L	Mins	GA	SO	Avg
1998-99	V.Frolunda Jr.	Swe-Jr.	35	....	....	....	2100	95	0	2.73	....	....	....	....	....	....	....
99-2000	V.Frolunda Jr.	Swe-Jr.	30	....	....	....	1726	73	0	2.54	5	4	1	300	7	2	1.40
2000-01	V.Frolunda U18	Swe-U18	2	....	....	....	120	5	0	2.50	3	2	1	182	5	0	1.62
	V.Frolunda Jr.	Swe-Jr.	19	....	....	....	1140	50	2	2.64	....	....	....	....	....	....	....
	IF Molndal Hockey	Sweden-2	7	....	....	....	420	29	0	4.22	....	....	....	....	....	....	....
	V.Frolunda	Sweden	4	....	....	....	190	11	0	3.47	....	....	....	....	....	....	....
2001-02	V.Frolunda	Sweden	20	....	....	....	1152	52	2	2.71	8	8	0	489	18	*2	2.21
	V.Frolunda Jr.	Swe-Jr.	1	1	0	0	60	4	0	4.00	....	....	....	....	....	....	....
2002-03	V.Frolunda	Sweden	28	....	....	....	1650	40	*6	*1.45	12	....	....	739	26	*2	2.11
	V.Frolunda Jr.	Swe-Jr.	1	1	0	0	60	4	0	4.00	....	....	....	....	....	....	....
2003-04	V.Frolunda	Sweden	*48	....	....	....	*2897	105	7	2.17	10	....	....	610	20	0	1.97
2004-05	Frolunda	Sweden	44	*33	8	3	2642	79	*6	*1.79	*14	*12	2	854	15	*6	*1.05
2005-06	**NY Rangers**	**NHL**	**53**	**30**	**12**	**9**	**3112**	**116**	**2**	**2.24**	**3**	**0**	**3**	**177**	**13**	**0**	**4.41**
	Sweden	Olympics	6	5	1	0	360	14	0	2.33	....	....	....	....	....	....	....
2006-07	**NY Rangers**	**NHL**	**70**	**37**	**22**	**8**	**4109**	**160**	**5**	**2.34**	**10**	**6**	**4**	**637**	**22**	**1**	**2.07**
2007-08	**NY Rangers**	**NHL**	**72**	**37**	**24**	**10**	**4305**	**160**	***10**	**2.23**	**10**	**5**	**5**	**608**	**26**	**1**	**2.57**
2008-09	**NY Rangers**	**NHL**	**70**	**38**	**25**	**7**	**4153**	**168**	**3**	**2.43**	**7**	**3**	**4**	**380**	**19**	**1**	**3.00**
2009-10	**NY Rangers**	**NHL**	**73**	**35**	**27**	**10**	**4204**	**167**	**4**	**2.38**	....	....	....	....	....	....	....
	Sweden	Olympics	3	2	1	0	179	4	*2	1.34	....	....	....	....	....	....	....
2010-11	**NY Rangers**	**NHL**	**68**	**36**	**27**	**5**	**4007**	**152**	***11**	**2.28**	**5**	**1**	**4**	**346**	**13**	**0**	**2.25**
2011-12	**NY Rangers**	**NHL**	**62**	**39**	**18**	**5**	**3754**	**123**	**8**	**1.97**	**20**	**10**	**10**	**1251**	**38**	***3**	**1.82**
2012-13	**NY Rangers**	**NHL**	**43**	***24**	**16**	**3**	**2575**	**88**	**2**	**2.05**	**12**	**5**	**7**	**756**	**27**	**2**	**2.14**
2013-14	**NY Rangers**	**NHL**	**63**	**33**	**24**	**5**	**3655**	**144**	**5**	**2.36**	**25**	**13**	**11**	**1516**	**54**	**1**	**2.14**
	Sweden	Olympics	6	5	1	0	360	9	2	1.50	....	....	....	....	....	....	....
2014-15	**NY Rangers**	**NHL**	**46**	**30**	**13**	**3**	**2743**	**103**	**5**	**2.25**	**19**	**11**	**8**	**1166**	**41**	**0**	**2.11**
2015-16	**NY Rangers**	**NHL**	**65**	**35**	**21**	**7**	**3772**	**156**	**4**	**2.48**	**5**	**1**	**3**	**205**	**15**	**0**	**4.39**
2016-17	**NY Rangers**	**NHL**	**57**	**31**	**20**	**4**	**3240**	**148**	**2**	**2.74**	**12**	**6**	**6**	**775**	**29**	**1**	**2.25**
	NHL Totals		**742**	**405**	**249**	**76**	**43629**	**1685**	**61**	**2.32**	**128**	**61**	**65**	**7817**	**297**	**10**	**2.28**

NHL All-Rookie Team (2006) • NHL First All-Star Team (2012) • Vezina Trophy (2012) • NHL Second All-Star Team (2013) • Olympic All-Star Team (2014)

Played in NHL All-Star Game (2009, 2011, 2012)

LUONGO, Roberto (loo-WAHN-goh, roh-BUHR-toh) FLA

Goaltender. Catches left. 6'3", 217 lbs. Born, Montreal, QC, April 4, 1979.
(NY Islanders' 1st pick, 4th overall, in 1997 NHL Draft).

			Regular Season								Playoffs						
Season	Club	League	GP	W	L	O/T	Mins	GA	SO	Avg	GP	W	L	Mins	GA	SO	Avg
1994-95	Montreal-Bourassa	QAAA	29	10	16	0	1526	94	2	3.85	4	1	3	240	17	0	4.25
1995-96	Val-d'Or Foreurs	QMJHL	23	6	11	4	1201	74	0	3.70	3	0	1	68	5	0	4.41
1996-97	Val-d'Or Foreurs	QMJHL	60	32	21	2	3305	171	2	3.10	13	8	5	777	44	0	3.40
1997-98	Val-d'Or Foreurs	QMJHL	54	27	20	5	3046	157	*7	3.09	*17	*14	3	*1020	37	*2	*2.18
1998-99	Val-d'Or Foreurs	QMJHL	21	6	10	2	1177	77	1	3.93	....	....	....	....	....	....	....
	Acadie-Bathurst	QMJHL	22	14	7	1	1341	74	0	3.31	*23	*16	6	*1400	64	0	2.74
99-2000	**NY Islanders**	**NHL**	**24**	**7**	**14**	**1**	**1292**	**70**	**1**	**3.25**	....	....	....	....	....	....	....
	Lowell	AHL	26	10	12	4	1517	74	1	2.93	6	3	3	359	18	0	3.01

2000-01	**Florida**	**NHL**	**47**	**12**	**24**	**7**	**2628**	**107**	**5**	**2.44**	....	....	....	....	....	....	....
	Louisville Panthers	AHL	3	1	2	0	178	10	0	3.38	....	....	....	....	....	....	....
2001-02	**Florida**	**NHL**	**58**	**16**	**33**	**4**	**3030**	**140**	**4**	**2.77**	....	....	....	....	....	....	....
2002-03	**Florida**	**NHL**	**65**	**20**	**34**	**7**	**3627**	**164**	**6**	**2.71**	....	....	....	....	....	....	....
2003-04	**Florida**	**NHL**	**72**	**25**	**33**	**14**	**4252**	**172**	**7**	**2.43**	....	....	....	....	....	....	....
2004-05								DID NOT PLAY									
2005-06	**Florida**	**NHL**	***75**	**35**	**30**	**9**	**4305**	**213**	**4**	**2.97**	....	....	....	....	....	....	....
	Canada	Olympics	2	1	1	0	119	3	0	1.51	....	....	....	....	....	....	....
2006-07	**Vancouver**	**NHL**	**76**	**47**	**22**	**6**	**4490**	**171**	**5**	**2.29**	**12**	**5**	**7**	**847**	**25**	**0**	**1.77**
2007-08	**Vancouver**	**NHL**	**73**	**35**	**29**	**9**	**4233**	**168**	**6**	**2.38**	....	....	....	....	....	....	....
2008-09	**Vancouver**	**NHL**	**54**	**33**	**13**	**7**	**3181**	**124**	**9**	**2.34**	**10**	**6**	**4**	**618**	**26**	**1**	**2.52**
2009-10	**Vancouver**	**NHL**	**68**	**40**	**22**	**4**	**3899**	**167**	**4**	**2.57**	**12**	**6**	**6**	**707**	**38**	**0**	**3.22**
	Canada	Olympics	5	5	0	0	308	9	1	1.76	....	....	....	....	....	....	....
2010-11	**Vancouver**	**NHL**	**60**	***38**	**15**	**7**	**3590**	**126**	**4**	**2.11**	***25**	**15**	**10**	**1427**	**61**	***4**	**2.56**
2011-12	**Vancouver**	**NHL**	**55**	**31**	**14**	**8**	**3162**	**127**	**5**	**2.41**	**2**	**0**	**2**	**117**	**7**	**0**	**3.59**
2012-13	**Vancouver**	**NHL**	**20**	**9**	**6**	**3**	**1197**	**51**	**2**	**2.56**	**3**	**0**	**2**	**140**	**6**	**0**	**2.57**
2013-14	**Vancouver**	**NHL**	**42**	**19**	**16**	**6**	**2418**	**96**	**3**	**2.38**	....	....	....	....	....	....	....
	Canada	Olympics	1	1	0	0	60	0	1	0.00	....	....	....	....	....	....	....
	Florida	**NHL**	**14**	**6**	**7**	**1**	**804**	**33**	**1**	**2.46**	....	....	....	....	....	....	....
2014-15	**Florida**	**NHL**	**61**	**28**	**19**	**12**	**3528**	**138**	**2**	**2.35**	....	....	....	....	....	....	....
2015-16	**Florida**	**NHL**	**62**	**35**	**19**	**6**	**3602**	**141**	**4**	**2.35**	**6**	**2**	**4**	**438**	**15**	**0**	**2.05**
2016-17	**Florida**	**NHL**	**40**	**17**	**15**	**6**	**2327**	**104**	**1**	**2.68**	....	....	....	....	....	....	....
	NHL Totals		**966**	**453**	**365**	**117**	**55565**	**2312**	**73**	**2.50**	**70**	**34**	**35**	**4294**	**178**	**5**	**2.49**

NHL Second All-Star Team (2004, 2007) • William M. Jennings Trophy (2011) (shared with Cory Schneider)

Played in NHL All-Star Game (2004, 2007, 2009, 2015, 2016)

Traded to **Florida** by **NY Islanders** with Olli Jokinen for Mark Parrish and Oleg Kvasha, June 24, 2000. Traded to **Vancouver** by **Florida** with Lukas Krajicek and Florida's 6th round pick (Sergei Shirokov) in 2006 NHL Draft for Todd Bertuzzi, Bryan Allen and Alex Auld, June 23, 2006. Traded to **Florida** by **Vancouver** with Steven Anthony for Jacob Markstrom and Shawn Matthias, March 4, 2014.

LUUKKONEN, Ukko-Pekka (LOO-KOH-nehn, OO-KOH-peh-KA) BUF

Goaltender. Catches left. 6'4", 198 lbs. Born, Espoo, Finland, September 3, 1999.
(Buffalo's 3rd pick, 54th overall, in 2017 NHL Draft).

			Regular Season								Playoffs						
Season	**Club**	**League**	**GP**	**W**	**L**	**O/T**	**Mins**	**GA**	**SO**	**Avg**	**GP**	**W**	**L**	**Mins**	**GA**	**SO**	**Avg**
2015-16	HPK U18	Fin-U18	31	....	....	....	....	77	....	....	....	....	....	....	....	....	....
	HPK Jr.	Fin-Jr.	15	....	....	....	880	29	....	1.98	8	....	....	433	14	....	1.94
2016-17	HPK Jr.	Fin-Jr.	35	....	....	....	1950	58	....	1.78	9	....	....	566	19	....	2.01

LYON, Alex (LIGH-uhn, AL-ehx) PHI

Goaltender. Catches left. 6'1", 200 lbs. Born, Baudette, MN, December 9, 1992.

			Regular Season								Playoffs						
Season	**Club**	**League**	**GP**	**W**	**L**	**O/T**	**Mins**	**GA**	**SO**	**Avg**	**GP**	**W**	**L**	**Mins**	**GA**	**SO**	**Avg**
2009-10	Lake of the Woods	High-MN	25	12	12	1	1291	71	3	2.80	1	0	1	51	4	0	4.00
2010-11	Team North	UMHSEL	14	7	3	1	630	29	0	2.76	2	0	2	87	5	0	3.43
	Lake of the Woods	High-MN	25	16	6	3	1273	37	6	1.48	2	1	1	101	6	0	3.03
	Cedar Rapids	USHL	1	0	1	0	60	5	0	5.00	....	....	....	....	....	....	....
2011-12	Omaha Lancers	USHL	48	28	15	3	2762	127	4	2.76	4	1	3	237	13	0	3.30
2012-13	Omaha Lancers	USHL	50	26	21	1	2894	128	1	2.65	....	....	....	....	....	....	....
2013-14	Yale	ECAC	30	14	11	5	1764	71	3	2.41	....	....	....	....	....	....	....
2014-15	Yale	ECAC	32	17	10	5	1925	52	*7	*1.62	....	....	....	....	....	....	....
2015-16	Yale	ECAC	31	19	8	4	1906	52	5	*1.64	....	....	....	....	....	....	....
2016-17	Lehigh Valley	AHL	47	27	14	5	2719	124	4	2.74	2	0	1	116	4	0	2.07

ECAC First All-Star Team (2015, 2016) • NCAA East First All-American Team (2015, 2016)

Signed as a free agent by **Philadelphia**, April 5, 2016.

MACHOVSKY, Matej (meh-HAWZ-kee, Ma-TAY) DET

Goaltender. Catches left. 6'2", 187 lbs. Born, Opava, Czech Rep., July 25, 1993.

			Regular Season								Playoffs						
Season	**Club**	**League**	**GP**	**W**	**L**	**O/T**	**Mins**	**GA**	**SO**	**Avg**	**GP**	**W**	**L**	**Mins**	**GA**	**SO**	**Avg**
2009-10	Opava Jr.	CzRep-Jr.	33	....	....	....	1917	127	1	3.97	....	....	....	....	....	....	....
2010-11	Guelph Storm	OHL	5	2	2	0	234	16	0	4.10	....	....	....	....	....	....	....
	Brampton Battalion	OHL	18	5	11	0	1088	48	1	2.65	2	0	0	64	3	0	2.80
2011-12	Brampton Battalion	OHL	42	24	13	0	2420	95	5	2.36	8	4	4	526	20	1	2.28
2012-13	Brampton Battalion	OHL	52	25	19	3	3023	127	3	2.52	4	1	2	197	11	0	3.35
2013-14	HC Skoda Plzen	CzRep	36	....	....	....	2046	57	6	1.67	6	....	....	362	14	0	2.32
2014-15	HC Skoda Plzen	CzRep	48	....	....	....	2678	108	2	2.42	4	....	....	239	14	0	3.51
2015-16	HC Skoda Plzen	CzRep	48	....	....	....	2737	111	4	2.43	11	....	....	647	26	1	2.41
2016-17	HC Skoda Plzen	CzRep	46	....	....	....	2695	101	2	2.25	11	....	....	692	33	0	2.86

Signed as a free agent by **Detroit**, May 2, 2017.

MADSEN, Merrick (MAD-sehn, MAIR-ihk) ARI

Goaltender. Catches left. 6'5", 192 lbs. Born, Preston, ID, August 22, 1995.
(Philadelphia's 5th pick, 162nd overall, in 2013 NHL Draft).

			Regular Season								Playoffs						
Season	**Club**	**League**	**GP**	**W**	**L**	**O/T**	**Mins**	**GA**	**SO**	**Avg**	**GP**	**W**	**L**	**Mins**	**GA**	**SO**	**Avg**
2011-12	Proctor Academy	High-NH	20	....	....	....	748	....	....	4.00	....	....	....	....	....	....	....
2012-13	Proctor Academy	High-NH	26	10	13	3	1171	82	1	3.19	....	....	....	....	....	....	....
2013-14	Minot Minotauros	NAHL	27	10	16	0	1571	72	1	2.75	3	1	2	171	7	....	2.45
2014-15	Harvard Crimson	ECAC	1	0	0	0	43	2	0	2.77	....	....	....	....	....	....	....
2015-16	Harvard Crimson	ECAC	29	18	7	3	1713	57	4	2.00	....	....	....	....	....	....	....
2016-17	Harvard Crimson	ECAC	*36	*28	6	2	*2104	74	3	2.11	....	....	....	....	....	....	....

• Missed majority of 2014-15 as a healthy reserve. Traded to **Arizona** by **Philadelphia** with Nick Cousins for Brendan Warren and Arizona's 5th round pick in 2018 NHL Draft, June 16, 2017.

MAGUIRE, Sean (muh-GWIGH-uhr, SHAWN) PIT

Goaltender. Catches left. 6'2", 202 lbs. Born, Edmonton, AB, February 2, 1993.
(Pittsburgh's 7th pick, 113th overall, in 2012 NHL Draft).

			Regular Season								Playoffs						
Season	**Club**	**League**	**GP**	**W**	**L**	**O/T**	**Mins**	**GA**	**SO**	**Avg**	**GP**	**W**	**L**	**Mins**	**GA**	**SO**	**Avg**
2009-10	North Island	BCMML	20	....	....	....	....	....	....	....	1	....	....	....	....	....	....
2010-11	Powell River Kings	BCHL	15	10	3	0	841	35	2	2.50	2	0	0	44	1	0	1.36
2011-12	Powell River Kings	BCHL	31	17	12	1	1774	69	3	2.33	15	7	6	808	28	2	2.08
2012-13	Boston University	H-East	21	13	8	0	1230	52	4	2.54	....	....	....	....	....	....	....
2013-14	Boston University	H-East	16	3	12	0	868	42	0	2.90	....	....	....	....	....	....	....
2014-15	Boston University	H-East						DID NOT PLAY – INJURED									
2015-16	Boston University	H-East	25	13	9	1	1372	55	1	2.41	....	....	....	....	....	....	....
	Wilkes-Barre	AHL	1	0	0	1	13	0	0	0.00	....	....	....	....	....	....	....
2016-17	Wheeling Nailers	ECHL	35	14	16	4	2025	108	2	3.20	....	....	....	....	....	....	....
	Wilkes-Barre	AHL	1	1	0	0	60	4	0	4.00	....	....	....	....	....	....	....

• Missed 2014-15 due to head injury in practice, March 2, 2014.

MAKINIEMI, Eetu (mak-ih-NEE-yehm-ee, AY-too) CAR

Goaltender. Catches left. 6'2", 184 lbs. Born, Vantaa, Finland, April 19, 1999.
(Carolina's 6th pick, 104th overall, in 2017 NHL Draft).

			Regular Season								Playoffs						
Season	**Club**	**League**	**GP**	**W**	**L**	**O/T**	**Mins**	**GA**	**SO**	**Avg**	**GP**	**W**	**L**	**Mins**	**GA**	**SO**	**Avg**
2014-15	Jokerit U18	Fin-U18	2	....	....	....	....	5	....	....	....	....	....	....	....	....	....
2015-16	Jokerit U18	Fin-U18	24	....	....	....	....	73	....	....	....	....	....	....	....	....	....
2016-17	Jokerit U18	Fin-U18	4	....	....	....	....	14	....	....	1	....	....	....	1	....	....
	Jokerit Helsinki Jr.	Fin-Jr.	26	....	....	....	1520	68	....	2.68	....	....	....	....	....	....	....

MARKSTROM, Jacob (MAHRK-struhm, JAY-kawb) VAN

Goaltender. Catches left. 6'6", 196 lbs. Born, Gavle, Sweden, January 31, 1990.
(Florida's 1st pick, 31st overall, in 2008 NHL Draft).

			Regular Season								Playoffs						
Season	**Club**	**League**	**GP**	**W**	**L**	**O/T**	**Mins**	**GA**	**SO**	**Avg**	**GP**	**W**	**L**	**Mins**	**GA**	**SO**	**Avg**
2006-07	Brynas U18	Swe-U18	13	....	....	....	789	27	0	2.05	3	....	....	193	6	1	1.86
	Brynas IF Gavle Jr.	Swe-Jr.	1	....	....	....	65	3	0	2.77	1	....	....	25	4	0	9.76
2007-08	Brynas U18	Swe-U18	1	....	....	....	60	3	0	3.00	....	....	....	....	....	....	....
	Brynas IF Gavle Jr.	Swe-Jr.	22	....	....	....	1320	44	2	2.00	....	....	....	....	....	....	....
	Brynas IF Gavle	Sweden	7	....	....	....	423	22	0	3.12	....	....	....	....	....	....	....
	Brynas IF Gavle	Sweden-Q	9	....	....	....	505	15	2	1.78	....	....	....	....	....	....	....
2008-09	Brynas IF Gavle	Sweden	35	....	....	....	1992	79	3	2.38	1	....	....	59	2	0	2.02
2009-10	Brynas IF Gavle	Sweden	43	....	....	....	2542	85	*5	*2.01	4	....	....	224	12	0	3.21
	Brynas IF Gavle Jr.	Swe-Jr.	....	....	....	....	....	....	....	....	2	....	....	119	6	0	3.03
2010-11	**Florida**	**NHL**	**1**	**0**	**1**	**0**	**40**	**2**	**0**	**3.00**	....	....	....	....	....	....	....
	Rochester	AHL	37	16	20	1	2174	108	1	2.98	....	....	....	....	....	....	....
2011-12	**Florida**	**NHL**	**7**	**2**	**4**	**1**	**383**	**17**	**0**	**2.66**	....	....	....	....	....	....	....
	San Antonio	AHL	32	17	12	1	1839	71	1	2.32	8	4	4	546	26	0	2.85
2012-13	San Antonio	AHL	33	16	15	2	1972	87	3	2.65	....	....	....	....	....	....	....
	Florida	**NHL**	**23**	**8**	**14**	**1**	**1266**	**68**	**0**	**3.22**	....	....	....	....	....	....	....
2013-14	**Florida**	**NHL**	**12**	**1**	**6**	**3**	**614**	**36**	**0**	**3.52**	....	....	....	....	....	....	....
	San Antonio	AHL	29	12	11	3	1688	72	2	2.56	....	....	....	....	....	....	....
	Vancouver	**NHL**	**4**	**1**	**2**	**0**	**200**	**10**	**0**	**3.00**	....	....	....	....	....	....	....
2014-15	**Vancouver**	**NHL**	**3**	**1**	**1**	**0**	**78**	**4**	**0**	**3.08**	....	....	....	....	....	....	....
	Utica Comets	AHL	32	22	7	2	1880	59	5	1.88	23	12	11	1450	51	2	2.11
2015-16	**Vancouver**	**NHL**	**33**	**13**	**14**	**4**	**1847**	**84**	**0**	**2.73**	....	....	....	....	....	....	....
	Utica Comets	AHL	2	1	0	1	125	5	0	2.40	....	....	....	....	....	....	....
2016-17	**Vancouver**	**NHL**	**26**	**10**	**11**	**3**	**1417**	**62**	**0**	**2.63**	....	....	....	....	....	....	....
	NHL Totals		**109**	**36**	**53**	**12**	**5845**	**283**	**0**	**2.91**	....	....	....	....	....	....	....

AHL Second All-Star Team (2015)

Traded to **Vancouver** by **Florida** with Shawn Matthias for Roberto Luongo and Steven Anthony, March 4, 2014.

MARTIN, Spencer (MAHR-tihn, SPEHN-suhr) COL

Goaltender. Catches left. 6'3", 210 lbs. Born, Oakville, ON, June 8, 1995.
(Colorado's 3rd pick, 63rd overall, in 2013 NHL Draft).

			Regular Season								Playoffs						
Season	**Club**	**League**	**GP**	**W**	**L**	**O/T**	**Mins**	**GA**	**SO**	**Avg**	**GP**	**W**	**L**	**Mins**	**GA**	**SO**	**Avg**
2010-11	Tor. Jr. Canadiens	GTHL	50	....	....	....	2250	115	5	2.27	....	....	....	....	....	....	....
2011-12	St. Michael's	OHL	15	2	7	1	753	50	0	3.98	....	....	....	....	....	....	....
2012-13	Mississauga	OHL	46	17	21	4	2504	126	0	3.02	2	0	1	90	9	0	6.01
2013-14	Mississauga	OHL	*64	24	33	5	*3562	210	3	3.54	4	1	3	270	18	0	3.99
2014-15	Mississauga	OHL	31	15	13	1	1713	85	1	2.98	....	....	....	....	....	....	....
2015-16	San Antonio	AHL	18	7	7	1	905	40	3	2.65	....	....	....	....	....	....	....
	Fort Wayne	ECHL	20	9	9	1	1113	60	2	3.23	1	0	1	44	5	0	6.87
2016-17	**Colorado**	**NHL**	**3**	**0**	**2**	**1**	**179**	**13**	**0**	**4.36**	....	....	....	....	....	....	....
	San Antonio	AHL	50	19	26	4	2812	136	2	2.90	....	....	....	....	....	....	....
	NHL Totals		**3**	**0**	**2**	**1**	**179**	**13**	**0**	**4.36**	....	....	....	....	....	....	....

MASON, Steve (MAY-sohn, STEEV) WPG

Goaltender. Catches right. 6'4", 210 lbs. Born, Oakville, ON, May 29, 1988.
(Columbus' 2nd pick, 69th overall, in 2006 NHL Draft).

			Regular Season								Playoffs						
Season	**Club**	**League**	**GP**	**W**	**L**	**O/T**	**Mins**	**GA**	**SO**	**Avg**	**GP**	**W**	**L**	**Mins**	**GA**	**SO**	**Avg**
2003-04	Oakville Rangers	Minor-ON	27	....	....	....	1209	41	5	1.58	....	....	....	....	....	....	....
2004-05	Grimsby	ON-Jr.C	45	....	....	....	2800	....	6	1.75	....	....	....	....	....	....	....
2005-06	Petrolia Jets	ON-Jr.B	9	6	3	0	522	22	1	2.53	5	3	2	348	9	0	1.55
	London Knights	OHL	12	5	3	0	497	22	0	2.66	4	0	1	150	7	0	2.80
2006-07	London Knights	OHL	*62	*45	13	4	*3733	199	2	3.20	16	9	7	931	54	0	3.48
2007-08	London Knights	OHL	26	19	4	3	1569	73	2	2.79	....	....	....	....	....	....	....
	Kitchener Rangers	OHL	16	13	3	0	961	33	1	2.06	5	5	0	313	10	1	1.92
2008-09	**Columbus**	**NHL**	**61**	**33**	**20**	**7**	**3664**	**140**	***10**	**2.29**	**4**	**0**	**4**	**239**	**17**	**0**	**4.27**
	Syracuse Crunch	AHL	3	2	1	0	184	5	0	1.63	....	....	....	....	....	....	....
2009-10	**Columbus**	**NHL**	**58**	**20**	**26**	**9**	**3201**	**163**	**5**	**3.06**	....	....	....	....	....	....	....
2010-11	**Columbus**	**NHL**	**54**	**24**	**21**	**7**	**3027**	**153**	**3**	**3.03**	....	....	....	....	....	....	....
2011-12	**Columbus**	**NHL**	**46**	**16**	**26**	**3**	**2534**	**143**	**1**	**3.39**	....	....	....	....	....	....	....
2012-13	**Columbus**	**NHL**	**13**	**3**	**6**	**1**	**712**	**35**	**0**	**2.95**	....	....	....	....	....	....	....
	Philadelphia	**NHL**	**7**	**4**	**2**	**0**	**378**	**12**	**0**	**1.90**	....	....	....	....	....	....	....

2013-14	**Philadelphia**	**NHL**	**61**	**33**	**18**	**7**	**3486**	**145**	**4**	**2.50**	**5**	**2**	**2**	**244**	**8**	**0**	**1.97**
2014-15	**Philadelphia**	**NHL**	**51**	**18**	**18**	**11**	**2885**	**108**	**3**	**2.25**	....	....	....	....	....	....	....
2015-16	**Philadelphia**	**NHL**	**54**	**23**	**19**	**10**	**3150**	**132**	**4**	**2.51**	**3**	**0**	**3**	**176**	**12**	**0**	**4.09**
2016-17	**Philadelphia**	**NHL**	**58**	**26**	**21**	**8**	**3225**	**143**	**3**	**2.66**	....	....	....	....	....	....	....
	NHL Totals		**463**	**200**	**177**	**63**	**26262**	**1174**	**33**	**2.68**	**12**	**2**	**9**	**659**	**37**	**0**	**3.37**

OHL First All-Star Team (2007) • OHL Second All-Star Team (2008) • NHL All-Rookie Team (2009) • NHL Second All-Star Team (2009) • Calder Memorial Trophy (2009)

Traded to **Philadelphia** by **Columbus** for Michael Leighton and Philadelphia's 3rd round pick (later traded to Toronto – Toronto selected Martins Dzierkals) in 2015 NHL Draft, April 3, 2013. Signed as a free agent by **Winnipeg**, July 1, 2017.

MAZANEC, Marek (muh-ZAN-ehk, MAHR-ehk) NSH

Goaltender. Catches right. 6'4", 187 lbs. Born, Pisek, Czech., July 18, 1991.
(Nashville's 9th pick, 179th overall, in 2012 NHL Draft).

			Regular Season								Playoffs						
Season	Club	League	GP	W	L	O/T	Mins	GA	SO	Avg	GP	W	L	Mins	GA	SO	Avg
2004-05	IHC Pisek U17	CzR-U17	1	....	....	....	30	7	0	14.00	....	....	....	....	....	....	....
2006-07	HC Plzen U17	CzR-U17	14	....	....	....	666	32	2	2.88	1	....	....	27	1	0	2.22
2007-08	HC Plzen U17	CzR-U17	41	....	....	....	2457	99	5	2.42	8	....	....	492	15	1	1.83
2008-09	HC Plzen Jr.	CzRep-Jr.	27	....	....	....	1577	68	0	2.59	5	....	....	309	9	0	1.75
2009-10	HC Plzen 1929	CzRep	1	....	....	....	20	3	0	9.00	....	....	....	....	....	....	....
	SHC Klatovy	CzRep-3	3	....	....	....	185	10	0	3.24	....	....	....	....	....	....	....
	HC Plzen Jr.	CzRep-Jr.	43	....	....	....	2560	111	3	2.60	2	....	....	120	7	0	3.50
2010-11	HC Plzen Jr.	CzRep-Jr.	30	....	....	....	1683	59	7	2.10	....	....	....	....	....	....	....
	HC Plzen 1929	CzRep	15	....	....	....	860	40	1	2.79	....	....	....	....	....	....	....
	IHC Komterm Pisek	CzRep-2	9	....	....	....	435	17	1	2.34	....	....	....	....	....	....	....
2011-12	HC Plzen Jr.	CzRep-Jr.	1	....	....	....	60	4	0	4.00	....	....	....	....	....	....	....
	HC Plzen 1929	CzRep	19	....	....	....	973	48	1	2.96	5	....	....	222	8	0	2.16
	SHC Klatovy	CzRep-3	17	....	....	....	1033	65	0	3.78	6	....	....	359	19	1	3.18
2012-13	HC Plzen Jr.	CzRep-Jr.	2	....	....	....	120	5	0	2.50	....	....	....	....	....	....	....
	IHC Pisek	CzRep-2	12	....	....	....	706	50	0	4.25	....	....	....	....	....	....	....
	HC Skoda Plzen	CzRep	21	....	....	....	1255	52	1	2.49	*20	....	....	*1241	44	2	2.13
2013-14	**Nashville**	**NHL**	**25**	**8**	**10**	**4**	**1370**	**64**	**2**	**2.80**	....	....	....	....	....	....	....
	Milwaukee	AHL	31	18	10	3	1866	76	0	2.44	3	0	3	178	9	0	3.03
2014-15	**Nashville**	**NHL**	**2**	**0**	**1**	**0**	**106**	**4**	**0**	**2.26**	....	....	....	....	....	....	....
	Milwaukee	AHL	48	18	18	9	2628	121	4	2.76	....	....	....	....	....	....	....
2015-16	Milwaukee	AHL	39	19	15	5	2349	96	4	2.45	1	0	1	56	4	0	4.26
2016-17	**Nashville**	**NHL**	**4**	**0**	**2**	**0**	**178**	**14**	**0**	**4.72**	....	....	....	....	....	....	....
	Milwaukee	AHL	47	27	17	3	2789	123	3	2.65	3	0	3	198	10	0	3.03
	NHL Totals		**31**	**8**	**13**	**4**	**1654**	**82**	**2**	**2.97**	....	....	....	....	....	....	....

McADAM, Eamon (muhk-A-duhm, AY-muhn) NYI

Goaltender. Catches left. 6'2", 200 lbs. Born, Doylestown, PA, September 24, 1994.
(NY Islanders' 2nd pick, 70th overall, in 2013 NHL Draft).

			Regular Season								Playoffs						
Season	Club	League	GP	W	L	O/T	Mins	GA	SO	Avg	GP	W	L	Mins	GA	SO	Avg
2010-11	Austin Bruins	NAHL	9	2	4	2	506	28	0	3.32	....	....	....	....	....	....	....
	Waterloo	USHL	4	2	2	0	190	11	0	3.48	....	....	....	....	....	....	....
2011-12	Waterloo	USHL	23	11	7	0	1149	67	0	3.50	....	....	....	....	....	....	....
2012-13	Waterloo	USHL	31	17	9	3	1806	104	2	3.45	....	....	....	....	....	....	....
2013-14	Penn State	Big Ten	10	0	9	0	558	38	0	4.09	....	....	....	....	....	....	....
2014-15	Penn State	Big Ten	12	5	4	1	653	34	0	3.13	....	....	....	....	....	....	....
2015-16	Penn State	Big Ten	22	13	8	1	1210	60	1	2.98	....	....	....	....	....	....	....
	Bridgeport	AHL	1	0	1	0	60	6	0	6.00	....	....	....	....	....	....	....
2016-17	Bridgeport	AHL	26	15	8	0	1407	68	0	2.90	....	....	....	....	....	....	....
	Missouri Mavericks	ECHL	17	11	3	1	943	49	1	3.12	....	....	....	....	....	....	....

Big Ten Second All-Star Team (2016)

McCOLLUM, Tom (muh-KAW-luhm, TAWM) DET

Goaltender. Catches left. 6'2", 226 lbs. Born, Amherst, NY, December 7, 1989.
(Detroit's 1st pick, 30th overall, in 2008 NHL Draft).

			Regular Season								Playoffs						
Season	Club	League	GP	W	L	O/T	Mins	GA	SO	Avg	GP	W	L	Mins	GA	SO	Avg
2005-06	Wheatfield Blades	EmJHL	24	2	19	3	1448	109	1	4.52	....	....	....	....	....	....	....
2006-07	Guelph Storm	OHL	55	26	18	10	3158	126	*5	2.39	4	0	4	233	17	0	4.38
2007-08	Guelph Storm	OHL	51	25	17	6	2978	124	*4	2.50	10	5	5	596	19	1	1.91
2008-09	Guelph Storm	OHL	31	17	10	4	1859	69	*3	2.23	....	....	....	....	....	....	....
	Brampton Battalion	OHL	23	17	6	0	1333	43	*4	1.94	*21	13	8	*1284	62	*1	2.90
2009-10	Grand Rapids	AHL	32	10	16	2	1741	101	0	3.48	....	....	....	....	....	....	....
	Toledo Walleye	ECHL	4	2	1	0	188	14	0	4.48	....	....	....	....	....	....	....
2010-11	**Detroit**	**NHL**	**1**	**0**	**0**	**0**	**15**	**3**	**0**	**12.00**	....	....	....	....	....	....	....
	Grand Rapids	AHL	22	6	12	2	1152	64	1	3.33	....	....	....	....	....	....	....
	Toledo Walleye	ECHL	23	11	9	2	1305	60	3	2.76	....	....	....	....	....	....	....
2011-12	Grand Rapids	AHL	28	11	16	0	1580	92	0	3.49	....	....	....	....	....	....	....
	Toledo Walleye	ECHL	15	6	6	2	870	38	0	2.62	....	....	....	....	....	....	....
2012-13	Grand Rapids	AHL	31	18	11	2	1846	81	2	2.63	....	....	....	....	....	....	....
2013-14	Grand Rapids	AHL	46	24	12	5	2561	98	2	2.30	1	0	0	34	2	0	3.50
2014-15	**Detroit**	**NHL**	**2**	**1**	**0**	**0**	**66**	**1**	**0**	**0.91**	....	....	....	....	....	....	....
	Grand Rapids	AHL	37	19	11	6	2171	87	1	2.40	15	9	6	895	38	0	2.55
2015-16	Grand Rapids	AHL	30	15	13	0	1686	68	1	2.42	7	3	3	401	16	0	2.39
	Toledo Walleye	ECHL	1	1	0	0	60	3	0	3.00	....	....	....	....	....	....	....
2016-17	Stockton Heat	AHL	1	1	0	0	40	1	0	1.50	....	....	....	....	....	....	....
	Adirondack	ECHL	5	3	1	1	303	15	0	2.97	....	....	....	....	....	....	....
	Charlotte Checkers	AHL	17	11	2	4	1030	36	1	2.10	5	2	2	251	12	1	2.87
	NHL Totals		**3**	**1**	**0**	**0**	**81**	**4**	**0**	**2.96**	....	....	....	....	....	....	....

OHL Second All-Star Team (2009)

Signed as a free agent by **Calgary**, October 16, 2016. • Loaned to **Charlotte** (AHL) by **Calgary**, March 8, 2017. Traded to **Detroit** by **Calgary** for a conditional 7th round pick in 2018 NHL Draft, July 1, 2017.

McDONALD, Mason (muhk-DAWN-uhld, MAY-suhn) CGY

Goaltender. Catches right. 6'4", 200 lbs. Born, Halifax, NS, April 23, 1996.
(Calgary's 2nd pick, 34th overall, in 2014 NHL Draft).

			Regular Season								Playoffs						
Season	Club	League	GP	W	L	O/T	Mins	GA	SO	Avg	GP	W	L	Mins	GA	SO	Avg
2010-11	Halifax Hawks	NSBHL	17	10	1	4	925	33	0	2.14	1	1	0	60	1	0	2.10
	Halifax Hawks	Other	....	....	....	....	....	....	....	....	5	3	0	257	9	0	2.10
2011-12	Halifax Titans	NSMHL	20	14	1	0	1162	39	1	2.01	6	5	1	325	11	0	2.03
2012-13	Acadie-Bathurst	QMJHL	26	6	8	3	1004	79	1	4.72	....	....	....	....	....	....	....
2013-14	Acadie-Bathurst	QMJHL	13	3	7	1	655	39	0	3.57	....	....	....	....	....	....	....
	Charlottetown	QMJHL	16	5	8	2	948	53	0	3.35	4	0	4	201	22	0	6.58
2014-15	Charlottetown	QMJHL	56	28	22	4	3194	163	1	3.06	3	1	1	121	8	0	3.98
2015-16	Charlottetown	QMJHL	39	21	15	3	2307	128	3	3.33	12	6	6	736	45	0	3.67
2016-17	Adirondack	ECHL	29	13	9	5	1678	76	1	2.72	....	....	....	....	....	....	....
	Stockton Heat	AHL	1	0	0	1	63	6	0	5.75	....	....	....	....	....	....	....

McELHINNEY, Curtis (MAK-ihl-ehn-ee, KUHR-tihs) TOR

Goaltender. Catches left. 6'3", 205 lbs. Born, London, ON, May 23, 1983.
(Calgary's 9th pick, 176th overall, in 2002 NHL Draft).

			Regular Season								Playoffs						
Season	Club	League	GP	W	L	O/T	Mins	GA	SO	Avg	GP	W	L	Mins	GA	SO	Avg
2000-01	Notre Dame	SJHL					STATISTICS NOT AVAILABLE										
2001-02	Colorado College	WCHA	9	6	0	1	441	15	1	2.04	....	....	....	....	....	....	....
2002-03	Colorado College	WCHA	*37	*25	6	5	*2147	85	*4	2.37	....	....	....	....	....	....	....
2003-04	Colorado College	WCHA	19	10	6	1	1015	41	2	2.42	....	....	....	....	....	....	....
2004-05	Colorado College	WCHA	26	*21	4	1	1550	58	2	2.24	....	....	....	....	....	....	....
2005-06	Omaha	AHL	33	9	14	2	1621	68	3	2.52	....	....	....	....	....	....	....
2006-07	Omaha	AHL	57	35	17	1	3181	113	*7	2.13	5	2	3	311	11	0	2.12
2007-08	**Calgary**	**NHL**	**5**	**0**	**2**	**0**	**150**	**5**	**0**	**2.00**	....	....	....	....	....	....	....
	Quad City Flames	AHL	41	20	18	2	2320	88	3	2.28	....	....	....	....	....	....	....
2008-09	**Calgary**	**NHL**	**14**	**1**	**6**	**1**	**518**	**31**	**0**	**3.59**	**1**	**0**	**0**	**34**	**1**	**0**	**1.76**
2009-10	**Calgary**	**NHL**	**10**	**3**	**4**	**0**	**502**	**27**	**0**	**3.23**	....	....	....	....	....	....	....
	Anaheim	**NHL**	**10**	**5**	**1**	**2**	**521**	**24**	**0**	**2.76**	....	....	....	....	....	....	....
2010-11	**Anaheim**	**NHL**	**21**	**6**	**9**	**1**	**996**	**57**	**2**	**3.43**	....	....	....	....	....	....	....
	Ottawa	**NHL**	**7**	**3**	**4**	**0**	**399**	**17**	**0**	**2.56**	....	....	....	....	....	....	....
2011-12	**Phoenix**	**NHL**	**2**	**1**	**0**	**0**	**72**	**2**	**0**	**1.67**	....	....	....	....	....	....	....
	Portland Pirates	AHL	25	10	13	0	1379	70	0	3.04	....	....	....	....	....	....	....
2012-13	Springfield Falcons	AHL	49	29	16	3	2926	113	*9	2.32	8	3	5	483	25	0	3.10
2013-14	**Columbus**	**NHL**	**28**	**10**	**11**	**1**	**1423**	**64**	**2**	**2.70**	....	....	....	....	....	....	....
2014-15	**Columbus**	**NHL**	**32**	**12**	**14**	**2**	**1710**	**82**	**0**	**2.88**	....	....	....	....	....	....	....
2015-16	**Columbus**	**NHL**	**18**	**2**	**7**	**3**	**835**	**46**	**0**	**3.31**	....	....	....	....	....	....	....
2016-17	**Columbus**	**NHL**	**7**	**2**	**1**	**2**	**376**	**15**	**0**	**2.39**	....	....	....	....	....	....	....
	Toronto	**NHL**	**14**	**6**	**7**	**0**	**759**	**36**	**1**	**2.85**	....	....	....	....	....	....	....
	NHL Totals		**168**	**51**	**66**	**12**	**8261**	**406**	**5**	**2.95**	**1**	**0**	**0**	**34**	**1**	**0**	**1.76**

WCHA First All-Star Team (2003, 2005) • NCAA West Second All-American Team (2003) • NCAA West First All-American Team (2005) • AHL Second All-Star Team (2007, 2013)

Traded to **Anaheim** by **Calgary** for Vesa Toskala, March 3, 2010. Traded to **Tampa Bay** by **Anaheim** for Dan Ellis, February 24, 2011. Claimed on waivers by **Ottawa** from **Tampa Bay**, February 28, 2011. Signed as a free agent by **Phoenix**, July 4, 2011. Traded to **Columbus** by **Phoenix** with Ottawa's 2nd round pick (previously acquired, later traded to Philadelphia – Philadelphia selected Anthony Stolarz) in 2012 NHL Draft and Phoenix's 4th round pick (later traded to Philadelphia, later traded to Los Angeles – Los Angeles selected Justin Auger) in 2013 NHL Draft for Antoine Vermette, February 22, 2012. Claimed on waivers by **Toronto** from **Columbus**, January 10, 2017.

McINTYRE, Zane (MAK-ihn-tigh-uhr, ZAYN) BOS

Goaltender. Catches left. 6'2", 206 lbs. Born, Grand Forks, ND, August 20, 1992.
(Boston's 6th pick, 165th overall, in 2010 NHL Draft).

			Regular Season								Playoffs						
Season	Club	League	GP	W	L	O/T	Mins	GA	SO	Avg	GP	W	L	Mins	GA	SO	Avg
2007-08	Thief River Falls	High-MN	....	14	12	0	....	....	....	2.15	....	....	....	....	....	....	....
2008-09	Thief River Falls	High-MN	27	20	5	2	1354	....	4	1.49	....	....	....	....	....	....	....
2009-10	Team Great Plains	UMHSEL	5	0	4	0	250	32	0	7.68	....	....	....	....	....	....	....
	Thief River Falls	High-MN	25	16	7	1	1281	46	3	1.83	3	2	1	153	5	0	1.67
2010-11	Fargo Force	USHL	23	14	8	0	1318	49	2	2.23	1	0	1	55	3	0	3.25
2011-12	Fargo Force	USHL	46	26	16	4	2758	102	*7	2.22	6	3	3	370	11	0	1.78
2012-13	North Dakota	WCHA	17	9	4	3	1001	41	0	2.46	....	....	....	....	....	....	....
2013-14	North Dakota	NCHC	33	*20	10	3	1930	64	3	*1.99	....	....	....	....	....	....	....
2014-15	North Dakota	NCHC	*42	*29	10	3	*2493	85	1	2.05	....	....	....	....	....	....	....
2015-16	Providence Bruins	AHL	31	14	8	7	1772	79	0	2.68	1	0	0	40	4	0	6.00
2016-17	**Boston**	**NHL**	**8**	**0**	**4**	**1**	**333**	**22**	**0**	**3.96**	....	....	....	....	....	....	....
	Providence Bruins	AHL	31	21	6	2	1777	60	2	2.03	16	8	7	933	40	0	2.57
	NHL Totals		**8**	**0**	**4**	**1**	**333**	**22**	**0**	**3.96**	....	....	....	....	....	....	....

USHL First All-Star Team (2012) • NCHC First All-Star Team (2015) • NCAA West Second All-American Team (2015) • AHL Second All-Star Team (2017)

McKENNA, Mike (mih-KEHN-ah, MIGHK) DAL

Goaltender. Catches right. 6'2", 190 lbs. Born, St. Louis, MO, April 11, 1983.
(Nashville's 4th pick, 172nd overall, in 2002 NHL Draft).

			Regular Season								Playoffs						
Season	Club	League	GP	W	L	O/T	Mins	GA	SO	Avg	GP	W	L	Mins	GA	SO	Avg
2001-02	St. Lawrence	ECAC	20	7	10	1	1121	59	0	3.16	....	....	....	....	....	....	....
2002-03	St. Lawrence	ECAC	15	1	7	2	618	38	0	3.69	....	....	....	....	....	....	....
2003-04	St. Lawrence	ECAC	27	9	10	3	1475	60	3	2.44	....	....	....	....	....	....	....
2004-05	St. Lawrence	ECAC	35	15	17	2	2022	92	3	2.73	....	....	....	....	....	....	....
2005-06	Norfolk Admirals	AHL	7	4	2	1	388	25	0	3.86	....	....	....	....	....	....	....
	Las Vegas	ECHL	25	19	2	1	1383	49	1	2.13	4	1	1	173	9	0	3.12
2006-07	Milwaukee	AHL	1	0	0	0	11	3	0	15.72	....	....	....	....	....	....	....
	Omaha	AHL	2	0	1	0	96	6	0	3.74	....	....	....	....	....	....	....
	Las Vegas	ECHL	38	27	4	7	2258	83	5	*2.21	6	3	3	358	15	0	2.51
2007-08	Portland Pirates	AHL	41	24	13	1	2269	103	3	2.72	6	2	4	320	18	0	3.38
2008-09	**Tampa Bay**	**NHL**	**15**	**4**	**8**	**1**	**776**	**46**	**1**	**3.56**	....	....	....	....	....	....	....
	Norfolk Admirals	AHL	24	11	10	1	1315	65	1	2.97	....	....	....	....	....	....	....
2009-10	Lowell Devils	AHL	50	24	17	6	2891	119	3	2.47	5	1	4	317	17	0	3.22
2010-11	Albany Devils	AHL	39	14	20	2	2062	124	1	3.61	....	....	....	....	....	....	....
	New Jersey	**NHL**	**2**	**0**	**1**	**0**	**118**	**6**	**0**	**3.05**	....	....	....	....	....	....	....
2011-12	Binghamton	AHL	41	14	22	1	2196	109	0	2.98	....	....	....	....	....	....	....
2012-13	Peoria Rivermen	AHL	39	19	18	1	2307	93	4	2.42	....	....	....	....	....	....	....
2013-14	**Columbus**	**NHL**	**4**	**1**	**1**	**1**	**219**	**11**	**0**	**3.01**	....	....	....	....	....	....	....
	Springfield Falcons	AHL	36	22	10	1	2106	89	3	2.54	5	2	2	245	14	0	3.43
2014-15	**Arizona**	**NHL**	**1**	**0**	**1**	**0**	**60**	**5**	**0**	**5.00**	....	....	....	....	....	....	....
	Portland Pirates	AHL	52	27	18	6	2979	111	7	2.24	2	0	1	41	6	0	8.89

2015-16	Portland Pirates	AHL	57	33	17	5	3256	133	3	2.45	5	2	3	338	12	0	2.13
2016-17	Springfield	AHL	26	9	10	7	1550	73	1	2.83	....	....	....	....	....	....	....
	Syracuse Crunch	AHL	14	5	5	3	796	38	0	2.87	*22	13	9	*1341	60	0	2.68
	NHL Totals		**22**	**5**	**11**	**2**	**1173**	**68**	**1**	**3.48**	....	....	....	....	....	....	....

ECHL Second All-Star Team (2007)

Signed as a free agent by **Tampa Bay**, February 3, 2009. Signed as a free agent by **Lowell** (AHL), October 7, 2009. Signed as a free agent by **New Jersey**, February 10, 2010. Signed as a free agent by **Ottawa**, July 8, 2011. Signed as a free agent by **St. Louis**, July 1, 2012. Signed as a free agent by **Columbus**, July 6, 2013. Signed as a free agent by **Arizona**, July 1, 2014. Signed as a free agent by **Florida**, July 1, 2015. Traded to **Tampa Bay** by **Florida** for Adam Wilcox, March 1, 2017. Signed as a free agent by **Dallas**, July 1, 2017.

McNIVEN, Michael (muhk-NIH-vehn, MIGH-kuhl) MTL

Goaltender. Catches left. 6'1", 218 lbs. Born, Winnipeg, MB, July 9, 1997.

			Regular Season								Playoffs						
Season	Club	League	GP	W	L	O/T	Mins	GA	SO	Avg	GP	W	L	Mins	GA	SO	Avg
2012-13	Halton Hurricanes	Minor-ON	22	11	9	2	....	....	....	1.48	....	....	....	....	....	....	....
2013-14	Georgetown	ON-Jr.A	35	21	10	0	1891	82	5	2.60	13	8	5	778	35	0	2.70
2014-15	Owen Sound	OHL	24	15	8	0	1334	62	2	2.79	....	....	....	....	....	....	....
2015-16	Owen Sound	OHL	53	21	18	10	2964	145	3	2.94	6	2	4	360	22	1	3.67
2016-17	Owen Sound	OHL	54	*41	9	4	3184	122	*6	*2.30	17	10	7	992	46	*2	2.78

OHL First All-Star Team (2017)

Signed as a free agent by **Montreal**, September 24, 2015.

MERZLIKINS, Elvis (muhrz-LIGH-kinz, EHL-vihs) CBJ

Goaltender. Catches left. 6'3", 183 lbs. Born, Riga, Latvia, April 13, 1994.
(Columbus' 3rd pick, 76th overall, in 2014 NHL Draft).

			Regular Season								Playoffs						
Season	Club	League	GP	W	L	O/T	Mins	GA	SO	Avg	GP	W	L	Mins	GA	SO	Avg
2009-10	HC Lugano U17	Swiss-U17	24	....	....	....	....	....	....	....	12	....	....	....	....	....	....
2010-11	HC Lugano U17	Swiss-U17	28	....	....	....	....	....	....	....	5	....	....	....	....	....	....
2011-12	HC Lugano Jr.	Swiss-Jr.	8	....	....	....	....	....	....	3.52	3	....	....	....	....	....	5.07
2012-13	HC Lugano Jr.	Swiss-Jr.	30	....	....	....	....	....	....	2.76	4	....	....	....	....	....	3.84
2013-14	HC Lugano Jr.	Swiss-Jr.	12	....	....	....	....	....	....	2.07	10	....	....	....	....	....	1.68
	HC Lugano	Swiss	22	12	10	0	1269	45	1	2.13	1	0	1	80	1	0	0.75
2014-15	HC Lugano	Swiss	22	14	9	0	1309	57	2	2.61	1	0	1	36	2	0	3.33
2015-16	HC Lugano	Swiss	44	23	13	5	2713	125	1	2.76	*15	8	6	*930	36	0	2.32
2016-17	HC Lugano	Swiss	40	19	17	0	2408	116	3	2.89	11	5	6	654	25	0	2.29

METCALF, Garrett (MEHT-caf, GAIR-eht) ANA

Goaltender. Catches left. 6'3", 193 lbs. Born, Salt Lake City, UT, March 5, 1996.
(Anaheim's 7th pick, 179th overall, in 2015 NHL Draft).

			Regular Season								Playoffs						
Season	Club	League	GP	W	L	O/T	Mins	GA	SO	Avg	GP	W	L	Mins	GA	SO	Avg
2012-13	Col. Rampage U16	T1EHL	13	2	9	1	647	40	0	3.34	2	2	0	102	3	0	1.50
	Om. Lancers U16	NAPHL	1	1	0	0	51	0	1	0.00	....	....	....	....	....	....	....
	Om. Lancers U18	NAPHL	1	0	1	0	51	4	0	4.00	....	....	....	....	....	....	....
2013-14	Col. Rampage U18	T1EHL	14	7	7	0	749	32	2	2.31	....	....	....	....	....	....	....
	Colorado Rampage	Other	1	1	0	0	51	2	0	2.00	....	....	....	....	....	....	....
2014-15	Madison Capitols	USHL	33	10	12	4	1529	83	1	3.26	....	....	....	....	....	....	....
2015-16	Madison Capitols	USHL	27	10	13	2	1484	79	1	3.19	....	....	....	....	....	....	....
	Waterloo	USHL	9	3	3	2	496	27	1	3.26	....	....	....	....	....	....	....
2016-17	U. Mass Lowell	H-East	4	1	0	1	208	9	0	2.59	....	....	....	....	....	....	....

MICHALEK, Steve (MIGH-KUHL-ehk, STEEV) MIN

Goaltender. Catches left. 6'3", 205 lbs. Born, Hartford, CT, August 6, 1993.
(Minnesota's 5th pick, 161st overall, in 2011 NHL Draft).

			Regular Season								Playoffs						
Season	Club	League	GP	W	L	O/T	Mins	GA	SO	Avg	GP	W	L	Mins	GA	SO	Avg
2009-10	Loomis Chaffee	High-CT	35	....	....	....	1121	106	....	....	....	....	....	....	....	....	....
2010-11	Loomis Chaffee	High-CT	23	2	19	2	1203	91	....	3.95	....	....	....	....	....	....	....
	Boston Little Bruins	Minor-MA	STATISTICS NOT AVAILABLE														
2011-12	Harvard Crimson	ECAC	24	7	7	8	1336	71	0	3.19	....	....	....	....	....	....	....
2012-13	Cedar Rapids	USHL	17	7	6	3	992	51	0	3.09	....	....	....	....	....	....	....
2013-14	Harvard Crimson	ECAC	18	5	8	2	970	40	2	2.47	....	....	....	....	....	....	....
2014-15	Harvard Crimson	ECAC	*37	21	13	3	*2232	85	3	2.28	....	....	....	....	....	....	....
2015-16	Iowa Wild	AHL	14	7	5	2	845	37	0	2.63	....	....	....	....	....	....	....
	Quad City Mallards	ECHL	24	12	8	4	1414	57	2	2.42	....	....	....	....	....	....	....
2016-17	Iowa Wild	AHL	30	13	14	1	1690	74	1	2.63	....	....	....	....	....	....	....

ECAC All-Rookie Team (2012)

MILLER, Ryan (MIH-luhr, RIGH-uhn) ANA

Goaltender. Catches left. 6'2", 168 lbs. Born, East Lansing, MI, July 17, 1980.
(Buffalo's 7th pick, 138th overall, in 1999 NHL Draft).

			Regular Season								Playoffs						
Season	Club	League	GP	W	L	O/T	Mins	GA	SO	Avg	GP	W	L	Mins	GA	SO	Avg
1997-98	Soo Indians	NAHL	37	21	14	0	2113	82	3	2.33	2	0	2	158	7	0	2.66
1998-99	Soo Indians	NAHL	47	31	14	1	2711	104	8	2.30	4	2	2	218	10	1	2.76
99-2000	Michigan State	CCHA	26	16	5	3	1525	39	*8	*1.53	....	....	....	....	....	....	....
2000-01	Michigan State	CCHA	40	*31	5	4	2447	54	*10	*1.32	....	....	....	....	....	....	....
2001-02	Michigan State	CCHA	40	26	9	5	2411	71	*8	*1.77	....	....	....	....	....	....	....
2002-03	**Buffalo**	**NHL**	**15**	**6**	**8**	**1**	**912**	**40**	**1**	**2.63**	....	....	....	....	....	....	....
	Rochester	AHL	47	23	18	5	2817	110	2	2.34	3	1	2	190	13	0	4.11
2003-04	**Buffalo**	**NHL**	**3**	**0**	**3**	**0**	**178**	**15**	**0**	**5.06**	....	....	....	....	....	....	....
	Rochester	AHL	60	27	25	7	3579	132	5	2.21	14	7	7	857	26	2	1.82
2004-05	Rochester	AHL	63	*41	17	4	3741	153	8	2.45	9	5	4	547	24	0	2.63
2005-06	**Buffalo**	**NHL**	**48**	**30**	**14**	**3**	**2862**	**124**	**1**	**2.60**	**18**	**11**	**7**	**1123**	**48**	**1**	**2.56**
	Rochester	AHL	2	1	1	0	120	5	0	2.50	....	....	....	....	....	....	....
2006-07	**Buffalo**	**NHL**	**63**	**40**	**16**	**6**	**3692**	**168**	**2**	**2.73**	**16**	**9**	**7**	**1029**	**38**	**0**	**2.22**
2007-08	**Buffalo**	**NHL**	**76**	**36**	**27**	**10**	**4474**	**197**	**3**	**2.64**	....	....	....	....	....	....	....
2008-09	**Buffalo**	**NHL**	**59**	**34**	**18**	**6**	**3443**	**145**	**5**	**2.53**	....	....	....	....	....	....	....
2009-10	**Buffalo**	**NHL**	**69**	**41**	**18**	**8**	**4047**	**150**	**5**	**2.22**	**6**	**2**	**4**	**384**	**15**	**0**	**2.34**
	United States	Olympics	6	5	1	0	355	8	1	1.35	....	....	....	....	....	....	....
2010-11	**Buffalo**	**NHL**	**66**	**34**	**22**	**8**	**3829**	**165**	**5**	**2.59**	**7**	**3**	**4**	**410**	**20**	**2**	**2.93**
2011-12	**Buffalo**	**NHL**	**61**	**31**	**21**	**7**	**3536**	**150**	**6**	**2.55**	....	....	....	....	....	....	....
2012-13	**Buffalo**	**NHL**	**40**	**17**	**17**	**5**	**2302**	**108**	**0**	**2.81**	....	....	....	....	....	....	....
2013-14	**Buffalo**	**NHL**	**40**	**15**	**22**	**3**	**2384**	**108**	**0**	**2.72**	....	....	....	....	....	....	....
	United States	Olympics	1	1	0	0	60	1	0	1.00	....	....	....	....	....	....	....
	St. Louis	**NHL**	**19**	**10**	**8**	**1**	**1117**	**46**	**1**	**2.47**	**6**	**2**	**4**	**422**	**19**	**0**	**2.70**
2014-15	**Vancouver**	**NHL**	**45**	**29**	**15**	**1**	**2542**	**107**	**6**	**2.53**	**3**	**1**	**1**	**156**	**6**	**0**	**2.31**
2015-16	**Vancouver**	**NHL**	**51**	**17**	**24**	**9**	**3043**	**137**	**1**	**2.70**	....	....	....	....	....	....	....
2016-17	**Vancouver**	**NHL**	**54**	**18**	**29**	**6**	**3212**	**150**	**3**	**2.80**	....	....	....	....	....	....	....
	NHL Totals		**709**	**358**	**262**	**74**	**41573**	**1810**	**39**	**2.61**	**56**	**28**	**27**	**3524**	**146**	**3**	**2.49**

CCHA Second All-Star Team (2000) • CCHA First All-Star Team (2001, 2002) • CCHA Player of the Year (2001, 2002) • NCAA West First All-American Team (2001, 2002) • Hobey Baker Memorial Award (Top U.S. Collegiate Player) (2001) • AHL First All-Star Team (2005) • Aldege "Baz" Bastien Memorial Award (AHL – Outstanding Goaltender) (2005) • Olympic All-Star Team (2010) • Best Goaltender – Olympics (2010) • MVP – Olympics (2010) • NHL First All-Star Team (2010) • NHL Foundation Player Award (2010) • Vezina Trophy (2010)

Played in NHL All-Star Game (2007)

Traded to **St. Louis** by **Buffalo** with Steve Ott for Jaroslav Halak, Chris Stewart, William Carrier, St. Louis' 1st round pick (later traded to Winnipeg – Winnipeg selected Jack Roslovic) in 2015 NHL Draft and St. Louis' 3rd round pick (later traded to Florida – Florida selected Linus Nassen) in 2016 NHL Draft, February 28, 2014. Signed as a free agent by **Vancouver**, July 1, 2014. Signed as a free agent by **Anaheim**, July 1, 2017.

MISKA, Hunter (MIS-kah, HUHN-tuhr) ARI

Goaltender. Catches left. 6'1", 174 lbs. Born, Stacy, MN, July 7, 1995.

			Regular Season								Playoffs						
Season	Club	League	GP	W	L	O/T	Mins	GA	SO	Avg	GP	W	L	Mins	GA	SO	Avg
2009-10	North Branch	High-MN	22	12	7	3	1100	83	1	3.85	2	1	1	102	17	0	8.50
2010-11	North Branch	High-MN	25	7	18	0	1248	110	0	4.50	1	0	1	51	7	0	7.00
2011-12	USAHNTDP	USHL	25	9	13	0	1305	78	0	3.59	2	0	2	119	12	0	6.06
	USAHNTDP	U-17	14	10	2	1	666	22	2	1.98	....	....	....	....	....	....	....
2012-13	USAHNTDP	USHL	13	3	7	1	745	38	0	3.06	....	....	....	....	....	....	....
	USAHNTDP	U-18	13	5	5	0	701	36	0	3.08	....	....	....	....	....	....	....
2013-14	Penticton Vees	BCHL	36	21	12	2	2107	81	2	2.31	6	3	1	284	16	0	3.38
2014-15	Penticton Vees	BCHL	46	*34	9	3	2775	87	*5	*1.88	21	*15	6	1365	52	*2	2.24
2015-16	Dubuque	USHL	46	32	13	1	2761	113	1	2.46	*12	6	5	*750	28	1	2.24
2016-17	U. Minn-Duluth	NCHC	*39	27	5	5	*2321	85	*5	2.20	....	....	....	....	....	....	....

NCHC Second All-Star Team (2017)

Signed as a free agent by **Arizona**, April 15, 2017.

MONTEMBEAULT, Sam (mawn-tehm-BOH, SAM) FLA

Goaltender. Catches left. 6'3", 192 lbs. Born, Quebec, QC, October 30, 1996.
(Florida's 2nd pick, 77th overall, in 2015 NHL Draft).

			Regular Season								Playoffs						
Season	Club	League	GP	W	L	O/T	Mins	GA	SO	Avg	GP	W	L	Mins	GA	SO	Avg
2012-13	Trois-Rivieres	QAAA	19	11	7	1	1110	47	1	2.54	6	4	2	....	....	....	....
2013-14	Blainville-Bois.	QMJHL	14	9	1	1	714	28	0	2.35	1	1	0	53	3	0	3.40
2014-15	Blainville-Bois.	QMJHL	52	33	11	7	3104	134	3	2.59	6	2	4	353	14	0	2.38
2015-16	Blainville-Bois.	QMJHL	47	17	19	8	2711	119	3	2.63	11	5	6	685	28	1	2.45
2016-17	Blainville-Bois.	QMJHL	41	28	9	1	2226	89	*6	2.40	*18	12	6	1070	42	0	2.35

QMJHL Second All-Star Team (2017)

MONTOYA, Al (mawn-TOI-uh, AL) MTL

Goaltender. Catches left. 6'2", 209 lbs. Born, Chicago, IL, February 13, 1985.
(NY Rangers' 1st pick, 6th overall, in 2004 NHL Draft).

			Regular Season								Playoffs						
Season	Club	League	GP	W	L	O/T	Mins	GA	SO	Avg	GP	W	L	Mins	GA	SO	Avg
99-2000	Loyola Academy	High-MN	28	12	13	3	1685	56	1	2.01	....	....	....	....	....	....	....
2000-01	Texas Tornado	NAHL	15	10	3	0	780	38	0	2.92	1	1	0	60	2	0	2.00
	United States	Nat-Tm	2	2	0	0	120	4	0	2.00	....	....	....	....	....	....	....
2001-02	USAHNTDP	U-17	10	5	5	0	570	24	0	2.53	....	....	....	....	....	....	....
	USAHNTDP	NAHL	24	6	11	4	1344	79	0	3.53	....	....	....	....	....	....	....
2002-03	U. of Michigan	CCHA	*43	*30	10	3	*2547	99	4	2.33	....	....	....	....	....	....	....
2003-04	U. of Michigan	CCHA	*40	*26	12	2	*2340	87	6	2.23	....	....	....	....	....	....	....
2004-05	U. of Michigan	CCHA	*40	*30	7	3	*2359	99	3	2.52	....	....	....	....	....	....	....
2005-06	Hartford Wolf Pack	AHL	40	23	9	1	2094	91	2	2.61	5	2	1	257	8	1	1.87
	Charlotte Checkers	ECHL	2	1	1	0	123	8	0	3.92	....	....	....	....	....	....	....
2006-07	Hartford Wolf Pack	AHL	48	27	17	0	2556	98	6	2.30	7	3	4	391	20	1	3.07
2007-08	Hartford Wolf Pack	AHL	31	16	8	3	1704	72	0	2.54	....	....	....	....	....	....	....
	San Antonio	AHL	14	8	6	0	789	34	1	2.59	1	0	1	59	4	0	4.04
2008-09	**Phoenix**	**NHL**	**5**	**3**	**1**	**0**	**259**	**9**	**1**	**2.08**	....	....	....	....	....	....	....
	San Antonio	AHL	29	7	17	2	1562	84	0	3.23	....	....	....	....	....	....	....
2009-10	San Antonio	AHL	14	4	7	1	771	34	0	2.65	....	....	....	....	....	....	....
2010-11	**NY Islanders**	**NHL**	**20**	**9**	**5**	**5**	**1154**	**46**	**1**	**2.39**	....	....	....	....	....	....	....
	San Antonio	AHL	21	11	8	0	1130	60	0	3.19	....	....	....	....	....	....	....
2011-12	**NY Islanders**	**NHL**	**31**	**9**	**11**	**5**	**1720**	**89**	**0**	**3.10**	....	....	....	....	....	....	....
2012-13	**Winnipeg**	**NHL**	**7**	**3**	**1**	**0**	**351**	**17**	**1**	**2.91**	....	....	....	....	....	....	....
2013-14	**Winnipeg**	**NHL**	**28**	**13**	**8**	**3**	**1541**	**59**	**2**	**2.30**	....	....	....	....	....	....	....
2014-15	**Florida**	**NHL**	**20**	**6**	**7**	**2**	**977**	**49**	**0**	**3.01**	....	....	....	....	....	....	....
2015-16	**Florida**	**NHL**	**25**	**12**	**7**	**3**	**1351**	**49**	**0**	**2.18**	....	....	....	....	....	....	....
2016-17	**Montreal**	**NHL**	**19**	**8**	**6**	**4**	**1125**	**50**	**2**	**2.67**	....	....	....	....	....	....	....
	NHL Totals		**155**	**63**	**46**	**22**	**8478**	**368**	**7**	**2.60**	....	....	....	....	....	....	....

CCHA All-Rookie Team (2003) • NCAA West Second All-American Team (2004)

Traded to **Phoenix** by **NY Rangers** with Marcel Hossa for Josh Gratton, David LeNeveu, Fredrik Sjostrom and Phoenix's 5th round pick (Roman Horak) in 2009 NHL Draft, February 26, 2008. Traded to **NY Islanders** by **Phoenix** for NY Islanders' 6th round pick (Andrew Fritsch) in 2011 NHL Draft, February 9, 2011. Signed as a free agent by **Winnipeg**, July 4, 2012. Signed as a free agent by **Florida**, July 1, 2014. Signed as a free agent by **Montreal**, July 1, 2016.

MRAZEK, Petr (M'RAZ-ihk, PEH-tuhr) DET

Goaltender. Catches left. 6'2", 183 lbs. Born, Ostrava, Czech., February 14, 1992.
(Detroit's 5th pick, 141st overall, in 2010 NHL Draft).

			Regular Season								Playoffs						
Season	Club	League	GP	W	L	O/T	Mins	GA	SO	Avg	GP	W	L	Mins	GA	SO	Avg
2006-07	HC Vitkovice U17	CzR-U17	23	....	....	....	1273	51	2	2.40	9	....	....	486	15	1	1.85
2007-08	HC Vitkovice U17	CzR-U17	34	....	....	....	1974	81	4	2.46	3	....	....	179	8	0	2.68
	HC Vitkovice Steel	CzRep	1	....	....	....	24	4	0	10.00	....	....	....	....	....	....	....
2008-09	HC Vitkovice U17	CzR-U17	28	....	....	....	1601	53	5	1.99	4	....	....	193	3	2	0.93
	HC Vitkovice Jr.	CzRep-Jr.	13	....	....	....	795	33	0	2.49	1	....	....	60	1	0	1.00
2009-10	Ottawa 67's	OHL	30	12	9	1	1562	78	2	3.00	8	4	4	451	18	0	2.39
2010-11	Ottawa 67's	OHL	52	33	15	3	3089	146	4	2.84	4	0	3	224	21	0	5.63
2011-12	Ottawa 67's	OHL	50	30	13	6	3016	143	3	2.84	17	9	8	1065	46	0	2.59
2012-13	Grand Rapids	AHL	42	23	16	2	2498	97	1	2.33	*24	*15	9	*1431	55	*4	2.31
	Toledo Walleye	ECHL	3	2	1	0	179	6	0	2.02	....	....	....	....	....	....	....
	Detroit	**NHL**	**2**	**1**	**1**	**0**	**119**	**4**	**0**	**2.02**	....	....	....	....	....	....	....

Season	Club	League	GP	W	L	O/T	Mins	GA	SO	Avg	GP	W	L	Mins	GA	SO	Avg
2013-14	Detroit	NHL	9	2	4	0	449	13	2	1.74							
	Grand Rapids	AHL	32	22	9	1	1830	64	3	2.10	10	5	5	600	28	0	2.80
2014-15	Detroit	NHL	29	16	9	2	1585	63	3	2.38	7	3	4	398	14	2	2.11
	Grand Rapids	AHL	13	9	2	1	757	26	3	2.06							
2015-16	Detroit	NHL	54	27	16	6	2961	115	4	2.33	3	1	2	177	4	1	1.36
2016-17	Detroit	NHL	50	18	21	9	2858	145	1	3.04							
	NHL Totals		144	64	51	17	7972	340	10	2.56	10	4	6	575	18	3	1.88

AHL Second All-Star Team (2014)

MURRAY, Matt (MUHR-ee, MAT) PIT

Goaltender. Catches left. 6'4", 178 lbs. Born, Thunder Bay, ON, May 25, 1994.
(Pittsburgh's 5th pick, 83rd overall, in 2012 NHL Draft).

			Regular Season								Playoffs						
Season	Club	League	GP	W	L	O/T	Mins	GA	SO	Avg	GP	W	L	Mins	GA	SO	Avg
2009-10	Thunder Bay Kings	Minor-ON	40	32	5	0	1975	75	6	1.71							
2010-11	Sault Ste. Marie	OHL	28	8	11	3	1377	87	1	3.79							
2011-12	Sault Ste. Marie	OHL	36	13	19	1	1912	130	0	4.08							
2012-13	Sault Ste. Marie	OHL	53	26	19	4	2910	178	2	3.67	6	2	4	381	17	1	2.67
2013-14	Sault Ste. Marie	OHL	49	32	11	1	2984	128	*6	2.57	9	4	3	547	24	1	2.63
	Wilkes-Barre	AHL	1	0	1	0	60	2	0	2.00	1	0	0	20	0	0	0.00
2014-15	Wilkes-Barre	AHL	40	25	10	3	2321	61	12	1.58	8	4	4	456	18	1	2.37
2015-16 ♦	Pittsburgh	NHL	13	9	2	1	749	25	1	2.00	21	*15	6	1267	44	1	2.08
	Wilkes-Barre	AHL	31	20	9	1	1827	64	4	2.10							
2016-17 ♦	Pittsburgh	NHL	49	32	10	4	2766	111	4	2.41	11	7	3	669	19	*3	*1.70
	NHL Totals		62	41	12	5	3515	136	5	2.32	32	22	9	1936	63	4	1.95

OHL Second All-Star Team (2014) • AHL All-Rookie Team (2015) • AHL First All-Star Team (2015) • Dudley "Red" Garrett Memorial Trophy (AHL – Rookie of the Year) (2015) • Harry "Hap" Holmes Memorial Award (AHL – fewest goals against) (2015) (shared with Jeff Zatkoff) • Aldege "Baz" Bastien Award (AHL – Outstanding Goaltender) (2015) • AHL Second All-Star Team (2016) • NHL All-Rookie Team (2017)

NALIMOV, Ivan (na-LEE-mawv, ee-VAHN) CHI

Goaltender. Catches left. 6'4", 210 lbs. Born, Novokuznetsk, Russia, March 12, 1994.
(Chicago's 8th pick, 179th overall, in 2014 NHL Draft).

			Regular Season								Playoffs						
Season	Club	League	GP	W	L	O/T	Mins	GA	SO	Avg	GP	W	L	Mins	GA	SO	Avg
2011-12	St. Petersburg Jr.	Russia-Jr.	20	7	6	3	966	36	1	2.24							
2012-13	St. Petersburg Jr.	Russia-Jr.	47	23	11	10	2772	98	4	2.12	7	3	4	388	21	0	3.25
2013-14	VMF	Russia-2	1	1	0	0	60	1	0	1.00							
	St. Petersburg Jr.	Russia-Jr.	12	5	7	0	634	30	0	2.84	1	0	0	12	2	0	10.06
2014-15	Vladivostok	KHL	30	10	10	0	1479	68	3	2.76							
2015-16	Vladivostok	KHL	39	20	13	0	2189	95	4	2.60	3	0	3	175	10	0	3.44
2016-17	Vladivostok	KHL	13	4	4	0	564	27	0	2.87							
	Novosibirsk	KHL	5	1	3	0	275	15	1	3.27							

NEDELJKOVIC, Alex (nuh-DEHL-koh-vihch, AL-ehx) CAR

Goaltender. Catches left. 6', 198 lbs. Born, Parma, OH, January 7, 1996.
(Carolina's 2nd pick, 37th overall, in 2014 NHL Draft).

			Regular Season								Playoffs						
Season	Club	League	GP	W	L	O/T	Mins	GA	SO	Avg	GP	W	L	Mins	GA	SO	Avg
2012-13	Plymouth Whalers	OHL	26	19	2	2	1371	52	2	2.28	15	9	4	864	39	1	2.71
2013-14	Plymouth Whalers	OHL	61	26	27	7	3436	165	1	2.88	5	1	4	272	20	0	4.41
2014-15	Plymouth Whalers	OHL	55	20	28	7	3206	167	5	3.13							
	Florida Everblades	ECHL	3	2	1	0	178	10	0	3.38							
2015-16	Flint Firebirds	OHL	19	9	7	2	1122	60	1	3.21							
	Niagara Ice Dogs	OHL	30	15	13	2	1766	80	1	2.72	17	12	5	1026	48	0	2.81
2016-17	Carolina	NHL	1	0	0	0	30	0	0	0.00							
	Charlotte Checkers	AHL	25	8	14	1	1287	73	1	3.40							
	Florida Everblades	ECHL	12	6	4	0	565	28	1	2.97	7	1	5	406	13	0	1.92
	NHL Totals		1	0	0	0	30	0	0	0.00							

OHL All-Rookie Team (2013) • OHL First All-Star Team (2014)

NELL, Chris (NEHL, KRIHS) NYR

Goaltender. Catches left. 6'1", 190 lbs. Born, Green Bay, WI, September 2, 1994.

			Regular Season								Playoffs						
Season	Club	League	GP	W	L	O/T	Mins	GA	SO	Avg	GP	W	L	Mins	GA	SO	Avg
2010-11	Notre Dame Acad.	High-WI	22	16	4	0	981	27	2	1.65	5	4	1	281	11	1	2.35
2011-12	Team Wisconsin	UMHSEL	17	5	6	3	915	60	0	3.93	1	0	1	60	11	0	11.00
	Notre Dame Acad.	High-WI	24	19	3	0	1045	34	4	1.66	6	6	0	307	8	1	1.56
2012-13	Chicago Steel	USHL	25	7	11	2	1214	70	0	3.46							
2013-14	Chicago Steel	USHL	43	16	22	3	2397	127	1	3.18							
2014-15	Bowling Green	WCHA	13	6	4	2	751	29	3	2.32							
2015-16	Bowling Green	WCHA	37	18	11	6	2167	69	4	1.91							
2016-17	Bemidji State	WCHA	34	17	14	2	2069	74	4	2.15							
	Hartford Wolf Pack	AHL	4	1	3	0	239	16	0	4.02							

WCHA First All-Star Team (2016)

Signed as a free agent by **NY Rangers**, March 23, 2017.

NEUVIRTH, Michal (NOI-vihrt, MIGHK-ahl) PHI

Goaltender. Catches left. 6'1", 209 lbs. Born, Usti nad Labem, Czech., March 23, 1988.
(Washington's 3rd pick, 34th overall, in 2006 NHL Draft).

			Regular Season								Playoffs						
Season	Club	League	GP	W	L	O/T	Mins	GA	SO	Avg	GP	W	L	Mins	GA	SO	Avg
2003-04	Sparta U17	CzR-U17	55				3137	96	5	1.84	3			180	13	0	4.33
2004-05	Sparta U17	CzR-U17	20				1178	49	3	2.50	8			482	17	0	2.12
	Sparta Jr.	CzRep-Jr.	10				501	20	1	2.40							
2005-06	Sparta Jr.	CzRep-Jr.	42				2516	82	5	1.96	3			179	9	0	3.02
2006-07	Plymouth Whalers	OHL	41	26	8	4	2223	86	4	*2.32	*18	*14	4	*1080	44	0	*2.44
2007-08	Plymouth Whalers	OHL	10	5	4	1	600	26	0	2.60							
	Windsor Spitfires	OHL	8	6	1	1	482	17	0	2.12							
	Oshawa Generals	OHL	15	6	2	6	844	57	0	4.05	9	7	2	507	21	0	2.49
2008-09	Washington	NHL	5	2	1	0	220	11	0	3.00							
	Hershey Bears	AHL	17	9	5	2	1001	45	1	2.70	*22	*16	6	*1346	43	*4	1.92
	South Carolina	ECHL	13	6	7	0	762	29	2	2.28							
2009-10	Washington	NHL	17	9	4	0	872	40	0	2.75							
	Hershey Bears	AHL	22	15	6	0	1231	46	1	2.24	*18	*14	4	*1133	39	1	2.07
2010-11	Washington	NHL	48	27	12	4	2689	110	4	2.45	9	4	5	590	23	1	2.34
2011-12	Washington	NHL	38	13	13	5	2020	95	3	2.82							
2012-13	HC Sparta Praha	CzRep	24				1342	55	1	2.46							
	Washington	NHL	13	4	5	2	723	33	0	2.74							
2013-14	Washington	NHL	13	4	6	2	767	36	0	2.82							
	Hershey Bears	AHL	1	1	0	0	60	4	0	4.02							
	Buffalo	NHL	2	0	2	0	117	5	0	2.56							
2014-15	Buffalo	NHL	27	6	17	3	1544	77	0	2.99							
	NY Islanders	NHL	5	1	3	1	306	15	0	2.94	1	0	0	11	0	0	0.00
2015-16	Philadelphia	NHL	32	18	8	4	1825	69	3	2.27	3	2	1	178	2	1	0.67
2016-17	Philadelphia	NHL	28	11	11	1	1364	64	0	2.82							
	NHL Totals		228	95	82	22	12447	555	10	2.68	13	6	6	779	25	2	1.93

OHL Second All-Star Team (2007) • Jack A. Butterfield Trophy (AHL – Playoff MVP) (2009)

Signed as a free agent by **Sparta Praha** (CzRep), September 20, 2012. Traded to **Buffalo** by **Washington** with Rostislav Klesla for Jaroslav Halak and Buffalo's 3rd round pick (later traded to NY Rangers – NY Rangers selected Robin Kovacs) in 2015 NHL Draft, March 5, 2014. Traded to **NY Islanders** by **Buffalo** for Chad Johnson and Vancouver's 3rd round pick (previously acquired, later traded to Pittsburgh, later traded back to Vancouver – Vancouver selected William Lockwood) in 2016 NHL Draft, March 2, 2015. Signed as a free agent by **Philadelphia**, July 1, 2015.

NIEMI, Antti (nee-YEH-mee, AN-tee) PIT

Goaltender. Catches left. 6'2", 210 lbs. Born, Vantaa, Finland, August 29, 1983.

			Regular Season								Playoffs						
Season	Club	League	GP	W	L	O/T	Mins	GA	SO	Avg	GP	W	L	Mins	GA	SO	Avg
2000-01	Kiekko-Vantaa Jr.	Fin-Jr.	4							6.86							
2001-02	Kiekko-Vantaa	Finland-2	24								3						
2002-03	Kiekko-Vantaa	Finland-2					364	16	0	2.63							
2003-04	Kiekko-Vantaa Jr.	Fin-Jr.	19				1095	58	2	3.18							
	Kiekko-Vantaa	Finland-2	19				1048	47	1	2.52	3			187	13	0	4.17
2004-05	Kiekko-Vantaa	Finland-2	38				2261	95	1	2.52	3			187	13	0	4.17
2005-06	Pelicans Lahti	Finland	40	12	17	8	2263	103	3	2.73							
2006-07	Pelicans Lahti	Finland	48	18	21	7	2780	119	3	2.57	6	2	4	371	9	1	1.46
2007-08	Pelicans Lahti	Finland	49	26	14	6	2778	109	4	2.35	6	2	3	327	21	0	3.85
2008-09	Chicago	NHL	3	1	1	1	141	8	0	3.40							
	Rockford IceHogs	AHL	38	18	14	3	2095	85	2	2.43	2	0	2	115	7	0	3.65
2009-10 ♦	Chicago	NHL	39	26	7	4	2190	82	7	2.25	*22	*16	6	*1322	58	2	2.63
2010-11	San Jose	NHL	60	35	18	6	3524	140	6	2.38	18	8	9	1044	56	0	3.22
2011-12	San Jose	NHL	68	34	22	9	3936	159	6	2.42	5	1	4	318	13	0	2.45
2012-13	Pelicans Lahti	Finland	10	3	5	2	597	31	0	3.11							
	San Jose	NHL	43	*24	12	6	*2581	93	4	2.16	11	7	4	673	21	0	1.87
2013-14	San Jose	NHL	64	39	17	7	3740	149	4	2.39	6	3	3	305	19	0	3.74
	Finland	Olympics	DID NOT PLAY – SPARE GOALTENDER														
2014-15	San Jose	NHL	61	31	23	7	3588	155	5	2.59							
2015-16	Dallas	NHL	48	25	13	7	2654	118	3	2.67	5	1	3	237	13	0	3.29
2016-17	Dallas	NHL	37	12	12	4	1729	95	0	3.30							
	NHL Totals		423	227	125	51	24083	999	35	2.49	67	36	29	3899	180	2	2.77

Signed as a free agent by **Chicago**, May 5, 2008. Signed as a free agent by **San Jose**, September 2, 2010. Signed as a free agent by **Lahti** (Finland), October 5, 2012. Traded to **Dallas** by **San Jose** for Dallas' 7th round pick (Jake Kupsky) in 2015 NHL Draft, June 27, 2015. Signed as a free agent by **Pittsburgh**, July 1, 2017.

NILSSON, Anders (NIHL-suhn, AN-duhrz) VAN

Goaltender. Catches left. 6'5", 229 lbs. Born, Lulea, Sweden, March 19, 1990.
(NY Islanders' 4th pick, 62nd overall, in 2009 NHL Draft).

			Regular Season								Playoffs						
Season	Club	League	GP	W	L	O/T	Mins	GA	SO	Avg	GP	W	L	Mins	GA	SO	Avg
2004-05	Lulea HF Jr.	Swe-Jr.	1				24	4	0	9.90							
2007-08	Lulea HF U18	Swe-U18	11				625	31	0	2.97							
	Lulea HF Jr.	Swe-Jr.	16				898	31	2	2.07	1			60	6	0	6.00
2008-09	Lulea HF Jr.	Swe-Jr.	37				2199	75	4	2.05	6			357	14	1	2.35
	Lulea HF	Sweden	1				28	0	0	0.00							
	Kalix Ungdoms HC	Sweden-3	1				59	3	0	3.05							
2009-10	Lulea HF Jr.	Swe-Jr.	4				244	12	0	2.95							
	Lulea HF	Sweden	27				1383	61	2	2.65							
2010-11	Lulea HF	Sweden	31				1876	60	6	*1.92	13			827	27	0	1.96
2011-12	NY Islanders	NHL	4	1	2	0	218	10	1	2.75							
	Bridgeport	AHL	25	15	8	2	1441	58	1	2.42							
2012-13	Bridgeport	AHL	21	8	11	0	1208	60	1	2.98							
2013-14	NY Islanders	NHL	19	8	7	2	1101	57	0	3.11							
	Bridgeport	AHL	29	12	14	2	1684	79	2	2.81							
2014-15	Ak Bars Kazan	KHL	38	20	9	0	2248	64	5	1.71	20	13	7	1207	31	*6	*1.54
2015-16	Edmonton	NHL	26	10	12	2	1413	74	0	3.14							
	Bakersfield	AHL	2	2	0	0	120	4	0	2.01							
	St. Louis	NHL	3	0	1	0	87	4	0	2.76							
2016-17	Buffalo	NHL	26	10	10	4	1484	66	1	2.67							
	NHL Totals		78	29	32	8	4303	211	2	2.94							

Signed as a free agent by **Kazan** (KHL), May 26, 2014. Traded to **Chicago** by **NY Islanders** with T.J. Brennan and Ville Pokka for Nick Leddy and Kent Simpson, October 4, 2014. Traded to **Edmonton** by **Chicago** for Liam Coughlin, July 6, 2015. Traded to **St. Louis** by **Edmonton** for Niklas Lundstrom and St. Louis' 5th round pick (Graham McPhee) in 2016 NHL Draft, February 27, 2016. Traded to **Buffalo** by **St. Louis** for Buffalo's 5th round pick (David Noel) in 2017 NHL Draft, July 2, 2016. Signed as a free agent by **Vancouver**, July 1, 2017.

O'CONNOR, Matt (OH-CAW-nuhr, MAT) NSH

Goaltender. Catches left. 6'6", 202 lbs. Born, Sault Ste. Marie, ON, February 14, 1992.

			Regular Season								Playoffs						
Season	Club	League	GP	W	L	O/T	Mins	GA	SO	Avg	GP	W	L	Mins	GA	SO	Avg
2008-09	Upper Canada	ON-Jr.A	27	3	19	1	1428	147	1	6.18							
2009-10	Upper Canada	ON-Jr.A	23	7	12	2	1325	89	1	4.03							
	Burlington	ON-Jr.A	5	2	2	0	237	18	0	4.55	4	2	1	164	8	0	2.92
2010-11	Youngstown	USHL	29	10	16	2	1713	98	0	3.43							
2011-12	Youngstown	USHL	50	28	16	5	2886	146	1	3.04	6	3	3	326	20	0	3.68
2012-13	Boston University	H-East	19	8	8	2	1110	53	0	2.86							
2013-14	Boston University	H-East	22	7	9	4	1225	59	0	2.89							
2014-15	Boston University	H-East	35	*25	4	4	2088	76	1	2.18							
2015-16	Ottawa	NHL	1	0	1	0	58	3	0	3.10							
	Binghamton	AHL	34	10	20	3	1921	106	0	3.31							

2016-17	Binghamton	AHL	37	14	18	2	2064	111	0	3.23	....	....	....	....	....	....	....
	Wichita Thunder	ECHL	2	0	2	0	90	7	0	4.63	....	....	....	....	....	....	....
	NHL Totals		**1**	**0**	**1**	**0**	**58**	**3**	**0**	**3.10**	....	....	....	....	....	....	....

Hockey East Second All-Star Team (2015)

Signed as a free agent by **Ottawa**, May 9, 2015. Signed as a free agent by **Nashville**, July 1, 2017.

OETTINGER, Jake (AW-tihn-juhr, JAYK) DAL

Goaltender. Catches left. 6'4", 218 lbs. Born, Lakeville, MN, December 18, 1998.
(Dallas' 2nd pick, 26th overall, in 2017 NHL Draft).

			Regular Season								Playoffs						
Season	Club	League	GP	W	L	O/T	Mins	GA	SO	Avg	GP	W	L	Mins	GA	SO	Avg
2013-14	Lakeville North	High-MN	9	7	2	0	465	17	2	1.86	6	4	1	263	13	1	2.52
2014-15	USAHNTDP	USHL	20	5	10	0	1058	57	1	3.23	....	....	....	....	....	....	....
	USAHNTDP	U-17	11	7	3	1	603	14	1	1.39	....	....	....	....	....	....	....
	USAHNTDP	U-18	1	1	0	0	30	2	0	4.00	....	....	....	....	....	....	....
2015-16	USAHNTDP	USHL	15	11	3	0	858	32	1	2.24	....	....	....	....	....	....	....
	USAHNTDP	U-18	22	14	5	1	1180	49	0	2.49	....	....	....	....	....	....	....
2016-17	Boston University	H-East	35	21	11	3	2131	75	4	2.11	....	....	....	....	....	....	....

Hockey East All-Rookie Team (2017) • Hockey East Second All-Star Team (2017)

OLDHAM, Kristian (OHL-duhm, KRIHS-ch'yehn) T.B.

Goaltender. Catches left. 6'2", 203 lbs. Born, Anchorage, AK, June 25, 1997.
(Tampa Bay's 8th pick, 153rd overall, in 2015 NHL Draft).

			Regular Season								Playoffs						
Season	Club	League	GP	W	L	O/T	Mins	GA	SO	Avg	GP	W	L	Mins	GA	SO	Avg
2012-13	Alaska All-Stars	Minor-AK	5	5	0	0	225	6	2	1.20	....	....	....	....	....	....	....
	Alaska All-Stars	Other	11	7	3	0	468	20	3	2.00	....	....	....	....	....	....	....
	Kenai River	NAHL	1	1	0	0	60	5	0	5.00	....	....	....	....	....	....	....
2013-14	Kenai River	NAHL	23	11	6	4	1288	68	1	3.17	....	....	....	....	....	....	....
2014-15	Omaha Lancers	USHL	33	21	6	4	1853	77	1	2.38	3	0	3	176	8	0	2.73
2015-16	Omaha Lancers	USHL	31	12	15	4	1744	82	1	2.82	....	....	....	....	....	....	....
2016-17	Nebraska-Omaha	NCHC	10	5	3	1	568	32	0	3.38	....	....	....	....	....	....	....

OPILKA, Luke (oh-PIHL-kuh, LOOK) ST.L.

Goaltender. Catches left. 6'1", 192 lbs. Born, Effingham, IL, February 27, 1997.
(St. Louis' 5th pick, 146th overall, in 2015 NHL Draft).

			Regular Season								Playoffs						
Season	Club	League	GP	W	L	O/T	Mins	GA	SO	Avg	GP	W	L	Mins	GA	SO	Avg
2012-13	St.L. AAA Blues	T1EHL	22	18	2	1	1184	34	4	1.55	3	3	0	153	1	2	0.33
2013-14	USAHNTDP	USHL	18	5	9	1	845	65	0	4.62	....	....	....	....	....	....	....
	USAHNTDP	U-17	12	9	0	0	587	21	0	2.14	....	....	....	....	....	....	....
2014-15	USAHNTDP	USHL	15	11	1	2	824	34	1	2.48	....	....	....	....	....	....	....
	USAHNTDP	U-18	21	14	5	0	1188	59	2	2.98	....	....	....	....	....	....	....
2015-16	Kitchener Rangers	OHL	44	27	11	5	2552	115	3	2.70	1	0	0	10	3	0	18.75
2016-17	Kitchener Rangers	OHL	31	13	13	3	1779	106	0	3.58	5	1	4	278	23	0	4.96

ORTIO, Joni (OHR-tee-oh, YOH-nee)

Goaltender. Catches left. 6'1", 190 lbs. Born, Turku, Finland, April 16, 1991.
(Calgary's 5th pick, 171st overall, in 2009 NHL Draft).

			Regular Season								Playoffs						
Season	Club	League	GP	W	L	O/T	Mins	GA	SO	Avg	GP	W	L	Mins	GA	SO	Avg
2007-08	TuTo Turku U18	Fin-U18	7	1	6	0	392	34	0	5.20	....	....	....	....	....	....	....
	TuTo Turku Jr.	Fin-Jr.	5	1	3	0	302	16	0	3.18	....	....	....	....	....	....	....
2008-09	TPS Turku U18	Fin-U18	1	1	0	0	60	4	0	4.00	....	....	....	....	....	....	....
	TPS Turku Jr.	Fin-Jr.	26	18	8	0	1573	69	1	2.63	12	6	6	716	23	0	1.93
2009-10	Suomi U20	Finland-2	5	3	2	0	312	11	0	2.12	....	....	....	....	....	....	....
	TuTo Turku	Finland-2	9	5	4	0	546	27	0	2.96	....	....	....	....	....	....	....
	TPS Turku Jr.	Fin-Jr.	16	8	6	0	935	45	1	2.89	....	....	....	....	....	....	....
	TPS Turku	Finland	3	1	0	0	108	8	0	4.45	....	....	....	....	....	....	....
2010-11	TPS Turku	Finland	15	2	7	3	730	38	1	3.12	....	....	....	....	....	....	....
	Abbotsford Heat	AHL	1	0	1	0	60	6	0	6.03	....	....	....	....	....	....	....
2011-12	Abbotsford Heat	AHL	9	1	4	0	387	19	0	2.94	....	....	....	....	....	....	....
	TPS Turku	Finland	14	3	6	3	753	33	2	2.63	2	0	1	87	3	0	2.06
2012-13	HIFK Helsinki	Finland	*54	23	20	9	*3120	126	4	2.42	8	3	5	481	20	0	2.49
2013-14	**Calgary**	**NHL**	**9**	**4**	**4**	**0**	**501**	**21**	**0**	**2.51**	....	....	....	....	....	....	....
	Abbotsford Heat	AHL	37	27	8	0	2133	83	2	2.33	4	1	3	250	12	0	2.88
	Alaska Aces	ECHL	4	3	1	0	238	4	2	1.01	....	....	....	....	....	....	....
2014-15	**Calgary**	**NHL**	**6**	**4**	**2**	**0**	**333**	**14**	**1**	**2.52**	....	....	....	....	....	....	....
	Adirondack Flames	AHL	37	21	13	1	2095	94	4	2.69	....	....	....	....	....	....	....
2015-16	**Calgary**	**NHL**	**22**	**7**	**9**	**5**	**1197**	**55**	**1**	**2.76**	....	....	....	....	....	....	....
	Stockton Heat	AHL	20	9	9	0	1055	59	0	3.36	....	....	....	....	....	....	....
2016-17	Skelleftea AIK	Sweden	*42	*26	15	0	*2458	90	5	2.20	7	3	4	368	13	1	2.12
	NHL Totals		**37**	**15**	**15**	**5**	**2031**	**90**	**2**	**2.66**	....	....	....	....	....	....	....

AHL All-Rookie Team (2014)

Signed as a free agent by **Skelleftea** (Sweden), September 7, 2016.

PAJPACH, Maximilian (PIGH-PAHKH, max-ih-MIHL-y'uhn) COL

Goaltender. Catches left. 6', 207 lbs. Born, Poprad, Slovakia, January 4, 1996.
(Colorado's 6th pick, 174th overall, in 2014 NHL Draft).

			Regular Season								Playoffs						
Season	Club	League	GP	W	L	O/T	Mins	GA	SO	Avg	GP	W	L	Mins	GA	SO	Avg
2010-11	Poprad U18	Svk-U18	1	....	....	....	50	1	0	1.19	....	....	....	....	....	....	....
2011-12	Poprad U18	Svk-U18	34	....	....	....	1760	128	1	4.36	....	....	....	....	....	....	....
2012-13	Poprad U18	Svk-U18	37	....	....	....	2049	105	4	3.07	3	....	....	182	10	0	3.30
	HK SKP Poprad Jr.	Slovak-Jr.	1	....	....	....	19	0	0	0.00	....	....	....	....	....	....	....
2013-14	Slovakia U20	Slovakia	2	....	....	....	93	11	0	7.06	....	....	....	....	....	....	....
	Slovakia U18	Slovak-2	14	....	....	....	736	53	0	4.32	....	....	....	....	....	....	....
	Poprad U18	Svk-U18	....	....	....	....	....	....	....	....	2	....	....	120	4	0	2.00
	HK SKP Poprad Jr.	Slovak-Jr.	2	....	....	....	120	5	0	2.50	3	....	....	185	12	0	3.89
2014-15							DID NOT PLAY – INJURED										
2015-16	Tappara Jr.	Fin-Jr.	22	....	....	....	1112	70	....	3.77	....	....	....	....	....	....	....
2016-17	HK SKP Poprad Jr.	Slovak-Jr.	4	....	....	....	229	13	0	3.41	....	....	....	....	....	....	....
	MHC Martin "B"	Slovak-2	5	....	....	....	145	17	0	7.05	....	....	....	....	....	....	....
	HK Poprad	Slovakia	9	....	....	....	370	26	0	4.22	1	....	....	14	0	0	0.00

• Missed 2014-15 due to lower-body injury in training camp with Tappara Tampere Jr. (Fin.-Jr.), September 15, 2014.

PARSONS, Tyler (PAHR-suhnz, TIGH-luhr) CGY

Goaltender. Catches left. 6'1", 185 lbs. Born, Mt. Clemas, MI, September 18, 1997.
(Calgary's 2nd pick, 54th overall, in 2016 NHL Draft).

			Regular Season								Playoffs						
Season	Club	League	GP	W	L	O/T	Mins	GA	SO	Avg	GP	W	L	Mins	GA	SO	Avg
2012-13	Det. L.C. U16	HPHL	12	4	6	1	565	42	0	3.79	....	....	....	....	....	....	....
2013-14	Det. L.C. U16	HPHL	1	1	0	0	51	2	0	2.00	....	....	....	....	....	....	....
	Det. L.C. U18	HPHL	16	8	4	1	722	36	1	2.54	....	....	....	....	....	....	....
2014-15	London Knights	OHL	33	15	10	2	1647	97	0	3.53	8	....	....	....	....	....	....
2015-16	London Knights	OHL	49	37	9	3	2835	110	4	*2.33	*18	*16	2	*1086	39	1	*2.15
2016-17	London Knights	OHL	34	23	6	5	2000	79	4	2.37	14	7	4	870	39	1	2.69

OHL Second All-Star Team (2017)

PASQUALE, Eddie (pas-KWAHL-ee, EH-dee) EDM

Goaltender. Catches left. 6'3", 215 lbs. Born, Toronto, ON, November 20, 1990.
(Atlanta's 4th pick, 117th overall, in 2009 NHL Draft).

			Regular Season								Playoffs						
Season	Club	League	GP	W	L	O/T	Mins	GA	SO	Avg	GP	W	L	Mins	GA	SO	Avg
2005-06	Tor. Red Wings	GTHL	53	....	....	....	2385	98	5	1.84	....	....	....	....	....	....	....
2006-07	Wellington Dukes	ON-Jr.A	18	13	3	2	1091	35	1	1.92	....	....	....	....	....	....	....
	Belleville Bulls	OHL	7	4	1	0	367	19	0	3.11	....	....	....	....	....	....	....
2007-08	Belleville Bulls	OHL	10	4	4	2	558	27	1	2.90	....	....	....	....	....	....	....
	Saginaw Spirit	OHL	13	8	5	0	661	39	0	3.54	2	0	1	97	5	0	3.09
2008-09	Saginaw Spirit	OHL	*61	32	21	6	*3536	178	0	3.02	8	4	4	530	34	0	3.85
2009-10	Saginaw Spirit	OHL	51	27	17	5	2898	153	1	3.17	6	2	4	361	14	0	2.33
2010-11	Chicago Wolves	AHL	24	11	11	1	1372	67	1	2.93	....	....	....	....	....	....	....
	Gwinnett	ECHL	12	7	4	0	715	44	0	3.69	....	....	....	....	....	....	....
2011-12	St. John's IceCaps	AHL	38	23	12	1	2163	87	4	2.41	15	7	8	917	37	0	2.42
2012-13	St. John's IceCaps	AHL	43	15	23	4	2453	114	4	2.79	....	....	....	....	....	....	....
2013-14	St. John's IceCaps	AHL	31	17	13	1	1851	75	1	2.43	....	....	....	....	....	....	....
2014-15	Hershey Bears	AHL					DID NOT PLAY – INJURED										
2015-16	St. John's IceCaps	AHL	30	13	10	....	1531	67	0	2.62	....	....	....	....	....	....	....
	Brampton Beast	ECHL	12	*4	6	2	691	40	1	3.47	....	....	....	....	....	....	....
2016-17	Grand Rapids	AHL	29	15	9	3	1654	67	4	2.43	1	0	0	41	0	0	0.00

AHL All-Rookie Team (2012)

• Transferred to **Winnipeg** after **Atlanta** franchise relocated, June 21, 2011. Traded to **Washington** by **Winnipeg** with Winnipeg's 6th round pick (Steven Spinner) in 2014 NHL Draft for Washington's 6th round pick (Pavel Kraskovsky) in 2014 NHL Draft, Nashville's 7th round pick (previously acquired, Winnipeg selected Matt Ustaski) in 2014 NHL Draft and Washington's 7th round pick (Matteo Gennaro) in 2015 NHL Draft, June 28, 2014. Signed as a free agent by **Detroit**, July 1, 2015. Signed as a free agent by **Edmonton**, July 1, 2017.

PATERA, Jiri (pa-TAIR-uh, YIH-ree) VGK

Goaltender. Catches left. 6'1", 202 lbs. Born, Prague, , February 24, 1999.
(Las Vegas' 11th pick, 161st overall, in 2017 NHL Draft).

			Regular Season								Playoffs						
Season	Club	League	GP	W	L	O/T	Mins	GA	SO	Avg	GP	W	L	Mins	GA	SO	Avg
2013-14	Slavia U18	CzR-U18	....	....	....	....	....	....	....	....	1	....	....	18	1	0	3.33
2014-15	Slavia U18	CzR-U18	5	....	....	....	295	18	0	3.66	2	....	....	120	2	1	1.00
2015-16	Slavia U18	CzR-U18	40	....	....	....	2350	121	3	3.09	5	....	....	294	16	0	3.27
	HC Slavia Praha Jr.	CzRep-Jr.	1	....	....	....	60	5	0	5.00	....	....	....	....	....	....	....
2016-17	C. Budejovice U18	CzR-U18	4	....	....	....	239	9	0	2.26	....	....	....	....	....	....	....
	C. Budejovice Jr.	CzRep-Jr.	38	....	....	....	2257	98	2	2.61	8	....	....	448	20	1	2.68

PAVELEC, Ondrej (pah-vah-LEK, AWN-dray) NYR

Goaltender. Catches left. 6'3", 215 lbs. Born, Kladno, Czech., August 31, 1987.
(Atlanta's 2nd pick, 41st overall, in 2005 NHL Draft).

			Regular Season								Playoffs						
Season	Club	League	GP	W	L	O/T	Mins	GA	SO	Avg	GP	W	L	Mins	GA	SO	Avg
2003-04	HC Kladno U17	CzR-U17	38	....	....	....	2079	77	3	2.22	2	....	....	67	7	0	6.27
2004-05	HC Kladno Jr.	CzRep-Jr.	39	....	....	....	2218	85	7	2.30	10	....	....	587	24	1	2.45
	HK LEV Slany	CzRep-3	1	....	....	....	60	4	0	4.00	....	....	....	....	....	....	....
2005-06	Cape Breton	QMJHL	47	27	18	0	2578	108	3	2.51	9	4	5	507	19	0	*2.25
2006-07	Cape Breton	QMJHL	43	28	11	0	2335	98	1	*2.52	16	11	5	970	37	*2	*2.29
2007-08	**Atlanta**	**NHL**	**7**	**3**	**3**	**0**	**347**	**18**	**0**	**3.11**	....	....	....	....	....	....	....
	Chicago Wolves	AHL	52	33	16	3	3033	140	2	2.77	*24	*16	8	*1438	56	*2	2.34
2008-09	**Atlanta**	**NHL**	**12**	**3**	**7**	**0**	**599**	**36**	**0**	**3.61**	....	....	....	....	....	....	....
	Chicago Wolves	AHL	40	18	20	2	2417	104	3	2.58	....	....	....	....	....	....	....
2009-10	**Atlanta**	**NHL**	**42**	**14**	**18**	**7**	**2317**	**127**	**2**	**3.29**	....	....	....	....	....	....	....
	Czech Republic	Olympics					DID NOT PLAY – SPARE GOALTENDER										
2010-11	**Atlanta**	**NHL**	**58**	**21**	**23**	**9**	**3225**	**147**	**4**	**2.73**	....	....	....	....	....	....	....
	Chicago Wolves	AHL	1	0	1	0	58	3	0	3.10	....	....	....	....	....	....	....
2011-12	**Winnipeg**	**NHL**	**68**	**29**	**28**	**9**	**3932**	**191**	**4**	**2.91**	....	....	....	....	....	....	....
2012-13	Liberec	CzRep	14	4	10	0	772	45	0	3.50	....	....	....	....	....	....	....
	Pelicans Lahti	Finland	6	....	....	....	....	....	....	2.68	....	....	....	....	....	....	....
	Winnipeg	**NHL**	***44**	**21**	**20**	**3**	**2553**	**119**	**0**	**2.80**	....	....	....	....	....	....	....
2013-14	**Winnipeg**	**NHL**	**57**	**22**	**26**	**7**	**3248**	**163**	**1**	**3.01**	....	....	....	....	....	....	....
	Czech Republic	Olympics	4	....	....	....	209	10	0	2.87	....	....	....	....	....	....	....
2014-15	**Winnipeg**	**NHL**	**50**	**22**	**16**	**8**	**2838**	**108**	**5**	**2.28**	**4**	**0**	**4**	**241**	**15**	**0**	**3.73**
2015-16	**Winnipeg**	**NHL**	**33**	**13**	**13**	**4**	**1899**	**88**	**1**	**2.78**	....	....	....	....	....	....	....
2016-17	**Winnipeg**	**NHL**	**8**	**4**	**4**	**0**	**440**	**26**	**0**	**3.55**	....	....	....	....	....	....	....
	Manitoba Moose	AHL	18	8	7	2	1059	49	0	2.78	....	....	....	....	....	....	....
	NHL Totals		**379**	**152**	**158**	**47**	**21398**	**1023**	**17**	**2.87**	**4**	**0**	**4**	**241**	**15**	**0**	**3.73**

QMJHL All-Rookie Team (2006) • QMJHL First All-Star Team (2006, 2007) • QMJHL Defensive Rookie of the Year (2006)

• Transferred to **Winnipeg** after **Atlanta** franchise relocated, June 21, 2011. Signed as a free agent by **Liberec** (CzRep), September 21, 2012. Signed as a free agent by **Lahti** (Finland), November 26, 2012. Signed as a free agent by **NY Rangers**, July 1, 2017.

PEETERS, Wouter (PEE-tuhrz, WOO-tuhr) CHI

Goaltender. Catches left. 6'4", 205 lbs. Born, Turnhout, Belgium, July 31, 1998.
(Chicago's 4th pick, 83rd overall, in 2016 NHL Draft).

			Regular Season								Playoffs						
Season	Club	League	GP	W	L	O/T	Mins	GA	SO	Avg	GP	W	L	Mins	GA	SO	Avg
2012-13	Turnhout	Belgium	5	....	....	....	....	....	....	....	....	....	....	....	....	....	....
2013-14	EC Salzburg U18	RBHRCU18	1	....	....	....	....	....	....	6.46	....	....	....	....	....	....	....
2014-15	EC Salzburg U18	Aust-U18	17	....	....	....	....	....	....	2.43	7	....	....	....	....	....	2.41
	EC Salzburg U18	RBHRCU18	6	....	....	....	....	....	....	4.07	....	....	....	....	....	....	....
	EC Salzburg Jr.	Austria Jr.	1	....	....	....	31	1	0	1.94	....	....	....	....	....	....	....

2015-16	EC Salzburg U18	RBHRCU18	5	....	....	....	....	....	....	3.80	....	....	....	....	....	....	....
	EC Salzburg Jr. II	RBHS-Jr.	24	....	....	....	....	....	....	3.27	2	....	....	....	....	....	0.96
2016-17	Jokerit Helsinki Jr.	Fin-Jr.	23	....	....	....	1381	74	....	3.21	....	....	....	....	....	....	....

PERRY, Chase (PAIR-ee, CHAYS) DET

Goaltender. Catches left. 6'3", 189 lbs. Born, Grand Forks, ND, February 8, 1996.
(Detroit's 4th pick, 136th overall, in 2014 NHL Draft).

			Regular Season								Playoffs						
Season	Club	League	GP	W	L	O/T	Mins	GA	SO	Avg	GP	W	L	Mins	GA	SO	Avg
2010-11	Andover Huskies	High-MN	16	4	9	0	704	51	2	3.69	....	....	....	....	....	....	....
2011-12	Team Northwest	UMHSEL	1	1	0	0	60	3	0	3.00	....	....	....	....	....	....	....
	Metro Northwest	MEPDL	12	2	1	2	153	20	0	7.83	....	....	....	....	....	....	....
	Andover Huskies	High-MN	25	16	6	2	1219	64	0	2.68	3	2	1	145	11	0	3.87
2012-13	Apple Valley	High-MN	25	10	10	2	1132	60	3	2.70	1	0	1	51	3	0	3.00
	Team Northwest	UMHSEL	18	7	3	3	772	25	0	1.94	3	0	2	103	6	0	3.50
2013-14	Wenatchee Wild	NAHL	35	15	12	6	2048	80	2	2.34	10	5	5	656	20	*3	1.83
2014-15	Colorado College	NCHC	15	1	8	1	695	46	0	3.97	....	....	....	....	....	....	....
2015-16	Wenatchee Wild	BCHL	43	23	16	2	2431	106	5	2.62	9	4	5	525	24	1	2.74
2016-17	RPI Engineers	ECAC	28	6	20	1	1575	88	1	3.35	....	....	....	....	....	....	....

PETERS, Justin (PEE-tuhrz, JUHS-tihn) DAL

Goaltender. Catches left. 6'1", 210 lbs. Born, Blyth, ON, August 30, 1986.
(Carolina's 2nd pick, 38th overall, in 2004 NHL Draft).

			Regular Season								Playoffs						
Season	Club	League	GP	W	L	O/T	Mins	GA	SO	Avg	GP	W	L	Mins	GA	SO	Avg
2001-02	Huron-Perth	Minor-ON	17	11	2	4	810	32	1	1.89	13	9	4	285	30	1	2.31
2002-03	St. Michael's	OHL	23	6	10	1	1052	54	0	3.08	7	1	0	126	4	0	1.90
2003-04	St. Michael's	OHL	53	30	16	6	3149	139	4	2.65	18	10	8	1109	37	4	2.00
2004-05	St. Michael's	OHL	58	23	23	5	3150	146	3	2.78	10	4	4	524	25	0	2.86
2005-06	St. Michael's	OHL	20	10	6	3	1174	75	0	3.83	....	....	....	....	....	....	....
	Plymouth Whalers	OHL	35	19	15	1	2073	95	1	2.75	13	6	7	789	42	0	3.19
2006-07	Albany River Rats	AHL	34	10	18	0	1765	96	1	3.26	....	....	....	....	....	....	....
	Florida Everblades	ECHL	1	0	0	1	65	6	0	5.54	....	....	....	....	....	....	....
2007-08	Albany River Rats	AHL	11	7	3	0	645	29	0	2.70	....	....	....	....	....	....	....
	Florida Everblades	ECHL	31	18	10	2	1846	79	1	2.57	....	....	....	....	....	....	....
2008-09	Albany River Rats	AHL	56	19	30	4	3178	153	4	2.89	....	....	....	....	....	....	....
2009-10	**Carolina**	**NHL**	**9**	**6**	**3**	**0**	**488**	**23**	**0**	**2.83**	....	....	....	....	....	....	....
	Albany River Rats	AHL	47	26	18	2	2763	117	1	2.54	8	4	4	509	29	0	3.42
2010-11	**Carolina**	**NHL**	**12**	**3**	**5**	**1**	**648**	**43**	**0**	**3.98**	....	....	....	....	....	....	....
2011-12	**Carolina**	**NHL**	**7**	**2**	**3**	**2**	**387**	**16**	**1**	**2.48**	....	....	....	....	....	....	....
	Charlotte Checkers	AHL	28	10	13	2	1604	74	1	2.77	....	....	....	....	....	....	....
2012-13	Charlotte Checkers	AHL	37	22	12	1	2072	79	6	2.29	....	....	....	....	....	....	....
	Carolina	**NHL**	**19**	**4**	**11**	**1**	**954**	**55**	**1**	**3.46**	....	....	....	....	....	....	....
2013-14	**Carolina**	**NHL**	**21**	**7**	**9**	**4**	**1225**	**51**	**1**	**2.50**	....	....	....	....	....	....	....
	Charlotte Checkers	AHL	6	4	1	1	364	13	0	2.14	....	....	....	....	....	....	....
2014-15	**Washington**	**NHL**	**12**	**3**	**6**	**1**	**647**	**35**	**0**	**3.25**	....	....	....	....	....	....	....
	Hershey Bears	AHL	2	1	1	0	119	3	1	1.51	....	....	....	....	....	....	....
2015-16	Hershey Bears	AHL	37	17	8	7	2055	104	1	3.04	*20	*11	9	*1242	44	*2	2.13
2016-17	**Arizona**	**NHL**	**3**	**0**	**1**	**0**	**133**	**7**	**0**	**3.16**	....	....	....	....	....	....	....
	Tucson	AHL	12	5	6	0	590	41	0	4.17	....	....	....	....	....	....	....
	Texas Stars	AHL	31	13	16	2	1760	91	2	3.10	....	....	....	....	....	....	....
	NHL Totals		**83**	**25**	**38**	**9**	**4482**	**230**	**3**	**3.08**	....	....	....	....	....	....	....

Signed as a free agent by **Washington**, July 1, 2014. Signed as a free agent by **Arizona**, July 1, 2016. Traded to **Dallas** by **Arizona** with Justin Hache for Brendan Ranford and Branden Troock, February 1, 2017.

PETERSEN, Cal (PEE-tuhr-suhn, KAL) L.A.

Goaltender. Catches right. 6'2", 189 lbs. Born, Waterloo, IA, October 19, 1994.
(Buffalo's 7th pick, 129th overall, in 2013 NHL Draft).

			Regular Season								Playoffs						
Season	Club	League	GP	W	L	O/T	Mins	GA	SO	Avg	GP	W	L	Mins	GA	SO	Avg
2010-11	Chi. Americans	T1EHL	24	13	6	5	1244	53	4	2.30	....	....	....	....	....	....	....
2011-12	Chi. Americans	HPHL	12	3	6	2	680	35	0	3.09	....	....	....	....	....	....	....
	Topeka	NAHL	2	1	0	1	129	4	0	1.86	....	....	....	....	....	....	....
	Waterloo	USHL	5	3	1	0	265	13	0	2.94	....	....	....	....	....	....	....
2012-13	Waterloo	USHL	35	21	11	1	1937	96	3	2.97	4	2	2	211	15	0	4.26
2013-14	Waterloo	USHL	37	*27	7	6	2229	93	2	2.50	*12	*8	4	*800	30	0	2.37
2014-15	U. of Notre Dame	H-East	33	13	16	3	1892	79	*4	2.51	....	....	....	....	....	....	....
2015-16	U. of Notre Dame	H-East	37	19	11	7	2232	82	1	2.20	....	....	....	....	....	....	....
2016-17	U. of Notre Dame	H-East	*40	23	12	5	*2375	88	*6	2.22	....	....	....	....	....	....	....

USHL All-Rookie Team (2013) • USHL Second All-Star Team (2014) • Hockey East All-Rookie Team (2015) • Hockey East First All-Star Team (2017)

Signed as a free agent by **Los Angeles**, July 1, 2017.

PETRUZZELLI, Keith (peh-truh-ZEHL-ee, KEETH) DET

Goaltender. Catches left. 6'5", 180 lbs. Born, Wilbraham, MA, September 2, 1999.
(Detroit's 5th pick, 88th overall, in 2017 NHL Draft).

			Regular Season								Playoffs						
Season	Club	League	GP	W	L	O/T	Mins	GA	SO	Avg	GP	W	L	Mins	GA	SO	Avg
2013-14	Springfield Cath.	High-MA	22	13	2	5	834	17	5	....	3	2	1	135	6	1	....
	Bos. Jr. Bruins U16	USPHL	14	8	1	0	458	12	2	1.34	....	....	....	....	....	....	....
2014-15	Springfield Cath.	High-MA	22	16	0	2	945	21	4	....	3	2	1	141	5	1	....
	Springfield U16	Minor-MA	5	2	1	0	....	4	....	1.31	....	....	....	....	....	....	....
2015-16	Selects Acad. U18	Minor-CT	38	30	4	7	1987	70	11	1.76	....	....	....	....	....	....	....
	Selects Acad. U18	USPHL	26	21	1	0	1110	25	9	1.13	3	3	0	160	5	1	1.59
2016-17	Muskegon	USHL	35	22	10	1	2052	82	2	2.40	2	0	1	138	6	0	2.61

• Signed Letter of Intent to attend **Quinnipiac University** (ECAC) in fall of 2017.

PHILLIPS, Jamie (FIHL-ihps, JAY-mee) WPG

Goaltender. Catches left. 6'3", 185 lbs. Born, Caledonia, ON, March 24, 1993.
(Winnipeg's 6th pick, 190th overall, in 2012 NHL Draft).

			Regular Season								Playoffs						
Season	Club	League	GP	W	L	O/T	Mins	GA	SO	Avg	GP	W	L	Mins	GA	SO	Avg
2008-09	St. Cath. Falcons	Minor-ON	41	....	....	....	1845	57	1	2.61	....	....	....	....	....	....	....
	Brantford	ON-Jr.B	....	....	....	....	....	....	....	....	1	0	1	60	3	0	3.00
2009-10	Welland	ON-Jr.B	6	0	2	0	202	16	0	4.76	....	....	....	....	....	....	....
	Brantford	ON-Jr.B	3	2	0	0	140	7	0	3.00	....	....	....	....	....	....	....
2010-11	Pembroke	ON-Jr.A	33	25	6	1	1857	66	*6	*2.13	2	2	0	12	3	1	1.50
2011-12	Powell River Kings	BCHL	26	16	6	1	....	....	....	2.01	....	....	....	....	....	....	....
	Tor. Canadiens	ON-Jr.A	11	4	4	0	637	33	1	3.11	10	5	5	581	29	0	2.99
2012-13	Michigan Tech	WCHA	9	2	2	0	324	13	1	2.40	....	....	....	....	....	....	....
2013-14	Michigan Tech	WCHA	13	4	6	1	681	32	0	2.82	....	....	....	....	....	....	....
2014-15	Michigan Tech	WCHA	*41	*28	9	2	2417	70	*6	1.74	....	....	....	....	....	....	....
2015-16	Michigan Tech	WCHA	36	*23	8	5	*2193	72	3	1.97	....	....	....	....	....	....	....
2016-17	Manitoba Moose	AHL	11	2	4	2	585	29	0	2.97	....	....	....	....	....	....	....
	Tulsa Oilers	ECHL	31	19	10	2	1871	82	1	2.63	....	....	....	....	....	....	....

WCHA First All-Star Team (2015) • WCHA Second All-Star Team (2016)

PICKARD, Calvin (pih-KARD, KAL-vihn) VGK

Goaltender. Catches left. 6'1", 200 lbs. Born, Moncton, NB, April 15, 1992.
(Colorado's 2nd pick, 49th overall, in 2010 NHL Draft).

			Regular Season								Playoffs						
Season	Club	League	GP	W	L	O/T	Mins	GA	SO	Avg	GP	W	L	Mins	GA	SO	Avg
2007-08	Winnipeg Wild	MMHL	40	....	....	....	....	....	....	1.91	....	....	....	....	....	....	....
2008-09	Seattle	WHL	47	23	16	5	2694	137	3	3.05	5	1	4	297	15	0	3.03
2009-10	Seattle	WHL	*62	16	34	12	*3688	190	3	3.09	....	....	....	....	....	....	....
2010-11	Seattle	WHL	*68	27	33	8	*4013	225	1	3.36	....	....	....	....	....	....	....
2011-12	Seattle	WHL	*64	25	37	2	*3630	217	*5	3.59	....	....	....	....	....	....	....
	Lake Erie Monsters	AHL	2	1	0	0	77	4	0	3.12	....	....	....	....	....	....	....
2012-13	Lake Erie Monsters	AHL	47	20	19	5	2749	113	5	2.47	....	....	....	....	....	....	....
2013-14	Lake Erie Monsters	AHL	43	16	18	7	2445	116	2	2.85	....	....	....	....	....	....	....
2014-15	**Colorado**	**NHL**	**16**	**6**	**7**	**3**	**895**	**35**	**0**	**2.35**	....	....	....	....	....	....	....
	Lake Erie Monsters	AHL	50	23	17	9	2943	128	3	2.61	....	....	....	....	....	....	....
2015-16	**Colorado**	**NHL**	**20**	**7**	**6**	**1**	**985**	**42**	**1**	**2.56**	....	....	....	....	....	....	....
	San Antonio	AHL	21	9	8	4	1264	58	1	2.75	....	....	....	....	....	....	....
2016-17	**Colorado**	**NHL**	**50**	**15**	**31**	**2**	**2820**	**140**	**2**	**2.98**	....	....	....	....	....	....	....
	NHL Totals		**86**	**28**	**44**	**6**	**4700**	**217**	**3**	**2.77**	....	....	....	....	....	....	....

WHL West First All-Star Team (2010) • WHL West Second All-Star Team (2011)

Claimed by **Vegas** from **Colorado** in Expansion Draft, June 21, 2017.

POINT, Colton (POYNT, KOHL-tuhn) DAL

Goaltender. Catches left. 6'3", 219 lbs. Born, North Bay, ON, March 4, 1998.
(Dallas' 4th pick, 128th overall, in 2016 NHL Draft).

			Regular Season								Playoffs						
Season	Club	League	GP	W	L	O/T	Mins	GA	SO	Avg	GP	W	L	Mins	GA	SO	Avg
2013-14	North Bay Trappers	Minor-ON	15	....	....	....	883	51	0	3.47	2	....	....	132	9	0	4.09
	North Bay Trappers	NOJHL	1	0	0	0	6	3	0	28.35	....	....	....	....	....	....	....
2014-15	North Bay Trappers	Minor-ON	25	....	....	....	1456	70	2	2.85	8	....	....	523	21	0	2.41
	Powassan	NOJHL	3	0	2	0	122	16	79	7.86	2	0	2	48	10	0	12.62
2015-16	Carleton Place	ON-Jr.A	33	23	6	2	1891	68	7	*2.16	16	*12	4	1024	31	*5	*1.82
2016-17	Colgate	ECAC	10	2	5	2	589	24	0	2.45	....	....	....	....	....	....	....

PRICE, Carey (PRIGHS, KAIR-ee) MTL

Goaltender. Catches left. 6'3", 226 lbs. Born, Anahim Lake, BC, August 16, 1987.
(Montreal's 1st pick, 5th overall, in 2005 NHL Draft).

			Regular Season								Playoffs						
Season	Club	League	GP	W	L	O/T	Mins	GA	SO	Avg	GP	W	L	Mins	GA	SO	Avg
2002-03	Williams Lake	Minor-BC	18	....	....	....	1050	48	1	2.70	....	....	....	....	....	....	....
	Tri-City Americans	WHL	1	0	0	0	20	2	0	6.00	....	....	....	....	....	....	....
2003-04	Tri-City Americans	WHL	28	8	9	3	1362	54	1	2.38	8	5	3	470	19	0	2.43
2004-05	Tri-City Americans	WHL	63	24	31	8	3712	145	8	2.34	5	1	4	324	12	0	2.22
2005-06	Tri-City Americans	WHL	55	21	25	6	3072	147	3	2.87	5	1	4	302	12	0	2.39
2006-07	Tri-City Americans	WHL	46	30	13	1	2722	111	3	2.45	6	2	4	348	17	0	2.93
	Hamilton Bulldogs	AHL	2	1	1	0	117	3	0	1.53	*22	*15	6	*1314	45	*2	2.06
2007-08	**Montreal**	**NHL**	**41**	**24**	**12**	**3**	**2413**	**103**	**3**	**2.56**	**11**	**5**	**6**	**648**	**30**	**2**	**2.78**
	Hamilton Bulldogs	AHL	10	6	4	0	581	26	1	2.69	....	....	....	....	....	....	....
2008-09	**Montreal**	**NHL**	**52**	**23**	**16**	**10**	**3036**	**143**	**1**	**2.83**	**4**	**0**	**4**	**219**	**15**	**0**	**4.11**
2009-10	**Montreal**	**NHL**	**41**	**13**	**20**	**5**	**2358**	**109**	**0**	**2.77**	**4**	**0**	**1**	**135**	**8**	**0**	**3.56**
2010-11	**Montreal**	**NHL**	**72**	***38**	**28**	**6**	**4206**	**165**	**8**	**2.35**	**7**	**3**	**4**	**455**	**16**	**1**	**2.11**
2011-12	**Montreal**	**NHL**	**65**	**26**	**28**	**11**	**3944**	**160**	**4**	**2.43**	....	....	....	....	....	....	....
2012-13	**Montreal**	**NHL**	**39**	**21**	**13**	**4**	**2249**	**97**	**3**	**2.59**	**4**	**1**	**2**	**239**	**13**	**0**	**3.26**
2013-14	**Montreal**	**NHL**	**59**	**34**	**20**	**5**	**3464**	**134**	**6**	**2.32**	**12**	**8**	**4**	**739**	**29**	**1**	**2.35**
	Canada	Olympics	5	5	0	0	303	3	2	0.59	....	....	....	....	....	....	....
2014-15	**Montreal**	**NHL**	**66**	**44**	**16**	**6**	**3977**	**130**	**9**	**1.96**	**12**	**6**	**6**	**752**	**28**	**1**	**2.23**
2015-16	**Montreal**	**NHL**	**12**	**10**	**2**	**0**	**698**	**24**	**2**	**2.06**	....	....	....	....	....	....	....
2016-17	**Montreal**	**NHL**	**62**	**37**	**20**	**5**	**3708**	**138**	**3**	**2.23**	**6**	**2**	**4**	**387**	**12**	**0**	**1.86**
	NHL Totals		**509**	**270**	**175**	**55**	**30053**	**1203**	**39**	**2.40**	**60**	**25**	**31**	**3574**	**151**	**5**	**2.53**

WHL West First All-Star Team (2007) • WHL Goaltender of the Year (2007) • Canadian Major Junior First All-Star Team (2007) • Canadian Major Junior Goaltender of the Year (2007) • Jack A. Butterfield Trophy (AHL – Playoff MVP) (2007) • NHL All-Rookie Team (2008) • Best Goaltender – Olympics (2014) • NHL First All-Star Team (2015) • William M. Jennings Trophy (2015) (tied with Corey Crawford) • Vezina Trophy (2015) • Ted Lindsay Award (2015) • Hart Memorial Trophy (2015)

Played in NHL All-Star Game (2009, 2011, 2012, 2015, 2017)

• Missed majority of 2015-16 due to knee injury at NY Rangers, November 25, 2015.

PRIMEAU, Cayden (PREE-moh, KAY-dehn) MTL

Goaltender. Catches left. 6'3", 187 lbs. Born, Voorhees, NJ, November 8, 1999.
(Montreal's 7th pick, 199th overall, in 2017 NHL Draft).

			Regular Season								Playoffs						
Season	Club	League	GP	W	L	O/T	Mins	GA	SO	Avg	GP	W	L	Mins	GA	SO	Avg
2013-14	Comcast U16	AYHL	15	....	....	....	726	31	3	2.18	....	....	....	....	....	....	....
	Comcast U16	T1EHL	17	9	7	0	897	28	3	1.69	....	....	....	....	....	....	....
	Bishop Eustace	High-NJ	5	....	....	....	....	....	....	....	....	....	....	....	....	....	....
2014-15	Phi. Rev. U19	Minor-PA	31	....	....	....	....	....	....	2.02	....	....	....	....	....	....	....
	Bishop Eustace	High-NJ	11	....	....	....	....	26	....	....	....	....	....	....	....	....	....
2015-16	Phi. Revolution	EHL	29	16	5	0	1224	38	5	1.86	4	2	2	249	15	0	3.62
2016-17	Lincoln Stars	USHL	30	14	11	2	1616	85	1	3.16	....	....	....	....	....	....	....
	USAHNTDP	U-18	1	0	0	....	20	0	0	0.00	....	....	....	....	....	....	....

• Signed Letter of Intent to attend **Northeastern University** (Hockey East) in fall of 2017.

QUICK, Jonathan (KWIHK, JAWN-ah-thuhn) L.A.

Goaltender. Catches left. 6'1", 218 lbs. Born, Milford, CT, January 21, 1986.
(Los Angeles' 4th pick, 72nd overall, in 2005 NHL Draft).

			Regular Season								Playoffs						
Season	Club	League	GP	W	L	O/T	Mins	GA	SO	Avg	GP	W	L	Mins	GA	SO	Avg
2002-03	Avon Old Farms	High-CT	13	8	5	0	780	38	0	2.92	....	....	....	....	....	....	....
2003-04	Avon Old Farms	High-CT	21	20	1	0	1260	26	2	1.71	....	....	....	....	....	....	....
2004-05	Avon Old Farms	High-CT	27	25	2	0	1413	27	9	1.14	....	....	....	....	....	....	....
2005-06	Massachusetts	H-East	17	4	10	1	905	45	0	2.98	....	....	....	....	....	....	....
2006-07	Massachusetts	H-East	37	19	12	5	2224	80	3	2.16	....	....	....	....	....	....	....
2007-08	**Los Angeles**	**NHL**	**3**	**1**	**2**	**0**	**141**	**9**	**0**	**3.83**	....	....	....	....	....	....	....
	Manchester	AHL	19	11	8	0	1085	42	3	2.32	1	0	1	59	1	0	1.02
	Reading Royals	ECHL	38	23	11	3	2257	105	1	2.79	....	....	....	....	....	....	....
2008-09	**Los Angeles**	**NHL**	**44**	**21**	**18**	**2**	**2495**	**103**	**4**	**2.48**	....	....	....	....	....	....	....
	Manchester	AHL	14	6	5	2	827	37	0	2.68	....	....	....	....	....	....	....
2009-10	**Los Angeles**	**NHL**	**72**	**39**	**24**	**7**	**4258**	**180**	**4**	**2.54**	**6**	**2**	**4**	**360**	**21**	**0**	**3.50**
	United States	Olympics	DID NOT PLAY – SPARE GOALTENDER														
2010-11	**Los Angeles**	**NHL**	**61**	**35**	**22**	**3**	**3591**	**134**	**6**	**2.24**	**6**	**2**	**4**	**380**	**20**	**1**	**3.16**
2011-12 ♦	**Los Angeles**	**NHL**	**69**	**35**	**21**	**13**	**4099**	**133**	***10**	**1.95**	**20**	***16**	**4**	**1238**	**29**	***3**	***1.41**
2012-13	**Los Angeles**	**NHL**	**37**	**18**	**13**	**4**	**2134**	**87**	**1**	**2.45**	**18**	**9**	**9**	**1099**	**34**	***3**	**1.86**
2013-14 ♦	**Los Angeles**	**NHL**	**49**	**27**	**17**	**4**	**2904**	**100**	**6**	**2.07**	***26**	***16**	**10**	***1605**	**69**	***2**	**2.58**
	United States	Olympics	5	....	....	....	304	11	0	2.17	....	....	....	....	....	....	....
2014-15	**Los Angeles**	**NHL**	**72**	**36**	**22**	**13**	**4184**	**156**	**6**	**2.24**	....	....	....	....	....	....	....
2015-16	**Los Angeles**	**NHL**	***68**	**40**	**23**	**5**	***4034**	**149**	**5**	**2.22**	**5**	**1**	**4**	**296**	**15**	**0**	**3.04**
2016-17	**Los Angeles**	**NHL**	**17**	**8**	**5**	**2**	**931**	**35**	**2**	**2.26**	....	....	....	....	....	....	....
	NHL Totals		**492**	**260**	**167**	**53**	**28771**	**1086**	**44**	**2.26**	**81**	**46**	**35**	**4978**	**188**	**9**	**2.27**

Hockey East Second All-Star Team (2007) • NCAA East Second All-American Team (2007) • NHL Second All-Star Team (2012) • Conn Smythe Trophy (2012) • William M. Jennings Trophy (2014)

Played in NHL All-Star Game (2012, 2016)

RAANTA, Antti (RAHN-tah, AN-tee) ARI

Goaltender. Catches left. 6', 193 lbs. Born, Rauma, Finland, May 12, 1989.

			Regular Season								Playoffs						
Season	Club	League	GP	W	L	O/T	Mins	GA	SO	Avg	GP	W	L	Mins	GA	SO	Avg
2007-08	Lukko Rauma Jr.	Fin-Jr.	13	....	....	....	....	....	....	3.23	....	....	....	....	....	....	....
2008-09	Lukko Rauma	Finland	2	....	....	....	....	....	....	2.51	....	....	....	....	....	....	....
2009-10	Lukko Rauma Jr.	Fin-Jr.	15	....	....	....	....	....	....	2.20	4	....	....	....	....	....	1.51
	Lukko Rauma	Finland	15	6	7	1	836	37	2	2.66	....	....	....	....	....	....	....
2010-11	Lukko Rauma	Finland	20	....	....	....	....	....	....	2.37	2	....	....	....	....	....	4.28
2011-12	Assat Pori	Finland	38	....	....	....	....	....	....	2.23	3	....	....	....	....	....	3.07
2012-13	Assat Pori	Finland	45	21	10	11	2595	80	5	*1.85	*16	*12	4	*1039	23	*4	*1.33
2013-14	**Chicago**	**NHL**	**25**	**13**	**5**	**4**	**1397**	**63**	**1**	**2.71**	....	....	....	....	....	....	....
	Rockford IceHogs	AHL	14	7	5	0	677	32	0	2.83	....	....	....	....	....	....	....
2014-15	**Chicago**	**NHL**	**14**	**7**	**4**	**1**	**792**	**25**	**2**	**1.89**	....	....	....	....	....	....	....
	Rockford IceHogs	AHL	11	8	1	1	604	24	2	2.39	....	....	....	....	....	....	....
2015-16	**NY Rangers**	**NHL**	**25**	**11**	**6**	**2**	**1150**	**43**	**1**	**2.24**	**3**	**0**	**1**	**94**	**4**	**0**	**2.55**
2016-17	**NY Rangers**	**NHL**	**30**	**16**	**8**	**2**	**1617**	**61**	**4**	**2.26**	....	....	....	....	....	....	....
	NHL Totals		**94**	**47**	**23**	**9**	**4956**	**192**	**8**	**2.32**	**3**	**0**	**1**	**94**	**4**	**0**	**2.55**

Signed as a free agent by **Chicago**, June 3, 2013. Traded to **NY Rangers** by **Chicago** for Ryan Haggerty, June 27, 2015. Traded to **Arizona** by **NY Rangers** with Derek Stepan for Tony DeAngelo and Arizona's 1st round pick (Lias Andersson) in 2017 NHL Draft, June 23, 2017.

RASK, Tuukka (RASK, TU-kah) BOS

Goaltender. Catches left. 6'2", 185 lbs. Born, Savonlinna, Finland, March 10, 1987.
(Toronto's 1st pick, 21st overall, in 2005 NHL Draft).

			Regular Season								Playoffs						
Season	Club	League	GP	W	L	O/T	Mins	GA	SO	Avg	GP	W	L	Mins	GA	SO	Avg
2003-04	Ilves Tampere U18	Fin-U18	9	4	3	2	533	25	0	2.81	....	....	....	....	....	....	....
	Ilves Tampere Jr.	Fin-Jr.	30	12	10	7	1767	65	2	2.21	3	1	2	178	6	0	2.02
2004-05	Ilves Tampere Jr.	Fin-Jr.	26	17	3	4	1517	47	2	1.86	10	9	1	619	9	6	0.87
	Ilves Tampere	Finland	4	0	1	1	201	15	0	4.46	....	....	....	....	....	....	....
2005-06	Ilves Tampere Jr.	Fin-Jr.	1	....	....	....	60	2	0	2.00	....	....	....	....	....	....	....
	Suomi U20	Finland-2	3	....	....	....	179	6	0	2.01	....	....	....	....	....	....	....
	Ilves Tampere	Finland	30	12	8	7	1724	60	2	2.09	3	0	3	180	7	0	2.33
2006-07	Suomi U20	Finland-2	1	0	1	0	58	4	0	4.14	....	....	....	....	....	....	....
	Ilves Tampere	Finland	49	18	18	10	2872	114	3	2.38	7	2	5	397	20	0	3.02
2007-08	**Boston**	**NHL**	**4**	**2**	**1**	**1**	**184**	**10**	**0**	**3.26**	....	....	....	....	....	....	....
	Providence Bruins	AHL	45	27	13	2	2570	100	1	2.33	10	6	4	605	22	*2	2.18
2008-09	**Boston**	**NHL**	**1**	**1**	**0**	**0**	**60**	**0**	**1**	**0.00**	....	....	....	....	....	....	....
	Providence Bruins	AHL	57	33	20	4	3340	139	4	2.50	16	9	7	977	36	0	2.21
2009-10	**Boston**	**NHL**	**45**	**22**	**12**	**5**	**2562**	**84**	**5**	***1.97**	**13**	**7**	**6**	**829**	**36**	**0**	**2.61**
2010-11 ♦	**Boston**	**NHL**	**29**	**11**	**14**	**2**	**1594**	**71**	**2**	**2.67**	....	....	....	....	....	....	....
2011-12	**Boston**	**NHL**	**23**	**11**	**8**	**3**	**1289**	**44**	**3**	**2.05**	....	....	....	....	....	....	....
2012-13	HC Skoda Plzen	CzRep	17	....	....	....	993	35	1	2.11	....	....	....	....	....	....	....
	Boston	**NHL**	**36**	**19**	**10**	**5**	**2104**	**70**	***5**	**2.00**	**22**	**14**	**8**	**1466**	**46**	***3**	**1.88**
2013-14	**Boston**	**NHL**	**58**	**36**	**15**	**6**	**3386**	**115**	***7**	**2.04**	**12**	**7**	**5**	**753**	**25**	***2**	***1.99**
	Finland	Olympics	4	3	1	0	243	7	1	1.73	....	....	....	....	....	....	....
2014-15	**Boston**	**NHL**	**70**	**34**	**21**	**13**	**4063**	**156**	**3**	**2.30**	....	....	....	....	....	....	....
2015-16	**Boston**	**NHL**	**64**	**31**	**22**	**8**	**3678**	**157**	**4**	**2.56**	....	....	....	....	....	....	....
2016-17	**Boston**	**NHL**	**65**	**37**	**20**	**5**	**3680**	**137**	**8**	**2.23**	**6**	**2**	**4**	**402**	**15**	**0**	**2.24**
	NHL Totals		**395**	**204**	**123**	**48**	**22600**	**844**	**38**	**2.24**	**53**	**30**	**23**	**3450**	**122**	**5**	**2.12**

NHL First All-Star Team (2014) • Vezina Trophy (2014)

Played in NHL All-Star Game (2017)

Traded to **Boston** by **Toronto** for Andrew Raycroft, June 24, 2006. Signed as a free agent by **Plzen** (CzRep), September 25, 2012.

REDMOND, Angus (REHD-muhnd, AN-guhs) ANA

Goaltender. Catches left. 6'1", 200 lbs. Born, Langley, BC, October 3, 1995.

			Regular Season								Playoffs						
Season	Club	League	GP	W	L	O/T	Mins	GA	SO	Avg	GP	W	L	Mins	GA	SO	Avg
2011-12	Valley West Hawks	BCMML	25	....	....	....	....	....	....	4.24	....	....	....	....	....	....	....
2012-13	Port Moody	PJHL	19	4	12	0	1029	72	0	4.20	....	....	....	....	....	....	....
	Salmon Arm	BCHL	9	4	3	1	486	21	0	2.59	3	0	2	137	6	0	2.63
2013-14	Salmon Arm	BCHL	32	11	18	0	1768	98	0	3.33	....	....	....	....	....	....	....
2014-15	Salmon Arm	BCHL	50	24	22	3	2959	134	5	2.72	....	....	....	....	....	....	....
2015-16	Salmon Arm	BCHL	41	21	17	3	2324	118	3	3.05	6	2	4	354	21	0	3.56
2016-17	Michigan Tech	WCHA	38	*22	10	5	2273	70	4	1.85	....	....	....	....	....	....	....

WCHA All-Rookie Team (2017)

Signed as a free agent by **Anaheim**, March 31, 2017.

REIMER, James (RIGH-muhr, JAYMZ) FLA

Goaltender. Catches left. 6'2", 217 lbs. Born, Morweena, MB, March 15, 1988.
(Toronto's 3rd pick, 99th overall, in 2006 NHL Draft).

			Regular Season								Playoffs						
Season	Club	League	GP	W	L	O/T	Mins	GA	SO	Avg	GP	W	L	Mins	GA	SO	Avg
2003-04	Interlake Lightning	MMHL	27	....	....	....	....	....	1	2.85	....	....	....	....	....	....	....
2004-05	Interlake Lightning	MMHL	37	....	....	....	....	....	4	2.11	....	....	....	....	....	....	....
2005-06	Red Deer Rebels	WHL	34	7	18	3	1709	80	0	2.81	....	....	....	....	....	....	....
2006-07	Red Deer Rebels	WHL	60	26	23	7	3339	148	3	2.66	7	3	4	417	27	0	3.88
2007-08	Red Deer Rebels	WHL	30	8	15	4	1668	76	1	2.73	....	....	....	....	....	....	....
2008-09	Toronto Marlies	AHL	3	1	2	0	183	10	0	3.28	....	....	....	....	....	....	....
	Reading Royals	ECHL	22	10	7	3	1236	68	0	3.30	....	....	....	....	....	....	....
	South Carolina	ECHL	6	6	0	0	363	8	2	1.32	8	4	3	497	18	1	2.17
2009-10	Toronto Marlies	AHL	26	14	8	2	1520	57	1	2.25	....	....	....	....	....	....	....
2010-11	**Toronto**	**NHL**	**37**	**20**	**10**	**5**	**2080**	**90**	**3**	**2.60**	....	....	....	....	....	....	....
	Toronto Marlies	AHL	15	9	5	1	858	37	3	2.59	....	....	....	....	....	....	....
2011-12	**Toronto**	**NHL**	**34**	**14**	**14**	**4**	**1879**	**97**	**3**	**3.10**	....	....	....	....	....	....	....
2012-13	**Toronto**	**NHL**	**33**	**19**	**8**	**5**	**1856**	**76**	**4**	**2.46**	**7**	**3**	**4**	**438**	**21**	**0**	**2.88**
2013-14	**Toronto**	**NHL**	**36**	**12**	**16**	**1**	**1785**	**98**	**1**	**3.29**	....	....	....	....	....	....	....
2014-15	**Toronto**	**NHL**	**35**	**9**	**16**	**1**	**1767**	**93**	**0**	**3.16**	....	....	....	....	....	....	....
2015-16	**Toronto**	**NHL**	**32**	**11**	**12**	**7**	**1809**	**75**	**0**	**2.49**	....	....	....	....	....	....	....
	San Jose	**NHL**	**8**	**6**	**2**	**0**	**481**	**13**	**3**	**1.62**	**1**	**0**	**0**	**29**	**1**	**0**	**2.07**
2016-17	**Florida**	**NHL**	**43**	**18**	**16**	**5**	**2325**	**98**	**3**	**2.53**	....	....	....	....	....	....	....
	NHL Totals		**258**	**109**	**94**	**28**	**13982**	**640**	**17**	**2.75**	**8**	**3**	**4**	**467**	**22**	**0**	**2.83**

ECHL Playoff MVP (2009)

Traded to **San Jose** by **Toronto** with Jeremy Morin for Alex Stalock, Ben Smith and San Jose's 3rd round pick in 2018 NHL Draft February 28, 2016. Signed as a free agent by **Florida**, July 1, 2016.

RINNE, Pekka (RIH-nay, PEH-kuh) NSH

Goaltender. Catches left. 6'5", 217 lbs. Born, Kempele, Finland, November 3, 1982.
(Nashville's 10th pick, 258th overall, in 2004 NHL Draft).

			Regular Season								Playoffs						
Season	Club	League	GP	W	L	O/T	Mins	GA	SO	Avg	GP	W	L	Mins	GA	SO	Avg
2000-01	Karpat Oulu Jr.	Fin-Jr.	20	9	4	5	1148	63	0	3.29	....	....	....	....	....	....	....
2001-02	Karpat Oulu Jr.	Fin-Jr.	30	19	7	3	1724	61	3	2.12	3	1	2	184	10	1	3.26
2002-03	Karpat Oulu Jr.	Fin-Jr.	25	14	8	3	1479	48	5	1.95	4	1	3	238	7	0	1.76
	Karpat Oulu	Finland	1	0	1	0	60	7	0	7.00	....	....	....	....	....	....	....
2003-04	Karpat Oulu	Finland	14	5	4	4	824	41	0	2.99	2	1	0	22	0	0	0.00
	Hokki Kajaani	Finland-2	8	5	2	1	463	16	2	2.07	....	....	....	....	....	....	....
2004-05	Karpat Oulu	Finland	10	8	0	1	571	16	0	1.68	....	....	....	....	....	....	....
2005-06	**Nashville**	**NHL**	**2**	**1**	**1**	**0**	**63**	**4**	**0**	**3.81**	....	....	....	....	....	....	....
	Milwaukee	AHL	51	30	18	2	2960	139	2	2.82	14	10	4	734	35	3	2.86
2006-07	Milwaukee	AHL	29	15	7	6	1670	65	3	2.34	4	0	4	247	12	0	2.91
2007-08	**Nashville**	**NHL**	**1**	**0**	**0**	**0**	**29**	**0**	**0**	**0.00**	....	....	....	....	....	....	....
	Milwaukee	AHL	*65	*36	24	3	*3840	158	5	2.47	6	2	4	358	15	1	2.51
2008-09	**Nashville**	**NHL**	**52**	**29**	**15**	**4**	**2999**	**119**	**7**	**2.38**	....	....	....	....	....	....	....
2009-10	**Nashville**	**NHL**	**58**	**32**	**16**	**5**	**3246**	**137**	**7**	**2.53**	**6**	**2**	**4**	**358**	**16**	**0**	**2.68**
2010-11	**Nashville**	**NHL**	**64**	**33**	**22**	**9**	**3789**	**134**	**6**	**2.12**	**12**	**6**	**6**	**748**	**32**	**0**	**2.57**
2011-12	**Nashville**	**NHL**	***73**	***43**	**18**	**8**	**4169**	**166**	**5**	**2.39**	**10**	**5**	**5**	**609**	**21**	**1**	**2.07**
2012-13	Dynamo Minsk	KHL	22	9	11	0	1327	68	1	3.08	....	....	....	....	....	....	....
	Nashville	**NHL**	**43**	**15**	**16**	**8**	**2444**	**99**	***5**	**2.43**	....	....	....	....	....	....	....
2013-14	**Nashville**	**NHL**	**24**	**10**	**10**	**3**	**1367**	**63**	**2**	**2.77**	....	....	....	....	....	....	....
	Milwaukee	AHL	2	2	0	0	121	2	0	0.99	....	....	....	....	....	....	....
2014-15	**Nashville**	**NHL**	**64**	**41**	**17**	**6**	**3851**	**140**	**4**	**2.18**	**6**	**2**	**4**	**425**	**19**	**0**	**2.68**
2015-16	**Nashville**	**NHL**	**66**	**34**	**21**	**10**	**3895**	**161**	**4**	**2.48**	**14**	**7**	**7**	**866**	**38**	**0**	**2.63**
2016-17	**Nashville**	**NHL**	**61**	**31**	**19**	**9**	**3568**	**144**	**3**	**2.42**	***22**	***14**	**8**	***1289**	**42**	**2**	**1.96**
	NHL Totals		**508**	**269**	**155**	**62**	**29420**	**1167**	**43**	**2.38**	**70**	**36**	**34**	**4295**	**168**	**3**	**2.35**

NHL Second All-Star Team (2011)

Played in NHL All-Star Game (2016)

Signed as a free agent by **Minsk** (KHL), September 25, 2012.

RITTICH, David (RIH-TIHK, DAY-vihd) CGY

Goaltender. Catches left. 6'3", 198 lbs. Born, Jihlava, Czech Rep., August 19, 1992.

			Regular Season								Playoffs						
Season	Club	League	GP	W	L	O/T	Mins	GA	SO	Avg	GP	W	L	Mins	GA	SO	Avg
2012-13	HC Dukla Jihlava	CzRep-2	24	....	....	....	....	2.26	....	....	2	....	....	....	2.67	....	....
2013-14	HC Dukla Jihlava	CzRep-2	41	....	....	....	....	2.07	....	....	9	....	....	....	2.11	....	....
2014-15	BK Mlada Boleslav	CzRep	23	8	15	0	1218	64	0	3.15	....	....	....	....	....	....	....
	HC Dukla Jihlava	CzRep-2	7	....	....	....	....	....	....	1.52	6	....	....	....	....	....	2.41
2015-16	BK Mlada Boleslav	CzRep	*48	....	....	....	*2849	120	5	2.53	10	....	....	642	34	*1	3.18
2016-17	**Calgary**	**NHL**	**1**	**0**	**0**	**0**	**20**	**1**	**0**	**3.00**	....	....	....	....	....	....	....
	Stockton Heat	AHL	31	15	11	4	1774	67	5	2.27	4	2	1	167	8	0	2.88
	NHL Totals		**1**	**0**	**0**	**0**	**20**	**1**	**0**	**3.00**	....	....	....	....	....	....	....

Signed as a free agent by **Calgary**, June 13, 2016.

ROBINSON, Mike (RAW-bihn-suhn, MIGHK) S.J.

Goaltender. Catches left. 6'3", 195 lbs. Born, Bedford, NH, March 27, 1997.
(San Jose's 3rd pick, 86th overall, in 2015 NHL Draft).

			Regular Season								Playoffs						
Season	Club	League	GP	W	L	O/T	Mins	GA	SO	Avg	GP	W	L	Mins	GA	SO	Avg
2013-14	Bos. Jr. Rangers	MtJHL	25	....	....	....	1417	....	....	1.99	....	....	....	....	....	....	....
2014-15	Bos. Jr. Rangers	EHL	8	4	4	0	459	18	0	2.35	....	....	....	....	....	....	....
	Lawrence	High-MA	23	....	....	....	1229	80	....	3.52	....	....	....	....	....	....	....
2015-16	Boston Jr. Bruins	USPHL	12	7	5	0	667	33	0	2.97	1	0	0	8	0	0	0.00
2016-17	Springfield-IL	NAHL	25	11	10	2	1425	71	0	2.99	....	....	....	....	....	....	....

• Signed Letter of Intent to attend **University of New Hampshire** (Hockey East) in fall of 2017.

RUUSU, Markus (ROO-SOO, MAHR-kuhs) DAL

Goaltender. Catches left. 6'2", 175 lbs. Born, Jamsa, Finland, August 23, 1997.
(Dallas' 5th pick, 163rd overall, in 2015 NHL Draft).

			Regular Season								Playoffs						
Season	Club	League	GP	W	L	O/T	Mins	GA	SO	Avg	GP	W	L	Mins	GA	SO	Avg
2013-14	JyP Jyvaskyla U18	Fin-U18	33	....	....	....	1979	121	....	3.67	....	....	....	....	....	....	....
2014-15	JyP Jyvaskyla U18	Fin-U18	34	....	....	....	....	101	....	....	7	....	....	....	13	....	....
	JyP Jyvaskyla Jr.	Fin-Jr.	12	....	....	....	649	32	....	2.96	....	....	....	....	....	....	....
2015-16	JyP Jyvaskyla Jr.	Fin-Jr.	18	....	....	....	961	64	....	3.99	....	....	....	....	....	....	....
	JYP-Akatemia	Finland-2	20	....	....	....	1164	60	....	3.09	....	....	....	....	....	....	....
	JyP Jyvaskyla U18	Fin-U18	....	....	....	....	....	....	....	....	5	....	....	320	15	....	2.81
2016-17	KooKoo Kouvola	Finland	2	0	1	1	121	2	1	0.99	....	....	....	....	....	....	....
	JYP Jyvaskyla	Finland	5	2	1	2	309	10	1	1.94	....	....	....	....	....	....	....
	JYP-Akatemia	Finland-2	25	....	....	....	1470	84	....	3.43	....	....	....	....	....	....	....

SAMSONOV, Ilya (sam-SAWN-awv, ihl-YAH) WSH

Goaltender. Catches left. 6'3", 200 lbs. Born, Magnitogorsk, Russia, February 22, 1997.
(Washington's 1st pick, 22nd overall, in 2015 NHL Draft).

			Regular Season								Playoffs						
Season	Club	League	GP	W	L	O/T	Mins	GA	SO	Avg	GP	W	L	Mins	GA	SO	Avg
2014-15	Magnitogorsk	KHL	1	0	0	0	22	2	0	5.50	....	....	....	....	....	....	....
	Magnitogorsk Jr.	Russia-Jr.	18	11	4	0	1039	46	2	2.66	2	1	1	127	6	0	2.83
2015-16	Magnitogorsk Jr.	Russia-Jr.	5	5	0	0	300	9	0	1.80	1	0	1	64	3	0	2.82
	Magnitogorsk	KHL	19	6	4	0	853	29	2	2.04	6	2	2	263	10	0	2.29
2016-17	Magnitogorsk	KHL	27	15	3	0	1128	40	2	2.13	3	1	0	94	2	0	1.28

SANDSTROM, Felix (SAND-struhm, FEH-lihx) PHI

Goaltender. Catches left. 6'2", 196 lbs. Born, Gavle, Sweden, January 12, 1997.
(Philadelphia's 3rd pick, 70th overall, in 2015 NHL Draft).

			Regular Season								Playoffs						
Season	Club	League	GP	W	L	O/T	Mins	GA	SO	Avg	GP	W	L	Mins	GA	SO	Avg
2011-12	Brynas U18	Swe-U18	1	....	....	....	60	1	0	1.00	....	....	....	....	....	....	....
2012-13	Brynas U18	Swe-U18	28	23	5	0	1706	49	9	1.72	1	0	1	59	4	0	4.10
2013-14	Brynas U18	Swe-U18	26	19	7	0	1568	52	3	1.99	5	3	2	310	10	1	1.94
	Brynas IF Gavle Jr.	Swe-Jr.	6	2	4	0	323	18	0	3.34	....	....	....	....	....	....	....
2014-15	Brynas U18	Swe-U18	4	3	1	0	238	10	1	2.52	4	4	0	244	8	0	1.96
	Brynas IF Gavle Jr.	Swe-Jr.	14	10	4	0	822	36	0	2.63	1	0	1	70	3	0	2.57
	Brynas IF Gavle	Sweden	2	1	0	0	55	1	0	1.09	1	0	0	20	1	0	3.00
2015-16	Brynas IF Gavle Jr.	Swe-Jr.	3	3	0	0	181	8	0	2.65	2	0	2	119	10	0	5.05
	Brynas IF Gavle	Sweden	25	10	14	0	1471	64	0	2.61	2	1	1	117	7	0	3.60
2016-17	Brynas IF Gavle	Sweden	22	14	7	0	1282	48	2	2.25	13	6	4	594	28	2	2.83

SAROS, Juuse (SA-ruhs, YOO-seh) NSH

Goaltender. Catches left. 5'11", 180 lbs. Born, Forssa, Finland, April 19, 1995.
(Nashville's 4th pick, 99th overall, in 2013 NHL Draft).

			Regular Season								Playoffs						
Season	Club	League	GP	W	L	O/T	Mins	GA	SO	Avg	GP	W	L	Mins	GA	SO	Avg
2011-12	HPK U18	Fin-U18	14	11	3	0	844	19	2	1.35	....	....	....	....	....	....	....
	HPK Jr.	Fin-Jr.	31	20	10	0	1804	76	2	2.53	10	6	4	630	22	0	2.10
2012-13	HPK Jr.	Fin-Jr.	37	24	13	0	2220	69	4	1.86	11	9	2	661	23	0	2.09
2013-14	HPK Hameenlinna	Finland	44	17	16	9	2625	77	7	1.76	6	2	4	367	14	0	2.29
2014-15	HPK Hameenlinna	Finland	47	13	18	16	2834	101	6	2.14	....	....	....	....	....	....	....
2015-16	**Nashville**	**NHL**	**1**	**0**	**1**	**0**	**58**	**3**	**0**	**3.10**	....	....	....	....	....	....	....
	Milwaukee	AHL	38	29	8	0	2248	84	4	2.24	2	0	2	117	5	0	2.57
2016-17	**Nashville**	**NHL**	**21**	**10**	**8**	**3**	**1200**	**47**	**1**	**2.35**	**2**	**0**	**0**	**57**	**3**	**0**	**3.16**
	Milwaukee	AHL	15	13	2	0	903	28	1	1.86	....	....	....	....	....	....	....
	NHL Totals		**22**	**10**	**9**	**3**	**1258**	**50**	**1**	**2.38**	**2**	**0**	**0**	**57**	**3**	**0**	**3.16**

AHL All-Rookie Team (2016)

SATERI, Harri (SA-teh-ree, HAR-ree) FLA

Goaltender. Catches left. 6'1", 205 lbs. Born, Toijala, Finland, December 29, 1989.
(San Jose's 3rd pick, 106th overall, in 2008 NHL Draft).

			Regular Season								Playoffs						
Season	Club	League	GP	W	L	O/T	Mins	GA	SO	Avg	GP	W	L	Mins	GA	SO	Avg
2005-06	HPK U18	Fin-U18	27	....	....	....	1515	66	5	2.61	2	....	....	118	10	0	5.08
	HPK Jr.	Fin-Jr.	1	....	....	....	50	3	0	3.60	....	....	....	....	....	....	....
2006-07	Tappara U18	Fin-U18	2	....	....	....	119	4	0	2.02	....	....	....	....	....	....	....
	Tappara Jr.	Fin-Jr.	23	....	....	....	1346	59	2	2.63	10	....	....	614	31	0	3.03
2007-08	Tappara Jr.	Fin-Jr.	34	13	17	0	2048	102	1	2.99	3	0	3	178	8	0	2.70
2008-09	Suomi U20	Finland-2	4	2	2	0	247	12	0	2.91	....	....	....	....	....	....	....
2009-10	Tappara Tampere	Finland	49	21	22	4	2836	129	2	2.73	9	4	5	572	27	0	2.83
2010-11	Tappara Tampere	Finland	37	9	19	8	2147	106	2	2.96	....	....	....	....	....	....	....
	Worcester Sharks	AHL	7	1	3	1	351	15	0	2.56	....	....	....	....	....	....	....
2011-12	Worcester Sharks	AHL	38	15	20	1	2116	101	2	2.86	....	....	....	....	....	....	....
2012-13	Worcester Sharks	AHL	39	14	21	3	2201	106	1	2.89	....	....	....	....	....	....	....
2013-14	Worcester Sharks	AHL	45	18	24	2	2646	130	1	2.95	....	....	....	....	....	....	....
2014-15	Podolsk	KHL	45	17	21	0	2603	128	3	2.95	....	....	....	....	....	....	....
2015-16	Podolsk	KHL	45	15	23	0	2565	104	4	2.43	....	....	....	....	....	....	....
2016-17	Podolsk	KHL	42	20	16	0	2424	101	2	2.50	4	0	4	216	20	0	5.56

Signed as a free agent by **Podolsk** (KHL), May 19, 2014. Signed as a free agent by **Florida**, July 1, 2017.

SCHNEIDER, Cory (SHNIGH-duhr, KOHR-ee) N.J.

Goaltender. Catches left. 6'3", 200 lbs. Born, Marblehead, MA, March 18, 1986.
(Vancouver's 1st pick, 26th overall, in 2004 NHL Draft).

			Regular Season								Playoffs						
Season	Club	League	GP	W	L	O/T	Mins	GA	SO	Avg	GP	W	L	Mins	GA	SO	Avg
2002-03	Andover	High-MA	23	13	7	2	1385	39	3	1.69	....	....	....	....	....	....	....
2003-04	Andover	High-MA	24	17	5	2	1336	32	6	1.42	....	....	....	....	....	....	....
	USAHNTDP	U-18	10	9	1	0	559	15	1	1.61	....	....	....	....	....	....	....
	USAHNTDP	NAHL	2	2	0	0	120	6	0	3.00	....	....	....	....	....	....	....
2004-05	Boston College	H-East	18	13	1	4	1102	35	1	1.90	....	....	....	....	....	....	....
2005-06	Boston College	H-East	*39	*24	13	2	*2362	83	*8	2.11	....	....	....	....	....	....	....
2006-07	Boston College	H-East	*42	*29	12	1	*2517	90	6	2.15	....	....	....	....	....	....	....
2007-08	Manitoba Moose	AHL	36	21	12	2	2054	78	3	2.28	6	1	4	375	12	0	1.92
2008-09	**Vancouver**	**NHL**	**8**	**2**	**4**	**1**	**355**	**20**	**0**	**3.38**	....	....	....	....	....	....	....
	Manitoba Moose	AHL	40	28	10	1	2324	79	5	*2.04	*22	14	7	1315	47	0	2.15
2009-10	**Vancouver**	**NHL**	**2**	**0**	**1**	**0**	**79**	**5**	**0**	**3.80**	....	....	....	....	....	....	....
	Manitoba Moose	AHL	60	35	23	2	*3557	149	4	2.51	6	2	4	366	19	0	3.12
2010-11	**Vancouver**	**NHL**	**25**	**16**	**4**	**2**	**1372**	**51**	**1**	**2.23**	**5**	**0**	**0**	**163**	**7**	**0**	**2.58**
2011-12	**Vancouver**	**NHL**	**33**	**20**	**8**	**1**	**1833**	**60**	**3**	**1.96**	**3**	**1**	**2**	**183**	**4**	**0**	**1.31**
2012-13	HC Ambri-Piotta	Swiss	8	4	4	0	485	26	0	3.22	....	....	....	....	....	....	....
	Vancouver	**NHL**	**30**	**17**	**9**	**4**	**1733**	**61**	***5**	**2.11**	**2**	**0**	**2**	**117**	**9**	**0**	**4.62**
2013-14	**New Jersey**	**NHL**	**45**	**16**	**15**	**12**	**2680**	**88**	**3**	**1.97**	....	....	....	....	....	....	....
2014-15	**New Jersey**	**NHL**	**69**	**26**	**31**	**9**	**3924**	**148**	**5**	**2.26**	....	....	....	....	....	....	....
2015-16	**New Jersey**	**NHL**	**58**	**27**	**25**	**6**	**3412**	**122**	**4**	**2.15**	....	....	....	....	....	....	....
2016-17	**New Jersey**	**NHL**	**60**	**20**	**27**	**11**	**3473**	**163**	**2**	**2.82**	....	....	....	....	....	....	....
	NHL Totals		**330**	**144**	**124**	**46**	**18861**	**718**	**23**	**2.28**	**10**	**1**	**4**	**463**	**20**	**0**	**2.59**

Hockey East All-Rookie Team (2005) (co-winners - Kevin Regan and Peter Vetri) • Hockey East Second All-Star Team (2006) • NCAA East First All-American Team (2006) • AHL First All-Star Team (2009) • Harry "Hap" Holmes Memorial Award (AHL – fewest goals against) (2009) (shared with Karl Goehring) • Aldege "Baz" Bastien Memorial Award (AHL – Outstanding Goaltender) (2009) • William M. Jennings Trophy (2011) (shared with Roberto Luongo)

Played in NHL All-Star Game (2016)

Signed as a free agent by **Ambri-Piotta** (Swiss), November 28, 2012. Traded to **New Jersey** by **Vancouver** for New Jersey's 1st round pick (Bo Horvat) in 2013 NHL Draft, June 30, 2013.

SCHNEIDER, Nick (SHNIGH-duhr, NIHK) CGY

Goaltender. Catches left. 6'2", 170 lbs. Born, Leduc, AB, July 21, 1997.

			Regular Season								Playoffs						
Season	Club	League	GP	W	L	O/T	Mins	GA	SO	Avg	GP	W	L	Mins	GA	SO	Avg
2012-13	PAC Saints	Minor-AB	....	6	7	1	932	43	1	2.77	3	3	0	180	3	1	1.00
2013-14	Leduc Oil Kings	AMHL	....	1	2	1	239	13	0	3.26	....	....	....	....	....	....	....
	Regina Pats	WHL	9	2	2	2	438	26	0	3.56	....	....	....	....	....	....	....
	Medicine Hat	WHL	8	6	0	0	380	9	1	142.00	....	....	....	....	....	....	....
2014-15	Medicine Hat	WHL	27	15	7	1	1426	67	0	2.82	....	....	....	....	....	....	....
2015-16	Medicine Hat	WHL	50	21	26	1	2771	167	2	3.62	....	....	....	....	....	....	....
	Stockton Heat	AHL	9	4	5	0	536	35	0	3.92	....	....	....	....	....	....	....
2016-17	Medicine Hat	WHL	47	32	11	1	2588	148	0	3.43	....	....	....	....	....	....	....

Signed as a free agent by **Calgary**, September 23, 2015.

SCOTT, Ian (SKAWT, EE-uhn) TOR

Goaltender. Catches left. 6'3", 169 lbs. Born, Calgary, AB, November 1, 1999.
(Toronto's 3rd pick, 110th overall, in 2017 NHL Draft).

			Regular Season								Playoffs						
Season	Club	League	GP	W	L	O/T	Mins	GA	SO	Avg	GP	W	L	Mins	GA	SO	Avg
2014-15	Calgary Northstars	AMHL	....	4	7	5	1030	46	1	2.75	....	....	....	....	....	....	....
2015-16	Prince Albert	WHL	26	13	9	2	1316	71	1	3.24	1	0	0	33	3	0	5.52
2016-17	Prince Albert	WHL	50	12	31	3	2649	163	2	3.69	....	....	....	....	....	....	....

SCRIVENS, Ben (SKRIH-vehnz, BEHN)

Goaltender. Catches left. 6'2", 181 lbs. Born, Spruce Grove, AB, September 11, 1986.

			Regular Season								Playoffs						
Season	Club	League	GP	W	L	O/T	Mins	GA	SO	Avg	GP	W	L	Mins	GA	SO	Avg
2004-05	Drayton Valley	AJHL	1	0	1	0	59	3	0	3.03	....	....	....	....	....	....	....
	Calgary Canucks	AJHL	16	7	3	3	857	43	1	3.01	....	....	....	....	....	....	....
2005-06	Spruce Grove	AJHL	45	27	12	2	2469	100	3	2.43	13	9	4	777	37	*2	2.86
2006-07	Cornell Big Red	ECAC	12	3	6	2	574	22	1	2.30	....	....	....	....	....	....	....
2007-08	Cornell Big Red	ECAC	35	*19	12	3	1965	66	4	*2.02	....	....	....	....	....	....	....
2008-09	Cornell Big Red	ECAC	36	*22	10	4	2153	65	*7	*1.81	....	....	....	....	....	....	....
2009-10	Cornell Big Red	ECAC	34	*21	9	4	*2018	63	*7	*1.87	....	....	....	....	....	....	....
2010-11	Toronto Marlies	AHL	33	13	12	5	1929	75	2	2.33	....	....	....	....	....	....	....
	Reading Royals	ECHL	13	10	3	0	779	29	0	2.23	3	0	1	107	9	0	5.04
2011-12	**Toronto**	**NHL**	**12**	**4**	**5**	**2**	**672**	**35**	**0**	**3.13**	....	....	....	....	....	....	....
	Toronto Marlies	AHL	39	22	15	1	2293	78	4	*2.04	*17	11	6	*1030	33	*3	1.92
2012-13	Toronto Marlies	AHL	22	14	7	1	1325	49	2	2.22	....	....	....	....	....	....	....
	Toronto	**NHL**	**20**	**7**	**9**	**0**	**1025**	**46**	**2**	**2.69**	....	....	....	....	....	....	....
2013-14	**Los Angeles**	**NHL**	**19**	**7**	**5**	**4**	**975**	**32**	**3**	**1.97**	....	....	....	....	....	....	....
	Edmonton	**NHL**	**21**	**9**	**11**	**0**	**1235**	**62**	**1**	**3.01**	....	....	....	....	....	....	....
2014-15	**Edmonton**	**NHL**	**57**	**15**	**26**	**11**	**3228**	**170**	**1**	**3.16**	....	....	....	....	....	....	....
2015-16	Bakersfield	AHL	10	2	6	1	554	32	1	3.47	....	....	....	....	....	....	....
	Montreal	**NHL**	**15**	**5**	**8**	**0**	**822**	**42**	**0**	**3.07**	....	....	....	....	....	....	....
	St. John's IceCaps	AHL	1	0	1	0	60	4	0	4.00	....	....	....	....	....	....	....
2016-17	Dynamo Minsk	KHL	*55	*28	18	0	*3232	123	8	2.28	5	1	4	271	16	0	3.55
	NHL Totals		**144**	**47**	**64**	**17**	**7957**	**387**	**7**	**2.92**	....	....	....	....	....	....	....

ECAC Second All-Star Team (2009) • ECAC First All-Star Team (2010) • NCAA East First All-American Team (2010) • Harry ''Hap'' Holmes Memorial Award (AHL – fewest goals against) (2012)

Signed as a free agent by **Toronto**, April 28, 2010. Traded to **Los Angeles** by **Toronto** with Matt Frattin and Toronto's 2nd round pick (later traded to Columbus, later traded back to Toronto – Toronto selected Travis Dermott) 2015 NHL Draft for Jonathan Bernier, June 23, 2013. Traded to **Edmonton** by **Los Angeles** for Edmonton's 3rd round pick (later traded to Columbus, later traded to Detroit – Detroit selected Dominic Turgeon) in 2014 NHL Draft, January 15, 2014. Traded to **Montreal** by **Edmonton** for Zack Kassian, December 28, 2015. Signed as a free agent by **Minsk** (KHL), July 25, 2016. Signed as a free agent by **Ufa** (KHL), July 5, 2017.

SENN, Gilles (SEHN, ZHEEL) N.J.

Goaltender. Catches left. 6'5", 190 lbs. Born, Saas-Almagell, Switz., January 3, 1996.
(New Jersey's 6th pick, 129th overall, in 2017 NHL Draft).

			Regular Season								Playoffs						
Season	Club	League	GP	W	L	O/T	Mins	GA	SO	Avg	GP	W	L	Mins	GA	SO	Avg
2009-10	EHC Visp U17	Swiss-U17	2	....	....	....	....	....	....	....	....	....	....	....	....	....	....
2010-11	EHC Visp U17	Swiss-U17	1	....	....	....	....	....	....	....	....	....	....	....	....	....	....
2011-12	HC Davos U17	Swiss-U17	5	....	....	....	....	....	....	5.74	....	....	....	....	....	....	....
2012-13	HC Davos U17	Swiss-U17	21	....	....	....	....	....	....	2.69	4	....	....	....	....	....	4.25
	HC Davos Jr.	Swiss-Jr.	8	....	....	....	....	....	....	3.43	3	....	....	....	....	....	4.75
2013-14	HC Davos Jr.	Swiss-Jr.	34	....	....	....	....	....	....	2.76	3	....	....	....	....	....	5.00
2014-15	HC Davos Jr.	Swiss-Jr.	32	....	....	....	....	....	....	2.52	9	....	....	567	22	....	2.33
	HC Davos	Swiss	4	1	0	0	85	3	0	2.12	....	....	....	....	....	....	....
2015-16	HC Davos Jr.	Swiss-Jr.	16	8	6	0	839	45	0	3.22	....	....	....	....	....	....	....
	HC Davos	Swiss	3	1	2	0	234	15	0	3.84	....	....	....	....	....	....	....
2016-17	HC Davos	Swiss	34	16	17	0	2000	88	1	2.64	10	6	4	639	29	0	2.72

SHESTERKIN, Igor (shehs-TUHR-kihn, EE-gohr) NYR

Goaltender. Catches left. 6'1", 187 lbs. Born, Moscow, Russia, December 30, 1995.
(NY Rangers' 4th pick, 118th overall, in 2014 NHL Draft).

			Regular Season								Playoffs						
Season	Club	League	GP	W	L	O/T	Mins	GA	SO	Avg	GP	W	L	Mins	GA	SO	Avg
2012-13	Spartak Jr.	Russia-Jr.	15	9	1	4	886	31	2	2.10	9	6	3	529	14	3	1.59
2013-14	Spartak Jr.	Russia-Jr.	23	14	5	4	1399	33	5	1.42	19	12	7	1134	33	4	1.75
	Spartak Moscow	KHL	9	1	5	0	428	20	1	2.80	....	....	....	....	....	....	....
2014-15	SKA St. Petersburg	KHL	6	3	0	0	231	9	0	2.33	....	....	....	....	....	....	....
	SKA-Kareliya	Russia-2	8	3	3	0	488	14	1	1.72	....	....	....	....	....	....	....
	St. Petersburg Jr.	Russia-Jr.	3	2	0	0	159	6	0	2.26	13	7	4	778	32	1	2.47
2015-16	St. Petersburg Jr.	Russia-Jr.	2	1	1	0	119	3	0	1.51	....	....	....	....	....	....	....
	SKA-Neva	Russia-2	25	16	6	0	1513	30	6	1.19	....	....	....	....	....	....	....
	SKA St. Petersburg	KHL	7	5	2	0	419	18	1	2.58	....	....	....	....	....	....	....
2016-17	SKA St. Petersburg	KHL	39	27	4	0	2191	60	8	1.64	5	4	1	228	7	0	1.84

SKINNER, Stuart (SKIH-nuhr, STEW-uhrt) EDM

Goaltender. Catches left. 6'3", 200 lbs. Born, Edmonton, AB, January 11, 1998.
(Edmonton's 2nd pick, 78th overall, in 2017 NHL Draft).

			Regular Season								Playoffs						
Season	Club	League	GP	W	L	O/T	Mins	GA	SO	Avg	GP	W	L	Mins	GA	SO	Avg
2013-14	SSAC Athletics	AMHL	20	13	5	0	1031	47	1	2.74	3	1	2	152	9	0	3.55
	Lethbridge	WHL	4	0	3	0	197	17	0	5.17	....	....	....	....	....	....	....
2014-15	Lethbridge	WHL	43	13	20	5	2327	143	1	3.69	....	....	....	....	....	....	....
2015-16	Lethbridge	WHL	44	27	10	1	2238	102	3	2.73	4	1	3	191	12	0	3.76
2016-17	Lethbridge	WHL	60	34	18	5	3386	184	2	3.26	20	10	10	1243	64	0	3.09

SMITH, Jeremy (SMIHTH, JAIR-eh-mee) CAR

Goaltender. Catches left. 6', 177 lbs. Born, Dearborn, MI, April 13, 1989.
(Nashville's 2nd pick, 54th overall, in 2007 NHL Draft).

			Regular Season								Playoffs						
Season	Club	League	GP	W	L	O/T	Mins	GA	SO	Avg	GP	W	L	Mins	GA	SO	Avg
2005-06	Det. Compuware	MWEHL	13	5	6	0	696	31	0	2.67	....	....	....	....	....	....	....
	Det. Compuware	Other	3	2	1	0	178	8	0	2.70	....	....	....	....	....	....	....
	Plymouth Whalers	OHL	5	0	2	0	111	11	0	5.95	....	....	....	....	....	....	....
2006-07	Plymouth Whalers	OHL	34	23	6	1	1901	82	4	2.59	3	2	0	149	8	0	3.22
2007-08	Plymouth Whalers	OHL	40	23	13	4	2431	116	3	2.86	4	0	4	224	29	0	7.77
2008-09	Plymouth Whalers	OHL	17	3	9	2	901	72	0	4.80	....	....	....	....	....	....	....
	Niagara Ice Dogs	OHL	26	12	9	3	1488	79	1	3.19	12	5	7	724	45	*1	3.73
2009-10	Milwaukee	AHL	1	0	0	0	5	0	0	0.00	....	....	....	....	....	....	....
	Cincinnati	ECHL	42	23	15	2	2468	108	2	2.63	*17	9	8	*988	44	1	2.67
2010-11	Milwaukee	AHL	28	16	8	2	1513	57	2	2.26	13	7	6	843	32	0	2.28
	Cincinnati	ECHL	1	0	0	1	65	3	0	2.78	....	....	....	....	....	....	....
2011-12	Milwaukee	AHL	*56	31	19	2	*3284	119	5	2.17	3	0	3	177	11	0	3.73
2012-13	Milwaukee	AHL	43	19	19	3	2471	114	1	2.77	....	....	....	....	....	....	....
2013-14	Springfield Falcons	AHL	38	21	14	3	2179	101	1	2.78	....	....	....	....	....	....	....
2014-15	Providence Bruins	AHL	39	22	11	5	2278	78	3	2.05	3	1	2	183	6	0	1.96
2015-16	Iowa Wild	AHL	23	5	14	3	1326	65	0	2.94	....	....	....	....	....	....	....
	Providence Bruins	AHL	20	13	5	1	1129	38	1	2.02	3	0	3	180	8	0	2.66
2016-17	**Colorado**	**NHL**	**10**	**1**	**6**	**1**	**543**	**32**	**0**	**3.54**	....	....	....	....	....	....	....
	San Antonio	AHL	17	5	8	1	841	36	0	2.57	....	....	....	....	....	....	....
	NHL Totals		**10**	**1**	**6**	**1**	**543**	**32**	**0**	**3.54**	....	....	....	....	....	....	....

ECHL Playoff MVP (2010) (co-winner - Robert Mayer)

Signed as a free agent by **Columbus**, July 5, 2013. Signed as a free agent by **Boston**, July 2, 2014. • Loaned to **Iowa** (AHL) by **Boston**, October 8, 2015. • Re-assigned to **Providence** (AHL) by **Boston**, February 7, 2016. Signed as a free agent by **Colorado**, July 1, 2016. Signed as a free agent by **Carolina**, July 1, 2017.

SMITH, Mike (SMIHTH, MIGHK) CGY

Goaltender. Catches left. 6'4", 215 lbs. Born, Kingston, ON, March 22, 1982.
(Dallas' 5th pick, 161st overall, in 2001 NHL Draft).

			Regular Season								Playoffs						
Season	Club	League	GP	W	L	O/T	Mins	GA	SO	Avg	GP	W	L	Mins	GA	SO	Avg
1998-99	Kingston	ON-Jr.A	16	....	....	....	906	53	0	3.51	....	....	....	....	....	....	....
99-2000	Kingston	OHL	15	4	5	0	666	42	0	3.78	....	....	....	....	....	....	....
2000-01	Kingston	OHL	3	0	0	2	136	8	0	3.53	....	....	....	....	....	....	....
	Sudbury Wolves	OHL	43	22	13	7	2571	108	3	2.52	12	7	5	735	26	2	*2.12
2001-02	Sudbury Wolves	OHL	53	19	28	5	3082	157	3	3.06	5	1	4	302	15	0	2.98
2002-03	Utah Grizzlies	AHL	11	5	5	0	614	33	0	3.23	....	....	....	....	....	....	....
	Lexington	ECHL	27	11	10	4	1553	66	1	2.55	2	0	1	93	8	0	5.14
2003-04	Utah Grizzlies	AHL	21	8	11	0	1186	56	2	2.83	....	....	....	....	....	....	....
2004-05	Houston Aeros	AHL	45	19	17	3	2408	97	5	2.42	3	1	2	181	4	0	1.33
2005-06	Iowa Stars	AHL	50	25	19	6	2998	125	3	2.50	7	3	4	417	19	0	2.74
2006-07	**Dallas**	**NHL**	**23**	**12**	**5**	**2**	**1213**	**45**	**3**	**2.23**	....	....	....	....	....	....	....
2007-08	**Dallas**	**NHL**	**21**	**12**	**9**	**0**	**1172**	**48**	**2**	**2.46**	....	....	....	....	....	....	....
	Tampa Bay	**NHL**	**13**	**3**	**10**	**0**	**774**	**36**	**1**	**2.79**	....	....	....	....	....	....	....
2008-09	**Tampa Bay**	**NHL**	**41**	**14**	**18**	**9**	**2471**	**108**	**2**	**2.62**	....	....	....	....	....	....	....
2009-10	**Tampa Bay**	**NHL**	**42**	**13**	**18**	**7**	**2273**	**117**	**2**	**3.09**	....	....	....	....	....	....	....
2010-11	**Tampa Bay**	**NHL**	**22**	**13**	**6**	**1**	**1202**	**58**	**1**	**2.90**	**3**	**1**	**1**	**120**	**2**	**0**	**1.00**
	Norfolk Admirals	AHL	5	1	4	0	296	9	1	1.83	....	....	....	....	....	....	....
2011-12	**Phoenix**	**NHL**	**67**	**38**	**18**	**10**	**3903**	**144**	**8**	**2.21**	**16**	**9**	**7**	**1027**	**34**	***3**	**1.99**
2012-13	**Phoenix**	**NHL**	**34**	**15**	**12**	**5**	**1956**	**84**	***5**	**2.58**	....	....	....	....	....	....	....
2013-14	**Phoenix**	**NHL**	**62**	**27**	**21**	**10**	**3610**	**159**	**3**	**2.64**	....	....	....	....	....	....	....
	Canada	Olympics	DID NOT PLAY – SPARE GOALTENDER														
2014-15	**Arizona**	**NHL**	**62**	**14**	**42**	**5**	**3556**	**187**	**0**	**3.16**	....	....	....	....	....	....	....
2015-16	**Arizona**	**NHL**	**32**	**15**	**13**	**2**	**1754**	**77**	**3**	**2.63**	....	....	....	....	....	....	....
2016-17	**Arizona**	**NHL**	**55**	**19**	**26**	**9**	**3202**	**156**	**3**	**2.92**	....	....	....	....	....	....	....
	NHL Totals		**474**	**195**	**198**	**60**	**27086**	**1219**	**33**	**2.70**	**19**	**10**	**8**	**1147**	**36**	**3**	**1.88**

NHL All-Rookie Team (2007)

Played in NHL All-Star Game (2017)

Traded to **Tampa Bay** by **Dallas** with Jussi Jokinen, Jeff Halpern and Dallas' 4th round pick (later traded to Minnesota, later traded to Edmonton – Edmonton selected Kyle Bigos) in 2009 NHL Draft for Brad Richards and Johan Holmqvist, February 26, 2008. Signed as a free agent by **Phoenix**, July 1, 2011. Traded to **Calgary** by **Arizona** for Chad Johnson, Brandon Hickey and a conditional 3rd round pick in 2018 NHL Draft, June 17, 2017.

SODERSTROM, Linus (SOH-duhr-strohm, LEE-nuhs) NYI

Goaltender. Catches left. 6'5", 196 lbs. Born, Stockholm, Sweden, August 23, 1996.
(NY Islanders' 4th pick, 95th overall, in 2014 NHL Draft).

			Regular Season								Playoffs						
Season	Club	League	GP	W	L	O/T	Mins	GA	SO	Avg	GP	W	L	Mins	GA	SO	Avg
2011-12	Djurgarden U18	Swe-U18	3	....	....	....	180	4	0	1.33	....	....	....	....	....	....	....
2012-13	Djurgarden U18	Swe-U18	18	13	5	0	1013	30	5	1.77	9	6	3	556	22	0	2.37
2013-14	Djurgarden Jr.	Swe-Jr.	23	12	11	0	1356	59	0	2.61	1	0	1	60	4	0	4.00
	Djurgarden U18	Swe-U18	....	....	....	....	....	....	....	....	1	0	1	59	3	0	3.03
2014-15	Almtuna	Sweden-2	5	1	4	0	253	11	0	2.61	....	....	....	....	....	....	....
	Sodertalje SK	Sweden-2	4	1	3	0	194	8	0	2.48	....	....	....	....	....	....	....
	Djurgarden Jr.	Swe-Jr.	14	10	4	0	850	41	0	2.89	....	....	....	....	....	....	....
2015-16	Vita Hasten	Sweden-2	17	7	10	0	1035	32	4	1.86	....	....	....	....	....	....	....
2016-17	HV 71 Jonkoping	Sweden	22	18	4	0	1341	30	6	*1.34	*16	*12	4	*993	35	0	2.11

SOROKIN, Ilya (saw-ROH-kihn, IHL-yah) NYI

Goaltender. Catches left. 6'2", 175 lbs. Born, Mezhdurechensk, Russia, August 4, 1995.
(NY Islanders' 3rd pick, 78th overall, in 2014 NHL Draft).

			Regular Season								Playoffs						
Season	Club	League	GP	W	L	O/T	Mins	GA	SO	Avg	GP	W	L	Mins	GA	SO	Avg
2012-13	Novokuznetsk Jr.	Russia-Jr.	27	11	8	3	1423	61	1	2.57	3	0	2	159	9	0	3.40
	Novokuznetsk	KHL	5	1	1	0	151	7	0	2.77	3	1	2	198	10	0	3.03
2013-14	Novokuznetsk Jr.	Russia-Jr.	4	2	1	1	245	11	0	2.69	2	0	2	104	7	0	4.04
	Novokuznetsk	KHL	27	5	12	0	1346	65	0	2.90	1	0	1	60	2	0	2.00
2014-15	Novokuznetsk	KHL	22	4	11	0	978	53	1	3.25	....	....	....	....	....	....	....
	CSKA Moscow	KHL	6	3	2	0	275	6	0	1.31	....	....	....	....	....	....	....
	CSKA Jr.	Russia-Jr.	3	1	1	0	184	4	1	1.31	7	2	4	363	13	1	2.15
2015-16	Zvezda Chekhov	Russia-2	1	0	1	0	60	2	0	2.01	....	....	....	....	....	....	....
	CSKA Moscow	KHL	28	17	7	0	1639	29	10	*1.06	*20	*15	5	*1270	28	3	*1.32
2016-17	CSKA Moscow	KHL	39	25	7	0	2276	61	5	1.61	7	5	2	443	15	1	2.03

SPARKS, Garret (SPARKS, GAIR-eht) TOR

Goaltender. Catches left. 6'2", 207 lbs. Born, Elmhurst, IL, June 28, 1993.
(Toronto's 8th pick, 190th overall, in 2011 NHL Draft).

			Regular Season								Playoffs						
Season	Club	League	GP	W	L	O/T	Mins	GA	SO	Avg	GP	W	L	Mins	GA	SO	Avg
2008-09	Team Illinois	T1EHL	18	9	6	2	854	51	0	3.05	....	....	....	....	....	....	....
2009-10	Chicago Mission	T1EHL	27	19	7	2	1392	51	3	1.98	....	....	....	....	....	....	....
2010-11	Guelph Storm	OHL	19	8	6	1	972	59	0	3.64	....	....	....	....	....	....	....
2011-12	Guelph Storm	OHL	59	27	25	4	3304	171	5	3.11	6	2	4	323	24	0	4.45
2012-13	Guelph Storm	OHL	*60	*36	17	4	*3440	152	*7	2.65	5	1	4	275	14	0	3.05
	Toronto Marlies	AHL	3	2	0	1	189	8	0	2.53	1	0	0	14	1	0	4.23
2013-14	Toronto Marlies	AHL	21	11	6	1	1094	48	0	2.63	....	....	....	....	....	....	....
	Orlando	ECHL	10	4	6	0	552	26	1	2.82	....	....	....	....	....	....	....
2014-15	Toronto Marlies	AHL	2	1	0	0	120	2	1	1.00	....	....	....	....	....	....	....
	Orlando	ECHL	36	21	7	3	1946	76	5	2.34	6	2	4	342	17	0	2.98
2015-16	**Toronto**	**NHL**	**17**	**6**	**9**	**1**	**975**	**49**	**1**	**3.02**	....	....	....	....	....	....	....
	Toronto Marlies	AHL	21	14	4	3	1212	47	3	2.33	5	2	2	235	9	1	2.30
	Orlando	ECHL	1	1	0	0	60	1	0	1.00	....	....	....	....	....	....	....
2016-17	Toronto Marlies	AHL	31	21	9	0	1774	64	5	2.16	2	1	1	98	4	0	2.46
	NHL Totals		**17**	**6**	**9**	**1**	**975**	**49**	**1**	**3.02**	....	....	....	....	....	....	....

• First goalie in Toronto Maple Leafs history to record a shutout in his 1st NHL game (November 30, 2015).

STALOCK, Alex (STAY-lahk, AL-ehx) MIN

Goaltender. Catches left. 6', 190 lbs. Born, St. Paul, MN, July 28, 1987.
(San Jose's 3rd pick, 112th overall, in 2005 NHL Draft).

			Regular Season								Playoffs						
Season	Club	League	GP	W	L	O/T	Mins	GA	SO	Avg	GP	W	L	Mins	GA	SO	Avg
2003-04	South St. Paul	High-MN	31	23	7	1	....	....	....	2.20	....	....	....	....	....	....	....
2004-05	Cedar Rapids	USHL	32	19	9	3	1801	82	1	2.73	9	7	2	582	14	*1	*1.44
2005-06	Cedar Rapids	USHL	44	*28	13	3	2641	112	4	2.54	8	3	5	472	25	0	3.18
2006-07	U. Minn-Duluth	WCHA	23	5	14	3	1364	76	1	3.34	....	....	....	....	....	....	....
2007-08	U. Minn-Duluth	WCHA	36	13	17	6	2170	85	3	2.35	....	....	....	....	....	....	....
2008-09	U. Minn-Duluth	WCHA	*42	21	13	8	*2534	90	*5	*2.13	....	....	....	....	....	....	....
2009-10	Worcester Sharks	AHL	*61	*39	19	2	3534	155	4	2.63	11	6	5	683	26	0	2.28
2010-11	**San Jose**	**NHL**	**1**	**1**	**0**	**0**	**30**	**0**	**0**	**0.00**	....	....	....	....	....	....	....
	Worcester Sharks	AHL	41	19	17	4	2397	105	0	2.63	....	....	....	....	....	....	....
2011-12	Stockton Thunder	ECHL	6	5	1	0	360	17	0	2.83	....	....	....	....	....	....	....
	Worcester Sharks	AHL	2	1	1	0	119	5	0	2.51	....	....	....	....	....	....	....
	Peoria Rivermen	AHL	3	2	0	0	106	2	1	1.13	....	....	....	....	....	....	....
2012-13	Worcester Sharks	AHL	38	17	16	4	2281	99	2	2.60	....	....	....	....	....	....	....
	San Jose	**NHL**	**2**	**0**	**0**	**1**	**42**	**2**	**0**	**2.86**	....	....	....	....	....	....	....
2013-14	**San Jose**	**NHL**	**24**	**12**	**5**	**2**	**1252**	**39**	**2**	**1.87**	**3**	**0**	**1**	**117**	**4**	**0**	**2.05**
2014-15	**San Jose**	**NHL**	**22**	**8**	**9**	**2**	**1237**	**54**	**2**	**2.62**	....	....	....	....	....	....	....
2015-16	**San Jose**	**NHL**	**13**	**3**	**5**	**2**	**674**	**33**	**0**	**2.94**	....	....	....	....	....	....	....
	San Jose Barracuda	AHL	2	2	0	0	122	4	0	1.96	....	....	....	....	....	....	....
	Toronto Marlies	AHL	3	1	2	0	181	8	0	2.66	....	....	....	....	....	....	....
2016-17	**Minnesota**	**NHL**	**2**	**1**	**1**	**0**	**119**	**3**	**0**	**1.51**	....	....	....	....	....	....	....
	Iowa Wild	AHL	50	23	17	8	2871	109	4	2.28	....	....	....	....	....	....	....
	NHL Totals		**64**	**25**	**20**	**7**	**3354**	**131**	**4**	**2.34**	**3**	**0**	**1**	**117**	**4**	**0**	**2.05**

USHL Playoff MVP (2005) • USHL First All-Star Team (2006) • USHL Goaltender of the Year (2006) • WCHA All-Rookie Team (2007) • WCHA First All-Star Team (2009) • NCAA West First All-American Team (2009) • AHL All-Rookie Team (2010)

Traded to **Toronto** by **San Jose** with Ben Smith and San Jose's 3rd round pick in 2018 NHL Draft for James Reimer and Jeremy Morin, February 28, 2016. Signed as a free agent by **Minnesota**, July 1, 2016.

STARRETT, Shane (STAIR-eht, SHAYN) EDM

Goaltender. Catches left. 6'5", 194 lbs. Born, Bellingham, MA, July 12, 1994.

			Regular Season								Playoffs						
Season	Club	League	GP	W	L	O/T	Mins	GA	SO	Avg	GP	W	L	Mins	GA	SO	Avg
2010-11	Catholic Memorial	High-MA	9	....	....	....	....	....	....	2.00	....	....	....	....	....	....	....
2011-12	Catholic Memorial	High-MA	20	....	....	....	....	40	4	2.00	....	....	....	....	....	....	....
2012-13	Selects Academy	Minor-CT	46	25	15	5	2310	90	11	1.96	....	....	....	....	....	....	....
2013-14	Sioux Falls	USHL	1	0	0	0	1	0	0	0.00	....	....	....	....	....	....	....
	Lincoln Stars	USHL	2	0	1	0	16	2	0	7.56	....	....	....	....	....	....	....
	Portland Jr. Pirates	USPHL	20	8	9	0	980	57	0	3.22	2	0	2	120	10	0	5.00

2014-15	South Shore Kings	USPHL	30	11	16	0	1554	75	2	2.90	4	1	3	155	13	0	4.17
2015-16	Air Force Falcons	AH	33	16	9	5	1782	57	*4	*1.92	....	....	....	....	....	....	....
2016-17	Air Force Falcons	AH	*37	*26	6	4	*2142	71	5	1.99	....	....	....	....	....	....	....

Signed as a free agent by **Edmonton**, April 10, 2017.

STEVENS, Colin (STEE-vehns, KAW-lihn) FLA

Goaltender. Catches left. 6'2", 185 lbs. Born, Niskayuna, NY, June 30, 1993.

			Regular Season								Playoffs						
Season	**Club**	**League**	**GP**	**W**	**L**	**O/T**	**Mins**	**GA**	**SO**	**Avg**	**GP**	**W**	**L**	**Mins**	**GA**	**SO**	**Avg**
2009-10	Boston Jr. Bruins	EmJHL	26	23	1	2	....	....	6	1.66	6	4	2	....	....	....	2.66
	USAHNTDP	USHL	1	0	0	0	40	2	0	3.00	....	....	....	....	....	....	....
	USAHNTDP	U-18	1	0	1	0	59	7	0	7.19	....	....	....	....	....	....	....
2010-11	Boston Jr. Bruins	EJHL	29	24	3	0	....	....	5	2.41	2	1	1	....	....	....	2.75
2011-12	Union College	ECAC	11	4	2	4	561	21	0	2.25	....	....	....	....	....	....	....
2012-13	Union College	ECAC	12	5	3	0	480	13	3	1.62	....	....	....	....	....	....	....
2013-14	Union College	ECAC	36	*28	4	2	2080	71	*6	2.05	....	....	....	....	....	....	....
2014-15	Union College	ECAC	31	16	15	0	1742	67	2	2.31	....	....	....	....	....	....	....
2015-16	Manchester	ECHL	28	15	9	2	1563	72	2	2.77	1	0	1	58	3	0	3.09
2016-17	Manchester	ECHL	9	3	5	1	470	28	0	3.58	....	....	....	....	....	....	....
	Tulsa Oilers	ECHL	24	7	13	4	1350	70	1	3.11	....	....	....	....	....	....	....

NCAA East Second All-American Team (2014) • NCAA Championship All-Tournament Team (2014)

Signed as a free agent by **Florida**, March 20, 2015. • Re-assigned to **Tulsa** (ECHL) by **Florida**, November 11, 2016.

STEZKA, Ales (STEHZH-kuh, ah-LEHSH) MIN

Goaltender. Catches left. 6'4", 190 lbs. Born, Liberec, Czech Rep., January 6, 1997.
(Minnesota's 3rd pick, 111th overall, in 2015 NHL Draft).

			Regular Season								Playoffs						
Season	**Club**	**League**	**GP**	**W**	**L**	**O/T**	**Mins**	**GA**	**SO**	**Avg**	**GP**	**W**	**L**	**Mins**	**GA**	**SO**	**Avg**
2012-13	HC Liberec U18	CzR-U18	25	....	....	....	1257	65	0	3.10	3	....	....	126	4	0	1.90
	HC Liberec Jr.	CzRep-Jr.	1	....	....	....	60	7	0	7.00	....	....	....	....	....	....	....
2013-14	HC Liberec U18	CzR-U18	24	....	....	....	1347	38	8	1.69	5	....	....	300	9	0	1.80
	HC Liberec Jr.	CzRep-Jr.	2	....	....	....	89	1	0	0.67	....	....	....	....	....	....	....
2014-15	HC Liberec U18	CzR-U18	7	....	....	....	420	10	2	1.42	3	....	....	189	2	2	0.63
	HC Liberec Jr.	CzRep-Jr.	40	....	....	....	2425	112	3	2.77	6	....	....	364	12	0	1.98
2015-16	Sioux Falls	USHL	19	6	10	1	1013	56	1	3.32	....	....	....	....	....	....	....
2016-17	Chicago Steel	USHL	37	22	10	2	2154	82	4	2.28	*13	*9	4	796	27	*3	2.04

STOLARZ, Anthony (STOHL-ahrz, AN-thuh-nee) PHI

Goaltender. Catches left. 6'6", 232 lbs. Born, Edison, NJ, January 20, 1994.
(Philadelphia's 2nd pick, 45th overall, in 2012 NHL Draft).

			Regular Season								Playoffs						
Season	**Club**	**League**	**GP**	**W**	**L**	**O/T**	**Mins**	**GA**	**SO**	**Avg**	**GP**	**W**	**L**	**Mins**	**GA**	**SO**	**Avg**
2010-11	Jersey Hitmen	EmJHL	....	12	4	0	884	47	0	3.19	3	1	2	153	8	0	3.13
2011-12	Corpus Christi	NAHL	50	23	22	4	2939	139	3	2.84	....	....	....	....	....	....	....
2012-13	Nebraska-Omaha	WCHA	8	2	5	0	421	18	1	2.56	....	....	....	....	....	....	....
2013-14	London Knights	OHL	35	25	5	2	1927	81	4	2.52	....	....	....	....	....	....	....
2014-15	Lehigh Valley	AHL	31	9	13	4	1592	87	2	3.28	....	....	....	....	....	....	....
2015-16	Lehigh Valley	AHL	47	21	18	7	2726	118	0	2.60	....	....	....	....	....	....	....
2016-17	**Philadelphia**	**NHL**	**7**	**2**	**1**	**1**	**376**	**13**	**1**	**2.07**	....	....	....	....	....	....	....
	Lehigh Valley	AHL	29	18	9	0	1645	80	1	2.92	....	....	....	....	....	....	....
	NHL Totals		**7**	**2**	**1**	**1**	**376**	**13**	**1**	**2.07**	....	....	....	....	....	....	....

SUBBAN, Malcolm (soo-BAN, MAL-kuhm) BOS

Goaltender. Catches left. 6'2", 222 lbs. Born, Toronto, ON, December 21, 1993.
(Boston's 1st pick, 24th overall, in 2012 NHL Draft).

			Regular Season								Playoffs						
Season	**Club**	**League**	**GP**	**W**	**L**	**O/T**	**Mins**	**GA**	**SO**	**Avg**	**GP**	**W**	**L**	**Mins**	**GA**	**SO**	**Avg**
2009-10	Mississauga Reps	GTHL	14	....	....	....	....	....	....	1.86	7	....	....	....	....	....	2.00
	Tor. Canadiens	ON-Jr.A	2	0	1	0	71	4	0	3.39	....	....	....	....	....	....	....
	Belleville Bulls	OHL	1	0	0	0	13	0	0	0.00	....	....	....	....	....	....	....
2010-11	Belleville Bulls	OHL	32	10	17	2	1785	94	0	3.16	3	0	3	178	6	0	2.02
2011-12	Belleville Bulls	OHL	39	25	14	0	2258	94	3	2.50	6	2	4	369	18	0	2.93
2012-13	Belleville Bulls	OHL	46	29	11	4	2695	96	5	*2.14	17	11	6	1021	34	*3	*2.00
2013-14	Providence Bruins	AHL	33	15	10	5	1920	74	1	2.31	6	2	2	244	12	0	2.96
2014-15	**Boston**	**NHL**	**1**	**0**	**1**	**0**	**31**	**3**	**0**	**5.81**	....	....	....	....	....	....	....
	Providence Bruins	AHL	35	16	13	4	2017	82	3	2.44	2	1	1	160	3	0	1.12
2015-16	Providence Bruins	AHL	27	14	8	5	1635	67	1	2.46	....	....	....	....	....	....	....
2016-17	**Boston**	**NHL**	**1**	**0**	**1**	**0**	**31**	**3**	**0**	**5.81**	....	....	....	....	....	....	....
	Providence Bruins	AHL	32	11	14	5	1779	72	1	2.41	3	0	2	113	4	0	2.12
	NHL Totals		**2**	**0**	**2**	**0**	**62**	**6**	**0**	**5.81**	....	....	....	....	....	....	....

OHL All-Rookie Team (2011)

SVEDBERG, Niklas (SVEHD-buhrg, NIHK-luhs) MIN

Goaltender. Catches left. 6', 176 lbs. Born, Sollentuna, Sweden, September 4, 1989.

			Regular Season								Playoffs						
Season	**Club**	**League**	**GP**	**W**	**L**	**O/T**	**Mins**	**GA**	**SO**	**Avg**	**GP**	**W**	**L**	**Mins**	**GA**	**SO**	**Avg**
2007-08	MODO	Sweden	1	0	0	0	8	7.11	....	....	....	....	....	....	....	....	....
2008-09	Huddinge IK	Sweden-2	24	....	....	....	....	....	....	....	....	....	....	....	....	....	....
	MODO	Sweden	3	....	....	....	178	16	0	5.41	....	....	....	....	....	....	....
2009-10	MODO	Sweden	21	....	....	....	1261	82	1	2.59	....	....	....	....	....	....	....
2010-11	Brynas IF Gavle	Sweden	21	....	....	....	1261	48	2	2.28	....	....	....	....	....	....	....
2011-12	Brynas IF Gavle	Sweden	29	....	....	....	1726	71	0	2.47	13	....	....	814	23	4	1.70
2012-13	Providence Bruins	AHL	48	37	8	2	2873	104	4	2.17	12	6	6	675	37	0	3.29
2013-14	**Boston**	**NHL**	**1**	**1**	**0**	**0**	**61**	**2**	**0**	**1.97**	....	....	....	....	....	....	....
	Providence Bruins	AHL	45	25	15	4	2602	114	2	2.63	9	4	4	510	23	1	2.70
2014-15	**Boston**	**NHL**	**18**	**7**	**5**	**1**	**900**	**35**	**2**	**2.33**	....	....	....	....	....	....	....
	Providence Bruins	AHL	4	3	1	0	239	11	0	2.76	....	....	....	....	....	....	....
2015-16	Ufa	KHL	*53	*29	19	0	*3058	121	5	2.37	19	9	10	1111	47	0	2.54
2016-17	Ufa	KHL	48	14	17	0	2528	126	1	2.99	5	1	4	272	8	0	1.76
	NHL Totals		**19**	**8**	**5**	**1**	**961**	**37**	**2**	**2.31**	....	....	....	....	....	....	....

AHL All-Rookie Team (2013) • AHL First All-Star Team (2013) • Aldege "Baz" Bastien Memorial Award (AHL – Outstanding Goaltender) (2013)

Signed as a free agent by **Boston**, May 29, 2012. Signed as a free agent by **Ufa** (KHL), May 10, 2015. Signed as a free agent by **Minnesota**, July 1, 2017.

SWAYMAN, Jeremy (SWAY-man, JAIR-ih-mee) BOS

Goaltender. Catches left. 6'2", 196 lbs. Born, Anchorage, Alaska, November 24, 1998.
(Boston's 3rd pick, 111th overall, in 2017 NHL Draft).

			Regular Season								Playoffs						
Season	**Club**	**League**	**GP**	**W**	**L**	**O/T**	**Mins**	**GA**	**SO**	**Avg**	**GP**	**W**	**L**	**Mins**	**GA**	**SO**	**Avg**
2013-14	Alaska Jr. Aces	Minor-AK	STATISTICS NOT AVAILABLE														
	Alaska U16	HPHL	2	1	1	0	102	2	1	1.00	....	....	....	....	....	....	....
2014-15	S. Anchorage	High-AK	28	17	3	6	1202	34	5	1.27	....	....	....	....	....	....	....
2015-16	Pikes Peak U18	NAPHL	18	9	8	1	914	32	*4	1.79	4	2	2	203	8	0	2.01
2016-17	Sioux Falls	USHL	32	7	18	5	1883	91	0	2.90	....	....	....	....	....	....	....

• Signed Letter of Intent to attend **University of Maine** (Hockey East) in fall of 2017.

TALBOT, Cam (TAL-buht, KAM) EDM

Goaltender. Catches left. 6'3", 199 lbs. Born, Caledonia, ON, June 5, 1987.

			Regular Season								Playoffs						
Season	**Club**	**League**	**GP**	**W**	**L**	**O/T**	**Mins**	**GA**	**SO**	**Avg**	**GP**	**W**	**L**	**Mins**	**GA**	**SO**	**Avg**
2005-06	Hamilton	ON-Jr.A	35	21	13	1	2046	87	1	2.55	14	8	6	903	52	1	3.46
2006-07	Hamilton	ON-Jr.A	28	19	5	2	1644	57	1	2.08	19	13	6	1243	51	0	2.46
2007-08	AL-Huntsville	CHA	13	1	10	0	583	45	0	4.63	....	....	....	....	....	....	....
2008-09	AL-Huntsville	CHA	24	2	16	3	1320	65	1	2.95	....	....	....	....	....	....	....
2009-10	AL-Huntsville	CHA	*33	12	18	3	*1958	85	1	2.61	....	....	....	....	....	....	....
	Hartford Wolf Pack	AHL	1	0	0	0	19	3	0	9.70	....	....	....	....	....	....	....
2010-11	Connecticut Whale	AHL	22	11	9	2	1308	62	2	2.84	1	0	1	38	2	0	3.13
	Greenville	ECHL	2	1	0	1	122	5	0	2.46	....	....	....	....	....	....	....
2011-12	Connecticut Whale	AHL	33	14	15	1	1865	81	4	2.61	9	5	4	571	20	2	2.10
2012-13	Connecticut Whale	AHL	55	25	28	1	3105	136	2	2.63	....	....	....	....	....	....	....
2013-14	**NY Rangers**	**NHL**	**21**	**12**	**6**	**1**	**1211**	**33**	**3**	**1.64**	**2**	**0**	**1**	**46**	**2**	**0**	**2.61**
	Hartford Wolf Pack	AHL	5	4	0	1	314	13	0	2.49	....	....	....	....	....	....	....
2014-15	**NY Rangers**	**NHL**	**36**	**21**	**9**	**4**	**2095**	**77**	**5**	**2.21**	....	....	....	....	....	....	....
2015-16	**Edmonton**	**NHL**	**56**	**21**	**27**	**5**	**3223**	**137**	**3**	**2.55**	....	....	....	....	....	....	....
2016-17	**Edmonton**	**NHL**	**73**	***42**	**22**	**8**	***4294**	**171**	**7**	**2.39**	**13**	**7**	**6**	**799**	**33**	**2**	**2.48**
	NHL Totals		**186**	**96**	**64**	**18**	**10823**	**418**	**18**	**2.32**	**15**	**7**	**7**	**845**	**35**	**2**	**2.49**

Signed as a free agent by **NY Rangers**, March 30, 2010. Traded to **Edmonton** by **NY Rangers** with NY Rangers' 7th round pick (Ziyat Paigin) in 2015 NHL Draft for Edmonton's 7th round pick (Adam Huska) in 2015 NHL Draft, Montreal's 2nd round pick (previously acquired, later traded to Washington – Washington selected Jonas Siegenthaler) in 2015 NHL Draft and Ottawa's 3rd round pick (previously acquired, NY Rangers selected Sergey Zborovskiy) in 2015 NHL Draft, June 27, 2015.

TARASOV, Daniil (tair-AW-sawv, da-NEEL) CBJ

Goaltender. Catches left. 6'4", 180 lbs. Born, Novokuznetsk, Russia, March 27, 1999.
(Columbus' 2nd pick, 86th overall, in 2017 NHL Draft).

			Regular Season								Playoffs						
Season	**Club**	**League**	**GP**	**W**	**L**	**O/T**	**Mins**	**GA**	**SO**	**Avg**	**GP**	**W**	**L**	**Mins**	**GA**	**SO**	**Avg**
2015-16	Tolpar Ufa Jr.	Russia-Jr.	9	3	0	0	282	12	0	2.55	2	0	2	72	2	0	1.52
2016-17	Tolpar Ufa Jr.	Russia-Jr.	DID NOT PLAY – INJURED														

TAYLOR, Danny (TAY-luhr, DA-nee) OTT

Goaltender. Catches left. 5'11", 179 lbs. Born, Plymouth, England, April 28, 1986.
(Los Angeles' 8th pick, 221st overall, in 2004 NHL Draft).

			Regular Season								Playoffs						
Season	**Club**	**League**	**GP**	**W**	**L**	**O/T**	**Mins**	**GA**	**SO**	**Avg**	**GP**	**W**	**L**	**Mins**	**GA**	**SO**	**Avg**
2002-03	Cumberland Grads	ON-Jr.A	23	13	3	1	1009	41	1	2.44	6	3	3	432	17	0	2.36
2003-04	Guelph Storm	OHL	26	16	4	3	1462	66	0	2.71	3	1	1	159	9	0	3.40
2004-05	Guelph Storm	OHL	31	13	14	3	1821	80	2	2.64	1	0	1	59	4	0	4.07
2005-06	Kingston	OHL	57	32	15	6	3319	172	3	3.11	....	....	....	....	....	....	....
2006-07	Bakersfield	ECHL	17	7	7	2	969	70	0	4.33	....	....	....	....	....	....	....
	Wheeling Nailers	ECHL	1	0	0	1	62	4	0	3.86	....	....	....	....	....	....	....
	Texas Wildcatters	ECHL	2	0	1	0	74	2	0	1.61	....	....	....	....	....	....	....
2007-08	**Los Angeles**	**NHL**	**1**	**0**	**0**	**0**	**20**	**2**	**0**	**6.00**	....	....	....	....	....	....	....
	Manchester	AHL	23	13	5	2	1275	51	4	2.40	....	....	....	....	....	....	....
	Reading Royals	ECHL	5	3	0	0	182	8	0	2.63	13	7	6	815	38	1	2.80
2008-09	Manchester	AHL	15	7	4	2	744	33	0	2.66	....	....	....	....	....	....	....
2009-10	Syracuse Crunch	AHL	9	2	4	0	397	24	0	3.63	....	....	....	....	....	....	....
	Gwinnett	ECHL	37	18	13	5	2181	126	1	3.47	....	....	....	....	....	....	....
2010-11	Springfield Falcons	AHL	4	2	2	0	230	9	0	2.35	....	....	....	....	....	....	....
	Hamburg Freezers	Germany	28	14	14	....	1679	81	1	2.90	....	....	....	....	....	....	....
2011-12	Springfield Falcons	AHL	10	5	3	0	512	22	0	2.58	....	....	....	....	....	....	....
	Abbotsford Heat	AHL	33	17	10	3	1815	67	5	2.21	7	4	3	426	16	0	2.26
2012-13	Abbotsford Heat	AHL	40	18	10	2	2108	72	3	2.05	....	....	....	....	....	....	....
	Calgary	**NHL**	**2**	**1**	**1**	**0**	**120**	**6**	**0**	**3.00**	....	....	....	....	....	....	....
2013-14	Farjestad	Sweden	16	4	11	0	958	37	0	2.32	....	....	....	....	....	....	....
2014-15	Dynamo Minsk	KHL	19	11	6	2	1146	53	1277.00		....	....	....	....	....	....	....
2015-16	Zagreb	KHL	38	16	14	3	2079	79	3	....	....	....	....	....	....	....	....
	HC Sparta Praha	CzRep	7	6	1	0	374	16	0	2.57	....	....	....	....	....	....	....
2016-17	Zagreb	KHL	17	7	5	3	968	36	1	2.23	....	....	....	....	....	....	....
	Novosibirsk	KHL	29	12	11	0	1540	45	5	1.75	....	....	....	....	....	....	....
	NHL Totals		**3**	**1**	**1**	**0**	**140**	**8**	**0**	**3.43**	....	....	....	....	....	....	....

Signed to a PTO (professional tryout) contract by **Springfield** (AHL), October, 2010. Signed as a free agent by **Hamburg** (Germany), November 14, 2010. Signed as a free agent by **Abbotsford** (AHL), December 1, 2011. Signed as a free agent by **Calgary**, February 6, 2013. Signed as a free agent by **Farjestad** (Sweden), May 22, 2013. Signed as a free agent by **Minsk** (KHL), October 21, 2014. Signed as a free agent by **Zagreb** (KHL), July 15, 2015. Signed as a free agent by **Sparta Praha** (CzRep), February 1, 2016. Signed as a free agent by **Zagreb** (KHL), July 6, 2016. Signed as a free agent by **Novosibirsk** (KHL), October 20, 2016. Signed as a free agent by **Ottawa**, July 1, 2017.

THIESSEN, Brad (THEE-suhn, BRAD)

Goaltender. Catches left. 6', 180 lbs. Born, Aldergrove, BC, March 19, 1986.

			Regular Season								Playoffs						
Season	**Club**	**League**	**GP**	**W**	**L**	**O/T**	**Mins**	**GA**	**SO**	**Avg**	**GP**	**W**	**L**	**Mins**	**GA**	**SO**	**Avg**
2003-04	Penticton Panthers	BCHL	42	13	17	1	2131	122	2	3.44	....	....	....	....	....	....	....
2004-05	Penticton Vees	BCHL	26	7	18	1	1492	86	1	3.46	....	....	....	....	....	....	....
	Prince George	BCHL	10	5	4	0	561	31	0	3.31	3	1	1	158	9	0	3.42
2005-06	Prince George	BCHL	36	14	17	4	2058	99	5	2.89	....	....	....	....	....	....	....
	Merritt	BCHL	13	8	4	0	754	36	2	2.87	6	3	3	261	16	1	3.68
2006-07	Northeastern	H-East	33	11	17	5	1985	82	4	2.48	....	....	....	....	....	....	....
2007-08	Northeastern	H-East	37	16	17	3	2180	96	2	2.64	....	....	....	....	....	....	....
2008-09	Northeastern	H-East	*41	25	12	4	*2496	88	*3	2.12	....	....	....	....	....	....	....
2009-10	Wilkes-Barre	AHL	30	14	14	1	1763	72	4	2.45	....	....	....	....	....	....	....
	Wheeling Nailers	ECHL	12	8	3	0	674	30	1	2.67	....	....	....	....	....	....	....

2010-11	Wilkes-Barre	AHL	46	*35	8	1	2567	83	7	1.94	12	6	6	720	20	2	*1.67
2011-12	Pittsburgh	NHL	5	3	1	0	258	16	0	3.72	....	....	....	....	....	....	....
	Wilkes-Barre	AHL	41	23	15	2	2321	109	2	2.82	12	6	6	756	27	0	2.14
2012-13	Wilkes-Barre	AHL	32	16	12	2	1793	80	4	2.68	12	6	4	654	15	2	*1.38
2013-14	HIFK Helsinki	Finland	8	2	5	1	353	18	1	3.06	....	....	....	....	....	....	....
	Norfolk Admirals	AHL	18	8	6	2	984	37	1	2.26	4	1	3	252	16	0	3.81
2014-15	Adirondack Flames	AHL	34	10	16	7	1908	99	2	3.11	....	....	....	....	....	....	....
2015-16	Lake Erie Monsters	AHL	22	12	4	4	1231	40	3	1.95	....	....	....	....	....	....	....
	Cincinnati	ECHL	19	10	4	4	1113	35	1	1.89	7	3	4	454	19	0	2.51
2016-17	Cleveland	AHL	12	5	6	1	666	26	3	2.34	....	....	....	....	....	....	....
	Cincinnati	ECHL	2	0	0	2	125	8	0	3.83	....	....	....	....	....	....	....
	NHL Totals		5	3	1	0	258	16	0	3.72	....	....	....	....	....	....	....

Hockey East First All-Star Team (2009) • Hockey East Player of the Year (2009) • NCAA East First All-American Team (2009) • AHL First All-Star Team (2011) • Harry ''Hap'' Holmes Memorial Award (AHL – fewest goals against) (2011) (shared with John Curry) • Aldege "Baz" Bastien Award (AHL – Outstanding Goaltender) (2011) • Harry ''Hap'' Holmes Memorial Award (AHL – fewest goals against) (2013) (shared with Jeff Zatkoff)

Signed as a free agent by **Pittsburgh**, April 8, 2009. Signed as a free agent by **HIFK Helsinki** (Finland), July 15, 2013. Signed as a free agent by **Norfolk** (AHL), November 28, 2013. Signed as a free agent by **Calgary**, July 3, 2014. Signed to a PTO (professional tryout) contract by **Columbus**, September 16, 2015. • Loaned to **Cincinnati** (ECHL) by **Lake Erie** (AHL), October 17, 2015. Signed as a free agent by **Cleveland** (AHL), May 24, 2016. • Loaned to **Cincinatti** (ECHL) by **Cleveland** (AHL), December 8, 2016.

THOME, Peter (TOW-mee, PEE-tuhr) CBJ

Goaltender. Catches left. 6'4", 202 lbs. Born, Minneapolis, MN, May 24, 1997.
(Columbus' 4th pick, 155th overall, in 2016 NHL Draft).

			Regular Season								Playoffs						
Season	Club	League	GP	W	L	O/T	Mins	GA	SO	Avg	GP	W	L	Mins	GA	SO	Avg
2013-14	Chi. Fury U16	T1EHL	17	7	10	0	883	67	0	4.10	....	....	....	....	....	....	....
2014-15	Chi. Fury U18	T1EHL	19	12	5	1	996	35	3	1.90	2	0	2	113	5	0	2.39
2015-16	Aberdeen Wings	NAHL	47	17	21	9	2788	113	4	2.43	....	....	....	....	....	....	....
	Omaha Lancers	USHL	1	0	1	0	32	1	0	1.89	....	....	....	....	....	....	....
2016-17	Omaha Lancers	USHL	14	7	3	0	741	44	0	3.56	....	....	....	....	....	....	....
	Chicago Steel	USHL	5	3	1	1	278	11	0	2.37	....	....	....	....	....	....	....
	Waterloo	USHL	15	11	4	0	898	41	1	2.74	2	....	....	37	3	0	4.89

• Signed Letter of Intent to attend **University of North Dakota** (NCHC) in fall of 2017.

TOKARSKI, Dustin (toh-KAHR-skee, DUHS-tihn) ANA

Goaltender. Catches left. 6', 205 lbs. Born, Watson, SK, September 16, 1989.
(Tampa Bay's 3rd pick, 122nd overall, in 2008 NHL Draft).

			Regular Season								Playoffs						
Season	Club	League	GP	W	L	O/T	Mins	GA	SO	Avg	GP	W	L	Mins	GA	SO	Avg
2006-07	Spokane Chiefs	WHL	30	13	11	2	1674	78	2	2.80	6	2	4	364	17	0	2.80
2007-08	Spokane Chiefs	WHL	45	30	10	3	2543	87	6	2.05	*21	*16	5	*1352	31	*3	*1.38
2008-09	Spokane Chiefs	WHL	54	34	18	2	3264	107	*7	*1.97	12	7	5	812	23	1	*1.70
2009-10	Tampa Bay	NHL	2	0	0	0	44	3	0	4.09	....	....	....	....	....	....	....
	Norfolk Admirals	AHL	55	27	25	3	3319	139	4	2.51	....	....	....	....	....	....	....
2010-11	Norfolk Admirals	AHL	46	21	20	4	2691	119	2	2.65	6	2	4	355	13	1	2.19
2011-12	Tampa Bay	NHL	5	1	3	1	244	14	0	3.44	....	....	....	....	....	....	....
	Norfolk Admirals	AHL	45	*32	11	0	2583	96	5	2.23	14	*12	2	866	21	*3	*1.46
2012-13	Syracuse Crunch	AHL	33	18	8	4	1881	77	3	2.46	....	....	....	....	....	....	....
	Hamilton Bulldogs	AHL	15	6	8	0	836	31	3	2.22	....	....	....	....	....	....	....
2013-14	Montreal	NHL	3	2	0	0	163	5	1	1.84	5	2	3	300	13	0	2.60
	Hamilton Bulldogs	AHL	41	20	16	3	2375	94	1	2.38	....	....	....	....	....	....	....
2014-15	Montreal	NHL	17	6	6	4	1005	46	0	2.75	....	....	....	....	....	....	....
	Hamilton Bulldogs	AHL	2	1	1	0	119	5	0	2.52	....	....	....	....	....	....	....
2015-16	Montreal	NHL	6	1	3	0	226	12	0	3.19	....	....	....	....	....	....	....
	St. John's IceCaps	AHL	10	3	3	4	613	29	0	2.84	....	....	....	....	....	....	....
	San Diego Gulls	AHL	2	1	1	0	102	4	0	2.35	....	....	....	....	....	....	....
2016-17	Anaheim	NHL	1	0	0	0	10	0	0	0.00	....	....	....	....	....	....	....
	San Diego Gulls	AHL	27	17	8	1	1578	77	1	2.93	2	0	0	30	0	0	0.00
	NHL Totals		34	10	12	5	1692	80	1	2.84	5	2	3	300	13	0	2.60

WHL West Second All-Star Team (2009)

Traded to **Montreal** by **Tampa Bay** for Cedrick Desjardins, February 14, 2013. Traded to **Anaheim** by **Montreal** for Max Friberg, January 7, 2016.

TOMEK, Matej (TOH-mehk, MAH-tay) PHI

Goaltender. Catches . 6'3", 180 lbs. Born, Bratislava, Slovakia, May 24, 1997.
(Philadelphia's 4th pick, 90th overall, in 2015 NHL Draft).

			Regular Season								Playoffs						
Season	Club	League	GP	W	L	O/T	Mins	GA	SO	Avg	GP	W	L	Mins	GA	SO	Avg
2012-13	Bratislava U18	Svk-U18	19	....	....	....	1052	36	3	2.05	4	....	....	212	7	0	1.98
2013-14	Slovakia U18	Slovak-2	14	....	....	....	778	31	1	2.39	....	....	....	....	....	....	....
	Poprad U18	Svk-U18	6	....	....	....	359	14	0	2.34	4	....	....	240	12	1	3.00
	HK SKP Poprad Jr.	Slovak-Jr.	2	....	....	....	120	3	0	1.50	....	....	....	....	....	....	....
2014-15	Topeka	NAHL	33	24	9	0	1938	59	6	1.83	7	4	2	375	20	0	3.20
2015-16	North Dakota	NCHC	DID NOT PLAY – FRESHMAN														
2016-17	North Dakota	NCHC	2	0	0	0	32	4	0	7.46	....	....	....	....	....	....	....

TOMKINS, Matt (TAWM-kihnz, MAT) CHI

Goaltender. Catches left. 6'3", 194 lbs. Born, Edmonton, AB, June 19, 1994.
(Chicago's 8th pick, 199th overall, in 2012 NHL Draft).

			Regular Season								Playoffs						
Season	Club	League	GP	W	L	O/T	Mins	GA	SO	Avg	GP	W	L	Mins	GA	SO	Avg
2008-09	Leduc Oil Kings	AMBHL	....	8	8	3	1093	75	0	4.12	1	0	1	60	5	0	5.00
2009-10	Sherwood Park	Minor-AB	18	8	5	5	1047	47	0	2.69	8	*8	0	490	17	1	2.08
2010-11	Sherwood Park	AMHL	16	6	8	1	1002	64	0	3.83	6	3	3	333	23	0	4.14
2011-12	Sherwood Park	AJHL	33	18	11	2	1898	108	0	3.41	10	4	6	595	35	1	3.53
2012-13	Sherwood Park	AJHL	44	22	14	6	2533	108	4	2.56	10	5	5	607	33	0	3.26
2013-14	Ohio State	Big Ten	17	6	7	2	929	43	0	2.78	....	....	....	....	....	....	....
2014-15	Ohio State	Big Ten	14	5	7	1	768	42	2	3.28	....	....	....	....	....	....	....
2015-16	Ohio State	Big Ten	14	5	7	1	775	50	0	3.87	....	....	....	....	....	....	....
2016-17	Ohio State	Big Ten	22	12	5	3	1136	47	1	*2.48	....	....	....	....	....	....	....

ULLMARK, Linus (UHL-mahrk, LEE-nuhs) BUF

Goaltender. Catches left. 6'4", 212 lbs. Born, Lugnvik, Sweden, July 31, 1993.
(Buffalo's 6th pick, 163rd overall, in 2012 NHL Draft).

			Regular Season								Playoffs						
Season	Club	League	GP	W	L	O/T	Mins	GA	SO	Avg	GP	W	L	Mins	GA	SO	Avg
2008-09	Kramfors U18	Swe-U18	14	....	....	....	824	54	0	3.93	....	....	....	....	....	....	....
2009-10	Kramfors U18	Swe-U18	2	....	....	....	120	11	0	5.50	....	....	....	....	....	....	....
	MODO U18	Swe-U18	8	....	....	....	484	26	1	3.22	2	....	....	120	7	0	3.50
2010-11	MODO U18	Swe-U18	24	....	....	....	1387	51	5	2.20	2	....	....	103	6	0	3.49
	MODO Jr.	Swe-Jr.	1	....	....	....	60	2	0	2.00	....	....	....	....	....	....	....
2011-12	MODO Jr.	Swe-Jr.	25	....	....	....	1521	70	1	2.76	5	....	....	242	9	1	2.24
	MODO	Sweden	3	....	....	....	148	8	0	3.24	....	....	....	....	....	....	....
2012-13	MODO Jr.	Swe-Jr.	23	18	5	0	1352	46	2	2.04	5	4	1	....	1	....	1.39
	Mora IK	Sweden-2	6	4	2	0	343	12	0	2.10	....	....	....	....	....	....	....
	MODO	Sweden	6	3	1	0	320	11	0	2.07	2	1	1	123	3	0	1.47
2013-14	MODO	Sweden	35	17	16	0	2043	71	3	2.08	2	0	2	127	9	0	4.24
2014-15	MODO	Sweden	35	12	20	0	1926	100	1	3.12	....	....	....	....	....	....	....
	MODO	Sweden-Q	....	....	....	....	....	....	....	....	4	4	0	240	2	2	0.50
2015-16	Buffalo	NHL	20	8	10	2	1131	49	0	2.60	....	....	....	....	....	....	....
	Rochester	AHL	28	10	16	0	1582	90	0	3.41	....	....	....	....	....	....	....
2016-17	Buffalo	NHL	1	0	1	0	59	3	0	3.05	....	....	....	....	....	....	....
	Rochester	AHL	*55	26	27	2	*3202	153	1	2.87	....	....	....	....	....	....	....
	NHL Totals		21	8	11	2	1190	52	0	2.62	....	....	....	....	....	....	....

USTIMENKO, Kirill (us-tih-MEHN-koh, kih-RIHL) PHI

Goaltender. Catches left. 6'3", 187 lbs. Born, Gomel, Belarus, January 29, 1999.
(Philadelphia's 4th pick, 80th overall, in 2017 NHL Draft).

			Regular Season								Playoffs						
Season	Club	League	GP	W	L	O/T	Mins	GA	SO	Avg	GP	W	L	Mins	GA	SO	Avg
2016-17	Dyn'o St. Pet. Jr.	Russia-Jr.	27	17	5	3	1515	44	3	1.74	5	2	3	282	17	1	3.61

VAN POTTELBERGHE, Joren (van paw-tehl-BAIRG, YOH-ruhn) DET

Goaltender. Catches left. 6'3", 187 lbs. Born, Zug, Switzerland, June 5, 1997.
(Detroit's 3rd pick, 110th overall, in 2015 NHL Draft).

			Regular Season								Playoffs						
Season	Club	League	GP	W	L	O/T	Mins	GA	SO	Avg	GP	W	L	Mins	GA	SO	Avg
2011-12	EV Zug U17	Swiss-U17	3	....	....	....	....	....	....	1.64	....	....	....	....	....	....	....
2012-13	EV Zug U17	Swiss-U17	14	....	....	....	....	....	....	2.62	4	....	....	....	....	....	2.71
	EV Zug Jr.	Swiss-Jr.	4	....	....	....	....	....	....	2.17	....	....	....	....	....	....	....
	EV Zug II Jr.	Swiss-Jr.	1	....	....	....	....	....	....	....	....	....	....	....	....	....	....
2013-14	Linkopings HC U18	Swe-U18	15	12	3	0	880	27	3	1.84	....	....	....	....	....	....	....
2014-15	Linkopings HC U18	Swe-U18	26	21	5	0	1577	40	4	1.52	5	2	3	299	12	1	2.41
	Linkopings HC Jr.	Swe-Jr.	5	4	1	0	312	16	0	3.08	....	....	....	....	....	....	....
2015-16	Linkopings HC Jr.	Swe-Jr.	19	11	8	0	1119	49	0	2.63	....	....	....	....	....	....	....
2016-17	HC Davos Jr.	Swiss-Jr.	1	0	1	0	60	3	0	3.02	4	2	2	238	11	0	2.77
	HC Davos	Swiss	16	10	6	0	1006	44	0	2.63	....	....	....	....	....	....	....

VANECEK, Vitek (va-NIH-chehk, VIH-tehk) WSH

Goaltender. Catches left. 6'1", 180 lbs. Born, Havlickuv Brod, Czech Rep., January 9, 1996.
(Washington's 2nd pick, 39th overall, in 2014 NHL Draft).

			Regular Season								Playoffs						
Season	Club	League	GP	W	L	O/T	Mins	GA	SO	Avg	GP	W	L	Mins	GA	SO	Avg
2010-11	Havl. Brod U18	CzR-U18	1	....	....	....	60	6	0	6.00	....	....	....	....	....	....	....
2011-12	Havl. Brod U18	CzR-U18	7	....	....	....	323	22	0	4.09	....	....	....	....	....	....	....
2012-13	Havl. Brod U18	CzR-U18	36	....	....	....	2011	108	1	3.22	....	....	....	....	....	....	....
	Havl. Brod Jr.	CzRep-Jr.	2	....	....	....	....	....	....	2.00	....	....	....	....	....	....	....
2013-14	HC Liberec Jr.	CzRep-Jr.	38	....	....	....	2156	95	2	2.64	4	....	....	213	15	0	4.23
2014-15	HC Liberec Jr.	CzRep-Jr.	4	....	....	....	200	12	1	3.60	....	....	....	....	....	....	....
	Liberec	CzRep	6	....	....	....	359	16	0	2.67	....	....	....	....	....	....	....
	Benatky	CzRep-2	20	....	....	....	1178	44	0	2.24	5	....	....	282	13	0	2.77
2015-16	Hershey Bears	AHL	1	1	0	0	65	1	0	0.92	....	....	....	....	....	....	....
	South Carolina	ECHL	32	18	7	6	1867	63	4	2.03	11	6	4	624	24	1	2.31
2016-17	Hershey Bears	AHL	39	18	10	7	2147	91	5	2.54	4	1	2	196	9	0	2.75

VARLAMOV, Semyon (vahr-LA-mawv, sehm-YAWN) COL

Goaltender. Catches left. 6'2", 209 lbs. Born, Kuybyshev, USSR, April 27, 1988.
(Washington's 2nd pick, 23rd overall, in 2006 NHL Draft).

			Regular Season								Playoffs						
Season	Club	League	GP	W	L	O/T	Mins	GA	SO	Avg	GP	W	L	Mins	GA	SO	Avg
2004-05	Yaroslavl 2	Russia-3	8	....	....	....	369	15	1	2.43	....	....	....	....	....	....	....
2005-06	Yaroslavl 2	Russia-3	33	....	....	....	1782	60	8	2.02	....	....	....	....	....	....	....
2006-07	Yaroslavl 2	Russia-3	2	....	....	....	120	3	0	1.50	....	....	....	....	....	....	....
	Yaroslavl	Russia	33	....	....	....	1936	70	3	2.17	6	....	....	368	18	0	2.94
2007-08	Yaroslavl	Russia	44	....	....	....	2592	106	3	2.45	*16	....	....	*924	25	*5	1.62
2008-09	Washington	NHL	6	4	0	1	329	13	0	2.37	13	7	6	759	32	*2	2.53
	Hershey Bears	AHL	27	19	7	1	1551	62	2	2.40	....	....	....	....	....	....	....
2009-10	Washington	NHL	26	15	4	6	1527	65	2	2.55	6	3	3	349	14	0	2.41
	Hershey Bears	AHL	3	3	0	0	185	6	0	1.95	....	....	....	....	....	....	....
	Russia	Olympics	DID NOT PLAY – SPARE GOALTENDER														
2010-11	Washington	NHL	27	11	9	5	1560	58	2	2.23	....	....	....	....	....	....	....
	Hershey Bears	AHL	3	2	1	0	179	10	0	3.36	....	....	....	....	....	....	....
2011-12	Colorado	NHL	53	26	24	3	3151	136	4	2.59	....	....	....	....	....	....	....
2012-13	Yaroslavl	KHL	16	8	4	3	928	27	3	*1.74	....	....	....	....	....	....	....
	Colorado	NHL	35	11	21	3	1950	98	3	3.02	....	....	....	....	....	....	....
2013-14	Colorado	NHL	63	*41	14	6	3640	146	2	2.41	7	3	4	432	20	0	2.78
	Russia	Olympics	3	....	....	....	152	5	....	1.99	....	....	....	....	....	....	....
2014-15	Colorado	NHL	57	28	20	8	3307	141	5	2.56	....	....	....	....	....	....	....
2015-16	Colorado	NHL	57	27	25	3	3159	148	2	2.81	....	....	....	....	....	....	....
2016-17	Colorado	NHL	24	6	17	0	1348	76	1	3.38	....	....	....	....	....	....	....
	NHL Totals		348	169	134	35	19971	881	21	2.65	26	13	13	1540	66	2	2.57

NHL Second All-Star Team (2014)

Traded to **Colorado** by **Washington** for Colorado's 1st round pick (Filip Forsberg) in 2012 NHL Draft and Boston's 2nd round pick (previously acquired, later traded to Dallas – Dallas selected Mike Winther) in 2012 NHL Draft, July 1, 2011. Signed as a free agent by **Yaroslavl** (KHL), September 27, 2012.

VASILEVSKIY, Andrei (va-sihl-EHV-skee, an-DRAY) T.B.

Goaltender. Catches left. 6'3", 207 lbs. Born, Tyumen, Russia, July 25, 1994.
(Tampa Bay's 2nd pick, 19th overall, in 2012 NHL Draft).

			Regular Season								Playoffs						
Season	Club	League	GP	W	L	O/T	Mins	GA	SO	Avg	GP	W	L	Mins	GA	SO	Avg
2010-11	Tolpar Ufa Jr.	Russia-Jr.	14	8	2	0	730	22	3	1.81	2	1	1	88	3	0	2.05
2011-12	Tolpar Ufa Jr.	Russia-Jr.	27	15	8	0	1477	55	3	2.23	2	0	2	120	5	0	2.50
2012-13	Ufa	KHL	8	4	1	0	298	11	1	2.22	....	....	....	....	....	....	....
	Tolpar Ufa Jr.	Russia-Jr.	27	17	6	0	1613	52	3	1.93	3	0	2	190	9	0	2.85
2013-14	Ufa	KHL	28	14	8	0	1601	59	3	2.21	18	9	9	1144	38	1	1.99
2014-15	**Tampa Bay**	**NHL**	**16**	**7**	**5**	**1**	**864**	**34**	**1**	**2.36**	**4**	**1**	**1**	**113**	**6**	**0**	**3.19**
	Syracuse Crunch	AHL	25	14	6	5	1469	60	2	2.45	....	....	....	....	....	....	....
2015-16	**Tampa Bay**	**NHL**	**24**	**11**	**10**	**0**	**1259**	**58**	**1**	**2.76**	**8**	**3**	**4**	**434**	**20**	**0**	**2.76**
	Syracuse Crunch	AHL	12	7	4	1	711	23	1	1.94	....	....	....	....	....	....	....
2016-17	**Tampa Bay**	**NHL**	**50**	**23**	**17**	**7**	**2831**	**123**	**2**	**2.61**	....	....	....	....	....	....	....
	NHL Totals		**90**	**41**	**32**	**8**	**4954**	**215**	**4**	**2.60**	**12**	**4**	**5**	**547**	**26**	**0**	**2.85**

VAY, Adam (VAY, A-duhm) MIN

Goaltender. Catches left. 6'5", 228 lbs. Born, Budapest, Hungary, March 22, 1994.

			Regular Season								Playoffs						
Season	Club	League	GP	W	L	O/T	Mins	GA	SO	Avg	GP	W	L	Mins	GA	SO	Avg
2011-12	HK Trnava U18	Svk-U18	24	....	....	....	1386	36	6	1.56	....	....	....	....	....	....	....
	HK Trnava Jr.	Slovak-Jr.	7	....	....	....	274	21	0	4.61	....	....	....	....	....	....	....
2012-13	Budapest Jr.	Russia-Jr.	9	0	7	0	412	35	0	5.10	....	....	....	....	....	....	....
2013-14	El Paso Rhinos	WSHL	26	25	1	0	1569	46	*5	*1.76	3	3	0	180	6	0	2.00
2014-15	El Paso Rhinos	WSHL	32	*28	4	0	1984	67	*5	2.03	9	5	2	457	21	0	2.75
2015-16	Debreceni HK	MOL	39	....	....	....	2235	103	2	2.76	3	....	....	141	12	0	5.11
2016-17	Quad City Mallards	ECHL	39	20	17	2	2298	116	3	3.03	....	....	....	....	....	....	....

Signed as a free agent by **Minnesota**, May 17, 2016.

VEJMELKA, Karel (vay-MEHL-kuh, KAHR-uhl) NSH

Goaltender. Catches right. 6'3", 202 lbs. Born, Trebic, Czech Rep., May 25, 1996.
(Nashville's 5th pick, 145th overall, in 2015 NHL Draft).

			Regular Season								Playoffs						
Season	Club	League	GP	W	L	O/T	Mins	GA	SO	Avg	GP	W	L	Mins	GA	SO	Avg
2010-11	Trebic U18	CzR-U18	7	....	....	....	....	....	....	2.18	....	....	....	....	....	....	....
2011-12	Trebic U18	CzR-U18	17	....	....	....	....	....	....	2.87	....	....	....	....	....	....	....
	Trebic Jr.	CzRep-Jr.	2	....	....	....	....	....	....	2.00	....	....	....	....	....	....	....
2012-13	Trebic U18	CzR-U18	1	....	....	....	....	....	....	0.00	....	....	....	....	....	....	....
	Trebic Jr.	CzRep-Jr.	5	....	....	....	....	....	....	2.17	....	....	....	....	....	....	....
	HC Pardubice U18	CzR-U18	17	....	....	....	993	43	3	2.60	1	....	....	60	4	0	4.00
2013-14	HC Pardubice U18	CzR-U18	4	....	....	....	247	10	0	2.43	....	....	....	....	....	....	....
	HC Pardubice Jr.	CzRep-Jr.	36	....	....	....	2053	88	1	2.57	....	....	....	....	....	....	....
2014-15	HC Pardubice Jr.	CzRep-Jr.	37	....	....	....	2222	94	2	2.54	....	....	....	....	....	....	....
	Pardubice	CzRep	7	....	....	....	419	20	0	2.86	6	....	....	338	17	1	3.02
	Trebic	CzRep-2	3	....	....	....	176	4	0	1.36	....	....	....	....	....	....	....
2015-16	Pardubice	CzRep	1	....	....	....	44	1	0	1.36	....	....	....	....	....	....	....
	HC Kometa Brno	CzRep	5	....	....	....	163	4	1	1.47	....	....	....	....	....	....	....
	Trebic	CzRep-2	44	....	....	....	2550	111	1	2.61	....	....	....	....	....	....	....
2016-17	Trebic	CzRep-2	10	....	....	....	595	23	1	2.32	....	....	....	....	....	....	....
	HC Kometa Brno	CzRep	31	....	....	....	1729	72	3	2.50	....	....	....	....	....	....	....

VILLALTA, Matt (vihl-AL-ta, MAT) L.A.

Goaltender. Catches left. 6'3", 165 lbs. Born, Kingston, ON, March 6, 1999.
(Los Angeles' 3rd pick, 72nd overall, in 2017 NHL Draft).

			Regular Season								Playoffs						
Season	Club	League	GP	W	L	O/T	Mins	GA	SO	Avg	GP	W	L	Mins	GA	SO	Avg
2014-15	Kingston Fr. MM	Minor-ON	33	....	....	....	1024	66	....	....	....	....	....	....	....	....	....
2015-16	Kingston Fr. Mid.	Minor-ON	STATISTICS NOT AVAILABLE														
	Napanee Raiders	ON-Jr.C	DID NOT PLAY – SPARE GOALTENDER														
2016-17	Sault Ste. Marie	OHL	33	25	3	0	1795	72	1	2.41	2	1	1	100	7	0	4.20

VLADAR, Dan (VLA-duhr, DAN) BOS

Goaltender. Catches left. 6'6", 192 lbs. Born, Prague, Czech Rep., August 20, 1997.
(Boston's 7th pick, 75th overall, in 2015 NHL Draft).

			Regular Season								Playoffs						
Season	Club	League	GP	W	L	O/T	Mins	GA	SO	Avg	GP	W	L	Mins	GA	SO	Avg
2012-13	HC Kladno U18	CzR-U18	36	....	....	....	2125	107	1	3.02	3	....	....	179	10	0	3.35
	HC KEB Kladno Jr.	CzRep-Jr.	1	....	....	....	60	3	0	3.00	....	....	....	....	....	....	....
2013-14	HC Kladno U18	CzR-U18	31	....	....	....	1829	69	4	2.26	3	....	....	178	10	0	3.37
	HC KEB Kladno Jr.	CzRep-Jr.	6	....	....	....	366	15	1	2.46	....	....	....	....	....	....	....
2014-15	HC KEB Kladno Jr.	CzRep-Jr.	29	....	....	....	1681	78	1	2.78	4	....	....	20	12	0	3.60
	Rytiri Kladno	CzRep-2	8	....	....	....	487	16	1	1.97	....	....	....	....	....	....	....
2015-16	Chicago Steel	USHL	30	12	12	4	1766	68	3	2.31	....	....	....	....	....	....	....
2016-17	Providence Bruins	AHL	8	4	0	2	390	17	1	2.62	....	....	....	....	....	....	....
	Atlanta Gladiators	ECHL	18	5	9	2	972	63	0	3.89	....	....	....	....	....	....	....

VOLKOV, Konstantin (VOHL-kawv, KAWN-stan-tihn) NSH

Goaltender. Catches left. 6'3", 211 lbs. Born, Murmansk, Russia, September 20, 1997.
(Nashville's 7th pick, 168th overall, in 2016 NHL Draft).

			Regular Season								Playoffs						
Season	Club	League	GP	W	L	O/T	Mins	GA	SO	Avg	GP	W	L	Mins	GA	SO	Avg
2014-15	St. Petersburg Jr.	Russia-Jr.	3	0	1	0	112	6	0	3.21	....	....	....	....	....	....	....
	SKA-Varyagi Jr.	Rus-Jr.B	28	13	11	0	1626	73	3	2.69	8	4	4	446	17	1	2.29
2015-16	St. Petersburg Jr.	Russia-Jr.	17	10	4	0	929	36	1	2.33	1	0	0	23	2	0	5.29
	SKA-Varyagi Jr.	Rus-Jr.B	6	3	3	0	337	12	1	2.14	....	....	....	....	....	....	....
2016-17	St. Petersburg Jr.	Russia-Jr.	36	27	8	0	2139	62	4	1.74	8	4	4	479	20	1	2.51

VOMACKA, Tomas (voh-MAHCH-ka, toh-MAHSH) NSH

Goaltender. Catches left. 6'3", 165 lbs. Born, Trutnov, Czech Rep., February 5, 1999.
(Nashville's 4th pick, 154th overall, in 2017 NHL Draft).

			Regular Season								Playoffs						
Season	Club	League	GP	W	L	O/T	Mins	GA	SO	Avg	GP	W	L	Mins	GA	SO	Avg
2014-15	Hr. Kralove U18	CzR-U18	7	....	....	....	359	17	0	2.84	....	....	....	....	....	....	....
2015-16	Hr. Kralove U18	CzR-U18	28	....	....	....	1592	63	4	2.37	3	....	....	190	11	0	3.47
	Hr. Kralove Jr.	CzRep-Jr.	4	....	....	....	212	15	0	4.25	1	....	....	13	1	0	4.62
2016-17	Corpus Christi	NAHL	41	19	13	2	2344	95	1	2.43	8	5	3	544	13	2	*1.43

• Signed Letter of Intent to attend **University of Connecticut** (Hockey East) in fall of 2018.

WALL, Tyler (WAWL, TIGH-luhr) NYR

Goaltender. Catches left. 6'3", 206 lbs. Born, Leamington, ON, January 14, 1998.
(NY Rangers' 5th pick, 174th overall, in 2016 NHL Draft).

			Regular Season								Playoffs						
Season	Club	League	GP	W	L	O/T	Mins	GA	SO	Avg	GP	W	L	Mins	GA	SO	Avg
2012-13	Sun County Bant.	Minor-ON	STATISTICS NOT AVAILABLE														
	Sun County MM	Minor-ON	....	....	....	....	....	....	....	....	1	0	1	45	3	0	3.00
2013-14	Sun County MM	Minor-ON	17	8	4	0	765	39	0	2.29	4	0	2	190	13	0	3.08
2014-15	Wind. Jr. Spitfires	Minor-ON	19	15	3	0	1139	44	1	2.32	5	3	2	306	13	1	2.55
	Leamington Flyers	ON-Jr.B	1	0	1	0	60	7	0	7.00	....	....	....	....	....	....	....
2015-16	Leamington Flyers	ON-Jr.B	31	27	2	0	1809	45	4	*1.49	12	7	5	720	31	1	2.58
2016-17	U. Mass Lowell	H-East	37	*26	10	1	2095	72	2	*2.06	....	....	....	....	....	....	....

WARD, Cam (WOHRD, KAM) CAR

Goaltender. Catches left. 6'1", 185 lbs. Born, Saskatoon, SK, February 29, 1984.
(Carolina's 1st pick, 25th overall, in 2002 NHL Draft).

			Regular Season								Playoffs						
Season	Club	League	GP	W	L	O/T	Mins	GA	SO	Avg	GP	W	L	Mins	GA	SO	Avg
1998-99	Sherwood Park	Minor-AB	24	13	7	4	1403	85	0	3.64	....	....	....	....	....	....	....
99-2000	Sherwood Park	AMHL	20	9	5	1	1194	71	0	3.57	7	4	3	262	22	0	3.57
2000-01	Sherwood Park	AMHL	25	14	6	3	1449	70	0	2.90	....	....	....	....	....	....	....
	Red Deer Rebels	WHL	1	1	0	0	60	0	1	0.00	....	....	....	....	....	....	....
2001-02	Red Deer Rebels	WHL	46	30	11	4	2695	102	1	*2.27	*23	14	9	*1503	52	*2	2.08
2002-03	Red Deer Rebels	WHL	57	*40	13	2	3367	118	5	2.10	*23	14	9	*1407	49	3	2.09
2003-04	Red Deer Rebels	WHL	56	31	16	8	3338	114	4	2.05	19	10	9	1199	37	3	1.85
2004-05	Lowell	AHL	50	27	17	3	2829	94	6	1.99	11	5	6	664	28	2	2.53
2005-06 ♦	**Carolina**	**NHL**	**28**	**14**	**8**	**2**	**1484**	**91**	**0**	**3.68**	***23**	***15**	**8**	***1320**	**47**	**2**	**2.14**
	Lowell	AHL	2	0	2	0	118	5	0	2.54	....	....	....	....	....	....	....
2006-07	**Carolina**	**NHL**	**60**	**30**	**21**	**6**	**3422**	**167**	**2**	**2.93**	....	....	....	....	....	....	....
2007-08	**Carolina**	**NHL**	**69**	**37**	**25**	**5**	**3930**	**180**	**4**	**2.75**	....	....	....	....	....	....	....
2008-09	**Carolina**	**NHL**	**68**	**39**	**23**	**5**	**3928**	**160**	**6**	**2.44**	**18**	**8**	**10**	**1101**	**49**	***2**	**2.67**
2009-10	**Carolina**	**NHL**	**47**	**18**	**23**	**5**	**2651**	**119**	**0**	**2.69**	....	....	....	....	....	....	....
2010-11	**Carolina**	**NHL**	***74**	**37**	**26**	**10**	***4318**	**184**	**4**	**2.56**	....	....	....	....	....	....	....
2011-12	**Carolina**	**NHL**	**68**	**30**	**23**	**13**	**3988**	**182**	**5**	**2.74**	....	....	....	....	....	....	....
2012-13	**Carolina**	**NHL**	**17**	**9**	**6**	**1**	**929**	**44**	**0**	**2.84**	....	....	....	....	....	....	....
2013-14	**Carolina**	**NHL**	**30**	**10**	**12**	**6**	**1645**	**84**	**0**	**3.06**	....	....	....	....	....	....	....
	Charlotte Checkers	AHL	2	1	1	0	119	4	0	2.02	....	....	....	....	....	....	....
2014-15	**Carolina**	**NHL**	**51**	**22**	**24**	**5**	**3026**	**121**	**1**	**2.40**	....	....	....	....	....	....	....
2015-16	**Carolina**	**NHL**	**52**	**23**	**17**	**10**	**3038**	**122**	**1**	**2.41**	....	....	....	....	....	....	....
2016-17	**Carolina**	**NHL**	**61**	**26**	**22**	**12**	**3618**	**162**	**2**	**2.69**	....	....	....	....	....	....	....
	NHL Totals		**625**	**295**	**230**	**80**	**35977**	**1616**	**25**	**2.70**	**41**	**23**	**18**	**2421**	**96**	**4**	**2.38**

WHL East First All-Star Team (2002, 2004) • Canadian Major Junior Second All-Star Team (2002) • WHL East Second All-Star Team (2003) • WHL Goaltender of the Year (2002, 2004) • WHL Player of the Year (2004) • Canadian Major Junior First All-Star Team (2004) • Canadian Major Junior Goaltender of the Year (2004) • AHL All-Rookie Team (2005) • Conn Smythe Trophy (2006)

Played in NHL All-Star Game (2011)

• Scored a goal vs. New Jersey, December 26, 2011.

WEDGEWOOD, Scott (WEHJ-wud, SKAWT) N.J.

Goaltender. Catches left. 6'2", 195 lbs. Born, Brampton, ON, August 14, 1992.
(New Jersey's 2nd pick, 84th overall, in 2010 NHL Draft).

			Regular Season								Playoffs						
Season	Club	League	GP	W	L	O/T	Mins	GA	SO	Avg	GP	W	L	Mins	GA	SO	Avg
2007-08	Miss. Senators	GTHL	29	....	....	....	1305	63	2	2.17	....	....	....	....	....	....	....
2008-09	Plymouth Whalers	OHL	6	0	2	0	158	12	0	4.56	3	0	0	26	2	0	4.62
2009-10	Plymouth Whalers	OHL	18	5	9	0	938	51	2	3.26	4	1	1	116	4	0	2.07
2010-11	Plymouth Whalers	OHL	55	28	18	2	3046	152	2	2.99	10	4	6	606	33	0	3.27
2011-12	Plymouth Whalers	OHL	43	28	10	3	2482	125	3	3.02	13	7	6	781	31	*2	2.38
2012-13	Trenton Titans	ECHL	48	20	22	5	2741	147	1	3.22	....	....	....	....	....	....	....
	Albany Devils	AHL	5	2	2	0	242	14	0	3.47	....	....	....	....	....	....	....
2013-14	Albany Devils	AHL	36	16	14	3	1980	79	4	2.39	....	....	....	....	....	....	....
2014-15	Albany Devils	AHL	36	13	14	6	2014	92	2	2.74	....	....	....	....	....	....	....
2015-16	**New Jersey**	**NHL**	**4**	**2**	**1**	**1**	**241**	**5**	**1**	**1.24**	....	....	....	....	....	....	....
	Albany Devils	AHL	22	14	3	3	1241	32	2	1.55	11	6	5	662	30	0	2.72
	Adirondack	ECHL	1	1	0	0	60	2	0	2.00	....	....	....	....	....	....	....
2016-17	Albany Devils	AHL	10	5	3	0	550	20	0	2.18	....	....	....	....	....	....	....
	NHL Totals		**4**	**2**	**1**	**1**	**241**	**5**	**1**	**1.24**	....	....	....	....	....	....	....

• Missed majority of 2016-17 due to shoulder injury vs. Binghamton (AHL), November 19, 2016 and resulting surgery.

WELLS, Dylan (WEHLZ, DIH-luhn) EDM

Goaltender. Catches left. 6'1", 182 lbs. Born, St. Catherines, ON, January 3, 1998.
(Edmonton's 6th pick, 123rd overall, in 2016 NHL Draft).

			Regular Season								Playoffs						
Season	Club	League	GP	W	L	O/T	Mins	GA	SO	Avg	GP	W	L	Mins	GA	SO	Avg
2013-14	Niagara N Stars	Minor-ON	17	....	....	....	....	....	....	2.29	4	....	....	....	....	....	3.08
2014-15	Peterborough	OHL	27	7	15	4	1471	97	0	3.96	....	....	....	....	....	....	....
2015-16	Peterborough	OHL	27	9	13	3	1516	116	0	4.59	....	....	....	....	....	....	....
2016-17	Peterborough	OHL	52	33	15	4	3026	155	1	3.07	12	8	4	764	32	0	2.51

WERNER, Adam (WUHR-nuhr, A-duhm) COL

Goaltender. Catches left. 6'5", 198 lbs. Born, Mariestad, Sweden, May 2, 1997.
(Colorado's 4th pick, 131st overall, in 2016 NHL Draft).

			Regular Season								Playoffs						
Season	Club	League	GP	W	L	O/T	Mins	GA	SO	Avg	GP	W	L	Mins	GA	SO	Avg
2011-12	Mariestads BoIS HC	Swe-U18	1	1	0	0	60	2	0	2.00	....	....	....	....	....	....	....
2012-13	Mariestads BoIS HC	Swe-U18	10	8	1	0	562	22	0	2.35	....	....	....	....	....	....	....
2013-14	Farjestad U18	Swe-U18	30	19	11	0	1749	64	4	2.19	4	2	2	242	10	0	2.48
	Farjestad Jr.	Swe-Jr.	9	6	3	0	527	26	1	2.96	....	....	....	....	....	....	....
2014-15	Farjestad U18	Swe-U18	1	0	1	0	60	4	0	4.00	....	....	....	....	....	....	....
	Farjestad Jr.	Swe-Jr.	28	15	13	0	1692	85	2	3.01	6	3	3	357	20	0	3.36
	Farjestad	Sweden	1	0	0	0	3	0	0	0.00	....	....	....	....	....	....	....
2015-16	Farjestad Jr.	Swe-Jr.	30	20	10	0	1783	74	3	2.49	5	2	3	306	13	1	2.55
	Koping HC	Sweden-3	1	0	1	0	65	2	0	1.85	....	....	....	....	....	....	....
	Forshaga IF	Sweden-3	2	1	1	0	119	5	0	2.53	....	....	....	....	....	....	....
2016-17	IF Bjorkloven Umea	Sweden-2	25	12	13	0	1471	73	2	2.98	....	....	....	....	....	....	....
	Farjestad Jr.	Swe-Jr.	....	....	....	....	....	....	....	....	1	0	1	58	3	0	3.08

WILCOX, Adam   (WIHL-cawx, A-duhm)   **BUF**

Goaltender. Catches left. 6', 171 lbs.   Born, South St. Paul, MN, November 26, 1992.
(Tampa Bay's 4th pick, 178th overall, in 2011 NHL Draft).

						Regular Season								Playoffs			
Season	Club	League	GP	W	L	O/T	Mins	GA	SO	Avg	GP	W	L	Mins	GA	SO	Avg
2009-10	South St. Paul	High-MN	23	11	11	0	1119	73	0	3.33	2	1	1	102	8	0	4.00
2010-11	Green Bay	USHL	24	16	6	1	1420	52	1	2.20	2	1	0	88	1	0	0.68
2011-12	Green Bay	USHL	9	7	2	0	529	20	2	2.27	….	….	….	….	….	….	….
	Tri-City Storm	USHL	34	16	17	1	1896	92	1	2.91	….	….	….	….	….	….	….
2012-13	U. of Minnesota	WCHA	39	*25	8	5	*2331	73	3	*1.88	….	….	….	….	….	….	….
2013-14	U. of Minnesota	Big Ten	*38	*26	6	6	*2282	75	*4	*1.97	….	….	….	….	….	….	….
2014-15	U. of Minnesota	Big Ten	*38	*22	12	3	*2252	91	*6	2.42	….	….	….	….	….	….	….
	Syracuse Crunch	AHL	2	0	2	0	113	6	0	3.18	1	0	0	32	1	0	1.86
2015-16	Syracuse Crunch	AHL	27	9	12	6	1455	81	0	3.34	….	….	….	….	….	….	….
2016-17	Syracuse Crunch	AHL	34	18	9	4	1842	88	1	2.87	….	….	….	….	….	….	….
	Springfield	AHL	13	7	4	1	713	24	3	2.02	….	….	….	….	….	….	….

Big Ten First All-Star Team (2014) • Big Ten Player of the Year (2014)
Traded to **Florida** by **Tampa Bay** for Mike McKenna, March 1, 2017. Signed as a free agent by **Buffalo**, July 1, 2017.

WILL, Roman   (WIHL, ROH-muhn)

Goaltender. Catches left. 6'1", 195 lbs.   Born, Plzen, Czech., May 22, 1992.

						Regular Season								Playoffs			
Season	Club	League	GP	W	L	O/T	Mins	GA	SO	Avg	GP	W	L	Mins	GA	SO	Avg
2008-09	Ml. Boleslav U17	CzR-U17	40	….	….	….	2332	104	2	2.68	2	….	….	120	6	0	3.00
2009-10	Ml. Boleslav U18	CzR-U18	23	….	….	….	1366	39	6	1.71	….	….	….	….	….	….	….
	Ml. Boleslav Jr.	CzRep-Jr.	23	….	….	….	1304	72	1	3.31	3	….	….	184	8	0	2.61
2010-11	Ml. Boleslav Jr.	CzRep-Jr.	48	….	….	….	2730	102	3	2.24	….	….	….	….	….	….	….
	BK Mlada Boleslav	CzRep-Q	1	….	….	….	40	5	0	7.50	….	….	….	….	….	….	….
2011-12	Moncton Wildcats	QMJHL	63	29	25	7	3592	166	1	2.77	4	0	4	205	19	0	5.56
2012-13	BK Mlada Boleslav	Czech-2	44	….	….	….	….	….	1.87	….	….	10	….	….	….	1.42	….
2013-14	BK Mlada Boleslav	Czech-2	20	….	….	….	….	….	1.84	….	….	10	….	….	….	1.81	….
	BK Mlada Boleslav	CzRep-Q	2	….	….	….	….	….	5.27	….	….	….	….	….	….	….	….
2014-15	Lake Erie Monsters	AHL	11	2	6	1	576	34	0	3.54	….	….	….	….	….	….	….
	Fort Wayne	ECHL	29	17	8	4	1745	70	1	2.41	7	4	3	417	19	1	2.74
2015-16	**Colorado**	**NHL**	**1**	**0**	**0**	**0**	**18**	**1**	**0**	**3.33**	….	….	….	….	….	….	….
	San Antonio	AHL	29	10	13	3	1527	87	0	3.42	….	….	….	….	….	….	….
2016-17	Bili Tygri Liberec	CzRep	30	….	….	….	1772	50	7	1.69	….	….	….	296	10	2	2.03
	NHL Totals		**1**	**0**	**0**	**0**	**18**	**1**	**0**	**3.33**							

Signed as a free agent by **Colorado**, May 13, 2014. Signed as a free agent by **Liberec** (CzRep), May 10, 2016.

WILLIAMS, Stephon   (WIHL-yuhms, STEH-fawn)

Goaltender. Catches left. 6'3", 200 lbs.   Born, Fairbanks, AK, April 28, 1993.
(NY Islanders' 4th pick, 106th overall, in 2013 NHL Draft).

						Regular Season								Playoffs			
Season	Club	League	GP	W	L	O/T	Mins	GA	SO	Avg	GP	W	L	Mins	GA	SO	Avg
2010-11	Sioux Falls	USHL	35	20	7	6	2042	88	1	2.59	5	4	1	298	11	0	2.21
2011-12	Sioux Falls	USHL	21	6	9	2	1113	50	1	2.70	….	….	….	….	….	….	….
	Waterloo	USHL	19	10	6	2	1054	49	1	2.79	*15	10	5	*895	34	*1	2.28
2012-13	Minnesota State	WCHA	35	21	12	2	2043	68	*4	2.00	….	….	….	….	….	….	….
2013-14	Minnesota State	WCHA	12	5	6	0	595	32	1	3.23	….	….	….	….	….	….	….
2014-15	Minnesota State	WCHA	35	25	6	3	1999	55	5	*1.65	….	….	….	….	….	….	….
	Bridgeport	AHL	5	3	1	0	255	9	0	2.12	….	….	….	….	….	….	….
2015-16	Bridgeport	AHL	29	15	13	1	1605	74	1	2.77	2	0	2	120	6	0	3.01
	Missouri Mavericks	ECHL	7	2	3	2	412	20	0	2.91	….	….	….	….	….	….	….
2016-17	Bridgeport	AHL	24	6	13	1	1265	65	1	3.08	….	….	….	….	….	….	….
	Missouri Mavericks	ECHL	8	3	4	0	424	19	0	2.69	….	….	….	….	….	….	….

WCHA All-Rookie Team (2013) • WCHA First All-Star Team (2013) • WCHA Rookie of the Year (2013) • WCHA Second All-Star Team (2015)

WOLL, Joseph   (WAHL, JOH-sehf)   **TOR**

Goaltender. Catches left. 6'2", 202 lbs.   Born, St.Louis, MO, July 12, 1998.
(Toronto's 4th pick, 62nd overall, in 2016 NHL Draft).

						Regular Season								Playoffs			
Season	Club	League	GP	W	L	O/T	Mins	GA	SO	Avg	GP	W	L	Mins	GA	SO	Avg
2013-14	St.L. AAA Blues	T1EHL	18	13	4	1	981	31	3	1.71	….	….	….	….	….	….	….
2014-15	USAHNTDP	USHL	18	3	15	0	983	69	0	4.21	….	….	….	….	….	….	….
	USAHNTDP	U-17	11	6	3	0	603	23	0	2.29	….	….	….	….	….	….	….
2015-16	USAHNTDP	USHL	12	6	4	1	670	29	0	2.60	….	….	….	….	….	….	….
	USAHNTDP	U-18	21	14	2	3	1182	37	2	1.88	….	….	….	….	….	….	….
2016-17	Boston College	H-East	34	17	13	3	1977	87	1	2.64	….	….	….	….	….	….	….

Hockey East All-Rookie Team (2017)

ZATKOFF, Jeff   (ZAT-kawf, JEHF)   **L.A.**

Goaltender. Catches left. 6'2", 179 lbs.   Born, Detroit, MI, June 9, 1987.
(Los Angeles' 4th pick, 74th overall, in 2006 NHL Draft).

						Regular Season								Playoffs			
Season	Club	League	GP	W	L	O/T	Mins	GA	SO	Avg	GP	W	L	Mins	GA	SO	Avg
2004-05	Sioux City	USHL	24	13	6	3	1271	54	1	2.55	2	0	0	68	10	0	8.88
2005-06	Miami U.	CCHA	20	14	5	1	1217	41	3	2.02	….	….	….	….	….	….	….
2006-07	Miami U.	CCHA	26	14	8	3	1542	58	1	2.26	….	….	….	….	….	….	….
2007-08	Miami U.	CCHA	36	27	8	1	2161	62	3	*1.72	….	….	….	….	….	….	….
2008-09	Manchester	AHL	3	1	2	0	182	7	0	2.31	….	….	….	….	….	….	….
	Ontario Reign	ECHL	37	17	15	3	2164	107	1	2.97	7	3	4	418	26	0	3.73
2009-10	Manchester	AHL	22	10	9	0	1170	57	2	2.92	….	….	….	….	….	….	….
2010-11	Manchester	AHL	45	20	17	5	2508	112	3	2.68	5	1	3	253	16	0	3.80
2011-12	Manchester	AHL	44	21	17	1	2432	101	3	2.49	2	0	2	97	7	0	4.34
2012-13	Wilkes-Barre	AHL	49	26	20	0	2799	90	5	*1.93	5	2	3	253	23	0	5.45
2013-14	**Pittsburgh**	**NHL**	**20**	**12**	**6**	**2**	**1171**	**51**	**1**	**2.61**	….	….	….	….	….	….	….
2014-15	**Pittsburgh**	**NHL**	**1**	**0**	**1**	**0**	**37**	**1**	**0**	**1.62**	….	….	….	….	….	….	….
	Wilkes-Barre	AHL	37	18	14	4	2155	88	3	2.45	2	0	0	59	1	0	1.03
2015-16 ◆	**Pittsburgh**	**NHL**	**14**	**4**	**7**	**1**	**732**	**34**	**0**	**2.79**	**2**	**1**	**1**	**117**	**6**	**0**	**3.08**
2016-17	**Los Angeles**	**NHL**	**13**	**2**	**7**	**1**	**550**	**27**	**0**	**2.95**	….	….	….	….	….	….	….
	Ontario Reign	AHL	8	2	3	2	458	23	0	3.01	….	….	….	….	….	….	….
	NHL Totals		**48**	**18**	**21**	**4**	**2490**	**113**	**1**	**2.72**	**2**	**1**	**1**	**117**	**6**	**0**	**3.08**

CCHA Second All-Star Team (2008) • Harry "Hap" Holmes Memorial Award (AHL – fewest goals against) (2013) (shared with Brad Thiessen) • Harry "Hap" Holmes Memorial Award (AHL – fewest goals against) (2015) (shared with Matt Murray).
Signed as a free agent by **Pittsburgh**, July 1, 2012. Signed as a free agent by **Los Angeles**, July 1, 2016.

ZHUKOV, Maxim   (ZHOO-kawv, MAK-sihm)   **VGK**

Goaltender. Catches left. 6'2", 187 lbs.   Born, Kaliningrad, Russia, July 22, 1999.
(Las Vegas' 7th pick, 96th overall, in 2017 NHL Draft).

						Regular Season								Playoffs			
Season	Club	League	GP	W	L	O/T	Mins	GA	SO	Avg	GP	W	L	Mins	GA	SO	Avg
2015-16	Loko-Yunior Jr.	Russia-Jr. B	4	4	0	0	212	7	0	1.98	2	1	0	80	3	0	2.25
2016-17	Green Bay	USHL	31	19	8	2	1736	65	4	2.25	….	….	….	….	….	….	….

Retired NHL Player Index

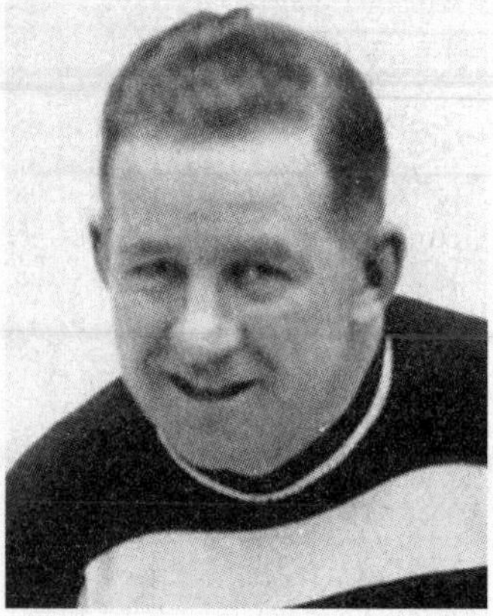

Jack Adams

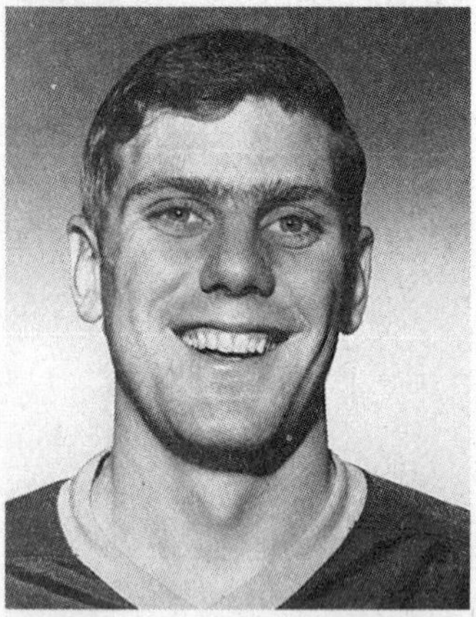

Ron Anderson

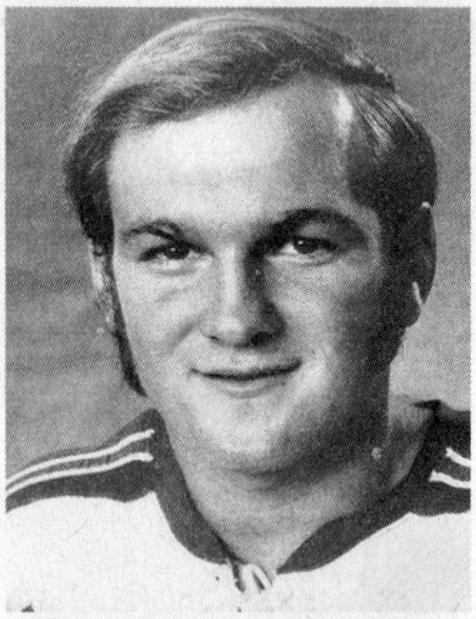

Steve Andrascik

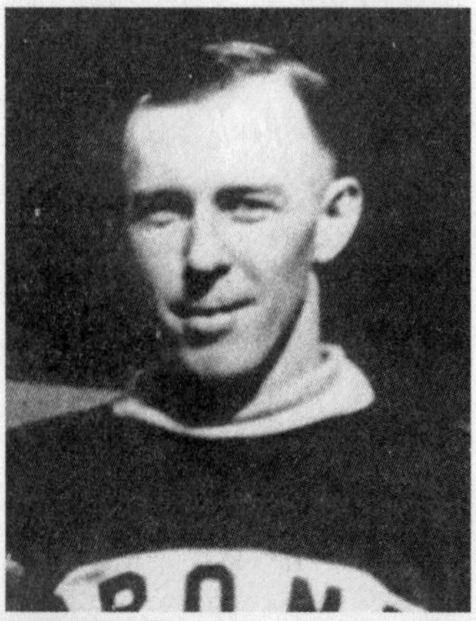

Lloyd Andrews

Abbreviations: Teams/Cities: – **Ana.** – Anaheim; **Atl.** – Atlanta; **Bos.** – Boston; **Bro.** – Brooklyn; **Buf.** – Buffalo; **Cgy.** – Calgary; **Cal.** – California; **Car.** – Carolina; **Chi.** – Chicago; **Cle.** – Cleveland; **Col.** – Colorado; **CBJ** – Columbus; **Dal.** – Dallas; **Det.** – Detroit; **Edm.** – Edmonton; **Fla.** – Florida; **Ham.** – Hamilton; **Hfd.** – Hartford; **K.C.** – Kansas City; **L.A.** – Los Angeles; **Min.** – Minnesota; **Mtl.** – Montreal; **Mtl.M.** – Montreal Maroons; **Mtl.W.** – Montreal Wanderers; **Nsh.** – Nashville; **N.J.** – New Jersey; **NYA** – NY Americans; **NYI** – NY Islanders; **NYR** – New York Rangers; **Oak.** – Oakland; **Ott.** – Ottawa; **Phi.** – Philadelphia; **Phx.** – Phoenix; **Pit.** – Pittsburgh; **Que.** – Quebec; **St.L.** – St. Louis; **S.J.** – San Jose; **T.B.** – Tampa Bay; **Tor.** – Toronto; **Van.** – Vancouver; **Wsh.** – Washington; **Wpg.** – Winnipeg

GP – games played; **G** – goals; **A** – assists; **TP** – total points; **PIM** – penalties in minutes.
• – deceased. ‡ – Remains active in other leagues. **Note:** Assists not recorded during 1917-18 season

NHL Seasons – A player or goaltender who does not play in a regular season but who does appear in that year's playoffs is credited with an NHL Season in this Index. Total seasons are rounded off to the nearest full season. **2015-16** – recently added to Retired Player Index.

			Regular Schedule					Playoffs							
Name	NHL Teams	NHL Seasons	GP	G	A	TP	PIM	GP	G	A	TP	PIM	NHL Cup Wins	First NHL Season	Last NHL Season
A															
Aalto, Antti	Ana.	4	151	11	17	28	52	4	0	0	0	2	....	1997-98	2000-01
Abbott, Reg	Mtl.	1	3	0	0	0	0	....	....	....	....	....	....	1952-53	1952-53
• Abel, Clarence	NYR, Chi.	8	333	19	18	37	359	38	1	1	2	58	2	1926-27	1933-34
Abel, Gerry	Det.	1	1	0	0	0	0	....	....	....	....	....	....	1966-67	1966-67
• Abel, Sid	Det., Chi.	14	612	189	283	472	376	97	28	30	58	79	3	1938-39	1953-54
Abgrall, Dennis	L.A.	1	13	0	2	2	4	....	....	....	....	....	....	1975-76	1975-76
Abid, Ramzi	Phx., Pit., Atl., Nsh.	4	68	14	16	30	78	2	0	0	0	0	....	2002-03	2006-07
Abrahamsson, Thommy	Hfd.	1	32	6	11	17	16	....	....	....	....	....	....	1980-81	1980-81
Achtymichuk, Gene	Mtl., Det.	4	32	3	5	8	2	....	....	....	....	....	....	1951-52	1958-59
Acomb, Doug	Tor.	1	2	0	1	1	0	....	....	....	....	....	....	1969-70	1969-70
Acton, Keith	Mtl., Min., Edm., Phi., Wsh., NYI	15	1023	226	358	584	1172	66	12	21	33	88	1	1979-80	1993-94
‡ Acton, Will	Edm.	2	33	3	2	5	26	....	....	....	....	....	....	2013-14	2014-15
• Adam, Douglas	NYR	1	4	0	1	1	0	....	....	....	....	....	....	1949-50	1949-50
‡ Adam, Luke	Buf., CBJ	5	90	15	11	26	36	....	....	....	....	....	....	2010-11	2014-15
Adam, Russ	Tor.	1	8	1	2	3	11	....	....	....	....	....	....	1982-83	1982-83
Adams, Bryan	Atl.	2	11	0	1	1	2	....	....	....	....	....	....	1999-00	2000-01
Adams, Craig	Car., Chi., Pit.	14	951	55	105	160	683	106	7	5	12	74	2	2000-01	2014-15
Adams, Greg	Phi., Hfd., Wsh., Edm., Van., Que., Det.	10	545	84	143	227	1173	43	2	11	13	153	....	1980-81	1989-90
Adams, Greg	N.J., Van., Dal., Phx., Fla.	17	1056	355	388	743	326	81	20	22	42	16	....	1984-85	2000-01
• Adams, Jack	Tor., Ott.	7	173	83	32	115	366	10	2	0	2	13	2	1917-18	1926-27
• Adams, John	Mtl.	1	42	6	12	18	11	3	0	0	0	0	....	1940-41	1940-41
Adams, Kevyn	Tor., CBJ, Fla., Car., Phx., Chi.	10	540	59	77	136	317	67	2	2	4	39	1	1997-98	2007-08
• Adams, Stew	Chi., Tor.	4	95	9	26	35	60	11	3	3	6	14	....	1929-30	1932-33
Adduono, Rick	Bos., Atl.	2	4	0	0	0	2	....	....	....	....	....	....	1975-76	1979-80
Afanasenkov, Dmitry	T.B., Phi.	5	227	27	27	54	52	28	1	3	4	8	1	2000-01	2006-07
Affleck, Bruce	St.L., Van., NYI	7	280	14	66	80	86	8	0	0	0	0	....	1974-75	1983-84
‡ Afinogenov, Maxim	Buf., Atl.	10	651	158	237	395	486	49	10	13	23	22	....	1999-00	2009-10
Agnew, Jim	Van., Hfd.	6	81	0	1	1	257	4	0	0	0	6	....	1986-87	1992-93
Ahern, Fred	Cal., Cle., Col.	4	146	31	30	61	130	2	0	1	1	2	....	1974-75	1977-78
• Ahlin, Rudy	Chi.	1	1	0	0	0	0	....	....	....	....	....	....	1937-38	1937-38
Ahola, Peter	L.A., Pit., S.J., Cgy.	3	123	10	17	27	137	6	0	0	0	2	....	1991-92	1993-94
Ahrens, Chris	Min.	6	52	0	3	3	84	1	0	0	0	0	....	1972-73	1977-78
• Ailsby, Lloyd	NYR	1	3	0	0	0	2	....	....	....	....	....	....	1951-52	1951-52
Aitken, Brad	Pit., Edm.	2	14	1	3	4	25	....	....	....	....	....	....	1987-88	1990-91
Aitken, Johnathan	Bos., Chi.	2	44	0	1	1	70	....	....	....	....	....	....	1999-00	2003-04
Aivazoff, Micah	Det., Edm., NYI	3	92	4	6	10	46	....	....	....	....	....	....	1993-94	1995-96
Alatalo, Mika	Phx.	2	152	17	29	46	58	5	0	0	0	2	....	1999-00	2000-01
Albelin, Tommy	Que., N.J., Cgy.	18	952	44	211	255	417	81	7	15	22	22	2	1987-88	2005-06
Alberts, Andrew	Bos., Phi., Car., Van.	9	459	8	47	55	492	31	0	2	2	45	....	2005-06	2013-14
• Albright, Clint	NYR	1	59	14	5	19	19	....	....	....	....	....	....	1948-49	1948-49
Aldcorn, Gary	Tor., Det., Bos.	5	226	41	56	97	78	6	1	2	3	4	....	1956-57	1960-61
Aldridge, Keith	Dal.	1	4	0	0	0	0	....	....	....	....	....	....	1999-00	1999-00
Alexander, Claire	Tor., Van.	4	155	18	47	65	36	16	2	4	6	4	....	1974-75	1977-78
• Alexandre, Art	Mtl.	2	11	0	2	2	8	4	0	0	0	0	....	1931-32	1932-33
Alexeev, Nikita	T.B., Chi.	3	159	20	17	37	28	11	1	0	1	0	....	2001-02	2006-07
Alfredsson, Daniel	Ott., Det.	18	1246	444	713	1157	510	124	51	49	100	76	....	1995-96	2013-14
‡ Aliu, Akim	Cgy.	2	7	2	1	3	26	....	....	....	....	....	....	2011-12	2012-13
Allan, Jeff	Cle.	1	4	0	0	0	2	....	....	....	....	....	....	1977-78	1977-78
Allen, Bobby	Edm., Bos.	3	51	0	3	3	12	....	....	....	....	....	....	2002-03	2007-08
Allen, Bryan	Van., Fla., Car., Ana., Mtl.	14	721	29	107	136	839	27	1	1	2	36	....	2000-01	2014-15
Allen, Chris	Fla.	2	2	0	0	0	2	....	....	....	....	....	....	1997-98	1998-99
• Allen, George	NYR, Chi., Mtl.	8	339	82	115	197	179	41	9	10	19	32	....	1938-39	1946-47
• Allen, Keith	Det.	2	28	0	4	4	8	5	0	0	0	0	1	1953-54	1954-55
Allen, Peter	Pit.	1	8	0	0	0	8	....	....	....	....	....	....	1995-96	1995-96
• Allen, Viv	NYA	1	6	0	1	1	0	....	....	....	....	....	....	1940-41	1940-41
Alley, Steve	Hfd.	2	15	3	3	6	11	3	0	1	1	0	....	1979-80	1980-81
Allison, Dave	Mtl.	1	3	0	0	0	12	....	....	....	....	....	....	1983-84	1983-84
Allison, Jamie	Cgy., Chi., CBJ, Nsh., Fla.	10	372	7	23	30	639	....	....	....	....	....	....	1994-95	2005-06
Allison, Jason	Wsh., Bos., L.A., Tor.	12	552	154	331	485	441	25	7	18	25	14	....	1993-94	2005-06
Allison, Mike	NYR, Tor., L.A.	10	499	102	166	268	630	82	9	17	26	135	....	1980-81	1989-90
Allison, Ray	Hfd., Phi.	7	238	64	93	157	223	12	2	3	5	20	....	1979-80	1986-87
• Allum, Bill	NYR	1	1	0	1	1	0	....	....	....	....	....	....	1940-41	1940-41
‡ Almond, Cody	Min.	3	25	2	0	2	26	....	....	....	....	....	....	2009-10	2011-12
‡ Almqvist, Adam	Det.	1	2	1	0	1	0	....	....	....	....	....	....	2013-14	2013-14
• Amadio, Dave	Det., L.A.	3	125	5	11	16	163	16	1	2	3	18	....	1957-58	1968-69
Ambroziak, Peter	Buf.	1	12	0	1	1	0	....	....	....	....	....	....	1994-95	1994-95
Amodeo, Mike	Wpg.	1	19	0	0	0	2	....	....	....	....	....	....	1979-80	1979-80
Amonte, Tony	NYR, Chi., Phx., Phi., Cgy.	16	1174	416	484	900	752	99	22	33	55	56	....	1990-91	2006-07
• Anderson, Bill	Bos.	1	....	....	....	....	....	1	0	0	0	0	....	1942-43	1942-43
• Anderson, Dale	Det.	1	13	0	0	0	6	2	0	0	0	0	....	1956-57	1956-57
Anderson, Doug	Mtl.	1	....	....	....	....	....	2	0	0	0	0	....	1952-53	1952-53
Anderson, Earl	Det., Bos.	3	109	19	19	38	22	5	0	1	1	0	....	1974-75	1976-77
Anderson, Glenn	Edm., Tor., NYR, St.L.	16	1129	498	601	1099	1120	225	93	121	214	442	6	1980-81	1995-96
• Anderson, Jim	L.A.	1	7	1	2	3	2	....	....	....	....	....	....	1967-68	1967-68
Anderson, John	Tor., Que., Hfd.	12	814	282	349	631	263	37	9	18	27	2	....	1977-78	1988-89
‡ Anderson, Matt	N.J.	1	2	0	1	1	0	....	....	....	....	....	....	2012-13	2012-13
Anderson, Murray	Wsh.	1	40	0	1	1	68	....	....	....	....	....	....	1974-75	1974-75
Anderson, Perry	St.L., N.J., S.J.	10	400	50	59	109	1051	36	2	1	3	161	....	1981-82	1991-92
Anderson, Ron	Det., L.A., St.L., Buf.	5	251	28	30	58	146	5	0	0	0	4	....	1967-68	1971-72
Anderson, Ron	Wsh.	1	28	9	7	16	8	....	....	....	....	....	....	1974-75	1974-75
Anderson, Russ	Pit., Hfd., L.A.	9	519	22	99	121	1086	10	0	3	3	28	....	1976-77	1984-85
Anderson, Shawn	Buf., Que., Wsh., Phi.	8	255	11	51	62	117	19	1	1	2	16	....	1986-87	1994-95
• Anderson, Tom	Det., NYA, Bro.	8	319	62	127	189	180	16	2	7	9	8	....	1934-35	1941-42
Andersson, Erik	Cgy.	1	12	2	1	3	8	....	....	....	....	....	....	1997-98	1997-98
‡ Andersson, Joakim	Det.	5	205	15	21	36	48	27	2	6	8	14	....	2011-12	**2015-16**
Andersson, Jonas	Nsh., Van.	2	9	0	0	0	2	....	....	....	....	....	....	2001-02	2010-11
Andersson, Kent-Erik	Min., NYR	7	456	72	103	175	78	50	4	11	15	4	....	1977-78	1983-84
Andersson, Mikael	Buf., Hfd., T.B., Phi., NYI	15	761	95	169	264	134	25	2	7	9	10	....	1985-86	1999-00
Andersson, Niklas	Que., NYI, S.J., Nsh., Cgy.	6	164	29	53	82	85	....	....	....	....	....	....	1992-93	2000-01
Andersson, Peter	Wsh., Que.	3	172	10	41	51	81	7	0	2	2	2	....	1983-84	1985-86
Andersson, Peter	NYR, Fla.	2	47	6	13	19	20	....	....	....	....	....	....	1992-93	1993-94
Andrascik, Steve	NYR	1	....	....	....	....	....	1	0	0	0	0	....	1971-72	1971-72
Andrea, Paul	NYR, Pit., Cal., Buf.	4	150	31	49	80	10	....	....	....	....	....	....	1965-66	1970-71
• Andrews, Lloyd	Tor.	4	53	8	5	13	10	2	0	0	0	0	1	1921-22	1924-25
Andreychuk, Dave	Buf., Tor., N.J., Bos., Col., T.B.	23	1639	640	698	1338	1125	162	43	54	97	162	1	1982-83	2005-06
Andrievski, Alexander	Chi.	1	1	0	0	0	0	....	....	....	....	....	....	1992-93	1992-93
Andruff, Ron	Mtl., Col.	5	153	19	36	55	54	2	0	0	0	0	....	1974-75	1978-79
Andrusak, Greg	Pit., Tor.	5	28	0	6	6	16	15	1	0	1	8	....	1993-94	1999-00

Name	NHL Teams	NHL Seasons	Regular Schedule GP	G	A	TP	PIM	Playoffs GP	G	A	TP	PIM	NHL Cup Wins	First NHL Season	Last NHL Season
Angelstad, Mel	Wsh.	1	2	0	0	0	2	....	....	....	....	....	....	2003-04	2003-04
Angotti, Lou	NYR, Chi., Phi., Pit., St.L.	10	653	103	186	289	228	65	8	8	16	17	....	1964-65	1973-74
Anholt, Darrel	Chi.	1	1	0	0	0	0	....	....	....	....	....	....	1983-84	1983-84
• Anslow, Hub	NYR	1	2	0	0	0	0	....	....	....	....	....	....	1947-48	1947-48
Antonovich, Mike	Min., Hfd., N.J.	5	87	10	15	25	37	....	....	....	....	....	....	1975-76	1983-84
Antoski, Shawn	Van., Phi., Pit., Ana.	8	183	3	5	8	599	36	1	3	4	74	....	1990-91	1997-98
Antropov, Nik	Tor., NYR, Atl., Wpg.	13	788	193	272	465	627	35	4	4	8	40	....	1999-00	2012-13
• Apps, Syl	Tor.	10	423	201	231	432	56	69	25	29	54	8	3	1936-37	1947-48
Apps, Syl	NYR, Pit., L.A.	10	727	183	423	606	311	23	5	5	10	23	....	1970-71	1979-80
• Arbour, Al	Det., Chi., Tor., St.L.	16	626	12	58	70	617	86	1	8	9	92	4	1953-54	1970-71
• Arbour, Amos	Mtl., Ham., Tor.	6	113	52	20	72	77	....	....	....	....	....	....	1918-19	1923-24
• Arbour, Jack	Det., Tor.	2	47	5	1	6	56	....	....	....	....	....	....	1926-27	1928-29
Arbour, John	Bos., Pit., Van., St.L.	5	106	1	9	10	149	5	0	0	0	0	....	1965-66	1971-72
• Arbour, Ty	Pit., Chi.	5	207	28	28	56	112	11	2	0	2	6	....	1926-27	1930-31
Archambault, Michel	Chi.	1	3	0	0	0	0	....	....	....	....	....	....	1976-77	1976-77
Archibald, Dave	Min., NYR, Ott., NYI	8	323	57	67	124	139	5	0	1	1	0	....	1987-88	1996-97
Archibald, Jim	Min.	3	16	1	2	3	45	....	....	....	....	....	....	1984-85	1986-87
Areshenkoff, Ron	Edm.	1	4	0	0	0	0	....	....	....	....	....	....	1979-80	1979-80
Arkhipov, Denis	Nsh., Chi.	5	352	56	82	138	128	....	....	....	....	....	....	2000-01	2006-07
Armstrong, Bill	Phi.	1	1	0	1	1	0	....	....	....	....	....	....	1990-91	1990-91
• Armstrong, Bob	Bos.	12	542	13	86	99	671	42	1	7	8	28	....	1950-51	1961-62
Armstrong, Chris	Min., Ana.	2	7	0	1	1	0	....	....	....	....	....	....	2000-01	2003-04
Armstrong, Colby	Pit., Atl., Tor., Mtl.	8	476	89	120	209	376	9	0	1	1	26	....	2005-06	2012-13
Armstrong, Derek	NYI, Ott., NYR, L.A., St.L.	14	477	72	149	221	355	....	....	....	....	....	....	1993-94	2009-10
Armstrong, George	Tor.	21	1187	296	417	713	721	110	26	34	60	52	4	1949-50	1970-71
• Armstrong, Murray	Tor., NYA, Bro., Det.	8	270	67	121	188	72	30	4	6	10	2	....	1937-38	1945-46
• Armstrong, Norm	Tor.	1	7	1	1	2	2	....	....	....	....	....	....	1962-63	1962-63
Armstrong, Riley	S.J.	1	2	0	0	0	2	....	....	....	....	....	....	2008-09	2008-09
Armstrong, Tim	Tor.	1	11	1	0	1	6	....	....	....	....	....	....	1988-89	1988-89
Arnason, Chuck	Mtl., Atl., Pit., K.C., Col., Cle., Min., Wsh.	8	401	109	90	199	122	9	2	4	6	4	....	1971-72	1978-79
Arnason, Tyler	Chi., Ott., Col.	7	487	88	157	245	140	13	2	3	5	2	....	2001-02	2008-09
‡ Arniel, Jamie	Bos.	1	1	0	0	0	0	....	....	....	....	....	....	2010-11	2010-11
Arniel, Scott	Wpg., Buf., Bos.	11	730	149	189	338	599	34	3	3	6	39	....	1981-82	1991-92
‡ Arnold, Bill	Cgy.	1	1	0	0	0	0	....	....	....	....	....	....	2013-14	2013-14
Arnott, Jason	Edm., N.J., Dal., Nsh., Wsh., St.L.	18	1244	417	521	938	1242	122	32	41	73	76	1	1993-94	2011-12
Arsene, Dean	Edm.	1	13	0	0	0	41	....	....	....	....	....	....	2009-10	2009-10
Arthur, Fred	Hfd., Phi.	3	80	1	8	9	49	4	0	0	0	2	....	1980-81	1982-83
‡ Artyukhin, Evgeny	T.B., Ana., Atl.	3	199	19	30	49	313	5	1	0	1	6	....	2005-06	2009-10
• Arundel, John	Tor.	1	3	0	0	0	9	....	....	....	....	....	....	1949-50	1949-50
Arvedson, Magnus	Ott., Van.	7	434	100	125	225	241	52	3	8	11	34	....	1997-98	2003-04
Asham, Arron	Mtl., NYI, N.J., Phi., Pit., NYR	15	789	94	114	208	1004	72	11	8	19	56	....	1998-99	2013-14
• Ashbee, Barry	Bos., Phi.	5	284	15	70	85	291	17	0	4	4	22	1	1965-66	1973-74
• Ashby, Don	Tor., Col., Edm.	6	188	40	56	96	40	12	1	0	1	4	....	1975-76	1980-81
Ashton, Brent	Van., Col., N.J., Min., Que., Det., Wpg., Bos., Cgy.	14	998	284	345	629	635	85	24	25	49	70	....	1979-80	1992-93
‡ Ashton, Carter	Tor.	3	54	0	3	3	32	....	....	....	....	....	....	2011-12	2014-15
Ashworth, Frank	Chi.	1	18	5	4	9	2	....	....	....	....	....	....	1946-47	1946-47
• Asmundson, Oscar	NYR, Det., St.L., NYA, Mtl.	5	111	11	23	34	30	9	0	2	2	4	1	1932-33	1937-38
• Astashenko, Kaspars	T.B.	2	23	1	2	3	8	....	....	....	....	....	....	1999-00	2000-01
Astley, Mark	Buf.	3	75	4	19	23	92	2	0	0	0	0	....	1993-94	1995-96
• Atanas, Walt	NYR	1	49	13	8	21	40	....	....	....	....	....	....	1944-45	1944-45
Atcheynum, Blair	Ott., St.L., Nsh., Chi.	5	196	27	33	60	36	23	1	3	4	8	....	1992-93	2000-01
• Atkinson, Steve	Bos., Buf., Wsh.	6	302	60	51	111	104	1	0	0	0	0	....	1968-69	1974-75
Attwell, Bob	Col.	2	22	1	5	6	0	....	....	....	....	....	....	1979-80	1980-81
Attwell, Ron	St.L., NYR	1	22	1	7	8	8	....	....	....	....	....	....	1967-68	1967-68
Aubin, Norm	Tor.	2	69	18	13	31	30	1	0	0	0	0	....	1981-82	1982-83
Aubin, Serge	Col., CBJ, Atl.	7	374	44	64	108	361	22	0	1	1	10	....	1998-99	2005-06
Aubry, Pierre	Que., Det.	5	202	24	26	50	133	20	1	1	2	32	....	1980-81	1984-85
• Aubuchon, Ossie	Bos., NYR	2	50	20	12	32	4	6	1	0	1	0	....	1942-43	1943-44
Aucoin, Adrian	Van., T.B., NYI, Chi., Cgy., Phx., CBJ	18	1108	121	278	399	793	62	6	15	21	44	....	1994-95	2012-13
‡ Aucoin, Keith	Car., Wsh., NYI, St.L.	9	145	17	32	49	22	20	0	5	5	12	....	2005-06	2013-14
Audet, Philippe	Det.	1	4	0	0	0	0	....	....	....	....	....	....	1998-99	1998-99
Audette, Donald	Buf., L.A., Atl., Dal., Mtl., Fla.	15	735	260	249	509	584	73	21	27	48	46	....	1989-90	2003-04
• Auge, Les	Col.	1	6	0	3	3	4	....	....	....	....	....	....	1980-81	1980-81
Augusta, Patrik	Tor., Wsh.	2	4	0	0	0	0	....	....	....	....	....	....	1993-94	1998-99
Aulin, Jared	L.A.	1	17	2	2	4	0	....	....	....	....	....	....	2002-03	2002-03
• Aurie, Larry	Det.	12	489	147	129	276	279	24	6	9	15	10	2	1927-28	1938-39
Avery, Sean	Det., L.A., NYR, Dal.	10	580	90	157	247	1533	28	5	10	15	69	....	2001-02	2011-12
Awrey, Don	Bos., St.L., Mtl., Pit., NYR, Col.	16	979	31	158	189	1065	71	0	18	18	150	3	1963-64	1978-79
Axelsson, P.J.	Bos.	11	797	103	184	287	276	54	4	3	7	24	....	1997-98	2008-09
• Ayres, Vern	NYA, Mtl.M., St.L., NYR	6	211	6	11	17	350	....	....	....	....	....	....	1930-31	1935-36

B

Name	NHL Teams	NHL Seasons	Regular Schedule GP	G	A	TP	PIM	Playoffs GP	G	A	TP	PIM	NHL Cup Wins	First NHL Season	Last NHL Season
Babando, Pete	Bos., Det., Chi., NYR	6	351	86	73	159	194	17	3	3	6	6	1	1947-48	1952-53
Babchuk, Anton	Chi., Car., Cgy.	7	289	36	71	107	108	13	0	1	1	10	1	2003-04	2012-13
Babcock, Bobby	Wsh.	2	2	0	0	0	2	....	....	....	....	....	....	1990-91	1992-93
Babe, Warren	Min.	3	21	2	5	7	23	2	0	0	0	0	....	1987-88	1990-91
Babenko, Yuri	Col.	1	3	0	0	0	0	....	....	....	....	....	....	2000-01	2000-01
Babin, Mitch	St.L.	1	8	0	0	0	0	....	....	....	....	....	....	1975-76	1975-76
Baby, John	Cle., Min.	2	26	2	8	10	26	....	....	....	....	....	....	1977-78	1978-79
Babych, Dave	Wpg., Hfd., Van., Phi., L.A.	19	1195	142	581	723	970	114	21	41	62	113	....	1980-81	1998-99
Babych, Wayne	St.L., Pit., Que., Hfd.	9	519	192	246	438	498	41	7	9	16	24	....	1978-79	1986-87
Baca, Jergus	Hfd.	2	10	0	2	2	14	....	....	....	....	....	....	1990-91	1991-92
Backman, Christian	St.L., NYR, CBJ	6	302	23	56	79	182	13	0	2	2	16	....	2002-03	2008-09
Backman, Mike	NYR	3	18	1	6	7	18	10	2	2	4	2	....	1981-82	1983-84
• Backor, Pete	Tor.	1	36	4	5	9	6	....	....	....	....	....	1	1944-45	1944-45
Backstrom, Ralph	Mtl., L.A., Chi.	17	1032	278	361	639	386	116	27	32	59	68	6	1956-57	1972-73
Bagnall, Drew	Min.	1	2	0	0	0	4	....	....	....	....	....	....	2010-11	2010-11
• Bailey, Ace	Tor.	8	313	111	82	193	472	21	3	4	7	12	1	1926-27	1933-34
• Bailey, Bob	Tor., Det., Chi.	5	150	15	21	36	207	15	0	4	4	22	....	1953-54	1957-58
• Bailey, Garnet	Bos., Det., St.L., Wsh.	10	568	107	171	278	633	15	2	4	6	28	2	1968-69	1977-78
Bailey, Reid	Phi., Tor., Hfd.	4	40	1	3	4	105	16	0	2	2	25	....	1980-81	1983-84
Baillargeon, Joel	Wpg., Que.	3	20	0	2	2	31	....	....	....	....	....	....	1986-87	1988-89
Baird, Ken	Cal.	1	10	0	2	2	15	....	....	....	....	....	....	1971-72	1971-72
Baker, Bill	Mtl., Col., St.L., NYR	3	143	7	25	32	175	6	0	0	0	0	....	1980-81	1982-83
Baker, Jamie	Que., Ott., S.J., Tor.	10	404	71	79	150	271	25	5	4	9	42	....	1989-90	1998-99
Bakovic, Peter	Van.	1	10	2	0	2	48	....	....	....	....	....	....	1987-88	1987-88
Bala, Chris	Ott.	1	6	0	1	1	0	....	....	....	....	....	....	2001-02	2001-02
Balastik, Jaroslav	CBJ	2	74	13	11	24	30	....	....	....	....	....	....	2005-06	2006-07
Balderis, Helmut	Min.	1	26	3	6	9	2	....	....	....	....	....	....	1989-90	1989-90
• Baldwin, Doug	Tor., Det., Chi.	3	24	0	1	1	8	....	....	....	....	....	....	1945-46	1947-48
‡ Balej, Jozef	Mtl., NYR, Van.	2	18	1	5	6	4	....	....	....	....	....	....	2003-04	2005-06
Balfour, Earl	Tor., Chi.	7	288	30	22	52	78	26	0	3	3	4	1	1951-52	1960-61
• Balfour, Murray	Mtl., Chi., Bos.	8	306	67	90	157	393	40	9	10	19	45	1	1956-57	1964-65
Ball, Terry	Phi., Buf.	4	74	7	19	26	26	....	....	....	....	....	....	1967-68	1971-72
Ballard, Keith	Phx., Fla., Van., Min.	10	604	38	137	175	612	17	0	1	1	8	....	2005-06	2014-15
Balmochnykh, Maxim	Ana.	1	6	0	1	1	2	....	....	....	....	....	....	1999-00	1999-00
• Balon, Dave	NYR, Mtl., Min., Van.	14	776	192	222	414	607	78	14	21	35	109	2	1959-60	1972-73
Baltimore, Bryon	Edm.	1	2	0	0	0	4	....	....	....	....	....	....	1979-80	1979-80
Baluik, Stan	Bos.	1	7	0	0	0	2	....	....	....	....	....	....	1959-60	1959-60
Bancroft, Steve	Chi., S.J.	2	6	0	1	1	2	....	....	....	....	....	....	1992-93	2001-02
Bandura, Jeff	NYR	1	2	0	1	1	0	....	....	....	....	....	....	1980-81	1980-81
Bang, Daniel	Nsh.	1	8	0	2	2	0	....	....	....	....	....	....	2012-13	2012-13
Banham, Frank	Ana., Phx.	4	32	9	2	11	16	....	....	....	....	....	....	1996-97	2002-03
Banks, Darren	Bos.	2	20	2	2	4	73	....	....	....	....	....	....	1992-93	1993-94
Bannister, Drew	T.B., Edm., Ana., NYR	6	164	5	25	30	161	12	0	0	0	30	....	1995-96	2001-02
Barahona, Ralph	Bos.	2	6	2	2	4	0	....	....	....	....	....	....	1990-91	1991-92
‡ Baranka, Ivan	NYR	1	1	0	1	1	0	....	....	....	....	....	....	2007-08	2007-08
• Barbe, Andy	Tor.	1	1	0	0	0	2	....	....	....	....	....	....	1950-51	1950-51
Barber, Bill	Phi.	12	903	420	463	883	623	129	53	55	108	109	2	1972-73	1983-84

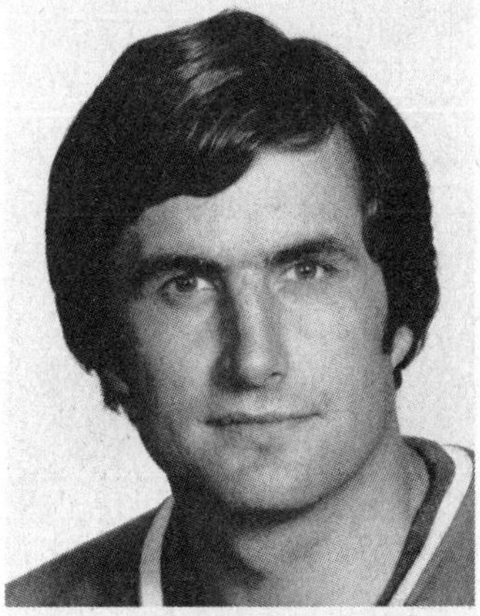

Syl Apps Jr.

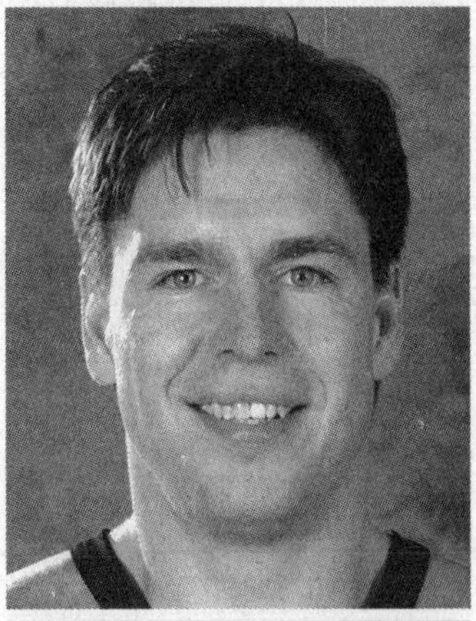

Blair Atcheynum

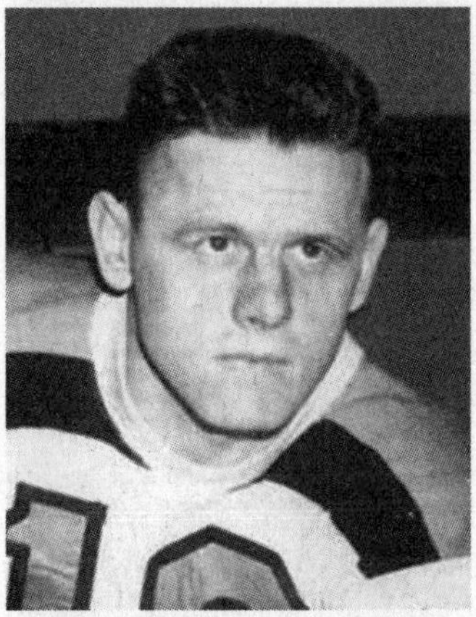

Ed Barry

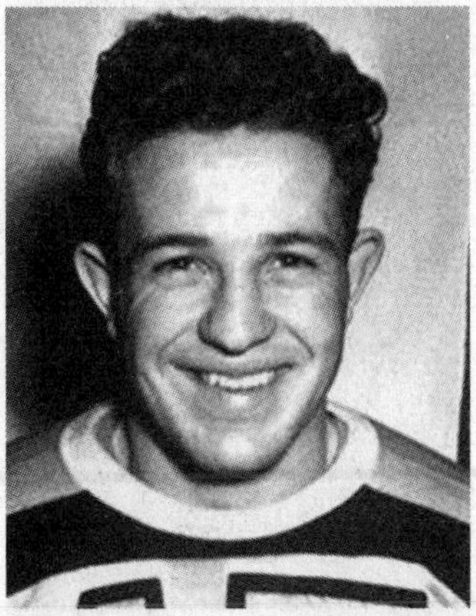

Bobby Bauer

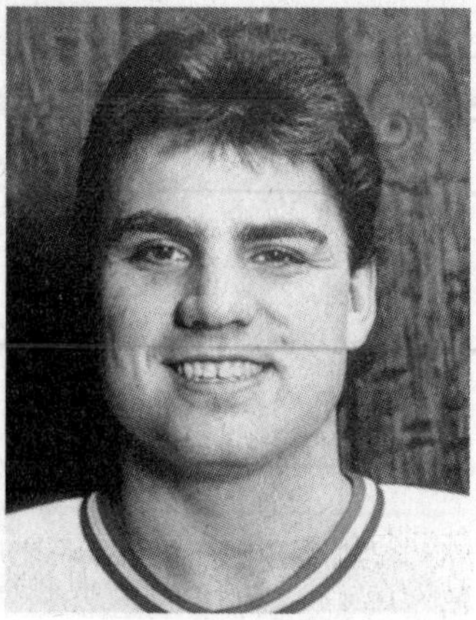

Bruce Bell

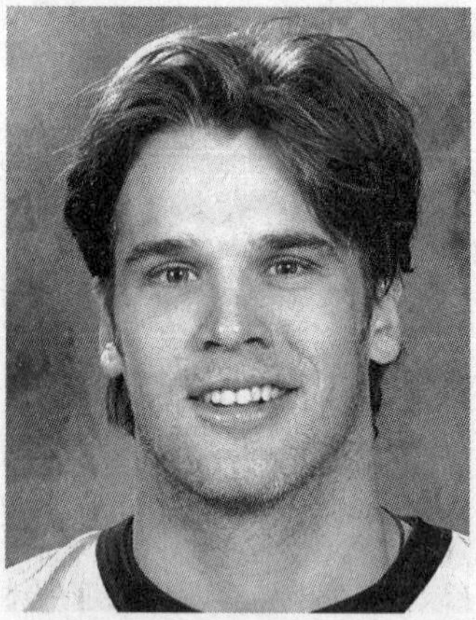

Drake Berehowsky

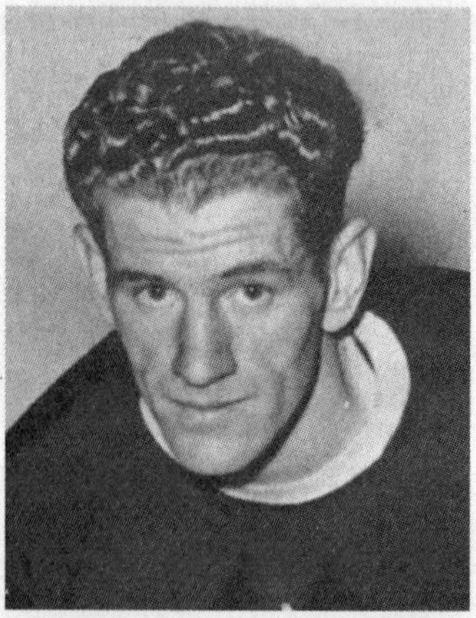

George Boothman

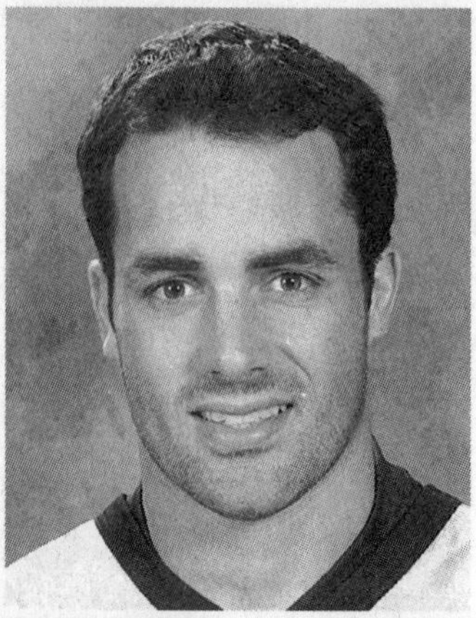

Sebastien Bordeleau

			Regular Schedule					Playoffs							
Name	NHL Teams	NHL Seasons	GP	G	A	TP	PIM	GP	G	A	TP	PIM	NHL Cup Wins	First NHL Season	Last NHL Season
Barber, Don	Min., Wpg., Que., S.J.	4	115	25	32	57	64	11	4	4	8	10	....	1988-89	1991-92
Barch, Krys	Dal., Fla., N.J.	8	381	12	23	35	812	3	0	0	0	2	....	2006-07	2013-14
• Barilko, Bill	Tor.	5	252	26	36	62	456	47	5	7	12	104	4	1946-47	1950-51
‡ Barinka, Michal	Chi.	2	34	0	2	2	26	....	....	....	....	....	....	2003-04	2005-06
‡ Barker, Cam	Chi., Min., Edm., Van.	8	310	21	75	96	290	17	3	6	9	2	....	2005-06	2012-13
Barkley, Doug	Chi., Det.	6	253	24	80	104	382	30	0	9	9	63	....	1957-58	1965-66
Barlow, Bob	Min.	2	77	16	17	33	10	6	2	2	4	6	....	1969-70	1970-71
Barnaby, Matthew	Buf., Pit., T.B., NYR, Col., Chi., Dal.	14	834	113	187	300	2562	62	7	15	22	170	....	1992-93	2006-07
• Barnes, Blair	L.A.	1	1	0	0	0	0	....	....	....	....	....	....	1982-83	1982-83
Barnes, Norm	Phi., Hfd.	5	156	6	38	44	178	12	0	0	0	8	....	1976-77	1981-82
Barnes, Ryan	Det.	1	2	0	0	0	0	....	....	....	....	....	....	2003-04	2003-04
Barnes, Stu	Wpg., Fla., Pit., Buf., Dal.	16	1136	261	336	597	438	116	30	32	62	24	....	1991-92	2007-08
‡ Barney, Scott	L.A., Atl.	3	27	5	6	11	4	....	....	....	....	....	....	2002-03	2005-06
Baron, Murray	Phi., St.L., Mtl., Phx., Van.	15	988	35	94	129	1309	73	2	8	10	78	....	1989-90	2003-04
Baron, Normand	Mtl., St.L.	2	27	2	0	2	51	3	0	0	0	22	....	1983-84	1985-86
Barr, Dave	Bos., NYR, St.L., Hfd., Det., N.J., Dal.	13	614	128	204	332	520	71	12	10	22	70	....	1981-82	1993-94
Barrault, Doug	Min., Fla.	2	4	0	0	0	2	....	....	....	....	....	....	1992-93	1993-94
Barrett, Fred	Min., L.A.	13	745	25	123	148	671	44	0	2	2	60	....	1970-71	1983-84
Barrett, John	Det., Wsh., Min.	8	488	20	77	97	604	16	2	2	4	50	....	1980-81	1987-88
Barrie, Doug	Pit., Buf., L.A.	3	158	10	42	52	268	....	....	....	....	....	....	1968-69	1971-72
Barrie, Len	Phi., Fla., Pit., L.A.	7	184	19	45	64	290	8	1	0	1	8	....	1989-90	2000-01
• Barry, Ed	Bos.	1	19	1	3	4	2	....	....	....	....	....	....	1946-47	1946-47
• Barry, Marty	NYA, Bos., Det., Mtl.	12	509	195	192	387	231	43	15	18	33	34	2	1927-28	1939-40
Barry, Ray	Bos.	1	18	1	2	3	6	....	....	....	....	....	....	1951-52	1951-52
Bartecko, Lubos	St.L., Atl.	5	257	46	65	111	107	12	1	1	2	2	....	1998-99	2002-03
Bartel, Robin	Cgy., Van.	2	41	0	1	1	14	6	0	0	0	16	....	1985-86	1986-87
Bartlett, Jim	Mtl., NYR, Bos.	5	191	34	23	57	273	2	0	0	0	0	....	1954-55	1960-61
• Barton, Cliff	Pit., Phi., NYR	3	85	10	9	19	22	....	....	....	....	....	....	1929-30	1939-40
Bartos, Peter	Min.	1	13	4	2	6	6	....	....	....	....	....	....	2000-01	2000-01
‡ Bartovic, Milan	Buf., Chi.	3	50	3	14	17	26	....	....	....	....	....	....	2002-03	2005-06
‡ Bartulis, Oskars	Phi.	2	66	1	8	9	32	7	0	0	0	4	....	2009-10	2010-11
Bashkirov, Andrei	Mtl.	3	30	0	3	3	0	....	....	....	....	....	....	1998-99	2000-01
Bassen, Bob	NYI, Chi., St.L., Que., Dal., Cgy.	15	765	88	144	232	1004	93	9	15	24	134	....	1985-86	1999-00
Bast, Ryan	Phi.	1	2	0	1	1	0	....	....	....	....	....	....	1998-99	1998-99
Bates, Shawn	Bos., NYI	10	465	72	126	198	266	29	3	4	7	19	....	1997-98	2007-08
Bathe, Frank	Det., Phi.	9	224	3	28	31	542	27	1	3	4	42	....	1974-75	1983-84
• Bathgate, Andy	NYR, Tor., Det., Pit.	17	1069	349	624	973	624	54	21	14	35	76	1	1952-53	1970-71
• Bathgate, Frank	NYR	1	2	0	0	0	2	....	....	....	....	....	....	1952-53	1952-53
Battaglia, Bates	Car., Col., Wsh., Tor.	9	580	80	118	198	385	42	5	16	21	28	....	1997-98	2007-08
• Batters, Jeff	St.L.	2	16	0	0	0	28	....	....	....	....	....	....	1993-94	1994-95
Batyrshin, Ruslan	L.A.	1	2	0	0	0	6	....	....	....	....	....	....	1995-96	1995-96
• Bauer, Bobby	Bos.	9	327	123	137	260	36	48	11	8	19	6	2	1936-37	1951-52
Baumgartner, Ken	L.A., NYI, Tor., Ana., Bos.	12	696	13	41	54	2244	51	1	2	3	106	....	1987-88	1998-99
Baumgartner, Mike	K.C.	1	17	0	0	0	0	....	....	....	....	....	....	1974-75	1974-75
Baumgartner, Nolan	Wsh., Chi., Van., Pit., Phi., Dal.	10	143	7	40	47	69	4	0	0	0	10	....	1995-96	2009-10
Baun, Bob	Tor., Oak., Det.	17	964	37	187	224	1493	96	3	12	15	171	4	1956-57	1972-73
Bautin, Sergei	Wpg., Det., S.J.	3	132	5	25	30	176	6	0	0	0	2	....	1992-93	1995-96
Bawa, Robin	Wsh., Van., S.J., Ana.	4	61	6	1	7	60	1	0	0	0	0	....	1989-90	1993-94
Baxter, Paul	Que., Pit., Cgy.	8	472	48	121	169	1564	40	0	5	5	162	....	1979-80	1986-87
Bayda, Ryan	Car.	5	179	16	24	40	94	15	2	2	4	18	....	2002-03	2008-09
Beadle, Sandy	Wpg.	1	6	1	0	1	2	....	....	....	....	....	....	1980-81	1980-81
Beaton, Frank	NYR	2	25	1	1	2	43	....	....	....	....	....	....	1978-79	1979-80
• Beattie, Red	Bos., Det., NYA	9	334	62	85	147	137	24	4	2	6	8	....	1930-31	1938-39
Beaudin, Norm	St.L., Min.	2	25	1	2	3	4	....	....	....	....	....	....	1967-68	1970-71
Beaudoin, Eric	Fla.	3	53	3	8	11	41	....	....	....	....	....	....	2001-02	2003-04
Beaudoin, Serge	Atl.	1	3	0	0	0	0	....	....	....	....	....	....	1979-80	1979-80
Beaudoin, Yves	Wsh.	3	11	0	0	0	5	....	....	....	....	....	....	1985-86	1987-88
Beaufait, Mark	S.J.	1	5	1	0	1	0	....	....	....	....	....	....	1992-93	1992-93
Beck, Barry	Col., NYR, L.A.	10	615	104	251	355	1016	51	10	23	33	77	....	1977-78	1989-90
Beckett, Bob	Bos.	4	68	7	6	13	18	....	....	....	....	....	....	1956-57	1963-64
Bedard, James	Chi.	2	22	1	1	2	8	....	....	....	....	....	....	1949-50	1950-51
Beddoes, Clayton	Bos.	2	60	2	8	10	57	....	....	....	....	....	....	1995-96	1996-97
‡ Bednar, Jaroslav	L.A., Fla.	3	102	10	25	35	30	3	0	0	0	0	....	2001-02	2003-04
Bednarski, John	NYR, Edm.	4	100	2	18	20	114	1	0	0	0	17	....	1974-75	1979-80
Beech, Kris	Wsh., Pit., Nsh., CBJ, Van.	7	198	25	42	67	113	....	....	....	....	....	....	2000-01	2007-08
Beers, Bob	Bos., T.B., Edm., NYI	8	258	28	79	107	225	21	1	1	2	22	....	1989-90	1996-97
Beers, Eddy	Cgy., St.L.	5	250	94	116	210	256	41	7	10	17	47	....	1981-82	1985-86
Begin, Steve	Cgy., Mtl., Dal., Bos., Nsh.	13	524	56	52	108	561	36	1	4	5	30	....	1997-98	2012-13
• Behling, Dick	Det.	2	5	1	0	1	2	....	....	....	....	....	....	1940-41	1942-43
• Beisler, Frank	NYA	2	2	0	0	0	0	....	....	....	....	....	....	1936-37	1939-40
Bekar, Derek	St.L., L.A., NYI	3	11	0	0	0	6	....	....	....	....	....	....	1999-00	2003-04
• Belak, Wade	Col., Cgy., Tor., Fla., Nsh.	14	549	8	25	33	1263	22	1	0	1	36	....	1996-97	2010-11
Belanger, Alain	Tor.	1	9	0	1	1	6	....	....	....	....	....	....	1977-78	1977-78
Belanger, Eric	L.A., Car., Atl., Min., Wsh., Phx., Edm.	12	820	138	220	358	361	41	2	5	7	28	....	2000-01	2012-13
Belanger, Francis	Mtl.	1	10	0	0	0	29	....	....	....	....	....	....	2000-01	2000-01
Belanger, Jesse	Mtl., Fla., Van., Edm., NYI	8	246	59	76	135	56	12	0	3	3	2	1	1991-92	2000-01
Belanger, Ken	Tor., NYI, Bos., L.A.	11	248	11	12	23	695	12	1	0	1	16	....	1994-95	2005-06
• Belanger, Roger	Pit.	1	44	3	5	8	32	....	....	....	....	....	....	1984-85	1984-85
Belisle, Danny	NYR	1	4	2	0	2	0	....	....	....	....	....	....	1960-61	1960-61
• Beliveau, Jean	Mtl.	20	1125	507	712	1219	1029	162	79	97	176	211	10	1950-51	1970-71
• Bell, Billy	Mtl.W., Mtl., Ott.	6	66	3	2	5	14	5	0	0	0	0	1	1917-18	1923-24
Bell, Brendan	Tor., Phx., Ott., NYR	5	102	7	21	28	51	....	....	....	....	....	....	2005-06	2011-12
Bell, Bruce	Que., St.L., NYR, Edm.	5	209	12	64	76	113	34	3	5	8	41	....	1984-85	1989-90
• Bell, Huddy	NYR	1	1	0	1	1	0	....	....	....	....	....	....	1946-47	1946-47
• Bell, Joe	NYR	2	62	8	9	17	18	....	....	....	....	....	....	1942-43	1946-47
Bell, Mark	Chi., S.J., Tor., Ana.	8	450	87	95	182	602	9	0	0	0	10	....	2000-01	2011-12
Belland, Neil	Van., Pit.	6	109	13	32	45	54	21	2	9	11	23	....	1981-82	1986-87
Belle, Shawn	Min., Mtl., Edm., Col.	3	20	0	1	1	2	....	....	....	....	....	....	2006-07	2010-11
Bellefeuille, Blake	CBJ	2	5	0	1	1	0	....	....	....	....	....	....	2001-02	2002-03
• Bellefeuille, Pete	Tor., Det.	4	92	26	4	30	58	....	....	....	....	....	....	1925-26	1929-30
• Bellemer, Andy	Mtl.M.	1	15	0	0	0	0	....	....	....	....	....	....	1932-33	1932-33
‡ Bellemore, Brett	Car.	3	121	4	16	20	79	....	....	....	....	....	....	2012-13	2014-15
Bellows, Brian	Min., Mtl., T.B., Ana., Wsh.	17	1188	485	537	1022	718	143	51	71	122	143	1	1982-83	1998-99
‡ Belov, Anton	Edm.	1	57	1	6	7	34	....	....	....	....	....	....	2013-14	2013-14
• Bend, Lin	NYR	1	8	3	1	4	2	....	....	....	....	....	....	1942-43	1942-43
Benda, Jan	Wsh.	1	9	0	3	3	6	....	....	....	....	....	....	1997-98	1997-98
Bennett, Adam	Chi., Edm.	3	69	3	8	11	69	....	....	....	....	....	....	1991-92	1993-94
Bennett, Bill	Bos., Hfd.	2	31	4	7	11	65	....	....	....	....	....	....	1978-79	1979-80
Bennett, Curt	St.L., NYR, Atl.	10	580	152	182	334	347	21	1	1	2	57	....	1970-71	1979-80
• Bennett, Frank	Det.	1	7	0	1	1	2	....	....	....	....	....	....	1943-44	1943-44
Bennett, Harvey	Pit., Wsh., Phi., Min., St.L.	5	268	44	46	90	347	4	0	0	0	2	....	1974-75	1978-79
• Bennett, Max	Mtl.	1	1	0	0	0	0	....	....	....	....	....	....	1935-36	1935-36
Bennett, Rick	NYR	3	15	1	1	2	13	....	....	....	....	....	....	1989-90	1991-92
Benning, Brian	St.L., L.A., Phi., Edm., Fla.	11	568	63	233	296	963	48	3	20	23	74	....	1984-85	1994-95
Benning, Jim	Tor., Van.	9	605	52	191	243	461	7	1	1	2	2	....	1981-82	1989-90
• Benoit, Joe	Mtl.	5	185	75	69	144	94	11	6	3	9	11	1	1940-41	1946-47
• Benson, Bill	NYA, Bro.	2	67	11	25	36	35	....	....	....	....	....	....	1940-41	1941-42
• Benson, Bobby	Bos.	1	8	0	1	1	4	....	....	....	....	....	....	1924-25	1924-25
Bentivoglio, Sean	NYI	1	1	0	0	0	2	....	....	....	....	....	....	2008-09	2008-09
• Bentley, Doug	Chi., NYR	13	566	219	324	543	217	23	9	8	17	12	....	1939-40	1953-54
• Bentley, Max	Chi., Tor., NYR	12	646	245	299	544	179	51	18	27	45	14	3	1940-41	1953-54
• Bentley, Reg	Chi.	1	11	1	2	3	2	....	....	....	....	....	....	1942-43	1942-43
Benysek, Ladislav	Edm., Min.	4	161	3	12	15	74	....	....	....	....	....	....	1997-98	2002-03
Beraldo, Paul	Bos.	2	10	0	0	0	4	....	....	....	....	....	....	1987-88	1988-89
Beranek, Josef	Edm., Phi., Van., Pit.	9	531	118	144	262	398	57	5	8	13	24	....	1991-92	2000-01
Berard, Bryan	NYI, Tor., NYR, Bos., Chi., CBJ	10	619	76	247	323	500	20	2	8	10	10	....	1996-97	2007-08
Berehowsky, Drake	Tor., Pit., Edm., Nsh., Van., Phx.	13	549	37	112	149	848	22	1	3	4	30	....	1990-91	2003-04
Berenson, Red	Mtl., NYR, St.L., Det.	17	987	261	397	658	305	85	23	14	37	49	1	1961-62	1977-78
Berenzweig, Bubba	Nsh.	4	37	3	7	10	14	....	....	....	....	....	....	1999-00	2002-03
Berezan, Perry	Cgy., Min., S.J.	9	378	61	75	136	279	31	4	7	11	34	....	1984-85	1992-93
Berezin, Sergei	Tor., Phx., Mtl., Chi., Wsh.	7	502	160	126	286	54	52	13	17	30	6	....	1996-97	2002-03
Berg, Aki	L.A., Tor.	9	606	15	70	85	374	54	1	7	8	47	....	1995-96	2005-06

Name	NHL Teams	NHL Seasons	Regular Schedule					Playoffs					NHL Cup Wins	First NHL Season	Last NHL Season
			GP	G	A	TP	PIM	GP	G	A	TP	PIM			
Berg, Bill	NYI, Tor., NYR, Ott.	10	546	55	67	122	488	61	3	4	7	34	....	1988-89	1998-99
• Bergdinon, Fred	Bos.	1	2	0	0	0	0	....	....	....	....	....	....	1925-26	1925-26
Bergen, Todd	Phi.	1	14	11	5	16	4	17	4	9	13	8	....	1984-85	1984-85
‡ Bergenheim, Sean	NYI, T.B., Fla., Min.	9	506	96	84	180	379	26	12	5	17	12	....	2003-04	2014-15
Berger, Mike	Min.	2	30	3	1	4	67	....	....	....	....	....	....	1987-88	1988-89
‡ Bergeron, Marc-Andre	Edm., NYI, Ana., Min., Mtl., T.B., Car.	10	490	82	153	235	214	57	7	8	15	39	....	2002-03	2012-13
Bergeron, Michel	Det., NYI, Wsh.	5	229	80	58	138	165	....	....	....	....	....	....	1974-75	1978-79
Bergeron, Yves	Pit.	2	3	0	0	0	0	....	....	....	....	....	....	1974-75	1976-77
Bergevin, Marc	Chi., NYI, Hfd., T.B., Det., St.L., Pit., Van.	20	1191	36	145	181	1090	80	3	6	9	52	....	1984-85	2003-04
‡ Bergfors, Niclas	N.J., Atl., Fla., Nsh.	5	173	35	48	83	20	....	....	....	....	....	....	2007-08	2011-12
Bergkvist, Stefan	Pit.	2	7	0	0	0	9	4	0	0	0	2	....	1995-96	1996-97
Bergland, Tim	Wsh., T.B.	5	182	17	26	43	75	26	2	2	4	22	....	1989-90	1993-94
Bergloff, Bob	Min.	1	2	0	0	0	5	....	....	....	....	....	....	1982-83	1982-83
Berglund, Bo	Que., Min., Phi.	3	130	28	39	67	40	9	2	0	2	6	....	1983-84	1985-86
Berglund, Christian	N.J., Fla.	3	86	11	16	27	42	3	0	0	0	2	....	2001-02	2003-04
• Bergman, Gary	Det., Min., K.C.	12	838	68	299	367	1249	21	0	5	5	20	....	1964-65	1975-76
Bergman, Thommie	Det.	6	246	21	44	65	243	7	0	2	2	2	....	1972-73	1979-80
Bergqvist, Jonas	Cgy.	1	22	2	5	7	10	....	....	....	....	....	....	1989-90	1989-90
• Berlinguette, Louis	Mtl., Mtl.M., Pit.	8	193	45	33	78	129	11	0	5	5	9	....	1917-18	1925-26
Bernier, Serge	Phi., L.A., Que.	7	302	78	119	197	234	5	1	1	2	0	....	1968-69	1980-81
Berry, Bob	Mtl., L.A.	8	541	159	191	350	344	26	2	6	8	6	....	1968-69	1976-77
Berry, Brad	Wpg., Min., Dal.	8	241	4	28	32	323	13	0	1	1	16	....	1985-86	1993-94
Berry, Doug	Col.	2	121	10	33	43	25	....	....	....	....	....	....	1979-80	1980-81
Berry, Fred	Det.	1	3	0	0	0	0	....	....	....	....	....	....	1976-77	1976-77
Berry, Ken	Edm., Van.	4	55	8	10	18	30	....	....	....	....	....	....	1981-82	1988-89
Berry, Rick	Col., Pit., Wsh.	4	197	2	13	15	314	....	....	....	....	....	....	2000-01	2003-04
Berti, Adam	Chi.	1	2	0	0	0	0	....	....	....	....	....	....	2007-08	2007-08
Bertrand, Eric	N.J., Atl., Mtl.	2	15	0	0	0	4	....	....	....	....	....	....	1999-00	2000-01
Bertuzzi, Todd	NYI, Van., Fla., Det., Ana., Cgy.	18	1159	314	456	770	1478	87	14	28	42	159	....	1995-96	2013-14
Berube, Craig	Phi., Tor., Cgy., Wsh., NYI	17	1054	61	98	159	3149	89	3	1	4	211	....	1986-87	2002-03
• Besler, Phil	Bos., Chi., Det.	2	30	1	4	5	18	....	....	....	....	....	....	1935-36	1938-39
• Bessone, Pete	Det.	1	6	0	1	1	6	....	....	....	....	....	....	1937-38	1937-38
Bethel, John	Wpg.	1	17	0	2	2	4	....	....	....	....	....	....	1979-80	1979-80
Betik, Karel	T.B.	1	3	0	2	2	2	....	....	....	....	....	....	1998-99	1998-99
Bets, Maxim	Ana.	1	3	0	0	0	0	....	....	....	....	....	....	1993-94	1993-94
• Bettio, Sam	Bos.	1	44	9	12	21	32	....	....	....	....	....	....	1949-50	1949-50
Betts, Blair	Cgy., NYR, Phi.	9	477	41	37	78	118	62	2	2	4	12	....	2001-02	2010-11
Beukeboom, Jeff	Edm., NYR	14	804	30	129	159	1890	99	3	16	19	197	4	1985-86	1998-99
Beverley, Nick	Bos., Pit., NYR, Min., L.A., Col.	11	502	18	94	112	156	7	0	1	1	0	....	1966-67	1979-80
‡ Bezina, Goran	Phx.	1	3	0	0	0	2	....	....	....	....	....	....	2003-04	2003-04
Bialowas, Dwight	Atl., Min.	4	164	11	46	57	46	....	....	....	....	....	....	1973-74	1976-77
Bialowas, Frank	Tor.	1	3	0	0	0	12	....	....	....	....	....	....	1993-94	1993-94
Bianchin, Wayne	Pit., Edm.	7	276	68	41	109	137	3	0	1	1	6	....	1973-74	1979-80
Bicanek, Radim	Ott., Chi., CBJ	7	122	1	11	12	62	7	0	0	0	8	....	1994-95	2001-02
‡ Bicek, Jiri	N.J.	4	62	6	7	13	29	7	0	0	0	0	1	2000-01	2003-04
Bidner, Todd	Wsh.	1	12	2	1	3	7	....	....	....	....	....	....	1981-82	1981-82
Biega, Danny	Car.	1	10	0	2	2	0	....	....	....	....	....	....	2014-15	2014-15
Biggs, Don	Min., Phi.	2	12	2	0	2	8	....	....	....	....	....	....	1984-85	1989-90
Bignell, Larry	Pit.	2	20	0	3	3	2	3	0	0	0	2	....	1973-74	1974-75
• Bilodeau, Gilles	Que.	1	9	0	1	1	25	....	....	....	....	....	....	1979-80	1979-80
• Bionda, Jack	Tor., Bos.	4	93	3	9	12	113	11	0	1	1	14	....	1955-56	1958-59
Biron, Mathieu	NYI, T.B., Fla., Wsh.	6	253	12	32	44	177	....	....	....	....	....	....	1999-00	2005-06
Bisaillon, Sebastien	Edm.	1	2	0	0	0	0	....	....	....	....	....	....	2006-07	2006-07
Bishai, Mike	Edm.	1	14	0	2	2	19	....	....	....	....	....	....	2003-04	2003-04
Bissett, Tom	Det.	1	5	0	0	0	0	....	....	....	....	....	....	1990-91	1990-91
‡ Bissonnette, Paul	Pit., Phx.	6	202	7	15	22	340	4	0	0	0	15	....	2008-09	2013-14
Bitz, Byron	Bos., Fla., Van.	3	97	10	12	22	65	6	1	1	2	17	....	2008-09	2011-12
Bjugstad, Scott	Min., Pit., L.A.	9	317	76	68	144	144	9	0	1	1	2	....	1983-84	1991-92
Black, James	Hfd., Min., Dal., Buf., Chi., Wsh.	11	352	58	57	115	84	13	2	1	3	4	....	1989-90	2000-01
• Black, Steve	Det., Chi.	2	113	11	20	31	77	13	0	0	0	13	1	1949-50	1950-51
Blackburn, Bob	NYR, Pit.	3	135	8	12	20	105	6	0	0	0	4	....	1968-69	1970-71
Blackburn, Don	Bos., Phi., NYR, NYI, Min.	6	185	23	44	67	87	12	3	0	3	10	....	1962-63	1972-73
‡ Blacker, Jesse	Ana.	1	1	0	0	0	0	....	....	....	....	....	....	2014-15	2014-15
• Blade, Hank	Chi.	2	24	2	3	5	2	....	....	....	....	....	....	1946-47	1947-48
Bladon, Tom	Phi., Pit., Edm., Wpg., Det.	9	610	73	197	270	392	86	8	29	37	70	2	1972-73	1980-81
• Blaine, Garry	Mtl.	1	1	0	0	0	0	....	....	....	....	....	....	1954-55	1954-55
• Blair, Andy	Tor., Chi.	9	402	74	86	160	323	38	6	6	12	32	1	1928-29	1936-37
• Blair, Chuck	Tor.	1	1	0	0	0	0	....	....	....	....	....	....	1948-49	1948-49
• Blair, Dusty	Tor.	1	2	0	0	0	0	....	....	....	....	....	....	1950-51	1950-51
Blaisdell, Mike	Det., NYR, Pit., Tor.	9	343	70	84	154	166	6	1	2	3	10	....	1980-81	1988-89
• Blake, Bob	Bos.	1	12	0	0	0	0	....	....	....	....	....	....	1935-36	1935-36
Blake, Jason	L.A., NYI, Tor., Ana.	13	871	213	273	486	455	30	6	5	11	19	....	1998-99	2011-12
• Blake, Mickey	Mtl.M., St.L., Tor.	3	10	1	1	2	4	....	....	....	....	....	....	1932-33	1935-36
Blake, Rob	L.A., Col., S.J.	20	1270	240	537	777	1679	146	26	47	73	166	1	1989-90	2009-10
• Blake, Toe	Mtl.M., Mtl.	14	577	235	292	527	272	58	25	37	62	23	3	1934-35	1947-48
Blanchard, Nicolas	Car.	1	9	0	0	0	20	....	....	....	....	....	....	2012-13	2012-13
Blatny, Zdenek	Atl., Bos.	3	25	3	0	3	8	....	....	....	....	....	....	2002-03	2005-06
• Blight, Rick	Van., L.A.	7	326	96	125	221	170	5	0	5	5	2	....	1975-76	1982-83
• Blinco, Russ	Mtl.M., Chi.	6	268	59	66	125	24	19	3	3	6	4	1	1933-34	1938-39
‡ Bliznak, Mario	Van.	2	6	1	0	1	0	....	....	....	....	....	....	2009-10	2010-11
Block, Ken	Van.	1	1	0	0	0	0	....	....	....	....	....	....	1970-71	1970-71
Bloemberg, Jeff	NYR	4	43	3	6	9	25	7	0	3	3	5	....	1988-89	1991-92
Blomqvist, Timo	Wsh., N.J.	5	243	4	53	57	293	13	0	0	0	24	....	1981-82	1986-87
Blomsten, Arto	Wpg., L.A.	3	25	0	4	4	8	....	....	....	....	....	....	1993-94	1995-96
Bloom, Mike	Wsh., Det.	3	201	30	47	77	215	....	....	....	....	....	....	1974-75	1976-77
Blouin, Sylvain	NYR, Mtl., Min.	6	115	3	4	7	336	....	....	....	....	....	....	1996-97	2002-03
Blum, John	Edm., Bos., Wsh., Det.	8	250	7	34	41	610	20	0	2	2	27	....	1982-83	1989-90
‡ Bochenski, Brandon	Ott., Chi., Bos., Ana., Nsh., T.B.	5	156	28	40	68	54	3	0	0	0	0	....	2005-06	2009-10
Bodak, Bob	Cgy., Hfd.	2	4	0	0	0	29	....	....	....	....	....	....	1987-88	1989-90
Boddy, Gregg	Van.	5	273	23	44	67	263	3	0	0	0	0	....	1971-72	1975-76
Bodger, Doug	Pit., Buf., S.J., N.J., L.A., Van.	16	1071	106	422	528	1007	47	6	18	24	25	....	1984-85	1999-00
Bodie, Troy	Ana., Car., Tor.	5	159	9	12	21	172	....	....	....	....	....	....	2008-09	2014-15
• Bodnar, Gus	Tor., Chi., Bos.	12	667	142	254	396	207	32	4	3	7	10	2	1943-44	1954-55
Boehm, Ron	Oak.	1	16	2	1	3	10	....	....	....	....	....	....	1967-68	1967-68
• Boesch, Garth	Tor.	4	197	9	28	37	205	34	2	5	7	18	3	1946-47	1949-50
Boguniecki, Eric	Fla., St.L., Pit., NYI	7	178	34	42	76	105	9	1	3	4	2	....	1999-00	2006-07
Boh, Rick	Min.	1	8	2	1	3	4	....	....	....	....	....	....	1987-88	1987-88
Bohonos, Lonny	Van., Tor.	4	83	19	16	35	22	9	3	6	9	2	....	1995-96	1998-99
Boikov, Alexandre	Nsh.	2	10	0	0	0	15	....	....	....	....	....	....	1999-00	2000-01
• Boileau, Marc	Det.	1	54	5	6	11	8	....	....	....	....	....	....	1961-62	1961-62
Boileau, Patrick	Wsh., Det., Pit.	5	48	5	11	16	26	....	....	....	....	....	....	1996-97	2003-04
• Boileau, Rene	NYA	1	7	0	0	0	0	....	....	....	....	....	....	1925-26	1925-26
Boimistruck, Fred	Tor.	2	83	4	14	18	45	....	....	....	....	....	....	1981-82	1982-83
Bois, Danny	Ott.	1	1	0	0	0	7	....	....	....	....	....	....	2006-07	2006-07
Boisvert, Serge	Tor., Mtl.	5	46	5	7	12	8	23	3	7	10	4	1	1982-83	1987-88
Boivin, Claude	Phi., Ott.	4	132	12	19	31	364	....	....	....	....	....	....	1991-92	1994-95
Boivin, Leo	Tor., Bos., Det., Pit., Min.	19	1150	72	250	322	1192	54	3	10	13	59	....	1951-52	1969-70
Boland, Mike	Phi.	1	2	0	0	0	0	....	....	....	....	....	....	1974-75	1974-75
Boland, Mike	K.C., Buf.	2	23	1	2	3	29	3	1	0	1	2	....	1974-75	1978-79
Boldirev, Ivan	Bos., Cal., Chi., Atl., Van., Det.	16	1052	361	505	866	507	48	13	20	33	14	1	1969-70	1984-85
‡ Bolduc, Alexandre	Van., Phx., Ari.	6	65	2	3	5	44	3	0	0	0	0	....	2008-09	2014-15
Bolduc, Danny	Det., Cgy.	3	102	22	19	41	33	1	0	0	0	0	....	1978-79	1983-84
Bolduc, Michel	Que.	2	10	0	0	0	6	....	....	....	....	....	....	1981-82	1982-83
• Boll, Buzz	Tor., NYA, Bro., Bos.	12	437	133	130	263	148	31	7	3	10	13	....	1932-33	1943-44
‡ Bolland, Dave	Chi., Tor., Fla.	10	433	85	123	208	299	67	17	26	43	84	2	2006-07	**2015-16**
Bolonchuk, Larry	Van., Wsh.	4	74	3	9	12	97	....	....	....	....	....	....	1972-73	1977-78
• Bolton, Hugh	Tor.	8	235	10	51	61	221	17	0	5	5	14	1	1949-50	1956-57
Bombardir, Brad	N.J., Min., Nsh.	7	356	8	46	54	127	16	0	1	1	2	1	1997-98	2003-04
Bonar, Dan	L.A.	3	170	25	39	64	208	14	3	4	7	22	....	1980-81	1982-83
Bondra, Peter	Wsh., Ott., Atl., Chi.	16	1081	503	389	892	761	80	30	26	56	60	....	1990-91	2006-07
Bonin, Brian	Pit., Min.	2	12	0	0	0	0	3	0	0	0	0	....	1998-99	2000-01

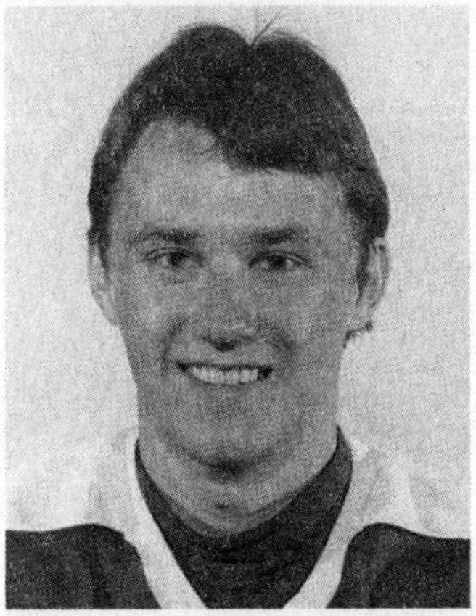

Laurie Boschman

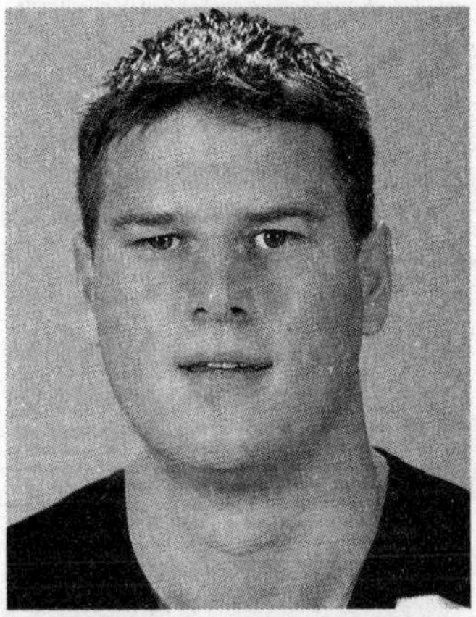

Jason Botterill

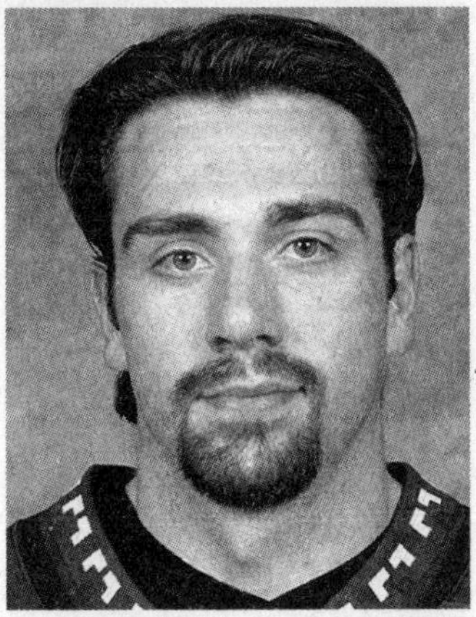

Joel Bouchard

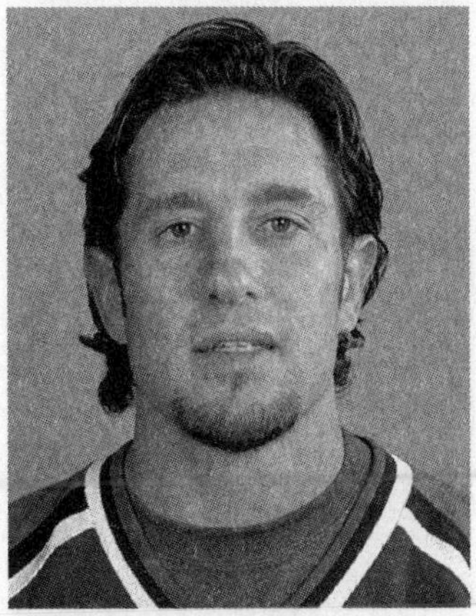

Bob Boughner

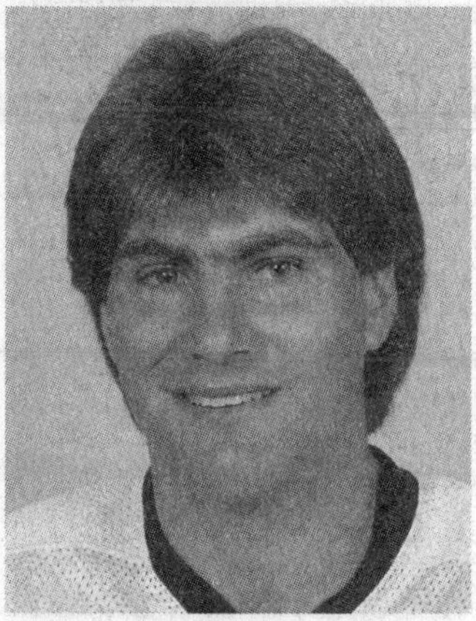

Raymond Bourque

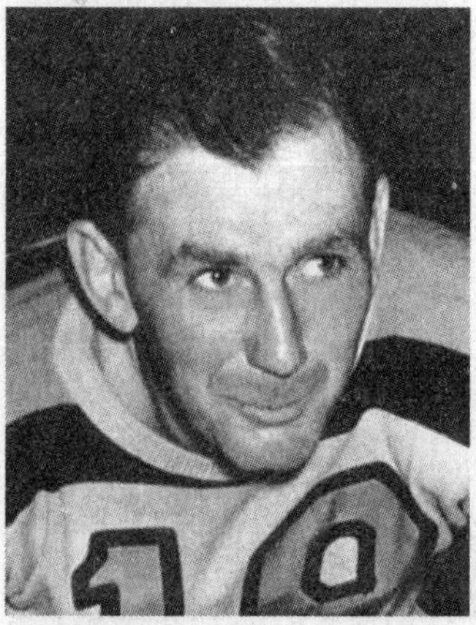

Irwin Boyd

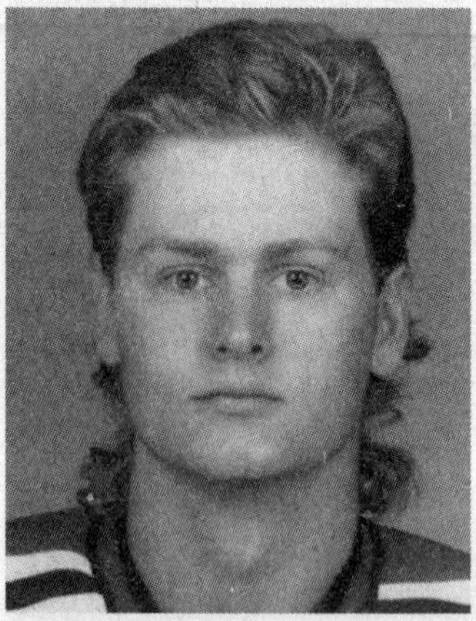

Neil Brady

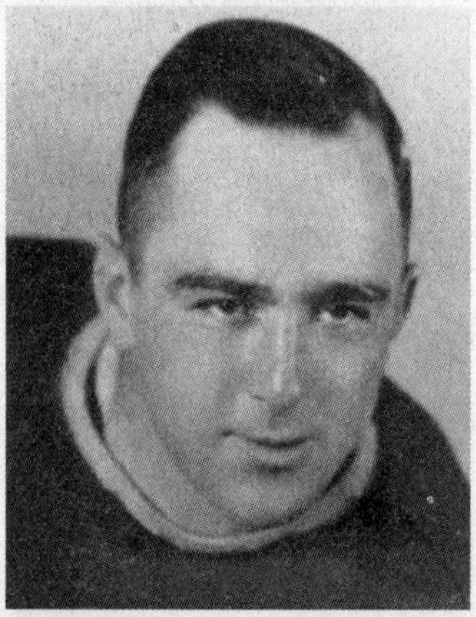

Doug Brennan

			Regular Schedule					Playoffs							
Name	NHL Teams	NHL Seasons	GP	G	A	TP	PIM	GP	G	A	TP	PIM	NHL Cup Wins	First NHL Season	Last NHL Season
Bonin, Marcel	Det., Bos., Mtl.	9	454	97	175	272	336	50	11	14	25	51	4	1952-53	1961-62
Bonk, Radek	Ott., Mtl., Nsh.	14	969	194	303	497	581	73	12	15	27	42	....	1994-95	2008-09
Bonni, Ryan	Van.	1	3	0	0	0	0	....	....	....	....	....	....	1999-00	1999-00
Bonsignore, Jason	Edm., T.B.	4	79	3	13	16	34	....	....	....	....	....	....	1994-95	1998-99
Bonvie, Dennis	Edm., Chi., Pit., Bos., Ott., Col.	9	92	1	2	3	311	1	0	0	0	0	....	1994-95	2003-04
Boo, Jim	Min.	1	6	0	0	0	22	....	....	....	....	....	....	1977-78	1977-78
● Boogaard, Derek	Min., NYR	6	277	3	13	16	589	10	0	1	1	44	....	2005-06	2010-11
● Boone, Buddy	Bos.	2	34	5	3	8	28	22	2	1	3	25	....	1956-57	1957-58
‡ Booth, David	Fla., Van., Tor.	9	502	120	111	231	206	5	0	1	1	0	....	2006-07	2014-15
● Boothman, George	Tor.	2	58	17	19	36	18	5	2	1	3	2	....	1942-43	1943-44
‡ Bootland, Darryl	Det., NYI	3	32	1	2	3	85	....	....	....	....	....	....	2003-04	2007-08
Bordeleau, Christian	Mtl., St.L., Chi.	4	205	38	65	103	82	19	4	7	11	17	1	1968-69	1971-72
Bordeleau, J.P.	Chi.	10	519	97	126	223	143	48	3	6	9	12	....	1969-70	1979-80
‡ Bordeleau, Patrick	Col.	3	129	8	8	16	185	7	0	0	0	10	....	2012-13	2014-15
Bordeleau, Paulin	Van.	3	183	33	56	89	47	5	2	1	3	0	....	1973-74	1975-76
Bordeleau, Sebastien	Mtl., Nsh., Min., Phx.	7	251	37	61	98	118	5	0	0	0	2	....	1995-96	2001-02
‡ Borer, Casey	Car.	3	16	1	2	3	9	....	....	....	....	....	....	2007-08	2009-10
Borotsik, Jack	St.L.	1	1	0	0	0	0	....	....	....	....	....	....	1974-75	1974-75
Borsato, Luciano	Wpg.	5	203	35	55	90	113	7	1	0	1	4	....	1990-91	1994-95
Borschevsky, Nikolai	Tor., Cgy., Dal.	4	162	49	73	122	44	31	4	9	13	4	....	1992-93	1995-96
Boschman, Laurie	Tor., Edm., Wpg., N.J., Ott.	14	1009	229	348	577	2265	57	8	13	21	140	....	1979-80	1992-93
Bossy, Mike	NYI	10	752	573	553	1126	210	129	85	75	160	38	4	1977-78	1986-87
● Bostrom, Helge	Chi.	4	96	3	3	6	58	13	0	0	0	16	....	1929-30	1932-33
Botell, Mark	Phi.	1	32	4	10	14	31	....	....	....	....	....	....	1981-82	1981-82
Bothwell, Tim	NYR, St.L., Hfd.	11	502	28	93	121	382	49	0	3	3	56	....	1978-79	1988-89
Botterill, Jason	Dal., Atl., Cgy., Buf.	6	88	5	9	14	89	....	....	....	....	....	....	1997-98	2003-04
Botting, Cam	Atl.	1	2	0	1	1	0	....	....	....	....	....	....	1975-76	1975-76
Boucha, Henry	Det., Min., K.C., Col.	6	247	53	49	102	157	....	....	....	....	....	....	1971-72	1976-77
● Bouchard, Butch	Mtl.	15	785	49	144	193	863	113	11	21	32	121	4	1941-42	1955-56
● Bouchard, Dick	NYR	1	1	0	0	0	0	....	....	....	....	....	....	1954-55	1954-55
● Bouchard, Edmond	Mtl., Ham., NYA, Pit.	8	211	19	21	40	117	....	....	....	....	....	....	1921-22	1928-29
Bouchard, Joel	Cgy., Nsh., Dal., Phx., N.J., NYR, Pit., NYI	11	364	22	53	75	264	....	....	....	....	....	....	1994-95	2005-06
Bouchard, Pierre	Mtl., Wsh.	12	595	24	82	106	433	76	3	10	13	56	5	1970-71	1981-82
Bouchard, Pierre-Marc	Min., NYI	11	593	110	246	356	190	21	4	5	9	4	....	2002-03	2013-14
● Boucher, Billy	Mtl., Bos., NYA	7	213	93	38	131	409	14	3	0	3	17	1	1921-22	1927-28
● Boucher, Bobby	Mtl.	1	11	1	0	1	0	2	0	0	0	0	1	1923-24	1923-24
● Boucher, Clarence	NYA	2	47	2	2	4	133	....	....	....	....	....	....	1926-27	1927-28
● Boucher, Frank	Ott., NYR	14	557	160	263	423	119	55	16	20	36	12	2	1921-22	1943-44
● Boucher, George	Ott., Mtl.M., Chi.	15	449	117	87	204	838	28	5	3	8	88	4	1917-18	1931-32
Boucher, Philippe	Buf., L.A., Dal., Pit.	16	748	94	206	300	702	65	4	10	14	39	1	1992-93	2008-09
Bouck, Tyler	Dal., Phx., Van.	5	91	4	8	12	93	2	0	0	0	0	....	2000-01	2006-07
Boudreau, Bruce	Tor., Chi.	8	141	28	42	70	46	9	2	0	2	0	....	1976-77	1985-86
Boudrias, Andre	Mtl., Min., Chi., St.L., Van.	12	662	151	340	491	216	34	6	10	16	12	....	1963-64	1975-76
Boughner, Barry	Oak., Cal.	2	20	0	0	0	11	....	....	....	....	....	....	1969-70	1970-71
Boughner, Bob	Buf., Nsh., Pit., Cgy., Car., Col.	10	630	15	57	72	1382	65	0	12	12	67	....	1995-96	2005-06
Bouillon, Francis	Mtl., Nsh.	14	776	32	117	149	536	55	4	7	11	50	....	1999-00	2013-14
Boulerice, Jesse	Phi., Car., St.L., Edm.	6	172	8	2	10	333	....	....	....	....	....	....	2001-02	2008-09
‡ Boulton, Eric	Buf., Atl., N.J., NYI	15	654	31	48	79	1421	4	0	0	0	24	....	2000-01	**2015-16**
Boumedienne, Josef	N.J., T.B., Wsh.	3	47	4	12	16	36	....	....	....	....	....	....	2001-02	2003-04
Bourbonnais, Dan	Hfd.	2	59	3	25	28	11	....	....	....	....	....	....	1981-82	1983-84
Bourbonnais, Rick	St.L.	3	71	9	15	24	29	4	0	1	1	0	....	1975-76	1977-78
● Bourcier, Conrad	Mtl.	1	6	0	0	0	0	....	....	....	....	....	....	1935-36	1935-36
● Bourcier, Jean	Mtl.	1	9	0	1	1	0	....	....	....	....	....	....	1935-36	1935-36
● Bourdon, Luc	Van.	2	36	2	0	2	24	....	....	....	....	....	....	2006-07	2007-08
Bourdon, Marc-Andre	Phi.	1	45	4	3	7	52	1	0	0	0	0	....	2011-12	2011-12
● Bourgeault, Leo	Tor., NYR, Ott., Mtl.	8	307	24	20	44	334	24	1	1	2	18	1	1926-27	1934-35
Bourgeois, Charlie	Cgy., St.L., Hfd.	7	290	16	54	70	788	40	2	3	5	194	....	1981-82	1987-88
Bourne, Bob	NYI, L.A.	14	964	258	324	582	605	139	40	56	96	108	4	1974-75	1987-88
Bourque, Phil	Pit., NYR, Ott.	12	477	88	111	199	516	56	13	12	25	107	2	1983-84	1995-96
Bourque, Raymond	Bos., Col.	22	1612	410	1169	1579	1141	214	41	139	180	171	1	1979-80	2000-01
Boutette, Pat	Tor., Hfd., Pit.	10	756	171	282	453	1354	46	10	14	24	109	....	1975-76	1984-85
Boutilier, Paul	NYI, Bos., Min., NYR, Wpg.	8	288	27	83	110	358	41	1	9	10	45	1	1981-82	1988-89
Bowen, Jason	Phi., Edm.	6	77	2	6	8	109	....	....	....	....	....	....	1992-93	1997-98
Bowler, Bill	CBJ	1	9	0	2	2	8	....	....	....	....	....	....	2000-01	2000-01
‡ Bowman, Drayson	Car., Mtl.	6	179	15	18	33	53	....	....	....	....	....	....	2009-10	2014-15
Bowman, Kirk	Chi.	3	88	11	17	28	19	7	1	0	1	0	....	1976-77	1978-79
● Bowman, Ralph	Ott., St.L., Det.	7	274	8	17	25	260	22	2	2	4	6	2	1933-34	1939-40
● Bownass, Jack	Mtl., NYR	4	80	3	8	11	58	....	....	....	....	....	....	1957-58	1961-62
Bowness, Rick	Atl., Det., St.L., Wpg.	7	173	18	37	55	191	5	0	0	0	2	....	1975-76	1981-82
‡ Boyce, Darryl	Tor., CBJ	3	84	6	12	18	68	....	....	....	....	....	....	2007-08	2011-12
‡ Boychuk, Zach	Car., Pit., Nsh.	7	127	12	18	30	16	....	....	....	....	....	....	2008-09	2014-15
● Boyd, Bill	NYR, NYA	4	138	15	7	22	72	10	0	0	0	4	1	1926-27	1929-30
‡ Boyd, Dustin	Cgy., Nsh., Mtl.	5	220	32	31	63	41	9	1	0	1	0	....	2006-07	2010-11
● Boyd, Irwin	Bos., Det.	4	96	10	10	20	30	5	0	1	1	4	....	1931-32	1943-44
Boyd, Randy	Pit., Chi., NYI, Van.	8	257	20	67	87	328	13	0	2	2	26	....	1981-82	1988-89
Boyer, Wally	Tor., Chi., Oak., Pit.	7	365	54	105	159	163	15	1	3	4	0	....	1965-66	1971-72
Boyer, Zac	Dal.	2	3	0	0	0	0	2	0	0	0	0	....	1994-95	1995-96
Boyes, Brad	S.J., Bos., St.L., Buf., NYI, Fla., Tor.	12	822	211	294	505	251	17	3	4	7	2	....	2003-04	**2015-16**
Boyko, Darren	Wpg.	1	1	0	0	0	0	....	....	....	....	....	....	1988-89	1988-89
Boyle, Dan	Fla., T.B., S.J., NYR	17	1093	163	442	605	693	130	17	64	81	70	1	1998-99	**2015-16**
Boynton, Nick	Bos., Phx., Fla., Ana., Chi., Phi.	11	605	34	110	144	862	21	1	5	6	16	1	1999-00	2010-11
Bozek, Steve	L.A., Cgy., St.L., Van., S.J.	11	641	164	167	331	309	58	12	11	23	69	....	1981-82	1991-92
Bozon, Philippe	St.L.	4	144	16	25	41	101	19	2	0	2	31	....	1991-92	1994-95
● Brackenborough, John	Bos.	1	7	0	0	0	0	....	....	....	....	....	....	1925-26	1925-26
Brackenbury, Curt	Que., Edm., St.L.	4	141	9	17	26	226	2	0	0	0	0	....	1979-80	1982-83
● Bradley, Bart	Bos.	1	1	0	0	0	0	....	....	....	....	....	....	1949-50	1949-50
Bradley, Brian	Cgy., Van., Tor., T.B.	13	651	182	321	503	528	13	3	7	10	16	....	1985-86	1997-98
Bradley, Lyle	Cal., Cle.	2	6	1	0	1	2	....	....	....	....	....	....	1973-74	1976-77
Bradley, Matt	S.J., Pit., Wsh., Fla.	11	675	59	90	149	562	47	3	8	11	8	....	2000-01	2011-12
Brady, Neil	N.J., Ott., Dal.	5	89	9	22	31	95	....	....	....	....	....	....	1989-90	1993-94
Bragnalo, Rick	Wsh.	4	145	15	35	50	46	....	....	....	....	....	....	1975-76	1978-79
Brandner, Christoph	Min.	1	35	4	5	9	8	....	....	....	....	....	....	2003-04	2003-04
● Branigan, Andy	NYA, Bro.	2	27	1	2	3	31	....	....	....	....	....	....	1940-41	1941-42
Brasar, Per-Olov	Min., Van.	5	348	64	142	206	33	13	1	2	3	0	....	1977-78	1981-82
Brashear, Donald	Mtl., Van., Phi., Wsh., NYR	16	1025	85	120	205	2634	60	3	6	9	121	....	1993-94	2009-10
● Brayshaw, Russ	Chi.	1	43	5	9	14	24	....	....	....	....	....	....	1944-45	1944-45
Breault, Francis	L.A.	3	27	2	4	6	42	....	....	....	....	....	....	1990-91	1992-93
● Breitenbach, Ken	Buf.	3	68	1	13	14	49	8	0	1	1	4	....	1975-76	1978-79
Bremberg, Fredrik	Edm.	1	8	0	0	0	2	....	....	....	....	....	....	1998-99	1998-99
Brendl, Pavel	Phi., Car., Phx.	4	78	11	11	22	16	2	0	0	0	0	....	2001-02	2005-06
Brennan, Dan	L.A.	2	8	0	1	1	9	....	....	....	....	....	....	1983-84	1985-86
● Brennan, Doug	NYR	3	123	9	7	16	152	16	1	0	1	21	1	1931-32	1933-34
Brennan, Kip	L.A., Atl., Ana., NYI	5	61	1	1	2	222	....	....	....	....	....	....	2001-02	2007-08
Brennan, Rich	Col., S.J., NYR, L.A., Nsh., Bos.	6	50	2	6	8	33	....	....	....	....	....	....	1996-97	2002-03
● Brennan, Tom	Bos.	2	12	2	2	4	2	....	....	....	....	....	....	1943-44	1944-45
Brenneman, John	Chi., NYR, Tor., Det., Oak.	5	152	21	19	40	46	....	....	....	....	....	1	1964-65	1968-69
Brent, Tim	Ana., Pit., Chi., Tor., Car.	7	207	21	27	48	76	....	....	....	....	....	....	2006-07	2012-13
● Bretto, Joe	Chi.	1	3	0	0	0	4	....	....	....	....	....	....	1944-45	1944-45
● Brewer, Carl	Tor., Det., St.L.	12	604	25	198	223	1037	72	3	17	20	146	3	1957-58	1979-80
Brewer, Eric	NYI, Edm., St.L., T.B., Ana., Tor.	16	1009	77	194	271	792	34	3	14	17	22	....	1998-99	2014-15
Brickley, Andy	Phi., Pit., N.J., Bos., Wpg.	11	385	82	140	222	81	17	1	4	5	4	....	1982-83	1993-94
● Briden, Archie	Bos., Det., Pit.	2	71	9	5	14	56	....	....	....	....	....	....	1926-27	1929-30
Bridgman, Mel	Phi., Cgy., N.J., Det., Van.	14	977	252	449	701	1625	125	28	39	67	298	....	1975-76	1988-89
Briere, Daniel	Phx., Buf., Phi., Mtl., Col.	17	973	307	389	696	744	124	53	63	116	98	....	1997-98	2014-15
● Briere, Michel	Pit.	1	76	12	32	44	20	10	5	3	8	17	....	1969-70	1969-70
Brigley, Travis	Cgy., Col.	3	55	3	6	9	16	....	....	....	....	....	....	1997-98	2003-04
Brimanis, Aris	Phi., NYI, Ana., St.L.	7	113	2	12	14	57	....	....	....	....	....	....	1993-94	2003-04
Brind'Amour, Rod	St.L., Phi., Car.	21	1484	452	732	1184	1100	159	51	60	111	97	1	1988-89	2009-10
Brindley, Doug	Tor.	1	3	0	0	0	0	....	....	....	....	....	....	1970-71	1970-71
Brine, David	Fla.	1	9	0	1	1	4	....	....	....	....	....	....	2007-08	2007-08
● Brink, Milt	Chi.	1	5	0	0	0	0	....	....	....	....	....	....	1936-37	1936-37

Name	NHL Teams	NHL Seasons	Regular Schedule					Playoffs					NHL Cup Wins	First NHL Season	Last NHL Season
			GP	G	A	TP	PIM	GP	G	A	TP	PIM			
Brisebois, Patrice	Mtl., Col.	18	1009	98	322	420	623	98	9	23	32	76	1	1990-91	2008-09
• Brisson, Gerry	Mtl.	1	4	0	2	2	4	....	....	....	....	....	....	1962-63	1962-63
Britz, Greg	Tor., Hfd.	3	8	0	0	0	4	....	....	....	....	....	....	1983-84	1986-87
• Broadbent, Punch	Ott., Mtl.M., NYA	11	303	121	51	172	564	23	4	6	10	60	4	1918-19	1928-29
Brochu, Stephane	NYR	1	1	0	0	0	0	....	....	....	....	....	....	1988-89	1988-89
• Broden, Connie	Mtl.	3	6	2	1	3	2	7	0	1	1	0	2	1955-56	1957-58
‡ Brookbank, Sheldon	Nsh., N.J., Ana., Chi.	8	351	7	37	44	473	25	0	2	2	32	1	2006-07	2013-14
Brookbank, Wade	Nsh., Van., Bos., Car.	5	127	6	3	9	345	....	....	....	....	....	....	2003-04	2008-09
Brooke, Bob	NYR, Min., N.J.	7	447	69	97	166	520	34	9	9	18	59	....	1983-84	1989-90
Brooks, Alex	N.J.	1	19	0	1	1	4	....	....	....	....	....	....	2006-07	2006-07
Brooks, Gord	St.L., Wsh.	3	70	7	18	25	37	....	....	....	....	....	....	1971-72	1974-75
Brophey, Evan	Chi., Col.	2	4	0	0	0	0	....	....	....	....	....	....	2010-11	2011-12
• Brophy, Bernie	Mtl.M., Det.	3	62	4	4	8	25	2	0	0	0	2	1	1925-26	1929-30
Brossart, Willie	Phi., Tor., Wsh.	6	129	1	14	15	88	1	0	0	0	0	....	1970-71	1975-76
Broten, Aaron	Col., N.J., Min., Que., Tor., Wpg.	12	748	186	329	515	441	34	7	18	25	40	....	1980-81	1991-92
Broten, Neal	Min., Dal., N.J., L.A.	17	1099	289	634	923	569	135	35	63	98	77	1	1980-81	1996-97
Broten, Paul	NYR, Dal., St.L.	7	322	46	55	101	264	38	4	6	10	18	....	1989-90	1995-96
Brousseau, Paul	Col., T.B., Fla.	4	26	1	3	4	29	....	....	....	....	....	....	1995-96	2000-01
• Brown, Adam	Det., Chi., Bos.	10	391	104	113	217	378	26	2	4	6	14	1	1941-42	1951-52
Brown, Arnie	Tor., NYR, Det., NYI, Atl.	12	681	44	141	185	738	22	0	6	6	23	....	1961-62	1973-74
Brown, Brad	Mtl., Chi., NYR, Min., Buf.	7	330	2	27	29	747	11	0	0	0	16	....	1996-97	2003-04
Brown, Cam	Van.	1	1	0	0	0	7	....	....	....	....	....	....	1990-91	1990-91
• Brown, Connie	Det.	5	73	15	24	39	12	14	2	3	5	0	1	1938-39	1942-43
Brown, Curtis	Buf., S.J., Chi.	13	736	129	171	300	398	87	14	15	29	58	....	1994-95	2007-08
Brown, Dave	Phi., Edm., S.J.	14	729	45	52	97	1789	80	2	3	5	209	1	1982-83	1995-96
Brown, Doug	N.J., Pit., Det.	15	854	160	214	374	210	109	23	23	46	26	2	1986-87	2000-01
• Brown, Fred	Mtl.M.	1	19	1	0	1	0	9	0	0	0	0	....	1927-28	1927-28
• Brown, George	Mtl.	3	79	6	22	28	34	7	0	0	0	2	....	1936-37	1938-39
• Brown, Gerry	Det.	2	23	4	5	9	2	12	2	1	3	4	....	1941-42	1945-46
Brown, Greg	Buf., Pit., Wpg.	4	94	4	14	18	86	6	0	1	1	4	....	1990-91	1994-95
• Brown, Harold	NYR	1	13	2	1	3	2	....	....	....	....	....	....	1945-46	1945-46
Brown, Jeff	Que., St.L., Van., Hfd., Car., Tor., Wsh.	13	747	154	430	584	498	87	20	45	65	59	....	1985-86	1997-98
Brown, Jim	L.A.	1	3	0	1	1	5	....	....	....	....	....	....	1982-83	1982-83
Brown, Keith	Chi., Fla.	16	876	68	274	342	916	103	4	32	36	184	....	1979-80	1994-95
Brown, Kevin	L.A., Hfd., Car., Edm.	6	64	7	9	16	28	1	0	0	0	0	....	1994-95	1999-00
Brown, Larry	NYR, Det., Phi., L.A.	9	455	7	53	60	180	35	0	4	4	10	....	1969-70	1977-78
Brown, Mike	Van., Ana., Chi.	4	34	1	2	3	130	....	....	....	....	....	....	2000-01	2005-06
‡ Brown, Mike	Van., Ana., Tor., Edm., S.J., Mtl.	9	407	19	17	36	778	19	1	3	4	51	....	2007-08	**2015-16**
Brown, Rob	Pit., Hfd., Chi., Dal., L.A.	11	543	190	248	438	599	54	12	14	26	45	....	1987-88	1999-00
Brown, Sean	Edm., Bos., N.J., Van.	9	436	14	43	57	907	9	0	0	0	37	....	1996-97	2005-06
• Brown, Stan	NYR, Det.	2	48	8	2	10	18	2	0	0	0	0	....	1926-27	1927-28
Brown, Wayne	Bos.	1	....	....	....	....	....	4	0	0	0	2	....	1953-54	1953-54
• Browne, Cecil	Chi.	1	13	2	0	2	4	....	....	....	....	....	....	1927-28	1927-28
Brownschidle, Jack	St.L., Hfd.	9	494	39	162	201	151	26	0	5	5	18	....	1977-78	1985-86
• Brownschidle, Jeff	Hfd.	2	7	0	1	1	2	....	....	....	....	....	....	1981-82	1982-83
Brubaker, Jeff	Hfd., Mtl., Cgy., Tor., Edm., NYR, Det.	8	178	16	9	25	512	2	0	0	0	27	....	1979-80	1988-89
Bruce, David	Van., St.L., S.J.	8	234	48	39	87	338	3	0	0	0	2	....	1985-86	1993-94
• Bruce, Gordie	Bos.	3	28	4	9	13	13	7	2	3	5	4	....	1940-41	1945-46
• Bruce, Morley	Ott.	4	71	8	3	11	27	3	0	0	0	2	2	1917-18	1921-22
‡ Brule, Gilbert	CBJ, Edm., Phx.	8	299	43	52	95	156	12	2	1	3	0	....	2005-06	2013-14
Brule, Steve	N.J., Col.	2	2	0	0	0	0	1	0	0	0	0	1	1999-00	2002-03
Brumwell, Murray	Min., N.J.	7	128	12	31	43	70	2	0	0	0	2	....	1980-81	1987-88
Brunet, Benoit	Mtl., Dal., Ott.	13	539	101	161	262	229	54	5	20	25	32	1	1988-89	2001-02
• Bruneteau, Eddie	Det.	7	180	40	42	82	35	31	7	6	13	0	....	1940-41	1948-49
• Bruneteau, Mud	Det.	11	411	139	138	277	80	77	23	14	37	22	3	1935-36	1945-46
Brunette, Andrew	Wsh., Nsh., Atl., Min., Col., Chi.	16	1110	268	465	733	314	49	17	18	35	14	....	1995-96	2011-12
‡ Brunner, Damien	Det., N.J.	3	121	25	33	58	46	14	5	4	9	4	....	2012-13	2014-15
‡ Brunnstrom, Fabian	Dal., Det.	3	104	19	22	41	22	....	....	....	....	....	....	2008-09	2011-12
• Brydge, Bill	Tor., Det., NYA	9	368	26	52	78	506	2	0	0	0	4	....	1926-27	1935-36
Brydges, Paul	Buf.	1	15	2	2	4	6	....	....	....	....	....	....	1986-87	1986-87
• Brydson, Glenn	Mtl.M., St.L., NYR, Chi.	8	299	56	79	135	203	11	0	0	0	8	....	1930-31	1937-38
• Brydson, Gord	Tor.	1	8	2	0	2	8	....	....	....	....	....	....	1929-30	1929-30
Brylin, Sergei	N.J.	13	765	129	179	308	273	109	15	19	34	32	3	1994-95	2007-08
Bubla, Jiri	Van.	5	256	17	101	118	202	6	0	0	0	7	....	1981-82	1985-86
• Buchanan, Al	Tor.	2	4	0	1	1	2	....	....	....	....	....	....	1948-49	1949-50
• Buchanan, Bucky	NYR	1	2	0	0	0	0	....	....	....	....	....	....	1948-49	1948-49
Buchanan, Jeff	Col.	1	6	0	0	0	6	....	....	....	....	....	....	1998-99	1998-99
• Buchanan, Mike	Chi.	1	1	0	0	0	0	....	....	....	....	....	....	1951-52	1951-52
Buchanan, Ron	Bos., St.L.	2	5	0	0	0	0	....	....	....	....	....	....	1966-67	1969-70
Buchberger, Kelly	Edm., Atl., L.A., Phx., Pit.	18	1182	105	204	309	2297	97	10	15	25	129	2	1986-87	2003-04
Bucyk, John	Det., Bos.	23	1540	556	813	1369	497	124	41	62	103	42	2	1955-56	1977-78
Bucyk, Randy	Mtl., Cgy.	2	19	4	2	6	8	2	0	0	0	0	....	1985-86	1987-88
• Buhr, Doug	K.C.	1	6	0	2	2	4	....	....	....	....	....	....	1974-75	1974-75
• Bukovich, Tony	Det.	2	17	7	3	10	6	6	0	1	1	0	....	1943-44	1944-45
Bulis, Jan	Wsh., Mtl., Van.	9	552	96	149	245	268	35	3	3	6	14	....	1997-98	2006-07
Bullard, Mike	Pit., Cgy., St.L., Phi., Tor.	11	727	329	345	674	703	40	11	18	29	44	....	1980-81	1991-92
• Buller, Hy	Det., NYR	5	188	22	58	80	215	....	....	....	....	....	....	1943-44	1953-54
Bulley, Ted	Chi., Wsh., Pit.	8	414	101	113	214	704	29	5	5	10	24	....	1976-77	1983-84
‡ Bulmer, Brett	Min.	3	17	0	3	3	15	....	....	....	....	....	....	2011-12	**2015-16**
Burakovsky, Robert	Ott.	1	23	2	3	5	6	....	....	....	....	....	....	1993-94	1993-94
• Burch, Billy	Ham., NYA, Bos., Chi.	11	390	137	61	198	255	2	0	0	0	0	....	1922-23	1932-33
• Burchell, Fred	Mtl.	2	4	0	0	0	2	....	....	....	....	....	....	1950-51	1953-54
Burdon, Glen	K.C.	1	11	0	2	2	0	....	....	....	....	....	....	1974-75	1974-75
Bure, Pavel	Van., Fla., NYR	12	702	437	342	779	484	64	35	35	70	74	....	1991-92	2002-03
Bure, Valeri	Mtl., Cgy., Fla., St.L., Dal.	10	621	174	226	400	221	22	0	7	7	16	....	1994-95	2003-04
Bureau, Marc	Cgy., Min., T.B., Mtl., Phi.	11	567	55	83	138	327	50	5	7	12	46	....	1989-90	1999-00
Burega, Bill	Tor.	1	4	0	1	1	4	....	....	....	....	....	....	1955-56	1955-56
Burish, Adam	Chi., Dal., S.J.	9	378	27	33	60	554	38	3	2	5	36	1	2006-07	2014-15
• Burke, Eddie	Bos., NYA	4	106	29	20	49	55	....	....	....	....	....	....	1931-32	1934-35
• Burke, Marty	Mtl., Pit., Ott., Chi.	11	494	19	47	66	560	31	2	4	6	44	2	1927-28	1937-38
• Burmister, Roy	NYA	3	67	4	3	7	2	....	....	....	....	....	....	1929-30	1931-32
Burnett, Garrett	Ana.	1	39	1	2	3	184	....	....	....	....	....	....	2003-04	2003-04
Burnett, Kelly	NYR	1	3	1	0	1	0	....	....	....	....	....	....	1952-53	1952-53
• Burns, Bobby	Chi.	3	20	1	0	1	8	....	....	....	....	....	....	1927-28	1929-30
Burns, Charlie	Det., Bos., Oak., Pit., Min.	11	749	106	198	304	252	31	5	4	9	6	....	1958-59	1972-73
Burns, Gary	NYR	2	11	2	2	4	18	5	0	0	0	2	....	1980-81	1981-82
• Burns, Norm	NYR	1	11	0	4	4	2	....	....	....	....	....	....	1941-42	1941-42
Burns, Robin	Pit., K.C.	5	190	31	38	69	139	....	....	....	....	....	....	1970-71	1975-76
• Burr, Shawn	Det., T.B., S.J.	16	878	181	259	440	1069	91	16	19	35	95	....	1984-85	1999-00
Burridge, Randy	Bos., Wsh., L.A., Buf.	13	706	199	251	450	458	107	18	34	52	103	....	1985-86	1997-98
Burrows, Dave	Pit., Tor.	10	724	29	135	164	373	29	1	5	6	25	....	1971-72	1980-81
• Burry, Bert	Ott.	1	4	0	0	0	0	....	....	....	....	....	....	1932-33	1932-33
Burt, Adam	Hfd., Car., Phi., Atl.	13	737	37	115	152	961	21	0	1	1	8	....	1988-89	2000-01
• Burton, Cummy	Det.	3	43	0	2	2	21	3	0	0	0	0	....	1955-56	1958-59
Burton, Nelson	Wsh.	2	8	1	0	1	21	....	....	....	....	....	....	1977-78	1978-79
• Bush, Eddie	Det.	2	26	4	6	10	40	11	1	6	7	23	....	1938-39	1941-42
Buskas, Rod	Pit., Van., L.A., Chi.	11	556	19	63	82	1294	18	0	3	3	45	....	1982-83	1992-93
Busniuk, Mike	Phi.	2	143	3	23	26	297	25	2	5	7	34	....	1979-80	1980-81
Busniuk, Ron	Buf.	2	6	0	3	3	13	....	....	....	....	....	....	1972-73	1973-74
• Buswell, Walt	Det., Mtl.	8	368	10	40	50	164	24	2	1	3	10	....	1932-33	1939-40
Butcher, Garth	Van., St.L., Que., Tor.	14	897	48	158	206	2302	50	6	5	11	122	....	1981-82	1994-95
Butenschon, Sven	Pit., Edm., NYI, Van.	8	140	2	12	14	86	4	0	0	0	0	....	1997-98	2005-06
‡ Butler, Bobby	Ott., N.J., Nsh., Fla.	5	130	20	29	49	28	3	0	0	0	0	....	2009-10	2013-14
• Butler, Dick	Chi.	1	7	2	0	2	0	....	....	....	....	....	....	1947-48	1947-48
Butler, Jerry	NYR, St.L., Tor., Van., Wpg.	11	641	99	120	219	515	48	3	3	6	79	....	1972-73	1982-83
Butsayev, Viacheslav	Phi., S.J., Ana., Fla., Ott., T.B.	6	132	17	26	43	133	....	....	....	....	....	....	1992-93	1999-00
Butsayev, Yuri	Det., Atl.	4	99	10	4	14	28	....	....	....	....	....	....	1999-00	2002-03
Butters, Bill	Min.	2	72	1	4	5	77	....	....	....	....	....	....	1977-78	1978-79
• Buttrey, Gord	Chi.	1	10	0	0	0	0	....	....	....	....	....	....	1943-44	1943-44
Buynak, Gord	St.L.	1	4	0	0	0	2	....	....	....	....	....	....	1974-75	1974-75
Buzek, Petr	Dal., Atl., Cgy.	6	157	9	22	31	94	....	....	....	....	....	....	1997-98	2002-03
Byakin, Ilja	Edm., S.J.	2	57	8	25	33	44	....	....	....	....	....	....	1993-94	1994-95

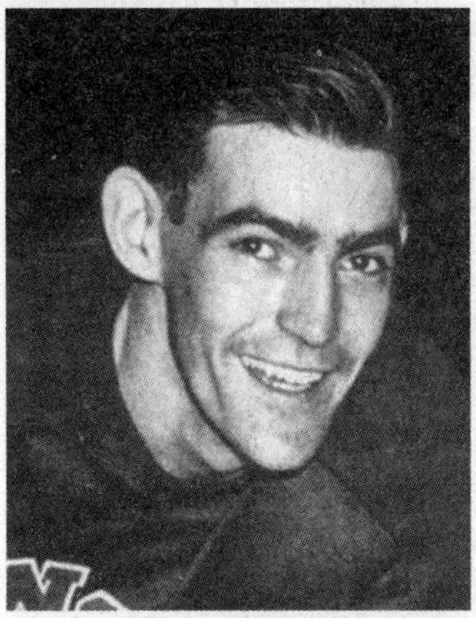

Harold Brown

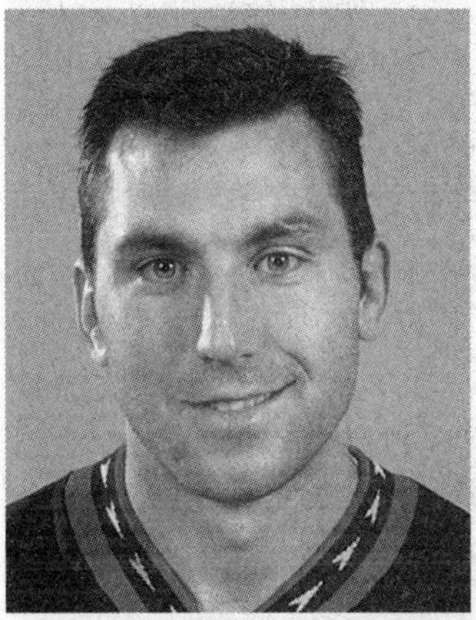

Andrew Brunette

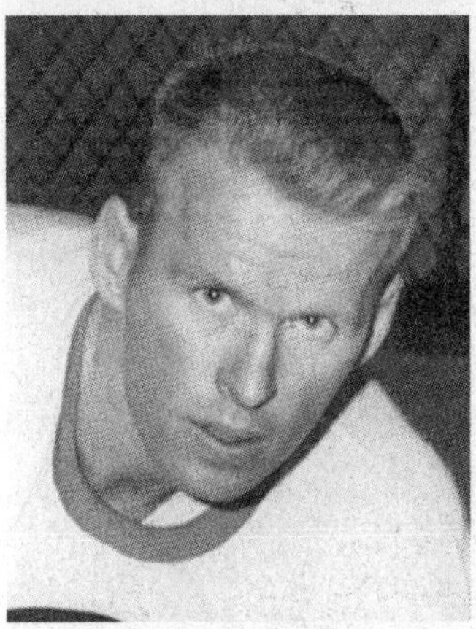

Mike Buchanan

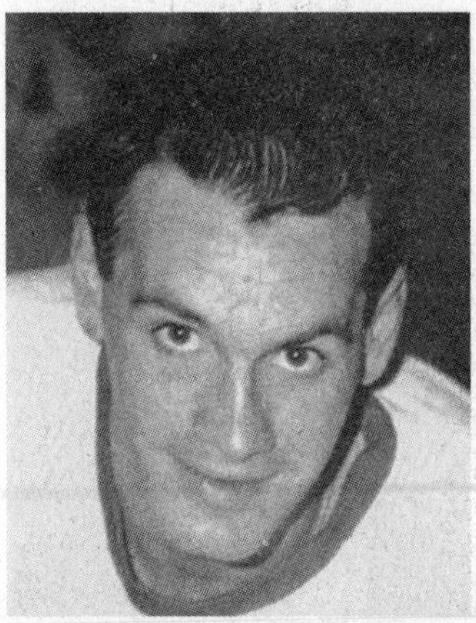

Charlie Burns

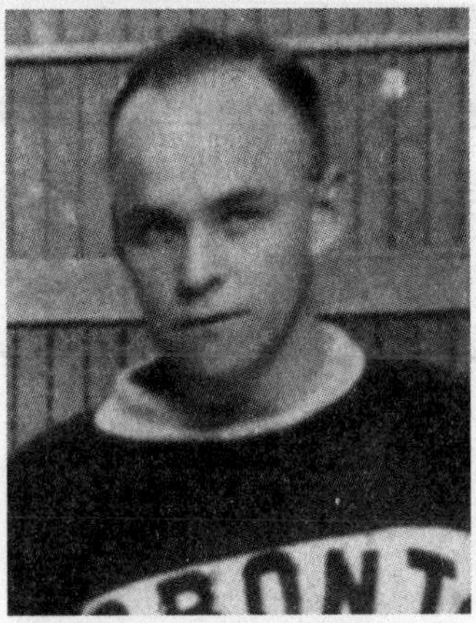

Harry Cameron

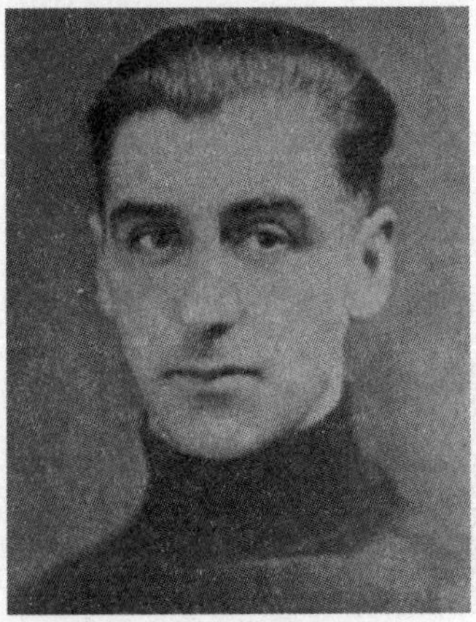

Earl Campbell

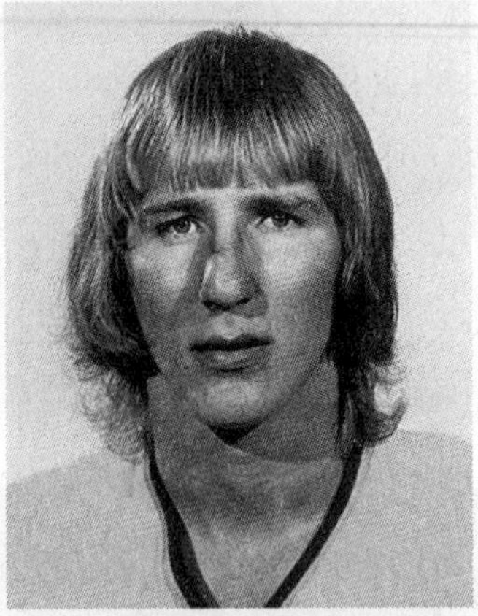

Jack Carlson

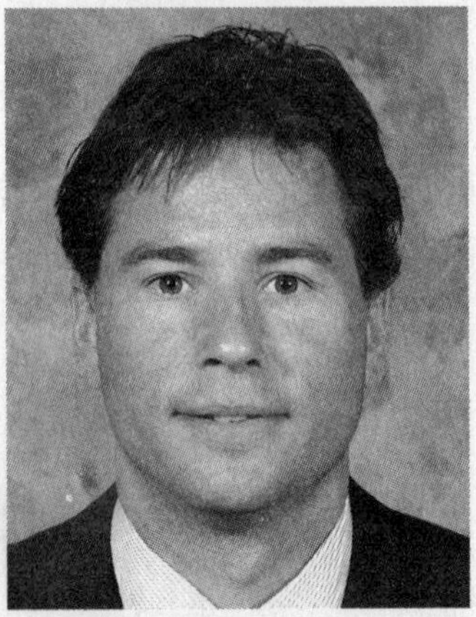

Bruce Cassidy

Name	NHL Teams	NHL Seasons	Regular Schedule GP	G	A	TP	PIM	Playoffs GP	G	A	TP	PIM	NHL Cup Wins	First NHL Season	Last NHL Season
Byce, John	Bos.	3	21	2	3	5	6	8	2	0	2	2	....	1989-90	1991-92
‡ Byers, Dane	NYR, CBJ	3	14	1	0	1	60	....	....	....	....	....	....	2007-08	2011-12
• Byers, Gord	Bos.	1	1	0	1	1	0	....	....	....	....	....	....	1949-50	1949-50
• Byers, Jerry	Min., Atl., NYR	4	43	3	4	7	15	....	....	....	....	....	....	1972-73	1977-78
Byers, Lyndon	Bos., S.J.	10	279	28	43	71	1081	37	2	2	4	96	....	1983-84	1992-93
• Byers, Mike	Tor., Phi., L.A., Buf.	4	166	42	34	76	39	4	0	1	1	0	....	1967-68	1971-72
Bykov, Dmitri	Det.	1	71	2	10	12	43	4	0	0	0	0	....	2002-03	2002-03
Bylsma, Dan	L.A., Ana.	9	429	19	43	62	184	16	0	1	1	2	....	1995-96	2003-04
Byram, Shawn	NYI, Chi.	2	5	0	0	0	14	....	....	....	....	....	....	1990-91	1991-92

C

Name	NHL Teams	NHL Seasons	Regular Schedule GP	G	A	TP	PIM	Playoffs GP	G	A	TP	PIM	NHL Cup Wins	First NHL Season	Last NHL Season
• Caffery, Jack	Tor., Bos.	3	57	3	2	5	22	10	1	0	1	4	....	1954-55	1957-58
Caffery, Terry	Chi., Min.	2	14	0	0	0	0	1	0	0	0	0	....	1969-70	1970-71
• Cahan, Larry	Tor., NYR, Oak., L.A.	13	666	38	92	130	700	29	1	1	2	38	....	1954-55	1970-71
• Cahill, Charles	Bos.	2	32	0	1	1	4	....	....	....	....	....	....	1925-26	1926-27
• Cain, Francis	Mtl.M., Tor.	2	61	4	0	4	35	....	....	....	....	....	....	1924-25	1925-26
• Cain, Herb	Mtl.M., Mtl., Bos.	13	570	206	194	400	178	67	16	13	29	13	2	1933-34	1945-46
Cairns, Don	K.C., Col.	2	9	0	1	1	2	....	....	....	....	....	....	1975-76	1976-77
Cairns, Eric	NYR, NYI, Fla., Pit.	10	457	10	32	42	1182	16	0	0	0	28	....	1996-97	2006-07
Cajanek, Petr	St.L.	4	269	46	107	153	144	7	0	2	2	4	....	2002-03	2006-07
Calder, Eric	Wsh.	2	2	0	0	0	0	....	....	....	....	....	....	1981-82	1982-83
Calder, Kyle	Chi., Phi., Det., L.A., Ana.	10	590	114	180	294	309	18	2	1	3	10	....	1999-00	2009-10
‡ Caldwell, Ryan	NYI, Phx.	2	4	0	0	0	4	....	....	....	....	....	....	2005-06	2007-08
• Calladine, Norm	Bos.	3	63	19	29	48	8	....	....	....	....	....	....	1942-43	1944-45
Callahan, Joe	NYI, S.J., Fla.	3	46	0	4	4	16	....	....	....	....	....	....	2008-09	2010-11
Callander, Drew	Phi., Van.	4	39	6	2	8	7	....	....	....	....	....	....	1976-77	1979-80
Callander, Jock	Pit., T.B.	5	109	22	29	51	116	22	3	8	11	12	1	1987-88	1992-93
Callighen, Brett	Edm.	3	160	56	89	145	132	14	4	6	10	8	....	1979-80	1981-82
• Callighen, Patsy	NYR	1	36	0	0	0	32	9	0	0	0	0	1	1927-28	1927-28
Caloun, Jan	S.J., CBJ	3	24	8	6	14	2	....	....	....	....	....	....	1995-96	2000-01
Camazzola, James	Chi.	2	3	0	0	0	0	....	....	....	....	....	....	1983-84	1986-87
Camazzola, Tony	Wsh.	1	3	0	0	0	4	....	....	....	....	....	....	1981-82	1981-82
Cameron, Al	Det., Wpg.	6	282	11	44	55	356	7	0	1	1	2	....	1975-76	1980-81
• Cameron, Billy	Mtl., NYA	2	39	0	0	0	2	2	0	0	0	0	1	1923-24	1925-26
• Cameron, Craig	Det., St.L., Min., NYI	9	552	87	65	152	196	27	3	1	4	17	....	1966-67	1975-76
Cameron, Dave	Col., N.J.	3	168	25	28	53	238	....	....	....	....	....	....	1981-82	1983-84
• Cameron, Harry	Tor., Ott., Mtl.	6	128	88	51	139	189	11	5	4	9	16	2	1917-18	1922-23
• Cameron, Scotty	NYR	1	35	8	11	19	0	....	....	....	....	....	....	1942-43	1942-43
Campanale, Matt	NYI	1	1	0	0	0	2	....	....	....	....	....	....	2010-11	2010-11
Campbell, Bryan	L.A., Chi.	5	260	35	71	106	74	22	3	4	7	2	....	1967-68	1971-72
Campbell, Colin	Pit., Col., Edm., Van., Det.	11	636	25	103	128	1292	45	4	10	14	181	....	1974-75	1984-85
Campbell, Darcy	CBJ	1	1	0	0	0	0	....	....	....	....	....	....	2006-07	2006-07
• Campbell, Dave	Mtl.	1	2	0	0	0	0	....	....	....	....	....	....	1920-21	1920-21
• Campbell, Don	Chi.	1	17	1	3	4	8	....	....	....	....	....	....	1943-44	1943-44
• Campbell, Earl	Ott., NYA	3	76	6	3	9	14	1	0	0	0	6	....	1923-24	1925-26
Campbell, Gregory	Fla., Bos., CBJ	12	803	71	116	187	696	59	4	9	13	19	1	2003-04	**2015-16**
Campbell, Jim	Ana., St.L., Mtl., Chi., Fla., T.B.	9	285	61	75	136	268	14	8	3	11	18	....	1995-96	2005-06
Campbell, Scott	Wpg., St.L.	3	80	4	21	25	243	....	....	....	....	....	....	1979-80	1981-82
Campbell, Wade	Wpg., Bos.	6	213	9	27	36	305	10	0	0	0	20	....	1982-83	1987-88
• Campeau, Tod	Mtl.	3	42	5	9	14	16	1	0	0	0	0	....	1943-44	1948-49
Campedelli, Dom	Mtl.	1	2	0	0	0	0	....	....	....	....	....	....	1985-86	1985-86
Campoli, Chris	NYI, Ott., Chi., Mtl.	7	440	35	111	146	200	18	1	4	5	8	....	2005-06	2011-12
Capuano, Dave	Pit., Van., T.B., S.J.	4	104	17	38	55	56	6	1	1	2	5	....	1989-90	1993-94
Capuano, Jack	Tor., Van., Bos.	3	6	0	0	0	0	....	....	....	....	....	....	1989-90	1991-92
Caputi, Luca	Pit., Tor.	3	35	3	6	9	20	....	....	....	....	....	....	2008-09	2010-11
• Carbol, Leo	Chi.	1	6	0	1	1	4	....	....	....	....	....	....	1942-43	1942-43
Carbonneau, Guy	Mtl., St.L., Dal.	19	1318	260	403	663	820	231	38	55	93	161	3	1980-81	1999-00
Carcillo, Daniel	Phx., Phi., Chi., L.A., NYR	9	429	48	52	100	1233	45	7	7	14	97	2	2006-07	2014-15
Card, Mike	Buf.	1	4	0	0	0	0	....	....	....	....	....	....	2006-07	2006-07
Cardin, Claude	St.L.	1	1	0	0	0	0	....	....	....	....	....	....	1967-68	1967-68
Cardwell, Steve	Pit.	3	53	9	11	20	35	4	0	0	0	2	....	1970-71	1972-73
• Carey, George	Que., Ham., Tor.	5	72	21	12	33	20	....	....	....	....	....	....	1919-20	1923-24
Carkner, Matt	S.J., Ott., NYI	7	237	4	23	27	556	14	1	2	3	35	....	2005-06	2013-14
Carkner, Terry	NYR, Que., Phi., Det., Fla.	13	858	42	188	230	1588	54	1	9	10	48	....	1986-87	1998-99
‡ Carle, Mathieu	Mtl.	1	3	0	0	0	4	....	....	....	....	....	....	2009-10	2009-10
Carleton, Wayne	Tor., Bos., Cal.	7	278	55	73	128	172	18	2	4	6	14	1	1965-66	1971-72
Carlin, Brian	L.A.	1	5	1	0	1	0	....	....	....	....	....	....	1971-72	1971-72
Carlson, Jack	Min., St.L.	6	236	30	15	45	417	25	1	2	3	72	....	1978-79	1986-87
Carlson, Kent	Mtl., St.L., Wsh.	5	113	7	11	18	148	8	0	0	0	13	....	1983-84	1988-89
Carlson, Steve	L.A.	1	52	9	12	21	23	4	1	1	2	7	....	1979-80	1979-80
Carlsson, Anders	N.J.	3	104	7	26	33	34	3	1	0	1	2	....	1986-87	1988-89
Carlyle, Randy	Tor., Pit., Wpg.	17	1055	148	499	647	1400	69	9	24	33	120	....	1976-77	1992-93
Carnback, Patrik	Mtl., Ana.	4	154	24	38	62	122	....	....	....	....	....	....	1992-93	1995-96
Carney, Keith	Buf., Chi., Phx., Ana., Van., Min.	16	1018	45	183	228	904	91	3	19	22	67	....	1991-92	2007-08
• Caron, Alain	Oak., Mtl.	2	60	9	13	22	18	....	....	....	....	....	....	1967-68	1968-69
Carpenter, Bob	Wsh., NYR, L.A., Bos., N.J.	18	1178	320	408	728	919	140	21	38	59	136	1	1981-82	1998-99
• Carpenter, Ed	Que., Ham.	2	45	10	5	15	41	....	....	....	....	....	....	1919-20	1920-21
Carr, Gene	St.L., NYR, L.A., Pit., Atl.	8	465	79	136	215	365	35	5	8	13	66	....	1971-72	1978-79
• Carr, Lorne	NYR, NYA, Tor.	13	580	204	222	426	132	53	10	9	19	13	2	1933-34	1945-46
• Carr, Red	Tor.	1	5	0	1	1	2	....	....	....	....	....	....	1943-44	1943-44
Carriere, Larry	Buf., Atl., Van., L.A., Tor.	7	367	16	74	90	462	27	0	3	3	42	....	1972-73	1979-80
• Carrigan, Gene	NYR, Det., St.L.	3	37	2	1	3	13	4	0	0	0	0	....	1930-31	1934-35
Carroll, Billy	NYI, Edm., Det.	7	322	30	54	84	113	71	6	12	18	18	4	1980-81	1986-87
• Carroll, George	Mtl.M., Bos.	1	16	0	0	0	11	....	....	....	....	....	....	1924-25	1924-25
Carroll, Greg	Wsh., Det., Hfd.	2	131	20	34	54	44	....	....	....	....	....	....	1978-79	1979-80
Carruthers, Dwight	Det., Phi.	2	2	0	0	0	0	....	....	....	....	....	....	1965-66	1967-68
• Carse, Bill	NYR, Chi.	4	124	28	43	71	38	13	3	2	5	0	....	1938-39	1941-42
• Carse, Bob	Chi., Mtl.	5	167	32	55	87	52	10	0	2	2	2	....	1939-40	1947-48
• Carson, Bill	Tor., Bos.	4	159	54	24	78	156	11	3	0	3	14	1	1926-27	1929-30
‡ Carson, Brett	Car., Cgy.	5	90	2	11	13	20	....	....	....	....	....	....	2008-09	2012-13
• Carson, Frank	Mtl.M., NYA, Det.	7	248	42	48	90	166	27	0	2	2	9	1	1925-26	1933-34
• Carson, Gerry	Mtl., NYR, Mtl.M.	6	261	12	11	23	205	22	0	0	0	12	1	1928-29	1936-37
Carson, Jimmy	L.A., Edm., Det., Van., Hfd.	10	626	275	286	561	254	55	17	15	32	22	....	1986-87	1995-96
Carson, Lindsay	Phi., Hfd.	7	373	66	80	146	524	49	4	10	14	56	....	1981-82	1987-88
Carter, Anson	Wsh., Bos., Edm., NYR, L.A., Van., CBJ, Car.	10	674	202	219	421	229	24	8	5	13	4	....	1996-97	2006-07
Carter, Billy	Mtl., Bos.	3	16	0	0	0	6	....	....	....	....	....	....	1957-58	1961-62
Carter, John	Bos., S.J.	8	244	40	50	90	201	31	7	5	12	51	....	1985-86	1992-93
Carter, Ron	Edm.	1	2	0	0	0	0	....	....	....	....	....	....	1979-80	1979-80
‡ Caruso, Michael	Fla.	1	2	0	0	0	0	....	....	....	....	....	....	2012-13	2012-13
• Carveth, Joe	Det., Bos., Mtl.	11	504	150	189	339	81	69	21	16	37	28	2	1940-41	1950-51
Cashman, Wayne	Bos.	17	1027	277	516	793	1041	145	31	57	88	250	2	1964-65	1982-83
Casselman, Mike	Fla.	1	3	0	0	0	0	....	....	....	....	....	....	1995-96	1995-96
Cassels, Andrew	Mtl., Hfd., Cgy., Van., CBJ, Wsh.	16	1015	204	528	732	410	21	4	7	11	8	....	1989-90	2005-06
Cassidy, Bruce	Chi.	6	36	4	13	17	10	1	0	0	0	0	....	1983-84	1989-90
Cassidy, Tom	Pit.	1	26	3	4	7	15	....	....	....	....	....	....	1977-78	1977-78
Cassolato, Tony	Wsh.	3	23	1	6	7	4	....	....	....	....	....	....	1979-80	1981-82
Caufield, Jay	NYR, Min., Pit.	7	208	5	8	13	759	17	0	0	0	42	2	1986-87	1992-93
Cavallini, Gino	Cgy., St.L., Que.	9	593	114	159	273	507	74	14	19	33	66	....	1984-85	1992-93
Cavallini, Paul	Wsh., St.L., Dal.	10	564	56	177	233	750	69	8	27	35	114	....	1986-87	1995-96
• Cavanagh, Tom	S.J.	2	18	1	2	3	4	....	....	....	....	....	....	2007-08	2008-09
• Ceresino, Ray	Tor.	1	12	1	1	2	2	....	....	....	....	....	....	1948-49	1948-49
Cernik, Frantisek	Det.	1	49	5	4	9	13	....	....	....	....	....	....	1984-85	1984-85
‡ Cervenka, Roman	Cgy.	1	39	9	8	17	14	....	....	....	....	....	....	2012-13	2012-13
Chabot, John	Mtl., Pit., Det.	8	508	84	228	312	85	33	6	20	26	2	....	1983-84	1990-91
• Chad, John	Chi.	3	80	15	22	37	29	10	0	1	1	2	....	1939-40	1945-46
• Chalmers, Chick	NYR	1	1	0	0	0	0	....	....	....	....	....	....	1953-54	1953-54
Chalupa, Milan	Det.	1	14	0	5	5	6	....	....	....	....	....	....	1984-85	1984-85
• Chamberlain, Murph	Tor., Mtl., Bro., Bos.	12	510	100	175	275	769	66	14	17	31	96	2	1937-38	1948-49
Chambers, Shawn	Min., Wsh., T.B., N.J., Dal.	13	625	50	185	235	364	94	7	26	33	72	2	1987-88	1999-00
Champagne, Andre	Tor.	1	2	0	0	0	0	....	....	....	....	....	....	1962-63	1962-63

			Regular Schedule					Playoffs					NHL	First	Last
Name	**NHL Teams**	**NHL Seasons**	**GP**	**G**	**A**	**TP**	**PIM**	**GP**	**G**	**A**	**TP**	**PIM**	**Cup Wins**	**NHL Season**	**NHL Season**
Chapdelaine, Rene	L.A.	3	32	0	2	2	32	....	....	....	....	....	....	1990-91	1992-93
• Chapman, Art	Bos., NYA	10	438	62	176	238	140	26	1	5	6	9	....	1930-31	1939-40
Chapman, Blair	Pit., St.L.	7	402	106	125	231	158	25	4	6	10	15	....	1976-77	1982-83
Chapman, Brian	Hfd.	1	3	0	0	0	29	....	....	....	....	....	....	1990-91	1990-91
Charbonneau, Jose	Mtl., Van.	4	71	9	13	22	67	11	1	0	1	8	....	1987-88	1994-95
Charbonneau, Stephane	Que.	1	2	0	0	0	0	....	....	....	....	....	....	1991-92	1991-92
Charlebois, Bob	Min.	1	7	1	0	1	0	....	....	....	....	....	....	1967-68	1967-68
Charlesworth, Todd	Pit., NYR	6	93	3	9	12	47	....	....	....	....	....	....	1983-84	1989-90
Charron, Eric	Mtl., T.B., Wsh., Cgy.	8	130	2	7	9	127	6	0	0	0	8	....	1992-93	1999-00
Charron, Guy	Mtl., Det., K.C., Wsh.	12	734	221	309	530	146	....	....	....	....	....	....	1969-70	1980-81
Chartier, Dave	Wpg.	1	1	0	0	0	0	....	....	....	....	....	....	1980-81	1980-81
Chartrand, Brad	L.A.	5	215	25	25	50	122	11	1	1	2	8	....	1999-00	2003-04
Chartraw, Rick	Mtl., L.A., NYR, Edm.	10	420	28	64	92	399	75	7	9	16	80	4	1974-75	1983-84
Chase, Kelly	St.L., Hfd., Tor.	11	458	17	36	53	2017	27	1	1	2	100	....	1989-90	1999-00
Chasse, Denis	St.L., Wsh., Wpg., Ott.	4	132	11	14	25	292	7	1	7	8	23	....	1993-94	1996-97
Chebaturkin, Vladimir	NYI, St.L., Chi.	5	62	2	7	9	52	3	0	0	0	2	....	1997-98	2001-02
• Check, Lude	Det., Chi.	2	27	6	2	8	4	....	....	....	....	....	....	1943-44	1944-45
‡ Cheechoo, Jonathan	S.J., Ott.	7	501	170	135	305	324	59	16	19	35	32	....	2002-03	2009-10
Chelios, Chris	Mtl., Chi., Det., Atl.	26	1651	185	763	948	2891	266	31	113	144	423	3	1983-84	2009-10
• Chernoff, Mike	Min.	1	1	0	0	0	0	....	....	....	....	....	....	1968-69	1968-69
Chernomaz, Rich	Col., N.J., Cgy.	7	51	9	7	16	18	....	....	....	....	....	....	1981-82	1991-92
Cherry, Dick	Bos., Phi.	3	145	12	10	22	45	4	1	0	1	4	....	1956-57	1969-70
Cherry, Don	Bos.	1	....	....	....	....	....	1	0	0	0	0	....	1954-55	1954-55
Chervyakov, Denis	Bos.	1	2	0	0	0	2	....	....	....	....	....	....	1992-93	1992-93
• Chevrefils, Real	Bos., Det.	8	387	104	97	201	185	30	5	4	9	20	....	1951-52	1958-59
• Chiasson, Steve	Det., Cgy., Hfd., Car.	13	751	93	305	398	1107	63	16	19	35	119	....	1986-87	1998-99
Chibirev, Igor	Hfd.	2	45	7	12	19	2	....	....	....	....	....	....	1993-94	1994-95
Chicoine, Dan	Cle., Min.	3	31	1	2	3	12	1	0	0	0	0	....	1977-78	1979-80
Chinnick, Rick	Min.	2	4	0	2	2	0	....	....	....	....	....	....	1973-74	1974-75
‡ Chipchura, Kyle	Mtl., Ana., Phx., Ari.	9	482	31	73	104	376	15	1	3	4	7	....	2007-08	**2015-16**
Chipperfield, Ron	Edm., Que.	2	83	22	24	46	34	....	....	....	....	....	....	1979-80	1980-81
Chisholm, Art	Bos.	1	3	0	0	0	0	....	....	....	....	....	....	1960-61	1960-61
Chisholm, Colin	Min.	1	1	0	0	0	0	....	....	....	....	....	....	1986-87	1986-87
• Chisholm, Lex	Tor.	2	54	10	8	18	19	3	1	0	1	0	....	1939-40	1940-41
‡ Chistov, Stanislav	Ana., Bos.	3	196	19	42	61	116	21	4	2	6	8	....	2002-03	2006-07
Chorney, Marc	Pit., L.A.	4	210	8	27	35	209	7	0	1	1	2	....	1980-81	1983-84
Chorske, Tom	Mtl., N.J., Ott., NYI, Wsh., Cgy., Pit.	11	596	115	122	237	225	50	5	12	17	10	1	1989-90	1999-00
‡ Chouinard, Eric	Mtl., Phi., Min.	4	90	11	11	22	16	....	....	....	....	....	....	2000-01	2005-06
• Chouinard, Gene	Ott.	1	8	0	0	0	0	....	....	....	....	....	....	1927-28	1927-28
Chouinard, Guy	Atl., Cgy., St.L.	10	578	205	370	575	120	46	9	28	37	12	....	1974-75	1983-84
Chouinard, Marc	Ana., Min., Van.	6	320	37	41	78	123	15	1	0	1	0	....	2000-01	2006-07
‡ Christensen, Erik	Pit., Atl., Ana., NYR, Min.	7	387	68	95	163	162	17	1	2	3	8	....	2005-06	2011-12
Christian, Dave	Wpg., Wsh., Bos., St.L., Chi.	15	1009	340	433	773	284	102	32	25	57	27	....	1979-80	1993-94
Christian, Jeff	N.J., Pit., Phx.	5	18	2	2	4	17	....	....	....	....	....	....	1991-92	1997-98
Christie, Mike	Cal., Cle., Col., Van.	7	412	15	101	116	550	2	0	0	0	0	....	1974-75	1980-81
Christie, Ryan	Dal., Cgy.	2	7	0	0	0	0	....	....	....	....	....	....	1999-00	2001-02
Christoff, Steve	Min., Cgy., L.A.	5	248	77	64	141	108	35	16	12	28	25	....	1979-80	1983-84
Chrystal, Bob	NYR	2	132	11	14	25	112	....	....	....	....	....	....	1953-54	1954-55
Chubarov, Artem	Van.	5	228	25	33	58	40	27	0	4	4	4	....	1999-00	2003-04
Chucko, Kris	Cgy.	1	2	0	0	0	2	....	....	....	....	....	....	2008-09	2008-09
Church, Brad	Wsh.	1	2	0	0	0	0	....	....	....	....	....	....	1997-98	1997-98
• Church, Jack	Tor., Bro., Bos.	5	130	4	19	23	154	25	1	1	2	18	....	1938-39	1945-46
Churla, Shane	Hfd., Cgy., Min., Dal., L.A., NYR	11	488	26	45	71	2301	78	5	7	12	282	....	1986-87	1996-97
Chychrun, Jeff	Phi., L.A., Pit., Edm.	8	262	3	22	25	744	19	0	2	2	65	1	1986-87	1993-94
Chynoweth, Dean	NYI, Bos.	9	241	4	18	22	667	6	0	0	0	26	....	1988-89	1997-98
Chyzowski, Dave	NYI, Chi.	6	126	15	16	31	144	2	0	0	0	0	....	1989-90	1996-97
Ciavaglia, Peter	Buf.	2	5	0	0	0	0	....	....	....	....	....	....	1991-92	1992-93
‡ Cibak, Martin	T.B.	3	154	5	18	23	60	11	0	1	1	0	1	2001-02	2005-06
Ciccarelli, Dino	Min., Wsh., Det., T.B., Fla.	19	1232	608	592	1200	1425	141	73	45	118	211	....	1980-81	1998-99
Ciccone, Enrico	Min., Wsh., T.B., Chi., Car., Van., Mtl.	9	374	10	18	28	1469	13	1	0	1	48	....	1991-92	2000-01
Cichocki, Chris	Det., N.J.	4	68	11	12	23	27	....	....	....	....	....	....	1985-86	1988-89
Ciernik, Ivan	Ott., Wsh.	5	89	12	14	26	32	2	0	1	1	6	....	1997-98	2003-04
Cierny, Jozef	Edm.	1	1	0	0	0	0	....	....	....	....	....	....	1993-94	1993-94
• Ciesla, Hank	Chi., NYR	4	269	26	51	77	87	6	0	2	2	0	....	1955-56	1958-59
Ciger, Zdeno	N.J., Edm., NYR, T.B.	7	352	94	134	228	101	13	2	6	8	4	....	1990-91	2001-02
Cimellaro, Tony	Ott.	1	2	0	0	0	0	....	....	....	....	....	....	1992-93	1992-93
Cimetta, Rob	Bos., Tor.	4	103	16	16	32	66	1	0	0	0	15	....	1988-89	1991-92
Cirella, Joe	Col., N.J., Que., NYR, Fla., Ott.	15	828	64	211	275	1446	38	0	13	13	98	....	1981-82	1995-96
Cirone, Jason	Wpg.	1	3	0	0	0	2	....	....	....	....	....	....	1991-92	1991-92
Cisar, Marian	Nsh.	3	73	13	17	30	57	....	....	....	....	....	....	1999-00	2001-02
Clackson, Kim	Pit., Que.	2	106	0	8	8	370	8	0	0	0	70	....	1979-80	1980-81
• Clancy, King	Ott., Tor.	16	592	136	147	283	914	55	8	8	16	88	3	1921-22	1936-37
Clancy, Terry	Oak., Tor.	4	93	6	6	12	39	....	....	....	....	....	....	1967-68	1972-73
• Clapper, Dit	Bos.	20	833	228	246	474	462	82	13	17	30	50	3	1927-28	1946-47
Clark, Brett	Mtl., Atl., Col., T.B., Min.	14	689	45	141	186	293	28	3	4	7	10	....	1997-98	2012-13
Clark, Chris	Cgy., Wsh., CBJ	11	607	103	111	214	700	34	4	3	7	38	....	1999-00	2010-11
Clark, Dan	NYR	1	4	0	1	1	6	....	....	....	....	....	....	1978-79	1978-79
Clark, Dean	Edm.	1	1	0	0	0	0	....	....	....	....	....	....	1983-84	1983-84
Clark, Gordie	Bos.	2	8	0	1	1	0	1	0	0	0	0	....	1974-75	1975-76
• Clark, Nobby	Bos.	1	5	0	0	0	0	....	....	....	....	....	....	1927-28	1927-28
Clark, Wendel	Tor., Que., NYI, T.B., Det., Chi.	15	793	330	234	564	1690	95	37	32	69	201	....	1985-86	1999-00
Clarke, Bobby	Phi.	15	1144	358	852	1210	1453	136	42	77	119	152	2	1969-70	1983-84
Clarke, Dale	St.L.	1	3	0	0	0	0	....	....	....	....	....	....	2000-01	2000-01
Clarke, Noah	L.A., N.J.	4	21	3	1	4	4	....	....	....	....	....	....	2003-04	2007-08
Classen, Greg	Nsh.	3	90	7	10	17	48	....	....	....	....	....	....	2000-01	2002-03
Cleary, Dan	Chi., Edm., Phx., Det.	17	938	165	222	387	492	121	24	28	52	76	1	1997-98	2014-15
• Cleghorn, Odie	Mtl., Pit.	10	181	95	34	129	142	12	7	2	9	5	1	1918-19	1927-28
• Cleghorn, Sprague	Ott., Tor., Mtl., Bos.	10	259	83	55	138	538	21	4	3	7	26	2	1918-19	1927-28
Clement, Bill	Phi., Wsh., Atl., Cgy.	11	719	148	208	356	383	50	5	3	8	26	2	1971-72	1981-82
Cline, Bruce	NYR	1	30	2	3	5	10	....	....	....	....	....	....	1956-57	1956-57
Clippingdale, Steve	L.A., Wsh.	2	19	1	2	3	9	1	0	0	0	0	....	1976-77	1979-80
Clitsome, Grant	CBJ, Wpg.	6	205	15	56	71	98	....	....	....	....	....	....	2009-10	2014-15
Cloutier, Real	Que., Buf.	6	317	146	198	344	119	25	7	5	12	20	....	1979-80	1984-85
Cloutier, Rejean	Det.	2	5	0	2	2	2	....	....	....	....	....	....	1979-80	1981-82
Cloutier, Roland	Det., Que.	3	34	8	9	17	2	....	....	....	....	....	....	1977-78	1979-80
Cloutier, Sylvain	Chi.	1	7	0	0	0	0	....	....	....	....	....	....	1998-99	1998-99
Clowe, Ryane	S.J., NYR, N.J.	10	491	112	197	309	618	70	18	28	46	97	....	2005-06	2014-15
• Clune, Wally	Mtl.	1	5	0	0	0	6	....	....	....	....	....	....	1955-56	1955-56
Clymer, Ben	T.B., Wsh.	7	438	52	77	129	367	16	0	2	2	6	1	1999-00	2006-07
Coalter, Gary	Cal., K.C.	2	34	2	4	6	2	....	....	....	....	....	....	1973-74	1974-75
Coates, Steve	Det.	1	5	1	0	1	24	....	....	....	....	....	....	1976-77	1976-77
Cochrane, Glen	Phi., Van., Chi., Edm.	10	411	17	72	89	1556	18	1	1	2	31	....	1978-79	1988-89
Coffey, Paul	Edm., Pit., L.A., Det., Hfd., Phi., Chi., Car., Bos.	21	1409	396	1135	1531	1802	194	59	137	196	264	4	1980-81	2000-01
Coflin, Hugh	Chi.	1	31	0	3	3	33	....	....	....	....	....	....	1950-51	1950-51
Cohen, Colby	Col.	1	3	0	0	0	4	....	....	....	....	....	....	2010-11	2010-11
‡ Colaiacovo, Carlo	Tor., St.L., Det., Phi., Buf.	13	470	34	123	157	231	20	0	4	4	20	....	2002-03	**2015-16**
Cole, Danton	Wpg., T.B., N.J., NYI, Chi.	7	318	58	60	118	125	1	0	0	0	0	1	1989-90	1995-96
Cole, Erik	Car., Edm., Mtl., Dal., Det.	13	892	265	267	532	659	46	6	8	14	54	1	2001-02	2014-15
Colley, Kevin	NYI	1	16	0	0	0	52	....	....	....	....	....	....	2005-06	2005-06
Colley, Tom	Min.	1	1	0	0	0	2	....	....	....	....	....	....	1974-75	1974-75
• Collings, Norm	Mtl.	1	1	0	1	1	0	....	....	....	....	....	....	1934-35	1934-35
Collins, Bill	Min., Mtl., Det., St.L., NYR, Phi., Wsh.	11	768	157	154	311	415	18	3	5	8	12	....	1967-68	1977-78
Collins, Gary	Tor.	1	....	....	....	....	....	2	0	0	0	0	....	1958-59	1958-59
Collins, Rob	NYI	1	8	1	1	2	0	....	....	....	....	....	....	2005-06	2005-06
Collins, Sean	Wsh.	3	21	2	1	3	12	1	0	0	0	0	....	2008-09	2011-12
‡ Collins, Sean	CBJ, Wsh.	4	21	0	3	3	10	....	....	....	....	....	....	2012-13	**2015-16**
Colliton, Jeremy	NYI	5	57	3	3	6	26	....	....	....	....	....	....	2005-06	2010-11
Collyard, Bob	St.L.	1	10	1	3	4	4	....	....	....	....	....	....	1973-74	1973-74
• Colman, Michael	S.J.	1	15	0	1	1	32	....	....	....	....	....	....	1991-92	1991-92
• Colville, Mac	NYR	9	353	71	104	175	130	40	9	10	19	14	1	1935-36	1946-47
• Colville, Neil	NYR	12	464	99	166	265	213	46	7	19	26	32	1	1935-36	1948-49

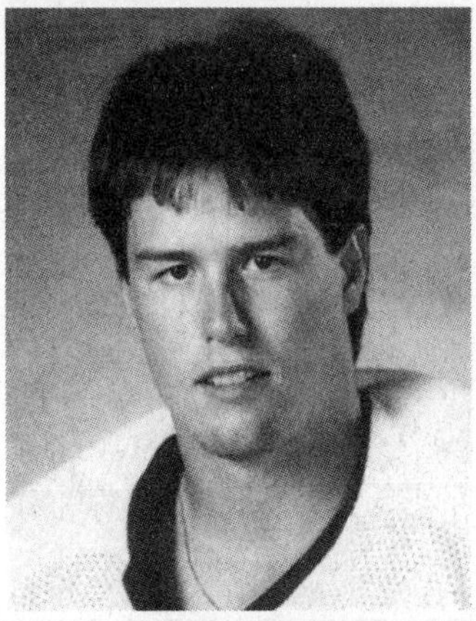

Todd Charlesworth

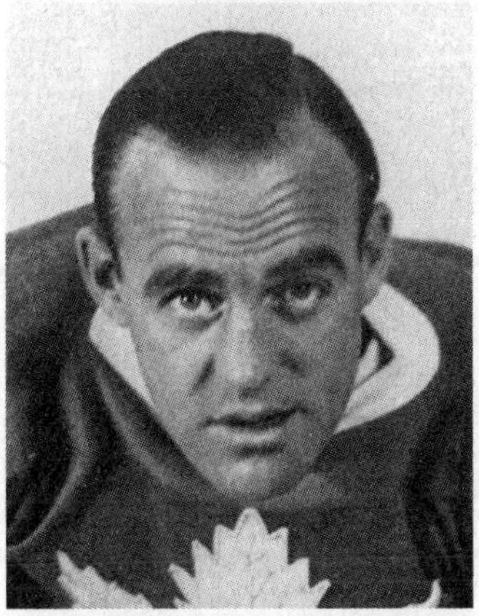

King Clancy

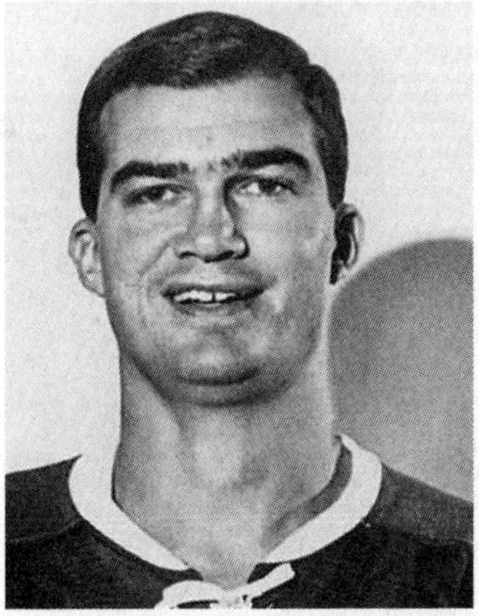

Brian Conacher

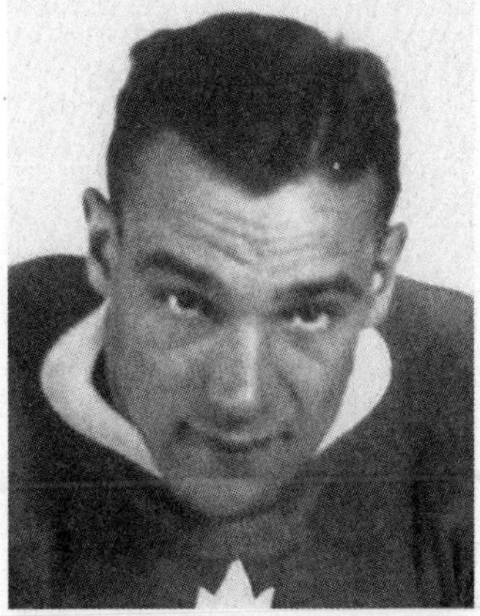

Charlie Conacher

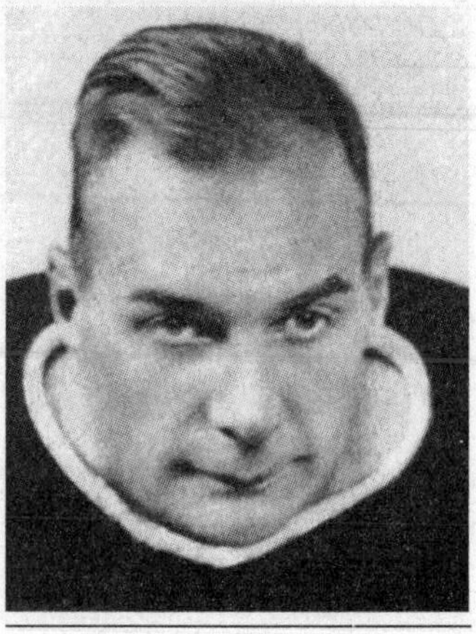

Lionel Conacher

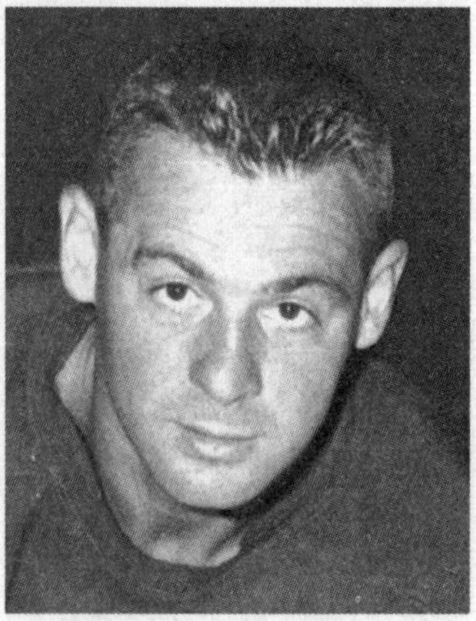

Pete Conacher

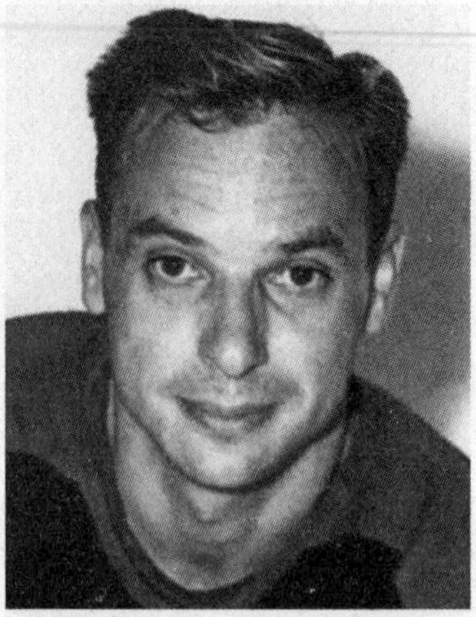

Roy Conacher

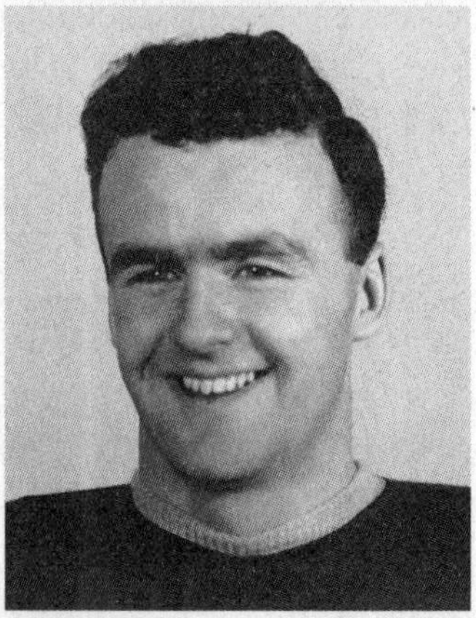

Les Costello

			Regular Schedule					Playoffs							
Name	NHL Teams	NHL Seasons	GP	G	A	TP	PIM	GP	G	A	TP	PIM	NHL Cup Wins	First NHL Season	Last NHL Season
Colwill, Les	NYR	1	69	7	6	13	16	....	....	....	....	....	....	1958-59	1958-59
Comeau, Rey	Mtl., Atl., Col.	9	564	98	141	239	175	9	2	1	3	8	....	1971-72	1979-80
Commodore, Mike	N.J., Cgy., Car., Ott., CBJ, Det., T.B.	11	484	23	83	106	683	53	2	6	8	70	1	2000-01	2011-12
Comrie, Mike	Edm., Phi., Phx., Ott., NYI, Pit.	10	589	168	197	365	443	32	4	6	10	27	....	2000-01	2010-11
Comrie, Paul	Edm.	1	15	1	2	3	4	....	....	....	....	....	....	1999-00	1999-00
Conacher, Brian	Tor., Det.	5	155	28	28	56	84	12	3	2	5	21	1	1961-62	1971-72
• Conacher, Charlie	Tor., Det., NYA	12	459	225	173	398	523	49	17	18	35	49	1	1929-30	1940-41
Conacher, Jim	Det., Chi., NYR	8	328	85	117	202	91	19	5	2	7	4	....	1945-46	1952-53
• Conacher, Lionel	Pit., NYA, Mtl.M., Chi.	12	498	80	105	185	882	35	2	2	4	34	2	1925-26	1936-37
Conacher, Pat	NYR, Edm., N.J., L.A., Cgy., NYI	13	521	63	76	139	235	67	11	10	21	40	1	1979-80	1995-96
Conacher, Pete	Chi., NYR, Tor.	6	229	47	39	86	57	7	0	0	0	0	....	1951-52	1957-58
• Conacher, Roy	Bos., Det., Chi.	11	490	226	200	426	90	42	15	15	30	14	2	1938-39	1951-52
Conboy, Tim	Car.	3	59	0	6	6	121	3	0	0	0	9	....	2007-08	2009-10
• Conn, Red	NYA	2	96	9	28	37	22	....	....	....	....	....	....	1933-34	1934-35
Conn, Rob	Chi., Buf.	2	30	2	5	7	20	....	....	....	....	....	....	1991-92	1995-96
• Connelly, Bert	NYR, Chi.	3	87	13	15	28	37	14	1	0	1	0	1	1934-35	1937-38
Connelly, Wayne	Mtl., Bos., Min., Det., St.L., Van.	10	543	133	174	307	156	24	11	7	18	4	....	1960-61	1971-72
Connolly, Mike	Col.	1	2	0	0	0	2	....	....	....	....	....	....	2011-12	2011-12
Connolly, Tim	NYI, Buf., Tor.	12	697	131	300	431	300	36	5	18	23	8	....	1999-00	2011-12
Connor, Cam	Mtl., Edm., NYR	5	89	9	22	31	256	20	5	0	5	6	1	1978-79	1982-83
• Connor, Harry	Bos., NYA, Ott.	4	134	16	5	21	149	10	0	0	0	2	....	1927-28	1930-31
• Connors, Bob	NYA, Det.	3	78	17	10	27	110	2	0	0	0	10	....	1926-27	1929-30
Conroy, Al	Phi.	3	114	9	14	23	156	....	....	....	....	....	....	1991-92	1993-94
Conroy, Craig	Mtl., St.L., Cgy., L.A.	16	1009	182	360	542	603	81	10	20	30	52	....	1994-95	2010-11
Contini, Joe	Col., Min.	3	68	17	21	38	34	2	0	0	0	0	....	1977-78	1980-81
Convery, Brandon	Tor., Van., L.A.	4	72	9	19	28	36	5	0	0	0	2	....	1995-96	1998-99
• Convey, Eddie	NYA	3	36	1	1	2	33	....	....	....	....	....	....	1930-31	1932-33
• Cook, Bill	NYR	11	474	229	138	367	386	46	13	11	24	68	2	1926-27	1936-37
• Cook, Bob	Van., Det., NYI, Min.	4	72	13	9	22	22	....	....	....	....	....	....	1970-71	1974-75
• Cook, Bud	Bos., Ott., St.L.	3	50	5	4	9	22	....	....	....	....	....	....	1931-32	1934-35
• Cook, Bun	NYR, Bos.	11	473	158	144	302	444	46	15	3	18	50	2	1926-27	1936-37
• Cook, Lloyd	Bos.	1	4	1	0	1	0	....	....	....	....	....	....	1924-25	1924-25
• Cook, Tom	Chi., Mtl.M.	9	349	77	98	175	184	24	2	4	6	19	1	1929-30	1937-38
‡ Cooke, Matt	Van., Wsh., Pit., Min.	16	1046	167	231	398	1135	110	13	25	38	141	1	1998-99	2014-15
• Cooper, Carson	Bos., Mtl., Det.	8	294	110	57	167	111	7	0	0	0	2	....	1924-25	1931-32
Cooper, David	Tor.	3	30	3	7	10	24	....	....	....	....	....	....	1996-97	2000-01
Cooper, Ed	Col.	2	49	8	7	15	46	....	....	....	....	....	....	1980-81	1981-82
• Cooper, Hal	NYR	1	8	0	0	0	2	....	....	....	....	....	....	1944-45	1944-45
• Cooper, Joe	NYR, Chi.	11	420	30	66	96	442	35	3	5	8	58	....	1935-36	1946-47
• Copp, Bobby	Tor.	2	40	3	9	12	26	....	....	....	....	....	....	1942-43	1950-51
Corazzini, Carl	Bos., Chi.	2	19	2	1	3	2	....	....	....	....	....	....	2003-04	2006-07
• Corbeau, Bert	Mtl., Ham., Tor.	10	258	63	49	112	629	9	2	2	4	38	....	1917-18	1926-27
Corbet, Rene	Que., Col., Cgy., Pit.	8	362	58	74	132	420	53	7	6	13	52	1	1993-94	2000-01
• Corbett, Mike	L.A.	1	....	....	....	....	....	2	0	1	1	2	....	1967-68	1967-68
• Corcoran, Norm	Bos., Det., Chi.	4	29	1	3	4	21	4	0	0	0	6	....	1949-50	1955-56
Corkum, Bob	Buf., Ana., Phi., Phx., L.A., N.J., Atl.	12	720	97	103	200	281	62	7	7	14	24	....	1989-90	2001-02
• Cormier, Roger	Mtl.	1	1	0	0	0	0	....	....	....	....	....	....	1925-26	1925-26
‡ Cornet, Philippe	Edm.	1	2	0	1	1	0	....	....	....	....	....	....	2011-12	2011-12
Cornforth, Mark	Bos.	1	6	0	0	0	4	....	....	....	....	....	....	1995-96	1995-96
Corrente, Matthew	N.J.	2	34	0	6	6	68	2	0	0	0	2	....	2009-10	2010-11
• Corrigan, Chuck	Tor., NYA	2	19	2	2	4	2	....	....	....	....	....	....	1937-38	1940-41
Corrigan, Mike	L.A., Van., Pit.	10	594	152	195	347	698	17	2	3	5	20	....	1967-68	1977-78
Corrinet, Chris	Wsh.	1	8	0	1	1	6	....	....	....	....	....	....	2001-02	2001-02
• Corriveau, Andre	Mtl.	1	3	0	1	1	0	....	....	....	....	....	....	1953-54	1953-54
Corriveau, Yvon	Wsh., Hfd., S.J.	9	280	48	40	88	310	29	5	7	12	50	....	1985-86	1993-94
Corso, Daniel	St.L., Atl.	4	77	14	11	25	20	14	0	1	1	0	....	2000-01	2003-04
Corson, Shayne	Mtl., Edm., St.L., Tor., Dal.	19	1156	273	420	693	2357	140	38	49	87	291	....	1985-86	2003-04
Corvo, Joe	L.A., Ott., Car., Wsh., Bos.	11	708	92	218	310	241	50	5	13	18	14	....	2002-03	2013-14
Cory, Ross	Wpg.	2	51	2	10	12	41	....	....	....	....	....	....	1979-80	1980-81
Cossette, Jacques	Pit.	3	64	8	6	14	29	3	0	1	1	4	....	1975-76	1978-79
• Costello, Les	Tor.	3	15	2	3	5	11	6	2	2	4	2	1	1947-48	1949-50
Costello, Murray	Chi., Bos., Det.	4	162	13	19	32	54	5	0	0	0	2	....	1953-54	1956-57
Costello, Rich	Tor.	2	12	2	2	4	2	....	....	....	....	....	....	1983-84	1985-86
• Cotch, Charlie	Ham., Tor.	1	12	1	0	1	0	....	....	....	....	....	....	1924-25	1924-25
Cote, Alain	Que.	10	696	103	190	293	383	67	9	15	24	44	....	1979-80	1988-89
Cote, Alain	Bos., Wsh., Mtl., T.B., Que.	9	119	2	18	20	124	11	0	2	2	26	....	1985-86	1993-94
‡ Cote, Jean-Philippe	Mtl., T.B.	2	27	0	4	4	26	....	....	....	....	....	....	2005-06	2013-14
Cote, Patrick	Dal., Nsh., Edm.	6	105	1	2	3	377	....	....	....	....	....	....	1995-96	2000-01
Cote, Ray	Edm.	3	15	0	0	0	4	14	3	2	5	0	....	1982-83	1984-85
Cote, Riley	Phi.	4	156	1	6	7	411	3	0	0	0	0	....	2006-07	2009-10
Cote, Sylvain	Hfd., Wsh., Tor., Chi., Dal.	19	1171	122	313	435	545	102	11	22	33	62	....	1984-85	2002-03
• Cotton, Baldy	Pit., Tor., NYA	12	503	101	103	204	419	43	4	9	13	46	1	1925-26	1936-37
• Coughlin, Jack	Tor., Que., Mtl., Ham.	3	19	2	0	2	3	....	....	....	....	....	1	1917-18	1920-21
Coulis, Tim	Wsh., Min.	4	47	4	5	9	138	3	1	0	1	2	....	1979-80	1985-86
Coulombe, Patrick	Van.	1	7	0	1	1	4	....	....	....	....	....	....	2006-07	2006-07
• Coulson, D'arcy	Phi.	1	28	0	0	0	103	....	....	....	....	....	....	1930-31	1930-31
• Coulter, Art	Chi., NYR	11	465	30	82	112	543	49	4	5	9	61	2	1931-32	1941-42
Coulter, Neal	NYI	3	26	5	5	10	11	....	....	....	....	....	....	1985-86	1987-88
• Coulter, Thomas	Chi.	1	2	0	0	0	0	....	....	....	....	....	....	1933-34	1933-34
Cournoyer, Yvan	Mtl.	16	968	428	435	863	255	147	64	63	127	47	10	1963-64	1978-79
Courteau, Yves	Cgy., Hfd.	3	22	2	5	7	4	1	0	0	0	0	....	1984-85	1986-87
Courtenay, Ed	S.J.	2	44	7	13	20	10	....	....	....	....	....	....	1991-92	1992-93
Courtnall, Geoff	Bos., Edm., Wsh., St.L., Van.	17	1048	367	432	799	1465	156	39	70	109	262	1	1983-84	1999-00
Courtnall, Russ	Tor., Mtl., Min., Dal., Van., NYR, L.A.	16	1029	297	447	744	557	129	39	44	83	83	....	1983-84	1998-99
Courville, Larry	Van.	3	33	1	2	3	16	....	....	....	....	....	....	1995-96	1997-98
• Coutu, Billy	Mtl., Ham., Bos.	10	244	33	21	54	478	19	1	1	2	39	1	1917-18	1926-27
• Couture, Gerry	Det., Mtl., Chi.	10	385	86	70	156	89	45	9	7	16	4	1	1944-45	1953-54
• Couture, Rosie	Chi., Mtl.	8	309	48	56	104	184	23	1	5	6	15	1	1928-29	1935-36
Couturier, Sylvain	L.A.	3	33	4	5	9	4	....	....	....	....	....	....	1988-89	1991-92
Cowan, Jeff	Cgy., Atl., L.A., Van.	8	413	47	34	81	695	10	2	0	2	22	....	1999-00	2007-08
Cowick, Bruce	Phi., Wsh., St.L.	3	70	5	6	11	43	8	0	0	0	9	1	1973-74	1975-76
Cowie, Rob	L.A.	2	78	7	12	19	52	....	....	....	....	....	....	1994-95	1995-96
• Cowley, Bill	St.L., Bos.	13	549	195	353	548	143	64	12	34	46	22	2	1934-35	1946-47
• Cox, Danny	Tor., Ott., Det., NYR	8	319	47	49	96	128	10	0	1	1	6	....	1926-27	1933-34
Coxe, Craig	Van., Cgy., St.L., S.J.	8	235	14	31	45	713	5	1	0	1	18	....	1984-85	1991-92
Crabb, Joey	Atl., Tor., Wsh., Fla.	5	179	20	33	53	100	....	....	....	....	....	....	2008-09	2013-14
Craig, Mike	Min., Dal., Tor., S.J.	9	423	71	97	168	550	26	2	2	4	49	....	1990-91	2001-02
Craig, Ryan	T.B., Pit., CBJ	8	198	32	31	63	148	11	0	0	0	22	....	2005-06	2014-15
Craighead, John	Tor.	1	5	0	0	0	10	....	....	....	....	....	....	1996-97	1996-97
Craigwell, Dale	S.J.	3	98	11	18	29	28	....	....	....	....	....	....	1991-92	1993-94
Crashley, Bart	Det., K.C., L.A.	6	140	7	36	43	50	....	....	....	....	....	....	1965-66	1975-76
Craven, Murray	Det., Phi., Hfd., Van., Chi., S.J.	18	1071	266	493	759	524	118	27	43	70	64	....	1982-83	1999-00
Crawford, Bob	St.L., Hfd., NYR, Wsh.	7	246	71	71	142	72	11	0	1	1	8	....	1979-80	1986-87
Crawford, Bobby	Col., Det.	2	16	1	3	4	6	....	....	....	....	....	....	1980-81	1982-83
• Crawford, Jack	Bos.	13	548	38	140	178	202	66	3	13	16	36	2	1937-38	1949-50
Crawford, Lou	Bos.	2	26	2	1	3	29	1	0	0	0	0	....	1989-90	1991-92
Crawford, Marc	Van.	6	176	19	31	50	229	20	1	2	3	44	....	1981-82	1986-87
• Crawford, Rusty	Ott., Tor.	2	38	10	8	18	117	2	2	1	3	9	1	1917-18	1918-19
Creighton, Adam	Buf., Chi., NYI, T.B., St.L.	14	708	187	216	403	1077	61	11	14	25	137	....	1983-84	1996-97
Creighton, Dave	Bos., Tor., Chi., NYR	12	616	140	174	314	223	51	11	13	24	20	....	1948-49	1959-60
• Creighton, Jimmy	Det.	1	11	1	0	1	2	....	....	....	....	....	....	1930-31	1930-31
Cressman, Dave	Min.	2	85	6	8	14	37	....	....	....	....	....	....	1974-75	1975-76
Cressman, Glen	Mtl.	1	4	0	0	0	2	....	....	....	....	....	....	1956-57	1956-57
Crisp, Terry	Bos., St.L., NYI, Phi.	11	536	67	134	201	135	110	15	28	43	40	2	1965-66	1976-77
Cristofoli, Ed	Mtl.	1	9	0	1	1	4	....	....	....	....	....	....	1989-90	1989-90
• Croghan, Maurice	Mtl.M.	1	16	0	0	0	4	....	....	....	....	....	....	1937-38	1937-38
Crombeen, B.J.	Dal., St.L., T.B., Ari.	8	445	34	46	80	850	18	1	0	1	43	....	2007-08	2014-15
Crombeen, Mike	Cle., St.L., Hfd.	8	475	55	68	123	218	27	6	2	8	32	....	1977-78	1984-85
Cronin, Shawn	Wsh., Wpg., Phi., S.J.	7	292	3	18	21	877	32	1	0	1	38	....	1988-89	1994-95
Cross, Cory	T.B., Tor., NYR, Edm., Pit., Det.	12	659	34	97	131	684	47	2	4	6	62	....	1993-94	2005-06
• Crossett, Stan	Phi.	1	21	0	0	0	10	....	....	....	....	....	....	1930-31	1930-31

Name	NHL Teams	NHL Seasons	Regular Schedule GP	G	A	TP	PiM	Playoffs GP	G	A	TP	PIM	NHL Cup Wins	First NHL Season	Last NHL Season
Crossman, Doug	Chi., Phi., L.A., NYI, Hfd., Det., T.B., St.L.	14	914	105	359	464	534	97	12	39	51	105	....	1980-81	1993-94
Croteau, Gary	L.A., Det., Cal., K.C., Col.	12	684	144	175	319	143	11	3	2	5	8	....	1968-69	1979-80
Crowder, Bruce	Bos., Pit.	4	243	47	51	98	156	31	8	4	12	41	....	1981-82	1984-85
Crowder, Keith	Bos., L.A.	10	662	223	271	494	1354	85	14	22	36	218	....	1980-81	1989-90
Crowder, Troy	N.J., Det., L.A., Van.	7	150	9	7	16	433	4	0	0	0	22	....	1987-88	1996-97
Crowe, Phil	L.A., Phi., Ott., Nsh.	6	94	4	5	9	173	3	0	0	0	16	....	1993-94	1999-00
Crowley, Mike	Ana.	3	67	5	15	20	44	....	....	....	....	....	....	1997-98	2000-01
Crowley, Ted	Hfd., Col., NYI	2	34	2	4	6	12	....	....	....	....	....	....	1993-94	1998-99
Crozier, Greg	Pit.	1	1	0	0	0	0	....	....	....	....	....	....	2000-01	2000-01
Crozier, Joe	Tor.	1	5	0	3	3	2	....	....	....	....	....	....	1959-60	1959-60
• Crutchfield, Nels	Mtl.	1	41	5	5	10	20	2	0	1	1	22	....	1934-35	1934-35
Culhane, Jim	Hfd.	1	6	0	1	1	4	....	....	....	....	....	....	1989-90	1989-90
Cullen, Barry	Tor., Det.	5	219	32	52	84	111	6	0	0	0	2	....	1955-56	1959-60
Cullen, Brian	Tor., NYR	7	326	56	100	156	92	19	3	0	3	2	....	1954-55	1960-61
Cullen, David	Phx., Min.	2	19	0	0	0	6	....	....	....	....	....	....	2000-01	2001-02
Cullen, John	Pit., Hfd., Tor., T.B.	11	621	187	363	550	898	53	12	22	34	58	....	1988-89	1998-99
Cullen, Mark	Chi., Phi., Fla.	3	38	7	10	17	4	....	....	....	....	....	....	2005-06	2011-12
Cullen, Ray	NYR, Det., Min., Van.	6	313	92	123	215	120	20	3	10	13	2	....	1965-66	1970-71
Cullimore, Jassen	Van., Mtl., T.B., Chi., Fla.	15	812	26	85	111	704	35	1	3	4	24	1	1994-95	2010-11
‡ Cuma, Tyler	Min.	1	1	0	0	0	2	....	....	....	....	....	....	2011-12	2011-12
‡ Cumiskey, Kyle	Col., Chi.	6	139	9	26	35	48	15	1	1	2	2	....	2006-07	2014-15
Cummins, Barry	Cal.	1	36	1	2	3	39	....	....	....	....	....	....	1973-74	1973-74
Cummins, Jim	Det., Phi., T.B., Chi., Phx., Mtl., Ana., NYI, Col.	12	511	24	36	60	1538	37	1	2	3	43	....	1991-92	2003-04
‡ Cundari, Mark	Cgy.	2	8	1	2	3	2	....	....	....	....	....	....	2012-13	2013-14
Cunneyworth, Randy	Buf., Pit., Wpg., Hfd., Chi., Ott.	16	866	189	225	414	1280	45	7	7	14	61	....	1980-81	1998-99
Cunningham, Bob	NYR	2	4	0	1	1	0	....	....	....	....	....	....	1960-61	1961-62
Cunningham, Craig	Bos., Ari.	3	63	3	5	8	6	....	....	....	....	....	....	2013-14	**2015-16**
• Cunningham, Jim	Phi.	1	1	0	0	0	4	....	....	....	....	....	....	1977-78	1977-78
• Cunningham, Les	NYA, Chi.	2	60	7	19	26	21	1	0	0	0	0	....	1936-37	1939-40
• Cupolo, Bill	Bos.	1	47	11	13	24	10	7	1	2	3	0	....	1944-45	1944-45
Curran, Brian	Bos., NYI, Tor., Buf., Wsh.	10	381	7	33	40	1461	24	0	1	1	122	....	1983-84	1993-94
Currie, Dan	Edm., L.A.	4	22	2	1	3	4	....	....	....	....	....	....	1990-91	1993-94
Currie, Glen	Wsh., L.A.	8	326	39	79	118	100	12	1	3	4	4	....	1979-80	1987-88
Currie, Hugh	Mtl.	1	1	0	0	0	0	....	....	....	....	....	....	1950-51	1950-51
Currie, Tony	St.L., Van., Hfd.	8	290	92	119	211	83	16	4	12	16	14	....	1977-78	1984-85
• Curry, Floyd	Mtl.	11	601	105	99	204	147	91	23	17	40	38	4	1947-48	1957-58
Curtale, Tony	Cgy.	1	2	0	0	0	0	....	....	....	....	....	....	1980-81	1980-81
Curtis, Paul	Mtl., L.A., St.L.	4	185	3	34	37	161	5	0	0	0	2	....	1969-70	1972-73
Cushenan, Ian	Chi., Mtl., NYR, Det.	5	129	3	11	14	134	....	....	....	....	....	1	1956-57	1963-64
Cusson, Jean	Oak.	1	2	0	0	0	0	....	....	....	....	....	....	1967-68	1967-68
Cutta, Jakub	Wsh.	3	8	0	0	0	0	....	....	....	....	....	....	2000-01	2003-04
Cyr, Denis	Cgy., Chi., St.L.	6	193	41	43	84	36	4	0	0	0	0	....	1980-81	1985-86
• Cyr, Paul	Buf., NYR, Hfd.	9	470	101	140	241	623	24	4	6	10	31	....	1982-83	1991-92
Czerkawski, Mariusz	Bos., Edm., NYI, Mtl., Tor.	12	745	215	220	435	274	42	8	7	15	18	....	1993-94	2005-06

D

Name	NHL Teams	NHL Seasons	Regular Schedule GP	G	A	TP	PiM	Playoffs GP	G	A	TP	PIM	NHL Cup Wins	First NHL Season	Last NHL Season
‡ Da Costa, Stephane	Ott.	4	47	7	4	11	10	....	....	....	....	....	....	2010-11	2013-14
Dackell, Andreas	Ott., Mtl.	8	613	91	159	250	162	44	5	5	10	10	....	1996-97	2003-04
Dagenais, Pierre	N.J., Fla., Mtl.	5	142	35	23	58	58	8	0	1	1	6	....	2000-01	2005-06
‡ D'Agostini, Matt	Mtl., St.L., N.J., Pit., Buf.	7	324	52	55	107	147	7	1	0	1	4	....	2007-08	2013-14
Dahl, Kevin	Cgy., Phx., Tor., CBJ	8	188	7	22	29	153	16	0	2	2	12	....	1992-93	2000-01
Dahlen, Ulf	NYR, Min., Dal., S.J., Chi., Wsh.	14	966	301	354	655	230	85	15	25	40	12	....	1987-88	2002-03
Dahlin, Kjell	Mtl.	3	166	57	59	116	10	35	6	11	17	6	1	1985-86	1987-88
Dahlman, Toni	Ott.	2	22	1	1	2	0	....	....	....	....	....	....	2001-02	2002-03
Dahlquist, Chris	Pit., Min., Cgy., Ott.	11	532	19	71	90	488	39	4	7	11	30	....	1985-86	1995-96
• Dahlstrom, Cully	Chi.	8	342	88	118	206	58	29	6	8	14	4	1	1937-38	1944-45
Daigle, Alain	Chi.	6	389	56	50	106	122	17	0	1	1	0	....	1974-75	1979-80
Daigle, Alexandre	Ott., Phi., T.B., NYR, Pit., Min.	10	616	129	198	327	186	12	0	2	2	2	....	1993-94	2005-06
Daigneault, J.J.	Van., Phi., Mtl., St.L., Pit., Ana., NYI, Nsh., Phx., Min.	16	899	53	197	250	687	99	5	26	31	100	1	1984-85	2000-01
Dailey, Bob	Van., Phi.	9	561	94	231	325	814	63	12	34	46	105	....	1973-74	1981-82
• Daley, Frank	Det.	1	5	0	0	0	0	2	0	0	0	0	....	1928-29	1928-29
Daley, Pat	Wpg.	2	12	1	0	1	13	....	....	....	....	....	....	1979-80	1980-81
Dalgarno, Brad	NYI	10	321	49	71	120	332	27	2	4	6	37	....	1985-86	1995-96
‡ Dallman, Kevin	Bos., St.L., L.A.	3	154	8	23	31	45	....	....	....	....	....	....	2005-06	2007-08
Dallman, Marty	Tor.	2	6	0	1	1	0	....	....	....	....	....	....	1987-88	1988-89
Dallman, Rod	NYI, Phi.	4	6	1	0	1	26	1	0	1	1	0	....	1987-88	1991-92
• Dame, Bunny	Mtl.	1	34	2	5	7	4	....	....	....	....	....	....	1941-42	1941-42
‡ D'Amigo, Jerry	Tor., Buf.	2	31	1	2	3	2	....	....	....	....	....	....	2013-14	2014-15
• Damore, Hank	NYR	1	4	1	0	1	2	....	....	....	....	....	....	1943-44	1943-44
Damphousse, Vincent	Tor., Edm., Mtl., S.J.	18	1378	432	773	1205	1190	140	41	63	104	144	1	1986-87	2003-04
Dandenault, Mathieu	Det., Mtl.	13	868	68	135	203	516	83	3	8	11	24	3	1995-96	2008-09
Daneyko, Ken	N.J.	20	1283	36	142	178	2516	175	5	17	22	296	3	1983-84	2002-03
Daniels, Jeff	Pit., Fla., Hfd., Car., Nsh.	12	425	17	26	43	83	41	3	5	8	2	1	1990-91	2002-03
Daniels, Kimbi	Phi.	2	27	1	2	3	4	....	....	....	....	....	....	1990-91	1991-92
Daniels, Scott	Hfd., Phi., N.J.	6	149	8	12	20	667	1	0	0	0	0	....	1992-93	1998-99
Danton, Mike	N.J., St.L.	3	87	9	5	14	182	5	1	0	1	2	....	2000-01	2003-04
Daoust, Dan	Mtl., Tor.	8	522	87	167	254	544	32	7	5	12	83	....	1982-83	1989-90
Darby, Craig	Mtl., NYI, Phi., N.J.	9	196	21	35	56	32	....	....	....	....	....	....	1994-95	2003-04
Darche, Mathieu	CBJ, Nsh., S.J., T.B., Mtl.	9	250	30	42	72	58	18	1	2	3	2	....	2000-01	2011-12
Dark, Michael	St.L.	2	43	5	6	11	14	....	....	....	....	....	....	1986-87	1987-88
• Darragh, Harold	Pit., Phi., Bos., Tor.	8	308	68	49	117	50	16	1	3	4	4	1	1925-26	1932-33
• Darragh, Jack	Ott.	6	121	66	46	112	113	11	3	0	3	9	3	1917-18	1923-24
‡ Datsyuk, Pavel	Det.	14	953	314	604	918	228	157	42	71	113	55	2	2001-02	**2015-16**
‡ Daugavins, Kaspars	Ott., Bos.	3	91	6	9	15	21	7	0	0	0	2	....	2009-10	2012-13
David, Richard	Que.	3	31	4	4	8	10	1	0	0	0	0	....	1979-80	1982-83
• Davidson, Bob	Tor.	12	491	94	160	254	398	79	5	17	22	76	2	1934-35	1945-46
• Davidson, Gord	NYR	2	51	3	6	9	8	....	....	....	....	....	....	1942-43	1943-44
Davidson, Matt	CBJ	3	56	5	7	12	28	....	....	....	....	....	....	2000-01	2002-03
Davidsson, Johan	Ana., NYI	2	83	6	9	15	16	1	0	0	0	0	....	1998-99	1999-00
• Davie, Bob	Bos.	3	41	0	1	1	25	....	....	....	....	....	....	1933-34	1935-36
• Davies, Buck	NYR	1	....	....	....	....	....	1	0	0	0	0	....	1947-48	1947-48
• Davis, Bob	Det.	1	3	0	0	0	0	....	....	....	....	....	....	1932-33	1932-33
Davis, Kim	Pit., Tor.	4	36	5	7	12	51	4	0	0	0	0	....	1977-78	1980-81
• Davis, Lorne	Mtl., Chi., Det., Bos.	6	95	8	12	20	20	18	3	1	4	10	1	1951-52	1959-60
Davis, Mal	Det., Buf.	6	100	31	22	53	34	7	1	0	1	0	....	1978-79	1985-86
Davis, Patrick	N.J.	2	9	1	0	1	0	....	....	....	....	....	....	2008-09	2009-10
• Davison, Murray	Bos.	1	1	0	0	0	0	....	....	....	....	....	....	1965-66	1965-66
Davison, Rob	S.J., NYI, Van., N.J.	7	219	3	15	18	321	6	0	2	2	4	....	2002-03	2009-10
Davydov, Evgeny	Wpg., Fla., Ott.	4	155	40	39	79	120	11	2	2	4	2	....	1991-92	1994-95
Daw, Jeff	Col.	1	1	0	1	1	0	....	....	....	....	....	....	2001-02	2001-02
Dawe, Jason	Buf., NYI, Mtl., NYR	8	366	86	90	176	162	22	4	3	7	18	....	1993-94	2001-02
• Dawes, Bob	Tor., Mtl.	4	32	2	7	9	6	10	0	0	0	2	1	1946-47	1950-51
‡ Dawes, Nigel	NYR, Phx., Cgy., Atl., Mtl.	5	212	39	45	84	43	11	2	2	4	0	....	2006-07	2010-11
• Day, Hap	Tor., NYA	14	581	86	116	202	601	53	4	7	11	56	1	1924-25	1937-38
Day, Joe	Hfd., NYI	3	72	1	10	11	87	....	....	....	....	....	....	1991-92	1993-94
Daze, Eric	Chi.	11	601	226	172	398	176	37	5	7	12	8	....	1994-95	2005-06
de Vries, Greg	Edm., Nsh., Col., NYR, Ott., Atl.	13	878	48	146	194	780	111	8	14	22	91	1	1995-96	2008-09
Dea, Billy	NYR, Det., Chi., Pit.	8	397	67	54	121	44	11	2	1	3	6	....	1953-54	1970-71
• Deacon, Don	Det.	3	30	6	4	10	6	2	2	1	3	0	....	1936-37	1939-40
Deadmarsh, Adam	Que., Col., L.A.	10	567	184	189	373	819	105	26	40	66	100	1	1994-95	2003-04
Deadmarsh, Butch	Buf., Atl., K.C.	5	137	12	5	17	155	4	0	0	0	17	....	1970-71	1974-75
Dean, Barry	Col., Phi.	3	165	25	56	81	146	....	....	....	....	....	....	1976-77	1978-79
Dean, Kevin	N.J., Atl., Dal., Chi.	7	331	7	48	55	138	16	2	2	4	2	1	1994-95	2000-01
Debenedet, Nelson	Det., Pit.	2	46	10	4	14	13	....	....	....	....	....	....	1973-74	1974-75
DeBlois, Lucien	NYR, Col., Wpg., Mtl., Que., Tor.	15	993	249	276	525	814	52	7	6	13	38	1	1977-78	1991-92
Debol, Dave	Hfd.	2	92	26	26	52	4	3	0	0	0	0	....	1979-80	1980-81
DeBrusk, Louie	Edm., T.B., Phx., Chi.	11	401	24	17	41	1161	15	2	0	2	10	....	1991-92	2002-03
DeFauw, Brad	Car.	1	9	3	0	3	2	....	....	....	....	....	....	2002-03	2002-03

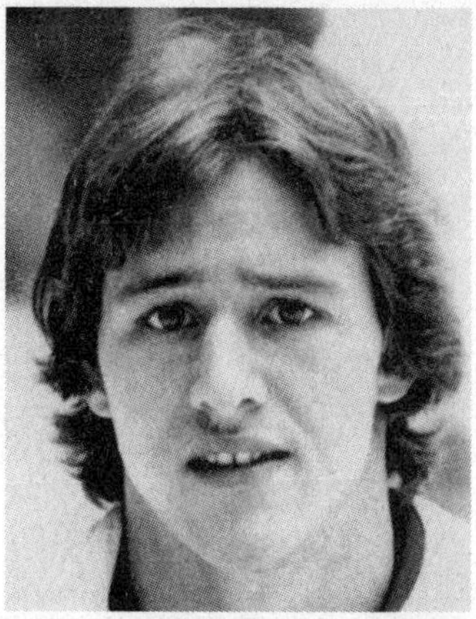
Bobby Crawford

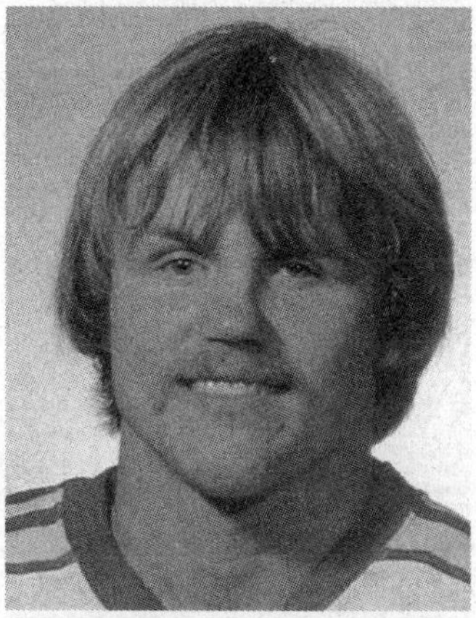
Tony Currie

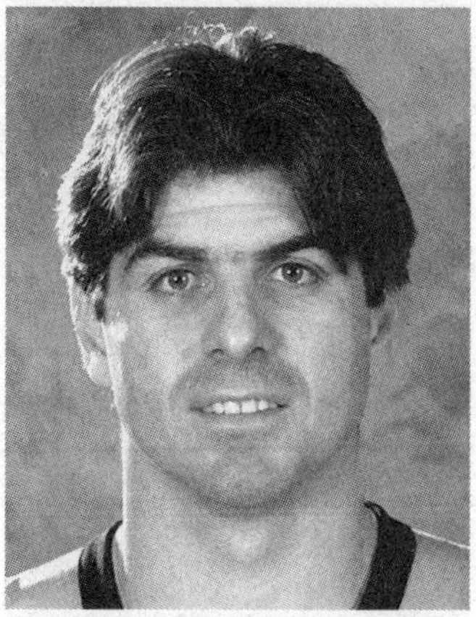
J.J. Daigneault

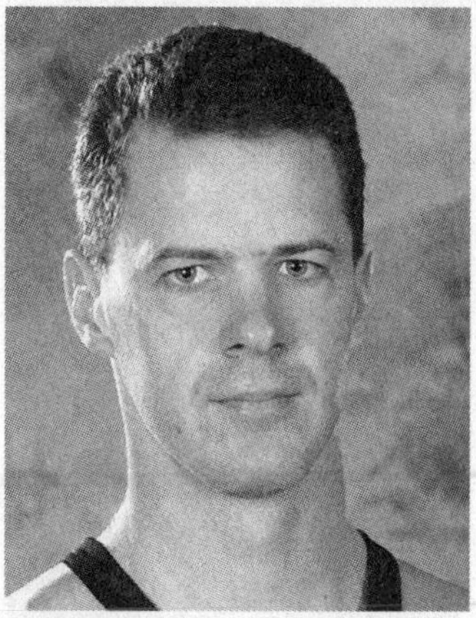
Jeff Daniels

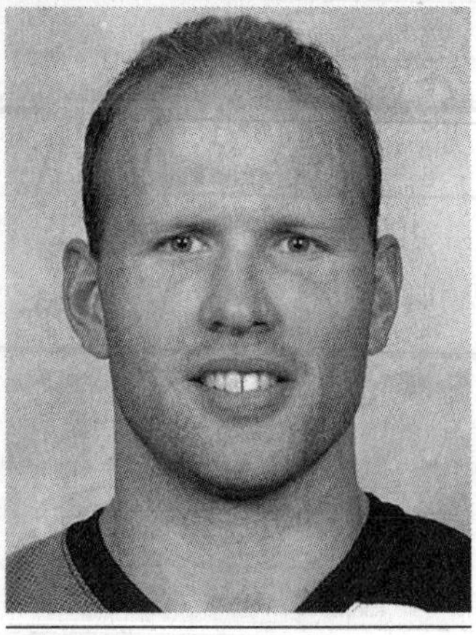

Greg de Vries

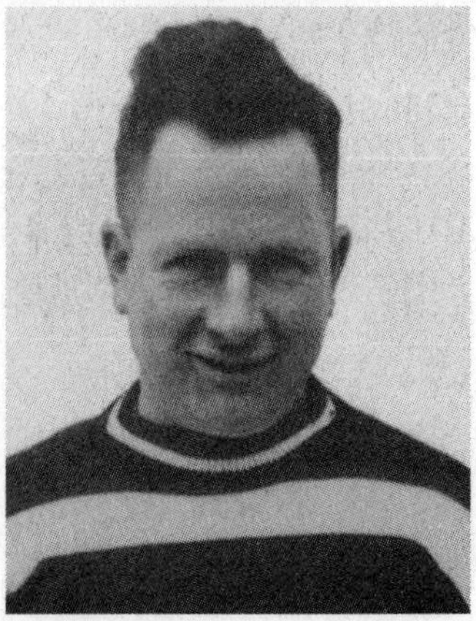

Cy Denneny

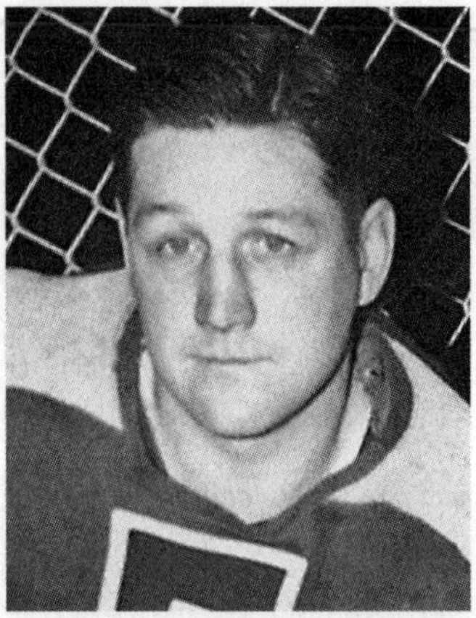

Bob Dill

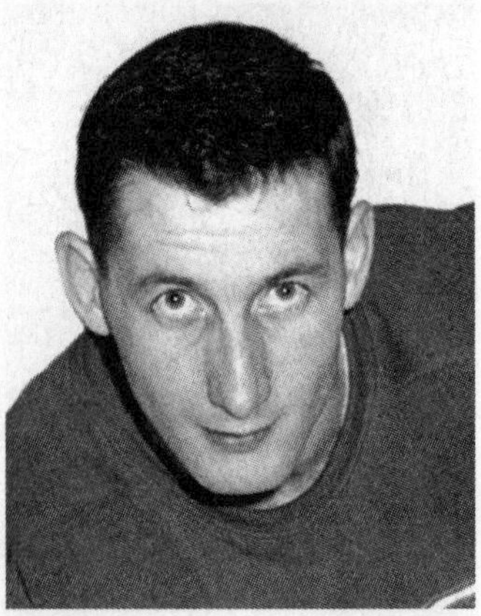

Bill Dineen

			Regular Schedule					Playoffs					NHL	First	Last
Name	**NHL Teams**	**NHL Seasons**	**GP**	**G**	**A**	**TP**	**PIM**	**GP**	**G**	**A**	**TP**	**PIM**	**Cup Wins**	**NHL Season**	**NHL Season**
‡ DeFazio, Brandon	Van.	1	2	0	0	0	0	....	....	....	....	....	....	2014-15	2014-15
Defazio, Dean	Pit.	1	22	0	2	2	28	....	....	....	....	....	....	1983-84	1983-84
DeGray, Dale	Cgy., Tor., L.A., Buf.	5	153	18	47	65	195	13	1	3	4	28	....	1985-86	1989-90
• Delisle, Jonathan	Mtl.	1	1	0	0	0	0	....	....	....	....	....	....	1998-99	1998-99
Delisle, Xavier	T.B., Mtl.	2	16	3	2	5	6	....	....	....	....	....	....	1998-99	2000-01
‡ Della Rovere, Stefan	St.L.	1	7	0	0	0	11	....	....	....	....	....	....	2010-11	2010-11
• Delmonte, Armand	Bos.	1	1	0	0	0	0	....	....	....	....	....	....	1945-46	1945-46
Delmore, Andy	Phi., Nsh., Buf., CBJ	7	283	43	58	101	105	20	6	2	8	16	....	1998-99	2005-06
Delorme, Gilbert	Mtl., St.L., Que., Det., Pit.	9	541	31	92	123	520	56	1	9	10	56	....	1981-82	1989-90
Delorme, Ron	Col., Van.	9	524	83	83	166	667	25	1	2	3	59	....	1976-77	1984-85
Delory, Val	NYR	1	1	0	0	0	0	....	....	....	....	....	....	1948-49	1948-49
Delparte, Guy	Col.	1	48	1	8	9	18	....	....	....	....	....	....	1976-77	1976-77
Delvecchio, Alex	Det.	24	1549	456	825	1281	383	121	35	69	104	29	3	1950-51	1973-74
• DeMarco, Ab	Chi., Tor., Bos., NYR	7	209	72	93	165	53	11	3	0	3	2	....	1938-39	1946-47
DeMarco, Ab	NYR, St.L., Pit., Van., L.A., Bos.	9	344	44	80	124	75	25	1	2	3	17	....	1969-70	1978-79
• Demers, Tony	Mtl., NYR	6	83	20	22	42	23	2	0	0	0	0	....	1937-38	1943-44
• Demitra, Pavol	Ott., St.L., L.A., Min., Van.	16	847	304	464	768	284	94	23	36	59	34	....	1993-94	2009-10
Dempsey, Nathan	Tor., Chi., L.A., Bos.	8	260	21	67	88	120	6	0	2	2	0	....	1996-97	2006-07
Denis, Jean-Paul	NYR	2	10	0	2	2	2	....	....	....	....	....	....	1946-47	1949-50
Denis, Lulu	Mtl.	2	3	0	1	1	0	....	....	....	....	....	....	1949-50	1950-51
• Denneny, Corb	Tor., Ham., Chi.	9	176	103	42	145	148	6	1	0	1	7	2	1917-18	1927-28
• Denneny, Cy	Ott., Bos.	12	328	248	85	333	301	25	16	2	18	23	5	1917-18	1928-29
Dennis, Norm	St.L.	4	12	3	0	3	11	5	0	0	0	2	....	1968-69	1971-72
• Denoird, Gerry	Tor.	1	17	0	1	1	0	....	....	....	....	....	....	1922-23	1922-23
DePalma, Larry	Min., S.J., Pit.	7	148	21	20	41	408	3	0	0	0	6	....	1985-86	1993-94
Derlago, Bill	Van., Tor., Bos., Wpg., Que.	9	555	189	227	416	247	13	5	0	5	8	....	1978-79	1986-87
• Desaulniers, Gerard	Mtl.	3	8	0	2	2	4	....	....	....	....	....	....	1950-51	1953-54
‡ Desbiens, Guillaume	Van., Cgy.	3	23	0	0	0	37	....	....	....	....	....	....	2009-10	2011-12
Deschamps, Nicolas	Wsh.	1	3	0	0	0	0	....	....	....	....	....	....	2013-14	2013-14
Descoteaux, Matthieu	Mtl.	1	5	1	1	2	4	....	....	....	....	....	....	2000-01	2000-01
• Desilets, Joffre	Mtl., Chi.	5	192	37	45	82	57	7	1	0	1	7	....	1935-36	1939-40
Desjardins, Eric	Mtl., Phi.	17	1143	136	439	575	757	168	23	57	80	93	1	1988-89	2005-06
Desjardins, Martin	Mtl.	1	8	0	2	2	2	....	....	....	....	....	....	1989-90	1989-90
• Desjardins, Vic	Chi., NYR	2	87	6	15	21	27	16	0	0	0	0	....	1930-31	1931-32
Deslauriers, Jacques	Mtl.	1	2	0	0	0	0	....	....	....	....	....	....	1955-56	1955-56
Deuling, Jarrett	NYI	2	15	0	1	1	11	....	....	....	....	....	....	1995-96	1996-97
‡ Deveaux, Andre	Tor., NYR	3	31	0	2	2	104	....	....	....	....	....	....	2008-09	2011-12
Devereaux, Boyd	Edm., Det., Phx., Tor.	11	627	67	112	179	205	27	3	4	7	4	1	1997-98	2008-09
Devine, Kevin	NYI	1	2	0	1	1	8	....	....	....	....	....	....	1982-83	1982-83
• Dewar, Tom	NYR	1	9	0	2	2	4	....	....	....	....	....	....	1943-44	1943-44
• Dewsbury, Al	Det., Chi.	9	347	30	78	108	365	14	1	5	6	16	1	1946-47	1955-56
Deziel, Michel	Buf.	1	....	....	....	....	....	1	0	0	0	0	....	1974-75	1974-75
• Dheere, Marcel	Mtl.	1	11	1	2	3	2	5	0	0	0	6	....	1942-43	1942-43
Diachuk, Edward	Det.	1	12	0	0	0	19	....	....	....	....	....	....	1960-61	1960-61
‡ Diaz, Raphael	Mtl., Van., NYR, Cgy.	5	201	8	41	49	62	13	0	1	1	0	....	2011-12	**2015-16**
Dibenedetto, Justin	NYI	1	8	0	1	1	2	....	....	....	....	....	....	2010-11	2010-11
• Dick, Harry	Chi.	1	12	0	1	1	12	....	....	....	....	....	....	1946-47	1946-47
• Dickens, Ernie	Tor., Chi.	6	278	12	44	56	98	13	0	0	0	4	1	1941-42	1950-51
Dickenson, Herb	NYR	2	48	18	17	35	10	....	....	....	....	....	....	1951-52	1952-53
Diduck, Gerald	NYI, Mtl., Van., Chi., Hfd., Phx., Tor., Dal.	17	932	56	156	212	1612	114	8	16	24	212	....	1984-85	2000-01
Dietrich, Don	Chi., N.J.	2	28	0	7	7	10	....	....	....	....	....	....	1983-84	1985-86
• Dill, Bob	NYR	2	76	15	15	30	135	....	....	....	....	....	....	1943-44	1944-45
• Dillabough, Bob	Det., Bos., Pit., Oak.	9	283	32	54	86	76	17	3	0	3	0	....	1961-62	1969-70
• Dillon, Cecil	NYR, Det.	10	453	167	131	298	105	43	14	9	23	14	1	1930-31	1939-40
Dillon, Gary	Col.	1	13	1	1	2	29	....	....	....	....	....	....	1980-81	1980-81
Dillon, Wayne	NYR, Wpg.	4	229	43	66	109	60	3	0	1	1	0	....	1975-76	1979-80
DiMaio, Rob	NYI, T.B., Phi., Bos., NYR, Car., Dal.	17	894	106	171	277	840	62	7	9	16	40	....	1988-89	2005-06
Dimitrakos, Niko	S.J., Phi.	4	158	24	38	62	95	20	1	8	9	10	....	2002-03	2006-07
• Dineen, Bill	Det., Chi.	5	323	51	44	95	122	37	1	1	2	18	2	1953-54	1957-58
• Dineen, Gary	Min.	1	4	0	1	1	0	....	....	....	....	....	....	1968-69	1968-69
Dineen, Gord	NYI, Min., Pit., Ott.	13	528	16	90	106	695	40	1	7	8	68	....	1982-83	1994-95
Dineen, Kevin	Hfd., Phi., Car., Ott., CBJ	19	1188	355	405	760	2229	59	23	18	41	127	....	1984-85	2002-03
Dineen, Peter	L.A., Det.	2	13	0	2	2	13	....	....	....	....	....	....	1986-87	1989-90
Dingman, Chris	Cgy., Col., Car., T.B.	8	385	15	19	34	769	52	2	5	7	100	2	1997-98	2005-06
• Dinsmore, Chuck	Mtl.M.	4	100	6	2	8	50	8	1	0	1	2	1	1924-25	1929-30
Dionne, Gilbert	Mtl., Phi., Fla.	6	223	61	79	140	108	39	10	12	22	34	1	1990-91	1995-96
Dionne, Marcel	Det., L.A., NYR	18	1348	731	1040	1771	600	49	21	24	45	17	....	1971-72	1988-89
DiPenta, Joe	Atl., Ana.	4	174	6	17	23	110	32	0	0	0	17	1	2002-03	2007-08
DiPietro, Paul	Mtl., Tor., L.A.	6	192	31	49	80	96	31	11	10	21	10	1	1991-92	1996-97
Dirk, Robert	St.L., Van., Chi., Ana., Mtl.	9	402	13	29	42	786	39	0	1	1	56	....	1987-88	1995-96
DiSalvatore, Jon	St.L., Min.	2	6	0	0	0	4	....	....	....	....	....	....	2005-06	2011-12
Divisek, Tomas	Phi.	2	5	1	0	1	0	....	....	....	....	....	....	2000-01	2001-02
Djoos, Per	Det., NYR	3	82	2	31	33	58	....	....	....	....	....	....	1990-91	1992-93
• Doak, Gary	Det., Bos., Van., NYR	16	789	23	107	130	908	78	2	4	6	121	1	1965-66	1980-81
Dobbin, Brian	Phi., Bos.	5	63	7	8	15	61	2	0	0	0	17	....	1986-87	1991-92
Dobson, Jim	Min., Col., Que.	4	12	0	0	0	6	....	....	....	....	....	....	1979-80	1983-84
Doell, Kevin	Atl.	1	8	0	1	1	4	....	....	....	....	....	....	2007-08	2007-08
• Doherty, Fred	Mtl.	1	1	0	0	0	0	....	....	....	....	....	....	1918-19	1918-19
Doig, Jason	Wpg., Phx., NYR, Wsh.	7	158	6	18	24	285	6	0	1	1	6	....	1995-96	2003-04
Dollas, Bobby	Wpg., Que., Det., Ana., Edm., Pit., Ott., Cgy., S.J.	16	646	42	96	138	467	47	2	1	3	41	....	1983-84	2000-01
Dome, Robert	Pit., Cgy.	3	53	7	7	14	12	....	....	....	....	....	....	1997-98	2002-03
Domenichelli, Hnat	Hfd., Cgy., Atl., Min.	7	267	52	61	113	104	....	....	....	....	....	....	1996-97	2002-03
Domi, Tie	Tor., NYR, Wpg.	16	1020	104	141	245	3515	98	7	12	19	238	....	1989-90	2005-06
Donaldson, Gary	Chi.	1	1	0	0	0	0	....	....	....	....	....	....	1973-74	1973-74
Donatelli, Clark	Min., Bos.	2	35	3	4	7	39	2	0	0	0	0	....	1989-90	1991-92
Donato, Ted	Bos., NYI, Ott., Ana., Dal., St.L., L.A., NYR	13	796	150	197	347	396	58	8	10	18	22	....	1991-92	2003-04
• Donnelly, Babe	Mtl.M.	1	34	0	1	1	14	2	0	0	0	0	....	1926-27	1926-27
Donnelly, Dave	Bos., Chi., Edm.	5	137	15	24	39	150	5	0	0	0	0	....	1983-84	1987-88
Donnelly, Gord	Que., Wpg., Buf., Dal.	12	554	28	41	69	2069	26	0	2	2	61	....	1983-84	1994-95
Donnelly, Mike	NYR, Buf., L.A., Dal., NYI	11	465	114	121	235	255	47	12	12	24	30	....	1986-87	1996-97
‡ Donovan, Matt	NYI	3	67	2	17	19	26	2	0	0	0	10	....	2011-12	2014-15
Donovan, Shean	S.J., Col., Atl., Pit., Cgy., Bos., Ott.	15	951	112	129	241	705	49	6	6	12	39	....	1994-95	2009-10
Doornbosch, Jamie	NYI	1	1	0	0	0	0	....	....	....	....	....	....	2010-11	2010-11
Dopita, Jiri	Phi., Edm.	2	73	12	21	33	19	....	....	....	....	....	....	2001-02	2002-03
• Doran, John	NYA, Det., Mtl.	5	98	5	10	15	110	3	0	0	0	0	....	1933-34	1939-40
• Doran, Lloyd	Det.	1	24	3	2	5	10	....	....	....	....	....	....	1946-47	1946-47
• Doraty, Ken	Chi., Tor., Det.	5	103	15	26	41	24	15	7	2	9	2	....	1926-27	1937-38
Dore, Andre	NYR, St.L., Que.	7	257	14	81	95	261	23	1	2	3	32	....	1978-79	1984-85
Dore, Daniel	Que.	2	17	2	3	5	59	....	....	....	....	....	....	1989-90	1990-91
Dorey, Jim	Tor., NYR	4	232	25	74	99	553	11	0	2	2	40	....	1968-69	1971-72
Dorion, Dan	N.J.	2	4	1	1	2	2	....	....	....	....	....	....	1985-86	1987-88
Dornhoefer, Gary	Bos., Phi.	14	787	214	328	542	1291	80	17	19	36	203	2	1963-64	1977-78
• Dorohoy, Eddie	Mtl.	1	16	0	0	0	6	....	....	....	....	....	....	1948-49	1948-49
Douglas, Jordy	Hfd., Min., Wpg.	6	268	76	62	138	160	6	0	0	0	4	....	1979-80	1984-85
• Douglas, Kent	Tor., Oak., Det.	7	428	33	115	148	631	19	1	3	4	33	3	1962-63	1968-69
• Douglas, Les	Det.	4	52	6	12	18	8	10	3	2	5	2	1	1940-41	1946-47
Doull, Doug	Bos., Wsh.	2	37	0	1	1	151	....	....	....	....	....	....	2003-04	2005-06
Douris, Peter	Wpg., Bos., Ana., Dal.	11	321	54	67	121	80	27	3	5	8	14	....	1985-86	1997-98
Dowd, Jim	N.J., Van., NYI, Cgy., Edm., Min., Mtl., Chi., Col., Phi.	16	728	71	168	239	390	99	9	17	26	50	1	1991-92	2007-08
Downey, Aaron	Bos., Chi., Dal., St.L., Mtl., Det.	9	243	8	10	18	494	5	0	0	0	8	1	1999-00	2008-09
• Downie, Dave	Tor.	1	11	0	1	1	2	....	....	....	....	....	....	1932-33	1932-33
Downie, Steve	Phi., T.B., Col., Pit., Ari.	9	434	76	120	196	1057	28	2	15	17	54	....	2007-08	**2015-16**
Doyon, Mario	Chi., Que.	3	28	3	4	7	16	....	....	....	....	....	....	1988-89	1990-91
Drake, Dallas	Det., Wpg., Phx., St.L.	15	1009	177	300	477	885	90	14	19	33	79	1	1992-93	2007-08
• Draper, Bruce	Tor.	1	1	0	0	0	0	....	....	....	....	....	....	1962-63	1962-63
Draper, Kris	Wpg., Det.	20	1157	161	203	364	790	222	24	22	46	160	4	1990-91	2010-11
Drazenovic, Nick	St.L., CBJ, Pit.	3	12	0	0	0	6	....	....	....	....	....	....	2010-11	2013-14
Drewiske, Davis	L.A., Mtl.	5	135	5	20	25	67	....	....	....	....	....	1	2008-09	2012-13

Name	NHL Teams	NHL Seasons	Regular Schedule GP	G	A	TP	PIM	Playoffs GP	G	A	TP	PIM	NHL Cup Wins	First NHL Season	Last NHL Season
• Drillon, Gordie	Tor., Mtl.	7	311	155	139	294	56	50	26	15	41	10	1	1936-37	1942-43
Driscoll, Peter	Edm.	2	60	3	8	11	97	3	0	0	0	0	....	1979-80	1980-81
Driver, Bruce	N.J., NYR	15	922	96	390	486	670	108	10	40	50	64	1	1983-84	1997-98
Drolet, Rene	Phi., Det.	2	2	0	0	0	0	....	....	....	....	....	....	1971-72	1974-75
Droppa, Ivan	Chi.	2	19	0	1	1	14	....	....	....	....	....	....	1993-94	1995-96
• Drouillard, Clarence	Det.	1	10	0	1	1	0	....	....	....	....	....	....	1937-38	1937-38
Drouin, Jude	Mtl., Min., NYI, Wpg.	12	666	151	305	456	346	72	27	41	68	33	....	1968-69	1980-81
Drouin, P.C.	Bos.	1	3	0	0	0	0	....	....	....	....	....	....	1996-97	1996-97
• Drouin, Polly	Mtl.	7	160	23	50	73	80	5	0	1	1	5	....	1934-35	1940-41
Druce, John	Wsh., Wpg., L.A., Phi.	10	531	113	126	239	347	53	17	6	23	38	....	1988-89	1997-98
Druken, Harold	Van., Car., Tor.	5	146	27	36	63	36	4	0	1	1	0	....	1999-00	2003-04
Drulia, Stan	T.B.	3	126	15	27	42	52	....	....	....	....	....	....	1992-93	2000-01
• Drummond, Jim	NYR	1	2	0	0	0	0	....	....	....	....	....	....	1944-45	1944-45
Drury, Chris	Col., Cgy., Buf., NYR	12	892	255	360	615	468	135	47	42	89	46	1	1998-99	2010-11
• Drury, Herb	Pit., Phi.	6	213	24	13	37	203	4	1	1	2	0	....	1925-26	1930-31
Drury, Ted	Cgy., Hfd., Ott., Ana., NYI, CBJ	8	414	41	52	93	367	14	1	0	1	4	....	1993-94	2000-01
Dube, Christian	NYR	2	33	1	1	2	4	3	0	0	0	0	....	1996-97	1998-99
• Dube, Gilles	Mtl., Det.	2	12	1	2	3	2	2	0	0	0	0	1	1949-50	1953-54
Dube, Norm	K.C.	2	57	8	10	18	54	....	....	....	....	....	....	1974-75	1975-76
Duberman, Justin	Pit.	1	4	0	0	0	0	....	....	....	....	....	....	1993-94	1993-94
Dubinsky, Steve	Chi., Cgy., Nsh., St.L.	10	375	25	45	70	164	10	1	0	1	14	....	1993-94	2002-03
• Duchesne, Gaetan	Wsh., Que., Min., S.J., Fla.	14	1028	179	254	433	617	84	14	13	27	97	....	1981-82	1994-95
Duchesne, Steve	L.A., Phi., Que., St.L., Ott., Det.	16	1113	227	525	752	824	121	16	61	77	96	1	1986-87	2001-02
Duco, Mike	Fla., Van.	3	18	0	2	2	65	....	....	....	....	....	....	2009-10	2011-12
Dudley, Rick	Buf., Wpg.	6	309	75	99	174	292	25	7	2	9	69	....	1972-73	1980-81
Duerden, Dave	Fla.	1	2	0	0	0	0	....	....	....	....	....	....	1999-00	1999-00
Duff, Dick	Tor., NYR, Mtl., L.A., Buf.	18	1030	283	289	572	743	114	30	49	79	78	6	1954-55	1971-72
Dufour, Luc	Bos., Que., St.L.	3	167	23	21	44	199	18	1	0	1	32	....	1982-83	1984-85
• Dufour, Marc	NYR, L.A.	3	14	1	0	1	2	....	....	....	....	....	....	1963-64	1968-69
Dufresne, Donald	Mtl., T.B., L.A., St.L., Edm.	9	268	6	36	42	258	34	1	3	4	47	1	1988-89	1996-97
• Duggan, John	Ott.	1	27	0	0	0	0	2	0	0	0	0	....	1925-26	1925-26
Duggan, Ken	Min.	1	1	0	0	0	0	....	....	....	....	....	....	1987-88	1987-88
Duguay, Ron	NYR, Det., Pit., L.A.	12	864	274	346	620	582	89	31	22	53	118	....	1977-78	1988-89
• Duguid, Lorne	Mtl.M., Det., Bos.	6	135	9	15	24	57	4	1	0	1	6	....	1931-32	1936-37
• Dukowski, Duke	Chi., NYA, NYR	5	200	16	30	46	172	6	0	0	0	6	....	1926-27	1933-34
• Dumart, Woody	Bos.	16	772	211	218	429	99	88	12	15	27	23	2	1935-36	1953-54
Dumont, J.P.	Chi., Buf., Nsh.	12	822	214	309	523	364	51	17	17	34	28	....	1998-99	2010-11
Dunbar, Dale	Van., Bos.	2	2	0	0	0	2	....	....	....	....	....	....	1985-86	1988-89
• Duncan, Art	Det., Tor.	5	156	18	16	34	225	5	0	0	0	4	....	1926-27	1930-31
Duncan, Iain	Wpg.	4	127	34	55	89	149	11	0	3	3	6	....	1986-87	1990-91
Duncanson, Craig	L.A., Wpg., NYR	7	38	5	4	9	61	....	....	....	....	....	....	1985-86	1992-93
Dundas, Rocky	Tor.	1	5	0	0	0	14	....	....	....	....	....	....	1989-90	1989-90
• Dunlap, Frank	Tor.	1	15	0	1	1	2	....	....	....	....	....	....	1943-44	1943-44
Dunlop, Blake	Min., Phi., St.L., Det.	11	550	130	274	404	172	40	4	10	14	18	....	1973-74	1983-84
Dunn, Dave	Van., Tor.	3	184	14	41	55	313	10	1	1	2	41	....	1973-74	1975-76
• Dunn, Richie	Buf., Cgy., Hfd.	12	483	36	140	176	314	36	3	15	18	24	....	1977-78	1988-89
Dupere, Denis	Tor., Wsh., St.L., K.C., Col.	8	421	80	99	179	66	16	1	0	1	0	....	1970-71	1977-78
Dupont, Andre	NYR, St.L., Phi., Que.	13	800	59	185	244	1986	140	14	18	32	352	2	1970-71	1982-83
‡ Dupont, Brodie	NYR	1	1	0	0	0	0	....	....	....	....	....	....	2010-11	2010-11
Dupont, Jerome	Chi., Tor.	6	214	7	29	36	468	20	0	2	2	56	....	1981-82	1986-87
DuPont, Micki	Cgy., Pit., St.L.	4	23	1	3	4	12	....	....	....	....	....	....	2001-02	2007-08
Dupont, Norm	Mtl., Wpg., Hfd.	5	256	55	85	140	52	13	4	2	6	0	....	1979-80	1983-84
• Dupre, Yanick	Phi.	3	35	2	0	2	16	....	....	....	....	....	....	1991-92	1995-96
Dupuis, Pascal	Min., NYR, Atl., Pit.	15	871	190	219	409	387	97	19	25	44	56	2	2000-01	**2015-16**
‡ Dupuis, Philippe	Col., Tor.	4	116	6	12	18	62	....	....	....	....	....	....	2008-09	2011-12
• Durbano, Steve	St.L., Pit., K.C., Col.	6	220	13	60	73	1127	5	0	2	2	8	....	1972-73	1978-79
Duris, Vitezslav	Tor.	2	89	3	20	23	62	3	0	1	1	2	....	1980-81	1982-83
Durno, Chris	Col.	2	43	4	4	8	47	1	0	0	0	0	....	2008-09	2009-10
Dusablon, Benoit	NYR	1	3	0	0	0	2	....	....	....	....	....	....	2003-04	2003-04
• Dussault, Norm	Mtl.	4	206	31	62	93	47	7	3	1	4	0	....	1947-48	1950-51
• Dutton, Red	Mtl.M., NYA	10	449	29	67	96	871	18	1	0	1	33	....	1926-27	1935-36
• Dvorak, Miroslav	Phi.	3	193	11	74	85	51	18	0	2	2	6	....	1982-83	1984-85
Dvorak, Radek	Fla., NYR, Edm., St.L., Atl., Dal., Ana., Car.	18	1260	227	363	590	449	39	2	5	7	4	....	1995-96	2013-14
Dwyer, Gordie	T.B., NYR, Mtl.	5	108	0	5	5	394	....	....	....	....	....	....	1999-00	2003-04
Dwyer, Mike	Col., Cgy.	4	31	2	6	8	25	1	1	0	1	0	....	1978-79	1981-82
• Dyck, Henry	NYR	1	1	0	0	0	0	....	....	....	....	....	....	1943-44	1943-44
• Dye, Babe	Tor., Ham., Chi., NYA	11	271	201	47	248	221	10	2	0	2	11	1	1919-20	1930-31
Dykhuis, Karl	Chi., Phi., T.B., Mtl.	12	644	42	91	133	495	62	8	10	18	50	....	1991-92	2003-04
Dykstra, Steve	Buf., Edm., Pit., Hfd.	5	217	8	32	40	545	1	0	0	0	2	....	1985-86	1989-90
• Dyte, Jack	Chi.	1	27	1	0	1	31	....	....	....	....	....	....	1943-44	1943-44
Dziedzic, Joe	Pit., Phx.	3	130	14	14	28	131	21	1	3	4	23	....	1995-96	1998-99
‡ Dziurzynski, David	Ott.	2	26	3	3	6	22	....	....	....	....	....	....	2012-13	**2015-16**

E

Name	NHL Teams	NHL Seasons	Regular Schedule GP	G	A	TP	PIM	Playoffs GP	G	A	TP	PIM	NHL Cup Wins	First NHL Season	Last NHL Season
Eager, Ben	Phi., Chi., Atl., S.J., Edm.	9	407	43	42	85	875	47	3	3	6	148	1	2005-06	2013-14
Eagles, Mike	Que., Chi., Wpg., Wsh.	16	853	74	122	196	928	44	2	6	8	34	....	1982-83	1999-00
Eakin, Bruce	Cgy., Det.	4	13	2	2	4	4	....	....	....	....	....	....	1981-82	1985-86
Eakins, Dallas	Wpg., Fla., St.L., Phx., NYR, Tor., NYI, Cgy.	10	120	0	9	9	208	5	0	0	0	4	....	1992-93	2001-02
‡ Earl, Robbie	Tor., Min.	3	47	6	1	7	6	....	....	....	....	....	....	2007-08	2010-11
Eastwood, Mike	Tor., Wpg., Phx., NYR, St.L., Chi., Pit.	13	783	87	149	236	354	97	8	11	19	64	....	1991-92	2003-04
Eaton, Mark	Phi., Nsh., Pit., NYI	13	650	24	61	85	242	68	4	9	13	24	1	1999-00	2012-13
Eatough, Jeff	Buf.	1	1	0	0	0	0	....	....	....	....	....	....	1981-82	1981-82
Eaves, Mike	Min., Cgy.	8	324	83	143	226	80	43	7	10	17	14	....	1978-79	1985-86
Eaves, Murray	Wpg., Det.	8	57	4	13	17	9	4	0	1	1	2	....	1980-81	1989-90
‡ Ebbett, Andrew	Ana., Chi., Min., Phx., Van., Pit.	8	224	26	45	71	50	19	1	2	3	8	....	2007-08	2014-15
Ecclestone, Tim	St.L., Det., Tor., Atl.	11	692	126	233	359	344	48	6	11	17	76	....	1967-68	1977-78
Eckford, Tyler	N.J.	2	7	0	1	1	4	....	....	....	....	....	....	2009-10	2010-11
Edberg, Rolf	Wsh.	3	184	45	58	103	24	....	....	....	....	....	....	1978-79	1980-81
• Eddolls, Frank	Mtl., NYR	8	317	23	43	66	114	31	0	2	2	10	1	1944-45	1951-52
Edestrand, Darryl	St.L., Phi., Pit., Bos., L.A.	10	455	34	90	124	404	42	3	9	12	57	....	1967-68	1978-79
• Edmundson, Garry	Mtl., Tor.	3	43	4	6	10	49	11	0	1	1	8	....	1951-52	1960-61
Edur, Tom	Col., Pit.	2	158	17	70	87	67	....	....	....	....	....	....	1976-77	1977-78
• Egan, Pat	NYA, Bro., Det., Bos., NYR	11	554	77	153	230	776	46	9	4	13	48	....	1939-40	1950-51
Egeland, Allan	T.B.	3	17	0	0	0	16	....	....	....	....	....	....	1995-96	1997-98
Egers, Jack	NYR, St.L., Wsh.	7	284	64	69	133	154	32	5	6	11	32	....	1969-70	1975-76
• Ehman, Gerry	Bos., Det., Tor., Oak., Cal.	9	429	96	118	214	100	41	10	10	20	12	1	1957-58	1970-71
‡ Ehrhoff, Christian	S.J., Van., Buf., Pit., L.A., Chi.	12	789	74	265	339	517	73	7	27	34	64	....	2003-04	**2015-16**
Eisenhut, Neil	Van., Cgy.	2	16	1	3	4	21	....	....	....	....	....	....	1993-94	1994-95
Eklund, Pelle	Phi., Dal.	9	594	120	335	455	109	66	10	36	46	8	....	1985-86	1993-94
Ekman, Nils	T.B., S.J., Pit.	5	264	60	91	151	188	28	2	5	7	16	....	1999-00	2006-07
Eldebrink, Anders	Van., Que.	2	55	3	11	14	29	14	0	0	0	10	....	1981-82	1982-83
Elias, Patrik	N.J.	20	1240	408	617	1025	549	162	45	80	125	89	2	1995-96	**2015-16**
Elich, Matt	T.B.	2	16	1	1	2	0	....	....	....	....	....	....	1999-00	2000-01
• Elik, Bo	Det.	1	3	0	0	0	0	....	....	....	....	....	....	1962-63	1962-63
Elik, Todd	L.A., Min., Edm., S.J., St.L., Bos.	8	448	110	219	329	453	52	15	27	42	48	....	1989-90	1996-97
‡ Elkins, Corey	L.A.	1	3	1	0	1	0	....	....	....	....	....	....	2009-10	2009-10
‡ Ellerby, Keaton	Fla., L.A., Wpg.	6	212	4	23	27	88	6	0	0	0	2	....	2009-10	2014-15
Ellett, Dave	Wpg., Tor., N.J., Bos., St.L.	16	1129	153	415	568	985	116	11	46	57	87	....	1984-85	1999-00
• Elliott, Fred	Ott.	1	43	2	0	2	6	....	....	....	....	....	....	1928-29	1928-29
Ellis, Matt	Det., L.A., Buf.	9	356	21	28	49	89	4	1	0	1	0	....	2006-07	2014-15
Ellis, Ron	Tor.	16	1034	332	308	640	207	70	18	8	26	20	1	1963-64	1980-81
‡ Ellison, Matt	Chi., Phi.	3	43	3	11	14	19	....	....	....	....	....	....	2003-04	2006-07
Elomo, Miika	Wsh.	1	2	0	1	1	2	....	....	....	....	....	....	1999-00	1999-00
Eloranta, Kari	Cgy., St.L.	5	267	13	103	116	155	26	1	7	8	19	....	1981-82	1986-87
Eloranta, Mikko	Bos., L.A.	4	264	32	44	76	186	7	1	1	2	2	....	1999-00	2002-03
Elynuik, Pat	Wpg., Wsh., T.B., Ott.	9	506	154	188	342	459	20	6	9	15	25	....	1987-88	1995-96
• Emberg, Eddie	Mtl.	1	....	....	....	....	....	2	1	0	1	0	....	1944-45	1944-45
Emerson, Nelson	St.L., Wpg., Hfd., Car., Chi., Ott., Atl., L.A.	12	771	195	293	488	575	40	7	15	22	33	....	1990-91	2001-02

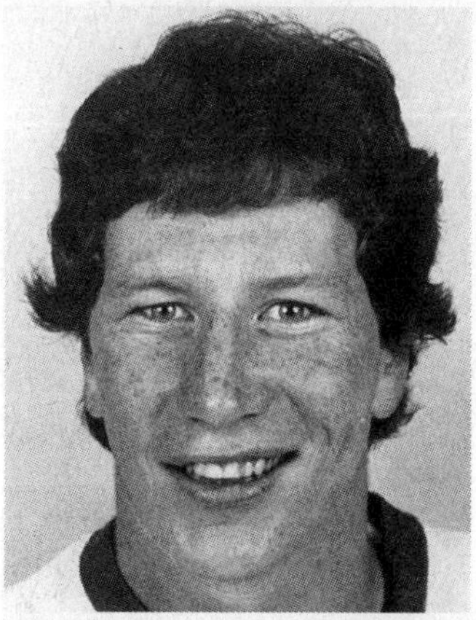

Gord Dineen

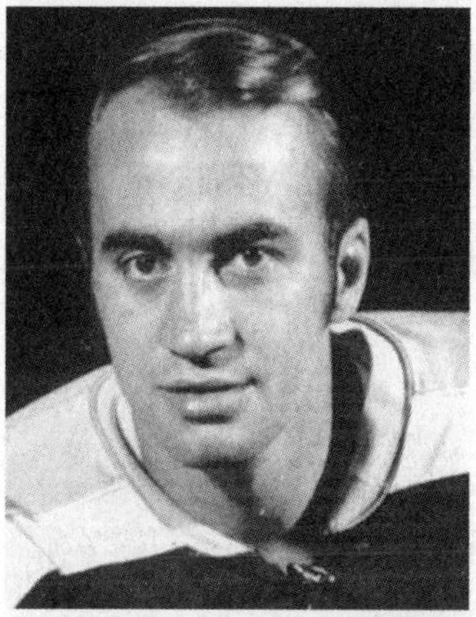

Gary Doak

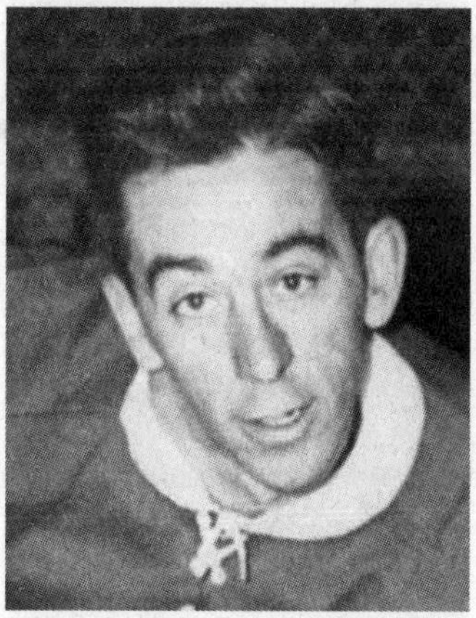

Gilles Dube

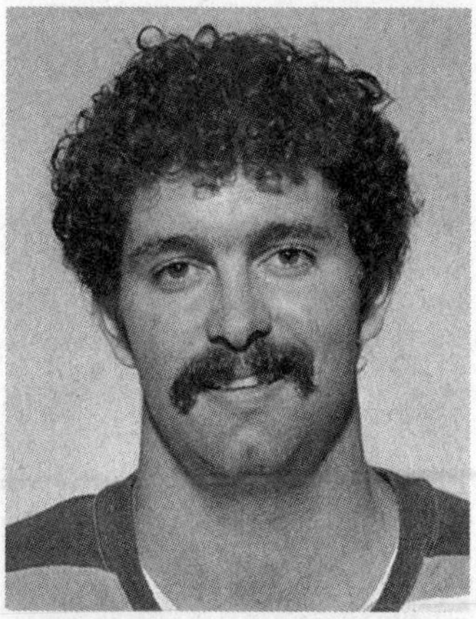

Richie Dunn

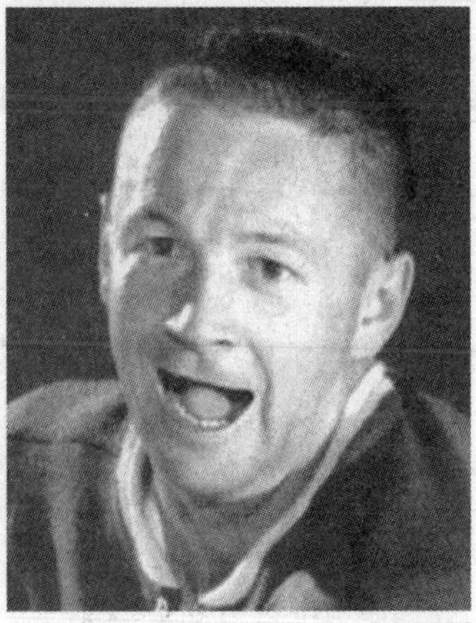

Garry Edmundson

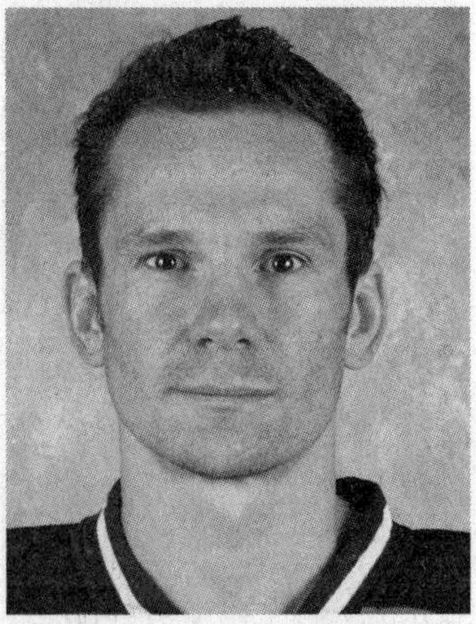

Patrik Elias

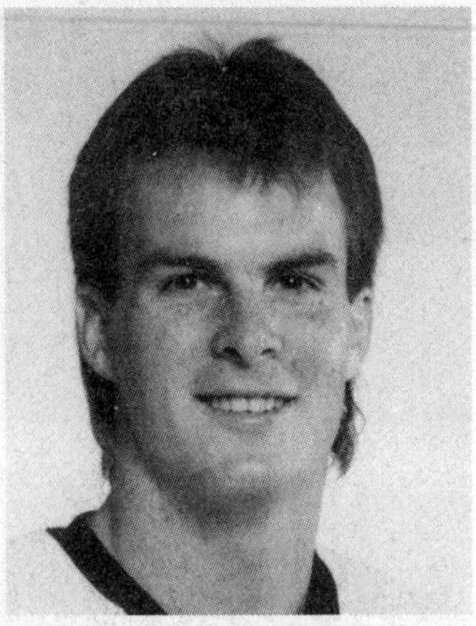

Bob Errey

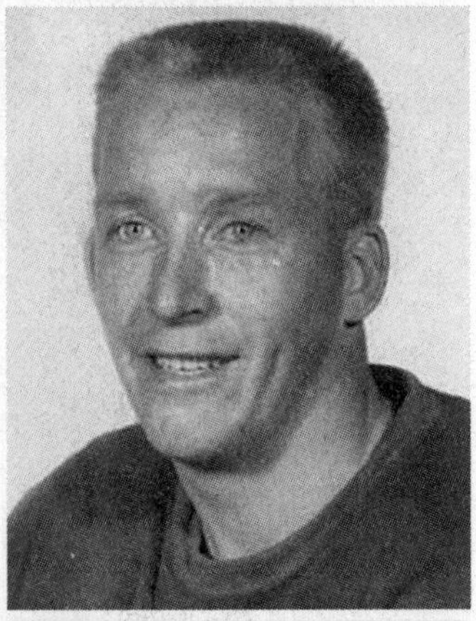

Alex Faulkner

			Regular Schedule					Playoffs							
Name	NHL Teams	NHL Seasons	GP	G	A	TP	PIM	GP	G	A	TP	PIM	NHL Cup Wins	First NHL Season	Last NHL Season
Eminger, Steve	Wsh., Phi., T.B., Fla., Ana., NYR	10	488	19	80	99	359	20	1	2	3	6	....	2002-03	2012-13
Emma, David	N.J., Bos., Fla.	5	34	5	6	11	2	....	....	....	....	....	....	1992-93	2000-01
‡ Emmerton, Cory	Det.	4	139	12	9	21	22	18	1	1	2	6	....	2010-11	2013-14
Emmons, Gary	S.J.	1	3	1	0	1	0	....	....	....	....	....	....	1993-94	1993-94
Emmons, John	Ott., T.B., Bos.	3	85	2	4	6	64	....	....	....	....	....	....	1999-00	2001-02
● Emms, Hap	Mtl.M., NYA, Det., Bos.	10	320	36	53	89	311	14	0	0	0	12	....	1926-27	1937-38
Endean, Craig	Wpg.	1	2	0	1	1	0	....	....	....	....	....	....	1986-87	1986-87
Endicott, Shane	Pit.	2	45	1	2	3	47	....	....	....	....	....	....	2001-02	2005-06
Engblom, Brian	Mtl., Wsh., L.A., Buf., Cgy.	11	659	29	177	206	599	48	3	9	12	43	2	1976-77	1986-87
Engele, Jerry	Min.	3	100	2	13	15	162	2	0	1	1	0	....	1975-76	1977-78
English, John	L.A.	1	3	1	3	4	4	1	0	0	0	0	....	1987-88	1987-88
‡ Engqvist, Andreas	Mtl.	2	15	0	0	0	4	....	....	....	....	....	....	2010-11	2011-12
Ennis, Jim	Edm.	1	5	1	0	1	10	....	....	....	....	....	....	1987-88	1987-88
‡ Erat, Martin	Nsh., Wsh., Phx., Ari.	13	881	176	369	545	506	50	8	15	23	40	....	2001-02	2014-15
● Erickson, Aut	Bos., Chi., Tor., Oak.	7	226	7	24	31	182	7	0	0	0	2	1	1959-60	1969-70
Erickson, Bryan	Wsh., L.A., Pit., Wpg.	9	351	80	125	205	141	14	3	4	7	7	....	1983-84	1993-94
Erickson, Grant	Bos., Min.	2	6	1	0	1	0	....	....	....	....	....	....	1968-69	1969-70
Eriksson, Anders	Det., Chi., Fla., Tor., CBJ, Cgy., Phx., NYR	13	572	22	154	176	242	36	0	6	6	18	1	1995-96	2009-10
Eriksson, Peter	Edm.	1	20	3	3	6	24	....	....	....	....	....	....	1989-90	1989-90
Eriksson, Roland	Min., Van.	3	193	48	95	143	26	2	1	0	1	0	....	1976-77	1978-79
Eriksson, Thomas	Phi.	5	208	22	76	98	107	19	0	3	3	12	....	1980-81	1985-86
Erixon, Jan	NYR	10	556	57	159	216	167	58	7	7	14	16	....	1983-84	1992-93
Errey, Bob	Pit., Buf., S.J., Det., Dal., NYR	15	895	170	212	382	1005	99	13	16	29	109	2	1983-84	1997-98
Erskine, John	Dal., NYI, Wsh.	12	491	15	39	54	865	39	1	6	7	32	....	2001-02	2013-14
Esau, Len	Tor., Que., Cgy., Edm.	4	27	0	10	10	24	....	....	....	....	....	....	1991-92	1994-95
Esposito, Phil	Chi., Bos., NYR	18	1282	717	873	1590	910	130	61	76	137	138	2	1963-64	1980-81
Evans, Brennan	Cgy.	1	....	....	....	....	....	2	0	0	0	0	....	2003-04	2003-04
● Evans, Chris	Tor., Buf., St.L., Det., K.C.	5	241	19	42	61	143	12	1	1	2	8	....	1969-70	1974-75
Evans, Daryl	L.A., Wsh., Tor.	6	113	22	30	52	25	11	5	8	13	12	....	1981-82	1986-87
Evans, Doug	St.L., Wpg., Phi.	8	355	48	87	135	502	22	3	4	7	38	....	1985-86	1992-93
● Evans, Jack	NYR, Chi.	14	752	19	80	99	989	56	2	2	4	97	1	1948-49	1962-63
Evans, Kevin	Min., S.J.	2	9	0	1	1	44	....	....	....	....	....	....	1990-91	1991-92
Evans, Paul	Tor.	2	11	1	1	2	21	2	0	0	0	0	....	1976-77	1977-78
Evans, Paul	Phi.	3	103	14	25	39	34	1	0	0	0	0	....	1978-79	1982-83
Evans, Shawn	St.L., NYI	2	9	1	0	1	2	....	....	....	....	....	....	1985-86	1989-90
● Evans, Stewart	Det., Mtl.M., Mtl.	8	367	28	49	77	425	26	0	0	0	20	1	1930-31	1938-39
Evason, Dean	Wsh., Hfd., S.J., Dal., Cgy.	13	803	139	233	372	1002	55	9	20	29	132	....	1983-84	1995-96
● Ewen, Todd	St.L., Mtl., Ana., S.J.	11	518	36	40	76	1911	26	0	0	0	87	1	1986-87	1996-97
Exelby, Garnet	Atl., Tor.	7	408	7	43	50	584	4	0	0	0	6	....	2002-03	2009-10
● Ezinicki, Bill	Tor., Bos., NYR	9	368	79	105	184	713	40	5	8	13	87	3	1944-45	1954-55

F

Name	NHL Teams	NHL Seasons	GP	G	A	TP	PIM	GP	G	A	TP	PIM	NHL Cup Wins	First NHL Season	Last NHL Season
Fahey, Brian	Wsh.	1	7	0	1	1	2	....	....	....	....	....	....	2010-11	2010-11
Fahey, Jim	S.J., N.J.	4	92	1	24	25	67	2	0	0	0	0	....	2002-03	2006-07
Fahey, Trevor	NYR	1	1	0	0	0	0	....	....	....	....	....	....	1964-65	1964-65
Fairbairn, Bill	NYR, Min., St.L.	11	658	162	261	423	173	54	13	22	35	42	....	1968-69	1978-79
‡ Fairchild, Cade	St.L.	1	5	0	1	1	0	....	....	....	....	....	....	2011-12	2011-12
Fairchild, Kelly	Tor., Dal., Col.	4	34	2	3	5	6	....	....	....	....	....	....	1995-96	2001-02
Falkenberg, Bob	Det.	5	54	1	5	6	26	....	....	....	....	....	....	1966-67	1971-72
Falloon, Pat	S.J., Phi., Ott., Edm., Pit.	9	575	143	179	322	141	66	11	7	18	16	....	1991-92	1999-00
Farkas, Jeff	Tor., Atl.	4	11	0	2	2	6	5	1	0	1	0	....	1999-00	2002-03
● Farrant, Walt	Chi.	1	1	0	0	0	0	....	....	....	....	....	....	1943-44	1943-44
Farrell, Mike	Wsh., Nsh.	3	13	0	0	0	2	....	....	....	....	....	....	2001-02	2003-04
Farrish, Dave	NYR, Que., Tor.	7	430	17	110	127	440	14	0	2	2	24	....	1976-77	1983-84
● Fashoway, Gordie	Chi.	1	13	3	2	5	14	....	....	....	....	....	....	1950-51	1950-51
Fast, Brad	Car.	1	1	1	0	1	0	....	....	....	....	....	....	2003-04	2003-04
Fata, Drew	NYI	2	8	1	1	2	9	1	0	0	0	0	....	2006-07	2007-08
Fata, Rico	Cgy., NYR, Pit., Atl., Wsh.	8	230	27	36	63	104	....	....	....	....	....	....	1998-99	2006-07
Faubert, Mario	Pit.	7	231	21	90	111	292	10	2	2	4	6	....	1974-75	1981-82
Faulkner, Alex	Tor., Det.	3	101	15	17	32	15	12	5	0	5	2	....	1961-62	1963-64
Fauss, Ted	Tor.	2	28	0	2	2	15	....	....	....	....	....	....	1986-87	1987-88
Faust, Andre	Phi.	2	47	10	7	17	14	....	....	....	....	....	....	1992-93	1993-94
Feamster, Dave	Chi.	4	169	13	24	37	154	33	3	5	8	61	....	1981-82	1984-85
Featherstone, Glen	St.L., Bos., NYR, Hfd., Cgy.	9	384	19	61	80	939	28	0	2	2	103	....	1988-89	1996-97
Featherstone, Tony	Oak., Cal., Min.	3	130	17	21	38	65	2	0	0	0	0	....	1969-70	1973-74
Federko, Bernie	St.L., Det.	14	1000	369	761	1130	487	91	35	66	101	83	....	1976-77	1989-90
Fedorov, Fedor	Van., NYR	3	18	0	2	2	14	....	....	....	....	....	....	2002-03	2005-06
Fedorov, Sergei	Det., Ana., CBJ, Wsh.	18	1248	483	696	1179	839	183	52	124	176	133	3	1990-91	2008-09
Fedoruk, Todd	Phi., Ana., Dal., Min., Phx., T.B.	9	545	32	65	97	1050	25	1	1	2	54	....	2000-01	2009-10
Fedotenko, Ruslan	Phi., T.B., NYI, Pit., NYR	12	863	173	193	366	472	108	22	18	40	66	2	2000-01	2012-13
Fedotov, Anatoli	Wpg., Ana.	2	4	0	2	2	0	....	....	....	....	....	....	1992-93	1993-94
Fedyk, Brent	Det., Phi., Dal., NYR	10	470	97	112	209	308	16	3	2	5	12	....	1987-88	1998-99
Felix, Chris	Wsh.	4	35	1	12	13	10	2	0	1	1	0	....	1987-88	1990-91
Felsner, Brian	Chi.	1	12	1	3	4	12	....	....	....	....	....	....	1997-98	1997-98
Felsner, Denny	St.L.	4	18	1	4	5	6	10	2	3	5	2	....	1991-92	1994-95
Feltrin, Tony	Pit., NYR	4	48	3	3	6	65	....	....	....	....	....	....	1980-81	1985-86
Fenton, Paul	Hfd., NYR, L.A., Wpg., Tor., Cgy., S.J.	8	411	100	83	183	198	17	4	1	5	27	....	1984-85	1991-92
Fenyves, David	Buf., Phi.	9	206	3	32	35	119	11	0	0	0	9	....	1982-83	1990-91
Ference, Andrew	Pit., Cgy., Bos., Edm.	16	907	43	182	225	753	120	8	30	38	122	1	1999-00	**2015-16**
Ference, Brad	Fla., Phx., Cgy.	6	250	4	30	34	565	....	....	....	....	....	....	1999-00	2006-07
Fergus, Tom	Bos., Tor., Van.	12	726	235	346	581	499	65	21	17	38	48	....	1981-82	1992-93
Ferguson, Craig	Mtl., Cgy., Fla.	5	27	1	1	2	6	....	....	....	....	....	....	1993-94	1999-00
Ferguson, George	Tor., Pit., Min.	12	797	160	238	398	431	86	14	23	37	44	....	1972-73	1983-84
● Ferguson, John	Mtl.	8	500	145	158	303	1214	85	20	18	38	260	5	1963-64	1970-71
● Ferguson, Lorne	Bos., Det., Chi.	8	422	82	80	162	193	31	6	3	9	24	....	1949-50	1958-59
Ferguson, Norm	Oak., Cal.	4	279	73	66	139	72	10	1	4	5	7	....	1968-69	1971-72
Ferguson, Scott	Edm., Ana., Min.	7	218	7	14	21	310	11	0	0	0	8	....	1997-98	2005-06
Ferland, Jonathan	Mtl.	1	7	1	0	1	2	....	....	....	....	....	....	2005-06	2005-06
Ferner, Mark	Buf., Wsh., Ana., Det.	6	91	3	10	13	51	....	....	....	....	....	....	1986-87	1994-95
Ferraro, Chris	NYR, Pit., Edm., NYI, Wsh.	6	74	7	9	16	57	....	....	....	....	....	....	1995-96	2001-02
Ferraro, Peter	NYR, Pit., Bos., Wsh.	6	92	9	15	24	58	2	0	0	0	0	....	1995-96	2001-02
Ferraro, Ray	Hfd., NYI, NYR, L.A., Atl., St.L.	18	1258	408	490	898	1288	68	21	22	43	54	....	1984-85	2001-02
Ferriero, Benn	S.J., NYR, Van.	5	98	14	9	23	25	8	1	0	1	6	....	2009-10	2013-14
‡ Festerling, Brett	Ana., Wpg.	4	88	0	8	8	35	1	0	0	0	0	....	2008-09	2011-12
Fetisov, Viacheslav	N.J., Det.	9	546	36	192	228	656	116	2	26	28	147	2	1989-90	1997-98
Fibiger, Jesse	S.J.	1	16	0	0	0	2	....	....	....	....	....	....	2002-03	2002-03
Fidler, Mike	Cle., Min., Hfd., Chi.	7	271	84	97	181	124	....	....	....	....	....	....	1976-77	1982-83
● Field, Wilf	NYA, Bro., Mtl., Chi.	6	219	17	25	42	151	2	0	0	0	2	....	1936-37	1944-45
Fielder, Guyle	Chi., Det., Bos.	4	9	0	0	0	2	6	0	0	0	2	....	1950-51	1957-58
‡ Filatov, Nikita	CBJ, Ott.	4	53	6	8	14	20	....	....	....	....	....	....	2008-09	2011-12
Filewich, Jonathan	Pit.	1	5	0	0	0	0	....	....	....	....	....	....	2007-08	2007-08
Filimonov, Dmitri	Ott.	1	30	1	4	5	18	....	....	....	....	....	....	1993-94	1993-94
● Fillion, Bob	Mtl.	7	327	42	61	103	84	33	7	4	11	10	2	1943-44	1949-50
● Fillion, Marcel	Bos.	1	1	0	0	0	0	....	....	....	....	....	....	1944-45	1944-45
● Filmore, Tommy	Det., NYA, Bos.	4	117	15	12	27	33	....	....	....	....	....	....	1930-31	1933-34
Finger, Jeff	Col., Tor.	4	199	17	40	57	114	5	0	2	2	4	....	2006-07	2009-10
● Finkbeiner, Lloyd	NYA	1	2	0	0	0	0	....	....	....	....	....	....	1940-41	1940-41
Finley, Jeff	NYI, Phi., Wpg., Phx., NYR, St.L.	15	708	13	70	83	457	52	1	6	7	38	....	1987-88	2003-04
‡ Finley, Joe	Buf., NYI	2	21	0	1	1	32	....	....	....	....	....	....	2011-12	2012-13
Finn, Steven	Que., T.B., L.A.	12	725	34	78	112	1724	23	0	4	4	39	....	1985-86	1996-97
● Finney, Sid	Chi.	3	59	10	7	17	4	7	0	2	2	0	....	1951-52	1953-54
● Finnigan, Ed	St.L., Bos.	2	15	1	1	2	2	....	....	....	....	....	....	1934-35	1935-36
● Finnigan, Frank	Ott., Tor., St.L.	14	553	115	88	203	407	38	6	9	15	22	2	1923-24	1936-37
Fiorentino, Peter	NYR	1	1	0	0	0	0	....	....	....	....	....	....	1991-92	1991-92
Fischer, Jiri	Det.	6	305	11	49	60	295	38	4	3	7	55	1	1999-00	2005-06
Fischer, Patrick	Phx.	1	27	4	6	10	24	....	....	....	....	....	....	2006-07	2006-07
Fischer, Ron	Buf.	2	18	0	7	7	6	....	....	....	....	....	....	1981-82	1982-83
● Fisher, Alvin	Tor.	1	9	1	0	1	4	....	....	....	....	....	....	1924-25	1924-25
Fisher, Craig	Phi., Wpg., Fla.	4	12	0	0	0	2	....	....	....	....	....	....	1989-90	1996-97
Fisher, Dunc	NYR, Bos., Det.	7	275	45	70	115	104	21	4	4	8	14	....	1947-48	1958-59

Name	NHL Teams	NHL Seasons	Regular Schedule					Playoffs					NHL Cup Wins	First NHL Season	Last NHL Season
			GP	G	A	TP	PIM	GP	G	A	TP	PIM			
• Fisher, Joe	Det.	4	65	8	12	20	13	12	2	1	3	6	1	1939-40	1942-43
Fistric, Mark	Dal., Edm., Ana.	8	325	4	30	34	284	14	0	0	0	12	....	2007-08	2014-15
Fitchner, Bob	Que.	2	78	12	20	32	59	3	0	0	0	10	....	1979-80	1980-81
Fitzgerald, Rusty	Pit.	2	25	2	2	4	12	5	0	0	0	4	....	1994-95	1995-96
Fitzgerald, Tom	NYI, Fla., Col., Nsh., Chi., Tor., Bos.	17	1097	139	190	329	776	78	7	12	19	90	....	1988-89	2005-06
‡ Fitzgerald, Zack	Van.	1	1	0	0	0	0	....	....	....	....	....	....	2007-08	2007-08
Fitzpatrick, Rory	Mtl., St.L., Nsh., Buf., Van., Phi.	10	287	10	25	35	201	20	1	5	6	22	....	1995-96	2007-08
Fitzpatrick, Ross	Phi.	4	20	5	2	7	0	....	....	....	....	....	....	1982-83	1985-86
Fitzpatrick, Sandy	NYR, Min.	2	22	3	6	9	8	12	0	0	0	0	....	1964-65	1967-68
• Flaman, Fern	Bos., Tor.	17	910	34	174	208	1370	63	4	8	12	93	1	1944-45	1960-61
Flatley, Pat	NYI, NYR	14	780	170	340	510	686	70	18	15	33	75	....	1983-84	1996-97
Fleischmann, Tomas	Wsh., Col., Fla., Ana., Mtl., Chi.	11	657	137	198	335	200	39	4	5	9	12	....	2005-06	**2015-16**
Fleming, Gerry	Mtl.	2	11	0	0	0	42	....	....	....	....	....	....	1993-94	1994-95
• Fleming, Reggie	Mtl., Chi., Bos., NYR, Phi., Buf.	12	749	108	132	240	1468	50	3	6	9	106	1	1959-60	1970-71
Flesch, John	Min., Pit., Col.	4	124	18	23	41	117	....	....	....	....	....	....	1974-75	1979-80
Fletcher, Steven	Mtl., Wpg.	2	3	0	0	0	5	1	0	0	0	5	....	1987-88	1988-89
• Flett, Bill	L.A., Phi., Tor., Atl., Edm.	11	689	202	215	417	501	52	7	16	23	42	1	1967-68	1979-80
Fleury, Theoren	Cgy., Col., NYR, Chi.	15	1084	455	633	1088	1840	77	34	45	79	116	1	1988-89	2002-03
Flichel, Todd	Wpg.	3	6	0	1	1	4	....	....	....	....	....	....	1987-88	1989-90
Flinn, Ryan	L.A.	3	31	1	0	1	84	....	....	....	....	....	....	2001-02	2005-06
Flockhart, Rob	Van., Min.	5	55	2	5	7	14	1	1	0	1	2	....	1976-77	1980-81
Flockhart, Ron	Phi., Pit., Mtl., St.L., Bos.	9	453	145	183	328	208	19	4	6	10	14	....	1980-81	1988-89
‡ Flood, Mark	NYI, Wpg.	2	39	3	5	8	10	....	....	....	....	....	....	2009-10	2011-12
Floyd, Larry	N.J.	2	12	2	3	5	9	....	....	....	....	....	....	1982-83	1983-84
Focht, Dan	Phx., Pit.	3	82	2	6	8	145	1	0	1	1	0	....	2001-02	2003-04
• Fogarty, Bryan	Que., Pit., Mtl.	6	156	22	52	74	119	....	....	....	....	....	....	1989-90	1994-95
• Fogolin, Lee	Det., Chi.	9	427	10	48	58	575	28	0	2	2	30	1	1947-48	1955-56
Fogolin, Lee	Buf., Edm.	13	924	44	195	239	1318	108	5	19	24	173	2	1974-75	1986-87
Folco, Peter	Van.	1	2	0	0	0	0	....	....	....	....	....	....	1973-74	1973-74
Foley, Gerry	Tor., NYR, L.A.	4	142	9	14	23	99	9	0	1	1	2	....	1954-55	1968-69
• Foley, Rick	Chi., Phi., Det.	3	67	11	26	37	180	4	0	1	1	4	....	1970-71	1973-74
Foligno, Mike	Det., Buf., Tor., Fla.	15	1018	355	372	727	2049	57	15	17	32	185	....	1979-80	1993-94
• Folk, Bill	Det.	2	12	0	0	0	4	....	....	....	....	....	....	1951-52	1952-53
Fontaine, Len	Det.	2	46	8	11	19	10	....	....	....	....	....	....	1972-73	1973-74
Fontas, Jon	Min.	2	2	0	0	0	0	....	....	....	....	....	....	1979-80	1980-81
Fonteyne, Val	Det., NYR, Pit.	13	820	75	154	229	26	59	3	10	13	8	....	1959-60	1971-72
• Fontinato, Lou	NYR, Mtl.	9	535	26	78	104	1247	21	0	2	2	42	....	1954-55	1962-63
Foote, Adam	Que., Col., CBJ	19	1154	66	242	308	1534	170	7	35	42	298	2	1991-92	2010-11
Forbes, Colin	Phi., T.B., Ott., NYR, Wsh.	9	311	33	28	61	213	13	1	0	1	16	....	1996-97	2005-06
Forbes, Dave	Bos., Wsh.	6	363	64	64	128	341	45	1	4	5	13	....	1973-74	1978-79
Forbes, Mike	Bos., Edm.	3	50	1	11	12	41	....	....	....	....	....	....	1977-78	1981-82
Forey, Connie	St.L.	1	4	0	0	0	2	....	....	....	....	....	....	1973-74	1973-74
Forsberg, Peter	Que., Col., Phi., Nsh.	14	708	249	636	885	690	151	64	107	171	163	2	1994-95	2010-11
• Forsey, Jack	Tor.	1	19	7	9	16	10	3	0	1	1	0	....	1942-43	1942-43
• Forslund, Gus	Ott.	1	48	4	9	13	2	....	....	....	....	....	....	1932-33	1932-33
Forslund, Tomas	Cgy.	2	44	5	11	16	12	....	....	....	....	....	....	1991-92	1992-93
Forsyth, Alex	Wsh.	1	1	0	0	0	0	....	....	....	....	....	....	1976-77	1976-77
Fortier, Dave	Tor., NYI, Van.	4	205	8	21	29	335	20	0	2	2	33	....	1972-73	1976-77
Fortier, Marc	Que., Ott., L.A.	6	212	42	60	102	135	....	....	....	....	....	....	1987-88	1992-93
Fortin, Jean-Francois	Wsh.	3	71	1	4	5	42	....	....	....	....	....	....	2001-02	2003-04
Fortin, Ray	St.L.	3	92	2	6	8	33	6	0	0	0	8	....	1967-68	1969-70
Foster, Alex	Tor.	1	3	0	0	0	0	....	....	....	....	....	....	2007-08	2007-08
Foster, Corey	N.J., Phi., Pit., NYI	4	45	5	6	11	24	3	0	0	0	4	....	1988-89	1996-97
Foster, Dwight	Bos., Col., N.J., Det.	10	541	111	163	274	420	35	5	12	17	4	....	1977-78	1986-87
• Foster, Herb	NYR	2	6	1	0	1	5	....	....	....	....	....	....	1940-41	1947-48
Foster, Kurtis	Atl., Min., T.B., Edm., Ana., N.J., Phi.	10	405	42	118	160	308	3	0	2	2	0	....	2002-03	2012-13
• Foster, Yip	NYR, Bos., Det.	4	83	3	2	5	32	....	....	....	....	....	....	1929-30	1934-35
Fotiu, Nick	NYR, Hfd., Cgy., Phi., Edm.	13	646	60	77	137	1362	38	0	4	4	67	....	1976-77	1988-89
‡ Foucault, Kris	Min.	1	1	0	0	0	0	....	....	....	....	....	....	2011-12	2011-12
• Fowler, Jimmy	Tor.	3	135	18	29	47	39	18	0	3	3	2	....	1936-37	1938-39
• Fowler, Tom	Chi.	1	24	0	1	1	18	....	....	....	....	....	....	1946-47	1946-47
Fox, Greg	Atl., Chi., Pit.	8	494	14	92	106	637	44	1	9	10	67	....	1977-78	1984-85
Fox, Jim	L.A.	9	578	186	293	479	143	22	4	8	12	0	....	1980-81	1989-90
Foy, Matt	Min.	3	56	6	7	13	48	1	0	0	0	0	....	2005-06	2007-08
• Foyston, Frank	Det.	2	64	17	7	24	32	....	....	....	....	....	....	1926-27	1927-28
• Frampton, Bob	Mtl.	1	2	0	0	0	0	3	0	0	0	0	....	1949-50	1949-50
Franceschetti, Lou	Wsh., Tor., Buf.	10	459	59	81	140	747	44	3	2	5	111	....	1981-82	1991-92
Francis, Bobby	Det.	1	14	2	0	2	0	....	....	....	....	....	....	1982-83	1982-83
Francis, Ron	Hfd., Pit., Car., Tor.	23	1731	549	1249	1798	979	171	46	97	143	95	2	1981-82	2003-04
• Fraser, Archie	NYR	1	3	0	1	1	0	....	....	....	....	....	....	1943-44	1943-44
• Fraser, Charles	Ham.	1	1	0	0	0	0	....	....	....	....	....	....	1923-24	1923-24
Fraser, Colin	Chi., Edm., L.A., St.L.	9	359	20	38	58	290	39	1	3	4	16	2	2006-07	2014-15
Fraser, Curt	Van., Chi., Min.	12	704	193	240	433	1306	65	15	18	33	198	....	1978-79	1989-90
• Fraser, Gord	Chi., Det., Mtl., Pit., Phi.	5	144	24	12	36	224	2	1	0	1	6	....	1926-27	1930-31
• Fraser, Harvey	Chi.	1	21	5	4	9	0	....	....	....	....	....	....	1944-45	1944-45
Fraser, Iain	NYI, Que., Dal., Edm., Wpg., S.J.	5	94	23	23	46	31	4	0	0	0	0	....	1992-93	1996-97
Fraser, Jamie	NYI	1	1	0	0	0	0	....	....	....	....	....	....	2008-09	2008-09
‡ Fraser, Matt	Dal., Bos., Edm.	4	87	11	6	17	27	4	1	1	2	0	....	2011-12	2014-15
Fraser, Scott	Mtl., Edm., NYR	3	72	16	15	31	24	11	1	1	2	0	....	1995-96	1998-99
Frawley, Dan	Chi., Pit.	6	273	37	40	77	674	1	0	0	0	0	....	1983-84	1988-89
Freadrich, Kyle	T.B.	2	23	0	1	1	75	....	....	....	....	....	....	1999-00	2000-01
Fredheim, Kris	Min.	1	3	0	0	0	2	....	....	....	....	....	....	2011-12	2011-12
• Fredrickson, Frank	Det., Bos., Pit.	5	161	39	34	73	206	10	2	3	5	24	....	1926-27	1930-31
Freer, Mark	Phi., Ott., Cgy.	7	124	16	23	39	61	....	....	....	....	....	....	1986-87	1993-94
• Frew, Irv	Mtl.M., St.L., Mtl.	3	96	2	5	7	146	4	0	0	0	6	....	1933-34	1935-36
Friday, Tim	Det.	1	23	0	3	3	6	....	....	....	....	....	....	1985-86	1985-86
Fridgen, Dan	Hfd.	2	13	2	3	5	2	....	....	....	....	....	....	1981-82	1982-83
Friedman, Doug	Edm., Nsh.	2	18	0	1	1	34	....	....	....	....	....	....	1997-98	1998-99
Friesen, Jeff	S.J., Ana., N.J., Wsh., Cgy.	12	893	218	298	516	488	84	18	15	33	48	1	1994-95	2006-07
Friest, Ron	Min.	3	64	7	7	14	191	6	1	0	1	7	....	1980-81	1982-83
Frig, Len	Chi., Cal., Cle., St.L.	7	311	13	51	64	479	14	2	1	3	0	....	1972-73	1979-80
Frischmon, Trevor	CBJ	1	3	0	0	0	4	....	....	....	....	....	....	2009-10	2009-10
Fritsch, Jamie	Phi.	1	1	0	0	0	0	....	....	....	....	....	....	2008-09	2008-09
Fritsche, Dan	CBJ, NYR, Min.	5	256	34	42	76	103	....	....	....	....	....	....	2003-04	2008-09
Fritz, Mitch	NYI	1	20	0	0	0	42	....	....	....	....	....	....	2008-09	2008-09
Frogren, Jonas	Tor.	1	41	1	6	7	28	....	....	....	....	....	....	2008-09	2008-09
Frolov, Alex	L.A., NYR	8	579	175	222	397	218	6	1	3	4	0	....	2002-03	2010-11
• Frost, Harry	Bos.	1	4	0	0	0	0	1	0	0	0	0	1	1938-39	1938-39
Frycer, Miroslav	Que., Tor., Det., Edm.	8	415	147	183	330	486	17	3	8	11	16	....	1981-82	1988-89
• Fryday, Bob	Mtl.	2	5	1	0	1	0	....	....	....	....	....	....	1949-50	1951-52
Ftorek, Robbie	Det., Que., NYR	8	334	77	150	227	262	19	9	6	15	28	....	1972-73	1984-85
Fullan, Larry	Wsh.	1	4	1	0	1	0	....	....	....	....	....	....	1974-75	1974-75
Funk, Michael	Buf.	2	9	0	2	2	0	....	....	....	....	....	....	2006-07	2007-08
Fusco, Mark	Hfd.	2	80	3	12	15	42	....	....	....	....	....	....	1983-84	1984-85
Fussey, Owen	Wsh.	1	4	0	1	1	0	....	....	....	....	....	....	2003-04	2003-04

G

• Gadsby, Bill	Chi., NYR, Det.	20	1248	130	438	568	1539	67	4	23	27	92	....	1946-47	1965-66
Gaetz, Link	Min., S.J.	3	65	6	8	14	412	....	....	....	....	....	....	1988-89	1991-92
Gage, Jody	Det., Buf.	6	68	14	15	29	26	....	....	....	....	....	....	1980-81	1991-92
• Gagne, Art	Mtl., Bos., Ott., Det.	6	228	67	33	100	257	11	2	1	3	20	....	1926-27	1931-32
Gagne, Paul	Col., N.J., Tor., NYI	8	390	110	101	211	127	....	....	....	....	....	....	1980-81	1989-90
Gagne, Pierre	Bos.	1	2	0	0	0	0	....	....	....	....	....	....	1959-60	1959-60
Gagne, Simon	Phi., T.B., L.A., Bos.	14	822	291	310	601	328	109	37	22	59	32	1	1999-00	2014-15
Gagner, Dave	NYR, Min., Dal., Tor., Cgy., Fla., Van.	15	946	318	401	719	1018	57	22	26	48	64	....	1984-85	1998-99
‡ Gagnon, Aaron	Dal., Wpg.	4	38	3	2	5	2	....	....	....	....	....	....	2009-10	2012-13
• Gagnon, Germain	Mtl., NYI, Chi., K.C.	5	259	40	101	141	72	19	2	3	5	2	....	1971-72	1975-76
• Gagnon, Johnny	Mtl., Bos., NYA	10	454	120	141	261	295	32	12	12	24	37	1	1930-31	1939-40
Gagnon, Sean	Phx., Ott.	3	12	0	1	1	34	....	....	....	....	....	....	1997-98	2000-01
Gainey, Bob	Mtl.	16	1160	239	262	501	585	182	25	48	73	151	5	1973-74	1988-89
Gainey, Steve	Dal., Phx.	4	33	0	2	2	34	....	....	....	....	....	....	2000-01	2005-06

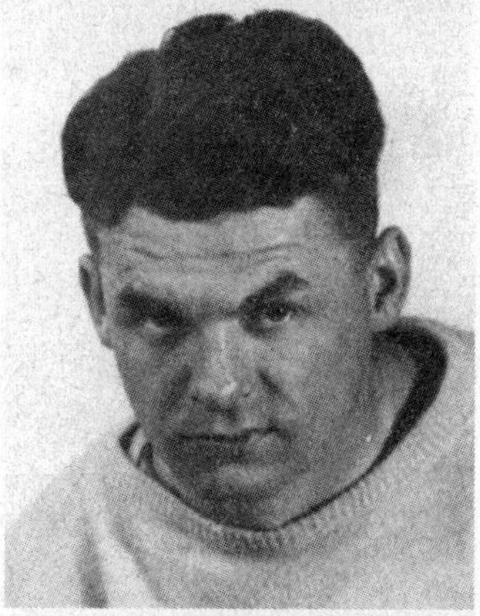
Frank Finnigan

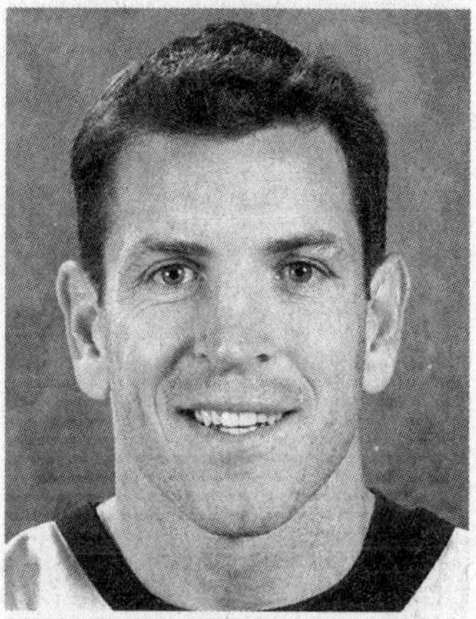
Tom Fitzgerald

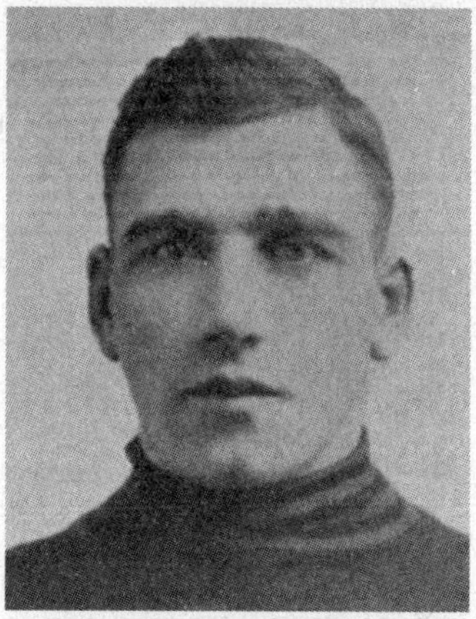
Charles Fraser

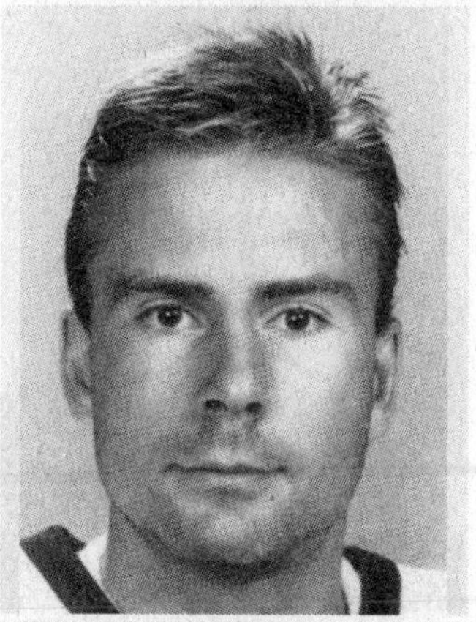
Mark Freer

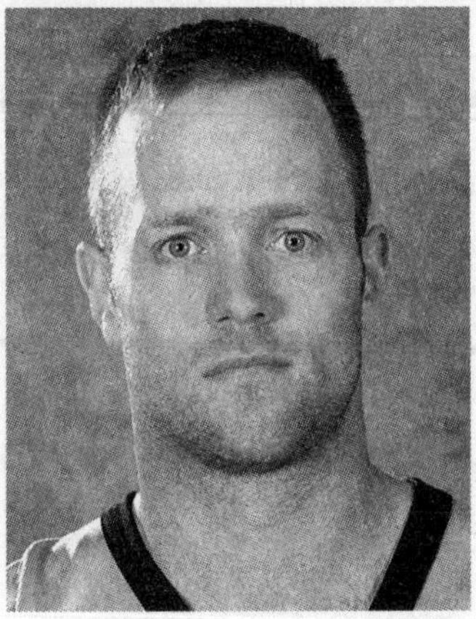

Doug Friedman

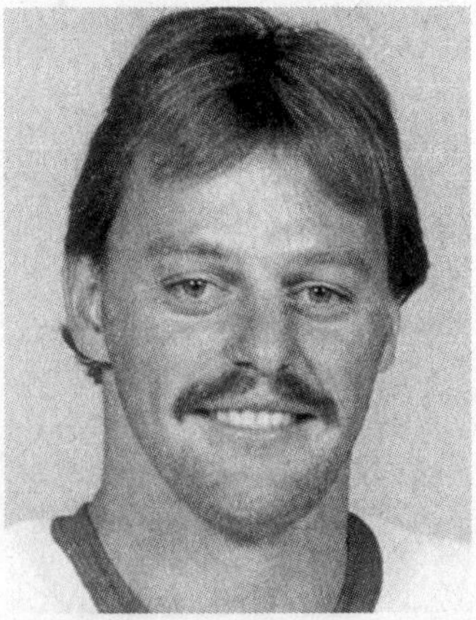

Gerard Gallant

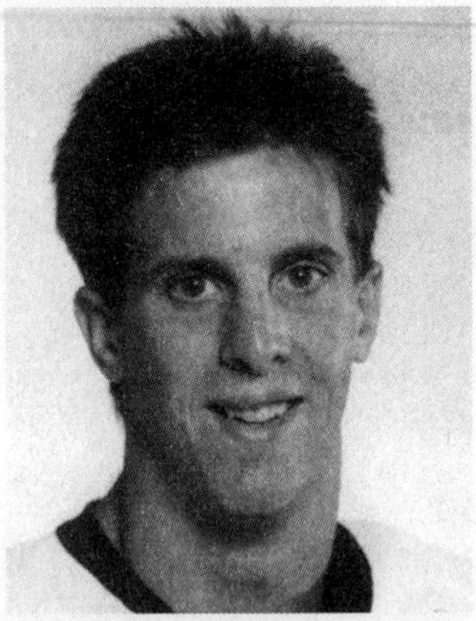

Lee Giffin

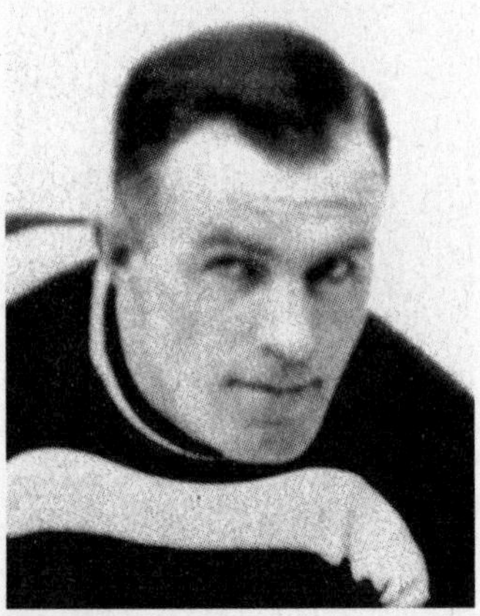

Ed Gorman

Name	NHL Teams	NHL Seasons	Regular Schedule					Playoffs					NHL Cup Wins	First NHL Season	Last NHL Season
			GP	G	A	TP	PIM	GP	G	A	TP	PIM			
• Gainor, Dutch	Bos., NYR, Ott., Mtl.M.	7	246	51	56	107	129	22	2	1	3	14	2	1927-28	1934-35
Galanov, Maxim	NYR, Pit., Atl., T.B.	4	122	8	12	20	44	1	0	0	0	0	....	1997-98	2000-01
Galarneau, Michel	Hfd.	3	78	7	10	17	34	....	....	....	....	....	....	1980-81	1982-83
• Galbraith, Percy	Bos., Ott.	8	347	29	31	60	224	31	4	7	11	24	1	1926-27	1933-34
‡ Galiardi, TJ	Col., S.J., Cgy., Wpg.	7	321	44	61	105	136	20	1	3	4	18	....	2008-09	2014-15
• Gallagher, John	Mtl.M., Det., NYA	7	205	14	19	33	153	24	2	3	5	27	1	1930-31	1938-39
Gallant, Gerard	Det., T.B.	11	615	211	269	480	1674	58	18	21	39	178	....	1984-85	1994-95
Galley, Garry	L.A., Wsh., Bos., Phi., Buf., NYI	17	1149	125	475	600	1218	89	7	23	30	119	....	1984-85	2000-01
Gallimore, Jamie	Min.	1	2	0	0	0	0	....	....	....	....	....	....	1977-78	1977-78
• Gallinger, Don	Bos.	5	222	65	88	153	89	23	5	5	10	19	....	1942-43	1947-48
Gamache, Simon	Atl., Nsh., St.L., Tor.	4	48	6	7	13	18	....	....	....	....	....	....	2002-03	2007-08
Gamble, Dick	Mtl., Chi., Tor.	8	195	41	41	82	66	14	1	2	3	4	1	1950-51	1966-67
Gambucci, Gary	Min.	2	51	2	7	9	9	....	....	....	....	....	....	1971-72	1973-74
Ganchar, Perry	St.L., Mtl., Pit.	4	42	3	7	10	36	7	3	1	4	0	....	1983-84	1988-89
Gans, Dave	L.A.	2	6	0	0	0	2	....	....	....	....	....	....	1982-83	1985-86
Gardiner, Bruce	Ott., T.B., CBJ, N.J.	6	312	34	54	88	263	21	1	4	5	8	....	1996-97	2001-02
• Gardiner, Herb	Mtl., Chi.	3	108	10	9	19	52	9	0	1	1	16	....	1926-27	1928-29
Gardner, Bill	Chi., Hfd.	9	380	73	115	188	68	45	3	8	11	17	....	1980-81	1988-89
• Gardner, Cal	NYR, Tor., Chi., Bos.	12	696	154	238	392	517	61	7	10	17	20	2	1945-46	1956-57
Gardner, Dave	Mtl., St.L., Cal., Cle., Phi.	7	350	75	115	190	41	....	....	....	....	....	....	1972-73	1979-80
Gardner, Paul	Col., Tor., Pit., Wsh., Buf.	10	447	201	201	402	207	16	2	6	8	14	....	1976-77	1985-86
Gare, Danny	Buf., Det., Edm.	13	827	354	331	685	1285	64	25	21	46	195	....	1974-75	1986-87
• Gariepy, Ray	Bos., Tor.	2	36	1	6	7	43	....	....	....	....	....	....	1953-54	1955-56
• Garland, Scott	Tor., L.A.	3	91	13	24	37	115	7	1	2	3	35	....	1975-76	1978-79
Garner, Rob	Pit.	1	1	0	0	0	0	....	....	....	....	....	....	1982-83	1982-83
Garpenlov, Johan	Det., S.J., Fla., Atl.	10	609	114	197	311	276	44	10	9	19	22	....	1990-91	1999-00
• Garrett, Red	NYR	1	23	1	1	2	18	....	....	....	....	....	....	1942-43	1942-43
Gartner, Mike	Wsh., Min., NYR, Tor., Phx.	19	1432	708	627	1335	1159	122	43	50	93	125	....	1979-80	1997-98
• Gassoff, Bob	St.L.	4	245	11	47	58	866	9	0	1	1	16	....	1973-74	1976-77
Gassoff, Brad	Van.	4	122	19	17	36	163	3	0	0	0	0	....	1975-76	1978-79
Gatzos, Steve	Pit.	4	89	15	20	35	83	1	0	0	0	0	....	1981-82	1984-85
Gaudreau, Rob	S.J., Ott.	4	231	51	54	105	69	14	2	0	2	0	....	1992-93	1995-96
• Gaudreault, Armand	Bos.	1	44	15	9	24	27	7	0	2	2	8	....	1944-45	1944-45
• Gaudreault, Leo	Mtl.	3	67	8	4	12	30	....	....	....	....	....	....	1927-28	1932-33
Gaul, Mike	Col., CBJ	2	3	0	0	0	4	....	....	....	....	....	....	1998-99	2000-01
Gaulin, Jean-Marc	Que.	4	26	4	3	7	8	1	0	0	0	0	....	1982-83	1985-86
Gaume, Dallas	Hfd.	1	4	1	1	2	0	....	....	....	....	....	....	1988-89	1988-89
Gaustad, Paul	Buf., Nsh.	12	727	89	142	231	778	68	2	9	11	64	....	2002-03	**2015-16**
• Gauthier, Art	Mtl.	1	13	0	0	0	0	1	0	0	0	0	....	1926-27	1926-27
Gauthier, Daniel	Chi.	1	5	0	0	0	0	....	....	....	....	....	....	1994-95	1994-95
Gauthier, Denis	Cgy., Phx., Phi., L.A.	10	554	17	60	77	748	12	0	2	2	23	....	1997-98	2008-09
• Gauthier, Fern	NYR, Mtl., Det.	6	229	46	50	96	35	22	5	1	6	7	....	1943-44	1948-49
Gauthier, Gabe	L.A.	2	8	0	0	0	2	....	....	....	....	....	....	2006-07	2007-08
Gauthier, Jean	Mtl., Phi., Bos.	10	166	6	29	35	150	14	1	3	4	22	1	1960-61	1969-70
Gauthier, Luc	Mtl.	1	3	0	0	0	2	....	....	....	....	....	....	1990-91	1990-91
Gauvreau, Jocelyn	Mtl.	1	2	0	0	0	0	....	....	....	....	....	....	1983-84	1983-84
Gavey, Aaron	T.B., Cgy., Dal., Min., Tor., Ana.	9	360	41	50	91	272	19	1	2	3	14	....	1995-96	2005-06
Gavin, Stew	Tor., Hfd., Min.	13	768	130	155	285	584	66	14	20	34	75	....	1980-81	1992-93
Geale, Bob	Pit.	1	1	0	0	0	2	....	....	....	....	....	....	1984-85	1984-85
• Gee, George	Chi., Det.	9	551	135	183	318	345	41	6	13	19	32	1	1945-46	1953-54
Geldart, Gary	Min.	1	4	0	0	0	5	....	....	....	....	....	....	1970-71	1970-71
Gelinas, Martin	Edm., Que., Van., Car., Cgy., Fla., Nsh.	19	1273	309	351	660	820	147	23	33	56	120	1	1988-89	2007-08
Gendron, Jean-Guy	NYR, Bos., Mtl., Phi.	14	863	182	201	383	701	42	7	4	11	47	....	1955-56	1971-72
Gendron, Martin	Wsh., Chi.	3	30	4	2	6	10	....	....	....	....	....	....	1994-95	1997-98
‡ Genoway, Chay	Min.	1	1	0	1	1	0	....	....	....	....	....	....	2011-12	2011-12
• Geoffrion, Bernie	Mtl., NYR	16	883	393	429	822	689	132	58	60	118	88	6	1950-51	1967-68
Geoffrion, Blake	Nsh., Mtl.	2	55	8	5	13	34	12	0	2	2	4	....	2010-11	2011-12
Geoffrion, Danny	Mtl., Wpg.	3	111	20	32	52	99	2	0	0	0	7	....	1979-80	1981-82
• Geran, Gerry	Mtl.W., Bos.	2	37	5	1	6	6	....	....	....	....	....	....	1917-18	1925-26
• Gerard, Eddie	Ott.	6	128	50	48	98	108	11	4	0	4	17	3	1917-18	1922-23
Germain, Eric	L.A.	1	4	0	1	1	13	1	0	0	0	4	....	1987-88	1987-88
Germyn, Carsen	Cgy.	2	4	0	0	0	0	....	....	....	....	....	....	2005-06	2006-07
Gernander, Ken	NYR	3	12	2	3	5	6	15	0	0	0	0	....	1995-96	2003-04
‡ Gervais, Bruno	NYI, T.B., Phi.	8	418	16	71	87	182	5	1	1	2	2	....	2005-06	2012-13
• Getliffe, Ray	Bos., Mtl.	10	393	136	137	273	250	45	9	10	19	30	2	1935-36	1944-45
Giallonardo, Mario	Col.	2	23	0	3	3	6	....	....	....	....	....	....	1979-80	1980-81
Gibbs, Barry	Bos., Min., Atl., St.L., L.A.	13	797	58	224	282	945	36	4	2	6	67	....	1967-68	1979-80
Gibson, Don	Van.	1	14	0	3	3	20	....	....	....	....	....	....	1990-91	1990-91
Gibson, Doug	Bos., Wsh.	3	63	9	19	28	0	1	0	0	0	0	....	1973-74	1977-78
Gibson, John	L.A., Tor., Wpg.	3	48	0	2	2	120	....	....	....	....	....	....	1980-81	1983-84
• Giesebrecht, Gus	Det.	4	135	27	51	78	13	17	2	3	5	0	....	1938-39	1941-42
Giffin, Lee	Pit.	2	27	1	3	4	9	....	....	....	....	....	....	1986-87	1987-88
Gilbert, Ed	K.C., Pit.	3	166	21	31	52	22	....	....	....	....	....	....	1974-75	1976-77
Gilbert, Greg	NYI, Chi., NYR, St.L.	15	837	150	228	378	576	133	17	33	50	162	3	1981-82	1995-96
Gilbert, Jeannot	Bos.	2	9	0	1	1	4	....	....	....	....	....	....	1962-63	1964-65
Gilbert, Rod	NYR	18	1065	406	615	1021	508	79	34	33	67	43	....	1960-61	1977-78
Gilbertson, Stan	Cal., St.L., Wsh., Pit.	6	428	85	89	174	148	3	1	1	2	2	....	1971-72	1976-77
Gilchrist, Brent	Mtl., Edm., Min., Dal., Det., Nsh.	15	792	135	170	305	400	90	17	14	31	48	1	1988-89	2002-03
Giles, Curt	Min., NYR, St.L.	14	895	43	199	242	733	103	6	16	22	118	....	1979-80	1992-93
Gilhen, Randy	Hfd., Wpg., Pit., L.A., NYR, T.B., Fla.	11	457	55	60	115	314	33	3	2	5	26	1	1982-83	1995-96
Gill, Hal	Bos., Tor., Pit., Mtl., Nsh., Phi.	16	1108	36	148	184	962	111	0	6	6	68	1	1997-98	2013-14
Gill, Todd	Tor., S.J., St.L., Det., Phx., Col., Chi.	19	1007	82	272	354	1214	103	7	30	37	193	....	1984-85	2002-03
Gillen, Don	Phi., Hfd.	2	35	2	4	6	22	....	....	....	....	....	....	1979-80	1981-82
• Gillie, Farrand	Det.	1	1	0	0	0	0	....	....	....	....	....	....	1928-29	1928-29
Gillies, Clark	NYI, Buf.	14	958	319	378	697	1023	164	47	47	94	287	4	1974-75	1987-88
‡ Gillies, Colton	Min., CBJ	4	154	6	12	18	72	....	....	....	....	....	....	2008-09	2012-13
‡ Gillies, Trevor	Ana., NYI	4	57	2	1	3	261	....	....	....	....	....	....	2005-06	2011-12
Gillis, Jere	Van., NYR, Que., Buf., Phi.	9	386	78	95	173	230	19	4	7	11	9	....	1977-78	1986-87
Gillis, Mike	Col., Bos.	6	246	33	43	76	186	27	2	5	7	10	....	1978-79	1983-84
Gillis, Paul	Que., Chi., Hfd.	11	624	88	154	242	1498	42	3	14	17	156	....	1982-83	1992-93
Gilmour, Doug	St.L., Cgy., Tor., N.J., Chi., Buf., Mtl.	20	1474	450	964	1414	1301	182	60	128	188	235	1	1983-84	2002-03
‡ Gilroy, Matt	NYR, T.B., Ott., Fla.	5	225	11	37	48	67	8	1	0	1	2	....	2009-10	2013-14
Gingras, Gaston	Mtl., Tor., St.L.	10	476	61	174	235	161	52	6	18	24	20	1	1979-80	1988-89
Girard, Bob	Cal., Cle., Wsh.	5	305	45	69	114	140	....	....	....	....	....	....	1975-76	1979-80
Girard, Jonathan	Bos.	5	150	10	34	44	46	3	0	1	1	2	....	1998-99	2002-03
Girard, Kenny	Tor.	3	7	0	1	1	2	....	....	....	....	....	....	1956-57	1959-60
‡ Giroux, Alexandre	NYR, Wsh., Edm., CBJ	6	48	6	6	12	26	....	....	....	....	....	....	2005-06	2011-12
• Giroux, Art	Mtl., Bos., Det.	3	54	6	4	10	14	2	0	0	0	0	....	1932-33	1935-36
Giroux, Larry	St.L., K.C., Det., Hfd.	7	274	15	74	89	333	5	0	0	0	4	....	1973-74	1979-80
Giroux, Pierre	L.A.	1	6	1	0	1	17	....	....	....	....	....	....	1982-83	1982-83
Giroux, Raymond	NYI, N.J.	4	38	0	13	13	22	4	0	0	0	0	....	1999-00	2003-04
Giuliano, Jeff	L.A.	2	101	3	10	13	40	....	....	....	....	....	....	2005-06	2007-08
Gladney, Bob	L.A., Pit.	2	14	1	5	6	4	....	....	....	....	....	....	1982-83	1983-84
• Gladu, Jean-Paul	Bos.	1	40	6	14	20	2	7	2	2	4	0	....	1944-45	1944-45
Gleason, Tim	L.A., Car., Tor., Wsh.	11	727	17	125	142	701	32	1	5	6	37	....	2003-04	2014-15
Glencross, Curtis	Ana., CBJ, Edm., Cgy., Wsh.	9	507	134	141	275	351	16	1	3	4	14	....	2006-07	2014-15
Glennie, Brian	Tor., L.A.	10	572	14	100	114	621	32	0	1	1	66	....	1969-70	1978-79
Glennie, Scott	Dal.	1	1	0	0	0	2	....	....	....	....	....	....	2011-12	2011-12
Glennon, Matt	Bos.	1	3	0	0	0	2	....	....	....	....	....	....	1991-92	1991-92
Globke, Rob	Fla.	3	46	1	1	2	8	....	....	....	....	....	....	2005-06	2007-08
Gloeckner, Lorry	Det.	1	13	0	2	2	6	....	....	....	....	....	....	1978-79	1978-79
Gloor, Dan	Van.	1	2	0	0	0	0	....	....	....	....	....	....	1973-74	1973-74
• Glover, Fred	Det., Chi.	5	92	13	11	24	62	8	0	0	0	0	1	1948-49	1952-53
Glover, Howie	Chi., Det., NYR, Mtl.	5	144	29	17	46	101	11	1	2	3	2	....	1958-59	1968-69
Glumac, Mike	St.L.	3	40	7	6	13	38	....	....	....	....	....	....	2005-06	2007-08
Glynn, Brian	Cgy., Min., Edm., Ott., Van., Hfd.	10	431	25	79	104	410	57	6	10	16	40	....	1987-88	1996-97
‡ Goc, Marcel	S.J., Nsh., Fla., Pit., St.L.	11	636	75	113	188	157	63	5	10	15	14	....	2003-04	2014-15
‡ Goc, Sascha	N.J., T.B.	2	22	0	0	0	4	....	....	....	....	....	....	2000-01	2001-02
Godard, Eric	NYI, Cgy., Pit.	8	335	6	12	18	833	7	0	1	1	6	1	2002-03	2010-11
Godden, Ernie	Tor.	1	5	1	1	2	6	....	....	....	....	....	....	1981-82	1981-82
• Godfrey, Warren	Bos., Det.	16	786	32	125	157	752	52	1	4	5	42	....	1952-53	1967-68
Godin, Eddy	Wsh.	2	27	3	6	9	12	....	....	....	....	....	....	1977-78	1978-79

Name	NHL Teams	NHL Seasons	Regular Schedule GP	G	A	TP	PIM	Playoffs GP	G	A	TP	PIM	NHL Cup Wins	First NHL Season	Last NHL Season
● Godin, Sam	Ott., Mtl.	3	83	4	3	7	36	....	....	....	....	....	....	1927-28	1933-34
Godynyuk, Alexander	Tor., Cgy., Fla., Hfd.	7	223	10	39	49	224	....	....	....	....	....	....	1990-91	1996-97
● Goegan, Pete	Det., NYR, Min.	11	383	19	67	86	365	33	1	3	4	61	....	1957-58	1967-68
Goertz, Dave	Pit.	1	2	0	0	0	2	....	....	....	....	....	....	1987-88	1987-88
Goertzen, Steven	CBJ, Phx., Car.	4	68	2	2	4	83	....	....	....	....	....	....	2005-06	2009-10
● Goldham, Bob	Tor., Chi., Det.	12	650	28	143	171	400	66	3	14	17	53	5	1941-42	1955-56
Goldmann, Erich	Ott.	1	1	0	0	0	0	....	....	....	....	....	....	1999-00	1999-00
● Goldsworthy, Bill	Bos., Min., NYR	14	771	283	258	541	793	40	18	19	37	30	....	1964-65	1977-78
● Goldsworthy, Leroy	NYR, Det., Chi., Mtl., Bos., NYA	10	336	66	57	123	79	24	1	0	1	4	1	1928-29	1938-39
Goldup, Glenn	Mtl., L.A.	9	291	52	67	119	303	16	4	3	7	22	....	1973-74	1981-82
● Goldup, Hank	Tor., NYR	6	202	63	80	143	97	26	5	1	6	6	1	1939-40	1945-46
Golubovsky, Yan	Det., Fla.	4	56	1	7	8	32	....	....	....	....	....	....	1997-98	2000-01
Gomez, Scott	N.J., NYR, Mtl., S.J., Fla., St.L., Ott.	16	1079	181	575	756	655	149	29	72	101	95	2	1999-00	**2015-16**
Gonchar, Sergei	Wsh., Bos., Pit., Ott., Dal., Mtl.	20	1301	220	591	811	981	141	22	68	90	102	1	1994-95	2014-15
Goneau, Daniel	NYR	3	53	12	3	15	14	....	....	....	....	....	....	1996-97	1999-00
● Gooden, Bill	NYR	2	53	9	11	20	15	....	....	....	....	....	....	1942-43	1943-44
Goodenough, Larry	Phi., Van.	6	242	22	77	99	179	22	3	15	18	10	1	1974-75	1979-80
● Goodfellow, Ebbie	Det.	14	557	134	190	324	511	45	8	8	16	65	3	1929-30	1942-43
Gordiouk, Viktor	Buf.	2	26	3	8	11	0	....	....	....	....	....	....	1992-93	1994-95
‡ Gordon, Andrew	Wsh., Ana., Van.	5	55	3	4	7	6	....	....	....	....	....	....	2008-09	2012-13
● Gordon, Fred	Det., Bos.	2	81	8	7	15	68	2	0	0	0	0	....	1926-27	1927-28
Gordon, Jack	NYR	3	36	3	10	13	0	9	1	1	2	7	....	1948-49	1950-51
Gordon, Robb	Van.	1	4	0	0	0	2	....	....	....	....	....	....	1998-99	1998-99
Goren, Lee	Bos., Fla., Van.	5	67	5	4	9	44	5	0	0	0	5	....	2000-01	2006-07
Gorence, Tom	Phi., Edm.	6	303	58	53	111	89	37	9	6	15	47	....	1978-79	1983-84
Goring, Butch	L.A., NYI, Bos.	16	1107	375	513	888	102	134	38	50	88	32	4	1969-70	1984-85
Gorman, Dave	Atl.	1	3	0	0	0	0	....	....	....	....	....	....	1979-80	1979-80
● Gorman, Ed	Ott., Tor.	4	111	14	6	20	108	8	0	0	0	2	1	1924-25	1927-28
Gosselin, Benoit	NYR	1	7	0	0	0	33	....	....	....	....	....	....	1977-78	1977-78
Gosselin, David	Nsh.	2	13	2	1	3	11	....	....	....	....	....	....	1999-00	2001-02
Gosselin, Guy	Wpg.	1	5	0	0	0	6	....	....	....	....	....	....	1987-88	1987-88
Gotaas, Steve	Pit., Min.	3	49	6	9	15	53	3	0	1	1	5	....	1987-88	1990-91
● Gottselig, Johnny	Chi.	16	589	176	195	371	203	43	13	13	26	18	2	1928-29	1944-45
Gould, Bobby	Atl., Cgy., Wsh., Bos.	11	697	145	159	304	572	78	15	13	28	58	....	1979-80	1989-90
Gould, John	Buf., Van., Atl.	9	504	131	138	269	113	14	3	2	5	4	....	1971-72	1979-80
Gould, Larry	Van.	1	2	0	0	0	0	....	....	....	....	....	....	1973-74	1973-74
Goulet, Michel	Que., Chi.	15	1089	548	604	1152	825	92	39	39	78	110	....	1979-80	1993-94
● Goupille, Red	Mtl.	8	222	12	28	40	256	8	2	0	2	6	....	1935-36	1942-43
● Gove, David	Car.	2	2	0	1	1	0	....	....	....	....	....	....	2005-06	2006-07
Govedaris, Chris	Hfd., Tor.	4	45	4	6	10	24	4	0	0	0	2	....	1989-90	1993-94
Goyer, Gerry	Chi.	1	40	1	2	3	4	3	0	0	0	2	....	1967-68	1967-68
Goyette, Phil	Mtl., NYR, St.L., Buf.	16	941	207	467	674	131	94	17	29	46	26	4	1956-57	1971-72
● Graboski, Tony	Mtl.	3	66	6	10	16	24	3	0	0	0	6	....	1940-41	1942-43
‡ Grachev, Evgeny	NYR, St.L.	2	34	1	3	4	2	....	....	....	....	....	....	2010-11	2011-12
● Gracie, Bob	Tor., Bos., NYA, Mtl.M., Mtl., Chi.	9	379	82	109	191	205	33	4	7	11	4	2	1930-31	1938-39
Gradin, Thomas	Van., Bos.	9	677	209	384	593	298	42	17	25	42	20	....	1978-79	1986-87
Graham, Dirk	Min., Chi.	12	772	219	270	489	917	90	17	27	44	92	....	1983-84	1994-95
● Graham, Leth	Ott., Ham.	6	27	3	0	3	0	1	0	0	0	0	1	1920-21	1925-26
Graham, Pat	Pit., Tor.	3	103	11	17	28	136	4	0	0	0	2	....	1981-82	1983-84
Graham, Rod	Bos.	1	14	2	1	3	7	....	....	....	....	....	....	1974-75	1974-75
● Graham, Ted	Chi., Mtl.M., Det., St.L., Bos., NYA	9	346	14	25	39	300	24	3	1	4	30	....	1927-28	1936-37
Granato, Tony	NYR, L.A., S.J.	13	773	248	244	492	1425	79	16	27	43	141	....	1988-89	2000-01
Grand-Pierre, Jean-Luc	Buf., CBJ, Atl., Wsh.	6	269	7	13	20	311	4	0	0	0	4	....	1998-99	2003-04
Grant, Danny	Mtl., Min., Det., L.A.	13	736	263	273	536	239	43	10	14	24	19	1	1965-66	1978-79
Grant, Triston	Phi., Nsh.	2	11	0	1	1	19	....	....	....	....	....	....	2006-07	2009-10
Gratton, Benoit	Wsh., Cgy., Mtl.	6	58	6	10	16	58	....	....	....	....	....	....	1997-98	2003-04
Gratton, Chris	T.B., Phi., Buf., Phx., Col., Fla., CBJ	15	1092	214	354	568	1638	40	8	7	15	82	....	1993-94	2008-09
Gratton, Dan	L.A.	1	7	1	0	1	5	....	....	....	....	....	....	1987-88	1987-88
Gratton, Josh	Phi., Phx.	4	86	3	3	6	294	....	....	....	....	....	....	2005-06	2008-09
Gratton, Norm	NYR, Atl., Buf., Min.	5	201	39	44	83	64	6	0	1	1	2	....	1971-72	1975-76
● Gravelle, Leo	Mtl., Det.	5	223	44	34	78	42	17	4	1	5	2	....	1946-47	1950-51
Graves, Adam	Det., Edm., NYR, S.J.	16	1152	329	287	616	1224	125	38	27	65	119	2	1987-88	2002-03
Graves, Hilliard	Cal., Atl., Van., Wpg.	9	556	118	163	281	209	2	0	0	0	0	....	1970-71	1979-80
Graves, Steve	Edm.	3	35	5	4	9	10	....	....	....	....	....	....	1983-84	1987-88
● Gray, Alex	NYR, Tor.	2	50	7	0	7	32	13	1	0	1	0	1	1927-28	1928-29
Gray, Terry	Bos., Mtl., L.A., St.L.	6	147	26	28	54	64	35	5	5	10	22	....	1961-62	1970-71
Grebeshkov, Denis	L.A., NYI, Edm., Nsh.	6	234	17	68	85	114	2	0	2	2	0	....	2003-04	2013-14
‡ Green, Josh	L.A., NYI, Edm., NYR, Wsh., Cgy., Van., Ana.	11	341	36	40	76	206	17	0	1	1	12	....	1998-99	2011-12
Green, Mike	Fla., NYR	1	24	1	3	4	4	....	....	....	....	....	....	2003-04	2003-04
● Green, Red	Ham., NYA, Bos., Det.	6	195	59	26	85	290	1	0	0	0	0	1	1923-24	1928-29
Green, Rick	Wsh., Mtl., Det., NYI	15	845	43	220	263	588	100	3	16	19	73	1	1976-77	1991-92
● Green, Shorty	Ham., NYA	4	103	33	20	53	151	....	....	....	....	....	....	1923-24	1926-27
Green, Ted	Bos.	11	620	48	206	254	1029	31	4	8	12	54	1	1960-61	1971-72
Green, Travis	NYI, Ana., Phx., Tor., Bos.	14	970	193	262	455	764	56	10	11	21	60	....	1992-93	2006-07
Greenlaw, Jeff	Wsh., Fla.	6	57	3	6	9	108	2	0	0	0	21	....	1986-87	1993-94
Greentree, Kyle	Phi., Cgy.	2	4	0	0	0	0	....	....	....	....	....	....	2007-08	2008-09
Gregg, Randy	Edm., Van.	10	474	41	152	193	333	137	13	38	51	127	5	1981-82	1991-92
● Greig, Bruce	Cal.	2	9	0	1	1	46	....	....	....	....	....	....	1973-74	1974-75
Greig, Mark	Hfd., Tor., Cgy., Phi.	9	125	13	27	40	90	5	0	1	1	0	....	1990-91	2002-03
Grenier, Lucien	Mtl., L.A.	4	151	14	14	28	18	2	0	0	0	0	....	1968-69	1971-72
Grenier, Martin	Phx., Van., Phi.	4	18	1	0	1	14	....	....	....	....	....	....	2001-02	2006-07
Grenier, Richard	NYI	1	10	1	1	2	2	....	....	....	....	....	....	1972-73	1972-73
Greschner, Ron	NYR	16	982	179	431	610	1226	84	17	32	49	106	....	1974-75	1989-90
Gretzky, Brent	T.B.	2	13	1	3	4	2	....	....	....	....	....	....	1993-94	1994-95
Gretzky, Wayne	Edm., L.A., St.L., NYR	20	1487	894	1963	2857	577	208	122	260	382	66	4	1979-80	1998-99
Grier, Mike	Edm., Wsh., Buf., S.J.	14	1060	162	221	383	510	101	14	14	28	72	....	1996-97	2010-11
Grieve, Brent	NYI, Edm., Chi., L.A.	4	97	20	16	36	87	....	....	....	....	....	....	1993-94	1996-97
● Grigor, George	Chi.	1	2	1	0	1	0	1	0	0	0	0	....	1943-44	1943-44
Grimson, Stu	Cgy., Chi., Ana., Det., Hfd., Car., L.A., Nsh.	14	729	17	22	39	2113	42	1	1	2	120	....	1988-89	2001-02
Grisdale, John	Tor., Van.	6	250	4	39	43	346	10	0	1	1	15	....	1972-73	1978-79
Groleau, Francois	Mtl.	3	8	0	1	1	6	....	....	....	....	....	....	1995-96	1997-98
Gron, Stanislav	N.J.	1	1	0	0	0	0	....	....	....	....	....	....	2000-01	2000-01
Gronman, Tuomas	Chi., Pit.	2	38	1	3	4	38	1	0	0	0	0	....	1996-97	1997-98
● Gronsdahl, Lloyd	Bos.	1	10	1	2	3	0	....	....	....	....	....	....	1941-42	1941-42
Gronstrand, Jari	Min., NYR, Que., NYI	5	185	8	26	34	135	3	0	0	0	4	....	1986-87	1990-91
Grosek, Michal	Wpg., Buf., Chi., NYR, Bos.	11	526	84	137	221	509	45	9	11	20	77	....	1993-94	2003-04
● Gross, Lloyd	Tor., NYA, Bos., Det.	3	52	11	5	16	20	1	0	0	0	0	....	1926-27	1934-35
● Grosso, Don	Det., Chi., Bos.	9	336	87	117	204	90	48	15	14	29	63	1	1938-39	1946-47
● Grosvenor, Len	Ott., NYA, Mtl.	6	149	9	11	20	78	4	0	0	0	2	....	1927-28	1932-33
Groulx, Wayne	Que.	1	1	0	0	0	0	....	....	....	....	....	....	1984-85	1984-85
Gruden, John	Bos., Ott., Wsh.	6	92	1	8	9	46	3	0	1	1	0	....	1993-94	2003-04
Gruen, Danny	Det., Col.	3	49	9	13	22	19	....	....	....	....	....	....	1972-73	1976-77
Gruhl, Scott	L.A., Pit.	3	20	3	3	6	6	....	....	....	....	....	....	1981-82	1987-88
Gryp, Bob	Bos., Wsh.	3	74	11	13	24	33	....	....	....	....	....	....	1973-74	1975-76
Guay, Francois	Buf.	1	1	0	0	0	0	....	....	....	....	....	....	1989-90	1989-90
Guay, Paul	Phi., L.A., Bos., NYI	7	117	11	23	34	92	9	0	1	1	12	....	1983-84	1990-91
Guerard, Daniel	Ott.	1	2	0	0	0	0	....	....	....	....	....	....	1994-95	1994-95
Guerard, Stephane	Que.	2	34	0	0	0	40	....	....	....	....	....	....	1987-88	1989-90
Guerin, Bill	N.J., Edm., Bos., Dal., St.L., S.J., NYI, Pit.	18	1263	429	427	856	1660	140	39	35	74	162	2	1991-92	2009-10
Guevremont, Jocelyn	Van., Buf., NYR	9	571	84	223	307	319	40	4	17	21	18	....	1971-72	1979-80
● Guidolin, Aldo	NYR	4	182	9	15	24	117	....	....	....	....	....	....	1952-53	1955-56
● Guidolin, Bep	Bos., Det., Chi.	9	519	107	171	278	606	24	5	7	12	35	....	1942-43	1951-52
Guindon, Bobby	Wpg.	1	6	0	1	1	0	....	....	....	....	....	....	1979-80	1979-80
Guite, Ben	Bos., Col., Nsh.	5	175	19	26	45	97	10	1	0	1	14	....	2005-06	2009-10
Guolla, Steve	S.J., T.B., Atl., N.J.	6	205	40	46	86	60	....	....	....	....	....	....	1996-97	2002-03
Guren, Miloslav	Mtl.	2	36	1	3	4	16	....	....	....	....	....	....	1998-99	1999-00
Gusarov, Alexei	Que., Col., NYR, St.L.	11	607	39	128	167	313	68	0	14	14	38	1	1990-91	2000-01
Gusev, Sergey	Dal., T.B.	4	89	4	10	14	34	....	....	....	....	....	....	1997-98	2000-01
Gusmanov, Ravil	Wpg.	1	4	0	0	0	0	....	....	....	....	....	....	1995-96	1995-96

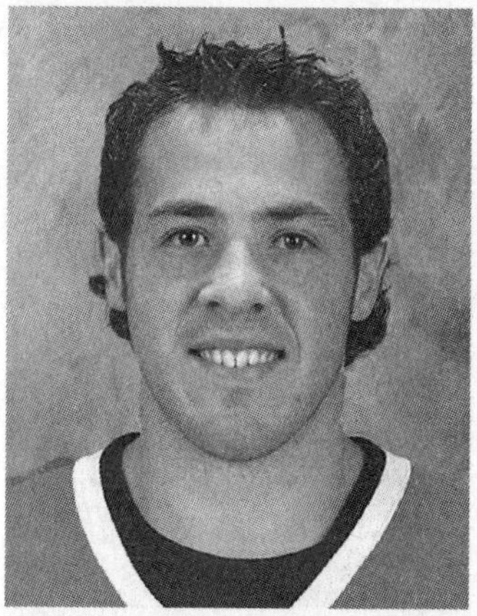

Dave Gove

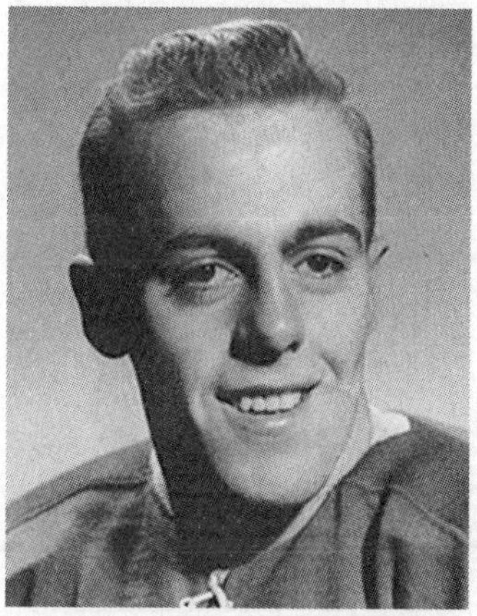

Leo Gravelle

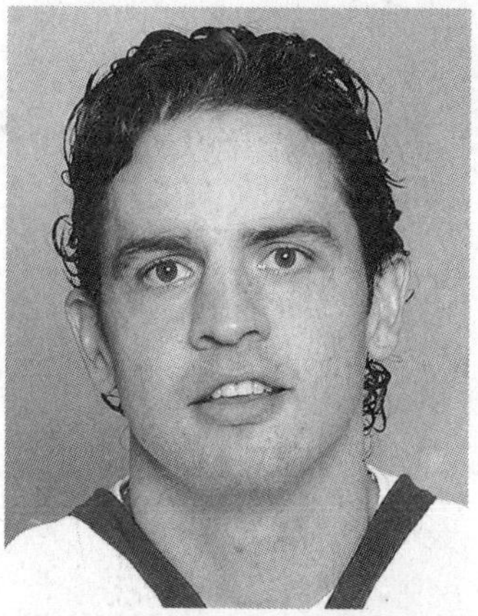

Travis Green

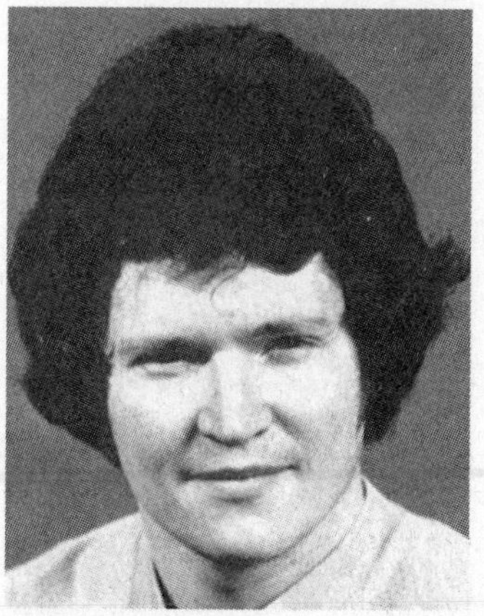

Bruce Greig

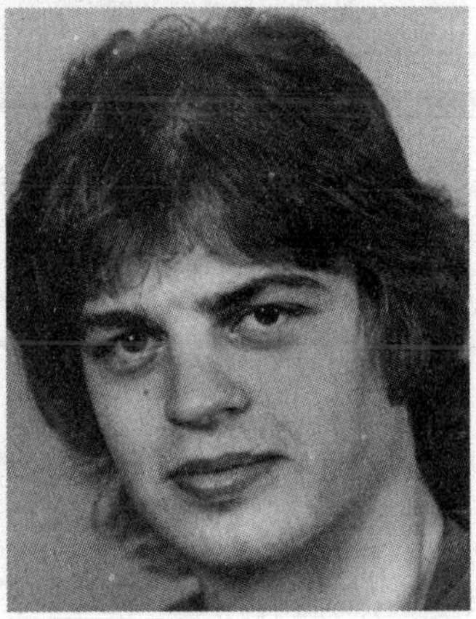

Bengt-Ake Gustafsson

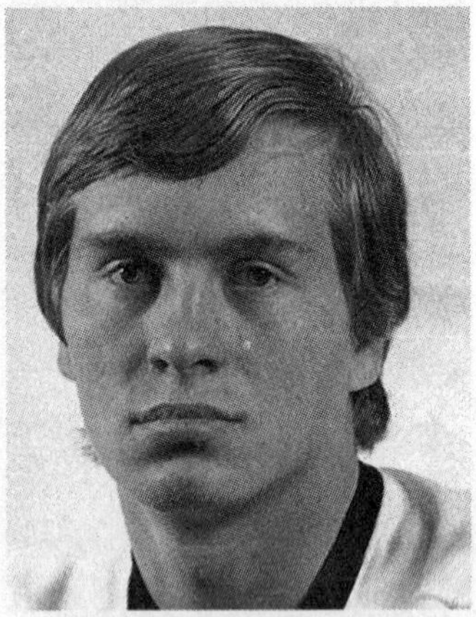

Matti Hagman

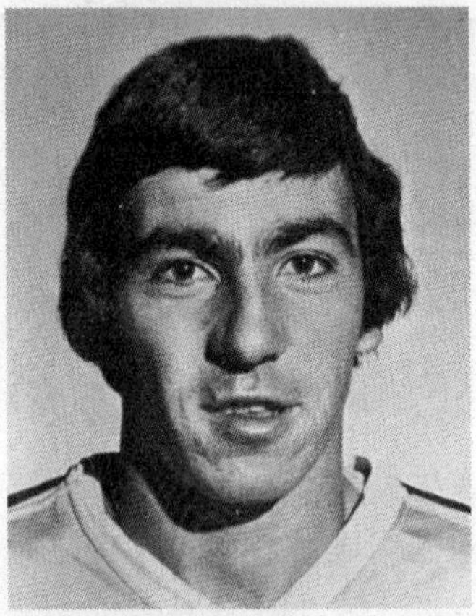

Del Hall

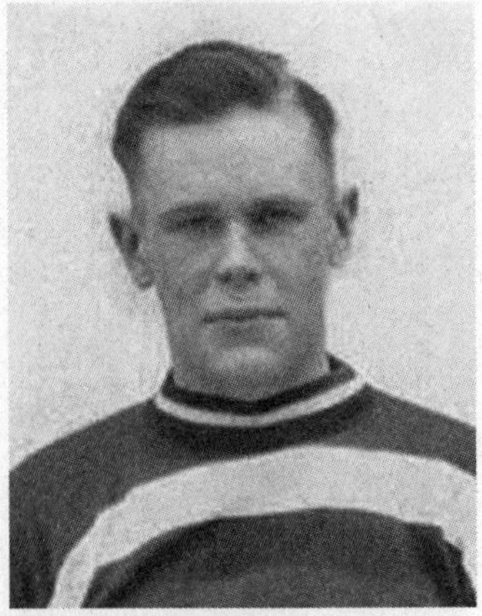

Milt Halliday

			Regular Schedule					Playoffs							
Name	NHL Teams	NHL Seasons	GP	G	A	TP	PIM	GP	G	A	TP	PIM	NHL Cup Wins	First NHL Season	Last NHL Season
Gustafsson, Bengt-Ake	Wsh.	9	629	196	359	555	196	32	9	19	28	16	....	1979-80	1988-89
‡ Gustafsson, Erik	Phi.	4	91	6	17	23	14	9	2	1	3	4	....	2010-11	2013-14
Gustafsson, Per	Fla., Tor., Ott.	2	89	8	27	35	38	1	0	0	0	0	....	1996-97	1997-98
Gustavsson, Peter	Col.	1	2	0	0	0	0	....	....	....	....	....	....	1981-82	1981-82
Guy, Kevan	Cgy., Van.	6	156	5	20	25	138	5	0	1	1	23	....	1986-87	1991-92
H															
Haakana, Kari	Edm.	1	13	0	0	0	4	....	....	....	....	....	....	2002-03	2002-03
Haanpaa, Ari	NYI	3	60	6	11	17	37	6	0	0	0	10	....	1985-86	1987-88
Haas, David	Edm., Cgy.	2	7	2	1	3	7	....	....	....	....	....	....	1990-91	1993-94
Habscheid, Marc	Edm., Min., Det., Cgy.	11	345	72	91	163	171	12	1	3	4	13	....	1981-82	1991-92
Hachborn, Len	Phi., L.A.	3	102	20	39	59	29	7	0	3	3	7	....	1983-84	1985-86
Haddon, Lloyd	Det.	1	8	0	0	0	2	1	0	0	0	0	....	1959-60	1959-60
Hadfield, Vic	NYR, Pit.	16	1002	323	389	712	1154	73	27	21	48	117	....	1961-62	1976-77
• Haggarty, Jim	Mtl.	1	5	1	1	2	0	3	2	1	3	0	....	1941-42	1941-42
Haggerty, Sean	Tor., NYI, Nsh.	4	14	1	2	3	4	....	....	....	....	....	....	1995-96	2000-01
• Hagglund, Roger	Que.	1	3	0	0	0	0	....	....	....	....	....	....	1984-85	1984-85
• Hagman, Matti	Bos., Edm.	4	237	56	89	145	36	20	5	2	7	6	....	1976-77	1981-82
‡ Hagman, Niklas	Fla., Dal., Tor., Cgy., Ana.	10	770	147	154	301	220	30	4	3	7	28	....	2001-02	2011-12
Hahl, Riku	Col.	3	92	5	8	13	38	34	2	4	6	4	....	2001-02	2003-04
• Haidy, Gord	Det.	1	....	....	....	....	....	1	0	0	0	0	....	1949-50	1949-50
Hajdu, Richard	Buf.	2	5	0	0	0	4	....	....	....	....	....	....	1985-86	1986-87
Hajt, Bill	Buf.	14	854	42	202	244	433	80	2	16	18	70	....	1973-74	1986-87
Hajt, Chris	Edm., Wsh.	2	6	0	0	0	2	....	....	....	....	....	....	2000-01	2003-04
Hakansson, Anders	Min., Pit., L.A.	5	330	52	46	98	141	6	0	0	0	2	....	1981-82	1985-86
• Halderson, Harold	Det., Tor.	1	44	3	2	5	65	....	....	....	....	....	....	1926-27	1926-27
Hale, David	N.J., Cgy., Phx., T.B., Ott.	7	327	4	25	29	242	17	0	2	2	20	....	2003-04	2010-11
Hale, Larry	Phi.	4	196	5	37	42	90	8	0	0	0	12	....	1968-69	1971-72
Haley, Len	Det.	2	30	2	2	4	14	6	1	3	4	6	....	1959-60	1960-61
‡ Halischuk, Matt	N.J., Nsh., Wpg.	8	280	33	42	75	57	18	2	1	3	4	....	2008-09	**2015-16**
Halkidis, Bob	Buf., L.A., Tor., Det., T.B., NYI	11	256	8	32	40	825	20	0	1	1	51	....	1984-85	1995-96
Halko, Steven	Car.	6	155	0	15	15	71	4	0	0	0	2	....	1997-98	2002-03
‡ Hall, Adam	Nsh., NYR, Min., Pit., T.B., Car., Phi.	11	682	69	87	156	282	56	7	7	14	32	....	2001-02	2013-14
• Hall, Bob	NYA	1	8	0	0	0	0	....	....	....	....	....	....	1925-26	1925-26
Hall, Del	Cal.	3	9	2	0	2	2	....	....	....	....	....	....	1971-72	1973-74
• Hall, Joe	Mtl.	2	37	15	9	24	235	7	0	1	1	38	....	1917-18	1918-19
Hall, Murray	Chi., Det., Min., Van.	9	164	35	48	83	46	6	0	0	0	0	....	1961-62	1971-72
Hall, Taylor	Van., Bos.	5	41	7	9	16	29	....	....	....	....	....	....	1983-84	1987-88
Hall, Wayne	NYR	1	4	0	0	0	0	....	....	....	....	....	....	1960-61	1960-61
Haller, Kevin	Buf., Mtl., Phi., Hfd., Car., Ana., NYI	13	642	41	97	138	907	64	7	16	23	71	1	1989-90	2001-02
• Halliday, Milt	Ott.	3	67	1	0	1	4	6	0	0	0	0	1	1926-27	1928-29
Hallin, Mats	NYI, Min.	5	152	17	14	31	193	15	1	0	1	13	1	1982-83	1986-87
Halpern, Jeff	Wsh., Dal., T.B., L.A., Mtl., NYR, Phx.	14	976	152	221	373	641	39	7	7	14	31	....	1999-00	2013-14
Halverson, Trevor	Wsh.	1	17	0	4	4	28	....	....	....	....	....	....	1998-99	1998-99
Halward, Doug	Bos., L.A., Van., Det., Edm.	14	653	69	224	293	774	47	7	10	17	113	....	1975-76	1988-89
Hamel, Denis	Buf., Ott., Atl., Phi.	7	192	19	12	31	77	....	....	....	....	....	....	1999-00	2006-07
Hamel, Gilles	Buf., Wpg., L.A.	9	519	127	147	274	276	27	4	5	9	10	....	1980-81	1988-89
• Hamel, Herb	Tor.	1	2	0	0	0	4	....	....	....	....	....	....	1930-31	1930-31
Hamel, Jean	St.L., Det., Que., Mtl.	12	699	26	95	121	766	33	0	2	2	44	....	1972-73	1983-84
• Hamill, Red	Bos., Chi.	12	419	128	94	222	160	24	1	2	3	20	1	1937-38	1950-51
‡ Hamill, Zach	Bos.	3	20	0	4	4	4	....	....	....	....	....	....	2009-10	2011-12
Hamilton, Al	NYR, Buf., Edm.	7	257	10	78	88	258	7	0	0	0	2	....	1965-66	1979-80
Hamilton, Chuck	Mtl., St.L.	2	4	0	2	2	2	....	....	....	....	....	....	1961-62	1972-73
‡ Hamilton, Curtis	Edm.	1	1	0	0	0	5	....	....	....	....	....	....	2014-15	2014-15
• Hamilton, Jack	Tor.	3	102	28	32	60	20	11	2	1	3	0	....	1942-43	1945-46
Hamilton, Jeff	NYI, Chi., Car., Tor.	5	157	32	45	77	44	....	....	....	....	....	....	2003-04	2008-09
Hamilton, Jim	Pit.	8	95	14	18	32	28	6	3	0	3	0	....	1977-78	1984-85
• Hamilton, Reg	Tor., Chi.	12	424	21	87	108	412	64	3	8	11	46	2	1935-36	1946-47
Hammarstrom, Inge	Tor., St.L.	6	427	116	123	239	86	13	2	3	5	4	....	1973-74	1978-79
Hammond, Ken	L.A., Edm., NYR, Tor., Bos., S.J., Van., Ott.	8	193	18	29	47	290	15	0	0	0	24	....	1984-85	1992-93
Hampson, Gord	Cgy.	1	4	0	0	0	5	....	....	....	....	....	....	1982-83	1982-83
Hampson, Ted	Tor., NYR, Det., Oak., Cal., Min.	12	676	108	245	353	94	35	7	10	17	2	....	1959-60	1971-72
Hampton, Rick	Cal., Cle., L.A.	6	337	59	113	172	147	2	0	0	0	0	....	1974-75	1979-80
Hamr, Radek	Ott.	2	11	0	0	0	0	....	....	....	....	....	....	1992-93	1993-94
Hamrlik, Roman	T.B., Edm., NYI, Cgy., Mtl., Wsh., NYR	20	1395	155	483	638	1408	113	3	38	41	87	....	1992-93	2012-13
Hamway, Mark	NYI	3	53	5	13	18	9	1	0	0	0	0	....	1984-85	1986-87
Handy, Ron	NYI, St.L.	2	14	0	3	3	0	....	....	....	....	....	....	1984-85	1987-88
‡ Handzus, Michal	St.L., Phx., Phi., Chi., L.A., S.J.	15	1009	185	298	483	498	116	16	30	46	52	1	1998-99	2013-14
Hangsleben, Al	Hfd., Wsh., L.A.	3	185	21	48	69	396	....	....	....	....	....	....	1979-80	1981-82
Hankinson, Ben	N.J., T.B.	3	43	3	3	6	45	2	1	0	1	4	....	1992-93	1994-95
Hankinson, Casey	Chi., Ana.	3	18	0	1	1	13	....	....	....	....	....	....	2000-01	2003-04
• Hanna, John	NYR, Mtl., Phi.	5	198	6	26	32	206	....	....	....	....	....	....	1958-59	1967-68
Hannan, Dave	Pit., Edm., Tor., Buf., Col., Ott.	16	841	114	191	305	942	63	6	7	13	46	2	1981-82	1996-97
Hannan, Scott	S.J., Col., Wsh., Cgy., Nsh.	16	1055	38	179	217	625	100	1	20	21	93	....	1998-99	2014-15
• Hannigan, Gord	Tor.	4	161	29	31	60	117	9	2	0	2	8	....	1952-53	1955-56
• Hannigan, Pat	Tor., NYR, Phi.	5	182	30	39	69	116	11	1	2	3	11	....	1959-60	1968-69
Hannigan, Ray	Tor.	1	3	0	0	0	2	....	....	....	....	....	....	1948-49	1948-49
‡ Hanowski, Ben	Cgy.	2	16	1	2	3	2	....	....	....	....	....	....	2012-13	2013-14
Hansen, Richie	NYI, St.L.	4	20	2	8	10	4	....	....	....	....	....	....	1976-77	1981-82
Hansen, Tavis	Wpg., Phx.	5	34	2	1	3	16	2	0	0	0	0	....	1994-95	2000-01
Hanson, Christian	Tor.	3	42	3	6	9	22	....	....	....	....	....	....	2008-09	2010-11
Hanson, Dave	Det., Min.	2	33	1	1	2	65	....	....	....	....	....	....	1978-79	1979-80
• Hanson, Emil	Det.	1	7	0	0	0	6	....	....	....	....	....	....	1932-33	1932-33
Hanson, Keith	Cgy.	1	25	0	2	2	77	....	....	....	....	....	....	1983-84	1983-84
• Hanson, Oscar	Chi.	1	8	0	0	0	0	....	....	....	....	....	....	1937-38	1937-38
• Harbaruk, Nick	Pit., St.L.	5	364	45	75	120	273	14	3	1	4	20	....	1969-70	1973-74
Harding, Jeff	Phi.	2	15	0	0	0	47	....	....	....	....	....	....	1988-89	1989-90
Hardy, Joe	Oak., Cal.	2	63	9	14	23	51	4	0	0	0	0	....	1969-70	1970-71
Hardy, Mark	L.A., NYR, Min.	15	915	62	306	368	1293	67	5	16	21	158	....	1979-80	1993-94
Hargreaves, Jim	Van.	2	66	1	7	8	105	....	....	....	....	....	....	1970-71	1972-73
‡ Harju, Johan	T.B.	1	10	1	2	3	2	....	....	....	....	....	....	2010-11	2010-11
Harkins, Brett	Bos., Fla., CBJ	4	78	6	30	36	22	....	....	....	....	....	....	1994-95	2001-02
Harkins, Todd	Cgy., Hfd.	3	48	3	3	6	78	....	....	....	....	....	....	1991-92	1993-94
Harlock, David	Tor., Wsh., NYI, Atl.	8	212	2	14	16	188	....	....	....	....	....	....	1993-94	2001-02
Harlow, Scott	St.L.	1	1	0	1	1	0	....	....	....	....	....	....	1987-88	1987-88
• Harmon, Glen	Mtl.	9	452	50	96	146	334	53	5	10	15	37	2	1942-43	1950-51
• Harms, John	Chi.	2	44	5	5	10	21	4	3	0	3	2	....	1943-44	1944-45
• Harnott, Walter	Bos.	1	6	0	0	0	2	....	....	....	....	....	....	1933-34	1933-34
Harper, Terry	Mtl., L.A., Det., St.L., Col.	19	1066	35	221	256	1362	112	4	13	17	140	5	1962-63	1980-81
Harrer, Tim	Cgy.	1	3	0	0	0	2	....	....	....	....	....	....	1982-83	1982-83
• Harrington, Hago	Bos., Mtl.	3	72	9	3	12	15	4	1	0	1	2	....	1925-26	1932-33
• Harris, Billy	Tor., Det., Oak., Pit.	13	769	126	219	345	205	62	8	10	18	30	3	1955-56	1968-69
Harris, Billy	NYI, L.A., Tor.	12	897	231	327	558	394	71	19	19	38	48	....	1972-73	1983-84
Harris, Duke	Min., Tor.	1	26	1	4	5	4	....	....	....	....	....	....	1967-68	1967-68
• Harris, Henry	Bos.	1	32	2	4	6	20	....	....	....	....	....	....	1930-31	1930-31
Harris, Hugh	Buf.	1	60	12	26	38	17	3	0	0	0	0	....	1972-73	1972-73
Harris, Ron	Det., Oak., Atl., NYR	11	476	20	91	111	474	28	4	3	7	33	....	1962-63	1975-76
• Harris, Smokey	Bos.	1	6	3	1	4	8	....	....	....	....	....	....	1924-25	1924-25
Harris, Ted	Mtl., Min., Det., St.L., Phi.	12	788	30	168	198	1000	100	1	22	23	230	5	1963-64	1974-75
• Harrison, Ed	Bos., NYR	4	194	27	24	51	53	9	1	0	1	2	....	1947-48	1950-51
Harrison, Jay	Tor., Car., Wpg.	9	372	23	52	75	360	....	....	....	....	....	....	2005-06	2014-15
Harrison, Jim	Bos., Tor., Chi., Edm.	8	324	67	86	153	435	13	1	1	2	43	....	1968-69	1979-80
Harrold, Peter	L.A., N.J.	9	274	13	29	42	74	19	0	4	4	6	....	2006-07	2014-15
Hart, Gerry	Det., NYI, Que., St.L.	15	730	29	150	179	1240	78	3	12	15	175	....	1968-69	1982-83
• Hart, Gizzy	Det., Mtl.	3	104	6	8	14	12	8	0	1	1	0	....	1926-27	1932-33
Hartigan, Mark	Atl., CBJ, Ana., Det.	6	102	19	11	30	58	5	0	1	1	4	1	2001-02	2007-08
‡ Hartikainen, Teemu	Edm.	3	52	6	7	13	16	....	....	....	....	....	....	2010-11	2012-13
Hartman, Mike	Buf., Wpg., T.B., NYR	9	397	43	35	78	1388	21	0	0	0	106	1	1986-87	1994-95
Hartsburg, Craig	Min.	10	570	98	315	413	818	61	15	27	42	70	....	1979-80	1988-89
• Harvey, Buster	Min., Atl., K.C., Det.	7	407	90	118	208	131	14	0	2	2	8	....	1970-71	1976-77

Name	NHL Teams	NHL Seasons	Regular Schedule					Playoffs					NHL Cup Wins	First NHL Season	Last NHL Season
			GP	G	A	TP	PIM	GP	G	A	TP	PIM			
• Harvey, Doug	Mtl., NYR, Det., St.L.	20	1113	88	452	540	1216	137	8	64	72	152	6	1947-48	1968-69
Harvey, Hugh	K.C.	2	18	1	1	2	4	....	....	....	....	....	....	1974-75	1975-76
Harvey, Todd	Dal., NYR, S.J., Edm.	11	671	91	132	223	950	68	3	6	9	52	....	1994-95	2005-06
• Hassard, Bob	Tor., Chi.	5	126	9	28	37	22	....	....	....	....	....	1	1949-50	1954-55
Hatcher, Derian	Min., Dal., Det., Phi.	16	1045	80	251	331	1581	133	7	26	33	248	1	1991-92	2007-08
Hatcher, Kevin	Wsh., Dal., Pit., NYR, Car.	17	1157	227	450	677	1392	118	22	37	59	252	....	1984-85	2000-01
Hatoum, Ed	Det., Van.	3	47	3	6	9	25	....	....	....	....	....	....	1968-69	1970-71
Hauer, Brett	Edm., Nsh.	3	37	4	4	8	38	....	....	....	....	....	....	1995-96	2001-02
Havelid, Niclas	Ana., Atl., N.J.	9	628	34	137	171	342	32	0	7	7	4	....	1999-00	2008-09
Havlat, Martin	Ott., Chi., Min., S.J., N.J., St.L.	15	790	242	352	594	404	75	21	31	52	52	....	2000-01	**2015-16**
Hawerchuk, Dale	Wpg., Buf., St.L., Phi.	16	1188	518	891	1409	730	97	30	69	99	67	....	1981-82	1996-97
Hawgood, Greg	Bos., Edm., Phi., Fla., Pit., S.J., Van., Dal.	12	474	60	164	224	426	42	2	8	10	37	....	1987-88	2001-02
Hawkins, Todd	Van., Tor.	3	10	0	0	0	15	....	....	....	....	....	....	1988-89	1991-92
Haworth, Alan	Buf., Wsh., Que.	8	524	189	211	400	425	42	12	16	28	28	....	1980-81	1987-88
Haworth, Gord	NYR	1	2	0	1	1	0	....	....	....	....	....	....	1952-53	1952-53
Hawryliw, Neil	NYI	1	1	0	0	0	0	....	....	....	....	....	....	1981-82	1981-82
Hay, Bill	Chi.	8	506	113	273	386	244	67	15	21	36	62	1	1959-60	1966-67
Hay, Dwayne	Wsh., Fla., T.B., Cgy.	4	79	2	4	6	22	....	....	....	....	....	....	1997-98	2000-01
• Hay, George	Chi., Det.	6	238	74	60	134	84	8	2	3	5	2	....	1926-27	1932-33
Hay, Jim	Det.	3	75	1	5	6	22	9	1	0	1	2	1	1952-53	1954-55
Haydar, Darren	Nsh., Atl., Col.	4	23	1	7	8	2	....	....	....	....	....	....	2002-03	2009-10
Hayek, Peter	Min.	1	1	0	0	0	0	....	....	....	....	....	....	1981-82	1981-82
Hayes, Chris	Bos.	1	....	....	....	....	....	1	0	0	0	0	....	1971-72	1971-72
Hayes, Eriah	S.J.	2	19	1	0	1	4	....	....	....	....	....	....	2013-14	2014-15
• Haynes, Paul	Mtl.M., Bos., Mtl.	11	391	61	134	195	164	24	2	8	10	13	....	1930-31	1940-41
Hayward, Rick	L.A.	1	4	0	0	0	5	....	....	....	....	....	....	1990-91	1990-91
Hazlett, Steve	Van.	1	1	0	0	0	0	....	....	....	....	....	....	1979-80	1979-80
Head, Galen	Det.	1	1	0	0	0	0	....	....	....	....	....	....	1967-68	1967-68
• Headley, Fern	Bos., Mtl.	1	30	1	3	4	10	1	0	0	0	0	....	1924-25	1924-25
Healey, Eric	Bos.	1	2	0	0	0	2	....	....	....	....	....	....	2005-06	2005-06
Healey, Paul	Phi., Tor., NYR, Col.	6	77	6	14	20	44	22	0	2	2	4	....	1996-97	2005-06
Healey, Rich	Det.	1	1	0	0	0	2	....	....	....	....	....	....	1960-61	1960-61
Heaphy, Shawn	Cgy.	1	1	0	0	0	0	....	....	....	....	....	....	1992-93	1992-93
Heaslip, Mark	NYR, L.A.	3	117	10	19	29	110	5	0	0	0	2	....	1976-77	1978-79
Heath, Randy	NYR	2	13	2	4	6	15	....	....	....	....	....	....	1984-85	1985-86
Heatley, Dany	Atl., Ott., S.J., Min., Ana.	13	869	372	419	791	620	77	16	47	63	63	....	2001-02	2014-15
Hebenton, Andy	NYR, Bos.	9	630	189	202	391	83	22	6	5	11	8	....	1955-56	1963-64
Hecht, Jochen	St.L., Edm., Buf.	14	833	186	277	463	458	59	14	18	32	24	....	1998-99	2012-13
Hecl, Radoslav	Buf.	1	14	0	0	0	2	....	....	....	....	....	....	2002-03	2002-03
Hedberg, Anders	NYR	7	465	172	225	397	144	58	22	24	46	31	....	1978-79	1984-85
Hedican, Bret	St.L., Van., Fla., Car., Ana.	17	1039	55	239	294	893	108	4	22	26	108	1	1991-92	2008-09
Hedin, Pierre	Tor.	1	3	0	1	1	0	....	....	....	....	....	....	2003-04	2003-04
Hedstrom, Jonathan	Ana.	2	83	13	14	27	48	3	0	1	1	2	....	2002-03	2005-06
Heerema, Jeff	Car., St.L.	2	32	4	2	6	6	....	....	....	....	....	....	2002-03	2003-04
• Heffernan, Frank	Tor.	1	19	0	1	1	10	....	....	....	....	....	....	1919-20	1919-20
• Heffernan, Gerry	Mtl.	3	83	33	35	68	27	11	3	3	6	8	1	1941-42	1943-44
Heidt, Mike	L.A.	1	6	0	1	1	7	....	....	....	....	....	....	1983-84	1983-84
‡ Heikkinen, Ilkka	NYR	1	7	0	0	0	0	....	....	....	....	....	....	2009-10	2009-10
• Heindl, Bill	Min., NYR	3	18	2	1	3	0	....	....	....	....	....	....	1970-71	1972-73
• Heinrich, Lionel	Bos.	1	35	1	1	2	33	....	....	....	....	....	....	1955-56	1955-56
Heins, Shawn	S.J., Pit., Atl.	6	125	4	12	16	154	2	0	0	0	0	....	1998-99	2003-04
Heinze, Steve	Bos., CBJ, Buf., L.A.	12	694	178	158	336	379	69	11	15	26	48	....	1991-92	2002-03
Heiskala, Earl	Phi.	3	127	13	11	24	294	....	....	....	....	....	....	1968-69	1970-71
Heisten, Barrett	NYR	1	10	0	0	0	2	....	....	....	....	....	....	2001-02	2001-02
Hejda, Jan	Edm., CBJ, Col.	9	627	25	110	135	317	10	0	0	0	8	....	2006-07	2014-15
Hejduk, Milan	Col.	14	1020	375	430	805	316	112	34	42	76	28	1	1998-99	2012-13
Helander, Peter	L.A.	1	7	0	1	1	0	....	....	....	....	....	....	1982-83	1982-83
‡ Helbling, Timo	T.B., Wsh.	2	11	0	1	1	8	....	....	....	....	....	....	2005-06	2006-07
Helenius, Sami	Cgy., T.B., Col., Dal., Chi.	6	155	2	4	6	260	1	0	0	0	0	....	1996-97	2002-03
• Heller, Ott	NYR	15	647	55	176	231	465	61	6	8	14	61	2	1931-32	1945-46
• Helman, Harry	Ott.	3	44	1	0	1	7	2	0	0	0	0	1	1922-23	1924-25
Helmer, Bryan	Phx., St.L., Van., Wsh.	7	146	8	18	26	135	6	0	0	0	0	....	1998-99	2008-09
Helminen, Dwight	Car., S.J.	2	27	2	1	3	0	8	1	0	1	4	....	2008-09	2009-10
Helminen, Raimo	NYR, Min., NYI	3	117	13	46	59	16	2	0	0	0	0	....	1985-86	1988-89
Hemingway, Colin	St.L.	1	3	0	0	0	0	....	....	....	....	....	....	2005-06	2005-06
• Hemmerling, Tony	NYA	2	22	3	3	6	4	....	....	....	....	....	....	1935-36	1936-37
Henderson, Archie	Wsh., Min., Hfd.	3	23	3	1	4	92	....	....	....	....	....	....	1980-81	1982-83
Henderson, Jay	Bos.	4	33	1	3	4	37	....	....	....	....	....	....	1998-99	2001-02
‡ Henderson, Kevin	Nsh.	1	4	1	0	1	0	....	....	....	....	....	....	2012-13	2012-13
Henderson, Matt	Nsh., Chi.	2	6	0	1	1	2	....	....	....	....	....	....	1998-99	2001-02
• Henderson, Murray	Bos.	8	405	24	62	86	305	41	2	3	5	23	....	1944-45	1951-52
Henderson, Paul	Det., Tor., Atl.	13	707	236	241	477	304	56	11	14	25	28	....	1962-63	1979-80
Hendrickson, Darby	Tor., NYI, Van., Min., Col.	11	518	65	64	129	370	25	3	3	6	6	....	1993-94	2003-04
Hendrickson, John	Det.	3	5	0	0	0	4	....	....	....	....	....	....	1957-58	1961-62
Hendry, Jordan	Chi., Ana.	5	131	4	9	13	40	15	0	0	0	2	1	2007-08	2012-13
‡ Hennessy, Josh	Ott., Bos.	5	23	1	0	1	6	....	....	....	....	....	....	2006-07	2011-12
Henning, Lorne	NYI	9	543	73	111	184	102	81	7	7	14	8	2	1972-73	1980-81
Henry, Alex	Edm., Wsh., Min., Mtl.	4	177	2	9	11	269	....	....	....	....	....	....	2002-03	2008-09
Henry, Burke	Chi.	2	39	2	6	8	33	....	....	....	....	....	....	2002-03	2003-04
• Henry, Camille	NYR, Chi., St.L.	14	727	279	249	528	88	47	6	12	18	7	....	1953-54	1969-70
Henry, Dale	NYI	6	132	13	26	39	263	14	1	0	1	19	....	1984-85	1989-90
Hentunen, Jukka	Cgy., Nsh.	1	38	4	5	9	4	....	....	....	....	....	....	2001-02	2001-02
Hepple, Alan	N.J.	3	3	0	0	0	7	....	....	....	....	....	....	1983-84	1985-86
Herbers, Ian	Edm., T.B., NYI	2	65	0	5	5	79	....	....	....	....	....	....	1993-94	1999-00
• Herbert, Jimmy	Bos., Tor., Det.	6	206	83	31	114	253	9	3	0	3	10	....	1924-25	1929-30
• Herchenratter, Art	Det.	1	10	1	2	3	2	....	....	....	....	....	....	1940-41	1940-41
• Hergerts, Fred	NYA	2	20	2	4	6	2	....	....	....	....	....	....	1934-35	1935-36
• Hergesheimer, Phil	Chi., Bos.	4	125	21	41	62	19	6	0	0	0	2	....	1939-40	1942-43
• Hergesheimer, Wally	NYR, Chi.	7	351	114	85	199	106	5	1	0	1	0	....	1951-52	1958-59
• Heron, Red	Tor., Bro., Mtl.	4	106	21	19	40	38	21	2	2	4	6	....	1938-39	1941-42
Heroux, Yves	Que.	1	1	0	0	0	0	....	....	....	....	....	....	1986-87	1986-87
Herperger, Chris	Chi., Ott., Atl.	4	169	18	25	43	75	....	....	....	....	....	....	1999-00	2002-03
Herr, Matt	Wsh., Fla., Bos.	4	58	4	5	9	25	....	....	....	....	....	....	1998-99	2002-03
Herter, Jason	NYI	1	1	0	1	1	0	....	....	....	....	....	....	1995-96	1995-96
Hervey, Matt	Wpg., Bos., T.B.	3	35	0	5	5	97	5	0	0	0	6	....	1988-89	1992-93
‡ Heshka, Shaun	Phx.	1	8	0	2	2	4	....	....	....	....	....	....	2009-10	2009-10
Hess, Bob	St.L., Buf., Hfd.	8	329	27	95	122	178	4	1	1	2	2	....	1974-75	1983-84
Heward, Jamie	Tor., Nsh., NYI, CBJ, Wsh., L.A., T.B.	9	394	38	86	124	221	....	....	....	....	....	....	1995-96	2008-09
• Heximer, Obs	NYR, Bos., NYA	3	84	13	7	20	16	5	0	0	0	2	....	1929-30	1934-35
• Hextall, Bryan	NYR	11	449	187	175	362	227	37	8	9	17	19	1	1936-37	1947-48
Hextall, Bryan	NYR, Pit., Atl., Det., Min.	8	549	99	161	260	738	18	0	4	4	59	....	1962-63	1975-76
Hextall, Dennis	NYR, L.A., Cal., Min., Det., Wsh.	13	681	153	350	503	1398	22	3	3	6	45	....	1967-68	1979-80
• Heyliger, Vic	Chi.	2	33	2	3	5	2	....	....	....	....	....	....	1937-38	1943-44
• Hicke, Bill	Mtl., NYR, Oak., Cal., Pit.	14	729	168	234	402	395	42	3	10	13	41	2	1958-59	1971-72
Hicke, Ernie	Cal., Atl., NYI, Min., L.A.	8	520	132	140	272	407	2	1	0	1	0	....	1970-71	1977-78
Hickey, Greg	NYR	1	1	0	0	0	0	....	....	....	....	....	....	1977-78	1977-78
Hickey, Pat	NYR, Col., Tor., Que., St.L.	10	646	192	212	404	351	55	5	11	16	37	....	1975-76	1984-85
Hicks, Alex	Ana., Pit., S.J., Fla.	5	258	25	54	79	247	15	0	2	2	8	....	1995-96	1999-00
Hicks, Doug	Min., Chi., Edm., Wsh.	9	561	37	131	168	442	18	2	1	3	15	....	1974-75	1982-83
Hicks, Glenn	Det.	2	108	6	12	18	127	....	....	....	....	....	....	1979-80	1980-81
• Hicks, Henry	Mtl.M., Det.	3	96	7	2	9	72	....	....	....	....	....	....	1928-29	1930-31
Hicks, Wayne	Chi., Bos., Mtl., Phi., Pit.	5	115	13	23	36	22	2	0	1	1	2	1	1959-60	1967-68
Hidi, Andre	Wsh.	2	7	2	1	3	9	2	0	0	0	0	....	1983-84	1984-85
Hiemer, Uli	N.J.	3	143	19	54	73	176	....	....	....	....	....	....	1984-85	1986-87
Higgins, Chris	Mtl., NYR, Cgy., Fla., Van.	12	711	165	168	333	220	62	11	10	21	10	....	2003-04	**2015-16**
Higgins, Matt	Mtl.	4	57	1	2	3	6	....	....	....	....	....	....	1997-98	2000-01
Higgins, Paul	Tor.	2	25	0	0	0	152	1	0	0	0	0	....	1981-82	1982-83
Higgins, Tim	Chi., N.J., Det.	11	706	154	198	352	719	65	5	8	13	77	....	1978-79	1988-89
Hilbert, Andy	Bos., Chi., Pit., NYI, Min.	8	307	42	62	104	132	10	1	0	1	2	....	2001-02	2009-10
• Hildebrand, Ike	NYR, Chi.	2	41	7	11	18	16	....	....	....	....	....	....	1953-54	1954-55
Hill, Al	Phi.	8	221	40	55	95	227	51	8	11	19	43	....	1976-77	1987-88

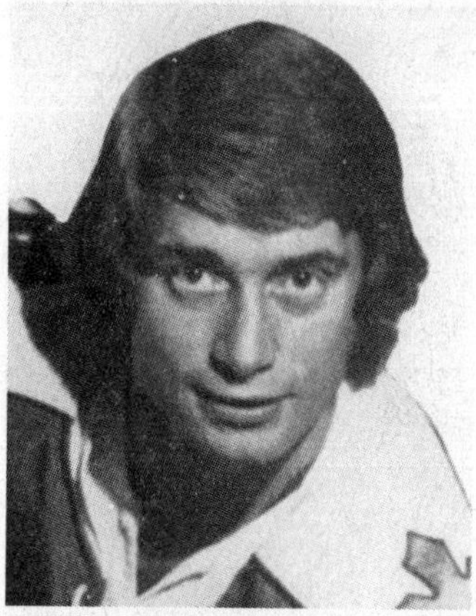
Inge Hammarstrom

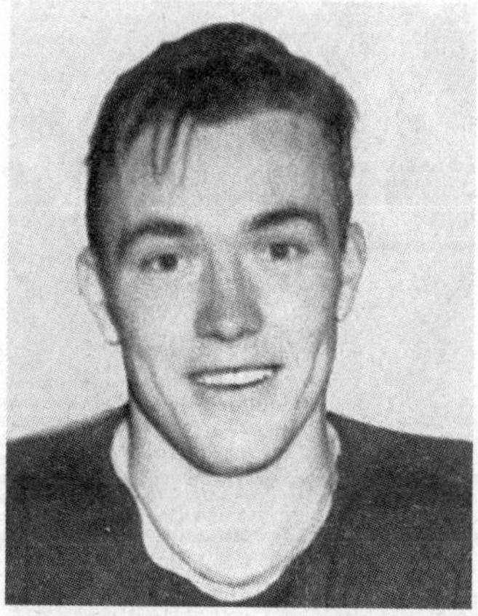
Gord Hannigan

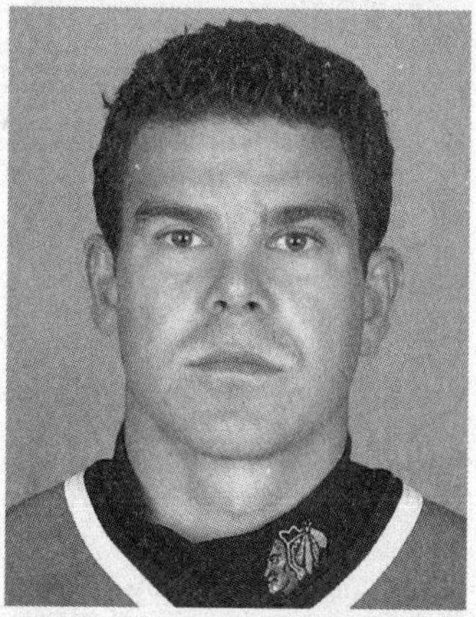
Matt Henderson

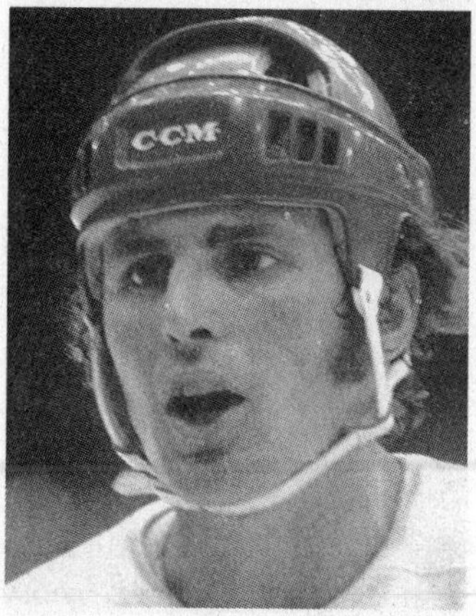
Paul Henderson

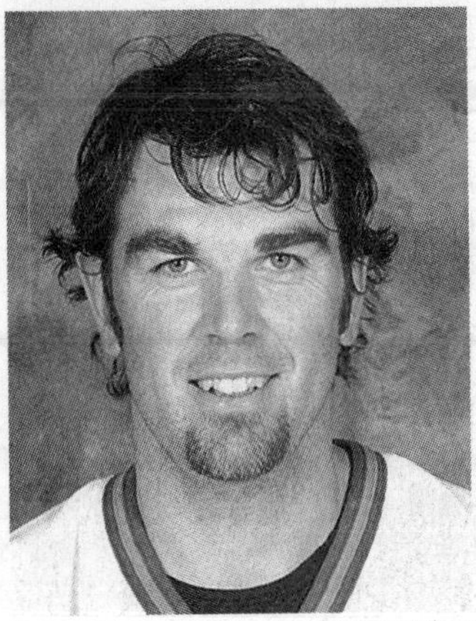

Jamie Heward

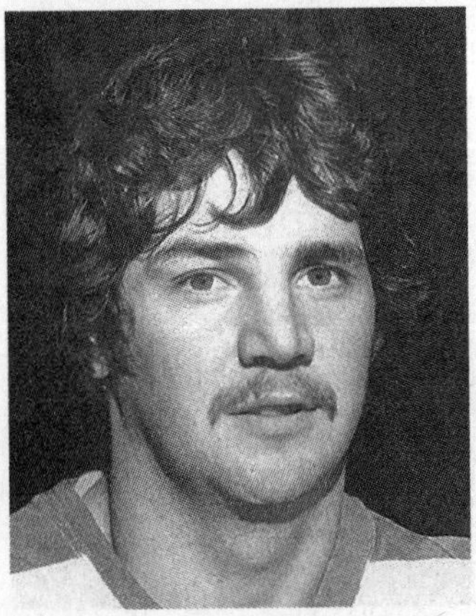

Rick Hodgson

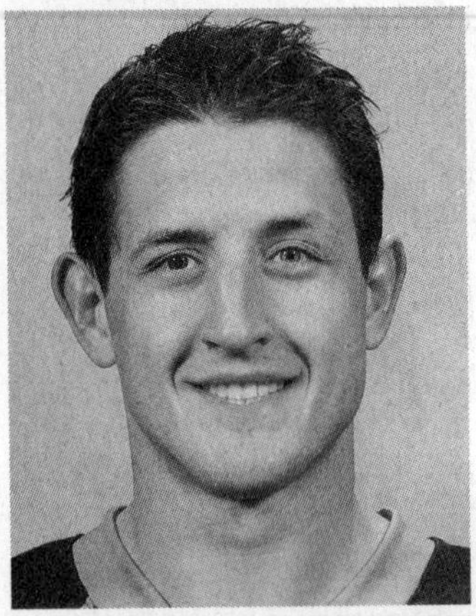

Shawn Horcoff

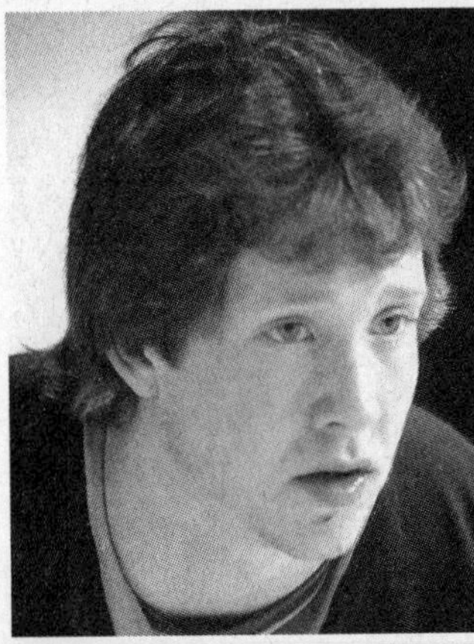

Phil Housley

			Regular Schedule					Playoffs							
Name	NHL Teams	NHL Seasons	GP	G	A	TP	PIM	GP	G	A	TP	PIM	NHL Cup Wins	First NHL Season	Last NHL Season
Hill, Brian	Hfd.	1	19	1	1	2	4	....	....	....	....	....	....	1979-80	1979-80
● Hill, Mel	Bos., Bro., Tor.	9	324	89	109	198	128	43	12	7	19	18	3	1937-38	1945-46
Hill, Sean	Mtl., Ana., Ott., Car., St.L., Fla., NYI, Min.	17	876	62	236	298	1008	55	5	5	10	42	1	1990-91	2007-08
Hillen, Jack	NYI, Nsh., Wsh., Car.	8	304	13	58	71	157	9	0	1	1	8	....	2007-08	2014-15
● Hiller, Dutch	NYR, Det., Bos., Mtl.	9	383	91	113	204	163	48	9	8	17	21	2	1937-38	1945-46
Hiller, Jim	L.A., Det., NYR	2	63	8	12	20	116	2	0	0	0	4	....	1992-93	1993-94
Hillier, Randy	Bos., Pit., NYI, Buf.	11	543	16	110	126	906	28	0	2	2	93	1	1981-82	1991-92
Hillman, Floyd	Bos.	1	6	0	0	0	10	....	....	....	....	....	....	1956-57	1956-57
Hillman, Larry	Det., Bos., Tor., Min., Mtl., Phi., L.A., Buf.	19	790	36	196	232	579	74	2	9	11	30	6	1954-55	1972-73
● Hillman, Wayne	Chi., NYR, Min., Phi.	13	691	18	86	104	534	28	0	3	3	19	1	1960-61	1972-73
Hilworth, John	Det.	3	57	1	1	2	89	....	....	....	....	....	....	1977-78	1979-80
● Himes, Normie	NYA	9	402	106	113	219	127	2	0	0	0	0	....	1926-27	1934-35
Hindmarch, Dave	Cgy.	4	99	21	17	38	25	10	0	0	0	6	....	1980-81	1983-84
Hinote, Dan	Col., St.L.	9	503	38	52	90	383	72	6	9	15	67	1	1999-00	2008-09
Hinse, Andre	Tor.	1	4	0	0	0	0	....	....	....	....	....	....	1967-68	1967-68
Hinton, Dan	Chi.	1	14	0	0	0	16	....	....	....	....	....	....	1976-77	1976-77
Hirsch, Tom	Min.	3	31	1	7	8	30	12	0	0	0	6	....	1983-84	1987-88
● Hirschfeld, Bert	Mtl.	2	33	1	4	5	2	5	1	0	1	0	....	1949-50	1950-51
‡ Hishon, Joey	Col.	2	13	1	1	2	0	3	0	1	1	2	....	2013-14	2014-15
Hislop, Jamie	Que., Cgy.	5	345	75	103	178	86	28	3	2	5	11	....	1979-80	1983-84
● Hitchman, Lionel	Ott., Bos.	12	417	28	34	62	523	35	2	2	4	73	2	1922-23	1933-34
‡ Hlavac, Jan	NYR, Phi., Van., Car., T.B., Nsh.	6	436	90	134	224	138	11	0	3	3	2	....	1999-00	2007-08
● Hlinka, Ivan	Van.	2	137	42	81	123	28	16	3	10	13	8	....	1981-82	1982-83
‡ Hlinka, Jaroslav	Col.	1	63	8	20	28	16	1	0	0	0	0	....	2007-08	2007-08
Hlushko, Todd	Phi., Cgy., Pit.	6	79	8	13	21	84	3	0	0	0	2	....	1993-94	1998-99
Hnidy, Shane	Ott., Nsh., Atl., Ana., Bos., Min.	10	550	16	55	71	633	40	4	2	6	34	....	2000-01	2010-11
Hocking, Justin	L.A.	1	1	0	0	0	0	....	....	....	....	....	....	1993-94	1993-94
Hodge, Ken	Chi., Bos., NYR	14	881	328	472	800	779	97	34	47	81	120	2	1964-65	1977-78
Hodge, Ken	Min., Bos., T.B.	4	142	39	48	87	32	15	4	6	10	6	....	1988-89	1992-93
‡ Hodgman, Justin	Ari.	1	5	1	0	1	2	....	....	....	....	....	....	2014-15	2014-15
Hodgson, Cody	Van., Buf., Nsh.	6	328	64	78	142	68	12	0	1	1	2	....	2010-11	**2015-16**
Hodgson, Dan	Tor., Van.	4	114	29	45	74	64	....	....	....	....	....	....	1985-86	1988-89
Hodgson, Rick	Hfd.	1	6	0	0	0	6	1	0	0	0	0	....	1979-80	1979-80
Hodgson, Ted	Bos.	1	4	0	0	0	0	....	....	....	....	....	....	1966-67	1966-67
Hoekstra, Cec	Mtl.	1	4	0	0	0	0	....	....	....	....	....	....	1959-60	1959-60
● Hoekstra, Ed	Phi.	1	70	15	21	36	6	7	0	1	1	0	....	1967-68	1967-68
Hoene, Phil	L.A.	3	37	2	4	6	22	....	....	....	....	....	....	1972-73	1974-75
● Hoffinger, Val	Chi.	2	28	0	1	1	30	....	....	....	....	....	....	1927-28	1928-29
Hoffman, Mike	Hfd.	3	9	1	3	4	2	....	....	....	....	....	....	1982-83	1985-86
Hoffmeyer, Bob	Chi., Phi., N.J.	6	198	14	52	66	325	3	0	1	1	25	....	1977-78	1984-85
Hofford, Jim	Buf., L.A.	3	18	0	0	0	47	....	....	....	....	....	....	1985-86	1988-89
Hogaboam, Bill	Atl., Det., Min.	8	332	80	109	189	100	2	0	0	0	0	....	1972-73	1979-80
Hoganson, Dale	L.A., Mtl., Que.	7	343	13	77	90	186	11	0	3	3	12	....	1969-70	1981-82
Hoggan, Jeff	St.L., Bos., Phx.	5	107	2	9	11	76	....	....	....	....	....	....	2005-06	2009-10
Hoglund, Jonas	Cgy., Mtl., Tor.	7	545	117	145	262	112	59	8	11	19	8	....	1996-97	2002-03
Hogue, Benoit	Buf., NYI, Tor., Dal., T.B., Phx., Bos., Wsh.	15	863	222	321	543	877	92	17	16	33	124	1	1987-88	2001-02
Holan, Milos	Phi., Ana.	3	49	5	11	16	42	....	....	....	....	....	....	1993-94	1995-96
Holbrook, Terry	Min.	2	43	3	6	9	4	6	0	0	0	0	....	1972-73	1973-74
‡ Holden, Josh	Van., Car., Tor.	6	60	5	9	14	16	....	....	....	....	....	....	1998-99	2003-04
Holik, Bobby	Hfd., N.J., NYR, Atl.	18	1314	326	421	747	1423	141	20	39	59	120	2	1990-91	2008-09
Holland, Jason	NYI, Buf., L.A.	7	81	4	5	9	36	1	0	0	0	0	....	1996-97	2003-04
Holland, Jerry	NYR	2	37	8	4	12	6	....	....	....	....	....	....	1974-75	1975-76
Holland, Patrick	Mtl.	1	5	0	0	0	0	....	....	....	....	....	....	2013-14	2013-14
● Hollett, Flash	Tor., Ott., Bos., Det.	13	562	132	181	313	358	79	8	26	34	38	2	1933-34	1945-46
Hollinger, Terry	St.L.	2	7	0	0	0	2	....	....	....	....	....	....	1993-94	1994-95
● Hollingworth, Gord	Chi., Det.	4	163	4	14	18	201	3	0	0	0	2	....	1954-55	1957-58
Holloway, Bruce	Van.	1	2	0	0	0	0	....	....	....	....	....	....	1984-85	1984-85
Holloway, Bud	Mtl.	1	1	0	0	0	0	....	....	....	....	....	....	**2015-16**	**2015-16**
Hollweg, Ryan	NYR, Tor., Phx.	5	228	5	9	14	349	14	0	1	1	23	....	2005-06	2010-11
● Holmes, Bill	Mtl., NYA	3	52	6	4	10	35	....	....	....	....	....	....	1925-26	1929-30
Holmes, Chuck	Det.	2	23	1	3	4	10	....	....	....	....	....	....	1958-59	1961-62
● Holmes, Lou	Chi.	2	59	1	4	5	6	2	0	0	0	2	....	1931-32	1932-33
Holmes, Warren	L.A.	3	45	8	18	26	7	....	....	....	....	....	....	1981-82	1983-84
Holmgren, Paul	Phi., Min.	10	527	144	179	323	1684	82	19	32	51	195	....	1975-76	1984-85
Holmqvist, Michael	Ana., Chi.	3	156	18	17	35	72	....	....	....	....	....	....	2003-04	2006-07
Holmstrom, Tomas	Det.	15	1026	243	287	530	769	180	46	51	97	162	4	1996-97	2011-12
‡ Holos, Jonas	Col.	1	39	0	6	6	10	....	....	....	....	....	....	2010-11	2010-11
● Holota, John	Det.	2	15	2	0	2	0	....	....	....	....	....	....	1942-43	1945-46
Holst, Greg	NYR	3	11	0	0	0	0	....	....	....	....	....	....	1975-76	1977-78
Holt, Gary	Cal., Cle., St.L.	5	101	13	11	24	133	....	....	....	....	....	....	1973-74	1977-78
Holt, Randy	Chi., Cle., Van., L.A., Cgy., Wsh., Phi.	10	395	4	37	41	1438	21	2	3	5	83	....	1974-75	1983-84
● Holway, Albert	Tor., Mtl.M., Pit.	5	112	7	2	9	48	6	0	0	0	0	1	1923-24	1928-29
Holzinger, Brian	Buf., T.B., Pit., CBJ	10	547	93	145	238	339	52	11	18	29	61	....	1994-95	2003-04
Homenuke, Ron	Van.	1	1	0	0	0	0	....	....	....	....	....	....	1972-73	1972-73
Hoover, Ron	Bos., St.L.	3	18	4	0	4	31	8	0	0	0	18	....	1989-90	1991-92
Hopkins, Dean	L.A., Edm., Que.	6	223	23	51	74	306	18	1	5	6	29	....	1979-80	1988-89
Hopkins, Larry	Tor., Wpg.	4	60	13	16	29	26	6	0	0	0	2	....	1977-78	1982-83
Horacek, Tony	Phi., Chi.	5	154	10	19	29	316	2	1	0	1	2	....	1989-90	1994-95
‡ Horak, Roman	Cgy., Edm.	3	84	6	13	19	16	....	....	....	....	....	....	2011-12	2013-14
Horava, Miloslav	NYR	3	80	5	17	22	38	2	0	1	1	0	....	1988-89	1990-91
Horbul, Doug	K.C.	1	4	1	0	1	2	....	....	....	....	....	....	1974-75	1974-75
Horcoff, Shawn	Edm., Dal., Ana.	15	1008	186	325	511	624	46	11	19	30	25	....	2000-01	**2015-16**
Hordichuk, Darcy	Atl., Phx., Fla., Nsh., Van., Edm.	12	542	20	21	41	1140	17	1	0	1	16	....	2000-01	2012-13
Hordy, Mike	NYI	2	11	0	0	0	7	....	....	....	....	....	....	1978-79	1979-80
● Horeck, Pete	Chi., Det., Bos.	8	426	106	118	224	340	34	6	8	14	43	....	1944-45	1951-52
● Horne, George	Mtl.M., Tor.	3	54	9	3	12	34	4	0	0	0	4	1	1925-26	1928-29
● Horner, Red	Tor.	12	490	42	110	152	1254	71	7	10	17	170	1	1928-29	1939-40
● Hornung, Larry	St.L.	2	48	2	9	11	10	11	0	2	2	2	....	1970-71	1971-72
● Horton, Tim	Tor., NYR, Pit., Buf.	24	1446	115	403	518	1611	126	11	39	50	183	4	1949-50	1973-74
Horvath, Bronco	NYR, Mtl., Bos., Chi., Tor., Min.	9	434	141	185	326	319	36	12	9	21	18	....	1955-56	1967-68
Hospodar, Ed	NYR, Hfd., Phi., Min., Buf.	9	450	17	51	68	1314	44	4	1	5	208	....	1979-80	1987-88
‡ Hossa, Marcel	Mtl., NYR, Phx.	6	237	31	30	61	106	14	2	2	4	10	....	2001-02	2007-08
Hostak, Martin	Phi.	2	55	3	11	14	24	....	....	....	....	....	....	1990-91	1991-92
Hotham, Greg	Tor., Pit.	6	230	15	74	89	139	5	0	3	3	6	....	1979-80	1984-85
Houck, Paul	Min.	3	16	1	2	3	2	....	....	....	....	....	....	1985-86	1987-88
Houda, Doug	Det., Hfd., L.A., Buf., NYI, Ana.	15	561	19	63	82	1104	18	0	3	3	21	....	1985-86	2002-03
Houde, Claude	K.C.	2	59	3	6	9	40	....	....	....	....	....	....	1974-75	1975-76
Houde, Eric	Mtl.	3	30	2	3	5	4	....	....	....	....	....	....	1996-97	1998-99
Hough, Mike	Que., Fla., NYI	14	707	100	156	256	675	44	5	5	10	38	....	1984-85	1998-99
Houlder, Bill	Wsh., Buf., Ana., St.L., T.B., S.J., Nsh.	16	846	59	191	250	412	30	5	6	11	14	....	1987-88	2002-03
Houle, Rejean	Mtl.	11	635	161	247	408	395	90	14	34	48	66	5	1969-70	1982-83
Housley, Phil	Buf., Wpg., St.L., Cgy., N.J., Wsh., Chi., Tor.	21	1495	338	894	1232	822	85	13	43	56	36	....	1982-83	2002-03
Houston, Ken	Atl., Cgy., Wsh., L.A.	9	570	161	167	328	624	35	10	9	19	66	....	1975-76	1983-84
● Howard, Jack	Tor.	1	2	0	0	0	0	....	....	....	....	....	....	1936-37	1936-37
Howatt, Garry	NYI, Hfd., N.J.	12	720	112	156	268	1836	87	12	14	26	289	2	1972-73	1983-84
● Howe, Gordie	Det., Hfd.	26	1767	801	1049	1850	1685	157	68	92	160	220	4	1946-47	1979-80
Howe, Mark	Hfd., Phi., Det.	16	929	197	545	742	455	101	10	51	61	34	....	1979-80	1994-95
Howe, Marty	Hfd., Bos.	6	197	2	29	31	99	15	1	2	3	9	....	1979-80	1984-85
● Howe, Syd	Ott., Phi., Tor., St.L., Det.	17	698	237	291	528	212	70	17	27	44	10	3	1929-30	1945-46
● Howe, Vic	NYR	3	33	3	4	7	10	....	....	....	....	....	....	1950-51	1954-55
Howell, Harry	NYR, Oak., Cal., L.A.	21	1411	94	324	418	1298	38	3	3	6	32	....	1952-53	1972-73
● Howell, Ron	NYR	2	4	0	0	0	4	....	....	....	....	....	....	1954-55	1955-56
Howse, Don	L.A.	1	33	2	5	7	6	2	0	0	0	0	....	1979-80	1979-80
Howson, Scott	NYI	2	18	5	3	8	4	....	....	....	....	....	....	1984-85	1985-86
● Hoyda, Dave	Phi., Wpg.	4	132	6	17	23	299	12	0	0	0	17	....	1977-78	1980-81
‡ Hrabarenka, Raman	N.J.	1	1	0	0	0	0	....	....	....	....	....	....	2014-15	2014-15
Hrdina, Jan	Pit., Phx., N.J., CBJ	7	513	101	196	297	341	45	12	14	26	24	....	1998-99	2005-06
Hrdina, Jiri	Cgy., Pit.	5	250	45	85	130	92	46	2	5	7	24	3	1987-88	1991-92

Name	NHL Teams	NHL Seasons	Regular Schedule GP	G	A	TP	PIM	Playoffs GP	G	A	TP	PIM	NHL Cup Wins	First NHL Season	Last NHL Season
• Hrechkosy, Dave	Cal., St.L.	4	140	42	24	66	41	3	1	0	1	2	....	1973-74	1976-77
Hrkac, Tony	St.L., Que., S.J., Chi., Dal., Edm., NYI, Ana., Atl.	13	758	132	239	371	173	41	7	7	14	12	1	1986-87	2002-03
Hrycuik, Jim	Wsh.	1	21	5	5	10	12	....	....	....	....	....	....	1974-75	1974-75
• Hrymnak, Steve	Chi., Det.	2	18	2	1	3	4	2	0	0	0	0	....	1951-52	1952-53
Hrynewich, Tim	Pit.	2	55	6	8	14	82	....	....	....	....	....	....	1982-83	1983-84
Huard, Bill	Bos., Ott., Que., Dal., Edm., L.A.	8	223	16	18	34	594	5	0	0	0	2	....	1992-93	1999-00
• Huard, Rolly	Tor.	1	1	1	0	1	0	....	....	....	....	....	....	1930-31	1930-31
‡ Hubacek, Petr	Phi.	1	6	1	0	1	2	....	....	....	....	....	....	2000-01	2000-01
• Huber, Willie	Det., NYR, Van., Phi.	10	655	104	217	321	950	33	5	5	10	35	....	1978-79	1987-88
Hubick, Greg	Tor., Van.	2	77	6	9	15	10	....	....	....	....	....	....	1975-76	1979-80
Huck, Fran	Mtl., St.L.	3	94	24	30	54	38	11	3	4	7	2	....	1969-70	1972-73
Hucul, Fred	Chi., St.L.	5	164	11	30	41	113	6	1	0	1	10	....	1950-51	1967-68
Huddy, Charlie	Edm., L.A., Buf., St.L.	17	1017	99	354	453	785	183	19	66	85	135	5	1980-81	1996-97
Hudson, Dave	NYI, K.C., Col.	6	409	59	124	183	89	2	1	1	2	0	....	1972-73	1977-78
Hudson, Lex	Pit.	1	2	0	0	0	0	2	0	0	0	0	....	1978-79	1978-79
Hudson, Mike	Chi., Edm., NYR, Pit., Tor., St.L., Phx.	9	416	49	87	136	414	49	4	10	14	64	1	1988-89	1996-97
Hudson, Ron	Det.	2	33	5	2	7	2	....	....	....	....	....	....	1937-38	1939-40
Huffman, Kerry	Phi., Que., Ott.	10	401	37	108	145	361	11	0	0	0	2	....	1986-87	1995-96
• Huggins, Al	Mtl.M.	1	20	1	1	2	2	....	....	....	....	....	....	1930-31	1930-31
• Hughes, Albert	NYA	2	60	6	8	14	22	....	....	....	....	....	....	1930-31	1931-32
Hughes, Brent	L.A., Phi., St.L., Det., K.C.	8	435	15	117	132	440	22	1	3	4	53	....	1967-68	1974-75
Hughes, Brent	Wpg., Bos., Buf., NYI	8	357	41	39	80	831	29	4	1	5	53	....	1988-89	1996-97
Hughes, Frank	Cal.	1	5	0	0	0	0	....	....	....	....	....	....	1971-72	1971-72
Hughes, Howie	L.A.	3	168	25	32	57	30	14	2	0	2	2	....	1967-68	1969-70
Hughes, Jack	Col.	2	46	2	5	7	104	....	....	....	....	....	....	1980-81	1981-82
• Hughes, James	Det.	1	40	0	1	1	48	....	....	....	....	....	....	1929-30	1929-30
Hughes, John	Van., Edm., NYR	2	70	2	14	16	211	7	0	1	1	16	....	1979-80	1980-81
Hughes, Pat	Mtl., Pit., Edm., Buf., St.L., Hfd.	10	573	130	128	258	646	71	8	25	33	77	3	1977-78	1986-87
Hughes, Ryan	Bos.	1	3	0	0	0	0	....	....	....	....	....	....	1995-96	1995-96
Hulbig, Joe	Edm., Bos.	5	55	4	4	8	16	6	0	1	1	2	....	1996-97	2000-01
Hull, Bobby	Chi., Wpg., Hfd.	16	1063	610	560	1170	640	119	62	67	129	102	1	1957-58	1979-80
Hull, Brett	Cgy., St.L., Dal., Det., Phx.	20	1269	741	650	1391	458	202	103	87	190	73	2	1985-86	2005-06
Hull, Dennis	Chi., Det.	14	959	303	351	654	261	104	33	34	67	30	....	1964-65	1977-78
Hull, Jody	Hfd., NYR, Ott., Fla., T.B., Phi.	16	831	124	137	261	156	69	4	5	9	14	....	1988-89	2003-04
Hulse, Cale	N.J., Cgy., Nsh., Phx., CBJ	10	619	16	79	95	1000	1	0	0	0	0	....	1995-96	2005-06
‡ Huml, Ivan	Bos.	3	49	6	12	18	36	....	....	....	....	....	....	2001-02	2003-04
• Hunt, Fred	NYA, NYR	2	59	15	14	29	6	....	....	....	....	....	....	1940-41	1944-45
Hunt, Jamie	Wsh.	1	1	0	0	0	0	....	....	....	....	....	....	2006-07	2006-07
Hunter, Dale	Que., Wsh., Col.	19	1407	323	697	1020	3565	186	42	76	118	729	....	1980-81	1998-99
Hunter, Dave	Edm., Pit., Wpg.	10	746	133	190	323	918	105	16	24	40	211	3	1979-80	1988-89
Hunter, Mark	Mtl., St.L., Cgy., Hfd., Wsh.	12	628	213	171	384	1426	79	18	20	38	230	1	1981-82	1992-93
Hunter, Tim	Cgy., Que., Van., S.J.	16	815	62	76	138	3146	132	5	7	12	426	1	1981-82	1996-97
Hunter, Trent	NYI, L.A.	10	497	101	135	236	209	14	4	1	5	6	....	2001-02	2011-12
Huras, Larry	NYR	1	2	0	0	0	0	....	....	....	....	....	....	1976-77	1976-77
Hurlburt, Bob	Van.	1	1	0	0	0	2	....	....	....	....	....	....	1974-75	1974-75
Hurlbut, Mike	NYR, Que., Buf.	5	29	1	8	9	20	....	....	....	....	....	....	1992-93	1999-00
Hurley, Paul	Bos.	1	1	0	1	1	0	....	....	....	....	....	....	1968-69	1968-69
Hurst, Ron	Tor.	2	64	9	7	16	70	3	0	2	2	4	....	1955-56	1956-57
Huscroft, Jamie	N.J., Bos., Cgy., T.B., Van., Phx., Wsh.	10	352	5	33	38	1065	21	0	1	1	46	....	1988-89	1999-00
Huselius, Kristian	Fla., Cgy., CBJ	10	662	190	261	451	256	24	3	11	14	18	....	2001-02	2011-12
Huska, Ryan	Chi.	1	1	0	0	0	0	....	....	....	....	....	....	1997-98	1997-98
Huskins, Kent	Ana., S.J., St.L., Det., Phi.	7	318	13	55	68	173	48	0	3	3	23	1	2006-07	2012-13
Hussey, Matt	Pit., Det.	3	21	2	2	4	2	....	....	....	....	....	....	2003-04	2006-07
Huston, Ron	Cal.	2	79	15	31	46	8	....	....	....	....	....	....	1973-74	1974-75
Hutchinson, Andrew	Nsh., Car., T.B., Dal., Pit.	5	140	12	27	39	70	....	....	....	....	....	1	2003-04	2010-11
Hutchinson, Ron	NYR	1	9	0	0	0	0	....	....	....	....	....	....	1960-61	1960-61
Hutchison, Dave	L.A., Tor., Chi., N.J.	10	584	19	97	116	1550	48	2	12	14	149	....	1974-75	1983-84
• Hutton, Bill	Bos., Ott., Phi.	2	64	3	2	5	8	2	0	0	0	0	....	1929-30	1930-31
• Hyland, Harry	Mtl.W., Ott.	1	17	14	2	16	65	....	....	....	....	....	....	1917-18	1917-18
Hynes, Dave	Bos.	2	22	4	0	4	2	....	....	....	....	....	....	1973-74	1974-75
Hynes, Gord	Bos., Phi.	2	52	3	9	12	22	12	1	2	3	6	....	1991-92	1992-93
Hyvonen, Hannes	S.J., CBJ	2	42	4	5	9	22	....	....	....	....	....	....	2001-02	2002-03

I

Name	NHL Teams	NHL Seasons	Regular Schedule GP	G	A	TP	PIM	Playoffs GP	G	A	TP	PIM	NHL Cup Wins	First NHL Season	Last NHL Season
Iafrate, Al	Tor., Wsh., Bos., S.J.	12	799	152	311	463	1301	71	19	16	35	77	....	1984-85	1997-98
Iggulden, Mike	S.J., NYI	2	12	1	4	5	4	....	....	....	....	....	....	2007-08	2008-09
Ignatjev, Victor	Pit.	1	11	0	1	1	6	1	0	0	0	2	....	1998-99	1998-99
Ihnacak, Miroslav	Tor., Det.	3	56	8	9	17	39	1	0	0	0	0	....	1985-86	1988-89
Ihnacak, Peter	Tor.	8	417	102	165	267	175	28	4	10	14	25	....	1982-83	1989-90
Imlach, Brent	Tor.	2	3	0	0	0	0	....	....	....	....	....	....	1965-66	1966-67
‡ Immonen, Jarkko	NYR	2	20	3	5	8	4	....	....	....	....	....	....	2005-06	2006-07
Ingarfield, Earl	NYR, Pit., Oak., Cal.	13	746	179	226	405	239	21	9	8	17	10	....	1958-59	1970-71
Ingarfield, Earl	Atl., Cgy., Det.	2	39	4	4	8	22	2	0	1	1	0	....	1979-80	1980-81
Inglis, Billy	L.A., Buf.	3	36	1	3	4	4	11	1	2	3	4	....	1967-68	1970-71
• Ingoldsby, Jack	Tor.	2	29	5	1	6	15	....	....	....	....	....	....	1942-43	1943-44
• Ingram, Frank	Chi.	3	101	24	16	40	69	11	0	1	1	2	....	1929-30	1931-32
• Ingram, John	Bos.	1	1	0	0	0	0	....	....	....	....	....	....	1924-25	1924-25
• Ingram, Ron	Chi., Det., NYR	4	114	5	15	20	81	2	0	0	0	0	....	1956-57	1964-65
Intranuovo, Ralph	Edm., Tor.	3	22	2	4	6	4	....	....	....	....	....	....	1994-95	1996-97
Irmen, Danny	Min.	1	2	0	0	0	0	....	....	....	....	....	....	2009-10	2009-10
• Irvin, Dick	Chi.	3	94	29	23	52	78	2	2	0	2	4	....	1926-27	1928-29
Irvine, Ted	Bos., L.A., NYR, St.L.	11	724	154	177	331	657	83	16	24	40	115	....	1963-64	1976-77
Irwin, Brayden	Tor.	1	2	0	0	0	2	....	....	....	....	....	....	2009-10	2009-10
Irwin, Ivan	Mtl., NYR	5	155	2	27	29	214	5	0	0	0	8	....	1952-53	1957-58
• Isaksson, Ulf	L.A.	1	50	7	15	22	10	....	....	....	....	....	....	1982-83	1982-83
Isbister, Brad	Phx., NYI, Edm., Bos., NYR, Van.	10	541	106	116	222	615	18	1	2	3	33	....	1997-98	2007-08
Issel, Kim	Edm.	1	4	0	0	0	0	....	....	....	....	....	....	1988-89	1988-89
Ivanans, Raitis	Mtl., L.A., Cgy.	7	282	12	6	18	569	1	0	0	0	0	....	2005-06	2011-12

J

Name	NHL Teams	NHL Seasons	Regular Schedule GP	G	A	TP	PIM	Playoffs GP	G	A	TP	PIM	NHL Cup Wins	First NHL Season	Last NHL Season
Jacina, Greg	Fla.	2	14	0	1	1	6	....	....	....	....	....	....	2005-06	2006-07
Jackman, Barret	St.L., Nsh.	14	876	29	157	186	1102	53	2	5	7	84	....	2001-02	**2015-16**
Jackman, Ric	Dal., Bos., Tor., Pit., Fla., Ana.	7	231	19	58	77	166	7	1	1	2	2	1	1999-00	2006-07
Jackman, Tim	CBJ, Phx., L.A., NYI, Cgy., Ana.	12	483	32	43	75	806	9	0	0	0	12	....	2003-04	**2015-16**
• Jackson, Art	Tor., Bos., NYA	11	468	123	178	301	144	52	8	12	20	29	2	1934-35	1944-45
• Jackson, Busher	Tor., NYA, Bos.	15	633	241	234	475	437	71	18	12	30	53	1	1929-30	1943-44
Jackson, Dane	Van., Buf., NYI	4	45	12	6	18	58	6	0	0	0	10	....	1993-94	1997-98
Jackson, Don	Min., Edm., NYR	10	311	16	52	68	640	53	4	5	9	147	2	1977-78	1986-87
• Jackson, Harold	Chi., Det.	8	219	17	34	51	208	31	1	2	3	33	2	1936-37	1946-47
• Jackson, Jack	Chi.	1	48	2	5	7	38	....	....	....	....	....	....	1946-47	1946-47
Jackson, Jeff	Tor., NYR, Que., Chi.	8	263	38	48	86	313	6	1	1	2	16	....	1984-85	1991-92
Jackson, Jim	Cgy., Buf.	4	112	17	30	47	20	14	3	2	5	6	....	1982-83	1987-88
• Jackson, Lloyd	NYA	1	14	1	1	2	0	....	....	....	....	....	....	1936-37	1936-37
Jackson, Scott	T.B.	1	1	0	0	0	0	....	....	....	....	....	....	2009-10	2009-10
• Jackson, Stan	Tor., Bos., Ott.	5	86	9	6	15	75	....	....	....	....	....	1	1921-22	1926-27
• Jackson, Walter	NYA, Bos.	4	84	16	11	27	18	....	....	....	....	....	....	1932-33	1935-36
• Jacobs, Paul	Tor.	1	1	0	0	0	0	....	....	....	....	....	....	1918-19	1918-19
Jacobs, Tim	Cal.	1	46	0	10	10	35	....	....	....	....	....	....	1975-76	1975-76
‡ Jacques, Jean-Francois	Edm., Ana.	7	166	9	8	17	197	....	....	....	....	....	....	2005-06	2011-12
‡ Jaffray, Jason	Van., Cgy., Wpg.	4	49	4	7	11	40	....	....	....	....	....	....	2007-08	2011-12
Jakopin, John	Fla., Pit., S.J.	6	113	1	6	7	145	....	....	....	....	....	....	1997-98	2002-03
Jalo, Risto	Edm.	1	3	0	3	3	0	....	....	....	....	....	....	1985-86	1985-86
Jalonen, Kari	Cgy., Edm.	2	37	9	6	15	4	5	1	0	1	0	....	1982-83	1983-84
James, Connor	L.A., Pit.	3	16	1	0	1	2	....	....	....	....	....	....	2005-06	2008-09
James, Gerry	Tor.	5	149	14	26	40	257	15	1	0	1	8	....	1954-55	1959-60
James, Val	Buf., Tor.	2	11	0	0	0	30	3	0	0	0	0	....	1981-82	1986-87
• Jamieson, Jim	NYR	1	1	0	1	1	0	....	....	....	....	....	....	1943-44	1943-44
Jancevski, Dan	Dal., T.B.	3	9	0	0	0	2	....	....	....	....	....	....	2005-06	2008-09

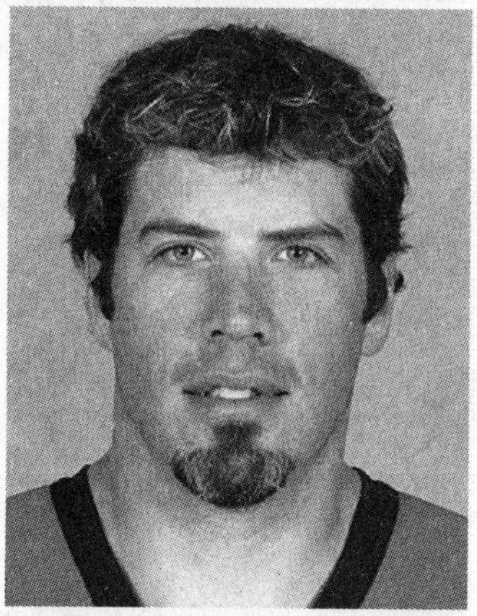
Jody Hull

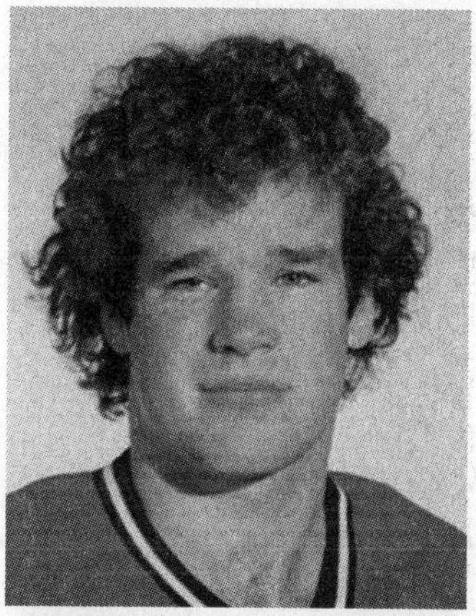
Mark Hunter

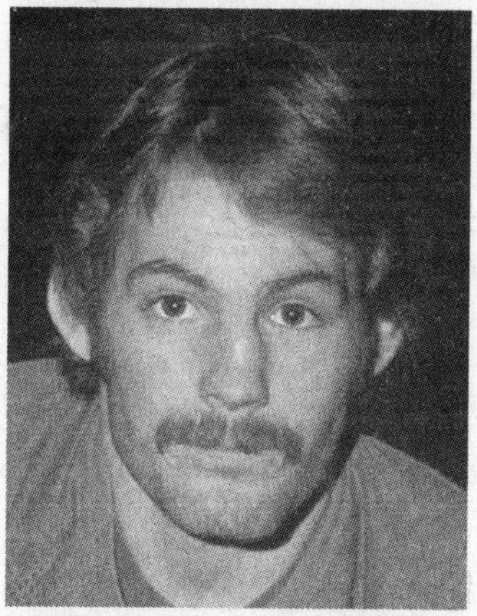
Earl Ingarfield

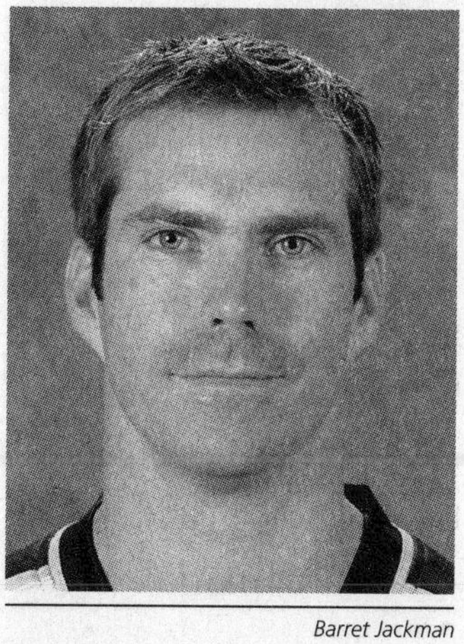
Barret Jackman

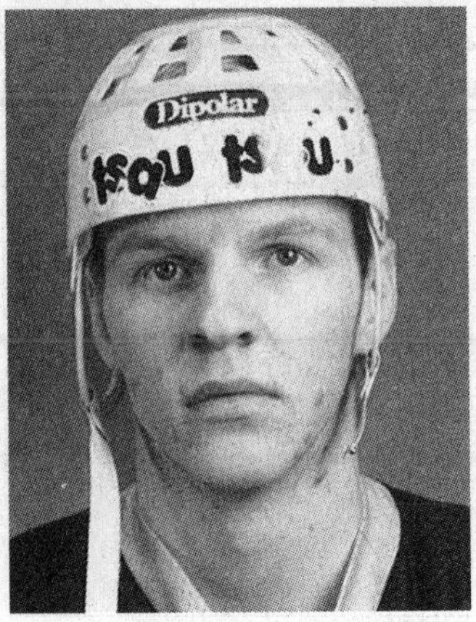

Kari Jalonen

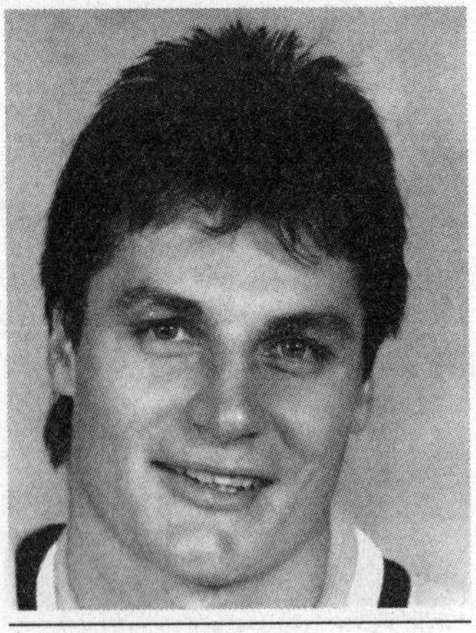

Grant Jennings

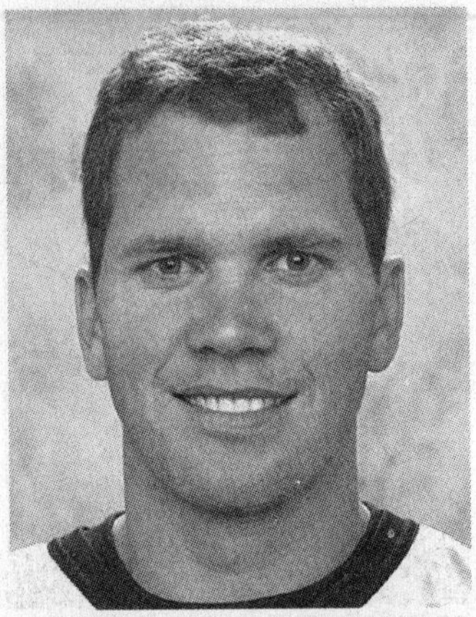

Greg Johnson

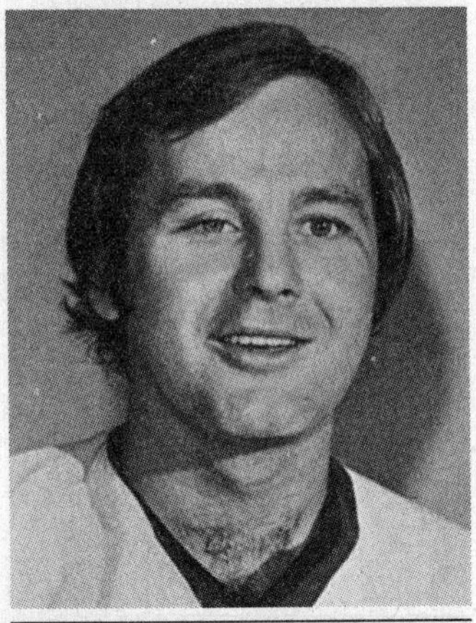

Joey Johnston

Name	NHL Teams	NHL Seasons	Regular Schedule GP	G	A	TP	PIM	Playoffs GP	G	A	TP	PIM	NHL Cup Wins	First NHL Season	Last NHL Season
Janik, Doug	Buf., T.B., Dal., Mtl., Det.	9	190	3	16	19	154	6	1	0	1	2	....	2002-03	2011-12
• Jankowski, Lou	Det., Chi.	4	127	19	18	37	15	1	0	0	0	0	....	1950-51	1954-55
Janney, Craig	Bos., St.L., S.J., Wpg., Phx., T.B., NYI	12	760	188	563	751	170	120	24	86	110	53	....	1987-88	1998-99
Janssen, Cam	N.J., St.L.	9	336	6	8	14	774	10	0	0	0	26	....	2005-06	2013-14
Janssens, Mark	NYR, Min., Hfd., Ana., NYI, Phx., Chi.	14	711	40	73	113	1422	27	5	1	6	33	....	1987-88	2000-01
Jantunen, Marko	Cgy.	1	3	0	0	0	0	....	....	....	....	....	....	1996-97	1996-97
Jardine, Ryan	Fla.	1	8	0	2	2	2	....	....	....	....	....	....	2001-02	2001-02
‡ Jarrett, Cole	NYI	1	1	0	0	0	0	....	....	....	....	....	....	2005-06	2005-06
• Jarrett, Doug	Chi., NYR	13	775	38	182	220	631	99	7	16	23	82	....	1964-65	1976-77
Jarrett, Gary	Tor., Det., Oak., Cal.	7	341	72	92	164	131	11	3	1	4	9	....	1960-61	1971-72
Jarry, Pierre	NYR, Tor., Det., Min.	7	344	88	117	205	142	5	0	1	1	0	....	1971-72	1977-78
Jarvenpaa, Hannu	Wpg.	3	114	11	26	37	83	....	....	....	....	....	....	1986-87	1988-89
Jarventie, Martti	Mtl.	1	1	0	0	0	0	....	....	....	....	....	....	2001-02	2001-02
Jarvi, Iiro	Que.	2	116	18	43	61	58	....	....	....	....	....	....	1988-89	1989-90
Jarvis, Doug	Mtl., Wsh., Hfd.	13	964	139	264	403	263	105	14	27	41	42	4	1975-76	1987-88
• Jarvis, James	Pit., Phi., Tor.	3	112	17	15	32	62	....	....	....	....	....	....	1929-30	1936-37
Jarvis, Wes	Wsh., Min., L.A., Tor.	9	237	31	55	86	98	2	0	0	0	2	....	1979-80	1987-88
‡ Jaspers, Jason	Phx.	3	9	0	1	1	6	....	....	....	....	....	....	2001-02	2003-04
• Javanainen, Arto	Pit.	1	14	4	1	5	2	....	....	....	....	....	....	1984-85	1984-85
Jay, Bob	L.A.	1	3	0	1	1	0	....	....	....	....	....	....	1993-94	1993-94
‡ Jeffrey, Dustin	Pit., Dal., Ari.	7	131	18	15	33	12	....	....	....	....	....	....	2008-09	**2015-16**
Jeffrey, Larry	Det., Tor., NYR	8	368	39	62	101	293	38	4	10	14	42	1	1961-62	1968-69
Jelinek, Tomas	Ott.	1	49	7	6	13	52	....	....	....	....	....	....	1992-93	1992-93
Jenkins, Dean	L.A.	1	5	0	0	0	2	....	....	....	....	....	....	1983-84	1983-84
• Jenkins, Roger	Chi., Tor., Mtl., Bos., Mtl.M., NYA	8	325	15	39	54	253	27	1	7	8	12	2	1930-31	1938-39
• Jennings, Bill	Det., Bos.	5	108	32	33	65	45	20	4	4	8	6	....	1940-41	1944-45
Jennings, Grant	Wsh., Hfd., Pit., Tor., Buf.	9	389	14	43	57	804	54	2	1	3	68	2	1987-88	1995-96
Jensen, Chris	NYR, Phi.	6	74	9	12	21	27	....	....	....	....	....	....	1985-86	1991-92
Jensen, David	Min.	3	18	0	2	2	11	....	....	....	....	....	....	1983-84	1985-86
Jensen, David	Hfd., Wsh.	4	69	9	13	22	22	11	0	0	0	2	....	1984-85	1987-88
Jensen, Joe	Car.	1	6	1	0	1	2	....	....	....	....	....	....	2007-08	2007-08
Jensen, Steve	Min., L.A.	7	438	113	107	220	318	12	0	3	3	9	....	1975-76	1981-82
• Jeremiah, Ed	NYA, Bos.	1	15	0	1	1	0	....	....	....	....	....	....	1931-32	1931-32
Jerrard, Paul	Min.	1	5	0	0	0	4	....	....	....	....	....	....	1988-89	1988-89
• Jerwa, Frank	Bos., St.L.	4	81	11	16	27	53	....	....	....	....	....	....	1931-32	1934-35
• Jerwa, Joe	NYR, Bos., NYA	7	234	29	58	87	309	17	2	3	5	16	....	1930-31	1938-39
Jessiman, Hugh	Fla.	1	2	0	0	0	5	....	....	....	....	....	....	2010-11	2010-11
Jillson, Jeff	S.J., Bos., Buf.	4	140	9	32	41	96	8	0	0	0	0	....	2001-02	2005-06
• Jirik, Jaroslav	St.L.	1	3	0	0	0	0	....	....	....	....	....	....	1969-70	1969-70
• Joanette, Rosario	Mtl.	1	2	0	1	1	4	....	....	....	....	....	....	1944-45	1944-45
Jodzio, Rick	Col., Cle.	1	70	2	8	10	71	....	....	....	....	....	....	1977-78	1977-78
‡ Joensuu, Jesse	NYI, Edm.	6	129	13	11	24	77	1	0	0	0	0	....	2008-09	2014-15
Johannesen, Glenn	NYI	1	2	0	0	0	0	....	....	....	....	....	....	1985-86	1985-86
Johannson, John	N.J.	1	5	0	0	0	0	....	....	....	....	....	....	1983-84	1983-84
• Johansen, Bill	Tor.	1	1	0	0	0	0	....	....	....	....	....	....	1949-50	1949-50
Johansen, Trevor	Tor., Col., L.A.	5	286	11	46	57	282	13	0	3	3	21	....	1977-78	1981-82
Johansson, Andreas	NYI, Pit., Ott., T.B., Cgy., NYR, Nsh.	8	377	81	88	169	190	9	0	0	0	0	....	1995-96	2003-04
Johansson, Bjorn	Cle.	2	15	1	1	2	10	....	....	....	....	....	....	1976-77	1977-78
Johansson, Calle	Buf., Wsh., Tor.	17	1109	119	416	535	519	105	12	43	55	44	....	1987-88	2003-04
Johansson, Jonas	Wsh.	1	1	0	0	0	2	....	....	....	....	....	....	2005-06	2005-06
Johansson, Magnus	Chi., Fla.	1	45	0	14	14	18	....	....	....	....	....	....	2007-08	2007-08
Johansson, Mathias	Cgy., Pit.	1	58	5	10	15	16	....	....	....	....	....	....	2002-03	2002-03
Johansson, Roger	Cgy., Chi.	4	161	9	34	43	163	5	0	1	1	2	....	1989-90	1994-95
• Johns, Don	NYR, Mtl., Min.	6	153	2	21	23	76	....	....	....	....	....	....	1960-61	1967-68
‡ Johnson, Aaron	CBJ, NYI, Chi., Cgy., Edm., Bos.	8	291	17	45	62	227	....	....	....	....	....	....	2003-04	2012-13
Johnson, Allan	Mtl., Det.	4	105	21	28	49	30	11	2	2	4	6	....	1956-57	1962-63
Johnson, Brian	Det.	1	3	0	0	0	5	....	....	....	....	....	....	1983-84	1983-84
• Johnson, Ching	NYR, NYA	12	436	38	48	86	808	61	5	2	7	161	2	1926-27	1937-38
Johnson, Craig	St.L., L.A., Ana., Tor., Wsh.	10	557	75	98	173	260	16	3	2	5	10	....	1994-95	2003-04
• Johnson, Danny	Tor., Van., Det.	3	121	18	19	37	24	....	....	....	....	....	....	1969-70	1971-72
• Johnson, Earl	Det.	1	1	0	0	0	0	....	....	....	....	....	1	1953-54	1953-54
Johnson, Greg	Det., Pit., Chi., Nsh.	12	785	145	224	369	345	37	7	6	13	14	....	1993-94	2005-06
Johnson, Jim	NYR, Phi., L.A.	8	302	75	111	186	73	7	0	2	2	2	....	1964-65	1971-72
Johnson, Jim	Pit., Min., Dal., Wsh., Phx.	13	829	29	166	195	1197	51	1	11	12	132	....	1985-86	1997-98
Johnson, Justin	NYI	1	2	0	0	0	7	....	....	....	....	....	....	2013-14	2013-14
Johnson, Mark	Pit., Min., Hfd., St.L., N.J.	11	669	203	305	508	260	37	16	12	28	10	....	1979-80	1989-90
Johnson, Matt	L.A., Atl., Min.	10	473	23	20	43	1523	16	0	0	0	31	....	1994-95	2003-04
Johnson, Mike	Tor., T.B., Phx., Mtl., St.L.	11	661	129	246	375	315	22	4	3	7	10	....	1996-97	2007-08
‡ Johnson, Nick	Pit., Min., Phx., Bos.	5	113	14	23	37	52	....	....	....	....	....	....	2009-10	2013-14
• Johnson, Norm	Bos., Chi.	3	61	5	20	25	41	14	4	0	4	6	....	1957-58	1959-60
Johnson, Ryan	Fla., T.B., St.L., Van., Chi.	13	701	38	84	122	250	29	1	4	5	12	....	1997-98	2010-11
Johnson, Terry	Que., St.L., Cgy., Tor.	9	285	3	24	27	580	38	0	4	4	118	....	1979-80	1987-88
• Johnson, Tom	Mtl., Bos.	17	978	51	213	264	960	111	8	15	23	109	6	1947-48	1964-65
• Johnson, Virgil	Chi.	3	75	1	11	12	27	19	0	3	3	4	1	1937-38	1944-45
Johnsson, Kim	NYR, Phi., Min., Chi.	10	739	67	217	284	406	43	2	10	12	38	....	1999-00	2009-10
Johnston, Bernie	Hfd.	2	57	12	24	36	16	3	0	1	1	0	....	1979-80	1980-81
• Johnston, George	Chi.	4	58	20	12	32	2	....	....	....	....	....	....	1941-42	1946-47
Johnston, Greg	Bos., Tor.	9	187	26	29	55	124	22	2	1	3	12	....	1983-84	1991-92
Johnston, Jay	Wsh.	2	8	0	0	0	13	....	....	....	....	....	....	1980-81	1981-82
Johnston, Joey	Min., Cal., Chi.	6	331	85	106	191	320	....	....	....	....	....	....	1968-69	1975-76
Johnston, Larry	L.A., Det., K.C., Col.	7	320	9	64	73	580	....	....	....	....	....	....	1967-68	1976-77
Johnston, Marshall	Min., Cal.	7	251	14	52	66	58	6	0	0	0	2	....	1967-68	1973-74
Johnston, Randy	NYI	1	4	0	0	0	4	....	....	....	....	....	....	1979-80	1979-80
Johnstone, Eddie	NYR, Det.	10	426	122	136	258	375	55	13	10	23	83	....	1975-76	1986-87
• Johnstone, Ross	Tor.	2	42	5	4	9	14	3	0	0	0	0	1	1943-44	1944-45
‡ Jokela, Mikko	Van.	1	1	0	0	0	0	....	....	....	....	....	....	2002-03	2002-03
Jokinen, Olli	L.A., NYI, Fla., Phx., Cgy., NYR, Wpg., Nsh., Tor., St.L.	17	1231	321	429	750	1071	6	2	3	5	4	....	1997-98	2014-15
• Joliat, Aurele	Mtl.	16	655	270	190	460	771	45	9	13	22	66	3	1922-23	1937-38
• Joliat, Rene	Mtl.	1	1	0	0	0	0	....	....	....	....	....	....	1924-25	1924-25
Joly, Greg	Wsh., Det.	9	365	21	76	97	250	5	0	0	0	8	....	1974-75	1982-83
Joly, Yvan	Mtl.	3	2	0	0	0	0	1	0	0	0	0	....	1979-80	1982-83
Jomphe, Jean-Francois	Ana., Phx., Mtl.	4	111	10	29	39	102	....	....	....	....	....	....	1995-96	1998-99
Jonathan, Stan	Bos., Pit.	8	411	91	110	201	751	63	8	4	12	137	....	1975-76	1982-83
‡ Jones, Blair	T.B., Cgy., Phi.	8	132	7	10	17	65	7	0	0	0	2	....	2006-07	2014-15
Jones, Bob	NYR	1	2	0	0	0	0	....	....	....	....	....	....	1968-69	1968-69
Jones, Brad	Wpg., L.A., Phi.	6	148	25	31	56	122	9	1	1	2	2	....	1986-87	1991-92
• Jones, Buck	Det., Tor.	4	50	2	2	4	36	12	0	1	1	18	....	1938-39	1942-43
Jones, David	Col., Cgy., Min.	9	462	104	87	191	122	27	2	5	7	8	....	2007-08	**2015-16**
Jones, Jim	Cal.	1	2	0	0	0	0	....	....	....	....	....	....	1971-72	1971-72
Jones, Jimmy	Tor.	3	148	13	18	31	68	19	1	5	6	11	....	1977-78	1979-80
Jones, Keith	Wsh., Col., Phi.	9	491	117	141	258	765	63	12	12	24	120	....	1992-93	2000-01
Jones, Matt	Phx.	3	106	1	10	11	63	....	....	....	....	....	....	2005-06	2007-08
Jones, Randy	Phi., L.A., T.B., Wpg.	8	365	20	85	105	185	31	0	4	4	8	....	2003-04	2011-12
Jones, Ron	Bos., Pit., Wsh.	5	54	1	4	5	31	....	....	....	....	....	....	1971-72	1975-76
‡ Jones, Ryan	Nsh., Edm.	6	334	54	46	100	181	....	....	....	....	....	....	2008-09	2013-14
Jones, Ty	Chi., Fla.	2	14	0	0	0	19	....	....	....	....	....	....	1998-99	2003-04
Jonsson, Hans	Pit.	4	242	10	38	48	92	27	0	1	1	14	....	1999-00	2002-03
Jonsson, Jorgen	NYI, Ana.	1	81	12	19	31	16	....	....	....	....	....	....	1999-00	1999-00
Jonsson, Kenny	Tor., NYI	10	686	63	204	267	298	19	1	3	4	6	....	1994-95	2003-04
Jonsson, Lars	Phi.	1	8	0	2	2	6	....	....	....	....	....	....	2006-07	2006-07
Jonsson, Tomas	NYI, Edm.	8	552	85	259	344	482	80	11	26	37	97	2	1981-82	1988-89
• Jordan, Michal	Car.	3	79	3	4	7	18	....	....	....	....	....	....	2012-13	**2015-16**
Joseph, Chris	Pit., Edm., T.B., Van., Phi., Phx., Atl.	14	510	39	112	151	567	31	3	4	7	24	....	1987-88	2000-01
Joseph, Tony	Wpg.	1	2	1	0	1	0	....	....	....	....	....	....	1988-89	1988-89
‡ Joslin, Derek	S.J., Car., Van.	5	116	4	12	16	63	....	....	....	....	....	....	2008-09	2012-13
‡ Joudrey, Andrew	CBJ	1	1	0	0	0	0	....	....	....	....	....	....	2011-12	2011-12
Jovanovski, Ed	Fla., Van., Phx.	18	1128	137	363	500	1491	76	11	19	30	102	....	1995-96	2013-14
Joyal, Eddie	Det., Tor., L.A., Phi.	9	466	128	134	262	103	50	11	8	19	18	....	1962-63	1971-72
Joyce, Bob	Bos., Wsh., Wpg.	6	158	34	49	83	90	46	15	9	24	29	....	1987-88	1992-93
Joyce, Duane	Dal.	1	3	0	0	0	0	....	....	....	....	....	....	1993-94	1993-94
• Juckes, Bing	NYR	2	16	2	1	3	6	....	....	....	....	....	....	1947-48	1949-50

Name	NHL Teams	NHL Seasons	Regular Schedule GP	G	A	TP	PIM	Playoffs GP	G	A	TP	PIM	NHL Cup Wins	First NHL Season	Last NHL Season
Juhlin, Patrik	Phi.	2	56	7	6	13	23	13	1	0	1	2	....	1994-95	1995-96
Julien, Claude	Que.	2	14	0	1	1	25	....	....	....	....	....	....	1984-85	1985-86
Juneau, Joe	Bos., Wsh., Buf., Ott., Phx., Mtl.	13	828	156	416	572	272	112	25	54	79	69	....	1991-92	2003-04
Junker, Steve	NYI	2	5	0	0	0	0	3	0	1	1	0	....	1992-93	1993-94
‡ Junland, Jonas	St.L.	2	4	0	2	2	2	....	....	....	....	....	....	2008-09	2009-10
‡ Jurcina, Milan	Bos., Wsh., CBJ, NYI	7	430	22	59	81	280	21	2	0	2	18	....	2005-06	2011-12
Jutila, Timo	Buf.	1	10	1	5	6	13	....	....	....	....	....	....	1984-85	1984-85
• Juzda, Bill	NYR, Tor.	9	398	14	54	68	398	42	0	3	3	46	2	1940-41	1951-52

K

Name	NHL Teams	NHL Seasons	Regular Schedule GP	G	A	TP	PIM	Playoffs GP	G	A	TP	PIM	NHL Cup Wins	First NHL Season	Last NHL Season
• Kabel, Bob	NYR	2	48	5	13	18	34	....	....	....	....	....	....	1959-60	1960-61
Kaberle, Frantisek	L.A., Atl., Car.	9	523	29	164	193	218	32	4	10	14	10	1	1999-00	2008-09
Kaberle, Tomas	Tor., Bos., Car., Mtl.	14	984	87	476	563	260	102	6	33	39	28	1	1998-99	2012-13
Kachowski, Mark	Pit.	3	64	6	5	11	209	....	....	....	....	....	....	1987-88	1989-90
• Kachur, Ed	Chi.	2	96	10	14	24	35	....	....	....	....	....	....	1956-57	1957-58
Kaese, Trent	Buf.	1	1	0	0	0	0	....	....	....	....	....	....	1988-89	1988-89
Kaigorodov, Alexei	Ott.	1	6	0	1	1	0	....	....	....	....	....	....	2006-07	2006-07
• Kaiser, Vern	Mtl.	1	50	7	5	12	33	2	0	0	0	0	....	1950-51	1950-51
• Kalbfleisch, Walter	Ott., St.L., NYA, Bos.	4	36	0	4	4	32	5	0	0	0	2	....	1933-34	1936-37
• Kaleta, Alex	Chi., NYR	7	387	92	121	213	190	17	1	6	7	2	....	1941-42	1950-51
Kaleta, Patrick	Buf.	9	348	27	27	54	542	12	2	3	5	28	....	2006-07	2014-15
‡ Kalinin, Dmitri	Buf., NYR, Phx.	9	539	36	126	162	321	37	2	7	9	20	....	1999-00	2008-09
Kalinski, Jon	Phi.	2	22	1	4	5	0	....	....	....	....	....	....	2008-09	2009-10
‡ Kallio, Tomi	Atl., CBJ, Phi.	3	140	24	31	55	48	....	....	....	....	....	....	2000-01	2002-03
Kallur, Anders	NYI	6	383	101	110	211	149	78	12	23	35	32	4	1979-80	1984-85
Kalus, Petr	Bos., Min.	2	11	4	1	5	6	....	....	....	....	....	....	2006-07	2009-10
Kamensky, Valeri	Que., Col., NYR, Dal., N.J.	11	637	200	301	501	383	66	25	35	60	72	1	1991-92	2001-02
Kaminski, Kevin	Min., Que., Wsh.	7	139	3	10	13	528	8	0	0	0	52	....	1988-89	1996-97
• Kaminsky, Max	Ott., St.L., Bos., Mtl.M.	4	130	22	34	56	38	4	0	0	0	0	....	1933-34	1936-37
Kaminsky, Yan	Wpg., NYI	2	26	3	2	5	4	2	0	0	0	4	....	1993-94	1994-95
• Kampman, Bingo	Tor.	5	189	14	30	44	287	47	1	4	5	38	1	1937-38	1941-42
Kana, Tomas	CBJ	1	6	0	2	2	2	....	....	....	....	....	....	2009-10	2009-10
Kane, Boyd	Phi., Wsh.	5	31	0	3	3	39	....	....	....	....	....	....	2003-04	2009-10
• Kane, Francis	Det.	1	2	0	0	0	0	....	....	....	....	....	....	1943-44	1943-44
Kanko, Petr	L.A.	1	10	1	0	1	0	....	....	....	....	....	....	2005-06	2005-06
Kannegiesser, Gord	St.L.	2	23	0	1	1	15	....	....	....	....	....	....	1967-68	1971-72
Kannegiesser, Sheldon	Pit., NYR, L.A., Van.	8	366	14	67	81	292	18	0	2	2	10	....	1970-71	1977-78
‡ Kapanen, Niko	Dal., Atl., Phx.	6	397	36	90	126	160	18	5	4	9	22	....	2001-02	2007-08
Kapanen, Sami	Hfd., Car., Phi.	12	831	189	269	458	175	87	13	22	35	22	....	1995-96	2007-08
Karabin, Ladislav	Pit.	1	9	0	0	0	2	....	....	....	....	....	....	1993-94	1993-94
Karalahti, Jere	L.A., Nsh.	3	149	8	19	27	97	17	0	1	1	20	....	1999-00	2001-02
Karamnov, Vitali	St.L.	3	92	12	20	32	65	2	0	0	0	2	....	1992-93	1994-95
Kariya, Paul	Ana., Col., Nsh., St.L.	15	989	402	587	989	399	46	16	23	39	12	....	1994-95	2009-10
Kariya, Steve	Van.	3	65	9	18	27	32	....	....	....	....	....	....	1999-00	2001-02
Karjalainen, Kyosti	L.A.	1	28	1	8	9	12	3	0	1	1	2	....	1991-92	1991-92
Karlander, Al	Det.	4	212	36	56	92	70	4	0	1	1	0	....	1969-70	1972-73
Karlsson, Andreas	Atl., T.B.	5	264	16	35	51	72	6	0	0	0	0	....	1999-00	2007-08
Karpa, Dave	Que., Ana., Car., NYR	12	557	18	80	98	1374	19	1	1	2	39	....	1991-92	2002-03
• Karpov, Valeri	Ana.	3	76	14	15	29	32	....	....	....	....	....	....	1994-95	1996-97
• Karpovtsev, Alexander	NYR, Tor., Chi., NYI, Fla.	12	596	34	154	188	430	74	4	14	18	52	1	1993-94	2005-06
‡ Karsums, Martins	Bos., T.B.	1	24	1	5	6	6	....	....	....	....	....	....	2008-09	2008-09
Kasatonov, Alexei	N.J., Ana., St.L., Bos.	7	383	38	122	160	326	33	4	7	11	40	....	1989-90	1995-96
‡ Kaspar, Lukas	S.J.	2	16	2	2	4	8	....	....	....	....	....	....	2007-08	2008-09
Kasparaitis, Darius	NYI, Pit., Col., NYR	14	863	27	136	163	1379	83	2	10	12	107	....	1992-93	2006-07
Kasper, Steve	Bos., L.A., Phi., T.B.	13	821	177	291	468	554	94	20	28	48	82	....	1980-81	1992-93
Kassian, Matt	Min., Ott.	4	76	4	1	5	177	5	0	2	2	17	....	2010-11	2013-14
Kastelic, Ed	Wsh., Hfd.	7	220	11	10	21	719	8	1	0	1	32	....	1985-86	1991-92
Kaszycki, Mike	NYI, Wsh., Tor.	5	226	42	80	122	108	19	2	6	8	10	....	1977-78	1982-83
‡ Katic, Mark	NYI	1	11	0	1	1	4	....	....	....	....	....	....	2010-11	2010-11
Kavanagh, Pat	Van., Phi.	4	14	2	0	2	4	3	0	0	0	2	....	2000-01	2005-06
• Kea, Ed	Atl., St.L.	10	583	30	145	175	508	32	2	4	6	39	....	1973-74	1982-83
Keane, Mike	Mtl., Col., NYR, Dal., St.L., Van.	16	1161	168	302	470	881	220	34	40	74	135	3	1988-89	2003-04
Kearns, Dennis	Van.	10	677	31	290	321	386	11	1	2	3	8	....	1971-72	1980-81
• Keating, Jack	Det.	2	11	3	0	3	4	....	....	....	....	....	....	1938-39	1939-40
• Keating, John	NYA	2	35	5	5	10	17	....	....	....	....	....	....	1931-32	1932-33
Keating, Mike	NYR	1	1	0	0	0	0	....	....	....	....	....	....	1977-78	1977-78
• Keats, Duke	Bos., Det., Chi.	3	82	30	19	49	113	....	....	....	....	....	....	1926-27	1928-29
Keczmer, Dan	Min., Hfd., Cgy., Dal., Nsh.	10	235	8	38	46	212	12	0	1	1	8	....	1990-91	1999-00
Keefe, Sheldon	T.B.	3	125	12	12	24	78	....	....	....	....	....	....	2000-01	2002-03
• Keeling, Butch	Tor., NYR	12	525	157	63	220	331	47	11	11	22	34	1	1926-27	1937-38
Keenan, Larry	Tor., St.L., Buf., Phi.	6	233	38	64	102	28	46	15	16	31	12	....	1961-62	1971-72
Kehoe, Rick	Tor., Pit.	14	906	371	396	767	120	39	4	17	21	4	....	1971-72	1984-85
Keith, Matt	Chi., NYI	4	27	2	3	5	14	....	....	....	....	....	....	2003-04	2007-08
Kekalainen, Jarmo	Bos., Ott.	3	55	5	8	13	28	....	....	....	....	....	....	1989-90	1993-94
Kelleher, Chris	Bos.	1	1	0	0	0	0	....	....	....	....	....	....	2001-02	2001-02
Keller, Ralph	NYR	1	3	1	0	1	6	....	....	....	....	....	....	1962-63	1962-63
Keller, Ryan	Ott.	1	6	0	0	0	0	....	....	....	....	....	....	2009-10	2009-10
Kellgren, Christer	Col.	1	5	0	0	0	0	....	....	....	....	....	....	1981-82	1981-82
Kelly, Bob	Phi., Wsh.	12	837	154	208	362	1454	101	9	14	23	172	2	1970-71	1981-82
Kelly, Bob	St.L., Pit., Chi.	6	425	87	109	196	687	23	6	3	9	40	....	1973-74	1978-79
Kelly, Dave	Det.	1	16	2	0	2	4	....	....	....	....	....	....	1976-77	1976-77
Kelly, John Paul	L.A.	7	400	54	70	124	366	18	1	1	2	41	....	1979-80	1985-86
• Kelly, Pep	Tor., Chi., Bro.	8	288	74	53	127	105	38	7	6	13	10	....	1934-35	1941-42
• Kelly, Pete	St.L., Det., NYA, Bro.	7	177	21	38	59	68	19	3	1	4	2	2	1934-35	1941-42
Kelly, Red	Det., Tor.	20	1316	281	542	823	327	164	33	59	92	51	8	1947-48	1966-67
Kelly, Steve	Edm., T.B., N.J., L.A., Min.	9	149	9	12	21	83	25	0	0	0	8	1	1996-97	2007-08
• Kemp, Kevin	Hfd.	1	3	0	0	0	4	....	....	....	....	....	....	1980-81	1980-81
• Kemp, Stan	Tor.	1	1	0	0	0	2	....	....	....	....	....	....	1948-49	1948-49
‡ Kemppainen, Joonas	Bos.	1	44	2	3	5	4	....	....	....	....	....	....	**2015-16**	**2015-16**
Kenady, Chris	St.L., NYR	2	7	0	2	2	0	....	....	....	....	....	....	1997-98	1999-00
• Kendall, Bill	Chi., Tor.	5	131	16	10	26	28	6	0	0	0	0	1	1933-34	1937-38
‡ Kenins, Ronalds	Van.	2	38	4	8	12	14	5	1	1	2	4	....	2014-15	**2015-16**
Kennedy, Dean	L.A., NYR, Buf., Wpg., Edm.	12	717	26	110	136	1118	36	1	7	8	59	....	1982-83	1994-95
Kennedy, Forbes	Chi., Det., Bos., Phi., Tor.	11	603	70	108	178	988	12	2	4	6	64	....	1956-57	1968-69
Kennedy, Mike	Dal., Tor., NYI	5	145	16	36	52	112	5	0	0	0	9	....	1994-95	1998-99
Kennedy, Sheldon	Det., Cgy., Bos.	8	310	49	58	107	233	24	6	4	10	20	....	1989-90	1996-97
• Kennedy, Ted	Tor.	14	696	231	329	560	432	78	29	31	60	32	5	1942-43	1956-57
‡ Kennedy, Tim	Buf., Fla., S.J., Phx.	6	162	15	24	39	60	9	1	2	3	6	....	2008-09	2013-14
Kennedy, Tyler	Pit., S.J., NYI, N.J.	9	527	89	126	215	239	79	12	15	27	27	1	2007-08	**2015-16**
• Kenny, Ernest	NYR, Chi.	2	10	0	0	0	18	....	....	....	....	....	....	1930-31	1934-35
Keon, Dave	Tor., Hfd.	18	1296	396	590	986	117	92	32	36	68	6	4	1960-61	1981-82
Kerch, Alexander	Edm.	1	5	0	0	0	2	....	....	....	....	....	....	1993-94	1993-94
Kerr, Alan	NYI, Det., Wpg.	9	391	72	94	166	826	38	5	4	9	70	....	1984-85	1992-93
Kerr, Reg	Cle., Chi., Edm.	6	263	66	94	160	169	7	1	0	1	7	....	1977-78	1983-84
Kerr, Tim	Phi., NYR, Hfd.	13	655	370	304	674	596	81	40	31	71	58	....	1980-81	1992-93
Kesa, Dan	Van., Dal., Pit., T.B.	4	139	8	22	30	66	13	1	0	1	0	....	1993-94	1999-00
Kessell, Rick	Pit., Cal.	5	135	4	24	28	6	....	....	....	....	....	....	1969-70	1973-74
Ketola, Veli-Pekka	Col.	1	44	9	5	14	4	....	....	....	....	....	....	1981-82	1981-82
Ketter, Kerry	Atl.	1	41	0	2	2	58	....	....	....	....	....	....	1972-73	1972-73
Kharin, Sergei	Wpg.	1	7	2	3	5	2	....	....	....	....	....	....	1990-91	1990-91
Kharitonov, Alexander	T.B., NYI	2	71	7	15	22	12	....	....	....	....	....	....	2000-01	2001-02
Khavanov, Alexander	St.L., Tor.	5	348	27	75	102	233	26	5	5	10	18	....	2000-01	2005-06
Khmylev, Yuri	Buf., St.L.	5	263	64	88	152	133	26	8	6	14	24	....	1992-93	1996-97
Khristich, Dmitri	Wsh., L.A., Bos., Tor.	12	811	259	337	596	422	75	15	25	40	41	....	1990-91	2001-02
Kidd, Ian	Van.	2	20	4	7	11	25	....	....	....	....	....	....	1987-88	1988-89
Kiessling, Udo	Min.	1	1	0	0	0	2	....	....	....	....	....	....	1981-82	1981-82
Kilger, Chad	Ana., Wpg., Phx., Chi., Edm., Mtl., Tor.	12	714	107	111	218	363	36	3	2	5	13	....	1995-96	2007-08
Kilrea, Brian	Det., L.A.	2	26	3	5	8	12	....	....	....	....	....	....	1957-58	1967-68
• Kilrea, Hec	Ott., Det., Tor.	15	633	167	129	296	438	48	8	7	15	18	3	1925-26	1939-40
• Kilrea, Ken	Det.	5	91	16	23	39	8	15	2	2	4	4	....	1938-39	1943-44
• Kilrea, Wally	Ott., Phi., NYA, Mtl.M., Det.	9	329	35	58	93	87	25	2	4	6	6	2	1929-30	1937-38

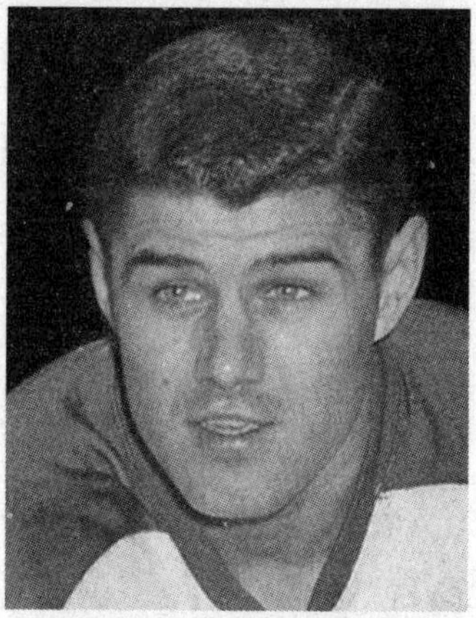

Bob Kabel

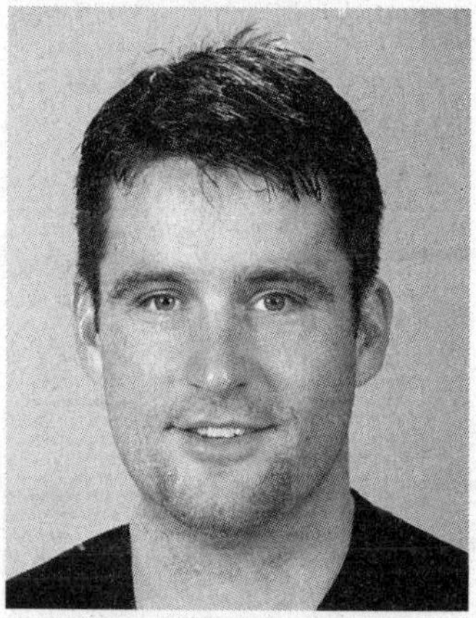

Dan Keczmer

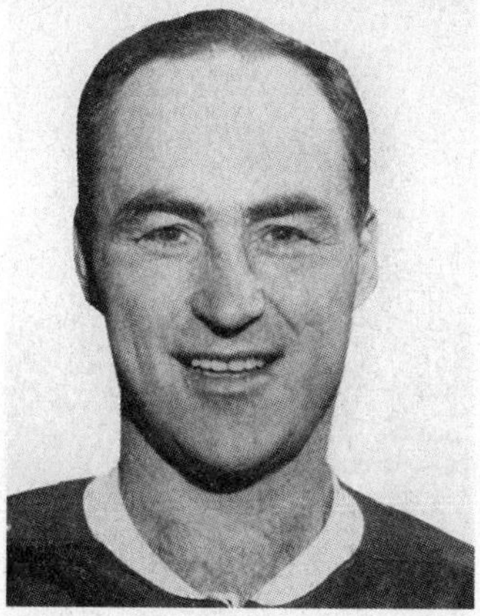

Red Kelly

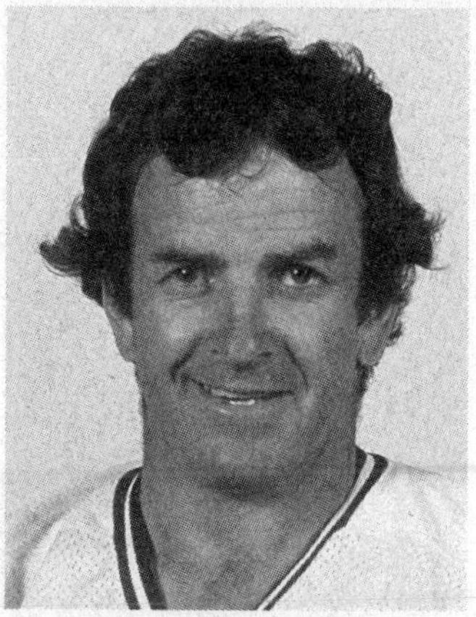

Dave Keon

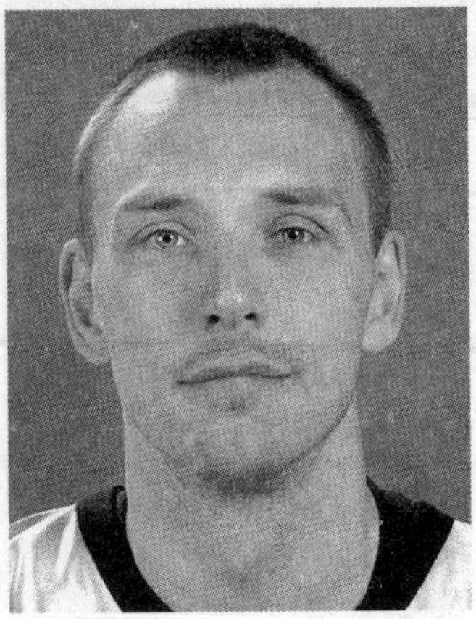

Patric Kjellberg

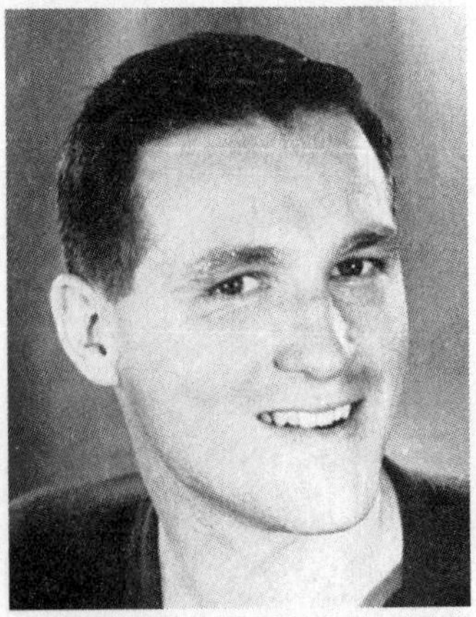

Bill Knibbs

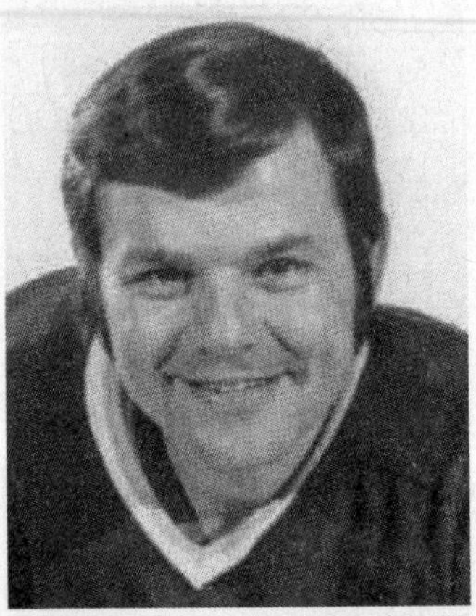

George Konik

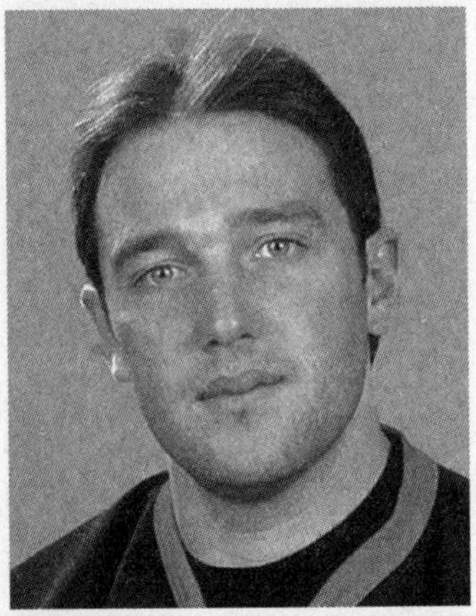

Sergei Krivokrasov

Name	NHL Teams	NHL Seasons	Regular Schedule GP	G	A	TP	PIM	Playoffs GP	G	A	TP	PIM	NHL Cup Wins	First NHL Season	Last NHL Season
Kimble, Darin	Que., St.L., Bos., Chi.	7	311	23	20	43	1082	23	0	0	0	52	....	1988-89	1994-95
Kindrachuk, Orest	Phi., Pit., Wsh.	10	508	118	261	379	648	76	20	20	40	53	2	1972-73	1981-82
King, D.J.	St.L., Wsh.	6	118	4	7	11	215	....	....	....	....	....	....	2006-07	2011-12
King, Derek	NYI, Hfd., Tor., St.L.	14	830	261	351	612	417	47	4	17	21	24	....	1986-87	1999-00
• King, Frank	Mtl.	1	10	1	0	1	2	....	....	....	....	....	....	1950-51	1950-51
King, Jason	Van., Ana.	3	59	12	11	23	8	1	0	0	0	0	....	2002-03	2007-08
King, Kris	Det., NYR, Wpg., Phx., Tor., Chi.	14	849	66	85	151	2030	67	8	5	13	142	....	1987-88	2000-01
King, Steven	NYR, Ana.	3	67	17	8	25	75	....	....	....	....	....	....	1992-93	1995-96
King, Wayne	Cal.	3	73	5	18	23	34	....	....	....	....	....	....	1973-74	1975-76
Kinnear, Geordie	Atl.	1	4	0	0	0	13	....	....	....	....	....	....	1999-00	1999-00
‡ Kinrade, Geoff	T.B.	1	1	0	0	0	0	....	....	....	....	....	....	2008-09	2008-09
Kinsella, Brian	Wsh.	2	10	0	1	1	0	....	....	....	....	....	....	1975-76	1976-77
• Kinsella, Ray	Ott.	1	14	0	0	0	0	....	....	....	....	....	....	1930-31	1930-31
Kiprusoff, Marko	Mtl., NYI	2	51	0	10	10	12	....	....	....	....	....	....	1995-96	2001-02
• Kirk, Bobby	NYR	1	39	4	8	12	14	....	....	....	....	....	....	1937-38	1937-38
• Kirkpatrick, Bob	NYR	1	49	12	12	24	6	....	....	....	....	....	....	1942-43	1942-43
Kirton, Mark	Tor., Det., Van.	6	266	57	56	113	121	4	1	2	3	7	....	1979-80	1984-85
Kisio, Kelly	Det., NYR, S.J., Cgy.	13	761	229	429	658	768	39	6	15	21	52	....	1982-83	1994-95
• Kitchen, Bill	Mtl., Tor.	4	41	1	4	5	40	3	0	1	1	0	....	1981-82	1984-85
• Kitchen, Hobie	Mtl.M., Det.	2	47	5	4	9	58	....	....	....	....	....	1	1925-26	1926-27
Kitchen, Mike	Col., N.J.	8	474	12	62	74	370	2	0	0	0	2	....	1976-77	1983-84
Kjellberg, Patric	Mtl., Nsh., Ana.	6	394	64	96	160	84	10	0	0	0	0	....	1992-93	2002-03
‡ Klasen, Linus	Nsh.	1	4	0	0	0	0	....	....	....	....	....	....	2010-11	2010-11
Klassen, Ralph	Cal., Cle., Col., St.L.	9	497	52	93	145	120	26	4	2	6	12	....	1975-76	1983-84
Klatt, Trent	Min., Dal., Phi., Van., L.A.	13	782	143	200	343	307	74	16	9	25	20	....	1991-92	2003-04
Klee, Ken	Wsh., Tor., N.J., Col., Atl., Ana., Phx.	14	934	55	140	195	880	51	2	2	4	50	....	1994-95	2008-09
• Klein, Lloyd	Bos., NYA	8	164	30	24	54	68	5	0	0	0	2	1	1928-29	1937-38
Kleinendorst, Scot	NYR, Hfd., Wsh.	8	281	12	46	58	452	26	2	7	9	40	....	1982-83	1989-90
Klementyev, Anton	NYI	1	1	0	0	0	0	....	....	....	....	....	....	2009-10	2009-10
Klemm, Jon	Que., Col., Chi., Dal., L.A.	15	773	42	100	142	436	105	7	7	14	47	2	1991-92	2007-08
‡ Klepis, Jakub	Wsh.	2	66	4	10	14	36	....	....	....	....	....	....	2005-06	2006-07
Klesla, Rostislav	CBJ, Phx.	13	659	48	111	159	620	23	2	7	9	11	....	2000-01	2013-14
Klima, Petr	Det., Edm., T.B., L.A., Pit.	13	786	313	260	573	671	95	28	24	52	83	1	1985-86	1998-99
Klimovich, Sergei	Chi.	1	1	0	0	0	2	....	....	....	....	....	....	1996-97	1996-97
• Klingbeil, Ike	Chi.	1	5	1	2	3	2	....	....	....	....	....	....	1936-37	1936-37
‡ Klingberg, Carl	Atl., Wpg.	4	12	1	0	1	4	....	....	....	....	....	....	2010-11	2014-15
‡ Klinkhammer, Rob	Chi., Ott., Phx., Ari., Pit., Edm.	6	193	22	21	43	64	....	....	....	....	....	....	2010-11	**2015-16**
‡ Kloucek, Tomas	NYR, Nsh., Atl.	5	141	2	8	10	250	....	....	....	....	....	....	2000-01	2005-06
• Klukay, Joe	Tor., Bos.	11	566	109	127	236	189	71	13	10	23	23	4	1942-43	1955-56
Kluzak, Gord	Bos.	7	299	25	98	123	543	46	6	13	19	129	....	1982-83	1990-91
• Knibbs, Bill	Bos.	1	53	7	10	17	4	....	....	....	....	....	....	1964-65	1964-65
Knipscheer, Fred	Bos., St.L.	3	28	6	3	9	18	16	2	1	3	6	....	1993-94	1995-96
• Knott, Nick	Bro.	1	14	3	1	4	9	....	....	....	....	....	....	1941-42	1941-42
Knox, Paul	Tor.	1	1	0	0	0	0	....	....	....	....	....	....	1954-55	1954-55
Knuble, Mike	Det., NYR, Bos., Phi., Wsh.	16	1068	278	270	548	641	65	14	16	30	38	1	1996-97	2012-13
Knutsen, Espen	Ana., CBJ	5	207	30	81	111	105	....	....	....	....	....	....	1997-98	2003-04
Koalska, Matt	NYI	1	3	0	0	0	2	....	....	....	....	....	....	2005-06	2005-06
Kobasew, Chuck	Cgy., Bos., Min., Col., Pit.	11	601	110	100	210	394	44	4	4	8	38	....	2002-03	2013-14
Koci, David	Chi., T.B., St.L., Col.	5	142	3	1	4	461	....	....	....	....	....	....	2006-07	2010-11
Kocur, Joe	Det., NYR, Van.	15	820	80	82	162	2519	118	10	12	22	231	3	1984-85	1998-99
Koehler, Greg	Car.	1	1	0	0	0	0	....	....	....	....	....	....	2000-01	2000-01
Kohn, Dustin	NYI	1	22	0	4	4	4	....	....	....	....	....	....	2009-10	2009-10
Kohn, Ladislav	Cgy., Tor., Ana., Atl., Det.	7	186	14	28	42	125	2	0	0	0	5	....	1995-96	2002-03
‡ Koistinen, Ville	Nsh., Fla.	3	103	8	24	32	40	....	....	....	....	....	....	2007-08	2009-10
Koivisto, Tom	St.L.	1	22	2	4	6	10	....	....	....	....	....	....	2002-03	2002-03
Koivu, Saku	Mtl., Ana.	18	1124	255	577	832	809	80	18	41	59	62	....	1995-96	2013-14
Kolanos, Krys	Phx., Edm., Min., Cgy.	6	149	20	22	42	94	2	0	0	0	6	....	2001-02	2011-12
‡ Kolarik, Chad	CBJ, NYR	2	6	0	1	1	2	....	....	....	....	....	....	2009-10	2010-11
Kolarik, Pavel	Bos.	2	23	0	0	0	10	....	....	....	....	....	....	2000-01	2001-02
Kolesar, Mark	Tor.	2	28	2	2	4	14	3	1	0	1	2	....	1995-96	1996-97
Kolnik, Juraj	NYI, Fla.	6	240	46	49	95	84	....	....	....	....	....	....	2000-01	2006-07
Kolstad, Dean	Min., S.J.	3	40	1	7	8	69	....	....	....	....	....	....	1988-89	1992-93
Koltsov, Konstantin	Pit.	3	144	12	26	38	50	....	....	....	....	....	....	2002-03	2005-06
Komadoski, Neil	L.A., St.L.	8	502	16	76	92	632	23	0	2	2	47	....	1972-73	1979-80
Komarniski, Zenith	Van., CBJ	3	21	1	1	2	10	....	....	....	....	....	....	1999-00	2003-04
Komisarek, Mike	Mtl., Tor., Car.	11	551	14	67	81	679	29	1	2	3	56	....	2002-03	2013-14
Konan, Matthew	Phi.	1	2	0	0	0	0	....	....	....	....	....	....	2012-13	2012-13
Kondratiev, Maxim	Tor., NYR, Ana.	3	40	1	2	3	24	....	....	....	....	....	....	2003-04	2007-08
• Konik, George	Pit.	1	52	7	8	15	26	....	....	....	....	....	....	1967-68	1967-68
Konopka, Zenon	Ana., CBJ, T.B., NYI, Ott., Min., Buf.	9	346	12	18	30	1082	8	0	2	2	2	....	2005-06	2013-14
Konowalchuk, Steve	Wsh., Col.	14	790	171	225	396	703	52	9	12	21	60	....	1991-92	2005-06
Konroyd, Steve	Cgy., NYI, Chi., Hfd., Det., Ott.	15	895	41	195	236	863	97	10	15	25	99	....	1980-81	1994-95
Konstantinov, Vladimir	Det.	6	446	47	128	175	838	82	5	14	19	107	1	1991-92	1996-97
‡ Kontiola, Petri	Chi.	1	12	0	5	5	6	....	....	....	....	....	....	2007-08	2007-08
Kontos, Chris	NYR, Pit., L.A., T.B.	8	230	54	69	123	103	20	11	0	11	12	....	1982-83	1992-93
• Kopak, Russ	Bos.	1	24	7	9	16	0	....	....	....	....	....	....	1943-44	1943-44
‡ Kopecky, Tomas	Det., Chi., Fla.	10	578	68	106	174	307	37	5	3	8	25	2	2005-06	2014-15
Korab, Jerry	Chi., Van., Buf., L.A.	15	975	114	341	455	1629	93	8	18	26	201	....	1970-71	1984-85
Kordic, Dan	Phi.	6	197	4	8	12	584	12	1	0	1	22	....	1991-92	1998-99
• Kordic, John	Mtl., Tor., Wsh., Que.	7	244	17	18	35	997	41	4	3	7	131	1	1985-86	1991-92
Korn, Jim	Det., Tor., Buf., N.J., Cgy.	10	597	66	122	188	1801	16	1	2	3	109	....	1979-80	1989-90
Korney, Mike	Det., NYR	4	77	9	10	19	59	....	....	....	....	....	....	1973-74	1978-79
‡ Korobov, Dmitry	T.B.	1	3	0	1	1	2	....	....	....	....	....	....	2013-14	2013-14
Korolev, Evgeny	NYI	3	42	1	4	5	20	2	0	0	0	0	....	1999-00	2001-02
• Korolev, Igor	St.L., Wpg., Phx., Tor., Chi.	12	795	119	227	346	330	41	0	8	8	6	....	1992-93	2003-04
Koroll, Cliff	Chi.	11	814	208	254	462	376	85	19	29	48	67	....	1969-70	1979-80
Korolyuk, Alexander	S.J.	6	296	62	80	142	140	34	6	8	14	18	....	1997-98	2003-04
Kortko, Roger	NYI	2	79	7	17	24	28	10	0	3	3	17	....	1984-85	1985-86
‡ Kostitsyn, Andrei	Mtl., Nsh.	7	398	103	119	222	181	49	14	9	23	24	....	2005-06	2011-12
‡ Kostitsyn, Sergei	Mtl., Nsh.	6	353	67	109	176	188	40	4	11	15	22	....	2007-08	2012-13
Kostynski, Doug	Bos.	2	15	3	1	4	4	....	....	....	....	....	....	1983-84	1984-85
Kotalik, Ales	Buf., Edm., NYR, Cgy.	9	542	136	148	284	348	34	6	9	15	16	....	2001-02	2010-11
• Kotanen, Dick	NYR	1	1	0	0	0	0	....	....	....	....	....	....	1950-51	1950-51
Kotsopoulos, Chris	NYR, Hfd., Tor., Det.	10	479	44	109	153	827	31	1	3	4	91	....	1980-81	1989-90
‡ Kovalchuk, Ilya	Atl., N.J.	11	816	417	399	816	516	32	11	16	27	31	....	2001-02	2012-13
Kovalenko, Andrei	Que., Col., Mtl., Edm., Phi., Car., Bos.	9	620	173	206	379	389	33	5	6	11	20	....	1992-93	2000-01
Kovalev, Alex	NYR, Pit., Mtl., Ott., Fla.	19	1316	430	599	1029	1304	123	45	55	100	114	1	1992-93	2012-13
Kowal, Joe	Buf.	2	22	0	5	5	13	2	0	0	0	0	....	1976-77	1977-78
Kozak, Don	L.A., Van.	7	437	96	86	182	480	29	7	2	9	69	....	1972-73	1978-79
Kozak, Les	Tor.	1	12	1	0	1	2	....	....	....	....	....	....	1961-62	1961-62
Kozlov, Viktor	S.J., Fla., N.J., NYI, Wsh.	14	897	198	339	537	248	35	4	8	12	10	....	1994-95	2008-09
Kozlov, Vyacheslav	Det., Buf., Atl.	18	1182	356	497	853	704	118	42	37	79	82	2	1991-92	2009-10
‡ Kozun, Brandon	Tor.	1	20	2	2	4	6	....	....	....	....	....	....	2014-15	2014-15
Kraft, Milan	Pit.	4	207	41	41	82	52	8	0	0	0	2	....	2000-01	2003-04
Kraft, Ryan	S.J.	1	7	0	1	1	0	....	....	....	....	....	....	2002-03	2002-03
• Kraftcheck, Stephen	Bos., NYR, Tor.	4	157	11	18	29	83	6	0	0	0	7	....	1950-51	1958-59
‡ Krajicek, Lukas	Fla., Van., T.B., Phi.	7	328	11	61	72	245	34	0	5	5	20	....	2001-02	2009-10
Krake, Skip	Bos., L.A., Buf.	7	249	23	40	63	182	10	1	0	1	17	....	1963-64	1970-71
Kravchuk, Igor	Chi., Edm., St.L., Ott., Cgy., Fla.	12	699	64	210	274	251	51	6	15	21	18	....	1991-92	2002-03
Kravets, Mikhail	S.J.	2	2	0	0	0	0	....	....	....	....	....	....	1991-92	1992-93
Krentz, Dale	Det.	3	30	5	3	8	9	2	0	0	0	0	....	1986-87	1988-89
‡ Kreps, Kamil	Fla.	4	232	18	42	60	71	....	....	....	....	....	....	2006-07	2009-10
Krestanovich, Jordan	Col.	2	22	0	2	2	6	....	....	....	....	....	....	2001-02	2003-04
Kristek, Jaroslav	Buf.	1	6	0	0	0	4	....	....	....	....	....	....	2002-03	2002-03
Krivokrasov, Sergei	Chi., Nsh., Cgy., Min., Ana.	10	450	86	109	195	288	21	2	0	2	14	....	1992-93	2001-02
Krog, Jason	NYI, Ana., Atl., NYR, Van.	7	202	22	37	59	46	21	3	1	4	4	....	1999-00	2008-09
• Krol, Joe	NYR, Bro.	3	26	10	4	14	8	....	....	....	....	....	....	1936-37	1941-42
Kromm, Richard	Cgy., NYI	9	372	70	103	173	138	36	2	6	8	22	....	1983-84	1992-93
Kron, Robert	Van., Hfd., Car., CBJ	12	771	144	194	338	119	16	3	2	5	2	....	1990-91	2001-02
‡ Kronwall, Staffan	Tor., Wsh., Cgy.	4	66	1	3	4	23	....	....	....	....	....	....	2005-06	2009-10
Krook, Kevin	Col.	1	3	0	0	0	2	....	....	....	....	....	....	1978-79	1978-79
Kroupa, Vlastimil	S.J., N.J.	5	105	4	19	23	66	20	1	2	3	25	....	1993-94	1997-98

Name	NHL Teams	NHL Seasons	Regular Schedule					Playoffs					NHL Cup Wins	First NHL Season	Last NHL Season
			GP	G	A	TP	PIM	GP	G	A	TP	PIM			
Krulicki, Jim	NYR, Det.	1	41	0	3	3	6	....	....	....	....	....	....	1970-71	1970-71
Krupp, Uwe	Buf., NYI, Que., Col., Det., Atl.	15	729	69	212	281	660	81	6	23	29	86	1	1986-87	2002-03
Kruppke, Gord	Det.	3	23	0	0	0	32	....	....	....	....	....	....	1990-91	1993-94
Kruse, Paul	Cgy., NYI, Buf., S.J.	11	423	38	33	71	1074	28	5	2	7	36	....	1990-91	2000-01
Krushelnyski, Mike	Bos., Edm., L.A., Tor., Det.	14	897	241	328	569	699	139	29	43	72	106	3	1981-82	1994-95
• Krutov, Vladimir	Van.	1	61	11	23	34	20	....	....	....	....	....	....	1989-90	1989-90
Krygier, Todd	Hfd., Wsh., Ana.	9	543	100	143	243	533	48	10	7	17	40	....	1989-90	1997-98
Kryskow, Dave	Chi., Wsh., Det., Atl.	4	231	33	56	89	174	12	2	0	2	4	....	1972-73	1975-76
• Kryzanowski, Ed	Bos., Chi.	5	237	15	22	37	65	18	0	1	1	4	....	1948-49	1952-53
Kuba, Filip	Fla., Min., T.B., Ott.	14	836	70	263	333	361	31	4	11	15	38	....	1998-99	2012-13
‡ Kubalik, Tomas	CBJ	2	12	1	3	4	6	....	....	....	....	....	....	2010-11	2011-12
Kubina, Pavel	T.B., Tor., Atl., Phi.	14	970	110	276	386	1123	51	3	7	10	110	1	1997-98	2011-12
Kucera, Frantisek	Chi., Hfd., Van., Phi., CBJ, Pit., Wsh.	9	465	24	95	119	251	12	0	1	1	0	....	1990-91	2001-02
Kudashov, Alexei	Tor.	1	25	1	0	1	4	....	....	....	....	....	....	1993-94	1993-94
Kudelski, Bob	L.A., Ott., Fla.	9	442	139	102	241	218	22	4	4	8	4	....	1987-88	1995-96
Kudroc, Kristian	T.B., Fla.	3	26	2	2	4	38	....	....	....	....	....	....	2000-01	2003-04
• Kuhn, Gord	NYA	1	12	1	1	2	4	....	....	....	....	....	....	1932-33	1932-33
‡ Kukkonen, Lasse	Chi., Phi.	4	159	6	16	22	90	14	0	2	2	6	....	2003-04	2008-09
• Kukulowicz, Aggie	NYR	2	4	1	0	1	0	....	....	....	....	....	....	1952-53	1953-54
Kulak, Stu	Van., Edm., NYR, Que., Wpg.	4	90	8	4	12	130	3	0	0	0	2	....	1982-83	1988-89
‡ Kulda, Arturs	Atl., Wpg.	3	15	0	2	2	8	....	....	....	....	....	....	2009-10	2011-12
Kuleshov, Mikhail	Col.	1	3	0	0	0	0	....	....	....	....	....	....	2003-04	2003-04
• Kullman, Arnie	Bos.	2	13	0	1	1	11	....	....	....	....	....	....	1947-48	1949-50
• Kullman, Eddie	NYR	6	343	56	70	126	298	6	1	0	1	2	....	1947-48	1953-54
Kultanen, Jarno	Bos.	3	102	2	11	13	59	....	....	....	....	....	....	2000-01	2002-03
Kumpel, Mark	Que., Det., Wpg.	6	288	38	46	84	113	39	6	4	10	14	....	1984-85	1990-91
‡ Kundratek, Tomas	Wsh.	2	30	1	6	7	10	....	....	....	....	....	....	2011-12	2012-13
• Kuntz, Alan	NYR	2	45	10	12	22	12	6	1	0	1	2	....	1941-42	1945-46
Kuntz, Murray	St.L.	1	7	1	2	3	0	....	....	....	....	....	....	1974-75	1974-75
Kurka, Tomas	Car.	2	17	3	2	5	2	....	....	....	....	....	....	2002-03	2003-04
Kurri, Jari	Edm., L.A., NYR, Ana., Col.	17	1251	601	797	1398	545	200	106	127	233	123	5	1980-81	1997-98
Kurtenbach, Orland	NYR, Bos., Tor., Van.	13	639	119	213	332	628	19	2	4	6	70	....	1960-61	1973-74
Kurtz, Justin	Van.	1	27	3	5	8	14	....	....	....	....	....	....	2001-02	2001-02
Kurvers, Tom	Mtl., Buf., N.J., Tor., Van., NYI, Ana.	11	659	93	328	421	350	57	8	22	30	68	1	1984-85	1994-95
Kuryluk, Merv	Chi.	1	....	....	....	....	....	2	0	0	0	0	....	1961-62	1961-62
Kushner, Dale	NYI, Phi.	3	84	10	13	23	215	....	....	....	....	....	....	1989-90	1991-92
‡ Kutlak, Zdenek	Bos.	3	16	1	2	3	4	....	....	....	....	....	....	2000-01	2003-04
Kuznetsov, Maxim	Det., L.A.	4	136	2	8	10	137	....	....	....	....	....	....	2000-01	2003-04
Kuznik, Greg	Car.	1	1	0	0	0	0	....	....	....	....	....	....	2000-01	2000-01
Kuzyk, Ken	Cle.	2	41	5	9	14	8	....	....	....	....	....	....	1976-77	1977-78
Kvartalnov, Dmitri	Bos.	2	112	42	49	91	26	4	0	0	0	0	....	1992-93	1993-94
Kvasha, Oleg	Fla., NYI, Phx.	7	493	81	136	217	335	21	1	2	3	8	....	1998-99	2005-06
Kwiatkowski, Joel	Ott., Wsh., Fla., Pit., Atl.	7	282	16	29	45	245	6	0	0	0	2	....	2000-01	2007-08
Kwong, Larry	NYR	1	1	0	0	0	0	....	....	....	....	....	....	1947-48	1947-48
• Kyle, Bill	NYR	2	3	0	3	3	0	....	....	....	....	....	....	1949-50	1950-51
• Kyle, Gus	NYR, Bos.	3	203	6	20	26	362	14	1	2	3	34	....	1949-50	1951-52
Kyllonen, Markku	Wpg.	1	9	0	2	2	2	....	....	....	....	....	....	1988-89	1988-89
Kypreos, Nick	Wsh., Hfd., NYR, Tor.	8	442	46	44	90	1210	34	1	3	4	65	1	1989-90	1996-97
Kyte, Jim	Wpg., Pit., Cgy., Ott., S.J.	13	598	17	49	66	1342	42	0	6	6	94	....	1982-83	1995-96
‡ Kytnar, Milan	Edm.	1	1	0	0	0	0	....	....	....	....	....	....	2011-12	2011-12
L															
‡ Laakso, Teemu	Nsh.	3	17	0	0	0	10	....	....	....	....	....	....	2009-10	2011-12
Laaksonen, Antti	Bos., Min., Col.	8	483	81	87	168	152	25	1	5	6	6	....	1998-99	2006-07
Labadie, Mike	NYR	1	3	0	0	0	0	....	....	....	....	....	....	1952-53	1952-53
Labatte, Neil	St.L.	2	26	0	2	2	19	....	....	....	....	....	....	1978-79	1981-82
L'Abbe, Moe	Chi.	1	5	0	1	1	0	....	....	....	....	....	....	1972-73	1972-73
Labelle, Marc	Dal.	1	9	0	0	0	46	....	....	....	....	....	....	1996-97	1996-97
• Labine, Leo	Bos., Det.	11	643	128	193	321	730	60	12	11	23	82	....	1951-52	1961-62
Labossiere, Gord	NYR, L.A., Min.	6	215	44	62	106	75	10	2	3	5	28	....	1963-64	1971-72
Labovitch, Max	NYR	1	5	0	0	0	4	....	....	....	....	....	....	1943-44	1943-44
Labraaten, Dan	Det., Cgy.	4	268	71	73	144	47	8	1	0	1	4	....	1978-79	1981-82
Labre, Yvon	Pit., Wsh.	9	371	14	87	101	788	....	....	....	....	....	....	1970-71	1980-81
• Labrie, Guy	Bos., NYR	2	42	4	9	13	16	....	....	....	....	....	....	1943-44	1944-45
• Lach, Elmer	Mtl.	14	664	215	408	623	478	76	19	45	64	36	3	1940-41	1953-54
Lachance, Michel	Col.	1	21	0	4	4	22	....	....	....	....	....	....	1978-79	1978-79
Lachance, Scott	NYI, Mtl., Van., CBJ	13	819	31	112	143	567	11	1	2	3	6	....	1991-92	2003-04
Lacombe, Francois	Oak., Buf., Que.	4	78	2	17	19	54	3	1	0	1	0	....	1968-69	1979-80
Lacombe, Normand	Buf., Edm., Phi.	7	319	53	62	115	196	26	5	1	6	49	1	1984-85	1990-91
LaCouture, Dan	Edm., Pit., NYR, Bos., N.J., Car.	9	337	20	25	45	348	6	0	0	0	2	....	1998-99	2008-09
Lacroix, Andre	Phi., Chi., Hfd.	6	325	79	119	198	44	16	2	5	7	0	....	1967-68	1979-80
Lacroix, Daniel	NYR, Bos., Phi., Edm., NYI	7	188	11	7	18	379	16	0	1	1	26	....	1993-94	1999-00
Lacroix, Eric	Tor., L.A., Col., NYR, Ott.	8	472	67	70	137	361	30	1	5	6	25	....	1993-94	2000-01
Lacroix, Pierre	Que., Hfd.	4	274	24	108	132	197	8	0	2	2	10	....	1979-80	1982-83
Ladouceur, Randy	Det., Hfd., Ana.	14	930	30	126	156	1322	40	5	8	13	59	....	1982-83	1995-96
LaFayette, Nathan	St.L., Van., NYR, L.A.	6	187	17	20	37	103	32	2	7	9	8	....	1993-94	1998-99
Laflamme, Christian	Chi., Edm., Mtl., St.L.	8	324	2	45	47	282	9	0	1	1	6	....	1996-97	2003-04
Lafleur, Guy	Mtl., NYR, Que.	17	1126	560	793	1353	399	128	58	76	134	67	5	1971-72	1990-91
• Lafleur, Roland	Mtl.	1	1	0	0	0	0	....	....	....	....	....	....	1924-25	1924-25
LaFontaine, Pat	NYI, Buf., NYR	15	865	468	545	1013	552	69	26	36	62	36	....	1983-84	1997-98
• Laforce, Ernie	Mtl.	1	1	0	0	0	0	....	....	....	....	....	....	1942-43	1942-43
LaForest, Bob	L.A.	1	5	1	0	1	2	....	....	....	....	....	....	1983-84	1983-84
Laforge, Claude	Mtl., Det., Phi.	8	193	24	33	57	82	5	1	2	3	15	....	1957-58	1968-69
Laforge, Marc	Hfd., Edm.	2	14	0	0	0	64	....	....	....	....	....	....	1989-90	1993-94
• Laframboise, Pete	Cal., Wsh., Pit.	4	227	33	55	88	70	9	1	0	1	0	....	1971-72	1974-75
• Lafrance, Adie	Mtl.	1	3	0	0	0	2	2	0	0	0	0	....	1933-34	1933-34
• Lafrance, Leo	Mtl., Chi.	2	33	2	0	2	6	....	....	....	....	....	....	1926-27	1927-28
Lafreniere, Jason	Que., NYR, T.B.	5	146	34	53	87	22	15	1	5	6	19	....	1986-87	1993-94
• Lafreniere, Roger	Det., St.L.	2	13	0	0	0	4	....	....	....	....	....	....	1962-63	1972-73
Lagace, Jean-Guy	Pit., Buf., K.C.	6	197	9	39	48	251	....	....	....	....	....	....	1968-69	1975-76
Laidlaw, Tom	NYR, L.A.	10	705	25	139	164	717	69	4	17	21	78	....	1980-81	1989-90
‡ Lain, Kellan	Van.	1	9	1	0	1	21	....	....	....	....	....	....	2013-14	2013-14
Laing, Quintin	Chi., Wsh.	4	79	3	8	11	31	....	....	....	....	....	....	2003-04	2009-10
Laird, Robbie	Min.	1	1	0	0	0	0	....	....	....	....	....	....	1979-80	1979-80
Lajeunesse, Serge	Det., Phi.	5	103	1	4	5	103	....	....	....	....	....	....	1970-71	1974-75
• Lakovic, Sasha	Cgy., N.J.	3	37	0	4	4	118	....	....	....	....	....	....	1996-97	1998-99
• Lalande, Hec	Chi., Det.	4	151	21	39	60	120	....	....	....	....	....	....	1953-54	1957-58
‡ Laliberte, David	Phi.	1	11	2	1	3	6	1	0	0	0	2	....	2009-10	2009-10
Lalonde, Bobby	Van., Atl., Bos., Cgy.	11	641	124	210	334	298	16	4	2	6	6	....	1971-72	1981-82
• Lalonde, Newsy	Mtl., NYA	6	99	125	41	166	183	7	15	4	19	32	....	1917-18	1926-27
Lalonde, Ron	Pit., Wsh.	7	397	45	78	123	106	....	....	....	....	....	....	1972-73	1978-79
‡ Lalonde, Shawn	Chi.	1	1	0	0	0	0	....	....	....	....	....	....	2012-13	2012-13
Lalor, Mike	Mtl., St.L., Wsh., Wpg., S.J., Dal.	12	687	17	88	105	677	92	5	10	15	167	1	1985-86	1996-97
• Lamb, Joe	Mtl.M., Ott., NYA, Bos., Mtl., St.L., Det.	11	443	108	101	209	601	18	1	1	2	51	....	1927-28	1937-38
Lamb, Mark	Cgy., Det., Edm., Ott., Phi., Mtl.	11	403	46	100	146	291	70	7	19	26	51	1	1985-86	1995-96
Lambert, Dan	Que.	2	29	6	9	15	22	....	....	....	....	....	....	1990-91	1991-92
Lambert, Denny	Ana., Ott., Nsh., Atl.	8	487	27	66	93	1391	17	0	1	1	28	....	1994-95	2001-02
Lambert, Lane	Det., NYR, Que.	6	283	58	66	124	521	17	2	4	6	40	....	1983-84	1988-89
Lambert, Yvon	Mtl., Buf.	10	683	206	273	479	340	90	27	22	49	67	4	1972-73	1981-82
Lamby, Dick	St.L.	3	22	0	5	5	22	....	....	....	....	....	....	1978-79	1980-81
• Lamirande, Jean-Paul	NYR, Mtl.	4	49	5	5	10	26	8	0	0	0	4	....	1946-47	1954-55
Lammens, Hank	Ott.	1	27	1	2	3	22	....	....	....	....	....	....	1993-94	1993-94
• Lamoureux, Leo	Mtl.	6	235	19	79	98	175	28	1	6	7	16	2	1941-42	1946-47
Lamoureux, Mitch	Pit., Phi.	3	73	11	9	20	59	....	....	....	....	....	....	1983-84	1987-88
Lampman, Bryce	NYR	3	10	0	0	0	2	....	....	....	....	....	....	2003-04	2006-07
Lampman, Mike	St.L., Van., Wsh.	4	96	17	20	37	34	....	....	....	....	....	....	1972-73	1976-77
• Lancien, Jack	NYR	4	63	1	5	6	35	6	0	1	1	2	....	1946-47	1950-51
Landon, Larry	Mtl., Tor.	2	9	0	0	0	2	....	....	....	....	....	....	1983-84	1984-85
Landry, Eric	Cgy., Mtl.	4	68	5	9	14	47	....	....	....	....	....	....	1997-98	2001-02
Lane, Gord	Wsh., NYI	10	539	19	94	113	1228	75	3	14	17	214	4	1975-76	1984-85

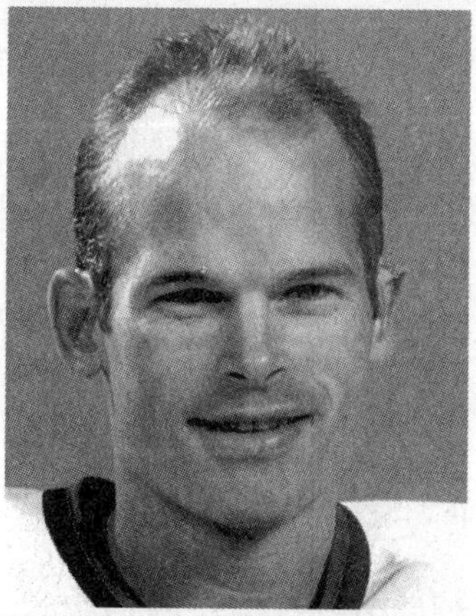
Jim Kyte

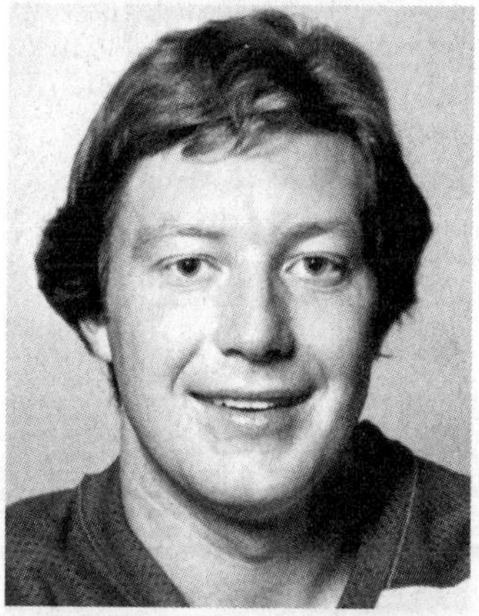
Dan Labraaten

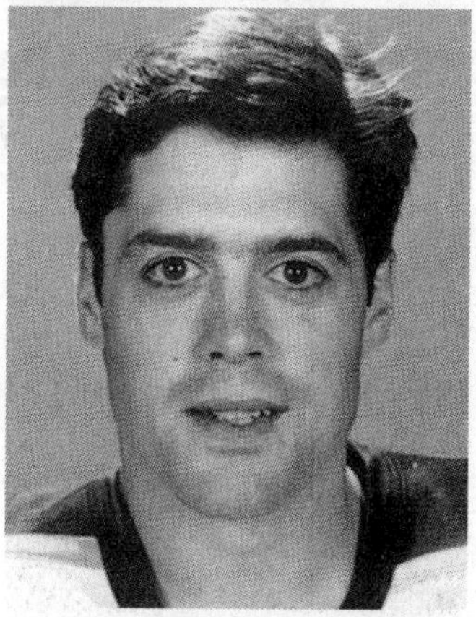
Pat LaFontaine

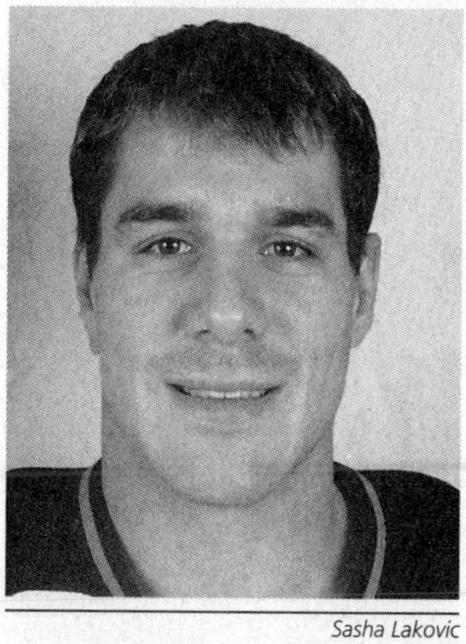
Sasha Lakovic

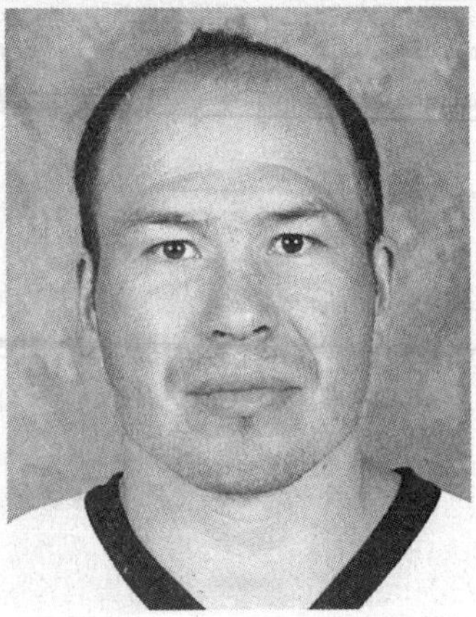

Denny Lambert

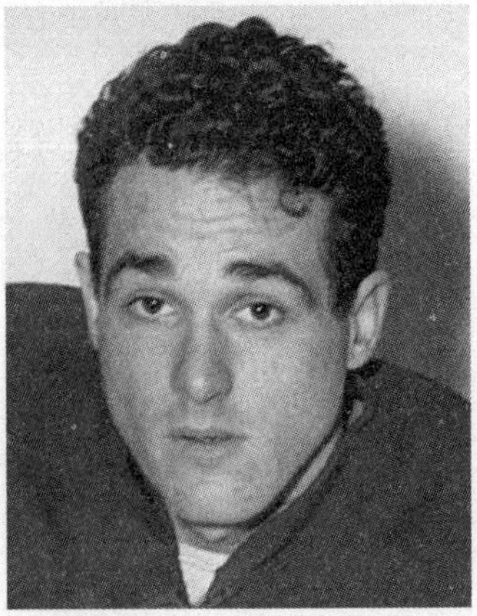

Jack Lancien

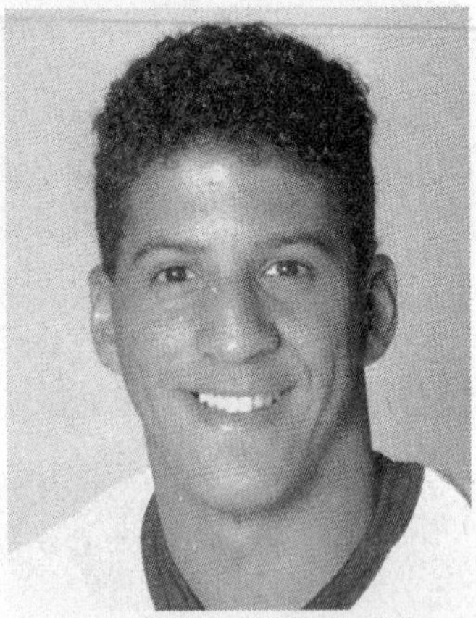

Jeff Lazaro

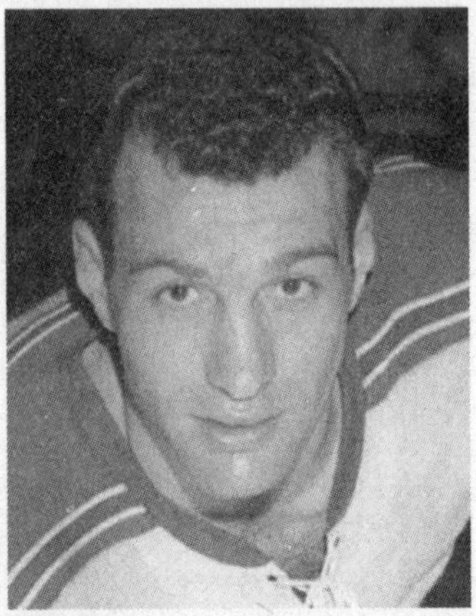

Al LeBrun

			Regular Schedule					Playoffs					NHL	First	Last
Name	NHL Teams	NHL Seasons	GP	G	A	TP	PIM	GP	G	A	TP	PIM	Cup Wins	NHL Season	NHL Season
• Lane, Myles	NYR, Bos.	3	71	4	1	5	41	11	0	0	0	0	1	1928-29	1933-34
Lang, Robert	L.A., Bos., Pit., Wsh., Det., Chi., Mtl., Phx.	16	989	261	442	703	422	91	18	28	46	24	....	1992-93	2009-10
Langdon, Darren	NYR, Car., Van., Mtl., N.J.	11	521	16	23	39	1251	25	1	0	1	20	....	1994-95	2005-06
Langdon, Steve	Bos.	3	7	0	1	1	2	4	0	0	0	0	....	1974-75	1977-78
• Langelle, Pete	Tor.	4	136	22	51	73	11	39	5	9	14	4	1	1938-39	1941-42
Langenbrunner, Jamie	Dal., N.J., St.L.	18	1109	243	420	663	837	146	34	53	87	138	2	1994-95	2012-13
Langevin, Chris	Buf.	2	22	3	1	4	22	....	....	....	....	....	....	1983-84	1985-86
Langevin, Dave	NYI, Min., L.A.	8	513	12	107	119	530	87	2	17	19	106	4	1979-80	1986-87
Langfeld, Josh	Ott., S.J., Bos., Det., Nsh.	6	143	9	23	32	60	1	0	0	0	0	....	2001-02	2007-08
Langkow, Daymond	T.B., Phi., Phx., Cgy.	16	1090	270	402	672	547	75	15	29	44	43	....	1995-96	2011-12
Langlais, Alain	Min.	2	25	4	4	8	10	....	....	....	....	....	....	1973-74	1974-75
Langlois, Albert	Mtl., NYR, Det., Bos.	9	497	21	91	112	488	53	1	5	6	50	3	1957-58	1965-66
• Langlois, Charlie	Ham., NYA, Pit., Mtl.	4	151	22	5	27	189	2	0	0	0	0	....	1924-25	1927-28
Langway, Rod	Mtl., Wsh.	15	994	51	278	329	849	104	5	22	27	97	1	1978-79	1992-93
Lank, Jeff	Phi.	1	2	0	0	0	2	....	....	....	....	....	....	1999-00	1999-00
Lanthier, Jean-Marc	Van.	4	105	16	16	32	29	....	....	....	....	....	....	1983-84	1987-88
• Lanyon, Ted	Pit.	1	5	0	0	0	4	....	....	....	....	....	....	1967-68	1967-68
Lanz, Rick	Van., Tor., Chi.	10	569	65	221	286	448	28	3	8	11	35	....	1980-81	1991-92
Laperriere, Daniel	St.L., Ott.	4	48	2	5	7	27	....	....	....	....	....	....	1992-93	1995-96
Laperriere, Ian	St.L., NYR, L.A., Col., Phi.	17	1083	121	215	336	1956	67	3	10	13	102	....	1993-94	2010-11
Laperriere, Jacques	Mtl.	12	691	40	242	282	674	88	9	22	31	101	6	1962-63	1973-74
‡ Lapierre, Maxim	Mtl., Ana., Van., St.L., Pit.	10	614	65	74	139	586	80	7	8	15	144	....	2005-06	2014-15
Laplante, Darryl	Det.	3	35	0	6	6	10	....	....	....	....	....	....	1997-98	1999-00
Lapointe, Claude	Que., Col., Cgy., NYI, Phi.	14	879	127	178	305	721	34	4	7	11	44	....	1990-91	2003-04
Lapointe, Guy	Mtl., St.L., Bos.	16	884	171	451	622	893	123	26	44	70	138	6	1968-69	1983-84
Lapointe, Martin	Det., Bos., Chi., Ott.	16	991	181	200	381	1417	108	19	24	43	202	2	1991-92	2007-08
• Lapointe, Rick	Det., Phi., St.L., Que., L.A.	11	664	44	176	220	831	46	2	7	9	64	....	1975-76	1985-86
Lappin, Peter	Min., S.J.	2	7	0	0	0	2	....	....	....	....	....	....	1989-90	1991-92
• Laprade, Edgar	NYR	10	500	108	172	280	42	18	4	9	13	4	....	1945-46	1954-55
• LaPrairie, Benjamin	Chi.	1	7	0	0	0	0	....	....	....	....	....	....	1936-37	1936-37
Laraque, Georges	Edm., Phx., Pit., Mtl.	12	695	53	100	153	1126	57	4	8	12	72	....	1997-98	2009-10
Larionov, Igor	Van., S.J., Det., Fla., N.J.	14	921	169	475	644	474	150	30	67	97	60	3	1989-90	2003-04
Lariviere, Garry	Que., Edm.	4	219	6	57	63	167	14	0	5	5	8	....	1979-80	1982-83
Larman, Drew	Fla., Bos.	3	26	2	1	3	4	....	....	....	....	....	....	2006-07	2009-10
Larmer, Jeff	Col., N.J., Chi.	5	158	37	51	88	57	5	1	0	1	2	....	1981-82	1985-86
Larmer, Steve	Chi., NYR	15	1006	441	571	1012	532	140	56	75	131	89	1	1980-81	1994-95
• Larochelle, Wildor	Mtl., Chi.	12	474	92	74	166	211	34	6	4	10	24	2	1925-26	1936-37
Larocque, Denis	L.A.	1	8	0	1	1	18	....	....	....	....	....	....	1987-88	1987-88
Larocque, Mario	T.B.	1	5	0	0	0	16	....	....	....	....	....	....	1998-99	1998-99
• Larose, Bonner	Bos.	1	6	0	0	0	0	....	....	....	....	....	....	1925-26	1925-26
LaRose, Chad	Car.	8	508	85	95	180	286	39	4	8	12	26	1	2005-06	2012-13
Larose, Claude	Mtl., Min., St.L.	16	943	226	257	483	887	97	14	18	32	143	5	1962-63	1977-78
Larose, Claude	NYR	2	25	4	7	11	2	2	0	0	0	0	....	1979-80	1981-82
Larose, Cory	NYR	1	7	0	1	1	4	....	....	....	....	....	....	2003-04	2003-04
Larose, Guy	Wpg., Tor., Cgy., Bos.	6	70	10	9	19	63	4	0	0	0	0	....	1988-89	1994-95
Larouche, Pierre	Pit., Mtl., Hfd., NYR	14	812	395	427	822	237	64	20	34	54	16	2	1974-75	1987-88
Larouche, Steve	Ott., NYR, L.A.	2	26	9	9	18	10	....	....	....	....	....	....	1994-95	1995-96
Larsen, Brad	Col., Atl., Ana.	9	294	19	29	48	134	25	1	3	4	13	....	1997-98	2008-09
• Larson, Norm	NYA, Bro., NYR	3	89	25	18	43	12	....	....	....	....	....	....	1940-41	1946-47
Larson, Reed	Det., Bos., Edm., NYI, Min., Buf.	14	904	222	463	685	1391	32	4	7	11	63	....	1976-77	1989-90
Larter, Tyler	Wsh.	1	1	0	0	0	0	....	....	....	....	....	....	1989-90	1989-90
Lashoff, Matt	Bos., T.B., Tor.	5	74	1	15	16	59	....	....	....	....	....	....	2006-07	2010-11
Latal, Jiri	Phi.	3	92	12	36	48	24	....	....	....	....	....	....	1989-90	1991-92
Latendresse, Guillaume	Mtl., Min., Ott.	7	341	87	60	147	185	15	1	2	3	37	....	2006-07	2012-13
Latos, James	NYR	1	1	0	0	0	0	....	....	....	....	....	....	1988-89	1988-89
Latreille, Phil	NYR	1	4	0	0	0	2	....	....	....	....	....	....	1960-61	1960-61
Latta, David	Que.	4	36	4	8	12	4	....	....	....	....	....	....	1985-86	1990-91
• Lauder, Martin	Bos.	1	3	0	0	0	2	....	....	....	....	....	....	1927-28	1927-28
Lauen, Mike	Wpg.	1	4	0	1	1	0	....	....	....	....	....	....	1983-84	1983-84
Lauer, Brad	NYI, Chi., Ott., Pit.	9	323	44	67	111	218	34	7	5	12	24	....	1986-87	1995-96
Laughlin, Craig	Mtl., Wsh., L.A., Tor.	8	549	136	205	341	364	33	6	6	12	20	....	1981-82	1988-89
Laughton, Mike	Oak., Cal.	4	189	39	48	87	101	11	3	4	7	0	....	1967-68	1970-71
Laukkanen, Janne	Que., Col., Ott., Pit., T.B.	9	407	22	99	121	335	59	7	9	16	46	....	1994-95	2002-03
Laurence, Don	Atl., St.L.	2	79	15	22	37	14	....	....	....	....	....	....	1978-79	1979-80
‡ Lauridsen, Oliver	Phi.	2	16	2	1	3	44	....	....	....	....	....	....	2012-13	2014-15
Laus, Paul	Fla.	9	530	14	58	72	1702	30	2	7	9	74	....	1993-94	2001-02
LaVallee, Kevin	Cgy., L.A., St.L., Pit.	7	366	110	125	235	85	32	5	8	13	21	....	1980-81	1986-87
LaVarre, Mark	Chi.	3	78	9	16	25	58	1	0	0	0	2	....	1985-86	1987-88
Lavender, Brian	St.L., NYI, Det., Cal.	4	184	16	26	42	174	3	0	0	0	2	....	1971-72	1974-75
Lavigne, Eric	L.A.	1	1	0	0	0	0	....	....	....	....	....	....	1994-95	1994-95
• Laviolette, Jack	Mtl.	1	18	2	1	3	6	2	0	0	0	0	....	1917-18	1917-18
Laviolette, Peter	NYR	1	12	0	0	0	6	....	....	....	....	....	....	1988-89	1988-89
Lavoie, Dominic	St.L., Ott., Bos., L.A.	6	38	5	8	13	32	....	....	....	....	....	....	1988-89	1993-94
Law, Kirby	Phi.	3	9	0	1	1	4	....	....	....	....	....	....	2000-01	2003-04
Lawless, Paul	Hfd., Phi., Van., Tor.	7	239	49	77	126	54	3	0	2	2	2	....	1982-83	1989-90
Lawrence, Mark	Dal., NYI	6	142	18	26	44	115	....	....	....	....	....	....	1994-95	2000-01
• Lawson, Danny	Det., Min., Buf.	5	219	28	29	57	61	16	0	1	1	2	....	1967-68	1971-72
Lawton, Brian	Min., NYR, Hfd., Que., Bos., S.J.	9	483	112	154	266	401	11	1	1	2	12	....	1983-84	1992-93
Laxdal, Derek	Tor., NYI	6	67	12	7	19	88	1	0	2	2	2	....	1984-85	1990-91
• Laycoe, Hal	NYR, Mtl., Bos.	11	531	25	77	102	292	40	2	5	7	39	....	1945-46	1955-56
Lazaro, Jeff	Bos., Ott.	3	102	14	23	37	114	28	3	3	6	32	....	1990-91	1992-93
Leach, Jamie	Pit., Hfd., Fla.	5	81	11	9	20	12	....	....	....	....	....	1	1989-90	1993-94
Leach, Jay	Bos., T.B., N.J., Mtl., S.J.	5	70	1	2	3	60	....	....	....	....	....	....	2005-06	2010-11
Leach, Larry	Bos.	3	126	13	29	42	91	7	1	1	2	8	....	1958-59	1961-62
Leach, Reggie	Bos., Cal., Phi., Det.	13	934	381	285	666	387	94	47	22	69	22	1	1970-71	1982-83
Leach, Stephen	Wsh., Bos., St.L., Car., Ott., Phx., Pit.	15	702	130	153	283	978	92	15	11	26	87	....	1985-86	1999-00
Leahy, Patrick	Bos., Nsh.	3	50	4	4	8	19	....	....	....	....	....	....	2003-04	2006-07
Leavins, Jim	Det., NYR	2	41	2	12	14	30	....	....	....	....	....	....	1985-86	1986-87
Lebda, Brett	Det., Tor., CBJ	7	397	20	56	76	229	62	0	10	10	40	1	2005-06	2011-12
Lebeau, Patrick	Mtl., Cgy., Fla., Pit.	4	15	3	2	5	6	....	....	....	....	....	....	1990-91	1998-99
Lebeau, Stephan	Mtl., Ana.	7	373	118	159	277	105	30	9	7	16	12	1	1988-89	1994-95
‡ LeBlanc, Drew	Chi.	1	2	0	0	0	0	....	....	....	....	....	....	2012-13	2012-13
LeBlanc, Fern	Det.	3	34	5	6	11	0	....	....	....	....	....	....	1976-77	1978-79
LeBlanc, J.P.	Chi., Det.	5	153	14	30	44	87	2	0	0	0	0	....	1968-69	1978-79
LeBlanc, John	Van., Edm., Wpg.	7	83	26	13	39	28	1	0	0	0	0	....	1986-87	1994-95
Leblanc, Louis	Mtl.	2	50	5	5	10	32	....	....	....	....	....	....	2011-12	2013-14
‡ Leblanc, Peter	Wsh.	1	1	0	0	0	0	....	....	....	....	....	....	2013-14	2013-14
LeBoutillier, Peter	Ana.	2	35	2	1	3	176	....	....	....	....	....	....	1996-97	1997-98
LeBrun, Al	NYR	2	6	0	2	2	4	....	....	....	....	....	....	1960-61	1965-66
Lecaine, Bill	Pit.	1	4	0	0	0	0	....	....	....	....	....	....	1968-69	1968-69
Lecavalier, Vincent	T.B., Phi., L.A.	17	1212	421	528	949	848	75	26	30	56	84	1	1998-99	**2015-16**
• Leclair, Jackie	Mtl.	3	160	20	40	60	56	20	6	1	7	6	2	1954-55	1956-57
LeClair, John	Mtl., Phi., Pit.	16	967	406	413	819	501	154	42	47	89	94	1	1990-91	2006-07
Leclerc, Mike	Ana., Phx., Cgy.	9	341	64	94	158	288	26	2	9	11	14	....	1996-97	2005-06
Leclerc, Rene	Det.	2	87	10	11	21	105	....	....	....	....	....	....	1968-69	1970-71
Lecuyer, Doug	Chi., Wpg., Pit.	4	126	11	31	42	178	7	4	0	4	15	....	1978-79	1982-83
‡ Ledin, Per	Col.	1	3	0	0	0	2	....	....	....	....	....	....	2008-09	2008-09
Ledingham, Walt	Chi., NYI	3	15	0	2	2	4	....	....	....	....	....	....	1972-73	1976-77
• Leduc, Albert	Mtl., Ott., NYR	10	383	57	35	92	614	28	5	6	11	32	2	1925-26	1934-35
LeDuc, Rich	Bos., Que.	4	130	28	38	66	69	5	0	0	0	9	....	1972-73	1980-81
Ledyard, Grant	NYR, L.A., Wsh., Buf., Dal., Van., Bos., Ott., T.B.	18	1028	90	276	366	766	83	6	12	18	96	....	1984-85	2001-02
• Lee, Bobby	Mtl.	1	1	0	0	0	0	....	....	....	....	....	....	1942-43	1942-43
Lee, Brian	Ott., T.B.	6	209	5	31	36	124	4	0	0	0	2	....	2007-08	2012-13
Lee, Edward	Que.	1	2	0	0	0	5	....	....	....	....	....	....	1984-85	1984-85
Lee, Peter	Pit.	6	431	114	131	245	257	19	0	8	8	4	....	1977-78	1982-83
Leeb, Brad	Van., Tor.	3	5	0	0	0	2	....	....	....	....	....	....	1999-00	2003-04
Leeb, Greg	Dal.	1	2	0	0	0	0	....	....	....	....	....	....	2000-01	2000-01
Leeman, Gary	Tor., Cgy., Mtl., Van., St.L.	14	667	199	267	466	531	36	8	16	24	36	1	1982-83	1996-97
Leetch, Brian	NYR, Tor., Bos.	18	1205	247	781	1028	571	95	28	69	97	36	1	1987-88	2005-06
Lefebvre, Guillaume	Phi., Pit., Bos.	4	39	2	4	6	13	....	....	....	....	....	....	2001-02	2009-10

Name	NHL Teams	NHL Seasons	Regular Schedule GP	G	A	TP	PIM	Playoffs GP	G	A	TP	PIM	NHL Cup Wins	First NHL Season	Last NHL Season
Lefebvre, Patrice	Wsh.	1	3	0	0	0	2	....	....	....	....	....	....	1998-99	1998-99
Lefebvre, Sylvain	Mtl., Tor., Que., Col., NYR	14	945	30	154	184	674	129	4	14	18	101	1	1989-90	2002-03
• Lefley, Bryan	NYI, K.C., Col.	5	228	7	29	36	101	2	0	0	0	0	....	1972-73	1977-78
Lefley, Chuck	Mtl., St.L.	9	407	128	164	292	137	29	5	8	13	10	2	1970-71	1980-81
• Leger, Roger	NYR, Mtl.	5	187	18	53	71	71	20	0	7	7	14	....	1943-44	1949-50
Legge, Barry	Que., Wpg.	3	107	1	11	12	144	....	....	....	....	....	....	1979-80	1981-82
Legge, Randy	NYR	1	12	0	2	2	2	....	....	....	....	....	....	1972-73	1972-73
Legwand, David	Nsh., Det., Ott., Buf.	17	1136	228	390	618	551	55	13	15	28	46	....	1998-99	**2015-16**
Lehman, Scott	Atl.	1	1	0	0	0	0	....	....	....	....	....	....	2008-09	2008-09
Lehman, Tommy	Bos., Edm.	3	36	5	5	10	16	....	....	....	....	....	....	1987-88	1989-90
Lehoux, Yanick	Phx.	2	10	2	2	4	6	....	....	....	....	....	....	2005-06	2006-07
Lehtinen, Jere	Dal.	14	875	243	271	514	210	108	27	22	49	12	1	1995-96	2009-10
Lehto, Petteri	Pit.	1	6	0	0	0	4	....	....	....	....	....	....	1984-85	1984-85
Lehtonen, Antero	Wsh.	1	65	9	12	21	14	....	....	....	....	....	....	1979-80	1979-80
Lehtonen, Mikko	Nsh.	1	15	1	2	3	8	....	....	....	....	....	....	2006-07	2006-07
‡ Lehtonen, Mikko	Bos.	2	2	0	0	0	0	....	....	....	....	....	....	2008-09	2009-10
Lehvonen, Henry	K.C.	1	4	0	0	0	0	....	....	....	....	....	....	1974-75	1974-75
Leier, Edward	Chi.	2	16	2	1	3	2	....	....	....	....	....	....	1949-50	1950-51
‡ Leino, Ville	Det., Phi., Buf.	6	286	40	79	119	70	37	10	18	28	6	....	2008-09	2013-14
Leinonen, Mikko	NYR, Wsh.	4	162	31	78	109	71	20	2	11	13	28	....	1981-82	1984-85
Leiter, Bobby	Bos., Pit., Atl.	10	447	98	126	224	144	8	3	0	3	2	....	1962-63	1975-76
Leiter, Ken	NYI, Min.	5	143	14	36	50	62	15	0	6	6	8	....	1984-85	1989-90
Lemaire, Jacques	Mtl.	12	853	366	469	835	217	145	61	78	139	63	8	1967-68	1978-79
Lemay, Moe	Van., Edm., Bos., Wpg.	8	317	72	94	166	442	28	6	3	9	55	1	1981-82	1988-89
Lemelin, Roger	K.C., Col.	4	36	1	2	3	27	....	....	....	....	....	....	1974-75	1977-78
Lemieux, Alain	St.L., Que., Pit.	6	119	28	44	72	38	19	4	6	10	0	....	1981-82	1986-87
Lemieux, Bob	Oak.	1	19	0	1	1	12	....	....	....	....	....	....	1967-68	1967-68
Lemieux, Claude	Mtl., N.J., Col., Phx., Dal., S.J.	21	1215	379	407	786	1777	234	80	78	158	529	4	1983-84	2008-09
Lemieux, Jacques	L.A.	3	19	0	4	4	8	1	0	0	0	0	....	1967-68	1969-70
Lemieux, Jean	Atl., Wsh.	5	204	23	63	86	39	3	1	1	2	0	....	1973-74	1977-78
Lemieux, Jocelyn	St.L., Mtl., Chi., Hfd., N.J., Cgy., Phx.	12	598	80	84	164	740	60	5	10	15	88	....	1986-87	1997-98
Lemieux, Mario	Pit.	18	915	690	1033	1723	834	107	76	96	172	87	2	1984-85	2005-06
• Lemieux, Real	Det., L.A., NYR, Buf.	8	456	51	104	155	262	18	2	4	6	10	....	1966-67	1973-74
Lemieux, Rich	Van., K.C., Atl.	5	274	39	82	121	132	2	0	0	0	0	....	1971-72	1975-76
Lenardon, Tim	N.J., Van.	2	15	2	1	3	4	....	....	....	....	....	....	1986-87	1989-90
Leopold, Jordan	Cgy., Col., Fla., Pit., Buf., St.L., CBJ, Min.	12	695	67	147	214	293	80	0	17	17	26	....	2002-03	2014-15
• Lepine, Hec	Mtl.	1	33	5	2	7	2	....	....	....	....	....	....	1925-26	1925-26
• Lepine, Pit	Mtl.	13	526	143	98	241	392	41	7	5	12	26	2	1925-26	1937-38
‡ Lepisto, Sami	Wsh., Phx., CBJ, Chi.	5	176	6	29	35	137	10	1	0	1	6	....	2007-08	2011-12
Leroux, Francois	Edm., Ott., Pit., Col.	10	249	3	20	23	577	33	1	3	4	34	....	1988-89	1997-98
• Leroux, Gaston	Mtl.	1	2	0	0	0	0	....	....	....	....	....	....	1935-36	1935-36
Leroux, Jean-Yves	Chi.	5	220	16	22	38	146	....	....	....	....	....	....	1996-97	2000-01
Leschyshyn, Curtis	Que., Col., Wsh., Hfd., Car., Min., Ott.	16	1033	47	165	212	669	68	2	6	8	34	1	1988-89	2003-04
• Lesieur, Art	Mtl., Chi.	4	100	4	2	6	50	14	0	0	0	4	1	1928-29	1935-36
Lessard, Francis	Atl., Ott.	5	115	1	3	4	346	....	....	....	....	....	....	2001-02	2010-11
Lessard, Junior	Dal., T.B.	3	27	3	1	4	23	....	....	....	....	....	....	2005-06	2007-08
Lessard, Rick	Cgy., S.J.	3	15	0	4	4	18	....	....	....	....	....	....	1988-89	1991-92
Lesuk, Bill	Bos., Phi., L.A., Wsh., Wpg.	8	388	44	63	107	368	9	1	0	1	12	1	1968-69	1979-80
• Leswick, Jack	Chi.	1	37	1	7	8	16	....	....	....	....	....	1	1933-34	1933-34
• Leswick, Pete	NYA, Bos.	2	3	1	0	1	0	....	....	....	....	....	....	1936-37	1944-45
• Leswick, Tony	NYR, Det., Chi.	12	740	165	159	324	900	59	13	10	23	91	3	1945-46	1957-58
Letang, Alan	Dal., Cgy., NYI	3	14	0	0	0	2	....	....	....	....	....	....	1999-00	2002-03
Letowski, Trevor	Phx., Van., CBJ, Car.	9	616	84	117	201	209	17	1	3	4	12	....	1998-99	2007-08
• Levandoski, Joe	NYR	1	8	1	1	2	0	....	....	....	....	....	....	1946-47	1946-47
Leveille, Normand	Bos.	2	75	17	25	42	49	....	....	....	....	....	....	1981-82	1982-83
• Leveque, Guy	L.A.	2	17	2	2	4	21	....	....	....	....	....	....	1992-93	1993-94
Lever, Don	Van., Atl., Cgy., Col., N.J., Buf.	15	1020	313	367	680	593	30	7	10	17	26	....	1972-73	1986-87
Levie, Craig	Wpg., Min., St.L., Van.	6	183	22	53	75	177	16	2	3	5	32	....	1981-82	1986-87
Levins, Scott	Wpg., Fla., Ott., Phx.	5	124	13	20	33	316	....	....	....	....	....	....	1992-93	1997-98
• Levinsky, Alex	Tor., NYR, Chi.	9	367	19	49	68	307	37	2	1	3	26	2	1930-31	1938-39
Levo, Tapio	Col., N.J.	2	107	16	53	69	36	....	....	....	....	....	....	1981-82	1982-83
Lewicki, Danny	Tor., NYR, Chi.	9	461	105	135	240	177	28	0	4	4	8	1	1950-51	1958-59
Lewis, Dale	NYR	1	8	0	0	0	0	....	....	....	....	....	....	1975-76	1975-76
Lewis, Dave	NYI, L.A., N.J., Det.	15	1008	36	187	223	953	91	1	20	21	143	....	1973-74	1987-88
• Lewis, Doug	Mtl.	1	3	0	0	0	0	....	....	....	....	....	....	1946-47	1946-47
Lewis, Grant	Atl.	1	1	0	0	0	0	....	....	....	....	....	....	2008-09	2008-09
• Lewis, Herbie	Det.	11	483	148	161	309	248	38	13	10	23	6	2	1928-29	1938-39
Ley, Rick	Tor., Hfd.	6	310	12	72	84	528	14	0	2	2	20	....	1968-69	1980-81
Liba, Igor	NYR, L.A.	1	37	7	18	25	36	2	0	0	0	2	....	1988-89	1988-89
Libby, Jeff	NYI	1	1	0	0	0	0	....	....	....	....	....	....	1997-98	1997-98
Libett, Nick	Det., Pit.	14	982	237	268	505	472	16	6	2	8	2	....	1967-68	1980-81
• Licari, Tony	Det.	1	9	0	1	1	0	....	....	....	....	....	....	1946-47	1946-47
Liddington, Bob	Tor.	1	11	0	1	1	2	....	....	....	....	....	....	1970-71	1970-71
Lidster, Doug	Van., NYR, St.L., Dal.	16	897	75	268	343	679	80	6	15	21	64	1	1983-84	1998-99
Lidstrom, Nicklas	Det.	20	1564	264	878	1142	514	263	54	129	183	76	4	1991-92	2011-12
‡ Liffiton, David	NYR, Col.	3	7	1	0	1	26	....	....	....	....	....	....	2005-06	2010-11
Lilja, Andreas	L.A., Fla., Det., Ana., Phi.	12	580	16	71	87	563	66	1	2	3	58	1	2000-01	2012-13
Lilley, John	Ana.	3	23	3	8	11	13	....	....	....	....	....	....	1993-94	1995-96
Lind, Juha	Dal., Mtl.	3	133	9	13	22	20	15	2	2	4	8	....	1997-98	2000-01
Lindberg, Chris	Cgy., Que.	3	116	17	25	42	47	2	0	1	1	2	....	1991-92	1993-94
Lindblad, Matt	Bos.	2	4	0	0	0	0	....	....	....	....	....	....	2013-14	2014-15
Lindbom, Johan	NYR	1	38	1	3	4	28	....	....	....	....	....	....	1997-98	1997-98
Linden, Jamie	Fla.	1	4	0	0	0	17	....	....	....	....	....	....	1994-95	1994-95
Linden, Trevor	Van., NYI, Mtl., Wsh.	19	1382	375	492	867	895	124	34	65	99	104	....	1988-89	2007-08
Lindgren, Lars	Van., Min.	6	394	25	113	138	325	40	5	6	11	20	....	1978-79	1983-84
Lindgren, Mats	Edm., NYI, Van.	7	387	54	74	128	146	24	1	5	6	10	....	1996-97	2002-03
‡ Lindgren, Perttu	Dal.	1	1	0	0	0	0	....	....	....	....	....	....	2009-10	2009-10
Lindholm, Mikael	L.A.	1	18	2	2	4	2	....	....	....	....	....	....	1989-90	1989-90
Lindros, Brett	NYI	2	51	2	5	7	147	....	....	....	....	....	....	1994-95	1995-96
Lindros, Eric	Phi., NYR, Tor., Dal.	14	760	372	493	865	1398	53	24	33	57	122	....	1992-93	2006-07
Lindsay, Bill	Que., Fla., Cgy., S.J., Mtl., Atl.	13	777	83	141	224	922	42	7	8	15	44	....	1991-92	2003-04
Lindsay, Ted	Det., Chi.	17	1068	379	472	851	1808	133	47	49	96	194	4	1944-45	1964-65
‡ Lindstrom, Joakim	CBJ, Phx., Col., St.L., Tor.	6	150	19	24	43	58	....	....	....	....	....	....	2005-06	2014-15
Lindstrom, Willy	Wpg., Edm., Pit.	8	582	161	162	323	200	57	14	18	32	24	2	1979-80	1986-87
Ling, David	Mtl., CBJ	5	93	4	4	8	191	....	....	....	....	....	....	1996-97	2003-04
‡ Linglet, Charles	Edm.	1	5	0	0	0	2	....	....	....	....	....	....	2009-10	2009-10
Linseman, Ken	Phi., Edm., Bos., Tor.	14	860	256	551	807	1727	113	43	77	120	325	1	1978-79	1991-92
Lintner, Richard	Nsh., NYR, Pit.	3	112	8	12	20	54	....	....	....	....	....	....	1999-00	2002-03
Lipuma, Chris	T.B., S.J.	5	72	0	9	9	146	....	....	....	....	....	....	1992-93	1996-97
• Liscombe, Carl	Det.	9	373	137	140	277	117	59	22	19	41	20	1	1937-38	1945-46
‡ Lisin, Enver	Phx., NYR	4	135	24	18	42	64	....	....	....	....	....	....	2006-07	2009-10
• Litzenberger, Ed	Mtl., Chi., Det., Tor.	12	618	178	238	416	283	40	5	13	18	34	4	1952-53	1963-64
Loach, Lonnie	Ott., L.A., Ana.	2	56	10	13	23	29	1	0	0	0	0	....	1992-93	1993-94
• Locas, Jacques	Mtl.	2	59	7	8	15	66	....	....	....	....	....	....	1947-48	1948-49
Lochead, Bill	Det., Col., NYR	6	330	69	62	131	180	7	3	0	3	6	....	1974-75	1979-80
‡ Locke, Corey	Mtl., NYR, Ott.	3	9	0	1	1	0	....	....	....	....	....	....	2007-08	2010-11
• Locking, Norm	Chi.	2	48	2	6	8	26	....	....	....	....	....	....	1934-35	1935-36
Loewen, Darcy	Buf., Ott.	5	135	4	8	12	211	....	....	....	....	....	....	1989-90	1993-94
Lofthouse, Mark	Wsh., Det.	6	181	42	38	80	73	....	....	....	....	....	....	1977-78	1982-83
Logan, Dave	Chi., Van.	6	218	5	29	34	470	12	0	0	0	10	....	1975-76	1980-81
Logan, Robert	Buf., L.A.	3	42	10	5	15	0	....	....	....	....	....	....	1986-87	1988-89
Loiselle, Claude	Det., N.J., Que., Tor., NYI	13	616	92	117	209	1149	41	4	11	15	58	....	1981-82	1993-94
Lojek, Martin	Fla.	2	5	0	1	1	0	....	....	....	....	....	....	2006-07	2007-08
‡ Loktionov, Andrei	L.A., N.J., Car.	5	155	22	26	48	22	2	0	0	0	0	....	2009-10	2013-14
• Lomakin, Andrei	Phi., Fla.	4	215	42	62	104	92	....	....	....	....	....	....	1991-92	1994-95
Lombardi, Matthew	Cgy., Phx., Nsh., Tor., Ana.	9	536	101	161	262	293	40	3	13	16	12	....	2003-04	2012-13
Loney, Brian	Van.	1	12	2	3	5	6	....	....	....	....	....	....	1995-96	1995-96
Loney, Troy	Pit., Ana., NYI, NYR	12	624	87	110	197	1091	67	8	14	22	97	2	1983-84	1994-95
Long, Barry	L.A., Det., Wpg.	5	280	11	68	79	250	5	0	1	1	18	....	1972-73	1981-82
• Long, Stan	Mtl.	1	....	....	....	....	....	3	0	0	0	0	....	1951-52	1951-52
• Lonsberry, Ross	Bos., L.A., Phi., Pit.	15	968	256	310	566	806	100	21	25	46	87	2	1966-67	1980-81

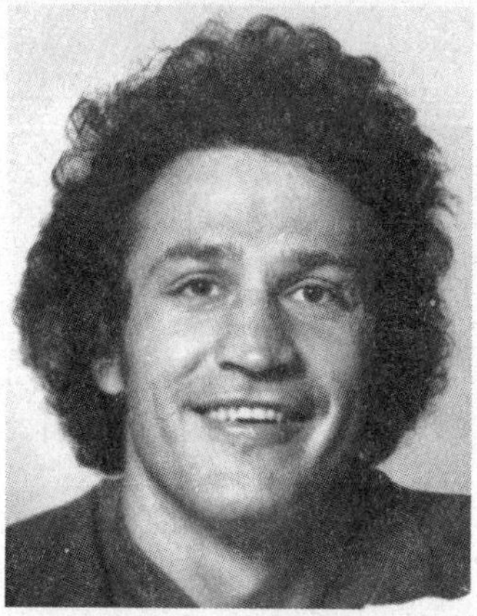

Bill Lesuk

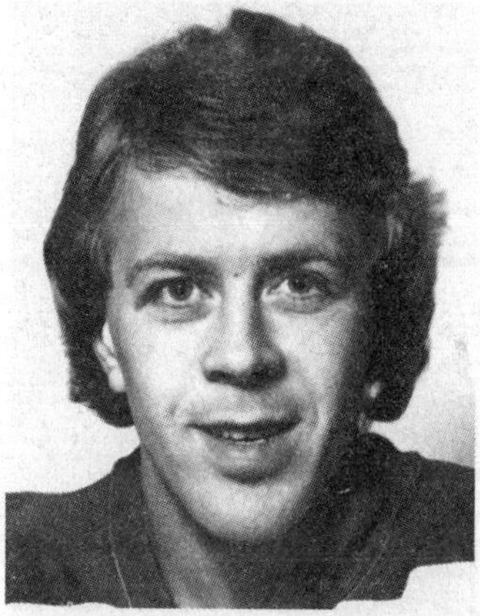

Willy Lindstrom

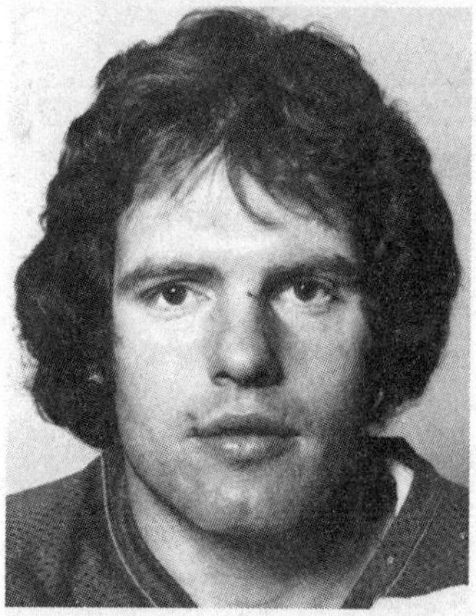

Barry Long

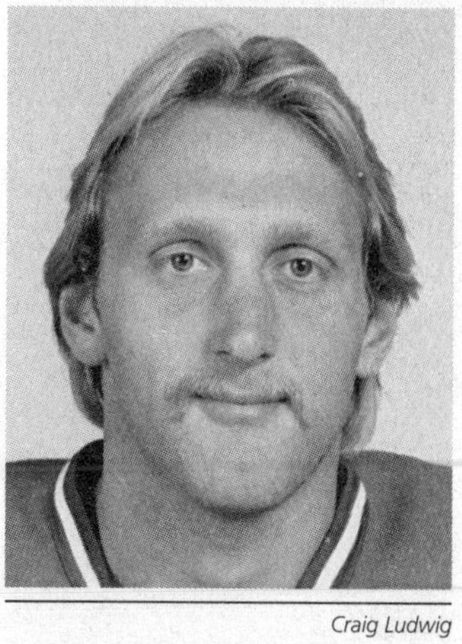

Craig Ludwig

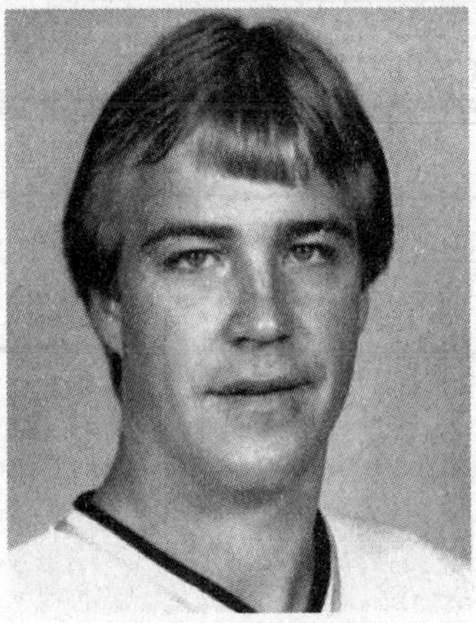

Brian Lundberg

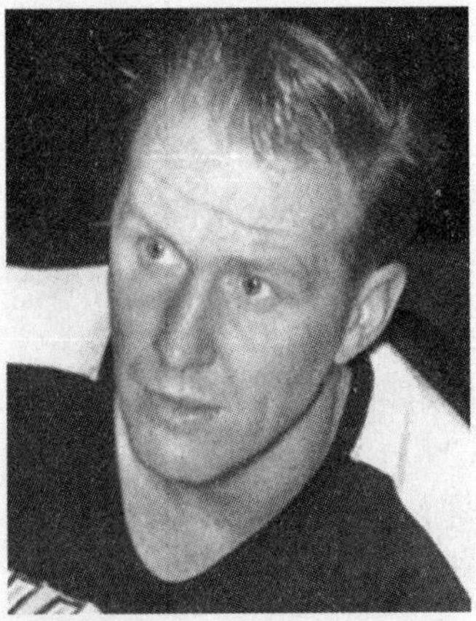

Kilby MacDonald

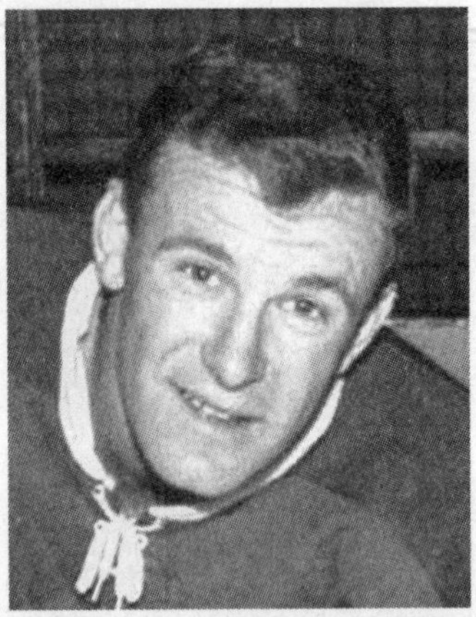

Barry MacKenzie

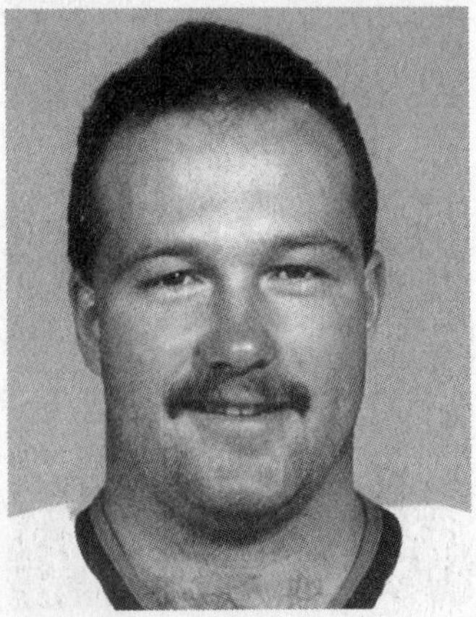

Jeff Madill

			Regular Schedule					Playoffs							
Name	NHL Teams	NHL Seasons	GP	G	A	TP	PIM	GP	G	A	TP	PIM	NHL Cup Wins	First NHL Season	Last NHL Season
Loob, Hakan	Cgy.	6	450	193	236	429	189	73	26	28	54	16	1	1983-84	1988-89
Loob, Peter	Que.	1	8	1	2	3	0	....	....	....	....	....	....	1984-85	1984-85
Lorentz, Jim	Bos., St.L., NYR, Buf.	10	659	161	238	399	208	54	12	10	22	30	1	1968-69	1977-78
Lorimer, Bob	NYI, Col., N.J.	10	529	22	90	112	431	49	3	10	13	83	2	1976-77	1985-86
• Lorrain, Rod	Mtl.	6	179	28	39	67	30	11	0	3	3	0	....	1935-36	1941-42
• Loughlin, Clem	Det., Chi.	3	101	8	6	14	77	....	....	....	....	....	....	1926-27	1928-29
• Loughlin, Wilf	Tor.	1	14	0	0	0	2	....	....	....	....	....	....	1923-24	1923-24
Lovsin, Ken	Wsh.	1	1	0	0	0	0	....	....	....	....	....	....	1990-91	1990-91
Low, Reed	St.L., Chi.	5	256	3	16	19	725	....	....	....	....	....	....	2000-01	2006-07
Lowdermilk, Dwayne	Wsh.	1	2	0	1	1	2	....	....	....	....	....	....	1980-81	1980-81
Lowe, Darren	Pit.	1	8	1	2	3	0	....	....	....	....	....	....	1983-84	1983-84
Lowe, Kevin	Edm., NYR	19	1254	84	347	431	1498	214	10	48	58	192	6	1979-80	1997-98
Lowe, Odie	NYR	1	4	1	1	2	0	....	....	....	....	....	....	1949-50	1949-50
• Lowe, Ross	Bos., Mtl.	3	77	6	8	14	82	2	0	0	0	0	....	1949-50	1951-52
• Lowrey, Ed	Ott., Ham.	3	27	2	2	4	6	....	....	....	....	....	....	1917-18	1920-21
• Lowrey, Fred	Mtl.M., Pit.	2	53	1	1	2	10	2	0	0	0	6	....	1924-25	1925-26
• Lowrey, Gerry	Tor., Pit., Phi., Chi., Ott.	6	211	48	48	96	148	2	1	0	1	2	....	1927-28	1932-33
Lowry, Dave	Van., St.L., Fla., S.J., Cgy.	19	1084	164	187	351	1191	111	16	20	36	181	....	1985-86	2003-04
Loyns, Lynn	S.J., Cgy.	3	34	3	2	5	21	....	....	....	....	....	....	2002-03	2005-06
Lucas, Danny	Phi.	1	6	1	0	1	0	....	....	....	....	....	....	1978-79	1978-79
Lucas, Dave	Det.	1	1	0	0	0	0	....	....	....	....	....	....	1962-63	1962-63
Luce, Don	NYR, Det., Buf., L.A., Tor.	13	894	225	329	554	364	71	17	22	39	52	....	1969-70	1981-82
Ludvig, Jan	N.J., Buf.	7	314	54	87	141	418	....	....	....	....	....	....	1982-83	1988-89
Ludwig, Craig	Mtl., NYI, Min., Dal.	17	1256	38	184	222	1437	177	4	25	29	244	2	1982-83	1998-99
Ludzik, Steve	Chi., Buf.	9	424	46	93	139	333	44	4	8	12	70	....	1981-82	1989-90
Luhning, Warren	NYI, Dal.	3	29	0	1	1	21	....	....	....	....	....	....	1997-98	1999-00
Lukowich, Bernie	Pit., St.L.	2	79	13	15	28	34	2	0	0	0	0	....	1973-74	1974-75
Lukowich, Brad	Dal., T.B., NYI, N.J., S.J., Van.	13	658	23	90	113	369	71	1	5	6	22	1	1997-98	2010-11
Lukowich, Morris	Wpg., Bos., L.A.	8	582	199	219	418	584	11	0	2	2	24	....	1979-80	1986-87
Luksa, Charlie	Hfd.	1	8	0	1	1	4	....	....	....	....	....	....	1979-80	1979-80
Lumley, Dave	Mtl., Edm., Hfd.	9	437	98	160	258	680	61	6	8	14	131	2	1978-79	1986-87
Lumme, Jyrki	Mtl., Van., Phx., Dal., Tor.	15	985	114	354	468	620	105	9	35	44	52	....	1988-89	2002-03
• Lund, Pentti	Bos., NYR	7	259	44	55	99	40	19	7	5	12	0	....	1946-47	1952-53
Lundberg, Brian	Pit.	1	1	0	0	0	2	....	....	....	....	....	....	1982-83	1982-83
• Lunde, Len	Det., Chi., Min., Van.	8	321	39	83	122	75	20	3	2	5	2	....	1958-59	1970-71
Lundholm, Bengt	Wpg.	5	275	48	95	143	72	14	3	4	7	14	....	1981-82	1985-86
‡ Lundin, Mike	T.B., Min., Ott.	6	252	4	32	36	54	18	0	2	2	2	....	2007-08	2012-13
Lundmark, Jamie	NYR, Phx., Cgy., L.A., Tor.	6	295	40	59	99	204	6	0	1	1	7	....	2002-03	2009-10
‡ Lundqvist, Joel	Dal.	3	134	7	19	26	56	25	4	5	9	14	....	2006-07	2008-09
Lundrigan, Joe	Tor., Wsh.	2	52	2	8	10	22	....	....	....	....	....	....	1972-73	1974-75
Lundstrom, Tord	Det.	1	11	1	1	2	0	....	....	....	....	....	....	1973-74	1973-74
• Lundy, Pat	Det., Chi.	5	150	37	32	69	31	16	2	2	4	2	....	1945-46	1950-51
‡ Luoma, Mikko	Edm.	1	3	0	1	1	0	....	....	....	....	....	....	2003-04	2003-04
Luongo, Chris	Det., Ott., NYI	5	218	8	23	31	176	....	....	....	....	....	....	1990-91	1995-96
Lupaschuk, Ross	Pit.	1	3	0	0	0	4	....	....	....	....	....	....	2002-03	2002-03
Lupien, Gilles	Mtl., Pit., Hfd.	5	226	5	25	30	416	25	0	0	0	21	2	1977-78	1981-82
• Lupul, Gary	Van.	7	293	70	75	145	243	25	4	7	11	11	....	1979-80	1985-86
• Lyashenko, Roman	Dal., NYR	4	139	14	9	23	55	17	2	1	3	0	....	1999-00	2002-03
Lydman, Toni	Cgy., Buf., Ana.	12	847	36	206	242	551	55	3	8	11	42	....	2000-01	2012-13
Lyle, George	Det., Hfd.	4	99	24	38	62	51	....	....	....	....	....	....	1979-80	1982-83
Lynch, Doug	Edm.	1	2	0	0	0	0	....	....	....	....	....	....	2003-04	2003-04
Lynch, Jack	Pit., Det., Wsh.	7	382	24	106	130	336	....	....	....	....	....	....	1972-73	1978-79
• Lynn, Vic	NYR, Det., Mtl., Tor., Bos., Chi.	11	327	49	76	125	274	47	7	10	17	46	3	1942-43	1953-54
Lyon, Steve	Pit.	1	3	0	0	0	2	....	....	....	....	....	....	1976-77	1976-77
• Lyons, Ron	Bos., Phi.	1	36	2	4	6	27	5	0	0	0	0	....	1930-31	1930-31
Lysak, Brett	Car.	1	2	0	0	0	2	....	....	....	....	....	....	2003-04	2003-04
• Lysiak, Tom	Atl., Chi.	13	919	292	551	843	567	76	25	38	63	49	....	1973-74	1985-86
M															
MacAdam, Al	Phi., Cal., Cle., Min., Van.	12	864	240	351	591	509	64	20	24	44	21	....	1973-74	1984-85
MacDermid, Lane	Bos., Dal., Cgy.	3	21	2	2	4	36	....	....	....	....	....	....	2011-12	2013-14
MacDermid, Paul	Hfd., Wpg., Wsh., Que.	14	690	116	142	258	1303	43	5	11	16	116	....	1981-82	1994-95
MacDonald, Blair	Edm., Van.	4	219	91	100	191	65	11	0	6	6	2	....	1979-80	1982-83
MacDonald, Brett	Van.	1	1	0	0	0	0	....	....	....	....	....	....	1987-88	1987-88
MacDonald, Craig	Car., Fla., Bos., Cgy., Chi., T.B., CBJ	8	233	11	24	35	91	7	0	0	0	2	....	1998-99	2008-09
MacDonald, Doug	Buf.	3	11	1	0	1	2	....	....	....	....	....	....	1992-93	1994-95
MacDonald, Jason	NYR	1	4	0	0	0	19	....	....	....	....	....	....	2003-04	2003-04
MacDonald, Kevin	Ott.	1	1	0	0	0	2	....	....	....	....	....	....	1993-94	1993-94
• MacDonald, Kilby	NYR	4	151	36	34	70	47	15	1	2	3	4	1	1939-40	1944-45
MacDonald, Lowell	Det., L.A., Pit.	13	506	180	210	390	92	30	11	11	22	12	....	1961-62	1977-78
MacDonald, Parker	Tor., NYR, Det., Bos., Min.	14	676	144	179	323	253	75	14	14	28	20	....	1952-53	1968-69
MacDougall, Kim	Min.	1	1	0	0	0	0	....	....	....	....	....	....	1974-75	1974-75
MacEachern, Shane	St.L.	1	1	0	0	0	0	....	....	....	....	....	....	1987-88	1987-88
‡ Macenauer, Maxime	Ana.	1	29	1	3	4	18	....	....	....	....	....	....	2011-12	2011-12
• Macey, Hub	NYR, Mtl.	3	30	6	9	15	0	8	0	0	0	0	....	1941-42	1946-47
MacGregor, Bruce	Det., NYR	14	893	213	257	470	217	107	19	28	47	44	....	1960-61	1973-74
MacGregor, Randy	Hfd.	1	2	1	1	2	2	....	....	....	....	....	....	1981-82	1981-82
MacGuigan, Garth	NYI	2	5	0	1	1	2	....	....	....	....	....	....	1979-80	1983-84
‡ Machacek, Spencer	Atl., Wpg.	3	25	2	7	9	7	....	....	....	....	....	....	2008-09	2011-12
Macias, Ray	Col.	2	8	0	1	1	2	....	....	....	....	....	....	2008-09	2010-11
MacInnis, Al	Cgy., St.L.	23	1416	340	934	1274	1511	177	39	121	160	255	1	1981-82	2003-04
• MacIntosh, Ian	NYR	1	4	0	0	0	4	....	....	....	....	....	....	1952-53	1952-53
MacIntyre, Steve	Edm., Fla., Pit.	5	91	2	2	4	175	....	....	....	....	....	....	2008-09	2012-13
MacIver, Don	Wpg.	1	6	0	0	0	2	....	....	....	....	....	....	1979-80	1979-80
Maciver, Norm	NYR, Hfd., Edm., Ott., Pit., Wpg., Phx.	12	500	55	230	285	350	56	3	11	14	32	....	1986-87	1997-98
MacKasey, Blair	Tor.	1	1	0	0	0	2	....	....	....	....	....	....	1976-77	1976-77
• MacKay, Calum	Det., Mtl.	8	237	50	55	105	214	38	5	13	18	20	1	1946-47	1954-55
MacKay, Dave	Chi.	1	29	3	0	3	26	5	0	1	1	2	....	1940-41	1940-41
• MacKay, Mickey	Chi., Pit., Bos.	4	147	44	19	63	79	11	0	0	0	6	1	1926-27	1929-30
• MacKay, Murdo	Mtl.	4	19	0	3	3	0	15	1	2	3	0	....	1945-46	1948-49
• MacKell, Fleming	Tor., Bos.	13	665	149	220	369	562	80	22	41	63	75	2	1947-48	1959-60
• MacKell, Jack	Ott.	2	45	4	2	6	59	2	0	0	0	0	2	1919-20	1920-21
MacKenzie, Aaron	Col.	1	5	0	0	0	0	....	....	....	....	....	....	2008-09	2008-09
MacKenzie, Barry	Min.	1	6	0	1	1	6	....	....	....	....	....	....	1968-69	1968-69
• MacKenzie, Bill	Mtl.M., NYR, Mtl., Chi.	6	228	11	10	21	132	21	1	1	2	11	1	1933-34	1939-40
• MacKenzie, Clarence	Chi.	1	36	4	4	8	13	....	....	....	....	....	....	1932-33	1932-33
Mackey, David	Chi., Min., St.L.	6	126	8	12	20	305	3	0	0	0	2	....	1987-88	1993-94
• Mackey, Reg	NYR	1	34	0	0	0	16	1	0	0	0	0	....	1926-27	1926-27
• Mackie, Howie	Det.	2	20	1	0	1	4	8	0	0	0	0	1	1936-37	1937-38
MacKinnon, Paul	Wsh.	5	147	5	23	28	91	....	....	....	....	....	....	1979-80	1983-84
Maclean, Brett	Phx., Wpg.	2	18	2	3	5	4	....	....	....	....	....	....	2010-11	2011-12
MacLean, Don	L.A., Tor., CBJ, Det., Phx.	6	41	8	5	13	6	3	0	0	0	0	....	1997-98	2006-07
MacLean, John	N.J., S.J., NYR, Dal.	18	1194	413	429	842	1328	104	35	48	83	152	1	1983-84	2001-02
MacLean, Paul	St.L., Wpg., Det.	11	719	324	349	673	968	53	21	14	35	110	....	1980-81	1990-91
• MacLeish, Rick	Phi., Hfd., Pit., Det.	14	846	349	410	759	434	114	54	53	107	38	2	1970-71	1983-84
MacLellan, Brian	L.A., NYR, Min., Cgy., Det.	10	606	172	241	413	551	47	5	9	14	42	1	1982-83	1991-92
MacLeod, Pat	Min., S.J., Dal.	4	53	5	13	18	14	....	....	....	....	....	....	1990-91	1995-96
MacMillan, Billy	Tor., Atl., NYI	7	446	74	77	151	184	53	6	6	12	40	....	1970-71	1976-77
MacMillan, Bob	NYR, St.L., Atl., Cgy., Col., N.J., Chi.	11	753	228	349	577	260	31	8	11	19	16	....	1974-75	1984-85
MacMillan, Jeff	Dal.	1	4	0	0	0	0	....	....	....	....	....	....	2003-04	2003-04
MacMillan, John	Tor., Det.	5	104	5	10	15	32	12	0	1	1	2	2	1960-61	1964-65
MacNeil, Al	Tor., Mtl., Chi., NYR, Pit.	11	524	17	75	92	617	37	0	4	4	67	....	1955-56	1967-68
MacNeil, Bernie	St.L.	1	4	0	0	0	0	....	....	....	....	....	....	1973-74	1973-74
MacNeil, Ian	Phi.	1	2	0	0	0	0	....	....	....	....	....	....	2002-03	2002-03
Macoun, Jamie	Cgy., Tor., Det.	16	1128	76	282	358	1208	159	10	32	42	169	2	1982-83	1998-99
• MacPherson, Bud	Mtl.	7	259	5	33	38	233	29	0	3	3	21	1	1948-49	1956-57
• MacSweyn, Ralph	Phi.	5	47	0	5	5	10	8	0	0	0	6	....	1967-68	1971-72
MacTavish, Craig	Bos., Edm., NYR, Phi., St.L.	17	1093	213	267	480	891	193	20	38	58	218	4	1979-80	1996-97
MacWilliam, Mike	NYI	1	6	0	0	0	14	....	....	....	....	....	....	1995-96	1995-96
Madden, John	N.J., Chi., Min., Fla.	13	898	165	183	348	219	141	21	22	43	26	3	1998-99	2011-12
Madigan, Connie	St.L.	1	20	0	3	3	25	5	0	0	0	4	....	1972-73	1972-73

Name	NHL Teams	NHL Seasons	Regular Schedule GP	G	A	TP	PIM	Playoffs GP	G	A	TP	PIM	NHL Cup Wins	First NHL Season	Last NHL Season
Madill, Jeff	N.J.	1	14	4	0	4	46	7	0	2	2	8	....	1990-91	1990-91
Magee, Dean	Min.	1	7	0	0	0	4	....	....	....	....	....	....	1977-78	1977-78
Maggs, Darryl	Chi., Cal., Tor.	3	135	14	19	33	54	4	0	0	0	0	....	1971-72	1979-80
Magnan, Marc	Tor.	1	4	0	1	1	5	....	....	....	....	....	....	1982-83	1982-83
Magnan, Olivier	N.J.	1	18	0	0	0	4	....	....	....	....	....	....	2010-11	2010-11
• Magnuson, Keith	Chi.	11	589	14	125	139	1442	68	3	9	12	164	....	1969-70	1979-80
Maguire, Kevin	Tor., Buf., Phi.	6	260	29	30	59	782	11	0	0	0	86	....	1986-87	1991-92
• Mahaffy, John	Mtl., NYR	3	37	11	25	36	4	1	0	1	1	0	....	1942-43	1944-45
Mahovlich, Frank	Tor., Det., Mtl	18	1181	533	570	1103	1056	137	51	67	118	163	6	1956-57	1973-74
Mahovlich, Pete	Det., Mtl., Pit.	16	884	288	485	773	916	88	30	42	72	134	4	1965-66	1980-81
Mailhot, Jacques	Que.	1	5	0	0	0	33	....	....	....	....	....	....	1988-89	1988-89
• Mailley, Frank	Mtl.	1	1	0	0	0	0	....	....	....	....	....	....	1942-43	1942-43
Mair, Adam	Tor., L.A., Buf., N.J.	12	615	38	76	114	829	35	3	5	8	36	....	1998-99	2010-11
Mair, Jim	Phi., NYI, Van.	5	76	4	15	19	49	3	1	2	3	4	....	1970-71	1974-75
• Majeau, Fern	Mtl.	2	56	22	24	46	43	1	0	0	0	0	1	1943-44	1944-45
‡ Majesky, Ivan	Fla., Atl., Wsh.	3	202	8	23	31	234	....	....	....	....	....	....	2002-03	2005-06
Major, Bruce	Que.	1	4	0	0	0	0	....	....	....	....	....	....	1990-91	1990-91
Major, Mark	Det.	1	2	0	0	0	5	....	....	....	....	....	....	1996-97	1996-97
Makarov, Sergei	Cgy., S.J., Dal.	7	424	134	250	384	317	34	12	11	23	8	....	1989-90	1996-97
Makela, Mikko	NYI, L.A., Buf., Bos.	7	423	118	147	265	139	18	3	8	11	14	....	1985-86	1994-95
• Maki, Chico	Chi.	15	841	143	292	435	345	113	17	36	53	43	1	1960-61	1975-76
‡ Maki, Tomi	Cgy.	1	1	0	0	0	0	....	....	....	....	....	....	2006-07	2006-07
• Maki, Wayne	Chi., St.L., Van.	6	246	57	79	136	184	2	1	0	1	2	....	1967-68	1972-73
Makkonen, Kari	Edm.	1	9	2	2	4	0	....	....	....	....	....	....	1979-80	1979-80
Malakhov, Vladimir	NYI, Mtl., N.J., NYR, Phi.	13	712	86	260	346	697	75	8	19	27	64	1	1992-93	2005-06
‡ Malec, Tomas	Car., Ott.	4	46	0	2	2	47	....	....	....	....	....	....	2002-03	2006-07
Maley, David	Mtl., N.J., Edm., S.J., NYI	9	466	43	81	124	1043	46	5	5	10	111	1	1985-86	1993-94
Malgunas, Stewart	Phi., Wpg., Wsh., Cgy.	7	129	1	5	6	144	....	....	....	....	....	....	1993-94	1999-00
Malhotra, Manny	NYR, Dal., CBJ, S.J., Van., Car., Mtl.	16	991	116	179	295	451	35	2	0	2	0	....	1998-99	2014-15
Malik, Marek	Hfd., Car., Van., NYR, T.B.	13	691	33	135	168	620	65	2	8	10	64	....	1994-95	2008-09
Malinowski, Merlin	Col., N.J., Hfd.	5	282	54	111	165	121	....	....	....	....	....	....	1978-79	1982-83
Malkoc, Dean	Van., Bos., NYI	4	116	1	3	4	299	....	....	....	....	....	....	1995-96	1998-99
Mallette, Troy	NYR, Edm., N.J., Ott., Bos., T.B.	9	456	51	68	119	1226	15	2	2	4	99	....	1989-90	1997-98
Malmivaara, Olli	N.J.	1	2	0	0	0	0	....	....	....	....	....	....	2007-08	2007-08
• Malone, Cliff	Mtl.	1	3	0	0	0	0	....	....	....	....	....	....	1951-52	1951-52
Malone, Greg	Pit., Hfd., Que.	11	704	191	310	501	661	20	3	5	8	32	....	1976-77	1986-87
• Malone, Joe	Mtl., Que., Ham.	7	126	143	32	175	57	9	6	2	8	6	1	1917-18	1923-24
Malone, Ryan	Pit., T.B., NYR	11	647	179	191	370	693	43	9	13	22	49	....	2003-04	2014-15
Maloney, Dan	Chi., L.A., Det., Tor.	11	737	192	259	451	1489	40	4	7	11	35	....	1970-71	1981-82
Maloney, Dave	NYR, Buf.	11	657	71	246	317	1154	49	7	17	24	91	....	1974-75	1984-85
Maloney, Don	NYR, Hfd., NYI	13	765	214	350	564	815	94	22	35	57	101	....	1978-79	1990-91
Maloney, Phil	Bos., Tor., Chi.	5	158	28	43	71	16	6	0	0	0	0	....	1949-50	1959-60
Maltais, Steve	Wsh., Min., T.B., Det., CBJ	6	120	9	18	27	53	1	0	0	0	0	....	1989-90	2000-01
Maltby, Kirk	Edm., Det.	16	1072	128	132	260	867	169	16	15	31	149	4	1993-94	2009-10
Maluta, Ray	Bos.	2	25	2	3	5	6	2	0	0	0	0	....	1975-76	1976-77
• Manastersky, Tom	Mtl.	1	6	0	0	0	11	....	....	....	....	....	....	1950-51	1950-51
‡ Mancari, Mark	Buf., Van.	5	42	3	10	13	22	1	0	0	0	0	....	2006-07	2011-12
• Mancuso, Gus	Mtl., NYR	4	42	7	9	16	17	....	....	....	....	....	....	1937-38	1942-43
Manderville, Kent	Tor., Edm., Hfd., Car., Phi., Pit.	12	646	37	67	104	348	67	3	3	6	44	....	1991-92	2002-03
Mandich, Dan	Min.	4	111	5	11	16	303	7	0	0	0	2	....	1982-83	1985-86
Maneluk, Mike	Phi., Chi., NYR, CBJ	3	85	11	10	21	57	....	....	....	....	....	....	1998-99	2000-01
Manery, Kris	Cle., Min., Van., Wpg.	4	250	63	64	127	91	....	....	....	....	....	....	1977-78	1980-81
Manery, Randy	Det., Atl., L.A.	10	582	50	206	256	415	13	0	2	2	12	....	1970-71	1979-80
Manlow, Eric	Bos., NYI	4	37	2	4	6	8	....	....	....	....	....	....	2000-01	2003-04
Mann, Cameron	Bos., Nsh.	5	93	14	10	24	40	1	0	0	0	0	....	1997-98	2002-03
• Mann, Jack	NYR	2	9	3	4	7	0	....	....	....	....	....	....	1943-44	1944-45
Mann, Jimmy	Wpg., Que., Pit.	8	293	10	20	30	895	22	0	0	0	89	....	1979-80	1987-88
Mann, Ken	Det.	1	1	0	0	0	0	....	....	....	....	....	....	1975-76	1975-76
• Mann, Norm	Tor.	3	31	0	3	3	4	2	0	0	0	0	....	1935-36	1940-41
• Manners, Rennison	Pit., Phi.	2	37	3	2	5	14	....	....	....	....	....	....	1929-30	1930-31
Manning, Paul	CBJ	1	8	0	0	0	2	....	....	....	....	....	....	2002-03	2002-03
Manno, Bob	Van., Tor., Det.	8	371	41	131	172	274	17	2	4	6	12	....	1976-77	1984-85
Manson, Dave	Chi., Edm., Wpg., Phx., Mtl., Dal., Tor.	16	1103	102	288	390	2792	112	7	24	31	343	....	1986-87	2001-02
• Manson, Ray	Bos., NYR	2	2	0	1	1	0	....	....	....	....	....	....	1947-48	1948-49
• Mantha, Georges	Mtl.	13	488	89	102	191	148	36	6	2	8	24	2	1928-29	1940-41
Mantha, Moe	Wpg., Pit., Edm., Min., Phi.	12	656	81	289	370	501	17	5	10	15	18	....	1980-81	1991-92
• Mantha, Sylvio	Mtl., Bos.	14	542	63	78	141	671	39	5	5	10	64	3	1923-24	1936-37
Mapletoft, Justin	NYI	2	38	3	6	9	8	2	0	0	0	0	....	2002-03	2003-04
Mara, Paul	T.B., Phx., Bos., NYR, Mtl., Ana.	12	734	64	189	253	776	33	3	4	7	50	....	1998-99	2010-11
• Maracle, Bud	NYR	1	11	1	3	4	4	4	0	0	0	0	....	1930-31	1930-31
• Marcetta, Milan	Tor., Min.	3	54	7	15	22	10	17	7	7	14	4	1	1966-67	1968-69
• March, Mush	Chi.	17	759	153	230	383	540	45	12	15	27	41	2	1928-29	1944-45
Marchant, Todd	NYR, Edm., CBJ, Ana.	17	1195	186	312	498	774	95	13	21	34	88	1	1993-94	2010-11
• Marchinko, Brian	Tor., NYI	4	47	2	6	8	0	....	....	....	....	....	....	1970-71	1973-74
Marchment, Bryan	Wpg., Chi., Hfd., Edm., T.B., S.J., Col., Tor., Cgy.	17	926	40	142	182	2307	83	4	3	7	102	....	1988-89	2005-06
Marcinyshyn, Dave	N.J., Que., NYR	3	16	0	1	1	49	....	....	....	....	....	....	1990-91	1992-93
Marcon, Lou	Det.	3	60	0	4	4	42	....	....	....	....	....	....	1958-59	1962-63
Marcotte, Don	Bos.	15	868	230	254	484	317	132	34	27	61	81	2	1965-66	1981-82
Marha, Josef	Col., Ana., Chi.	6	159	21	32	53	32	....	....	....	....	....	....	1995-96	2000-01
Marini, Hector	NYI, N.J.	5	154	27	46	73	246	10	3	6	9	14	2	1978-79	1983-84
Marinucci, Chris	NYI, L.A.	2	13	1	4	5	2	....	....	....	....	....	....	1994-95	1996-97
• Mario, Frank	Bos.	2	53	9	19	28	24	....	....	....	....	....	....	1941-42	1944-45
• Mariucci, John	Chi.	5	223	11	34	45	308	12	0	3	3	26	....	1940-41	1947-48
Marjamaki, Masi	NYI	1	1	0	0	0	0	....	....	....	....	....	....	2005-06	2005-06
Mark, Gordon	N.J., Edm.	4	85	3	10	13	187	....	....	....	....	....	....	1986-87	1994-95
Markell, John	Wpg., St.L., Min.	4	55	11	10	21	36	....	....	....	....	....	....	1979-80	1984-85
• Marker, Gus	Det., Mtl.M., Tor., Bro.	10	322	64	69	133	133	46	5	7	12	36	1	1932-33	1941-42
Markham, Ray	NYR	1	14	1	1	2	21	7	1	0	1	24	....	1979-80	1979-80
• Markle, Jack	Tor.	1	8	0	1	1	0	....	....	....	....	....	....	1935-36	1935-36
Markov, Danny	Tor., Phx., Car., Phi., Nsh., Det.	9	538	29	118	147	456	81	2	12	14	84	....	1997-98	2006-07
• Marks, Jack	Mtl.W., Tor., Que.	2	7	0	0	0	4	....	....	....	....	....	1	1917-18	1919-20
Marks, John	Chi.	10	657	112	163	275	330	57	5	9	14	60	....	1972-73	1981-82
Markwart, Nevin	Bos., Cgy.	8	309	41	68	109	794	19	1	0	1	33	....	1983-84	1991-92
Marois, Daniel	Tor., NYI, Bos., Dal.	8	350	117	93	210	419	19	3	3	6	28	....	1987-88	1995-96
Marois, Mario	NYR, Van., Que., Wpg., St.L.	15	955	76	357	433	1746	100	4	34	38	182	....	1977-78	1991-92
• Marotte, Gilles	Bos., Chi., L.A., NYR, St.L.	12	808	56	265	321	919	29	3	3	6	26	....	1965-66	1976-77
• Marquess, Mark	Bos.	1	27	5	4	9	6	4	0	0	0	0	....	1946-47	1946-47
Marsh, Brad	Atl., Cgy., Phi., Tor., Det., Ott.	15	1086	23	175	198	1241	97	6	18	24	124	....	1978-79	1992-93
Marsh, Gary	Det., Tor.	2	7	1	3	4	4	....	....	....	....	....	....	1967-68	1968-69
Marsh, Peter	Wpg., Chi.	5	278	48	71	119	224	26	1	5	6	33	....	1979-80	1983-84
Marshall, Bert	Det., Oak., Cal., NYR, NYI	14	868	17	181	198	926	72	4	22	26	99	....	1965-66	1978-79
Marshall, Don	Mtl., NYR, Buf., Tor.	19	1176	265	324	589	127	94	8	15	23	14	5	1951-52	1971-72
Marshall, Grant	Dal., CBJ, N.J.	11	700	92	147	239	793	90	6	11	17	95	2	1994-95	2005-06
Marshall, Jason	St.L., Ana., Wsh., Min., S.J.	12	526	16	51	67	1004	43	2	3	5	55	....	1991-92	2005-06
‡ Marshall, Kevin	Phi.	1	10	0	0	0	8	....	....	....	....	....	....	2011-12	2011-12
Marshall, Paul	Pit., Tor., Hfd.	4	95	15	18	33	17	1	0	0	0	0	....	1979-80	1982-83
Marshall, Willie	Tor.	4	33	1	5	6	2	....	....	....	....	....	....	1952-53	1958-59
Marson, Mike	Wsh., L.A.	6	196	24	24	48	233	....	....	....	....	....	....	1974-75	1979-80
‡ Martensson, Tony	Ana.	1	6	1	1	2	0	....	....	....	....	....	....	2003-04	2003-04
• Martin, Clare	Bos., Det., Chi., NYR	6	237	12	28	40	78	27	0	2	2	6	1	1941-42	1951-52
Martin, Craig	Wpg., Fla.	2	21	0	1	1	24	....	....	....	....	....	....	1994-95	1996-97
• Martin, Frank	Bos., Chi.	6	282	11	46	57	122	10	0	2	2	2	....	1952-53	1957-58
Martin, Grant	Van., Wsh.	4	44	0	4	4	55	1	1	0	1	2	....	1983-84	1986-87
Martin, Jack	Tor.	1	1	0	0	0	0	....	....	....	....	....	....	1960-61	1960-61
Martin, Matt	Tor.	4	76	0	5	5	71	....	....	....	....	....	....	1993-94	1996-97
• Martin, Pit	Det., Bos., Chi., Van.	17	1101	324	485	809	609	100	27	31	58	56	....	1961-62	1978-79
• Martin, Rick	Buf., L.A.	11	685	384	317	701	477	63	24	29	53	74	....	1971-72	1981-82
• Martin, Ron	NYA	2	94	13	16	29	36	....	....	....	....	....	....	1932-33	1933-34
Martin, Terry	Buf., Que., Tor., Edm., Min.	10	479	104	101	205	202	21	4	2	6	26	....	1975-76	1984-85
Martin, Tom	Tor.	1	3	1	0	1	0	....	....	....	....	....	....	1967-68	1967-68
Martin, Tom	Wpg., Hfd., Min.	6	92	12	11	23	249	4	0	0	0	6	....	1984-85	1989-90

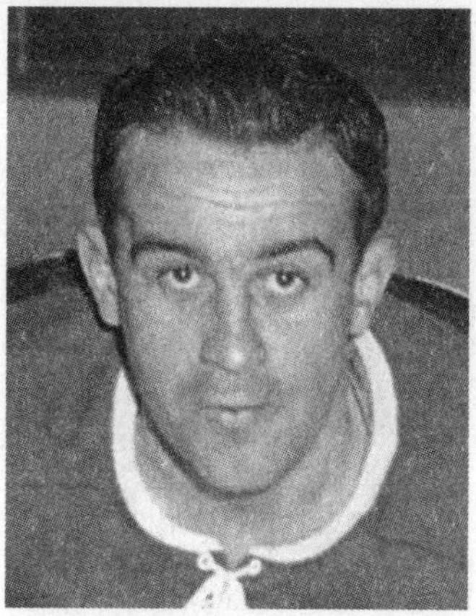

Cliff Malone

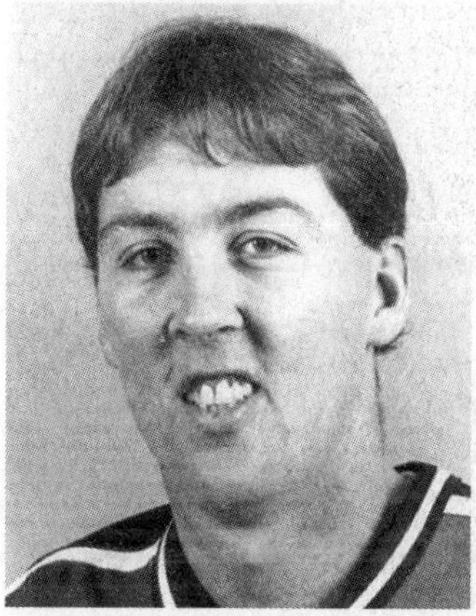

Gordon Mark

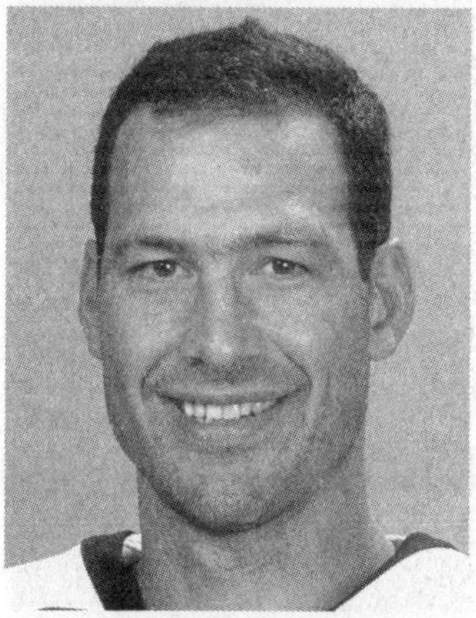

Brad Marsh

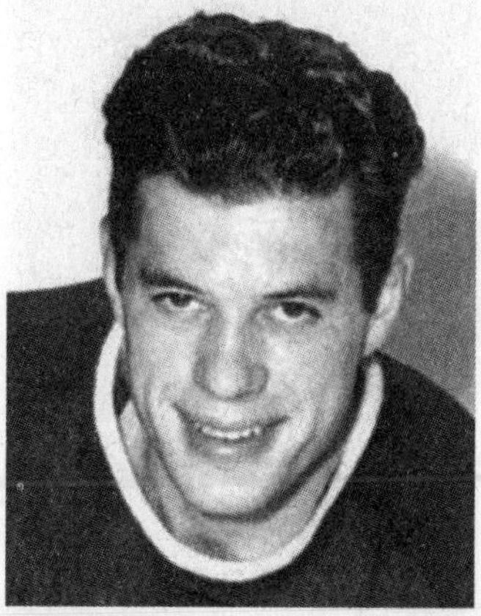

Frank Mathers

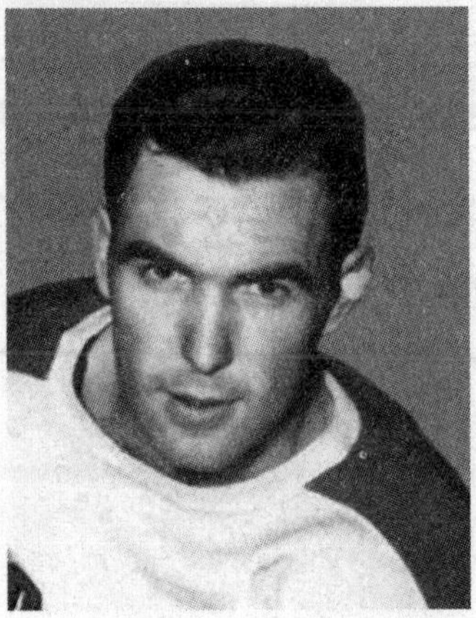

Hazen McAndrew

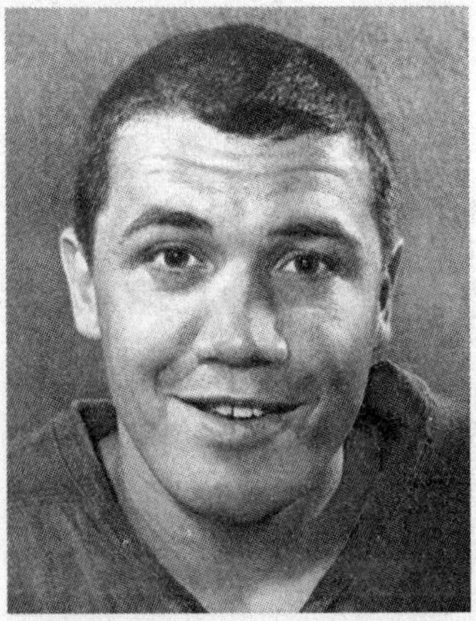

Bob McCord

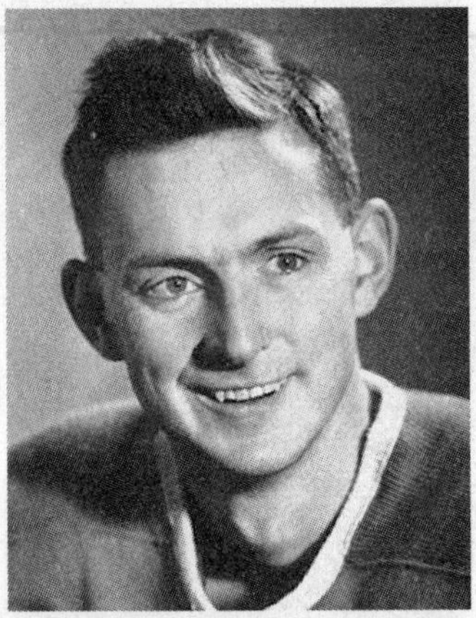

John McCormack

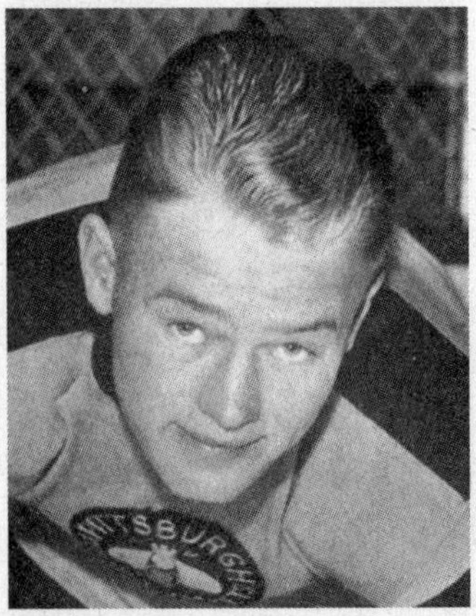

Butch McDonald

			Regular Schedule					Playoffs					NHL	First	Last
Name	NHL Teams	NHL Seasons	GP	G	A	TP	PIM	GP	G	A	TP	PIM	Cup Wins	NHL Season	NHL Season
● Martineau, Don	Atl., Min., Det.	4	90	6	10	16	63	....	....	....	....	....	....	1973-74	1976-77
Martinek, Radek	NYI, CBJ	12	486	25	85	110	280	11	0	1	1	6	....	2001-02	2013-14
Martini, Darcy	Edm.	1	2	0	0	0	0	....	....	....	....	....	....	1993-94	1993-94
Martins, Steve	Hfd., Car., Ott., T.B., NYI, St.L.	10	267	21	25	46	142	5	0	1	1	0	....	1995-96	2005-06
Martinson, Steve	Det., Mtl., Min.	4	49	2	1	3	244	1	0	0	0	10	....	1987-88	1991-92
Maruk, Dennis	Cal., Cle., Min., Wsh.	14	888	356	522	878	761	34	14	22	36	26	....	1975-76	1988-89
Masnick, Paul	Mtl., Chi., Tor.	6	232	18	41	59	139	33	4	5	9	27	1	1950-51	1957-58
● Mason, Charley	NYR, NYA, Det., Chi.	4	95	7	18	25	44	4	0	1	1	0	....	1934-35	1938-39
● Massecar, George	NYA	3	100	12	11	23	46	....	....	....	....	....	....	1929-30	1931-32
Masters, Jamie	St.L.	3	33	1	13	14	2	2	0	0	0	0	....	1975-76	1978-79
● Masterton, Bill	Min.	1	38	4	8	12	4	....	....	....	....	....	....	1967-68	1967-68
● Mathers, Frank	Tor.	3	23	1	3	4	4	....	....	....	....	....	....	1948-49	1951-52
Mathiasen, Dwight	Pit.	3	33	1	7	8	18	....	....	....	....	....	....	1985-86	1987-88
Mathieson, Jim	Wsh.	1	2	0	0	0	4	....	....	....	....	....	....	1989-90	1989-90
Mathieu, Marquis	Bos.	3	16	0	2	2	14	....	....	....	....	....	....	1998-99	2000-01
Matsumoto, Jon	Car., Fla.	2	14	2	0	2	4	....	....	....	....	....	....	2010-11	2011-12
Matte, Christian	Col., Min.	5	25	2	3	5	12	....	....	....	....	....	....	1996-97	2000-01
● Matte, Joe	Tor., Ham., Bos., Mtl.	4	68	17	15	32	54	....	....	....	....	....	....	1919-20	1925-26
● Matte, Joe	Det., Chi.	2	24	0	3	3	8	....	....	....	....	....	....	1929-30	1942-43
Matteau, Stephane	Cgy., Chi., NYR, St.L., S.J., Fla.	13	848	144	172	316	742	109	12	22	34	80	1	1990-91	2002-03
Matteucci, Mike	Min.	2	6	0	0	0	4	....	....	....	....	....	....	2000-01	2001-02
Mattiussi, Dick	Pit., Oak., Cal.	4	200	8	31	39	124	8	0	1	1	6	....	1967-68	1970-71
Matvichuk, Richard	Min., Dal., N.J.	14	796	39	139	178	624	123	5	19	24	128	1	1992-93	2006-07
● Matz, Johnny	Mtl.	1	30	2	3	5	0	1	0	0	0	0	....	1924-25	1924-25
‡ Mauldin, Greg	CBJ, NYI, Col.	3	36	5	5	10	12	....	....	....	....	....	....	2003-04	2010-11
Maxner, Wayne	Bos.	2	62	8	9	17	48	....	....	....	....	....	....	1964-65	1965-66
‡ Maxwell, Ben	Mtl., Atl., Wpg., Ana.	4	47	2	6	8	19	1	0	0	0	0	....	2008-09	2011-12
Maxwell, Brad	Min., Que., Tor., Van., NYR	10	612	98	270	368	1292	79	12	49	61	178	....	1977-78	1986-87
Maxwell, Bryan	Min., St.L., Wpg., Pit.	8	331	18	77	95	745	15	1	1	2	86	....	1977-78	1984-85
Maxwell, Kevin	Min., Col., N.J.	3	66	6	15	21	61	16	3	4	7	24	....	1980-81	1983-84
Maxwell, Wally	Tor.	1	2	0	0	0	0	....	....	....	....	....	....	1952-53	1952-53
May, Alan	Bos., Edm., Wsh., Dal., Cgy.	8	393	31	45	76	1348	40	1	2	3	80	....	1987-88	1994-95
May, Brad	Buf., Van., Phx., Col., Ana., Tor., Det.	18	1041	127	161	288	2248	88	4	9	13	112	1	1991-92	2009-10
Mayer, Derek	Ott.	1	17	2	2	4	8	....	....	....	....	....	....	1993-94	1993-94
Mayer, Jim	NYR	1	4	0	0	0	0	....	....	....	....	....	....	1979-80	1979-80
Mayer, Pat	Pit.	1	1	0	0	0	4	....	....	....	....	....	....	1987-88	1987-88
● Mayer, Shep	Tor.	1	12	1	2	3	4	....	....	....	....	....	....	1942-43	1942-43
Mayers, Jamal	St.L., Tor., Cgy., S.J., Chi.	15	915	90	129	219	1200	63	5	8	13	32	1	1996-97	2012-13
Mayorov, Maksim	CBJ	4	22	2	1	3	2	....	....	....	....	....	....	2008-09	2011-12
● Mazur, Eddie	Mtl., Chi.	6	107	8	20	28	120	25	4	5	9	22	1	1950-51	1956-57
Mazur, Jay	Van.	4	47	11	7	18	20	6	0	1	1	8	....	1988-89	1991-92
McAdam, Gary	Buf., Pit., Det., Cgy., Wsh., N.J., Tor.	11	534	96	132	228	243	30	6	5	11	16	....	1975-76	1985-86
● McAdam, Sam	NYR	1	5	0	0	0	0	....	....	....	....	....	....	1930-31	1930-31
McAllister, Chris	Van., Tor., Phi., Col., NYR	7	301	4	17	21	634	9	0	1	1	4	....	1997-98	2003-04
McAlpine, Chris	N.J., St.L., T.B., Atl., Chi., L.A.	8	289	6	24	30	245	28	0	1	1	18	1	1994-95	2002-03
McAmmond, Dean	Chi., Edm., Phi., Cgy., Col., St.L., Ott., NYI, N.J.	17	996	186	262	448	490	46	6	7	13	35	....	1991-92	2009-10
● McAndrew, Hazen	Bro.	1	7	0	1	1	6	....	....	....	....	....	....	1941-42	1941-42
McAneeley, Ted	Cal.	3	158	8	35	43	141	....	....	....	....	....	....	1972-73	1974-75
McArdle, Kenndal	Fla., Wpg.	4	42	1	2	3	51	....	....	....	....	....	....	2008-09	2011-12
● McAtee, Jud	Det.	3	46	15	13	28	6	14	2	1	3	0	....	1942-43	1944-45
● McAtee, Norm	Bos.	1	13	0	1	1	0	....	....	....	....	....	....	1946-47	1946-47
● McAvoy, George	Mtl.	1	....	....	....	....	....	4	0	0	0	0	....	1954-55	1954-55
McBain, Andrew	Wpg., Pit., Van., Ott.	11	608	129	172	301	633	24	5	7	12	39	....	1983-84	1993-94
McBain, Jason	Hfd.	2	9	0	0	0	0	....	....	....	....	....	....	1995-96	1996-97
McBain, Mike	T.B.	2	64	0	7	7	22	....	....	....	....	....	....	1997-98	1998-99
McBean, Wayne	L.A., NYI, Wpg.	6	211	10	39	49	168	2	1	1	2	0	....	1987-88	1993-94
● McBride, Cliff	Mtl.M., Tor.	2	2	0	0	0	0	....	....	....	....	....	....	1928-29	1929-30
McBurney, Jim	Chi.	1	1	0	1	1	0	....	....	....	....	....	....	1952-53	1952-53
McCabe, Bryan	NYI, Van., Chi., Tor., Fla., NYR	15	1135	145	383	528	1732	56	10	18	28	84	....	1995-96	2010-11
● McCabe, Stan	Det., Mtl.M.	4	78	9	4	13	49	....	....	....	....	....	....	1929-30	1933-34
● McCaffrey, Bert	Tor., Pit., Mtl.	7	260	43	30	73	202	8	2	1	3	10	1	1924-25	1930-31
McCahill, John	Col.	1	1	0	0	0	0	....	....	....	....	....	....	1977-78	1977-78
● McCaig, Doug	Det., Chi.	7	263	8	21	29	255	7	0	1	1	10	....	1941-42	1950-51
● McCallum, Dunc	NYR, Pit.	5	187	14	35	49	230	10	1	2	3	12	....	1965-66	1970-71
● McCalmon, Eddie	Chi., Phi.	2	39	5	0	5	14	....	....	....	....	....	....	1927-28	1930-31
● McCann, Rick	Det.	6	43	1	4	5	6	....	....	....	....	....	....	1967-68	1974-75
McCarthy, Dan	NYR	1	5	4	0	4	4	....	....	....	....	....	....	1980-81	1980-81
McCarthy, Kevin	Phi., Van., Pit.	10	537	67	191	258	527	21	2	3	5	20	....	1977-78	1986-87
McCarthy, Sandy	Cgy., T.B., Phi., Car., NYR, Bos.	11	736	72	76	148	1534	23	0	2	2	61	....	1993-94	2003-04
McCarthy, Steve	Chi., Van., Atl.	8	302	17	38	55	168	....	....	....	....	....	....	1999-00	2007-08
● McCarthy, Thomas	Que., Ham.	2	35	22	7	29	10	....	....	....	....	....	....	1919-20	1920-21
● McCarthy, Tom	Det., Bos.	4	60	8	9	17	8	....	....	....	....	....	....	1956-57	1960-61
McCarthy, Tom	Min., Bos.	9	460	178	221	399	330	68	12	26	38	67	....	1979-80	1987-88
● McCartney, Walt	Mtl.	1	2	0	0	0	0	....	....	....	....	....	....	1932-33	1932-33
McCarty, Darren	Det., Cgy.	15	758	127	161	288	1477	174	23	26	49	228	4	1993-94	2008-09
● McCaskill, Ted	Min.	1	4	0	2	2	0	....	....	....	....	....	....	1967-68	1967-68
McCauley, Alyn	Tor., S.J., L.A.	9	488	69	97	166	116	52	7	12	19	18	....	1997-98	2006-07
McClanahan, Rob	Buf., Hfd., NYR	5	224	38	63	101	126	34	4	12	16	31	....	1979-80	1983-84
McCleary, Trent	Ott., Bos., Mtl.	4	192	8	15	23	134	....	....	....	....	....	....	1995-96	1999-00
McClelland, Kevin	Pit., Edm., Det., Tor., Wpg.	12	588	68	112	180	1672	98	11	18	29	281	4	1981-82	1993-94
McCord, Bob	Bos., Det., Min., St.L.	7	316	10	58	68	262	14	2	5	7	10	....	1963-64	1972-73
● McCord, Dennis	Van.	1	3	0	0	0	6	....	....	....	....	....	....	1973-74	1973-74
● McCormack, John	Tor., Mtl., Chi.	8	311	25	49	74	35	22	1	1	2	0	2	1947-48	1954-55
McCormick, Cody	Col., Buf., Min.	11	405	21	44	65	550	27	2	3	5	37	....	2003-04	2014-15
McCosh, Shawn	L.A., NYR	2	9	1	0	1	6	....	....	....	....	....	....	1991-92	1994-95
McCourt, Dale	Det., Buf., Tor.	7	532	194	284	478	124	21	9	7	16	6	....	1977-78	1983-84
McCreary, Bill	NYR, Det., Mtl., St.L.	8	309	53	62	115	108	48	6	16	22	14	....	1953-54	1970-71
McCreary, Bill	Tor.	1	12	1	0	1	4	....	....	....	....	....	....	1980-81	1980-81
● McCreary, Keith	Mtl., Pit., Atl.	10	532	131	112	243	294	16	0	4	4	6	....	1961-62	1974-75
● McCreedy, John	Tor.	2	64	17	12	29	25	21	4	3	7	16	2	1941-42	1944-45
● McCrimmon, Brad	Bos., Phi., Cgy., Det., Hfd., Phx.	18	1222	81	322	403	1416	116	11	18	29	176	1	1979-80	1996-97
McCrimmon, Jim	St.L.	1	2	0	0	0	0	....	....	....	....	....	....	1974-75	1974-75
● McCulley, Bob	Mtl.	1	1	0	0	0	0	....	....	....	....	....	....	1934-35	1934-35
● McCurry, Duke	Pit.	4	148	21	11	32	119	4	0	2	2	2	....	1925-26	1928-29
McCutcheon, Brian	Det.	3	37	3	1	4	7	....	....	....	....	....	....	1974-75	1976-77
McCutcheon, Darwin	Tor.	1	1	0	0	0	2	....	....	....	....	....	....	1981-82	1981-82
● McDill, Jeff	Chi.	1	1	0	0	0	0	....	....	....	....	....	....	1976-77	1976-77
McDonagh, Bill	NYR	1	4	0	0	0	2	....	....	....	....	....	....	1949-50	1949-50
McDonald, Ab	Mtl., Chi., Bos., Det., Pit., St.L.	15	762	182	248	430	200	84	21	29	50	42	4	1957-58	1971-72
McDonald, Andy	Ana., St.L.	12	685	182	307	489	280	56	18	19	37	28	1	2000-01	2012-13
McDonald, Brian	Chi., Buf.	2	12	0	0	0	29	8	0	0	0	2	....	1967-68	1970-71
● McDonald, Bucko	Det., Tor., NYR	11	446	35	88	123	206	50	6	1	7	24	3	1934-35	1944-45
● McDonald, Butch	Det., Chi.	2	66	8	20	28	2	5	0	2	2	10	....	1939-40	1944-45
McDonald, Gerry	Hfd.	2	8	0	0	0	4	....	....	....	....	....	....	1981-82	1983-84
● McDonald, Jack	Mtl.W., Mtl., Que., Tor.	5	69	26	14	40	30	7	1	3	4	3	....	1917-18	1921-22
● McDonald, Jack	NYR	1	43	10	9	19	6	....	....	....	....	....	....	1943-44	1943-44
McDonald, Lanny	Tor., Col., Cgy.	16	1111	500	506	1006	899	117	44	40	84	120	1	1973-74	1988-89
● McDonald, Robert	NYR	1	1	0	0	0	0	....	....	....	....	....	....	1943-44	1943-44
McDonald, Terry	K.C.	1	8	0	1	1	6	....	....	....	....	....	....	1975-76	1975-76
McDonell, Kent	CBJ	2	32	1	2	3	36	....	....	....	....	....	....	2002-03	2003-04
McDonnell, Joe	Van., Pit.	3	50	2	10	12	34	....	....	....	....	....	....	1981-82	1985-86
● McDonnell, Moylan	Ham.	1	22	1	2	3	2	....	....	....	....	....	....	1920-21	1920-21
McDonough, Al	L.A., Pit., Atl., Det.	5	237	73	88	161	73	8	0	1	1	2	....	1970-71	1977-78
McDonough, Hubie	L.A., NYI, S.J.	5	195	40	26	66	67	5	1	0	1	4	....	1988-89	1992-93
McDougal, Mike	NYR, Hfd.	4	61	8	10	18	43	....	....	....	....	....	....	1978-79	1982-83
McDougall, Bill	Det., Edm., T.B.	3	28	5	5	10	12	1	0	0	0	0	....	1990-91	1993-94
McEachern, Shawn	Pit., L.A., Bos., Ott., Atl.	14	911	256	323	579	506	97	12	25	37	62	1	1991-92	2005-06
McElmury, Jim	Min., K.C., Col.	5	180	14	47	61	49	....	....	....	....	....	....	1972-73	1977-78
McEwen, Mike	NYR, Col., NYI, L.A., Wsh., Det., Hfd.	12	716	108	296	404	460	78	12	36	48	48	3	1976-77	1987-88
● McFadden, Jim	Det., Chi.	8	412	100	126	226	89	49	10	9	19	30	1	1946-47	1953-54
● McFadyen, Don	Chi.	4	179	12	33	45	77	11	2	2	4	5	1	1932-33	1935-36

Name	NHL Teams	NHL Seasons	Regular Schedule					Playoffs					NHL Cup Wins	First NHL Season	Last NHL Season
			GP	G	A	TP	PIM	GP	G	A	TP	PIM			
McFall, Dan	Wpg.	2	9	0	1	1	0	....	....	....	....	....	....	1984-85	1985-86
• McFarlane, Gord	Chi.	1	2	0	0	0	0	....	....	....	....	....	....	1926-27	1926-27
McGeough, Jim	Wsh., Pit.	4	57	7	10	17	32	....	....	....	....	....	....	1981-82	1986-87
• McGibbon, Irv	Mtl.	1	1	0	0	0	2	....	....	....	....	....	....	1942-43	1942-43
McGill, Bob	Tor., Chi., S.J., Det., NYI, Hfd.	13	705	17	55	72	1766	49	0	0	0	88	....	1981-82	1993-94
• McGill, Jack	Mtl.	3	134	27	10	37	71	3	2	0	2	0	....	1934-35	1936-37
• McGill, Jack	Bos.	4	97	23	36	59	42	27	7	4	11	17	....	1941-42	1946-47
McGill, Ryan	Chi., Phi., Edm.	4	151	4	15	19	391	....	....	....	....	....	....	1991-92	1994-95
McGillis, Dan	Edm., Phi., S.J., Bos., N.J.	9	634	56	182	238	570	64	8	14	22	76	....	1996-97	2005-06
‡ McGrattan, Brian	Ott., Phx., Cgy., Nsh.	9	317	10	17	27	609	....	....	....	....	....	....	2005-06	2014-15
McGregor, Sandy	NYR	1	2	0	0	0	2	....	....	....	....	....	....	1963-64	1963-64
• McGuire, Mickey	Pit.	2	36	3	0	3	6	....	....	....	....	....	....	1926-27	1927-28
McHugh, Mike	Min., S.J.	4	20	1	0	1	16	....	....	....	....	....	....	1988-89	1991-92
McIlhargey, Jack	Phi., Van., Hfd.	8	393	11	36	47	1102	27	0	3	3	68	....	1974-75	1981-82
• McInenly, Bert	Det., NYA, Ott., Bos.	6	166	19	15	34	144	4	0	0	0	2	....	1930-31	1935-36
McInnis, Marty	NYI, Cgy., Ana., Bos.	12	796	170	250	420	330	22	3	2	5	4	....	1991-92	2002-03
McIntosh, Bruce	Min.	1	2	0	0	0	0	....	....	....	....	....	....	1972-73	1972-73
McIntosh, Paul	Buf.	2	48	0	2	2	66	2	0	0	0	7	....	1974-75	1975-76
‡ McIntyre, David	Min.	1	7	1	1	2	2	....	....	....	....	....	....	2011-12	2011-12
• McIntyre, Jack	Bos., Chi., Det.	11	499	109	102	211	173	29	7	6	13	4	....	1949-50	1959-60
McIntyre, John	Tor., L.A., NYR, Van.	6	351	24	54	78	516	44	0	6	6	54	....	1989-90	1994-95
McIntyre, Larry	Tor.	2	41	0	3	3	26	....	....	....	....	....	....	1969-70	1972-73
McIver, Nathan	Van., Ana.	3	36	0	1	1	95	....	....	....	....	....	....	2006-07	2008-09
McKay, Doug	Det.	1	....	....	....	....	....	1	0	0	0	0	1	1949-50	1949-50
McKay, Randy	Det., N.J., Dal., Mtl.	15	932	162	201	363	1731	123	20	23	43	123	2	1988-89	2002-03
McKay, Ray	Chi., Buf., Cal.	6	140	2	16	18	102	1	0	0	0	0	....	1968-69	1973-74
McKay, Scott	Ana.	1	1	0	0	0	0	....	....	....	....	....	....	1993-94	1993-94
McKechnie, Walt	Min., Cal., Bos., Det., Wsh., Cle., Tor., Col.	16	955	214	392	606	469	15	7	5	12	7	....	1967-68	1982-83
McKee, Jay	Buf., St.L., Pit.	14	802	21	104	125	622	60	3	6	9	66	....	1995-96	2009-10
McKee, Mike	Que.	1	48	3	12	15	41	....	....	....	....	....	....	1993-94	1993-94
McKegney, Ian	Chi.	1	3	0	0	0	2	....	....	....	....	....	....	1976-77	1976-77
McKegney, Tony	Buf., Que., Min., NYR, St.L., Det., Chi.	13	912	320	319	639	517	79	24	23	47	56	....	1978-79	1990-91
McKendry, Alex	NYI, Cgy.	4	46	3	6	9	21	6	2	2	4	0	1	1977-78	1980-81
McKenna, Sean	Buf., L.A., Tor.	9	414	82	80	162	181	15	1	2	3	2	....	1981-82	1989-90
McKenna, Steve	L.A., Min., Pit., NYR	8	373	18	14	32	824	3	0	1	1	8	....	1996-97	2003-04
McKenney, Don	Bos., NYR, Tor., Det., St.L.	13	798	237	345	582	211	58	18	29	47	10	1	1954-55	1967-68
McKenny, Jim	Tor., Min.	14	604	82	247	329	294	37	7	9	16	10	....	1965-66	1978-79
McKenzie, Brian	Pit.	1	6	1	1	2	4	....	....	....	....	....	....	1971-72	1971-72
McKenzie, Jim	Hfd., Dal., Pit., Wpg., Phx., Ana., Wsh., N.J., Nsh.	15	880	48	52	100	1739	51	0	0	0	38	1	1989-90	2003-04
McKenzie, John	Chi., Det., NYR, Bos.	12	691	206	268	474	917	69	15	32	47	133	2	1958-59	1971-72
McKim, Andrew	Bos., Det.	3	38	1	4	5	6	....	....	....	....	....	....	1992-93	1994-95
• McKinnon, Alex	Ham., NYA, Chi.	5	193	19	11	30	237	....	....	....	....	....	....	1924-25	1928-29
• McKinnon, John	Mtl., Pit., Phi.	6	208	28	11	39	224	2	0	0	0	4	....	1925-26	1930-31
McLaren, Frazer	S.J., Tor.	5	102	4	7	11	264	1	0	0	0	2	....	2009-10	2013-14
McLaren, Kyle	Bos., S.J.	12	719	46	161	207	671	70	1	13	14	78	....	1995-96	2007-08
McLaren, Steve	St.L.	1	6	0	0	0	25	....	....	....	....	....	....	2003-04	2003-04
‡ McLean, Brett	Chi., Col., Fla.	6	385	56	106	162	204	8	0	1	1	4	....	2002-03	2008-09
McLean, Don	Wsh.	1	9	0	0	0	6	....	....	....	....	....	....	1975-76	1975-76
• McLean, Fred	Que., Ham.	2	8	0	0	0	2	....	....	....	....	....	....	1919-20	1920-21
• McLean, Jack	Tor.	3	67	14	24	38	76	13	2	2	4	8	1	1942-43	1944-45
• McLean, Jeff	S.J.	1	6	1	0	1	0	....	....	....	....	....	....	1993-94	1993-94
‡ McLean, Kurtis	NYI	1	4	1	0	1	0	....	....	....	....	....	....	2008-09	2008-09
• McLellan, John	Tor.	1	2	0	0	0	0	....	....	....	....	....	....	1951-52	1951-52
McLellan, Scott	Bos.	1	2	0	0	0	0	....	....	....	....	....	....	1982-83	1982-83
McLellan, Todd	NYI	1	5	1	1	2	0	....	....	....	....	....	....	1987-88	1987-88
• McLenahan, Rollie	Det.	1	9	2	1	3	10	2	0	0	0	0	....	1945-46	1945-46
McLeod, Al	Det.	1	26	2	2	4	24	....	....	....	....	....	....	1973-74	1973-74
McLeod, Jackie	NYR	5	106	14	23	37	12	7	0	0	0	0	....	1949-50	1954-55
McLlwain, Dave	Pit., Wpg., Buf., NYI, Tor., Ott.	10	501	100	107	207	292	20	0	2	2	2	....	1987-88	1996-97
• McMahon, Mike	Mtl., Bos.	3	57	7	18	25	102	13	1	2	3	30	1	1942-43	1945-46
• McMahon, Mike	NYR, Min., Chi., Det., Pit., Buf.	8	224	15	68	83	171	14	3	7	10	4	....	1963-64	1971-72
McManama, Bob	Pit.	3	99	11	25	36	28	8	0	1	1	6	....	1973-74	1975-76
• McManus, Sammy	Mtl.M., Bos.	2	26	0	1	1	8	1	0	0	0	0	1	1934-35	1936-37
‡ McMillan, Brandon	Ana., Phx., Ari., Van.	5	171	14	22	36	60	8	2	1	3	4	....	2010-11	2014-15
‡ McMillan, Carson	Min.	3	16	2	3	5	11	....	....	....	....	....	....	2010-11	2013-14
McMorrow, Sean	Buf.	1	1	0	0	0	0	....	....	....	....	....	....	2002-03	2002-03
McMurchy, Tom	Chi., Edm.	4	55	8	4	12	65	....	....	....	....	....	....	1983-84	1987-88
• McNab, Max	Det.	4	128	16	19	35	24	25	1	0	1	4	1	1947-48	1950-51
McNab, Peter	Buf., Bos., Van., N.J.	14	954	363	450	813	179	107	40	42	82	20	....	1973-74	1986-87
• McNabney, Sid	Mtl.	1	....	....	....	....	....	5	0	1	1	2	....	1950-51	1950-51
• McNamara, Howard	Mtl.	1	10	1	0	1	4	....	....	....	....	....	....	1919-20	1919-20
• McNaughton, George	Que.	1	1	0	0	0	0	....	....	....	....	....	....	1919-20	1919-20
• McNeill, Billy	Det.	6	257	21	46	67	142	4	1	1	2	4	....	1956-57	1963-64
McNeill, Grant	Fla.	1	3	0	0	0	5	....	....	....	....	....	....	2003-04	2003-04
McNeill, Mike	Chi., Que.	2	63	5	11	16	18	....	....	....	....	....	....	1990-91	1991-92
McNeill, Stu	Det.	3	10	1	1	2	2	....	....	....	....	....	....	1957-58	1959-60
McPhee, George	NYR, N.J.	7	115	24	25	49	257	29	5	3	8	69	....	1982-83	1988-89
McPhee, Mike	Mtl., Min., Dal.	11	744	200	199	399	661	134	28	27	55	193	1	1983-84	1993-94
McRae, Basil	Que., Tor., Det., Min., T.B., St.L., Chi.	16	576	53	83	136	2457	78	8	4	12	349	....	1981-82	1996-97
McRae, Chris	Tor., Det.	3	21	1	0	1	122	....	....	....	....	....	....	1987-88	1989-90
McRae, Ken	Que., Tor.	7	137	14	21	35	364	6	0	0	0	4	....	1987-88	1993-94
• McReavy, Pat	Bos., Det.	4	55	5	10	15	4	22	3	3	6	9	1	1938-39	1941-42
McReynolds, Brian	Wpg., NYR, L.A.	3	30	1	5	6	8	....	....	....	....	....	....	1989-90	1993-94
McSheffrey, Bryan	Van., Buf.	3	90	13	7	20	44	....	....	....	....	....	....	1972-73	1974-75
McSorley, Marty	Pit., Edm., L.A., NYR, S.J., Bos.	17	961	108	251	359	3381	115	10	19	29	374	2	1983-84	1999-00
McSween, Don	Buf., Ana.	5	47	3	10	13	55	....	....	....	....	....	....	1987-88	1995-96
McTaggart, Jim	Wsh.	2	71	3	10	13	205	....	....	....	....	....	....	1980-81	1981-82
McTavish, Dale	Cgy.	1	9	1	2	3	2	....	....	....	....	....	....	1996-97	1996-97
McTavish, Gord	St.L., Wpg.	2	11	1	3	4	2	....	....	....	....	....	....	1978-79	1979-80
• McVeigh, Charley	Chi., NYA	9	397	84	88	172	138	4	0	0	0	2	....	1926-27	1934-35
• McVicar, Jack	Mtl.M.	2	88	2	4	6	63	6	0	0	0	2	....	1930-31	1931-32
Meagher, Rick	Mtl., Hfd., N.J., St.L.	12	691	144	165	309	383	62	8	7	15	41	....	1979-80	1990-91
Meech, Derek	Det., Wpg.	6	144	4	13	17	45	2	0	0	0	0	....	2006-07	2012-13
Meehan, Gerry	Tor., Phi., Buf., Van., Atl., Wsh.	10	670	180	243	423	111	10	0	1	1	0	....	1968-69	1978-79
Meeke, Brent	Cal., Cle.	5	75	9	22	31	8	....	....	....	....	....	....	1972-73	1976-77
Meeker, Howie	Tor.	8	346	83	102	185	329	42	6	9	15	50	4	1946-47	1953-54
Meeker, Mike	Pit.	1	4	0	0	0	5	....	....	....	....	....	....	1978-79	1978-79
• Meeking, Harry	Tor., Det., Bos.	3	64	18	12	30	66	9	3	0	3	6	....	1917-18	1926-27
Meger, Paul	Mtl.	6	212	39	52	91	118	35	3	8	11	16	1	1949-50	1954-55
Meighan, Ron	Min., Pit.	2	48	3	7	10	18	....	....	....	....	....	....	1981-82	1982-83
Meissner, Barrie	Min.	2	6	0	1	1	4	....	....	....	....	....	....	1967-68	1968-69
• Meissner, Dick	Bos., NYR	5	171	11	15	26	37	....	....	....	....	....	....	1959-60	1964-65
Melametsa, Anssi	Wpg.	1	27	0	3	3	2	....	....	....	....	....	....	1985-86	1985-86
Melanson, Dean	Buf., Wsh.	2	9	0	0	0	8	....	....	....	....	....	....	1994-95	2001-02
Melichar, Josef	Pit., Car., T.B.	7	349	7	42	49	300	5	0	0	0	2	....	2000-01	2008-09
Melin, Bjorn	Ana.	1	3	1	0	1	0	....	....	....	....	....	....	2006-07	2006-07
Melin, Roger	Min.	2	3	0	0	0	0	....	....	....	....	....	....	1980-81	1981-82
Mellanby, Scott	Phi., Edm., Fla., St.L., Atl.	21	1431	364	476	840	2479	136	24	29	53	220	....	1985-86	2006-07
Mellor, Tom	Det.	2	26	2	4	6	25	....	....	....	....	....	....	1973-74	1974-75
• Melnyk, Gerry	Det., Chi., St.L.	6	269	39	77	116	34	53	6	6	12	6	....	1955-56	1967-68
Melnyk, Larry	Bos., Edm., NYR, Van.	10	432	11	63	74	686	66	2	9	11	127	1	1980-81	1989-90
Meloche, Eric	Pit., Phi.	4	74	9	11	20	36	....	....	....	....	....	....	2001-02	2006-07
Melrose, Barry	Wpg., Tor., Det.	6	300	10	23	33	728	7	0	2	2	38	....	1979-80	1985-86
Menard, Hillary	Chi.	1	1	0	0	0	0	....	....	....	....	....	....	1953-54	1953-54
Menard, Howie	Det., L.A., Chi., Oak.	4	151	23	42	65	87	19	3	7	10	36	....	1963-64	1969-70
Mercier, Justin	Col.	1	9	1	1	2	0	....	....	....	....	....	....	2009-10	2009-10
Mercredi, Vic	Atl.	1	2	0	0	0	0	....	....	....	....	....	....	1974-75	1974-75
Meredith, Greg	Cgy.	2	38	6	4	10	8	5	3	1	4	4	....	1980-81	1982-83
Merkosky, Glenn	Hfd., N.J., Det.	5	66	5	12	17	22	....	....	....	....	....	....	1981-82	1989-90
• Meronek, Bill	Mtl.	2	19	5	8	13	0	1	0	0	0	0	....	1939-40	1942-43

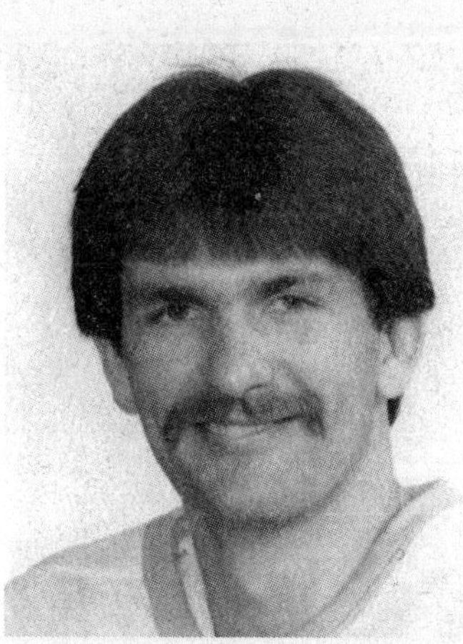

Joe McDonnell

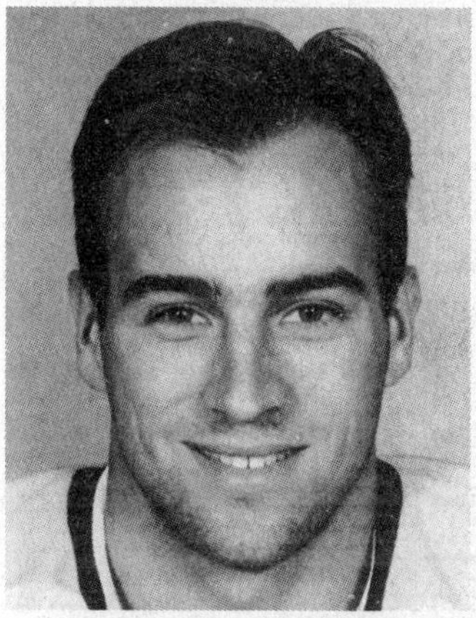

Shawn McEachren

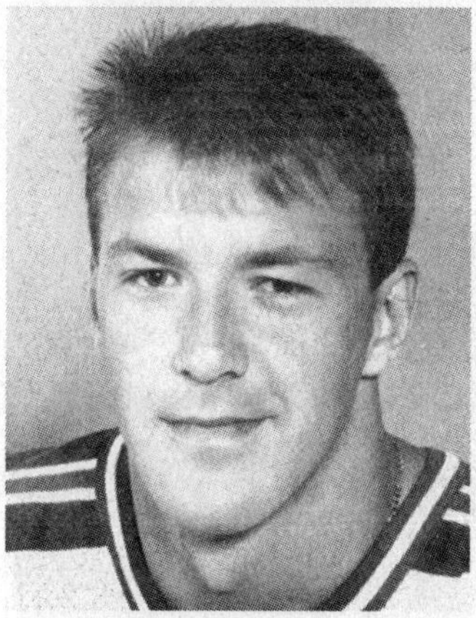

Brian McReynolds

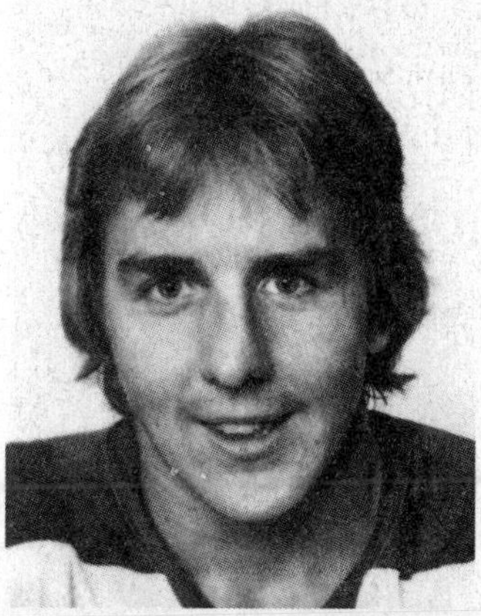

Perry Miller

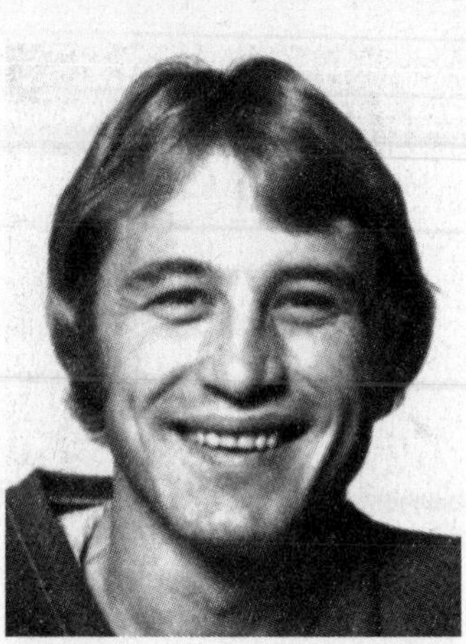

Lyle Moffatt

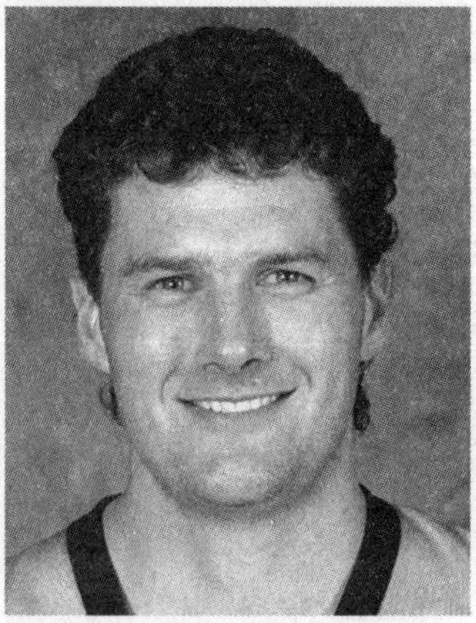

Jay More

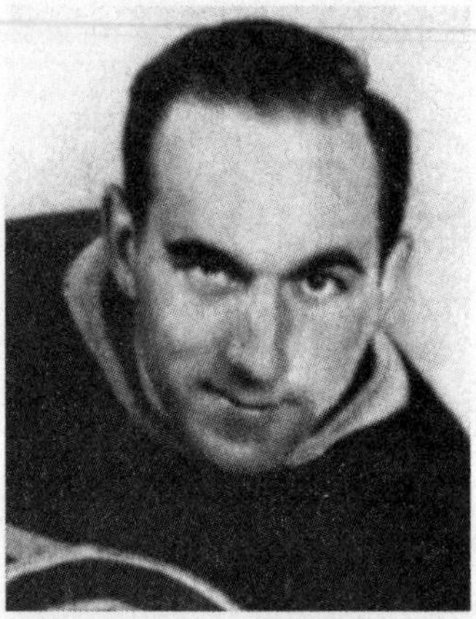

Howie Morenz

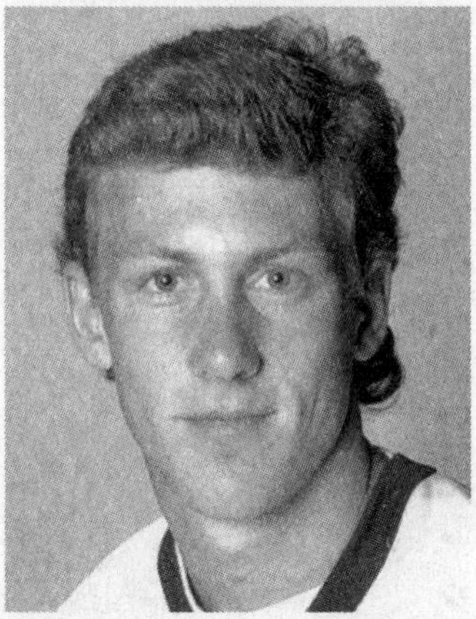

Scott Morrow

			Regular Schedule					Playoffs							
Name	NHL Teams	NHL Seasons	GP	G	A	TP	PIM	GP	G	A	TP	PIM	NHL Cup Wins	First NHL Season	Last NHL Season
Merrick, Wayne	St.L., Cal., Cle., NYI	12	774	191	265	456	303	102	19	30	49	30	4	1972-73	1983-84
• Merrill, Horace	Ott.	2	8	0	0	0	3	....	....	....	....	....	1	1917-18	1919-20
Mertzig, Jan	NYR	1	23	0	2	2	8	....	....	....	....	....	....	1998-99	1998-99
Messier, Eric	Col., Fla.	8	406	25	50	75	146	72	3	5	8	22	1	1996-97	2003-04
Messier, Joby	NYR	3	25	0	4	4	24	....	....	....	....	....	....	1992-93	1994-95
Messier, Mark	Edm., NYR, Van.	25	1756	694	1193	1887	1910	236	109	186	295	244	6	1979-80	2003-04
Messier, Mitch	Min.	4	20	0	2	2	11	....	....	....	....	....	....	1987-88	1990-91
Messier, Paul	Col.	1	9	0	0	0	4	....	....	....	....	....	....	1978-79	1978-79
‡ Meszaros, Andrej	Ott., T.B., Phi., Bos., Buf.	10	645	63	175	238	457	50	4	13	17	46	....	2005-06	2014-15
Metcalfe, Scott	Edm., Buf.	3	19	1	2	3	18	....	....	....	....	....	....	1987-88	1989-90
‡ Metropolit, Glen	Wsh., T.B., Atl., St.L., Bos., Phi., Mtl.	8	407	57	102	159	148	30	1	4	5	12	....	1999-00	2009-10
• Metz, Don	Tor.	9	172	20	35	55	42	42	7	8	15	12	5	1938-39	1948-49
• Metz, Nick	Tor.	12	518	131	119	250	149	76	19	20	39	31	4	1934-35	1947-48
Meyer, Freddy	Phi., NYI, Phx., Atl.	7	281	20	53	73	155	6	0	1	1	8	....	2003-04	2010-11
Meyer, Stefan	Fla., Cgy.	2	20	0	2	2	17	....	....	....	....	....	....	2007-08	2010-11
‡ Mezei, Branislav	NYI, Fla.	7	240	5	19	24	311	....	....	....	....	....	....	2000-01	2007-08
• Michaluk, Art	Chi.	1	5	0	0	0	0	....	....	....	....	....	....	1947-48	1947-48
• Michaluk, John	Chi.	1	1	0	0	0	0	....	....	....	....	....	....	1950-51	1950-51
Michayluk, Dave	Phi., Pit.	3	14	2	6	8	8	7	1	1	2	0	1	1981-82	1991-92
Micheletti, Joe	St.L., Col.	3	158	11	60	71	114	11	1	11	12	10	....	1979-80	1981-82
Micheletti, Pat	Min.	1	12	2	0	2	8	....	....	....	....	....	....	1987-88	1987-88
• Mickey, Larry	Chi., NYR, Tor., Mtl., L.A., Phi., Buf.	11	292	39	53	92	160	9	1	0	1	10	....	1964-65	1974-75
• Mickoski, Nick	NYR, Chi., Det., Bos.	13	703	158	185	343	319	18	1	6	7	6	....	1947-48	1959-60
Middendorf, Max	Que., Edm.	4	13	2	4	6	6	....	....	....	....	....	....	1986-87	1990-91
Middleton, Rick	NYR, Bos.	14	1005	448	540	988	157	114	45	55	100	19	....	1974-75	1987-88
Miehm, Kevin	St.L.	2	22	1	4	5	8	2	0	1	1	0	....	1992-93	1993-94
Miettinen, Antti	Dal., Min., Wpg.	9	539	97	133	230	234	24	2	3	5	10	....	2003-04	2012-13
• Migay, Rudy	Tor.	10	418	59	92	151	293	15	1	0	1	20	....	1949-50	1959-60
‡ Mihalik, Vladimir	T.B.	2	15	0	3	3	8	....	....	....	....	....	....	2008-09	2009-10
Mika, Petr	NYI	1	3	0	0	0	0	....	....	....	....	....	....	1999-00	1999-00
‡ Mikhnov, Alexei	Edm.	1	2	0	0	0	0	....	....	....	....	....	....	2006-07	2006-07
Mikita, Stan	Chi.	22	1394	541	926	1467	1270	155	59	91	150	169	1	1958-59	1979-80
Mikkelson, Bill	L.A., NYI, Wsh.	4	147	4	18	22	105	....	....	....	....	....	....	1971-72	1976-77
‡ Mikkelson, Brendan	Ana., Cgy., T.B.	5	131	1	9	10	59	....	....	....	....	....	....	2008-09	2012-13
• Mikol, Jim	Tor., NYR	2	34	1	4	5	8	....	....	....	....	....	....	1962-63	1964-65
Mikulchik, Oleg	Wpg., Ana.	3	37	0	3	3	33	....	....	....	....	....	....	1993-94	1995-96
Milbury, Mike	Bos.	12	754	49	189	238	1552	86	4	24	28	219	....	1975-76	1986-87
• Milks, Hib	Pit., Phi., NYR, Ott.	8	317	87	41	128	179	11	0	0	0	2	....	1925-26	1932-33
Millar, Craig	Edm., Nsh., T.B.	5	114	8	14	22	73	....	....	....	....	....	....	1996-97	2000-01
• Millar, Hugh	Det.	1	4	0	0	0	0	1	0	0	0	0	....	1946-47	1946-47
Millar, Mike	Hfd., Wsh., Bos., Tor.	5	78	18	18	36	12	....	....	....	....	....	....	1986-87	1990-91
Millen, Corey	NYR, L.A., N.J., Dal., Cgy.	8	335	90	119	209	236	47	5	7	12	22	....	1989-90	1996-97
Miller, Aaron	Que., Col., L.A., Van.	14	677	25	94	119	422	80	3	9	12	40	....	1993-94	2007-08
• Miller, Bill	Mtl.M., Mtl.	3	95	7	3	10	16	12	0	0	0	0	1	1934-35	1936-37
Miller, Bob	Bos., Col., L.A.	6	404	75	119	194	220	36	4	7	11	27	....	1977-78	1984-85
Miller, Brad	Buf., Ott., Cgy.	6	82	1	5	6	321	....	....	....	....	....	....	1988-89	1993-94
• Miller, Earl	Chi., Tor.	5	109	19	14	33	124	10	1	0	1	6	1	1927-28	1931-32
• Miller, Jack	Chi.	2	17	0	0	0	4	....	....	....	....	....	....	1949-50	1950-51
Miller, Jason	N.J.	3	6	0	0	0	0	....	....	....	....	....	....	1990-91	1992-93
Miller, Jay	Bos., L.A.	7	446	40	44	84	1723	48	2	3	5	243	....	1985-86	1991-92
Miller, Kelly	NYR, Wsh.	15	1057	181	282	463	512	119	20	34	54	65	....	1984-85	1998-99
Miller, Kevin	NYR, Det., Wsh., St.L., S.J., Pit., Chi., NYI, Ott.	13	620	150	185	335	429	61	7	10	17	49	....	1988-89	2003-04
Miller, Kip	Que., Min., S.J., NYI, Chi., Pit., Ana., Wsh.	12	449	74	165	239	105	25	6	11	17	23	....	1990-91	2003-04
Miller, Paul	Col.	1	3	0	3	3	0	....	....	....	....	....	....	1981-82	1981-82
Miller, Perry	Det.	4	217	10	51	61	387	....	....	....	....	....	....	1977-78	1980-81
Miller, Tom	Det., NYI	4	118	16	25	41	34	....	....	....	....	....	....	1970-71	1974-75
Miller, Warren	NYR, Hfd.	4	262	40	50	90	137	6	1	0	1	0	....	1979-80	1982-83
Milley, Norm	Buf., T.B.	4	29	2	4	6	12	....	....	....	....	....	....	2001-02	2005-06
Mills, Brad	N.J., Chi.	3	34	1	1	2	37	....	....	....	....	....	....	2010-11	2013-14
Mills, Craig	Wpg., Chi.	3	31	0	5	5	36	1	0	0	0	0	....	1995-96	1998-99
Milroy, Duncan	Mtl.	1	5	0	1	1	0	....	....	....	....	....	....	2006-07	2006-07
Minard, Chris	Pit., Edm.	3	40	2	4	6	14	....	....	....	....	....	....	2007-08	2009-10
Miner, John	Edm.	1	14	2	3	5	16	....	....	....	....	....	....	1987-88	1987-88
Mink, Graham	Wsh.	3	7	0	0	0	2	....	....	....	....	....	....	2003-04	2008-09
Minor, Gerry	Van.	5	140	11	21	32	173	12	1	3	4	25	....	1979-80	1983-84
Mironov, Boris	Wpg., Edm., Chi., NYR	11	716	76	231	307	891	25	5	11	16	45	....	1993-94	2003-04
Mironov, Dmitri	Tor., Pit., Ana., Det., Wsh.	10	556	54	206	260	568	75	10	26	36	48	1	1991-92	2000-01
Miszuk, John	Det., Chi., Phi., Min.	6	237	7	39	46	232	19	0	3	3	19	....	1963-64	1969-70
• Mitchell, Bill	Det.	1	1	0	0	0	0	....	....	....	....	....	....	1963-64	1963-64
• Mitchell, Herb	Bos.	2	44	6	0	6	36	....	....	....	....	....	....	1924-25	1925-26
Mitchell, Jeff	Dal.	1	7	0	0	0	7	....	....	....	....	....	....	1997-98	1997-98
• Mitchell, Red	Chi.	3	83	4	5	9	67	....	....	....	....	....	....	1941-42	1944-45
Mitchell, Roy	Min.	1	3	0	0	0	0	....	....	....	....	....	....	1992-93	1992-93
Mitchell, Willie	N.J., Min., Dal., Van., L.A., Fla.	16	907	34	146	180	787	89	4	12	16	90	2	1999-00	**2015-16**
Modano, Mike	Min., Dal., Det.	22	1499	561	813	1374	930	176	58	88	146	128	1	1988-89	2010-11
Modin, Fredrik	Tor., T.B., CBJ, L.A., Atl., Cgy.	14	898	232	230	462	453	57	14	12	26	42	1	1996-97	2010-11
Modry, Jaroslav	N.J., Ott., L.A., Atl., Dal., Phi.	13	725	49	201	250	510	28	1	5	6	6	....	1993-94	2007-08
• Moe, Bill	NYR	5	261	11	42	53	163	1	0	0	0	0	....	1944-45	1948-49
Moen, Travis	Chi., Ana., S.J., Mtl., Dal.	12	747	59	77	136	801	83	11	8	19	61	1	2003-04	**2015-16**
Moffat, Lyle	Tor., Wpg.	3	97	12	16	28	51	....	....	....	....	....	....	1972-73	1979-80
• Moffat, Ron	Det.	3	37	1	1	2	8	7	0	0	0	0	....	1932-33	1934-35
Moger, Sandy	Bos., L.A.	5	236	41	38	79	212	5	2	2	4	12	....	1994-95	1998-99
Mogilny, Alexander	Buf., Van., N.J., Tor.	16	990	473	559	1032	432	124	39	47	86	58	1	1989-90	2005-06
Moher, Mike	N.J.	1	9	0	1	1	28	....	....	....	....	....	....	1982-83	1982-83
• Mohns, Doug	Bos., Chi., Min., Atl., Wsh.	22	1390	248	462	710	1250	94	14	36	50	122	....	1953-54	1974-75
• Mohns, Lloyd	NYR	1	1	0	0	0	0	....	....	....	....	....	....	1943-44	1943-44
‡ Mojzis, Tomas	Van., St.L., Min.	3	17	1	2	3	14	....	....	....	....	....	....	2005-06	2008-09
Mokosak, Carl	Cgy., L.A., Phi., Pit., Bos.	6	83	11	15	26	170	1	0	0	0	0	....	1981-82	1988-89
Mokosak, John	Det.	2	41	0	2	2	96	....	....	....	....	....	....	1988-89	1989-90
Molin, Lars	Van.	3	172	33	65	98	37	19	2	9	11	7	....	1981-82	1983-84
Moller, Mike	Buf., Edm.	7	134	15	28	43	41	3	0	1	1	0	....	1980-81	1986-87
‡ Moller, Oscar	L.A.	3	87	12	14	26	22	1	0	0	0	0	....	2008-09	2010-11
Moller, Randy	Que., NYR, Buf., Fla.	14	815	45	180	225	1692	78	6	16	22	197	....	1981-82	1994-95
Molloy, Mitch	Buf.	1	2	0	0	0	10	....	....	....	....	....	....	1989-90	1989-90
• Molyneaux, Larry	NYR	2	45	0	1	1	20	10	0	0	0	8	....	1937-38	1938-39
Momesso, Sergio	Mtl., St.L., Van., Tor., NYR	13	710	152	193	345	1557	119	18	26	44	311	....	1983-84	1996-97
Monahan, Garry	Mtl., Det., L.A., Tor., Van.	12	748	116	169	285	484	22	3	1	4	13	....	1967-68	1978-79
Monahan, Hartland	Cal., NYR, Wsh., Pit., L.A., St.L.	7	334	61	80	141	163	6	0	0	0	4	....	1973-74	1980-81
• Mondou, Armand	Mtl.	12	386	47	71	118	99	32	3	5	8	12	2	1928-29	1939-40
Mondou, Pierre	Mtl.	9	548	194	262	456	179	69	17	28	45	26	3	1976-77	1984-85
• Mongeau, Michel	St.L., T.B.	4	54	6	19	25	10	2	0	1	1	0	....	1989-90	1992-93
Mongrain, Bob	Buf., L.A.	6	81	13	14	27	14	11	1	2	3	2	....	1979-80	1985-86
• Montador, Steve	Cgy., Fla., Ana., Bos., Buf., Chi.	10	571	33	98	131	807	43	3	5	8	36	....	2001-02	2011-12
Monteith, Hank	Det.	3	77	5	12	17	6	4	0	0	0	0	....	1968-69	1970-71
Montgomery, Jim	St.L., Mtl., Phi., S.J., Dal.	6	122	9	25	34	80	8	1	0	1	2	....	1993-94	2002-03
Moore, Barrie	Buf., Edm., Wsh.	3	39	2	6	8	18	....	....	....	....	....	....	1995-96	1999-00
• Moore, Dickie	Mtl., Tor., St.L.	14	719	261	347	608	652	135	46	64	110	122	6	1951-52	1967-68
Moore, Greg	NYR, CBJ	2	10	0	0	0	0	....	....	....	....	....	....	2007-08	2009-10
Moore, Steve	Col.	3	69	5	7	12	41	....	....	....	....	....	....	2001-02	2003-04
• Moran, Amby	Mtl., Chi.	2	35	1	1	2	24	....	....	....	....	....	....	1926-27	1927-28
Moran, Brad	CBJ, Van.	3	8	1	2	3	4	....	....	....	....	....	....	2001-02	2006-07
Moran, Ian	Pit., Bos., Ana.	12	489	21	50	71	321	66	1	7	8	24	....	1994-95	2006-07
Moravec, David	Buf.	1	1	0	0	0	0	....	....	....	....	....	....	1999-00	1999-00
More, Jay	NYR, Min., S.J., Phx., Chi., Nsh.	10	406	18	54	72	702	31	0	6	6	45	....	1988-89	1998-99
Moreau, Ethan	Chi., Edm., CBJ, L.A.	16	928	147	140	287	1110	46	3	6	9	52	....	1995-96	2011-12
• Morenz, Howie	Mtl., Chi., NYR	14	550	271	201	472	546	39	13	9	22	58	3	1923-24	1936-37
Moretto, Angelo	Cle.	1	5	1	2	3	2	....	....	....	....	....	....	1976-77	1976-77
Morgan, Gavin	Dal.	1	6	0	0	0	21	....	....	....	....	....	....	2003-04	2003-04
Morgan, Jason	L.A., Cgy., Nsh., Chi., Min.	5	44	2	5	7	18	....	....	....	....	....	....	1996-97	2006-07
• Morin, Pete	Mtl.	1	31	10	12	22	7	1	0	0	0	0	....	1941-42	1941-42

Name	NHL Teams	NHL Seasons	Regular Schedule GP	G	A	TP	PIM	Playoffs GP	G	A	TP	PIM	NHL Cup Wins	First NHL Season	Last NHL Season
• Morin, Stephane	Que., Van.	5	90	16	39	55	52	....	....	....	....	....	....	1989-90	1993-94
Morisset, Dave	Fla.	1	4	0	0	0	5	....	....	....	....	....	....	2001-02	2001-02
Morissette, Dave	Mtl.	2	11	0	0	0	57	....	....	....	....	....	....	1998-99	1999-00
Mormina, Joey	Car.	1	1	0	0	0	0	....	....	....	....	....	....	2007-08	2007-08
Moro, Marc	Ana., Nsh., Tor.	4	30	0	0	0	77	....	....	....	....	....	....	1997-98	2001-02
Morozov, Aleksey	Pit.	7	451	84	135	219	98	39	4	5	9	8	....	1997-98	2003-04
• Morris, Bernie	Bos.	1	6	1	0	1	0	....	....	....	....	....	....	1924-25	1924-25
Morris, Derek	Cgy., Col., Phx., NYR, Bos.	16	1107	92	332	424	1004	37	3	12	15	41	....	1997-98	2013-14
Morris, Jon	N.J., S.J., Bos.	6	103	16	33	49	47	11	1	7	8	25	....	1988-89	1993-94
• Morris, Moe	Tor., NYR	4	135	13	29	42	58	18	4	2	6	16	1	1943-44	1948-49
Morrison, Brendan	N.J., Van., Ana., Dal., Wsh., Cgy., Chi.	14	934	200	401	601	452	61	9	21	30	40	....	1997-98	2011-12
Morrison, Dave	L.A., Van.	4	39	3	3	6	4	....	....	....	....	....	....	1980-81	1984-85
• Morrison, Don	Det., Chi.	3	112	18	28	46	12	3	0	1	1	0	....	1947-48	1950-51
Morrison, Doug	Bos.	4	23	7	3	10	15	....	....	....	....	....	....	1979-80	1984-85
Morrison, Gary	Phi.	3	43	1	15	16	70	5	0	1	1	2	....	1979-80	1981-82
• Morrison, George	St.L.	2	115	17	21	38	13	3	0	0	0	0	....	1970-71	1971-72
Morrison, Jim	Bos., Tor., Det., NYR, Pit.	12	704	40	160	200	542	36	0	12	12	38	....	1951-52	1970-71
• Morrison, John	NYA	1	18	0	0	0	0	....	....	....	....	....	....	1925-26	1925-26
Morrison, Kevin	Col.	1	41	4	11	15	23	....	....	....	....	....	....	1979-80	1979-80
Morrison, Lew	Phi., Atl., Wsh., Pit.	9	564	39	52	91	107	17	0	0	0	2	....	1969-70	1977-78
Morrison, Mark	NYR	2	10	1	1	2	0	....	....	....	....	....	....	1981-82	1983-84
• Morrison, Rod	Det.	1	34	8	7	15	4	3	0	0	0	0	....	1947-48	1947-48
‡ Morrisonn, Shaone	Bos., Wsh., Buf.	8	480	11	64	75	455	27	0	2	2	18	....	2002-03	2010-11
Morrow, Brenden	Dal., Pit., St.L., T.B.	15	991	265	310	575	1362	118	19	27	46	130	....	1999-00	2014-15
Morrow, Ken	NYI	10	550	17	88	105	309	127	11	22	33	97	4	1979-80	1988-89
Morrow, Scott	Cgy.	1	4	0	0	0	0	....	....	....	....	....	....	1994-95	1994-95
Morton, Dean	Det.	1	1	1	0	1	2	....	....	....	....	....	....	1989-90	1989-90
• Mortson, Gus	Tor., Chi., Det.	13	797	46	152	198	1380	54	5	8	13	68	4	1946-47	1958-59
• Mosdell, Ken	Bro., Mtl., Chi.	16	693	141	168	309	475	80	16	13	29	48	4	1941-42	1958-59
‡ Moser, Simon	Nsh.	1	6	1	1	2	2	....	....	....	....	....	....	2013-14	2013-14
• Mosienko, Bill	Chi.	14	711	258	282	540	121	22	10	4	14	15	....	1941-42	1954-55
Moss, Dave	Cgy., Phx., Ari.	9	501	78	100	178	157	17	4	2	6	4	....	2006-07	2014-15
Motin, Johan	Edm.	1	1	0	0	0	0	....	....	....	....	....	....	2009-10	2009-10
Mott, Morris	Cal.	3	199	18	32	50	49	....	....	....	....	....	....	1972-73	1974-75
Mottau, Mike	NYR, Cgy., N.J., NYI, Bos., Fla.	9	321	7	51	58	164	19	2	2	4	0	....	2000-01	2013-14
• Motter, Alex	Bos., Det.	8	255	39	64	103	135	41	3	9	12	41	1	1934-35	1942-43
Motzko, Joe	CBJ, Ana., Wsh., Atl.	5	25	4	2	6	0	3	0	0	0	2	1	2003-04	2008-09
‡ Mouillierat, Kael	NYI, Pit.	2	7	1	1	2	10	....	....	....	....	....	....	2014-15	**2015-16**
Mowers, Mark	Nsh., Det., Bos., Ana.	7	278	18	44	62	70	3	0	0	0	0	....	1998-99	2007-08
Moxey, Jim	Cal., Cle., L.A.	3	127	22	27	49	59	....	....	....	....	....	....	1974-75	1976-77
Mrozik, Rick	Cgy.	1	2	0	0	0	0	....	....	....	....	....	....	2002-03	2002-03
Muckalt, Bill	Van., NYI, Ott., Min.	5	256	40	57	97	204	5	0	0	0	0	....	1998-99	2002-03
Mueller, Marcel	Tor.	1	3	0	0	0	2	....	....	....	....	....	....	2010-11	2010-11
‡ Mueller, Peter	Phx., Col., Fla.	5	297	63	97	160	98	....	....	....	....	....	....	2007-08	2012-13
Muir, Bryan	Edm., N.J., Chi., T.B., Col., L.A., Wsh.	11	279	16	37	53	281	29	0	0	0	6	1	1995-96	2006-07
Mulhern, Richard	Atl., L.A., Tor., Wpg.	6	303	27	93	120	217	7	0	3	3	5	....	1975-76	1980-81
Mulhern, Ryan	Wsh.	1	3	0	0	0	0	....	....	....	....	....	....	1997-98	1997-98
Mullen, Brian	Wpg., NYR, S.J., NYI	11	832	260	362	622	414	62	12	18	30	30	....	1982-83	1992-93
Mullen, Joe	St.L., Cgy., Pit., Bos.	17	1062	502	561	1063	241	143	60	46	106	42	3	1979-80	1996-97
Muller, Kirk	N.J., Mtl., NYI, Tor., Fla., Dal.	19	1349	357	602	959	1223	127	33	36	69	153	1	1984-85	2002-03
Muloin, Wayne	Det., Oak., Cal., Min.	3	147	3	21	24	93	11	0	0	0	2	....	1963-64	1970-71
Mulvenna, Glenn	Pit., Phi.	2	2	0	0	0	4	....	....	....	....	....	....	1991-92	1992-93
Mulvey, Grant	Chi., N.J.	10	586	149	135	284	816	42	10	5	15	70	....	1974-75	1983-84
Mulvey, Paul	Wsh., Pit., L.A.	4	225	30	51	81	613	....	....	....	....	....	....	1978-79	1981-82
• Mummery, Harry	Tor., Que., Mtl., Ham.	6	106	33	19	52	226	2	1	1	2	17	....	1917-18	1922-23
Muni, Craig	Tor., Edm., Chi., Buf., Wpg., Pit., Dal.	16	819	28	119	147	775	113	0	17	17	108	3	1981-82	1997-98
• Munro, Dunc	Mtl.M., Mtl.	8	239	28	18	46	172	21	2	2	4	18	1	1924-25	1931-32
• Munro, Gerry	Mtl.M., Tor.	2	34	1	0	1	37	....	....	....	....	....	....	1924-25	1925-26
Murdoch, Bob	Mtl., L.A., Atl., Cgy.	12	757	60	218	278	764	69	4	18	22	92	2	1970-71	1981-82
Murdoch, Bob	Cal., Cle., St.L.	4	260	72	85	157	127	....	....	....	....	....	....	1975-76	1978-79
Murdoch, Don	NYR, Edm., Det.	6	320	121	117	238	155	24	10	8	18	16	....	1976-77	1981-82
• Murdoch, Murray	NYR	11	508	84	108	192	197	55	9	12	21	28	2	1926-27	1936-37
‡ Murley, Matt	Pit., Phx.	3	62	2	7	9	38	....	....	....	....	....	....	2003-04	2007-08
Murphy, Brian	Det.	1	1	0	0	0	0	....	....	....	....	....	....	1974-75	1974-75
‡ Murphy, Cory	Fla., T.B., N.J.	3	91	9	27	36	38	....	....	....	....	....	....	2007-08	2009-10
Murphy, Curtis	Min.	1	1	0	0	0	0	....	....	....	....	....	....	2002-03	2002-03
Murphy, Gord	Phi., Bos., Fla., Atl.	14	862	85	238	323	668	53	3	16	19	35	....	1988-89	2001-02
Murphy, Joe	Det., Edm., Chi., St.L., S.J., Bos., Wsh.	15	779	233	295	528	810	120	34	43	77	185	1	1986-87	2000-01
Murphy, Larry	L.A., Wsh., Min., Pit., Tor., Det.	21	1615	287	929	1216	1084	215	37	115	152	201	4	1980-81	2000-01
Murphy, Mike	St.L., NYR, L.A.	12	831	238	318	556	514	66	13	23	36	54	....	1971-72	1982-83
Murphy, Rob	Van., Ott., L.A.	7	125	9	12	21	152	4	0	0	0	2	....	1987-88	1993-94
• Murphy, Ron	NYR, Chi., Det., Bos.	18	889	205	274	479	460	53	7	8	15	26	2	1952-53	1969-70
• Murray, Allan	NYA	7	271	5	9	14	163	14	0	0	0	10	....	1933-34	1939-40
Murray, Andrew	CBJ, S.J., St.L.	6	221	24	16	40	36	....	....	....	....	....	....	2007-08	2012-13
Murray, Bob	Atl., Van.	4	194	6	16	22	98	10	1	1	2	15	....	1973-74	1976-77
Murray, Bob	Chi.	15	1008	132	382	514	873	112	19	37	56	106	....	1975-76	1989-90
Murray, Brady	L.A.	1	4	1	0	1	6	....	....	....	....	....	....	2007-08	2007-08
Murray, Chris	Mtl., Hfd., Car., Ott., Chi., Dal.	6	242	16	18	34	550	15	1	0	1	12	....	1994-95	1999-00
Murray, Douglas	S.J., Pit., Mtl.	9	518	7	57	64	412	75	4	9	13	78	....	2005-06	2013-14
Murray, Garth	NYR, Mtl., Fla., Phx.	5	116	8	2	10	131	6	0	0	0	0	....	2003-04	2008-09
Murray, Glen	Bos., Pit., L.A.	16	1009	337	314	651	679	94	20	22	42	66	....	1991-92	2007-08
Murray, Jim	L.A.	1	30	0	2	2	14	....	....	....	....	....	....	1967-68	1967-68
Murray, Ken	Tor., NYI, Det., K.C.	5	106	1	10	11	135	....	....	....	....	....	....	1969-70	1975-76
• Murray, Leo	Mtl.	1	6	0	0	0	2	....	....	....	....	....	....	1932-33	1932-33
Murray, Marty	Cgy., Phi., Car., L.A.	8	261	31	42	73	41	9	0	1	1	4	....	1995-96	2006-07
Murray, Mike	Phi.	1	1	0	0	0	0	....	....	....	....	....	....	1987-88	1987-88
Murray, Pat	Phi.	2	25	3	1	4	15	....	....	....	....	....	....	1990-91	1991-92
Murray, Randy	Tor.	1	3	0	0	0	2	....	....	....	....	....	....	1969-70	1969-70
Murray, Rem	Edm., NYR, Nsh.	9	560	94	121	215	161	62	5	12	17	18	....	1996-97	2005-06
Murray, Rob	Wsh., Wpg., Phx.	8	107	4	15	19	111	9	0	0	0	18	....	1989-90	1998-99
Murray, Terry	Cal., Phi., Det., Wsh.	8	302	4	76	80	199	18	2	2	4	10	....	1972-73	1981-82
Murray, Troy	Chi., Wpg., Ott., Pit., Col.	15	915	230	354	584	875	113	17	26	43	145	1	1981-82	1995-96
‡ Mursak , Jan	Det.	3	46	2	2	4	8	....	....	....	....	....	....	2010-11	2012-13
Murzyn, Dana	Hfd., Cgy., Van.	14	838	52	152	204	1571	82	9	10	19	166	1	1985-86	1998-99
Musil, Frantisek	Min., Cgy., Ott., Edm.	15	797	34	106	140	1241	42	2	4	6	47	....	1986-87	2000-01
Myers, Hap	Buf.	1	13	0	0	0	6	....	....	....	....	....	....	1970-71	1970-71
Myhres, Brantt	T.B., Phi., S.J., Nsh., Wsh., Bos.	7	154	6	2	8	687	....	....	....	....	....	....	1994-95	2002-03
• Myles, Vic	NYR	1	45	6	9	15	57	....	....	....	....	....	....	1942-43	1942-43
Myrvold, Anders	Col., Bos., NYI, Det.	4	33	0	5	5	12	....	....	....	....	....	....	1995-96	2003-04

N

Name	NHL Teams	NHL Seasons	GP	G	A	TP	PIM	GP	G	A	TP	PIM	NHL Cup Wins	First NHL Season	Last NHL Season
Nabokov, Dmitri	Chi., NYI	3	55	11	13	24	28	....	....	....	....	....	....	1997-98	1999-00
Nachbaur, Don	Hfd., Edm., Phi.	8	223	23	46	69	465	11	1	1	2	24	....	1980-81	1989-90
‡ Nagy, Ladislav	St.L., Phx., Dal., L.A.	8	435	115	196	311	358	18	2	2	4	23	....	1999-00	2007-08
Nahrgang, Jim	Det.	3	57	5	12	17	34	....	....	....	....	....	....	1974-75	1976-77
Namestnikov, John	Van., NYI, Nsh.	6	43	0	9	9	24	2	0	0	0	2	....	1993-94	1999-00
Nanne, Lou	Min.	11	635	68	157	225	356	32	4	10	14	8	....	1967-68	1977-78
Nantais, Rich	Min.	3	63	5	4	9	79	....	....	....	....	....	....	1974-75	1976-77
Napier, Mark	Mtl., Min., Edm., Buf.	11	767	235	306	541	157	82	18	24	42	11	2	1978-79	1988-89
‡ Nash, Brendon	Mtl.	1	2	0	0	0	0	....	....	....	....	....	....	2010-11	2010-11
Nash, Tyson	St.L., Phx.	7	374	27	37	64	673	23	3	2	5	52	....	1998-99	2005-06
Naslund, Markus	Pit., Van., NYR	15	1117	395	474	869	736	52	14	22	36	56	....	1993-94	2008-09
Naslund, Mats	Mtl., Bos.	9	651	251	383	634	111	102	35	57	92	33	1	1982-83	1994-95
Nasreddine, Alain	Chi., Mtl., NYI, Pit.	5	74	1	4	5	84	....	....	....	....	....	....	1998-99	2007-08
• Nattrass, Ralph	Chi.	4	223	18	38	56	308	....	....	....	....	....	....	1946-47	1949-50
Nattress, Ric	Mtl., St.L., Cgy., Tor., Phi.	11	536	29	135	164	377	67	5	10	15	60	1	1982-83	1992-93
Natyshak, Mike	Que.	1	4	0	0	0	0	....	....	....	....	....	....	1987-88	1987-88
Nazarov, Andrei	S.J., T.B., Cgy., Ana., Bos., Phx., Min.	12	571	53	71	124	1409	9	0	0	0	11	....	1993-94	2005-06
Ndur, Rumun	Buf., NYR, Atl.	4	69	2	3	5	137	....	....	....	....	....	....	1996-97	1999-00
Neaton, Pat	Pit.	1	9	1	1	2	12	....	....	....	....	....	....	1993-94	1993-94
Nechayev, Viktor	L.A.	1	3	1	0	1	0	....	....	....	....	....	....	1982-83	1982-83

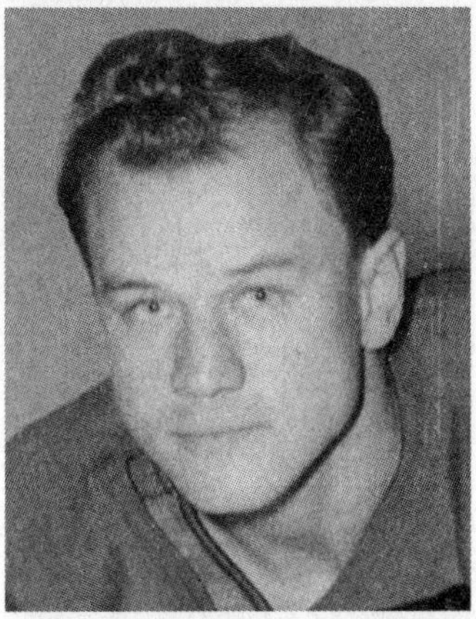
Bill Mosienko

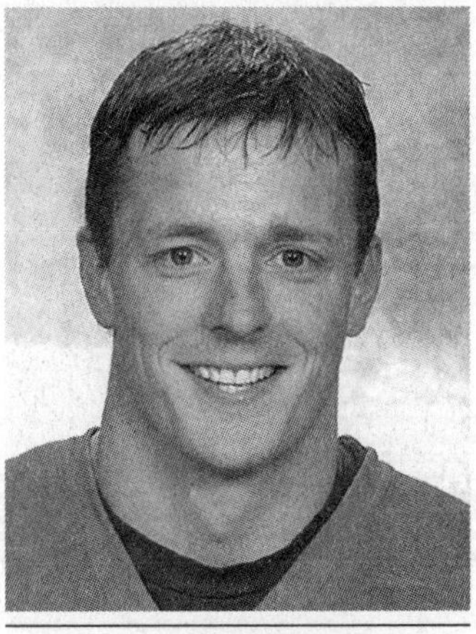
Mark Mowers

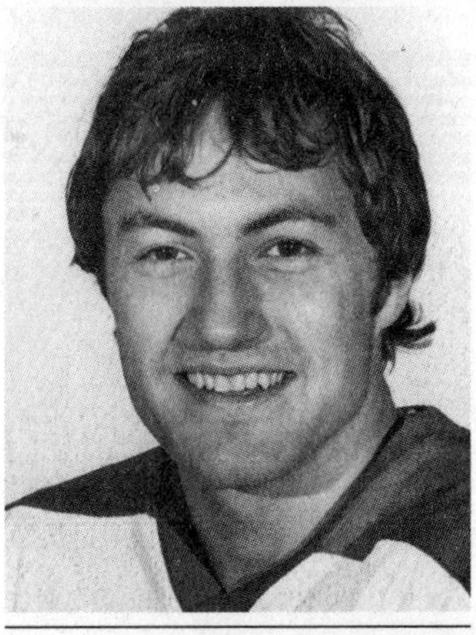
Richard Mulhern

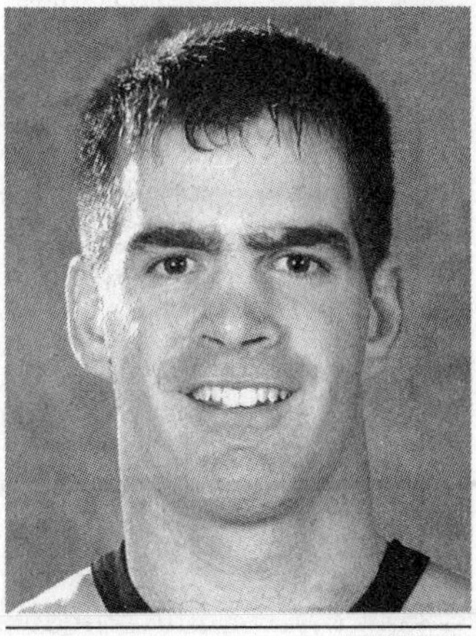
Jeff Nelson

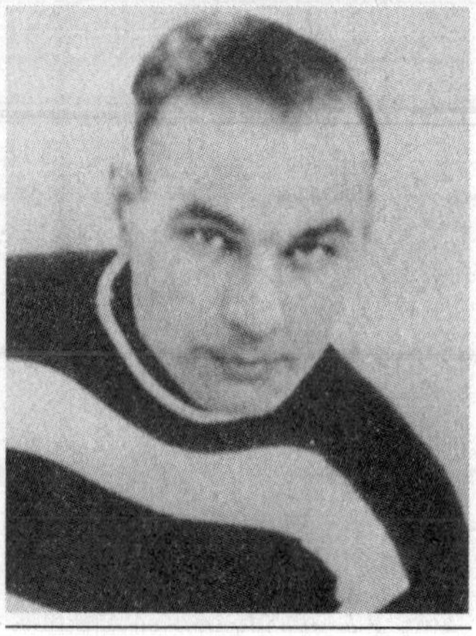

Frank Nighbor

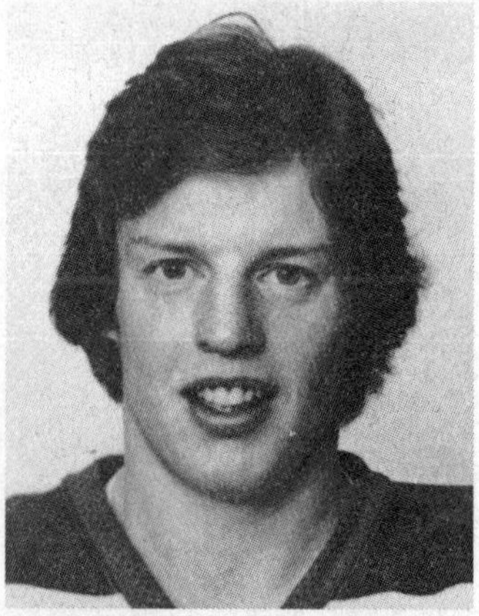

Ulf Nilsson

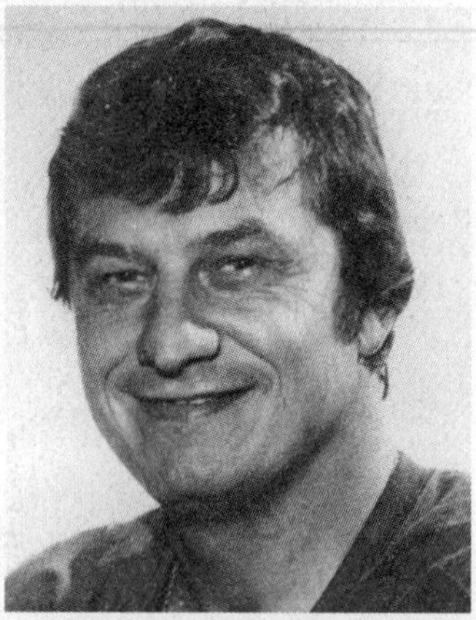

Simon Nolet

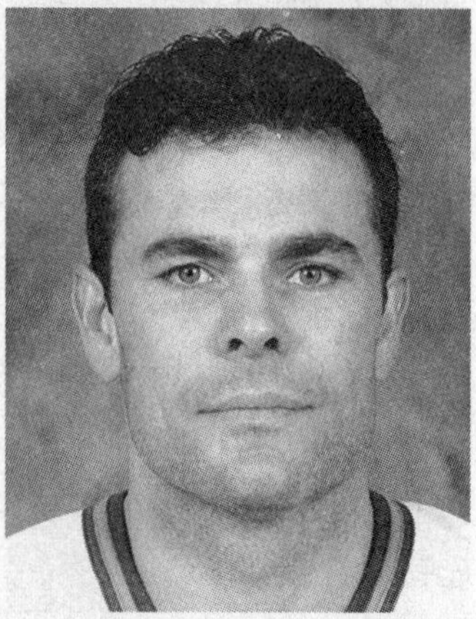

Adam Oates

			Regular Schedule					Playoffs							
Name	NHL Teams	NHL Seasons	GP	G	A	TP	PIM	GP	G	A	TP	PIM	NHL Cup Wins	First NHL Season	Last NHL Season
Neckar, Stan	Ott., NYR, Phx., T.B., Nsh.	10	510	12	41	53	316	29	0	3	3	8	1	1994-95	2003-04
Nedomansky, Vaclav	Det., NYR, St.L.	6	421	122	156	278	88	7	3	5	8	0	....	1977-78	1982-83
Nedorost, Andrej	CBJ	3	28	2	3	5	12	....	....	....	....	....	....	2001-02	2003-04
‡ Nedorost, Vaclav	Col., Fla.	3	99	10	10	20	34	....	....	....	....	....	....	2001-02	2003-04
Nedved, Petr	Van., St.L., NYR, Pit., Edm., Phx., Phi.	15	982	310	407	717	708	71	19	23	42	64	....	1990-91	2006-07
Nedved, Zdenek	Tor.	3	31	4	6	10	14	....	....	....	....	....	....	1994-95	1996-97
Needham, Mike	Pit., Dal.	3	86	9	5	14	16	14	2	0	2	4	1	1991-92	1993-94
Neely, Bob	Tor., Col.	5	283	39	59	98	266	26	5	7	12	15	....	1973-74	1977-78
Neely, Cam	Van., Bos.	13	726	395	299	694	1241	93	57	32	89	168	....	1983-84	1995-96
‡ Negrin, John	Cgy.	1	3	0	1	1	2	....	....	....	....	....	....	2008-09	2008-09
Neilson, Jim	NYR, Cal., Cle.	16	1023	69	299	368	904	65	1	17	18	61	....	1962-63	1977-78
Nelson, Gordie	Tor.	1	3	0	0	0	11	....	....	....	....	....	....	1969-70	1969-70
Nelson, Jeff	Wsh., Nsh.	3	52	3	8	11	20	3	0	0	0	4	....	1994-95	1998-99
Nelson, Todd	Pit., Wsh.	2	3	1	0	1	2	4	0	0	0	0	....	1991-92	1993-94
Nemchinov, Sergei	NYR, Van., NYI, N.J.	11	761	152	193	345	251	105	11	20	31	24	2	1991-92	2001-02
Nemecek, Jan	L.A.	2	7	1	0	1	4	....	....	....	....	....	....	1998-99	1999-00
Nemeth, Steve	NYR	1	12	2	0	2	2	....	....	....	....	....	....	1987-88	1987-88
Nemirovsky, David	Fla.	4	91	16	22	38	42	3	1	0	1	0	....	1995-96	1998-99
Nemisz, Greg	Cgy.	2	15	0	1	1	0	....	....	....	....	....	....	2010-11	2011-12
Nesterenko, Eric	Tor., Chi.	21	1219	250	324	574	1273	124	13	24	37	127	1	1951-52	1971-72
Nethery, Lance	NYR, Edm.	2	41	11	14	25	14	14	5	3	8	9	....	1980-81	1981-82
Neufeld, Ray	Hfd., Wpg., Bos.	11	595	157	200	357	816	28	8	6	14	55	....	1979-80	1989-90
• Neville, Mike	Tor., NYA	3	65	5	5	10	14	2	0	0	0	0	....	1924-25	1930-31
Nevin, Bob	Tor., NYR, Min., L.A.	18	1128	307	419	726	211	84	16	18	34	24	2	1957-58	1975-76
Newberry, John	Mtl., Hfd.	4	22	0	4	4	6	2	0	0	0	0	....	1982-83	1985-86
Newell, Rick	Det.	2	6	0	0	0	0	....	....	....	....	....	....	1972-73	1973-74
Newman, Dan	NYR, Mtl., Edm.	4	126	17	24	41	63	3	0	0	0	4	....	1976-77	1979-80
• Newman, John	Det.	1	8	1	1	2	0	....	....	....	....	....	....	1930-31	1930-31
Nichol, Scott	Buf., Cgy., Chi., Nsh., S.J., St.L.	13	662	56	71	127	916	49	1	2	3	76	....	1995-96	2012-13
Nicholls, Bernie	L.A., NYR, Edm., N.J., Chi., S.J.	18	1127	475	734	1209	1292	118	42	72	114	164	....	1981-82	1998-99
• Nicholson, Al	Bos.	2	19	0	1	1	4	....	....	....	....	....	....	1955-56	1956-57
• Nicholson, Ed	Det.	1	1	0	0	0	0	....	....	....	....	....	....	1947-48	1947-48
• Nicholson, Hickey	Chi.	1	2	1	0	1	0	....	....	....	....	....	....	1937-38	1937-38
Nicholson, Neil	Oak., NYI	4	39	3	1	4	23	2	0	0	0	0	....	1969-70	1977-78
• Nicholson, Paul	Wsh.	3	62	4	8	12	18	....	....	....	....	....	....	1974-75	1976-77
Nickulas, Eric	Bos., St.L., Chi.	6	118	15	23	38	82	1	0	0	0	2	....	1998-99	2005-06
Nicolson, Graeme	Bos., Col., NYR	3	52	2	7	9	60	....	....	....	....	....	....	1978-79	1982-83
Nieckar, Barry	Hfd., Cgy., Ana.	4	8	0	0	0	21	....	....	....	....	....	....	1992-93	1997-98
Niedermayer, Rob	Fla., Cgy., Ana., N.J., Buf.	17	1153	186	283	469	904	116	18	25	43	111	1	1993-94	2010-11
Niedermayer, Scott	N.J., Ana.	18	1263	172	568	740	784	202	25	73	98	155	4	1991-92	2009-10
Niekamp, Jim	Det.	2	29	0	2	2	37	....	....	....	....	....	....	1970-71	1971-72
Nielsen, Chris	CBJ	2	52	6	8	14	8	....	....	....	....	....	....	2000-01	2001-02
Nielsen, Jeff	NYR, Ana., Min.	5	252	20	27	47	70	4	0	0	0	2	....	1996-97	2000-01
Nielsen, Kirk	Bos.	1	6	0	0	0	0	....	....	....	....	....	....	1997-98	1997-98
Niemi, Antti-Jussi	Ana.	2	29	1	1	2	22	....	....	....	....	....	....	2000-01	2001-02
Nieminen, Ville	Col., Pit., Chi., Cgy., NYR, S.J., St.L.	7	385	48	69	117	333	58	8	12	20	99	1	1999-00	2006-07
Nienhuis, Kraig	Bos.	3	87	20	16	36	39	2	0	0	0	14	....	1985-86	1987-88
Nieuwendyk, Joe	Cgy., Dal., N.J., Tor., Fla.	20	1257	564	562	1126	677	158	66	50	116	91	3	1986-87	2006-07
• Nighbor, Frank	Ott., Tor.	13	349	139	98	237	249	20	4	9	13	13	4	1917-18	1929-30
Nigro, Frank	Tor.	2	68	8	18	26	39	3	0	0	0	2	....	1982-83	1983-84
Niinimaa, Janne	Phi., Edm., NYI, Dal., Mtl.	10	741	54	265	319	733	59	3	21	24	60	....	1996-97	2006-07
‡ Nikitin, Nikita	St.L., CBJ, Edm.	6	259	17	59	76	85	5	0	0	0	0	....	2010-11	**2015-16**
Nikolishin, Andrei	Hfd., Wsh., Chi., Col.	10	628	93	187	280	270	43	1	17	18	22	....	1994-95	2003-04
‡ Nikulin, Alexander	Ott., Phx.	2	3	0	0	0	0	....	....	....	....	....	....	2007-08	2008-09
Nikulin, Igor	Ana.	1	....	....	....	....	....	1	0	0	0	0	....	1996-97	1996-97
Nilan, Chris	Mtl., NYR, Bos.	13	688	110	115	225	3043	111	8	9	17	541	1	1979-80	1991-92
Nill, Jim	St.L., Van., Bos., Wpg., Det.	9	524	58	87	145	854	59	10	5	15	203	....	1981-82	1989-90
Nilson, Marcus	Fla., Cgy.	9	521	67	101	168	270	34	4	7	11	14	....	1998-99	2007-08
Nilsson, Kent	Atl., Cgy., Min., Edm.	9	553	264	422	686	116	59	11	41	52	14	1	1979-80	1994-95
‡ Nilsson, Robert	NYI, Edm.	5	252	37	81	118	90	....	....	....	....	....	....	2005-06	2009-10
Nilsson, Ulf	NYR	4	170	57	112	169	85	25	8	14	22	27	....	1978-79	1982-83
‡ Niskala, Janne	T.B.	1	6	1	2	3	6	....	....	....	....	....	....	2008-09	2008-09
Nistico, Lou	Col.	1	3	0	0	0	0	....	....	....	....	....	....	1977-78	1977-78
• Noble, Reg	Tor., Mtl.M., Det.	16	510	168	106	274	916	18	2	2	4	33	3	1917-18	1932-33
Nodl, Andreas	Phi., Car.	5	183	15	21	36	28	12	0	0	0	0	....	2008-09	2012-13
Noel, Claude	Wsh.	1	7	0	0	0	0	....	....	....	....	....	....	1979-80	1979-80
Nokelainen, Petteri	NYI, Bos., Ana., Phx., Mtl.	5	245	20	21	41	103	21	0	2	2	8	....	2005-06	2011-12
Nolan, Brandon	Car.	1	6	0	1	1	0	....	....	....	....	....	....	2007-08	2007-08
Nolan, Owen	Que., Col., S.J., Tor., Phx., Cgy., Min.	18	1200	422	463	885	1793	65	21	19	40	66	....	1990-91	2009-10
• Nolan, Paddy	Tor.	1	2	0	0	0	0	....	....	....	....	....	....	1921-22	1921-22
Nolan, Ted	Det., Pit.	3	78	6	16	22	105	....	....	....	....	....	....	1981-82	1985-86
Nolet, Simon	Phi., K.C., Pit., Col.	10	562	150	182	332	187	34	6	3	9	8	1	1967-68	1976-77
Noonan, Brian	Chi., NYR, St.L., Van., Phx.	12	629	116	159	275	518	71	17	19	36	77	1	1987-88	1998-99
Nordgren, Niklas	Car., Pit.	1	58	4	2	6	34	....	....	....	....	....	....	2005-06	2005-06
Nordmark, Robert	St.L., Van.	4	236	13	70	83	254	7	3	2	5	8	....	1987-88	1990-91
Nordqvist, Jonas	Chi.	1	3	0	2	2	2	....	....	....	....	....	....	2006-07	2006-07
Nordstrom, Peter	Bos.	1	2	0	0	0	0	....	....	....	....	....	....	1998-99	1998-99
‡ Noreau, Maxim	Min.	2	6	0	0	0	0	....	....	....	....	....	....	2009-10	2010-11
Noris, Joe	Pit., St.L., Buf.	3	55	2	5	7	22	....	....	....	....	....	....	1971-72	1973-74
Norris, Dwayne	Que., Ana.	3	20	2	4	6	8	....	....	....	....	....	....	1993-94	1995-96
Norrish, Rod	Min.	2	21	3	3	6	2	....	....	....	....	....	....	1973-74	1974-75
Norstrom, Mattias	NYR, L.A., Dal.	14	903	18	147	165	661	56	2	5	7	54	....	1993-94	2007-08
• Northcott, Baldy	Mtl.M., Chi.	11	446	133	112	245	273	31	8	5	13	14	1	1928-29	1938-39
Norton, Brad	Fla., L.A., Wsh., Ott., Det., S.J.	6	124	3	8	11	287	....	....	....	....	....	....	2001-02	2007-08
Norton, Jeff	NYI, S.J., St.L., Edm., T.B., Fla., Pit., Bos.	15	799	52	332	384	615	65	4	21	25	89	....	1987-88	2001-02
Norwich, Craig	Wpg., St.L., Col.	2	104	17	58	75	60	....	....	....	....	....	....	1979-80	1980-81
Norwood, Lee	Que., Wsh., St.L., Det., N.J., Hfd., Cgy.	12	503	58	153	211	1099	65	6	22	28	171	....	1980-81	1993-94
‡ Novak, Filip	Ott., CBJ	2	17	0	0	0	6	....	....	....	....	....	....	2005-06	2006-07
Novoseltsev, Ivan	Fla., Phx.	5	234	31	44	75	112	....	....	....	....	....	....	1999-00	2003-04
‡ Novotny, Jiri	Buf., Wsh., CBJ	4	189	20	31	51	66	4	0	0	0	0	....	2005-06	2008-09
Novy, Milan	Wsh.	1	73	18	30	48	16	2	0	0	0	0	....	1982-83	1982-83
Nowak, Hank	Pit., Det., Bos.	4	180	26	29	55	161	13	1	0	1	8	....	1973-74	1976-77
‡ Nummelin, Petteri	CBJ, Min.	3	139	9	36	45	34	7	1	2	3	0	....	2000-01	2007-08
Numminen, Teppo	Wpg., Phx., Dal., Buf.	20	1372	117	520	637	513	82	9	14	23	28	....	1988-89	2008-09
Nurminen, Kai	L.A., Min.	2	69	17	11	28	24	....	....	....	....	....	....	1996-97	2000-01
Nycholat, Lawrence	NYR, Wsh., Ott., Van., Col.	4	50	2	7	9	24	....	....	....	....	....	....	2003-04	2008-09
Nykoluk, Mike	Tor.	1	32	3	1	4	20	....	....	....	....	....	....	1956-57	1956-57
Nylander, Michael	Hfd., Cgy., T.B., Chi., Wsh., Bos., NYR	15	920	209	470	679	468	47	12	22	34	14	....	1992-93	2008-09
Nylund, Gary	Tor., Chi., NYI	11	608	32	139	171	1235	24	0	6	6	63	....	1982-83	1992-93
• Nyrop, Bill	Mtl., Min.	4	207	12	51	63	101	35	1	7	8	22	3	1975-76	1981-82
Nystrom, Bob	NYI	14	900	235	278	513	1248	157	39	44	83	236	4	1972-73	1985-86
‡ Nystrom, Eric	Cgy., Min., Dal., Nsh.	10	593	75	48	123	401	14	2	2	4	4	....	2005-06	**2015-16**

O

Name	NHL Teams	NHL Seasons	GP	G	A	TP	PIM	GP	G	A	TP	PIM	NHL Cup Wins	First NHL Season	Last NHL Season
Oates, Adam	Det., St.L., Bos., Wsh., Phi., Ana., Edm.	19	1337	341	1079	1420	415	163	42	114	156	66	....	1985-86	2003-04
• Oatman, Russell	Det., Mtl.M., NYR	3	120	20	9	29	100	15	1	0	1	18	....	1926-27	1928-29
Oberg, Evan	Van., T.B.	3	7	0	0	0	0	....	....	....	....	....	....	2009-10	2011-12
O'Brien, Dennis	Min., Col., Cle., Bos.	10	592	31	91	122	1017	34	1	2	3	101	....	1970-71	1979-80
O'Brien, Doug	T.B.	1	5	0	0	0	2	....	....	....	....	....	....	2005-06	2005-06
• O'Brien, Ellard	Bos.	1	2	0	0	0	0	....	....	....	....	....	....	1955-56	1955-56
‡ O'Brien, Shane	Ana., T.B., Van., Nsh., Col., Cgy., Fla.	9	537	13	79	92	916	40	2	3	5	79	....	2006-07	2014-15
Obsut, Jaroslav	St.L., Col.	2	7	0	0	0	2	....	....	....	....	....	....	2000-01	2001-02
O'Byrne, Ryan	Mtl., Col., Tor.	6	308	5	34	39	369	25	0	0	0	16	....	2007-08	2012-13
O'Callahan, Jack	Chi., N.J.	7	389	27	104	131	541	32	4	11	15	41	....	1982-83	1988-89
O'Connell, Mike	Chi., Bos., Det.	13	860	105	334	439	605	82	8	24	32	64	....	1977-78	1989-90
• O'Connor, Buddy	Mtl., NYR	10	509	140	257	397	34	53	15	21	36	6	2	1941-42	1950-51
O'Connor, Myles	N.J., Ana.	4	43	3	4	7	69	....	....	....	....	....	....	1990-91	1993-94
Oddleifson, Chris	Bos., Van.	9	524	95	191	286	464	14	1	6	7	8	....	1972-73	1980-81
Odelein, Lyle	Mtl., N.J., Phx., CBJ, Chi., Dal., Fla., Pit.	16	1056	50	202	252	2316	86	5	13	18	209	1	1989-90	2005-06

Name	NHL Teams	NHL Seasons	Regular Schedule GP	G	A	TP	PIM	Playoffs GP	G	A	TP	PIM	NHL Cup Wins	First NHL Season	Last NHL Season
Odelein, Selmar	Edm.	3	18	0	2	2	35	....	....	....	....	....	....	1985-86	1988-89
‡ O'Dell, Eric	Wpg.	2	41	3	5	8	29	....	....	....	....	....	....	2013-14	2014-15
Odgers, Jeff	S.J., Bos., Col., Atl.	12	821	75	70	145	2364	47	2	1	3	73	....	1991-92	2002-03
Odjick, Gino	Van., NYI, Phi., Mtl.	12	605	64	73	137	2567	44	4	1	5	142	....	1990-91	2001-02
O'Donnell, Fred	Bos.	2	115	15	11	26	98	5	0	1	1	5	....	1972-73	1973-74
O'Donnell, Sean	L.A., Min., N.J., Bos., Phx., Ana., Phi., Chi.	17	1224	31	198	229	1809	106	6	13	19	129	1	1994-95	2011-12
• O'Donoghue, Don	Oak., Cal.	3	125	18	17	35	35	3	0	0	0	0	....	1969-70	1971-72
Odrowski, Gerry	Det., Oak., St.L.	6	309	12	19	31	111	30	0	1	1	16	....	1960-61	1971-72
O'Dwyer, Bill	L.A., Bos.	5	120	9	13	22	108	10	0	0	0	2	....	1983-84	1989-90
O'Flaherty, Gerry	Tor., Van., Atl.	8	438	99	95	194	168	7	2	2	4	6	....	1971-72	1978-79
• O'Flaherty, Peanuts	NYA, Bro.	2	21	5	1	6	0	....	....	....	....	....	....	1940-41	1941-42
Ogilvie, Brian	Chi., St.L.	6	90	15	21	36	29	....	....	....	....	....	....	1972-73	1978-79
• O'Grady, George	Mtl.W.	1	4	0	0	0	0	....	....	....	....	....	....	1917-18	1917-18
Ogrodnick, John	Det., Que., NYR	14	928	402	425	827	260	41	18	8	26	6	....	1979-80	1992-93
Ohlund, Mattias	Van., T.B.	13	909	93	250	343	885	70	10	21	31	63	....	1997-98	2010-11
Ojanen, Janne	N.J.	4	98	21	23	44	28	3	0	2	2	0	....	1988-89	1992-93
Okerlund, Todd	NYI	1	4	0	0	0	2	....	....	....	....	....	....	1987-88	1987-88
Oksiuta, Roman	Edm., Van., Ana., Pit.	4	153	46	41	87	100	10	2	3	5	0	....	1993-94	1996-97
Olausson, Fredrik	Wpg., Edm., Ana., Pit., Det.	16	1022	147	434	581	450	71	6	23	29	28	1	1986-87	2002-03
Olczyk, Ed	Chi., Tor., Wpg., NYR, L.A., Pit.	16	1031	342	452	794	874	57	19	15	34	57	1	1984-85	1999-00
‡ Olesz, Rostislav	Fla., Chi., N.J.	8	365	57	77	134	118	....	....	....	....	....	....	2005-06	2013-14
Oliver, David	Edm., NYR, Ott., Phx., Dal.	9	233	49	49	98	84	10	0	0	0	2	....	1994-95	2005-06
• Oliver, Harry	Bos., NYA	11	463	127	85	212	147	35	10	6	16	24	1	1926-27	1936-37
• Oliver, Murray	Det., Bos., Tor., Min.	17	1127	274	454	728	320	35	9	16	25	10	....	1957-58	1974-75
Oliwa, Krzysztof	N.J., CBJ, Pit., NYR, Bos., Cgy.	9	410	17	28	45	1447	32	2	0	2	47	1	1996-97	2005-06
• Olmstead, Bert	Chi., Mtl., Tor.	14	848	181	421	602	884	115	16	43	59	101	5	1948-49	1961-62
Olsen, Darryl	Cgy.	1	1	0	0	0	0	....	....	....	....	....	....	1991-92	1991-92
Olsen, Dylan	Chi., Fla.	4	124	5	17	22	36	1	0	0	0	0	....	2011-12	**2015-16**
Olson, Dennis	Det.	1	4	0	0	0	0	....	....	....	....	....	....	1957-58	1957-58
Olson, Josh	Fla.	1	5	1	0	1	0	....	....	....	....	....	....	2003-04	2003-04
Olsson, Christer	St.L., Ott.	2	56	4	12	16	24	3	0	0	0	0	....	1995-96	1996-97
‡ Olvecky, Peter	Min., Nsh.	2	32	2	5	7	12	....	....	....	....	....	....	2008-09	2009-10
‡ Olver, Mark	Col.	3	74	10	12	22	39	....	....	....	....	....	....	2010-11	2012-13
Olvestad, Jimmie	T.B.	2	111	3	14	17	40	....	....	....	....	....	....	2001-02	2002-03
‡ Omark, Linus	Edm., Buf.	3	79	8	24	32	40	....	....	....	....	....	....	2010-11	2013-14
O'Marra, Ryan	Edm., Ana.	3	33	1	6	7	17	....	....	....	....	....	....	2009-10	2011-12
Ondrus, Ben	Tor.	4	52	0	2	2	77	....	....	....	....	....	....	2005-06	2008-09
• O'Neil, Jim	Bos., Mtl.	6	156	6	30	36	109	9	1	1	2	13	....	1933-34	1941-42
O'Neil, Paul	Van., Bos.	2	6	0	0	0	0	....	....	....	....	....	....	1973-74	1975-76
‡ O'Neill, Brian	N.J.	1	22	0	2	2	8	....	....	....	....	....	....	**2015-16**	**2015-16**
O'Neill, Jeff	Hfd., Car., Tor.	11	821	237	259	496	670	34	9	8	17	37	....	1995-96	2006-07
• O'Neill, Tom	Tor.	2	66	10	12	22	53	4	0	0	0	6	1	1943-44	1944-45
O'Neill, Wes	Col.	2	5	0	0	0	6	....	....	....	....	....	....	2008-09	2009-10
Orban, Bill	Chi., Min.	3	114	8	15	23	67	3	0	0	0	0	....	1967-68	1969-70
O'Ree, Willie	Bos.	2	45	4	10	14	26	....	....	....	....	....	....	1957-58	1960-61
O'Regan, Tom	Pit.	3	61	5	12	17	10	....	....	....	....	....	....	1983-84	1985-86
O'Reilly, Terry	Bos.	14	891	204	402	606	2095	108	25	42	67	335	....	1971-72	1984-85
Oreskovic, Phil	Tor.	1	10	1	1	2	21	....	....	....	....	....	....	2008-09	2008-09
Oreskovich, Victor	Fla., Van.	3	67	2	7	9	41	19	0	0	0	12	....	2009-10	2011-12
Orlando, Gates	Buf.	3	98	18	26	44	51	5	0	4	4	14	....	1984-85	1986-87
• Orlando, Jimmy	Det.	6	199	6	25	31	375	36	0	9	9	105	1	1936-37	1942-43
Orleski, Dave	Mtl.	2	2	0	0	0	0	....	....	....	....	....	....	1980-81	1981-82
Orr, Bobby	Bos., Chi.	12	657	270	645	915	953	74	26	66	92	107	2	1966-67	1978-79
Orr, Colton	Bos., NYR, Tor.	11	477	12	12	24	1186	19	0	0	0	48	....	2003-04	2014-15
Orszagh, Vladimir	NYI, Nsh., St.L.	7	289	54	65	119	194	6	2	0	2	4	....	1997-98	2005-06
Ortmeyer, Jed	NYR, Nsh., S.J., Min.	8	345	22	31	53	161	17	1	1	2	6	....	2003-04	2011-12
‡ Osala, Oskar	Wsh., Car.	2	3	0	0	0	0	....	....	....	....	....	....	2008-09	2009-10
Osborne, Keith	St.L., T.B.	2	16	1	3	4	16	....	....	....	....	....	....	1989-90	1992-93
Osborne, Mark	Det., NYR, Tor., Wpg.	14	919	212	319	531	1152	87	12	16	28	141	....	1981-82	1994-95
Osburn, Randy	Tor., Phi.	2	27	0	2	2	0	....	....	....	....	....	....	1972-73	1974-75
O'Shea, Danny	Min., Chi., St.L.	5	369	64	115	179	265	39	3	7	10	61	....	1968-69	1972-73
• O'Shea, Kevin	Buf., St.L.	3	134	13	18	31	85	12	2	1	3	10	....	1970-71	1972-73
Osiecki, Mark	Cgy., Ott., Wpg., Min.	2	93	3	11	14	43	....	....	....	....	....	....	1991-92	1992-93
O'Sullivan, Chris	Cgy., Van., Ana.	5	62	2	17	19	16	....	....	....	....	....	....	1996-97	2002-03
O'Sullivan, Patrick	L.A., Edm., Car., Min., Phx.	6	334	58	103	161	116	....	....	....	....	....	....	2006-07	2011-12
Otevrel, Jaroslav	S.J.	2	16	3	4	7	2	....	....	....	....	....	....	1992-93	1993-94
Otto, Joel	Cgy., Phi.	14	943	195	313	508	1934	122	27	47	74	207	1	1984-85	1997-98
Ouellet, Michel	Pit., T.B., Van.	4	190	52	64	116	58	5	0	2	2	6	....	2005-06	2008-09
• Ouellette, Eddie	Chi.	1	43	3	2	5	11	1	0	0	0	0	....	1935-36	1935-36
Ouellette, Gerry	Bos.	1	34	5	4	9	0	....	....	....	....	....	....	1960-61	1960-61
Owchar, Dennis	Pit., Col.	6	288	30	85	115	200	10	1	1	2	8	....	1974-75	1979-80
• Owen, George	Bos.	5	183	44	33	77	151	21	2	5	7	25	1	1928-29	1932-33
Oystrick, Nathan	Atl., Ana., St.L.	3	65	5	10	15	61	....	....	....	....	....	....	2008-09	2010-11
Ozolinsh, Sandis	S.J., Col., Car., Fla., Ana., NYR	15	875	167	397	564	638	137	23	67	90	131	1	1992-93	2007-08

P

Name	NHL Teams	NHL Seasons	Regular Schedule GP	G	A	TP	PIM	Playoffs GP	G	A	TP	PIM	NHL Cup Wins	First NHL Season	Last NHL Season
Pachal, Clayton	Bos., Col.	3	35	2	3	5	95	....	....	....	....	....	....	1976-77	1978-79
Paddock, Cam	St.L.	1	16	2	1	3	0	....	....	....	....	....	....	2008-09	2008-09
Paddock, John	Wsh., Phi., Que.	5	87	8	14	22	86	5	2	0	2	0	....	1975-76	1982-83
Paek, Jim	Pit., L.A., Ott.	5	217	5	29	34	155	27	1	4	5	8	2	1990-91	1994-95
Pahlsson, Samuel	Bos., Ana., Chi., CBJ, Van.	11	798	68	131	199	356	86	10	19	29	58	1	2000-01	2011-12
Paiement, Rosaire	Phi., Van.	5	190	48	52	100	343	3	3	0	3	0	....	1967-68	1971-72
Paiement, Wilf	K.C., Col., Tor., Que., NYR, Buf., Pit.	14	946	356	458	814	1757	69	18	17	35	185	....	1974-75	1987-88
• Palangio, Pete	Mtl., Det., Chi.	5	71	13	10	23	28	7	0	0	0	0	1	1926-27	1937-38
• Palazzari, Aldo	Bos., NYR	1	35	8	3	11	4	....	....	....	....	....	....	1943-44	1943-44
Palazzari, Doug	St.L.	4	108	18	20	38	23	2	0	0	0	0	....	1974-75	1978-79
Palffy, Ziggy	NYI, L.A., Pit.	12	684	329	384	713	322	24	9	10	19	8	....	1993-94	2005-06
Palmer, Brad	Min., Bos.	3	168	32	38	70	58	29	9	5	14	16	....	1980-81	1982-83
Palmer, Jarod	Min.	1	6	1	0	1	4	....	....	....	....	....	....	2011-12	2011-12
Palmer, Rob	Chi.	3	16	0	3	3	2	....	....	....	....	....	....	1973-74	1975-76
Palmer, Robert	L.A., N.J.	7	320	9	101	110	115	8	1	2	3	6	....	1977-78	1983-84
‡ Palmieri, Nick	N.J., Min.	3	87	13	12	25	20	....	....	....	....	....	....	2009-10	2011-12
‡ Palushaj, Aaron	Mtl., Col., Car.	4	68	3	11	14	18	....	....	....	....	....	....	2010-11	2013-14
• Panagabko, Ed	Bos.	2	29	0	3	3	38	....	....	....	....	....	....	1955-56	1956-57
Pandolfo, Jay	N.J., NYI, Bos.	15	899	100	126	226	164	131	11	22	33	12	2	1996-97	2012-13
Pandolfo, Mike	CBJ	1	3	0	0	0	0	....	....	....	....	....	....	2003-04	2003-04
Pankewicz, Greg	Ott., Cgy.	2	21	0	3	3	22	....	....	....	....	....	....	1993-94	1998-99
Panteleev, Grigori	Bos., NYI	4	54	8	6	14	12	....	....	....	....	....	....	1992-93	1995-96
• Papike, Joe	Chi.	3	20	3	3	6	4	5	0	2	2	0	....	1940-41	1944-45
Papineau, Justin	St.L., NYI	3	81	11	8	19	12	1	0	0	0	0	....	2001-02	2003-04
Pappin, Jim	Tor., Chi., Cal., Cle.	14	767	278	295	573	667	92	33	34	67	101	2	1963-64	1976-77
Paradise, Bob	Min., Atl., Pit., Wsh.	8	368	8	54	62	393	12	0	1	1	19	....	1971-72	1978-79
Parent, Ryan	Phi., Van.	5	106	1	6	7	36	27	1	1	2	8	....	2006-07	2010-11
• Pargeter, George	Mtl.	1	4	0	0	0	0	....	....	....	....	....	....	1946-47	1946-47
• Parise, J.P.	Bos., Tor., Min., NYI, Cle.	14	890	238	356	594	706	86	27	31	58	87	....	1965-66	1978-79
Parizeau, Michel	St.L., Phi.	1	58	3	14	17	18	....	....	....	....	....	....	1971-72	1971-72
Park, Brad	NYR, Bos., Det.	17	1113	213	683	896	1429	161	35	90	125	217	....	1968-69	1984-85
Park, Richard	Pit., Ana., Phi., Min., Van., NYI	14	738	102	139	241	266	40	3	6	9	12	....	1994-95	2011-12
Parker, Jeff	Buf., Hfd.	5	141	16	19	35	163	5	0	0	0	26	....	1986-87	1990-91
Parker, Scott	Col., S.J.	8	308	7	14	21	699	5	0	0	0	4	1	1998-99	2007-08
• Parkes, Ernie	Mtl.M.	1	17	0	0	0	2	....	....	....	....	....	....	1924-25	1924-25
• Parks, Greg	NYI	3	23	1	2	3	6	2	0	0	0	0	....	1990-91	1992-93
Parrish, Mark	Fla., NYI, L.A., Min., Dal., T.B., Buf.	12	722	216	171	387	246	27	5	4	9	10	....	1998-99	2010-11
Parros, George	L.A., Col., Ana., Fla., Mtl.	9	474	18	18	36	1092	19	0	0	0	35	1	2005-06	2013-14
Parse, Scott	L.A.	3	73	14	16	30	36	6	0	0	0	0	1	2009-10	2011-12
• Parsons, George	Tor.	3	78	12	13	25	20	7	3	2	5	11	....	1936-37	1938-39
Parssinen, Timo	Ana.	1	17	0	3	3	2	....	....	....	....	....	....	2001-02	2001-02
• Pasek, Dusan	Min.	1	48	4	10	14	30	2	1	0	1	0	....	1988-89	1988-89
Pasin, Dave	Bos., L.A.	2	76	18	19	37	50	3	0	1	1	0	....	1985-86	1988-89
Paslawski, Greg	Mtl., St.L., Wpg., Buf., Que., Phi., Cgy.	11	650	187	185	372	169	60	19	13	32	25	....	1983-84	1993-94

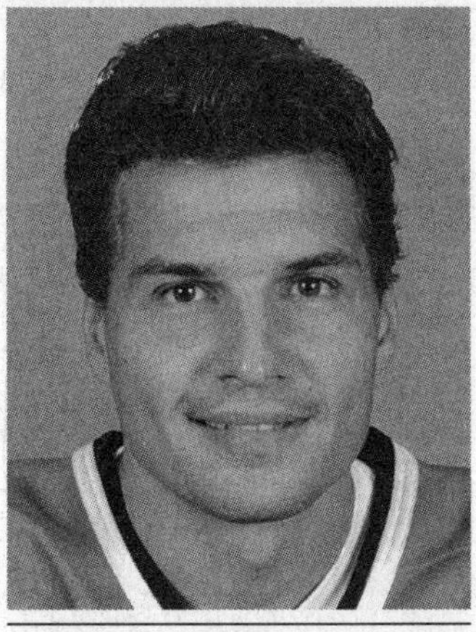
Ed Olczyk

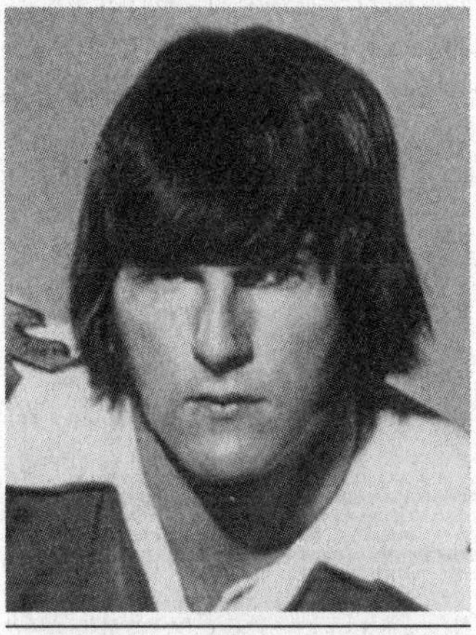
Randy Osburn

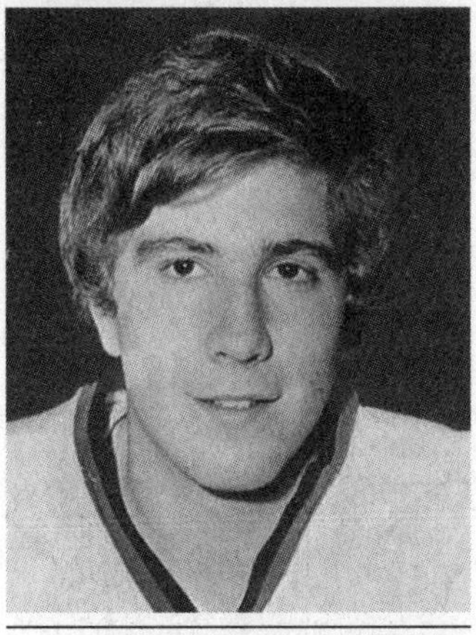
Rob Palmer

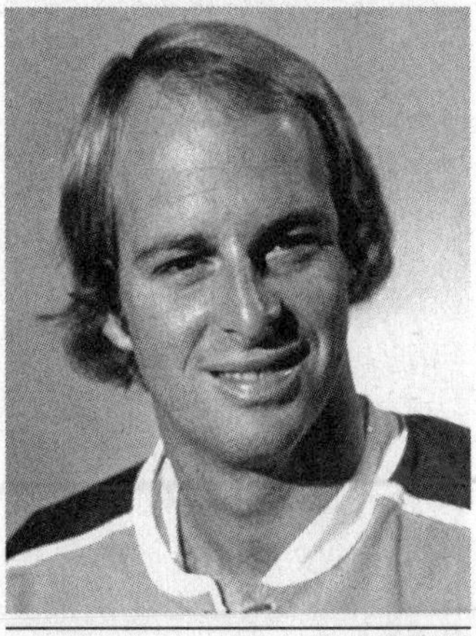
Craig Patrick

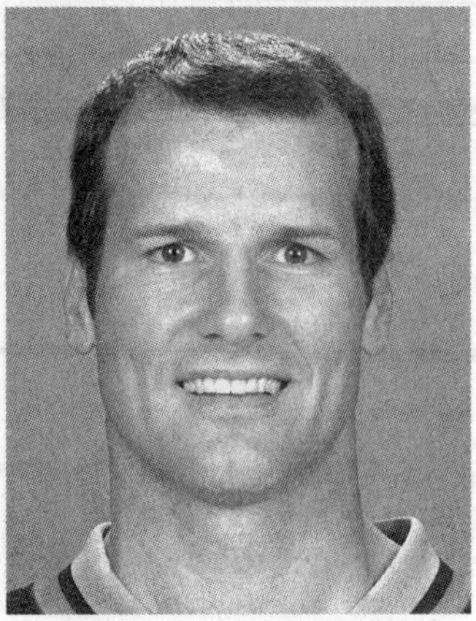

James Patrick

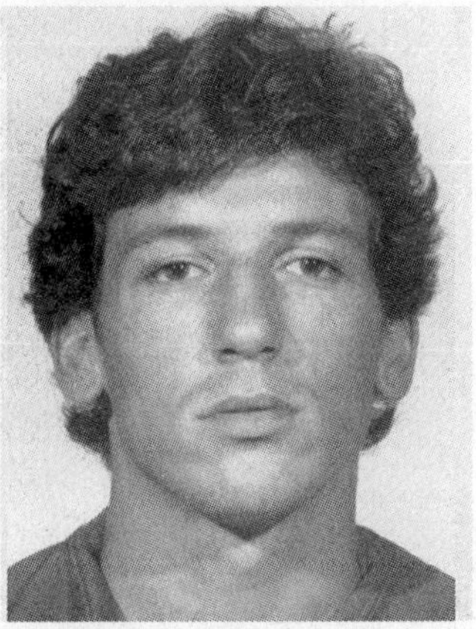

Steve Patrick

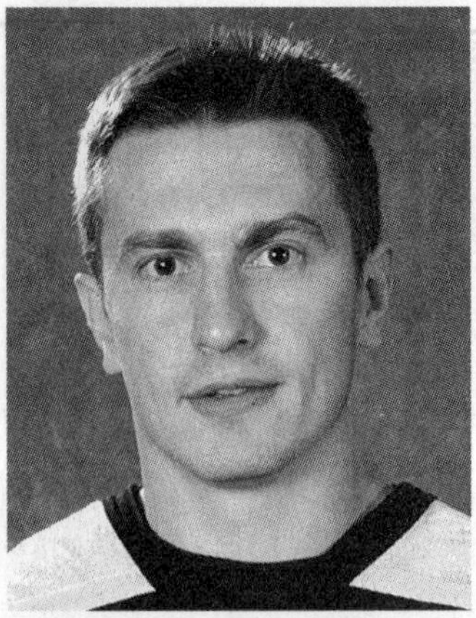

Ville Peltonen

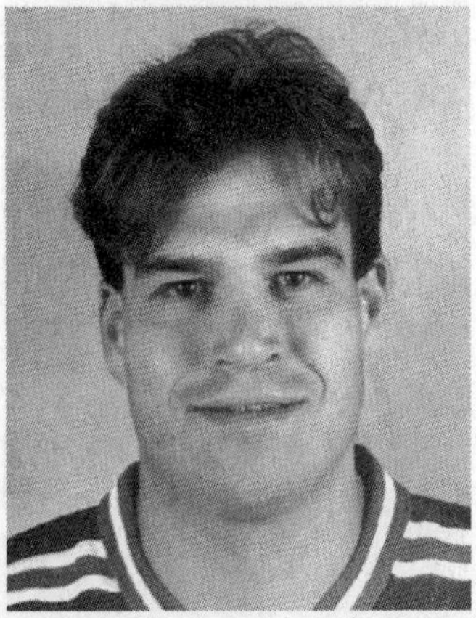

Mike Peluso

Name	NHL Teams	NHL Seasons	Regular Schedule GP	G	A	TP	PIM	Playoffs GP	G	A	TP	PIM	NHL Cup Wins	First NHL Season	Last NHL Season
Patera, Pavel	Dal., Min.	2	32	2	7	9	8	....	....	....	....	....	....	1999-00	2000-01
Paterson, Joe	Det., Phi., L.A., NYR	9	291	19	37	56	829	22	3	4	7	77	....	1980-81	1988-89
Paterson, Mark	Hfd.	4	29	3	3	6	33	....	....	....	....	....	....	1982-83	1985-86
Paterson, Rick	Chi.	9	430	50	43	93	136	61	7	10	17	51	....	1978-79	1986-87
Patey, Doug	Wsh.	3	45	4	2	6	8	....	....	....	....	....	....	1976-77	1978-79
Patey, Larry	Cal., St.L., NYR	12	717	153	163	316	631	40	8	10	18	57	....	1973-74	1984-85
Patrick, Craig	Cal., St.L., K.C., Wsh.	8	401	72	91	163	61	2	0	1	1	0	....	1971-72	1978-79
Patrick, Glenn	St.L., Cal., Cle.	4	38	2	3	5	72	....	....	....	....	....	....	1973-74	1976-77
Patrick, James	NYR, Hfd., Cgy., Buf.	21	1280	149	490	639	759	117	6	32	38	86	....	1983-84	2003-04
• Patrick, Lester	NYR	1	1	0	0	0	2	....	....	....	....	....	....	1926-27	1926-27
• Patrick, Lynn	NYR	10	455	145	190	335	240	44	10	6	16	22	1	1934-35	1945-46
• Patrick, Muzz	NYR	5	166	5	26	31	133	25	4	0	4	34	1	1937-38	1945-46
Patrick, Steve	Buf., NYR, Que.	6	250	40	68	108	242	12	0	1	1	12	....	1980-81	1985-86
Patterson, Colin	Cgy., Buf.	10	504	96	109	205	239	85	12	17	29	57	1	1983-84	1992-93
Patterson, Dennis	K.C., Phi.	3	138	6	22	28	67	....	....	....	....	....	....	1974-75	1979-80
Patterson, Ed	Pit.	3	68	3	3	6	56	....	....	....	....	....	....	1993-94	1996-97
• Patterson, George	Tor., Mtl., NYA, Bos., Det., St.L.	9	284	51	27	78	218	3	0	0	0	2	....	1926-27	1934-35
• Paul, Butch	Det.	1	3	0	0	0	0	....	....	....	....	....	....	1964-65	1964-65
Paul, Jeff	Col.	1	2	0	0	0	7	....	....	....	....	....	....	2002-03	2002-03
• Paulhus, Rollie	Mtl.	1	33	0	0	0	0	....	....	....	....	....	....	1925-26	1925-26
Pavelich, Mark	NYR, Min., S.J.	7	355	137	192	329	340	23	7	17	24	14	....	1981-82	1991-92
Pavelich, Marty	Det.	10	634	93	159	252	454	91	13	15	28	74	4	1947-48	1956-57
Pavese, Jim	St.L., NYR, Det., Hfd.	8	328	13	44	57	689	36	0	6	6	81	....	1981-82	1988-89
• Payer, Evariste	Mtl.	1	1	0	0	0	0	....	....	....	....	....	....	1917-18	1917-18
Payer, Serge	Fla., Ott.	4	124	7	6	13	49	....	....	....	....	....	....	2000-01	2006-07
Payne, Davis	Bos.	2	22	0	1	1	14	....	....	....	....	....	....	1995-96	1996-97
Payne, Steve	Min.	10	613	228	238	466	435	71	35	35	70	60	....	1978-79	1987-88
Paynter, Kent	Chi., Wsh., Wpg., Ott.	7	37	1	3	4	69	4	0	0	0	10	....	1987-88	1993-94
Peake, Pat	Wsh.	5	134	28	41	69	105	13	2	2	4	20	....	1993-94	1997-98
• Pearson, Mel	NYR, Pit.	5	38	2	6	8	25	....	....	....	....	....	....	1959-60	1967-68
Pearson, Rob	Tor., Wsh., St.L.	6	269	56	54	110	645	33	4	2	6	94	....	1991-92	1996-97
Pearson, Scott	Tor., Que., Edm., Buf., NYI	10	292	56	42	98	615	10	2	0	2	14	....	1988-89	1999-00
Peat, Stephen	Wsh.	4	130	8	2	10	234	....	....	....	....	....	....	2001-02	2005-06
Peca, Michael	Van., Buf., NYI, Edm., Tor., CBJ	14	864	176	289	465	798	97	15	19	34	80	....	1993-94	2008-09
Peckham, Theo	Edm.	6	160	4	13	17	388	....	....	....	....	....	....	2007-08	2012-13
Pedersen, Allen	Bos., Min., Hfd.	8	428	5	36	41	487	64	0	0	0	91	....	1986-87	1993-94
Pederson, Barry	Bos., Van., Pit., Hfd.	12	701	238	416	654	472	34	22	30	52	25	1	1980-81	1991-92
Pederson, Denis	N.J., Van., Phx., Nsh.	8	435	57	71	128	398	27	1	5	6	8	....	1995-96	2002-03
Pederson, Mark	Mtl., Phi., S.J., Det.	5	169	35	50	85	77	2	0	0	0	0	....	1989-90	1993-94
Pederson, Tom	S.J., Tor.	5	240	20	49	69	142	24	1	11	12	10	....	1992-93	1996-97
• Peer, Bert	Det.	1	1	0	0	0	0	....	....	....	....	....	....	1939-40	1939-40
Peirson, Johnny	Bos.	11	545	153	173	326	315	49	10	16	26	26	....	1946-47	1957-58
‡ Pelech, Matt	Cgy., S.J.	3	13	1	3	4	38	....	....	....	....	....	....	2008-09	2013-14
Pelensky, Perry	Chi.	1	4	0	0	0	5	....	....	....	....	....	....	1983-84	1983-84
Pellerin, Scott	N.J., St.L., Min., Car., Bos., Dal., Phx.	11	536	72	126	198	320	37	1	2	3	26	....	1992-93	2003-04
‡ Pelletier, Pascal	Bos., Chi., Van.	3	16	0	0	0	0	....	....	....	....	....	....	2007-08	2013-14
Pelletier, Roger	Phi.	1	1	0	0	0	0	....	....	....	....	....	....	1967-68	1967-68
Peloffy, Andre	Wsh.	1	9	0	0	0	0	....	....	....	....	....	....	1974-75	1974-75
Peltier, Derek	Col.	2	14	0	0	0	2	....	....	....	....	....	....	2008-09	2009-10
Peltonen, Ville	S.J., Nsh., Fla.	8	382	52	96	148	119	....	....	....	....	....	....	1995-96	2008-09
Peluso, Mike	Chi., Ott., N.J., St.L., Cgy.	9	458	38	52	90	1951	62	3	4	7	107	1	1989-90	1997-98
Peluso, Mike	Chi., Phi.	2	38	4	2	6	19	....	....	....	....	....	....	2001-02	2003-04
Pelyk, Mike	Tor.	9	441	26	88	114	566	40	0	3	3	41	....	1967-68	1977-78
Penner, Dustin	Ana., Edm., L.A., Wsh.	9	589	151	159	310	354	78	13	22	35	58	2	2005-06	2013-14
Penner, Jeff	Bos.	1	2	0	0	0	0	....	....	....	....	....	....	2009-10	2009-10
Penney, Chad	Ott.	1	3	0	0	0	2	....	....	....	....	....	....	1993-94	1993-94
Pennington, Cliff	Mtl., Bos.	3	101	17	42	59	6	....	....	....	....	....	....	1960-61	1962-63
Peplinski, Jim	Cgy.	11	711	161	263	424	1467	99	15	31	46	382	1	1980-81	1994-95
‡ Perezhogin, Alexander	Mtl.	2	128	15	19	34	86	6	1	1	2	4	....	2005-06	2006-07
Perlini, Fred	Tor.	2	8	2	3	5	0	....	....	....	....	....	....	1981-82	1983-84
Perrault, Joel	Phx., St.L., Van.	6	96	12	14	26	68	....	....	....	....	....	....	2005-06	2010-11
Perreault, Fern	NYR	2	3	0	0	0	0	....	....	....	....	....	....	1947-48	1949-50
Perreault, Gilbert	Buf.	17	1191	512	814	1326	500	90	33	70	103	44	....	1970-71	1986-87
Perreault, Yanic	Tor., L.A., Mtl., Nsh., Phx., Chi.	14	859	247	269	516	402	54	11	19	30	18	....	1993-94	2007-08
‡ Perrin, Eric	T.B., Atl.	4	245	32	72	104	92	18	1	2	3	8	1	2003-04	2008-09
Perrott, Nathan	Nsh., Tor., Dal.	4	89	4	5	9	251	....	....	....	....	....	....	2001-02	2005-06
Perry, Brian	Oak., Buf.	3	96	16	29	45	24	8	1	1	2	4	....	1968-69	1970-71
‡ Persson, John	NYI	1	10	1	0	1	6	....	....	....	....	....	....	2013-14	2013-14
Persson, Ricard	N.J., St.L., Ott.	7	229	10	44	54	262	26	1	3	4	59	....	1995-96	2001-02
Persson, Stefan	NYI	9	622	52	317	369	574	102	7	50	57	69	4	1977-78	1985-86
‡ Pesonen, Harri	N.J.	1	4	0	0	0	2	....	....	....	....	....	....	2012-13	2012-13
‡ Pesonen, Janne	Pit.	1	7	0	0	0	0	....	....	....	....	....	....	2008-09	2008-09
Pesut, George	Cal.	2	92	3	22	25	130	....	....	....	....	....	....	1974-75	1975-76
Peters, Andrew	Buf., N.J.	6	229	4	3	7	650	....	....	....	....	....	....	2003-04	2009-10
• Peters, Frank	NYR	1	43	0	0	0	59	4	0	0	0	2	....	1930-31	1930-31
Peters, Garry	Mtl., NYR, Phi., Bos.	8	311	34	34	68	261	9	2	2	4	31	1	1964-65	1971-72
• Peters, Jimmy	Mtl., Bos., Det., Chi.	9	574	125	150	275	186	60	5	9	14	22	3	1945-46	1953-54
Peters, Jimmy	Det., L.A.	9	309	37	36	73	48	11	0	2	2	2	....	1964-65	1974-75
Peters, Steve	Col.	1	2	0	1	1	0	....	....	....	....	....	....	1979-80	1979-80
Peters, Warren	Cgy., Dal., Min.	4	96	4	4	8	72	4	0	0	0	0	....	2008-09	2011-12
Petersen, Toby	Pit., Edm., Dal.	10	398	33	48	81	50	18	1	0	1	2	....	2000-01	2012-13
Peterson, Brent	Det., Buf., Van., Hfd.	11	620	72	141	213	484	31	4	4	8	65	....	1978-79	1988-89
Peterson, Brent	T.B.	3	56	9	1	10	6	....	....	....	....	....	....	1996-97	1998-99
‡ Petersson, Andre	Ott.	1	1	0	0	0	0	....	....	....	....	....	....	2011-12	2011-12
Petiot, Richard	L.A., T.B., Edm.	3	15	0	3	3	25	....	....	....	....	....	....	2005-06	2010-11
Petit, Michel	Van., NYR, Que., Tor., Cgy., L.A., T.B., Edm., Phi., Phx.	16	827	90	238	328	1839	19	0	2	2	61	....	1982-83	1997-98
Petrecki, Nicholas	S.J.	1	1	0	0	0	0	....	....	....	....	....	....	2012-13	2012-13
‡ Petrell, Lennart	Edm.	2	95	7	11	18	49	....	....	....	....	....	....	2011-12	2012-13
Petrenko, Sergei	Buf.	1	14	0	4	4	0	....	....	....	....	....	....	1993-94	1993-94
Petrov, Oleg	Mtl., Nsh.	8	382	72	115	187	101	20	1	6	7	2	....	1992-93	2002-03
Petrovicky, Robert	Hfd., Dal., St.L., T.B., NYI	8	208	27	38	65	118	2	0	0	0	0	....	1992-93	2000-01
Petrovicky, Ronald	Cgy., NYR, Atl., Pit.	6	342	41	51	92	429	3	0	0	0	2	....	2000-01	2006-07
‡ Petruzalek, Jakub	Car.	1	2	0	1	1	0	....	....	....	....	....	....	2008-09	2008-09
Pettersson, Jorgen	St.L., Hfd., Wsh.	6	435	174	192	366	117	44	15	12	27	4	....	1980-81	1985-86
Pettinen, Tomi	NYI	3	24	0	0	0	18	....	....	....	....	....	....	2002-03	2005-06
• Pettinger, Eric	Bos., Tor., Ott.	3	98	7	12	19	83	4	1	0	1	8	....	1928-29	1930-31
• Pettinger, Gord	NYR, Det., Bos.	8	292	42	74	116	77	47	4	5	9	11	4	1932-33	1939-40
Pettinger, Matt	Wsh., Van., T.B.	9	422	65	58	123	210	1	0	0	0	0	....	2000-01	2009-10
Peverley, Rich	Nsh., Atl., Bos., Dal.	8	442	84	157	241	167	59	9	12	21	33	1	2006-07	2013-14
Phair, Lyle	L.A.	3	48	6	7	13	12	1	0	0	0	0	....	1985-86	1987-88
Phillipoff, Harold	Atl., Chi.	3	141	26	57	83	267	6	0	2	2	9	....	1977-78	1979-80
• Phillips, Bill	Mtl.M.	1	27	1	1	2	6	4	0	0	0	2	....	1929-30	1929-30
• Phillips, Charlie	Mtl.	1	17	0	0	0	6	....	....	....	....	....	....	1942-43	1942-43
Phillips, Chris	Ott.	17	1179	71	217	288	756	114	6	9	15	105	....	1997-98	2014-15
• Phillips, Merlyn	Mtl.M., NYA	8	302	52	31	83	232	24	5	1	6	19	1	1925-26	1932-33
‡ Picard, Alexandre	Phi., T.B., Ott., Car., Mtl., Pit.	7	253	19	50	69	86	....	....	....	....	....	....	2005-06	2011-12
‡ Picard, Alexandre	CBJ	5	67	0	2	2	58	....	....	....	....	....	....	2005-06	2009-10
Picard, Michel	Hfd., S.J., Ott., St.L., Edm., Phi.	9	166	28	42	70	103	5	0	0	0	2	....	1990-91	2000-01
Picard, Noel	Mtl., St.L., Atl.	7	335	12	63	75	616	50	2	11	13	167	1	1964-65	1972-73
Picard, Robert	Wsh., Tor., Mtl., Wpg., Que., Det.	13	899	104	319	423	1025	36	5	15	20	39	....	1977-78	1989-90
Picard, Roger	St.L.	1	15	2	2	4	21	....	....	....	....	....	....	1967-68	1967-68
Pichette, Dave	Que., St.L., N.J., NYR	7	322	41	140	181	348	28	3	7	10	54	....	1980-81	1987-88
• Picketts, Hal	NYA	1	48	3	1	4	32	....	....	....	....	....	....	1933-34	1933-34
• Pidhirny, Harry	Bos.	1	2	0	0	0	0	....	....	....	....	....	....	1957-58	1957-58
Pierce, Randy	Col., N.J., Hfd.	8	277	62	76	138	223	2	0	0	0	0	....	1977-78	1984-85
‡ Pihlman, Tuomas	N.J.	3	15	1	1	2	12	....	....	....	....	....	....	2003-04	2006-07
‡ Pihlstrom, Antti	Nsh.	2	54	2	5	7	10	....	....	....	....	....	....	2007-08	2008-09
• Pike, Alf	NYR	6	234	42	77	119	145	21	4	2	6	12	1	1939-40	1946-47
‡ Pikkarainen, Ilkka	N.J.	1	31	1	3	4	10	....	....	....	....	....	....	2009-10	2009-10
‡ Pilar, Karel	Tor.	3	90	6	24	30	42	12	1	4	5	12	....	2001-02	2003-04
Pilon, Rich	NYI, NYR, St.L.	14	631	8	69	77	1745	15	0	0	0	50	....	1988-89	2001-02

Name	NHL Teams	NHL Seasons	Regular Schedule					Playoffs					NHL Cup Wins	First NHL Season	Last NHL Season
			GP	G	A	TP	PIM	GP	G	A	TP	PIM			
Pilote, Pierre	Chi., Tor.	14	890	80	418	498	1251	86	8	53	61	102	1	1955-56	1968-69
Pinder, Gerry	Chi., Cal.	3	223	55	69	124	135	17	0	4	4	6	....	1969-70	1971-72
Pineault, Adam	CBJ	1	3	0	0	0	0	....	....	....	....	....	....	2007-08	2007-08
‡ Pinizzotto, Steve	Van., Edm.	3	36	2	4	6	74	1	0	0	0	0	....	2012-13	2014-15
Pirjeta, Lasse	CBJ, Pit.	3	146	23	27	50	50	....	....	....	....	....	....	2002-03	2005-06
Pirnes, Esa	L.A.	1	57	3	8	11	12	....	....	....	....	....	....	2003-04	2003-04
Piros, Kamil	Atl., Fla.	3	28	4	4	8	10	....	....	....	....	....	....	2001-02	2003-04
Pirus, Alex	Min., Det.	4	159	30	28	58	94	2	0	1	1	2	....	1976-77	1979-80
Pisa, Ales	Edm., NYR	2	53	1	3	4	26	....	....	....	....	....	....	2001-02	2002-03
Pisani, Fernando	Edm., Chi.	8	462	87	82	169	200	33	15	4	19	12	....	2002-03	2010-11
Piskula, Joe	L.A., Cgy., Nsh.	4	13	0	0	0	10	....	....	....	....	....	....	2006-07	2014-15
Pitkanen, Joni	Phi., Edm., Car.	9	535	57	225	282	484	39	0	13	13	24	....	2003-04	2012-13
Pitlick, Lance	Ott., Fla.	8	393	16	33	49	298	24	0	2	2	21	....	1994-95	2001-02
• Pitre, Didier	Mtl.	6	127	64	33	97	87	9	2	4	6	19	....	1917-18	1922-23
Pittis, Domenic	Pit., Buf., Edm., Nsh.	7	86	5	11	16	71	3	0	0	0	2	....	1996-97	2003-04
Pivko, Libor	Nsh.	1	1	0	0	0	0	....	....	....	....	....	....	2003-04	2003-04
Pivonka, Michal	Wsh.	13	825	181	418	599	478	95	19	36	55	86	....	1986-87	1998-99
• Plager, Barclay	St.L.	10	614	44	187	231	1115	68	3	20	23	182	....	1967-68	1976-77
• Plager, Bill	Min., St.L., Atl.	9	263	4	34	38	294	31	0	2	2	26	....	1967-68	1975-76
Plager, Bob	NYR, St.L.	14	644	20	126	146	802	74	2	17	19	195	....	1964-65	1977-78
Plamondon, Gerry	Mtl.	5	74	7	13	20	10	11	5	2	7	2	1	1945-46	1950-51
‡ Plante, Alex	Edm.	3	10	0	2	2	15	....	....	....	....	....	....	2009-10	2011-12
Plante, Cam	Tor.	1	2	0	0	0	0	....	....	....	....	....	....	1984-85	1984-85
Plante, Dan	NYI	4	159	9	14	23	135	1	1	0	1	2	....	1993-94	1997-98
Plante, Derek	Buf., Dal., Chi., Phi.	8	450	96	152	248	138	41	6	10	16	18	1	1993-94	2000-01
Plante, Pierre	Phi., St.L., Chi., NYR, Que.	9	599	125	172	297	599	33	2	6	8	51	....	1971-72	1979-80
Plantery, Mark	Wpg.	1	25	1	5	6	14	....	....	....	....	....	....	1980-81	1980-81
‡ Platt, Geoff	CBJ, Ana.	3	46	4	10	14	28	....	....	....	....	....	....	2005-06	2007-08
Plavsic, Adrien	St.L., Van., T.B., Ana.	8	214	16	56	72	161	13	1	7	8	4	....	1989-90	1996-97
• Plaxton, Hugh	Mtl.M.	1	15	1	2	3	4	....	....	....	....	....	....	1932-33	1932-33
Playfair, Jim	Edm., Chi.	3	21	2	4	6	51	....	....	....	....	....	....	1983-84	1988-89
Playfair, Larry	Buf., L.A.	12	688	26	94	120	1812	43	0	6	6	111	....	1978-79	1989-90
Pleau, Larry	Mtl.	3	94	9	15	24	27	4	0	0	0	0	....	1969-70	1971-72
Pletka, Vaclav	Phi.	1	1	0	0	0	0	....	....	....	....	....	....	2001-02	2001-02
• Pletsch, Charles	Ham.	1	1	0	0	0	0	....	....	....	....	....	....	1920-21	1920-21
Plett, Willi	Atl., Cgy., Min., Bos.	13	834	222	215	437	2572	83	24	22	46	466	....	1975-76	1987-88
‡ Plihal, Tomas	S.J.	3	89	7	9	16	26	4	0	0	0	0	....	2006-07	2008-09
‡ Plotnikov, Sergei	Pit., Ari.	1	45	0	3	3	24	....	....	....	....	....	....	**2015-16**	**2015-16**
Plumb, Rob	Det.	2	14	3	2	5	2	....	....	....	....	....	....	1977-78	1978-79
Plumb, Ron	Hfd.	1	26	3	4	7	14	....	....	....	....	....	....	1979-80	1979-80
Poapst, Steve	Wsh., Chi., Pit., St.L.	7	307	8	28	36	173	11	0	0	0	0	....	1995-96	2005-06
‡ Pock, Thomas	NYR, NYI	5	118	8	9	17	55	4	0	3	3	4	....	2003-04	2008-09
Pocza, Harvie	Wsh.	2	3	0	0	0	2	....	....	....	....	....	....	1979-80	1981-82
• Poddubny, Walt	Edm., Tor., NYR, Que., N.J.	11	468	184	238	422	454	19	7	2	9	12	....	1981-82	1991-92
Podein, Shjon	Edm., Phi., Col., St.L.	11	699	100	106	206	439	127	14	13	27	132	1	1992-93	2002-03
Podkonicky, Andrej	Fla., Wsh.	2	8	1	0	1	2	....	....	....	....	....	....	2000-01	2003-04
Podloski, Ray	Bos.	1	8	0	1	1	17	....	....	....	....	....	....	1988-89	1988-89
Podollan, Jason	Fla., Tor., L.A., NYI	4	41	1	5	6	19	....	....	....	....	....	....	1996-97	2001-02
• Podolsky, Nels	Det.	1	1	0	0	0	0	7	0	0	0	4	....	1948-49	1948-49
Poeschek, Rudy	NYR, Wpg., T.B., St.L.	12	364	6	25	31	817	5	0	0	0	18	....	1987-88	1999-00
• Poeta, Tony	Chi.	1	1	0	0	0	0	....	....	....	....	....	....	1951-52	1951-52
Pohl, John	St.L., Tor.	4	115	17	21	38	24	....	....	....	....	....	....	2003-04	2007-08
• Poile, Bud	Tor., Chi., Det., NYR, Bos.	7	311	107	122	229	91	23	4	5	9	8	1	1942-43	1949-50
Poile, Don	Det.	2	66	7	9	16	12	4	0	0	0	0	....	1954-55	1957-58
• Poirier, Gordie	Mtl.	1	10	0	0	0	0	....	....	....	....	....	....	1939-40	1939-40
‡ Polak, Vojtech	Dal.	2	5	0	0	0	0	....	....	....	....	....	....	2005-06	2006-07
Polanic, Tom	Min.	2	19	0	2	2	53	5	1	1	2	4	....	1969-70	1970-71
• Polich, John	NYR	2	3	0	1	1	0	....	....	....	....	....	....	1939-40	1940-41
Polich, Mike	Mtl., Min.	5	226	24	29	53	57	23	2	1	3	2	1	1976-77	1980-81
Polis, Greg	Pit., St.L., NYR, Wsh.	10	615	174	169	343	391	7	0	2	2	6	....	1970-71	1979-80
Poliziani, Dan	Bos.	1	1	0	0	0	0	3	0	0	0	0	....	1958-59	1958-59
Pollock, Jame	St.L.	1	9	0	0	0	6	....	....	....	....	....	....	2003-04	2003-04
Polonich, Dennis	Det.	8	390	59	82	141	1242	7	1	0	1	19	....	1974-75	1982-83
‡ Ponikarovsky, Alexei	Tor., Pit., L.A., Car., N.J., Wpg.	12	678	139	184	323	419	62	4	15	19	28	....	2000-01	2012-13
Pooley, Paul	Wpg.	2	15	0	3	3	0	....	....	....	....	....	....	1984-85	1985-86
Popein, Larry	NYR, Oak.	8	449	80	141	221	162	16	1	4	5	6	....	1954-55	1967-68
Popiel, Poul	Bos., L.A., Det., Van., Edm.	7	224	13	41	54	210	4	1	0	1	4	....	1965-66	1979-80
‡ Popovic, Mark	Ana., Atl.	5	81	2	5	7	20	....	....	....	....	....	....	2003-04	2009-10
Popovic, Peter	Mtl., NYR, Pit., Bos.	8	485	10	63	73	291	35	1	4	5	18	....	1993-94	2000-01
• Portland, Jack	Mtl., Bos., Chi.	10	381	15	56	71	323	33	1	3	4	25	1	1933-34	1942-43
Porvari, Jukka	Col., N.J.	2	39	3	9	12	4	....	....	....	....	....	....	1981-82	1982-83
Posa, Victor	Chi.	1	2	0	0	0	2	....	....	....	....	....	....	1985-86	1985-86
Posavad, Mike	St.L.	2	8	0	0	0	0	....	....	....	....	....	....	1985-86	1986-87
Posmyk, Marek	T.B.	2	19	1	2	3	20	....	....	....	....	....	....	1999-00	2000-01
Pothier, Brian	Atl., Ott., Wsh., Car.	9	362	26	92	118	202	29	2	3	5	18	....	2000-01	2009-10
Poti, Tom	Edm., NYR, NYI, Wsh.	13	824	69	258	327	586	51	2	17	19	29	....	1998-99	2012-13
• Potomski, Barry	L.A., S.J.	3	68	6	5	11	227	....	....	....	....	....	....	1995-96	1997-98
‡ Potter, Corey	NYR, Pit., Edm., Bos., Cgy., Nsh.	8	130	8	24	32	53	3	0	0	0	0	....	2008-09	**2015-16**
‡ Potulny, Ryan	Phi., Edm., Chi., Ott.	6	126	22	27	49	54	....	....	....	....	....	....	2005-06	2010-11
Potvin, Denis	NYI	15	1060	310	742	1052	1356	185	56	108	164	253	4	1973-74	1987-88
Potvin, Jean	L.A., Phi., NYI, Cle., Min.	11	613	63	224	287	478	39	2	9	11	17	2	1970-71	1980-81
• Potvin, Marc	Det., L.A., Hfd., Bos.	6	121	3	5	8	456	13	0	1	1	50	....	1990-91	1995-96
Poudrier, Daniel	Que.	3	25	1	5	6	10	....	....	....	....	....	....	1985-86	1987-88
• Poulin, Daniel	Min.	1	3	1	1	2	2	....	....	....	....	....	....	1981-82	1981-82
Poulin, Dave	Phi., Bos., Wsh.	13	724	205	325	530	482	129	31	42	73	132	....	1982-83	1994-95
Poulin, Patrick	Hfd., Chi., T.B., Mtl.	11	634	101	134	235	299	32	6	2	8	8	....	1991-92	2001-02
‡ Pouliot, Marc	Edm., T.B., Phx.	7	192	21	36	57	76	8	1	1	2	2	....	2005-06	2011-12
Pouzar, Jaroslav	Edm.	4	186	34	48	82	135	29	6	4	10	16	3	1982-83	1986-87
Powe, Darroll	Phi., Min., NYR	6	329	28	28	56	214	43	1	4	5	17	....	2008-09	2013-14
• Powell, Ray	Chi.	1	31	7	15	22	2	....	....	....	....	....	....	1950-51	1950-51
• Powis, Geoff	Chi.	1	2	0	0	0	0	....	....	....	....	....	....	1967-68	1967-68
Powis, Lynn	Chi., K.C.	2	130	19	33	52	25	1	0	0	0	0	....	1973-74	1974-75
Prajsler, Petr	L.A., Bos.	4	46	3	10	13	51	4	0	0	0	0	....	1987-88	1991-92
• Pratt, Babe	NYR, Tor., Bos.	12	517	83	209	292	463	63	12	17	29	90	2	1935-36	1946-47
• Pratt, Jack	Bos.	2	37	2	0	2	42	4	0	0	0	0	....	1930-31	1931-32
Pratt, Kelly	Pit.	1	22	0	6	6	15	....	....	....	....	....	....	1974-75	1974-75
Pratt, Nolan	Hfd., Car., Col., T.B., Buf.	11	592	9	56	65	537	38	0	1	1	22	2	1996-97	2007-08
Pratt, Tracy	Oak., Pit., Buf., Van., Col., Tor.	10	580	17	97	114	1026	25	0	1	1	62	....	1967-68	1976-77
Preissing, Tom	S.J., Ott., L.A., Col.	6	326	31	101	132	78	42	3	12	15	14	....	2003-04	2009-10
Prentice, Dean	NYR, Bos., Det., Pit., Min.	22	1378	391	469	860	484	54	13	17	30	38	....	1952-53	1973-74
• Prentice, Eric	Tor.	1	5	0	0	0	4	....	....	....	....	....	....	1943-44	1943-44
Presley, Wayne	Chi., S.J., Buf., NYR, Tor.	12	684	155	147	302	953	83	26	17	43	142	....	1984-85	1995-96
Preston, Rich	Chi., N.J.	8	580	127	164	291	348	47	4	18	22	56	....	1979-80	1986-87
Preston, Yves	Phi.	2	28	7	3	10	4	....	....	....	....	....	....	1978-79	1980-81
Priakin, Sergei	Cgy.	3	46	3	8	11	2	3	0	0	0	0	....	1988-89	1990-91
• Price, Jack	Chi.	3	57	4	6	10	24	4	0	0	0	0	....	1951-52	1953-54
Price, Noel	Tor., NYR, Det., Mtl., Pit., L.A., Atl.	14	499	14	114	128	333	12	0	1	1	8	1	1957-58	1975-76
Price, Pat	NYI, Edm., Pit., Que., NYR, Min.	13	726	43	218	261	1456	74	2	10	12	195	....	1975-76	1987-88
Price, Tom	Cal., Cle., Pit.	5	29	0	2	2	12	....	....	....	....	....	....	1974-75	1978-79
Priestlay, Ken	Buf., Pit.	6	168	27	34	61	63	14	0	0	0	21	1	1986-87	1991-92
• Primeau, Joe	Tor.	9	310	66	177	243	105	38	5	18	23	12	1	1927-28	1935-36
Primeau, Keith	Det., Hfd., Car., Phi.	15	909	266	353	619	1541	128	18	39	57	213	....	1990-91	2005-06
Primeau, Kevin	Van.	1	2	0	0	0	4	....	....	....	....	....	....	1980-81	1980-81
Primeau, Wayne	Buf., T.B., Pit., S.J., Bos., Cgy., Tor.	15	774	69	125	194	789	90	7	14	21	42	....	1994-95	2009-10
• Pringle, Ellie	NYA	1	6	0	0	0	0	....	....	....	....	....	....	1930-31	1930-31
‡ Printz, David	Phi.	2	13	0	0	0	4	....	....	....	....	....	....	2005-06	2006-07
• Probert, Bob	Det., Chi.	16	935	163	221	384	3300	81	16	32	48	274	....	1985-86	2001-02
Prochazka, Martin	Tor., Atl.	2	32	2	5	7	8	....	....	....	....	....	....	1997-98	1999-00
• Prodger, Goldie	Tor., Ham.	6	111	63	29	92	39	....	....	....	....	....	....	1919-20	1924-25
Prokhorov, Vitali	St.L.	3	83	19	11	30	35	4	0	0	0	0	....	1992-93	1994-95
Prokopec, Mike	Chi.	2	15	0	0	0	11	....	....	....	....	....	....	1995-96	1996-97
Pronger, Chris	Hfd., St.L., Edm., Ana., Phi.	18	1167	157	541	698	1590	173	26	95	121	326	1	1993-94	2011-12

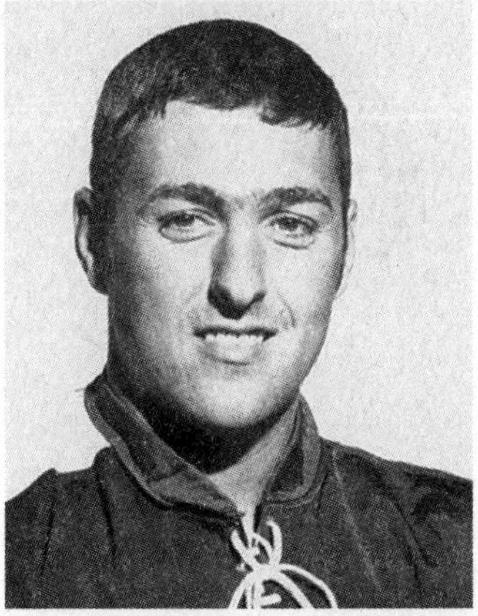
Brian Perry

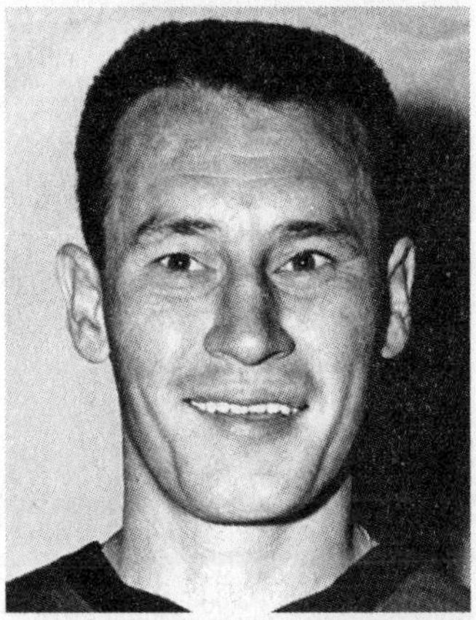
Pierre Pilote

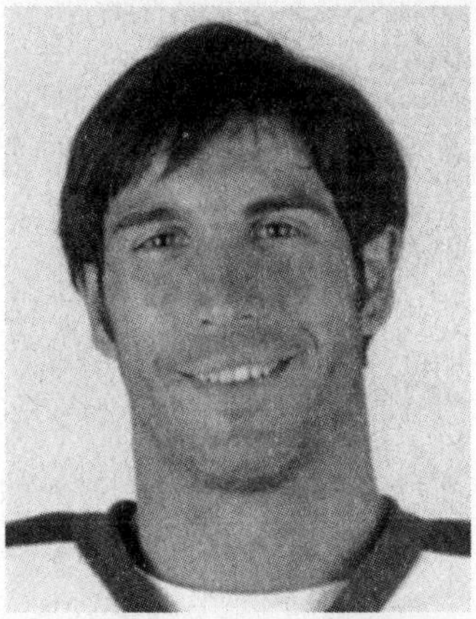
Adrien Plavsic

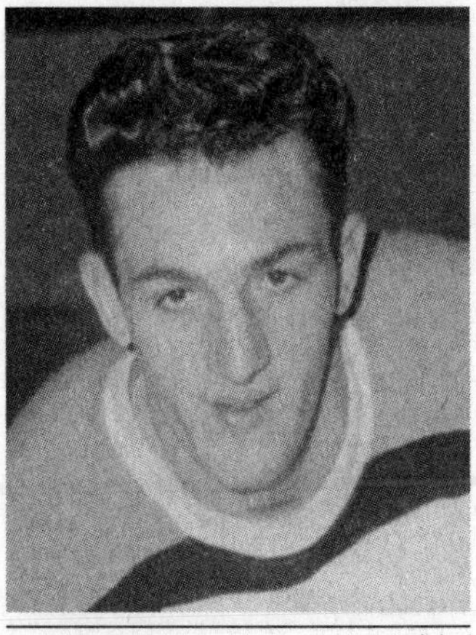
Dan Poliziani

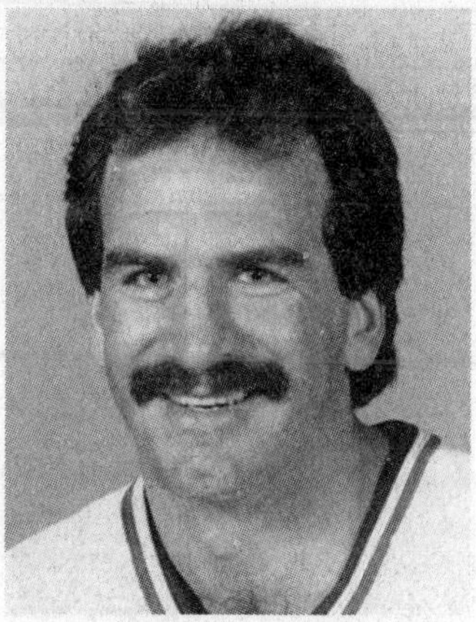

Joel Quenneville

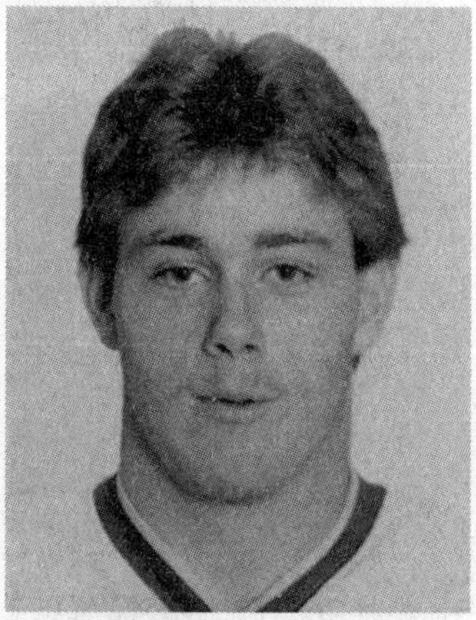

Herb Raglan

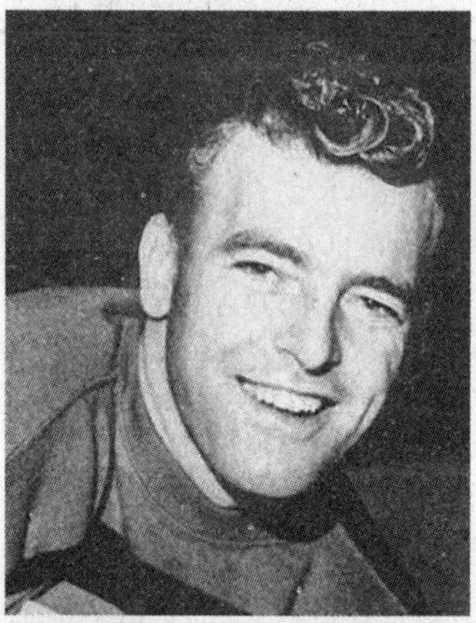

Mel Read

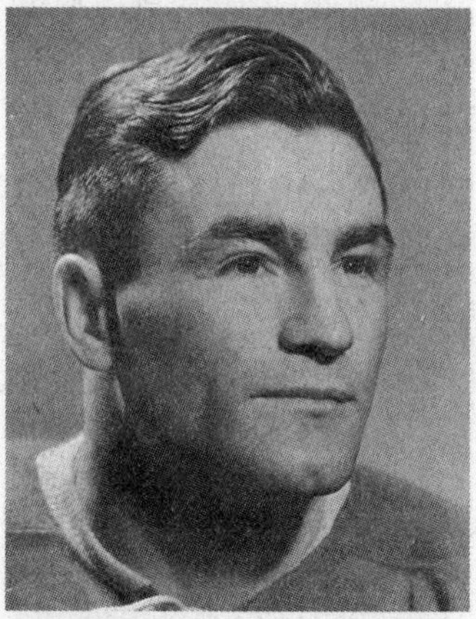

Ken Reardon

			Regular Schedule					Playoffs					NHL	First	Last
Name	NHL Teams	NHL Seasons	GP	G	A	TP	PIM	GP	G	A	TP	PIM	Cup Wins	NHL Season	NHL Season
Pronger, Sean	Ana., Pit., NYR, L.A., Bos., CBJ, Van.	8	260	23	36	59	159	14	0	2	2	8	....	1995-96	2003-04
Pronovost, Andre	Mtl., Bos., Det., Min.	10	556	94	104	198	408	70	11	11	22	58	4	1956-57	1967-68
Pronovost, Jean	Pit., Atl., Wsh.	14	998	391	383	774	413	35	11	9	20	14	....	1968-69	1981-82
• Pronovost, Marcel	Det., Tor.	21	1206	88	257	345	851	134	8	23	31	104	5	1949-50	1969-70
Propp, Brian	Phi., Bos., Min., Hfd.	15	1016	425	579	1004	830	160	64	84	148	151	....	1979-80	1993-94
Prospal, Vinny	Phi., Ott., Fla., T.B., Ana., NYR, CBJ	16	1108	255	510	765	581	65	10	25	35	26	....	1996-97	2012-13
Proulx, Christian	Mtl.	1	7	1	2	3	20	....	....	....	....	....	....	1993-94	1993-94
• Provost, Claude	Mtl.	15	1005	254	335	589	469	126	25	38	63	86	9	1955-56	1969-70
Prpic, Joel	Bos., Col.	3	18	0	3	3	4	....	....	....	....	....	....	1997-98	2000-01
Prucha, Petr	NYR, Phx.	6	346	78	68	146	133	24	2	3	5	8	....	2005-06	2010-11
Pryor, Chris	Min., NYI	6	82	1	4	5	122	....	....	....	....	....	....	1984-85	1989-90
• Prystai, Metro	Chi., Det.	11	674	151	179	330	231	43	12	14	26	8	2	1947-48	1957-58
• Pudas, Al	Tor.	1	4	0	0	0	0	....	....	....	....	....	....	1926-27	1926-27
Pulford, Bob	Tor., L.A.	16	1079	281	362	643	792	89	25	26	51	126	4	1956-57	1971-72
Pulkkinen, Dave	NYI	1	2	0	0	0	0	....	....	....	....	....	....	1972-73	1972-73
Purinton, Dale	NYR	5	181	4	16	20	578	....	....	....	....	....	....	1999-00	2003-04
• Purpur, Fido	St.L., Chi., Det.	5	144	25	35	60	46	16	1	2	3	4	....	1934-35	1944-45
Purves, John	Wsh.	1	7	1	0	1	0	....	....	....	....	....	....	1990-91	1990-91
‡ Pushkarev, Konstantin	L.A.	2	17	2	3	5	8	....	....	....	....	....	....	2005-06	2006-07
Pushor, Jamie	Det., Ana., Dal., CBJ, Pit., NYR	10	521	14	46	60	648	14	0	1	1	16	1	1995-96	2005-06
• Pusie, Jean	Mtl., NYR, Bos.	5	61	1	4	5	28	7	0	0	0	0	1	1930-31	1935-36
Pyatt, Nelson	Det., Wsh., Col.	7	296	71	63	134	69	....	....	....	....	....	....	1973-74	1979-80
Pyatt, Taylor	NYI, Buf., Van., Phx., NYR, Pit.	13	859	140	140	280	430	69	10	14	24	26	....	2000-01	2013-14
‡ Pyorala, Mika	Phi.	1	36	2	2	4	10	....	....	....	....	....	....	2009-10	2009-10
Q															
• Quackenbush, Bill	Det., Bos.	14	774	62	222	284	95	80	2	19	21	8	....	1942-43	1955-56
Quackenbush, Max	Bos., Chi.	2	61	4	7	11	30	6	0	0	0	4	....	1950-51	1951-52
Quenneville, Joel	Tor., Col., N.J., Hfd., Wsh.	13	803	54	136	190	705	32	0	8	8	22	....	1978-79	1990-91
• Quenneville, Leo	NYR	1	25	0	3	3	10	3	0	0	0	0	....	1929-30	1929-30
‡ Quick, Kevin	T.B.	1	6	0	1	1	0	....	....	....	....	....	....	2008-09	2008-09
• Quilty, John	Mtl., Bos.	4	125	36	34	70	81	13	3	5	8	9	....	1940-41	1947-48
Quinn, Dan	Cgy., Pit., Van., St.L., Phi., Min., Ott., L.A.	14	805	266	419	685	533	65	22	26	48	62	....	1983-84	1996-97
• Quinn, Pat	Tor., Van., Atl.	9	606	18	113	131	950	11	0	1	1	21	....	1968-69	1976-77
Quinney, Ken	Que.	3	59	7	13	20	23	....	....	....	....	....	....	1986-87	1990-91
‡ Quint, Deron	Wpg., Phx., N.J., CBJ, Chi., NYI	10	463	46	97	143	166	7	0	2	2	0	....	1995-96	2006-07
Quintal, Stephane	Bos., St.L., Wpg., Mtl., NYR, Chi.	16	1037	63	180	243	1320	52	2	10	12	51	....	1988-89	2003-04
Quintin, Jean-Francois	S.J.	2	22	5	5	10	4	....	....	....	....	....	....	1991-92	1992-93
R															
• Rachunek, Karel	Ott., NYR, N.J.	7	371	22	118	140	227	26	1	7	8	16	....	1999-00	2007-08
Racine, Yves	Det., Phi., Mtl., S.J., Cgy., T.B.	9	508	37	194	231	439	25	5	4	9	37	....	1989-90	1997-98
‡ Radivojevic, Branko	Phx., Phi., Min.	6	393	52	68	120	252	31	2	1	3	36	....	2001-02	2007-08
• Radley, Yip	NYA, Mtl.M.	2	18	0	1	1	13	....	....	....	....	....	....	1930-31	1936-37
‡ Radulov, Igor	Chi.	2	43	9	7	16	22	....	....	....	....	....	....	2002-03	2003-04
Raduns, Nate	Phi.	1	1	0	0	0	0	....	....	....	....	....	....	2008-09	2008-09
Rafalski, Brian	N.J., Det.	11	833	79	436	515	282	165	29	71	100	66	3	1999-00	2010-11
Raglan, Herb	St.L., Que., T.B., Ott.	9	343	33	56	89	775	32	3	6	9	50	....	1985-86	1993-94
• Raglan, Rags	Det., Chi.	3	100	4	9	13	52	3	0	0	0	0	....	1950-51	1952-53
Ragnarsson, Marcus	S.J., Phi.	9	632	37	140	177	482	68	2	13	15	60	....	1995-96	2003-04
‡ Rakhshani, Rhett	NYI	2	7	0	0	0	2	....	....	....	....	....	....	2010-11	2011-12
• Raleigh, Don	NYR	10	535	101	219	320	96	18	6	5	11	6	....	1943-44	1955-56
‡ Rallo, Greg	Fla.	2	11	1	0	1	2	....	....	....	....	....	....	2011-12	2012-13
Ralph, Brad	Phx.	1	1	0	0	0	0	....	....	....	....	....	....	2000-01	2000-01
Ramage, Rob	Col., St.L., Cgy., Tor., Min., T.B., Mtl., Phi.	15	1044	139	425	564	2226	84	8	42	50	218	2	1979-80	1993-94
‡ Ramholt, Tim	Cgy.	1	1	0	0	0	0	....	....	....	....	....	....	2007-08	2007-08
• Ramsay, Beattie	Tor.	1	43	0	2	2	10	....	....	....	....	....	....	1927-28	1927-28
Ramsay, Craig	Buf.	14	1070	252	420	672	201	89	17	31	48	27	....	1971-72	1984-85
• Ramsay, Les	Chi.	1	11	2	2	4	2	....	....	....	....	....	....	1944-45	1944-45
Ramsey, Mike	Buf., Pit., Det.	18	1070	79	266	345	1012	115	8	29	37	176	....	1979-80	1996-97
Ramsey, Wayne	Buf.	1	2	0	0	0	0	....	....	....	....	....	....	1977-78	1977-78
• Randall, Ken	Tor., Ham., NYA	10	218	68	50	118	533	6	2	1	3	27	2	1917-18	1926-27
Ranger, Paul	T.B., Tor.	6	323	24	82	106	254	11	2	5	7	4	....	2005-06	2013-14
Ranheim, Paul	Cgy., Hfd., Car., Phi., Phx.	15	1013	161	199	360	288	36	3	8	11	6	....	1988-89	2002-03
Ranieri, George	Bos.	1	2	0	0	0	0	....	....	....	....	....	....	1956-57	1956-57
‡ Rask, Joonas	Nsh.	1	2	0	1	1	0	....	....	....	....	....	....	2012-13	2012-13
Rasmussen, Erik	Buf., L.A., N.J.	9	545	52	76	128	305	52	2	7	9	46	....	1997-98	2006-07
Ratchuk, Peter	Fla.	2	32	1	1	2	10	....	....	....	....	....	....	1998-99	2000-01
Ratelle, Jean	NYR, Bos.	21	1281	491	776	1267	276	123	32	66	98	24	....	1960-61	1980-81
Rathje, Mike	S.J., Phi.	13	768	30	150	180	491	77	9	14	23	51	....	1993-94	2006-07
Rathwell, Jake	Bos.	1	1	0	0	0	0	....	....	....	....	....	....	1974-75	1974-75
Ratushny, Dan	Van.	1	1	0	1	1	2	....	....	....	....	....	....	1992-93	1992-93
‡ Rau, Chad	Min.	1	9	2	0	2	0	....	....	....	....	....	....	2011-12	2011-12
Rausse, Errol	Wsh.	3	31	7	3	10	0	....	....	....	....	....	....	1979-80	1981-82
Rautakallio, Pekka	Atl., Cgy.	3	235	33	121	154	122	23	2	5	7	8	....	1979-80	1981-82
Ravlich, Matt	Bos., Chi., Det., L.A.	10	410	12	78	90	364	24	1	5	6	16	....	1962-63	1972-73
Ray, Rob	Buf., Ott.	15	900	41	50	91	3207	55	3	2	5	169	....	1989-90	2003-04
• Raymond, Armand	Mtl.	2	22	0	2	2	10	....	....	....	....	....	....	1937-38	1939-40
• Raymond, Paul	Mtl.	4	76	2	3	5	6	5	0	0	0	2	....	1932-33	1938-39
• Read, Mel	NYR	1	1	0	0	0	0	....	....	....	....	....	....	1946-47	1946-47
Ready, Ryan	Phi.	1	7	0	1	1	0	....	....	....	....	....	....	2005-06	2005-06
• Reardon, Ken	Mtl.	7	341	26	96	122	604	31	2	5	7	62	1	1940-41	1949-50
• Reardon, Terry	Bos., Mtl.	7	193	47	53	100	73	30	8	10	18	12	1	1938-39	1946-47
Reasoner, Marty	St.L., Edm., Bos., Atl., Fla., NYI	14	798	97	169	266	379	24	6	2	8	23	....	1998-99	2012-13
Reaume, Marc	Tor., Det., Mtl., Van.	9	344	8	43	51	273	21	0	2	2	8	....	1954-55	1970-71
• Reay, Billy	Det., Mtl.	10	479	105	162	267	202	63	13	16	29	43	2	1943-44	1952-53
Recchi, Mark	Pit., Phi., Mtl., Car., Atl., T.B., Bos.	22	1652	577	956	1533	1033	189	61	86	147	93	3	1988-89	2010-11
‡ Rechlicz, Joel	NYI, Wsh.	3	26	0	1	1	105	....	....	....	....	....	....	2008-09	2011-12
• Redahl, Gord	Bos.	1	18	0	1	1	2	....	....	....	....	....	....	1958-59	1958-59
Redden, Wade	Ott., NYR, St.L., Bos.	14	1023	109	348	457	665	106	13	36	49	55	....	1996-97	2012-13
• Redding, George	Bos.	2	55	3	2	5	23	....	....	....	....	....	....	1924-25	1925-26
‡ Reddox, Liam	Edm.	4	100	6	18	24	34	....	....	....	....	....	....	2007-08	2010-11
Redmond, Craig	L.A., Edm.	5	191	16	68	84	134	3	1	0	1	2	....	1984-85	1988-89
Redmond, Dick	Min., Cal., Chi., St.L., Atl., Bos.	13	771	133	312	445	504	66	9	22	31	27	....	1969-70	1981-82
Redmond, Keith	L.A.	1	12	1	0	1	20	....	....	....	....	....	....	1993-94	1993-94
Redmond, Mickey	Mtl., Det.	9	538	233	195	428	219	16	2	3	5	2	2	1967-68	1975-76
• Reeds, Mark	St.L., Hfd.	8	365	45	114	159	135	53	8	9	17	23	....	1981-82	1988-89
Reekie, Joe	Buf., NYI, T.B., Wsh., Chi.	17	902	25	139	164	1326	51	3	4	7	63	....	1985-86	2001-02
‡ Reese, Dylan	NYI, Pit., Ari.	5	78	3	14	17	40	....	....	....	....	....	....	2009-10	2014-15
• Regan, Bill	NYR, NYA	3	67	3	2	5	67	8	0	0	0	2	....	1929-30	1932-33
• Regan, Larry	Bos., Tor.	5	280	41	95	136	71	42	7	14	21	18	....	1956-57	1960-61
‡ Regehr, Richie	Cgy.	2	20	1	3	4	6	....	....	....	....	....	....	2005-06	2006-07
Regehr, Robyn	Cgy., Buf., L.A.	15	1089	36	163	199	972	67	3	15	18	41	1	1999-00	2014-15
Regier, Darcy	Cle., NYI	3	26	0	2	2	35	....	....	....	....	....	....	1977-78	1983-84
Regier, Steve	NYI, St.L.	4	26	3	1	4	8	....	....	....	....	....	....	2005-06	2008-09
‡ Regin, Peter	Ott., NYI, Chi.	7	243	23	44	67	64	11	3	1	4	6	....	2008-09	2014-15
• Reibel, Dutch	Det., Chi., Bos.	6	409	84	161	245	75	39	6	14	20	4	2	1953-54	1958-59
Reich, Jeremy	CBJ, Bos.	3	99	2	4	6	161	4	0	0	0	8	....	2003-04	2007-08
Reichel, Robert	Cgy., NYI, Phx., Tor.	11	830	252	378	630	388	70	8	23	31	20	....	1990-91	2003-04
Reichert, Craig	Ana.	1	3	0	0	0	0	....	....	....	....	....	....	1996-97	1996-97
Reid, Brandon	Van.	3	13	2	4	6	0	10	0	2	2	0	....	2002-03	2006-07
Reid, Darren	T.B., Phi.	2	21	0	1	1	18	....	....	....	....	....	....	2005-06	2006-07
• Reid, Dave	Tor.	3	7	0	0	0	0	....	....	....	....	....	....	1952-53	1955-56
Reid, Dave	Bos., Tor., Dal., Col.	18	961	165	204	369	253	118	9	26	35	34	2	1983-84	2000-01
• Reid, Gerry	Det.	1	....	....	....	....	....	2	0	0	0	2	....	1948-49	1948-49
• Reid, Gord	NYA	1	1	0	0	0	2	....	....	....	....	....	....	1936-37	1936-37
• Reid, Reg	Tor.	2	39	1	0	1	4	2	0	0	0	0	....	1924-25	1925-26

Name	NHL Teams	NHL Seasons	Regular Schedule GP	G	A	TP	PIM	Playoffs GP	G	A	TP	PIM	NHL Cup Wins	First NHL Season	Last NHL Season
Reid, Tom	Chi., Min.	11	701	17	113	130	654	42	1	13	14	49	....	1967-68	1977-78
Reierson, Dave	Cgy.	1	2	0	0	0	2	....	....	....	....	....	....	1988-89	1988-89
● Reigle, Ed	Bos.	1	17	0	2	2	25	....	....	....	....	....	....	1950-51	1950-51
Reinhart, Paul	Atl., Cgy., Van.	11	648	133	426	559	277	83	23	54	77	42	....	1979-80	1989-90
● Reinikka, Ollie	NYR	1	16	0	0	0	0	....	....	....	....	....	....	1926-27	1926-27
‡ Reinprecht, Steve	L.A., Col., Cgy., Phx., Fla.	11	663	140	242	382	186	50	10	10	20	10	1	1999-00	2010-11
Reirden, Todd	Edm., St.L., Atl., Phx.	5	183	11	35	46	181	5	0	1	1	0	....	1998-99	2003-04
● Reise, Leo	Ham., NYA, NYR	8	223	36	29	65	181	6	0	0	0	16	....	1920-21	1929-30
● Reise, Leo	Chi., Det., NYR	9	494	28	81	109	399	52	8	5	13	68	2	1945-46	1953-54
Reitz, Erik	Min., NYR	4	48	1	1	2	69	2	0	0	0	0	....	2005-06	2008-09
Renaud, Mark	Hfd., Buf.	5	152	6	50	56	86	....	....	....	....	....	....	1979-80	1983-84
Renberg, Mikael	Phi., T.B., Phx., Tor.	10	661	190	274	464	372	67	16	22	38	42	....	1993-94	2003-04
‡ Repik, Michal	Fla.	4	72	9	11	20	36	....	....	....	....	....	....	2008-09	2011-12
Reynolds, Bobby	Tor.	1	7	1	1	2	0	....	....	....	....	....	....	1989-90	1989-90
Rheault, Jon	Fla.	1	5	0	0	0	0	....	....	....	....	....	....	2012-13	2012-13
Rheaume, Pascal	N.J., St.L., Chi., Atl., NYR, Phx.	9	318	39	52	91	144	45	3	6	9	27	1	1996-97	2005-06
Ribble, Pat	Atl., Chi., Tor., Wsh., Cgy.	8	349	19	60	79	365	8	0	1	1	12	....	1975-76	1982-83
Ricci, Mike	Phi., Que., Col., S.J., Phx.	16	1099	243	362	605	974	110	23	43	66	77	1	1990-91	2006-07
Rice, Steven	NYR, Edm., Hfd., Car.	8	329	64	61	125	275	2	2	1	3	6	....	1990-91	1997-98
Richard, Henri	Mtl.	20	1256	358	688	1046	928	180	49	80	129	181	11	1955-56	1974-75
● Richard, Jacques	Atl., Buf., Que.	10	556	160	187	347	307	35	5	5	10	34	....	1972-73	1982-83
Richard, Jean-Marc	Que.	2	5	2	1	3	2	....	....	....	....	....	....	1987-88	1989-90
● Richard, Maurice	Mtl.	18	978	544	421	965	1285	133	82	44	126	188	8	1942-43	1959-60
Richard, Mike	Wsh.	2	7	0	2	2	0	....	....	....	....	....	....	1987-88	1989-90
Richards, Brad	T.B., Dal., NYR, Chi., Det.	15	1126	298	634	932	251	146	37	68	105	65	2	2000-01	**2015-16**
Richards, Mike	Phi., L.A., Wsh.	11	749	181	306	487	585	136	26	61	87	95	2	2005-06	**2015-16**
Richards, Todd	Hfd.	2	8	0	4	4	4	11	0	3	3	6	....	1990-91	1991-92
Richards, Travis	Dal.	2	3	0	0	0	2	....	....	....	....	....	....	1994-95	1995-96
Richardson, Dave	NYR, Chi., Det.	4	45	3	2	5	27	....	....	....	....	....	....	1963-64	1967-68
Richardson, Glen	Van.	1	24	3	6	9	19	....	....	....	....	....	....	1975-76	1975-76
Richardson, Ken	St.L.	3	49	8	13	21	16	....	....	....	....	....	....	1974-75	1978-79
Richardson, Luke	Tor., Edm., Phi., CBJ, T.B., Ott.	21	1417	35	166	201	2055	69	0	8	8	130	....	1987-88	2008-09
Richer, Bob	Buf.	1	3	0	0	0	0	....	....	....	....	....	....	1972-73	1972-73
Richer, Stephane	Mtl., N.J., T.B., St.L., Pit.	17	1054	421	398	819	614	134	53	45	98	61	2	1984-85	2001-02
Richer, Stephane	T.B., Bos., Fla.	3	27	1	5	6	20	3	0	0	0	0	....	1992-93	1994-95
Richmond, Danny	Car., Chi.	3	49	0	3	3	75	....	....	....	....	....	....	2005-06	2007-08
Richmond, Steve	NYR, Det., N.J., L.A.	5	159	4	23	27	514	4	0	0	0	12	....	1983-84	1988-89
Richter, Barry	NYR, Bos., NYI, Mtl.	5	151	11	34	45	76	....	....	....	....	....	....	1995-96	2000-01
Richter, Dave	Min., Phi., Van., St.L.	9	365	9	40	49	1030	22	1	0	1	80	....	1981-82	1989-90
Ridley, Mike	NYR, Wsh., Tor., Van.	12	866	292	466	758	424	104	28	50	78	70	....	1985-86	1996-97
Riesen, Michel	Edm.	1	12	0	1	1	4	....	....	....	....	....	....	2000-01	2000-01
Riley, Bill	Wsh., Wpg.	5	139	31	30	61	320	....	....	....	....	....	....	1974-75	1979-80
● Riley, Jack	Det., Mtl., Bos.	4	104	10	22	32	8	4	0	3	3	0	....	1932-33	1935-36
● Riley, Jim	Chi., Det.	1	9	0	2	2	14	....	....	....	....	....	....	1926-27	1926-27
● Riopelle, Rip	Mtl.	3	169	27	16	43	73	8	1	1	2	2	....	1947-48	1949-50
Rioux, Gerry	Wpg.	1	8	0	0	0	6	....	....	....	....	....	....	1979-80	1979-80
Rioux, Pierre	Cgy.	1	14	1	2	3	4	....	....	....	....	....	....	1982-83	1982-83
● Ripley, Vic	Chi., Bos., NYR, St.L.	7	278	51	49	100	173	20	4	1	5	10	....	1928-29	1934-35
Risebrough, Doug	Mtl., Cgy.	13	740	185	286	471	1542	124	21	37	58	238	4	1974-75	1986-87
‡ Rissanen, Rasmus	Car.	1	6	0	0	0	4	....	....	....	....	....	....	2014-15	2014-15
Rissling, Gary	Wsh., Pit.	7	221	23	30	53	1008	5	0	1	1	4	....	1978-79	1984-85
Rissmiller, Patrick	S.J., NYR, Atl., Fla.	6	192	18	28	46	60	30	3	4	7	10	....	2003-04	2010-11
Rita, Jani	Edm., Pit.	4	66	9	5	14	10	....	....	....	....	....	....	2001-02	2005-06
Ritchie, Bob	Phi., Det.	2	29	8	4	12	10	....	....	....	....	....	....	1976-77	1977-78
‡ Ritchie, Byron	Car., Fla., Cgy., Van.	8	324	25	33	58	373	8	0	0	0	10	....	1998-99	2007-08
● Ritchie, Dave	Mtl.W., Ott., Tor., Que., Mtl.	6	58	15	6	21	50	1	0	0	0	0	....	1917-18	1925-26
‡ Ritola, Mattias	Det., T.B.	4	43	4	5	9	17	2	0	0	0	0	....	2007-08	2011-12
● Ritson, Alex	NYR	1	1	0	0	0	0	....	....	....	....	....	....	1944-45	1944-45
Rittinger, Alan	Bos.	1	19	3	7	10	0	....	....	....	....	....	....	1943-44	1943-44
Rivard, Bob	Pit.	1	27	5	12	17	4	....	....	....	....	....	....	1967-68	1967-68
● Rivers, Gus	Mtl.	3	88	4	5	9	12	16	2	0	2	2	2	1929-30	1931-32
Rivers, Jamie	St.L., NYI, Ott., Bos., Fla., Det., Phx.	11	454	17	49	66	385	15	1	1	2	8	....	1995-96	2006-07
Rivers, Shawn	T.B.	1	4	0	2	2	2	....	....	....	....	....	....	1992-93	1992-93
Rivers, Wayne	Det., Bos., St.L., NYR	7	108	15	30	45	94	....	....	....	....	....	....	1961-62	1968-69
Rivet, Craig	Mtl., S.J., Buf., CBJ	16	923	50	187	237	1171	69	4	19	23	69	....	1994-95	2010-11
Rizzuto, Garth	Van.	1	37	3	4	7	16	....	....	....	....	....	....	1970-71	1970-71
Roach, Andy	St.L.	1	5	1	2	3	10	....	....	....	....	....	....	2005-06	2005-06
● Roach, Mickey	Tor., Ham., NYA	8	211	77	34	111	54	....	....	....	....	....	....	1919-20	1926-27
Roberge, Mario	Mtl.	5	112	7	7	14	314	15	0	0	0	24	1	1990-91	1994-95
Roberge, Serge	Que.	1	9	0	0	0	24	....	....	....	....	....	....	1990-91	1990-91
● Robert, Claude	Mtl.	1	23	1	0	1	9	....	....	....	....	....	....	1950-51	1950-51
Robert, Rene	Tor., Pit., Buf., Col.	12	744	284	418	702	597	50	22	19	41	73	....	1970-71	1981-82
Roberto, Phil	Mtl., St.L., Det., K.C., Col., Cle.	8	385	75	106	181	464	31	9	8	17	69	1	1969-70	1976-77
Roberts, David	St.L., Edm., Van.	5	125	20	33	53	85	9	0	0	0	16	....	1993-94	1997-98
Roberts, Doug	Det., Oak., Cal., Bos.	10	419	43	104	147	342	16	2	3	5	46	....	1965-66	1974-75
Roberts, Gary	Cgy., Car., Tor., Fla., Pit., T.B.	22	1224	438	472	910	2560	130	32	61	93	332	1	1986-87	2008-09
Roberts, Gordie	Hfd., Min., Phi., St.L., Pit., Bos.	15	1097	61	359	420	1582	153	10	47	57	273	2	1979-80	1993-94
Roberts, Jim	Min.	3	106	17	23	40	33	2	0	0	0	0	....	1976-77	1978-79
● Roberts, Jimmy	Mtl., St.L.	15	1006	126	194	320	621	153	20	16	36	160	5	1963-64	1977-78
● Robertson, Fred	Tor., Det.	2	34	1	0	1	35	7	0	0	0	0	1	1931-32	1933-34
Robertson, Geordie	Buf.	1	5	1	2	3	7	....	....	....	....	....	....	1982-83	1982-83
Robertson, George	Mtl.	2	31	2	5	7	6	....	....	....	....	....	....	1947-48	1948-49
Robertson, Torrie	Wsh., Hfd., Det.	10	442	49	99	148	1751	22	2	1	3	90	....	1980-81	1989-90
Robertsson, Bert	Van., Edm., NYR	4	123	4	10	14	75	5	0	0	0	0	....	1997-98	2000-01
Robidas, Stephane	Mtl., Dal., Chi., Ana., Tor.	15	937	57	201	258	713	47	3	12	15	44	....	1999-00	2014-15
Robidoux, Florent	Chi.	3	52	7	4	11	75	....	....	....	....	....	....	1980-81	1983-84
Robins, Bobby	Bos.	1	3	0	0	0	14	....	....	....	....	....	....	2014-15	2014-15
Robinson, Doug	Chi., NYR, L.A.	7	239	44	67	111	34	11	4	3	7	0	....	1963-64	1970-71
● Robinson, Earl	Mtl.M., Chi., Mtl.	11	417	83	98	181	133	25	5	4	9	0	1	1928-29	1939-40
Robinson, Larry	Mtl., L.A.	20	1384	208	750	958	793	227	28	116	144	211	6	1972-73	1991-92
Robinson, Moe	Mtl.	1	1	0	0	0	0	....	....	....	....	....	....	1979-80	1979-80
Robinson, Nathan	Det., Bos.	2	7	0	0	0	2	....	....	....	....	....	....	2003-04	2005-06
Robinson, Rob	St.L.	1	22	0	1	1	8	....	....	....	....	....	....	1991-92	1991-92
Robinson, Scott	Min.	1	1	0	0	0	2	....	....	....	....	....	....	1989-90	1989-90
Robitaille, Louis	Wsh.	1	2	0	0	0	5	....	....	....	....	....	....	2005-06	2005-06
Robitaille, Luc	L.A., Pit., NYR, Det.	19	1431	668	726	1394	1177	159	58	69	127	174	1	1986-87	2005-06
Robitaille, Mike	NYR, Det., Buf., Van.	8	382	23	105	128	280	13	0	1	1	4	....	1969-70	1976-77
Robitaille, Randy	Bos., Nsh., L.A., Pit., NYI, Atl., Min., Phi., Ott.	11	531	84	172	256	201	13	1	4	5	8	....	1996-97	2007-08
Roche, Dave	Pit., Cgy., NYI	5	171	15	15	30	334	16	2	7	9	26	....	1995-96	2001-02
● Roche, Des	Mtl.M., Ott., St.L., Mtl., Det.	4	113	20	18	38	44	....	....	....	....	....	....	1930-31	1934-35
● Roche, Earl	Mtl.M., Bos., Ott., St.L., Det.	4	147	25	27	52	48	2	0	0	0	0	....	1930-31	1934-35
Roche, Ernie	Mtl.	1	4	0	0	0	2	....	....	....	....	....	....	1950-51	1950-51
Roche, Travis	Min., Phx.	4	60	6	14	20	24	....	....	....	....	....	....	2000-01	2006-07
Rochefort, Dave	Det.	1	1	0	0	0	0	....	....	....	....	....	....	1966-67	1966-67
Rochefort, Leon	NYR, Mtl., Phi., L.A., Det., Atl., Van.	15	617	121	147	268	93	39	4	4	8	16	2	1960-61	1975-76
Rochefort, Normand	Que., NYR, T.B.	13	598	39	119	158	570	69	7	5	12	82	....	1980-81	1993-94
● Rockburn, Harvey	Det., Ott.	3	94	4	2	6	254	....	....	....	....	....	....	1929-30	1932-33
● Rodden, Eddie	Chi., Tor., Bos., NYR	4	97	6	14	20	60	2	0	1	1	0	....	1926-27	1930-31
Rodgers, Marc	Det.	1	21	1	1	2	10	....	....	....	....	....	....	1999-00	1999-00
Rodney, Bryan	Car., Edm.	4	34	1	12	13	12	....	....	....	....	....	....	2008-09	2011-12
Roenick, Jeremy	Chi., Phx., Phi., L.A., S.J.	20	1363	513	703	1216	1463	154	53	69	122	115	....	1988-89	2008-09
Roest, Stacy	Det., Min.	5	244	28	48	76	54	3	0	0	0	0	....	1998-99	2002-03
Rogers, John	Min.	2	14	2	4	6	0	....	....	....	....	....	....	1973-74	1974-75
Rogers, Mike	Hfd., NYR, Edm.	7	484	202	317	519	184	17	1	13	14	6	....	1979-80	1985-86
Rohlicek, Jeff	Van.	2	9	0	0	0	8	....	....	....	....	....	....	1987-88	1988-89
Rohlin, Leif	Van.	2	96	8	24	32	40	5	0	0	0	0	....	1995-96	1996-97
Rohloff, Jon	Bos.	3	150	7	25	32	129	10	1	2	3	8	....	1994-95	1996-97
Rohloff, Todd	Wsh., CBJ	2	75	0	6	6	40	....	....	....	....	....	....	2001-02	2003-04
Rolfe, Dale	Bos., L.A., Det., NYR	9	509	25	125	150	556	71	5	24	29	89	....	1959-60	1974-75
Rolston, Brian	N.J., Col., Bos., Min., NYI	17	1256	342	419	761	472	77	20	14	34	38	1	1994-95	2011-12
Romanchych, Larry	Chi., Atl.	6	298	68	97	165	102	7	2	2	4	4	....	1970-71	1976-77

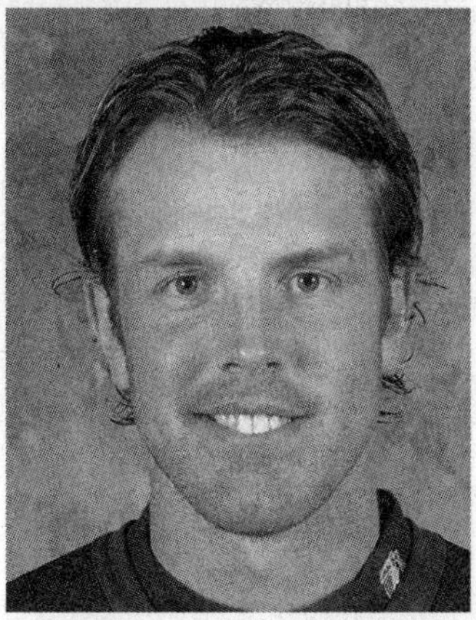
Brad Richards

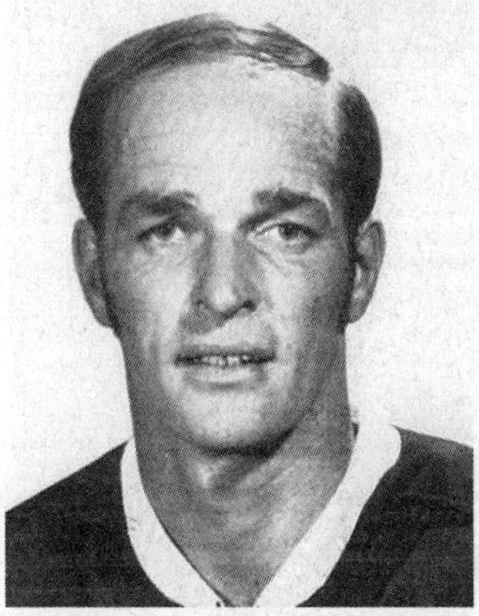
Leon Rochefort

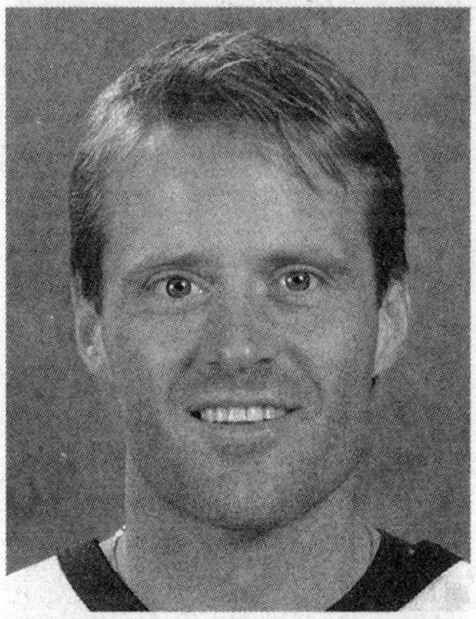
Cliff Ronning

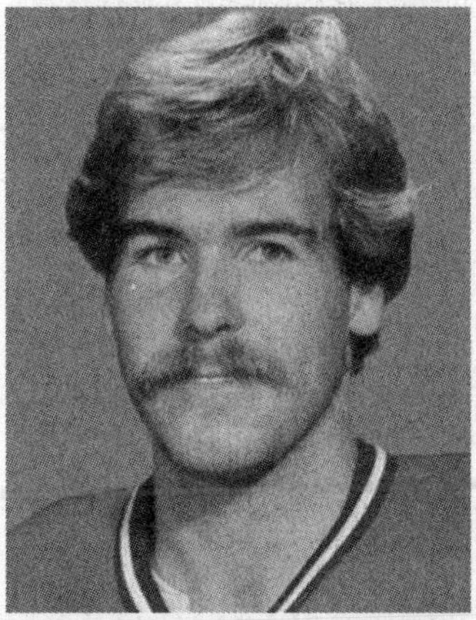
Bill Root

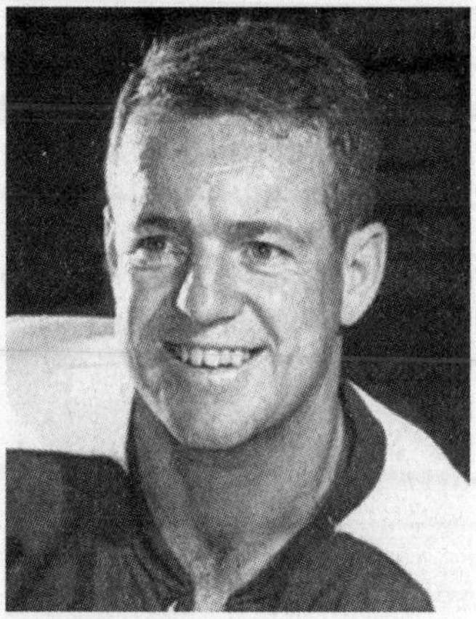

Guy Rousseau

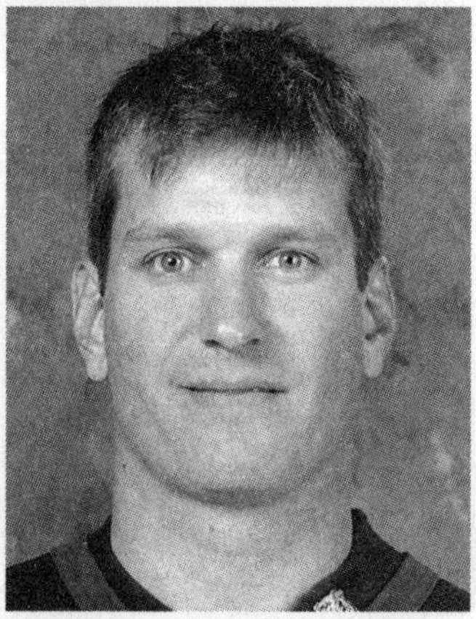

Darren Rumble

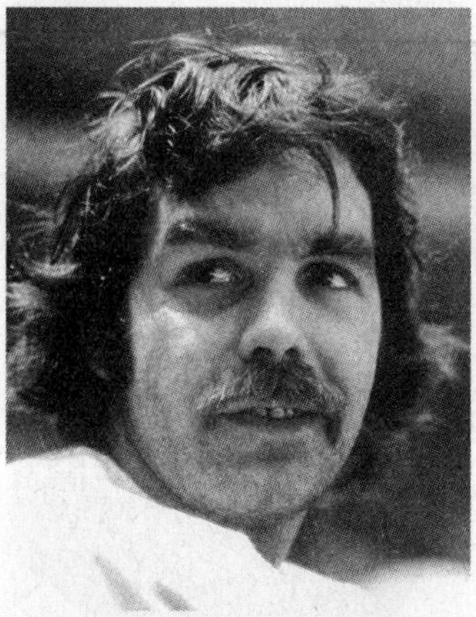

Derek Sanderson

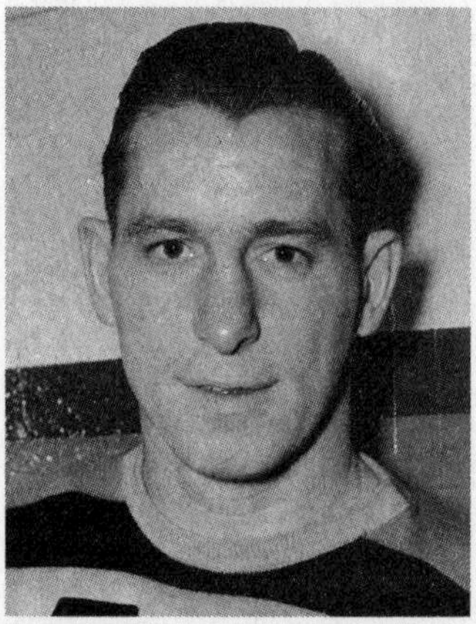

Milt Schimdt

Name	NHL Teams	NHL Seasons	Regular Schedule GP	G	A	TP	PIM	Playoffs GP	G	A	TP	PIM	NHL Cup Wins	First NHL Season	Last NHL Season
Romaniuk, Russell	Wpg., Phi.	5	102	13	14	27	63	2	0	0	0	0	....	1991-92	1995-96
• Rombough, Doug	Buf., NYI, Min.	4	150	24	27	51	80	....	....	....	....	....	....	1972-73	1975-76
Rome, Aaron	Ana., CBJ, Van., Dal.	8	226	6	22	28	185	19	1	1	2	37	1	2006-07	2013-14
Rominski, Dale	T.B.	1	3	0	1	1	2	....	....	....	....	....	....	1999-00	1999-00
• Romnes, Doc	Chi., Tor., NYA	10	360	68	136	204	42	43	7	18	25	4	2	1930-31	1939-40
Ronan, Ed	Mtl., Wpg., Buf.	6	182	13	23	36	101	27	4	3	7	16	1	1991-92	1996-97
• Ronan, Skene	Ott.	1	11	0	0	0	6	....	....	....	....	....	....	1918-19	1918-19
Ronning, Cliff	St.L., Van., Phx., Nsh., L.A., Min., NYI	18	1137	306	563	869	453	126	29	57	86	72	....	1985-86	2003-04
Ronnqvist, Jonas	Ana.	1	38	0	4	4	14	....	....	....	....	....	....	2000-01	2000-01
• Ronson, Len	NYR, Oak.	2	18	2	1	3	10	....	....	....	....	....	....	1960-61	1968-69
Ronty, Paul	Bos., NYR, Mtl.	8	488	101	211	312	103	21	1	7	8	6	....	1947-48	1954-55
Rooney, Steve	Mtl., Wpg., N.J.	5	154	15	13	28	496	25	3	2	5	86	1	1984-85	1988-89
Root, Bill	Mtl., Tor., St.L., Phi.	6	247	11	23	34	180	22	1	2	3	25	....	1982-83	1987-88
Rosa, Pavel	L.A.	4	36	5	13	18	6	....	....	....	....	....	....	1998-99	2003-04
‡ Rosehill, Jay	Tor., Phi.	5	117	5	3	8	352	....	....	....	....	....	....	2009-10	2013-14
• Ross, Art	Mtl.W.	1	3	1	0	1	12	....	....	....	....	....	....	1917-18	1917-18
‡ Ross, Jared	Phi.	2	13	0	0	0	2	9	1	0	1	0	....	2008-09	2009-10
• Ross, Jim	NYR	2	62	2	11	13	29	....	....	....	....	....	....	1951-52	1952-53
• Rossignol, Roly	Det., Mtl.	3	14	3	5	8	6	1	0	0	0	2	....	1943-44	1945-46
Rossiter, Kyle	Fla., Atl.	3	11	0	1	1	9	....	....	....	....	....	....	2001-02	2003-04
Rota, Darcy	Chi., Atl., Van.	11	794	256	239	495	973	60	14	7	21	147	....	1973-74	1983-84
Rota, Randy	Mtl., L.A., K.C., Col.	5	212	38	39	77	60	5	0	1	1	0	....	1972-73	1976-77
• Rothschild, Sam	Mtl.M., Pit., NYA	4	100	8	6	14	25	6	0	0	0	0	1	1924-25	1927-28
• Roulston, Rolly	Det.	3	24	0	6	6	10	....	....	....	....	....	1	1935-36	1937-38
Roulston, Tom	Edm., Pit.	5	195	47	49	96	74	21	2	2	4	2	....	1980-81	1985-86
Roupe, Magnus	Phi.	2	40	3	5	8	42	....	....	....	....	....	....	1987-88	1988-89
Rourke, Allan	Car., NYI, Edm.	4	55	1	4	5	31	....	....	....	....	....	....	2003-04	2007-08
Rouse, Bob	Min., Wsh., Tor., Det., S.J.	17	1061	37	181	218	1559	136	7	21	28	198	2	1983-84	1999-00
Rousseau, Bobby	Mtl., Min., NYR	15	942	245	458	703	359	128	27	57	84	69	4	1960-61	1974-75
Rousseau, Guy	Mtl.	2	4	0	1	1	0	....	....	....	....	....	....	1954-55	1956-57
• Rousseau, Roland	Mtl.	1	2	0	0	0	0	....	....	....	....	....	....	1952-53	1952-53
Routhier, Jean-Marc	Que.	1	8	0	0	0	9	....	....	....	....	....	....	1989-90	1989-90
• Rowe, Bobby	Bos.	1	4	1	0	1	0	....	....	....	....	....	....	1924-25	1924-25
Rowe, Mike	Pit.	3	11	0	0	0	11	....	....	....	....	....	....	1984-85	1986-87
• Rowe, Ron	NYR	1	5	1	0	1	0	....	....	....	....	....	....	1947-48	1947-48
Rowe, Tom	Wsh., Hfd., Det.	7	357	85	100	185	615	3	2	0	2	0	....	1976-77	1982-83
Roy, Andre	Bos., Ott., T.B., Pit., Cgy.	11	515	35	33	68	1169	41	1	3	4	98	1	1995-96	2008-09
‡ Roy, Derek	Buf., Dal., Van., St.L., Nsh., Edm.	11	738	189	335	524	391	49	7	20	27	36	....	2003-04	2014-15
Roy, Jean-Yves	NYR, Ott., Bos.	4	61	12	16	28	26	....	....	....	....	....	....	1994-95	1997-98
Roy, Mathieu	Edm., CBJ, T.B.	6	66	2	11	13	76	....	....	....	....	....	....	2005-06	2012-13
Roy, Stephane	Min.	1	12	1	0	1	0	....	....	....	....	....	....	1987-88	1987-88
Royer, Gaetan	T.B.	1	3	0	0	0	2	....	....	....	....	....	....	2001-02	2001-02
Royer, Remi	Chi.	1	18	0	0	0	67	....	....	....	....	....	....	1998-99	1998-99
• Rozzini, Gino	Bos.	1	31	5	10	15	20	6	1	2	3	6	....	1944-45	1944-45
Rucchin, Steve	Ana., NYR, Atl.	12	735	171	318	489	164	37	9	8	17	12	....	1994-95	2006-07
Rucinski, Mike	Chi.	2	1	0	0	0	0	2	0	0	0	0	....	1987-88	1988-89
Rucinski, Mike	Car.	3	26	0	2	2	10	....	....	....	....	....	....	1997-98	2000-01
Rucinsky, Martin	Edm., Que., Col., Mtl., Dal., NYR, St.L., Van.	16	961	241	371	612	821	37	9	5	14	24	....	1991-92	2007-08
• Ruelle, Bernie	Det.	1	2	1	0	1	0	....	....	....	....	....	....	1943-44	1943-44
Ruff, Jason	St.L., T.B.	2	14	3	3	6	10	....	....	....	....	....	....	1992-93	1993-94
Ruff, Lindy	Buf., NYR	12	691	105	195	300	1264	52	11	13	24	193	....	1979-80	1990-91
Ruhnke, Kent	Bos.	1	2	0	1	1	0	....	....	....	....	....	....	1975-76	1975-76
Rumble, Darren	Phi., Ott., St.L., T.B.	8	193	10	26	36	216	....	....	....	....	....	1	1990-91	2003-04
‡ Rundblad, David	Ott., Phx., Chi.	5	113	4	21	25	30	8	0	0	0	4	1	2011-12	**2015-16**
Rundqvist, Thomas	Mtl.	1	2	0	1	1	0	....	....	....	....	....	....	1984-85	1984-85
• Runge, Paul	Bos., Mtl.M., Mtl.	7	140	18	22	40	57	7	0	0	0	6	....	1930-31	1937-38
Ruotsalainen, Reijo	NYR, Edm., N.J.	7	446	107	237	344	180	86	15	32	47	44	2	1981-82	1989-90
Rupp, Duane	NYR, Tor., Min., Pit.	10	374	24	93	117	220	10	2	2	4	8	....	1962-63	1972-73
Rupp, Mike	N.J., Phx., CBJ, Pit., NYR, Min.	11	610	54	45	99	855	67	2	6	8	83	1	2002-03	2013-14
Ruskowski, Terry	Chi., L.A., Pit., Min.	10	630	113	313	426	1354	21	1	6	7	86	....	1979-80	1988-89
Russell, Cam	Chi., Col.	10	396	9	21	30	872	44	0	5	5	16	....	1989-90	1998-99
• Russell, Church	NYR	3	90	20	16	36	12	....	....	....	....	....	....	1945-46	1947-48
Russell, Phil	Chi., Atl., Cgy., N.J., Buf.	15	1016	99	325	424	2038	73	4	22	26	202	....	1972-73	1986-87
Russell, Ryan	CBJ	1	41	2	0	2	2	....	....	....	....	....	....	2011-12	2011-12
Ruuttu, Christian	Buf., Chi., Van.	9	621	134	298	432	714	42	4	9	13	49	....	1986-87	1994-95
Ruutu, Jarkko	Van., Pit., Ott., Ana.	11	652	58	84	142	1078	58	5	5	10	114	....	1999-00	2010-11
‡ Ruutu, Tuomo	Chi., Car., N.J.	12	735	148	198	346	596	16	1	3	4	8	....	2003-04	**2015-16**
‡ Ruzicka, Stefan	Phi.	3	55	4	13	17	47	....	....	....	....	....	....	2005-06	2007-08
Ruzicka, Vladimir	Edm., Bos., Ott.	5	233	82	85	167	129	30	4	14	18	2	....	1989-90	1993-94
Ryan, Matt	L.A.	1	12	0	1	1	2	....	....	....	....	....	....	2005-06	2005-06
Ryan, Michael	Buf., Car.	3	83	7	8	15	34	....	....	....	....	....	....	2006-07	2008-09
Ryan, Prestin	Van.	1	1	0	0	0	2	....	....	....	....	....	....	2005-06	2005-06
Ryan, Terry	Mtl.	3	8	0	0	0	36	....	....	....	....	....	....	1996-97	1998-99
Rychel, Warren	Chi., L.A., Tor., Col., Ana.	9	406	38	39	77	1422	70	8	13	21	121	1	1988-89	1998-99
Rycroft, Mark	St.L., Col.	4	226	21	25	46	113	3	0	0	0	2	....	2001-02	2006-07
Ryder, Michael	Mtl., Bos., Dal., N.J.	11	806	237	247	484	353	75	21	24	45	26	1	2003-04	2014-15
Rymsha, Andy	Que.	1	6	0	0	0	23	....	....	....	....	....	....	1991-92	1991-92
• Rypien, Rick	Van.	6	119	9	7	16	226	17	0	3	3	47	....	2005-06	2010-11
Ryznar, Jason	N.J.	1	8	0	0	0	2	....	....	....	....	....	....	2005-06	2005-06

S

Name	NHL Teams	NHL Seasons	Regular Schedule GP	G	A	TP	PIM	Playoffs GP	G	A	TP	PIM	NHL Cup Wins	First NHL Season	Last NHL Season
Saarinen, Simo	NYR	1	8	0	0	0	0	....	....	....	....	....	....	1984-85	1984-85
Sabol, Shaun	Phi.	1	2	0	0	0	0	....	....	....	....	....	....	1989-90	1989-90
Sabourin, Bob	Tor.	1	1	0	0	0	2	....	....	....	....	....	....	1951-52	1951-52
Sabourin, Gary	St.L., Tor., Cal., Cle.	10	627	169	188	357	397	62	19	11	30	58	....	1967-68	1976-77
Sabourin, Ken	Cgy., Wsh.	4	74	2	8	10	201	12	0	0	0	34	....	1988-89	1991-92
Sacco, David	Tor., Ana.	3	35	5	13	18	22	....	....	....	....	....	....	1993-94	1995-96
Sacco, Joe	Tor., Ana., NYI, Wsh., Phi.	13	738	94	119	213	421	26	2	0	2	8	....	1990-91	2002-03
Sacharuk, Larry	NYR, St.L.	5	151	29	33	62	42	2	1	1	2	2	....	1972-73	1976-77
Safronov, Kirill	Phx., Atl.	2	35	2	2	4	16	....	....	....	....	....	....	2001-02	2002-03
Saganiuk, Rocky	Tor., Pit.	6	259	57	65	122	201	6	1	0	1	15	....	1978-79	1983-84
Sakic, Joe	Que., Col.	20	1378	625	1016	1641	614	172	84	104	188	78	2	1988-89	2008-09
‡ Salcido, Brian	Ana.	1	2	0	1	1	0	....	....	....	....	....	....	2008-09	2008-09
• Salei, Ruslan	Ana., Fla., Col., Det.	14	917	45	159	204	1065	62	7	9	16	52	....	1996-97	2010-11
Saleski, Don	Phi., Col.	9	543	128	125	253	629	82	13	17	30	131	2	1971-72	1979-80
‡ Salmela, Anssi	N.J., Atl.	3	112	4	17	21	44	....	....	....	....	....	....	2008-09	2010-11
Salmelainen, Tony	Edm., Chi.	2	70	6	12	18	30	....	....	....	....	....	....	2003-04	2006-07
Salming, Borje	Tor., Det.	17	1148	150	637	787	1344	81	12	37	49	91	....	1973-74	1989-90
Salo, Sami	Ott., Van., T.B.	15	878	99	240	339	286	102	12	19	31	18	....	1998-99	2013-14
Salomonsson, Andreas	N.J., Wsh.	2	71	5	9	14	36	4	0	1	1	0	....	2001-02	2002-03
Salovaara, Barry	Det.	2	90	2	13	15	70	....	....	....	....	....	....	1974-75	1975-76
Salvador, Bryce	St.L., N.J.	13	786	24	86	110	696	74	7	11	18	64	....	2000-01	2014-15
Salvian, Dave	NYI	1	....	....	....	....	....	1	0	1	1	2	....	1976-77	1976-77
Samis, Phil	Tor.	2	2	0	0	0	0	5	0	1	1	2	1	1947-48	1949-50
Sampson, Gary	Wsh.	4	105	13	22	35	25	12	1	0	1	0	....	1983-84	1986-87
‡ Samson, Jerome	Car.	3	46	2	7	9	18	....	....	....	....	....	....	2009-10	2011-12
Samsonov, Sergei	Bos., Edm., Mtl., Chi., Car., Fla.	13	888	235	336	571	209	76	18	29	47	20	....	1997-98	2010-11
Samuelsson, Kjell	NYR, Phi., Pit., T.B.	14	813	48	138	186	1225	123	4	20	24	178	1	1985-86	1998-99
Samuelsson, Martin	Bos.	2	14	0	1	1	2	....	....	....	....	....	....	2002-03	2003-04
Samuelsson, Mikael	S.J., NYR, Pit., Fla., Det., Van.	13	699	149	197	346	370	104	23	37	60	62	1	2000-01	2013-14
Samuelsson, Ulf	Hfd., Pit., NYR, Det., Phi.	16	1080	57	275	332	2453	132	7	27	34	272	2	1984-85	1999-00
Sandelin, Scott	Mtl., Phi., Min.	4	25	0	4	4	2	....	....	....	....	....	....	1986-87	1991-92
Sanderson, Derek	Bos., NYR, St.L., Van., Pit.	13	598	202	250	452	911	56	18	12	30	187	2	1965-66	1977-78
Sanderson, Geoff	Hfd., Car., Van., Buf., CBJ, Phx., Phi., Edm.	17	1104	355	345	700	511	55	9	10	19	32	....	1990-91	2007-08
Sandford, Ed	Bos., Det., Chi.	9	502	106	145	251	355	42	13	11	24	27	....	1947-48	1955-56
Sandlak, Jim	Van., Hfd.	11	549	110	119	229	821	33	7	10	17	30	....	1985-86	1995-96
• Sands, Charlie	Tor., Bos., Mtl., NYR	12	427	99	109	208	58	34	6	6	12	4	1	1932-33	1943-44
Sandstrom, Tomas	NYR, L.A., Pit., Det., Ana.	15	983	394	462	856	1193	139	32	49	81	183	1	1984-85	1998-99
Sandwith, Terran	Edm.	1	8	0	0	0	6	....	....	....	....	....	....	1997-98	1997-98

Name	NHL Teams	NHL Seasons	Regular Schedule GP	G	A	TP	PIM	Playoffs GP	G	A	TP	PIM	NHL Cup Wins	First NHL Season	Last NHL Season
‡ Sanguinetti, Bobby	NYR, Car.	3	45	2	4	6	8	....	....	....	....	....	....	2009-10	2012-13
Sanipass, Everett	Chi., Que.	5	164	25	34	59	358	5	2	0	2	4	....	1986-87	1990-91
‡ Santala, Tommi	Atl., Van.	2	63	2	7	9	46	1	0	0	0	0	....	2003-04	2006-07
Santorelli, Mike	Nsh., Fla., Wpg., Van., Tor., Ana.	8	406	64	74	138	78	4	1	0	1	0	....	2008-09	**2015-16**
Saprykin, Oleg	Cgy., Phx., Ott.	7	325	55	82	137	240	41	4	4	8	18	....	1999-00	2006-07
Sarault, Yves	Mtl., Cgy., Col., Ott., Atl., Nsh.	8	106	10	10	20	51	5	0	0	0	2	....	1994-95	2001-02
Sargent, Gary	L.A., Min.	8	402	61	161	222	273	20	5	7	12	8	....	1975-76	1982-83
Sarich, Cory	Buf., T.B., Cgy., Col.	15	969	21	137	158	1089	57	0	7	7	45	1	1998-99	2013-14
Sarner, Craig	Bos.	1	7	0	0	0	0	....	....	....	....	....	....	1974-75	1974-75
Sarno, Peter	Edm., CBJ	2	7	1	0	1	2	....	....	....	....	....	....	2003-04	2005-06
Sarrazin, Dick	Phi.	3	100	20	35	55	22	4	0	0	0	0	....	1968-69	1971-72
Sasakamoose, Fred	Chi.	1	11	0	0	0	6	....	....	....	....	....	....	1953-54	1953-54
Sasser, Grant	Pit.	1	3	0	0	0	0	....	....	....	....	....	....	1983-84	1983-84
Satan, Miroslav	Edm., Buf., NYI, Pit., Bos.	14	1050	363	372	735	464	86	21	33	54	41	1	1995-96	2009-10
Sather, Glen	Bos., Pit., NYR, St.L., Mtl., Min.	10	658	80	113	193	724	72	1	5	6	86	....	1966-67	1975-76
Sauer, Kurt	Ana., Col., Phx.	7	357	5	28	33	250	43	2	1	3	18	....	2002-03	2009-10
Sauer, Michael	NYR	3	98	4	14	18	96	5	0	1	1	0	....	2008-09	2011-12
Saunders, Bernie	Que.	2	10	0	1	1	8	....	....	....	....	....	....	1979-80	1980-81
Saunders, David	Van.	1	56	7	13	20	10	....	....	....	....	....	....	1987-88	1987-88
• Saunders, Ted	Ott.	1	18	1	3	4	4	....	....	....	....	....	....	1933-34	1933-34
Sauve, Jean-Francois	Buf., Que.	7	290	65	138	203	114	36	9	12	21	10	....	1980-81	1986-87
Sauve, Max	Bos.	1	1	0	0	0	0	....	....	....	....	....	....	2011-12	2011-12
‡ Sauve, Yann	Van.	2	8	0	0	0	0	....	....	....	....	....	....	2010-11	2013-14
Savage, Andre	Bos., Phi.	4	66	10	14	24	14	....	....	....	....	....	....	1998-99	2002-03
Savage, Brian	Mtl., Phx., St.L., Phi.	12	674	192	167	359	321	39	3	8	11	12	....	1993-94	2005-06
Savage, Joel	Buf.	1	3	0	1	1	0	....	....	....	....	....	....	1990-91	1990-91
Savage, Reggie	Wsh., Que.	3	34	5	7	12	28	....	....	....	....	....	....	1990-91	1993-94
• Savage, Tony	Bos., Mtl.	1	49	1	5	6	6	2	0	0	0	0	....	1934-35	1934-35
Savard, Andre	Bos., Buf., Que.	12	790	211	271	482	411	85	13	18	31	77	....	1973-74	1984-85
Savard, Denis	Chi., Mtl., T.B.	17	1196	473	865	1338	1336	169	66	109	175	256	1	1980-81	1996-97
Savard, Jean	Chi., Hfd.	3	43	7	12	19	29	....	....	....	....	....	....	1977-78	1979-80
Savard, Marc	NYR, Cgy., Atl., Bos.	13	807	207	499	706	737	25	8	14	22	22	1	1997-98	2010-11
Savard, Serge	Mtl., Wpg.	17	1040	106	333	439	592	130	19	49	68	88	8	1966-67	1982-83
Savoia, Ryan	Pit.	1	3	0	0	0	0	....	....	....	....	....	....	1998-99	1998-99
Sawada, Raymond	Dal.	3	11	1	0	1	0	....	....	....	....	....	....	2008-09	2010-11
Sawyer, Kevin	St.L., Bos., Phx., Ana.	6	110	3	3	6	403	....	....	....	....	....	....	1995-96	2002-03
Scamurra, Peter	Wsh.	4	132	8	25	33	59	....	....	....	....	....	....	1975-76	1979-80
Scatchard, Dave	Van., NYI, Bos., Phx., Nsh., St.L.	11	659	128	141	269	1040	17	2	2	4	34	....	1997-98	2010-11
Sceviour, Darin	Chi.	1	1	0	0	0	0	....	....	....	....	....	....	1986-87	1986-87
Schaefer, Peter	Van., Ott., Bos.	9	572	99	162	261	200	63	6	18	24	34	....	1998-99	2010-11
• Schaeffer, Butch	Chi.	1	5	0	0	0	6	....	....	....	....	....	....	1936-37	1936-37
Schamehorn, Kevin	Det., L.A.	3	10	0	0	0	17	....	....	....	....	....	....	1976-77	1980-81
Schastlivy, Petr	Ott., Ana.	5	129	18	22	40	30	1	0	0	0	0	....	1999-00	2003-04
Schella, John	Van.	2	115	2	18	20	224	....	....	....	....	....	....	1970-71	1971-72
• Scherza, Chuck	Bos., NYR	2	36	6	6	12	35	....	....	....	....	....	....	1943-44	1944-45
Schinkel, Ken	NYR, Pit.	12	636	127	198	325	163	19	7	2	9	4	....	1959-60	1972-73
Schlegel, Brad	Wsh., Cgy.	3	48	1	8	9	10	7	0	1	1	2	....	1991-92	1993-94
Schliebener, Andy	Van.	3	84	2	11	13	74	6	0	0	0	0	....	1981-82	1984-85
Schmautz, Bobby	Chi., Van., Bos., Edm., Col.	13	764	271	286	557	988	84	28	33	61	92	....	1967-68	1980-81
• Schmautz, Cliff	Buf., Phi.	1	56	13	19	32	33	....	....	....	....	....	....	1970-71	1970-71
Schmidt, Chris	L.A.	1	10	0	2	2	5	....	....	....	....	....	....	2002-03	2002-03
• Schmidt, Clarence	Bos.	1	7	1	0	1	2	....	....	....	....	....	....	1943-44	1943-44
• Schmidt, Jackie	Bos.	1	45	6	7	13	6	5	0	0	0	0	....	1942-43	1942-43
• Schmidt, Milt	Bos.	16	776	229	346	575	466	86	24	25	49	60	2	1936-37	1954-55
Schmidt, Norm	Pit.	4	125	23	33	56	73	....	....	....	....	....	....	1983-84	1987-88
• Schmidt, Otto	Bos.	1	2	0	0	0	0	....	....	....	....	....	....	1943-44	1943-44
Schnabel, Robert	Nsh.	3	22	0	3	3	34	....	....	....	....	....	....	2001-02	2003-04
• Schnarr, Werner	Bos.	2	26	0	0	0	0	....	....	....	....	....	....	1924-25	1925-26
Schneider, Andy	Ott.	1	10	0	0	0	15	....	....	....	....	....	....	1993-94	1993-94
Schneider, Mathieu	Mtl., NYI, Tor., NYR, L.A., Det., Ana., Atl., Van., Phx.	21	1289	223	520	743	1245	114	11	43	54	155	1	1987-88	2009-10
• Schock, Danny	Bos., Phi.	2	20	1	2	3	0	1	0	0	0	0	1	1969-70	1970-71
Schock, Ron	Bos., St.L., Pit., Buf.	15	909	166	351	517	260	55	4	16	20	29	....	1963-64	1977-78
Schoenfeld, Jim	Buf., Det., Bos.	13	719	51	204	255	1132	75	3	13	16	151	....	1972-73	1984-85
Schofield, Dwight	Det., Mtl., St.L., Wsh., Pit., Wpg.	7	211	8	22	30	631	9	0	0	0	55	....	1976-77	1987-88
Schreiber, Wally	Min.	2	41	8	10	18	12	....	....	....	....	....	....	1987-88	1988-89
Schremp, Rob	Edm., NYI, Atl.	5	114	20	34	54	26	....	....	....	....	....	....	2006-07	2010-11
• Schriner, Sweeney	NYA, Tor.	11	484	201	204	405	148	59	18	11	29	54	2	1934-35	1945-46
Schubert, Christoph	Ott., Atl.	5	315	25	47	72	263	31	0	2	2	34	....	2005-06	2009-10
Schulte, Paxton	Que., Cgy.	2	2	0	0	0	4	....	....	....	....	....	....	1993-94	1996-97
Schultz, Dave	Phi., L.A., Pit., Buf.	9	535	79	121	200	2294	73	8	12	20	412	2	1971-72	1979-80
‡ Schultz, Jesse	Van.	1	2	0	0	0	0	....	....	....	....	....	....	2006-07	2006-07
Schultz, Ray	NYI	6	45	0	4	4	155	2	0	0	0	2	....	1997-98	2002-03
Schurman, Maynard	Hfd.	1	7	0	0	0	0	....	....	....	....	....	....	1979-80	1979-80
Schutt, Rod	Mtl., Pit., Tor.	8	286	77	92	169	177	22	8	6	14	26	....	1977-78	1985-86
Scissons, Scott	NYI	3	2	0	0	0	0	1	0	0	0	0	....	1990-91	1993-94
• Sclisizzi, Enio	Det., Chi.	6	81	12	11	23	26	13	0	0	0	6	1	1946-47	1952-53
• Scott, Ganton	Tor., Ham., Mtl.M.	3	57	1	1	2	0	....	....	....	....	....	....	1922-23	1924-25
Scott, John	Min., Chi., NYR, Buf., S.J., Ari., Mtl.	8	286	5	6	11	544	4	0	0	0	22	....	2008-09	**2015-16**
• Scott, Laurie	NYA, NYR	2	62	6	3	9	28	....	....	....	....	....	....	1926-27	1927-28
Scott, Richard	NYR	2	10	0	0	0	28	....	....	....	....	....	....	2001-02	2003-04
Scoville, Darrel	Cgy., CBJ	3	16	0	1	1	12	....	....	....	....	....	....	1999-00	2003-04
Scremin, Claudio	S.J.	2	17	0	1	1	29	....	....	....	....	....	....	1991-92	1992-93
Scruton, Howard	L.A.	1	4	0	4	4	9	....	....	....	....	....	....	1982-83	1982-83
Seabrooke, Glen	Phi.	3	19	1	6	7	4	....	....	....	....	....	....	1986-87	1988-89
Secord, Al	Bos., Chi., Tor., Phi.	12	766	273	222	495	2093	102	21	34	55	382	....	1978-79	1989-90
Sedlbauer, Ron	Van., Chi., Tor.	7	430	143	86	229	210	19	1	3	4	27	....	1974-75	1980-81
Seftel, Steve	Wsh.	1	4	0	0	0	2	....	....	....	....	....	....	1990-91	1990-91
‡ Segal, Brandon	T.B., L.A., Dal., NYR	5	103	11	11	22	85	....	....	....	....	....	....	2008-09	2012-13
Seguin, Dan	Min., Van.	2	37	2	6	8	50	....	....	....	....	....	....	1970-71	1973-74
Seguin, Steve	L.A.	1	5	0	0	0	9	....	....	....	....	....	....	1984-85	1984-85
• Seibert, Earl	NYR, Chi., Det.	15	645	89	187	276	746	66	11	8	19	76	2	1931-32	1945-46
Seiling, Ric	Buf., Det.	10	738	179	208	387	573	62	14	14	28	36	....	1977-78	1986-87
Seiling, Rod	Tor., NYR, Wsh., St.L., Atl.	17	979	62	269	331	601	77	4	8	12	55	....	1962-63	1978-79
Sejba, Jiri	Buf.	1	11	0	2	2	8	....	....	....	....	....	....	1990-91	1990-91
Sejna, Peter	St.L.	4	49	7	4	11	12	....	....	....	....	....	....	2002-03	2006-07
‡ Sekac, Jiri	Mtl., Ana., Chi., Ari.	2	108	10	19	29	38	7	0	0	0	2	....	2014-15	**2015-16**
Sekeras, Lubomir	Min., Dal.	4	213	18	53	71	122	15	1	1	2	6	....	2000-01	2003-04
Selanne, Teemu	Wpg., Ana., S.J., Col.	21	1451	684	773	1457	660	130	44	44	88	62	1	1992-93	2013-14
Selby, Brit	Tor., Phi., St.L.	8	350	55	62	117	163	16	1	1	2	8	....	1964-65	1971-72
Self, Steve	Wsh.	1	3	0	0	0	0	....	....	....	....	....	....	1976-77	1976-77
Selivanov, Alex	T.B., Edm., CBJ	7	459	121	114	235	379	13	2	3	5	16	....	1994-95	2000-01
Sellars, Luke	Atl.	1	1	0	0	0	2	....	....	....	....	....	....	2001-02	2001-02
Selmser, Sean	CBJ	1	1	0	0	0	5	....	....	....	....	....	....	2000-01	2000-01
Selwood, Brad	Tor., L.A.	3	163	7	40	47	153	6	0	0	0	4	....	1970-71	1979-80
Semak, Alexander	N.J., T.B., NYI, Van.	6	289	83	91	174	187	8	1	1	2	0	....	1991-92	1996-97
Semchuk, Brandy	L.A.	1	1	0	0	0	2	....	....	....	....	....	....	1992-93	1992-93
• Semenko, Dave	Edm., Hfd., Tor.	9	575	65	88	153	1175	73	6	6	12	208	2	1979-80	1987-88
‡ Semenov, Alexei	Edm., Fla., S.J.	6	211	7	26	33	249	8	0	0	0	2	....	2002-03	2008-09
Semenov, Anatoli	Edm., T.B., Van., Ana., Phi., Buf.	8	362	68	126	194	122	49	9	13	22	12	....	1989-90	1996-97
‡ Semin, Alexander	Wsh., Car., Mtl.	11	650	239	278	517	582	51	15	19	34	46	....	2003-04	**2015-16**
• Senick, George	NYR	1	13	2	3	5	8	....	....	....	....	....	....	1952-53	1952-53
Seppa, Jyrki	Wpg.	1	13	0	2	2	6	....	....	....	....	....	....	1983-84	1983-84
Serafini, Ron	Cal.	1	2	0	0	0	2	....	....	....	....	....	....	1973-74	1973-74
Serowik, Jeff	Tor., Bos., Pit.	3	28	0	6	6	16	....	....	....	....	....	....	1990-91	1998-99
Servinis, George	Min.	1	5	0	0	0	0	....	....	....	....	....	....	1987-88	1987-88
‡ Sestito, Tim	Edm., N.J.	7	101	0	8	8	55	1	0	0	0	0	....	2008-09	2014-15
Sevcik, Jaroslav	Que.	1	13	0	2	2	2	....	....	....	....	....	....	1989-90	1989-90
Severson, Cam	Ana., CBJ	3	37	3	0	3	63	1	0	0	0	0	....	2002-03	2005-06
Severyn, Brent	Que., Fla., NYI, Col., Ana., Dal.	7	328	10	30	40	825	8	0	0	0	12	1	1989-90	1998-99
Sevigny, Pierre	Mtl., NYR	4	78	4	5	9	64	3	0	1	1	0	....	1993-94	1997-98
‡ Sexton, Dan	Ana.	2	88	13	19	32	20	1	0	0	0	2	....	2009-10	2010-11

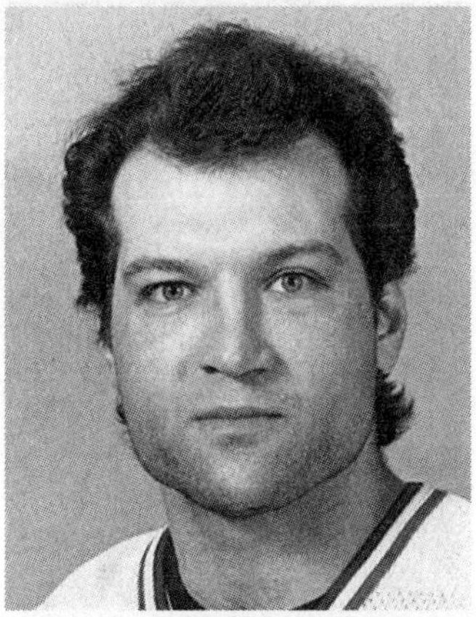

Dave Semenko

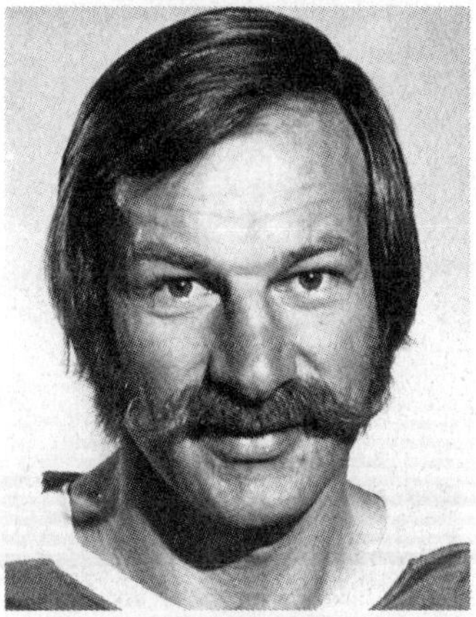

Eddie Shack

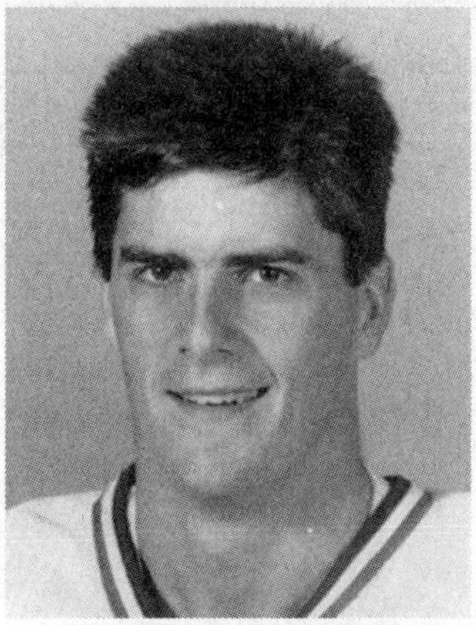

Brad Shaw

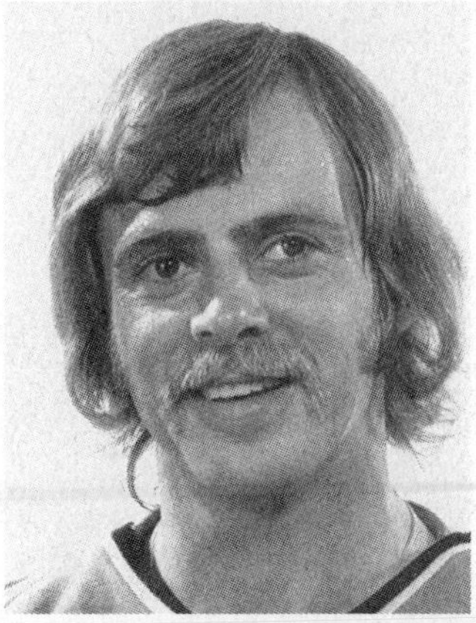

Danny Shock

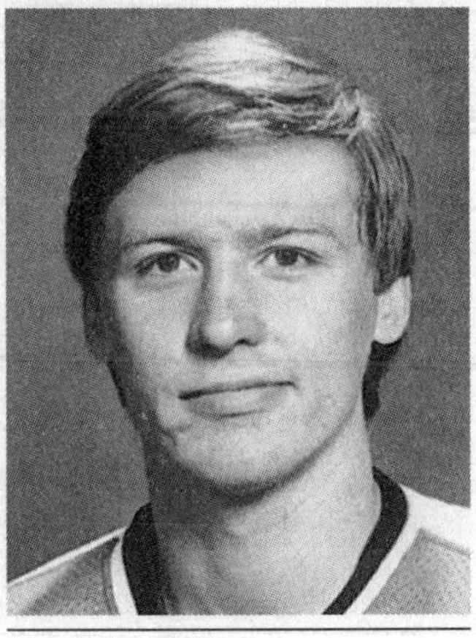

Ilkka Sinisalo

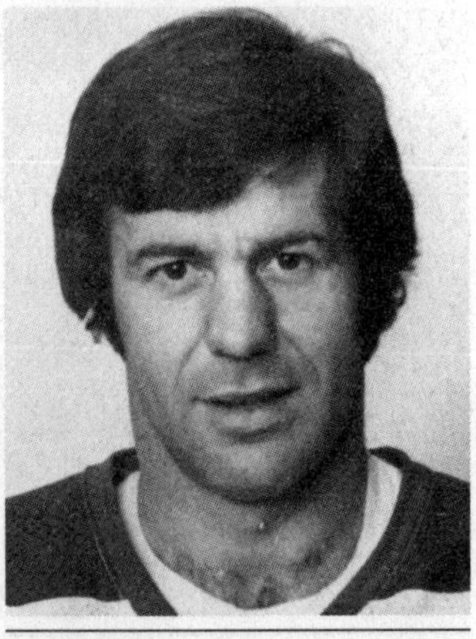

Lars-Erik Sjoberg

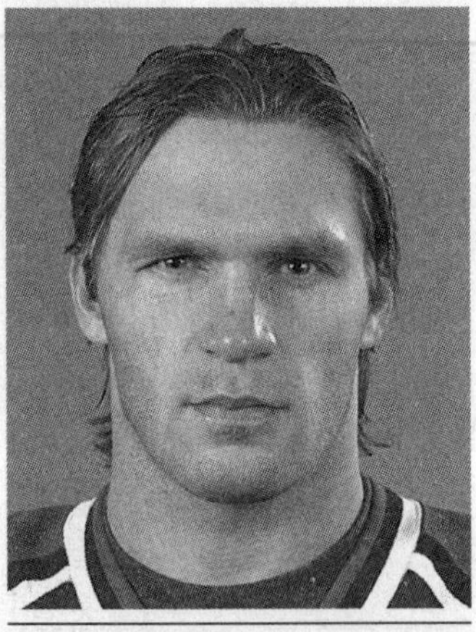

Karlis Skrastins

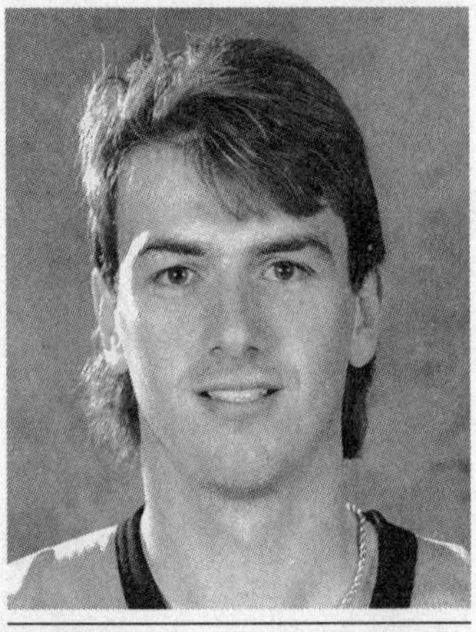

John Slaney

			Regular Schedule					Playoffs							
Name	NHL Teams	NHL Seasons	GP	G	A	TP	PIM	GP	G	A	TP	PIM	NHL Cup Wins	First NHL Season	Last NHL Season
Shack, Eddie	NYR, Tor., Bos., L.A., Buf., Pit.	17	1047	239	226	465	1437	74	6	7	13	151	4	1958-59	1974-75
• Shack, Joe	NYR	2	70	9	27	36	20	....	....	....	....	....	....	1942-43	1944-45
Shafranov, Konstantin	St.L.	1	5	2	1	3	0	....	....	....	....	....	....	1996-97	1996-97
Shakes, Paul	Cal.	1	21	0	4	4	12	....	....	....	....	....	....	1973-74	1973-74
Shaldybin, Yevgeny	Bos.	1	3	1	0	1	0	....	....	....	....	....	....	1996-97	1996-97
Shanahan, Brendan	N.J., St.L., Hfd., Det., NYR	21	1524	656	698	1354	2489	184	60	74	134	279	3	1987-88	2008-09
Shanahan, Sean	Mtl., Col., Bos.	3	40	1	3	4	47	....	....	....	....	....	....	1975-76	1977-78
Shand, Dave	Atl., Tor., Wsh.	8	421	19	84	103	544	26	1	2	3	83	....	1976-77	1984-85
Shank, Daniel	Det., Hfd.	3	77	13	14	27	175	5	0	0	0	22	....	1989-90	1991-92
• Shannon, Chuck	NYA	1	4	0	0	0	2	....	....	....	....	....	....	1939-40	1939-40
Shannon, Darrin	Buf., Wpg., Phx.	10	506	87	163	250	344	45	7	10	17	38	....	1988-89	1997-98
Shannon, Darryl	Tor., Wpg., Buf., Atl., Cgy., Mtl.	13	544	28	111	139	523	29	4	7	11	16	....	1988-89	2000-01
• Shannon, Gerry	Ott., St.L., Bos., Mtl.M.	5	180	23	29	52	80	9	0	1	1	2	....	1933-34	1937-38
‡ Shannon, Ryan	Ana., Van., Ott., T.B.	6	305	35	64	99	90	13	0	0	0	6	1	2006-07	2011-12
Shantz, Jeff	Chi., Cgy., Col.	10	642	72	139	211	341	44	5	8	13	24	....	1993-94	2002-03
Sharifijanov, Vadim	N.J., Van.	3	92	16	21	37	50	4	0	0	0	0	....	1996-97	1999-00
Sharp, MacGregor	Ana.	1	8	0	0	0	0	....	....	....	....	....	....	2009-10	2009-10
Sharples, Jeff	Det.	3	105	14	35	49	70	7	0	3	3	6	....	1986-87	1988-89
Sharpley, Glen	Min., Chi.	6	389	117	161	278	199	27	7	11	18	24	....	1976-77	1981-82
Shaunessy, Scott	Que.	2	7	0	0	0	23	....	....	....	....	....	....	1986-87	1988-89
Shaw, Brad	Hfd., Ott., Wsh., St.L.	11	377	22	137	159	208	23	4	8	12	6	....	1985-86	1998-99
Shaw, David	Que., NYR, Edm., Min., Bos., T.B.	16	769	41	153	194	906	45	3	9	12	81	....	1982-83	1997-98
• Shay, Norm	Bos., Tor.	2	53	5	3	8	34	....	....	....	....	....	....	1924-25	1925-26
• Shea, Pat	Chi.	1	10	1	0	1	0	....	....	....	....	....	....	1931-32	1931-32
Shearer, Rob	Col.	1	2	0	0	0	0	....	....	....	....	....	....	2000-01	2000-01
Shedden, Doug	Pit., Det., Que., Tor.	8	416	139	186	325	176	....	....	....	....	....	....	1981-82	1990-91
Sheehan, Bobby	Mtl., Cal., Chi., Det., NYR, Col., L.A.	9	310	48	63	111	40	25	4	3	7	8	1	1969-70	1981-82
Sheehy, Neil	Cgy., Hfd., Wsh.	9	379	18	47	65	1311	54	0	3	3	241	....	1983-84	1991-92
Sheehy, Tim	Det., Hfd.	2	27	2	1	3	0	....	....	....	....	....	....	1977-78	1979-80
Shelley, Jody	CBJ, S.J., NYR, Phi.	12	627	18	36	54	1538	9	0	0	0	4	....	2000-01	2012-13
Shelton, Doug	Chi.	1	5	0	1	1	2	....	....	....	....	....	....	1967-68	1967-68
• Sheppard, Frank	Det.	1	8	1	1	2	0	....	....	....	....	....	....	1927-28	1927-28
Sheppard, Gregg	Bos., Pit.	10	657	205	293	498	243	82	32	40	72	31	....	1972-73	1981-82
‡ Sheppard, James	Min., S.J., NYR	6	394	23	68	91	192	37	3	6	9	22	....	2007-08	2014-15
• Sheppard, Johnny	Det., NYA, Bos., Chi.	8	308	68	58	126	224	10	0	0	0	0	1	1926-27	1933-34
Sheppard, Ray	Buf., NYR, Det., S.J., Fla., Car.	13	817	357	300	657	212	81	30	20	50	21	....	1987-88	1999-00
• Sherf, John	Det.	5	19	0	0	0	8	8	0	1	1	2	1	1935-36	1943-44
• Shero, Fred	NYR	3	145	6	14	20	137	13	0	2	2	8	....	1947-48	1949-50
• Sherritt, Gordon	Det.	1	8	0	0	0	12	....	....	....	....	....	....	1943-44	1943-44
Sherven, Gord	Edm., Min., Hfd.	5	97	13	22	35	33	3	0	0	0	0	....	1983-84	1987-88
Shevalier, Jeff	L.A., T.B.	3	32	5	9	14	8	....	....	....	....	....	....	1994-95	1999-00
• Shewchuk, Jack	Bos.	6	187	9	19	28	160	20	0	1	1	19	1	1938-39	1944-45
• Shibicky, Alex	NYR	8	324	110	91	201	161	39	12	12	24	12	1	1935-36	1945-46
• Shields, Al	Ott., Phi., NYA, Mtl.M., Bos.	11	459	42	46	88	637	17	0	1	1	14	1	1927-28	1937-38
• Shill, Bill	Bos.	3	79	21	13	34	18	7	1	2	3	2	....	1942-43	1946-47
• Shill, Jack	Tor., Bos., NYA, Chi.	6	160	15	20	35	70	25	1	6	7	23	1	1933-34	1938-39
‡ Shinnimin, Brendan	Ari.	1	12	0	1	1	8	....	....	....	....	....	....	2014-15	2014-15
• Shinske, Rick	Cle., St.L.	3	63	5	16	21	10	....	....	....	....	....	....	1976-77	1978-79
Shires, Jim	Det., St.L., Pit.	3	56	3	6	9	32	....	....	....	....	....	....	1970-71	1972-73
‡ Shirokov, Sergei	Van.	2	8	1	0	1	2	....	....	....	....	....	....	2009-10	2010-11
Shishkanov, Timofei	Nsh., St.L.	2	24	3	2	5	6	....	....	....	....	....	....	2003-04	2005-06
• Shmyr, Paul	Chi., Cal., Min., Hfd.	7	343	13	72	85	528	34	3	3	6	44	....	1968-69	1981-82
Shoebottom, Bruce	Bos.	4	35	1	4	5	53	14	1	2	3	77	....	1987-88	1990-91
• Shore, Eddie	Bos., NYA	14	550	105	179	284	1047	55	7	12	19	181	2	1926-27	1939-40
• Shore, Hamby	Ott.	1	18	3	8	11	51	....	....	....	....	....	....	1917-18	1917-18
Short, Steve	L.A., Det.	2	6	0	0	0	2	....	....	....	....	....	....	1977-78	1978-79
Shuchuk, Gary	Det., L.A.	5	142	13	26	39	70	20	2	2	4	12	....	1990-91	1995-96
Shudra, Ron	Edm.	1	10	0	5	5	6	....	....	....	....	....	....	1987-88	1987-88
‡ Shugg, Justin	Car.	1	3	0	0	0	2	....	....	....	....	....	....	2014-15	2014-15
Shutt, Steve	Mtl., L.A.	13	930	424	393	817	410	99	50	48	98	65	5	1972-73	1984-85
Shvidki, Denis	Fla.	4	76	11	14	25	30	....	....	....	....	....	....	2000-01	2003-04
• Siebert, Babe	Mtl.M., NYR, Bos., Mtl.	14	592	140	156	296	982	49	7	5	12	62	2	1925-26	1938-39
‡ Sigalet, Jonathan	Bos.	1	1	0	0	0	4	....	....	....	....	....	....	2006-07	2006-07
Siklenka, Mike	Phi., NYR	2	2	0	0	0	0	....	....	....	....	....	....	2002-03	2003-04
Silk, Dave	NYR, Bos., Det., Wpg.	7	249	54	59	113	271	13	2	4	6	13	....	1979-80	1985-86
Sillinger, Mike	Det., Ana., Van., Phi., T.B., Fla., Ott., CBJ, Phx., St.L., Nsh., NYI	18	1049	240	308	548	644	43	11	7	18	28	....	1990-91	2008-09
Siltala, Mike	Wsh., NYR	3	7	1	0	1	2	....	....	....	....	....	....	1981-82	1987-88
Siltanen, Risto	Edm., Hfd., Que.	8	562	90	265	355	266	32	6	12	18	30	....	1979-80	1986-87
Sim, Jon	Dal., Nsh., L.A., Pit., Phi., Fla., Atl., NYI	12	469	75	64	139	314	15	1	0	1	6	1	1998-99	2010-11
Sim, Trevor	Edm.	1	3	0	1	1	2	....	....	....	....	....	....	1989-90	1989-90
Simard, Martin	Cgy., T.B.	3	44	1	5	6	183	....	....	....	....	....	....	1990-91	1992-93
Simicek, Roman	Pit., Min.	2	63	7	10	17	59	....	....	....	....	....	....	2000-01	2001-02
Simmer, Charlie	Cal., Cle., L.A., Bos., Pit.	14	712	342	369	711	544	24	9	9	18	32	....	1974-75	1987-88
Simmons, Al	Cal., Bos.	3	11	0	1	1	21	1	0	0	0	0	....	1971-72	1975-76
Simon, Ben	Atl., CBJ	4	81	3	1	4	47	....	....	....	....	....	....	2001-02	2005-06
Simon, Chris	Que., Col., Wsh., Chi., NYR, Cgy., NYI, Min.	15	782	144	161	305	1824	75	10	7	17	191	1	1992-93	2007-08
• Simon, Cully	Det., Chi.	3	130	4	11	15	121	14	1	0	1	6	1	1942-43	1944-45
Simon, Jason	NYI, Phx.	2	5	0	0	0	34	....	....	....	....	....	....	1993-94	1996-97
• Simon, Thain	Det.	1	3	0	0	0	0	....	....	....	....	....	....	1946-47	1946-47
Simon, Todd	Buf.	1	15	0	1	1	0	5	1	0	1	0	....	1993-94	1993-94
Simonetti, Frank	Bos.	4	115	5	8	13	76	12	0	1	1	8	....	1984-85	1987-88
Simpson, Bobby	Atl., St.L., Pit.	5	175	35	29	64	98	6	0	1	1	2	....	1976-77	1982-83
• Simpson, Cliff	Det.	2	6	0	1	1	0	2	0	0	0	2	....	1946-47	1947-48
Simpson, Craig	Pit., Edm., Buf.	10	634	247	250	497	659	67	36	32	68	56	2	1985-86	1994-95
• Simpson, Joe	NYA	6	228	21	19	40	156	2	0	0	0	0	....	1925-26	1930-31
Simpson, Reid	Phi., Min., N.J., Chi., T.B., St.L., Mtl., Nsh., Pit.	12	301	18	18	36	838	10	0	0	0	31	....	1991-92	2003-04
Simpson, Todd	Cgy., Fla., Phx., Ana., Ott., Chi., Mtl.	10	580	14	63	77	1357	9	0	2	2	10	....	1995-96	2005-06
Sims, Al	Bos., Hfd., L.A.	10	475	49	116	165	286	41	0	2	2	14	....	1973-74	1982-83
Sims, Shane	NYI	1	1	0	0	0	0	....	....	....	....	....	....	2010-11	2010-11
• Sinclair, Reg	NYR, Det.	3	208	49	43	92	139	3	1	0	1	0	....	1950-51	1952-53
• Singbush, Alex	Mtl.	1	32	0	5	5	15	3	0	0	0	4	....	1940-41	1940-41
• Sinisalo, Ilkka	Phi., Min., L.A.	11	582	204	222	426	208	68	21	11	32	6	....	1981-82	1991-92
Siren, Ville	Pit., Min.	5	290	14	68	82	276	7	0	0	0	6	....	1985-86	1989-90
Sirois, Bob	Phi., Wsh.	6	286	92	120	212	42	....	....	....	....	....	....	1974-75	1979-80
Sittler, Darryl	Tor., Phi., Det.	15	1096	484	637	1121	948	76	29	45	74	137	....	1970-71	1984-85
Sivek, Michal	Pit.	1	38	3	3	6	14	....	....	....	....	....	....	2002-03	2002-03
• Sjoberg, Lars-Erik	Wpg.	1	79	7	27	34	48	....	....	....	....	....	....	1979-80	1979-80
Sjodin, Tommy	Min., Dal., Que.	2	106	8	40	48	52	....	....	....	....	....	....	1992-93	1993-94
Sjostrom, Fredrik	Phx., NYR, Cgy., Tor.	7	489	46	58	104	190	17	0	2	2	2	....	2003-04	2010-11
• Skaare, Bjorn	Det.	1	1	0	0	0	0	....	....	....	....	....	....	1978-79	1978-79
Skalde, Jarrod	N.J., Ana., Cgy., S.J., Chi., Dal., Atl., Phi.	9	115	13	21	34	62	....	....	....	....	....	....	1990-91	2001-02
Skarda, Randy	St.L.	2	26	0	5	5	11	....	....	....	....	....	....	1989-90	1991-92
• Skilton, Raymie	Mtl.W.	1	1	0	0	0	0	....	....	....	....	....	....	1917-18	1917-18
• Skinner, Alf	Tor., Bos., Mtl.M., Pit.	4	71	26	10	36	87	2	0	1	1	9	1	1917-18	1925-26
Skinner, Brett	NYI	1	11	0	0	0	4	....	....	....	....	....	....	2008-09	2008-09
Skinner, Larry	Col.	4	47	10	12	22	8	2	0	0	0	0	....	1976-77	1979-80
Skolney, Wade	Phi.	1	1	0	0	0	2	....	....	....	....	....	....	2005-06	2005-06
Skopintsev, Andrei	T.B., Atl.	3	40	2	4	6	32	....	....	....	....	....	....	1998-99	2000-01
Skoula, Martin	Col., Ana., Dal., Min., Pit., N.J.	10	776	44	152	196	328	83	1	13	14	22	1	1999-00	2009-10
• Skov, Glen	Det., Chi., Mtl.	12	650	106	136	242	413	53	7	7	14	48	3	1949-50	1960-61
• Skrastins, Karlis	Nsh., Col., Fla., Dal.	12	832	32	104	136	375	20	0	3	3	12	....	1998-99	2010-11
‡ Skrbek, Pavel	Pit., Nsh.	3	12	0	0	0	8	....	....	....	....	....	....	1998-99	2001-02
Skriko, Petri	Van., Bos., Wpg., S.J.	9	541	183	222	405	246	28	5	9	14	4	....	1984-85	1992-93
Skrlac, Rob	N.J.	1	8	1	0	1	22	....	....	....	....	....	....	2003-04	2003-04
Skrudland, Brian	Mtl., Cgy., Fla., NYR, Dal.	15	881	124	219	343	1107	164	15	46	61	323	2	1985-86	1999-00
Slaney, John	Wsh., Col., L.A., Phx., Nsh., Pit., Phi.	9	268	22	69	91	99	14	2	1	3	4	....	1993-94	2003-04

	Name	NHL Teams	NHL Seasons	Regular Schedule GP	G	A	TP	PIM	Playoffs GP	G	A	TP	PIM	NHL Cup Wins	First NHL Season	Last NHL Season
‡	Slater, Jim	Atl., Wpg.	10	584	67	71	138	407	8	0	0	0	2	....	2005-06	2014-15
•	Sleaver, John	Chi.	2	13	1	0	1	6	....	....	....	....	....	....	1953-54	1956-57
	Slegr, Jiri	Van., Edm., Pit., Atl., Det., Bos.	11	622	56	193	249	838	42	4	14	18	39	1	1992-93	2005-06
	Sleigher, Louis	Que., Bos.	6	194	46	53	99	146	17	1	1	2	64	....	1979-80	1985-86
	Sloan, Blake	Dal., CBJ, Cgy.	6	290	11	32	43	162	35	0	2	2	20	1	1998-99	2003-04
•	Sloan, Tod	Tor., Chi.	13	745	220	262	482	831	47	9	12	21	47	2	1947-48	1960-61
	Sloan, Tyler	Wsh.	3	99	4	13	17	50	4	0	1	1	0	....	2008-09	2010-11
	Sloane, David	Phi.	1	1	0	0	0	0	....	....	....	....	....	....	2008-09	2008-09
•	Slobodian, Peter	NYA	1	41	3	2	5	54	....	....	....	....	....	....	1940-41	1940-41
•	Slowinski, Ed	NYR	6	291	58	74	132	63	16	2	6	8	6	....	1947-48	1952-53
•	Sly, Darryl	Tor., Min., Van.	4	79	1	2	3	20	....	....	....	....	....	....	1965-66	1970-71
	Smaby, Matt	T.B.	4	122	0	6	6	106	....	....	....	....	....	....	2007-08	2010-11
	Smail, Doug	Wpg., Min., Que., Ott.	13	845	210	249	459	602	42	9	2	11	49	....	1980-81	1992-93
•	Smart, Alex	Mtl.	1	8	5	2	7	0	....	....	....	....	....	....	1942-43	1942-43
	Smedsmo, Dale	Tor.	1	4	0	0	0	0	....	....	....	....	....	....	1972-73	1972-73
	Smehlik, Richard	Buf., Atl., N.J.	10	644	49	146	195	415	88	1	14	15	40	1	1992-93	2002-03
	Smid, Ladislav	Edm., Cgy.	10	583	12	60	72	472	....	....	....	....	....	....	2006-07	**2015-16**
•	Smillie, Don	Bos.	1	12	2	2	4	4	....	....	....	....	....	....	1933-34	1933-34
	Smirnov, Alexei	Ana.	2	52	3	3	6	20	4	0	0	0	2	....	2002-03	2003-04
•	Smith, Alex	Ott., Det., Bos., NYA	11	443	41	50	91	645	19	0	2	2	26	1	1924-25	1934-35
•	Smith, Art	Tor., Ott.	4	144	15	10	25	249	4	1	1	2	8	....	1927-28	1930-31
•	Smith, Barry	Bos., Col.	3	114	7	7	14	10	....	....	....	....	....	....	1975-76	1980-81
	Smith, Bobby	Min., Mtl.	15	1077	357	679	1036	917	184	64	96	160	245	1	1978-79	1992-93
	Smith, Brad	Van., Atl., Cgy., Det., Tor.	9	222	28	34	62	591	20	3	3	6	49	....	1978-79	1986-87
	Smith, Brandon	Bos., NYI	4	33	3	4	7	10	....	....	....	....	....	....	1998-99	2002-03
	Smith, Brian	Det.	3	61	2	8	10	12	5	0	0	0	0	....	1957-58	1960-61
•	Smith, Brian	L.A., Min.	2	67	10	10	20	33	7	0	0	0	0	....	1967-68	1968-69
•	Smith, Carl	Det.	1	7	1	1	2	2	....	....	....	....	....	....	1943-44	1943-44
•	Smith, Clint	NYR, Chi.	11	483	161	236	397	24	42	10	14	24	2	1	1936-37	1946-47
	Smith, D.J.	Tor., Col.	3	45	1	1	2	67	....	....	....	....	....	....	1996-97	2002-03
	Smith, Dallas	Bos., NYR	16	890	55	252	307	959	86	3	29	32	128	2	1959-60	1977-78
	Smith, Dan	Col., Edm.	3	22	0	0	0	16	....	....	....	....	....	....	1998-99	2005-06
	Smith, Dennis	Wsh., L.A.	2	8	0	0	0	4	....	....	....	....	....	....	1989-90	1990-91
	Smith, Derek	Buf., Det.	8	335	78	116	194	60	30	9	14	23	13	....	1975-76	1982-83
‡	Smith, Derek	Ott., Cgy.	5	94	2	12	14	24	....	....	....	....	....	....	2009-10	2013-14
	Smith, Derrick	Phi., Min., Dal.	10	537	82	92	174	373	82	14	11	25	79	....	1984-85	1993-94
•	Smith, Des	Mtl.M., Mtl., Chi., Bos.	5	196	22	25	47	236	25	1	4	5	18	1	1937-38	1941-42
•	Smith, Don	Mtl.	1	12	1	0	1	6	....	....	....	....	....	....	1919-20	1919-20
•	Smith, Don	NYR	1	11	1	1	2	0	1	0	0	0	0	....	1949-50	1949-50
	Smith, Doug	L.A., Buf., Edm., Van., Pit.	9	535	115	138	253	624	18	4	2	6	21	....	1981-82	1989-90
	Smith, Floyd	Bos., NYR, Det., Tor., Buf.	13	616	129	178	307	207	48	12	11	23	16	....	1954-55	1971-72
	Smith, Geoff	Edm., Fla., NYR	10	462	18	73	91	282	13	0	1	1	8	1	1989-90	1998-99
•	Smith, Glen	Chi.	1	2	0	0	0	0	....	....	....	....	....	....	1950-51	1950-51
•	Smith, Glenn	Tor.	1	9	0	0	0	0	....	....	....	....	....	....	1921-22	1921-22
	Smith, Gord	Wsh., Wpg.	6	299	9	30	39	284	....	....	....	....	....	....	1974-75	1979-80
	Smith, Greg	Cal., Cle., Min., Det., Wsh.	13	829	56	232	288	1110	63	4	7	11	106	....	1975-76	1987-88
•	Smith, Hooley	Ott., Mtl.M., Bos., NYA	17	715	200	225	425	1013	54	11	8	19	109	2	1924-25	1940-41
	Smith, Jason	N.J., Tor., Edm., Phi., Ott.	15	1008	41	128	169	1099	68	1	10	11	60	....	1993-94	2008-09
•	Smith, Ken	Bos.	7	331	78	93	171	49	30	8	13	21	6	....	1944-45	1950-51
	Smith, Mark	S.J., Cgy.	7	377	23	47	70	457	24	4	0	4	21	....	2000-01	2007-08
•	Smith, Nakina	Det.	1	10	1	2	3	0	....	....	....	....	....	....	1943-44	1943-44
	Smith, Nathan	Van., Pit., Min.	5	26	0	0	0	14	4	0	0	0	0	....	2003-04	2009-10
	Smith, Nick	Fla.	1	15	0	0	0	0	....	....	....	....	....	....	2001-02	2001-02
	Smith, Randy	Min.	2	3	0	0	0	0	....	....	....	....	....	....	1985-86	1986-87
	Smith, Rick	Bos., Cal., St.L., Det., Wsh.	11	687	52	167	219	560	78	3	23	26	73	1	1968-69	1980-81
•	Smith, Rodger	Pit., Phi.	6	210	20	4	24	172	4	3	0	3	0	....	1925-26	1930-31
	Smith, Ron	NYI	1	11	1	1	2	14	....	....	....	....	....	....	1972-73	1972-73
•	Smith, Sid	Tor.	12	601	186	183	369	94	44	17	10	27	2	3	1946-47	1957-58
•	Smith, Stan	NYR	2	9	2	1	3	0	1	0	0	0	0	....	1939-40	1940-41
	Smith, Steve	Phi., Buf.	6	18	0	1	1	15	....	....	....	....	....	....	1981-82	1988-89
	Smith, Steve	Edm., Chi., Cgy.	16	804	72	303	375	2139	134	11	41	52	288	3	1984-85	2000-01
•	Smith, Stu	Mtl.	2	4	2	2	4	2	1	0	0	0	0	....	1940-41	1941-42
	Smith, Stu	Hfd.	4	77	2	10	12	95	....	....	....	....	....	....	1979-80	1982-83
•	Smith, Tommy	Que.	1	10	0	1	1	11	....	....	....	....	....	....	1919-20	1919-20
	Smith, Vern	NYI	1	1	0	0	0	0	....	....	....	....	....	....	1984-85	1984-85
	Smith, Wayne	Chi.	1	2	1	1	2	2	1	0	0	0	0	....	1966-67	1966-67
	Smith, Wyatt	Phx., Nsh., NYI, Min., Col.	8	211	10	22	32	65	5	0	0	0	0	....	1999-00	2007-08
	Smithson, Jerred	L.A., Nsh., Fla., Edm., Tor.	11	606	39	57	96	363	36	2	2	4	39	....	2002-03	2013-14
‡	Smolenak, Radek	T.B., Chi.	2	7	0	1	1	15	....	....	....	....	....	....	2008-09	2009-10
	Smolinski, Bryan	Bos., Pit., NYI, L.A., Ott., Chi., Van., Mtl.	15	1056	274	377	651	606	123	23	29	52	60	....	1992-93	2007-08
	Smotherman, Jordan	Atl.	2	4	1	1	2	0	....	....	....	....	....	....	2007-08	2008-09
	Smrek, Peter	St.L., NYR	2	28	2	4	6	18	....	....	....	....	....	....	2000-01	2001-02
	Smrke, John	St.L., Que.	3	103	11	17	28	33	....	....	....	....	....	....	1977-78	1979-80
•	Smrke, Stan	Mtl.	2	9	0	3	3	0	....	....	....	....	....	....	1956-57	1957-58
	Smyl, Stan	Van.	13	896	262	411	673	1556	41	16	17	33	64	....	1978-79	1990-91
•	Smylie, Rod	Tor., Ott.	6	74	4	2	6	12	4	0	0	0	2	1	1920-21	1925-26
	Smyth, Brad	Fla., L.A., NYR, Nsh., Ott.	6	88	15	13	28	109	....	....	....	....	....	....	1995-96	2002-03
	Smyth, Greg	Phi., Que., Cgy., Fla., Tor., Chi.	10	229	4	16	20	783	12	0	0	0	40	....	1986-87	1996-97
	Smyth, Kevin	Hfd.	3	58	6	8	14	31	....	....	....	....	....	....	1993-94	1995-96
	Smyth, Ryan	Edm., NYI, Col., L.A.	19	1270	386	456	842	976	93	28	31	59	88	....	1994-95	2013-14
	Sneep, Carl	Pit.	1	1	0	1	1	0	....	....	....	....	....	....	2011-12	2011-12
	Snell, Chris	Tor., L.A.	2	34	2	7	9	24	....	....	....	....	....	....	1993-94	1994-95
	Snell, Ron	Pit.	2	7	3	2	5	6	....	....	....	....	....	....	1968-69	1969-70
	Snell, Ted	Pit., K.C., Det.	2	104	7	18	25	22	....	....	....	....	....	....	1973-74	1974-75
	Snepsts, Harold	Van., Min., Det., St.L.	17	1033	38	195	233	2009	93	1	14	15	231	....	1974-75	1990-91
	Snow, Sandy	Det.	1	3	0	0	0	2	....	....	....	....	....	....	1968-69	1968-69
	Snuggerud, Dave	Buf., S.J., Phi.	4	265	30	54	84	127	12	1	3	4	6	....	1989-90	1992-93
•	Snyder, Dan	Atl.	3	49	11	5	16	64	....	....	....	....	....	....	2000-01	2002-03
	Sobchuk, Dennis	Det., Que.	2	35	5	6	11	2	....	....	....	....	....	....	1979-80	1982-83
	Sobchuk, Gene	Van.	1	1	0	0	0	0	....	....	....	....	....	....	1973-74	1973-74
	Solheim, Ken	Chi., Min., Det., Edm.	5	135	19	20	39	34	3	1	1	2	2	....	1980-81	1985-86
•	Solinger, Bob	Tor., Det.	5	99	10	11	21	19	....	....	....	....	....	....	1951-52	1959-60
•	Somers, Art	Chi., NYR	6	222	33	56	89	189	30	1	5	6	20	1	1929-30	1934-35
	Somik, Radovan	Phi.	2	113	12	20	32	27	15	2	2	4	10	....	2002-03	2003-04
	Sommer, Roy	Edm.	1	3	1	0	1	7	....	....	....	....	....	....	1980-81	1980-81
	Songin, Tom	Bos.	3	43	5	5	10	22	....	....	....	....	....	....	1978-79	1980-81
•	Sonmor, Glen	NYR	2	28	2	0	2	21	....	....	....	....	....	....	1953-54	1954-55
	Sonnenberg, Martin	Pit., Cgy.	3	63	2	3	5	21	7	0	0	0	0	....	1998-99	2003-04
	Sopel, Brent	Van., NYI, L.A., Chi., Atl., Mtl.	12	659	44	174	218	309	71	4	14	18	20	1	1998-99	2010-11
	Sorochan, Lee	Cgy.	2	3	0	0	0	0	....	....	....	....	....	....	1998-99	1999-00
•	Sorrell, John	Det., NYA	11	490	127	119	246	100	42	12	15	27	10	2	1930-31	1940-41
	Souray, Sheldon	N.J., Mtl., Edm., Dal., Ana.	14	758	109	191	300	1145	40	3	8	11	69	....	1997-98	2012-13
	Spacek, Jaroslav	Fla., Chi., CBJ, Edm., Buf., Mtl., Car.	13	880	82	273	355	618	61	4	14	18	44	....	1998-99	2011-12
	Spanhel, Martin	CBJ	2	10	2	0	2	4	....	....	....	....	....	....	2000-01	2001-02
•	Sparrow, Emory	Bos.	1	8	0	0	0	4	....	....	....	....	....	....	1924-25	1924-25
•	Speck, Fred	Det., Van.	3	28	1	2	3	2	....	....	....	....	....	....	1968-69	1971-72
•	Speer, Bill	Pit., Bos.	4	130	5	20	25	79	8	1	0	1	4	1	1967-68	1970-71
	Speers, Ted	Det.	1	4	1	1	2	0	....	....	....	....	....	....	1985-86	1985-86
•	Spence, Gordon	Tor.	1	3	0	0	0	0	....	....	....	....	....	....	1925-26	1925-26
•	Spencer, Brian	Tor., NYI, Buf., Pit.	10	553	80	143	223	634	37	1	5	6	29	....	1969-70	1978-79
•	Spencer, Irv	NYR, Bos., Det.	8	230	12	38	50	127	16	0	0	0	8	....	1959-60	1967-68
•	Speyer, Chris	Tor., NYA	3	14	0	0	0	0	....	....	....	....	....	....	1923-24	1933-34
	Spiller, Matthew	Phx., NYI	3	68	0	2	2	74	....	....	....	....	....	....	2003-04	2007-08
	Spring, Corey	T.B.	2	16	1	1	2	12	....	....	....	....	....	....	1997-98	1998-99
	Spring, Don	Wpg.	4	259	1	54	55	80	6	0	0	0	10	....	1980-81	1983-84
	Spring, Frank	Bos., St.L., Cal., Cle.	5	61	14	20	34	12	....	....	....	....	....	....	1969-70	1976-77
•	Spring, Jesse	Ham., Pit., Tor., NYA	6	133	11	4	15	74	2	0	2	2	2	....	1923-24	1929-30
	Spruce, Andy	Van., Col.	3	172	31	42	73	111	2	0	2	2	0	....	1976-77	1978-79
‡	Sprukts, Janis	Fla.	2	14	1	2	3	2	....	....	....	....	....	....	2006-07	2008-09
	Srsen, Tomas	Edm.	1	2	0	0	0	0	....	....	....	....	....	....	1990-91	1990-91
	St. Amour, Martin	Ott.	1	1	0	0	0	2	....	....	....	....	....	....	1992-93	1992-93

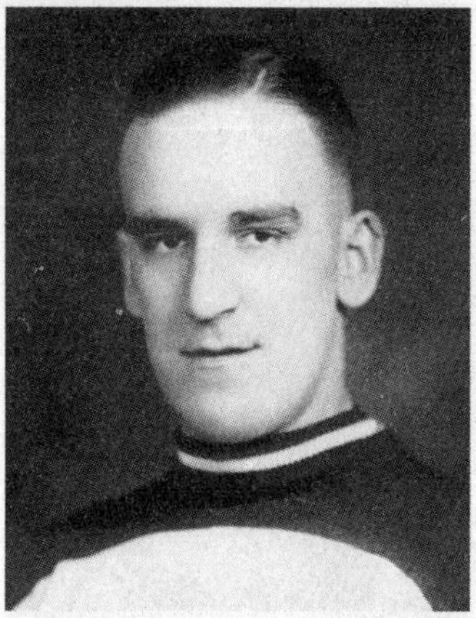
Alex Smith

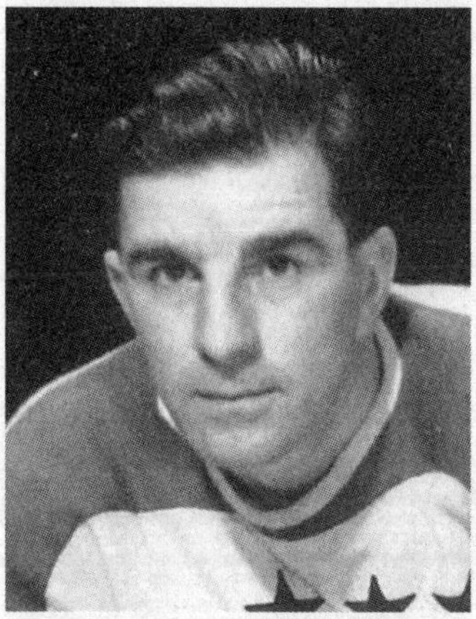
Hooley Smith

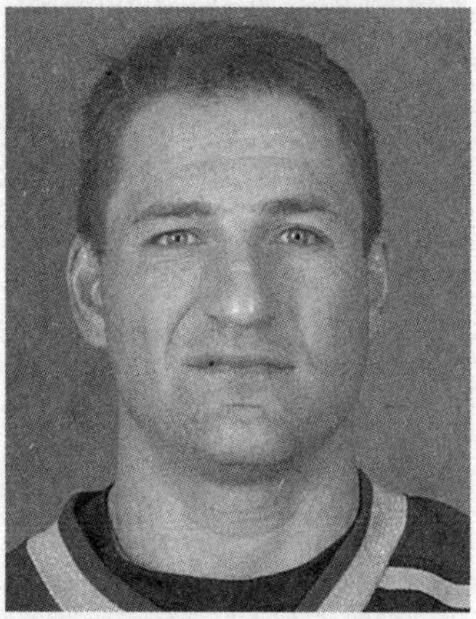
Brad Smyth

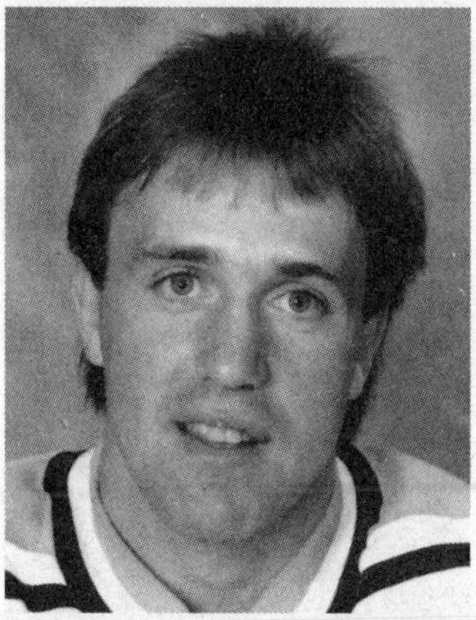
Mike Stapleton

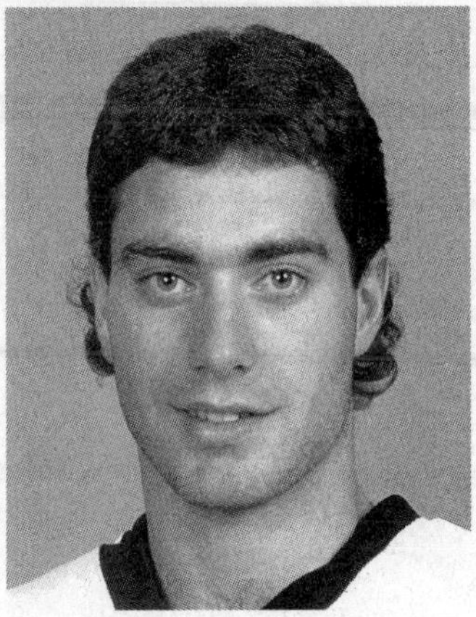

John Stevens

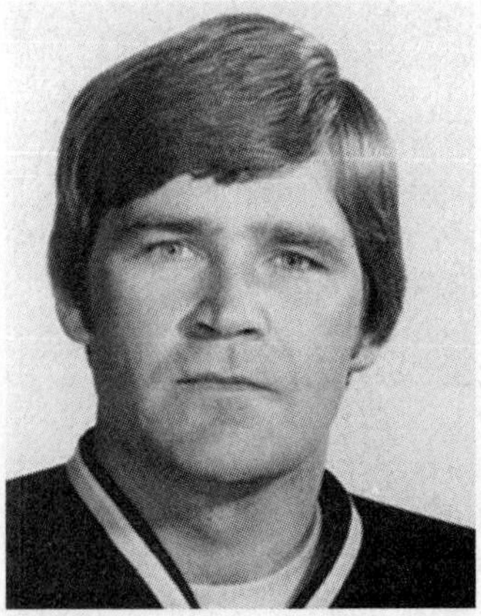

Bob Stewart

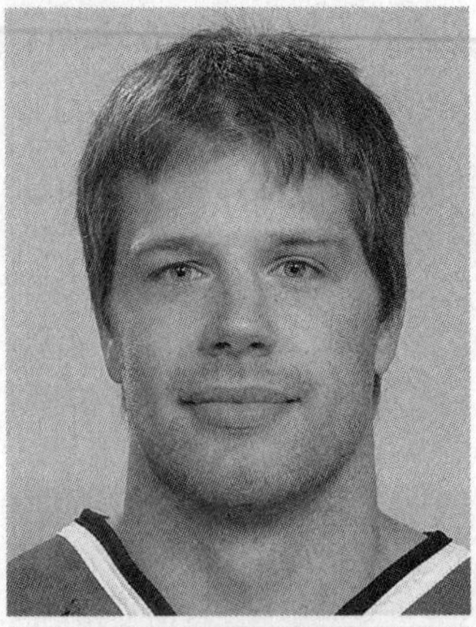

Brad Stuart

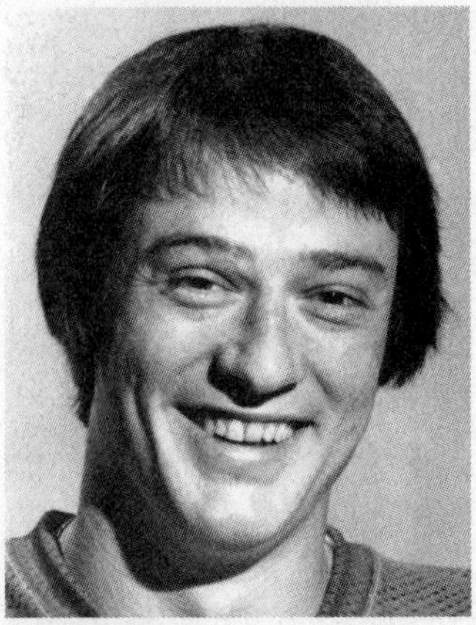

Peter Sullivan

			Regular Schedule					Playoffs					NHL	First	Last
Name	NHL Teams	NHL Seasons	GP	G	A	TP	PIM	GP	G	A	TP	PIM	Cup Wins	NHL Season	NHL Season
‡ St. Denis, Frederic	Mtl., CBJ	2	21	1	3	4	10	....	....	....	....	....	....	2011-12	2014-15
St. Jacques, Bruno	Phi., Car., Ana.	4	67	3	7	10	47	....	....	....	....	....	....	2001-02	2005-06
St. Laurent, Andre	NYI, Det., L.A., Pit.	11	644	129	187	316	749	59	8	12	20	48	....	1973-74	1983-84
• St. Laurent, Dollard	Mtl., Chi.	12	652	29	133	162	496	92	2	22	24	87	5	1950-51	1961-62
St. Louis, Martin	Cgy., T.B., NYR	16	1134	391	642	1033	310	107	42	48	90	34	1	1998-99	2014-15
St. Marseille, Frank	St.L., L.A.	10	707	140	285	425	242	88	20	25	45	18	....	1967-68	1976-77
‡ St. Pierre, Martin	Chi., Bos., Ott., Mtl.	6	39	3	5	8	12	....	....	....	....	....	....	2005-06	2013-14
St. Sauveur, Claude	Atl.	1	79	24	24	48	23	2	0	0	0	0	....	1975-76	1975-76
‡ Staal, Jared	Car.	1	2	0	0	0	2	....	....	....	....	....	....	2012-13	2012-13
Stackhouse, Ron	Cal., Det., Pit.	12	889	87	372	459	824	32	5	8	13	38	....	1970-71	1981-82
• Stackhouse, Ted	Tor.	1	13	0	0	0	2	1	0	0	0	0	1	1921-22	1921-22
Stafford, Garrett	Det., Dal., Phx.	3	7	0	2	2	0	....	....	....	....	....	....	2007-08	2010-11
• Stahan, Butch	Mtl.	1	....	....	....	....	....	3	0	1	1	2	....	1944-45	1944-45
Staios, Steve	Bos., Van., Atl., Edm., Cgy., NYI	16	1001	56	164	220	1322	33	1	5	6	32	....	1995-96	2011-12
Stajduhar, Nick	Edm.	1	2	0	0	0	4	....	....	....	....	....	....	1995-96	1995-96
Staley, Al	NYR	1	1	0	1	1	0	....	....	....	....	....	....	1948-49	1948-49
Stamler, Lorne	L.A., Tor., Wpg.	4	116	14	11	25	16	....	....	....	....	....	....	1976-77	1979-80
Standing, George	Min.	1	2	0	0	0	0	....	....	....	....	....	....	1967-68	1967-68
Stanfield, Fred	Chi., Bos., Min., Buf.	14	914	211	405	616	134	106	21	35	56	10	2	1964-65	1977-78
Stanfield, Jack	Chi.	1	....	....	....	....	....	1	0	0	0	0	....	1965-66	1965-66
• Stanfield, Jim	L.A.	3	7	0	1	1	0	....	....	....	....	....	....	1969-70	1971-72
Stankiewicz, Ed	Det.	2	6	0	0	0	2	....	....	....	....	....	....	1953-54	1955-56
Stankiewicz, Myron	St.L., Phi.	1	35	0	7	7	36	1	0	0	0	0	....	1968-69	1968-69
• Stanley, Allan	NYR, Chi., Bos., Tor., Phi.	21	1244	100	333	433	792	109	7	36	43	80	4	1948-49	1968-69
• Stanley, Barney	Chi.	1	1	0	0	0	0	....	....	....	....	....	....	1927-28	1927-28
Stanley, Daryl	Phi., Van.	6	189	8	17	25	408	17	0	0	0	30	....	1983-84	1989-90
• Stanowski, Wally	Tor., NYR	10	428	23	88	111	160	60	3	14	17	13	4	1939-40	1950-51
Stanton, Paul	Pit., Bos., NYI	5	295	14	49	63	262	44	2	10	12	66	2	1990-91	1994-95
Stapleton, Brian	Wsh.	1	1	0	0	0	0	....	....	....	....	....	....	1975-76	1975-76
Stapleton, Mike	Chi., Pit., Edm., Wpg., Phx., Atl., NYI, Van.	14	697	71	111	182	342	34	1	0	1	39	....	1986-87	2000-01
Stapleton, Pat	Bos., Chi.	10	635	43	294	337	353	65	10	39	49	38	....	1961-62	1972-73
‡ Stapleton, Tim	Tor., Atl., Wpg.	4	118	19	18	37	24	....	....	....	....	....	....	2008-09	2011-12
Starikov, Sergei	N.J.	1	16	0	1	1	8	....	....	....	....	....	....	1989-90	1989-90
• Starr, Harold	Ott., Mtl.M., Mtl., NYR	7	205	6	5	11	186	15	1	0	1	4	....	1929-30	1935-36
• Starr, Wilf	NYA, Det.	4	87	8	6	14	25	7	0	2	2	2	....	1932-33	1935-36
Stasiuk, Vic	Chi., Det., Bos.	14	745	183	254	437	669	69	16	18	34	40	3	1949-50	1962-63
Stastny, Anton	Que.	9	650	252	384	636	150	66	20	32	52	31	....	1980-81	1988-89
Stastny, Marian	Que., Tor.	5	322	121	173	294	110	32	5	17	22	7	....	1981-82	1985-86
Stastny, Peter	Que., N.J., St.L.	15	977	450	789	1239	824	93	33	72	105	123	....	1980-81	1994-95
Stastny, Yan	Edm., Bos., St.L.	5	91	6	10	16	58	....	....	....	....	....	....	2005-06	2009-10
Staszak, Ray	Det.	1	4	0	1	1	7	....	....	....	....	....	....	1985-86	1985-86
Staubitz, Brad	S.J., Min., Mtl., Ana.	5	230	10	11	21	521	....	....	....	....	....	....	2008-09	2012-13
‡ Steckel, David	Wsh., N.J., Tor., Ana.	9	425	33	46	79	129	31	5	4	9	8	....	2005-06	2013-14
• Steele, Frank	Det.	1	1	0	0	0	0	....	....	....	....	....	....	1930-31	1930-31
Steen, Anders	Wpg.	1	42	5	11	16	22	....	....	....	....	....	....	1980-81	1980-81
Steen, Thomas	Wpg.	14	950	264	553	817	753	56	12	32	44	62	....	1981-82	1994-95
Stefan, Patrik	Atl., Dal.	7	455	64	124	188	158	....	....	....	....	....	....	1999-00	2006-07
Stefaniw, Morris	Atl.	1	13	1	1	2	2	....	....	....	....	....	....	1972-73	1972-73
Stefanski, Bud	NYR	1	1	0	0	0	0	....	....	....	....	....	....	1977-78	1977-78
Stemkowski, Pete	Tor., Det., NYR, L.A.	15	967	206	349	555	866	83	25	29	54	136	1	1963-64	1977-78
Stenlund, Vern	Cle.	1	4	0	0	0	0	....	....	....	....	....	....	1976-77	1976-77
Stephens, Charlie	Col.	2	8	0	2	2	4	....	....	....	....	....	....	2002-03	2003-04
Stephenson, Bob	Hfd., Tor.	1	18	2	3	5	4	....	....	....	....	....	....	1979-80	1979-80
Stephenson, Shay	L.A.	1	2	0	0	0	0	....	....	....	....	....	....	2006-07	2006-07
‡ Sterling, Brett	Atl., Pit., St.L.	4	30	5	4	9	32	....	....	....	....	....	....	2007-08	2011-12
Stern, Ron	Van., Cgy., S.J.	12	638	75	86	161	2077	43	7	7	14	119	....	1987-88	1999-00
Sterner, Ulf	NYR	1	4	0	0	0	0	....	....	....	....	....	....	1964-65	1964-65
Stevens, John	Phi., Hfd.	5	53	0	10	10	48	....	....	....	....	....	....	1986-87	1993-94
Stevens, Kevin	Pit., Bos., L.A., NYR, Phi.	15	874	329	397	726	1470	103	46	60	106	170	2	1987-88	2001-02
Stevens, Mike	Van., Bos., NYI, Tor.	4	23	1	4	5	29	....	....	....	....	....	....	1984-85	1989-90
• Stevens, Phil	Mtl.W., Mtl., Bos.	3	25	1	0	1	3	....	....	....	....	....	....	1917-18	1925-26
Stevens, Scott	Wsh., St.L., N.J.	22	1635	196	712	908	2785	233	26	92	118	402	3	1982-83	2003-04
Stevenson, Grant	S.J.	1	47	10	12	22	14	5	0	0	0	4	....	2005-06	2005-06
Stevenson, Jeremy	Ana., Nsh., Min., Dal.	9	207	19	19	38	451	21	0	5	5	20	....	1995-96	2005-06
Stevenson, Shayne	Bos., T.B.	3	27	0	2	2	35	....	....	....	....	....	....	1990-91	1992-93
Stevenson, Turner	Mtl., N.J., Phi.	13	644	75	115	190	969	67	6	12	18	66	1	1992-93	2005-06
Stewart, Allan	N.J., Bos.	6	64	6	4	10	243	....	....	....	....	....	....	1985-86	1991-92
Stewart, Anthony	Fla., Atl., Car.	6	262	27	44	71	123	....	....	....	....	....	....	2005-06	2011-12
Stewart, Bill	Buf., St.L., Tor., Min.	8	261	7	64	71	424	13	1	3	4	11	....	1977-78	1985-86
Stewart, Blair	Det., Wsh., Que.	7	229	34	44	78	326	....	....	....	....	....	....	1973-74	1979-80
• Stewart, Bob	Bos., Cal., Cle., St.L., Pit.	9	575	27	101	128	809	5	1	1	2	2	....	1971-72	1979-80
Stewart, Cam	Bos., Fla., Min.	7	202	16	23	39	120	13	1	3	4	9	....	1993-94	2001-02
• Stewart, Gaye	Tor., Chi., Det., NYR, Mtl.	11	502	185	159	344	274	25	2	9	11	16	2	1941-42	1953-54
Stewart, Greg	Mtl.	3	26	0	1	1	48	2	0	0	0	2	....	2007-08	2009-10
• Stewart, Jack	Det., Chi.	12	565	31	84	115	765	80	5	14	19	143	2	1938-39	1951-52
Stewart, John	Pit., Atl., Cal.	5	258	58	60	118	158	4	0	0	0	10	....	1970-71	1974-75
Stewart, John	Que.	1	2	0	0	0	0	....	....	....	....	....	....	1979-80	1979-80
Stewart, Karl	Atl., Pit., Chi., T.B.	4	69	2	4	6	68	....	....	....	....	....	....	2003-04	2007-08
• Stewart, Ken	Chi.	1	6	1	1	2	2	....	....	....	....	....	....	1941-42	1941-42
• Stewart, Nels	Mtl.M., Bos., NYA	15	650	324	191	515	953	50	9	12	21	47	1	1925-26	1939-40
Stewart, Paul	Que.	1	21	2	0	2	74	....	....	....	....	....	....	1979-80	1979-80
Stewart, Ralph	Van., NYI	7	252	57	73	130	28	19	4	4	8	2	....	1970-71	1977-78
• Stewart, Ron	Tor., Bos., St.L., NYR, Van., NYI	21	1353	276	253	529	560	119	14	21	35	60	3	1952-53	1972-73
Stewart, Ryan	Wpg.	1	3	1	0	1	0	....	....	....	....	....	....	1985-86	1985-86
Stienburg, Trevor	Que.	4	71	8	4	12	161	1	0	0	0	0	....	1985-86	1988-89
Stiles, Tony	Cgy.	1	30	2	7	9	20	....	....	....	....	....	....	1983-84	1983-84
Stillman, Cory	Cgy., St.L., T.B., Car., Ott., Fla.	16	1025	278	449	727	489	82	19	32	51	43	2	1994-95	2010-11
‡ Stoa, Ryan	Col., Wsh.	3	40	4	3	7	20	1	0	0	0	2	....	2009-10	2013-14
Stock, P.J.	NYR, Mtl., Phi., Bos.	7	235	5	21	26	523	8	1	0	1	19	....	1997-98	2003-04
• Stoddard, Jack	NYR	2	80	16	15	31	31	....	....	....	....	....	....	1951-52	1952-53
Stojanov, Alek	Van., Pit.	3	107	2	5	7	222	14	0	0	0	21	....	1994-95	1996-97
Stoll, Jarret	Edm., L.A., NYR, Min.	13	872	144	244	388	618	97	10	16	26	72	2	2002-03	**2015-16**
Stoltz, Roland	Wsh.	1	14	2	2	4	14	....	....	....	....	....	....	1981-82	1981-82
Stone, Ryan	Pit., Edm.	3	35	0	7	7	55	....	....	....	....	....	....	2007-08	2009-10
Stone, Steve	Van.	1	2	0	0	0	0	....	....	....	....	....	....	1973-74	1973-74
Storm, Jim	Hfd., Dal.	3	84	7	15	22	44	....	....	....	....	....	....	1993-94	1995-96
Stothers, Mike	Phi., Tor.	4	30	0	2	2	65	5	0	0	0	11	....	1984-85	1987-88
Stoughton, Blaine	Pit., Tor., Hfd., NYR	8	526	258	191	449	204	8	4	2	6	2	....	1973-74	1983-84
Stoyanovich, Steve	Hfd.	1	23	3	5	8	11	....	....	....	....	....	....	1983-84	1983-84
• Strain, Neil	NYR	1	52	11	13	24	12	....	....	....	....	....	....	1952-53	1952-53
Straka, Martin	Pit., Ott., NYI, Fla., L.A., NYR	15	954	257	460	717	360	106	26	44	70	52	....	1992-93	2007-08
Strate, Gord	Det.	3	61	0	0	0	34	....	....	....	....	....	....	1956-57	1958-59
Stratton, Art	NYR, Det., Chi., Pit., Phi.	4	95	18	33	51	24	5	0	0	0	0	....	1959-60	1967-68
Strbak, Martin	L.A., Pit.	1	49	5	11	16	46	....	....	....	....	....	....	2003-04	2003-04
• Strobel, Art	NYR	1	7	0	0	0	0	....	....	....	....	....	....	1943-44	1943-44
Strong, Ken	Tor.	3	15	2	2	4	6	....	....	....	....	....	....	1982-83	1984-85
Stroshein, Garret	Wsh.	1	3	0	0	0	14	....	....	....	....	....	....	2003-04	2003-04
Struch, David	Cgy.	1	4	0	0	0	4	....	....	....	....	....	....	1993-94	1993-94
Strudwick, Jason	NYI, Van., Chi., NYR, Edm.	14	674	13	42	55	811	7	0	0	0	0	....	1995-96	2010-11
Strueby, Todd	Edm.	3	5	0	1	1	2	....	....	....	....	....	....	1981-82	1983-84
• Stuart, Billy	Tor., Bos.	7	195	30	20	50	151	12	1	1	2	6	1	1920-21	1926-27
Stuart, Brad	S.J., Bos., Cgy., L.A., Det., Col.	16	1056	80	255	335	565	142	10	30	40	77	1	1999-00	**2015-16**
Stuart, Colin	Atl., Buf.	4	56	8	5	13	26	....	....	....	....	....	....	2007-08	2011-12
Stuart, Mike	St.L.	2	3	0	0	0	0	....	....	....	....	....	....	2003-04	2005-06
‡ Stumpel, Jozef	Bos., L.A., Fla.	16	957	196	481	677	245	55	6	24	30	24	....	1991-92	2007-08
Stumpf, Bob	St.L., Pit.	1	10	1	1	2	20	....	....	....	....	....	....	1974-75	1974-75
Sturgeon, Peter	Col.	2	6	0	1	1	2	....	....	....	....	....	....	1979-80	1980-81
Sturm, Marco	S.J., Bos., L.A., Wsh., Van., Fla.	14	938	242	245	487	446	68	9	13	22	30	....	1997-98	2011-12
Stutzel, Mike	Phx.	1	9	0	0	0	0	....	....	....	....	....	....	2003-04	2003-04
‡ Suchy, Radoslav	Phx., CBJ	6	451	13	58	71	104	10	1	1	2	0	....	1999-00	2005-06
Suglobov, Alexander	N.J., Tor.	3	18	1	0	1	4	....	....	....	....	....	....	2003-04	2006-07

			Regular Schedule					Playoffs							
Name	NHL Teams	NHL Seasons	GP	G	A	TP	PIM	GP	G	A	TP	PIM	NHL Cup Wins	First NHL Season	Last NHL Season
Suikkanen, Kai	Buf.	2	2	0	0	0	0	....	....	....	....	....	....	1981-82	1982-83
Sulliman, Doug	NYR, Hfd., N.J., Phi.	11	631	160	168	328	175	16	1	3	4	2	....	1979-80	1989-90
• Sullivan, Barry	Det.	1	1	0	0	0	0	....	....	....	....	....	....	1947-48	1947-48
Sullivan, Bob	Hfd.	1	62	18	19	37	18	....	....	....	....	....	....	1982-83	1982-83
Sullivan, Brian	N.J.	1	2	0	1	1	0	....	....	....	....	....	....	1992-93	1992-93
• Sullivan, Frank	Tor., Chi.	4	8	0	0	0	2	....	....	....	....	....	....	1949-50	1955-56
Sullivan, Mike	S.J., Cgy., Bos., Phx.	11	709	54	82	136	203	34	4	8	12	14	....	1991-92	2001-02
Sullivan, Peter	Wpg.	2	126	28	54	82	40	....	....	....	....	....	....	1979-80	1980-81
Sullivan, Red	Bos., Chi., NYR	11	557	107	239	346	441	18	1	2	3	6	....	1949-50	1960-61
Sullivan, Steve	N.J., Tor., Chi., Nsh., Pit., Phx.	17	1011	290	457	747	587	50	9	14	23	30	....	1995-96	2012-13
‡ Sulzer, Alexander	Nsh., Fla., Van., Buf.	6	131	7	15	22	44	....	....	....	....	....	....	2008-09	2013-14
Summanen, Raimo	Edm., Van.	5	151	36	40	76	35	10	2	5	7	0	....	1983-84	1987-88
• Summerhill, Bill	Mtl., Bro.	4	72	14	17	31	70	3	0	0	0	2	....	1937-38	1941-42
Sundblad, Niklas	Cgy.	1	2	0	0	0	0	....	....	....	....	....	....	1995-96	1995-96
Sundin, Mats	Que., Tor., Van.	18	1346	564	785	1349	1093	91	38	44	82	74	....	1990-91	2008-09
Sundin, Ronnie	NYR	1	1	0	0	0	0	....	....	....	....	....	....	1997-98	1997-98
‡ Sundstrom, Johan	NYI	1	11	0	1	1	6	....	....	....	....	....	....	2013-14	2013-14
Sundstrom, Niklas	NYR, S.J., Mtl.	10	750	117	232	349	256	59	6	22	28	22	....	1995-96	2005-06
Sundstrom, Patrik	Van., N.J.	10	679	219	369	588	349	37	9	17	26	25	....	1982-83	1991-92
Sundstrom, Peter	NYR, Wsh., N.J.	6	338	61	83	144	120	23	3	3	6	8	....	1983-84	1989-90
• Suomi, Al	Chi.	1	5	0	0	0	0	....	....	....	....	....	....	1936-37	1936-37
Surma, Damian	Car.	2	2	1	1	2	0	....	....	....	....	....	....	2002-03	2003-04
‡ Surovy, Tomas	Pit.	3	126	27	32	59	71	....	....	....	....	....	....	2002-03	2005-06
Sushinsky, Maxim	Min.	1	30	7	4	11	29	....	....	....	....	....	....	2000-01	2000-01
Suter, Gary	Cgy., Chi., S.J.	17	1145	203	641	844	1349	108	17	56	73	120	1	1985-86	2001-02
Sutherby, Brian	Wsh., Ana., Dal.	9	460	41	49	90	533	10	0	0	0	12	....	2001-02	2010-11
• Sutherland, Bill	Mtl., Phi., Tor., St.L., Det.	6	250	70	58	128	99	14	2	4	6	0	....	1962-63	1971-72
• Sutherland, Max	Bos.	1	2	0	0	0	0	....	....	....	....	....	....	1931-32	1931-32
Sutter, Brent	NYI, Chi.	18	1111	363	466	829	1054	144	30	44	74	164	2	1980-81	1997-98
Sutter, Brian	St.L.	12	779	303	333	636	1786	65	21	21	42	249	....	1976-77	1987-88
Sutter, Darryl	Chi.	8	406	161	118	279	288	51	24	19	43	26	....	1979-80	1986-87
Sutter, Duane	NYI, Chi.	11	731	139	203	342	1333	161	26	32	58	405	4	1979-80	1989-90
Sutter, Rich	Pit., Phi., Van., St.L., Chi., T.B., Tor.	13	874	149	166	315	1411	78	13	5	18	133	....	1982-83	1994-95
Sutter, Ron	Phi., St.L., Que., NYI, Bos., S.J., Cgy.	19	1093	205	329	534	1352	104	8	32	40	193	....	1982-83	2000-01
Sutton, Andy	S.J., Min., Atl., NYI, Ott., Ana., Edm.	14	676	38	112	150	1185	11	0	0	0	20	....	1998-99	2012-13
Sutton, Ken	Buf., Edm., St.L., N.J., S.J., NYI	11	388	23	80	103	338	32	3	4	7	29	1	1990-91	2001-02
Suzor, Mark	Phi., Col.	2	64	4	16	20	60	....	....	....	....	....	....	1976-77	1977-78
Svartvadet, Per	Atl.	4	247	17	34	51	58	....	....	....	....	....	....	1999-00	2002-03
• Svatos, Marek	Col., Nsh., Ott.	7	344	100	72	172	217	14	2	5	7	4	....	2003-04	2010-11
Svehla, Robert	Fla., Tor.	9	655	68	267	335	649	38	1	14	15	42	....	1994-95	2002-03
Svejkovsky, Jaroslav	Wsh., T.B.	4	113	23	19	42	56	1	0	0	0	2	....	1996-97	1999-00
Svensson, Leif	Wsh.	2	121	6	40	46	49	....	....	....	....	....	....	1978-79	1979-80
Svensson, Magnus	Fla.	2	46	4	14	18	31	....	....	....	....	....	....	1994-95	1995-96
‡ Svitov, Alexander	T.B., CBJ	3	179	13	24	37	223	7	0	0	0	6	....	2002-03	2006-07
‡ Svoboda, Jaroslav	Car., Dal.	4	134	12	17	29	62	25	1	4	5	30	....	2001-02	2005-06
Svoboda, Petr	Mtl., Buf., Phi., T.B.	17	1028	58	341	399	1605	127	4	45	49	140	1	1984-85	2000-01
Svoboda, Petr	Tor.	1	18	1	2	3	10	....	....	....	....	....	....	2000-01	2000-01
Swain, Garry	Pit.	1	9	1	1	2	0	....	....	....	....	....	....	1968-69	1968-69
Swanson, Brian	Edm., Atl.	4	70	4	13	17	16	....	....	....	....	....	....	2000-01	2003-04
Swarbrick, George	Oak., Pit., Phi.	4	132	17	25	42	173	....	....	....	....	....	....	1967-68	1970-71
‡ Sweatt, Bill	Van.	2	3	0	0	0	0	....	....	....	....	....	....	2011-12	2012-13
Sweatt, Lee	Van.	1	3	1	1	2	2	....	....	....	....	....	....	2010-11	2010-11
• Sweeney, Bill	NYR	1	4	1	0	1	0	....	....	....	....	....	....	1959-60	1959-60
Sweeney, Bob	Bos., Buf., NYI, Cgy.	10	639	125	163	288	799	103	15	18	33	197	....	1986-87	1995-96
Sweeney, Don	Bos., Dal.	16	1115	52	221	273	681	108	9	10	19	81	....	1988-89	2003-04
Sweeney, Tim	Cgy., Bos., Ana., NYR	8	291	55	83	138	123	4	0	0	0	2	....	1990-91	1997-98
Sydor, Darryl	L.A., Dal., CBJ, T.B., Pit., St.L.	18	1291	98	409	507	755	155	9	47	56	73	2	1991-92	2009-10
Sykes, Bob	Tor.	1	2	0	0	0	0	....	....	....	....	....	....	1974-75	1974-75
Sykes, Phil	L.A., Wpg.	10	456	79	85	164	519	26	0	3	3	29	....	1982-83	1991-92
Sykora, Michal	S.J., Chi., T.B., Phi.	7	267	15	54	69	185	7	0	1	1	0	....	1993-94	2000-01
Sykora, Petr	N.J., Ana., NYR, Edm., Pit., Min.	15	1017	323	398	721	455	133	34	40	74	62	2	1995-96	2011-12
‡ Sykora, Petr	Nsh., Wsh.	2	12	2	2	4	6	....	....	....	....	....	....	1998-99	2005-06
Sylvester, Dean	Buf., Atl.	3	96	21	16	37	32	4	0	0	0	0	....	1998-99	2000-01
‡ Syvret, Danny	Edm., Phi., Ana.	5	59	3	4	7	30	10	0	0	0	0	....	2005-06	2010-11
‡ Szczechura, Paul	T.B., Buf.	3	92	10	10	20	34	....	....	....	....	....	....	2008-09	2011-12
• Szura, Joe	Oak.	2	90	10	15	25	30	7	2	3	5	2	....	1967-68	1968-69

T

‡ Taffe, Jeff	Phx., NYR, Pit., Fla., Chi., Min.	9	180	21	25	46	40	....	....	....	....	....	....	2002-03	2011-12
Taft, John	Det.	1	15	0	2	2	4	....	....	....	....	....	....	1978-79	1978-79
Taglianetti, Peter	Wpg., Min., Pit., T.B.	11	451	18	74	92	1106	53	2	8	10	103	2	1984-85	1994-95
Talafous, Dean	Atl., Min., NYR	8	497	104	154	258	163	21	4	7	11	11	....	1974-75	1981-82
• Talakoski, Ron	NYR	2	9	0	1	1	33	....	....	....	....	....	....	1986-87	1987-88
Talbot, Jean-Guy	Mtl., Min., Det., St.L., Buf.	17	1056	43	242	285	1006	150	4	26	30	142	7	1954-55	1970-71
‡ Talbot, Max	Pit., Phi., Col., Bos.	11	704	91	113	204	495	84	18	21	39	101	1	2005-06	**2015-16**
‡ Tallackson, Barry	N.J.	4	20	1	1	2	2	....	....	....	....	....	....	2005-06	2008-09
‡ Tallinder, Henrik	Buf., N.J.	12	678	28	114	142	378	39	2	10	12	28	....	2001-02	2013-14
Tallon, Dale	Van., Chi., Pit.	10	642	98	238	336	568	33	2	10	12	45	....	1970-71	1979-80
‡ Tambellini, Jeff	L.A., NYI, Van.	6	242	27	36	63	88	6	0	0	0	2	....	2005-06	2010-11
Tambellini, Steve	NYI, Col., N.J., Cgy., Van.	10	553	160	150	310	105	2	0	1	1	0	1	1978-79	1987-88
Tamer, Chris	Pit., NYR, Atl.	11	644	21	64	85	1183	37	0	8	8	52	....	1993-94	2003-04
Tanabe, David	Car., Phx., Bos.	8	449	30	84	114	245	7	2	1	3	12	....	1999-00	2007-08
Tancill, Chris	Hfd., Det., Dal., S.J.	8	134	17	32	49	54	11	1	1	2	8	....	1990-91	1997-98
Tanguay, Alex	Col., Cgy., Mtl., T.B., Ari.	16	1088	283	580	863	527	98	19	40	59	42	1	1999-00	**2015-16**
Tanguay, Christian	Que.	1	2	0	0	0	0	....	....	....	....	....	....	1981-82	1981-82
Tannahill, Don	Van.	2	111	30	33	63	25	....	....	....	....	....	....	1972-73	1973-74
Tanti, Tony	Chi., Van., Pit., Buf.	11	697	287	273	560	661	30	3	12	15	27	....	1981-82	1991-92
Tapper, Brad	Atl.	3	71	14	11	25	72	....	....	....	....	....	....	2000-01	2002-03
‡ Tardif, Jamie	Bos.	1	2	0	0	0	0	....	....	....	....	....	....	2012-13	2012-13
Tardif, Marc	Mtl., Que.	8	517	194	207	401	443	62	13	15	28	75	2	1969-70	1982-83
Tardif, Patrice	St.L., L.A.	2	65	7	11	18	78	....	....	....	....	....	....	1994-95	1995-96
‡ Tarnasky, Nick	T.B., Nsh., Fla.	5	245	13	17	30	297	6	0	0	0	10	....	2005-06	2009-10
Tarnstrom, Dick	NYI, Pit., Edm., CBJ	5	306	35	105	140	254	17	0	2	2	12	....	2001-02	2007-08
Tatarinov, Mikhail	Wsh., Que., Bos.	4	161	21	48	69	184	....	....	....	....	....	....	1990-91	1993-94
• Tatchell, Spence	NYR	1	1	0	0	0	0	....	....	....	....	....	....	1942-43	1942-43
‡ Taticek, Petr	Fla.	1	3	0	0	0	0	....	....	....	....	....	....	2005-06	2005-06
• Taylor, Billy	Tor., Det., Bos., NYR	7	323	87	180	267	120	33	6	18	24	13	1	1939-40	1947-48
• Taylor, Billy	NYR	1	2	0	0	0	0	....	....	....	....	....	....	1964-65	1964-65
• Taylor, Bob	Bos.	1	8	0	0	0	6	....	....	....	....	....	....	1929-30	1929-30
Taylor, Chris	NYI, Bos., Buf.	8	149	11	21	32	48	2	0	0	0	2	....	1994-95	2003-04
Taylor, Dave	L.A.	17	1111	431	638	1069	1589	92	26	33	59	145	....	1977-78	1993-94
• Taylor, Harry	Tor., Chi.	3	66	5	10	15	30	1	0	0	0	0	1	1946-47	1951-52
Taylor, Mark	Phi., Pit., Wsh.	5	209	42	68	110	73	6	0	0	0	0	....	1981-82	1985-86
• Taylor, Ralph	Chi., NYR	3	99	4	1	5	169	4	0	0	0	10	....	1927-28	1929-30
Taylor, Ted	NYR, Det., Min., Van.	6	166	23	35	58	181	....	....	....	....	....	....	1964-65	1971-72
Taylor, Tim	Det., Bos., NYR, T.B.	13	746	73	94	167	433	89	2	12	14	73	2	1993-94	2006-07
Teal, Jeff	Mtl.	1	6	0	1	1	0	....	....	....	....	....	....	1984-85	1984-85
• Teal, Skip	Bos.	1	1	0	0	0	0	....	....	....	....	....	....	1954-55	1954-55
Teal, Vic	NYI	1	1	0	0	0	0	....	....	....	....	....	....	1973-74	1973-74
Tebbutt, Greg	Que., Pit.	2	26	0	3	3	35	....	....	....	....	....	....	1979-80	1983-84
‡ Tedenby, Mattias	N.J.	4	120	10	20	30	42	....	....	....	....	....	....	2010-11	2013-14
Tenkrat, Petr	Ana., Nsh., Bos.	3	177	22	30	52	84	....	....	....	....	....	....	2000-01	2006-07
Tenute, Joey	Wsh.	1	1	0	0	0	0	....	....	....	....	....	....	2005-06	2005-06
Tepper, Stephen	Chi.	1	1	0	0	0	0	....	....	....	....	....	....	1992-93	1992-93
• Terbenche, Paul	Chi., Buf.	5	189	5	26	31	28	12	0	0	0	0	....	1967-68	1973-74
Terrion, Greg	L.A., Tor.	8	561	93	150	243	339	35	2	9	11	41	....	1980-81	1987-88
Terry, Bill	Min.	1	5	0	0	0	0	....	....	....	....	....	....	1987-88	1987-88
• Tertyshny, Dmitri	Phi.	1	62	2	8	10	30	1	0	0	0	0	....	1998-99	1998-99
Tessier, Orval	Mtl., Bos.	3	59	5	7	12	6	....	....	....	....	....	....	1954-55	1960-61
Tetarenko, Joey	Fla., Ott., Car.	4	73	4	1	5	176	....	....	....	....	....	....	2000-01	2003-04
‡ Teubert, Colten	Edm.	1	24	0	1	1	25	....	....	....	....	....	....	2011-12	2011-12

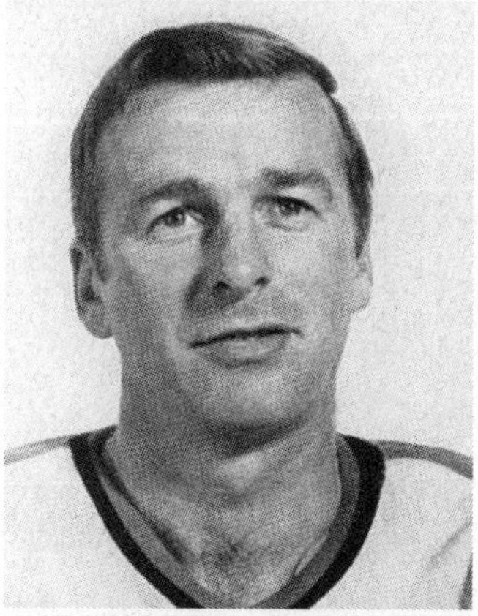
Bill Sutherland

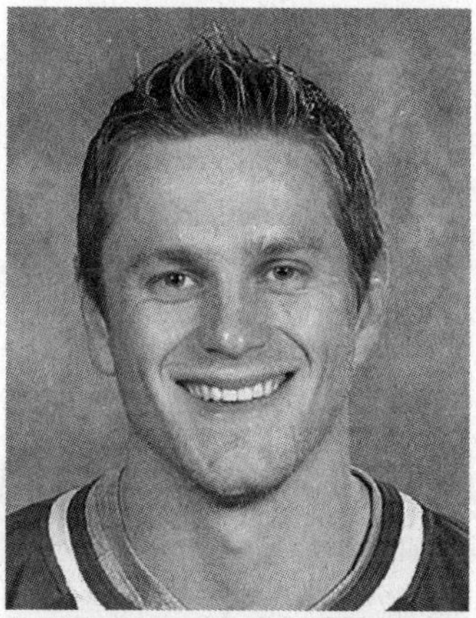
Marek Svatos

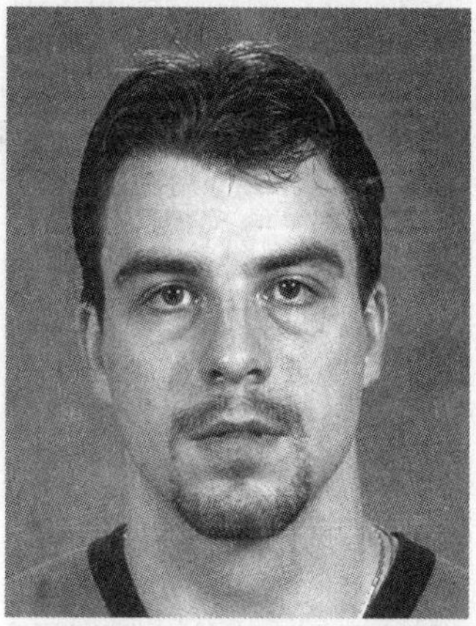
Michal Sykora

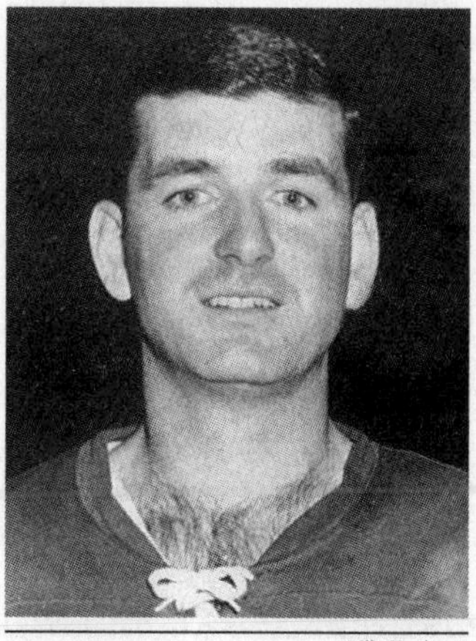
Billy Taylor Jr.

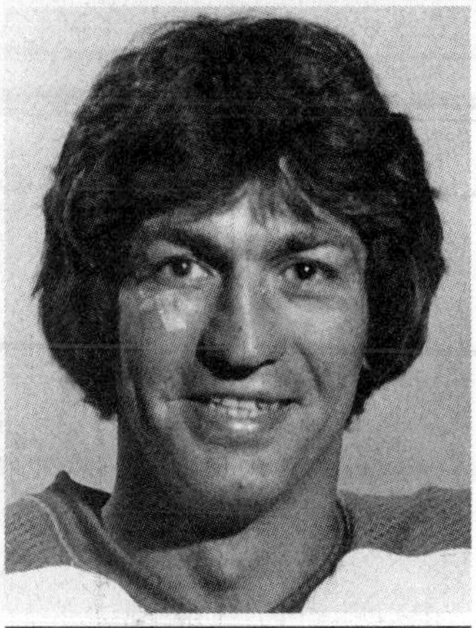

Paul Terbenche

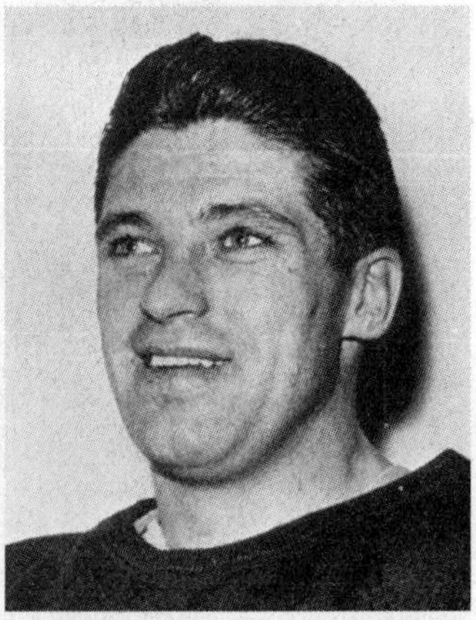

Lorrain Thibeault

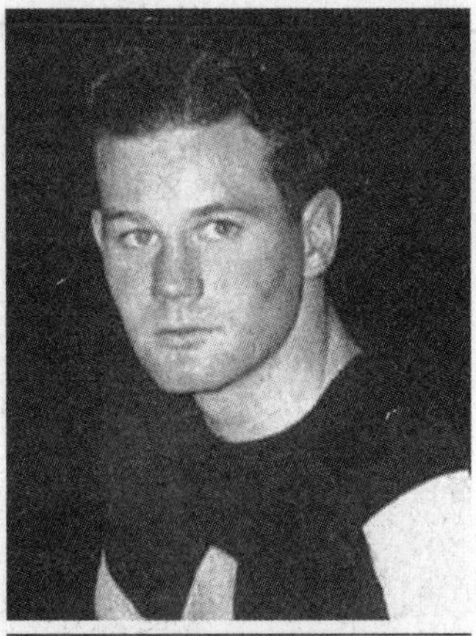

Rhys Thomson

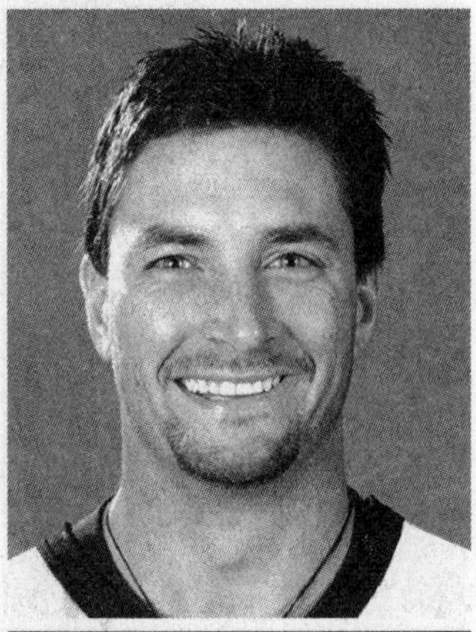

Darren Turcotte

			Regular Schedule					Playoffs							
Name	NHL Teams	NHL Seasons	GP	G	A	TP	PIM	GP	G	A	TP	PIM	NHL Cup Wins	First NHL Season	Last NHL Season
Tezikov, Alexei	Wsh., Van.	3	30	1	1	2	2	....	....	....	....	....	....	1998-99	2001-02
Thang, Ryan	Nsh.	1	1	0	0	0	0	....	....	....	....	....	....	2011-12	2011-12
Theberge, Greg	Wsh.	5	153	15	63	78	73	4	0	1	1	0	....	1979-80	1983-84
Thelin, Mats	Bos.	3	163	8	19	27	107	5	0	0	0	6	....	1984-85	1986-87
Thelven, Michael	Bos.	5	207	20	80	100	217	34	4	10	14	34	....	1985-86	1989-90
Therien, Chris	Phi., Dal.	11	764	29	130	159	585	104	4	10	14	68	....	1994-95	2005-06
Therrien, Gaston	Que.	3	22	0	8	8	12	9	0	1	1	4	....	1980-81	1982-83
Thibaudeau, Gilles	Mtl., NYI, Tor.	5	119	25	37	62	40	8	3	3	6	2	....	1986-87	1990-91
• Thibeault, Lorrain	Det., Mtl.	2	5	0	2	2	2	....	....	....	....	....	....	1944-45	1945-46
Thiffault, Leo	Min.	1	....	....	....	....	....	5	0	0	0	0	....	1967-68	1967-68
‡ Thomas, Bill	Phx., Pit., Fla.	6	87	16	12	28	18	....	....	....	....	....	....	2005-06	2011-12
• Thomas, Cy	Chi., Tor.	1	14	2	2	4	12	....	....	....	....	....	....	1947-48	1947-48
Thomas, Reg	Que.	1	39	9	7	16	6	....	....	....	....	....	....	1979-80	1979-80
Thomas, Scott	Buf., L.A.	3	63	6	4	10	32	12	1	0	1	4	....	1992-93	2000-01
Thomas, Steve	Tor., Chi., NYI, N.J., Ana., Det.	20	1235	421	512	933	1306	174	54	53	107	187	....	1984-85	2003-04
Thomlinson, Dave	St.L., Bos., L.A.	5	42	1	3	4	50	9	3	1	4	4	....	1989-90	1994-95
Thompson, Brent	L.A., Wpg., Phx.	6	121	1	10	11	352	4	0	0	0	4	....	1991-92	1996-97
• Thompson, Cliff	Bos.	2	13	0	1	1	2	....	....	....	....	....	....	1941-42	1948-49
Thompson, Errol	Tor., Det., Pit.	10	599	208	185	393	184	34	7	5	12	11	....	1970-71	1980-81
• Thompson, Ken	Mtl.W.	1	1	0	0	0	0	....	....	....	....	....	....	1917-18	1917-18
• Thompson, Paul	NYR, Chi.	13	582	153	179	332	336	48	11	11	22	54	3	1926-27	1938-39
Thompson, Rocky	Cgy., Fla.	4	25	0	0	0	117	....	....	....	....	....	....	1997-98	2001-02
• Thoms, Bill	Tor., Chi., Bos.	13	548	135	206	341	154	44	6	10	16	6	....	1932-33	1944-45
• Thomson, Bill	Det.	2	9	2	2	4	0	2	0	0	0	0	....	1938-39	1943-44
Thomson, Floyd	St.L.	8	411	56	97	153	341	10	0	2	2	6	....	1971-72	1979-80
Thomson, Jim	Wsh., Hfd., N.J., L.A., Ott., Ana.	7	115	4	3	7	416	1	0	0	0	0	....	1986-87	1993-94
• Thomson, Jimmy	Tor., Chi.	13	787	19	215	234	920	63	2	13	15	135	4	1945-46	1957-58
• Thomson, Rhys	Mtl., Tor.	2	25	0	2	2	38	....	....	....	....	....	....	1939-40	1942-43
‡ Thoresen, Patrick	Edm., Phi.	2	106	6	18	24	66	14	0	2	2	4	....	2006-07	2007-08
Thornbury, Tom	Pit.	1	14	1	8	9	16	....	....	....	....	....	....	1983-84	1983-84
Thornton, Scott	Tor., Edm., Mtl., Dal., S.J., L.A.	17	941	144	141	285	1459	79	13	14	27	82	....	1990-91	2007-08
• Thorsteinson, Joe	NYA	1	4	0	0	0	0	....	....	....	....	....	....	1932-33	1932-33
‡ Thuresson, Andreas	Nsh.	2	25	1	2	3	6	....	....	....	....	....	....	2009-10	2010-11
• Thurier, Fred	NYA, Bro., NYR	3	80	25	27	52	18	....	....	....	....	....	....	1940-41	1944-45
Thurlby, Tom	Oak.	1	20	1	1	2	4	....	....	....	....	....	....	1967-68	1967-68
Thyer, Mario	Min.	1	5	0	0	0	0	1	0	0	0	2	....	1989-90	1989-90
Tibbetts, Billy	Pit., Phi., NYR	3	82	2	8	10	269	....	....	....	....	....	....	2000-01	2002-03
Tichy, Milan	Chi., NYI	3	23	0	5	5	40	....	....	....	....	....	....	1992-93	1995-96
Tidey, Alex	Buf., Edm.	3	9	0	0	0	8	2	0	0	0	0	....	1976-77	1979-80
‡ Tikhonov, Viktor	Phx., Chi., Ari.	2	111	11	11	22	40	....	....	....	....	....	....	2008-09	**2015-16**
Tikkanen, Esa	Edm., NYR, St.L., N.J., Van., Fla., Wsh.	15	877	244	386	630	1077	186	72	60	132	275	5	1984-85	1998-99
Tiley, Brad	Phx., Phi.	3	11	0	0	0	0	1	0	0	0	0	....	1997-98	2000-01
Tilley, Tom	St.L.	4	174	4	38	42	89	14	1	3	4	19	....	1988-89	1993-94
Timander, Mattias	Bos., CBJ, NYI, Phi.	8	419	13	57	70	165	23	3	5	8	8	....	1996-97	2003-04
• Timgren, Ray	Tor., Chi.	6	251	14	44	58	70	30	3	9	12	6	2	1948-49	1954-55
‡ Timmins, Scott	Fla.	2	24	1	0	1	12	....	....	....	....	....	....	2010-11	2012-13
‡ Timonen, Jussi	Phi.	1	14	0	4	4	6	....	....	....	....	....	....	2006-07	2006-07
Timonen, Kimmo	Nsh., Phi., Chi.	16	1108	117	454	571	654	105	4	31	35	109	1	1998-99	2014-15
Tinordi, Mark	NYR, Min., Dal., Wsh.	12	663	52	148	200	1514	70	7	11	18	165	....	1987-88	1998-99
Tippett, Dave	Hfd., Wsh., Pit., Phi.	12	721	93	169	262	317	62	6	16	22	34	....	1983-84	1993-94
Titanic, Morris	Buf.	2	19	0	0	0	0	....	....	....	....	....	....	1974-75	1975-76
Titov, German	Cgy., Pit., Edm., Ana.	9	624	157	220	377	311	34	11	12	23	18	....	1993-94	2001-02
Tjarnqvist, Daniel	Atl., Min., Edm., Col.	6	352	18	72	90	130	....	....	....	....	....	....	2001-02	2008-09
Tjarnqvist, Mathias	Dal., Phx.	4	173	13	19	32	60	....	....	....	....	....	....	2003-04	2007-08
Tkachuk, Keith	Wpg., Phx., St.L., Atl.	18	1201	538	527	1065	2219	89	28	28	56	176	....	1991-92	2009-10
Tkaczuk, Daniel	Cgy.	1	19	4	7	11	14	....	....	....	....	....	....	2000-01	2000-01
Tkaczuk, Walt	NYR	14	945	227	451	678	556	93	19	32	51	119	....	1967-68	1980-81
‡ Tlusty, Jiri	Tor., Car., Wpg., N.J.	9	446	89	88	177	126	4	0	0	0	0	....	2007-08	**2015-16**
Toal, Mike	Edm.	1	3	0	0	0	0	....	....	....	....	....	....	1979-80	1979-80
Tobler, Ryan	T.B.	1	4	0	0	0	5	....	....	....	....	....	....	2001-02	2001-02
Tocchet, Rick	Phi., Pit., L.A., Bos., Wsh., Phx.	18	1144	440	512	952	2972	145	52	60	112	471	1	1984-85	2001-02
Todd, Kevin	N.J., Edm., Chi., L.A., Ana.	9	383	70	133	203	225	12	3	2	5	16	....	1988-89	1997-98
‡ Tollefsen, Ole-Kristian	CBJ, Phi.	5	163	4	8	12	296	....	....	....	....	....	....	2005-06	2009-10
‡ Tolpeko, Denis	Phi.	1	26	1	5	6	24	....	....	....	....	....	....	2007-08	2007-08
Tomalty, Glenn	Wpg.	1	1	0	0	0	0	....	....	....	....	....	....	1979-80	1979-80
Tomlak, Mike	Hfd.	4	141	15	22	37	103	10	0	1	1	4	....	1989-90	1993-94
Tomlinson, Dave	Tor., Wpg., Fla.	4	42	1	3	4	28	....	....	....	....	....	....	1991-92	1994-95
Tomlinson, Kirk	Min.	1	1	0	0	0	0	....	....	....	....	....	....	1987-88	1987-88
Toms, Jeff	T.B., Wsh., NYI, NYR, Pit., Fla.	8	236	22	33	55	59	1	0	0	0	0	....	1995-96	2002-03
• Tomson, Jack	NYA	3	15	1	1	2	0	2	0	0	0	0	....	1938-39	1940-41
Tonelli, John	NYI, Cgy., L.A., Chi., Que.	14	1028	325	511	836	911	172	40	75	115	200	4	1978-79	1991-92
Tookey, Tim	Wsh., Que., Pit., Phi., L.A.	7	106	22	36	58	71	10	1	3	4	2	....	1980-81	1988-89
Toomey, Sean	Min.	1	1	0	0	0	0	....	....	....	....	....	....	1986-87	1986-87
Toporowski, Shayne	Tor.	1	3	0	0	0	7	....	....	....	....	....	....	1996-97	1996-97
• Toppazzini, Jerry	Bos., Chi., Det.	12	783	163	244	407	436	40	13	9	22	13	....	1952-53	1963-64
• Toppazzini, Zellio	Bos., NYR, Chi.	5	123	21	22	43	49	2	0	0	0	0	....	1948-49	1956-57
Torgaev, Pavel	Cgy., T.B.	2	55	6	14	20	20	1	0	0	0	0	....	1995-96	1999-00
Torkki, Jari	Chi.	1	4	1	0	1	0	....	....	....	....	....	....	1988-89	1988-89
Tormanen, Antti	Ott.	1	50	7	8	15	28	....	....	....	....	....	....	1995-96	1995-96
Torres, Raffi	NYI, Edm., CBJ, Buf., Van., Phx., S.J.	12	635	137	123	260	497	68	11	17	28	80	....	2001-02	2013-14
• Touhey, Bill	Mtl.M., Ott., Bos.	7	280	65	40	105	107	2	1	0	1	0	....	1927-28	1933-34
• Toupin, Jacques	Chi.	1	8	1	2	3	0	4	0	0	0	0	....	1943-44	1943-44
• Townsend, Art	Chi.	1	5	0	0	0	0	....	....	....	....	....	....	1926-27	1926-27
Townshend, Graeme	Bos., NYI, Ott.	5	45	3	7	10	28	....	....	....	....	....	....	1989-90	1993-94
Trader, Larry	Det., St.L., Mtl.	4	91	5	13	18	74	3	0	0	0	0	....	1982-83	1987-88
• Trainor, Wes	NYR	1	17	1	2	3	6	....	....	....	....	....	....	1948-49	1948-49
• Trapp, Bob	Chi., Mtl.	3	83	4	4	8	129	2	0	0	0	4	....	1926-27	1932-33
Trapp, Doug	Buf.	1	2	0	0	0	0	....	....	....	....	....	....	1986-87	1986-87
• Traub, Percy	Chi., Det.	3	130	3	3	6	217	4	0	0	0	6	....	1926-27	1928-29
Traverse, Patrick	Ott., Ana., Bos., Mtl., Dal.	7	279	14	51	65	113	6	0	0	0	2	....	1995-96	2005-06
Trebil, Dan	Ana., Pit., St.L.	5	85	4	4	8	32	10	0	1	1	8	....	1996-97	2000-01
Tredway, Brock	L.A.	1	....	....	....	....	....	1	0	0	0	0	....	1981-82	1981-82
Tremblay, Brent	Wsh.	2	10	1	0	1	6	....	....	....	....	....	....	1978-79	1979-80
• Tremblay, Gilles	Mtl.	9	509	168	162	330	161	48	9	14	23	4	4	1960-61	1968-69
• Tremblay, J.C.	Mtl.	13	794	57	306	363	204	108	14	51	65	58	5	1959-60	1971-72
• Tremblay, Marcel	Mtl.	1	10	0	2	2	0	....	....	....	....	....	....	1938-39	1938-39
Tremblay, Mario	Mtl.	12	852	258	326	584	1043	101	20	29	49	187	5	1974-75	1985-86
• Tremblay, Nils	Mtl.	2	3	0	1	1	0	2	0	0	0	0	....	1944-45	1945-46
Tremblay, Yannick	Tor., Atl., Van.	9	390	38	87	125	178	....	....	....	....	....	....	1996-97	2006-07
Trepanier, Pascal	Col., Ana., Nsh.	6	229	12	22	34	252	2	0	0	0	0	....	1997-98	2002-03
Trimper, Tim	Chi., Wpg., Min.	6	190	30	36	66	153	2	0	0	0	2	....	1979-80	1984-85
Tripp, John	NYR, L.A.	2	43	2	7	9	35	....	....	....	....	....	....	2002-03	2003-04
Trnka, Pavel	Ana., Fla.	7	411	14	63	77	323	4	0	1	1	2	....	1997-98	2003-04
Trotter, Brock	Mtl.	1	2	0	0	0	0	....	....	....	....	....	....	2009-10	2009-10
Trottier, Bryan	NYI, Pit.	18	1279	524	901	1425	912	221	71	113	184	277	6	1975-76	1993-94
• Trottier, Dave	Mtl.M., Det.	11	446	121	113	234	517	31	4	3	7	39	1	1928-29	1938-39
• Trottier, Guy	NYR, Tor.	3	115	28	17	45	37	9	1	0	1	16	....	1968-69	1971-72
Trottier, Rocky	N.J.	2	38	6	4	10	2	....	....	....	....	....	....	1983-84	1984-85
Trudel, Jean-Guy	Phx., Min.	3	5	0	0	0	4	....	....	....	....	....	....	1999-00	2002-03
• Trudel, Lou	Chi., Mtl.	8	306	49	69	118	122	24	1	3	4	4	2	1933-34	1940-41
• Trudell, Rene	NYR	3	129	24	28	52	72	5	0	0	0	2	....	1945-46	1947-48
Tselios, Nikos	Car.	1	2	0	0	0	6	....	....	....	....	....	....	2001-02	2001-02
Tsulygin, Nikolai	Ana.	1	22	0	1	1	8	....	....	....	....	....	....	1996-97	1996-97
• Tsygurov, Denis	Buf., L.A.	3	51	1	5	6	45	....	....	....	....	....	....	1993-94	1995-96
Tsyplakov, Vladimir	L.A., Buf.	6	331	69	101	170	90	18	1	2	3	16	....	1995-96	2000-01
Tucker, Darcy	Mtl., T.B., Tor., Col.	14	947	215	261	476	1410	68	10	11	21	81	....	1995-96	2009-10
Tucker, John	Buf., Wsh., NYI, T.B.	12	656	177	259	436	285	31	10	18	28	24	....	1983-84	1995-96
• Tudin, Connie	Mtl.	1	4	0	1	1	4	....	....	....	....	....	....	1941-42	1941-42
Tudor, Rob	Van., St.L.	3	28	4	4	8	19	3	0	0	0	0	....	1978-79	1982-83
Tuer, Allan	L.A., Min., Hfd.	4	57	1	1	2	208	....	....	....	....	....	....	1985-86	1989-90
‡ Tukonen, Lauri	L.A.	2	5	0	0	0	0	....	....	....	....	....	....	2006-07	2007-08
Tuomainen, Marko	Edm., L.A., NYI	4	79	9	9	18	84	1	0	0	0	0	....	1994-95	2001-02

Name	NHL Teams	NHL Seasons	Regular Schedule GP	G	A	TP	PIM	Playoffs GP	G	A	TP	PIM	NHL Cup Wins	First NHL Season	Last NHL Season
Turcotte, Alfie	Mtl., Wpg., Wsh.	7	112	17	29	46	49	5	0	0	0	0	....	1983-84	1990-91
Turcotte, Darren	NYR, Hfd., Wpg., S.J., St.L., Nsh.	12	635	195	216	411	301	35	6	8	14	12	....	1988-89	1999-00
Turgeon, Pierre	Buf., NYI, Mtl., St.L., Dal., Col.	19	1294	515	812	1327	452	109	35	62	97	36	....	1987-88	2006-07
Turgeon, Sylvain	Hfd., N.J., Mtl., Ott.	12	669	269	226	495	691	36	4	7	11	22	....	1983-84	1994-95
Turlick, Gord	Bos.	1	2	0	0	0	2	....	....	....	....	....	....	1959-60	1959-60
Turnbull, Ian	Tor., L.A., Pit.	10	628	123	317	440	736	55	13	32	45	94	....	1973-74	1982-83
Turnbull, Perry	St.L., Mtl., Wpg.	9	608	188	163	351	1245	34	6	7	13	86	....	1979-80	1987-88
Turnbull, Randy	Cgy.	1	1	0	0	0	2	....	....	....	....	....	....	1981-82	1981-82
‡ Turnbull, Travis	Buf.	1	3	1	0	1	5	....	....	....	....	....	....	2011-12	2011-12
• Turner, Bob	Mtl., Chi.	8	478	19	51	70	307	68	1	4	5	44	5	1955-56	1962-63
Turner, Brad	NYI	1	3	0	0	0	0	....	....	....	....	....	....	1991-92	1991-92
Turner, Dean	NYR, Col., L.A.	4	35	1	0	1	59	....	....	....	....	....	....	1978-79	1982-83
• Tustin, Norm	NYR	1	18	2	4	6	0	....	....	....	....	....	....	1941-42	1941-42
• Tuten, Aud	Chi.	2	39	4	8	12	48	....	....	....	....	....	....	1941-42	1942-43
Tutt, Brian	Wsh.	1	7	1	0	1	2	....	....	....	....	....	....	1989-90	1989-90
Tuttle, Steve	St.L.	3	144	28	28	56	12	17	1	6	7	2	....	1988-89	1990-91
Tuzzolino, Tony	Ana., NYR, Bos.	3	9	0	0	0	7	....	....	....	....	....	....	1997-98	2001-02
Tverdovsky, Oleg	Ana., Wpg., Phx., N.J., Car., L.A.	11	713	77	240	317	291	45	0	14	14	6	2	1994-95	2006-07
Tvrdon, Roman	Wsh.	1	9	0	1	1	2	....	....	....	....	....	....	2003-04	2003-04
Twist, Tony	St.L., Que.	10	445	10	18	28	1121	18	1	1	2	22	....	1989-90	1998-99
Tyrell, Dana	T.B., CBJ	5	135	7	17	24	26	7	0	0	0	2	....	2010-11	2014-15

U V

Name	NHL Teams	NHL Seasons	Regular Schedule GP	G	A	TP	PIM	Playoffs GP	G	A	TP	PIM	NHL Cup Wins	First NHL Season	Last NHL Season
Ubriaco, Gene	Pit., Oak., Chi.	3	177	39	35	74	50	11	2	0	2	4	....	1967-68	1969-70
‡ Uher, Dominik	Pit.	1	2	0	0	0	0	....	....	....	....	....	....	2014-15	2014-15
Ulanov, Igor	Wpg., Wsh., Chi., T.B., Mtl., Edm., NYR, Fla.	14	739	27	135	162	1151	39	1	4	5	84	....	1991-92	2005-06
Ullman, Norm	Det., Tor.	20	1410	490	739	1229	712	106	30	53	83	67	....	1955-56	1974-75
‡ Ullstrom, David	NYI	2	49	6	7	13	12	3	0	1	1	0	....	2011-12	2012-13
Ulmer, Jeff	NYR	1	21	3	0	3	8	....	....	....	....	....	....	2000-01	2000-01
Ulmer, Layne	NYR	1	1	0	0	0	0	....	....	....	....	....	....	2003-04	2003-04
Umberger, RJ	Phi., CBJ	11	779	180	212	392	312	30	14	6	20	14	....	2005-06	**2015-16**
Unger, Garry	Tor., Det., St.L., Atl., L.A., Edm.	16	1105	413	391	804	1075	52	12	18	30	105	....	1967-68	1982-83
‡ Urbom, Alexander	N.J., Wsh.	4	34	3	1	4	28	....	....	....	....	....	....	2010-11	2013-14
Ustorf, Stefan	Wsh.	2	54	7	10	17	16	5	0	0	0	0	....	1995-96	1996-97
Vaananen, Ossi	Phx., Col., Phi., Van.	7	479	13	55	68	482	20	0	1	1	26	....	2000-01	2008-09
Vachon, Nick	NYI	1	1	0	0	0	0	....	....	....	....	....	....	1996-97	1996-97
• Vadnais, Carol	Mtl., Oak., Cal., Bos., NYR, N.J.	17	1087	169	418	587	1813	106	10	40	50	185	2	1966-67	1982-83
Vaic, Lubomir	Van.	2	9	1	1	2	2	....	....	....	....	....	....	1997-98	1999-00
Vail, Eric	Atl., Cgy., Det.	9	591	216	260	476	281	20	5	6	11	6	....	1973-74	1981-82
• Vail, Sparky	NYR	2	50	4	1	5	18	10	0	0	0	2	....	1928-29	1929-30
Vaive, Rick	Van., Tor., Chi., Buf.	13	876	441	347	788	1445	54	27	16	43	111	....	1979-80	1991-92
‡ Valabik, Boris	Atl.	3	80	0	7	7	210	....	....	....	....	....	....	2007-08	2009-10
Valentine, Chris	Wsh.	3	105	43	52	95	127	2	0	0	0	4	....	1981-82	1983-84
Valicevic, Rob	Nsh., L.A., Ana., Dal.	6	193	28	20	48	61	....	....	....	....	....	....	1998-99	2003-04
Valiquette, Jack	Tor., Col.	7	350	84	134	218	79	23	3	6	9	4	....	1974-75	1980-81
Valk, Garry	Van., Ana., Pit., Tor., Chi.	13	777	100	156	256	747	61	6	7	13	79	....	1990-91	2002-03
Vallis, Lindsay	Mtl.	1	1	0	0	0	0	....	....	....	....	....	....	1993-94	1993-94
Van Allen, Shaun	Edm., Ana., Ott., Dal., Mtl.	13	794	84	185	269	481	61	1	7	8	45	....	1990-91	2003-04
Van Boxmeer, John	Mtl., Col., Buf., Que.	11	588	84	274	358	465	38	5	15	20	37	1	1973-74	1983-84
Van Der Gulik, David	Cgy., Col., L.A.	6	49	2	11	13	10	....	....	....	....	....	....	2008-09	2014-15
Van Dorp, Wayne	Edm., Pit., Chi., Que.	6	125	12	12	24	565	27	0	1	1	42	....	1986-87	1991-92
Van Drunen, David	Ott.	1	1	0	0	0	0	....	....	....	....	....	....	1999-00	1999-00
Van Guilder, Mark	Nsh.	1	1	0	0	0	0	....	....	....	....	....	....	2013-14	2013-14
Van Impe, Darren	Ana., Bos., NYR, Fla., NYI, CBJ	9	411	25	90	115	397	33	3	9	12	28	....	1994-95	2002-03
Van Impe, Ed	Chi., Phi., Pit.	11	700	27	126	153	1025	66	1	12	13	131	2	1966-67	1976-77
Van Ryn, Mike	St.L., Fla., Tor.	9	353	30	99	129	260	9	0	0	0	0	....	2000-01	2009-10
VandenBussche, Ryan	NYR, Chi., Pit.	9	310	10	10	20	702	1	0	0	0	0	....	1996-97	2005-06
Vandermeer, Jim	Phi., Chi., Cgy., Phx., Edm., S.J.	9	461	25	80	105	664	21	0	2	2	17	....	2002-03	2011-12
Vandermeer, Peter	Phx.	1	2	0	0	0	0	....	....	....	....	....	....	2007-08	2007-08
Varada, Vaclav	Buf., Ott.	10	493	58	125	183	410	87	11	19	30	82	....	1995-96	2005-06
Varis, Petri	Chi.	1	1	0	0	0	0	....	....	....	....	....	....	1997-98	1997-98
Varlamov, Sergei	Cgy., St.L.	4	63	8	7	15	26	1	0	0	0	2	....	1997-98	2002-03
Varvio, Jarkko	Dal.	2	13	3	4	7	4	....	....	....	....	....	....	1993-94	1994-95
• Vasicek, Josef	Car., Nsh., NYI	7	460	77	106	183	311	37	5	2	7	14	1	2000-01	2007-08
Vasilevski, Alexander	St.L.	2	4	0	0	0	2	....	....	....	....	....	....	1995-96	1996-97
Vasiliev, Alexei	NYR	1	1	0	0	0	2	....	....	....	....	....	....	1999-00	1999-00
Vasiljevs, Herbert	Fla., Atl., Van.	4	51	8	7	15	22	....	....	....	....	....	....	1998-99	2001-02
Vasilyev, Andrei	NYI, Phx.	4	16	2	5	7	6	....	....	....	....	....	....	1994-95	1998-99
Vaske, Dennis	NYI, Bos.	9	235	5	41	46	253	22	0	7	7	16	....	1990-91	1998-99
• Vasko, Moose	Chi., Min.	13	786	34	166	200	719	78	2	7	9	73	1	1956-57	1969-70
Vasko, Rick	Det.	3	31	3	7	10	29	....	....	....	....	....	....	1977-78	1980-81
• Vasyunov, Alexander	N.J.	1	18	1	4	5	0	....	....	....	....	....	....	2010-11	2010-11
‡ Vauclair, Julien	Ott.	1	1	0	0	0	2	....	....	....	....	....	....	2003-04	2003-04
Vautour, Yvon	NYI, Col., N.J., Que.	6	204	26	33	59	401	....	....	....	....	....	....	1979-80	1984-85
Vaydik, Greg	Chi.	1	5	0	0	0	0	....	....	....	....	....	....	1976-77	1976-77
Veilleux, Stephane	Min., T.B., N.J.	11	506	50	56	106	348	17	0	0	0	35	....	2002-03	2014-15
Veitch, Darren	Wsh., Det., Tor.	10	511	48	209	257	296	33	4	11	15	33	....	1980-81	1990-91
Velischek, Randy	Min., N.J., Que.	10	509	21	76	97	401	44	2	5	7	32	....	1982-83	1991-92
Vellucci, Mike	Hfd.	1	2	0	0	0	11	....	....	....	....	....	....	1987-88	1987-88
Venasky, Vic	L.A.	7	430	61	101	162	66	21	1	5	6	12	....	1972-73	1978-79
Veneruzzo, Gary	St.L.	2	7	1	1	2	0	9	0	2	2	2	....	1967-68	1971-72
Verbeek, Pat	N.J., Hfd., NYR, Dal., Det.	20	1424	522	541	1063	2905	117	26	36	62	225	1	1982-83	2001-02
Vermette, Mark	Que.	4	67	5	13	18	33	....	....	....	....	....	....	1988-89	1991-92
Vernace, Mike	Col., T.B.	2	22	0	1	1	10	....	....	....	....	....	....	2008-09	2010-11
Vernarsky, Kris	Bos.	2	17	1	0	1	2	....	....	....	....	....	....	2002-03	2003-04
Verot, Darcy	Wsh.	1	37	0	2	2	135	....	....	....	....	....	....	2003-04	2003-04
Verret, Claude	Buf.	2	14	2	5	7	2	....	....	....	....	....	....	1983-84	1984-85
Verstraete, Leigh	Tor.	3	8	0	1	1	14	....	....	....	....	....	....	1982-83	1987-88
Ververgaert, Dennis	Van., Phi., Wsh.	8	583	176	216	392	247	8	1	2	3	6	....	1973-74	1980-81
‡ Vesce, Ryan	S.J.	2	19	3	2	5	4	....	....	....	....	....	....	2008-09	2009-10
Vesey, Jim	St.L., Bos.	3	15	1	2	3	7	....	....	....	....	....	....	1988-89	1991-92
Veysey, Sid	Van.	1	1	0	0	0	0	....	....	....	....	....	....	1977-78	1977-78
Vial, Dennis	NYR, Det., Ott.	8	242	4	15	19	794	....	....	....	....	....	....	1990-91	1997-98
Vickers, Steve	NYR	10	698	246	340	586	330	68	24	25	49	58	....	1972-73	1981-82
Vigier, J.P.	Atl.	6	213	23	23	46	97	....	....	....	....	....	....	2000-01	2006-07
Vigneault, Alain	St.L.	2	42	2	5	7	82	4	0	1	1	26	....	1981-82	1982-83
Viitakoski, Vesa	Cgy.	3	23	2	4	6	8	....	....	....	....	....	....	1993-94	1995-96
Vilgrain, Claude	Van., N.J., Phi.	5	89	21	32	53	78	11	1	1	2	17	....	1987-88	1993-94
Vincelette, Dan	Chi., Que.	6	193	20	22	42	351	12	0	0	0	4	....	1986-87	1991-92
‡ Vincour, Tomas	Dal., Col.	4	95	7	10	17	12	....	....	....	....	....	....	2010-11	2014-15
Vipond, Pete	Cal.	1	3	0	0	0	0	....	....	....	....	....	....	1972-73	1972-73
Virta, Hannu	Buf.	5	245	25	101	126	66	17	1	3	4	6	....	1981-82	1985-86
Virta, Tony	Min.	1	8	2	3	5	0	....	....	....	....	....	....	2001-02	2001-02
Virtue, Terry	Bos., NYR	2	5	0	0	0	0	....	....	....	....	....	....	1998-99	1999-00
Visheau, Mark	Wpg., L.A.	2	29	1	3	4	107	....	....	....	....	....	....	1993-94	1998-99
Vishnevski, Vitaly	Ana., Atl., Nsh., N.J.	8	552	16	52	68	494	40	0	5	5	18	....	1999-00	2007-08
Vishnevskiy, Ivan	Dal.	2	5	0	2	2	2	....	....	....	....	....	....	2008-09	2009-10
Visnovsky, Lubomir	L.A., Edm., Ana., NYI	14	883	128	367	495	373	28	0	8	8	4	....	2000-01	2014-15
Vitale, Joe	Pit., Ari.	6	234	11	33	44	156	23	0	1	1	22	....	2010-11	**2015-16**
Vitolinsh, Harijs	Wpg.	1	8	0	0	0	4	....	....	....	....	....	....	1993-94	1993-94
Viveiros, Emanuel	Min.	3	29	1	11	12	6	....	....	....	....	....	....	1985-86	1987-88
Vlasak, Tomas	L.A.	1	10	1	3	4	2	....	....	....	....	....	....	2000-01	2000-01
• Vokes, Ed	Chi.	1	5	0	0	0	0	....	....	....	....	....	....	1930-31	1930-31
Volcan, Mickey	Hfd., Cgy.	4	162	8	33	41	146	....	....	....	....	....	....	1980-81	1983-84
‡ Volchenkov, Anton	Ott., N.J., Nsh.	12	696	19	114	133	438	86	4	13	17	60	....	2002-03	2014-15
Volchkov, Alexandre	Wsh.	1	3	0	0	0	0	....	....	....	....	....	....	1999-00	1999-00
Volek, David	NYI	6	396	95	154	249	201	15	5	5	10	2	....	1988-89	1993-94
Volmar, Doug	Det., L.A.	4	62	13	8	21	26	2	1	0	1	0	....	1969-70	1972-73
Volpatti, Aaron	Van., Wsh.	5	114	5	2	7	137	....	....	....	....	....	....	2010-11	2014-15
Von Arx, Reto	Chi.	1	19	3	1	4	4	....	....	....	....	....	....	2000-01	2000-01

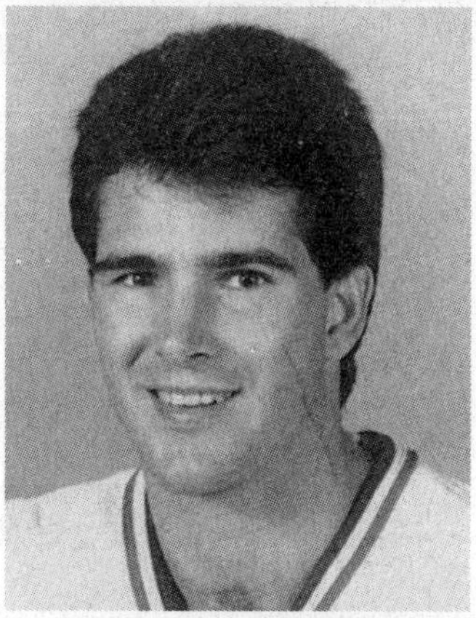

Sylvain Turgeon

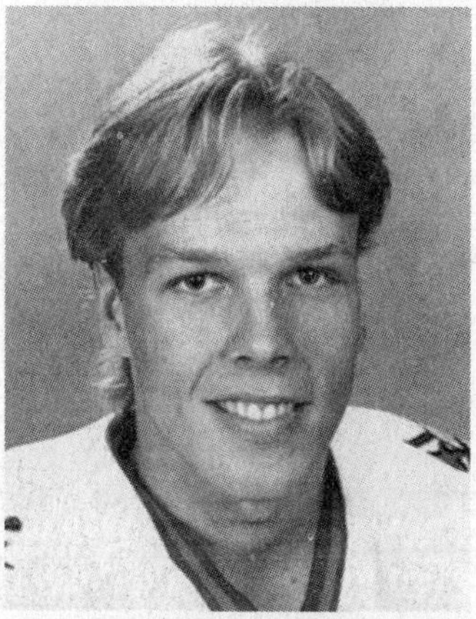

Stefan Ustorf

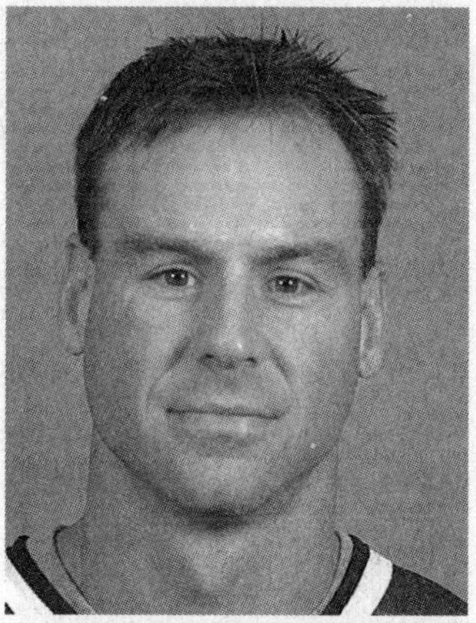

Rob Valicevic

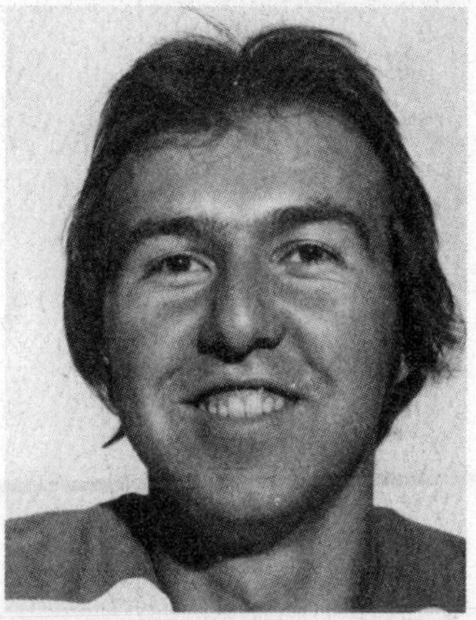

Jack Valiquette

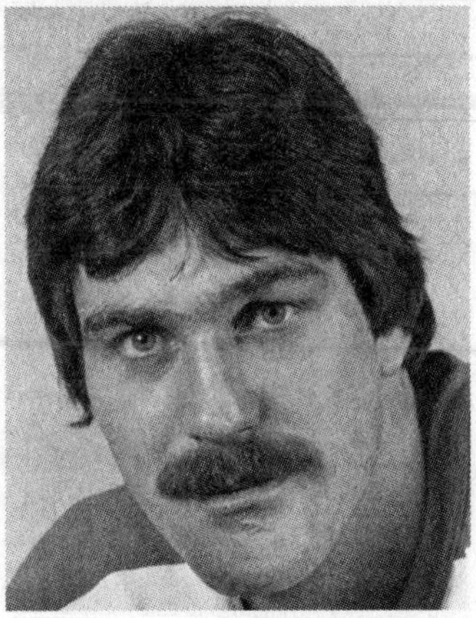

Dennis Ververgaert

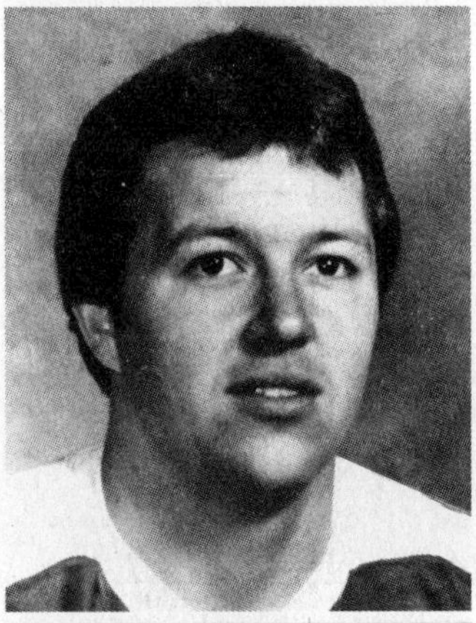

Kurt Walker

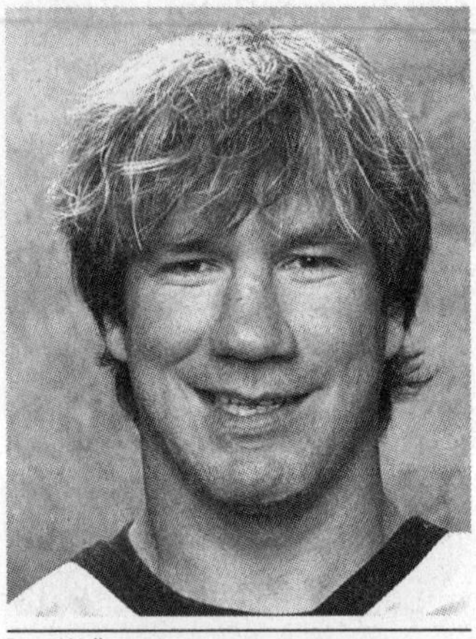

Scott Walker

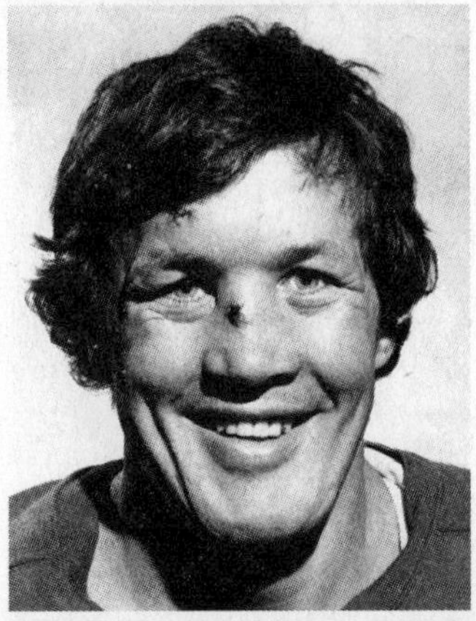

Bryan Watson

Name	NHL Teams	NHL Seasons	Regular Schedule GP	G	A	TP	PIM	Playoffs GP	G	A	TP	PIM	NHL Cup Wins	First NHL Season	Last NHL Season
Von Stefenelli, Phil	Bos., Ott.	2	33	0	5	5	23	....	....	....	....	....	....	1995-96	1996-97
Vopat, Jan	L.A., Nsh.	5	126	11	20	31	70	2	0	1	1	2	....	1995-96	1999-00
Vopat, Roman	St.L., L.A., Chi., Phi.	4	133	6	14	20	253	....	....	....	....	....	....	1995-96	1998-99
Vorobiev, Pavel	Chi.	2	57	10	15	25	38	....	....	....	....	....	....	2003-04	2005-06
Vorobiev, Vladimir	NYR, Edm.	3	33	9	7	16	14	1	0	0	0	0	....	1996-97	1998-99
Voros, Aaron	Min., NYR, Ana.	4	162	18	19	37	395	9	1	0	1	30	....	2007-08	2010-11
• Voss, Carl	Tor., NYR, Det., Ott., St.L., NYA, Mtl.M., Chi.	8	261	34	70	104	50	24	5	3	8	0	1	1926-27	1937-38
‡ Voynov, Slava	L.A.	4	190	18	63	81	72	64	9	16	25	20	2	2011-12	2014-15
‡ Vrana, Petr	N.J.	1	16	1	0	1	2	....	....	....	....	....	....	2008-09	2008-09
Vujtek, Vladimir	Mtl., Edm., T.B., Atl., Pit.	6	110	7	30	37	38	....	....	....	....	....	....	1991-92	2002-03
Vukota, Mick	NYI, T.B., Mtl.	11	574	17	29	46	2071	23	0	0	0	73	....	1987-88	1997-98
• Vyazmikin, Igor	Edm.	1	4	1	0	1	0	....	....	....	....	....	....	1990-91	1990-91
Vyborny, David	CBJ	7	543	113	204	317	228	....	....	....	....	....	....	2000-01	2007-08
Vyshedkevich, Sergei	Atl.	2	30	2	5	7	16	....	....	....	....	....	....	1999-00	2000-01

W

Name	NHL Teams	NHL Seasons	Regular Schedule GP	G	A	TP	PIM	Playoffs GP	G	A	TP	PIM	NHL Cup Wins	First NHL Season	Last NHL Season
Waddell, Don	L.A.	1	1	0	0	0	0	....	....	....	....	....	....	1980-81	1980-81
Wagner, Steve	St.L.	2	46	4	8	12	26	....	....	....	....	....	....	2007-08	2008-09
• Waite, Frank	NYR	1	17	1	3	4	4	....	....	....	....	....	....	1930-31	1930-31
Walker, Gord	NYR, L.A.	4	31	3	4	7	23	....	....	....	....	....	....	1986-87	1989-90
Walker, Howard	Wsh., Cgy.	3	83	2	13	15	133	....	....	....	....	....	....	1980-81	1982-83
• Walker, Jack	Det.	2	80	5	8	13	18	....	....	....	....	....	....	1926-27	1927-28
Walker, Kurt	Tor.	3	71	4	5	9	142	16	0	0	0	34	....	1975-76	1977-78
Walker, Matt	St.L., Chi., T.B., Phi.	9	314	4	26	30	464	21	0	2	2	14	....	2002-03	2011-12
Walker, Russ	L.A.	2	17	1	0	1	41	....	....	....	....	....	....	1976-77	1977-78
Walker, Scott	Van., Nsh., Car., Wsh.	15	829	151	246	397	1162	30	1	7	8	31	....	1994-95	2009-10
Wall, Bob	Det., L.A., St.L.	8	322	30	55	85	155	22	0	3	3	2	....	1964-65	1971-72
‡ Wallace, Tim	Pit., NYI, T.B., Car.	5	101	4	9	13	45	....	....	....	....	....	....	2008-09	2012-13
Wallin, Jesse	Det.	4	49	0	2	2	34	....	....	....	....	....	....	1999-00	2002-03
Wallin, Niclas	Car., S.J.	10	614	21	58	79	460	93	4	8	12	44	1	2000-01	2010-11
Wallin, Peter	NYR	2	52	3	14	17	14	14	2	6	8	6	....	1980-81	1981-82
Wallin, Rickard	Min., Tor.	3	79	8	11	19	34	....	....	....	....	....	....	2002-03	2009-10
‡ Walser, Derrick	CBJ	4	91	8	21	29	56	....	....	....	....	....	....	2001-02	2006-07
Walsh, Jim	Buf.	1	4	0	1	1	4	....	....	....	....	....	....	1981-82	1981-82
Walsh, Mike	NYI	2	14	2	0	2	4	....	....	....	....	....	....	1987-88	1988-89
‡ Walter, Ben	Bos., NYI, N.J.	5	24	1	0	1	6	....	....	....	....	....	....	2005-06	2009-10
Walter, Ryan	Wsh., Mtl., Van.	15	1003	264	382	646	946	113	16	35	51	62	1	1978-79	1992-93
• Walton, Bobby	Mtl.	1	4	0	0	0	0	....	....	....	....	....	....	1943-44	1943-44
Walton, Mike	Tor., Bos., Van., St.L., Chi.	12	588	201	247	448	357	47	14	10	24	45	2	1965-66	1978-79
Walz, Wes	Bos., Phi., Cgy., Det., Min.	13	607	109	151	260	343	32	10	7	17	20	....	1989-90	2007-08
‡ Wandell, Tom	Dal.	5	229	20	23	43	52	....	....	....	....	....	....	2008-09	2012-13
Wanvig, Kyle	Min., T.B.	5	75	6	9	15	94	....	....	....	....	....	....	2002-03	2007-08
Wappel, Gord	Atl., Cgy.	3	20	1	1	2	10	2	0	0	0	4	....	1979-80	1981-82
Ward, Aaron	Det., Car., NYR, Bos., Ana.	15	839	44	107	151	736	95	4	6	10	73	3	1993-94	2009-10
Ward, Dixon	Van., L.A., Tor., Buf., Bos., NYR	10	537	95	129	224	431	62	14	20	34	46	....	1992-93	2002-03
• Ward, Don	Chi., Bos.	2	34	0	1	1	16	....	....	....	....	....	....	1957-58	1959-60
Ward, Ed	Que., Cgy., Atl., Ana., N.J.	8	278	23	26	49	354	....	....	....	....	....	....	1993-94	2000-01
Ward, Jason	Mtl., NYR, L.A., T.B.	8	336	36	45	81	171	12	0	3	3	10	....	1999-00	2008-09
• Ward, Jimmy	Mtl.M., Mtl.	12	527	147	127	274	455	36	4	4	8	26	1	1927-28	1938-39
Ward, Joe	Col.	1	4	0	0	0	2	....	....	....	....	....	....	1980-81	1980-81
Ward, Lance	Fla., Ana.	4	209	4	12	16	391	....	....	....	....	....	....	2000-01	2003-04
Ward, Ron	Tor., Van.	2	89	2	5	7	6	....	....	....	....	....	....	1969-70	1971-72
Ware, Jeff	Tor., Fla.	3	21	0	1	1	12	....	....	....	....	....	....	1996-97	1998-99
Ware, Michael	Edm.	2	5	0	1	1	15	....	....	....	....	....	....	1988-89	1989-90
• Wares, Eddie	NYR, Det., Chi.	9	321	60	102	162	161	45	5	7	12	34	1	1936-37	1946-47
Warner, Bob	Tor.	2	10	1	1	2	4	4	0	0	0	0	....	1975-76	1976-77
Warner, Jim	Hfd.	1	32	0	3	3	10	....	....	....	....	....	....	1979-80	1979-80
Warrener, Rhett	Fla., Buf., Cgy.	12	714	24	82	106	899	101	1	7	8	68	....	1995-96	2007-08
Warriner, Todd	Tor., T.B., Phx., Van., Phi., Nsh.	9	453	65	89	154	249	21	2	1	3	6	....	1994-95	2002-03
• Warwick, Billy	NYR	2	14	3	3	6	16	....	....	....	....	....	....	1942-43	1943-44
• Warwick, Grant	NYR, Bos., Mtl.	9	395	147	142	289	220	16	2	4	6	6	....	1941-42	1949-50
Washburn, Steve	Fla., Van., Phi.	6	93	14	15	29	42	1	0	1	1	0	....	1995-96	2000-01
• Wasnie, Nick	Chi., Mtl., NYA, Ott., St.L.	7	248	57	34	91	176	20	6	3	9	20	2	1927-28	1934-35
Wathier, Francis	Dal.	4	10	0	0	0	5	....	....	....	....	....	....	2009-10	2012-13
Watkins, Matt	Phx.	1	1	0	0	0	0	....	....	....	....	....	....	2011-12	2011-12
Watson, Bill	Chi.	4	115	23	36	59	12	6	0	2	2	0	....	1985-86	1988-89
Watson, Bryan	Mtl., Det., Oak., Pit., St.L., Wsh.	16	878	17	135	152	2212	32	2	0	2	70	1	1963-64	1978-79
Watson, Dave	Col.	2	18	0	1	1	10	....	....	....	....	....	....	1979-80	1980-81
• Watson, Harry	Bro., Det., Tor., Chi.	14	809	236	207	443	150	62	16	9	25	27	5	1941-42	1956-57
Watson, Jim	Det., Buf.	8	221	4	19	23	345	....	....	....	....	....	....	1963-64	1971-72
Watson, Jimmy	Phi.	10	613	38	148	186	492	101	5	34	39	89	2	1972-73	1981-82
Watson, Joe	Bos., Phi., Col.	14	835	38	178	216	447	84	3	12	15	82	2	1964-65	1978-79
• Watson, Phil	NYR, Mtl.	13	590	144	265	409	532	54	10	25	35	67	2	1935-36	1947-48
Watt, Mike	Edm., NYI, Nsh., Car.	5	157	15	26	41	41	....	....	....	....	....	....	1997-98	2002-03
Watters, Tim	Wpg., L.A.	14	741	26	151	177	1289	82	1	5	6	115	....	1981-82	1994-95
Watts, Brian	Det.	1	4	0	0	0	0	....	....	....	....	....	....	1975-76	1975-76
Weaver, Mike	Atl., L.A., Van., St.L., Fla., Mtl.	13	633	8	89	97	227	28	2	3	5	14	....	2001-02	2014-15
Webb, Steve	NYI, Pit.	8	321	5	13	18	532	14	0	0	0	28	....	1996-97	2003-04
• Webster, Aubrey	Phi., Mtl.M.	2	5	0	0	0	0	....	....	....	....	....	....	1930-31	1934-35
• Webster, Don	Tor.	1	27	7	6	13	28	5	0	0	0	12	....	1943-44	1943-44
Webster, John	NYR	1	14	0	0	0	4	....	....	....	....	....	....	1949-50	1949-50
Webster, Tom	Bos., Det., Cal.	5	102	33	42	75	61	1	0	0	0	0	....	1968-69	1979-80
Weight, Doug	NYR, Edm., St.L., Car., Ana., NYI	20	1238	278	755	1033	970	97	23	49	72	94	1	1990-91	2010-11
• Weiland, Cooney	Bos., Ott., Det.	11	509	173	160	333	147	45	12	10	22	12	2	1928-29	1938-39
Weinhandl, Mattias	NYI, Min.	4	182	19	37	56	70	5	0	0	0	2	....	2002-03	2006-07
Weinrich, Eric	N.J., Hfd., Chi., Mtl., Bos., Phi., St.L., Van.	17	1157	70	318	388	825	81	6	23	29	67	....	1988-89	2005-06
Weir, Stan	Cal., Tor., Edm., Col., Det.	10	642	139	207	346	183	37	6	5	11	4	....	1972-73	1982-83
Weir, Wally	Que., Hfd., Pit.	6	320	21	45	66	625	23	0	1	1	96	....	1979-80	1984-85
Weiss, Stephen	Fla., Det.	13	732	156	267	423	341	9	3	2	5	6	....	2001-02	2014-15
‡ Welch, Noah	Pit., Fla., T.B., Atl.	5	75	4	5	9	58	....	....	....	....	....	....	2005-06	2010-11
Weller, Craig	Phx., Min.	2	95	4	10	14	127	....	....	....	....	....	....	2007-08	2008-09
• Wellington, Alex	Que.	1	1	0	0	0	0	....	....	....	....	....	....	1919-20	1919-20
‡ Wellman, Casey	Min., Wsh.	4	54	6	10	16	4	....	....	....	....	....	....	2009-10	2013-14
Wells, Chris	Pit., Fla.	5	195	9	20	29	193	3	0	0	0	0	....	1995-96	1999-00
Wells, Jay	L.A., Phi., Buf., NYR, St.L., T.B.	18	1098	47	216	263	2359	114	3	14	17	213	1	1979-80	1996-97
Wellwood, Eric	Phi.	3	31	5	5	10	4	11	0	0	0	2	....	2010-11	2012-13
Wellwood, Kyle	Tor., Van., S.J., Wpg.	9	489	92	143	235	36	40	4	16	20	0	....	2003-04	2012-13
‡ Welsh, Jeremy	Car., Van., St.L.	4	27	1	1	2	12	....	....	....	....	....	....	2011-12	**2015-16**
Wensink, John	St.L., Bos., Que., Col., N.J.	8	403	70	68	138	840	43	2	6	8	86	....	1973-74	1982-83
• Wentworth, Cy	Chi., Mtl.M., Mtl.	13	575	39	68	107	355	35	5	6	11	20	1	1927-28	1939-40
Werenka, Brad	Edm., Que., Chi., Pit., Cgy.	7	320	19	61	80	299	19	2	1	3	14	....	1992-93	2000-01
Wesenberg, Brian	Phi.	1	1	0	0	0	5	....	....	....	....	....	....	1998-99	1998-99
Wesley, Blake	Phi., Hfd., Que., Tor.	7	298	18	46	64	486	19	2	2	4	30	....	1979-80	1985-86
Wesley, Glen	Bos., Hfd., Car., Tor.	20	1457	128	409	537	1045	169	15	37	52	141	1	1987-88	2007-08
Westcott, Duvie	CBJ	6	201	11	45	56	299	....	....	....	....	....	....	2001-02	2007-08
Westfall, Ed	Bos., NYI	18	1226	231	394	625	544	95	22	37	59	41	2	1961-62	1978-79
Westgarth, Kevin	L.A., Car., Cgy.	5	169	7	9	16	266	6	0	2	2	14	1	2008-09	2013-14
Westlund, Tommy	Car.	4	203	9	13	22	48	25	1	0	1	17	....	1999-00	2002-03
Westrum, Erik	Phx., Min., Tor.	3	27	1	2	3	22	....	....	....	....	....	....	2003-04	2006-07
Wey, Patrick	Wsh.	1	9	0	3	3	5	....	....	....	....	....	....	2013-14	2013-14
• Wharram, Kenny	Chi.	14	766	252	281	533	222	80	16	27	43	38	1	1951-52	1968-69
• Wharton, Len	NYR	1	1	0	0	0	0	....	....	....	....	....	....	1944-45	1944-45
Wheeldon, Simon	NYR, Wpg.	3	15	0	2	2	10	....	....	....	....	....	....	1987-88	1990-91
• Wheldon, Don	St.L.	1	2	0	0	0	0	....	....	....	....	....	....	1974-75	1974-75
Whelton, Bill	Wpg.	1	2	0	0	0	0	....	....	....	....	....	....	1980-81	1980-81
Whistle, Rob	NYR, St.L.	2	51	7	5	12	16	4	0	0	0	2	....	1985-86	1987-88
• White, Bill	L.A., Chi.	9	604	50	215	265	495	91	7	32	39	76	....	1967-68	1975-76
White, Brian	Col.	1	2	0	0	0	0	....	....	....	....	....	....	1998-99	1998-99
White, Colin	N.J., S.J.	12	797	21	108	129	869	114	3	14	17	125	2	1999-00	2011-12

Name	NHL Teams	NHL Seasons	Regular Schedule GP	G	A	TP	PIM	Playoffs GP	G	A	TP	PIM	NHL Cup Wins	First NHL Season	Last NHL Season
White, Ian	Tor., Cgy., Car., S.J., Det.	8	503	45	134	179	254	22	2	8	10	8	....	2005-06	2012-13
• White, Moe	Mtl.	1	4	0	1	1	2	....	....	....	....	....	....	1945-46	1945-46
White, Peter	Edm., Tor., Phi., Chi.	9	220	23	37	60	36	19	0	2	2	0	....	1993-94	2003-04
• White, Sherman	NYR	2	4	0	2	2	0	....	....	....	....	....	....	1946-47	1949-50
• White, Tex	Pit., NYA, Phi.	6	203	33	12	45	141	4	0	0	0	4	....	1925-26	1930-31
White, Todd	Chi., Phi., Ott., Min., Atl., NYR	13	653	141	240	381	228	43	8	3	11	16	....	1997-98	2010-11
White, Tony	Wsh., Min.	5	164	37	28	65	104	....	....	....	....	....	....	1974-75	1979-80
• Whitelaw, Bob	Det.	2	32	0	2	2	2	8	0	0	0	0	....	1940-41	1941-42
Whitfield, Trent	Wsh., NYR, St.L., Bos.	9	194	11	18	29	104	18	0	0	0	12	....	1999-00	2011-12
Whitlock, Bob	Min.	1	1	0	0	0	0	....	....	....	....	....	....	1969-70	1969-70
‡ Whitmore, Derek	Buf.	1	2	0	0	0	0	....	....	....	....	....	....	2011-12	2011-12
Whitney, Ray	S.J., Edm., Fla., CBJ, Det., Car., Phx., Dal.	22	1330	385	679	1064	465	108	21	32	53	48	1	1991-92	2013-14
Whitney, Ryan	Pit., Ana., Edm., Fla.	9	481	50	209	259	383	38	3	11	14	40	....	2005-06	2013-14
Whyte, Sean	L.A.	2	21	0	2	2	12	....	....	....	....	....	....	1991-92	1992-93
‡ Wick, Roman	Ott.	1	7	0	0	0	0	....	....	....	....	....	....	2010-11	2010-11
• Wickenheiser, Doug	Mtl., St.L., Van., NYR, Wsh.	10	556	111	165	276	286	41	4	7	11	18	....	1980-81	1989-90
• Widing, Juha	NYR, L.A., Cle.	8	575	144	226	370	208	8	1	2	3	2	....	1969-70	1976-77
Widmer, Jason	NYI, S.J.	3	7	0	1	1	7	....	....	....	....	....	....	1994-95	1996-97
• Wiebe, Art	Chi.	11	414	14	27	41	201	31	1	3	4	10	1	1932-33	1943-44
Wiemer, Jason	T.B., Cgy., Fla., NYI, Min., N.J.	11	726	90	112	202	1420	19	1	0	1	67	....	1994-95	2005-06
Wiemer, Jim	Buf., NYR, Edm., L.A., Bos.	11	325	29	72	101	378	62	5	8	13	63	....	1982-83	1993-94
• Wilcox, Archie	Mtl.M., Bos., St.L.	6	208	8	14	22	158	12	1	0	1	8	....	1929-30	1934-35
Wilcox, Barry	Van.	2	33	3	2	5	15	....	....	....	....	....	....	1972-73	1974-75
• Wilder, Arch	Det.	1	18	0	2	2	2	....	....	....	....	....	....	1940-41	1940-41
Wiley, Jim	Pit., Van.	5	63	4	10	14	8	....	....	....	....	....	....	1972-73	1976-77
Wilkie, Bob	Det., Phi.	2	18	2	5	7	10	....	....	....	....	....	....	1990-91	1993-94
Wilkie, David	Mtl., T.B., NYR	6	167	10	26	36	165	8	1	2	3	14	....	1994-95	2000-01
• Wilkins, Barry	Bos., Van., Pit.	9	418	27	125	152	663	6	0	1	1	4	....	1966-67	1975-76
• Wilkinson, John	Bos.	1	9	0	0	0	6	....	....	....	....	....	....	1943-44	1943-44
Wilkinson, Neil	Min., S.J., Chi., Wpg., Pit.	10	460	16	67	83	813	53	3	6	9	41	....	1989-90	1998-99
Wilks, Brian	L.A.	4	48	4	8	12	27	....	....	....	....	....	....	1984-85	1988-89
Willard, Rod	Tor.	1	1	0	0	0	0	....	....	....	....	....	....	1982-83	1982-83
• Williams, Burr	Det., St.L., Bos.	3	19	0	1	1	28	7	0	0	0	8	....	1933-34	1936-37
Williams, Butch	St.L., Cal.	3	108	14	35	49	131	....	....	....	....	....	....	1973-74	1975-76
Williams, Darryl	L.A.	1	2	0	0	0	10	....	....	....	....	....	....	1992-93	1992-93
Williams, David	S.J., Ana.	4	173	11	53	64	157	....	....	....	....	....	....	1991-92	1994-95
Williams, Fred	Det.	1	44	2	5	7	10	....	....	....	....	....	....	1976-77	1976-77
Williams, Gord	Phi.	2	2	0	0	0	2	....	....	....	....	....	....	1981-82	1982-83
‡ Williams, Jason	Det., Chi., Atl., CBJ, Dal., Pit.	11	455	94	133	227	157	27	1	2	3	12	1	2000-01	2011-12
Williams, Jeremy	Tor., NYR	5	32	9	2	11	6	....	....	....	....	....	....	2005-06	2010-11
Williams, Sean	Chi.	1	2	0	0	0	4	....	....	....	....	....	....	1991-92	1991-92
Williams, Tiger	Tor., Van., Det., L.A., Hfd.	14	962	241	272	513	3966	83	12	23	35	455	....	1974-75	1987-88
Williams, Tom	NYR, L.A.	8	397	115	138	253	73	29	8	7	15	4	....	1971-72	1978-79
• Williams, Tommy	Bos., Min., Cal., Wsh.	13	663	161	269	430	177	10	2	5	7	2	....	1961-62	1975-76
Willis, Shane	Car., T.B.	5	174	31	43	74	77	2	0	0	0	0	....	1998-99	2003-04
‡ Willsie, Brian	Col., Wsh., L.A.	10	381	52	57	109	217	10	1	1	2	4	....	1999-00	2010-11
• Willson, Don	Mtl.	2	22	2	7	9	0	3	0	0	0	0	....	1937-38	1938-39
Wilm, Clarke	Cgy., Nsh., Tor.	7	455	37	60	97	336	5	0	1	1	2	....	1998-99	2005-06
Wilson, Behn	Phi., Chi.	9	601	98	260	358	1480	67	12	29	41	190	....	1978-79	1987-88
• Wilson, Bert	NYR, St.L., L.A., Cgy.	8	478	37	44	81	646	21	0	2	2	42	....	1973-74	1980-81
Wilson, Bob	Chi.	1	1	0	0	0	0	....	....	....	....	....	....	1953-54	1953-54
Wilson, Carey	Cgy., Hfd., NYR	10	552	169	258	427	314	52	11	13	24	14	....	1983-84	1992-93
‡ Wilson, Clay	CBJ, Atl., Fla., Cgy.	5	36	4	4	8	12	....	....	....	....	....	....	2007-08	2011-12
• Wilson, Cully	Tor., Mtl., Ham., Chi.	5	127	59	28	87	243	2	1	0	1	6	....	1919-20	1926-27
Wilson, Doug	Chi., S.J.	16	1024	237	590	827	830	95	19	61	80	88	....	1977-78	1992-93
• Wilson, Gerry	Mtl.	1	3	0	0	0	2	....	....	....	....	....	....	1956-57	1956-57
Wilson, Gord	Bos.	1	....	....	....	....	....	2	0	0	0	0	....	1954-55	1954-55
• Wilson, Hub	NYA	1	2	0	0	0	0	....	....	....	....	....	....	1931-32	1931-32
• Wilson, Johnny	Det., Chi., Tor., NYR	13	688	161	171	332	190	66	14	13	27	11	4	1949-50	1961-62
‡ Wilson, Kyle	Wsh., CBJ, Nsh.	3	39	4	9	13	12	....	....	....	....	....	....	2009-10	2011-12
Wilson, Landon	Col., Bos., Phx., Pit., Dal.	10	375	53	66	119	352	13	1	1	2	20	....	1995-96	2008-09
• Wilson, Larry	Det., Chi.	6	152	21	48	69	75	4	0	0	0	0	1	1949-50	1955-56
Wilson, Mike	Buf., Fla., Pit., NYR	8	336	16	41	57	264	29	0	2	2	15	....	1995-96	2002-03
Wilson, Mitch	N.J., Pit.	2	26	2	3	5	104	....	....	....	....	....	....	1984-85	1986-87
Wilson, Murray	Mtl., L.A.	7	386	94	95	189	162	53	5	14	19	32	4	1972-73	1978-79
Wilson, Rick	Mtl., St.L., Det.	4	239	6	26	32	165	3	0	0	0	0	....	1973-74	1976-77
• Wilson, Rik	St.L., Cgy., Chi.	6	251	25	65	90	220	22	0	4	4	23	....	1981-82	1987-88
Wilson, Roger	Chi.	1	7	0	2	2	6	....	....	....	....	....	....	1974-75	1974-75
Wilson, Ron	Tor., Min.	7	177	26	67	93	68	20	4	13	17	8	....	1977-78	1987-88
Wilson, Ron	Wpg., St.L., Mtl.	14	832	110	216	326	415	63	10	12	22	64	....	1979-80	1993-94
‡ Wilson, Ryan	Col.	6	230	7	60	67	157	8	0	3	3	2	....	2009-10	2014-15
• Wilson, Wally	Bos.	1	53	11	8	19	18	1	0	0	0	0	....	1947-48	1947-48
Winchester, Brad	Edm., Dal., St.L., Ana., S.J.	7	390	37	31	68	552	24	1	2	3	26	....	2005-06	2011-12
Winchester, Jesse	Ott., Fla.	6	285	20	50	70	159	10	0	0	0	0	....	2007-08	2013-14
Wing, Murray	Det.	1	1	0	1	1	0	....	....	....	....	....	....	1973-74	1973-74
Winnes, Chris	Bos., Phi.	4	33	1	6	7	6	1	0	0	0	0	....	1990-91	1993-94
‡ Wirtanen, Petteri	Ana.	1	3	1	0	1	2	....	....	....	....	....	....	2007-08	2007-08
Wiseman, Brian	Tor.	1	3	0	0	0	0	....	....	....	....	....	....	1996-97	1996-97
Wiseman, Chad	S.J., NYR	3	9	1	1	2	8	1	0	0	0	2	....	2002-03	2005-06
• Wiseman, Eddie	Det., NYA, Bos.	10	456	115	165	280	136	43	10	10	20	16	1	1932-33	1941-42
‡ Wishart, Ty	T.B., NYI	3	26	1	5	6	10	....	....	....	....	....	....	2008-09	2011-12
‡ Wisniewski, James	Chi., Ana., NYI, Mtl., CBJ, Car.	11	552	53	221	274	459	24	1	6	7	27	....	2005-06	**2015-16**
Wiste, Jim	Chi., Van.	3	52	1	10	11	8	....	....	....	....	....	....	1968-69	1970-71
Witehall, Johan	NYR, Mtl.	3	54	2	5	7	16	....	....	....	....	....	....	1998-99	2000-01
Witherspoon, Jim	L.A.	1	2	0	0	0	2	....	....	....	....	....	....	1975-76	1975-76
Witiuk, Steve	Chi.	1	33	3	8	11	14	....	....	....	....	....	....	1951-52	1951-52
Witt, Brendan	Wsh., Nsh., NYI	14	890	25	96	121	1424	41	4	1	5	44	....	1995-96	2009-10
Woit, Benny	Det., Chi.	7	334	7	26	33	170	41	2	6	8	18	3	1950-51	1956-57
Wojciechowski, Steve	Det.	2	54	19	20	39	17	6	0	1	1	0	....	1944-45	1946-47
Wolanin, Craig	N.J., Que., Col., T.B., Tor.	13	695	40	133	173	894	35	4	6	10	67	1	1985-86	1997-98
Wolf, Bennett	Pit.	3	30	0	1	1	133	....	....	....	....	....	....	1980-81	1982-83
‡ Wolf, David	Cgy.	1	3	0	0	0	2	1	0	0	0	0	....	2014-15	2014-15
‡ Wolski, Wojtek	Col., Phx., NYR, Fla., Wsh.	8	451	99	168	267	113	29	8	9	17	8	....	2005-06	2012-13
Wong, Mike	Det.	1	22	1	1	2	12	....	....	....	....	....	....	1975-76	1975-76
Wood, Dody	S.J.	5	106	8	10	18	471	....	....	....	....	....	....	1992-93	1997-98
Wood, Randy	NYI, Buf., Tor., Dal.	11	741	175	159	334	603	51	8	9	17	40	....	1986-87	1996-97
• Wood, Robert	NYR	1	1	0	0	0	0	....	....	....	....	....	....	1950-51	1950-51
Woodley, Dan	Van.	1	5	2	0	2	17	....	....	....	....	....	....	1987-88	1987-88
Woods, Paul	Det.	7	501	72	124	196	276	7	0	5	5	4	....	1977-78	1983-84
Woolley, Jason	Wsh., Fla., Pit., Buf., Det.	14	718	68	246	314	430	79	11	36	47	44	....	1991-92	2005-06
Worrell, Peter	Fla., Col.	7	391	19	27	46	1554	4	1	0	1	8	....	1997-98	2003-04
Wortman, Kevin	Cgy.	1	5	0	0	0	2	....	....	....	....	....	....	1993-94	1993-94
Wotton, Mark	Van., Dal.	4	43	3	6	9	25	5	0	0	0	4	....	1994-95	2000-01
• Woytowich, Bob	Bos., Min., Pit., L.A.	8	503	32	126	158	352	24	1	3	4	20	....	1964-65	1971-72
Woywitka, Jeff	St.L., Dal., NYR	7	278	9	46	55	149	4	0	0	0	0	....	2005-06	2011-12
Wozniewski, Andy	Tor., St.L., Bos.	5	79	2	10	12	81	....	....	....	....	....	....	2005-06	2009-10
Wren, Bob	Ana., Tor.	3	5	0	0	0	0	1	0	0	0	0	....	1997-98	2001-02
‡ Wright, James	T.B., Wpg.	4	146	4	8	12	64	....	....	....	....	....	....	2009-10	2013-14
Wright, Jamie	Dal., Cgy., Phi.	6	124	12	20	32	54	5	0	0	0	0	....	1997-98	2002-03
Wright, John	Van., St.L., K.C.	3	127	16	36	52	67	....	....	....	....	....	....	1972-73	1974-75
Wright, Keith	Phi.	1	1	0	0	0	0	....	....	....	....	....	....	1967-68	1967-68
Wright, Larry	Phi., Cal., Det.	5	106	4	8	12	19	....	....	....	....	....	....	1971-72	1977-78
Wright, Tyler	Edm., Pit., CBJ, Ana.	13	613	79	70	149	854	30	3	2	5	40	....	1992-93	2005-06
• Wycherley, Ralph	NYA, Bro.	2	28	4	7	11	6	....	....	....	....	....	....	1940-41	1941-42
• Wylie, Bill	NYR	1	1	0	0	0	0	....	....	....	....	....	....	1950-51	1950-51
Wylie, Duane	Chi.	2	14	3	3	6	2	....	....	....	....	....	....	1974-75	1976-77
‡ Wyman, J.T.	Mtl., T.B.	3	44	2	9	11	8	....	....	....	....	....	....	2009-10	2012-13
Wyrozub, Randy	Buf.	4	100	8	10	18	10	....	....	....	....	....	....	1970-71	1973-74

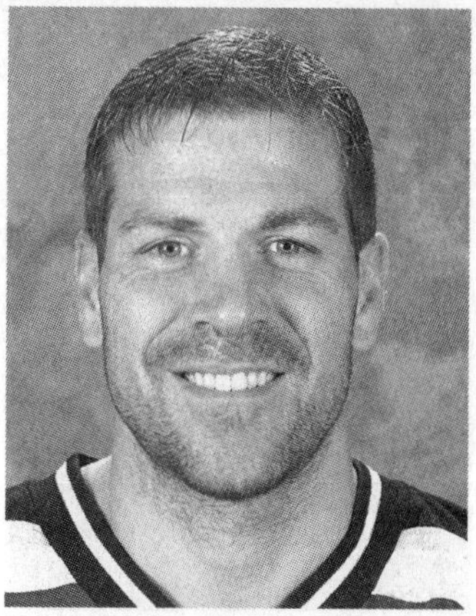

Doug Weight

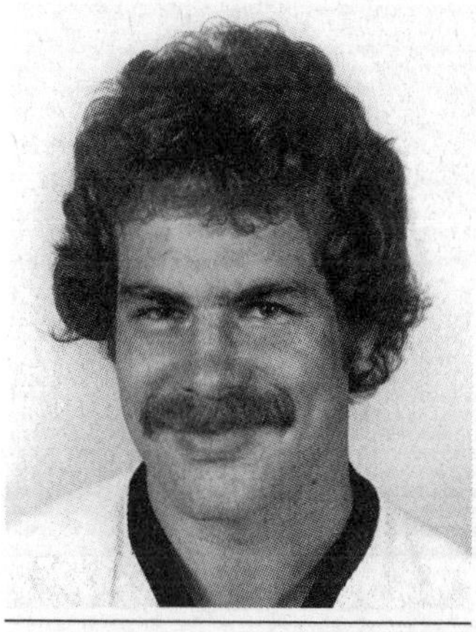

John Wensink

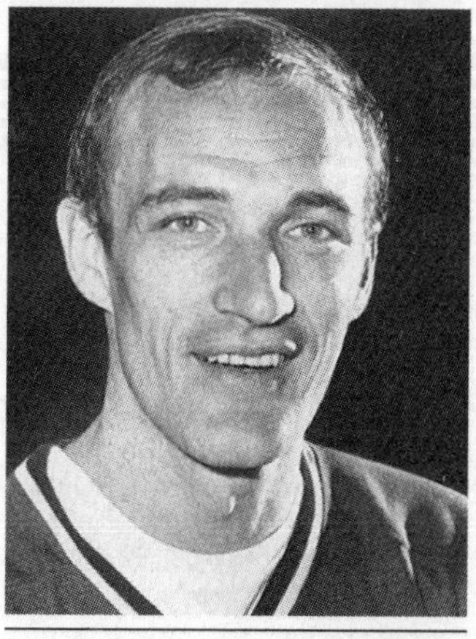

Bill White

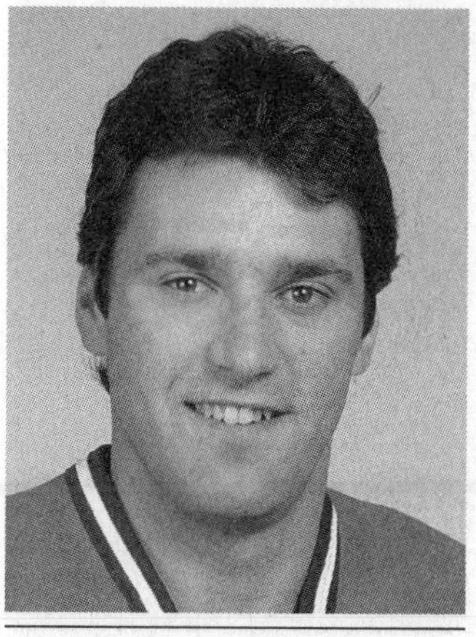

Doug Wickenheiser

Benny Woit

Vitali Yachmenev

Miles Zaharko

Rob Zettler

Y Z

Name	NHL Teams	NHL Seasons	Regular Schedule					Playoffs					NHL Cup Wins	First NHL Season	Last NHL Season
			GP	G	A	TP	PIM	GP	G	A	TP	PIM			
‡ Yablonski, Jeremy	St.L.	1	1	0	0	0	5	....	....	....	....	....	....	2003-04	2003-04
Yachmenev, Vitali	L.A., Nsh.	8	487	83	133	216	88	....	....	....	....	....	....	1995-96	2002-03
● Yackel, Ken	Bos.	1	6	0	0	0	2	2	0	0	0	2	....	1958-59	1958-59
‡ Yake, Terry	Hfd., Ana., Tor., St.L., Wsh.	11	403	77	120	197	220	32	4	4	8	36	....	1988-89	2000-01
‡ Yakubov, Mikhail	Chi., Fla.	2	53	2	10	12	20	....	....	....	....	....	....	2003-04	2005-06
Yakushin, Dmitri	Tor.	1	2	0	0	0	2	....	....	....	....	....	....	1999-00	1999-00
Yaremchuk, Gary	Tor.	4	34	1	4	5	28	....	....	....	....	....	....	1981-82	1984-85
Yaremchuk, Ken	Chi., Tor.	6	235	36	56	92	106	31	6	8	14	49	....	1983-84	1988-89
Yashin, Alexei	Ott., NYI	12	850	337	444	781	401	48	11	16	27	24	....	1993-94	2006-07
Yates, Ross	Hfd.	1	7	1	1	2	4	....	....	....	....	....	....	1983-84	1983-84
Yawney, Trent	Chi., Cgy., St.L.	12	593	27	102	129	783	60	9	17	26	81	....	1987-88	1998-99
● Yegorov, Alexei	S.J.	2	11	3	3	6	2	....	....	....	....	....	....	1995-96	1996-97
Yelle, Stephane	Col., Cgy., Bos., Car.	14	991	96	169	265	490	171	11	21	32	90	2	1995-96	2009-10
‡ Yip, Brandon	Col., Nsh., Phx.	5	174	29	27	56	130	16	3	3	6	12	....	2009-10	2013-14
Ylonen, Juha	Phx., T.B., Ott.	6	341	26	76	102	90	15	0	7	7	4	....	1996-97	2001-02
‡ Yonkman, Nolan	Wsh., Phx., Fla., Ana.	7	76	1	9	10	140	....	....	....	....	....	....	2001-02	2013-14
York, Harry	St.L., NYR, Pit., Van.	4	244	29	46	75	99	5	0	0	0	2	....	1996-97	1999-00
York, Jason	Det., Ana., Ott., Nsh., Bos.	13	757	42	187	229	621	34	2	7	9	25	....	1992-93	2006-07
York, Mike	NYR, Edm., NYI, Phi., Phx., CBJ	9	579	127	195	322	135	6	0	2	2	2	....	1999-00	2008-09
● Young, B.J.	Det.	1	1	0	0	0	0	....	....	....	....	....	....	1999-00	1999-00
Young, Brian	Chi.	1	8	0	2	2	6	....	....	....	....	....	....	1980-81	1980-81
Young, Bryan	Edm.	2	17	0	0	0	10	....	....	....	....	....	....	2006-07	2007-08
Young, C.J.	Cgy., Bos.	1	43	7	7	14	32	....	....	....	....	....	....	1992-93	1992-93
● Young, Doug	Det., Mtl.	10	388	35	45	80	303	28	1	5	6	16	2	1931-32	1940-41
● Young, Howie	Det., Chi., Van.	8	336	12	62	74	851	19	2	4	6	46	....	1960-61	1970-71
Young, Scott	Hfd., Pit., Que., Col., Ana., St.L., Dal.	17	1181	342	415	757	448	141	44	43	87	64	2	1987-88	2005-06
Young, Tim	Min., Wpg., Phi.	10	628	195	341	536	438	36	7	24	31	27	....	1975-76	1984-85
Young, Warren	Min., Pit., Det.	7	236	72	77	149	472	....	....	....	....	....	....	1981-82	1987-88
Younghans, Tom	Min., NYR	6	429	44	41	85	373	24	2	1	3	21	....	1976-77	1981-82
Ysebaert, Paul	N.J., Det., Wpg., Chi., T.B.	11	532	149	187	336	217	30	4	3	7	20	....	1988-89	1998-99
Yushkevich, Dmitry	Phi., Tor., Fla., L.A.	11	786	43	182	225	659	72	4	19	23	52	....	1992-93	2002-03
Yzerman, Steve	Det.	22	1514	692	1063	1755	924	196	70	115	185	84	3	1983-84	2005-06
Zabransky, Libor	St.L.	2	40	1	6	7	50	....	....	....	....	....	....	1996-97	1997-98
Zaharko, Miles	Atl., Chi.	4	129	5	32	37	84	3	0	0	0	0	....	1977-78	1981-82
Zaine, Rod	Pit., Buf.	2	61	10	6	16	25	....	....	....	....	....	....	1970-71	1971-72
Zalapski, Zarley	Pit., Hfd., Cgy., Mtl., Phi.	12	637	99	285	384	684	48	4	23	27	47	....	1987-88	1999-00
Zalesak, Miroslav	S.J.	2	12	1	2	3	0	....	....	....	....	....	....	2002-03	2003-04
‡ Zalewski, Steven	S.J., N.J.	2	10	0	0	0	0	....	....	....	....	....	....	2009-10	2011-12
Zamuner, Rob	NYR, T.B., Ott., Bos.	13	798	139	172	311	467	34	4	5	9	26	....	1991-92	2003-04
Zanon, Greg	Nsh., Min., Bos., Col.	8	493	12	50	62	230	18	0	5	5	6	....	2005-06	2012-13
Zanussi, Joe	NYR, Bos., St.L.	3	87	1	13	14	46	4	0	1	1	2	....	1974-75	1976-77
Zanussi, Ron	Min., Tor.	5	299	52	83	135	373	17	0	4	4	17	....	1977-78	1981-82
Zavisha, Brad	Edm.	1	2	0	0	0	0	....	....	....	....	....	....	1993-94	1993-94
Zednik, Richard	Wsh., Mtl., NYI, Fla.	13	745	200	179	379	563	48	16	10	26	41	....	1995-96	2008-09
Zehr, Jeff	Bos.	1	4	0	0	0	2	....	....	....	....	....	....	1999-00	1999-00
● Zeidel, Larry	Det., Chi., Phi.	5	158	3	16	19	198	12	0	1	1	12	1	1951-52	1968-69
Zeiler, John	L.A.	4	90	1	4	5	87	....	....	....	....	....	....	2006-07	2010-11
Zelepukin, Valeri	N.J., Edm., Phi., Chi.	10	595	117	177	294	527	85	13	13	26	48	1	1991-92	2000-01
Zemlak, Richard	Que., Min., Pit., Cgy.	5	132	2	12	14	587	1	0	0	0	10	....	1986-87	1991-92
● Zeniuk, Ed	Det.	1	2	0	0	0	0	....	....	....	....	....	....	1954-55	1954-55
Zent, Jason	Ott., Phi.	3	27	3	3	6	13	....	....	....	....	....	....	1996-97	1998-99
Zetterstrom, Lars	Van.	1	14	0	1	1	2	....	....	....	....	....	....	1978-79	1978-79
Zettler, Rob	Min., S.J., Phi., Tor., Nsh., Wsh.	14	569	5	65	70	920	14	0	0	0	4	....	1988-89	2001-02
● Zezel, Peter	Phi., St.L., Wsh., Tor., Dal., N.J., Van.	15	873	219	389	608	435	131	25	39	64	83	....	1984-85	1998-99
Zhamnov, Alex	Wpg., Chi., Phi., Bos.	13	807	249	470	719	668	35	6	13	19	18	....	1992-93	2005-06
‡ Zharkov, Vladimir	N.J.	3	82	2	12	14	10	....	....	....	....	....	....	2009-10	2011-12
‡ Zherdev, Nikolai	CBJ, NYR, Phi.	6	421	115	146	261	225	15	1	2	3	4	....	2003-04	2010-11
‡ Zhitnik, Alexei	L.A., Buf., NYI, Phi., Atl.	15	1085	96	375	471	1268	98	9	30	39	168	....	1992-93	2007-08
‡ Zholtok, Sergei	Bos., Ott., Mtl., Edm., Min., Nsh.	10	588	111	147	258	166	45	4	14	18	0	....	1992-93	2003-04
Zidlicky, Marek	Nsh., Min., N.J., Det., NYI	12	836	89	328	417	680	49	1	15	16	44	....	2003-04	**2015-16**
Ziegler, Thomas	T.B.	1	5	0	0	0	0	....	....	....	....	....	....	2000-01	2000-01
Zigomanis, Mike	Car., St.L., Phx., Pit., Tor.	7	197	21	19	40	89	....	....	....	....	....	1	2002-03	2010-11
Zinger, Dwayne	Wsh.	1	7	0	1	1	9	....	....	....	....	....	....	2003-04	2003-04
Zinovjev, Sergei	Bos.	1	10	0	1	1	2	....	....	....	....	....	....	2003-04	2003-04
‡ Zizka, Tomas	L.A.	2	25	2	6	8	16	....	....	....	....	....	....	2002-03	2003-04
Zmolek, Doug	S.J., Dal., L.A., Chi.	8	467	11	53	64	905	14	0	1	1	16	....	1992-93	1999-00
● Zoborosky, Marty	Chi.	1	1	0	0	0	2	....	....	....	....	....	....	1944-45	1944-45
Zombo, Rick	Det., St.L., Bos.	12	652	24	130	154	728	60	1	11	12	127	....	1984-85	1995-96
‡ Zubarev, Andrei	Atl.	1	4	0	1	1	4	....	....	....	....	....	....	2010-11	2010-11
‡ Zubov, Ilya	Ott.	2	11	0	2	2	0	....	....	....	....	....	....	2007-08	2008-09
Zubov, Sergei	NYR, Pit., Dal.	16	1068	152	619	771	337	164	24	93	117	62	2	1992-93	2008-09
Zubrus, Dainius	Phi., Mtl., Wsh., Buf., N.J., S.J.	19	1293	228	363	591	791	106	12	25	37	78	....	1996-97	**2015-16**
Zuke, Mike	St.L., Hfd.	8	455	86	196	282	220	26	6	6	12	12	....	1978-79	1985-86
● Zunich, Rudy	Det.	1	2	0	0	0	2	....	....	....	....	....	....	1943-44	1943-44
Zyuzin, Andrei	S.J., T.B., N.J., Min., Cgy., Chi.	10	496	38	82	120	446	29	2	1	3	30	....	1997-98	2007-08

Retired Players, Goaltenders and Coaches Research Project

Throughout the Retired Players and Retired Goaltenders sections of this book, you will notice many players with a bullet (•) by their names. These players, according to our records, are deceased. The editors recognize that our information on the death dates of NHLers is incomplete. If you have documented information on the passing of any player not marked with a bullet (•) in this edition, we would like to hear from you. We also welcome information on deceased NHL head coaches. Please send this information to:

Ralph Dinger • ralph.dda@sympatico.ca

or by mail to:
Retired Player Research Project
194 Dovercourt Road
Toronto, Ontario
M6J 3C8   Canada

Many thanks to the following contributors . . .

Tim Bateman, Corey Bryant, Paul R. Carroll, Jr., Bob Duff, Peter Fillman, Ernie Fitzsimmons, Gary J. Pearce, Martin Schmid, Chuck Scott, Andreas Szabo.

Retired NHL Goaltender Index

Abbreviations: Teams/Cities: – **Ana**. – Anaheim; **Atl**. – Atlanta; **Bos**. – Boston; **Bro**. – Brooklyn; **Buf**. – Buffalo; **Cgy**. – Calgary; **Cal**. – California; **Car**. – Carolina; **Chi**. – Chicago; **Cle**. – Cleveland; **Col**. – Colorado; **CBJ** – Columbus; **Dal**. – Dallas; **Det**. – Detroit; **Edm**. – Edmonton; **Fla**. – Florida; **Ham**. – Hamilton; **Hfd**. – Hartford; **K.C.** – Kansas City; **L.A.** – Los Angeles; **Min**. – Minnesota; **Mtl**. – Montreal; **Mtl.M.** – Montreal Maroons; **Mtl.W.** – Montreal Wanderers; **Nsh**. – Nashville; **N.J.** – New Jersey; **NYA** – NY Americans; **NYI** – NY Islanders; **NYR** – New York Rangers; **Oak**. – Oakland; **Ott**. – Ottawa; **Phi**. – Philadelphia; **Phx**. – Phoenix; **Pit**. – Pittsburgh; **Que**. – Quebec; **St.L.** – St. Louis; **S.J.** – San Jose; **T.B.** – Tampa Bay; **Tor**. – Toronto; **Van**. – Vancouver; **Wsh**. – Washington; **Wpg**. – Winnipeg

GP – games played; **W** – wins; **L** – losses; **T** – ties; **Mins** – minutes played; **GA** – goals against; **SO** – shutouts; **Avg** – goals against average per 60 minutes played.
• – deceased. § – Forward, defenseman or coach who appeared in goal. For complete career, see Retired Player Index. ‡ – Remains active in other leagues.

NHL Seasons – A player or goaltender who does not play in a regular season but who does appear in that year's playoffs is credited with an NHL Season in this Index. Total seasons are rounded off to the nearest full season. **2015-16** – recently added to Retired Goaltender Index.

Name	NHL Teams	NHL Seasons	Regular Schedule								Playoffs								NHL Cup Wins	First NHL Season	Last NHL Season
			GP	W	L	T	Mins	GA	SO	Avg	GP	W	L	T	Mins	GA	SO	Avg			
• Abbott, George	Bos.	1	1	0	1	0	60	7	0	7.00	....	....	....	....	....	....	....	....		1943-44	1943-44
Adams, John	Bos., Wsh.	3	22	9	10	1	1180	85	1	4.32	....	....	....	....	....	....	....	....	1	1969-70	1974-75
Aebischer, David	Col., Mtl., Phx.	7	214	106	74	17	12230	513	13	2.52	13	6	5	....	697	24	1	2.07	1	2000-01	2007-08
Aiken, Don	Mtl.	1	1	0	1	0	34	6	0	10.59	....	....	....	....	....	....	....	....		1957-58	1957-58
• Aitkenhead, Andy	NYR	3	106	47	43	16	6570	257	11	2.35	10	6	2	2	608	15	3	1.48	1	1932-33	1934-35
‡ Aittokallio, Sami	Col.	2	2	0	1	0	89	5	0	3.37	....	....	....	....	....	....	....	....		2012-13	2013-14
• Almas, Red	Det., Chi.	3	3	0	2	1	180	13	0	4.33	5	1	3	....	263	13	0	2.97		1946-47	1952-53
• Anderson, Lorne	NYR	1	3	1	2	0	180	18	0	6.00	....	....	....	....	....	....	....	....		1951-52	1951-52
Askey, Tom	Ana.	2	7	0	1	2	273	12	0	2.64	1	0	1	....	30	2	0	4.00		1997-98	1998-99
Astrom, Hardy	NYR, Col.	3	83	17	44	12	4456	278	0	3.74	....	....	....	....	....	....	....	....		1977-78	1980-81
Aubin, Jean-Sebastien	Pit., Tor., L.A.	9	218	80	83	16	11197	547	7	2.93	1	0	0	0	1	0	0	0.00		1998-99	2007-08
Auld, Alex	Van., Fla., Phx., Bos., Ott., Dal., NYR, Mtl.	10	237	91	88	32	12986	606	6	2.80	4	1	2	0	242	10	0	2.48		2001-02	2011-12
‡ Bacashihua, Jason	St.L.	2	38	7	17	4	1860	99	0	3.19	....	....	....	....	....	....	....	....		2005-06	2006-07
Bach, Ryan	L.A.	1	3	0	3	0	108	8	0	4.44	....	....	....	....	....	....	....	....		1998-99	1998-99
Backlund, Johan	Phi.	1	1	0	1	0	40	2	0	3.00	1	0	0	....	1	0	0	0.00		2009-10	2009-10
‡ Backstrom, Niklas	Min., Cgy.	10	413	196	144	50	23481	975	28	2.49	11	3	8	....	658	28	0	2.55		2006-07	**2015-16**
Bailey, Scott	Bos.	2	19	6	6	2	965	55	0	3.42	....	....	....	....	....	....	....	....		1995-96	1996-97
Baker, Steve	NYR	4	57	20	20	11	3081	190	3	3.70	14	7	7	....	826	55	0	4.00		1979-80	1982-83
Bales, Mike	Bos., Ott.	4	23	2	15	1	1120	77	0	4.13	....	....	....	....	....	....	....	....		1992-93	1996-97
Bannerman, Murray	Van., Chi.	8	289	116	125	33	16470	1051	8	3.83	40	20	18	....	2322	165	0	4.26		1977-78	1986-87
Baron, Marco	Bos., L.A., Edm.	6	86	34	38	9	4822	292	1	3.63	1	0	1	....	20	3	0	9.00		1979-80	1984-85
Barrasso, Tom	Buf., Pit., Ott., Car., Tor., St.L.	19	777	369	277	86	44180	2385	38	3.24	119	61	54	....	6953	349	6	3.01	2	1983-84	2002-03
• Bassen, Hank	Chi., Det., Pit.	9	156	46	66	31	8759	434	5	2.97	5	1	3	....	274	11	0	2.41		1954-55	1967-68
• Bastien, Baz	Tor.	1	5	0	4	1	300	20	0	4.00	....	....	....	....	....	....	....	....		1945-46	1945-46
• Bauman, Garry	Mtl., Min.	3	35	5	16	6	1719	102	0	3.56	....	....	....	....	....	....	....	....		1966-67	1968-69
Beaupre, Don	Min., Wsh., Ott., Tor.	17	667	268	277	75	37396	2151	17	3.45	72	33	31	....	3943	220	3	3.35		1980-81	1996-97
Beauregard, Stephane	Wpg., Phi.	5	90	19	39	11	4402	268	2	3.65	4	1	3	....	238	12	0	3.03		1989-90	1993-94
Beckford-Tseu, Chris	St.L.	1	1	0	0	0	27	1	0	2.22	....	....	....	....	....	....	....	....		2007-08	2007-08
Bedard, Jim	Wsh.	2	73	17	40	13	4232	278	1	3.94	....	....	....	....	....	....	....	....		1977-78	1978-79
Behrend, Marc	Wpg.	3	39	12	19	3	1991	160	1	4.82	7	1	3	....	312	19	0	3.65		1983-84	1985-86
Belanger, Yves	St.L., Atl., Bos.	6	78	29	33	6	4134	259	2	3.76	....	....	....	....	....	....	....	....		1974-75	1979-80
Belfour, Ed	Chi., S.J., Dal., Tor., Fla.	18	963	484	320	125	55695	2317	76	2.50	161	88	68	....	9945	359	14	2.17	1	1988-89	2006-07
Belhumeur, Michel	Phi., Wsh.	3	65	9	36	7	3306	254	0	4.61	1	0	0	....	10	1	0	6.00		1972-73	1975-76
• Bell, Gordie	Tor., NYR	2	8	3	5	0	480	31	0	3.88	2	1	1	....	120	9	0	4.50		1945-46	1955-56
• Benedict, Clint	Ott., Mtl.M.	13	362	190	143	28	22367	863	57	2.32	28	11	12	5	1707	53	9	1.86	4	1917-18	1929-30
• Bennett, Harvey	Bos.	1	25	10	12	2	1470	103	0	4.20	....	....	....	....	....	....	....	....		1944-45	1944-45
Bergeron, Jean-Claude	Mtl., T.B., L.A.	6	72	21	33	7	3772	232	1	3.69	....	....	....	....	....	....	....	....		1990-91	1996-97
Berkhoel, Adam	Atl.	1	9	2	4	1	473	30	0	3.81	....	....	....	....	....	....	....	....		2005-06	2005-06
Bernhardt, Tim	Cgy., Tor.	4	67	17	36	7	3748	267	0	4.27	....	....	....	....	....	....	....	....		1982-83	1986-87
Berthiaume, Daniel	Wpg., Min., L.A., Bos., Ott.	9	215	81	90	21	11662	714	5	3.67	14	5	9	....	807	50	0	3.72		1985-86	1993-94
Bester, Allan	Tor., Det., Dal.	10	219	73	99	17	11773	786	7	4.01	11	2	6	....	508	37	0	4.37		1983-84	1995-96
• Beveridge, Bill	Det., Ott., St.L., Mtl.M., NYR	9	297	87	166	42	18375	879	18	2.87	5	2	3	....	300	11	0	2.20		1929-30	1942-43
• Bibeault, Paul	Mtl., Tor., Bos., Chi.	7	214	81	107	25	12890	785	10	3.65	20	6	14	....	1237	71	2	3.44		1940-41	1946-47
Bierk, Zac	T.B., Min., Phx.	6	47	9	20	5	2135	113	1	3.18	....	....	....	....	....	....	....	....		1997-98	2003-04
Billington, Craig	N.J., Ott., Bos., Col., Wsh.	15	332	110	149	31	17097	1034	9	3.63	8	0	2	....	213	15	0	4.23		1985-86	2002-03
Binette, Andre	Mtl.	1	1	1	0	0	60	4	0	4.00	....	....	....	....	....	....	....	....		1954-55	1954-55
Binkley, Les	Pit.	5	196	58	94	34	11046	575	11	3.12	7	5	2	....	428	15	0	2.10		1967-68	1971-72
Biron, Martin	Buf., Phi., NYI, NYR	16	508	230	191	52	28614	1247	28	2.61	23	11	12	....	1424	68	2	2.87		1995-96	2013-14
• Bittner, Richard	Bos.	1	1	0	0	1	60	3	0	3.00	....	....	....	....	....	....	....	....		1949-50	1949-50
Blackburn, Dan	NYR	2	63	20	32	4	3499	188	1	3.22	....	....	....	....	....	....	....	....		2001-02	2002-03
Blake, Mike	L.A.	3	40	13	15	5	2117	150	0	4.25	....	....	....	....	....	....	....	....		1981-82	1983-84
Blue, John	Bos., Buf.	3	46	16	18	7	2521	126	1	3.00	2	0	1	....	96	5	0	3.13		1992-93	1995-96
Boisvert, Gilles	Det.	1	3	0	3	0	180	9	0	3.00	....	....	....	....	....	....	....	....		1959-60	1959-60
Bouchard, Dan	Atl., Cgy., Que., Wpg.	14	655	286	232	113	37919	2061	27	3.26	43	13	30	....	2549	147	1	3.46		1972-73	1985-86
Boucher, Brian	Phi., Phx., Cgy., Chi., CBJ, S.J., Car.	13	328	120	139	45	18220	822	17	2.71	43	21	18	....	2388	94	2	2.36		1999-00	2012-13
• Bourque, Claude	Mtl., Det.	2	62	16	38	8	3830	193	4	3.02	3	1	2	....	188	8	1	2.55		1938-39	1939-40
Boutin, Rollie	Wsh.	3	22	7	10	1	1137	75	0	3.96	....	....	....	....	....	....	....	....		1978-79	1980-81
• Bouvrette, Lionel	NYR	1	1	0	1	0	60	6	0	6.00	....	....	....	....	....	....	....	....		1942-43	1942-43
Bower, Johnny	NYR, Tor.	15	552	250	195	90	32016	1340	37	2.51	74	35	34	....	4378	180	5	2.47	4	1953-54	1969-70
§ • Branigan, Andy	NYA	1	1	0	0	0	7	0	0	0.00	....	....	....	....	....	....	....	....		1940-41	1940-41
Brathwaite, Fred	Edm., Cgy., St.L., CBJ	9	254	81	99	37	13840	629	15	2.73	1	0	0	0	1	0	0	0.00		1993-94	2003-04
• Brimsek, Frank	Bos., Chi.	10	514	252	182	80	31210	1404	40	2.70	68	32	36	....	4395	186	2	2.54	2	1938-39	1949-50
Brochu, Martin	Wsh., Van., Pit.	3	9	0	5	0	369	22	0	3.58	....	....	....	....	....	....	....	....		1998-99	2003-04
• Broda, Turk	Tor.	14	629	302	224	101	38167	1609	62	2.53	101	60	39	....	6389	211	13	1.98	5	1936-37	1951-52
• Broderick, Ken	Min., Bos.	3	27	11	12	1	1464	74	1	3.03	....	....	....	....	....	....	....	....		1969-70	1974-75
Broderick, Len	Mtl.	1	1	1	0	0	60	2	0	2.00	....	....	....	....	....	....	....	....		1957-58	1957-58
Brodeur, Martin	N.J., St.L.	22	1266	691	397	154	74439	2781	125	2.24	205	113	91	....	12719	428	24	2.02	3	1991-92	2014-15
Brodeur, Mike	Ott.	2	7	3	1	0	277	10	1	2.17	....	....	....	....	....	....	....	....		2009-10	2010-11
Brodeur, Richard	NYI, Van., Hfd.	9	385	131	175	62	21968	1410	6	3.85	33	13	20	....	2009	111	1	3.32		1979-80	1987-88
Bromley, Gary	Buf., Van.	6	136	54	44	28	7427	425	7	3.43	7	2	5	....	360	25	0	4.17		1973-74	1980-81
• Brooks, Art	Tor.	1	4	2	2	0	220	23	0	6.27	....	....	....	....	....	....	....	....		1917-18	1917-18
Brooks, Ross	Bos.	3	54	37	7	6	3047	134	4	2.64	1	0	0	....	20	3	0	9.00		1972-73	1974-75
• Brophy, Frank	Que.	1	21	3	18	0	1249	148	0	7.11	....	....	....	....	....	....	....	....		1919-20	1919-20
Brown, Andy	Det., Pit.	3	62	22	26	9	3373	213	1	3.79	....	....	....	....	....	....	....	....		1971-72	1973-74
Brown, Ken	Chi.	1	1	0	0	0	18	1	0	3.33	....	....	....	....	....	....	....	....		1970-71	1970-71
Brunetta, Mario	Que.	3	40	12	17	1	1967	128	0	3.90	....	....	....	....	....	....	....	....		1987-88	1989-90
‡ Brust, Barry	L.A.	1	11	2	4	1	486	30	0	3.70	....	....	....	....	....	....	....	....		2006-07	2006-07
Bryzgalov, Ilya	Ana., Phx., Phi., Edm., Min.	12	465	221	162	54	26550	1141	34	2.58	47	20	25	....	2700	125	4	2.78	1	2001-02	2014-15
Bullock, Bruce	Van.	3	16	3	9	3	927	74	0	4.79	....	....	....	....	....	....	....	....		1972-73	1976-77
Bunz, Tyler	Edm.	1	1	0	0	0	20	3	0	9.00	....	....	....	....	....	....	....	....		2014-15	2014-15
Burke, Sean	N.J., Hfd., Car., Van., Phi., Fla., Phx., T.B., L.A.	18	820	324	341	110	46442	2290	38	2.96	38	12	23	....	2151	119	1	3.32		1987-88	2006-07
• Buzinski, Steve	NYR	1	9	2	6	1	560	55	0	5.89	....	....	....	....	....	....	....	....		1942-43	1942-43
Caley, Don	St.L.	1	1	0	0	0	30	3	0	6.00	....	....	....	....	....	....	....	....		1967-68	1967-68
Caprice, Frank	Van.	6	102	31	46	11	5589	391	1	4.20	....	....	....	....	....	....	....	....		1982-83	1987-88
Carey, Jim	Wsh., Bos., St.L.	5	172	79	65	16	9668	416	16	2.58	10	2	5	....	455	35	0	4.62		1994-95	1998-99
Caron, Jacques	L.A., St.L., Van.	5	72	24	29	11	3846	211	2	3.29	12	4	7	....	639	34	0	3.19		1967-68	1973-74
Caron, Sebastien	Pit., Chi., Ana., T.B.	5	95	26	48	12	5156	296	4	3.44	....	....	....	....	....	....	....	....		2002-03	2011-12
Carter, Lyle	Cal.	1	15	4	7	0	721	50	0	4.16	....	....	....	....	....	....	....	....		1971-72	1971-72
Casey, Jon	Min., Bos., St.L.	12	425	170	157	55	23255	1246	16	3.21	66	32	31	....	3743	192	3	3.08		1983-84	1996-97
Cassivi, Frederic	Atl., Wsh.	4	13	3	6	1	628	38	0	3.63	....	....	....	....	....	....	....	....		2001-02	2006-07
Cechmanek, Roman	Phi., L.A.	4	212	110	64	28	12085	419	25	2.08	23	9	14	....	1441	56	3	2.33		2000-01	2003-04
Centomo, Sebastien	Tor.	1	1	0	0	0	40	3	0	4.50	....	....	....	....	....	....	....	....		2001-02	2001-02

Name	NHL Teams	NHL Seasons	Regular Schedule								Playoffs								NHL Cup Wins	First NHL Season	Last NHL Season
			GP	W	L	T	Mins	GA	SO	Avg	GP	W	L	T	Mins	GA	SO	Avg			
Chabot, Frederic	Mtl., Phi., L.A.	5	32	4	8	4	1262	62	0	2.95	....	....	....	....	....	....	....	....		1990-91	1998-99
• Chabot, Lorne	NYR, Tor., Mtl., Chi., Mtl.M., NYA	11	412	201	147	62	25411	859	71	2.03	37	13	17	6	2498	64	5	1.54	2	1926-27	1936-37
Chadwick, Ed	Tor., Bos.	6	184	57	92	35	11040	541	14	2.94	....	....	....	....	....	....	....	....		1955-56	1961-62
Champoux, Bob	Det., Cal.	2	17	2	11	3	923	80	0	5.20	1	1	0	....	55	4	0	4.36		1963-64	1973-74
Charpentier, Sebastien	Wsh.	3	26	6	14	1	1350	66	0	2.93	....	....	....	....	....	....	....	....		2001-02	2003-04
Cheevers, Gerry	Tor., Bos.	13	418	230	102	74	24394	1174	26	2.89	88	53	34	....	5396	242	8	2.69	2	1961-62	1979-80
Cheveldae, Tim	Det., Wpg., Bos.	9	340	149	136	37	19172	1116	10	3.49	25	9	15	....	1418	71	2	3.00		1988-89	1996-97
Chevrier, Alain	N.J., Wpg., Chi., Pit., Det.	6	234	91	100	14	12202	845	2	4.16	16	9	7	....	1013	44	0	2.61		1985-86	1990-91
Chiodo, Andy	Pit.	1	8	3	4	1	486	28	0	3.46	....	....	....	....	....	....	....	....		2003-04	2003-04
Chouinard, Mathieu	L.A.	1	1	0	0	0	3	0	0	0.00	....	....	....	....	....	....	....	....		2003-04	2003-04
§ • Clancy, King	Ott., Tor.	2	2	0	0	0	3	1	0	20.00	....	....	....	....	....	....	....	....		1924-25	1931-32
§ • Cleghorn, Odie	Pit.	1	1	1	0	0	60	2	0	2.00	....	....	....	....	....	....	....	....		1925-26	1925-26
§ • Cleghorn, Sprague	Ott., Mtl.	2	2	0	0	0	5	0	0	0.00	....	....	....	....	....	....	....	....		1918-19	1921-22
Clemmensen, Scott	N.J., Tor., Fla.	12	191	73	59	24	10059	468	7	2.79	4	1	2	....	186	7	0	2.26		2001-02	2014-15
Clifford, Chris	Chi.	2	2	0	0	0	24	0	0	0.00	....	....	....	....	....	....	....	....		1984-85	1988-89
‡ Climie, Matt	Dal., Phx.	3	5	2	2	0	277	15	0	3.25	....	....	....	....	....	....	....	....		2008-09	2010-11
Cloutier, Dan	NYR, T.B., Van., L.A.	10	351	139	142	37	18927	874	15	2.77	25	10	13	0	1361	75	0	3.31		1997-98	2007-08
Cloutier, Jacques	Buf., Chi., Que.	12	255	82	102	24	12826	778	3	3.64	8	1	5	....	413	18	1	2.62		1981-82	1993-94
Coleman, Gerald	T.B.	1	2	0	0	1	43	2	0	2.79	....	....	....	....	....	....	....	....		2005-06	2005-06
• Colvin, Les	Bos.	1	1	0	1	0	60	4	0	4.00	....	....	....	....	....	....	....	....		1948-49	1948-49
§ • Conacher, Charlie	Tor., Det.	3	4	0	0	0	10	0	0	0.00	....	....	....	....	....	....	....	....		1932-33	1938-39
Conklin, Ty	Edm., CBJ, Buf., Pit., Det., St.L.	9	215	96	67	21	11527	516	17	2.69	2	0	1	0	26	1	0	2.31		2001-02	2011-12
• Connell, Alec	Ott., Det., NYA, Mtl.M.	12	417	193	156	67	26050	830	81	1.91	21	8	5	8	1309	26	4	1.19	2	1924-25	1936-37
Corsi, Jim	Edm.	1	26	8	14	3	1366	83	0	3.65	....	....	....	....	....	....	....	....		1979-80	1979-80
• Courteau, Maurice	Bos.	1	6	2	4	0	360	33	0	5.50	....	....	....	....	....	....	....	....		1943-44	1943-44
Cousineau, Marcel	Tor., NYI, L.A.	4	26	4	10	1	1047	51	1	2.92	....	....	....	....	....	....	....	....		1996-97	1999-00
Cowley, Wayne	Edm.	1	1	0	1	0	57	3	0	3.16	....	....	....	....	....	....	....	....		1993-94	1993-94
• Cox, Abbie	Mtl.M., NYA, Det., Mtl.	3	5	1	1	2	263	11	0	2.51	....	....	....	....	....	....	....	....		1929-30	1935-36
Craig, Jim	Atl., Bos., Min.	3	30	11	10	7	1588	100	0	3.78	....	....	....	....	....	....	....	....		1979-80	1983-84
Crha, Jiri	Tor.	2	69	28	27	11	3942	261	0	3.97	5	0	4	....	186	21	0	6.77		1979-80	1980-81
• Crozier, Roger	Det., Buf., Wsh.	14	518	206	197	70	28567	1446	30	3.04	32	14	16	....	1789	82	1	2.75		1963-64	1976-77
• Cude, Wilf	Phi., Bos., Chi., Mtl., Det.	10	282	100	132	49	17586	798	24	2.72	19	7	11	1	1257	51	1	2.43		1930-31	1940-41
Curry, John	Pit., Min.	4	8	3	2	1	326	20	0	3.68	....	....	....	....	....	....	....	....		2008-09	2014-15
Cutts, Don	Edm.	1	6	1	2	1	269	16	0	3.57	....	....	....	....	....	....	....	....		1979-80	1979-80
• Cyr, Claude	Mtl.	1	1	0	0	0	20	1	0	3.00	....	....	....	....	....	....	....	....		1958-59	1958-59
Dadswell, Doug	Cgy.	2	27	8	8	3	1346	99	0	4.41	....	....	....	....	....	....	....	....		1986-87	1987-88
Dafoe, Byron	Wsh., L.A., Bos., Atl.	12	415	171	170	56	23478	1051	26	2.69	27	10	16	....	1686	65	3	2.31		1992-93	2003-04
D'Alessio, Corrie	Hfd.	1	1	0	0	0	11	0	0	0.00	....	....	....	....	....	....	....	....		1992-93	1992-93
Daley, Joe	Pit., Buf., Det.	4	105	34	44	19	5836	326	3	3.35	....	....	....	....	....	....	....	....		1968-69	1971-72
• Damore, Nick	Bos.	1	1	1	0	0	60	3	0	3.00	....	....	....	....	....	....	....	....		1941-42	1941-42
D'Amour, Marc	Cgy., Phi.	2	16	2	4	2	579	32	0	3.32	....	....	....	....	....	....	....	....		1985-86	1988-89
Damphousse, Jean-Fr.	N.J.	1	6	1	3	0	294	12	0	2.45	....	....	....	....	....	....	....	....		2001-02	2001-02
§ • Darragh, Jack	Ott.	1	1	0	0	0	2	0	0	0.00	....	....	....	....	....	....	....	....		1919-20	1919-20
Daskalakis, Cleon	Bos.	3	12	3	4	1	506	41	0	4.86	....	....	....	....	....	....	....	....		1984-85	1986-87
Davidson, John	St.L., NYR	10	301	123	124	39	17109	1004	7	3.52	31	16	14	....	1862	77	1	2.48		1973-74	1982-83
• DeCourcy, Bob	NYR	1	1	0	1	0	29	6	0	12.41	....	....	....	....	....	....	....	....		1947-48	1947-48
• Defelice, Norm	Bos.	1	10	3	5	2	600	30	0	3.00	....	....	....	....	....	....	....	....		1956-57	1956-57
DeJordy, Denis	Chi., L.A., Mtl., Det.	12	316	124	128	51	17798	929	15	3.13	18	6	9	....	946	55	0	3.49	1	1960-61	1973-74
‡ Dekanich, Mark	Nsh.	1	1	0	0	0	50	3	0	3.60	....	....	....	....	....	....	....	....		2010-11	2010-11
DelGuidice, Matt	Bos.	2	11	2	5	1	434	28	0	3.87	....	....	....	....	....	....	....	....		1990-91	1991-92
Denis, Marc	Col., CBJ, T.B., Mtl.	11	349	112	179	31	19526	982	16	3.02	....	....	....	....	....	....	....	....		1996-97	2008-09
DeRouville, Philippe	Pit.	2	3	1	2	0	171	9	0	3.16	....	....	....	....	....	....	....	....		1994-95	1996-97
Desjardins, Cedrick	T.B.	3	6	2	4	0	298	12	0	2.42	....	....	....	....	....	....	....	....		2010-11	2013-14
Desjardins, Gerry	L.A., Chi., NYI, Buf.	10	331	122	153	44	19014	1042	12	3.29	35	15	15	....	1874	108	0	3.46		1968-69	1977-78
Deslauriers, Jeff	Edm., Ana.	3	62	23	32	4	3579	193	3	3.24	....	....	....	....	....	....	....	....		2008-09	2011-12
DesRochers, Patrick	Phx., Car.	2	11	2	6	1	540	33	0	3.67	....	....	....	....	....	....	....	....		2001-02	2002-03
• Dickie, Bill	Chi.	1	1	1	0	0	60	3	0	3.00	....	....	....	....	....	....	....	....		1941-42	1941-42
• Dion, Connie	Det.	2	38	23	11	4	2280	119	1	3.13	5	1	4	....	300	17	0	3.40		1943-44	1944-45
Dion, Michel	Que., Wpg., Pit.	6	227	60	118	32	12695	898	2	4.24	5	2	3	....	304	22	0	4.34		1979-80	1984-85
DiPietro, Rick	NYI	11	318	130	136	36	18199	871	16	2.87	10	2	7	....	554	24	1	2.60		2000-01	2012-13
Divis, Reinhard	St.L.	4	28	6	9	3	1212	67	0	3.32	1	0	0	....	18	0	0	0.00		2001-02	2005-06
• Dolson, Dolly	Det.	3	93	35	41	17	5820	192	16	1.98	2	0	2	0	120	7	0	3.50		1928-29	1930-31
Dopson, Rob	Pit.	1	2	0	0	0	45	3	0	4.00	....	....	....	....	....	....	....	....		1993-94	1993-94
Dowie, Bruce	Tor.	1	2	0	1	0	72	4	0	3.33	....	....	....	....	....	....	....	....		1983-84	1983-84
Draper, Tom	Wpg., Buf., NYI	6	53	19	23	5	2807	173	1	3.70	7	3	4	....	433	19	1	2.63		1988-89	1995-96
Dryden, Dave	NYR, Chi., Buf., Edm.	9	203	66	76	31	10424	555	9	3.19	3	0	2	....	133	9	0	4.06		1961-62	1979-80
Dryden, Ken	Mtl.	8	397	258	57	74	23352	870	46	2.24	112	80	32	....	6846	274	10	2.40	6	1970-71	1978-79
Dubielewicz, Wade	NYI, CBJ, Min.	6	43	18	16	2	2196	97	0	2.65	1	0	1	....	59	4	0	4.07		2003-04	2009-10
Duchesne, Jeremy	Phi.	1	1	0	0	0	17	1	0	3.53	....	....	....	....	....	....	....	....		2009-10	2009-10
Duffus, Parris	Phx.	1	1	0	0	0	29	1	0	2.07	....	....	....	....	....	....	....	....		1996-97	1996-97
Dumas, Michel	Chi.	3	8	2	1	2	362	24	0	3.98	1	0	0	....	19	1	0	3.16		1974-75	1976-77
Dunham, Mike	N.J., Nsh., NYR, Atl., NYI	10	394	141	178	44	21653	989	19	2.74	....	....	....	....	....	....	....	....		1996-97	2006-07
Dupuis, Bob	Edm.	1	1	0	1	0	60	4	0	4.00	....	....	....	....	....	....	....	....		1979-80	1979-80
• Durnan, Bill	Mtl.	7	383	208	112	62	22945	901	34	2.36	45	27	18	....	2871	99	2	2.07	2	1943-44	1949-50
• Dyck, Ed	Van.	3	49	8	28	5	2453	178	1	4.35	....	....	....	....	....	....	....	....		1971-72	1973-74
Edwards, Don	Buf., Cgy., Tor.	10	459	208	155	74	26181	1449	16	3.32	42	16	21	....	2302	132	1	3.44		1976-77	1985-86
Edwards, Gary	St.L., L.A., Cle., Min., Edm., Pit.	13	286	88	125	51	16002	973	10	3.65	11	5	4	....	537	34	0	3.80		1968-69	1981-82
Edwards, Marv	Pit., Tor., Cal.	4	61	15	34	7	3467	218	2	3.77	....	....	....	....	....	....	....	....		1968-69	1973-74
• Edwards, Roy	Chi., Det., Pit.	8	236	97	88	38	13109	637	12	2.92	4	0	3	....	206	11	0	3.20	1	1960-61	1973-74
Eklund, Brian	T.B.	1	1	0	1	0	58	3	0	3.10	....	....	....	....	....	....	....	....		2005-06	2005-06
Eliot, Darren	L.A., Det., Buf.	5	89	25	41	12	4931	377	1	4.59	1	0	0	....	40	7	0	10.50		1984-85	1988-89
Ellacott, Ken	Van.	1	12	2	3	4	555	41	0	4.43	....	....	....	....	....	....	....	....		1982-83	1982-83
Ellis, Dan	Dal., Nsh., T.B., Ana., Car., Fla.	9	212	87	79	18	11306	526	15	2.79	7	2	5	....	398	19	0	2.86		2003-04	2014-15
Emery, Ray	Ott., Phi., Ana., Chi.	11	287	145	86	28	15488	697	16	2.70	39	21	17	0	2344	103	3	2.64	1	2002-03	2014-15
Erickson, Chad	N.J.	1	2	1	1	0	120	9	0	4.50	....	....	....	....	....	....	....	....		1991-92	1991-92
‡ Eriksson, Joacim	Van.	1	1	0	0	0	36	6	0	10.00	....	....	....	....	....	....	....	....		2013-14	2013-14
Ersberg, Erik	L.A.	3	53	18	19	10	2827	120	2	2.55	1	0	0	....	13	2	0	9.23		2007-08	2009-10
Esche, Robert	Phx., Phi.	8	186	78	64	22	10139	464	10	2.75	25	13	11	....	1405	64	1	2.73		1998-99	2006-07
Esposito, Tony	Mtl., Chi.	16	886	423	306	151	52585	2563	76	2.92	99	45	53	....	6017	308	6	3.07	1	1968-69	1983-84
Essensa, Bob	Wpg., Det., Edm., Phx., Van., Buf.	12	446	173	176	47	24215	1270	18	3.15	16	4	9	....	864	51	0	3.54		1988-89	2001-02
• Evans, Claude	Mtl., Bos.	2	5	1	2	1	260	16	0	3.69	....	....	....	....	....	....	....	....		1954-55	1957-58
Exelby, Randy	Mtl., Edm.	2	2	0	1	0	63	5	0	4.76	....	....	....	....	....	....	....	....		1988-89	1989-90
Fankhouser, Scott	Atl.	2	23	4	12	2	1180	65	0	3.31	....	....	....	....	....	....	....	....		1999-00	2000-01
Farr, Rocky	Buf.	3	19	2	6	3	722	42	0	3.49	....	....	....	....	....	....	....	....		1972-73	1974-75
‡ Fasth, Viktor	Ana., Edm.	3	63	26	26	7	3465	161	4	2.79	....	....	....	....	....	....	....	....		2012-13	2014-15
Favell, Doug	Phi., Tor., Col.	12	373	123	153	69	20771	1096	18	3.17	21	6	15	....	1270	66	1	3.12		1967-68	1978-79
Fernandez, Manny	Dal., Min., Bos.	13	325	143	123	35	18580	775	15	2.50	11	3	4	....	571	19	0	2.00		1994-95	2008-09
Fichaud, Eric	NYI, Nsh., Car., Mtl.	6	95	22	47	10	4799	251	2	3.14	....	....	....	....	....	....	....	....		1995-96	2000-01
Finley, Brian	Nsh., Bos.	3	4	0	2	0	166	13	0	4.70	....	....	....	....	....	....	....	....		2002-03	2006-07
Fiset, Stephane	Que., Col., L.A., Mtl.	13	390	164	153	44	21785	1114	16	3.07	14	1	7	....	563	37	0	3.94	1	1989-90	2001-02
Fitzpatrick, Mark	L.A., NYI, Fla., T.B., Chi., Car.	12	329	113	136	49	18329	953	8	3.12	9	0	3	....	289	23	0	4.78		1988-89	1999-00
Flaherty, Wade	S.J., NYI, T.B., Fla., Nsh.	11	120	27	56	9	5941	348	5	3.51	7	2	3	....	377	31	0	4.93		1991-92	2002-03
• Forbes, Jake	Tor., Ham., NYA, Phi.	13	210	85	114	11	12922	594	19	2.76	2	0	2	0	120	7	0	3.50		1919-20	1932-33
Ford, Brian	Que., Pit.	2	11	3	7	0	580	61	0	6.31	....	....	....	....	....	....	....	....		1983-84	1984-85
Foster, Brian	Fla.	1	1	0	0	0	5	0	0	0.00	....	....	....	....	....	....	....	....		2011-12	2011-12
Foster, Norm	Bos., Edm.	2	13	7	4	0	623	34	0	3.27	....	....	....	....	....	....	....	....		1990-91	1991-92
Fountain, Mike	Van., Car., Ott.	4	11	2	6	0	483	28	1	3.48	....	....	....	....	....	....	....	....		1996-97	2000-01
• Fowler, Hec	Bos.	1	7	1	6	0	409	42	0	6.16	....	....	....	....	....	....	....	....		1924-25	1924-25
Francis, Emile	Chi., NYR	6	95	31	52	11	5660	355	1	3.76	....	....	....	....	....	....	....	....		1946-47	1951-52
• Franks, Jimmy	Det., NYR, Bos.	4	42	12	23	7	2520	181	1	4.31	1	0	1	....	30	2	0	4.00	1	1936-37	1943-44
Frazee, Jeff	N.J.	1	1	0	0	0	19	0	0	0.00	....	....	....	....	....	....	....	....		2012-13	2012-13

			Regular Schedule								Playoffs										
Name	NHL Teams	NHL Seasons	GP	W	L	T	Mins	GA	SO	Avg	GP	W	L	T	Mins	GA	SO	Avg	NHL Cup Wins	First NHL Season	Last NHL Season
• Frederick, Ray	Chi.	1	5	0	4	1	300	22	0	4.40	....	....	....	....	....	....	....	....		1954-55	1954-55
Friesen, Karl	N.J.	1	4	0	2	1	130	16	0	7.38	....	....	....	....	....	....	....	....		1986-87	1986-87
Froese, Bob	Phi., NYR	8	242	128	72	20	13451	694	13	3.10	18	3	9	....	830	55	0	3.98		1982-83	1989-90
Fuhr, Grant	Edm., Tor., Buf., L.A., St.L., Cgy.	19	868	403	295	114	48945	2756	25	3.38	150	92	50	....	8834	430	6	2.92	5	1981-82	1999-00
Fukufuji, Yutaka	L.A.	1	4	0	3	0	96	7	0	4.38	....	....	....	....	....	....	....	....		2006-07	2006-07
Gage, Joaquin	Edm.	3	23	4	12	1	1076	67	0	3.74	....	....	....	....	....	....	....	....		1994-95	2000-01
Gagnon, Dave	Det.	1	2	0	1	0	35	6	0	10.29	....	....	....	....	....	....	....	....		1990-91	1990-91
• Gamble, Bruce	NYR, Bos., Tor., Phi.	10	327	110	150	46	18442	988	22	3.21	5	0	4	....	206	25	0	7.28		1958-59	1971-72
Gamble, Troy	Van.	4	72	22	29	9	3804	229	1	3.61	4	1	3	....	249	16	0	3.86		1986-87	1991-92
• Gardiner, Bert	NYR, Mtl., Chi., Bos.	6	144	49	68	27	8760	554	3	3.79	9	4	5	....	647	20	0	1.85		1935-36	1943-44
• Gardiner, Charlie	Chi.	7	316	112	152	52	19687	664	42	2.02	21	12	6	3	1472	35	5	1.43	1	1927-28	1933-34
• Gardner, George	Det., Van.	5	66	16	30	6	3313	207	0	3.75	....	....	....	....	....	....	....	....		1965-66	1971-72
Garner, Tyrone	Cgy.	1	3	0	2	0	139	12	0	5.18	....	....	....	....	....	....	....	....		1998-99	1998-99
‡ Garnett, Michael	Atl.	1	24	10	7	4	1271	73	2	3.45	....	....	....	....	....	....	....	....		2005-06	2005-06
Garon, Mathieu	Mtl., L.A., Edm., Pit., CBJ, T.B.	12	341	144	131	31	18342	865	20	2.83	2	0	0	....	36	0	0	0.00	1	2000-01	2012-13
Garrett, John	Hfd., Que., Van.	6	207	68	91	37	11763	837	1	4.27	9	4	3	....	461	33	0	4.30		1979-80	1984-85
Gatherum, Dave	Det.	1	3	2	0	1	180	3	1	1.00	....	....	....	....	....	....	....	....	1	1953-54	1953-54
• Gauthier, Paul	Mtl.	1	1	0	0	1	70	2	0	1.71	....	....	....	....	....	....	....	....		1937-38	1937-38
Gauthier, Sean	S.J.	1	1	0	0	0	3	0	0	0.00	....	....	....	....	....	....	....	....		1998-99	1998-99
• Gelineau, Jack	Bos., Chi.	4	143	46	64	33	8580	447	7	3.13	4	1	2	....	260	7	1	1.62		1948-49	1953-54
‡ Gerber, Martin	Ana., Car., Ott., Tor., Edm.	7	229	113	78	21	12920	566	10	2.63	12	1	5	....	479	28	1	3.51	1	2002-03	2010-11
Giacomin, Ed	NYR, Det.	13	609	289	209	96	35633	1672	54	2.82	65	29	35	....	3838	180	1	2.81		1965-66	1977-78
Giguere, Jean-Sebastien	Hfd., Cgy., Ana., Tor., Col.	16	597	262	216	75	33717	1423	38	2.53	52	33	17	....	3167	110	6	2.08	1	1996-97	2013-14
Gilbert, Gilles	Min., Bos., Det.	14	416	192	143	60	23677	1290	18	3.27	32	17	15	....	1919	97	3	3.03		1969-70	1982-83
• Gill, Andre	Bos.	1	5	3	2	0	270	13	1	2.89	....	....	....	....	....	....	....	....		1967-68	1967-68
• Goodman, Paul	Chi.	3	52	23	20	9	3240	117	6	2.17	3	0	3	....	187	10	0	3.21	1	1937-38	1940-41
Gordon, Scott	Que.	2	23	2	16	0	1082	101	0	5.60	....	....	....	....	....	....	....	....		1989-90	1990-91
Gosselin, Mario	Que., L.A., Hfd.	9	241	91	107	14	12857	801	6	3.74	32	16	15	....	1816	99	0	3.27		1983-84	1993-94
Goverde, David	L.A.	3	5	1	4	0	278	29	0	6.26	....	....	....	....	....	....	....	....		1991-92	1993-94
Grahame, John	Bos., T.B., Car.	8	224	97	86	18	12363	574	12	2.79	6	1	4	0	333	19	0	3.42	1	1999-00	2007-08
Grahame, Ron	Bos., L.A., Que.	4	114	50	43	15	6472	409	5	3.79	4	2	1	....	202	7	0	2.08		1977-78	1980-81
• Grant, Benny	Tor., NYA, Bos.	6	52	17	27	4	3036	188	4	3.72	....	....	....	....	....	....	....	....		1928-29	1943-44
Grant, Doug	Det., St.L.	7	77	27	34	8	4199	280	2	4.00	....	....	....	....	....	....	....	....		1973-74	1979-80
Gratton, Gilles	St.L., NYR	2	47	13	18	9	2299	154	0	4.02	....	....	....	....	....	....	....	....		1975-76	1976-77
Gray, Gerry	Det., NYI	2	8	1	5	1	440	35	0	4.77	....	....	....	....	....	....	....	....		1970-71	1972-73
Gray, Harrison	Det.	1	1	0	1	0	40	5	0	7.50	....	....	....	....	....	....	....	....		1963-64	1963-64
Greenlay, Mike	Edm.	1	2	0	0	0	20	4	0	12.00	....	....	....	....	....	....	....	....		1989-90	1989-90
Guenette, Steve	Pit., Cgy.	5	35	19	16	0	1958	122	1	3.74	....	....	....	....	....	....	....	....		1986-87	1990-91
Gustafson, Derek	Min.	2	5	1	3	0	265	10	0	2.26	....	....	....	....	....	....	....	....		2000-01	2001-02
Hackett, Jeff	NYI, S.J., Chi., Mtl., Bos., Phi.	15	500	166	244	56	28125	1361	26	2.90	12	3	7	....	610	36	0	3.54		1988-89	2003-04
• Hainsworth, George	Mtl., Tor.	11	465	246	145	74	29087	937	94	1.93	52	22	25	5	3486	112	8	1.93	2	1926-27	1936-37
Hall, Glenn	Det., Chi., St.L.	19	906	407	326	163	53484	2222	84	2.49	115	49	65	....	6899	320	6	2.78	2	1951-52	1970-71
Hamel, Pierre	Tor., Wpg.	4	69	13	41	7	3766	276	0	4.40	....	....	....	....	....	....	....	....		1974-75	1980-81
Hanlon, Glen	Van., St.L., NYR, Det.	14	477	167	202	61	26037	1561	13	3.60	35	11	15	....	1756	92	4	3.14		1977-78	1990-91
Harding, Josh	Min.	9	151	60	59	11	7995	327	10	2.45	6	1	4	....	265	12	0	2.72		2005-06	2013-14
Harrison, Paul	Min., Tor., Pit., Buf.	7	109	28	59	9	5806	408	2	4.22	4	0	1	....	157	9	0	3.44		1975-76	1981-82
Hasek, Dominik	Chi., Buf., Det., Ott.	16	735	389	223	95	42837	1572	81	2.20	119	65	49	0	7318	246	14	2.02	2	1990-91	2007-08
Hauser, Adam	L.A.	1	1	0	0	0	51	6	0	7.06	....	....	....	....	....	....	....	....		2005-06	2005-06
Hayward, Brian	Wpg., Mtl., Min., S.J.	11	357	143	156	37	20025	1242	8	3.72	37	11	18	....	1803	104	0	3.46		1982-83	1992-93
Head, Don	Bos.	1	38	9	26	3	2280	158	2	4.16	....	....	....	....	....	....	....	....		1961-62	1961-62
Healy, Glenn	L.A., NYI, NYR, Tor.	15	437	166	190	47	24256	1361	13	3.37	37	13	15	....	1930	108	0	3.36	1	1985-86	2000-01
Hebert, Guy	St.L., Ana., NYR	10	491	191	222	56	27889	1307	28	2.81	14	4	7	....	744	33	1	2.66		1991-92	2000-01
• Hebert, Sammy	Tor., Ott.	2	4	2	1	0	200	19	0	5.70	....	....	....	....	....	....	....	....	1	1917-18	1923-24
Hedberg, Johan	Pit., Van., Dal., Atl., N.J.	12	373	161	143	36	20758	977	22	2.82	23	10	13	....	1374	53	2	2.31		2000-01	2012-13
‡ Heeter, Cal	Phi.	1	1	0	0	1	64	5	0	4.69	....	....	....	....	....	....	....	....		2013-14	2013-14
Heinz, Rick	St.L., Van.	5	49	14	19	5	2356	159	2	4.05	1	0	0	....	8	1	0	7.50		1980-81	1984-85
‡ Helenius, Riku	T.B.	1	1	0	0	0	7	0	0	0.00	....	....	....	....	....	....	....	....		2008-09	2008-09
Henderson, John	Bos.	2	46	15	15	15	2688	113	5	2.52	2	0	2	....	120	8	0	4.00		1954-55	1955-56
• Henry, Gord	Bos.	4	3	1	2	0	180	5	1	1.67	5	0	4	....	283	21	0	4.45		1948-49	1952-53
• Henry, Jim	NYR, Chi., Bos.	9	406	161	173	70	24355	1166	28	2.87	29	11	18	....	1741	81	2	2.79		1941-42	1954-55
Herron, Denis	Pit., K.C., Mtl.	14	462	146	203	76	25608	1579	10	3.70	15	5	10	....	901	50	0	3.33		1972-73	1985-86
Hextall, Ron	Phi., Que., NYI	13	608	296	214	69	34750	1723	23	2.97	93	47	43	....	5456	276	2	3.04		1986-87	1998-99
• Highton, Hec	Chi.	1	24	10	14	0	1440	108	0	4.50	....	....	....	....	....	....	....	....		1943-44	1943-44
§ • Himes, Normie	NYA	2	2	0	1	0	79	3	0	2.28	....	....	....	....	....	....	....	....		1927-28	1928-29
Hirsch, Corey	NYR, Van., Wsh., Dal.	7	108	34	45	14	5775	301	4	3.13	6	2	3	....	338	21	0	3.73		1992-93	2002-03
Hnilicka, Milan	NYR, Atl., L.A.	5	121	29	67	13	6509	359	5	3.31	....	....	....	....	....	....	....	....		1999-00	2003-04
• Hodge, Charlie	Mtl., Oak., Van.	14	358	150	125	61	20573	925	24	2.70	16	7	8	....	804	32	2	2.39	6	1954-55	1970-71
Hodson, Kevin	Det., T.B.	6	71	17	18	10	2910	134	4	2.76	1	0	0	....	1	0	0	0.00	2	1995-96	2002-03
Hoffort, Bruce	Phi.	2	9	4	0	3	368	22	0	3.59	....	....	....	....	....	....	....	....		1989-90	1990-91
Hoganson, Paul	Pit.	1	2	0	1	0	57	7	0	7.37	....	....	....	....	....	....	....	....		1970-71	1970-71
Hogosta, Goran	NYI, Que.	2	22	5	12	3	1208	83	1	4.12	....	....	....	....	....	....	....	....		1977-78	1979-80
Holden, Mark	Mtl., Wpg.	4	8	2	2	1	372	25	0	4.03	....	....	....	....	....	....	....	....		1981-82	1984-85
Holland, Ken	Hfd., Det.	2	4	0	2	1	206	17	0	4.95	....	....	....	....	....	....	....	....		1980-81	1983-84
Holland, Rob	Pit.	2	44	11	22	9	2513	171	1	4.08	....	....	....	....	....	....	....	....		1979-80	1980-81
• Holmes, Hap	Tor., Det.	4	103	39	54	10	6510	264	17	2.43	2	1	1	0	120	7	0	3.50	1	1917-18	1927-28
‡ Holmqvist, Johan	NYR, T.B., Dal.	5	99	48	34	9	5264	262	3	2.99	6	2	4	....	370	18	0	2.92		2000-01	2007-08
Holt, Chris	NYR, St.L.	2	2	0	0	0	29	0	0	0.00	....	....	....	....	....	....	....	....		2005-06	2008-09
§ • Horner, Red	Tor.	2	2	0	0	0	3	1	0	20.00	....	....	....	....	....	....	....	....		1928-29	1931-32
Houle, Martin	Phi.	1	1	0	0	0	2	1	0	30.00	....	....	....	....	....	....	....	....		2006-07	2006-07
Hrivnak, Jim	Wsh., Wpg., St.L.	5	85	34	30	3	4217	262	0	3.73	....	....	....	....	....	....	....	....		1989-90	1993-94
Hrudey, Kelly	NYI, L.A., S.J.	15	677	271	265	88	38084	2174	17	3.43	85	36	46	....	5163	283	0	3.29		1983-84	1997-98
‡ Huet, Cristobal	L.A., Mtl., Wsh., Chi.	7	272	129	90	32	15260	625	24	2.46	17	6	10	....	987	44	0	2.67	1	2002-03	2009-10
Hunwick, Shawn	CBJ	1	1	0	0	0	3	0	0	0.00	....	....	....	....	....	....	....	....		2011-12	2011-12
Hurme, Jani	Ott., Fla.	4	76	29	25	11	4041	176	6	2.61	....	....	....	....	....	....	....	....		1999-00	2002-03
Ing, Peter	Tor., Edm., Det.	4	74	20	37	9	3941	266	1	4.05	....	....	....	....	....	....	....	....		1989-90	1993-94
Inness, Gary	Pit., Phi., Wsh.	7	162	58	61	27	8710	494	2	3.40	9	5	4	....	540	24	0	2.67		1973-74	1980-81
Irbe, Arturs	S.J., Dal., Van., Car.	13	568	218	236	79	32066	1513	33	2.83	51	23	27	....	2981	142	1	2.86		1991-92	2003-04
Ireland, Randy	Buf.	1	2	0	0	0	30	3	0	6.00	....	....	....	....	....	....	....	....		1978-79	1978-79
Irons, Robbie	St.L.	1	1	0	0	0	3	0	0	0.00	....	....	....	....	....	....	....	....		1968-69	1968-69
• Ironstone, Joe	Ott., NYA, Tor.	3	2	0	0	1	110	3	1	1.64	....	....	....	....	....	....	....	....		1924-25	1927-28
‡ Irving, Leland	Cgy.	2	13	3	4	4	664	36	0	3.25	....	....	....	....	....	....	....	....		2011-12	2012-13
Jablonski, Pat	St.L., T.B., Mtl., Phx., Car.	8	128	28	62	18	6634	413	1	3.74	4	0	0	....	139	6	0	2.59		1989-90	1997-98
• Jackson, Doug	Chi.	1	6	2	3	1	360	42	0	7.00	....	....	....	....	....	....	....	....		1947-48	1947-48
• Jackson, Percy	Bos., NYA, NYR	4	7	1	3	1	392	26	0	3.98	....	....	....	....	....	....	....	....		1931-32	1935-36
Jaks, Pauli	L.A.	1	1	0	0	0	40	2	0	3.00	....	....	....	....	....	....	....	....		1994-95	1994-95
Janaszak, Steve	Min., Col.	2	3	0	1	1	160	15	0	5.63	....	....	....	....	....	....	....	....		1979-80	1981-82
Janecyk, Bob	Chi., L.A.	6	110	43	47	13	6250	432	2	4.15	3	0	3	....	184	10	0	3.26		1983-84	1988-89
§ • Jenkins, Roger	NYA	1	1	0	1	0	30	7	0	14.00	....	....	....	....	....	....	....	....		1938-39	1938-39
Jensen, Al	Det., Wsh., L.A.	7	179	95	53	18	9974	557	8	3.35	12	5	5	....	598	32	0	3.21		1980-81	1986-87
Jensen, Darren	Phi.	2	30	15	10	1	1496	95	2	3.81	....	....	....	....	....	....	....	....		1984-85	1985-86
Johnson, Bob	St.L., Pit.	2	24	9	9	1	1059	66	0	3.74	....	....	....	....	....	....	....	....		1972-73	1974-75
Johnson, Brent	St.L., Phx., Wsh., Pit.	12	309	140	112	31	16978	744	14	2.63	15	5	6	0	737	27	3	2.20		1998-99	2011-12
Johnston, Eddie	Bos., Tor., St.L., Chi.	16	592	234	257	80	34216	1852	32	3.25	18	7	10	....	1023	57	1	3.34	2	1962-63	1977-78
Joseph, Curtis	St.L., Edm., Tor., Det., Phx., Cgy.	19	943	454	352	96	54054	2516	51	2.79	133	63	66	....	8106	327	16	2.42		1989-90	2008-09
• Junkin, Joe	Bos.	1	1	0	0	0	8	0	0	0.00	....	....	....	....	....	....	....	....		1968-69	1968-69
Kaarela, Jari	Col.	1	5	2	2	0	220	22	0	6.00	....	....	....	....	....	....	....	....		1980-81	1980-81
Kamppuri, Hannu	N.J.	1	13	1	10	1	645	54	0	5.02	....	....	....	....	....	....	....	....		1984-85	1984-85
• Karakas, Mike	Chi., Mtl.	8	336	114	169	53	20614	1002	28	2.92	23	11	12	0	1434	72	3	3.01	1	1935-36	1945-46
‡ Karlsson, Henrik	Cgy.	2	26	5	9	8	1292	60	0	2.79	....	....	....	....	....	....	....	....		2010-11	2011-12
Keans, Doug	L.A., Bos.	9	210	96	64	26	11388	666	4	3.51	9	2	6	....	432	34	0	4.72		1979-80	1987-88

Name	NHL Teams	NHL Seasons	Regular Schedule GP	W	L	T	Mins	GA	SO	Avg	Playoffs GP	W	L	T	Mins	GA	SO	Avg	NHL Cup Wins	First NHL Season	Last NHL Season
• Keenan, Don	Bos.	1	1	0	1	0	60	4	0	4.00	....	....	....	....	....	....	....	....		1958-59	1958-59
Keetley, Matt	Cgy.	1	1	0	0	0	9	0	0	0.00	....	....	....	....	....	....	....	....		2007-08	2007-08
• Kerr, Dave	Mtl.M., NYA, NYR	11	427	203	148	75	26639	954	51	2.15	40	18	19	3	2616	76	8	1.74	1	1930-31	1940-41
Khabibulin, Nikolai	Wpg., Phx., T.B., Chi., Edm.	18	799	333	334	97	45609	2071	46	2.72	72	39	31	....	4345	174	6	2.40	1	1994-95	2013-14
Kidd, Trevor	Cgy., Car., Fla., Tor.	12	387	140	162	52	21426	1014	19	2.84	10	3	5	....	550	36	1	3.93		1991-92	2003-04
King, Scott	Det.	2	2	0	0	0	61	3	0	2.95	....	....	....	....	....	....	....	....		1990-91	1991-92
Kiprusoff, Miikka	S.J., Cgy.	12	623	319	213	71	36169	1500	44	2.49	56	25	28	....	3284	127	6	2.32		2000-01	2012-13
Kleisinger, Terry	NYR	1	4	0	2	0	191	14	0	4.40	....	....	....	....	....	....	....	....		1985-86	1985-86
Klymkiw, Julian	NYR	1	1	0	0	0	19	2	0	6.32	....	....	....	....	....	....	....	....		1958-59	1958-59
‡ Knapp, Connor	Buf.	1	2	0	0	1	77	4	0	3.12	....	....	....	....	....	....	....	....		2013-14	2013-14
Knickle, Rick	L.A.	2	14	7	6	0	706	44	0	3.74	....	....	....	....	....	....	....	....		1992-93	1993-94
Kochan, Dieter	T.B., Min.	4	21	1	11	1	849	56	0	3.96	....	....	....	....	....	....	....	....		1999-00	2002-03
‡ Kolesnik, Vitali	Col.	1	8	3	3	0	370	20	0	3.24	....	....	....	....	....	....	....	....		2005-06	2005-06
Kolzig, Olie	Wsh., T.B.	17	719	303	297	87	41671	1885	35	2.71	45	20	24	....	2799	100	6	2.14		1989-90	2008-09
Konstantinov, Evgeny	T.B.	2	2	0	0	0	21	1	0	2.86	....	....	....	....	....	....	....	....		2000-01	2002-03
‡ Koskinen, Mikko	NYI	1	4	2	1	0	208	15	0	4.33	....	....	....	....	....	....	....	....		2010-11	2010-11
Krahn, Brent	Dal.	1	1	0	0	0	20	3	0	9.00	....	....	....	....	....	....	....	....		2008-09	2008-09
Kuntar, Les	Mtl.	1	6	2	2	0	302	16	0	3.18	....	....	....	....	....	....	....	....		1993-94	1993-94
Kurt, Gary	Cal.	1	16	1	7	5	838	60	0	4.30	....	....	....	....	....	....	....	....		1971-72	1971-72
LaBarbera, Jason	NYR, L.A., Van., Phx., Edm., Ana.	11	187	62	73	20	9615	457	6	2.85	....	....	....	....	....	....	....	....		2000-01	2014-15
Labbe, Jean-Francois	NYR, CBJ	3	15	3	6	0	628	36	0	3.44	....	....	....	....	....	....	....	....		1999-00	2002-03
Labrecque, Patrick	Mtl.	1	2	0	1	0	98	7	0	4.29	....	....	....	....	....	....	....	....		1995-96	1995-96
Lacher, Blaine	Bos.	2	47	22	16	4	2636	123	4	2.80	5	1	4	....	283	12	0	2.54		1994-95	1995-96
LaCosta, Dan	CBJ	2	4	2	0	0	169	4	1	1.42	....	....	....	....	....	....	....	....		2007-08	2008-09
• Lacroix, Frenchy	Mtl.	2	5	1	4	0	280	16	0	3.43	....	....	....	....	....	....	....	....		1925-26	1926-27
LaFerriere, Rick	Col.	1	1	0	0	0	20	1	0	3.00	....	....	....	....	....	....	....	....		1981-82	1981-82
LaForest, Mark	Det., Phi., Tor., Ott.	6	103	25	54	4	5032	354	2	4.22	2	1	0	....	48	1	0	1.25		1985-86	1993-94
Lajeunesse, Simon	Ott.	1	1	0	0	0	24	0	0	0.00	....	....	....	....	....	....	....	....		2001-02	2001-02
Lalime, Patrick	Pit., Ott., St.L., Chi., Buf.	12	444	200	174	48	25241	1085	35	2.58	41	21	20	....	2549	75	5	1.77		1996-97	2010-11
Lamothe, Marc	Chi., Det.	2	4	2	1	1	241	13	0	3.24	....	....	....	....	....	....	....	....		1999-00	2003-04
Langkow, Scott	Wpg., Phx., Atl.	4	20	3	12	1	943	68	0	4.33	....	....	....	....	....	....	....	....		1995-96	1999-00
• Larocque, Michel	Mtl., Tor., Phi., St.L.	11	312	160	89	45	17615	978	17	3.33	14	6	6	....	759	37	1	2.92	4	1973-74	1983-84
Larocque, Michel	Chi.	1	3	0	2	0	152	9	0	3.55	....	....	....	....	....	....	....	....		2000-01	2000-01
‡ Lasak, Jan	Nsh.	2	6	0	4	0	267	18	0	4.04	....	....	....	....	....	....	....	....		2001-02	2002-03
Laskoski, Gary	L.A.	2	59	19	27	5	2942	228	0	4.65	....	....	....	....	....	....	....	....		1982-83	1983-84
‡ Lawson, Nathan	NYI, Ott.	2	11	1	4	2	396	28	0	4.24	....	....	....	....	....	....	....	....		2010-11	2013-14
Laxton, Gord	Pit.	4	17	4	9	0	800	74	0	5.55	....	....	....	....	....	....	....	....		1975-76	1978-79
LeBlanc, Ray	Chi.	1	1	1	0	0	60	1	0	1.00	....	....	....	....	....	....	....	....		1991-92	1991-92
Leclaire, Pascal	CBJ, Ott.	7	173	61	76	15	9406	453	10	2.89	3	1	2	....	211	10	0	2.84		2003-04	2010-11
§ • Leduc, Albert	Mtl.	1	1	0	0	0	2	1	0	30.00	....	....	....	....	....	....	....	....		1931-32	1931-32
Legace, Manny	L.A., Det., St.L., Car.	11	365	187	99	41	20140	809	24	2.41	11	4	6	....	639	27	0	2.54	1	1998-99	2009-10
Legris, Claude	Det.	2	4	0	1	1	91	4	0	2.64	....	....	....	....	....	....	....	....		1980-81	1981-82
• Lehman, Hugh	Chi.	2	48	20	24	4	3047	136	6	2.68	2	0	1	1	120	10	0	5.00		1926-27	1927-28
Lemelin, Reggie	Atl., Cgy., Bos.	15	507	236	162	63	28006	1613	12	3.46	59	23	25	....	3119	186	2	3.58		1978-79	1992-93
Lenarduzzi, Mike	Hfd.	2	4	1	1	1	189	10	0	3.17	....	....	....	....	....	....	....	....		1992-93	1993-94
LeNeveu, David	Phx., CBJ	3	22	5	9	2	1067	61	0	3.43	....	....	....	....	....	....	....	....		2005-06	2010-11
Lessard, Mario	L.A.	6	240	92	97	39	13529	843	9	3.74	20	6	12	....	1136	83	0	4.38		1978-79	1983-84
Levasseur, Jean-Louis	Min.	1	1	0	1	0	60	7	0	7.00	....	....	....	....	....	....	....	....		1979-80	1979-80
§ • Levinsky, Alex	Tor.	1	1	0	0	0	1	1	0	60.00	....	....	....	....	....	....	....	....		1931-32	1931-32
Lieuwen, Nathan	Buf.	1	7	1	4	0	363	18	0	2.98	....	....	....	....	....	....	....	....		2013-14	2013-14
• Lindbergh, Pelle	Phi.	5	157	87	49	15	9150	503	7	3.30	23	12	10	....	1214	63	3	3.11		1981-82	1985-86
• Lindsay, Bert	Mtl.W., Tor.	2	20	6	14	0	1238	118	0	5.72	....	....	....	....	....	....	....	....		1917-18	1918-19
Little, Neil	Phi.	2	2	0	2	0	93	6	0	3.87	....	....	....	....	....	....	....	....		2001-02	2003-04
Littman, David	Buf., T.B.	3	3	0	2	0	141	14	0	5.96	....	....	....	....	....	....	....	....		1990-91	1992-93
Liut, Mike	St.L., Hfd., Wsh.	13	664	294	271	74	38215	2221	25	3.49	67	29	32	....	3814	215	2	3.38		1979-80	1991-92
Lockett, Ken	Van.	2	55	13	15	8	2348	131	2	3.35	1	0	1	....	60	6	0	6.00		1974-75	1975-76
• Lockhart, Howard	Tor., Que., Ham., Bos.	5	59	16	41	0	3413	287	1	5.05	....	....	....	....	....	....	....	....		1919-20	1924-25
LoPresti, Pete	Min., Edm.	6	175	43	102	20	9858	668	5	4.07	2	0	2	....	77	6	0	4.68		1974-75	1980-81
• LoPresti, Sam	Chi.	2	74	30	38	6	4530	236	4	3.13	8	3	5	....	530	17	1	1.92		1940-41	1941-42
Lorenz, Danny	NYI	3	8	1	5	0	357	25	0	4.20	....	....	....	....	....	....	....	....		1990-91	1992-93
Loustel, Ron	Wpg.	1	1	0	1	0	60	10	0	10.00	....	....	....	....	....	....	....	....		1980-81	1980-81
Low, Ron	Tor., Wsh., Det., Que., Edm., N.J.	11	382	102	203	38	20502	1463	4	4.28	7	1	6	....	452	29	0	3.85		1972-73	1984-85
Lozinski, Larry	Det.	1	30	6	11	7	1459	105	0	4.32	....	....	....	....	....	....	....	....		1980-81	1980-81
• Lumley, Harry	Det., NYR, Chi., Tor., Bos.	16	803	330	329	142	48044	2206	71	2.75	76	29	47	....	4778	198	7	2.49	1	1943-44	1959-60
‡ MacDonald, Joey	Det., Bos., NYI, Tor., Cgy.	8	133	44	61	15	7331	367	2	3.00	....	....	....	....	....	....	....	....		2006-07	2013-14
‡ MacIntyre, Drew	Van., Buf., Tor.	3	6	0	2	0	199	8	0	2.41	....	....	....	....	....	....	....	....		2007-08	2013-14
MacKenzie, Shawn	N.J.	1	4	0	1	0	130	15	0	6.92	....	....	....	....	....	....	....	....		1982-83	1982-83
Madeley, Darrin	Ott.	3	39	4	23	5	1928	140	0	4.36	....	....	....	....	....	....	....	....		1992-93	1994-95
‡ Makarov, Andrey	Buf.	1	1	0	1	0	60	3	0	3.00	....	....	....	....	....	....	....	....		2014-15	2014-15
Malarchuk, Clint	Que., Wsh., Buf.	10	338	141	130	45	19030	1100	12	3.47	15	2	9	....	781	56	0	4.30		1981-82	1991-92
Maneluk, George	NYI	1	4	1	1	0	140	15	0	6.43	....	....	....	....	....	....	....	....		1990-91	1990-91
Maniago, Cesare	Tor., Mtl., NYR, Min., Van.	15	568	190	257	97	32569	1773	30	3.27	36	15	21	....	2247	100	3	2.67		1960-61	1977-78
Mannino, Peter	NYI, Atl., Wpg.	3	6	1	1	0	226	15	0	3.98	....	....	....	....	....	....	....	....		2008-09	2011-12
Maracle, Norm	Det., Atl.	5	66	14	33	8	3430	177	1	3.10	2	0	0	....	58	3	0	3.10		1997-98	2001-02
‡ Markkanen, Jussi	Edm., NYR	5	128	43	47	15	6610	297	7	2.70	7	3	3	....	374	14	1	2.25		2001-02	2006-07
• Marois, Jean	Tor., Chi.	2	3	1	2	0	180	15	0	5.00	....	....	....	....	....	....	....	....		1943-44	1953-54
• Martin, Seth	St.L.	1	30	8	10	7	1552	67	1	2.59	2	0	0	....	73	5	0	4.11		1967-68	1967-68
Mason, Bob	Wsh., Chi., Que., Van.	8	145	55	65	16	7988	500	1	3.76	5	2	3	....	369	12	1	1.95		1983-84	1990-91
Mason, Chris	Nsh., St.L., Atl., Wpg.	11	317	137	113	32	17004	754	23	2.66	9	1	8	....	552	27	0	2.93		1998-99	2012-13
Mattsson, Markus	Wpg., Min., L.A.	4	92	21	46	14	5007	343	6	4.11	....	....	....	....	....	....	....	....		1979-80	1983-84
May, Darrell	St.L.	2	6	1	5	0	364	31	0	5.11	....	....	....	....	....	....	....	....		1985-86	1987-88
• Mayer, Gilles	Tor.	4	9	2	6	1	540	24	0	2.67	....	....	....	....	....	....	....	....		1949-50	1955-56
• McAuley, Ken	NYR	2	96	17	64	15	5740	537	1	5.61	....	....	....	....	....	....	....	....		1943-44	1944-45
McCartan, Jack	NYR	2	12	2	7	3	680	42	1	3.71	....	....	....	....	....	....	....	....		1959-60	1960-61
• McCool, Frank	Tor.	2	72	34	31	7	4320	242	4	3.36	13	8	5	....	807	30	4	2.23	1	1944-45	1945-46
McDuffe, Peter	St.L., NYR, K.C., Det.	5	57	11	36	6	3207	218	0	4.08	1	0	1	....	60	7	0	7.00		1971-72	1975-76
McGrattan, Tom	Det.	1	1	0	0	0	8	1	0	7.50	....	....	....	....	....	....	....	....		1947-48	1947-48
McKay, Ross	Hfd.	1	1	0	0	0	35	3	0	5.14	....	....	....	....	....	....	....	....		1990-91	1990-91
McKenzie, Bill	Det., K.C., Col.	6	91	18	49	13	4776	326	2	4.10	....	....	....	....	....	....	....	....		1973-74	1979-80
McKichan, Steve	Van.	1	1	0	0	0	20	2	0	6.00	....	....	....	....	....	....	....	....		1990-91	1990-91
McLachlan, Murray	Tor.	1	2	0	1	0	25	4	0	9.60	....	....	....	....	....	....	....	....		1970-71	1970-71
McLean, Kirk	N.J., Van., Car., Fla., NYR	16	612	245	262	72	35090	1904	22	3.26	68	34	34	....	4189	198	6	2.84		1985-86	2000-01
McLelland, Dave	Van.	1	2	1	1	0	120	10	0	5.00	....	....	....	....	....	....	....	....		1972-73	1972-73
McLennan, Jamie	NYI, St.L., Min., Cgy., NYR, Fla.	11	254	80	109	36	13834	617	13	2.68	5	0	2	....	134	7	0	3.13		1993-94	2006-07
• McLeod, Don	Det., Phi.	2	18	3	10	1	879	74	0	5.05	....	....	....	....	....	....	....	....		1970-71	1971-72
McLeod, Jim	St.L.	1	16	6	6	4	880	44	0	3.00	....	....	....	....	....	....	....	....		1971-72	1971-72
McNamara, Gerry	Tor.	2	7	2	2	1	323	14	0	2.60	....	....	....	....	....	....	....	....		1960-61	1969-70
• McNeil, Gerry	Mtl.	8	276	119	105	52	16535	649	28	2.36	35	17	18	....	2284	72	5	1.89	3	1947-48	1957-58
McRae, Gord	Tor.	5	71	30	22	10	3799	221	1	3.49	8	2	5	....	454	22	0	2.91		1972-73	1977-78
McVicar, Rob	Van.	1	1	0	0	0	3	0	0	0.00	....	....	....	....	....	....	....	....		2005-06	2005-06
Melanson, Roland	NYI, Min., L.A., N.J., Mtl.	11	291	129	106	33	16452	995	6	3.63	23	4	9	....	801	59	0	4.42	3	1980-81	1991-92
Meloche, Gilles	Chi., Cal., Cle., Min., Pit.	18	788	270	351	131	45401	2756	20	3.64	45	21	19	....	2464	143	2	3.48		1970-71	1987-88
Micalef, Corrado	Det.	5	113	26	59	15	5794	409	2	4.24	3	0	0	....	49	8	0	9.80		1981-82	1985-86
Michaud, Alfie	Van.	1	2	0	1	0	69	5	0	4.35	....	....	....	....	....	....	....	....		1999-00	1999-00
Michaud, Olivier	Mtl.	1	1	0	0	0	18	0	0	0.00	....	....	....	....	....	....	....	....		2001-02	2001-02
Middlebrook, Lindsay	Wpg., Min., N.J., Edm.	4	37	3	23	6	1845	152	0	4.94	....	....	....	....	....	....	....	....		1979-80	1982-83
• Millar, Al	Bos.	1	6	1	4	1	360	25	0	4.17	....	....	....	....	....	....	....	....		1957-58	1957-58
Millen, Greg	Pit., Hfd., St.L., Que., Chi., Det.	14	604	215	284	89	35377	2281	17	3.87	59	27	29	....	3383	193	0	3.42		1978-79	1991-92
• Miller, Joe	NYA, NYR, Pit., Phi.	4	127	24	87	16	7871	383	16	2.92	3	2	1	0	180	3	1	1.00	1	1927-28	1930-31
Minard, Mike	Edm.	1	1	1	0	0	60	3	0	3.00	....	....	....	....	....	....	....	....		1999-00	1999-00
Mio, Eddie	Edm., NYR, Det.	7	192	64	73	30	10428	705	4	4.06	17	9	7	....	986	63	0	3.83		1979-80	1985-86

Name	NHL Teams	NHL Seasons	Regular Schedule GP	W	L	T	Mins	GA	SO	Avg	Playoffs GP	W	L	T	Mins	GA	SO	Avg	NHL Cup Wins	First NHL Season	Last NHL Season
● Mitchell, Mike	Tor.	3	22	10	9	0	1190	88	0	4.44	....	....	....	....	....	....	....	....	1	1919-20	1921-22
Moffat, Mike	Bos.	3	19	7	7	2	979	70	0	4.29	11	6	5	....	663	38	0	3.44		1981-82	1983-84
Moog, Andy	Edm., Bos., Dal., Mtl.	18	713	372	209	88	40151	2097	28	3.13	132	68	57	....	7452	377	4	3.04	3	1980-81	1997-98
● Moore, Alfie	NYA, Chi., Det.	4	21	7	14	0	1290	81	1	3.77	3	1	2	....	180	7	0	2.33	1	1936-37	1939-40
Moore, Robbie	Phi., Wsh.	2	6	3	1	1	257	8	2	1.87	5	3	2	....	268	18	0	4.03		1978-79	1982-83
● Morissette, Jean-Guy	Mtl.	1	1	0	1	0	36	4	0	6.67	....	....	....	....	....	....	....	....		1963-64	1963-64
Morrison, Mike	Edm., Ott., Phx.	2	29	11	7	3	1226	67	0	3.28	....	....	....	....	....	....	....	....		2005-06	2006-07
Moss, Tyler	Cgy., Car., Van.	4	30	6	16	1	1496	81	0	3.25	....	....	....	....	....	....	....	....		1997-98	2002-03
● Mowers, Johnny	Det.	4	152	65	61	26	9350	399	15	2.56	32	19	13	....	2000	85	2	2.55	1	1940-41	1946-47
Mrazek, Jerome	Phi.	1	1	0	0	0	6	1	0	10.00	....	....	....	....	....	....	....	....		1975-76	1975-76
§ ● Mummery, Harry	Que., Ham.	2	4	2	1	0	192	20	0	6.25	....	....	....	....	....	....	....	....		1919-20	1921-22
Munro, Adam	Chi.	2	17	4	10	3	927	51	1	3.30	....	....	....	....	....	....	....	....		2003-04	2005-06
§ ● Munro, Dunc	Mtl.M.	1	1	0	0	0	2	0	0	0.00	....	....	....	....	....	....	....	....		1924-25	1924-25
● Murphy, Hal	Mtl.	1	1	1	0	0	60	4	0	4.00	....	....	....	....	....	....	....	....		1952-53	1952-53
Murphy, Mike	Car.	1	2	0	1	0	36	0	0	0.00	....	....	....	....	....	....	....	....		2011-12	2011-12
● Murray, Mickey	Mtl.	1	1	0	1	0	60	4	0	4.00	....	....	....	....	....	....	....	....		1929-30	1929-30
Muzzatti, Jason	Cgy., Hfd., NYR, S.J.	5	62	13	25	10	3014	167	1	3.32	....	....	....	....	....	....	....	....		1993-94	1997-98
Myllys, Jarmo	Min., S.J.	4	39	4	27	1	1846	161	0	5.23	....	....	....	....	....	....	....	....		1988-89	1991-92
● Mylnikov, Sergei	Que.	1	10	1	7	2	568	47	0	4.96	....	....	....	....	....	....	....	....		1989-90	1989-90
Myre, Phil	Mtl., Atl., St.L., Phi., Col., Buf.	14	439	149	198	76	25220	1482	14	3.53	12	6	5	....	747	41	1	3.29		1969-70	1982-83
Nabokov, Evgeni	S.J., NYI, T.B.	14	697	353	227	86	40152	1630	59	2.44	86	42	42	0	5144	208	7	2.43		1999-00	2014-15
Naumenko, Gregg	Ana.	1	2	0	1	0	70	7	0	6.00	....	....	....	....	....	....	....	....		2000-01	2000-01
Newton, Cam	Pit.	2	16	4	7	1	814	51	0	3.76	....	....	....	....	....	....	....	....		1970-71	1972-73
Niittymaki, Antero	Phi., T.B., S.J.	7	234	95	86	31	13113	645	5	2.95	4	1	0	....	164	6	0	2.20		2003-04	2010-11
Nilstorp, Cristopher	Dal.	2	6	1	3	1	330	18	0	3.27	....	....	....	....	....	....	....	....		2012-13	2013-14
Noronen, Mika	Buf., Van.	5	71	23	32	6	3652	163	3	2.68	....	....	....	....	....	....	....	....		2000-01	2005-06
Norrena, Fredrik	CBJ	3	100	35	45	11	5235	243	5	2.79	....	....	....	....	....	....	....	....		2006-07	2008-09
Norris, Jack	Bos., Chi., L.A.	4	58	20	25	4	3119	202	2	3.89	....	....	....	....	....	....	....	....		1964-65	1970-71
Nurminen, Pasi	Atl.	3	125	48	54	12	7059	338	5	2.87	....	....	....	....	....	....	....	....		2001-02	2003-04
Oleschuk, Bill	K.C., Col.	4	55	7	28	10	2835	188	1	3.98	....	....	....	....	....	....	....	....		1975-76	1979-80
● Olesevich, Dan	NYR	1	1	0	0	1	29	2	0	4.14	....	....	....	....	....	....	....	....		1961-62	1961-62
O'Neill, Mike	Wpg., Ana.	4	21	0	9	2	855	61	0	4.28	....	....	....	....	....	....	....	....		1991-92	1996-97
Osgood, Chris	Det., NYI, St.L.	17	744	401	216	95	42564	1768	50	2.49	129	74	49	....	7651	267	15	2.09	3	1993-94	2010-11
Ouellet, Maxime	Phi., Wsh., Van.	3	12	2	6	2	663	34	1	3.08	....	....	....	....	....	....	....	....		2000-01	2005-06
Ouimet, Ted	St.L.	1	1	0	1	0	60	2	0	2.00	....	....	....	....	....	....	....	....		1968-69	1968-69
Pageau, Paul	L.A.	1	1	0	1	0	60	8	0	8.00	....	....	....	....	....	....	....	....		1980-81	1980-81
● Paille, Marcel	NYR	7	107	32	52	22	6342	362	2	3.42	....	....	....	....	....	....	....	....		1957-58	1964-65
Palmateer, Mike	Tor., Wsh.	8	356	149	138	52	20131	1183	17	3.53	29	12	17	....	1765	89	2	3.03		1976-77	1983-84
Pang, Darren	Chi.	3	81	27	35	7	4252	287	0	4.05	6	1	3	....	250	18	0	4.32		1984-85	1988-89
Parent, Bernie	Bos., Phi., Tor.	13	608	271	198	121	35136	1493	54	2.55	71	38	33	....	4302	174	6	2.43	2	1965-66	1978-79
Parent, Bob	Tor.	2	3	0	2	0	160	15	0	5.63	....	....	....	....	....	....	....	....		1981-82	1982-83
Parent, Rich	St.L., T.B., Pit.	4	32	7	11	5	1561	82	1	3.15	....	....	....	....	....	....	....	....		1997-98	2000-01
Parro, Dave	Wsh.	4	77	21	36	10	4015	274	2	4.09	....	....	....	....	....	....	....	....		1980-81	1983-84
Passmore, Steve	Edm., Chi., L.A.	6	93	23	44	12	5045	235	2	2.79	3	0	2	....	138	6	0	2.61		1998-99	2003-04
§ ● Patrick, Lester	NYR	1	....	....	....	....	....	....	....	....	1	1	0	0	46	1	0	1.30	1	1927-28	1927-28
‡ Patzold, Dimitri	S.J.	1	3	0	0	0	44	4	0	5.45	....	....	....	....	....	....	....	....		2007-08	2007-08
Pechurski, Alexander	Pit.	1	1	0	0	0	36	1	0	1.67	....	....	....	....	....	....	....	....		2009-10	2009-10
Peeters, Pete	Phi., Bos., Wsh.	13	489	246	155	51	27699	1424	21	3.08	71	35	35	....	4200	232	2	3.31		1978-79	1990-91
Pelletier, Jean-Marc	Phi., Phx.	3	7	1	4	0	354	23	0	3.90	....	....	....	....	....	....	....	....		1998-99	2003-04
● Pelletier, Marcel	Chi., NYR	2	8	1	6	0	395	32	0	4.86	....	....	....	....	....	....	....	....		1950-51	1962-63
Penney, Steve	Mtl., Wpg.	5	91	35	38	12	5194	313	1	3.62	27	15	12	....	1604	72	4	2.69		1983-84	1987-88
● Perreault, Bob	Mtl., Det., Bos.	3	31	8	16	7	1827	103	3	3.38	....	....	....	....	....	....	....	....		1955-56	1962-63
Pettie, Jim	Bos.	3	21	9	7	2	1157	71	1	3.68	....	....	....	....	....	....	....	....		1976-77	1978-79
‡ Pielmeier, Timo	Ana.	1	1	0	0	0	40	5	0	7.50	....	....	....	....	....	....	....	....		2010-11	2010-11
Pietrangelo, Frank	Pit., Hfd.	7	141	46	59	6	7141	490	1	4.12	12	7	5	....	713	34	1	2.86	1	1987-88	1993-94
● Plante, Jacques	Mtl., NYR, St.L., Tor., Bos.	18	837	437	246	145	49533	1964	82	2.38	112	71	36	....	6651	237	14	2.14	6	1952-53	1972-73
● Plasse, Michel	St.L., Mtl., K.C., Pit., Col., Que.	11	299	92	136	54	16760	1058	2	3.79	4	1	2	....	195	9	1	2.77	1	1970-71	1981-82
§ ● Plaxton, Hugh	Mtl.M.	1	1	0	1	0	57	5	0	5.26	....	....	....	....	....	....	....	....		1932-33	1932-33
Pogge, Justin	Tor.	1	7	1	4	1	372	27	0	4.35	....	....	....	....	....	....	....	....		2008-09	2008-09
‡ Popperle, Tomas	CBJ	1	2	0	0	0	45	1	0	1.33	....	....	....	....	....	....	....	....		2006-07	2006-07
Potvin, Felix	Tor., NYI, Van., L.A., Bos.	13	635	266	260	85	36765	1694	32	2.76	72	35	37	....	4435	195	8	2.64		1991-92	2003-04
‡ Poulin, Kevin	NYI	5	50	18	25	3	2735	140	0	3.07	2	0	0	....	52	1	0	1.15		2010-11	2014-15
Pronovost, Claude	Bos., Mtl.	2	3	1	1	0	120	7	1	3.50	....	....	....	....	....	....	....	....		1955-56	1958-59
Prusek, Martin	Ott., CBJ	4	57	31	12	4	2898	114	3	2.36	1	0	0	....	40	1	0	1.50		2001-02	2005-06
Puppa, Daren	Buf., Tor., T.B.	15	429	179	161	54	23819	1204	19	3.03	16	4	9	....	786	51	0	3.89		1985-86	1999-00
Pusey, Chris	Det.	1	1	0	0	0	40	3	0	4.50	....	....	....	....	....	....	....	....		1985-86	1985-86
Racicot, Andre	Mtl.	5	68	26	23	8	3357	196	2	3.50	4	0	1	....	31	4	0	7.74	1	1989-90	1993-94
Racine, Bruce	St.L.	1	11	0	3	0	230	12	0	3.13	1	0	0	....	1	0	0	0.00		1995-96	1995-96
Ram, Jamie	NYR	1	1	0	0	0	27	0	0	0.00	....	....	....	....	....	....	....	....		1995-96	1995-96
‡ Ramo, Karri	T.B., Cgy.	6	159	60	63	18	8722	414	5	2.85	7	2	3	....	336	16	0	2.86		2006-07	**2015-16**
Ranford, Bill	Bos., Edm., Wsh., T.B., Det.	15	647	240	279	76	35936	2042	15	3.41	53	28	25	....	3110	159	4	3.07	2	1985-86	1999-00
Raycroft, Andrew	Bos., Tor., Col., Van., Dal.	11	280	113	114	27	15191	732	9	2.89	8	3	4	....	472	17	1	2.16		2000-01	2011-12
Raymond, Alain	Wsh.	1	1	0	1	0	40	2	0	3.00	....	....	....	....	....	....	....	....		1987-88	1987-88
● Rayner, Chuck	NYA, Bro., NYR	10	424	138	208	77	25491	1294	25	3.05	18	9	9	....	1135	46	1	2.43		1940-41	1952-53
Reaugh, Daryl	Edm., Hfd.	3	27	8	9	1	1246	72	1	3.47	....	....	....	....	....	....	....	....		1984-85	1990-91
Reddick, Pokey	Wpg., Edm., Fla.	6	132	46	58	16	7162	443	0	3.71	4	0	2	....	168	10	0	3.57	1	1986-87	1993-94
§ ● Redding, George	Bos.	1	1	0	0	0	11	1	0	5.45	....	....	....	....	....	....	....	....		1924-25	1924-25
Redquest, Greg	Pit.	1	1	0	0	0	13	3	0	13.85	....	....	....	....	....	....	....	....		1977-78	1977-78
Reece, Dave	Bos.	1	14	7	5	2	777	43	2	3.32	....	....	....	....	....	....	....	....		1975-76	1975-76
Reese, Jeff	Tor., Cgy., Hfd., T.B., N.J.	11	174	53	65	17	8667	529	5	3.66	11	3	5	....	515	35	0	4.08		1987-88	1998-99
Resch, Glenn	NYI, Col., N.J., Phi.	14	571	231	224	82	32279	1761	26	3.27	41	17	17	....	2044	85	2	2.50	1	1973-74	1986-87
● Rheaume, Herb	Mtl.	1	31	10	20	1	1889	92	0	2.92	....	....	....	....	....	....	....	....		1925-26	1925-26
Rhodes, Damian	Tor., Ott., Atl.	10	309	99	140	48	17339	820	12	2.84	13	5	7	....	741	27	0	2.19		1990-91	2001-02
Ricci, Nick	Pit.	4	19	7	12	0	1087	79	0	4.36	....	....	....	....	....	....	....	....		1979-80	1982-83
Richardson, Terry	Det., St.L.	5	20	3	11	0	906	85	0	5.63	....	....	....	....	....	....	....	....		1973-74	1978-79
Richter, Mike	NYR	15	666	301	258	73	38183	1840	24	2.89	76	41	33	....	4514	202	9	2.68	1	1988-89	2002-03
Ridley, Curt	NYR, Van., Tor.	6	104	27	47	16	5498	355	1	3.87	2	0	2	....	120	8	0	4.00		1974-75	1980-81
Riendeau, Vincent	Mtl., St.L., Det., Bos.	8	184	85	65	20	10423	573	5	3.30	25	11	12	....	1277	71	1	3.34		1987-88	1994-95
● Riggin, Dennis	Det.	2	18	6	10	2	999	52	1	3.12	....	....	....	....	....	....	....	....		1959-60	1962-63
Riggin, Pat	Atl., Cgy., Wsh., Bos., Pit.	9	350	153	120	52	19872	1135	11	3.43	25	8	13	....	1336	72	0	3.23		1979-80	1987-88
● Ring, Bob	Bos.	1	1	0	0	0	33	4	0	7.27	....	....	....	....	....	....	....	....		1965-66	1965-66
● Rivard, Fern	Min.	4	55	9	27	11	2865	190	2	3.98	....	....	....	....	....	....	....	....		1968-69	1974-75
● Roach, John Ross	Tor., NYR, Det.	14	492	219	204	68	30444	1246	58	2.46	29	12	14	3	1901	60	7	1.89	1	1921-22	1934-35
● Roberts, Moe	Bos., NYA, Chi.	4	10	3	5	0	501	31	0	3.71	....	....	....	....	....	....	....	....		1925-26	1951-52
● Robertson, Earl	Det., NYA, Bro.	6	190	60	95	34	11820	575	16	2.92	15	7	7	....	995	29	2	1.75	1	1936-37	1941-42
● Rollins, Al	Tor., Chi., NYR	9	430	141	205	83	25723	1192	28	2.78	13	6	7	....	755	30	0	2.38	1	1949-50	1959-60
Roloson, Dwayne	Cgy., Buf., Min., Edm., NYI, T.B.	14	606	227	257	82	34297	1552	29	2.72	50	28	18	....	2860	121	2	2.54		1996-97	2011-12
Romano, Roberto	Pit., Bos.	6	126	46	63	8	7111	471	4	3.97	....	....	....	....	....	....	....	....		1982-83	1993-94
Rosati, Mike	Wsh.	1	1	1	0	0	28	0	0	0.00	....	....	....	....	....	....	....	....		1998-99	1998-99
Roussel, Dominic	Phi., Wpg., Ana., Edm.	8	205	77	70	23	10665	555	7	3.12	1	0	0	....	23	0	0	0.00		1991-92	2000-01
Roy, Patrick	Mtl., Col.	19	1029	551	315	131	60235	2546	66	2.54	247	151	94	....	15209	584	23	2.30	4	1984-85	2002-03
Rudkowsky, Cody	St.L.	1	1	1	0	0	30	0	0	0.00	....	....	....	....	....	....	....	....		2002-03	2002-03
● Rupp, Pat	Det.	1	1	0	1	0	60	4	0	4.00	....	....	....	....	....	....	....	....		1963-64	1963-64
Rutherford, Jim	Det., Pit., Tor., L.A.	13	457	151	227	59	25895	1576	14	3.65	8	2	5	....	440	28	0	3.82		1970-71	1982-83
● Rutledge, Wayne	L.A.	3	82	28	37	9	4325	241	2	3.34	8	2	4	....	378	20	0	3.17		1967-68	1969-70
‡ Rynnas, Jussi	Tor., Dal.	3	5	0	2	0	201	14	0	4.18	....	....	....	....	....	....	....	....		2011-12	2014-15
Sabourin, Dany	Cgy., Pit., Van.	5	57	18	25	4	2901	139	2	2.87	2	0	0	....	14	1	0	4.29		2003-04	2008-09
St. Croix, Rick	Phi., Tor.	8	130	49	54	18	7295	451	2	3.71	11	4	6	....	562	29	1	3.10		1977-78	1984-85
St. Laurent, Sam	N.J., Det.	5	34	7	12	4	1572	92	1	3.51	1	0	0	....	10	1	0	6.00		1985-86	1989-90
‡ Salak, Alexander	Fla.	1	2	0	1	0	67	6	0	5.37	....	....	....	....	....	....	....	....		2009-10	2009-10

			Regular Schedule								Playoffs								NHL	First	Last
Name	NHL Teams	NHL Seasons	GP	W	L	T	Mins	GA	SO	Avg	GP	W	L	T	Mins	GA	SO	Avg	Cup Wins	NHL Season	NHL Season
Salo, Tommy	NYI, Edm., Col.	10	526	210	225	73	30436	1296	37	2.55	22	5	16	....	1369	58	0	2.54		1994-95	2003-04
§ • Sands, Charlie	Mtl.	1	1	0	0	0	25	5	0	12.00	....	....	....	....	....	....	....	....		1939-40	1939-40
Sands, Mike	Min.	2	6	0	5	0	302	26	0	5.17	....	....	....	....	....	....	....	....		1984-85	1986-87
Sanford, Curtis	St.L., Van., CBJ	6	144	47	55	15	7354	333	6	2.72	....	....	....	....	....	....	....	....		2002-03	2011-12
Sarjeant, Geoff	St.L., S.J.	2	8	1	2	1	291	20	0	4.12	....	....	....	....	....	....	....	....		1994-95	1995-96
Sauve, Bob	Buf., Det., Chi., N.J.	13	420	182	154	54	23711	1377	8	3.48	34	15	16	....	1850	95	4	3.08		1976-77	1988-89
Sauve, Philippe	Col., Cgy., Phx., Bos.	3	32	10	14	3	1616	93	0	3.45	....	....	....	....	....	....	....	....		2003-04	2006-07
• Sawchuk, Terry	Det., Bos., Tor., L.A., NYR	21	971	447	330	172	57194	2389	103	2.51	106	54	48	....	6290	266	12	2.54	4	1949-50	1969-70
• Schaefer, Joe	NYR	2	2	0	2	0	86	8	0	5.58	....	....	....	....	....	....	....	....		1959-60	1960-61
Schaefer, Nolan	S.J.	1	7	5	1	0	352	11	1	1.88	....	....	....	....	....	....	....	....		2005-06	2005-06
Schafer, Paxton	Bos.	1	3	0	0	0	77	6	0	4.68	....	....	....	....	....	....	....	....		1996-97	1996-97
Schwab, Corey	N.J., T.B., Van., Tor.	8	147	42	63	13	7476	360	6	2.89	3	0	0	....	40	0	0	0.00	1	1995-96	2003-04
‡ Schwarz, Marek	St.L.	3	6	0	2	0	125	9	0	4.32	....	....	....	....	....	....	....	....		2006-07	2008-09
Scott, Ron	NYR, L.A.	5	28	8	13	4	1450	91	0	3.77	1	0	0	....	32	4	0	7.50		1983-84	1989-90
Scott, Travis	L.A.	1	1	0	0	0	25	3	0	7.20	....	....	....	....	....	....	....	....		2000-01	2000-01
Sevigny, Richard	Mtl., Que.	9	176	80	54	20	9485	507	5	3.21	4	0	3	....	208	13	0	3.75	1	1978-79	1986-87
Sharples, Scott	Cgy.	1	1	0	0	1	65	4	0	3.69	....	....	....	....	....	....	....	....		1991-92	1991-92
§ • Shields, Al	NYA	1	2	0	0	0	41	9	0	13.17	....	....	....	....	....	....	....	....		1931-32	1931-32
Shields, Steve	Buf., S.J., Ana., Bos., Fla., Atl.	10	246	80	104	40	13630	606	10	2.67	25	9	16	....	1445	74	1	3.07		1995-96	2005-06
Shtalenkov, Mikhail	Ana., Edm., Phx., Fla.	7	190	62	82	19	9966	480	8	2.89	4	0	3	....	211	10	0	2.84		1993-94	1999-00
Shulmistra, Richard	N.J., Fla.	2	2	1	1	0	122	3	0	1.48	....	....	....	....	....	....	....	....		1997-98	1999-00
Sidorkiewicz, Peter	Hfd., Ott., N.J.	8	246	79	128	27	13884	832	8	3.60	15	5	10	....	912	55	0	3.62		1987-88	1997-98
Sigalet, Jordan	Bos.	1	1	0	0	0	1	0	0	0.00	....	....	....	....	....	....	....	....		2005-06	2005-06
• Simmons, Don	Bos., Tor., NYR	11	249	101	101	41	14555	701	20	2.89	24	13	11	....	1436	62	3	2.59	3	1956-57	1968-69
Simmons, Gary	Cal., Cle., L.A.	4	107	30	57	15	6162	366	5	3.56	1	0	0	....	20	1	0	3.00		1974-75	1977-78
‡ Simpson, Kent	Chi.	1	1	0	0	0	20	2	0	6.00	....	....	....	....	....	....	....	....		2013-14	2013-14
‡ Skapski, Mackenzie	NYR	1	2	2	0	0	119	1	1	0.50	....	....	....	....	....	....	....	....		2014-15	2014-15
Skidmore, Paul	St.L.	1	2	1	1	0	120	6	0	3.00	....	....	....	....	....	....	....	....		1981-82	1981-82
Skorodenski, Warren	Chi., Edm.	5	35	12	11	4	1732	100	2	3.46	2	0	0	....	33	6	0	10.91		1981-82	1987-88
Skudra, Peter	Pit., Buf., Bos., Van.	6	146	51	47	20	7162	326	6	2.73	3	0	1	....	116	6	0	3.10		1997-98	2002-03
• Smith, Al	Tor., Pit., Det., Buf., Hfd., Col.	10	233	74	99	36	12752	735	10	3.46	6	1	4	....	317	21	0	3.97		1965-66	1980-81
Smith, Billy	L.A., NYI	18	680	305	233	105	38431	2031	22	3.17	132	88	36	....	7645	348	5	2.73	4	1971-72	1988-89
Smith, Gary	Tor., Oak., Cal., Chi., Van., Min., Wsh., Wpg.	14	532	173	261	74	29619	1675	26	3.39	20	5	13	....	1153	62	1	3.23		1965-66	1979-80
• Smith, Normie	Mtl.M., Det.	8	199	81	83	35	12357	479	17	2.33	12	9	2	0	820	18	3	1.32	2	1931-32	1944-45
Sneddon, Bob	Cal.	1	5	0	2	0	225	21	0	5.60	....	....	....	....	....	....	....	....		1970-71	1970-71
Snow, Garth	Que., Phi., Van., Pit., NYI	12	368	135	147	44	19837	925	16	2.80	20	9	8	....	1040	48	1	2.77		1993-94	2005-06
Soderstrom, Tommy	Phi., NYI	5	156	45	69	19	8189	496	10	3.63	....	....	....	....	....	....	....	....		1992-93	1996-97
Soetaert, Doug	NYR, Wpg., Mtl.	12	284	110	104	42	15583	1030	6	3.97	5	1	2	....	180	14	0	4.67	1	1975-76	1986-87
Soucy, Christian	Chi.	1	1	0	0	0	3	0	0	0.00	....	....	....	....	....	....	....	....		1993-94	1993-94
• Spooner, Red	Pit.	1	1	0	1	0	60	6	0	6.00	....	....	....	....	....	....	....	....		1929-30	1929-30
§ • Spring, Jesse	Ham.	1	1	0	0	0	2	0	0	0.00	....	....	....	....	....	....	....	....		1924-25	1924-25
Stana, Rastislav	Wsh.	1	6	1	2	0	211	11	0	3.13	....	....	....	....	....	....	....	....		2003-04	2003-04
Staniowski, Ed	St.L., Wpg., Hfd.	10	219	67	104	21	12075	818	2	4.06	8	1	6	....	428	28	0	3.93		1975-76	1984-85
§ • Starr, Harold	Mtl.M.	1	1	0	0	0	3	0	0	0.00	....	....	....	....	....	....	....	....		1931-32	1931-32
Stauber, Robb	L.A., Buf.	4	62	21	23	9	3295	209	1	3.81	4	3	1	....	240	16	0	4.00		1989-90	1994-95
Stefan, Greg	Det.	9	299	115	127	30	16333	1068	5	3.92	30	12	17	....	1681	99	1	3.53		1981-82	1989-90
• Stein, Phil	Tor.	1	1	0	0	1	70	2	0	1.71	....	....	....	....	....	....	....	....		1939-40	1939-40
‡ Stephan, Tobias	Dal.	2	11	1	3	2	499	29	0	3.49	....	....	....	....	....	....	....	....		2007-08	2008-09
• Stephenson, Wayne	St.L., Phi., Wsh.	10	328	146	103	49	18343	937	14	3.06	26	11	12	....	1522	79	2	3.11	1	1971-72	1980-81
• Stevenson, Doug	NYR, Chi.	3	8	2	6	0	480	39	0	4.88	....	....	....	....	....	....	....	....		1944-45	1945-46
• Stewart, Charles	Bos.	3	77	30	41	5	4742	194	10	2.45	....	....	....	....	....	....	....	....		1924-25	1926-27
Stewart, Jim	Bos.	1	1	0	1	0	20	5	0	15.00	....	....	....	....	....	....	....	....		1979-80	1979-80
Storr, Jamie	L.A., Car.	10	219	85	86	23	11512	488	16	2.54	5	0	3	....	182	11	0	3.63		1994-95	2003-04
• Stuart, Herb	Det.	1	3	1	2	0	180	5	0	1.67	....	....	....	....	....	....	....	....		1926-27	1926-27
Sylvestri, Don	Bos.	1	3	0	0	2	102	6	0	3.53	....	....	....	....	....	....	....	....		1984-85	1984-85
Tabaracci, Rick	Pit., Wpg., Wsh., Cgy., T.B., Atl., Col.	11	286	93	125	30	15255	760	15	2.99	17	4	12	....	1025	53	0	3.10		1988-89	1999-00
Takko, Kari	Min., Edm.	6	142	37	71	14	7317	475	1	3.90	4	0	1	....	109	7	0	3.85		1985-86	1990-91
Tallas, Robbie	Bos., Chi.	6	99	28	42	10	5069	246	3	2.91	....	....	....	....	....	....	....	....		1995-96	2000-01
Tanner, John	Que.	3	21	2	11	5	1084	65	1	3.60	....	....	....	....	....	....	....	....		1989-90	1991-92
Tarkki, Iiro	Ana.	1	1	1	0	0	41	3	0	4.39	....	....	....	....	....	....	....	....		2011-12	2011-12
Tataryn, Dave	NYR	1	2	1	1	0	80	10	0	7.50	....	....	....	....	....	....	....	....		1976-77	1976-77
Taylor, Bobby	Phi., Pit.	5	46	15	17	6	2268	155	0	4.10	....	....	....	....	....	....	....	....	2	1971-72	1975-76
‡ Tellqvist, Mikael	Tor., Phx., Buf.	6	113	45	41	10	6034	303	6	3.01	....	....	....	....	....	....	....	....		2002-03	2008-09
• Teno, Harvey	Det.	1	5	2	3	0	300	15	0	3.00	....	....	....	....	....	....	....	....		1938-39	1938-39
Terreri, Chris	N.J., S.J., Chi., NYI	14	406	151	172	43	22369	1143	9	3.07	29	12	12	....	1523	86	0	3.39	2	1986-87	2000-01
Theodore, Jose	Mtl., Col., Wsh., Min., Fla.	17	648	286	254	69	36607	1635	33	2.68	56	21	30	0	3185	148	2	2.79		1995-96	2012-13
Thibault, Jocelyn	Que., Col., Mtl., Chi., Pit., Buf.	14	586	238	238	75	32892	1508	39	2.75	18	4	11	....	848	50	0	3.54		1993-94	2007-08
Thomas, Tim	Bos., Fla., Dal.	9	426	214	145	49	24448	1027	31	2.52	51	29	21	0	3115	108	6	2.08	1	2002-03	2013-14
Thomas, Wayne	Mtl., Tor., NYR	9	243	103	93	34	13768	766	10	3.34	15	6	8	....	849	50	1	3.53		1972-73	1980-81
• Thompson, Tiny	Bos., Det.	12	553	284	194	75	34175	1183	81	2.08	44	20	24	0	2974	93	7	1.88	1	1928-29	1939-40
‡ Toivonen, Hannu	Bos., St.L.	3	61	18	24	10	3259	183	1	3.37	....	....	....	....	....	....	....	....		2005-06	2007-08
§ • Toppazzini, Jerry	Bos.	1	1	0	0	0	1	0	0	0.00	....	....	....	....	....	....	....	....		1960-61	1960-61
Torchia, Mike	Dal.	1	6	3	2	1	327	18	0	3.30	....	....	....	....	....	....	....	....		1994-95	1994-95
Tordjman, Josh	Phx.	1	2	0	2	0	118	8	0	4.07	....	....	....	....	....	....	....	....		2008-09	2008-09
Toskala, Vesa	S.J., Tor., Cgy.	8	266	129	82	30	14767	679	13	2.76	11	6	5	....	686	28	1	2.45		2001-02	2009-10
Trefilov, Andrei	Cgy., Buf., Chi.	7	54	12	25	4	2663	153	2	3.45	1	0	0	....	5	0	0	0.00		1992-93	1998-99
Tremblay, Vincent	Tor., Pit.	5	58	12	26	8	2785	223	1	4.80	....	....	....	....	....	....	....	....		1979-80	1983-84
‡ Treutle, Niklas	Ari.	1	2	0	1	0	50	5	0	6.00	....	....	....	....	....	....	....	....		**2015-16**	**2015-16**
Tucker, Ted	Cal.	1	5	1	1	1	177	10	0	3.39	....	....	....	....	....	....	....	....		1973-74	1973-74
Tugnutt, Ron	Que., Edm., Ana., Mtl., Ott., Pit., CBJ, Dal.	16	537	186	239	62	29486	1497	26	3.05	25	9	13	....	1482	56	3	2.27		1987-88	2003-04
Turco, Marty	Dal., Chi., Bos.	11	543	275	167	66	30957	1216	41	2.36	47	21	26	....	3103	112	4	2.17		2000-01	2011-12
Turek, Roman	Dal., St.L., Cgy.	8	328	159	115	43	19095	734	27	2.31	22	12	9	....	1342	50	0	2.24	1	1996-97	2003-04
• Turner, Joe	Det.	1	1	0	0	1	70	3	0	2.57	....	....	....	....	....	....	....	....		1941-42	1941-42
Underhill, Matt	Chi.	1	1	0	1	0	61	4	0	3.93	....	....	....	....	....	....	....	....		2003-04	2003-04
Vachon, Rogie	Mtl., L.A., Det., Bos.	16	795	355	291	127	46298	2310	51	2.99	48	23	23	....	2876	133	2	2.77	3	1966-67	1981-82
Valiquette, Steve	NYI, Edm., NYR	6	46	16	14	5	2256	103	4	2.74	2	0	0	....	40	0	0	0.00		1999-00	2009-10
Vanbiesbrouck, John	NYR, Fla., Phi., NYI, N.J.	20	882	374	346	119	50475	2503	40	2.98	71	28	38	....	3969	177	5	2.68		1981-82	2001-02
Veisor, Mike	Chi., Hfd., Wpg.	10	139	41	62	26	7806	532	5	4.09	4	0	2	....	180	15	0	5.00		1973-74	1983-84
Vernon, Mike	Cgy., Det., S.J., Fla.	19	781	385	273	92	44449	2206	27	2.98	138	77	56	....	8214	367	6	2.68	2	1982-83	2001-02
• Vezina, Georges	Mtl.	9	190	103	81	5	11592	633	13	3.28	13	10	3	0	780	35	2	2.69	1	1917-18	1925-26
Villemure, Gilles	NYR, Chi.	10	205	100	64	29	11581	542	13	2.81	14	5	5	....	656	32	0	2.93		1963-64	1976-77
‡ Visentin, Mark	Phx.	1	1	0	1	0	59	3	0	3.05	....	....	....	....	....	....	....	....		2013-14	2013-14
Vokoun, Tomas	Mtl., Nsh., Fla., Wsh., Pit.	15	700	300	288	78	39695	1688	51	2.55	22	9	13	....	1365	51	2	2.24		1996-97	2012-13
Waite, Jimmy	Chi., S.J., Phx.	11	106	28	41	12	5253	293	4	3.35	6	0	3	....	211	14	0	3.98		1988-89	1998-99
Wakaluk, Darcy	Buf., Min., Dal., Phx.	8	191	67	75	21	9756	524	9	3.22	8	4	2	....	364	18	0	2.97		1988-89	1996-97
Wakely, Ernie	Mtl., St.L.	7	113	41	42	17	6244	290	8	2.79	10	2	6	....	509	37	1	4.36	2	1962-63	1971-72
Wall, Michael	Ana.	1	4	2	2	0	202	10	0	2.97	....	....	....	....	....	....	....	....		2006-07	2006-07
• Walsh, Flat	Mtl.M., NYA	7	108	48	43	16	6641	256	12	2.31	8	2	4	2	570	16	2	1.68		1926-27	1932-33
Wamsley, Rick	Mtl., St.L., Cgy., Tor.	13	407	204	131	46	23123	1287	12	3.34	27	7	18	....	1397	81	0	3.48	1	1980-81	1992-93
Watt, Jim	St.L.	1	1	0	0	0	20	2	0	6.00	....	....	....	....	....	....	....	....		1973-74	1973-74
Weekes, Kevin	Fla., Van., NYI, T.B., Car., NYR, N.J.	11	348	105	163	39	18837	903	19	2.88	9	3	3	....	468	15	2	1.92		1997-98	2008-09
Weeks, Steve	NYR, Hfd., Van., NYI, L.A., Ott.	13	290	111	119	33	15879	989	5	3.74	12	3	5	....	486	27	0	3.33		1980-81	1992-93
Weiman, Tyler	Col.	1	1	0	0	0	16	0	0	0.00	....	....	....	....	....	....	....	....		2007-08	2007-08
Wetzel, Carl	Det., Min.	2	7	1	4	1	301	22	0	4.39	....	....	....	....	....	....	....	....		1964-65	1967-68
Whitmore, Kay	Hfd., Van., Bos., Cgy.	9	155	60	64	16	8596	508	4	3.55	4	0	2	....	174	13	0	4.48		1988-89	2001-02
Wilkinson, Derek	T.B.	4	22	3	12	3	933	57	0	3.67	....	....	....	....	....	....	....	....		1995-96	1998-99
Willis, Jordan	Dal.	1	1	0	1	0	19	1	0	3.16	....	....	....	....	....	....	....	....		1995-96	1995-96
Wilson, Dunc	Phi., Van., Tor., NYR, Pit.	10	287	80	150	33	15851	988	8	3.74	....	....	....	....	....	....	....	....		1969-70	1978-79

Name	NHL Teams	NHL Seasons	GP	W	L	T	Mins	GA	SO	Avg	GP	W	L	T	Mins	GA	SO	Avg	NHL Cup Wins	First NHL Season	Last NHL Season
• Wilson, Lefty	Det., Tor., Bos.	3	3	0	0	1	81	1	0	0.74	....							....		1953-54	1957-58
• Winkler, Hal	NYR, Bos.	2	75	35	26	14	4739	126	21	1.60	10	2	3	5	640	18	2	1.69		1926-27	1927-28
Wolfe, Bernie	Wsh.	4	120	20	61	21	6104	424	1	4.17	....							....		1975-76	1978-79
• Wood, Alex	NYA	1	1	0	1	0	70	3	0	2.57	....							....		1936-37	1936-37
• Worsley, Gump	NYR, Mtl., Min.	21	861	335	352	150	50183	2407	43	2.88	70	40	26		4084	189	5	2.78	4	1952-53	1973-74
• Worters, Roy	Pit., NYA, Mtl.	12	484	171	229	83	30175	1143	67	2.27	11	3	6	2	690	24	3	2.09		1925-26	1936-37
• Worthy, Chris	Oak., Cal.	3	26	5	10	4	1326	98	0	4.43	....							....		1968-69	1970-71
Wregget, Ken	Tor., Phi., Pit., Cgy., Det.	17	575	225	248	53	31663	1917	9	3.63	56	28	25		3341	160	3	2.87	1	1983-84	1999-00
Yeats, Matthew	Wsh.	1	5	1	3	0	258	13	0	3.02	....							....		2003-04	2003-04
Yeremeyev, Vitali	NYR	1	4	0	4	0	212	16	0	4.53	....							....		2000-01	2000-01
York, Allen	CBJ	1	11	3	2	0	417	16	0	2.30	....							....		2011-12	2011-12
§ • Young, Doug	Det.	1	1	0	0	0	21	1	0	2.86	....							....		1933-34	1933-34
Young, Wendell	Van., Phi., Pit., T.B.	10	187	59	86	12	9410	618	2	3.94	2	0	1		99	6	0	3.64	2	1985-86	1994-95
Zaba, Matt	NYR	1	1	0	0	0	34	2	0	3.53	....							....		2009-10	2009-10
Zanier, Mike	Edm.	1	3	1	1	1	185	12	0	3.89	....							....		1984-85	1984-85
Zepp, Rob	Phi.	1	10	5	2	0	519	25	0	2.89	....							....		2014-15	2014-15

Late Additions

BUTCHER, Will — (see page 288 for data panel)
Defense — Drafted by Colorado in 2013. Not signed.
Acquired free agent status, August 16, 2017.

CULLEN, Matt — (see page 394 for data panel) — **MIN**
Center — Signed as a free agent by **Minnesota**, August 16, 2017.

DRAISAITAL Leon — (see page 402 for data panel) — **EDM**
Center — Restricted Free Agent re-signed with **Edmonton**, August 16, 2017.

GIRGENSONS, Zemgus — (see page 425 for data panel) — **BUF**
Center — Restricted Free Agent re-signed with **Buffalo**, August 17, 2017.

MARCHENKO, Alexey — (see page 482 for data panel)
Defense — Signed as a free agent by **CSKA Moscow** (KHL), August 16, 2017.

TONINATO, Dominic — (see page 344 for data panel) — **COL**
Center — Signed as a free agent by **Colorado**, August 16, 2017.

Additional On-Ice Officials

Referee

#	Name	*Age	Birthplace
42	Corey Syvret	28	Millgrove, ON

Linesmen

#	Name	*Age	Birthplace
67	Travis Gawryletz	32	Kelowna, BC
61	James Tobias	22	West Seneca, NY

*Age at start of 2017-18 season.

Roster of 2017-18 NHL On-Ice Officials is found on page 8

continued from page 120
Mike Babcock
Head Coach, Toronto Maple Leafs
Born: Manitouwadge, ON, April 29, 1963.

Coaching Record

Season	Team	League	GC	W	L	O/T	GC	W	L	T
1988-89	Red Deer	ACAC	24	18	4	2	6	5	1	....
1988-89	Red Deer	CCAA	....	....	....	....	4	3	1	....
1989-90	Red Deer	ACAC	24	11	12	1	5	2	3	....
1990-91	Red Deer	ACAC	25	19	6	0	3	1	2	....
1991-92	Moose Jaw	WHL	72	33	36	3	4	0	4	....
1992-93	Moose Jaw	WHL	72	27	42	3	....	....	....	....
1993-94	U of Lethbridge	CIAU	28	19	7	2	....	....	....	....
1994-95	Spokane	WHL	72	32	36	4	11	6	5	....
1995-96	Spokane	WHL	72	50	18	4	9	3	6	....
1996-97	Spokane	WHL	72	35	33	4	9	4	5	....
1997-98	Spokane	WHL	72	45	23	4	18	10	8	....
1998-99	Spokane	WHL	72	19	44	9	....	....	....	....
99-2000	Spokane	WHL	72	47	19	6	20	15	5	....
2000-01	Cincinnati	AHL	80	41	26	13	4	1	3	....
2001-02	Cincinnati	AHL	80	33	33	14	3	1	2	....
2002-03	**Anaheim**	**NHL**	82	40	27	15	21	15	6	....
2003-04	**Anaheim**	**NHL**	82	29	35	18	....	....	....	....
2004-05	**Anaheim**		SEASON CANCELLED							
2005-06	**Detroit**	**NHL**	82	58	16	8	6	2	4	....
2006-07	**Detroit**	**NHL**	82	50	19	13	18	10	8	....
2007-08•	**Detroit**	**NHL**	82	54	21	7	22	16	6	....
2008-09	**Detroit**	**NHL**	82	51	21	10	23	15	8	....
2009-10	**Detroit**	**NHL**	82	44	24	14	12	5	7	....
2010-11	**Detroit**	**NHL**	82	47	25	10	11	7	4	....
2011-12	**Detroit**	**NHL**	82	48	28	6	5	1	4	....
2012-13	**Detroit**	**NHL**	48	24	16	8	14	7	7	....
2013-14	**Detroit**	**NHL**	82	39	28	15	5	1	4	....
2014-15	**Detroit**	**NHL**	82	43	25	14	7	3	4	....
2015-16	**Toronto**	**NHL**	82	29	42	11	....	....	....	....
2016-17	**Toronto**	**NHL**	82	40	27	15	6	2	4	....
	NHL Totals		1114	596	354	164	150	84	66	....

• Stanley Cup win.

2016-17
NHL Three Stars of the Week/Month
Award Winners

Three Stars

Period Ending	First Star	Second Star	Third Star
Oct. 16	Connor McDavid, Edm.	Auston Matthews, Tor.	Roberto Luongo, Fla.
Oct. 23	Cam Talbot, Edm.	Artem Anisimov, Chi.	Mike Green, Det.
Oct. 30	Craig Anderson, Ott.	Devan Dubnyk, Min.	Shea Weber, Mtl.
October	**Connor McDavid, Edm.**	**Shea Weber, Mtl.**	**Jonathan Marchessault, Fla.**
Nov. 6	Nikita Kucherov, T.B.	Corey Crawford, Chi.	Kevin Hayes, NYR
Nov. 13	Tuukka Rask, Bos.	Mark Scheifele, Wpg.	Pekka Rinne, Nsh.
Nov. 20	Jeff Carter, L.A.	Cam Ward, Car.	Nicklas Backstrom, Wsh.
Nov. 27	Craig Anderson, Ott.	Michael Cammalleri, N.J.	Brent Burns, S.J.
November	**Pekka Rinne, Nsh.**	**Nikita Kucherov, T.B.**	**Connor McDavid, Edm.**
Dec. 4	Steve Mason, Phi.	Vladimir Tarasenko, St.L.	Martin Jones, S.J.
Dec. 11	Jakub Voracek, Phi.	Antti Raanta, NYR	Sam Gagner, CBJ
Dec. 18	Artemi Panarin, Chi.	Henrik Lundqvist, NYR	Eric Staal, Min.
Dec. 25	Jaromir Jagr, Fla.	Jeff Carter, L.A.	Cam Talbot, Edm.
December	**Sergei Bobrovsky, CBJ**	**Evgeni Malkin, Pit.**	**Devan Dubnyk, Min.**
Jan. 1	Auston Matthews, Tor.	Chris Kreider, NYR	Marc-Andre Fleury, Pit.
Jan. 8	Michael Grabner, NYR	Patrick Maroon, Edm.	Braden Holtby, Wsh.
Jan. 15	Nicklas Backstrom, Wsh.	Brad Marchand, Bos.	Brock McGinn, Car.
Jan. 22	Conor Sheary, Pit.	Thomas Greiss, NYI	T.J. Oshie, Wsh.
Jan. 29	Wayne Simmonds, Phi.	Patrick Marleau, S.J.	Frederik Andersen, Tor.
January	**Evgeny Kuznetsov, Wsh.**	**Brad Marchand, Bos.**	**Brent Burns, S.J.**
Feb. 5	Sebastian Aho, Car.	Mikael Granlund, Min.	Peter Budaj, L.A.
Feb. 12	Jason Pominville, Min.	Jake Allen, St.L.	Viktor Arvidsson, Nsh.
Feb. 19	Patrik Laine, Wpg.	Nazem Kadri, Tor.	Connor McDavid, Edm.
Feb. 26	Filip Forsberg, Nsh.	Jonathan Toews, Chi.	Johnny Gaudreau, Cgy.
February	**Jonathan Toews, Chi.**	**Filip Forsberg, Nsh.**	**Braden Holtby, Wsh.**
Mar. 5	Nikita Kucherov, T.B.	Sergei Bobrovsky, CBJ	Carey Price, Mtl.
Mar. 12	Joe Pavelski, S.J.	Jonathan Bernier, Ana.	Erik Karlsson, Ott.
Mar. 19	Brad Marchand, Bos.	Sidney Crosby, Pit.	Brian Elliott. Cgy.
Mar. 26	Nikita Kucherov, T.B.	Kari Lehtonen, Dal.	Ryan Getzlaf, Ana.
March	**Nikita Kucherov, T.B.**	**Sergei Bobrovsky, CBJ**	**Patrick Kane, Chi.**
Apr. 2	Artemi Panarin, Chi.	Marcus Johansson, Wsh.	Cam Talbot, Edm.
Apr. 9	Craig Anderson, Ott.	Oscar Klefbom, Edm.	Brayden Point, T.B.

Rookies of the Month

Month	Player	Month	Playe
October	William Nylander, Tor.	January	Mitch Marner, Tor.
November	Zach Werenski, CBJ	February	Patrik Laine, Wpg.
December	Auston Matthews, Tor.	March	William Nylander, Tor.

William Nylander (top) of the Toronto Maple Leafs was the NHL's Rookie of the Month for October and March in 2016-17. Nylander ranked among the league's rookie leaders with 22 goals, 39 assists, and 61 points.

Pekka Rinne (right) of Nashville was the NHL's First Star of the Month for November. Rinne was 9-1-2 with a league-best 1.49 goals-against average and .949 save percentage in 12 appearances. He later put up 14 wins in the postseason to help the Predators reach the Stanley Cup Final for the first time in franchise history.

Sergei Bobrovsky (far right) was the First Star of the Month for December and the Second Star in March. The Columbus netminder went on to win the Vezina Trophy for the second time in his career, leading the NHL with a 2.06 goals-against average and .931 save percentage to guide the Blue Jackets to their best season in club history.

Hockey Hall of Fame,
U.S. Hockey Hall of Fame and IIHF Hall of Fame
2017 Inductees and Award Winners

Dave Andreychuk
Hockey Hall of Fame
2017 Inductee

Cam Cole
2017 Foster Hewitt
Memorial Award Winner

Kevin Collins
U.S. Hockey Hall of Fame
2017 Inductee • Referee

Clare Drake
Hockey Hall of Fame
2017 Inductee • Builder

Patrick Francheterre
IIHF Hall of Fame
2017 Paul Loicq Award Winner

Danielle Goyette
Hockey Hall of Fame
2017 Inductee

Tony Hand
IIHF 2017 Bibi Torriani
Award Winner

Jeremy Jacobs
Hockey Hall of Fame
2017 Inductee • Builder

Dieter Kalt
IIHF Hall of Fame
2017 Inductee • Builder

Paul Kariya
Hockey Hall of Fame
2017 Inductee

Saku Koivu
IIHF Hall of Fame
2017 Inductee

Uwe Krupp
IIHF Hall of Fame
2017 Inductee

Jack Parker
U.S. Hockey Hall of Fame
2017 Inductee • Coach

Mark Recchi
Hockey Hall of Fame
2017 Inductee

Angela Ruggiero
IIHF Hall of Fame
2017 Inductee

Joe Sakic
IIHF Hall of Fame
2017 Inductee

Teemu Selanne
Hockey & IIHF Hall of Fame
2017 Inductee

Ben Smith
U.S. Hockey Hall of Fame
2017 Inductee • Coach

Dave Strader
2017 Elmer Ferguson
Memorial Award Winner

Ron Wilson
U.S. Hockey Hall of Fame
2017 Inductee • Coach

Scott Young
U.S. Hockey Hall of Fame
2017 Inductee

Free Agent Signing Register, 2017

PLAYER	POS.	SIGNED BY	PREVIOUS ORGANIZATION	SIGNING DATE	PLAYER	POS.	SIGNED BY	PREVIOUS ORGANIZATION	SIGNING DATE
Karl Alzner	D	Montreal	Washington	July 1	Ales Hemsky	RW	Montreal	Dallas	July 3
Viktor Arvidsson	RW	Nashville	Nashville	July 22	Peter Holland	C	Montreal	Arizona	July 1
Nathan Beaulieu	D	Buffalo	Buffalo	July 31	Matt Hunwick	D	Pittsburgh	Toronto	July 1
Beau Bennett	RW	St. Louis	New Jersey	July 1	Zach Hyman	LW	Toronto	Toronto	July 5
Andre Benoit	D	Columbus	Malmo (Sweden)	July 1	Ryan Johansen	C	Nashville	Nashville	July 28
Jonathan Bernier	G	Colorado	Anaheim	July 1	Chad Johnson	G	Buffalo	Calgary	July 1
Reto Berra	G	Anaheim	Florida	July 5	Tyler Johnson	C	Tampa Bay	Tampa Bay	July 10
Joseph Blandisi	C/RW	New Jersey	New Jersey	July 25	Jussi Jokinen	C	Edmonton	Florida	July 7
Brandon Bollig	LW	San Jose	Calgary	July 4	Martin Jones	G	San Jose	San Jose	July 1
Nick Bonino	C	Nashville	Pittsburgh	July 1	Josh Jooris	C	Carolina	Arizona	July 1
Reid Boucher	LW	Vancouver	Vancouver	July 24	Jacob Josefson	C/LW	Buffalo	New Jersey	July 1
Lance Bouma	C	Chicago	Calgary	July 1	Darcy Kuemper	G	Los Angeles	Minnesota	July 1
Michael Bournival	LW	Tampa Bay	Tampa Bay	July 14	Dmitry Kulikov	D	Winnipeg	Buffalo	July 1
Gabriel Bourque	LW	Colorado	Columbus	July 18	Chris Kunitz	LW	Tampa Bay	Pittsburgh	July 1
Brian Boyle	C	New Jersey	Toronto	July 18	Evgeny Kuznetsov	C	Washington	Washington	July 2
Andre Burakovsky	C/LW	Washington	Washington	July 4	Johan Larsson	LW	Buffalo	Buffalo	July 8
Alexander Burmistrov	C	Vancouver	Arizona	July 1	Michael Latta	C	Arizona	Los Angeles	July 4
Michael Cammalleri	LW	Los Angeles	New Jersey	July 1	Scott Laughton	C	Philadelphia	Philadelphia	July 11
Michael Chaput	C	Vancouver	Vancouver	July 13	Curtis Lazar	C/RW	Calgary	Calgary	July 14
Adam Clendening	D	Arizona	NY Rangers	July 1	Robin Lehner	G	Buffalo	Buffalo	July 25
Brett Connolly	RW	Washington	Washington	July 1	Michael Leighton	G	Tampa Bay	Carolina	July 1
Andrew Copp	C	Winnipeg	Winnipeg	July 12	Anders Lindback	G	Nashville	Rogle (Sweden)	July 1
Frank Corrado	D	Pittsburgh	Pittsburgh	July 1	Oscar Lindberg	C	Vegas	NY Rangers	July 4
Nick Cousins	C	Arizona	Arizona	July 1	Brad Malone	C/LW	Edmonton	Washington	July 3
Evgeni Dadonov	LW/RW	Florida	St. Petersburg (KHL)	July 1	Patrick Marleau	C	Toronto	San Jose	July 2
Trevor Daley	D	Detroit	Pittsburgh	July 1	Jordan Martinook	LW	Arizona	Arizona	July 22
Calvin De Haan	D	NY Islanders	NY Islanders	Aug. 1	Steve Mason	G	Winnipeg	Philadelphia	July 1
Michael Del Zotto	D	Vancouver	Philadelphia	July 1	Stefan Matteau	LW	Vegas	Montreal	July 1
David Desharnais	C	NY Rangers	Edmonton	July 5	Jamie McBain	D	Tampa Bay	Arizona	July 1
Phil Di Giuseppe	LW	Carolina	Carolina	July 27	Connor McDavid	C	Edmonton	Edmonton	July 5
Brian Dumoulin	D	Pittsburgh	Pittsburgh	July 24	Curtis McElhinney	G	Toronto	Toronto	July 1
Ryan Dzingel	RW	Ottawa	Ottawa	July 21	Greg McKegg	C	Pittsburgh	Tampa Bay	July 1
Brian Elliott	G	Philadelphia	Calgary	July 1	Ryan Miller	G	Anaheim	Vancouver	July 1
Emerson Etem	LW/RW	Arizona	Anaheim	July 5	Dominic Moore	C	Toronto	Boston	July 1
Radek Faksa	C	Dallas	Dallas	July 10	Joe Morrow	D	Montreal	Boston	July 1
Jesper Fast	LW/RW	NY Rangers	NY Rangers	July 5	Chris Mueller	C	Toronto	Arizona	July 1
Michael Ferland	LW	Calgary	Calgary	July 13	Mirco Mueller	D	New Jersey	New Jersey	July 25
Landon Ferraro	C/RW	Minnesota	St. Louis	July 1	Ryan Murphy	D	Minnesota	Carolina	July 1
Brian Flynn	RW	Dallas	Montreal	July 1	Patrik Nemeth	D	Dallas	Dallas	July 1
Christian Folin	D	Los Angeles	Minnesota	July 1	Nino Niederreiter	RW	Minnesota	Minnesota	July 30
Cam Fowler	D	Anaheim	Anaheim	July 1	Antti Niemi	G	Pittsburgh	Dallas	July 1
Byron Froese	C	Montreal	Tampa Bay	July 1	Matt Nieto	LW	Colorado	Colorado	July 25
Sam Gagner	C	Vancouver	Columbus	July 1	Anders Nilsson	G	Vancouver	Buffalo	July 1
Alex Galchenyuk	C	Montreal	Montreal	July 5	Johnny Oduya	D	Ottawa	Chicago	July 24
Brendan Gaunce	C	Vancouver	Vancouver	Aug. 9	Jamie Oleksiuk	D	Dallas	Dallas	Aug. 4
Luke Gazdic	LW	Calgary	New Jersey	July 2	Steve Oleksy	D	Anaheim	Toronto	July 2
Brian Gibbons	C	New Jersey	New Jersey	July 1	Cal O'Reilly	C	Minnesota	Buffalo	July 1
Stephen Gionta	C	NY Islanders	NY Islanders	Aug. 9	Xavier Ouellet	D	Detroit	Detroit	July 3
Dan Girardi	D	Tampa Bay	NY Rangers	July 1	Jean-Gabriel Pageau	C	Ottawa	Ottawa	July 17
Barclay Goodrow	RW	San Jose	San Jose	Aug. 7	Ondrej Palat	LW	Tampa Bay	Tampa Bay	July 14
Mikael Granlund	C	Minnesota	Minnesota	Aug. 1	Colton Parayko	D	St. Louis	St. Louis	July 18
Derek Grant	C	Anaheim	Buffalo	July 2	Ondrej Pavelec	G	NY Rangers	Winnipeg	July 1
Kevin Gravel	D	Los Angeles	Los Angeles	July 14	Adam Pelech	D	NY Islanders	NY Islanders	July 24
Colin Greening	LW	Toronto	Toronto	July 1	Anthony Peluso	RW	Washington	Winnipeg	July 1
Seth Griffith	C/RW	Buffalo	Toronto	July 1	Brett Pesce	D	Carolina	Carolina	Aug. 1
Philipp Grubauer	G	Washington	Washington	July 3	Alex Petrovic	D	Florida	Florida	July 1
Ron Hainsey	D	Toronto	Pittsburgh	July 1	Tyler Pitlick	RW	Dallas	Edmonton	July 1
Michael Haley	C	Florida	San Jose	July 1	Kevin Porter	C	Buffalo	Pittsburgh	July 1
Martin Hanzal	C	Dallas	Minnesota	July 1	Paul Postma	D	Boston	Winnipeg	July 1
Scott Hartnell	LW	Nashville	Columbus	July 1	Benoit Pouliot	LW	Buffalo	Edmonton	July 1
Seth Helgeson	D	NY Islanders	New Jersey	July 1	Derrick Pouliot	D	Pittsburgh	Pittsburgh	July 12
Connor Hellebuyck	G	Winnipeg	Winnipeg	July 24	Carey Price	G	Montreal	Montreal	July 2

PLAYER	POS.	SIGNED BY	PREVIOUS ORGANIZATION	SIGNING DATE	PLAYER	POS.	SIGNED BY	PREVIOUS ORGANIZATION	SIGNING DATE
Nate Prosser	D	St. Louis	Minnesota	Aug. 3	Brandon Tanev	LW	Winnipeg	Winnipeg	July 10
Teemu Pulkkinen	LW	Vegas	Arizona	July 6	Matt Taormina	D	Montreal	Tampa Bay	July 1
Mark Pysyk	D	Florida	Florida	July 6	Tomas Tatar	C	Detroit	Detroit	July 21
Kyle Quincey	D	Minnesota	Columbus	July 1	Matt Tennyson	D	Buffalo	Carolina	July 1
Alexander Radulov	RW	Dallas	Montreal	July 3	Nate Thompson	C	Ottawa	Anaheim	July 1
Dennis Rasmussen	C	Anaheim	Chicago	July 7	Chris Thorburn	RW	St. Louis	Winnipeg	July 1
Zac Rinaldo	C	Arizona	Boston	July 1	Joe Thornton	C	San Jose	San Jose	July 2
Brett Ritchie	RW	Dallas	Dallas	July 6	Jarred Tinordi	D	PIttsburgh	Arizona	July 1
Tim Schaller	C	Boston	Boston	July 5	Zach Trotman	D	PIttsburgh	Los Angeles	July 1
Nate Schmidt	D	Vegas	Vegas	Aug. 4	Phil Varone	C	Philadelphia	Ottawa	July 1
Justin Schultz	D	Pittsburgh	Pittsburgh	July 1	Marc-Edouard Vlasic	D	San Jose	San Jose	July 1
Tom Sestito	LW	PIttsburgh	Pittsburgh	July 1	Radim Vrbata	RW	Florida	Arizona	July 1
Patrick Sharp	LW	Chicago	Dallas	July 1	Austin Watson	LW	Nashville	Nashville	July 24
Kevin Shattenkirk	D	NY Rangers	Washington	July 1	Patrick Wiercioch	D	Vancouver	Colorado	July 1
Conor Sheary	LW	PIttsburgh	Pittsburgh	July 30	Justin Williams	RW	Carolina	Washington	July 1
Nick Shore	C	Los Angeles	Los Angeles	July 6	Tommy Wingels	LW/RW	Chicago	Ottawa	July 1
Jaccob Slavin	D	Carolina	Carolina	July 12	Luke Witkowski	D	Detroit	Tampa Bay	July 1
Devante Smith-Pelly	LW/RW	Washington	New Jersey	July 3	Nail Yakupov	LW/RW	Colorado	St. Louis	July 4
Ryan Spooner	C	Boston	Boston	July 26	Mika Zibanejad	C	NY Rangers	NY Rangers	July 25
Ryan Stanton	D	Edmonton	Colorado	July 1					
Brian Strait	D	New Jersey	Winnipeg	July 1					
Mark Streit	D	Montreal	Pittsburgh	July 25					
Chris Summers	D	PIttsburgh	NY Rangers	July 1					

Trades and free agent signings after August 12, 2017 are listed on page 671.

Kevin Shattenkirk (above), who was dealt from St. Louis to Washington prior to the 2017 trade deadline, signed a four-year contract with the New York Rangers as a free agent on July 1.

Sam Gagner (left), who collected a career-high 50 points for Columbus in 2016-17, signed with Vancouver for three years.

Trade Register, 2016-17

AUGUST 2016

25 – Arizona traded Arizona's 3rd round pick (D **Max Gildon**) in 2017 NHL Draft and Arizona's 2nd round pick in 2018 NHL Draft to Florida for C **Dave Bolland** and LW **Lawson Crouse**.

OCTOBER 2016

7 – Edmonton traded D **Nail Yakupov** to St. Louis for LW **Zach Pochiro** and St. Louis's 3rd round pick (later traded to Arizona – Arizona selected D **Cameron Crotty**) in 2017 NHL Draft.

8 – Florida traded D **Jonathan Racine** to Montreal for LW **Tim Bozon**.

11 – Carolina traded C **Brody Sutter** to Florida for C **Connor Brickley**.

NOVEMBER 2016

2 – Ottawa traded Ottawa's 5th round pick (LW **Jan Drozg**) in 2017 NHL Draft to Pittsburgh for G **Mike Condon**.

8 – Florida traded D **Steven Kampfer** and a conditional 7th round pick in 2018 NHL Draft (conditions not met) to NY Rangers for D **Dylan McIlrath**.

12 – New Jersey traded a conditional 7th round pick in 2017 NHL Draft (conditions not met) to Philadelphia for RW **Petr Straka**.

16 – Anaheim traded C **Michael Sgarbossa** to Florida for LW **Logan Shaw**.

19 – Pittsburgh traded D **Reid McNeill** to St. Louis for RW **Danny Kristo**.

28 – Colorado traded D **Ryan Stanton** to Columbus for D **Cody Goloubef**.

DECEMBER 2016

9 – Arizona traded a conditional pick in 2018 NHL Draft (conditions not met) to Toronto for C **Peter Holland**.

JANUARY 2017

11 – Anaheim traded Anaheim's 7th round pick in 2018 NHL Draft to Toronto for G **Jhonas Enroth**.

13 – Colorado traded LW **Cody McLeod** to Nashville for C **Felix Girard**.

19 – Anaheim traded D **Andrew O'Brien** to Los Angeles for RW **Max Gortz**.

21 – Chicago traded D **Cameron Schilling** to Los Angeles for C **Michael Latta**.

24 – Ottawa traded RW **Buddy Robinson**, RW **Zach Stortini** and Ottawa's 7th round pick (later traded to New Jersey – New Jersey selected D **Matthew Hellickson**) in 2017 NHL Draft to San Jose for C **Tommy Wingels**.

26 – Montreal traded D **Jonathan Racine** and Montreal's 6th round pick (C **Cole Guttman**) in 2017 NHL Draft to Tampa Bay for D **Nikita Nesterov**.

FEBRUARY 2017

1 – Minnesota traded future considerations to Ottawa for RW **Marc Hagel**.

– Arizona traded D **Justin Hache** and G **Justin Peters** to Edmonton for LW **Brendan Ranford** and RW **Brendan Troock**.

– Arizona traded C/RW **Henrik Samuelsson** to Edmonton for C **Mitch Moroz**.

4 – Nashville traded Nashville's 4th round pick (later traded to San Jose, later traded to NY Rangers – NY Rangers selected D **Brandon Crawley**) in 2017 NHL Draft to New Jersey for C **Vernon Fiddler**.

15 – Los Angeles traded D **Tom Gilbert** to Washington for future considerations (conditions not met).

18 – New Jersey traded RW **Sergey Kalinin** to Toronto for D **Viktor Loov**.

20 – Arizona traded D **Michael Stone** to Calgary for Calgary's 3rd round pick (later traded to Edmonton – Edmonton selected G **Stuart Skinner**) in 2017 NHL Draft and Calgary's 5th round pick in 2018 NHL Draft.

21 – Carolina traded D **Keegan Lowe** to Montreal for D **Philip Samuelsson**.

23 – Carolina traded D **Ron Hainsey** to Pittsburgh for RW **Danny Kristo** and Pittsburgh's 2nd round pick (later traded to Vegas – Vegas selected C **Jake Leschyshyn**) in 2017 NHL Draft.

24 – Anaheim traded Anaheim's 1st round pick (later traded to Chicago – Chicago selected D **Henri Jokiharju**) in 2017 NHL Draft to Dallas for RW **Patrick Eaves**.

– Chicago traded Chicago's 3rd round pick (G **Keith Petruzzelli**) in 2017 NHL Draft to Detroit for RW **Tomas Jurco**.

26 – Los Angeles traded C **Peter Budaj**, D **Erik Cernak** and Los Angeles' 7th round pick (later traded to Philadelphia – Philadelphia selected D **Wyatt Kalynuk**) in 2017 NHL Draft to Tampa Bay for G **Ben Bishop** and Tampa Bay's 5th round pick (C **Drake Rymsha**) in 2017 NHL Draft.

– Arizona traded C **Martin Hanzal**, C **Ryan White** and Arizona's 4th round pick (C **Mason Shaw**) in 2017 NHL Draft to Minnesota for C **Grayson Downing**, Minnesota's 1st round pick (D **Pierre-Olivier Joseph**) in 2017 NHL Draft, Minnesota's 2nd round pick in 2018 NHL Draft and Minnesota's 4th round pick in 2019 NHL Draft.

27 – Arizona traded future considerations to Minnesota for LW **Teemu Pulkkinen**.

– Tampa Bay traded C **Brian Boyle** to Toronto for C **Bryan Froese** and

Toronto's 2nd round pick (RW **Alexander Volkov**) in 2017 NHL Draft.

– Dallas traded D **Jordie Benn** to Montreal for D **Greg Pateryn** and Montreal's 4th round pick (later traded to Los Angeles – Los Angeles selected D **Markus Phillips**) in 2017 NHL Draft.

– Ottawa traded LW **Jonathan Dahlen** to Vancouver for LW **Alexandre Burrows**.

– St. Louis traded D **Kevin Shattenkirk** and G **Pheonix Copley** to Washington for LW **Zach Sanford**, C/LW **Brad Malone** and Washington's 1st round pick (later traded to Philadelphia – Philadelphia selected C **Morgan Frost**) in 2017 NHL Draft.

28 – Detroit traded D **Brendan Smith** to NY Rangers for NY Rangers' 3rd round pick (D **Zach Gallant**) in 2017 NHL Draft and NY Rangers' 2nd round pick in 2018 NHL Draft.

– Carolina traded LW **Viktor Stalberg** to Ottawa for Ottawa's 3rd round pick (later traded to Chicago – Chicago selected C **Evan Barratt**) in 2017 NHL Draft.

– Buffalo traded C **Daniel Catenacci** to NY Rangers for D **Mat Bodie**.

– Chicago traded RW **Mark McNeill** and a conditional 4th round pick in 2018 NHL Draft to Dallas for D **Johnny Oduya**.

– Edmonton traded D **Brandon Davidson** to Montreal for C **David Desharnais**.

MARCH 2017

1 – Anaheim traded LW **Kenton Helgesen** and Anaheim's 7th round pick in 2019 NHL Draft to Chicago for C **Sam Carrick** and LW **Spencer Abbott**.

– Arizona traded LW **Brendan Ranford** to Colorado for RW **Joe Whitney**.

– Boston traded Boston's 5th round pick in 2018 NHL Draft to Winnipeg for RW **Drew Stafford**.

– Calgary traded D **Jyrki Jokipakka** and Calgary's 2nd round pick (LW **Alex Formenton**) in 2017 NHL Draft to Ottawa for RW **Curtis Lazar** and D **Michael Kostka**.

– Colorado traded RW **Jarome Iginla** to Los Angeles for a conditional 4th round pick in 2018 NHL Draft.

– Colorado traded D **Cody Corbett** to Washington for G **Joe Cannata**.

– Colorado traded LW **Andreas Martinsen** to Montreal for RW **Sven Andrighetto**.

– Columbus traded D **Dalton Prout** to New Jersey for D **Kyle Quincey**.

– Columbus traded D **Dillon Heatherington** to Dallas for LW **Lauri Korpikoski**.

– Detroit traded LW **Tomas Vanek** to Florida for D **Dylan McIlrath** and Florida's 3rd round pick (D **Kasper Kotkansalo**) in 2017 NHL Draft.

– Detroit traded C **Steve Ott** to Montreal for Montreal's 6th round pick in 2018 NHL Draft.

– Edmonton traded LW **Taylor Beck** to NY Rangers for RW **Justin Fontaine**.

– Florida traded G **Mike McKenna** to Tampa Bay for G **Adam Wilcox**.

– Florida traded RW **Shane Harper** to New Jersey for D **Reece Scarlett**.

– Los Angeles traded LW **Dwight King** to Montreal for Montreal's 4th round pick in 2018 NHL Draft.

– New Jersey traded LW **PA Parenteau** to Nashville for Nashville's 6th round pick (later traded to San Jose – San Jose selected C **Alexander Chmelevski**) in 2017 NHL Draft.

– Philadelphia traded D **Mark Streit** to Tampa Bay for C **Valtteri Filpulla**, Tampa Bay's 4th round pick (RW **Maksim Sushko**) in 2017 NHL Draft and Los Angeles' 7th round pick (previously acquired, Philadelphia selected D **Wyatt Kalynuk**) in 2017 NHL Draft.

– Pittsburgh traded C **Eric Fehr**, D **Steve Oleksy** and Pittsburgh's 4th round pick (LW **Vladislav Kara**) in 2017 NHL Draft to Toronto for D **Frank Corrado**.

– Pittsburgh traded Pittsburgh' 4th round pick (later traded to Vegas) in 2018 NHL Draft to Tampa Bay for D **Mark Streit**.

– San Jose traded RW **Nikolay Goldobin** and San Jose's 4th round pick (later traded to Chicago – Chicago selected C/LW **Tim Soderlund**) in 2017 NHL Draft to Vancouver for RW **Jannik Hanse**n.

6 – New Jersey traded D **Brandon Gormley** to Ottawa for future considerations.

APRIL 2017

28 – Carolina traded Ottawa's 3rd round pick (previously acquired, Chicago selected C **Evan Barratt**) in 2017 NHL Draft to Chicago for G **Scott Darling**.

MAY 2017

9 – Dallas traded Montreal's 4th round pick (previously acquired, Los Angeles selected D **Markus Phillips**) in 2017 NHL Draft to Los Angeles for G **Ben Bishop**.

31 – Los Angeles traded Los Angeles' 7th round pick in 2018 NHL Draft to Tampa Bay for LW **Boko Imama**.

JUNE 2017

14 – Minnesota traded C **Tyler Graovac** to Washington for Washington's 5th round pick in 2018 NHL Draft.

15 – Montreal traded D **Mikhail Sergachev** and a conditional 2nd round pick in 2018 NHL Draft to Tampa Bay for LW **Jonathan Drouin** and a conditional 6th round pick in 2018 NHL Draft.

16 – Arizona traded LW **Brendan Warren** and Arizona's 5th round pick in 2018 NHL Draft to Philadelphia for C **Nick Cousins** and G **Merrick Madsen**.

17 – Buffalo traded Buffalo's 3rd round pick (C **Scott Walford**) in 2017 NHL Draft to Montreal for D **Nathan Beaulieu**.

– Arizona traded G **Mike Smith** to Calgary for G **Chad Johnson**, D **Brandon Hickey** and a conditional 3rd round pick in 2018 NHL Draft.

– New Jersey traded Boston's 2nd round pick (previously acquired, San Jose selected D **Mario Ferraro**) in 2017 NHL Draft and Nashville's 4th round pick (previously acquired, later traded to NY Rangers – NY Rangers selected D **Brandon Crawley**) in 2017 NHL Draft to San Jose for D **Mirco Mueller** and San Jose's 5th round pick (RW **Marian Studenic**) in 2017 NHL Draft.

21 – Florida traded RW **Reilly Smith** to Vegas for Vegas' 4th round pick in 2018 NHL Draft and Expansion Draft considerations.

– Tampa Bay traded LW **Nikita Gusev**, Tampa Bay's 2nd round pick (later traded to Columbus – Columbus selected C **Alexandre Texier**) in 2017 NHL Draft and Pittsburgh's 4th round pick (previously acquired) in 2018 NHL Draft to Vegas for Expansion Draft considerations.

– NY Islanders traded RW **Mikhail Grabovski**, D **Jake Bischoff**, NY Islanders' 1st round pick (D **Erik Brannstrom**) in 2017 NHL Draft and NY Islanders' 2nd round pick in 2019 NHL Draft to Vegas for Expansion Draft considerations.

– Anaheim traded D **Shea Theodore** to Vegas for Expansion Draft considerations.

– Minnesota traded RW **Alex Tuch** to Vegas for Vegas' 3rd round pick in 2018 NHL Draft and Expansion Draft considerations.

– Columbus traded RW **David Clarkson**, Winnipeg's 1st round pick (previously acquired. Vegas selected C **Nick Suzuki**) in 2017 NHL Draft and Columbus' 2nd round pick in 2019 NHL Draft to Vegas for Expansion Draft considerations.

22 – Carolina traded Pittsburgh's 2nd round pick (previously acquired, Vegas selected C **Jake Leschyshyn**) in 2017 NHL Draft to Vegas for D **Trevor Van Riemsdyk** and Vegas' 7th round pick in 2018 NHL Draft.

– Montreal traded Montreal's 5th round pick in 2019 NHL Draft to Vegas for D **David Schlemko**.

– Edmonton traded RW **Jordan Eberle** to NY Islanders for C **Ryan Strome**.

23 – Arizona traded D **Connor Murphy** and C **Laurent Dauphin** to Chicago for D **Niklas Hjalmarsson**.

– Chicago traded LW **Artemi Panarin**, C **Tyler Motte** and NY Islander's 6th round pick (previousy acquired, Columbus selected RW **Jonathan Davidson**) in 2017 NHL Draft to Columbus for LW **Brandon Saad**, G **Anton Forsberg** and Columbus' 5th round pick in 2018 NHL Draft.

– Philadelphia traded C **Brayden Schenn** to St. Louis for C **Jori Lehtera** and Washington's 1st round pick (previously acquired, Philadelphia selected C **Morgan Frost**) in 2017 NHL Draft.

– Arizona traded D **Tony DeAngelo** and Arizona's 1st round pick (C **Lias Andersson**) in 2017 NHL Draft to NY Rangers for C **Derek Stepan** and G **Antti Raanta**.

– Columbus traded C **Dante Salituro** to Minnesota for C **Jordan Schroeder**.

– Pittsburgh traded C **Oskar Sundqvist** and Pittsburgh's 1st round pick (C/LW **Klim Kostin**) in 2017 NHL Draft to St. Louis for RW **Ryan Reaves** and St. Louis' 2nd round pick (D **Zachary Lauzon**) in 2017 NHL Draft.

24 – Columbus traded RW **Keegan Kolesar** to Vegas for Tampa Bay's 2nd round pick (previously acquired, Columbus selected C **Alexandre Texier**) in 2017 NHL Draft.

– Calgary traded Calgary's 1st and 2nd round picks in 2018 NHL Draft and Calgary's 2nd round pick in 2019 or 2020 NHL Draft to NY Islanders for D **Travis Hamonic** and NY Islanders' 4th round pick in 2019 or 2020 NHL Draft.

26 – Dallas traded G **Dylan Ferguson** and Dallas' 2nd round pick in 2020 NHL Draft to Vegas for D **Marc Methot**.

29 – Calgary traded D **Keegan Kanzig** and Calgary's 6th round pick in 2019 NHL Draft to Carolina for G **Eddie Lack**, D **Ryan Murphy** and Carolina's 7th round pick in 2019 NHL Draft.

30 – Buffalo traded LW **Tyler Ennis**, LW **Marcus Foligno** and Buffalo's 3rd round pick in 2018 NHL Draft to Minnesota for RW **Jason Pominville**, D **Marco Scandella** and Minnesota's 4th round pick in 2018 NHL Draft.

JULY 2017

1 – NY Islanders traded C **Carter Verhaeghe** to Tampa Bay for G **Kristers Gudlevskis**.

– Colorado traded Colorado's 4th round pick in 2019 NHL Draft to Nashville for C **Colin Wilson**.

– Calgary traded G **Tom McCollum** to Detroit for a conditional 7th round pick in 2018 NHL Draft.

– Nashville traded Nashville's 3rd round pick in 2019 NHL Draft to Vegas for D **Alexei Emelin**.

2 – Chicago traded C **Marcus Kruger** to Vegas for future considerations.

– New Jersey traded Florida's 2nd round pick (previously acquired) in 2018 NHL Draft and Toronto's 3rd round pick (previously acquired) in 2018 NHL Draft to Washington for LW **Marcus Johansson**.

4 – Carolina traded Carolina's 5th round pick in 2018 NHL Draft to Vegas for C **Marcus Kruger**.

Trades and free agent signings after August 12, 2017 are listed on page 671.

Arizona dealt goalie Mike Smith (left) to Calgary on June 17, 2017 for a package that included the rights to unrestricted free agent goalie Chad Johnson (right). Johnson later signed with the Buffalo Sabres.

League Abbreviations

AHA ....Alberta Amateur Hockey Association
AAHL ....Alaska Amateur Hockey League
AASHA ....Alaska All-Stars Hockey Association
ACAC ....Alberta Colleges Athletic Conference
ACHA...........American Collegiate Hockey Association
ACHL ....Atlantic Coast Hockey League
AFHL............American Frontier Hockey League
AH ....Atlantic Hockey
AHL ....American Hockey League
AJHL ....Alberta Junior Hockey League
ALIH ....Asia League Ice Hockey
Alpenliga.......Alpenliga (Austria, Italy, Slovenia 1994-1999)
AMHA ....Alberta Minor Hockey Association
AMHL ....Alberta Midget AAA Hockey League
AMBHL.........Alberta Major Bantam Hockey League
AtJHL...........Atlantic Junior Hockey League
AUAA...........Atlantic University Athletic Association
AUS ....Atlantic University Sport
AWHL ....American West Hockey League
AYHL............Atlantic Youth Hockey League
BCAHA ....British Columbia Amateur Hockey Association
BCHL ....British Columbia (Junior) Hockey League
        (also BCJHL)
BCMML.........British Columbia Major Midget League
BigTen..........Big Ten Conference
CABHL ....Central Alberta Bantam Hockey League
CaJHL...........Calgary Junior Hockey League
CapJHL.........Capital Junior Hockey League
CBHL ....Calgary Bantam Hockey League
CCAA...........Canadian Colleges Athletic Association
CCHA...........Central Collegiate Hockey Association
CEGEP ....Quebec College Prep
CHA.............College Hockey America
CHL ....Central Hockey League
CIS................Commonwealth of Independent States
CIS................Canadian Interuniversity Sport
CISAA ....Conference of Independent Schools Athletic
        Association (Ontario)
CJHL ....Central Junior A Hockey League
CMHA...........Calgary Minor Hockey Association
ColHL...........Colonial Hockey League
CSHL............Central States Hockey League
CSJHL ....Central States Junior Hockey League
CSSHL..........Canadian Sport School Hockey League
CWUAA ....Canada West Unversities Athletic Assoc.
ECAC ....Eastern College Athletic Conference
ECACHL........ECAC Hockey League
ECHL............East Coast Hockey League
EEHL ....Eastern European Hockey League
EJEPL...........Eastern Junior Elite Prospects League
EHL...............Eastern Hockey League
EJHL.............Eastern Junior Hockey League
EMHA ....Edmonton Minor Hockey Association
EmJHL..........Empire Junior B Hockey League
EuroHL.........European Hockey League
Exhib. ....Exhibition Games, Series or Season
GLHL............Great Lakes Hockey League
GNML...........Greater North Midget League
GPAC ....Great Plains Athletic Conference

GTHL ....Greater Toronto Hockey League
H-East...........Hockey East
High-XX.........High School (state/province)
HJHL ....Heritage Junior Hockey League
HPHL ....High Performance Hockey League
IEHL ....Internationale Eishockey Liga
IHL ....International Hockey League
JIHL..............Japan Ice Hockey League
KIJHL ....Kootenay International Jr. B Hockey League
LCJHL............Little Caesar's Junior Hockey League
MAAC...........Metro Atlantic Athletic Conference
MAHA ....Manitoba Amateur Hockey Association
MAHL ....Mid America Hockey League
MBAHL.........Metropolitan Boston Amateur Hockey League
MBHL ....Metropolitan Boston Hockey League
MEHL............Midwest Elite Hockey League
MEPDL.........Minnesota Elite Prep Development League
Metro-HL.......Metro Hockey League
MIAC ....Minnesota Intercollegiate Athletic Conference
Minor-XX.......Minor/Youth hockey (state/province)
MJHL............Manitoba Junior Hockey League
MJrHL...........Maritime Junior A Hockey League
MMBHL.........Manitoba Major Bantam Hockey League
MMHL ....Manitoba Midget AAA Hockey League
MMHL ....Michigan Minor Hockey League
MMMHL.........Manitoba Minor Midget Hockey League
MNHL............Michigan National Hockey League
MNJHL..........Minnesota Junior Hockey League
MPHL............Midwest Prep Hockey League
MtJHL...........Metropolitan Junior Hockey League (NY)
MTJHL..........Metropolitan Toronto Junior Hockey League
MTHL............Metro Toronto Hockey League
MWEHL ....Midwest Elite Hockey League
NAHL............North American Hockey League (Tier I Junior)
NAJHL...........North American Junior Hockey League
NA3HL..........North American Hockey League (Tier III)
NAPHL...........North American Prospects Hockey League
Nat-Team ....National Team (also Nt.-Team)
NBAHA ....New Brunswick Amateur Hockey Association
NBMHL..........New Brunswick Midget Hockey League
NBPEI ....New Brunswick Prince Edward Island
        Midget Hockey League
NCAA ....National Collegiate Athletic Association
NCHA ....Northern Collegiate Hockey Association
NCHC............National Collegiate Hockey Conference
NEJHL...........New England Junior Hockey League
NFAHA..........Newfoundland Amateur Hockey Association
NHL ....National Hockey League
NJCAA ....National Junior Collegiate Athletic Assoc.
NOBHL..........Northern Ontario Bantam Hockey League
NOHA...........Northern Ontario Hockey Association
NOJHA..........Northern Ontario Junior Hockey Association
NOJHL..........Northern Ontario Junior Hockey League
NORPAC ....Northern Pacific Hockey League
NSBHL...........Nova Scotia Bantam Hockey League
NSMHL ....Nova Scotia Midget AAA Hockey League
NTHL ....North Texas Hockey League
NWJHL...........Northwest Junior B Hockey League
NYJHL...........New York Junior Hockey League

OCJHL...........Ontario Central Junior A Hockey League
OHA..............Ontario Hockey Association
OHL..............Ontario Hockey League
OMJHL..........Ontario Major Junior Hockey League
ON-Jr.A ....Ontario Junior A Hockey Leagues
ON-Jr.B ....Ontario Junior B Hockey Leagues
OPJHL..........Ontario Provincial Junior A Hockey League
Other ....Tournament and Exhibition Games
OUAA ....Ontario Universities Athletic Association
PAHA ....Pennsylvania Amateur Hockey Association
PCJHL............Pacific Coast Junior Hockey League
PEIHA ....Prince Edward Island Hockey Association
PIJHL............Pacific International Junior Hockey League
PJHL.............Pacific Junior Hockey League
QAA..............Quebec Junior AA
QAAA ....Quebec Midget AAA Hockey League
QAHA ....Quebec Amateur Hockey Association
QCHL ....Quebec Collegial Hockey League
QJHL............Quebec Junior Hockey League
QMJHL..........Quebec Major Junior Hockey League
QNAHL ....(Quebec) North American Hockey League
Q-RHL..........(Quebec) Richelieu Elite Hockey League
QSPHL...........Quebec Semi-Pro Hockey League
RAMHL.........Rural Alberta Midget Hockey League
RMJHL..........Rocky Mountain Junior Hockey League
SAHA ....Saskatchewan Amateur Hockey Association
SAMHL ....Southern Alberta Midget Hockey League
SBHL.............Saskatchewan Bantam Hockey League
SCAHA...........Southern California Amateur Hockey Assoc.
SIJHL............Superior International Junior Hockey League
SJHL.............Saskatchewan Junior Hockey League
SMBHL..........Saskatchewan Major Bantam Hockey League
SMHL............Saskatchewan Midget AAA Hockey League
SMMHL ....Saskatchewan Minor Midget Hockey League
SPHL.............Southern Professional Hockey League
SSJHL............South Saskatchewan Junior B Hockey League
SSMHL...........South Saskatchewan Minor Hockey League
SunHL...........Sunshine Hockey League
T1EHL ....Tier 1 Elite Hockey League
TBAHA...........Thunder Bay Amateur Hockey Association
TBJHL............Thunder Bay Junior Hockey League
TBMHL...........Thunder Bay Midget Hockey League
U-17 ....Under 17
U-18 ....Under 18
UHL ....United Hockey League
UMEHL ....Upper Midwest Elite Hockey League
UMHSEL ....Upper Midwest High School Elite League
USAHA ....United States Amateur Hockey Association
USHL.............United States (Junior A) Hockey League
USPHL...........United State Premier Hockey League
VIJHL............Vancouver Island Junior Hockey League
WCHA...........Western Collegiate Hockey Association
WCHL ....West Coast Hockey League
WHL.............Western Hockey League
WNYHA ....Western New York Hockey Association
WPHL............Western Professional Hockey League
WSHL............Western States Hockey League
WSJHL ....Western States Junior Hockey League

Pittsburgh Penguins / Joe Sargent photo

Back-to-back Cup wins: Sidney Crosby and Evgeny Malkin strike a pose that pays homage to a 1992 photo (at right) of earlier Penguin superstars and two-time Cup winners Mario Lemieux and Jaromir Jagr.

Contributors

The NHL Official Guide & Record Book is produced with the help of many.

Special thanks to: Dave Andjelic, Joe Babik (ECHL), Cam Baccanale (Quebec Midget AAA), Rod Brind'Amour, Craig Campbell, www.capfriendly.com, Jason Chaimovitch (AHL), Carl Champagne, Kyle Chase, John Clarke, Ken Coleman (Manitoba Midget AAA), Rick Comfort, Brad Cook, Clay Cotie, Joshua Dawson, Denis Demers (QMJHL), Jason Deskins, Pat Devlin, Shawn Dietrich, Daniel Doyon, Bob Duff, Tim Droogsma, Elias Sports Bureau, Peter Fillman, Dave Fischer (USA Hockey), Ernie Fitzsimmons, Jon Frape, Jeremy Freeborn, Ryan Gage, Byron Hackett, Mike Hartwick, Steve Henley, www.hockey-reference.com, www.hockeydb.com, Eric Hornick, Geoff Jones, John Kay, Tyler King, Mike Klein (U.S. Premier Hockey League), Alex Kryias, (NAHL), Allen Lacroix, Jason LaRose (Hockey Canada), Eric Lind, John MacArthur, Sam Malkin, Doug Mathison, Pat McIver, Taylor Medak, Rickey Michel, Neil Moffatt (Alberta Midget Hockey League), Stephen Moore, Herb Morell (OHL), Scott Murray, Brent Mutis (BCHL), Cody Nidesh (Saskatchewan Midget AAA), Kris Nolt (USA Hockey National Team Development Program), Dwayne Norris, Charles O'Brien, Dave Peters, Matt Plante, www.pointstreak.com, Len Ralph, Devin Rask, Gino Riffle, Rita Rocys, Dan Ruoho, Martin Schmid, Chuck Scott, Steven Steinsaltz, Dave Strader, Matthew E. Thomas, Dean A. Tripp, www.ushl.com, Martin Walker, Jeff Wallace (WHL), Izak Westgate, Scott Whitcomb, Lyle Wildgoose, Travis Wight.

Photo Credits

Hockey Hall of Fame: Various Collections.

Chase Agnello-Dean, Justin K. Aller, Claus Andersen, Scott Audette, Brian Babineau, Steve Babineau, Brian Bahr, Al Bello, Mike Blinch, Denis Brodeur, Mark Buckner, Brandon Colston, Jonathan Daniel, Andy Devlin, Melchior DiGiacomo, Elsa, Darcy Finley, Gregg Forwerck, Norm Hall, Tim Heitman, Kirk Irwin, Scott Iskowitz, Glenn James George Kalinsky, Bruce Kluckhohn, Jonathan Kozub, Robert Laberge, S. Levy, Andy Marlin, Michael Martin, Ronald Martinez, Patrick McDermott, Codie McLachlan, Maddie Meyer, NHL Images, Minas Panagiotakis, Aaron Poole, Len Redkoles Dave Reginek, Andre Ringuette (Freestyle Photography), Debora Robinson, Jim Rogash, Scott Rovak, John Russell, Jamie Sabau, Dave Sandford, Joe Sargent, Eliot J. Schechter, Gregory Shamus, Jared Silber, Lyndon Slewidge, Don Smith, Kevin Sousa, Jamie Squire, Gerry Thomas, Jeff Vinnick, Dilip Vishwanat, Rocky Widner, Bill Wippert.

Special Thanks to Bruce Bennett, Martha McClintock and Getty Images.

Researchers and historians: contact the Society for International Hockey Research (www.sihrhockey.org) and/or Hockey Reference (www.hockey-reference.com).

100 years of NHL history. In the photo above, Glen Harmon of the Montreal Canadiens stands above Tony Leswick of the New York Rangers while Ken Reardon and goalie Bill Durnan look on, December 16, 1945.

Right: Toronto goalie Frederik Andersen keeps an eye on the puck amidst a crowd of Maple Leafs and Detroit Red Wings during the NHL Centennial Classic on January 1, 2017.